S0-AZQ-144

HALLIWELL'S FILM GUIDE

By the same author

Halliwell's Filmgoer's Companion
Halliwell's Television Companion (with Philip Purser)
The Filmgoer's Book of Quotes
Halliwell's Movie Quiz
Mountain of Dreams
The Clapperboard Book of the Cinema (with Graham Murray)
Halliwell's Hundred
Halliwell's Harvest
The Ghost of Sherlock Holmes (fiction)
Seats in All Parts: Half a Lifetime at the Movies
Return to Shangri-La (fiction)
The Dead That Walk
Double Take and Fade Away

LESLIE HALLIWELL

HALLIWELL'S FILM GUIDE

SEVENTH EDITION

1817

Harper & Row, Publishers, New York
Grand Rapids, Philadelphia, St. Louis, San Francisco
London, Singapore, Sydney, Tokyo, Toronto

This book is published in Great Britain by Grafton Books,
a division of the Collins Publishing Group.

Library of Congress Catalog Card Number 89-45159

ISBN 0-06-016322-4

89 90 91 92 93 10 9 8 7 6 5 4 3 2 1

CONTENTS

Publisher's Note for the Seventh Edition

Leslie Halliwell died on 21 January 1989, shortly after completing work on this new edition. It seems appropriate that, in spite of serious illness, he devoted the last months of his life to the *Film Guide* which, together with *Halliwell's Filmgoer's Companion*, is the fruit of his lifelong passion for the cinema, and which made him known to thousands of appreciative film enthusiasts throughout the world.

Both reference books will continue to be updated and will appear in subsequent editions under the existing titles.

Preface to the Sixth Edition

A thousand new entries appear in this edition. They include all the new films which seem worth noting, but I have also ransacked the forties for items of interest which were previously omitted; I have taken a keen look at Australian films; and I have said something about each and every one of the two hundred-odd serials produced since the coming of sound. You have to be of a certain age to remember the serial, a twenty-minute chunk of which, until the early fifties, was added even to double bills at the lesser cinemas, to reappear in due course at the Saturday morning kids' matinées. Art was not involved in their production, but they featured a willing repertory of familiar actors (the player most often featured may have been Dale Van Sickel or I. Stanford Jolley) and at their best they provided lively entertainment for children of all ages, with explosions galore and a cliffhanger at the end of each chapter.

My favourites were those which featured a masked villain, who usually went by some such name as The Lightning or The Black Tiger or The Clutching Hand. Sometimes the dauntless hero masked himself as well, conducting his exploits as The Green Hornet or The Phantom, or as an old friend like Batman or Zorro. At the end of chapter twelve or thirteen the villain would be exposed as Eduardo Ciannelli or George Macready or Lionel Atwill, and fed to the fishes so that we could all go home happy in the knowledge that the world was safe for another generation. The hero meanwhile would re-assume his rightful identity and marry the girl, not that anybody cared. The last serials were made in 1955, and cinemas have been duller places without them.

As usual, nothing has been deleted from the last edition. Countless amendments and additions have also been made to existing entries and the illustrations are all new. If the book gets much bigger, it will need a shelf to itself, or the type face will become too small to read. It is now roughly the length of twenty novels and covers 16,000 films.

Leslie Halliwell
London, January 1987

Preface to the Fifth Edition

The fourth edition was such a rapid sell-out that a revision is offered two years later. The films and awards of the intervening period are of course fully represented, but the opportunity has been taken to improve the work in a number of ways, in addition to the obvious corrections which have come to hand.

The three-column setting has reduced the number of pages, which means that there is still room for expansion, and so I have decided to bring the past into sharper focus than at one time seemed possible. My plan is to explore one decade per edition, and to bring in many more titles of moderate interest, which were previously omitted for reasons of space. In the current edition, the period chosen for this thickening of texture is the thirties, and approximately one thousand new entries have resulted. If many of them are unimportant historically, most do involve well-known actors, writers and directors and so have a strong claim to be recorded.

I have aimed to increase the number of critical quotes, especially those given at the time of release by the American trade paper *Variety*, whose reviews were often a key to commercial success and whose pithy comments give a significant edge to changing film fashions. Other opinions, however, have not been neglected.

Another means of judging a film is the way in which it is promoted. I have therefore collected a thousand or more original publicity taglines, which apart from being amusing in themselves tell us much about the audiences of their time. These, in the manner of trailers, precede their entries, and I shall be grateful to hear of others for future editions.

Films made for television – including those commissioned by Channel Four – will continue to be consigned to my *Television Companion*, a bulkier edition of which is due for publication at the end of 1986. In this present volume, however, I have done my best to indicate what films readers may hope to enjoy again on their television screens by means of video cassettes. Alas, this information may date rather quickly. Video distributors tend to take on films for shortish periods, and titles which prove uncommercial may be quickly withdrawn; but the information has been asked for and I am pleased to make it as complete as I can. Bear in mind only that I have concentrated on major films of all countries which are available in Great Britain at the end of 1984. American distributors differ in the main, in their title selection; to my American friends I apologize for being unable to cover their country in the same way, but at least the information I give may be a useful guide, for I find that fans have much the same interests in both countries. All video users should note that I am neither willing nor able to comment on the plethora of independently made, low-budget productions which fill video shop shelves. If they have not been good enough to warrant a cinema release, I assume that I may overlook them too. Even the most casual enquirer will know that the vast majority of available videos harp on horror and sex themes, a nauseous flood of celluloid with which no commentator could hope to keep up, even if he wanted to.

Once again I am grateful for unsolicited advice from correspondents, especially E. A. Layzell and Richard Chatten. Please note, however, that I cannot agree to insert every piece of information submitted, for too much emphasis on small-part players or silent films would upset the balance of the book, which as ever aims to be convenient and amiable but is not intended to replace the detailed research which must be undertaken by specialists. A review of the last edition dismissed my comments as 'increasingly weary and blimpish'! I feel myself to be neither, but I remain suspicious of the films of the last fifteen years or so, which have followed fashion to the exclusion of permanent value. Just as poetry was once said to be emotion recollected in tranquillity, my evaluations are intended to set films in their historical context, which is impossible until they have some years on them; and I reserve the right in each edition to add or subtract from the number of stars previously given.

The illustrations as usual are mainly nostalgic; but bear in mind that they are reminders of films which many viewers are seeing for the first time through the courtesy of Channel Four.

Leslie Halliwell
January 1985

Preface to the Fourth Edition

In the first edition of this work, published in 1977, I wrote as follows:

> During the twelve years which have elapsed since *The Filmgoer's Companion* first appeared, I have often been asked why I do not produce a complete compendium of all the films ever made, giving a minimum of useful information for each title. Some people even complain because the *Companion* does not provide all this. Plainly, with more than 25,000 English-speaking titles alone to contend with – and I am speaking here of feature-length films only – no one volume could hope to be comprehensive, and even if it were possible the attempt would be fairly pointless, for the book would be cluttered up with endless lists of routine second features of long ago, which no one in his right mind would even wish to remember, let alone see again.
>
> In the *Companion* I do treat separately some seven or eight hundred titles which I consider significant either historically or as pure entertainment, and some readers have been annoyed when looking up films they consider memorable to discover that their titles have not accorded with my prejudices. Ever anxious to please, I have rearranged and amplified the information given in these entries, and multiplied the number of entries tenfold: hence the volume you hold in your hand, which I hope will provide an instant reference when what you want to look up is a movie rather than a person, a theme or a technical expression.
>
> The key to the volume must still be selection, even with a goal of eight thousand entries. To some extent the selection must be personal, but readers of the *Companion* will be helped by having sensed the extent of my memory and the balance of my inclinations. (I think I may claim to have as reasonable a set of hang-ups as anyone now writing about films, except that I tend to hark back towards the old rather than the new, which is not a bad qualification for the job in hand.) I did feel it necessary, however, to restrict myself, at least in the first edition, to films wholly or partly financed in America or Britain. Obviously there are many foreign-language films which demanded inclusion, but it would have been impossible to select them on the same level: I could have given only a smattering of the better-known ones, which seemed unfair. The same is true of silent films, so I firmly put both problems aside for another day and limited myself to English-speaking talking films, which gave me fifty years of product to play with.
>
> I have tried to include every film which seemed likely or worthy to be remembered by the keen filmgoer or student, whether with affection for its own sake as good entertainment, for showcasing memorable work by a particular talent, for sheer curiosity value or for box office success. This brings in virtually everything which played as a main feature in Britain or America. Co-features, 'programmers' and second features are included if they are known to have special merit or to show promise in some department; I have tried to omit the

absolutely routine, and specifically excluded a few hundred westerns on the Audie Murphy and Randolph Scott level or below. Another way of looking at my choice is to say that the main studios to suffer are Republic, Monogram, PRC, Nettlefold and Mancunian. Other deliberate exclusions are porno films (hard or soft); underground films; documentaries and shorts; features below fifty-five minutes; exploitation and horror films from independent sources; from-the-stalls versions of ballet, opera and Shakespeare; and pop concerts on film.

I shall be disappointed if the regular reader of the *Companion* cannot find in this volume any film he is likely to require, unless he is a specialist in the early work of Edgar G. Ulmer, Maurice Elvey, or Harry d'Abbabie d'Arrast. Complaints of omissions will nevertheless be welcome: if only one reader sees merit in an excluded film, it has to be worthy of reconsideration next time. Be assured, however, that I already have another three thousand titles half researched . . .

Well, the modest enterprise was more successful than could have been anticipated. Six years have elapsed, and we are up to the fourth edition, making the book far bigger, and much faster in expansion, than *The Filmgoer's Companion*, which however is in the works for a major overhaul. The *Film Guide* in fact seems in danger of bursting its covers, its horizons having been gradually extended to take in a generous selection of silent classics, widely shown foreign-language entertainments, some shorts, and nearly six thousand more English-speaking films (including those Audie Murphy and Randolph Scott westerns). These additions involved the transfer of TV movie entries to the *Television Companion*, and the devising of a compressed form of entry for less outstanding films. Correction and amendment is a constant process, and in the last editions I have added thousands of critical quotes, as well as listing not only Academy Awards but nominations, which in my view are equally important, since the best man doesn't always win.

The film industry is frequently reported to be dying, and certainly it seems unlikely that the cinema in the High Street can survive much longer on a ration of one *E.T.* a year followed by many months with little to play but reissues. My own home town, Bolton, once boasted twenty-seven cinemas; it now has one, and I recently witnessed the closure of its proud 2,600-seater Odeon, which in 1937 I watched step by step as it rose from the slums. At the time I write there is a new villain of the piece, not television but video, which has enjoyed astonishing success, not surprisingly since one can hire a favourite movie for the evening at a cost less than that of a cinema ticket. Soon the industry will be blaming cable and satellite channels for a further step in its demise. At least we can be pleased that more British films are being made, but with a couple of exceptions a year they are unglamorous hybrids, made on low budgets for a quick press showing, three weeks at an art house, and a second première on Channel Four. This may well become the accepted state of things in the future, and to people who know no better it may work well enough for films which do not depend on audible audience reaction. To my mind, however, home viewing, though undeniably the most comfortable form of filmgoing, can never quite equal the thrill of my first timorous entry all those years ago into the scented cathedral-like atmosphere of the Bolton Odeon, with the air of excitement which rose from a packed house when the house grew dimmer and footlights shone on red velour curtains which seemed to stretch upwards to the sky. Those were the great days of cinema, and most of the films in this book were made for that kind of presentation. Even without it, many of them can still provide more quiet pleasure than the aggressive, sexy, violent and mindless sideshows with which the industry for the last fifteen years has been vainly trying to save itself.

As for the book itself, it seems to fill a need, and proves the phenomenon of the snowball, which grows in size as it gathers momentum. When I pick it up, with something of an effort, I can scarcely believe that I typed every word with my two overworked and untrained index fingers. But I did.

Leslie Halliwell
January 1983

The great Mr Hitchcock on the set of *Psycho*.

Alphabetical Index of Alternative Titles

If the film you seek does not appear in the main section of the book and you suspect it to have more than one title, check it here. (NB: Foreign-language films are listed here only if they have more than one foreign- or English-language title. See the following lists for original titles or English-language versions.)

Abandon Ship *see* Seven Waves Away
Abbott and Costello Meet the Ghosts *see* Abbott and Costello Meet Frankenstein
Abdulla's Harem *see* Abdulla the Great
Absinthe *see* Madame X (1929)
Adamson of Africa *see* The Killers of Kilimanjaro
Adventure for Two *see* The Demi-Paradise
Adventures of a Young Man *see* Hemingway's Adventures of a Young Man
The Adventures of Huckleberry Finn *see* Huckleberry Finn (1960)
The Adventures of Quentin Durward *see* Quentin Durward
The Adventuress *see* I See a Dark Stranger
Affair at the Villa Fiorita *see* The Battle of the Villa Fiorita
Affair in Monte Carlo *see* Twenty-Four Hours of a Woman's Life
Affairs of a Rogue *see* The First Gentleman
Affairs of Sally *see* The Fuller Brush Girl
African Fury *see* Cry the Beloved Country
After Eight Hours *see* Society Doctor
After Midnight *see* Captain Carey USA
Agent 8¾ *see* Hot Enough for June
Ah! Les Belles Bacchantes *see* Femmes de Paris
Airport '80: The Concorde *see* The Concorde: Airport '79
Alias Bulldog Drummond *see* Bulldog Jack
All at Sea *see* Barnacle Bill
All These Women *see* Now About All These Women. . .
All This and Glamour Too *see* Vogues of 1938
All This and Money Too *see* Love is a Ball
Along Came Sally *see* Aunt Sally
Almost a Bride *see* A Kiss for Corliss
The Amazing Mr Beecham *see* The Chiltern Hundreds
The Amazing Mr Forrest *see* The Gang's All Here (1939)
The Anatolian Smile *see* America, America
And Woman . . . Was Created *see* And God Created Woman
Andy Warhol's Dracula *see* Dracula
Angel Street *see* Gaslight (1939)
Angels and the Pirates *see* Angels in the Outfield
April Romance *see* Blossom Time
Armored Attack *see* North Star
Arms and the Girl *see* Red Salute
Arms and the Woman *see* Mr Winkle Goes to War
Arouse and Beware *see* The Man from Dakota
Arrivederci Baby *see* Drop Dead Darling
The Assassin (1947) *see* Gunfighters
The Assassin (1952) *see* Venetian Bird
At Dawn We Die *see* Tomorrow We Live
Atlantic Episode *see* Catch As Catch Can
Atoll K *see* Robinson Crusoeland
The Avengers *see* The Day Will Dawn
Baby Be Good *see* Brother Rat and a Baby
The Baby Vanishes *see* Broadway Limited
Bachelor Bait *see* Adventure in Baltimore
Bachelor Girl Apartment *see* Any Wednesday
Bachelor Girls *see* The Bachelor's Daughter
Bachelor Knight *see* The Bachelor and the Bobbysoxer
Bad Man of Wyoming *see* Wyoming (1940)
Bad Sister *see* The White Unicorn
The Baited Trap *see* The Trap
The Ballad of Tam-Lin *see* Tam-Lin
The Bank Breaker *see* Kaleidoscope
The Bank Detective *see* The Bank Dick
Basil, The Great Mouse Detective *see* The Great Mouse Detective
The Battle for Anzio *see* Anzio
Battle Hell *see* Yangtse Incident
The Battle of City Hall *see* Angels Wash Their Faces
The Battle of Gallipoli *see* Tell England
The Battle of Midway *see* Midway
Battle of Powder River *see* Tomahawk
Battle on the Beach *see* The Battle at Bloody Beach
Battle Stripe *see* The Men
Battling Bellhop *see* Kid Galahad (1937)
The Beachcomber *see* Vessel of Wrath
Beau Chumps *see* Beau Hunks
Beautiful but Dangerous *see* She Couldn't Say No
The Beautiful Cheat *see* What a Woman
The Beautiful Rebel *see* Janice Meredith
Behemoth the Sea Monster *see* The Giant Behemoth
Behind the Door *see* The Man with Nine Lives
Bengal Rifles *see* Bengal Brigade
Betrayed *see* When Strangers Marry
Beware of Children *see* No Kidding
Beyond the Limit *see* The Honorary Consul
Beyond the River *see* The Bottom of the Bottle
The Big Bankroll *see* King of the Roaring Twenties
The Big Carnival *see* Ace in the Hole
Big Deal at Dodge City *see* A Big Hand for the Little Lady
Big Deal on Madonna Street *see* Persons Unknown
The Big Heart *see* Miracle on 34th Street
The Big Story *see* Appointment with a Shadow
Big Time Operators *see* The Smallest Show on Earth
Billy Rose's Diamond Horseshoe *see* Diamond Horseshoe
Billy Rose's Jumbo *see* Jumbo
The Birds and the Bees *see* Three Daring Daughters
The Bishop's Misadventures *see* The Bishop Misbehaves
The Black Arrow Strikes *see* The Black Arrow

Black Bart, Highwayman *see* Black Bart
Black Flowers for the Bride *see* Something for Everyone
Blackout *see* Contraband
Blonde Bombsell *see* Bombshell
A Blonde in Love *see* Loves of a Blonde
Blonde Sinner *see* Yield to the Night
Blood Beast from Outer Space *see* The Night Caller
Blood Money *see* Requiem for a Heavyweight
Blood on My Hands *see* Kiss the Blood Off My Hands
The Bloody Bushido Blade *see* The Bushido Blade
The Blue and the Gold *see* An Annapolis Story
Blue Jeans *see* Blue Denim
Blues for Lovers *see* Ballad in Blue
Bombsight Stolen *see* Cottage to Let
Bonaventure *see* Thunder on the Hill
Bosambo *see* Sanders of the River
Borderlines *see* The Caretakers
Born for Glory *see* Brown on Resolution
Born for Trouble *see* Murder in the Big House
Born to Kill *see* Cockfighter
Both Ends of the Candle *see* The Helen Morgan Story
Both Sides of the Law *see* Street Corner
The Boy from Barnardo's *see* Lord Jeff
A Boy Ten Feet Tall *see* Sammy Going South
The Boyars' Plot *see* Ivan the Terrible
The Brain (1962) *see* Vengeance
The Brave and the Beautiful *see* The Magnificent Matador
Break to Freedom *see* Albert RN
Breakdance *see* Breakin'
Breakdance 2: Electric Boogaloo *see* Breakin' 2: Electric Boogaloo
Breaking the Sound Barrier *see* The Sound Barrier
Breakout *see* Danger Within
Breath of Scandal *see* His Glorious Night
The Bride Wasn't Willing *see* Frontier Gal
Brink of Hell *see* Toward the Unknown
Broadway Singer *see* Torch Singer
Brotherly Love *see* Country Dance
Build My Gallows High *see* Out of the Past
Burn! *see* Queimada!
Burn, Witch, Burn *see* Night of the Eagle
By Hook or by Crook *see* I Dood It

Cactus in the Snow *see* You Can't Have Everything
Cactus Jack *see* The Villain
Café of Seven Sinners *see* Seven Sinners
The California Dolls *see* All the Marbles
California Holiday *see* Spinout
Call Harry Crown *see* 99 and 44/100 Per Cent Dead
Call it Murder *see* Midnight
Call Me Genius *see* The Rebel
Canyon Pass *see* Raton Pass
Captain Blood, Fugitive *see* Captain Pirate
Cardigan's Last Case *see* State's Attorney
Cargo of Innocents *see* Stand By for Action
Caribbean Gold *see* Caribbean
Carnival of Thieves *see* The Caper of the Golden Bulls
Carquake *see* Cannonball
Carry On, Follow That Camel *see* Follow That Camel
The Case of Mrs Pembroke *see* Two Against the World
The Case of the Missing Blonde *see* Lady in the Morgue
C.A.S.H. *see* W.H.I.F.F.S.
Cash and Carry *see* Maisie (Ringside Maisie)
Casino de Paree *see* Go Into Your Dance
Cast Iron *see* The Virtuous Sin
The Cave Dwellers *see* One Million BC
Chained to Yesterday *see* Limbo
The Chairman *see* The Most Dangerous Man in the World
Chamber of Horrors *see* The Door with Seven Locks
Champagne for Everybody *see* Here Come the Girls
Chance Meeting (1954) *see* The Young Lovers
Chance Meeting (1959) *see* Blind Date
The Charge is Murder *see* Twilight of Honor
Charley's American Aunt *see* Charley's Aunt
Chicago, Chicago *see* Gaily, Gaily
Chicago Masquerade *see* Little Egypt
Chilly Scenes of Winter *see* Head Over Heels
China Caravan *see* A Yank on the Burma Road
Chinese Den *see* The Chinese Bungalow
Choice of Weapons *see* Trial by Combat
Choose Your Partner *see* Two Girls on Broadway
The Chosen *see* Holocaust 2000
The Circle *see* The Vicious Circle
Citizens' Band *see* FM
City After Midnight *see* That Woman Opposite
The City Is Dark *see* Crime Wave
The City Jungle *see* The Young Philadelphians
Clouds Over Europe *see* Q Planes
A Clown Must Laugh *see* Pagliacci
Code of Scotland Yard *see* The Shop at Sly Corner
Colonel Blimp *see* The Life and Death of Colonel Blimp
Colossus, The Forbin Project *see* The Forbin Project
Come Back to Me *see* Doll Face
A Coming-Out Party *see* Very Important Person
Company of Cowards *see* Advance to the Rear
Concealment *see* The Secret Bride
Concerto *see* I've Always Loved You
The Concrete Jungle *see* The Criminal
Condemned to Devil's Island *see* Condemned
Condemned to Life *see* Life for Ruth
The Confession (1965) *see* Quick Let's Get Married
Confessions of a Counterspy *see* Man on a String
The Conqueror Worm *see* Witchfinder General
The Contact Man *see* Alias Nick Beal
Contest Girl *see* The Beauty Jungle
The Courageous Mr Penn *see* Penn of Pennsylvania
Court Martial *see* Carrington VC
The Courtney Affair *see* The Courtneys of Curzon Street
The Cowboy and the Girl *see* A Lady Takes a Chance
The Crash of Silence *see* Mandy
The Crawling Eye *see* The Trollenberg Terror
Crazy to Kill *see* Dr Gillespie's Criminal Case
The Creeping Unknown *see* The Quatermass Experiment
Crest of the Wave *see* Seagulls over Sorrento
The Crime of the Century *see* Walk East on Beacon
The Crimson Blade *see* The Scarlet Blade
The Crimson Cult *see* Curse of the Crimson Altar
Crooks in Clover *see* Penthouse
Crossed Swords *see* The Prince and the Pauper (1977)
Curse of the Demon *see* Night of the Demon
The Curse of the Ellanbys *see* She Wolf of London
Cutter's Way *see* Cutter and Bone
Cynthia's Secret *see* Dark Delusion
Czar of the Slot Machines *see* King of Gamblers
Czarina *see* A Royal Scandal

Damn the Defiant *see* HMS Defiant
Dance of the Vampires *see* The Fearless Vampire Killers
Dancing Fool *see* Harold Teen
Dangerous Days *see* Wild Boys of the Road
Dangerous Female *see* The Maltese Falcon (1931)
Dangerous Youth *see* These Dangerous Years
Daniel and the Devil *see* All That Money Can Buy
Dark of the Sun *see* The Mercenaries
The Dark Page *see* Scandal Sheet
Dark Sands *see* Jericho
Darling I am Growing Younger *see* Monkey Business
A Date with a Lonely Girl *see* T. R. Baskin
A Date with Destiny (1948) *see* The Return of October
A Date with Destiny (1941) *see* The Mad Doctor
Daughter of Luxury *see* Five and Ten
Daughters of Destiny *see* Love, Soldiers and Women
The Day They Gave Babies Away *see* All Mine to Give

G Man's Wife *see* Public Enemy's Wife
Gaiety Girls *see* Paradise for Two
Gang War *see* Odd Man Out
The Gay Divorce *see* The Gay Divorcee
The Gay Duellist *see* Meet Me at Dawn
The Gay Imposters *see* Gold Diggers in Paris
The Gay Lady *see* Trottie True
The Gay Mrs Trexel *see* Susan and God
The Gay Nineties *see* The Floradora Girl
A Genius in the Family *see* So Goes My Love
The Gentle Sergeant *see* Three Stripes in the Sun
Gentleman for a Day *see* Union Depot
Georgia's Friends *see* Four Friends
Gestapo *see* Night Train to Munich
Get Charlie Tully *see* Ooh, You Are Awful
Get off My Back *see* Synanon
Gideon of Scotland Yard *see* Gideon's Day
The Girl Getters *see* The System (GB)
Girl in Distress *see* Jeannie
The Girl in Overalls *see* Maisie (Swing Shift Maisie)
The Girl in Pawn *see* Little Miss Marker
The Girl in Room 17 *see* Vice Squad
The Girl in the Painting *see* Portrait from Life
Girl of the Year *see* The Petty Girl
The Girl on the Canal *see* Painted Boats
A Girl Was Young *see* Young and Innocent
The Girls He Left Behind *see* The Gang's All Here (1943)
Girls in the Street *see* London Melody
Girls Never Tell *see* Her First Romance
Girly *see* Mumsy, Nanny, Sonny and Girly
Glory at Sea *see* The Gift Horse
God Gave Him a Dog *see* The Biscuit Eater (1940)
The Golden Heist *see* Inside Out
The Golden Horde of Genghis Khan *see* The Golden Horde
The Golden Hour *see* Pot o' Gold
The Golden Mask *see* South of Algiers
The Golden Virgin *see* The Story of Esther Costello
Good Girl *see* Good Dame
Good Morning Doctor *see* You Belong to Me
Good Old Schooldays *see* Those Were the Days
The Grace Moore Story *see* So This Is Love
Grand Rue *see* Calle Mayor
The Great Adventure *see* The Adventurers
The Great Awakening *see* New Wine
The Great Manhunt (1949) *see* The Doolins of Oklahoma
The Great Manhunt (1950) *see* State Secret
The Great Spy Mission *see* Operation Crossbow
Green Eyed Woman *see* Take a Letter Darling
The Grip of Fear *see* Experiment in Terror
The Guest *see* The Caretaker
The Gun Runner *see* Santiago
Gunpoint *see* At Gunpoint
Guns in the Afternoon *see* Ride the High Country
Guns of Wyoming *see* Cattle King
Gypsy Girl *see* Sky West and Crooked

Hallelujah I'm a Tramp *see* Hallelujah I'm a Bum
The Hammond Mystery *see* The Undying Monster
A Handful of Clouds *see* Doorway to Hell
The Hands of Orlac (1935) *see* Mad Love
Happy Family *see* The Merry Frinks
Happy Landing *see* Flying High
Happy Times *see* The Inspector General
Hara Kiri *see* The Battle
Hard Driver *see* The Last American Hero
The Hardcore Life *see* Hardcore
Harem Holiday *see* Harum Scarum
Harmony Parade *see* Pigskin Parade
The Harp of Burma *see* The Burmese Harp
Harry Black *see* Harry Black and the Tiger
The Haunted and the Hunted *see* Dementia 13
Haunted Honeymoon *see* Busman's Honeymoon
The Haunted Strangler *see* Grip of the Strangler
Having a Wild Weekend *see* Catch Us If You Can
Head Over Heels in Love *see* Head Over Heels
Hearts in Springtime *see* Glamour Boy
The Heir to Genghis Khan *see* Storm Over Asia
The Heist *see* Dollars
Hell Bent for Glory *see* Lafayette Escadrille
Hell, Heaven and Hoboken *see* I Was Monty's Double
Hell in Korea *see* A Hill in Korea
Hello Beautiful *see* The Powers Girl
He or She *see* Glen or Glenda
Her Man Gilbey *see* English without Tears
Her Panelled Door *see* The Woman with No Name
Her Sweetheart *see* Christopher Bean
Here Is a Man *see* All That Money Can Buy
The Hero *see* Bloomfield
The Heroin Gang *see* Sol Madrid
The Hidden Room *see* Obsession (1948)
The Hideout *see* The Small Voice
Hideout in the Alps *see* Dusty Ermine
High and Dry *see* The Maggie
The High Commissioner *see* Nobody Runs Forever
High Encounters of the Ultimate Kind *see* Cheech and Chong's Next Movie
High Fury *see* White Cradle Inn
High Vermilion *see* Silver City
The High Window *see* The Brasher Doubloon
Highway to Freedom *see* Joe Smith American
Hill's Angels *see* The North Avenue Irregulars
His Affair *see* This is My Affair
His Majesty Bunker Bean *see* Bunker Bean
His Other Woman *see* Desk Set
Hit Parade of 1943 *see* Change of Heart
Hitler's Gold *see* Inside Out
Hitler's Hangman *see* Hitler's Madman
Hold That Girl *see* Hold That Co-Ed
Holiday in Spain *see* Scent of Mystery
Hollow Triumph *see* The Scar
Hollywood Cowboy *see* Hearts of the West
The Honourable Mr Wong *see* The Hatchet Man
Hoppity Goes to Town *see* Mr Bug Goes to Town
Horror Hotel *see* City of the Dead
Horror of Dracula *see* Dracula (1958)
The Hot One *see* Corvette Summer
Hot Spot *see* I Wake Up Screaming
Hounded *see* Johnny Allegro
The Hounds of Zaroff *see* The Most Dangerous Game
Hour of Glory *see* The Small Back Room
House of Connelly *see* Carolina
House of Doom *see* The Black Cat
House of Fright *see* The Two Faces of Dr Jekyll
House of Menace *see* Kind Lady
House of Mystery *see* Night Monster
House of Settlement *see* Mr Soft Touch
The House of Tao Lin *see* Dangerous Millions
Howard, a New Breed of Hero *see* Howard the Duck
How to Rob a Bank *see* A Nice Little Bank That Should Be Robbed
How to Steal a Diamond in Four Uneasy Lessons *see* The Hot Rock
The Human Monster *see* Dark Eyes of London
The Hypnotist *see* London After Midnight

I Became a Criminal *see* They Made Me a Fugitive
I Changed My Sex *see* Glen or Glenda
I Even Knew Happy Gypsies *see* Happy Gypsies
I Led Two Lives *see* Glen or Glenda
I Like Money *see* Mr Topaze
I Live for You *see* I Live for Love
I Married a Communist *see* The Woman on Pier 13
I Married a Nazi *see* The Man I Married
I Shall Return *see* An American Guerrilla in the Philippines

I Stand Condemned *see* Moscow Nights
I Was a Fireman *see* Fires Were Started
Idols in the Dust *see* Saturday's Hero
If This Be Sin *see* That Dangerous Age
If You Feel Like Singing *see* Summer Stock
I'll Never Forget You *see* The House in the Square
Imaginary Sweetheart *see* Professional Sweetheart
Immortal Battalion *see* The Way Ahead
The Imperfect Lady *see* The Perfect Gentleman
The Impossible Lover *see* Huddle
In Old Oklahoma *see* War of the Wildcats
In Rosie's Room *see* Rosie the Riveter
Indian Summer *see* The Judge Steps Out
Indiscretion (1954) *see* Indiscretion of an American Wife
Indiscretion (1945) *see* Christmas in Connecticut
The Inheritance *see* Uncle Silas
Innocence is Bliss *see* Miss Grant Takes Richmond
Intrigue in Paris *see* Miss V from Moscow
The Invaders *see* 49th Parallel
An Investigation of Murder *see* The Laughing Policeman
The Iron Road *see* Buckskin Frontier
Island Escape *see* No Man is an Island
Island of Desire *see* Saturday Island
Island Rescue *see* Appointment with Venus
It Happened One Summer *see* State Fair (1945)
It Hurts Only When I Laugh *see* Only When I Laugh
It's a Dog's Life *see* The Bar Sinister
It's Hot in Hell *see* A Monkey in Winter
It's Magic *see* Romance on the High Seas
It's Only Money *see* Double Dynamite
Ivory Hunter *see* Where No Vultures Fly

Jacqueline Susann's Once is Not Enough *see* Once is Not Enough
Jailbirds *see* Pardon Us
The James Brothers *see* The True Story of Jesse James
The Janitor *see* Eye Witness (1981)
Jennie *see* Portrait of Jennie
Jenny Lind *see* A Lady's Morals
Jet Men of the Air *see* Air Cadet
Joan Medford Is Missing *see* House of Horrors
Joe Hill *see* The Ballad of Joe Hill
Johnny in the Clouds *see* The Way to the Stars
Johnny Vagabond *see* Johnny Come Lately
Jungle Fighters *see* The Long and the Short and the Tall
Justice for Sale *see* Night Court

Katina *see* Iceland
Kidnapped *see* Miss Fane's Baby is Stolen
The Kid's Last Fight *see* The Life of Jimmy Dolan
Killer Grizzly *see* Grizzly
Killer Meets Killer *see* Each Dawn I Die
Killer on a Horse *see* Welcome to Hard Times
Killer of Killers *see* The Mechanic
Kisenga, Man of Africa *see* Men of Two Worlds
Kiss of Evil *see* Kiss of the Vampire
Knockout *see* Knute Rockne, All American

The Lady and the Doctor *see* The Lady and the Monster
The Lady and the Outlaw *see* Billy Two Hats
Lady Hamilton *see* That Hamilton Woman
Lady in Distress *see* A Window in London
Lady of Deceit *see* Born to Kill
Lady Godiva of Coventry *see* Lady Godiva
Lady of the Boulevards *see* Nana
A Lady Surrenders *see* Love Story (1944)
Lady Windermere's Fan *see* The Fan
Land of Fury *see* The Seekers
Larceny Lane *see* Blonde Crazy
The Last Days of Man on Earth *see* The Final Programme
The Last Frontier *see* Savage Wilderness
The Last Gangster *see* Roger Touhy, Gangster
The Last Warrior *see* Flap
Laurel and Hardy in Toyland *see* Babes in Toyland (1934)
The Law *see* Where the Hot Wind Blows
Law and Disorder *see* Spies of the Air
Lazy Bones *see* Hallelujah I'm a Bum
Lest We Forget *see* Hangmen Also Die
Let's Make Up *see* Lilacs in the Spring
Life After Dark *see* Girls in the Night
The Light Fantastic *see* Love Is Better Than Ever
The Light of Heart *see* Life Begins at Eight-Thirty
The Light Touch *see* Touch and Go
Lights Out *see* Bright Victory
Lisa *see* The Inspector
The Little Kidnappers *see* The Kidnappers
Live Today for Tomorrow *see* An Act of Murder (1964)
Lock Your Doors *see* The Ape Man
Lola *see* Twinky
The Lolly Madonna War *see* Lolly Madonna XXX
Long Ago Tomorrow *see* The Raging Moon
The Long Ride Home *see* A Time for Killing
Loss of Innocence *see* The Greengage Summer
The Lost Illusion *see* The Fallen Idol
Lost Treasure of the Amazon *see* Jivaro
The Loudest Whisper *see* The Children's Hour
Love and Sacrifice *see* America
The Love Ban *see* It's a 2′ 6″ Above the Ground World
The Love Cage *see* Joy House
Love Finds a Way *see* Alias French Gertie
Love in Las Vegas *see* Viva Las Vegas
Love Never Dies *see* Lilac Time
Lovely to Look At (1937) *see* Thin Ice
A Lovely Way to Go *see* A Lovely Way to Die
Lover Boy *see* Knave of Hearts
Lovers Must Learn *see* Rome Adventure
The Loves of a Dictator *see* The Dictator
The Loves of Isadora *see* Isadora
Lucky Mascot *see* The Brass Monkey
Lucky Nick Cain *see* I'll Get You for This
The Lullaby *see* The Sin of Madelon Claudet
Lulu *see* Pandora's Box

MacDonald of the Canadian Mounties *see* Pony Soldier
McGuire Go Home *see* The High Bright Sun
Mad Little Island *see* Rockets Galore
Mad Masquerade *see* Washington Masquerade
Madame Pimpernel *see* Paris Underground
Mademoiselle France *see* Reunion in France
Magic Night *see* Goodnight Vienna
The Magician *see* The Face
The Magnificent Showman *see* Circus World
Maiden Voyage *see* Bridal Suite
Mail Train *see* Inspector Hornleigh Goes To It
Malaga (1962) *see* Moment of Danger
A Man Alone *see* The Killers (1946)
Man and His Mate *see* One Million BC
The Man from Nevada *see* The Nevadan
A Man Called Sullivan *see* The Great John L.
The Man from the Folies Bergère *see* Folies Bergère
The Man I Killed *see* Broken Lullaby
Man in a Cocked Hat *see* Carlton-Browne of the FO
The Man in Possession *see* Personal Property
A Man Is Ten Feet Tall *see* Edge of the City
Man of Affairs *see* His Lordship
Man of Bronze *see* Jim Thorpe, All American
Man of Evil *see* Fanny by Gaslight
Man of the Hour *see* Colonel Effingham's Raid
The Man on America's Conscience *see* Tennessee Johnson
The Man Who Came Back *see* Swamp Water
The Man Who Lived Again *see* The Man Who Changed His Mind
The Man with a Hundred Faces *see* Crackerjack
Man with a Million *see* The Million Pound Note
The Man with the Deadly Lens *see* Wrong Is Right
The Man with the Green Carnation *see* The Trials of Oscar Wilde
The Man with Thirty Sons *see* The Magnificent Yankee

The Man with X-Ray Eyes *see* X—The Man with X-Ray Eyes
Manbait *see* The Last Page
Manhattan Madness *see* Adventure in Manhattan
Manhunt *see* From Hell to Texas
Maniacs on Wheels *see* Once a Jolly Swagman
March of the Wooden Soldiers *see* Babes in Toyland
Marching Along *see* Stars and Stripes Forever
Marco the Magnificent *see* The Fabulous Adventures of Marco Polo
Marie Walewska *see* Conquest
Married but Single *see* This Thing Called Love
Marshmallow Moon *see* Aaron Slick from Punkin Creek
The Marx Brothers at the Circus *see* At The Circus
Massacre Hill *see* Eureka Stockade
Master of Lassie *see* The Hills of Home
Master of the Islands *see* The Hawaiians
A Matter of Innocence *see* Pretty Polly
The Mean Machine *see* The Longest Yard
Medals *see* Seven Days Leave (1929)
Meet Whiplash Willie *see* The Fortune Cookie
Melody Inn *see* Riding High
Melody of Life *see* Symphony of Six Million
Melody of Youth *see* They Shall Have Music
The Memory Expert *see* The Man on the Flying Trapeze
Men Behind Bars *see* Duffy of San Quentin
Men of the Sea *see* Midshipman Easy
Men on Her Mind *see* The Girl from Tenth Avenue
The Message *see* Mohammed, Messenger of God
MGM's Big Parade of Comedy *see* The Big Parade of Comedy
Michael Strogoff *see* The Soldier and the Lady
Middle of Nowhere *see* The Webster Boy
Midnight Melody *see* Murder in the Music Hall
Military Policemen *see* Off Limits
Millionaire Merry Go Round *see* Kicking the Moon Around
A Minute to Pray, a Second to Die *see* Dead or Alive
A Miracle Can Happen *see* On Our Merry Way
The Miracle of Fatima *see* The Miracle of our Lady of Fatima
Missiles from Hell *see* The Battle of the V1
Missing Ten Days *see* Ten Days in Paris
Mr Arkadin *see* Confidential Report
Mr Ashton Was Indiscreet *see* The Senator Was Indiscreet
Mr Griggs Returns *see* The Cockeyed Miracle
Mr Hobo *see* The Guvnor
Mr Lord Says No *see* The Happy Family
Mr Mum *see* Mr Mom
Mr Potts Goes to Moscow *see* Top Secret
Mister V *see* Pimpernel Smith
Mrs Loring's Secret *see* The Imperfect Lady
The Model Murder Case *see* The Girl in the Headlines
A Modern Hero *see* Knute Rockne, All American
The Modern Miracle *see* The Story of Alexander Graham Bell
Money for Jam *see* It Ain't Hay
Monsieur Ripois et Son Nemesis *see* Knave of Hearts
Monster *see* Humanoids of the Deep
Monte Carlo or Bust *see* Those Daring Young Men in Their Jaunty Jalopies
Morituri: The Saboteur *see* The Saboteur, Code Name Morituri
Mother Joan of the Angels *see* The Devil and the Nun
Mother Knows Best *see* Mother Is a Freshman
Mother, Sir! *see* Navy Wife
Movietone Follies of 1929 *see* Fox Follies of 1929
The Moving Target *see* Harper
La Mura de Malapaga *see* Au dela des Grilles
Murder at the Baskervilles *see* Silver Blaze
Murder by Illusion *see* F/X
The Murder in Thornton Square *see* Gaslight (1944)
Murder Inc *see* The Enforcer
Murder Is News *see* The Delavine Affair
Murder My Sweet *see* Farewell My Lovely (1944)
Murder on Diamond Row *see* The Squeaker
Murder on Monday *see* Home at Seven
Murder Will Out *see* The Voice of Merrill
My Heart Goes Crazy *see* London Town
My Hero *see* A Southern Yankee
My Old Man's a Fireman *see* The Chief
My Son Alone *see* American Empire
My Son the Vampire *see* Mother Riley meets the Vampire
My Two Husbands *see* Too Many Husbands
My World Dies Screaming *see* Terror in the Haunted House
Mysterious Invader *see* The Astounding She-Monster
The Mystery of the Wentworth Castle *see* Doomed to Die

The Naked Night *see* Sawdust and Tinsel
Naked Under Leather *see* Girl on a Motorcycle
A Natural Born Salesman *see* Earthworm Tractors
Naughty Arlette *see* The Romantic Age
The Navy Steps Out *see* A Girl a Guy and a Gob
The Nelson Affair *see* Bequest to the Nation
The Nelson Touch *see* Corvette K 225
The Neptune Disaster *see* The Neptune Factor
Never Give an Inch *see* Sometimes a Great Notion
Never to Love *see* A Bill of Divorcement (1940)
The New Adventures of Don Juan *see* The Adventures of Don Juan
New Face in Hell *see* P.J.
Next Time We Live *see* Next Time We Love
Nick's Movie *see* Lightning Over Water
Night Ambush *see* Ill Met by Moonlight
Night Club Hostess *see* Unmarried
Night Creatures *see* Captain Clegg
Night Fighters *see* A Terrible Beauty
A Night in Cairo *see* The Barbarian
A Night in Havana *see* The Big Boodle
The Night Is Ending *see* Paris After Dark
The Night They Invented Striptease *see* The Night They Raided Minsky's
Night Train *see* Night Train to Munich
Nine Days a Queen *see* Tudor Rose
No Highway in the Sky *see* No Highway
No Sleep Till Dawn *see* Bombers B52
None But the Brave *see* For the Love of Mike (1960)
Notorious Gentleman *see* The Rake's Progress
A Novel Affair *see* The Passionate Stranger
Now Barabbas Was a Robber *see* Now Barabbas . . .

Obsessed *see* The Late Edwina Black
Off the Beaten Track *see* Behind the Eight Ball
Oh! For a Man! *see* Will Success Spoil Rock Hunter?
OK Connery *see* Operation Kid Brother
Old and New *see* The General Line
The Old Curiosity Shop *see* Mister Quilp
Old Dracula *see* Vampira
On My Way to the Crusades I Met a Girl Who . . . *see* The Chastity Belt
On the Carpet *see* Little Giant
On Wings of Song *see* Love Me Forever
Once Upon A Thursday *see* The Affairs Of Martha
One Against Seven *see* Counterattack
One Born Every Minute *see* The Flim Flam Man
One for the Book *see* The Voice of the Turtle
One Hour with You *see* The Marriage Circle
One Hundred Per cent Pure *see* The Girl from Missouri
One Man Mutiny *see* The Court Martial of Billy Mitchell
The One Piece Bathing Suit *see* Million Dollar Mermaid
One Woman's Story *see* The Passionate Friends
Only the Best *see* I Can Get It for You Wholesale
Operation Disaster *see* Morning Departure
Operation Snafu *see* On the Fiddle
Operation Undercover *see* Report to the Commissioner
Operation X *see* My Daughter Joy
Oriental Dream *see* Kismet (1944)
O'Rourke of the Royal Mounted *see* Saskatchewan
The Outcast *see* Man in the Saddle

Outpost in Malaya *see* The Planter's Wife
The Outsider (US 1948) *see* The Guinea Pig
Over the River *see* One More River

Palm Springs Affair *see* Palm Springs
Panic in the Parlor *see* Sailor Beware (1956)
Panther's Moon *see* Spy Hunt
Paradise Lagoon *see* The Admirable Crichton
Paratrooper *see* The Red Beret
Paris Express *see* The Man Who Watched Trains Go By
Paris Love Song *see* Paris in Spring
Passing Clouds *see* Spellbound (GB)
Passion *see* Madame Dubarry
The Passionate Sentry *see* Who Goes There?
Passport to Fame *see* The Whole Town's Talking
The Patient Vanishes *see* This Man Is Dangerous
Patterns of Power *see* Patterns
Patton—Lust for Glory *see* Patton
Paula *see* Framed
Pay the Devil *see* Man in the Shadow
Paying the Penalty *see* Underworld
Pearl of the South Pacific *see* South Sea Woman
Penalty of Fame *see* Okay America
A Perfect Weekend *see* The St Louis Kid
The Persecution and Assassination of Jean-Paul Marat . . . *see* The Marat/Sade
Personal Column *see* Lured
Peter Rabbit and the Tales of Beatrix Potter *see* Tales of Beatrix Potter
The Phantom Carriage *see* Thy Soul Shall Bear Witness
The Phantom Fiend *see* The Lodger
Phantom Ship *see* The Mystery of the Marie Celeste
The Phantom Strikes *see* The Gaunt Stranger
Pickup Alley *see* Interpol
Pier 13 (1932) *see* Me and My Gal
Pioneer Builders *see* The Conquerors
The Playboy *see* Kicking the Moon Around
The Playgirl and the War Minister *see* The Amorous Prawn
The Plot to Kill Roosevelt *see* Teheran
Pluck of the Irish *see* Great Guy
The Politic Flapper *see* The Patsy
Polly Fulton *see* BF's Daughter
Pookie *see* The Sterile Cuckoo
Portrait in Smoke *see* Wicked as They Come
Portrait of a Sinner *see* The Rough and the Smooth
Postmark for Danger *see* Portrait of Alison
Power *see* Jew Suss (1934)
Precinct 45: Los Angeles Police *see* The New Centurions
Prehistoric Women *see* Slave Girls
Present Arms *see* Leathernecking
Pride of Kentucky *see* The Story of Seabiscuit
Prison *see* The Devil's Wanton
The Private Wore Skirts *see* Never Wave at a WAC
Profession: Reporter *see* The Passenger
Project M 7 *see* The Net
The Promoter *see* The Card
The Public Eye *see* Follow Me
Pursuit of the Graf Spee *see* The Battle of the River Plate
Pussycat Alley *see* The World Ten Times Over

Q, The Winged Serpent *see* The Winged Serpent
Queen of Destiny *see* Sixty Glorious Years
The Queen of Spies *see* Joan of Ozark
The Queen's Husband *see* The Royal Bed

Race Gang *see* The Green Cockatoo
Raging Waters *see* Green Promise
The Raider *see* Western Approaches
The Raiders *see* Riders of Vengeance
The Randolph Family *see* Dear Octopus
The Rape of Malaya *see* A Town Like Alice
Rasputin the Mad Monk *see* Rasputin and the Empress
The Red Baron *see* Von Richthofen and Brown
Reign of Terror *see* The Black Book
The Remarkable Mr Kipps *see* Kipps
Remember That Face *see* The Mob
Rendezvous *see* Darling How Could You?
Reprieve *see* Convicts Four
Reputation *see* Lady with a Past
Reserved for Ladies *see* Service for Ladies
The Return of the Corsican Brothers *see* Bandits of Corsica
Rhodes *see* Rhodes of Africa
Rhythm Romance *see* Some Like it Hot
The Rich Full Life *see* Cynthia
Rich, Young and Deadly *see* Platinum High School
Richer than the Earth *see* The Whistle at Eaton Falls
Ring of Treason *see* Ring of Spies
Ring Up the Curtain *see* Broadway to Hollywood
The Rise of Helga *see* Susan Lenox, Her Fall and Rise
The Road to Frisco *see* They Drive by Night
The Road Warrior *see* Mad Max 2
Rocket to the Moon *see* Cat Women of the Moon
Romance and Riches *see* The Amazing Quest of Ernest Bliss
Romance for Three *see* Paradise for Three
Romance Is Sacred *see* The King and the Chorus Girl
Romeo in Pajamas *see* Parlor, Bedroom and Bath
Rommel Desert Fox *see* The Desert Fox
Rookies *see* Buck Privates
Rookies Come Home *see* Buck Privates Come Home
Rough Company *see* The Violent Men
Royal Flush *see* Two Guys from Milwaukee
Rudyard Kipling's Jungle Book *see* The Jungle Book
A Run on Gold *see* Midas Run
Runaway Daughter *see* Red Salute

The Sabre and the Arrow *see* Last of the Comanches
Sabrina Fair *see* Sabrina
The Sacred Flame *see* The Right to Live
Salt to the Devil *see* Give Us This Day
Sandy Takes a Bow *see* Unexpected Father
Saraband *see* Saraband for Dead Lovers
Satan's Skin *see* Blood on Stan's Claw
The Scarlet Buccaneer *see* Swashbuckler
Scotch on the Rocks *see* Laxdale Hall
Scream of Fear *see* Taste of Fear
The Sea Wall *see* This Angry Age
Sealed Lips *see* After Tonight
Season of Passion *see* Summer of the Seventeenth Doll
The Seaweed Children *see* Malachi's Cove
The Second Best Secret Agent in the Whole Wide World *see* Licensed to Kill
Secret Flight *see* School for Secrets
The Secret Four *see* The Four Just Men (1939)
The Secret Four *see* Kansas City Confidential
Secret Interlude *see* The View from Pompey's Head (1955)
Secret Interlude (1936) *see* Private Number
Secret Motive *see* The London Blackout Murders
Secrets of G32 *see* Fly By Night
The Seduction of Julia *see* Adorable Julia
See No Evil *see* Blind Terror
See You in Hell Darling *see* An American Dream
The Selling of America *see* Beer
Separate Beds *see* The Wheeler Dealers
Serenade *see* Broadway Serenade
Seven Different Ways *see* Quick Let's Get Married
The Shame of a Nation *see* Scarface
She Got Her Man *see* Maisie (Maisie Gets Her Man)
She Played with Fire *see* Fortune is a Woman
Sherlock Holmes (1939) *see* The Adventures of Sherlock Holmes
Sherlock Holmes and the Secret Code *see* Dressed to Kill (1946)
She's My Lovely *see* Get Hep to Love
Shoot First *see* Rough Shoot
The Shop on the High Street *see* The Shop on Main Street

Showtime *see* Gaiety George
Sidewalks of London *see* St Martin's Lane
Silent Night, Evil Night *see* Black Christmas
The Silent Stranger *see* Step Down to Terror
The Silent Voice (1932) *see* The Man Who Played God
The Silent Voice (1952) *see* Paula
The Singing Musketeer *see* The Three Musketeers (1939)
Sinners' Holiday *see* Christmas Eve
Six Inches Tall *see* Attack of the Puppet People
Slade *see* Jack Slade
Smiling Along *see* Keep Smiling
Smoke Jumpers *see* Red Skies of Montana
Smokey and the Bandit Ride Again *see* Smokey and the Bandit II
The Smugglers *see* The Man Within
Snow Job *see* The Ski Raiders
Snow White and the Three Clowns *see* Snow White and the Three Stooges
So Bright the Flame *see* The Girl in White
Somewhere in France *see* The Foreman Went to France
Son of Blob *see* Beware! The Blob
Sons of the Musketeers *see* At Sword's Point
Sons of the Sea *see* Atlantic Ferry
Sophie's Place *see* Crooks and Coronets
The Sound of Fury *see* Try and Get Me
The Soul Kiss *see* A Lady's Morals
Southwest to Sonora *see* The Appaloosa
The Spell of Amy Nugent *see* Spellbound (GB)
Spin of a Coin *see* The George Raft Story
Spinster *see* Two Loves
Spirit of the People *see* Abe Lincoln in Illinois
The Spiritualist *see* The Amazing Dr X
Spitfire *see* The First of the Few
Splitface *see* Dick Tracy
Sport of a Nation *see* The All-American
Spot *see* Dogpound Shuffle
Spy in the Pantry *see* Ten Days in Paris
The Spy in White *see* The Secret of Stamboul
Spy 13 *see* Operator 13
Spylarks *see* The Intelligence Men
Stairway to Heaven *see* A Matter of Life and Death
Stampeded *see* The Big Land
The Star Said No *see* Callaway Went Thataway
Stop Me before I Kill *see* The Full Treatment
Storm over Africa *see* Royal African Rifles
The Story of Dr Ehrlich's Magic Bullet *see* Dr Ehrlich's Magic Bullet
Stowaway Girl *see* Manuela
Stranded in Paris *see* Artists and Models Abroad
Strange Confession *see* The Imposter
Strange Conspiracy *see* The President Vanishes
Strange Incident *see* The Ox Bow Incident
Strange Interval *see* Strange Interlude
The Stranger *see* The Intruder (1961)
The Stranger in Between *see* Hunted
A Stranger Walked In *see* Love from a Stranger
The Strangler *see* East of Piccadilly
Strauss's Great Waltz *see* Waltzes from Vienna
The Streetfighter *see* Hard Times
Street Fleet *see* D. C. Cab
Strictly Confidential *see* Broadway Bill
Strictly for Pleasure *see* The Perfect Furlough
Striptease Lady *see* Lady of Burlesque
Stronger than Fear *see* Edge of Doom
Submarine Zone *see* Escape to Glory
Such Men Are Dangerous *see* The Racers
The Suicide Club *see* Trouble for Two
Suicide Squadron *see* Dangerous Moonlight
Summer Lightning *see* Scudda Hoo Scudda Hay
Summer Madness *see* Summertime
Surrounded by Women *see* Between Two Women
S.W.A.L.K. *see* Melody
Sweet Aloes *see* Give Me Your Heart
Sweet Revenge *see* Dandy the All-American Girl
Swing, Teacher, Swing *see* College Swing
The Swinging Maiden *see* The Iron Maiden
Swirl of Glory *see* Sugarfoot
Sword of Lancelot *see* Lancelot and Guinevere

Tainted Money *see* Show Them No Mercy
Take the Stage *see* Curtain Call at Cactus Creek
A Tale of Five Women *see* A Tale of Five Cities
Tammy *see* Tammy and the Bachelor Girl
Target for Scandal *see* Washington Story
Tartu *see* The Adventures of Tartu
Tears for Simon *see* Lost
Teenage Frankenstein *see* I Was a Teenage Frankenstein
Teenage Bad Girl *see* My Teenage Daughter
Ten Little Niggers *see* And Then There Were None (1945)
Terminus Station *see* Indiscretion of an American Wife
Terror House *see* The Night Has Eyes
Terror on a Train *see* Time Bomb
The Terrorists *see* Ransom (1975)
Texas Kid, Outlaw *see* The Kid from Texas
Texas to Tokyo *see* We've Never Been Licked
Thank You All Very Much *see* A Touch of Love
That Mad Mr Jones *see* The Fuller Brush Man
Theatre Royal *see* The Royal Family of Broadway
Their Secret Affair *see* Top Secret Affair
Thelma Jordon *see* The File on Thelma Jordon
These Are the Damned *see* The Damned (GB)
They All Died Laughing *see* A Jolly Bad Fellow
They Passed This Way *see* Four Faces West
They're Off *see* Straight, Place and Show
Thieves' Holiday *see* A Scandal in Paris
The Thing from Another World *see* The Thing (1951)
The Third Key *see* The Long Arm
This is Dynamite! *see* The Turning Point
This Is My Affair *see* I Can Get It for You Wholesale
This Man Reuter *see* A Dispatch from Reuter's
This Rebel Age *see* The Beat Generation
Three Cockeyed Sailors *see* Sailors Three
Three Men and a Girl *see* Golden Arrow (1949)
Three on a Weekend *see* Bank Holiday
Thunder Across the Pacific *see* The Wild Blue Yonder
Thunder Birds *see* Thunderbirds
Thunder in the East *see* The Battle
Thundercloud *see* Colt 45
Tiger in the Sky *see* The McConnell Story
Tiger Man *see* The Lady and the Monster
Tight Little Island *see* Whisky Galore
Time for Action *see* Tip on a Dead Jockey
A Time for Giving *see* Generation
Time Lost and Time Remembered *see* I Was Happy Here
To the Victor *see* Owd Bob
Toast of the Legion *see* Kiss Me Again (1931)
The Tomahawk and the Cross *see* Pillars of the Sky
Tonight's the Night *see* Happy Ever After (1954)
Too Many Chefs *see* Who Is Killing the Great Chefs of Europe?
Too Dangerous to Love *see* Perfect Strangers (1950)
Tops is the Limit *see* Anything Goes
Torment *see* Frenzy
Torpedoed *see* Our Fighting Navy
A Town Called Hell *see* A Town Called Bastard
Transatlantic Tunnel *see* The Tunnel
The Transvestite *see* Glen or Glenda
Treason *see* Guilty of Treason
The Tree of Liberty *see* The Howards of Virginia
Trelawny of the Wells *see* The Actress
Trial and Error *see* The Dock Brief
Triple Trouble *see* Kentucky Kernels
Troopship *see* Farewell Again
Tropicana *see* The Heat's On
Trouble in the Sky *see* Cone of Silence
The Trouble Shooter *see* The Man with the Gun

The Trunk Mystery *see* One New York Night
Try and Find It *see* Hi Diddle Diddle
Tunnel 28 *see* Escape from East Berlin
Twist of Fate *see* Beautiful Stranger
Two Men and a Girl *see* Honeymoon (US)
Two Minds for Murder *see* Someone Behind the Door
Two Texas Knights *see* Two Guys from Texas
Two Who Dared *see* A Woman Alone

U Boat 29 *see* The Spy in Black
The Ultimate Solution of Grace Quigley *see* Grace Quigley
Uncle Harry *see* The Strange Affair of Uncle Harry
Unconventional Linda *see* Holiday (1938)
Under the Clock *see* The Clock
Undercover Girl *see* Maisie (Undercover Maisie)
Undercovers Hero *see* Soft Beds, Hard Battles
Underworld Informers *see* The Informers
The Unholy Four *see* The Stranger Came Home
Unidentified Flying Oddball *see* The Spaceman and King Arthur
Unseen Heroes *see* The Battle of the V1
Up She Goes *see* Maisie (Up Goes Maisie)
USS Teakettle *see* You're in the Navy Now
Utopia *see* Robinson Crusoeland

Vacation from Marriage *see* Perfect Strangers (GB)
Valley of Fury *see* Chief Crazy Horse
Vaudeville *see* Variety
The Violent Hour *see* Dial 1119
Violent Streets *see* Thief
Viva Las Vegas! (1956) *see* Meet Me in Las Vegas
A Voice in the Night *see* Freedom Radio

Wages of Fear *see* Sorcerer
Walking Down Broadway *see* Hello Sister
War Correspondent *see* The Story of GI Joe
War Gods of the Deep *see* City under the Sea
The Warriors *see* The Dark Avenger
Waterfront Women *see* Waterfront
We Humans *see* Young America
Web of Evidence *see* Beyond This Place
Wedding Bells *see* Royal Wedding
Wedding Breakfast *see* The Catered Affair
Wee Geordie *see* Geordie
Welcome Home *see* SNAFU
We're in the Army Now *see* Pack Up Your Troubles
West of Montana *see* Mail Order Bride
What a Man *see* Never Give a Sucker an Even Break
What Lola Wants *see* Damn Yankees
What Shall It Profit *see* Hard Steel
When Boys Leave Home *see* Downhill
When New York Sleeps *see* Now I'll Tell
When the Door Opened *see* Escape (1940)
When Thief Meets Thief *see* Jump for Glory
Where the River Bends *see* Bend of the River
White Blood *see* The Planter's Wife
White Captive *see* White Savage
The White Man *see* The Squaw Man
White Savage *see* South of Tahiti
Whoever Slew Auntie Roo? *see* Who Slew Auntie Roo?
Why Bother to Knock *see* Don't Bother to Knock
The Wicked Wife *see* Grand National Night
The Wild Heart *see* Gone to Earth
Wild Seed *see* Fargo
Wildcat *see* The Great Scout and Cathouse Thursday
Will Tomorrow Ever Come? *see* That's My Man
A Window to the Sky *see* The Other Side of the Mountain
Wings and the Woman *see* They Flew Alone
The Winning Way *see* The All American
Witch Doctor *see* Men of Two Worlds
Within the Law *see* Paid
A Woman Alone *see* Sabotage
The Woman Between *see* The Woman I Love
A Woman Destroyed *see* Smash-Up, The Story of a Woman
A Woman in Her Thirties *see* Side Streets
The Woman in His House *see* The Animal Kingdom
Woman of Dolwyn *see* The Last Days of Dolwyn
Woman of Summer *see* The Stripper
A Woman of the World *see* Outcast Lady
Woman without a Face *see* Mister Buddwing
Wonderful to Be Young *see* The Young Ones
Wooden Soldiers *see* Babes in Toyland (1934)
The World and His Wife *see* State of the Union
The World in My Pocket *see* On Friday at Eleven
The Wrong Kind of Girl *see* Bus Stop
The Wyoming Kid *see* Cheyenne

X, Y and Zee *see* Zee and Co

A Yank in Dutch *see* The Wife Takes a Flyer
A Yank in London *see* I Live in Grosvenor Square
A Yankee in King Arthur's Court *see* A Connecticut Yankee in King Arthur's Court
Years without Days *see* Castle on the Hudson
The Yellow Passport *see* The Yellow Ticket
You Belong to My Heart *see* Mr Imperium
You Can't Do That to Me *see* Maisie (Maisie Goes to Reno)
You Can't Sleep Here *see* I Was a Male War Bride
You Can't Take Money *see* Internes Can't Take Money
You Don't Need Pajamas at Rosie's *see* The First Time
You Never Know *see* You Never Can Tell
Young and Eager *see* Claudelle Inglish
Young and Willing *see* The Wild and the Willing
The Young Invaders *see* Darby's Rangers
Young Man of Music *see* Young Man with a Horn
Young Scarface *see* Brighton Rock
Your Past is Showing *see* The Naked Truth
You're in the Army Now *see* O.H.M.S.

Zoltan, Hound of Dracula *see* Dracula's Dog
Zombies *see* Dawn of the Dead

Basil Rathbone and Nigel Bruce pursuing *The Hound of the Baskervilles.*

English-Language Titles of Foreign Films

The American Beauty *see* La Belle Américaine
The Apple Fell *see* Der Apfel ist ab
Are We All Murderers? *see* Nous Sommes Tous Les Assassins
An Artist with Ladies *see* Coiffeur pour Dames

The Baker's Wife *see* La Femme du Boulanger
The Ballad of Berlin *see* Berliner Ballade
The Battle of Austerlitz *see* Austerlitz
Bay of Angels *see* La Baie des Anges
Beyond the Gates *see* Au dela des Grilles
Birds of a Feather *see* La Cage aux Folles
Bizarre, Bizarre *see* Drôle de Drame
Bluebeard *see* Landru
Boudu Saved from Drowning *see* Boudu Sauvé des Eaux
Breathless *see* A Bout de Souffle
The Butcher *see* Le Boucher

A Cage of Nightingales *see* La Cage aux Rossignols
Carnival in Flanders *see* La Kermesse Héroïque
Children of Paradise *see* Les Enfants du Paradis
Clean Slate *see* Coup de Torchon
Cold Cuts *see* Buffet Froid
Comradeship *see* Kameradschaft
The Crazy Ray *see* Paris Qui Dort
The Cry *see* Il Grido

A Day in the Country *see* Une Partie de Campagne
Daybreak *see* Le Jour Se Lève
Days of Hope *see* Espoir
Devil in the Flesh *see* Le Diable au Corps
The Devil's Envoys *see* Les Visiteurs du Soir
Dirty Hands *see* Les Mains Sales
The Does *see* Les Biches
A Dog's Life *see* Mondo Cane
Doomed *see* Ikiru
The Double *see* Kagemusha

The Earrings of Madame de *see* Madame de
Ecstasy *see* Extase
Empire of the Passions *see* Ai No Corrida
Empire of the Senses *see* Ai No Corrida
Every Second Counts *see* Les Assassins du Dimanche

Father and Master *see* Padre Padrone
The Fiends *see* Les Diaboliques
Film without Title *see* Film ohne Titel
Forbidden Games *see* Les Jeux Interdits
Françoise Steps Out *see* Rue de l'Estrapade
Frontier *see* Aerograd

Gate of Lilacs *see* Porte des Lilas
Gates of Night *see* Les Portes de la Nuit
The Girl Friends *see* Le Amiche
Girls in Uniform *see* Maedchen in Uniform
God Needs Men *see* Dieu a Besoin des Hommes
The Goddess *see* Devi
Golden Marie *see* Casque d'Or
A Good Marriage *see* Le Beau Mariage

Hands off the Loot *see* Touchez pas au Grisbi
Handsome Antonio *see* Il Bell'Antonio
Hanged Man's Farm *see* La Ferme du Pendu
Heroism *see* Eroica
The Hole *see* Onibaba
Holiday for Henrietta *see* La Fête à Henriette
Honour Among Thieves *see* Touchez pas au Grisbi
The Human Beast *see* La Bête Humaine
Hungry for Love *see* Adua e le Compagne

I Have a New Master *see* L'Ecole Buissonière
In the Woods *see* Rashomon
The Inquisitor *see* Garde a Vue
Isle of Sinners *see* Dieu a Besoin des Hommes
It Happened at the Inn *see* Goupi Mains Rouges
It's in the Bag *see* L'Affaire est dans le Sac

Judas Was a Woman *see* La Bête Humaine

Keep an Eye on Amelia *see* Occupe-Toi d'Amélie

Life Dances on *see* Un Carnet de Bal
Living *see* Ikiru
The Long Absence *see* Une Aussi Longue Absence
Love Is My Profession *see* En Cas de Malheur
Love Story *see* Une Histoire d'Amour
The Lovers *see* Les Amants
The Lovers of Verona *see* Les Amants de Vérone
The Lower Depths *see* Les Bas-fonds

Madame *see* Madame Sans-Gène (1962)
Man's Hope *see* Espoir
Moscow Distrusts Tears *see* Moskva Slezam Ne Verit
The Murderer Lives at 21 *see* L'Assassin habite au 21
My Night at Maud's *see* Ma Nuit chez Maud

Nights of Cabiria *see* Cabiria

One Woman or Two *see* Une Femme ou Deux
The Outsiders *see* Bande à Part

The Phantom Baron *see* Le Baron Fantôme
Port of Shadows *see* Quai des Brumes

The Raven *see* Le Corbeau
The Road *see* La Strada
The Road to Hope *see* Il Cammino della Speranza
The Rules of the Game *see* La Règle du Jeu

The Saga of Anatahan *see* Anatahan
Savage Princess *see* Aan
Scarlet and Black *see* Le Rouge et le Noir
The Secret Game *see* Les Jeux Interdits
Secret Meeting *see* Marie Octobre
Shadow Warrior *see* Kagemusha
The Spies *see* Les Espions
Spivs *see* I Vitelloni
Stormy Waters *see* Remorques

The Story of a Cheat *see* Le Roman d'un Tricheur
The Strange Adventure of David Gray *see* Vampyr
The Strange Ones *see* Les Enfants Terribles
Such a Pretty Little Beach *see* Une Si Jolie Petite Plage
Summer Manoeuvres *see* Les Grandes Manoeuvres
Sunday in August *see* Domenico d'Agosto
The Sweet Life *see* La Dolce Vita
The Swindlers *see* Il Bidone
Swords of Blood *see* Cartouche

The Testament of Orpheus *see* Le Testament d'Orphée
These Things Happen *see* Les Choses de la Vie
They Loved Life *see* Kanal
The Things of Life *see* Les Choses de la Vie
This Strange Passion *see* El
The Threepenny Opera *see* Die Dreigroschenoper
A Time to Live and a Time to Die *see* Le Feu Follet
Tomorrow Is Too Late *see* Domani e Troppo Tardi
Torments *see* El
The Tragic Pursuit *see* Caccia Tragica
Two Pennyworth of Hope *see* Due Soldi de Speranza

The Umbrellas of Cherbourg *see* Les Parapluies de Cherbourg
The Unfaithful Wife *see* La Femme Infidèle
The Unvanquished *see* Aparajito

Volcano *see* Les Rendezvous du Diable

The Wanton *see* Manèges
The Wanton Countess *see* Senso
The War Is Over *see* La Guerre Est Finie
Web of Passion *see* À Double Tour
The Well-Digger's Daughter *see* La Fille du Puisatier
What a Chassis *see* La Belle Américaine
The Wild Child *see* L'Enfant Sauvage
Wild Stallion *see* Crin Blanc
Will o' the Wisp *see* Le Feu Follet
A Woman Disappeared, Portrait of a Woman *see* Une Femme Disparait
The Woman from Nowhere *see* La Femme de Nulle Part
Woman Hunt *see* Au Royaume des Cieux
Woman of Antwerp *see* Dédée d'Anvers

Yesterday Girl *see* Abschied von Gestern
The Young and the Damned *see* Los Olvidados

Original Titles of Foreign-Language Films Listed in English

Aimez-Vous les Femmes? *see* Do You Like Women?
Akahige *see* Redbeard
Akasen Chitai *see* Street of Shame
Alice au Pays de Merveilles *see* Alice in Wonderland
Alskande Par *see* Loving Couples
Les Amants du Tage *see* The Lovers of Lisbon
Un Amour de Swann *see* Swann in Love
Les Amours de la Reine Elisabeth *see* Queen Elizabeth
El Angel Exterminador *see* The Exterminating Angel
Ansiktet *see* The Face
L'Argent de Poche *see* Small Change
Ascenseur pour l'Echafaud *see* Lift to the Scaffold
Attilo Flagello di Dio *see* Attila the Hun
Au Hasard, Balthazar *see* Balthazar
L'Auberge Rouge *see* The Red Inn
Un Autre Homme, une Autre Chance *see* Another Man, Another Chance
L'Aveu *see* The Confession

Babette S'en Va-t-en Guerre *see* Babette Goes to War
Baisers Volés *see* Stolen Kisses
Ballada o Soldate *see* Ballad of a Soldier
Banditi a Orgoloso *see* Bandits of Orgoloso
Baron Prasil *see* Baron Münchhausen
La Battaglia di Algeri *see* The Battle of Algiers
Berlin, die Symphonie einer Grosstadt *see* Berlin, Symphony of a Great City
Betrogen bis zum Jungsten Tag *see* Duped Till Doomsday
Bezhin Lug *see* Bezhin Meadow
Bij de Beesten Af *see* Ape and Super Ape
Les Bijoutiers du Clair de Lune *see* Heaven Fell That Night
Biruma no Tategoto *see* The Burmese Harp
Die Blechtrommel *see* The Tin Drum
Die Bleierne Zeit *see* The German Sisters
Den Blodiga Tiden *see* Mein Kampf
La Bonne Année *see* Happy New Year
Das Boot *see* The Boat
Bronenosets Potemkin *see* Battleship Potemkin
El Bruto *see* The Brute
Die Büchse der Pandora *see* Pandora's Box
Il Buono, il Bruto, il Cattivo *see* The Good, the Bad and the Ugly

Cadaveri Eccellenti *see* Illustrious Corpses
La Caida *see* The Fall
O'Cangaceiro *see* The Bandit
Le Caporal Epinglé *see* The Vanishing Corporal
Les Carnets de Major Thompson *see* The Diary of Major Thompson
Le Carrosse d'Or *see* The Golden Coach
La Casa del Angel *see* The House of the Angel
La Casse *see* The Burglars
Celui Qui Doit Mourir *see* He Who Must Die
Un Chapeau de Paille d'Italie *see* An Italian Straw Hat
Le Charme Discret de la Bourgeoisie *see* The Discreet Charm of the Bourgeoisie
Chelovek s Kinoapparatom *see* The Man with the Movie Camera
La Ciociara *see* Two Women
La Città delle Donne *see* City of Women
Compartiment Tueurs *see* The Sleeping Car Murders
Il Conformista *see* The Conformist
Cybèle ou les Dimanches de Ville d'Avray *see* Sundays and Cybèle

Dama s Sobachkoi *see* The Lady with the Little Dog
Déjeuner sur l'Herbe *see* Lunch on the Grass
Les Demoiselles de Rochefort *see* The Young Girls of Rochefort
La Dentellière *see* The Lacemaker
Il Deserto Rosso *see* The Red Desert
Destinées *see* Love, Soldiers and Women
Le Diable, Probablement *see* The Devil, Probably
La Diga sul Pacifico *see* This Angry Age
Un Dimanche à la Campagne *see* Sunday in the Country
Ditte Menneskebarn *see* Ditte, Child of Man
Divorzio all'Italiana *see* Divorce Italian Style
En Djungelsaga *see* The Flute and the Arrow
Doktor Mabuse, der Spieler *see* Doctor Mabuse
Don Camillo e l'Onorevolo Peppone *see* Don Camillo's Last Round
Dorp aan de Rivier *see* Doctor in the Village
Dyrygent *see* The Conductor

L'Eclisse *see* The Eclipse
E la Nave Va *see* And the Ship Sails On
En Compagnie de Max Linder *see* Laugh with Max Linder
Eine Reise ins Licht *see* Despair
Ensayo de un Crimen *see* The Criminal Life of Archibaldo de la Cruz
Ercole e la Regina di Lidia *see* Hercules Unchained
Es Geschah am 20 Juli *see* Jackboot Mutiny
L'Espion *see* The Defector
L'Eté Meurtrier *see* One Deadly Summer
Et Dieu Créa la Femme *see* And God Created Woman
Et Mourir de Plaisir *see* Blood and Roses
L'Eternel Retour *see* Love Eternal

Die Fälschung *see* Circle of Deceit
Fängelse *see* The Devil's Wanton
Le Fatiche di Ercole *see* Hercules
Faustrecht der Freiheit *see* Fox
La Femme de l'Aviateur *see* The Aviator's Wife
Une Femme Mariée *see* A Married Woman
La Fin du Monde *see* End of the World
Frau im Mond *see* The Woman in the Moon
Die Freudlose Gasse *see* Joyless Street
Le Fruit Défendu *see* Forbidden Fruit

Il Gattopardo *see* The Leopard
Giulietta degli Spiriti *see* Juliet of the Spirits
Gosta Berlings Saga *see* The Atonement of Gosta Berling
Götterdämmerung *see* The Damned (1969)
La Grande Vadrouille *see* Don't Look Now . . . We're Being Shot At!
Gruppo di Famiglia in un Interno *see* Conversation Piece
Gycklarnas Afton *see* Sawdust and Tinsel

Hadaka no Shima *see* The Island
Haxan *see* Witchcraft through the Ages
Les Héros Sont Fatigués *see* The Heroes Are Tired
Hets *see* Frenzy
L'Homme de Rio *see* That Man from Rio
Un Homme et une Femme *see* A Man and a Woman
Hori, Ma Panenko *see* The Firemen's Ball
L'Horloger de St Paul *see* The Watchmaker of St Paul
Las Hurdes *see* Land without Bread

Im Lauf der Zeit *see* Kings of the Road
Ivan Groznyi *see* Ivan the Terrible

Jigokumon *see* Gate of Hell
Journal d'un Curé de Campagne *see* The Diary of a Country Priest
Le Journal d'une Femme de Chambre *see* The Diary of a Chambermaid
Jujiro *see* Crossroads
Jungfraukällan *see* The Virgin Spring

Kakushi Toride No San-Akunin *see* The Hidden Fortress
Käre John *see* Dear John
Der Kongress Tanzt *see* Congress Dances
Konyets Sankt-Peterburga *see* The End of St Petersburg
To Koritsi me ta Mavra *see* The Girl in Black
Korkalen *see* Thy Soul Shall Bear Witness
Kumonosu-Jo *see* Throne of Blood
Kvinnodrom *see* Journey into Autumn

Ladri di Biciclette *see* Bicycle Thieves
Lasky Jedne Plavovlasky *see* Loves of a Blonde
Lenin v Octiabrye *see* Lenin in October
Les Favoris de la Lune *see* Favourites of the Moon
Letyat Zhuravli *see* The Cranes are Flying
Der Letzte Mann *see* The Last Laugh
Le Locataire *see* The Tenant
La Loi *see* Where the Hot Wind Blows
La Lumière d'en Face *see* The Light across the Street
Luna de Miel *see* Honeymoon

Das Mädchen Rosemarie *see* The Girl Rosemarie
Il Maestro di Don Giovanni *see* Crossed Swords
Mahanagar *see* The Big City (1963)
Le Mani sulla Città *see* Hands over the City
Mannen pa Taket *see* The Man on the Roof
Mano della Straniero *see* The Stranger's Hand
La Mariée Etait en Noir *see* The Bride Wore Black
Mat *see* Mother
Matka Joanna od Aniolow *see* The Devil and the Nun
Les Maudits *see* The Damned
Menschen am Sonntag *see* People on Sunday
Mon Oncle Américain *see* My American Uncle
Die Mörder Sind Unter Uns *see* The Murderers Are Among Us
Morte a Venezia *see* Death in Venice
La Motocyclette *see* Girl on a Motorcycle
Le Mouton a Cinq Pattes *see* The Sheep Has Five Legs
Der Müde Tod *see* Destiny
Muerte de un Ciclista *see* Death of a Cyclist
Muriel, ou le Temps d'un Retour *see* Muriel
Musik I Mörker *see* Night Is My Future

Nattlek *see* Night Games
Nattvardsgasterna *see* Winter Light
Nobi *see* Fires on the Plain
La Noia *see* The Empty Canvas
Nosferatu, Phantom der Nacht *see* Nosferatu The Vampyre
Le Notti di Cabiria *see* Cabiria
Novecento *see* 1900
Novyi Vavilon *see* The New Babylon
Noz w Wodzie *see* Knife in the Water
La Nuit Américaine *see* Day for Night
Nuit et Brouillard *see* Night and Fog

Oberst Redl *see* Colonel Redl
Obchod na Korze *see* The Shop on Main Street
Ad Ogni Costo *see* Grand Slam
Orfeu Negro *see* Black Orpheus
L'Oro di Napoli *see* Gold of Naples
Ostatni Etap *see* The Last Stage
Otto e Mezzo *see* Eight and a Half

Pánico en el Transiberiano *see* Horror Express
Pasazerka *see* Passenger
Pasqualino Settebellezze *see* Seven Beauties
Le Passage du Rhin *see* The Crossing of the Rhine
La Peau Douce *see* Silken Skin
Piatka z Ulicy Barskiej *see* Five Boys from Barska Street
Pokolenie *see* Generation
Popiol y Diament *see* Ashes and Diamonds
Il Posto *see* The Job
Pote tin Kyriaki *see* Never on Sunday
Potomok Chingis-Khana *see* Storm over Asia
Prividenie, Kotoroe ne Vozvrashchaetsya *see* The Ghost That Never Returns
Le Procès *see* The Trial
I Pugni in Tasca *see* Fists in the Pocket
Puss och Kram *see* Hugs and Kisses

Les Quatre Cents Coups *see* The Four Hundred Blows
Quattro Passi fra le Nuvole *see* Four Steps in the Clouds

Regain *see* Harvest
La Resa dei Conti *see* The Big Gundown
Le Retour de Martin Guerre *see* The Return of Martin Guerre
Le Rideau Cramoisi *see* The Crimson Curtain
Riso Amaro *see* Bitter Rice
La Rivière du Hibou *see* Incident at Owl Creek
Le Roi de Coeur *see* King of Hearts
Roma, Città Aperta *see* Open City
Ruba al Prossimo Tua *see* A Fine Pair

Saiyu-ki *see* Alakazam the Great
Le Salaire de la Peur *see* The Wages of Fear
Le Sang d'un Poète *see* The Blood of a Poet
Le Scandale *see* The Champagne Murders
Sciuscià *see* Shoeshine
Seemabadha *see* Company Ltd
Sei Donne per l'Assassino *see* Blood and Black Lace
Seppuku *see* Hara Kiri
Shichi-nin no Samurai *see* Seven Samurai
Shinjuku Dorobo Nikki *see* Diary of a Shinjuku Thief
Si Tùtte le Donne del Mondo *see* Kiss the Girls and Make Them Cry
Signore e Signori *see* The Birds, the Bees and the Italians
Un Singe en Hiver *see* A Monkey in Winter
La Sirène du Mississippi *see* The Mississippi Mermaid
Det Sjunde Inseglet *see* The Seventh Seal
Smultronstället *see* Wild Strawberries
Solange Du da bist *see* As Long as You're Near Me
I Soliti Ignoti *see* Persons Unknown
Sommarlek *see* Summer Interlude
Sommarnattens Leende *see* Smiles of a Summer Night
Les Sorcières de Salem *see* The Witches of Salem
Sorok Pervyi *see* The Forty First
Le Soupirant *see* The Suitor
La Spina Dorsale del Diavolo *see* The Deserter
Staroye i Novoye *see* The General Line
Sudba Cheloveka *see* Destiny of a Man
Suna no Onna *see* Woman of the Dunes
Il Suo Modo di Fari *see* The Girl Who Couldn't Say No
Sylvie et la Fantôme *see* Sylvia and the Ghost

Tagebuch einer Verliebten *see* The Diary of a Married Woman
Tagebuch einer Verlorenen *see* Diary of a Lost Girl
Taiheiyo Hitoribochi *see* Alone on the Pacific
Tendre Poulet *see* Dear Inspector

Michael Caine in sombre mood.

Explanatory Notes

Please stop here and read!

Alternative titles

Three lists are given at the front of the book, immediately preceding this section. Readers are recommended to consult them before wading in exasperation through the book for films which are in fact listed under apparently unfamiliar titles, i.e. those used in their country of origin at the time of release. Any subsequently-used titles (unless they are at least as well known as the original) will be found only in the alternative title lists. British readers in particular should consult these lists with care: *Lady Hamilton*, for instance, is to be found in the main section under 'T'; for *That Hamilton Woman*, the correct and original American title of this film which was made in America. Please note also that in all cases the complete title is given as billed, though the definite and indefinite articles are not counted in the alphabetical arrangement. The spelling of the country of origin is invariably used, e.g. *My Favorite Blonde* and not *My Favourite Blonde*.

Alphabetical order

This too has caused occasional problems. Some books in formulating the sequence take the complete title into account, as though there were no gaps between words. We have always persevered with the old-fashioned word-at-a-time arrangement: for instance, all the titles starting with *In*, including *In Which We Serve*, are used up before one goes on to titles beginning *Incredible*, *Inspector*, *Intolerance*. Hyphenated or apostrophized words are counted as one word. Compressions such as *Dr* and *St* are treated as though they had been spelled out, as *Doctor* and *Saint*. *Mac* and *Mc* are regarded as interchangeable under *Mac*.

The remaining explanatory notes are only slightly changed from previous editions and are set out below in the order in which they will be encountered in the fuller entry format. (There are also compressed entries for the less outstanding films.)

Publicity tags These were used in the original promotion for the film and, in the manner of trailers, precede the entry.

Ratings It would be absurd to classify films selected from a period of eighty years as to which are the best or the worst. Techniques improve, standards change, and personal preferences have to be accounted for. I have tried, however, to give credit for what seemed excellent or innovative at the time, even though it may have been overtaken by imitators; I have tried to judge each film by its own standards (how could one sensibly compare *Frankenstein Meets the Wolf Man* with *Gone with the Wind*?), and I have rescrutinized it now to see what historical or artistic interest it retains. Mere entertainment value has not been derided, nor have films which may seem naive but give an accurate picture of the standards of their own time. To sum up in one word, the ratings indicate how much *interest* a film is thought to have for the modern viewer, whether he be a student or a reasonably alert seeker of entertainment.

Four stars, then, indicate a film outstanding in many ways, a milestone in cinema history, remarkable for acting, direction, writing, photography or some other aspect of technique. Three stars indicate a very high standard of professional excellence or high historical interest: or if you like, three strong reasons for admiring it. Two stars indicate a good level of competence and a generally entertaining film. One star draws attention to minor points of merit, usually in a film not very satisfactory as a whole; it could be a failed giant or a second feature with a few interesting ideas among the dross. No stars at all indicates a totally routine production or worse; such films may be watchable but are at least equally missable.

It will be seen that my judgements are fairly harsh, but I hope they are consistent. For further elucidation of my personal prejudices see the essay, 'The Decline and Fall of the Movie', at the end of the book.

Country of origin First item on second line.

Year of release Comes after country of origin, and is intended to be the year in which the film was first shown. If it was made earlier and held back, I have tried to indicate the fact. Dating is sometimes an onerous task, and the result debatable; please be sympathetic.

Running time In minutes, signified by 'm'. So far as possible this is the original release time. Very many films are cut when they cross the water, sometimes by twenty minutes or more, but I have not tried to indicate this, as when the film appears on television a new print is usually taken from the original negative (but may be cut again). Remember, however, that an engineering function of British television results in an imperceptible speeding-up of projection and a consequent loss of one minute in every twenty-five. A hundred-minute film, therefore, will run only ninety-six minutes on the box, so check your facts before complaining.

Black and white or colour I have given the colour process where known (it is not always stated these days) and have coined the single word Eastmancolor to equate with Technicolor.

Other notable points are given at the end of the second line: whether the film is in some special process (3-D, Vistavision, etc). See separate essay on screen shape.

Production credit The central credit on the third line is the production company. To the left, however, comes the distributor if different from the production company, in brackets if his rights subsequently lapsed. To the right is the actual producer, except for early thirties films in which he was seldom credited. He is also in brackets unless he has a stake in the production, in which case he follows an oblique.

Alternative title This is given on a separate line, usually with a note of the country in which it was used. If no such fine line exists, I have used the formula *aka* (also known as). Indexes of alternative titles will be found at the beginning of the book, and should be consulted if any film for which the reader is looking cannot at first be found.

Synopsis Self-explanatory, with brevity and accuracy the keynote.

Assessment Again very brief, so flippancy will inevitably be suspected. Not so, but for more considered judgements look for books which have more space.

Writer credit (*w*) It seems to me that this is, at least sometimes, more important than the director credit, and as script in any case precedes direction, it comes first in this book. The author of the screenplay is always given; if this derives from a novel, play or story, this is given next, together with the original author.

Director credit *d.*

Photography credit *ph.*

Music credit (*m*) This means the composer of the background music score. Sometimes there is only a music director (*md*) who orchestrates library or classical music.

Other credits Production designer (*pd*), music and lyrics (*m / ly*), art director (*ad*), special effects (*sp*), editor (*ed*), etc, are given when they seem important and can be found. In some cases it has not been possible to track down all the credits one would wish.

Cast The principal actors are given, where possible, roughly in order of importance. I have stopped before the bit parts, and given fewer names in the case of foreign films, where the actors tend to be less well known.

Italics These denote a contribution of a particularly high standard. Arguments are expected and additions welcomed.

Comments from critics To approximately half the items I have appended brief quotes from well-known professional critics, sometimes because they wittily confirm my own findings, and sometimes because they disagree with me entirely. I hope these will be enjoyable and illuminating; the absence of a quote casts no reflection whatever on the film, only on my own ability as a researcher.

Additional notes Any other significant remarks about the film are given after the symbol †.

Academy Awards Awards (AA) and also nominations (AAN) are listed for all principal categories, including acting, direction, photography, music score, songs and best picture.

Video References to video availability have been omitted from this edition because the shelf life of a video is short and therefore video information can quickly become out of date and mislead the reader.

The Film Guide
A–Z

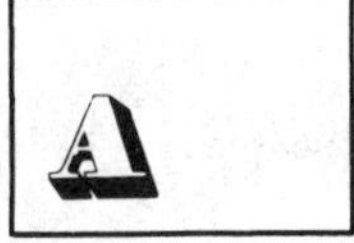

À Bout de Souffle**
France 1959 90m bw
SNC (Georges de Beauregard)
aka: *Breathless*

A young car thief kills a policeman and goes on the run with his American girl friend.
Casual, influential, New Wave reminiscence of both *Quai des Brumes* and innumerable American gangster thrillers. (The film is dedicated to Monogram.)

w François Truffaut d Jean-Luc Godard
ph Raoul Coutard *m* Martial Solal

Jean-Paul Belmondo, Jean Seberg, Daniel Boulanger, Jean-Pierre Melville

'A film all dressed up for rebellion but with no real tangible territory on which to stand and fight.'—*Peter John Dyer*

† See also *Breathless*, American remake.

À Double Tour
France / Italy 1959 110m Eastmancolor
Paris / Panitalia (Robert and Raymond Hakim)
aka: *Web of Passion*

A wealthy wine grower has trouble with his wife, his children, his best friend, and his mistress across the way, who is murdered.
Talented but irritating mixture of Hitchcock and *Les Parents Terribles*; rather an undergraduatish romp.

w Paul Gégauff, *novel* La Clé de la Rue Saint-Nicolas *d* Claude Chabrol *ph* Henri Decaë *m* Paul Misraki

Jacques Dacqmine, Madeleine Robinson, Jean-Paul Belmondo, Bernadette Lafont, Antonella Lualdi, André Jocelyn

A-Haunting We Will Go*
US 1942 68m bw
TCF (Sol M. Wurtzel)

Gangsters dupe Laurel and Hardy into escorting a coffin, which is accidentally switched with one used in a magic act.
Nothing whatever to do with haunting: a poor comedy with no typical material for the stars, but interesting as a record of the touring show of Dante the Magician.

w Lou Breslow *d* Alfred Werker *ph* Glen MacWilliams *m* Glen MacWilliams

Stan Laurel, Oliver Hardy, *Dante*, Sheila Ryan, John Shelton, Elisha Cook Jnr

'The comedians' lack of enthusiasm for their material is rather evident.'—*William K. Everson, 1967*

À Nous la Liberté****
France 1931 95m bw
Tobis
US title: *Freedom for Us*

A factory owner is blackmailed about his past, and helped by an old prison friend, with whom he finally takes to the road.
Operetta-style satirical comedy with leftish attitudes and several famous sequences later borrowed by Chaplin for *Modern Times*. In terms of sheer film flair, a revelation, though the plot has its tedious turns.

wd René Clair ph Georges Périnal m Georges Auric pd Lazare Meerson

Raymond Cordy, Henri Marchand, Rolla France, Paul Olivier

'Different from the usual run . . . easily understandable even to those who do not know French.'—*Variety*

'He demonstrates that sound pictures can be as fluid as silents were, and the picture is rightly considered a classic.'—*Pauline Kael, 1970s*

'I was close to the extreme left . . . I wanted to attack the Machine, which led men into starvation instead of adding to their happiness.'—*René Clair*

À Propos de Nice*
France 1930 30m bw

A satirical documentary on the millionaire's paradise of the French Riviera.
Cheaply made and rather naive-looking after fifty years, this amusingly belligerent lampoon still has its striking moments.

wd Jean Vigo ph Boris Kaufman

Aan*
India 1952 190m approx (English version 130m) Technicolor
All India Film Corporation / Mehboob Productions
aka: *Savage Princess*

A usurping young prince and his sister are tamed by an athletic peasant and his girl friend.
One of the few examples to reach the west of Indian costume melodrama with music, spectacle and swashbuckling. Distinctly intriguing, if overpowering.

w Chaudary, Ali Raza *d* Mehboob
ph Faredoon A. Irani *m* Naushad Dilip Kumar, Nimmi, Premnath, Nadira

'Disarmingly enthusiastic . . . exotic and yet charmingly naive.'—*MFB*

Aaron Slick from Punkin Crick*
US 1952 95m Technicolor
Paramount (William Perlberg, George Seaton)
GB title: *Marshmallow Moon*

A small-town girl is tricked into selling her farm and moving to the city, but eventually marries the simple farmer who rescues her.
Homespun entertainment based on a staple success of the American provincial theatre, with pleasant songs added.

wd Claude Binyon, *play* Walter Benjamin Hare *ph* Charles B. Lang Jnr *m / ly* Jay Livingston, Ray Evans *ch* Charles O'Curran

Alan Young, Dinah Shore, Robert Merrill, Adele Jergens, Minerva Urecal

Abandon Ship: see Seven Waves Away

Abandoned
US 1949 79m bw

Reporter breaks baby-farming racket.
Competent action thriller for double billing. Dennis O'Keefe, Gale Storm, Raymond Burr (and young Jeff Chandler). Written by Irwin Gielgud; directed by Joseph Newman; for Universal-International.

'They're too wild for one world!'
Abbott and Costello Go to Mars
US 1953 76m bw
U-I (Howard Christie)

Two incompetents accidentally launch a space ship and land first in Louisiana, then on Venus.
Dismal knockabout, badly made.

w John Grant, D. D. Beauchamp *d* Charles Lamont
ph Clifford Stine *m* Joseph Gershenson

Bud Abbott, Lou Costello, Mari Blanchard, Robert Paige, Martha Hyer

Abbott and Costello in Hollywood*
US 1945 85m bw
MGM (Martin Gosch)

Two agents have hectic adventures in a film studio.
Tolerable star romp on one of their biggest budgets, climaxing in a roller coaster ride.

w Nat Perrin, Lou Breslow *d* S. Sylvan Simon *ph* Charles Schoenbaum *m* George Bassman

Bud Abbott, Lou Costello, Francis Rafferty, Warner Anderson, Robert Z. Leonard

Abbott and Costello in the Foreign Legion
US 1950 80m bw
U-I (Robert Arthur)

Incompetent legionnaires become heroes to the fury of their sergeant.

Dull star vehicle on ramshackle sets, with no memorable routines.

w John Grant, Leonard Stern, Martin Ragaway *d* Charles Lamont *ph* George Robinson *m* Joseph Gershenson

Bud Abbott, Lou Costello, Patricia Medina, Walter Slezak, Douglass Dumbrille

Abbott and Costello Lost in Alaska

US 1952 76m bw
U-I (Howard Christie)

Two San Francisco firemen take a melancholy prospector back to Alaska to find a gold mine.
Sub-standard comedy vehicle with poor production.

w Martin Ragaway, Leonard Stern *d* Jean Yarbrough
ph George Robinson *m* Joseph Gershenson

Bud Abbott, Lou Costello, *Tom Ewell*, Mitzi Green, Bruce Cabot

Abbott and Costello Meet Captain Kidd*

US 1952 70m Supercinecolor
Warner / Woodley (Alex Gottlieb)

Two servants have a treasure map, and a fearsome pirate wants it.
Crude knockabout: the stars are way below their best, and a famous actor is embarrassed.

w Howard Dimsdale, John Grant *d* Charles Lamont
ph Stanley Cortez *m* Raoul Kraushaar

Bud Abbott, Lou Costello, Charles Laughton, Hillary Brooke, Leif Erickson

Abbott and Costello Meet Dr Jekyll and Mr Hyde*

US 1953 77m bw
U-I (Howard Christie)

In Victorian London, two rookie policemen catch a monster.
Quite a lively spoof with some well-paced comedy sequences.

w John Grant, Lee Loeb *d* Charles Lamont
ph George Robinson *m* Hans Salter

Bud Abbott, Lou Costello, Boris Karloff, Reginald Denny, Craig Stevens, Helen Westcott, John Dierkes

'Gracious Boris Karloff is superior to his surroundings.'—*MFB*. (Though it is doubtful whether he ever got behind the Hyde make-up.)

† In Britain, the film was given an 'X' certificate, though it later played on children's television.

eepers! the creepers are after somebody—and guess who! More howls than you can shake a shiver at!!!'

Abbott and Costello Meet Frankenstein**

US 1948 83m bw
U-I (Robert Arthur)
GB title: *Abbott and Costello Meet the Ghosts*

Two railway porters deliver crates containing the Frankenstein monster, Dracula, and the Wolf Man.
Fairly lively spoof which put an end to Universal's monsters for a while. Good typical sequences for the stars, a few thrills, and some good lines. Dracula to Costello, lovingly: 'What we need is young blood . . . and brains . . .'

w Robert Lees, Frederic I. Rinaldo, John Grant *d* Charles Barton *ph* Charles van Enger *m* Frank Skinner

Bud Abbott, Lou Costello, Bela Lugosi, Lon Chaney Jnr, Glenn Strange, Lenore Aubert, Jane Randolph

WOLF MAN: 'You don't understand. Every night when the moon is full, I turn into a wolf.'

COSTELLO: 'You and fifty million other guys!'

† Probably the Abbott and Costello film which survives best.

Abbott and Costello Meet the Invisible Man*

US 1951 82m bw
U-I (Howard Christie)

A boxer accused of murder makes himself invisible while two detectives clear him.
Quite a bright comedy with good trick effects.

w Robert Lees, Frederic I. Rinaldo, John Grant *d* Charles Lamont *ph* George Robinson *m* Hans Salter

Bud Abbott, Lou Costello, Arthur Franz, Nancy Guild, Adele Jergens, Sheldon Leonard

'When every face wore a custard pie, and vamps broke hearts with a winking eye!'

Abbott and Costello Meet the Keystone Kops*

US 1954 79m bw
U-I (Howard Christie)

In pioneer film days, two incompetents are sold a dud studio by a con man, but succeed as stunt men.
Flabby comedy which never seems to get going until the chase finale; notable chiefly for a guest appearance by Mack Sennett.

w John Grant *d* Charles Lamont *ph* Reggie Lanning *m* Joseph Gershenson

Bud Abbott, Lou Costello, Lynn Bari, Fred Clark, Frank Wilcox, Maxie Rosenbloom

'More ghoulish glee than when they met Frankenstein!'

Abbott and Costello Meet the Killer, Boris Karloff*

US 1948 84m bw
U-I (Robert Arthur)

Two bellboys help to solve mysterious murders in a remote hotel.
This clumsily titled comedy really does not work until the last sequence in a cavern. Boris Karloff is not the killer and appears very little.

w Hugh Wedlock Jnr, Howard Snyder, John Grant *d* Charles Barton *ph* Charles van Enger *md* Milton Schwarzwald

Bud Abbott, Lou Costello, Boris Karloff, Gar Moore, Lenore Aubert, Alan Mowbray

'It has been said that a man's best friend is his mummy . . .'

Abbott and Costello Meet the Mummy*

US 1955 77m bw
U-I (Howard Christie)

A missing medallion leads to a lost tomb and a living mummy.
The comedians show their age in this one, but there is some typical if predictable humour and a thrill or two.

w John Grant *d* Charles Lamont *ph* George Robinson *m* Hans Salter

Bud Abbott, Lou Costello, Kurt Katch, Marie Windsor, Michael Ansara, Dan Seymour

'How stupid can you get?'
—'How stupid do you want me to be?'

The Abdication

GB 1974 102m Technicolor
Warner (Robert Fryer, James Cresson)

17th-century Queen Christina of Sweden journeys to Rome to embrace the Catholic church and falls in love with a cardinal.
Sombre historical fantasia, more irritating than interesting.

w Ruth Wolff, from her play *d* Anthony Harvey *ph* Geoffrey Unsworth *m* Nino Rota

Liv Ullmann, Peter Finch, Cyril Cusack, Paul Rogers, Graham Crowden, Michael Dunn, Lewis Fiander, Harold Goldblatt

'Dainty debauchery and titillating tease straight from twenties women's pulp magazines.'—*Variety*

'Embalmed in such reverence for its own cultural elevation that it loses all contact with the audience.'—*Pauline Kael*

The Abductors*

US 1957 80m bw Regalscope
TCF / Regal (Ray Wander)

Around 1870, criminals steal Lincoln's body as ransom to effect a convict's release.
Interesting minor melodrama, but not sufficiently well made.

w Ray Wander *d* Andrew V. McLaglen
ph Joseph La Shelle

Victor McLaglen, Gavin Muir, George Macready

Abdul the Damned*

GB 1935 111m bw
BIP / Capitol (Max Schach)

In 1900 Turkey, an opera star gives herself to a villainous sultan to protect her fiancé.
Thoroughgoing hokum, well produced, which pleased some people in its day.

w Ashley Dukes, Warren Chetham Strode, Robert Burford *d* Karl Grune *ph* Otto Kanturek

Fritz Kortner, Adrienne Ames, Nils Asther, John Stuart, Esme Percy, Walter Rilla, Patric Knowles, Eric Portman

Abdulla the Great
GB / Egypt 1954 103m Technicolor
(Gregory Ratoff)
aka: *Abdulla's Harem*

A pleasure-loving Egyptian potentate sets his sights on an English girl.
Feeble satire on King Farouk, inept and relentlessly boring.

w George St George, Boris Ingster *d* Gregory Ratoff *ph* Lee Garmes

Gregory Ratoff, Kay Kendall, Sydney Chaplin

Abe Lincoln in Illinois**
US 1940 110m bw
RKO (Max Gordon)
GB title: *Spirit of the People*

Episodes in the political and domestic life of Abraham Lincoln.
Pleasant, muted, careful film based on a Broadway success: generally informative and interesting.

w Grover Jones, *play* Robert E. Sherwood *d* John Cromwell *ph James Wong Howe* *m* Roy Webb

Raymond Massey, Ruth Gordon, Gene Lockhart, Mary Howard, Dorothy Tree, Minor Watson, Howard da Silva

'If you want attitudes, a five gallon hat, famous incidents, and One Nation Indivisible, they're all here. As a picture and as a whole, it just doesn't stick.'—*Otis Ferguson*

AAN: Raymond Massey, James Wong Howe

Abie's Irish Rose
US 1946 96m bw
(UA) Bing Crosby Productions (Edward A. Sutherland)

Flat filming of the twenties Broadway play about Irish girl marrying Jewish boy, leading to a clash of families.

w Anne Nichols, from her play *d* Edward A. Sutherland *ph* William Mellor *m* John Scott Trotter

Joanne Dru, Richard Norris, Michael Chekhov, Eric Blore, Art Baker

† There had been a silent version in 1928, and the plot was borrowed, to say the least, for the 1972 TV series *Bridget Loves Bernie*.

Abilene Town*
US 1946 89m bw

An upright marshal routs crooked cattlemen.
Vigorous, enjoyable Western programmer with Randolph Scott and Ann Dvorak on the side of the law. Written by Harold Shumate; directed by Edwin L. Marin; for Jules Levey / UA.

'Love means never having to say you're ugly!'
The Abominable Dr Phibes*
GB 1971 94m Movielab
AIP (Louis M. Heyward, Ron Dunas)

A disfigured musical genius devises a series of horrible murders, based on the ten curses of Pharaoh, for the surgeons who failed to save his wife.
Brisk but uninspired treatment of a promising theme, with more unintended nastiness than intended laughs. Some good moments and interesting low-budget thirties sets.

w James Whiton, William Goldstein *d* Robert Fuest *ph* Norman Warwick *m* Basil Kirchen, Jack Nathan *pd* Brian Eatwell

Vincent Price, Joseph Cotten, Hugh Griffith, Terry-Thomas, Peter Jeffrey, Virginia North, Aubrey Woods

'The sets are awful, the plot ludicrous and the dialogue inane—what more could a horror freak desire?'—*Motion Picture Guide*

† Sequel: *Dr Phibes Rises Again* (1973).

'See it with someone brave!'
The Abominable Snowman*
GB 1957 91m bw Hammerscope
Hammer / Clarion (Aubrey Baring)

Himalayan explorers are attacked one by one by the Yeti and their own fear.
A thin horror film with intelligent scripting: more philosophizing and characterization than suspense. The briefly glimpsed Yeti are disappointing creations.

w Nigel Kneale, from his TV play *d* Val Guest *ph* Arthur Grant *m* Humphrey Searle

Peter Cushing, Forrest Tucker, Maureen Connell, Richard Wattis, Robert Brown, *Arnold Marle*

About Face
US 1952 96m Technicolor
Warner (William Jacobs)

Moronic remake of *Brother Rat* (qv), shorn of all wit, pace and style.

w Peter Milne *d* Roy del Ruth *ph* Bert Glennon *songs* Charles Tobias, Peter de Rose

Eddie Bracken, Gordon Macrae, Dick Wesson, Virginia Gibson, Phyllis Kirk, Joel Grey

About Last Night
US 1986 113m MGM colour
Tri-Star (Jason Brett, Stuart Oken)

The ups and downs of an unmarried relationship.
Smart, slick, up-to-the minute account of human coupling and uncoupling in the eighties . . . but no plot.

w Tim Kazurinsky, Denise DeClue, *play* Sexual Perversity in Chicago by David Mamet *d* Edward Zwick *ph* Andrew Dintenfass *m* Miles Goodman *pd* Ida Random

Rob Lowe, Demi Moore, Jim Belushi, Eizabeth Perkins, George DiCenzo

'Savvy enough to recognize points of conflict but not daring enough to look beneath the surface.'—*Variety*

About Mrs Leslie*
US 1954 104m bw
Paramount (Hal B. Wallis)

An ageing nightclub singer has a platonic affair with a mysterious wealthy man, who leaves her enough money to buy a boarding house.
Odd, likeable romantic drama tailored for an unusual star; but its plot is too thin and its direction too drab for real success.

w Ketti Frings, Hal Kanter *d* Daniel Mann *ph* Ernest Laszlo *m* Victor Young

Shirley Booth, Robert Ryan, Alex Nicol, Marjie Miller, Eilene Janssen

'This quiet and curious film has an unexpectedly gentle, civilized flavour.'—*Gavin Lambert*

'It's all sunny disposition and sweet sadness for Miss Booth.'—*Judith Crist*

'One is reminded alternately of Chekhov and of *Back Street*.'—*Sight and Sound*

'The love story behind the billion dollar secret!'
Above and Beyond*
US 1952 122m bw
MGM (Melvin Frank, Norman Panama)

The training of Colonel Paul Tibbetts, who dropped the first atomic bomb on Japan.
Overstretched flagwaver with laborious domestic interludes. Of little real interest then or now.

w Melvin Frank, Norman Panama, *story* Beirne Lay Jnr *d* Melvin Frank, Norman Panama *ph* Ray June *m* Hugo Friedhofer

Robert Taylor, Eleanor Parker, James Whitmore, Larry Keating, Larry Gates

AAN: Beirne Lay Jnr, Hugo Friedhofer

Above Suspicion*
US 1943 91m bw
MGM (Victor Saville)

Just before World War II, an Oxford professor on a continental honeymoon is asked to track down a missing agent.
Patchy, studio-bound spy comedy-drama with a couple of good sequences. Notable also for Mr MacMurray's impersonation of a professor who hails a Nazi as 'Hiya, dope!'

w Keith Winter, Melville Baker, Patricia Coleman, *novel* Helen MacInnes *d* Richard Thorpe *ph* Robert Planck *m* Bronislau Kaper

Fred MacMurray, Joan Crawford, Conrad Veidt, *Basil Rathbone*, Reginald Owen, Felix Bressart, Richard Ainley

'Will need more than strong support for passable biz.'—*Variety*

'A story of impudent gallantry!'
Above Us the Waves
GB 1955 99m bw
(Rank) London Independent Producers (William Macquitty)

In World War II, midget submarines attack a German battleship in a Norwegian fjord.
Archetypal stiff-upper-lip war drama with disappointing action sequences and jumbled continuity.

w Robin Estridge *d* Ralph Thomas *ph* Ernest Steward *m* Arthur Benjamin

John Mills, John Gregson, Donald Sinden, James Robertson Justice, Michael Medwin, Lee Patterson, Lyndon Brook

'It tells a heroic story without any flowery effects at all.'—*Manchester Guardian*

'The wonder film of the century, about the most romantic figure who ever lived!'

Abraham Lincoln**

US 1930 97m bw
(UA) D. W. Griffith / Art Cinema Corporation

An account of Lincoln's entry into politics and his years of power.
Rather boring even at the time, this straightforward biopic has the virtues of sincerity and comparative fidelity to the facts.

w Stephen Vincent Benet, Gerrit Lord *d D. W. Griffith* *ph* Karl Struss *m* Hugo Riesenfeld *pd* William Cameron Menzies

Walter Huston, Una Merkel, Edgar Dearing, Russell Simpson, Henry B. Walthall

'A startlingly superlative accomplishment, one rejuvenating a greatest Griffith . . . one smooth roll of literally pulsating passion, pathos, laughter . . . it should be his greatest contribution to the exhibitor.'—*Variety*

'It brings to us—with a curious finality ot disappointment, a sentimental sense of the closing of a chapter—the impression of a director who has nowhere made a valid contact with the condition of the screen today.'—*C. A. Lejeune*

'A treasure trove of magnificent moments.'—*MFB, 1973*

'Dull, episodic, overlong . . . it is difficult to understand why contemporary critics were so impressed.'—*Anthony Slide, 70s*

† There was a silent biopic in 1924 starring George A. Billings, but it lacked cinematic interest. Written by Frances Marion and directed by Phil Rosen, for Rocket / Lincoln / AFN.

'Two roaring Romeos who thought even the dames were on lend lease!'

Abroad with Two Yanks*

US 1944 80m bw
Edward Small

Adventures around the Pacific with two woman-chasing sailors.
This simple-minded farce with its punny title was a great success in its day, and still generates a laugh or two.

w Charles Rogers, Wilkie Maholey, Fred Redsills *d* Allan Dwan *ph* Charles Lawton *m* Lud Gluskin

Dennis O'Keefe, William Bendix, Helen Walker, John Abbott, John Loder

Abschied von Gestern*

West Germany 1966 90m bw
Kairos Film / Alexander Kluge / Independent
aka: *Yesterday Girl*

A Jewish girl escapes from East to West Germany but is disillusioned and gives herself up.
Witty and remarkably light-hearted satirical comedy which can be fully understood only by those living in Germany in the sixties.

wd Alexander Kluge *ph* Edgar Reitz, Thomas Mauch

Alexandra Kluge, Gunther Mack, Hans Korte, Eva Marie Meinecke

Absence of Malice*

US 1981 116m De Luxe
Columbia / Mirage (Sydney Pollack)

When a longshoremen's union leader disappears, a lady journalist throws an unfair spotlight on an innocent suspect.
Well-meaning but overwritten attack on journalistic abuses, hampered by unsuitable leading performances.

w Kurt Luedtke *d* Sydney Pollack *ph* Owen Roizman *m* Dave Grusin *pd* Terence Marsh

Paul Newman, Sally Field, Bob Balaban, Melinda Dillon, Luther Adler, Barry Primus

'Pollack seems to be carving out a new niche for himself as an updater of Hollywood's most tried and true methods of sugaring a message.'—*Richard Combs, MFB*

'A thoroughly craftsmanlike movie that never quite delivers on the commercial or the artistic front.'—*Guardian*

'The story is perfunctory and disappointing in a movie that promises but does not deliver.'—*Motion Picture Guide*

AAN: screenplay; Paul Newman; Melinda Dillon

'It's all about a wacky prof who invents an anti-gravity goo that flew!'

The Absent-Minded Professor*

US 1960 97m bw
Walt Disney (Bill Walsh)

A lighter-than-air substance called flubber enables its inventor to drive his Model-T through the sky and catch some spies.
Foolishly engaging fantasy comedy with goodish trick effects.

w Bill Walsh *d* Robert Stevenson *ph* Edward Colman *m* George Bruns *sp* Robert A. Mattey, Peter Ellenshaw, Eustace Lycett

Fred MacMurray, Tommy Kirk, Keenan Wynn, Nancy Olson, Leon Ames, Ed Wynn, Edward Andrews

† Sequel: *Son of Flubber* (1964).

AAN: Edward Colman

'Welcome to the world of your dreams!'

Absolute Beginners

GB 1986 107m Rank colour SuperTechniscope
Virgin / Goldcrest / Palace (Stephen Woolley, Chris Brown)

Teen life and pop fashion in 1958 London.
Deafening, mindless, musical, multi-screen pot-pourri of teen culture which sadly needs narrative links not to mention better music and firmer control.

w Richard Burridge, Christopher Wicking, Don MacPherson, *novel* Colin MacInnes *d* Julien Temple *ph* Oliver Stapleton *m* David Bowie, Ray Davies, *et al.* *pd* John Beard

Eddie O'Connell, Patsy Kensit, David Bowie, Ray Davies, James Fox, Lionel Blair, Steven Berkoff, Mandy Rice Davies

'All that noise, all that energy, so little governing thought.'—*Time Out*

Absolute Quiet*

US 1936 71m bw

Interestingly-cast programmer about a murder plot after a planeload of strangers is forced down on a financier's ranch. Lionel Atwill, Louis Hayward, Raymond Walburn, Stuart Erwin, Wallace Ford, J. Carrol Naish. Written by Harry Clark; directed by Edwin L. Marin; for MGM.

Absolution*

GB 1978 95m Technicolor
Bulldog (Danny O'Donovan, Elliott Kastner)
TV title: *Murder by Confession*

A schoolmaster priest at a Roman Catholic boarding school is taunted by a malicious pupil into committing murder.
Interesting and suspenseful, though finally too complicated compromise between a thriller of the *Sleuth* type and a downbeat character study.

w Anthony Shaffer *d* Anthony Page *ph* John Coquillon *m* Stanley Myers

Richard Burton, Dominic Guard, Dai Bradley, Billy Connolly, Andrew Keir

'A dire slice of clever-clever narrative trickery.'—*Paul Taylor, MFB*

'You can't make real bricks from this kind of straw, since a potentially interesting study of character and environment is gradually weakened by the constraints of a second-rate murder mystery.'—*Guardian*

The Abysmal Brute

US 1924 80m approx bw silent

Remembered more for its title than anything else, this is not a horror film but a comedy about a mild and naive young mountain man who comes to the big city, becomes a hero of the fight game under the titular pseudonym, and still contrives to make a society marriage. A star was created, but failed to follow through. Reginald Danny, Mabel Julienne Scott, Hayden Stevenson, Charles French. Written by A. P. Younger from the novel by Jack London; directed by Hobart Henley; for Universal.

Accattone*

Italy 1961 120m bw
Cino del Duca / Arco (Alfredo Bini)

A Roman pimp and thief is beset by troubles, and is finally killed escaping from the police.
Sordid and rough-edged but vividly realistic melodrama.

wd Pier Paolo Pasolini *ph* Tonino delli Colli *md* Carlo Rustichelli

Franco Citti, Franca Pasut, Roberto Scaringella, Adele Cambria

Accent on Love

US 1941 61m bw

A real estate executive walks out to become spokesman for his former underprivileged tenants. Thin Capraesque romantic comedy. George Montgomery, Osa Massen, J. Carrol Naish, Cobina Wright Jnr, Stanley Clements, Thurston Hall, Minerva Urecal. Written by John Larkin, from a story by Dalton Trumbo; directed by Ray McCarey; for TCF.

Accent on Youth*
US 1935 77m bw
Paramount (Douglas Maclean)

A secretary falls in love with her middle-aged playwright employer.
Reasonably sparkling comedy from a popular play, later remade as *Mr Music* and *But Not for Me.*

w Herbert Fields, Claude Binyon, *play* Samson Raphaelson *d* Wesley Ruggles *ph* Leon Shamroy

Herbert Marshall, Sylvia Sidney, Philip Reed, Astrid Allwyn, Holmes Herbert

'Well adapted, presented and produced for box office satisfaction.'—*Variety*

Accident**
GB 1967 105m Eastmancolor
London Independent Producers (Joseph Losey, Norman Priggen)

An Oxford undergraduate is killed in a car crash; his tutor looks back over the tangle of personal relationships that contributed to his death.
Ascetic drama in which the audience is too often left to observe at length and draw its own conclusions; good characterizations nevertheless.

w Harold Pinter, *novel* Nicholas Mosley *d* Joseph Losey *ph* Gerry Fisher *m* Johnny Dankworth

Dirk Bogarde, Stanley Baker, Jacqueline Sassard, Vivien Merchant, Michael York

'The whole thing is such a teapot tempest, and it is so assiduously underplayed that it is neither strong drama nor stinging satire. It is just a sad little story of a wistful don.'—*Bosley Crowther*

'Everything is calm, unruffled, lacquered in a veneer of civilization, yet underneath it all, one gradually begins to realize, the characters are tearing each other emotionally to shreds.'—*MFB*

'Uneven, unsatisfying, but with virtuoso passages of calculated meanness.'—*New Yorker, 1977*

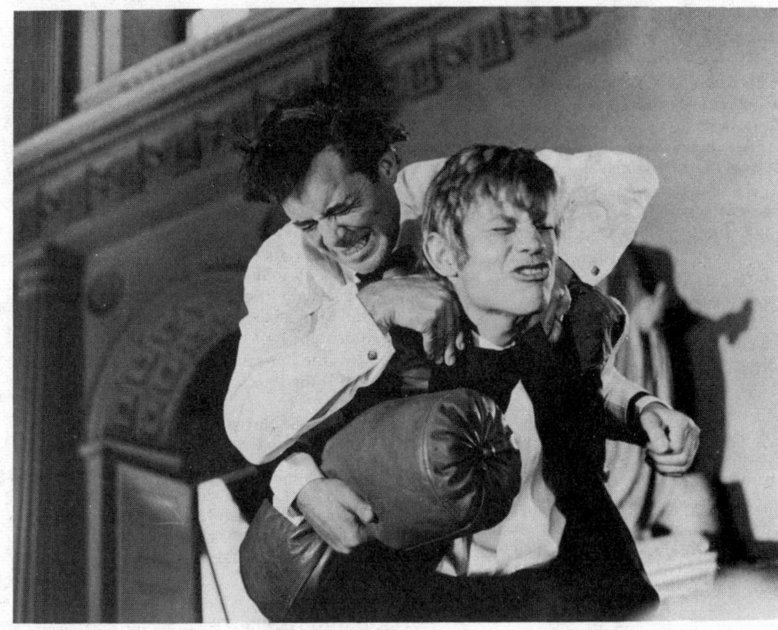

ACCIDENT. Dirk Bogarde and Michael York in a rare red-blooded moment from the coldly cerebral second Pinter-Losey screen collaboration.

Accidents Will Happen
US 1938 62m bw

An insurance claims adjuster takes to crime. Slack little programmer. Ronald Reagan, Dick Purcell, Gloria Blondell, Addison Richards, Hugh O'Connell. Written by George Bricker and Anthony Coldeway; directed by William Clemens; for Bryan Foy / Warner.

According to Mrs Hoyle
US 1951 60m bw

A retired schoolteacher lives in a hotel run by criminals, and becomes involved. Uninspired sentimental comedy providing a rare star part for a well-liked character actress. Spring Byington, Anthony Caruso, Brett King, Tanis Chandler. Written by W. Scott Darling and Barney Gerard; directed by Jean Yarbrough; for Monogram.

Account Rendered
GB 1957 59m bw

A man is suspected of the murder of his unfaithful wife. Adequate lower-billed suspenser. Griffith Jones, Ursula Howells, Honor Blackman, Ewen Solon, John Van Eyssen. Written by Barbara S. Harper, from a novel by Pamela Barrington; directed by Peter Graham Scott; for Major / RFD.

Accused
GB 1936 85m bw

In Paris, a dancer is stabbed and his wife is thought guilty. Overwrought melodrama, chiefly interesting for cast: Douglas Fairbanks Jnr, Dolores del Rio, Googie Withers, Florence Desmond, Basil Sydney. Written by Zoe Akins, George Barraud and Harold French; directed by Thornton Freeland; for Criterion / UA.

'The standout suspense triumph of the year!'
The Accused*
US 1948 101m bw
Paramount (Hal B. Wallis)
aka: *Strange Deception*

In self-defence a lady professor kills a student who has sexually attacked her.
Dullish suspenser with the outcome never in doubt, though the production values are beyond reproach.

w Ketti Frings *d* William Dieterle *ph* Milton Krasner *m* Victor Young

Loretta Young, Robert Cummings, Wendell Corey, Sam Jaffe, Douglas Dick

Accused of Murder
US 1956 76m Trucolor (and 'Naturama')

When a crooked lawyer is murdered, his mistress is suspected. Flat little mystery with unappetizing characters. Vera Ralston, David Brian, Sidney Blackmer, Virginia Grey, Warren Stevens, Lee Van Cleef. Written by Bob Williams and W. R. Burnett, from the novel *Vanity Row* by W. R. Burnett; directed by Joe Kane; for Republic.

Ace Drummond
US 1936 bw serial: 13 eps

John King as a civil aviation pioneer hampered by an evil power named The Dragon. With Jean Rogers, Noah Beery Jnr, Guy Bates Post; directed by Ford Beebe and Cliff Smith; for Universal.

Ace Eli and Roger of the Skies
US 1973 92m De Luxe Panavision
TCF (Robert Fryer, James Cresson)

Adventures of a father-and-son aerial barnstorming act after World War I.
Poorly written melodrama, very tame apart from the flying shots.

w Claudia Salter, *story* Steven Spielberg *d* John Erman *ph* David M. Walsh, Bill Birch, Don Morgan *m* Jerry Goldsmith

Cliff Robertson, Pamela Franklin, Eric Shea, Rosemary Murphy, Bernadette Peters, Alice Ghostley

'A tediously inane flop. Nostalgia isn't what it used to be.'—*Variety*

Ace High
Italy 1969 120m Techniscope

A condemned outlaw is offered an opportunity to save his neck. Violent spaghetti western with vestiges of a sense of humour. Eli Wallach, Brock Peters, Terence Hill, Bud Spencer, Kevin McCarthy. Written and directed by Giuseppe Colizzi; for Paramount.

Ace in the Hole***
US 1951 111m bw
Paramount (Billy Wilder)
aka: *The Big Carnival*

In order to prolong the sensation and boost newspaper sales, a self-seeking journalist delays the rescue of a man trapped in a cave. An incisive, compelling melodrama taking a sour look at the American scene; one of its director's masterworks.

w Billy Wilder, Lesser Samuels, Walter Newman d Billy Wilder ph Charles B. Lang Jnr *m* Hugo Friedhofer

Kirk Douglas (Chuck Tatum), Jan Sterling (Lorraine), *Porter Hall* (Boot), Bob Arthur (Herbie), Richard Benedict (Leo), Ray Teal (Sheriff), Frank Cady (Federber)

LORRAINE to Tatum: 'I've met some hard-boiled eggs, but you—you're twenty minutes!'

LORRAINE: 'I don't go to church. Kneeling bags my nylons.'

TATUM to editor: 'I've done a lot of lying in my time. I've lied to men who wear belts. I've lied to men who wear suspenders. But I'd never be so stupid as to lie to a man who wears both belt and suspenders.'

TATUM, dying, to editor: 'How'd you like to make a thousand dollars a day, Mr Boot? I'm a thousand-dollar-a-day newspaperman. You can have me for nothing.'

'Few of the opportunities for irony, cruelty and horror are missed.'—*Gavin Lambert*

'Style and purpose achieve for the most part a fusion even more remarkable than in *Sunset Boulevard*.'—*Penelope Houston*

'As stimulating as black coffee.'—*Richard Mallett, Punch*

'Americans expected a cocktail and felt I was giving them a shot of vinegar instead.'—*Billy Wilder*

'Some people have tried to claim some sort of satirical brilliance for it, but it's really rather nasty, in a sociologically pushy way.'—*New Yorker, 1980*

'A brilliant arrangement of cause and effect . . . unique as a mirror of the morbid psychology of crowds . . . revolting but incontrovertibly true.'—*New York Times*

† Locations were at Gallup, New Mexico.

AAN: script

Ace of Aces*
US 1933 76m bw

On the outbreak of World War I an American sculptor is branded a coward when he does not immediately enlist; but he disappears and turns up in France a hero, though with a sour taste in his mouth. Melodrama of disillusion, dated in many respects but interesting to compare with *The Dawn Patrol* and *The Last Flight*. Richard Dix, Elizabeth Allan, Theodore Newton, Ralph Bellamy, Joseph Sawyer, Frank Conroy, William Cagney. Written by John Monk Saunders and H. W. Hannemann from the story 'Bird of Prey' by John Monk Saunders; directed by J. Walter Ruben; for RKO.

'It's the fine photography and crashes that provide the thrills.'—*Variety*

The Ace of Scotland Yard
US 1929 bw serial: 10 eps

The first talking serial: Blake of the Yard thwarts a jewel thief called The Queen of Diamonds. With Crawford Kent, Grace Cunard, Florence Allen; directed by Ray Taylor; for Universal.

Aces High*
GB 1976 114m Technicolor
EMI / S. Benjamin Fisz / Jacques Roitfeld

In the air force during World War I, young pilots are needlessly sacrificed.
Spirited if rather unnecessary remake of *Journey's End* transposed to the air war, which makes it almost identical to *The Dawn Patrol*.

w Howard Barker *d* Jack Gold *ph* Gerry Fisher, Peter Allwork *m* Richard Hartley

Malcolm McDowell, Christopher Plummer, Simon Ward, Peter Firth, John Gielgud, Trevor Howard, Richard Johnson, Ray Milland

Across 110th Street*
US 1972 102m De Luxe
UA / Film Guarantors (Fouad Said, Ralph Serpe)

A tough New York cop loses his own life tracking down three Harlem criminals who have robbed the Mafia.
Brutish, noisy, incoherent police melodrama, with fashionable sadism and predictable performances. Good location work, though.

w Luther Davis, *novel* Wally Ferris *d* Barry Shear *ph* Jack Priestley *m* J. J. Johnson

Anthony Quinn, Anthony Franciosa, Yaphet Kotto, Paul Benjamin, Ed Bernard

'Not for the squeamish . . . a virtual blood bath, leaving no relief from depression and oppression.'—*Variety*

Across the Bridge*
GB 1957 103m bw
Rank / IPF (John Stafford)

A fugitive financier kills his pursuer, finds he was a murderer, and tries to hide out across the Mexican border.
This star *tour de force* is unconvincing in detail and rather unattractive to watch (British films never could cope with American settings), but the early sequences have suspense.

w Guy Elmes, Denis Freeman, *novel* Graham Greene *d* Ken Annakin *ph* Reg Wyer *m* James Bernard

Rod Steiger, David Knight, Marla Landi, Noel Willman, Bernard Lee

Across the Pacific***
US 1942 99m bw
Warner (Hal B. Wallis)

Just before Pearl Harbor, an army officer is cashiered by arrangement in order to contact pro-Japanese sympathizers.
Hasty, easy-going and very enjoyable hokum, partly ship-set and successfully reteaming three stars of *The Maltese Falcon*.

w Richard Macauley, *serial* Aloha Means Goodbye by Robert Carson *d* John Huston *ph* Arthur Edeson *m* Adolph Deutsch

Humphrey Bogart (Rick Leland), *Mary Astor* (Alberta Marlow), *Sydney Greenstreet* (Dr Lorenz), *Sen Yung* (Joe Totsuiko); and Charles Halton, Monte Blue, Richard Loo, Chester Gan, Kam Tong

'A spy picture which tingles with fearful uncertainties and glints with the sheen of blue steel.'—*Bosley Crowther*

† Huston was called up before the film was completed, and allegedly reshaped the script before leaving in order to put the hero in an impossible situation. Direction was eventually completed by Vincent Sherman.

†† Monte Blue, who has a tiny last-reel part as the heroine's drunken father, starred in a 1926 silent film with the same title but a totally different plot. He played an army officer fighting Philippine guerrillas. Darryl F. Zanuck wrote the script, and Roy del Ruth directed, for Warners.

Across the Wide Missouri*
US 1951 77m Technicolor
MGM (Robert Sisk)

In the 1820s, a trapper marries an Indian girl and lives with her people.
Promising credits produce an unsatisfactory western: despite honest efforts, the elements do not jell into a convincing whole.

w Talbot Jennings *d* William Wellman *ph* William C. Mellor *m* David Raksin

Clark Gable, Ricardo Montalban, John Hodiak, Adolphe Menjou, Maria Elena Marques, J. Carrol Naish, Jack Holt, Alan Napier, Howard Keel (narrator)

Act of Love *
US 1954 104m bw
UA / Benagoss (Anatole Litvak)

In Paris in 1944, an American with the liberation army falls in love with a French girl, who commits suicide when he is posted and cannot make their rendezvous.
Cheerless romantic drama, rather thin and unmemorable despite the efforts of all concerned.

w Irwin Shaw, *novel* The Girl on the Via Flaminia by Alfred Hayes *d* Anatole Litvak *ph* Armand Thirard *m* Michael Emer, Joe Hajos *pd* Alexander Trauner

Kirk Douglas, Dany Robin, Barbara Laage, Robert Strauss, Gabrielle Dorziat, Gregoire Aslan, Fernand Ledoux, Serge Reggiani, Brigitte Bardot
† Made in France, an early Hollywood foreign location film.

An Act of Murder*
US 1948 90m bw
U-I (Jerry Bresler)
aka: *Live Today for Tomorrow*

A judge insists on being tried for the mercy killing of his incurably ill wife.
Earnest social drama which despite excellent acting can only reach an inconclusive ending.

w Michael Blankfort, Robert Thoeren, *novel* The Mills of God by Ernst Lothar *d* Michael Gordon *ph* Hal Mohr *m* Daniele Amfitheatrof

Fredric March, Florence Eldridge, Edmond O'Brien, Geraldine Brooks

Act of Murder**
GB 1964 62m bw
Merton Park (Jack Greenwood)

A couple arrange a holiday by swapping houses with strangers, and a complex plot ensues.
Slick, superior example of the Edgar Wallace second feature series.

w Lewis Davidson *d Alan Bridges* *ph* James Wilson *m* Bernard Ebbinghouse

John Carson, Anthony Bate, Justine Lord, Duncan Lewis, Dandy Nichols

'This uncommonly intelligent little thriller is just the sort of film which is likely to arouse critical sneers for reaching too high on a low budget.'—*Tom Milne*

Act of the Heart
Canada 1970 103m colour

An innocent country girl falls for a priest with doubts, and they both commit suicide. Glum stuff with nary a flicker of hope or real feeling. 'For extremely tolerant psychiatrists only.'—*Motion Picture Guide*. Genevieve Bujold, Donald Sutherland, Monique Leyrac, Sharon Acker. Written, directed and produced by Paul Almond for Quest/CIC.

Act of Violence**
US 1948 82m bw
MGM (William Wright)

After the war, an ex-GI tracks down a prison camp informer.
Moody, glossy melodrama with tension well sustained, though the sentimental ending is a cop-out.

w Robert I. Richards, *story* Collier Young *d Fred Zinnemann* *ph Robert Surtees* *m* Bronislau Kaper

Van Heflin, Robert Ryan, Janet Leigh, Mary Astor

'Strong characterization, fine direction and good photography combine to put this film high among its kind.'—*MFB*

'An effortless narrative control and a real power to maintain tension.'—*Richard Winnington*

Act One*
US 1963 110m bw
Warner (Dore Schary)

Poor Brooklyn boy Moss Hart rises to Broadway eminence via his writing partnership with George S. Kaufman.
Incredibly stilted film version of an excellent autobiography, notable only for fragments of acting and the fact that a film so totally uncommercial was made at all.

wd Dore Schary *ph* Arthur J. Ornitz *m* Skitch Henderson

George Hamilton (Hart), Jason Robards Jnr (Kaufman), Jack Klugman, Sam Levene, George Segal, Ruth Ford, Eli Wallach

'From the moment young Hart takes pencil in hand, we have nowhere to go except to that happy ending; and despite all the painstaking detail, we don't believe a word of it.'—*Judith Crist*

Action for Slander*
GB 1937 83m bw
London Films / Saville (Victor Saville)

A bankrupt officer, accused of cheating at cards, defends his honour with a writ.
Lively melodrama of the old school.

w Ian Dalrymple, Miles Malleson, *novel* Mary Borden *d* Tim Whelan *ph* Harry Stradling *md* Muir Mathieson

Clive Brook, Ann Todd, Margaretta Scott, Arthur Margetson, Ronald Squire, Athole Stewart, Percy Marmont, Frank Cellier, Morton Selten

'Hollywood in its most lavish spurt of extravagance never went to such pains to assemble a cast . . . general run of patrons however will chafe under the lack of physical movement.'—*Variety*

Action in Arabia
US 1944 75m bw

Nazis and Frenchmen of both persuasions clash in the Damascus desert. Formula war melodrama using stock footage originally shot by Cooper and Schoedsack. George Sanders (as an American war correspondent), Virginia Bruce, Lenore Aubert, Gene Lockhart, Robert Armstrong, H. B. Warner, Alan Napier, André Charlot, Marcel Dalio. Written by Philip MacDonald and Herbert Biberman; directed by Leonide Moguy; for Maurice Geraghty / RKO.

Action in the North Atlantic*
US 1943 127m bw
Warner (Jerry Wald)

An American convoy bound for Russia comes under U-boat attack.
Efficient propaganda potboiler; studio bound, but still works as a war actioner.

w John Howard Lawson, *story* Guy Gilpatric *d* Lloyd Bacon *ph* Ted McCord *m* Adolph Deutsch

Humphrey Bogart, Raymond Massey, Alan Hale, Julie Bishop, Ruth Gordon, Sam Levene, Dane Clark

'The production has interludes of tremendous power. What is lacking is dramatic cohesion.'—*Howard Barnes*

'Directly in line of descent from *The Perils of Pauline*.'—*Time*

'The American equivalent of our war documentaries . . . tough, exciting, with no concession to flim flam.'—*New Statesman*

'I cannot think I have ever seen such realistic battles, or lived so intimately with the characters who comprise the crew.'—*Evening Standard*

AAN: Guy Gilpatric

Action of the Tiger
GB 1957 93m Technicolor Cinemascope
MGM / Claridge (Kenneth Harper)

An adventurer helps a French girl to rescue her brother from political imprisonment in Albania.
Dull and poorly constructed action melodrama.

w Robert Carson, *novel* James Wellard *d* Terence Young *ph* Desmond Dickinson *m* Humphrey Searle

Van Johnson, Martine Carol, Herbert Lom, Gustavo Rocco, Anthony Dawson, Helen Haye, Sean Connery

Actors and Sin*
US 1952 91m bw
(UA) Sid Kuller (Ben Hecht)

Two short stories. When an unsuccessful actress commits suicide, her father makes it look like murder so that for once she shall get attention.
The authoress of a romantic script bought by Hollywood is discovered to be a horrid little 9-year-old.
Interesting but incompetent compendium which descends almost to the home movie level and leaves the actors struggling.

wd Ben Hecht *ph* Lee Garmes *m* George Antheil

Edward G. Robinson, Marsha Hunt, Dan O'Herlihy, Rudolph Anders, Eddie Albert, Alan Reed, Jenny Hecht

'A depressing double bill.'—*Lindsay Anderson*

An Actor's Revenge*
Japan 1963 113m Daieicolor Daieiscope
Daiei (Masaichi Nagata)
original title: *Yukinojo Henge*

In the early 19th century, a touring actor comes upon the rich merchant who had ruined his parents, and his revenge involves several deaths.
Complex, fascinating period melodrama, both rich and strange, with strong echoes of Jacobean melodrama.

w Daisuke Ito, Teinosuke Kinugasa, Natto Wada, *novel* Otokichi Mikami *d Kon Ichikawa* *ph* Setsuo Kobayashi *m* Yasushi Akutagawa

Kazuo Hasegawa, Fujiko Yamamoto, Ayako Wakao, Ganjiro Nakamura

The Actress*
US 1928 90m approx (24 fps) bw silent
MGM
GB title: *Trelawny of the Wells*

A young Victorian actress marries a rich admirer.
Pleasing, well-cast version of a celebrated play.

w Albert Lewin, Richard Schayer, *play* Sir Arthur Wing Pinero *d* Sidney Franklin *ph* William Daniels

Norma Shearer, Ralph Forbes, O. P. Heggie, Owen Moore, Roy D'Arcy

'A thoughtful, rounded and provocative entertainment.'—*New York Times*

† Opening attraction at London's Empire Theatre, Leicester Square.

The Actress
US 1953 91m bw
MGM (Lawrence Weingarten)

Ruth Jones becomes an actress against the wishes of her stubborn seafaring father.
Episodes from Ruth Gordon's early life, based on her Broadway play *Years Ago*, make a pleasant though scarcely engrossing film: it is all a shade too discreet and wanly winning, and the few key events take place offscreen.

w Ruth Gordon *d* George Cukor *ph* Harold Rosson *m* Bronislau Kaper *ad* Cedric Gibbons, Arthur Lonergan

Jean Simmons, Spencer Tracy, Teresa Wright, Anthony Perkins, Ian Wolfe, Mary Wickes

Ada*
US 1961 109m Metrocolor Cinemascope
MGM / Avon / Chalmar (Lawrence Weingarten)

A political candidate marries a call girl who becomes his strong right arm and weathers a threat to reveal her past.
Indecisive romantic drama which pulls too many punches but has interesting background detail.

w Arthur Sheekman, William Driskill, *novel* Ada Dallas by Wirt Williams *d* Daniel Mann *ph* Joseph Ruttenberg *m* Bronislau Kaper

Susan Hayward, Dean Martin, Wilfrid Hyde White, Ralph Meeker, Martin Balsam

'A bonanza for connoisseurs of perfectly awful movies.'—*Judith Crist*

'Its characterizations are sketchy, its political setting routine and symbolic.'—*New York Herald Tribune*

Adalen 31**
Sweden 1969 115m Technicolor Techniscope
Svensk Filmindustri

A prolonged strike at a small-town paper mill ends in tragedy when the troops move in.
Effective period piece which emphasizes the idyllic qualities of the backgrounds rather than the foreground terrors.

wd Bo Widerberg ph Jorgen Persson

Peter Schildt, Kerstin Tidelius, Roland Hedlund, Stefan Feierbach, Anita Bjork

AA: best foreign film

Adam and Eva*
US 1923 83m approx bw silent

An extravagant girl reforms when her father goes bust. Moral comedy with a happy ending: a hit of its day. Marion Davies, T. Roy Barnes, Tom Lewis, William Norris, Percy Ames. Written by Luther Reed from a play by Guy Middleton and George Bolton; directed by Robert G. Vignola; for Cosmopolitan/MGM.

Adam and Evelyne
GB 1949 92m bw
Rank / Two Cities (Harold French)

A society playboy adopts his dead friend's daughter, and falls in love with her.
Undernourished romantic drama, a mild variation on *Daddy Longlegs*.

w Noel Langley, Lesley Storm, George Barraud, Nicholas Phipps *d* Harold French *ph* Guy Green *m* Mischa Spoliansky

Stewart Granger, Jean Simmons, Helen Cherry, Edwin Styles, Beatrice Varley, Wilfrid Hyde White

Adam Had Four Sons*
US 1941 81m bw
Columbia (Robert Sherwood)

A widower's family is cared for by a governess.
Modest magazine fiction which established Ingrid Bergman as an American star.

w Michael Blankfort, William Hurlbut, *novel* Legacy by Charles Bonner *d* Gregory Ratoff *ph* Peverell Marley *m* W. Franke Harling

Warner Baxter, *Ingrid Bergman,* Susan Hayward, Richard Denning, Fay Wray

Adam's Rib*
US 1922 86m bw silent

By offering herself in her stead, an American girl tries to prevent her mother's adultery with a European ex-monarch. One of its director's 'sin in high life' melodramas, which packed 'em in at the time, this has nothing but decoration to offer to a modern audience. Milton Sills, Elliott Dexter, Theodore Kosloff, Anna Q. Nilsson, Pauline Garon, Julia Fay. Written by Jeanie MacPherson, directed and produced by Cecil B. De Mille; for Paramount.

Adam's Rib**
US 1949 101m bw
MGM (Lawrence Weingarten)

Husband and wife lawyers are on opposite sides of an attempted murder case.
A superior star vehicle which also managed to introduce four promising personalities; slangily written and smartly directed, but perhaps a shade less funny than it once seemed.

w Ruth Gordon, Garson Kanin d George Cukor ph George J. Folsey *m* Miklos Rozsa

Spencer Tracy, Katharine Hepburn, David Wayne, Tom Ewell, Judy Holliday, Jean Hagen, Hope Emerson, Clarence Kolb

'Hepburn and Tracy are again presented as the ideal US Mr and Mrs of upper-middle income. This time, as well as being wittily urbane, both are lawyers.'—*Time*

'It isn't solid food but it certainly is meaty and juicy and comically nourishing.'—*Bosley Crowther*

† A 1972 TV series of the same title provided a boring imitation, with Ken Howard and Blythe Danner.
AAN: Ruth Gordon and Garson Kanin

Adam's Woman
Australia 1970 115m colour Panavision

In the 1840s an American finds himself a prisoner in an antipodean penal colony, and schemes to get out. Oddball period drama, unreleased in Britain. Beau Bridges, Jane Merrow, James Booth, John Mills. Written by Richard Fielder; directed by Philip Leacock; for Warner / EMI.

The Adding Machine*
GB 1968 99m Technicolor
Universal / Associated London (Jerome Epstein)

Downtrodden clerk Mr Zero rebels against society by murdering his boss. Tried and executed, he spends thirty years in heaven before being 'laundered' and sent back to start again as another nonentity.
Elmer Rice's satirical fantasy of the twenties is here robbed of its expressionist staging and presented naturalistically, a fatal error from which the film never for one moment recovers.

wd Jerome Epstein *ph* Walter Lassally *m* Mike Leander, Lambert Williamson

Phyllis Diller, Milo O'Shea, Billie Whitelaw, Sydney Chaplin, Julian Glover, Raymond Huntley, Phil Brown, Libby Morris

Address Unknown**
US 1944 72m bw
Columbia (William Cameron Menzies)

A German-American becomes a Nazi and is incriminated by false letters from his one-time friend.
Reasonably engrossing, cheaply-made adaptation of a slim little thriller which was widely read during World War II.

w Kressman Taylor, Herbert Dalmass, *novel* Kressman Taylor *d* William Cameron Menzies *ph* Rudolph Maté *m* Ernst Toch

Paul Lukas, Carl Esmond, Peter Van Eyck, Mady Christians, Emory Parnell

AAN: Ernst Toch

Adieu Philippine*
France / Italy 1962 106m bw
Unitec / Alpha / Rome-Paris (Georges de Beauregard)

A young TV cameraman is torn between two girls.
Flimsy but attractive romantic comedy, slightly marred by New Wave improvisation with consequent rough edges.

w Michèle O'Glor, Jacques Rozier *d* Jacques Rozier *ph* René Mathelin *m* various

Jean-Claude Aimini, Yveline Céry, Stefania Sabatini, Vittorio Caprioli

The Admirable Crichton*
GB 1957 93m Technicolor Vistavision
Columbia / Modern Screenplays (Ian Dalrymple)
US title: *Paradise Lagoon*

Lord Loam and his family are shipwrecked on a desert island, where his manservant proves the undisputed leader.
Few laughs are to be had from this blunt, sentimental version of a famous play, but the photography and decor are excellent.

w Vernon Harris, *play* J. M. Barrie *d* Lewis Gilbert *ph* Wilkie Cooper *m* Douglas Gamley, Richard Addinsell *ad* William Kellner *costumes* Bernard Nevill *devices* Emmett

Kenneth More, Cecil Parker, Sally Ann Howes, Diane Cilento, Martita Hunt, Jack Watling, Peter Graves, Gerald Harper

'Barrie's play now seems more remote than Gammer Gurton.'—*David Robinson*

The Admiral Was a Lady
US 1950 87m bw

Four ex-airmen and an ex-Wac try to live on their wits. Unappealing comedy which gives the impression that it has tried to find a new style, and failed. Edmond O'Brien, Wanda Hendrix, Rudy Vallee, Johnny Sands, Steve Brodie, Richard Erdman, Hillary Brooke, Richard Lane. Written by Sidney Salkow and John O'Dea; directed and produced by Albert S. Rogell; photographed by Stanley Cortez; for Roxbury (Albert S. Rogell / Jack M. Warner).

Adolf Hitler—My Part in His Downfall*
GB 1972 102m Technicolor
UA / Norcon (Gregory Smith, Norman Cohen)

Episodes in the life of a conscript at the beginning of World War II.
Lumbering anarchic comedy based on Spike Milligan's own sidesplitting memoirs; an enfeebled British *M*A*S*H*.

w Johnny Byrne *d* Norman Cohen *ph* Terry Maher *m* Wilfred Burns

Jim Dale, Spike Milligan (as his own father), Arthur Lowe, Bill Maynard, Windsor Davies, Pat Coombs, Tony Selby, Geoffrey Hughes

'A convincing period shabbiness and sleaziness which are endearing when they're not being overstated.'—*MFB*

Adorable*
US 1933 85m bw
Fox

A Ruritanian princess falls in love with a naval officer.
Charming, lightweight romance of the old school.

w George Marion Jr, Jane Storm, *story* Paul Frank, Billy Wilder *d* William Dieterle *ph* John Seitz *songs* Werner Richard Heymann, George Marion, Richard Whiting

Janet Gaynor, Henri Garat, C. Aubrey Smith, Herbert Mundin, Blanche Friderici, Hans von Twardowski

'Not strong b.o. . . . even the neighbourhood fans have caught up with the musical comedy kingdom idea.'—*Variety*

† The film was remade from German–French originals under a title which translated as *Her Majesty Commands*. The German version starred Kaethe von Nagy and Willy Fritsch, the French Lillian Harvey and Henri Garat.

Adorable Creatures
France 1952 105m bw
Jacques Roitfeld / Sirius

A Paris fashion executive recalls his love affairs.
A collection of four short sex comedies which did well on the heels of *La Ronde*.

w Charles Spaak, Jacques Companeez *d* Christian-Jaque *ph* Christian Matras *m* Georges Van Parys

Daniel Gélin, *Danielle Darrieux*, Edwige Feuillère, Antonella Lualdi, Martine Carol, Marilyn Buferd

Adorable Julia
Austria / France 1962 97m bw

A middle-aged actress takes on a lover. Moderately pleasing sex comedy, rather more heavily directed than Maugham would have liked. Lilli Palmer, Charles Boyer, Jean Sorel, Jeanne Valerie. Written by Johanna Sibelius and Eberhard Keindorff from the novel Theatre by Somerset Maugham; directed by Alfred Weidenmann; for Wiener Mundus / Etoile. (GB title: *The Seduction of Julia*.)

Adua e le Compagne
Italy 1960 150m bw

When brothels in Italy are officially closed, four of the old girls open a restaurant. Immensely overlong comedy drama whose rewards come entirely from the actors. Simone Signoret, Marcello Mastroianni, Sanda Milo, Emmanuelle Riva, Gina Rovere. Written by Ruggero Maccari, Ettore Scola, Antonio Pietrangeli, Tullio Pinelli; directed by Antonio Pietrangeli; for Zebra Film. 'The script becomes increasingly episodic, and clichés abound.'—*MFB*. (GB title: *Hungry for Love*.)

Advance to the Rear*
US 1964 97m bw Panavision
MGM / Ted Richmond
GB title: *Company of Cowards?*

After the Civil War, a troop of misfits is sent west out of harm's way, but manages to capture a rebel spy and save a gold shipment.
Semi-satirical western action comedy with a farcical climax; quite sharply made.

w Samuel A. Peeples, William Bowers *d* George Marshall *ph* Milton Krasner *m* Randy Sparks

Glenn Ford, *Melvyn Douglas*, Stella Stevens, Jim Backus, Joan Blondell, Andrew Prine, Alan Hale, James Griffith, Preston Foster

'Gable's back and Garson's got him!'
Adventure*
US 1945 126m bw
MGM (Sam Zimbalist)

A roughneck sailor marries a librarian, but only settles down to love her when their child is born.
Uniquely embarrassing (and fascinating) mishmash of pretentious dialogue and cardboard characters.

w Frederick Hazlitt Brennan, Vincent Lawrence, *novel* Clyde Brion Davis *d* Victor Fleming *ph* Joseph Ruttenberg *m* Herbert Stothart

Clark Gable, Greer Garson, Thomas Mitchell, Joan Blondell, John Qualen, Richard Haydn

'MGM proudly announce *Adventure* as the meeting of a red-blooded man with a blue-blooded woman. Its impact on the bloodstream of your critic was a chilling one. Fifty years of the cinema, he thought, and this is where we've landed.'—*Richard Winnington*

Adventure in Baltimore
US 1949 89m bw
RKO (Richard H. Berger)
GB title: *Bachelor Bait*

In 1905, a young society girl becomes a suffragette.
Inconsequential period comedy which did nothing for its young star's fading career.

w Lionel Houser, *story* Christopher Isherwood, Lesser Samuels *d* Richard Wallace *ph* Robert de Grasse *m* Frederick Hollander

Shirley Temple, Robert Young, John Agar, Albert Sharpe, Josephine Hutchinson, Johnny Sands, John Miljan, Norma Varden

Adventure in Diamonds
US 1940 76m bw
Paramount (George Fitzmaurice)

A British adventurer in South Africa falls in love with a lady diamond thief.
Acceptable romantic comedy-drama.

w Leonard Lee, Franz Schultz *d* George Fitzmaurice *ph* Charles Lang *m* Leo Shuken

George Brent, Isa Miranda, John Loder, Nigel Bruce, Elizabeth Patterson, Matthew Boulton, Cecil Kellaway, Ernest Truex, E. E. Clive

Adventure in Iraq
US 1943 65m bw

Wartime second feature about Americans who fall into Nazi–Arab hands. Interesting only as a remake of *The Green Goddess*, with Paul Cavanagh in the George Arliss role. Also featuring John Loder, Ruth Ford. Written by George Bilson and Robert E. Kent; directed by D. Ross Lederman; for Warner.

Adventure in Manhattan
US 1936 73m bw
Columbia
GB title: *Manhattan Madness*

An actress helps an ace reporter to foil a bank robbery by a master criminal.
Flat romantic mystery comedy which wastes a good cast.

w Sidney Buchman, Harry Sauber, Jack Kirkland *d* Edward Ludwig *ph* Henry Freulich

Jean Arthur, Joel McCrea, Thomas Mitchell, Reginald Owen, Herman Bing

Adventure in Washington
US 1941 82m bw

A Senate page sells government secrets in Wall Street. Unlikely melodrama with senators getting together to hush up a scandal. Herbert Marshall, Virginia Bruce, Gene Reynolds, Samuel S. Hinds, Ralph Morgan, Vaughan Glaser. Written by Lewis R. Foster and Arthur Caesar; directed by Alfred E. Green; for Columbia.

Adventure Island
US 1947 67m Cinecolor

Seafarers chance on an uncharted island, ruled by a deadly fanatic. Hokum rehash of Stevenson's *Ebb Tide*, with Paul Kelly as the madman; also featuring Rory Calhoun, Rhonda Fleming. Written by Maxwell Shane; directed by Peter Stewart; for Paramount.

The Adventure of Sherlock Holmes' Smarter Brother
GB 1975 91m De Luxe
TCF / Jouer (Richard A. Roth)

More by good luck than good management, Sherlock's younger brother solves one of his cases.
Infuriating parody with little sense of the original and a hit-or-miss style all of its own. Amusing moments fail to atone for the general waste of opportunity.

wd Gene Wilder *ph* Gerry Fisher *m* John Morris *pd* Terry Marsh

Gene Wilder, Marty Feldman, Madeleine Kahn, Leo McKern, Dom De Luise, Roy Kinnear, John Le Mesurier, Douglas Wilmer, Thorley Walters

'Like a compilation of the kind of numbers actors like to do at parties.'—*Howard Kissel*

'He has bitten off more than he can chew or I can swallow.'—*John Simon*

'A few stray chuckles but nothing more.'—*Sight and Sound*

'There's no mystery, and since you can't have a parody of a mystery without a mystery, there's no comic suspense.'—*New Yorker, 1980*

The Adventurer***
US 1917 21m approx (24 fps) bw silent
Mutual

An escaped convict rescues two wealthy women from drowning and is invited to their home.
Hilarious early Chaplin knockabout, with his physical gags at their most streamlined.

wd Charles Chaplin ph William C. Foster, Rollie Totheroh

Charles Chaplin, Edna Purviance, Eric Campbell, Henry Bergman

The Adventurers
GB 1950 86m bw
Rank / Mayflower (Maxwell Setton, Aubrey Baring)
US title: *The Great Adventure*

In 1902, two Boers and a cashiered English officer set out to recover stolen diamonds.
Lethargic South African western in the wake of *Treasure of the Sierra Madre*; clumsy and unconvincing, with cardboard characters.

w Robert Westerby *d* David MacDonald *ph* Oswald Morris *m* Cedric Thorpe Davie

Dennis Price, Jack Hawkins, Siobhan McKenna, Peter Hammond, Bernard Lee, Grégoire Aslan

The Adventurers*
US 1970 170m Technicolor Panavision
Paramount / Avco Embassy / Adventurers Film (Lewis Gilbert)

A sensualist brought up amid Europe's luxuries returns to his Central American homeland to take vengeance on the brutal security chief who raped and murdered his mother.
Sprawling, sexy, bloodstained extravaganza from a Harold Robbins novel. Expensive to look at and riddled with sensation, but that's about all.

w Michael Hastings, Lewis Gilbert *d* Lewis Gilbert *ph* Claude Renoir *m* Antonio Carlos Jobim *pd* Tony Masters

Bekim Fehmiu, Alan Badel, Candice Bergen, Ernest Borgnine, Olivia de Havilland, Rossano Brazzi, Charles Aznavour, Sidney Tafler, Fernando Rey, Leigh Taylor-Young, Thommy Berggren, John Ireland

'A three-hour slog through every imaginable cliché of writing and direction . . . in addition to an abundance of flaccid sex and violence, it offers drugs, sadism, orchids, fireworks, orgies, lesbianism, a miscarriage, a private torture chamber, and the hell of several fashion shows with loud pop music accompaniment. This might well be described as the film with everything; trouble is, it is difficult to imagine anybody wanting any of it.'—*MFB*

'Lovers of rotten movies and close-up violence can revel in it.'—*Judith Crist*

Adventures of a Rookie
US 1943 64m bw

Modest attempt to launch a new comedy team in a threadbare army farce. Wally Brown, Alan Carney, Erford Gage, Richard Martin. Written by Edward James, William Bowers, M. Coates Webster; directed by Leslie Goodwins; for RKO. 'Sufficiently corny to get through the subsequent duals where the customers are not too particular.'—*Variety*

The Adventures of Arsène Lupin*
France / Italy 1956 103m Eastmancolor
Chavane-SNE-Gaumont / Lambor-Costellazione (Robert Sussfeld)

In 1912, the famous jewel thief conducts several successful robberies and outwits the Kaiser.
The most stylish Lupin film, though not based on the original stories.

w Jacques Becker, Albert Simonin, based on the character created by Maurice Leblanc *d Jacques Becker ph Edmond Séchan ad* Rino Mondellini

Robert Lamoureux, Lisolotte Pulver, Otto Hasse, Henri Rolland

The Adventures of Barry Mackenzie*
Australia 1972 114m Eastmancolor
Columbia / Longford (Philip Adams)

A sex-hungry Australian gets into all kinds of trouble on a visit to the Old Country.
Occasionally funny, defiantly crude and tasteless, but poorly produced comedy-misadventure from the *Private Eye* comic strip. Australian slang combines with bad sound recording to make much of the film unintelligible.

w Barry Humphries, Bruce Beresford *d* Bruce Beresford *ph* Don McAlpine *m* Peter Best

Barry Crocker, Barry Humphries (as Dame Edna Everage), Peter Cook, Spike Milligan, Dennis Price, Avice Landon, Dick Bentley, Joan Bakewell, William Rushton

'A wildly uneven concoction of antipodean bad taste, probably only fully appreciated by Earls Court exiles.'—*Sight and Sound*

† Sequel 1974: *Barry Mackenzie Holds His Own.*

The Adventures of Bullwhip Griffin*
US 1965 110m Technicolor
Walt Disney (Bill Anderson)

In the 1849 California Gold Rush, two aristocrats and their butler head west.
Rather splendid spoof western with careful attention to detail and comedy pointing, well above the average Disney standard.

w Lowell S. Hawley, novel By the Great Horn Spoon by Sid Fleischman *d* James Neilson *ph* Edward Colman *m* George Bruns *titles Ward Kimball*

Roddy McDowall, Suzanne Pleshette, Bryan Russell, Karl Malden, Harry Guardino, Richard Haydn, Mike Mazurki, Hermione Baddeley, Cecil Kellaway

Adventures of Captain Africa
US 1955 bw serial: 15 eps

A wild animal trapper combats rebels who have kidnapped an African prime minister. Routine hokum. John Hart, Rick Vallin, Ben Welden. Directed by Spencer Bennet; for Columbia.

The Adventures of Captain Fabian
US 1951 100m bw
Republic / Silver (William Marshall)

A sea captain returns to New Orleans to revenge himself on the family which had defrauded his father.
Stilted, old-fashioned *Monte Cristo*ish melodrama with some curiosity value but little verve in the playing or production. An awful warning to independent producers.

w Errol Flynn, *novel* Fabulous Ann Medlock by Robert Shannon *d* William Marshall *ph* Marcel Grignon *m* René Cloerec

Errol Flynn, Micheline Presle, Agnes Moorehead, Vincent Price, Victor Francen, Jim Gerald

† Made in France.

Adventures of Captain Marvel*
US 1941 bw serial: 12 eps

When a scientific expedition goes to Siam, the assistant radio operator is endowed by the mysterious Shazam with the power to transform himself into Captain Marvel, and to defeat the evil Scorpion. Modest classic serial, good for more than a few laughs. Tom Tyler, Frank Coghlan Jnr, William Benedict, Louise Currie. Directed by William Witney and John English; for Republic.

Adventures of Casanova
US 1948 83m bw

Casanova returns to Sicily and helps overthrow the tyrannical rule of the King of Naples. Robin Hood transplanted, with a few amorous asides; but this is a totally stilted production which fails to entertain. Arturo de Cordova, Lucille Bremer, Turhan Bey. Written by Crane Wilbur, Walter Bullock and Ken de Wolf; directed by Roberto Gavaldon; for Eagle-Lion.

The Adventures of Don Juan**
US 1949 110m Technicolor
Warner (Jerry Wald)
GB title: *The New Adventures of Don Juan*

A reformed 17th-century rake saves his queen from the machinations of her first minister. Expensive, slightly uneasy, but generally very entertaining swashbuckler with elements of self-spoofery. Flynn's last big-budget extravaganza.

w George Oppenheimer, Harry Kurnitz *d* Vincent Sherman *ph* Elwood Bredell *m* Max Steiner

Errol Flynn, Viveca Lindfors, Romney Brent, Robert Douglas, Alan Hale, Ann Rutherford, Robert Warwick, Jerry Austin, Douglas Kennedy, Una O'Connor, Aubrey Mather, Raymond Burr

'A lavish film on a truly magnificent scale.'—*The Times*

Adventures of Frank and Jesse James
US 1948 bw serial: 13 eps

Supposed outlaws pay back the money their gang has stolen. A new but not very interesting twist on history. Clayton Moore, Steve Darrell, Noel Neill. Directed by Fred Brannon and Yakima Canutt; for Republic.

Adventures of Frank Merriwell
US 1936 bw serial: 12 eps

A star baseball pitcher, armed with a mysterious ring, goes in search of his missing father. Ho-hum adventures with sporting asides. Don Briggs, Jean Rogers, Don King. Directed by Cliff Smith; for Universal.

The Adventures of Gallant Bess
US 1984 71m Cinecolor

The master of a trained rodeo horse becomes a range wanderer. Easy-going animal interest saga with a pleasant ending. Cameron Mitchell, Audrey Long, Fuzzy Knight, James Millican, Ed Gargan. Written by Matthew Rapf; directed by Lew Larders; for Eagle Lion.

The Adventures of Gerard*
GB 1970 91m De Luxe Panavision
UA / Sir Nigel Films (Peter Beale)

A hussar of Napoleon becomes involved in a double spy game but comes out trumps and wins a fair lady.
A lighthearted historical spoof of military pomp, with plenty of attractive elements which unfortunately fail to jell into a satisfying film.

w H. A. L. Craig and others, from stories by Arthur Conan Doyle *d* Jerzy Skolimowski *ph* Witold Sobocinski *m* Riz Ortolani

Peter McEnery, Claudia Cardinale, Eli Wallach, Jack Hawkins, Mark Burns, Norman Rossington, John Neville

'Enormously graceful and witty . . . picks its way with amazing delicacy through the reefs of facetiousness.'—*Tom Milne*

The Adventures of Hajji Baba*
US 1954 93m De Luxe Cinemascope
Allied Artists / Walter Wanger

In ancient Arabia, a barber helps and falls in love with an escaping princess.
A reasonably dashing sword and sandal romp which no one takes very seriously.

w Richard Collins *d* Don Weis *ph* Harold Lipstein *m* Dmitri Tiomkin *pd* Gene Allen

John Derek, Elaine Stewart, Thomas Gomez, Amanda Blake, Paul Picerni, Rosemarie Bowe

The Adventures of Huckleberry Finn:
see Huckleberry Finn

Adventures of Kitty O'Day
US 1944 63m bw

A snoopy phone operator solves three murders before the police get started. Predictable stuff, but tolerable and bright in its way. Jean Parker, Peter Cookson, Tim Ryan, Ralph Sanford. Written by Tim Ryan, George Callahan, Victor Hammond; directed by William Beaudine; for Monogram.

The Adventures of Marco Polo*
US 1938 100m bw
Samuel Goldwyn

The medieval Italian explorer discovers China, fireworks, and a beautiful maiden.
One gets the impression that this began as a standard adventure and that during production it switched to comedy; whatever the cause, lively and amusing scenes fail to add up to more than a thinly scripted pantomime.

w Robert E. Sherwood *d* Archie Mayo *ph* Rudolph Maté *m* Hugo Friedhofer *md* Alfred Newman *ad* Richard Day

Gary Cooper, Sigrid Gurie, Basil Rathbone, Ernest Truex, Binnie Barnes, Alan Hale, George Barbier

'In spite of its elaborate settings and the presence of Gary Cooper, it never quite lives up to its promises.'—*New York Sun*

'Goldwyn's most ambitious endeavour . . . deserves and will get enthusiastic exhibitor plugging. Sherwood's more concerned with entertainment than with history.'—*Variety*
† Release prints were in sepiatone.

The Adventures of Mark Twain**
US 1944 130m bw
Warner (Jesse L. Lasky)

The life of America's foremost humorous writer, from a Mississippi riverboat to his becoming an honorary fellow of Oxford University.
Conventional biopic, quite watchable and with unusual side turnings, but eventually lacking the zest of the subject.

w Harold M. Sherman, Alan le May, Harry Chandler *d* Irving Rapper *ph Sol Polito* *m* Max Steiner

Fredric March, Alexis Smith, Donald Crisp, Alan Hale, C. Aubrey Smith, John Carradine, William Henry, Robert Barrat, Walter Hampden

'It's not that it's much worse than most cinematized biographies, because it does have its good moments. It's just that once more biographical inaccuracy is rampant, and once more the best dramatic possibilities have been overlooked, so it's hard to think of anything new, in the line of protest, to say.'—*David Lardner, New Yorker*

AAN: Max Steiner

The Adventures of Martin Eden
US 1942 87m bw

An American seaman fights a brutal captain and wins better conditions for his comrades. Routine actioner based on what are virtually the author's memoirs. Glenn Ford, Evelyn Keyes, Claire Trevor, Stuart Erwin, Dickie Moore. Written by W. L. River from the story by Jack London; directed by Sidney Salkow; for B. P. Schulberg / Columbia.

Adventures of Red Ryder
US 1940 bw serial: 12 eps

Our hero forms an organization to drive gunfighters out of Santa Fe. Unsurprising serialized shenanigans. Don Barry, Noah Beery Jnr, Tommy Cook, William Farnum. Directed by William Witney and John English; for Republic.

Adventures of Rex and Rinty
US 1935 bw serial: 12 eps

A stolen prize horse teams up with a wandering dog to help oust various villains. Slightly unusual chapter play with 'the king of wild horses' and 'Rin Tin Tin Jnr'. Kane Richmond, Mischa Auer, Norma Taylor, Smiley Burnette. Directed by Ford Beebe and B. Reeves Eason; for Mascot.

'Only the rainbow can duplicate its brilliance!'

The Adventures of Robin Hood****
US 1938 102m Technicolor
Warner (Hal B. Wallis)

Rebel outlaw Robin Hood outwits Guy of Gisbourne and the Sheriff of Nottingham, and saves the throne for the absent King Richard.
A splendid adventure story, rousingly operatic in treatment, with dashing action highlights, fine comedy balance, and incisive acting all round. Historically notable for its use of early three-colour Technicolor; also for convincingly recreating Britain in California.

w Seton I. Miller, Norman Reilly Raine d William Keighley, Michael Curtiz ph Tony Gaudio, Sol Polito, Howard Green m Erich Wolfgang Korngold ad Carl Jules Weyl

Errol Flynn (Sir Robin of Locksley), *Basil Rathbone* (Sir Guy of Gisbourne), *Claude Rains* (Prince John), Olivia de Havilland (Maid Marian), *Alan Hale* (Little John), Patric Knowles (Will Scarlet), *Eugene Pallette* (Friar Tuck), *Ian Hunter* (King Richard), *Melville Cooper* (Sheriff of Nottingham), Una O'Connor (Bess), Herbert Mundin (Much the Miller's Son), Montagu Love (Bishop of Black Canons), Howard Hill (Captain of Archers)

PRINCE JOHN: 'Any objections to the new tax, from our Saxon friends?'

ROBIN to Gisbourne during duel: 'Did I upset your plans?'

GISBOURNE: 'You've come to Nottingham once too often!'

ROBIN: 'When this is over, my friend, there'll be no need for me to come again!'

PRINCE JOHN: 'Ho, varlets, bring Sir Robin food! Such insolence must support a healthy appetite!'

ROBIN: 'It's injustice I hate, not the Normans!'

'Magnificent, unsurpassable . . . the film is lavish, brilliantly photographed, and has a great Korngold score.'—*NFT, 1974*

'Mostly the picture is full of movement, some of it dashing in fine romantic costume style, some of it just sprightly. The excitement comes from fast action – galloping steeds, men swinging Tarzan-like from the trees, hurling tables and chairs, rapid running swordplay, the sudden whiz of Robin's arrows coming from nowhere to startle his enemies – more than from any fear that Robin might be worsted. Somehow the whole thing has the air of being a costume party, a jolly and rather athletic one, with a lot of well-bred Englishmen playing at being in the greenwood.'—*James Shelley Hamilton, National Board of Review*

† At the time of its release this was Warners' most expensive film, costing more than two million dollars. Chico, California, stood in for Sherwood Forest; the archery contest was shot at Busch Gardens, Pasadena. Curtiz took over direction when it was felt that the action lacked impact.

AA: Erich Wolfgang Korngold; Carl Jules Weyl

AAN: best picture

The Adventures of Robinson Crusoe***

Mexico 1953 89m Pathecolor
Tepeyac (Oscar Dancigers, Henry F. Ehrlich)

A 17th-century mariner is shipwrecked on an uninhabited tropical island.
Fascinating version of a famous story, with only one character on screen until the belated arrival of Friday and the escape to civilization. Subtle and compelling, with only the colour unsatisfactory.

w Luis Bunuel, Phillip Roll, novel Daniel Defoe *d Luis Bunuel ph* Alex Phillips *m* Anthony Collins

Dan O'Herlihy, James Fernandez

'A film of which the purity, the tense poetic style, evokes a kind of wonder.'—*Gavin Lambert*

'Free of that deadly solicitude which usually kills off classics.'—*New Yorker, 1977*

AAN: Dan O'Herlihy

The Adventures of Sherlock Holmes**

US 1939 83m bw
TCF (Gene Markey)
GB title: *Sherlock Holmes*

Moriarty sends Holmes on a false trail while he plots to steal the Crown jewels.
An engaging piece of pseudo-Victoriana: all elements smooth save an unconvincing plot.

w Edwin Blum, William Drake *d* Alfred Werker *ph Leon Shamroy m* Cyril Mockridge

Basil Rathbone (Holmes), *Nigel Bruce* (Dr Watson), *George Zucco* (Moriarty), Ida Lupino (Ann Brandon), Alan Marshal (Jerrold Hunter), Terry Kilburn (Billy), E. E. Clive (Inspector Bristol), Henry Stephenson (Sir Ronald Ramsgate), Mary Gordon (Mrs Hudson)

'The "elementary my dear Watson" type of dialogue is soft-pedalled for more modern phrases or understandable patter.'—*Variety*

'Told with more movie art per foot than seven reels of anything the intellectual men have been finding good this whole year or more.'—*Otis Ferguson*

† This was the second and last of Rathbone's costume outings as Holmes, and the one in which he sang a comic song in disguise.

Adventures of Sir Galahad

US 1949 bw serial: 15 eps

King Arthur's knight goes in search of the missing magic sword Excalibur. Predictably stiff-necked medieval goings-on with American accents. George Reeves, Charles King, William Fawcett. Directed by Spencer Bennet; for Columbia.

Adventures of Smilin' Jack

US 1943 bw serial: 12 eps

On an Eastern island, an American adventurer helps the Chinese to prevent a Japanese takeover. Standard rough stuff with a rather interesting cast. Tom Brown, Marjorie Lord, Philip Ahn, Sidney Toler, Turhan Bey, Rose Hobart, Keye Luke, Nigel de Brulier. Directed by Ray Taylor and Lewis D. Collins; for Universal.

The Adventures of Tartu*

GB 1943 103m bw
MGM (Irving Asher)
US title: *Tartu*

During World War II, a British spy goes to Czechoslovakia to dismantle a poison gas factory.
Halting and artificial comedy-thriller, saved only by a graceful star performance.

w Howard Emmett Rogers, John Lee Mahin, Miles Malleson *d* Harold S. Bucquet *ph* John J. Cox *m* Hubert Bath *md* Louis Levy

Robert Donat, Valerie Hobson, Walter Rilla, Glynis Johns, Martin Miller

'You are seeing all it has, and bald spots as well, first time around, whereas with a good Hitchcock or even a good Carol Reed, the pleasures visible at a first seeing stand up, or intensify, at a third or a fifth.'—*James Agee*

Adventures of the Flying Cadets

US 1943 bw serial: 13 eps

Flying students fight a Nazi agent called the Black Hangman. Spirited thick-ear with a competent cast. Johnny Downs, Bobby Jordan, Ward Wood, Robert Armstrong, Eduardo Ciannelli, Billy Benedict, Regis Toomey. Directed by Ray Taylor and Lewis D. Collins; for Universal.

Adventures of the Wilderness Family

US 1975 101m colour

An urban family runs into trouble when it takes to the wilds. Naïve little four-wall family movie in which the pretty scenery (Utah and the Canadian Rockies) and the animals compensate for the dramatic inadequacies. Robert Logan, Susan Damante Shaw. Written and directed by Stewart Raffil; for Pacific International. (*Further Adventures of the Wilderness Family* appeared in 1977.)

The Adventures of Tom Sawyer***

US 1938 91m Technicolor
David O. Selznick (William H. Wright)

Small-town Mississippi boy tracks down a murderer, Injun Joe.
Set-bound but excellent version of the children's classic by Mark Twain.

w John Weaver d Norman Taurog *ph* James Wong Howe, Wilfrid Cline *m* Max Steiner *ad William Cameron Menzies*

Tommy Kelly (Tom), *May Robson* (Aunt Polly), Walter Brennan (Muff Potter), Victor Jory (Injun Joe), Victor Kilian (Sheriff), Jackie Moran (Huckleberry Finn), Ann Gillis (Becky Thatcher), Donald Meek (Sunday School Superintendent), Margaret Hamilton (Mrs Sawyer), Marcia Mae Jones (Mary Sawyer)

'Another Selznick box office clean-up, an attraction destined for extended first runs, repeat bookings and heavy matinée take.'—*Variety*

'The familiar characters emerge in all their old amiability, the atmosphere is there and so is the excitement.'—*MFB*

'Should make Mark Twain circulate in his grave like a trout in a creel.'—*Otis Ferguson*

'Another Selznick International box office clean-up . . . that there exists a broad audience for films whose essential appeal is to the family trade has always been true. *Snow White* touched a source of almost unlimited audience draw: *Tom Sawyer* follows to the same customers.'—*Variety*

Advice to the Lovelorn*

US 1933 62m bw

A reporter is demoted to the lonelyhearts column and becomes absorbed in it. Springy vehicle for *Lee Tracy*, with Sally Blane, Sterling Holloway, Isabel Jewell, Jean Adair; written by Leonard Praskins from the novel Miss Lonelyhearts by Nathanael West; directed by Alfred Werker; for Darryl F. Zanuck/Twentieth Century. (Compare the Paul Muni vehicle *Hi Nellie*.)

'Are the men and women of Washington really like this?'

Advise and Consent**
US 1962 139m bw Panavision
Columbia / Alpha-Alpina / Otto Preminger

The President's choice of an unpopular secretary of state leads to divisions in the Senate and the blackmail and suicide of a senator.
Absorbing political melodrama from a novel which aimed to lift the lid off Washington. Many character actors make their mark, but the harsh-contrast photography seems misjudged.

w Wendell Mayes, *novel* Allen Drury *d* Otto Preminger *ph* Sam Leavitt *m* Jerry Fielding *titles* Saul Bass

Don Murray, *Charles Laughton,* Henry Fonda, Walter Pidgeon, Lew Ayres, Edward Andrews, Burgess Meredith, Gene Tierney, Franchot Tone, George Grizzard, Paul Ford, Peter Lawford, Inga Swenson, Will Geer

'The result is supremely ambivalent, a battle between fascinatingly real props and procedures and melodramatically unreal characters and situations.'—*Peter John Dyer*

'The parade of people helps to take one's mind off the overwrought melodrama.'—*New Yorker, 1980*

Aelita*
USSR 1924 70m approx bw silent
Mezhrabpom

Two Russian rocket pioneers land on Mars and start a revolution against the planet's queen.
Notable early space fiction, with footage of twenties Moscow as well as interesting set designs.

w Fedor Ozep, Alexei Faiko, *novel* Alexei Tolstoy *d* Yakov Protazanov *ph* Yuri Zhelabuzhsky *pd* Sergei Kozlovsky

Yulia Solntseva, Nikolai Batalov, Igor Ilinsky

Aerial Gunner
US 1943 78m bw

A US air force pilot in hospital thinks back to his training and his young brother's problems.
A watered-down *Wings* (with process footage to match) which also starred Arlen. Richard Arlen, Chester Morris, Jimmy Lydon, Lita Ward, Dick Purcell. Written by Maxwell Shane, produced and directed by William H. Pine and William G. Thomas, for Pine-Thomas (Paramount).

Aerograd**
USSR 1935 81m bw
Mosfilm-Ukrainfilm
aka: *Frontier*

Guards keep Japanese spies out of Siberia, where an airport is being built.
An action film with style and pretensions.

wd Alexander Dovzhenko ph Edouard Tissé, Mikhail Gindin *m* Dmitri Kabalevsky

Semyon Shagaida, Stepan Shkurat, Sergei Stolyarov

Affair in Trinidad*
US 1952 98m bw
Columbia / Beckworth (Vincent Sherman)

A nightclub singer whose husband is killed by gangsters works undercover for the police and routs the gang with the help of her husband's brother.
A tired tropical melodrama intended to follow up the success of *Gilda*, but without the verve. Some routine pleasures, though.

w Oscar Saul, James Gunn *d* Vincent Sherman *ph* Joseph Walker *m* Morris Stoloff, George Dunning

Rita Hayworth, Glenn Ford, Alexander Scourby, Torin Thatcher, Valerie Bettis, Steve Geray, Karel Stepanek, George Voskovec

'Improbable, foolish, but glossy.'—*Penelope Houston*

An Affair to Remember**
US 1957 114m Eastmancolor Cinemascope
TCF (Jerry Wald)

An ex-nightclub singer falls in love with a wealthy bachelor on a transatlantic liner, but an accident prevents her from attending their subsequent rendezvous.
Remake of *Love Affair*, a surprisingly successful mixture of smart lines, sentiment and tears, all applied with style and assurance.

w Delmer Daves, Leo McCarey *d* Leo McCarey *ph* Milton Krasner *m* Hugo Friedhofer

Cary Grant, Deborah Kerr, Cathleen Nesbitt, Richard Denning, Neva Patterson

'A lush slice of Hollywood romanticism.'—*MFB*

'90 masterly minutes of entrancing light comedy and 25 beastly minutes of beastly, melodramatic, pseudo-tragic guff.'—*Paul Dehn*

AAN: Milton Krasner; Hugo Friedhofer; title song (*m* Harry Warren, *ly* Harold Adamson, Leo McCarey)

Affair with a Stranger*
US 1953 87m bw
RKO (Robert Sparks)

Five friends reminisce about a marriage which seems about to break up.
This would-be-smart comedy has a good idea unsatisfactorily worked out, and could have used a more sparkling cast.

w Richard Flournoy *d* Roy Rowland *ph* Harry J. Wild *m* Roy Webb

Jean Simmons, Victor Mature, Mary Jo Tarola, Monica Lewis, Jane Darwell, Nicholas Joy, Wally Vernon, Dabbs Greer

L'Affaire est dans le Sac*
France 1932 47m bw
Pathé / Nathan
aka: *It's in the Bag*

Two would-be kidnappers end up (a) married to and (b) employed by their intended victims.
Semi-professional nonsense comedy with political jokes.

w Jacques Prévert *d* Pierre Prévert *ph* A. Giboury, Eli Lotar *m* Maurice Jaubert

J.-P. Le Chanois, Jacques Brunius, Etienne Decroux, Lucien Raimbourg, Julien Carette, Lora Hays

Affairs of a Gentleman
US 1934 68m bw

A novelist who has used all his love affairs in his novels holds a reunion. Mild star vehicle which wastes an amusing idea. Paul Lukas, Leila Hyams, Onslow Stevens. Written by Cyril Hume, Peter Ruric and Milton Krims; directed by Edwin L. Marin; for Universal.

The Affairs of Anatol*
US 1921 95m approx (24 fps) bw silent
Famous Players–Lasky / de Mille–Paramount

A socialite interrupts his honeymoon to go looking for romance.
Dated but historically very interesting sophisticated farce from a time when Hollywood was aping Viennese naughtiness.

w Jeanie MacPherson, Beulah Marie Dix, Lorna Moon, Elmer Harris, from Granville Barker's paraphrase of the play Anatol by Arthur Schnitzler *d* Cecil B. de Mille *ph* Alvin Wyckoff, Karl Struss *ed* Anne Bauchens

Wallace Reid, Gloria Swanson, Bebe Daniels, Elliott Dexter, Monte Blue, Wanda Hawley, Theodore Roberts

'Should be enormously popular, especially with those who think Schnitzler is a cheese.'—*Robert E. Sherwood*

'The man who doesn't sell out for every performance of a double run should turn his show shop into a Quaker meeting house.'—*Motion Picture Herald*

The Affairs of Annabel*
US 1938 69m bw
RKO (Lee Marcus, Lou Lusty)

A crackpot Hollywood press agent sends his star to jail as a publicity stunt.
An amusing frenetic comedy of its time, successful enough to warrant a sequel, *Annabel Takes a Tour*, in the same year.

w Bert Granet, Paul Yawitz *d* Lew Landers *ph* Russell Metty *m* Roy Webb

Lucille Ball, Jack Oakie, Ruth Donnelly, Bradley Page, Fritz Feld, Thurston Hall, Elizabeth Risdon, Granville Bates, James Burke

The Affairs of Cellini*
US 1934 90m bw
Twentieth Century (Darryl F. Zanuck)

The complex amours of a 16th-century Florentine rake.
Lively period bedroom farce somewhat hampered by censorship.

w Bess Meredyth, *play* The Firebrand by Edwin Justus Mayer *d* Gregory La Cava *ph* Charles Rosher *m* Alfred Newman

Fredric March, Constance Bennett, *Frank Morgan,* Fay Wray, Vince Barnett, Louis Calhern, Jessie Ralph

'Gay and entertaining though whipped up synthetically like circus ice cream.'—*Variety*

AAN: Charles Rosher; Frank Morgan

The Affairs of Dobie Gillis
US 1953 74m bw
MGM (Arthur M. Loew Jnr)

Adventures of an indolent and accident-prone university student.
Scatty comedy with good talent and musical numbers encased in a tatty production.

w Max Shulman *d* Don Weis *ph* William Mellor *md* Jeff Alexander

Bobby Van, Debbie Reynolds, Hans Conried, Barbara Ruick, Bob Fosse

The Affairs of Martha
US 1942 66m bw

A servant writes a scandalous book about her employers. Fairly amusing comedy with an ingratiating cast: Marsha Hunt, Richard Carlson, Spring Byington, Allyn Joslyn, Frances Drake, Margaret Hamilton, Melville Cooper, Virginia Weidler, Ernest Truex, Marjorie Main. Written by Isobel Lennart and Lee Gold; directed by Jules Dassin; for MGM. (GB title: *Once Upon a Thursday*.)

'She's so romantic she drives four men frantic!'

The Affairs of Susan**
US 1945 110m bw
Paramount (Hal B. Wallis)

Four men in Susan's life see her differently. Occasionally witty comedy designed as a champagne vehicle for its star. It seemed quite good at the time.

w Richard Flournoy, *original story* Laszlo Gorog, T. Monroe *d* William A. Seiter *ph* David Abel *m* Frederick Hollander

Joan Fontaine, George Brent, Walter Abel, Don Defore, Dennis O'Keefe

'The cast enters into the irresponsibilities with gusto.'—*MFB*

'A bright thing, a bit too long.'—*Richard Mallett, Punch*

AAN: Laszlo Gorog, T. Monroe

Affectionately Yours
US 1941 88m bw
Warner (Mark Hellinger)

A foreign correspondent hurries home when he hears that his wife plans to divorce him. Thin lightweight comedy, unsuitably cast.

w Edward Kaufman *d* Lloyd Bacon *ph* Tony Gaudio *m* Heinz Roemheld

Merle Oberon, Dennis Morgan, *Rita Hayworth*, George Tobias, Ralph Bellamy, James Gleason, Hattie McDaniel

Africa Screams
US 1949 79m bw

Two dumbbells go on safari with a treasure map. Lower-case Abbott and Costello comedy, with Hillary Brooke, Max Baer, Shemp Howard. Written by Earl Baldwin; directed by Charles Barton; for Edward Nassour / UA.

Africa Texas Style*
GB 1967 109m Eastmancolor
Paramount / Vantors (Andrew Marton)

A Kenyan settler hires two Texas cowboys to help in his scheme of wild game ranching. Excellent location sequences are dragged down by a very boring script, but it's a good family film nevertheless.

w Andy White *d* Andrew Marton *ph* Paul Beeson *m* Malcolm Arnold

John Mills, Hugh O'Brian, Nigel Green, Tom Nardini, Adrienne Corri, Ronald Howard

† Forerunner of TV series, *Cowboy in Africa.*

'They never dreamed of being in each other's arms, yet the mystic spell of the jungle swept them to primitive, hungry embrace! The greatest adventure a man ever had . . . with a woman!'

The African Queen***
GB 1951 103m Technicolor
IFD / Romulus–Horizon (Sam Spiegel)

In 1915, a gin-drinking river trader and a prim missionary make odd companions for a boat trip down a dangerous river, culminating in an attack on a German gunboat.
Despite some unfortunate studio sets mixed in with real African footage achieved through great hardship by all concerned, this is one of those surprising films that really work, a splendidly successful mixture of comedy, character and adventure.

w James Agee, novel C. S. Forester *d John Huston ph Jack Cardiff m Allan Gray*

Humphrey Bogart (Charlie Allnutt), *Katharine Hepburn* (Rose Sayer), Robert Morley (The Rev. Samuel Sayer), Peter Bull (Captain), Theodore Bikel (2nd Officer)

ROSE: 'I never dreamed that any experience could be so stimulating!'

'Entertaining but not entirely plausible or original.'—*Robert Hatch*

'The movie is not great art but it is great fun, essentially one long, exciting, old-fashioned movie chase.'—*Time*

'A Technicolor Cook's Tour of jungle wonders, enriched by performances unmatched by anything Hepburn or Bogart have yet contributed to the screen.'—*Cue*

† Peter Viertel's book, *White Hunter Black Heart*, is basically about Huston during the making of this film.

AA: Humphrey Bogart
AAN: James Agee; John Huston; Katharine Hepburn

'When it's after midnight in New York City, you don't have to look for love, laughter and trouble. They'll all find you!'

After Hours**
US 1985 97m Duart Color
Warner / Geffen / Double Play (Amy Robinson, Griffin Dunne, Robert F. Colesberry)

Through a chapter of accidents, a mild-mannered computer programmer has a bad time in the night streets of New York.
An unsettling kind of black comedy with moments of malaise: nobody denies its touches of brilliance, but few people want to see it again.

w Joseph Minion *d Martin Scorsese*
ph Michael Ballhaus *m* Howard Shore
pd Jeffrey Townsend ed Thelma Schoonmaker

Griffin Dunne, Rosanna Arquette, Verna Bloom, Thomas Chong, Teri Garr, Cheech Marin

'The cinema of paranoia and persecution reaches an apogee . . . would have been pretty funny if it didn't play like a confirmation of everyone's worst fears about contemporary urban life.'—*Variety*

'A film so original, so particular, that one is uncertain from moment to moment exactly how to respond to it. Interesting.'—*Roger Ebert*

After Office Hours
GB 1932 78m bw

A bird's-eye view of life in a City of London office. Popular film version of a popular play which would now seem almost Dickensian. Frank Lawton, Heather Angel, Viola Lyel, Garry Marsh, Eileen Peel, Frank Royde, Katie Johnson. Written by Thomas Bentley and Frank Launder, from the play *London Wall* by John Van Druten; directed by Thomas Bentley; for British International.

After Office Hours*
US 1935 75m bw
MGM (Bernard H. Hyman)

A newspaperman and his socialite reporter solve a murder mystery.
Crisply-written, fast-moving comedy melodrama; good stuff of its time and type.

w Herman J. Mankiewicz d Robert Z. Leonard *ph* Charles Rosher

Clark Gable, Constance Bennett, Stuart Erwin, Billie Burke, Harvey Stephens, Katherine Alexander, Henry Travers, Henry Armetta

'One of the best balanced pix of the season; it has practically everything.'—*Film Daily*

'Mildly satisfactory entertainment . . . story deficiencies are surprising . . . Gable and Bennett will have to carry this one.'—*Variety*

After the Ball*
GB 1957 89m Eastmancolor
IFD / Beaconsfield (Peter Rogers)

The life and loves of music-hall singer Vesta Tilley, who married into the nobility.
Adequate if uninspired biopic with entertaining detail and songs.

w Hubert Gregg *d* Compton Bennett *ph* Jack Asher *ad* Norman Arnold *md* Muir Mathieson

Pat Kirkwood, Laurence Harvey, Clive Morton, Jerry Verno, June Clyde

After the Fox*
US / Italy 1966 103m Technicolor Panavision
UA / Nancy / CCM (John Bryan)

The Fox escapes from jail to execute a gold bullion caper and save his young sister from the streets.
Unlikeable and unfunny farce which sets its star among excitable Italians and hopes for the best, adding a few wild stabs at satire on movie-making styles.

w Neil Simon, Cesare Zavattini *d* Vittorio de Sica *ph* Leonida Barboni *m* Burt Bacharach

Peter Sellers, *Victor Mature* (agreeably sending up his old image), Britt Ekland, Lilia Brazzi, Paola Stoppa, Akim Tamiroff, Martin Balsam

'Never even begins to get off the ground.'—*MFB*

Written and directed by Ingmar Bergman

After the Rehearsal**
Sweden colour 72m

After a rehearsal for Strindberg's Dream Play, the director sits and remembers the circumstances surrounding an earlier production. Typical but satisfyingly unpretentious Bergman piece of the second rank. Erland Josephson, Ingrid Thulin, Lena Olin. Written and directed by Bergman, for Svenskfilmindustri/SV2. 'What we are left with is the very strong sense of an artist who has satisfied many lives for the sake of his art, and now wonders if perhaps one of those lives was his own.'—*Roger Ebert*

After the Thin Man**
US 1936 113m bw
MGM (Hunt Stromberg)

Nick and Nora Charles, not forgetting Asta, solve another murder.
Overlong but well-carpentered sequel to *The Thin Man*, developing the thesis that a married couple, even if they are detectives and drink too much, can be interesting and lovable.

w Frances Goodrich, Albert Hackett *d* W. S. Van Dyke II *ph* Oliver T. Marsh *m* Herbert Stothart, Edward Ward

William Powell, Myrna Loy, James Stewart, Elissa Landi, Joseph Calleia, Jessie Ralph, Alan Marshal, Sam Levene

'It is evident that it was almost impossible to make a better mystery comedy than *The Thin Man*. Early speed would have helped, but . . . few films this season have contained more risibles.'—*Variety*

AAN: Frances Goodrich; Albert Hackett

After Tomorrow
US 1932 70m bw

Family troubles and small salaries prevent a young couple from getting married. Rather curious drama which was sold on the fact that it retained the sex discussion from its stage original. Charles Farrell, Marian Nixon, Minna Gombell, Josephine Hull, William Collier Snr, William Pawley. Written by Sonia Levien from the play by John Golden and Hugh Strange; directed by Frank Borzage; for Fox. 'In several sequences it pioneers for the picture business. That financial success is doubtful is rather unfortunate.'—*Variety*

After Tonight
US 1933 71m bw

During World War I a Russian lady spy falls for an Austrian officer. Tediously talky romantic vehicle which barely gets started before it bogs down. Constance Bennett, Gilbert Roland, Edward Ellis, Mischa Auer. Written by Jane Murfin; directed by George Archainbaud; for RKO. (GB title: *Sealed Lips*.)

Against a Crooked Sky
US 1975 colour 89m

Two westerners set out to find the sister of one of them, who has been kidnapped by Indians. Very ordinary variation on *The Searchers*, which in itself was a bit tedious at times. Richard Boone, Stewart Petersen, Geoffrey Land, Jewel Blanch, Henry Wilcoxon. Written by Douglas G. Stewart, Eleanor Lamb; directed by Earl Bellamy; for Doty/Dayton.

Against All Flags*
US 1952 83m Technicolor
U-I (Howard Christie)

A daring British seaman routs Spanish ships at the request of the king.
Standard pirate yarn, almost Flynn's last swashbuckler; production below par.

w Aeneas Mackenzie, Joseph Hoffman *d* George Sherman *ph* Russell Metty *m* Hans Salter

Errol Flynn, Maureen O'Hara, Anthony Quinn, Mildred Natwick

† Remade as *The King's Pirate* (qv).

†† Though Flynn did most of his own stunts for this picture, he balked at the one involving sliding down through a sail on a rapier blade, which was originated by Douglas Fairbanks in *The Black Pirate*; it was performed by a stunt double.

Against All Odds
US 1984 121m Metrocolor
Columbia / Delphi (Jerry Bick)

An unemployed football player is hired by a bookmaker to find his missing wife.
Complex and lugubrious remake of *Out of the Past* (qv), which long outstays its welcome.

w Eric Hughes *d* Taylor Hackford *ph* Donald Thorin, E. Pershing Flynn *m* Michel Colombier, Larry Carlton *ad* Richard James Lawrence

Jeff Bridges, Rachel Ward, James Woods, Richard Widmark, Jane Greer (from the original cast), Alex Karras, Dorian Harewood, Swoosie Kurtz

'It has so many convoluted double crosses that each time you are told what was really going on behind the scene you just witnessed, you care less.'—*Time Out*

'A tedious concatenation of narrative twists.'—*MFB*

'The best thing to do is accept the plot, then disregard it, and pay attention to the scenes of passion.'—*Roger Ebert*.

AAN: title song (Phil Collins)

Against the Wind*
GB 1947 96m bw
Ealing (Sidney Cole)

In London during World War II, men and women are trained as saboteurs, and one of them is a traitor.
Thoughtful, well-made spy thriller with good performances; but a bit dour.

w T. E. B. Clarke, Michael Pertwee *d* Charles Crichton *ph* Lionel Banes *m* Leslie Bridgewater

Simone Signoret, Robert Beatty, Jack Warner, Gordon Jackson, Paul Dupuis, Gisele Preville, John Slater, Peter Illing, James Robertson Justice

Agatha*
GB 1978 105m Technicolor
Warner / First Artists / Sweetall / Casablanca (Jarvis Astaire, Gavrik Losey)

In 1926, Agatha Christie disappears after marital difficulties and tries to commit suicide in a Harrogate hotel under a pseudonym.
Lushly recreated but still imaginary and unconvincing solution to a real-life disappearance, complete with romantic encounter with an American newspaperman.

w Kathleen Tynan, Arthur Hopcraft *d* Michael Apted *ph Vittorio Storaro* *m* Johnny Mandel *pd Shirley Russell*

Vanessa Redgrave, Dustin Hoffman, Timothy Dalton, Helen Morse, Timothy West, Tony Britton, Alan Badel

'With its shadowy characters, paucity of plot, and an abundance of stylistic red herrings, one doubts whether *Agatha* would have met Mrs Christie's own requirements for a thriller, though she may well have enjoyed its sumptuous recreation of hotel interiors in the 1920s.'—*Geoff Brown, MFB*

'It has a general air of knowingness, but seems to be missing the scenes which would explain why it was made.'—*New Yorker*

'There is no suspense, no tension and not even one good scene in this preposterous and ostentatious mess.'—*Motion Picture Guide*

L'Âge d'Or**
France 1930 63m bw
Vicomte de Noailles

A collection of strange events satirizing religion and the social order.
Deliberately shocking and possibly quite meaningless, this truly surrealist film is chiefly interesting now for its flashforwards to Bunuel's later work.

w Luis Bunuel, Salvador Dali d Luis Bunuel *ph* Albert Dubergen

Gaston Modot, Lya Lys, Max Ernst, Pierre Prévert, Jacques Brunius

'In some way the juxtaposition of images causes in almost every spectator a train of reactions of unprecedented violence.'—*Basil Wright, 1972*

'The story is also a sequence of moral and surrealist aesthetic. The sexual instinct and the sense of death form its substance.'—*Luis Buñuel*

'It retains its outrageous anarchic vitality, as though unwilling to admit its age.'—*Observer 1980*

The Age for Love
US 1931 81m bw
(UA) Howard Hughes

A wife does not want children; her husband leaves her and marries a woman who does. Shapeless and would-be shocking, this forgotten film was written off as soon as it was made.

w Robert E. Sherwood, Frank Lloyd, Ernest Pascal, from the latter's novel *d* Frank Lloyd *m* Alfred Newman

Billie Dove, Adrian Morris, Charles Starrett, Lois Wilson, Edward Everett Horton, Mary Duncan

'Everybody makes mistakes, and this is one by Howard Hughes.'—*Variety*

Age of Consent*
Australia 1969 103m Technicolor
Columbia / Nautilus (James Mason, Michael Powell)

An artist seduces the granddaughter of a drunken harridan with whom he shares a Barrier Reef island.
Mildly likeable but self-conscious and overlong South Pacific idyll.

w Peter Yeldham, *novel* Norman Lindsay *d* Michael Powell *ph* Hannes Staudinger *m* Stanley Myers

James Mason, Helen Mirren, Jack McGowran, Neva Carr-Glyn, Frank Thring

Age of Indiscretion
US 1935 80m bw

A high-minded publisher finds that his wife is unfaithful. Tolerable marital drama about child custody. Paul Lukas, Helen Vinson, May Robson, Madge Evans, Ralph Forbes. Written by Lenore Coffee; directed by Edward Ludwig; for MGM.

Age of Innocence
US 1934 71m bw

In the 1870s, a young attorney's career is threatened when he falls in love with a divorcee. Dated romantic drama, rather thinly performed and presented. Irene Dunne, John Boles, Lionel Atwill, Laura Hope Crews, Helen Westley, Julie Haydon. Written by Sarah Y. Mason, Victor Heerman, from the novel by Edith Wharton; directed by Philip Moeller; for RKO. 'It will take smart selling to protect it at the box office, especially away from the social registers of the land.'—*Variety*

Age of Innocence
Canada / GB 1977 101m Eastmancolor
Judson / Willoughby (Henning Jacobsen)

After World War I, an English teacher in Canada develops pacifist views which stir up local resentment and lead to violence.
Rather uninteresting melodrama which never really comes to the boil despite care all round.

w Ratch Wallace *d* Alan Bridges *ph* Brian West *m* Lucio Agostini

David Warner, Honor Blackman, Trudy Young, Cec Linder, Tim Henry, Lois Maxwell, Robert Hawkins

Agency
Canada 1981 94m colour

An advertising agency gets into political hands which send out messages through special tv packs. Faded melodrama which did nothing for anyone involved in it. Robert Mitchum, Lee Majors, Valerie Perrine, Saul Rubinek, Alexandra Stewart. Written by Noel Hynd from a novel by Paul Gottlieb; directed by George Kaczender; for Farley.

Agent for Harm
US 1966 84m colour

A Washington agency prevents the Russians from abducting a scientist. Spy spoof somewhat below the level of the tv UNCLE films. Wendell Corey, Mark Richman, Martin Kosleck, Carl Esmond, Barbara Bouchet. Written by Blair Robertson; directed by Gerd Oswald; produced by Joseph F. Robertson for Universal.

Aggie Appleby Maker of Men
US 1933 73m bw

An eccentric girl can't decide between a wimp she has turned into a roughneck and a tough guy she has turned into a sissy. Dim comedy which doesn't seem to know its own mind. Wynne Gibson, Charles Farrell, William Gargan, Betty Furness, Blanche Friderici, Zasu Pitts. Written by Humphrey Pearson, Edward Kaufman, from a play by Joseph Kesselring; directed by Mark Sandrich; for RKO. (GB title: *Cupid in the Rough*.)

The Agitator*
GB 1944 98m bw
British National (Louis H. Jackson)

An embittered mechanic becomes a loud-mouthed union spokesman, but fate eventually takes him into management.
Fairly absorbing, modest narrative of the flaws of socialism.

w Edward Dryhurst, *novel* Peter Pettinger by William Riley *d* John Harlow *ph* James Wilson

William Hartnell (then being built into a star), Mary Morris, John Laurie, Moore Marriott, George Carney, Edward Rigby, Elliot Mason, Frederick Leister, Cathleen Nesbitt, Moira Lister

Agnes of God*
US 1985 98m Metrocolor
Columbia / Delphi IV (Patrick Palmer, Norman Jewison)

A young nun is accused of giving birth and then killing her baby.
Heavy hysterical weather with no clear solution, but a field day for three actresses.

w John Pielmeier, from his play *d* Norman Jewison *ph* Sven Nykvist *m* Georges Delerue *pd* Ken Adam *ed* Anthony Gibbs

Jane Fonda, Anne Bancroft, Meg Tilly

'Predictably, religion and reason play to something like a draw.'—*Variety*

AAN: Anne Bancroft, Meg Tilly (supporting actress), music

The Agony and the Ecstasy*
US 1965 140m De Luxe Todd-AO
TCF / International Classics Inc (Carol Reed)

Pope Julius II persuades Michelangelo to leave his sculptures and paint the ceiling of the Sistine Chapel.
Dully reverent comic strip approach to art and history; generally heavy going, but good looking.

w Philip Dunne, *novel* Irving Stone *d* Carol Reed *ph* Leon Shamroy *m* Alex North *pd* John de Cuir

Charlton Heston, Rex Harrison, Diane Cilento, Harry Andrews, Alberto Lupo, Adolfo Celi

JULIUS: 'You dare to dicker with your pontiff?'

'The vulgarity of the whole concept has none of the joyfully enthusiastic philistinism of a de Mille; rather its tone is a dry, almost cynical, condescension.'—*Brenda Davies*

'All agony, no ecstasy.'—*Judith Crist*

'Not a strong and soaring drama but an illustrated lecture of a slow artist at work.'—*Bosley Crowther*

'Heston hits the ceiling.'—*New York Times.*

† The film is said to have cost 12 million dollars and earned 4.

†† Michelangelo was apparently both a dwarf and a homosexual. He is played by Charlton Heston.

AAN: Leon Shamroy; Alex North

Aguirre, Wrath of God**
West Germany 1972 95m colour
Werner Herzog / Hessicher Rundfunk

In 1560, one of Pizarro's lieutenants takes a party of forty down river by raft, and succumbs to megalomania.
Absorbing conquistador melodrama, vividly assembled and impossible to forget.

wd Werner Herzog *ph* Thomas Mauch *m* Popol Vuh

Klaus Kinski, Ruy Guerra, Helena Rojo, Cecilia Rivera

'It ingeniously combines Herzog's gift for deep irony, his strong social awareness, and his worthy ambition to fashion a whole new visual perspective on the world around us via mystical, evocative, yet oddly direct imagery. It is a brilliant cinematic achievement.'—*David Skerritt, Christian Science Monitor*

'The play that startled the nation!'

Ah, Wilderness**
US 1935 101m bw
MGM (Hunt Stromberg)

Problems of a small-town family at the turn of the century.
Well-acted, affectionately remembered version of a play later musicalized as *Summer Holiday*. The commercial success of this film led to the Hardy family series.

w Albert Hackett, Frances Goodrich, *play* Eugene O'Neill *d* Clarence Brown *ph* Clyde de Vinna *m* Herbert Stothart

Wallace Beery, Lionel Barrymore, Eric Linden, Spring Byington, Mickey Rooney, Aline MacMahon, Charley Grapewin, Cecilia Parker, Frank Albertson, Bonita Granville

'A job of picture making, in craftsmanship and feeling, that is wonderful to see.'—*Otis Ferguson*

'That it is a fine artistic effort will not be denied anywhere, but for the public at large it will need all the boosting it can get.'—*Variety*

Ai No Corrida*
France / Japan 1976 105m Eastmancolor
Argos / Oshima / Shibata (Anatole Dauman)
French title: *L'Empire des Sens*
aka: *Empire of the Passions; Empire of the Senses*

A sexually complicated servant girl has an intense affair with the master of the house, and finally murders and mutilates him.
Strong but stylish stuff, a kind of Japanese *Last Tango in Paris*. Those who like this kind of thing will like it a lot.

wd Nagisa Oshima *ph* Hideo Ito *m* Minoru Miki

Tatsuya Fuji, Eiko Matsuda, Aoi Nakajima, Meika Seri

'By the final sequence, we are all implicated in the continuing social system which makes such love impossible. It is not Sade, but the censor in all of us who ultimately wields the knife.'—*Jan Dawson, MFB*

Aida
Italy 1953 95m Ferraniacolor
Oscar Film (Ferrucio de Martino, Federico Teti)

A young Egyptian army officer loves the captive princess of the Ethiopians.
Stuffy, over-dressed, pantomimish version of the opera, with some pretension to cinematic vitality.

w various, from Verdi's opera *d* Clemente Fracassi *ph* Piero Portalupi *ad* Flavio Mogherini

Sophia Loren (sung by Renata Tebaldi), Lois Maxwell, Luciano della Marra

Ain't Misbehavin'*
US 1955 81m Technicolor
U-I (Samuel Marx)

A young millionaire marries a cabaret girl, who determines to improve her mind and manners.
Lively American version of *Pygmalion*, with musical numbers and some bright lines.

w Edward Buzzell, Philip Rapp, Devery Freeman *d* Edward Buzzell *ph* Wilfrid Cline *m* Joseph Gershenson *ch* Kenny Williams, Lee Scott

Rory Calhoun, *Piper Laurie, Reginald Gardiner*, Jack Carson, Barbara Britton, Mamie Van Doren

'Are you going to let that boy go up alone?'
Air Cadet
US 1951 94m bw

THE AGONY AND THE ECSTASY. Charlton Heston as Michelangelo furrows his brow to approximate the creative process: audiences were less than ecstatic.

Problems of an air force flight instructor.
Routine flagwaver. Stephen McNally, Alex Nicol, Gail Russell, Richard Long, Charles Drake, Rock Hudson. Written by Robert L. Richards; directed by Joseph Pevney; for Universal-International. (GB title: *Jet Men of the Air*.)

Air Force*
US 1943 124m bw
Warner (Hal B. Wallis)

A Flying Fortress and its crew see action in Manila, Pearl Harbor and the Coral Sea.
Propaganda piece concentrating on the characters of the crew members, with action set pieces largely provided by newsreel; but skilled direction still conveys plenty of punch.

w Dudley Nichols *d Howard Hawks* *ph* James Wong Howe, Elmer Dyer, Charles Marshall *m* Franz Waxman

John Garfield, Gig Young, Arthur Kennedy, Charles Drake, John Ridgley, Harry Carey,

George Tobias, Stanley Ridges, Moroni Olsen, Edward Brophy

'Maybe the story is high-flown, maybe it overdraws a recorded fact a bit. We'd hate to think it couldn't happen—or didn't—because it leaves you feeling awfully good.'—*Bosley Crowther*

'The film is one crisis after another, and the director stages the air battles handsomely, but for the rest it helps if you're interested in the factors involved in getting a bomber somewhere and back.'—*Pauline Kael, 70s*

AAN: Dudley Nichols; James Wong Howe, Elmer Dyer, Charles Marshall

Air Hawks
US 1935 68m bw

Two aviation firms battle for airmail contracts. Routine low-budget action drama inspired by the stratosphere cross-continent flights of Wiley Post (who appears as himself and was killed later in the year along with Will Rogers). Ralph Bellamy, Wiley Post, Tala Birell, Douglass Dumbrille, Victor Kilian. Written by Griffin Jay and Grace Neville; directed by Albert Rogell; for Columbia. 'Word-of-mouth bally should help in face of marquee weakness.'—*Variety*

Air Mail*
US 1932 84m bw

Brash young pilot effects a daring rescue and gets the mail through. Moderate actioner of its time. Pat O'Brien, Ralph Bellamy, Russell Hopton, Gloria Stuart, Lillian Bond, Slim Summerville. Written by Dale Van Every and Frank Wead; directed by John Ford; for Universal. 'Far short of a smash . . . it has no sock name, it is weak on the romantic side and the story material is directed at men.'—*Variety*

† There was also a good silent version in 1925, with Warner Baxter and Douglas Fairbanks Jnr, written by James Shelley Hamilton and directed by Irvin Williat; both had remarkable similarities to *Only Angels Have Wings* (1938).

Air Raid Wardens
US 1943 67m bw
MGM (B. F. Zeidman)

Rejected by the armed services, two incompetent air raid wardens accidentally round up Nazi spies.
Well below par star comedy: their incomparable dignity has disappeared.

w Jack Jevne, Martin Rackin, Charles Rogers, Harry Crane *d* Edward Sedgwick *ph* Walter Lundin *m* Nathaniel Shilkret

Stan Laurel, Oliver Hardy, Edgar Kennedy, Jacqueline White, Stephen McNally, Nella Walker, Donald Meek

The Airmail Mystery
US 1932 bw serial: 12 eps

An airmail pilot owns a gold mine which interests the evil Black Hawk. Reasonably lively fisticuff saga in which the villain has devised an 'aerial catapult' for launching planes. James Flavin (later familiar as an Irish cop), Lucile Browne, Wheeler Oakman, Walter Brennan. Directed by Ray Taylor; for Universal.

Airplane**
US 1980 88m Metrocolor
Paramount / Howard W. Koch (Jan Davison)

A former pilot gets his nerve back when called upon to land a passenger plane because the crew all have food poisoning.
Arthur Hailey's play *Flight into Danger* and the film *Zero Hour* which was made from it get the zany parody treatment in this popular movie which is often funny but sometimes merely crude. It rang the box office bell more loudly than most expensive epics of its year.

wd Jim Abrahams, David and Jerry Zucker *ph* Joseph Biroc *m* Elmer Bernstein *pd* Ward Preston

Robert Stack, Lloyd Bridges, Robert Hays, Julie Hegerty, Peter Graves, Leslie Nielsen, Lorna Paterson, Ethel Merman, Kareem Abdul-Jabbar

'Parody may be the lowest form of humour, but few comedies in ages have rocked the laugh meter this hard.'—*Variety*

'It keeps going, like a dervish with skids on.'—*Derek Malcolm, Guardian*

'Proof that the cinema is alive and well and bursting with ingenuity.'—*David Hughes, Sunday Times*

'It's compiled like a jokebook and has the kind of pacing that goes with a laugh track.'—*Pauline Kael*

'All pretty juvenile really, though the relentless pace and sheer poor taste make up for a lack of originality.'—*Time Out, 1984*

'Practically a satirical anthology of movie clichés . . . it compensates for its lack of original comic invention by its utter willingness to steal, beg, borrow and rewrite from anywhere.'—*Roger Ebert*

Airplane II: The Sequel
US 1982 85m Metrocolor
Paramount (Howard W. Koch)

A space shuttle gets into trouble but is rescued in the nick of time.
Palsied sequel to a funny film, with some of the same cast and some of the same jokes.

wd Ken Finkleman *ph* Joe Biroc *m* Elmer Bernstein *pd* William Sandell *ed* Dennis Virkler

Robert Hays, Julie Hagerty, Lloyd Bridges, Peter Graves, William Shatner, Chad Everett, Steven Stucker, Sonny Bono, Raymond Burr, Chuck Connors, Rip Torn, John Dehner, Kent McCord, John Vernon

'All the pleasure lies in the humour's weakness.'—*Observer*

Airport***
US 1970 136m Technicolor Todd-AO
Universal / Ross Hunter (Jaque Mapes)

Events of one snowy night at a midwestern international airport, culminating in airborne melodrama when a mad bomber is killed and the damaged plane has to be talked down.
Glossy, undeniably entertaining, all-star version of a popular novel, with cardboard characters skilfully deployed in Hollywood's very best style.

w George Seaton, *novel* Arthur Hailey
d George Seaton *ph* Ernest Laszlo *m* Alfred Newman

Burt Lancaster, Dean Martin, Jean Seberg, *Helen Hayes*, Van Heflin, Jacqueline Bisset, George Kennedy, Maureen Stapleton, Barry Nelson, Dana Wynter, Lloyd Nolan, Barbara Hale, Gary Collins, Jessie Royce Landis

'The best film of 1944.'—*Judith Crist*

'For sheer contentment there is nothing to beat the sight of constant catastrophe happening to others.'—*Alexander Walker*

'A *Grand Hotel* in the sky . . . every few years or so some more show-biz types would crowd onto a plane that would threaten to crash, collide with another, meet with terrorists, or otherwise be subjected to the perils of Pauline.'—*Les Keyser, Hollywood in the Seventies*

† The film cost 10 million dollars and earned 45.

AA: Helen Hayes
AAN: best picture; George Seaton; Ernest Laszlo; Alfred Newman; Maureen Stapleton

Airport 1975
US 1974 105m Technicolor Panavision
Universal (Jennings Lang, William Frye)

A private aircraft collides with a jet plane and kills or immobilizes its crew, so a stewardess has to manoeuvre the jumbo to safety.
Inept airborne suspenser loaded with stars who do nothing and marred by continuity lapses and boring dialogue.

w Don Ingalls *d* Jack Smight *ph* Philip Lathrop *m* John Cacavas

Charlton Heston, *Karen Black*, George Kennedy, Helen Reddy, Efrem Zimbalist Jnr, Susan Clark, Myrna Loy, Gloria Swanson, Linda Blair, Dana Andrews, Roy Thinnes, Sid Caesar, Ed Nelson, Nancy Olson, Martha Scott

'Aimed squarely for the yahoo trade.'—*Variety*

'Processed schlock. One can have a fairly good time laughing at it, but it doesn't sit too well as a joke, because the people on the screen are being humiliated.'—*Pauline Kael, New Yorker*

'Good exciting corny escapism, and the kind of movie you would *not* want to watch as an inflight film.'—*Roger Ebert*

Airport '77
US 1977 114m Technicolor Panavision
Universal (William Frye)

A private airliner loaded with guests and art treasures hits an oil rig and settles underwater on a sandbank.
Hysteria, rescue, and guest stars with nothing to do; the mixture as before.

w Michael Scheff, David Spector *d* Jerry Jameson *ph* Philip Lathrop *m* John Cacavas *pd* George C. Webb

Jack Lemmon, James Stewart, Brenda Vaccaro, Joseph Cotten, Olivia de Havilland, Lee Grant, Darren McGavin, Christopher Lee, Robert Foxworth, Robert Hooks, Monte Markham, Kathleen Quinlan, James Booth

'Neither as riveting as it should be, nor as much fun as its absurd plotline would suggest.'—*Verina Glaessner, MFB*

† See also: *The Concorde—Airport '79.*

Akenfield
GB 1974 98m Techniscope

Semi-dramatized film version of a book which documented a Suffolk village by interviewing its older inhabitants. An interesting venture ruined by imprecision, misty photography, lack of narrative drive or any compensating detail, and the appalling error of using a cheap wide screen process. Written by Ronald Blythe, from his book; directed by Peter Hall; for Angle Films and London Weekend Television.

Al Capone**
US 1959 105m bw
Allied Artists (John H. Burrows, Leonard J. Ackerman)

An account of Chicago's most famous gangster, up to his arrest for income tax evasion.
Only slightly overplayed, semi-documentary retelling of a larger-than-life true story.

w Marvin Wald, Henry Greenberg *d* Richard Wilson *ph* Lucien Ballard *m* David Raksin

Rod Steiger (a clever impersonation on the border of caricature), Fay Spain, Murvyn Vye, Nehemiah Persoff, Martin Balsam, James Gregory, Joe de Santis

'The most remarkable thing about it is its truth.'—*Daily Telegraph*

'This powerful production may turn out to be the definitive gangster film of all time.'—*Film Daily*

Al Jennings of Oklahoma
US 1950 78m Technicolor

A lawyer becomes a western outlaw. Tolerable co-feature which strays from the truth. Dan Duryea, Gale Storm, Dick Foran, Gloria Henry, Guinn Williams. Written by George Bricker; directed by Ray Nazarro; for Columbia.

Alakazam the Great*
Japan 1960 88m Eastmancolor
Toei (Hiroshi Okawa)
original title: *Saiyu-ki*

The arrogant monkey king of the animals is sent by his human master on a pilgrimage; he defeats evil King Gruesome and returns a hero.
Smartly animated, Disney-inspired cartoon based on the same legend as *Monkey*, translated by Arthur Waley.

w Osamu Tezuka, Keinosuke Uekusa *d* Taiji Yabushita

The Alamo*
US 1960 193m Technicolor Todd-AO
UA / John Wayne

In 1836 a small southern fort becomes the centre of Texas' fight for independence, but it is suddenly annihilated by a Mexican raid, and all its defenders killed.
Sprawling historical epic with many irrelevant episodes and distracting changes of mood.

w James Edward Grant *d* John Wayne *ph* William H. Clothier *m* Dmitri Tiomkin

John Wayne (as Crockett), Richard Widmark (Bowie), Laurence Harvey (Travis), Richard Boone (Houston), Frankie Avalon, Patrick Wayne, Linda Cristal, Chill Wills, Joseph Calleia

CROCKETT: 'Republic. I like the sound of the word. It means people can live free, talk free, go or come, buy or sell, be drunk or sober, however they choose. Some words give you a feeling. Republic is one of those words that makes me tight in the throat—the same tightness a man gets when his baby takes his first step or his first baby shaves and makes his first sound like a man. Some words can give you a feeling that makes your heart warm. Republic is one of those words.'

'Its sole redeeming feature lies in one of those crushing climaxes of total massacre which Hollywood can still pull off thunderingly well.'—*Peter John Dyer*

AAN: best picture; William H. Clothier; Dmitri Tiomkin; Chill Wills; song 'The Green Leaves of Summer' (*m* Dmitri Tiomkin, *ly* Paul Francis Webster)

Alamo Bay
US 1985 98m Metrocolor
Tri-Star / Delphi III (Louis and Vincent Malle)

Fisherfolk in Galveston Bay resent the intrusion of refugee Vietnamese.
Unsympathetic, slow-paced melodrama which ends up seeming pointless despite a Ku Klux Klan confrontation.

w Alice Arlen *d* Louis Malle *ph* Curtis Clark *m* Ry Cooder *pd* Trevor Williams *ed* James Bruce

Amy Madigan, Ed Harris, Donald Moffat, Rudy Young, Ho Nguyen

'A failed piece of social consciousness.'—*Variety*

Alaska Highway
US 1943 66m bw

Engineer brothers blaze a trail for the Army Engineer Corps, and fall for the same girl. Routine sock-it-to-me adventure romance with process photography. Richard Arlen, Jean Parker, Ralph Sanford, Bill Henry. Written by Maxwell Shane and Lewis R. Foster; directed by Frank McDonald; for Pine-Thomas (Paramount).

The Alaskan*
US 1924 80m approx bw

An Alaskan defies robber barons intent on corrupting the new state. Tough, effective and straightforward action drama, one of its star's best roles. *Thomas Meighan*, Estelle Taylor, John Sainpolis, Anna May Wong. Written by Willis Goldbeck from the novel by James Oliver Curwood; directed by Herbert Brenon; for Famous Players/Paramount.

Alaska Seas
US 1953 78m bw
Paramount (Mel Epstein)

Alaska fishermen oppose the crooked owner of the local cannery.
Insipid remake of *Spawn of the North (qv)*.

w Geoffrey Homes, Walter Doniger *d* Jerry Hopper *ph* William C. Mellor *md* Irvin Talbot

Robert Ryan, Gene Barry, Jan Sterling, Brian Keith, Richard Shannon

Albert RN**
GB 1953 88m bw
Dial (Daniel M. Angel)
US title: *Break to Freedom*

Prisoners of war construct a lifelike dummy to cover the absence of escaping prisoners.
Competent, entertaining version of a successful play: an archetypal POW comedy drama.

w Guy Morgan, Vernon Harris, *play* Guy Morgan, Edward Sammis *d* Lewis Gilbert *ph* Jack Asher *m* Malcolm Arnold

Jack Warner, Anthony Steel, Robert Beatty, William Sylvester, Anton Diffring, Eddie Byrne, Guy Middleton, Paul Carpenter, Frederick Valk

Albuquerque
US 1947 89m Cinecolor

The nephew of a town tyrant steps in to save an independent wagon line. Formula western with adequate action. Randolph Scott; Barbara Britton, George 'Gabby' Hayes, George Cleveland, Lon Chaney Jnr, Russell Hayden. Written by Gene Lewis and Clarence Upson Young, from novel by Luke Short; directed by Ray Enright; for Pine-Thomas / Paramount. (GB title: *Silver City*.)

Alcatraz Island
US 1937 64m bw

The federal government decides to build a top-security prison on a rock in San Francisco Bay. Cheap routine treatment of what might have been an interesting subject. Ann Sheridan, Mary Maguire, Dick Purcell, Addison Richards, *George E. Stone*, Doris Lloyd, John Litel. Written by Crane Wilbur; directed by William McGann; for Warners / Cosmopolitan. 'Should about complete the Warner file on prisons.'—*Variety*

Alex and the Gypsy
US 1976 99m De Luxe
TCF / Richard Shepherd

A cynical California bailbondsman involved in illicit activities chooses romantic freedom with a gypsy girl.
Incoherent hardbitten romance with an unconvincing set of characters.

w Lawrence B. Marcus, *novel* The Bailbondsman by Stanley Elkin *d* John Korty *ph* Bill Butler *m* Henry Mancini

Jack Lemmon, Genevieve Bujold, James Woods, Gino Ardito, Robert Emhardt

'Even if it were well done (which it is not) it would be banal, predictable and cloying.'—*Frank Rich*

'Off the beaten track, but that's just about the only thing you can give it points for.'—*Pauline Kael*

Alex in Wonderland
US 1970 109m colour
MGM (Larry Tucker)

A Hollywood director finds life tedious.
So did the small paying audiences who saw this pale imitation of Fellini. (Some wags called it *One and a Half.*)

w Paul Mazursky, Larry Tucker *d* Paul Mazursky

Donald Sutherland, Jeanne Moreau, Ellen Burstyn, Federico Fellini

'The Fellini elements are laid onto the film and don't quite sink in . . . but the human story does work, remarkably well.'—*Roger Ebert*

Alexander Hamilton*
US 1931 73m bw
Warner

The life of America's 18th-century financier.
Star biopic, highly satisfying in its day.

w Julian Josephson, Maude Howell, George Arliss *d* John G. Adolfi *ph* James Van Trees

George Arliss, Doris Kenyon, Montagu Love, Dudley Digges, Lionel Belmore, Ralf Harolde, Alan Mowbray

Alexander Nevsky****
USSR 1938 112m bw
Mosfilm

In 1242, Prince Alexander Nevsky defeats the invading Teutonic Knights in a battle on the ice of Lake Peipus.
A splendid historical pageant which shows the director at his most inventively pictorial and climaxes in a superb battle sequence using music instead of natural sound.

w Pyotr Pavlenko, Sergei Eisenstein *d Sergei Eisenstein ph Edouard Tissé m Prokofiev ad* I. Shpinel, N. Soloviov, K. Yeliseyev

Nikolai Cherkassov, Nikolai Okhlopkov, Andrei Abrikosov, Dmitri Orlov

'The picture will meet with good results wherever its political sentiments find established adherents. Otherwise it's almost nil for general appeal.'—*Variety*

'Superb sequences of cinematic opera that pass from pastoral to lamentation and end in a triumphal cantata.'—*Georges Sadoul*

'The colossus who conquered the world! The most colossal motion picture of all time!'

Alexander the Great*
US 1956 135m Technicolor Cinemascope
UA / Robert Rossen

The life and early death at thirty-three of the Macedonian warrior who conquered the entire known world.
Dour impassive epic which despite good intelligent stretches makes one long for Hollywood's usual more ruthless view of history.

wd Robert Rossen *m* Mario Nascimbene *ph* Robert Krasker *ad* Andrei Andreiev

Richard Burton, Fredric March, Danielle Darrieux, Claire Bloom, Barry Jones, Harry Andrews, Peter Cushing, Stanley Baker, Michael Hordern, Niall MacGinnis

'Not a scene is held for a second longer than it is worth; greatness is pictured in constant dissolve.'—*Alexander Walker*

'Rossen has aimed for greatness and lost honourably.'—*Andrew Sarris*

Alexander's Ragtime Band***
US 1938 106m bw
TCF (Darryl F. Zanuck, Harry Joe Brown)

Between 1911 and 1939, two songwriters vie for the affections of a rising musical comedy star.
Archetypal chronicle musical with 26 songs: well-paced, smartly made, and bursting with talent.

w Kathryn Scola, Lamar Trotti, Richard Sherman *d Henry King ph Peverell Marley m / ly Irving Berlin md Alfred Newman*

Tyrone Power, *Alice Faye*, Don Ameche, *Ethel Merman, Jack Haley*, Jean Hersholt, Helen Westley, John Carradine, Paul Hurst, Wally Vernon, Ruth Terry, Eddie Collins, Douglas Fowley, Chick Chandler

'A grand filmusical which stirs and thrills, finding response in the American heart to memories of the exciting, sentimental and patriotic moments of the past quarter of a century.'—*Variety*

AA: Alfred Newman

AAN: best picture; Irving Berlin (for original story); Irving Berlin (for song, 'Now It Can Be Told')

Alf, Bill and Fred*
GB 1964 8m Eastmancolor

A man, a duck and a dog enjoy bouncing together. Bittersweet cartoon fable which pleases much more than its synopsis might suggest. Written by Stan Hayward; produced, directed and animated by *Bob Godfrey*; for Biographic 4.

The Alf Garnett Saga
GB 1972 90m colour
Columbia / Associated London Films (Ned Sherrin, Terry Glinwood)

Bigoted Alf is exasperated by his council flat, his son-in-law, and the possibility that his daughter is pregnant by a black man.
Second inflation of the TV series, *Till Death Us Do Part*, even cruder and less funny than the first; listlessly written and developed.

w Johnny Speight *d* Bob Kellett *ph* Nic Knowland *m* Georgie Fame

Warren Mitchell, Dandy Nichols, Adrienne Posta, Mike Angelis, John Le Mesurier, Joan Sims, John Bird, Roy Kinnear

'One long, repetitive and unfunny diatribe.'—*MFB*

Alfie**
GB 1966 114m Techniscope
Paramount / Sheldrake (Lewis Gilbert)

A Cockney Lothario is proud of his amorous conquests, but near-tragedy finally makes him more mature.
Garish sex comedy, an immense box office success because of its frankness and an immaculate performance from its star.

w Bill Naughton, from his play *d* Lewis Gilbert *ph* Otto Heller *m* Sonny Rollins

Michael Caine, Vivien Merchant, Shirley Anne Field, Millicent Martin, Jane Asher, Julia Foster, Shelley Winters, Eleanor Bron, Denholm Elliott

'Paramount thought it was a good bet because it was going to be made for 500,000 dollars, normally the sort of money spent on executives' cigar bills.'—*Lewis Gilbert*

AAN: best picture; Bill Naughton; Michael Caine; Vivien Merchant; title song

Alfie Darling
GB 1975 102m Technicolor
EMI / Signal (Dugald Rankin)

Further repetitive amorous exploits of the Cockney Lothario, now a continental truck driver.
Soft porn adventures quite unworthy of the writer–director, and tedious to sit through; the touch of tragedy at the end only makes matters worse.

wd Ken Hughes *ph* Ousama Rawi *m* Alan Price

Alan Price, Jill Townsend, Paul Copley, Joan Collins, Sheila White, Annie Ross, Hannah Gordon, Rula Lenska

Alfred the Great*
GB 1969 122m Metrocolor Panavision
MGM / Bernard Smith

In AD 871 Alfred takes over kingship from his weak elder brother.
A 'realistic' youth-oriented view of history: blood and four-letter words alternate with cliché to make a dispiriting, disunified whole, though the background detail is interesting and the battle scenes vivid.

w Ken Taylor, James R. Webb *d* Clive Donner *ph* Alex Thomson *m* Ray Leppard *pd* Michael Stringer

David Hemmings, Michael York, Prunella Ransome, Colin Blakely, Julian Glover, Ian McKellen, Alan Dobie

Alf's Button
GB 1930 96m bw

Not the first version (there was one in 1920 with Leslie Henson) but the first in sound of W. A. Darlington's play about a soldier whose button, when rubbed, summons an all-powerful genie. It even had a colour sequence, and featured Nervo and Knox (see below), with Tubby Edlin, Alf Goddard, Nora Swinburne and Polly Ward. Written by L'Estrange Fawcett; directed by W. P. Kellino; for Gaumont.

Alf's Button Afloat**
GB 1938 89m bw
Gainsborough (Edward Black)

Six itinerants encounter a genie, whose granting of their wishes brings riches and embarrassment.
Archetypal music hall farce descending at moments into surrealism (the lovers are eaten by a bear). All concerned are on top form.

w Marriott Edgar, Val Guest, Ralph Smart, novel Alf's Button by W. A. Darlington *d Marcel Varnel ph* Arthur Crabtree *md* Louis Levy

Bud Flanagan, Chesney Allen, Jimmy Nervo, Teddy Knox, Charles Naughton, Jimmy Gold (the six original members of the Crazy Gang), *Alastair Sim,* Wally Patch, Peter Gawthorne

Algiers**
US 1938 95m bw
Walter Wanger

A romantic Casbah thief makes the mistake of falling in love.
Seminal Hollywood romantic drama based closely on a French original, *Pepe le Moko*; laughed at for years because of the alleged line 'Come with me to the Casbah' (which is never actually said), it holds up remarkably well in its fashion.

w John Howard Lawson, James M. Cain *d John Cromwell ph James Wong Howe m* Vincent Scott, Mohammed Igorbouchen

Charles Boyer, Hedy Lamarr, Sigrid Gurie, Gene Lockhart, Joseph Calleia, Alan Hale, Johnny Downs

'A quality of sustained suspense and excitement . . . there is nothing makeshift about the production.'—*Variety*

'Few films this season, or any other, have sustained their mood more brilliantly.'—*New York Times*

'The general tone is that of the decent artistry we must demand and enjoy in pictures, which should someday be as respectable as books, only more near and vivid.'—*Otis Ferguson*

'This version is pure Hollywood, sacrificing everything to glamour, and the heavy make-up and studio lighting make it seem so artificial one can get giggly.'—*New Yorker, 1977*
† Remake: *Casbah* (qv).

AAN: James Wong Howe; Charles Boyer; Gene Lockhart

'Wild nights of sheer delights! Burning days of bold adventure! When beauty was the booty and the prize of all was love!'

Ali Baba and the Forty Thieves*
US 1943 87m Technicolor
U-I (Paul Malvern)

A deposed prince pretending to be a bandit regains his rightful throne.
Absurd but likeable wartime pantomime without much humour: a typical big-budget production of its studio and period.

w Edmund L. Hartmann *d* Arthur Lubin *ph* George Robinson *m* Edward Ward

Jon Hall, Maria Montez, Scotty Beckett, Turhan Bey, Frank Puglia, Andy Devine, Kurt Katch
† Remake: *Sword of Ali Baba*, which over twenty years later used much of the same footage.

Ali Baba and the Forty Thieves*
France 1954 90m Eastmancolor
Films du Cyclope

Ali Baba is sent to buy a new wife for his master, and accidentally finds a thieves' treasure cave . . .
Sporadically amusing but finally disappointing version of the Arabian Nights story; it looks hasty.

w Jacques Becker, Marc Maurette, Maurice Griffe *d* Jacques Becker *ph* Robert Le Fèbvre *m* Paul Misraki

Fernandel, Samia Gamal, Dieter Borsche, Henri Vilbert

Ali Baba Goes to Town*
US 1937 81m bw
TCF (Lawrence Schwab)

A hobo falls off a train into a film set and thinks he is back in the Arabian Nights.
Rather flat star vehicle with a few compensations.

w Harry Tugend, Jack Yelten *d* David Butler *ph* Ernest Palmer *m* Louis Silvers *songs* Mack Gordon, Harry Revel

Eddie Cantor, Tony Martin, Roland Young, John Carradine, June Lang

'An elaborately produced filmusical which satirizes the New Deal policies, politicians and politics.'—*Variety*

Alias a Gentleman
US 1947 76m bw

An ex-convict tries to find his daughter and go straight. Sudsy star vehicle. Wallace Beery, Gladys George, Tom Drake, Leon Ames. Written by William Lipman; directed by Harry Beaumont; for MGM.

Alias French Gertie
US 1934 68m bw

A 'French maid' and her accomplice work a high society racket. Faded society comedy drama with Bebe Daniels and Ben Lyon in a rare teaming before their exile to England. Written by Bayard Veiller; directed by George Archainbaud; for RKO. (GB title: *Love Finds a Way.*)

Alias Jesse James*
US 1958 92m De Luxe
Hope Enterprises (Jack Hope)

An incompetent insurance salesman sells a policy to Jesse James and has to protect his client until he can get it back.
Ho-hum star comedy saved by a climax in which Hope is protected by every cowboy star in Hollywood.

w William Bowers, D. D. Beauchamp *d* Norman Z. McLeod *ph* Lionel Lindon *m* Joseph J. Lilley

Bob Hope, Rhonda Fleming, Wendell Corey, Jim Davis, Will Wright

Alias Jimmy Valentine
US 1928 75m bw

Crook comedy drama previously made in 1920; this version is notable only as the first MGM sound film. William Haines, Karl Dane, Lionel Barrymore. Written by Sarah Y. Mason and A. P. Younger; directed by Jack Conway; for MGM.

Alias John Preston
GB 1956 66m bw

A stranger with amnesia arrives in a small community, only to find that his frequent nightmares have a sinister reason. Watchable second feature. Christopher Lee, Alexander Knox, Betta St John, Patrick Holt, Sandra Dorne, Betty Anne Davies, John Stuart, John Longden, Bill Fraser. Written by Paul Tabori; directed by David MacDonald; for the Danzigers.

Alias Mary Dow
US 1935 65m bw

A millionaire persuades a chorus girl to pose as his long-lost kidnapped daughter, to satisfy his wife. Obvious audience-pleaser of its time. Ray Milland, Sally Eilers, Henry O'Neill, Katherine Alexander. Written by Gladys Unger, Rose Franken and Arthur Caesar; directed by Kurt Neumann; for Universal.

'Not a bad picture . . . small towns should like it best.'—*Variety*

'No man ever held more terrible power over women than this tall dark handsome stranger from nowhere! The shock-filled story of a man whose love was more dangerous than a loaded gun!'

Alias Nick Beal***
US 1949 93m bw
Paramount (Endre Boehm)
GB title: *The Contact Man*

A politician is nearly corrupted by a mysterious stranger offering wealth and power.
Highly satisfactory modern version of *Faust*, done in gangster terms but not eschewing a supernatural explanation. Acting, photography and direction all in the right key.

w Jonathan Latimer, story Mindret Lord *d John Farrow ph Lionel Lindon m* Franz Waxman

Ray Milland, Thomas Mitchell, Audrey Totter, George Macready, Fred Clark

Alias the Deacon
US 1940 74m bw

A sentimental cardsharp is mistaken by smalltown folk for their new deacon. Modest rural comedy from a well-worn play. Bob Burns, Mischa Auer, Peggy Moran, Dennis O'Keefe, Edward Brophy, Thurston Hall, Jack Carson. Written by Nat Perrin and Charles Grayson from play by John B. Hymer and Leroy Clemens; directed by Christy Cabanne; for Ben Pivar / Universal.

Alias the Doctor
US 1932 70m bw

A natural man of the soil tries to follow his mother's wish that he should become a doctor. Dated drama of family sentiment. Richard Barthelmess, Laura la Plante, Marian Marsh, Norman Foster, Oscar Apfel. Written by Benjamin McGill, Houston Branch; directed by Michael Curtiz; for First National / Warners. 'It misses big league rating, but will satisfy on the average programme.'—*Variety*

Alibi*
US 1929 90m bw
Roland West

An ex-convict marries a policeman's daughter and uses her in his plan for the perfect murder.
Early talkie drama, mostly risible now but with interesting fragments of technique and imagination.

w Roland West, C. Gardner Sullivan, from the play Nightstick by Elaine Sterne Carrington, John Wray, J. C. Nugent; *d Roland West* *ph* Ray June *m* Hugo Riesenfeld *ad William Cameron Menzies*

Chester Morris, Eleanor Griffith, Regis Toomey, Mae Busch, Harry Stubbs
AAN: best picture; Chester Morris

Alibi
GB 1931 75m bw

Hercule Poirot proves that an apparent suicide was murder. Tame adaptation, without the narrative gimmick, of Agatha Christie's *The Murder of Roger Ackroyd.* Austin Trevor, Franklin Dyall, Elizabeth Allan, J. H. Roberts, Mary Jerrold. Written by H. Fowler Mear; directed by Leslie Hiscott; for Twickenham.

Alibi*
GB 1942 82m bw
Corona (Josef Somlo)

A nightclub mindreader forces the lady owner to give him a murder alibi.
Interesting but disappointing minor suspenser copied from a sharper French original.

w uncredited, *novel* Marcel Achard *d* Brian Desmond Hurst *ph* Otto Heller *m* Jack Beaver

Margaret Lockwood, Hugh Sinclair, James Mason, *Raymond Lovell,* Enid Stamp-Taylor, Hartley Power, Jane Carr, Rodney Ackland, Edana Romney, Elizabeth Welch, Olga Lindo, Muriel George
† The French film, *L'Alibi*, was made in 1939 by B-N Films. The girl was Jany Holt, with Erich Von Stroheim as the villain and Louis Jouvet as the inspector. Pierre Chenal directed.

Alibi Ike*
US 1935 73m bw
Warner (Edward Chodorov)

A baseball pitcher gets involved in all kinds of trouble.
Above average star comedy vehicle.

w William Wister Haines, *story* Ring Lardner *d* Ray Enright *ph* Arthur Todd *md* Leo F. Forbstein

Joe E. Brown, Olivia de Havilland, Ruth Donnelly, Roscoe Karns, William Frawley

Alice Adams**
US 1935 99m bw
RKO (Pandro S. Berman)

A social-climbing small-town girl falls in love. Dated but interesting star vehicle with good production values.

w Dorothy Yost, Mortimer Offner, *novel* Booth Tarkington *d George Stevens* *ph* Robert de Grasse *m* Max Steiner, Roy Webb

Katharine Hepburn, Fred MacMurray, Evelyn Venable, Frank Albertson, Fred Stone, Ann Shoemaker, Charles Grapewin, Grady Sutton, Hedda Hopper

'Sturdy cinematic substance, virtually audience proof.'—*Variety*

'A nice middle-class film, as trivial as a schoolgirl's diary, and just about as pathetically true.'—*C. A. Lejeune*

'What was in 1922 a biting and observant novel emerges in 1935 as a bitingly satiric portrait of an era.'—*Time*

AAN: best picture; Katharine Hepburn

'A picture for anyone who has ever dreamed of a second chance!'

Alice Doesn't Live Here Any More**
US 1974 112m Technicolor
Warner (David Susskind, Audrey Maas)

A widow sets off with her young son for Monterey and a singing career.
Realistically squalid and foul-mouthed but endearing look at a slice of America today, with firm handling and excellent performances in a surprisingly old-fashioned theme.

w Robert Getchell *d Martin Scorsese* *ph* Kent L. Wakeford *m* various *md* Richard La Salle *pd* Toby Carr Rafelson

Ellen Burstyn, Alfred Lutter, Kris Kristofferson, Billy Green Bush, *Diane Ladd*, Lelia Goldoni, Jodie Foster

'What Scorsese has done is to rescue an American cliché from the bland, flat but much more portentous naturalism of such as *Harry and Tonto* and restore it to an emotional and intellectual complexity through his particular brand of baroque realism.'—*Richard Combs*

'Full of funny malice and breakneck vitality.'—*New Yorker*

'A tough weepie, redeemed by its picturesque locations and its eye for social detail.'—*Michael Billington, Illustrated London News*

AA: Ellen Burstyn
AAN: Robert Getchell; Diane Ladd

Alice in the Cities
West Germany 1974 110m bw

A German journalist in America reluctantly escorts a small girl back to Germany. Interesting but overlong collection of modern metaphors, occasionally reminiscent of *Paper Moon.* Rudiger Vogeler, Yella Röttlander. Written and directed by Wim Wenders; for Filmverlag der Autoren.

Alice in Wonderland**
US 1933 75m bw
Paramount (Louis D. Lighton)

Intriguing but disappointing version of the nonsense classic, keeping to the Tenniel drawings by dressing an all-star cast in masks, thereby rendering them ineffective.

w Joseph L. Mankiewicz, William Cameron Menzies, *novel* Lewis Carroll *d* Norman Z. McLeod *ph* Henry Sharp, Bert Glennon *m* Dmitri Tiomkin

Charlotte Henry, W. C. Fields (Humpty Dumpty), Cary Grant (Mock Turtle), Gary Cooper (White Knight), Edward Everett Horton (Mad Hatter), Edna May Oliver (Red Queen), Jack Oakie (Tweedledum), Leon Errol (Uncle), Charles Ruggles (March Hare), May Robson (Queen of Hearts), Louise Fazenda (White Queen), Ned Sparks (Caterpillar), Alison Skipworth (Duchess)

'Nothing grows out of anything else in this phantasmagoria. It's like reading a whole volume of separate four-line gags.'—*Variety*

'Lavishly produced, with great care given to costumes and settings and make-up, but the spirit is missing.'—*New Yorker, 1977*

† Ida Lupino was brought from the UK for the title role, but not used.

Alice in Wonderland*
US 1951 75m Technicolor
Walt Disney

Fully animated cartoon version which has good moments but modernizes and Americanizes the familiar characters.

w various *d* Clyde Geronomi, Hamilton Luske, Wilfred Jackson *supervisor* Ben Sharpsteen *m* Oliver Wallace

AAN: Oliver Wallace

Alice in Wonderland*
aka: *Alice au Pays de Merveilles*
USA / France / Great Britain 1951 83m Ansco-color
Lou Bunin / UGC / Rank

Often interesting if sometimes crude version with Bunin's puppets, filmed in Nice; the simultaneous Disney cartoon version effectively kept it off the world's screens. Carol Marsh, Stephen Murray (as Lewis Carroll), Pamela Brown (as Queen Victoria), Felix Aylmer (as Dr Liddell)

Alice's Adventures in Wonderland*
GB 1972 101m Eastmancolor Todd-AO
TCF / Josef Shaftel (Derek Horne)

Live-action version which starts amiably enough but soon becomes flat and uninventive, with a star cast all at sea and tedium replacing the wit of the original.

wd William Sterling *ph* Geoffrey Unsworth *m* John Barry *pd* Michael Stringer

Fiona Fullerton, Michael Crawford (White Rabbit), Robert Helpmann (Mad Hatter), Dudley Moore (Dormouse), Spike Milligan (Gryphon), Peter Sellers (March Hare), Dennis Price (King of Hearts), Flora Robson (Queen of Hearts), Rodney Bewes (Knave of Hearts), Peter Bull (Duchess), Michael Hordern (Mock Turtle), Ralph Richardson (Caterpillar), etc

Alice's Restaurant*
US 1969 110m De Luxe
UA / Florin (Harold Levanthal)

Folk singer Arlo Guthrie, on the verge of being drafted, gets some varied experience of life among the drop-outs of Montana, Massachusetts and New York.
Typical of the freakish, anti-Vietnam, do-as-you-please movies which splurged from Hollywood in the wake of *Easy Rider*, this has the minor benefits of good production values and a few jokes.

w Venable Herndon, Arthur Penn *d* Arthur Penn *ph* Michael Nebbia *m / songs* Arlo Guthrie

Arlo Guthrie, Pat Quinn, James Broderick, Michael McClanathan, Geoff Outlaw

AAN: Arthur Penn

'In space, no one can hear you scream!'
Alien*
GB 1979 117m Eastmancolor Panavision
TCF / Brandywine (Walter Hill, Gordon Carroll, David Giler)

Astronauts returning to earth visit an apparently dead planet and are infected by a violent being which has unexpected behaviour patterns and eliminates them one by one.
Deliberately scarifying and highly commercial shocker with little but its art direction to commend it to connoisseurs.

w Dan O'Bannon *d Ridley Scott ph* Derek Vanlint, Denys Ayling *m* Jerry Goldsmith *chief designer H. R. Giger*

Tom Skerritt, Sigourney Weaver, John Hurt, Veronica Cartwright, Harry Dean Stanton, Ian Holm, Yaphet Kotto

'A sort of inverse relationship to *The Thing* invites unfavourable comparisons.'—*Sight and Sound*

'Empty bag of tricks whose production values and expensive trickery cannot disguise imaginative poverty.'—*Time Out*

'It was not, as its co-author admitted, a think piece. The message he intended was simple: Don't close your eyes or it will get ya.'—*Les Keyser, Hollywood in the Seventies*

Aliens*
US 1986 137m De Luxe
TCF / Brandywine (Gale Anne Hurd)

The sole survivor of the space team in *Alien* goes back with another team to the mystery planet, and finds more monsters.
Frightening but mechanical sequel with none of the half-assed poetry of the original.

w James Cameron, Walter Hill, David Giler *d* James Cameron *ph* Adrian Biddle *m* James Horner *pd* Peter Lamont *ed* Ray Lovejoy

Sigourney Weaver, Carrie Henn, Michael Biehn, Paul Reiser

'Audiences will be riveted to their seats with drooling dread in anticipation of the next horrifying attack.'—*Variety*

'I'm giving the movie a high rating for its skill and professionalism, and because it does the job it says it will do. I am also advising you not to eat before you see it.'—*Roger Ebert*

AA: special visual effects (Robert Skotak, Stan Winston, John Richardson, Suzanne Benson)

AAN: Music; production design; Ray Lovejoy; Sigourney Weaver

Alive and Kicking*
GB 1958 94m bw
ABP (Victor Skuzetsky)

Three old ladies escape from a home to an Irish island.
Agreeable minor comedy, a showcase for its elderly but vigorous stars.

w Denis Cannan *d* Cyril Frankel *ph* Gilbert Taylor *m* Philip Green

Sybil Thorndike, Kathleen Harrison, Estelle Winwood, Stanley Holloway, Joyce Carey, Eric Pohlmann, Colin Gordon

'The most provocative picture of the year!'
All About Eve***
US 1950 138m bw
TCF (Darryl F. Zanuck)

An ageing Broadway star suffers from the hidden menace of a self-effacing but secretly ruthless and ambitious young actress.
A basically unconvincing story with thin characters is transformed by a screenplay scintillating with savage wit and a couple of waspish performances into a movie experience to treasure.

wd Joseph L. Mankiewicz ph Milton Krasner *m* Alfred Newman

Bette Davis (Margo Channing), *George Sanders* (Addison de Witt), Anne Baxter (Eve), Celeste Holm (Karen Richards), Thelma Ritter (Birdie), Gary Merrill (Bill Sampson), Hugh Marlowe (Lloyd Richards), Gregory Ratoff (Max Fabian), Marilyn Monroe (Miss Caswell), Barbara Bates (Girl at Mirror), Walter Hampden (Speaker at dinner)

MARGO: 'Fasten your seat belts, it's going to be a bumpy night!'

ADDISON: 'That I should want you at all suddenly strikes me as the height of improbability . . . you're an improbable person, Eve, but so am I. We have that in common. Also a contempt for humanity, an inability to love or be loved, insatiable ambition—and talent. We deserve each other.'

BIRDIE: 'The bed looks like a dead animal act.'

ADDISON: 'That's all television is, dear—just auditions.'

BIRDIE: 'What a story! Everything but the bloodhounds snappin' at her rear end!'

ADDISON: 'I have lived in the theatre as a Trappist monk lives in his faith. In it I toil not, neither do I spin. I am a critic and a commentator. I am essential to the theatre—as ants to a picnic, as the boll weevil to a cotton field.'

'The wittiest, the most devastating, the most adult and literate motion picture ever made that had anything to do with the New York Stage.'—*Leo Mishkin*

'The dialogue and atmosphere are so peculiarly remote from life that they have sometimes been mistaken for art.'—*Pauline Kael, 1968*

'Plenty of surface cynicism, but no detachment, no edge and no satire. Boiled down it is a plush backstage drama.'—*Richard Winnington*

'Long, but continuously, wonderfully entertaining in a way I had almost forgotten was possible for films.'—*Richard Mallett, Punch*

'Someone remarked of this witty, exaggerated, cruel and yet wildly funny film that the secret of its success was the extreme bad taste shown throughout by all concerned (though I hope they didn't mean to include Milton Krasner's tactful camerawork in this).'—*Basil Wright, 1972*

'The picture seemed long—though it was not by today's standards of length—and the crispness of the dialogue was not matched by equally crisp editing.'—*Hollis Alpert, 1962*

† The idea for the film came from a short story, 'The Wisdom of Eve', by Mary Orr.

AA: best picture; Joseph L. Mankiewicz (as writer); Joseph L. Mankiewicz (as director); George Sanders
AAN: Milton Krasner; Alfred Newman; Bette Davis; Anne Baxter; Celeste Holm; Thelma Ritter

The All-American
US 1932 73m bw

A college football star finds his fame of little use to him in the outside world. Lively drama of its day, but with little permanent interest. Richard Arlen, Andy Devine, Gloria Stuart, James Gleason, Preston Foster. Written by Frank Wead, Ferdinand Reyney, Richard Schayer, Dale Van Every; directed by Russell Mack; for Universal. 'A pleaser for all audiences, having more than the football stuff to recommend it.'—*Variety*. (GB title: *Sport of a Nation*.)

The All-American
US 1952 83m bw
U-I (Aaron Rosenberg)
GB title: *The Winning Way*

When his parents are killed on the way to a match, a college football hero rejects sport for the groves of *academe*.
Very modest formula drama.

w D. D. Beauchamp *d* Jesse Hibbs *ph* Maury Gertsman *m* Joseph Gershenson

Tony Curtis, Mamie Van Doren, Lori Nelson, Gregg Palmer, Richard Long, Paul Cavanagh

The All-American Boy
US 1973 118m colour Panavision

A young boxer has got to the top too fast, and is depressed by the future. Uninteresting character study. Jon Voight, Carol Androsky, Anne Archer. Written and directed by Charles Eastman; for Warner.

ALIEN. The plot comes as no surprise to anyone who remembers *It! The Terror from Beyond Space* but H. R. Giger's extraordinary designs give the familiar tale an unsettling visual style to compensate for the clichés.

All Ashore
US 1952 80m Technicolor
Columbia (Jonie Taps)

Three sailors on shore leave work their passage to Catalina.
Very lightweight musical, no rival for *On the Town.*

w Blake Edwards, Richard Quine *d* Richard Quine *ph* Charles Lawton Jnr *m* Morris Stoloff, George Duning *ly* Robert Wells

Mickey Rooney, Dick Haymes, Ray McDonald, Peggy Ryan, Barbara Bates, Jody Lawrance

All Coppers Are . . .
GB 1972 87m colour

A crook and a cop both fancy the same girl.
Pointlessly titled lowlife melodrama with no style whatever; any episode of *Z Cars* would be vastly preferable. Nicky Henson, Martin Potter, Julia Foster, Ian Hendry. Written by Allan Prior; directed by Sidney Hayers; for Peter Rogers / Rank.

All Creatures Great and Small*
GB 1974 92m Eastmancolor
EMI / Venedon (David Susskind, Duane Bogie)

The pre-war Yorkshire life of a country vet.
Simple-minded popular entertainment of a long-forgotten kind, oddly sponsored by American TV in the shape of Readers' Digest and the Hallmark Hall of Fame.

w Hugh Whitemore, *novel* James Herriot
d Claude Whatham *ph* Peter Suschitzky
m Wilfred Josephs

Anthony Hopkins, Simon Ward, Lisa Harrow, Freddie Jones, Brian Stirner, T. P. McKenna, Brenda Bruce, John Collin
† 1976 sequel: *It Shouldn't Happen to a Vet.*

All Fall Down*
US 1962 111m bw Panavision
MGM (John Houseman)

A young man reveres his ne'er-do-well elder brother but determines to shoot him when he causes a girl's death.
Another gallery of middle American failures, competently portrayed by a writer and actors very practised at this sort of thing.

w William Inge, *novel* James Leo Herlihy
d John Frankenheimer *ph* Lionel Lindon
m Alex North

Warren Beatty, Brandon de Wilde, Angela Lansbury, Karl Malden, Eva Marie Saint

'That strange area of nostalgic Americana where the familiar is the Freudian grotesque.'—*New Yorker, 1982*

All for Mary*
GB 1955 82m Eastmancolor
Rank / Paul Soskin

Two rivals for the hand of the pretty daughter of a Swiss hotelier are struck down by chicken pox and cared for by the old nanny of one of them.
Simple-minded farce in which two grown men quail like children before a forceful old lady; on the strength of the latter characterization and a few funny lines the original play was a considerable West End success.

w Peter Blackmore, Paul Soskin, *play* Harold Brooke, Kay Bannerman *d* Wendy Toye *ph* Reg Wyer *m* Robert Farnon

Kathleen Harrison, Nigel Patrick, David Tomlinson, Jill Day, David Hurst, Leo McKern

All Hands on Deck
US 1961 98m De Luxe Cinemascope
TCF (Oscar Brodney)

Romantic and farcical adventures of sailors on leave.
Tired musical comedy romp with a second team cast.

w Jay Sommars, *novel* Donald R. Morris *d* Norman Taurog *ph* Leo Tover *m* Cyril Mockridge *songs* Jay Livingston, Ray Evans

Pat Boone, Buddy Hackett, Dennis O'Keefe, Barbara Eden, Warren Berlinger, Gale Gordon, Joe E. Ross

All I Desire
US 1953 79m bw
U-I (Ross Hunter)

A woman who had deserted her husband and family for a life on the stage returns for her daughter's graduation and is reconciled.
Resilient star melodrama with all stops out.

w James Gunn, Robert Blees *d* Douglas Sirk *ph* Carl Guthrie *m* Joseph Gershenson

Barbara Stanwyck, Richard Carlson, Lyle Bettger, Maureen O'Sullivan, Richard Long, Lori Nelson

All In
GB 1936 71m bw

A young man whose rich aunt opposes gambling finds himself the owner of a wrestling arena as well as a racing stable. Ralph Lynn, Gina Malo, Jack Barty, Claude Dampier, Sydney Fairbrother, Garry Marsh. Written by Leslie Arliss, Val Guest from the play Tattenham Corner by Bernard Merivale and Brandon Fleming; directed by Val Guest; for Gainsborough.

All in a Night's Work
US 1961 94m Technicolor
Paramount / Hal B. Wallis–Joseph Hazen

A publishing heir falls for a girl he suspects of having been his uncle's mistress.
Unpolished and not very amusing comedy which falters after an intriguing start.

w Edmund Beloin, Maurice Richlin, Sidney Sheldon *d* Joseph Anthony *ph* Joseph La Shelle *m* André Previn

Shirley Maclaine, Dean Martin, Charles Ruggles, Cliff Robertson, Norma Crane, Gale Gordon, Jerome Cowan, Jack Weston

'Tame and aimless sex-and-big-business comedy.'—*MFB*

All Men Are Enemies
US 1934 78m bw

Sweethearts parted by the war are reunited at last, despite another woman. Tedious romantic drama which failed to make a Hollywood star of its British lead. Hugh Williams, Helen Twelvetrees, Mona Barrie, Herbert Mundin, Henry Stephenson, Walter Byron, Una O'Connor, Halliwell Hobbes. Written by Samuel Hoffenstein, Lenore Coffee from the novel by Richard Aldington; directed by George Fitzmaurice; for Rocket / Fox.

All Mine To Give*
US 1956 102m Technicolor RKOscope
RKO (Sam Wiesenthal)
GB title: *The Day They Gave Babies Away*

In 1856, a pioneer couple in Wisconsin train their children to carry on the family after their own deaths.
Weird sentimental sob story, even odder under its English title. Surprisingly, some of it works quite well.

w Dale and Katherine Eunson (apparently about their own ancestors) *d* Allen Reisner *ph* William Skall *m* Max Steiner

Glynis Johns, Cameron Mitchell, Patty McCormack, Rex Thompson, Ernest Truex, Hope Emerson, Alan Hale

'A strong mood of folksy western reminiscence.'—*MFB*

All My Sons*
US 1948 94m bw
U-I (Chester Erskine)

A young man establishes that his father sold defective airplanes during the war.
Heady family melodrama from a taut and topical stage play. The film is well-meaning but artificial and unconvincing.

w Chester Erskine, *play* Arthur Miller *d* Irving Reis *ph* Russell Metty *m* Leith Stevens

Edward G. Robinson, Burt Lancaster, Mady Christians, Howard Duff

All Neat in Black Stockings
GB 1969 99m Eastmancolor
Anglo Amalgamated / Miton (Leon Clore)

Sex adventures of an amorous window cleaner.
Modish comedy drama with surface entertainment of a sort, but no depth.

w Jane Gaskell, Hugh Whitemore *d* Christopher Morahan *ph* Larry Pizer *m* Robert Cornford

Victor Henry, Susan George, Jack Shepherd, Anna Cropper, Clare Kelly, Terence de Marney

All Night*
US 1918 57m approx bw silent

A bright young entrepreneur throws a dinner for would-be investors. Theatrical farce, with most characters pretending to be what they're not, this must have worked better on the stage but by all accounts did pretty well on film. *Rudolph Valentino*, Carmel Myers, Charles Dorian, Mary Warren. Written by Fred Myton; directed by Paul Powell; for Bluebird Films.

All Night Long*
GB 1961 95m bw
Rank / Bob Roberts (Michael Relph, Basil Dearden)

Because of rumour set about by a jealous rival, a jazz trumpeter at an all-night party tries to strangle his wife.
Cheeky updating of *Othello* with jazz accompaniment, played a shade too grimly by an excellent cast. An interesting misfire.

w Nel King, Peter Achilles *d* Basil Dearden *ph* Ted Scaife *m* Philip Green

Patrick McGoohan, Richard Attenborough, Keith Michell, Betsy Blair, Marti Stevens, Paul Harris, Bernard Braden; and on the sound track Dave Brubeck, Tubby Hayes, Johnny Dankworth etc

All Night Long
US 1981 87m Technicolor
Universal (Leonard Goldberg, Jerry Weintraub)

The wife of the night manager of a supermarket has a hyperactive sex life.
Curiously misjudged and outdated farce which offers very few laughs.

w W. D. Richter *d* Jean-Claude Tramont *ph* Philip Lathrop *m* Ira Newborn, Richard Hazard *pd* Peter Jamison

Barbra Streisand, Gene Hackman, Diane Ladd, Dennis Quaid, Kevin Dobson, William Daniels, Ann Doran

'Neither screenplay nor direction seem very clear what they're trying to say, and large chunks of it make no sense at all.'—*Daily Mail*

'There are two kinds of women, but only one kind of love!'

All of Me
US 1934 70m bw
Paramount (Louis Lighton)

An engineering professor on his way to Boulder Dam finds his life affected by the problems of a criminal.
Confused and uninteresting romantic melodrama with a good cast all at sea.

w Sidney Buchman, Thomas Mitchell, *play* Chrysalis by Rose Porter *d* James Flood *ph* Victor Milner *m / ly* Ralph Rainger, Leo Robin

Fredric March, Miriam Hopkins, George Raft, Helen Mack, Nella Walker, William Collier Jnr, Gilbert Emery, Blanche Friderici, Edgar Kennedy

'The most startling glorification of criminals that even the movies have ever dared.'—*New York Sun*

'The gags aren't thought out visually in terms of the L.A. locations, and the film has the bland ugliness of sitcoms.'—*Pauline Kael, New Yorker*

All of Me
US 1984 91m Technicolor

A guru accidentally transfers a woman's soul after death into her lawyer's body. Curiously vulgar sitcom with a familiar team trying and failing to go one better on *The Man With Two Brains*. Steve Martin, Lily Tomlin, Victoria Tennant, Madolyn Smith, Dana Elcar. Written by Phil Alden Robinson; directed by Carl Reiner; for Old Time/Universal.

All Over Town
US 1937 62m bw

A pair of vaudevillians with a trained seal save a theatre on the skids. Routine knockabout comedy. Ole Olsen, Chic Johnson, Mary Howard, Harry Stockwell, James Finlayson, Franklin Pangborn. Written by Jack Townley, Jerome Chodorov; directed by James Horne; for Republic.

All Over the Town*
GB 1949 88m bw
Rank / Wessex (Ian Dalrymple)

Two reporters revivify a West of England local newspaper, and expose local corruption. Fresh, agreeable romantic comedy on sub-Ealing lines.

w Derek Twist and others *d* Derek Twist *ph* C. Pennington-Richards *m* Temple Abady

Norman Wooland, Sarah Churchill, *Fabia Drake* (as a local gorgon), Cyril Cusack, James Hayter

All Quiet on the Western Front****
US 1930 130m approx. bw
Universal (Carl Laemmle Jnr)

In 1914, a group of German teenagers volunteer for action on the Western Front, but they become disillusioned, and none of them survives.
A landmark of American cinema and Universal's biggest and most serious undertaking until the sixties, this highly emotive war film with its occasional outbursts of bravura direction fixed in millions of minds the popular image of what it was like in the trenches, even more so than *Journey's End* which had shown the Allied viewpoint. Despite dated moments, it retains its overall power and remains a great pacifist work.

w Lewis Milestone, Maxwell Anderson, Del Andrews, George Abbott, *novel* Erich Maria Remarque *d Lewis Milestone* (in a manner reminiscent of Eisenstein and Lang) *ph Arthur Edeson* *m* David Broekman

Lew Ayres (Paul Baumer), Louis Wolheim (Katczinsky), Slim Summerville (Tjaden), John Wray (Himmelstoss), Raymond Griffith (Gerard Duval), Russell Gleason (Muller), Ben Alexander (Kemmerick), Beryl Mercer (Mrs Baumer)

TJADEN: 'Me and the Kaiser, we are both fighting. The only difference is, the Kaiser isn't here.'

KATCZINSKY: 'At the next war let all the Kaisers, Presidents and Generals and diplomats go into a big field and fight it out first among themselves. That will satisfy us and keep us at home.'

PAUL: 'We live in the trenches out there. We fight. We try not to be killed, but sometimes we are. That's all.'

'A magnificent cinematic equivalent of the book . . . to Mr Milestone goes the credit of effecting the similitude in united and dynamic picture terms. The sound and image mediums blend as one, as a form of artistic expression that only the motion screen can give.'—*National Board of Review*

'Nothing passed up for the niceties; nothing glossed over for the women. Here exhibited is war as it is, butchery. The League of Nations could make no better investment than to buy up the master-print, reproduce it in every language to be shown to every nation every year until the word war is taken out of the dictionaries.'—*Variety*

'A trenchant and imaginative audible picture . . . most of the time the audience was held to silence by its realistic scenes.'—*New York Times*

AA: best picture; Lewis Milestone (as director)
AAN: Lewis Milestone, Maxwell Anderson, Del Andrews, George Abbott; Arthur Edeson

All That Heaven Allows
US 1955 89m Technicolor
U-I (Ross Hunter)

A sad widow falls in love with the gardener at her winter home, and marries him despite local prejudice.
Standard tearjerker in the tradition of *Magnificent Obsession*, reuniting the same stars, producer and director in the same rich musical and photographic sauce.

w Peg Fenwick *d* Douglas Sirk *ph* Russell Metty *m* Frank Skinner

Jane Wyman, Rock Hudson, Agnes Moorehead, Conrad Nagel, Virginia Grey, Charles Drake

'As laboriously predictable as it is fatuously unreal.'—*MFB*

All That Jazz**
US 1979 123m Technicolor
COL/TCF (Robert Alan Aurthur, Daniel Melnick)

A stage musical director pushes himself too hard, and dies of a surfeit of wine, women and work.
Self-indulgent, semi-autobiographical tragi-comic extravaganza complete with heart operations and a recurring angel of death. Flashes of brilliant talent make it a must for Fosse fans.

w Robert Alan Aurthur, Bob Fosse *d Bob Fosse* *ph* Giuseppe Rotunno *m* Ralph Burns *pd* Philip Rosenberg, Tony Walton

Roy Scheider, Jessica Lange, Ann Rainking, Leland Palmer, Ben Vereen, Cliff Gorman

'Egomaniacal, wonderfully choreographed, often compelling . . . more an art item than a broad commercial prospect.'—*Variety*

'An improbable mixture of crass gags, song 'n' dance routines and open heart surgery. Not for the squeamish.'—*Time Out*

'By the end I felt I'd learned more about Fosse than I actually cared to know.'—*Daily Mail*

'High cholesterol hokum. Enjoyable, but probably not good for you.'—*Pauline Kael, New Yorker*

AAN: best picture

BFA: cinematography; editing (Alan Heim); sound

All That Money Can Buy****
US 1941 106m bw
RKO / William Dieterle (Charles L. Glett)
aka: *The Devil and Daniel Webster; Daniel and the Devil; Here Is a Man*

A hard-pressed farmer gives in to the Devil's tempting, but is saved from the pit by a famous lawyer's pleading at his 'trial'.
A brilliant Germanic *Faust* set in 19th-century New Hampshire and using historical figures, alienation effects, comedy asides and the whole cinematic box of tricks which Hollywood had just learned again through *Citizen Kane*. A magic act in more ways than one.

w Dan Totheroh, based on The Devil and Daniel Webster by Stephen Vincent Benet *d William Dieterle* *ph Joseph August* *m Bernard Herrmann* *ad Van Nest Polglase* *sp Vernon L. Walker*

Walter Huston ('Mr Scratch', a great performance), James Craig, Anne Shirley, Simone Simon, *Edward Arnold* (Daniel Webster), Jane Darwell, Gene Lockhart, John Qualen, H. B. Warner

MR SCRATCH: 'A soul. A soul is nothing. Can you see it, smell it, touch it? No. Think of it—this soul—your soul—a nothing, against seven whole years of good luck! You will have money and all that money can buy.'

'Some of those in the movie industry who saw it restively called it a dog; but some of them cried it was another catapult hurling the cinema up to its glorious destiny.'—*Cecilia Ager*

AA: Bernard Herrmann
AAN: Walter Huston

All the Brothers Were Valiant*
US 1953 94m Technicolor
MGM (Pandro S. Berman)

Rivalry between brothers on a whaling schooner.
Remake of a silent melodrama with predictable vengefulness and formula heroism, capably but unmemorably portrayed.

w Harry Brown, *novel* Ben Ames Williams *d* Richard Thorpe *ph* George Folsey *m* Miklos Rozsa

Stewart Granger, Robert Taylor, Ann Blyth, Betta St John, Keenan Wynn, James Whitmore, Kurt Kasznar, Lewis Stone

AAN: George Folsey

All the Fine Young Cannibals
US 1960 122m Metrocolor
Cinemascope
MGM / Avon (Pandro S. Berman)

The son of a country clergyman loves the daughter of another clergyman; they both find the realities of life in New York a horrid shock.
The glum joys of sex and dope in the big city are revealed in this boring rather than daring farrago which is not even unintentionally funny.

w Robert Thom, *novel* The Bixby Girls by Rosamond Marshall *d* Michael Anderson *ph* William H. Daniels *m* Jeff Alexander

Robert Wagner, Natalie Wood, Pearl Bailey, Susan Kohner, George Hamilton, Jack Mullaney, Onslow Stevens, Anne Seymour

All the King's Horses
US 1935 87m bw

A Hollywood star revisiting his native Langenstein turns out to be a double of the king, and finds himself romancing the queen. Operetta-style entertainment grafted onto the plot of *The Prisoner of Zenda*; by no means unacceptable even now. Carl Brisson, Mary Ellis, Edward Everett Horton, Eugene Pallette, Katherine de Mille. Written by Frank Tuttle and Frederick Stephani, from a play by Lawrence Clark and Max Giersberg; directed by Frank Tuttle; for Paramount.

'He thought he had the world by the tail—till it exploded in his face, with a bullet attached!'

All the King's Men***
US 1949 109m bw
Columbia (Robert Rossen)

An honest man from a small town is elected mayor and then governor, but power corrupts him absolutely and he ruins his own life and those of his friends before being assassinated.
Archetypal American political melodrama based on the life of southern senator Huey Long. The background is well sketched in and there are excellent performances, but the overall narrative is rather flabby.

w Robert Rossen, *novel* Robert Penn Warren *d Robert Rossen ph* Burnett Guffey *m* Louis Gruenberg *ad* Sturges Carne

Broderick Crawford, John Ireland, Mercedes McCambridge, Joanne Dru, John Derek, Anne Seymour, Shepperd Strudwick

'More conspicuous for scope and worthiness of intention than for inspiration.'—*Gavin Lambert*

'A superb pictorialism which perpetually crackles and explodes.'—*Bosley Crowther*

'Realism comes from within as well as without and the core of meaning that might have made this film a step forward from *Boomerang* does not exist amid all the courageous camera-work.'—*Richard Winnington*

'Broderick Crawford's Willie Stark might just make you feel better about the President you've got . . . By no means a great film, but it moves along.'—*Pauline Kael, New Yorker*

AA: best picture; Broderick Crawford; Mercedes McCambridge
AAN: Robert Rossen (as writer); Robert Rossen (as director); John Ireland

All the Marbles . . .
US 1981 113m Metrocolor
MGM / Aldrich Company (William Aldrich)
GB title: *The California Dolls*

Problems of a women's wrestling team in the midwest.
Tasteless and tedious exploitation comedy with just a few flashes of the director's old flair.

w Mel Frohman *d* Robert Aldrich *ph* Joseph Biroc *m* Frank de Vol *pd* Carl Anderson *ed* Irving C. Rosenblum, Richard Lane

Peter Falk, Vicki Frederick, Laurene Landon, Burt Young, Tracy Reed

'The most devastating detective story of the century!'

All the President's Men***
US 1976 138m Technicolor
Warner / Wildwood (Robert Redford, Walter Coblenz)

A reconstruction of the discovery of the White House link with the Watergate affair by two young reporters from the *Washington Post*.
An absorbing drama from the headlines which despite its many excellences would have been better with a more audible dialogue track, less murky photography and a clearer introduction of the characters concerned. The acting however is a treat.

w William Goldman, *book* Carl Bernstein, Bob Woodward *d* Alan J. Pakula *ph* Gordon Willis *m* David Shire *pd* George Jenkins

Robert Redford, Dustin Hoffman, Jason Robards Jnr, Martin Balsam, Hal Holbrook, Jack Warden, Jane Alexander, Meredith Baxter

'It works as a detective thriller (even though everyone knows the ending), as a credible (if occasionally romanticized) primer on the prosaic fundamentals of big league investigative journalism, and best of all, as a chilling tone poem that conveys the texture of the terror in our nation's capital during that long night when an aspiring fascist regime held our democracy under siege.'—*Frank Rich, New York Post*

AA: William Goldman; Jason Robards Jnr
AAN: best picture; Alan J. Pakula; Jane Alexander

All The Right Moves
US 1983 91m colour

An ambitious high school football star is helped to get an athletics scholarship. Rather dislikeable melodrama with specifically American atmosphere. Tom Cruise, Craig T. Nelson, Lea Thomson, Charles Cioffi, Christopher Penn. Written by Michael Kane, directed by Michael Chapman, for Stephen Deutsch/20th Century Fox.

All the Right Noises*
GB 1969 91m Eastmancolor
(TCF) Trigon (Anthony Hope)

The electrician of a touring company has an affair with a 15-year-old actress, but finally returns to his wife.
Sharp, sensible treatment of a cliché situation, as watchable as a superior television play.

wd Gerry O'Hara ph Gerry Fisher *m* John Cameron

Tom Bell, Judy Carne, Olivia Hussey, John Standing

'Built on a solid framework of disciplined direction and animated performances.'—*MFB*

'Love is not a thing that grows only in the dark!'

All the Way Home**
US 1963 107m bw
Paramount / Talent Associates (David Susskind)

In 1916 Tennessee, the beloved father of a family is killed in a car crash, and after the trauma wears off, mother helps the children to rebuild their lives.
Tactful, charming though finally depressing slice of small town period Americana, with generally eloquent performances.

w Philip Reisman Jnr, *play* Tad Mosel, *novel* A Death in the Family by James Agee *d* Alex Segal *ph Boris Kaufman m* Bernard Green

Robert Preston, Jean Simmons, Aline MacMahon, Pat Hingle, Michael Kearney

'A heart-wrenching blend of nostalgia and sorrow.'—*Judith Crist*

'Terribly earnest, pictorial, and well intentioned. And a terrible mistake.'—*Pauline Kael, New Yorker*

All the Way Up*
GB 1970 97m Technicolor
Granada / EMI (Philip Mackie)

Social-climbing Dad makes his way by treachery and blackmail, but gets his come-uppance when his son takes after him.
Crudely farcical adaptation of a thoughtful comedy of its time; the treatment works in fits and starts but leaves one in no mood for the talkative finale.

w Philip Mackie, *play* Semi Detached by David Turner *d* James MacTaggart *ph* Dick Bush *m* Howard Blake

Warren Mitchell, Pat Heywood, Elaine Taylor, Kenneth Cranham, Vanessa Howard, Richard Briers, Adrienne Posta, Bill Fraser

All the Young Men
US 1960 87m bw
Columbia (Hall Bartlett / Jaguar)

A marine patrol in Korea is commanded by a black man, and racial tensions take precedence over fighting the enemy.
Simple-minded, parsimoniously-budgeted war melodrama.

wd Hall Bartlett *ph* Daniel Fapp *m* George Duning

Alan Ladd, Sidney Poitier, Ingemar Johansson, Glenn Corbett, James Darren, Mort Sahl

'Strenuously engaged in exploiting the entertainment values of nostalgia, fear, suspense, hatred and sex.'—*MFB*

ALL THIS AND HEAVEN TOO. Charles Boyer and Bette Davis pull out every dramatic stop in a smooth and typically elaborate Warner production.

All This and Heaven Too**
US 1940 143m bw
Warner (Jack L. Warner, Hal B. Wallis)

A 19th-century French nobleman falls in love with his governess and murders his wife.
Romantic, melodramatic soap opera from a mammoth best seller; well made for those who can stomach it, with excellent acting and production values.

w Casey Robinson, *novel* Rachel Field
d Anatole Litvak *ph* Ernest Haller *m* Max Steiner

Charles Boyer, Bette Davis, Barbara O'Neil, Virginia Weidler, Jeffrey Lynn, Helen Westley, Henry Daniell, Harry Davenport, Walter Hampden, George Coulouris, Janet Beecher, Montagu Love

'Deserves extended runs and upped admissions . . . completely shorn of spectacle, but replete with finely drawn characters in absorbingly dramatic situations.'—*Variety*

'Litvak had it all on paper: he planned every move. There is not the spontaneity or flexibility.'—*Bette Davis*

AAN: best picture; Ernest Haller; Barbara O'Neil

All This and World War Two*
US 1977 88m De Luxe / bw

Wartime newsreels are interwoven with pop songs and clips from feature films. A messy mélange with obvious items of interest, but totally confusing and uninformative for the young historian. No writer credit; directed by Susan Winslow for Lou Reizner Productions / TCF. 'Desperately straining to make any kind of sense, it is reduced to making parallels that are either glib or facetious.'—*MFB*

'Killer Bogart takes the Gestapo for a ride!'
All Through the Night*
US 1942 107m bw
Warner (Jerry Wald)

Gangsters help to track down fifth columnists in World War II New York.
Highly entertaining muddle of several styles which somehow works well and allows several favourites to do their thing.

w Leonard Spiegelgass, Edwin Gilbert
d Vincent Sherman *ph* Sid Hickox *m* Adolph Deutsch

Humphrey Bogart, Conrad Veidt, Peter Lorre, Karen Verne, Judith Anderson, Jane Darwell, Frank McHugh, Jackie Gleason, William Demarest, Phil Silvers

'Exciting slaphappy stuff.'—*Kine Weekly*

'The thrills and the jokes have both been sharpened to a pin point.'—*New Statesman*

Allan Quatermain and the Lost City of Gold
US 1987 99m colour JDC

A mysterious old gold piece sends Quatermain looking for his brother, missing in Africa after seeking a lost white race. Abysmal follow-up to 1985's ghastly *King Solomon's Mines*. Richard Chamberlain, Sharon Stone, James Earl Jones, Henry Silva, Robert Ronner. 'The embarrassing screenplay jettisons Haggard's enduring fantasy and myth-making in favour of a back-of-the-envelope plotline and anachronistic jokes about Cleveland.'—*Daily Variety*. Written by Gene Quintano, directed by Gary Nelson, for Avi Lerner/Cannon.

Allegheny Uprising
US 1939 98m bw
RKO (P. J. Wolfson)
GB title: *The First Rebel*

A young frontiersman smashes liquor traffic with the Indians.
Modestly efficient western with an impressive cast.

w P. J. Wolfson, *story* Neil Swanson
d William A. Seiter *ph* Nicholas Musuraca

John Wayne, Claire Trevor, Brian Donlevy, George Sanders, Wilfrid Lawson, Robert Barrat, Moroni Olsen, Eddie Quillan, Chill Wills

'Long on horsemanship and action, short on romance and suspense.'—*Variety*

Allegro Ma Troppo*
France 1963 16m Eastmancolor
Films Je Vois Tout

One night in Paris viewed through accelerated motion.
An amusing if not original conceit, smartly executed.

w, d, ph Paul de Roubaix m François de Roubaix *ed* Robert Enrico

Allegro Non Troppo*
Italy 1977 85m colour

Animated feature, a modernistic version of *Fantasia*, e.g. Ravel's 'Bolero' is danced by a Coca-Cola bottle. Directed by Bruno Bozzetto, written and produced by a group including himself, Guido Manuli and Maurizio Nichetti.

Alligator*
US 1980 91m De Luxe
Group 1 / Alligator Associates (Brandon Chase)

A pet baby alligator is flushed down the toilet and later, grown to enormous size, goes on the rampage.
Jaws-type monster movie made tolerable by occasional flashes of humour but not otherwise remarkable.

w John Sayles *d* Lewis Teague *ph* Joseph Mangine *m* Craig Hundley *sp* Richard O. Helmer

Robert Forster, Robin Ryker, Michael Gazzo, Dean Jagger, Jack Carter, Henry Silva

'Hair raising, funny, shrewdly scripted and politically telling.'—*Margaret Hinxman, Daily Mail*

An Alligator Named Daisy
GB 1955 88m Technicolor Vistavision
Rank (Raymond Stross)

A young songwriter finds himself saddled with a pet alligator.
The ultimate in silly animal comedies, this does score a few laughs.

w Jack Davies, *novel* Charles Terrot *d* J. Lee-Thompson *ph* Reg Wyer *m* Stanley Black

Donald Sinden, Diana Dors, Jean Carson, James Robertson Justice, Stanley Holloway,

Roland Culver, Margaret Rutherford, Avice Landone, Richard Wattis, Frankie Howerd, Jimmy Edwards, Gilbert Harding

'Apart from a fairly Kafkaesque scene in which Daisy is discovered in an upright piano, the situation is treated with little wit or comic invention.'—*MFB*

The Alligator People
US 1959 73m bw Cinemascope

A doctor uses a revolutionary serum which unfortunately turns patients into the alligators from which it was derived. Moderately inventive 'B' chiller. George Macready, Frieda Inescort, Beverly Garland, Bruce Bennett, Lon Chaney Jnr. Written by Orville H. Hampton; directed by Roy del Ruth; for TCF.

Almonds and Raisins*
GB 1983 90m bw

The story of the Yiddish cinema in thirties New York. Interesting documentary compilation majoring in the work of Edgar G. Ulmer. Written by Wolf Mankowitz; directed by Russ Karel; for Willowgold / Brook Productions and the National Center for Jewish Film.

Almost Angels
US 1962 93m colour

A boy joins the Vienna Boys' Choir. The singing outweighs the story in this overlong but often pleasing filler. Vincent Winter, Peter Weck, Sean Scully, Hans Holt. Written by Vernon Harris from a story by R. A. Stemmle, directed by Steven Previn, for Buena Vista.

Almost Married
US 1932 50m bw

An insane Bolshevik breaks out of hospital when he hears of his wife's bigamous marriage. Oddly-titled melodrama with flashes of interest, previously filmed by MGM in 1919. Violet Heming, Ralph Bellamy, Alexander Kirkland, Alan Dinehart. Written by Wallace Smith from the novel Devil's Triangle by Andrew Soutar; directed by William Cameron Menzies; for TCF.

An Almost Perfect Affair*
US 1979 93m De Luxe
Paramount / Terry Carr

A young film producer at the Cannes Festival falls for the wife of an Italian impresario. Lively detail lifts many scenes of this eccentric romance, but the routine plot is a downer.

w Walter Bernstein, Don Peterson *d Michael Ritchie* *ph* Henri Decae *m* Georges Delerue

Keith Carradine, Monica Vitti, Raf Vallone, Christian de Sica

Aloha Bobby and Rose
US 1975 89m Metrocolor
(Warner) Cine Artists International (Fouad Said)

A Los Angeles motor mechanic becomes unwittingly involved in crime and finds himself fleeing for the Mexican border with a girl friend.

Warmed-over retread of *They Live By Night*, not badly done but of no abiding interest.

wd Floyd Mutrux *ph* William A. Fraker

Paul Le Mat, Dianne Hull, Tim McIntire, Leigh French, Noble Willingham, Robert Carradine

'As accurate a picture of Southern California as I've yet seen.'—*Guardian*

'Pagan love—in an exotic, exciting tropic paradise!'

Aloma of the South Seas
US 1941 77m Technicolor
Paramount (Monte Bell)

A young Polynesian chieftain returns to quell trouble on his island after being educated in the US.
Hoary goings-on in gory colour, a remake of a silent epic devised to display the star's sarong and the backlot's expensive volcano.

w Frank Butler, Seena Owen, Lillie Hayward *d* Alfred Santell *ph* Karl Struss, Wilfrid M. Cline, William Snyder *m* Victor Young *sp* Gordon Jennings

Dorothy Lamour, Jon Hall, Lynne Overman, Philip Reed, Katherine de Mille, Fritz Leiber, Dona Drake, Esther Dale

'The mountain has the privilege of belching when it is dissatisfied, which is something no well-bred critic should do.'—*C. A. Lejeune*

† A silent version in 1926 had starred Gilda Gray. Directed by Maurice Tourneur, it adhered more closely to the original play (by John B. Hymer and Leroy Clemens).

AAN: Karl Struss, Wilfrid M. Cline, William Snyder

Alone in the Dark
US 1982 93m Cineffects

Maximum-security prisoners in a mental hospital are liberated by a power failure. Pretentious but incompetent horror flick of the Halloween school, with a plot partly borrowed from *Spellbound*. Jack Palance, Donald Pleasence, Martin Landau, Dwight Schultz, Deborah Hedwall. Written and directed by Jack Shoder; for New Line / Masada.

Alone on the Pacific**
Japan 1963 104m Eastmancolor Cinemascope
Ishihara-Nikkatsu (Akira Nakai)
original title: *Taiheiyo Hitoribochi*

A young man crosses from Osaka to San Francisco in a small yacht.
Fascinating Robinson-Crusoe-like exercise, with flashbacks to life on dry land.

w Natto Wada, based on the experiences of Kenichi Horie *d Kon Ichikawa* *ph* Yoshihiro Yamazaki *m* Yasushi Akatagawa, Tohru Takemitsu

Yujiro Ishihara, Masayuki Mori, Kinuyo Tanaka, Ruriko Asaoko

'Wonderfully comic moments emerge, but they never overshadow the film's sheer pictorial value.'—*Brenda Davies, MFB*

Along Came Jones*
US 1945 90m bw
(UA) Cinema Artists Corporation (Gary Cooper)

Two cowboys are mistaken for killers.
Very mild western comedy melodrama, with the star at his most self-effacing and production only mediocre.

w Nunnally Johnson, *novel* Alan le May *d* Stuart Heisler *ph* Milton Krasner *m* Charles Maxwell, Arthur Lange, Hugo Friedhofer

Gary Cooper, Loretta Young, William Demarest, Dan Duryea, Russell Simpson

Along the Great Divide
US 1950 88m bw
Warner (Anthony Veiller)

A marshal prevents an old man from being hanged for murder, and eventually discovers the real culprit.
Adequate, modest western with an unusual detective element.

w Walter Doniger, Lewis Meltzer *d* Raoul Walsh *ph* Sid Hickox *m* David Buttolph

Kirk Douglas, Virginia Mayo, Walter Brennan, John Agar, Ray Teal

The Alphabet Murders
GB 1965 90m bw
MGM (Ben Arbeid)

Hercule Poirot solves a series of murders by an apparent lunatic choosing his victims in alphabetical order.
Ruination of a classic whodunnit novel, misguided both in its attempt to mix slapstick with detection and in its terrible central performance.

w David Pursall, Jack Seddon, *novel* The ABC Murders by Agatha Christie *d* Frank Tashlin *ph* Desmond Dickinson *m* Ron Goodwin

Tony Randall, Robert Morley, Anita Ekberg, Maurice Denham, Guy Rolfe, James Villiers, Clive Morton

Alphaville*
France / Italy 1965 98m bw
Chaumiane / Filmstudio (André Michelin)

A special agent travels across space to find out what happened to his predecessor, and finds himself in a loveless society.
A rather chill futuristic fantasy on the lines of *1984* but with an outer space background and a hero borrowed from Peter Cheyney. Interesting but not endearing.

wd Jean-Luc Godard *ph* Raoul Coutard *m* Paul Misraki

Eddie Constantine, Anna Karina, Akim Tamiroff, Howard Vernon, Laszlo Szabo

Altered States*
US 1980 102m Technicolor
Warner / Howard Gottfried, Daniel Melnick

A psychophysiologist uses a sensory deprivation tank to hallucinate himself back into primitive states of human evolution, in which guise he emerges to kill. . . .
Amusing elaboration of Jekyll and Hyde, not to mention the Karloff mad doctor second features of the forties. All very po-faced now, and certainly impeccably done.

w Sidney Aaron, *novel* Paddy Chayevsky *d Ken Russell ph* Jordan Cronenweth *m* John Corigliano *pd* Richard McDonald

William Hurt, Blair Brown, Bob Balaban, Charles Haid

'Russell clomps from one scene to the next, the psychedelic visions come at you like choppy slide shows, and the picture has a dismal, tired, humanistic ending.'—*Pauline Kael, New Yorker*

'A feast for special effects lovers and drugged philosophy majors only.'—*Roger Ebert*

'A herd of cattle against a herd of cannon!'

Alvarez Kelly
US 1966 116m Technicolor Panavision
Columbia / Ray David (Sol C. Siegel)

The owner of a herd of 2500 cattle finds himself between two sides in the American Civil War.
Unusual if rather tepid western which balances historical interest against social conscience and throws in a variety of other elements.

w Franklin Coen *d* Edward Dmytryk *ph* Joseph MacDonald *m* John Green

William Holden, Richard Widmark, Janice Rule, Patrick O'Neal, Victoria Shaw, Roger C. Carmel, Richard Rust

Alvin Purple
Australia 1973 97m colour

A young man who finds himself irresistible to women finally lands a job as gardener in a convent. Dismal sex farce which nevertheless helped to start the present world-wide popularity of Australian cinema. Graeme Blundell, Abigail, Lynette Curran, Christine Amor, Dina Mann. Written by Alan Hopgood; directed by Tim Burstall; for Hexagon.

Always Goodbye
US 1931 62m Fox

A much-jilted girl finally believes she has met Mr Right. Fairly pointless romantic comedy which must have pleased some people in the early days of talkies. Elissa Landi, Lewis Stone, Paul Cavanagh, John Garrick, Frederick Kerr. Written by Kate MacLaurin; directed by William Cameron Menzies and Kenneth MacKenna; for Fox.

Always Goodbye
US 1938 75m bw
TCF (Raymond Griffith)

An unwed mother gives up her baby and later wants it back.
Tired sentimental warhorse, a remake of *Gallant Lady* (qv).

w Kathryn Scola, Edith Skouras *d* Sidney Lanfield *ph* Robert Planck *md* Louis Silvers

Barbara Stanwyck, Herbert Marshall, Ian Hunter, Cesar Romero, Lynn Bari, Binnie Barnes

'A fair summer attraction . . . should do satisfactorily on the strength of its cast.'—*Variety*

Always in My Heart*
US 1942 92m bw
Warner (Walter McEwen, William Jacobs)

A convict returns home to find his daughter a stranger and his wife about to marry again.
Well acted sentimental drama.

w Adele Commandini, *play* Fly Away Home by Dorothy Bennett, Irving White *d* Joe Graham *ph* Sid Hickox *m* Heinz Roemheld

Walter Huston, Kay Francis, Gloria Warren, Frankie Thomas, Sidney Blackmer, Una O'Connor

AAN: title song (*m* Ernest Lucuona, *ly* Kim Gannon)

Always Leave Them Laughing*
US 1949 116m bw
Warner (Jerry Wald)

A vaudeville comedian craves the spotlight at the expense of his private life.
Raucous backstage vehicle, crammed with sentimental and melodramatic cliché but affording tantalizing glimpses of the stage acts of its two stars.

w Jack Rose, Mel Shavelson *d* Roy del Ruth *ph* Ernest Haller *ly* Sammy Cahn *md* Ray Heindorf

Milton Berle, Bert Lahr, Virginia Mayo, Ruth Roman, Alan Hale, Jerome Cowan

Always Together*
US 1947 78m bw

Dying millionaire bequeaths his all to a working girl, then recovers and tries to retrieve it. Oddball comedy about a girl who has film fantasies, killed by dull title. Joyce Reynolds, Robert Hutton, Cecil Kellaway, Ernest Truex; guest appearances by Bogart and Flynn (among others). Written by Henry and Phoebe Ephron and I. A. L. Diamond; directed by Frederick de Cordova; for Warner.

Amadeus***
US 1984 160m Technicolor Panavision
Saul Zaentz

Dying in 1823, the jealous composer Salieri claims to have murdered Mozart.
A musical legend performed with success and economy on stage now becomes an exciting baroque film, like an opera in high-pitched dialogue. Great to look at, and only the American accents jar the ear.

w Peter Shaffer from his play *d Milos Forman ph Miroslav Ondricek md* Neville Marriner *pd Patrizia Van Brandenstein* *ed* Nena Danevic, Michael Chandler

F. Murray Abraham, Tom Hulce, Elizabeth Berridge, Simon Callow, Roy Dotrice, Christine Ebersole

AA: best picture, direction, F. Murray Abraham, adapted screenplay
AAN: Tom Hulce, photography, editing, art direction
BFA: Miroslav Ondricek

Les Amants*
France 1958 88m bw Dyaliscope
Nouvelles Editions
aka: *The Lovers*

A rich provincial wife has a secret life in Paris, but finds real satisfaction in an affair with a young man.
A passionate romance which had some censorship difficulties at the time, this rather gloomy film never quite whirls one away as it should, and it doesn't have the eye for detail of *Brief Encounter*.

wd Louis Malle, *novel* Point de Lendemain by Dominique Vivant, Baron de Denon *ph* Henri Decaë *m* Brahms

Jeanne Moreau, Alain Cluny, Jean-Marc Bory, Judith Magre

Les Amants de Vérone*
France 1948 110m bw
CICC (Raymond Borderie)
aka: *The Lovers of Verona*

In modern Venice a film is being made of *Romeo and Juliet*, and the stand-ins for the stars feel they are re-enacting the old story.
A superbly stylish if rather empty piece, the dazzling detail being much more interesting than the main story.

w André Cayatte, Jacques Prévert *d André Cayatte ph* Henri Alekan *m* Joseph Kosma *ad* Moulaert

Pierre Brasseur, Serge Reggiani, Anouk Aimée, Louis Salou, Marcel Dalio

'Visually exciting, immaculately made.'—*Penelope Houston*

Amarcord**
Italy / France 1973 123m Technicolor
FC Produzione / PECF (Franco Cristaldi)

Memories of a small Italian town during the fascist period.
A bizarre, intriguing mixture of fact, fantasy and obscurity, generally pleasing to watch though hardly satisfying. The title means 'I remember'.

w Federico Fellini, Tonino Guerra *d Federico Fellini ph* Giuseppe Rotunno *m Nino Rota* *ad* Danilo Donati

Puppela Maggio, Magali Noel, Armando Brancia, Ciccio Ingrassia

'A rich surface texture and a sense of exuberant melancholia.'—*Michael Billington, Illustrated London News*

'Peaks of invention separated by raucous valleys of low comedy.'—*Sight and Sound*

'Some idea of attitudes within the film business may be conveyed by the fact that this witty, tender, humane, marvellously photographed picture has been booked into a cinema with 132 seats.'—*Benny Green, Punch*

'Hitchcock once said that he wanted to play his audiences like a piano. Fellini requires the entire orchestra.'—*Roger Ebert*

AA: best foreign film
AAN: script; direction

The Amateur
US 1982 111m Technicolor
TCF / Joel B. Michaels, Garth B. Drabinsky

A computer expert goes into action on his own account when his girl friend is killed in the Munich consulate and the CIA takes no reprisals.
Ho-hum espionage adventure which has its moments but barely got released.

THE AMAZING DR CLITTERHOUSE. Edward G. Robinson relished playing a role played on stage by Cedric Hardwicke although the critics thought he was miscast. Bogart, on the other hand, hated his part as a gangster.

w Robert Littell, Diana Maddox, *novel* Robert Littell *d* Charles Jarrott *ph* John Coquillon *m* Ken Wannberg

John Savage, Christopher Plummer, Marthe Keller, Arthur Hill, Ed Lauter

'Ill constructed and largely implausible, with occasional atmospheric touches.'—*Guardian*

Amateur Daddy
US 1932 71m bw

A promise to a dying friend leaves a construction engineer with four orphans to look after. Sentimental drama of the *Daddy Longlegs* school, with backwoods atmosphere which makes it seem even more dated than it is. Warner Baxter, Marian Nixon, Rita LaRoy, William Pawley, David Landau. Written by William Conselman, Doris Malloy and Frank Dolan, from the novel Scotch Valley by Mildred Cram; directed by John Blystone; for Fox. 'Strikes a strong human interest note . . . more than often very agreeable entertainment.'—*Variety*

The Amateur Gentleman*
GB 1936 102m bw
Criterion (Marcel Hellman, Douglas Fairbanks Jnr)

A Regency innkeeper's son poses as a travelling pugilist in order to clear his father's name of theft.

Dated but rather fascinating period adventure, quite a lively production of its time.

w Clemence Dane, Edward Knoblock, Sergei Nolbandov from novel by Jeffrey Farnol *d* Thornton Freeland *ph* Gunther Krampf *m* Richard Addinsell

Douglas Fairbanks Jnr, Elissa Landi, Gordon Harker, Basil Sydney, Hugh Williams, Irene Browne, Margaret Lockwood, Coral Browne, Frank Pettingell, Athole Stewart, Esmé Percy

'Growing! growing! growing! When will it stop?'

The Amazing Colossal Man*
US 1957 80m bw
AIP / Malibu (Bert I. Gordon)

A plutonium explosion causes an army colonel to grow at the rate of ten feet a day.
Modest, quite well written sci-fi let down by shaky trick work.

w Bert I. Gordon, Mark Hanna *d* Bert I. Gordon *ph* Joe Biroc *m* Albert Glasser

Glenn Langan, Cathy Downs, William Hudson, James Seay

† Sequel: *War of the Colossal Beast* (GB: *The Terror Strikes*).

The Amazing Dobermans
US 1976 99m colour

Most ambitious of three low-budget independent movies (others, *The Daring Dobermans* and *The Doberman Gang*) about a group of trained dogs; this one concerns an ex-con who hires them out for guard duty. A fair low-budget production for family audiences. Fred Astaire, James Franciscus, Parley Baer, Billy Barty. Written by Richard Chapman; directed by Byron Chudnow; for Doberman Associates.

The Amazing Dr Clitterhouse**
US 1938 87m bw
Warner (Robert Lord)

A criminologist researcher joins a gangster's mob and becomes addicted to crime.
Amusing, suspenseful, well acted comedy-melodrama.

w John Huston, John Wexley, *play* Barre Lyndon *d* Anatole Litvak *ph* Tony Gaudio *m* Max Steiner

Edward G. Robinson, Humphrey Bogart, Claire Trevor, Allen Jenkins, Gale Page, Donald Crisp, Maxie Rosebloom

'An unquestionable winner . . . the picture inculcates a bit of the sherlocking theme and modified romance.'—*Variety*

'The story is ingenious, but Anatole Litvak and his producing-acting crew have so thoroughly kept the larky mood of it while setting up the necessary mood of interest and suspense that it is hard to see where conception leaves off and the shaping of it into motion begins.'—*Otis Ferguson*

The Amazing Dr X
US 1948 78m bw
Eagle–Lion
GB title: *The Spiritualist*

A widow seeks comfort from a fraudulent medium.
An interesting subject for a thriller is muffed by naïve handling.

w Muriel Roy Bolton, Ian McLellan Hunter, *story* Crane Wilbur *d* Bernard Vorhaus *ph* John Alton

Lynn Bari, Richard Carlson, Turhan Bey, Cathy O'Donnell

Amazing Grace and Chuck
US 1987 115m colour

On both sides of the Iron Curtain, a weird selection of public personalities stand up in favour of the elimination of nuclear weapons. Expensive but inept propaganda apparently motivated by Ted Turner. Jamie Lee Curtis, Alex English, Gregory Peck, William L. Petersen, Joshua Zuehike. Written and produced by David Field; directed by Mike Newell; for Tri-Star / Rastar. 'As amazingly bad as it is audacious.'—*Daily Variety*

The Amazing Mr Blunden**
GB 1972 99m Eastmancolor
Hemdale / Hemisphere (Barry Levinson)

In 1918, a widow and her two children meet a kindly gentleman who offers them work in his old mansion. Here they meet two ghost children, discover that he is a ghost too, and travel a hundred years back in time to right a wicked wrong.

Involved ghost story for intellectual children, made generally palatable by oodles of period charm and good acting.

wd Lionel Jeffries, story The Ghosts by Antonia Baker *ph* Gerry Fisher *m* Elmer Bernstein *pd* Wilfrid Shingleton

Laurence Naismith, Diana Dors, James Villiers, David Lodge, Lynne Frederick, Dorothy Alison, Rosalyn Lander, Marc Granger

'Easy period charm . . . fills every crevice.'—*Clyde Jeavons*

The Amazing Mr Williams*
US 1939 86m bw
Columbia (Everett Riskin)

About-to-be-marrieds investigate a murder.
Brisk comedy-thriller on *Thin Man* lines.

w Dwight Taylor, Sy Bartlett, Richard Maibaum *d* Alexander Hall *ph* Arthur Todd *md* Morris Stoloff

Melvyn Douglas, Joan Blondell, Ruth Donnelly, Clarence Kolb, Ed Brophy, Donald MacBride, Don Beddoe

The Amazing Mrs Holliday
US 1943 98m bw
Universal (Bruce Manning, Frank Shaw)

Torpedoed in mid-Pacific, a missionary's daughter arrives in San Francisco with eight Chinese orphans.
Unusual sentimental vehicle for its star; of no particular interest or merit in itself, but with the usual interludes for song.

w Frank Ryan, John Jacoby *d* Bruce Manning *ph* Elwood Bredell *m* Hans Salter, Frank Skinner *md* Charles Previn

Deanna Durbin, Edmond O'Brien, Frieda Inescort, Barry Fitzgerald, Arthur Treacher, Harry Davenport, Grant Mitchell

'Timely drama with human interest angles.'—*Variety*

AAN: Hans Salter, Frank Skinner

The Amazing Quest of Ernest Bliss
GB 1936 80m bw
Garrett–Klement (Robert Garrett, Otto Klement)
US title: *Romance and Riches*

A millionaire accepts a wager that he can live independently of his riches for one year.
Formulary comedy drama of its era on the theme that money isn't everything. Very dated.

w John L. Balderston from novel by E. Phillips Oppenheim *d* Alfred Zeisler *ph* Otto Heller

Cary Grant (on home leave after his first Hollywood success), Mary Brian, Henry Kendall, Leon M. Lion, Garry Marsh, Moore Marriott, Peter Gawthorne, Ralph Richardson

The Amazing Spiderman

The films released theatrically in the late seventies were 'stretchouts' of television episodes. See *Halliwell's Television Companion*.

The Ambassador
US 1984 95m TVC colour
Cannon / Northbrook (Isaac Kol)

An American ambassador to Israel gets in the line of fire with the Arabs; meanwhile his wife is having an affair with a man who is secretly a leader of the PLO.
Aged stars go gloomily through some tasteless paces in this politically unwise pseudo-thriller.

w Max Jack *novel* 52 Pick Up by Elmore Leonard *d* J. Lee Thompson *ph* Avi Karpik, Ofer Yanov, Rami Siman Tov *m* Dov Seltzer

Robert Mitchum, Ellen Burstyn, Rock Hudson, Fabio Testi, Donald Pleasence

'Not wild enough to be funny.'—*Sight and Sound*

† Not much more than a year later, the original novel was filmed under its own title in its original setting.

Ambassador Bill
US 1931 68m bw

An Oklahoma cattle man is appointed US ambassador to a foreign country ruled by a regency. Poorly tailored star vehicle. Will Rogers, Marguerite Churchill, Greta Nissen, Gustav Von Seyffertitz, Ray Milland. Written by Guy Bolton, from a story by Vincent Sheean; directed by Sam Taylor; for Fox. 'Wilting yarn, illogical hoke.'—*Variety*

The Ambassador's Daughter*
US 1956 102m Technicolor Cinemascope
UA / Norman Krasna

An American senator in Paris decides that the presence of US forces in Paris constitutes a moral danger. The ambassador's daughter decides to investigate.
Thin comedy of the old-fashioned type: smart lines and intimate playing not helped by the vast screen.

wd Norman Krasna *ph* Michael Kelber *m* Jacques Metehen

Olivia de Havilland, John Forsythe, Edward Arnold, Adolphe Menjou, Myrna Loy, Francis Lederer, Tommy Noonan, Minor Watson

'An experienced cast approach the story's frivolities with poise and style.'—*MFB*

Ambush*
US 1938 62m bw

A girl proves her brother innocent and brings gangsters to book. Brisk second feature with an unexpected writing credit. Gladys Swarthout, Lloyd Nolan, Ernest Truex. Written by S. J. and Laura Perelman; directed by Kurt Neumann; for Paramount. 'Hard hitting, fast moving and at all times plausible.'—*Variety*

Ambush*
US 1949 89m bw
MGM (Armand Deutsch)

An army scout leads a posse to capture an Indian chief who is holding a white woman hostage.
Good, clean, robust western, well produced and acted.

w Marguerite Roberts *d* Sam Wood *ph* Harold Lipstein *m* Rudolph Kopp

Robert Taylor, John Hodiak, Arlene Dahl, Don Taylor, Jean Hagen, Leon Ames

'One man against the west!'
Ambush at Tomahawk Gap
US 1953 73m Technicolor
Columbia (Wallace MacDonald)

Four ex-convicts seek hidden loot in a ghost town.
Standard co-feature western with rather more violence than usual for its date.

w David Lang *d* Fred F. Sears *ph* Henry Freulich *m* Ross Di Maggio

John Hodiak, John Derek, David Brian, Maria Elena Marques, Ray Teal, John Qualen

Ambush Bay
US 1966 109m De Luxe
UA / Aubrey Schenck

In 1944, nine Marines try to escape from a Japanese-held island.
Routine, lengthy, sub-standard heroics for action addicts.

w Marve Feinberg, Ib Melchior *d* Ron Winston *ph* Emanuel Rojas *m* Richard La Salle

Hugh O'Brian, Mickey Rooney, James Mitchum, Tisa Chang, Harry Lauter

The Ambushers
US 1967 102m Technicolor
Columbia / Meadway / Claude (Irving Allen)

An experimental flying disc disappears on a test run, and the trail leads Matt Helm to the Mexican jungle.
The third Matt Helm adventure had such a stupid script that all concerned decided to send it up, unfortunately with too obvious a tendency to smirk at their own bravado.

w Herbert Baker *d* Henry Levin *ph* Burnett Guffey, Edward Colman *m* Hugo Montenegro

Dean Martin, Senta Berger, Janice Rule, Kurt Kasznar, James Gregory, Albert Salmi

'Plot, jokes and gadgets all well below par.'—*MFB*

'Love of tender girlhood! Passionate deeds of heroes! A rushing, leaping drama of charm and excitement!'
America*
US 1924 122m (24 fps) bw silent
(UA) D. W. Griffith

Various characters experience the Revolutionary War.
The Birth of a Nation, one war back. Much of interest, but nothing new; Griffith was basically repeating himself.

w John Pell *d D. W. Griffith ph* Billy Bitzer, Hendrick Sartow, Marcel le Picard, Hal Sintzenich

Neil Hamilton, Carol Dempster, Lionel Barrymore, Erville Alderson

'Here is the romance of one hundred million people, told in heartthrobs!'—*D. W. Griffith*

† As the English were the villains, the film was banned in Britain, but later released under the title *Love and Sacrifice*.

America, America*
US 1963 177m bw
Warner (Elia Kazan)
GB title: *The Anatolian Smile*

In 1896 Turkey, a young Greek dreams of emigrating to America, and finally does so.
A massive piece of self-indulgence by a one-man band, fascinating for his family circle but so poorly constructed as to be of very limited interest elsewhere.

wd Elia Kazan *ph* Haskell Wexler *m* Manos Hadjidakis

Stathis Giallelis, Frank Wolff, Harry Davis, Elena Karam, Estelle Hemsley, Lou Antonio

'Kazan has failed to film the adventure implicit in his material, and a potentially exciting story has gone to waste.'—*MFB*

'If he sinks his teeth in a scene or a sequence that he enjoys, the audience can just sit around and be damned.'—*Stanley Kauffmann*

'Every episode, almost every shot, has its own beginning, middle and end, and the numberless playlets are cemented together into a strip which after the first two hours threatens to stretch grimly into eternity.'—*Robert Hatch, The Nation*

AAN: best picture; Elia Kazan (as writer); Elia Kazan (as director)

An American Dream
US 1966 103m Technicolor
Warner (William Conrad)
GB title: *See You in Hell, Darling*

A TV commentator is goaded into murdering his wife, becomes involved with gangsters and, tortured by guilt, allows them to kill him for shielding the girl friend of one of them.
Ludicrously heavy-handed version of a semi-surrealist book which presumably had something to say about modern America, at least in its author's mind. Nothing comes through but relentless boredom at watching sordid and unlikely events, and sympathy for those involved.

w Mann Rubin, *novel* Norman Mailer *d* Robert Gist *ph* Sam Leavitt *m* Johnny Mandel

Stuart Whitman, Janet Leigh, Eleanor Parker (in a one-scene role of screaming bitchery that has to be seen to be believed), J. D. Cannon, Lloyd Nolan, Barry Sullivan, Murray Hamilton

AAN: song, 'A Time for Love' (*m* Johnny Mandel, *ly* Paul Francis Webster)

American Dreamer
US 1984 105m Technicolor
CBS / Krest / Chaplin (Doug Chapin)

An Ohio housewife writes a novel, wins a trip to Paris, and finds her romantic dreams coming true.
A kind of lower-case reprise of *Romancing the Stone*, this modest comedy works only in fits and starts.

w Jim Kouf, David Greenwalt *story* Ann Biderman *d* Rick Rosenthal *ph* Giuseppe Rotunno *m* Lewis Furey *pd* Brian Eatwell *ed* Anne Goursand

JoBeth Williams, Tom Conti, Giancarlo Giannini, Coral Browne, James Staley

'A pleasant throwback to earlier forms of Hollywood farce.'—*Variety*

'The nation-blazing epic of America's westward march!'

American Empire
US 1942 82m bw

Brothers fall out over management of their Texas ranch. Reasonable but forgettable semi-western. Richard Dix, Preston Foster, Frances Gifford, Leo Carrillo. Written by Ben Grauman Kohn, Gladys Atwater, Robert Bren; directed by William McGann; for Harry Sherman / UA. (GB title: *My Son Alone*.)

American Flyers
US 1985 114m / Panavision Technicolor
Warner / Gareth Wigan, Paula Weinstein

Two brothers compete in a gruelling bicycle race.
Ambitious but ineffective drama with too much effort to explore personal dramas instead of getting on with the action.

w Steve Tesich *d* John Badham *ph* Don Peterman *m* Lee Ritenour, Greg Mathieson *pd* Laurence G. Paull *ed* Frank Morriss

Kevin Costner, David Grant, Rae Dawn Chong, Alexandra Paull, Janice Rule

'Overblown production just pumps hot air in too many directions and comes up limp.'—*Variety*

The American Friend*
West Germany 1977 127m colour

A Hamburg picture-framer thinks he is dying and is persuaded to become a Mafia hitman. Strange melodrama which got the ear of the cognoscenti. Dennis Hopper, Bruno Ganz, Lisa Kreuzer, Gerard Blain, Nicholas Ray, Samuel Fuller. Written and directed by *Wim Wenders* from the novel The Amazing Mr Ripley by Patricia Highsmith; for Road Movies/Filmverlag der Autoren.

'He's the highest paid lover in Beverly Hills!'

American Gigolo
US 1980 117m Metrocolor
Paramount / Pierre Associates (Freddie Fields)

A male prostitute finds that a client won't clear him when he is falsely charged with murder.
Thoroughly unattractive wallow on the seamy side of Los Angeles, with none of *Midnight Cowboy*'s compassion.

wd Paul Schraeder *ph* John Bailey *m* Giorgio Moroder

Richard Gere, Lauren Hutton, Hector Elizondo, Nina Van Pallandt

'A hot subject, cool style and overly contrived plotting don't all mesh.'—*Variety*

'A perverse film devoted to perversity, typical of Schrader's apparently sadistic intent to pillory his audience with every kind of degenerate act he can manufacture.'—*Motion Picture Guide*

† Christopher Reeve allegedly refused one million dollars to play the lead.

American Gothic
US 1988 89m colour

Survivors of a plane crash are terrorized by a psychotic family. Routine grotesquerie. Rod Steiger, Yvonne De Carlo, Sarah Torgov, Mark Ericksen. Written and directed by John Hough; for Pinetalk (John Quested).

'Where were you in '62?'

American Graffiti**
US 1973 110m Techniscope
Universal / Lucasfilm / Coppola Company (Francis Ford Coppola, Gary Kurtz)

In 1962 California, four young men about to leave for college gather for a night's girl-chasing and police-baiting.
Nostalgic comedy recalling many sights and sounds of the previous generation and carefully crystallizing a particular time and place. Successful in itself, it led to many imitations.

wd George Lucas *ph* Ron Eveslage, Jan D'Alquen *m* popular songs

Richard Dreyfuss, Ronny Howard, Paul le Mat, Charlie Martin Smith, Cindy Williams, Candy Clark, Mackenzie Philips

† The film cost 750,000 dollars, and grossed 55 million.

AAN: best picture; George Lucas (as writer); George Lucas (as director); Candy Clark

An American Guerrilla in the Philippines*
US 1950 105m Technicolor
TCF (Lamar Trotti)
GB title: *I Shall Return*

World War II, Pacific Zone: two American sailors try to make their way to Australia after MacArthur's surrender at Bataan.
Rather dull adventure story shot in the actual locations.

w Lamar Trotti, *novel* Ira Wolfert *d* Fritz Lang *ph* Harry Jackson *m* Cyril Mockridge

Tyrone Power, Micheline Presle, Tom Ewell, Bob Pattern, Tommy Cook, Robert Barrat (as MacArthur), Jack Elam

'Cannot be regarded as a serious war film.'—*Penelope Houston*

American Hot Wax
US 1978 91m Metrocolor
Paramount (Art Linson)

The early days of rock and roll as seen by a prominent disc jockey of the time.
Mildly entertaining ragbag of semi-historical facts and authentic music, strictly for the youth market.

w John Kaye *d* Floyd Mutrux *ph* William A. Fraker *md* Kenny Vance

Tim McIntire (as Alan Freed), Fran Drescher, Jay Lena, Laraine Newman, Chuck Berry, Jerry Lee Lewis, Screamin' Jay Hawkins

An American in Paris****
US 1951 113m Technicolor
MGM (*Arthur Freed*)

A carefree young artist scorns a rich woman's patronage and wins the love of a gamine.
Altogether delightful musical holiday, one of the highspots of the Hollywood genre, with infectious enthusiasm and an unexpected sense of the Paris that was.

w Alan Jay Lerner d Vincente Minnelli ph Al Gilks, John Alton m George Gershwin ly Ira Gershwin ch Gene Kelly ad Cedric Gibbons, Preston Ames

Gene Kelly, Oscar Levant, Nina Foch, Leslie Caron, Georges Guetary

Songs include 'I Got Rhythm'; 'Embraceable You'; 'By Strauss'; 'Swonderful'; 'Tra La La'; 'Our Love Is Here to Stay'; 'Stairway to Paradise'; 'Concerto in F' (instrumental); 'An American in Paris' (ballet)

'Too fancy and overblown, but the principal performers are in fine form and the Gershwin music keeps everything good-spirited.'—*New Yorker, 1977*

† Chevalier was originally paged for the Georges Guetary role, but turned it down because he lost the girl. The production cost $2,723,903, of which $542,000 went on the final ballet.

AA: best picture; Alan Jay Lerner; Al Gilks, John Alton; musical arrangements (Saul Chaplin, Johnny Green)
AAN: Vincente Minnelli

American Madness**
US 1932 80m bw
Columbia

When a bank failure threatens, hundreds of small savers increase their deposits to save the situation.
Vivid, overstressed topical melodrama with crowd scenes typical of its director's later output.

w Robert Riskin *d Frank Capra ph* Joseph Walker

Walter Huston, Pat O'Brien, Kay Johnson, Constance Cummings, Gavin Gordon, Berton Churchill

'It's a money picture. That goes both ways. It's about money and banks and spells dough for the box office. It's timely, topical, human, dramatic, punchy and good entertainment at one and the same time.'—*Variety*

'The sequence of the mounting panic and the storming of the bank are effectively staged, but the resolution is the usual Capra / Riskin populist hokum.'—*New Yorker, 1977*

An American Romance*
US 1944 151m Technicolor
MGM (King Vidor)

The life of a European immigrant who becomes a master of industry.
Mind-boggling pageant of the American dream, coldly presented and totally humourless. Its saving grace is its smooth physical presentation.

w Herbert Dalmas, William Ludwig *d* King Vidor *ph* Harold Rosson *m* Louis Gruenberg

Brian Donlevy, Ann Richards, John Qualen, Walter Abel, Stephen McNally

'A thousand chances to inform, excite or even interest have been flung away.'—*Richard Winnington*

'The whole aim of it is to boost The American Way.'—*Richard Mallett, Punch*

The American Success Company*
US 1980 94m colour

The inexperienced son of a credit card tycoon becomes a tough guy. Tilts at the American myth: not a notable success. Jeff Bridges, Belinda Bauer, Ned Beatty, Steven Keats, Bianca Jagger. Written by William Richert and Larry Cohen; directed by William Richert; produced by Edgar J. Scherick and Daniel H. Blatt for Columbia.

An American Tail*
US 1986 80m De Luxe
Universal / Steven Spielberg (Don Bluth, John Pomeroy, Gary Goldman)

Russian mice encounter all kinds of trouble when in the 1880s they emigrate to the United States.
Expensive cartoon feature with old-fashioned full animation but not much in the way of narrative interest or indeed humour.

w Judy Freudberg, Tony Geiss *d* Don Bluth (also designer)
voices: Cathianne Blore, Christopher Plummer, Dom DeLuise, Madeline Kahn

'Every character and every situation have been presented a thousand times before . . . anyone over the age of 12 will likely experience more boredom than pleasure.'—*Variety*

AAN: song, 'Somewhere Out There' by James Horner, Barry Mann, Cynthia Weil

'Drama that happens around you every day—when the wild life of impetuous youth burns away age-old barriers!'

An American Tragedy**
US 1931 95m bw
Paramount

An ambitious young man murders his pregnant fiancée when he has a chance to marry a rich girl.
Dated but solidly satisfying adaptation of a weighty novel, more compelling than the 1951 remake *A Place in the Sun.*

wd Josef Von Sternberg, novel Theodore Dreiser *ph* Lee Garmes *ad* Hans Dreier

Phillips Holmes, *Sylvia Sidney*, Frances Dee, Irving Pichel, Frederick Burton, Claire McDowell

'It unreels as an ordinary programme effort with an unhappy ending . . . as Sternberg has seen fit to present it the celluloid structure is slow, heavy and not always interesting drama. Its box office success is very doubtful.'—*Variety*

'It is the first time, I believe, that the subjects of sex, birth control and murder have been put into a picture with sense, taste and reality.'—*Pare Lorentz*

'An aimless, lugubrious mess. The fireworks may dazzle to schoolboys of criticism, but they will add no permanent color to the motion picture.'—*Harry Alan Potamkin*

An American Werewolf in London*
GB 1981 97m Technicolor
Polygram / Lycanthrope (Peter Guber, Jon Peters)

Two American tourists are bitten by a werewolf.
Curious but oddly endearing mixture of horror film and spoof, of comedy and shock, with everything grist to its mill including tourist Britain and the wedding of Prince Charles. The special effects are notable, and signalled new developments in this field.

wd John Landis ph Robert Paynter *m* Elmer Bernstein *sp Effects Associates, Rick Baker*

David Naughton, Jenny Agutter, Griffin Dunne, John Woodvine

'The gear changes of tone and pace make for a very jerkily driven vehicle.'—*Sunday Times*

'Seems curiously unfinished, as though Landis spent all his energy on spectacular set-pieces and then didn't want to bother with things like transitions, character development, or an ending.'—*Roger Ebert*

The Americanization of Emily*
US 1964 115m bw
MGM / Filmways (John Calley)

World War II: just before the Normandy landings, a war widow driver falls for an American commander who is a self-confessed coward.
Bizarre comedy full of eccentric characters, an uneasy choice for its female star but otherwise successful in patches in its random distillation of black comedy, sex and the tumbling of old-fashioned virtues.

w Paddy Chayevsky, *novel* William Bradford Huie *d* Arthur Hiller *ph Philip Lathrop, Chris Challis m* Johnny Mandel

Julie Andrews, James Garner, *Melvyn Douglas*, James Coburn, Liz Fraser, Joyce Grenfell, Edward Binns, Keenan Wynn, William Windom

'Out of it all there comes the definite feeling that Hitler's war is incidental to Paddy Chayevsky's war of ideas . . . no plot synopsis could begin to suggest how much the characters talk.'—*MFB*

AAN: Philip Lathrop

The Americano
US 1916 60m approx (24 fps) bw silent
Triangle (D. W. Griffith)

A young American engineer becomes involved in a revolution in Patagonia.
Early star adventure vehicle, an immense popular success; the last film Fairbanks made for Griffith.

w Anita Loos, John Emerson, *novel* Blaze Derringer by Eugene P. Lyle Jnr *d* John Emerson *ph* Victor Fleming

Douglas Fairbanks, Alma Rubens, Spottiswoode Aitken, Lillian Langdon

The Americano
US 1955 85m Technicolor
(RKO) Robert Stillman

A westerner takes three prize bulls to Brazil, but finds the buyer has been murdered.
A western with a twist, but otherwise extremely dull, with poor pace, colour and use of settings.

w Guy Trosper *d* William Castle *ph* William Snyder *m* Roy Webb

Glenn Ford, Frank Lovejoy, Abbe Lane, Cesar Romero, Ursula Thiess

Un Ami Viendra ce Soir
France 1946 111m bw
CGC (R. Artus)

During World War II a French patriot uses a lunatic asylum as a resistance headquarters.
Rather glum wartime melodrama, lacking in tension.

w Jacques Companeez, Raymond Bernard *d* Raymond Bernard *ph* Robert Le Fèbvre *m* Arthur Honegger

Michel Simon, Louis Salou, Saturnin Fabre, Paul Bernard, Madeleine Sologne, Marcel André

Le Amiche*
Italy 1955 90m bw
Trionfalcine (Giovanni Addessi)
aka: *The Girl Friends*

The interaction of five girls living together in Turin.
Highbrow lending library stuff, quite watchable but equally forgettable.

w Suso Cecchi d'Amico, Alba de Cespedes, *story* Tra Donne Sole by Cesare Pavese *d* Michelangelo Antonioni *ph* Gianni di Venanzo *m* Giovanni Fusco

Eleanora Rossi Drago, Valentina Cortese, Yvonne Furneaux, Gabriele Ferzetti, Franco Fabrizi, Madeleine Fischer

The Amityville Horror
US 1979 118m Movielab
AIP / Cinema 77 (Ronald Saland, Elliot Geisinger)

Newlyweds move into a house where a murder was committed, and experience strange manifestations which drive them away.
Sub-*Exorcist* goings on, a shameless exaggeration of some of the alleged facts retailed in the best-selling book. A shocker for the uncritical.

w Sandor Stern, *book* Jay Anson *d* Stuart Rosenberg *ph* Fred J. Koenekamp *m* Lalo Schifrin

James Brolin, Margot Kidder, Rod Steiger, Don Stroud, Murray Hamilton

Amityville II: The Possession
US 1982 104m De Luxe

The haunted house at Amityville gives the jitters to a second family. Everything but the kitchen sink is thrown into this ghoulish brew, and most of it is red; but the script is hopeless from the start. Burt Young, Rutanya Alda, James Olson, Jack Magner, Andrew Prine. Written by Tommy Lee Wallace; directed by Damiano Damiani; for Dino de Laurentiis / Orion. 'There probably isn't a more unsympathetic bunch on screen this year. They're sure to make audiences root for the house.'—*Variety*.

Amityville 3-D
US 1984 93m colour Arrivision

A sceptical journalist moves into the haunted house but is jolted out of his complacency. Ragbag of supernatural incident with neither cohesion nor plausibility, but good 3-D. Tony Roberts, Tess Harper, Robert Joy, Candy Clark, John Beal, Leora Dana. Written by William Wales; directed by Richard Fleischer; for Dino de Laurentiis / Orion. 'An assortment of unrelated happenings precedes the final appearance of a crude bug-eyed monster.'—*MFB*

Among the Living*
US 1941 68m bw
Paramount (Sol C. Siegel)

In a small town live twin brothers, one of whom is a murderer.
Offbeat suspenser with effective performances.

w Lester Cole, Garrett Fort *d* Stuart Heisler *ph* Theodor Sparkuhl

Albert Dekker, Susan Hayward, Frances Farmer, Harry Carey, Gordon Jones

'Head and shoulders above all the filler shows ground out by Hollywood to perpetuate the double feature system.'—*Howard Barnes, New York Herald Tribune*

L'Amore*
Italy 1948 79m bw
Tevere Film (Roberto Rossellini)

Two short films. *The Human Voice*: a woman talks on the phone to the man who has forsaken her. *The Miracle*: a peasant woman is seduced and is convinced she will give birth to a new Messiah.
A *tour de force* by an actress to be reckoned with; but hardly compulsive as cinema.

play Jean Cocteau *original script* Tullio Pinelli, Roberto Rossellini, Federico Fellini *d* Roberto Rossellini *ph* Robert Juillard, Aldo Tonti *m* Renzo Rossellini

Anna Magnani, Federico Fellini

† *The Miracle* was separately released in some countries.

'The rollicking story of a ribald century that should have been ashamed of itself!'

The Amorous Adventures of Moll Flanders
GB 1965 125m Technicolor Panavision
Paramount / Winchester (Marcel Hellman)

An ambitious servant girl loses her virtue to a succession of rich gentlemen but finally settles for a highwayman.
The aim was to make a female *Tom Jones*, but this bawdy romp never achieves the freewheeling fluency of that surprise success, and a vacuous central performance makes the constant couplings more boring than exciting.

w Dennis Cannan, Roland Kibbee, *novel* Daniel Defoe *d* Terence Young *ph* Ted Moore *m* John Addison *pd* Syd Cain

Kim Novak, Richard Johnson, George Sanders, Lilli Palmer, Angela Lansbury, Leo McKern, Vittorio de Sica, Cecil Parker, Daniel Massey

'Further from Defoe than *Tom Jones* was from Fielding, but with much the same combination of crude table manners and clean sets to stand in for period flavour.'—*MFB*

The Amorous Prawn*
GB 1962 89m bw
BL / Covent Garden (Leslie Gilliat)
US title: *The Playgirl and the War Minister* (an attempt to cash in on the Profumo case)

A hard-up general's wife invites American paying guests to their official highland home.
This film version of a stage success seems very mild, but the cast is eager to please: the result is a frantic high class farce.

w Anthony Kimmins, Nicholas Phipps, *play* Anthony Kimmins *d* Anthony Kimmins *ph* Wilkie Cooper *m* John Barry

Joan Greenwood, Ian Carmichael, Cecil Parker, Dennis Price, Robert Beatty, Finlay Currie, Liz Fraser, Derek Nimmo

L'Amour à Mort*
France 1984 90m colour
Dussart / Ariane / A2 (Philippe Dussart)

An archaeologist and his mistress come to the conclusion that their love will reach its fullest expression in death.
Chilly symbolic drama, a continuation of the same team's preoccupations with the meaning of life which were previously explored (via the same four actors) in *Mon Oncle d'Amérique* and *La Vie est un Roman*. Interesting but not especially rewarding.

w Jean Gruault d Alain Resnais ph Sacha Vierny *m* Hans Werner Henze

Sabine Azema, Fanny Ardant, Pierre Arditi, André Dussolier

Amsterdam Affair
GB 1968 91m Eastmancolor
LIP / Trio / Group W (Gerry Willoughby)

Inspector Van der Valk investigates when a writer is accused of murdering his mistress.
Tolerable *roman policier*.

w Edmund Ward, *novel* Love in Amsterdam by Nicholas Freeling *d* Gerry O'Hara *ph* Gerry Fisher *m* Patrick John Scott

Wolfgang Kieling, William Marlowe, Caterina Von Schell

The Amsterdam Kill
Hong Kong 1977 93m Technicolor Panavision
Golden Harvest / Fantastic Films / Raymond Chow

An American ex-Drug Enforcement Agency officer tries to protect an old friend caught in the Hong Kong drug wars.
Roughly made and uninventive thriller in which the Hong Kong film makers fail to consolidate the international ground they gained with kung fu films.

w Robert Clouse, Gregory Teifer *d* Robert Clouse *ph* Alan Hume *m* Hal Schaffer

Robert Mitchum, Bradford Dillman, Richard Egan, Leslie Nielsen, Keye Luke

Amy
US 1981 100m Technicolor

A spinster is taught a little about life and love. Unmemorable family comedy drama. Jenny Agutter, Barry Newman, Kathleen Nolan, Chris Robinson, Margaret O'Brien, Nanette Fabray. Written by Noreen Stone; directed by Vincent McEveety; for Walt Disney.

'The most amazing conspiracy the world has ever known, and love as it never happened to a man and woman before!'

Anastasia**
GB 1956 105m Eastmancolor Cinemascope
TCF (Buddy Adler)

In 1928 Paris, a group of exiled White Russians claim to have found the living daughter of the Tsar, presumed executed in 1918; but the claimant is a fake schooled by a general, with whom she falls in love.
Slick, highly theatrical entertainment for the upper classes; it dazzles and satisfies without throwing any light on history.

w Arthur Laurents, *play* Marcelle Maurette, Guy Bolton *d* Anatole Litvak *ph* Jack Hildyard *m* Alfred Newman *ad* Andrei Andreiev, Bill Andrews

Ingrid Bergman (her Hollywood comeback after some years in Europe under a cloud for her 'immoral' behaviour), Yul Brynner, *Helen Hayes,* Martita Hunt, Akim Tamiroff, Felix Aylmer, Ivan Desny

'Little weight but considerable and urbane charm.'—*John Cutts*

AA: Ingrid Bergman
AAN: Alfred Newman

Anatahan
Japan 1953 92m bw
Daiwa (K. Takimura)
aka: *The Saga of Anatahan*

During World War II, Japanese seamen are shipwrecked on the same deserted island as a man and a woman; the latter causes jealousy and murder.
Downright peculiar studio-set melodrama, based on true events and directed by its creator through interpreters, with results far from happy.

wd, ph Josef Von Sternberg *m* A. Ifukube

Akemi Negishi, T. Sugunuma, K. Onoe, T. Bandoh

'The main impression is of tedium relieved by moments of far from intentional humour.'—*Penelope Houston*

'Last year's number one best seller. This year's (we hope) number one motion picture!'

Anatomy of a Murder**
US 1959 161m bw
Columbia / Carlyle / Otto Preminger

A small-town lawyer successfully defends an army officer accused of murdering a bartender who had assaulted his wife.
Overlong and over-faithful version of a highly detailed courtroom bestseller. The plot is necessarily equivocal, the characterizations overblown, but the trial commands some interest, and the use of 'daring' words in evidence caused controversy at the time.

w Wendell Mayes, *novel* Robert Traver *d* Otto Preminger *ph* Sam Leavitt *m* Duke Ellington *pd* Boris Leven

James Stewart, Ben Gazzara, Lee Remick, *Eve Arden,* Arthur O'Connell, *George C. Scott* (his first notable role, as the prosecutor), Kathryn Grant, Orson Bean, Murray Hamilton

† The trial judge was played by Joseph N. Welch, a real-life judge who had gained fame in 1954 by representing the army against Senator McCarthy.

AAN: best picture; Wendell Mayes; Sam Leavitt; James Stewart; Arthur O'Connell; George C. Scott

Anchors Aweigh**
US 1945 139m Technicolor
MGM (Joe Pasternak)

Two sailors on leave in Los Angeles get involved with a small boy who wants to join the navy.
Rather droopy musical most notable as a forerunner of *On the Town*, though on much more conventional lines. Amiable performances, and a brilliant dance with a cartoon mouse, save the day.

w Isobel Lennart *d* George Sidney *ph* Robert Planck, Charles Boyle *principal songs* Jule Styne *ly* Sammy Cahn *m* George Stoll *pd* Cedric Gibbons

Frank Sinatra, Gene Kelly, Kathryn Grayson, Jose Iturbi, Sharon McManus, Carlos Ramirez, Dean Stockwell, Pamela Britton
Songs include 'We Hate to Leave'; 'What Makes the Sun Set?'; 'The Charm of You'; 'I Begged Her'; 'I Fall in Love Too Easily'; 'The Worry Song'

AA: George Stoll
AAN: best picture; Robert Planck; Gene Kelly; song 'I Fall in Love Too Easily' (*m* Jule Styne, *ly* Sammy Cahn)

And Baby Makes Three
US 1950 83m bw
Columbia (Robert Lord)

A wife divorces her compromised husband before discovering that she is pregnant.
Thin marital comedy with minor compensations.

w Lou Breslow, Joseph Hoffman *d* Henry Levin *ph* Burnett Guffey *m* George Duning

Robert Young, Barbara Hale, Billie Burke, Robert Hutton, Janis Carter, Nicholas Joy, Lloyd Corrigan

'It has everything but a story that hangs together.'—*New York Herald Tribune*

And God Created Woman
France 1956 92m Eastmancolor Cinemascope
Iena / UCIL / Cocinor (Raoul Lévy)
original title: *Et Dieu Créa la Femme;* aka: *And Woman . . . Was Created*

An 18-year-old finds herself fatally attracted towards men.
Rather a feeble excuse for its star to strip on the St Tropez beach.

w Roger Vadim, Raoul Lévy *d* Roger Vadim *ph* Armand Thirard *m* Paul Misraki

Brigitte Bardot, Curt Jurgens, Jean-Louis Trintignant, Christian Marquand, Georges Poujouly, Jane Marken, Paul Faivre

'An open violation of conventional morality.'—*Catholic Legion of Decency*

'I'm prepared to bet an overcoat to a bikini that this film will make its star Miss Sex of the Universe.'—*Sketch*

† Vadim made a second film with this title (US 1987) but a different plot, in which the stripping was done by Rebecca De Mornay.

And Hope To Die
US / Fr / Canada 1972 104m bw
Original title: *La Course du lièvre à travers les champs*

A fugitive Frenchman in Canada runs foul of criminals and gypsies and causes several deaths. Muddled melodrama of the worst 'international' kind. Jean-Louis Trintignant, Robert Ryan, Aldo Ray, Tisa Farrow, Lea Massari. Written by Sebastien Japrisot; directed by René Clément; for Serge Silberman / TCF.

And Justice For All
US 1979 119m Metrocolor
Columbia / Walton (Joe Wizan)

An American lawyer gets into all kinds of trouble, including the defence of a judge on a rape charge.
Not so much a satire as a series of random pot-shots at the legal system, sometimes funny but cumulatively stultifying.

w Valerie Curtin, Barry Levinson *d* Norman Jewison *ph* Frank Holgate *m* Dave Grusin

Al Pacino, Jack Warden, John Forsythe, Lee Strasberg, Christine Lahti, Sam Levene, Jeffrey Taybor

'Most incriminating is its own hysterical imprecision and sentimental pleading.'—*Sight and Sound*

And Now For Something Completely Different*
GB 1971 88m colour
(Columbia) Kettledrum / Python (Victor Lownes / GSF) (Patricia Casey)

Useful round-up of the more famous sketches from BBC TV's zany comedy series *Monty Python.*
Side-splitting for those who want Groucho Marx updated; baffling for reactionaries; movie presentation perfunctory.

Written by and starring *John Cleese, Graham Chapman, Terry Gilliam, Eric Idle, Michael Palin, Terry Jones* *d* Ian Macnaughton *ph* David Muir

And Now Miguel*
US 1965 95m Technicolor
Universal / Robert B. Radnitz

A 10-year-old Mexican boy proves himself worthy to work on the mountain with the sheep.
A children's film typical of its producer: good to look at, documentarily convincing, but too slight and too slow.

w Ted Sherdeman, Jane Clove, *novel* Joseph Krumgold *d* James B. Clark *ph* Clifford Stine *m* Phillip Lambro

Pat Cardi, Guy Stockwell, Clu Gulager, Michael Ansara, Joe de Santis

And Now The Screaming Starts
GB 1973 91m colour
Amicus (Max J. Rosenberg, Milton Subotsky)

A new bride in a country house is haunted by hallucinations of the past.
Grisly ghost story which overplays its hand and outstays its welcome.

w Roger Marshall, *novel* Fengriffen by David Case *d* Roy Ward Baker *ph* Denys Coop *m* Douglas Gamley

Peter Cushing, Stephanie Beacham, Herbert Lom, Patrick Magee, Ian Ogilvy, Geoffrey Whitehead, Guy Rolfe, Rosalie Crutchley

'Who are you that a man can't make love to you?'

And Now Tomorrow*
US 1944 86m bw
Paramount (Fred Kohlmar)

A rich girl goes deaf, loses her fiancé, but wins the poor doctor who cares for her.
Bestselling slush turned into a routine star romance.

w Frank Partos, Raymond Chandler (!), *novel* Rachel Field *d* Irving Pichel *ph* Daniel L. Fapp *m* Victor Young

Loretta Young, Alan Ladd (his first film in confirmed top-star status after a meteoric rise interrupted by war service), Susan Hayward, Beulah Bondi, Cecil Kellaway, Barry Sullivan.

'A vernal sign of the boys getting back to one of their favourite legends after the wintry days of war.'—*Richard Winnington*

And One Was Beautiful
US 1940 68m bw

A girl sets a trap for a playboy, who falls for her sister. Cinderella-style second feature, quite unremarkable. Robert Cummings, Laraine Day, Jean Muir, Billie Burke, Esther Dale. Written by Harry Clork from story by Alice Duer Miller; directed by Robert Sinclair; for Frederick Stephani / MGM.

And So They Were Married
US 1935 74m bw
Columbia (B. P. Schulberg)

A widow and a widower try to get married despite the ill-feeling of their children.
Predictable romantic farce.

w Doris Anderson, Joseph Anthony *d* Elliott Nugent *ph* Henry Freulich *m* Howard Jackson

Melvyn Douglas, Mary Astor, Edith Fellows, Jackie Moran, Donald Meek, Dorothy Stickney

And Soon the Darkness*
GB 1970 99m Technicolor
Associated British (Albert Fennell, Brian Clemens)

Of two young nurses on a cycling holiday in France, one is murdered by a local sex maniac and the other almost shares her fate.
Slow, overstretched, often risible suspenser on vanishing lady lines; long on red herrings and short on humour, but with some pretension to style. The action all takes place along a mile or two of sunlit country road.

w Brian Clemens, Terry Nation *d* Robert Fuest *ph* Ian Wilson *m* Laurie Johnson

Pamela Franklin, Michele Dotrice, Sandor Eles, John Nettleton

And Sudden Death
US 1936 60m bw

A young man denies a hit and run charge but confesses on his death bed. Preachy melodrama with little entertainment value. Randolph Scott (as the cop in the case), Tom Brown, Frances Drake, Billy Lee, Fuzzy Knight, Porter Hall. Written by Joseph Moncure March, directed by Charles Barton; for Paramount.

'There's nothing but trouble in Paradise when the bandleader tries to make love to a whole sister act—simultaneously!'

And the Angels Sing*
US 1943 95m bw
Paramount (E. D. Leshin)

Four singing sisters have hectic adventures with a bandleader.
Mildly disarming romantic comedy with music, more firmly set in a recognizable social milieu than the usual fan product from this studio.

w Melvin Frank, Norman Panama, Claude Binyon *d* George Marshall *ph* Karl Struss *m* Victor Young *songs* Johnny Burke, Jimmy Van Heusen

Dorothy Lamour, Diana Lynn, Betty Hutton, Mimi Chandler, Fred MacMurray, Raymond Walburn, Eddie Foy Jnr, Frank Albertson, Mikhail Rasumny

'Slapstick sophistication in a sub-Sturges manner.'—*MFB*

'Cruel, soggily professional, over-elaborate, and inclined towards snobbish whimsy.'—*James Agee*

And the Same To You
GB 1960 70m bw

A clergyman's nephew decides to become a boxer. Uninventive and unfunny comedy. Brian Rix, Leo Franklyn, William Hartnell, Vera Day, Tommy Cooper, Dick Bentley, Sid James. Written by John Paddy Carstairs and John Junkin from a play by A. P. Dearsley; directed by George Pollock; for Monarch.

And the Ship Sails On*
Italy / France 1983 132m Technicolor
RAI / Vides / Gaumont (Franco Cristaldi)
original title: *E la Nave Va*

From Naples in 1914 a luxurious liner sets forth to scatter the ashes of an opera singer. Less a Ship of Fools than a theatre of the absurd, with familiar Fellini caricatures going through their paces against studio sets. Fascination alternates with boredom.

w Federico Fellini, Tonino Guerra *d* Federico Fellini *ph* Giuseppe Rotunno *m* Gianfranco Plenizio *ad* Dante Ferretti

Freddie Jones, Barbara Jefford, Victor Poletti, Peter Cellier, Elisa Mainardi, Norma West

And Then There Were None****
US 1945 97m bw
Popular Pictures / Harry M. Popkin (René Clair)
GB title: *Ten Little Niggers*

Ten people are invited to a house party on a lonely island, and murdered one by one.
A classic mystery novel is here adapted and directed with the utmost care to provide playful black comedy, stylish puzzlement, and some splendid acting cameos.

w Dudley Nichols, novel Agatha Christie (aka Ten Little Niggers) *d René Clair ph Lucien Andriot m Mario Castelnuovo-Tedesco*

Walter Huston, Barry Fitzgerald, Louis Hayward, June Duprez, *Roland Young, Richard Haydn,* C. Aubrey Smith, Judith Anderson, Queenie Leonard, Mischa Auer

MISS BRENT: 'Very stupid to kill the only servant in the house. Now we don't even know where to find the marmalade.'

JUDGE QUINCANNON: 'Mr Owen could only come to the island in one way. It's perfectly clear. Mr Owen is one of us.'

ROGERS: 'Never in my life have I been accused of any crime, sir—and if that's what you think of me, I shan't serve any dinner.'

'Rich in the elements which have made mystery melodramas popular, yet not in the precise form of any previously made.'—*Hollywood Reporter*

'The efforts at sprightly, stylish comedy don't gain much momentum.'—*Pauline Kael, New Yorker, 70s*

And Then There Were None
GB 1974 98m Technicolor
EMI / Filibuster (Harry Alan Towers)
US title: *Ten Little Indians*

Ten people are lured to an isolated Persian hotel and murdered one by one.
Listless remake, often so inept you could scream.

w Peter Welbeck (Harry Alan Towers) *d* Peter Collinson *ph* Fernando Arribas *m* Bruno Nicolai

Oliver Reed, Richard Attenborough, Elke Sommer, Herbert Lom, Gert Froebe, Stéphane Audran, Charles Aznavour, Adolfo Celi, Alberto de Mendoza, Maria Rohm

The Anderson Tapes*
US 1971 98m Technicolor Panavision
Columbia / Robert M. Weitman

An ex-con forms a gang to rob a building, not knowing that police and others, for various purposes, are making tape recordings of his conversations.
Superficially slick and fashionable crime thriller, marred by unnecessarily flashy direction, a failure to explain enough about the tapes, and a climax which oddly mixes bloodshed and farce.

w Frank R. Pierson, *novel* Lawrence Sanders *d* Sidney Lumet *ph* Arthur J. Ornitz *m* Quincy Jones

Sean Connery, *Martin Balsam*, Dyan Cannon, Alan King, Ralph Meeker

Andrei Rublev**
USSR 1966 181m colour (part) Cinemascope
Mosfilm

Imaginary episodes from the life of a 15th-century icon painter.
A superb recreation of medieval life dramatizes the eternal problem of the artist, whether to take part in the life around him or merely comment on it.

w Andrei Mikhalkov-Konchalovsky, Andrei Tarkovsky *d Andrei Tarkovsky ph Vadim Yusov m* Vyacheslav Tcherniaiev

'The one indisputable Russian masterpiece of the last decade.'—*Nigel Andrews, MFB, 1973*

'With the exception of the great Eisenstein, I can't think of any film which has conveyed a feeling of the remote past with such utter conviction . . . a durable and unmistakable masterpiece.'—*Michael Billington, Illustrated London News*

Androcles and the Lion**
US 1952 96m bw
RKO (Gabriel Pascal)

A slave takes a thorn from the paw of a lion which later, in the arena, refuses to eat him.
Shavian drollery, with interpolated discussions on faith, is scarcely ideal cinema material, but gusto in the performances keeps it going despite stolid direction.

w Chester Erskine, *play* Bernard Shaw *d* Chester Erskine *ph* Harry Stradling *m* Frederick Hollander *ad* Harry Horner

Alan Young, Jean Simmons, Robert Newton, Victor Mature, Maurice Evans (as Caesar), Reginald Gardiner, Elsa Lanchester, Alan Mowbray, Gene Lockhart

† Production had previously begun with Harpo Marx as Androcles and Rex Harrison as Caesar.

Android*
US 1982 80m De Luxe
New World / Android (Mary Ann Fisher)

In 2036, a police transport vehicle is hijacked in space, and the scientists on board, some of them androids, react in unexpected ways.
Cheaply made, but a bobby dazzler for science fiction addicts.

w James Reigle, Don Opper *d Aaron Lipstadt ph* Tim Suhrstedt *m* Don Preston

Klaus Kinski, Brie Howard, Norbert Weisser, Crofton Hardester, Kendra Kirchner, Don Opper

'The best first feature since *Dark Star*.'—*Tom Milne, MFB*

The Andromeda Strain**
US 1970 131m Technicolor Panavision
Universal / Robert Wise

Scientists work frantically to neutralize an infected village, knowing that the least infection will cause their laboratory to self-destruct.
Solemn and over-detailed but generally suspenseful thriller, with a sense of allegory about man's inhumanity to man.

w Nelson Gidding, *novel* Michael Crichton *d* Robert Wise *ph* Richard H. Kline *m* Gil Melle *ad* Boris Leven

Arthur Hill, David Wayne, James Olson, Kate Reid, Paula Kelly

Andy Hardy Comes Home*
US 1958 81m bw
MGM (Red Doff)

Fortyish Andy returns to Carvel, his home town, to negotiate a land deal.
Rather dismal sequel to the celebrated series of Hardy family comedies which were enormously popular in the early forties: a thirteen-year gap is too long, and although most of the family is reunited the old Judge is sadly missed.

w Edward Everett Hutshing, Robert Morris Donley *d* Howard W. Koch *ph* William W. Spencer, Harold E. Wellman *m* Van Alexander

Mickey Rooney, Fay Holden, Cecilia Parker, Patricia Breslin, Sara Haden, Jerry Colonna

† See also under *Hardy Family*.

'I want love—and I'm going to get it!'

Angel*
US 1937 98m bw
Paramount (Ernst Lubitsch)

The wife of an English diplomat finds herself neglected and almost has an affair with his old friend.
A curious romantic comedy in many ways typical of its time, yet with very few laughs, showing none of its director's usual cinematic sense, and compromised by the censor's refusal to let a spade be called a spade. Underplaying, and a sense that we watch a way of life about to be swept away, just about save it.

w Samson Raphaelson, *play* Melchior Lengyel *d* Ernst Lubitsch *ph* Charles Lang *m* Frederick Hollander

Marlene Dietrich, Herbert Marshall, Melvyn Douglas, Edward Everett Horton, Laura Hope Crews, Ernest Cossart

MARIA: 'What's the matter, darling? Is it France?'
SIR FREDERICK: 'No, no. Jugoslavia.'
MARIA: 'Oh. I see.'

'A rich Hollywood dish that copies foreign recipes. It's a good picture and in the keys, especially for the carriage trade, it can't miss.'—*Variety*

'Very sophisticated, very subtle, very chic, vastly polished and entertaining.'—*Literary Digest*

'The production is performed with studied deliberation.'—*New York Times*

'This movie isn't essentially different from the best of Lubitsch, but it's attenuated. It's the sort of cultivated triangular love affair in which each of the three has a turn at the piano.'—*Pauline Kael, 70s*

Angel*
Eire 1982 92m Technicolor
Motion Picture Company of Ireland / Irish Film Board / Channel 4 (John Boorman)

Against a background of the Irish troubles, a saxophonist is drawn into a maze of violence when he attempts to avenge the murder of a mute girl.
Glumly Irish thriller with metaphysical overtones as well as references to the state of Ireland. Keen narrative style is dissipated by overkill.

wd Neil Jordan *ph* Chris Menges *m* Verdi

Stephen Rea, Veronica Quilligan, Alan Devlin, Peter Caffrey

'Honor student by day—hooker by night!'
'You're young, attractive and healthy—and swimming in a toilet bowl!'

Angel
US 1983 93m CFI colour
New World / Adam's Apple / Angel (Sandy Howard)

A 15-year-old student doubles as a Hollywood hooker and takes on a psychopathic killer.
Yucky melodrama with no holds barred, not even moments of humour.

w Robert Vincent O'Neil, Joseph M. Cala *d* Robert Vincent O'Neil *ph* Andrew Davis *m* Craig Safan

Cliff Gorman, Donna Wilkes, Rory Calhoun, Susan Tyrrell, Dick Shawn, John Diehl, Elaine Giftos

'A tasteless blend of realism and farce.'—*Sunday Times*

† A sequel appeared in 1985 under the title *Avenging Angel*. Betsy Russell was the girl, now hunting down her mentor.

Angel and the Badman*
US 1947 100m bw
Republic (John Wayne)

The love of a Quaker girl converts a wounded gunslinger to an honourable life.
Thoughtful western with good background detail and a fair measure of action.

wd James Edward Grant *ph* Archie Stout *m* Richard Hageman *pd* Ernest Fegte

John Wayne, Gail Russell, Harry Carey, Bruce Cabot, Irene Rich, Tom Powers

'Unpretentious, sweet-tempered and quite likeable.'—*James Agee*

Angel, Angel, Down We Go
US 1969 93m colour
Decadence in Hollywood: rock and rollers invade the lives of a rich family. Unpleasant blather with a star well past her prime. Jennifer Jones, Jordan Christopher, Roddy McDowall, Lou Rawls, Holly Near, Charles Aidman. Written and directed by Robert Thom, for Jerome F. Katzman/AIP.

Angel Baby*
US 1960 97m bw
Madera (Thomas F. Woods)
A mute girl is cured by an evangelist, and renounces her sins.
Strident, vigorous low-budget melodrama.
w Oris Borstem, Samuel Roeca, Paul Mason, *novel* Jenny Angel by Elsie Oaks Barbour *d Paul Wendkos* *ph* Haskell Wexler, Jack Marta *m* Wayne Shanklin
Salome Jens, George Hamilton, Joan Blondell, Mercedes McCambridge, Henry Jones, Burt Reynolds

Angel Face*
US 1952 91m bw
RKO (Otto Preminger)
A demented girl murders her father and stepmother, involving her chauffeur, whom she finally kills, and commits suicide.
Outrageous melodrama, so absurd as to be almost endearing.
w Frank Nugent, Oscar Millard *d* Otto Preminger *ph* Harry Stradling *m* Dmitri Tiomkin
Jean Simmons, Robert Mitchum, Herbert Marshall, Barbara O'Neil, Leon Ames, Mona Freeman, Kenneth Tobey, Raymond Greenleaf
'The one lyrical nightmare in the cinema.'—*Ian Cameron*

An Angel from Texas*
US 1940 69m bw
Warner (Robert Fellows)
Misadventures of a country boy in New York.
Modest revamping of a much filmed farce, also made as *The Tenderfoot* (1928) and *Dance Charlie Dance* (1937).
w Fred Niblo Jnr, Bertram Millhauser, *play* The Butter and Egg Man by George F. Kaufman *d* Ray Enright *ph* Arthur L. Todd *m* Howard Jackson
Eddie Albert, Rosemary Lane, Wayne Morris, Ronald Reagan, Milburn Stone

Angel Heart*
US 1987 113m Technicolor
Tri-Star/Kassar-Vajna/Carolco/Winkast-Union (Alan Marshall, Elliott Kastner)
In 1955, a New York private eye descends into Hell.
He does, literally, in pursuit of a missing person who's opted out of a pact with the devil.
Thoroughly unpleasant in detail, this wallow in the private eye cult constantly takes the eye with its pictorial qualities, even at its most nauseating.
w,d Alan Parker from the novel Falling Angel by William Hjortsberg *ph* Michael Seresin *m* Trevor Jones *pd* Brian Morris
Mickey Rourke, Robert De Niro, Lisa Bonet, Charlotte Rampling, Stocker Fontelieu, Brownie McGhee
'Faustian theme, heavy bloodletting and pervasive grimness may represent barriers too great for general audiences to surmount.'—*Daily Variety*

Angel in Exile
US 1948 90m bw
Republic
An ex-con heads for an abandoned Arizona mine to recover stolen gold.
Modest, effective western about a baddie who reforms.
w Charles Larson *d* Allan Dwan, Philip Ford *ph* Reggie Lanning *m* Nathan Scott
John Carroll, Adele Mara, Thomas Gomez

Angel in My Pocket
US 1969 105m Technicolor
Universal (Ed Montagne)
A minister and his family arrive in a small town.
Simplistic comedy–drama with nothing to distinguish it from a dozen others in similar vein.
w Jim Fritzell, Everett Greenbaum *d* Alan Rafkin
Andy Griffith, Jerry Van Dyke, Kay Medford, Edgar Buchanan, Margaret Hamilton, Gary Collins, Lee Meriwether, Henry Jones

The Angel Levine*
US 1970 105m De Luxe
UA/Belafonte Enterprises (Chiz Schultz)
An elderly Jewish tailor complains to God of his bad luck; a black angel appears and seems to help him for a while.
Muddled and seemingly pointless parable with occasional felicities.
w Bill Gunn, Ronald Ribman, *story* Bernard Malamud *d* Jan Kadar *ph* Richard Kratina *pd* George Jenkins *m* Zdenek Linka
Zero Mostel, Harry Belafonte, Ida Kaminska, Milo O'Shea, Eli Wallach, Anne Jackson, *Gloria Foster*
'A prolonged variation on the theme that faith can produce miracles, but only if there is enough of it.'—*John Gillett*

The Angel of Broadway*
US 1927 82m approx bw silent
A nightclub entertainer haunts Salvation Army missions in search of material, but ultimately joins the cause. Fairly impressive propaganda piece of its time. Leatrice Joy, Victor Varconi, May Robson, Alice Lake. Written by Lenore J. Coffee; directed by Lois Weber; for DeMille/Pathe.

Angel on My Shoulder**
US 1946 101m bw
UA/Charles R. Rogers
The devil promises leniency to a dead gangster if he will return to earth and take over the body of a judge who is stamping out evil.
Crude but lively fantasy on the tail-end of the *Here Comes Mr Jordan* cycle, and by the same author.
w Harry Segall, Roland Kibbee *d* Archie Mayo *ph* James Van Trees *m* Dmitri Tiomkin
Paul Muni, Claude Rains, Anne Baxter, Erskine Sanford, Hardie Albright
'The story is so imitative that it's hard to feel any more towards it than a mildly nostalgic regard.'—*Bosley Crowther*
'Witty, caustic and exciting.'—*Motion Picture Guide*

Angel on the Amazon
US 1948 86m bw
Republic (John H. Auer)
GB title: *Drums Along the Amazon*
An elderly white lady resident of the Amazon jungle looks only 25 after being scared by a panther . . .
Ludicrous melodrama which the actors take seriously.
w Lawrence Kimble *d* John H. Auer *ph* Reggie Lanning *m* Nathan Scott
George Brent, Constance Bennett, Vera Hruba Ralston, Brian Aherne, Fortunio Bonanova, Alfonso Bedoya, Gus Schilling

The Angel Who Pawned Her Harp*
GB 1954 76m bw
Group Three (Sidney Cole)
A real angel arrives on a goodwill visit to seamy Islington, and manages to right a few wrongs.
Simple-minded whimsy, spottily effective, with good performances.
w Charles Terrot, Sidney Cole *d* Alan Bromly *ph* Arthur Grant *m* Antony Hopkins
Diane Cilento, Felix Aylmer, Robert Eddison, Jerry Desmonde, Sheila Sweet, Alfie Bass

The Angel with the Trumpet
GB 1949 98m bw
British Lion/London Films (Karl Hartl)
An Austrian lady has an affair with a crown prince but marries for security and dies in defiance of the Nazis.
Curious European cavalcade, dully directed to keep the budget down and accommodate long stretches of an Austrian original. An eccentricity.
w Karl Hartl, Franz Tassie, *novel* Ernst Lothar *d* Anthony Bushell *ph* Robert Krasker *m* Willy Schmidt-Gentner
Eileen Herlie, Basil Sydney, Norman Wooland, Anthony Bushell, Maria Schell, John Justin, Oskar Werner, Andrew Cruickshank

The Angel Wore Red
US 1960 105m bw
MGM/Titanus/Spectator (Gottfredo Lombardo)
The love story of a priest and a prostitute in the Spanish Civil War.
Turgid farrago, unsatisfactory both romantically and politically.

wd Nunnally Johnson *ph* Giuseppe Rotunno *m* Bronislau Kaper

Ava Gardner, Dirk Bogarde, Joseph Cotten, Vittorio de Sica, Aldo Fabrizi, Finlay Currie

'The stars show no apparent surprise that a film so empty of reward should take itself so seriously.'—*Peter John Dyer*

Angelina*
Italy 1947 98m bw
Lux-Ora (Paulo Frasca)

An impoverished housewife becomes the spokeswoman for her community on flooding, housing and other slum problems.
Reasonably rewarding star vehicle in the neo-realist tradition, this time angled for comedy.

w Suso Cecchi d'Amico, Piero Tellini, Luigi Zampa *d* Luigi Zampa *ph* Mario Craveri *m* Enzio Masetti

Anna Magnani, Nando Bruno, Gianni Glori, Franco Zeffirelli

Angélique
France / West Germany / Italy 1964
116m Eastmancolor Dyaliscope
Francos / CICC / Gloria / Fona Roma (Francis Cosne)
Original title: *Angélique Marquise des Anges*

Adventures of a nobleman's daughter at the court of Louis XIV.
Watchable swashbuckling nonsense, a kind of French *Forever Amber*. Several sequels were made.

w Claude Brûlé, Bernard Borderie, Francis Cosne, *novel* Serge and Anne Golon *d* Bernard Borderie *ph* Henri Persin *m* Michel Magne

Michèle Mercier, Robert Hossein, Giuliano Gemma, Jean Rochefort, François Maistre, Jacques Toja

Angelo My Love
US 1982 116m colour

Adventures of an eight-year-old gypsy boy in Manhattan. Angelo is a precocious little rogue, but two hours is a long haul for this kind of ethnic medley. Angelo Evans, Michael Evans, Ruthie Evans, Steve Tsigonoff. Written and directed by Robert Duvall; for Lorton. 'Duvall has done wonders with his actors and then robbed them of their glory by mishandling the tempo of the piece.'—*Sunday Times*

Angel's Holiday
US 1937 74m bw

The niece of a newspaper editor rounds up a gang of racketeers. Smart comedy vehicle for Shirley Temple's only rival. Jane Withers, Robert Kent, Joan Davis, Sally Blane, Harold Huber, Frank Jenks, John Qualen, Lon Chaney Jnr. Written by Frank Fenton, Lynn Root; directed by James Tinling; for John Stone / TCF.

Angels in the Outfield
US 1952 99m bw
MGM (Clarence Brown)
GB title: *Angels and the Pirates*

The profane and bad-tempered manager of an unsuccessful baseball team gets help from an angel.
Unamusing, saccharine whimsy which does not deserve its excellent production values.

w Dorothy Kingsley, George Wells *d* Clarence Brown *ph* Paul C. Vogel *m* Daniele Amfitheatrof

Paul Douglas, Janet Leigh, Keenan Wynn, Lewis Stone, Donna Corcoran, Spring Byington, Bruce Bennett

Angels One Five*
GB 1952 98m bw
Templar (John W. Gossage)

A slice of life in an RAF fighter station during the Battle of Britain.
Underplayed semi-documentary drama with stiff upper lips all round and the emphasis on characterization rather than action. A huge commercial success in Britain.

w Derek Twist *d* George More O'Ferrall *ph* Christopher Challis, Stanley Grant (air scenes) *m* John Wooldridge

Jack Hawkins, John Gregson, Michael Denison, Andrew Osborn, Cyril Raymond, Humphrey Lestocq, Dulcie Gray, Veronica Hurst

Angels Over Broadway
US 1940 80m bw
Columbia / Ben Hecht

During one rainy New York night, three of life's failures have one last stab at success.
Would-be poetic, moralizing melodrama very typical of its author; interesting but not a success.

w Ben Hecht *d* Ben Hecht, Lee Garmes *ph* Lee Garmes *m* George Antheil

Douglas Fairbanks Jnr, Rita Hayworth, Thomas Mitchell, John Qualen, George Watts, Ralph Theodore

'There's a genial, original spirit to it.'—*New Yorker, 1978*

'It has excitement, fast talk, some knowable people, cynicism and sentiment.'—*Otis Ferguson*

† Sample dialogue: 'This town's a giant dice game . . . come on, seven!'

AAN: Ben Hecht (as writer)

Angels Wash Their Faces*
US 1939 86m bw
Warner (Max Siegel)

A bad boy joins the Dead End Kids, but they all reform in the end.
Routine programmer, hastily concocted after the success of *Angels with Dirty Faces*.

w Michael Fessier, Niven Busch, Robert Buckner *d* Ray Enright *ph* Arthur Todd *m* Adolph Deutsch

Ann Sheridan, Ronald Reagan, the Dead End Kids, Bonita Granville, Frankie Thomas, Henry O'Neill, Berton Churchill, Eduardo Ciannelli

'Ray Enright's terrific meller pace makes it the sort of fare the average audience will eat up . . . he has an eye for the spectacular, including a thrilling fire sequence and a dramatic courtroom scene.'—*Variety*

† Original title: *The Battle of City Hall*.

Angels with Dirty Faces****
US 1938 97m bw
Warner (Sam Bischoff)

A Brooklyn gangster is admired by slum boys, but for their sake pretends to be a coward when he goes to the electric chair.
A shrewd, slick entertainment package and a seminal movie for all kinds of reasons. It combined gangster action with fashionable social conscience; it confirmed the Dead End Kids as stars; it provided archetypal roles for its three leading players and catapulted the female lead into stardom. It also showed the Warner style of film-making, all cheap sets and shadows, at its most effective.

w John Wexley, Warren Duff, *original story* Rowland Brown *d Michael Curtiz* *ph Sol Polito* *m* Max Steiner

James Cagney (gangster with redeeming features), *Pat O'Brien* (priest), *Humphrey Bogart* (gangster with no redeeming features), *The Dead End Kids*, *Ann Sheridan*, George Bancroft, Edward Pawley

'Should do fair business, but the picture itself is no bonfire.'—*Variety*

'A rousing, bloody, brutal melodrama.'—*New York Mirror*

AAN: Rowland Brown; Michael Curtiz; James Cagney

Les Anges du Péché*
France 1943 73m bw
Synops / Robert Paul

A novice nun has trouble with the mother superior because of her obsessive interest in a rebellious delinquent girl, and dies before taking her vows.
Interesting study of an enclosed society, notable as its director's first film.

w R. P. Bruckberger, Jean Giraudoux, Robert Bresson *d Robert Bresson* *ph* Philippe Agostini *m* Jean-Jacques Grunenwald

Renée Faure, Jany Holt, Sylvie, Mila Parély, Marie-Hélène Dasté

Angora Love**
US 1929 20m bw silent

Laurel and Hardy keep a goat in their lodgings. Lively L & H comedy, even funnier when remade two years later as *Laughing Gravy*. With Edgar Kennedy, Charlie Hall. Written by Leo McCarey and H. M. Walker; directed by Lewis R. Foster; for Hal Roach.

The Angry Hills
GB 1959 105m bw
MGM / Raymond Stross

In 1940, an American war correspondent is helped by Greek freedom fighters.
Laboured war melodrama with pretentious dialogue but little characterization.

w A. I. Bezzerides, *novel* Leon Uris *d* Robert Aldrich *ph* Stephen Dade *m* Richard Rodney Bennett *ad* Ken Adam

Robert Mitchum, Gia Scala, Elisabeth Mueller, Stanley Baker, Donald Wolfit, Kieron Moore, Theodore Bikel, Sebastian Cabot, Peter Illing, Marius Goring, Leslie Phillips

The Angry Silence**
GB 1960 94m bw
British Lion / Beaver (Richard Attenborough, Bryan Forbes)

A worker who refuses to join an unofficial strike is 'sent to Coventry' by his mates; the matter hits national headlines, and the communists use it to their own advantage.
Irresistibly reminding one of a po-faced *I'm All Right Jack*, this remains a fresh and urgent film which unfortunately lost excitement in its domestic scenes.

w Bryan Forbes, *story* Michael Craig, Richard Gregson *d* Guy Green *ph* Arthur Ibbetson *m* Malcolm Arnold

Richard Attenborough, Michael Craig, Pier Angeli, Bernard Lee, Alfred Burke, Laurence Naismith, Geoffrey Keen

'Vastly entertaining as well as thought-provoking. Matter and manner are for once wholly in harmony.'—*Daily Mail*

AAN: Bryan Forbes

Animal Crackers***
US 1930 98m bw
Paramount

Thieves covet a valuable oil painting unveiled at a swank party.
An excuse for the Marx Brothers, and a lively one in patches, though sedate and stage bound in treatment. The boys are all in top form, and many of the dialogue exchanges are classics.

w Morrie Ryskind, from musical play by himself and *George F. Kaufman* *d* Victor Heerman *ph* George Folsey *m / ly Bert Kalmar, Harry Ruby*

Groucho, Chico, Harpo, Zeppo, *Margaret Dumont*, Lillian Roth, Louis Sorin, Robert Greig, Hal Thompson

GROUCHO: 'You're the most beautiful woman I've ever seen, which doesn't say much for you.'

GROUCHO: 'One morning I shot an elephant in my pajamas. How he got into my pajamas I'll never know.'

GUESTS: 'Hooray for Captain Spaulding, the African explorer!'

GROUCHO: 'Did someone call me schnorrer?'

GUESTS: 'Hooray, hooray, hooray!'

ZEPPO: 'He went into the jungle, where all the monkeys *throw* nuts.'

GROUCHO: 'If I stay here, I'll *go* nuts.'

GUESTS: 'Hooray, hooray, hooray!
He put all his reliance
In courage and defiance
And risked his life for science.'

GROUCHO: 'Hey, hey!'

MRS RITTENHOUSE: 'He is the only white man who covered every acre . . .'

GROUCHO: 'I think I'll try and make her . . .'

GUESTS: 'Hooray, hooray, hooray!'

'A hit on the screen before it opened, and in the money plenty.'—*Variety*

Animal Farm**
GB 1955 75m Technicolor
Louis de Rochemont / Halas and Batchelor

Oppressed by the cruelty and inefficiency of their master, the animals take over a farm but find fresh tyrants among themselves.
George Orwell's political fable—'all animals are equal but some animals are more equal than others'—is faithfully followed in this ambitious but rather disappointingly flat cartoon version.

w,p,d John Halas and Joy Batchelor *m* Matyas Seiber *voices* Maurice Denham

'A melodramatic fantasy that is mordant, tender and quixotic, shot with ironic humour.'—*New York Times*

The Animal Kingdom*
US 1932 95m bw
RKO (David O. Selznick)
GB title: *The Woman in His House*

An intellectual publisher tries to justify keeping both a wife and a mistress.
Smart comedy-drama from a Broadway success, later bowdlerized as *One More Tomorrow* (qv).

w Horace Jackson, *play* Philip Barry *d* Edward H. Griffith *ph* Lucien Andriot *m* Max Steiner

Leslie Howard, Ann Harding, Myrna Loy, Neil Hamilton, William Gargan, Henry Stephenson, Ilka Chase

'A wise and engaging picture addressed to the upper levels of fandom.'—*Variety*

'Two billion years in the making!'
The Animal World*
US 1956 80m Technicolor
Warner / Windsor (Irwin Allen)

The evolution of animals from their primitive beginnings.
Ambitious documentary with a popular science approach; very variable, with poorish model work.

wd Irwin Allen *ph* Harold Wellman *m* Paul Sawtell *sp* Willis O'Brien, Ray Harryhausen

The Animals Film*
GB / US 1981 136m colour / bw

A hard-hitting documentary recording human ill-treatment of animals, with obvious hints that humans themselves will be next. Not for the squeamish. Narrated by Julie Christie; written and directed by Victor Schonfeld; for Slick Pix.

Animated Genesis*
GB 1952 22m Technicolor (blown up from 16mm)

Greed and the machine enslave mankind.
Ambitious and decorative cartoon conceived and drawn by *Joan and Peter Foldes*, from whom little was subsequently heard. Music by Thomas Henderson; distributed by Korda / British Lion.

Ann Vickers*
US 1933 72m bw
RKO (Pandro S. Berman)

A feminist social worker is taught a thing or two by life and settles down with a corrupt judge.
Reasonably effective version of a popular though heavy-going novel of the time.

w Jane Murfin, *novel* Sinclair Lewis *d* John Cromwell *ph* David Abel, Edward Cronjager *m* Max Steiner

Irene Dunne, Walter Huston, Conrad Nagel, Bruce Cabot, Edna May Oliver, Mitchell Lewis, Murray Kinnell

'Her sufferings are bearable and her ultimate happiness is assured, so this is vicarious enjoyment for any woman. Lovely romance, moderate penance, final respectability. All of which suggests that Ann Vickers should do moderately good biz.'—*Variety*

Anna
Italy 1952 100m bw
Lux (Ponti / de Laurentiis)

A novice nun recalls her former life and almost gives up her vocation.
Soupy woman's picture of no particular merit.

w various *d* Alberto Lattuada *ph* Otello Martelli *m* Nino Rota

Silvana Mangano, Raf Vallone, Vittorio Gassman, Gaby Morlay, Jacques Dumesnil

Anna
US 1987 100m TVC colour
Magnus (Zanne Devine, Yurek Bogayevicz)

A Czech-born actress in the New York fringe theatre is betrayed by a young female admirer.
Echoes of *All About Eve* seem less important than the political asides, and the whole thing is a bit of a muddle.

w Agnieszka Holland *d* Yurek Bogayevicz *ph* Bobby Bukowski *m* Greg Hawkes

Sally Kirkland, Robert Fields, Paulina Porizkova

AAN: Sally Kirkland

Anna and the King of Siam**
US 1946 128m bw
TCF (Louis D. Lighton)

In 1862 an English governess arrives in Bangkok to teach the 67 children of the king.
Unusual and lavish drama, tastefully handled and generally absorbing despite miscasting and several slow passages.

w Talbot Jennings, Sally Benson, *book* Margaret Landon *d* John Cromwell *ph Arthur Miller* *m* Bernard Herrmann *ad Lyle Wheeler, William Darling*

Irene Dunne, Rex Harrison, Linda Darnell, Gale Sondergaard, Lee J. Cobb, Mikhail Rasumny

'A film that never touches the imagination, a film that leaves the mind uninformed and the memory unburdened.'—*Richard Winnington*

'It's pitifully unauthentic, and not a very good movie either, but the story itself holds considerable interest.'—*Pauline Kael, 70s*

AA: Arthur Miller
AAN: Talbot Jennings, Sally Benson; Bernard Herrmann; Gale Sondergaard

'Garbo talks!'
Anna Christie**
US 1930 86m bw
MGM

A waterfront prostitute falls in love with a young seaman.
Primitive sound version of an earthy theatrical warhorse: it has a niche in history as the film in which Garbo first talked.

w Frances Marion, *play* Eugene O'Neill *d* Clarence Brown *ph* William Daniels

Greta Garbo, Charles Bickford, *Marie Dressler*, James T. Mack, Lee Phelps

'Great artistically and tremendous commercially . . . in all respects a wow picture.'—*Variety*

'A very talkie, uncinematic affair, more old-fashioned than the silent movies. If it were not so well acted it would be pretty tiresome.'—*National Board of Review*

† A 1923 silent version starred Blanche Sweet and was directed by John Wray.

AAN: Clarence Brown; William Daniels; Greta Garbo

Anna Karenina**
US 1935 95m bw
MGM (David O. Selznick)

The wife of a Russian aristocrat falls for a dashing cavalry officer.
Well-staged but finally exasperating romantic tragedy, sparked by good performances and production.

w Clemence Dane, Salka Viertel, *novel* Leo Tolstoy *d Clarence Brown ph William Daniels m* Herbert Stothart
Greta Garbo (Anna), Fredric March (Vronsky), *Basil Rathbone* (Karenin), Freddie Bartholomew (Sergei), Maureen O'Sullivan (Kitty), May Robson (Countess), Reginald Owen (Silva), Reginald Denny (Yashvin)

'Cinch b.o. anywhere. In the foreign markets it should come close to establishing modern-day highs.'—*Variety*

'A dignified and effective drama which becomes significant because of that tragic, lonely and glamorous blend which is the Garbo personality.'—*André Sennwald*

'It reaches no great heights of tragedy or drama but rather moves forward relentlessly and a little coldly.'—*The Times*
† Previously filmed as a 1928 silent called *Love*, with Garbo and John Gilbert.

AAN: William Daniels

Anna Karenina*
GB 1947 139m bw
London Films (Alexander Korda)

Tiresomely overlong but very handsomely staged remake marred by central miscasting.

w Jean Anouilh, Guy Morgan, Julien Duvivier *d* Julien Duvivier *ph Henri Alekan m* Constant Lambert

Vivien Leigh, Kieron Moore, *Ralph Richardson*, Marie Lohr, Sally Ann Howes, Niall MacGinnis, Michael Gough, Helen Haye, Mary Kerridge

'Vivien Leigh is lashed about by the tremendous role of Anna like a pussy cat with a tigress by the tail. She is not helped by a script which insists on sentimentally ennobling one of fiction's most vehemently average women.'—*James Agee*

Anna Lucasta*
US 1949 86m bw
Columbia / Security (Philip Yordan)

The bad girl of a farming family comes home to marry, but her past catches up with her.
Polish immigrant melodrama, a touring company staple, adequately transferred to the screen.

w Philip Yordan, Arthur Laurents, *play* Philip Yordan *d* Irving Rapper *ph* Sol Polito *m* David Diamond

Paulette Goddard, Oscar Homolka, Broderick Crawford, William Bishop, Gale Page, Mary Wickes

Anna Lucasta*
US 1958 97m bw
(UA) Longridge Enterprises (Sidney Harmon)

Black version of the long-running play; performances standard.

w Philip Yordan *d* Arnold Laven *ph* Lucien Ballard *m* Elmer Bernstein

Eartha Kitt, Frederick O'Neal, Sammy Davis Jnr, Henry Scott, Rex Ingram, James Edwards

Anna of Brooklyn
Italy / France / US 1958 106m Technirama
Circeo Cinematografica / France Cinema / RKO (Milko Skofic)

An attractive widow returns from New York to her native Italian village in search of a husband.
Footling romantic drama which wastes its cast and budget.

w Ettore Margadonna, Dino Risi *d* Reginald Denham, Carlo Lasticati *ph* Giuseppe Rotunno *m* Alessandro Cicognini, Vittorio de Sica

Gina Lollobrigida, Dale Robertson, Vittorio de Sica, Amedeo Nazzari, Peppino de Felippo, Gabriella Palotta

Annabelle's Affairs
US 1931 74m bw

When her husband disappears, a young bride becomes head cook at his rival's home. Then the husband turns up. Standard farce which worked pretty well in its day. Jeanette MacDonald, Victor McLaglen, Roland Young, Sam Hardy, William Collier Snr. Written by anonymous hands from the play Good Gracious Annabelle by Clare Kummer; directed by Alfred Werker; for Fox.

Annabel Takes a Tour
US 1939 69m bw

A star on a publicity tour balks at the stunts she is expected to perform. Thinnish sequel to *The Affairs of Annabel*. Lucille Ball, Jack Oakie, Ruth Donnelly, Bradley Page, Ralph Forbes. Written by Bert Granet and Oliver Cooper; directed by Lew Landers; for RKO.

Annapolis Farewell
US 1935 75m bw

An old officer so loves the service that he continues to live near the Naval Academy. Tolerable sentimentality of a familiar kind. Sir Guy Standing, Tom Brown, Richard Cromwell, Rosalind Keith, John Howard, Benny Baker, Louise Beavers, Samuel S. Hinds, Minor Watson. Written by Dale Van Every, Frank Craven, Grover Jones, William Slavens McNutt; directed by Alexander Hall; for Louis D. Lighton / Paramount. (GB title: *Gentlemen of the Navy*.)

An Annapolis Story
US 1953 81m colour
Allied Artists / Walter Mirisch
GB title: *The Blue and the Gold*

Two cadets at the naval academy love the same girl.
Artless recruiting poster heroics.

w Dan Ullman *d* Don Siegel *ph* Sam Leavitt *m* Marlin Skiles
Diana Lynn, John Derek, Kevin McCarthy, Pat Dooley, L. Q. Jones

'Seldom have so many scrubbed, wholesome-looking young people thronged any picture.'—*New York Times*

Annapolis Farewell
US 1935 75m bw

A retired naval officer goes down with his ship in college manoeuvres. Fairly absurd stiff-upper-lip propaganda drama. *Sir Guy Standing*, Rosalind Keith, Tom Brown, Richard Cromwell, John Howard, Benny Baker, Louise Beavers, Minor Watson, Samuel S. Hinds. Written by Dale Van Every, Frank Craven, Grover Jones, William Slavens McNutt; directed by Alexander Hall; for Paramount.

Anne of Green Gables*
US 1934 79m bw
RKO (Kenneth MacGowan)

An orphan girl goes to the country to live with her aunt.
Standard version of the classic for young girls.

w Sam Mintz, *novel* L. M. Montgomery *d* George Nicholls Jnr *ph* Lucien Andriot *m* Max Steiner

Anne Shirley (who had been known as Dawn O'Day and legally adopted the name of her character in this, her first starring role), Tom Brown, O. P. Heggie, Helen Westley, Sara Haden, Charley Grapewin

'Made up and monotonous—tragedy having its breakfast in bed.'—*Otis Ferguson*

† *Anne of Windy Willows*, with the same stars and production team, followed in 1940.

Anne of the Indies*
US 1951 87m Technicolor
TCF (George Jessel)

Lady pirate Anne Bonney, the terror of the Caribbean, is at odds with her former master Blackbeard.
Routine swashbuckler, generally well handled.

w Philip Dunne, Arthur Caesar *d* Jacques Tourneur *ph* Harry Jackson *m* Franz Waxman

Jean Peters, Louis Jourdan, Debra Paget, Herbert Marshall, Thomas Gomez, James Robertson Justice, Sean McClory, Francis Pierlot

Anne of the Thousand Days*
GB 1969 146m Technicolor Panavision
Universal / Hal B. Wallis

Henry VIII divorces his wife to marry Anne Boleyn, but soon finds evidence of adultery.
A somewhat unlikely view of history, rather boringly presented on a woman's magazine level, but with occasional good moments from a cast of British notables.

w John Hale, Bridget Boland, *play* Maxwell Anderson *d* Charles Jarrott *ph* Arthur Ibbetson *pd* Maurice Carter *m* Georges Delerue

Richard Burton, Geneviève Bujold, John Colicos (as Cromwell), Irene Papas, Anthony Quayle, Michael Hordern, Katharine Blake, Peter Jeffrey, William Squire, Esmond Knight, Nora Swinburne

'The costumes, beautiful in themselves, have that unconvincing air of having come straight off the rack at Nathan's.'—*Brenda Davies*

'A decent dullness is, alas, the keynote.'—*Michael Billington, Illustrated London News*

'The quintessential work of art for people who haven't the foggiest notion of what art is.'—*John Simon*

'Intelligent from line to line, but the emotions supplied seem hypocritical, and the conception lacks authority . . . Burton's performance is colourless. It's as though he *remembered* how to act but couldn't work up much enthusiasm or involvement.'—*Pauline Kael*

AAN: best picture; John Hale, Bridget Boland; Arthur Ibbetson; Georges Delerue; Richard Burton; Geneviève Bujold; Anthony Quayle

Annie
US 1982 128m Metrocolor Panavision
Columbia / Ray Stark (Joe Layton)

In 1933 an orphan waif charms a munitions millionaire and is adopted by him.
Misguided opening-out of a charming stage musical based on the comic strip which is basically a reversal of *Oliver Twist*. Some of the best numbers have been discarded, the dancing is ponderous, the acting distinctly uneasy, and the choice of director stupefying. None of it works at all.

w Carol Sobieski, from the stage play, *book* Thomas Meehan, *lyrics* Martin Charnin, *music* Charles Strouse; *comic strip* Harold Gray *d* John Huston *ph* Richard Moore *pd* Dale Hennesy *m* Ralph Burns

Albert Finney, Carol Burnett, Aileen Quinn, Ann Reinking, Bernadette Peters, Tim Curry, Geoffrey Holder, Edward Herrman (as Franklin D. Roosevelt)

'Whatever indefinable charm the stage show had is completely lost in this lumbering and largely uninteresting and uninvolving exercise, where the obvious waste reaches almost Pentagonian proportions.'—*Variety*

'The whole thing has the air of a vast, hollow Christmas tree bauble intended not so much for children as for the infantile-minded middle-aged.'—*Sunday Times*

'This is the film I want on my tombstone.'—*Ray Stark.*

'Funeral services may be held starting this week at a theatre near you.'—*Time*

† The cost of *Annie*, starting with $9,000,000 for the rights, rose to $42,000,000. It was not recovered.

AAN: art direction; original song score

Annie Get Your Gun*
US 1950 107m Technicolor
MGM (Arthur Freed)

A young female hillbilly joins Frank Butler's sharpshooting act, and is sophisticated by her love for him.
Gaudy, stagey, generally uninspired screen version of the famous musical show based remotely on a historical character of post-wild-west days. There is a lack of dancing, the direction is stodgy, and in general flair the production falls disappointingly below MGM's usual standard.

w Sidney Sheldon, *musical play* Herbert and Dorothy Fields *d* George Sidney *ph* Charles Rosher *m / ly Irving Berlin md* Adolph Deutsch, Roger Edens *ch* Robert Alton *ad* Cedric Gibbons, Paul Grosse

Betty Hutton, *Howard Keel*, Edward Arnold, J. Carrol Naish, Louis Calhern

Songs include 'Colonel Buffalo Bill'; 'Doing What Comes Naturally'; 'The Girl That I Marry'; 'You Can't Get a Man with a Gun'; 'There's No Business Like Show Business'; 'My Defenses Are Down'; 'I'm an Indian Too'; 'I Got the Sun in the Morning'; 'Anything You Can Do'; 'They Say It's Wonderful'.

† The real Annie Oakley was born Phoebe Ann Oakley Mozie in 1860, and died in 1926. The role was to have been played by Judy Garland, who was fired after displays of temperament; also considered were Doris Day, Judy Canova and Betty Garrett.

†† Louis Calhern replaced Frank Morgan, who died during production

AA: music direction
AAN: Charles Rosher

Annie Hall***
US 1977 93m De Luxe
UA / Jack Rollins-Charles H. Joffe (Fred T. Gallo)
Sub-title: *A Nervous Romance*

Against the neuroses of New York and Los Angeles, a Jewish comedian has an affair with a midwestern girl.
Semi-serious collage of jokes and bits of technique, some of the former very funny and some of the latter very successful. For no very good reason it hit the box office spot and turned its creator, of whom it is very typical, from a minority performer to a superstar.

w Woody Allen, Marshall Brickman *d* Woody Allen *ph* Gordon Willis *m* various

Woody Allen, Diane Keaton, Tony Roberts, Carol Kane, Paul Simon, Shelly Duvall

ALLEN: 'Hey, don't knock masturbation. It's sex with someone I love.'

'The film's priceless vignettes about the difficulties in chitchatting with strangers, the awkward moments in family visits, and the frequent breakdowns in communication and failures in intimacy, its reminiscences about the palpable horrors of growing up in Brooklyn, and its comic encounters with lobsters in the kitchen or spiders in the bathroom, all seem like snapshots from Allen and Keaton's own romance.'—*Les Keyser, Hollywood in the Seventies*

† The narrative supposedly mirrors the real-life affair of the stars, who separated before the film came out. (Diane Keaton's family name is Hall.)

AA: best picture; script; direction; Diane Keaton
AAN: Woody Allen (as actor)

Annie Oakley*
US 1935 90m bw
RKO (Cliff Reid)

The historical story, more or less, of the lady later immortalized in *Annie Get Your Gun*. Lively semi-western with good dialogue but gluey plot development.

w Joel Sayre, John Twist *d George Stevens ph* J. Roy Hunt *m* Alberto Columbo *ad* Van Nest Polglase

Barbara Stanwyck, Preston Foster, Melvyn Douglas, Moroni Olsen, Pert Kelton, Andy Clyde, Chief Thunderbird

'A swell idea that doesn't quite come through.'—*Variety*

Annie's Coming Out*
Australia 1984 93m Eastmancolor
Film Australia (Don Murray)

A physically handicapped child, wrongly characterized as mentally retarded also, is brought out by a devoted teacher.
Fictionalized version of a true story: predictably well intentioned, shocking, and consistently watchable.

w John Patterson, Chris Borthwick, *book* Rosemary Crossley *d* Gil Brealey *ph* Mick Van Borneman *m* Simon Walker

Angela Punch McGregor, Drew Forsythe, Tina Arhondis, Liddy Clark, Monica Maughan

The Anniversary*
GB 1968 95m Technicolor
Hammer (Jimmy Sangster)

A malevolent one-eyed widow will stop at nothing to prevent her grown sons from

leaving the family orbit, and they meet each year to mourn the death of the husband she really hated.
Agreeable but over-talkative black comedy with a splendid role for its star and some good scattered moments, marred by a general lack of style.

w Jimmy Sangster, *play Bill MacIlwraith*
d Roy Ward Baker *ph* Harry Waxman
m Philip Martell

Bette Davis, Jack Hedley, *James Cossins*, Sheila Hancock, Elaine Taylor, Christian Roberts, Timothy Bateson

'It all reminds one of a love scene in a funeral parlour.'—*Variety*

'Magisterially grotesque in elegantly tailored eye-patch and exotic gown, she snaps out her bitchy insults with all 57 varieties of relish.'—*MFB*

'Convention outraged . . . a class abandoned . . . a country betrayed!'

Another Country*
GB 1984 90m colour
TCF / Virgin / Goldcrest (Alan Marshall)

A homosexual defector to Russia reflects on the public school pressures which influenced him.
Upper-crust militarism, arrogance, sadism and homosexuality rolled up in a package which pleased the West End theatre crowds but seems faintly absurd on film. Not much of a recruiting poster for Eton.

w Julian Mitchell, from his play *d* Marek Kanievska *ph* Peter Biziou *m* Michael Storey *pd* Brian Morris

Rupert Everett, Colin Firth, Michael Jenn, Robert Addie, Anna Massey, Rupert Wainwright, Betsy Brantley

'Inevitably it went down well at the Cannes Film Festival, where movies critical of their own country's shortcomings are always favoured.'—*Margaret Hinxman, Daily Mail*

Another Dawn
US 1937 73m bw
Warner (Harry Joe Brown)

In a British army post in Africa, a wife is torn between duty and romance.
Absurdly sudsy melodrama, a potboiler for stars between more important assignments.

w Laird Doyle *d* William Dieterle *ph* Tony Gaudio *m* Erich Wolfgang Korngold

Errol Flynn, Kay Francis, Ian Hunter, Frieda Inescort, Herbert Mundin

† In every Warner film where a cinema canopy was shown, the title advertised was *Another Dawn*, so its use here as an actual title is presumably a piece of cynicism.

Another Face
US 1935 72m bw

A gangster has his face lifted and becomes a film star. Rather heavy comedy with some good laughs. *Brian Donlevy*, Wallace Ford, Phyllis Brooks, Erik Rhodes, Molly Lamont, Alan Hale. Written by Garrett Graham, John Twist, Ray Mayer, Thomas Dugan; directed by Christy Cabanne; for RKO. (GB title: *It Happened in Hollywood*.)

Another Fine Mess**
US 1930 30m bw

On the run from a cop, Stan and Ollie masquerade as master and maid. Elaborate star comedy with spoken introduction instead of titles; very satisfying but not quite vintage. Laurel and Hardy, James Finlayson, Thelma Todd, Charles Gerrard. Written by H. M. Walker, from a sketch by Stan Laurel's father; directed by James Parrott; for Hal Roach.

Another Language
US 1933 75m bw
MGM (Walter Wanger)

A young wife does not fit in with her husband's snobby family and falls in love with his nephew.
Flat treatment of a dated play.

w Herman J. Mankiewicz, Gertrude Purcell, Donald Ogden Stewart, *play* Rose Franken
d Edward H. Griffith *ph* Ray June

Helen Hayes, Robert Montgomery, John Beal, Louise Closser Hale, Henry Travers, Margaret Hamilton

'A very good picture that will get more than average box office attention . . . everything is handled with intellect and due restraint.'—*Variety*

Another Man, Another Chance
France / US 1977 132m Eastmancolor
UA / Films 13 / Ariane (Alexandre Mnouchkine, George Dancigers)
French title: *Un Autre Homme, une Autre Chance*
aka: *Another Man, Another Woman*

A Yank vet and a French widow meet and fall in love in the old west.
Pretty, overlong, rather enervating romance with an unusual and not entirely convincing setting.

wd Claude Lelouch *ph* Jacques Lefrançois
m Francis Lai

James Caan, Geneviève Bujold, Francis Huster, Susan Tyrrell

Another Man's Poison*
GB 1951 89m bw
Douglas Fairbanks Jnr / Daniel M. Angel

A lady novelist poisons her husband and lover, then unwittingly takes a fatal dose herself.
Hysterical vehicle for a fading Hollywood star reduced to repeating her tantrums in an English studio on a low budget; she should have stayed home, as should her director.

w Val Guest, *play* Deadlock by Leslie Sands
d Irving Rapper *ph* Robert Krasker *m* John Greenwood

Bette Davis, Anthony Steel, Gary Merrill, Emlyn Williams, Barbara Murray, Reginald Beckwith, Edna Morris

'Barnstormers as rich and improbable as this are rare . . . the general atmosphere takes one back to 1935.'—*Gavin Lambert*

'Like reading Ethel M. Dell by flashes of lightning.'—*Frank Hauser*

'The melodramatic gamut has seldom experienced such a workout.'—*Hollywood Reporter*

Another Part of the Forest*
US 1948 108m bw
U-I (Jerry Bresler)

In the post-Civil War years, Marcus Hubbard leads his family to worldly success by cheating and the misuse of power: he lives to regret it, as the children learn their lessons all too well.
This backwards sequel to *The Little Foxes*, showing how the characters of that play got to be their nasty selves, is quite absorbingly acted but stagily presented, with plenty of care but no style.

w Vladimir Pozner, *play Lillian Hellman*
d Michael Gordon *ph* Hal Mohr *m* Daniele Amfitheatrof

Fredric March, Florence Eldridge, Ann Blyth, Dan Duryea, Edmond O'Brien, John Dall

'The Hubbards are the greatest collection of ghouls since *The Old Dark House*.'—*Pauline Kael, 70s*

Another Shore*
GB 1948 77m bw
Ealing (Ivor Montagu)

A young Irishman dreams of life in the South Seas but gives up his fancies for love.
Curiously whimsical, artificial and unconvincing comedy drama from a famous studio, but not without its moments of interest.

w Walter Meade, *novel* Kenneth Reddin
d Charles Crichton *ph* Douglas Slocombe
m Georges Auric

Robert Beatty, Stanley Holloway, Moira Lister, Michael Medwin, Dermot Kelly, Wilfred Brambell, Irene Worth

'It's a blessed event!'

Another Thin Man
US 1939 102m bw
MGM (Hunt Stromberg)

Nick Charles solves a murder on a Long Island weekend.
Overwritten and distinctly tedious star sequel to *The Thin Man* and *After the Thin Man*. The title refers (erroneously) to Nick and Nora's baby.

w Dashiell Hammett *d* W. S. Van Dyke II
ph Oliver T. Marsh, William Daniels
m Edward Ward

William Powell, Myrna Loy, Otto Kruger, C. Aubrey Smith, Virginia Grey, Nat Pendleton, Tom Neal, Ruth Hussey, Sheldon Leonard

'The screenplay tosses shootings and skulduggery and repartee at us before we're ready, and then Nick Charles takes an unconscionable amount of time sorting things out.'—*Pauline Kael, 70s*

Another Time, Another Place
GB 1958 98m bw Vistavision
Paramount / Kaydor (Lewis Allen, Smedley Aston)

During World War II an American newspaperwoman has an affair with a British war correspondent; when he is killed in action, she consoles his widow.
Drippy romance, unsympathetically played and artificially set in a Cornish village.

w Stanley Mann, *novel* Lenore Coffee
d Lewis Allen *ph* Jack Hildyard *m* Douglas Gamley

Lana Turner, Barry Sullivan, Glynis Johns, Sean Connery, Sidney James

Anthony Adverse*
US 1936 141m bw
Warner (Henry Blanke)

Adventures of an ambitious young man in early 19th-century America.
A rousing spectacle of its day, from a bestselling novel, this award-winning movie quickly dated and now seems very thin and shadowy despite the interesting talents involved.

w Sheridan Gibney, *novel* Hervey Allen
d Mervyn Le Roy *ph Tony Gaudio ad Anton Grot m Erich Wolfgang Korngold*

Fredric March, Olivia de Havilland, Gale Sondergaard, Edmund Gwenn, Claude Rains, Anita Louise, Louis Hayward, Steffi Duna, Donald Woods, Akim Tamiroff, Ralph Morgan, Henry O'Neill

'A bulky, rambling and indecisive photoplay which has not merely taken liberties with the letter of the original but with its spirit.'—*Frank S. Nugent, New York Times*

'In the dramatizing there is shown no relish or conviction, only a retentive memory for all the old clothes of show business.'—*Otis Ferguson*

'A lavish gold-leaf from Hervey Allen's book, an earnest cinema endeavour, taxing alike its studio's purse and artistry.'—*Douglas Gilbert, New York World Telegraph*

'The show is fairly glutted with plot and counter-plot and is apt to make one feel that one is witnessing a serial run off continuously at a single performance.'—*Howard Barnes, New York Herald Tribune*

'It goes on too long, otherwise it might have been the funniest film since *The Crusades*.'—*Graham Greene*

AA: Tony Gaudio; Erich Wolfgang Korngold; Gale Sondergaard
AAN: best picture; Anton Grot

Antoine et Antoinette*
France 1947 87m bw
SNEG / Gaumont

A young married couple find they have won a lottery but lost the ticket.
A bubbly soufflé, most expertly served but leaving one still a little hungry; not quite in the Clair class.

w Françoise Giroud, M. Griffe, Jacques Becker *d Jacques Becker ph* Pierre Montazel *m Jean-Jacques Grunenwald*

Roger Pigaut, Clair Maffei

ANTHONY ADVERSE. Fredric March puts his best profile forward, Olivia de Havilland does likewise, while Anton Grot's Oscar-nominated art direction threatens to upstage them both.

Antony and Cleopatra*
GB 1972 170m Technicolor Todd-AO 35
Transac (Zurich) / Izaro (Madrid) / Folio Films (London) (Peter Snell)

Well-meaning, well-mounted, but quite uninspired rendering.

wd Charlton Heston, *play* William Shakespeare *ph* Rafael Pacheco *m* John Scott *pd* Maurice Pelling

Charlton Heston, Hildegarde Neil, Eric Porter, *John Castle* (as Octavius), Fernando Rey, Freddie Jones, Peter Arne, Roger Delgado

† Olivier and Orson Welles were both sought for the lead.

Any Number Can Play*
US 1949 103m bw
MGM (Arthur Freed)

A gambling casino owner has health problems, is reconciled with his son and retires from the game.
Rather boring drama redeemed by slightly offbeat dialogue and excellent star acting, albeit in routine roles.

w Richard Brooks, *novel* E. H. Heth
d Mervyn Le Roy *ph* Harold Rosson
m Lennie Hayton

Clark Gable, Alexis Smith, Mary Astor, Wendell Corey, Audrey Totter, Lewis Stone, Frank Morgan, *Marjorie Rambeau*, Barry Sullivan

Any Old Port*
US 1932 20m bw

Stan and Ollie are sailors on leave, and Ollie enters Stan for a boxing match. Minor star comedy with good moments but a weak finish.
Laurel and Hardy, Walter Long. Written by H. M. Walker; directed by James W. Horne; for Hal Roach.

Any Wednesday*
US 1966 109m Technicolor
Warner (Julius J. Epstein)
GB title: *Bachelor Girl Apartment*

A millionaire businessman spends every Wednesday with his mistress, but complications arise when his young associate is accidentally sent to use the company flat.
Overlong screen version of a thinly scripted Broadway success in which yawns gradually overtake laughs.

w Julius J. Epstein, *play* Muriel Resnik
d Robert Ellis Miller *ph* Harold Lipstein
m George Duning

Jane Fonda, Dean Jones, Jason Robards Jnr, *Rosemary Murphy* (a breath of air as the deceived wife who doesn't mind), Ann Prentiss, King Moody

Any Which Way You Can

US 1980 116m De Luxe

The hero of *Every Which Way But Loose* becomes involved in further brawls and car crashes, with the help of his friendly orang-utan. A sequel designed entirely for the box office, its tone set by the scene in which the villains on motorcycles are covered in tar. Clint Eastwood, Ruth Gordon, Sondra Locke, Geoffrey Lewis, William Smith, Harry Guardino. Written by Stanford Sherman; directed by Buddy Van Horn; for Malpaso / Warner. 'This kind of thing is clearly beyond or beneath criticism.'—*Variety*.

'Where the previous comedy set up a zany situation, this one ploughs it into the ground.'—*Daily Mail*

Anybody's Woman

US 1930 80m bw

A drunken lawyer marries a chorus girl and regrets it, but she reforms him. Tedious matrimonial drama. Ruth Chatterton, Clive Brook, Paul Lukas, Huntley Gordon, Virginia Hammond. Written by Zoe Akins, Doris Anderson, Gouverneur Morris; directed by Dorothy Arzner; for Paramount. 'It can't lose through that title and the stars.'—*Variety*

Anything Can Happen*

US 1952 93m bw
Paramount / William Perlberg, George Seaton

Adventures of a Russian immigrant family in New York.
A standard Hollywood product based on a sentimental best-seller.

w George Seaton, George Oppenheimer, *book* George and Helen Papashvily *d* George Seaton *ph* Daniel L. Fapp *m* Victor Young

Jose Ferrer, Kim Hunter, Kurt Kasznar, Alex Danaroff, Oscar Beregi

'Exploits to the hilt the somewhat limited possibilities of quaintness and whimsicality with a broken accent.'—*Penelope Houston*

Anything Goes**

US 1936 92m bw
Paramount (Benjamin Glazer)
TV title: *Tops is the Limit*

Romantic adventures on board a transatlantic liner.
Amiably batty musical comedy, zestfully directed and blithely performed.

w Guy Bolton, P. G. Wodehouse, Howard Lindsay, Russell Crouse, from their Broadway show *d* Lewis Milestone *ph* Karl Struss *songs* Cole Porter *md* Victor Young *ad* Hans Dreier

Bing Crosby, Ethel Merman, Charles Ruggles, Grace Bradley, Ida Lupino, Chill Wills, the Avalon Boys, Arthur Treacher

† Only three of Cole Porter's songs were retained from the Broadway show: 'Anything Goes', 'You're the Top' and 'I Get a Kick out of You'. Others by various hands include 'Moonburn', 'Sailor Beware', 'My Heart and I', 'Am I Awake?', 'Hopelessly in Love'.

Anything Goes*

US 1956 106m Technicolor Vistavision
Paramount (Robert Emmett Dolan)

The male stars of a musical comedy each sign a girl to play the female lead; resulting complications are ironed out during a transatlantic voyage.
Below-par reworking of the 1936 film in which technical gloss and dull sets virtually reduce the characters to puppets. A few good moments transcend the general lack of imagination.

w Sidney Sheldon, from show as credited in 1936 version *d* Robert Lewis *ph* John F. Warren *songs* Cole Porter *md* Joseph J. Lilley *ch* Nick Castle, Roland Petit *ad* Hal Pereira, Joseph M. Johnson

Bing Crosby, Donald O'Connor, Zizi Jeanmaire, Mitzi Gaynor, Phil Harris, Kurt Kasznar

Anzio

Italy 1968 117m Technicolor Panavision
(Columbia) Dino de Laurentiis (Marcel Bebert)
GB title: *The Battle for Anzio*

A war correspondent joins American and British troops preparing for the 1944 landing in Italy.
Threadbare war film which wastes an all-star American cast.

w H. A. L. Craig, *book* Anzio by Wynford Vaughan Thomas *d* Edward Dmytryk *ph* Giuseppe Rotunno *m* Riz Ortolani

Robert Mitchum, Peter Falk, Arthur Kennedy, Robert Ryan, Earl Holliman, Mark Damon, Reni Santoni, Anthony Steel, Patrick Magee

'It must be a long time since a script managed to pack in so many crassly portentous statements about why men fight wars.'—*MFB*

Apache*

US 1954 91m Technicolor
UA / Hecht–Lancaster (Harold Hecht)

After the surrender of Geronimo, one Apache leader is unconquered; after creating much havoc, he settles for domesticity, and the white men let him go unharmed.
Sober western in the wake of *Broken Arrow*, with a predictably sympathetic star performance and a surprising happy ending. More decency than excitement along the way.

w James R. Webb, *novel* Bronco Apache by Paul I. Wellman *d* Robert Aldrich *ph* Ernest Laszlo *m* David Raksin

Burt Lancaster, Jean Peters, John McIntire, Charles Bronson, John Dehner, Paul Guilfoyle, Walter Sande, Monte Blue

'The picture was seriously compromised. You make a picture about one thing, the inevitability of Massai's death. His courage is measured against the inevitable. The whole previous two hours becomes reduced if at the end he can just walk away.'—*Robert Aldrich*

Apache Drums

US 1951 75m Technicolor
U-I (Val Lewton)

A gambler helps a town under Indian attack. Standard co-feature western, perfectly adequate but showing no sign of its producer's former tastes and skills.

w David Chandler *d* Hugo Fregonese *ph* Charles Boyle *m* Hans Salter

Stephen McNally, Willard Parker, Coleen Gray, Arthur Shields, James Griffith

Apache Rifles

US 1964 92m De Luxe

In 1879 Arizona, an Indian-hating officer falls for a half-caste. Tolerable mid-budget western. Audie Murphy, Michael Dante, Linda Lawson, L. Q. Jones. Written by Charles B. Smith; directed by William H. Witney; for Admiral Pictures / TCF.

Apache Trail

US 1942 66m bw

A highwayman's brother guards the stagecoach mail box. Routine western support, quite watchable. Lloyd Nolan, Donna Reed, William Lundigan, Ann Ayars, Connie Gilchrist, Chill Wills, Miles Mander, Gloria Holden. Written by Maurice Geraghty from story by Ernest Haycox; directed by Richard Thorpe; for Sam Marx / MGM.

Apache Uprising

US 1965 90m Techniscope
Paramount / A. C. Lyles

Assorted passengers in a stagecoach survive an Indian attack at a way station.
It sounds like a remake, and almost is, but the handling is lively enough and the producer's usual cast of nostalgic stars is in evidence.

w Harry Sanford, Max Lamb *d* R. G. Springsteen *ph* W. Wallace Kelley *m* Jimmie Haskell

Rory Calhoun, Corinne Calvet, John Russell, Lon Chaney Jnr, Gene Evans, DeForest Kelley, Arthur Hunnicutt, Richard Arlen, Johnny Mack Brown, Jean Parker

Apache War Smoke

US 1952 67m bw

An Indian killer is among those sheltering in a desert outpost before an Apache raid. Talkative but tense lower-berth western. Gilbert Roland, Robert Horton, Glenda Farrell, Barbara Ruick, Henry Morgan. Written by Jerry Davis, from a story by Ernest Haycox; directed by Harold Kress; for MGM.

Aparajito**

India 1956 113m bw
Epic Films Private Ltd (Satyajit Ray)
aka: *The Unvanquished*

After his father's death, a poor country boy is helped by his mother to study for the university.

A detailed and moving study of two characters who are universally familiar despite an unusual background.

wd Satyajit Ray *ph* Subrata Mitra *m* Ravi Shankar

Pinaki Sen Gupta, Karuna Banerjee, Kanu Banerjee

† This was the sequel to *Pather Panchali*, and was itself followed by *The World of Apu*

'Movie-wise, there has never been anything like it—laugh-wise, love-wise, or otherwise-wise!'

The Apartment**
US 1960 125m bw Panavision
UA / Mirisch (Billy Wilder)

A lonely, ambitious clerk rents out his apartment to philandering executives and finds that one of them is after his own girl.
Overlong and patchy but agreeably mordant and cynical comedy with a sparkling view of city office life and some deftly handled individual sequences.

w Billy Wilder, I. A. L. Diamond d Billy Wilder ph Joseph La Shelle *m* Adolph Deutsch *ad* Alexander Trauner

Jack Lemmon (C. C. Baxter), *Shirley Maclaine* (Miss Kubelik), *Fred MacMurray* (Jeff D. Sheldrake), Ray Walston (Joe Dobisch), Jack Kruschen (Dr Dreyfuss), Joan Shawlee (Sylvia), Edie Adams (Miss Olsen), David Lewis (Al Kirkeby)

Baxter's opening narration: 'On November 1st, 1959, the population of New York City was 8,042,753. If you laid all these people end to end, figuring an average height of five feet six and a half inches, they would reach from Times Square to the outskirts of Karachi, Pakistan. I know facts like this because I work for an insurance company—Consolidated Life of New York. We are one of the top five companies in the country. Last year we wrote nine point three billion dollars worth of policies. Our home office has 31,259 employees, which is more than the entire population of Natchez, Mississippi, or Gallup, New Mexico. I work on the 19th floor—Ordinary Policy department—Premium Accounting division—Section W—desk number 861.'

BAXTER: 'Miss Kubelik, one doesn't get to be a second administrative assistant around here unless he's a pretty good judge of character, and as far as I'm concerned you're tops. I mean, decency-wise and otherwise-wise.'

BAXTER: 'You know, I used to live like Robinson Crusoe—shipwrecked among eight million people. Then one day I saw a footprint in the sand and there you were. It's a wonderful thing, dinner for two.'

MISS KUBELIK: 'Shut up and deal.' (*Last line of film.*)

'Without either style or taste, shifting gears between pathos and slapstick without any transition.'—*Dwight MacDonald*

'Billy Wilder directed this acrid story as if it were a comedy, which is a cheat, considering that it involves pimping and a suicide attempt and many shades of craven ethics.'—*New Yorker, 1980*

AA: best picture; Billy Wilder, I. A. L. Diamond (as writers); Billy Wilder (as director)
AAN: Joseph La Shelle; Jack Lemmon; Shirley Maclaine; Jack Kruschen

Apartment for Peggy*
US 1948 98m Technicolor
TCF (William Perlberg)

A retired professor finds a new lease of life through caring for the homeless family of an ex-GI.
Sentimental comedy with serious undertones (the professor twice attempts suicide). Signs of enterprise are smothered by regulation charm.

wd George Seaton, *story* Faith Baldwin *ph* Harry Jackson *m* David Raksin

Edmund Gwenn, Jeanne Crain, William Holden, Gene Lockhart, Henri Letondal, Charles Lane, Houseley Stevenson

'A first rate experience for observers with comprehending minds.'—*Bosley Crowther, New York Times*

The Ape
US 1940 61m bw
Monogram (Scott R. Dunlop)

Dr Adrian seeks to cure polio by means of a serum which can only be obtained from the spinal fluid of a human being. He kills an escaped ape and dresses in its skin to seek victims.
Silly and rather boring addition to the mad doctor cycle.

w Curt Siodmak, Richard Carroll, *play* Adam Shirk *d* William Nigh *ph* Harry Neumann *m* Edward Kay

Boris Karloff, Maris Wrixon, Gertrude Hoffman, Henry Hall

Ape and Super Ape
Netherlands / USA 1972 103m
Technicolor

An alleged documentary comparing human and animal behaviour seems regrettably to turn into a series of episodes depicting animal savagery in close-up. Written, directed, edited and produced by Bert Haanstra; photographed by Anton Van Munster; for Bert Haanstra Films / Unicorn. (Original title: *Bij de Beesten Af.*) 'It lacks even associational interest for the wild-life enthusiast, and is best written off as an inconclusive, unoriginal and often repellent exercise unworthy of its maker.'—*John Baxter, MFB*

The Ape Man
US 1943 64m bw
Monogram (Sam Katzman, Jack Dietz)
GB title: *Lock Your Doors*

A scientist injects himself with spinal fluid which turns him into an ape creature.
Cheap rubbish shot in a couple of corners and offering no thrill whatever.

w Barney A. Sarecky, *story* They Creep in the Dark by Karl Brown *d* William Beaudine *ph* Mack Stengler *m* Edward Kay

Bela Lugosi, Wallace Ford, Louise Currie, Minerva Urecal

'Bela Lugosi, rigged out in a shaggy beard and formal morning attire, ambling like an ape and sharing a cage with a gorilla, scares nobody. It's strictly a dual support.'—*Variety*

† A supposed sequel the following year, *Return of the Ape Man*, had in fact no plot connection. In this Lugosi thawed out a neanderthal man, inserted John Carradine's brain, and the composite turned into George Zucco!

Der Apfel ist ab**
West Germany 1949 105m bw
Camera Film / Helmut Beck-Herzog
Translated title: *The Apple Fell*

Adam and Eve have marital problems in Paradise, and consult a psychiatrist.
Lively sophisticated fantasy, perhaps a bit arch for general consumption, but almost as interesting in post-war Nazi Germany as *Caligari* was in 1919.

w Kurd E. Heyne, Helmut Kautner, Bobby Todd, from their musical comedy *d Helmut Kautner ph* Igor Oberberg *m* Bernhard Eichhorn

Bobby Todd, Bettina Moissi, Joana Maria Gorvin

'Hollywood should look over this Kautner. He has a Lubitsch touch that runs all over this picture.'—*Variety*

Apocalypse Now**
US 1979 153m Technicolor
Technovision
Omni Zoetrope (Francis Coppola)

A Vietnam captain is instructed to eliminate a colonel who has retired to the hills and is fighting his own war.
Pretentious war movie, made even more hollow-sounding by the incomprehensible performance of Brando as the mad martinet. Some vivid scenes along the way, and some interesting parallels with Conrad's *Heart of Darkness*, but these hardly atone for the director's delusion that prodigal expenditure of time and money will result in great art. (The movie took so long to complete that it was dubbed *Apocalypse Later.*)

w John Milius, Francis Coppola *d* Francis Coppola *ph Vittorio Storaro m* Carmine Coppola, Francis Coppola *pd* Dean Tavoularis

Martin Sheen, Robert Duvall, Frederic Forrest, Marlon Brando, Sam Bottoms, Dennis Hopper

'The characters are living through Vietnam as pulp adventure fantasy, as movie, as stoned humour.'—*New Yorker*

† Coppola admitted the following at the Cannes Film Festival: 'It's more of an experience than a movie. At the beginning there's a story. Along the river the story becomes less important and the experience more important.'

AA: Vittorio Storaro
AAN: best picture; best writing; best direction; Robert Duvall

The Appaloosa*
US 1966 99m Techniscope
Universal (Alan Miller)
GB title: *Southwest to Sonora*

A cowboy's plan to start a stud farm with his magnificent horse is interrupted by badmen who think he has molested their girl.
Mannered, slow western set on the Mexican border, with star and director apparently striving to upstage each other.

w James Bridges, Roland Kibbee, *novel* Robert MacLeod *d* Sidney J. Furie *ph Russell Metty* *m* Frank Skinner

Marlon Brando, Anjanette Comer, John Saxon, Rafael Campos, Frank Silvera

'Seems intent less on telling a story than in carving out the incidental details.'—*MFB*

'The camerawork concentrates on beady eyes, sweaty foreheads, spurred boots and anonymous midriffs being studied through a variety of frames, ranging from tequila bottles to cook fires to grillwork to fingers to feet.'—*Judith Crist*

'A dog of a movie about a horse.'—*Pauline Kael*

'Is Kitty a mother?'
Applause**
US 1929 78m bw
Paramount (Jesse L. Lasky, Walter Wanger)

A vaudeville star gradually loses the love of her daughter.
Absorbing treatment of a hasbeen tearjerking theme, full of cinematic touches and with unusual use of New York locations.

w Garrett Fort, *novel* Beth Brown *d Rouben Mamoulian* *ph* George Folsey

Helen Morgan, Joan Peers, Henry Wadsworth, Fuller Mellish Jnr

'An oasis of filmic sophistication in a desert of stage-bound early talkies.'—*William Everson, 1966*

'A cohesive, well integrated series of pictures. Its intensity, its sharp projection of tragedy, emerge from the eye of the camera: an omniscient, omnipresent eye that slides easily over the links of the story and emphasizes only the true and the relevant.'—*Thornton Delehanty, The Arts*

The Apple Dumpling Gang
US 1974 100m Technicolor
Walt Disney (Bill Anderson)

Three orphan children strike gold in 1878 California.
Better-than-average Disney romp.

w Don Tait, *novel* Jack M. Bickham *d* Norman Tokar *ph* Frank Phillips *m* Buddy Baker

Bill Bixby, Susan Clark, David Wayne, Don Knotts, Tim Conway, Slim Pickens, Harry Morgan, John McGiver, Marie Windsor, Iris Adrian

† *The Apple Dumpling Gang Rides Again*, a shoddy sequel under the direction of Vincent McEveety, appeared in 1979 with fragments of the old cast but no panache.

The Appointment*
US 1969 100m colour
MGM (Martin Poll)

A businessman suspects his wife of spare time prostitution.
Unusual sophisticated fable, dressed to kill but rather stretched out for its substance. Shades of *El* and *The Chinese Room*.

w James Salter *d* Sidney Lumet *m* John Barry, Don Walker

Omar Sharif, Anouk Aimée, Lotte Lenya

Appointment for Love*
US 1941 89m bw
Universal (Bruce Manning)

A doctor and a playwright agree to marry 'without love'.
A familiar theme quite amusingly explored by a practised cast.

w Bruce Manning, Felix Jackson *d* William A. Seiter *ph* Joseph Valentine *m* Frank Skinner, Charles Previn

Charles Boyer, Margaret Sullavan, Eugene Pallette, Rita Johnson, Gus Schilling, Reginald Denny, Ruth Terry

Appointment in Berlin
US 1943 77m bw
Columbia (Sam Bischoff)

An RAF wing commander expresses unpopular views and is recruited by the Nazis as a 'voice of truth' broadcaster.
World War II potboiler.

w Horace McCoy, Michael Hogan *d* Alfred E. Green *ph* Franz Planer *m* Werner Heymann

George Sanders, Marguerite Chapman, Gale Sondergaard, Onslow Stevens, Alan Napier, H. P. Sanders (the star's father)

Appointment in Honduras
US 1953 79m Technicolor print
RKO / Benedict Bogeaus

Three assorted types and four criminals escape through the jungle from a revolution.
Predictable adventure drama sabotaged by poor colour.

w Karen deWolf *d* Jacques Tourneur *ph* Joseph Biroc *m* Louis Forbes

Glenn Ford, Ann Sheridan, Zachary Scott, Rodolfo Acosta, Jack Elam

Appointment in London*
GB 1952 96m bw
Mayflower (Aubrey Baring, Maxwell Setton)

The exploits of a squadron of Bomber Command during one month in 1943.
Dullish war film with standard credits.

w John Wooldridge, Robert Westerby *d* Philip Leacock *ph* Stephen Dade *m* John Wooldridge

Dirk Bogarde, Ian Hunter, Dinah Sheridan, Bill Kerr, Bryan Forbes, William Sylvester, Charles Victor

Appointment with a Shadow
US 1957 72m bw CinemaScope

An alcoholic reporter redeems himself by capturing a criminal single-handed. Maudlin melodrama which takes itself too seriously. George Nader, Joanna Moore, Brian Keith, Virginia Field. Written by Alec Coppel and Norman Jolley; directed by Richard Carlson; for Universal-International. (GB title: *The Big Story*.)

Appointment with Crime
GB 1945 97m bw

Ex-convict revenges himself on the former friends who shopped him. Stodgy melodrama which seemed about to make a big star of William Hartnell. Robert Beatty, Joyce Howard, Raymond Lovell, Herbert Lom. Written and directed by John Harlow; for British National.

Appointment with Danger*
US 1949 89m bw
Paramount (Robert Fellows)

A nun becomes the government's chief witness in identifying the murderers of a US postal inspector.
Routine but entertaining star thick-ear.

w Richard Breen, Warren Duff *d* Lewis Allen *ph* John Seitz *m* Victor Young

Alan Ladd, Phyllis Calvert, Paul Stewart, Jan Sterling, Jack Webb, Henry Morgan

Appointment With Death
GB 1988 108m colour

Another starry Hercule Poirot tale, this time in 30s Palestine. Peter Ustinov, Lauren Bacall, Carrie Fisher, John Gielgud, Piper Laurie. Written by Peter Shaffer and others, from novel by Agatha Christie; directed by Michael Winner; for Golan-Globus.

'They came home with the milk!'
Appointment with Venus**
GB 1951 89m bw
GFD / British Film Makers (Betty E. Box)
US title: *Island Rescue*

During World War II, a pedigree cow is rescued from the German-occupied Channel Islands.
Curious but generally agreeable mixture of comedy and war adventure, pleasantly shot on Sark.

w Nicholas Phipps, *novel* Jerrard Tickell *d* Ralph Thomas *ph* Ernest Steward *m* Benjamin Frankel

David Niven, Glynis Johns, George Coulouris, Barry Jones, Kenneth More, Noel Purcell, Bernard Lee, Jeremy Spenser

The Apprenticeship of Duddy Kravitz*
Canada 1974 121m Bellevue-Pathé Panavision
Duddy Kravitz Syndicate (Gerald Schneider)

An ambitious young Jew finds that it is best to be liked.
Amusing adventures of an anti-hero; good scenes but rather patchy technique.

w Mordecai Richler, from his novel *d* Ted Kotcheff *ph* Miklos Lente *m* Stanley Myers

Richard Dreyfuss, Micheline Lanctot, Jack Warden, Randy Quaid, Denholm Elliott, Joseph Wiseman

AAN: Mordecai Richler

The April Fools*
US 1969 95m Technicolor Panavision
Cinema Center / Jalem (Gordon Carroll)

An unhappy New York husband elopes to Paris with an unhappy wife.
Whimsical romantic comedy which rather strains its resources without giving full value for money in romance, humour or simple charm. Good moments, though.

w Hal Dresner *d* Stuart Rosenberg *ph* Michel Hugo *m* Marvin Hamlisch *pd* Richard Sylbert

Jack Lemmon, Catherine Deneuve, Myrna Loy, Charles Boyer, Peter Lawford, Jack Weston, Harvey Korman, Sally Kellerman

'Painfully modish, from the opening party in an apartment filled with fashionable objets d'art to the final mad dash to the airport in an expensive sports car.'—*MFB*

April in Paris*
US 1952 100m Technicolor
Warner (William Jacobs)

A chorus girl is mistakenly invited to a US Arts Festival in Paris, and bewitches the bureaucrat in charge.
Poorly produced star musical with a thin plot and a few redeeming wisps of wit.

w Jack Rose, Melville Shavelson *d* David Butler *ph* Wilfrid Cline *md* Ray Heindorf *ch* Le Roy Prinz *songs* Sammy Cahn, Vernon Duke, E. Y. Harburg

Doris Day, *Ray Bolger*, Claude Dauphin, Eve Miller, George Givot

April Love
US 1957 99m Eastmancolor Cinemascope
TCF (David Weisbart)

For stealing a car, a teenager is sent on probation to his uncle's stud farm, where circumstances seem once again to put him in trouble with the law.
Easygoing star vehicle with little to recommend it to adults.

w Winston Miller, *novel* George Agnew Chamberlain *d* Henry Levin *ph* Wilfrid Cline *songs* Sammy Fain, Paul Francis Webster

Pat Boone, Shirley Jones, Dolores Michaels, Arthur O'Connell, Jeanette Nolan
† A remake of *Home in Indiana*.

AAN: title song (*m* Sammy Fain, *ly* Paul Francis Webster)

April Showers*
US 1948 94m bw
Warner (William Jacobs)

In a family vaudeville act, Dad takes to drink.
Hoary musical melodrama enlivened by occasional acts.

w Peter Milne *d* James V. Kern *ph* Carl Guthrie *md* Ray Heindorf *m adaptation* Max Steiner *songs* various

Jack Carson, Robert Alda, Ann Sothern, Robert Ellis, S. Z. Sakall

The Arab see The Barbarian

Arabella
US / Italy 1969 91m Technicolor

A female confidence trickster needs the money to pay her grandmother's back taxes. Floppy, tedious comedy adventure with an international cast all at sea. Virna Lisi, James Fox, Terry-Thomas, Margaret Rutherford. Written by Adriano Barocco; directed by Mauro Bolognini; for Cram Film / Universal.

Arabesque**
US 1966 118m Technicolor Panavision
Universal (Stanley Donen)

An Oxford professor is asked by Middle Eastern oil magnates to decipher a hieroglyphic, and finds afterwards that he is marked for assassination.
The ultimate in sixties spy kaleidoscopes, in which the working out of the plot matters much less than the stars, the jokes and the lavish backgrounds. Fast moving, amusing and utterly forgettable.

w Julian Mitchell, Stanley Price, Pierre Marton, *novel* The Cipher by Gordon Votler *d* Stanley Donen *ph Christopher Challis* *ad* Reece Pemberton *m* Henry Mancini

Gregory Peck, Sophia Loren, *Alan Badel*, Kieron Moore, Carl Duering

'Nothing could look more "with it", or somehow matter less.'—*MFB*

'A strikingly visual chase and intrigue yarn.'—*Robert Windeler*

'All rather too flashy for comfort.'—*Sight and Sound*

† Pierre Marton was a pen name for Peter Stone.

Arabian Adventure
GB 1979 98m colour
Badger Films / John Dark

The dictator of Jadur promises his daughter's hand in marriage if a young prince will seek and find a magic rose.
Artless juggling of elements from *The Thief of Baghdad*, including magic carpets, monsters and a bottle djinn.

w Brian Hayles *d* Kevin Connor *ph* Alan Hume *m* Ken Thorne *pd* Elliot Scott
Christopher Lee, Oliver Tobias, Mickey Rooney, Milo O'Shea, Elizabeth Welch, Peter Cushing, Capucine

'Resolutely well mounted, but somehow lacking that necessary fillip of Hollywood vulgarity or exuberance.'—*John Pym, MFB*

Arabian Nights*
US 1942 86m Technicolor
Universal (Walter Wanger)

The Caliph of Baghdad is deposed by his half-brother but wins back his throne with the help of a dancer and an acrobat.
Well presented oriental adventure which has nothing to do with its source material but entertained multitudes in search of relief from total war and was followed by several vaguely similar slices of hokum with the same stars.

w Michael Hogan *d John Rawlins* *ph* Milton Krasner, William V. Skall, W. Howard Greene *m* Frank Skinner

Jon Hall, Maria Montez, Sabu, Leif Erickson, Thomas Gomez, Turhan Bey, John Qualen, Billy Gilbert, Shemp Howard

AAN: Milton Krasner, William V. Skall, W. Howard Greene; Frank Skinner

Arabian Nights
Italy 1980 155m Technicolor

A travelling prince listens to three erotic stories. Unappealing, too realistic trilogy which the director saw as a companion to his *Canterbury Tales* and *The Decameron*. The public saw it as a lengthy bore. Ninetto Davoli, Franco Merli, Ines Pellegrini, Luiginia Rocci. Written and directed by Pier Paolo Pasolini; for Alberto Grimaldi

'The story of an outcast and a killer!'
Arch of Triumph*
US 1948 120m bw
Enterprise (Lewis Milestone)

In postwar Paris, an embittered refugee seeks his former Nazi tormentor and has a tragic romance with a would-be suicide.
Doleful, set-bound melodrama knee-deep in misery and artificial melodramatics. An expensive, ambitious failure, both commercially and artistically, but an interesting one.

w Lewis Milestone, Harry Brown, *novel* Erich Maria Remarque *d* Lewis Milestone *ph* Russell Metty *m* Leonard Gruenberg *md* Morris Stoloff

Ingrid Bergman, Charles Boyer, Charles Laughton, Louis Calhern

† The film cost 5 million dollars and grossed 1.5 million.
†† The story was remade for TV in 1984.

Are Husbands Necessary?
US 1942 79m bw
Paramount

A bickering couple decide to adopt a baby. Mild marital comedy in a familiar mould.

w Tess Slesinger, Frank Davis, *novel* Mr and Mrs Cugat by Isabel Scott Rorick *d* Norman Taurog *ph* Charles Lang *m* Robert Emmett Dolan

Ray Milland, Betty Field, Patricia Morison, Eugene Pallette, Charles Dingle, Cecil Kellaway, Leif Erickson, Richard Haydn, Elizabeth Risdon

'A chaos of farcical situations, conceived without gusto and played without conviction.'—*Richard Mallett, Punch*

Are These Our Children?
US 1931 75m bw

A teenager gets into bad company and ends up facing the electric chair. Shapeless and uncompelling moralistic farrago of no entertainment value. Eric Linden, Rochelle Hudson, Arline Judge, Ben Alexander, Robert Quirk, Beryl Mercer. Written and directed by Wesley Ruggles (screenplay by Howard Estabrook); for RKO.

Are These Our Parents?
US 1944 74m bw

Parents neglect their children, who become suspects in a murder case. Cheap yellow press sensationalism without much production expertise to back it up. Helen Vinson, Lyle Talbot, Ivan Lebedeff, Addison Richards. Written by Michel Jacoby and Hilary Lynn; directed by William Nigh for Jeffrey Bernerd / Monogram. 'Juvenile delinquency yarn is a dualer, twenty years too late; must rely on exploitation for biz.'—*Variety*
(GB title: *They Are Guilty*)

Are You a Mason?
GB 1934 70m bw
Real Art

A stockbroker has been pretending to be a Masonic grand master so that he can get out nights. Fairly simple-minded farce which could have done with slicker production. Sonnie Hale, Robertson Hare, Davy Burnaby, Gwyneth Lloyd, Bertha Belmore. Written by H. Fowler Mear from the farce by Leo Dietrichstein and Emmanuel Lederer; directed by Henry Edwards; for Twickenham.

Are You Being Served?
GB 1977 95m Technicolor
EMI (Andrew Mitchell)

The staff of the clothing section of a department store go on holiday to the Costa Plonka.
Feeble enlargement of an old-fashioned but very popular TV series relying heavily on sexual badinage and ancient jokes.

w Jeremy Lloyd, David Croft *d* Bob Kellett *ph* Jack Atcheler *m* various

John Inman, Frank Thornton, Mollie Sugden, Trevor Bannister, Wendy Richard, Arthur Brough, Nicholas Smith, Arthur English, Harold Bennett, Glyn Houston

'A withering selection of patent British puns.'—*John Pym, MFB*

Are You Listening?
US 1932 73m bw

A radio continuity announcer accidentally kills his wife. Curious disjointed melodrama, the sidelights on the new radio business being its main interest. William Haines, Karen Morley, Madge Evans, Anita Page, Neil Hamilton, Wallace Ford, Jean Hersholt. Written by Dwight Taylor from the Collier's serial by J. P. McEvoy; directed by Harry Beaumont; for MGM.

Are You With It?*
US 1948 90m bw
Universal-International (Robert Arthur)

An insurance executive with doubts joins a fun fair and has a whale of a time.
Pleasantly lively low-budget musical.

w Oscar Brodney, *musical comedy* Sam Perrin, George Balzer *d* Jack Hively *ph* Maury Gertsman *md* Walter Scharf *songs* Sidney Miller, Inez James

Donald O'Connor, Olga San Juan, Martha Stewart, Lew Parker

Arena
US 1953 83m Anscocolor 3-D
MGM (Arthur M. Loew Jnr)

A rodeo rider regains his wife and his sense when his best friend is killed.
Routine actioner, distinguished by 3-D camerawork.

w Harold Jack Bloom *d* Richard Fleischer *ph* Paul C. Vogel *m* Rudolph G. Kopp

Gig Young, Jean Hagen, Polly Bergen, Henry Morgan, Barbara Lawrence, Robert Horton, Lee Van Cleef

Aren't Men Beasts!*
GB 1937 66m bw
BIP (Walter Mycroft)

A dentist poses as his aunt to stop a plot to prevent his son's marriage.
Archetypal British star farce.

w Marjorie Deans, William Freshman, *play* Vernon Sylvaine *d* Graham Cutts *ph* Roy Kellino

Robertson Hare, Alfred Drayton, June Clyde, Billy Milton, Judy Kelly

Aren't We All?
GB 1932 67m bw

A society wife commits a momentary indiscretion. A pale shadow of the theatrical success of the twenties. Gertrude Lawrence, Hugh Wakefield, Owen Nares, Harold Huth, Marie Lohr, Renée Gadd, Aubrey Mather. Written by Basil Mason from the play by Frederick Lonsdale; directed by Harry Lachman and Rudolf Maté; for Paramount British.

L'Argent*
Switzerland / France 1983 84m colour
EOS / Marion's Films / FR3 (Jean-Marc Henchoz)

A tragic chain of events is started when a forged note is passed in a photographer's shop.
A bleak Bressonian study of conscience, fate and atonement.

w,d Robert Bresson, *story* The False Note by Leo Tolstoy *ph* Emmanuel Machuel, Pasqualino de Santis *m* from Bach

Christian Patey, Sylvie Van Den Elsen, Michel Briguet, Caroline Lang

Argentine Nights
US 1940 75m bw

The Ritz Brothers and the Andrews Sisters head for Argentina to avoid their creditors. Fair low-budget musical. Written by Arthur Horman, Ray Golden and Sid Kuller; directed by Albert S. Rogell; for Universal.

Ariane
Germany 1931 78m bw

An innocent young girl falls for a man of the world and makes him think she is a cocotte. Sophisticated comedy later remade as *Love in the Afternoon*; this version is interesting chiefly for its presentation of a new star. *Elisabeth Bergner*, Rudolf Forster, Annemarie Steinsieck, Hertha Guthmar. Written by Paul Czinner and Carl Mayer from the novel by Claude Anet; directed by Paul Czinner; for Nerofilm.

'Here's the gay, glorious story of a war correspondent and a war ace . . . a romance that could happen only in 1940!'

Arise My Love***
US 1940 113m bw
Paramount (Arthur Hornblow Jnr)

American reporters in Europe and in love survive the Spanish Civil War, a wrathful editor in Paris and the sinking of the *Athenia*. Unique sophisticated entertainment gleaned from the century's grimmest headlines, ending with a plea against American isolationism. A significant and stylish comedy melodrama.

w Charles Brackett, Billy Wilder d Mitchell Leisen ph Charles Lang *m* Victor Young

Claudette Colbert, Ray Milland, Walter Abel (who as the harassed editor inaugurated his celebrated line 'I'm not happy. I'm not happy at all . . .'), Dennis O'Keefe, George Zucco, Dick Purcell

'Against the background of European fisticuffs, Paramount brings forth a film of absorbing romantic interest, proving that love will find a way through the hazards of air raids, torpedo attacks and enemy invasions.'—*Variety*

† Joel McCrea was originally cast for the Milland role.

AA: original story (Benjamin Glazer, John S. Toldy)
AAN: Charles Lang; Victor Young

The Aristocats**
US 1970 78m Technicolor
Walt Disney

Two cats are deliberately lost by a butler who fears they will inherit his mistress's wealth; but a variety of animal friends restore them to their rightful place.
Cartoon feature, a moderate example of the studio's work after Disney's death, with rather too few felicitous moments.

w Larry Clemmons and others *d* Wolfgang Reitherman

Arizona
US 1941 125m bw
Columbia (Wesley Ruggles)

A Tucson wildcat meets her match in a travelling Missourian who helps her outwit villains who are sabotaging her wagon trains. Loosely built, deliberately paced western which for all its pretensions makes very little impact.

w Claude Binyon *d* Wesley Ruggles *ph* Joseph Walker, Harry Hollenberger, Fayte Brown *m* Victor Young

Jean Arthur, William Holden, Warren William, Porter Hall, Paul Harvey, George Chandler, Byron Foulger, Regis Toomey, Edgar Buchanan

'Lacks the sweep and dramatic impulse that would have made it a great picture.'—*Variety*

AAN: Victor Young

Arizona Bushwhackers
US 1968 86m Techniscope
Paramount (A. C. Lyles)

A Confederate prisoner is given a chance as a western sheriff.
Stolid western, notable only, as is usual with this producer, for its gallery of ageing but still reliable familiar faces.

w Steve Fisher *d* Lesley Selander *ph* Lester Shorr *m* Jimmie Haskell

Howard Keel, Yvonne de Carlo, Brian Donlevy, John Ireland, Marilyn Maxwell, Scott Brady, Barton Maclane, James Craig

The Arizona Kid
US 1930 84m bw

A wanted bandit finds a secret gold mine in Utah. Disappointing semi-sequel to *In Old Arizona*: same star, much less talent to back him up. Warner Baxter, Mona Maris, Carole Lombard, Theodore Von Eltz. Written by Ralph Block; directed by Alfred Santell; for Fox.

Arizona Raiders
US 1965 88m Techniscope

Two of Quantrell's Raiders are offered a pardon if they will round up renegades. Stereotyped western, poorly processed. Audie Murphy, Michael Dante, Ben Cooper, Buster Crabbe, Gloria Talbott. Written by Alex Gottleib and Mary and Willard Willingham; directed by William Witney; for Admiral / Columbia.

Arizona to Broadway
US 1933 66m bw

A small-town girl in the big city is changed by a con man. Fast-moving support which has its moments. James Dunn, Joan Bennett, Herbert Mundin, Sammy Cohen, Theodore von Eltz, J. Carrol Naish, Walter Catlett. Written by William Conselman, Henry Johnson; directed by James Tinling; for Fox.

The Arizonian
US 1935 72m bw

Lawless Silver City gets a reform marshal. Adequate first feature western, but not a spectacular. Richard Dix, Margot Grahame, Preston Foster, Louis Calhern. Written by Dudley Nichols; directed by Charles Vidor; for RKO. 'Through the names it can slip into the keys where westerns rarely treat, and where, therefore, horse operas are regarded as refreshing novelties.'—*Variety*

The Arkansas Traveller
US 1938 85m bw

A small-town widow is helped to keep her newspaper going by a stranger who happens to be passing through. Archetypal mid-American fantasy. Bob Burns, Fay Bainter, Jean Parker, Irvin S. Cobb. Written by Viola Brothers Shore, George Sessions Perry, from a story by Jack Cunningham; directed by Alfred Santell; for Paramount.

'It will get over nicely in the key spots, but its biggest b.o. will be in the nabes and smaller communities.'—*Variety*

ARISE MY LOVE. In spite of a screenplay which was continually revised during shooting to keep up with volatile world events, Ray Milland and Claudette Colbert memorably kept up with Mitchell Leisen's smooth direction. George Zucco looks quizzical.

Armed Response
US 1986 85m United Color

A private eye retrieves a jade antique for a Japanese gangster. Violent low budgeter with allusions for film buffs.

David Carradine, Lee Van Cleef, Mako, Lois Hamilton, Ross Hagen. Written by T. L. Lankford; directed by Fred Olen Ray; for Paul Hertzberg / Cintel.

Armored Car Robbery*
US 1950 67m bw
RKO (Herman Schlom)

A police lieutenant leads the recovery of half a million dollars stolen by gangsters.
Good competent second feature with Los Angeles locations and detailed observation of police methods.

w Earl Felton, Gerald Drayson Adams
d Richard Fleischer *ph* Guy Roe
m Constantin Bakaleinikoff

Charles McGraw, Adele Jergens, William Talman, Douglas Fowley, Steve Brodie

Armored Command
US 1961 105m bw
Allied Artists (Ron W. Alcorn)

During the Battle of the Bulge, a ravishing Nazi spy is infiltrated into an American army outpost.
Incredible Mata Hari melodrama posing as a war film, nicely shot in bleak snowscapes. Not exactly rewarding, but unusual.

w Ron W. Alcorn *d* Byron Haskin *ph* Ernest Haller *m* Bert Grund

Howard Keel, Tina Louise, Burt Reynolds, Earl Holliman, Warner Anderson, Carleton Young, Marty Ingels

Arms and the Man
GB 1932 85m bw

A soldier who finds discretion the better part of valour hides in a girl's bedroom. Faithful but uninspired version of Bernard Shaw's play. Barry Jones, Anne Grey, Angela Baddeley. Directed by Cecil Lewis; for BIP / Wardour.

Army Girl
US 1938 90m bw

Old loyalties flare at an army post when tanks replace cavalry troops. Modest flagwaver which got by at the time. Madge Evans, Preston Foster, James Gleason, H. B. Warner, Ruth Donnelly, Neil Hamilton, Billy Gilbert, Heather Angel, Ralph Morgan. Written by Barry Trivers and Sam Ornitz; directed by George Nicholls Jnr; for Republic.

(GB title: *The Last of the Cavalry*.)

'Thoroughly entertaining . . . suitable as single in smaller spots, or action half of double bill in keys.'—*Variety*. AAN: Ernest Miller, photography; Victor Young, music.

The Arnelo Affair
US 1946 86m bw

Lawyer's wife gets involved with nightclub owner. Yawnworthy murder melodrama. George Murphy, Frances Gifford, John Hodiak, Eve Arden. Written and directed by Arch Oboler; for MGM.

Arnold
US 1973 95m De Luxe
Avco / Fenady (Charles A. Pratt, Andrew Fenady)

Via cassette recordings, a dead man toys with his would-be heirs, and several are murdered. Unpleasant and very laboured black comedy on the lines of *And Then There Were None* and a hundred others, all better than this.

w Jameson Brewer, John Fenton Murray *d* Georg Fenady *ph* William Jurgenson *m* George Duning

Stella Stevens, Roddy McDowell, Elsa Lanchester, Shani Wallis, Farley Granger, Victor Buono, John McGiver, Bernard Fox, Patric Knowles

† Apparently made back to back with *Terror in the Wax Museum*, which has very similar credits.

Around the World
US 1943 81m bw
RKO (Allan Dwan)

Kay Kyser's band goes on a world tour to entertain troops overseas.
Typical wartime patriotic musical, now of sociological interest.

w Ralph Spence *d* Allan Dwan *ph* Russell Metty *md* Constantin Bakaleinikoff *m* George Duning *songs* Jimmy McHugh, Harold Adamson

Kay Kyser, Ish Kabibble, Ginny Simms, Joan Davis, Mischa Auer

'It's a wonderful world, if you'll only take the time to go around it!'

Around the World in Eighty Days***
US 1956 178m Technicolor Todd-AO
UA / *Michael Todd*

A Victorian gentleman and his valet win a bet that they can go round the world in eighty days.
Amiable large-scale pageant resolving itself into a number of sketches, which could have been much sharper, separated by wide screen spectacle. What was breathtaking at the time seems generally slow and blunted in retrospect, but the fascination of recognizing 44 cameo stars remains. The film is less an exercise in traditional skills than a tribute to its producer's energy.

w James Poe, John Farrow, S. J. Perelman, *novel* Jules Verne *d* Michael Anderson, Kevin McClory *ph Lionel Lindon m Victor Young titles Saul Bass*

David Niven, Cantinflas, Robert Newton, Shirley Maclaine, Charles Boyer, Joe E. Brown, Martine Carol, John Carradine, Charles Coburn, *Ronald Colman*, Melville Cooper, *Noel Coward*, Finlay Currie, Reginald Denny, Andy Devine, Marlene Dietrich, Luis Dominguin, Fernandel, *John Gielgud*, Hermione Gingold, Jose Greco, Cedric Hardwicke, Trevor Howard, Glynis Johns, *Buster Keaton*, Evelyn Keyes, Beatrice Lillie, Peter Lorre, Edmund Lowe, A. E. Matthews, Mike Mazurki, Tim McCoy, Victor McLaglen, John Mills, Alan Mowbray, Robert Morley, Jack Oakie, George Raft, Gilbert Roland, Cesar Romero, Frank Sinatra, *Red Skelton*, Ronald Squire, Basil Sidney, *Harcourt Williams*, Ed Murrow

'Michael Todd's "show", shorn of the ballyhoo and to critics not mollified by parties and sweetmeats, is a film like any other, only twice as long as most . . . the shots of trains and boats seem endless.'—*David Robinson*

AA: best picture; James Poe, John Farrow, S. J. Perelman; Lionel Lindon; Victor Young
AAN: Michael Anderson

Around the World in Eighty Minutes
US 1931 80m bw

An account of Douglas Fairbanks' travels, mainly in the Far East. Awfully padded travelogue which seems to have been a bore even at the time, despite a few magic-carpet tricks. Written by Robert E. Sherwood; directed by Douglas Fairbanks and Victor Fleming; for United Artists. 'Fairbanks enlivens much of the drab footage with his acrobatics.'—*Variety*

Around the World under the Sea
US 1966 110m Metrocolor Panavision
MGM / Ivan Tors (Andrew Marton)

An ultra-modern underwater craft travels around the seabed fixing sensors to give early warning of volcanoes.
Earnest, dullish, elementary sci-fi with cardboard characters providing routine five men-one woman skirmishes.

w Arthur Weiss, Art Arthur *d* Andrew Marton, Ricou Browning *ph* Clifford Poland, Lamar Boren *m* Harry Sukman

Lloyd Bridges, Shirley Eaton, Brian Kelly, David McCallum, Keenan Wynn, Marshall Thompson, Gary Merrill

The Arrangement**
US 1969 127m Technicolor Panavision
Warner / Athena (Elia Kazan)

A wealthy advertising man fails in a suicide attempt and spends his convalescence reflecting on his unsatisfactory emotional life. A lush, all-American melodrama, rich in technique but peopled by characters who have nothing to say; the film makes no discernible point except as a well-acted tirade against the compromises of modern urban living.

wd Elia Kazan, from his own novel *ph Robert Surtees m* David Amram *pd* Malcolm C. Bert

Kirk Douglas, Faye Dunaway, Deborah Kerr, Richard Boone, Hume Cronyn

'The sort of collage that won't fit together, no matter where you stand.'—*PS*

'As dead as a flower arrangement in an undertaker's parlour . . . all possible cinematic clevernesses—usually yesterday's—are dragged out in an endless parade, to illustrate a senseless and banal story that reels from platitude to platitude.'—*John Simon*

Arrest Bulldog Drummond: see Bulldog Drummond

Arrowhead
US 1953 105m Technicolor 3D
Paramount (Nat Holt)

Enmity between an army scout and an Indian chief is resolved by single combat.
Standard western, good-looking but rather lifeless.

w Charles Marquis Warren, *novel* W. R. Burnett *d* Charles Marquis Warren *ph* Ray Rennahan *m* Paul Sawtell

Charlton Heston, Jack Palance, Katy Jurado, Brian Keith, Milburn Stone

Arrowsmith*
US 1931 108m bw
Samuel Goldwyn

The self-sacrificing career of a doctor. Emotionally satisfactory, dramatically slow and unsurprising variation on a theme which has since been treated far too often.

w Sidney Howard, *novel* Sinclair Lewis *d* John Ford *ph* Ray June *m* Alfred Newman

Ronald Colman, Helen Hayes, Richard Bennett, Myrna Loy, Charlotte Henry, Beulah Bondi, A. E. Anson

'Pictures would do better to stay clear of these elaborately biographical novels with their wealth of actionless detail. . . . That portion of the citizenry which read the Sinclair Lewis novel will probably be in sympathy with the film, those who didn't will not be prone to deem this macabre tale entertainment.'—*Variety*

† The negative was later cut to about 89m for reissue, and this version, virtually eliminating Myrna Loy, is the only one now available.

AAN: best picture; Sidney Howard; Ray June

Arsenal**
USSR 1929 99m (16 fps) bw silent
VUFKU

The 1914 war is made worse by strikes at home.
Patchy propagandist drama with brilliant sequences.

wd Alexander Dovzhenko ph Danylo Demutsky

S. Svashenko, A. Buchma, M. Nademsky

'A romantic and lyrical masterpiece.'—*Georges Sadoul*

The Arsenal Stadium Mystery
GB 1939 85m bw

A footballer is poisoned during a match. Brisk little mystery, with an amiable star performance. *Leslie Banks*, Greta Gynt, Esmond Knight, Brian Worth. Written by Thorold Dickinson and Donald Bull, from the novel by Leonard Gribble; directed by Thorold Dickinson; for G&S / GFD.

'This picture is as good to watch as either of the *Thin Man* films, and Dickinson gives us wit instead of facetiousness—wit of cutting and wit of angle.'—*Graham Greene*

Arsène Lupin**
US 1932 75m bw
MGM

The Parisian gentleman thief accomplishes some daring robberies and is almost caught stealing the Mona Lisa.
Amusing crook comedy with a few flat passages but much sparkle in between, and a lively finale.

w Carey Wilson, Lenore Coffee, Bayard Veiller *d* Jack Conway *ph* Oliver Marsh

John Barrymore, Lionel Barrymore, Karen Morley, Tully Marshall, John Miljan

'First screen appearance of John and Lionel together and their acting of this old standard detective story ensures its box office in spite of the absence of other qualities that make for notable screen successes. . . . At least it addresses itself to a higher class of fans than the lurid type of dime novel subject.'—*Variety*

Arsène Lupin Returns
US 1938 81m bw
MGM (John W. Considine Jnr)

The reformed jewel thief helps an American detective to track down a French criminal.
Smooth but disappointingly scripted sequel which never quite rises to a climax despite sympathetic casting.

w James Kevin McGuinness, Howard Emmett Rogers, George Harmon Coxe *d* George Fitzmaurice *ph* George Folsey *m* Franz Waxman

Melvyn Douglas, Warren William, Virginia Bruce, John Halliday, Nat Pendleton, Monty Woolley, George Zucco, E. E. Clive

'A first-class mystery jewel theft combo . . . for the top side of the marquee pairing, missing A classification quite a little, but still being okay.'—*Variety*

Arsenic and Old Lace***
US 1942 (released 1944) 118m bw
Warner (Frank Capra)

Two dear, well-meaning old ladies invite lonely old men to their Brooklyn home, poison them with elderberry wine, and have their mad brother, who believes the corpses are yellow fever victims, bury them in the cellar. A homicidal nephew then turns up with bodies of his own.
A model for stage play adaptations, this famous black farce provided a frenzy of hilarious activity, and its flippant attitude to death was better received in wartime than would have been the case earlier or later. The director coaxes some perfect if overstated performances from his star cast, and added his own flair for perpetuating a hubbub.

w Julius J. and Philip G. Epstein, from the play by Joseph Kesselring with help from Howard Lindsay and Russell Crouse *d Frank Capra ph Sol Polito m* Max Steiner

Cary Grant (Mortimer Brewster), *Josephine Hull* (Abby Brewster), *Jean Adair* (Martha Brewster), Priscilla Lane (Elaine Harper), Raymond Massey (Jonathan Brewster), *John Alexander* (Teddy Brewster), Peter Lorre (Dr Einstein), James Gleason (Lt Rooney), Jack Carson (Officer O'Hara), Edward Everett Horton (Mr Witherspoon), Grant Mitchell (Reverend Harper)

MORTIMER: 'Insanity runs in my family. It practically gallops.'

MARTHA: 'One of our gentlemen found time to say "How delicious!" before he died. . . .'

The Art of Love
US 1965 99m Technicolor
Universal / Cherokee / Ross Hunter

To stimulate interest in his work, a penniless artist fakes suicide, subsequently becoming so famous that he finds it difficult to reappear.
A pleasant black comedy idea is buried under lush production, dull direction and a host of unattractive Parisian sets.

w Carl Reiner *d* Norman Jewison *ph* Russell Metty *m* Cy Coleman

James Garner, Dick Van Dyke, Angie Dickinson, Elke Sommer, Ethel Merman, Pierre Olaf

'I race cars, I play tennis, I fondle women, but I have weekends off and I am my own boss!'

Arthur*
US 1981 97m Technicolor
Warner / Orion (Robert Greenhut)

A rich New York layabout is forced to moderate his life style in order to qualify for his inheritance.
An unattractive excuse for the star to do his drunk act. In effect his thunder was stolen by Gielgud as the valet who is not above a few choice four-letter words; but over the whole enterprise hung a pall of desperation. It is a sign of its times that it made a lot of money.

wd Steve Gordon *ph* Fred Schuler *m* Burt Bacharach *pd* Stephen Hendrikson

Dudley Moore, *John Gielgud*, Liza Minnelli, Geraldine Fitzgerald, Jill Eikenberry, Stephen Elliott

'It comes as no surprise to find the funniest sequences packed into the first half-hour.'—*Martyn Auty, MFB*

'Gielgud may be the most poised and confident funnyman you'll ever see.'—*New Yorker*

'Arthur may be the surprise hit of 1981, but to me he's a pain in the neck.'—*Margaret Hinxman, Daily Mail*

† In *Arthur II: On the Rocks* (1988, 113m, directed by Bud Yorkin) the character tried to sober up with the aid of Liza Minnelli.

AA: John Gielgud (supporting actor)
AAN: screenplay; Dudley Moore

Artistes at the Top of the Big Top: Disorientated**
West Germany 1968 103m bw / colour
Kairos Film

The daughter of a dead trapezist dreams of creating the ideal circus with a moral for mankind but step by step gives up her ambition.
A melancholy satire, told in fragmented fashion with some brilliant tricks and memorable sequences.

wd Alexander Kluge ph Gunther Hörmann, Thomas Mauch

Hannelore Hoger, Siegfried Graue, Alfred Edel, Bernd Höltz

'Those who interpret it simply as an allegory of German politics or of the present crisis in film-making narrow it unnecessarily.'—*Jan Dawson, MFB*

Artists and Models*
US 1937 97m bw
Paramount (Lewis E. Gensler)

An advertising man has to find the right girl as symbol for a silverware company.
Fairly stylish comedy musical with many elements typical of its studio.

w Walter de Leon, Francis Martin *d* Raoul Walsh *ph* Victor Milner *m* Victor Young *songs* various

Jack Benny, Ida Lupino, Richard Arlen, Gail Patrick, Ben Blue, Judy Canova, Martha Raye, Donald Meek, Hedda Hopper, André Kostelanetz and his Orchestra, Louis Armstrong and his Orchestra

'Should be a box-office bonanza for exhibitors. It holds enough variety, comedy, colour, spectacle, flash, dash and novelty for a couple of pictures.'—*Variety*

AAN: song 'Whispers in the Dark' (*m* Frederick Hollander, *ly* Leo Robin)

Artists and Models*
US 1955 109m Technicolor Vistavision
Paramount / Hal B. Wallis

A goonish young man receives telepathic top secret information in his nightmares, which are used by his artist friend in comic strips; foreign agents and the CIA get interested.
A good zany idea is worked into an overlong dyspeptic comedy which neither the stars nor frantic treatment can hope to save.

w Frank Tashlin, Don McGuire *d* Frank Tashlin *ph* Daniel Fapp *m* Walter Scharf

Dean Martin, Jerry Lewis, Shirley Maclaine, Dorothy Malone, Eddie Mayehoff, Eva Gabor, Anita Ekberg, George 'Foghorn' Winslow, Jack Elam

'It's an ooh-la-lalapalooza!'

Artists and Models Abroad*
US 1938 90m bw
Paramount (Arthur Hornblow Jnr)
GB title: *Stranded in Paris*

Stranded in Paris, a troupe of girls and their manager are helped by a Texas oil millionaire. Generally agreeable comedy musical with emphasis on fashion.

w Howard Lindsay, Russell Crouse, Ken Englund *d Mitchell Leisen* *ph* Ted Tetzlaff *md* Borris Morros *songs* various *ad Hans Dreier, Ernest Fegte*

Jack Benny, Joan Bennett, Mary Boland, Charley Grapewin, Joyce Compton, the Yacht Club Boys, Fritz Feld, G. P. Huntley, Monty Woolley

'Straight farce comedy. The models are in a fashion show and the artists are missing entirely.'—*Variety*

The Aryan*
US 1916 75m (16 fps) bw silent
Triangle (Thomas Ince)

A gold prospector is cheated by a woman and becomes an outlaw.
Striking early star western.

w C. Gardner Sullivan *d* William S. Hart, Clifford Smith *ph* Joseph August, Clyde de Vinna

William S. Hart, Bessie Love, Louise Glaum, Hershall Mayall

As Husbands Go
US 1934 65m bw

Lover and husband become friends, making infidelity impossible. Minor smart-set comedy from a then popular play. Warner Baxter, Helen Vinson, Warner Oland, G. P. Huntley Jnr, Catherine Doucet. Written by Sam Behrman and Sonia Levien from the play by Rachel Crothers; directed by Hamilton McFadden; for Jesse Lasky / Fox. 'Pleasant entertainment all the way, but a lack of action will bore children and annoy that not inconsiderable body of Americans who violently resent too much suavity of speech and manner.'—*Variety*

As Long as They're Happy*
GB 1955 91m Eastmancolor
Rank / Regroup (Raymond Stross)

The suburban home of a London stockbroker is invaded by an American sob singer.
Frantic farce expanded from a stage satire of the Johnnie Ray cult; a patchy but sometimes funny star vehicle.

w Alan Melvile, *play* Vernon Sylvaine *d* J. Lee-Thompson *ph* Gilbert Taylor *m* Stanley Black

Jack Buchanan, Brenda de Banzie, Diana Dors, Jean Carson, Janette Scott, Susan Stephen, Jerry Wayne, Hugh McDermott

As Long as You're Near Me
West Germany 1954 94m colour

A film director almost ruins a small-part actress's life by insisting on making her a star. Reasonably absorbing drama (original title: *Solange Du da bist*), chiefly remarkable for being a great hit in the US when dubbed. O. W. Fischer, Hardy Kruger, Maria Schell. Written by Jochen Huth; directed by Harold Braun; for Warner.

As the Earth Turns
US 1934 73m bw

The problems of three farming families in Maine. Reliable rustic soap opera, pretty well presented. Jean Muir, Donald Woods, Emily Lowry, William Janney, David Landau, Dorothy Peterson. Written by Ernest Pascal from the book by Gladys Hasty Carroll; directed by Alfred E. Green; for Warners. 'What it may lack in box office, it makes up in entertainment . . . the sort of story that commands attention and favour.'—*Variety*

'You don't need us to tell you not to miss this film. You couldn't be kept away!'

As You Desire Me*
US 1931 71m bw
MGM (George Fitzmaurice)

The amnesiac mistress of a novelist rediscovers her real husband and falls in love with him again.
Interesting star vehicle with good cast and production.

w Gene Markey, *play* Luigi Pirandello *d* George Fitzmaurice *ph* William Daniels

Greta Garbo, Melvyn Douglas, Erich Von Stroheim, Owen Moore, Hedda Hopper, Rafaela Ottiano

'Pretty subtle for the generality of fans. It was more of a courageous gesture towards production ideals than good business judgement that dictated its choice for filming in the first place.'—*Variety*

As You Like It*
GB 1936 96m bw
TCF / Inter-Allied (Joseph M. Schenck, Paul Czinner)

The fortunes of an exiled king take a turn in the Forest of Arden.
Stylized, rather effete but often amusing version of Shakespeare's pastoral comedy.

w J. M. Barrie, Robert Cullen, *play* William Shakespeare *d* Paul Czinner *ph* Harold Rosson *m* William Walton

Elisabeth Bergner, Laurence Olivier, Sophie Stewart, Leon Quartermaine, Henry Ainley, Richard Ainley, Felix Aylmer, Mackenzie Ward, Aubrey Mather, John Laurie, Peter Bull

'Rather too respectably lighthearted, but by no means a contemptible production.'—*New Yorker, 1978*

'There are far too many dull middle-length shots from a fixed camera, so that we might just as well be seated in the circle above the deep wide stage at Drury Lane.'—*Graham Greene*

As Young as You Feel*
US 1951 77m bw
TCF (Lamar Trotti)

An elderly employee, forced to retire, impersonates the company president, saves the firm from bankruptcy, and proves his continued worth.
Good-natured comedy, ably presented.

w Lamar Trotti, *story* Paddy Chayevsky *d* Harmon Jones *ph* Joe MacDonald *m* Cyril Mockridge

Monty Woolley, Constance Bennett, Thelma Ritter, David Wayne, Jean Peters, Marilyn Monroe, Allyn Joslyn, Albert Dekker

Ascendancy*
GB 1982 85m colour
British Film Institute Production Board (Penny Clark, Ian Elsey)

In 1920 Belfast a shipyard owner's daughter, shocked by the death of her brother in the war, cannot come to terms with the sectarian slaughter around her.
Unilluminatingly argumentative character study which fails to make its purpose very clear despite a stunning central performance.

w Edward Bennett, Nigel Gearing *d* Edward Bennett *ph* Clive Tickner *m* Ronnie Leahy

Julie Covington, Ian Charleson, John Phillips, Susan Engel, Philip Locke

Ash Wednesday
US 1973 99m Technicolor
Sagittarius (Dominick Dunne)

An ageing American beauty rejuvenates herself via plastic surgery, leads a vivid sex life, and leaves her stolid husband.
The bloodthirsty operation scenes are revolting, yet this joyless saga seems meant as a celebration of the wonders of cosmetic surgery and Sex for the Aged. Hypnotic but hardly rewarding.

w Jean Claude Tramont *d* Larry Peerce *ph* Ennio Guarnieri *m* Maurice Jarre

Elizabeth Taylor, Henry Fonda, Helmut Berger, Keith Baxter, Maurice Teynac

'Endless shots of Elizabeth Taylor expensively attired against the plush background of Cortina.'—*Michael Billington, Illustrated London News*

'A long-drawn-out ghoulish commercial for cosmetic surgery—made apparently for people who can't think of anything to do with their lives but go backwards.'—*Pauline Kael*

Ashanti
Switzerland 1979 117m Panavision Technicolor
Columbia / Beverly (Luciano Sacripanti)

In West Africa, the wife of a member of the World Health Organization is seized by slave traders.
Absurd and rather unattractively brutal adventure story, decked out with appearances by guest stars.

w Stephen Geller, *novel* Ebano by Alberto Vasquez-Figueroa *d* Richard Fleischer *ph* Aldo Tonti *m* Michael Melvoin

Michael Caine, Omar Sharif, Peter Ustinov, Rex Harrison, Kabir Bedi, William Holden, Zia Mohyeddin, Beverly Johnson

Ashes and Diamonds**
Poland 1958 104m bw
Film Polski
original title: *Popiol y Diament*

A Polish partisan is confused by the apparent need to continue killing after the war is over.
A chilling account of the intellectual contradictions to which war leads, and a moving and sensitive film in its own right.

*w*d *Andrzej Wajda*, *novel* Jerzy Andrzejewski *ph* Jerzy Wojcik

Zbigniew Cybulski, Ewa Krzyzanowska, Adam Pawlikowski

Ask a Policeman**
GB 1938 82m bw
Gainsborough (Edward Black)

In a small coastal village, incompetent policemen accidentally expose smugglers who are scaring the locals with a headless horseman legend.
One of the best comedies of an incomparable team, with smart dialogue, good situations and a measure of suspense.

w Marriott Edgar, Val Guest, J. O. C. Orton d Marcel Varnel ph Derek Williams *md* Louis Levy

Will Hay, Moore Marriott, Graham Moffatt, Glennis Lorimer, *Peter Gawthorne*, *Herbert Lomas*, Charles Oliver

'A good laugh getter and safe second feature on any programme.'—*Variety*

Ask Any Girl*
US 1959 98m Metrocolor
Cinemascope
MGM / Euterpe (Joe Pasternak)

A husband-hunting receptionist in New York catches the eye of a wealthy playboy but finally settles for his elder brother.
Predictable Cinderella story with a lively but forgettable script and actors going through familiar paces.

w George Wells, *novel* Winifred Wolfe *d* Charles Walters *ph* Robert Bronner *m* Jeff Alexander

David Niven, Shirley Maclaine, Gig Young, Rod Taylor, Jim Backus, Claire Kelly

'Like a comic strip transposed to the glossy pages of *Vogue*'.—*MFB*

Asking for Trouble*
GB 1941 81m bw

A bookie poses as a big game hunter. The last opportunity to see a great music hall comic on film, his style admittedly bowdlerized. *Max Miller*, Carole Lynne, Wilfrid Hyde White, Mark Lester. Written by Oswald Mitchell and Con West; directed by Oswald Mitchell; for British National.

Aspern*
Portugal 1981 96m colour
VO / Oxala (Paulo Branco)

The French biographer of a deceased poet goes to Venice to get unpublished papers from his aged mistress.
This very well-known story (see also *The Lost Moment* and various theatrical versions) is styled with exceeding solemnity in this well-acted but boring version.

w Michael Graham, *story* Henry James *d* Eduardo de Grigorio *ph* Acacio de Almeida *m* mainly from Mozart
Alida Valli, Jean Sorel, Bulle Ogier, Ana Marta

Asphalt*
Germany 1929 101m bw
UFA

A young policeman accidentally kills his rival for a worthless girl.
Heavily expressionist melodrama, overlong but good to watch.

w Rolf Vanloo, Fred Majo, Hans Szekely *d Joe May ph* Günther Rittau

Gustav Fröhlich, Betty Amann, Else Heller, Louise Brooks

'So well produced that it is good entertainment in spite of itself.'—*Variety*

The Asphalt Jungle***
US 1950 112m bw
MGM (Arthur Hornblow Jnr)

An elderly crook comes out of prison and assembles a gang for one last robbery.
Probably the very first film to show a 'caper' from the criminals' viewpoint (a genre which has since been done to death several times over), this is a clever character study rather than a thriller, extremely well executed and indeed generally irreproachable yet somehow not a film likely to appear on many top ten lists; perhaps the writer-director stands too far back from everybody, or perhaps he just needed Humphrey Bogart.

w Ben Maddow, John Huston, *novel* W. R. Burnett *d John Huston ph* Harold Rosson *m* Miklos Rozsa

Sterling Hayden (Dix Handley), Louis Calhern (Alonzo D Emmerich), *Sam Jaffe* (Doc Erwin Riedenschneider), Jean Hagen (Doll Conovan), James Whitmore (Gus Minissi), John McIntire (Police Commissioner Hardy), Marc Lawrence (Cobby), Marilyn Monroe (Angela Phinlay), Barry Kelley (Lt Ditrich)

RIEDENSCHNEIDER: 'Crime is a left-handed form of human endeavour.'

'Where this film excels is in the fluency of its narration, the sharpness of its observation of character and the excitement of its human groupings.'—*Dilys Powell*

'That Asphalt Pavement thing is full of nasty, ugly people doing nasty things. I wouldn't walk across the room to see a thing like that.'—*Louis B. Mayer* (who was head of the studio which made it)

† Apart from imitations, the film has been directly remade as *The Badlanders*, *Cairo* and *A Cool Breeze*.

AAN: Ben Maddow, John Huston (writers); John Huston (as director); Harold Rosson; Sam Jaffe

The Asphyx
GB 1973 99m Eastmancolor
Todd AO 35
Glendale (John Brittany)

A Victorian aims to become immortal by separating the spirit of death from his body.
Interminable hocus pocus with a plethora of talk, seldom exciting but watchable because of its remarkable cast and other credits.

w Brian Comport *d* Peter Newbrook *ph* Freddie Young *m* Bill McGuffie *sp* Ted Samuels

Robert Stephens, Robert Powell, Jane Lapotaire

The Assam Garden
GB 1985 90m colour
Contemporary / Moving Picture Company (Nigel Stafford-Clark)

A widow returns from Assam to the English house where many years previously her husband had created a garden full of eastern plants, and where events now help her to free herself of the past.
Muted and somewhat ineffective treatment of a familiar television theme. Not unpleasant to watch despite obvious economies, but instantly forgettable.

w Elisabeth Bond *d* Mary McMurray *ph* Bryan Loftus *m* Richard Harvey

Deborah Kerr, Madhur Jaffrey, Alec McCowen, Zia Mohyeddin, Iain Cuthbertson

The Assassin**
Italy / France 1961 105m bw
Titanus-Vides-SGC (Franco Cristaldi)

A prosperous antique dealer is accused of murder and his unsavoury past is revealed; but when he is freed, he prides himself on his new personality.
A careful, detailed and wholly enjoyable character study, somewhere between comedy and drama.

w Elio Petri and others *d Elio Petri ph* Carlo di Palma *m* Piero Piccioni

Marcello Mastroianni, Salvo Randone, Micheline Presle, Andrea Checci

Assassin
GB 1973 83m Technicolor
Pemini (David M. Jackson)

MI5 arranges the liquidation of an Air Ministry spy.
Old hat espionage melodrama, topheavy with artiness which makes it look like an endless TV commercial.

w Michael Sloan *d* Peter Crane *ph* Brian Jonson *m* Zack Lawrence

Ian Hendry, Edward Judd, Frank Windsor, Ray Brooks, John Hart Dyke

Assassin for Hire*
GB 1951 67m bw
Merton Park

A professional killer is trapped into admitting a murder he didn't do. Taut little suspenser, quite watchable. Sydney Tafler, Ronald Howard, John Hewer, Martin Benson. Written by Rex Rienits; directed by *Michael McCarthy*; for Julian Wintle / Anglo Amalgamated.

L'Assassin habite au 21**
France 1947 83m bw
Mage / Liote
aka: *The Murderer Lives at 21*

A police detective assumes the guise of a clergyman to investigate mass killings which seem to centre on a boarding house.
Agreeable, straight-faced but tongue-in-cheek comedy thriller which was probably even funnier in French.

w,d Henri-Georges Clouzot novel S. A. Steerman *ph* Armand Thirard

Pierre Fresnay, Suzy Delair, Pierre Larquey, Noel Roquevert

Assassination
US 1986 88m TVC Color

A White House secret service man finds himself on the run with the first lady. Mildly diverting but over-mysterious chase movie, less violent than the Bronson norm. Charles Bronson, Jill Ireland, Stephen Elliott, Joe Gan Boyd, Randy Brooks, Michael Ansara. Written by Richard Sale; directed by Peter Hunt; for Pancho Kohner/Cannon.

The Assassination Bureau*
GB 1968 110m Technicolor
Paramount / Heathfield (Michael Relph)

In 1906 a lady journalist breaks up an international gang of professional killers by falling in love with their leader.
Black comedy period pastiche which resolves itself into a series of sketches leading up to a spectacular zeppelin climax. Plenty going on, but the level of wit is not high.

w Michael Relph, with Wolf Mankowitz *d* Basil Dearden *ph Geoffrey Unsworth* *m* Ron Grainer

Oliver Reed, Diana Rigg, Telly Savalas, Curt Jurgens, Philippe Noiret, Warren Mitchell, Clive Revill, Beryl Reid, Kenneth Griffith

The Assassination of the Duc de Guise*
France 1908 15m (16 fps) bw silent
Film d'Art

Henry III arranges the killing of the Duc de Guise when he comes to court.
Influential early story film.

w Henri Lavedan *d* Charles le Bargy *m* Saint-Saëns

Charles le Bargy, Albert Lambert, Gabrielle Lavinne

'For one moment, they hold history in their hands. With one terrible blow, they make it'

The Assassination of Trotsky
Italy / GB / France 1972 103m Technicolor
Dino de Laurentiis / Josef Shaftel / Cinetel (Norman Priggen, Joseph Losey)

In 1940, Trotsky is hiding out in Mexico; a Stalinist infiltrates his presence and kills him with an ice pick.
Glum historical reconstruction with much fictitious padding; basically undramatic.

w Nicholas Mosley, Masolino d'Amico *d* Joseph Losey *ph* Pasquale de Santis *m* Egisto Macchi

Richard Burton, Alain Delon, Romy Schneider, Valentina Cortese, Jean Desailly

'Not for anyone who knows, or cares, anything about Leon Trotsky.'—*New Yorker, 1977*

Les Assassins du Dimanche
France 1956 94m bw Cinepanoramic
EDIC
aka: *Every Second Counts*

Dozens of people help to track down a holiday car which has been driven away from a garage in a dangerous condition.
Watchable but artificial suspenser.

w Alex Joffe, Gabriel Arout *d* Alex Joffe *ph* Jean Bourgoin

Barbara Laage, Jean-Marc Thibault, Dominique Wilms, Paul Frankeur

Assault
GB 1970 91m Eastmancolor
Rank / Peter Rogers (George H. Brown)

An art mistress helps police to solve a case of multiple rape in an English village.
Old-fashioned police mystery with new-fangled shock treatment. Routine excitements.

w John Kruse, *novel* Kendal Young *d* Sidney Hayers *ph* Ken Hodges *m* Eric Rogers

Frank Finlay, Suzy Kendall, James Laurenson, Lesley-Anne Down, Freddie Jones, Tony Beckley, Anthony Ainley, Dilys Hamlett

'All right for that wet afternoon.'—*Michael Billington, Illustrated London News*

Assault on a Queen
US 1966 106m Technicolor Panavision
Paramount / Seven Arts / Sinatra Enterprises (William Goetz)

Crooks dredge up a submarine and use it to hi-jack the *Queen Mary*.
Strained caper film which remains uncertain whether to play for drama or thrills, and achieves neither. Special effects unconvincing.

w Rod Serling, *novel* Jack Finney *d* Jack Donohue *ph* William Daniels *m* Duke Ellington

Frank Sinatra, Virna Lisi, Tony Franciosa, Alf Kjellin, Errol John, Richard Conte, Murray Matheson, Reginald Denny

'Just about as enthralling as plastic boats in the bath.'—*MFB*

Assault on Precinct 13**
US 1976 91m Metrocolor Panavision
CKK (Joseph Kaufman)

Gang members on a vendetta attack a police station.
Violent but basically efficient and old-fashioned programmer which shows that not all the expertise of the forties in this then-familiar field has been lost.

wd / m John Carpenter *ph* Douglas Knapp

Austin Stoker, Darwin Joston, Laurie Zimmer, Martin West

'One of the most effective exploitation movies of the last ten years . . . Carpenter scrupulously avoids any overt socio-political pretensions, playing instead for laughs and suspense in perfectly balanced proportions.'—*Time Out*

Assignment in Brittany
US 1943 96m bw
MGM (J. Walter Ruben)

A Free French soldier stays in occupied France to fight the Nazis.
Routine propagandist actioner, totally unbelievable.

w Anthony Veiller, William Wright, Howard Emmett Rogers, *novel* Helen MacInnes *d* Jack Conway *ph* Charles Rosher *m* Lennie Hayton

Jean Pierre Aumont, Signe Hasso, Susan Peters, Reginald Owen, Richard Whorf, Margaret Wycherly, John Emery, Miles Mander, George Coulouris

'Any moment the world might blow up in their double faces!'

Assignment K
GB 1968 97m Techniscope
Columbia / Mazurka (Ben Arbeid, Maurice Foster)

The European head of a toy firm is also head of a special spy unit.
Dreary espionage thriller, instantly forgettable, and only watchable at odd moments while it's on.

w Val Guest, Bill Strutton, Maurice Foster, *novel* Hartley Howard *d* Val Guest *ph* Ken Hodges *m* Basil Kirchen

Stephen Boyd, Michael Redgrave, Camilla Sparv, Leo McKern, Jeremy Kemp

Assignment Paris
US 1952 85m bw
Columbia (Sam Marx, Jerry Bresler)

A reporter on the Paris staff of the *New York Herald-Tribune* goes to Yugoslavia, is arrested as a spy, and has to be exchanged.
Dim cold war melodrama with occasional entertaining moments.

w William Bowers, *novel* Trial by Terror by Paul Gallico *d* Robert Parrish *ph* Burnett Guffey, Ray Cory *m* George Duning

George Sanders, Dana Andrews, Sandra Giglio, Marta Toren, Audrey Totter, Herbert Berghof

Assignment Redhead
GB 1956 79m bw

An international criminal gang arrives in London looking for counterfeit dollars printed by the Nazis during the war. Initially sharp but eventually yawnworthy thick ear on the smallest scale. Richard Denning, Ronald Adam, Carole Matthews, Danny Green, Brian Worth, Jan Holden. Written and directed by

Maclean Rogers from a story by Lindsay Hardy; for W. G. Chalmers/Butcher's. (US title: *Million Dollar Manhunt*.)

Assignment to Kill
US 1967 99m Technicolor Panavision
Warner Seven Arts (William Conrad)

A New York insurance company hires a private eye to investigate a dubious European financier.
Routine international intrigue with muddled plot and unusual cast. A nice production wasted.

wd Sheldon Reynolds *ph* Harold Lipstein *m* William Lava

Patrick O'Neal, John Gielgud, Peter Van Eyck, Joan Hackett, Herbert Lom, Eric Portman, Oscar Homolka, Leon Greene

The Assisi Underground
Italy/US 1985 178m colour
Cannon (Menahem Golan, Yoram Globus)

During World War II, Assisi monasteries hide Jewish refugees.
Expansive but generally abysmal war adventure which was released in various forms, including a television miniseries. No amount of re-editing can disguise an empty script and incompetent direction.

w,d Giuseppe Ramati, from his novel *ph* Giuseppe Rotunno *m* Dov Seltzer *pd* Luciano Spadoni

Ben Cross, James Mason, Irene Papas, Maximilian Schell

'There is simply not enough story to fill three hours, so the scenery upstages the actors.'—*Variety*

The Astonished Heart*
GB 1949 89m bw
Gainsborough / Sydney Box (Antony Darnborough)

A psychiatrist is permitted by his wife to fall in love with another woman but finds the situation intolerable and kills himself.
The star, looking like a Chinese mandarin, reached his nadir in this unwise screen adaptation, inelegantly directed, of one of his slightest short plays about boring and effete people. It sank without trace.

w Noel Coward, from his play *d* Terence Fisher, Antony Darnborough *ph* Jack Asher *m* Noel Coward

Noel Coward, Margaret Leighton, Celia Johnson, Graham Payn, Joyce Carey, Ralph Michael, Michael Hordern

The Astounding She-Monster
US 1957 59m bw

In a remote spot, some crooks and a scientist combat a female space visitor with remarkable powers. An early sub-Corman pot-boiler with only its camp qualities to recommend it. Robert Clarke, Kenne Duncan, Marilyn Harvey. Written by Frank Hall; directed and produced by Ronnie Ashcroft; for Hollywood International. (GB title: *Mysterious Invader*.)

'You have nothing to lose but your mind!'
Asylum*
GB 1972 88m Eastmancolor
Amicus (Max J. Rosenberg, Milton Subotsky)
aka: *House of Crazies*

A doctor applies for a job at an asylum, hears weird stories from four patients, and finds himself in the middle of a weirder one.
Lively horror compilation with echoes of *Caligari* and *Dead of Night*. Gruesomeness sometimes overdone.

w Robert Bloch *d* Roy Ward Baker *ph* Denys Coop *m* Douglas Gamley

Patrick Magee, Robert Powell, Geoffrey Bayldon, Barbara Parkins, Sylvia Syms, Richard Todd, Peter Cushing, Barry Morse, Britt Ekland, Charlotte Rampling, James Villiers, Megs Jenkins, Herbert Lom

At Close Range
US 1986 111m CFI color Panavision
Orion / Hemdale (Elliott Llewitt, Don Guest)

In Pennsylvania, a gang of young robbers is picked off one by one by the father of one of them, who feels they know too much about his own criminal activities.
Relentlessly brutal, dispiriting and quite pointless melodrama, even with the saving grace of a factual basis.

w Nicholas Kazan *d* James Foley *ph* Jean Ruiz-Anchia *m* Patrick Leonard

Sean Penn, Christopher Walken, Mary Stuart Masterson, Christopher Penn, Millie Perkins, Eileen Ryan, Candy Clark

'A very tough picture . . . runs the risk of being an audience turnoff.'—*Variety*

At Gunpoint
US 1955 80m Technicolor Cinemascope

A western storekeeper accidentally kills a bank robber, whose brothers seek revenge; will the townsfolk come to his aid? Fair western on the lines of *High Noon*. Fred MacMurray, Dorothy Malone, Walter Brennan, John Qualen, Skip Homeier. Written by Dan Ullman; directed by Alfred Werker; for Allied Artists. (GB title: *Gunpoint*.)

'A new kind of musical!'
At Long Last Love
US 1975 114m Technicolor
TCF / Copa de Oro (Peter Bogdanovich)

The 1935 romance of a New York millionaire and a musical star.
An attempt to recapture the simple pleasures of an Astaire–Rogers musical; unfortunately true professionalism is lacking and the wrong kind of talent is used. The result is awful to contemplate.

wd Peter Bogdanovich *ph* Laszlo Kovacs *m* Cole Porter *pd* Gene Allen

Burt Reynolds, Cybill Shepherd, Eileen Brennan, Madeleine Kahn, Duilio del Prete, John Hillerman, Mildred Natwick

'He works hard at reducing all his sets and costumes to variations of black against silver or white on white, and uncovers in his most oft-repeated visual motif—the elegant mirrors before which his cast seem at all times to be posed—the perfect metaphor for this endlessly narcissistic, thoroughly calcified enterprise.'—*Richard Combs*

'It just lies there, and it dies there.'—*Variety*

'Studios bury more films than the public or the critics. Fox gave up on *At Long Last Love* instantly. A six million dollar film was written off while it was doing well because their lawyers told them they could make more money that way.'—*Peter Bogdanovich*

'It is justly included on most lists of the ten worst films ever made.'—*Les Keyser, Hollywood in the Seventies*

'Stillborn . . . a relentlessly vapid pastiche.'—*Pauline Kael*

At Sword's Point*
US 1951 81m Technicolor
RKO (Jerrold T. Brandt)
GB title: *Sons of the Musketeers*

The sons of the three musketeers rally round their ageing queen to prevent her daughter's marriage to a villain.
Adequate swashbuckler with plenty of pace and a sound cast.

w Walter Ferris, Joseph Hoffman *d* Lewis Allen *ph* Ray Rennahan *m* Roy Webb

Cornel Wilde, Maureen O'Hara, Gladys Cooper, Robert Douglas, Dan O'Herlihy, Alan Hale Jnr, Blanche Yurka, Nancy Gates

At the Circus**
US 1939 87m bw
MGM (Mervyn Le Roy)
aka: *The Marx Brothers at the Circus*

A shyster lawyer and two incompetents save a circus from bankruptcy.
This film began the decline of the Marx Brothers; in it nothing is ill done but nothing is very fresh either apart from the rousing finale which shows just what professionalism meant in the old Hollywood. Highlights include Groucho singing about Lydia the tattooed lady, his seduction of Mrs Dukesbury, and the big society party.

w Irving Brecher *d* Edward Buzzell *ph* Leonard M. Smith *m / ly* Harold Arlen, E. Y. Harburg *m* Franz Waxman

Groucho, Chico, Harpo, Margaret Dumont, Florence Rice, Kenny Baker, Eve Arden, Nat Pendleton, Fritz Feld

Songs include 'Lydia', 'Two Blind Loves', 'Step up and Take a Bow'.

GROUCHO: 'I don't know what I'm doing here when I could be at home in bed with a hot toddy. That's a drink.'

'Rousing physical comedy and staccato gag dialogue . . . geared for fine b.o. and general audience appeal.'—*Variety*

'We must regretfully accept the fact that, thanks to the Metro millions, the Marx Brothers are finally imprisoned in the Hollywood world.'—*Graham Greene*

At the Earth's Core
GB 1976 90m Technicolor
Amicus (John Dark)

Scientists testing a geological excavator are carried by it to the centre of the earth, and find a prehistoric land inhabited by feuding tribes.
Mainly feeble science fiction for kids, with occasional amusing moments..

w Milton Subotsky, *novel* Edgar Rice Burroughs *d* Kevin Connor *ph* Alan Hume *m* Mike Vickers *sp* Ian Wingrove *pd* Maurice Carter

Doug McClure, Peter Cushing, Caroline Munro, Cy Grant, Godfrey James, Keith Barron

'Papier mâché people-eaters, idiotic situations, and a frequent sense of confusion as to what is going on.'—*David Stewart, Christian Science Monitor*

At the Stroke of Nine
GB 1957 72m bw

A mad concert pianist plots to murder a young girl reporter. Absurd and rather endearing melodrama of the very old school. Stephen Murray, Patricia Dainton, Patrick Barr, Dermot Walsh. Written by Tony O'Grady, Harry Booth, Jon Pennington and Michael Deeley; directed by Lance Comfort; for Tower / Grand National.

At the Villa Rose
This murder mystery by A. E. W. Mason has had three British filmings: in 1920 with Teddy Arundell as Inspector Hanaud; in 1930 with Austin Trevor; in 1939 with Keneth Kent. All were adequate to their time. The story concerns a medium framed for the murder of a rich widow.

At War with the Army
US 1951 93m bw
Paramount / Fred K. Finklehoffe

A couple of song and dance men have trouble as army recruits.
American service farce, based on a play and confined largely to one set; rather untypical of Martin and Lewis, yet oddly enough the film which sealed their success.

w Fred K. Finkelhoffe, *play* James Allardice *d* Hal Walker *ph* Stuart Thompson *m* Joseph Lilley

Dean Martin, Jerry Lewis, Mike Kellin, Polly Bergen, Jimmie Dundee

L'Atalante*
France 1934 89m bw
J. L. Nounez-Gaumont

A barge captain takes his new wife down river. One of those classics which no longer provides the authentic thrill; its lack of incident and plot leads quickly to boredom.

w Jean Guinée, Jean Vigo, Albert Riera *d Jean Vigo* *ph* Boris Kaufman, Louis Berger *m* Maurice Jaubert

Jean Dasté, Dita Parlo, *Michel Simon*, Giles Margarites

Athena
US 1954 96m Eastmancolor
MGM (Joe Pasternak)

A young lawyer falls in love with the eldest of seven sisters brought up to high standards of moral conduct and physical fitness.
Promising but unfulfilling light musical which smothers a good idea in routine treatment.

w William Ludwig, Leonard Spiegelgass *d* Richard Thorpe *ph* Robert Planck *md* George Stoll *songs* Hugh Martin, Ralph Blane

Edmund Purdom, Jane Powell, Debbie Reynolds, Louis Calhern, Evelyn Varden, Vic Damone, Linda Christian, Ray Collins

Atlantic
GB 1929 90m bw

A passenger liner sinks in mid-Atlantic. Veiled retelling of the *Titanic* story, here in a clumsy Anglo-German version with extremely primitive sound and a plethora of pregnant silences. Franklin Dyall, Madeleine Carroll, Monty Banks, John Stuart, John Longden, Ellaline Terriss. Written by Victor Kendall, from the play *The Berg* by Ernest Raymond; directed by E. A. Dupont; for BIP.

'If you want to be mentally shipwrecked or lost at sea, see Atlantic. . . . It's something unnecessary to see; something no one wants to see; something horrible to even think of.

'. . . It will draw to and drive away from the box office. Draw to because it holds horror, thrills and suspense; drive away through children not being permitted to see it and the suggested gruesomeness too strong for many, not only women.

'. . . A faint try at comedy with a valet was like a ghoul in a cemetery . . . but Franklin Dyall excelled as an aged invalid with John . Longden as a ship's officer, making a splendid appearance.'—*Variety*

Atlantic Adventure*
US 1935 68m bw

A reporter captures a murderer on an ocean liner. Lively double-biller, better than average in all departments. Nancy Carroll, Lloyd Nolan, Harry Langdon, Arthur Hohl, Robert Middlemass, John Wray, E. E. Clive. Written by John T. Neville and Nat Dorfman; directed by Albert Rogell; for Columbia. 'Only lack of cast names keeps this in dual pix classification.'—*Variety*

Atlantic City*
US 1944 87m bw
Republic (Albert J. Cohen)

Before World War I, a young showman aims to make Atlantic City the entertainment centre of the world.
Simple-minded romantic musical, quite pacy and effectively staged for a Republic product.

w Doris Gilbert, Frank Gill Jnr, George Carlton Brown *d* Ray McCarey *ph* John Alton *m / ly* various

Constance Moore, Brad Taylor, Jerry Colonna, Charley Grapewin

Atlantic City USA*
Canada / France 1981 105m colour
Cine-Neighbour / Selta Films (Denis Heroux)

Small-time crooks congregate round Atlantic City's new casinos.
Elegiac character drama which often achieves the mood it seeks but on the whole remains too understated for its own good.

w John Guare *d Louis Malle* *ph* Richard Ciupka *m* Michel Legrand *pd* Anne Pritchard

Burt Lancaster, Susan Sarandon, Kate Reid, Michel Piccoli, Hollis McLaren

AAN: best picture; John Guare; Burt Lancaster; Susan Sarandon
BFA: best direction; Burt Lancaster; Louis Malle

Atlantic Ferry*
GB 1941 108m bw
Warner (Max Milder)
US title: *Sons of the Sea*

In 1837 Liverpool, two brothers build the first steamship to cross the Atlantic.
Ponderous historical romance with points of interest.

w Gordon Wellesley, Edward Dryhurst, Emeric Pressburger *d* Walter Forde *ph* Basil Emmott *m* Jack Beaver

Michael Redgrave, Valerie Hobson, Griffith Jones, Margaretta Scott, Hartley Power, Bessie Love, Milton Rosmer

'Probably the finest collection of model shots in captivity.'—*C. A. Lejeune*

L'Atlantide*
France 1921 125m approx (16 fps) bw silent
Thalman

Two explorers find the lost continent of Atlantis and fall in love with its queen.
Highly commercial adventure fantasy of its day; it cost two million francs and ran in Paris for a year. Some scenes still sustain, and the desert scenes are impressive.

wd Jacques Feyder, *novel* Pierre Benoît *ph* Georges Specht, Victor Morin

Jean Angelo, Stacia Napierkowska, Georges Melchior

† Other versions include *Queen of Atlantis* (Germany 1932, *d* G. W. Pabst, with Brigitte Helm); *Siren of Atlantis* (US 1948, *d* Gregg Tallas, with Maria Montez); *L'Atlantide* (France / Italy 1961, *d* Edgar G. Ulmer).

Atlantis, the Lost Continent
US 1961 91m Metrocolor
MGM / Galaxy / George Pal

A Greek fisherman is imprisoned when he returns a maiden he has rescued to her island home of Atlantis, but escapes just before volcanic eruption overtakes the decadent nation.
Penny-pinching fantasy spectacle with very little entertainment value.

w Daniel Mainwaring, *play* Sir Gerald Hargreaves *d* George Pal *ph* Harold E. Wellman *m* Russell Garcia

ATLANTIC CITY USA. Only his jacket betrays the fact that Burt Lancaster (here with Kate Reid) was once a gangster.

Anthony Hall, Joyce Taylor, John Dall, Edward Platt, Frank de Kova, Jay Novello

Atom Man vs Superman
US 1950 bw serial: 15 eps

The evil Luthor threatens Metropolis with mad and dangerous devices. Absurd but still quite watchable adventures for those experiencing second childhood. Kirk Alyn, Noel Neill, Lyle Talbot, Tommy Bond, Pierre Watkin. Directed by Spencer Bennet; for Columbia.

The Atomic City*
US 1952 85m bw
Paramount (Joseph Sistrom)

The young son of a leading atomic scientist is kidnapped but his father and the FBI rescue him.
Routine but well-paced thriller with a documentary background of research at Los Alamos.

w Sidney Boehm *d* Jerry Hopper *ph* Charles B. Lang Jnr *m* Leith Stevens

Gene Barry, Lydia Clarke, Lee Aaker, Nancy Gates, Milburn Stone

AAN: Sidney Boehm

The Atomic Kid
US 1954 86m bw
Republic / Mickey Rooney (Maurice Duke)

After an atomic blast, a prospector accidentally left in the area proves immune to uranium, and after various adventures rounds up some communist spies.
Inane romp which raises a few laughs.

w Benedict Freeman, John Fenton Murray, *story* Blake Edwards *d* Leslie H. Martinson *ph* John L. Russell Jnr *m* Van Alexander

Mickey Rooney, Robert Strauss, Elaine Davis, Bill Goodwin, Whit Bissell

The Atonement of Gosta Berling**
Sweden 1924 200m approx (16 fps) bw silent
Svensk Filmindustri
original title: *Gosta Berlings Saga*

A pastor is defrocked for drinking, becomes a tutor, and has various love affairs.
Lumpy but often engrossing picturization of a famous novel, veering mostly into melodrama but finding its way to a happy ending.

w Mauritz Stiller, Ragnar Hylten-Cavallius, *novel* Selma Lagerlof *d* Mauritz Stiller *ph* Julius Jaenzon

Lars Hanson, Gerda Lundeqvist, Ellen Cederstrom, Mona Martensson, Jenny Hasselqvist, Otto Elg-Lundberg, Greta Garbo.

'Stiller was a master at unifying visual beauty and emotional effect; the complicated narrative is blurry, but there are sequences as lovely and expressive as any on film.'—*New Yorker, 1980*

† It was her small role in this film which led directly to Greta Garbo's American stardom.

Attack**
US 1956 104m bw
UA / Associates and Aldrich

In 1944 Belgium, an American infantry command is led by a coward.
High-pitched, slick, violent and very effective war melodrama, even though by the end we seem to be in the company of raving lunatics rather than soldiers.

w James Poe, play Fragile Fox by Norman Brooks *d Robert Aldrich ph Joseph Biroc m* Frank de Vol

Jack Palance, Eddie Albert, Lee Marvin, Buddy Ebsen, Robert Strauss, Richard Jaeckel, William Smithers, Peter Van Eyck

'The film does not so much tackle a subject as hammer it down.'—*Penelope Houston*

Attack of the Crab Monsters
US 1957 65m bw

25-foot mutant crabs cause landslides on a Pacific island. Bottom-of-the-barrel monster mayhem from this tongue-in-cheek producer; now a cult. Richard Garland, Pamela Duncan, Russell Johnson. Written by Charles B. Griffith; produced and directed by Roger Corman; for Allied Artists.

The Attack of the Fifty Foot Woman
US 1958 72m bw

A neurotic woman is lured inside a space ship, becomes radio-active, and grows to alarming proportions. Hilarious tailpiece to the fifties monster cycle, a dismal movie worth remembering only for its title. Allison Hayes, William Hudson, Roy Gordon. Written by Mark Hanna; directed by Nathan Hertz; for Allied Artists.

Attack of the Giant Leeches
US 1959 62m bw

A bar owner forces his wife and her lover into a swamp to be eaten by monsters. The bottom of the Corman / AIP barrel, good only for a few unintentional laughs. Ken Clark, Michael Emmet, Yvette Vickers, Bruno De Sota. Written by Leo Gordon; directed by Bernard Kowalski; for Corman / AIP.

Attack of the Killer Tomatoes
US 1978 87m colour

Vegetables go berserk in the big city. Apparently a cult film made deliberately as such, which is a contradiction in terms. Nothing for the ordinary audience, anyway. David Miller, George Wilson, Sharon Taylor, Jack Riley. Written by Costa Dillon, Steve Peace, John de Bello; directed by John de Bello; for Four Square / NAI. 'Though the idea sounds funny, actually sitting through nearly 90 minutes of it is enough to make anyone long for *Attack of the Fifty Foot Woman*.'—*Motion Picture Guide*.

Attack of the Puppet People
US 1957 79m bw

A doll-maker has also learned to shrink people. Inferior entry in the *Dr Cyclops* mould; mildly amusing moments are sandwiched between chunks of tedium. John Hoyt, John Agar, June Kenny. Written by George Worthing Yates; directed and produced by Bert I. Gordon; for Alta Vista. (GB title: *Six Inches Tall*.)

Attack on the Iron Coast
GB 1967 90m De Luxe
US / Mirisch (John Champion)

In World War II, a Canadian commando unit destroys a German installation on the French coast.
Stagey low-budgeter with modest action sequences.

w Herman Hoffman *d* Paul Wendkos *ph* Paul Beeson *m* Gerard Schurmann

Lloyd Bridges, Andrew Keir, Mark Eden, Sue Lloyd

Attila the Hun
Italy / France 1954 79m Technicolor
Lux Ponti de Laurentiis / LCCF (Georgio Andriani)
original title: *Attilo Flagello di Dio*

The barbarian chief attacks the forces of the Emperor Valentinian and marches on Rome. Predictably violent adventures after de Mille; a bit slow to start.

w Ennio de Concini, Primo Zeglio *d* Pietro Francisci *ph* Aldo Tonti *m* Enzo Masetti

Anthony Quinn, Sophia Loren, Henri Vidal, Irene Papas, Ettore Manni, Claude Laydu

Attorney for the Defense
US 1932 70m bw

A prosecutor's wiles result in an innocent man being executed, so he turns crusader and takes on defence cases. Punchy if unconvincing courtroom melodrama which would certainly satisfy at the time. Edmund Lowe, Evelyn Brent, Constance Cummings, Donald Dillaway, Dorothy Peterson, Dwight Frye, Nat Pendleton, Clarence Muse. Written by Jo Swerling and J. K. McGuinness; directed by Irving Cummings; for Columbia.

Au dela des Grilles
Italy / France 1949 90m bw
Italia Produzione / Francinex (Alfredo Guarini)
aka: *Beyond the Gates*; Italian title: *La mura de Malapaga*

A murderer on the run in Genoa falls in love with a waitress and loses his chance of escape. *Quai des Brumes* reworked against an Italian neo-realist setting; dramatic values less interesting now than historical ones.

w Jean Aurenche, Pierre Bost, Cesare Zavattini, Suso Cecchi d'Amico *d* René Clément *ph* Louis Page *m* Roman Vlad

Jean Gabin, *Isa Miranda*, Vera Talchi, Andrea Checci

AA: best foreign film

Au Royaume des Cieux
France 1949 108m bw
Regina (Julien Duvivier)
aka: *Woman Hunt*

An 18-year-old girl suffers at a reform school. Shoddy melodrama, more sensational than Hollywood ever dared to be.

wd Julien Duvivier *ph* Victor Armenise

Suzanne Cloutier, Serge Reggiani, Monique Mélinand, Suzy Prim, Jean Davy, Juliette Greco

'A depressing exhibit from a director who once had a serious reputation.'—*Gavin Lambert*

Audrey Rose*
US 1977 113m De Luxe Panavision
United Artists / Robert Wise

A man believes that a 12-year-old girl is the reincarnation of his dead daughter.
Rather painful and not very persuasive spiritualist thriller in the wake of *The Exorcist*; only moments of dramaturgy survive.

w Frank de Felitta, from his novel *d* Robert Wise *ph* Victor J. Kemper *m* Michael Small *pd* Harry Horner

Anthony Hopkins, Marsha Mason, John Beck, Susan Swift, Norman Lloyd, John Hillerman, Robert Walden

Aunt Clara
GB 1954 84m bw
London Films (Colin Lesslie, Anthony Kimmins)

A pious old person inherits from a reprobate uncle five greyhounds, a pub and a brothel. Extremely mild star vehicle with a gallery of comedy character cameos.

w Kenneth Horne, *novel* Noel Streatfeild *d* Anthony Kimmins *ph* C. Pennington-Richards *m* Benjamin Frankel

Margaret Rutherford, Ronald Shiner, A. E. Matthews, Fay Compton, Nigel Stock, Jill Bennett, Reginald Beckwith, Raymond Huntley

Aunt Sally
GB 1933 84m bw
Gainsborough
US title: *Along Came Sally*

A fake French star saves a nightclub owner from gangsters. Predictable star vehicle. Cicely Courtneidge, Sam Hardy, Billy Milton, Phyllis Clare, Hartley Power. Written by Austin Melford, Guy Bolton and A. R. Rawlinson; directed by Tim Whelan; for Gaumont.

Auntie Mame*
US 1958 144m Technirama
Warner (Morton da Costa)

An orphan boy is adopted by his volatile extravagant aunt, whose giddy escapades fill his memory of the twenties and thirties.
A rather unsatisfactory star revue from a book and play later turned into a musical, *Mame*. A few splendid moments, otherwise rather dull and irritating.

w Betty Comden, Adolph Green, *novel* Patrick Dennis, *play* Jerome Lawrence, Robert E. Lee *d* Morton da Costa *ph* Harry Stradling *m* Bronislau Kaper *ad* Malcolm Bert

Rosalind Russell, Forrest Tucker, *Coral Browne*, *Fred Clark*, Roger Smith, Patric Knowles, Peggy Cass, Lee Patrick, Joanna Barnes

AAN: best picture; Harry Stradling; Rosalind Russell; Peggy Cass

Une Aussi Longue Absence*
France / Italy 1961 96m bw
Procinex / Lyre / Galatea (Jacques Nahum)
aka: *The Long Absence*

A widow who owns a Paris café meets an amnesiac tramp who may be her long-lost husband.
Romantic character study which just about comes off thanks to good acting.

w Marguerite Duras, Gérald Jarlot *d* *Henri Colpi* *ph* Marcel Weiss *m* Georges Delerue

Alida Valli, Georges Wilson, Jacques Harden

Austerlitz
France / Italy / Liechtenstein / Yugoslavia 1959 166m Eastmancolor Dyaliscope
CFPI / SCLF / Galatea / Michael Arthur / Dubrava (Alexander and Michael Salkind)
aka: *The Battle of Austerlitz*

Napoleon defeats the Austro-Russian army. Elaborate pageant with a hopelessly cluttered narrative line arranged to take in a roster of guest stars who merely distract from the central theme.

wd Abel Gance *ph* Henri Alekan, Robert Juillard *m* Jean Ledrut

Pierre Mondy, Jean Mercure, Jack Palance, Orson Welles, Michel Simon, Jean-Louis Trintignant, Martine Carol, Leslie Caron, Claudia Cardinale, Rossano Brazzi, Ettore Manni, Jean Marais, Vittorio de Sica

'Strictly for connoisseurs of Gance's brand of hyperbolic history.'—*Peter John Dyer, MFB*

Author, Author!*
US 1982 109m TVC
TCF (Irwin Winkler)

A Broadway playwright has worries about his wife's fidelity.
Like a sixties update of *All About Eve*, this thin but sometimes witty sex-behind-the-footlights comedy has nothing to offer the general audience of the eighties, and one can only speculate as to why it was made. The acting does help, but it's a long haul.

w Israel Horovitz *d* Arthur Hiller *ph* Victor J. Kemper *m* Dave Grusin *pd* Gene Rudolf *ed* William Reynolds

Al Pacino, Dyan Cannon, Tuesday Weld, Bob Dishy, Bob Elliott

'In trying to dig a little deeper than the average Neil Simon comedy, it only prepares its own grave.'—*Observer*

Automania 2000**
GB 1963 10m Eastmancolor

New cars have the ability to reproduce themselves: city dwellers of the future consequently live in stationary vehicles piled on top of each other. Amusing cartoon fantasy, neatly executed. Written by Joy Batchelor; directed by John Halas; for Halas and Batchelor.

Autumn Crocus
GB 1934 86m bw

A British schoolmistress on holiday falls for her Tyrolean innkeeper. Difficult now to conceive the popularity in its day of this novelettish romance, which seems frozen in amber. Ivor Novello, Fay Compton, Jack Hawkins, Diana Beaumont, Muriel Aked, George Zucco. Written and directed by Basil Dean, from the play by C. L. Anthony; for ATP.

'In the dark, when I feel his heart pounding against mine—is it love? or frenzy? or terror?'
Autumn Leaves*
US 1956 108m bw
Columbia / William Goetz

A middle-aged spinster marries a young man who turns out to be a pathological liar and tries to murder her.
Skilfully tailored star vehicle for female audiences.

w Jack Jevne, Lewis Meltzer, Robert Blees *d* Robert Aldrich *ph* Charles Lang *m* Hans Salter

Joan Crawford, Cliff Robertson, Lorne Greene, Vera Miles, Ruth Donnelly, Shepperd Strudwick

Autumn Sonata*
Sweden / West Germany / GB 1978 97m colour
Personafilm / ITC (Ingmar Bergman)

When her lover dies, a concert pianist visits the daughter she has not seen for many years.
Typically Bergmanesque, understated conversation piece with no obvious happy ending for anybody.

wd Ingmar Bergman *ph* Sven Nykvist
m Chopin, Handel, Bach

Ingrid Bergman, Liv Ullmann, Halvar Bjork
'Professional gloom.'—*Time*
'It fills these middle-class rooms with the deep music of conflict and reconciliation that must strike home to any audiences in any culture or society.'—*Jack Kroll, Newsweek*

AAN: script; Ingrid Bergman

'Six million tons of icy terror!'
Avalanche
US 1978 91m Metrocolor
New World (Roger Corman)

Snow threatens holidaymakers at a ski lodge.
A disaster movie which, while quite competent in most ways, is no better than TV movies of this kind, especially as it resorts for its climaxes to scratched old stock film.

w Claude Pola, Corey Allen *d* Corey Allen *ph* Pierre-William Glenn *m* William Kraft

Rock Hudson, Mia Farrow, Robert Forster, Jeanette Nolan, Rick Moses, Steve Franken, Barry Primus

Avalanche Express
Eire 1979 88m De Luxe Panavision
TCF / Lorimar (Mark Robson)

Spies of all nations converge on a train from Milan to Rotterdam.
Fitfully amusing hodgepodge which had to be finished off in a hurry following the death of its star and director in mid-production.

w Abraham Polonsky, *novel* Colin Forbes *d* Mark Robson *ph* Jack Cardiff *m* Allyn Ferguson

Robert Shaw, Lee Marvin, Linda Evans, Maximilian Schell, Mike Connors, Joe Namath, Horst Buchholz
'The most impressive work of montage to emerge from a big-budget adventure movie.'—*Richard Combs, MFB*
'Pell-mell direction and editing perform a precarious, oddly suspenseful balancing act.'—*Sight and Sound*

'When someone knocks at your door and says "Permesso?", be careful before you say . . .'
Avanti!**
US 1972 144m De Luxe
UA / Mirisch / Phalanx / Jalem (Billy Wilder)

A young American goes to Ischia to collect the body of his father who has died on holiday. He finds that the fatal accident had also killed his father's mistress, and amid overwhelming bureaucratic problems proceeds to fall in love with her daughter.
Absurdly overlong black comedy, with compensations in the shape of a generally witty script and some fine breakneck sequences of culminating confusion.

w Billy Wilder, I. A. L. Diamond, play Samuel Taylor *d Billy Wilder ph* Luigi Kuveiller *m* Carlo Rustichelli

Jack Lemmon, Juliet Mills, Clive Revill, Edward Andrews, Gianfranco Barra

The Avenging Conscience*
US 1914 58m (24 fps) bw silent

An elaboration of Poe's *The Tell Tale Heart* in which Griffith first shows his ability to control a feature-length movie, with many cinematic devices. Henry B. Walthall, Blanche Sweet, Spottiswoode Aiken, Mae Marsh. Written and directed by D. W. Griffith; photographed by Billy Bitzer; for Mutual.

The Aviator
US 1930 73m bw

A timid clerk lends his name to a technical book on aviation, and finds himself having to back up the pretence by flying. Predictable star comedy. Edward Everett Horton, Patsy Ruth Miller, Johnny Arthur, Lee Moran. From the play by James Montgomery; directed by Roy del Ruth; for Warners. 'Peg this as a good one.'—*Variety*

The Aviator
US 1985 96m Metrocolor
MGM-UA / Mace Neufeld

In 1928, a spoiled rich girl is cared for by a sullen pilot when they crashland in the Sierras.
Drawn-out, actionless adventure concerning unattractive characters; it has been seen before in at least two TV movies.

w Marc Norman *novel* Ernest Gann
d George Miller *ph* David Connell
m Dominic Frontiere *pd* Brenton Swift
ed Duane Hartzell

Christopher Reeve, Rosanna Arquette, Jack Warden, Sam Wanamaker, Scott Wilson, Tyne Daly
'Doesn't fly.'—*Variety*

The Aviator's Wife*
France 1980 106m Eastmancolor (blown up from 16mm)
Les Films du Losange (Margaret Menegoz)
original title: *La Femme de L'Aviateur*

Anne and François are having an affair, but each has other entanglements.
Meticulously arranged conversations in this director's best style, but this time not seeming to amount to very much.

wd Eric Rohmer *ph* Bernard Lutic *m* Jean-Louis Valero

Philippe Marlaud, Marie Rivière, Anne-Laure Maeury, Matthieu Carrière
'Does the aviator Christian's wife exist? It really does not matter: she is a formal device in a play of formalist devices.'—*Jill Forbes, MFB*

L'Avventura**
Italy / France 1960 145m bw
Cino del Duca / PCE / Lyre (Amato Pennasilico)

Young people on a yachting holiday go ashore on a volcanic island. One of them disappears; this affects the life of the others, but she is never found.
Aimless, overlong parable with lots of vague significance; rather less entertaining than the later *Picnic at Hanging Rock* (qv), it made its director a hero of the highbrows.

w Michelangelo Antonioni, Elio Bartolini, Tonino Guerra *d Michelangelo Antonioni ph* Aldo Scavarda *m* Giovanni Fusco

Monica Vitti, Lea Massari, Gabriele Ferzetti, Dominique Blanchar, James Addams, Lelio Luttazi
'A film of complete maturity, sincerity and creative intuition.'—*Peter John Dyer, MFB*

The Awakening
GB 1980 105m Technicolor
EMI / Orion (Robert Solo)

An obsessed archaeologist believes that the spirit of a long-dead Egyptian queen has entered into the soul of his daughter.

Unpersuasive and humourless mumbo jumbo from the same intractably complex novel which provided the basis for *Blood from the Mummy's Tomb*.

w Allan Scott, Chris Bryant, Clive Exton, *novel* Jewel of the Seven Stars by Bram Stoker *d* Mike Newell *ph* Jack Cardiff *m* Claude Bolling *pd* Michael Stringer

Charlton Heston, Susannah York, Jill Townsend, Stephanie Zimbalist, Patrick Drury, Bruce Myers

'An almost total waste of the talents involved.'—*Sunday Times*

'It is difficult to imagine a film more likely to put you to sleep.'—*Guardian*

Away All Boats!
US 1956 114m Technicolor Vistavision
U-I (Howard Christie)

Adventures of a small transport boat during the Pacific War.

Competent drum-beating war heroics with expensive action sequences.

w Ted Sherdeman *d* Joseph Pevney *ph* William Daniels, Clifford Stine *m* Frank Skinner

Jeff Chandler, George Nader, Julie Adams, Lex Barker, Keith Andes, Richard Boone, Frank Faylen

The Awful Truth***
US 1937 90m bw
Columbia (Leo McCarey)

A divorcing couple endure various adventures which lead to reconciliation.
Classic crazy comedy of the thirties, marked by a mixture of sophistication and farce and an irreverent approach to plot.

w Vina Delmar play Arthur Richman *wd Leo McCarey ph* Joseph Walker *md* Morris Stoloff

Irene Dunne, Cary Grant, Ralph Bellamy, Alexander D'Arcy, Cecil Cunningham, Molly Lamont, Esther Dale, Joyce Compton

IRENE DUNNE: 'You've come back and caught me in the truth, and there's nothing less logical than the truth.'

CARY GRANT: 'In the spring a young man's fancy lightly turns to what he's been thinking about all winter.'

'Fast, smart comedy that will please everywhere and do strong general biz.'—*Variety*

'The funniest picture of the season.'—*Otis Ferguson*

'Among the ingredients the raising powder is the important thing and out of the oven comes a frothy bit of stuff that leaves no taste in the mouth and is easy on the stomach.'—*Marion Fraser, World Film News*

'Delightfully effective entertainment.'—*Time Out, 1985*

† Remade 1953 as *Let's Do It Again* (qv).

AA: Leo McCarey
AAN: best picture; script; Irene Dunne; Ralph Bellamy

B.F.'s Daughter*
US 1948 106m bw
MGM (Edwin A. Knopf)
GB title: *Polly Fulton*

The wife of a penniless lecturer secures her husband's rise to fame without his knowing that she is the daughter of a millionaire.
Solid upper class romantic drama with a touch of Peg's Paper.

w Luther Davis, *novel* John P. Marquand *d* Robert Z. Leonard *ph* Joseph Ruttenberg *m* Bronislau Kaper

Barbara Stanwyck, Van Heflin, Charles Coburn, Richard Hart, Keenan Wynn, Margaret Lindsay, Spring Byington, Marshall Thompson

B.S. I Love You
US 1970 98m De Luxe

A director of TV commercials is beset by passionate women. Tiresomely trendy sex comedy with a visual style that never lets up. Peter Kastner, Joanna Cameron, Louise Sorel, Gary Burghoff, Joanna Barnes, Richard B. Shull. Written and directed by Steven Hillard Stern; for Motion Pictures International / TCF. (NB: The initials in the title are short for bullshit.)

Babbitt*
US 1934 74m bw
Warner (Sam Bischoff)

Problems of a middle-aged man in a small American town.
A minor attempt to film a major novel: quite tolerable but lacking density.

w Mary McCall Jnr, *novel* Sinclair Lewis *d* William Keighley *ph* Arthur Todd

Guy Kibbee, Aline MacMahon, Claire Dodd, Maxine Doyle, Minor Watson, Minna Gombell, Alan Hale, Berton Churchill, Russell Hicks, Nan Grey

'Smooth, pleasant but trite.'—*Variety*

† Previously filmed in 1924 with Willard Louis.

The Babe Ruth Story
US 1948 107m bw
Allied Artists (Roy del Ruth)

The biography of a baseball player who was thought of as something of a saint.
Dim, sentimental and faintly mystical biopic, throughout which the star presents his familiar image.

w Bob Considine, George Callahan *d* Roy del Ruth *ph* Philip Tunnura, James Van Trees *m* Edward Ward

William Bendix, Claire Trevor, Charles Bickford

Babes in Arms**
US 1939 96m bw
MGM (Arthur Freed)

The teenage sons and daughters of retired vaudevillians put on a big show.
Simple-minded backstage musical which marked the first enormously successful teaming of its two young stars.

w Jack McGowan, Kay Van Riper, from the Broadway show by Rodgers and Hart *d / ch* Busby Berkeley *ph* Ray June *songs* Rodgers and Hart and others *m* Roger Edens, George Stoll

Judy Garland, Mickey Rooney, Charles Winninger, Douglas Macphail, Leni Lynn, June Preisser

Songs include 'Where or When'; 'The Lady Is a Tramp'; 'Babes in Arms'; 'I Cried for You'; 'God's Country'; 'Good Morning'; 'You Are my Lucky Star'

'A topflight filmusical entertainment. It will click mightily in the key deluxers, and roll up hefty profits for exhibs in the subsequent runs and smaller situations.'—*Variety*

AAN: Roger Edens, George Stoll; Mickey Rooney

Babes in Baghdad
US 1952 77m Exotic Color

Harem ladies go on strike. Embarrassing attempt at satire by stars who are over the hill and not helped by abysmal technique. Paulette Goddard, Gypsy Rose Lee, Richard Ney, John Boles, Sebastian Cabot. Written by Felix E. Feist and Joe Anson; directed by Edgar G. Ulmer; for the Danzigers.

Babes in Toyland**
US 1934 77m bw
Hal Roach
aka: *Wooden Soldiers; March of the Wooden Soldiers; Laurel and Hardy in Toyland*

Santa Claus's incompetent assistants accidentally make some giant wooden soldiers, which come in useful when a villain tries to take over Toyland.
Comedy operetta in which the stars have pleasant but not outstanding material; the style and decor are however sufficient to preserve the film as an eccentric minor classic.

w Nick Grinde, Frank Butler, *original book / ly* Glen MacDonough *d* Gus Meins, Charles Rogers *ph* Art Lloyd, Francis Corby *m* Victor Herbert

Stan Laurel, Oliver Hardy, Charlotte Henry, Henry Brandon, Felix Knight, Florence Roberts, Johnny Downs, Marie Wilson

'It is amusing enough to entertain older persons who remember when they were young.'—*Variety*

Babes in Toyland
US 1961 105m Technicolor
Walt Disney

A misfiring remake, all charm and no talent apart from some excellent special effects at the climax.

w Ward Kimball, Joe Rinaldi, Lowell S. Hawley *d* Jack Donohue *ph* Edward Colman *md* George Bruns *sp* Eustace Lycett, Robert A. Mattey, Bill Justice, Xavier Atencio, Yale Gracey

Ray Bolger (miscast as the villain), Annette Funicello, Tommy Kirk, Gene Sheldon (imitating Stan Laurel), Henry Calvin (imitating Oliver Hardy), Ed Wynn, Kevin Corcoran

AAN: George Bruns

Babes on Broadway**
US 1941 118m bw
MGM (Arthur Freed)

A sequel to *Babes in Arms*, in which the kids get to Broadway and share some disillusion. Inflated and less effective than the original, but with good numbers.

w Fred Finkelhoffe, Elaine Ryan *d / ch* Busby Berkeley *ph* Lester White *songs* Burton Lane and Ralph Freed

Judy Garland, Mickey Rooney, Virginia Weidler, Ray Macdonald, Richard Quine, Fay Bainter

'Enough energy and enthusiasm to make older people wish they were young, and young people glad that they are.'—*Monthly Film Bulletin*

† The Virginia Weidler role was originally intended for Shirley Temple, but TCF wouldn't loan her.

AAN: song 'How About You' (*m* Burton Lane, *ly* Ralph Freed)

Babette Goes to War
France 1959 103m Eastmancolor Cinemascope
Iéna (Raoul Lévy)
original title: *Babette S'en Va-t-en Guerre*

In 1940 a French refugee girl is sent by British intelligence from London to Paris as bait in a plot to kidnap a German general and delay the Nazi invasion of England.
Witless war farce which goes on for ever.

w Raoul Lévy, Gérard Oury *d* Christian-Jaque *ph* Armand Thirard *m* Gilbert Bécaud

Brigitte Bardot, Jacques Charrier, Hannes Messemer, Yves Vincent, Ronald Howard, Francis Blanche

'A kind of *Private's Progress* without comedians.'—*MFB*

Babette's Feast*
Denmark 1987 103m Eastmancolor
Panorama / Nordisk / Danish Film Institute

A French refugee in 19th-century Norway wins 10,000 francs in a lottery and spends it all on preparing a sumptuous banquet for her Lutheran employers and their friends.
Ironic and elegant fable juxtaposing bacchanalian extravagance with narrow piety.

w Gabriel Axel, from story by Isak Dinesen *d* Gabriel Axel *ph* Henning Kristiansen *m* Per Norgard *ad* Sven Wichman

Stéphane Audran, Jean-Philippe Lafont, Jarl Kulle, Bibi Andersson, Bodil Kjer, Birgitte Federspiel

Baboona
US 1935 78m bw

Africa photographed from the air as well as the jungle; one of the better documentary features of the mid-thirties. Mr and Mrs Martin Johnson. Photographed and directed by Martin Johnson; for Fox.

The Baby and the Battleship
GB 1956 96m Eastmancolor
British Lion / Jay Lewis

Two sailors hide an Italian baby on their battleship.
Simple-minded lower decks farce, with lots of confusion and cooing over the baby, but not much to laugh at.

w Jay Lewis, Gilbert Hackforth-Jones, Bryan Forbes *d* Jay Lewis *ph* Harry Waxman *m* James Stevens

John Mills, Richard Attenborough, André Morell, Bryan Forbes, Michael Howard, Lisa Gastoni, Ernest Clark, Lionel Jeffries, Thorley Walters

Baby Blue Marine*
US 1976 90m Metrocolor
Columbia / Spelling–Goldberg (Robert LaVigne)

In 1943, a failed marine returns home and pretends to be a war hero.
Careful small-town drama with good period feel but not much dramatic punch: *Hail the Conquering Hero* did it better.

w Stanford Whitmore *d* John Hancock *ph* Laszlo Kovacs *m* Fred Karlin

Jan-Michael Vincent, Glynnis O'Connor, Katherine Helmond, Dana Elcar, Bert Remsen, Richard Gere

'A rickety structure of strange events.'—*New York Post*

'19 years old and married . . . but not really!'

Baby Doll**
US 1956 116m bw
Warner / Elia Kazan

In the deep South, the child wife of a broken-down cotton miller is seduced by her husband's revenge-seeking rival.
An incisive, cleverly-worked-out study of moral and physical decay; whether it was worth doing is another question, for it's a film difficult to remember with affection.

w Tennessee Williams from his play 27 Wagonloads of Cotton *d* Elia Kazan *ph Boris Kaufman* *m* Kenyon Hopkins *ad* Richard Sylbert

Karl Malden, Eli Wallach, Carroll Baker, Mildred Dunnock, Lonny Chapman

'Just possibly the dirtiest American-made motion picture that has ever been legally exhibited, with Priapean detail that might well have embarrassed Boccaccio.'—*Time*

'He views southern pretensions with sardonic humor, and builds an essentially minor story into a magnificently humorous study of the grotesque and the decadent.'—*Hollis Alpert*

'A droll and engrossing carnal comedy.'—*Pauline Kael, 1968*

'A film in which everything works: narration, casting, tempo, rhythm, dramatic tension.'—*Basil Wright, 1972*

† Another publicity tag read: 'Condemned by Cardinal Spellman!'

AAN: script; Boris Kaufman; Carroll Baker; Mildred Dunnock

'She climbed the ladder of success—wrong by wrong!'

Baby Face**
US 1933 70m bw
Warner (Ray Griffith)

Amorous adventures of an ambitious working girl.
Sharp melodrama very typical of its time, with fast pace and good performances.

w Gene Markey, Kathryn Scola, Mark Canfield (Darryl F. Zanuck) *d* Alfred E. Green *ph* James Van Trees

Barbara Stanwyck, George Brent, Donald Cook, Margaret Lindsay, Arthur Hohl, John Wayne, Henry Kolker, Douglass Dumbrille

'Blue and nothing else. It possesses no merit for general or popular appeal, is liable to offend the family trade and can't count on any juve attendance.

'. . . This is reputed to be a remake on the first print, which was considered too hot. Anything hotter than this for public showing would call for an asbestos audience blanket.'—*Variety*

Baby Face Harrington
US 1935 63m bw

A timid man is mistakenly identified as a public enemy, and chased by both cops and rival gangsters. Thin but appealing comedy. Charles Butterworth, Una Merkel, Nat Pendleton, Eugene Pallette, Donald Meek. Written by Nunnally Johnson and Edwin Knopf; directed by Raoul Walsh; for MGM.

'Weak satire, grievously overacted.'—*Variety*

Baby Face Morgan
US 1942 60m bw

The son of a racketeer is made a figurehead by his father's old mob. Curious comedy of non-violent crime; also non-entertaining. Richard Cromwell, Mary Carlisle, Robert Armstrong, Chick Chandler, Warren Hymer, Vince Barnett. Written by Edward Dein, Jack Rubin, Oscar Brodney; directed by Arthur Dreifuss; for Jack Schwartz / PRC.

'Don't see it unless your nerves are bullet proof!'

Baby Face Nelson*
US 1957 85m bw
UA / Fryman–ZS (Al Zimbalist)

Fragmentary account of the life of a thirties public enemy, with the star over the top and the technicians doing what they can on an obviously low budget.

w Irving Shulman, Daniel Mainwaring *d* Don Siegel *ph* Hal Mohr *m* Van Alexander

Mickey Rooney, Cedric Hardwicke, Carolyn Jones, Chris Dark, Ted de Corsia, Leo Gordon, John Hoyt, Anthony Caruso, Jack Elam

Baby It's You*
US 1982 104m colour
Paramount / Double Play (Griffin Dunne, Andy Robinson)

In the sixties, a well-heeled high school girl is wooed and won by a greasy street sheik with ambitions.
Curious sweet-and-sour romance with a determination to be modern; agreeable in parts but basically empty, and rather undermined by a torrent of rock music on the sound track.

w,d John Sayles, from a story by Amy Robinson *ph* Michael Ballhaus *md* Joel Dorn *pd* Jeffrey Townsend

Rosanna Arquette, Vincent Spano, Joanna Merlin, Jack Davidson, Nick Ferrari, Leora Dana

Baby Love
GB 1968 93m Eastmancolor
(Avco) Avton / Michael Klinger (Guido Coen)

An orphaned nymphet causes trouble among the men in her foster home.
Ludicrous sexploiter which embarrasses a good cast and descends into bathos.

w Alastair Reid, Guido Coen, Michael Klinger, *novel* Tina Chad Christian *d* Alastair Reid *ph* Desmond Dickinson *m* Max Harris

Linda Hayden, Ann Lynn, Keith Barron, Derek Lamden, Diana Dors, Patience Collier, Dick Emery

The Baby Maker
US 1970 109m Technicolor

A freewheeling girl agrees to have a baby for a childless couple. Stretched-out fable for our time which refrains from pointing a moral and is generally tastefully done but nevertheless outstays its welcome. Barbara Hershey, Collin Wilcox-Horne, Sam Groom, Scott Glenn, Jeannie Berlin. Written and directed by James Bridges; for National General.

Baby—Secret of the Lost Legend
US 1985 95m Technicolor
Supertechnirama
Touchstone (Jonathan T. Taplin)

Palaeontologists in the African jungle discover a family of living dinosaurs.
Technically and dramatically less than effective, this latter-day *King Kong* demonstrates yet again the Disney company's difficulties in hitting the right note for the modern family audience.

w Clifford and Ellen Green *d* B. W. L. Norton *ph* John Alcott *m* Jerry Goldsmith *sp* Philip Meador, Peter Anderson

William Katt, Sean Young, Patrick McGoohan, Julian Fellowes

Baby Take a Bow*
US 1934 76m bw

An ex-convict is accused of theft, but his small daughter unmasks the real culprit. *Shirley Temple*'s first star vehicle was a solid enough commercial property to take her right to the top. James Dunn, Claire Trevor, Alan Dinehart. Written by Philip Klein and E. E. Paramore Jnr; directed by Harry Lachman; for Fox. 'A pretty obvious and silly melodrama, but it has Shirley Temple, so it can go down in the books as a neat and sure b.o. hit.'—*Variety*

'The more he gets into trouble, the more he gets under her skin!'

Baby, the Rain Must Fall
US 1964 100m bw
Columbia / Pakula–Mulligan (Alan Pakula)

A parolee rejoins his wife and daughter in a Southern town, but his outbursts of violence separate them again.
Hard work by all concerned scarcely produces absorbing interest in this filmed play of the Tennessee Williams school.

w Horton Foote, from his play The Travelling Lady *d* Robert Mulligan *ph* Ernest Laszlo *m* Elmer Bernstein

Steve McQueen, Lee Remick, Don Murray, Paul Fix, Josephine Hutchinson, Ruth White, Charles Watts

The Bachelor and the Bobbysoxer***
US 1947 95m bw
RKO (Dore Schary)
GB title: *Bachelor Knight*

A lady judge allows her impressionable young sister to get over her crush on an errant playboy by forcing them together.
Simple but unexpectedly delightful vehicle for top comedy talents, entirely pleasant and with several memorable moments.

w Sidney Sheldon *d* Irving Reis *ph* Robert de Grasse, Nicholas Musuraca *m* Leigh Harline

Cary Grant, Myrna Loy, Shirley Temple, *Ray Collins*, Rudy Vallee, *Harry Davenport*, Johnny Sands, Don Beddoe

'Sure-fire stuff guaranteed to do no conceivable harm . . . the audience laughed so loud I missed some of the lines.'—*Shirley O'Hara, New Republic*

AA: Sidney Sheldon

Bachelor Apartment
US 1931 77m bw
RKO (William Le Baron)

A virtuous working girl in New York falls for a rich woman-chasing bachelor.
Mildly agreeable early talking romantic comedy.

w J. Walter Ruben, John Howard Lawson *d* Lowell Sherman *ph* Leo Tover

Irene Dunne, Lowell Sherman, Mae Murray, Norman Kerry, Claudia Dell, Ivan Lebedeff

'It oversteps the reasonable limits of sophisticated art . . . thus the film is doubtful for small towns.'—*Variety*

Bachelor Daddy*
US 1941 61m bw

Three bachelors find themselves in charge of a baby. Best of the comedies starring Baby Sandy. Edward Everett Horton, Franklin Pangborn, Raymond Walburn, Donald Woods, Evelyn Ankers. Written by Robert Lees and Fred Rinaldo; directed by Harold Young; for Universal.

Bachelor Father
US 1931 90m bw
MGM (B. P. Fineman)

A much-married elderly man visits his grown children.
Unremarkable star comedy of its day.

w Laurence E. Johnson, *play* Edward Childs Carpenter *d* Robert Z. Leonard *ph* Oliver T. Marsh

Marion Davies, *C. Aubrey Smith*, Ray Milland, Ralph Forbes, Halliwell Hobbes, Guinn Williams, David Torrence

'Where they have used the old hoke they have masked it with commendable skill.'—*Variety*

Bachelor Flat
US 1961 91m De Luxe Cinemascope
TCF / Jack Cummings

An English professor at an American university is unrelentingly pursued by girls.
Flat one-joke comedy which simply hasn't the style to sustain itself.

w Frank Tashlin, Budd Grossman, from Grossman's play *d* Frank Tashlin *ph* Daniel L. Fapp *m* Johnny Williams

Terry-Thomas, Richard Beymer, Tuesday Weld, Celeste Holm, Francesca Bellini, Howard McNear

Bachelor in Paradise
US 1961 109m Metrocolor
Cinemascope
MGM / Ted Richmond

A famous writer of advice to the lovelorn settles incognito in a well-heeled Californian community to observe its social habits.
Mildly amusing satire is too frequently interrupted by unsuitable romantic interludes in this rather ill-considered star comedy.

w Valentine Davies, Hal Kanter *d* Jack Arnold *ph* Joseph Ruttenberg *m* Henry Mancini

Bob Hope, Lana Turner, Janis Paige, Don Porter, Paula Prentiss, Jim Hutton, Virginia Grey, Reta Shaw, John McGiver, Agnes Moorehead

AAN: title song (*m* Henry Mancini, *ly* Mack David)

'Just ten tiny fingers and ten tiny toes . . . Trouble? Scandal? Gosh, nobody knows!'

Bachelor Mother***
US 1939 82m bw
RKO (B. G. De Sylva)

A shopgirl finds an abandoned baby and is thought to be its mother; the department store owner's son is then thought to be the father.
Blithely-scripted comedy which stands the test of time and provided several excellent roles.

w Norman Krasna d Garson Kanin
ph Robert de Grasse *m* Roy Webb

Ginger Rogers, David Niven, Charles Coburn, Frank Albertson, E. E. Clive, Ernest Truex

'Carries some rather spicy lines aimed at the adult trade, but broad enough in implication to catch the fancy of general audiences . . . a surprise laugh hit that will do biz generally and overcome hot weather box office lethargy.'—*Variety*

'An excellent comedy, beautifully done.'—*Richard Mallett, Punch*

'This is the way farce should be handled, with just enough conviction to season its extravagances.'—*New York Times*

† Remade as *Bundle of Joy* (qv).

AAN: Felix Jackson (for original story)

Bachelor of Hearts
GB 1958 94m Technicolor
Rank / Independent Artists (Vivian A. Cox)

Adventures of a German student at Cambridge University.
Sometimes agreeable, sometimes annoying, especially when romance gets in the way of the possibilities for fun.

w Leslie Bricusse, Frederic Raphael *d* Wolf Rilla *ph* Geoffrey Unsworth *m* Hubert Clifford

Hardy Kruger, Sylvia Syms, Ronald Lewis, Eric Barker, Newton Blick

The Bachelor Party***
US 1957 93m bw
UA / Norma (Harold Hecht)

New York book-keepers throw a wedding eve party for one of their fellows, but drink only brings to the fore their own private despairs. Though the last half-hour lets it down, most of this is a brilliantly observed social study of New York life at its less attractive, and the acting matches the incisiveness of the script.

w Paddy Chayevsky, from his TV play *d* Delbert Mann *ph* Joseph La Shelle *m* Alex North

Don Murray, E. G. Marshall, Jack Warden, Philip Abbott, Larry Blyden, Patricia Smith, Carolyn Jones

AAN: Carolyn Jones

Bachelor Party
US 1984 105m De Luxe

A bachelor party is beset by a series of disasters. Crude, exploitative farce full of physical mess and tending to get most of its humour from the destruction of order and some teetering on the brink of pornography. Tom Hanks, Tawny Kitaen, Adrian Zmed, George Grizzard, Barbara Stuart, Robert Prescott. Written by Neal Israel, Pat Proft; directed by Neal Israel; for Aspect Ratio / Twin Continental / TCF.

Bachelor's Affairs
US 1931 64m bw

A middle-aged bachelor thinks he needs a young wife, but can't keep up with the one he gets. Strained star comedy of no surviving interest. Adolphe Menjou, Minna Gombell, Arthur Pierson, Joan Marsh, Alan Dinehart. Written by Barry Conners and Philip Klein from the play Precious by James Forbes; directed by Alfred Werker; for Fox. 'Neither farce nor a social problem development, it misses throughout.'—*Variety*

The Bachelor's Daughters*
US 1946 90m bw
UA / Andrew Stone
GB title: *Bachelor Girls*

Four shopgirls and a floorwalker rent a Long Island house and pass themselves off as a wealthy family in order to lure suitable husbands for the girls.
Mildly amusing comedy with good performances.

wd Andrew Stone *ph* Theodor Sparkuhl *m* Heinz Roemheld

Adolphe Menjou, Gail Russell, Claire Trevor, Billie Burke

Back Door to Heaven
US 1939 81m bw

A boy born on the wrong side of the tracks is prevented from going straight, and having escaped execution for murder, he is bumped off by gangsters. Heavy-going indictment of society; too glum to work, it seems to have finished off the career of its talented director. Wallace Ford, Aline MacMahon, Stuart Erwin, Jimmy Lydon, William Harrigan, Bert Frohman. Written by John Bright and Robert Tasker; produced, directed and original story by *William K. Howard* (who also appears as the prosecuting attorney); for Odessco / Paramount. 'Artistic drama, too heavy and slow-tempoed for general b.o.'—*Variety*

Back from Eternity
US 1956 97m bw
RKO (John Farrow)

An airliner is forced to crashland in headhunter country, and when repairs are made only five of the eight survivors can be carried.
Remake by the same producer-director of his own 1939 'B', *Five Came Back*, this time to considerably less effect despite superior production.

w Jonathan Latimer *d* John Farrow *ph* William Mellor *m* Franz Waxman

Robert Ryan, Anita Ekberg, Rod Steiger, Phyllis Kirk, Gene Barry, Keith Andes, Beulah Bondi, Fred Clark, Cameron Prud'homme, Jesse White

Back from the Dead
US 1957 78m bw Regalscope
TCF / Regal (Robert Stabler)

A girl on honeymoon becomes possessed by the spirit of her husband's first wife.
Blithe Spirit played for real but getting just as many laughs, unintentional this time.

w Catherine Turney, from her novel The Other One *d* Charles Marquis Warren *ph* Ernest Haller *m* Raoul Kraushaar

Peggie Castle, Arthur Franz, Marsha Hunt, Don Haggerty

Back in Circulation
US 1937 80m bw

Girl news reporter wins her editor's attention by solving a murder. Sub-*Front Page* melodrama, of no intrinsic interest. Pat O'Brien, Joan Blondell, Margaret Lindsay. Written by Warren Duff; directed by Ray Enright; for Warner. 'The newspaper boys, the goofy photographers and the hysterical city editor are on the murder trail, relentlessly pursuing the accused, telling coroners, district attorneys and defence counsel how to conduct their business.'—*Variety*

Back Roads
US 1981 95m De Luxe Panavision
CBS Theatrical / Meta Films (Ronald Shedlo)

A hooker and an ex-boxer hitch-hike to California.
Tiresomely with-it update of *It Happened One Night*; the humour and romance of the original are preferable to this dollop of bad language, boring people and bed-hopping.

w Gary Devore *d* Martin Ritt *ph* John A. Alonzo *m* Henry Mancini

Sally Field, Tommy Lee Jones, David Keith, Miriam Colon, Michael Gazzo

'Decidedly sticky, and instantly forgettable.'—*Guardian*

Back Room Boy*
GB 1942 82m bw
GFD / Gainsborough (Edward Black)

A timid meteorologist is sent to an Orkney lighthouse and unmasks a bunch of spies. Fairly spirited star comedy of interest as a shameless rip-off of *The Ghost Train* and *Oh Mr Porter*, whose plotlines are milked but not improved: note also that Askey took over Will Hay's discarded stooges.

w Val Guest, Marriott Edgar *d* Herbert Mason *ph* Jack Cox

Arthur Askey, Moore Marriott, Graham Moffatt, Googie Withers, Vera Frances, John Salew

Back Street*
US 1932 93m bw
Universal (Carl Laemmle Jnr)

A married man has a sweet-tempered mistress who effaces herself for twenty years.
Popular version of a sudsy bestselling novel.

w Gladys Lehman, Lynn Starling, *novel* Fannie Hurst *d* John M. Stahl *ph* Karl Freund

Irene Dunne, John Boles, June Clyde, George Meeker, Zasu Pitts, Doris Lloyd

'Swell romance, a little tear-jerking, and a woman's picture—which means a money production.'—*Variety*

Back Street*
US 1941 89m bw
Universal (Bruce Manning)

Competent remake.

w Bruce Manning, Felix Jackson *d* Robert Stevenson *ph* William Daniels *m* Frank Skinner

Margaret Sullavan, Charles Boyer, Richard Carlson, Frank McHugh, Tim Holt, Frank Jenks, Esther Dale, Samuel S. Hinds

AAN: Frank Skinner

Back Street*
US 1961 107m Technicolor
U-I / Ross Hunter / Carrollton

Glossy remake typical of its producer: unfortunately it fails to work because the heroine suffers too luxuriously.

w Eleanore Griffin, William Ludwig *d* David Miller *ph* Stanley Cortez *m* Frank Skinner

Susan Hayward, John Gavin, Vera Miles, Virginia Grey, Charles Drake, Reginald Gardiner

'Though there is a lot to be said for this new version's thesis that one can be just as lonely in a series of apartments and lovers' nests apparently never less than a hundred yards wide, the illusion is quickly shattered the moment one gets the impression that the lovers prefer to keep much the same distance during their moments of passion.'—*Peter John Dyer*

'Ross Hunter has updated this old faithful and given it a contemporary lack of significance.'—*Hollis Alpert, Saturday Review*

'The bathrooms look like the lobby of the

Beverly Hilton . . . the fallen woman falls, not into the pit of shame, but into the lap of luxury.'—*Time*

Back to Bataan
US 1945 97m bw
RKO (Robert Fellows)

When Bataan is cut off, a Marine colonel organizes guerrilla resistance.
Modestly made and rather dislikeable flagwaver.

w Ben Barzman, Richard Landau *d* Edward Dmytryk *ph* Nicholas Musuraca *m* Roy Webb

John Wayne, Anthony Quinn, Beulah Bondi, Fely Franquelli, Leonard Strong, Richard Loo, Philip Ahn, Lawrence Tierney, Paul Fix

Back to God's Country
US 1953 78m Technicolor
U-I (Howard Christie)

A sea captain battles the Canadian winter and a villain who wants his wife and his cargo of furs.
Old-fashioned adventure story, moderately well presented.

w Tom Reed, *novel* James Oliver Curwood *d* Joseph Pevney *ph* Maury Gertsman *m* Frank Skinner

Rock Hudson, Steve Cochran, Marcia Henderson, Hugh O'Brian

Back to School
US 1986 94m colour
Orion / Paper Clip

A millionaire enrols in university as a freshman so as to teach his son the ropes. Crass and ineptly made comedy vehicle for a star with distinct limitations. Rodney Dangerfield, Sally Kellerman, Burt Young, Keith Gordon, Paxton Whitehead. Written by Steven Kampmann, Harold Ramis, Will Porter, Peter Torokvei; directed by Alan Metter; for Chuck Russell.

Back to the Beach
US 1987 92m colour

Former teenage surfers return to the beach in middle age and help kids with problems. Not so bad as it sounds, but for cultists only. Annette Funicello, Frankie Avalon, Connie Stevens, Lori Loughlin, Tommy Hinkley. Plus Don Adams, Bob Denver, Jerry Mathers, Pee Wee Herman. Written by Peter Krikes, Steve Meerson, Christopher Thompson; directed by Lyndall Hobbs; for Frank Mancuso Jnr/Paramount. 'A wonderfully campy trip down pop culture's trash-filled memory lane.'—*Daily Variety*

Back to the Future***
US 1985 116m Technicolor
Universal / Steven Spielberg (Bob Gale, Neil Canton)

With the help of a not-so-crazy scientist, a teenager goes back thirty years to make a man out of his dimwit father.
Lighthearted Twilight Zone fantasy which certainly pleased the international multitudes.

w Robert Zemeckis, Bob Gale d Robert Zemeckis ph Dean Cundey *m* Alan Silvestri *pd* Lawrence G. Paull *ed* Arthur Schmidt, Harry Keramidas

Michael J. Fox, Christopher Lloyd, Crispin Glover, Lea Thompson, Claudia Wells

'Accelerates with wit, ideas, and infectious, wide-eyed wonder.'—*Variety*

AAN: original screenplay

Backfire
US 1949 90m bw
Warner (Anthony Veiller)

A war veteran solves the murder of which his best friend is accused.
Confusing murder mystery of a very familiar kind, adequately made but with no particular style. Flashbacks don't help.

w Larry Marcus, Ivan Goff, Ben Roberts *d* Vincent Sherman *ph* Carl Guthrie *ad* Anton Grot *m* Ray Heindorf

Gordon Macrae, Virginia Mayo, Edmond O'Brien, Dane Clark, Viveca Lindfors, Ed Begley

Backfire
US 1987 91m colour

A Vietnam veteran with nightmares seems to be in the middle of a murder plot. Too-murky thriller which takes an awful long time to come clean. Karen Allen, Keith Carradine, Jeff Fahey, Bernie Casey, Dean Paul Martin. Written by Larry Brand, Rebecca Reynolds; directed by Gilbert Cates; for Danton Rissner/ITC.

Background*
GB 1953 82m bw
Group Three (Herbert Mason)
US title: *Edge of Divorce*

Two people decide on divorce, but thoughts of their children bring them together again.
Low budget, stiff-upper-lip marriage guidance tract, well acted but more well-intentioned than memorable.

w Warren Chetham Strode, from his play, with Don Sharp *d* Daniel Birt *ph* Arthur Grant

Valerie Hobson, Philip Friend, Norman Wooland, Janette Scott, Mandy Miller, Jeremy Spenser, Richard Wattis

Background to Danger
US 1943 80m bw
Warner (Jerry Wald)

An adventurer thwarts Nazi intrigue in Turkey.
Flat, studio-bound wartime potboiler with a good cast all at sea.

w W. R. Burnett, *novel* Uncommon Danger by Eric Ambler *d* Raoul Walsh *ph* Tony Gaudio *m* Frederick Hollander

George Raft, Brenda Marshall, Sydney Greenstreet, Peter Lorre, Osa Massen, Turhan Bey, Kurt Katch

'You could use this film for one kind of measurement of the unconquerable difference between a good job by Hitchcock and a good job of the Hitchcock type.'—*James Agee*

'There's nothing for the cast to do other than concentrate on the display of melodramatics.'—*Variety*

Backlash*
US 1956 84m Technicolor
U-I (Aaron Rosenberg)

A gunman seeks the father he has never met, who turns out to be a villain who sold his partners for gold to attacking Indians.
Rather unusual suspense western, very watchable for its mystery elements.

w Borden Chase d John Sturges ph Irving Glassberg *m* Herman Stein

Richard Widmark, Donna Reed, John McIntire, William Campbell, Barton Maclane

The Bacon Grabbers*
US 1929 20m bw silent

Bailiffs fail to recover a radio on which the instalments are overdue. Modestly pleasing star comedy on the lines of *Big Business*. Laurel and Hardy, Edgar Kennedy, Jean Harlow, Charlie Hall. Written by Leo McCarey and H. M. Walker; directed by Lewis R. Foster; for Hal Roach.

'The story of a blonde who wanted to go places, and a brute who got her there—the hard way!'

The Bad and the Beautiful**
US 1952 118m bw
MGM (John Houseman)

A director, a star, a screenwriter and an executive recall their experiences at the hands of a go-getting Hollywood producer.
Very much a Hollywood 'in' picture, this rather obvious flashback melodrama offers good acting chances and a couple of intriguing situations; never quite finding the style it seeks, it offers good bitchy entertainment along the way, and there are references back to it in *Two Weeks in Another Town*, made ten years later.

w Charles Schnee *d* Vincente Minnelli *ph* Robert Surtees *m* David Raksin *ad* Cedric Gibbons, Edward Carfagno

Kirk Douglas (Jonathan Shields), Lana Turner (Georgia Lorrison), Walter Pidgeon (Harry Pebbel), Dick Powell (James Lee Bartlow), Barry Sullivan (Fred Amiel), Gloria Grahame (Rosemary Bartlow), Gilbert Roland (Victor Ribera), Leo G. Carroll (Henry Whitfield), Vanessa Brown (Kay Amiel), Paul Stewart (Syd Murphy)

'For all the cleverness of the apparatus, it lacks a central point of focus.'—*Penelope Houston*

'Clever, sharply observed little scenes reflect the Hollywood surface: the egotistic babble at a party, the affectations of European directors, the sneak preview, the trying on of suits for catmen in a B picture.'—*MFB*

'It is a crowded and colourful picture, but it is choppy, episodic and vague. There does not emerge a clear picture of exactly how movies are made.'—*Bosley Crowther*

AA: Charles Schnee; Robert Surtees; art direction; Gloria Grahame
AAN: Kirk Douglas

Bad Bascomb*
US 1946 110m bw
MGM (Orville Dull)

A sentimental bank robber becomes the hero of a group of travelling Mormons.
Pleasing though overlong star western, with good production values.

w William Lipman, Grant Garrett *d* S. Sylvan Simon *ph* Charles Schoenbaum *m* David Snell

Wallace Beery, Margaret O'Brien, Marjorie Main, J. Carrol Naish, Russell Simpson, Sara Haden

Bad Boys
US 1983 123m Astro Color
EMI / Robert Solo

Delinquents get out of control in a Juvenile Correctional Facility.
Ugly but yawnworthy saga of up-to-date Dead End Kids.

w Richard di Lello *d* Rick Rosenthal *ph* Bruce Surtees, Don Thorin *m* Bill Conti

Sean Penn, Reni Santoni, Jim Moody, Eric Gurry, Esai Morales, Ally Sheedy

Bad Company**
US 1972 92m Technicolor
Paramount (Stanley R. Jaffe)

During the Civil War, two youths on the run team up and become outlaws.
A successful attempt to recreate the feeling of past time, by the writers of another criminal myth, *Bonnie and Clyde*.

w David Newman, Robert Benton d Robert Benton *ph* Gordon Willis *m* Harvey Schmidt

Jeff Bridges, Barry Brown, Jim Davis, David Huddleston, John Savage

Bad Day at Black Rock****
US 1955 81m Eastmancolor Cinemascope
MGM (Dore Schary)

A one-armed stranger gets off the train at a sleepy desert hamlet and is greeted with hostility by the townsfolk, who have something to hide.
Seminal suspense thriller—the guilty town motif became a cliché—with a terse script and professional presentation. The moments of violence, long awaited, are electrifying.

w Millard Kaufman, story Bad Time at Hondo by Howard Briskin *d John Sturges ph William C. Mellor m* André Previn

Spencer Tracy, Robert Ryan, Dean Jagger, Walter Brennan, Ernest Borgnine, Lee Marvin, Anne Francis, John Ericson, Russell Collins

'A very superior example of motion picture craftsmanship.'—*Pauline Kael*

'The movie takes place within twenty-four hours. It has a dramatic unity, an economy of word and action, that is admirable in an age of flabby Hollywood epics that maunder on forever.'—*William K. Zinsser, New York Herald Tribune*

'The skill of some sequences, the mood and symbiosis between man and nature makes this film sometimes superior to *High Noon*.'—*G. N. Fenin*

AAN: Millard Kaufman; John Sturges; Spencer Tracy

Bad for Each Other
US 1954 83m bw
Columbia (William Fadiman)

A doctor back from the army scorns his home town for high society, but a mine disaster reverses his decision.
Misleadingly titled cliché drama, patterned after *The Citadel*. Actors ill at ease, handling competent but routine.

w Irving Wallace, Horace McCoy, from the latter's novel *d* Irving Rapper *ph* Franz Planer *md* Mischa Bakaleinikoff

Charlton Heston, Lizabeth Scott, Dianne Foster, Mildred Dunnock, Arthur Franz, Ray Collins, Marjorie Rambeau

Bad Girl*
US 1931 90m bw
Fox

Two New York youngsters have to get married and find life bewildering.
Typical Borzage sentiment which was well received at the time.
w Edwin Burke, *novel* Vina Delmar *d Frank Borzage ph* Chester Lyons

Sally Eilers, James Dunn, Minna Gombell, William Pawley, Frank Darien

AAN: Frank Borzage; Edwin Burke; best picture

Bad Little Angel
US 1939 72m bw

A sad little girl flees an orphanage and brightens up several lives in a small town. Pollyanna-type period drama, definitely for small-town audiences but well enough done. Virginia Weidler, Gene Reynolds, Guy Kibbee, Ian Hunter, Elizabeth Patterson, Reginald Owen, Henry Hull, Lois Wilson. Written by Dorothy Yost from the novel Looking after Sandy by Margaret Turnbull; directed by William Thiele; for MGM. 'Homespunner for the nabes.'—*Variety*

The Bad Lord Byron*
GB 1948 85m bw
Triton (Aubrey Baring)

Byron lies dying, and imagines his life and loves under review in a heavenly court.
Thought risible at the time, this historical romance in flashback now seems no worse and even a little more stylish than most, though the script suffers from too many cooks.

w Terence Young, Anthony Thorne, Peter Quennell, Laurence Kitchin, Paul Holt *d* David MacDonald *ph* Stephen Dade *m* Cedric Thorpe Davie

Dennis Price, Mai Zetterling, Linden Travers, *Joan Greenwood*, Sonia Holm, Raymond Lovell, Leslie Dwyer
† The end of the British costume cycle which began with *The Man in Grey*.

The Bad Man
US 1940 70m sepia
MGM (J. Walter Ruben)
GB title: *Two Gun Cupid*

A Mexican outlaw helps a former friend and unites two lovers.
Forgettable western comedy drama with a sterling cast.

w Wells Root, *play* Porter Emerson Brown *d* Richard Thorpe *ph* Clyde de Vinna *m* Franz Waxman

Wallace Beery, Lionel Barrymore, Laraine Day, Ronald Reagan, Henry Travers

Bad Man of Brimstone
US 1937 89m bw

An old bandit discovers his long-lost son and sees the light. Hilariously predictable but enjoyable star vehicle, quite palatable when it isn't too lachrymose. Wallace Beery, Virginia Bruce, Noah Beery, Dennis O'Keefe, Lewis Stone, Guy Kibbee, Joseph Calleia. Written by Richard Maibaum and Cyril Hume; directed by J. Walter Ruben; for MGM.

Bad Man's River
Spain / Italy / France 1972 90m Eastmancolor Franscope
Zurbano / Apollo / Roitfeld (Bernard Gordon)

Four outlaws accept the job of blowing up a government arsenal in Mexico.
Lurid western with comedy leanings and a somewhat eccentric cast.

w Philip Yordan, Eugenio Martin *d* Eugenio Martin *ph* Alexander Ulloa *m* Waldo de Los Rios

Lee Van Cleef, James Mason, Gina Lollobrigida, Simon Andreu, Diana Lorys

'When shooting a western in Spain one should not say to oneself, "Never mind, no one is going to see it," because that will be just the film which the Rank Organization will choose to release in England.'—*James Mason*

Bad Medicine
US 1985 96m De Luxe
TCF / Lantana (Alex Winitsky, Arlene Sellers)

A student goes to medical school in Mexico. Condescending farce which the Mexicans certainly won't like. Nothing much in it for general audiences either.

w,d Harvey Miller *novel* Steven Horowitz *ph* Kelvin Pike *m* Lalo Schifrin *pd* Les Dilley

Steve Guttenberg, Alan Arkin, Julie Hegerty, Bill Macy

'With the tone shifting constantly from realistic to slapstick, the film has no center and just sprawls on.'–*Variety*

Bad Men of Missouri
US 1941 72m bw

The Younger brothers become outlaws when they fight the influence of carpetbaggers.
Whitewashing of a family of western criminals; good double-bill entertainment. Dennis Morgan, Arthur Kennedy, Wayne Morris, Jane Wyman, Victor Jory, Walter Catlett. Written by Charles Grayson; directed by Ray Enright; for Warner.

Bad Men of Tombstone
US 1949 75m bw

Adventurers clash during gold rush days.
Workaday western with some vigour. Broderick Crawford, Barry Sullivan, Marjorie Reynolds, Julie Gibson. Written by Philip Yordan and Arthur Strawn; directed by Kurt Neumann; for King Brothers / Allied Artists.

The Bad News Bears
US 1976 103m Movielab
Paramount (Stanley Jaffe)

An ex-baseball professional coaches a team of tough kids.
Rough-tongued, sentimental star comedy.

w Bill Lancaster *d* Michael Ritchie *ph* John A. Alonzo *m* Jerry Fielding (after Bizet)

Walter Matthau, Tatum O'Neal, Vic Morrow, Joyce Van Patten

The Bad News Bears in Breaking Training
US 1977 100m Movielab
Paramount / Leonard Goldberg (Fred T. Gallo)

The Bears are invited to play in the Houston Astrodome but have trouble finding a coach.
Dimwitted and alarmingly sentimental sequel to a raucously vulgar oncer which should have been left alone.

w Paul Brickman *d* Michael Pressman *ph* Fred J. Koenekamp *m* Craig Safan from Tchaikovsky's 1812 Overture *ed* John W. Wheeler

William Devane, Clifton James, Jackie Earle Haley, Jimmy Baio, Chris Barnes

The Bad News Bears Go to Japan
US 1978 91m Movielab
Paramount

Yet another unnecessary sequel with a self-explanatory title.

w Bill Lancaster *d* John Berry *ph* Gene Polito *m* Paul Chihara

Tony Curtis, Jackie Earle Haley, Tomisaburo Wayakama, George Wyner

The Bad One
US 1930 70m bw

A prostitute falls for a client and saves him from prison. Artificial to the point of risibility, this incredible melodrama demeans all concerned with it. Dolores del Rio, Edmund Lowe, Don Alvarado, Blanche Friderici. Written by Carey Wilson, Howard E. Rogers and John Farrow; directed by George Fitzmaurice; for Art Cinema Corporation / UA.

The Bad Seed*
US 1956 129m bw
Warner (Mervyn Le Roy)

A sweet-looking 8-year-old girl is a liar and a murderess; her mother finds out and attempts to kill her and commit suicide.
A real curiosity from an unexpected stage hit: absurd melodrama treated with astonishing high literary style and some censor-induced levity: at the end, after the little villainess has been struck by lightning, a curtain call shows her being soundly spanked.

w John Lee Mahin, *play* Maxwell Anderson, *novel* William March *d* Mervyn Le Roy *ph* Harold Rosson *m* Alex North

Nancy Kelly (rather uneasily recreating her stage role as the mother), *Patty McCormack*, Henry Jones, Eileen Heckart, Evelyn Varden, William Hopper, Paul Fix, Jesse White

AAN: Harold Rosson; Nancy Kelly; Patty McCormack; Eileen Heckart

Bad Sister
US 1931 71m bw
Universal (Carl Laemmle Jnr)

A small-town coquette falls for a city slicker, and her quiet sister gets her steady boy friend.
A teenage potboiler of its day, remarkable only for its cast.

w Raymond L. Schrock, Tom Reed, *story* The Flirt by Booth Tarkington *d* Hobart Henley *ph* Karl Freund

Conrad Nagel, Sidney Fox, Bette Davis, Humphrey Bogart, Zasu Pitts, Slim Summerville, Emma Dunn, Bert Roach

Bad Timing
GB 1980 123m colour Technovision
Rank / Recorded Picture Company (Jeremy Thomas)

In Vienna, an American divorcee has a strange and unhappy affair with a psychoanalyst.
Weird and unsympathetic sex melodrama, presented with the disconnected style expected from this director as a series of flashbacks from the heroine's near-deathbed.

w Yale Udoff *d* Nicolas Roeg *ph* Anthony Richmond *m* Richard Hartley

Art Garfunkel, Theresa Russell, Harvey Keitel, Denholm Elliott, Daniel Massey

'An enervating experience. Technically flashy, and teeming with degenerate chic, the downbeat tale is unrelieved by its tacked-on thriller ending, and deals purely in despair.'—*Variety*

The Badge of Marshal Brennan
US 1957 75m bw

A man on the run takes on the identity of a dying marshal, and cleans up a corrupt town.
Satisfying lower-case western. Jim Davis, Arleen Whelan, Louis Jean Heydt, Lee Van Cleef. Written by Thomas G. Hubbard; directed by Albert C. Gannoway; for Allied Artists.

Badge 373
US 1973 116m Technicolor
Paramount (Howard W. Koch)

A police detective is enraged by the murder of his partner and his own suspension after the death of a suspect.
'Realistic' (i.e. violent and foul-mouthed) cop thriller in the wake of *The French Connection*, tolerable only for action highlights.

w Pete Hamill, from the exploits of Eddie Egan *d* Howard W. Koch *ph* Arthur J. Ornitz *m* J. J. Johnson

Robert Duvall, Verna Bloom, Henry Darrow, Eddie Egan, Felipe Luciano, Tina Christiana, Marina Durell

'A deeply divided and scarcely reassuring addition to the movies' composite portrait of the American police force.'—*John Gillett*

'Nasty, violent and humourless.'—*Sight and Sound*

'A movie well worth protesting about.'—*Michael Billington, Illustrated London News*

The Badlanders*
US 1958 83m Metrocolor Cinemascope
MGM / Arcola (Aaron Rosenberg)

Crooked westerners plan to rob a goldmine.
Rather sloppy western remake of *The Asphalt Jungle*.

w Richard Collins *d* Delmer Daves *ph* John Seitz

Alan Ladd, Ernest Borgnine, Katy Jurado, Claire Kelly, Kent Smith, *Nehemiah Persoff*, Robert Emhardt

Badlands**
US 1973 94m Consolidated Color
(Warner) Pressman / Williams / Badlands (Terrence Malick)

A teenage girl and a young garbage collector wander across America leaving a trail of murder behind them.
A violent folk tale for moderns; very well put together if somewhat lacking in point, it quickly became a cult film.

wd Terrence Malick *ph* Brian Probyn, Tak Fujimoto, Stevan Larner *m* George Tipton

Martin Sheen, Sissy Spacek, Warren Oates, Ramon Bieri

'One of the finest literate examples of narrated cinema since the early days of Welles and Polonsky.'—*Jonathan Rosenbaum*

'So preconceived that there's nothing left to respond to.'—*New Yorker*

Badlands of Dakota
US 1941 75m bw

A young man steals his elder brother's girl and becomes sheriff of a corrupt western town.
Standard family fare. Robert Stack, Richard Dix, Broderick Crawford, Ann Rutherford, Frances Farmer, Hugh Herbert, Andy Devine, Lon Chaney Jnr. Written by Gerald Geraghty; directed by Alfred E. Green; for Universal.

Badman's Country
US 1958 72m bw

Pat Garrett, Wyatt Earp, Buffalo Bill Cody and Bat Masterson have a showdown with Butch Cassidy. Wildly unhistorical western. George Montgomery, Buster Crabbe,

BADLANDS. A legend in the making—Martin Sheen strides towards an uncertain future.

Malcolm Attenbury, Gregory Walcott, Neville Brand. Written by Orville H. Hampton; directed by Fred F. Sears; for Warner.

'The west's worst killers strike again!'

Badman's Territory
US 1946 97m bw

The brutality of the Texas state police forces a sheriff to seek help from outlaws.
Unconvincing western with good moments. Randolph Scott, Steve Brodie, Gabby Hayes, Ann Richards. Written by Jack Nettlefold and Luci Ward; directed by Tim Whelan; for RKO.

Bagdad
US 1949 81m Technicolor
U-I (Robert Arthur)

A chieftain's daughter seeks revenge for her father's death.
Thinly-conceived Arabian Nights modernization, unsure whether to take itself seriously.

w Robert Hardy Andrews *d* Charles Lamont *ph* Russel Metty *m* Frank Skinner, Jack Brooks

Maureen O'Hara, Vincent Price, Paul Christian, John Sutton, Jeff Corey, Frank Puglia

'The two most gorgeous humans you've ever beheld—caressed by soft tropic winds—tossed by the tides of love!'

Bahama Passage
US 1941 82m Technicolor
Paramount (Edward H. Griffith)

A sophisticated girl is determined to live on a salt-mining island in the West Indies.
Forgettable tropical romance in very pleasing early colour.

w Virginia Van Upp, *novel* Nelson Hayes *d* Edward H. Griffith *ph* Leo Tover *m* David Buttolph

Madeleine Carroll, Sterling Hayden, Flora Robson, Leo G. Carroll, Cecil Kellaway, Dorothy Dandridge

La Baie des Anges**
France 1962 85m bw
Sud-Pacifique (Paul-Edmond Decharme)
GB title: *Bay of Angels*

A bank clerk who has had unexpected winnings at the Nice Casino falls in love with a compulsive gambler.
Good-looking romantic drama utilizing many of the cinema's most dazzling resources.

wd Jacques Demy ph Jean Rabier m Michel Legrand

Jeanne Moreau, Claude Mann, Paul Guers, Henri Nassiet

'Immense lightness, speed and gaiety . . . stunning visual texture.'—*Tom Milne, MFB*
'It's like a French attempt to purify, to get to the essence of, a Warners' movie of the 30s.'—*Pauline Kael*

Bail Out at 43,000
US 1957 82m bw

Airmen test ejection seats for jet bombers. Humdrum flagwaver. John Payne, Paul Kelly, Karen Steele, Richard Eyer. Written by Paul Monash; directed by Francis D. Lyon; for Pine-Thomas-Shane / UA.

Bait
US 1954 79m bw
Columbia (Hugo Haas)

Gold prospectors fall out over a mine and a woman.
Antediluvian melodrama typical of this director, made more risible than usual by Cedric Hardwicke's introduction in the shape of Satan.

w Samuel W. Taylor *d* Hugo Haas *ph* Edward P. Fitzgerald *m* Vaclav Divina

Hugo Haas, Cleo Moore, John Agar, Emmett Lynn

Baker's Hawk*
US 1976 96m colour

A reclusive westerner becomes the victim of hoodlum vigilantes and is helped by a boy and his father. Refreshingly simple-minded western for the family audience. Clint Walker, Burl Ives, Diane Baker, Lee H. Montgomery, Alan Young. Written by Dan Greer, Hal Harrison Jnr, from the novel by Jack Bickham; directed by Lyman D. Dayton; for Doty-Dayton.

Le Bal**
France / Italy / Algeria 1982 112m Fujicolor
S.A. / A2 / Massfil / Oncic (Giorgio Silvagni)

Scenes from the history of a small Paris ballroom between 1936 and 1983.
Striking if overlong attempt at a totally speechless drama, with handling very nearly good enough to meet the challenge, though the result will not be to everyone's taste, and one's reaction in any case will depend very much on mood.

w Jean-Claude Penchenat, Ruggero Maccari, Furio Scarpelli, Ettore Scola, from an idea by the first-named and the stage production by the Théâtre du Campagnol *d Ettore Scola ph* Ricardo Aranovich *m Vladimir Cosma*

Jean-Claude Penchenat, Chantal Capron, Etienne Guichard and large company each playing several roles

Balalaika*
US 1939 102m bw
MGM (Lawrence Weingarten)

Russian exiles gather in Paris.
Mildly pleasing star musical.

w Jacques Deval, Leon Gordon, *play* Eric Maschwitz *d* Reinhold Schunzel *ph* Joseph Ruttenberg, Karl Freund *m* Herbert Stothart

Nelson Eddy, Ilona Massey, Charles Ruggles, Frank Morgan, C. Aubrey Smith, Lionel Atwill, Walter Woolf King, Joyce Compton
Songs include 'At the Balalaika'; 'Tanya'; 'Ride, Cossack, Ride'; 'Shadows on the Sand'; 'Tale of the Tailors'; 'Beneath the Winter's Snows'; 'In a Heart as Brave as Your Own'; 'Soldiers of the Czar'; 'How Many Miles to Go'; 'The Magic of Your Love'; 'My Heart Is a Gypsy'

'A sumptuously produced operetta in the opulent MGM tradition.'—*Variety*

† Only the title song was retained from the original score.

The Balcony*
US 1963 86m bw
Walter Reade / Sterling / Allen Hodgdon / City Film (Joseph Strick, Ben Maddow)

In a war-torn world, a brothel continues to attract customers of every variety.
Low-budget adaptation of a rather confused allegorical play: vivid moments hardly atone for reels of surrealist groping.

w Ben Maddow, *play* Jean Genet *d* Joseph Strick *ph* George Folsey *m* Igor Stravinsky

Shelley Winters, Peter Falk, Lee Grant, Peter Brocco, Kent Smith, Ruby Dee, Jeff Corey, Leonard Nimoy

'Relentlessly funny, shaggy, shocking.'—*Times*

'Unfit for exhibition to man, woman or child.'—*The People*

AAN: George Folsey

Ball of Fire*
US 1942 111m bw
Samuel Goldwyn
working title: *The Professor and the Burlesque Queen*

Seven professors compiling a dictionary give shelter to a stripteaser on the run from gangsters.
Rather overstretched but fitfully amusing romp inspired by *Snow White and the Seven Dwarfs.*

w Charles Brackett, Billy Wilder d Howard Hawks *ph* Gregg Toland *m* Alfred Newman

Barbara Stanwyck, Gary Cooper, Oscar Homolka, Henry Travers, S. Z. Sakall, Tully Marshall, Leonid Kinskey, Richard Haydn, Aubrey Mather, Allen Jenkins, Dana Andrews, Dan Duryea

'It's played as if it were terribly bright, but it's rather shrill and tiresome.'—*New Yorker, 1982*

† Ginger Rogers was first choice for the Stanwyck role.

AAN: original story (Theodore Monroe, Billy Wilder); Alfred Newman; Barbara Stanwyck

Ballad in Blue
GB 1964 88m bw
(Warner) Alexander and Miguel Salkind (Herman Blaser)
US title: *Blues for Lovers*

A famous pianist becomes friendly with a blind boy and helps reconcile his parents.
Curious sentimental drama with the star playing himself; competent but hardly rousing.

w Burton Wohl *d* Paul Henreid *ph* Ron Taylor *m* Ray Charles, Stanley Black

Ray Charles, Mary Peach, Dawn Addams, Tom Bell, Piers Bishop, Betty McDowell

Ballad of a Soldier**
USSR 1959 89m bw
Mosfilm
original title: *Ballada o Soldate*

A soldier is granted four days' home leave before returning to be killed at the front.
Lyrical tear-jerker most notable for its impeccably photographed detail of Russian domestic and everyday life.

w Valentin Yoshov, Grigori Chukrai *d Grigori Chukrai ph Vladimir Nikolayev, Era Saveleva m* Mikhail Ziv

Vladimir Ivashev, Sharma Prokhorenko, Antonina Maximova

'In an epoch when the entertainment in most entertainment films is little more than offensive, its persuasive charm is particularly welcome.'—*MFB*

AAN: Valentin Yoshov, Grigori Chukrai

The Ballad of Cable Hogue*
US 1970 121m Technicolor
Warner / Phil Feldman (Sam Peckinpah)

A gold prospector takes a lengthy and ineffectual revenge on men who robbed him, and dies trying to be a hero.
Curious peripatetic western with the director in uncharacteristically experimental and comparatively non-violent mood. All concerned seem to be enjoying themselves, but the fun is not always communicated.

w John Crawford, Edward Penney *d Sam Peckinpah ph Lucien Ballard m* Jerry Goldsmith

Jason Robards, David Warner, Strother Martin, Slim Pickens, L. Q. Jones, Peter Whitney, R. G. Armstrong, Gene Evans, Stella Stevens

The Ballad of Joe Hill**
Sweden 1971 115m Eastmancolor
Bo Widerberg Film (Waldemar Bergendahl)
aka: *Joe Hill*

In 1902, a Swedish immigrant in New York becomes a revolutionary and is executed for the murder of a grocer.
Romantic propaganda which incidentally gives a delightfully detailed outsider's view of period America.

w,d Bo Widerberg *ph* Peter Davidsson, Jorgen Persson *m* Stefan Grossman *ad* Ulf Axen

Thommy Berggren, Anja Schmidt, Evert Anderson, Cathy Smith

The Ballad of Josie
US 1967 102m Techniscope
Universal (Marty Melcher)

Cleared of the manslaughter of her husband, a western widow renovates a derelict ranch and sets up as a sheep farmer.
Tediously whimsical, unsuitably cast women's lib comedy with so few laughs that it may require to be taken seriously.

w Harold Swanton *d* Andrew V. McLaglen *ph* Milton Krasner *m* Frank de Vol

Doris Day, Peter Graves, George Kennedy, William Talman, Andy Devine, Audrey Christie

The Ballad of Narayama*
Japan 1983 130m colour
Toei

In a remote village, local traditions include burying alive for the theft of food, and this is the fate of a pregnant woman and her family.
Primitivist ritual drama, totally distasteful to those new to the myths. On its own terms, some sort of classic.

w,d Shohei Imamura, from novels by Shichiro Fukazawa *ph* Masao Tochizawa *m* Shinichiro Ikebe

Ken Ogata, Sumiko Sakamoto, Tonpei Hidari

'One of the most intense portraits of personal fulfilment in all cinema.'—*Tony Rayns, MFB*

Ballet Mécanique*
France 1924 10m bw silent

Famous experimental short in which everyday images form abstract patterns. A key to all subsequent surrealist experiments in the cinema. Music by Georges Antheil; written, directed and produced by *Fernand Léger* and *Dudley Murphy.*

Balthazar*
France / Sweden 1966 95m bw
Parc / Ardos / Athos / Svenska Filminstitutet (Mag Bodard)
original title: *Au Hasard, Balthazar*

The life of a talented donkey, born in the Swiss alps and eventually killed during a smuggling escapade.
Something between *Black Beauty* and a Christian parable, this quiet, episodic film is counted by some as its director's best work.

wd Robert Bresson ph Ghislain Cloquet *m* Jean Wiener (and Schubert)

Anne Wiazemsky, François Lafarge, Walter Green (amateur cast)

Baltic Deputy*
USSR 1937 100m bw
Lenfilm

An old professor is finally reconciled to the 1917 revolution.
Propagandist biography (of scientist K. A. Timiriazev) with interesting scenes and a strong central performance.

w the directors and others *d* Alexander Zharki, Josef Heifits *ph* M. Kaplan *m* M. Timofeyev

Nikolai Cherkassov, M. Damasheva, A. Melnikov

The Baltimore Bullet
US 1980 103m Eastmancolor
Avco Embassy / Filmfair (John F. Brescia)

Adventures of a pair of pool sharks.
Flabby comedy attempting a lighthearted version of *The Hustler*. The rewards are meagre.

w John F. Brescia, Robert Vincent O'Neill *d* Robert Ellis Miller *ph* James A. Crabe *m* Johnny Mandel

James Coburn, Omar Sharif, Bruce Boxleitner, Ronee Blakely, Calvin Lockhart

'It manages to be stupidly macho and hopelessly incompetent at one and the same time.'—*Guardian*

La Bamba*
US 1987 108m colour

The brief life of 1950s rock-and-roller Ritchie Valens, who at 17 was killed in the Buddy Holly plane crash. Palatable biopic, for those who can stand the kind of music. Lou Diamond Philips, Esai Morales, Rosana de Soto, Elizabeth Pena, Danielle von Zerneck. Written and directed by Luis Valdez; for Taylor Hackford–Bill Borden/New Visions/Columbia.

Bambi****
US 1942 72m Technicolor
Walt Disney

The story of a forest deer, from the book by Felix Salten.
Anthropomorphic cartoon feature, one of Disney's most memorable and brilliant achievements, with a great comic character in Thumper the rabbit and a climactic forest fire sequence which is genuinely thrilling. A triumph of the animator's art.

supervisor David Hand *m* Frank Churchill, Edward Plumb

'The ultimate stag movie.'—*anon.*

AA: song 'Love Is a Song' (*m* Frank Churchill, *ly* Larry Morey)
AAN: Frank Churchill, Edward Plumb

The Bamboo Blonde
US 1946 68m bw

A night club singer falls for a B29 pilot who christens her—and his plane—The Bamboo Blonde. Mediocre filler with the star ill at ease except when singing. Frances Langford, Ralph Edwards, Russell Wade, Iris Adrian, Jane Greer. Written by Olive Cooper, Lawrence Kimble, Wayne Williams; directed by Anthony Mann; for Herman Schlom / RKO.

The Bamboo Prison
US 1955 80m bw

An American prisoner-of-war in Korea poses as a collaborator in order to get secret information. Forlorn war drama which makes little impact. Robert Francis, Brian Keith, E. G. Marshall, Dianne Foster, Jerome Courtland. Written by Edwin Blum and Jack de Witt; directed by Lewis Seiler; for Columbia.

Banana Ridge
GB 1941 87m bw

A business man's old flame presents him with an alleged son. Stagey farce salvaged by star performances. Robertson Hare, Alfred Drayton, Isabel Jeans, Nova Pilbeam, Adele Dixon, Stewart Rome. Written by Walter C. Mycroft, Lesley Storm, Ben Travers, from the play by Ben Travers; directed by Walter C. Mycroft; for ABPC.

Bananas*
US 1971 81m De Luxe
UA / Rollins and Joffe (Jack Grossberg)

A meek and mild product tester for a New York corporation accidentally becomes a South American rebel hero.
Disjointed anarchic comedy with a few good jokes typical of their author.

w Woody Allen with Mickey Rose *d* Woody Allen *ph* Andrew M. Costikyan *m* Marvin Hamlisch

Woody Allen, Louise Lasser, Carlos Montalban, Jacobo Morales

'Full of hilarious comic ideas and lines, supplied by Allen and his collaborator; then Allen, the director and actor, murders them.'—*Stanley Kauffmann*

† Asked why his film was called *Bananas*, Allen replied: 'Because there are no bananas in it.'

'You're no blue blood any more, honey. The master bought you . . . and now he's waitin'!'

Band of Angels
US 1957 127m Warnercolor
Warner (no producer credited)

In 1865, a Kentucky girl learns that her mother was black and is sold as a slave, but quickly becomes her owner's mistress.
Long-winded romantic adventure, rather lamely scripted and developed. The star's presence reinforces the impression of sitting through the ghost of *Gone with the Wind*.

w John Twist, Ivan Goff, Ben Roberts, *novel* Robert Penn Warren *d* Raoul Walsh *ph* Lucien Ballard *m* Max Steiner

Clark Gable, Yvonne de Carlo, Sidney Poitier, Efrem Zimbalist Jnr, Patric Knowles, Rex Reason, Torin Thatcher, Andrea King

'Too absurd to be dislikeable.'—*MFB*

The Band Plays On
US 1934 87m bw

Four street kids are saved by football and eventually become national stars. Ho-hum sentimental melodrama with plot trouble. Robert Young, Stuart Erwin, Leo Carrillo, Betty Furness, Ted Healy, Preston Foster, Russell Hardie, William Tannen. Written by Bernard Schubert, Ralph Spence, Harvey Gates; directed by Russell Mack; for MGM.
'Slow, long, and weak on cast names.'—*Variety*

Band Waggon*
GB 1939 85m bw
Gainsborough (Edward Black)

Comedians running a pirate TV station in a ghostly castle round up a gang of spies.
Film version of a long-running radio comedy series; quite a serviceable record of a phenomenon.

w Marriott Edgar, Val Guest *d* Marcel Varnel

Arthur Askey, Richard Murdoch, Jack Hylton and his band, Pat Kirkwood, Moore Marriott, Peter Gawthorne, Wally Patch, Donald Calthrop

The Band Wagon****
US 1953 112m Technicolor
MGM (Arthur Freed)

A has-been Hollywood dancer joins forces with a temperamental stage producer to put on a Broadway musical.
Simple but sophisticated musical with the bare minimum of plot, told mostly in jokes, and the maximum of music and song. Numbers include those listed below, as well as a spoof Mickey Spillane ballet finale. Level of technical accomplishment very high.

w Adolph Green, Betty Comden d Vincente Minnelli ph Harry Jackson *songs Howard Dietz, Arthur Schwarz m* Adolph Deutsch *ad Cedric Gibbons, Preston Ames*

Fred Astaire, Jack Buchanan, Oscar Levant, Cyd Charisse, Nanette Fabray

'The best musical of the month, the year, the decade, or for all I know of all time.'—*Archer Winsten*

† The Jack Buchanan character, Jeffrey Cordova, was first offered to Clifton Webb. It was loosely based on Jose Ferrer, who in the early fifties produced four Broadway shows all running at the same time, and acted in a fifth.
†† Songs include: 'A Shine on Your Shoes', 'By Myself', 'That's Entertainment', 'Dancing in the Dark', 'Triplets', 'New Sun in the Sky', 'I Guess I'll Have to Change My Plan', 'Louisiana Hayride', 'I Love Louisa', 'Girl Hunt' ballet.

AAN: Adolph Green, Betty Comden; Adolph Deutsch

Bande à Part
France 1964 95m bw
Anouchka / Orsay (Philippe Dussart)
aka: *The Outsiders*

Aimless young people plan a robbery which ends in murder.
Despite the plot, the emphasis is on fragments of lyricism, and the film is not among its director's greatest successes.

wd Jean-Luc Godard, *novel* Fool's Gold by Dolores and B. Hitchens *ph* Raoul Coutard *m* Michel Legrand

Anna Karina, Claude Brasseur, Sami Frey, Louisa Colpeyn

'In a sense, the whole film is a metaphor illustrating this glancing collision, when fantasy and reality merge but one may still remain unsure which is which.'—*Tom Milne, MFB*

Bandido
US 1956 92m De Luxe Cinemascope
UA / Robert L. Jacks

Mexico 1916: an American adventurer helps a rebel leader to defeat a gun runner.
Standard action fare, rather slackly handled.

w Earl Felton *d* Richard Fleischer *ph* Ernest Laszlo *m* Max Steiner

Robert Mitchum, Gilbert Roland, Zachary Scott, Ursula Thiess

The Bandit*
Brazil 1953 119m bw
Companhia Cinematographica (Cid Leite da Silva)
original title: *O'Cangaceiro*

The leader of a gang of outlaws comes to grief after falling out with his second in command over a woman.
One of the few Brazilian films to achieve international popularity, mainly because of its memorable theme tune. The film itself looks attractive but becomes a bit of a bore.

wd Lima Barreto *ph* Chick Fowle *m Gabriel Migliori*

Alberto Ruschel, Milton Ribeiro, Marisa Prado

The Bandit of Sherwood Forest*
US 1946 87m Technicolor
Columbia (Leonard S. Picker, Clifford Sanforth)

Robin Hood frustrates the Regent who plans to usurp the throne from the boy king.
A lively romp through Sherwood Forest with a capable cast.

w Wilfrid H. Pettit, Melvin Levy, *novel* Son of Robin Hood by Paul A. Castleton *d* George Sherman, Henry Levin *ph* Tony Gaudio, William Snyder, George Meehan *m* Hugo Friedhofer

Cornel Wilde, Anita Louise, Edgar Buchanan, Jill Esmond, Henry Daniell, George Macready, Russell Hicks, John Abbott, Lloyd Corrigan

The Bandit of Zhobe
GB 1959 81m Technicolor Cinemascope

An Indian chieftain kidnaps a British major's daughter in retaliation for the death of his wife. Tinpot action melodrama in the wake of the rather better *Zarak*. Victor Mature, Anthony Newley, Anne Aubrey, Norman Wooland. Written and directed by John Gilling; for Warwick / Columbia.

The Bandit Queen
US 1950 69m bw

The daughter of murdered Spaniards in California takes revenge against violent settlers from the east. Predictable western adventure on a low budget. Barbara Britton, Willard Parker, Barton Maclane, Philip Reed, Victor Kilian, Thurston Hall. Written by Victor West and Budd Lesser; directed and produced by William Berke; for Lippert.

Bandits of Corsica*
US 1951 83m bw

Mario and his gypsy twin get together to unseat a tyrant. Rather muffled actioner with adequate highlights. Richard Greene, Paula Raymond, Raymond Burr, Dona Drake, Raymond Greenleaf, Lee Van Cleef. Written by Richard Schayer; directed by Ray Nazarro; for Global/UA. (GB title: *The Return of the Corsican Brothers*. See also: *The Corsican Brothers*.)

Bandits of Orgosolo
Italy 1961 98m bw
Titanus

A Sardinian shepherd shelters some bandits and becomes one of them.
Rather slow character adventure which achieved some international reputation in its first release.

w Vittorio de Seta, Vera Gherarducci *d,p,ph* Vittorio de Seta *m* Valentino Bucci

Michele Cossu, Peppeddu Cuccu, and amateur cast

Bandolero!*
US 1968 108m De Luxe Panavision
TCF (Robert L. Jacks)

In Texas, fugitive outlaw brothers run into trouble with their Mexican counterparts.
Dour and downbeat but well-staged western with emphasis on hanging and rape; an unusual mixture but smoothly assembled.

w James Lee Barrett *d* Andrew V. McLaglen *ph* William H. Clothier *m* Jerry Goldsmith

James Stewart, Dean Martin, Raquel Welch, George Kennedy, Will Geer, Andrew Prine

Bang the Drum Slowly
US 1973 96m Movielab
Paramount (Maurice and Lois Rosenfield)

A baseball star finds that he is dying of leukemia.
Cliché-ridden tearjerker in the modern style.

w Mark Harris, from his novel *d* John Hancock *ph* Richard Shore *m* Stephen Lawrence

Michael Moriarty, Robert de Niro, Vincent Gardenia, Phil Foster

AAN: Vincent Gardenia

Bang, You're Dead
GB 1954 88m bw
British Lion / Wellington (Lance Comfort)
US title: *Game of Danger*

A small boy accidentally shoots a local villain, and another man is arrested.
Singularly pointless and unattractive melodrama, a long way behind *The Window* and *The Yellow Balloon*.

w Guy Elmes, Ernest Borneman *d* Lance Comfort *ph* Brendan J. Stafford *m* Eric Spear

Jack Warner, Derek Farr, Veronica Hurst, Gordon Harker, Michael Medwin, Anthony Richmond, Philip Saville

Banjo on my Knee**
US 1936 95m bw
TCF (Nunnally Johnson)

In a Mississippi riverboat shanty town, a wedding night is interrupted when the groom is arrested during a brawl.
Unusual, easy-going comedy in which the stars sing and dance as well as fool around.

w Nunnally Johnson, novel Harry Hamilton *d John Cromwell ph* Ernest Palmer *m* Arthur Lange *songs* Jimmy McHugh, Harold Adamson

Barbara Stanwyck, Joel McCrea, Buddy Ebsen, Walter Brennan, Helen Westley, Walter Catlett, Tony Martin, Katherine de Mille

'Too complicated for any better than moderate reception.'—*Variety*

The Bank Dick***
US 1940 73m bw
Universal
GB title: *The Bank Detective*

In Lompoc, California, a ne'er-do-well accidentally stops a hold-up, is made a bank detective, acquires deeds to a worthless mine and interferes in the production of a film.
Imperfect, but probably the best Fields vehicle there is: the jokes sometimes end in mid-air, but there are delicious moments and very little padding. The character names are sometimes funnier than the script: they include Egbert Sousè (accent grave over the 'e'), J. Pinkerton Snoopington, Ogg Oggilbie and Filthy McNasty.

w Mahatma Kane Jeeves (W. C. Fields) *d* Eddie Cline *ph* Milton Krasner *md* Charles Previn

W. C. Fields, Franklin Pangborn, Shemp Howard, Jack Norton, Grady Sutton, Cora Witherspoon

'One of the great classics of American comedy.'—*Robert Lewis Taylor*

'When the man is funny he is terrific . . . but the story is makeshift, the other characters are stock types, the only pace discernible is the distance between drinks or the rhythm of the fleeting seconds it takes Fields to size up trouble coming and duck the hell out.'—*Otis Ferguson*

'Individualistic display of broad comedy . . . adequate program supporter.'—*Variety*

† Fields's writing nom-de-plume was allegedly borrowed from noble characters in old English plays he squirmed through as a youth. They kept saying: 'M'hat, m'cane, Jeeves.'

Bank Holiday*
GB 1938 86m bw
Gainsborough (Edward Black)
US title: *Three on a Weekend*

The lives of various people intertwine during a day out in Brighton.
Simple but effective slice-of-life comedy-drama, establishing several actors and a director. Still quite refreshing.

w Hans Wilhelm, Rodney Ackland, Roger Burford *d Carol Reed ph* Arthur Crabtree

Margaret Lockwood, Hugh Williams, Kathleen Harrison, Wally Patch, Rene Ray, Linden Travers, Garry Marsh, Wilfrid Lawson

'Ranges from pathos to farce with a nice avoidance of overstatement.'—*Daily Telegraph*

The Bank Shot*
US 1974 83m De Luxe
UA / Hal Landers, Bobby Roberts

Using house-moving equipment, an escaped convict steals a whole bank.
Extended chase comedy with scenes of gleeful destruction. Acceptable for those in the mood, but a shade overdone.

w Wendell Mayes, *novel* Donald E. Westlake *d* Gower Champion *ph* Harry Stradling Jnr *m* John Morris

George C. Scott, Joanna Cassidy, Sorrell Brooke, G. Wood, Clifton James

Bannerline*
US 1951 87m bw
MGM (Henry Berman)

To comfort a dying old man, a young reporter prints a fake newspaper showing the indictment of the old man's gangster enemy. By an odd chain of events, the story becomes true.
Worthy but rather dull MGM 'B', typical of the regime of Dore Schary, boasting a pleasing small-town atmosphere and a remarkable cast of old actors.

w Charles Schnee, *story* Samson Raphaelson *d* Don Weis *ph* Harold Lipstein *m* Rudolph Kopp

Lionel Barrymore, Keefe Brasselle, Sally Forrest, Lewis Stone, Elizabeth Risdon, J. Carrol Naish, Spring Byington, Larry Keating

Banning
US 1967 102m Techniscope
Universal (Dick Berg)

A golf pro has sporting and amorous adventures at a country club.
Tedious, complexly plotted melodrama of life among the idle rich; handling generally laboured. A showcase for the studio's young contract talent.

w James Lee *d* Ron Winston *ph* Loyal Griggs *m* Quincy Jones

Robert Wagner, Anjanette Comer, Jill St John, Guy Stockwell, James Farentino, Susan Clark, Howard St John, Mike Kellin, Sean Garrison, Gene Hackman

AAN: song 'The Eyes of Love' (*m* Quincy Jones, *ly* Bob Russell)

The Bar Sinister
US 1955 87m Eastmancolor Cinemascope
MGM (Henry Berman)
GB title: *It's a Dog's Life*

The rise in lifestyle of a Bowery bull terrier, as told by himself.
Tolerable whimsy, in MGM's best family manner; ten years earlier it might have been a hit.

w John Michael Hayes, *story* Richard Harding Davis *d* Herman Hoffman *ph* Paul Vogel *m* Elmer Bernstein

Edmund Gwenn, Jeff Richards, Jarma Lewis, Dean Jagger

Barabbas*
Italy / US 1962 144m Technirama
Columbia / Dino de Laurentiis

Pardoned instead of Christ, Barabbas is sentenced to the silver mines, turns Christian, and becomes a gladiator.
Overblown epic which starts with a genuine eclipse of the sun and has nowhere to go but down. The cast sparks a few moments, but it is generally a gaudy display of carnage.

w Christopher Fry, Nigel Balchin, Diego Fabbri, Ivo Perilli, *novel* Pär Lagerkvist *d* Richard Fleischer *ph* Aldo Tonti *m* Mario Nascimbene *ad* Mario Chiari

Anthony Quinn, Silvana Mangano, Vittorio Gassman, Ernest Borgnine, Jack Palance, Arthur Kennedy, Norman Wooland, Valentina Cortese, Harry Andrews, Katy Jurado, Michael Gwynn

'Unacceptable in its pain-preoccupation and its religiosity.'—*Peter John Dyer*

† The eclipse of the sun at the beginning is a real one, photographed at Nice.

'See her do her thing!'
Barbarella*
France / Italy 1967 98m Technicolor Panavision
Marianne / Dino de Laurentiis

A beautiful young 40th-century astronaut prevents the positronic ray from getting into the wrong hands.
Campy and slightly sick adventures with angels and other space people, from a highly censorable comic strip; some ingenious gadgetry and design, but not much of interest in the foreground.

w Terry Southern, *book* Jean-Claude Forest *d* Roger Vadim *ph* Claude Renoir *pd Mario Garbuglia* *m* Bob Crewe, Charles Fox

Jane Fonda, John Phillip Law, Anita Pallenberg, Milo O'Shea, David Hemmings, Marcel Marceau, Ugo Tognazzi, Claude Dauphin

'A leading science fiction authority has claimed that if Lewis Carroll were alive today he would inevitably have written not *Alice's Adventures in Wonderland* but *Lolita*. He might perhaps equally well have written *Barbarella*.'—*Jack Ibberson*

'A flaccid, jaded appeal to our baser appetites, always liberally doused with essence of cop-out, resulting in elucubrated, anaemic pornography.'—*John Simon*

The Barbarian
US 1933 82m approx bw
MGM
GB title: *A Night in Cairo*

An American lady travelling in the Middle East falls for a local potentate.
Shades of *The Sheik*. Actually this version was first filmed in 1915 by Edgar Selwyn from his own play, then again in 1924. Any version would seem fairly hysterical now.

w Anita Loos, Elmer Harris, *play* Edgar Selwyn *d* Sam Wood *ph* Harold Rosson

Ramon Novarro, Myrna Loy, Reginald Denny, C. Aubrey Smith, Louise Closser Hale, Edward Arnold

'An abrupt switch to melodrama at the halfway mark makes this a maudlin, doubtful desert melodrama.'—*Variety*

The Barbarian and the Geisha*
US 1958 105m Eastmancolor Cinemascope
TCF (Eugene Frenke)

In 1856 the first US diplomat to visit Japan meets local opposition but is helped by a geisha.
Episodic semi-historical romance which scarcely suits the talents of those involved.

w Charles Grayson *d* John Huston *ph* Charles G. Clarke *m* Hugo Friedhofer

John Wayne, Eiko Ando, Sam Jaffe, So Yamamura

'It is saddening to think that the director of *The Asphalt Jungle* has gained professional freedom and international celebrity to become, at 51, yet another taskmaster who goes out in the midday sun.'—*Arlene Croce*

Barbarosa*
US 1981 90m Eastmancolor
ITC / Wittliff–Nelson–Busey (Paul N. Lazarus III)

An outlaw's legend grows along with his enemies.
Undercast but interestingly directed western, with more than enough elegiac qualities mixed with some nods to the old enjoyable style.

w William D. Wittliff *d Fred Schepsi* *ph* Ian Baker *m* Bruce Smeaton

Willie Nelson, Gary Busey, Isela Vega, Gilbert Roland, George Voskovec

'The most spirited and satisfying new western epic in several years.'—*New Yorker*

'More than its share of artistic merit.'—*Variety*

Barbary Coast**
US 1935 91m bw
Samuel Goldwyn

During San Francisco's gold rush days a ruthless club owner builds a lonely girl into a star attraction but cannot win her love.
Juicy melodrama tailored for its stars, but with excellent background detail, sets and lighting.

w Ben Hecht, Charles MacArthur *d Howard Hawks* *ph* Ray June *m* Alfred Newman

Edward G. Robinson, Miriam Hopkins, Joel McCrea, Walter Brennan, Frank Craven, Brian Donlevy, Donald Meek

'More than a year ago Sam Goldwyn picked Barbary Coast as a title and called in Hecht and MacArthur to write a story to fit. Result is a picture that has all it takes to get along in thoroughbred company.'—*Variety*

† David Niven made his first screen appearance as an extra.

AAN: Ray June

Barbary Coast Gent
US 1944 87m bw
MGM (Orville Dull)

A bandit from the Californian goldfields tries to go straight in San Francisco.
Star comedy drama, somewhat below par despite attractive settings and good production.
w William Lipman, Grant Garrett, Harry Ruskin *d* Roy del Ruth *ph* Charles Salerno Jnr *m* David Snell
Wallace Beery, Binnie Barnes, Frances Rafferty, Chill Wills, Ray Collins, John Carradine, Noah Beery, Morris Ankrum, Henry O'Neill, Donald Meek, Paul Hurst, Louise Beavers

Barbed Wire*
US 1927 85m approx bw silent
A French girl falls for a German prisoner of war. Almost forgotten war film which seems at least worthy of comparison with *All Quiet on the Western Front*, which was made three years later. Pola Negri, Clive Brook, Einar Hanson, Claude Gillingwater, Gustav von Seyffertitz. Written by Jules Furthman and Rowland V. Lee from the novel The Woman of Knockaloe by Hall Caine; directed by Rowland V. Lee; photographed by Bert Glennon; for Paramount.

Bardelys the Magnificent
US 1926 88m at 24 fps bw silent
A sixteenth-century French adventurer finally wins his fair lady. Laboured swashbuckler. John Gilbert, Eleanor Boardman, George K. Arthur. Written by Dorothy Farnum, from the novel by Rafael Sabatini; directed by King Vidor; for MGM.

Barefaced Flatfoot***
US 1952 7m Technicolor
Mr Magoo battles shortsightedly to save his nephew from the underworld. Archetypal Magoo cartoon. ('Didn't we meet in Heidelberg?' he murmurs to the dummy he is duelling with his umbrella.) The title is a spoof on a contemporary Columbia movie, *The Barefoot Mailman*. Designed by *John Hubley*; produced by *Stephen Bosustow*; for UPA.

Barefoot Battalion
Greece 1954 89m bw
Peter Boudoures
War orphans inhabit a derelict barge and band together to harass the Germans.
Unlikely true story, roughly dramatized and poorly produced.
w Nico Katsiotes *d* Gregg Tallas *ph* Mixalis Gaziadis *m* Mikis Theodorakis
Maria Costi, Nico Fermas, Stavros Krozos

'The world's most beautiful animal!'
The Barefoot Contessa*
US 1954 128m Technicolor
UA / Figaro (Forrest E. Johnston)
A glamorous barefoot dancer in a Spanish cabaret is turned into a Hollywood star, but her sexual frustrations lead to a tragic end.
A fascinating farrago of addled philosophy and lame wisecracks, very typical of a writer-director here not at his best, decorated by a splendid gallery of actors and some attractive settings.
wd Joseph L. Mankiewicz ph Jack Cardiff
m Mario Nascimbene
Humphrey Bogart (Harry Dawes), Ava Gardner (Maria Vargas), Edmond O'Brien (Oscar Muldoon), Marius Goring (Alberto Bravano), Valentina Cortesa (Eleonora Torlato-Favrini), Rossano Brazzi (Vincenzo Torlato-Favrini), Elizabeth Sellars (Jerry), Warren Stevens (Kirk Edwards), Franco Interlenghi (Pedro), Mari Aldon (Myrna)

HARRY: 'Life, every now and then, behaves as though it had seen too many bad movies, when everything fits too well—the beginning, the middle, the end—from fade-in to fade-out.'

'This example of the Higher Lunacy must vie with *Johnny Guitar* for the silliest film of the year.'—*Gavin Lambert*

'A trash masterpiece: a Cinderella story in which the prince turns out to be impotent.'—*Pauline Kael, 1968*

AA: Edmond O'Brien
AAN: Joseph L. Mankiewicz (as writer)

The Barefoot Executive*
US 1970 96m Technicolor
Walt Disney (Bill Anderson)
A TV network discovers that its most infallible average viewer is a chimpanzee.
Quite a beguiling little farcical comedy with mild doses of satire.
w Joseph L. McEveety *d* Robert Butler
ph Charles F. Wheeler *m* Robert F. Brunner
Kurt Russell, Harry Morgan, Joe Flynn, Wally Cox, Heather North, Alan Hewitt, Hayden Rorke

'Break the rules! Make love! Fall over laughing!'
Barefoot in the Park**
US 1967 109m Technicolor
Paramount / Hal B. Wallis
A pair of New York newlyweds rent a cold water flat at the top of a liftless building, and manage to marry the bride's mother to an eccentric neighbour.
Breezy but overlong adaptation of a stage play which succeeded through audience response to its one-liners, which on the screen sometimes fall flat. The people are nice, though.
w Neil Simon, from his play *d* Gene Saks
ph Joseph La Shelle *m* Neal Hefti
Robert Redford (Paul Bratter), Jane Fonda (Corie Bratter), *Mildred Natwick* (Ethel Banks), *Charles Boyer* (Victor Velasco), Herb Edelman (Harry Pepper), Mabel Albertson (Aunt Harriet), Fritz Feld (restaurant owner)

ETHEL: 'Make him feel important. If you do that, you'll have a happy and wonderful marriage—like two out of every ten couples.'

ETHEL: 'I feel like we've died and gone to heaven—only we had to climb up.'

AAN: Mildred Natwick

The Barefoot Mailman
US 1951 82m Supercinecolor
Columbia (Robert Cohn)
In 19th-century Florida, the mailman is joined by a confidence trickster who later has a change of heart.
Inept comedy adventure which never really gets started.
w James Gunn, Francis Swann, *novel* Theodore Pratt *d* Earl McEvoy
ph Ellis W. Carter *m* George Duning
Robert Cummings, Jerome Courtland, Terry Moore, John Russell, Will Geer, Arthur Shields, Trevor Bardette
† This is the title parodied by the Magoo cartoon *Barefaced Flatfoot*.

Barfly*
US 1987 99m TVC Color
Cannon / Barbet Schroeder, Fred Roos, Tom Luddy
A self-styled poet of the bottle lords it over a Los Angeles bar.
Unrelieved serio-comic wallow in the underside of American life. For connoisseurs and idiots as well as star fans.
w Charles Bukowski *d* Barbet Schroeder
ph Robby Muller *m* none *pd* Bob Ziembicki
Mickey Rourke, Faye Dunaway, Alice Krige, Jack Nance

The Bargee*
GB 1964 106m Techniscope
AB / Galton–Simpson (W. A. Whitaker)
A canal barge Casanova is trapped into marriage.
The long-awaited comedy which was supposed to make a film star out of TV's Young Steptoe turned out to be rough and vulgar but not very funny.
w Ray Galton, Alan Simpson *d* Duncan Wood *ph* Harry Waxman *m* Frank Cordell
Harry H. Corbett, Ronnie Barker, Hugh Griffith, Eric Sykes, Julia Foster, Miriam Karlin, Eric Barker, Derek Nimmo, Norman Bird, Richard Briers

The Barkleys of Broadway*
US 1949 109m Technicolor
MGM (Arthur Freed)
A quarrelling couple of musical comedy stars split up, and she becomes a serious actress.
A rather flat and unattractive reunion for a famous pair, with a witless script, poorish numbers and very little style. The compensations are minor.
w Adolph Green, Betty Comden *d* Charles Walters *ph* Harry Stradling *songs* Harry Warren, Ira Gershwin *md* Lennie Hayton
Fred Astaire, Ginger Rogers, Oscar Levant, Jacques François, Billie Burke
AAN: Harry Stradling
† Ginger Rogers was in fact second choice; Judy Garland was cast but withdrew through illness.
†† Songs include: 'They Can't Take That Away from Me', 'Shoes with Wings On', 'My

One and Only Highland Fling', 'Swing Trot', 'Manhattan Downbeat', 'You'd be So Hard to Replace', 'A Weekend in the Country', 'Sabre Dance'.

Barnacle Bill
US 1941 90m bw
MGM (Milton Bren)

A fishing boat skipper gets romantic in the hope of financing his enterprises.
Adequate waterfront comedy on *Min and Bill* lines, consolidating a popular star teaming.

w Jack Jevne, Hugo Butler *d* Richard Thorpe *ph* Clyde de Vinna *m* Bronislau Kaper

Wallace Beery, Marjorie Main, Leo Carrillo, Virginia Weidler, Donald Meek, Barton Maclaine, Connie Gilchrist, Sara Haden

Barnacle Bill*
GB 1957 87m bw
Ealing (Michael Balcon)
US title: *All at Sea*

The last of a long line of sailors suffers from seasickness, and takes command of a decaying Victorian pier at an English seaside resort.
Quite an amusing comedy which had the misfortune to come at the tag-end of the Ealing classics and so seemed too mild and predictable. Perhaps it was a little staid.

w T. E. B. Clarke *d* Charles Frend *ph* Douglas Slocombe *m* John Addison

Alec Guinness, Irene Browne, Percy Herbert, Harold Goodwin, Maurice Denham, George Rose, Lionel Jeffries, Victor Maddern

Le Baron Fantôme*
France 1943 100m bw
Consortium de Productions de Films (Robert Florat)
GB title: *The Phantom Baron*

In the early 19th-century, the disappearance of a nobleman causes problems for his heirs.
Macabre fairy tale with effective scenes which seem to relate to Cocteau's later fantasies; the film as a whole is less effective.

wd Serge de Poligny *dialogue* Jean Cocteau *ph* Roger Hubert *m* Louis Beydts

Jany Holt, Odette Joyeux, Alain Cuny, Gabrielle Dorziat

Baron Münchhausen*
Czechoslovakia 1962 81m Agfacolor
Ceskoslovensky Film
original title: *Baron Prasil*

An astronaut finds on the moon the famous liar Baron Münchhausen, who takes him back to earth and a variety of exaggerated adventures.
Amusing variation on the old stories, using live action against deliberately artificial backgrounds.

wd Karel Zeman, from the novel by Gottfried Burger and the illustrations by Gustave Doré *ph* Jiri Tarantik *m* Zdenek Liska

Milos Kopecky, Rudolf Jelinek, Jana Becjchova

The Baron of Arizona
US 1950 85m bw
Lippert (Carl Hittleman)

In the 19th century a clerk tries to claim the whole of Arizona by false land grants.
Initially appealing but basically rather feeble tall tale, ineffectively worked out and decidedly undernourished as a production.

wd Samuel Fuller *ph* James Wong Howe *m* Paul Dunlap

Vincent Price, Ellen Drew, Beulah Bondi, Vladimir Sokoloff, Reed Hadley, Robert Barrat

The Baroness and the Butler
US 1938 75m bw
TCF (Raymond Griffith)

The Hungarian prime minister's butler is loved by a princess.
Thin mittel-European romantic star whimsy.

w Sam Hellman, Lamar Trotti, Kathryn Scola, *play* The Lady Has a Heart by Ladislaus Bus-Fekete *d* Walter Lang *ph* Arthur Miller *md* Louis Silvers

William Powell, Annabella, Henry Stephenson, Nigel Bruce, Helen Westley, Joseph Schildkraut, J. Edward Bromberg, Lynn Bari

Barquero!
US 1970 114m De Luxe
Aubrey Schenck (Hal Klein)

A western ferryman is taken prisoner by bandits but turns the tables.
Long, violent, rather uninteresting western in the Spanish manner.

w George Schenck, William Marks *d* Gordon Douglas *ph* Jerry Finnermann *m* Dominic Frontiere

Lee Van Cleef, Forrest Tucker, Warren Oates, Kerwin Mathews, Mariette Hartley, Brad Weston, John Davis Chandler

'When poets love, heaven and earth fall back to watch!'

The Barretts of Wimpole Street**
US 1934 109m bw
MGM (Irving Thalberg)
TV title: *Forbidden Alliance*

Invalid Elizabeth Barrett plans to marry poet Robert Browning, against her tyrannical father's wishes.
Claustrophobic but well-acted adaptation of a stage play which has become more forceful than history. Stilted now, but still better than the remake.

w Ernst Vajda, Claudine West, Donald Ogden Stewart, *play* Rudolf Besier *d* Sidney Franklin *ph* William Daniels *m* Herbert Stothart

Norma Shearer (Elizabeth Barrett), Fredric March (Robert Browning), *Charles Laughton* (Edward Moulton-Barrett), Maureen O'Sullivan (Henrietta), Katherine Alexander (Arabel), Una O'Connor (Wilson), Ralph Forbes (Captain Surtees-Cook), Ian Wolfe (Harry Bevan)

'Box office for all its celluloid lethargy . . . truly an actor's picture, with long speeches and verbose philosophical observations.'—*Variety*

AAN: best picture; Norma Shearer

The Barretts of Wimpole Street
GB 1956 105m Metrocolor Cinemascope
MGM (Sam Zimbalist)

Dreadful, miscast remake of the above, with emphasis on the Freudian father-daughter relationship. An unattractive and boring film.

w John Dighton *d* Sidney Franklin *ph* Frederick A. Young *m* Bronislau Kaper

Jennifer Jones, Bill Travers, John Gielgud, Virginia McKenna

Barricade
US 1939 71m bw
TCF (Edward Kaufman)

A newsman and a girl with a past fight Mongolian bandits in North China.
A bagful of clichés which does not quite add up to entertainment.

w Granville Walker *d* Gregory Ratoff *ph* Karl Freund *m* David Buttolph

Warner Baxter, Alice Faye, Charles Winninger, Arthur Treacher, Keye Luke, Willie Fung, Doris Lloyd

'Inadequate and confusing . . . it was launched as an A, but winds up as a B that will have to groove generally in the supporting spots.'—*Variety*

Barricade
US 1949 75m Technicolor
Warner (Saul Elkins)

A tough mine-owner who runs a camp miles from civilization meets his come-uppance when three strangers are forced to accept his hospitality.
Rough western only notable as an (almost) scene-for-scene steal from *The Sea Wolf*: a text-book adaptation.

w William Sackheim *d* Peter Godfrey *ph* Carl Guthrie *m* William Lava

Raymond Massey, Dane Clark, Ruth Roman, Robert Douglas, Morgan Farley

The Barrier
US 1926 79m at 24 fps bw silent

A brutal sea captain tries to prevent his protégé's marriage. Brooding melodrama climaxing in an Alaskan storm. Lionel Barrymore (in his first film for the studio where he spent the rest of his career), Henry B. Walthall, Marceline Day, Norman Kerry. Written by Rex Beach; directed by George Hill; for MGM.

The Barrier
US 1937 90m bw

A gold rush prospector kidnaps a child and brings her up in the belief that she is a half-breed. Lyceum-like melodrama against spectacular natural settings; somehow not of interest. Leo Carrillo, Jean Parker, Robert Barrat, James Ellison, Otto Kruger, Andy Clyde, Addison Richards, Sara Haden. Written by Bernard Schubert, Mordaunt Shairp, Harrison Jacobs, from the novel by Rex Beach; directed by Lesley Selander; for Harry Sherman (Paramount).

Barry Lyndon**
GB 1975 187m Eastmancolor
Warner / Hawk / Peregrine (Stanley Kubrick)

Adventures of an 18th-century Irish gentleman of fortune.
A curiously cold-hearted enterprise, like an art gallery in which the backgrounds are sketched in loving detail and the human figures totally neglected; there is much to enjoy, but script and acting are variable to say the least, and the point of it all is obscure, as it certainly does not tell a rattling good story.

wd Stanley Kubrick, novel W. M. Thackeray *ph John Alcott md* Leonard Rosenman *pd Ken Adam*

Ryan O'Neal, Marisa Berenson, Patrick Magee, Hardy Kruger, Steven Berkoff, Gay Hamilton, Marie Kean, Murray Melvin, André Morell, Leonard Rossiter, Philip Stone *narrator* Michael Hordern

'The motion picture equivalent of one of these very large, very expensive, very elegant and very dull books that exist solely to be seen on coffee tables.'—*Charles Champlin*

'Watching the movie is like looking at illustrations for a work that has not been supplied.'—*John Simon*

'All art and no matter: a series of still pictures which will please the retina while denying our hunger for drama. And far from re-creating another century, it more accurately embalms it.'—*Michael Billington, Illustrated London News*

AA: John Alcott; Leonard Rosenman
AAN: best picture; Stanley Kubrick (as writer); Stanley Kubrick (as director)

Bartleby*
GB 1970 79m Eastmancolor
Pantheon (Rodney Carr-Smith)

A young clerk gradually refuses to take part in life.
A non-action film from an independent source, praiseworthy but overlong and fairly lacking in any kind of appeal except to literary connoisseurs.

w Anthony Friedmann, Rodney Carr-Smith, *story* Herman Melville *d* Anthony Friedmann *ph* Ian Wilson *m* Roger Webb

Paul Scofield, John McEnery, Thorley Walters, Colin Jeavons

Les Bas-fonds*
France 1936 92m bw
Albatros (Alexander Kamenka)
aka: *The Lower Depths*

A clash of temperaments flares up between derelicts in a dosshouse.
Uneven transposition of a famous work, with patches of good acting.

w Jean Renoir, Charles Spaak and others, *play* Maxim Gorky *d Jean Renoir ph* Jean Bachelet *m* Jean Wiener

Jean Gabin, Louis Jouvet, Vladimir Sokoloff, Robert Le Vigan, Suzy Prim

'When it flies, someone dies!'
The Bat
US 1959 78m bw
AA / Liberty (C. J. Tevlin)

A lady mystery writer rents a spooky old house and finds herself and her guests at the mercy of a maniac in search of hidden loot.
Poor remake of a standard twenties stage thriller; everyone chews the scenery.

wd Crane Wilbur, *play* Mary Roberts Rinehart *ph* Joseph Biroc *m* Louis Forbes

Vincent Price, Agnes Moorehead, Gavin Gordon, John Sutton, Lenita Lane, Darla Hood

The Bat Whispers**
US 1930 82m bw
UA / Roland West

Classic early sound version of *The Bat* (qv) by the director of the 1926 silent version.
Excellent use of camera, sets, and unusual models.

wd Roland West ph Ray June, Robert Planck

Chester Morris, Una Merkel, Chancer Ward, Grayce Hampton, Maude Eburne, Spencer Charters, Gustav Von Seyffertitz

† Originally released in a 'wide screen' process.
†† West had also made a silent version in 1926.

'The story America will never forget!'
Bataan*
US 1943 114m bw
MGM (Irving Starr)

Thirteen soldiers holding a bridge against the Japanese die one by one.
Uncredited remake of *The Lost Patrol* (qv) transposed to the Pacific war, with stereotyped characters and much flagwaving. Very dated, but a big box office film of its time, despite its studio jungles.

w Robert D. Andrews *d* Tay Garnett *ph* Sidney Wagner *m* Bronislau Kaper

Robert Taylor, George Murphy, Thomas Mitchell, Lloyd Nolan, Lee Bowman, Robert Walker, Desi Arnaz, Barry Nelson, Philip Terry

'Naïve, coarse-grained, primitive, honest, accomplished and true.'—*James Agee*

'One of the most convincing attempts I have ever seen to show a bit of hell on the screen.'—*Observer*

La Bataille du Rail**
France 1945 87m bw
CGCF

Reconstructions of heroic resistance work by the French railwaymen during World War II.
Reasonably compulsive documentary fiction which was plainly more inspiring at the time than it seems now.

wd René Clément ph Henri Alekan *m* Yves Baudrier

Salina, Daurand, Lozach, Tony Laurent

Bathing Beauty
US 1944 101m Technicolor
MGM (Jack Cummings)

A songwriter plans to retire and settle down, but his publisher schemes to set his fiancée against him.
Witless, artificial aqua-musical, with plenty of unpersuasive high jinks but no real style despite a capable cast.

w Dorothy Kingsley, Allen Boretz, Frank Waldman *d* George Sidney *ph* Harry Stradling *m* Johnny Green *ch* John Murray Anderson

Esther Williams, Red Skelton, Basil Rathbone, Keenan Wynn, Ethel Smith, Xavier Cugat, Bill Goodwin
Songs include 'Faculty Row'; 'Tico Tico'; 'Echo of a Serenade'; 'I Cried for You'; 'Bim Bam Boom'; 'By the Waters of Minnetonka'; 'I've Got a Problem'; 'I'll Take the High Note'

'I could not resist the wish that MGM had topped its aquatic climax—a huge pool full of girls, fountains and spouts of flame—by suddenly draining the tank and ending the show with the entire company writhing like goldfish on a rug.'—*James Agee*

Batman
US 1943 bw serial: 15 eps

With the help of the Boy Wonder, the Caped Crusader battles an enemy underground ring led by Dr Daka. Reasonably spirited romp marred by the usual tinpot sets. Lewis Wilson, Douglas Croft, J. Carrol Naish, William Austin. Directed by Lambert Hillyer; for Columbia. *Batman and Robin* (15 eps) followed in 1948, directed by Spencer Bennet: the leads were played by Robert Lowery and John Duncan: they combated The Wizard with the help of Lyle Talbot as the police commissioner.

Batman*
US 1966 105m De Luxe
TCF / Greenlawn / National Periodical Publications (William Dozier)

The cloaked avenger saves an important executive from the clutches of four of the world's most notorious criminals.
Glossy feature version of the old and new serials about the comic strip hero who scurries around in his Batmobile making sure that justice is done. The scriptwriter's invention unfortunately flags halfway, so that despite a fairly sharp production the result is more childish than camp.

w Lorenzo Semple Jnr *d* Leslie Martinson *ph* Howard Schwarz *m* Nelson Riddle

Adam West, Burt Ward, Cesar Romero, Frank Gorshin, Burgess Meredith, Lee Meriwether, Alan Napier, Neil Hamilton

Battement de Coeur**
France 1940 100m bw

A poor Parisienne joins a school for pickpockets but falls for the ambassador she robs. Amusing romance later remade in the US as *Heartbeat* (qv). Danielle Darrieux, André Luguet, Claude Dauphin, Julien Carette, Saturnin Fabre. Written by Jean Villeme, Max Colpet, Michel Duran; directed by Henri Decoin; for Ciné Alliance / Osso. 'Dauphin fails to rate in hero roles . . . he lacks personality, is short of stature, and dresses like a bank clerk.'—*Variety*

Batteries Not Included
US 1987 106m DeLuxe
Universal (Robert L. Schwarz)

A Manhattan neighbourhood where everyone has problems is helped out by miniature flying saucers with angelic intentions.
Frank Capra would have done it much better.

w Matthew Robbins and others *d* Matthew Robbins *ph* John McPherson *m* James Horner *pd* Ted Haworth

Hume Cronyn, Jessica Tandy, Frank McRae, Elizabeth Pena, Michael Carmine

'Forced by her husband to love another man . . . to exchange her kisses for naval secrets!'

The Battle*
France 1934 85m bw
Lionofilm (Leon Garganoff)
English language version aka: *Thunder in the East, Hara Kiri*

A Japanese aristocrat urges his wife to befriend an English naval attaché and steal secrets from him; she does, and falls in love.
Stagey but discreet melodrama of the old school, quite well made and acted.

w Nicolas Farkas, Bernard Zimmer, Robert Stevenson, *novel* Claude Farrère *d* Nicolas Farkas *ph* Roger Hubert

Charles Boyer, Merle Oberon, John Loder, Betty Stockfield, Miles Mander

The Battle at Apache Pass
US 1952 85m Technicolor

Cochise negotiates peace with the whites, but Geronimo won't agree. Standard cavalry-versus-Indians western, with Jeff Chandler repeating his famous Cochise impersonation. John Lund, Susan Cabot, Bruce Cowling, Richard Egan. Written by Gerald Drayson Adams; directed by George Sherman; for U-I.

The Battle at Bloody Beach
US 1961 80m bw Cinemascope
TCF / API (Richard Maibaum)
GB title: *Battle on the Beach*

Guerrillas fight Japs in the Philippines.
Tedious war melodrama with interludes for an eternal triangle.

w Richard Maibaum, Willard Willingham *d* Herbert Coleman *ph* Kenneth Peach *m* Henry Vars

Audie Murphy, Gary Crosby, Dolores Michaels, Alejandro Rey

Battle beneath the Earth*
GB 1967 92m Technicolor
MGM / Reynolds / Vetter (Charles Reynolds)

Enemy agents burrow under the US by means of a giant laser.
Agreeable schoolboy science fiction with fair special effects.

w L. Z. Hargeaves *d* Montgomery Tully *ph* Kenneth Talbot *m* Ken Jones *sp* Tom Howard

Kerwin Mathews, Vivienne Ventura, Robert Ayres, Peter Arne, Martin Benson

Battle beyond the Stars*
US 1980 104m Metrocolor
New World / Roger Corman (Ed Carlin)

A small planet hires help to repel invaders.
Impertinent and sometimes amusing space fiction rip-off of *Seven Samurai*, with plenty of in-jokes and quite pleasant special effects.

w John Sayles *d* Jimmy T. Murakami *ph* Daniel Lacambre *m* James Horner *ad* Jim Cameron, Charles Breen

Richard Thomas, Robert Vaughn, John Saxon, George Peppard, Sam Jaffe, Morgan Woodward, Darlanne Fluegel, Sybil Danning

Battle Circus
US 1952 90m bw
MGM (Pandro S. Berman)

A patriotic nurse and a disillusioned major fall in love at a mobile army hospital in Korea.
A flat, studio-bound potboiler with miscast stars, bound to provoke hilarity now as a serious version of *M*A*S*H*.

wd Richard Brooks *ph* John Alton *m* Lennie Hayton

Humphrey Bogart, June Allyson, Keenan Wynn, Robert Keith, William Campbell
'It is disappointing that Brooks, whose early work . . . suggested considerable promise, should have descended to such a glib, uninteresting piece of film-making.'—*MFB*

Battle Cry
US 1955 148m Warnercolor Cinemascope
Warner (producer not credited)

During World War II, marines endure tough training before combat in Saipan; their sex lives come a close second to the war.
Interminable cheapie epic with both eyes on the box office: the cast salvages an odd moment or two, but violence of all kinds is the key to the entertainment.

w Leon Uris, from his novel *d* Raoul Walsh *ph* Sid Hickox *m* Max Steiner

Van Heflin, Aldo Ray, Mona Freeman, Dorothy Malone, Raymond Massey, Nancy Olson, James Whitmore, Tab Hunter, Anne Francis, William Campbell

AAN: Max Steiner

The Battle Cry of Peace*
US 1915 120m approx bw silent

Lost film in which New York was invaded by forces of apparently German origin. It caused great political unrest and was followed by Thomas Ince's *Civilisation* which took the pacifist point of view. Charles Richman, L. Rogers Lytton, Charles Kent, James Morrison. Written by J. Stuart Blackton from the book Defenceless America by Hudson Maxim; directed by Wilfred North; for Blackton/VIT.

Battle for Music*
GB 1943 87m bw
Strand Films (Donald Taylor)

The story of the wartime ups and downs of the London Philharmonic Orchestra.
Not many films feature a classical orchestra, and this simple tribute, a mediocre production at best, has considerable historical interest.

w St John L. Clowes *d* Donald Taylor

Hay Petrie, Joss Ambler, Charles Carson, Jack Hylton. J. B. Priestley, Eileen Joyce, Moiseiwitch, Sir Adrian Boult, Sir Malcolm Sargent

Battle for Russia***
US 1943 80m bw

Fifth of Frank Capra's Why We Fight documentaries, and like the others a brilliant compilation of carefully selected footage. Produced by Anatole Litvak, with commentary by Anthony Veiller and music by Dimitri Tiomkin. For the US Army Signal Corps.

Battle for the Planet of the Apes
US 1973 86m De Luxe Panavision
TCF / APJAC (Frank Capra Jnr)

Following a nuclear war, apes are the only surviving leaders of society, but begin to fight among themselves.
Fifth and last in an increasingly confusing chronology, this is at least more thoughtful than violent.

w John William Corrington, Joyce Hooper Corrington *d* J. Lee Thompson *ph* Richard H. Kline *m* Leonard Rosenman *make-up* John Chambers

Roddy McDowall, Claude Akins, John Huston, Natalie Trundy, Severn Darden, Lew Ayres, Paul Williams
† See *Planet of the Apes*.

Battle Hymn
US 1957 108m Technicolor Cinemascope
U-I (Ross Hunter)

An American preacher with a guilt complex volunteers to help the South Koreans and after many adventures founds an orphanage.
Earnest, somnolent biopic of one Dean Hess; its mixture of drama, comedy, religion and war heroics is indigestible despite professional handling.

w Charles Grayson, Vincent B. Evans *d* Douglas Sirk *ph* Russell Metty *m* Frank Skinner

Rock Hudson, Anna Kashfi, Dan Duryea, Don Defore, Martha Hyer, Jock Mahoney, James Edwards, Carl Benton Reid

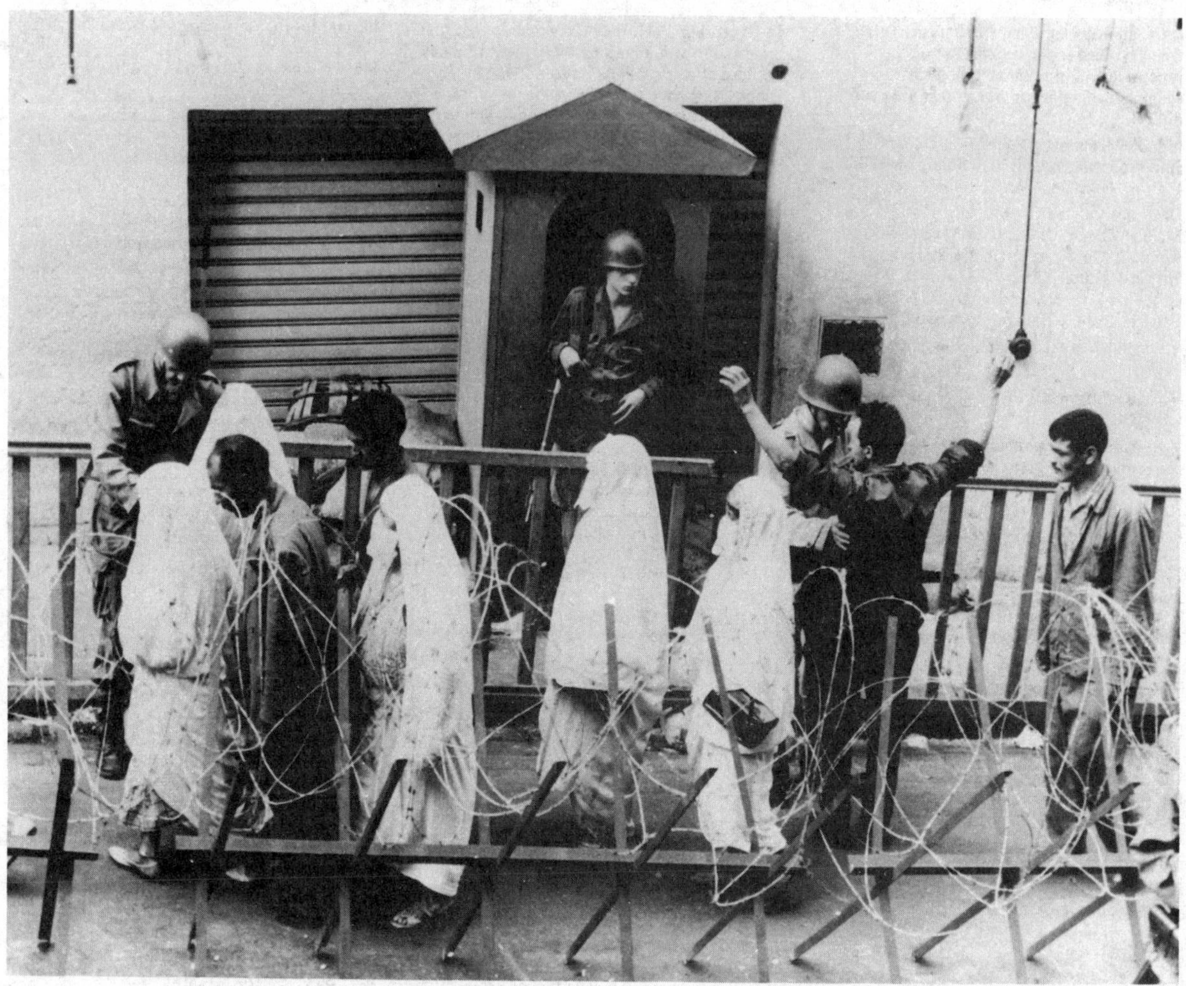

THE BATTLE OF ALGIERS. Actors and real-life participants used to excellent effect by director Gillo Pontecorvo in his drama-documentary reconstruction of violent events, without recourse to newsreel footage. He was rewarded with the Best Film award at Venice in 1966.

'The film seems to infer that heroic self-sacrifice, a little homely Eastern philosophy and a capacity for combining battle experience with an awareness of spiritual values are enough to overcome all emergencies.'—*John Gillett*

The Battle of Algiers*
Algeria / Italy 1965 135m bw
Casbah / Igor (Antonio Musi, Yacef Saadi)
original title: *La Battaglia di Algeri*

In 1954 Algiers, an ex-convict joins the terrorists in rebellion against the French government.

Politically oriented reconstruction of a bitter period of French colonial history, made better propaganda by its wealth of effective detail.

w Franco Solinas *d Gillo Pontecorvo*
ph Marcello Gatti *m* Ennio Morricone, Gillo Pontecorvo

Brahim Haggiag, Jean Martin, Yacef Saadi, Tommaso Neri

AAN: best foreign film; Franco Solinas; Gillo Pontecorvo (as director)

Battle of Britain***
US 1943 52m bw

Fourth of the Why We Fight series. (See *Battle for Russia*.)

'It will emerge as one of the vital documents depicting a people's courage when the torch of freedom flickered at its lowest.'—*Variety*

Battle of Britain*
GB 1969 131m Technicolor Panavision
UA / Spitfire (Harry Saltzman, Ben Fisz)

Summer 1940: England defends itself against aerial onslaught.

Plodding attempt to cover an historic event from too many angles and with too many guest stars, all indistinguishable from each other when masked in the cockpit during the repetitive and interminable dogfight sequences. On the ground, things are even duller.

w James Kennaway, Wilfrid Greatorex *d* Guy Hamilton *ph Frederick A. Young* *m* William Walton, Ron Goodwin

Laurence Olivier (as Dowding), Robert Shaw, Michael Caine, Christopher Plummer, Kenneth More, Susannah York, Trevor Howard, Ralph Richardson, Patrick Wymark, Curt Jurgens, Michael Redgrave, Nigel Patrick, Robert Flemyng, Edward Fox

† The film lost ten million dollars worldwide.

Battle of Broadway
US 1938 84m bw

Two American legionnaires at a New York convention try to break up the infatuation of their boss's son with a showgirl. Amiably rowdy Flagg-and-Quirt imitation. Victor McLaglen, Brian Donlevy, Gypsy Rose Lee, Raymond Walburn, Lynn Bari, Jane Darwell, Hattie McDaniel. Written by Lou Breslow and John Patrick; directed by George Marshall; for TCF. 'Flagg and Quirt shenanigans . . . rowdy, good-natured fun.'—*Variety*

The Battle of Neretva
Yugoslavia 1969 106m in dubbed version colour Cinemascope

In 1943, Yugoslav partisans resist German and Italian invaders. War spectacular with international cast; despite brilliant handling of the climaxes it didn't travel. Yul Brynner, Orson Welles, Hardy Kruger, Franco Nero. Written by Ugo Pirro and others; directed by Veljko Bulajic; for Jadran-Bosna.

AA: best foreign film

The Battle of Paris
US 1929 71m bw
Paramount

A lady music seller teams up with a pickpocket and falls for an American artist.
Primitive sound musical notable chiefly for its cast.

w Gene Markey *d* Robert Florey *ph* Bill Steiner *songs* Cole Porter

Gertrude Lawrence, Charles Ruggles, Walter Petrie, Arthur Treacher, Gladys du Bois

The Battle of Rogue River
US 1954 71m Technicolor

A disciplinarian major at a western fort discovers that his friend is fanning hatred between Indians and whites, for personal reasons. Tatty western with little action, and that very lame. George Montgomery, Richard Denning, Martha Hyer, John Crawford. Written by Douglas Heyes; directed by William Castle; for Columbia.

Battle of the Bulge**
US 1965 167m Technicolor Ultra Panavision
Warner / United States Pictures (Sidney Harmon, Milton Sperling, Philip Yordan)

In December 1944, the Allies take longer than expected to win a land battle in the Ardennes because of a crack Nazi Panzer commander. Bloody and unbowed war spectacle, quite literate and handsome but deafeningly noisy and with emphasis on strategy rather than character.

w Philip Yordan, Milton Sperling, John Melson *d* Ken Annakin *ph* Jack Hildyard *m* Benjamin Frankel

Henry Fonda, Robert Shaw, Robert Ryan, Telly Savalas, Dana Andrews, George Montgomery, Ty Hardin, Pier Angeli, Barbara Werle, Charles Bronson, James MacArthur, Werner Peters

The Battle of the Century**
US 1927 20m bw silent

The manager of an unsuccessful boxer accidentally starts a marathon pie fight. The first reel is lost, but the pie sequence is what matters, being one of the most celebrated pieces of slapstick in cinema history. Laurel and Hardy, Eugene Pallette. Written by Hal Roach and H. M. Walker; directed by Clyde Bruckman; for Hal Roach.

Battle of the Coral Sea
US 1959 85m bw

During World War II a submarine commander, sent to photograph the Japanese fleet, is captured but escapes. Routine, unconvincing war heroics. Cliff Robertson, Gia Scala, Patricia Cutts. Written by Dan Ullman and Stephen Kandel; directed by Paul Wendkos; for Charles H. Schneer / Columbia.

The Battle of the River Plate*
GB 1956 119m Technicolor Vistavision
Rank / Powell and Pressburger
US title: *Pursuit of the Graf Spee*

Semi-documentary account of the 1939 trapping of the German pocket battleship *Graf Spee* in Montevideo Harbour, and of her subsequent scuttling.
A sympathetic view of a German hero, Commander Langsdorff (not unexpected from these producers) is the most notable feature of this disappointingly patchy and studio-bound war epic, with too many actors in ill-defined bit parts, too undisciplined a storyline, and too confusing scenes of battle.

wd Michael Powell, Emeric Pressburger *ph* Christopher Challis *m* Brian Easdale

John Gregson, Anthony Quayle, Peter Finch, Bernard Lee, Ian Hunter, Jack Gwillim, Lionel Murton, Anthony Bushell, Peter Illing

'It is difficult to understand how English film-makers can have done thus badly with material so apt to their gifts.'—*Stanley Kauffmann*

The Battle of the Sexes
US 1914 60m approx bw silent

A wealthy middle-aged man is taken in by a fortune-hunting couple. A commercial potboiler from D. W. Griffith, made on the cheap but enormously successful. Lillian Gish, Owen Moore, Mary Alden, Fay Tincher, Robert Harron. Directed (from the play The Single Standard by Daniel Carson) by D. W. Griffith; for Mutual.

† In 1928 Griffith remade the property with Phyllis Haver, Jean Hersholt, Belle Bennett, Sally O'Neil and Don Alvarado.

The Battle of the Sexes*
GB 1960 83m bw
Prometheus (Monja Danischewsky)

A lady efficiency expert upsets the even tenor of life at an Edinburgh tweed manufactory, and the chief accountant plans to eliminate her.
Sub-Ealing black comedy which tends to misfire despite effort all round.

w Monja Danischewsky, from James Thurber's story The Catbird Seat *d* Charles Crichton *ph* Freddie Francis *m* Stanley Black

Peter Sellers, Constance Cummings, Robert Morley, Jameson Clark, Moultrie Kelsall, Alex Mackenzie, Roddy McMillan, Donald Pleasance, Ernest Thesiger

The Battle of the V1
GB 1958 109m bw
Criterion (George Maynard)
US titles: *Unseen Heroes; Missiles from Hell*

Polish patriots sabotage the German rocket installation at Peenemunde.
Effective though schoolboyish war adventure shot on a low budget: story development reasonably brisk though predictable.

w Jack Hanley, Eryk Wlodek, *book* Bernard Newman *d* Vernon Sewell *ph* Basil Emmott *m* Robert Sharples

Michael Rennie, Patricia Medina, Milly Vitale, David Knight, Esmond Knight, Christopher Lee

The Battle of the Villa Fiorita
GB 1964 111m Technicolor Panavision
Warner (Delmer Daves)
US title: *Affair at the Villa Fiorita*

Two children aim to break up their mother's romance with an Italian concert pianist.
Quite lively, old-fashioned romantic comedy-drama largely set in a splendid Mediterranean villa; happy ending never in doubt.

wd Delmer Daves, *novel* Rumer Godden *ph* Oswald Morris *m* Mischa Spoliansky

Maureen O'Hara, Rossano Brazzi, Richard Todd, Phyllis Calvert, Olivia Hussey, Martin Stephens, Elizabeth Dear

Battle Stations
US 1956 81m bw

Life on an aircraft carrier as seen by the padre. Cliché-strewn, mini-budgeted war thriller. John Lund, William Bendix, Keefe Brasselle, Richard Boone. Written by Crane Wilbur; directed by Lewis Seiler; for Columbia.

Battle Taxi
US 1954 82m bw

A newcomer to the helicopter rescue service in Korea resents his non-combatant status, but becomes a hero. The story takes second place to one damned rescue after another in this lively but overlong second feature. Sterling Hayden, Arthur Franz, Marshall Thompson. Written by Malvin Wald; directed by Herbert L. Strock; for Ivan Tors / UA.

Battle Zone
US 1952 81m bw

Two official war photographers in Korea fall out over a girl. Very conventional war programmer. John Hodiak, Stephen McNally, Linda Christian, Martin Milner, Dave Willcock. Written by Steve Fisher; directed by Lesley Selander; for Walter Wanger / Allied Artists.

'The guts! The girls! The glory! of a lot of wonderful guys!'
Battleground*
US 1949 118m bw
MGM (Dore Schary)

How a group of American soldiers in 1944 endured the Battle of the Bulge.
Enormously successful at the box office, this studio-bound production now seems stilted and unpersuasive, despite some good writing and direction.

w Robert Pirosh *d* William Wellman *ph* Paul C. Vogel *m* Lennie Hayton

Van Johnson, John Hodiak, Ricardo Montalban, George Murphy, Marshall Thompson, Jerome Courtland, Don Taylor, Bruce Cowling, James Whitmore, Douglas Fowley, Leon Ames

'Engrossingly well done.'—*Richard Mallett, Punch*

AA: Robert Pirosh; Paul C. Vogel
AAN: best picture; William Wellman; James Whitmore

Battles of Chief Pontiac
US 1953 75m bw

In the mid-18th century, peace talks with the Detroit Indians are sabotaged. Slightly unusual but undistinguished slice of western history. Lon Chaney Jnr, Lex Barker, Helen Westcott, Barry Kroeger, Roy Roberts. Written by Jack de Witt; directed by Felix E. Feist; for Jack Broder.

The Battleship Potemkin****
USSR 1925 75m approx (16 fps) silent; sound version 65m
Goskino
original title: *Bronenosets Potemkin*

A partly fictitious account of the mutiny at Odessa, an episode in the 1905 revolution. (The film was made as part of the 20th anniversary celebrations.)
A textbook cinema classic, and masterpiece of creative editing, especially in the famous Odessa Steps sequence in which innocent civilians are mown down in the bloodshed; the happenings of a minute are drawn into five by frenzied cross-cutting. The film contains 1,300 separate shots, and was judged the best film ever made in 1948 and 1958 by a panel of international judges.

wd Sergei Eisenstein ph Edouard Tissé, V. Popov

A. Antonov, Grigori Alexandrov, Vladimir Barsky, Levshin

Battling Butler*
US 1926 68m approx (24 fps) bw silent
MGM (Joseph M. Schenck)

A young millionaire pretends to be a boxer in order to win a sweetheart.
Middling star comedy.

w Al Boasberg, Charles Smith, Paul Gerard Smith, Lex Neal *d* Buster Keaton
ph J. Devereux Jennings, Bert Haines

Buster Keaton, Sally O'Neil

Battling with Buffalo Bill
US 1931 bw serial: 12 eps

Buffalo Bill rids a town of a murderous gambler and also calms down hostile Indians. Elementary serial stuff. Tom Tyler, Rex Bell, Francis Ford, Lucile Browne, William Desmond, Jim Thorpe, Yakima Canutt. Directed by Ray Taylor; for Universal.

The Bawdy Adventures of Tom Jones
GB 1976 94m Technicolor
Universal / Robert Sadoff

See *Tom Jones*, of which this is a musical version.
Not quite as bad as one would expect, but not up to the original.

w Jeremy Lloyd, *play* Don McPherson
songs Paul Holden *d* Cliff Owen *ph* Douglas Slocombe *m* Ron Grainer

Nicky Henson, Trevor Howard, Terry-Thomas, Arthur Lowe, Georgia Brown, Joan Collins, William Mervyn, Murray Melvin, Geraldine McEwan, Michael Bates, James Hayter, Isabel Dean, Gladys Henson

'A cheap, crude, sexed-up rehash with only three actual musical numbers . . . more boring than bawdy.'—*Kevin Thomas, Los Angeles Times*

Baxter*
GB 1972 100m Technicolor
(EMI) Performing Arts (Arthur Lewis)

An American son of divorced parents comes to London with his mother, meets tragedy in the shape of a friend's death, and responds to treatment for a speech defect.
Slight, appealing case history of a maladjusted 12-year-old; a rather unnecessarily uncommercial slice of life with no easy solution offered.

w Reginald Rose *d* Lionel Jeffries
ph Geoffrey Unsworth *m* Michael J. Lewis

Patricia Neal (as the therapist), Scott Jacoby, Britt Ekland, Jean-Pierre Cassel, Lynn Carlin, Paul Eddington

The Bay Boy
Canada / France 1984 101m colour

In 1937 Nova Scotia, a 16-year-old boy is distracted by real-life problems from his supposed vocation as a priest. Doleful, weatherbeaten slice of autobiography which remains of interest only to those who know the country and the people. Liv Ullmann, Kiefer Sutherland, Peter Donat, Allan Scarfe, Chris Wiggins. Written and directed by Daniel Petrie; for Bay Boy / Hachette-Fox.

The Bay of St Michel
GB 1963 73m bw

Commandos return to Normandy to seek hidden Nazi loot. Uninspired hokum programmer. Keenan Wynn, Mai Zetterling, Ronald Howard, Rona Anderson, Trader Faulkner, Edward Underdown. Written by Christopher David; produced and directed by John Ainsworth; for Trionyx / Rank.

Be Big*
US 1931 20m bw

Ollie feigns illness to avoid a trip with his wife, but Stan's help proves disastrous. Comedy warm-up for *Sons of the Desert*; Ollie spends most of the second reel trying to rid himself of a tight boot. Laurel and Hardy, Anita Garvin, Isabelle Keith. Written by H. M. Walker; directed by James Parrott; for Hal Roach.

The Beach Girls and the Monster
US 1966 70m bw

An oceanographer finds something very strange emerging from the waters of Waikiki Beach. Elementary horror flick which fails to scare and is only notable for the re-emergence of its star. Jon Hall, Sue Casey, Walker Edmiston, Arnold Lessing. Written by Joan Gardner; directed by Jon Hall; for Edward Janis/Films.

Beach Party*
US 1963 104m Pathecolor Panavision
AIP / Alta Vista (James H. Nicholson)

An anthropologist sets up house on a California beach to study the mating habits of young people but becomes personally involved when one of them falls for him.
Vaguely satirical pop musical with relaxed performances; quite tolerable in itself, it started an excruciating trend.

w Lou Rusoff *d* William Asher *ph* Kay Norton *m* Les Baxter

Robert Cummings, Dorothy Malone, Annette Funicello, Frankie Avalon, Vincent Price, Harvey Lembeck, Morey Amsterdam, Jody McCrea

Beach Red*
US 1967 105m Technicolor
UA / Theodora (Cornel Wilde)

In 1943, American assault craft take a Jap-held Pacific island.
Brutal, pacifist war film, simply and clearly portrayed but not exactly entertaining.

w Clint Johnston, Donald A. Peters, Jefferson Pascal *d Cornel Wilde* *ph* Cecil R. Cooney *m* Antonio Buenaventura

Cornel Wilde, Rip Torn, Burr de Benning, Jean Wallace

The Beachcomber*
GB 1954 90m Technicolor
GFD / London Independent (William MacQuitty)

An alcoholic ne'er-do-well in the Dutch East Indies reforms after an unexpected adventure with a lady missionary.
Styleless remake of *Vessel of Wrath* (qv); the acting just about holds the interest, but all other contributions are flat.

w Sydney Box, from Somerset Maugham's story *d* Muriel Box *ph* Reg Wyer *m* Francis Chagrin

Robert Newton, Glynis Johns, Donald Sinden, Paul Rogers, Donald Pleasence, Walter Crisham, Michael Hordern, Ronald Lewis

Beachhead
US 1953 90m print by Technicolor

American marines land on a Pacific island to bring back a planter who has supplied information. World War II jungle thriller, not too badly done. Tony Curtis, Frank Lovejoy, Mary Murphy, Eduard Franz. Written by Richard Alan Simmons; directed by Stuart Heisler; for Aubrey Schenck / UA.

Bear Country see The Living Desert

Bear Island
GB / Canada 1979 118m colour Panavision
Columbia / Bear Island / Selkirk (Peter Snell)

Meteorological experts on an Arctic island are menaced by neo-Nazis.
Highly implausible adventure yarn, indifferently presented.

w David Butler, Don Sharp, *novel* Alistair MacLean *d* Don Sharp *ph* Alan Hume *m* Robert Farnon

Vanessa Redgrave, Donald Sutherland, Richard Widmark, Christopher Lee, Barbara Parkins, Lloyd Bridges

The Bears and I
US 1974 89m Technicolor
Walt Disney (Winston Hibler)

An army veteran goes to live near an Indian settlement and adopts three bear cubs, later becoming a Park Ranger.
Simple, pleasing outdoor family film.

w John Whedon, *novel* Robert Franklin Leslie *d* Bernard McEveety *ph* Ted D. Landon *m* Buddy Baker

Patrick Wayne, Chief Dan George, Andrew Duggan, Michael Ansara

The Beast from Twenty Thousand Fathoms
US 1953 80m bw
Warner (Hal Chester, Jack Dietz)

Heat generated by an atomic bomb test in the Arctic thaws out a prehistoric rhedosaurus which travels down the American coast to cause havoc in New York until cornered and destroyed on Coney Island.
Flat-footed addition to the monster cycle, with an interminable wait for the beast's appearance and inferior trick work when he goes on the rampage.

w Lou Morheim, Fred Freiburger *d* Eugène Lourié *ph* Jack Russell *m* David Buttolph *sp* Ray Harryhausen

Paul Christian, Paula Raymond, Cecil Kellaway (as a professor gobbled up in a bathysphere), Kenneth Tobey, Donald Woods, Lee Van Cleef

The Beast in the Cellar
GB 1970 87m Eastmancolor
Tigon-Leander (Tony Tenser, Graham Harris)

A rampaging killer in the Lancashire woods turns out to be the deranged ex-soldier brother of two elderly spinsters who have kept him locked up for thirty years.
Idiotically boring farrago, totally lacking in suspense and wasting good talent.

wd James Kelly *ph* Harry Waxman, Desmond Dickinson *m* Tony Macaulay

Flora Robson, Beryl Reid, Tessa Wyatt, John Hamill, T. P. McKenna

The Beast Must Die*
GB 1974 93m Technicolor
BL / Amicus (Milton Subotsky)

A millionaire big game hunter holds a weekend party to track down a werewolf, but his guest list rapidly gets smaller . . .
A savage variation on *Ten Little Niggers*, not badly done, with such gimmicks as a 'guess who' break near the end.

w Michael Winder, *story* James Blish *d* Paul Annett *ph* Jack Hildyard *m* Douglas Gamley

Calvin Lockhart, Peter Cushing, Charles Gray, Anton Diffring, Marlene Clark, Ciaran Madden, Michael Gambon

Beast of the City
US 1932 80m bw
MGM

A police captain is determined to get a ruthless racketeer by fair means or foul.
Curiously dour little crime melodrama with a high death rate; the cast does not quite save it.

w John Lee Mahin, *story* W. R. Burnett *d* Charles Brabin *ph* Barney McGill

Walter Huston, Jean Harlow, Wallace Ford, Jean Hersholt, Dorothy Petersen, Tully Marshall, John Miljan

'A gang story for rural and home circle consumption, preaching the gospel of civic righteousness and the glory of steadfast purpose. Aiming at domestic patronage, they even make Miss Harlow keep her skirts down.'—*Variety*

'Endowed with vitality and realism.'—*New York Times*

The Beast with a Million Eyes
US 1955 84m bw

A malicious space creature lands in the desert but is defeated by human love. Semi-professional would-be horror story, on a level with the Corman horrors of the period. Paul Birch, Lorna Thayer, Dick Sargent. Written by Tom Filer; directed by David Karminsky; for San Matteo / AIP.

The Beast with Five Fingers*
US 1946 88m bw
Warner (William Jacobs)

A famous pianist dies and his severed hand returns to commit murder.
Slow-moving, Italian-set horror thriller which wastes an excellent original; a superb central performance and clever trick effects can hardly redeem the stodgy script or the ending which reveals the hauntings as an hallucination.

w Curt Siodmak, *story* W. F. Harvey *d* Robert Florey *ph* Wesley Anderson *m* Max Steiner

Peter Lorre, Andrea King, Robert Alda, J. Carrol Naish, Victor Francen, Charles Dingle

The Beastmaster
US 1982 118m colour

A royal child, stolen at birth by a witch, is rescued by a peasant who brings him up skilled in the martial arts. Comic strip sword and sorcery: fairly high budget but very low intelligence. Marc Singer, Tanya Roberts, Rip Torn, John Amos, Rod Loomis. Written by Don Coscarelli and Paul Pepperman; directed by Don Coscarelli; for Leisure Investments.

The Beat Generation
US 1959 95m bw Cinemascope
Albert Zugsmith
aka: *This Rebel Age*

A vicious rapist joins the beatniks.
Bankrupt exploitation melodrama, not easy to sit through.

w Richard Matheson, Lewis Meltzer *d* Charles Haas *ph* Walter H. Castle *m* Albert Glasser

Ray Danton, Steve Cochran, Fay Spain, Mamie Van Doren, Jackie Coogan, Louis Armstrong, Maggie Hayes, Jim Mitchum, Irish McCalla, Maxie Rosenbloom

'An enervating mixture of slapstick, religiosity, psychological hokum and grubby sensationalism.'—*MFB*

Beat Girl
GB 1960 85m bw

An architect's teenage daughter goes to the dogs. Risible exposé-style melodrama. David Farrar, Noelle Adam, Christopher Lee, Gillian Hills, Adam Faith. Written by Dail Ambler; directed by Edmond T. Greville; for Renown.
(US title: *Wild for Kicks*).

Beat Street
US 1984 106m Movielab

An aspiring DJ from South Bronx has trouble getting into showbiz. For teenagers only; a rehash of *Saturday Night Fever* applied to the new fad of break-dancing. Rae Dawn Chong, Guy Davis, Jon Chardiet, Leon W. Grant, Saundra Santiago. Written by Andy Davis, David Gilbert, Paul Golding; directed by Stan Lathan; for Orion.

'Adventure at its boldest! Bogart at his best!'

Beat the Devil*
GB 1953 100m bw
Romulus / Santana (Jack Clayton)

In a small Mediterranean port, and subsequently on a boat bound for the African coast, oddly assorted travellers plan to acquire land known to contain uranium deposits.
Unsatisfactory, over-talkative and inconsequential burlesque of the director's own *The Maltese Falcon* and *Across the Pacific*. Good fun was obviously had by the cast, but audiences were mostly baffled by the in-jokes, the extra-strange characters, and the lack of attention to pace, suspense and plot development.

w Truman Capote, John Huston, *novel* James Helvick *d* John Huston *ph* Oswald Morris *m* Franco Mannino

Humphrey Bogart (Billy Dannreuther), *Jennifer Jones* (Gwendolen Chelm), Gina Lollobrigida (Maria Dannreuther), *Edward Underdown* (Harry Chelm), Peter Lorre (O'Hara), Robert Morley (Petersen), *Ivor Barnard* (Major Ross), Bernard Lee (Inspector), Marco Tulli (Ravello)

GWENDOLEN: 'Harry, we must beware of these men. They're desperate characters. Not one of them looked at my legs.'

DANNREUTHER: 'Trouble with England, it's all pomp and no circumstance. You're very wise to get out of it, escape while you can.'

O'HARA: 'Time! Time! What is time? The Swiss manufacture it. The French hoard it. Italians want it. Americans say it is money. Hindus say it does not exist. Do you know what I say? I say time is a crook.'

'A potential treat emerged as a wet firecracker . . . the incidents remain on a naggingly arch and lagging verbal keel.'—*New York Times*

'Each of its cinematic clichés appears to be placed in the very faintest of mocking quotation marks.'—*Time*

'Only the phonies liked it. It's a mess!'—*Humphrey Bogart*

'The formula of *Beat the Devil* is that everyone is slightly absurd.'—*John Huston*

† James Helvick was the pseudonym of Claud Cockburn.

Beau Brummell*
US 1924 104m approx at 24 fps bw silent

A Regency dandy becomes the right-hand man of the Prince of Wales, but falters through his own arrogance. Elegant period romance which marked the beginning of its star's great movie decade. *John Barrymore*, Mary Astor, Carmel Myers, Willard Louis. Written by Dorothy Farnum; directed by Harry Beaumont; for Warners.

Beau Brummell*
GB 1954 111m Eastmancolor
MGM (Sam Zimbalist)

A Regency dandy enjoys a close relationship with the Prince of Wales, and when this is eventually withdrawn he dies in penury.
Stodgy historical romance with entertaining patches; the main story is too graceful and conventional to be believed.

w Karl Tunberg, *play* Clyde Fitch *d* Curtis Bernhardt *ph* Oswald Morris *m* Richard Addinsell *ad* Alfred Junge

Stewart Granger, Elizabeth Taylor, *Peter Ustinov* (as the Prince), *Robert Morley* (as George III), James Donald, James Hayter, Rosemary Harris, Paul Rogers, Noel Willman, Peter Bull, Peter Dyneley

'Hard lives, quick deaths, undying love!'

Beau Geste**
US 1926 120m approx (24 fps) bw (colour sequences) silent
Paramount (Herbert Brenon)

Three English brothers join the Foreign Legion, suffer under a brutal sergeant, and die fighting the Arabs.
Although outmoded even when first filmed, this tale of derring-do and self sacrifice usually works, and in this case it gave its star a fresh image. One of the best remembered silents of the twenties.

w Paul Schofield, *novel* P. C. Wren *d Herbert Brenon* *ph* Roy Hunt *ad* Julian Boone Fleming

Ronald Colman, Neil Hamilton, Ralph Forbes, Alice Joyce, Mary Brian, *Noah Beery*, William Powell, Victor McLaglen

† Remade 1939 and 1966; sequel, *Beau Ideal*, 1931.

'Three against the world! Brothers and soldiers all!'

Beau Geste**
US 1939 120m bw
Paramount (William Wellman)

Spirited remake, with the famous flashback opening of the desert fort defended by corpses. Style and acting generally satisfactory.

w Robert Carson *d* William Wellman *ph* Theodor Sparkuhl, Archie Stout *m* Alfred Newman *ad* Hans Dreier, Robert Odell

Gary Cooper, Ray Milland, Robert Preston, *Brian Donlevy*, *J. Carrol Naish*, Susan Hayward, Heather Thatcher, James Stephenson, Donald O'Connor, G. P. Huntley Jnr, Albert Dekker, Broderick Crawford

FOREWORD: 'The love of a man for a woman waxes and wanes like the moon, but the love of brother for brother is steadfast as the stars and endures like the word of the prophet . . .' *Arabian proverb*

MARKOFF: 'Keep shooting, you scum! You'll get a chance yet to die with your boots on!'

'Its melodrama is sometimes grim but never harrowing, its pace is close to hectic and its suspense is constant.'—*Herbert Cohn, Brooklyn Daily Eagle*

'A morbid picture, but I doubt whether any morality council will take action, the whole story being so wrapped up in the school colours—in comradeship and loyalty and breeding, and the pure girl left behind; morbid because the brutality has no relation whatever to the real world; it is uncriticized day-dreaming.'—*Graham Greene*

'A handsome treatment of a well-loved adventure tale.'—*New York Daily Mirror*

'Will do nominal biz, but lacks punch for smash proportions.'—*Variety*

† Shot in Buttercup Valley, west of Yuma.
†† The nasty sergeant, originally Lejeune, became Markoff to avoid offending the French.

AAN: Brian Donlevy; Hans Dreier, Robert Odell

Beau Geste
US 1966 105m Techniscope
Universal (Walter Seltzer)

The central desert section of the story is here augmented, with violence stressed, and Beau allowed to survive at the end.
A cheap leery melodrama is what results from the jettisoning of all the romantic portions of the original.

wd Douglas Heyes *ph* Bud Thackery *m* Hans Salter

Telly Savalas (rampant as the sadistic sergeant), Guy Stockwell, Doug McClure, Leslie Nielsen, Leon Gordon, Michael Constantine

Beau Hunks**
US 1931 40m bw

A fool and his friend join the Foreign Legion to forget. Patchy but amiable star comedy with memorable high spots. In-joke: the woman the whole legion wants to forget is Jean Harlow. Laurel and Hardy, Charles Middleton. Written by H. M. Walker; directed by James W. Horne; for Hal Roach. (GB title: *Beau Chumps*.)

Beau Ideal
US 1931 75m bw
RKO (William Le Baron)

John Geste and a new legionnaire friend become involved in a religious war started by a rascally emir.
Lame sequel to *Beau Geste*, fettered by primitive dialogue.

w Paul Schofield, *novel* P. C. Wren *d* Herbert Brenon *ph* J. Roy Hunt *m* Max Steiner

Lester Vail, Ralph Forbes, Don Alvarado, Loretta Young, Irene Rich

'Ordinary programme picture with slight romance. Doubtful draw for women.'—*Variety*

'He took New York for its wildest joy ride!'

Beau James*
US 1957 107m Technicolor Vistavision
Paramount / Hope Enterprises (Jack Rose)

The vaguely crooked career of Jimmy Walker, mayor of New York in the twenties.
Romanticized biopic with few funny moments:

Hope cannot cope with the drama, and the result is a creaking vehicle apart from a well-recreated twenties atmosphere and excellent production values.

w Jack Rose, Melville Shavelson, *book* Gene Fowler *d* Melville Shavelson *ph* John F. Warren *m* Joseph J. Lilley

Bob Hope, Paul Douglas, Vera Miles, Alexis Smith, Darren McGavin, Joe Mantell, Walter Catlett *guest stars* Jack Benny, George Jessel, Jimmy Durante *narrator* Walter Winchell (Alistair Cooke in GB)

Le Beau Mariage*
France 1981 97m colour
Les Films du Losange / Les Films du Carrosse (Margaret Menegoz)
GB title: *A Good Marriage*

An art student abandons her many affairs and announces her intention of getting married, but her intended proves reluctant . . .
Quietly amusing conversation piece in the style expected of this director; an after-dinner entertainment for the *Sunday Times* set.

wd Eric Rohmer ph Bernard Lutic *m* Ronan Girre, Simon des Innocents

Beatrice Ronand, André Dussollier, Feodor Atkine, Arielle Dombasle

Beau Sabreur
US 1928 85m (24 fps) bw silent

A French officer is sent to the Sahara to negotiate a treaty with a powerful sheik. Romantic adventure concocted to use up bits and pieces left over from *Beau Geste*. Not a hit. Gary Cooper, Evelyn Brent, Noah Beery, William Powell, Roscoe Karns. Written by Tom Geraghty; directed by John Waters; for Paramount.

Le Beau Serge*
France 1958 97m bw
AYJM (Jean Cotet)

A student returns to his home town and tries to redeem his old friend who has become a drunkard.
Enjoyable character drama with well observed village backgrounds. Credited with being the spearhead of the 'new wave'.

wd Claude Chabrol ph Henri Decaë m Emile Delpierre

Gérard Blain, Jean-Claude Brialy, Michèle Meritz, Bernadette Lafont

La Beauté du Diable***
Italy / France 1949 96m bw
AYJM

The Faust story with the protagonists agreeing to change places.
Dazzling plot twists and cinematic virtuosity make this a richly enjoyable fantasy, though perhaps not among Clair's greatest works.

w René Clair, Armand Salacrou *d René Clair ph* Michel Kelber *m* Roman Vlad *ad* Léon Barsacq

Michel Simon, Gérard Philipe, Raymond Cordy, Nicole Besnard, Gaston Modot, Paolo Stoppa

'She's got the biggest six-shooters in the west!'

The Beautiful Blonde from Bashful Bend*
US 1949 77m Technicolor
TCF (Preston Sturges)

A temperamental saloon entertainer accidentally shoots the sheriff and takes refuge as a schoolmistress.
A dishevelled western farce unworthy of its creator, but with the advantage of appearances by many of his usual repertory of players.

wd Preston Sturges *ph* Harry Jackson *m* Cyril Mockridge

Betty Grable, Cesar Romero, El Brendel, Hugh Herbert, Rudy Vallee, Olga San Juan, Sterling Holloway, Porter Hall, Esther Howard, Margaret Hamilton

'It erects a fabric of roaring slapstick on a conventional western foundation, and from time to time it succeeds in being very funny.'—*Richard Mallett, Punch*

'Somehow the ramshackle air of Bashful Bend itself seems to have permeated the whole film.'—*MFB*

Beautiful but Broke
US 1944 74m bw

An agent and a girls' band get romantically marooned on the way to a date in Cleveland. Haphazard comedy with music; just an occasional smile amid the tedium. Joan Davis, Jane Frazee, John Hubbard, Judy Clark, Willie West and McGinty. Written by Manny Seff and Arthur Housman; directed by Charles Barton; for Irving Briskin / Columbia. 'Commonplace B entry.'—*Variety*

Beautiful Stranger
GB 1954 89m bw
Marksman (Maxwell Setton, John R. Sloan)
US title: *Twist of Fate*

On the Riviera, an actress discovers that her fiancé is a criminal.
Tawdry star melodrama of virtually no interest.

w Robert Westerby, Carl Nystrom *d* David Miller *ph* Robert Day, Ted Scaife *m* Malcolm Arnold

Ginger Rogers, Jacques Bergerac, Herbert Lom, Stanley Baker, Margaret Rawlings, Eddie Byrne, Coral Browne

Beauty and the Boss
US 1932 75m bw

A girl down on her luck becomes secretary to an amorous banker and eventually becomes his wife. Artless Cinderella story in an uneasy Viennese setting. Warren William, Marian Marsh, Charles Butterworth, Frederick Kerr, Lillian Bond. Written by Joseph Jackson from the play The Church Mouse by Ladislas Fodor and Paul Frank; directed by Roy del Ruth; for Warners. 'Elementary stuff for the B houses, titularly phrased for flap appeal.'—*Variety*

Beauty for Sale
US 1933 85m bw

An innocent girl snares a rich man while working in a beauty parlour. Well-mounted romantic comedy-drama with most of the elements the 1933 public wanted. Madge Evans, Alice Brady, Una Merkel, Otto Kruger, May Robson, Phillips Holmes, Eddie Nugent, Hedda Hopper. Written by Zelda Sears and Eve Greene from the novel Beauty by Faith Baldwin; directed by Richard Boleslawski; for MGM. 'Pulp magazine fiction made for subway-riding stenographers . . . romantic hoke skilfully dressed up.'—*Variety*

Beauty for the Asking
US 1939 68m bw

Jealousies flourish among the women in a cosmetics showroom. Average supporting drama for female audiences. Lucille Ball, Frieda Inescort, Patric Knowles, Donald Woods, Inez Courtney. Written by Doris Anderson and Paul Jarrico; directed by Glenn Tryon; for RKO.

The Beauty Jungle*
GB 1964 114m Eastmancolor Cinemascope
Rank / Val Guest
US title: *Contest Girl*

A typist enters a beauty contest and step by step becomes Miss Globe; but her descent is equally rapid.
Wicked show biz and the road to ruin in one glossy package, predictable, but not badly done; always something going on, and performed with gusto.

w Robert Muller, Val Guest *d Val Guest ph* Arthur Grant *m* Laurie Johnson

Janette Scott, Ian Hendry, Ronald Fraser, Edmund Purdom, Kay Walsh, Norman Bird, Janina Faye, Tommy Trinder, Francis Matthews

Because of Him*
US 1945 88m bw
Universal (Felix Jackson)

A waitress pesters a Broadway author and actor for a leading role in their new show. Moderately sprightly star vehicle with bonuses in the leading men; handling disappointingly routine.

w Edmund Beloin *d* Richard Wallace *ph* Hal Mohr *m* Miklos Rozsa

Deanna Durbin, Charles Laughton, Franchot Tone, Helen Broderick, Stanley Ridges, Donald Meek

'Even in the first wild joy of his arms, she realized that she would be . . . an unfit mother!'

Because of You
US 1952 95m bw
U-I (Albert J. Cohen)

A female ex-convict marries on parole but does not tell her husband of her past. Her old associates involve her innocently in another crime, and her husband divorces her; but years later she gets him and their child back.
Soap opera of the stickiest kind, made quite tolerable by good production.

w Ketti Frings *d* Joseph Pevney *ph* Russell Metty *m* Frank Skinner

Loretta Young, Jeff Chandler, Alex Nicol, Frances Dee, Lynne Roberts, Alexander Scourby, Mae Clarke

'Shows the most whole-hearted devotion to woman's magazine conventions.'—*MFB*

'Whoever you are, you're in this picture! Because this tells of youth's challenge to grown-ups who can't understand!'

Because They're Young
US 1960 98m bw
Columbia / Drexel (Jerry Bresler)

A high school teacher helps one of his tougher pupils not to slip into crime.
Routine sentimental melodrama, slightly redeemed by directorial expertise.

w James Gunn, *novel* Harrison High by John Farris *d Paul Wendkos ph* Wilfrid Cline *m* Johnny Williams

Dick Clark, Michael Callan, Tuesday Weld, Victoria Shaw, Warren Berlinger, Doug McClure

Because You're Mine
US 1952 103m Technicolor
MGM (Joe Pasternak)

An opera singer becomes a GI and wins the sergeant's sister.
Lumberingly inept star vehicle, giving the impression of nothing at all happening between the songs.

w Leonard Spiegelgass, Karl Tunberg *d* Alexander Hall *ph* Joseph Ruttenberg *md* Johnny Green

Mario Lanza, Doretta Morrow, James Whitmore, Dean Miller, Paula Corday, Jeff Donnell, Spring Byington

'On a dull day in Manchester it will bring colour to the greyness of life.'—*Sunday Express*

AAN: title song (*m* Nicholas Brodszky, *ly* Sammy Cahn)

'The screen explodes with rage and passion and greatness!'

Becket**
GB 1964 149m Technicolor Panavision
(Paramount) Hal B. Wallis

Henry II leans on his boisterous Saxon friend Thomas à Becket, but when the latter is made first chancellor and then archbishop a rift between them widens and ends in Becket's assassination by Henry's over-eager knights.
Jean Anouilh's bitter stage comedy is filmed literally and soberly as a rather anaemic epic, so that the point is lost and the edge blunted. The paucity of physical action causes good scenes to alternate with long stretches of tedium.

w Edward Anhalt *d* Peter Glenville *ph Geoffrey Unsworth m* Laurence Rosenthal

Richard Burton, Peter O'Toole, Donald Wolfit, *John Gielgud*, Martita Hunt, Pamela Brown, Sian Phillips, Paolo Stoppa

'Handsome, respectable and boring.'—*John Simon*

AA: Edward Anhalt
AAN: best picture; Peter Glenville; Geoffrey Unsworth; Laurence Rosenthal; Richard Burton; Peter O'Toole; John Gielgud

Becky Sharp**
US 1935 83m Technicolor
(RKO) Kenneth MacGowan

An ambitious girl makes her way into Regency society.
Chiefly notable as the first feature in three-colour Technicolor, this rather theatrical piece has its civilized enjoyments and the director made a few predictable cinematic experiments; the overall effect, however, is patchy.

w Francis Edward Faragoh, *play* Landon Mitchell, *novel* Vanity Fair by W. M. Thackeray *d Rouben Mamoulian ph Ray Rennahan m* Roy Webb *pd Robert Edmond Jones*

Miriam Hopkins, *Cedric Hardwicke*, Frances Dee, Billie Burke, Alison Skipworth, Nigel Bruce, Alan Mowbray, Colin Tapley, G. P. Huntley Jnr

'Beautiful cinematographically but weak on story. No cinch, and should be sold on colour angle.'—*Variety*

'As pleasing to the eye as a fresh fruit sundae, but not much more.'—*Otis Ferguson*

'If colour is to be of permanent importance a way must be found to use it realistically, not only as a beautiful decoration. It must be made to contribute to our sense of truth. The machine gun, the cheap striped tie, the battered Buick and the shabby bar will need a subtler colour sense than the Duchess of Richmond's ball, the girls of Miss Pinkerton's Academy, the Marquess of Steyne's dinner for two. Can Technicolor reproduce with the necessary accuracy the suit that has been worn too long, the oily hat?'—*Graham Greene*

AAN: Miriam Hopkins

'The girl who took a short cut down the primrose path!'

Bed of Roses
US 1933 67m bw

A reform-school graduate determines to be a scarlet woman but falls for an upright riverboat captain. Adequate vehicle for a fading star who had played too many such roles. Constance Bennett, Joel McCrea, Pert Kelton, Samuel S. Hinds, John Halliday. Written by Wanda Tuchok, Eugene Thackrey; directed by Gregory La Cava; for RKO.

The Bed Sitting Room*
GB 1969 91m De Luxe
UA / Oscar Lewenstein (Richard Lester)

Surrealist romance; after a nuclear war, motley survivors in the waste lands turn into bed sitting rooms, cupboards and parakeets.
Arrogantly obscure fantasy, a commercial flop which kept its director in the wilderness for four years. Fans of Monty Python may salvage a joke or two.

w John Antrobus, from the play by himself and Spike Milligan *d* Richard Lester *ph* David Watkin *m* Ken Thorne *pd* Assheton Gorton

Ralph Richardson, Rita Tushingham, Michael Hordern, Arthur Lowe, Mona Washbourne, Peter Cook, Dudley Moore, Spike Milligan, Harry Secombe, Marty Feldman, Jimmy Edwards

Bedazzled*
GB 1967 96m De Luxe Panavision
TCF / Stanley Donen

A short order cook is saved from suicide by Mr Spiggott, who offers him seven wishes in exchange for his soul.
A camped-up version of *Faust* which resolves itself into a series of threadbare sketches for the stars. All rather desperate apart from the leaping nuns.

w Peter Cook *d* Stanley Donen *ph* Austin Dempster *m* Dudley Moore

Peter Cook, Dudley Moore, Michael Bates, Raquel Welch, Eleanor Bron

Bedelia
GB 1946 90m bw
John Corfield (Isadore Goldsmith)

A psychotic woman is discovered to have poisoned three husbands.
Dreary upper-class British murder drama, totally devoid of style or suspense but a big star hit of the time.

w Vera Caspary, Moie Charles, Herbert Victor, Roy Ridley, Isadore Goldsmith, *novel* Vera Caspary *d* Lance Comfort *ph* F. A. Young

Margaret Lockwood, Ian Hunter, Barry K. Barnes, Anne Crawford, Jill Esmond, Ellen Pollock

Bedevilled
US 1955 86m Eastmancolor Cinemascope
MGM (Henry Berman)

In Paris, a novice priest befriends a girl on the run from gangsters. She turns out to be a murderess and is shot by her victim's brother.
Absurd high-flown bosh, unsuitably cinemascoped in ugly colour, and surprisingly badly handled by old professionals.

w Jo Eisinger *d* Mitchell Leisen *ph* Frederick A. Young *m* William Alwyn

Anne Baxter, Steve Forrest, Simone Renant, Victor Francen, Maurice Teynac, Joseph Tomelty

'This mixture of melodrama and religion provides a most unedifying entertainment.'—*MFB*

The Bedford Incident***
GB 1965 102m bw
Columbia / Bedford Productions (James B. Harris)

A ruthlessly efficient US destroyer captain in the Arctic chases a Russian submarine and accidentally fires an atomic weapon.
Gripping mixture of themes from *Dr Strangelove* and *The Caine Mutiny*, very tense and forceful, with excellent acting.

w James Poe, novel Mark Rascovitch *d James B. Harris ph* Gilbert Taylor *m* Gerald Schurrmann

Richard Widmark, Sidney Poitier (his first role with no reference to his colour), James MacArthur, Eric Portman, Wally Cox, Martin Balsam, Phil Brown, Michael Kane, Garry Cockrell, Donald Sutherland

'Strong on virtues of a rather negative kind.'—*Penelope Houston*

Bedknobs and Broomsticks
US 1971 117m Technicolor
Walt Disney (Bill Walsh)

In 1940 three evacuee children and a kindly witch ride on a magic bedstead and defeat the invasion of England.
Extraordinarily dishevelled and incompetent Disney follow-up to *Mary Poppins*, a very muddled narrative with few high points and evidence of much cutting. Redeemed occasionally by camera trickery.

w Bill Walsh, Don DaGradi *d* Robert Stevenson *ph* Frank Philips *m / ly* Richard M. Sherman, Robert B. Sherman *sp* Eustace Lycett, Alan Maley, Danny Lee

Angela Lansbury, David Tomlinson, Roy Snart, Cindy O'Callaghan, Sam Jaffe, Roddy McDowall, Bruce Forsyth, Tessie O'Shea, Reginald Owen

AAN: Richard M. Sherman, Robert B. Sherman; song 'The Age of Not Believing' by the Shermans

Bedlam**
US 1946 80m bw
RKO (*Val Lewton*)

In 18th-century London, a sane girl is confined by the malevolent asylum master.
Interesting but rather flatly handled addition to the Val Lewton gallery of horrors, perhaps too carefully and discreetly done for pace or suspense.

w Mark Robson, Carlos Keith *d* Mark Robson *ph* Nicholas Musuraca *m* Roy Webb

Boris Karloff, Anna Lee, Billy House, Richard Fraser, Glenn Vernon

† Carlos Keith was Val Lewton's pseudonym.
†† *Bedlam* was never granted a certificate in Britain.

The Bedroom Window
US 1986 115m colour JDC Widescreen
De Laurentiis (Robert Towne, Martha Schumacher)

From her boyfriend's apartment window, an adulterous wife witnesses an assault, and sends her boyfriend to the police in her place.
Sub-Hitchcock thriller, almost as creaky as it sounds.

w,d Curtis Hanson *ph* Gil Taylor *m* Michael Shrieve, Patrick Gleeson *ed* Scott Conrad

Steve Guttenberg, Elizabeth McGovern, Isabelle Huppert, Paul Shenar, Frederick Coffin, Wallace Shawn

'Less than riveting entertainment.'—*Daily Variety*

Bedside Manner
US 1945 79m bw

A lady doctor falls for a war worker. Flat and contrived comedy which just about manages to keep going. Ruth Hussey, John Carroll, Charles Ruggles, Ann Rutherford, Claudia Drake, Grant Mitchell, Frank Jenks, Charles Drake. Written by Frederick Jackson and Malcolm Stuart Boylan from story by Robert Carson; directed by Andrew Stone; produced by him for UA.

Bedtime for Bonzo
US 1951 83m bw
U-I (Michael Kraike)

To prove that environment determines character, a chimpanzee is brought up as a human baby.
Very moderate fun and games which proved successful enough for a sequel, *Bonzo Goes to College*.

w Val Burton, Lou Breslow *d* Frederick de Cordova *ph* Carl Guthrie *m* Frank Skinner

Ronald Reagan, Diana Lynn, Walter Slezak, Lucille Berkely, Herbert Heyes

A Bedtime Story*
US 1933 89m bw
Paramount (Emmanuel Cohen)

A breezy Frenchman has to interrupt his romances to look after an abandoned baby.
Mild star vehicle in which the agreeable comedy is largely supplanted by sentimental cooing.

w Benjamin Glazer, *novel* Bellamy the Magnificent by Roy Horniman *d* Norman Taurog *ph* Charles Lang *songs* Ralph Rainger, Leo Robin

Maurice Chevalier, Helen Twelvetrees, Baby LeRoy, Edward Everett Horton, Adrienne Ames

Bedtime Story*
US 1941 85m bw
Columbia (B. P. Schulberg)

A playwright's wife wants to retire instead of acting in his next play.
Pleasantly sparkling comedy with good performances.

w Horace Jackson, Grant Garrett, Richard Flournoy *d* Alexander Hall *ph* Joseph Walker *m* Werner Heymann

Fredric March, Loretta Young, Robert Benchley, Allyn Joslyn, Eve Arden, Helen Westley, Joyce Compton, Tim Ryan

Bedtime Story*
US 1964 99m Eastmancolor
U-I / Lankershim / Pennebaker (Stanley Shapiro)

Two Riviera confidence tricksters outwit each other.
A fairly lively script is defeated by dull handling, but performances and backgrounds are attractive.

w Stanley Shapiro, Paul Henning *d* Ralph Levy *ph* Clifford Stine *m* Hans Salter

David Niven, Marlon Brando, Shirley Jones, Dody Goodman, Aram Stephan, Marie Windsor

'The most vulgar and embarrassing film of the year.'—*Daily Express*

Beer
US 1985 82m De Luxe

A lady executive on Madison Avenue promotes a brand of beer by promoting three honest Joes from the street and turning them into macho media figures. Another shred of proof that satire is what closes Saturday night. A few smiles, but no release. Loretta Swit, Rip Torn, Kenneth Mars, David Alan Grier, William Russ. Written by Allan Weissbecker; directed by Patrick Kelly; for Robert Chartoff / Orion. (Original title: *The Selling of America*.)

Bees in Paradise
GB 1943 75m bw

Four airmen find themselves on a South Sea island ruled by women who kill their spouses after the honeymoon. Saucy farce, too talkative to be very interesting even in the dark days of war. Arthur Askey, Peter Graves, Max Bacon, Anne Shelton, Jean Kent. Written by Val Guest and Marriott Edgar; directed by Val Guest; for Gainsborough.

Beetlejuice
US 1988 92m Technicolor
Warner Bros / Geffen (Michael Bender)

The newly dead at a New England barn try to scare off objectionable new buyers.
Mainly unpleasant and seldom funny fantasy.

w Michael McDowell, Warren Skaaren *d* Tim Burton *ph* Thomas Ackerman *m* Danny Elfman *pd* Bo Welch

Alec Baldwin, Geena Davis, Michael Keaton, Catherine O'Hara, Glenn Shadix

Before Dawn*
US 1933 60m bw

Three murders take place in a mysterious mansion. Lively comedy-thriller which won't bore anybody: good in its class. Warner Oland, Stuart Erwin, Dorothy Wilson, Dudley Digges, Oscar Apfel. Written by Garrett Fort, Marian Dix, Ralph Block from a story by Edgar Wallace; directed by *Irving Pichel*; music by Max Steiner; for RKO.

Before Hindsight**
GB 1977 78m Eastmancolor
Elizabeth Taylor-Mead

Interviews and clips show how inadequately cinema newsreels covered world events in the 1930s.
Hard tack for entertainment seekers, but a clear exposition of a proven case of importance to film-makers and politicians.

w Elizabeth Taylor-Mead *d* Jonathan Lewis

'Certainly not the kind of picture people will pay money to see.'—*Variety*

Before I Hang*
US 1940 71m bw
Columbia (Wallace MacDonald)

A research scientist experiments with a new serum which turns him into a murderer.
Archetypal Karloff mad doctor flick, Jekyll and Hyde model: still quite tolerable.

w Robert D. Andrews *d* Nick Grinde *ph* Benjamin Kline *md* Morris Stoloff

Boris Karloff, Evelyn Keyes, Bruce Bennett, Pedro de Cordoba, Edward Van Sloan, Don Beddoe

Before the Nickelodeon**
US 1982 60m bw / colour

The life, times and films of the pioneer Edwin S. Porter. Valuable documentary on a little-known figure, with films ranging from 1896 to 1907. Written by Warren D. Leight, Charles Musser; directed by Charles Musser; for Film for Thought.

Before Winter Comes*
GB 1968 107m Technicolor
Columbia / Windward (Robert Emmett Ginna)

Austria 1945: a British major in charge of displaced persons is helped and hindered by a cheerful Yugoslav refugee who turns out to be a Russian deserter.
Likeable, well-produced drama hampered by a plot which becomes unnecessarily schematic, coincidental and downbeat in its attempts to tug at the heartstrings.

w Andrew Sinclair, *novel* The Interpreter by Frederick L. Keefe *d* J. Lee-Thompson *ph* Gilbert Taylor *m* Ron Grainer

David Niven, Topol, Ori Levi, Anna Karina, John Hurt, Anthony Quayle

'One of those films with a message on every page of its script.'—*MFB*

Beg, Borrow or Steal
US 1937 70m bw

An American expatriate lives by his wits in Paris. Flabby comedy which misses on all cylinders. Frank Morgan, Florence Rice, John Beal, Janet Beecher, Herman Bing, Erik Rhodes, E. E. Clive, Reginald Denny, George Givot. Written by Leonard Lee, Harry Ruskin, Marion Parsonnet; directed by William Thiele; for MGM. 'Nothing quite so incredible as this story has been tossed to the double bills since the major studios started competing among themselves to turn out low-grade entertainment for the filler-in spots.'—*Variety*

Beggars in Ermine
US 1934 70m bw

A steelworker who loses his legs and his livelihood organizes beggars into a wealthy union. Curious semi-fantasy, probably worth a mark for trying. Lionel Atwill, Henry B. Walthall, Betty Furness, Jameson Thomas, Astrid Allwyn. Written by Tristam Tupper from the novel by Esther Lynd Daly; directed by Phil Rosen; for Monogram.

Beggars of Life*
US 1928 80m bw part-talkie

Adventures of a hobo. Curious melodramatic farrago notable chiefly for technical advances but far from boring to watch for its own sake. Richard Arlen, Wallace Beery, Louise Brooks, Edgar Blue Washington, H. A. Morgan, Roscoe Karns. Written by Benjamin Glazer, Jim Tully; directed by William Wellman; for Paramount.

The Beggar's Opera*
GB 1952 94m Technicolor
British Lion / Imperadio (Herbert Wilcox, Laurence Olivier)

A highwayman in Newgate jail devises an opera based on his own exploits.
Exuberant potted version of the 1728 low opera, generally likeable but lacking a strong coherent approach and marred by violent colour and raggedly theatrical presentation. It nearly but not quite comes off.

w Dennis Cannan, Christopher Fry, *opera* John Gay *d* Peter Brook *ph* Guy Green *ad* George Wakhevitch, William C. Andrews *musical arrangement and additions* Arthur Bliss

Laurence Olivier, Stanley Holloway, Dorothy Tutin, Daphne Anderson, Mary Clare, George Devine, Athene Seyler, Hugh Griffith, Margot Grahame, Sandra Dorne, Laurence Naismith

'The failure is equalled only by the ambition.'—*Gavin Lambert*

The Beginning of the End
US 1957 73m bw

Radiation breeds giant grasshoppers which are only stopped when they can't withstand the waters of Lake Michigan.
Bottom-of-the-sci-fi-barrel rubbish, very boring to watch. Peggie Castle, Peter Graves, Morris Ankrum, James Seay, Richard Benedict, Pierre Watkin. Written by Fred Freiberger, Lester Corn; produced and directed by Bert I. Gordon; for ABPT/Republic.

The Beginning or the End
US 1947 112m bw
MGM (Samuel Marx)

During World War II American scientists continue to perfect the atom bomb despite their own misgivings, and one dies in an explosion.
Semi-documentary marred by sentimental personal asides and of very little continuing interest.

w Robert Considine *d* Norman Taurog *ph* Ray June *m* Daniele Amfitheatrof

Brian Donlevy, Robert Walker, Tom Drake, Beverly Tyler, Hume Cronyn, Audrey Totter, *Godfrey Tearle* (as Roosevelt)

Begone Dull Care****
Canada 1953 9m colour
National Film Board (Norman McLaren)

Abstract images drawn directly onto the film are accompanied by three pieces of jazz performed by the Oscar Peterson Trio.
The central movement is a little too slow, but the first piece is witty and the climax is an irresistible frenzy of sound and image. Undeniably a classic short, and probably McLaren's best.

conceived and made by Norman McLaren

'One man . . . seven women . . . in a strange house!'

The Beguiled*
US 1971 109m Technicolor
Universal / Malpaso (Don Siegel)

A wounded Unionist soldier hides out in a Confederate ladies' school; the teachers fend for him until he causes trouble among the sexually frustrated women, who eventually kill him.
Eccentric melodrama which does not really work despite its credentials and patient work all round.

w John B. Sherry, Grimes Grice, *novel* Thomas Cullinan *d* Don Siegel *ph* Bruce Surtees *m* Lalo Schifrin *pd* Ted Haworth

Clint Eastwood, Geraldine Page, Elizabeth Hartman, Jo Ann Harris, Darleen Carr, Mae Mercer

'A must for sadists and woman-haters.'—*Judith Crist*

Behave Yourself*
US 1951 81m bw
RKO (Jerry Wald, Norman Krasna)

A young married couple and their dog get mixed up in a chain of murders.
Zany black comedy in the wake of *A Slight Case of Murder* and *The Thin Man*. The humour is spread too thin for success.

wd George Beck *ph* James Wong Howe *m* Leigh Harline

Farley Granger, Shelley Winters, William Demarest, Francis L. Sullivan, Margalo Gillmore, Lon Chaney, Hans Conried, Elisha Cook Jnr

Behind Green Lights
US 1945 64m bw

A murderer is spotted during one night in the press room of a police station. A pale shadow of *The Front Page*, with inferior work all round. Carole Landis, William Gargan, Richard Crane, Mary Anderson, John Ireland, Roy Roberts, Mabel Paige. Written by W. Scott Darling and Charles G. Booth; directed by Otto Brower; for TCF.

Behind Prison Gates
US 1939 63m bw

A secret agent follows bank robbers into prison. Standard undercover crime support. Brian Donlevy, Jacqueline Wells, Joseph Crehan, Paul Fix. Written by Arthur T. Horman, Leslie T. White; directed by Charles Barton; for Columbia.

Behind Prison Walls
US 1943 64m bw

Too-honest son gets his tycoon father sent to prison, but ends up there himself. Curious moral comedy drama which can't work on a low budget. Alan Baxter, Tully Marshall, Gertrude Michael, Edwin Maxwell, Matt Willis. Written by Van Norcross, W. A. Ulman Jnr; directed by Steve Sekely; for Arthur Ripley/PRC. (GB title: *Youth Takes a Hand*.)

Behind That Curtain
US 1929 91m bw
Murder follows when a ne'er-do-well aspires to marry an heiress. Nominally the third Charlie Chan film, but Chan, played by E. L. Parks, is whittled down to a tiny role. As it stands, a clumsy effort, but could be worth remaking. Warner Baxter, Lois Moran, Gilbert Emery, Claude King, Philip Strange, Boris Karloff. Written by Sonya Levien, Clarke Silvernail from the novel by Earl Derr Biggers; directed by Irving Cummings; for Fox.

Behind the Eight Ball
US 1942 60m bw
Actors are mistaken for spies. Very patchy but commendably brief star comedy. The Ritz Brothers, Carol Bruce, Dick Foran, William Demarest. Written by Stanley Roberts and Mel Ronson; directed by Edward F. Cline; for Universal. (GB title: *Off the Beaten Track.*)

Behind the High Wall
US 1956 85m bw
U-I (Stanley Rubin)
A prison warder, taken as hostage by escaping convicts, steals some of the money they have taken.
Glum melodrama, capably presented.
w Harold Jack Bloom *d* Abner Biberman *ph* Maury Gertsman *m* Joseph Gershenson
Tom Tully, Sylvia Sidney, John Gavin, Betty Lynn, John Larch, Barney Phillips, Don Beddoe

Behind the Iron Mask: see The Fifth Musketeer

Behind the Make-up
US 1930 65m bw
A talented clown is constantly frustrated by the ill-advised schemes of his partner. Seamy melodrama from another age; barely playable now. Hal Skelly, William Powell, Fay Wray, Kay Francis, E. H. Calvert, Paul Lukas. Written by George Manker Watters, Howard Estabrook, from a story by Mildred Cram; directed by Robert Milton; for Paramount.

Behind the Mask
US 1932 68m bw
A crazy doctor operates fatally on those who know too much. Semi-horror mystery using two members of the Frankenstein cast. Jack Holt, Constance Cummings, Edward Van Sloan, Boris Karloff. Written by Jo Swerling; directed by John Francis Dillon; for Columbia.

Behind the Mask*
GB 1958 99m Eastmancolor
BL / GW Films (Sergei Nolbandov, Josef Somlo)
Political infighting causes tension on the board of a local hospital.
Oddly titled social drama with interesting detail but not much tension or conclusion.
w John Hunter, *novel* The Pack by John Rowan Wilson *d* Brian Desmond Hurst *ph* Robert Krasker *m* Geoffrey Wright
Michael Redgrave, Tony Britton, Carl Mohner, Niall MacGinnis, Vanessa Redgrave, Ian Bannen, Brenda Bruce, Lionel Jeffries, Miles Malleson, John Welsh, Ann Firbank

Behind the Rising Sun*
US 1943 88m bw
RKO
An American-educated Japanese goes home in the thirties, comes under the influence of war-mongers, and causes his father to commit hara-kiri.
Outrageous wartime flagwaver designed to vilify 'Uncle Tojo's dogs', from the writer and director of the similar *Hitler's Children* (qv).
w Emmet Lavery, *novel* James R. Young *d* Edward Dmytryk *ph* Russell Metty *m* Roy Webb
J. Carrol Naish, Tom Neal, Margo, Robert Ryan, Gloria Holden, Don Douglas, Adeline de Walt Reynolds

Behold a Pale Horse*
US 1964 121m bw
Columbia / Highland / Brentwood (Fred Zinnemann, Alexander Trauner)
A Spanish guerrilla goes into exile at the end of the Civil War. Twenty years later he is persuaded to return and kill a brutal police chief.
An action film which unfortunately insists on saying something significant about morality, destiny and death. Impeccably made, but somehow not very interesting apart from the action sequences.
w J. P. Miller, *novel* Killing a Mouse on Sunday by Emeric Pressburger *d Fred Zinnemann* *ph* Jean Badal *m* Maurice Jarre *ad* Alexander Trauner
Gregory Peck, Omar Sharif, Anthony Quinn, Raymond Pellegrin, Paolo Stoppa, Mildred Dunnock, Daniela Rocca, Christian Marquand
'A fine example of a high class failure.'—*Judith Crist*

'Her savage heart pounded with revenge when her love went unwanted!'
Behold My Wife
US 1934 79m bw
Paramount (B. P. Schulberg)
A wealthy young man brings back and marries a New Mexico Indian girl to show up his snobbish family.
Dated melodrama, of interest solely for its racial theme.
w William R. Lippman, Oliver LaFarge, *novel* The Translation of a Savage by Sir Gilbert Parker *d* Mitchell Leisen *ph* Leon Shamroy
Sylvia Sidney, Gene Raymond, Juliette Compton, Laura Hope Crews, H. B. Warner, Monroe Owsley, Ann Sheridan
'Frank melodrama of the hokiest sort.'—*Variety*

'Getting there is half the fun; being there is all of it!'
Being There**
US 1979 130m Metrocolor
Lorimar / North Star / CIP (Andrew Braunsberg)
An illiterate gardener is taken for a homespun philosopher and becomes a national celebrity.
Overlong serio-comic parable hinging on a somewhat dubious star performance. Chance made it a popular urban success, but few who saw it were enthused.
w Jerzy Kosinski, from his novel *d* Hal Ashby *ph* Dianne Schroeder *m* John Mandel *pd* Michael Haller
Peter Sellers, Shirley Maclaine, *Melvyn Douglas*, Jack Warden, Richard Dysart, Richard Basehart
'It pulls off its long shot and is a confoundingly provocative movie.'—*Roger Ebert*
AA: Melvyn Douglas
AAN: Peter Sellers
BFA: screenplay

Bela Lugosi Meets a Brooklyn Gorilla
US 1952 74m bw
A tropical island scientist turns one half of a stranded comedy team into a gorilla. Stupid farce which never rises to the occasion. Bela Lugosi, Duke Mitchell, Sammy Petrillo, Ray 'Crash' Corrigan, Muriel Landers. Written by Tim Ryan; directed by William Beaudine; for Jack Broder. (GB title: *The Monster Meets the Gorilla.*) 'Neighbourhood and small-town audiences will get some laughs.'—*Box Office*

Believe in Me
US 1971 90m colour
MGM (Irwin Winkler, Robert Chartoff)
Two young marrieds take to drugs.
Tedious and unenlightening modern drama which seems to think it's saying something new.
w Israel Horovitz *d* Stuart Hagmann *ph* Dick Kratina, Richard C. Brooks *m* Fred Karlin
Michael Sarrazin, Jacqueline Bisset, Jon Cypher, Allen Garfield

The Believers*
US 1987 114m De Luxe
Orion / John Schlesinger, Michael Childers, Beverly Camhe
New York's occult underworld is permeated by a sinister Catholic ritual.
Most of the time it's hard to say what's going on in this intensely melodramatic thriller, but there are the odd rewards along the way. Not too many, actually.
w Mark Frost from the book The Religion by Nicholas Conde *d* John Schlesinger *ph* Bobby Muller *m* J. Peter Robinson *pd* Simon Holland *ed* Peter Honess
Martin Sheen, Helen Shaver, Harley Cross, Robert Loggia, Elizabeth Wilson, Harris Yulin
'If nothing else, Schlesinger knows how to produce a film where pain and horror are beautiful to watch.'—*Daily Variety*

'A bewitching comedy about an enchanting subject!'
Bell, Book and Candle*
US 1958 103m Technicolor
Columbia / Phoenix (Julian Blaustein)

A publisher slowly becomes aware that his new girl friend is a witch.
A gossamer stage comedy has been fatally flattened in translation; most of the actors are miscast, and sentiment soaks the script. But it remains a civilized entertainment.

w Daniel Taradash, *play* John Van Druten *d* Richard Quine *ph* James Wong Howe *m* George Duning

James Stewart, Kim Novak, Jack Lemmon, Ernie Kovacs, *Hermione Gingold*, Elsa Lanchester, Janice Rule

Bell Bottom George
GB 1943 97m bw

A medically exempt waiter dons uniform and catches a ring of spies. Formula star comedy, too long and too familiar. George Formby, Anne Firth, Reginald Purdell, Peter Murray Hill. Written by Peter Fraser and Edward Dryhurst; directed by Marcel Varnel; for Columbia.

A Bell for Adano*
US 1945 104m bw
TCF (Louis D. Lighton, Lamar Trotti)

An American major takes over an Italian town and wins affection by replacing the local bell.
Slight end-of-war mood piece, still quite pleasant but without the undercurrents of feeling it had at the time.

w Lamar Trotti, Norman Reilly Raine, *novel* John Hersey *d* Henry King *ph* Joseph La Shelle *m* Alfred Newman

John Hodiak, Gene Tierney, William Bendix, Glenn Langan, Richard Conte, Stanley Prager, Henry Morgan

The Bell Jar
US 1979 107m colour

A teenage girl becomes mentally ill when her father dies. Numbingly tedious case history without much apparent point. Marilyn Hassett, Julie Harris, Anne Jackson, Barbara Barrie. Written by Marjorie Kellog, from the novel by Sylvia Plath; directed by Larry Peerce; for Peerce-Goldston / Avco.

Belladonna
GB 1934 91m bw

A selfish woman tries to poison her husband for love of an Egyptian. Intriguingly-cast version of the Robert Hichens novel dramatized by J. B. Fagan; later filmed in Hollywood as *Temptation* (qv). Mary Ellis, Conrad Veidt, Cedric Hardwicke, John Stuart, Michael Shepley. Written by H. Fowler Mear; directed by Robert Milton; for Twickenham.

Il Bell'Antonio*
Italy / France 1960 105m bw
Cina del Duca–Arco / Lyre Cinématographique (Alfredo Bini)
GB title: *Handsome Antonio*

A youngish man returns to his native town with the reputation of a lady-killer, but when married turns out to be impotent.
Amusing but finally exhausting Sicilian comedy with all the expected exaggeration of speech and gesture.

w Pier Paolo Pasolini, Gino Visentini, *novel* Vitaliano Brancati *d* Piero Piccioni

Marcello Mastroianni, Claudia Cardinale, Pierre Brasseur, Rina Morelli, Tomas Milian

The Bellboy*
US 1960 72m bw
Paramount / Jerry Lewis Productions (Jerry Lewis)

An incompetent bellboy causes havoc in a Miami hotel.
Plotless essence of a comedian who divides opinion and will never be better than variable. This ragbag of old gags at least prevents his usual sentimental excesses, and is mercifully short.

wd Jerry Lewis *ph* Haskell Boggs *m* Walter Scharf

Jerry Lewis, Alex Gerry, Bob Clayton, Herkie Styles, Milton Berle

La Belle Américaine*
France 1961 101m bw (colour finale)
CCFC / Film d'Art / Panorama / Corflor (Henri Diamant-Berger, Arthur Lesser)
GB / US titles: *What a Chassis; The American Beauty*

A Parisian factory worker gets into all kinds of trouble when he buys an American supercar for a ridiculously low price.
Some brilliant gags are separated by long dull spots of unnecessary storytelling.

w Robert Dhéry, Pierre Tchernia, Alfred Adam *d* Robert Dhéry *ph* Ghislain Cloquet *m* Gérard Calvi

Robert Dhéry, Louis de Funes, Colette Brosset, Alfred Adam, Bernard Lavalette, Annie Ducaux

Belle de Jour***
France / Italy 1967 100m Eastmancolor
Paris Film / Five Film (Robert and Raymond Hakim)

A surgeon's wife finds herself drawn to afternoon work in a brothel.
Fascinating Bunuel mixture of fact and fantasy, impeccably woven into a rich fabric.

w Luis Bunuel, Jean-Claude Carrière d Luis Bunuel ph Sacha Vierny m none

Catherine Deneuve, Jean Sorel, Michel Piccoli, Genevieve Page, Pierre Clémenti

La Belle Equipe*
France 1936 74m bw
Ciné Arts

Five unemployed Parisians win the lottery and open a restaurant, but things do not go smoothly.
Interesting but rather lumpy star drama which finally descends into melodrama; alternative tragic and happy endings were originally offered.

w Charles Spaak, Julien Duvivier *d* Julien Duvivier *ph* Jules Kruger, Marc Fessard *m* Maurice Yvain

Jean Gabin, Charles Vanel, Viviane Romance, Raymond Aimes, Robert Lynen, Raymond Cordy, Raphael Medina

La Belle et la Bête**
France 1946 95m bw
André Paulvé

Beauty gives herself to the Beast who has kidnapped her father; through love the monster turns into a handsome prince.
Slightly heavy-handed though usually stunning-looking adaptation of the fairy tale.

wd Jean Cocteau ph Henri Alekan *m* Georges Auric *ad Christian Bérard*

Jean Marais, Josette Day, Mila Parély, Marcel André, Michel Auclair

'Perhaps the most sumptuously elegant of all filmed fairy tales.'—*New Yorker, 1980*

'Absolute magic: diamond cold and lunar bright.'—*CBS*

Belle le Grand
US 1951 89m bw
Republic

The proprietress of a Barbary Coast gambling house is plagued by an ex-husband on whose account she served a prison term.
Confused and incompetent period melodrama.

w D. D. Beauchamp *d* Allan Dwan *ph* Reggie Lanning *m* Victor Young

Vera Ralston, John Carroll, William Ching, Hope Emerson, Stephen Chase, Grant Withers, John Qualen

The Belle of New York*
US 1952 82m Technicolor
MGM (Arthur Freed)

A nineties playboy falls for a Salvation Army girl.
A rather dreary version of the old musical, with undistinguished additions.

w Robert O'Brien, Irving Elinson *d* Charles Walters *ph* Robert Planck *m / ly* Johnny Mercer, Harry Warren *md* Adolph Deutsch *ad Jack Martin Smith*

Fred Astaire, Vera-Ellen, Marjorie Main, Keenan Wynn, Alice Pearce, Clinton Sundberg, Gale Robbins

Songs include 'When I'm Out with the Belle of New York'; 'Oops'; 'Baby Doll'; 'Naughty but Nice'; 'Seeing's Believing'; 'Thank You Mr Currier, Thank You Mr Ives'; 'I Love to Beat a Big Bass Drum'; 'I Wanna Be a Dancing Man'; 'Let a Little Love Come In'

Belle of the Nineties*
US 1934 75m bw
Paramount (William Le Baron)

A saloon entertainer loves two men, one of whom is a crook.
Much-laundered star vehicle which despite superior production seems a pale shadow of the star's better pieces.

w Mae West *d* Leo McCarey *ph* Karl Struss *songs* Arthur Johnston, Sam Coslow

Mae West, Roger Pryor, John Miljan, John Mack Brown, Katherine de Mille, Duke Ellington and his Orchestra

'It's been sufficiently denatured from within, yet not completely emasculated.'—*Variety*

Belle of the Yukon*
US 1945 84m Technicolor
International

A troupe of saloon entertainers in the Yukon become involved with a bank robbery.
Threads of plot support comedy, dancing and songs in this thin but reasonably fresh musical imitation of *The Spoilers*.

w James Edward Grant *d* William A. Seiter *ph* Ray Rennahan *md* Arthur Lange

Gypsy Rose Lee, Randolph Scott, Dinah Shore, Charles Winninger, Bob Burns

AAN: Arthur Lange; song 'Sleigh Ride in July' (*m* Jimmy Van Heusen, *ly* Johnny Burke)

Belle Starr
US 1941 87m Technicolor
TCF (Kenneth MacGowan)

Absurdly laundered version of the life of the west's most notorious female outlaw, with the star laughably miscast.

w Lamar Trotti *d* Irving Cummings *ph* Ernest Palmer, Ray Rennahan *m* Alfred Newman

Gene Tierney, Randolph Scott, Dana Andrews, Shepperd Strudwick, Elizabeth Patterson, Chill Wills, Louise Beavers

Les Belles de Nuit**
France / Italy 1952 89m bw
Franco London / Rizzoli

A discontented music teacher dreams of beautiful women through the ages.
Charming but very slight dream fantasy with many of the master's touches. (He claims to have intended a comic *Intolerance*.)

wd René Clair ph Armand Thirard, Robert Juilliard, Louis Née *m Georges Van Parys ad* Léon Barsacq

Gérard Philipe, Gina Lollobrigida, Martine Carol, Magali Vendeuil, Paolo Stoppa, Raymond Bussières, Raymond Cordy

The Belles of St Trinian's*
GB 1954 91m bw
BL / London Films / Launder and Gilliat

At an unruly and bankrupt school for girls, more time is spent backing horses than studying subjects, and the headmistress's bookmaker brother has a scheme or two of his own.
Fairly successful film version of Ronald Searle's awful schoolgirl cartoons, the emphasis shifted to a grotesque older generation with the star in drag. An enormous commercial success, but the three sequels *Blue Murder at St Trinian's, The Pure Hell of St Trinian's, The Great St Trinian's Train Robbery* went from bad to awful.

w Frank Launder, Sidney Gilliat, Val Valentine *d* Frank Launder *ph* Stan Pavey *m* Malcolm Arnold

Alastair Sim, George Cole, Joyce Grenfell, Hermione Baddeley, Betty Ann Davies, Renée Houston, Beryl Reid, Irene Handl, Mary Merrall

'Not so much a film as an entertainment on celluloid, a huge charade, a rich pile of idiot and splendidly senseless images.'—*David Robinson*

Belles on Their Toes
US 1952 89m Technicolor
TCF (Samuel G. Engel)

Further adventures in the growing up of the twelve Gilbreth children.
Flat sequel to *Cheaper by the Dozen* (qv) with sentimentality instead of Clifton Webb. Period atmosphere attractive.

w Phoebe and Henry Ephron, *book* Frank B. Gilbreth Jnr and Ernestine Gilbreth Carey *d* Henry Levin *ph* Arthur E. Arling *m* Cyril Mockridge

Myrna Loy, Jeanne Crain, Debra Paget, Jeffrey Hunter, Edward Arnold, Hoagy Carmichael, Barbara Bates, Robert Arthur

Bellissima*
Italy 1951 100m bw
Bellissima Films (Salvo d'Angelo)

A mother struggles to get a part in a film for her 7-year-old daughter.
Highly detailed, very noisy star vehicle with neo-realist working-class backgrounds. Exhausting.

w Suso Cecchi d'Amico, Francesco Rosi, Luchino Visconti, Cesare Zavattini *d* Luchino Visconti *ph* Piero Portalupi *m* Franco Mannino

Anna Magnani, Walter Chiari, Tina Apicella, Gastone Renzelli, Alessandro Blasetti

Bellman and True*
GB 1987 122m Technicolor
Handmade / Euston

A young burglar in a heist is protected by an older crook's computer skills.
Good crime drama with television derivation.

w Desmond Lowder and others, from Lowder's novel *d* Richard Loncraine *ph* Ken Westbury *pd* Jon Bunker

Bernard Hill, Kieran O'Brien, Richard Hope, Frances Tomelty

The Bells
GB 1931 75m bw

An Alsatian burgomaster is forced by conscience to confess to the killing of a Jew.
Only sound version of a famous melodrama played on stage by Henry Irving. Donald Calthrop, Jane Welsh, Edward Sinclair. (In a 1926 silent version Lionel Barrymore played the murderer and Boris Karloff the mesmerist.) Written by C. H. Dand, from the play by Erckmann and Chatrian; directed by Oscar M. Werndorff and Harcourt Templeman; in three language versions; for Isidore Schlesinger / BSFP.

Bells are Ringing*
US 1960 126m Metrocolor Cinemascope
MGM (Arthur Freed)

A telephone answering service operator becomes passionately involved in the lives of her clients.
Dull, rather ugly and boring transcription of a Broadway musical, with all talents below par, not enough dancing and too much plot.

w / ly Betty Comden, Adolph Green, from their play *d* Vincente Minnelli *ph* Milton Krasner *m* Jule Styne *md* André Previn *ad* George W. Davis, Preston Ames *ch* Charles O'Curran

Judy Holliday, Dean Martin, Fred Clark, Eddie Foy Jnr, Jean Stapleton, Ruth Storey, Frank Gorshin

AAN: André Previn

The Bells Go Down*
GB 1943 89m bw
Ealing (S. C. Balcon)

The exploits of a London firefighting unit during World War II.
Tragi-comedy with lively scenes, a good record of the historical background of the blitz.

w Roger Macdougall, Stephen Black *d* Basil Dearden *ph* Ernest Palmer *m* Roy Douglas

Tommy Trinder, James Mason, Mervyn Johns, Philippa Hyatt, Finlay Currie, Philip Friend, Meriel Forbes, Beatrice Varley, Billy Hartnell

'Your heart will be wearing a smile!'

The Bells of St Mary's**
US 1945 126m bw
RKO / Rainbow (Leo McCarey)

At a big city Catholic school, Father O'Malley and Sister Benedict indulge in friendly rivalry, and succeed in extending the school through the gift of a building.
Sentimental and very commercial sequel to *Going My Way*, with the stars at their peak and the handling as cosy and well-paced as might be expected.

w Dudley Nichols *d* Leo McCarey *ph* George Barnes *m* Robert Emmett Dolan

Bing Crosby, Ingrid Bergman, Henry Travers, William Gargan, Ruth Donnelly, Rhys Williams, Una O'Connor, Eva Novak

'The picture is full of shrewd and pleasant flashes. It is also fascinating to watch as a talented, desperate effort to repeat the unrepeatable. But on the whole it is an unhappy film.'—*James Agee*

AAN: best picture; Leo McCarey; Robert Emmett Dolan; Bing Crosby; Ingrid Bergman; song 'Aren't You Glad You're You' (*m* Jimmy Van Heusen, *ly* Johnny Burke)

The Belly of an Architect
GB / Italy 1987 118m Technicolor
Mondial / Tangram

An American architect in Rome discovers he is terminally ill, is deserted by his wife, and commits suicide.
Ravishing evocation of 18th-century Roman architecture is no compensation for the multi-layered psychological complexity.

w,d Peter Greenaway *ph* Sach Vierny *m* Wim Mertens *ad* Luciana Vedovelli

Brian Dennehy, Chloe Webb, Lambert Wilson

Beloved
US 1933 80m bw

A composer ages from 10 to 90 while trying to place his symphony; he dies happy. Curious fictional biopic with plenty of incident but no plot. John Boles, Gloria Stuart, Albert Conti, Dorothy Peterson, Morgan Farley. Written by Paul Gangelin and George O'Neil; directed by Victor Schertzinger; for Bennie F. Zeidman / Universal. 'Too hopelessly muddled in conception to reach the important money class.'—*Variety*

The Beloved Bachelor
US 1931 72m bw

A man falls in love with his adopted daughter. Innocuous tearjerker made with some style. Paul Lukas, Dorothy Jordan, Betty Van Allen, Charles Ruggles, Vivienne Osborne. Written by Sidney Buchman, Raymond Griffith and Agnes Brand Leahy, from the play by Edward H. Peple; directed by Lloyd Corrigan; for Paramount. 'A particularly femme appealing yarn with apt dialogue and natural continuity.'—*Variety*

Beloved Enemy*
US 1936 90m bw
Samuel Goldwyn (George Haight)

During the 1921 Irish rebellion, the fiancée of a British army officer falls in love with the leading revolutionary.
Dreamy-eyed romance with little relevance to the real situation; not badly done of its kind.

w John Balderston, Rose Franken, William Brown Meloney, David Hart *d* H. C. Potter *ph* Gregg Toland *m* Alfred Newman

Brian Aherne, Merle Oberon, David Niven, Karen Morley, Jerome Cowan, Henry Stephenson, Donald Crisp

'One of the most incredible screen yarns which has been shown in many a day. . . . If when the film is shown in Dublin a tidal wave engulfs Hollywood, it will be caused by the Emerald Isle turning somersaults.'—*Variety*

Beloved Infidel*
US 1959 123m De Luxe Cinemascope
TCF / Company of Artists (Jerry Wald)

Sheilah Graham, a British chorus girl turned Hollywood columnist, lives with Scott Fitzgerald but fails to cure him of alcoholism.
A bitter and even sordid true story becomes a slice of Hollywood romance, with stars unsuitably cast. On all levels it falls between two stools, satisfying nobody.

w Sy Bartlett, *book* Sheilah Graham and Gerald Frank *d* Henry King *ph* Leon Shamroy *m* Franz Waxman

Gregory Peck, Deborah Kerr, Eddie Albert, Philip Ober, Herbert Rudley, Karin Booth, Ken Scott

'Catastrophically misguided.'—*Penelope Houston*

The Beloved Rogue*
US 1927 99m at 24 fps bw silent

Fifteenth-century poet and thief François Villon becomes a friend of the king, but is banished when he falls for a lady of the court. Stylish star vehicle remade as *If I Were King* (qv). John Barrymore, Conrad Veidt, Marceline Day, Mack Swain, Slim Summerville. Written by Paul Bern; directed by Alan Crosland; production design by William Cameron Menzies; for Art Cinema Corporation.

'He kissed many but loved one!'
The Beloved Vagabond*
GB 1936 78m bw
Ludovico Toeplitz

At the turn of the century, a jilted French artist becomes a vagabond and falls in love with an orphan girl.
Mildly amusing bi-lingual production from a bestselling picaresque novel; production quite lively.

w Wells Root, Arthur Wimperis, Hugh Mills, Walter Creighton, *novel* W. J. Locke *d* Curtis Bernhardt *ph* Franz Planer

Maurice Chevalier, Margaret Lockwood, Betty Stockfield, Desmond Tester, Austin Trevor, Peter Haddon, Cathleen Nesbitt

'A weak sister, mostly for the duals.'—*Variety*

Below Zero**
US 1930 20m bw

Street musicians treat a policeman to lunch on the contents of a found wallet which turns out to be his. Slow-paced but likeable star comedy from their best period. Laurel and Hardy, Frank Holliday, Tiny Sandford. Written by H. M. Walker; directed by James Parrott; for Hal Roach.

The Belstone Fox*
GB 1973 103m Eastmancolor Todd-AO 35
Rank / Independent Artists (Sally Shuter)

A fox and a hound grow up together but the fox leads to tragedy for its masters.
Good animal and countryside photography barely compensate for a fragmentary story with unpleasant moments or for a muddled attitude towards humans and animals; one is not clear what audience the result is supposed to appeal to.

wd James Hill, *novel* David Rook *ph* John Wilcox, James Allen *m* Laurie Johnson

Eric Porter, Rachel Roberts, Jeremy Kemp, Bill Travers, Dennis Waterman

Ben
US 1972 92m De Luxe
Cinerama / Bing Crosby (Mort Briskin)

A sickly boy inherits an army of trained rats.
Boring reprise of *Willard* in which the audience knows only too well what to expect. Production and development quite routine.

w Gilbert A. Ralston *d* Phil Karlson *ph* Russell Metty *m* Walter Scharf

Lee Harcourt Montgomery, Arthur O'Connell, Rosemary Murphy, Meredith Baxter, Kaz Garas, Paul Carr, Kenneth Tobey, Joseph Campanella

AAN: title song (*m* Walter Scharf, *ly* Don Black)

'The great decade (1915–25) of the progress of motion picture art reaches its summit! A cast of 125,000!'

'The inspired love of the prince of Hur for the gentle lovely Esther!'

Ben Hur***
US 1926 170m approx (16 fps) bw (colour sequence) silent
MGM

In the time of Christ, a Jew suffers mightily under the Romans.
The American silent screen's biggest epic; the sea battle and the chariot race are its most famous sequences.

w Bess Meredyth, Carey Wilson, *novel* Lew Wallace *d Fred Niblo* *ph* Karl Struss, Clyde de Vinna, and others *ad* Horace Jackson, Ferdinand Pinney Earle

Ramon Novarro, Francis X. Bushman, Carmel Myers, May McAvoy, Betty Bronson

'Masterpiece of study and patience, a photodrama filled with artistry.'—*New York Times*

† Previously filmed in 1907.

Ben Hur**
US 1959 217m Technicolor Camera 65
MGM (Sam Zimbalist)

Solid, expensive, surprisingly unimaginative remake; generally less sprightly than the silent version.

w Karl Tunberg *d* William Wyler, *Andrew Marton* *ph* Robert L. Surtees *m* Miklos Rozsa *ad* William A. Horning, Edward Carfagno

Charlton Heston, Haya Harareet, Jack Hawkins, Stephen Boyd, Hugh Griffith, Martha Scott, Sam Jaffe, Cathy O'Donnell, Finlay Currie, Frank Thring, Terence Longdon, André Morell, George Relph

'Watching it is like waiting at a railroad crossing while an interminable freight train lumbers by, sometimes stopping altogether.'—*Dwight MacDonald*

'A Griffith can make a hundred into a crowd while a Wyler can reduce a thousand to a confused cocktail party.'—*Ibid.*

'The most tasteful and visually exciting film spectacle yet produced by an American company.'—*Albert Johnson, Film Quarterly*

'Spectacular without being a spectacle . . . not only is it not simple-minded, it is downright literate.'—*Saturday Review*

'A major motion picture phenomenon.'—*Films in Review*

† The production cost four million dollars, twice the maximum at the time. Rock Hudson, Marlon Brando and Burt Lancaster were all sought in vain for the lead before Heston was selected.

†† This version was subtitled 'A Tale of the Christ'.

AA: best picture; William Wyler; Robert L. Surtees; Miklos Rozsa; Charlton Heston; Hugh Griffith
AAN: Karl Tunberg

Benchley

The one-reel shorts in which Robert Benchley, sitting behind a desk, delivered nonsensical lectures on aspects of modern life were very popular with better-class audiences, and launched Benchley onto his movie career as a light actor. Here is a list of them:
1928: THE TREASURER'S REPORT; THE SEX LIFE OF THE POLYP; THE SPELLBINDER.
1929: LESSON NUMBER ONE (2 reels); FURNACE TROUBLE (2 reels); STEWED, FRIED AND BOILED (2 reels).
1933: YOUR TECHNOCRACY AND MINE (2 reels).
1935: HOW TO BREAK 90 AT CROQUET; HOW TO SLEEP.
1936: HOW TO BEHAVE; HOW TO TRAIN A DOG; HOW TO VOTE; HOW TO BE A DETECTIVE.
1937: THE ROMANCE OF DIGESTION; HOW TO START THE DAY; A NIGHT AT THE MOVIES.
1938: HOW TO FIGURE INCOME TAX; MUSIC MADE SIMPLE; AN EVENING ALONE; HOW TO RAISE A BABY; THE COURTSHIP OF THE NEWT; HOW TO READ; HOW TO WATCH FOOTBALL; OPENING DAY; MENTAL POISE; HOW TO SUBLET.
1939: AN HOUR FOR LUNCH; DARK MAGIC; HOME EARLY; HOW TO EAT; THE DAY OF REST; SEE YOUR DOCTOR.
1940: THAT INFERIOR FEELING; HOME MOVIES; THE TROUBLE WITH HUSBANDS.
1941: WAITING FOR BABY; CRIME CONTROL; THE FORGOTTEN MAN; HOW TO TAKE A VACATION.
1942: NOTHING BUT NERVES; THE WITNESS; KEEPING IN SHAPE; THE MAN'S ANGLE.
1943: MY TOMATO; NO NEWS IS GOOD NEWS.
1944: IMPORTANT BUSINESS; WHY, DADDY?
1945: BOOGIE WOOGIE (2 reels); I'M A CIVILIAN HERE MYSELF.
In the late seventies a feature compilation was made under the title *Those Wonderful Benchley Shorts*.

Bend of the River*

US 1952 91m Technicolor
U-I (Aaron Rosenberg)
GB title: *Where the River Bends*

1880 wagon trains arrive in Oregon, and the pioneers have trouble with the local bad man.
Good standard western with pace and period feeling but not much plot sense.

w Borden Chase, *novel* Bend of the Snake by William Gulick *d* Anthony Mann *ph* Irving Glassberg *m* Hans Salter

James Stewart, Arthur Kennedy, Rock Hudson, Julia Adams, Lori Nelson, Jay C. Flippen, Henry Morgan, Royal Dano, Stepin Fetchit

Beneath the Planet of the Apes*

US 1969 94m De Luxe Panavision
TCF / APJAC (Mort Abrahams)

Astronauts on the ape planet discover that it is really Earth and that subterranean human mutants are nursing a live atom bomb.
Violence replaces the thoughtfulness of the original, but this is not at all a bad sequel as sequels go.

w Paul Dehn, Mort Abrahams *d* Ted Post *ph* Milton Krasner *m* Leonard Rosenman

James Franciscus, Charlton Heston, Linda Harrison, Kim Hunter, Maurice Evans, Paul Richards, Victor Buono, Jeff Corey, James Gregory, Thomas Gomez

† See *Planet of the Apes*.

Beneath the Twelve Mile Reef

US 1953 102m Technicolor Cinemascope
TCF (Robert Bassler)

Jealousy, tragedy and romance among the Florida sponge fishers.
Fox's early Cinemascope production involved much underwater shooting, a trick octopus, and predictable plot devices.

w A. I. Bezzerides *d* Robert D. Webb *ph* Edward Cronjager *m* Bernard Herrmann

Robert Wagner, Terry Moore, Gilbert Roland, Peter Graves, J. Carrol Naish, Richard Boone, Angela Clarke, Jay Novello

'The dead weight of a melodramatic script overtaxes the gallant attempts at conviction.'—*MFB*

AAN: Edward Cronjager

Bengal Brigade

US 1954 87m Technicolor
U-I (Ted Richmond)
GB title: *Bengal Rifles*

In 19th-century India, an officer is cashiered through false evidence, and becomes an undercover man with the wicked local rajah.
Routine Hollywood heroics with a few unintended laughs.

w Richard Alan Simmons, *novel* Bengal Tiger by Hall Hunter *d* Laslo Benedek *ph* Maury Gertsman *m* Hans Salter

Rock Hudson, Arlene Dahl, Dan O'Herlihy, Ursula Thiess, Torin Thatcher, Michael Ansara, Arnold Moss

Bengazi

US 1955 79m bw Superscope
RKO / Panamint (Sam Wiesenthal, Eugene Tevlin)

Various unsavoury characters set out into the African desert to look for gold hidden by the Nazis.
Poor potboiler on predictable lines.

w Endre Boehm, Louis Vittes *d* John Brahm *ph* Joseph Biroc *m* Roy Webb

Richard Conte, Victor McLaglen, Richard Carlson, Mala Powers, Richard Erdman, Gonzales Gonzales, Hillary Brooke

Benjamin, or The Diary of an Innocent Young Man

France 1966 104m Eastmancolor
Paramount / Parc / Marianne (Mag Bodard)

In the 18th century, a 17-year-old orphan is taken in hand by his wealthy aunt and initiated into the mysteries of sex.
Imitation *Tom Jones*, quite good to look at but rather boring.

w Nina Companeez *d* Michel Déville *ph* Ghislain Cloquet

Pierre Clémenti, Michèle Morgan, Catherine Deneuve, Michel Piccoli, Francine Bergé, Anna Gaël, Odile Versois

'Heavy with Gallic naughtiness rather than airy charm . . . a plethora of colourful costumes, foliage and fireworks.'—*MFB*

'A marathon tease . . . an unending series of interrupted coitions . . . a gorgeously wrapped and beribboned Christmas package containing an empty box.'—*John Simon*

Benji*

US 1974 86m CFI color
Mulberry Square (Joe Camp)

A stray mongrel dog saves two kidnapped children.
Family film par excellence which rang the box office bell in a big way in the US. Its modest merits are rather beside the point.

wd Joe Camp *ph* Don Reddy *m* Euel Box

Peter Breck, Edgar Buchanan, Terry Carter, Christopher Connelly

† A sequel, *For the Love of Benji,* followed in 1977.
In 1980 came the curious *Oh Heavenly Dog* (qv). Then in 1987 the same team presented a quirky movie of a different kind: *Benji the Hunted* (qv).

AAN: song 'I Feel Love' (*m* Euel Box, *ly* Betty Box)

Benji the Hunted

US 1987 88m CFI Color

A mongrel dog is shipwrecked and fosters a pack of cougar cubs. Freaky fable about a dog with a high IQ; but the training is remarkable.
Benji, Frank Inn (trainer). Written and directed by Joe Camp; for Mulberry Square/Embark/Buena Vista.

The Benny Goodman Story*

US 1955 117m Technicolor
U-I (Aaron Rosenberg)

A clarinettist from the Jewish section of Chicago becomes internationally famous.
Sentimental biopic of a familiar figure which comes to life when the sound track is given its head (and the real Goodman's clarinet).

wd Valentine Davies *ph* William Daniels *md* Joseph Gershenson

Steve Allen, Donna Reed, *Berta Gersten*, Herbert Anderson, Robert F. Simon, Sammy Davis Snr, Harry James, Martha Tilton, Gene Krupa

'The customary fictional liberties appear to have been taken.'—*MFB*

Benvenuta*

Belgium / France / Italy 1982 106m Eastmancolor
La Nouvelle Imagerie / UGC / FR3 / Opéra Film (Jean-Claude Batz)

A filmscript writer interviews a reclusive female novelist about a work which may be autobiographical.
Stylish but fairly incomprehensible romantic drama which makes the audience work rather harder than the material seems to warrant.

w,d André Delvaux, *novel* La Confession Anonyme by Suzanne Lilar *ph* Charlie Van Damme *m* Frédéric Devreese

Fanny Ardant, Vittorio Gassman, Françoise Fabian, Mathieu Carrière

Bequest to the Nation*
GB 1973 116m Technicolor
Universal / Hal B. Wallis
US title: *The Nelson Affair*

The story of Nelson's long affair with the tempestuous Lady Hamilton.
Undistinguished historical drama from a thin play which despite hard work all round makes very ordinary screen entertainment.

w Terence Rattigan, from his play *d* James Cellan Jones *ph* Gerry Fisher *pd* Carmen Dillon *m* Michel Legrand

Peter Finch, Glenda Jackson (way over the top), Michael Jayston, Anthony Quayle, Margaret Leighton, Dominic Guard, Nigel Stock, Roland Culver

'As empty as an out-of-town matinee.'—*MFB*

Berkeley Square**
US 1933 87m bw
Fox (Jesse L. Lasky)

A London house reincarnates its owner as his 18th-century ancestor.
Romantic fantasy on a time lapse theme, the first of many and perhaps the most stylish and self-assured. Remade as *The House on the Square* (qv).

w Sonya Levien, John Balderston, from Balderston's play *d* Frank Lloyd *ph* Ernest Palmer *m* Louis de Francesco *ad* William Carling

Leslie Howard, Heather Angel, Valerie Taylor, Irene Browne, Beryl Mercer, Colin Keith-Johnson, Alan Mowbray

'Too far above the heads of ordinary theatregoers and too British in tempo and execution to break any box office records.'—*Variety*

AAN: Leslie Howard

Berlin Correspondent
US 1942 70m bw
TCF (Bryan Foy)

In pre-war Germany an American reporter is kidnapped by the Nazis and replaced by a double . . .
Preposterous melodrama, so silly as to be often quite funny.

w Steve Fisher, Jack Andrews *d* Eugene Forde *ph* Virgil Miller *md* Emil Newman

Dana Andrews, Virginia Gilmore, Mona Maris, Martin Kosleck, Sig Rumann, Kurt Katch, Torben Meyer

Berlin Express*
US 1948 87m bw
RKO (Bert Granet)

Police of four nations guard a German VIP on a crack train to Berlin.
Rather muddled suspenser with attempts at political moralizing; the cast provides some good moments.

w Harold Medford *d* Jacques Tourneur *ph* Lucien Ballard *m* Frederick Hollander

Merle Oberon, Robert Ryan, Charles Korvin, Paul Lukas, Robert Coote

Berlin, Symphony of a Great City***
Germany 1927 78m bw silent
Fox-Europa
original title: *Berlin, die Symphonie einer Grosstadt*

An impression of the life of a city from dawn to midnight, expressed by cinematic montages, angles, sequences, etc, and set to music.
A leader in the field of 'impressionistic' documentaries which are now so familiar (*Rien que les Heures* did a similar job for Paris at around the same time), this still has moments of poetry which have seldom been equalled.

w Walter Ruttman, Karl Freund, Carl Mayer d Walter Ruttman ph Reimar Kuntze, Robert Baberske, Laszlo Schäffer m Edmund Meisel ed Walter Ruttman

Berliner Ballade*
Germany 1948 77m bw
Comedia Film (Alf Teichs)
aka: *The Ballad of Berlin*

Otto Nobody, an unwilling soldier, returns home to find himself at the mercy of bureaucrats and black marketeers.
Melancholy satire presented as a series of sketches, almost a forerunner of *That Was the Week That Was.*

w Gunter Neumann *d* Robert Stemmle *ph* Georg Krause *m / ly* Gunter Neumann, Werner Eisbrenner

Gert Fröbe, Anton Zeithammer, Tatjana Sais, O. E. Hasse

'Very much the film of a defeated people.'—*Penelope Houston*

Bermuda Affair
GB 1956 77m bw

The pilot of a West Indian airline falls for his partner's wife but dies in an air accident.
Tedious and unconvincing marital drama with back-projected local colour. Kim Hunter, Gary Merrill, Ron Randell, Zena Marshall. Written by Robert J. Shaw and Edward Sutherland; directed by Edward Sutherland; for Bermuda Studio Productions.

The Bermuda Mystery
US 1944 65m bw

Friends who have invested in a joint insurance policy are murdered one by one. Competent lower-berth murder mystery. Preston Foster, Ann Rutherford, Charles Butterworth, Helene Reynolds, Richard Lane. Written by W. Scott Darling, from a story by John Larkin; directed by Ben Stoloff; for TCF.

Bernardine*
US 1957 95m Eastmancolor Cinemascope
TCF (Samuel G. Engel)

A college student forced to swot for exams asks a friend's elder brother to look after his girl.
Henry Aldrich-style high school comedy, showing the lighter side of *Rebel without a Cause.* Notable for the clean-living hero played by a clean-living singing star, and the reappearance of Janet Gaynor for the only time since 1939, in a routine mother role.

w Theodore Reeves, *play* Mary Chase *d* Henry Levin *ph* Paul Vogel *m* Lionel Newman

Pat Boone, Richard Sargent, Terry Moore, *Janet Gaynor*, Walter Abel, Dean Jagger, Natalie Schaefer, James Drury

Berserk!
GB 1967 96m Technicolor
Columbia (Herman Cohen)

A lady circus owner revels in the publicity brought about by a series of murders.
Grisly and unattractive thriller with an ageing star in a series of unsuitably abbreviated costumes; the script is beyond redemption.

w Herman Cohen, Aben Kandel *d* Jim O'Connolly *ph* Desmond Dickinson *m* Patrick John Scott

Joan Crawford, Diana Dors, Ty Hardin, Judy Geeson, Michael Gough, Robert Hardy, Geoffrey Keen, Sidney Tafler, Philip Madoc

Berth Marks
US 1929 20m bw silent

Stan and Ollie, on a train, have to share an upper berth. Overstretched single-situation comedy, one of the team's poorest. Laurel and Hardy. Written by Leo McCarey and H. M. Walker; directed by Lewis R. Foster; for Hal Roach.

The Bespoke Overcoat**
GB 1956 33m bw
Remus (Jack Clayton)

A clerk in a clothing warehouse is refused a coat and asks a tailor friend to make him one. But he dies of cold and his ghost persuades the tailor to steal the coat he deserved.
The story seems stiff, but the production has a rich Dickensian feel and may be the best short drama filmed in Britain.

w Wolf Mankowitz, *story* Gogol *d Jack Clayton ph Wolfgang Suschitzky m* Georges Auric

Alfie Bass, David Kossoff

'A triumph of talent, small means and originality.'—*New Statesman*

Best Boy*
US 1979 111m colour 16mm

A documentary, shot by his cousin, of the problems of a mentally retarded 53-year-old man whose elderly parents are ailing. A film with very moving elements, though they would have been even sharper at half the length. Written, directed and produced by *Ira Wohl.*

Best Defense
US 1984 94m Movielab
Paramount (Gloria Katz)

A US tank goes hopelessly out of control in Kuwait; intercut with this are some of the problems which confronted its designer two years earlier.
Weird, unappetizing and disjointed farce, composed mainly of irrelevancies.

w Gloria Katz, Willard Huyck *novel* Easy and Hard Ways Out by Robert Grossbach *d* Willard Huyck *ph* Don Peterman *m* Patrick Williams *pd* Peter Jamison

Dudley Moore, Eddie Murphy, Kate Capshaw, George Dzundza, Helen Shaver

'As bereft of charm and spontaneity as it is overburdened with tedious gesticulation.'—*Tim Pulleine, Monthly Film Bulletin*

'About as funny as getting hi-jacked by a group of kamikaze terrorists.'—*Derek Malcolm, Guardian*

'How did I get involved? The door opened, and four men came in carrying a cheque.'—*Eddie Murphy*

Best Foot Forward
US 1943 94m Technicolor
MGM (Arthur Freed)

A glamorous publicity-seeking film star accepts an invitation to a military college ball.
Old-fashioned formula musical based on a lightweight Broadway success.

w Irving Brecher, Fred Finkelhoffe, *play* John Cecil Holmes *d* Edward Buzzell *ph* Leonard Smith *md* Lennie Hayton *songs* Hugh Martin, Ralph Blane *ch* Charles Walters

Lucille Ball, William Gaxton, Virginia Weidler, Harry James and his Orchestra, June Allyson, Gloria de Haven

Best Friends*
US 1982 116m Technicolor
Warner / Joe Wizan / Norman Jewison

Two writers who have enjoyed a peaceful professional relationship find problems when they get married and visit their respective families.
Rather a heavy comedy which seems to have no real point, this gets by on enjoyable sequences and star performances.

w Valerie Curtin, Barry Levinson *d* Norman Jewison *ph* Jordan Cronenweth *m* Michel Legrand *ad* Joe Russo *ed* Don Zimmerman

Burt Reynolds, Goldie Hawn, Jessica Tandy, Barnard Hughes, Audra Lindley, Keenan Wynn

'A print-out of a script conference at which everyone collapsed at everyone else's contributory sally.'—*Sunday Times*

AAN: song 'How Do You Keep the Music Playing?' by Michel Legrand, Alan and Marilyn Bergman

The Best House in London*
GB 1968 96m Eastmancolor
MGM / Bridge / Carlo Ponti (Philip Breen, Kurt Unger)

A Victorian publicity agent tries to organize a government-sponsored brothel.
Cheerful slam-bang historical send-up with as many dull thuds of banality as pleasant witticisms.

w Denis Norden *d* Philip Savile *ph* Alex Thompson *m* Mischa Spoliansky *pd* Wilfrid Shingleton

David Hemmings, George Sanders, Joanna Pettet, Warren Mitchell, Dany Robin, William Rushton

The Best Little Whorehouse in Texas
US 1982 114m Technicolor Panavision
Universal / RKO (Thomas L. Miller, Edward K. Milkis, Robert L. Boyett)

A long-established Texas whorehouse becomes the object of a clean-up campaign.
Flat and feeble screen version of a limp and tuneless musical which astonishingly was a Broadway hit, perhaps because people thought it was naughty. Onscreen the acting is too easy-going and the script too coy for anybody to have a good time.

w Larry L. King, Peter Masterson from their stage play *m / ly* Carol Hall *d* Colin Higgins *ph* William A. Fraker *m* Patrick Williams *pd* Robert F. Boyle

Burt Reynolds, Dolly Parton, Charles Durning, Dom DeLuise, Jim Nabors, Robert Mandan, Lois Nettleton, Noah Beery Jnr

'Rancid, self-deceiving, hypocritical stuff.'—*Observer*

'A sanitized, coyly predictable piece of brothel creeping, set to musak by a poorly programmed computer.'—*Guardian*

'Almost everything about it is misjudged.'—*Daily Mail*

'High on jollity, low on country and western, and very uncertainly directed.'—*Sight and Sound*

'Never gets beyond the concept stage.'—*Roger Ebert*

AAN: Charles Durning

The Best Man***
US 1964 104m bw
UA / Stuart Millar, Lawrence Turman

Two contenders for a presidential nomination seek the support of the dying ex-president.
Brilliant political melodrama, ingeniously adapted on a low budget from an incisive play, with splendid dramatic scenes, memorable performances and good convention detail.

w Gore Vidal from his play *d Franklin Schaffner ph* Haskell Wexler *m* Mort Lindsey

Henry Fonda, Cliff Robertson, *Lee Tracy*, Margaret Leighton, Edie Adams, Kevin McCarthy, *Shelley Berman*, Ann Sothern, Gene Raymond, Mahalia Jackson

'A fine opportunity to watch pros at work in a hard-hitting and cogent drama that seems to become more topical and have more relevance with each showing.'—*Judith Crist*

'Some of the wittiest lines since *Strangelove* . . . the acting fairly crackled with authenticity.'—*Isabel Quigly*

'You are left gasping at its sheer professionalism.'—*Evening News*

AAN: Lee Tracy

The Best Man Wins
US 1934 75m bw

A harbour cop finds himself tracking down the friend who had saved his life. Predictable tough-guy programmer. Edmund Lowe, Jack Holt, Bela Lugosi, Florence Rice, Forrester Harvey. Written by Ethel Hill and Bruce Manning; directed by Erle C. Kenton; for Columbia.

The Best of Enemies
US / Italy 1961 104m Technirama
Columbia / Dino de Laurentiis

During the Abyssinian campaign of 1941, an Italian and a British officer learn mutual respect.
Mild satirical comedy drama with a few points to make about war; the elements blend rather obviously and dispiritingly.

w Jack Pulman *d* Guy Hamilton *ph Giuseppe Rotunno m* Nino Rota

David Niven, Alberto Sordi, Michael Wilding, Amedeo Nazzari, Harry Andrews, David Opatoshu, Kenneth Fortescue, Duncan Macrae

The Best of Everything*
US 1959 121m De Luxe Cinemascope
TCF (Jerry Wald)

Personal problems of a New York publisher's female staff.
Slick novelette on the lines of a naughty Peg's Paper; pure Hollywood gossamer.

w Edith Sommer, Mann Rubin, *novel* Rona Jaffe *d* Jean Negulesco *ph* William C. Mellor *m* Alfred Newman

Hope Lange, Stephen Boyd, Joan Crawford, Louis Jourdan, Suzy Parker, Martha Hyer, Diane Baker, Brian Aherne, Robert Evans, Brett Halsey, Donald Harron

'A cautionary tale sensationally told.'—*Alexander Walker*

AAN: title song (*m* Alfred Newman, *ly* Sammy Cahn)

Best of the Badmen*
US 1951 84m Technicolor
RKO (Herman Schlom)

At the end of the Civil War Jeff Clanton organizes the break-up of Quantrell's Raiders, but is himself arrested on a trumped-up charge and needs the Raiders' help.
Standard western notable for a good cast and for bringing in a remarkable number of historical outlaws, doing rather unhistorical things.

w Robert Hardy Andrews, John Twist *d* William D. Russell *ph* Edward Cronjager *m* Paul Sawtell

Robert Ryan, Claire Trevor, Jack Buetel, Robert Preston, Walter Brennan, Bruce Cabot, John Archer, Lawrence Tierney

The Best of Times
US 1985 104m Technicolor
Universal / Kings Road (Gordon Carroll)

A small-town loser determines to have one more shot at the big time.
Curious, almost plotless comedy drama with nothing to draw the punters.

w Ron Shelton *d* Roger Spottiswoode *ph* Charles F. Wheeler *m* Arthur B. Rubinstein

Robin Williams, Kurt Russell, Pamela Reed, Holly Palance, Donald Moffat, M. Emmet Walsh

'Required magic is in too short supply and box office returns should be also.'—*Variety*

Best Seller*
US 1987 110m CFI Color
Orion / Hemdale (Carter de Haven)

A former hit-man helps an ex-cop write a book based on an old unsolved case.
Tortuous but generally lively and interesting melodrama which at least tries to be different.

w Larry Cohen *d* John Flynn *ph* Fred Murphy *m* Jay Ferguson *pd* Gene Rudolf *ed* David Rosenbloom

James Woods, Brian Dennehey, Victoria Tennant, Allison Balson, Paul Shenar, George Coe

The Best Things in Life Are Free*
US 1956 103m Eastmancolor Cinemascope
TCF (Henry Ephron)

From Broadway to Hollywood in the twenties, the story of songwriting team De Sylva, Brown and Henderson.
Gangsters, movie studios and the writing of 'Sonny Boy' for Al Jolson all figure in this amiable musical which spends more time on jokes than romance; the numbers are disappointing despite good tunes.

w William Bowers, Phoebe Ephron *d* Michael Curtiz *ph* Leon Shamroy *md* Lionel Newman

Ernest Borgnine, Gordon Macrae, Dan Dailey, Sheree North, Jacques d'Amboise, Norman Brooks, Murvyn Vye

AAN: Lionel Newman

'Three wonderful loves in the best picture of the year!'
The Best Years of Our Lives****
US 1946 182m bw
Samuel Goldwyn

Three men come home from war to a small middle-American community, and find it variously difficult to pick up where they left off.
The situations and even some of the characters now seem a little obvious, but this was a superb example of high-quality film-making in the forties, with smiles and tears cunningly spaced, and a film which said what was needed on a vital subject.

w Robert Sherwood, novel Glory for Me by Mackinlay Kantor *d William Wyler ph Gregg Toland m* Hugo Friedhofer

Fredric March, Myrna Loy, Teresa Wright, Dana Andrews, Virginia Mayo, Cathy O'Donnell, *Hoagy Carmichael, Harold Russell* (a non-actor-trained handless veteran whose only film this was until *Inside Moves* in 1980), Gladys George, Roman Bohnen, Ray Collins

'One of the best pictures of our lives!'—*Variety*

'The result is a work of provocative and moving insistence and beauty.'—*Howard Barnes*

'One recognizes everything and in the end this recognition is all the excitement, for what is on the screen becomes finally as accustomed and undramatic as the shabby decor of the theatre itself.'—*Robert Warshow, The Immediate Experience*

'One of the very few American studio-made movies in years that seem to me profoundly pleasing, moving and encouraging.'—*James Agee*

'Easily the best film from Hollywood on the warrior's return.'—*Sunday Graphic*

† In 1977 came a TV remake *Returning Home* but it did not lead to the expected series.

AA: best picture; Robert Sherwood; William Wyler; Hugo Friedhofer; Fredric March; Harold Russell

La Bête Humaine**
France 1938 99m bw
Paris Films (Robert Hakim)
aka: *The Human Beast; Judas Was a Woman*

A psychopathic train driver falls for a married woman, plans with her to kill her husband, but finally strangles her instead.
Curious melodrama with strong visual sequences, flawed by its ambivalent attitude to its hero-villain.

wd Jean Renoir, novel Emile Zola *ph Curt Courant m Joseph Kosma*

Jean Gabin, Simone Simon, Julien Carette, Fernand Ledoux, Jean Renoir

'French production at its best.'—*Variety*

'Marvellous atmosphere and a fine cast, but the material turns oppressive.'—*New Yorker, 1978*

'What is most deft is the way Renoir works the depot and the man's job into every scene—conversations on platforms, in washrooms and canteens, views from the station master's window over the steaming metal waste: the short sharp lust worked out in a wooden platelayer's shed among shunted trucks under the steaming rain.'—*Graham Greene*

† Remade in Hollywood as *Human Desire.*

Betrayal*
GB 1982 95m colour
Horizon / Sam Spiegel (Eric Rattray)

The story of a publisher, his wife and her lover is told in scenes that go backwards in time.
Sharply acted stuff very typical of its author, for audiences with wideawake minds; but more theatrical than cinematic.

w Harold Pinter from his play *d* David Jones *ph* Mike Fash *m* Dominic Muldowney

Jeremy Irons, Ben Kingsley, Patricia Hodge, Avril Elgar

AAN: Screenplay adaptation

Betrayal from the East
US 1945 83m bw
RKO (Herman Schlom)

Japanese out to sabotage the Panama Canal are thwarted by a carnival showman.
Extravagant but penny-pinching flagwaver.

w Kenneth Gamet, Aubrey Wisberg, *novel* Alan Hynd *d* William Berke *ph* Russell Metty *m* Roy Webb

Lee Tracy, Nancy Kelly, Richard Loo, Abner Biberman, Regis Toomey, Philip Ahn, Addison Richards, Sen Yung, Drew Pearson

Betrayed
US 1954 108m Eastmancolor
MGM (Gottfried Reinhardt)

In 1943 a Dutch intelligence officer works with a resistance leader who turns out to be a traitor.
Slow-moving, studio-set romantic melodrama of the old school; not very lively.

w Ronald Millar, George Froeschel *d* Gottfried Reinhardt *ph* Frederick A. Young *m* Walter Goehr

Clark Gable, Victor Mature, Lana Turner, Louis Calhern, O. E. Hasse, Wilfrid Hyde White, Ian Carmichael, Niall MacGinnis, Nora Swinburne

Betrayed*
US 1988 128m Alpha / Astro
MGM / UA / Irwin Winkler (Joe Eszterhas)

Following the murder of a radio talk show hostess, a couple on the run find themselves in a web of political intrigue.
Heavygoing piece with Something to Say, but not much to watch.

w Joe Eszterhas *d* Costa-Gavras *ph* Patrick Blossier *m* Bill Conti *pd* Patrizia Von Brandenstein

Debra Winger, Tom Berenger, John Heard, Betsy Blair, John Mahoney

'The Harold Robbins people: what you dream, they do!'
The Betsy
US 1977 125m Technicolor
Allied Artists / Harold Robbins International (Robert R. Weston)

Jockeying for power in the boardroom and the family life of an aged car manufacturer.
Rather tame and obvious melodrama enlivened by its star performance.

w William Bast, Walter Bernstein, *novel* Harold Robbins *d* Daniel Petrie *ph* Mario Tosi *m* John Barry

Laurence Olivier, Robert Duvall, Tommy Lee Jones, Katharine Ross, Jane Alexander, Lesley-Anne Down, Joseph Wiseman, Edward Herrmann

'Almost compulsively dreadful.'—*Derek Malcolm, Guardian*

Better Late Than Never
US 1983 87m colour

From two possibilities, an heiress selects her true grandfather. (Her grandmother wasn't sure.) Would-be risqué comedy which fails to spark despite the talents involved. David Niven, Art Carney, Maggie Smith, Kimberley

Partridge, Catherine Hicks, Lionel Jeffries. Written and directed by Bryan Forbes; music by Henry Mancini; for Jack Haley Jnr, David Niven Jnr (Warner). 'As predictable as a rumbling stomach after a bowl of chili.'—*Motion Picture Guide*

Better Off Dead
US 1985 98m Technicolor
Warner / A&M (Michael Jaffe)

When his fickle girlfriend leaves him, a lonely teenager becomes despondent, but the sun shines when another girl shows interest.
Plotless, almost legless comedy drama with no direction whatever.

w,d Savage Steve Holland *ph* Isidore Mankovsky *m* Rupert Hine *pd* Herman Zimmerman

John Cusack, David Ogden Stiers, Kim Darby, Demian Slade, Scotter Stevens, Diane Franklin

'Kids deserve better than this.'—*Variety*

The Better 'Ole
US 1926 97m (24 fps) bw silent

A British sergeant in Flanders proves that his major is actually a German spy. Comedy–drama based on the cartoons of Old Bill by Bruce Bairnsfather. (The title comes from one in which Old Bill, in the trenches, is saying to a disgruntled soldier: 'If yer knows of a better 'ole, go to it.'). Criticism is irrelevant now, but the piece has historical interest.

w Charles Reisner, Darryl F. Zanuck
d Charles Reisner *ph* Ed Du Par, Walter Robinson

Syd Chaplin, Doris Hill, Harold Goodwin, Edgar Kennedy

Betty Blue*
France 1986 120m Fujicolor
Gaumont / Constellation / Cargofilms (Claudie Ossard)

Original title: *37.2°au matin*

A waitress indulges her animal attraction for an odd job man but discovers him to be a literary genius.
What virtues this film has are more in style than content, but most people will find it over the top anyway.

w,d Jean-Jacques Beineix *novel* Philippe Dijan *ph* Jean-François Robin *m* Gabriel Yared *ed* Monique Prim

Béatrice Dalle, Jean-Hugues Anglade, Consuelo de Haviland

Between Heaven and Hell
US 1956 94m Eastmancolor Cinemascope
TCF (David Weisbart)

After Pearl Harbor a young southern landowner is called up and finds himself on active service with mixed racial types.
Vaguely anti-war, pro-understanding action thriller which ends up going through predictable heroics in a professional but not too sympathetic manner.

w Harry Brown, *novel* The Day the Century Ended by Francis Gwaltney *d* Richard Fleischer *ph* Leo Tover *m* Hugo Friedhofer

Robert Wagner, Buddy Ebsen, Broderick Crawford, Brad Dexter, Mark Damon, Robert Keith, Ken Clark, Skip Homeier, Harvey Lembeck

AAN: Hugo Friedhofer

Between Midnight and Dawn
US 1950 89m bw
Columbia (Hunt Stromberg)

Radio policemen track down a racketeer.
Competent, undistinguished programmer.

w Eugene Ling *d* Gordon Douglas
ph George E. Diskant *m* George Duning

Mark Stevens, Edmond O'Brien, Gale Storm, Donald Buka, Gale Robbins, Roland Winters

Between the Lines*
US 1977 101m TVC colour

Workers on a Boston newspaper are worried by rumours of an impending sale. Sharply observed but slackly structured slice of provincial life. John Heard, Lindsay Crouse, Jeff Goldblum, Jill Eikenberry, Stephen Collins. Written by Fred Barron; directed by Joan Micklin Silver; for Midwest Film Productions.

Between Two Women
US 1937 88m bw

Romance between doctor and nurse is interrupted by her alcoholic husband and his infatuation with a patient. Incident-packed men-in-white melodrama. Franchot Tone, Maureen O'Sullivan, Virginia Bruce, Edward Norris, Cliff Edwards, Janet Beecher. Written by Carey Wilson, from a story by Erich Von Stroheim; directed by George B. Seitz; for MGM. (NB: Title later changed to *Surrounded by Women* to avoid confusion with a Dr Kildare episode.) 'Class B that almost grew up. Eternal triangle in a hospital; okay dualler for nabes.'—*Variety*

Between Two Worlds*
US 1944 112m bw
Warner (Mark Hellinger)

A number of air-raid victims, and two lovers who have committed suicide, find themselves on a luxury ship en route to the next world.
Nice-looking but slow and turgid remake of *Outward Bound* (qv), largely sunk in its own misery but redeemed by two performances.

w Daniel Fuchs, *play* Sutton Vane *d* Edward A. Blatt *ph* Carl Guthrie *m* Erich Wolfgang Korngold

John Garfield, *Edmund Gwenn*, Eleanor Parker, Paul Henreid, *Sydney Greenstreet*, Sara Allgood, George Tobias, Faye Emerson, George Coulouris, Dennis King, Isobel Elsom

'For ferry service from a world so saturated with death, the ship seems strangely empty—a fact that was not obtrusive in a day when death was not intrusive.'—*James Agee*

Between Us Girls
US 1942 89m bw
Universal (Henry Koster, Phil Karlson)

BEVERLY HILLS COP. Eddie Murphy finds stardom with a flip wisecrack and appropriate action for every unlikely situation. But his language had to be sanitized for TV. The sequel proves the law of diminishing returns.

A mother and daughter are both involved in romances which tend to cross.
Mild comedy, a disappointing bid for stardom for a disappointing young star.

w Myles Connolly, True Boardman, *play* Le Fruit Vert by Regis Gignoux, Jacques Thery *d* Henry Koster *ph* Joseph Valentine *m* Frank Skinner

Diana Barrymore, Kay Francis, Robert Cummings, John Boles, Scotty Beckett, Ethel Griffies

Beverly Hills Cop**
US 1984 105m Technicolor
Paramount / Don Simpson / Jerry Bruckheimer

A Detroit cop races to Los Angeles to track down the killers of his best friend.
Filled with foul language and frenetic action, this rough-edged action comedy became one of the top box office grossers of its year. So much for its year.

w Daniel Petrie Jnr *d* Martin Brest *ph* Bruce Surtees *m* Harold Faltermeyer *pd* Angelo Graham *ed* Billy Weber, Arthur O. Coburn

Eddie Murphy, Judge Reinhold, Lisa Elibacher, John Ashton, Ronny Cox, Steven Berkoff

† The role was originally tailored for Sylvester Stallone.

AAN: original screenplay

Beverly Hills Cop 2
US 1987 102m Technicolor Panavision

Further helpings from the same bowl. In no respect is the second film an improvement on the first. Eddie Murphy, Judge Reinhold, Jurgen Prochnow, Ronnie Cox, Allen Garfield, Brigitte Nielsen, Dean Stockwell, Paul Guilfoyle. Written by Larry Ferguson, Warren Skaaren, with help from others; directed by Tony Scott; for Don Simpson-Harry Bruckheimer/Eddie Murphy/Paramount. 'A noisy, numbing, unimaginative, heartless remake . . . all has gone sour and cold.'—*Daily Variety*

Beverly of Graustark
US 1926 85m approx at 24 fps bw silent

When a prince falls ill, his girl cousin impersonates him at an important ceremony. Cheerful Ruritanian comedy. Marion Davies, Antonio Moreno, Roy D'Arcy, Creighton Hale. Written by Agnes Christine Johnson; directed by Sidney Franklin; for MGM.

Beware My Lovely
US 1952 77m bw
RKO / Filmmakers (Collier Young)

A handyman employed by a widow turns out to be a mental defective who imprisons and threatens to rape and murder her.
Dismal suspenser with a lot of screaming and running around but very little flair.

w Mel Dinelli, from his play The Man *d* Harry Horner *ph* George E. Diskant *m* Leith Stevens

Ida Lupino, Robert Ryan, Taylor Holmes, Barbara Whiting

'Inept characterization and ludicrously repetitive situations will surely rank this among the silliest films of the year.'—*MFB*

Beware of Pity*
GB 1946 106m bw
Two Cities (W. P. Lipscomb)

An officer courts a crippled girl out of pity. She finds out and kills herself.
Ambitious but rather artificial and dreary drama, a shade too pleased with its own literariness; performances straitjacketed by production.

w W. P. Lipscomb, Elizabeth Baron, Margaret Steen, *novel* Stefan Zweig *d* Maurice Elvey *ph* Derick Williams

Lilli Palmer, Albert Lieven, Cedric Hardwicke, Gladys Cooper, Linden Travers, Ernest Thesiger, Emrys Jones

Beware Spooks!
US 1939 65m bw

A nervous policeman routs crooks operating from a fairground. Standard star comedy with some funny moments. Joe E. Brown, Mary Carlisle, Clarence Kolb, Marc Lawrence, Don Beddoe. Written by Richard Flournoy, Albert Duffy, Brian Marlow; directed by Edward Sedgwick; for Robert Sparks / Columbia.

Beware! The Blob
US 1971 88m De Luxe
Jack H. Harris
GB title: *Son of Blob*

A mysterious jelly from outer space consumes most of the population of a small town. Spoofy sequel to one of the original space monster movies of the fifties. It's all too laboured to raise a thrill or a smile.

w Jack Woods, Anthony Harris *d* Larry Hagman *ph* Al Hamm *m* Mort Garson *sp* Tim Baar

Robert Walker, Gwynne Gilford, Godfrey Cambridge, Richard Webb, Shelley Berman, Carol Lynley, Burgess Meredith, Gerrit Graham, Larry Hagman

Bewitched
US 1945 65m bw
MGM (Arch Oboler)

A girl with twin personalities has her murderous element exorcized by a spiritualist. Hilarious nonsense, ancestor of the Eve and Lizzie schizos of the fifties.

wd Arch Oboler, from his story Alter Ego *ph* Charles Salerno Jnr *m* Bronislau Kaper

Phyllis Thaxter, Edmund Gwenn, Addison Richards, Kathleen Lockhart

'Oboler manages the first persuasive imitations of stream of consciousness I know of in a movie. Much more often, he bores to desperation with the vulgarity and mere violence of his effects.'—*James Agee*

Beyond a Reasonable Doubt*
US 1956 80m bw
RKO (Bert Friedlob)

A novelist is persuaded by a crusading newspaper proprietor to fake circumstantial evidence incriminating himself in a murder, thus proving the uselessness of such evidence. He does it so well that he is convicted . . . but that doesn't matter as he was guilty all the time.
Ingenious but rather cheerless and mechanical thriller. The actors extract what they can from a script intent on sleight of hand, but the distinguished director is at his most flatulent.

w Douglas Morrow *d* Fritz Lang *ph* William Snyder *m* Herschel Burke Gilbert

Dana Andrews, Joan Fontaine, Sidney Blackmer, Philip Bourneuf, Shepperd Strudwick, Arthur Franz, Edward Binns

'An adventure which cowards quit early and weaklings never finish at all!'

Beyond Glory
US 1948 82m bw
Paramount (Robert Fellows)

The honour of a West Point cadet is vindicated.
Proficient but dramatically turgid vehicle for an absurdly over-age star.

w Jonathan Latimer, Charles Marquis Warren, William Wister Haines *d* John Farrow *ph* John F. Seitz *m* Victor Young

Alan Ladd, Donna Reed, George Coulouris, George Macready, Audie Murphy

Beyond Mombasa
GB1955 90m Technicolor
Columbia / Hemisphere (Adrian Worker)

In East Africa, an American avenges his brother's death at the hands of the Mau Mau (here called the Leopard Men and revealed to be run by a mad English missionary).
Tasteless and rather humdrum jungle adventure using real-life problems purely as a backdrop.

w Richard English, Gene Levitt, *novel* Mark of the Leopard by James Eastwood *d* George Marshall *ph* Frederick A. Young *m* Humphrey Searle

Cornel Wilde, Donna Reed, Leo Genn, Ron Randell, Christopher Lee

Beyond Reasonable Doubt
New Zealand 1980 108m colour
Endeavour / New Zealand Film Commission (John Barnett)

A vengeful inspector convicts a farmer who may or may not be guilty of a triple murder. Sometimes striking but generally muddled crime story, which is based rather remotely on a real case but keeps shifting its angle.

w David Yallop, from his book *d* John Laing *ph* Alun Bollinger *m* Dave Fraser

David Hemmings, John Hargreaves, Tony Barry, Martyn Sanderson

'The queen of the tropics finds a new jungle man!'

Beyond the Blue Horizon*
US 1942 76m Technicolor
Paramount (Monta Bell)

An orphan white girl grows up on a tropical island with a chimpanzee and a swimming tiger; when rescued and her story doubted, she leads an expedition back to prove it.
The most tongue-in-cheek of the Lamour jungle extravaganzas, with plenty of simple fun.

w Frank Butler *d* Alfred Santell *ph* Charles Boyle *m* Victor Young

Dorothy Lamour, Richard Denning, Jack Haley, Patricia Morison, Walter Abel, Helen Gilbert, Elizabeth Patterson

Beyond the Curtain
GB 1960 88m bw
Rank / Welbeck (John Martin)

A flying officer rescues a stewardess whose plane has been forced down in East Germany. Inept, penny-pinching cold war melodrama in which very little happens.

w John Cresswell, Compton Bennett, *novel* Thunder Above by Charles F. Blair *d* Compton Bennett *ph* Eric Cross *m* Kenneth Pakeman

Richard Greene, Eva Bartok, Marius Goring, Lucie Mannheim, Andree Melly, George Mikell, John Welsh

'A twelve o'clock girl in a nine o'clock town!'

Beyond the Forest
US 1949 96m bw
Warner (Henry Blanke)

The discontented wife of a small-town doctor has an affair with a wealthy Chicagoan,

murders a witness, attempts suicide, and dies of fever.
The star caricatures herself in this overblown melodrama which marked the unhappy end of her association with the studio. The rest of the cast suffer more dumbly from the script's unintentional hilarities.

w Lenore Coffee, *novel* Stuart Engstrandt *d* King Vidor *ph* Robert Burks *m* Max Steiner

Bette Davis (Rosa Moline), Joseph Cotten (Dr Lewis Moline), David Brian (Neil Latimer); and Ruth Roman, Minor Watson, Dona Drake, Regis Toomey

ROSA: 'What a dump!'

ROSA: 'If I don't get out of here, I'll just die! Living here is like waiting for the funeral to begin.'

'Nobody's as good as Bette when she's bad!'—*publicity*

'This peerless piece of camp.'—*New Yorker, 1978*

'Miss Davis makes a regrettably melodramatic mess of what is undoubtedly one of the most unfortunate stories she has ever tackled.'—*Newsweek*

AAN: Max Steiner

Beyond the Poseidon Adventure
US 1979 114m Technicolor Panavision
Warner / Irwin Allen

When rescuers reach the topsy-turvy passenger liner, one of them is intent on plunder.
Dreary alternative ending to *The Poseidon Adventure,* with cardboard character studies, cut-price action, and tenth-rate technicalities.

w Nelson Gidding *d* Irwin Allen *ph* Joseph Biroc *m* Jerry Fielding *md* Preston Ames

Michael Caine, Telly Savalas, Karl Malden, Sally Field, Peter Boyle, Jack Warden, Shirley Knight, Shirley Jones, Slim Pickens

Beyond the Time Barrier
US 1959 75m bw
AIP / Pacific International / Miller-Consolidated (Robert Clarke)

A test pilot crosses the fifth dimension and finds himself in 2024 when civilization has gone underground to avoid nuclear contamination.
Crude science fiction, roughly on the level of Flash Gordon but less entertaining.

w Arthur G. Pierce *d* Edgar G. Ulmer *ph* Meredith Nicholson *m* Darrell Calker

Robert Clarke, Darlene Tompkins, Adrienne Arden, Vladimir Sokoloff, Stephen Bekassy

Beyond the Valley of the Dolls
US 1970 109m De Luxe Panavision
TCF (Russ Meyer)

Three girls in Hollywood enjoy the wilder reaches of show biz high life.
The skinflick director's first film for a major studio, with positively no connection with *Valley of the Dolls*, is not explicitly pornographic but pussyfoots around with as many general excesses as can be crammed into two hours. If taken as high camp it provides a laugh or two, but is chiefly notable as marking a major studio's deepest dip into muddy waters.

w Roger Ebert *d* Russ Meyer *ph* Fred J. Koenekamp *m* Stu Phillips, William Loose

Dolly Read, Cynthia Myers, Marcia McBroom, John La Zar, Michael Blodgett, Edy Williams

'If one can resist walking out, the last half hour is quite manic.'—*MFB*

'A film whose total, idiotic, monstrous badness raises it to the pitch of near-irresistible entertainment.'—*Alexander Walker*

'Awful, stupid and preposterous . . . also weirdly funny and a real curio, rather like a Grandma Moses illustration for a work by the Marquis de Sade.'—*John Simon*

Beyond Therapy
US 1986 93m colour

Psychiatrists become personally involved in the hang-ups of young New Yorkers. Unfunny film version of a play which may have had something. Glenda Jackson, Tom Conti, Julie Hagerty, Jeff Goldblum, Christopher Guest, Genevieve Page. Directed by Robert Altman from the play by Christopher Durang; for Sandcastle 5 / Roger Berlind / New World.

Beyond This Place*
GB 1959 90m bw
Renown / Georgefield (Maxwell Setton, John R. Sloan)
US title: *Web of Evidence*

An American visiting London finds his supposedly dead father in prison serving a life sentence for murder; he delves into history and finds the real culprit.
Spiritless murder mystery with less serious intent than the original novel; tolerable entertainment.

w Kenneth Taylor, *novel* A. J. Cronin *d* Jack Cardiff *ph* Wilkie Cooper *m* Douglas Gamley *ad* Ken Adam

Van Johnson, Vera Miles, Bernard Lee, Emlyn Williams, Jean Kent, Moultrie Kelsall, Leo McKern, Ralph Truman

Beyond Tomorrow
US 1940 84m bw

Two elderly ghosts return at Christmas to help young lovers. An amiably modest example of the kind they don't do any more. Richard Carlson, Jean Parker, C. Aubrey Smith, Charles Winninger. Written by Adele Comandini from a story by Mildred Cram; directed by Edward Sutherland; for RKO.

Bezhin Meadow**
USSR 1937 31m bw
Mosfilm
original title: *Bezhin Lug*

Fragments from an incomplete Eisenstein film are held together by freeze frames.
Even this collection of bits and pieces shows the power of the master.

w Alexander Rozhdestvenski, *story* Ivan Turgenev *d Sergei Eisenstein* *ph* Edouard Tissé

Vitya Kartashov, Boris Zakhava, Igor Pavlenko
† The film was reconstructed in 1966.

Bhowani Junction*
GB 1956 110m Eastmancolor Cinemascope
MGM (Pandro S. Berman)

Adventures of an Anglo-Indian girl during the last years of British India.
Disappointingly anaemic semi-epic from a gutsy novel, variably handled by all concerned.

w Sonya Levien, Ivan Moffat, *novel* John Masters *d* George Cukor *ph* Frederick A. Young *m* Miklos Rozsa

Ava Gardner, Stewart Granger, *Francis Matthews*, Bill Travers, Abraham Sofaer, Marne Maitland, Peter Illing, Freda Jackson, Edward Chapman

'An unwieldy, flatly-conceived charade.'—*MFB*

'One may believe with Henry Ford that history is bunk; if so, be assured that the labour pains of India are not half as much bunk as the romance of Victoria Jones, daughter of a Hindu lady, and a Welsh engine driver.'—*Alexander Walker*

The Bible*
US / Italy 1966 174m De Luxe Dimension 150 (70mm)
TCF / Dino de Laurentiis (Luigi Luraschi)

Through the Old Testament from Adam to Isaac.
A portentous creation with whispered commentary gives way to a dull misty Eden with decorous nudes, a sprightly Noah's Ark, a spectacular Babel, a brooding Sodom and a turgid Abraham. The pace is killingly slow and the script has little religious sense, but the pictures are often pretty.

w Christopher Fry and others *d* John Huston *ph Giuseppe Rotunno* *m* Toshiro Mayuzumi *ad* Mario Chiari

Michael Parks (Adam), Ulla Bergryd (Eve), Richard Harris (Cain), *John Huston* (Noah), Stephen Boyd (Nimrod), George C. Scott (Abraham), Ava Gardner (Sarah), Peter O'Toole (the three angels)

'An Old Testament spectacular like any other.'—*David Robinson*

'At a time when religion needs all the help it can get, John Huston may have set its cause back a couple of thousand years.'—*Rex Reed*

AAN: Toshiro Mayuzumi

Les Biches**
France / Italy 1968 99m Eastmancolor
La Boétie / Alexandra (André Génovès)
aka: *The Does*

Two lesbians form an uneasy *ménage à trois* with a young architect, who loves both of them.
Fascinating and well-detailed character study with more depth than at first appears.

w Paul Gégauff, Claude Chabrol d Claude Chabrol ph Jean Rabier m Pierre Jansen

Stéphane Audran, Jacqueline Sassard, Jean-Louis Trintignant

'You can almost see tubes attached to the heels of all the characters, through which the meaning has been sucked out of them and Chabrol pumped in.'—*John Simon*

Bicycle Thieves***
Italy 1948 90m bw
PDS-ENIC (Umberto Scarparelli)
original title: *Ladri di Biciclette*

An Italian workman, long unemployed, is robbed of the bicycle he needs for his new job, and he and his small son search Rome for it. The epitome of Italian neo-realism, the slight human drama is developed so that it has all the force of *King Lear*, and both the acting and the backgrounds are vividly compelling.

w Cesare Zavattini d Vittorio de Sica ph Carlo Montuori *m* Alessandro Cicognini

Lamberto Maggiorani, Enzo Staiola

'A film of rare humanity and sensibility.'—*Gavin Lambert*

'A memorable work of art with the true flavour of reality. To see it is an experience worth having.'—*Richard Mallett, Punch*

'My idea is to de-romanticize the cinema.'—*Vittorio de Sica*

AA: best foreign film; Cesare Zavattini

Les Bicyclettes de Belsize*
GB 1969 29m Eastmancolor
Delmore / Ullustria (Jacques de Lane Lea)

The way to true love for a Hampstead shop owner is found through his bicycle.
Mildly attractive whimsy, obviously patterned after *Les Parapluies de Cherbourg* but not quite hitting the spot.

w Michael Newling *d* Douglas Hickox *ph* Wolfgang Suschitzky *m / ly* Les Reed, Barry Mason

Anthony May, Judy Huxtable

Il Bidone**
Italy / France 1955 109m bw
Titanus / SGC
aka: *The Swindlers*

A group of petty swindlers fails to move into the higher criminal bracket.
Sharply observed but rather sentimental melodrama with tragic pretensions.

w Federico Fellini, Ennio Flaiano, Tullio Pinelli *d Federico Fellini ph* Otello Martelli *m* Nino Rota

Broderick Crawford, Richard Basehart, Franco Fabrizi, Giulietta Masina

Big**
US 1988 102m DuArt / DeLuxe
TCF (James L. Brooks, Robert Greenhut, Anne Spielberg, Gary Ross)

A 13-year-old boy has his wish to grow 'big' granted by a carnival wishing machine.
Magic fun, better done than it has been since *Turnabout* in 1940.

w Gary Ross, Anne Spielberg *d Penny Marshall ph* Barry Sonnenfeld *pd* Santo Loquasto

Tom Hanks, Elizabeth Perkins, John Heard, Jared Rushton, Robert Loggia, David Moscow

'Men, money and moonshine . . . when it comes to vice, Mama knows best!'

Big Bad Mama
US 1974 85m Metrocolor
Santa Cruz (Roger Corman)

In 1932 Texas, a desirable widow becomes a bank robber. Fast moving, violent nonsense, like a caricature of *Bonnie and Clyde*, which was itself a caricature.

w William Norton, Frances Doel *d* Steve Carver *ph* Bruce Logan *m* David Grisman

Angie Dickinson, William Shatner, Tom Skerritt, Susan Sennett, Robbie Lee.

The Big Blockade*
GB 1941 73m bw
Ealing (Alberto Cavalcanti)

A semi-documentary showing the importance of blockading Germany in winning the war.
A curious all-star propaganda revue with some sketches more effective than others.

w Charles Frend, Angus Macphail *d* Charles Frend *ph* Wilkie Cooper *m* Richard Addinsell

Leslie Banks, Michael Redgrave, John Mills, Will Hay (his only serious role), Frank Cellier, Robert Morley, Alfred Drayton, Michael Rennie, Marius Goring, Bernard Miles

'Topical subject matter, graphic descriptive work, pungent commentary, thrilling spectacle, clever characterisation.'—*Kine Weekly*

The Big Boodle
US 1957 83m bw
UA / Monteflor (Lewis F. Blumberg)
GB Title: *Night in Havana*

A croupier in an Havana gambling casino is suspected of knowing where counterfeited plates are hidden . . .
An undistinguished chase film with the star very tired and a long way from home.

w Jo Eisinger, *novel* Robert Sylvester *d* Richard Wilson *ph* Lee Garmes *m* Raoul Lavista

Errol Flynn, Pedro Armendariz, Gia Scala, Rossana Rory

The Big Bounce
US 1969 102m Technicolor Panavision
Warner / Greenway (Wiliam Dozier)

An ex-GI with a criminal record gets into sexual and criminal trouble while working at a Californian motel.
Unattractive melodrama with no discernible point, certainly not to entertain.

w Robert Dozier, *novel* Elmore Leonard *d* Alex March *ph* Howard R. Schwartz *m* Michael Curb

Ryan O'Neal, Leigh Taylor Young, Van Heflin, James Daly, Robert Webber, Lee Grant

Big Boy
US 1930 68m approx bw

A negro jockey wins a big race. Star musical from a Broadway original; routine except that Jolson plays in blackface, then comes on as himself for the finale. Al Jolson. Lousie Closser Hale, Noah Beery. Written by William K. Wells and Perry Vekroff; directed by Alan Crosland; for Warner. 'Comedy entertaining in hoke way, but production inferior to previous Jolson pictures.'—*Variety*

The Big Brawl
US 1980 95m Technicolor Panavision
Warner Brothers / Golden Harvest (Raymond Chow)

The son of a Chinese restaurateur in Chicago outwits gangsters.
Silly but quite entertaining chopsocky melodrama laced with comedy.

wd Robert Clouse *ph* Robert Jessup *m* Lalo Schifrin

Jackie Chan, Jose Ferrer, Kristine de Bell, Mako, David Sheiner

The Big Broadcast**
US 1932 78m bw
Paramount

A failing radio station is saved by an all-star show.
Revue-style show with a minimum of plot, valuable as archive material covering many stars of the time.

w George Marion Jnr, *novel* Wild Waves by William Ford Manley *d* Frank Tuttle *ph* George Folsey

Bing Crosby, Kate Smith, George Burns, Gracie Allen, Stuart Erwin, Leila Hyams, Cab Calloway, the Mills Brothers, the Boswell Sisters
Songs include 'Please'; 'Here Lies Love'; 'Hot Toddy'; 'In the Blue of the Night'; 'Tiger Rag'; 'Crazy People'; 'It Was So Beautiful'; 'Kicking the Gong Around'

'Flock of radio names ensures b.o. interest, especially in hinterland.'—*Variety*

'A musical meteor of songs, comedy and romance!'

The Big Broadcast of 1936*
US 1935 97m bw
Paramount (Ben Glazer)

The 'radio lover' of a small radio station is kidnapped by a man-hungry countess.
Zany comedy with interpolated variety acts and a totally Marxian climax.

w Walter de Leon, Francis Martin, Ralph Spence *d* Norman Taurog *ph* Leo Tover *songs* various *ch* LeRoy Prinz

Jack Oakie, George Burns, Gracie Allen, Henry Wadsworth, Wendy Barrie, Lyda Roberti, C. Henry Gordon, Benny Baker, Bing Crosby, Ethel Merman, Richard Tauber, Amos 'n Andy, Mary Boland, Charles Ruggles, Virginia Weidler, Guy Standing, Gail Patrick, Bill Robinson, the Nicholas Brothers, the Vienna Boys Choir, Akim Tamiroff
Songs include 'Miss Brown to You'; 'Through

the Doorway of Dreams'; 'Double Trouble'; 'Why Dream?'; 'Amargura'; 'I Wished on the Moon'; 'Crooner's Lullaby'; 'Why Stars Come Out at Night'

'Names are in and out as fast and as often as a firefly's tail light.'—*Variety*

'It hasn't much story, but the lack won't bother.'—*Variety*

The Big Broadcast of 1937**
US 1936 100m bw
Paramount (Lewis Gensler)

A radio station manager has trouble with his sponsors.
More recorded acts separated by a measure of plot.

w Edwin Gelsey, Arthur Kober, Barry Travers, Walter de Leon, Francis Martin *d* Mitchell Leisen *ph* Theodor Sparkuhl *songs* various

Jack Benny, George Burns, Gracie Allen, Bob Burns, Martha Raye, Shirley Ross, Ray Milland, Benny Fields, Benny Goodman and his Orchestra, Leopold Stokowski and the Philadelphia Orchestra, Eleanore Whitney, Larry Adler, Louis da Pron

'It isn't a comedy and it isn't a musical, but it has a lot of laughs, the best in several types of music, and I don't know where in the world you will see anything like it.'—*Otis Ferguson*

The Big Broadcast of 1938**
US 1937 90m bw
Paramount (Harlan Thompson)

A steamship owner engaged in a transatlantic race is hampered by his practical joking twin brother.
Glamorous, empty-headed all-star nonsense with the expected bevy of interpolated acts.

w Walter de Leon, Francis Martin, Ken Englund, Frederick Hazlitt Brennan *d* Mitchell Leisen *ph* Harry Fischbeck *songs* Ralph Rainger, Leo Robin

W. C. Fields, Bob Hope (debut), Martha Raye, Dorothy Lamour, Shirley Ross, Lynne Overman, Ben Blue, Leif Erickson, Kirsten Flagstad, Tito Guizar, Shep Fields and his Rippling Rhythm Orchestra
Songs include 'Thanks for the Memory'; 'Don't Tell a Secret to a Rose'; 'You Took the Words Right Out of My Heart'; 'Mama That Moon Is Here Again'; 'This Little Ripple Has Rhythm'; 'The Waltz Lives On': 'Zuni Zuni'; 'Sawing a Woman in Half'

'Pictorially original and alluring, with the rejuvenated W. C. Fields at his inimitable best.'—*Variety*

AA: song 'Thanks for the Memory' (*m* Ralph Rainger, *ly* Leo Robin)

Big Brown Eyes
US 1936 76m bw
Paramount (Walter Wanger)

A private detective and his wisecracking girl friend catch a jewel thief.
Minor league *Thin Man* stuff, quite acceptably done.

w Raoul Walsh, Bert Hanlon *d* Raoul Walsh *ph* George Clemens *m* Gerald Carbonara *md* Morris Stoloff

BIG BUSINESS. Stan and Ollie's favourite foil James Finlayson is drawn into joyous comic mayhem. He should have bought a Christmas tree from the immortal duo.

Cary Grant, Joan Bennett, Walter Pidgeon, Lloyd Nolan, Alan Baxter, Marjorie Gateson, Isabel Jewell, Douglas Fowley

The Big Bus
US 1976 88m Movielab Panavision
Paramount (Fred Freeman, Lawrence J. Cohen)

Misadventures of a giant atomic-powered bus on its first cross-country trip.
Rather feeble spoof on disaster pictures, with some good moments.

w Fred Freeman, Lawrence J. Cohen *d* James Frawley *ph* Harry Stradling Jnr *m* David Shire *pd* Joel Schiller

Joseph Bologna, Stockard Channing, John Beck, René Auberjonois, Ned Beatty, Bob Dishy, Jose Ferrer, Ruth Gordon, Harold Gould, Larry Hagman, Sally Kellerman, Richard Mulligan, Lynn Redgrave

'It's all fast, bright, surface stuff, almost obsessively intent on never letting a laugh get away, misfiring, backfiring, skidding and crashing gears gaily all the way, often quite as thrilling, if not always as ludicrous, as some of the films it mocks.'—*Alan Brien, Sunday Times*

'It has been produced with such consummate bad taste, schlock acting and feeble attempts at verbal and visual humour that whatever laughs are engendered are at it rather than with it.'—*Dave Pomeroy, Film Information*

Big Business****
US 1929 20m silent

Stan and Ollie fail to sell a Christmas tree to a belligerent householder. Classic silent comedy consisting largely of a brilliant tit-for-tat routine of reciprocal destruction, to which scripting, acting and editing equally combine. Laurel and Hardy, James Finlayson. Written by Leo McCarey and H. M. Walker; directed by James W. Horne; edited by Richard Currier; for Hal Roach.

Big Business
US 1988 97m Metrocolor
Buena Vista / Touchstone / Silver Screen Partners III

Big business complexities are made more so by the fact that the principals are discovered to have been exchanged at birth.
Loud-shouting farce which just about gets by on star value.

w Dori Pierson, Marc Rubel *d* Jim Abrahams *ph* Dean Cundey *m* Lee Holdridge

Bette Midler, Lily Tomlin, Fred Ward, Edward Herrmann

The Big Cage
US 1933 71m bw

A lion tamer is worshipped by an orphan boy. Pretty awful programme filler capitalizing on the animal act from the Ringling Brothers circus. Clyde Beatty, Andy Devine, Mickey Rooney, Anita Page, Vince Barnett, Wallace Ford, Raymond Hatton. Written by Edward Anthony and Ferdinand Reyher; directed by Kurt Neumann; for Universal.

The Big Cat
US 1949 75m Technicolor

Feuding mountain families combine to track a marauding lion. Standard outdoor melodrama, almost a straight version of *Track of the Cat*. Peggy Ann Garner, Lon McCallister, Preston Foster, Forrest Tucker, Skip Homeier, Sara Haden. Written by Morton Grant and Dorothy Yost; directed by Phil Karlson; for Eagle-Lion.

'How much love, sex, fun and friendship can a person take?'

'In a cold world, you need your friends to keep you warm!'

The Big Chill**
US 1983 105m Metrocolor
Columbia / Carson Productions (Michael Shamberg)

University contemporaries try to comfort each other after the death of a friend.
Wry satirical comedy which seems to be nostalgic for the sixties, but is funny anyway.

w Lawrence Kasdan, Barbara Benedek d Lawrence Kasdan ph John Bailey *m* various *pd* Ida Random *ed* Carol Littleton

Tom Berenger, Glenn Close, Jeff Goldblum, William Hurt, Kevin Kline, Mary Kay Place, Meg Tilly, JoBeth Williams, Don Galloway

'The final impression left is of a collage of small relishable moments.'—*Kim Newman, MFB*

'An entertainment in which humour and sentiment are finely balanced and profundities are artfully skirted.'—*Sight and Sound*

'A splendid technical exercise . . . but there's no pay-off and it doesn't lead anywhere.'—*Roger Ebert*

AAN: best picture; Glenn Close; screenplay

The Big Circus*
US 1959 109m Technicolor Cinemascope
AA (Irwin Allen)

A bankrupt circus owner tries to get his show back on the road despite the murderous schemes of his ex-partners.
Fast-paced melodrama which makes little sense but generally provides the expected thrills.

w Irwin Allen, Charles Bennett, Irving Wallace *d* Joseph Newman *ph* Winton C. Hoch *m* Paul Sawtell, Bert Shefter

Victor Mature, Red Buttons, Rhonda Fleming, Kathryn Grant, Vincent Price, Peter Lorre, *Gilbert Roland*, David Nelson, Adele Mara, Steve Allen

The Big City
US 1927 80m approx (24 fps) bw silent
MGM

A cabaret owner has a jewel robbery gang as a sideline.
Minor star melodrama.

w Waldemar Young, Tod Browning *d* Tod Browning

Lon Chaney, Betty Compson, James Murray, Marceline Day

The Big City*
US 1937 80m bw
MGM (Norman Krasna)

An honest cab driver and his wife hold out against corruption.
Sentimental realism of the type expected of its director. Smooth and syrupy.

w Dore Schary, Hugo Butler *d* Frank Borzage *ph* Joseph Ruttenberg *m* William Axt

Spencer Tracy, Luise Rainer, Charley Grapewin, Janet Beecher, Irving Bacon, William Demarest, Eddie Quillan

Big City
US 1948 103m bw
MGM (Joe Pasternak)

In New York's East Side, a little girl is the adopted daughter of three bachelors, but trouble looms when they all get ideas of romance.
Later-day star vehicle for which the young star is really too old and all else is excessively sentimental and sprawling.

w Whitfield Cook, Ann Morrison *d* Norman Taurog *ph* Robert Surtees

Margaret O'Brien, Robert Preston, Danny Thomas, George Murphy, Karin Booth, Jackie Butch Jenkins, Betty Garrett

The Big City**
India 1963 131m bw
R. D. Bansal
original title: *Mahanagar*

A poverty-stricken Calcutta bank accountant sends his wife out to work; then the bank crashes, and she becomes the sole breadwinner.
Immensely detailed, overlong, but mainly fascinating account of modern urban India and its attitudes.

wd, m Satyajit Ray, novel Narendra Nath Mitra *ph* Subrata Mitra

Madhabi Mukherjee, Anil Chatterjee, Haren Chatterjee, Haradhan Banerjee

Big City Blues
US 1932 65m bw

A country boy gets into trouble on his first trip to New York. Predictable comedy drama which seems to have no point other than the obvious one. Joan Blondell, Eric Linden, Inez Courtney, Evalyn Knapp, Guy Kibbee, Walter Catlett, Humphrey Bogart, Ned Sparks. Written by Ward Morehouse and Lillie Hayward; directed by Mervyn Le Roy; for Warners.

'The strangest and most savage manhunt in history!'

The Big Clock*
US 1947 95m bw
Paramount (John Farrow)

A publishing magnate murders his mistress and assigns one of his editors to solve the crime.
Slick but rather empty thriller with judicious use of adequate talent.

w Jonathan Latimer, *novel* Kenneth Fearing *d* John Farrow *ph* John Seitz *m* Victor Young

Charles Laughton, Ray Milland, Maureen O'Sullivan, Rita Johnson, Elsa Lanchester

The Big Combo*
US 1955 80m bw
Allied Artists / Security-Theodora (Sidney Harmon)

The police crush a crime syndicate.
An otherwise uninspired thriller memorable for starting the new violence, with some ugly scenes of torture which suffered at the time from the censor.

w Philip Yordan *d* Joseph H. Lewis *ph* John Alton *m* David Raksin

Cornel Wilde, Richard Conte, Jean Wallace, Brian Donlevy, Robert Middleton, Lee Van Cleef, Ted de Corsia, Helen Walker, John Hoyt

The Big Country***
US 1958 165m Technirama
UA / Anthony / Worldwide (William Wyler, Gregory Peck)

The Terills and the Hannesseys feud over water rights, and peace is brought about only with the deaths of the family heads.
Big-scale western with a few pretensions to say something about the Cold War. All very fluent, star-laden and easy to watch.

w James R. Webb, Sy Bartlett, Robert Wilder, *novel* Donald Hamilton *d William Wyler ph Franz Planer m Jerome Moross*

Gregory Peck, Jean Simmons, Charlton Heston, Carroll Baker, *Burl Ives, Charles Bickford*, Alfonso Bedoya, Chuck Connors

AA: Burl Ives
AAN: Jerome Moross

The Big Cube
US 1969 98m Technicolor

Girl tries to murder her actress stepmother by feeding her overdoses of LSD. Stultifyingly boring melodrama. Lana Turner, George Chakiris, Dan O'Herlihy, Karin Mossberg, Richard Egan. Written by William Douglas Lansford; directed by Tito Davison; for Francisco Diez Barroso / Warner.

The Big Easy*
US 1986 108m De Luxe
Kings Road (Stephen Friedman)

A New Orleans homicide detective is persuaded by a lady investigator from the DA's office to look into irregularities in the department.
Sassy, easy-going melodrama with comedy asides.

w Dan Petrie Jr *d* Jim McBride *ph* Afonso Beato *m* Brad Feidel *pd* Jeannine Claudia Oppewall

Dennis Quaid, Ellen Barkin, Ned Beatty, John Goodman, Ebbe Roe Smith

'The cooks did the best they could with ingredients that tasted good but were a little tough to chew.'—*Daily Variety*

Big Executive
US 1933 70m bw

A go-getting market operator finds himself competing with the grandfather of the girl he loves. Ho-hum melodrama with no compelling angles. Ricardo Cortez, Richard Bennett, Elizabeth Young, Sharon Lynn, Dorothy Peterson, Barton MacLane. Written by Laurence Stallings from a story by Alice Duer Miller; directed by Erle C. Kenton; for Paramount. 'It will be anything but big at the box office.'—*Variety*

Big Fella*
GB 1937 73m bw
Fortune (J. Elder Wills)

In Marseilles, a black man returns a lost child to his English parents.
Pleasant light vehicle with the star in typical easy form.

w Fenn Sherie, Ingram d'Abbes, *novel* Banjo by Claude McKay *d* J. Elder Wills *ph* Cyril Bristow

Paul Robeson, Elizabeth Welch, Roy Emerton, Marcelle Rogez

'A very unpretentious vehicle.'—*Variety*

The Big Fisherman
US 1959 166m Technicolor Panavision
Centurion (Rowland V. Lee)

An Arab princess meets disciple Simon Peter, who dissuades her from her plan to assassinate her stepfather Herod.
Well-meaning but leaden adaptation of a bestselling novel which followed on from *The Robe*. Too reverent by half, and in many respects surprisingly incompetent.

w Howard Estabrook, Rowland V. Lee, *novel* Lloyd C. Douglas *d* Frank Borzage *ph* Lee Garmes *m* Albert Hay Malotte *pd* John de Cuir

Howard Keel, Alexander Scourby, Susan Kohner, John Saxon, Martha Hyer, Herbert Lom, Ray Stricklyn, Beulah Bondi

'Its overall flatness of conception and execution is a stiff price to pay for the lack of spectacular sensationalism characterizing its fellow-epics.'—*MFB*

'The picture is three hours long, and, except for those who can be dazzled by big gatherings of props, horses and camels, it is hard to find three minutes of entertainment in it.'—*Hollywood Reporter*

AAN: Lee Garmes

The Big Fix
US 1978 108m Technicolor
Universal (Carl Borack, Richard Dreyfuss)

An industrial investigator fancies himself as a private eye and gets involved in a political corruption case.
Hard to follow and harder still to care about, this rather sloppy, with-it movie is a little too pleased with itself from the word go.

w Roger L. Simon, from his novel *d* Jeremy Paul Kagan *ph* Frank Stanley *m* Bill Conti *pd* Robert F. Boyle

Richard Dreyfuss, Susan Anspach, Bonnie Bedelia, John Lithgow

'The strength of this film lies in the cool, meandering discretion with which its central theme is fleshed out: regret for lost illusions as the protest generation of the sixties finds its arteries hardening.'—*Tom Milne, MFB*

The Big Gamble*
US 1960 100m De Luxe Cinemascope
TCF / Darryl F. Zanuck

Three people drive an ailing truck to a remote African township where they hope to start a haulage business.
Curious comedy-drama-adventure which starts off with family matters in Dublin and gradually develops into a lighter-hearted *Wages of Fear*. It has its moments.

w Irwin Shaw *d* Richard Fleischer, Elmo Williams *ph* William Mellor, Henri Persin *m* Maurice Jarre

Stephen Boyd, Juliette Greco, David Wayne, *Gregory Ratoff*, Sybil Thorndike, Fernand Ledoux

The Big Gundown
Italy / Spain 1966 105m Techniscope
PEA / PC (Alberto Grimaldi)
Italian title: *La Resa dei Conti*

A Texas lawman is hired to catch a Mexican outlaw, who repeatedly escapes and finally proves his innocence.
Violent but moderately enjoyable spaghetti western.

w Sergio Donati, Sergio Sollima *d* Sergio Sollima *ph* Carlo Carlini *m* Ennio Morricone

Lee Van Cleef, Tomas Milian, Walter Barnes, Luisa Rivelli

The Big Guy
US 1939 78m bw

A young convict becomes involved in a prison break which leads to murder. Suspenseful routine melodrama with adequate production values. Victor McLaglen, Jackie Cooper, Edward Brophy, Peggy Moran, Ona Munson, Russell Hicks, Jonathan Hale, Edward Pawley. Written by Lester Cole; directed by Arthur Lubin; for Universal.

'All the action you can take . . . all the adventure you can wish for!'

A Big Hand for the Little Lady**
US 1966 96m Technicolor
Warner / Eden (Fielder Cook)
GB title: *Big Deal at Dodge City* (though the action clearly takes place in Laredo)

Five rich poker players are outwitted by a family of confidence tricksters.
Diverting but thinly stretched acting-piece from a much shorter TV original; still, suspense builds nicely until the disappointingly handled revelation.

w Sidney Carroll, from his own TV play *d Fielder Cook* *ph* Lee Garmes *m* David Raksin

Henry Fonda, *Joanne Woodward*, Jason Robards, Paul Ford, Kevin McCarthy, *Charles Bickford*, Robert Middleton, *Burgess Meredith*, John Qualen

The Big Hangover
US 1950 82m bw
MGM (Norman Krasna)

A lawyer struggling to mingle with the mighty finds he is allergic to strong drink.
Woefully unfunny comedy with virtually no plot.

wd Norman Krasna *ph* George Folsey *m* Adolph Deutsch

Van Johnson, Elizabeth Taylor, Percy Waram, Fay Holden, Leon Ames, Edgar Buchanan, Rosemary de Camp, Gene Lockhart, Selena Royle

Big Hearted Herbert
US 1934 60m bw

A prosperous plumber becomes more concerned with money than with his family's happiness. Pleasing moral comedy, well cast. Guy Kibbee, Aline MacMahon, Patricia Ellis, Philip Reed, George Chandler. Written by Lillie Hayward and Ben Markson, from the play by Sophie Kerr and Anna Steese Richardson; directed by William Keighley; for Warners. (NB: 1940 brought a remake under the title *Father Is a Prince*, with Grant Mitchell.)

'A hard cop and a soft dame!'

The Big Heat**
US 1953 90m bw
Columbia (Robert Arthur)

A police detective's wife is killed by a bomb meant for himself; he goes undercover to track down the gangsters responsible.
Considered at the time to reach a new low in violence (boiling coffee in the face), this dour little thriller also struck a new note of realism in crime films and produced one of Glenn Ford's most typical performances.

w Sydney Boehm, *novel* William P. McGivern *d* Fritz Lang *ph* Charles Lang *m* Arthur Morton *md* Mischa Bakaleinikoff

Glenn Ford, Gloria Grahame, Alexander Scourby, Jocelyn Brando, Lee Marvin, Jeanette Nolan, Peter Whitney

'The main impression is of violence employed arbitrarily, mechanically and in the long run pointlessly.'—*Penelope Houston*

The Big House**
US 1930 88m bw
MGM (Irving Thalberg)

Tensions in prison lead to an attempted break-out and a massacre.

Archetypal prison melodrama and a significant advance in form for early talkies.

w Frances Marion d George Hill ph Harold Wenstrom

Chester Morris, Wallace Beery, Robert Montgomery, Lewis Stone, Leila Hyams, George F. Marion, J. C. Nugent, Karl Dane

'Not a two-dollar talker, but virile, realistic melodrama, a cinch for any week-stand and hold-overable generally.'—*Variety*

'We all gave our roles the best that was in us, and the virility and truthfulness of the picture were more satisfying than anything else I've done.'—*Chester Morris, 1953*

† The role played by Wallace Beery had been intended for Lon Chaney, who died during preparation

AA: Frances Marion
AAN: best picture; Wallace Beery

Big House USA
US 1954 82m bw
UA / Bel Air (Aubrey Schenck)

Convicts stage a break-out to get at hidden loot.
Though less explicit in its violence than many later films, this is a singularly unpleasant melodrama with not one attractive character.

w John C. Higgins *d* Howard W. Koch
ph Gordon Avil *m* Paul Dunlap

Broderick Crawford, Ralph Meeker, Lon Chaney, Charles Bronson, William Talman, Reed Hadley

Big Jack
US 1949 85m bw
MGM (Gottfried Reinhardt)

Adventures of a couple of amiable scoundrels in 1890 Virginia.
The elements don't jell in this outdoor comedy-drama, which was its star's last film.

w Gene Fowler, Marvin Borowsky, Otto Van Eyss *d* Richard Thorpe *ph* Robert Surtees *m* Herbert Stothart

Wallace Beery, Marjorie Main, Richard Conte, Edward Arnold, Vanessa Brown, Clinton Sundberg, Charles Dingle, Clem Bevans

Big Jake*
US 1971 110m Technicolor Panavision
Batjac / Cinema Center (Michael A. Wayne)

An elderly Texas cattleman swings into action when his grandson is kidnapped.
Satisfactory example of the star's later vehicles, with efficient production and familiar cast and brawling.

w Harry Julian Fink, R. M. Fink *d* George Sherman *ph* William Clothier *m* Elmer Bernstein

John Wayne, Richard Boone, Maureen O'Hara, Patrick Wayne, Chris Mitchum, Bobby Vinton, Bruce Cabot, Glenn Corbett, Harry Carey Jnr, John Agar

'Another genial celebration of Big John's ability to carry a film practically single-handed.'—*MFB*

Big Jim McLain
US 1952 90m bw
Wayne / Fellows (Robert Fellows)

A special agent for the House of UnAmerican Activities Committee routs communists in Hawaii.
Curious and rather offensive star vehicle in which the right-wing political shading interferes seriously with the entertainment value.

w James Edward Grant *d* Edward Ludwig *ph* Archie Stout *m* Paul Dunlap *md* Emil Newman

John Wayne, Nancy Olson, James Arness, Alan Napier, Veda Ann Borg, Hans Conried, Gayne Whitman

'Brings to the screen all the unattractively hysterical mentality of the witch hunt.'—*Penelope Houston*

The Big Knife*
US 1955 111m bw
UA / Aldrich and Associates

A depressed Hollywood star who wants better things for himself is blackmailed into signing a new contract.
Overheated argument between Art and Mammon, with rather disagreeable people shouting at each other, for too long a time. Limited interest is provided by the acting.

w James Poe, *play* Clifford Odets *d* Robert Aldrich *ph* Ernest Laszlo *m* Frank de Vol

Jack Palance, Ida Lupino, *Rod Steiger*, Everett Sloane, Jean Hagen, Shelley Winters, Wendell Corey, Ilka Chase, Wesley Addy

'Everything in it is garish and overdone: it's paced too fast and pitched too high, immorality is attacked with almost obscene relish, the knife turns into a buzz saw.'—*Pauline Kael, 1968*

The Big Land
US 1957 92m Warnercolor
(Warner) Jaguar
GB title: *Stampeded*

Cattlemen encourage the building of a rail link for Texas.
Undistinguished star western.

w David Dortort, Martin Rackin, *novel* Buffalo Grass by Frank Gruber *d* Gordon Douglas *ph* John F. Seitz *m* David Buttolph

Alan Ladd, Virginia Mayo, Edmond O'Brien, Anthony Caruso, Julie Bishop, John Qualen

'Hackneyed, humdrum western.'—*Howard Thompson*

Big Leaguer
US 1953 73m bw
MGM (Matthew Rapf)

An ageing baseball player is given the job of running a youth training camp.
Even the synopsis is boring. A routine job from the doldrums of the star's career.

w Herbert Baker *d* Robert Aldrich
ph William Mellor *md* Alberto Colombo

Edward G. Robinson, Vera-Ellen, Jeff Richards, William Campbell, Richard Jaeckel

'The film treats its subject with an almost hushed reverence and its appeal is restricted almost entirely to baseball enthusiasts.'—*MFB*

The Big Lift*
US 1950 119m bw
TCF (William Perlberg)

When the Russians blockade Berlin, British and American airmen get supplies there via a massive airlift; two men on one plane hold opposite views of the matter, and both have chastening experiences.
Rather heavy-going fiction based on fact, with earnest performances and good production.

wd George Seaton *ph* Charles G. Clarke *m* Alfred Newman

Montgomery Clift, Paul Douglas, Cornell Borchers, O. E. Hasse, Bruni Lobel

'There are some acute touches . . . just enough to make the slick evasions of the rest all the more regrettable.'—*Gavin Lambert*

The Big Money
GB 1956 86m Technicolor Vistavision
Rank (Joseph Janni)

A family of petty crooks is ashamed of its eldest son, who is an incompetent thief.
A would-be high-spirited lark in which none of the jokes comes off, and a note of forced artificiality hangs over the whole production.

w John Baines *d* John Paddy Carstairs
ph Jack Cox *m* Van Phillips

Ian Carmichael, Belinda Lee, Kathleen Harrison, Robert Helpmann, James Hayter, George Coulouris, Jill Ireland, Renée Houston, Leslie Phillips

The Big Mouth
US 1967 107m Pathecolor
Columbia (Jerry Lewis)

A meek bank auditor finds he is the double of a dying gangster and is put on the trail of stolen diamonds.
The comedian at his worst, most repetitive and long drawn out.

w Jerry Lewis, Bill Richmond *d* Jerry Lewis
ph W. Wallace Kelley, Ernest Laszlo
m Harry Betts

Jerry Lewis, Harold J. Stone, Susan Day, Buddy Lester, Del Moore

The Big Night
US 1951 75m bw
(UA) Philip A. Waxman

A 17-year-old youth goes on the rampage in the underworld to avenge the beating up of his father by gangsters.
Hysterical melodrama presenting a rather false and dismal view of the world. Amazingly typical of its director's later output.

w Stanley Ellin, Joseph Losey, *novel* Dreadful Summit by Stanley Ellin *d* Joseph Losey
ph Hal Mohr *m* Lyn Murray

John Barrymore Jnr, Preston Foster, Howard St John, Philip Bourneuf, Howland Chamberlin, Emile Meyer, Dorothy Comingore, Joan Lorring

'We are in that familiar underworld of the American cinema: dark streets gleaming with rain, sleazy apartments, garish night clubs, with Negro singers, drunks who spout philosophy, discontented blondes and fierce pock-marked thugs.'—*Gavin Lambert*

The Big Noise
US 1944 74m bw
TCF (Sol M. Wurtzel)

Two incompetent detectives accidentally round up a spy gang.
Very thin star vehicle consisting largely of poorly staged and warmed up versions of a few old routines.

w Scott Darling *d* Mal St Clair *ph* Joe MacDonald *m* Cyril Mockridge

Stan Laurel, Oliver Hardy, Doris Merrick, Arthur Space, Jack Norton

The Big Operator
US 1959 91m bw Cinemascope
MGM / Albert Zugsmith-Fryman (Red Doff)

The racketeer head of a labour union goes berserk when the government has him investigated.
Unpleasant gangster exploitation melodrama from the bottom of the barrel.

w Robert Smith, Allen Rivkin *d* Charles Haas *ph* Walter H. Castle *m* Van Alexander

Mickey Rooney, Steve Cochran, Mamie Van Doren, Mel Tormé, Ray Danton, Jim Backus, Jackie Coogan, Ray Anthony, Charles Chaplin Jnr

'The epic of the American doughboy!'

The Big Parade***
US 1925 115m approx (24 fps) bw silent
MGM

A young American enlists in 1917, learns the realities of war, is wounded but survives.
Enormously successful commercially, this 'anti-war' film survives best as a thrilling spectacle and a well-considered piece of film-making.

w Lawrence Stallings, Harry Behn *d King Vidor ph John Arnold m* William Axt, David Mendoza

John Gilbert, Renee Adoree, Hobart Bosworth, Karl Dane, George K. Arthur

'The human comedy emerges from a terrifying tragedy.'—*King Vidor*

'A cinegraphically visualized result of a cinegraphically imagined thing . . . something conceived in terms of a medium and expressed by that medium as only that medium could properly express it.'—*National Board of Review*

'The extraordinary impression of the rush of lorries, the queer terror of the woods . . . it was amazing how much fear could be felt in the mere continuous pace of movement.'—*Bryher, Close Up*

† The biggest grossing silent film of all.

The Big Parade of Comedy**
US 1964 90m approx bw
MGM (Robert Youngson)
aka: *MGM's Big Parade of Comedy*

A compilation by Robert Youngson, including material as diverse as *Ninotchka*, Laurel and Hardy and the Marx Brothers.
One is grateful for the excerpts but the assembly of them is somewhat graceless.

The Big Pond*
US 1930 79m bw
Paramount (Monta Bell)

The son of an important French family acts as a tourist guide in Venice.
Reasonably lively, semi-satirical early musical with Americans the butt of the jokes.

w Robert Presnell, Garrett Fort, Preston Sturges, *play* George Middleton, A. E. Thomas *d* Hobart Henley *ph* George Folsey *songs* various *m* arranged by John Green

Maurice Chevalier, Claudette Colbert, George Barbier, Nat Pendleton, Marion Ballou

'An amiable and ingratiating comedy that will give the Chevalier momentum another good shove.'—*Variety*

AAN: Maurice Chevalier

The Big Punch
US 1948 80m bw

A boxer refuses to throw a fight and is framed for murder. Routine time-passer with a second team before and behind the camera. Gordon MacRae, Wayne Morris, Lois Maxwell, Mary Stewart. Written by Bernard Girard; directed by Sherry Shourds; for Warner.

Big Red
US 1962 89m Technicolor
Walt Disney (Winston Hibler)

An orphan boy protects a dog which later saves him from a mountain lion.
Simple boy-and-dog yarn with impressive Canadian settings.

w Louis Pelletier *d* Norman Tokar *ph* Edward Colman *m* Oliver Wallace

Walter Pidgeon, Gilles Payant, Emile Genest

The Big Red One*
US 1980 111m colour
UA / Lorimar (Gene Corman)

Five foot-soldiers survive action in several theatres of war between 1940 and 1945
Symbolic action drama, very well made but finally lacking a cumulative impact.

wd Samuel Fuller ph Adam Greenberg *m* Dana Kaproff

Lee Marvin, Mark Hamill, Robert Carradine, Bobby DiCicco, Kelly Ward, Stéphane Audran, Serge Marquand

'A picture of palpable raw power which manages both intense intimacy and great scope at the same time.'—*Variety*

'Like all Fuller movies, about an inch from cliché all the way.'—*Guardian*

The Big Shakedown
US 1934 64m bw
Warner (Sam Bischoff)

A racketeer finds a new gimmick: cut-price medicine.
Action programmer with emphasis on the young couple forced into helping the racket.

w Niven Busch, Rian James *d* John Francis Dillon *ph* Sid Hickox

Bette Davis, Ricardo Cortez, Charles Farrell, Glenda Farrell, Allen Jenkins, Henry O'Neill, Samuel S. Hinds

'A routine assortment of gang-film impedimenta.'—*New York Times*

The Big Shot*
US 1942 82m bw
Warner (Walter MacEwen)

An ill-fated criminal has trouble with women and his former companions.
Dullish star vehicle.

w Bertram Millhauser, Aben Finkel, Daniel Fuchs *d* Lewis Seiler *ph* Sid Hickox *m* Adolph Deutsch

Humphrey Bogart, Irene Manning, Richard Travis, Donald Crisp, Stanley Ridges, Henry Hull, Susan Peters, Howard da Silva

The Big Show
US 1961 113m De Luxe Cinemascope
TCF / API (Ted Sherdeman)

A circus proprietor dominates his sons; after his death they fight for supremacy.
Another remake of *House of Strangers*, which was also remodelled as *Broken Lance*. Not too bad as circus melodramas go.

w Ted Sherdeman *d* James B. Clark *ph* Otto Heller *m* Paul Sawtell, Bert Shefter

Esther Williams, Cliff Robertson, *Nehemiah Persoff*, Robert Vaughn, Carol Christensen, Margia Dean, David Nelson

The Big Sky*
US 1952 122m bw
RKO / Winchester (Howard Hawks)

In 1830 two Kentucky mountain men join an exploration up the Missouri and become preoccupied with Indian trouble.
A large-scale adventure, loaded with talent, which becomes oddly tedious.

w Dudley Nichols, *novel* A. B. Guthrie Jnr *d* Howard Hawks *ph* Russell Harlan *m* Dmitri Tiomkin

Kirk Douglas, Arthur Hunnicutt, Elizabeth Threatt, Dewey Martin, Buddy Baer, Steve Geray, Jim Davis

'It has the timeless, relentless quality of the long American historical novel.'—*Penelope Houston*

AAN: Russell Harlan; Arthur Hunnicutt

The Big Sleep***
US 1946 114m bw
Warner (Howard Hawks)

Private eye Philip Marlowe is hired to protect General Sternwood's wild young daughter from her own indiscretions, and finds several murders later that he has fallen in love with her elder sister.
Inextricably complicated, moody thriller from a novel whose author claimed that even he did not know 'who done it'. The film is

nevertheless vastly enjoyable along the way for its slangy script, star performances and outbursts of violence, suspense and sheer fun.

w William Faulkner, Leigh Brackett, Jules Furthman, novel Raymond Chandler
d Howard Hawks *ph* Sid Hickox *m Max Steiner*
Humphrey Bogart (Philip Marlowe), *Lauren Bacall* (Vivian Sherwood Rutledge), John Ridgely (Eddie Mars), Martha Vickers (Carmen Sternwood), Dorothy Malone (Proprietress), Regis Toomey (Bernie Ohls), Charles Waldron (General Sternwood), Charles D. Brown (Norris), Elisha Cook Jr (Harry Jones), Louis Jean Heydt (Joe Brody), Bob Steele (Canino), Peggy Knudsen (Mona Mars), Sonia Darrin (Agnes)

MARLOWE: 'My, my, my. Such a lot of guns around town and so few brains.'

GENERAL: 'You may smoke, too. I can still enjoy the smell of it. Nice thing when a man has to indulge his vices by proxy.'

VIVIAN: 'So you're a private detective. I didn't know they existed, except in books—or else they were greasy little men snooping around hotel corridors. My, you're a mess, aren't you?'

MARLOWE: 'I don't mind if you don't like my manners. I don't like 'em myself. They're pretty bad. I grieve over 'em on long winter evenings.'

GENERAL: 'If I seem a bit sinister as a parent, Mr Marlowe, it's because my hold on life is too slight to include any Victorian hypocrisy. I need hardly add that any man who has lived as I have and indulges for the first time in parenthood at the age of 55 deserves all he gets.'

MARLOWE: 'Speaking of horses . . . you've got a touch of class, but I don't know how far you can go.'

VIVIAN: 'A lot depends on who's in the saddle. Go ahead Marlowe. I like the way you work. In case you don't know it, you're doing all right.'

'A sullen atmosphere of sex saturates the film, which is so fast and complicated you can hardly catch it.'—*Richard Winnington*

'A violent, smoky cocktail shaken together from most of the printable misdemeanours and some that aren't.'—*James Agee*

'Harder, faster, tougher, funnier and more laconic than any thriller since.'—*NFT, 1974*

'Wit, excitement and glamour in generous doses.'—*Francis Wyndham*

'Some days business is good—and some days it's murder!'

The Big Sleep
GB 1977 99m De Luxe
Winkast (Elliott Kastner, Michael Winner)

Straight remake of the 1946 film, curiously and ineffectively set in London.

wd Michael Winner *ph* Robert Paynter *m* Jerry Fielding

Robert Mitchum, Sarah Miles, Richard Boone, Candy Clark, Edward Fox, Joan Collins, John Mills, James Stewart, Oliver Reed, Harry Andrews, Richard Todd, James Donald, Colin Blakely

'The 1946 film takes on even more stature in light of this. For a Winner film, however, it's quite good.'—*Variety*

The Big Steal**
US 1949 72m bw
RKO (Jack J. Gross)

An army officer is framed for the theft of a payroll, and sets off across Mexico in hectic pursuit of the real culprit.
Unexpectedly enjoyable comedy melodrama with a plethora of twists and a pace that never lets up. Routine Hollywood at a level seldom achieved, and short enough to leave one asking for more.

w Gerald Drayson Adams, Geoffrey Homes, story The Road to Carmichael's by Richard Wormser *d Don Siegel* *ph* Harry J. Wild *m* Leigh Harline

Robert Mitchum, Jane Greer, William Bendix, Ramon Novarro, Patric Knowles, Don Alvarado, John Qualen

'Vigour and excellent craftsmanship.'—*Gavin Lambert*

The Big Store*
US 1941 83m bw
MGM (Louis K. Sidney)

An eccentric private eye saves a department store from the hands of crooks.
Reckoned to be the Marx Brothers' weakest MGM vehicle, but it has its moments, especially the first reel and the bedding department scene, also Groucho's rendering of 'Sing While You Sell'.

w Sid Kuller, Hal Fimberg, Ray Golden *d* Charles Reisner *ph* Charles Lawton *m* George Stoll

Groucho, Chico, Harpo, Margaret Dumont, Douglass Dumbrille, Tony Martin, Virginia Grey, Virginia O'Brien, Henry Armetta

The Big Street*
US 1942 88m bw
RKO (Damon Runyon)

A Broadway nightclub waiter falls in love with a crippled singer who selfishly accepts his help without loving him in return.
Unusual but mawkish material from an author who never really suited the screen; a mixture of laughs, tears and sentimentality, with a comic gangster background.

w Leonard Spiegelgass, *story* Little Pinks by Damon Runyon *d* Irving Reis *ph* Russell Metty *m* Roy Webb

Henry Fonda, Lucille Ball, Eugene Pallette, Virginia Weidler, Agnes Moorehead, Barton MacLane, Ozzie Nelson and his Orchestra, Sam Levene, Ray Collins, Marion Martin

Big Town
US 1947 59m bw

Adventures of the crusading editor of a city newspaper. Anaemic support which surprisingly started a series. Philip Reed, Hillary Brooke, Robert Lowery, Byron Barr, Veda Ann Borg. Written by Geoffrey Homes from radio scripts; directed by William Thomas; for Pine-Thomas / Paramount.

Big Town Girl
US 1937 66m bw

A night-club singer adopts a disguise to elude her escaped convict husband. Satisfactory supporting comedy-melodrama. Claire Trevor, Donald Woods, Alan Dinehart, Alan Baxter, Murray Alper, Spencer Charters. Written by Lou Breslow, John Patrick, Robert Ellis, Helen Logan; directed by Alfred Werker; for Milton H. Feld / TCF. 'First-class dualler which should please everywhere.'—*Variety*

The Big Trail*
US 1930 125m bw
Fox

A wagon train struggles along the Oregon trail.
Simple-minded early talkie western spectacular with a new young star who took another nine years to make it big. Originally shown on a giant 70mm gauge and intended for big screens.

w Jack Peabody, Marie Boyle, Florence Postal *d* Raoul Walsh *ph* Lucien Andriot, Arthur Edeson

John Wayne, Marguerite Churchill, El Brendel, Tully Marshall, Tyrone Power Snr, David Rollins, Ward Bond, Helen Parrish

'Failing to own a kick or a punch, other than scenically, and with no outstanding cast names, it remains only a western of the pioneering sort, so thoroughly made familiar by those pioneering epics preceding it.'—*Variety*

'Printed upon the new wide film and projected upon the vastly large Grandeur screen, the landscapes, wagon trains, vistas and camp scenes achieve an incredibly greater sweep [than *The Covered Wagon*]. *The Big Trail* is often stagey, melodramatic, ranty.'—*Theatre Magazine*

The Big Trees**
US 1952 89m Technicolor
Warner (Louis F. Edelmann)

An unscrupulous lumberman tries to exploit California's giant redwood forests but is won over by the local Quakers who hold the trees in awe.
Pleasing, old-fashioned outdoor drama with a plot which allows the star much opportunity for derring-do.

w John Twist, James R. Webb *d* Felix Feist *ph* Bert Glennon *m* Heinz Roemheld

Kirk Douglas, Eve Miller, Patrice Wymore, Edgar Buchanan, John Archer, Alan Hale Jnr
† A remake of *Valley of the Giants* (qv)

Big Trouble
US 1984 / 86 93m Metrocolor
Columbia / Delphi III (Michael Lobell)

Two incompetent con men try to swindle an insurance company.

Witless comic farrago apparently designed to cash in on the success of *The In-Laws* by utilizing the plot of *Double Indemnity*. Not a goer.

w Warren Bogle (Andrew Bergman) *d* John Cassavetes *ph* Bill Butler *m* Bill Conti

Peter Falk, Alan Arkin, Beverly D'Angelo, Charles Durning, Paul Dooley, Robert Stack, Valerie Curtin

Big Trouble in Little China
US 1986 99m De Luxe Panavision
TCF / Paul Monash, Keith Barish (Larry J. Franco)

A philosophizing truck driver in San Francisco finds himself combating an ancient, evil Chinese magician.
Misfiring attempt to equal the nonsense of the Indiana Jones sagas; occasional effective action moments don't stop the whole from being tiresome.

w W. D. Richter, Gary Goldman, David Z. Weinstein *d* John Carpenter *ph* Dean Cundey *m* John Carpenter *pd* John J. Lloyd

Kurt Russell, Kim Cattrall, Dennis Dun, James Hong, Victor Wong, Kate Burton

'Glitzy sets, vacuous characters, limping fantasy.'—*Sight and Sound*

Big Wednesday*
US 1978 119m Metrocolor Panavision
Warner / A-Team (Alex Rose, Tamara Asseyev)

Three California surfing friends of the early sixties get back together after the Vietnam war.
It isn't clear whether the intent is to extol or deride the mystical camaraderie of surfing, but for those who can stand rumbustious beach behaviour this curious movie may have at least as much to say as *The Deer Hunter*.

w John Milius, Dennis Aaberg *d* John Milius *ph* Bruce Surtees *surfing ph Greg MacGillivray* *m* Basil Poledouris

Jan-Michael Vincent, William Katt, Gary Busey, Darell Fetty

The Big Wheel
US 1949 92m bw
(UA) Popkin / Stiefel / Dempsey (Samuel H. Stiefel)

The son of a racing driver is determined to follow in father's footsteps.
Grubby star actioner.

w Robert Smith *d* Edward Ludwig *ph* Ernest Laszlo *m* Nat W. Finston

Mickey Rooney, Spring Byington, Thomas Mitchell, Mary Hatcher, Allen Jenkins

'Wanted by two women!'

The Bigamist*
US 1953 80m bw
Filmmakers (Collier Young)

A travelling salesman has two wives.
Minor melodrama which took its subject seriously but failed to make absorbing drama of it. Very much a family affair, starring the producer's present and past wives, the latter also directing.

w Collier Young *d* Ida Lupino *ph* George Diskant *m* Leith Stevens

Edmond O'Brien, Joan Fontaine, Ida Lupino, Edmund Gwenn, Jane Darwell

'The film seems to have summoned all its energy to shout defiantly that bigamous marriages exist and, finding no one to defy, retires deflated.'—*MFB*

The Bigamist*
Italy / France 1956 97m bw
Royal / Filmel / Alba

An innocent young salesman is accused of bigamy and dragged into court.
Noisy comedy of mistaken identity; some laughs, but the talents are not at their best.

w Sergio Amidei, Age Scarpelli, Franco Rosi, Elio Talarico *d* Luciano Emmer *ph* Mario Montuori *m* Alessandro Cicognini

Marcello Mastroianni, Vittorio de Sica, Franca Valeri, Giovanna Ralli

Bigger than Life*
US 1956 95m Eastmancolor Cinemascope
TCF / James Mason

A small-town schoolteacher is prescribed cortisone for arthritis; it gradually turns him into a bullying megalomaniac full of grandiose schemes.
Exaggerated and sensationalized but still not very dramatic expansion of a genuine case history. A curious choice for all concerned.

w Cyril Hume, Richard Maibaum *d* Nicholas Ray *ph* Joe MacDonald *m* David Raksin

James Mason, Barbara Rush, Walter Matthau, Robert Simon, Roland Winters

'This is the world's sexiest robbery!'

The Biggest Bundle of Them All
US 1967 110m Metrocolor Panavision
MGM / Shaftel–Stewart

A retired gangster is kidnapped by other gangsters and shows them how to steal five million dollars worth of platinum.
Very moderately amusing international comedy caper.

w Josef Shaftel, Sy Salkowitz *d* Ken Annakin *ph* Piero Portalupi *m* Riz Ortolani

Raquel Welch, Robert Wagner, Vittorio de Sica, Edward G. Robinson, Godfrey Cambridge, Davy Kaye

'It begins like one of these really bad movies that are unintentionally funny. Then it becomes clear that it intends to be funny, and it isn't.'—*Renata Adler*

Biggles
GB 1986 92m Technicolor
(UIP) Compact Yellowbill / Tambarle (Kent Walwin, Pom Oliver)

A young New York businessman is transported back in time to 1917, and his help solicited by a daredevil airman.
The bookends set a spoofy tone, but most of the movie is the same old teenage gunge.

w John Groves, Kent Walwin, characters created by Captain W. E. Johns *d* John Hough *ph* Ernest Vincze *m* Stanislas *pd* Terry Pritchard

Neil Dickson, Alex Hyde-White, Peter Cushing, Fiona Hutchison, Marcus Gilbert, William Hootkins

Bikini Beach
US 1964 100m Pathecolor

A California beach is disputed by surfers, motor bikers, and a businessman who wants to build a retirement community. Mindless youth nonsense with flashes of satire. Frankie Avalon, Annette Funicello, Martha Hyer, Don Rickles, Harvey Lembeck, Keenan Wynn, John Ashley, (guest appearance) Boris Karloff. Written by William Asher, Leo Townsend and Robert Diller; directed by William Asher; for American International.

Bill and Coo
US 1947 61m colour

Trials and tribulations of the inhabitants of Chirpendale are enacted entirely by birds, mostly wearing hats and neckties. An eccentricity which won its creator, Ken Murray, a special Academy Award. For Republic. 'By conservative estimate, the god-damnedest thing ever seen.'—*James Agee.*

A Bill of Divorcement**
US 1932 76m bw
RKO / David O. Selznick

A middle-aged man, released from a mental institution, comes home and meets his strong-willed daughter.
Pattern play which became a celebrated star vehicle; now very dated but the performances survive.

w Howard Estabrook, Harry Wagstaff Gribble, *play* Clemence Dane *d* George Cukor *ph* Sid Hickox *m* Max Steiner, W. Franke Harling

John Barrymore, Katharine Hepburn (her debut), Billie Burke, David Manners, Paul Cavanagh, Henry Stephenson, Elizabeth Patterson

'A money picture for all classes of houses . . . the most potent tear jerker in many a moon.'—*Variety*

'A very good picture, tender, emotional and intensely gripping.'—*Picturegoer*

A Bill of Divorcement*
US 1940 69m bw
RKO
GB title: *Never To Love*

Virtually a scene-for-scene remake of the above. Again the acting holds the material together.

w Dalton Trumbo *d* John Farrow *ph* Nicholas Musuraca *m* Roy Webb

Adolphe Menjou, Maureen O'Hara, Patric Knowles, Herbert Marshall, C. Aubrey Smith, Dame May Whitty

Billie
US 1965 87m Techniscope
UA / Peter Lawford (Don Weis)

A teenage tomboy runs into trouble because she is better at sport than her boy friends.
Routine American college / domestic comedy with a young star and good comedy support.

w Ronald Alexander, from his play Time Out for Ginger *d* Don Weis *ph* John Russell *m* Dominic Frontière

Patty Duke, Jim Backus, Jane Greer, Warren Berlinger, Billy de Wolfe, Charles Lane, Dick Sargent, Richard Deacon

Billion Dollar Brain
GB 1967 111m Technicolor Panavision
UA / Lowndes (Harry Saltzman)

Ex-secret agent Harry Palmer agrees to take a mysterious canister to Finland and becomes involved in an American megalomaniac's bid to take over the world.
Incomprehensible spy story smothered in the kind of top dressing now expected from this director, but which almost killed his career at the time. Occasional pictorial pleasures, but the total kaleidoscopic effect is enough to drive most audiences to the exit.

w John McGrath, *novel* Len Deighton *d* Ken Russell *ph Billy Williams m* Richard Rodney Bennett *pd* Syd Cain

Michael Caine, *Oscar Homolka*, Françoise Dorléac, Karl Malden, Ed Begley

Billion Dollar Scandal
US 1932 81m bw

Ex-convicts are involved by a millionaire in a shady oil deal. Competent but complex and talky melodrama 'from the headlines'. Robert Armstrong, Constance Cummings, Frank Morgan, Olga Baclanova, James Gleason, Irving Pichel. From a story by Gene Towne and Graham Baker; directed by Harry Joe Brown; for Paramount.

Billy Budd*
GB 1962 125m bw Cinemascope
Anglo-Allied (A. Ronald Lubin, Peter Ustinov)

In 1797 the sadistic master at arms of a British warship terrorizes the crew and is killed by young Billy Budd, who must hang for his unpremeditated crime.
Handsomely photographed but obtusely scripted and variously acted attempt at the impossible, an allegory of good and evil more suited to opera or the printed page than film: in any case, a hopelessly and defiantly uncommercial enterprise. Some actors bore, others chew the scenery.

w Peter Ustinov, Robert Rossen, *novel* Herman Melville *d* Peter Ustinov *ph* Robert Krasker *m* Antony Hopkins

Peter Ustinov, Robert Ryan, Terence Stamp, Melvyn Douglas, Paul Rogers, John Neville, Ronald Lewis, David McCallum, Lee Montague, John Meillon, Thomas Heathcote, Niall MacGinnis, Cyril Luckham

'A beautiful, terrifying and heartbreaking film.'—*Time*

AAN: Terence Stamp

Billy Galvin*
US 1986 94m bw

Frictions develop between father and son in blue collar Boston. Old-fashioned family drama, quite rewarding for old-fashioned audiences. Karl Malden, Lenny Von Dohlen, Joyce Van Patten, Toni Kalem, Paul Guilfoyle. Written and directed by John Gray; for American Playhouse/Vestron.

Billy Jack*
US 1971 113m Technicolor
Warner / National Student Film Corporation (Mary Rose Solti)

A half-breed Vietnam veteran roams the Arizona desert protecting wild mustangs and a runaway teenager.
A trendy radical drama, virtually a one-man show which had an enormous success in the US and led to a sequel, *The Trial of Billy Jack*.

w Tom Laughlin, Delores Taylor *d* Tom Laughlin (T. C. Frank) *ph* Fred Koenekamp, John Stephens *m* Mundell Lowe

Tom Laughlin, Delores Taylor, Bert Freed, Clark Howat, Julie Webb, Ken Tobey, Victor Izay

'A plea for the alternative society with a format of the crudest melodrama.'—*MFB*

Billy Liar***
GB 1963 98m bw Cinemascope
Vic Films (Joe Janni)

In a drab North Country town, an undertaker's clerk lives in a world of fantasy.
Flawed only by its unsuitable Cinemascope ratio, this is a brilliant urban comedy of its time, seminal in acting, theme, direction and permissiveness. From a novel and play no doubt inspired by Thurber's Walter Mitty, it was later turned into a TV series and a successful stage musical, making Billy a universal figure of the period.

w Keith Waterhouse, Willis Hall, from KW's novel and their play *d John Schlesinger ph* Denys Coop *m* Richard Rodney Bennett

Tom Courtenay, Julie Christie, Wilfred Pickles, Mona Washbourne, *Ethel Griffies*, Finlay Currie, Rodney Bewes, Leonard Rossiter

Billy the Kid*
US 1930 90m bw
MGM

A young western outlaw is relentlessly pursued by Sheriff Pat Garrett.
Mildly interesting early talkie western with the usual romanticized view of Billy. Originally made and shown in 70mm.

w Wanda Tuchock, Laurence Stallings, Charles MacArthur *d* King Vidor *ph* Gordon Avil

Johnny Mack Brown, Wallace Beery, Kay Johnson, Karl Dane, Roscoe Ates

'Should stand up for slightly better than average business where shown on Realife. Otherwise just an ordinary western.'—*Variety*

Billy the Kid*
US 1941 95m Technicolor
MGM (Irving Asher)

Remake of the above, equally false and rather less well acted, but a striking outdoor colour film of its period.

w Gene Fowler *d* David Miller *ph* Leonard Smith, William V. Skall *m* David Snell

Robert Taylor, Brian Donlevy, Ian Hunter, Mary Howard, Gene Lockhart, Henry O'Neill, Frank Puglia Cy Kendall, Ethel Griffies

AAN: Leonard Smith, William V. Skall

Billy the Kid and the Green Baize Vampire
GB 1985 93m colour
ITC / Zenith (Simon Mallin)

A hustling young snooker player takes on a formidable opponent.
Predictable sporting melodrama with curious supernatural overtones; not a coherent whole.

w Trevor Preston *d* Alan Clarke *ph* Clive Tickner *m* George Fenton *pd* Jamie Leonard

Phil Daniels, Alun Armstrong, Bruce Payne, Louise Gold, Eve Ferret

'Weird, not to say downright perverse.'—*Sight and Sound*

Billy Two Hats
US 1973 99m Technicolor
UA / Algonquin (Norman Jewison, Patrick Palmer, Mitchell Lifton)
aka: *The Lady and the Outlaw*

The friendship of an old Scottish outlaw and a young half-breed is broken only by the old man's death.
Curiously miscast western shot in Israel; it makes no discernible point and is not very entertaining.

w Alan Sharp *d* Ted Kotcheff *ph* Brian West *m* John Scott

Gregory Peck, Desi Arnaz Jnr, Jack Warden, Sian Barbara Allen, David Huddleston

Biloxi Blues*
US 1988 106m colour Panavision
Universal/Raster

Standard, quite pleasing version of a Broadway comedy about a conscript called up in 1945 when World War Two was ending.

w Neil Simon, from his play *d* Mike Nichols *ph* Bill Butler *m* Georges Delerue

Matthew Broderick, Christopher Walken, Matt Mulhern, Corey Parker

The Bingo Long Traveling All-Stars and Motor Kings
US 1976 111m Technicolor
Universal (Rob Cohen)

Adventures of a black baseball team in the 1940s.
High-spirited japes and exhibitions of athleticism which dramatically do not add up to very much.

w Hal Barwood, Matthew Robbins, *novel* William Brashler *d* John Badham *ph* Bill Butler *m* William Goldstein

Billy Dee Williams, James Earl Jones, Richard Pryor, Rico Dawson

'Modest pleasures and dull stretches co-exist in equal abundance.'—*Frank Rich, New York Times*

Biography (of a Bachelor Girl)*
US 1935 84m bw
MGM

The biography of a sophisticated lady portrait painter reveals surprising details of her love life.
Leaden, bowdlerized screen version of a sparkling Broadway play, fragments of which do however survive.

w Anita Loos, *play* S. N. Behrman *d* Edward H. Griffith *ph* James Wong Howe *m* Herbert Stothart

Ann Harding (miscast), Robert Montgomery, Edward Everett Horton, Edward Arnold, Una Merkel, Charles Richman, Donald Meek

'Smart entertainment for top houses. Possibly too smart for the other end.'—*Variety*

Birch Interval
US 1976 105m colour

A twelve-year-old girl goes to live with her Amish relations in the country. Simple-minded moral tale which needed some old-fashioned style to bring it off. Eddie Albert, Rip Torn, Susan McClung, Ann Wedgeworth, Bill Lucking. Written by Joanna Crawford, from her novel; directed by Delbert Mann; for Robert B. Radnitz / Gamma III.

Bird*
US 1988 161m Technicolor
Warner / Malpaso (Clint Eastwood)

The life of Charlie Parker.
Long, downbeat, heavygoing treatment of America's greatest black saxophonist; but not a popular choice.

w Joel Oliansky *d* Clint Eastwood *ph* Jack N. Green *m* Lennie Niehaus

Forest Whitaker, Diane Venora, Michael Zelnikar

Bird of Paradise
US 1932 80m bw
RKO (David O. Selznick)

An adventurer on a South Sea island marries a native girl and causes trouble.
Never-never romance which remains stilted despite care obviously taken.

w Wells Root *d* King Vidor *ph* Clyde de Vinna *m* Max Steiner

Joel McCrea, John Halliday, *Dolores del Rio*, Skeets Gallagher

'The old tropical romance nicely done. OK for the main stem stands.'—*Variety*

Bird of Paradise
US 1951 100m Technicolor
TCF (Harmon Jones)

Opulent remake of the above; the trappings make it even more absurd, and the ritual sacrifice of the heroine seems misplaced in what is otherwise a pantomime.

wd Delmer Daves *ph* Winton Hoch
m Daniele Amfitheatrof

Louis Jourdan, Jeff Chandler, Debra Paget, Maurice Schwartz, Everett Sloane, Jack Elam

'The Kahuna is a naively grotesque figure, with a Central European accent and carrying what appears to be an outsize radish: he personifies the film's dubious approach to Polynesian myth and culture.'—*Gavin Lambert*

The Bird with the Crystal Plumage
Italy 1969 98m colour

A supposed murderer is vindicated when his alleged next victim turns out to be a psychopath. Tolerable shocker which was popular in dubbed version. Suzy Kendall, Tony Musante. Written and directed by Dario Argento; for Salvatore Argento.

Birdman of Alcatraz*
US 1961 148m bw
UA / Hecht–Lancaster (Stuart Millar, Guy Trosper)

An imprisoned murderer makes a name for himself as an ornithologist.
Overlong and rather weary biopic of Robert Stroud, who spent nearly sixty years in prison and became a *cause célèbre*. One cannot deny many effective moments, notably of direction, but it's a long haul.

w Guy Trosper, *book* Thomas E. Gaddis
d John Frankenheimer *ph* Burnett Guffey
m Elmer Bernstein

Burt Lancaster, Karl Malden, Thelma Ritter, Edmond O'Brien, Betty Field, Neville Brand, Hugh Marlowe, Telly Savalas, James Westerfield

AAN: Burnett Guffey; Burt Lancaster; Thelma Ritter; Telly Savalas

'Suspense and shock beyond anything you have ever seen or imagined!'

The Birds***
US 1963 119m Technicolor
Universal / Alfred Hitchcock

In a Californian coastal area, flocks of birds unaccountably make deadly attacks on human beings.
A curiously absorbing work which begins as light comedy and ends as apocalyptic allegory, this piece of Hitchcockery has no visible point except to tease the audience and provide plenty of opportunity for shock, offbeat humour and special effects (which despite the drumbeating are not quite as good as might be expected). The actors are pawns in the master's hand.

w Evan Hunter, *story* Daphne du Maurier
d Alfred Hitchcock *ph Robert Burks* *sound consultant* Bernard Herrmann *sp* Lawrence A. Hampton

Rod Taylor, Tippi Hedren, Jessica Tandy, Suzanne Pleshette, Ethel Griffies

'Enough to make you kick the next pigeon you come across.'—*Judith Crist*

'The dialogue is stupid, the characters insufficiently developed to rank as clichés, the story incohesive.'—*Stanley Kauffmann*

'We must sit through half an hour of pachydermous flirtation between Rod and Tippi before the seagull attacks, and another fifteen minutes of tedium . . . before the birds attack again. If one adds later interrelations between mother, girl friend and a particularly repulsive child actress, about two-thirds of the film is devoted to extraneous matters. Poe would have been appalled.'—*Dwight MacDonald*

The Birds and the Bees
US 1956 94m Technicolor Vistavision
Paramount (Paul Jones)

On a transatlantic voyage a wealthy simpleton is fleeced by a card sharp and his daughter; but the latter falls in love with her victim.
Competent but uninspired reworking of *The Lady Eve* as a vehicle for a rather charmless comic. Lacking Preston Sturges at the helm, the mixture of slapstick and sentiment fails to jell.

w Sidney Sheldon after Preston Sturges
d Norman Taurog *ph* Daniel Fapp *m* Walter Scharf

George Gobel, David Niven, Mitzi Gaynor, Fred Clark, Reginald Gardiner, Harry Bellaver, Hans Conried

'Beneath her icy composure lay a deep desire to love!'

Birds Come to Die in Peru
France 1968 98m Technicolor Franscope
Universal France (Jacques Natteau)

On a Peruvian beach a tormented nymphomaniac makes love to several men and attempts suicide, but is rescued by her true love.
Elaborate high-flown bosh, quite fun to watch.

wd Romain Gary *ph* Christian Matras
m Kenton Coe

Jean Seberg, Maurice Ronet, Danielle Darrieux, Pierre Brasseur

Birds Do It
US 1966 88m colour
Columbia (Ivan Tors, Stanley Colbert)

A janitor at an atomic plant is accidentally ionized and finds he can fly, which enables him to catch a spy or two.
Childish stunt comedy.

w Arnie Kogen *d* Andrew Marton
ph Howard Winner *m* Samuel Maltovsky

Soupy Sales, Tab Hunter, Arthur O'Connell, Edward Andrews, Doris Dowling, Beverly Adams, Louis Quinn

The Birds, the Bees and the Italians
Italy / France 1965 98m colour
Dear Film / Films du Siècle (Robert Haggiag, Pietro Germi)
original title: *Signore e Signori*

Stories of adultery in an Italian provincial town.
Mainly tedious sex comedy full of gesticulating actors.

w Furio Scarpelli, Luciano Vincenzoni, Pietro Germi *d* Pietro Germi *ph* Aiace Parolin *m* Carlo Rustichelli

Gastone Moschin, Virna Lisi, Alberto Lionello, Gigi Ballista, Beba Loncar, Franco Fabrizi

Birdy
US 1984 120m Metrocolor
Tri-Star (Alan Marshall)

A psychologically disturbed war veteran thinks he can fly like a bird.
A case history which somewhat lacks plot advancement. Too self-indulgent even to earn marks for trying.

w Sandy Kroopf, Jack Behr *novel* William Wharton *d* Alan Parker *ph* Michael Seresin *m* Peter Gabriel *pd* Geoffrey Kirkland

Matthew Modine, Nicolas Cage, John Harkins, Sandy Baron

'Likely will fall short of taking full flight at the box office.'—*Variety*

Birth of a Legend*
US 1966 26m bw

Sprightly compilation of clips from the films of Mary Pickford and Douglas Fairbanks; the treatment is cursory but sympathetic. Written and directed by Matty Kemp; for the Mary Pickford Corporation.

'The dawn of a new art!'
The Birth of a Nation****
US 1915 approx 185m (16 fps) bw silent
Epoch (D. W. Griffith, Harry E. Aitken)

Northern and southern families are caught up in the Civil War.
The cinema's first and still most famous epic, many sequences of which retain their mastery despite negro villains, Ku Klux Klan heroes, and white actors in blackface. Originally shown as *The Clansman*; a shorter version with orchestral track was released in 1931.

w D. W. Griffith, Frank E. Woods, *novel* The Klansman by Thomas Dixon Jnr *d D. W. Griffith ph G. W. Bitzer*

Henry B. Walthall, Mae Marsh, Miriam Cooper, Lillian Gish, Robert Harron, Wallace Reid, Donald Crisp, Joseph Henaberry, Raoul Walsh, Eugene Pallette, Walter Long

'A film version of some of the melodramatic and inflammatory material contained in *The Clansman* . . . a great deal might be said concerning the sorry service rendered by its plucking at old wounds. But of the film as a film, it may be reported simply that it is an impressive new illustration of the scope of the motion picture camera.'—*New York Times*

The Birth of the Blues*
US 1941 85m bw
Paramount (B. G. De Sylva, Monta Bell)

Trials and tribulations of a jazz band in New Orleans.
Thin fiction on which is strung a multitude of dark brown musical entertainment. Not bad, even now.

w Harry Tugend, Walter de Leon *d* Victor Schertzinger *ph* William C. Mellor *md* Robert Emmett Dolan

Bing Crosby, Mary Martin, Brian Donlevy, Jack Teagarden, Eddie Rochester Anderson, Carolyn Lee

AAN: Robert Emmett Dolan

The Birthday Party*
GB 1968 126m Technicolor
Palomar (Max Rosenberg, Milton Subotsky)

The down-at-heel lodger in a seaside boarding house is menaced by two mysterious strangers, who eventually take him away.
Overlong but otherwise satisfactory film record of an entertaining if infuriating play, first of the black absurdities which proliferated in the sixties to general disadvantage, presenting structure without plot and intelligence without meaning.

w Harold Pinter, from his play *d* William Friedkin *ph* Denys Coop *m* none *pd* Edward Marshall

Sidney Tafler, Patrick Magee, Robert Shaw, *Dandy Nichols*, Moultrie Kelsall

The Birthday Present*
GB 1957 100m bw
BL / Jack Whittingham

A toy salesman's life is changed when he is charged with smuggling a watch through the customs.
Downcast, prolonged and rather uninteresting domestic drama; attention is held by generally good acting.

w Jack Whittingham *d* Pat Jackson *ph* Ted Scaife *m* Clifton Parker

Tony Britton, Sylvia Syms, Jack Watling, Walter Fitzgerald, Geoffrey Keen, Howard Marion Crawford, John Welsh

The Biscuit Eater

Two versions exist of this story by James Street about a white and a black boy who turn a stray into a crack hunting dog. The first was by Stuart Heisler for Paramount in 1940; it starred Billy Lee and made quite a box-office impact. The second was by Vincent McEveety for Disney in 1972, with Johnny Whittaker; despite the presence of Earl Holliman and Lew Ayres it made no impact at all. (GB title, 1940 version: *God Gave Him a Dog*.)

The Bishop Misbehaves*
US 1935 87m bw

A bishop gets on the wrong side of the law when he helps a young girl to see justice done. Amusing trifle with strong cast. Edmund Gwenn, Maureen O'Sullivan, Lucile Watson, Reginald Owen, Robert Greig, Reginald Owen, Dudley Digges, Melville Cooper, Lillian Bond. Written by Leon Gordon and George Auerbach, from the play by Frederick Jackson; directed by E. A. Dupont; for MGM. (GB title: *The Bishop's Misadventures*.) 'Reaches a grade above the average programmer, but points mainly to sophisticated patronage.'—*Variety*

The Bishop Murder Case
US 1930 91m bw

Philo Vance unmasks a killer who sends warning notes in rhyme. Mildly interesting early talkie detection which moves at too stately a pace. Basil Rathbone, Leila Hyams, Alec B. Francis, Roland Young, George Marion. Written by Lenore Coffee, from the novel by S. S. Van Dine; directed by Nick Grinde and David Burton; for MGM.

The Bishop's Wife**
US 1947 108m bw
Samuel Goldwyn

An angel is sent down to mend the ways of a bishop whose absorption with cathedral buildings has put him out of touch with his wife and parishioners.
Whimsical, stolid and protracted light comedy saved by its actors and its old-fashioned Hollywood style.

w Robert E. Sherwood, Leonardo Bercovici, *novel* Robert Nathan *d* Henry Koster *ph* Gregg Toland *m* Hugo Friedhofer

Cary Grant, Loretta Young, David Niven, Monty Woolley, James Gleason, Gladys Cooper, Elsa Lanchester, Sara Haden, Regis Toomey

'It is the Protestant comeback to the deadly successful RC propaganda of *Going My Way* and *The Bells of St Mary's*. It surpasses in tastelessness, equals in whimsy and in technique falls well below those crooning parables. It is really quite a monstrous film.'—*Richard Winnington, News Chronicle*

'When a film undertakes to bring audiences a spiritual message, we wonder whether the director doesn't owe it to us to clothe such messages in less muddled characterizations and to dispense with caricature.'—*Scholastic Magazine*

'A sophisticated *Christmas Carol*.'—*Philip Hartung*

'As cheerful an invasion of the realm of conscience as we have seen.'—*New York Times*

† Director William A. Seiter was replaced when the film was half complete; this caused nearly one million dollars to be wasted.

AAN: best picture; Henry Koster; Hugo Friedhofer

The Bitch
GB 1979 94m colour

A woman of much influence in London's underworld has a temporary liaison with a young gangster wanted by the Mafia.
Intolerable sexed-up sequel to *The Stud*, hard on both eyes and ears. Joan Collins, Kenneth Haigh, Michael Coby, Ian Hendry, Carolyn Seymour, Sue Lloyd, Mark Burns. Written and directed by Gerry O'Hara; for Brent Walker. 'Appropriately enough for a film whose sole rationale seems to be its chic consumerist decoration (and of course its disco soundtrack), *The Bitch* ruthlessly pares away any other elements of interest.'—*Richard Combs, MFB.*

Bite the Bullet*
US 1975 131m Metrocolor Panavision
Columbia / Persky–Bright / Vista (Richard Brooks)

Several cowboys compete in a 700-mile endurance horse race.
Episodic adventure story with too much muddled chat and a very thin connecting story line; good to look at, though.

wd Richard Brooks *ph* Harry Stradling *m* Alex North

Gene Hackman, Candice Bergen, James Coburn, Ben Johnson, Ian Bannen, Jan-Michael Vincent, Paul Stewart

AAN: Alex North

'I want something good to happen to me before I die!'

Bitter Harvest
GB 1963 96m Eastmancolor
Rank / Independent Artists (Albert Fennell)

An innocent Welsh girl comes to London, is deflowered, and sets off in search of wealth and luxury at any price.
Naive sixties version of the road to ruin, quite well done if you like that kind of thing.

w Ted Willis *d* Peter Graham Scott *ph* Ernest Steward *m* Laurie Johnson

Janet Munro, John Stride, Anne Cunningham, Alan Badel, Thora Hird, Vanda Godsell, Terence Alexander

Bitter Rice*
Italy 1949 108m bw
Lux Films
original title: *Riso Amaro*

In the rice fields of the Po valley, a thief on the run meets a girl who tries to steal his loot.
Well-made exploitation melodrama which made a star of the well-endowed Mangano but is not otherwise more memorable than its innumerable American counterparts.

w Carlo Lizzani, Carlo Musso, Gianni Puccini, Corrado Alvaro, Ivo Perillo, Giuseppe de Santis *d* Giuseppe de Santis *ph* Otello Martelli *m* Goffredo Petrassi

Silvana Mangano, Raf Vallone, Doris Dowling, Vittorio Gassman

AAN: original story

Bitter Springs*
GB 1950 89m bw
Ealing (Leslie Norman)

A pioneer family in Australia buys a patch of ground but has trouble with aborigines.
Thinnest of the Ealing attempts to make movies down under, suffering from a lack of pace and sharpness as well as obvious studio settings.

w Monja Danischewsky, W. P. Lipscomb *d* Ralph Smart *ph* George Heath *m* Vaughan Williams

Chips Rafferty, Tommy Trinder, Gordon Jackson, Jean Blue, Charles Tingwell

Bitter Sweet
GB 1933 93m bw
British and Dominion (Herbert Wilcox)

In 1875 Vienna, a violinist marries a girl dancer and is later killed by a gambler.
Rather feeble filming of Noel Coward's operetta: it pleased a lot of people at the time.

w Lydia Hayward, Herbert Wilcox, Monckton Hoffe *d* Herbert Wilcox *ph* F. A. Young

Anna Neagle, Fernand Gravet, Ivy St Helier, Miles Mander, Esmé Percy, Hugh Williams, Pat Paterson, Kay Hammond

Bitter Sweet
US 1940 94m Technicolor
MGM (Victor Saville)

Remake of the above, retailored for unsuitable leads and with the story and music unattractively rearranged.

w Lesser Samuels, *operetta* Noel Coward *d* W. S. Van Dyke II *ph* Oliver T. Marsh, Allen Davey

Jeanette Macdonald, Nelson Eddy, George Sanders, Felix Bressart, Ian Hunter, Fay Holden, Sig Rumann, Herman Bing, Curt Bois

'It's now chiefly eye-and-ear entertainment, with the original sentimental charm and romance missing.'—*Variety*

AAN: Oliver T. Marsh, Allen Davey

The Bitter Tea of General Yen**
US 1932 89m bw
Columbia (Walter Wanger)

An American lady missionary in Shanghai is captured by a Chinese warlord and falls in love with him.
Arty miscegenation story which bids fair to become a cult film and certainly has a number of interesting sequences.

w Edward Paramore, *story* Grace Zaring Stone *d Frank Capra* *ph* Joseph Walker *m* W. Frank Harling

Barbara Stanwyck, Nils Asther, Toshia Mori, Walter Connolly, Gavin Gordon, Lucien Littlefield

'It is doubtful whether this picture can make the grade without support . . . photographic advantages cannot overcome the queer story.'—*Variety*

† The film chosen to open Radio City Music Hall.

The Bitter Tears of Petra Von Kant
West Germany 1975 124m colour

Lesbian jealousies in the fashion world. Interesting but exhausting hothouse confection, no more likeable than the Hollywood kind for being more intelligent about its perversions. Margit Carstensen, Irm Hermann, Hanna Schygull. Written and directed by Rainer Werner Fassbinder for his own company. 'Dazzling in the brittle brilliance of its execution, the precision of its structure and movement, the total hermetic self-containment of the little world it creates.'—*David Robinson, The Times*.

Bitter Victory
US / France 1957 100m bw Cinemascope
Columbia / Transcontinental / Robert Laffont

Two officers sent on a document raid in Libya during World War II become poor soldiers because one suspects the other of an affair with his wife.
Glum desert melodrama, turgidly scripted and boringly made.

w René Hardy, Nicholas Ray, Gavin Lambert, *novel* Bitter Victory by René Hardy *d* Nicholas Ray *ph* Michel Kelber *m* Maurice Le Roux

Richard Burton, Curt Jurgens, Ruth Roman, Raymond Pellegrin, Anthony Bushell, Andrew Crawford, Nigel Green, Christopher Lee

Bittersweet Love
US 1976 92m colour

Newlyweds discover that they both had the same father. Old-fashioned family shocker which needed a lot more zip if it was going to shock anybody. Lana Turner, Robert Alda, Celeste Holm, Robert Lansing, Scott Hylands, Denise DeMirjian. Written by Adrian Morrall and D. A. Kellogg; directed by David Miller; for Zappala-Slott. 'Performances and settings are all very high class. I mean, when you have all that money and those great surroundings you can still suffer, but you do have multiple choices.'—*Archer Winsten, New York Post.*

Black and White in Colour*
France / Switzerland / Ivory Coast 1976 100m Eastmancolor
Reggance / SFP / Artco / Société Ivorienne de Production (Arthur Cohn, Jacques Perrin, Giorgio Silvagni)
original title: *La Victoire en Chantant*

In French West Africa in 1915, easy-going colonials learn of the outbreak of war and prepare to attack a neighbouring German garrison.
Curious mixture of Ealing-style comedy and mordant satire; interesting without being wholly engaging.

w Georges Conchon, Jean-Jacques Annaud *d* Jean-Jacques Annaud *ph* Claude Agostini, Eduardo Serra, Nanamoudou Magassouda *m* Pierre Bachelet, Mat Camison

Jean Carmet, Jacques Dufilho, Catherine Rouvel, Jacques Spiesser, Dora Doll

AA: best foreign film

Black Angel*
US 1946 80m bw
U-I (Roy William Neill, Tom McKnight)

A drunk sets out to find the murderer of his wife, and finds it was himself.
Stylish but empty version of a tired theme, interesting for performances and atmosphere.

w Roy Chanslor, *novel* William Irish *d* Roy William Neill *ph* Paul Ivano *m* Frank Skinner

Dan Duryea, Peter Lorre, Broderick Crawford, June Vincent, Wallace Ford, Hobart Cavanaugh, Constance Dowling

Black Arrow
US 1944 bw serial: 15 eps

A young Indian chief turns out to be the son of a white man. Rather tedious chapter play with few of the regular western excitements. Robert Scott, Adele Jergens, Robert Williams, Charles Middleton. Directed by B. Reeves Eason; for Columbia.

The Black Arrow
US 1948 76m bw
Columbia
GB title: *The Black Arrow Strikes*

During the Wars of the Roses, an English knight seeks the murderer of his father.
Pennypinching swashbuckler which contrives to entertain despite total disregard of probability.

w Richard Schayer, David P. Sheppard, Thomas Seller, *novel* R. L. Stevenson *d* Gordon Douglas *ph* Charles Lawton Jnr

Louis Hayward, Janet Blair, George Macready, Edgar Buchanan, Paul Cavanaugh

Black Bart
US 1948 80m Technicolor
U-I (Leonard Goldstein)
GB title: *Black Bart, Highwayman*

Lola Montez, on an American tour, falls for an American bandit.
Acceptable western programmer with historical trimmings and some evidence of tongue-in-cheek attitudes.

w Luci Ward, Jack Natteford, William Bowers *d* George Sherman *ph* Irving Glassberg *m* Frank Skinner

Yvonne de Carlo, Dan Duryea, Jeffrey Lynn, Percy Kilbride, Lloyd Gough, Frank Lovejoy, John McIntire, Don Beddoe

Black Beauty
US 1946 74m bw
(TCF) Edward L. Alperson

In Victorian England, a girl searches for her lost colt.
Stilted children's film with little relation to the book.

w Lillie Hayward, Agnes Christie Johnson, *novel* Anna Sewell *d* Max Nosseck *ph* J. Roy Hunt *m* Dmitri Tiomkin

Mona Freeman, Richard Denning, Evelyn Ankers, J. M. Kerrigan, Terry Kilburn

Black Beauty*
GB 1971 106m colour
Tigon / Chilton (Tony Tenser)

A luckless horse passes from hand to hand but is finally restored to its original young master and has a happy retirement.
Pleasant, episodic animal story which stays pretty close to the book. A shade yawn-inducing for adults, but fine for children.

w Wolf Mankowitz, *novel* Anna Sewell *d* James Hill *ph* Chris Menges *m* Lionel Bart, John Cameron

Mark Lester, Walter Slezak, Peter Lee Lawrence, Patrick Mower, John Nettleton, Maria Rohm

The Black Bird
US 1975 98m colour
Columbia / Rastar (Michael Levee, Lou Lombardo)

Sam Spade's son finds himself beset by crooks still after the Maltese falcon.
Dismal, witless, boring parody of a classic crime film, with none of the humour of the original.

wd David Giler *ph* Philip Lathrop *m* Jerry Fielding

George Segal, Stéphane Audran, *Lee Patrick*, Elisha Cook Jnr, Lionel Stander, John Abbott, Signe Hasso, Felix Silla

'A dumb comedy with an insecure tone and some good ideas mixed up with some terrible ones.'—*Variety*

'It doesn't work because it has nothing to say.'—*Michael Billington, Illustrated London News*

The Black Book*
US 1949 88m bw
Eagle–Lion
GB title: *Reign of Terror*

A member of a secret organization which plans to replace Robespierre with a moderate goes undercover with the French Revolutionaries.
Moderate period melodrama with an attractive though artificial look.

w Philip Yordan, Aeneas Mackenzie *d* Anthony Mann *ph* John Alton *m* Sol Kaplan

Robert Cummings, Arlene Dahl, Richard Basehart, Richard Hart, Arnold Moss

The Black Camel
US 1931 67m bw

Charlie Chan solves the murder of a film starlet in Honolulu. Second in the Oland series (see under Charlie Chan), not easy to see these days. Warner Oland, Dorothy Revier, Bela Lugosi, Sally Eilers, Victor Varconi, Robert Young. Written by Barry Conners, Philip Klein; directed by Hamilton McFadden; for Fox.

The Black Castle
US 1952 80m bw
Universal-International (William Alland)

An 18th-century knight avenges the deaths of two friends who have attended a hunting party at the castle of a sadistic Viennese count.
A variation on *The Most Dangerous Game*, and not a good one: the pace is far too plodding and the atmosphere unpleasant.

w Jerry Sackheim *d* Nathan Juran *ph* Irving Glassberg *md* Joseph Gershenson *m* Hans Salter

Richard Greene, Stephen McNally, Boris Karloff, Lon Chaney Jnr, Paula Corday, John Hoyt, Michael Pate

'It's tremonstrous! The absolute apex of the super-shivery!'

The Black Cat*
US 1934 65m bw
Universal (Carl Laemmle Jnr)
GB title: *House of Doom*

A revengeful doctor seeks out the Austrian architect and devil-worshipper who betrayed his country in World War I.
Absurd and dense farrago set in a modernistic but crumbling castle which is eventually blown to bits just as its owner is skinned alive.
Mostly rather dull despite the extraordinary plot, but the thing has moments of style, a delightful cod devil worship sequence (especially for audiences with a rudimentary knowledge of Latin) and nothing at all to do with the title or Edgar Allan Poe.

w Peter Ruric *d* Edgar G. Ulmer *ph John Mescall* *m* Heinz Roemheld *ad* Charles D. Hall

Boris Karloff, *Bela Lugosi*, David Manners, Jacqueline Wells, Egon Brecher

'On the counts of story, novelty, thrills and distinction, the picture is sub-normal.'—*Variety*

'A truly bizarre concoction of mayhem, necrophilia, sadism and satanism.'—*Clive Hirschhorn, 1980s*

The Black Cat*
US 1941 70m bw
Universal (Burt Kelly)

Murder follows the summoning of the family to the spooky house of a cat-loving recluse.
Disappointing mystery which squanders a splendid cast on a script full of non-sequiturs and makes heavy weather of its light relief.

w Robert Lees, Fred Rinaldo, Eric Taylor, Robert Neville *d* Albert S. Rogell *ph* Stanley Cortez

Basil Rathbone, Gladys Cooper, Broderick Crawford, Hugh Herbert, Gale Sondergaard, Anne Gwynne, Alan Ladd, Cecilia Loftus, Bela Lugosi

HUGH HERBERT (reading inscription): 'That house is doubly blest, Which to our feline friends gives rest.'
BRODERICK CRAWFORD (not impressed): 'Her hats are full of bats, For spending all her dough on cats.'

The Black Cauldron*
US 1985 80m Technicolor
Walt Disney Productions (Joe Hale)

A medieval hero combats magic swords, wicked witches and skeletal tyrants.
Assured but somehow quite forgettable Disney cartoon feature.

w David Jonas, Vance Gerry, Ted Berman, Richard Rich, Al Wilson, Roy Morita, Peter Young, Art Stevens, Joe Hale, from The Chronicles of Prydain by Lloyd Alexander *d* Ted Berman, Richard Rich *key animator* Walt Stanchfield *m* Elmer Bernstein

voices include Freddie Jones, Nigel Hawthorne, John Hurt, John Huston, John Byner, Arthur Malet

† Production allegedly took ten years and cost 25 million dollars

'If this doesn't make your skin crawl . . . it's on too tight!'

Black Christmas
Canada 1974 97m Technicolor
aka: *Silent Night, Evil Night*

Girls in a college sorority house are attacked by a lurking psychopath. Moderate suspense chiller. Olivia Hussey, Keir Dullea, Margot Kidder, Andre Martin, John Saxon, Marian Waldman, Art Hindle. Written by Roy Moore; directed by Robert Clark; for Film Funding / Vision IV.

The Black Coin
US 1936 bw serial: 15 eps

American secret agents try to intercept papers which hold the key to a smuggling ring. Archetypal serial hokum during which the 'McGuffin' is quickly forgotten. Dave O'Brien, Ralph Graves, Ruth Mix, Matthew Betz, Snub Pollard, Bryant Washburn. Directed by Albert Herman; for Weiss-Mintz.

Black Eyes
GB 1939 72m bw

A Moscow head waiter has raised his daughter to believe he's a big wheel in the business world. Well-made comedy drama from a French original. Otto Kruger, Mary Maguire, Walter Rilla, John Wood. Written by Dudley Leslie (from the French original); directed by Herbert Brenon; for Associated British.

Black Eyes**
Italy 1987 117m colour

At the turn of the century, an aged Italian recounts his lapses. Highly amusing star vehicle based on stories by Chekhov. *Marcello Mastroianni*, Silvana Mangano, Marthe Keller, Elena Sofonova. Written by Nikita Mikhalkov, Alexander Adabachian, Suso Cecchi d'Amico; directed by *Nikita Mikhalkov*; for Excelsior/RAI. (GB title: *Dark Eyes*.) 'The film effortlessly swings from farce to tenderness, love to betrayal, exuberance to poignancy without missing a beat.'—*Daily Variety*. AAN: Marcello Mastroianni.

Black Fox
US 1962 89m bw

Slick documentary on the rise of Hitler, using the expected newsreels reinforced not too artfully by references to art and to the medieval folk tale of Reynard the Fox. Narrated by Marlene Dietrich. Written and directed by Louis Clyde Stoumen; for Jack Le Vien. (AA 1963; best documentary.)

Black Friday*
US 1940 70m bw
Universal (Burt Kelly)

After an accident, a college professor is given a gangster's brain, and the surgeon encourages him to believe that he is the gangster so as to find hidden loot.
Plot-packed melodrama which fails to provide the chills suggested by the cast, but passes the time agreeably enough.

w Curt Siodmak, Eric Taylor *d* Arthur Lubin *ph* Woody Bredell *m* Hans Salter

Boris Karloff, Bela Lugosi, *Stanley Ridges*, Anne Nagel, Anne Gwynne, Virginia Brissac, Paul Fix

† Lugosi was originally cast as the professor, but proved wrong for the part; Stanley Ridges replaced him and walked off with the movie.

Black Fury*
US 1935 95m bw
Warner (Robert Lord)

A coal miner comes up against union problems, unsafe conditions and corruption. Typical Warner social drama, good for its time but now very obvious.

w Abem Finkel, Carl Erickson, *play* Bohunk by Harry R. Irving *d* Michael Curtiz *ph* Byron Haskin *md* Leo Forbstein

Paul Muni, Karen Morley, William Gargan, Barton MacLane, John Qualen, J. Carrol Naish, Vince Barnett, Tully Marshall, Henry O'Neill

'Basic box office, packed with promotional potentialities.'—*Variety*

'The most powerful strike picture that has yet been made, and I am aware of the better-known Soviet jobs in the field.'—*Otis Ferguson*

Black Gold
US 1947 90m Cinecolor

An Indian couple on the reservation adopt a Chinese boy who becomes a famous jockey. Tears all round in this enterprising if rather muddled B picture with a social conscience. Anthony Quinn, Katherine de Mille, Elyse Knox, Kane Richmond, Ducky Louie, Raymond Hatton, Thurston Hall, Alan Bridge. Written by Agnes Christine Johnson from a story by Caryl Coleman; directed by Phil Karlson; for Allied Artists.

Black Gold
US 1963 98m bw

Novice wildcatter makes it rich in Oklahoma despite villains on every side. Absolutely predictable actioner which unspools like a remake even if it isn't. Philip Carey, Diane McBain, Claude Akins, Iron Eyes Cody, James Best. Written by Bob and Wanda Duncan; directed by Leslie H. Martinson; for Warner.

Black Hand*
US 1949 92m bw
MGM (William H. Wright)

In New York at the turn of the century, an Italian boy avenges his father's death at the hands of the Mafia.
Neatly produced, studio-set melodrama, unusual in subject but very stereotyped and artificial in treatment.

w Luther Davis *d* Richard Thorpe *ph* Paul C. Vogel *m* Alberto Colombo

Gene Kelly, J. Carrol Naish, Teresa Celli, Marc Lawrence, Frank Puglia, Barry Kelley

'A journey that begins where everything ends!'

The Black Hole*
US 1979 98m Technicolor Technovision
Walt Disney (Ron Miller)

A research team in space is welcomed aboard a mysterious survey ship poised on the edge of a black hole.
The special effects are superb, though achieved through a general gloom which is barely acceptable. But the story is an ill-worked-out remake of *Twenty Thousand Leagues Under the Sea*, the characterization is ridiculously inept, and the final disclosure that black holes are doorways to hell sends one home rather bemused.

w Jeb Rosebrook, Gerry Day *d* Gary Nelson *ph* Frank Phillips *pd Peter Ellenshaw* *m* John Barry

Maximilian Schell, Robert Forster, Anthony Perkins, Joseph Bottoms, Yvette Mimieux, Ernest Borgnine

'As pastiche, it sounds promising; as drama, encumbered with references to Cicero and Goethe, it is merely tedious.'—*John Halford, MFB*

'Rated PG, but the only danger to children is that it may make them think that outer space is not much fun any more.'—*New Yorker*

Black Horse Canyon
US 1954 81m Technicolor

Two cowpunchers help a lady rancher to capture and train a wild black stallion. Slight but agreeable outdoor programmer. Joel McCrea, Mari Blanchard, Race Gentry, Murvyn Vye, Irving Bacon. Written by Geoffrey Homes; directed by Jesse Hibbs; for Universal-International.

Black Jack
GB 1979 110m colour

In 1750 Yorkshire, a rascally French sailor recovers from a hanging and has adventures on the road with a young apprentice. The purpose of this costume adventure, from these creators, is obscure, but the execution of it is muddled and amateurish. Jean Franval, Stephen Hirst, Louise Cooper. From the novel by Leon Garfield; directed by Kenneth Loach; for Tony Garnett / Kestrel. 'Ploddingly unpersuasive. Not only narrative clarity but simple credibility is lacking.'—*Tim Pulleine, MFB*

Black Joy*
GB 1977 109m Eastmancolor
Winkast / West One (Elliott Kastner, Martin Campbell)

A Guyanan immigrant in Brixton is tricked by a Jamaican good-for-nothing but later goes into partnership with him and learns to stand up for his rights.
Vivid but eventually wearying ethnic comedy-melodrama.

w Anthony Simmons, Jamal Ali, from the latter's play Dark Days and Light Nights *d* Anthony Simmons *ph* Philip Meheux *md* Lou Reizner from reggae songs

Norman Beaton, Trevor Thomas, Floella Benjamin, Dawn Hope

'I wanted to show the reality of life in an immigrant area, angry and frustrated like so many parts of Britain—but full of hope and humour.'—*Anthony Simmons*

The Black Knight
GB 1954 85m Technicolor
Warwick (Irving Allen, Albert R. Broccoli)

A humble swordmaker reveals a traitor to King Arthur.
Hilarious travesty of English historical legend, meant seriously for Anglo-American consumption. Shades of *Zorro, Babes in the Wood* and *1066 and All That.*

w Alec Coppel *d* Tay Garnett *ph* John Wilcox *m* John Addison

Alan Ladd, Peter Cushing, Patricia Medina, Harry Andrews, André Morell, Anthony Bushell, Patrick Troughton, Laurence Naismith, John Laurie

'Alan Ladd galahads with wild west *gentillesse* in this Technicolored rampage through British history.'—*MFB*

'Unmasking America's brotherhood of butchery!'
Black Legion**
US 1936 83m bw
Warner (Robert Lord)

A factory worker becomes involved with the Ku Klux Klan.
Social melodrama typical of its studio, and good of its kind.

w Robert Lord, Abem Finkel, William Wister Haines *d* Archie Mayo *ph* George Barnes

Humphrey Bogart, Erin O'Brien Moore, Dick Foran, Ann Sheridan, Robert Barrat, John Litel, Charles Halton

'Powerful story of the horror spread by the hooded order; Surefire man's picture.'—*Variety*

'An honest job of film work, and one of the most direct social pieces released from Hollywood.'—*Otis Ferguson*

AAN: Robert Lord (original story)

Black Limelight*
GB 1938 70m bw
ABPC (Walter C. Mycroft)

The wife of a man convicted of killing his mistress proves that a 'moon murderer' did it.
Naive but effective little chiller.

w Dudley Leslie, Walter Summers, *play* Gordon Sherry *d* Paul Stein *ph* Claude Friese-Greene

Raymond Massey, Joan Marion, Walter Hudd, Henry Oscar, Coral Browne

'The biggest picture in ten years! The greatest cavalcade of intrigue, spectacle, adventure and excitement you'll ever see on the screen'
Black Magic*
US 1949 105m bw
Edward Small (Gregory Ratoff)

Cagliostro the magician becomes involved in a plot to supply a double for Marie Antoinette.
Deliriously complicated historical romp which unfortunately suffers from a stolid script and production which kill all the flights of fancy.

w Charles Bennett *d* Gregory Ratoff *ph* Ubaldo Arata, Anchise Brizzi *m* Paul Sawtell

Orson Welles, Nancy Guild, Akim Tamiroff, Valentina Cortese, Margot Grahame, Charles Goldner, Frank Latimore, Stephen Bekassy

The Black Marble
US 1980 113m De Luxe
Avco / Frank Capra Jnr

A drunken cop redeems himself when teamed with a policewoman who is less cynical about the work.
Curious cop show with emphasis on child murders and dog torturing. An unhappy film with a garbled message.

w Joseph Wambaugh, from his novel *d* Harold Becker *ph* Owen Roizman *m* Maurice Jarre

Robert Foxworth, Paula Prentiss, Harry Dean Stanton, Barbara Babcock, John Hancock

Black Market Babies
US 1946 71m bw

An ex-medico runs a baby farm for illegitimate offspring. Routine exploitationer with no surprises. Ralph Morgan, Kane Richmond, Teala Loring, George Meeker. Written by George Morris, George W. Sayre; directed by William Beaudine; for Jeffrey Bernerd / Monogram. 'Should bring fair returns on double bills.'—*Variety*

Black Moon Rising
US 1985 100m CFI colour

An adventurer in the pay of the US government hides much-wanted evidence in the back of a super-high-powered car. Absurd, almost impenetrable action shenanigans with more than enough violent action. Tommy Lee Jones, Linda Hamilton, Robert Vaughn, Richard Jaeckel, Keenan Wynn. Written by John Carpenter, Desmond Nakano, William Gray; directed by Harley Cokliss; for Joel B. Michaels and Douglas Curtiss / New World.

Black Narcissus***
GB 1946 100m Technicolor
GFD / The Archers (Michael Powell, Emeric Pressburger)

Anglo-Catholic nuns in the Himalayas have trouble with climate, morale, and one of their number who goes mad of sex frustration.
An unlikely theme produces one of the cinema's most beautiful films, a visual and emotional stunner despite some narrative uncertainty.

wd Michael Powell, Emeric Pressburger, *novel* Rumer Godden *ph Jack Cardiff* *m* Brian Easdale

Deborah Kerr, David Farrar, Sabu, Jean Simmons, Kathleen Byron, Flora Robson, Esmond Knight, Jenny Laird, May Hallatt, Judith Furse

AA: Jack Cardiff

Black on White*
Finland 1967 95m Eastmancolor
Jorn Donner / FJ Film
Original title: *Mustaa Valkoisella.*

A successful young executive falls in love with a girl hitch-hiker, but when his wife leaves him the girl is no longer interested.
Showy romantic melodrama which tries to make rather too much of a slender theme.

wd Jorn Donner *ph* Esko Nevaleinen *m* George Riedel

Jorn Donner, Kristina Halkola, Liisamaija Laaksonen

The Black Orchid*
US 1958 95m bw Vistavision
Paramount (Carlo Ponti, Marcello Girosi)

A widower incurs hostility from his daughter when he plans to marry a gangster's widow.
Rather solemn New York / Italian romantic melodrama, with much gesticulation all round.

w Joseph Stefano *d* Martin Ritt *ph* Robert Burks *m* Alessandro Cicognini

Sophia Loren, Anthony Quinn, Ina Balin, Jimmy Baird, Mark Richman

Black Orpheus*
France / Italy / Brazil 1958 106m Eastmancolor Cinemascope
Dispatfilm / Gemma / Tupan (Sacha Gordine)
original title: *Orfeu Negro*

Against a background of the Rio carnival, a black tram driver accidentally kills his girl friend, and after seeking her in the nether regions kills himself to be with her.
Rather irritating and noisy attempt to update a legend, without showing very much reason for doing so.

w Vinitius de Moraes *d* Marcel Camus *ph* Jean Bourgoin *m* Luis Bonfa, Antonio Carlos Jobim

Breno Mello, Marpessa Dawn, Ademar da Silva, Lourdes de Oliviera

AA: best foreign film

The Black Panther
GB 1977 98m Technicolor

A small-time post office robber becomes a kidnapper and murderer. Tasteless re-enactment of a case which made headlines in 1975. Donald Sumpter, Debbie Farrington, Marjorie Yates, David Swift. Written by Michael Armstrong; directed and produced by Ian Merrick; for Impics.

The Black Parachute
US 1944 65m bw

An American soldier parachutes into a mythical European kingdom to free its king from the Nazis. Thick-ear propaganda fare; it has its moments. Larry Parks, John Carradine, Osa Massen, Jeanne Bates, Jonathan Hale. Written by Clarence Upson Young; directed by Lew Landers; for Jack Fier / Columbia.

Black Patch
US 1957 84m bw

A marshal is wrongly suspected of murder. Dour, dark western, occasionally worth looking at. George Montgomery, Diane Brewster, Tom Pittman, Leo Gordon. Written and directed by Allen H. Miner; for Montgomery / Warner.

The Black Pirate***
US 1926 76m approx (24 fps)
Technicolor silent
Douglas Fairbanks

A shipwrecked mariner swears revenge on the pirates who blew up his father's ship.
Cheerful swashbuckler with the star in top form.

w Douglas Fairbanks, Jack Cunningham *d* Albert Parker *ph Henry Sharp* *ad* Oscar Borg, Dwight Franklin

Douglas Fairbanks, Billie Dove, Donald Crisp, Sam de Grasse

The Black Room*
US 1935 70m bw
Columbia

A nobleman's power is claimed by his evil twin brother.
Rather splendid old barnstormer with touches of horror, a neatly produced star vehicle.

w Henry Myers, from the writings of Arthur Strawn *d Roy William Neill* *ph* Al Siegler

Boris Karloff, Marian Marsh, Katherine de Mille, Thurston Hall

'Eerie affair, dull and destined for negative results. Its best qualities are scenic investiture and photography, which do not excite dollars to elope from people's pokes.'—*Variety*

'Mrs Radcliffe would not have been ashamed of this wild and exciting film, of the bones in the oubliette, the scene at the altar when the dog leaps and the paralysed arm comes to life in self-defence, of the Count's wild drive back to the castle, of the rearing horses, the rocketing coach, the strange valley of rocks with its leaning cross and neglected Christ, the graveyard with its owls and ivy.'—*Graham Greene*

The Black Rose*
GB 1950 120m Technicolor
TCF (Louis D. Lighton)

A 13th-century English scholar journeys to the land of the Mongols, and after many adventures returns to a knighthood for his scientific discoveries.
Portentous and slow-moving adventure with good things along the way.

w Talbot Jennings, *novel* Thomas B. Costain *d* Henry Hathaway *ph Jack Cardiff* *m* Richard Addinsell *ad* Paul Sheriff

Tyrone Power, Orson Welles, Cecile Aubry, Jack Hawkins, Finlay Currie, Henry Oscar, Michael Rennie

Black Sabbath
Italy 1963 99m Pathecolor

Three supernatural stories introduced by Boris Karloff. Tolerable horror portmanteau. *The Drop of Water* (Jacqueline Pierreux); *The Telephone* (Michele Mercier); *The Wurdelak* (Boris Karloff, Mark Damon). From stories by Anton Chekhov, Howard Snyder, Leo Tolstoy; directed by Mario Bava; for American International.

'The management reserves the right to put up the lights any time the audience becomes too emotionally disturbed. We urge you not to panic or bolt from your seats.'

The Black Scorpion
US 1957 88m bw
Warner (Frank Melford, Jack Dietz)

Volcanic explosions uncover a nest of prehistoric giant scorpions near a Mexican village.
Apart from a genuinely terrifying sequence in the scorpion's lair, this is a poor monster movie in which excessively dark photography seems intended to cover up very variable trick work.

w David Duncan, Robert Bless *d* Edward Ludwig *ph* Lionel Lindon *m* Paul Sawtell *sp* Willis O'Brien

Richard Denning, Mara Corday, Carlos Rivas, Mario Navarro

Black Sheep
US 1935 70m bw

A high-class gambler finds his forgotten son on a transatlantic liner. Mouldy compromise of sophistication and soul-searching. Edmund Lowe, Claire Trevor, Tom Brown, Eugene Pallette, Herbert Mundin, Adrienne Ames. Written and directed by Allan Dwan; for Fox. 'It doesn't rate as a solo performer.'—*Variety*

The Black Sheep of Whitehall*
GB 1941 80m bw
Ealing (S. C. Balcon)

An incompetent teacher is mistaken for an economics expert and saves the real expert from spies who run a nursing home.
Pretty good wartime star comedy, with a succession of briskly timed gags.

w Angus Macphail, John Dighton *d* Basil Dearden, Will Hay *ph* Gunther Krampf

Will Hay, John Mills, Basil Sydney, Frank Cellier, Felix Aylmer

The Black Shield of Falworth*
US 1954 99m Technicolor
Cinemascope
U-I (Robert Arthur, Melville Tucker)

The film in which Tony Curtis says 'Yonda lies the castle of my fodda' (or something like it) is an amiable romp which alternates between comic strip dialogue and a surprisingly convincing sense of medieval custom. The training scenes are as sharp as the romantic asides are pallid.

w Oscar Brodney, *novel* Men of Iron by Howard Pyle *d* Rudolph Maté *ph* Irving Glassberg *m* Herman Stein, Hans Salter

Tony Curtis, Janet Leigh, David Farrar, Barbara Rush, Herbert Marshall, Rhys Williams, Dan O'Herlihy, Torin Thatcher

'A straightforward piece of hokum with no pretensions, and spoken in a variety of accents that only Hollywood could muster.'—*John Gillett*

'A horror horde of monster mutants walk the earth!'

The Black Sleep
US 1956 81m bw
UA / Bel Air (Howard W. Koch)

A Victorian brain surgeon experiments on human beings and produces freaks who eventually turn on him.
Gruesome and humourless horror film notable only for its gallery of wasted talent.

w John C. Higgins *d* Reginald Le Borg *ph* Gordon Avil *m* Les Baxter

Basil Rathbone, Bela Lugosi, Lon Chaney Jnr, John Carradine, Akim Tamiroff, Tor Johnson, Herbert Rudley, Patricia Blake

The Black Stallion*
US 1979 117m Technicolor
UA / Omni Zoetrope (Francis Coppola)

After a 1946 shipwreck, a boy and a stallion are cast up on the African shore; many years later, he rides the horse to victory at Santa Anita.
1980 seems a bit late for boy-and-horse pictures, but this one is so beautifully directed and photographed, if drastically overlong, that most adults thought their children should see it.

w Melissa Mathison, Jeanne Rosenberg, William D. Witliff, *novel* Walter Farley *d Carroll Ballard* *ph Caleb Deschanel* *m* Carmine Coppola

Kelly Reno, Mickey Rooney, Teri Garr, Clarence Muse, Hoyt Axton

'A perfect gem—the beautiful craftsmanship alone makes it a joy to behold.'—*Variety*

AAN: Mickey Rooney

The Black Stallion Returns
US 1983 93m Technicolor

Rather desperate sequel in which a teenager loses his horse in Morocco and gets him back after various daredevil adventures. Tame, predictable and boring. Kelly Reno, Ferdy Mayne, Woody Strode, Vincent Spano, Allen Goorwitz. Written by Richard Kletter and Jerome Kass; directed by Robert Dalva; for Coppola / Zoetrope / MGM-UA. 'Well-intentioned, but overall it doesn't look like a winner.'—*Variety*

'The undead demons of hell terrorize the world!'

Black Sunday*
Italy 1960 83m bw

A beautiful witch is put to death in an iron maiden but rises from the dead to wreak vengeance. Stylish horror comic which started the Italian cult for such things. Barbara Steele, John Richardson, Ivo Garrani. From a story by Gogol; written and directed by Mario Bava; for Galatra / Jolly.

(aka: *Mask of the Demon*.)

Black Sunday*
US 1977 143m Movielab Panavision
Paramount (Robert Evans)

The Black September movement threatens a football game to be held in Miami's Superbowl.

Spectacular, heavily detailed, but somehow unexciting disaster melodrama.

w Ernest Lehman, Kenneth Ross, Ivan Moffat, *novel* Thomas Harris *d* John Frankenheimer *ph* John A. Alonzo *m* John Williams

Robert Shaw, Marthe Keller, Bruce Dern, Fritz Weaver, Steven Keats, Bekim Fehmiu, Michael V. Gazzo, William Daniels, Walter Gotell

'There's only one real motivation for this movie, and that's the desire to make money. Why else would anyone make an ostensibly anti-terrorist film that in actuality could end up promoting terrorism?'—*Frank Rich, New York Post*

The Black Swan***
US 1942 85m Technicolor
TCF (Robert Bassler)

Morgan the pirate is made governor of Jamaica and enlists the help of his old friends to rid the Caribbean of buccaneers.
Rousing adventure story with comic asides: just what action hokum always aimed to be, with a spirited gallery of heroes and villains and an entertaining narrative taken at a spanking pace.

w Ben Hecht, Seton I. Miller, novel Rafael Sabatini *d Henry King ph Leon Shamroy* *m* Alfred Newman

Tyrone Power, Maureen O'Hara, *Laird Cregar, Thomas Mitchell, George Sanders*, Anthony Quinn, George Zucco, Edward Ashley

'Performed by actors as though to the hokum born.'—*Time*

'Battles between sailing ships, realistic sword fights, assaults, abductions, tortures and love making.'—*CEA Report*

AA: Leon Shamroy
AAN: Alfred Newman

The Black Tent
GB 1956 93m Technicolor Vistavision
Rank / William MacQuitty

During a Libyan battle a wounded army captain is cared for by Arabs and marries the sheik's daughter. Ten years later, after his death, his son elects to live with the tribe.
Pleasantly shot but otherwise dull, formless and interminable romantic drama, all very stiff upper lip.

w Robin Maugham, Bryan Forbes *d* Brian Desmond Hurst *ph Desmond Dickinson* *m* William Alwyn

Anthony Steel, Donald Sinden, *André Morell*, Anna Maria Sandri, Ralph Truman, Donald Pleasence, Anthony Bushell, Michael Craig

'What was the deadly power that desired and devoured the women of Fordyke?'

The Black Torment*
GB 1964 85m Eastmancolor
Compton-Tekli (Robert Hartford-Davis)

The second wife of an 18th-century baronet investigates the hauntings which have followed the apparent suicide of his first.

BLACK WIDOW (1954). A glossy gathering of suspects in a glamorous 20th Century-Fox setting. George Raft (on the side of the law for once) would like to know whodunnit.

Agreeably unpretentious period ghost story (with a rational explanation). Not exactly good, but better than one might expect.

w Donald and Derek Ford *d* Robert Hartford-Davis *ph* Peter Newbrook *m* Robert Richards

John Turner, Heather Sears, Ann Lynn, Joseph Tomelty, Peter Arne, Raymond Huntley

Black Tuesday*
US 1954 80m bw
UA / Leonard Goldstein (Robert Goldstein)

A killer escapes from Death Row and hides out with hostages in a disused warehouse.
Starkly melodramatic gangster vehicle with the star up to his oldest tricks. Good tension, but generally rather unpleasant.

w Sydney Boehm *d* Hugo Fregonese *ph* Stanley Cortez *m* Paul Dunlap

Edward G. Robinson, Jean Parker, Peter Graves, Milburn Stone, Warren Stevens, Jack Kelly, James Bell

The Black Widow
US 1947 bw serial: 13 eps

An Asian king sends his daughter to America to steal an atomic rocket engine. Lively hokum with a lady villain for a change. Bruce Edwards, Virginia Lindley, Carol Forman, Anthony Warde, I. Stanford Jolley. Directed by Spencer Bennet and Fred C. Brannon; for Republic.

The Black Widow
GB 1951 62m bw

A man succeeds in killing his would-be murderer; his wife schemes to bury the body as her real husband so that she can marry again. A whole lot less interesting than it sounds, acting and direction being alike laborious. Christine Norden, Robert Ayres, Anthony Forwood, John Longden. Written by Alan MacKinnon, from Lester Powell's BBC serial *Return from Darkness*; directed by Vernon Sewell; for Hammer / Exclusive.

'An electrifying drama about a predatory female! All the suspense your system can take!'

Black Widow*
US 1954 95m De Luxe Cinemascope
TCF (Nunnally Johnson)

A Broadway producer is suspected of the murder of an ambitious young girl.
Reasonably classy whodunnit with glamorous settings and an able cast, but a little lacking in wit and pace.

wd Nunnally Johnson, *novel* Fatal Woman by Patrick Quentin *ph* Charles G. Clarke *m* Leigh Harline

Ginger Rogers, Van Heflin, George Raft, Gene Tierney, Peggy Ann Garner, Reginald Gardiner, Virginia Leith, Otto Kruger, Hilda Simms, Cathleen Nesbitt

Black Widow*
US 1986 103m colour
TCF / Laurence Mark (Harold Schneider)

A lady cop tracks down a lady murderer in Hawaii.
Watchable but overlong cop show with nothing very surprising about it once the plot is clear: TV movies have done just as well.

w Ronald Bass *d* Bob Rafelson *ph* Conrad Hall *m* Michael Small *pd* Gene Callahan

Debra Winger, Theresa Russell, Sami Frey, Dennis Hopper, Nicol Williamson, Lois Smith

'A moderately interesting tale of one woman's obsession for another's glamorous and criminal lifestyle.'—*Daily Variety*

The Black Windmill*
GB 1974 106m Technicolor Panavision
Universal / Zanuck–Brown (Don Siegel)

A secret service agent has to fight a lone battle when his young son is kidnapped by spies.
Unconvincing variant on *The Man Who Knew Too Much*, with an unwieldy and incoherent plot and more borrowings from Hitchcock than you can count. It ends up as fair predictable fun despite its jaded air.

w Leigh Vance, *novel* Seven Days to a Killing by Clive Egleton *d* Don Siegel *ph* Ousama Rawi *m* Roy Budd

Michael Caine, Janet Suzman, Joseph O'Conor, Donald Pleasence, Delphine Seyrig, John Vernon, Joss Ackland

'A flaccid spy thriller, vaguely reminiscent of Hitchcock and *Foreign Correspondent*, with direction as blank as the expression on Michael Caine's face throughout.'—*Sight and Sound*

Black Zoo
US 1962 88m Eastmancolor Panavision
Allied Artists / Herman Cohen

The owner of a private Los Angeles zoo trains his animals to kill his enemies.
Stultifyingly inept and uninteresting horror film.

w Herman Cohen *d* Robert Gordon *ph* Floyd Crosby *m* Paul Dunlap

Michael Gough, Jeanne Cooper, Rod Lauren, Virginia Grey, Jerome Cowan, Elisha Cook Jnr, Marianna Hill

Blackbeard the Pirate*
US 1952 99m Technicolor
RKO (Edmund Grainger)

In the 17th century, reformed pirate Sir Henry Morgan is commissioned to rid the Caribbean of the rascally Blackbeard.
A farrago of action clichés with the star giving his eye-rolling all. The romantic element is dreary and the whole a shade bloodthirsty for family fare.

w Alan le May *d* Raoul Walsh *ph* William E. Snyder *m* Victor Young

Robert Newton, Linda Darnell, Keith Andes, William Bendix, Torin Thatcher, Irene Ryan, Alan Mowbray, Richard Egan

Blackbeard's Ghost
US 1967 107m Technicolor
Walt Disney (Bill Walsh)

The famous pirate returns as a ghost to help the old ladies who own a hotel he loved.
Ponderous and lengthy comedy, partially salvaged by performances.

w Bill Walsh, Ben Da Gradi *d* Robert Stevenson *ph* Edward Colman *m* Robert F. Brunner

Peter Ustinov, Dean Jones, Suzanne Pleshette, Elsa Lanchester, Richard Deacon

The Blackbird
US 1925 70m at 24 fps bw silent

A Limehouse thief pretends to be a cripple, and after committing a murder finds that he is. Standard star vehicle with recollections of several others. Lon Chaney, Renee Adoree, Owen Moore, Doris Lloyd. Written and directed by Tod Browning; for MGM.

'I'm a teacher. My pupils are the kind you don't turn your back on, even in class!'

The Blackboard Jungle*
US 1955 101m bw
MGM (Pandro S. Berman)

In a slum school, a teacher finally gains the respect of his class of young hooligans.
Seminal fifties melodrama more notable for its introduction of 'Rock Around the Clock' behind the credits than for any intrinsic interest.

wd Richard Brooks, *novel* Evan Hunter *ph* Russell Harlan *m* *Bill Haley and the Comets*

Glenn Ford, Anne Francis, Louis Calhern, Margaret Hayes, John Hoyt, Richard Kiley, Emile Meyer, Warner Anderson, Basil Ruysdael, *Sidney Poitier, Vic Morrow*, Rafael Campos

'It could just as well have been the first good film of this kind. Actually, it will be remembered chiefly for its timely production and release.'—*G. N. Fenin, Film Culture*

AAN: Richard Brooks (as writer); Russell Harlan

Blackhawk
US 1952 bw serial: 15 eps

An organization dedicated to the freedom of mankind uncovers a saboteur. Fast-moving chapter play. Kirk Alyn, Carol Forman, John Crawford, Michael Fox. Directed by Spencer Bennet; for Columbia.

Blackjack Ketchum, Desperado
US 1956 76m bw

A former gunslinger turns sheriff and defeats the local badman. Standard lower-case western with predictable excitements. Howard Duff, Victor Jory, Maggie Mahoney, Angela Stevens. Written by Luci Ward and Jack Natteford, from a novel by Louis L'Amour; directed by Earl Bellamy; for Sam Katzman / Columbia.

Blackmail***
GB 1929 78m bw
BIP (John Maxwell)

A Scotland Yard inspector finds that his girl is involved in a murder; he conceals the fact and is blackmailed.
Hitchcock's first talkie is now a very hesitant entertainment but fully bears the director's stamp and will reward patient audiences in several excitingly staged sequences.

w Alfred Hitchcock, Benn W. Levy, Charles Bennett, *play* Charles Bennett *d* *Alfred Hitchcock* *ph* Jack Cox *m* Campbell and Connelly

Anny Ondra, Sara Allgood, John Longden, Charles Paton, Donald Calthrop, Cyril Ritchard

'Hitchcock's ending was to have been ironic, the detective seeing the cell door shut on the arrested girl, going home and then being asked if he was going out with his girl friend that evening. His answer: "Not tonight." This was unacceptable commercially and a happy ending was substituted.'—*George Perry*

Blackmail
US 1939 81m bw
MGM (John Considine Jnr)

A man is released from prison after serving a sentence for a crime he did not commit. Immediately a blackmailer pounces . . .
Co-feature drama for a star marking time; not bad in its way.

w David Hertz, William Ludwig *d* H. C. Potter *ph* Clyde de Vinna *m* David Snell, Edward Ward

Edward G. Robinson, Ruth Hussey, Gene Lockhart, Guinn Williams, Esther Dale

'The family circuit will accept it as sufficient entertainment for a suspenseful evening.'—*Variety*

Blackmailed
GB 1950 85m bw
GFD / Harold Huth

Several victims of a blackmailer are involved in his murder.
Interestingly plotted and well cast melodrama which suffers from a flat script and production.

w Hugh Mills, Roger Vadim, *novel* Mrs Christopher by Elizabeth Myers *d* Marc Allégret *ph* George Stretton *m* John Wooldridge

Dirk Bogarde, Mai Zetterling, Fay Compton, Robert Flemyng, Michael Gough, James Robertson Justice, Joan Rice, Wilfrid Hyde White, Harold Huth

Blackout
GB 1950 73m bw
A man supposedly killed in an air crash turns out to be the head of a counterfeiting ring. Fairly entertaining British support of its time. Dinah Sheridan, Maxwell Reed, Patrick Doonan, Eric Pohlman.
Written by John Gilling; directed and produced by Robert S. Baker and Monty Berman; for Tempean / Eros.

Blackwell's Island
US 1939 71m bw
Warner (Bryan Foy)
A reporter goes to jail to get the goods on a smart gangster.
Forgettable exposé of the lighter kind.
w Crane Wilbur *d* William McGann *ph* Sid Hickox
John Garfield, Rosemary Lane, Dick Purcell, Victor Jory, Stanley Fields
'An exploitation natural . . . a portrayal of incredible events taken from real life.'—*Variety*

Blacula
US 1972 93m Movielab
AIP (Joseph T. Naar)
In 1815 in Transylvania, an African prince falls victim to Dracula. A hundred and fifty years later, his body is shipped to Los Angeles and accidentally revivified.
Jaded semi-spoof notable chiefly as the first black horror film. The star's performance is as stately as could be wished in the circumstances.
w Joan Torres, Raymond Koenig *d* William Crain *ph* John Stevens *m* Gene Page
William Marshall, Vonetta McGee, Denise Nicholas, Gordon Pinsent, Charles Macaulay

Blade Runner*
US 1982 117m Technicolor Panavision
Warner / Ladd / Blade Runner Partnership (Michael Deeley, Ridley Scott)
Los Angeles, AD 2019; a licensed-to-kill policeman tracks down and destroys a group of intelligent robots who have hijacked a space shuttle and returned to earth.
Gloomy futuristic thriller, looking like a firework display seen through thick fog, and for all the tiring tricks and expense adding up to little more than an updated Philip Marlowe case.
w Hampton Fancher, David People, *novel* Do Androids Dream of Electric Sheep? by Philip K. Dick *d* Ridley Scott *ph* Jordan Cronenweth *pd* Lawrence G. Paull *m* Vangelis
Harrison Ford, Rutger Hauer, Sean Young, Edward James Olmos, M. Emmet Walsh, Daryl Hannah
'The sets are indeed impressive, but they are no compensation for a narrative so lame that it seems in need of a wheelchair.'—*Tom Milne, MFB*
'A richly detailed and visually overwhelming trip to 2019 which sticks with you like a recurrent nightmare.'—*Sunday Times*
'A massive assault on the senses which seems to have been launched from a madhouse equipped with all computerized mod cons.'—*Daily Mail*
'Glitteringly and atmospherically designed; but ultimately mechanics win out over philosophizing.'—*Sight and Sound*
AAN: art direction; visual effects (Douglas Trumbull, Richard Yuricich, David Dryer)

Blake of Scotland Yard
US 1937 bw serial: 15 eps
A munitions millionaire offers The Scorpion a fabulous sum to steal a death ray. Just what you expect from an old-time serial. Ralph Byrd, Joan Barclay, Dickie Jones, Herbert Rawlinson. Directed by Bob Hill; for Victory.

'She's the hottest thing on the beach. She's also his best friend's daughter!'
Blame It on Rio
US 1983 100m Metrocolor
Sherwood (Stanley Donen)
A businessman is enlisted by his best friend to find his daughter's seducer, who is in fact himself.
Totally joyless and witless comedy with a South American background which is supposedly presumed to take away the bad taste.
w Charlie Peters, Larry Gelbart, from Claude Berri's 1977 film Un Moment d'Egarement *d* Stanley Donen *ph* Reynaldo Villalobos *md* Ken Wannberg
Michael Caine, Joseph Bologna, Valerie Harper, Michelle Johnson

Blame It on the Night
US 1984 85m Technicolor
A rock star tries to make friends with the 13-year-old son he's only just met. Resolutely uninteresting pattern play which slouches its way to a predictable ending. Nick Mancuso, Byron Thames, Leslie Ackerman, Dick Bakalyan. Written by Len Jenkin; directed and produced by Gene Taft; for Tri-Star.

Blanche*
France 1971 92m Eastmancolor
Telepresse / Abel et Charton (Dominique Duvergé, Philippe d'Argila)
In 13th-century France, a baron's beautiful young wife excites dark passions in her stepson and in the king.
An adult fairy tale full of symbols for those who seek them; but its main virtue is its highly decorative pictorialism.
wd Walerian Borowczyk, *novel* Mazepa by Juliusz Slowacki *ph* Guy Durban *m* 13th-century music
Ligia Branice, Michel Simon, Lawrence Trimble, Jacques Perrin
'Live-action *Jeux des Anges*, a brilliant, terrifying ballad of imprisonment.'—*Philip Strick, MFB*

Blanche Fury
GB 1948 95m Technicolor
GFD / Cineguild (Anthony Havelock-Allan)
A governess marries a wealthy heir, then with a steward connives at his murder.
Chilly Victorian melodrama without much interest outside the decor: the actors have unplayable roles and the handling is very flat.
w Audrey Erskine Lindop, Hugh Mills, Cecil McGivern, *novel* Joseph Shearing *d* Marc Allégret *ph* Guy Green, Geoffrey Unsworth *m* Clifton Parker
Valerie Hobson, Stewart Granger, Walter Fitzgerald, Michael Gough, Maurice Denham, Sybilla Binder

'She kept her love for one—by sharing it with all!'
Blaze of Noon
US 1947 91m bw
Paramount (John Farrow)
Three stunt flier brothers in the twenties leave their circus to start a commercial air-line.
Predictable romantic drama with little flying: tragic pretensions, routine performances.
w Frank Wead, Arthur Sheekman *d* John Farrow *ph* William C. Mellor *m* Adolph Deutsch
William Holden, Anne Baxter, Sonny Tufts, Sterling Hayden, William Bendix, Howard da Silva
'So long as it sticks to stunt flying and mild comedy it is pleasant enough, but the last half, during which the obsessed brothers come one by one to grief and the little woman waits it out, gets pretty monotonous.'—*James Agee*

The Blazing Forest
US 1952 90m Technicolor
Paramount / Pine–Thomas (William H. Pine, William C. Thomas)
A lady landowner has trouble with her rival timber bosses.
Fair period programmer.
w Lewis R. Foster, Winston Miller *d* Edward Ludwig *ph* Lionel Lindon *m* Lucien Caillet
John Payne, Agnes Moorehead, William Demarest, Richard Arlen, Susan Morrow, Roscoe Ates, Lynne Roberts

Blazing Magnum
Canada 1976 99m colour Panavision
A tough cop solves his sister's murder. Tired rehash of the *Dirty Harry* formula, with plenty of violent action. Stuart Whitman, John Saxon, Martin Landau, Tisa Farrow, Gayle Hunnicutt, Carole Laure. Written by Vincent Mann and Frank Clark; directed by Martin Herbert; for Security Investment Trust Inc.

Blazing Saddles*
US 1974 93m Technicolor Panavision
Warner / Crossbow (Michael Herzberg)
A black railroad worker and an alcoholic ex-gunfighter foil a crooked attorney and his henchmen.

Wild western parody in which the action eventually shifts to the Warner backlot, after which the actors repair to Grauman's Chinese Theatre to find out what happened at the end of the story. At least as many misses as hits, and all aimed squarely at film buffs.

w Norman Steinberg, Mel Brooks, Andrew Bergman, Richard Pryor, Alan Unger *d* Mel Brooks *ph* Joseph Biroc *m* John Morris

Cleavon Little, Gene Wilder, Slim Pickens, Harvey Korman, Madeline Kahn, Mel Brooks, Burton Gilliam, Alex Karras

'One suspects that the film's gradual disintegration derives not from the makers' inability to end it, so much as from their inability to stop laughing at their own jokes.'—*Jan Dawson*

'A surfeit of chaos and a scarcity of comedy.'—*Judith Crist*

' "I just about got everything out of me," said Brooks, "all my furor, my frenzy, my insanity, my love of life and hatred of death." Audiences flocked to this insane affirmation of dancing girls, Hollywood production numbers, stomach gas around the campfire, and gallows humor. Brooks had found the perfect vehicle for the age.'—*Les Keyser, Hollywood in the Seventies*

AAN: Madeline Kahn; title song (*m* John Morris, *ly* Mel Brooks)

Blazing the Overland Trail
US 1952 bw serial: 15 eps

An unscrupulous outlaw raids wagon trains and blames the Indians. One of the last of all serials, but by no means the best. Lee Roberts, Dennis Moore, Norma Brooks, Gregg Barton. Directed by Spencer Bennet; for Columbia.

Bleak Moments*
GB 1971 110m Eastmancolor
Autumn / Memorial / BFI (Leslie Blair)

Scenes from drab lives in a south London suburb.
Clearly not likely to appeal to the entertainment-seeking masses, and undeniably overlong, this small movie nevertheless has plenty of telling and even amusing detail about life as most of us recognize it.

wd Mike Leigh ph Bahram Manoochehri *songs* Mike Bradwell

Anne Raitt, Sarah Stephenson, Eric Allan, Mike Bradwell

'A prolonged poem to inhibitions, speechlessness, and social unease.'—*John Coleman, New Statesman*

Bless the Beasts and Children*
US 1973 110m colour
Columbia / Stanley Kramer

Six boys on an adventure holiday try to free a herd of buffalo earmarked for destruction. Rather obviously pointed melodrama, well enough done but not very interesting.

w Mac Benoff, *novel* Glendon Swarthout *d* Stanley Kramer

Bill Mumy, Barry Robins, Miles Chapin, Jesse White, Ken Swofford

AAN: title song (*m / ly* Barry de Vorzon, Perry Botkin Jnr)

Bless This House
GB 1972 89m Eastmancolor

A suburbanite's multifarious frustrations culminate in preparations for his son's wedding. This tedious spin-off from a TV sitcom virtually abandons plot in favour of an endless series of slapstick gags which could have been better presented. Sid James, Diana Coupland, Terry Scott, June Whitfield, Peter Butterworth, Sally Geeson, Robin Askwith, Bill Maynard. Written by Dave Freeman; directed by Gerald Thomas; for Peter Rogers / Rank.

Blessed Event**
US 1932 84m bw
Warner (Ray Griffith)

A gossip columnist gets himself into hot water. Amusing vehicle for a fast-talking star, and quite an interesting historical document.

w Howard Green, *play* Manuel Seff, Forest Wilson *d* Roy del Ruth *ph* Sol Polito

Lee Tracy, Ned Sparks, Mary Brian, Dick Powell, Ruth Donnelly, Frank McHugh, Allen Jenkins

'A potential clean-up . . . a sustained hour and a half or so of smart entertainment.'—*Variety*

'Quick and pacy and very likeable.'—*Pauline Kael, 70s*

† A historically interesting note was small-part actress Emma Dunn's use of the expression 'Well I'll be damned', which was technically forbidden at the time.

Blighty*
GB 1926 93m (24 fps) bw silent
Gainsborough–Piccadilly (Michael Balcon, Carlyle Blackwell)

A chauffeur becomes an officer and after the war finds himself looking after the master's family.
Fairly unwatchable in a normal sense, but of historical interest as one of the key British films of the twenties to make a comment about the war.

w Eliot Stannard, Charles McEvoy, Ivor Montagu *d* Adrian Brunel

Jameson Thomas, Ellaline Terriss, Lilian Hall Davis, Godfrey Winn, Wally Patch, Seymour Hicks

Blind Adventure
US 1933 65m bw

An American in London gets mixed up with blackmailers and kidnappers. Light-hearted but ill-explained second feature. Robert Armstrong, Helen Mack, Roland Young, Ralph Bellamy, John Miljan, Laura Hope Crews, Henry Stephenson, Phyllis Barry. Written by Ruth Rose; directed by Ernest B. Schoedsack; music by Max Steiner; for RKO.

'Has some fine things but won't mean much more than a programmer in the split spots.'—*Variety*

†The film seems to have been undertaken as a diversion by the makers of *King Kong*.

Blind Alley**
US 1939 68m bw
Columbia

An escaped killer takes refuge in the home of a psychiatrist, who explores his subconscious and tames him.
Unusual lowercase thriller with effective dream sequences; it was much imitated.

w Michael Blankfort, Albert Duffy, *play* James Warwick *d Charles Vidor ph* Lucien Ballard *m* Morris Stoloff

Chester Morris, Ralph Bellamy, Ann Dvorak, Melville Cooper, Rose Stradner, Marc Lawrence

'Psychoanalysis of a criminal provides a new twist to what would otherwise be another crime picture of general trend.'—*Variety*

'As un-Hollywood as anything that has come from France this year.'—*New York Daily News*

'Survive a sticky ten minutes and you have a thriller of quite unusual merit.'—*Graham Greene*

† Remake: *The Dark Past* (qv).

A Blind Bargain*
US 1922 60m approx bw silent

A demented scientist creates an ape monster. Interesting star vehicle, a precursor of many hokum thrillers. Lon Chaney, Jacqueline Logan, Raymond McKee, Virginia True Boardman. Written by J. G. Hawks from The Octave of Claudius by Barry Pain; directed by Wallace Worsley; for Goldwyn.

Blind Date
US 1934 71m bw

A working girl jilts a man because he is not the marrying kind, then regrets it. Tedious homespun drama. Ann Sothern, Neil Hamilton, Paul Kelly, Mickey Rooney, Jane Darwell, Spencer Charters. Written by Ethel Hill; directed by Roy Willian Neill; for Columbia. 'Vida Hurst is credited with the basic story, but a lot of others used it before her. Used to be a favourite with Corinne Griffith.'—*Variety*

Blind Date*
GB 1959 95m bw
Rank / Sydney Box / Independent Artists (David Deutsch)
US title: *Chance Meeting*

A young Dutch painter in London discovers his mistress's body and finds himself in a web of deceit.
Tolerable, comparatively sophisticated murder puzzle; rather glum looking, but the plot holds the interest.

w Ben Barzman, Millard Lampell, *novel* Leigh Howard *d* Joseph Losey *ph* Christopher Challis *m* Richard Rodney Bennett

Hardy Kruger, Stanley Baker, Micheline Presle, Robert Flemyng, Gordon Jackson, John Van Eyssen

Blind Date*
US 1987 93m Metrocolor
Tri-Star / Blake Edwards (Tony Adams)

A company executive needs a date for a company function, and takes a remote relative who turns out to be an easy drunk.
One-note gag movie which spurs some laughs but wears out its welcome.

w Dale Launer *d* Blake Edwards *ph* Harry Stradling *m* Henry Mancini

Kim Basinger, Bruce Willis, John Larroquette, William Daniels, Phil Hartman, Alice Hirson
'In short, hokey and hip—which in this case is a foolproof formula.'—*Daily Variety*

The Blind Goddess
GB 1947 88m bw
Gainsborough (Betty Box)

The private secretary to a public figure finds that his idol has feet of clay, and suffers in court for his discovery.
Courtroom drama from an old-fashioned stage play: surefire for addicts, but routine as a film.

w Muriel and Sydney Box, *play Patrick Hastings* *d* Harold French *ph* Ray Elton

Eric Portman, Anne Crawford, Hugh Williams, Michael Denison, Nora Swinburne, Claire Bloom, Raymond Lovell, Frank Cellier

Blind Husbands**
US 1919 90m approx (24 fps) bw silent
Universal (Erich Von Stroheim)

An Austrian officer, on holiday in the Alps, seduces the wife of a rich American.
Stroheim's first comedy of sexual manners, now of mainly archival interest.

w, d, ad Erich Von Stroheim *ph* Ben Reynolds

Erich Von Stroheim, Sam de Grasse, Gibson Gowland, Francella Billington

Blind Man's Buff
GB 1936 72m bw

A doctor jealous of his wife does not reveal the fact that he has been cured of blindness.
Yawnworthy melodrama. Basil Sydney, James Mason, Enid Stamp-Taylor, Barbara Greene, Iris Ashley. Written by Cecil Maiden, from the play *Smoked Glasses* by William Foster and B. Scott-Elder; directed by Albert Parker; for Present Day / Fox British.

Blind Terror
GB 1971 89m colour
Columbia / Filmways / Genesis (Basil Appleby)
US title: *See No Evil*

A blind girl is the sole, hunted survivor of a maniac's rampage on a lonely estate.
Shocks, screams and starts fill a cliché-ridden but still effective script which is faithfully turned into a competent but routine heart-stopper.

w Brian Clemens *d* Richard Fleischer *ph* Gerry Fisher *m* Elmer Bernstein

Mia Farrow, Robin Bailey, Dorothy Alison, Diane Grayson, Norman Eshley, Brian Rawlinson
'For those who like to watch folks pull the wings off flies.'—*Judith Crist*

Blindfold**
US 1965 102m Technicolor Panavision
Universal (Marvin Schwarz)

A society psychiatrist is enlisted by the CIA to make regular blindfold journeys to a secret destination where he treats a neurotic physicist. Discovering that his contacts are really enemy agents, he tracks down the destination by sound and guesswork, and routs the villains.
Lively spy spoof with rather too much knockabout between the Hitchcockian suspense sequences; it has indeed the air of a script which Hitchcock rejected, but provides reliable entertainment.

w Philip Dunne, W. H. Menger, *novel* Lucile Fletcher *d* Philip Dunne *ph* Joseph MacDonald *m* Lalo Schifrin

Rock Hudson, Claudia Cardinale, Jack Warden, Guy Stockwell, Brad Dexter

The Bliss of Mrs Blossom
GB 1968 93m Technicolor
Paramount (Josef Shaftel)

The wife of a bra manufacturer keeps her lover in the attic.
Silly, wild-eyed sex comedy decorated with the flashy tinsel of swinging London's dying fall.

w Alec Coppel, Denis Norden *d* Joe McGrath *ph* Geoffrey Unsworth *m* Riz Ortolani *pd* Assheton Gorton

Richard Attenborough, Shirley Maclaine, James Booth, Freddie Jones, William Rushton, Bob Monkhouse, Patricia Routledge

Blithe Spirit***
GB 1945 96m Technicolor
Two Cities / Cineguild (Anthony Havelock-Allan)

A cynical novelist's second marriage is disturbed when the playful ghost of his first wife materializes during a séance.
Direction and acting carefully preserve a comedy which on its first West End appearance in 1941 achieved instant classic status. The repartee scarcely dates, and altogether this is a most polished job of film-making.

w Noel Coward, from his play *scenario* David Lean, Anthony Havelock-Allan, Ronald Neame *d* David Lean *ph* Ronald Neame *m* Richard Addinsell

Rex Harrison, Kay Hammond, Constance Cummings, Margaret Rutherford, Hugh Wakefield, Joyce Carey, Jacqueline Clark
† After seeing this, Noël Coward reputedly told Rex Harrison: 'After me you're the best light comedian in the world.'

Blitz on Britain*
GB 1960 71m bw

A very acceptable record of the Battle of Britain as it affected the home front, narrated by Alistair Cooke. Written by Patrick Brawn; directed and edited by Harry Booth; for Anglo-Continental / British Lion.

The Blob
US 1958 83m De Luxe
Tonylyn / Jack H. Harris

A small town combats a slimy space invader.
Padded hokum for drive-ins, with a few effective moments.

w Theodore Simonson, Kate Phillips *d* Irwin S. Yeaworth Jnr *ph* Thomas Spalding *m* Ralph Carmichael

Steve McQueen, Aneta Corseaut, Olin Howlin, Earl Rowe
† Sequel 1971: *Beware! The Blob* (GB: *Son of Blob*).

The Blob
US 1988 92m Technicolor

Fifties sci-fi horror dressed up for the 80s. Shawnee Smith, Kevin Dillon, Donovan Leitch. Written and directed by Chuck Russell; for Tri-Star (Jack H. Harris/Elliott Kastner).
'A great B-movie with an A-pic budget.'—*Variety*

Blockade*
US 1938 84m bw
Walter Wanger

During the Spanish Civil War, a peace-loving young farmer has to take up arms to defend his land.
Much touted as Hollywood's first serious contribution to international affairs, this dogged drama was in fact so bland that audiences had difficulty ascertaining which side it was on, especially as neither Franco nor the Fascists were mentioned. As a romantic action drama, however, it passed muster.

w John Howard Lawson *d* William Dieterle *m* Werner Janssen *ph* Rudolf Maté

Henry Fonda, Madeleine Carroll, Leo Carrillo, John Halliday, Vladimir Sokoloff, Robert Warwick, Reginald Denny
'It misses any claim to greatness because it pulls its punches . . . and it's going to be tough to sell.'—*Variety*
'The film has a curious unreality considering the grim reality behind it.'—*Frank S. Nugent*
'There is achieved a deadly numb level of shameless hokum out of which anything true or decent rises only for a second to confound itself.'—*Otis Ferguson*

† Original publicity carried this disclaimer: NOTE: Care has been taken to prevent any costume of the production from being accurately that of either side in the Spanish Civil War. The story does not attempt to favour any cause in the present conflict.

AAN: John Howard Lawson; Werner Janssen

Blockheads***
US 1938 60m bw
Hal Roach / Stan Laurel

Twenty years after World War I, Stan is still guarding a trench because nobody told him to stop. Olly takes him home to meet the wife, with disastrous consequences.
The last first-class Laurel and Hardy comedy is shapeless but hilarious, a fragmented reworking of earlier ideas, all of which work beautifully. Gags include encounters with a tip-up truck and an automatic garage, and a brilliantly worked out sequence up and down several flights of stairs.

w James Parrott, Harry Langdon, Felix Adler, Charles Rogers, Arnold Belgard *d* John G. Blystone *ph* Art Lloyd *m* Marvin Hatley

Stan Laurel, Oliver Hardy, Billy Gilbert, Patricia Ellis, Minna Gombell, James Finlayson

'Hodge-podge of old-fashioned slapstick and hoke.'—*Variety*

AAN: Marvin Hatley

Blonde Crazy*
US 1931 74m bw
Warner
GB title: *Larceny Lane*

A bellhop and a chambermaid set out to fleece all-comers.
Smart con man comedy with the star in excellent form.

w Kubec Glasmon, John Bright *d* Roy del Ruth *ph* Sid Hickox

James Cagney, Joan Blondell, Ray Milland, Louis Calhern, Guy Kibbee, Polly Walters, Charles Lane, Maude Eburne

'Naughty cracks galore, and one says "Nuts". But he doesn't push a grapefruit in the girl friend's face, though they expect it any time.'—*Variety*

'A chipper, hard-boiled, amusing essay in petty thieving.'—*Time*

Blonde Fever
US 1944 69m bw

A middle-aged husband falls for a blonde waitress. Very ho-hum comedy on familiar lines. Philip Dorn, Mary Astor, Gloria Grahame, Felix Bressart, Marshall Thompson, Curt Bois. Written by Patricia Coleman from play by Ferenc Molnar; directed by Richard Whorf; for MGM.

The Blonde from Peking
US / France 1968 80m colour

The CIA thinks that a girl with amnesia may know Chinese nuclear secrets. Witless international spy stuff, neither funny nor thrilling. Mireille Darc, Claudio Brook, Edward G. Robinson, Pascale Roberts. Written by Nicolas Gessner and Marc Behm, from a story by James Hadley Chase; directed by Nicolas Gessner; for Paramount.

A Blonde in Love: see *Loves of a Blonde*

'What could she do but flee from love? She loved two men at once!'
Blonde Venus*
US 1932 97m bw
Paramount

A German café singer marries an English research chemist, but their marriage doesn't run smoothly.
Rather dreary, fragmented star vehicle with good moments, notably the star's opening appearance as a gorilla.

w Jules Furthman, S. K. Lauren *d* Josef Von Sternberg *ph* Bert Glennon *m* Oscar Poteker

Marlene Dietrich, Herbert Marshall, Cary Grant, Dickie Moore

'Weak story, inept direction and generally sluggish total count heavily against it . . . it'll require plenty of bally.'—*Variety*

'The story has all the dramatic integrity of a sashweight murderer's tabloid autobiography.'—*Pare Lorentz*

'There is more pleasure for the eye in *Blonde Venus* than in a hundred of its fellows. But what does beauty ornament? The story of a wife who becomes a kept woman for the sake of her husband, and a prostitute for the sake of her child.'—*Forsyth Hardy, Cinema Quarterly*

Blondes for Danger
GB 1938 68m bw

A cockney taxi driver takes an unwanted fare and becomes involved in a deep dark plot. Modest but effective vehicle for *Gordon Harker*; with Enid Stamp Taylor, Ivan Brandt. Written by Gerald Elliott, from the novel *Red for Danger* by Evadne Price; directed by Jack Raymond; for Herbert Wilcox.

Blondie*
US 1938 68m bw
Columbia

Misadventures of a harassed suburban family man.
Dagwood Bumstead and his wife Blondie were Mr and Mrs Small Town America throughout the thirties and forties, and received their perfect screen incarnations in this unambitious but quite watchable series, which provided familiar and often quite observant fun.

w Richard Flournoy, from the comic strip by *Chic Young* *d* Frank R. Strayer *ph* Henry Freulich

Arthur Lake, Penny Singleton, Larry Simms, Daisy the Dog, *Jonathan Hale* (as the boss, Mr Dithers), Gene Lockhart, Ann Doran, Irving Bacon (as the mailman)

'Light fare, but universal in appeal . . . could be clicko series.'—*Variety*

Other episodes were as follows:
1939: BLONDIE MEETS THE BOSS, BLONDIE TAKES A VACATION, BLONDIE BRINGS UP BABY
1940: BLONDIE ON A BUDGET, BLONDIE HAS SERVANT TROUBLE, BLONDIE PLAYS CUPID
1941: BLONDIE GOES LATIN, BLONDIE IN SOCIETY
1942: BLONDIE GOES TO COLLEGE, BLONDIE'S BLESSED EVENT, BLONDIE FOR VICTORY
1943: IT'S A GREAT LIFE, FOOTLIGHT GLAMOUR
1945: LEAVE IT TO BLONDIE
1946: BLONDIE KNOWS BEST, LIFE WITH BLONDIE, BLONDIE'S LUCKY DAY
1947: BLONDIE'S BIG MOMENT, BLONDIE'S HOLIDAY, BLONDIE IN THE DOUGH, BLONDIE'S ANNIVERSARY
1948: BLONDIE'S REWARD
1949: BLONDIE'S SECRET, BLONDIE'S BIG DEAL, BLONDIE HITS THE JACKPOT
1950: BLONDIE'S HERO, BEWARE OF BLONDIE
† TV series were started in the fifties and sixties, but both failed.

Blondie Johnson
US 1933 67m bw

The career of a female larcenist who eventually takes her medicine. Competent programmer very typical of its studio and year. Joan Blondell, Chester Morris, Allen Jenkins, Claire Dodd. Written by Earl Baldwin; directed by Ray Enright; for Warner. 'After she departs for the pen, she lets the public in on the fact that crime doesn't pay. Neither will the picture.'—*Variety*

Blondie of the Follies*
US 1932 97m bw
MGM (Marion Davies)

Two New York showgirls graduate from tenements to luxury.
Adequate comedy-melodrama with an interesting cast and good dialogue.

w Frances Marion, Anita Loos *d* Edmund Goulding *ph* George Barnes *m* William Axt

Marion Davies, Jimmy Durante, Robert Montgomery, Billie Dove, James Gleason, Zasu Pitts, Sidney Toler, Douglass Dumbrille

'Not bad, but not very good, with chances that it will just get by. Length and slow pace the drawbacks. . . . It isn't padded out, it's just flatfooted.'—*Variety*

'An unjustly forgotten film.'—*New Yorker, 1979*

Blood Alley
US 1955 115m Warnercolor Cinemascope
Warner / Batjac (no producer credited)

An American sailor is helped by local people to escape from a Chinese jail; he then escorts them to Hong Kong.
Rudimentary anti-Red heroics with expensive spectacle punctuating a tacky script.

w A. S. Fleischmann, from his novel *d* William Wellman *ph* William H. Clothier *m* Roy Webb *pd* Alfred Ybarra

John Wayne, Lauren Bacall, Paul Fix, Joy Kim, Berry Kroger, Mike Mazurki, Anita Ekberg

Blood and Black Lace
Italy 1964 90m Eastmancolor

Six women are nastily murdered in a fashion house. Vaguely necrophiliac but trendy suspense-horror flick in the wake of *Psycho*. Cameron Mitchell, Thomas Reiner, Mary

Arden. Written by Marcel Fondato, Giuseppe Barilla and Mario Bava; directed by Mario Bava; for Emmepi. (Original title: *Sei Donne per l'Assassino.*)

Blood and Roses
France / Italy 1960 87m Technirama
Eger / Documento (Raymond Eger)
original title: *Et Mourir de Plaisir*

Carmilla takes on the vampiric personality of her ancestress Millarca, whom she closely resembles.
A rather half-hearted attempt to make an elegant horror story; boring rather than charming or frightening.

w Claude Brûlé, Claude Martin, Roger Vadim *d* Roger Vadim *ph* Claude Renoir *m* Jean Prodromidès

Mel Ferrer, Elsa Martinelli, Annette Vadim, Marc Allégret

Blood and Sand*
US 1922 80m (24 fps) bw silent
Paramount

A matador falls under the spell of an aristocratic woman.
Elegant star vehicle which established his image.

w June Mathis, *novel* Vicente Blasco Ibanez *d* Fred Niblo

Rudolph Valentino, Nita Naldi, Lila Lee, Walter Long

'Love flamed in the shadow of death!'
Blood and Sand*
US 1941 123m Technicolor
TCF (Darryl F. Zanuck, Robert T. Kane)

Rather boring remake, fine to look at but dramatically deadly.

w Jo Swerling, *novel* Vicente Blasco Ibanez *d* Rouben Mamoulian *ph* Ernest Palmer, Ray Rennahan *m* Alfred Newman *ad Richard Day, Joseph C. Wright*

Tyrone Power, Rita Hayworth, Linda Darnell, Nazimova, Anthony Quinn, J. Carrol Naish, John Carradine, Lynn Bari, Laird Cregar, Monty Banks

AA: Ernest Palmer, Ray Rennahan

The Blood Beast Terror
GB 1967 88m Eastmancolor
Tigon (Arnold L. Miller, Tony Tenser)

A Victorian entomologist creates human beings who can change themselves into monster death's-head moths.
Unpersuasive and totally idiotic cheapjack horror fare.

w Peter Bryan *d* Vernon Sewell *ph* Stanley A. Long *m* Paul Ferris

Robert Flemyng, Peter Cushing, Wanda Ventham, Vanessa Howard, David Griffin, John Paul, Kevin Stoney, Roy Hudd

Blood from the Mummy's Tomb*
GB 1971 94m Technicolor
Hammer (Howard Brandy)

Twenty years after a female mummy is brought back to England, members of the expedition are killed one by one, and their leader's daughter is possessed by the spirit of the dead princess.
Interesting but over-complicated and hard-to-enjoy attempt to maintain the mummy saga without an actual marauding mummy. Intelligently handled but sadly lacking in a sense of humour.

w Christopher Wicking, *novel* Jewel of the Seven Stars by Bram Stoker *d Seth Holt* *ph* Arthur Grant *m* Tristam Cary

Andrew Keir, Valerie Leon, James Villiers, Hugh Burden, George Coulouris, Mark Edwards, Rosalie Crutchley, Aubrey Morris, David Markham

'Makes the genre seem like new.'—*Tony Rayns*

† Seth Holt died when the shooting was still incomplete, and Michael Carreras took over for the last few days

Blood Money*
US 1933 66m bw

The decline of a bail-bond racketeer. Smartly made melodrama with good work all round. George Bancroft, Judith Anderson, Chick Chandler, Frances Dee, Blossom Seeley. Written and directed by Rowland Brown; for Darryl F. Zanuck / Twentieth Century.

The Blood of a Poet**
France 1930 58m bw
Vicomte de Noailles
original title: *Le Sang d'un Poète*

Aspects of a poet's vision, taking place while a chimney is falling down.
An indescribable film full of striking imagery which may, or may not, be meaningful. Its author claims that it is not surrealist, but that label for most people will do as well as any other.

wd Jean Cocteau *ph* Georges Périnal *m* Georges Auric *ad* Jean Gabriel d'Aubonne

Lee Miller, Pauline Carton, Odette Talazac

'It must be placed among the classic masterpieces of the seventh art.'—*Revue du Cinéma*

Blood of the Vampire
GB 1958 85m Eastmancolor

An asylum keeper turns inmates into vampires. Heavy-handed, crudely made horror comic. Donald Wolfit, Barbara Shelley, Vincent Ball, Victor Maddern, Andrew Faulds. Written by Jimmy Sangster; directed by Henry Cass; for Baker-Berman / Artistes Alliance.

Blood on Satan's Claw
GB 1970 93m Eastmancolor
Tigon-Chilton (Tony Tenser, Malcolm B. Heyworth, Peter L. Andrews)
aka: *Satan's Skin*

A devil's claw wreaks havoc among children in a 17th-century English village.
Moderately frightening, rather silly but at least original period horror comic.

w Robert Wynne-Simmons *d* Piers Haggard *ph* Dick Bush *m* Marc Wilkinson

Patrick Wymark, Linda Hayden, Barry Andrews, Avice Landon, Simon Williams, Tamara Ustinov, Anthony Ainley

Blood on the Arrow
US 1964 91m De Luxe

An outlaw is the only survivor of an Indian raid, and later becomes a hero when the Indians attack again. Unremarkable western, with every turn of plot to order. Dale Robertson, Martha Hyer, Wendell Corey, Paul Mantee, Ted de Corsia. Written by Robert E. Kent; directed by Sidney Salkow; for Leon Fromkess / Allied Artists.

Blood on the Moon*
US 1948 88m bw
RKO (Sid Rogell, Theron Warth)

A homesteader finds that his best friend is the villainous leader of a group of cattlemen.
Good-looking but rather pedestrian western, generally well handled.

w Lillie Hayward *novel* Gunman's Choice by Luke Short *d* Robert Wise *ph* Nicholas Musuraca *m* Roy Webb

Robert Mitchum, Barbara Bel Geddes, Robert Preston, Walter Brennan

Blood on the Sun*
US 1945 94m bw
Cagney Productions (William Cagney)

In the twenties, the American editor of a Tokyo newspaper reveals a Japanese militarist plan for world conquest.
Satisfactory star actioner with good production and exciting highlights.

w Lester Cole *d* Frank Lloyd *ph* Theodor Sparkuhl *m* Miklos Rozsa

James Cagney, Sylvia Sidney, Wallace Ford, Rosemary de Camp, Robert Armstrong, John Emery, Leonard Strong, Frank Puglia

'It ought to be fine for those who enjoy a good ninety-minute massacre.'—*New Yorker*

'Tough, hard-hitting and explosive, with just enough rudimentary suspense.'—*Bosley Crowther*

'Pure unadulterated melodrama has a safe niche in cinematic offerings, but this folderol is more pretentious than persuasive.'—*Howard Barnes*

Blood Simple*
US 1983 99m DuArt

A saloon owner hires a hit man to kill his unfaithful wife and her lover, but the plot rebounds on him. Yet another variation on *The Postman Always Rings Twice*, and one with strong moments. John Getz, Frances McDormand, Dan Hedaya, M. Emmet Walsh. Written by Joel and Ethan Coen; directed by *Joel Coen*; for River Road.

Bloodbath at the House of Death
GB 1983 92m colour
EMI / Wildwood (Ray Cameron)

Scientists investigate a haunted house.
Spoof tailored to the requirements of a zany television comedian who never knows when enough is enough. Too much gore and far too much smut.

w Ray Cameron, Barry Cryer *d* Ray Cameron *ph* Brian West, Dusty Miller *m* Mike Moran, Mark London

Kenny Everett, Pamela Stephenson, Vincent Price, Gareth Hunt, Don Warrington, John Fortune, Sheila Steafel, Graham Stark

'Presumably intended as high camp; looks like low-grade Carry On.'—*Martyn Auty, MFB*

Bloodbrothers
US 1978 116m Technicolor
Warner / Stephen Friedman / Kings Road

The disintegration through failure and inadequacy of a noisy Italian-American family. The kind of self-indulgence that has one seeking the exit before it's half over.

w Walter Newman, *novel* Richard Price *d* Robert Mulligan *ph* Robert Surtees *m* Elmer Bernstein *pd* Gene Callahan

Paul Sorvino, Tony Lo Bianco, Richard Gere, Lelia Goldoni

'Why should filmgoers pay to see what they can already hear in the next apartment?'—

'The director is trying for something crude, powerful, volatile . . . but it goes terribly wrong. People laugh with hysterical heartiness, or say things like: "Life can hurt. It's made me feel close to all those doing the hurting dance." '—*Pauline Kael, New Yorker*

AAN: Walter Newman

Bloodhounds of Broadway*
US 1952 90m Technicolor
TCF (George Jessel)

With the help of a gangster, an orphan girl and her pet bloodhounds make a big hit in cabaret.
Absurd but sporadically amusing gangster burlesque, typical of its author. Lively production values.

w Sy Gomberg, *story* Damon Runyon *d* Harmon Jones *ph* Edward Cronjager *md* Lionel Newman *m* David Raksin

Mitzi Gaynor, Scott Brady, Mitzi Green, Marguerite Chapman, Michael O'Shea, Wally Vernon, George E. Stone

Bloodline
US 1979 117m Movielab
Paramount / Geria (David V. Bicker, Sidney Beckerman)

A pharmaceutical tycoon is murdered and his daughter seems likely to be the next victim.
Involved all-star suspense shocker which seems constantly about to be better than it ever is.

w Laird Koenig, *novel* Sidney Sheldon *d* Terence Young *ph* Freddie Young *m* Ennio Morricone *pd* Ted Haworth

Audrey Hepburn, Ben Gazzara, James Mason, Claudia Mori, Omar Sharif, Irene Papas, Maurice Ronet, Romy Schneider, Beatrice Straight, Gert Frobe, Micheline Phillips

'Unutterably chic, inexpressibly absurd, and saved from being painfully tedious only by a personable cast doing their damnedest.'—*Tom Milne, MFB*

'The family that stays together slays together!'

Bloody Mama*
US 1969 90m Movielab
AIP (Roger Corman)

In the thirties, outlaw Kate Barker and her four sons conduct a reign of terror until what's left of the gang is riddled with machine gun bullets.
Violent gangster story with a star on the rampage; the attempt to philosophize is more than the facts will bear, but the production moves smartly enough.

w Robert Thom *d* Roger Corman *ph* John Alonzo *m* Don Randi

Shelley Winters, Pat Hingle, Don Stroud, Diane Varsi, Bruce Dern, Clint Kimbrough, Robert de Niro, Robert Walden, Alex Nicol

Bloomfield
GB 1969 95m Technicolor
World Film Services / Limbridge (John Heyman, Wolf Mankowitz)
US title: *The Hero*

A 10-year-old Israeli boy hitchhikes to Jaffa to see his football idol play his last game.
Sentimental whimsy, unattractively interpreted.

w Wolf Mankowitz *d* Richard Harris *ph* Otto Heller *m* Johnny Harris

Richard Harris, Romy Schneider, Kim Burfield, Maurice Kaufmann, Yossi Yadin

Blossom Time
GB 1934 90m bw

In old Vienna, a composer stands by while the girl he loves weds a dragoon. Stilted musical romance redeemed by its star's singing presence. Richard Tauber, Jane Baxter, Carl Esmond, Athene Seyler. Written by John Drinkwater, Walter Burford, Paul Perez and G. H. Clutsam; directed by Paul Stein; for BIP. (US title: *April Romance*.)

Blossoms in the Dust**
US 1941 99m Technicolor
MGM (Irving Asher)

A woman who loses her husband and child founds a state orphanage.
Archetypal tearjerker of the forties, a glossy 'woman's picture' which distorts the facts into a star vehicle. Excellent colour helped to make it an enormous success.

w Anita Loos, based on the life of Edna Gladney *d* Mervyn Le Roy *ph* Karl Freund, W. Howard Greene *m* Herbert Stothart

Greer Garson, Walter Pidgeon, Felix Bressart, Marsha Hunt, Fay Holden, Samuel S. Hinds

AAN: best picture; Karl Freund, W. Howard Greene; Greer Garson

'Heading for the laff round-up!'

Blossoms on Broadway
US 1937 88m bw

A girl who owns a Death Valley gold mine comes to New York and is hounded by confidence men. Tolerably fast-moving comedy. Edward Arnold, Shirley Ross, John Trent, Weber and Fields, Frank Craven, Rufe David, William Frawley. Written by Theodore Reeves; directed by Richard Wallace; for B. P. Schulberg / Paramount. 'Won't do much b.o. blossoming. Good songs, but story stumbles badly.'—*Variety*

Blotto*
US 1930 20m bw

Ollie helps Stan escape his wife for a night on the town, but the lady takes revenge. Palatable star comedy with a strained second half following a splendidly typical opening. Laurel and Hardy, Anita Garvin. Written by Leo McCarey and H. M. Walker; directed by James Parrott; for Hal Roach.

'Murder has a sound all of its own!'

Blow Out
US 1981 108m Technicolor Panavision
Filmways / Cinema 77 / Geria (George Litto)

A sound effects man accidentally captures on film what turns out to be a murder.
Showily unpleasant thriller concocted of equal parts of *The Conversation*, *Blow Up*, and Kennedy at Chappaquiddick; the work of a copycat talent operating below par.

wd Brian de Palma *ph* Vilmos Szigmond *m* Pino Donaggio *pd* Paul Sylbert

John Travolta, Nancy Allen, John Lithgow, Dennis Franz, John McMartin, John Aquino

'The camera is better deployed than the script.'—*Guardian*

Blow Up**
GB 1966 110m Eastmancolor
MGM / Carlo Ponti

A London fashion photographer thinks he sees a murder, but the evidence disappears.
Not a mystery but a fashionable think-in on the difference (if any) between fantasy and reality. Agreeable to look at for those who can stifle their irritation at the non-plot and non-characters; a huge audience was lured by flashes of nudity and the trendy 'swinging London' setting.

wd Michelangelo Antonioni *ph* Carlo di Palma *m* Herbert Hancock *ad* Assheton Gorton

David Hemmings, Sarah Miles, Vanessa Redgrave

AAN: Michelangelo Antonioni (as writer and director)

Blowing Wild*
US 1953 88m bw
(Warner) United States (Milton Sperling)

A Mexican oil driller becomes involved with the psychotic wife of an old friend; the triangle leads to murder and retribution.
Pot-boiling star vehicle with adequate melodramatic interest, full of reminiscences of other movies, with a wicked lady to end them all.

w Philip Yordan *d* Hugo Fregonese *ph* Sid Hickox *m* Dmitri Tiomkin

Gary Cooper, Barbara Stanwyck, Anthony Quinn, Ruth Roman, Ward Bond

Blue
US 1968 113m Technicolor Panavision
Paramount / Kettledrum (Judd Bernard, Irwin Winkler)

The white adopted son of a Mexican bandit prevents his cohorts from raping a white girl, and falls in love with her.
Pretentious, self-conscious, literary western without much zest.

w Meade Roberts, Ronald M. Cohen *d* Silvio Narizzano *ph Stanley Cortez* *m* Manos Hadjidakis

Terence Stamp, Joanna Pettet, Karl Malden, Ricardo Montalban

'I don't know which is worse—bad cowboy movies or bad *arty* cowboy movies. *Blue* is both.'—*Rex Reed*

The Blue Angel****
Germany 1930 98m bw
UFA (Erich Pommer)

A fuddy-duddy professor is infatuated with a tawdry night-club singer. She marries him but is soon bored and contemptuous; humiliated, he leaves her and dies in his old classroom.
A masterwork of late twenties German grotesquerie, and after a slowish beginning an emotional powerhouse, set in a dark nightmare world which could be created only in the studio. Shot also in English, it was highly popular and influential in Britain and America.

w Robert Liebmann, Karl Zuckmayer, Karl Vollmoeller, *novel* Professor Unrath by Heinrich Mann *d* Josef Von Sternberg *ph* Günther Rittau, Hans Schneeberger *m* Frederick Hollander (inc 'Falling in Love Again', 'They Call Me Wicked Lola') *ad* Otto Hunte, Emil Hasler

Emil Jannings, Marlene Dietrich (who was instantly catapulted to international stardom), Kurt Gerron, Hans Albers

'It will undoubtedly do splendidly in the whole of Europe and should also appeal strongly in the States . . . only fault is a certain ponderousness of tempo which tends to tire.'—*Variety*

'At the time I thought the film was awful and vulgar and I was shocked by the whole thing. Remember, I was a well brought up German girl.'—*Marlene Dietrich*

The Blue Angel
US 1959 107m De Luxe Cinemascope
TCF (Jack Cummings)

Ill-advised attempt at a 'realistic', updated remake of the above; the result is a total travesty, with the actors aware that stylized melodrama is turning before their eyes into unintentional farce.

w Nigel Balchin *d* Edward Dmytryk *ph* Leon Shamroy *m* Hugo Friedhofer

Curt Jurgens, May Britt, Theodore Bikel, John Banner

'It totally lacks the stifling atmosphere of sordid and oppressive sexuality which is essential to give conviction to the German sadism of the story.'—*Brenda Davies*

The Blue Bird***
US 1940 98m Technicolor (bw prologue)
TCF (Gene Markey)

In a Grimm's Fairy Tale setting, the two children of a poor woodcutter seek the bluebird of happiness in the past, the future and the Land of Luxury, but eventually discover it in their own back yard.
An imaginative and often chilling script clarifies Maurice Maeterlinck's fairy play, and the art direction is outstanding, but the children are necessarily unsympathetic and the expensive production paled beside the success of the more upbeat *Wizard of Oz*, which was released almost simultaneously. Slashed for re-release, the only existing prints now open with confusing abruptness and no scene-setting before the adventures begin.

w Ernest Pascal d Walter Lang ph Arthur Miller, Ray Rennahan m Alfred Newman *ad Richard Day, Wiard B. Ihnen*

Shirley Temple, Johnny Russell, *Gale Sondergaard* (as the cat), *Eddie Collins* (as the dog), Nigel Bruce, Jessie Ralph, Spring Byington, Sybil Jason, Helen Ericson, Russell Hicks, Al Shean, Cecilia Loftus

'One of the most deliciously lovely productions to be brought to the screen.'—*Monthly Film Bulletin*

AAN: Arthur Miller, Ray Rennahan

The Blue Bird
US / USSR 1976 83m Technicolor Panavision
TCF / Edward Lewis / Lenfilm

Abortive remake of the above, widely touted as the first Russian–American co-production, but sabotaged by a flabby script, unsuitable casting and unresolved production problems.

w Hugh Whitemore, Alfred Hayes *d* George Cukor *ph* Freddie Young, Ionas Gritzus *m* Irwin Kostal, Andrei Petrov

Elizabeth Taylor (as Mother, Maternal Love, Light and the Witch), Ava Gardner, Cicely Tyson, Jane Fonda, Harry Andrews, Will Geer, Mona Washbourne, George Cole

'It works so hard at making history that it forgets to make sense.'—*David Sterritt, Christian Science Monitor*

'If you have any naughty children you want to punish, take them to *The Blue Bird* and make them sit all the way through it.'—*William Wolf, Cue*

'It turns a work for adults that children can enjoy into a charade for children that must sicken adults.'—*John Simon, New Yorker*

'Senile and interminable.'—*Stephen Farber, New West*

'Lavishly done; limited box office.'—*Variety*

Blue Blood
GB 1973 86m Technicolor
Mallard-Impact Quadrant

A German governess arrives at an English stately home and finds the malevolent butler plotting to show his supremacy over his effete master.
An extremely unattractive, would-be satirical melodrama which plays like a Grand Guignol version of *The Servant*.

wd Andrew Sinclair, *novel* The Carry-Cot by Alexander Thynne *ph* Harry Waxman *m* Brian Gascoigne

Oliver Reed, Derek Jacobi, Fiona Lewis, Anna Gael, Meg Wynn Owen

Blue Collar*
US 1978 114m Technicolor
Universal / TAT (Don Guest)

Three car factory workers try to improve their lot by unionization and robbery.
Salty, rough, downbeat but impressively realistic modern drama, a belated American equivalent of *Saturday Night and Sunday Morning*.

w Paul Schraeder, Leonard Schraeder *d* Paul Schraeder *ph* Bobby Byrne *m* Jack Nitzche

Richard Pryor, Harvey Keitel, Yaphet Kotto, Ed Begley Jnr, Harry Bellaver

'Tamed by a brunette—framed by a blonde—blamed by the cops!'
The Blue Dahlia**
US 1946 99m bw
Paramount (John Houseman)

A returning war veteran finds his faithless wife murdered and himself suspected.
Hailed on its first release as sharper than average, this mystery suspenser is now only moderately compelling despite the screenplay credit; direction and editing lack urgency and the acting lacks bounce.

w Raymond Chandler d George Marshall *ph* Lionel Lindon *m* Victor Young

Alan Ladd, Veronica Lake, William Bendix, Howard da Silva, Doris Dowling, Tom Powers, Hugh Beaumont, Howard Freeman, Will Wright

'It threatens to turn into something, but it never does.'—*New Yorker, 1978*

'The picture is as neatly stylized and synchronized, and as uninterested in moral excitement, as a good ballet; it knows its own weight and size perfectly and carries them gracefully and without self-importance; it is, barring occasional victories and noble accidents, about as good a movie as can be expected from the big factories.'—*James Agee*

AAN: Raymond Chandler

Blue Denim*
US 1959 89m bw Cinemascope
TCF (Charles Brackett)
GB title: *Blue Jeans*

Teenagers confronted with the prospect of illegitimate parenthood consult an abortionist, but all ends with wedding bells.
First of its rather dreary kind but better than most, this only slightly mawkish domestic drama has its heart in the right place and steers surprisingly towards a nick-of-time chase climax.

w Edith Sommer, Philip Dunne, *play* James Leo Herlihy, William Noble *d* Philip Dunne *ph* Leo Tover *m* Bernard Herrmann

THE BLUE BIRD. Has Shirley Temple finally found the Blue Bird of Happiness? Gale Sondergaard, Laura Hope Crews, Claire Du Brey, Brandon Hurst and Johnny Russell join the diminutive superstar.

Carol Lynley, Brandon de Wilde, Macdonald Carey, Marsha Hunt, Nina Shipman, Warren Berlinger

The Blue Gardenia
US 1953 90m bw
Warner / Gloria / Blue Gardenia (Alex Gottlieb)

A girl gets drunk and wakes up in a strange apartment with a dead man by her side. Totally undistinguished mystery which leaves egg on the actors' faces.

w Charles Hoffman *d* Fritz Lang *ph* Nicholas Musuraca *m* Raoul Krashaar

Anne Baxter, Richard Conte, Ann Sothern, Raymond Burr, Jeff Donnell, Richard Erdman, Nat King Cole

Blue Hawaii
US 1961 101m Technicolor Panavision
Hal B. Wallis

A GI comes home to Honolulu and becomes a beachcomber. Lifeless star vehicle shot on glamorous locations.

w Hal Kanter *d* Norman Taurog *ph* Charles Lang Jnr *m* Joseph J. Lilley

Elvis Presley, Joan Blackman, Nancy Walters, Roland Winters, Angela Lansbury, John Archer, Howard McNear

The Blue Lagoon*
GB 1949 103m Technicolor
GFD / Individual (Frank Launder, Sidney Gilliat)

A shipwrecked boy and girl grow up on a desert island, ward off smugglers, have a baby, and eventually sail away in search of civilization.
Rather lifeless, though pretty, treatment of a famous novel: the story never becomes vivid despite splendid Fijian locations.

w Frank Launder, John Baines, Michael Hogan, *novel* H. de Vere Stacpoole *d* Frank Launder *ph Geoffrey Unsworth* *m* Clifton Parker

Jean Simmons, Donald Houston, Noel Purcell, Cyril Cusack, James Hayter

The Blue Lagoon
US 1980 102m Colorfilm
Columbia / Randal Kleiser

Remake of the above with poor narrative balance and a great deal of nudity and adolescent frankness about sex. Adolescents are probably its only audience.

w Douglas Day Stewart *d* Randal Kleiser *ph* Nestor Almendros *m* Basil Poledouris

Brooke Shields, Christopher Atkins, Leo McKern, William Daniels

'At best a damp dream, a Sunday school fairy tale which makes the story of Adam and Eve seem like hard porn, as hygienically sanitized as a Hilton Hotel lavatory seat.'—*Sunday Times*

'A total fraud from beginning to end.'—*Guardian*

'The film has an inevitable, built-in prurience. All we have to look forward to is: when are these two going to discover fornication?'—*Pauline Kael, New Yorker*

'This movie made me itch.'—*Roger Ebert*

AAN: Nestor Almendros

The Blue Lamp***
GB 1949 84m bw
Ealing (Michael Relph)

A young man joins London's police force. The elderly copper who trains him is killed in a shootout, but the killer is apprehended.
Seminal British police film which spawned not only a long line of semi-documentary imitations but also the twenty-year TV series *Dixon of Dock Green* for which the shot PC was happily revived. As an entertainment, pacy but dated; more important, it burnished the image of the British copper for generations.

w T. E. B. Clarke *d Basil Dearden* *ph* Gordon Dines *md* Ernest Irving

Jack Warner, Jimmy Hanley, Dirk Bogarde, Meredith Edwards, Robert Flemyng, Bernard Lee, Patric Doonan, Peggy Evans, Gladys Henson, Dora Bryan

'The mixture of coyness, patronage and naive theatricality which has vitiated British films for the last ten years.'—*Gavin Lambert*

'A soundly made crime thriller which would not be creating much of a stir if it were American.'—*Richard Mallett, Punch*

The Blue Light*
Germany 1932 68m bw
H. R. Sokal / Leni Riefenstahl

In the early 19th century, a painter defies a local legend to climb a Dolomite mountain.
Romantic fairy tale with a story more suited to a ballet. It still takes the eye, and is recognizable as the work of its director.

wd Leni Riefenstahl *ph* Hans Schneeberger, Henry Jaworsky *m* Giuseppe Becce

Leni Riefenstahl, Matthias Wieman, Max Holsboer

† This version was put together in 1950 after the original negative had been lost; among other things, a flashback frame was removed.

'There was no quiet on the western front for the heroes and cowards who flew to their rendezvous with hell!'

The Blue Max*
US 1966 156m De Luxe Cinemascope
TCF (Christian Ferry)

In Germany after World War I an ambitious and skilful pilot causes the death of his comrades and steals the wife of his High Command superior, who eventually finds a means of revenge.
For once, an action spectacular not too badly let down by its connecting threads of plot, apart from some hilarious and unnecessary bedroom scenes in which the female star's bath towel seems to become conveniently adhesive.

w David Pursall, Jack Seddon, Gerald Hanley, *novel* Jack Hunter *d John Guillermin* *ph* Douglas Slocombe *m* Jerry Goldsmith

George Peppard, *James Mason*, Ursula Andress, Jeremy Kemp, Karl Michael Vogler, Anton Diffring, Derren Nesbitt

'Addicts of flying movies swear by this one, but for others, the monoplanes and biplanes can't smash or burn fast enough'—*Pauline Kael*

Blue Murder at St Trinians*
GB 1957 86m bw
British Lion / John Marvel (Launder and Gilliat)

The awful schoolgirls win a UNESCO prize trip which takes them to Rome where they become involved with a jewel thief.
Possibly the best of this series, which isn't saying much. See *The Belles of St Trinians.*

w Frank Launder, Val Valentine, Sidney Gilliat *d* Frank Launder *ph* Gerald Gibbs *m* Malcolm Arnold

Terry-Thomas, George Cole, Joyce Grenfell, Alistair Sim, Judith Furse, Sabrina, Lionel Jeffries, Lloyd Lamble, Thorley Walters, Kenneth Griffith, Eric Barker, Richard Wattis

The Blue Peter
GB 1955 93m Eastmancolor
British Lion / Beaconsfield (Herbert Mason)
US title: *Navy Heroes*

A confused war hero becomes a trainer at an Outward Bound school for boys.
Pleasant but uninspired open air adventure for young people.

w Don Sharp, John Pudney *d* Wolf Rilla *ph* Arthur Grant *m* Antony Hopkins

Kieron Moore, Greta Gynt, Sarah Lawson, Mervyn Johns, Ram Gopal, Edwin Richfield, Harry Fowler, John Charlesworth

'It's the nearest thing to heaven!'

Blue Skies*
US 1946 104m Technicolor
Paramount (Sol C. Siegel)

A dancing star and a nightclub owner fight for years over the same girl.
Thin musical with splendid Irving Berlin tunes and lively individual numbers.

w Arthur Sheekman *d* Stuart Heisler *ph* Charles Lang *md* Robert Emmett Dolan

Fred Astaire (dancing 'Putting On the Ritz'), Bing Crosby, Joan Caulfield, Billy de Wolfe, Olga San Juan, Robert Benchley, Frank Faylen, Victoria Horne, Jack Norton

AAN: Robert Emmett Dolan; song 'You Keep Coming Back Like a Song' (*m* / *ly* Irving Berlin)

Blue Thunder*
US 1983 110m Technicolor Panavision
Columbia / Rastar / Gordon Carroll

A policeman in Los Angeles' Astro Division is haunted by memories of Vietnam and goes berserk when using his new ultra-sophisticated helicopter to wage war against crime.
Slick but hollow thriller most remarkable for its helicopter stunting between city skyscrapers. Otherwise, it is too often fashionably inaudible and almost invisible.

w Dan O'Bannon, Don Jakoby *d* John Badham *ph* John A. Alonzo *m* Arthur B. Rubenstein *aerial ph Frank Holgate*

Roy Scheider, Warren Oates, Candy Clark, Daniel Stern, Malcolm McDowell

† A watered-down TV version was quickly assembled, but its comic-strip dialogue grounded it after 13 episodes.

AAN: editing (Frank Morriss, Edward Abroms)

The Blue Veil*
US 1951 114m bw
(RKO) Wald–Krasna (Raymond Hakim)

The vocational career of a children's nurse who descends into poverty but is rescued by one of her own charges, now grown up.
Sober American remake of a French tearjerker (*Le Voile bleu*) with the star suffering nobly but being upstaged by the cameo players.

w Norman Corwin, from the original by François Campaux *d* Curtis Bernhardt *ph* Franz Planer *m* Franz Waxman

Jane Wyman, Charles Laughton, Richard Carlson, Joan Blondell, Agnes Moorehead, Don Taylor, Audrey Totter, Everett Sloane, Cyril Cusack, Natalie Wood, Warner Anderson

AAN: Jane Wyman; Joan Blondell

Blue Velvet
US 1986 120m colour
De Laurentiis (Richard Roth)

Murder, mutilation and sexual perversion in Middle America.
Bizarrely stylish exercise by the director of *The Elephant Man*, popular at the box office.

w,d David Lynch *ph* Frederick Elmes
m Angelo Badalamenti *pd* Patricia Norris

Kyle MacLachlan, Isabella Rossellini, Dennis Hopper, Laura Dern, Hope Lange, Dean Stockwell

AAN: David Lynch

Blue Water, White Death*
US 1971 99m Techniscope

A skilful and quite frightening documentary about the habits of the Great White Shark, with a lead-up showing events on the expedition which set out in search of it. Written and directed by Peter Gimbel; photographed by James Lipscomb; for Blue Water Films / Cinema Center.

Bluebeard*
US 1944 73m bw
PRC

A strangler of young girls is at large in Paris.
Poverty Row chiller with effective moments; possibly the most interesting film ever to come from PRC (which isn't saying *very* much).

w Pierre Gendron *d Edgar G. Ulmer*
ph Jockey Feindel

John Carradine, Jean Parker, Ludwig Stossel, Nils Asther, Iris Adrian

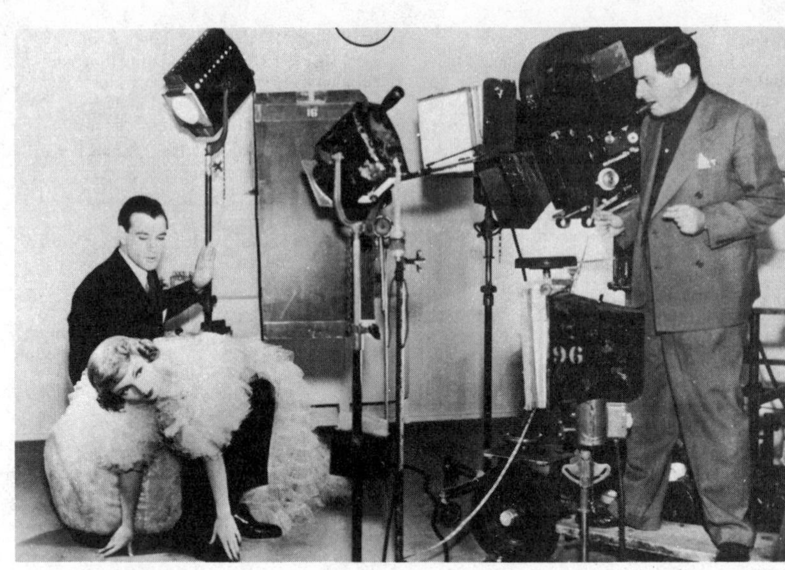

BLUEBEARD'S EIGHTH WIFE. In a painfully posed set-up, director Ernst Lubitsch supervises Gary Cooper's chastisement of Claudette Colbert.

Bluebeard
France / Italy / Germany 1972 124m Technicolor
Barnabé / Gloria / Geiselgasteig (Alexander Salkind)

The lady killer in this case is an Austrian aristocrat who has been driven to desperation and murder by a long line of mistresses whose bodies he keeps frozen in his cellar.
Would-be macabre comedy which becomes totally off-putting by its emphasis on close-up death agonies.

w Ennio di Concini, Edward Dmytryk, Maria Pia Fusco *d* Edward Dmytryk *ph* Gabor Pogany *m* Ennio Morricone

Richard Burton, Raquel Welch, Joey Heatherton, Virna Lisi, Nathalie Delon, Marilu Tolo

'Somewhere between (and a long way behind) *Kind Hearts and Coronets* and *The Abominable Dr Phibes*.'—*Clyde Jeavons, MFB*

Bluebeard's Eighth Wife*
US 1938 85m bw
Paramount (Ernst Lubitsch)

The daughter of an impoverished French aristocrat marries for money a millionaire who has had seven previous wives, and determines to teach him a lesson.
Very thin sophisticated comedy with unsympathetic characters and little wit after the first scene; a disappointment from the talent involved.

w Charles Brackett, Billy Wilder, *play* Alfred Savoir *d* Ernst Lubitsch *ph* Leo Tover
m Werner Heymann, Frederick Hollander

Claudette Colbert, Gary Cooper, David Niven, Edward Everett Horton, Elizabeth Patterson, Herman Bing, Warren Hymer, Franklin Pangborn

'Light and sometimes bright, but it gets a bit tiresome.'—*Variety*

'In these days it is bad enough to have to admire millionaires in any circumstances; but a millionaire with a harem complex simply can't help starting the bristles on the back of a sensitive neck.'—*New York Times*

† A previous version, released by Paramount in 1923 and directed by Sam Wood, starred Gloria Swanson and Huntley Gordon.

Bluebeard's Seven Wives*
US 1926 94m approx bw silent

A bank teller becomes a film star and is transformed, notably by seven imaginary marriages. Amusing spoof on the film industry that was. Ben Lyon, Lois Wilson, Blanche Sweet, Dorothy Sebastian, Sam Hardy. Written by Blanche Merrill, Paul Scofield; directed by Alfred Santell; for First National.

Bluebeard's Ten Honeymoons
GB 1960 93m bw
Anglo-Allied (Roy Parkinson)

Another version of the story of Landru, alternating wildly between fantasy, farce and melodrama. Not a success in any of its moods.

w Myles Wilder *d* W. Lee Wilder
ph Stephen Dade *m* Albert Elms

George Sanders, Corinne Calvet, Patricia Roc, Ingrid Hafner, Jean Kent, Greta Gynt, Maxine Audley, Selma Vaz Diaz, George Coulouris

'The unedifying narrative is developed along the most obvious lines imaginable.'—*MFB*

The Bluebird see *The Blue Bird*

A Blueprint for Murder*
US 1953 77m bw
TCF (Michael Abel)

After the death of his brother and niece, a man proves that his sister-in-law is a murderess.
Unpleasant but efficient murder story with enough twists to keep one watching.

wd Andrew Stone *ph* Leo Tover *m* David Raksin *md* Lionel Newman

Jean Peters, Joseph Cotten, Gary Merrill, Catherine McLeod, Jack Kruschen

Blueprint for Robbery*
US 1960 87m bw
Paramount (Bryan Foy)

Crooks plan and execute a robbery, agreeing not to touch the proceeds for two and a half years. But some get tired of waiting. . .
Minor but effective crime melodrama in semi-documentary vein.

w Irwin Winehouse, A. Sanford Wolf *d* Jerry Hopper *ph* Loyal Griggs *m* Van Cleave

J. Pat O'Malley, Robert Gist, Romo Vincent, Marion Ross, Tom Duggan

'A not uninteresting entry in the screen log-book on crime.'—*MFB*

The Blues Brothers
US 1980 133m Technicolor
Universal (Robert K. Weiss)

A massive car chase develops when two brothers collect money for their old orphanage without too much regard for law and order.
Fashionable chase comedy with so many stunts that its cost ran up to 33,000,000 dollars. The public stayed away.

w Dan Aykroyd, John Landis *d* John Landis *ph* Stephen M. Katz *md* Ira Newborn *pd* John Lloyd

John Belushi, Dan Aykroyd, Kathleen Freeman, James Brown, Henry Gibson, Cab Calloway, Carrie Fisher

'It meanders expensively like some pedigreed shaggy dog through 70s / 80s American cinema and 50s / 60s American rock, cocking its leg happily at every popular landmark on the way.'—*Paul Taylor, MFB*

'There's not a *soupçon* of wit or ingenuity in this brainless exercise in overspending.'—*Daily Mail*

'There's even room, in the midst of the carnage and mayhem, for a surprising amount of grace, humor and whimsy.'—*Roger Ebert*

Blues in the Night*
US 1941 88m bw
Warner (Henry Blanke)

Career and romantic problems for the members of a travelling jazz band.
Atmospheric little melodrama with good score and smart dialogue.

w Robert Rossen, play Hot Nocturne by Edwin Gilbert *d* Anatole Litvak *ph* Ernest Haller *songs* Harold Arlen, Johnny Mercer

Priscilla Lane, Richard Whorf, Lloyd Nolan, Betty Field, Jack Carson, Elia Kazan, Wallace Ford, Billy Halop, Peter Whitney

AAN: title song (*m* Harold Arlen, *ly* Johnny Mercer)

Blume in Love*
US 1973 116m Technicolor
Warner (Paul Mazursky)

A divorced American lawyer in Venice reminisces about his love life.
Shapeless but enjoyable 'serious comedy' with star and director in good form.

wd Paul Mazursky ph Bruce Surtees *m* various

George Segal, Susan Anspach, Kris Kristofferson, Marsha Mason, Shelley Winters

BMX Bandits
Australia 1983 90m colour Panavision

Bike enthusiasts become unpopular when they cause havoc in the streets, but become heroes when they capture bank robbers. Lively action piece with unacceptable behaviour followed by reformation and an old-fashioned moral for early teenagers. David Argue, John Ley, Nicole Brian Sloman, Peter Browne. Written by Patrick Edgeworth; directed by Brian Trenchard Smith; for BMX / Nilsen.

Boardwalk
US 1979 100m Eastmancolor
ITC / Stratford (Gerald T. Herrod)

An old couple in Coney Island are affected by escalating violence.
Well-meaning but somewhat absurd moral tale for our times, in which the harassed septuagenarian finally chokes the young punk leader to death.

w Stephen Verona, Leigh Chapman *d* Stephen Verona *ph* Billy Williams *m* various

Ruth Gordon, Lee Strasberg, Janet Leigh, Joe Silver, Eddie Barth

'One would probably have to reach as far back as *The Birth of a Nation* to find a more direct incitement to racial hatred.'—*Richard Combs, MFB*

The Boat**
West Germany 1981 149m Fujicolor
Columbia / Bavaria Atelier / Radiant Film (Gunter Röhrbach)
original and US title: *Das Boot*

Adventures of a German U-boat during World War II.
Well-crafted but totally unsurprising saga of heroism and self-sacrifice; a decent view of war from the German side, designed to impress world markets. It did so only moderately.

wd Wolfgang Petersen ph Jost Vacano m Klaus Doldinger *pd* Rolf Zehetbauer

Jürgen Prochnow, Herbert Grönemeyer, Klaus Wennemann, Hubertus Bengsch, Martin Semmelrogge

AAN: direction; screenplay (adaptation); cinematography; editing; sound; sound editing.

The Boatniks*
US 1970 100m Technicolor
Walt Disney (Ron Miller)

An accident-prone coastguard officer creates havoc at a yachting marina but is acclaimed a hero after catching three jewel thieves.
Simple fresh-air farce for the family, pleasantly set but flatly directed.

w Arthur Julian *d* Norman Tokar *ph* William Snyder *m* Robert F. Brunner

Phil Silvers, Robert Morse, Stefanie Powers, Norman Fell, Mickey Shaughnessey, Wally Cox, Don Ameche, Joey Forman

Bob and Carol and Ted and Alice**
US 1969 105m Technicolor
Columbia / M. J. Frankovich (Larry Tucker)

Two California couples, influenced by a group therapy session advocating natural spontaneous behaviour, decide to admit their extra-marital affairs and narrowly avoid a wife-swapping party.
Fashionable comedy without the courage of its convictions: it starts and finishes very bashfully, but there are bright scenes in the middle. An attempt to extend it into a TV series was a failure.

w Paul Mazursky, Larry Tucker *d* Paul Mazursky *ph* Charles E. Lang *m* Quincy Jones

Natalie Wood, Robert Culp, Elliott Gould, Dyan Cannon, Horst Ebersberg

'An old-fashioned romantic comedy disguised as a blue picture.'—*Arthur Schlesinger Jnr*

AAN: Paul Mazursky, Larry Tucker; Charles E. Lang; Elliott Gould; Dyan Cannon

The Bob Mathias Story
US 1954 80m bw

The biography of an American athlete who won the Decathlon in the 1952 Olympics.
Predictable low-budgeter of no abiding interest. Bob Mathias, Ward Bond, Melba Mathias, Ann Doran, Howard Petrie. Written by Richard Collins; directed by Francis D. Lyon; for Allied Artists. (GB title: *The Flaming Torch*.)

Bobbikins
GB 1959 90m bw Cinemascope
TCF (Oscar Brodney, Bob McNaught)

A downtrodden variety artist finds that his baby can not only talk but also give him tips on the stock exchange.
Not at all a good idea, and feebly executed.

w Oscar Brodney *d* Robert Day *ph* Geoffrey Faithfull *m* Philip Green

Max Bygraves, Shirley Jones, Billie Whitelaw, Barbara Shelley, Colin Gordon, Charles Tingwell, Lionel Jeffries, Rupert Davies

'He had to meet her—to find himself!'

Bobby Deerfield
US 1977 123m Metrocolor Panavision
Warner / First Artists (Sydney Pollack)

A depressive motor racing driver falls for a girl with an incurable illness.
A kind of understated *Love Story* for intellectuals; nicely made, but nothing that anybody will be wildly concerned about.

w Alvin Sargent, *novel* Heaven Has No Favourites by Erich Maria Remarque *d* Sydney Pollack *ph* Henri Decaë *m* Dave Grusin *pd* Stephen Grimes

Al Pacino, Marthe Keller, Anny Duperey, Walter McGinn, Romolo Valli, Jaime Sanchez

The Bobo
US 1967 105m Technicolor
Warner / Gina (Elliott Kastner, Jerry Gershwin) (David R. Schwarz)

An unsuccessful and timid bullfighter is offered a contract if within three days he can seduce the local belle.
Stylized, silly and boring comedy from an obviously dated play; Chaplinesque pathos was not this star's strong suit.

w David R. Schwarz, from his play and the novel *Olimpia* by Burt Cole *d* Robert Parrish *ph* Gerry Turpin *m* Francis Lai

Peter Sellers, Britt Ekland, Rossano Brazzi, Adolfo Celi, Hattie Jacques, Ferdy Mayne, Kenneth Griffith, John Wells

Boccaccio '70*
Italy / France 1962 210m Eastmancolor
TCF / CCC / Cineriz / Francinex / Gray Films (Antonio Cervi, Carlo Ponti)

Four modern stories which Boccaccio might have written (on an off day).
Overlong portmanteau with inevitable bright moments but many more longueurs.

'The Temptation of Dr Antonio': *w* Federico Fellini, Tullio Pinelli, Ennio Flaiano *d* Federico Fellini *ph* Otello Martelli; with Anita Ekberg
'The Job': *w* Suso Cecchi d'Amico, Luchino Visconti *d* Luchino Visconti *ph* Giuseppe Rotunno; with Romy Schneider, Tomas Milian
'The Raffle': *w* Cesare Zavattini *d* Vittorio de Sica *ph* Otello Martelli; with Sophia Loren
'Renzo and Luciana': *d* Mario Monichelli

Body and Soul
US 1931 82m bw

In the 1914–1918 war, a flier falls for the wife of his dead buddy. Tedious and often risible romantic melodrama. Charles Farrell, Elissa Landi, Humphrey Bogart, Myrna Loy, Donald Dillaway. From the play Squadrons by E. W. Springs and A. E. Thomas; directed by Alfred Santell; for Fox. 'Kidding is almost bound to creep in.'—*Variety*

Body and Soul*
US 1947 104m bw
Enterprise (Bob Roberts)

A young boxer fights his way unscrupulously to the top.
Melodramatic but absorbing study of prizefighting's seamy side. (Is there any other?) Inventively studio-bound and almost impressionist in treatment.

w Abraham Polonsky d Robert Rossen ph James Wong Howe md Rudolph Polk *m* Hugo Friedhofer

John Garfield, Lilli Palmer, Hazel Brooks, Anne Revere, William Conrad, Joseph Pevney, Canada Lee

'Here are the gin and tinsel, squalor and sables of the depression era, less daring than when first revealed in *Dead End* or *Golden Boy* but more valid and mature because shown without sentiment or blur.'—*National Board of Review*

AAN: Abraham Polonsky; John Garfield

Body and Soul
US 1981 122m colour
Cannon–Golan–Globus (Cliff Roquemore)

An amateur boxer turns professional to earn money for medical treatment for his kid sister.
Blood in the ring, sentimentality on the sidelines. Despite the credit, this repellent movie has virtually no connection with the previous 'version'.

w Leon Isaac Kennedy, from a *screenplay* by Abraham Polonsky *d* George Bowers *ph* James Forrest *m* Webster Lewis

Leon Isaac Kennedy, Jayne Kennedy, Muhammed Ali, Michael Gazzo, Perry Lang, Kim Hamilton, Peter Lawford

The Body Disappears
US 1941 72m bw
Warner (Ben Stoloff)

A professor invents an invisibility formula.
Uninspired comedy switch on a familiar theme.

w Scott Darling, Erna Lazarus *d* D. Ross Lederman *ph* Allen G. Seigler *m* Howard Jackson
Edward Everett Horton, Jeffrey Lynn, Jane Wyman, Herbert Anderson, Marguerite Chapman, Craig Stevens, David Bruce, Willie Best

Body Double
US 1984 114m Metrocolor
Columbia / Delphi II (Brian de Palma)

An out-of-work actor finds himself drawn into a nightmare when he spies on a lady stripteaser across the street.
Semi-porno melodrama with many echoes of Hitchcock overlaid with fashionable extremes of violence.

w Robert J. Avrech, Brian de Palma *d* Brian de Palma *ph* Stephen H. Burum *m* Pino Donaggio *pd* Ida Random *ed* Jerry Greenberg, Bill Pankow

Craig Wasson, Gregg Henry, Melanie Griffith

'De Palma lets all his obsessions hang out.'—*Variety*

'She taught him everything he knew—about passion and murder!'

Body Heat**
US 1981 113m Technicolor
Warner / Ladd (Fred T. Gallo)

A Florida lawyer becomes involved with a married woman and they plot to kill her businessman husband.
Oversexed and superfluous, not to mention uncredited, revamp of *Double Indemnity*. Some evidence of flair does not relieve that 'I have been here before' feeling.

wd Lawrence Kasdan ph Richard H. Kline *m* John Barry *pd* Bill Kenney *ed* Carol Littleton

William Hurt, *Kathleen Turner*, Richard Crenna, Ted Danson

'Film noir, if it is to be successfully reworked, needs to be approached with a sense of analysis, rather than simple excess.'—*Steve Jenkins, MFB*

Body Slam
US 1987 89m CFI color

A promoter on the skids accidentally creates the rock'n wrestling craze. Easy-going comedy which would have benefited from more confident production. Dirk Benedict, Tanya Roberts, Roddy Piper, Lou Albano, Charles Nelson Reilly, Billy Barty, Barry Gordon, John Astin. Written by Shel Lytton, Steve Burkow; directed by Hal Needham; for Musifilm / Hemdale.

The Body Snatcher***
US 1945 77m bw
RKO (Val Lewton)

In 19th-century Edinburgh a doctor obtains 'specimens' from grave-robbers, and murder results when supplies run short.
A familiar theme very imaginatively handled, and well acted, though the beginning is slow. The best of the Lewton thrillers.

w Philip MacDonald, Carlos Keith (Val Lewton), *story* R. L. Stevenson *d Robert Wise ph Robert de Grasse m* Roy Webb

Henry Daniell, Boris Karloff, Bela Lugosi, Edith Atwater, Russell Wade

'A humane sincerity and a devotion to good cinema . . . However, most of the picture is more literary than lively.'—*Time*

Boeing-Boeing
US 1965 102m Technicolor
(Paramount) Hal B. Wallis

By successfully juggling with plane schedules, a Paris journalist manages to live with three air hostesses at the same time.
Frenetic, paper-thin sex comedy from a one-joke play; film style generally undistinguished.

w Edward Anhalt, *play* Marc Camoletti *d* John Rich *ph* Lucien Ballard *m* Neal Hefti

Tony Curtis, Jerry Lewis (his only 'straight' part), Dany Saval, Christiane Schmidtner, Suzanna Leigh, *Thelma Ritter*

'A sort of jet-age French farce.'—*Judith Crist*

'The big comedy of nineteen sexty-sex!'—*publicity*

The Bofors Gun*
GB 1968 105m Technicolor
Rank / Everglades (Robert A. Goldson, Otto Plaschkes)

In 1954 Germany a British army unit runs into trouble when a violent and unstable Irish private picks on a weakly National Service corporal.
Keen, fascinating, but often crude and eventually rather silly expansion of a TV play chiefly notable for the excellent acting opportunities provided by its unattractive but recognizable characters.

w John McGrath *d* Jack Gold *ph* Alan Hume *m* Carl Davis

Nicol Williamson, John Thaw, *David Warner*, Ian Holm

La Bohème
US 1926 75m approx at 24 fps bw silent

Mimi starves to death in a Paris garret.
Overacted straight version of the opera, with two passionate star performances. Lillian Gish, John Gilbert, Renee Adoree, Edward Everett Horton. Written by Harry Behn and Ray Doyle, after Murger; directed by King Vidor; for MGM.

The Bohemian Girl*
US 1936 74m bw
Hal Roach

Gypsies kidnap a nobleman's daughter and bring her up as their own.
One of several operettas reworked for Laurel and Hardy, this is an inoffensive entertainment which devotes too little care to their need for slowly built-up gag structure; their sequences tend to fizzle out and the singing is a bore.

w Alfred Bunn, *operetta* William Balfe *d* James Horne, Charles Rogers *ph* Art Lloyd, Francis Corby

Stan Laurel, Oliver Hardy, Mae Busch, Antonio Moreno, Jacqueline Wells, Darla Hood, Zeffie Tilbury, James Finlayson, Thelma Todd (for one song, apparently dubbed: presumably before her sudden death she had been cast as the heroine)
† There was in 1922 a British silent version with a splendid cast including Ivor Novello, Gladys Cooper, C. Aubrey Smith, Ellen Terry and Constance Collier.

The Bold and the Brave
US 1956 87m bw Superscope
RKO / Hal E. Chester

An assortment of American types come together in the Italian campaign of 1944.
Routine war heroics chiefly remembered (if at all) for a crap game sequence.

w Robert Lewin *d* Lewis Foster *ph* Sam Leavitt *m* Herschel Burke Gilbert

Wendell Corey, *Mickey Rooney*, Nicole Maurey, Don Taylor

AAN: Robert Lewin; Mickey Rooney

'He rose to fame on a ladder of dancing ladies!'
Bolero*
US 1934 85m bw
Paramount

A New York dancer neglects his personal life to become king of the European night club circuit.
Lively romantic drama which performed remarkably at the box office and led to a kind of sequel, *Rumba*.

w Carey Wilson, Kubec Glasmon, Ruth Ridenour, Horace Jackson *d Wesley Ruggles* *ph* Leo Tover

George Raft, Carole Lombard, Sally Rand (doing her fan dance), Frances Drake, William Frawley, Ray Milland, Gertrude Michael

'A studio conference product: lots of surefire elements. On screen it's a little enervating . . . depends on Raft's popularity with the women.'—*Variety*

Bolero
US 1984 104m colour
Cannon / City (Bo Derek)

In 1926, a wealthy romantic girl travels the world in search of a man worthy of the sacrifice of her virginity.
Ludicrous sexual charade with unpleasant overtones resulting from the fact that the star's husband wrote and photographed this embarrassing piece of near-pornography.

w,ph,d John Derek *m* Peter Bernstein *pd* Alan Roderick-Jones

Bo Derek, George Kennedy, Andrea Occhipinti, Greg Bensen, Ana Obregon

'The only ecstatic moment a filmgoer might derive will be at the discovery that it's over.'—*Philip Strick, MFB*

Bomba the Jungle Boy
US 1949 71m bw or sepia
Monogram (Walter Mirisch)

Photographers in Africa meet a junior Tarzan who rescues their girl friend.
Cut-rate hokum starring the lad who had played Johnny Weissmuller's 'son' in earlier Tarzan movies; it led to several tedious sequels.

w Jack de Witt, from the comic strip by Roy Rockwell *d* Ford Beebe *ph* William Sickner *m* Edward Kay

Johnny Sheffield, Peggy Ann Garner, Onslow Stevens, Charles Irwin
† Sequels were as follows:
1948: BOMBA ON PANTHER ISLAND (76m) with Allene Roberts
1949: BOMBA AND THE LOST VOLCANO (76m) with Donald Woods; BOMBA AND THE HIDDEN CITY (71m) with Paul Guilfoyle
1950: BOMBA AND THE ELEPHANT STAMPEDE (71m) with Myron Sealey
1951: BOMBA AND THE AFRICAN TREASURE (70m) with Lyle Talbot; BOMBA AND THE JUNGLE GIRL (70m) with Karen Sharpe; BOMBA AND THE LION HUNTERS (75m) with Morris Ankrum
1953: SAFARI DRUMS (71m) with Douglas Kennedy
1954: THE GOLDEN IDOL (71m) with Paul Guilfoyle; KILLER LEOPARD (70m) with Beverly Garland
1955: LORD OF THE JUNGLE (69m) with Wayne Morris

Bombardier
US 1943 99m bw
RKO (Robert Fellows)

Cadet bombardiers learn the realities of war on raids over Japan.
Totally routine recruiting poster heroics.

w John Twist *d* Richard Wallace *ph* Nicholas Musuraca *m* Roy Webb

Pat O'Brien, Randolph Scott, Anne Shirley, Eddie Albert, Walter Reed, Robert Ryan, Barton Maclane

Bombay Clipper
US 1941 54m bw

On a clipper bound for Bombay, a reporter becomes involved in mystery and romance. Capsule actioner with stock studio talent. William Gargan, Irene Hervey, Maria Montez, Charles Lang, Turhan Bey, Lloyd Corrigan, Mary Gordon. Written by Roy Chanslor and Stanley Rubin; directed by John Rawlins; for Universal.

Bombay Mail
US 1933 66m bw

On a train between Calcutta and Bombay a Scotland Yard detective solves the murder of the Governor of Bengal. Very tolerable mystery filler. Edmund Lowe, Shirley Grey, Onslow Stevens, Ralph Forbes, Hedda Hopper. Written by Tom Reed and L. G. Blochman; directed by Edwin L. Marin; for Universal. 'It mixes a colourful set of characters and maintains a moderately absorbing pace.'—*Variety*

Bombay Talkie*
India 1970 105m Eastmancolor
Merchant-Ivory (Ismail Merchant)

A sophisticated American woman comes to Bombay and falls for two men involved in film-making.
Interesting but unsatisfactory romantic drama, rather pointlessly set against film studio backgrounds.

w Ruth Prawer Jhabvala, James Ivory *d* James Ivory *ph* Subrata Mitra *m* Shankar Jaikishan

Jennifer Kendal, Shashi Kapoor, Zia Mohyeddin

Bombers B-52
US 1957 106m Warnercolor Cinemascope
Warner (Richard Whorf)
GB title: *No Sleep till Dawn*

A USAF sergeant considers applying for a discharge so that he can earn more money in civilian life.
Glossy domestic melodrama punctuated by aircraft shots.

w Irving Wallace *d* Gordon Douglas *ph* William Clothier *m* Leonard Rosenman

Karl Malden, Marsha Hunt, Natalie Wood, Efrem Zimbalist Jnr, Don Kelly

'No one questions the basic assumption—that the good life consists of servicing bigger and better bombers.'—*MFB*

Bomber's Moon
US 1943 70m bw

An American pilot crashlands into Germany and makes for the coast. Modestly budgeted war adventure with conventional thrills. George Montgomery, Annabella, Kent Taylor, Walter Kingsford, Martin Kosleck. Written by Kenneth Gamet; directed by 'Charles Fuhr' (Edward Ludwig and Harold Schuster); for TCF.

Bombs Over Burma
US 1942 67m bw

Chinese carry out intelligence work on the Burma road. Cheapjack heroics, almost unwatchable even at the time. Anna May Wong, Noel Madison, Leslie Denison, Nedrick Young. Written by Milton Ralson, Joseph H. Lewis; directed by Joseph H. Lewis; for Alfred Stern-Arthur Alexander / PRC.

Bombshell***
US 1933 91m bw
MGM (Hunt Stromberg)
GB and aka title: *Blonde Bombshell*

A glamorous film star yearns for a new image. Crackpot farce which even by today's standards moves at a fair clip and enabled the star to give her best comedy performance.

w Jules Furthman, John Lee Mahin, play Caroline Francke, Mack Crane *d Victor Fleming ph* Chester Lyons, Hal Rosson

Jean Harlow, Lee Tracy, Frank Morgan, Franchot Tone, Pat O'Brien, Ivan Lebedeff, Una Merkel, Ted Healy, Isabel Jewell, C. Aubrey Smith, Louise Beavers, Leonard Carey, Mary Forbes

'Bound to click and the best legitimate comedy in a long time.'—*Variety*

Bon Voyage*
US 1962 133m Technicolor
Walt Disney (Bill Walsh, Ron Miller)

An American family spends a holiday in Paris. Simple-minded, overlong comedy of mishaps, with daddy finally trapped in the sewer. Smoothly done of its kind.

w Bill Walsh, *novel* Marrijane and Joseph Hayes *d* James Neilson *ph* William Snyder *m* Paul Smith

Fred MacMurray, Jane Wyman, Michael Callan, Deborah Walley, Jessie Royce Landis, Tommy Kirk, Ivan Desny

Bond Street
GB 1948 107m bw
ABP / World Screenplays (Anatole de Grunwald)

Four stories, each concerning an item of an expensive wedding trousseau.
Mild and laboured short story compendium.

w Anatole de Grunwald *d* Gordon Parry *ph* Otto Heller *m* Benjamin Frankel

Roland Young, Jean Kent, Paula Valenska, Kathleen Harrison, Derek Farr, *Kenneth Griffith*, Hazel Court, Ronald Howard

'Even a glimpse of actual Bond Street makes little contact with reality.'—*MFB*

Le Bonheur*
France 1965 79m Eastmancolor
Parc / Mag Bodard

A young carpenter is happy with his wife and family, happier still when he finds a mistress, whom he marries when his wife is found drowned.
Slight, good looking, ambivalent little fable which finally expires in a surfeit of style.

wd Agnès Varda *ph* Jean Rabier, Claude Beausoleil *m* Mozart

Jean-Claude Drouot, Claire Drouot, Marie-France Boyer

Bonjour Tristesse*
GB 1957 93m Technicolor Cinemascope
(Columbia) Wheel Films (Otto Preminger)

A teenage girl becomes involved with her sophisticated father's amours and causes the death of his would-be mistress.
The novel's rather repellent characters are here played like royal personages against a background of Riviera opulence. The result is very odd but often entertaining, especially when it slips into self-parody.

w Arthur Laurents, *novel* Françoise Sagan *d* Otto Preminger *ph Georges Périnal m* Georges Auric *pd* Roger Furse

David Niven, Deborah Kerr, Jean Seberg, Mylene Demongeot, Geoffrey Horne, Juliette Greco, Martita Hunt, Walter Chiari, Jean Kent, Roland Culver

'An elegant, ice-cold charade of emotions.'—*Judith Crist*

'Sagan not so much translated as traduced—opened out, smartened up, the sickness overlaid with Riviera suntan.'—*Alexander Walker*

'Long, untidy, muddled and mushy.'—*Financial Times*

† Shot in monochrome for Paris, colour for the Riviera.

Bonne Chance
France 1935 75m bw

An artist who wins a lottery takes on holiday with him, on a purely platonic basis, the girl who gave him half her ticket. Modest star comedy which pleased at the time. Sacha Guitry, Jacqueline Delubac, Robert Darthez. Written and directed by Sacha Guitry for his own company.

La Bonne Soupe
France / Italy 1963 97m bw
Belstar / Du Siècle / Dear Film (André Hakim)

A high-class prostitute tells her life story.
A saucy frolic complete with three-in-a-bed and rapidly closing doors; quite enjoyable of its kind.

wd Robert Thomas, *play* Félicien Marceau *ph* Roger Hubert *m* Raymond le Sénéchal

Annie Girardot, Marie Bell, Gérard Blain, Bernard Blier, Jean-Claude Brialy, Claude Dauphin, Sacha Distel, Daniel Gélin, Blanchette Brunoy, Jane Marken, Raymond Péllégrin, Franchot Tone

'They're young . . . they're in love . . . and they kill people!'

Bonnie and Clyde****
US 1967 111m Technicolor
Warner / Seven Arts / Tatira / Hiller (*Warren Beatty*)

In the early thirties, a car thief and the daughter of his intended victim team up to become America's most feared and ruthless bank robbers.
Technically brilliant evocation of sleepy mid-America at the time of the public enemies, using every kind of cinematic trick including fake snapshots, farcical interludes, dreamy soft-focus and a jazzy score. For all kinds of reasons a very influential film which even made extreme violence quite fashionable (and very bloody it is).

w David Newman, Robert Benton d Arthur Penn ph Burnett Guffey m Charles Strouse, using 'Foggy Mountain Breakdown' by Flatt and Scruggs

Warren Beatty, Faye Dunaway, Gene Hackman, Estelle Parsons, *Michael J. Pollard*, Dub Taylor, Denver Pyle, Gene Wilder

'It is a long time since we have seen an American film so perfectly judged.'—*MFB*

'. . . all to the rickety twang of a banjo and a saturation in time and place.'—*Judith Crist*

'The formula is hayseed comedy bursting sporadically into pyrotechnical bloodshed and laced with sentimental pop-Freudianism.'—*John Simon*

'A film from which we shall date reputations and innovations in the American cinema.'—*Alexander Walker*

'It works as comedy, as tragedy, as entertainment, as a meditation on the place of guns and violence in American society.'—*Roger Ebert*

AA: Burnett Guffey; Estelle Parsons
AAN: best picture; David Newman, Robert Benton; Arthur Penn; Warren Beatty; Faye Dunaway; Gene Hackman; Michael J. Pollard

The Bonnie Parker Story
US 1958 80m bw

A waitress joins up with a cheap crook in a series of bank raids. Tinpot 'B' gangster film chiefly notable for comparison with the later *Bonnie and Clyde*. All it really has is a certain exuberance in the action sequences. Dorothy Provine, Jack Hogan, Richard Bakalyan, Joseph Turkel. Written and produced by Stan Shpetner; directed by William Witney; for James H. Nicholson and Sam Arkoff.

Bonnie Prince Charlie
GB 1948 140m approx (later cut to 118m) Technicolor
British Lion / London Films (Edward Black)

The hope of the Stuarts returns from exile but is eventually forced to flee again.
Good highland photography combines with appalling studio sets, an initially confused narrative, a draggy script and uneasy performances to produce an ill-fated attempt at a British historical epic. Alexander Korda, who masterminded it, sulked in public at the critical roasting, but on this occasion the critics were right.

w Clemence Dane *d* Anthony Kimmins *ph* Robert Krasker *m* Ian Whyte

David Niven, Margaret Leighton, Jack Hawkins, Judy Campbell, Morland Graham, Finlay Currie, John Laurie

'I have a sense of wonder about this film, beside which *The Swordsman* seems like a dazzling work of veracity and art. It is that London Films, having surveyed the finished thing, should not have quietly scrapped it.'—*Richard Winnington*

'The picture is not lacking in moments of unconscious levity, what with David Niven rallying his hardy Highlanders to his standard in a voice hardly large enough to summon a waiter.'—*New Yorker*

'Time has made it the film industry's biggest joke. But the joke turns a little sour when one reflects how extravagance, recklessness and sheer bungling administration during the fat and prosperous years left the British film industry so poor and vulnerable when the hard times came along.'—*Gerald Garrett, 1975*

Bonnie Scotland*
US 1935 80m bw
MGM / Hal Roach

Two Americans journey to Scotland to collect a non-existent inheritance, then follow their friend in the army and wind up in India.
Generally disappointing star comedy which still contains excellent sequences when it is not vainly trying to preserve interest in a boring plot. An obvious parody on *Lives of a Bengal Lancer*, released earlier that year; Scotland has almost nothing to do with it.

w Frank Butler, Jeff Moffitt *d* James Horne *ph* Art Lloyd, Walter Lundin

Stan Laurel, Oliver Hardy, James Finlayson, Daphne Pollard, William Janney, June Lang

'You'll be tickled to death over this gay chiller diller!'

The Boogie Man Will Get You
US 1944 66m bw
Columbia (Colbert Clark)

Bodies accumulate when mad doctors get to work creating supermen in a small village.
Desperately unfunny spoof notable only for the fact that it was attempted with these players and at that time.

w Edwin Blum *d* Lew Landers *ph* Henry Freulich *md* Morris Stoloff

Boris Karloff, Peter Lorre, Maxie Rosenbloom, Jeff Donnell, Larry Parks, Maude Eburne, Don Beddoe

'She outlived six rich men!'

Boom!
GB 1968 113m Technicolor Panavision
Universal / World Film Services / Moon Lake Productions (John Heyman, Norman Priggen)

On the volcanic Mediterranean island which she owns, a dying millionairess plans to take as her last lover a wandering poet who is the angel of death.
Pretentious, boring nonsense, showing that when talent goes awry it certainly goes boom.

w Tennessee Williams, from his play *The Milk Train Doesn't Stop Here Any More* *d* Joseph Losey *ph* Douglas Slocombe *m* John Barry

Elizabeth Taylor, Richard Burton, *Noel Coward*, Michael Dunn, Joanna Shimkus

'It's a beautiful picture, the best ever made of one of my plays.'—*Tennessee Williams*

'A pointless, pompous nightmare.'—*Paul D. Zimmermann, Newsweek*

'An ordeal in tedium,'—*Hollywood Reporter*

'Outright junk.'—*Saturday Review*

'The title could not be more apt: it is precisely the sound of a bomb exploding.'—*Richard Schickel, Life*

'Boom! isn't doing little business; it's doing no business at all.'—*Universal executive*

Boom Town**
US 1940 120m bw
MGM (Sam Zimbalist)

Two friendly oil drillers strike it rich.
Enjoyable four-star, big-studio product of its time: world-wide entertainment of assured success, with a proven mix of romance, action, drama and comedy.

w John Lee Mahin, *story* James Edward Grant *d Jack Conway* *ph* Harold Rosson *m* Franz Waxman *ad* Cedric Gibbons

Clark Gable, Spencer Tracy, Claudette Colbert, Hedy Lamarr, *Frank Morgan,* Lionel Atwill, Chill Wills

'Western high jinks, a wee child, and courtroom speeches about individual enterprise constitute the various come-ons in a scrambled and inept picture.'—*New York Herald Tribune*

'More colourful action in the oil fields and less agitation indoors might have made it a great picture.'—*Bosley Crowther*

AAN: Harold Rosson

Boomerang***
US 1947 88m bw
TCF (Louis de Rochemont)

In a New England town, a clergyman is shot dead on the street. The DA prevents an innocent man from being convicted, but cannot track down the guilty party.
Incisive real life thriller: based on a true case, it was shot in an innovative documentary style which was much copied, and justice is not seen to be done, though the murderer is known to the audience. A milestone movie of its kind.

w Richard Murphy *d Elia Kazan* *ph* Norbert Brodine *m* David Buttolph

Dana Andrews, Jane Wyatt, Lee J. Cobb, Cara Williams, Arthur Kennedy, Sam Levene, Taylor Holmes, Robert Keith, Ed Begley

'A study of integrity, beautifully developed by Dana Andrews against a background of political corruption and chicanery that is doubly shocking because of its documentary understatement.'—*Richard Winnington*

'For the first time in many a moon we are treated to a picture that gives a good example of a typical small American city—the people, their way of living, their mode of government, the petty politics practised, the power of the press.'—*Frank Ward, National Board of Review*

AAN: Richard Murphy

Boots Malone
US 1952 103m bw
Columbia (Milton Holmes)

A would-be jockey tags along with a down-at-heel agent who gets him work and finally persuades him not to throw a crooked race.
Dullish racetrack melodrama bogged down by repetitive and unsympathetic plot twists.

w Milton Holmes *d* William Dieterle *ph* Charles Lawton *m* Elmer Bernstein

William Holden, Johnny Stewart, Stanley Clements, Basil Ruysdael, Carl Benton Reid, Ed Begley, Henry Morgan

The Border
US 1981 108m Technicolor Panavision
Universal / RKO (Neil Hartley)

A Los Angeles cop joins the border patrol in El Paso and becomes involved in the squalor, violence and double-dealing.
A rather solemn elaboration on a well-worn theme, with nothing very memorable except its excesses.

w Deric Washburn, Walon Green, David Freeman *d* Tony Richardson *ph* Ric Waite *m* Ry Cooder *pd* Toby Rafelson *ed* Robert K. Lambert

Jack Nicholson, Harvey Keitel, Valerie Perrine, Warren Oates, Elpidia Carrillo

Border Incident
US 1949 93m bw
MGM (Nicholas Nayfack)

Police stop the illegal immigration of labourers from Mexico.
Routine semi-documentary cops and robbers, well enough made.

w John C. Higgins *d* Anthony Mann *ph* John Alton *m* André Previn

Ricardo Montalban, George Murphy, Howard da Silva, James Mitchell, Alfonso Bedoya

Border River
US 1953 80m Technicolor

At the end of the Civil War, an ex-Confederate officer gets involved with a gold war in the Mexican free zone. Slightly unusual western programmer. Joel McCrea, Yvonne de Carlo, Pedro Armendariz, Ivan Triesault, Alfonso Bedoya, Howard Petrie. Written by William Sackheim and Louis Stevens; directed by George Sherman; for Universal–International.

Borderline
US 1980 97m colour
ITC (Martin Starger)

A Mexican border patrolman chases illegal immigrants and the big time crooks making money out of them.
Routine, quite effective action programmer.

w Steve Kline, Jerrold Freedman *d* Jerrold Freedman *ph* Tak Fujimoto *m* Gil Melle

Charles Bronson, Bruno Kirby, Karmin Murcelo, Michael Learner, Ed Harris

Bordertown*
US 1934 80m bw
Warner (Robert Lord)

In a North Mexican town, a shabby lawyer becomes infatuated with the neurotic wife of a businessman.
Satisfying melodrama whose plot climax was later borrowed for *They Drive by Night.*

w Laird Doyle, Wallace Smith, *novel* Carroll Graham *d* Archie Mayo *ph* Tony Gaudio *md* Leo Forbstein

Paul Muni, Bette Davis, Margaret Lindsay, Eugene Pallette, Robert Barrat, Henry O'Neill, Hobart Cavanaugh

'A strictly box office film, well written and paced.'—*Variety*

† *Blowing Wild* (qv) was also a partial uncredited remake.

Born Again
US 1978 110m Technicolor
Robert L. Munger / Frank Capra Jnr

Charles Colson, sent to prison after Watergate, becomes a devout Christian.
Part evangelism, part reconstruction through rose-tinted spectacles; not particularly entertaining or instructive as either.

w Walter Block *d* Irving Rapper *ph* Harry Stradling Jnr *m* Les Baxter

Dean Jones, Anne Francis, Jay Robinson, Dana Andrews, Raymond St Jacques, George Brent, Harry Spillman (as Nixon)

Born Free**
GB 1965 95m Technicolor Panavision
Columbia / Open Road (Carl Foreman) / High Road / Atlas (Sam Jaffe, Paul Radin)

A Kenyan game warden and his wife rear three lion cubs, one of which eventually presents them with a family.
Irresistible animal shots salvage this rather flabbily put together version of a bestselling book. An enormous commercial success, it was followed by the even thinner *Living Free*, by a TV series, and by several semi-professional documentaries.

w Gerald L. C. Copley, *book* Joy Adamson *d* James Hill *ph* Kenneth Talbot *m John Barry*

Virginia McKenna, Bill Travers, Geoffrey Keen

AA: John Barry; title song (*m* John Barry, *ly* Don Black)

Born Losers
US 1967 112m colour
AIP (Delores Taylor)

California teeny-boppers claim to have been gang-raped by wandering motorcyclists.
Teenage shocker, only notable for its credits, and for being the first Billy Jack film.

wd Tom Laughlin *ph* Gregory Sandor *m* Mike Curb

Tom Laughlin, Jane Russell, Elizabeth James, Jeremy Slate, William Wellman Jnr

'It's so pokey and crudely obvious that it seems almost guileless—helplessly inept.'—*Pauline Kael*

Born Reckless
US 1930 73m bw

Doings of an Italian gangster bootlegger. A generally poorly regarded early work of its director. Edmund Lowe, Catherine Dale Owen, Lee Tracy, Marguerite Churchill, Warren Hymer, Frank Albertson. Written from the novel Louis Beretti by Donald Henderson Clarke; directed by John Ford; for Fox. 'A singularly full and sprawling scenario . . . Fox originally intended the yarn for Paul Muni. It's possible the script got kicked around the lot and came out as beef stew.'—*Variety*

Born Reckless
US 1937 60m bw

Big-town taxi drivers start a war among themselves. Second-feature actioner, well enough done. Brian Donlevy, Richelle Hudson, Barton MacLane, Robert Kent, Harry Carey, Pauline Moore, Chick Chandler. Written by John Patrick, Helen Logan, Robert Ellis; directed by Malcolm St Clair; for TCF. 'Houses in the knuckle districts will give it its best play.'—*Variety*

Born to be Bad
US 1934 70m bw
Twentieth Century (William Goetz, Raymond Griffith)

A girl schemes to seduce the man who has adopted her illegitimate son.
Batty mother-love melodrama.

w Ralph Graves *d* Lowell Sherman *ph* Barney McGill *m* Alfred Newman

Loretta Young, Cary Grant, Jackie Kelk, Henry Travers, Russell Hopton, Andrew Tombes, Harry Green

Born to be Bad
US 1950 70m bw
RKO (Robert Sparks)

An ambitious girl marries a millionaire but continues her affair with a novelist; finally both men discover her true character.
Tentative bad girl novelette, just about passable.

w Edith Sommer, *novel* All Kneeling by Anne Parrish *d* Nicholas Ray *ph* Nicholas Musuraca *m* Frederick Hollander

Joan Fontaine, Robert Ryan, Zachary Scott, Joan Leslie, Mel Ferrer

'Trash story too much for cast and director to live down.'—*Variety*

Born to Dance*
US 1936 108m bw
MGM (Jack Cummings)

A sailor meets a girl in New York.
Well remembered musical with good numbers but a rather lame look.

w Jack McGowan, Sid Silvers, B. G. De Sylva *d* Roy del Ruth *ph* Ray June *songs* Cole Porter *md* Alfred Newman

Eleanor Powell, James Stewart, Virginia Bruce, Una Merkel, Sid Silvers, Frances Langford, Raymond Walburn, *Reginald Gardiner*, Buddy Ebsen

Songs include 'I've Got You under My Skin'; 'Easy to Love'; 'I'm Nuts about You'; 'Rap Tap on Wood'; 'Swinging the Jinx Away'; 'Rolling Home'; 'Hey Babe Hey'; 'Love Me Love My Pekinese'

'Corking entertainment. . . . Cast is youthful, sight stuff is lavish, the specialties are meritorious, and as for songs, the picture is positively filthy with them.'—*Variety*

'The plot is a half-hearted reprise of *42nd Street* . . . this time Eleanor Powell is the understudy who replaces the star . . . and by the time she finishes the finale, you're overpowered and feel you should cheer.'—*Pauline Kael, 70s*

AAN: song 'I've Got You Under My Skin'

Born to Kill*
US 1947 92m bw
RKO
GB title: *Lady of Deceit*

A psychotic involves his new wife in his criminal pursuits.
Unusual, heavy-going, well acted melodrama.

w Eve Greene, Richard Macauley *d* Robert Wise *ph* Robert de Grasse *m* Paul Sawtell

Lawrence Tierney, Claire Trevor, Walter Slezak, Philip Terry, Elisha Cook Jnr

Born to Love
US 1931 84m bw
RKO

During World War I a nurse bears the child of an army pilot who is reported missing; but he turns up after she has married an English milord.
A useful compendium of thirties romantic clichés, quite attractively packaged.

w Ernest Pascal *d* Paul Stein *ph* John Mescall

Constance Bennett, Joel McCrea, Paul Cavanagh, Frederick Kerr, Anthony Bushell, Louise Closser Hale, Edmond Breon, Mary Forbes

Born to Sing
US 1941 82m bw

Kids put together a patriotic show. Curiously undernourished family musical in the wake of *Babes in Arms*: lots of talent but no star. Virginia Weidler, Douglas McPhail, Leo Gorcey, Ray McDonald, Rags Ragland, Sheldon Leonard, Margaret Dumont, Larry Nunn, Henry O'Neill. Written by Franz Spencer and Harry Clark; directed by Edward Ludwig; for Frederick Stephani / MGM.

Born to Win
US 1971 89m colour

A Times Square junkie with delusions of grandeur runs out of luck. Dim low-life drama unworthy of its talent. George Segal, Paula Prentiss, Karen Black, Hector Elizondo. Written by David Scott Milton; directed by Ivan Passer; for UA.

'A perfectly swell motion picture!'
Born Yesterday**
US 1950 103m bw
Columbia (S. Sylvan Simon)

The ignorant ex-chorus girl mistress of a scrap iron tycoon takes English lessons, falls for her tutor, and politically outmanoeuvres her bewildered lover.
Pleasant film version of a cast-iron box office play, subtle and intelligent in all departments yet with a regrettable tendency to wave the flag.

w Albert Mannheimer, *play Garson Kanin* *d George Cukor* *ph* Joseph Walker *m* Frederick Hollander

Judy Holliday, Broderick Crawford, William Holden, Howard St John

† The original choices for the Judy Holliday role were Rita Hayworth and Jean Parker (who had played it on tour):

AA: Judy Holliday
AAN: best picture; Albert Mannheimer; George Cukor

Borsalino*
France / Italy 1970 126m Eastmancolor
Adel-Marianne-Mars (Alain Delon)

In the thirties two Marseilles gangsters become firm friends and join forces.
Semi-spoof, but with 'real' blood, and period atmosphere laid on thick. The stars just about keep it ticking over.

w Jean-Claude Carrière, Claude Sautet, Jacques Deray, Jean Cau *d* Jacques Deray *ph* Jean-Jacques Tarbès *m* Claude Bolling

Jean-Paul Belmondo, Alain Delon, Michel Bouquet, Catherine Rouvel, Corinne Marchand

'Rather like a Hollywood musical where someone has forgotten to insert the production numbers.'—*MFB*

The Boss*
US 1956 89m bw
UA / Frank N. Seltzer

After World War I, a ne'er-do-well becomes a corrupt small town political boss.
Low budgeted, complexly plotted, occasionally quite powerful and efficient crime melodrama.

w Ben L. Parry *d* Byron Haskin *ph* Hal Mohr *m* Albert Glasser

John Payne, William Bishop, Gloria McGhee, Doe Avedon, Joe Flynn

Boston Blackie

An American second feature series made by Columbia between 1941 and 1949. There had been silent films about the character, a reformed crook and con man who has to solve crimes because he is suspected by the law. Cheap but sometimes vigorous productions, they had a loyal following, and starred Chester Morris with George E. Stone as his assistant the Runt.

The titles were:

1941: MEET BOSTON BLACKIE, CONFESSIONS OF BOSTON BLACKIE
1942: ALIAS BOSTON BLACKIE, BOSTON BLACKIE GOES TO HOLLYWOOD
1943: AFTER MIDNIGHT WITH BOSTON BLACKIE
1944: ONE MYSTERIOUS NIGHT
1945: BOSTON BLACKIE BOOKED ON SUSPICION, BOSTON BLACKIE'S RENDEZVOUS
1946: A CLOSE CALL FOR BOSTON BLACKIE, THE PHANTOM THIEF
1947: BOSTON BLACKIE AND THE LAW
1948: TRAPPED BY BOSTON BLACKIE
1949: BOSTON BLACKIE'S CHINESE VENTURE
† A television series starring Kent Taylor followed in 1951.

The Boston Strangler**
US 1968 118m De Luxe Panavision
TCF (Robert Fryer)

A semi-factual account of the sex maniac who terrified Boston in the mid-sixties.
Ambitious *policier* rendered less effective by pretentious writing and flashy treatment, including multi-image sequences; the investigation is more interesting than the psychoanalysis.

w Edward Anhalt, *book* Gerold Frank *d* Richard Fleischer *ph* Richard Kline *m* Lionel Newman

Henry Fonda, *Tony Curtis* (as the murderer), George Kennedy, Mike Kellin, Hurd Hatfield, Murray Hamilton, Sally Kellerman, Jeff Corey, George Voskovec

The Bostonians
GB 1984 122m colour
Merchant Ivory / WGBH / Rediffusion / Almi (Ismail Merchant)

In 1876 Boston, the cause of female emancipation wrecks Verena Tarrant's relationship with the determined Basil Ransome.
Another sluggish literary adaptation from the heavily meaningful Merchant Ivory team: the material, one feels would have worked better as a TV bestseller.

w Ruth Prawer Jhabvala, *novel* Henry James *d* James Ivory *ph* Walter Lassally *m* Richard Robbins *pd* Leo Austin

Christopher Reeve, Vanessa Redgrave, Madeleine Potter, Jessica Tandy, Nancy Marchand, Linda Hunt, Wesley Addy.

'Although it's not so limp as some of their other collaborations, they don't dramatize the material, and Ivory doesn't shape the performances.'—*Pauline Kael, New Yorker*

AAN: Vanessa Redgrave

Botany Bay
US 1952 94m Technicolor
Paramount (Joseph Sistrom)

On a convict ship in 1787 an American student unjustly accused of robbery clashes with the brutal captain for the favours of the only woman aboard.
Cramped and brutal action melodrama, a let-down considering the talent involved.

w Jonathan Latimer, *novel* Charles Nordhof and James Hall *d* John Farrow *ph* John Seitz *m* Franz Waxman

James Mason, Alan Ladd, Patricia Medina, Cedric Hardwicke, Murray Matheson, Jonathan Harris

The Bottom of the Bottle
US 1956 86m Eastmancolor Cinemascope
TCF (Buddy Adler)
GB title: *Beyond the River*

A wealthy attorney is visited by his drunken brother, on the run from the police and needing help to escape into Mexico.
Dreary drama in muddy colour, a clearly misguided enterprise.

w Sydney Boehm, *novel* Georges Simenon *d* Henry Hathaway *ph* Lee Garmes *m* Leigh Harline

Joseph Cotten, Van Johnson, Ruth Roman, Jack Carson

'For those who like to laugh and sing when tears get in their eyes!'

Bottoms Up
US 1934 85m bw
Fox (B. G. De Sylva)

A slick promoter in Hollywood disguises his pals as British nobility and gets them lucrative jobs.
Mild musical with a rather interesting cast.

w B. G. De Sylva, David Butler, Sid Silvers *d* David Butler *ph* Arthur Miller *md* Constantin Bakaleinikoff

Spencer Tracy, Pat Patterson, John Boles, Harry Green, Herbert Mundin, Sid Silvers, Thelma Todd, Robert Emmett O'Connor

'In the best 1934 filmusical manner and contributes handily toward the perpetuation of the cycle.'—*Variety*

Bottoms Up
GB 1960 89m bw

A seedy schoolmaster passes off his bookie's son as an eastern prince. Rambling film version of a successful TV series, *Whacko!* Jimmy Edwards, Arthur Howard. Written by Frank Muir and Denis Norden; directed by Mario Zampi; for Transocean / Warner.

Le Boucher**
France / Italy 1969 94m Eastmancolor
La Boétie / Euro International (André Génoves)
aka: *The Butcher*

Murders in a small French town are traced to the inoffensive-seeming young butcher who is courting the local schoolmistress.
Curious, mainly charming film which can't make up its mind whether to be an eccentric character study or a Hitchcock thriller, but has its moments as each.

wd Claude Chabrol ph Jean Rabier m Pierre Jansen

Stéphane Audran, Jean Yanne, Antonio Passalia, Mario Beccaria

'A thriller, but a superlative example of the genre.'—*Times*

Boudu Sauvé des Eaux***
France 1932 87m bw
Michel Simon / Jean Gehret
aka: *Boudu Saved from Drowning*

A scruffy tramp is not grateful for being rescued from suicide, and plagues the family who invite him to stay.
A minor classic of black comedy, interesting equally for its characterizations, its acting, and its film technique.

wd Jean Renoir, play René Fauchois *ph* Marcel Lucien *m* from Raphael and Johann Strauss

Michel Simon, Charles Grandval, Marcelle Hainia, Séverine Lerczinska, Jean Dasté, Jacques Becker

'A beautifully rhythmed film that makes one nostalgic for the period when it was made.'—*New Yorker, 1977*

† Remade 1985, more or less, as *Down and Out in Beverly Hills.*

Bought
US 1931 70m bw
Warner

An ambitious working girl rebels against her slum existence and seeks a rich man.
Typical star vehicle of its time, with a predictable and unlikely change of heart for a finale.

w Charles Kenyon, Raymond Griffith, *novel* Jackdaw's Strut by Harriet Henry *d* Archie Mayo *ph* Ray June

Constance Bennett, Ben Lyon, Richard Bennett, Dorothy Peterson, Ray Milland, Doris Lloyd, Maude Eburne

'It's an entertainment in itself to be seated among women auditors during a Constance Bennett picture. They love that girl and she mustn't be worsted by men.'—*Variety*

Boulder Dam
US 1936 70m bw

A mechanic accidentally kills a man and seeks anonymity among the crews building Boulder Dam. Routine melo with an unusual setting. Ross Alexander, Patricia Ellis, Lyle Talbot, Eddie Acuff, Henry O'Neill. Written by Sy Bartlett and Ralph Block; directed by Frank McDonald; for Sam Bischoff / Warner.

Bound for Glory*
US 1976 148m De Luxe Panavision
UA / Robert F. Blumhofe, Harold Leventhal

In 1936 Woody Guthrie leaves the Texas dust bowl for California, and after various hardships his musical talent is recognized.
Care and occasional beauty in the photography do not obscure memories of *The Grapes of Wrath*, which told much the same story more dramatically and succinctly, and with less earnestness and self-pity.

w Robert Getchell, from Guthrie's autobiography *d* Hal Ashby *ph Haskell Wexler* *m* Leonard Rosenman *songs* Woody Guthrie *pd* Michael Haller

David Carradine, Ronny Cox, Melinda Dillon, Gail Strickland, John Lehne

'The movie spends two-and-a-half hours and seven million dollars gazing wistfully at a little man and a big country, and it ends up prettily embalming them both.'—*Janet Massin, Newsweek*

AA: Haskell Wexler; Leonard Rosenman
AAN: best picture; Robert Getchell

The Bounty*
GB 1984 133m Technicolor
Dino de Laurentiis (Bernard Williams)

William Bligh is summoned before a court martial to explain the events leading up to the famous mutiny.
Rather independent version of the twice-told movie tale, and the least compelling of all. Despite the emphasis on character, only occasionally interesting.

w Robert Bolt *d* Roger Donaldson
ph Arthur Ibbetson *m* Vangelis *pd* John Graysmark

Anthony Hopkins (Bligh), Mel Gibson (Fletcher Christian), Laurence Olivier (Admiral Hood), Edward Fox (Captain Greetham), Daniel Day-Lewis (John Fryer), Bernard Hill (Cole)

'A long voyage to nowhere.'—*Nick Roddick, MFB*

'This misshapen movie doesn't work as an epic—it doesn't have the scope or the emotional surge.'—*Pauline Kael, New Yorker*

'A great adventure, a lush romance, and a good movie.'—*Roger Ebert*

The Bounty Hunter
US 1954 79m WarnerColor

Three respectable citizens are unmasked as masterminds behind a series of train robberies.
Predictable but enjoyable star action fare.
Randolph Scott, Dolores Dorn, Marie Windsor, Ernest Borgnine. Written by Winston Miller; directed by André de Toth; for Warners.

The Bowery***
US 1933 92m bw
Twentieth Century (Darryl F. Zanuck)
(Raymond Griffith, William Goetz)

In nineties New York, two boisterous rivals settle their differences after one has jumped off the Brooklyn Bridge for a bet.
Roistering saga of cross and double cross on the seamy side, splendidly vigorous in acting and treatment.

w Howard Estabrook, James Gleason *d Raoul Walsh* *ph* Barney McGill *m* Alfred Newman *ad Richard Day*

Wallace Beery, George Raft, Pert Kelton, Jackie Cooper, Fay Wray, Herman Bing

'It delivers as entertainment. It should draw by itself, while the cast will be a considerable help.'—*Variety*

'A model of skilful reconstruction and ingenious research.'—*Times*

'Fairly reeking with authentic, rowdy, hurdy-gurdy atmosphere . . . a grand evening of fun for everybody.'—*Photoplay*

† *The Bowery* was the first production of Twentieth Century.
†† Gable was sought for the Raft role, but proved unavailable.

Bowery at Midnight
US 1942 61m bw

A criminal by night doubles as a mission proprietor by day. Star horror cheapie with echoes of his previous *Dark Eyes of London.* Bela Lugosi, John Archer, Wanda McKay, Tom Neal, Dave O'Brien, Vince Barnett. Written by Gerald Schnitzer; directed by Wallace Fox; for Monogram.

The Bowery Boys

A cheap and cheerful series of American second features, immensely popular between 1946 and 1958, these adventures of a group of ageing Brooklyn layabouts had their origin in the 1937 film *Dead End*, from which the Dead End Kids graduated to other features at Warner: *Crime School, They Made Me a Criminal, Angels with Dirty Faces, Angels Wash their Faces*, etc. A couple of the 'boys' then defected to Universal and made *Little Tough Guy* and a series of half a dozen subsequent pictures; while in 1940 Monogram took a couple more and built up another group called the East Side Kids. In 1946 a formal merger of talent at Monogram consolidated the remaining members into the Bowery Boys. The members were Leo Gorcey, Huntz Hall, Bobby Jordan, Gabriel Dell (all from the Dead End Kids), Bernard Gorcey, David Gorcey, Billy Benedict, and Bennie Bartlett.

The films are:

1946: IN FAST COMPANY, BOWERY BOMBSHELL, LIVE WIRES, SPOOK BUSTERS, MR HEX
1947: BOWERY BUCKAROOS, HARD BOILED MAHONEY, NEWS HOUNDS, ANGELS' ALLEY
1948: JINX MONEY, SMUGGLER'S COVE, TROUBLE MAKERS
1949: ANGELS IN DISGUISE, FIGHTING FOOLS, HOLD THAT BABY, MASTER MINDS
1950: BLONDE DYNAMITE, BLUES BUSTERS, LUCKY LOSERS, TRIPLE TROUBLE
1951: BOWERY BATALLION, CRAZY OVER HORSES, GHOST CHASERS, LET'S GO NAVY
1952: FEUDIN' FOOLS, HERE COME THE MARINES, HOLD THAT LINE, NO HOLDS BARRED
1953: CLIPPED WINGS, JALOPY, LOOSE IN LONDON, PRIVATE EYES
1954: THE BOWERY BOYS MEET THE MONSTERS, JUNGLE GENTS, PARIS PLAYBOYS
1955: BOWERY TO BAGDAD, HIGH SOCIETY, JAIL BUSTERS, SPY CHASERS
1956: DIG THAT URANIUM, CRASHING LAS VEGAS, FIGHTING TROUBLE, HOT SHOTS
1957: SPOOK CHASERS, HOLD THAT HYPNOTIST, LOOKING FOR DANGER
1958: UP IN SMOKE, IN THE MONEY.

Bowery to Broadway
US 1944 94m bw
Universal (John Grant)

In the nineties, a Bowery songstress makes it to the big time.
Simple-minded musical in which the drama has no drive and the guest stars are given inferior material.

w Joseph Lytton, Arthur T. Horman
d Charles Lamont *ph* Charles Van Enger
md Edward Ward

Maria Montez, Turhan Bey, Susanna Foster, Jack Oakie, Donald Cook, Louise Allbritton, Andy Devine, Rosemary de Camp, Ann Blyth, Donald O'Connor, Peggy Ryan, Frank McHugh, Leo Carrillo, Evelyn Ankers, Mantan Moreland
Songs include 'The Love Waltz'; 'There'll Always Be a Moon'; 'My Song of Romance'; 'Montevideo'; 'Coney Island Waltz' (plus standards)

Boxcar Bertha*
US 1972 88m De Luxe
AIP (Roger Corman)

In early thirties Arkansas, an unhappy girl falls in with gangsters and train robbers.
Competent imitation of *Bonnie and Clyde*.

w Joyce H. and John W. Corrington *d Martin Scorsese ph* John Stephens *m* Gilb Guilbeau, Thad Maxwell

Barbara Hershey, David Carradine, Barry Primus, Bernie Casey, John Carradine

A Boy a Girl and a Bike
GB 1947 92m bw
Gainsborough (Ralph Keene)

Romantic jealousies arise between members of a Yorkshire cycling club.
Mild comedy drama with the advantage of fresh air locations.

w Ted Willis *d* Ralph Smart *ph* Ray Elton *m* Kenneth Pakeman

John McCallum, Honor Blackman, Patrick Holt, Diana Dors, Leslie Dwyer, Thora Hird, Anthony Newley, Megs Jenkins, Maurice Denham

The Boy and the Bridge
GB 1959 91m bw
Xanadu (Kevin McClory)

A boy who believes he has committed a murder hides in the ramparts of Tower Bridge.
This tiny fable adds up to very weak entertainment, despite inventive photography, because it has virtually no plot development.

w Geoffrey Orme, Kevin McClory, Desmond O'Donovan *d* Kevin McClory *ph Ted Scaife m* Malcolm Arnold

Ian MacLaine, Liam Redmond, James Hayter, Norman Macowan, Geoffrey Keen, Jack MacGowran, Royal Dano, Rita Webb

The Boy and the Pirates
US 1960 84m Eastmancolor Perceptovision

A small boy finds an old bottle on the seashore, wishes he could live in pirate days, and hey presto. Modest juvenile fantasy on the lines of *The Wizard of Oz* but without the talent. Charles Herbert, Susan Gordon, Murvyn Vye, Paul Guilfoyle. Written by Lillie Hayward and Jerry Sackheim; directed and produced by Bert I. Gordon; for United Artists.

The Boy Cried Murder
GB / West Germany / Yugoslavia 1965
86m Eastmancolor

A small boy has such a vivid imagination that nobody except the criminal believes him when he says he has witnessed a murder. Flat and unnecessary remake of *The Window* (which was later done again as *Eye Witness*). Frazer MacIntosh, Veronica Hurst, Phil Brown, Tim Barrett. Written by Robin Estridge, from the story by Cornell Woolrich; directed by George Breakston; for CCC / Carlos / Avala.

'No more bubble bath, she screamed!'

Boy, Did I Get a Wrong Number
US 1966 99m De Luxe
UA / Edward Small (George Beck)

Trying to phone his wife, an estate agent gets involved with a runaway actress.
Lifeless and generally resistible star comedy, the first of several hard and unfunny vehicles for an ageing Bob Hope seeming to hark back to the least attractive aspects of burlesque rather than the sympathetic wisecracking which suits him best.

w Burt Styler, Albert E. Lewin, George Kennett *d* George Marshall *ph* Lionel Lindon *m* Richard Lasalle *ly* By Dunham

Bob Hope, Elke Sommer, Phyllis Diller, Marjorie Lord, Cesare Danova, Benny Baker

The Boy Friend*
GB 1971 125m Metrocolor Panavision
MGM / Russflix (Ken Russell)

On a wet Wednesday afternoon in Portsmouth in the late twenties, a tatty company with backstage problems puts on an empty-headed musical.
Russell the mastermind effectively destroys Sandy Wilson's charming period pastiche, sending up all the numbers (via badly staged dream sequences on the wrong shape screen) in a Busby Berkeley manner which had not yet been invented. Moments do work, but a non-star doesn't help, and the whole thing is an artistic disaster of some significance both to Russell's career and to the cinema of the early seventies.

w Ken Russell, from Sandy Wilson's musical play *d* Ken Russell *ph* David Watkin *md* Ian Whittaker, Peter Greenwell, Peter Maxwell Davies *pd* Tony Walton

Twiggy, Christopher Gable, *Max Adrian*, Tommy Tune, Barbara Windsor, Moyra Fraser, Bryan Pringle, Vladek Sheybal, *Antonia Ellis, Glenda Jackson*

'The glittering, joyless numbers keep coming at you: you never get any relief from Russell's supposed virtuosity.'—*New Yorker, 1977*

AAN: Ian Whittaker, Peter Greenwell, Peter Maxwell Davies

The Boy from Oklahoma*
US 1953 88m Warnercolor
Warner (David Weisbart)

A genial plainsman studying law becomes sheriff of a small town and uncovers its mayor as a killer.
Modest, pleasing western with the star imitating his father.

w Frank David, Winston Miller *d* Michael Curtiz *ph* Robert Burks *m* Max Steiner

Will Rogers Jnr, Nancy Olson, Lon Chaney Jnr, Anthony Caruso, Wallace Ford, Clem Bevans, Merv Griffin

Boy Meets Girl*
US 1938 86m bw
Warner (George Abbott)

Two crazy Hollywood scenario writers make a star of an infant yet unborn.
Freewheeling film version of a hilarious play: fine crazy comedy and excellent Hollywood satire.

w Bella and Sam Spewack, from their play *d* Lloyd Bacon *ph* Sol Polito *m* Leo Forbstein

James Cagney, Pat O'Brien, Marie Wilson, Ralph Bellamy, Frank McHugh, Dick Foran, Bruce Lester, Ronald Reagan, James Stephenson

'Satisfactory, but not socko.'—*Variety*

'It bounces from one hilarious absurdity to another with all the resilience of a rubber ball.'—*Monthly Film Bulletin*

Boy of the Streets
US 1937 75m bw

A city youngster falls in with racketeers. Ho-hum Dead End melodrama. Jackie Cooper, Maureen O'Connor, Kathleen Byrke, Marjorie Main, Robert Emmett O'Connor. Written by Scott Darling and Wilson Brown; directed by William Nigh; for Monogram.
'Will do biz for independents . . . easily Monogram's most ambitious production effort to date.'—*Variety*

Boy on a Dolphin*
US 1957 111m Eastmancolor Cinemascope
TCF (Samuel G. Engel)

A Greek girl diver discovers a sunken artifact of great value and the news spreads to an American archaeologist and an unscrupulous collector.
Likeable, sunswept Mediterranean adventure romance marred by the miscasting of the male lead.

w Ivan Moffatt, Dwight Taylor, *novel* David Divine *d* Jean Negulesco *ph Milton Krasner m* Hugo Friedhofer *md* Lionel Newman

Alan Ladd, Sophia Loren, *Clifton Webb*, Laurence Naismith, Alexis Minotis, Jorge Mistral

AAN: Hugo Friedhofer

Boy Slaves
US 1938 70m bw

A boy leaves home and ends up in a forced labour camp. Topical preachment drama which kicked up a bit of dust at the time. Anne Shirley, Roger Daniel, James McCallion, Alan Baxter. Written by Albert Bein and Ben Orkow; directed by P. J. Wolfson; for RKO.
'Devoid of essential entertainment factors for general theatre showings.'—*Variety*

Boy Trouble
US 1939 75m bw

A small-towner finds his life upset when his wife adopts two orphans. Sentimental comedy which caused a few tears to trickle. *Charles Ruggles*, Mary Boland, Donald O'Connor, Joyce Matthews, Billy Lee, Andrew Tombes. Written by Laura and S. J. Perelman from a story by Lloyd Corrigan and Monte Brice; directed by George Archainbaud; for

Paramount. 'Good old hokum with an emotional wallop . . . Exhibitors can use more pictures of this type.'—*Variety*

'Those who don't believe—are dead!'

The Boy who Cried Werewolf
US 1973 93m Technicolor

On a camping trip, a boy and his father are attacked by a werewolf, and later on dad starts acting mighty strange . . . Disappointingly straight rewrite of the old hokum. Kerwin Mathews, Elaine Devry, Scott Sealey. Written by Bob Homel; directed by Nathan Juran; for Universal.

The Boy Who Had Everything
Australia 1984 94m colour
Multi Films Alfred Roads (Richard Mason, Julia Overton)

In 1965, as Australian troops are about to be sent to Vietnam, a university freshman submits to initiation rites but renounces his mother and his future.
Angry, rather muddled character study which seems to be drawn from life but doesn't know what moral to point.

w,d Stephen Wallace *ph* Geoff Burton
m Ralph Schneider

Jason Connery, Diane Cilento, Laura Williams, Lewis Fitzgerald

The Boy Who Stole a Million
GB 1960 81m bw

A young page in a Spanish bank 'borrows' some money to help his father but finds Dad, police and crooks all after him. Half-hearted attempt at a British *Bicycle Thieves*, oddly set in Spain and never quite managing to convince or interest us. Maurice Reyna, Virgilia Texera, Harold Kasket, George Coulouris, Edwin Richfield. Written by John Eldridge and Charles Crichton; directed by Charles Crichton; for Fanfare / George H. Brown / British Lion.

The Boy with Green Hair
US 1948 82m Technicolor
RKO (Stephen Ames)

When he hears that his parents were killed in an air raid, a boy's hair turns green; other war orphans encourage him to parade himself publicly as an image of the horror and futility of war.
Muddled, pretentious and unpersuasive fantasy, typical of this producer's do-goodery. One of those oddities which make Hollywood endearing, but not very entertaining apart from Pat O'Brien's garrulous grandpa.

w Ben Barzman, Alfred Lewis Levitt, *story* Betsy Beaton *d* Joseph Losey *ph* George Barnes *m* Leigh Harline
Dean Stockwell, Pat O'Brien, Robert Ryan, Barbara Hale

The Boys
GB 1962 123m Cinemascope
Gala / Columbia (Sidney J. Furie)

Four boys are on trial for killing a garage attendant.

THE BOY FRIEND. Twiggy and Christopher Gable trip the light fantastic: director Ken Russell merely trips and crushes Sandy Wilson's whimsical stage success with lumpen handling.

Elaborate courtroom drama with flashbacks, stars for counsel, a tricksy director, and about forty minutes too much footage.

w Stuart Douglass *d* Sidney J. Furie
ph Gerald Gibbs *m* The Shadows

Richard Todd, Robert Morley, Felix Aylmer, Dudley Sutton, Ronald Lacey, Tony Garnett, Jess Conrad, Wilfrid Brambell, Allan Cuthbertson, Colin Gordon

'94 men must die to keep alive a dream—or a nightmare!'

The Boys From Brazil*
US / GB 1978 124m De Luxe
ITC / Producer Circle (Martin Richards, Stanley O'Toole)

A renegade Nazi in hiding has a sinister plot to reconquer the world.
Suspense fantasy firmly based on a gripping book; excellent performances, but a shade too long.

w Heywood Gould, *novel* Ira Levin
d Franklin Schaffner *ph* Henri Decaë
m Jerry Goldsmith *pd* Gil Parrando

Gregory Peck, Laurence Olivier, James Mason, Lilli Palmer, Uta Hagen, Steven Buttenberg, Denholm Elliott, Rosemary Harris, John Dehner, John Rubenstein, Anne Meara, David Hurst, Michael Gough

AAN: Jerry Goldsmith; Laurence Olivier

The Boys from Syracuse*
US 1940 74m bw
Universal (Jules Levey)

The Comedy of Errors with modern wisecracks, and a few songs.
Predictable well-drilled confusion arises from master and slave having identical twins, but the general tone is a bit flat for an adaptation from a hilarious Broadway success. Still, the songs are lively and the chariot race finale shows spirit.

w Leonard Spiegelgass, Charles Grayson, Paul Gerard Smith, from the play by George Abbott and William Shakespeare *d* Edward A. Sutherland *ph* Joseph Valentine *m* Frank Skinner *md* Charles Previn *songs* Rodgers and Hart

Allan Jones, Joe Penner, Charles Butterworth, Rosemary Lane, Irene Hervey, Martha Raye, Alan Mowbray
Songs include 'Who Are You?'; 'This Can't be Love'; 'Falling in Love with Love'; 'The Greeks Have no Word for It'; 'Sing for Your Supper'; 'He and She'

† The writing credit on screen ends: 'After a play by William Shakespeare . . . long, long after!'

The Boys in Blue
GB 1983 91m colour

Village policemen catch art thieves. Horribly incompetent remake of *Ask a Policeman*, with a totally untalented star team. Tommy Cannon, Bobby Ball, Suzanne Danielle, Roy Kinnear, Eric Sykes, Jack Douglas, Edward Judd, Jon Pertwee, Arthur English. Written and directed by Val Guest; for Elstree / Rank.
'The perfect antidote to sweeping claims about the British renaissance.'—*Geoff Brown, MFB*

Boys in Brown
GB 1949 84m bw
Gainsborough (Antony Darnborough)

Life in a Borstal institution.
The stars make elderly boys, but Jack Warner is a cuddly governor. Boring and unpersuasive non-documentary fiction in Britain's most tiresome style.

wd Montgomery Tully, *play* Reginald Beckwith *ph* Gordon Lang, Cyril Bristow *m* Doreen Carwithen

Jack Warner, Dirk Bogarde, Michael Medwin, Jimmy Hanley, Richard Attenborough, Alfie Bass, Barbara Murray, Thora Hird
† Made by the Independent Frame method, which blended real backgrounds with studio sets.

The Boys in Company C
Hong Kong 1977 125m Technicolor Panavision
Golden Harvest (Andre Morgan)

Five marines find their lives changed by the Vietnam war.
Crude action melodrama.

w Rick Natkin, Sidney J. Furie *d* Sidney J. Furie *ph* Godfrey Godar *m* Jaime Mendoza-Nava

Stan Shaw, Andrew Stevens, James Canning, Michael Lembeck, Craig Wasson, James Whitmore Jnr

'Laden with barrack room dialogue and played at the enlisted man's level.'—*Variety*

'An exploitation war movie, like dirty TV.'—*New Yorker*

The Boys in the Band*
US 1970 120m Technicolor
Cinema Center / Leo (Mart Crowley, Kenneth Utt)

Tempers fray and true selves are revealed when a heterosexual is accidentally invited to a homosexual party.
Careful but claustrophobic filming of a Broadway play, which at the screen's closer quarters becomes overpowering well before the end.

w Mart Crowley, from his play *d* William Friedkin *ph* Arthur J. Ornitz *m* none

Leonard Frey, Kenneth Nelson, Cliff Gorman, Frederick Combs, Reuben Greene, Robert La Tourneaux, Laurence Luckinbill, Keith Prentice, Peter White

'They crack jokes while their hearts are breaking.'—*New Yorker*

Boys' Night Out
US 1962 115m Metrocolor Cinemascope
MGM / Filmways (Martin Ransohoff)

Three married men and their bachelor friend share a flat and a 'mistress'.
Would-be saucy comedy in which nothing sexy ever happens and the helpless players are as witless as the script.

w Ira Wallach *d* Michael Gordon *ph* Arthur E. Arling *m* Frank de Vol

James Garner, Kim Novak, Tony Randall, Howard Duff, Howard Morris, Oscar Homolka, Janet Blair, Patti Page, Jessie Royce Landis

Boys' Ranch
US 1946 97m bw

A baseball player persuades Texas millionaires to finance a ranch where deprived city youngsters can learn life's true values. Predictable sentimental hogwash without much pace or star value. James Craig, Jackie 'Butch' Jenkins, Skip Homeier, Dorothy Patrick, Ray Collins, Darryl Hickman. Written by William Ludwig; directed by Roy Rowland; for Robert Sisk / MGM.

Boys' Town*
US 1938 93m bw
MGM (John W. Considine Jnr)

The story of Father Flanagan and his school for juvenile delinquents.
Well-made, highly successful, but sentimental crowd pleaser.

w John Meehan, Dore Schary, *original story* Eleanor Griffin, Dore Schary *d* Norman Taurog *ph* Sidney Wagner *m* Edward Ward

Spencer Tracy, Mickey Rooney, Henry Hull, Gene Reynolds, Sidney Miller, Frankie Thomas, Bobs Watson, Tommy Noonan

'More laughs than Laurel and Hardy! More thrills than *Test Pilot*! More tears than *Captains Courageous*!'—*publicity*

'A production that should build goodwill for the whole industry.'—*Variety*

AA: Eleanor Griffin, Dore Schary; Spencer Tracy
AAN: best picture; John Meehan, Dore Schary; Norman Taurog

Boys Will Be Boys**
GB 1935 75m bw
Gaumont / Gainsborough (Michael Balcon)

An incompetent headmaster thwarts a jewel robber.
The first recognizable Will Hay vehicle, based in part on J. B. Morton's Narkover sketches.

w Will Hay, Robert Edmunds *d* William Beaudine *ph* Charles Van Enger *m* Louis Levy

Will Hay, Gordon Harker, Jimmy Hanley, Davy Burnaby, Norma Varden, Claude Dampier, Charles Farrell, Percy Walsh

'It is hard to see how his distinctive sketch writing could have found a satisfactory screen equivalent. Nevertheless, a good augury of the films to come.'—*Ray Seaton and Roy Martin, 1978*

The Brain
France / US 1969 115m colour
Paramount (Alain Poire)
Original title: *Le Cerveau*

A British colonel leads an international crew in an attempt to rob NATO.
Exhausting and generally misfiring international crook comedy.

w Gérard Oury, Marcel Julian, Daniele Thompson *d* Gérard Oury *ph* Vladimir Ivanov, Armand Thirard *m* Georges Delerue

David Niven, Jean-Paul Belmondo, Bourvil, Eli Wallach, Silvia Monti

The Brain Machine*
GB 1954 83m bw

Through an electroencephalograph, a hospital psychiatrist recognizes a patient as a dangerous psychopath. Very tolerable crime thriller with a fresh angle. Elizabeth Allan, Patrick Barr, Maxwell Reed, Russell Napier, Vanda Gosell, Gibb McLaughlin. Written and directed by Ken Hughes; for Alec Snowden / Merton Park.

Brainstorm
US 1965 110m bw Panavision
Warner / Kodima (William Conrad)

A passer-by saves a married woman from suicide, has an affair with her, and conspires to murder her husband. This accomplished, she leaves him and he goes insane.
Overlong thriller which starts off agreeably in the *Double Indemnity* vein; but goes slow and solemn around the half way mark.

w Mann Rubin *d* William Conrad *ph* Sam Leavitt *m* George Duning

Jeffrey Hunter, Anne Francis, Dana Andrews, Viveca Lindfors, Stacy Harris

'A sub-B potboiler for those who find comic books too intellectual.'—*Judith Crist*

Brainstorm
US 1983 106m Metrocolor Super Panavision
MGM / UA / JF (Douglas Trumbull)

A technological device records emotions so faithfully as to make other people feel them through each of the five senses. The enemy is discovered to be using it for brainwashing purposes; but it has recorded the experience of death . . .
Scientific mumbo jumbo which went far too far as an attack on the audience's senses, and was jinxed by the death of its star during production.

w Robert Stitzel, Philip Frank Messina, Bruce Joel Rubin *d* Douglas Trumbull *ph* Richard Yuricich *m* James Horner *pd* John Vallone

Natalie Wood, Christopher Walken, Louise Fletcher, Cliff Roberston, Jordan Christopher, Alan Fudge

'A monstrous bore, with uninteresting characters buried beneath a mass of even less interesting technology.'—*Tom Milne, MFB*

The Bramble Bush
US 1960 105m Technicolor
Warner / United States (Milton Sperling)

A doctor returns to his home town and finds himself involved in old tragedies including the mercy killing of his friend.
Sordid small-town melodrama in the *Peyton Place* vein, with adequate production values but dispiriting treatment.

w Milton Sperling, Philip Yordan, *novel* Charles Mergendahl *d* Daniel Petrie *ph* Lucien Ballard *m* Leonard Rosenman

Richard Burton, Barbara Rush, Jack Carson, Angie Dickinson, James Dunn, Tom Drake, Henry Jones, Frank Conroy, Carl Benton Reid, William Hansen

Branded
US 1950 104m Technicolor
Paramount (Mel Epstein)

A gunman poses as a rancher's lost heir, but redeems himself by finding the real one.
Competent, brisk western.

w Sydney Boehm, Cyril Hume *d* Rudolph Maté *ph* Charles Lang Jnr *m* Roy Webb

Alan Ladd, Charles Bickford, Mona Freeman, Robert Keith, Joseph Calleia, Peter Hansen, Selena Royle, Tom Tully

Brandy for the Parson*
GB 1951 79m bw
Group Three (Alfred O'Shaughnessy)

A couple on a yachting holiday find themselves unwittingly smuggling brandy into Britain.
Pleasant little sub-Ealing comedy with agreeable locations but not much drive.

w John Dighton, Walter Meade, *story* Geoffrey Household *d* John Eldridge *ph* Martin Curtis *m* John Addison

James Donald, Kenneth More, Jean Lodge, Frederick Piper, Charles Hawtrey, Michael Trubshawe, Alfie Bass, Reginald Beckwith

'Detective-Lieutenant Brannigan is in London . . . God save the Queen!'

Brannigan*
GB 1975 111m De Luxe Panavision
UA / Wellborn (Jules Levy, Arthur Gardner)

A Chicago policeman is sent to London to pick up a gangster.
Cheerful crime pastiche and tour of London, quite an agreeable entertainment despite its obviously over-age star.

w Christopher Trumbo, Michael Butler, William P. McGivern, William Norton *d* Douglas Hickox *ph* Gerry Fisher *m* Dominic Frontière

John Wayne, Richard Attenborough, Judy Geeson, Mel Ferrer, John Vernon, Daniel Pilon, John Stride, James Booth, Barry Dennen

The Brasher Doubloon*
US 1946 72m bw
TCF
GB title: *The High Window*

Philip Marlowe investigates the theft of a rare coin and finds himself involved in a series of murders.
The poorest of the Chandler adaptations, previously filmed as *Time to Kill*, still contains good moments, though the star is lightweight and the production low-budget.

w Dorothy Bennett, *novel* The High Window by Raymond Chandler *d* John Brahm *ph* Lloyd Ahern *m* David Buttolph

George Montgomery, Nancy Guild, Florence Bates, Conrad Janis, Fritz Kortner

The Brass Bottle
US 1964 89m Eastmancolor
U-I / Scarus (Robert Arthur)

A young architect finds an old brass bottle which contains a troublesome genie.
Simple-minded farce with little invention and poor trickwork.

w Oscar Brodney, *novel* F. Anstey *d* Harry Keller *ph* Clifford Stine *m* Bernard Green *sp* Roswell Hoffman

Tony Randall, Burl Ives, Barbara Eden, Edward Andrews, Ann Doran

The Brass Legend
US 1956 79m bw

A sheriff finds himself in trouble when he tries to protect his fiancée's young brother. Stolid programmer of the *High Noon* school, but without the flair. Hugh O'Brian, Nancy Gates, Raymond Burr, Reba Tassell. Written by Don Martin; directed by Gerd Oswald; for Herman Cohen / Bob Goldstein / UA.

The Brass Monkey
GB 1948 84m bw

A radio singer thwarts the theft of a Buddhist idol. Flat thriller based round a radio 'discovery' programme. Carole Landis, Carroll Levis, Herbert Lom, Avril Angers, Ernest Thesiger. Written by Alec Coppel and Thornton Freeland; directed by Thornton Freeland; for Diadem / Alliance / UA. (Aka: *Lucky Mascot*.)

Brass Target
US 1978 111m Metrocolor
MGM (Berle Adams)

The alleged story behind the death of General Patton, who according to these sources was eliminated because he had discovered a bullion robbery attempt.
Good-looking but interminably complex and talkative, with nothing much for its star cast to do.

w Alvin Boretz, *novel* The Algonquin Project by Frederick Nolan *d* John Hough *ph* Tony Imi *m* Laurence Rosenthal

Sophia Loren, George Kennedy, Max Von Sydow, John Cassavetes, Patrick McGoohan, Robert Vaughn, Bruce Davison, Edward Herrmann, Ed Bishop

Brats*
US 1930 20m bw

Stan and Ollie have trouble baby-sitting their own mischievous kids. Fairly ambitious star comedy with trick sets and photography enabling Laurel and Hardy to play their own sons. About half the gags come off. Written by Leo McCarey, H. M. Walker and Hal Roach; directed by James Parrott; for Hal Roach.

The Bravados*
US 1958 98m Eastmancolor Cinemascope
TCF (Herbert B. Swope)

A widower chases four killers who, he believes, raped and murdered his wife.
Dour western with a downbeat ending; production good, but entertainment uneasy.

w Philip Yordan, *novel* Frank O'Rourke *d* Henry King *ph* Leon Shamroy *m* Hugo Friedhofer *md* Emil Newman

Gregory Peck, Stephen Boyd, Joan Collins, Albert Salmi, Henry Silva, George Voskovec, Barry Coe, Lee Van Cleef

The Brave Bulls
US 1951 108m bw
Columbia (Robert Rossen)

A Mexican matador regains his courage but loses his girl in a car crash.
Muddled narrative with dollops of bull-fighting mystique; a rather miserable movie despite effort all round.

w John Bright, *novel* Tom Lea *d* Robert Rossen *ph* James Wong Howe, Floyd Crosby

Mel Ferrer, Miroslava, Anthony Quinn, Eugene Iglesias

The Brave Don't Cry*
GB 1952 90m bw
Group Three (John Baxter)

Over a hundred men are rescued in a Scottish mine disaster.
Semi-documentary based on a real incident: well done on a small budget, but hardly memorable.

w Montagu Slater *d* Philip Leacock *ph* Arthur Grant *m* none

John Gregson, Meg Buchanan, John Rae, Fulton Mackay, Andrew Keir, Russell Waters, Jameson Clark, Jean Anderson, Eric Woodburn

The Brave One*
US 1956 100m Technicolor Cinemascope
King Brothers

A small boy saves the life of his pet bull when it is sent into the ring.
Mildly beguiling minor drama for those who adore small boys and bulls.

w Harry Franklin, Merrill G. White, *original story* Robert Rich *d* Irving Rapper *ph* Jack Cardiff *m* Victor Young

Michel Ray, Rodolfo Hoyos, Elsa Cardenas, Joi Lansing, Carlos Navarro

AA: Robert Rich. (There was much confusion when the mysterious Rich turned out to be

Dalton Trumbo, who was blacklisted at the time.)

Brazil
US 1944 91m bw
Republic (Robert North)

A lady novelist goes to Brazil for material; a local composer poses as her guide in order to pay her back for her previous remarks about his country.
Acceptable lower case musical with pleasant tunes and humour.

w Frank Gill Jnr, Laura Kerr *d* Joseph Santley *ph* Jack Marta *songs* Bob Russell and others *m* Walter Scharf

Virginia Bruce, Tito Guizar, Edward Everett Horton, Roy Rogers

AAN: song 'Rio de Janeiro' (*m* Ary Barrosa, *ly* Ned Washington); Walter Scharf

Brazil*
GB 1985 142m colour
Embassy (Arnon Milchan)

A comically pessimistic view of the future, seen through the eyes of a dutiful civil servant who is eventually crushed by the system.
An expensive, wild, overlong, hit-or-miss Orwellian satire: enough good jabs to please the intelligentsia, but a turnoff for patrons at the local Odeon.

w Terry Gilliam, Tom Stoppard, Charles McKeown *d* Terry Gilliam *ph* Roger Pratt *m* Michael Kamen *pd* Norman Garwood *ed* Julian Doyle

Jonathan Pryce, Robert de Niro, Michael Palin, Kim Greist, Katherine Helmond, Ian Holm, Ian Richardson, Peter Vaughan, Bob Hoskins

'It will not be everybody's cup of poisoned tea.'—*Variety*

'Exuberantly violent, cruelly funny and sometimes sickeningly scatological . . . the whole is wrapped up in a melancholy wistfulness.'—*Sight and Sound*

AAN: original screenplay, art direction

Breach of Promise
GB 1941 79m bw

A girl chases the man she wants by filing a breach of promise suit against him. Dated but lively comedy with agreeable playing. Clive Brook, Judy Campbell, C. V. France, Margaret Allan, Percy Walsh. Written by Roland Pertwee; directed by Harold Huth and Roland Pertwee; for British Mercury / MGM. (US Title: *Adventure in Blackmail.*)

Bread and Chocolate*
Italy 1973 112m Eastmancolor
Verona Cinematografica (Maurizio Lodo-Fe)

An Italian waiter in Switzerland is accused of murder and indecent exposure.
Amusing and often pathetic account of an inveterate loser, its flavour impossible to define.

w Franco Brusati, Iaia Fiastri, Nino Manfredi *d* Franco Brusati *ph* Luciano Tovoli *md* Daniele Patrucchi

Nino Manfredi, Anna Karina, Johnny Dorelli, Paolo Turco

Bread, Love and Dreams*
Italy 1953 90m bw
Titanus (Marcello Girosi)

The new sergeant of police in a small rural village comes looking for a wife.
Pleasant rather than exciting rural comedy which spun off a number of vaguely related sequels (*Bread, Love and Jealousy*, etc).

w Luigi Comencini, *original story* Ettore Margadonna *d* Luigi Comencini *ph* Arturo Gallea *m* Alessandro Cicognini

Vittorio de Sica, Gina Lollobrigida, Marisa Merlini, Roberto Risso

AAN: Ettore Margadonna

Break in the Circle
GB 1955 91m Eastmancolor

The owner of a cabin cruiser is hired to smuggle a scientist out of Germany. Routine action yarn of cross and double-cross, tolerably staged. Forrest Tucker, Eva Bartok, Marius Goring, Eric Pohlmann, Guy Middleton, Arnold Marle. Written and directed by Val Guest, from a novel by Philip Loraine; for Hammer / Exclusive.

Break of Hearts
US 1935 80m bw
RKO (Pandro S. Berman)

A girl composer falls in love with a distinguished conductor who becomes a dipsomaniac.
Well acted soap opera, not really worthy of its stars.

w Sarah Y. Mason, Victor Heerman, Anthony Veiller *d* Philip Moeller *ph* Robert de Grasse *m* Max Steiner

Katharine Hepburn, Charles Boyer, Jean Hersholt, John Beal, Sam Hardy

'A stale turnip story that relies entirely upon characterization to hide the basic dullness.'—*Variety*

'In spite of some capable acting, it lacks a certain compelling warmth. The audience's heart never breaks.'—*Eileen Creelman, New York Sun*

Break the News*
GB 1938 78m bw
GFD / Jack Buchanan

A dancer arranges his partner's 'death' for publicity reasons but is sent to jail when the partner disappears.
Thin but lively comedy with a remarkable couple of song and dance men. Negative apparently lost.

w Geoffrey Kerr, *novel* La Mort en Fuite by Loid de Gouriadec *d* René Clair *ph* Phil Tannura

Jack Buchanan, Maurice Chevalier, June Knight, Marta Labarr, Garry Marsh, Felix Aylmer, Robb Wilton
† Various remakes include *The Art of Love* (qv).

Breaker Morant*
Australia 1980 107m Eastmancolor Panavision
South Australian Film Corporation (Matthew Carroll)

During the Boer War three Australian officers are courtmartialled for murdering prisoners.
Careful, moving military drama which gives a more sympathetic view of the facts than history does.

w Jonathan Hardy, Bruce Beresford, David Stevens, *play* Kenneth Ross *d* Bruce Beresford *ph* Donald McAlpine *md* Phil Cuneen

Edward Woodward, Jack Thompson, John Waters, Charles Tingwell, Terence Donovan, Vincent Ball

'It is impossible to suppress a feeling that the spirit of Stanley Kramer is abroad on the veldt.'—*Tim Pulleine, MFB*

AAN: screenplay

Breakfast at Tiffany's*
US 1961 115m Technicolor
Paramount (Martin Jurow, Richard Shepherd)

A young New York writer has as neighbour the volatile Holly Golightly, a slightly crazy call girl with an exotic social and emotional life.
Impossibly cleaned up and asexual version of a light novel which tried to be the American *I Am a Camera.* Wild parties, amusing scenes and good cameos, but the pace is slow, the atmosphere is unconvincingly clean and luxurious, and the sentimentality kills it.

w George Axelrod, *novel* Truman Capote *d* Blake Edwards *ph* Franz Planer *m Henry Mancini*

Audrey Hepburn, George Peppard, Patricia Neal, Buddy Ebsen, Martin Balsam, *John McGiver* (as the Tiffany salesman), Mickey Rooney

AA: Henry Mancini; *song* 'Moon River' (*m* Henry Mancini, *ly* Johnny Mercer)
AAN: George Axelrod; Audrey Hepburn

The Breakfast Club
US 1985 97m Technicolor

Five rebellious students at Shermer High blame their parents for their misfortunes. Abysmal apologia for loutish teenage behaviour. Emilio Estevez, Judd Nelson, Molly Ringwald, Anthony Michael Hall, Ally Sheedy. Written and directed by John Hughes: for A&M / Universal.

Breakfast for Two*
US 1937 65m bw
RKO (Edward Kaufman)

A Texas heiress turns a playboy into a businessman.
Star crazy comedy with some wildly funny scenes.

w Charles Kaufman, Paul Yawitz, Viola Brothers Shore *d* Alfred Santell *ph* J. Roy Hunt

Barbara Stanwyck, Herbert Marshall, Donald Meek, Glenda Farrell, Eric Blore, Etienne Girardot

'Heaps of laughs in a breezily-paced farce.'—*Variety*

Breakfast in Hollywood
US 1945 90m bw

A day in the life of a radio breakfast show host. Topical programme filler, more interesting historically than entertaining. Tom Breneman, Bonita Granville, Beulah Bondi, Eddie Ryan, Raymond Walburn, Billie Burke, ZaSu Pitts, Spike Jones and his City Slickers, Andy Russell, Hedda Hopper. Written by Earl W. Baldwin; directed by Harold Schuster; for Golden Pictures / United Artists. (GB title: *The Mad Hatter*.)

Breakheart Pass*
US 1975 94m De Luxe
UA / Elliott Kastner (Jerry Gershwin)

Various mysterious passengers on an 1873 train across the frozen west to Fort Humboldt turn out to have smuggling and murder in mind.
Botched murder mystery on wheels: there are some exciting scenes, but the plot makes little sense and the 'action finale' is muddled.

w Alistair MacLean, from his book *d* Tom Gries *ph* Lucien Ballard *m* Jerry Goldsmith

Charles Bronson, Ben Johnson, Richard Crenna, Jill Ireland, Charles Durning, Archie Moore, Ed Lauter

Breakin'
US 1984 87m Metrocolor

Youngsters promote a new form of dancing. Minor exploitation item, the form little improved on *Rock around the Clock* thirty years earlier. Lucinda Dickey, Adolfo Shabba-Doo Quinones, Michael Boogaloo-Shrimp Chambers, Ben Lokey, Phineas Newborn III. Written by Charles Parker, Allen DeBevoise, Gerald Scaife; directed by Joel Silberg; for Cannon. (GB title: *Breakdance*.)

Breakin' 2: Electric Boogaloo
US 1984 94m TVC

Youngsters raise 200,000 dollars to save their local community centre; a dance show does it. Hurried sequel of no interest apart from the briefly popular musical gyrations. Lucinda Dickey, Adolfo Quinones, Michael Chambers, Susie Bono. Written by Jan Ventura, Julie Reichert; directed by Sam Firstenberg; for Cannon. (GB title: *Breakdance 2: Electric Boogaloo*.)

Breaking Away*
US 1979 101m De Luxe
TCF (Peter Yates)

An imaginative teenager has trouble adjusting to adult life after high school.
Andy Hardy would have felt at home in this fragmented comedy of the American hinterland; 1979 audiences found it a welcome relief from the stronger brews to which they had become accustomed.

w Steve Tesich d Peter Yates *ph* Matthew F. Leonetti *md* Lionel Newman
m Paul Williams, Lionel Newman

Dennis Christopher, Dennis Quaid, Daniel Stern, Jackie Earle Haley, Barbara Barrie, Paul Dooley

'Affection for the middle classes, the landscapes of Indiana, and bicycle racing.'—*New Yorker*

'It is not devoid of pleasures . . . but it fatally lacks a clear purpose and identity.'—*Geoff Brown, MFB*

'Here's a sunny, goofy, intelligent little film about coming of age in Bloomington, Indiana.'—*Roger Ebert*

† An unsuccessful TV series followed in 1980.
AAN: best picture

'The experience is shattering!'
Breaking Glass
GB 1980 104m Technicolor Panavision
GTO / Film and General (Dodi Fayed)

Vicissitudes of a pop band and of its singer who can't stand the pace.
Garish, freakish musical with unattractive characters strung along an oft-told tale. Some commendable vigour in the presentation, but it won't appeal to anybody over 21.

wd Brian Gibson *ph* Stephen Goldblatt *md* Tony Visconti

Hazel O'Connor, Phil Daniels, Jon Finch, Jonathan Pryce

'There's nothing more deadly than a gentle man pushed too far!'
The Breaking Point*
US 1950 97m bw
Warner (Jerry Wald)

A charterboat owner becomes involved with crooks but turns them in when they have killed his friend.
Adequate if slightly humdrum attempt by Warners to atone for what they had done to a Hemingway novel, the infidelity of *To Have and Have Not* and the unauthorized variation of *Key Largo*. (See also: *The Gun Runners*.)

w Ranald MacDougall, *novel* To Have and Have Not by Ernest Hemingway *d* Michael Curtiz *ph* Ted McCord *m* (uncredited) William Lava, Max Steiner

John Garfield, Patricia Neal, Phyllis Thaxter, Juano Hernandez, Wallace Ford, Edmon Ryan, William Campbell

'Innocence and fury don't mix—they explode!'
Breaking Point
Canada 1976 92m colour Panavision
TCF / Astral Belle Vue (Harold Greenberg, Harold Pariser)

An innocent witness against the Mafia takes off against them vigilante style when his partner is murdered and his own life threatened.
Comic strip thuggery with performances to match; plenty of excitement for toughies.

w Roger E. Swaybill, Stanley Mann *d* Bob Clark *ph* Marc Champion *m* David McLey

Bo Svenson, Robert Culp, John Colicos, Belinda J. Montgomery, Stephen Young

Breaking the Ice
US 1938 80m bw
(RKO) Sol Lesser

A Pennsylvania Dutch boy runs away to the city so that his mother can afford her own farm.
Slim star musical which had its pleasing moments.

w Mary McCall Jnr, Manuel Seff, Bernard Schubert *d* Edward F. Cline *ph* Jack MacKenzie *m* Victor Young

Bobby Breen, Charles Ruggles, Dolores Costello, Robert Barrat, Dorothy Peterson, John King, Billy Gilbert, Margaret Hamilton

'Moderately engrossing, combination folk drama and musical.'—*Variety*

AAN: Victor Young

Breakout
US 1975 96m colour Panavision
Columbia / Persky–Bright (Robert Chartoff, Irwin Winkler)

A professional rescuer gets an innocent man out of a Mexican jail.
Rough and ready adventure thriller which starts slowly and confusingly but later works up a fair head of steam.

w Howard B. Kreitsek, Frank Kowalski, from their novel Ten Second Jailbreak *d* Tom Gries *ph* Lucien Ballard *m* Jerry Goldsmith

Charles Bronson, Robert Duvall, John Huston, Jill Ireland, Randy Quaid, Sheree North

Breakthrough
US 1950 91m bw
Warner (Bryan Foy)

Adventures of a US army unit in Normandy after D-Day.
Routine low-budgeter which improves after a slow start.

w Bernard Girard, Ted Sherdeman, Joseph I. Breen Jnr *d* Lewis Seiler *ph* Edwin DuPar *m* William Lava

David Brian, John Agar, Frank Lovejoy, William Campbell, Paul Picerni, Greg McClure, Edward Norris, Matt Willis, Dick Wesson

A Breath of Scandal
US 1960 98m Technicolor
Paramount / Titanus / Ponti–Girosi (Carlo Ponti, Marcello Girosi)

A spirited Ruritanian princess falls for an American industrialist.
Exceedingly flat-footed and boring international co-production of an old Molnar play; if anyone concerned had bright ideas, they don't show.

w Sidney Howard (presumably in the thirties, for he died in 1939), *play* Olimpia by Ferenc Molnar *d* Michael Curtiz, Mario Russo *ph* Mario Montuori *m* Alessandro Cicognini

Sophia Loren, Maurice Chevalier, John Gavin, Isabel Jeans, Angela Lansbury, Roberto Risso, Frederick Ledebur, Tullio Carminati, Milly Vitale

Breathless
US 1983 101m De Luxe
Miko / Breathless Associates / Greenberg Brothers (Martin Erlichman)

A street-smart hustler steals a car in Las Vegas and heads for the coast.
Fashionable amalgam of sex and violence, borrowed from *À Bout de Souffle* but far too long after the event.

w L. M. Kit Carson, James McBride *d* James McBride *ph* Richard H. Kline *m* Jack Nitzsche *pd* Richard Sylbert

Richard Gere, Valerie Kaprinsky, William Tepper, John P. Ryan, Art Metrano

'Not much more than an ego trip for a bankable star.'—*Daily Mail*

Breezy
US 1973 107m Technicolor
Universal / Malpaso (Robert Daley)

A divorced 50-year-old real estate agent is rejuvenated by an affair with a young girl hippy.
An abrasive veneer covers the most stereotyped of January/May love stories. Technically an attractive piece of work.

w Jo Heims *d* Clint Eastwood *ph* Frank Stanley *m* Michel Legrand

William Holden, Kay Lenz, Roger C. Carmel, Marj Dusay, Joan Hotchkis

Brenda Starr, Reporter
US 1945 bw serial: 15 eps

A girl reporter traces a dead gangster's loot. Adequate who's-following-who melodramatics. Joan Woodbury, Kane Richmond, Sid Saylor, Joe Devin, George Meeker, Wheeler Oakman. Directed by Wallace W. Fox; for Columbia.

Brewster McCloud
US 1970 105m Metrocolor Panavision
MGM / Adler–Phillips / Lion's Gate (Lou Adler)

A man hides out under the roof of the Houston Astrodrome, prepares to learn to fly with man-made wings, and refuses all offers of help; when he launches himself, he falls to his death.
Anarchic, allegorical fantasy, a delight no doubt for connoisseurs of way-out humour. Everyone else, forget it.

w Doran William Cannon *d* Robert Altman *ph* Lamar Boren, Jordan Cronenweth *m* Gene Page

Bud Cort, Sally Kellerman, Michael Murphy, William Windom, Shelley Duvall, René Auberjonois, Stacy Keach, John Shuck, Margaret Hamilton

'Amorphous and rather silly . . . the idea seems to be left over from a Victorian fable, but the style is like a Road Runner cartoon.'—*New Yorker, 1974*

Brewster's Millions*
GB 1935 84m bw
British and Dominion (Herbert Wilcox)

If he can spend a million pounds within two months, a playboy will inherit many millions more.
Artless but lively version of a famous comedy which provided a good role for its star.

w Arthur Wimperis, Paul Gangelin, Douglas Furber, Clifford Grey, Donovan Pedelty, Wolfgang Wilhelm, *play* George Barr McCutcheon and Winchell Smith, *original novel* George Barr McCutcheon *d* Thornton Freeland *ph* Henry Harris, Barney McGill

Jack Buchanan, Lili Damita, Nancy O'Neil, Amy Veness, Sydney Fairbrother, Fred Emney, Sebastian Shaw

'As near 100% film entertainment as can be expected.'—*Variety*

† There had been silent versions in 1916 (with Edward Abeles) and 1921 (with Roscoe Arbuckle).

Brewster's Millions*
US 1945 79m bw
Edward Small

Competent American remake of the above.

w Sig Herzig, Charles Rogers *d* Allan Dwan *ph* Charles Lawton Jnr *m* Hugo Friedhofer

Dennis O'Keefe, Eddie 'Rochester' Anderson, Helen Walker

Gail Patrick, Mischa Auer, June Havoc, Joe Sawyer, Nana Bryant, John Litel, Thurston Hall, Byron Foulger

† Remade as *Three on a Spree* (GB 1961).

AAN: Lou Forbes

Brewster's Millions
US 1985 97m Technicolor

A baseball player learns that in order to inherit 30 million dollars he must spend one million a day for 30 days. Frantically noisy remake of an old chestnut. Richard Pryor, John Candy, Louette McKee, Stephen Collins, Jerry Orbach, Pat Hingle, Tovah Feldshuh. Written by Herschel Weingrod and Timothy Harris; directed by Walter Hill; for Lawrence Gordon, Joel Silver / Universal.

The Bribe*
US 1949 98m bw
MGM (Pandro S. Berman)

A US agent tracks down a group of criminals in Central America.
Steamy melodrama with pretensions but only moderate entertainment value despite high gloss. The rogues' gallery, however, is impressive.

w Marguerite Roberts *d* Robert Z. Leonard *ph* Joseph Ruttenberg *m* Miklos Rozsa

Robert Taylor, Ava Gardner, Charles Laughton, Vincent Price, John Hodiak

Brick Bradford
US 1947 bw serial: 15 eps

A tough crusader is asked by the United Nations to protect the Interceptor Ray. No holds are barred for typical serial action. Kane Richmond, Rick Vallin, Linda Johnson, Pierre Watkin. Directed by Spencer Bennet; for Columbia.

The Bridal Path*
GB 1959 95m Technicolor
Vale (Sidney Gilliat, Frank Launder)

A stalwart Hebridean islander journeys to the mainland in search of a wife.
Mild, episodic, very pleasant open-air comedy set amid splendid locations.

w Frank Launder, Geoffrey Willans, *novel* Nigel Tranter *d* Frank Launder *ph* Arthur Ibbetson *m* Cedric Thorpe Davie

Bill Travers, Fiona Clyne, George Cole, Duncan Macrae, Gordon Jackson, Dilys Laye, Bernadette O'Farrell

Bridal Suite
US 1939 70m bw

A playboy seldom turns up for his own weddings, but his new intended takes him and his mother in hand. Frothy comedy with dependable cast. Robert Young, Annabella, Walter Connolly, Billie Burke, Reginald Owen, Arthur Treacher. Written by Samuel Hoffenstein; directed by William Thiele; for MGM. 'Dull and uninteresting, with static direction, commonplace story and situations, and inability to catch audience attention except for brief moments.'—*Variety* (First known as *Maiden Voyage*.)

'A woman born of electricity . . . a man driven by passion!'

The Bride
US 1985 118m Rank colour
Columbia / Victor Drai

Frankenstein creates a bride for his monster, but she falls for him instead, and the monster goes off with a garrulous dwarf.
Insane romantic–feminist remake of *The Bride of Frankenstein*, extremely dull and aimless after an arresting start.

w Lloyd Fonvielle *d* Franc Roddam *ph* Stephen H. Burum *m* Maurice Jarre *pd* Michael Seymour *ed* Michael Ellis

Sting, Jennifer Beals, Clancy Brown, David Rappaport, Geraldine Page, Anthony Higgins, Quentin Crisp

'A misbegotten exercise.'—*Sight and Sound*

Bride by Mistake
US 1944 84m bw

An heiress tests her suitors by posing as her own secretary. Pleasant little comedy with hard-working cast. Laraine Day, Alan Marshall, Allyn Joslyn, Marsha Hunt. Written by Phoebe and Henry Ephron; directed by Richard Wallace; for RKO.

The Bride Came C.O.D.*
US 1941 92m bw
Warner (Hal B. Wallis)

A charter pilot agrees to kidnap a temperamental heiress, but is stuck with her when they crashland in the desert.

Feeble comedy with a script totally unworthy of its stars. The mass of talent does however provide a smile or two towards the end.

w Julius J. and Philip G. Epstein *d* William Keighley *ph* Ernest Haller *m* Max Steiner

Bette Davis, James Cagney, Harry Davenport, Stuart Erwin, Eugene Pallette, Jack Carson, George Tobias, William Frawley, Edward Brophy, Chick Chandler

'Neither the funniest comedy ever made, nor the shortest distance between two points, but for the most part a serviceable romp.'—*Theodore Strauss*

'Both of them mug good-naturedly, and it's pleasantly fast.'—*New Yorker, 1977*

The Bride Comes Home*
US 1935 82m bw
Paramount (Wesley Ruggles)

A penniless socialite helps a wealthy man and his roughneck bodyguard in a magazine venture.
Slight but freshly handled romantic comedy, still worth a look.

w Elizabeth Sanxay Holding, Claude Binyon *d* Wesley Ruggles *ph* Leo Tover

Claudette Colbert, Robert Young, Fred MacMurray, William Collier Snr, Donald Meek, Edgar Kennedy, Richard Carle, Jimmy Conlin

'Another galloping lithograph off the boy-and-girl-always-fighting woodblock.'—*Variety*

Bride for Sale
US 1949 87m bw
RKO (Jack H. Skirball)

A practical-minded businesswoman has two admirers.
Skittish romantic comedy for ageing stars.

w Bruce Manning, Islin Auster *d* William D. Russell *ph* Joseph Valentine *m* Frederick Hollander

Claudette Colbert, George Brent, Robert Young, Max Baer, Gus Schilling, Charles Arnt, Thurston Hall

The Bride Goes Wild
US 1948 98m bw
MGM (William H. Wright)

As his lady illustrator finds out, a writer of children's books is not quite the sober uncle she expected, especially when he has to pretend to adopt an unruly orphan.
Scatty comedy with farcical interludes, quite pleasantly played but lacking style.

w Albert Beich *d* Norman Taurog *ph* Ray June *m* Rudolf Kopp

June Allyson, Van Johnson, Jackie 'Butch' Jenkins, Hume Cronyn, Richard Derr

'The monster demands a mate!'
The Bride of Frankenstein****
US 1935 85–90m bw
Universal (Carl Laemmle Jnr)

Baron Frankenstein is blackmailed by Dr Praetorious into reviving his monster and building a mate for it.

Frankenstein was startlingly good in a primitive way; this sequel is the screen's sophisticated masterpiece of black comedy, with all the talents working deftly to one end. Every scene has its own delights, and they are woven together into a superb if wilful cinematic narrative which, of its gentle mocking kind, has never been surpassed.

w John L. Balderston, William Hurlbut d James Whale ph John Mescall m Franz Waxman

Boris Karloff, Colin Clive, *Ernest Thesiger*, Valerie Hobson, *E. E. Clive*, Dwight Frye, O. P. Heggie, Una O'Connor, *Elsa Lanchester* (as Mary Shelley and the monster's mate), Gavin Gordon (as Byron), Douglas Walton (as Shelley)

FRANKENSTEIN: 'I've been cursed for delving into the mysteries of life!'

'It is perhaps because Whale was by now master of the horror film that this production is the best of them all.'—*John Baxter, 1968*

'An extraordinary film, with sharp humour, macabre extravagance, and a narrative that proceeds at a fast, efficient pace.'—*Gavin Lambert, 1948*

'A great deal of art has gone into it, but it is the kind of art that gives the healthy feeling of men with their sleeves rolled up and working, worrying only about how to put the thing over in the best manner of the medium—no time for nonsense and attitudes and long hair.'—*Otis Ferguson*

† The regular release version runs 75m, having dropped part of the Mary Shelley prologue and a sequence in which the monster becomes unsympathetic by murdering the burgomaster.
†† The title was originally to have been *The Return of Frankenstein.*

Bride of the Gorilla
US 1951 65m bw

The manager of a rubber plantation is poisoned by a native woman and turns into a gorilla. Incredibly inane two-bit shocker, a strong contender for any list of the worst films of all time. Barbara Payton, Lon Chaney Jnr, Raymond Burr, Tom Conway, Paul Cavanagh (a rare cast of non-actors). Written and directed by Curt Siodmak; for Jack Broder Productions.

Bride of the Monster
US 1953 69m bw

Dr Vornoff has an atomic machine which will convert people into beings of superhuman strength; it is turned on himself, but a giant octopus, also with superoctopus strength, gets him. A perfectly terrible movie, on a par with this director's other works. Written by Edward D. Wood Jnr and Alex Gordon; directed and produced by Edward D. Wood Jnr; for Rolling M.

Bride of the Regiment
US 1930 79m Technicolor
First National
GB title: *Lady of the Rose*

In northern Italy a band of aristocrats rises against the invading Austrians.
Early talkie operetta, well received at the time. No colour material survives.

w Ray Harris, *operetta* The Lady in Ermine by Rudolph Schanzer and Ernest Wellsch *d* John Francis Dillon *ph* Dev Jennings, Charles Schoenbaum *ch* Jack Haskell *songs* Al Bryan, Ed Ward

Vivienne Segal, Allan Prior, Walter Pidgeon, Louise Fazenda, Ford Sterling, Myrna Loy, Lupino Lane

'Entertaining all the way, deserves returns above the average.'—*Variety*

Bride of Vengeance*
US 1948 91m bw
Paramount (Richard Maibaum)

The story of the Borgias (whitewashing Lucretia) and the Duke of Ferrara.
Superb looking but appallingly acted and rather stodgily directed piece of historical melodrama. Totally studio-bound, but one of these days it could find a sympathetic audience.

w Cyril Hume, Michael Hogan *d* Mitchell Leisen *ph* Daniel L. Fapp *m* Hugo Friedhofer *ad* Hans Dreier, Roland Anderson, Albert Nozaki

Paulette Goddard, John Lund, Macdonald Carey, Albert Dekker, Raymond Burr

'A dud . . . it just couldn't be that bad by accident.'—*Los Angeles Times*

The Bride Walks Out
US 1936 81m bw
RKO (Edward Small)

A successful mannequin tries to manage on her engineer husband's lowly salary.
Thin, pleasant marital comedy with no surprises.

w P. J. Wolfson, Philip G. Epstein *d* Leigh Jason *ph* J. Roy Hunt *m* Roy Webb

Barbara Stanwyck, Gene Raymond, Robert Young, Ned Sparks, Helen Broderick, Willie Best, Robert Warwick, Billy Gilbert, Hattie McDaniel, Irving Bacon

The Bride Wore Black*
France / Italy 1967 107m Eastmancolor
Films du Carrosse / Artistes Associés / Dino de Laurentiis (Marcel Bébert)
original title: *La Mariée Était en Noir*

A melancholy lady traces and kills the five men responsible for her fiancé's death.
Uncertain and not very entertaining attempt to turn a Hitchcock situation into a character study.

w François Truffaut, Jean-Louis Richard, *novel* William Irish *d* François Truffaut *ph* Raoul Coutard *m* Bernard Herrmann

Jeanne Moreau, Jean-Claude Brialy, Michel Bouquet, Charles Denner, Claude Rich, Michel Lonsdale

'Truffaut has called the film a love story; others have taken it as a tribute to his master, a Hitchcockian thriller. In fact it is neither; it is a piece of junk.'—*John Simon*

The Bride Wore Boots
US 1946 86m bw
Paramount (Seton I. Miller)

A woman who loves horses is married to a man who does not.
Flimsy, silly, but mainly quite tolerable light comedy sustained by its stars.

w Dwight Mitchell Wiley *d* Irving Pichel *ph* Stuart Thompson *m* Frederick Hollander

Barbara Stanwyck, Robert Cummings, Diana Lynn, Patric Knowles, Peggy Wood, Robert Benchley, Willie Best, Natalie Wood

The Bride Wore Crutches
US 1941 55m bw

A young reporter witnesses a bank robbery and tracks down the criminals. Lightweight support. Ted North, Lynne Roberts, Edgar Kennedy, Lionel Stander, Richard Lane, Grant Mitchell, Horace MacMahon. Written by Ed Verdier; directed by Shepherd Traube; for TCF.

The Bride Wore Red*
US 1937 103m bw
MGM (Joseph L. Mankiewicz)

A whimsical count arranges for a chorus girl to spend two weeks at an aristocratic Tyrol resort, where she is pursued by two rich men.
Cinderella retold in fancy dress; a typically unreal but quite entertaining star confection of its day.

w Tess Slesinger, Bradbury Foote, *play* The Girl from Trieste by Ferenc Molnar *d* Dorothy Arzner *ph* George Folsey *m* Franz Waxman

Joan Crawford, Robert Young, Franchot Tone, Billie Burke, Reginald Owen, George Zucco, Lynne Carver, Mary Phillips, Paul Porcasi

'Marquee values will have to bolster this one.'—*Variety*

'In the privacy of a girls' school he sought his prey—turning innocent beauty into a thing of unspeakable horror!'

Brides of Dracula**
GB 1960 85m Technicolor
U-I / Hammer / Hotspur (Anthony Hinds)

Baron Meinster, a disciple of Dracula, is locked up by his mother; but a servant lets him out and he goes on the rampage in a girls' school.
The best of the Hammer *Draculas*, with plenty of inventive action, some classy acting and a good sense of place and period.

w Jimmy Sangster, Peter Bryan, Edward Percy *d Terence Fisher ph* Jack Asher *m* Malcolm Williamson

David Peel (as Meinster), *Peter Cushing*, Freda Jackson, *Martita Hunt*, Yvonne Monlaur, Andrée Melly, Mona Washbourne, Henry Oscar, Miles Malleson

The Brides of Fu Manchu*
GB 1966 94m Eastmancolor

The yellow peril kidnaps twelve young women in order to blackmail their influential boy friends. Very adequate sequel to *The Face of Fu Manchu* (qv for details of series), after which Fu Manchu went rapidly downhill. Christopher Lee, Douglas Wilmer, Howard Marion Crawford, Marie Versini, Tsai Chin, Rupert Davies. Written and produced by Harry Alan Towers (Peter Welbeck); directed by Don Sharp; for Anglo Amalgamated.

The Bridge*
West Germany 1959 106m bw
Fono / Jochen Severin (Hermann Schwerin)

In 1945, only a handful of 16-year-old schoolboys is left to defend the bridge of a small German town.
Painful but memorable war vignette, almost an updating of *All Quiet on the Western Front.*

w Michael Mansfield, Karl-Wilhelm Vivier, *novel* Manfred Gregor *d Bernhard Wicki ph* Gerd Von Bonen *m* Hans-Martin Majewski

Vokler Bohnet, Fritz Wepper, Michael Hinz, Frank Glaubrecht, Karl Michael Balzer, Gunther Hoffman

The Bridge at Remagen*
US 1968 116m De Luxe Panavision
UA / Wolper (David L. Wolper)

February 1945: Germans and Americans fight over a Rhine bridge.
Disenchanted, violent war film in which incessant bang-bang, adroitly staged, is all that matters.

w Richard Yates, William Roberts *d* John Guillermin *ph* Stanley Cortez *m* Elmer Bernstein

George Segal, Robert Vaughn, Ben Gazzara, Bradford Dillman, E. G. Marshall, Peter Van Eyck

'Viable viewing if explosions and clichés are your shtick and exciting if you're not sure who won that war.'—*Judith Crist*

The Bridge of San Luis Rey*
US 1944 85m bw
(UA) Benedict Bogeaus

Five people die when a Peruvian rope bridge collapses; the film investigates why they were each on the bridge at the time.
An intriguing novel is turned into tedious film drama, with actors, director, scenarist and production designer all making heavy weather.

w Howard Estabrook, *novel* Thornton Wilder *d* Rowland V. Lee *ph* John Boyle *m* Dmitri Tiomkin

Lynn Bari, Francis Lederer, Nazimova, Louis Calhern, Akim Tamiroff, Blanche Yurka, Donald Woods

† A silent version, with a few minutes of hasty talk, was made in 1929 by Charles Brabin for MGM, from a script by Alice Duer Miller, Ruth Cummings and Marian Ainslee. The cast included Lili Damita, Ernest Torrence, Don Alvarado, Raquel Torres, and Henry B. Walthall.

'As a remake for present-day audiences, up to their ears in war news, this picture will be a welcome divertissement.'—*Variety*

AAN: Dmitri Tiomkin

'It spans a whole new world of entertainment!'

The Bridge on the River Kwai***
GB 1957 161m Technicolor Cinemascope
Columbia / Sam Spiegel

British POWs in Burma are employed by the Japs to build a bridge; meanwhile British agents seek to destroy it.
Ironic adventure epic with many fine moments but too many centres of interest and an unforgivably confusing climax. It is distinguished by Guinness' portrait of the English CO who is heroic in his initial stand against the Japs but finally cannot bear to see his bridge blown up: and the physical detail of the production is beyond criticism.

w Carl Foreman, *novel* Pierre Boulle *d David Lean ph* Jack Hildyard *m* Malcolm Arnold

Alec Guinness (Colonel Nicholson), William Holden (Shears), Jack Hawkins (Major Warden), Sessue Hayakawa (Colonel Saito), James Donald (Major Clipton), Geoffrey Horne (Lieut. Joyce), Andre Morell (Col. Green), Percy Herbert (Grogan)

'It may rank as the most rousing adventure film inspired by the last World War.'—*Alton Cook, New York World Telegram*

† Cary Grant was originally sought for the William Holden role.

†† The script was actually written by Michael Wilson, who was blacklisted by the anti-communists

AA: best picture; best adaptation (now credited to Carl Foreman, Michael Wilson and Pierre Boulle); David Lean; Jack Hildyard; Malcolm Arnold; Alec Guinness

AAN: Sessue Hayakawa

Bridge to the Sun*
France / US 1961 112m bw
MGM / Cité Films (Jacques Bar)

Just before Pearl Harbor, an American girl marries a Japanese diplomat and goes to live in Tokyo.
Romantic drama which oddly sides with the Japanese and shows America in a poor light. Interesting if not very compelling, with some unfamiliar views of Japan.

w Charles Kaufman, *autobiography* Gwendolen Terasaki *d* Etienne Périer *ph* Marcel Weiss, Seiichi Kizuka, Bill Kelly *m* Georges Auric

Carroll Baker, James Shigeta, James Yagi, Tetsuro Tamba

'In yet another burst of national flagellation, Hollywood turns on itself and unthinking Americans for being so beastly about the wartime Japanese.'—*MFB*

A Bridge Too Far**
US / GB 1977 175m Technicolor Panavision
UA / Joseph E. Levine (John Palmer)

The story of the Allied defeat at Arnhem in 1944.

A BRIDGE TOO FAR. A rare intimate moment in Richard Attenborough's solidly-staged war epic.

Like all large-scale military films, this one fails to make its tactics clear, and its sober intent conflicts with its roster of guest stars. For all that, there are impressive moments of acting and production.

w William Goldman, *book* Cornelius Ryan *d* Richard Attenborough (and Sidney Hayers) *ph Geoffrey Unsworth, Harry Waxman, Robin Browne* *m* John Addison *pd* Terence Marsh

Dirk Bogarde, James Caan, Michael Caine, Sean Connery, Edward Fox, Elliott Gould, Gene Hackman, Anthony Hopkins, Hardy Kruger, *Laurence Olivier*, Ryan O'Neal, Robert Redford, Maximilian Schell, Liv Ullmann, Arthur Hill, Wolfgang Preiss

'A film too long.'—*Anon.*

'So wearily, expensively predictable that by the end the viewer will in all likelihood be too enervated to notice Attenborough's prosaic moral epilogue.'—*John Pym, MFB*

The Bridges at Toko-Ri*
US 1954 104m Technicolor
Paramount / Perlberg–Seaton

The comradeship and death of two jet pilots during the Korean War.
Ambitiously staged action thriller with points to make about war, death and politics: a well-worn American formula pitched very hard.

w Valentine Davies, *novel* James E. Michener *d* Mark Robson *ph* Loyal Griggs *m* Lyn Murray

William Holden, Mickey Rooney, Grace Kelly, Fredric March, Robert Strauss, Charles McGraw, Earl Holliman, Willis Bouchey

'A taut, thrilling, top flight documentary drama of men, war, ships and planes.'—*Cue*

Brief Encounter****
GB 1945 86m bw
Cineguild (Anthony Havelock-Allan, Ronald Neame)

A suburban housewife on her weekly shopping visits develops a love affair with a local doctor; but he gets a job abroad and they agree not to see each other again.
An outstanding example of good middle-class cinema turned by sheer professional craft into a masterpiece; even those bored by the theme must be riveted by the treatment, especially the use of a dismal railway station and its trains.

w Noel Coward, from his one-act play Still Life *d David Lean* *ph Robert Krasker* *m* Rachmaninov

Celia Johnson, Trevor Howard, Stanley Holloway, Joyce Carey, Cyril Raymond

'Both a pleasure to watch as a well-controlled piece of work, and deeply touching.'—*James Agee*

'Polished as is this film, its strength does not lie in movie technique, of which there is plenty, so much as in the tight realism of its detail.'—*Richard Winnington*

'A celebrated, craftsmanlike tearjerker, and incredibly neat. There's not a breath of air in it.'—*Pauline Kael, 70s*

† A TV film version was made in 1975 by ITC, starring Richard Burton and Sophia Loren and directed by Alan Bridges. It was an unqualified disaster.
AAN: script; David Lean; Celia Johnson

Brigadoon*
US 1954 108m Anscocolor Cinemascope
MGM (Arthur Freed)

Two Americans in Scotland find a ghost village which awakens only once every hundred years.
Likeable but disappointing adaptation of a Lost Horizonish Broadway musical, marred by artificial sets and jaded direction.

w Alan Jay Lerner, from his play *d* Vincente Minnelli *ph* Joseph Ruttenberg *md* Johnny Green *songs* Frederick Loewe, Alan Jay Lerner

Gene Kelly, Cyd Charisse, Van Johnson, Jimmy Thompson, Elaine Stewart, Barry Jones, Eddie Quillan

'The whimsical dream world it creates holds no compelling attractions.'—*Penelope Houston*

The Brigand*
US 1952 93m Technicolor
Columbia

A Moroccan adventurer looks like the king and is reprieved from execution if he will impersonate the latter and root out his enemies.
Cheeky revamp of *The Prisoner of Zenda*, quite acceptably done.

w Jesse Lasky Jnr *d* Phil Karlson *ph* W. Howard Greene *m* Mario Castelnuovo-Tedesco

Anthony Dexter, Jody Lawrance, Gale Robbins, Anthony Quinn, Carl Benton Reid, Ron Randell

The Brigand of Kandahar
GB 1965 81m Technicolor 'Scope
EMI / Hammer (Anthony Nelson Keys)

A cashiered Bengal Lancer officer throws in his lot with a troublesome bandit.
Feeble frontier adventure with nothing ringing true.

wd John Gilling *ph* Reg Wyer *m* Don Banks *pd* Bernard Robinson

Oliver Reed, Ronald Lewis, Duncan Lamont, Yvonne Romain, Catherine Woodville, Glyn Houston

Brigham Young*
US 1940 112m bw
TCF (Kenneth MacGowan)

The story of the Mormon trek to Utah.
Ambitious but rather dull interpretation of history, seen as a western with romantic fictional trimmings.

w Lamar Trotti, *story* Louis Bromfield *d* Henry Hathaway *ph Arthur Miller* *m* Alfred Newman

Dean Jagger, Tyrone Power, Linda Darnell, Brian Donlevy, Jane Darwell, John Carradine, Mary Astor, Vincent Price, Moroni Olsen

'A big picture in every respect.'—*Variety*

'One of the year's outstanding films.'—*Newsweek*

† The production had a 133-day schedule, and cost 2,700,000 dollars

Bright Eyes*
US 1934 84m bw
TCF (Sol M. Wurtzel)

An orphan finds herself torn between foster-parents.
The first of Shirley Temple's genuine star vehicles has a liveliness and cheerfulness hard to find today. As a production, however, it is decidedly economical.

w William Conselman *d* David Butler *ph* Arthur Miller *m* Samuel Kaylin

Shirley Temple, James Dunn, Lois Wilson, *Jane Withers*, Judith Allen

'It seems a cinch to please generally, the family and sentimental strata particularly.'—*Variety*

Bright Leaf
US 1950 110m bw
Warner (Henry Blanke)

A 19th-century tobacco farmer builds a cigarette empire.
Quite agreeable but disjointed fictional biopic, more about love than tobacco.

w Ranald MacDougall, *novel* Robert Wilder *d* Michael Curtiz *ph* Karl Freund *m* Victor Young

Gary Cooper, Lauren Bacall, Patricia Neal, Jack Carson, Donald Crisp, Gladys George, Elizabeth Patterson, Jeff Corey, Taylor Holmes

Bright Lights*
US 1935 86m bw

A vaudevillian lets success go to his head. The plot served for a score or more of thirties musicals, but this had Busby Berkeley routines and an unusual star role for Joe E. Brown; with Ann Dvorak, Patricia Ellis, William Gargan. Written by Bert Kalmar and Harry Ruby; directed by Busby Berkeley; for Warner. (GB title: *Funny Face*.) (The same title covered a 1925 MGM silent with Charles Ray as a country boy in love with a Broadway star, also a 1930 Warners film with Frank Fay.)
'Practically an 86-minute monologue, with the star doing everything but taking tickets.'—*Variety*

Bright Road*
US 1953 69m bw
MGM (Sol Baer Fielding)

In an all-black school, a problem child finds himself when he helps to rid the school of a swarm of bees.
Slight but attractive second feature, unostentatiously set in a black community.

w Emmet Lavery *d* Gerald Mayer *ph* Alfred Gilks *m* David Rose

Dorothy Dandridge, Harry Belafonte, Robert Horton, Philip Hepburn, Barbara Ann Sanders

Bright Victory*
US 1951 97m bw
Universal (Robert Buckner)
GB title: *Lights Out*

A blinded soldier adjusts to civilian life. Well-meaning if rather slow and sticky, this drama is more sentimental than realistic but has good performances.

w Robert Buckner, *novel* Bayard Kendrick *d* Mark Robson *ph* William Daniels *m* Frank Skinner

Arthur Kennedy, Peggy Dow, Julia Adams, James Edwards, Will Geer, Minor Watson, Jim Backus

AAN: Arthur Kennedy

Brighton Beach Memoirs*
US 1986 108m colour
Universal / Rastar (David Chasman)

In 1937 Brooklyn, a lower middle class Jewish family has assorted crises.
Standard picturization of a Neil Simon play, somewhat flattened out in the process but with funny moments.

w Neil Simon, from his play *d* Gene Saks *ph* John Bailey *m* Michael Small

Blythe Danner, Bob Dishy, Brian Drillinger, Stacey Glick, Judith Ivey, Lisa Waltz

Brighton Rock***
GB 1947 92m bw
Associated British (Roy Boulting)
US title: *Young Scarface*

The teenage leader of a racetrack gang uses a waitress as alibi to cover a murder, and marries her. He later decides to be rid of her, but fate takes a hand in his murder plot.
A properly 'seedy' version of Graham Greene's 'entertainment', very flashily done for the most part but with a trick ending which allows the heroine to keep her illusions.

w Graham Greene, Terence Rattigan *d John Boulting ph* Harry Waxman *m* Hans May

Richard Attenborough, Hermione Baddeley, *Harcourt Williams*, William Hartnell, Alan Wheatley, Carol Marsh

'The film is slower, much less compelling, and, if you get me, less cinematic than the book, as a child's guide to which I hereby offer it.'—*Richard Winnington*

'It proceeds with the efficiency, the precision and the anxiety to please of a circular saw.'—*Dilys Powell*

The Brighton Strangler
US 1945 67m bw

An actor takes over in real life the part he is playing – of a murderer. This hoary plot had seen better days even in 1945, and was not helped by an establishing shot which put Parliament on the wrong side of the Thames. John Loder, June Duprez. Written by Arnold Philips and Max Nosseck; directed by Max Nosseck; for RKO.

Brimstone
US 1949 90m Trucolor

A US Marshal tracks down Public Outlaw Number One. High-spirited western co-feature. Rod Cameron, Walter Brennan, Adrian Booth, Forrest Tucker, Jack Holt, Jim Davis, James Brown, Guinn Williams. Written by Thames Williamson; directed and produced by Joseph Kane for Republic.

Brimstone and Treacle*
GB 1982 87m Technicolor
Namara / Alan E. Salke / Herbert Solow

A strange young man has a sinister effect on the family of a middle-aged writer of doggerel, whose crippled daughter he finally rapes.
Similar in mood to *Pennies from Heaven*, this is basically a television play very typical of its author. (Some years ago it was taped and then banned by the BBC.) In substance no more than a reversal of *The Passing of the Third Floor Back*, its points of interest are mainly technical.

w Dennis Potter, from his play *d* Richard Loncraine *ph* Peter Hannan *m* Sting *pd* Milly Burns

Sting, Denholm Elliott, Joan Plowright, Suzanna Hamilton, Benjamin Whitrow, Dudley Sutton

Bring 'Em Back Alive
US 1932 65m bw

A documentary showing how animal hunter Frank Buck scoured Malayan jungles for specimens to stock the world's zoos. Very dated now, but quite an attraction in its day. The title was used again in 1982 for a TV series in which Bruce Boxleitner played Buck; the emphasis now, however, was on serial-like intrigue. 'Will get money but needs alert exploitation.'—*Variety*

'It's got guts!'
Bring Me the Head of Alfredo Garcia
US 1974 112m De Luxe
UA / Optimus / Churubusco (Martin Baum)

A wealthy Mexican offers a million dollars for the head of a man who seduced his daughter, and claimants find that grave robbing is involved.
Gruesome, sickly action melodrama with revolting detail; the nadir of a director obsessed by violence.

w Gordon Dawson, Sam Peckinpah *d* Sam Peckinpah *ph* Alex Phillips Jnr *m* Jerry Fielding

Warren Oates, Gig Young, Isela Vega, Robert Webber, Helmut Dantine, Emilio Fernandez, Kris Kristofferson

'Few movies are as tedious. Bring me the head of the studio that released this one.'—*Gene Shalit*

'The only kind of analysis it really invites is psychoanalysis.'—*Wall Street Journal*

'Peckinpah clearly doesn't lack talent—what he lacks is brains.'—*John Simon*

Bring On the Girls
US 1945 92m Technicolor
Paramount (Fred Kohlmar)

A millionaire joins the navy in the hope that a girl will love him for himself.
A good example of the gaily-coloured but witless drivel which occasionally came out of the big studios towards the end of the war.

w Karl Tunberg, Darrell Ware *d* Sidney Lanfield *ph* Karl Struss *md* Robert Emmett Dolan

Veronica Lake, Eddie Bracken, Sonny Tufts, Marjorie Reynolds, Grant Mitchell, Alan Mowbray, Porter Hall

Bring Your Smile Along
US 1955 83m Technicolor

A lady schoolteacher goes to New York to write songs. Amiable musical filler with rather flat jokes. Frankie Laine, Keefe Brasselle, Constance Towers, Lucy Marlow. Written and directed by Blake Edwards; for Columbia.

Bringing Up Baby***
US 1938 102m bw
RKO (Howard Hawks)

A zany girl causes a zoology professor to lose a dinosaur bone and a pet leopard in the same evening.
Outstanding crazy comedy which barely pauses for romance and ends up with the whole splendid cast in jail.

w Dudley Nichols, Hagar Wilde d Howard Hawks ph Russell Metty *m* Roy Webb

Katharine Hepburn, Cary Grant, May Robson, Charles Ruggles, Walter Catlett, Fritz Feld, Jonathan Hale, Barry Fitzgerald

'Harum-scarum farce comedy . . . definite box-office.'—*Variety*

'I am happy to report that it is funny from the word go, that it has no other meaning to recommend it . . . and that I wouldn't swap it for practically any three things of the current season.'—*Otis Ferguson*

'It may be the American movies' closest equivalent to Restoration comedy.'—*Pauline Kael*

'Crazy comedies continue to become crazier, and there will soon be few actors and actresses left who have no straw in their hair.'—*Basil Wright*

† The dog George was played by Asta from *The Thin Man* movies.

Bringing Up Father
US 1928 approx 70m at 24 fps bw silent

Mild domestic comedy about a henpecked husband, from the famous comic strip; it marked the successful comeback of Marie Dressler (as the maid). J. Farrell MacDonald, Polly Moran, Gertrude Olmsted, Grant Withers. Written by Frances Marion; directed by Jack Conway; for MGM. (Two or three second features about Jiggs and Maggie, featuring Renie Riano and Joe Yule, appeared in the late forties.)

The Brinks Job
US 1978 103m Technicolor
Universal / Dino de Laurentiis (Ralph Serpe)

In 1944, amateur criminals bring off a raid on the vaults of a Boston security company.
Farcical variation of a much-told true tale. Despite much mugging by the stars and a frantic narrative style, it does not come off.
w Walon Green from the book Big Stick-Up at Brinks by Noel Behn *d* William Friedkin *ph* Norman Leigh *m* Richard Rodney Bennett *pd* Dean Tavoularis
Peter Falk, Warren Oates, Peter Boyle, Allen Goorwitz, Gena Rowlands, Paul Sorvino, Sheldon Leonard

Britannia Hospital
GB 1982 116m colour
EMI / Film and General / NFFC (Davina Belling, Clive Parsons)
Problems besetting a British hospital celebrating its 500th anniversary include strikes, demonstrators, and a mad doctor who transplants heads.
Looking as crummy as a Carry On at the end of its tether, this intended lampoon of the state of the nation never warms up and can only fire off stale jokes in all directions while repelling the eye with its Frankenstein scenes.
w David Sherwin *d* Lindsay Anderson *ph* Mike Fash *pd* Norris Spencer *m* Alan Price
Malcolm McDowell, Leonard Rossiter, Graham Crowden, Fulton Mackay, Vivian Pickles, Joan Plowright, Peter Jeffrey, Robin Askwith, Dandy Nichols, Valentine Dyall, Roland Culver, Alan Bates, Arthur Lowe, Marsha Hunt
'It has all the intensity, along with the flailing incoherence, of a soapbox jeremiah.'—*Richard Combs, MFB*
'Having once created a general shambles, the film is at a loss to clean it up.'—*Margaret Hinxman, Daily Mail*
'Inexplicably muddled and inconclusive.'—*Guardian*
'It mentholates the tubes and oxygenates the brain.'—*Sunday Telegraph*

Britannia Mews
GB 1948 91m bw
TCF (William Perlberg)
US title: *The Forbidden Street*
In Victorian times, the widow of a puppetmaster eventually marries his lookalike who rebuilds their puppet theatre.
Curious and uncertain comedy drama set among yesterday's high society, with poorly played leads but an interesting supporting cast and technical assurance.
w Ring Lardner Jnr, *novel* Margery Sharp *d* Jean Negulesco *ph* Georges Périnal *ad* Andrei Andreiev *m* Malcolm Arnold
Dana Andrews, Maureen O'Hara, Sybil Thorndike, Wilfrid Hyde White, Fay Compton, A. E. Matthews

British Agent*
US 1934 75m bw
Warner (Henry Blanke)
In 1910 Russia, a Britisher falls in love with a lady spy.
Sluggish and dated romantic melodrama, notable only for Howard's performance and some directional felicities.
w Laird Doyle, *novel* H. Bruce Lockhart *d* Michael Curtiz *ph* Ernest Haller *ad* Anton Grot
Leslie Howard, Kay Francis, William Gargan, *Irving Pichel*, Philip Reed, Walter Byron, J. Carrol Naish, Halliwell Hobbes
'One of those rare cases of a film both artistically and cinematically good entertainment . . . an exciting story well told, excellent acting, draw names and production value.'—*Variety*

British Intelligence
US 1940 63m bw
Warner (Bryan Foy)
GB title: *Enemy Agent*
During World War I a German lady spy becomes a guest in the house of a British war official, the butler of which is the leader of a German spy ring.
Second feature remake of *Three Faces East* (qv); still quite an entertaining melodrama.
w Lee Katz, *play* Anthony Paul Kelly *d* Terry Morse *ph* Sid Hickox *m* Heinz Roemheld
Boris Karloff, Margaret Lindsay, Maris Wrixon, Bruce Lester, Leonard Mudie, Holmes Herbert

Broadcast News*
US 1987 131m DeLuxe
TCF / James L. Brooks (Polly Platt)
Mildly satirical look at the world of television journalism that slips into romantic comedy.
w,d James L. Brooks *ph* Michael Balhaus *m* Bill Conti *pd* Charles Rosen
William Hurt, Albert Brooks, Holly Hunter, Robert Prosky, Lois Chiles

Broadminded*
US 1931 65m bw
A bashful swain leaves town after a misunderstanding and becomes involved in an intercontinental chase. Modest star farce with some hilarious moments. *Joe E. Brown*, Ona Munson, William Collier Jnr, Marjorie White, Holmes Herbert, Bela Lugosi. Written by Bert Kalmar and Harry Ruby; directed by Mervyn Le Roy; for First National. 'Best he has ever done . . . any audience will enjoy it.'—*Variety*

Broadway
US 1942 90m bw
Universal (Bruce Manning)
George Raft recalls his days as a hoofer in a New York speakeasy, and in particular a murder involving gangsters and chorus girls.
Minor crime melodrama which after interminable scene-setting paints an effective picture of the twenties but has too slack a grip on narrative.
w Felix Jackson, John Bright, *play* Philip Dunning, George Abbott *d* William A. Seiter *ph* George Barnes *md* Charles Previn
George Raft, Pat O'Brien, S. Z. Sakall, Janet Blair, Broderick Crawford, Marjorie Rambeau

Broadway Bad
US 1933 59m bw
A scheming chorus girl makes a rich marriage. Paper-thin melodrama, one of a hundred on similar lines. Joan Blondell, Ginger Rogers, Ricardo Cortez, Adrienne Ames, Spencer Charters, Donald Crisp. Written by Arthur Kober and Maude Fulton; directed by Sidney Lanfield; for Fox.

Broadway Bill**
US 1934 104m bw
Columbia (Frank Capra)
GB title: *Strictly Confidential*
A cheerful horse trainer finds he has a winner.
Easygoing romantic comedy with the energetic Capra style in fairly full bloom.
w Robert Riskin, *story* Mark Hellinger *d Frank Capra* *ph* Joseph Walker
Warner Baxter, Myrna Loy, Walter Connolly, Helen Vinson, Douglass Dumbrille, Raymond Walburn, Lynne Overman, Clarence Muse, Margaret Hamilton, Paul Harvey, Claude Gillingwater, Charles Lane, Ward Bond
'The effect of capable direction is discernible in every foot.'—*Variety*
'It will be a long day before we see so little made into so much: it is gay and charming and will make you happy, and I am sorry to say I do not know recommendations much higher.'—*Otis Ferguson*
† Remade as *Riding High* (qv).

Broadway Danny Rose*
US 1984 84m De Luxe
Orion (Robert Greenhut)
An artists' agent and former comic falls foul of the Mafia while promoting a client.
Generally appealing comedy-melodrama with rather less self-examination than has latterly been typical of its star.
w,d Woody Allen *ph* Gordon Willis *md* Nick Hyman *pd* Mel Bourne *ed* Susan E. Morse
Woody Allen, Mia Farrow, Nick Apollo Forte, Craig Vandenbergh, Herb Reynolds
AAN: direction, original screenplay
BFA: original screenplay

Broadway Gondolier
US 1935 98m bw
A taxi driver wants to become a radio singer. Rather tedious musical with second-rate elements. Dick Powell, Adolphe Menjou, Joan Blondell, Louise Fazenda, the Mills Brothers, Judy Canova, Ted Fiorito and his band. Written by Warren Duff and Sig Herzig; songs by Al Dubin and Harry Warren; directed by Lloyd Bacon; for Warner. 'Loose on story and even lethargic, it holds enough for gate values.'—*Variety*

Broadway Hostess
US 1935 69m bw
A small-town girl becomes a night-club singer. Modest musical which failed to create a new star. Wini Shaw, Genevieve Tobin, Lyle Talbot, Allen Jenkins, Phil Regan, Marie

Wilson, Spring Byington. Written by George Bricker; directed by Frank McDonald; for Warners. 'Adequate for family audience consumption.'—*Variety*

Broadway Limited*
US 1941 75m bw
Hal Roach
GB title: *The Baby Vanishes*

On an express train, a Hollywood publicity stunt backfires.
Wild farce which is not very funny as a whole but has entertaining comic performances.

w Rian James *d* Gordon Douglas *ph* Henry Sharp *m* Charles Previn

Victor McLaglen, Patsy Kelly, *Leonid Kinskey*, Marjorie Woodworth, Dennis O'Keefe, Zasu Pitts, George E. Stone

'The pulsating drama of Broadway's bared heart speaks and sings with a voice to stir your soul!'
'The new wonder of the screen!'

Broadway Melody*
US 1929 110m bw (Technicolor scenes)
MGM (Lawrence Weingarten)

Chorus girls try to make it big on Broadway.
The screen's very first musical, exceedingly primitive by the standards of even a year later, but rather endearing and with a splendid score.

w James Gleason, Norman Houston, Edmund Goulding *d* Harry Beaumont *ph* John Arnold *songs Nacio Herb Brown, Arthur Freed*

Charles King, Anita Page, Bessie Love, Jed Prouty, Kenneth Thomson, Mary Doran, Eddie Kane

'A basic story with some sense to it, action, excellent direction, laughs, a tear, a couple of great performances and plenty of sex.'—*Variety*

AA: best picture
AAN: Harry Beaumont, Bessie Love

'You have waited seven years for this!'

Broadway Melody of 1936**
US 1935 103m bw
MGM (John W. Considine Jnr)

A Broadway producer is at loggerheads with a columnist.
Fairly lively musical with lavish numbers.

w Jack McGowan, Sid Silvers, *original story* Moss Hart *d* Roy del Ruth *ph* Charles Rosher *songs Nacio Herb Brown, Arthur Freed*

Jack Benny, Robert Taylor, Una Merkel, *Eleanor Powell*, June Knight, Vilma and Buddy Ebsen, Nick Long Jnr

Songs include 'You Are My Lucky Star'; 'I've Gotta Feelin' You're Foolin' '; 'Broadway Rhythm'; 'On a Sunday Afternoon'; 'Sing Before Breakfast'

'Smash musical with strong dancing and comedy framework.'—*Variety*

AAN: best picture; Moss Hart

Broadway Melody of 1938*
US 1937 110m bw
MGM (Jack Cummings)

Backstage problems threaten the opening of a musical show.
Lavish but fairly forgettable musical with top talent.

w Jack McGowan, Sid Silvers *d* Roy del Ruth *ph* William Daniels *songs* Nacio Herb Brown, Arthur Freed

Eleanor Powell, George Murphy, *Sophie Tucker*, Judy Garland, Robert Taylor, Buddy Ebsen, Sid Silvers, Billy Gilbert, Raymond Walburn

Songs include 'Your Broadway and My Broadway'; 'A Pair of New Shoes'; 'Yours and Mine'; 'Sun Showers'; 'I'm Feeling Like a Million'

'Explosion in the cash drawers . . . will do smash business everywhere.'—*Variety*

Broadway Melody of 1940*
US 1939 102m bw
MGM (Jack Cummings)

A dance team gets to the top.
Splendidly produced but thinly plotted extravaganza with good numbers.

w Leon Gordon, George Oppenheimer *d* Norman Taurog *ph* Oliver T. Marsh, Joseph Ruttenberg *songs* Cole Porter *md* Alfred Newman

Fred Astaire, Eleanor Powell, George Murphy, Douglas Macphail, Florence Rice, Frank Morgan, Ian Hunter

Broadway Musketeers
US 1938 62m bw

Three girls from the same orphanage meet again in New York. Uninspired remake of *Three on a Match*. Ann Sheridan, Marie Wilson, Margaret Lindsay, John Litel, Dick Purcell. Written by Don Ryan and Ken Gamet; directed by John Farrow; for Bryan Foy / Warner. 'A programmer of average distinction . . . ought to get by satisfactorily.'—*Variety*

Broadway Rhythm*
US 1943 113m Technicolor
MGM (Jack Cummings)

Originally intended as *Broadway Melody of 1944*, this putting-on-a-show extravaganza had only the numbers to commend it.

w Dorothy Kingsley, Harry Clark, from the Kern / Hammerstein operetta Very Warm for May *d* Roy del Ruth *ph* Leonard Smith *songs* various *md* John Green

George Murphy, Ginny Simms, Charles Winninger, Gloria de Haven, Lena Horne, Nancy Walker, Hazel Scott, Eddie Anderson, Ben Blue, Tommy Dorsey and his Orchestra

'It contains perhaps three minutes of good acrobatic dancing and lasts nearly two hours.'—*James Agee*

Broadway Serenade
US 1939 114m bw
MGM (Robert Z. Leonard)
GB title: *Serenade*

Career problems split the marriage of a songwriter and his singing wife.
Lavish but rather dull romantic drama with music.

w Charles Lederer, Lew Lipton, John T. Foote, Hans Kraly *d* Robert Z. Leonard *ph* Oliver T. Marsh *md* Herbert Stothart

Jeanette MacDonald, Lew Ayres, Frank Morgan, Ian Hunter, Rita Johnson, Virginia Grey, William Gargan, Katherine Alexander

Songs include 'No Time to Argue'; 'Time Changes Everything but Love'; 'For Every Lonely Heart'; 'Broadway Serenade'; 'High Flyin''; 'One Look at You'

'With all its lavishness, it impresses as only mild box office material.'—*Variety*

Broadway thru a Keyhole*
US 1933 90m bw
UA / William Goetz, Raymond Griffith

A tough New York gangster falls for a singer in his nightclub.
Reputed acid observation of the New York scene distinguishes this low-budget gangster drama.

w Gene Towne and Graham Baker *story* Walter Winchell *d* Lowell Sherman *ph* Barney McGill *songs* Mack Gordon, Harry Revel

Constance Cummings, Russ Columbo, Paul Kelly, *Blossom Seeley*, Gregory Ratoff, *Texas Guinan*, Hobart Cavanaugh, C. Henry Gordon

'Not a big picture, but good entertainment.'—*Variety*

Broadway to Hollywood
US 1933 90m bw

A vaudeville family makes it in movies. Cliché-strewn rags-to-riches saga with songs; good moments. Frank Morgan, Alice Brady, Jackie Cooper, Madge Evans, Jimmy Durante, Nelson Eddy, May Robson, Una Merkel, Mickey Rooney. Written and directed by Willard Mack; for MGM. (GB title: *Ring Up the Curtain*.) 'A saga of the theatre that will please.'—*Variety*

† Some material was salvaged from an abandoned MGM musical of 1929, *The March of Time*.

Broken Arrow*
US 1950 92m Technicolor
TCF (Julian Blaustein)

A US army scout brings about peace between white man and Apache.
Solemn western which at the time was acclaimed for giving the Indian's point of view (something which had scarcely happened since silent days). As entertainment it was not exciting, but it set Jeff Chandler off on a career playing Cochise with variations, and a TV series of the same name surfaced in 1956.

w Michael Blankfort, *novel* Blood Brother by Elliott Arnold *d* Delmer Daves *ph* Ernest Palmer *m* Hugo Friedhofer *md* Alfred Newman

James Stewart, Jeff Chandler, Debra Paget, Basil Ruysdael, Will Geer, Arthur Hunnicutt, Jay Siverheels

'It has probably done more to soften racial hostilities than most movies designed to instruct, indict and inspire.'—*Pauline Kael*

AAN: Michael Blankfort; Ernest Palmer; Jeff Chandler

Broken Blossoms**
US 1919 105m (16 fps) bw silent
UA / D. W. Griffith

In slummy Limehouse, a young Chinaman loves the daughter of a brute, who kills her; the Chinaman then kills him and commits suicide.
Victorian-style melodrama presented by Griffith with all the stops out; sometimes striking, but very dated even on its first appearance.

wd D. W. Griffith, story The Chink and the Child in Thomas Burke's Limehouse Nights *ph* G. W. Bitzer, Hendrik Sartov, Karl Brown

Lillian Gish, Donald Crisp, Richard Barthelmess

'This is a Limehouse which neither Mr Burke nor anybody else who knows his East End of London will be able to recognize . . . but *Broken Blossoms* is a genuine attempt to bring real tragedy onto the screen as opposed to machine-made drama, and for that Mr Griffith deserves the thanks of all who are convinced of the potentialities of the film.'—*The Times*

'I know of no other picture in which so much screen beauty is obtained . . . attributable to the Whistlerian fogs and shadows, with that dock in Limehouse recurring like some pedal point.'—*James Agate, 1928*

† Leslie Henson appeared in a parody, *Broken Bottles*, in 1920.

Broken Blossoms*
GB 1936 84m bw
Twickenham (Julius Hagen)

A remake originally intended to be directed by Griffith. Quite stylish, and in some ways more interesting than its predecessor.

w Emlyn Williams *d* John Brahm *ph* Curt Courant

Dolly Haas, Arthur Margetson, Emlyn Williams, Donald Calthrop, Ernest Sefton, Kathleen Harrison, Basil Radford

'There isn't much reason for this one.'—*Variety*

Broken Journey
GB 1948 89m bw
Gainsborough (Sydney Box)

A plane crashes in the Alps, and the survivors take different attitudes to their situation.
Unpersuasive and stagey melodrama which wastes some good talent.

w Robert Westerby *d* Ken Annakin *ph* Jack Cox *m* John Greenwood

Phyllis Calvert, James Donald, Margot Grahame, Francis L. Sullivan, Raymond Huntley, Derek Bond, Guy Rolfe, David Tomlinson

Broken Lance*
US 1954 96m De Luxe Cinemascope
TCF (Sol C. Siegel)

An autocratic cattle baron causes dissension among his sons.
Western remake of *House of Strangers*, quite well done.

w Richard Murphy, *original story* Philip Yordan *d* Edward Dmytryk *ph* Joe MacDonald *m* Leigh Harline

Spencer Tracy, Richard Widmark, Robert Wagner, Jean Peters, Katy Jurado, Earl Holliman, Hugh O'Brian, Eduard Franz, E. G. Marshall

AA: Philip Yordan
AAN: Katy Jurado

Broken Lullaby*
US 1931 77m bw
Paramount
GB and original title: *The Man I Killed*

A young Frenchman goes to Germany to seek out the family of the man he killed in the war, and is accepted by them as a friend.
This most untypical Lubitsch film now seems very dated but was deeply felt at the time and has plenty of cinematic grip.

w Ernest Vajda, Samson Raphaelson, *play* L'Homme que J'ai Tué by Maurice Rostand *d Ernst Lubitsch ph* Victor Milner *ad* Hans Dreier *m* W. Franke Harling

Lionel Barrymore, Phillips Holmes, Nancy Carroll, Tom Douglas, Zasu Pitts, Lucien Littlefield, Lois Carver, Emma Dunn

'Well made, but heavy themes and actionless . . . hardly attuned to film patronage as a whole.'—*Variety*

'The best talking picture that has yet been seen and heard.'—*Robert E. Sherwood*

'I cannot remember a film so beautifully made, so completely fine in its execution.'—*John Grierson*

'Lubitsch can't entirely escape his own talent, and the film is beautifully crafted, but he mistook drab, sentimental hokum for ironic, poetic tragedy.'—*Pauline Kael, 70s*

Broken Mirrors
Holland 1984 116m Eastmancolor
Sigma (Matthijs van Heijningen)

Brothel girls consider the worthlessness of their lives.
Would-be symbolic melodrama with feminist overtones. Hard to take from beginning to end.

w,d Marleen Gorris *ph* Frans Bromet *m* Lodewijk De Boer

Lineke Rijxman, Henriette Tol, Edda Barends, Coby Stunnenberg

The Broken Wing
US 1932 71m bw
Paramount

A Mexican girl jilts a bandit for an American pilot.
Hokey romantic melodrama.

w Gordon Jones, William Slavens McNutt, *play* Paul Dickey, Charles Goddard *d* Lloyd Corrigan *ph* Henry Sharp

Lupe Velez, Leo Carrillo, Melvyn Douglas, George Barbier, Willard Robertson

'Too much of a monologue to get far as a talker. Entire first half is just a stage-setter for what follows, and what follows isn't important.'—*Variety*

Bronco Billy*
US 1980 116m De Luxe Panavision
Warner / Second Street (Neal Dubrovsky, Dennis Hackin)

A New Jersey shoe salesman takes over a rundown wild west show.
Enjoyable, sentimental, satirical comedy which unaccountably let down its star's box office record.

w Dennis Hackin *d* Clint Eastwood *ph* David Worth *md* Snuff Garrett, Steve Dorff *ad* Eugene Lourie

Clint Eastwood, Sondra Locke, Geoffrey Lewis, Scatman Crothers, Bill McKinney, Sam Bottoms

'Eastwood seems to have most enjoyed toying with some distinctly old-fashioned materials: a runaway heiress, a murder plot that isn't, some consequent punning on points of identity, and the most mischievously brittle set of greedy Eastern sophisticates since Frank Capra.'—*Richard Combs, MFB*

Bronco Buster
US 1952 80m Technicolor

A champion rodeo rider meets a challenge from a younger man. Totally routine programmer. John Lund, Scott Brady, Joyce Holden, Chill Wills, Don Haggerty. Written by Horace McCoy and Lillie Hayward; directed by Budd Boetticher; for Ted Richmond / Universal-International.

The Brood
Canada 1979 91m colour

The rage of a mentally disturbed woman produces homicidal 'babies'. Idiotic and repellent shocker. Oliver Reed, Samantha Eggar, Art Hindle, Cindy Hinds. Written and directed by David Cronenberg; for Mutual / Elgin.

Broth of a Boy
Eire 1958 77m bw
Emmet Dalton (Alec Snowden)

TV covers the village festivities celebrating an old poacher's 110th birthday.
Mildly amusing regional comedy.

w Patrick Kirwan, Blanaid Irvine, *play* The Big Birthday by Hugh Leonard *d* George Pollock *ph* Walter J. Harvey *m* Stanley Black

Barry Fitzgerald, June Thorburn, Tony Wright, Harry Brogan, Eddie Golden, Maire Kean, Godfrey Quigley, Dermot Kelly

Brother Can You Spare a Dime?
GB 1975 109m bw

A 'documentary' picture of America in the thirties, attempted by an apparently random collage of newsreel and feature film extracts, sometimes difficult to tell one from the other. Sometimes entertaining but mainly unpardonable. Written and directed by Philippe Mora; for VPS / Goodtimes.

The Brother from Another Planet
US 1984 108m Movielab

An alien lands in Harlem and is protected by locals from the horrors he finds there. Moderately amusing combination of science fiction, farce and satire, which outstays its welcome by at least half an hour. Joe Morton, Tom Wright, Caroline Aaron, Randy Sue Carter. Written and directed by John Sayles; for A-Train Films.

Brother John*
US 1970 94m Eastmancolor
Columbia / E and R (Joel Glickman)

A mysterious black man comes to town for a family funeral and is suspected by the townsfolk of various sinister motives, but when they imprison him he is freed by a sympathizer.
The humans are all mean-minded, the saintly visitor is either Christ or an emissary from another planet. Either way, we have been here before, but although this little fantasy has nothing clear to say it is quite enjoyable on the surface.

w Ernest Kinoy *d* James Goldstone *ph* Gerald Perry Finnerman *m* Quincy Jones

Sidney Poitier, Bradford Dillman, Will Geer, Beverly Todd, Ramon Pieri, Warren J. Kemmerling, Paul Winfield, Lincoln Kilpatrick

'It starts out as an engaging mystery with sociological overtones but ends up as a muddle-headed doomsday parable.'—*Judith Crist, 1977*

Brother Orchid*
US 1940 91m bw
Warner (Hal B. Wallis)

A gangster, 'taken for a ride' by his former friends, escapes and becomes a monk.
Rather uneasy blend of comedy, drama and religion, with some good scenes.

w Earl Baldwin, *story* Richard Connell *d* Lloyd Bacon *ph* Tony Gaudio *m* Heinz Roemheld

Edward G. Robinson, Humphrey Bogart, Donald Crisp, Ann Sothern, Ralph Bellamy, Allen Jenkins, Cecil Kellaway

Brother Rat*
US 1938 89m bw
Warner (Robert Lord)

Fun and games with the cadets at a military academy.
Brisk but dated farce from a highly successful Broadway original; remade as *About Face*.

w Richard Macaulay, Jerry Wald, *play* Fred Finklehoffe, John Monks *d* William Keighley *ph* Ernest Haller

Wayne Morris, Eddie Albert, Ronald Reagan, Priscilla Lane, Jane Bryan, Jane Wyman, Johnnie Davis, Henry O'Neill

'Exhibs who dig into exploitation fields will hit paydirt.'—*Variety*

Brother Rat and a Baby
US 1939 87m bw
Warner (Robert Lord)
GB title: *Baby Be Good*

Scatty follow-up to the above, with the cadets graduating.

w Jerry Wald, Richard Macauley *d* Ray Enright *ph* Charles Rosher *m* Heinz Roemheld

Wayne Morris, Eddie Albert, Ronald Reagan, Priscilla Lane, Jane Wyman, Jane Bryan, Arthur Treacher, Moroni Olsen

Brother Sun, Sister Moon
GB / Italy 1972 122m Technicolor Panavision
Paramount / Vic Films / Euro International (Luciano Perugia)

The life of Francis of Assisi.
Good-looking but relentlessly boring view of a medieval saint as a kind of early flower person.

w Suso Cecchi d'Amico, Kenneth Ross, Lina Wertmuller, Franco Zeffirelli *d* Franco Zeffirelli *ph* Ennio Guarnieri *m* Riz Ortolani

Graham Faulkner, Judi Bowker, Alec Guinness (as Pope Innocent III), Leigh Lawson, Kenneth Cranham, Lee Montague, Valentina Cortese

'If I were Pope, I would burn it.'—*Stanley Kauffmann*

The Brotherhood*
US 1968 96m Technicolor
Paramount / Brotherhood Company (Kirk Douglas)

A Mafia executive welcomes his younger brother into the syndicate, but is finally executed by him.
Dour melodrama with tragic pretensions: well made but rather tedious and violent.

w Lewis John Carlino *d* Martin Ritt *ph* Boris Kaufman *m* Lalo Schifrin

Kirk Douglas, Alex Cord, *Luther Adler*, Irene Papas, Susan Strasberg, Murray Hamilton, Eduardo Ciannelli

The Brotherhood of Satan*
US 1970 93m Techniscope
Columbia / LQJAF / Four Star Excelsior (L. Q. Jones, Alvy Moore)

A village is isolated by an outbreak of diabolism.
Fresh and intriguing minor horror film with imaginative touches.

w William Welch *d Bernard McEveety* *ph* John Arthur Morril *m* Jaime Mendoza-Nava

Strother Martin, L. Q. Jones, Charles Bateman, Anna Capri, Charles Robinson, Alvy Moore, Geri Reischl

The Brothers**
GB 1947 98m bw
Triton (Sydney Box)

An orphan girl comes to a Skye fishing family at the turn of the century, and causes superstition, sexual jealousy and tragedy.
Wildly melodramatic but good-looking open-air melodrama, a surprising and striking British film of its time.

w Muriel and Sydney Box, *novel* L. A. G. Strong *d David Macdonald* *ph Stephen Dade*

Patricia Roc, Maxwell Reed, *Duncan Macrae* (a splendidly malevolent performance), Will Fyffe, Andrew Crawford, Finlay Currie

'Heavy breathing, heavier dialect, and any number of quaint folk customs . . . the island and its actual inhabitants are all right; the rest is Mary Webb with hair on her chest.'—*James Agee*

Brothers in Law*
GB 1957 97m bw
British Lion / the Boultings (John Boulting)

A young barrister has comic misdemeanours in and out of court.
The lighter side of the law, from a bestseller by a judge; mechanically amusing and not in the same street as its predecessor *Private's Progress*, though it seemed hilarious at the time.

w Roy Boulting, Frank Harvey, Jeffrey Dell, *novel Henry Cecil* *d* Roy Boulting *ph* Max Greene *m* Benjamin Frankel

Ian Carmichael, Terry-Thomas, Richard Attenborough, *Miles Malleson, Eric Barker*, Irene Handl, John Le Mesurier, Olive Sloane, Kynaston Reeves

FOREWORD: If all the characters in this film were not fictitious—it would be alarming!

CLERK: 'You start with a blue robing bag, sir. Then if you do good work for counsel, he'll give you a red one. If at the end of seven years you haven't been given a red bag—use a suitcase.'

The Brothers Karamazov*
US 1958 146m Metrocolor
MGM / Avon (Pandro S. Berman)

In 19th-century Russia, the father of three sons is murdered and the wrong brother is found guilty.
Decent but decidedly unenthralling Hollywood compression of a classic, faithful to the letter but not the spirit of the book, and with few memorable moments or performances.

w Richard Brooks, *novel* Fedor Dostoievsky *d* Richard Brooks *ph* John Alton *m* Bronislau Kaper *ad* William A. Horning, Paul Groesse

Yul Brynner, Maria Schell, Richard Basehart, Claire Bloom, Lee J. Cobb, Albert Salmi, William Shatner, Judith Evelyn

'A picture full of ferocity and passion, with streaks of genius in the lighting, mounting and music.'—*News of the World*

† In 1968 came Ivan Pyryev's massive 220m Russian version, little seen in the west. See also *The Murder of Dmitri Karamazov*.

AAN: Lee J. Cobb

The Brothers Rico
US 1957 91m bw
Columbia / William Goetz (Lewis J. Rachmil)

An accountant fails to retrieve his brothers from a life of crime.
Moderate gangster fare with good credentials but more talk than action.

w Lewis Meltzer, Ben Perry, *novel* Georges Simenon *d* Phil Karlson *ph* Burnett Guffey *m* George Duning

Richard Conte, James Darren, Dianne Foster, Kathryn Grant, Larry Gates, Lamont Johnson, Harry Bellaver

Brown of Harvard
US 1926 approx 70m at 24 fps bw silent

Two college students, one academic and one sporty, love the same girl. Best-known version of a 1909 play first filmed in 1917: archetypal campus drama. William Haines, Jack Pickford, Mary Brian. Written by Donald Ogden Stewart and A. P. Younger, from a play by Rida Johnson Young; directed by Jack Conway; for MGM.

Brown on Resolution*
GB 1935 80m bw
Gaumont (Michael Balcon)
Later retitled: *Forever England*; US title: *Born for Glory*

In the 1914 war in the Mediterranean, a seaman holds a German warship at bay with a rifle.
Uneasy amalgam of adventure heroics and character study, interesting for its effort. Remade as *Singlehanded* (qv).

w Michael Hogan, Gerard Fairlie, J. O. C. Orton, *novel* C. S. Forester *d* Walter Forde *ph* Bernard Knowles

John Mills, Betty Balfour, Barry Mackay, Jimmy Hanley, Howard Marion Crawford, H. G. Stoker

'A milestone in British pictures . . . an attractive and interesting feature anywhere.'—*Variety*

The Browning Version*
GB 1951 90m bw
GFD / Javelin (Teddy Baird)

Retiring through ill health, a classics master finds that he is hated by his unfaithful wife, his headmaster and his pupils. An unexpected act of kindness gives him courage to face the future.
A rather thin extension of a one-act play, capped by a thank-you speech which is wildly out of character. Dialogue and settings are smooth, but the actors are not really happy with their roles.

w Terence Rattigan, from his play *d* Anthony Asquith *ph* Desmond Dickinson

Michael Redgrave, Jean Kent, Nigel Patrick, Wilfrid Hyde White, Bill Travers, Ronald Howard

'If the sustained anguish of the role does not allow Redgrave a great deal of room to move around in, it does give him a chance to show what he can do in tight quarters, and that, it turns out, is considerable.'—*Pauline Kael, 70s*

Brubaker*
US 1980 130m De Luxe
TCF (Ron Silverman)

A new governor fails to make much headway with his reform plan at Wakefield Prison Farm.
Fairly brutal but unsurprising prison drama which takes itself somewhat too seriously.

w W. D. Richter *d* Stuart Rosenberg *ph* Bruno Nuytten *m* Lalo Schifrin

Robert Redford, Yaphet Kotto, Jane Alexander, Murray Hamilton, David Keith, Morgan Freeman

'It's hard to imagine a broad audience wanting to share the two hours of agony.'—*Variety*

AAN: screenplay

Bruce Gentry—Daredevil of the Skies
US 1949 bw serial: 15 eps

A scientist's assistant sets out to unmask a villain called The Recorder, who controls an electronic flying disc. Routine serial exploits. Tom Neal, Judy Clark, Ralph Hodges, Forrest Taylor. Directed by Spencer Bennet and Thomas Carr; for Columbia.

Brushfire!
US 1961 80m bw

Planters in south-east Asia are attacked by rebel forces. Exploitation melodrama with a flat-footed script. John Ireland, Jo Morrow, Everett Sloane, Al Avalon, Carl Esmond. Written by Irwin R. Blacker; directed and produced by Jack Warner Jnr; for Obelisk / Paramount.

The Brute*
Mexico 1952 83m bw
International Cinematografica
original title: *El Bruto*

Victimized slum tenants call for help to a slow-witted giant, who kills the landlord and falls in love with his daughter.
Eccentric melodrama which doesn't quite seem to make its point.

wd Luis Bunuel *ph* Augustin Jiminez *m* Rafael Larista

Pedro Armendariz, *Katy Jurado*, Rosita Arenas, Andres Soler

Brute Force**
US 1947 96m bw
U-I (Mark Hellinger)

Six violent convicts revolt against a sadistic warden and try to escape.
Vivid and rather repellent prison melodrama leading up to an explosive climax; its savagery seemed at the time to break fresh ground.

w Richard Brooks d Jules Dassin ph William Daniels *m* Miklos Rozsa

Burt Lancaster, Charles Bickford, Hume Cronyn, Ella Raines, Yvonne de Carlo

The Brute Man
US 1946 60m bw

A disfigured paranoic is helped by a blind pianist and kills again to help her. Schlock horror programmer. Rondo Hatton, Tom Neal, Jane Adams. Written by George Bricker and M. Coates Webster; directed by Jean Yarborough; for Universal (who were so ashamed of it that they farmed it out to PRC).

The Buccaneer*
US 1937 125m bw
Paramount (Cecil B. de Mille)

During the 1812 war, pirate Jean Lafitte helps president Andrew Jackson to repel the British.
Sprightly adventure romance with generally good production and acting.

w Jeanie Macpherson, Edwin Justus Mayer, Harold Lamb, C. Gardner Sullivan *d* Cecil B. de Mille *ph* Victor Milner *md* Boris Morros *m* Georges Antheil

Fredric March, Franciska Gaal, *Akim Tamiroff*, Margot Grahame, Walter Brennan, Ian Keith, Spring Byington, Douglass Dumbrille, Robert Barrat, Hugh Sothern, Beulah Bondi, Anthony Quinn, Montagu Love

'A cinch for big box-office returns around the world.'—*Variety*

'From de Mille's skilled craftsmanship have come other pictures quite as ambitious, none more adroitly fabricated, skilfully adjusted to the norm of appeal to the world audience that such imposing and costly productions must command.'—*Terry Ramsaye*

AAN: Victor Milner

The Buccaneer
US 1958 121m Technicolor Vistavision
Paramount / Cecil B. de Mille (Henry Wilcoxon)

Slow, slack and stolid remake of the 1938 film, with practically no excitement or interest and very obvious studio sets.

w Jesse L. Lasky Jnr, Berenice Mosk, from the earlier screenplay *d* Anthony Quinn *ph* Loyal Griggs *m* Elmer Bernstein

Yul Brynner, Claire Bloom, Charles Boyer, Inger Stevens, Henry Hull, Charlton Heston, E. G. Marshall, Douglass Dumbrille, Lorne Greene, Ted de Corsia, Robert F. Simon

Buccaneer's Girl
US 1949 77m Technicolor

A New Orleans entertainer helps to free a pirate who was her friend. Cheerful action programmer. Yvonne de Carlo, Philip Friend, Robert Douglas, Elsa Lanchester. Written by Harold Shumate and Joseph Hoffman; directed by Frederick de Cordova; for Universal-International.

Buchanan Rides Alone
US 1958 78m colour

A wandering Texan helps a young Mexican accused of murder. Very moderate star western. Randolph Scott, Craig Stevens, Barry

Kelley, Peter Whitney. Written by Charles Lang; directed by Budd Boetticher; for Columbia.

Buck and the Preacher
US 1971 103m colour
Columbia / E and R / Belafonte (Joel Glickman)

Nightriders chasing escaped slaves are outwitted by a wagon train guide and a con man.
Lively, easygoing western with a largely black cast, and a message of militancy sugar-coated by Hollywood hokum.

w Ernest Kinoy *d* Sidney Poitier *ph* Alex Phillips *m* Benny Carter

Sidney Poitier, Harry Belafonte, Ruby Dee, Cameron Mitchell, Denny Miller, Nita Talbot, John Kelly

Buck Benny Rides Again*
US 1940 82m bw

A radio comedian goes west but finds he's no cowboy. Moderate filming of episodes and characters from the star's weekly radio show. Jack Benny, Ellen Drew, Eddie Anderson, Andy Devine, Phil Harris, Dennis Day. Written by William Morrow, Edmund Beloin; directed and produced by Mark Sandrich for Paramount. 'Swell mass entertainment.'—*Variety*

Buck Privates*
US 1941 84m bw
Universal (Alex Gottlieb)
GB title: *Rookies*

Two incompetents in the army accidentally become heroes.
Abbott and Costello's first starring vehicle is a tired bundle of army jokes and old routines separated by plot and romance, but it sent the comedians right to the top, where they stayed for ten years.

w Arthur T. Horman *d* Arthur Lubin *ph* Milton Krasner *md* Charles Previn

Bud Abbott, Lou Costello, Lee Bowman, Alan Curtis, Jane Frazee, *The Andrews Sisters, Nat Pendleton*, Samuel S. Hinds, Shemp Howard

AAN: Charles Previn; song 'The Boogie Woogie Bugle Boy of Company B' (*m* Hugh Prince, *ly* Don Raye)

Buck Privates Come Home
US 1946 77m bw
U-I (Robert Arthur)
GB title: *Rookies Come Home*

Incompetent war veterans are demobilized and find civilian life tough.
Thin star comedy with a good final chase.

w John Grant, Frederic I. Rinaldo, Robert Lees *d* Charles T. Barton *ph* Charles Van Enger

Bud Abbott, Lou Costello, Beverly Simmons,Tom Brown, Nat Pendleton

Buck Rogers*
US 1939 bw serial: 12 eps

After crashing in the Arctic and being preserved by gas for five hundred years, Buck discovers that the world has been conquered by gangsters led by Killer Kane. Acceptable science fiction hokum with moments of ingenuity. Buster Crabbe, Constance Moore, Jackie Moran, Jack Mulhall, Anthony Warde. Directed by Ford Beebe and Saul Goodkind; for Universal.

'You'll be sick—from laughing!'

A Bucket of Blood
US 1959 65m bw

A waiter becomes a renowned sculptor when he hits on the idea of moulding clay round corpses. Heavy-handed spoof with a few choice if bloody moments. Dick Miller, Barboura Morris, Anthony Carbone, Ed Nelson. Written by Charles B. Griffith; directed and produced by Roger Corman; for American International.

Buckskin
US 1968 97m Pathecolor
Paramount / A. C. Lyles

In the frontier town of Gloryhole a gambler is routed by the new marshal.
Routine old-fashioned western with this producer's predictable gallery of weatherbeaten familiar faces.

w Michael Fisher *d* Michael Moore *ph* W. Wallace Kelley *m* Jimmie Haskell

Barry Sullivan, Joan Caulfield, Lon Chaney Jnr, John Russell, Richard Arlen, Barbara Hale, Bill Williams, Barton Maclane

Buckskin Frontier
US 1943 75m bw

In the 1860s, cattle empires are born as the railroad stretches west. Ambitious mini-western; a bit stodgy. Richard Dix, Jane Wyatt, Lee J. Cobb, Albert Dekker, Victor Jory. Written by Norman Houston, from the novel *Buckskin Empire* by Harry Sinclair Drago; directed by Lesley Selander; for United Artists / George Sherman. (GB title: *The Iron Road.*)

Buddy Buddy
US 1981 96m Metrocolor Panavision
MGM (Jay Weston)

A hit man on a job is hampered by a woebegone fellow intent on committing suicide.
Painful remake of the French *L'Emmerdeur* (A Pain in the A . . .). Lugubriously funny at times, but generally much less attractive than the original.

w Billy Wilder, I. A. L. Diamond, *play* Francis Veber *d* Billy Wilder *ph* Harry Stradling Jnr *m* Lalo Schifrin *pd* Daniel A. Lomino

Walter Matthau, Jack Lemmon, Paula Prentiss, Klaus Kinski, Dana Elcar

'The saddest episode in Wilder's career.'—*Richard Combs, MFB*

The Buddy Holly Story
US 1978 113m colour
Columbia / Innavisions / ECA (Fred Bauer)

The life of a fifties rock-and-roller who died young in an accident.
Solidly carpentered showbiz biopic for the youth market.

w Robert Gitler *d* Steve Rash *ph* Stevan Larner *md* Joe Renzetti

Gary Busey, Dan Stroud, Charles Martin Smith, Bill Jordan, Maria Rochwine

'A B movie leavened by grade-A talent.'—*Les Keyser, Hollywood in the Seventies*

AA: Joe Renzetti
AAN: Gary Busey

Buffalo Bill*
US 1944 89m Technicolor
TCF (Harry Sherman)

A moderately fictitious account of the life of William Cody, from buffalo hunter to wild west showman.
Easygoing entertainment which turns from western excitements to domestic drama. Generally watchable.

w Aeneas Mackenzie, Clements Ripley, Cecile Kramer *d* William Wellman *ph* Leon Shamroy *m* David Buttolph

Joel McCrea, Maureen O'Hara, Linda Darnell, Thomas Mitchell, Edgar Buchanan, Anthony Quinn, Moroni Olsen

Buffalo Bill and the Indians, or Sitting Bull's History Lesson
US 1976 118m colour Panavision
UA / Robert Altman

During winter camp for his wild west show, Buffalo Bill Cody and his friends discuss life and his own myth.
Anti-action, alienation-effect talk piece which has some points of interest for sophisticates but is likely to set western addicts asking for their money back.

w Alan Rudolph, Robert Altman, *play* Indians by Arthur Kopit *d* Robert Altman *ph* Paul Lohmann *m* Richard Baskin

Paul Newman, Burt Lancaster, Joel Grey, Kevin McCarthy, Geraldine Chaplin, Harvey Keitel, John Considine, Denver Pyle

'The western is an enormously resilient form, but never has that resilience been tested quite so much as in this movie . . . it isn't really a movie, it's a happening.'—*Arthur Knight*

'Whereas Kopit's play offered a hallucinatory mosaic, Altman's script has the one-dimensional clarity of a cartoon.'—*Michael Billington, Illustrated London News*

'That American history is the creation of flamboyant lies and showmanship strikes us at first as an amusing trifle and then quickly becomes an epigram shaggy-dogging its way across two hours of eccentric Altmanship.'—*Will Aitken, Take One*

Buffet Froid
France 1979 93m Eastmancolor
Sara Films / Antenne 2 (Alain Sarde)
US title: *Cold Cuts*

A police inspector joins up with two new acquaintances: they discover that they all like killing people.

Satirical black comedy which goes on a little too long for its own good; invention gives way to glumness.

wd Bertrand Blier *ph* Jean Penzer *m* classical extracts

Gérard Depardieu, Bernard Blier, Jean Carmet, Geneviève Page

Bug
US 1975 101m Movielab
Paramount / William Castle

Large rocklike insects appear after an earthquake and set fire to themselves and their victims.
Absurd, overlong and rather nasty horror film with no visible redeeming features.

w William Castle, Thomas Page, *novel* The Hephaestus Plague by Thomas Page *d* Jeannot Szwarc *ph* Michel Hugo, Ken Middleham *m* Charles Fox

Bradford Dillman, Joanna Miles, Richard Gilliland, Jamie Smith Jackson, Alan Fudge, Patty McCormack

'The finer scientific points are to say the least elusive.'—*David Robinson*

The Bugle Sounds
US1941 101m bw
MGM (J. Walter Ruben)

An old cavalry sergeant, discharged for insubordination, rounds up fifth columnists and is reinstated.
Ho-hum star vehicle on familiar lines but at undue length.

w Cyril Hume *d* S. Sylvan Simon *ph* Clyde de Vinna *m* Lennie Hayton

Wallace Beery, Marjorie Main, Lewis Stone, George Bancroft, William Lundigan, Henry O'Neill, Donna Reed, Chill Wills, Roman Bohnen, Jerome Cowan, Tom Dugan, Guinn Williams, Jonathan Hale.

Bugles in the Afternoon
US 1952 85m Technicolor
William Cagney

In the US army at the time of Custer's last stand, a young officer is victimized by a jealous rival.
Modest, adequate western with nice scenery but no surprises.

w Geoffrey Homes, Harry Brown, *novel* Ernest Haycox *d* Roy Rowland *ph* Wilfrid Cline *m* Dmitri Tiomkin

Ray Milland, Hugh Marlowe, Helena Carter, Forrest Tucker, Barton Maclane, George Reeves, James Millican, Gertrude Michael

Bugsy Malone**
GB 1976 93m Eastmancolor
Rank / Bugsy Malone Productions (David Puttnam, Allan Marshall)

New York 1929: gangster Fat Sam fights it out with Dandy Dan, and the best man wins the girl.
Extremely curious musical gangster spoof with all the parts played by children and the guns shooting ice cream. Very professionally done, but one wonders to whom it is supposed to appeal.

wd Alan Parker ph Michael Seresin, Peter Biziou *m / songs* Paul Williams *pd* Geoffrey Kirkland

Scott Baio, Jodie Foster, Florrie Digger, John Cassisi

'If for nothing else, you would have to admire it for the sheer doggedness of its eccentricity.'—*David Robinson, The Times*

'All the pizazz in the world couldn't lift it above the level of empty camp.'—*Frank Rich, New York Post*

'I only wish the British could make adult movies as intelligent as this one.'—*Michael Billington, Illustrated London News*

'In an uncanny way the movie works as a gangster movie and we remember that the old Bogart and Cagney classics had a childlike innocence too. The world was simpler then. Now it's so complicated maybe only a kid can understand the Bogart role.'—*Roger Ebert*

AAN: Paul Williams

The Bulldog Breed
GB 1960 97m bw

A grocer joins the navy. Elementary raw recruit comedy with many familiar ruses. Norman Wisdom, Edward Chapman, Ian Hunter, David Lodge, Robert Urquhart, Eddie Byrne, Peter Jones. Written by Jack Davies, Henry Blyth, Norman Wisdom; directed by Robert Asher; for Hugh Stewart / Rank. 'A farce which ought never to have put to sea.'—*Monthly Film Bulletin*

Bulldog Drummond*
US 1929 90m bw
Samuel Goldwyn

After advertising for adventure, ex-war hero Drummond is approached by an American girl whose uncle is being held prisoner in a fake nursing home by villainous Carl Petersen.
This is the closest the screen ever came to the original Drummond character, debonair yet taking personal and unnecessary vengeance on the chief villain. A fairly primitive talkie with little movement, yet consistently interesting.

w Sidney Howard, *play* 'Sapper' (H. C. McNeile) *d* F. Richard Jones *ph* George Barnes, Gregg Toland *ad William Cameron Menzies*

Ronald Colman, Joan Bennett, *Claud Allister* (as Algy), Lilyan Tashman, Montagu Love, Lawrence Grant

AA: William Cameron Menzies
AAN: Ronald Colman

Bulldog Drummond at Bay
GB 1937 78m bw

Foreign spies use a peace club as a front, but are routed by Drummond the adventurer. A very poor entry in this occasional series: production, directing and acting are as bad as the dialogue. John Lodge, Dorothy Mackaill, Victor Jory, Claude Allister, Richard Bird. Written by Patrick Kirwan and James Parrish; directed by Norman Lee; for Wardour / ABPC.

Bulldog Drummond Strikes Back*
US 1934 83m bw
UA / Twentieth Century (Darryl F. Zanuck)

Drummond gets married, but delays his honeymoon to investigate a mysterious London house with a disappearing body.
Slow-starting, then intriguing light mystery which becomes repetitive and silly.
Performances and production enjoyable.

w Nunnally Johnson *d* Roy del Ruth *ph* Peverell Marley *m* Alfred Newman

Ronald Colman, Loretta Young, C. Aubrey Smith, *Charles Butterworth* (Algy), Warner Oland, Mischa Auer, Una Merkel

'Zippy, snappy comedy melodrama with a swashbuckling flavour. Packed with what it takes.'—*Variety*

† The full complement of Drummond films is as follows:
BULLDOG DRUMMOND (GB 1922); silent with Carlyle Brackwell.
THE THIRD ROUND (GB 1925); silent with Jack Buchanan.
BULLDOG DRUMMOND (US 1929); see above.
TEMPLE TOWER (US 1930); lost Fox film with Kenneth MacKenna.
THE RETURN OF BULLDOG DRUMMOND (GB 1934); perhaps the most Fascist of the series, with Ralph Richardson.
BULLDOG JACK (GB 1934); amiable spoof with Jack Hulbert (and Richardson as the Moriarty-like villain). Finale in an Underground tunnel.
BULLDOG DRUMMOND STRIKES BACK (US 1934); see above.
BULLDOG DRUMMOND AT BAY (GB 1937); see above
BULLDOG DRUMMOND ESCAPES (US 1937); start of minor series with Ray Milland, later replaced by John Howard (and Guy Standing as Colonel Neilson).
BULLDOG DRUMMOND COMES BACK (US 1937); John Howard takes over from Milland, John Barrymore from Standing.
BULLDOG DRUMMOND'S REVENGE (US 1938); Howard and Barrymore.
BULLDOG DRUMMOND'S PERIL (US 1938); ditto.
BULLDOG DRUMMOND IN AFRICA (US 1938); Howard and H. B. Warner.
ARREST BULLDOG DRUMMOND (US 1938); ditto.
BULLDOG DRUMMOND'S SECRET POLICE (US 1939); ditto.
BULLDOG DRUMMOND'S BRIDE (US 1939); ditto.
BULLDOG SEES IT THROUGH (GB 1939); imitation with Jack Buchanan.
BULLDOG DRUMMOND AT BAY (US 1947); second feature with Ron Randell.
BULLDOG DRUMMOND STRIKES BACK (US 1947); see above.
THE CHALLENGE (US 1948); with Tom Conway.
THIRTEEN LEAD SOLDIERS (US 1948); ditto.
CALLING BULLDOG DRUMMOND (GB 1951); with Walter Pidgeon.
DEADLIER THAN THE MALE (GB 1967); Richard Johnson as a Bond-like Drummond.
SOME GIRLS DO (GB 1970); Johnson again in a feeble sequel.

Bulldog Jack*
GB 1934 72m bw
Gaumont (Michael Balcon)
US title: *Alias Bulldog Drummond*

A playboy poses as Bulldog Drummond when the real man is injured, and manages to foil the thieves and save the girl.
After a slowish start, this comedy thriller works up into a fine frenzy with exciting scenes on the London Underground and in the British Museum.

w H. C. McNeile, Gerard Fairlie, J. O. C. Orton, Sidney Gilliat *d Walter Forde ph* Mutz Greenbaum (Max Greene) *md* Louis Levy

Jack Hulbert, Ralph Richardson, Claude Hulbert, Fay Wray, Athole Fleming, Paul Graetz

'There is . . . a mad train ride towards the terminus and destruction, as good as anything in screen melodrama.'—*Peter John Dyer, 1965*

'A sense of showmanship that is rewarded in a full quota of thrills and laughs.'—*Kine Weekly*

Bullet for a Badman
US 1964 80m Technicolor

An ex-Texas Ranger escapes from prison to prove his innocence of murder. Lively western programmer. Audie Murphy, Darren McGavin, Ruta Lee, Skip Homeier, George Tobias. Written by Mary and Willard Winningham; directed by R. G. Springsteen; for Universal-International.

BULLITT. A rare opportunity to see Steve McQueen apparently keeping to the speed limit in Peter Yates's first American film. Jacqueline Bisset at the wheel.

A Bullet for Joey
US 1955 85m bw
UA / Sam Bischoff, David Diamond

A Canadian policeman prevents the murder of an atomic scientist.
Listless low-budgeter with familiar stars below par.

w Geoffrey Homes, A. I. Bezzerides *d* Lewis Allen *ph* Harry Neumann *m* Harry Sukman

Edward G. Robinson, George Raft, Audrey Totter, George Dolenz, Peter Hanson, Peter Van Eyck

A Bullet is Waiting
US 1954 82m Technicolor
Columbia / Welsch (Howard Welsch)

A plane accident brings a policeman and his prisoner to a lonely farm, where a girl and her father bring a fresh twist to the situation.
Disappointing melodrama full of pretentious moralizing and fey characterization.

w Thames Williamson, Casey Robinson *d* John Farrow *ph* Franz Planer *m* Dmitri Tiomkin

Jean Simmons, Rory Calhoun, Stephen McNally, Brian Aherne

Bullet Scars
US 1942 59m bw

A doctor is kidnapped to patch up a bullet-scarred gunman. Just another second feature. Regis Toomey, Adele Longmire, Howard da Silva, John Ridgley. Written by Robert E. Kent; directed by D. Ross Lederman; for Warner.

Bullets for O'Hara
US 1941 50m bw

A gangster's wife helps an FBI man to trap her husband. Fast-moving filler with action scenes lifted from its original, *Public Enemy's Wife* (qv). Roger Pryor, Anthony Quinn, Joan Perry, Maris Wrixon, Dick Purcell. Written by Raymond L. Schrock; directed by William K. Howard; for Warner.

'Every real citizen should see it!'
Bullets or Ballots*
US 1936 81m bw
Warner (Lou Edelman)

A city cop goes undercover to break the mob.
Vivid routine gangster thriller, not quite of the top flight, but nearly.

w Seton I. Miller *d* William Keighley *ph* Hal Mohr *m* Heinz Roemheld

Edward G. Robinson, Joan Blondell, Humphrey Bogart, Barton Maclane, Frank McHugh, Dick Purcell, George E. Stone

'A good gangster film of the second class . . . all the old chivalrous situations of *Chums* and the *Boy's Own Paper* are agreeably translated into sub-machine gun terms.'—*Graham Greene*

The Bullfighter and the Lady
US 1950 87m bw
Republic / John Wayne (Budd Boetticher)

A young American in Mexico is fascinated by bullfighting but during training accidentally causes the death of a great matador.
Predictable, rather boring plot given routine treatment: for aficionados only.

w James Edward Grant *d* Budd Boetticher *ph* Jack Draper *m* Victor Young

Robert Stack, Gilbert Roland, Joy Page, Katy Jurado, Virginia Grey, John Hubbard

AAN: original story (Budd Boetticher, Ray Nazarro)

The Bullfighters*
US 1945 60m bw
TCF (William Girard)

Two detectives in Mexico find that one of them resembles a famous matador.
Laurel and Hardy's last American feature is poor enough as a whole, but at least has a few sequences in their earlier style.

w Scott Darling *d* Mal St Clair *ph* Norbert Brodine *m* David Buttolph

Stan Laurel, Oliver Hardy, Richard Lane, Carol Woode

Bullitt**
US 1968 113m Technicolor
Warner / Solar (Philip D'Antoni)

A San Francisco police detective conceals the death of an underground witness in his charge, and goes after the killers himself.
Routine cop thriller with undoubted charisma, distinguished by a splendid car chase which

takes one's mind off the tedious plot. Technical credits first class.

w Harry Kleiner, Alan R. Trustman, *novel* Mute Witness by Robert L. Pike *d Peter Yates ph William A. Fraker m* Lalo Schifrin

Steve McQueen, Jacqueline Bisset, Robert Vaughn, Don Gordon, Robert Duvall, Simon Oakland

'It has energy, drive, impact, and above all, style.'—*Hollis Alpert*

Bullshot
GB 1983 88m Technicolor
HandMade (Ian La Frenais)

In the twenties, Bullshot Crummond is pitted against his arch enemy Count Otto von Bruno. Very flat-footed spoof which belies the talents involved.

w Ron House, Diz White, Alan Shearman *d* Dick Clement *ph* Alex Thomson *m* John Du Prez *pd* Norman Garwood

Alan Shearman, Diz White, Ron House, Frances Tomelty, Michael Aldridge, Ron Pember, Mel Smith, Billy Connelly, Geoffrey Bayldon, Bryan Pringle

'Unrelievedly ghastly . . . even canned laughter would be hard pressed to raise a titter.'—*Gilbert Adair, MFB*

'Behind every mannered line you can hear technicians laughing the fun to death on the studio floor.'—*Sunday Times*

Bunco Squad
US 1950 67m bw

The police expose a fake medium. Slightly unusual cop caper. Robert Sterling, Ricardo Cortez, Joan Dixon. Written by George E. Callahan; directed by Herbert Leeds; for RKO.

Bundle of Joy
US 1956 98m Technicolor RKOscope
RKO / Edmund Grainger

A shopgirl finds an abandoned baby and everyone thinks it is hers.
Tame musical remake of *Bachelor Mother*; some laughs, but poor numbers.

w Norman Krasna, Arthur Sheekman, Robert Carson *d* Norman Taurog *ph* William Snyder *m* Josef Myrow

Debbie Reynolds, Eddie Fisher, Adolphe Menjou, Melville Cooper, Tommy Noonan, Nita Talbot, Una Merkel, Robert H. Harris

Bunker Bean
US 1936 67m bw

A meek office clerk rises to power after a personality course. Old-fashioned comedy previously filmed in 1917 and 1924. Owen Davis Jnr, Lucille Ball, Berton Churchill, Louise Latimer, Jessie Ralph, Hedda Hopper. Written by Edmund North, James Gow and Dorothy Yost, from the novel by Harry Leon Wilson; directed by William Hamilton and Edward Killy; for RKO. (Also known as *His Majesty Bunker Bean*.)

Bunny Lake is Missing**
GB 1965 107m bw Panavision
Columbia / Wheel (Otto Preminger)

The 4-year-old illegitimate daughter of an American girl in London disappears, and no one can be found to admit that she ever existed.
A nightmarish gimmick story, with more gimmicks superimposed along the way to say nothing of a *Psycho*ish ending; some of the decoration works and makes even the unconvincing story compelling, while the cast is alone worth the price of admission.

w John and Penelope Mortimer, *novel* Evelyn Piper *d* Otto Preminger *ph* Denys Coop *m* Paul Glass *pd* Don Ashton *titles* Saul Bass

Laurence Olivier, Carol Lynley, Keir Dullea, Noel Coward, Martita Hunt, Finlay Currie, Clive Revill, Anna Massey, Lucie Mannheim

'It has the enjoyable hallmarks of really high calibre professionalism.'—*Penelope Houston*

Bunny O'Hare
US 1971 92m Movielab
AIP (Gerd Oswald, Norman T. Herman)

A middle-aged widow and an ex-con plumber become bank robbers, dressed as hippies and escaping on a motor cycle.
Unappealing, ill-thought-out comedy with pretensions to satire, an unhappy venture for both stars.

w Stanley Z. Cherry, Coslough Johnson *d* Gerd Oswald *ph* Loyal Griggs, John Stephens *m* Billy Strange

Bette Davis, Ernest Borgnine, Jack Cassidy, Joan Delaney, Jay Robinson, John Astin

Buona Sera Mrs Campbell*
US 1968 113m Technicolor
UA / Connaught (Melvin Frank)

Wartime USAF comrades reassemble twenty years later in an Italian village, and three find that they have been paying paternity money to the same local glamour girl.
Agreeably cast, pleasantly set and photographed, quite funny in parts, this comedy of middle age unfortunately outstays its welcome and lets its invention peter out.

w Melvin Frank, Denis Norden, Sheldon Keller *d* Melvin Frank *ph* Gabor Pogany *m* Riz Ortolani

Gina Lollobrigida, Telly Savalas, Phil Silvers, Peter Lawford, Lee Grant, Marian Moses, Shelley Winters

Bureau of Missing Persons*
US 1933 73m bw

Police chief helps a girl find her husband, who turns out to have been murdered. Fast-moving potboiler typical of its studio. Pat O'Brien, Bette Davis, Lewis Stone, Glenda Farrell, Allen Jenkins, Hugh Herbert. Written by Robert Presnell; directed by Roy del Ruth; for Warner. 'Pretty fair entertainment. Nothing socko, but it will please.'—*Variety*

The Burglar*
US 1957 80m bw
Columbia (Louis W. Kellerman)

A burglar is shadowed by a policeman who is also after the loot.
Slightly pretentious but watchable low-budgeter.

w David Goodis from his novel *d / ed Paul Wendkos ph* Don Malkames *m* Sol Kaplan

Dan Duryea, Jayne Mansfield, Martha Vickers, Peter Capell

Burglar
US 1967 102m Technicolor
Warner / Nelvana (Kevin McCormick, Michael Hirsch)

An ex-con turns tec to avoid arrest as a cat burglar.
Strained comedy which is too goofy to sustain its mystery elements.

w Joseph Loeb III, Matthew Weisman, Hugh Wilson, from the books by Lawrence Block *d* Hugh Wilson *ph* William A. Fraker *m* Sylvester Levay

Whoopi Goldberg, Bob Goldthwait, G. W. Bailey, Lesley Ann Warren, James Handy, Anne De Salvo

The Burglars
France / Italy 1971 120m Eastmancolor Panavision
Columbia / Vides (Henri Verneuil)
original title: *La Casse*

A determined policeman chases three burglars and their girl accomplice.
Expensive, camped-up version of *The Burglar*, with plenty going on, most of it borrowed from other films.

w Vahe Katcha, Henri Verneuil, *novel* The Burglar by David Goodis *d* Henri Verneuil *ph* Claude Renoir *m* Ennio Morricone

Omar Sharif, Jean-Paul Belmondo, Dyan Cannon, Robert Hossein, Nicole Calfan, Renato Salvatori

'Electronic equipment, wild action, exotic locales and bland villainy.'—*Tom Milne, MFB*

Burke and Hare
GB 1971 91m De Luxe
UA / Kenneth Shipman / Armitage (Guido Coen)

The story of anatomist Dr Knox and his body snatchers, retold with emphasis on the local brothel. Depressing in its childish attempts to be gruesome and perverted.

w Ernie Bradford *d* Vernon Sewell *ph* Desmond Dickinson *m* Roger Webb

Harry Andrews, Derren Nesbitt, Glynn Edwards, Yootha Joyce, Dee Sjendery, Alan Tucker

Burke and Wills*
Australia 1985 140m Eastmancolor Panavision
Hoyts Edgley (Graeme Clifford, John Sexton)

An account of the 1860 expedition across Australia.
Downbeat epic with interesting highlights; but the length is against it.

w Michael Thomas *d* Graeme Clifford *ph* Russell Boyd *m* Peter Sculthorpe *pd* Ross Major

Jack Thompson, Nigel Havers, Greta Scacchi, Matthew Fargher

† A parody film, *Wills and Burke*, appeared simultaneously.

Burma Convoy
US 1941 72m bw

A trucking convoy on the Burma Road is terrorized by enemy smugglers. Adequately two-fisted second feature. Charles Bickford, Evelyn Ankers, Cecil Kellaway, Frank Albertson, Keye Luke, Turhan Bey, Willie Fung. Written by Stanley Rubin and Roy Chanslor; directed by Noel M. Smith; for Universal.

The Burmese Harp***
Japan 1956 116m bw
Nikkatsu (Masayuki Takagi)
original title: *Biruma no tategoto*

A shell-shocked Japanese soldier stays in the Burmese jungle to bury the unknown dead. Deeply impressive and horrifying war film with an epic, folk-tale quality, emphasized by superbly controlled direction.

w Natto Wada, novel Michio Takeyama *d Kon Ichikawa ph Minoru Yokoyama m* Akira Ifukube

Shoji Yasui, Rentaro Mikuni, Tatsuya Mihashi

AA: best foreign film

Burn 'Em Up Barnes
US 1934 bw serial: 12 eps

A racing driver and his adopted son combat racketeers. Routine serial hokum. Jack Mulhall, Frankie Darro, Lola Lane, Julian Rivero, Edwin Maxwell. Directed by Colbert Clark and Armand Schaefer; for Mascot.

Burn 'Em Up O'Connor
US 1938 70m bw

The life and loves of a speedway ace. Modestly effective second from the time when the studios were trying to make a star of Dennis O'Keefe. Harry Carey, Cecilia Parker, Nat Pendleton, Charley Grapewin. Written by Milton Merlin and Byron Morgan, from Sir Malcolm Campbell's *Salute to the Gods*; directed by Edward Sedgwick; for MGM. 'Will fill better half of duals for good b.o.'—*Variety*

Burning an Illusion
GB 1981 111m Eastmancolor
BFI (Vivien Pottersman)

A black secretary in London, reluctantly intrigued by the activities of her political boy friend, becomes a political militant.
Most people would sigh at the thought of sitting through this decently made but rather earnest document which preaches only to the converted.

wd Menelik Shabazz *ph* Roy Cornwall *songs* various

Cassie McFarlane, Victor Romero, Beverley Martin, Angela Wynter

The Burning Cross
US 1947 79m bw

A frustrated war veteran succumbs temporarily to the wiles of the Ku Klux Klan. Cheap semi-documentary with a clear exploitation purpose. Hank Daniels, Virginia Patton, Raymond Bond. Written by Aubrey Wisberg; directed by Walter Colmes; for Screen Guild.

The Burning Hills
US 1956 92m Warnercolor
Cinemascope

A young rancher gets even with a cattle baron who had his brother killed. Reasonable but unexciting star vehicle. Natalie Wood, Tab Hunter, Skip Homeier, Eduard Franz, Earl Holliman. Written by Irving Wallace, from a novel by Louis L'Amour; directed by Stuart Heisler; for Warner.

Burnt Offerings
US 1976 115m De Luxe
UA / PEA-Dan Curtis (Robert Singer)

An evil house restores itself by feeding on its tenants.
An agreeably macabre idea for a five-page story is dragged out to interminable length, and seizes the attention only by a few shock moments. The title is mysteriously irrelevant.

w William F. Nolan, Dan Curtis, *novel* Robert Marasco *d* Dan Curtis *ph* Jacques Marquette *m* Robert Colbert *pd* Eugene Lourie

Oliver Reed, Karen Black, Bette Davis, Lee Montgomery, Burgess Meredith, Eileen Heckart, Dub Taylor

'Before the ludicrous dénouement, the movie merely piles on one special effect after another—none of them too special—and stalls for time.'—*Janet Maslin, Newsweek*

Bury Me Dead*
US 1947 68m bw

A girl reappears on the day of her 'funeral', and determines to discover who is being buried in her name. Complex mystery which might have been worthy of a Grade A production. Cathy O'Donnell, June Lockhart, Hugh Beaumont, Mark Daniels, Greg McClure. Written by Karen de Wolf, Dwight V. Babcock, from story by Irene Winston; directed by Bernard Vorhaus; for Charles F. Reisner / Eagle Lion.

Bus Riley's Back in Town*
US 1965 93m Eastmancolor
U-I (Elliott Kastner)

An ex-sailor wants to settle back into small-town life but finds that his girl friend has married.
Watchable, middling, routine small-town drama in the style of *Picnic*.

w Walter Gage (William Inge) *d Harvey Hart ph* Russell Metty *m* Richard Markowitz

Michael Parks, Ann-Margret, Jocelyn Brando, Janet Margolin, Kim Darby, Brad Dexter, Larry Storch, Crahan Denton, Mimsy Farmer, David Carradine

Bus Stop**
US 1956 96m Eastmancolor
Cinemascope
TCF (Buddy Adler)
TV title: *The Wrong Kind of Girl*

In a rodeo town, a simple-thinking cowboy meets a café singer and asks her to marry him. Sex comedy-drama, a modest entertainment in familiar American vein, very well done but rather over-inflated by its star.

w George Axelrod, *play* William Inge *d* Joshua Logan *ph* Milton Krasner *m* Alfred Newman, Cyril Mockridge

Marilyn Monroe, Don Murray, Betty Field, Arthur O'Connell, Eileen Heckart, Robert Bray, Hope Lange, Hans Conried, Casey Adams

'The film demands of its principal performers a purely physical display of their bodies viewed as sexual machinery.'—*David Robinson*

AAN: Don Murray

Bush Christmas
GB 1947 77m bw

Australian children on holiday help catch horse thieves. Rather stolid family feature which got a reputation it hardly deserved. Chips Rafferty, John Fernside. Written and directed by Ralph Smart; for ABFD

The Bushido Blade
GB / US 1978 92m colour
Trident / Rankin–Bass (Arthur Rankin Jnr)
aka: *The Bloody Bushido Blade*

Yokohama 1854; a US–Japanese treaty is in jeopardy because the Shogun's gift of a ceremonial sword has been stolen.
Unappealing hybrid with much beheading and other random action, but little sense.

w William Overgard *d* Tom Katani *ph* Shaji Uedo *m* Maury Laws

Richard Boone, Frank Converse, Laura Gemser, Toshiro Mifune, Sonny Chibo, James Earl Jones, Mako

Business and Pleasure
US 1931 76m bw

A down-to-earth husband is tempted by a *femme fatale*. Mild star comedy for his regular fans. Will Rogers, Jetta Goudal, Joel McCrea, Dorothy Peterson, Jed Prouty. Written by Gene Towne and William Conselman, from the novel The Plutocrat by Booth Tarkington; directed by David Butler; for Fox. 'West of Albany, perhaps, it will see some good business.'—*Variety*

Busman's Honeymoon*
GB 1940 99m bw
MGM (Harold Huth)
US title: *Haunted Honeymoon*

Lord Peter Wimsey finds a murder to be solved in his honeymoon cottage.
Pleasant, slightly flat film version of a favourite old-fashioned detective novel.

w Monckton Hoffe, Angus Macphail, Harold Goldman, *novel* Dorothy L. Sayers *d* Arthur Woods *ph* F. A. Young

Robert Montgomery, Constance Cummings, Leslie Banks, *Seymour Hicks*, Robert Newton, Googie Withers, Frank Pettingell, Joan Kemp-Welch

Busses Roar
US 1942 61m bw

A saboteur fixes a bomb to explode on a bus as it passes through an oilfield. Passable time-filler. Richard Travis, Eleanor Parker, Julie Bishop, Charles Drake. Written by Anthony Coldeway and George Bilson; directed by D. Ross Lederman; for Warner.

Buster
GB 1988 102m colour

True story of Great Train Robber, actually a small-time thief, on the run. Uneasy combination of romantic comedy and chase thriller. Phil Collins, Julie Walters, Larry Lamb, Stephanie Lawrence. Written by David Schindler; directed by David Green; for Frank Giustra/Peter Strauss.

Buster and Billie
US 1973 99m CFI colour

A sensitive high school senior elects to marry the school's derided 'easy lay', with tragic results. Unattractive reminiscences of rural Georgia with a rather desperate appeal to oversexed teenagers. Jan-Michael Vincent, Pamela Sue Martin, Joan Goodfellow, Clifton James. Written by Ron Turbeville; directed by Daniel Petrie; for Black Creek Billie / Columbia.

The Buster Keaton Story*
US 1957 91m bw Vistavision
Paramount (Sidney Sheldon, Robert Smith)

A biopic of the great silent comedian, with the emphasis on his years of downfall through drink.
An interesting recreation of Hollywood in the twenties and thirties is the main asset of this otherwise dismal tribute to a man whose greatness the star is unable to suggest apart from a few acrobatic moments.

w Robert Smith, Sidney Sheldon *d* Sidney Sheldon *ph* Loyal Griggs *m* Victor Young

Donald O'Connor, Rhonda Fleming, Ann Blyth, Peter Lorre, Larry Keating, Richard Anderson, Dave Willock

Busting
US 1973 92m De Luxe
UA / Chartoff-Winkler (Henry Gellis)

Two Los Angeles vice squad officers fight corruption inside and outside the force.
Violent, exhausting, but totally routine police caper of the seventies.

wd Peter Hyams *ph* Earl Rath *m* Billy Goldenberg

Elliott Gould, Robert Blake, Allen Garfield, Antonio Fargas

'The farcical version of *Serpico*.'—*Michael Billington, Illustrated London News*

Bustin' Loose
US 1981 94m Technicolor
Universal / Richard Pryor (William Greaves)

A thief on parole learns to look after a school for maladjusted children en route to a mountain retreat.
A fairly nauseous compendium of pratfalls and sentiment, not too bad while it keeps on the move.

w Roger L. Simon *d* Oz Scott *ph* Dennis Dalzell *m* Mark Davis, Roberta Flack

Richard Pryor, Cicely Tyson, Angel Ramirez, Jimmy Hughes

'The sort of forties-style warm experience I could well do without.'—*Derek Malcolm, Guardian*

Busy Bodies**
US 1933 20m bw

Stan and Ollie are involved in various disasters in a sawmill. Though not among their most sympathetic comedies, this is a sustained and brilliantly contrived slapstick sequence. Laurel and Hardy, Tiny Sandford, Charlie Hall. Written by Anon (and Stan Laurel); directed by Lloyd French; for Hal Roach.

The Busy Body
US 1966 102m Techniscope
Paramount / William Castle

A gangster is buried in a suit with a million dollar lining which various people are out to get.
Unfunny black comedy; laboured handling makes it a joke in poor taste.

w Ben Starr, *novel* Donald E. Westlake *d* William Castle *ph* Hal Stine *m* Vic Mizzy

Robert Ryan, Sid Caesar, Arlene Golonka, Anne Baxter, Kay Medford, Charles McGraw

But Not for Me
US 1959 105m bw
Paramount (William Perlberg, George Seaton)

An ageing, washed-up Broadway producer is loved by his young drama student secretary.
Rather heavy-going remake of *Accent on Youth*, efficiently performed but lacking the original gaiety.

w John Michael Hayes *d* Walter Lang *ph* Robert Burks *m* Leith Stevens

Clark Gable, Carroll Baker, Lilli Palmer, Lee J. Cobb, Barry Coe, Thomas Gomez

But The Flesh Is Weak
US 1932 82m bw

A widower and his son both decide to marry wealthy widows. Amusing high society comedy from Ivor Novello's *The Truth Game*. Robert Montgomery, C. Aubrey Smith, Heather Thatcher, Edward Everett Horton, Nils Asther. Written by Ivor Novello; directed by Jack Conway; for MGM.

Butch and Sundance: The Early Days*
US 1979 112m De Luxe
TCF (Gabriel Katzka, Stephen Bach)

Early episodes in the careers of the famous outlaws, culminating in a train robbery.
'Prequel' to a more celebrated but not a fresher or more lyrical western.

w Allan Burns *d Richard Lester* *ph* Laszlo Kovacs *m* Patrick Williams *pd* Brian Eatwell

Tom Berenger, William Katt, Jeff Corey, John Schuck, Michael C. Gwynne, Brian Dennehy, Peter Weller

'Not that it matters, but most of it is true!'
Butch Cassidy and the Sundance Kid***
US 1969 110m De Luxe Panavision
TCF / Campanile (John Foreman)

A hundred years ago, two western train robbers keep one step ahead of the law until finally tracked down to Bolivia.
Humorous, cheerful, poetic, cinematic account of two semi-legendary outlaws, winningly acted and directed. One of the decade's great commercial successes, not least because of the song 'Raindrops Keep Fallin' on My Head'.

w William Goldman *d George Roy Hill* *ph Conrad Hall* *m Burt Bacharach*

Paul Newman, Robert Redford, Katharine Ross, Strother Martin, Henry Jones, Jeff Corey, Cloris Leachman, Ted Cassidy, Kenneth Mars

'A mere exercise in smart-alecky device-mongering, chock-full of out of place and out of period one-upmanship, a battle of wits at a freshman smoker.'—*John Simon*

AA: William Goldman; Conrad Hall; Burt Bacharach; song 'Raindrops Keep Fallin' on My Head' (*m* Burt Bacharach, *ly* Hal David)
AAN: best picture; George Roy Hill

The Butler's Dilemma
GB 1943 83m bw
British National / Shaftesbury (Elizabeth Hiscott)

A jewel thief has to pose as his fiancée's butler.
Predictable comedy of pretence and mistaken identity; a tolerable co-feature of its day.

w Michael Barringer *d* Leslie Hiscott *ph* Erwin Hillier

Richard Hearne, Francis L. Sullivan, Judy Kelly, Hermione Gingold, Henry Kendall, Wally Patch

Butley*
US / GB 1973 130m Eastmancolor
American Express / Ely Landau / Cinevision

Personal problems assail an English lecturer at a university college.
Adequate but not outstanding transcription (for the American Film Theatre) of a successful and percipient play.

w Simon Gray, from his play *d* Harold Pinter *ph* Gerry Fisher *m* none

Alan Bates, Jessica Tandy, Richard O'Callaghan, Susan Engel, Michael Byrne

The Butter and Egg Man
US

This pleasant George S. Kaufman comedy about a cowboy in New York was filmed as a silent in 1928, with Jack Mulhall; in 1932 as *The Tenderfoot* with Joe E. Brown; in 1937 as *Dance Charlie Dance* with Stuart Erwin; and in 1940 as *An Angel from Texas* with Eddie Albert; all for Warner in Hollywood.

The Buttercup Chain*
GB 1970 95m Technicolor Panavision
Columbia (Leslie Gilliat, John Whitney, Philip Waddilove)

A hothouse sex quartet changes partners with bewildering rapidity against a background of European splendour.
Chi-chi romance with a fashionably disillusioned and tragic ending. As watchable as the best TV commercials, but totally empty.

w Peter Draper, *novel* Janice Elliott *d* Robert Ellis Miller *ph* Douglas Slocombe *m* Richard Rodney Bennett

Hywel Bennett, Leigh Taylor-Young, Jane Asher, Sven-Bertil Taube, Clive Revill, Roy Dotrice

'British bathos about the unhappy overprivileged.'—*Variety*

'The most desirable woman in town, and the easiest to find!'
Butterfield Eight
US 1960 108m Metrocolor Cinemascope
MGM / Afton / Linebrook (Pandro S. Berman)

A society call girl has a complex love life.
This coy sex drama seemed mildly daring in 1960, but has since been well outclassed in that field and certainly has nothing else going for it except good production values.

w Charles Schnee, John Michael Hayes, *novel* John O'Hara *d* Daniel Mann *ph* Joseph Ruttenberg, Charles Harten *m* Bronislau Kaper

Elizabeth Taylor, Laurence Harvey, Eddie Fisher, Dina Merrill, Mildred Dunnock, Betty Field, Jeffrey Lynn, Kay Medford, Susan Oliver

'The mixture resolutely refuses to come to the boil.'—*John Gillett*

AA: Elizabeth Taylor
AAN: Joseph Ruttenberg, Charles Harten

Butterflies are Free
US 1972 109m Eastmancolor
Columbia / M. J. Frankovich

An aspiring actress falls for a blind neighbour but is handicapped by his possessive mother.
Three-character comedy-drama from a slight, sentimental but successful Broadway play.

w Leonard Gershe, from his play *d* Milton Katselas *ph* Charles B. Lang *m* Bob Alcivar

Goldie Hawn, Edward Albert, Eileen Heckart

AA: Eileen Heckart
AAN: Charles B. Lang

Butterfly
US 1981 108m Metrocolor
Par Par (Matt Cimber)

A 17-year-old sexpot reappears in her father's life, commits incest with him, and sets in train a grotesque series of plot developments.
Risible concatenation of murders, repentances, illegitimate sex and various kinds of lust, all revolving round butterfly marks and set in 1937 backwoods Arizona. *Tobacco Road* it ain't, though.

w John Goff, Matt Cimber, *novel* The Butterfly by James M. Cain *d* Matt Cimber *ph* Eddy Van Der Enden *m* Ennio Morricone

Stacy Keach, Pia Zadora, Orson Welles, Lois Nettleton, Edward Albert, Stuart Whitman, Ed MacMahon, June Lockhart, James Franciscus

Buy Me That Town*
US 1941 70m bw
Paramount (Sol C. Siegel)

Gangsters take over a small town and pull the community out of bankruptcy.
Unusual comedy-drama, quite well done for a second feature.

w Gordon Kahn *d* Eugene Forde *ph* Theodor Sparkuhl

Lloyd Nolan, Albert Dekker, Constance Moore, Sheldon Leonard, Vera Vague, Edward Brophy, Horace MacMahon, Warren Hymer

Bwana Devil
US 1952 79m Anscocolor 3D
(UA) Arch Oboler

At the turn of the century, two man-eating lions threaten an African railroad.
Inept actioner notable only as the first film in 3-D ('Natural Vision'), advertised with the famous slogan 'A lion in your lap'.

wd Arch Oboler *ph* Joseph Biroc *m* Gordon Jenkins

Robert Stack, Barbara Britton, Nigel Bruce, Ramsay Hill

By Candlelight*
US 1933 70m bw
Universal (Carl Laemmle Jnr)

On a transcontinental train a woman meets a butler and takes him for a prince; he does not disillusion her.
Moderately pleasing romantic comedy of the old school.

w Hans Kraly, F. Hugh Herbert, Karen de Wolf, Ruth Cummings, *play* Siegfried Geyer *d James Whale*

Elissa Landi, *Paul Lukas,* Nils Asther

'A nice little class picture that should make money all round.'—*Variety*

'A dazzling display of romantic confidence trickery which takes on Lubitsch in his own territory.'—*Tom Milne, 1978*

By Love Possessed*
US 1961 116m De Luxe Panavision
UA / Miral (Walter Mirisch)

A Massachusetts lawyer reflects on the outlandish sexual mores of himself, his family and friends.
Peyton Place moved up in the social scale; a reasonably absorbing melodrama but hardly memorable.

w John Dennis, *novel* James Gould Cozzens *d* John Sturges *ph* Russell Metty *m* Elmer Bernstein

Lana Turner, Efrem Zimbalist Jnr, Jason Robards Jnr, Barbara Bel Geddes, George Hamilton, Susan Kohner, Thomas Mitchell, Yvonne Craig, Everett Sloane

'A talky succession of soap opera situations.'—*Robert Windeler*

By the Light of the Silvery Moon*
US 1953 101m Technicolor
Warner (William Jacobs)

In a small American town in 1918, the Winfield family has several problems arising from the return of daughter Marjorie's soldier boyfriend.
A sequel to *On Moonlight Bay* (qv), presenting further situations from the Penrod stories retailored for Doris Day. Inoffensive, well-made, old-fashioned entertainment with nostalgic songs and an archetypal family.

w Robert O'Brien, Irving Elinson, from stories by Booth Tarkington *d* David Butler *ph* Wilfrid M. Cline *m* Max Steiner

Doris Day, Gordon Macrae, *Leon Ames, Rosemary de Camp, Mary Wickes*

By Whose Hand?
US 1932 63m bw

Murder on a train between Los Angeles and San Francisco. Brisk little 'B' thriller. Ben Lyon, Barbara Weeks, Ethel Kenyon, Kenneth Thomson, Tom Dugan, Dwight Frye. Written by Isadore Bernstein, Stephen Roe, Harry Adler; directed by Ben Stoloff; for Columbia. 'The answer to a grind house exhib's prayer.'—*Variety*

By Your Leave
US 1934 81m bw

A restless husband tries to be a Don Juan. Very mild domestic comedy. Frank Morgan, Genevieve Tobin, Neil Hamilton, Marian Nixon, Glenn Anders, Gene Lockhart, Margaret Hamilton, Betty Grable, Charles Ray. Written by Allan Scott from the play by Gladys Hurlbut and Emma B. C. Wells; directed by Lloyd Corrigan; for RKO. 'Once the customers are in they'll get some laughs, but they're not going to be easy to entice.'—*Variety*

Bye Bye Birdie
US 1963 112m Eastmancolor Panavision
Columbia / Fred Kohlmar / George Sidney

Havoc suffuses the last TV show of a pop star before he goes into the army.
Noisy, frenetic musical, hard to follow and even harder to like, with all the satire of the stage original subtracted. For young audiences who enjoy incoherence.

w Irving Brecher, from musical by Michael Stewart *d* George Sidney *ph* Joseph Biroc *md* Johnny Green *songs* Charles Strouse, Lee Adams

Janet Leigh, Dick Van Dyke, Maureen Stapleton, Ann-Margret, Bobby Rydell, Jesse Pearson, Ed Sullivan, Paul Lynde, Robert Paige

AAN: Johnny Green

Bye Bye Braverman*
US 1968 92m Technicolor
Warner / Sidney Lumet

New Yorkers get drunk and disillusioned on their way home from the funeral of a friend. Witty, downbeat Jewish comedy which does not quite come off and would in any case be caviare to the general.

w Herbert Sargent, *novel* To an Early Grave by Wallace Markfield *d* Sidney Lumet *ph* Boris Kaufman *m* Peter Matz

George Segal, Jack Warden, Joseph Wiseman, Sorrell Booke, Jessica Walter, Phyllis Newman, Zohra Lampert, Alan King, Godfrey Cambridge

'You don't have to be Jewish to love it, but it helps a lot to be a New Yorker.'—*Robert Hatch, The Nation*

C.C. and Company
US 1971 84m colour

Adventures of a motorcycle gang. Bottom of the barrel programme-filler. Joe Namath, Ann-Margret, William Smith, Jennifer Billingsley, Don Chastain. Written by William Smith; directed by Seymour Robbie; for Allan Carr–Roger Smith/Avco Embassy.

C.H.O.M.P.S.: see Chomps

C Man
US 1949 75m bw

Customs agents track down a murderer. Lively little independent co-feature of its day. Dean Jagger, John Carradine, Lotte Elwen, Harry Landers. Written by Berne Giler; directed and produced by Irving Lerner; for Film Classics.

Cabaret***
US 1972 123m Technicolor
ABC Pictures / Allied Artists (Cy Feuer)

In the early thirties, Berlin is a hotbed of vice and anti-semitism. In the Kit Kat Klub, singer Sally Bowles shares her English lover with a homosexual German baron, and her Jewish friend Natasha has troubles of her own.
This version of Isherwood's Berlin stories regrettably follows the plot line of the play *I Am a Camera* rather than the Broadway musical on which it is allegedly based, and it lacks the incisive remarks of the MC, but the very smart direction creates a near-masterpiece of its own, and most of the songs are intact.

w Jay Presson Allen, from Goodbye to Berlin by Christopher Isherwood *d / ch Bob Fosse m John Kander ly Fred Ebb ph Geoffrey Unsworth md* Ralph Burns *pd Rolf Zehetbauer*

Liza Minnelli, Joel Grey, Michael York, Helmut Griem, Fritz Wepper, Marisa Berenson

'A stylish, sophisticated entertainment for grown-up people.'—*John Russell Taylor*

'Film journals will feast for years on shots from this picture; as it rolled along, I saw page after illustrated page from a not-too-distant book called *The Cinema of Bob Fosse*.'—*Stanley Kauffmann*

AA: Bob Fosse (as director); Geoffrey Unsworth; Ralph Burns; Liza Minnelli; Joel Grey
AAN: best picture; Jay Presson Allen

Cabin in the Cotton*
US 1932 79m bw
Warner (Hal B. Wallis)

A sharecropper is almost ruined by a southern belle.
Dated melodrama with interesting style and performances.

w Paul Green, *novel* Harry Harrison Knoll
d Michael Curtiz *ph* Barney McGill

Richard Barthelmess, Dorothy Jordan, Bette Davis, David Landau, Tully Marshall, Henry B. Walthall, Hardie Albright

'Not well done . . . less than a moderate grosser all round.'—*Variety*

† The film in which Bette Davis drawled: 'Ah'd love to kiss yuh, but Ah just washed mah hair.'

'Broadway's big, fun-jammed music show is on the screen at last—crowded with stars and songs and spectacle in the famed MGM manner!'

Cabin in the Sky**
US 1943 99m bw
MGM (Arthur Freed)

An idle, gambling husband is reformed by a dream of his own death, with God and Satan battling for his soul.
Consistently interesting, often lively, but generally rather stilted all-black musical which must have seemed a whole lot fresher on the stage. Still, a good try.

w Joseph Schrank, *musical play* Lynn Root
d Vincente Minnelli *ph Sidney Wagner*
md George Stoll *new songs: m* Harold Arlen, *ly* E. Y. Harburg *show songs: m* Vernon Duke, *ly* John Latouche, Ted Fetter

Eddie 'Rochester' Anderson, Ethel Waters, Lena Horne, Cab Calloway, Louis Armstrong, John W. Bublett

'Whatever its box office fate, a worthwhile picture for Metro to have made, if only as a step toward Hollywood recognition of the place of the colored man in American life.'—*Variety*

AAN: song 'Happiness Is Just a Thing Called Joe' (*m* Harold Arlen, *ly* E. Y. Harburg)
Other songs: 'Li'l Black Sheep'; 'Ain't It De Truth'; 'Dat Ole Debbil Consequence'; 'Honey in the Honeycomb'; 'Taking a Chance on Love'; 'In My Old Virginia Home'; 'Going Up'; 'Things Ain't What They Used to be'; 'Shine'

'No one permitted out or in during the last thirteen nerve-shattering minutes!'

The Cabinet of Caligari
US 1962 105m bw Cinemascope
TCF / Lippert (Roger Kay)

A young woman whose car breaks down near a country house is held prisoner by the sinister Caligari. Eventually it transpires that the mystery is all in her imagination: he is a psychiatrist and she an old lady whose sexual fantasies he has been curing.
Interminably talkative and frequently (unintentionally) funny trick film with the odd moment of effective suspense. The original ending, which cast some doubt on who was mad and who sane, is no longer available. The actors do not entirely escape absurdity.

w Robert Bloch *d* Roger Kay *ph* John Russell *m* Gerald Fried

Glynis Johns, Dan O'Herlihy, Constance Ford, Dick Davalos, Lawrence Dobkin

'It is impossible to be grateful for the film on any of its levels.'—*MFB*

'The most complete essay in the décor of delirium.'—*New Yorker, 1979*

† The fact that the story is told through the eyes of a mad person is the only link with the 1919 classic.

'See the sleepwalker, floating down the street, ripped from some nightmare! A street of misshapen houses with brooding windows, streaked by dagger strokes of light and darkened by blots of shadow! You will immediately feel the terror in the movements of that floating grotesque!' (American advertising)

The Cabinet of Dr Caligari****
Germany 1919 90m approx (16 fps) bw silent
Decla-Bioscop (Erich Pommer)

A fairground showman uses a somnambulist for purposes of murder and is finally revealed to be the director of a lunatic asylum; but the whole story is only the dream of a madman.
Faded now, but a film of immense influence on the dramatic art of cinema, with its odd angles, stylized sets and hypnotic acting, not to mention the sting in the tail of its story (added by the producer).

w Carl Mayer, Hans Janowitz d Robert Wiene ph Willy Hameister ad Hermann Warm, Walter Röhrig, Walter Reiman

Werner Krauss, Conrad Veidt, Lil Dagover, Friedrich Feher, Hans von Twardowski

'The first hundred shocks are the hardest.'—*New York Evening Post*, 1924

† The film cost 18,000 dollars to make.

Cabiria**
Italy / France 1957 110m bw
Dino de Laurentiis / Les Films Marceau
original title: *Le Notti di Cabiria*; aka: *Nights of Cabiria*

A Roman prostitute has dreams of romance and respectability.
A bitter Cinderella story which was later turned into the Broadway musical *Sweet Charity*. Much of interest, but the leading lady is too Chaplinesque.

w Federico Fellini, Ennio Flaiano, Tullio Pinelli *d Federico Fellini ph* Aldo Tonti *m* Nino Rota

Giulietta Masina, François Périer, Amedeo Nazzari, Franca Marzi, Dorian Gray

'Any nobility in the original conception slowly suffocates in an atmosphere of subjective indulgence bordering dangerously on self-pity.'—*Peter John Dyer*

AA: best foreign film

Caboblanco
US 1981 87m colour Panavision
Avco / Martin V. Smith

A café proprietor in the Caribbean dodges various groups of criminals.
Witless spoof of Casablanca which seems to have been cobbled together from a half-finished negative.

w Mort Fine, Milton Gelman *d* J. Lee Thompson *ph* Alex Phillips Jnr *m* Jerry Goldsmith

Charles Bronson, Jason Robards Jnr, Dominique Sanda, Fernando Rey, Simon MacCorkindale, Camilla Sparv, Denny Miller, Gilbert Roland

Caccia Tragica*
Italy 1947 89m bw
Lux / ANPI
aka: *The Tragic Pursuit*

A bandit is hunted through the Po valley but finally allowed to escape.
Minor peripatetic melodrama, well-handled and exciting but uncertain in mood.

w Giuseppe de Santis, Michelangelo Antonioni, Cesare Zavattini, Carlo Lizzani, Unberto Barbaro *d Giuseppe de Santis ph* Otello Martelli *m* Giuseppe Rosati

Massimo Girotti, Andrea Checci, Vivi Gioi

Cactus Flower*
US 1969 103m Technicolor
Columbia / M. J. Frankovich

To deceive his mistress, a dentist employs his starchy secretary to pose as his wife, and falls for her when she loosens up.
Amusing sophisticated comedy, generally well handled.

w I. A. L. Diamond, *play* Abe Burrows, French original by Pierre Barillet, Jean Pierre Gredy *d* Gene Saks *ph* Charles E. Lang *m* Quincy Jones *pd* Robert Clatworthy

Ingrid Bergman, Walter Matthau, Goldie Hawn, Jack Weston, Rick Lenz, Vito Scotti, Irene Hervey

AA: Goldie Hawn

Caddie*
Australia 1978 106m Eastmancolor
Roadshow / Anthony Buckley

A deceived wife takes off with her two children and becomes a barmaid.
Desultory account of aimless low life to which Caddie brings a spark of sunshine. Watchable but forgettable.

w Joan Long, from the autobiography by 'Caddie' *d* Donald Crombie *ph* Peter James *m* Peter Flynn

Helen Morse, Takis Emmanuel, Kirrily Nolan, Jacki Weaver, Jack Thompson

The Caddy
US 1953 95m bw
Paramount (Paul Jones)

A music hall comedy act recall how they got together.
Less a feature than a series of short sketches, this ragbag has its choice moments, but they are few.

w Edmund Hartmann, Danny Arnold *d* Norman Taurog *ph* Daniel L. Fapp *m* Joseph L. Lilley

Dean Martin, Jerry Lewis, Donna Reed, Barbara Bates, Joseph Calleia, Fred Clark, Clinton Sundberg, Marshall Thompson

AAN: song 'That's Amore' (*m* Harry Warren, *ly* Jack Brooks)

Caddyshack
US 1980 98m Technicolor

Misadventures at a golf club. A relentlessly crude and lumbering series of farcical incidents which mainly fail to raise laughs. Chevy Chase, Rodney Dangerfield, Ted Knight, Michael O'Keefe. Written by Brian Doyle-Murray, Harold Ramis and Douglas Kenney; directed by Harold Ramis; for Jon Peters / Orion. 'There are jests about vomiting and nose-picking, while the most elaborate gag sequence involves a chocolate bar falling into a swimming pool and being mistaken for a turd . . . a sustained exercise in tiresomeness.'—*Tim Pulleine, MFB*

'Days of magnificent adventure . . . nights of maddest revelry . . . a temptation in Technicolor!'

Caesar and Cleopatra**
GB 1945 135m Technicolor
Rank / Gabriel Pascal

An elaborate screen treatment of Bernard Shaw's comedy about Caesar's years in Alexandria.
Britain's most expensive film is an absurd extravaganza for which the producer actually took sand to Egypt to get the right colour. It has compensations however in the sets, the colour, the performances and the witty lines, though all its virtues are theatrical rather than cinematic and the play is certainly not a major work.

w Bernard Shaw *d* Gabriel Pascal *ph* F. A. Young, Robert Krasker, Jack Hildyard, Jack Cardiff *m* Georges Auric *decor, costumes Oliver Messel sets John Bryan*

Claude Rains, Vivien Leigh, Cecil Parker, Stewart Granger, Flora Robson, Francis L. Sullivan, Raymond Lovell, Anthony Harvey, Anthony Eustrel, Basil Sydney, Ernest Thesiger, Stanley Holloway, Leo Genn, Jean Simmons, Esmé Percy, Michael Rennie

'It cost over a million and a quarter pounds, took two and a half years to make, and well and truly bored one spectator for two and a quarter hours.'—*Richard Winnington*

'It is so wonderful as to make my other films look naive.'—*Bernard Shaw*

'When Rains played a small part he sometimes gave the impression that he was carrying the movie, but here his impish grin and his equanimity aren't enough.'—*Pauline Kael, 70s*

Café Colette
GB 1936 73m bw

A diplomat in charge of a secret formula falls for a Russian princess. Old-hat spy melodrama, quite neatly staged. Paul Cavanagh, Greta Nissen, Sally Gray, Bruce Seton, Donald Calthrop, Dino Galvani. Written by Val Valentine and others; directed by Paul L. Stein; for Garrick. (US title: *Danger in Paris*.)

Café Metropole
US 1937 83m bw
TCF (Nunnally Johnson)

An heiress in Paris romances a Russian nobleman who is actually a penniless American.
Lighter-than-air romance which passed the time at the time.

w Jacques Duval *d* Edward H. Griffith *ph* Lucien Andriot *md* Louis Silvers

Loretta Young, Adolphe Menjou, Tyrone Power, Charles Winninger, Gregory Ratoff, Christian Rub, Helen Westley

'It's smart, sophisticated (not too much so), has the proper romantic ingredients, and will pull 'em in almost anywhere.'—*Variety*

'Here is a very amusing script, admirable acting . . . all thrown away by inferior direction. The camera is planked down four-square before the characters like a plain, honest, inexpressibly dull guest at a light and loony party.'—*Graham Greene*

Café Society
US 1939 84m bw
Paramount

A publicity-seeking socialite impulsively marries a reporter who has annoyed her, but instead of making a fool of him she falls in love.
Faded light comedy which was never outstanding.

w Virginia Van Upp *d* Edward H. Griffith *ph* Ted Tetzlaff

Madeleine Carroll, Fred MacMurray, Shirley Ross, Claude Gillingwater

'Good cast will carry it nicely into okay if not wow business.'—*Variety*

La Cage aux Folles*
France / Italy 1978 91m Eastmancolor
UA / PAA / Da Ma (Marcello Danon)
aka: *Birds of a Feather*

A homosexual nightclub owner is persuaded by his straight son to behave properly in front of his girl friend's parents, but chaos comes on the night of the party.
Internationally popular near-the-knuckle farce with excellent moments and some *longueurs*.

w Francis Veber, Edouard Molinaro, Marcello Danon, Jean Poiret, *play* Jean Poiret
d Edouard Molinaro *ph* Armando Nannuzzi
m Ennio Morricone

Ugo Tognazzi, Michel Serrault, Michel Galabru, Claire Maurier, Remi Laurent
AAN: Edouard Molinaro (as director)

La Cage aux Folles II
France / Italy 1980 99m Technicolor
UA / PAA / DAMA (Marcello Danon)

An ageing homosexual tells his partner he is too old to be an effective female impersonator. Trying to prove the opposite, the partner becomes involved in a spy search for hidden microfilm.
Rather dimwitted sequel to a comedy which though deliberately 'naughty' showed some restraint; here, all is noise and excess.

w Jean Poiret, Francis Veber, Marcello Danon *d* Edouard Molinaro *ph* Armando Nannuzzi *m* Ennio Morricone

Ugo Tognazzi, Michel Serrault, Marcel Bozzuffi, Paola Borboni

'The juxtaposition of campy histrionics with the dreariest kind of espionage comedy offers quickly diminishing returns.'—*Gilbert Adair, MFB*

La Cage Aux Folles III
France / Italy 1985 87m Eastmancolor

In order to inherit a fortune, Albin must marry and produce an heir. Yawnworthy attempt to milk more gags out of a formula which exhausted itself with number one. Ugo Tognazzi, Michel Serrault. Written by Philippe Nicaud, Christine Carere, Marcello Danon, Jacques Audiard, Michel Audiard, Georges Lautner, Gerald Lamballe; directed by Georges Lautner; for DaMa / Columbia. 'Lots of cooks but not much broth.'—*Variety*

La Cage aux Rossignols*
France 1947 88m bw

A reform school teacher fires difficult pupils with new hope. Low-key star vehicle with moderately pleasing results. *Noel-Noel*, Micheline Francey, Georges Biscot, René Blancard. Written by Noel-Noel, René Wheeler; directed by Jean Dreville; for Gaumont. (GB title: *A Cage of Nightingales*.)

Cage of Gold*
GB 1950 83m bw
Ealing (Michael Relph)

A girl's philandering ex-husband comes back into her life and is murdered.
Mild mystery melodrama in which the puzzle comes too late.

w Jack Whittingham *d* Basil Dearden
ph Douglas Slocombe *m* Georges Auric

Jean Simmons, David Farrar, James Donald, Madeleine Lebeau, Maria Mauban, Herbert Lom, Bernard Lee, Gladys Henson, Harcourt Williams, Grégoire Aslan

'Will she come out woman or wildcat?'
Caged*
US 1950 96m bw
Warner (Jerry Wald)

After being involved in a robbery a 19-year-old girl is sent to prison, and finds the staff more terrifying than the inmates.
Slick, superficial, hysterically harrowing women-in-prison melodrama; predictably overblown but also effective and powerful.

w Virginia Kellogg, Bernard Schoenfeld
d John Cromwell *ph* Carl Guthrie *m* Max Steiner

Eleanor Parker, Agnes Moorehead, Ellen Corby, *Hope Emerson*, Betty Garde, Jan Sterling, Lee Patrick, Olive Deering, Jane Darwell, Gertrude Michael, Joan Miller

† Remade in 1962 as *House of Women*, directed by Walter Doniger, with Shirley Knight.

AAN: Virginia Kellogg, Bernard Schoenfeld; Eleanor Parker; Hope Emerson

'Break the law and he's the last man you'll want to see. And the last man you ever will!'
Cahill, US Marshal
US 1973 103m Technicolor Panavision
Warner / Batjac (Michael A. Wayne)

A stalwart western marshal finds that his own young sons are involved in a robbery he is investigating.
Satisfactory but sentimental John Wayne vehicle with the star too often yielding place to the rather boring young folk.

w Harry Julian Fink, Rita M. Fink *d* Andrew V. McLaglen *ph* Joseph Biroc *m* Elmer Bernstein

John Wayne, George Kennedy, Gary Grimes, Neville Brand, Clay O'Brien, Marie Windsor, Royal Dano, Denver Pyle, Jackie Coogan

'It's unlike any musical you've ever seen before—Timed to the Tantalizing Tempo of Today!'

Cain and Mabel*
US 1936 90m bw
Warner (Sam Bischoff)

Tribulations of a prizefighter in love with a showgirl.
Generously produced but weakly written comedy drama with rather unexpected musical numbers; not a successful whole, but interesting.

w Laird Doyle, H. C. Witwer *d* Lloyd Bacon
ph George Barnes

Clark Gable, Marion Davies, Allen Jenkins, Roscoe Karns, Walter Catlett, Hobart Cavanaugh, Pert Kelton, Ruth Donelly, E. E. Clive

'As big as the ocean!'
The Caine Mutiny**
US 1954 125m Technicolor
Columbia / Stanley Kramer

Jealousies and frustrations among the officers of a peacetime destroyer come to a head when the neurotic captain panics during a typhoon and is relieved of his post. At the resulting trial the officers learn about themselves.
Decent if lamely paced version of a bestseller which also made a successful play; the film skates too lightly over the characterizations and even skimps the courtroom scene, but there are effective scenes and performances.

w Stanley Roberts, *novel* Herman Wouk
d Edward Dmytryk *ph* Franz Planer *m* Max Steiner

Humphrey Bogart (Captain Queeg), Jose Ferrer (Lt Barney Greenwald), Van Johnson (Lt Steve Maryk), Fred MacMurray (Lt Tom Keefer), Robert Francis (Ensign Willie Keith), May Wynn (May), Tom Tully (Captain DeVriess), E. G. Marshall (Lt Cdr Challee), Lee Marvin (Meatball), Claude Akins (Horrible)

QUEEG: 'There are four ways of doing things on board my ship. The right way, the wrong way, the navy way, and my way. If they do things my way, we'll get along.'

QUEEG: 'Ah, but the strawberries! That's where I had them. They laughed and made jokes, but I proved beyond the shadow of a doubt, and with geometric logic, that a duplicate key to the wardroom icebox did exist. And I'd have produced that key if they hadn't pulled the *Caine* out of action. I know now they were out to protect some fellow officer.'

KEEFER: 'There is no escape from the *Caine*, save death. We're all doing penance, sentenced to an outcast ship, manned by outcasts, and named after the greatest outcast of them all.'

AAN: best picture; Stanley Roberts; Max Steiner; Humphrey Bogart; Tom Tully

Cairo*
US 1942 100m bw
MGM (Joseph L. Mankiewicz)

An American war reporter in Egypt meets a screen star and thinks she is a spy.
Mildly pleasing light comedy-drama with self-spoofing elements.

w John McClain *d* W. S. Van Dyke II
ph Ray June *md* Herbert Stothart

Jeanette MacDonald, Robert Young, Ethel Waters, Reginald Owen, Lionel Atwill, Mona Barrie, Eduardo Ciannelli, Dennis Hoey, Dooley Wilson

'Confusing if not amusing.'—*Variety*

Cairo
GB 1963 91m bw
MGM (Ronald Kinnoch)

Crooks plan to steal Tutankhamun's jewels from the Cairo Museum.
Spiritless remake of *The Asphalt Jungle* (qv).

w Joanne Court *d* Wolf Rilla *ph* Desmond Dickinson *m* Kenneth V. Jones

George Sanders, Richard Johnson, Faten Hamama, John Meillon, Eric Pohlmann, Walter Rilla

Cairo Road
GB 1950 95m bw
ABP (Aubrey Baring)

An Egyptian police chief lays traps for drug smugglers.
Oddly cast, reasonably lively but routine police adventure in an unfamiliar setting.

w Robert Westerby *d* David MacDonald *ph* Oswald Morris *m* Robert Gill

Eric Portman, Laurence Harvey, Maria Mauban, Karel Stepanek, Harold Lang, Camelia, Grégoire Aslan, Oscar Quitak

Cal*
GB 1984 102m colour
Warner / Goldcrest / Enigma (Stuart Craig, David Puttnam)

A young Catholic in Ulster falls for the widow of the policeman in whose murder he has been an accomplice.
More clichés about the troubles: the film belies its publicity as 'a love story which happens to take place in Northern Ireland'. But it has style.

w Bernard MacLaverty, from his novel *d* Pat O'Connor *ph* Jerzy Zielinski *m* Mark Knopfler *pd* Stuart Craig

Helen Mirren, John Lynch, Donal McCann, John Kavanagh, Ray McAnally

Calabuch*
Spain / Italy 1956 93m bw
Aguila / Constellaxione (Jose Luis Jerez)

An atomic scientist settles delightedly in a peaceful Spanish village, but sacrifices his own privacy when he invents a sky rocket.
Semi-satirical Ealing-type comedy which starts engagingly but runs out of steam.

w Leonardo Martin, Ennio Flaiano, Florentino Soria, Luis Berlanga *d* Luis Berlanga *ph* Francisco Sempere *m* Francesco Lavagnino

Edmund Gwenn, Valentina Cortese, Franco Fabrizi

Calamity Jane**
US 1953 101m Technicolor
Warner (William Jacobs)

Calamity helps a saloon owner friend find a star attraction, and wins the heart of Wild Bill Hickok.
Agreeable, cleaned-up, studio-set western musical patterned after *Annie Get Your Gun*, but a much friendlier film, helped by an excellent score.

w James O'Hanlon *d* David Butler *ph* Wilfrid Cline *songs Sammy Fain, Paul Francis Webster* *md* Ray Heindorf *ch* Jack Donohue

Doris Day, Howard Keel, Allyn McLerie, Phil Carey, Dick Wesson, Paul Harvey

AA: song 'Secret Love' (*m* Sammy Fain, *ly* Paul Francis Webster)
AAN: Ray Heindorf

Calamity Jane and Sam Bass
US 1949 85m Technicolor

Sam Bass murders the man who poisoned his horse, becomes an outlaw, and tangles with Jane Carraway. Routine western programmer from this stable. Yvonne de Carlo, Howard Duff, Dorothy Hart, Willard Parker, Houseley Stevenson, Ann Doran, Norman Lloyd. Written by Maurice Geraghty and Melvin Levy; directed by George Sherman; for Universal-International.

Calcutta
US 1946 83m bw
Paramount (Seton I. Miller)

Two fliers seek the murderer of their friend in the hotels and bazaars of Calcutta.
Studio-bound action potboiler, simple-minded but quite good fun.

w Seton I. Miller *d* John Farrow *ph* John F. Seitz *m* Victor Young

Alan Ladd, Gail Russell, William Bendix, June Duprez, Lowell Gilmore

The Calendar
GB 1948 80m bw

A girl trainer helps an owner to prove he didn't nobble his horse. Very average racecourse melodrama from a novel by Edgar Wallace, previously filmed in 1932 with Herbert Marshall and Edna Best. Here with Greta Gynt, John McCallum, Leslie Dwyer, Raymond Lovell, Charles Victor, Barry Jones. Written by Geoffrey Kerr; directed by Arthur Crabtree; for Gainsborough.

Calendar Girl
US 1947 88m bw

In New York at the turn of the century, young boarding-house residents hope for fame and fortune. Dim, uncertain musical with fair talents. Jane Frazee, William Marshall, Gail Patrick, Kenny Baker, Victor McLaglen, Irene Rich, James Ellison, Franklin Pangborn, Gus Schilling. Written by Mary Loos, Richard Sale, Lee Loeb; produced and directed by Allan Dwan; for Republic.

'No town would have her! No man could tame her!'
California
US 1946 97m Technicolor
Paramount (Seton I. Miller)

An army deserter joins the 1848 California gold rush.
Standard glamorized star western; not bad if you accept the conventions.

w Frank Butler, Theodore Strauss *d* John Farrow *ph* Ray Rennahan *m* Victor Young

Ray Milland, Barbara Stanwyck, Barry Fitzgerald, Albert Dekker, George Coulouris, Anthony Quinn

'It quickly loses its stirrups and ends up caught by the chaps in a bed of cactus.'—*Newsweek*

California Conquest
US 1952 79m Technicolor

Spanish Californians band together against Russian would-be invaders. Tedious and unsympathetic historical western on a 'B' budget. Cornel Wilde, Teresa Wright, Alfonso Bedoya, Lisa Ferraday, Ivan Lebedeff, John Dehner. Written by Robert E. Kent; directed by Lew Landers; for Sam Katzman / Columbia.

California Split*
US 1974 109m Metrocolor Panavision
Columbia / Persky–Bright / Reno (Robert Altman, Joseph Walsh)

Two cheerful gamblers get drunk, laid, cheated and happy.
Sporadically entertaining character comedy sunk in a sea of chatter.

w Joseph Walsh *d* Robert Altman *ph* Paul Lohmann *m* Phyllis Shotwell

Elliott Gould, George Segal, Gwen Welles, Ann Prentiss, Joseph Walsh

'The film seems to be being improvised . . . we catch at events and personalities by the ends of threads.'—*New Yorker*

† An end title reads: FOR BARBARA, 1933–1973. This was Barbara Ruick, who played the barmaid and died on location.

California Straight Ahead*
US 1937 57m bw
Universal (Trem Carr)

A nationwide race is held between a special train and a convoy of high-powered trucks.
Unusual and quite lively second feature shot on location.

w Herman Boxer *d* Arthur Lubin *ph* Harry Neumann *m* Charles Previn

John Wayne, Louise Latimer, Robert McWade, Tully Marshall

'Everything happens as the audience expects and wishes, so in its field it will do okay.'—*Variety*

California Suite*
US 1978 103m colour
Columbia / Ray Stark

Misadventures of four groups of guests at the Beverly Hills Hotel.
Two hits, two misses; closer intercutting might have helped. No doubt that Maggie Smith and Michael Caine come off best, with bitcheries about the Academy Awards; Walter Matthau and Elaine May also raise laughs in Jewish farce. But Alan Alda and Jane Fonda in stiff-upper-lip divorce drama are a bore; and the black farce with Richard Pryor and Bill Cosby is scuppered before it starts.

w Neil Simon, from his play *d* Herbert Ross *ph* David M. Walsh *m* Claude Bolling *pd* Albert Brenner

'By turns silly and thoughtful, tedious and charming, broad and delicate.'—*Frank Rich, Time*

AA: Maggie Smith

'What would you have done if you had been given absolute power of life and death over everyone else in the whole wide world?'

Caligula
Italy / US 1979 150m Eastmancolor
Penthouse Films (Bob Guccione)

The violent life and times of a decadent Roman emperor. What would have been a dull and worthless pseudo-epic has been perked up by violence and hardcore sex. The result is a vile curiosity of interest chiefly to sado-masochists.

w Bob Guccione, after a screenplay by Gore Vidal *d* Tinto Brass and others *ph* Silvano Ippoliti *m* Paul Clemente *ph* Danilo Donati

Malcolm McDowell, John Gielgud, Peter O'Toole, Helen Mirren, Teresa Ann Savoy, John Steiner

'An anthology of sexual aberrations in which incest is the only face-saving relationship . . . far more Gore than Vidal.'—*Variety*

'It just keeps rolling along at inordinate length, suggesting de Mille grinding slowly to a frequent stoppage for a display of bums, breasts and pubic hair.'—*Time Out*

Call a Messenger
US 1939 65m bw

Working as telegraph messengers, the Little Tough Guys prevent a hold-up. Second-feature offshoot of the Dead End Kids, some of whom had now departed to become the East Side Kids (who later blossomed forth as the Bowery Boys). Billy Halop, Huntz Hall, Billy Benedict, David Gorcey, Robert Armstrong, Mary Carlisle, Anne Nagel, Victor Jory, El Brendel, Larry 'Buster' Crabbe. Written by Arthur T. Horman; directed by Arthur Lubin; for Universal. 'A rowdy, gripping production patterned as heavy bolstering in dual set-ups.'—*Variety*

Call Her Savage
US 1932 88m bw
Paramount (Sam E. Rork)

Trials and tribulations of a half-breed Indian girl who marries a cad and later takes to the streets.
Rough and ready melodrama for female audiences; the penultimate appearance of a star who did not take to talkies.

w Edwin Burke, *novel* Tiffany Thayer *d* John Francis Dillon *ph* Lee Garmes

Clara Bow, Gilbert Roland, Monroe Owsley, Thelma Todd, Estelle Taylor

'The return of Clara Bow in a madcap role makes a natural . . . the result is bound to be money.'—*Variety*

Call It a Day*
US 1937 89m bw
Warner (Henry Blanke)

An upper-class British family has problems during a single day.
Surprising, and not very effective, Hollywood treatment of a very British comedy.

w Casey Robinson, *play* Dodie Smith *d* Archie Mayo *ph* Ernest Haller

Olivia de Havilland, Ian Hunter, Anita Louise, Alice Brady, Roland Young, Frieda Inescort, Bonita Granville, Peggy Wood, Walter Woolf King, Una O'Connor, Beryl Mercer

'A fine cast rowing a very thin boat . . . charm, many a giggle but nary a sock laugh.'—*Variety*

Call Me Bwana*
GB 1962 93m Eastmancolor
Rank / Eon (Harry Saltzman, Albert R. Broccoli)

A fake African explorer is sent to the jungle to recover a space capsule.
Moderate star farce with occasional bright moments.

w Nate Monaster, Johanna Harwood *d* Gordon Douglas *ph* Ted Moore *m* Monty Norman

Bob Hope, Anita Ekberg, Edie Adams, Lionel Jeffries, Percy Herbert, Paul Carpenter, Orlando Martins

Call Me Madam***
US 1953 114m Technicolor
TCF (Sol C. Siegel)

A Washington hostess is appointed Ambassador to Lichtenberg and marries the foreign minister.
Studio-bound but thoroughly lively transcription of Irving Berlin's last big success, with most of the performers at their peak and some topical gags which may now be mystifying.

w Arthur Sheekman, *play* Howard Lindsay, Russel Crouse *m / ly Irving Berlin* *md* Alfred Newman *ph* Leon Shamroy *d* Walter Lang *ch* Robert Alton

Ethel Merman, Donald O'Connor, George Sanders, Vera-Ellen, Billy de Wolfe, Helmut Dantine, Walter Slezak, Steve Geray, Ludwig Stossel

AA: Alfred Newman

Call Me Mister
US 1951 95m Technicolor
TCF (Fred Kohlmar)

A husband-and-wife dance team entertain the troops in Japan and after the war.
Passable musical of a very predictable kind.

w Albert E. Lewin, Burt Styler *d* Lloyd Bacon *ph* Arthur E. Arling *m* Leigh Harline *ch* Busby Berkeley *songs* various *original show credits: m* Harold Rome, *book* Arnold Auerbach, Arnold B. Horwitt

Betty Grable, Dan Dailey, Danny Thomas, Dale Robertson, Richard Boone

Call Northside 777**
US 1948 111m bw
TCF (Otto Lang)

A Chicago reporter helps a washerwoman prove her son not guilty of murdering a policeman.
Overlong semi-documentary crime thriller based on a real case. Acting and detail excellent, but the sharp edge of *Boomerang* is missing.

w Jerome Cady, Jay Dratler *d* Henry Hathaway *ph Joe MacDonald* *m* Alfred Newman

James Stewart, Lee J. Cobb, Helen Walker, *Kazia Orzazewski*, Betty Garde, Richard Conte

'A most satisfying thriller, generously streaked with class.'—*Daily Mail*

'Absorbing, exciting, realistic.'—*Star*

Call of the Blood
GB 1947 88m bw

A Sicilian fisherman takes revenge on his daughter's seducer. Antediluvian melodrama with stiff-upper-lip English looking on. John Clements, Kay Hammond, John Justin, Lea Padovani, Robert Rietti. Written by John Clements, Akos Tolnay and Basil Mason, from the novel by Robert Hichens; directed by John Clements and Ladislas Vajda; for Pendennis.

Call of the Flesh
US 1930 100m bw (colour sequence)

A convent girl falls for a man of the world. Would-be tempestuous melodrama which fails through lack of pace. Ramon Novarro, Dorothy Jordan, Ernest Torrence, Nance O'Neil, Renee Adoree. Written by Dorothy Farnum and John Colton; directed by Charles Brabin; for MGM. 'Money picture, but can stand a lot of cutting.'—*Variety*

The Call of the Savage
US 1935 bw serial: 13 eps

A scientist's baby son survives a disaster in Africa and grows up with chimpanzees. Or, how to play Tarzan without paying royalties. Fair serial hokum about the wiles of a wicked prince. Noah Beery Jnr, Dorothy Short, H. L. Woods, Bryant Washburn. Directed by Louis Friedlander; for Universal.

Call of the Wild*
US 1935 81m bw
Twentieth Century (Darryl F. Zanuck)

A young widow falls in love with a wild Yukon prospector.
Inaccurate but pleasing adaptation of an adventure novel with dog interest.

w Gene Fowler, Leonard Praskins, *novel* Jack London *d* William Wellman *ph* Charles Rosher *m* Alfred Newman

Clark Gable, Loretta Young, Jack Oakie, Reginald Owen, Frank Conroy

'The lion-hearted dog emerges as a stooge for a rather conventional pair of human love-birds . . . looks like box office.'—*Variety*

Call of the Wild
GB / Ger / Sp / It / Fr 1972 105m Eastmancolor
Massfilms / CCC / Izaro / Oceania / UPF (Harry Alan Towers)

During the Klondike gold rush, a stolen dog becomes a miner's best friend before joining the wolf-pack.
Closer to the book than the previous version, but curiously scrappy and unsatisfactory.

w Harry Alan Towers, Wyn Wells, Peter Yeldman *d* Ken Annakin *ph* John Vabrera, Dudley Lovell *m* Carlo Rustichelli

Charlton Heston, Michèle Mercier, Raimund Harmstorf, George Eastman

Call Out the Marines*
US 1942 67m bw

Two adventurers re-enlist in the Marines and foil a spy plot. The last of many action comedies featuring the original Flagg and Quirt from *What Price Glory?* Victor McLaglen, Edmund Lowe, Binnie Barnes, Paul Kelly, Franklin Pangborn. Written and directed by Frank Ryan and William Hamilton; for RKO.

Callan*
GB 1974 106m Eastmancolor
EMI / Magnum (Derek Horne)

A former secret agent is seconded to a government section devoted to the elimination of undesirables.
Expanded rewrite of the first episode of a long-running TV series, quite fresh and vivid in the circumstances, especially as it comes at the tail end of ten years of similar bouts of blood and thunder.

w James Mitchell, from A Magnum for Schneider *d Don Sharp* *ph* Ernest Steward *m* Wilfred Josephs

Edward Woodward, Eric Porter, Carl Mohner, Catherine Schell, Peter Egan, Russell Hunter, Kenneth Griffith

Callaway Went Thataway*
US 1951 81m bw
MGM (Melvin Frank, Norman Panama)
GB title: *The Star Said No*

The old movies of a Hollywood cowboy become popular on TV, but the star has become a hopeless drunk and an actor is hired to pose as him for public appearances.
Reasonably engaging comedy using charm rather than acid.

wd Melvin Frank, Norman Panama *ph* Ray June *m* Marlin Skiles

Dorothy McGuire, Fred MacMurray, Howard Keel, Jesse White, Natalie Schaefer

Calle Mayor*
Spain / France 1956 95m bw
Play Art Iberia / Cesareo Gonzales
aka: *Grande Rue*

In a small Spanish town, a young stud pretends for a bet to be in love with a plain spinster.
Interesting but rather unattractive and certainly unconvincing little comedy-drama, rather too obviously styled for its American star after her success in *Marty*.

wd Juan Antonio Bardem *ph* Michel Kelber *m* Joseph Kosma

Betsy Blair, Yves Massard, René Blancard, Lila Kedrova

Calling Bulldog Drummond
GB 1951 80m bw
MGM (Hayes Goetz)

Drummond goes undercover to catch a gang of thieves.
Minor-league quota quickie addition to the exploits of a long-running character (see *Bulldog Drummond*).

w Howard Emmett Rogers, Gerard Fairlie, Arthur Wimperis *d* Victor Saville *ph* F. A. Young *m* Rudolph Kopp

Walter Pidgeon, Margaret Leighton, Robert Beatty, David Tomlinson, Peggy Evans, Charles Victor, Bernard Lee, James Hayter

'Terror strikes as a madman rules!'
Calling Doctor Death
US 1943 63m bw

A doctor's wife is murdered; her lover is arrested; but did the doctor himself do it? Probably not, as the tendency of the tinpot *Inner Sanctum* series, of which this was the first, was to make its star look anguished for six reels and then show him to be as innocent as the film was (mercifully) short. Lon Chaney, Patricia Morison, Fay Helm, David Bruce, Ramsay Ames, J. Carrol Naish. Written by Edward Dein; directed by Reginald Le Borg; for Universal.

Calling Dr Gillespie*
US 1942 84m bw

A deranged ex-patient breaks into Blair Hospital for the purpose of killing Dr Gillespie. The point at which cranky old wheelchair-bound Dr Gillespie took over the Kildare series, its star (Lew Ayres) having effectually abdicated from acting by declaring himself a conscientious objector. Production values up to par. Lionel Barrymore, Philip Dorn, Phil Brown, Donna Reed, Nat Pendleton, Mary Nash, Alma Kruger, Walter Kingsford. Written by Kubec Glasmon, Willis Goldbeck and Harry Ruskin; directed by Harold S. Bucquet; for MGM. (See *Dr Kildare* for titles in series.)

Calling Dr Kildare*
US 1939 86m bw

Kildare becomes innocently involved in murder and needs Dr Gillespie's help. The second in the Kildare series had the confidence that comes of box-office approval. Lew Ayres, Lionel Barrymore, Lana Turner, Nat Pendleton, Samuel S. Hinds, Laraine Day, Alma Kruger. Written by Harry Ruskin and Willis Goldbeck; directed by Harold S. Bucquet; for MGM.

Calling Philo Vance
US 1939 62m bw

A manufacturer is murdered and foreign agents are discovered among his servants. Essentially a remake of *The Kennel Murder Case*; inferior as a whole, but with an excellent new Vance in *James Stephenson*. Margot Stevenson, Henry O'Neill, Ed Brophy, Ralph Forbes, Martin Kosleck. Written by Tom Reed; directed by William Clemens; for Warner.

Calm Yourself
US 1935 70m bw

An advertising man helps solve a kidnapping. Spoofy comedy-drama which simply doesn't work. Robert Young, Madge Evans, Betty Furness, Nat Pendleton, Hardie Albright, Ralph Morgan. Written by Edward Hope, Arthur Kober; directed by George B. Seitz; for MGM. 'Strictly for the not too particular nabe clientele.'—*Variety*

Camelot**
US 1967 181m Technicolor
Panavision 70
Warner (Jack L. Warner)

King Arthur marries Guinevere, loses her to Lancelot, and is forced into war.
A film version of a long-running Broadway show with many excellent moments. Unfortunately the director cannot make up his mind whether to go for style or realism, and has chosen actors who cannot sing. The result is cluttered and overlong, with no real sense of period or sustained imagination, but the photography and the music linger in the mind.

w Alan Jay Lerner *m Frederick Loewe*
d Joshua Logan *ph Richard H. Kline*
pd / costumes John Truscott *ad Edward Carere* *md* Ken Darby, Alfred Newman

Richard Harris, Vanessa Redgrave, David Hemmings, Lionel Jeffries, Laurence Naismith, Franco Nero
Songs include 'The Merry Month of May'; 'Camelot'; 'If Ever I Would Leave You'; 'Take Me to the Fair'; 'C'est Moi'

'One wonders whether the fashion for musicals in which only the chorus can actually sing may be reaching its final stage.'—*MFB*

'Three hours of unrelieved glossiness, meticulous inanity, desperate and charmless striving for charm.'—*John Simon*

'The sets and costumes and people seem to be sitting there on the screen, waiting for the unifying magic that never happens.'—*New Yorker, 1977*

AA: art direction; costumes; music direction
AAN: cinematography

The Camels are Coming
GB 1934 80m bw

An officer in the camel corps catches Egyptian drug smugglers. Light, bouncy star vehicle. Jack Hulbert, Anna Lee, Hartley Power, Harold Huth, Allan Jeayes. Written by Jack Hulbert, Guy Bolton and W. P. Lipscomb; directed by Tim Whelan; for Gainsborough.

The Cameraman***
US 1928 78m approx (24 fps) bw
silent
MGM (Lawrence Weingarten)

In order to woo a film star, a street photographer becomes a newsreel cameraman.
Highly regarded chapter of farcical errors, among the star's top features.

w Clyde Bruckman, Lex Lipton, Richard Schayer *d* Edward Sedgwick *ph* Elgin Lessley, Reggie Manning

Buster Keaton, Marceline Day, Harry Gribbon, Harold Goodwin

† The film was remade in 1948 for Red Skelton as *Watch the Birdie*, with Keaton sadly supervising the gags but getting no credit.

'You who are so young—where can you have learned all you know about women like me?'

Camille**
US 1936 108m bw
MGM (Irving Thalberg, Bernard Hyman)

A dying courtesan falls for an innocent young man who loves her, and dies in his arms.
This old warhorse is an unsuitable vehicle for Garbo but magically she carries it off, and the production is elegant and pleasing.

w Frances Marion, James Hilton, Zoe Akins, *novel* Alexandre Dumas *d George Cukor* *ph William Daniels* *m* Herbert Stothart

Greta Garbo, Robert Taylor, Lionel Barrymore, *Henry Daniell*, Elizabeth Allan, Lenore Ulric, Laura Hope Crews, Rex O'Malley, Jessie Ralph, E. E. Clive

'Pretty close to the top mark in showmanship, direction, photography and box office names.'—*Variety*

'The slow, solemn production is luxuriant in its vulgarity: it achieves that glamor which MGM traditionally mistook for style.'—*Pauline Kael, 1968*

'The surprise is to find a story that should by rights be old hat coming to such insistent life on the screen.'—*Otis Ferguson*

'It steadily builds up an impression of being a spectacle of manners and fashions, a socially true background for its characters to move against.'—*National Board of Review*

'Their lips meet for the first time . . . a superb thrill seared in your memory forever!'—*publicity*

'This is not death as mortals know it. This is but the conclusion of a romantic ritual.'—*Bosley Crowther*

'Luxuriant in its vulgarity, it achieves that glamour which MGM traditionally mistook for style.'—*New Yorker 1982*

† A 1927 silent version starred Norma Talmadge with Gilbert Roland.

AAN: Greta Garbo

Il Cammino della Speranza*
Italy 1950 105m bw
Lux (Luigi Rovere)
aka: *The Road to Hope*

Unemployed Sicilian miners travel to France in search of work.
Episodic location melodrama with a social conscience, a kind of Italian *Grapes of Wrath*. Very watchable, but not moving.

w Federico Fellini, Tullio Pinelli *d Pietro Germi* *ph* Leonido Barboni *m* Carlo Rustichelli

Raf Vallone, Elena Varzi, Saro Urzi, Franco Navarra

The Camp on Blood Island
GB 1958 81m bw Megascope
Columbia / Hammer (Anthony Hinds)

The sadistic commandant of a Japanese POW camp swears to kill all the inmates. Japan surrenders, and a great effort is made to prevent the news from reaching him.
Dubious melodrama parading sadism and brutality as entertainment.

w Jon Manchip White, Val Guest *d* Val Guest *ph* Jack Asher *m* Gerard Schurmann

André Morell, Carl Mohner, Edward Underdown, Michael Goodliffe, Ronald Radd, Walter Fitzgerald, Phil Brown, Barbara Shelley, Michael Gwynn, Richard Wordsworth, Marne Maitland, Mary Merrall

Campbell's Kingdom*
GB 1957 102m Eastmancolor
Rank (Betty E. Box)

A young man who thinks he is dying arrives in the Canadian Rockies to take over his father's oil valley, but a scheming contractor opposes him.
Competent and entertaining romantic thick-ear.

w Robin Estridge, *novel* Hammond Innes *d* Ralph Thomas *ph* Ernest Steward *m* Clifton Parker

Dirk Bogarde, Michael Craig, Stanley Baker, Barbara Murray, Athene Seyler, Mary Merrall, James Robertson Justice

Can Can
US 1960 131m De Luxe Todd-AO
TCF / Suffolk–Cummings (Jack Cummings)

A Parisian nightclub dancer in the nineties is sued for performing the Can Can.
Flat film of a dull musical, with just a few plums in the pudding.

w Dorothy Kingsley, Charles Lederer, *play* Abe Burrows *songs* Cole Porter *d* Walter Lang *ph* William Daniels *ch* Hermes Pan *md* Nelson Riddle

Frank Sinatra, Shirley Maclaine, Maurice Chevalier, Louis Jourdan, Juliet Prowse, Marcel Dalio, Leon Belasco

AAN: Nelson Riddle

Can Heironymus Merkin Ever Forget Mercy Humppe and Find True Happiness?
GB 1969 117m Technicolor
Universal / Taralex (Anthony Newley)

A performer on a beach assembles a huge pile of personal bric-à-brac and reminisces about his life in the style of a variety show.
Obscure and pointless personal fantasy, financed at great expense by a major film company as a rather seedy monument to Anthony Newley's totally uninteresting sex life, and to the talent which he obviously thinks he possesses. The few mildly amusing moments are not provided by him.

w Herman Raucher, Anthony Newley *d* Anthony Newley *ph* Otto Heller *m* Anthony Newley

Anthony Newley, Joan Collins, George Jessel, Milton Berle, Bruce Forsyth, Stubby Kaye, Patricia Hayes, Victor Spinetti

'If I'd been Anthony Newley I would have opened it in Siberia during Christmas week and called it a day.'—*Rex Reed*

'The kindest thing for all concerned would be that every available copy should be quietly and decently buried.'—*Michael Billington, Illustrated London News*

Can She Bake a Cherry Pie?
US 1983 90m Du Art

An abandoned wife has an experimental affair with a hypochondriac divorcé. What the writer-director calls 'a bitter-sweet comedy about loneliness and love' has more to say to him than to an audience; but there are wryly amusing moments. Karen Black, Michael Emil Jaglom, Michael Margotta, Frances Fisher. Written and directed by Henry Jaglom; for Jagfilm / International Rainbow.

Can This Be Dixie?
US 1936 68m bw

In the old south, a medicine showman and his daughter help a bankrupt Kentucky colonel. Agreeable supporting material, with elements of satire, spoof and musical comedy. Jane Withers, Slim Summerville, Claude Gillingwater, Helen Wood, Thomas Beck, Sara Haden, Donald Cook, Hattie McDaniel. Written by Lamar Trotti; directed by George Marshall; for Sol M. Wurtzel / TCF. 'Plenty of ingredients were thrown into the soup . . . it will hold its own in the duals.'—*Variety*

Canadian Mounties vs Atomic Invaders
US 1953 bw serial: 12 eps

Foreign agents build rocket-launching platforms in the Arctic. The title suggests that serials were near the end of their tether by now; this was about ten from the end. Bill Henry, Susan Morrow, Arthur Space, Dale Van Sickel, Pierre Watkin. Directed by Franklin Adreon; for Republic.

'The blazing saga of untamed men and a savage wilderness!'

Canadian Pacific
US 1949 95m Cinecolor

A surveyor discovers the vital pass through the Rockies, and chooses between a lady doctor and a wilful half-breed. Fairly unhistorical western; watchable, though. Randolph Scott, Jane Wyatt, Nancy Olson, J. Carrol Naish, Victor Jory, Robert Barrat. Written by Jack De Witt and Kenneth Gamet; directed by Edwin L. Marin; for Nat Holt (TCF).

The Canadians
GB / Canada 1961 85m De Luxe Cinemascope
TCF (Herman E. Webber)

After Custer's defeat at Little Big Horn, 6,000 Sioux flee north and are victimized by villainous Canadians; but the Mounties come to the rescue.

Dreary, stumbling semi-western which set back Canadian production by a year or two. The blame seems to be equally shared by all concerned.

wd Burt Kennedy *ph* Arthur Ibbetson *m* none

Robert Ryan, John Dehner, Torin Thatcher, Burt Metcalfe, Teresa Stratas, Michael Pate, John Sutton

Canaries Sometimes Sing
GB 1930 90m bw

Two unhappily married couples change partners. Mild sophisticated comedy, a shade daring for its time, but only in concept. Tom Walls, Yvonne Arnaud, Athole Stewart, Cathleen Nesbitt. Written by W. P. Lipscomb from the play by Frederick Lonsdale; directed by Tom Walls; for British and Dominions.

Cancel My Reservation
US 1972 99m Technicolor

A TV talk show host retreats to his ranch and finds himself mixed up with murder. Bob Hope's last film, though it reverted to farce and his bumbling coward persona, proved a sorry affair with egg on the face of everybody concerned. Bob Hope, Eva Marie Saint, Ralph Bellamy, Forrest Tucker, Anne Archer, Keenan Wynn, Doodles Weaver. Written by Arthur Marx and Robert Fisher, from the novel *The Broken Gun* by Louis L'Amour; directed by Paul Bogart; for Naho Enterprises.

The Candidate**
US 1972 110m Technicolor
Warner / Redford–Ritchie (Walter Coblenz)

A young Californian lawyer is persuaded to run for senator; in succeeding, he alienates his wife and obscures his real opinions.
Put together in a slightly scrappy but finally persuasive style, this joins a select band of rousing, doubting American political films.

w Jeremy Larner *d Michael Ritchie* *ph* Victor J. Kemper *m* John Rubinstein

Robert Redford, Peter Boyle, *Don Porter*, Allen Garfield, Karen Carlson, Quinn Redeker, Morgan Upton, *Melvyn Douglas*

'Decent entertainment . . . it is never boring, but it is never enlarging, informationally or emotionally or thematically.'—*Stanley Kauffmann*

AA: Jeremy Larner

Candide
France 1960 90m bw
CLM / SN Pathé (Clément Duhour)

Ever optimistic, a 20th-century Candide tours Nazi prison camps, communist countries and various South American revolutions.
Scrappily-made satire which soon overstays its welcome.

wd Norbert Carbonneaux, from Voltaire *ph* Robert Le Fèbvre *m* Hubert Rostaing

Jean-Pierre Cassel, Daliah Lavi, Pierre Brasseur, Nadia Gray, Michel Simon, Louis de Funès

Candlelight in Algeria
GB 1943 85m bw

Spies seek whereabouts of Allied rendezvous. Elementary spy thriller using modest talents. Carla Lehmann, James Mason, Walter Rilla, Raymond Lovell, Enid Stamp Taylor. Written by Katherine Strueby and Brock Williams; directed by George King; for British Aviation.

Candles at Nine
GB 1944 86m bw

A young heiress in her benefactor's old mansion is menaced by his housekeeper. Elementary *Cat and the Canary* reprise; cast understandably uneasy. Jessie Matthews, John Stuart, Beatrix Lehmann, Winifred Shotter, Reginald Purdell. Written by John Harlow and Basil Mason, from a novel by Anthony Gilbert; directed by John Harlow; for British National.

Candleshoe
GB 1977 101m Technicolor
Walt Disney Productions (Hugh Attwooll)

An attempt to pass off a fake heiress to an English stately home is prevented by the resourceful butler.
Slackly handled comedy adventure full of easy targets and predictable incidents.

w David Swift, Rosemary Anne Sisson, *novel* Christmas at Candleshoe by Michael Innes *d* Norman Tokar *ph* Paul Beeson *m Ron Goodwin*

David Niven, Helen Hayes, Jodie Foster, Leo McKern, Veronica Quilligan, Ian Sharrock, Vivian Pickles

'It might have been conceived by a computer called upon to produce the definitive pastiche of a Disney film of the 1970s.'—*Financial Times*

Candy
US 1968 124m Technicolor
Selmur / Dear / Corona (Robert Haggiag)

An innocent girl defends herself from a fate worse than death in a variety of international situations.
Witless and charmless perversion of a sex satire in which the point (if any) was that the nymphet gladly surrendered herself to all the gentlemen for their own good. A star cast flounders helplessly in a morass of bad taste, bad film-making, and boredom.

w Buck Henry, *novel* Terry Southern *d* Christian Marquand *ph* Giuseppe Rotunno *m* Dave Grusin

Ewa Aulin, Richard Burton, Marlon Brando, James Coburn, Walter Matthau, Charles Aznavour, John Huston, Elsa Martinelli, Ringo Starr, John Astin

'Hippy psychedelics are laid on with the self-destroying effect of an overdose of garlic.'—*MFB*

'As an emetic, liquor is dandy, but *Candy* is quicker.'—*John Simon*

The Candy Man
US 1968 98m Eastmancolor

A British drug pusher in Mexico City plots the kidnap of an American film star's child. Abysmal independent thriller with a star at the end of his tether. George Sanders, Leslie Parrish, Gina Roman, Manolo Fabregas. Written, produced and directed by Herbert J. Leder; for Sagittarius.

Cannery Row
US 1982 120m Metrocolor
MGM / Michael Philips

Incidents in the life of a 1940s marine biologist who lives on the waterfront with bums and floozies.
Badly out of its time, this curious attempt at sentimental realism was long in the works but emerged as a bloodless, stultifying entertainment.

wd David S. Ward, *novel* John Steinbeck *ph* Sven Nykvist *m* Jack Nitzsche *ed* David Betherton *pd* Richard MacDonald

Nick Nolte, Debra Winger, Audra Lindley, Frank McRae, M. Emmet Walsh, John Huston (narrator)

'Another MGM item in which the entertainment values are difficult to locate.'—*Variety*

† Raquel Welch, originally cast for the Winger role, was fired in mid-production.

Cannon for Cordoba
US 1970 104m De Luxe Panavision
UA / Mirisch (Stephen Kandel, Vincent Fenelly)

In 1912, the Mexican bandit Cordoba is outgunned and outwitted by a US army captain.
Fast-moving but rather uninteresting action adventure.

w Stephen Kandel *d* Paul Wendkos *ph* Antonio Macasoli *m* Elmer Bernstein

George Peppard, Raf Vallone, Giovanna Ralli, Pete Duel, Don Gordon, Nico Minardos, John Russell

Cannonball
US / Hong Kong 1976 93m Metrocolor
Harbor / Shaw Brothers (Samuel W. Gelfman)
GB title: *Carquake*

Aggressive drivers compete in the Trans-American Grand Prix.
The plot is a thin excuse for multiple pile-ups and other road disasters. Moments amuse, but the violence quickly palls.

w Paul Bartel, Donald C. Simpson *d* Paul Bartel *ph* Tak Fujimoto *m* David A. Axelrod

David Carradine, Bill McKinney, Veronica Hamel, Gerrit Graham, Judy Canova

'A free-wheeling, stunt-studded, dented and demented story of a road racer without rules.'—*publicity*

The Cannonball Run
US 1980 95m Technicolor
Golden Harvest (Albert S. Ruddy)

The adventures of ill-assorted contestants in the illegal Cannonball coast-to-coast race.

Well-known stars are all at sea in this comedy / disaster extravaganza, which seems to have begun as a joke rather than a script.

w Brock Yates *d* Hal Needham *ph* Michael Butler *md* Al Capps

Burt Reynolds, Roger Moore, Farrah Fawcett, Dom DeLuise, Dean Martin, Sammy Davis Jnr, Adrienne Barbeau, Jack Elam, Bert Convy, Jamie Farr, Peter Fonda, Molly Picon, Bianca Jagger

'Lacking any recognizable plot or characterization, or indeed incidental invention, it merely offers a parade of inept whimsy and lame intra-mural reference.'—*Tim Pulleine, MFB*

'Moviegoers who relish the screech of tyres taking a fast turn on a narrow bend should have a whale of a time.'—*Daily Mail*

Cannonball Run II
US 1983 108m Technicolor

An Arab sheik puts up a million-dollar prize for the Cannonball Run. Dispirited rehash of number one, with poor technique and non-performances by stars who should have known better than to get involved. Burt Reynolds, Dom DeLuise, Sammy Davis Jnr, Dean Martin, Jamie Farr, Telly Savalas, Shirley Maclaine, Frank Sinatra, Susan Anton, Catherine Bach, Richard Kiel, Tim Conway, Sid Caesar, Don Knotts, Ricardo Montalban, Jim Nabors, Henry Silva. Written by Hal Needham, Albert S. Ruddy, Harvey Miller; directed by Hal Needham; for Golden Harvest / Warners.

Canon City*
US 1948 82m bw
Eagle Lion / Bryan Foy (Robert T. Kane)

Convicts break out of the Colorado State Prison.
Minor semi-documentary melodrama, quite effectively presented.

wd Crane Wilbur *ph* John Alton

Scott Brady, Jeff Corey, Whit Bissell, Stanley Clements, De Forrest Kelley

Can't Help Singing*
US 1944 90m Technicolor
Universal (Frank Ross)

A Washington heiress chases her army lieutenant lover across the wild west to California.
Lively star musical which could have used a little more wit in its lighthearted script.

w Lewis Foster, Frank Ryan *d* Frank Ryan
ph Woody Bredell, W. Howard Greene
m Jerome Kern *ly* E. Y. Harburg
md Jerome Kern, Hans Salter

Deanna Durbin, David Bruce, Robert Paige, *Akim Tamiroff*, *Leonid Kinskey*, Ray Collins, Thomas Gomez

'This could have been a beautiful and gay picture, but it is made without much feeling for beauty or gaiety.'—*James Agee*

'She can carry a simple part charmingly; she looks very well; her manners are impeccable; and she can sing a role just short of grand opera better than any actress on the screen.'—*Observer*

AAN: Jerome Kern, Hans Salter; song 'More and More' (*m* Jerome Kern, *ly* E. Y. Harburg)
Other songs: 'Elbow Room'; 'Any Moment Now'; 'Californ-i-ay'; 'Swing Your Sweetheart round the Fire'; 'Finale Ultimo'

Can't Stop the Music
US 1980 124m Metrocolor Panavision
EMI / Allan Carr

A Greenwich Village pop group hits the bigtime.
Curiously old-fashioned youth musical, unwisely touted as something special, which it isn't.

w Bronte Woodward, Allan Carr *d* Nancy Walker
ph Bill Butler *m* Jacques Morali

The Village People, Valerie Perrine, Paul Sand, Bruce Jenner, Tammy Grimes, June Havoc, Barbara Rush, Jack Weston

'The hype disaster of the 80s, a grisly rehash of the let's-start-a-group-of-our-own plot, peopled with butch gay stereotypes of both sexes pretending to be straight. The pervasive tackiness is unrelieved.'—*Time Out*

'Desperately knowing about the eighties but fixed remorselessly in a time warp of fifties hokum.'—*Guardian*

'All noise, lights, slogans, movement and dazzle, like a 124m commercial devoted to selling you a product you can't use.'—*Sunday Times*

'One doesn't watch it, one is attacked by it.'—*New England Entertainment Digest*

'Considering the low level of wit, perhaps the Village People should consider renaming themselves the Village Idiots.'—*Los Angeles Magazine*

'This shamefully tacky musical extravaganza fails on every aesthetic level.'—*Los Angeles Herald Examiner*

'A forced marriage between the worst of sitcom plotting and the highest of high camp production numbers.'—*New West*

A Canterbury Tale**
GB 1944 124m bw
Rank / Archers (Michael Powell, Emeric Pressburger)

A batty magistrate is unmasked by a land girl, an army sergeant and a GI.
Curious would-be propaganda piece with Old England bathed in a roseate wartime glow, but the plot seems to have little to do with Chaucer. Indeed, quite what Powell and Pressburger thought they were up to is hard to fathom, but the detail is interesting.

wd Michael Powell and Emeric Pressburger
ph Erwin Hillier

Eric Portman, Sheila Sim, John Sweet, Dennis Price, Esmond Knight, Charles Hawtrey, Hay Petrie, George Merritt, Edward Rigby

'To most people the intentions of the film-makers remained highly mysterious; nor did this picture of the British administration of justice commend itself to the authorities, who showed some reluctance to encourage its export to our allies.'—*Basil Wright, 1972*

The Canterbury Tales
Italy / France 1971 109m (English version) Technicolor
UA / PEA / PAA (Alberto Grimaldi)

Medieval pilgrims amuse each other by telling stories on the way to Canterbury.
A sweaty selection of the tales in their more prurient aspects, with relentless emphasis on excrement and sex perversions.

wd Pier Paolo Pasolini, after Chaucer
ph Tonino Delli Colli *m* Ennio Morricone

Pier Paolo Pasolini (as Chaucer), Hugh Griffith, Laura Betti, Tom Baker, Ninetto Davoli, Franco Citti

'Caricature Chaucer, with pilgrims losing the way to Canterbury amid a forest of male genitalia.'—*Sight and Sound*

'The vivid depiction of taboo subjects emerges less as an affirmation of the Chaucerian belief that all human activity lies within the artist's scope, than as a bludgeoning over-emphasis on physical appetite as man's primal motive for action.'—*Nigel Andrews, MFB*

The Canterville Ghost*
US 1943 95m bw
MGM (Arthur Field)

The young girl heiress of an English castle introduces GIs to the resident ghost.
Leaden comedy a long way after Oscar Wilde, sunk by slow script and direction, but partly salvaged by the respective roguishness and infant charm of its stars.

w Edwin Blum *d* Jules Dassin *ph* Robert Planck *m* George Bassman

Charles Laughton, *Margaret O'Brien*, Robert Young, William Gargan, Rags Ragland, Peter Lawford, Una O'Connor, Mike Mazurki
† In the mid 1970s, a television version starring David Niven was made by HTV.

Canyon Crossroads
US 1954 84m bw

A uranium prospector is trailed by thieves. Acceptable modern western. Richard Basehart, Phyllis Kirk, Stephen Elliott, Russell Collins, Charles Wagenheim. Written by Emmett Murphy and Leonard Heideman; directed by Alfred Werker; for MPT / UA.

Canyon Passage*
US 1946 99m Technicolor
Universal (Walter Wanger)

In the 1850s along the pioneering tracks the west's first towns were being built . . .
Simple, scrappy but generally pleasing film which gives a vivid picture of pioneering life while minimizing its hardships.

w Ernest Pascal, William Fosche *d* Jacques Tourneur *ph* Edward Cronjager *m* Frank Skinner

Dana Andrews, Patricia Roc, Hoagy Carmichael, Brian Donlevy, Susan Hayward, Ward Bond, Andy Devine, Lloyd Bridges

'Miles of beautiful scenery, lavishly punctuated with rough-and-tumble episodes, moments of tender romance and a smattering of folk customs.'—*New York Times*

AAN: song 'Ole Buttermilk Sky' (*m* Hoagy Carmichael, *ly* Jack Brooks)

Cape Fear
US 1962 106m bw
U-I / Melville–Talbot (Sy Bartlett)

An ex-convict blames a lawyer for his sentence and threatens to rape the lawyer's wife.
Unpleasant and drawn out suspenser with characters of cardboard and situations from stock.

w James R. Webb, *novel* The Executioners by John D. MacDonald *d* J. Lee-Thompson *ph* Sam Leavitt *m* Bernard Herrmann

Gregory Peck, Robert Mitchum, Polly Bergen, Martin Balsam, Lori Martin, Jack Kruschen, Telly Savalas

The Caper of the Golden Bulls
US 1966 104m Pathecolor
Embassy (Clarence Greene)
GB title: *Carnival of Thieves*

Ex-air-aces rob banks in order to pay for the restoration of a French cathedral they had to bomb; to avoid incrimination they are blackmailed into doing one last job in Pamplona.
Ingeniously plotted, flatly executed suspenser set in Pamplona during the bull run.

w Ed Waters, William Moessinger, *novel* William P. McGivern *d* Russel Rouse *ph* Hal Stine *m* Vic Mizzy

Stephen Boyd, Giovanna Ralli, Yvette Mimieux, Walter Slezak, Vito Scotti

Capetown Affair
US / SA 1967 100m De Luxe
TCF / Killarney (Robert D. Webb)

A pickpocket on a South African bus steals a purse containing secret microfilm.
Flatulent remake of *Pickup on South Street* with nothing but the unfamiliar locale to recommend it.

w Harold Medford, Samuel Fuller *d* Robert D. Webb *ph* David Millin *m* Bob Adams

James Brolin, Jacqueline Bisset, Claire Trevor, Bob Courtney, Jon Whiteley

'The man who made the twenties roar! Now, after 45 years, his true story can be told!'

Capone
US 1975 101m De Luxe
TCF / Santa Fe (Roger Corman)

Exploitation version of the Capone story, with the emphasis on unpleasant violence.

w Howard Browne *d* Steve Carver *ph* Vilis Lapenieks *m* David Grisman

Ben Gazzara, Sylvester Stallone, Susan Blakely, Harry Guardino, John Cassavetes, John Davis Chandler, Peter Maloney, Royal Dano

† See also: *Al Capone*.

Caprice*
US 1967 98m De Luxe Cinemascope
TCF / Aaron Rosenberg, Marty Melcher

A career girl investigating the death of her boss discovers that a cosmetics empire is the front for international drug smuggling.
Incoherent kaleidoscope which switches from farce to suspense and Bond-style action, scattering in-jokes along the way. Bits of it however are funny, and it looks good.

w Jay Jayson, Frank Tashlin *d* Frank Tashlin *ph* Leon Shamroy (who also appears) *m* Frank de Vol

Doris Day, Richard Harris, Edward Mulhare, Ray Walston, Jack Kruschen, Lilia Skala, Irene Tsu, Michael Romanoff, Michael J. Pollard

Capricious Summer*
Czechoslovakia 1968 75m Eastmancolor
Ceskoslovensky Film (Jan Libora)

The beautiful assistant of a wandering tightrope walker sets up sexual tensions when they stop at a sleepy riverside town.
Amusing little period comedy in a period setting.

wd Jiri Menzel ph Jaromir Sofr *m* Jiri Sust

Rudolf Hrusinksy, Vlastimil Brodsky, Frantisek Rehak, Jana Drchalova, Jiri Menzel

Capricorn One
US 1978 128m CFI colour Panavision
Associated General / Lew Grade (Paul N. Lazarus III)

A reporter discovers that the first manned space flight to Mars was a hoax.
Smartly packaged topical adventure thriller rather marred by its all star cast.

wd Peter Hyams ph Bill Butler *m* Jerry Goldsmith *pd* Albert Brenner

Elliott Gould, James Brolin, Brenda Vaccaro, Sam Waterston, O. J. Simpson, Hal Holbrook, Telly Savalas, Karen Black, David Huddleston

'After weighing in with some Watergate / Bernstein pretensions, the makers then opt for boring, Bondish derring-do.'—*Sight and Sound*

Captain America*
US 1944 bw serial: 15 eps

A masked avenger who is really a district attorney combats a museum curator who is really The Scarab. Serial elements in fairly fine fettle: one for sociologists of the future to work over. Dick Purcell, Lionel Atwill, Lorna Gray, Charles Trowbridge, Russell Hicks, Frank Reicher. Directed by John English and Elmer Clifton; for Republic.

Captain Apache
US / Spain 1971 94m Technicolor 'Scope
Benmar (Milton Sperling, Philip Yordan, Irving Lerner)

An Indian serving with US army intelligence tracks down a gun runner.
An old formula tarted up with the new violence. Very ho-hum.

w Philip Yordan, Milton Sperling, *novel* S. E. Whitman *d* Alexander Singer *ph* John Cabrera *m* Dolores Claman

Lee Van Cleef, Carroll Baker, Stuart Whitman, Percy Herbert, Tony Vogel

Captain Applejack
US 1931 70m bw

A timid man turns the tables on crooks who plan to find treasure beneath his ancestral home. Early talkie version of a well-worn play previously filmed in 1923. John Halliday, Kay Strozzi, Arthur Edmund Carewe, Mary Brian, Louise Closser Hale. Written by Maude Fulton, from *Ambrose Applejohn's Adventure* by Walter Hackett; directed by Hobart Henley; for Warner.

Captain Bill
GB 1935 81m bw

A bargee saves a schoolmistress from trouble with crooks. By reputation the best of its star's modest comedies, which have not yet been rediscovered. Leslie Fuller, Georgie Harris, Judy Kelly, Hal Gordon, O. B. Clarence. Written by Val Valentine, Syd Courtenay and George Harris; directed by Ralph Ceder; for Leslie Fuller.

Captain Black Jack
US / France 1952 90m bw

A Riviera socialite pretends to be an undercover agent but is really a smuggler; she is unmasked by a doctor who is really a detective. Trashy hodgepodge with a remarkable cast of ageing stars: George Sanders, Agnes Moorehead, Herbert Marshall, Patricia Roc, Marcel Dalio. Written by Julien Duvivier and Charles Spaak; directed by Julien Duvivier; for Walter Gould.

'A million dollars worth of adventure! To do justice in words to its fascination is impossible!'
'His sword carved his name across the continents—and his glory across the seas!'

Captain Blood**
US 1935 119m bw
Warner (Harry Joe Brown)

A young British surgeon, wrongly condemned by Judge Jeffreys for helping rebels, escapes and becomes a Caribbean pirate.
Modestly produced but quite exhilarating pirate adventure notable for making a star of Errol Flynn. Direction makes the most of very limited production values.

w Casey Robinson, *novel* Rafael Sabatini *d Michael Curtiz ph Hal Mohr m Erich Wolfgang Korngold ad Anton Grot*

Errol Flynn, Olivia de Havilland, *Basil Rathbone*, Lionel Atwill, Guy Kibbee, Ross Alexander, Henry Stephenson, Forrester Harvey, Hobart Cavanaugh, Donald Meek

'A lavish, swashbuckling saga of the Spanish Main . . . it can't fail at the wickets.'—*Variety*

'Here is a fine spirited mix-up with clothes and wigs which sometimes hark back to the sixteenth century and sometimes forward to the period of Wolfe . . . one is quite prepared for the culminating moment when the Union Jack breaks proudly, anachronistically forth at Peter Blood's masthead.'—*Graham Greene*

'Magnificently photographed, lavishly produced, and directed with consummate skill.'—*Picturegoer*

AAN: best picture

Captain Boycott*
GB 1947 93m bw
GFD / Individual (Frank Launder, Sidney Gilliat)

In 1880, poor Irish farmers rebel against their tyrannical English landlords.
Modest historical drama in which a splendid cast is rather subdued.

w Wolfgang Wilhelm, Frank Launder, Paul Vincent Carroll, Patrick Campbell, *novel* Philip Rooney *d* Frank Launder *ph* Wilkie Cooper *m* William Alwyn

Stewart Granger, Kathleen Ryan, Alastair Sim, Robert Donat (a cameo as Parnell), Cecil Parker, Mervyn Johns, Noel Purcell, Niall MacGinnis

'It is said that no actor can survive playing opposite a child or a dog. Let me add here that it is just as lethal playing with the Abbey Players. Apart from being able to act you off the stage, they can also drink you under the table.'—*Sidney Gilliat, 1982*

Captain Carey USA
US 1950 83m bw
Paramount (Richard Maibaum)
GB title: *After Midnight*

After the war, a military officer returns to an Italian village to expose the informer who betrayed his comrades.
Muddled and rather boring melodrama with a labyrinthine plot which seems to have stultified all concerned. It did produce a hit song, 'Mona Lisa'.

w Robert Thoeren, *novel* Dishonoured by Martha Albrand *d* Mitchell Leisen *ph* John F. Seitz *m* Hugo Friedhofer

Alan Ladd, Francis Lederer, Wanda Hendrix, Joseph Calleia, Celia Lovsky, Angela Clarke, Jane Nigh, Frank Puglia, Luis Alberni

AA: song 'Mona Lisa' (*m / ly* Ray Evens, Jay Livingston)

Captain Caution
US 1940 84m bw
Hal Roach

In 1812, a girl takes over her dead father's ship and fights the British.
Lively though unconvincing adventure with emphasis on comedy.

w Grover Jones, *novel* Kenneth Roberts *d* Richard Wallace *ph* Norbert Brodine *m* Phil Ohman

Victor Mature, Louise Platt, Bruce Cabot, Leo Carrillo, Robert Barrat, Vivienne Osborne, Alan Ladd

Captain China
US 1949 97m bw
Paramount / Pine-Thomas (William H. Pine, William C. Thomas)

A wandering seafarer seeks the mate who betrayed him.
Action melodrama with a second team look; all rather listless.

w Lewis R. Foster, Gwen Bagni *d* Lewis R. Foster *ph* John Alton *m* Lucien Caillet

John Payne, Gail Russell, Jeffrey Lynn, Lon Chaney Jnr, Michael O'Shea, Ellen Corby

Captain Clegg*
GB 1962 82m Technicolor
Universal / Hammer (John Temple-Smith)
US title: *Night Creatures*

The vicar of an 18th-century village in Romney Marsh is really a retired pirate, now doing a little smuggling on the side.
Mild remake of *Dr Syn* with a few moments of violence added; watchable for those who like totally predictable plot development.

w John Elder *d* Peter Graham Scott *ph* Arthur Grant *m* Don Banks

Peter Cushing, Patrick Allen, Michael Ripper, Oliver Reed, Derek Francis, Milton Reid, Martin Benson, David Lodge, Yvonne Romain

Captain Eddie
US 1945 107m bw
TCF / Eureka

Eddie Rickenbacker, adrift on a life raft after a plane crash in the Pacific, thinks back on his adventurous life in aviation.
Flat and surprisingly poorly made biopic with little to hold the attention.

w John Tucker Battle *d* Lloyd Bacon *ph* Joe MacDonald *m* Cyril Mockridge

Fred MacMurray, Lynn Bari, Thomas Mitchell, Lloyd Nolan, Charles Bickford

Captain from Castile
US 1947 140m Technicolor
TCF (Lamar Trotti)

A young 15th-century Spaniard hopés for fame and fortune in the New World.
Rather empty and boring adventure epic from a bestseller; high production values produce moments of interest.

w Lamar Trotti, *novel* Samuel Shellabarger *d* Henry King *ph* Charles Clarke, Arthur E. Arling *m* Alfred Newman *ad* Richard Day, James Basevi

Tyrone Power, Jean Peters, Lee J. Cobb, Cesar Romero, John Sutton, Antonio Moreno, Thomas Gomez, Alan Mowbray, Barbara Lawrence, George Zucco, Roy Roberts, Marc Lawrence

'The first few reels have flow and a kind of boy's-book splendour; the rest is locomotor ataxia.'—*James Agee*

AAN: Alfred Newman

Captain Fury*
US 1939 91m bw
Hal Roach

In 19th-century Australia, an adventurer fights the evil head of a penal colony.
Shades of Zorro and Robin Hood in a brawling, comic actioner typical of this producer.

w Grover Jones, Jack Jevne, William de Mille *d* Hal Roach *ph* Norbert Brodine *m* Marvin Hatley

Brian Aherne, Victor McLaglen, Paul Lukas, June Lang, John Carradine

'Action, fast riding, gunplay, surprise attacks, some broad comedy and a few dashes of romance . . . will do pretty good biz in the keys, but will hit a more profitable stride in the subsequents.'—*Variety*

The Captain Hates the Sea*
US 1934 92m bw
Columbia

Crime and comedy on an ocean voyage.
Zany, rather endearing comedy which gave the star his last role.

w Wallace Smith *d* Lewis Milestone *ph* Joseph August

John Gilbert, Victor McLaglen, Walter Connolly, Alison Skipworth, Wynne Gibson, Helen Vinson, Leon Errol, Walter Catlett, Donald Meek, Arthur Treacher, Akim Tamiroff

'A fine cast, excellent comedy relief and expert direction.'—*Variety*

'The best neglected picture in two years.'—*Otis Ferguson, 1936*

Captain Horatio Hornblower RN
GB 1951 117m Technicolor
Warner (Raoul Walsh)

Events from the adventure novels about a 19th-century sailor who outwits the Spaniards and the French and marries his admiral's widow.
Sprawling, plotless sea saga with the cast ill at ease in highly unconvincing sets: no air seems to blow across the decks of the *Lydia*.

w Ivan Goff, Ben Roberts, Aeneas Mackenzie, *novels* C. S. Forester *d* Raoul Walsh *ph* Guy Green *m* Robert Farnon *ad* Tom Morahan

Gregory Peck, Virginia Mayo, Robert Beatty, James Robertson Justice, Terence Morgan, Moultrie Kelsall, Richard Hearne, Denis O'Dea

'No point makes a strong enough impression to suggest a main line of criticism.'—*Richard Mallett, Punch*

The Captain Is a Lady*
US 1940 63m bw

A sea captain is forced by ill-fortune to send his wife to an old ladies' home, but he dresses as a woman to be with her. Absurd-sounding comedy not without a certain lunatic charm. Charles Coburn, Billie Burke, Beulah Bondi, Dan Dailey, Virginia Grey, Helen Broderick, Helen Westley. Written by Harry Clark, from a play by Rachel Crothers; directed by Robert Sinclair; for MGM.

Captain January*
US 1936 74m bw
TCF (Darryl F. Zanuck)

A little girl is rescued from a shipwreck by a lighthouse keeper.

Standard Shirley Temple vehicle with pleasing dialogue and numbers.

w Sam Hellman, Gladys Lehman, Harry Tugend, *novel* Laura E. Richards *d* David Butler *ph* John F. Seitz *m* Louis Silvers *songs* Lew Pollack, Sidney Mitchell, Jack Yellen

Shirley Temple, Guy Kibbee, Buddy Ebsen, Slim Summerville, June Lang, Sara Haden, Jane Darwell

Captain Kidd
US 1945 90m bw
Benedict Bogeaus

A pirate tricks King William III into giving him royal orders, but enemies he believes dead return to see him hanged.
Rather poorly produced vehicle for a star who however rants and raves to some effect.

w Norman Reilly Raine *d* Rowland V. Lee *ph* Archie Stout *m* Werner Janssen

Charles Laughton, Randolph Scott, Barbara Britton, Reginald Owen, John Carradine, Gilbert Roland, Sheldon Leonard

AAN: Werner Janssen

Captain Kidd and the Slave Girl
US 1954 82m CFI Color

A scheming earl reprieves Captain Kidd so that he can steal his treasure. Cut-price swashbuckler with more vigour than some. Anthony Dexter, Eva Gabor, Alan Hale Jnr, James Seay. Written by Aubrey Wisberg and Jack Pollexfen; directed by Lew Landers; for Reliance / UA.

Captain Kronos, Vampire Hunter*
GB 1974 91m colour

The title explains almost all; in this case he tackles an old vampire crone who becomes young when she sucks blood. Lively horror yarn with amusing asides. Horst Janson, John Carson, Shane Briant, Caroline Munro, John Cater, Wanda Ventham. Written and directed by *Brian Clemens* for Albert Fennell-Brian Clemens/Hammer.

Captain Lash*
US 1929 72m approx bw silent

Late silent adventure: a stoker gets involved with smuggling for a society girl. Mildly amusing goings-on with a star in good form. Victor McLaglen, Claire Windsor, Arthur Stone, Albert Conti, Clyde Cook. Written by John Stone and Daniel G. Tomlinson; directed by John Blystone; for Fox.

Captain Lightfoot
US 1955 92m Technicolor print Cinemascope
U-I (Ross Hunter)

Adventures of a 19th-century Irish rebel. Dullish adventure story with the star ill at ease.

w W. R. Burnett, Oscar Brodney *d* Douglas Sirk *ph* Irving Glassberg *m* Hans Salter

Rock Hudson, Barbara Rush, Jeff Morrow, Kathleen Ryan, Finlay Currie, Denis O'Dea, Geoffrey Toone

Captain Midnight
US 1942 bw serial: 15 eps

Ivan Shark terrifies the nation with night bombing planes, but an intrepid aviator comes to the rescue. Serial elements topically adopted to wartime sabotage. Fair fun. Dave O'Brien, Dorothy Short, James Craven, Bryant Washburn. Directed by James W. Horne; for Columbia.

Captain Nemo and the Underwater City
GB 1969 106m Metrocolor Panavision
MGM / Omnia (Steven Pallos, Bertram Ostrer)

Six survivors from an Atlantic shipwreck are picked up by a mysterious submarine and have adventures in a spectacular underwater city.
Further adventures of Jules Verne's engaging Victorian character from *Twenty Thousand Leagues under the Sea*. Here however the general production values are stolid rather than solid, and the script makes heavy weather.

w Pip Baker, Jane Baker, R. Wright Campbell *d* James Hill *ph* Alan Hume, Egil Woxholt *m* Walter Stott *ad* Bill Andrews

Robert Ryan, Chuck Connors, Bill Fraser, Kenneth Connor, Nanette Newman, John Turner, Luciana Paluzzi, Allan Cuthbertson

Captain Newman MD*
US 1963 126m Eastmancolor
Universal–Brentwood–Reynard (Robert Arthur)

At an army air base during World War II, a psychiatrist has varied success with his patients.
A decidedly curious comedy drama on the fringe of bad taste; it should have turned out better than it does, but will entertain those who like hospital heroics drenched in bitter-sweet sentimentality.

w Richard L. Breen, Phoebe and Henry Ephron, *novel* Leo Rosten *d* David Miller *ph* Russell Metty *m* Joseph Gershenson

Gregory Peck, Tony Curtis, Angie Dickinson, Eddie Albert, Bobby Darin, James Gregory, Jane Withers, Bethel Leslie, Robert Duvall, Larry Storch, Robert F. Simon, Dick Sargent

AAN: script; Bobby Darin

Captain of the Guard
US 1930 83m bw

During the French Revolution, a guards captain changes sides. Unexciting historical melodrama which failed to make the intended impression. John Boles, Laura La Plante, Lionel Belmore, Sam de Grasse, James Marcus, Otis Harlan. Written by Arthur Ripley, from a story by Houston Branch; directed by Paul Fejos and John S. Robertson; music and songs by Charles Wakefield Cedman; for Carl Laemmle / Universal.

'Universal's most pretentious release of the season . . . liberal expenditure shows on the screen.'—*Variety*

'Passions run hot and blood runs cold!'
Captain Pirate
US 1952 85m Technicolor
Columbia (Harry Joe Brown)
GB title: *Captain Blood, Fugitive*

A reformed pirate, accused of sacking Cartagena, returns to piracy to discover the perpetrators.
Lively buccaneering programmer with an adequate budget and plenty of high spirits.

w Robert Libbott, Frank Burt, John Meredyth Lucas, *novel* Captain Blood Returns by Rafael Sabatini *d* Ralph Murphy *ph* Charles Lawton Jnr *m* George Duning

Louis Hayward, Patricia Medina, John Sutton, George Givot, Rex Evans, Ted de Corsia, Charles Irwin

Captain Scarlett
US 1952 75m Technicolor
UA / Craftsman (Howard Dimsdale)

After the Napoleonic wars, southern France is in need of a protector against the villainous Duke of Corlaine. Captain Scarlett rides into action . . .
Robin Hood in all but name, an old tale retold without much flair.

w Howard Dimsdale *d* Thomas Carr *ph* Charles Carbajal *m* Elias Breeskin

Richard Greene, Leonora Amar, Nedrick Young, Eduardo Norriega

Captain Sinbad*
US / Germany 1963 88m Eastmancolor Wonderscope
King Brothers

Sinbad returns to Baristan and by means of magic deposes a sultan.
Rather splendid adventure fantasy with a European flavour, good trick effects and full-blooded performances.

w Samuel B. West, Harry Relis *d* Byron Haskin *ph* Gunther Senftleben, Eugen Shuftan *m* Michel Michelet *sp* Tom Howard *ad* Werner and Isabell Schlicting

Guy Williams, Pedro Armendariz, Heidi Bruhl, Abraham Sofaer

Captain Tugboat Annie
US 1945 70m bw

Annie wants to adopt a small boy but by clerical error gets a young man instead. A silly story which prevented this reworking of the old Dressler–Beery vehicle from becoming a series. Jane Darwell, Edgar Kennedy, Charles Gordon. Written by C. Callahan; directed by Phil Rosen; for Republic.

Captains Courageous**
US 1937 116m bw
MGM (Louis D. Lighton)

A spoiled rich boy falls off a cruise liner and lives for a while among fisherfolk who teach him how to live.

Semi-classic Hollywood family film which is not all that enjoyable while it's on but is certainly a good example of the prestige picture of the thirties. (It also happened to be good box office.)

w John Lee Mahin, Marc Connelly, Dale Van Every, *novel* Rudyard Kipling *d* Victor Fleming *ph* Harold Rosson *m* Franz Waxman

Spencer Tracy, Lionel Barrymore, Freddie Bartholomew, Mickey Rooney, Melvyn Douglas, Charley Grapewin, Christian Rub, John Carradine, Walter Kingsford, Leo G. Carroll, Charles Trowbridge

'Will not have to go begging for patronage . . . one of the best pictures of the sea ever made.'—*Variety*

'Another of those grand jobs of movie-making we have come to expect from Hollywood's most profligate studio.'—*Frank S. Nugent, New York Times*

† 1977 brought a TV movie remake.

AA: Spencer Tracy
AAN: best picture; script

The Captain's Kid
US 1936 72m bw

In New England, a retired sea captain's blood-chilling tales thrill a little girl and involve him in a real-life court case. Slightly unusual tale which deserved better handling than this routine second feature allows. Guy Kibbee, May Robson, Sybil Jason, Jane Bryan, Dick Purcell. Written by Tom Reed; directed by Nick Grinde; for Warner.

Captains of the Clouds
US 1942 113m Technicolor
Warner (Hal. B. Wallis, William Cagney)

A flippant Canadian Air Force pilot proves his worth under fire.
Recruiting poster heroics, reasonably well done but lacking the vital spark.

w Arthur T. Horman, Richard Macaulay, Norman Reilly Raine *d* Michael Curtiz *ph* Sol Polito, Wilfrid M. Cline *m* Max Steiner

James Cagney, Dennis Morgan, Brenda Marshall, George Tobias, Alan Hale, Reginald Gardiner, Reginald Denny, Paul Cavanagh, Clem Bevans, J. M. Kerrigan

'Pure tribute to the unchanging forcefulness of James Cagney.'—*New York Post*

AAN: Sol Polito, Wilfrid M. Cline

The Captain's Paradise*
GB 1953 89m bw
BL / London (Anthony Kimmins)

The captain of a steamer plying between Gibraltar and Tangier has a wife in each port, one to suit each of his personalities.
Over-dry comedy in which the idea is much funnier than the script. One is left with the memory of a pleasant star performance.

w Alec Coppel, Nicholas Phipps *d* Anthony Kimmins *ph* Ted Scaife *m* Malcolm Arnold

Alec Guinness, Celia Johnson, Yvonne de Carlo, Charles Goldner, Miles Malleson, Bill Fraser, Nicholas Phipps, Ferdy Mayne, George Benson

AAN: original story (Alec Coppel)

The Captain's Table*
GB 1958 89m Eastmancolor
Rank (Joseph Janni)

A cargo skipper is given command of a luxury liner and has to watch his manners.
Lively adaptation of a frivolous book of obvious jokes, most of which come up quite funny amid the luxurious surroundings.

w John Whiting, Bryan Forbes, Nicholas Phipps, *novel* Richard Gordon *d* Jack Lee *ph* Christopher Challis *m* Frank Cordell

John Gregson, Peggy Cummins, *Donald Sinden, Reginald Beckwith,* Nadia Gray, Richard Wattis, Maurice Denham, Nicholas Phipps, Joan Sims, Miles Malleson

The Captive City**
US 1951 91m bw
UA / Aspen (Theron Warth)

Small-town corruption imposed by the Mafia is revealed by a crusading editor who defies threats to his wife and family and tells all to the Kefauver Commission.
Excellent documentary melodrama made in a style then original, also notable for use of the Hoge deep focus lens.

w Karl Lamb, Alvin Josephy Jnr d Robert Wise ph Lee Garmes m Jerome Moross

John Forsythe, Joan Camden, Harold J. Kennedy, Marjorie Crossland, Victor Sutherland, Ray Teal, Martin Milner, Hal K. Dawson

The Captive City
Italy 1963 110m bw

Rebels keep an assorted group of people captive in an Athens hotel. Dim would-be thriller which rambles on far too long. David Niven, Lea Massari, Ben Gazzara, Daniela Rocca, Martin Balsam, Michael Craig, Percy Herbert. Written by Guy Elmes, Eric Bercovici, Marc Brandel, from the novel by John Appleby; directed by Joseph Anthony; for Paramount. (Italian title: *La Città Prigionera.*)

The Captive Heart**
GB 1946 108m bw
Ealing (Michael Relph)

Stories of life among British officers in a German POW camp, especially of a Czech who has stolen the papers of a dead Britisher.
Archetypal POW drama lacing an almost poetic treatment with humour and melodrama.

w Angus Macphail, Guy Morgan *d Basil Dearden ph* Lionel Banes, Douglas Slocombe *m* Alan Rawsthorne

Michael Redgrave, *Jack Warner*, Basil Radford, Mervyn Johns, Jimmy Hanley, Gordon Jackson, Ralph Michael, Derek Bond, Karel Stepanek, Guy Middleton, Jack Lambert, Gladys Henson, Rachel Kempson, Meriel Forbes

'A warm, emotional, intensely human document, entitled to rate among the best twenty films of the last ten years.'—*News of the World*

'A human form with animal instincts!'

Captive Wild Woman
US 1943 60m bw

A doctor finds a way of developing the glands of an ape and turning it into a beautiful girl. Lamebrain horror item which amazingly spawned two sequels, *Jungle Woman* (1944) and *Jungle Captive* (1945). Evelyn Ankers, Aquanetta, John Carradine, Martha Vickers, Milburn Stone. Written by Griffin Jay and Henry Sucher; directed by Edward Dmytryk; for Universal.

Captured
US 1933 72m bw

A prisoner-of-war discovers that his best friend was his wife's lover. Turgid and heavy-going early variation on a theme which would become very familiar indeed; the stars couldn't save it. Leslie Howard, Paul Lukas, Douglas Fairbanks Jnr, Margaret Lindsay, J. Carrol Naish, Arthur Hohl. Written by Edward Chodorov, from a novel by Sir Philip Gibbs; directed by Roy Del Ruth; for Warner. 'Too many obviously adverse ingredients, chiefly story, to chalk this one up as a winner . . . at best its earnings shape up as spotty.'—*Variety*

'Is it a phantom, a demon, or the devil himself?'

The Car
US 1977 98m Technicolor Panavision
Universal (Peter Saphier)

A small southwestern town is terrorized by a driverless car which may be a creation of the devil.
Silly suspenser with a draggy midsection.

w Dennis Shyrack, Michael Butler, Lane Slate *d* Elliot Silverstein *ph* Gerald Hirschfeld *m* Leonard Rosenman

James Brolin, Kathleen Lloyd, John Marley, R. G. Armstrong, John Rubenstein

Car 99
US 1935 70m bw

A novice state trooper redeems early failure by capturing bank robbers. Competent routine programmer which helped to establish its star. Fred MacMurray, Ann Sheridan, Sir Guy Standing. Written by Karl Ditzer and C. Gardner Sullivan; directed by Charles Barton; for Paramount. 'Heaps of excitement and comedy make a swell hour of entertainment for the nabe element.'—*Variety*

Car of Dreams
GB 1935 72m bw

A rich man's son buys a car for one of his father's factory girls. Silly comedy with sillier music, remade from a German original. John Mills, Grete Mosheim, Mark Lester, Robertson Hare, Norah Howard. Written by Austin Melford; directed by Austin Melford and Graham Cutts; for Gaumont British.

Car Trouble
GB 1986 93m colour
Thorn EMI / GTO / Goldfarb (Howard Malin, Gregory J. DeSantis)

A woman having an affair with a car salesman finds herself sexually locked to him in her husband's new vehicle.
This weird premise for a comedy rings up remarkably few laughs.

w James Whaley, A. J. Tipping *d* David Green *ph* Michael Garfath

Julie Walters, Ian Charleson, Stratford Johns, Vincenzo Ricotta

Car Wash
US 1976 96m Technicolor

Various eccentrics congregate around the Dee Luxe Car Wash. Zany ethnic (black) comedy with little rhyme or reason in its development but a certain vigour in some of its sketches. A subsequent TV series didn't last. Franklyn Ajaye, Sully Boyar, Richard Pryor, Ivan Dixon, Antonio Fargas, Tracy Reed. Written by Joel Schumacher; directed by Michael Schultz; for Universal. 'Its specialty is yanking laughs by having blacks do dirtier versions of the standard pranks that naughty kids used to do in comedies.'—*Pauline Kael*

Caravaggio*
GB 1986 89m Technicolor
BFI / Channel 4 / Nicholas Ward-Jackson (Sarah Radclyffe)

An imaginary biopic of the Italian painter who died in 1610, with emphasis on homosexual models, a variety of scandals, and jokey anachronisms.
A classic for the gay crowd; something of a mystery for everyone else.

w,d Derek Jarman *ph* Gabriel Beristain *m* Simon Fisher Turner *pd* Christopher Hobbs

Nigel Terry, Sean Bean, Garry Cooper, Spencer Leigh

'It rises above its financial restrictions to prove that less can be a lot more.'—*Variety*

Caravan
US 1934 101m bw
Fox

A countess marries a gypsy.
Odd romantic drama with music: too whimsical to succeed.

w Samson Raphaelson *d* Erik Charell *ph* Ernest Palmer, Theodor Sparkuhl *songs* Werner B. Heymann, Gus Kahn

Loretta Young, Charles Boyer, Jean Parker, Phillips Holmes, Louise Fazenda, Eugene Pallette, C. Aubrey Smith, Charley Grapewin, Noah Beery, Dudley Digges

'Big, beautiful and boring . . . peasants come popping out of nowhere, in pairs, tens, hundreds, thousands, and burst into song.'—*Variety*

Caravan
GB 1946 122m bw
Gainsborough (Harold Huth)

THE CAPTIVE HEART. Location filming in Germany and the realistic art direction of producer Michael Relph enhanced this telling Ealing omnibus drama.

A young man on a mission in Spain is left for dead by emissaries of his rival in love; he is nursed back to health by a gypsy girl who falls in love with him.
Artificial, romantic, high-flown period tosh without the courage of its lack of convictions. At the time, an exhibitor's dream.

w Roland Pertwee, *novel* Lady Eleanor Smith *d* Arthur Crabtree *ph* Stephen Dade

Stewart Granger, Jean Kent, Anne Crawford, *Robert Helpmann*, Dennis Price, Gerard Heinz, Enid Stamp-Taylor, David Horne, John Salew

Caravan to Vaccares
GB / France 1974 98m Eastmancolor Panavision
Crowndale (Geoffrey Reeve)

An American drifter on the Riviera is employed to escort a mysterious Hungarian to New York.
Lumpy Alistair MacLean action thriller, all a bit *déjà vu*.

w Paul Wheeler *d* Geoffrey Reeve *ph* Frederic Tammes *m* Stanley Myers

David Birney, Charlotte Rampling, Michel Lonsdale, Marcel Bozzuff, Michael Bryant

'An undernourished plot advanced only by a series of venerable clichés.'—*MFB*

'The biggest load of schoolboy hokum since Boy's Own Paper ceased circulation.'—*Michael Billington, Illustrated London News*

Caravans
US / Iran 1978 123m Technicolor Panavision
Ibex / FIDCI (Elmo Williams)

In the Middle East in 1948, a junior diplomat is sent to bring back the daughter of a US politician, who has married an arab, left him, and joined a Bedouin caravan.
Curiously halting succession of pretty pictures and not much plot; what there is tends to take second place to philosophy and eastern promise.

w Nancy Voyles Crawford, Thomas A. MacMahon, Lorraine Williams, *novel* James Michener *d* James Fargo *ph* Douglas Slocombe *m* Mike Batt

Anthony Quinn, Michael Sarrazin, Jennifer O'Neill, Christopher Lee, Joseph Cotten, Barry Sullivan, Jeremy Kemp

'A tiresome exercise in anti-climax.'—*Tim Pulleine, MFB*

† The film cost 14 million dollars and is said to have been financed by the Shah of Iran.

Carbine Williams
US 1952 93m bw
MGM (Armand Deutsch)

An imprisoned bootlegger perfects a new gun and is pardoned.
Flat fictionalization of a true story, with the star miscast.

w Art Cohn *d* Richard Thorpe *ph* William Mellor *m* Conrad Salinger

James Stewart, Jean Hagen, Wendell Corey, Carl Benton Reid, Paul Stewart, Otto Hulett, James Arness

Carbon Copy
US 1981 91m Metrocolor
Hemdale / RKO (Stanley Shapiro, Carter de Haven)

An executive is shocked when his long-lost son turns out to be black.
Stale comedy. The producers clearly think the basic idea worth ramming home a score of times; the characterization is thin and the production undernourished.

w Stanley Shapiro *d* Michael Schultz *ph* Fred J. Koenekamp *m* Bill Conti

George Segal, Susan Saint James, Jack Warden, Dick Martin, Densel Washington, Paul Winfield

'It makes *Guess Who's Coming to Dinner?* look like a tract for the nineties.'—*Derek Malcolm, Guardian*

'He's the cheekiest man in town!'
The Card**
GB 1952 91m bw
Rank / British Film Makers (John Bryan)
US title: *The Promoter*

A bright young clerk from the potteries finds many ingenious ways of improving his bank account and his place in society.
Pleasing period comedy with the star in a made-to-measure role and excellent production values.

w Eric Ambler, *novel* Arnold Bennett *d Ronald Neame* *ph* Oswald Morris *ad T. Hopwell Ash* *m* William Alwyn

Alec Guinness, Glynis Johns, Petula Clark, *Valerie Hobson*, Edward Chapman, Veronica Turleigh, Gibb McLaughlin, Frank Pettingell

Card of Fate see Le Grand Jeu

Cardboard Cavalier*
GB 1949 96m bw
Rank / Two Cities (Walter Forde)

In Cromwellian England, royalists commission a barrow boy to carry a secret letter. Helped by Nell Gwynn, he succeeds after encounters with a castle ghost and custard pies.
A pantomime crossed with an Aldwych farce in a period setting. It failed at the time but now seems a brave try, with nice judgment all round.

w Noel Langley *d Walter Forde* *ph* Jack Hildyard *m* Lambert Williamson

Sid Field, Margaret Lockwood, Mary Clare, Jerry Desmonde, Claude Hulbert, Irene Handl, Brian Worth, Edmund Willard (as Cromwell)

The Cardinal*
US 1963 175m Technicolor Panavision 70
Gamma / Otto Preminger

A 1917 ordinand becomes a Boston curate, a fighter of the Ku Klux Klan, a Rome diplomat, and finally gets a cardinal's hat.
Heavy-going documentary melodrama with many interesting sequences marred by lack of cohesion, too much grabbing at world problems, and over-sensational personal asides.

w Robert Dozier, *novel* Henry Morton Robinson *d Otto Preminger* *ph* Leon Shamroy *m* Jerome Moross *pd* Lyle Wheeler *titles* Saul Bass

Tom Tryon, *Carol Lynley*, Dorothy Gish, Maggie Macnamara, Cecil Kellaway, John Saxon, *John Huston*, Robert Morse, Burgess Meredith, Jill Haworth, Raf Vallone, Tullio Carminati, Ossie Davis, Chill Wills, Arthur Hunnicutt, Murray Hamilton, Patrick O'Neal, Romy Schneider

'Very probably the last word in glossy dishonesty posturing as serious art.'—*John Simon*

'Mere and sheer wide screen Technicolor movie.'—*Stanley Kauffmann*

AAN: Otto Preminger; Leon Shamroy; John Huston

'To thwart a king's passion, he gambled the fate of a nation!'
Cardinal Richelieu*
US 1935 83m bw
Twentieth Century (Darryl F. Zanuck)

Fictionalized biography of the unscrupulous cardinal who was the grey eminence behind Louis XIII.
One of George Arliss' better star vehicles, with not much conviction but excellent production values.

w Maude Howell, Cameron Rogers, W. P. Lipscomb *d* Rowland V. Lee *ph* Peverell Marley *m* Alfred Newman

George Arliss, Maureen O'Sullivan, Edward Arnold, Cesar Romero

'In selecting the churchly cardinal of Bulwer-Lytton rather than the cavalier-cardinal beloved of Dumas, they have lost romance and dash but gained compensating dignity . . . a fine technical production.'—*Variety*

The Care Bears Movie
US 1985 75m colour

Magical bears combat an evil spirit who aims to make everybody miserable. Cartoon feature, sluggishly animated and narrated, with appeal to nobody over five years old. Produced as a back-up to a range of toys. Written by Peter Sauder; directed by Arna Selznick; for Nelvana.

Career
US 1939 80m bw
RKO (Robert Sisk)

A respected small-town storekeeper has old scores to settle against the local banker.
Modest, pleasing, rather faded 'B' picture.

w Dalton Trumbo, Bert Granet, *novel* Phil Stong *d* Leigh Jason *ph* Frank Redman

Edward Ellis, Samuel S. Hinds, Anne Shirley, Janet Beecher, Leon Errol, Raymond Hatton, Hobart Cavanaugh

'Small-town story will sell better outside major playdates.'—*Variety*

† The film featured the winners of the Gateway to Hollywood talent contest, John Archer and Alice Eden.

Career*
US 1959 105m bw
Paramount / Hal B. Wallis (Paul Nathan)

An actor from the midwest finally gets his chance in New York.
A location melodrama with the feel of a documentary, well played but slow and rather indeterminate.

w James Lee, from his play *d* Joseph Anthony *ph* Joseph La Shelle *m* Franz Waxman

Anthony Franciosa, Dean Martin, Shirley Maclaine, Carolyn Jones, Joan Blackman, Robert Middleton, Frank McHugh, Donna Douglas

AAN: Joseph La Shelle

Career Woman
US 1936 75m bw

A shyster lawyer helps a girl student to win a murder case. Passable programme material which didn't bore. Michael Whalen, Claire Trevor, Isabel Jewell, Eric Linden, Virginia Field, Gene Lockhart, Ed Brophy, El Brendel. Written by Lamar Trotti from a story by Gene Fowler; directed by Lewis Seiler; for TCF. 'Teeters between farce and stark realism . . . not exactly for the family trade.'—*Variety*

Carefree*
US 1938 85m bw
RKO (Pandro S. Berman)

A humourless lawyer sends his undecided girl friend to an alienist, with whom she falls in love.
Slight, frothy comedy musical; quite palatable, but it signalled the end of the Astaire–Rogers series.

w Allan Scott, Ernest Pagano *d* Mark Sandrich *ph* Robert de Grasse *m / ly* Irving Berlin *ch* Hermes Pan *md* Victor Baravelle

Fred Astaire, Ginger Rogers, Ralph Bellamy, Luella Gear, Clarence Kolb, Jack Carson, Franklin Pangborne, Walter Kingsford, Hattie McDaniel

Songs: 'I Used to Be Colour Blind'; 'The Yam'; 'The Night Is Filled with Music'; 'Change Partners'

'Perhaps their poorest musical . . . a disappointing story and the stars alone may save it.'—*Variety*

AAN: Victor Baravelle; song 'Change Partners' (*m / ly* Irving Berlin)

Careful, Soft Shoulders*
US 1942 69m bw
TCF (Walter Morosco)

A Washington socialite becomes a spy for both sides.
Modest, slightly unusual second feature which over the years has gathered for itself more reputation than it really deserves.

wd Oliver H. P. Garrett *ph* Charles Clarke *m* Leigh Harline

Virginia Bruce, James Ellison, Aubrey Mather, Sheila Ryan, Ralph Byrd

Careless Lady
US 1932 76m bw

A young girl from the country pretends to be a married society woman and finds herself with a husband she doesn't want. It was the scriptwriter who was careless: the story doesn't make much sense. Joan Bennett, John Boles, Minna Gombell, Weldon Heyburn, Raul Roulien, Fortunio Bonanova, Josephine Hull. Written by Guy Bolton from a story by Reita Lambert; directed by Kenneth MacKenna; for Fox. 'Reaching house averages will be beyond expectations regardless of campaign.'—*Variety*

The Caretaker*
GB 1964 105m bw
Caretaker Films (Michael Birkett)
US title: *The Guest*

Two brothers invite a revolting tramp to share their attic.
Rather doleful filming of the fashionable play with its non-plot, irregular conceits and interesting interplay of character. It remains a theatrical experience.

w Harold Pinter *d* Clive Donner *ph* Nicolas Roeg *m* Ron Grainer

Alan Bates, Robert Shaw, Donald Pleasence

'Now the screen tells what makes a woman—and what breaks her!'

The Caretakers*
US 1963 97m bw
UA / Hall Bartlett
GB title: *Borderlines*

The interrelationship of several cases in a state mental hospital.
Rather hysterical melodrama, lacking in the stature required for its subject, but sometimes perversely entertaining.

w Henry F. Greenberg, *novel* Daniel Telfer *d* Hall Bartlett *ph Lucien Ballard* *m* Elmer Bernstein

Polly Bergen, Robert Stack, Joan Crawford, Diane McBain, Janis Paige, Van Williams, Robert Vaughn, Herbert Marshall, Constance Ford

AAN: Lucien Ballard

The Carey Treatment*
US 1972 101m Metrocolor Panavision
MGM (William Belasco)

A Boston pathologist investigating the death of an abortion victim becomes the potential murder victim of a father turned killer.
Pretentious thriller with a tendency to make moral points among the bloodshed; vigorously but variably made.

w James P. Bonner, *novel* A Case of Need by Jeffrey Hudson *d* Blake Edwards *ph* Frank Stanley *m* Roy Budd

James Coburn, Jennifer O'Neill, Skye Aubrey, Pat Hingle, Dan O'Herlihy, Elizabeth Allen, Alex Dreier, Regis Toomey

Cargo to Capetown
US 1950 84m bw

A merchant ship captain Shanghais his friend on a long voyage. Routine, competently staged thick ear. Broderick Crawford, John Ireland, Ellen Drew, Edgar Buchanan, Ted de Corsia. Written by Lionel Houser; directed by Earl McEvoy; for Columbia.

Caribbean
US 1952 94m Technicolor
(Paramount) Pine–Thomas (William H. Pine, William C. Thomas)
GB title: *Caribbean Gold*

An 18th-century pirate captures the nephew of his old enemy.
Adequate but not very exciting swashbuckler with fair production values.

w Frank L. Moss, Edward Ludwig *d* Edward Ludwig *ph* Lionel Lindon *m* Lucien Cailliet

John Payne, Arlene Dahl, Cedric Hardwicke (incredibly cast as the pirate), Francis L. Sullivan, Dennis Hoey

The Caribbean Mystery
US 1945 65m bw

A retired cop investigates the disappearance of several geologists on an oil company payroll. Modest mystery, previously filmed as *Murder in Trinidad*. James Dunn, Sheila Ryan, Edward Ryan, Jackie Paley, Reed Hadley. Written by W. Scott Darling from novel by John W. Vandercook; directed by Robert Webb; for William Girard / TCF.

The Cariboo Trail
US 1949 80m Cinecolor

Prospectors get involved in a cattle war. Standard western full of predictable elements. Randolph Scott, Gabby Hayes, Bill Williams, Karin Booth, Victor Jory. Written by Frank Gruber; directed by Edwin L. Marin; for Nat Holt (TCF).

Carlton-Browne of the FO
GB 1958 88m bw
British Lion / Charter Films (John Boulting)
US title: *Man in a Cocked Hat*

When valuable mineral deposits are found in a small British colony, the diplomat sent to cement good relations does quite the reverse. Hit-or-miss farcical comedy several rungs below the Ealing style, with all concerned in poor form.

wd Jeffrey Dell, Roy Boulting *ph* Max Greene *m* John Addison

Terry-Thomas, Peter Sellers, Ian Bannen, Thorley Walters, Raymond Huntley, John Le Mesurier, Luciana Paluzzi, Miles Malleson, Kynaston Reeves, Marie Lohr

Carmen**
Spain 1983 101m Eastmancolor

A rehearsal for the ballet *Carmen* finds dancers playing out in reality the parts of the drama. Enjoyable but exhausting melodrama with elements of *The Red Shoes*; meticulous choreography and direction are its chief assets. Antonio Gades, Laura del Sol, Paco de Lucia, Cristina Hoyos. Written by Carlos Saura, Antonio Gades; directed by *Carlos Saura*; for Emiliano Piedra Productions / Television Espanola. 'Extremely enjoyable, but lacks the edge that would make it in any way compelling.'—*Jill Forbes, MFB*
AAN: best foreign film

Carmen**
Italy / France 1984 152m Eastmancolor Panavision
Opera / Gaumont (Patrice Ledoux)

A luxuriantly filmed version of Bizet's opera, generally received with critical rapture.

d Francesco Rosi *ph Pasqualino de Santis* *pd Enrico Job*

Julia Migenes-Johnson, Placido Domingo, Ruggiero Raimondi

† Silent versions stretch back to 1915—that one starred Geraldine Farrar the opera singer (in a silent movie, by producer Cecil B. De Mille's whim).

Carmen Jones*
US 1954 105m De Luxe Cinemascope
TCF (Otto Preminger)

A factory girl marries a pilot, and is strangled by him for infidelity.
Black American updating of Bizet's opera, not really satisfactory but given full marks for trying, though the main singing is dubbed and the effect remains doggedly theatrical.

w Harry Kleiner *d* Otto Preminger *ph* Sam Leavitt *ly* Oscar Hammerstein II *titles Saul Bass* *md* Herschel Burke Gilbert

Dorothy Dandridge, Harry Belafonte, *Pearl Bailey*, Olga James, Joe Adams, Roy Glenn, Nick Stewart, Diahann Carroll, Brock Peters

'All one regrets is that the director has been unable to impose a unifying style on this promising material.'—*Gavin Lambert*

AAN: Herschel Burke Gilbert; Dorothy Dandridge

Carnal Knowledge*
US 1971 97m Technicolor Panavision
Avco Embassy / Icarus (Mike Nichols)

A college student embarks on an enthusiastic and varied sex life but by middle age is bored and empty.
Hampered by an unsuitable wide screen, this pretentious but fragmented comedy drama is embarrassingly conscious of its own daring in subject and language, and good performances are weighed down by an unsubtle script and tricksy direction.

w Jules Feiffer *d* Mike Nichols *ph* Giuseppe Rotunno *m* various songs *pd* Richard Sylbert

Jack Nicholson, *Arthur Garfunkel*, Candice Bergen, *Ann-Margret*, Rita Moreno

AAN: Ann-Margret

Carnegie Hall
US 1947 134m bw
Federal Films (Boris Morros, William Le Baron)

The story of New York's music centre, based on a fiction about a cleaner who finally becomes a concert organizer when her son is a famous pianist.
Slim and risible excuse for a classical concert, featuring among others Bruno Walter, Leopold Stokowski, Artur Rubenstein, Jascha Heifitz, Lily Pons, Rise Stevens, Ezio Pinza, Jan Peerce, Harry James, Vaughn Monroe and the New York Philharmonic Symphony Orchestra.

w Karl Lamb *d* Edgar G. Ulmer *ph* William Miller

Marsha Hunt, William Prince, Frank McHugh, Martha O'Driscoll

'The thickest and sourest mess of musical mulligatawny I have yet had to sit down to.'—*James Agee*

Un Carnet de Bal**
France 1937 135m bw
Lévy / Strauss / Sigma
aka: *Life Dances On*

A rich widow seeks her partners at a ball she remembers from her youth, finding that they are all failures and the ball a village hop.
Considering its fame, this is a lumpy porridge of a picture, good in parts but often slow, pretentious and banal. Its gallery of actors is, however, unique.

w Jean Sarment, Pierre Wolff, Bernard Zimmer, Henri Jeanson, Julien Duvivier *d* Julien Duvivier *ph* Michel Kelber, Philippe Agostini *m* Maurice Jaubert

Marie Bell, Françoise Rosay, *Louis Jouvet, Raimu, Harry Baur, Fernandel, Pierre Blanchar*

'Recent winner of the Mussolini Cup is loaded with top names, but it is not the film of the year . . . it tries to take in too much and takes too long to put across.'—*Variety*

† The film's international success took Duvivier to Hollywood, where he half-remade it as *Lydia* and went on to other multi-story films such as *Tales of Manhattan* and *Flesh and Fantasy*.

Carnival
US 1934 77m bw

A widowed puppeteer takes custody of his child, which is sought by the maternal grandfather, and seeks anonymity in a circus.
Curious sentimental melodrama with the stars shown in an unusual light. Lee Tracy, Jimmy Durante, Sally Eilers, Dickie Walters, Thomas Jackson, Florence Rice, Lucille Ball. Written by Robert Riskin; directed by Walter Lang; for Columbia. 'This should hold its own, though it probably will not climb to big grosses.'—*Variety*

Carnival
GB 1946 93m bw
Rank / Two Cities (John Sutro, William Sassoon)

In the nineties, a ballet dancer marries a dour Cornish farmer, who shoots her when her erstwhile lover comes after her.
Flimsy screen version of a solidly old-fashioned romantic drama.

w Eric Maschwitz, *novel* Compton Mackenzie *d* Stanley Haynes *ph* Guy Green

Sally Gray, Michael Wilding, Bernard Miles, Cathleen Nesbitt, Stanley Holloway, Jean Kent, Nancy Price, Hazel Court, Brenda Bruce, Catherine Lacey

† The story was previously filmed in 1931, as *Dance Pretty Lady*, with Ann Casson and Carl Harbord. The 1931 film *Carnival*, with Matheson Lang, is based on a story identical to *Men Are Not Gods* and *A Double Life:* an actor becomes obsessed with the part of Othello and strangles his wife.

Carnival in Costa Rica
US 1947 97m Technicolor
TCF (William A. Bacher)

A young Costa Rican, engaged to an American singer, returns home to find that his parents expect him to marry his childhood sweetheart.
Decidedly rundown musical in which incessant carnival largely supplants the wispy plot.

w John Larkin, Samuel Hoffenstein, Elizabeth Reinhardt *d* Gregory Ratoff *ph* Harry Jackson *ch* Leonide Massine *m / ly* Harry Ruby, Ernesto Lecuona

Dick Haymes, Vera-Ellen, Celeste Holm, J. Carrol Naish, Cesar Romero

Carnival in Flanders: see La Kermesse Héroique

Carnival of Souls
US 1962 80m bw

After an accident, a lady ghost emerges to become the new church organist. Absurd but occasionally compelling independently made horror film which would have been better in half-hour form. Candace Hilligoss, Herk Harvey, Francis Feist, Sidney Berger. Written by John Clifford; directed by Herk Harvey; for Herts-Lion. (Made in Kansas, allegedly for less than 100,000 dollars.)

Carnival Story
US / Germany 1954 95m Technicolor
The King Brothers

A starving girl becomes a trapezist at a German circus and stirs up jealousy among her partners.
Bleak reworking of *The Three Maxims* (qv), reworked again with more expertise in *Trapeze* (qv); this version is a cheap and unattractive co-production.

w Kurt Neumann, Hans Jacoby *d* Kurt Neumann *ph* Ernest Haller *m* Willi Schmidt-Genter

Anne Baxter, Steve Cochran, Lyle Bettger, George Nader, Jay C. Flippen

Carny
US 1980 105m Technicolor
Lorimar / Jonathan Taplin (Robbie Robertson)

Three wacky characters join a travelling carnival.
Sordid, sexy melodrama which seems to be doing a *Jules and Jim* with no holds barred. Not badly made, but full of people one would cross the road to avoid.

w Thomas Baum *d* Robert Kaylor *ph* Harry Stradling Jnr *m* Alex North

Gary Busey, Jodie Foster, Robbie Robertson, Kenneth McMillan, Meg Foster, Elisha Cook Jnr

'Too dark and turbulent a vision to be palatable to a large public.'—*Variety*

Carolina
US 1934 85m bw
Fox (Darryl F. Zanuck)
GB title: *House of Connelly*

A Yankee farmer's daughter falls in love with a Southern plantation owner.
Mildly pleasing period piece.

w Reginald Berkeley, *play* The House of Connelly by Paul Green *d* Henry King *ph* Hal Mohr *m* Louis de Francesco

Janet Gaynor, Lionel Barrymore, Robert Young, Henrietta Crosman, Mona Barrie, Richard Cromwell, Steppin Fetchit

'An arresting saga of a proud old southern family that starts out threateningly strong but peters to the point where it misses being another *State Fair*.'—*Variety*

Carolina Blues
US 1944 81m bw

A bandleader needs a new singer. Wispy comedy musical towards the end of Kyser's unlikely popularity. Kay Kyser and his band, Ann Miller, Victor Moore. Written by M. M. Musselman, Kenneth Earl, Joseph Hoffman and Al Martin; directed by Leigh Jason; for Columbia.

Caroline Chérie
France 1951 115m approx bw
SNEG / Cinéphonie

Adventures of an attractive and willing young French girl in the days of the revolution.
A cheerful French imitation of *Forever Amber*; witless and not very entertaining despite good period sense and a certain amount of self-mockery.

w Jean Anouilh, *novel* Cécil Saint-Laurent *d* Richard Poitier *ph* Maurice Barry *m* Georges Auric

Martine Carol, Jacques Dacqmine, Marie Déa, Paul Bernard, Pierre Cressoy

† After several sequels, a colour remake appeared in 1967.

Carousel*
US 1956 128m Eastmancolor Cinemascope 55
TCF (Henry Ephron)

A ne'er-do-well dies while committing a hold-up. Fifteen years later he returns from heaven to set his family's affairs in order.
Based on a fantasy play with an honourable history, this super-wide-screen version of an

effective stage musical is hollow and boring, a humourless whimsy in which even the songs seem an intrusion.

w Phoebe and Henry Ephron, from the musical based on Ferenc Molnar's play Liliom *d* Henry King *ph* Charles G. Clarke *m / ly* Rodgers and Hammerstein *ch* Rod Alexander, Agnes de Mille

Gordon Macrae, Shirley Jones, Cameron Mitchell,Gene Lockhart, Barbara Ruick, Robert Rounseville

'This is adult entertainment!'

The Carpetbaggers**
US 1964 150m Technicolor Panavision
Paramount / Embassy (Joseph E. Levine)

A young playboy inherits an aircraft business, becomes a megalomaniac tycoon, and moves to Hollywood in his search for power.
Enjoyable pulp fiction clearly suggested by the career of Howard Hughes. Lashings of old-fashioned melodrama, quite well pointed by all concerned.

w John Michael Hayes, *novel* Harold Robbins *d Edward Dmytryk* *ph* Joseph MacDonald *m* Elmer Bernstein *ad* Hal Pereira, Walter Tyler

George Peppard, Carroll Baker, *Alan Ladd* (his last film), *Martin Balsam*, Bob Cummings, Martha Hyer, Elizabeth Ashley, Lew Ayres, Ralph Taeger, Archie Moore, Leif Erickson, Audrey Totter

'One of those elaborate conjuring tricks in which yards and yards of coloured ribbon are spread all over the stage merely to prove that the conjuror has nothing up his sleeve.'—*Tom Milne*

Carrefour*
France 1938 75m bw

A French manufacturer, wounded during the war, finds himself the centre of blackmail plots. Intriguing melodrama which was later rather flatly remade in Hollywood as *Crossroads*. Charles Vanel, Jules Berry, Suzy Prim, Tania Fedor. Written by Hans Kofka; directed by Kurt Bernhardt; for BUP Tuscherer. 'One of the best French films of the late season, and worthy of American attention.'—*Variety*

Carrie**
US 1952 122m bw
Paramount (William Wyler)

In the early 1900s a country girl comes to Chicago, loses her innocence and goes on the stage, meanwhile reducing a wealthy restaurant manager to penury through love for her.
A famous satirical novel is softened into an unwieldy narrative with scarcely enough dramatic power to sustain interest despite splendid production values. Heavy pre-release cuts remain obvious, and the general effect is depressing; but it is very good to look at.

w Ruth and Augustus Goetz, *novel* Sister Carrie by Theodore Dreiser *d William Wyler* *ph Victor Milner* *m* David Raksin *ad Hal Pereira, Roland Anderson*

Laurence Olivier, Jennifer Jones, Miriam Hopkins, Eddie Albert, Basil Ruysdael, Ray Teal, Barry Kelley, Mary Murphy

'Olivier is so impassioned and so painfully touching that everything else in the movie, including the girl whose story it's meant to be, fades into insignificance.'—*Variety*

'They shot the later episodes for the strongest dramatic effect only, despite the fact that the story had stopped following a melodramatic line and become a sociological study . . . each additional episode exploits the audience's hope that things will be brought to a satisfactory conclusion, but they never are.'—*Films in Review*

Carrie*
US 1976 98m MGM-De Luxe
UA / Red Bank (Paul Monash)

A repressed teenager with remarkable mental powers takes a macabre revenge on classmates who taunt and persecute her.
Stylish but unattractive shocker which works its way up to a fine climax of gore and frenzy, and takes care to provide a final frisson just when the audience thinks it can safely go home.

w Laurence D. Cohen, *novel* Stephen King *d Brian de Palma* *ph* Mario Tosi *m* Pino Donaggio

Sissy Spacek, *Piper Laurie*, Amy Irving, William Katt, John Travolta

'Combining Gothic horror, offhand misogyny and an air of studied triviality, *Carrie* is de Palma's most enjoyable movie in a long while, and also his silliest.'—*Janet Maslin, Newsweek*

'The horror is effective only once, and the attempts at humour are never very successful and come almost when one is inclined to be moved by somebody's plight, so that the non-jokes yield authentic bad taste.'—*John Simon, New York*

AAN: Sissy Spacek; Piper Laurie

Carrington VC*
GB 1954 106m bw
British Lion / Romulus (Teddy Baird)
US title: *Court Martial*

An army major is courtmartialled for embezzling mess funds.
Good courtroom drama with a few plot surprises, convincing characters, and very serviceable acting and direction.

w John Hunter, *play* Dorothy and Campbell Christie *d* Anthony Asquith *ph* Desmond Dickinson

David Niven, Margaret Leighton, Noelle Middleton, Laurence Naismith, Clive Morton, Mark Dignam, Allan Cuthbertson, Victor Maddern, John Glyn-Jones, Raymond Francis, Newton Blick, John Chandos

Carry on Sergeant
GB 1958 83m bw
Anglo Amalgamated / Insignia (Peter Rogers)

An army training sergeant accepts a bet that his last platoon of raw recruits will win the Star Squad award.
Shabby farce with humdrum script and slack direction, saved by energetic performances.

w Norman Hudis, *play* The Bull Boys by R. F. Delderfield *d* Gerald Thomas *ph* Peter Hennessy *m* Bruce Montgomery

Bob Monkhouse, William Hartnell, Kenneth Williams, Charles Hawtrey, Shirley Eaton, Eric Barker, Dora Bryan, Bill Owen, Kenneth Connor

† From this unlikely beginning sprang almost twenty years of *Carry Ons*, their plots gradually disappearing under an accumulation of old jokes which grew steadily bluer. Colour did little to disguise their makeshift construction, and they never raised their sights as high as satire, but they became a British institution like fish and chips, and many of the regulars became stars. Apart from Williams, Hawtrey and Connor, those most regularly featured in the sequels were Sid James, Bernard Bresslaw, Jim Dale, Joan Sims, Hattie Jacques, Peter Butterworth, and Jack Douglas, with occasional guests such as Harry H. Corbett, Juliet Mills and even Phil Silvers. All were produced by Peter Rogers and directed by Gerald Thomas; most were written (or recollected) by Talbot Rothwell. Delivered at the rate of roughly two a year, the sequence of titles was CARRY ON NURSE (a surprising hit in the US), CARRY ON TEACHER, CARRY ON CONSTABLE, CARRY ON REGARDLESS, CARRY ON CRUISING, CARRY ON CABBY, CARRY ON JACK, CARRY ON SPYING, CARRY ON CLEO, CARRY ON COWBOY, CARRY ON SCREAMING, FOLLOW THAT CAMEL (Beau Geste), DON'T LOSE YOUR HEAD (the Scarlet Pimpernel), CARRY ON DOCTOR, CARRY ON UP THE KHYBER, CARRY ON CAMPING, CARRY ON AGAIN DOCTOR, CARRY ON LOVING, CARRY ON UP THE JUNGLE, CARRY ON HENRY (Henry VIII), CARRY ON AT YOUR CONVENIENCE, CARRY ON MATRON, CARRY ON ABROAD, CARRY ON GIRLS, CARRY ON DICK, CARRY ON BEHIND, CARRY ON ENGLAND, CARRY ON EMMANUELLE.
‡ CARRY ON ADMIRAL and WHAT A CARRY ON are not part of the series.

The Cars That Ate Paris*
Australia 1974 88m Eastmancolor Panavision
Saltpan / AFDC / Royce Smeal (Jim and Howard McElroy)

Car travellers become victims of a small town whose youthful inhabitants live on the pickings of engineered road accidents.
Another small town with a guilty secret, in this case more suitable to a half-hour than a feature, but with rewarding attention to detail.

wd Peter Weir *ph* John McLean *m* Bruce Smeaton

Terry Camillieri, John Meillon, Melissa Jaffa, Kevin Miles

Carson City*
US 1952 87m Warnercolor
Warner (David Weisbart)

A stagecoach service suffers from bandit raids, so a local banker finances a railroad.
Agreeably conventional western with plenty of reliable plot and a satisfactory outcome for the goodies.

w Sloan Nibley, Winston Miller *d* André de Toth *ph* John Boyle *m* David Buttolph

Randolph Scott, Raymond Massey, Lucille Norman, Richard Webb, James Millican, Larry Keating, George Cleveland

Cartouche
Italy / US 1954 85m approx bw
Venturini / RKO (John Nasht)

A French prince clears himself of a murder charge and brings the villain to book.
Flat costume drama.

w Louis Stevens, Tullio Pinelli *d* Steve Sekely, Gianni Vernuccio *ph* Massimo Dallamano *m* Bruce Montgomery

Richard Basehart, Patricia Roc, Massimo Serato, Akim Tamiroff

Cartouche**
France / Italy 1961 114m
Eastmancolor Dyaliscope
Ariane / Filmsonor / Vides (Georges Danciger)
aka: *Swords of Blood*

An 18th-century cooper's son becomes a quick-witted and gallant thief.
Slightly bitter fairy tale based on a French legend, vigorously encompassing tragedy, farce, violence and high-flown adventure.

w Daniel Boulanger, Philippe de Broca *d Philippe de Broca ph* Christian Matras *m* Georges Delerue

Jean-Paul Belmondo, Claudia Cardinale, Odile Versois, Marcel Dalio, Philippe Lemaire, Jean Rochefort

'A tour de force of virtuosity.'—*Peter John Dyer, MFB*

Carve Her Name with Pride*
GB 1958 119m bw
Rank / Keyboard (Daniel M. Angel)

In 1940, the young British widow of a French officer is enlisted as a spy, and after various adventures dies before a German firing squad.
Slightly muddled if ultimately moving biopic in which initial light comedy gives way to romance, documentary, character study, blazing war action and finally tragedy. Generally well made.

w Vernon Harris, Lewis Gilbert, *book* R. J. Minney *d Lewis Gilbert ph* John Wilcox *m* William Alwyn

Virginia McKenna (as Violette Szabo), *Paul Scofield*, Jack Warner, Sidney Tafler, Denise Grey, Alain Saury, Maurice Ronet, Nicole Stéphane, Noel Willman, Bill Owen, William Mervyn, Anne Leon

'What is missing is the deeply charged passion which would have gone beyond the quietly decent statement intermittently achieved.'—*John Gillett*

'As big and timely a picture as ever you've seen! You can tell by the cast it's important! gripping! big!'

Casablanca****
US 1942 102m bw
Warner *(Hal B. Wallis)*

Rick's Café in Casablanca is a centre for war refugees awaiting visas for America. Rick abandons his cynicism to help an old love escape the Nazis with her underground leader husband.
Cinema par excellence: a studio-bound Hollywood melodrama which after various chances just fell together impeccably into one of the outstanding entertainment experiences of cinema history, with romance, intrigue, excitement, suspense and humour cunningly deployed by master technicians and a perfect cast.

w Julius J. Epstein, Philip G. Epstein, Howard Koch, from an unproduced play, Everybody Comes to Rick's, by Murray Burnett and Joan Alison *d Michael Curtiz ph Arthur Edeson m Max Steiner*

Humphrey Bogart (Rick Blaine), *Ingrid Bergman* (Ilse Lund), Paul Henreid (Victor Laszlo), *Claude Rains* (Captain Louis Renault), Sydney Greenstreet (Ferrari), Peter Lorre (Ugarte), S. Z. Sakall (Carl), *Conrad Veidt* (Major Strasser), *Dooley Wilson* (Sam), *Marcel Dalio* (Croupier) and Madeleine LeBeau, Joy Page, John Qualen, Ludwig Stossel, Leonid Kinskey, Helmut Dantine, Ilka Gruning

Songs: 'As Time Goes By', 'Knock on Wood'

RICK: 'I stick out my neck for nobody. I'm the only cause I'm interested in.'

LOUIS: 'How extravagant you are, throwing away women like that. Someday they may be scarce.'

RICK: 'Ilse, I'm no good at being noble, but it doesn't take much to see that the problems of three little people don't amount to a hill of beans in this crazy world. Someday you'll understand that. Not now. Here's looking at you, kid.'

RICK: 'I came to Casablanca for the waters.'
LOUIS: 'What waters? We're in the desert.'
RICK: 'I was misinformed.'
RICK: 'Louis, I think this is the beginning of a beautiful friendship.'

'A picture which makes the spine tingle and the heart take a leap . . . they have so combined sentiment, humour and pathos with taut melodrama and bristling intrigue that the result is a highly entertaining and even inspiring film.'—*New York Times*

'Its humour is what really saves it, being a mixture of Central European irony of attack and racy Broadway–Hollywood Boulevard cynicism.'—*Herman G. Weinberg*

'The happiest of happy accidents, and the most decisive exception to the *auteur* theory.'—*Andrew Sarris, 1968*

'A film which seems to have been frozen in time . . . the sum of its many marvellous parts far exceeds the whole.'—*NFT, 1974*

'It's far from a great film, but it has an appealingly schlocky romanticism, and you're never really pressed to take its melodramatic twists and turns seriously.'—*Pauline Kael, 70s*

† Originally named for the leads were Ronald Reagan, Ann Sheridan and Dennis Morgan.

AA: best picture; Julius J. and Philip G. Epstein, Howard Koch; Michael Curtiz
AAN: Arthur Edeson; Max Steiner; Humphrey Bogart; Claude Rains

Casanova
Italy 1976 163m (English version)
Technicolor Scope
TCF / PEA (Alberto Grimaldi)
aka: *Fellini's Casanova*

Episodes from the life of the eighteenth-century libertine, in the course of which he seduces, among others, a nun, a mechanical doll, and a hunchbacked nymphomaniac.
A curiously rarefied spectacle which seldom comes to anything like life and despite its vast expense seems more likely to provoke yawns than lust.

w Federico Fellini, Barnadino Zapponi *d* Federico Fellini *ph* Giuseppe Rotunno *m* Nino Rota *pd* Danilo Donati, Federico Fellini

Donald Sutherland, Tina Aumont, Cicely Browne, Carmen Scarpitta

'It may well be the most ponderous specimen of imaginative vacuity ever devised.'—*John Simon, New York*

Casanova Brown
US 1944 99m bw
International / Christie (Nunnally Johnson)

Just as his divorce comes through, a man discovers that his wife is pregnant.
Very mild star comedy which tiptoes round its subject.

w Nunnally Johnson, *play* Bachelor Father by Floyd Dell, Thomas Mitchell *d* Sam Wood *ph* John F. Seitz *m* Arthur Lange *ad* Perry Ferguson

Gary Cooper, Teresa Wright, Frank Morgan, Anita Louise, Patricia Collinge, Edmond Breon, Jill Esmond, Isobel Elsom, Mary Treen, Halliwell Hobbes

'There is so much clowning with so little subject that one is exposed to the impression that anything went for a laugh.'—*Bosley Crowther, New York Times*

AAN: Arthur Lange; Perry Ferguson

Casanova in Burlesque
US 1944 74m bw

A professor has a secret summer life as a burlesque performer. Unusual, amiable comedy. Joe E. Brown, June Havoc. Written by Frank Gill; directed by Leslie Goodwins; for Republic.

Casanova's Big Night
US 1954 86m Technicolor
Paramount (Paul Jones)

In old Italy, the great lover is fleeing from his creditors and changes places with a tailor's apprentice.

The last of Bob Hope's big-budget, big-studio burlesques is a lumbering vehicle which wastes its star cast and mistimes its laughs.

w Hal Kanter, Edmund Hartmann *d* Norman Z. McLeod *ph* Lionel Lindon *m* Lynn Murray

Bob Hope, Joan Fontaine (an unhappy comedy foil), Basil Rathbone, Vincent Price, Audrey Dalton, Hugh Marlowe, John Carradine, Primo Carnera, Arnold Moss, Lon Chaney Jnr

Casbah
US 1948 94m bw
Universal (Erik Charell)

Remake of *Algiers* (qv) with songs added. Not too bad in the circumstances, but a wholly artificial exercise, and another version was really not needed. The sets seem overlit and claustrophobic.

w (not credited) *d* John Berry *ph* Irving Glassberg *m* Harold Arlen

Tony Martin, Yvonne de Carlo, Marta Toren, *Peter Lorre,* Hugo Haas

AAN: song 'For Every Man There's a Woman' (*m* Harold Arlen, *ly* Leo Robin)

The Case against Brooklyn
US 1958 81m bw

An undercover cop smashes a gambling syndicate. Competent second feature treatment of a story we have heard somewhere before. Darren McGavin, Marrie Hayes, Warren Stevens, Emile Meyer, Nestor Paiva. Written by Raymond T. Marcus; directed by Paul Wendkos; for Charles H. Schneer/ Columbia.

'Is she an unfit mother?'
The Case against Mrs Ames
US 1936 85m bw
Paramount (Walter Wanger)

The prosecutor in a murder case is convinced of the defendant's innocence.
Tired rehash of a familiar theme.

w Gene Towne, Graham Baker *d* William A. Seiter *ph* Lucien Andriot *m* Gerard Carbonara

Madeleine Carroll, George Brent, Arthur Treacher, Alan Baxter, Beulah Bondi, Alan Mowbray, Esther Dale, Ed Brophy

A Case for P.C.49
GB 1950 80m bw

A police constable solves a millionaire's murder. Incompetent and virtually unwatchable transcription of a juvenile tv series. Brian Reece, Joy Shelton, Christine Norden, Leslie Bradley, Gordon McLeod. Written by Alan Stranks and Vernon Harris from their series; directed by Francis Searle; for Hammer.

The Case of Charles Peace
GB 1949 88m bw

The story of a burglar and murderer of the 1870s whose career caught the public fancy. Antediluvian and largely fictitious treatment of a Victorian *cause célèbre*. Michael Martin Harvey, Chili Bouchier, Valentine Dyall, Bruce Belfrage, Ronald Adam. Written by Doris Davison and Norman Lee; directed by Norman Lee; for John Argyle.

The Case of Sergeant Grischa
US 1930 82m bw

A Russian no-good escapes from a German prison camp and after many adventures is shot as a spy. Oddball entertainment to come from Hollywood at any time, this seems to have no intent to please. Chester Morris, Betty Compson, Alec B. Francis, Gustav Von Seyffertitz, Jean Hersholt, Leyland Hodgson. From the story by Arnold Zweig; directed by Herbert Brenon; for RKO. 'No sympathy, no fan appeal and no entertainment. Can only be exploited as "a fine production" or "a new era in pictures".'—*Variety*

The Case of the Black Cat
US 1936 66m bw

An old man is murdered after changing his will: Perry Mason investigates. One of the better tales of the lawyer sleuth, here impersonated by Ricardo Cortez; with Harry Davenport, June Travis, Jane Bryan. Written by F. Hugh Herbert; directed by William McGann; for Warner.

The Case of the Black Parrot
US 1941 60m bw

Was it the butler who murdered to steal a case of diamonds? This sounds like a Perry Mason but is not; William Lundigan stars as a reporter who solves the puzzle; with Maris Wrixon, Eddie Foy Jnr, Paul Cavanagh. Written by Robert E. Kent, from a play by Burton Stevenson; directed by Noel Smith; for Warner.

The Case of the Curious Bride
US 1935 80m bw

Perry Mason helps a woman who is being blackmailed by her 'dead' husband. Smoothish mystery, with Warren William, Margaret Lindsay, Donald Woods, Claire Dodd, Allen Jenkins and—briefly—Errol Flynn. Written by Tom Reed, from an Erle Stanley Gardner original; directed by Michael Curtiz; for Warner.

The Case of the Frightened Lady
GB 1940 81m bw

A dowager knows that her son is mad and tries to prevent him from strangling his cousin. Quite a lively suspenser of its time. Marius Goring, Penelope Dudley Ward, Helen Haye, Patrick Barr, Felix Aylmer. Written by Edward Dryhurst, from the novel by Edgar Wallace; directed by George King; for Pennant. A previous version was released in 1932 as *The Frightened Lady* (qv).

The Case of the Howling Dog
US 1934 75m bw

Two men claim the same woman as their wife. Adequate Perry Mason mystery. Warren William, Mary Astor, Allen Jenkins, Grant Mitchell, Helen Twelvetrees. Written by Ben Markson, from an Erle Stanley Gardner original; directed by Alan Crosland; for Warner.

The Case of the Lucky Legs
US 1935 77m bw

Perry Mason chases a beauty contest promoter who skips town with the winnings. Fair light-hearted mystery, with Warren William as a somewhat dissipated sleuth; also Genevieve Tobin, Allen Jenkins, Patricia Ellis, Lyle Talbot, Barton Maclane. Written by Ben Markson and Brown Holmes, from an Erle Stanley Gardner original; directed by Archie Mayo; for Warner.

The Case of the Stuttering Bishop
US 1937 70m bw

Perry Mason investigates an heiress who may be an impostor. Thin mystery with another different star in the lead: Donald Woods. Also Ann Dvorak, Anne Nagel, Linda Perry. Written by Don Ryan and Kenneth Gamet, from an Erle Stanley Gardner original; directed by William Clemens; for Warner.

The Case of the Velvet Claws
US 1936 63m bw

Perry Mason's honeymoon is postponed when he finds himself on a murder charge. Moderate light-hearted mystery, but they should have awarded prizes to anyone who could explain the title. Warren William, Claire Dodd, Wini Shaw, Gordon Elliott, Addison Richards. Written by Tom Reed, from an Erle Stanley Gardner original; directed by William Clemens; for Warner.

Casey's Shadow
US 1978 116m Metrocolor Panavision
Columbia / Ray Stark (Michael Levee)

A Cajun family in New Mexico breeds a champion horse which wins the annual race. Shades of *Maryland*: an old-fashioned movie of the kind which absolutely nobody should want to revive, at least not so ineptly or at such length.

w Carol Sobieski, *story* Ruidoso by John McPhee *d* Martin Ritt *ph* John A. Alonzo *m* Patrick Williams

Walter Matthau, Alexis Smith, Robert Webber, Murray Hamilton, Andrew A. Rubin, Stephan Burns, Michael Hershewe

Cash McCall
US 1960 102m Technicolor
Warner (Henry Blanke)

A Napoleon of the stock market gets into trouble for the first time when love interferes with business.
Slightly unusual comedy drama, quite sharply made and played, but not adding up to much.

w Lenore Coffee, Marion Hargrove, *novel* Cameron Hawley *d* Joseph Pevney *ph* George Folsey *m* Max Steiner

James Garner, Natalie Wood, Nina Foch, Dean Jagger, E. G. Marshall, Henry Jones, Otto Kruger, Roland Winters

Cash on Demand*
GB 1963 86m bw
Columbia / Woodpecker / Hammer (Michael Carreras)

A fussy bank manager outwits a classy robber. Quietly effective suspenser with an admirable middle-aged cast and no love interest.

w Lewis Greifer, David T. Chantler, from Jacques Gillies' TV play *d* Quentin Lawrence *ph* Arthur Grant *m* Wilfred Josephs

Peter Cushing, André Morell, Richard Vernon, Norman Bird, Edith Sharpe

The Casino Murder Case
US 1935 85m bw

Philo Vance solves a murder in a family of neurotics. Rather heavy-going detection. Paul Lukas, Rosalind Russell, Eric Blore, Donald Cook, Louise Fazenda, Ted Healy, Isabel Jewell, Leo G. Carroll. Written by Florence Ryerson and Edgar Allen Woolf, from an S. S. Van Dine original; directed by Edwin Marin; for MGM.

Casino Royale
GB 1967 130m Technicolor Panavision
Columbia / Famous Artists (Charles K. Feldman, Jerry Bresler)

The heads of the allied spy forces call Sir James Bond out of retirement to fight the power of *SMERSH*.
Woeful all-star kaleidoscope, a way-out spoof which generates far fewer laughs than the original. One of the most shameless wastes of time and talent in screen history.

w Wolf Mankowitz, John Law, Michael Sayers, *novel* Ian Fleming *d* John Huston, Ken Hughes, Val Guest, Robert Parrish, Joe McGrath, Richard Talmadge *ph* Jack Hildyard *m* Burt Bacharach *pd* Michael Stringer

David Niven, Deborah Kerr, Orson Welles, Peter Sellers, Ursula Andress, Woody Allen, William Holden, Charles Boyer, John Huston, Joanna Pettet, Daliah Lavi, Kurt Kasznar, Jacqueline Bisset, Derek Nimmo, George Raft, Ronnie Corbett, Peter O'Toole, Jean-Paul Belmondo, Geoffrey Bayldon, Duncan Macrae

'One of those wild wacky extravaganzas in which the audience is expected to have a great time because everybody making the film did. It seldom works out that way, and certainly doesn't here.'—*John Russell Taylor*

'The dialogue is witless and unhampered by taste, and the interminable finale is a collection of clichés in a brawl involving the cavalry, parachuted Indians, split-second appearances by George Raft and Jean-Paul Belmondo, every variety of mayhem, and Woody Allen burping radiation as a walking atom bomb.'—*Judith Crist*

'The worst film I ever enjoyed.'—*Donald Zec*

AAN: song 'The Look of Love' (*m* Burt Bacharach, *ly* Hal David)

Casque d'Or***
France 1952 96m bw
Speva / Paris (Robert Hakim)
aka: *Golden Marie*

1898. In the Paris slums, an Apache finds passionate love but is executed for murder.
A tragic romance which on its first release seemed bathed in a golden glow and is certainly an impeccable piece of film-making.

w Jacques Becker, Jacques Companeez *d Jacques Becker ph Robert Le Fèbvre* *m* Georges Van Parys

Simone Signoret, Serge Reggiani, Claude Dauphin, Raymond Bussières, Gaston Modot

'Takes its place alongside *Le Jour Se Lève* among the masterpieces of the French cinema.'—*Karel Reisz*

'A screen alive with sensuousness and luminous figures.'—*Dilys Powell*

Cass Timberlane*
US 1947 119m bw
MGM (Arthur Hornblow Jnr)

A judge marries a working class girl, who is unsettled at first but finally comes to realize her good fortune.
Solid drama with an understanding star performance and good production values.

w Donald Ogden Stewart, *novel* Sinclair Lewis *d* George Sidney *ph* Robert Planck *m* Roy Webb

Spencer Tracy, Lana Turner, Zachary Scott, Tom Drake, Mary Astor, Albert Dekker, Selena Royle, Josephine Hutchinson, Margaret Lindsay

The Cassandra Crossing
GB / Italy / West Germany 1976 129m Technicolor Panavision
AGF / CCC / International Cine (Lew Grade, Carlo Ponti)

A terrorist carrying a deadly plague virus boards a transcontinental train.
Disaster spectacular with a number of fashionable interests but no observable film-making technique.

w Tom Mankiewicz, Robert Katz, George Pan Cosmatos *d* George Pan Cosmatos *ph* Ennio Guarnieri *m* Jerry Goldsmith *pd* Aurelio Crugnola

Sophia Loren, Richard Harris, Ava Gardner, Burt Lancaster, Martin Sheen, Ingrid Thulin, Lee Strasberg, John Phillip Law, Lionel Stander, Ann Turkel, O. J. Simpson, Alida Valli

Cast a Dark Shadow*
GB 1955 82m bw
Frobisher / Daniel M. Angel (Herbert Mason)

A wife-murderer marries an ex-barmaid and tries again.
Unambitious but enjoyable melodrama, well acted though with directorial opportunities missed.

w John Cresswell, *play* Murder Mistaken by Janet Green *d* Lewis Gilbert *ph* Jack Asher *m* Antony Hopkins

Dirk Bogarde, *Margaret Lockwood*, Kay Walsh, Kathleen Harrison, Robert Flemyng, Mona Washbourne, Walter Hudd

'Outnumbered—unarmed—unprepared—they hurled back their answer in flesh and flame!'

Cast a Giant Shadow*
US 1966 141m De Luxe Panavision
UA / Mirisch / Llenroc / Batjac (Melville Shavelson)

An American military lawyer and ex-colonel goes to Israel in 1947 to help in the fight against the Arabs.
Spectacular war biopic with all concerned in good form but lacking the clarity and narrative control of a real smash.

w Melville Shavelson, from Ted Berkman's biography of Col. David Marcus *d* Melville Shavelson *ph Aldo Tonti* *m* Elmer Bernstein *pd* Michael Stringer

Kirk Douglas, Angie Dickinson, Senta Berger, Luther Adler, Stathis Giallelis, Chaim Topol, John Wayne, Frank Sinatra, Yul Brynner, James Donald, Gordon Jackson, Michael Hordern, Gary Merrill, Allan Cuthbertson, Jeremy Kemp

Cast a Long Shadow
US 1959 82m colour

A hard-drinking drifter thinks he may be the illegitimate son of a dead cattle baron. Would-be psychological western with not enough going for it. Audie Murphy, John Dehner, Terry Moore, James Best, Denver Pyle. Written by Martin H. Goldsmith and John McGreevey, from the novel by Wayne D. Overholser; directed by Thomas Carr; for Mirisch / UA.

Castaway
GB 1986 118m Fujicolor

A bored London girl answers an ad placed by a man who wants a wife to take to a tropical island for a year; but he expects sex and she doesn't. Extended absurdity uncharacteristic of its director. Oliver Reed, Amanda Donohue, Georgina Hale. Written by Allan Scott from the book by Lucy Irvine; directed by Nicolas Roeg; photogaphed by Harvey Harrison; for Rick McCallum/United British Artists/Cannon. 'Prospects are good for those interested in beautiful scenery and naked bodies.'—*Daily Variety*

The Castaway Cowboy*
US 1974 91m Technicolor
Walt Disney (Ron Miller, Winston Hibler)

In 1850, a Shanghaied sailor on Hawaii helps a lady potato farmer to turn her land into a cattle ranch.
Unexciting and unexceptional family fare.

w Don Tait *d* Vincent McEveety *ph* Andrew Jackson *m* Robert F. Brunner

James Garner, Vera Miles, Robert Culp, Eric Shea, Elizabeth Smith

The Castle
West Germany 1969 93m colour

A surveyor is summoned to a remote castle but prevented by the villagers from getting there. Attempt, partly successful, to film an unfinished Kafka obscurity. Marks all round for trying. Maximilian Schell, Cordula Trantow, Trudik Daniel, Franz Misar. Written and directed by Rudolf Noelte; for Maximilian Schell/Alfa/Glarus/Rudolf Noelte.

Castle in the Air
GB 1952 90m bw

A nobleman fails to turn his castle into a hotel but hopes to sell it to the Coal Board. Topical comedy which sparkled rather more on the stage. David Tomlinson, Helen Cherry, Margaret Rutherford, Barbara Kelly, A. E. Matthews, Pat Dainton, Brian Oulton, Ewan Roberts. Written by Alan Melville and Edward Dryhurst from the play by Alan Melville; directed by Henry Cass; for Hallmark/ABP.

Castle in the Desert*
US 1942 62m bw

Murders take place at the remote castle of an eccentric millionaire. One of the sharpest Charlie Chan mysteries, with a lively plot and some good lines. Sidney Toler, Arleen Whelan, Richard Derr, Douglass Dumbrille, Henry Daniell, Steve Geray, Sen Yung, Ethel Griffies, Milton Parsons. Written by John Larkin; directed by Harry Lachman; for TCF.

'A one-eyed major and his oddball heroes fight a twentieth-century war in a tenth-century castle!'

Castle Keep*
US 1969 107m Technicolor Panavision
Columbia / Filmways (Martin Ransohoff, John Calley)

During World War II seven battle-weary American soldiers occupy a 10th-century castle filled with art treasures, then die defending it. Or are they dead all the time? The film version of this fantastic novel never seems quite sure, and the uncertainty finally deadens it despite careful work all round.

w Daniel Taradash, David Rayfiel, *novel* William Eastlake *d* Sydney Pollack *ph* Henri Decaë *m* Michel Legrand

Burt Lancaster, Peter Falk, Jean Pierre Aumont, Patrick O'Neal, Al Freeman Jnr, Scott Wilson, Tony Bill, Bruce Dern, Astrid Heeren

Castle of Evil
US 1966 81m Eastmancolor

A disfigured industrialist summons six people to a remote Caribbean island for the reading of his will. Tedious variation on *Ten Little Niggers* and *The Cat and the Canary*, with horror asides and the lowest of budgets. Virginia Mayo, Scott Brady, David Brian, Lisa Gaye, Hugh Marlowe. Written by Charles A. Wallace; directed by Francis D. Lyon; for NTA.

Castle of Fu Manchu
West Germany / Spain / Italy / GB 1968 92m Eastmancolor

The yellow peril wrecks an ocean-going liner by turning water into ice, and keeps the inventor a prisoner. Extraordinarily tatty entry in a series which started off well. (See *Fu Manchu* for list.) Christopher Lee, Richard Greene, Howard Marion Crawford, Gunther Stoll, Maria Perschy. Written by Harry Alan Towers (Peter Welbeck); directed by Jesus Franco; for Terra Finkunst / Balcazar / Italian International / Towers of London.

Castle on the Hudson*
US 1940 77m bw
Warner (Sam Bischoff)
GB title: *Years without Days*

A hardened criminal is not helped by his years in prison.
Adequate, gloomy remake of *Twenty Thousand Years in Sing Sing*.

w Seton I. Miller, Brown Holmes, Courtney Terrett *d* Anatole Litvak *ph* Arthur Edeson *m* Adolph Deutsch

John Garfield, Pat O'Brien, Ann Sheridan, Burgess Meredith, Jerome Cowan, Henry O'Neill, Guinn Williams, John Litel

The Cat*
France 1973 88m colour

After twenty-five years of marriage an embittered trapeze star and her husband simply don't talk to each other. Absorbing drama for two characters, brilliantly acted by Jean Gabin and Simone Signoret, but with a somewhat unsatisfactory conclusion. Written by Pascal Jardin; directed by Pierre Granier-Deferre; for Raymond Danon.

Cat and Mouse*
GB 1958 79m bw
(Eros) Anvil (Paul Rotha)

The daughter of a man executed for murder is threatened by criminals seeking hidden loot. Interesting rather than exciting second feature thriller directed by a documentary maker.

wd Paul Rotha, *novel* Michael Halliday *ph* Wolfgang Suschitsky

Lee Patterson, Ann Sears, Hilton Edwards, Victor Maddern, George Rose, Roddy McMillan

The Cat and the Canary***
US 1927 84m (24 fps) bw silent
Universal

Greedy relatives assemble in an old house to hear an eccentric's will, and a young girl's sanity is threatened.
Archetypal spooky house comedy horror, here given an immensely stylish production which influenced Hollywood through the thirties and was spoofed in *The Old Dark House*.

w Alfred Cohn, Robert F. Hill, play John Willard d Paul Leni ph Gilbert Warrenton ad Charles D. Hall

Creighton Hale, Laura La Plante, Forrest Stanley, Tully Marshall, Flora Finch, Gertrude Astor, Arthur Carewe

The Cat and the Canary***
US 1939 72m bw
Paramount (Arthur Hornblow Jnr)

A superbly staged remake, briskly paced, perfectly cast and lusciously photographed. The comedy-thriller par excellence, with Bob Hope fresh and sympathetic in his first big star part.

w Walter de Leon, Lynn Starling d Elliott Nugent ph Charles Lang m Dr Ernst Toch ad Hans Dreier, Robert Usher

Bob Hope (Wally Campbell), *Paulette Goddard* (Joyce Norman), *Gale Sondergaard* (Miss Lu), Douglass Montgomery (Charlie Wilder), John Beal (Fred Blythe), *George Zucco* (Lawyer Crosby), *Nydia Westman* (Cicily), *Elizabeth Patterson* (Aunt Susan), John Wray (Hendricks)

CICILY: 'Do you believe people come back from the dead?'
WALLY: 'You mean like republicans?'

CICILY: 'Don't these big empty houses scare you?'
WALLY: 'Not me, I was in vaudeville.'

WALLY: 'I get goose pimples. Even my goose pimples have goose pimples'.

'The objective is carried out briskly and to our complete satisfaction.'—*New York Times*

'A top programmer for upper-bracket bookings in the keys, and will hit a consistent stride down the line in the subsequents.'—*Variety*

'Beautifully shot, intelligently constructed.'—*Peter John Dyer, 1966*

The Cat and the Canary
GB 1979 98m Technicolor
Gala / Grenadier (Richard Gordon)

An overpoweringly cast but half-heartedly scripted remake of the above, which after a spirited beginning bores more than it thrills.

wd Radley Metzger *ph* Alex Thomson *m* Steven Cagan

Honor Blackman, Michael Callan, Edward Fox, Wendy Hiller, Beatrix Lehmann, Olivia Hussey, Daniel Massey, Carol Lynley, Peter McEnery, Wilfrid Hyde-White

'So mechanically are characters shunted through the indistinguishable rooms and corridors that one is surprised not to see the parquet marked off in neat little squares, as on a Cluedo board.'—*Gilbert Adair, MFB*

The Cat and the Fiddle
US 1933 90m bw (colour sequence)

In a taxi in Brussels, a leading lady of Broadway musicals meets a European composer. Very lightweight musical comedy. Jeanette MacDonald, Ramon Novarro, Charles Butterworth, Frank Morgan, Jean Hersholt, Vivienne Segal, Henry Armetta. Written by Sam and Bella Spewack, from the show by Jerome Kern and Otto Harbach; directed by William K. Howard; for MGM.

'The only thing remaining of merit is the music.'—*Variety*

Cat Ballou**
US 1965 96m Technicolor
Columbia (Harold Hecht)

Young Catherine Ballou hires a drunken gunfighter to protect her father from a vicious gunman, but despite her efforts he is shot, so she turns outlaw.
Sometimes lively, sometimes somnolent western spoof which considering the talent involved should have been funnier than it is. The linking ballad helps.

w Walter Newman, Frank R. Pierson, *novel* Roy Chanslor *d* Eliot Silverstein *ph* Jack Marta *m* Frank de Vol

Jane Fonda, *Lee Marvin*, Michael Callan, Dwayne Hickman, Nat King Cole, Stubby Kaye, Tom Nardini, John Marley, Reginald Denny

'Uneven, lumpy, coy and obvious.'—*Pauline Kael*

AA: Lee Marvin
AAN: Walter Newman, Frank R. Pierson; Frank de Vol; song 'The Ballad of Cat Ballou' (*m* Jerry Livingston, *ly* Mack David)

The Cat Creeps*
US 1930 71m bw

A sound remake of the 1927 *Cat and the Canary*. Not too bad on its own account. Helen Twelvetrees, Raymond Hackett, Neil Hamilton, Jean Hersholt, Montagu Love, Blanche Friderici, Elisabeth Patterson, Theodore Von Eltz, Lilyan Tashman, Lawrence Grant. Written by Gladys Lehman and William Hurlbut; directed by Rupert Julian; for Universal.

THE CAT AND THE CANARY. For once Bob Hope (with Paulette Goddard) seems lost for a wisecrack when faced by the archetypal menace of George Zucco and Gale Sondergaard.

The Cat Creeps
US 1946 58m bw

A reporter and photographer solve a murder and uncover missing millions. Terrible programme filler, nothing to do with *The Cat and the Canary*. Noah Beery Jnr, Lois Collier, Paul Kelly, Douglass Dumbrille, Rose Hobart, Jonathan Hale. Written by Edward Dein and Jerry Warner; directed by Erle C. Kenton; for Universal.

The Cat from Outer Space
US 1978 103m Technicolor
Walt Disney Productions (Ron Miller)

A superintelligent extraterrestrial cat is forced to land on earth for running repairs.
Fairly modest studio offering which pleased its intended market but could have been sharper.

w Ted Key *d* Norman Tokar *ph* Charles F. Wheeler *m* Lalo Schifrin *sp* Eustace Lycett, Art Cruickshank, Danny Dee

Ken Berry, Roddy McDowall, Sandy Duncan, Harry Morgan, McLean Stevenson, Jesse White, Alan Young, Hans Conried

Cat o'Nine Tails
Italy / France / Germany 1971 112m Techniscope

A blind reporter overhears an industrial espionage plot that turns into murder. Smart surface mechanics camouflage poor storytelling. Karl Malden, James Franciscus, Catherine Spaak. Written and directed by Dario Argento; for Spettacoli / Mondial / Terra / Labrador.

Cat on a Hot Tin Roof**
US 1958 108m Metrocolor
MGM / Avon (Lawrence Weingarten)

A rich plantation owner, dying of cancer, finds his two sons unsatisfactory: one is a conniver, the other a neurotic who refuses to sleep with his wife.
Slightly bowdlerized version of Tennessee Williams' most straightforward melodrama, watchable for the acting but still basically a theatrical experience.

w Richard Brooks, James Poe *d* Richard Brooks *ph* William Daniels *m* uncredited

Paul Newman, Burl Ives, Elizabeth Taylor, Jack Carson, Judith Anderson, Madeleine Sherwood, Larry Gates

BIG DADDY: 'Truth is pain and sweat and paying bills and making love to a woman that you don't love any more. Truth is dreams that don't come true and nobody prints your name in the paper until you die.'

MAGGIE: 'Win what? What is the victory of a cat on a hot tin roof?'
BRICK: 'Just staying on it, I guess.'

AAN: best picture; Richard Brooks, James Poe; Richard Brooks (as director); William Daniels; Paul Newman; Elizabeth Taylor

'Kiss me and I'll claw you to death!'

Cat People**
US 1942 73m bw
RKO (*Val Lewton*)

A beautiful Yugoslavian girl believes she can turn into a panther; before she is found mysteriously dead, several of her acquaintances are attacked by such a beast.
The first of Lewton's famous horror series for RKO is a slow starter but has some notable suspense sequences. It was also the first monster film to refrain from showing its monster.

w De Witt Bodeen *d Jacques Tourneur* *ph* Nicholas Musuraca *m* Roy Webb

Simone Simon, Kent Smith, Tom Conway, Jane Randolph, Jack Holt

'(Lewton) revolutionized scare movies with suggestion, imaginative sound effects and camera angles, leaving everything to the fear-filled imagination.'—*Pauline Kael, 1968*

† *Curse of the Cat People* (qv) was a very unrelated sequel.

Cat People
US 1982 118m Technicolor
Universal (Charles Fries)

A kinky version of the 1942 horrorpic. The feline lady now has an incestuous relationship with her brother, only changes after sex, and then must kill to become human again. (It is therefore safe to mate only with relatives.) One presumes that among the eroticism and bloodlust a statement is being made, but it is never evident.

w Alan Ormsby *d* Paul Schraeder *ph* John Bailey *m* Giorgio Moroder *ed* Jacqueline Cambas *sp* Tom Burman, Albert Whitlock *visual consultant* Ferdinando Scarfiotti

Nastassja Kinski, Malcolm McDowell, John Heard, Annette O'Toole, Ruby Dee, Ed Begley Jnr

'The final impression is of a phantasmagoric indulgence in sound and vision by a film-maker who fears sex and is excited by violence.'—*Sunday Times*

'The hobgoblins of an actual horror movie aren't easily translatable into the demons that haunt a Schrader hero on his way to a religious transcendence that is also a renunciation.'—*Richard Combs, MFB*

The Cat That Hated People**
US 1948 7m Technicolor

A weary Manhattan cat rockets to the moon but finds it even noisier and is glad to come home. Violent but dazzlingly inventive cartoon from this madcap director; a little classic of its kind. Written by Heck Allen; directed by *Tex Avery*; for MGM.

Cat Women of the Moon
US 1953 63m bw 3D

Five American astronauts find the moon inhabited solely by ravenous cat women. One of the top claimants to film history's booby prize, along with such other space fiction entrants as *Fire Maidens from Outer Space*, *Planet Seven from Outer Space* and *Santa Claus Conquers the Martians*. It has more than a chance. Sonny Tufts, Victor Jory, Marie Windsor, William Phipps, Douglas Fowley. Written by Roy Hamilton; directed by Arthur Hilton; for Three Dimensional Pictures. (Aka: *Rocket to the Moon*.)

Catacombs
GB 1964 90m bw

A rich woman is murdered by her husband and her male secretary. Involved melodrama with rather too many twists. Gary Merrill, Neil McCallum, Georgina Cookson, Jane Merrow, Rachel Thomas, Jack Train. Written by Dan Mainwaring; directed by Gordon Hessler; for Parroch / McCallum.

Catch As Catch Can
GB 1937 71m bw

Crooks after a valuable diamond converge on a transatlantic liner. Modest comedy-thriller. James Mason, Viki Dobson, Eddie Pola, Finlay Currie. Written by Richard Llewellyn; directed by Roy Kellino; for Fox British. (Aka: *Atlantic Episode*.)

Catch Me a Spy
GB 1971 94m Technicolor
Rank / Ludgate / Capitol / Films de la Pleiade (Steven Pallos)

A British agent smuggling Russian manuscripts into England falls for the wife of a Russian spy and finally gets his money as well. Complex, patchy comedy thriller with dispirited action scenes in Bucharest and Scotland. Technical credits rather dim.

w Dick Clement, Ian La Frenais, *novel* George Marton, Tibor Meray *d* Dick Clement *ph* Christopher Challis *m* Claude Bolling

Kirk Douglas, Trevor Howard, Tom Courtenay, Marlene Jobert, Patrick Mower, Bernadette Lafont, Bernard Blier

Catch 22*
US 1970 122m Technicolor Panavision
Paramount / Filmways (John Calley, Martin Ransohoff)

At a US Air Force base in the Mediterranean during World War II, one by one the officers are distressingly killed; a survivor paddles towards neutral Sweden.
Intensely black comedy, more so than *M*A*S*H* and less funny, effectively mordant in places but too grisly and missing several tricks.

w Buck Henry, *novel* Joseph Heller *d* Mike Nichols *ph* David Watkin *m* none *pd* Richard Sylbert

Alan Arkin, Martin Balsam, Richard Benjamin, Art Garfunkel, Jack Gilford, Buck Henry, Bob Newhart, Anthony Perkins, Paula Prentiss, Jon Voight, Martin Sheen, Orson Welles

'There are startling effects and good revue touches here and there, but the picture keeps going on and on, as if it were determined to impress us.'—*New Yorker, 1977*

'As hot and heavy as the original was cool and light.'—*Richard Schickel*

'It goes on so long that it cancels itself out, even out of people's memories; it was long awaited and then forgotten almost instantly.'—*Pauline Kael*

'Dr Strangelove out of Alice in Wonderland.'—*Daily Mail*

Catch Us If You Can
GB 1965 91m bw
Anglo Amalgamated / Bruton (David Deutsch)
US title: *Having a Wild Weekend*

Freelance stuntmen have various adventures in the west of England.
The first film of a pretentious director is a bright but wearisomely high-spirited imitation of *A Hard Day's Night*.

w Peter Nichols *d* John Boorman *ph Manny Wynn* *m* Dave Clark

The Dave Clark Five, Barbara Ferris, David Lodge, Robin Bailey, Yootha Joyce

The Catered Affair*
US 1956 93m bw
MGM (Sam Zimbalist)
GB title: *Wedding Breakfast*

When the daughter of a New York taxi driver gets married, her mother insists on a bigger function than they can afford.
Rather heavy-going comedy with amusing dialogue, from the period when Hollywood was seizing on TV plays like *Marty* and *Twelve Angry Men*.

w Gore Vidal, TV play Paddy Chayevsky *d* Richard Brooks *ph* John Alton *m* André Previn

Bette Davis, Ernest Borgnine, Debbie Reynolds, Barry Fitzgerald, Rod Taylor, Robert Simon, Madge Kennedy, Dorothy Stickney

Catherine the Great*
GB 1934 93m bw
Alexander Korda

How Catherine married the mad prince and slowly conquered the Russian court.
Dated but well acted and written account, sober by comparison with *The Scarlet Empress* which came out at the same time.

w Lajos Biro, Arthur Wimperis, Marjorie Deans, *play* The Czarina by Melchior Lengyel, Lajos Biro *d* Paul Czinner *ph* Georges Périnal *md* Muir Matheson

Elisabeth Bergner, Douglas Fairbanks Jnr, Flora Robson, Gerald du Maurier, Irene Vanbrugh, Griffith Jones, Joan Gardner, Diana Napier

'It rates no raves but is a good piece of merchandise.'—*Variety*

† The style is typified by a speech given to Grand Duke Peter: 'If she wasn't on the throne she'd be on the street.'

Catlow*
GB 1971 101m Metrocolor
MGM / Euan Lloyd

A likeable outlaw tries to avoid problems while recovering his hidden gold.
Light-hearted, cheerfully cast, fast-moving, Spanish-located western.

w Scot Finch, J. J. Griffith, *novel* Louis L'Amour *d* Sam Wanamaker *ph* Ted Scaife *m* Roy Budd

Yul Brynner, Leonard Nimoy, Richard Crenna, Daliah Lavi, Jo Ann Pflug, Jeff Corey, Bessie Love, David Ladd

Catman of Paris
US 1946 63m bw

An amnesia victim may be the mad killer who prowls the boulevards. Poverty Row thriller with a few sharp moments. Carl Esmond, Lenore Aubert, Adele Mara, Douglass Dumbrille, Gerald Mohr, Fritz Feld. Written by Sherman L. Lowe; directed by Lesley Selander; for Marek M. Libkov / Republic. 'Settings have solid mahogany look but the script has only a literate veneer.'—*Variety*

Cat's Eye
US 1985 93m Technicolor
Famous Films / Dino de Laurentiis (Martha J. Schumacher)

Three semi-horror stories about cats.
This poorly-linked omnibus is weak in every department.

w Stephen King *d* Lewis Teague *ph* Jack Cardiff *m* Alan Silvestri *pd* Giorgio Postiglione

Drew Barrymore, James Woods, Alan King, Kenneth McMillan, Robert Hays, Candy Clark, James Naughton

'It creeps in on foggy feet.'—*Variety*

The Cat's Paw*
US 1936 101m bw
Harold Lloyd

The son of a Chinese missionary returns home and finds himself in the middle of a Tong war. Very moderate star comedy from the time when he was considering himself a character comedian rather than a slapstick ace.
w Harold Lloyd, Sam Taylor, *story* Clarence Budington Kelland *d* Sam Taylor

Harold Lloyd, George Barbier, Una Merkel, Nat Pendleton, Grant Mitchell, Vince Barnett

'The picture gets its laughs all right, but it approaches them at a crawl.'—*Variety*

Cattle Annie and Little Britches
US 1980 98m CFI colour
Hemdale / UATC (David Korda)

In 1893, two girls head west in search of adventure.
Rather winsome family western, with too little real action and too much romping about.
w Robert Ward, from his novel *d* Lamont Johnson *ph* Larry Pizer *m* Sanh Berti, Tom Slocum

Burt Lancaster, John Savage, Rod Steiger, Diane Lane, Amanda Plummer, Scott Glenn, Steven Ford

Cattle Drive
US 1951 78m Technicolor

The spoiled teenage son of a magnate finds humanity and friendship with a cowhand during a cattle drive. *Captains Courageous* out west, not badly done. Joel McCrea, Dean Stockwell, Chill Wills, Leon Ames, Bob Steele. Written by Jack Natteford and Lillie Hayward; directed by Kurt Neumann; for Aaron Rosenberg / Universal-International.

Cattle Empire
US 1958 82m De Luxe Cinemascope

A trail boss out of prison gets a new assignment and signs up helpers who had previously made life difficult for him. Fair general western, entirely dependent on its star. Joel McCrea, Gloria Talbott, Don Haggerty, Phyllis Coates, Paul Brinegar. Written by Endre Boehm and Eric Norden; directed by Charles Marquis Warren; for TCF.

Cattle King
US 1963 90m Metrocolor
MGM / Missouri (Nat Holt)
GB title: *Guns of Wyoming*

A big rancher opposes a cattle trail and starts a range war.
Moderately expert but very familiar star western.
w Thomas Thompson *d* Tay Garnett *ph* William E. Snyder *m* Paul Sawtell

Robert Taylor, Joan Caulfield, Robert Middleton, Robert Loggia, Larry Gates, Malcolm Atterbury

Cattle Queen of Montana
US 1954 88m Technicolor

A tough woman inherits her father's rangeland and resists cattle rustlers. A western which runs in predictable grooves, and could have done with more vigour. Barbara Stanwyck, Ronald Reagan, Gene Evans, Lance Fuller, Anthony Caruso, Jack Elam. Written by Robert Blees and Howard Estabrook; directed by Allan Dwan; for RKO / Benedict Bogeaus.

Cattle Town
US 1952 71m bw

After the Civil War, returning ranch owners find their land appropriated by squatters. Reach-me-down western programmer. Dennis Morgan, Amanda Blake, Rita Moreno, Ray Teal, Philip Carey. Written by Tom Blackburn; directed by Noel Smith; for Warner.

Caught!
US 1931 71m bw

A US cavalry officer discovers that Calamity Jane is his mother. Curious mother-love western. Richard Arlen, Louise Dresser, Frances Dee. Written by Agnes Brand Leahy, Keane Thompson, Sam and Bella Spewack; directed by Edward Sloman; for Paramount.

Caught*
US 1948 88m bw
Enterprise (Wolfgang Reinhardt)

The ill-treated wife of a vicious millionaire leaves him for a doctor, but finds she is to have the millionaire's baby.
Pretentious *film noir*, rather typical of its time, with much talent squandered on a very boring plot.
w Arthur Laurents, *novel* Wild Calendar by Libbie Block *d Max Ophuls ph Lee Garmes m* Frederick Hollander

James Mason (the doctor), Robert Ryan (the millionaire), Barbara Bel Geddes, Natalie Schaefer, Curt Bois

'Ophuls had suffered at Hughes' hands . . . had wasted time on worthless projects . . . and had been referred to as "the oaf". Laurents built the script on stories which Ophuls told him about Hughes, and on the accounts given by one of Hughes' girls.'—*Pauline Kael*

Caught in the Draft**
US 1941 82m bw
Paramount (B. G. De Sylva)

A nervous film star cannot avoid being drafted into the army.
Sprightly comedy from the star's best period, with gags and supporting cast well up to form.
w Harry Tugend *d* David Butler *ph* Karl Struss *m* Victor Young

Bob Hope, Lynne Overman, Dorothy Lamour, Clarence Kolb, Eddie Bracken, Paul Hurst, Irving Bacon

Caught Plastered
US 1931 68m bw

In helping an old lady save her drug store, two hams get mixed up with bootleggers. Tedious star farce. Bert Wheeler, Robert Woolsey, Dorothy Lee, Lucy Beaumont, Jason Robards. Written by Ralph Spence, Douglas MacLean; directed by William Seiter; for RKO. 'Best for combo and three-dayers.'—*Variety*.

Caught Short
US 1930 approx 75m bw

Feuding boarding house landladies play the stock market—and win. Lumbering comedy which marked the first big success for the team of Marie Dressler and Polly Moran; featuring Charles Morton, Anita Page. Written by Willard Mack and Robert Hopkins; directed by Charles Reisner; for Cosmopolitan / MGM. 'A gold mine . . . the apex of the career of this pair of sublimated film-makers . . . a box office smash for all classes anywhere.'—*Variety*
† A credit reads: Story suggested by Eddie Cantor's gag book.

Cause for Alarm*
US 1951 74m bw
MGM (Tom Lewis)

A housewife tries frantically to retrieve a posted letter containing manufactured evidence which may put her on a murder charge.
Minor-league suspenser, watchable but disappointingly handled.
w Mel Dinelli, Tom Lewis *d* Tay Garnett *ph* Joe Ruttenberg *m* André Previn

Loretta Young, Barry Sullivan, Bruce Cowling, Margalo Gillmore, Irving Bacon

'A love that suffered and rose triumphant above the crushing events of this modern age! The march of time measured by a mother's heart!'

Cavalcade**
US 1932 109m bw
Fox (Winfield Sheehan)

The story of an upper-class English family between the Boer War and World War I. Rather static version of the famous stage spectacular, very similar in setting and style to TV's later *Upstairs Downstairs*. Good performances, flat handling.
w Reginald Berkeley, *play Noel Coward d* Frank Lloyd *ph* Ernest Palmer *war scenes* William Cameron Menzies *ad* William Darling *m* Louis de Francesco

Clive Brook, Diana Wynyard, Ursula Jeans, Herbert Mundin, Una O'Connor, Irene Browne, Merle Tottenham, Beryl Mercer, Frank Lawton, Billy Bevan

'Dignified and beautiful spectacle that will demand respect.'—*Variety*

'If there is anything that moves the ordinary American to uncontrollable tears, it is the plight—the constant plight—of dear old England . . . a superlative newsreel, forcibly strengthened by factual scenes, good music, and wonderful photography.'—*Pare Lorentz*

'Greater even than *Birth of a Nation*!'—*Louella Parsons*

'An orgy of British self-congratulation.'—*Pauline Kael, 70s*

AA: best picture; Frank Lloyd; William Darling
AAN: Diana Wynyard

The Cave Man
US 1926 approx 78m at 24 fps bw silent

A bored socialite cuts a high denomination note in half, throws one half away, and offers riches to the first man to find it. Typical twenties comedy which seemed very modern at the time. Marie Prevost, Matt Moore, Phyllis Haver, Myrna Loy. Written by Darryl F. Zanuck; directed by Lewis Milestone; for Warner.

Cave of Outlaws
US 1951 76m Technicolor

After surviving a long prison term, a bandit returns to the caves where his partners hid their booty. Modest western with scenes shot in the Carlsbad Caverns. Macdonald Carey, Alexis Smith, Edgar Buchanan, Victor Jory, Hugh O'Brian, Houseley Stevenson. Written by Elizabeth Wilson; directed by William Castle; for Universal-International.

Caveman
US 1981 91m Technicolor

Adventures of a prehistoric man. Witless farrago of puns and farts on a lower level than Mel Brooks, if such a thing were possible. Ringo Starr, Dennis Quaid, Jack Gilford, Barbara Bach, Avery Schreiber. Written by Rudy de Luca and Carl Gottlieb; directed by Carl Gottlieb; for Laurence Turman, David Foster / UA. 'Too gross and leery for children and not nearly sprightly or sly enough for adults.'—*Daily Mail.* 'Worth about half an hour of anybody's time. Unfortunately it runs 97 minutes.'—*Guardian*

The Cavern
US / Italy 1966 96m bw

In the last days of World War II, six soldiers and a girl are trapped by aerial bombardment in a cave in the Italian mountains. Enervating psychological drama, glum to look at and listen to. John Saxon, Rosanna Schiaffino, Larry Hagman, Brian Aherne, Nino Castelnuovo. Written by Michael Pertwee and Jack Davis; directed and produced by Edgar G. Ulmer; for Ulmer / TCF.

Cease Fire
US 1985 97m Continental Color

Ex-Vietnam vets in Miami have trouble getting work and forgetting the past. Honest but predictable drama from behind the headlines. Don Johnson, Lisa Blount, Robert F. Lyons, Richard Chaves, Rick Richards. Written by George Fernandez from his play *Vietnam Trilogy*; directed by David Nutter; for Double Helix / Cineworld.

Ceiling Zero*
US 1935 95m bw
Warner / Cosmopolitan (Harry Joe Brown)

Amorous and airborne adventures of an irresponsible but brilliant civil airlines pilot.
Splendid star vehicle which turns maudlin in the last reel but until then provides crackling entertainment.

w Frank 'Spig' Wead, from his play *d Howard Hawks ph* Arthur Edeson

James Cagney, Pat O'Brien, June Travis, Stuart Erwin, Henry Wadsworth, Isabel Jewell, Barton Maclane

'An entertainment wallop of extraordinary power.'—*Variety*

'The best of all airplane pictures.'—*Otis Ferguson, 1939*

'Directed at a breakneck pace which emphasizes its lean fibre and its concentration on the essentials of its theme.'—*Andrew Sarris, 1963*

† Remade in 1939 as *International Squadron*.

Cela s'appelle l'Aurore*
France / Italy 1955 108m bw
Marceau / Laetitia

A Corsican company doctor falls for a young widow while his wife is on holiday, and events lead to tragedy.
Efficient melodrama, given an extra dimension by its *auteur*.

w Luis Bunuel, Jean Ferry, *novel* Emmanuel Robles *d* Luis Bunuel *ph* Robert Le Fèbvre *m* Joseph Kosma

Georges Marchal, Lucia Bose, Gianni Esposito, Julien Bertheau, *Henri Nassiet*

Céleste*
West Germany 1981 106m Eastmancolor
Pelemele / Bayerische Rundfunk (Eleonore Adlon)

During his last years, Marcel Proust is looked after by his voluntary housekeeper.
Subdued and only partially effective memoir from Céleste's biography; not for action seekers, but with a fascination of its own if one can give in to its pace.

wd Percy Adlon, *book* Monsieur Proust by Céleste Albaret, *ph* Jurgen Martin, Horst Becker, Helmo Sahliger, Hermann Ramelow, *m* César Franck

Eva Mattes, Jürgen Arndt

Celine and Julie Go Boating*
France 1974 192m Eastmancolor
Les Films du Losange (Barbet Schroeder)

Two girls change the outcome of a drama played daily in a haunted house.
Odd, dreamlike, absurdly long and semi-improvisational mood piece, with reverberations from *Alice in Wonderland* and *Orphée*. Not an unpleasant experience, but sometimes a tiresome one.

w Eduardo de Gregorio, Juliet Berto, Dominique Labourier, Bulle Ogier, Marie-France Pisier, Jacques Rivette, partly suggested by two stories by Henry James *d* Jacques Rivette *ph* Jacques Renard *m* Jean-Marie Senia

Juliet Berto, Dominique Labourier, Bulle Ogier, Marie-France Pisier, Barbet Schroeder

'Rivette uncannily combines slapstick, suspense and tears in his most watchable assault on the narrative form.'—*Jan Dawson*

† Shot in 16mm.

Cell 2455 Death Row
US 1955 77m bw
Columbia (Wallace MacDonald)

A convicted murderer staves off execution with appeal after appeal.
Cheap run-off of the case of Caryl Chessman, who was executed ten years after his trial for rape and murder. Retold in a 1977 TV movie, *Kill Me If You Can*.

w Jack de Witt, *book* Caryl Chessman *d* Fred F. Sears *ph* Fred Jackman Jnr *md* Mischa Bakaleinikoff

William Campbell, Kathryn Grant, Harvey Stephens, Marian Carr, Vince Edwards

Centennial Summer**
US 1946 102m Technicolor
TCF (Otto Preminger)

A Philadelphia family responds to the Great Exposition of 1876.
Pleasing family comedy with music, the kind of harmless competence Hollywood used to throw off with ease but can no longer manage.

w Michael Kanin, *novel* Albert E. Idell *d* Otto Preminger *ph* Ernest Palmer *m* Alfred Newman *songs* Jerome Kern, Oscar Hammerstein II, E. Y. Harburg, Leo Robin

Jeanne Crain, Cornel Wilde, Linda Darnell, William Eythe, Walter Brennan, *Constance Bennett*, Dorothy Gish

AAN: Alfred Newman; song 'All Through the Day' (*m* Jerome Kern, *ly* Oscar Hammerstein II)

Central Airport
US 1933 75m bw

After the war the only job an ace pilot can get is as 'chauffeur' to a lady parachutist. Rather stiff romantic drama with aeronautics thrown in. Richard Barthelmess, Sally Eilers, Tom Brown, Glenda Farrell, Harold Huber. Written by Rian James and James Seymour; directed by William A. Wellman; for Warner.

'The aerial excitement should bring sufficient response to bring it over to the right side of the box office.'—*Variety*

Central Park
US 1932 57m bw

Stories of life in New York's park. Nifty portmanteau which moves fast and does not bore. Joan Blondell, Guy Kibbee, Wallace Ford, Henry B. Walthall, Patricia Ellis,

Spencer Charters. Written by Ward Morehouse and Earl Baldwin; directed by John Adolfi; for Warner.

The Ceremony
US / Spain 1963 107m bw
UA / Magla (Laurence Harvey)

In a Tangier jail, a bank robber awaits the firing squad, but he and his brother have an escape plan.
Murky and pretentious melodrama with aspirations to high style and symbolism. A bore.

w Ben Barzman, *novel* Frederic Grendel *d* Laurence Harvey *ph* Oswald Morris *m* Gerard Schurmann

Laurence Harvey, Sarah Miles, Robert Walker, John Ireland, Ross Martin, Lee Patterson, Jack McGowran, Murray Melvin, Fernando Rey

A Certain Smile*
US 1958 105m Eastmancolor Cinemascope
TCF (Henry Ephron)

A girl student falls in love with her philandering uncle.
Another sordid novella by Françoise Sagan (see *Bonjour Tristesse*), transformed by Hollywood into a glowing romantic saga of life among the Riviera rich. On this level, very competent.

w Frances Goodrich, Albert Hackett *d* Jean Negulesco *ph* Milton Krasner *m* Alfred Newman

Christine Carere, Rossano Brazzi, Joan Fontaine, Bradford Dillman, Eduard Franz, Kathryn Givney, Steve Geray

AAN: title song (*m* Sammy Fain, *ly* Paul Francis Webster)

Cervantes
Spain / Italy / France 1968 119m Eastmancolor Supertotalvision
Prisma / Protor / Procinex (Alexander Salkind)

Cervantes, an assistant papal envoy, helps persuade Philip of Spain to join the Holy League, then turns soldier and has various adventures.
Rather boring spectacular with conventional set pieces.

w Enrique Llovet, Enrico Bomba, *novel* Bruno Frank *d* Vincent Sherman *ph* Edmond Richard *m* Jean Ledrut

Horst Buchholz, Gina Lollobrigida, Louis Jourdan, Jose Ferrer, Fernando Rey, Francisco Rabal

César see Marius

César and Rosalie*
France / Italy / West Germany 1972 105m Eastmancolor
Fildebroc / UPS / Mega Paramount / Orion (Michèle de Broca)

A divorcee living with a rich merchant becomes attracted to a young artist. Unexpectedly, the two men become friends . . .
Wryly amusing comedy for adults.

w Jean-Loup Dabadie, Claude Sautet *d* Claude Sautet *ph* Jean Boffety *m* Philippe Sarde

Yves Montand, Romy Schneider, Sami Frey, Umberto Orsini

Chad Hanna*
US 1940 86m Technicolor
TCF (Darryl F. Zanuck, Nunnally Johnson)

Life in a New York state circus in the 1840s.
Mild romantic drama from a bestseller; local colour excellent, dramatic interest thin.

w Nunnally Johnson, *novel* Red Wheels Rolling by Walter D. Edmonds *d* Henry King *ph* Ernest Palmer *m* David Buttolph

Henry Fonda, Dorothy Lamour, Linda Darnell, Guy Kibbee, Jane Darwell, John Carradine, Ted North, Roscoe Ates

The Chain*
GB 1984 100m Eastmancolor
Quintet / County Bank / Channel Four (Victor Glynn)

Seven groups of people, corresponding to the seven deadly sins, are involved in a house-moving chain.
Rather tedious and predictable 'all star' comedy with effective moments but no narrative command.

w Jack Rosenthal *d* Jack Gold *ph* Wolfgang Suschitzky *m* Stanley Myers

Denis Lawson, Maurice Denham, Nigel Hawthorne, Billie Whitelaw, Judy Parfitt, Leo McKern, Warren Mitchell, Gary Waldhorn, Anna Massey

'When she's in his arms—it's the grandest thrill the screen can give!'

Chain Lightning
US 1950 94m bw
Warner (Anthony Veiller)

After World War II a bomber pilot learns how to control the new jets.
Absolutely routine romance and heroics.

w Liam O'Brien, Vincent Evans *d* Stuart Heisler *ph* Ernest Haller *m* David Buttolph

Humphrey Bogart, Eleanor Parker, Raymond Massey, Richard Whorf, James Brown, Roy Roberts, Morris Ankrum

'When she's in his arms, it's the grandest thrill the screen can give!'

Chained*
US 1934 77m bw
MGM (Hunt Stromberg)

A devoted wife has a shipboard romance with another man.
Moderate star romantic drama.

w John Lee Mahin *d* Clarence Brown *ph* George Folsey *m* Herbert Stothart

Joan Crawford, Clark Gable, Otto Kruger, Stuart Erwin, Una O'Connor, Akim Tamiroff

'Simple in story and unoriginal in idea, its weight is in words rather than action and dramatic potency.'—*Variety*

Chained for Life
US 1950 70m bw

One of two girl Siamese twins is accused of murder. Real life freak show starring Violet and Daisy Hilton, English twins (1908–64) who were joined at the hip. Hard to watch because of the subject but otherwise a routine lower-case effort. With Allen Jenkins. Written by Nat Tanchuck; directed by Harry L. Fraser; for Classic films.

A Chairy Tale**
Canada 1957 10m bw

A young man finds that a kitchen chair is unwilling for him to sit on it, but they arrive at a compromise. The simplest and most effective of fantasies is told at somewhat excessive length but remains among its director's more memorable creations. Written and directed by *Norman McLaren* (with Claude Jutra, who plays the young man); for the National Film Board of Canada.

The Chalk Garden*
GB 1964 106m Technicolor
U-I / Quota Rentals (Ross Hunter)

The governess in a melancholy household has an effect on the lives of her aged employer and the young granddaughter.
Sub-Chekhovian drama in a house by the sea, flattened by routine handling into something much less interesting than it was on the stage.

w John Michael Hayes, *novel* Enid Bagnold *d* Ronald Neame *ph* Arthur Ibbetson *m* Malcolm Arnold

Edith Evans, Deborah Kerr, Hayley Mills, John Mills, Felix Aylmer, Elizabeth Sellars, Lally Bowers, Toke Townley

'Crashing symbolism, cracker-motto sententiousness.'—*MFB*

AAN: Edith Evans

The Challenge
GB 1938 75m bw
London Films

On the Matterhorn in 1865, a guide proves that an English climber did not sacrifice his friends. Fictionalized mountain climbing history, a little dull. Luis Trenker, Robert Douglas, Joan Gardner, Mary Clare, Ralph Truman. Written by Emeric Pressburger, Milton Rosmer and Patrick Kirwan; directed by Milton Rosmer and Luis Trenker; for Alexander Korda. 'A rather simple story, yet seldom dull.'—*Variety*

The Challenge
US 1948 69m bw

Bulldog Drummond solves the mystery of a yacht which is stolen after its owner is murdered. Modest addition to a long-running series. Tom Conway, June Vincent, Richard Stapley. Written by Frank Gruber and Irving Elman; directed by Jean Yarbrough; for Reliance (TCF).

The Challenge
GB 1960 89m bw

In search of buried loot, a lady gangster kidnaps a convict's son. Murky and unsympathetic melodrama. Jayne Mansfield, Anthony Quayle, Carl Mohner, Barbara Mullen, Peter Reynolds, Dermot Walsh. Written and directed by John Gilling; for John Temple-Smith / Alexandra.

(US title: *It Takes a Thief*.)

The Challenge
US 1982 112m Eastmancolor
CBS Theatrical Film Group (Lyle Poncher, Robert L. Rosen, Ron Beckman)

An American boxer in Japan becomes involved in a feud between two brothers.
Belated martial arts saga with a good deal of head-lopping and plenty of pretensions but no apparent message to spike its dismal entertainment values.

w Richard Maxwell, John Sayles *d* John Frankenheimer *ph* Kozo Okazaki *m* Jerry Goldsmith *pd* Yoshiyuki Ishida *ed* Jack Wheeler

Scott Glenn, Toshiro Mifune, Donna Kei Benz, Atsuo Nakamura, Calvin Young, Clyde Kusatsu

'Ridiculous, demeaning stuff.'—*Guardian*

A Challenge for Robin Hood*
GB 1967 96m Technicolor
Hammer (Clifford Parkes)

A retelling of the original Robin Hood legend.
Unassuming, lively, predictable adventure hokum.

w Peter Bryan *d* C. Pennington-Richards *ph* Arthur Grant *m* Gary Hughes

Barrie Ingham, James Hayter, Leon Greene, John Arnatt, Peter Blythe, Gay Hamilton, William Squire

'The unspeakable vengeance of the crazed Baltimore strangler!'

Chamber of Horrors
US 1966 99m Warnercolor
Warner (Hy Averback)

A maniacal murderer is finally trapped by two amateur criminologists who run a wax museum in Baltimore.
Zany horror thriller originally meant for TV; it turned out a shade too harrowing. Advertised as 'the picture with the Fear Flasher and the Horror Horn', shock gimmicks which proved much more startling than the crude events they heralded.

w Stephen Kandel *d* Hy Averback *ph* Richard Kline *m* William Lava

Patrick O'Neal, Cesare Danova, Wilfrid Hyde White, Laura Devon, Patrice Wymore, Suzy Parker, Jeanette Nolan, Tony Curtis (guest)

'Don't fail to get a ringside seat!'

The Champ*
US 1931 87m bw
MGM (Harry Rapf)

A young boy has faith in a washed-up prizefighter.
Maudlin drama, highly commercial in its day and a box office tonic for its two stars.
Remade as *The Clown* (qv).

w Leonard Praskins, Frances Marion *d* King Vidor *ph* Gordon Avil

Wallace Beery, Jackie Cooper, Irene Rich, Roscoe Ates, Edward Brophy

'The knockout picture of the year!'—*publicity*

'This picture will hit 'em all, large or small, and that means lots of money.'—*Variety*

AA: original story (Frances Marion); Wallace Beery
AAN: best picture; King Vidor

The Champ*
US 1979 122m Metrocolor
MGM (Dyson Lovell)

A remake of the above, with Florida racetrack asides.
A lush version, so little updated in mood that its tearfulness seems to have strayed from another age.

w Walter Newman *d* Franco Zeffirelli *ph* Fred J. Koenekamp *m* Dave Grusin *pd* Herman A. Blumenthal

Jon Voight, Faye Dunaway, *Ricky Schroeder*, Jack Warden, Arthur Hill, Strother Martin, Joan Blondell, Elisha Cook

Champagne
GB 1928 90m (24 fps) bw silent

A millionaire pretends to be bankrupt so that his daughter won't marry. Tedious comedy drama with very few of the master's touches. Betty Balfour, Jean Bradin, Gordon Harker, Theodore Von Alten. Written by Eliot Stannard, Walter C. Mycroft and Alfred Hitchcock; directed by Alfred Hitchcock; for BIP 'Dreadful.'—*Alfred Hitchcock*

Champagne Charlie*
GB 1944 107m bw
Ealing (John Croydon)

The life of Victorian music hall singer George Leybourne and his rivalry with the Great Vance.
Careful period reconstruction and good songs and acting are somehow nullified by unsympathetic handling and photography.

w Austin Melford, Angus Macphail, John Dighton *d* Alberto Cavalcanti *ph* Wilkie Cooper *md* Ernest Irving

Tommy Trinder, Stanley Holloway, Betty Warren, Austin Trevor, Jean Kent, Guy Middleton, Frederick Piper, Harry Fowler

'Cavalcanti's taste for the bizarre and the vigour of the performances make it something more than a museum piece.'—*Time Out, 1984*

Champagne for Caesar*
US 1950 99m bw
Cardinal (George Moskov)

A self-confessed genius with a grudge against a soap company determines to win astronomical sums on its weekly radio quiz.
Agreeable, mildly satirical star comedy which tends to peter out halfway.

w Hans Jacoby, Fred Brady *d* Richard Whorf *ph* Paul Ivano *m* Dmitri Tiomkin

Ronald Colman, Vincent Price, Celeste Holm, Barbara Britton, Art Linkletter

The Champagne Murders
France 1967 107m Techniscope
Universal (France) (Jacques Natteau)
original title: *Le Scandale*

A disturbed champagne millionaire thinks he may be a murderer.
Complex but uninvolving mystery story in which the director's eye seems to be more on satire than on narrative.

w Claude Brûlé, Derek Prouse, Paul Gégauff *d* Claude Chabrol *ph* Jean Rabier *m* Pierre Jansen

Anthony Perkins, Maurice Ronet, Stéphane Audran, Yvonne Furneaux, Suzanne Lloyd

'As gay and sparkling as a champagne cocktail!'

Champagne Waltz
US 1937 90m bw

A press agent takes a swing band to Vienna. Rather tedious romantic comedy with music. Fred MacMurray, Gladys Swarthout, Jack Oakie. Written by Don Hartman, Frank Butler from a story by Billy Wilder, H. S. Kraft and Vienna Hall; directed by Edward Sutherland; for Paramount. 'On the slow side, but should do fairly.'—*Variety*

'This is the only sport in the world where two guys get paid for doing something they'd be arrested for if they got drunk and did it for nothing.'

Champion**
US 1949 99m bw
Stanley Kramer

An ambitious prizefighter alienates his friends and family, and dies of injuries received in the ring.
Interesting exposé of the fight racket, presented in good cinematic style and acted with great bravura.

w Carl Foreman, story Ring Lardner *d Mark Robson ph* Franz Planer *m* Dmitri Tiomkin

Kirk Douglas, Arthur Kennedy, Marilyn Maxwell, Paul Stewart, Ruth Roman, Lola Albright, Luis Van Rooten

AAN: Carl Foreman; Franz Planer; Dmitri Tiomkin; Kirk Douglas: Arthur Kennedy

Champions*
GB 1983 115m colour
Embassy / Archerwest / Ladbroke / United British Artists (Peter Shaw, Eva Monley)

A leading jockey develops cancer and his horse receives a leg injury, but both survive to win the Grand National.
Gruelling factual story which could have done with a little more drama, not to mention a more sympathetic hero.

w Evan Jones, *book* Bob Champion and Jonathan Powell *d* John Irvin *ph* Ronnie Taylor *m* Carl Davis

John Hurt, Edward Woodward, Ben Johnson, Jan Francis, Peter Barkworth, Ann Bell, Judy Parfitt

'It ignores any inner aspect, the better to concentrate on tearjerking externals.'—*Tom Milne, MFB*

'Told as an indecent tearjerker, directed with the discretion of a rampaging steamroller.'—*Sight and Sound*

Chance of a Lifetime*
GB 1950 93m bw
Pilgrim Pictures (Bernard Miles)

The owner of a small engineering works, impatient with the unionism of his men, gives them a chance to run the factory themselves. Quiet comedy-drama on sub-Ealing lines; always interesting, it never quite catches fire despite a reliable cast.

w Walter Greenwood, Bernard Miles
d Bernard Miles *ph* Eric Cross

Bernard Miles, Basil Radford, Niall MacGinnis, Geoffrey Keen, Julien Mitchell, Josephine Wilson, Kenneth More, Hattie Jacques

Chances*
US 1931 72m bw

In wartime London, two soldiers on leave fall for the same girl. Unexpectedly sensitive and pleasing romance, generally well handled. Douglas Fairbanks Jnr, Anthony Bushell, Rose Hobart. Written by Waldemar Young, from a novel by Hamilton Gibbs; directed by Allan Dwan; for Warner. 'Enough contributing sidelights to keep the emphasis away from the combat . . . should be pleasant b.o.'—*Variety*

Chandler
US 1971 88m Metrocolor Panavision

An ex-private eye becomes a security guard and an alcoholic but even worse befalls when he agrees to keep an eye on a government witness. Downbeat, generally unamusing and little seen piece of thick ear which harks back unsuccessfully to the forties. Warren Oates, Leslie Caron, Alex Dreier, Mitchell Ryan, Gordon Pinsent, Charles McGraw, Richard Loo, Walter Burke, Gloria Grahame, Royal Dano, Scatman Crothers. Written by John Sacret Young; directed by Paul Magwood; for MGM.

Chandu the Magician*
US 1932 74m bw
Fox

A spiritualist battles against a madman with a death ray which could destroy the world. Rather dim serial-like thriller, with interesting talent not at its best.

w Philip Klein, Barry Conners *d* Marcel Varnel, William Cameron Menzies *ph* James Wong Howe *m* Louis de Francesco

Edmund Lowe, Bela Lugosi, Irene Ware, Herbert Mundin, Henry B. Walthall

† Sequels (whittled down from serials) include *The Return of Chandu* and *Chandu and the Magic Isle*.

Chanel Solitaire
France / GB 1981 124m colour
Gardenia / Todrest (Larry G. Spangler)

Fashion designer Coco Chanel thinks back on her long career.
Moderately elegant but frigid autobiopic with very little entertainment value.

w Julian More, *novel* Claude Dulay
d George Kaczender *ph* Ricardo Aronovich
m Jean Musy

Marie-France Pisier, Timothy Dalton, Rutger Hauer, Karen Black, Brigitte Fossey

'The producer says the film is devoted to providing what every woman wants—men, money, jewellery, castles, caviare, champagne and love, love, love. I never realized they could be so boring.'—*Sunday Times*

Chang**
US 1927 71m (24 fps) bw silent
Paramount

The life of a rice-grower in Thailand.
Influential but now rather boring documentary with animal interest.

wd, ph, ed Merian C. Cooper, Ernest B. Schoedsack

Change of Habit
US 1969 97m colour

A young doctor working in a ghetto has his opinions changed by three nuns. A notably unsuccessful attempt by a star to change his image. Elvis Presley, Mary Tyler Moore, Barbara McNair, Ed Asner, Leora Dana, Jane Elliot, Robert Emhardt. Written by James Lee, S. S. Schweltzer and Eric Bercovici; directed by William Graham; for Universal.

Change of Heart
US 1934 74m bw
Fox

Four young California students make good in New York.
Minor fairy tale which marked the last of twelve teamings for Gaynor and Farrell.

w Sonya Levien, James Gleason, Samuel Hoffenstein, *novel* Kathleen Norris *d* John G. Blystone *ph* Hal Mohr *m* Louis de Francesco

Janet Gaynor, Charles Farrell, Ginger Rogers, James Dunn, Beryl Mercer, Gustav Von Seyffertitz, Shirley Temple

'They are on the back of a nag that never quite gets started . . . most of the time it causes that tired feeling.'—*Variety*

Change of Heart
US 1937 65m bw

A bored man and wife go their separate ways but are eventually reconciled. Bright little comedy on a tired old theme. Michael Whalen, Gloria Stuart, Lyle Talbot, Jane Darwell. Written by Frances Hyland, Albert Ray; directed by James Tinling; for Sol M. Wurtzel / TCF. 'More originality, freshness of treatment and solid entertainment than in half the more expensive efforts from the Hollywood studios.'—*Variety*

Change of Heart
US 1943 87m bw

A country girl writes songs and a publisher steals them. Slim basis for a so-so musical. Susan Hayward, John Carroll, Eve Arden, Gail Patrick, Walter Catlett, Melville Cooper, Count Basie and his Orchestra. Written by Frank Gill Jnr; directed by Albert S. Rogell; for Republic. (Original title: *Hit Parade of 1943*.)

Change of Mind
US 1969 98m Eastmancolor
Sagittarius (Seeleg Lester, Richard Wesson)

The life of a liberal white DA can only be 'saved' by transplanting his brain into the body of a dead black man.
Fantasy melodrama with a social conscience, about a half-and-half which is acceptable to neither whites nor blacks. Very obvious and rather boring.

w Seeleg Lester, Richard Wesson *d* Robert Stevens *ph* Arthur J. Ornitz *m* Duke Ellington

Raymond St Jacques, Susan Oliver, Janet McLachlan, Leslie Nielsen

A Change of Seasons
US 1980 102m De Luxe
TCF / Martin Ransohoff / Film Finance Group Ltd

A college professor takes a mistress and his wife retaliates.
Zestless and unhumorous rehash of *Who's Afraid of Virginia Woolf?* and *Bob and Carol and Ted and Alice*. Not a new thought anywhere.

w Erich Segal, Ronni Kern, Fred Segal
d Richard Lang *ph* Philip Lathrop *m* Henry Mancini *pd* Bill Kenney

Shirley Maclaine, Anthony Hopkins, Bo Derek, Michael Brandon, Mary Beth Hurt, Ed Winter

'A tired rehash of themes that might have been provocative a decade ago . . . it would take a Lubitsch to do justice to the incredibly tangled relationships.'—*Variety*

'The situation soon melts into a gooey mess, like a Mars bar left too long in a trouser pocket.'—*Sunday Times*

The Changeling
Canada 1979 107m colour Panavision
Chessman Palk Productions (Joel B. Michaels, Garth H. Drabinsky)

A widowed academic takes on an old house haunted by the spirit of a murdered child.
Tedious and not very brief, this uninspired ghost story comes very late in the horror stakes and contains very little to make one care about its outcome.

w William Gray, Diana Maddox *d* Peter Medak *ph* John Coquillon *m* Rick Wilkins

George C. Scott, Melvyn Douglas, Trish Van Devere, John Colicos, Jean Marsh, Barry Morse

'None of its most eerily untoward occurrences proceed from any spectral intervention, but from the worst abuses of Peter Medak's infuriatingly fidgety camera.'—*Gilbert Adair, MFB*

Channel Crossing*
GB 1933 70m bw

Various characters converge on a ferry boat to France. Somewhat stilted potboiler with interesting cast: Matheson Lang, Max Miller, Constance Cummings, Edmund Gwenn, Anthony Bushell, Dorothy Dickson, Nigel Bruce. Written by W. P. Lipscomb and Cyril Campion; directed by Milton Rosmer; for Gaumont.

The Chant of Jimmie Blacksmith
Australia 1978 122m Eastmancolor Panavision

In 1900, a half-caste mingles with high class whites, goes berserk, and slaughters several of them with an axe. Hard-to-take moral tale for philosophers with strong stomachs. Tommy Lewis, Ray Barrett, Jack Thompson, Freddy Reynolds. Written and directed by Fred Schepsi, from the novel by Thomas Keneally; for Film House.

Chapayev*
USSR 1934 94m bw
Lenfilm

Exploits of a Red Army commander during the 1919 battles.
Moderately striking propaganda piece.

wd Sergei and Georgy Vasiliev *ph* Alexander Sigayev *m* Gavril Popov

Boris Babochkin, B. Blinov, Leonid Kmit

'Easily the best film turned out in Russia since sound.'—*Variety*

The Chapman Report
US 1962 125m Technicolor
(Warner) Darryl F. Zanuck (Richard D. Zanuck)

Dr Chapman conducts a study of female sex behaviour in an American suburb.
Influenced by the Kinsey report, this melodramatic compendium takes itself far too seriously, and the director's smooth style is barely in evidence.

w Wyatt Cooper, Don M. Mankiewicz, *novel* Irving Wallace *d* George Cukor *ph* Harold Lipstein *m* Leonard Rosenman

Shelley Winters, Claire Bloom, *Glynis Johns*, Efrem Zimbalist Jnr, Jane Fonda, Ray Danton, Ty Hardin, Andrew Duggan, John Dehner, Henry Daniell, Corey Allen, Harold J. Stone

'We had a preview which went very well, and then it was sent over to Mr Zanuck, who did what I thought was a most horrendous job of cutting it up.'—*George Cukor*

Chapter Two
US 1979 127m Metrocolor
Columbia / Rastar (Margaret Booth)

A widowed novelist reluctantly embarks on an affair with a divorcee.
Simon in sad mood means that the wisecracks are still there but the pauses between them are longer. The thin but heavy-going plot finally militates against enthusiasm.

w Neil Simon *d* Robert Moore *ph* David M. Walsh, Richard Kratina *m* Marvin Hamlisch *pd* Gene Callahan

James Caan, Marsha Mason, Joseph Bologna, Valerie Harper, Alan Fudge

'The regular Neil Simon Broadway takeaway for people who watch movies with their ears. Over two hours of theatrical smart talk and unfailing wit-under-pressure as Simon-surrogate Caan and the real Mrs Simon swap marital repartee in front of a reverent camera.'—*Time Out*

'All the couple have to do is swap wisecracks and nurse their rather pretty emotional bruises.'—*Observer*

'More than two hours of discussions, arguments, debates, reconciliations and accusations that quickly become tedious.'—*Roger Ebert*

Charade
US 1952 83m bw

Three stories conceived and produced by the stars. Everything about this triptych is on the dull side, and Mason himself later regretted embarking on it. James Mason, Pamela Mason, Scott Forbes, Paul Cavanagh, Bruce Lester. Written by James and Pamela Mason; directed by Roy Kellino (Pam's brother); for Portland (James's company).

Charade**
US 1963 113m Technicolor
Universal / Stanley Donen

A Parisienne finds her husband murdered. Four strange men are after her, and she is helped by a handsome stranger . . . but is he hero, spy or murderer?
Smoothly satisfying sub-Hitchcock nonsense, effective both as black romantic comedy and macabre farce.

w Peter Stone d Stanley Donen ph Charles Lang Jnr *m* Henry Mancini

Cary Grant (sixty but concealing the fact by taking a shower fully clothed), *Audrey Hepburn, Walter Matthau*, James Coburn, George Kennedy, Ned Glass, Jacques Marin

'One hesitates to be uncharitable to a film like *Charade*, which seeks only to provide a little innocent merriment and make a pot of money. . . . Of itself, it is a stylish and amusing melodrama, but in the context of the bloodlust that seems unloosed in our land it is as sinister as the villains who stalk Miss Hepburn through the cobbled streets of Paris.'—*Arthur Knight*

AAN: song 'Charade' (*m* Henry Mancini, *ly* Johnny Mercer)

The Charge at Feather River*
US 1953 96m Warnercolor
Warner (David Weisbart)

An army platoon composed of men from the guardhouse tries to rescue two women kidnapped by Indians.
Formula western distinguished by 3-D photography, probably the best to be achieved in the brief life of the medium. Warnerphonic sound was less successfully added; the sum total would be trying for nervous people.

w James R. Webb *d* Gordon Douglas *ph Peverell Marley m* Max Steiner

Guy Madison, Frank Lovejoy, Vera Miles, Helen Westcott, Dick Wesson, Onslow Stevens, Steve Brodie

'From the start we are involved in a whirl of frenzied activity: a cavalry charge, knife throwing, sabre practice, flaming arrows—not a trick missed.'—*MFB*

Charge of the Lancers
US 1953 74m Technicolor

During the Crimean War, the Russians capture an English major who knows the details of a new cannon. Action cheapie which seems to be largely shot in the producer's back garden but provides a laugh or two. Paulette Goddard, Jean-Pierre Aumont, Richard Stapley, Karin Booth, Lester Matthews. Written by Robert E. Kent; directed by William Castle; for Sam Katzman / Columbia.

'The reckless lancers sweep on and on—so that a woman's heart might not be broken! You're not fighting a single legion—you're fighting the entire British army, Surat Khan!'

The Charge of the Light Brigade***
US 1936 115m bw
Warner (Hal B. Wallis, Sam Bischoff)

An army officer deliberately starts the Balaclava charge to even an old score with Surat Khan, who's on the other side.
Though allegedly 'based on the poem by Alfred Lord Tennyson', this is no more than a travesty of history, most of it taking place in India. As pure entertainment however it is a most superior slice of Hollywood hokum and the film which set the seal on Errol Flynn's superstardom.

w Michael Jacoby, Rowland Leigh *d Michael Curtiz ph Sol Polito, Fred Jackman m Max Steiner*

Errol Flynn, Olivia de Havilland, Patric Knowles, Donald Crisp, C. Aubrey Smith, David Niven, Henry Stephenson, Nigel Bruce, *C. Henry Gordon*, Spring Byington, E. E. Clive, Lumsden Hare, Robert Barrat, J. Carrol Naish

AAN: Max Steiner

The Charge of the Light Brigade*
GB 1968 141m De Luxe Panavision
UA / Woodfall (Neil Hartley)

An historical fantasia with comic, sociological and cartoon embellishments.
This version for the swinging sixties has a few splendid moments but apes *Tom Jones* all too obviously and leaves audiences with an even dimmer view of history than they started with.

w Charles Wood *d* Tony Richardson *ph* David Watkin, Peter Suschitsky *m* John Addison *animation Richard Williams* *ad* Edward Marshall

Trevor Howard, *John Gielgud*, David Hemmings, Vanessa Redgrave, Jill Bennett, Harry Andrews, Peter Bowles, Mark Burns

'Considering the lucid book on which it is largely based, it is almost as inexcusably muddled as the British commanders at Balaclava.'—*John Simon*

'The point of the film is to recreate mid-Victorian England in spirit and detail.'—*Stanley Kauffmann*

'Notions for at least three interesting films are on view . . . what seems signally lacking is a guiding hand, an overriding purpose.'—*John Coleman*

'This epic has so little feeling for the courage that went with the idiocies of the past that it diminishes itself along with its targets.'—*Pauline Kael*

Charing Cross Road
GB 1935 72m bw

Struggling boy and girl singers try to move into high society. Dated and artificial filler. John Mills, June Clyde, Derek Oldham, Jean Colin, Judy Kelly. Written by Con West and Clifford Grey; directed by Albert de Courville; for British Lion.

'Two men chasing dreams of glory!'
Chariots of Fire***
GB 1981 121m colour
TCF / Allied Stars / Enigma (David Puttnam)

In the 1924 Paris Olympics, a Jew and a Scotsman run for Britain.
A film of subtle qualities, rather like those of a BBC classic serial. Probably not quite worth the adulation it received, but full of pleasant romantic touches and sharp glimpses of the wider issues involved.

w Colin Welland *d* Hugh Hudson *ph* David Watkin *m* Vangelis

Ben Cross, *Ian Charleson*, Nigel Havers, Nicholas Farrell, Daniel Gerroll, Cheryl Campbell, Alice Krige, John Gielgud, Lindsay Anderson, Nigel Davenport, *Ian Holm*, Patrick Magee

'The whole contradictory bundle is unexpectedly watchable.'—*Jo Imeson, MFB*

'A piece of technological lyricism held together by the glue of simple-minded heroic sentiment.'—*Pauline Kael*

AA: best picture; Colin Welland; Vangelis; costume design (Milera Canonero)
AAN: Hugh Hudson; editing (Terry Rawlings); Ian Holm (supporting actor)
BFA: best picture; costume design; Ian Holm

Charley and the Angel*
US 1974 93m Technicolor
Walt Disney (Bill Anderson)

A small-town sporting goods storekeeper in the thirties escapes death three times and finds an impatient angel waiting for him.
Mild sentimental whimsy on the lines of *On Borrowed Time*, but with a happy ending and attractive period trappings.

w Roswell Rogers, *novel* The Golden Evenings of Summer by Will Stanton *d* Vincent McEveety *ph* Charles F. Wheeler *m* Buddy Baker

Fred MacMurray, Cloris Leachmann, Harry Morgan, Kurt Russell, Kathleen Cody, Edward Andrews, Barbara Nichols

Charley Moon*
GB 1956 92m Eastmancolor
Colin Lesslie, Aubrey Baring

A music hall comic becomes swollen-headed but returns to his home village and marries his childhood sweetheart.
Faltering musical lacking the gusto of its background, but providing a generally believable impression of life on the halls.

w / songs Leslie Bricusse, *novel* Reginald Arkell *d* Guy Hamilton *ph* Jack Hildyard *m* Francis Chagrin

Max Bygraves, Dennis Price, Michael Medwin, Florence Desmond, Shirley Eaton, Patricia Driscoll, Reginald Beckwith

'When he runs out of dumb luck he always has genius to fall back on!'
Charley Varrick**
US 1973 111m Technicolor Panavision
Universal (Don Siegel)

A bank robber discovers he has stolen Mafia money, and devises a clever scheme to get himself off the hook.
Sharp, smart, well-observed but implausible thriller, astringently handled and agreeably set in Californian backlands. Accomplished, forgettable entertainment.

w Howard Rodman, Dean Reisner, *novel* The Looters by John Reese *d Don Siegel* *ph* Michael Butler *m* Lalo Schifrin

Walter Matthau, Joe Don Baker, Felicia Farr, Andy Robinson, John Vernon, Sheree North, Norman Fell

'It proves there is nothing wrong with an *auteur* director that a good script can't cure.'—*Stanley Kauffmann*

'The narrative line is clean and direct, the characterizations economical and functional, and the triumph of intelligence gloriously satisfying.'—*Andrew Sarris*

Charley's Aunt**
US 1941 81m bw
TCF (William Perlberg)
GB title: *Charley's American Aunt*

For complicated reasons, an Oxford undergraduate has to impersonate his own rich aunt from Brazil (where the nuts come from).
Very adequate version of the Victorian farce, with all concerned in excellent form.

w George Seaton, *play* Brandon Thomas *d* Archie Mayo *ph* Peverell Marley *m* Alfred Newman *ad* Richard Day, Nathan Juran

Jack Benny, Kay Francis, James Ellison, Anne Baxter, *Laird Cregar*, Edmund Gwenn, Reginald Owen, Richard Haydn, Arleen Whelan, Ernest Cossart.

† See also: *Where's Charley?*

Charley's Big-Hearted Aunt
GB 1940 76m bw
Gainsborough (Edward Black)

Rather disappointing British version of the famous farce, dully assembled and rather unsuitably cast.

w Marriott Edgar, Val Guest *d* Walter Forde *ph* Jack Cox

Arthur Askey, Phyllis Calvert, Moore Marriott, Graham Moffatt, Richard Murdoch, Jeanne de Casalis, J. H. Roberts, Felix Aylmer, Wally Patch

Charlie Bubbles***
GB 1968 91m Technicolor
Universal / Memorial (Michael Medwin, George Pitcher)

A successful novelist loathes the pointlessness of the good life and tries unsuccessfully to return to his northern working class background.
A little arid and slow in its early stages, and with a rather lame end (our hero escapes by air balloon), this is nevertheless a fascinating, fragmentary character study with a host of wry comedy touches and nimbly sketched characters; in its unassuming way it indicts many of the symbols people lived by in the sixties.

w Shelagh Delaney *d Albert Finney* *ph Peter Suschitsky* *m* Mischa Donat

Albert Finney, Billie Whitelaw, Liza Minnelli, Colin Blakely, Timothy Garland, Diana Coupland, Alan Lake, Yootha Joyce, Joe Gladwin

'A modest thing, but like all good work in minor keys it has a way of haunting the memory.'—*Richard Schickel*

'The supreme deadweight is Liza Minnelli, whose screen debut proves easily the most inauspicious since Turhan Bey's.'—*John Simon*

Charlie Chan
The Oriental detective created by Earl Derr Biggers began his film career as a minor character (played by George Kuwa) in a 1926 serial called HOUSE WITHOUT A KEY. In 1928 Kamiyama Sojin had a bigger role in THE CHINESE PARROT, but in 1929 E. L. Park did almost nothing in BEHIND THAT CURTAIN. In 1931 however began the fully-fledged Chan movies, which entertained a generation. Chan, based on a real-life Chinese detective named Chang Apana, became a citizen of Honolulu and was developed as a polite family man, aided by his impulsive number one or number two son (out of a family of fourteen), in solving murder puzzles. He had a treasury of aphorisms (a whole book of which has been published), and his technique was to gather all the suspects into one room before unmasking one as the murderer. The films built to a peak around 1936–9, but tailed off disastrously in the mid-forties. They were never noted for production values, but many retain interest for their scripts, their puzzles, and their casts of budding stars, as well as the central character. This is a complete list:

For Fox (later Twentieth Century Fox), with *Warner Oland* as Chan:
1931: CHARLIE CHAN CARRIES ON*, THE BLACK CAMEL
1932: CHARLIE CHAN'S CHANCE

1933: CHARLIE CHAN'S GREATEST CASE
1934: CHARLIE CHAN'S COURAGE, CHARLIE CHAN IN LONDON
1935: CHARLIE CHAN IN PARIS*, CHARLIE CHAN IN EGYPT, CHARLIE CHAN IN SHANGHAI
1936: CHARLIE CHAN'S SECRET*, CHARLIE CHAN AT THE CIRCUS*, CHARLIE CHAN AT THE RACE TRACK, CHARLIE CHAN AT THE OPERA**
1937: CHARLIE CHAN AT THE OLYMPICS, CHARLIE CHAN ON BROADWAY*, CHARLIE CHAN AT MONTE CARLO

For Twentieth Century Fox, with *Sidney Toler*:
1938: CHARLIE CHAN IN HONOLULU
1939: CHARLIE CHAN IN RENO, CHARLIE CHAN ON TREASURE ISLAND**, CITY OF DARKNESS
1940: CHARLIE CHAN IN PANAMA, CHARLIE CHAN'S MURDER CRUISE, CHARLIE CHAN AT THE WAX MUSEUM*, MURDER OVER NEW YORK
1941: DEAD MEN TELL, CHARLIE CHAN IN RIO, CASTLE IN THE DESERT*

For Monogram, with Sidney Toler:
1944: CHARLIE CHAN IN THE SECRET SERVICE, THE CHINESE CAT, BLACK MAGIC
1945: THE SCARLET CLUE, THE JADE MASK, SHANGHAI COBRA, RED DRAGON
1946: SHADOWS OVER CHINATOWN, DANGEROUS MONEY
1947: THE TRAP

For Monogram, with Roland Winters:
1947: THE CHINESE RING
1948: DOCKS OF NEW ORLEANS, SHANGHAI CHEST, THE GOLDEN EYE, THE FEATHERED SERPENT
1949: SKY DRAGON

In the late fifties J. Carrol Naish appeared in a half-hour TV series as Chan, but the episodes were dull. In 1971 Universal tried to revive the character in a 96-minute pilot film *Happiness is a Warm Clue*, but Ross Martin was woefully miscast. See also below.

Charlie Chan and the Curse of the Dragon Queen
US 1980 95m CFI Color
UA / American Cinema / Jerry Sherlock

The villainous Dragon Queen puts a curse on Chan and his descendants, and works it out some years later in San Francisco.
The targets in this spoof are somewhat elementary (the sinister housekeeper is Mrs Danvers, the wheelchair-bound butler Gillespie) and almost all the jokes fall flat on their faces.

w Stan Burns, David Axelrod *d* Clive Donner *ph* Paul Lohmann *m* Patrick Williams

Peter Ustinov, Angie Dickinson, Richard Hatch, Brian Keith, Roddy McDowall, Rachel Roberts, Johnny Sekka

Charlie McCarthy, Detective
US 1939 65m bw

Ventriloquist Edgar Bergen helps to solve a murder. Slightly tiresome mystery comedy with no real place for the wisecracking dummy. Edgar Bergen, Robert Cummings, Constance Moore, John Sutton, Louis Calhern, Edgar Kennedy, Samuel S. Hinds, Warren Hymer, Harold Huber. Written by Edward Eliscu; directed and produced by Frank Tuttle; for Universal. 'Looks like a corner-cutter . . . will have to struggle as top half of the duallers.'—*Variety*

Charlie the Lonesome Cougar*
US 1967 75m colour

The growing-up of a cougar. Amiable true-life adventure. Written by Jack Speirs; directed by Winston Hibler; for Disney.

Charlotte's Web
US 1972 96m Technicolor
Hanna-Barbera for Sagittarius

Farmyard animals who sense their fate are stimulated and encouraged by a resourceful spider.
Interesting but overlong and rather plodding version of a stylish book for children; the animation has no style at all.

w Earl Hanmer Jnr, *novel* E. B. White
d Charles A. Nichols, Iwao Takamoto
m / ly Richard and Robert Sherman

Charly*
US 1968 106m Techniscope
Selmur / Robertson Associates (Ralph Nelson)

New methods of surgery cure a mentally retarded young man, who becomes a genius, but the effects wear off.
Smooth, unconvincing, rather pointless fantasy which ultimately leaves a bad taste in the mouth.

w Sterling Silliphant, *novel* Flowers for Algernon by Daniel Keyes *d* Ralph Nelson *ph* Arthur J. Ornitz *m* Ravi Shankar

Cliff Robertson, Claire Bloom, Leon Janney, Lilia Skala

'The most distressing thing about *Charly* is not its ticklish subject, nor yet its clumsily modish surface, but its insistent, persistent sentimentality.'—*Tom Milne*

AA: Cliff Robertson

Charming Sinners
US 1929 66m bw

A society wife schemes to regain the attention of her wayward husband. Early talkie version of Somerset Maugham's *The Constant Wife*; of historical interest only. Ruth Chatterton, Clive Brook, William Powell, Mary Nolan, Florence Eldridge. Written by Doris Anderson; directed by Robert Milton; for Paramount.

Charro
US 1969 98m Technicolor Panavision
National General (Charles Marquis Warren)

A reformed outlaw is framed for the theft of a cannon.
Dismal western with a singing star playing straight. A bad experience.

wd Charles Marquis Warren *ph* Ellsworth Fredericks *m* Hugo Montenegro

Elvis Presley, Ina Balin, Barbara Werle, Lynn Kellogg, Victor French, Solomon Sturges

Chartroose Caboose
US 1960 76m Eastmancolor Panavision

A runaway couple take refuge with a retired train conductor in his converted rolling stock home. Old-fashioned to the point of seeming half-witted, this comedy has little to offer but geniality. Molly Bee, Ben Cooper, Edgar Buchanan, O. Z. Whitehead, Slim Pickens. Written by Rod Peterson; directed by William Reynolds; for Red-Bill / U-I.

The Chase*
US 1947 84m bw
Nero Pictures (Seymour Nebenzal)

A shell-shocked ex-serviceman foils a criminal and falls for his wife.
Weird Cuban-set *film noir* with a strange cast and stranger atmosphere. A genuine bomb, but worth a look for its pretensions, its cast, and its trick ending.

w Philip Yordan, *novel* The Black Path of Fear by Cornell Woolrich *d Arthur Ripley* *ph* Franz Planer *m* Michel Michelet

Robert Cummings, Michèle Morgan, Peter Lorre, Steve Cochran, Lloyd Corrigan, Jack Holt

The Chase*
US 1966 135m Technicolor Panavision
Columbia / Sam Spiegel

When a convict escapes and heads for his small Texas home town, almost all the inhabitants are affected in one way or another.
Expensive but shoddy essay in sex and violence, with Brando as a masochistic sheriff lording it over Peyton-Place-in-all-but-name. Literate moments do not atone for the general pretentiousness, and we have all been here once too often.

w Lillian Hellman, *novel* Horton Foote
d Arthur Penn *ph* Joseph La Shelle
pd Richard Day *m* John Barry

Marlon Brando, Jane Fonda, Robert Redford, Angie Dickinson, Janice Rule, James Fox, Robert Duvall, E. G. Marshall, Miriam Hopkins, Henry Hull

'The worst thing that has happened to movies since Lassie played a war veteran with amnesia.'—*Rex Reed*

'Considering all the talent connected with it, it is hard to imagine how *The Chase* went so haywire.'—*Philip T. Hartung*

Chase a Crooked Shadow**
GB 1957 87m bw
ABP / Associated Dragon Films (Douglas Fairbanks Jnr)

An heiress finds her home invaded by a stranger posing as her dead brother.
Tricksy, lightly controlled suspense melodrama with a perfectly fair surprise ending. Handling equivocal but competent.

w David D. Osborn, Charles Sinclair
d Michael Anderson *ph* Erwin Hillier
m Matyas Seiber

Richard Todd, Anne Baxter, Faith Brook, Herbert Lom, Alexander Knox, Alan Tilvern

'It'll lead the wisest guessers up the garden and give them the surprise of their life!'—*Kine Weekly*

† The plot was borrowed from an episode in *The Whistler* TV series, and later reversed for a 1975 TV film, *One of my Wives is Missing*.

The Chaser
US 1938 73m bw

An ambulance-chasing lawyer falls for the girl whose intent is to show him up. Tolerable second feature. Dennis O'Keefe, Ann Morriss, Lewis Stone, Nat Pendleton, Henry O'Neill, John Qualen. Written by Everett Freeman, Bella and Sam Spewack, Harry Ruskin; directed by Edwin L. Marin; for MGM.

Chasing Rainbows
US 1929 100m bw (colour sequence)

True love finds a way while a big musical is rehearsing. Naïve attempt to repeat the success of *Broadway Melody*. Bessie Love, Charles King, Marie Dressler, Polly Moran, Jack Benny. Written by Bess Meredyth; directed by Charles Riesner; for MGM.

Songs include 'Happy Days Are Here Again'; 'Everybody Tap'; 'Lucky Me, Loveable You'; 'Poor but Honest'; 'Dynamic Personality'; 'Love Ain't Nothing but the Blues'; 'Gotta Feeling for You'

'Numerous exploitable names and a snappy set of tunes.'—*Variety*

Chasing Yesterday
US 1935 78m bw

An elderly archaeologist seeks to renew his lost youth through the daughter of the woman he once loved but lost. Slow and old-fashioned melodrama. O. P. Heggie, Anne Shirley, Elizabeth Patterson, Helen Westley, John Qualen, Etienne Girardot. Written by Francis E. Faragoh from The Crime of Sylvestre Bonnard by Anatole France; directed by George Nicholls Jnr; for RKO. 'Prospects not bright.'—*Variety*

The Chastity Belt
Italy 1967 110m Eastmancolor
Warner / Julia (Francesco Mazzei)
aka: *On My Way to the Crusades I Met a Girl Who . . .*

A 12th-century knight is called to the Crusades just as he is consummating his marriage, and when he locks his wife in a chastity belt she follows him.
Abysmal international romp which looks nice but is killed stone dead by writing, dubbing and direction.

w Luigi Magni, Larry Gelbart *d* Pasquale Festa Campanile *ph* Carlo di Palma *m* Riz Ortolani

Tony Curtis, Virna Lisi, Hugh Griffith, John Richardson, Nino Castelnuovo

Chato's Land
GB 1971 100m Technicolor
UA / Scimitar (Michael Winner)

An Apache half-breed kills a man in self-defence, subsequently eluding and destroying the sheriff's posse.
Exhaustingly violent western in which the audience is spared no gory detail; efficiently put together for those who like this kind of fracas.

w Gerald Wilson *d* Michael Winner
ph Robert Paynter *m* Jerry Fielding

Charles Bronson, Jack Palance, Richard Basehart, James Whitmore, Simon Oakland, Richard Jordan, Ralph Waite, Victor French, Lee Patterson

Chatterbox
US 1935 68m bw

A country maiden aspires to the stage. Mildly likeable comedy for family audiences. Anne Shirley, Phillips Holmes, Edward Ellis, Erik Rhodes, Margaret Hamilton, Granville Bates. Written by Sam Mintz from a play by David Carb; directed by George Nicholls Jnr; for RKO. 'Discounting the nice job all around, the picture isn't there.'—*Variety*

Chatterbox
US 1943 77m bw
Republic (Albert J. Cohen)

A radio cowboy gets a film contract but can't stand horses.
Flat star comedy which borrows some well-worn situations but handles them badly.

w George Carleton Brown, Frank Gill Jnr
d Joseph Santley *ph* Ernest Miller
md Walter Scharf

Joe E. Brown, Judy Canova, Rosemary Lane, John Hubbard, Chester Clute

'With a dream of justice, he created a nightmare of violence!'

Che!
US 1969 94m De Luxe Panavision
TCF (Sy Bartlett)

Fidel Castro is helped in his subversion of Batista's Cuban regime by an Argentinian doctor named Che Guevara.
Fictionalized biography, and a dull one, of a man who became a myth.

w Michael Wilson, Sy Bartlett *d* Richard Fleischer *ph* Charles Wheeler *m* Lalo Schifrin

Omar Sharif, Jack Palance (as Castro), Cesare Danova, Robert Loggia, Woody Strode, Barbara Luna

'It goes at the pace of a drugged ox, and hasn't an ounce of political or historical sense in its nut.'—*New Yorker*

The Cheap Detective
US 1978 92m Metrocolor Panavision
Columbia / Ray Stark

Forties private eye Lou Peckinpaugh is involved in a complex case with echoes of *Casablanca, The Big Sleep, The Maltese Falcon* and *Farewell My Lovely*.
Lame spoof which might have seemed funnier on a small screen in black and white; as it is, the strain is evident and desperate.

w Neil Simon *d* Robert Moore *ph* John A. Alonzo *m* Patrick Williams

Peter Falk (Bogart), John Houseman (Greenstreet), Nicol Williamson (Veidt), *Louise Fletcher* (Bergman), Fernando Lamas (Henreid), Madeline Kahn (Astor), Dom de Luise (Lorre), Paul Williams (Cook), Marsha Mason (Gladys George), Ann-Margret (Claire Trevor), Eileen Brennan (Bacall), Stockard Channing (Lee Patrick), Sid Caesar (Miles Mander), Scatman Crothers (Dooley Wilson); and James Coco, Phil Silvers, Abe Vigoda, Vic Tayback

'Frankly they did this sort of thing just as well, and a lot more quickly, on *The Carol Burnett Show*.'—*Richard Shickel, Time*

'There is about enough talent around for a twenty-minute sketch at the Edinburgh fringe.'—*Derek Malcolm, Guardian*

† The film was a follow-up to the not much more effective but at least more controlled *Murder by Death*.

Cheaper by the Dozen**
US 1950 86m Technicolor
TCF (Lamar Trotti)

Efficiency expert Frank Gilbreth and his wife Lillian have twelve children, a fact which requires mathematical conduct of all their lives.
Amusing family comedy set in the twenties, unconvincing in detail though based on a book by two of the children. A great commercial success and a Hollywood myth-maker. Sequel: *Belles on their Toes* (qv).

w Lamar Trotti, *book* Frank B. Gilbreth Jnr, Ernestine Gilbreth Carey *d Walter Lang*
ph Leon Shamroy *m* Cyril Mockridge
md Lionel Newman *ad* Lyle Wheeler, Leland Fuller

Clifton Webb, Myrna Loy, Jeanne Crain, Edgar Buchanan, Barbara Bates, Betty Lynn, Mildred Natwick, Sara Allgood

The Cheat*
US 1915 95m (16 fps) bw silent
Famous Players Lasky / Paramount

A society lady borrows from a rich Japanese, and he brands her when she refuses to become his mistress.
Hoary melodrama which caused a sensation in its day.

w Hector Turnbull *d Cecil B. de Mille*
ph Alvin Wyckoff

Fanny Ward, Jack Dean, Sessue Hayakawa, James Neill

† Remade in 1923 by George Fitzmaurice, in 1931 by George Abbott, and in 1937 (in France, as *Forfaiture*) by Marcel L'Herbier.

The Cheaters*
US 1945 86m bw
Republic

A selfish and ostentatious family is reformed by the ministrations of a down-and-out actor.

Fairly engaging variation on *The Passing of the Third Floor Back*, with sweetness and light brought into people's lives by a fireside recital of *A Christmas Carol*.

w Francis Hyland *d* Joseph Kane *ph* Reggie Lanning *m* Walter Scharf

Joseph Schildkraut, Billie Burke, Eugene Pallette, Ona Munson, Raymond Walburn

Cheating Cheaters
US 1934 67m bw

Two groups of jewel thieves clash when posing as society swells. Tolerable programmer from an old stage hit. Fay Wray, Cesar Romero, Minna Gombell, Hugh O'Connell, Henry Armetta, Francis L. Sullivan, Ann Shoemaker. Written by Gladys Unger and Allen Rivkin, from the play by Max Marcin; directed by Richard Thorpe; for Universal. 'Rather creaky entertainment, but it will about get by.'—*Variety*

Check and Double Check
US 1930 71m bw
RKO

Comic adventures of a couple of black handymen.
Feeble comedy notable only for the film appearance of radio's immensely popular Amos 'n Andy, played by white actors in blackface.

w Bert Kalmar, Harry Ruby, J. Walter Ruben *d* Melville Brown *ph* William Marshall *m* Max Steiner

Freeman F. Gosden, Charles V. Correll, Sue Carol, Charles Morton, Irene Rich, Ralf Harolde, Duke Ellington and his Orchestra

'The best picture for children ever put on the screen . . . as a freak talking picture it's in the money immediately.'—*Variety*

The Checkered Coat
US 1948 66m bw

A psychopathic killer is captured during one of his cataleptic seizures. Fairly routine programme filler which manages to keep the attention. Tom Conway, Hurd Hatfield, Noreen Nash, James Seay. Written by John C. Higgins; directed by Edward L. Cahn; for Sam Baerwitz / TCF.

Checkers
US 1937 79m bw

The niece of a ne'er-do-well horse owner brings him success. One of the most successful vehicles of Shirley Temple's arch rival. Jane Withers, Stuart Erwin, Una Merkel, Marvin Stephens, Andrew Tombes, Minor Watson. Written by Lynn Root, Frank Fenton and Karen de Wolf, from the play by Rida Johnson Young; directed by H. Bruce Humberstone; for TCF. 'Will delight the moppet's following . . . due for heavy dual booking.'—*Variety*

Checkpoint*
GB 1956 84m Eastmancolor
Rank (Betty Box)

A tycoon sends an industrial spy to Italy in search of new motor racing car designs.
Acceptable hokum, cleanly assembled, with motor race highlights.

w Robin Estridge *d* Ralph Thomas *ph* Ernest Steward *m* Bruce Montgomery

Anthony Steel, Stanley Baker, James Robertson Justice, Odile Versois, Maurice Denham, Michael Medwin, Lee Patterson

Cheech and Chong's Next Movie
US 1980 95m Technicolor

Two dopers have various rude adventures. Totally repulsive comedy which gives a bad name to self-indulgence. Richard Marin, Thomas Chong, Evelyn Guerrero, Betty Kennedy, Sy Kramer. Written by Cheech and Chong; directed by Chong; for Howard Brown / Universal. (GB title: *High Encounters of the Ultimate Kind*.)

Cheer Boys Cheer
GB 1939 84m bw

Brewery owners hate each other but their children fall in love. A highly predictable plot provides some incidental pleasures in this modest precursor of the Ealing comedies. Nova Pilbeam, Edmund Gwenn, Jimmy O'Dea, Moore Marriott, Graham Moffatt, C. V. France, Alexander Knox. Written by Roger MacDougall and Allan MacKinnon; directed by Walter Forde; for ATP.

Cheers for Miss Bishop*
US 1941 94m bw
(UA) Richard A. Rowland

The life of a schoolmistress in a small midwestern town.
Acceptable sentimental hokum, quite pleasantly done.

w Adelaide Heinbron, *novel* Bess Streeter Aldrich *d* Tay Garnett *ph* Hal Mohr *m* Edward Ward

Martha Scott, William Gargan, Edmund Gwenn, Sterling Holloway, Sidney Blackmer, Mary Anderson, Dorothy Petersen

AAN: Edward Ward

'America's favourite two-gun star battles for love and glory!'
Cherokee Strip
US 1940 86m bw

A marshal brings law and order to a frontier town. Competent western programmer. Richard Dix, Florence Rice, William Henry, Victor Jory, Andy Clyde. Written by Herman Houston and Bernard McConville; directed by Lesley Selander; for Harry Sherman / Paramount.

Chess Fever*
USSR 1925 20m (24 fps) bw silent

A chess fanatic is so absorbed that he misses his wedding. Spirited visual comedy which still raises the intended laughs. Vladimir Fogel, Anna Zemtsova. Written and co-directed by Nikolai Shpikovsky; co-directed by Vsevolod Pudovkin; for Mezhrabpom-Russ.

The Chess Players*
India 1977 129m Eastmancolor

In 1856 Lucknow, two noblemen are more interested in playing chess than in their state's imminent annexation by the British. Patchy but frequently charming historical piece with more specifically Indian elements than are usual from its director. Sanjeev Kumar, Saeed Jaffrey, Richard Attenborough, Amjad Khan. Written and directed by Satyajit Ray; for Devki Chitra.

Chetniks—The Fighting Guerrillas
US 1942 73m bw

Yugoslav freedom fighters oppose the Nazi occupation. Standard co-feature wartime heroics. Philip Dorn, Anna Sten, John Shepperd, Frank Lackteen, Virginia Gilmore, Martin Kosleck. Written by Jack Andrews and Ed Paramore; directed by Louis King; for Sol M. Wurtzel / TCF.

Cheyenne
US 1947 100m bw

A gambler turns lawman, catches a robber and marries his wife. Rather sluggish western which later inspired a long-running TV series. Dennis Morgan, Bruce Bennett, Jane Wyman, Arthur Kennedy, Janis Paige, Alan Hale. Written by Alan Le May and Thames Williamson; directed by Raoul Walsh; for Warner. (Later retitled: *The Wyoming Kid*.)

Cheyenne Autumn*
US 1964 170m Technicolor Panavision 70
Warner / Ford-Smith (Bernard Smith)

In the 1860s, Cheyenne Indians are moved to a new reservation 1500 miles away; wanting aid, they begin a trek back home, and various battles follow.
Dispirited, shapeless John Ford western with little of the master's touch; good to look at, however, with effective cameos, notably an irrelevant and out-of-key comic one featuring James Stewart as Wyatt Earp.

w James R. Webb, *novel* Mari Sandoz *d* John Ford *ph William H. Clothier* *m* Alex North

Richard Widmark, Carroll Baker, Karl Malden, *Dolores del Rio*, Sal Mineo, Edward G. Robinson, *James Stewart*, Ricardo Montalban, Gilbert Roland, Arthur Kennedy, Patrick Wayne, Elizabeth Allen, Victor Jory, John Carradine, Mike Mazurki, John Qualen, George O'Brien

'Although one would like to praise the film for its high-minded aims, it is hard to forget how ponderous and disjointed it is.'—*Moira Walsh*

'The acting is bad, the dialogue trite and predictable, the pace funereal, the structure fragmented and the climaxes puny.'—*Stanley Kauffmann*

AAN: William H. Clothier

The Cheyenne Social Club*
US 1970 102m Technicolor Panavision
National General (James Lee Barrett, Gene Kelly)

Two itinerant cowboys inherit a high-class brothel.
Disappointing star comedy western with pleasing moments and a lively climactic shoot-out. Perhaps the girls are just a shade too winsome.

w James Lee Barrett *d* Gene Kelly *ph* William H. Clothier *m* Walter Scharf

James Stewart, Henry Fonda, Shirley Jones, Sue Ane Langdon, Robert Middleton, Arch Johnson

'Co-starring Shirley Jones and Rigor Mortis, who enters early and stays through the very last scene.'—*Rex Reed*

Chicago Calling*
US 1951 75m bw
UA / Arrowhead / Joseph Justman (Peter Berneis)

A drunk cannot pay his phone bill and is waiting for a vital call about his daughter's involvement in a car crash.
Moderate, location-shot minor melodrama with a few good ideas.

w John Reinhardt, Peter Berneis *d* John Reinhardt *ph* Robert de Grasse *m* Heinz Roemheld

Dan Duryea, Mary Anderson, Gordon Gebert, Ross Elliot

Chicago Confidential
US 1957 74m bw

A gambling syndicate takes over a labour union and frames its incorruptible president for murder. Very routine gangster potboiler. Brian Keith, Beverly Garland, Dick Foran, Elisha Cook Jnr. Written by Raymond T. Marcus; directed by Sidney Salkow; for Peerless / UA.

Chicago Deadline
US 1949 87m bw
Paramount (Robert Fellows)

A reporter researches the life of a lonely girl who died of tuberculosis.
Flat star vehicle consisting mainly of overplayed cameos.

w Warren Duff, Tiffany Thayer *d* Lewis Allen *ph* John F. Seitz *m* Victor Young

Alan Ladd, Donna Reed, *June Havoc*, Berry Kroeger, Arthur Kennedy, Gavin Muir, Shepperd Strudwick

† Remade as the TV pilot of *The Name of the Game*.

Chicago Syndicate
US 1955 86m bw

A young accountant breaks up an outwardly respectable crime syndicate. Formula racket-busting melodrama. Dennis O'Keefe, Abbe Lane, Paul Stewart, Xavier Cugat, Alison Hayes. Written by Joseph Hoffman; directed by Fred F. Sears; for Clover / Columbia.

Chick Carter, Detective
US 1946 bw serial: 15 eps

A private eye finds himself in deep water when he investigates a jewel robbery at a night club. Unsuitable serial material, thinly stretched and with not enough action highpoints. Lyle Talbot, Douglas Fowley, Julie Gibson, Pamela Blake, Eddie Acuff. Directed by Derwin Abrahams; for Columbia.

The Chicken Chronicles
US 1977 94m CFI Color

Problems of a teenager in an American small town. Extremely boring comedy drama, obsessed with sex and lacking background detail. Phil Silvers, Ed Lauter, Steven Guttenberg, Meridith Baer, Lisa Reeves. Written by Paul Diamond; directed by Francis Simon; for Chicken Enterprises / Avco Embassy.

Chicken Every Sunday*
US 1949 94m bw
TCF

The Hefferans have run a boarding house for twenty years, but dad's wild schemes run away with any possible profit.
Archetypal, folksy, American small-town chronicle, reasonably well made, for an audience that later watched *The Waltons.*

w George Seaton, Valentine Davies *d* George Seaton *ph* Harry Jackson *m* Alfred Newman

Dan Dailey, Celeste Holm, Colleen Townsend, Alan Young, Natalie Wood

The Chicken Wagon Family
US 1939 81m bw

Louisiana backwooders make a trip to New York. Feeble country cousin comedy. Jane Withers, Leo Carrillo, Marjorie Weaver, Spring Byington, Kane Richmond, Hobart Cavanaugh. Written by Viola Brothers Shore; directed by Herbert I. Leeds; for TCF. 'Nabes and second runs will write best ledger marks.'—*Variety*

Chickens Come Home*
US 1931 30m bw

Stan helps his boss Ollie to evade the attentions of an old flame. Rather heavy and untypical, but mainly very enjoyable star comedy, a remake of *Love 'Em and Weep* in which all three leading players had appeared four years earlier in different roles. Laurel and Hardy, James Finlayson, Mae Busch, Thelma Todd. Written by H. M. Walker, from a story by Hal Roach; directed by James W. Horne; for Hal Roach.

The Chief
US 1933 80m bw

A fireman's son becomes a Bowery candidate for alderman. Feeble comedy with the star ill at ease. Ed Wynn, Dorothy Mackaill, Charles 'Chic' Sale, William Boyd, George Givot, C. Henry Gordon. Written by Arthur Caesar and R. E. Hopkins; directed by Charles F. Reisner; for MGM. (GB title: *My Old Man's a Fireman.*) 'With the radio draw angle discarded it is weak entertainment.'—*Variety*

Chief Crazy Horse
US 1954 86m Technicolor Cinemascope
U-I (William Alland)
GB title: *Valley of Fury*

The tribal problems of the Indian chief who defeated Custer at Little Big Horn.
Competent pro-Indian western.

w Franklin Coen, Gerald Drayson Adams *d* George Sherman *ph* Harold Lipstein *m* Frank Skinner

Victor Mature, Suzan Ball, John Lund, Ray Danton, Keith Larsen, Paul Guilfoyle, David Janssen

Un Chien Andalou*
France 1928 17m bw silent
Luis Bunuel

Famous surrealist short which includes dead donkeys on pianos and starts with a woman's eyeball being cut by a razor blade.
It had meaning for its makers, but very few other people saw anything in it but sensationalism.

w Luis Bunuel, Salvador Dali d, ed Luis Bunuel ph Albert Dubergen

Simone Mareuil, Pierre Batcheff, Jaime Miravilles, Salvador Dali, Luis Bunuel

La Chienne*
France 1931 85m bw
Braunberger-Richebé

A bank clerk falls for a prostitute and later kills her; her pimp is executed for the crime and the bank clerk becomes a tramp.
Heavy-going, old-fashioned melodrama with some interesting detail.

wd Jean Renoir, novel Georges de la Fouchardière *ph* Theodor Sparkuhl, Roger Hubert

Michel Simon, Janie Marèze, Georges Flament, Jean Gehret

'If the English translation of the title is unfit to print, the film's dialogue cannot be translated into English. Okay for sophisticated audiences that look for a taste of spice in a ritzy spot.'—*Variety*

† Remade as *Scarlet Street* (qv).

Child in the House
GB 1956 88m bw
Eros / Golden Era (Ben Fisz)

When her mother is ill and her father in hiding from the police, a 12-year-old girl goes to stay with her fussy uncle and aunt.
Modest family drama of the novelette type in which adult problems are put right by the wisdom of a child.

wd C. Raker Endfield, *novel* Janet McNeill *ph* Otto Heller *m* Mario Nascimbene *ad* Ken Adam

Eric Portman, Phyllis Calvert, Stanley Baker, Mandy Miller, Dora Bryan, Joan Hickson, Victor Maddern, Percy Herbert

A Child is Born
US 1939 79m bw
Warner (Sam Bischoff)

A slice of life in the maternity ward.
Adequately dramatic sequence of cameos, with mothers-to-be including a gangster's moll: a remake of *Life Begins*.

w Robert Rossen, *play* Mary M. Axelson *d* Lloyd Bacon *ph* Charles Rosher *m* Heinz Roemheld

Geraldine Fitzgerald, Jeffrey Lynn, Gladys George, Gale Page, Spring Byington, Henry O'Neill, John Litel, Gloria Holden, Eve Arden, Nanette Fabares, Hobart Cavanaugh, Johnny Downs, Johnnie Davis

A Child is Waiting**
US 1963 104m bw
UA / Stanley Kramer

A mixed-up spinster joins the staff of a school for mentally handicapped children.
Worthy semi-documentary marred by having a normal boy play the central character (albeit very well). A little over-dramatized but cogent and unsentimental.

w Abby Mann *d* John Cassavetes *ph* Joseph La Shelle *m* Ernest Gold

Burt Lancaster, *Judy Garland, Bruce Ritchey*, Steven Hill, Gena Rowlands, *Paul Stewart*, Lawrence Tierney

Child of Manhattan
US 1933 70m bw

A night-club hostess has an affair with a millionaire, but her baby dies. Hokey melodrama on familiar lines (at the time). John Boles, Nancy Carroll, Warburton Gamble, Clara Blandick, Jane Darwell, Betty Grable. Written by Gertrude Purcell from a play by Preston Sturges; directed by Edward Buzzell; for Columbia. 'Programme fodder, with more simplicity than purity.'—*Variety*

The Childhood of Maxim Gorky***
USSR 1938–40 bw
Soyuzdetfilm

Orphan Gorky is raised by his grandparents, and becomes a ship's cook and a painter before going on to university.
This simple and direct story is told in three beautifully detailed if rather overlong films:
'The Childhood of Maxim Gorky': 101m
'Out in the World': 98m
'My Universities': 104m

w Mark Donskoi, I. Grudzev *d Mark Donskoi ph* Pyotr Yermolov *m* Lev Schwartz *ad* I. Stepanov

Alexei Lyarsky, Y. Valbert, M. Troyanovski, Valeria Massalitinova

Children of a Lesser God*
US 1986 110m Film Lab Color

A deaf woman falls in love with her speech therapist. Sluggish adaptation of a play which meant more on the stage. William Hurt, Marlee Matlin, Piper Laurie, Philip Bosco. Written by Hesper Anderson and Mark Medoff, from the latter's play; directed by Randa Haines; for Burt Sugarman, Patrick Palmer / Paramount.

AA: Marlee Matlin
AAN: Best picture; William Hurt; Piper Laurie

Children of Hiroshima**
Japan 1952 97m bw
Kendai Eiga Lyokai / Gekidan Mingei

A young teacher returns to Hiroshima seven years after the bomb.
Restrained yet harrowing social documentary in fiction form, with the most effective use of flashbacks to show the horror of the bomb and its aftermath.

wd Kaneto Shindo, novel Arata Osada *ph Takeo Itoh m* Akira Ifukube

Nobuko Otowa, Chikako Hoshawa, Niwa Saito

The Children of Sanchez
US / Mexico 1978 126m colour
Hall Bartlett

A macho Mexican and one of his daughters have ideas above the semi-slum in which they live.
The star is still looking for another *Zorba the Greek*, but this isn't it. Glum, glum, glum.

w Cesare Zavattini, Hall Bartlett, *novel* Oscar Lewis *d* Hall Bartlett *ph* Gabriel Figueroa *m* Chuck Mangione

Anthony Quinn, Dolores del Rio, Lupita Ferrer, Katy Jurado, Stathis Giallelis

Children of the Corn
US 1984 92m CFI colour
New World / Angeles / Cinema Group (Donald P. Borchers, Terence Kirby)

A doctor and his girl friend run down a child, discover that his throat has been cut, and find themselves in a community of murderous adolescents.
Nightmarish modern fantasy with style but very little to like.

w George Goldsmith, *story* Stephen King *d* Fritz Kiersch *ph* Raoul Lomas *m* Jonathan Elias

Peter Horton, Linda Hamilton, R. G. Armstrong, John Franklin

'The aim seems to be to reassure rather than to disturb.'—*Robert Murphy, MFB*

'So young, so innocent, so deadly—they came to conquer the world!'

Children of the Damned*
GB 1964 90m bw
MGM (Ben Arbeid)

Six super-intelligent children of various nations are brought to London by UNESCO, and turn out to be invaders from another planet.
Moderate sequel to *Village of the Damned*, well made but with no new twists.

w John Briley *d* Anton M. Leader *ph* David Boulton *m* Ron Goodwin

Ian Hendry, Alan Badel, Barbara Ferris, Alfred Burke, Sheila Allen, Ralph Michael, Martin Miller, Harold Goldblatt

The Children's Hour*
US 1961 108m bw
UA / Mirisch (William Wyler)
GB title: *The Loudest Whisper*

A spoilt schoolgirl spreads a rumour that her schoolmistresses are lesbians.
Frank sixties version of a play originally filmed in a much bowdlerized version as *These Three*. Unfortunately frankness in this case leads to dullness, as nothing is done with the theme once it is stated, and the treatment is heavy-handed.

w Lillian Hellman, from her play *d* William Wyler *ph* Franz Planer *m* Alex North

Audrey Hepburn, Shirley Maclaine, James Garner, Miriam Hopkins, Fay Bainter, Karen Balkin

'All very exquisite, and dead as mutton.'—*Tom Milne*

AAN: Franz Planer; Fay Bainter

Child's Play*
US 1972 100m Movielab
Paramount (David Merrick)

In a Catholic boarding school for boys, an unpopular master is hounded and discredited by another whose motives may be diabolic.
Enjoyable overblown melodrama with hints of many nasty goings on, rather spoiled by too much talk and too little local colour.

w Leon Prochnik, *play* Robert Marasco *d* Sidney Lumet *ph* Gerald Hirschfeld *m* Michael Small

James Mason, *Robert Preston*, Beau Bridges, Ronald Weyand

Chilly Scenes of Winter: see Head Over Heels (1980)

The Chiltern Hundreds*
GB 1949 84m bw
Rank / Two Cities (George H. Brown)
US title: *The Amazing Mr Beecham*

An aged earl is bewildered when his son fails to be elected to parliament as a socialist but his butler gets in as a tory.
Satisfactory filming of an amusing stage comedy, with the aged A. E. Matthews repeating his delightful if irrelevant act as the dotty earl.

w William Douglas Home, Patrick Kirwan, *play William Douglas Home d* John Paddy Carstairs *ph* Jack Hildyard *m* Benjamin Frankel

A. E. Matthews, Cecil Parker, David Tomlinson, Marjorie Fielding, Joyce Carey

Chimes at Midnight*
Spain / Switz 1966 119m bw
Internacional Films Espanola / Alpine (Alessandro Tasca)
aka: *Falstaff*

Prince Hal becomes King Henry V and rejects his old friend Falstaff.
Clumsy adaptation of Shakespeare with brilliant flashes and the usual Welles vices of hasty production, poor synchronization and recording, etc. One wonders why, if he wanted to make a telescoped version of the plays, he did not spare the time and patience to make it better.

w Orson Welles *d* Orson Welles *ph* Edmond Richard *m* Angelo Francesco Lavagnino

Orson Welles, Keith Baxter, John Gielgud (Henry IV), Margaret Rutherford (Mistress Quickly), Jeanne Moreau (Doll Tearsheet), Norman Rodway, Alan Webb, Marina Vlady, Tony Beckley, Fernando Rey

The Chimp*
US 1932 30m bw

Stan and Ollie try to get lodgings without revealing that their friend is a chimp, their share of a bankrupt circus. The circus scenes are better than the rather tired farce which follows, especially as it is so similar to *Laughing Gravy*. Laurel and Hardy, James Finlayson, Billy Gilbert, Tiny Sandford. Written by H. M. Walker; directed by James Parrott; for Hal Roach.

'Alan Ladd and twenty girls—trapped by the rapacious Japs!'

China
US 1943 79m bw
Paramount (Richard Blumenthal)

An oil salesman joins a Chinese guerrilla force and sacrifices himself.
Solemnly hilarious propaganda piece tailored to its star, showing the immense superiority of one lone American to the entire Japanese army.

w Frank Butler, *novel* The Fourth Brother by Reginald Forbes *d* John Farrow *ph* Leo Tover *m* Victor Young

Alan Ladd, Loretta Young, William Bendix, Philip Ahn, Iris Wong, Sen Yung, Richard Loo, Tala Birell

China Clipper*
US 1936 89m bw
Warner (Sam Bischoff)

An aviator neglects his wife while building up a trans-Pacific civil aviation link.
Solid entertainment feature of its day, with adequate production and performance.

w Frank 'Spig' Wead *d* Ray Enright *ph* Arthur Edeson *m* Bernhard Kaun, W. Franke Harling

Pat O'Brien, Beverly Roberts, Ross Alexander, Humphrey Bogart, Marie Wilson, Henry B. Walthall, Joseph Crehan, Addison Richards

China Corsair
US 1951 76m bw

An American ship's engineer is stranded on an island off the China coast. Routine escapist hokum. Jon Hall, Lisa Ferraday, Ron Randell, Douglas Kennedy, Ernest Borgnine. Written by Harold R. Greene; directed by Ray Nazarro; for Columbia.

China Doll
US 1958 99m bw
Romina / Batjac (Frank Borzage)

In 1943 an American air force officer accidentally buys the services of a young Chinese housekeeper. He marries her but they are both killed in action; years later their daughter is welcomed to America by members of his old air crew.
Incurably sentimental and icky romantic drama in the style of the director's silent films; something of a curiosity for historians.

w Kitty Buhler *d* Frank Borzage *ph* William H. Clothier *m* Henry Vars

Victor Mature, Li Li Hua, Bob Mathias, Ward Bond, Stuart Whitman

'An American dynamiter love-locked in war-locked China!'

China Gate
US 1957 90m bw Cinemascope
TCF (Samuel Fuller)

A Eurasian girl guides her American husband to a communist arms dump.
Anti-Red thick ear, slick but undistinguished.

wd Samuel Fuller *ph* Joseph Biroc *m* Victor Young, Max Steiner

Gene Barry, Angie Dickinson, Nat King Cole, Paul Dubov, Lee Van Cleef, George Givot

China Girl
US 1943 95m bw
TCF (Ben Hecht)

A newsreel cameraman in China falls in love with a Eurasian schoolteacher.
Routine adventure romance with splodges of love and self-sacrifice.

w Ben Hecht *d* Henry Hathaway *ph* Lee Garmes *m* Hugo Friedhofer

Gene Tierney, George Montgomery, *Lynn Bari*, Victor McLaglen, Alan Baxter, Sig Rumann, Myron McCormick, Philip Ahn

China Seas**
US 1935 89m bw
MGM (Albert Lewin)

Luxury cruise passengers find themselves involved with piracy.
Omnibus shipboard melodrama, tersely scripted and featuring a splendid cast all somewhere near their best; slightly dated but very entertaining.

w Jules Furthman, James Kevin McGuinness, *novel* Crosbie Garstin *d Tay Garnett* *ph* Ray June *m* Herbert Stothart

Clark Gable, Jean Harlow, Wallace Beery, Rosalind Russell, Lewis Stone, C. Aubrey Smith, Dudley Digges, Robert Benchley

'It will do double-barrelled duty, drawing business and providing ace entertainment.'—*Variety*

'The hell with art this time. I'm going to produce a picture that will make money.'—*Irving Thalberg*

China Sky
US 1945 78m bw
RKO (Maurice Geraghty)

Two American doctors live with Chinese guerrillas; the jealousy of the wife of one of them causes problems.
Routine adventure romance with generally unconvincing production and performance.

w Brenda Weisberg, Joseph Hoffman, *novel* Pearl Buck *d* Ray Enright *ph* Nicholas Musuraca *m* Roy Webb

Randolph Scott, Ellen Drew, Ruth Warrick, Anthony Quinn, Carol Thurston, Richard Loo, Philip Ahn

The China Syndrome**
US 1979 122m Metrocolor
Columbia / IPC (Bruce Gilbert)

The controller of a nuclear power plant discovers an operational flaw which could lead to disaster, but the unscrupulous authorities want to cover it up.
Topical thriller-with-a-moral, absorbingly done in the old style but perhaps in the end a shade too hysterical and self-congratulatory.

w Mike Gray, T. S. Cook, James Bridges *d James Bridges* *ph* James Crabe *m* various *pd* George Jenkins

Jane Fonda, *Jack Lemmon*, Michael Douglas, Scott Brady, Peter Donat, James Hampton

'The performances are so good, and the screen so bombarded with both action and informative images . . . that it's only with considerable hindsight that one recovers sufficient breath to reproach the script with the occasional glib symmetry.'—*Jan Dawson, MFB*

China Venture
US 1953 83m bw

In 1945, American marines are sent into the Chinese jungle to recover a Japanese admiral held captive there. Topical thick-ear, played and presented without conviction. Edmond O'Brien, Barry Sullivan, Jocelyn Brando, Richard Loo. Written by George Worthing Yates and Richard Collins; directed by Don Siegel; for Anson Bond / Columbia.

Chinatown***
US 1974 131m Technicolor Panavision
Paramount / Long Road (Robert Evans)

In 1937, a Los Angeles private eye takes on a simple case and burrows into it until it leads to murder and a public scandal.
Pretentious melodrama which is basically no more serious than the Raymond Chandler mysteries from which it derives; the tragic ending is merely an irritation, and the title only allusive. Superficially, however, it is eminently watchable, with effective individual scenes and performances and photography which is lovingly composed though tending to suggest period by use of an orange filter.

w Robert Towne d Roman Polanski ph John A. Alonso m Jerry Goldsmith pd Richard Sylbert

Jack Nicholson, Faye Dunaway, John Huston, Perry Lopez, John Hillerman, Roman Polanski, Darrell Zwerling, Diane Ladd

AA: Robert Towne
AAN: best picture; Roman Polanski; John A. Alonso; Jerry Goldsmith; Jack Nicholson; Faye Dunaway

Chinatown at Midnight
US 1949 67m bw

Police seek a killer in Chinatown. Efficient lower-case police thriller. Hurd Hatfield, Jean

Willes, Tom Powers, Ray Walker. Written by Robert Libott and Frank Burt; directed by Seymour Friedman; for Columbia.

The Chinese Bungalow
GB 1939 72m bw
George King
US title: *Chinese Den*

A Chinese merchant plots to kill the lover of his English wife.
Stolid version of an old melodrama which can hardly fail; previously filmed in 1926 with Matheson Lang and Geneviève Townsend (directed by Sinclair Hill) and in 1930 with Matheson Lang and Anna Neagle (directed by J. B. Williams).

w A. R. Rawlinson, George Wellesley, *play* Matheson Lang, Marian Osmond *d* George King *ph* Hone Glendinning

Paul Lukas, Jane Baxter, Robert Douglas, Kay Walsh, Jerry Verno

Chinese Roulette*
West Germany / France 1976 86m Eastmancolor
Albatros / Losange (Rainer Werner Fassbinder)

Various related people, mainly adulterous, meet in a country château and play a truth game which ends in violence.
Interestingly enigmatic character melodrama reminiscent of Bergman at his prime, but concerning people who barely seem to matter.

wd Rainer Werner Fassbinder ph Michael Ballhaus *m* Peer Raben

Margit Carstensen, Andrea Schober, Ulli Lommel, Anna Karina, Macha Meril

'Locked into their private hell . . . this vicious octet form their own coherent and compelling universe.'—*Jan Dawson, MFB*

Chino
US / Italy 1973 98m colour

A runaway boy helps a half-breed run a ranch in New Mexico. Undistinguished western. Charles Bronson, Jill Ireland, Vincent Van Petten. Written by Clair Huffaker, from a novel by Lee Hoffman; directed by John Sturges; for Dino de Laurentiis.

Chip off the Old Block
US 1944 76m bw

The son of a seafaring family gets into expected romantic trouble. Lightweight comedy-musical which performed adequately at the time. Donald O'Connor, Peggy Ryan, Ann Blyth, Patrick Knowles, Helen Broderick, Helen Vinson, Arthur Treacher, J. Edward Bromberg, Ernest Truex. Written by Eugene Conrad, Leo Townsend; directed by Charles Lamont; for Bernard W. Burton / Universal. 'Effervescing juvenile comedy-drama for wide audience appeal.'—*Variety*

Chisum*
US 1970 110m Technicolor Panavision
Warner / Batjac (Michael Wayne, Andrew J. Fenady)

A corrupt businessman plots against the head of a vast cattle empire, who is saved by the intervention of numerous friends including Pat Garrett and Billy the Kid.
Desultory, overlong, friendly western in the Ford manner. Easy to watch and easier to forget.

w Andrew J. Fenady *d* Andrew V. McLaglen *ph William H. Clothier* *m* Dominic Frontière

John Wayne, Forrest Tucker, Christopher George, Ben Johnson, Glenn Corbett, Bruce Cabot, Andrew Prine, Patric Knowles, Richard Jaeckel, Linda Day George, John Agar, Ray Teal, Glenn Langan, Alan Baxter, Abraham Sofaer, Pete Duel

'A curious mixture of styles and myths.'—*John Gillett*

Chitty Chitty Bang Bang
GB 1968 145m Technicolor Super Panavision 70
UA / Warfield / DFI (Albert R. Broccoli)

An unsuccessful inventor rescues a derelict car and gives it magical properties, then helps the children who own it to overthrow the government of a country which hates children.
A bumpy ride. Sentiment, slapstick, whimsy and mild scares do not combine but are given equal shares of the limelight, while poor trickwork prevents the audience from being transported.

w Roald Dahl, Ken Hughes *d* Ken Hughes *ph* Christopher Challis *m* Irwin Kostal *songs* the Sherman Brothers *ad* Ken Adam *decor* Rowland Emmett

Dick Van Dyke, Sally Ann Howes (as Truly Scrumptious), Lionel Jeffries, Robert Helpmann, Gert Frobe, Benny Hill, James Robertson Justice

AAN: title song

Chronicle of a Death Foretold*
Italy / France 1987 110m Eastmancolor Panavision

A whole town colludes in the murder of an innocent man.
Rosi gives epic sweep to a South American tragedy of vendetta and machismo, in spite of some oddity in the international casting.

w Francesco Rosi, Tonino Guerra, from novel by Gabriel Garcia Marquez *d Francesco Rosi* *ph* Pasqualino De Santis *m* Piero Piccioni *pd* Andrea Crisanti

Rupert Everett, Ornella Muti, Gian Maria Volonte, Irene Papas

The Chocolate Soldier*
US 1941 102m bw
MGM (Victor Saville)

Married opera singers fall out backstage.
Talky musical remake of *The Guardsman*: nearly comes off but not quite.

w Keith Winter, Leonard Lee *d* Roy del Ruth *ph* Karl Freund *songs* Oscar Straus *m* Herbert Stothart, Bronislau Kaper

Nelson Eddy, Rise Stevens, Nigel Bruce, Florence Bates, Nydia Westman

AAN: Karl Freund; Herbert Stothart, Bronislau Kaper

The Choirboys
US 1978 119m Technicolor
Lorimar / Airone (Lee Rich, Merv Adelson)

Members of a police department are if anything more delinquent, vicious and mentally retarded than their quarries.
A vulgar and repellent anti-establishment display, apparently intended as black comedy. Just the thing to put an end to the art of the movie once and for all.

w Christopher Knopf, *novel* Joseph Wambaugh *d* Robert Aldrich *ph* Joseph Biroc *m* Frank de Vol

Charles Durning, Lou Gossett Jnr, Perry King, Stephen Macht, Tim McIntyre, Clyde Kusatu, Randy Quaid, Don Stroud, Robert Webber, Blair Brown

Chomps
US 1979 89m colour

A young inventor is successful with a robot dog (Canine Home Protection System). Rather feeble family-oriented comedy. Jim Backus, Valerie Bertinelli, Chuck McCann, Regis Toomey, Red Buttons. Written by Dick Robbins, Duane Poole; directed by Don Chaffey; for Joseph Barbera / American International.

Choose Me
US 1984 106m Movielab

Two lonely people in LA become a couple. Even for those not irritated by the director's style and interests, this is an entertainment which goes around in circles and gets nowhere, except Las Vegas. Genevieve Bujold, Keith Carradine, Lesley Ann Warren, Patrick Bachau, Rae Dawn Chong. Written and directed by Alan Rudolf; for Carolyn Pfeiffer, David Blocker / Island and Alive.

A Chorus Line
US 1985 111m Technicolor Panavision
Embassy / Polygram (Cy Feuer, Ernest Martin)

A Broadway musical chorus is selected.
Overpraised musical drama which took nine years to reach the screen because nobody could figure out how to 'open it up', despite Universal's payment of 5.5 million dollars for the rights. The present team has not solved the problem.

w Arnold Schulman *play* Nicholas Dante, James Kirkwood *d* Richard Attenborough *ph* Ronnie Taylor *m / ly* Marvin Hamlisch, Edward Kleban *pd* Patrizia von Brandenstein *ed* John Bloom

Michael Douglas, Terence Mann, Alyson Reed, Cameron English, Vicki Frederick

'Static and confined, rarely venturing beyond the immediate.'—*Variety*

'He makes his camera fly like a bird around the near-deserted theatre.'—*Shaun Usher, Daily Mail*

AAN: editing

The Chosen
US 1981 108m Movielab
The Chosen Film Company (Edie and Ely Landau)

In New York in the early forties, a family feud between Zionist and Hassidic Jews interferes with a friendship between two boys.
A sentimental minority piece which does what it has to do quite effectively.

w Edwin Gordon, *novel* Chaim Potok *d* Jeremy Paul Kagan *ph* Arthur Ornitz *m* Elmer Bernstein *pd* Stuart Wurtzel

Maximilian Schell, Rod Steiger, Robby Benson, Barry Miller, Hildy Brooks, Kaethe Fine

Chosen Survivors
US 1974 98m colour
Alpine / Metromedia (Charles Fries)

Ten people with special skills are chosen to test human reaction to thermo-nuclear war, but find themselves at the mercy of vampire bats.
Another misfit group united by disaster; more shocks than suspense, and not much characterization, but for adventure / horror addicts it will pass the time.

w H. B. Cross, Joe Red Moffly *d* Sutton Roley *ph* Gabriel Torres *m* Fred Karlin

Jackie Cooper, Alex Cord, Richard Jaeckel, Diana Muldaur, Lincoln Kilpatrick, Bradford Dillman, Pedro Armendariz Jnr, Gwen Mitchell, Barbara Babcock, Christina Moreno

Les Choses de la Vie*
France / Italy 1969 89m Eastmancolor
Lira / Fida (Raymond Danon)
aka: *These Things Happen; The Things of Life*

An architect has his wife and mistress neatly balanced when an accident upsets his scheme of things.
Nicely observed tragi-comedy in the best French manner; since it starts with the car crash, a mini-*Bridge of San Luis Rey*.

w Paul Guimard, Claude Sautet, Jean-Loup Dabadie, *novel* Paul Guimard *d Claude Sautet* *ph* Jean Boffety *m* Philippe Sarde

Michel Piccoli, Romy Schneider, Lea Massari, Gérard Lartigau, Jean Bouise

Christ Stopped at Eboli*
Italy / France 1979 155m Technospes colour
Vides Cinematografica / RAI / Action Film / Gaumont (Franco Cristaldi, Nicola Carraro)

In 1935 an Italian doctor is exiled because of his political views to a remote southern part of the country.
An attractively faithful account of a book which was part personal statement, part symbolism, part political opinion and part local colour. Non-Italians will be unable to extract the full flavour.

w Francesco Rosi, Tonino Guerra, Raffaele La Capria, *book* Carlo Levi *d* Francesco Rosi *ph* Pasqualino de Santis *m* Piero Piccioni

Gian Maria Volonte, Alain Cuny, Paolo Bonacelli, Lea Massari, Irene Papas, François Simon

BFA: best foreign film

The Christian Liquorice Store
US 1971 90m colour

A Hollywood tennis player succumbs to corrupting influences. Odd item with interesting credits but not much flesh on the bones. Beau Bridges, Maud Adams, Gilbert Roland, Alan Arbus, Monte Hellman. Written by Floyd Mutrux; directed by James Frawley; for National General.

Christiane F*
West Germany 1981 131m colour

A teenage girl becomes a drug addict. Slick melodrama hoked up from 'true' confessions with excellent background detail. Natja Brunckhorst, Thomas Haustein, Jens Kuphal. Written by Herman Weigel; directed by Ulrich Edel; for Maran Film / Popular Film / Hans H. Kaden / TCF.

'How do you kill something that can't possibly be alive?'

Christine
US 1983 110m Technicolor Panavision
Columbia / Delphi (Richard Kobritz)

A diabolical car maims and kills its owner's girl friends.
Thin and gruesomely extended horror flick which never begins to be convincing. For teenagers only.

w Bill Phillips, *novel* Stephen King *d* John Carpenter *ph* Donald M. Morgan *m* John Carpenter *pd* Daniel Lomino

Keith Gordon, John Stockwell, Alexandra Paul, Robert Prosky, Harry Dean Stanton, Christine Belford

'The kind of movie where you walk out with a silly grin, get in your car, and lay rubber halfway down the freeway.' *Roger Ebert*

A Christmas Carol*
US 1938 69m bw
MGM (Joseph L. Mankiewicz)

Scrooge the miser is reformed when four ghosts visit him on Christmas Eve.
Standard Dickensian frolic, quite well mounted.

w Hugo Butler *d* Edwin L. Marin *ph* Sidney Wagner *m* Franz Waxman

Reginald Owen, Gene Lockhart, Kathleen Lockhart, Terry Kilburn, Leo G. Carroll, Lynne Carver

'Top production, inspired direction, superb acting.'—*Variety*

† See also *Scrooge*.

Christmas Eve*
US 1947 92m bw
Benedict Bogeaus
aka: *Sinners' Holiday*

An old lady needs the help of her three adopted sons to prevent herself from being swindled.
Basically three short stories sealed by a Christmas Eve reunion, this is old-fashioned sentimental stuff, but it works on its level and the cast is interesting.

w Lawrence Stallings *d* Edwin L. Marin *ph* Gordon Avil *m* Heinz Roemheld

Ann Harding, George Raft, Randolph Scott, George Brent, Joan Blondell, Virginia Field, Reginald Denny

Christmas Holiday
US 1944 93m bw
Universal (Felix Jackson)

A young girl marries a murderer, and later, as a shady songstress in a nightclub, is forced to help him escape.
A weird change of pace for Deanna Durbin, whose forte had been sweetness and light, this relentlessly grim and boring melodrama was also a travesty of the novel on which it was based.

w Herman J. Mankiewicz, *novel* Somerset Maugham *d* Robert Siodmak *ph* Elwood Bredell *m* Hans Salter

Deanna Durbin, Gene Kelly, Dean Harens, Gladys George, Richard Whorf, Gale Sondergaard

AAN: Hans Salter

Christmas in Connecticut*
US 1945 101m bw
Warner (William Jacobs)
GB title: *Indiscretion*

The spinster writer of a successful column about love and marriage has to conjure up a family for herself in the cause of publicity.
Predictable but fairly brisk comedy with excellent talent well deployed.

w Lionel Houser, Adele Commandini *d* Peter Godfrey *ph* Carl Guthrie *m* Frederick Hollander

Barbara Stanwyck, Dennis Morgan, Sydney Greenstreet, Reginald Gardiner, S. Z. Sakall, Robert Shayne, Una O'Connor, Frank Jenks

'If you can't sleep at night, it isn't the coffee—it's the bunk!'

Christmas in July**
US 1940 67m bw
Paramount

A young clerk and his girl win first prize in a big competition.
Slightly unsatisfactory as a whole, this Preston Sturges comedy has echoes of Clair and a dully predictable plot line, but is kept alive by inventive touches and a gallery of splendid character comedians.

wd Preston Sturges *ph* Victor Milner *m* Sigmund Krumgold

Dick Powell, Ellen Drew, Ernest Truex, *Al Bridge*, Raymond Walburn, William Demarest

'The perfect restorative for battered humors and jangled nerves.'—*Bosley Crowther*

'Agreeable enough, but it lacks the full-fledged Sturges lunacy.'—*New Yorker, 1977*

A Christmas Story*
US 1983 93m colour
MGM / UA (René Dupont, Bob Clark)

In an Indiana suburb during the 1940s, a schoolboy hopes to get a rifle for Christmas.
Curious, almost plotless family comedy of the old school, with the difference that some grotesquerie and tastelessness is added. On the whole, however, an amusing entertainment for adults who don't mind their mood of sentimental nostalgia being tilted at by the director of *Porky's*.

w Jean Shepherd, Leigh Brown, Bob Clark *d* Bob Clark

Peter Billingsley, Melinda Dillon, Darren McGavin, Ian Petrella

The Christmas Tree
France / Italy 1969 110m Eastmancolor
Corona / Jupiter (Robert Dorfmann)

The small son of a millionaire widower is fatally infected by radioactivity.
Painfully sentimental and overdrawn weepie, the most lachrymose film of the sixties.

wd Terence Young, *novel* Michel Bataille *ph* Henri Alekan *m* Georges Auric

William Holden, Virna Lisi, Brook Fuller, Bourvil

'Depending on your taste threshold, there may not be a dry eye—nor a full stomach—in the house.'—*Judith Crist*

Christopher Bean*
US 1933 80m bw
aka: *Her Sweetheart*

A dying artist appoints his housekeeper as his executor. Solid family entertainment very typical of its studio. *Marie Dressler* (her last film), Lionel Barrymore, Beulah Bondi, Helen Mack, George Coulouris, H. B. Warner, Jean Hersholt. Written by Laurence Johnson and Sylvia Thalberg, from Sidney Howard's play *The Late Christopher Bean*; directed by Sam Wood; for MGM.

Christopher Columbus
US 1949 104m Technicolor
Rank / Gainsborough / Sydney Box (Betty E. Box)

Columbus seeks and receives the patronage of the Spanish court for his voyage to the west.
An extraordinarily tediously paced historical account of basically undramatic events; interesting without being stimulating.

w Muriel and Sydney Box, Cyril Roberts *d* David MacDonald *ph* Stephen Dade *m* Arthur Bliss

Fredric March, Florence Eldridge, Francis L. Sullivan, Linden Travers

'Even ten-year-olds will find it about as thrilling as an afternoon spent looking at Christmas cards.'—*Time*

'She gave herself to the great God speed, and tried to run away from the fires within her!'
'The personal story of a million daughters!'
Christopher Strong*
US 1933 72m bw
RKO (Pandro S. Berman)

A daring lady aviator has an affair with a married businessman and commits suicide when she finds herself pregnant.
A curious and unsatisfactory yarn for Hepburn's second film; well enough made, it died at the box office.

w Zoe Akins, *novel* Gilbert Frankau *d* Dorothy Arzner *ph* Bert Glennon *m* Max Steiner

Katharine Hepburn, Colin Clive, Billie Burke, Helen Chandler, Ralph Forbes, Irene Browne, Jack La Rue

'Draggy society play with circusy aeroplane stunt incidentals . . . interest in the star will outweigh other elements.'—*Variety*

Chronique d'un Eté*
France 1961 90m bw
Argos

Parisians talk about their lives.
Curious but rather stimulating acted documentary, with two interviewers pontificating; saved by shrewd editing to keep interest at its maximum.

wd Jean Rouch, Edgar Morin ph various

Chu Chin Chow*
GB 1934 102m bw
Gaumont British / Gainsborough (Michael Balcon)

In old Arabia, a slave girl foils a robber posing as a dead mandarin.
Second screen version (the first was silent) of the old Arabian Nights stage musical. A curiosity.

w Edward Knoblock, L. DuGarde Peach, Sidney Gilliat, *play* Oscar Asche and Frederick Norton *d* Walter Forde *songs* Frederick Norton *md* Louis Levy *ph* Max Greene *ch* Anton Dolin

George Robey, Fritz Kortner, Anna May Wong, John Garrick, Pearl Argyle, Malcolm MacEachern, Dennis Hoey, Francis L. Sullivan, Sydney Fairbrother

'A colourful, extravagant costume film that makes its bid for attention purely on an extravaganza platform, and makes the grade.'—*Variety*

'Gaumont British have broken away for the first time from their careful refinement, and produced something that has guts as well as grace.'—*C. A. Lejeune*

Chu Chu and the Philly Flash
US 1981 100m colour

A one-woman band performer and a drunken ex-baseball player lay claim to the same lost briefcase. Weird comedy which doesn't come off except at odd moments. Carol Burnett, Alan Arkin, Jack Warden, Danny Aiello, Adam Arkin, Ruth Buzzi. Written by Barbara Dana; directed by David Lowell Rich; for Jay Weston/Twentieth Century Fox.

Chubasco
US 1967 100m Technicolor Panavision
Warner Seven Arts (William Conrad)

A wild beach boy takes a job on a tuna fishing boat.
Old-fashioned boy-makes-good melodrama à la Captains Courageous. Excellent action sequences at sea.

wd Allen H. Miner *ph* Louis Jennings, Paul Ivano *m* William Lava

Chris Jones, Richard Egan, Susan Strasberg, Ann Sothern, Simon Oakland, Preston Foster, Audrey Totter, Peter Whitney

Chuka
US 1967 105m Technicolor
Paramount / Rod Taylor

A wandering gunfighter defends the inhabitants of a fort against Indian attack.
Ill-assorted characters under stress is the theme of this rather pedestrian and slightly pretentious western.

w Richard Jessup *d* Gordon Douglas *ph* Harold Stine *m* Leith Stevens

Rod Taylor, Ernest Borgnine, John Mills, Luciana Paluzzi, James Whitmore, Louis Hayward, Angela Dorian

A Chump at Oxford**
US 1939 63m bw
Hal Roach

Two street cleaners foil a bank hold-up and are presented with an Oxford education.
Patchy but endearing Laurel and Hardy romp, starting with an irrelevant two reels about their playing butler and maid, but later including Stan's burlesque impersonation of Lord Paddington.

w Charles Rogers, Harry Langdon, Felix Adler *d* Alfred Goulding *ph* Art Lloyd *m* Marvin Hatley

Stan Laurel, Oliver Hardy, James Finlayson, Forrester Harvey, Wilfrid Lucas, Peter Cushing

'Ranks with their best pictures—which, to one heretic, are more agreeable than Chaplin's. Their clowning is purer; they aren't out to better an unbetterable world; they've never wanted to play Hamlet.'—*Graham Greene*

'Earth-shaking in its grandeur! A titanic canvas sprung to life!'
Cimarron*
US 1930 130m bw
RKO (Louis Sarecky)

The life of an Oklahoma homesteader from 1890 to 1915.
Sprawling western family saga; a big early talkie, it dates badly.

w Howard Estabrook, *novel* Edna Ferber *d* Wesley Ruggles *ph* Edward Cronjager *m* Max Steiner

Richard Dix, Irene Dunne, Estelle Taylor, Nance O'Neill, William Collier Jnr, Roscoe Ates, George E. Stone, Stanley Fields, Edna May Oliver

'An elegant example of super film-making . . . big money feature for all classes.'—*Variety*

AA: best picture; Howard Estabrook
AAN: Wesley Ruggles; Edward Cronjager; Richard Dix; Irene Dunne

Cimarron*
US 1961 147m Metrocolor Cinemascope
MGM (Edmund Grainger)

Flabby, relentlessly boring remake of the above.

w Arnold Schulman *d* Anthony Mann *ph* Robert L. Surtees *m* Franz Waxman

Glenn Ford, Maria Schell, Anne Baxter, Lili Darvas, Russ Tamblyn, Henry Morgan, David Opatoshu, Charles McGraw, Aline MacMahon, Edgar Buchanan, Arthur O'Connell, Mercedes McCambridge, Vic Morrow, Robert Keith, Mary Wickes, Royal Dano, Vladimir Sokoloff

The Cincinnati Kid**
US 1965 113m Metrocolor
MGM / Filmways (Martin Ransohoff, John Calley)

In New Orleans in the late thirties, stud poker experts compete for supremacy.
This is to poker what *The Hustler* was to pool, a fascinating suspense study of experts at work; as before, the romantic asides let down the effectiveness of the others.

w Ring Lardner Jnr, Terry Southern, *novel* Richard Jessup *d Norman Jewison ph* Philip Lathrop *m* Lalo Schifrin

Steve McQueen, *Edward G. Robinson*, Karl Malden, Ann-Margret, Tuesday Weld, Joan Blondell, Rip Torn, Jack Weston, Cab Calloway, Jeff Corey

'I took out all the primaries. There are no reds, greens, whites or blues in the film outside of the red cards and the cockfight.'—*Norman Jewison*

Cinderella**
US 1950 75m Technicolor
Walt Disney

The Perrault fairy tale embroidered with animal characters.
A feature cartoon rather short on inspiration, though with all Disney's solid virtues. The mice are lively and the villainous cat the best character.

supervisor Ben Sharpsteen *d* Wilfred Jackson, Hamilton Luske, Clyde Geronomi *m* Oliver Wallace, Paul J. Smith

AAN: Oliver Wallace, Paul J. Smith; song 'Bibbidy Bobbidy Boo' (*m / ly* Mack David, Al Hoffman, Jerry Livingston)

Cinderella Jones
US 1946 89m bw
Warner (Alex Gottlieb)

To collect an inheritance, a girl must marry a brainy man.
Witless comedy for the easily pleased.

w Charles Hoffman, *story* Philip Wylie *d* Busby Berkeley *ph* Sol Polito *m* Frederick Hollander

Joan Leslie, Robert Alda, S. Z. Sakall, Edward Everett Horton, Julie Bishop, William Prince, Charles Dingle, Ruth Donnelly, Elisha Cook Jnr, Hobart Cavanaugh, Chester Clute

'A movie for every woman who thinks she can never fall in love again!'

Cinderella Liberty
US 1974 117m De Luxe Panavision
TCF / Sanford (Mark Rydell)

A sailor on shore leave picks up a prostitute and falls in love with her.
Assertively 'modern' yet glutinously sentimental love story in squalid settings. It presumably has an audience.

w Darryl Ponicsan, from his novel *d* Mark Rydell *ph* Vilmos Zsigmond *m* John Williams

James Caan, Marsha Mason, Eli Wallach, Kirk Calloway, Allyn Ann McLerie

'A sordid, messy affair which wants to jerk tears but just doesn't have the knack.'—*New Yorker*

AA: song 'You're So Nice To Be Around' (*m* John Williams, *ly* Paul Williams)
AAN: John Williams; Marsha Mason

Cinderfella
US 1960 91m Technicolor
Paramount / Jerry Lewis

Luxury pantomime featuring a male Cinderella.
Annoyingly lavish and empty star vehicle with precious little to laugh at: Lewis' own jokes are strung out to snapping point and no one else gets a look in.

wd Frank Tashlin *ph* Haskell Boggs *m* Walter Scharf

Jerry Lewis, Ed Wynn, Judith Anderson, Anna Maria Alberghetti, Henry Silva, Robert Hutton, Count Basie

'A drought of comic inspiration, followed by a flood of mawkish whimsy, gradually increases one's early misgivings to a degree which finally verges on revulsion.'—*Peter John Dyer*

The Circle

Somerset Maugham's brittle play contrasting noble breeding with vulgar riches was filmed by Frank Borzage as a Hollywood silent, in 1925 for MGM, with Elinor Boardman, Creighton Hale and Alec B. Francis. In 1930 the same studio made it as a talkie under the title *Strictly Unconventional*, with Catherine Dale Owen, Tyrrell Davis and Lewis Stone; directed by David Burton. Neither version really worked.

Circle of Danger*
GB 1951 89m bw
Coronado / David Rose (Joan Harrison)

An American in England investigates the strange death some years earlier of his brother during a commando raid.
Individual scenes are well milked for suspense and dramatic emphasis, but the plot line has virtually no mystery and absolutely no danger. It all seems mildly reminiscent of several Hitchcock films.

w Philip MacDonald *d Jacques Tourneur ph* Oswald Morris *m* Robert Farnon

Ray Milland, Patricia Roc, Marius Goring, Hugh Sinclair, Naunton Wayne, Marjorie Fielding, Edward Rigby, Colin Gordon, Dora Bryan

Circle of Deceit*
West Germany / France 1981 109m Eastmancolor
Bioskop / Artemis / Hessicher Rundfunk / Argos (Eberhard Junkersdorf)
original title: *Die Fälschung*

A German journalist has a crisis of conscience while covering the war in Beirut.
Fashionable self-scrutiny based on a published 'faction'. As a film, quite engrossing and occasionally hair-raising.

w Volker Schlöndorff and others, *book* Nicolas Born *d* Volker Schlöndorff *ph* Igor Luther *m* Maurice Jarre

Bruno Ganz, Hanna Schygulla, Jerzy Skolimowski, Gila von Weitershausen

'Rarely can a fiction film about war have had such a vividly authentic background, with real corpses and real destruction lending a bleak chill never captured by staged reconstructions.'—*Tom Milne, MFB*

Circle of Deception
GB 1960 100m bw Cinemascope
TCF (T. H. Morahan)

An officer is parachuted into Germany with the intention that he should crack under interrogation and reveal false information.
Depressing World War II tall tale, with suspense sacrificed by flashback structure.

w Nigel Balchin, Robert Musel, *novel* Alec Waugh *d* Jack Lee *ph* Gordon Dines *m* Clifton Parker

Bradford Dillman, Harry Andrews, Suzy Parker, Robert Stephens, John Welsh, Paul Rogers, Duncan Lamont, Michael Ripper

Circle of Two
Canada 1980 105m colour
Film Consortium of Canada (Henk Van der Kolk)

A 60-year-old artist falls for a teenage student.
Dreary and uninteresting star drama which never really gets going.

w Thomas Hedley, from A Lesson in Love by Marie Terese Baird *d* Jules Dassin *ph* Lazlo George *m* Paul Hoffert

Richard Burton, Tatum O'Neal, Nuala Fitzgerald, Kate Reid, Robin Gammell, Patricia Collins

Circonstances Attenuantes*
France 1939 85m bw

A retired magistrate becomes innocently involved with a gang of crooks. Nimble farce, most skilfully acted. Michel Simon, Arletty, Suzanne Dantes, Arnoux, Mila Parely. Written by Jean-Pierre Feydeau from a novel by Marcel Arnac; directed by Jean Boyer; for CCFC.

The Circus*
US 1928 72m (24 fps) bw silent
(UA) Charles Chaplin

A tramp on the run from the police takes refuge in a circus and falls for an equestrienne. Pathos often descends to bathos in this self-constructed star vehicle which has far too few laughs.

wd Charles Chaplin ph Rollie Totheroh, Jack Wilson, Mark Marlott

Charles Chaplin, Merna Kennedy, Allan Garcia, Harry Crocker

AAN: Charles Chaplin (as actor and director)

'One man's lust turns men into beasts, strips women of their souls!'

Circus of Horrors

GB 1960 91m Eastmancolor
Anglo Amalgamated / Lynx / Independent Artists (Norman Priggen)

A plastic surgeon staffs a semi-derelict circus with criminals whose faces he has altered, and murders any who try to flee.
Stark horror comic; quite professionally made, but content-wise a crude concoction of sex and sadism.

w George Baxt *d* Sidney Hayers *ph* Douglas Slocombe *m* Franz Reizenstein, Muir Mathieson

Anton Diffring, Erika Remberg, Yvonne Monlaur, Donald Pleasance, Jane Hylton, Kenneth Griffith, Conrad Phillips, Jack Gwyllim

The Circus Queen Murder*

US 1933 63m bw

Thatcher Colt solves murders in a travelling circus. Reasonably slick second feature of its period. *Adolphe Menjou*, Greta Nissen, Ruthelma Stevens, Dwight Frye, Donald Cook. Written by Jo Swerling from a novel by Anthony Abbott; directed by Roy William Neill; for Columbia.

Circus World

US 1964 138m Super Technirama
Bronston / Midway (Samuel Bronston)
GB title: *The Magnificent Showman*

An American circus owner tours Europe in search of his alcoholic ex-wife who left him when her lover fell to death from the trapeze. Lethargic big-screen epic which exhausts its spectacle in the first hour and then settles down to a dreary will-daughter-guess-who-the-strange-lady-is plot, without even the plus of an exciting finale.

w Ben Hecht, Julian Halevy, James Edward Grant *d* Henry Hathaway *ph* Jack Hildyard *pd* John de Cuir *m* Dmitri Tiomkin

John Wayne, *Rita Hayworth*, Claudia Cardinale, John Smith, Lloyd Nolan, Richard Conte, Wanda Rotha, Kay Walsh

'To sit through this film is something like holding an elephant on your lap for two hours and fifteen minutes.'—*Time*

The Cisco Kid

The Cisco Kid, a ruthless Mexican bandit originally created by O. Henry in a short story, was turned by Hollywood into a dashing wild western Robin Hood in twenty-three sound features (following a few silent ones) and a long-running TV series. In most of them he was accompanied by his fat side-kick Pancho.

For Fox:
1929: IN OLD ARIZONA (Warner Baxter)
1931: THE CISCO KID (Baxter)

For Twentieth Century Fox:
1939: THE RETURN OF THE CISCO KID (Baxter), THE CISCO KID AND THE LADY (Cesar Romero: who played the role in all the remaining TCF movies).
1940: VIVA CISCO KID, LUCKY CISCO KID, THE GAY CABALLERO
1941: ROMANCE OF THE RIO GRANDE, RIDE ON, VAQUERO

For Monogram:
1945: THE CISCO KID RETURNS (Duncan Renaldo), THE CISCO KID IN OLD NEW MEXICO (Renaldo), SOUTH OF THE RIO GRANDE (Renaldo)
1946: THE GAY CAVALIER (Gilbert Roland), SOUTH OF MONTEREY (Roland), BEAUTY AND THE BANDIT (Roland)
1947: RIDING THE CALIFORNIA TRAIL (Roland), ROBIN HOOD OF MONTEREY (Roland), KING OF THE BANDITS (Roland)

For United Artists (all with Renaldo):
1949: THE VALIANT HOMBRE, THE GAY AMIGO, THE DARING CABALLERO, SATAN'S CRADLE
1950: THE GIRL FROM SAN LORENZO

† The fifties TV series starred Renaldo with Leo Carrillo.

Cisco Pike

US 1971 94m Eastmancolor
Columbia / Acrobat (Gerald Ayres)

A former pop group leader and drug pusher is blackmailed by a cop into selling heroin. Low-key, would-be realistic study of a section of life in seventies LA. Flashy, boring and almost plotless.

wd Bill L. Norton *ph* Vilis Lapenieks *m* various

Kris Kristofferson, Gene Hackman, Karen Black, Harry Dean Stanton

'A moody, melancholy little film whose strength lies in its evocation of the rootless, aimless, irresponsible life-style of the pop / drug culture.'—*Brenda Davies*

'Secrets of a doctor as told by a doctor!'

The Citadel**

GB 1938 113m bw
MGM (Victor Saville)

A young doctor has a hard time in the mining villages but is later swayed by the easy rewards of a Mayfair practice.
Solidly produced adaptation of a bestseller; the more recent deluge of doctors on television make it appear rather elementary, but many scenes work in a classical way. One of the first fruits of MGM's British studios which were closed by World War II.

w Elizabeth Hill, Ian Dalrymple, Emlyn Williams, Frank Wead, *novel* A. J. Cronin *d* King Vidor *ph* Harry Stradling *m* Louis Levy

Robert Donat, Rosalind Russell, Ralph Richardson, Emlyn Williams, Penelope Dudley Ward, Francis L. Sullivan, Rex Harrison

'General audience limited . . . strong for the Anglo market.'—*Variety*

'I think any doctor will agree that here is a medical picture with no *Men in White* hokum, no hysterical, incredible melodrama, but with an honest story, honestly told. And that's a rare picture.'—*Pare Lorentz*

'We are grateful that a worthy idea has been handled with intelligence and imagination, that Vidor has shown respect both for his talent and for the sensibilities of the audience.'—*Robert Stebbins*

'Numerous passages shine brilliantly with those deft touches that first brought Vidor to prominence.'—*Variety*

'The pace of Hollywood, the honest characterization of England's best.'—*New York Times*

† The parts played by Russell and Richardson were originally intended for Elizabeth Allan and Spencer Tracy

AAN: best picture; script; King Vidor; Robert Donat

Citizen Kane****

US 1941 119m bw
RKO (Orson Welles)

A newspaper tycoon dies, and a magazine reporter interviews his friends in an effort to discover the meaning of his last words.
A brilliant piece of Hollywood cinema using all the resources of the studio; despite lapses of characterization and gaps in the narrative, almost every shot and every line is utterly absorbing both as entertainment and as craft. See *The Citizen Kane Book* by Pauline Kael, and innumerable other writings.

w Herman J. Mankiewicz, Orson Welles d Orson Welles ph Gregg Toland m Bernard Herrmann ad Van Nest Polglase sp Vernon L. Walker

Orson Welles (Kane), *Joseph Cotten* (Jedediah Leland), *Dorothy Comingore* (Susan Alexander), *Everett Sloane* (Bernstein), *Ray Collins* (Boss Jim Geddes), *Paul Stewart* (Raymond), *Ruth Warrick* (Emily Norton), *Erskine Sanford* (Herbert Carter), *Agnes Moorehead* (Kane's mother), *Harry Shannon* (Kane's father), *George Coulouris* (Walter Parks Thatcher), *William Alland* (Thompson), *Fortunio Bonanova* (music teacher)

'What is his name? It's Charlie Kane!
I'll bet you five you're not alive if you don't know his name!'

NEWSREEL: 'Then, last week, as it must to all men, death came to Charles Foster Kane.'

BERNSTEIN: 'Old age . . . it's the only disease you don't look forward to being cured of.'

THOMPSON: 'Mr Kane was a man who got everything he wanted, and then lost it. Maybe

Rosebud was something he couldn't get, or something he lost. Anyway, I don't think it would have explained everything. I don't think any word can explain a man's life. No, I guess Rosebud is just a piece in a jigsaw puzzle . . . a missing piece.'

SUSAN: 'Forty-nine acres of nothing but scenery and statues. I'm lonesome.'

KANE: 'You're right, Mr Thatcher. I did lose a million dollars last year. I expect to lose a million dollars this year. I expect to lose a million dollars next year. You know, Mr Thatcher, at the rate of a million dollars a year, I'll have to close this place—in sixty years.'

KANE: 'I run a couple of newspapers. What do you do?'

BERNSTEIN: 'One day back in 1896 I was crossing over to Jersey on the ferry, and as we pulled out, there was another ferry pulling in, and on it there was a girl waiting to get off. A white dress she had on. She was carrying a white parasol. I only saw her for one second. She didn't see me at all, but I'll bet a month hasn't gone by since that I haven't thought of that girl.'

'On seeing it for the first time, one got a conviction that if the cinema could do that, it could do anything.'—*Penelope Houston*

'What may distinguish *Citizen Kane* most of all is its extracting the mythic from under the humdrum surface of the American experience.'—*John Simon, 1968*

'Probably the most exciting film that has come out of Hollywood for twenty-five years. I am not sure it isn't the most exciting film that has ever come out of anywhere.'—*C. A. Lejeune*

'At any rate Orson Welles has landed in the movies, with a splash and a loud yell.'—*James Shelley Hamilton*

'More fun than any great movie I can think of.'—*Pauline Kael, 1968*

'It is a fascinating picture, but because of its congestion of technical stunts, it fails to move us.'—*Egon Larsen*

'A quite good film which tries to run the psychological essay in harness with the detective thriller, and doesn't quite succeed.'—*James Agate*

AA: Herman J. Mankiewicz, Orson Welles (script)
AAN: best picture; Orson Welles (as director); Gregg Toland; Bernard Herrmann; Orson Welles (as actor)

La Città Si Difende
Italy 1951 90m bw
Cines (Carlo Civallero)

A gang is recruited to rob a football stadium. Moderate forerunner of *The Good Die Young, The Killing*, and a hundred other caper films.

w Federico Fellini, Tullio Pinelli, Luigi Comencini *d* Pietro Germi *ph* Carlo Montuori *m* Carlo Rustichelli

Fausto Tozzi, Gina Lollobrigida, Patrizia Manca, Enzo Maggio

'As anonymous as the average B picture.'—*Gavin Lambert*

The City*
US 1939 32m bw

A historical, social and psychoanalytical study of urban living. Slightly guarded but convention-breaking documentary which though of its time still fascinates mildly by its style. Written by Henwar Rodakiewicz, from the book *The Culture of Cities* by Lewis Mumford; photographed and directed by Ralph Steiner and Willard Van Dyke; for the American Institute of Planners.

City across the River
US 1949 91m bw
U-I (Howard Christie)

Brooklyn delinquents get involved in murder. Semi-documentary throwback to the Dead End Kids, with location shooting influenced by *The Naked City*. Dull.

w Maxwell Shane, Dennis Cooper, *novel* The Amboy Dukes by Irving Shulman *d* Maxwell Shane *ph* Maury Gertsman *m* Walter Scharf

Stephen McNally, Barbara Whiting, Peter Fernandez, Al Ramsen, Joshua Shelley, Anthony Curtis (Tony Curtis in his first film role)

City beneath the Sea
US 1953 87m Technicolor
U-I (Albert J. Cohen)

Deep sea divers fall out over a sunken treasure.
Adequate double-biller with little to stir the interest.

w Jack Harvey, Ramon Romero *d* Budd Boetticher *ph* Charles P. Boyle *md* Joseph Gershenson

Robert Ryan, Anthony Quinn, Mala Powers, Suzan Ball, George Mathews, Karel Stepanek, Lalo Rios

City beneath the Sea
US 1970 98m De Luxe
Warner / Kent / Motion Pictures International (Irwin Allen)
GB theatrical release title: *One Hour to Doomsday*

An undersea city is threatened by an errant planetoid.
Futuristic adventure from a familiar stable; it will satisfy followers of *Voyage to the Bottom of the Sea*. Originally made for TV.

w John Meredyth Lucas *d* Irwin Allen *ph* Kenneth Peach *m* Richard La Salle *ad* Roger E. Maus, Stan Jolley

Stuart Whitman, Robert Wagner, Rosemary Forsyth, Robert Colbert, Burr de Benning, Richard Basehart, Joseph Cotten, James Darren, Sugar Ray Robinson, Paul Stewart

City for Conquest**
US 1940 106m bw
Warner (Anatole Litvak)

An East Side truck driver becomes a boxer but is blinded in a fight; meanwhile his composer brother gives up pop music for symphonies. Phony but oddly persuasive melodrama set in a studio in New York and heavily influenced by the pretensions of the Group theatre.

w John Wexley, *novel* Aben Kandel *d Anatole Litvak* *ph* Sol Polito, James Wong Howe *m* Max Steiner

James Cagney, Ann Sheridan, Frank Craven, Donald Crisp, *Arthur Kennedy*, Frank McHugh, George Tobias, Anthony Quinn, Jerome Cowan, Lee Patrick, Blanche Yurka, Thurston Hall

'Sometimes we wonder whether it wasn't really the Warner brothers who got New York from the Indians, so diligent and devoted have they been in feeling the great city's pulse, picturing its myriad facets and recording with deep compassion the passing life of its seething population.'—*Bosley Crowther*

City Girl*
US 1930 77m bw
Fox

A city girl finds rural life has its own drama. Rural drama distinguished by directorial touches.

w Berthold Viertel, Marion Orth, *play* The Mud Turtle by Elliot Lester *d F. W. Murnau* *ph* Ernest Palmer *m* Arthur Kay

Charles Farrell, Mary Duncan, David Torrence, Edith Yorke, Dawn O'Day

City Girl
US 1937 60m bw

A slightly dumb waitress becomes a gangster's moll. Fast-moving B picture which undoubtedly gave satisfaction. Phyllis Brooks, Ricardo Cortez, Robert Wilcox, Douglas Fowley, Chick Chandler, Esther Muir. Written by Frances Hyland, Robin Harris, Lester Ziffren; directed by Alfred Werker; for TCF.

City Heat
US 1984 97m Technicolor
Warner / Malpaso / Deliverance (Fritz Manes)

In the early thirties, a private eye's partner is bumped off, and he teams against the baddies with an old cop friend.
A tedious teaming for two tired stars who seem to imagine that all they have to do is show up.

w Sam O. Brown (Blake Edwards), Joseph C. Stinson *d* Richard Benjamin *ph* Nick McLean *m* Lennie Niehaus *pd* Edward Carfagno

Clint Eastwood, Burt Reynolds, Jane Alexander, Madeline Kahn, Rip Torn, Irene Cara, Richard Roundtree, Tony Lo Bianco

'It evaporates from the mind instantly upon its conclusion.'—*Variety*

City Lights***
US 1931 87m bw silent (with music and effects)
(UA) Charles Chaplin

A tramp befriends a millionaire and falls in love with a blind girl.
Sentimental comedy with several delightful sequences in Chaplin's best manner.

wd, m Charles Chaplin *ph* Rollie Totheroh, Mark Marlott, Gordon Pollock

Charles Chaplin, Virginia Cherrill, Harry Myers

'Chaplin has another good picture, but it gives indications of being short-winded, and may tire fast after a bombastic initial seven days . . . he has sacrificed speed to pathos, and plenty of it.'—*Variety*

'Even while laughing, one is aware of a faint and uneasy feeling that Chaplin has been pondering with more than a bit of solemnity on conventional story values, and it has led him further than ever into the realms of what is often called pathetic.'—*National Board of Review*

City of Bad Men*
US 1953 82m Technicolor
TCF (Leonard Goldstein)

In Carson City during the Corbett/ Fitzsimmons boxing match, outlaws plan to rob the arena of its receipts.
Slightly unusual western suspenser with generally accomplished handling.

w George W. George, George Slavin
d Harmon Jones *ph* Charles G. Clarke
md Lionel Newman

Dale Robertson, Jeanne Crain, Richard Boone, Lloyd Bridges, Carl Betz, Carole Mathews, Whitfield Connor

The City of Beautiful Nonsense
GB 1935 88m bw

A poor composer wins the girl he loves from a rich man. Thin and dated version of a fashionable novel by E. Temple Thurston. Emlyn Williams, Sophie Stewart, Eve Lister, George Carney. Written by Donovan Pedelty; directed by Adrian Brunel; for Butcher's.

City of Chance*
US 1939 57m bw

A girl reporter crusades against gangster gamblers. Smart little second feature with no time to be boring. Lynn Bari, C. Aubrey Smith, Donald Woods, Amanda Duff, June Gale, Richard Lane. Written by John Larkin, Barry Trivers; directed by Ricardo Cortez; for Sol M. Wurtzel / TCF.

'A half crazed man in a terror crazed town!'
City of Fear
US 1958 81m bw
Columbia / Orbit (Leon Chooluck)

A convict escapes with a canister of radioactive cobalt, which he believes to be heroin. After terrifying the city, he finally dies of exposure to it.
Rough-edged but occasionally gripping minor thriller from an independent company.

w Steven Ritch, Robert Dillon *d Irving Lerner* *ph* Lucien Ballard *m Jerry Goldsmith*

Vince Edwards, John Archer, Patricia Blair, Steven Ritch, Lyle Talbot

City of Gold**
Canada 1957 23m bw

The story of Dawson City, capital of the Klondike in 1897–8, is told by an accumulation of details from still photographs. A film with much to answer for, being the first documentary exclusively using the rostrum camera, a technique later adopted extensively by television. The subject matter is fascinating. Written and narrated by Pierre Berton; photographed and directed by Colin Low and Wolf Koenig; for National Film Board of Canada.

City of Silent Men
US 1942 64m bw

Two ex-convicts finally get work but are hounded by a newspaper publisher. Decent second feature, a cut above the average for its source. Frank Albertson, June Lang, Jan Wiley, Richard Clarke. Written by Joseph Hoffman, Robert E. Kent; directed by William Nigh; for Dixon R. Harwin / PRC.

City of the Dead*
GB 1960 78m bw
Vulcan (Donald Taylor)
US title: *Horror Hotel*

In Massachusetts, a woman burned as a witch 250 years ago is still 'alive', running a local hotel and luring unwary strangers into becoming sacrificial victims.
A deadly first half gives way to splendid cinematic terror when the scene shifts to the village by night, all dry ice and limpid fog, and the heroine becomes a human sacrifice. A superior horror comic.

w George Baxt *d John Moxey* *ph Desmond Dickinson* *m* Douglas Gamley, Ken Jones

Patricia Jessel, Betta St John, Christopher Lee, Dennis Lotis, Valentine Dyall, Venetia Stevenson, Norman Macowan, Fred Johnson

City of Women*
Italy-France 1980 140m Eastmancolor
Opera Film-Gaumont (Renzo Rossellini)
Original title: *La Città delle Donne*

A businessman finds himself trapped and threatened by women en masse.
Often leaden but sometimes spectacular fantasy in which the director spews out his views of the war between men and women. Fascinating in patches, but generally indigestible.

w Federico Fellini, Bernardino Zapponi
d Federico Fellini *ph* Giuseppe Rotunno
m Luis Bacalov

Marcello Mastroianni, Anna Prucnal, Bernice Stegers, Ettore Manni, Donatella Damiani

'Another visual tour de force in an elaborate dream framework; narrative thin, overlong, and finally overweight.'—*Variety*

City on Fire
Canada / US 1979 106m colour

A slum fire threatens an entire city. Shoddy disaster movie which does its cast no favour. Barry Newman, Susan Clark, Shelley Winters, Henry Fonda, Leslie Nielsen, James Franciscus, Ava Gardner. Written by Jack Hill, David P. Lewis and Celine La Freniere; directed by Alvin Rakoff; for Astral-Bellevue-Pathe / Sandy Howard.

'Love and courage pitted against a ruthless hate!'
City Streets**
US 1931 86m bw
Paramount (Rouben Mamoulian)

A gangster's daughter is sent to jail for a murder she did not commit, and on release narrowly escapes being 'taken for a ride'.
Tense, dated gangland melodrama of primary interest because of its director's very cinematic treatment.

w Max Marcin, Oliver H. P. Garrett, Dashiell Hammett, *story* Ladies of the Mob by Ernest Booth *d Rouben Mamoulian* *ph Lee Garmes*

Sylvia Sidney, Gary Cooper, Paul Lukas, Guy Kibbee, William (Stage) Boyd, Stanley Fields, Wynne Gibson

TYPICAL GANGSTER DIALOGUE OF THE TIME:
Who's running this show, anyhow?
—I am.
Who says so?
—I say so, for one. And when you talk to me, take that toothpick outa your mouth!

'So many brilliant touches that anyone who sees it will have to predict for Mamoulian a brilliant career.'—*Film Spectator*

'Too much attempt to artify hurts though the sophisticated treatment and elegant settings will help.'—*Variety*

'A love story in a gangster setting which got carried away into so much fancy expressionism and symbolism that it seems stylized out of all relationship to the actual world.'—*Pauline Kael, 70s*

City That Never Sleeps
US 1953 90m bw
Republic (John H. Auer)

The work of the Chicago police force during one night.
Adequate minor semi-documentary police yarn.

w Steve Fisher *d* John H. Auer *ph* John I. Russell *m* R. Dale Butts

Gig Young, Mala Powers, William Talman, Edward Arnold, Chill Wills, Paula Raymond, Marie Windsor

'They dared the most romantic journey that has ever challenged the imagination!'
City under the Sea
GB 1965 84m Eastmancolor Colorscope
Bruton / AIP (Daniel Haller)
US title: *War Gods of the Deep*

An American heiress in Cornwall meets Victorian smugglers who have lived a hundred years under the sea in Lyonesse.
Childlike, unpersuasive nonsense which wastes some good talent.

w Charles Bennett, Louis M. Heyward
d Jacques Tourneur *ph* Stephen Dade
m Stanley Black

Vincent Price, David Tomlinson, Susan Hart, Tab Hunter, Henry Oscar, John Le Mesurier

City Without Men
US 1943 75m bw

A boarding house near a prison is filled with women awaiting the parole of their menfolk. Stereotyped programmer. Linda Darnell, Michael Duane, Sara Allgood, Edgar Buchanan, Glenda Farrell, Leslie Brooks, Margaret Hamilton, Sheldon Leonard. Written by W. L. River, George Skier and Donald Davis; directed by Sidney Salkow; for Columbia.

The City's Edge
Australia 1983 86m colour

A troubled man takes a room in a Bondi boarding house and finds others worse off than himself. Dreary mini-dramas, somewhat arbitrarily linked and without a shred of hope in sight for anybody. Hugo Weaving, Tommy Lewis, Shirley Cameron, Mark Lee, Ralph Cotterill. Written by Robert J. Merritt and Ken Quinnell, from novel by W. A. Harbinson; directed by Ken Quinnell; for CB / Oliver Sullivan.

Civilization***
US 1916 68m (1931 'sound' version) bw silent
Triangle

A mythical country starts war, but one of the principals has a vision of Christ on the battlefields and the king is persuaded to sign a peace treaty.
Surprisingly impressive parable showing this early director at his best; intended as a pacifist tract in the middle of World War I.

w C. Gardner Sullivan *d Thomas Ince* *ph* Irwin Willat

Enid Markey, Howard Hickman, J. Barney Sherry

The Clairvoyant*
GB 1934 80m bw
Gainsborough (Michael Balcon)

A fraudulent mindreader predicts a disaster which comes true.
Effective minor suspenser on predictable but enjoyable lines.

w Charles Bennett, Bryan Edgar Wallace, Robert Edmunds *d* Maurice Elvey *ph* Glen MacWilliams

Claude Rains, Fay Wray, Jane Baxter, Mary Clare, Athole Stewart, Ben Field, Felix Aylmer, Donald Calthrop

Clambake
US 1967 98m Techniscope
UA / Rhodes (Laven–Gardner–Levy)

The son of an oil millionaire sets out to see life.
Painless, forgettable star vehicle.

w Arthur Browne Jnr *d* Arthur H. Nadel *ph* William Margulies *m* Jeff Alexander

Elvis Presley, Shelley Fabares, Bill Bixby, James Gregory, Will Hutchins, Gary Merrill

Clan of the Cave Bear
US 1985 98m Technicolor Technovision
Warner / PSO / Guber-Peters / Jozak-Decade / Jonesfilm (Gerald I. Isenberg)

In Neanderthal days, a blonde outcast girl is adopted by a swarthy tribe who think her ugly.
Comic-strip prehistory: better revive *One Million BC* or even the 1912 Griffith epic *Man's Genesis*.

w John Sayles *novel* Jean M. Auel *d* Michael Chapman *ph* Jan De Bont *m* Alan Silvestri *pd* Anthony Masters

Daryl Hannah, Pamela Reed, James Remar, Thomas G. Waites

AAN: make-up (Michael G. Westmore, Michele Burke)

Clancy of the Mounted
US 1933 bw serial: 12 eps

Clancy saves his brother, who has been framed for murder. Tolerable western serial. Tom Tyler, Jacqueline Wells, Earl McCarthy, William Desmond. Directed by Ray Taylor; for Universal.

Clarence the Cross-Eyed Lion
US 1965 98m Metrocolor
MGM (Leonard Kaufman)

Adventures of animal farmers in Africa.
Amiable theatrical 'pilot' for the *Daktari* TV series.

w Alan Caillou, Marshall Thompson, Art Arthur *d* Andrew Marton *ph* Lamar Boren

Marshall Thompson, Betsy Drake, Richard Haydn, Cheryl Miller

'Livin' in my house! Lovin' another man! Is that what you call honest? That's just givin' it a nice name!'

Clash by Night*
US 1952 105m bw
RKO (Harriet Parsons) (A Wald–Krasna Production)

In a northern fishing village, jealousy and near-tragedy are occasioned by the return home of a hardened girl from the big city.
Absurdly overblown melodrama of the *Anna Christie* school, burdened with significance and doggedly acted by a remarkable cast.

w Alfred Hayes, *play* Clifford Odets *d* Fritz Lang *ph* Nicholas Musuraca *m* Roy Webb

Barbara Stanwyck, Paul Douglas, Robert Ryan, Marilyn Monroe, J. Carrol Naish, Keith Andes

'When Stanwyck snarls into a pub and belts down a straight shot, we think we're watching a remake of *Anna Christie*; when she is shyly and ineptly courted by Douglas we think it's a remake of *Min and Bill*; a sub-plot involving Monroe and Andes plays like *Gidget Faces an Identity Crisis*.'—*Kit Parker catalogue*

Clash of the Titans
GB 1981 118m Metrocolor Dynarama
MGM / Charles H. Schneer, Ray Harryhausen

Perseus sets out to win Andromeda despite the impossible obstacles set for him by Thetis, which include a number of mythical monsters.
Star-packed but feebly imagined mythological spectacular, further hampered by gloomy photography which is presumably required to offset the jerkiness of the monsters. A very few moments provide the right kind of elation.

w Beverley Cross *d* Desmond Davis *ph* Ted Moore *m* Laurence Rosenthal *sp* Ray Harryhausen *pd* Frank White

Laurence Olivier, Claire Bloom, Maggie Smith, Ursula Andress, Jack Gwyllim, Harry Hamlin, Judy Bowker, Burgess Meredith, Siân Phillips, Flora Robson, Freda Jackson, Donald Houston

'There's a real possibility some audiences will be turned to stone before Medusa even appears.'—*Geoff Brown, MFB*

'Unspeakable dialogue, muddy photography and a motley, lacklustre cast.'—*Sight and Sound*

'The good news is, Jonathan's having his first affair. The bad news is, she's his roommate's mother!'

Class
US 1983 98m Astro Color
Orion / Martin Ransohoff

A shy student has an affair with an older woman who turns out to be his best friend's mother.
Ghastly travesty of *The Graduate* which aspires to every kind of sophistication it can think of but ends nowhere.

w Jim Kouf, David Greenwalt *d* Lewis John Carlino *ph* Ric Waite *m* Elmer Bernstein *ad* Jack Poplin

Jacqueline Bisset, Cliff Robertson, Rob Lowe, Andrew McCarthy, Stuart Margolin, John Cusack.

'It is not often that one comes across a film of such muddled aspirations and widely divergent achievements.'—*Nick Roddick, MFB*

Class of '44
US 1973 95m Technicolor Panavision
Warner (Paul Bogart)

Sex problems of college students during World War II.
Thin sequel to *Summer of '42*, nostalgic to Americans over forty but not much of a trip for anyone else.

w Herman Raucher *d* Paul Bogart *ph* Andrew Laszlo *m* David Shire

Gary Grimes, Jerry Houser, Oliver Conant, William Atherton, Sam Bottoms, Deborah Winters

Class of 84
Canada 1981 98m colour

A new teacher finds his students involved in drug and vice rackets. *The Blackboard Jungle* goes several steps further, to general indifference. Perry King, Merrie Lynn Ross, Timothy Van Patten, Roddy McDowall. Written by Mark Lester, John Saxton, Tom Holland; directed by Mark Lester; for Guerrilla High.

The Class of Miss McMichael
GB 1978 90m colour
Brut / Kettledrum (Judd Bernard)

CLASH BY NIGHT. Not for the first time Marilyn Monroe holds centre screen in spite of the fact that comedy, not melodrama, was her forte. Robert Ryan is the man causing the problem.

A dedicated schoolmistress has no chance against her slum surroundings.
The Blackboard Jungle lives on, very boringly.

w Judd Bernard, *novel* Sandy Hutson
d Silvio Narizzano *ph* Alex Thomson
m Stanley Myers

Glenda Jackson, Oliver Reed, John Standing, Michael Murphy, Rosalind Cash

'Poorly mannered, simple minded, badly disciplined . . . gives social science a bad name.'—*Variety*

Claudelle Inglish
US 1961 99m bw
Warner (Leonard Freeman)
GB title: *Young and Eager*

A poor farmer's daughter scorns a wealthy man for a succession of young studs.
Would-be sensational novelette from the author of *Tobacco Road*; it does not begin to be interesting.

w Leonard Freeman, *novel* Erskine Caldwell
d Gordon Douglas *ph* Ralph Woolsey
m Howard Jackson

Diane McBain, Arthur Kennedy, Constance Ford, Chad Everett, Claude Akins, Will Hutchins, Robert Colbert, Ford Rainey, James Bell

Claudia**
US 1943 92m bw
TCF (William Perlberg)

A middle-class husband helps his child-wife to mature.

Typical of the best of Hollywood's 'woman's pictures' of the period, this is a pleasant domestic comedy-drama featuring recognizably human characters in an agreeable setting.

w Morrie Ryskind, *novel* and *play Rose Franken* *d* Edmund Goulding *ph* Leon Shamroy *m* Alfred Newman

Dorothy McGuire (her film debut), *Robert Young, Ina Claire*, Reginald Gardiner, Olga Baclanova, Jean Howard, Elsa Janssen

'It won't leave a dry eye in the house.'—*Variety*

† Cary Grant was sought for the Robert Young part.

Claudia and David*
US 1946 78m bw
TCF (William Perlberg)

Claudia and her husband survive assorted crises including their son's illness and David's involvement in a car crash.
Patchwork sequel to *Claudia*, quite pleasant but obviously contrived quickly from scraps.

w Rose Franken, William Brown Meloney *d* Walter Lang *ph* Joseph La Shelle *m* Cyril Mockridge

Dorothy McGuire, Robert Young, Mary Astor, John Sutton, Gail Patrick, Florence Bates

The Clay Pigeon**
US 1949 63m bw
RKO (Herman Schlom)

An amnesiac sailor finds himself courtmartialled for treason, but discovers the real culprit.
Tidily efficient second feature thriller; good enjoyable stuff of its kind.

w Carl Foreman d Richard Fleischer ph Robert de Grasse *m* Paul Sawtell

Bill Williams, Barbara Hale, Richard Quine, Richard Loo, Frank Fenton

Cleo from Five to Seven*
France / Italy 1961 90m part colour
Rome / Paris (Bruno Drigo)

A girl waiting for the result of a medical examination wanders around Paris thinking she has cancer.
Impressively handled character sketch with gratifying attention to detail.

wd Agnès Varda ph Jean Rabier m Michel Legrand

Corinne Marchand, Antoine Bourseiller, Dorothée Blanck, Michel Legrand

'The love affair that shook the world!'
Cleopatra**
US 1934 101m bw
Paramount / Cecil B. de Mille

After Julius Caesar's death, Cleopatra turns her attention to Mark Antony.
More of the vices than the virtues of its producer are notable in this fustian epic, which is almost but not quite unwatchable because of its stolid pace and miscasting. Some of the action montages and the barge scene, however, are superb cinema.

w Waldemar Young, Vincent Lawrence *d Cecil B. de Mille ph Victor Milner m* Rudolph Kopp

Claudette Colbert, Henry Wilcoxon (Antony), Warren William (Caesar), Gertrude Michael, Joseph Schildkraut, Ian Keith, C. Aubrey Smith, Leonard Mudie, Irving Pichel, Arthur Hohl

'He has certainly made the most sumptuous of Roman circuses out of Roman history . . . a constant succession of banquets, dancers, triumphs, and a fleet set on fire.'—*The Times*

'Gorgeous optically but mentally weak . . . . a handpicked audience was polite but not over-enthusiastic.'—*Variety*

'A great cinematic achievement, a spectacle of breathtaking brilliance.'—*Daily Express*

'It is remarkable how Cecil B. de Mille can photograph so much on such a vast scale and still say nothing . . . it reeks of so much pseudo-artistry, vulgarity, philistinism, sadism, that it can only be compared with the lowest form of contemporary culture: Hitlerism. This is the type of "culture" that will be fed to the audience of Fascist America.'—*Irving Lerner, 1968*

AA: Victor Milner
AAN: best picture

'The motion picture the world has been waiting for!'
Cleopatra
US 1963 243m De Luxe Todd-AO
TCF (Walter Wanger)

The unsurprising story is told at inordinate length and dullness in this ill-starred epic, one of the most heralded, and mismanaged, in film history. (Its story is best told in the producer's *My Life with Cleopatra.*) The most expensive film ever made, for various reasons which do not appear on the screen.

w Joseph L. Mankiewicz, Ranald MacDougall, Sidney Buchman, and others *d* Joseph L. Mankiewicz (and others) *ph* Leon Shamroy *m* Alex North *ad* John de Cuir, Jack Martin Smith, and others

Elizabeth Taylor, Richard Burton, Rex Harrison, Pamela Brown, George Cole, Hume Cronyn, Cesare Danova, Kenneth Haigh, Andrew Keir, Martin Landau, Roddy McDowall, Robert Stephens, Francesca Annis, Martin Benson, Herbert Berghof, Grégoire Aslan, Richard O'Sullivan

'Whatever was interesting about it clearly ended up somewhere else: on the cutting room floor, in various hotel rooms, in the newspaper columns . . . it lacks not only the intelligent spectacle of *Lawrence of Arabia* but the spectacular unintelligence of a Cecil B. de Mille product . . .'—*John Simon*

'The small screen does more than justice to this monumental mouse.'—*Judith Crist*

'I only came to see the asp.'—*Charles Addams*

'Surely the most bizarre piece of entertainment ever to be perpetrated.'—*Elizabeth Taylor*

AA: Leon Shamroy
AAN: best picture; Alex North; Rex Harrison

Cleopatra Jones
US 1973 89m Technicolor Panavision

A black female CIA agent eliminates a ring of dope peddlers. Grotesque comic strip fantasy with a high mortality rate. Tamara Dobson, Shelley Winters, Bernie Casey, Brenda Sykes. Written by Max Julien and Sheldon Keller; directed by Jack Starrett; for Warner. 'It hampers the cause of racial entente more effectively than any work since *Uncle Tom's Cabin.*'—*John Baxter, MFB.*

The Climax*
US 1944 86m Technicolor
Universal (George Waggner)

A young opera singer is hypnotized by a mad doctor, who has kept his murdered mistress embalmed for ten years.
Gothic romantic melodrama invented to capitalize on the success—and the sets—of *Phantom of the Opera*. Curiously endearing, with a good eye-rolling part for Karloff.

w Curt Siodmak, Lynn Starling, *play* Edward Cochran *d* George Waggner *ph* Hal Mohr, W. Howard Greene *m* Edward Ward

Boris Karloff, Susanna Foster, Gale Sondergaard, Turhan Bey, Thomas Gomez, Scotty Beckett

'All quite unalarming, which is a bit of a handicap.'—*New Yorker, 1978*

Climbing High*
GB 1938 78m bw
Gaumont (Michael Balcon)

A rich man pretends to be a male model in order to win a girl.
Light-hearted romantic musical with interesting credits.

w Stephen Clarkson, *story* Lesser Samuels, Marian Dix *d* Carol Reed *ph* Mutz Greenbaum (Max Greene)

Jessie Matthews, Michael Redgrave, Noel Madison, Alistair Sim, Margaret Vyner, Mary Clare, Francis L. Sullivan

The Clinging Vine*
US 1926 71m (24 fps) bw silent
Cecil B. de Mille

The president's secretary is the real driving force of a paint company, but finds that love is more important than business.
Interesting silent predecessor of many career girl comedies of the thirties and forties.

w Jeannie McPherson *d* Paul Sloane

Leatrice Joy, Tom Moore, Toby Claude, Robert Edeson

'People are going to **** whether you like it or not—and this place is here to see that they enjoy it!'
The Clinic*
Australia 1982 92m colour

One day in the life of a clinic for venereal diseases. Slightly dishevelled comedy-drama which will be generally remembered as a very naughty carry-on. Chris Haywood, Simon Burke, Gerda Nicolson, Rona McLeod, Suzanne Roylance. Written by Greg Millin; directed by David Stevens; for Film House / Generation Films.

'Six words from a woman changed the map of Asia!'
Clive of India*
US 1934 90m bw
Twentieth Century (Darryl F. Zanuck, William Goetz, Raymond Griffith)

The life of the 18th-century empire builder, with special emphasis on his marriage.
A very tame and now faded epic, with more romance than adventure. The production relies more on stars than technique, but it works.

w W. P. Lipscomb, R. J. Minney, from their play *d* Richard Boleslawski *ph* Peverell Marley *m* Alfred Newman

Ronald Colman, Loretta Young, Colin Clive, Francis Lister, Montagu Love, Robert Greig, Leo G. Carroll, C. Aubrey Smith, Mischa Auer

'It may be spoken of as another of the best British pictures made in Hollywood. . . . Should be strong b.o.'—*Variety*

'Patriotic pageantry, undistorted by facts.'—*J. R. Parish*

'The moment he fell in love was his moment of greatest danger!'

Cloak and Dagger*
US 1946 106m bw
United States Pictures (Milton Sperling)

A physics professor joins the secret service and is parachuted into Germany to interview a kidnapped scientist.
Supposedly authoritative espionage adventure which turned out dull and humourless; plot routine, direction absent-minded.

w Albert Maltz, Ring Lardner Jnr *d* Fritz Lang *ph* Sol Polito *m* Max Steiner

Gary Cooper, Lilli Palmer, Robert Alda, Vladimir Sokoloff, J. Edward Bromberg, Ludwig Stossel, Helene Thimig, Marc Lawrence

'Just a B plot dressed up in A trimmings.'—*Newsweek*

Clochemerle
France 1948 93m bw
Cinéma Productions (Ralph Baum)

The progressive mayor of a French village erects a gentlemen's convenience in the main street and shocks the local reactionaries.
Most of the book's political satire was ironed out in this cheap and opportunist production which got a few easy laughs but failed to sustain itself.

w Gabriel Chevalier, from his novel *d* Pierre Chénal *ph* Robert Le Fèbvre *m* Henri Sauguet

Brochard, Maximilienne, Simone Michels, Jane Marken, Paul Demange, Felix Oudart, Saturnin Fabre

The Clock**
US 1945 90m bw
MGM (Arthur Freed)
GB title: *Under the Clock*

A girl meets a soldier at New York's Grand Central Station and marries him during his 24-hour leave.
Everyone now seems far too nice in this winsome romance full of comedy cameos and real New York locations, but if you can relive the wartime mood it still works as a corrective to the Betty Grable glamour pieces.

w Robert Nathan, Joseph Schrank, *story* Paul and Pauline Gallico *d Vincente Minnelli* *ph* George Folsey *m* George Bassman

Judy Garland, Robert Walker, James Gleason, Lucile Gleason, Keenan Wynn, Marshall Thompson, Chester Clute

'Sweetly charming, if maybe too irresistible . . . fortunately the director fills the edges with comic characters.'—*New Yorker, 1978*

'The emotion may have been honest, but the method was too rich for my eyes, and the writing as used on the screen too weak for my mind.'—*Stephen Longstreet*

'Strictly a romance . . . safely told, disappointing and angering in the thought of the great film it might have been.'—*James Agee*

'Amazingly, it was all shot in the studio, using street sets and back projection; even the old Penn Station, where so much of the action takes place, is a set.'—*Pauline Kael, 70s*

Clockwise*
GB 1986 97m Technicolor
EMI / Moment (Michael Codron)

A headmaster on his way to a conference is delayed by circumstance.
What was intended as an escalating climax of comic chaos falls away as the script runs out of steam, but the nation's need for comedy ensured box office success.

w Michael Frayn *d* Christopher Morahan *ph* John Coquillon *m* George Fenton *pd* Roger Murray-Leach *ed* Peter Boyle

John Cleese, Alison Steadman, Penelope Wilton, Stephen Moore, Joan Hickson, Charon Maiden

'The adventures of a young man whose interests are rape, ultra-violence, and Beethoven!'

A Clockwork Orange*
GB 1971 136m colour
Warner / Polaris (Bernard Williams)

In a future Britain of desolation and violence, a young gangster guilty of rape and murder obtains a release from prison after being experimentally brainwashed: he finds society more violent than it was in his time.
A repulsive film in which intellectuals have found acres of social and political meaning; the average judgement is likely to remain that it is pretentious and nasty rubbish for sick minds who do not mind jazzed-up images and incoherent sound.

wd Stanley Kubrick, *novel* Anthony Burgess *ph* John Alcott *m* Walter Carlos *pd* John Barry

Malcolm McDowell, Michael Bates, Adrienne Corri, Patrick Magee, Warren Clarke

'Very early there are hints of triteness and insecurity, and before half an hour is over it begins to slip into tedium . . . Inexplicably the script leaves out Burgess' reference to the title.'—*Stanley Kauffmann*

'It might be the work of a strict and exacting German professor who set out to make a porno violent sci-fi comedy.'—*New Yorker, 1980*

AAN: best picture; Stanley Kubrick (as writer and director)

'We are not alone . . .'

Close Encounters of the Third Kind*
US 1977 135m Metrocolor Panavision
Columbia / EMI (Julia and Michael Phillips)

A series of UFOs takes Indiana by surprise, and a workman is led by intuition and detection to the landing site which has been concealed from the public.
There's a lot of padding in this slender fantasy, which has less plot and much less suspense than *It Came from Outer Space* which was made on a tiny budget in 1955; but the technical effects are masterly though their exposure is over-prolonged, and the benevolent mysticism filled a current requirement of popular taste, accounting for the enormous box-office success of a basically flawed film. Much of the dialogue is inaudible.

wd Steven Spielberg *ph* Vilmos Zsigmond *m* John Williams *sp Douglas Trumbull* *pd* Joe Alves

Richard Dreyfuss, Françoise Truffaut, Teri Garr, Melinda Dillon, Cary Guffey

'It somehow combines Disney and 1950s SF and junk food into the most persuasive (if arrested) version of the American dream yet.'—*Time Out*

† The cost of this film was estimated at 20,000,000 dollars.

†† In 1980 a 'special edition' was released with some success: this pared down the idiotic middle section and extended the final scenes of the space ship, including some new interiors.

††† This film used the largest set in film history: the inside of an old dirigible hangar.

Of the special edition, Derek Malcolm in the *Guardian* wrote: 'One is inclined to feel that with all the money at his disposal, Spielberg might have got it right the first time.'

AA: Vilmos Zsigmond
AAN: direction; John Williams; Melinda Dillon

Close to My Heart
US 1951 90m bw
Warner (William Jacobs)

An adopted baby is discovered to have a murderer for a father; but environment is proved to be more important than heredity.
Routine sentimental drama.

wd William Keighley, *story* A Baby for Midge by James R. Webb *ph* Robert Burks *m* Max Steiner

Ray Milland, Gene Tierney, Fay Bainter, Howard St John, Mary Beth Hughes

Closely Observed Trains**
Czechoslovakia 1966 92m bw
Ceskoslovensky Film (Zdenek Oves)

During World War II, an apprentice railway guard at a country station falls in love and becomes a saboteur.
Warm, amusingly detailed comedy with a disconcerting downbeat ending.

wd Jiri Menzel, novel Bohumil Hrabal *ph* Jaromir Sofr *m* Jiri Pavlik

Vaclav Neckar, Jitka Bendova, Vladimir Valenta, Josef Somr

'Like Forman, Menzel seems incapable of being unkind to anybody.'—*Tom Milne*

AA: best foreign film

Cloud Dancer
US 1977 108m colour

Episodes in the life of a stunt flyer.
Technically proficient, loosely assembled amble through the problems of a man with an obsession for danger; not a great crowd-puller. David Carradine, Jennifer O'Neill, Joseph Bottoms, Albert Salmi, Salome Jens, Colleen Camp. Written by William Goodhart; directed by Barry Brown; for Melvin Simon.

Cloudburst
GB 1951 92m bw

A vengeful code expert goes after the criminals who ran down his wife in making a getaway. Watchable potboiler. Robert Preston, Elizabeth Sellars, Colin Tapley, Sheila Burrell, Harold Lang. Written by Leo Marks; directed by Francis Searle; for Hammer.

The Clouded Yellow*
GB 1950 96m bw
Sydney Box / Carillon (Betty Box)

A sacked secret service agent gets work tending a butterfly collection and finds that this involves him in a murder plot.
Implausible but quite engaging thriller in the Hitchcock style, involving a chase across the Lake District.

w Janet Green, Eric Ambler *d* Ralph Thomas *ph* Geoffrey Unsworth

Trevor Howard, Jean Simmons, Barry Jones, Sonia Dresdel, Maxwell Reed, Kenneth More, André Morell

The Clown
US 1952 91m bw
MGM (William H. Wright)

A drunken clown, once a great star, is idolized by his son who believes in a comeback.
Maudlin reworking of *The Champ* (qv), with not a surprise in the plot and a star way over the top.

w Martin Rackin *d* Robert Z. Leonard *ph* Paul C. Vogel *m* David Rose

Red Skelton, Jane Greer, Tim Considine, Loring Smith, Philip Ober

Club Havana
US 1946 62m bw

Several stories come to a head in a night club. Slight musical multi-drama with moments of interest. Tom Neal, Margaret Lindsay, Don Douglas, Isabelita, Ernest Truex, Renee Riano, Paul Cavanagh, Marc Lawrence. Written by Raymond L. Schrock and Fred Jackson; directed by Edgar G. Ulmer; for PRC.

Clue
US 1985 87m Metrocolor
Paramount / Guber-Peters / Debra Hill / Polygram

A murder game becomes reality.
A rather arch attempt to film an internationally popular board game; those not in on the joke may tend to restlessness.

w,d Jonathan Lynn *ph* Victor J. Kemper *m* John Morris *pd* John Lloyd

Eileen Brennan, Tim Curry, Madeline Kahn, Christopher Lloyd, Michael McKean, Lesley Ann Warren

'Enough wit, neuroses and motive to intrigue even the most inept whodunnit solver.'—*Variety*

† Three alternative solutions were originally provided.

Cluny Brown**
US 1946 100m bw
TCF (Ernst Lubitsch)

A plumber's niece goes into service and falls for a Czech refugee guest.
Romantic comedy in a never-never pre-war England; it does no more than poke casual fun at upper-class conventions, but the smooth direction and some excellent character comedy keep it well afloat.

w Samuel Hoffenstein, Elizabeth Reinhardt, *novel* Margery Sharp *d Ernst Lubitsch* *ph* Joseph La Shelle *m* Cyril Mockridge, Emil Newman

Jennifer Jones, Charles Boyer, *Richard Haydn, Una O'Connor*, Peter Lawford, Helen Walker, Reginald Gardiner, Reginald Owen, C. Aubrey Smith, Sara Allgood, Ernest Cossart, Florence Bates, Billy Bevan

'A lovely, easygoing comedy, full of small surprising touches.'—*Pauline Kael, 70s*

The Clutching Hand*
US 1936 bw serial: 15 eps

A scientist with a formula for synthetic gold is kidnapped, and rescue attempts are hampered by a sinister shadowy figure. Archetypal spooky house serial. Jack Mulhall, Marion Shilling, Yakima Canutt, Reed Howes, William Farnum. Directed by Albert Herman; for Stage and Screen.

Coal Miner's Daughter*
US 1980 124m Technicolor
Universal (Bob Larson)

The wife of a Kentucky hillbilly becomes a pop star.
'With-it' version of the old show business story: gradual success, stardom, nervous breakdown, reconciliation. Based on the life of Loretta Lynn, but mainly notable for its depiction of backwoods Kentucky.

w Tom Rickman *d Michael Apted* *ph* Ralf D. Bode *md* Owen Bradley *pd* John W. Corso

Sissy Spacek, Tommy Lee Jones, Levon Helm, Jennifer Beasley, Phyllis Boyens

AA: Sissy Spacek
AAN: best film; Tom Rickman; Ralf D. Bode; editing (Arthur Schmidt); art direction (John W. Corso, John M. Dwyer)

Coast to Coast
US 1980 94m Movielab
Paramount (Terry Carr)

A Los Angeles wife flees her husband and hitches a lift from a truck driver with problems.
Comedy for easy watching: pleasant characters are given very little of interest to do.

w Stanley Weiser *d* Joseph Sargent *ph* Joel King *m* Charles Bernstein

Dyan Cannon, Robert Blake, Quinn Redeker, Michael Lerner, Bill Lucking, Maxine Stuart

Cobra
US 1925 85m approx bw silent

An impoverished Italian nobleman collects women as a hobby. The star's first independent production won no plaudits and was thought to be a mistake conceived by his wife Natacha Rambova, who appeared in a dance act with him. Rudolph Valentino, Nita Naldi, Casson Ferguson, Gertrude Olmstead, Hector V. Samo. Written by Anthony Coldeway; directed by Joseph Henabery; for Ritz-Carlton.

Cobra
US 1986 87m Technicolor
Warner / Cannon (James D. Brubaker)

A tough LA cop tracks down a serial killer.
Relentless but unsurprising carbon of *Dirty Harry*, a bit too tough for its own good.

w Sylvester Stallone *novel* Fair Game by Paula Gosling *d* George Pan Cosmatos *ph* Ric Waite *m* Sylvester Levay *ed* Don Zimmerman, James Symons *pd* Bill Kenney

Sylvester Stallone, Brigitte Nielsen, Reni Santoni, Andrew Robinson

† 2,131 prints were made for the launch

Cobra Woman
US 1944 71m Technicolor
U-I (George Waggner)

A South Seas girl is abducted by snake worshippers ruled by her evil twin.
A monument of undiluted hokum with some amusing sets and performances but not enough self-mockery in the script.

w Richard Brooks, Gene Lewis *d* Robert Siodmak *ph* George Robinson, W. Howard Greene *m* Edward Ward

Maria Montez, Jon Hall, Sabu, Lon Chaney Jnr, Mary Nash, Edgar Barrier, Lois Collier, Samuel S. Hinds, Moroni Olsen

'Among the exotic treats: a rumbling volcano, a pet chim, ominous gong sounds, forest glade love scenes, human sacrifices, handmaidens in high-heeled pumps, Tollea's imperious writhing during a demonic dance, and the good Nadja's plea for the symbol of the power that is rightly hers: "Gif me the cobra jool." '—*Pauline Kael, 70s*

The Cobweb
US 1955 124m Eastmancolor Cinemascope
MGM (John Houseman)

Tensions among the staff of a private mental clinic reach a new high over the purchase of curtains.
The patients seem saner than the doctors in this strained and verbose character drama which despite its cast and big studio look never begins to engage the interest.

w John Paxton, *novel* William Gibson
d Vincente Minnelli *ph* George Folsey
m Leonard Rosenman

Richard Widmark, Lauren Bacall, Charles Boyer, *Lillian Gish*, Gloria Grahame, John Kerr, Susan Strasberg, *Oscar Levant*, Tommy Rettig, Paul Stewart, Adèle Jergens

'An overwrought and elaborately artificial exercise, made scarcely more plausible by reliance on the basic jargon of psychiatry.'—*Penelope Houston*

'By the mid-50s, nobody was surprised that the new variant on *Grand Hotel* was an expensive, exclusive loony bin.'—*Pauline Kael, 70s*

The Coca Cola Kid
Australia 1985 94m Eastmancolor

A Coca Cola rep is sent to Australia to combat a remote land baron who brews and distributes his own brand. Flaccid drama with an eventually mystifying superabundance of style.

Eric Roberts, Greta Scacchi, Bill Kerr, Max Gillies. Written by Frank Moorhouse; directed by Dusan Makavejev; for Cinema Enterprises/Film Gallery/Columbia.

Cockeyed Cavaliers
US 1934 72m bw

Two idiots have various adventures in medieval England. Fairly tolerable slapstick from a team which never seemed quite at its best. Bert Wheeler, Robert Woolsey, Thelma Todd, Noah Beery, Dorothy Lee, Franklyn Pangborn, Robert Greig. Written by Edward Kaufman, Ben Holmes; directed by Mark Sandrich; for RKO. 'With a fair quota of laughs, it eclipses their previous releases.'—*Variety*

The Cockeyed Cowboys of Calico County
US 1969 99m Technicolor

A western blacksmith stops working when his mail order bride doesn't arrive. Styleless American rehash of *La Femme du Boulanger*, with all concerned trying too hard. Dan Blocker, Nanette Fabray, Mickey Rooney. Written by Ranald MacDougall; directed by Tony Leader; for Universal.

The Cockeyed Miracle
US 1946 92m bw

Family ghosts return to sort out domestic chaos. Moderate 'Topper'-style comedy with amiable cast: Frank Morgan, Cecil Kellaway, Gladys Cooper, Audrey Totter, Marshall Thompson, Leon Ames. Written by Karen de Wolf, from a play by George Seaton; directed by S. Sylvan Simon; for MGM. (GB title: *Mr Griggs Returns*.)

The Cockeyed World*
US 1929 115m bw
Fox

Further adventures of Sergeants Flagg and Quirt, the boisterous heroes of *What Price Glory*.

Lively early talkie; the adventure comedy remains interesting, though the technique is badly faded.

w William K. Wells, Laurence Stallings, Michael Anderson, Wilson Mizner, Tom Barry *d* Raoul Walsh *ph* Arthur Edeson

Victor McLaglen, Edmund Lowe, Lili Damita, Lelia Karnelly, El Brendel, Bobby Burns, Stuart Erwin

Cockfighter
US 1974 83m Metrocolor
Rio Pinto / New World / Artists Entertainment Complex (Roger Corman)
aka: *Born to Kill*

A professional cockfighter ends a run of bad luck but loses his girl.
Not badly made but rather seedy film about appalling people.

w Charles Willeford, from his novel *d* Monte Hellman *ph* Nestor Almendros *m* Michael Franks

Warren Oates, Richard B. Shull, Harry Dean Stanton, Ed Begley Jnr, Laurie Bird, Troy Donahue

Cockleshell Heroes
GB 1955 97m Technicolor Cinemascope
Columbia / Warwick (Phil C. Samuel)

During World War II, ten marines are trained to travel by canoe into Bordeaux harbour and attach limpet mines to German ships.
Absolutely predictable semi-documentary war heroics, with barrack-room humour turning eventually into tragedy. The familiar elements, including a display of stiff upper lips, ensured box office success.

w Bryan Forbes, Richard Maibaum *d* Jose Ferrer *ph* John Wilcox, Ted Moore *m* John Addison

Jose Ferrer, *Trevor Howard*, Dora Bryan, Victor Maddern, Anthony Newley, Peter Arne, David Lodge, Walter Fitzgerald, Beatrice Campbell

Cocoanut Grove
US 1938 85m bw
Paramount (George Arthur)

A band is fired from an excursion boat but makes it big in a Los Angeles night club. Vacuous comedy musical with a watchable number or two.

w Sy Bartlett, Olive Cooper *d* Alfred Santell *ph* Leo Tover *songs* various

Fred MacMurray, Harriet Hilliard, The Yacht Club Boys, Ben Blue, Eve Arden, Billy Lee, Rufe Davis

'No mind-wearier as to plot, it shapes up as nice summer film fare.'—*Variety*

The Cocoanuts**
US 1929 96m bw
Paramount (Walter Wanger, James R. Cown)

A chiselling hotel manager tries to get in on the Florida land boom.

Considering its age and the dismal prints which remain, this is a remarkably lively if primitive first film by the Marxes, with some good routines among the excess footage.

w George S. Kaufman, Morrie Ryskind
d Robert Florey, Joseph Santley *ph* George Folsey *m / ly* Irving Berlin

The Four Marx Brothers, Margaret Dumont, Oscar Shaw, Mary Eaton, Kay Francis, Basil Ruysdael

'The camerawork showed all the mobility of a concrete fire hydrant caught in a winter freeze.'—*Paul D. Zimmermann*

Cocoon**
US 1985 117m De Luxe
TCF / Zanuck-Brown (Lili Zanuck)

Aliens from another galaxy leave pods in the pool of a Florida retirement home, whose bathers are rejuvenated.
Unusual, amusing and sentimentally effective movie of the kind which gets hearty word-of-mouth recommendation.

w Tom Benedek novel David Saperstein
d Ron Howard ph Don Peterman *m* James Horner *pd* Jack T. Collis *ed* Daniel Hanley, Michael J. Hill

Don Ameche, Wilford Brimley, Hume Cronyn, Brian Dennehy, Jack Gilford, Steve Guttenberg, Maureen Stapleton, Jessica Tandy, Gwen Verdon

'A mesmerizing tale that's a certified audience pleaser.'—*Variety*

AA: best supporting actor, Don Ameche

Code Name: Emerald
US 1985 93m Metrocolor

A double agent is sent to Paris in 1944 to make sure that a captured American officer doesn't talk about the D-Day plans. Plodding, old hat war melodrama with no specific virtues. Ed Harris, Max von Sydow, Horst Buchholz, Helmut Berger, Graham Crowden. Written by Ronald Bass, from his novel *The Emerald Illusion*; directed by Jonathan Sanger; for NBC / MGM-UA.

Code of Silence
US 1985 101m AstroColor

A Chicago cop raids a drug den and sets off a gang war. Routine tough stuff which just about avoids self-parody. Chuck Norris, Henry Silva, Bert Remsen, Molly Hagan. Written by Michael Butler, Dennis Shryack, Mike Gray; directed by Andy Davis; for Raymond Wagner / Orion.

Code of the Secret Service
US 1939 58m bw

Agents track a gang who stole treasury banknote plates. Serial-like adventures, one of several from the same stable, all featuring the future president of the US. Ronald Reagan, Eddie Foy Jnr, Rosella Towne, Moroni Olsen, Edgar Edwards. Written by Lee Katz, Dean Franklin; directed by Noel Smith; for Warners. 'Filler fodder; a wild actioner for lower dual bookings.'—*Variety*

Cody of the Pony Express
US 1950 bw serial: 15 eps

An express rider exposes an apparently respectable attorney as an outlaw leader. Pretty fair western serial. Jock O'Mahoney, Dickie Moore, Peggy Stewart, William Fawcett, George J. Lewis. Directed by Spencer Bennet; for Columbia.

Code Two
US 1953 69m bw

Three young men join the police academy. Predictable second biller. Ralph Meeker, Sally Forrest, Keenan Wynn, James Craig, Robert Hortu, Elaine Stewart, Jeff Richards. Written by Marcel Klauber; directed by Fred M. Wilcox; for MGM.

The Cohens and the Kellys

Seven comedies were made, all for Universal, about the friendly rivalry of Jewish and Irish neighbours. They were:
1927: THE COHENS AND KELLYS IN NEW YORK
1928: THE COHENS AND KELLYS IN PARIS
1929: THE COHENS AND KELLYS IN ATLANTIC CITY
1930: THE COHENS AND KELLYS IN SCOTLAND, THE COHENS AND KELLYS IN AFRICA,
1932: THE COHENS AND KELLYS IN HOLLYWOOD
1933: THE COHENS AND KELLYS IN TROUBLE
In all cases the leading roles were played by Charles Murray and George Sidney

Coiffeur pour Dames
France 1952 87m approx bw
Hoche (Jean Boyer)
GB title: *An Artist with Ladies*

A Provençal sheep shearer becomes a fashionable ladies' hairdresser with a Champs-Élysées salon, and finds that his clients are all susceptible to his charms.
Obvious star comedy with a fair measure of laughs; more in fact than the much later *Shampoo*.

w Serge Véber, Jean Boyer, *play* P. Armont, M. Gerbidon *d* Jean Boyer *ph* Charles Suin *m* Paul Misraki

Fernandel, Blanchette Crunoy, Renée Devillers, Arlette Poirier

Cold Sweat
Italy / France 1974 94m colour

An American living peaceably on the Riviera is forced into drug smuggling. Reliable tough stuff for those who like that sort of thing. Charles Bronson, James Mason, Liv Ullman, Jill Ireland, Jean Topart. Written by Shimon Wincelberg and Albert Simonin from a novel Ride the Nightmare by Richard Matheson; directed by Terence Young; for Emerson. (Aka: *The Man With Two Shadows*)

Cold Turkey*
US 1970 102m De Luxe
UA / Tandem / DFI (Bud Yorkin, Norman Lear)

A tobacco company offers 25 million dollars to any town which can give up smoking for thirty days.
Rather wild and strained but sporadically amusing satirical comedy, aggressively littered with unpleasant detail.

w Norman Lear, *novel* I'm Giving Them Up for Good by Margaret and Neil Rau
d Norman Lear *ph* Charles F. Wheeler
m Randy Newman

Dick Van Dyke, Pippa Scott, Tom Poston, Edward Everett Horton, Bob Newhart, Vincent Gardenia, Jean Stapleton
'An eager desire to debunk and shock at the same time.'—*David McGillivray*

A Cold Wind in August*
US 1960 77m bw
UA / Troy Films (Robert L. Ross, Philip Hazleton)

An ageing stripper seduces a 17-year-old janitor but the affair ends when he sees her do her act.
Roughly-made, well-acted sex drama which at the time seemed mildly shocking but can only survive for its central acting performance.

w Burton Wohl, from his novel *d* Alexander Singer *ph* Floyd Crosby *m* Gerald Fried

Lola Albright, Scott Marlowe, Joe de Santis, Herschel Bernardi

The Colditz Story**
GB 1954 97m bw
British Lion / Ivan Foxwell

Adventures of British POWs in the German maximum security prison in Saxony's Colditz Castle during World War II.
Probably the most convincing of the British accounts of POW life, with a careful balance of tragedy and comedy against a background of humdrum, boring daily existence. A TV series followed in 1972.

w Guy Hamilton, Ivan Foxwell, *book* P. R. Reid *d* Guy Hamilton *ph* Gordon Dines
m Francis Chagrin

John Mills, Eric Portman, Christopher Rhodes, Lionel Jeffries, Bryan Forbes, Ian Carmichael, Richard Wattis, Frederick Valk, Anton Diffring, Eugene Deckers, Theodore Bikel
'It has all the realism, dignity and courage of the men it commemorates.'—*News of the World*

'You won't dare open your mouth, but you'll be screaming for her to escape!'
The Collector*
US 1965 119m Technicolor
Columbia (Jud Kinberg, John Kohn)

An inhibited young butterfly specialist kidnaps a girl to add to his collection.
Talkative and unrewarding suspenser with pretensions, sluggishly handled and not very interestingly acted.

w Stanley Mann, John Kohn, *novel* John Fowles *d* William Wyler *ph* Robert L. Surtees, Robert Krasker *m* Maurice Jarre

Terence Stamp, Samantha Eggar, Mona Washbourne

AAN: Stanley Mann, John Kohn; William Wyler; Samantha Eggar

Colleen*
US 1936 89m bw
Warner (Robert Lord)

Boy meets Irish girl in New York.
Typical light musical of the period with standard studio talent.

w Peter Milne, F. Hugh Herbert, Sig Herzig
d Alfred E. Green *ph* Byron Haskin, Sol Polito *m / ly* Harry Warren, Al Dubin
ch Bobby Connolly *gowns* Orry-Kelly

Dick Powell, Ruby Keeler, Jack Oakie, Joan Blondell, Hugh Herbert, Louise Fazenda, Paul Draper, Marie Wilson, Luis Alberni, Hobart Cavanaugh, Berton Churchill

'You'll graduate with a perpetual smile!'
College*
US 1927 65m (24 fps) bw silent
Buster Keaton Productions (Joseph M. Schenck)

A brainy high school student becomes a college football star.
Disappointing comedy from this great stone-faced clown: the plums are there, but few and far between.

w Carl Harbaugh, Bryan Foy *d* James W. Horne *ph* J. Devereux Jennings, Bert Haines

Buster Keaton, Ann Cornwall, Harold Goodwin, Snitz Edwards, Florence Turner

College Coach
US 1933 75m bw

A tough football coach finds that his best star is a timid chemistry student. Unremarkable studio programmer despite a strong cast. Dick Powell, Pat O'Brien, Ann Dvorak, Arthur Byron, Lyle Talbot, Hugh Herbert, Guinn Williams, Donald Meek. Written by Niven Busch, Manuel Seff; directed by William A. Wellman; for Warners. 'Hasn't enough punch for real sock grosses.'—*Variety*

College Confidential
US 1960 91m bw

A professor surveys the sexual habits of his students. Tinpot exposé of a highly dubious kind. Steve Allen, Jayne Meadows, Mamie Van Doren, Rocky Marciano, Mickey Shaughnessy, Herbert Marshall, Conway Twitty. Written by Irvin Shulman; directed and produced by Albert Zugsmith; for Universal.

College Holiday
US 1936 87m bw
Paramount (Harlan Thompson)

Bright young specimens are invited to spend a summer with a lady hotelier interested in eugenics.
Boisterous fun and games which may have seemed funny at the time.

w J. P. McEvoy, Harlan Ware, Jay Gorney, Henry Myers *d* Frank Tuttle *ph* Theodor Sparkuhl *songs* various

Jack Benny, George Burns, Gracie Allen, Mary Boland, Martha Raye, Etienne Girardot, Marsha Hunt, Leif Erickson, Eleanore Whitney, Johnny Downs, Olympe Bradna, Ben Blue, Jed Prouty

'For a picture that permits the cast to run around practically on the loose, it gets along remarkably well.'—*Variety*

College Humor
US 1933 84m bw
Paramount

A freshman discovers that football and necking are at least as important as studies. Easy-going comedy-musical which helped to establish its star.

w Claude Binyon, Frank Butler, *story* Dean Fales *d* Wesley Ruggles *ph* Leo Tover *songs* Arthur Johnston, Sam Coslow

Bing Crosby, Jack Oakie, George Burns, Gracie Allen, Richard Arlen, Mary Carlisle

'A light frothy musical that doesn't give the customers much of a mental workout.'—*Variety*

College Rhythm
US 1934 75m bw

A college football team fights to help an old-fashioned department store to modernize itself. Of its time, a pleasant 'youth' movie, but with nothing for posterity. Jack Oakie, Joe Penner, Mary Brian, Lanny Ross, Helen Mack, Lyda Roberti, George Barbier, Franklin Pangborn, Dean Jagger. Written by Walter De Leon, John McDermott, Francis Martin, George Marion Jnr; directed by Norman Taurog; for Paramount. 'Entertaining semi-musical with bright box-office possibilities.'—*Variety*

† Songs, composed by Mack Gordon and Harry Revel, include: 'Stay as Sweet as you Are'; 'Goo Goo'; 'Let's Give Three Cheers for Love'; 'Take a Number from One to Ten'.

College Scandal
US 1935 75m bw

A killer attacks three male students. After *College Humor* and *College Rhythm*, this amounts to College Murder. With stars, it could have been memorable. Arline Judge, Kent Taylor, Wendy Barrie, Mary Nash, William Stack, William Frawley, Benny Baker, Johnny Downs. Written by Frank Partos, Charles Brackett, Marguerite Roberts; directed by Elliott Nugent; for Paramount. 'Worthwhile summer fare for high-grade dual houses.'—*Variety*

College Swing
US 1938 86m bw
Paramount (Lewis Gensler)
GB title: *Swing, Teacher, Swing*

A dumb girl must graduate if a college is to inherit a fortune.
Mild comedy more notable for its cast than its script.

w Walter de Leon, Francis Martin *d* Raoul Walsh *ph* Victor Milner *songs* various

George Burns, Gracie Allen, Martha Raye, Bob Hope, Edward Everett Horton, Florence George, Ben Blue, Betty Grable, Jackie Coogan, John Payne, Cecil Cunningham, Robert Cummings

'A medley of vaude specialties, bits and numbers strung together in not too happy a manner.'—*Variety*

Collegiate
US 1935 80m bw

A girls' college is kept going by the whim of an amnesiac. Mild comedy in the vein of *College Rhythm*. Jack Oakie, Joe Penner, Frances Langford, Ned Sparks, Betty Grable, Lynne Overman, Mack Gordon, Harry Revel, Julius Tannen. Written by Walter de Leon, Francis Martin, from the play The Charm School by Alice Duer Miller; directed by Ralph Murphy; for Paramount. 'Light, diverting, no sock, but no bore.'—*Variety*

Colonel Effingham's Raid
US 1946 70m bw
TCF (Lamar Trotti)
GB title: *Man of the Hour*

A retired southern colonel tries to straighten out a corrupt Georgia town.
Competent, unsurprising programmer.

w Kathryn Scola, *novel* Berry Fleming *d* Irving Pichel *ph* Edward Cronjager *m* Cyril Mockridge

Charles Coburn, Joan Bennett, William Eythe, Allyn Joslyn, Elizabeth Patterson, Donald Meek, Frank Craven, Thurston Hall, Cora Witherspoon, Emory Parnell, Henry Armetta, Roy Roberts, Charles Trowbridge

Colonel Redl**
Hungary / West Germany / Austria 1984 149m Eastmancolor
Mafilm / Mokep / Manfred Durniok / ZDF / ORF
Original title: *Oberst Redl*

The career of a railwayman's son who in the early years of the century rises high in the military but is condemned by his own insecurities and forced to commit suicide as a spy.
Whether or not one cares for the ironic parable (also treated by John Osborne in his play *A Patriot for Me*) this is a handsome film full of brilliant visuals.

w Istvan Szabo, Peter Dobai *d Istvan Szabo ph Lajos Koltai m* Zdenko Tamassy

Klaus Maria Brandauer, Hans-Christian Blech, Armin Müller-Stahl, Gudrun Landgrebe, Jan Niklas

AAN: best picture

BFA: best foreign film

The Color of Money**
US 1986 119m DuArt
Touchstone (Irving Axelrod, Barbara de Fina)

Twenty-five years later, the hero of *The Hustler* teaches a young man his skills.
Slackly told but consistently enjoyable adventures of Fast Eddie Felson in his older age.

w Richard Price, from characters in the novel by Walter Tevis *d Martin Scorsese ph* Michael Ballhaus *m* Robbie Robertson

Paul Newman, *Tom Cruise*, Mary Elizabeth Mastrantonio, Helen Shaver, Bill Cobbs, John Turturro

AA: Paul Newman

AAN: Michael Balhaus; Boris Leven (art direction); Kevin J. O'Hara (sound); Mary Elizabeth Mastrantonio

The Color Purple**
US 1985 152m De Luxe
Warner / Amblin (Steven Spielberg, Kathleen Kennedy, Frank Marshall, Quincy Jones)

The growth of a southern black family during the first half of the century.
Well-intentioned and gracious but not always dramatically cohesive generation saga from a director trying to prove he has depth.

w Menno Meyjes *novel* Alice Walker *d Steven Spielberg ph Allen Daviau m* Quincy Jones *pd* J. Michael Riva *ed* Michael Kahn

Whoopi Goldberg, Danny Glover, Margaret Avery, Oprah Winfrey, Willard Pugh, Adolph Caesar

AAN: best picture, Whoopi Goldberg, Margaret Avery (supporting actress), Oprah Winfrey (supporting actress), adapted screenplay, photography, music, editing

Colorado Territory*
US 1949 93m bw
Warner (Anthony Veiller)

An outlaw escapes from prison planning one last robbery but is shot in the attempt.
Moderate western remake of *High Sierra*.

w John Twist, Edmund H. North *d* Raoul Walsh *ph* Sid Hickox *m* David Buttolph

Joel McCrea, Virginia Mayo, Dorothy Malone, Henry Hull, John Archer, James Mitchell, Morris Ankrum, Basil Ruysdael, Frank Puglia

The Colossus of New York
US 1958 70m bw

An international scientist is killed in an accident; his father puts his brain into a robot, which goes on the rampage. Absurd horror comic for kids, with hilariously unexplained detail and poor technical effects. Otto Kruger, Ross Martin, Robert Hutton, John Baragrey, Mala Powers. Written by Thelma Schnee; directed by Eugene Lourie; for William Alland / Paramount.

The Colossus of Rhodes
Italy 1960 129m Technicolor SuperTotalScope

In 300 BC, a huge statue doubles as a fortress to prevent the Phoenicians from invading. Good-looking spectacle with the usual muddled script. Rory Calhoun, Lea Massari, Georges Marchal. Written by Sergio Leone and seven others; directed by Sergio Leone; for Michele Scaglione / MGM.

Colour Me Dead
Australia 1969 97m colour

An accountant discovers that he had been given a slow-acting poison. Poor remake of the 1949 semi-classic *D.O.A.*: no reason to see it. Tom Tryon, Carolyn Jones, Rick Jason, Patricia Connolly. Written by Russel Rouse and Clarence Greene, from their original; directed and produced by Eddie Davis; for Goldsworthy.

Colt 45
US 1950 74m Technicolor

A new kind of gun, intended to bring law and order to the west, gets into the wrong hands. Routine, watchable western which achieved a surprising popularity. Randolph Scott, Zachary Scott, Ruth Roman, Lloyd Bridges. Written by Thomas Blackburn; directed by Edwin L. Marin; for Warner. (American TV title: *Thundercloud.*)

Column South
US 1953 84m colour

A cavalry officer shows how to live peaceably with Indians. Tolerable co-feature western. Audie Murphy, Joan Evans, Robert Sterling, Ray Collins, Dennis Weaver. Written by William Sackheim; directed by Frederick de Cordova; for Universal.

Coma*
US 1978 113m Metrocolor
MGM (Martin Erlichman)

A lady doctor suspects that patients are being put deliberately into coma so that their organs can be sold, and finds herself in deadly peril. Hitchcockian suspense thriller with nobody but the audience believing the heroine; the fact that there are more dead than living characters makes it slightly too ghoulish at times.

wd Michael Crichton, *novel* Robin Cook *ph* Victor J. Kemper, Gerald Hirschfeld *m* Jerry Goldsmith *pd* Albert Brenner

Geneviève Bujold, Michael Douglas, Richard Widmark, Elizabeth Ashley, Rip Torn, Lois Chiles, Harry Rhodes

Comanche
US 1955 87m De Luxe Cinemascope

In 1875 New Mexico, a renegade Indian prevents peace between white and red man. Cheerful action western, satisfying to the easily pleased. Dana Adrews, Kent Smith, Nestor Paiva, Henry Brandon, John Litel, Lowell Gilmore, Mike Mazurki. Written by Carl Krueger; directed by George Sherman; for Carl Krueger / UA.

Comanche Station
US 1960 74m Technicolor Cinemascope

A man seeks his wife, taken prisoner by Indians. Below par star western, indifferently plotted. Randolph Scott, Nancy Gates, Claude Akins, Skip Homeier. Written by Burt Kennedy; directed by Budd Boetticher; for Harry Joe Brown / Columbia.

Comanche Territory
US 1950 76m Technicolor

Jim Bowie assists the Comanches against treacherous whites. Double bill western, adequate for its purpose. Maureen O'Hara, Macdonald Carey, Will Geer, Charles Drake. Written by Oscar Brodney and Louis Meltzer; directed by George Sherman; for Universal-International.

The Comancheros**
US 1961 107m De Luxe Cinemascope
TCF (George Sherman)

A Texas Ranger and his gambler prisoner join forces to clean up renegade gunmen operating from a remote armed compound.
Easy-going, cheerfully violent western with lively roughhouse sequences.

w James Edward Grant, Clair Huffaker *d* Michael Curtiz *ph* William H. Clothier *m* Elmer Bernstein

John Wayne, Stuart Whitman, Nehemiah Persoff, Lee Marvin, Ina Balin, Bruce Cabot

Come and Get It*
US 1936 99m bw
Samuel Goldwyn (Merritt Hulburd)

The life and loves of a lumber tycoon in 19th-century Wisconsin.
Disappointingly conventional, mainly studio-bound action drama using top talent of the period.

w Jules Furthman, Jane Murfin, *novel* Edna Ferber *d* Howard Hawks, William Wyler *ph* Gregg Toland, Rudolph Maté *m* Alfred Newman

Edward Arnold, Joel McCrea, Frances Farmer, Walter Brennan, Andrea Leeds

AA: Walter Brennan

Come Back Charleston Blue*
US 1972 101m Technicolor
Warner / Formosa (Samuel Goldwyn Jnr)

Harlem detectives Coffin Ed Johnson and Gravedigger Jones investigate the case of a long-dead gangster who seems to be still taking vengeance.
Occasionally funny but disturbingly violent crime kaleidoscope with a black ambience, more sophisticated and therefore more generally acceptable than its predecessor *Cotton Comes to Harlem* (qv).

w Bontche Schweig, Peggy Elliott, *novel* The Heat's On by Chester Himes *d* Mark Warren *ph* Dick Kratina *m* Donny Hathaway

Godfrey Cambridge, Raymond St Jacques, Peter de Anda, Jonelle Allen, Percy Rodrigues, Minny Gentry

'That girl in their house spelled trouble!'

Come Back Little Sheba*
US 1952 99m bw
Paramount (Hal B. Wallis)

An ex-alcoholic is let down not only by his slovenly wife but by the young girl he idolizes.
Stagey but theatrically effective transcription of a popular domestic drama, with one outstanding performance.

w Ketti Frings, *play William Inge* *d* Daniel Mann *ph* James Wong Howe *m* Franz Waxman

Shirley Booth, Burt Lancaster, Terry Moore, Richard Jaeckel

AA: Shirley Booth
AAN: Terry Moore

Come Back to the Five and Dime, Jimmy Dean, Jimmy Dean
US 1983 110m Du Art Color
Sandcastle 5 / Mark Goodman / Viacom

Misfits meet to celebrate the twentieth anniversary of the death of James Dean.
Filmed play which descends from cynicism through gloom to hysteria and is never very revealing.

w Ed Graczyk, from his play *d* Robert Altman *ph* Pierre Mignot *m* various

Sandy Dennis, Karen Black, Cher, Sudie Bond, Kathy Bates

'It may seem perverse to describe as Altman's masterpiece so self-contained and "alien" a work, with an existence pre-dating his own involvement and a thrusting (if perverse) biological life that owes nothing to the audience's willingness to participate. But the irony depends solely on which side of Altman's own two-way world one stands.'—*Richard Combs, MFB*

Come Blow Your Horn*
US 1962 112m Technicolor Panavision
Paramount / Lear and Yorkin

A country boy in New York is envious of his older brother's sophisticated life.
Amusing characters and funny lines permeate this stolid transcription of an early Neil Simon success; the big screen is not the place for them.

w Norman Lear, *play Neil Simon* *d* Bud Yorkin *ph* William Daniels *m* Nelson Riddle

Frank Sinatra, Tony Bill, Lee J. Cobb, Molly Picon, Jill St John, Barbara Rush, Dan Blocker

Come Clean**
US 1931 20m bw

Two much-married men go out for ice-cream and bring back a woman of the streets they have saved from suicide. Splendid star comedy with the famous characterizations fully rounded. Laurel and Hardy, Mae Busch, Charlie Hall, Gertrude Astor, Linda Loredo. Written by H. M. Walker; directed by James W. Horne; for Hal Roach. (NB: Remade in 1942 as *Brooklyn Orchid*, with William Bendix and Joe Sawyer.)

Come Fill the Cup*
US 1951 113m bw
Warner (Henry Blanke)

An alcoholic newspaperman cures himself, then his boss's alcoholic son who is involved with gangsters.
Unlikely but solidly entertaining melodrama, powerfully cast.

w Ivan Goff, Ben Roberts, *novel* Harlan Ware *d* Gordon Douglas *ph Robert Burks* *m* Ray Heindorf

James Cagney, Gig Young, Raymond Massey, Phyllis Thaxter, James Gleason, Selena Royle, Larry Keating

AAN: Gig Young

Come Fly with Me
US 1962 109m Metrocolor Panavision
MGM / Anatole de Grunwald

The romantic adventures of three air hostesses.
Good-looking girls and airplanes but little else make thin entertainment.

w William Roberts *d* Henry Levin *ph* Oswald Morris *m* Lyn Murray

Hugh O'Brian, Dolores Hart, Karl Malden, Pamela Tiffin, Lois Nettleton, Karl Boehm

Come Live with Me*
US 1941 86m bw
MGM (Clarence Brown)

In order to stay in America, a girl refugee from Vienna arranges a strictly platonic marriage with a struggling author.
Hypnotically predictable comedy, quite well presented and performed.

w Patterson McNutt, Virginia Van Upp *d* Clarence Brown *ph* George Folsey *m* Herbert Stothart

James Stewart, Hedy Lamarr, Ian Hunter, Verree Teasdale, Donald Meek, Barton MacLane, *Adeline de Walt Reynolds*

Come Next Spring*
US 1955 92m Trucolor
Republic

A drunkard returns to his Arkansas farm family and wins the respect of them and the community.
D. W. Griffith-type pastoral melodrama which surprisingly works pretty well and leaves one with the intended warm glow.

w Montgomery Pittman *d* R. G. Springsteen *ph* Jack Marta *m* Max Steiner

Ann Sheridan, Steve Cochran, Walter Brennan, Sherry Jackson, Richard Eyer, Edgar Buchanan, Sonny Tufts, Mae Clarke

'An unpretentious film with a good deal of charm.'—*MFB*

The Come On
US 1956 83m bw Superscope
AA (Lindley Parsons)

Husband and wife confidence tricksters get homicidal when she falls in love.
In trade parlance, strictly a lower berth item; but with points of mild interest.

w Warren Douglas, *novel* Whitman Chambers *d* Russell Birdwell *ph* Ernest Haller *m* Paul Dunlap

Anne Baxter, Sterling Hayden, John Hoyt, Jesse White, Paul Picerni

Come on George*
GB 1939 88m bw
ATP / Ealing (Jack Kitchin)

A stableboy calms a nervous racehorse and rides him to victory.
Standard comedy vehicle, well mounted, with the star at his box office peak.

w Anthony Kimmins, Leslie Arliss, Val Valentine *d* Anthony Kimmins *ph* Ronald Neame, Gordon Dines *m* Ernest Irving

George Formby, Pat Kirkwood, Joss Ambler, Meriel Forbes, Cyril Raymond, George Carney, Ronald Shiner

Come Out of the Pantry
GB 1935 73m bw

An English milord is forced by circumstance to take a job as his boss's footman. Pleasing if obvious comedy, later remodelled as *Spring in Park Lane*. Jack Buchanan, Fay Wray, James Carew, Ronald Squire, Olive Blakeney, Fred Emney. Written by Austin Parker from a story by Alice Duer Miller; directed by Jack Raymond; for British and Dominions.

Come September
US 1961 112m Technicolor CinemaScope
Universal / 7 Pictures Corporation / Raoul Walsh Enterprises (Robert Arthur)

A wealthy American discovers that his Italian villa is being used as a hotel by his once-a-year mistress, who is about to marry.
Clumsy sex farce with lush trimmings and generation gap asides; effort more noticeable than achievement.

w Stanley Shapiro, Maurice Richlin *d* Robert Mulligan *ph* William Daniels *m* Hans J. Salter

Rock Hudson, Gina Lollobrigida, Sandra Dee, Bobby Darin, Walter Slezak, Brenda de Banzie, Joel Grey, Rosanna Rory, Ronald Howard

Come to the Stable*
US 1949 94m bw
TCF (Samuel G. Engel)

Two French nuns arrive in New England to build a local hospital, and melt the hearts of the local grumps.
This old-time charmer simply brims with sweetness and light and is produced with high-class studio efficiency.

w Oscar Millard, Sally Benson, *story* Clare Boothe Luce *d* Henry Koster *ph* Joseph La Shelle *md* Lionel Newman *m* Cyril Mockridge

Loretta Young, Celeste Holm, Hugh Marlowe, Elsa Lanchester, Thomas Gomez, Dorothy Patrick, Basil Ruysdael, Dooley Wilson, Regis Toomey, Henri Letondal

AAN: Clare Boothe Luce; Joseph La Shelle; Loretta Young; Celeste Holm; Elsa Lanchester: song 'Through a Long and Sleepless Night' (*m* Alfred Newman, *ly* Mack Gordon)

The Comeback
GB 1978 100m colour

An American singer in London deals with the murder of his wife—and with her ghost. Dim mixture of mystery and horror, not at all persuasive. Jack Jones, Sheila Keith, Pamela Stephenson, David Doyle, Bill Owen, Richard Johnson. Written by Murray Smith; produced and directed by Pete Walker. (Aka: *The Day the Screaming Stopped*.)

The Comedians*
US / Bermuda / France 1967 160m Metrocolor Panavision
MGM / Maximilian / Trianon (Peter Glenville)

A variety of English-speaking eccentrics are caught up in the violent events of Haiti under Papa Doc Duvalier.
Clumsy and heavy-going compression of a too-topical novel, with most of the plot left in at the expense of character. Neither entertaining nor instructive, but bits of acting please.

w Graham Greene, from his novel *d* Peter Glenville *ph* Henri Decaë *m* Laurence Rosenthal

Richard Burton, Elizabeth Taylor, *Alec Guinness*, Peter Ustinov, Lillian Gish, Paul Ford, Roscoe Lee Browne, James Earl Jones, Raymond St Jacques, Cicely Tyson

'So thick and fast do the clichés come that one feels the script can only have been salvaged from some *New Statesman* competition.'—*Tom Milne*

'It's pleasant to spend two hours again in Greeneland, still well-stocked with bilious minor crucifixions, furtive fornication, cynical politics, and reluctant hope.'—*Stanley Kauffmann*

The Comedy Man*
GB 1964 92m bw
British Lion–Gray–Consort (Jon Pennington)

A middle-aged actor on the skids desperately rounds up his contacts and becomes the star of a TV commercial.
Determinedly depressing satirical melodrama with engaging moments; comedy emphasis would have better suited the talents.

w Peter Yeldham, *novel* Douglas Hayes *d* Alvin Rakoff *ph* Ken Hodges *m* Bill McGuffie

Kenneth More, Cecil Parker, Dennis Price, Billie Whitelaw, Norman Rossington, Angela Douglas, Edmund Purdom, Frank Finlay, Alan Dobie

'Humour and intelligent irony.'—*Sunday Express*

'A merciless and accurate picture of the brave band of actors who live from hand to mouth and commute between the Salisbury Arms pub and the Poland Street Labour exchange.'—*Evening News*

The Comedy of Terrors*
US 1963 88m Pathecolor Panavision
Alta Vista / AIP (Anthony Carras, Richard Matheson)

Two impecunious funeral directors decide to speed up the demise of their prospective clients.

Disappointingly slackly-handled and rather tiresome macabre frolic, notable for a few splendid moments and an imperishable cast.

w Richard Matheson *d* Jacques Tourneur *ph* Floyd Crosby *m* Les Baxter

Vincent Price, Peter Lorre, Boris Karloff, Basil Rathbone, Joe E. Brown, Joyce Jameson

Comes a Horseman
US 1978 118m Technicolor Panavision
UA / Chartoff-Winkler (Robert Caan)

In the forties, Montana ranchers have a hard time holding onto their land against the pressures of progress and a villainous cattle baron.
Portentous and wholly unexciting modern western, not helped by a loftily unexplained title and show-off photography.

w Dennis Lynton Clark *d* Alan J. Pakula *ph* Gordon Willis *m* Michael Small *pd* George Jenkins

Jane Fonda, Jason Robards Jnr, James Caan, George Grizzard, Richard Farnsworth, Jim Davis

'It's a film of few words (and about a quarter of them mangled by the sound recording). The melodrama is smothered under sullen, overcast skies. How can you get involved in the conflict between the good guys and the bad guys if you can't even see them?'—*Pauline Kael*

AAN: Richard Farnsworth

Comet over Broadway
US 1938 65m bw

An actress, having been involved in a murder, is torn between burning ambition and mother love. Arrant melodrama which overtaxes its star. Kay Francis, Ian Hunter, John Litel, Donald Crisp, Minna Gombell, Sybil Jason, Melville Cooper. Written by Mark Hellinger and Robert Buckner, from a story by Faith Baldwin; directed by Busby Berkeley; for Warners. 'A backstage yarn that goes overboard on assorted heartbreaks.'—*Variety*

Comfort and Joy*
GB 1984 106m colour
Lake / EMI / STV (Davina Belling, Clive Parsons)

A Scottish radio disc jockey becomes involved in a war between two ice-cream firms.
Heavy comedy, short of laughs and sympathy; a distinct descent from *Local Hero*, which was a comedown after *Gregory's Girl*.

w,d Bill Forsyth *ph* Chris Menges *m* Mark Knopfler

Bill Paterson, Eleanor David, C. P. Grogan, Alex Norton

The Comic*
US 1969 95m Technicolor
Columbia (Carl Reiner)

The success, downfall and old age of a silent film comedian in Hollywood.
Remarkably bright and cinematic tragi-comedy obviously based on Buster Keaton, with a *Citizen Kane*-type framework. Not a commercial success, but a must for professionals.

w Carl Reiner, Aaron Rubin *d* Carl Reiner *ph* W. Wallace Kelley *m* Jack Elliott

Dick Van Dyke, Mickey Rooney (more or less playing Ben Turpin), Cornel Wilde, Carl Reiner, Michele Lee, Pert Kelton

'Offers a variety of delights.'—*Judith Crist*

'A furious editorial about a business that treats its veterans like over-exposed celluloid.'—*Variety*

Comin' at Ya!
US 1981 101m Technicolor 3D

An ex-outlaw goes in search of three outlaws who kidnapped his wife-to-be. Determined three-dimensional attack on the sensibilities, with nothing to interest in story or acting. Tony Anthony, Gene Quintano, Victoria Abril. Written by Wolf Lowenthal, Lloyd Battista and Gene Quintano; directed by Ferdinando Baldi; for CAU.

Comin' Thro' the Rye
GB 1923 approx 85m (24 fps) bw silent
Hepworth Picture Plays

In Victorian England, lovers meet periodically in a rye field, but events move against them. Statuesque romantic drama whose reputation may be largely due to its accidental survival. (There was a previous version from the same producer in 1916, with the same leading actress.)

w Blanche McIntosh, *novel* Helen Mathers *d* Cecil M. Hepworth *ph* Geoffrey Faithfull

Alma Taylor, Shayle Garner, Eileen Dennes, Ralph Forbes, Francis Lister

'My best and most important film.'—*Cecil M. Hepworth*

'Hepworth's directorial style matches his material in simplicity.'—*Geoff Brown, MFB, 1976*

'A man who believed in war! A man who believed in nothing! And a woman who believed in both of them!'

Coming Home*
US 1978 128m De Luxe
UA / Jerome Hellman

An embittered Vietnam veteran falls for the wife of a serving soldier.
Self-pitying romantic wallow which must mean more to American audiences than to others. Goodish acting.

w Waldo Salt, Robert C. Jones, *story* Nancy Dowd *d* Hal Ashby *ph* Haskell Wexler *pd* Mike Haller *m* various

Jane Fonda, Jon Voight, Bruce Dern, Robert Carradine, Penelope Milford

AA: Jon Voight; Jane Fonda

AAN: best picture; best screenplay; Hal Ashby; Bruce Dern; Penelope Milford

Coming Up Roses*
GB 1986 93m Eastmancolor
Red Rooster / S4C
Welsh Title: *Rhosyn a Rhith*

When the local cinema closes down the local community take it over for mushroom-growing. Charming curiosity in Welsh with English subtitles, reminiscent of Ealing in its heyday.

w Ruth Carter *d* Stephen Bayley *ph* Dick Pope *m* Michael Story *pd* Hildegard Bechtler

Dafydd Hywel, Iola Gregory, Olive Michael, Mari Emlyn

The Command
US 1954 94m Warnercolor Cinemascope
Warner (David Weisbart)

A cavalry troop escorts a wagon train through Indian country.
Competent but unsurprising 'second team' western.

w Russell Hughes, *novel* James Warner Bellah *d* David Butler *ph* Wilfrid M. Cline *m* Dmitri Tiomkin

Guy Madison, Joan Weldon, James Whitmore, Carl Benton Reid, Harvey Lembeck, Ray Teal, Bob Nichols

'Heroes, cowards, fighters, braggarts, liars . . . and what goes on in their hearts!'

Command Decision*
US 1949 111m bw
MGM (Sidney Franklin)

War among the back-room boys; a general, his staff and his peers debate the aerial bombardment of Germany.
Plainly reproduced version of a determinedly serious play, with a remarkable cast partly at sea.

w William R. Laidlaw, George Froeschel, *play* William Wister Haines *d* Sam Wood *ph* Harold Rosson *m* Miklos Rozsa

Clark Gable, Walter Pidgeon, Van Johnson, Brian Donlevy, John Hodiak, Charles Bickford, Edward Arnold, Marshall Thompson, Richard Quine, Cameron Mitchell, Clinton Sundberg, Ray Collins, Warner Anderson, John McIntire, Moroni Olsen

Commando
US 1985 88m De Luxe

Unlikely mates are thrown together in pursuit of a deadly Latin dictator. Hard action nonsense with the saving grace of humour. Arnold Schwarzenegger, Rae Dawn Chong, Dan Hedaya, Vernon Wells, David Patrick Kelly. Written by Steven de Souza; directed by Mark L. Lester; for Joel Silver / TCF. 'Palatable actioner, inoffensively silly.'—*Variety*

The Commandos Strike at Dawn*
US 1942 98m bw
Columbia (Lester Cowan)

Norwegian commandos outwit the Nazis with the help of the British navy.
Standard war adventure shot on Vancouver Island.

w Irwin Shaw, *story* C. S. Forester *d* John Farrow *ph* William C. Mellor *m* Louis Gruenberg

Paul Muni, Anna Lee, Lillian Gish, Cedric Hardwicke, Robert Coote, Ray Collins, Rosemary de Camp, Richard Derr, Alexander Knox, Rod Cameron

AAN: Louis Gruenberg

Common Clay
US 1930 68m bw
Fox

A speakeasy hostess becomes maid in a wealthy household and falls in love with her betters.
Archetypal soap opera which caused a mild sensation and sent its star into half a dozen imitations.

w Jules Furthman, *novel* Cleves Kincaid *d* Victor Fleming *ph* Glen MacWilliams

Constance Bennett, Lew Ayres, Tully Marshall, Matty Kemp, Purnell Pratt, Beryl Mercer

'Emotional play of 1916 bearing the marks of that artificial school . . . heavy for fan diet.'—*Variety*

The Common Touch*
GB 1941 104m bw
British National (John Baxter)

A rich young man poses as a tramp to save a dosshouse from destruction.
Naive drama with a social conscience, remade from the 1932 talkie *Dosshouse.* A brave try.

w Barbara K. Emery, Geoffrey Orme, *novel* Herbert Ayres *d* John Baxter *ph* James Wilson

Geoffrey Hibbert, Greta Gynt, Joyce Howard, Harry Welchman, Edward Rigby, George Carney, Bransby Williams, Wally Patch, Eliot Makeham, Bernard Miles, Bill Fraser, John Longden; *guests* Sandy Macpherson, Scott Sanders, Mark Hambourg, Carrol Gibbons

Company Limited*
India 1971 112m bw
Chilrangali (B. S. Rama)
original title: *Seemabadha*

The young export sales manager of a firm of Delhi electrical appliance manufacturers is saved from boredom by his wife's younger sister.
Quietly pleasing but overlong comedy-drama of modern urban India, very typical of its director.

wd Satyajit Ray, novel Shankar *ph* Soumendu Roy *m* Satyajit Ray

Barun Chanda, Sharmilla Tagore, Parumita Chowdhary

'Subtle, witty, intelligent, and beautifully acted.'—*Michael Billington, Illustrated London News*

The Company of Wolves**
GB 1984 95m colour
ITC / Palace (Chris Brown, Stephen Woolley)

A young girl dreams of wolves and werewolves.
Fragmentary adult fantasy which had an unexpected box office success, chiefly because of its sexual allusiveness, its clever make-up and its pictorial qualities.

w Angela Carter, Neil Jordan, from stories by Angela Carter *d Neil Jordan ph Bryan Loftus m* George Fenton *special make-up effects* Christopher Tucker *pd* Anton Furst

Angela Lansbury, David Warner, Graham Crowden, Brian Glover, Sarah Patterson, Micha Bergese, Stephen Rea

The Company She Keeps
US 1950 83m bw
RKO (John Houseman)

A self-sacrificing parole officer allows a parolee to steal her fiancé.
Considering the credits, a dismally novelettish drama of almost no interest.

w Ketti Frings *d* John Cromwell *ph* Nicholas Musuraca *m* Leigh Harline

Lizabeth Scott, *Jane Greer,* Dennis O'Keefe, Fay Baker, John Hoyt, James Bell, Don Beddoe, Bert Freed

The Competition*
US 1980 129m Metrocolor
Columbia / Rastar / William Sackheim

An ageing piano prodigy has one last shot at fame in a San Francisco piano competition.
Slightly curious, old-fashioned but heavy-handed romance which aims to do for the piano what *The Turning Point* did for ballet. It doesn't sustain its length but at least the milieu is interesting.

wd Joel Oliansky *ph* Richard H. Kline *m,md* Lalo Schifrin *pd* Dale Hennesy

Richard Dreyfuss, Lee Remick, Amy Irving, Sam Wanamaker, Joseph Cali

AAN: editing (David Blewitt); best song ('People Alone')

Compromising Positions
US 1985 98m colour

The murder of a philandering dentist has repercussions among his many mistresses.
Combination sex comedy and whodunnit which never seems to hit the right groove.
Susan Sarandon, Raul Julia, Edward Herrmann, Judith Ivey, Mary Beth Hurt. Written by Susan Isaacs from her novel; directed by Frank Perry; for Paramount.

Compulsion*
US 1959 103m bw Cinemascope
TCF / Darryl F. Zanuck Productions (Richard F. Zanuck)

In the twenties, two Chicago students kidnap and murder a young boy for kicks.
Rather dogged but earnest fictionalization of the Leopold-Loeb case with solid performances and production.

w Richard Murphy, *play* Meyer Levin *d* Richard Fleischer *ph* William C. Mellor *m* Lionel Newman

Dean Stockwell, Bradford Dillman, Orson Welles (in a cameo court appearance as Clarence Darrow), Diane Varsi, E. G. Marshall, Martin Milner, Richard Anderson, Robert Simon

The Computer Wore Tennis Shoes
US 1970 90m Technicolor

While mending a computer a college student gets an electric shock and becomes omniscient.
Ho-hum Disney comedy, eager to please but instantly forgotten. Kurt Russell, Cesar Romero, Joe Flynn, William Schallert, Alan Hewitt. Written by Joseph L. McEveety; directed by Robert Butler; for Disney.

Comrade X*
US 1940 89m bw
MGM (Gottfried Reinhardt)

An American correspondent in Russia is blackmailed into smuggling a girl out of the country.
Lame satirical comedy in the wake of *Ninotchka*; a few good moments, but generally heavy-handed.

w Ben Hecht, Charles Lederer, *original story* Walter Reisch *d* King Vidor *ph* Joseph L. Ruttenberg *m* Bronislau Kaper

Clark Gable, Hedy Lamarr, Felix Bressart, Oscar Homolka, Eve Arden, Sig Rumann

'Broadest comedic strokes and not-too-subtle satire . . . a smacko entry for topflight biz.'—*Variety*

AAN: Walter Reisch

Comradeship*
GB 1919 67m (24 fps) bw silent

Two friends endure varying fortunes during World War I. An early British 'A' feature which was highly popular in its day. Lily Elsie, Gerald Ames, Guy Newall, Peggy Carlisle. Written by Jeffrey Bernerd; directed by Maurice Elvey; for Stoll.

Conan the Barbarian
US 1981 129m Technicolor Todd AO
Dino de Laurentiis / Edward R. Pressman (Buzz Feitshans, Raffaella de Laurentiis)

In the Dark Ages, a young stalwart seeks out the barbarian tribe which murdered his parents.
Intolerably doomladen, slow-moving and mainly unintelligible rubbish which failed to put a lift into the long-announced sword-and-sorcery cycle.

w John Milius, Oliver Stone, from a character created by Robert E. Howard *d* John Milius *ph* Duke Callaghan *m* Basil Poedouris *pd* Ron Cobb *ed* C. Timothy O'Meara

Arnold Schwarzenegger, James Earl Jones, Max Von Sydow, Sandahl Bergman, Ben Davidson, Mako, Gerry Lopez

'A ragbag of half-witted kitsch, where even locations resemble a set, actors look like extras, violence like a stunt and life a bad dream.'—*Sunday Times*

'An indigestible blend of anti-liberal braggadocio, post-60s mysticism and echt-60s blockbusting.'—*Sight and Sound*

Conan the Destroyer
US 1984 101m Technicolor Scope

An evil queen offers to bring Conan's last love back to life, if he will undertake a magical quest for her. More heavy-handed and unpleasant nonsense, with a slightly better pace than before. Arnold Schwarzenegger, Grace Jones, Wilt Chamberlain, Mako, Tracey Walter, Sarah Douglas. Written by Stanley Mann; directed by Richard Fleischer; photographed by Jack Cardiff; for Dino de Laurentiis.

The Concorde: Airport '79
US 1979 113m Technicolor
Universal (Jennings Lang)
GB title: *Airport '80: The Concorde*

Various disasters befall the Concorde on its way from Washington to Paris.
Stultified final (one presumes) effort in the *Airport* series; it could hardly be funnier if it were intended as a comedy, but somehow it entertains.

w Eric Roth *d* David Lowell Rich *ph* Philip Lathrop *m* Lalo Schifrin

Alain Delon, Susan Blakely, Robert Wagner, Sylvia Kristel, George Kennedy, Eddie Albert, Bibi Andersson, John Davidson, Martha Raye, Cicely Tyson, Mercedes McCambridge

'Larger-than-life characters are thrown together on a storyboard and must fend for themselves against attacks, chases and assorted escapades . . . this would be soporific even as a transatlantic inflight movie.'—*Martyn Auty, MFB*

'A kiss that cannot be forgotten!'
Condemned*
US 1930 86m bw
Samuel Goldwyn
aka: *Condemned to Devil's Island*

A bank robber is sent to Devil's Island and falls in love with the wife of the brutal warden.
Slow-moving but pictorially attractive melodrama with old-style performances.

w Sidney Howard, *novel* Condemned to Devil's Island by Blair Niles *d* Wesley Ruggles *ph George Barnes, Gregg Toland sets William Cameron Menzies*

Ronald Colman, Ann Harding, Louis Wolheim, Dudley Digges, William Elmer

'A piece of nonsense from which it would appear that French convicts on Devil's Island live a life consisting entirely of hot-towel shaves and flirtations with the governor's wife.'—*James Agate*

AAN: Ronald Colman

The Condemned of Altona*
Italy / France 1962 113m bw
(TCF) Titanus / SGC (Carlo Ponti)

The head of a German shipping empire discovers he has only a few months to live and tries to bring his family to order.
Strident intellectual melodrama whose credits tell all. Watchable for the acting, but very glum.

w Abby Mann, Cesare Zavattini, *play* Jean-Paul Sartre *d* Vittorio de Sica *ph* Roberto Gerardi *m* Dmitri Shostakovich

Fredric March, Sophia Loren, Robert Wagner, Maximilian Schell, Françoise Prévost, Alfredo Franchi

'This film is such a hopeless mess that it is difficult to know where to begin criticizing it.'—*Tom Milne*

Condemned to Death*
GB 1932 75m bw
Twickenham (Julius Hagen)

A condemned killer hypnotizes a judge into murdering those who turned him in.
Irresistible nonsense of the old school, with spirited direction and a good cast.

w Bernard Merivale, Harry Fowler Mear, Brock Williams, *play* Jack O'Lantern by George Goodchild and James Dawson *d Walter Forde ph* Sidney Blythe, William Luff

Arthur Wontner, Gillian Lind, Edmund Gwenn, Gordon Harker, Jane Welsh, Cyril Raymond

'A weak daily changer with double-headed programming its merited rating.'—*Variety*

'It would be difficult to find a dull moment.'—*The Bioscope*

Condemned Women
US 1938 77m bw

Murder in a prison for women. Rough-and-tumble melodrama with predictable elements. Sally Eilers, Anne Shirley, Louis Hayward, Esther Dale, Lee Patrick. Written by Lionel Houser; directed by Lew Landers; for RKO.
'Indelicate stuff and doubtful b.o.'—*Variety*

Condorman
US 1981 90m Technicolor Panavision
Walt Disney (Jan Williams)

The author of a 'superman' comic tries to act like his hero in real life.
Very mildly amusing spy spoof with inadequate special effects.

w Marc Sturdivant, Glen Caron, Mickey Rose, *novel* The Game of X by Robert Sheckley *d* Charles Jarrott *ph* Charles F. Wheeler *m* Henry Mancini *ph* Albert Witherick *sp* Art Cruickshank

Michael Crawford, Oliver Reed, Barbara Carrera, James Hampton, Jean-Pierre Kalfon

Conduct Unbecoming
GB 1975 107m Technicolor
British Lion / Crown (Michael Deeley, Barry Spikings)

In an officers' mess in India in the nineties, a cadet is accused of assault on a lady but the real culprit is a paranoic who has taken to pigsticking in quite the wrong way.
Disappointingly flatly-handled and quite unatmospheric picturization of an absorbing West End melodrama. The cast is largely wasted, but stretches of dialogue maintain their interest.

w Robert Enders, *play* Barry England *d* Michael Anderson *ph* Bob Huke *m* Stanley Myers

Michael York, Stacy Keach, Trevor Howard, Christopher Plummer, Richard Attenborough, Susannah York, James Faulkner, James Donald

The Conductor*
Poland 1979 102m Orwocolor
PRF / X Films of Poland
original title: *Dyrygent*

A Polish girl violinist finds her life affected when an elderly international conductor returns to her town.
Initially interesting but finally tedious and muddled allegory, further handicapped by stilted post-synching of the English version.

w Andrzej Kijowski *d* Andrzej Wajda *ph* Slawomir Idziak *m* from Beethoven

John Gielgud, Krystyna Janda, Andrzej Seweryn

Cone of Silence*
GB 1960 92m bw
British Lion / Bryanston (Aubrey Baring)
US title: *Trouble in the Sky*

A seasoned pilot is condemned for an error which caused a crash and later dies in similar circumstances. A flying examiner discovers scientific reasons for exonerating him.
Tolerable suspense drama let down by thin dialogue and confused characterization.

w Robert Westerby, *novel* David Beaty *d* Charles Frend *ph* Arthur Grant *m* Gerhard Schurmann

Michael Craig, Bernard Lee, Peter Cushing, George Sanders, Elizabeth Seal, André Morell, Gordon Jackson, Delphi Lawrence, Noel Willman, Charles Tingwell

Coney Island**
US 1943 96m Technicolor
TCF (William Perlberg)

Two fairground showmen vie for the affections of a songstress.
Brassy, simple-minded, entertaining musical. Very typical of its time; later remade as *Wabash Avenue* (qv).

w George Seaton *d Walter Lang ph* Ernest Palmer *songs* Leo Robin, Ralph Rainger *m* Alfred Newman *ch* Hermes Pan *ad* Richard Day, Joseph C. Wright

Betty Grable, George Montgomery, Cesar Romero, Charles Winninger, Phil Silvers, Matt Briggs, Paul Hurst, Frank Orth, Andrew Tombes, Alec Craig, Hal K. Dawson

AAN: Alfred Newman

Confession
US 1937 90m bw
Warner (Henry Blanke)

An errant mother shoots her former lover to protect her daughter.
Stilted romantic melodrama copied scene for scene from a 1936 German film *Mazurka*.

w Julius J. Epstein, Margaret Le Vino, *original screenplay* Hans Rameau *d* Joe May *ph* Sid Hickox *m* Peter Kreuder *md* Leo F. Forbstein *ad* Anton Grot

Kay Francis, Ian Hunter, Basil Rathbone, Jane Bryan, Donald Crisp, Dorothy Peterson, Laura Hope Crews, Robert Barrat

'Distinctly in the upper bracket and made to order for important first runs.'—*Variety*

Confession
GB 1955 90m bw

A murderer stalks the priest who knows his guilt through the confessional but may not reveal it. So-so reworking of the theme that daunted Hitchcock in *I Confess*; some pleasant touches are nullified by slow pacing. Sydney Chaplin, Audrey Dalton, John Welsh, John Bentley, Peter Hammond. Written and directed by Ken Hughes; for Anglo Guild. (US title: *The Deadliest Sin*.)

The Confession*
France / Italy 1970 160m Eastmancolor
Films Corona / Films Pomereu / Selena Cinematografica (Robert Dorfmann)
original title: *L'Aveu*

In Prague in 1951, a minister is secretly imprisoned and interrogated, and finally confesses under duress to anti-communist activities.
Brutally long but frequently impressive anti-Soviet tract, extremely well acted but less exciting than *Z*. Based on a true account.

w Jorge Semprun, *book* Lise and Artur London *d Costa-Gavras* *ph* Raoul Coutard *m* not credited

Yves Montand, Simone Signoret, Gabriele Ferzetti, Michel Vitold

Confessions of a Nazi Spy***
US 1939 110m bw
Warner (Robert Lord)

How G-men ferreted out Nazis in the United States.
Topical exposé with all concerned in top form; a semi-documentary very typical of Warner product throughout the thirties and forties, from *G-Men* to *Mission to Moscow* and *I Was a Communist for the FBI*: well made, punchy, and smartly edited, with a loud moral at the end.

w Milton Krims, John Wexley, from materials gathered by former FBI agent Leon G. Turrou *d Anatole Litvak* *ph Sol Polito* *m* Max Steiner

Edward G. Robinson, Paul Lukas, George Sanders, Francis Lederer, Henry O'Neill, Lya Lys, James Stephenson, Sig Rumann, Dorothy Tree, Joe Sawyer

'Its social implications are far more important than the immediate question of how much money the release makes for Warner Brothers.'—*Variety*

'The Warner brothers have declared war on Germany with this one . . . with this precedent there is no way any producer could argue against dramatizing any social or political theme on the grounds that he's afraid of domestic or foreign censorship. Everybody duck.'—*Pare Lorentz*

'Has a remarkable resemblance to a full-length *Crime Does Not Pay*.'—*David Wolff*

'One of the most sensational movie jobs on record, workmanlike in every respect and sprang across the headlines.'—*Otis Ferguson*

Confessions of an Opium Eater
US 1962 85m bw
Albert Zugsmith
GB title: *Evils of Chinatown*

In San Francisco in the nineties, a seaman falls into the clutches of a tong.
The hero is called De Quincey, but that is the only association with the famous book of the same title. This absurd melodrama is just about bad enough to be funny, but not very.

w Robert Hill *d* Albert Zugsmith *ph* Joseph Biroc *m* Albert Glasser *ad Eugene Lourié*

Vincent Price, Linda Ho, Richard Loo, Philip Ahn, June Kim

'Has to be seen to be believed . . . starved girls captive in cages, secret panels, sliding doors, sewer escape routes, opium dens and nightmares . . .'—*MFB*

Confidential Agent**
US 1945 122m bw
Warner (Robert Buckner)

An emissary of Franco's Spain comes to England in the late thirties to make a munitions deal, and falls in love with the tycoon's daughter.
Heavy-going simplification of Graham Greene's lowering novel, with cast and (especially) set designers all at sea but nevertheless providing striking moments.

w Robert Buckner *d* Herman Shumlin *ph James Wong Howe* *m* Franz Waxman

Charles Boyer, Lauren Bacall, Katina Paxinou, Peter Lorre, Victor Francen, George Coulouris, Wanda Hendrix, George Zucco, Miles Mander

'In some ways an exciting and good picture, the best attempt yet, though still inadequate, to make the best of a Greene novel.'—*James Agee*

Confidential Report
Spain 1955 99m bw
Sevilla Studios (Louis Dolivet, Orson Welles)
aka: *Mr Arkadin*

A wealthy and powerful financier employs a young American to seek out figures from his own past, who are soon found dead . . .
Silly melodrama which might have been suspenseful if done by Hitchcock, or even by Welles at his peak; as it is, weak writing and sloppy production remove most of the interest and reveal it as a very obvious bag of tricks.

wd Orson Welles *ph* Jean Bourgoin *m* Paul Misraki

Orson Welles, Michael Redgrave, Katina Paxinou, Akim Tamiroff, Mischa Auer, Patricia Medina, Jack Watling, Peter Van Eyck, Paola Mori, Robert Arden, Grégoire Aslan, Suzanne Flon

'Tilted camera angles, heavy atmospheric shots, overlapping dialogue—all the trademarks are here, sometimes over-used to an almost hysterical degree, but they have little significance . . . (the film) springs not from life but from the earlier cinematic world of Welles himself and from the kind of thriller written about thirty years ago by E. Philips Oppenheim.'—*Gavin Lambert*

'The quality of the soundtrack is quite disastrous, but there is a certain grandeur about the carelessness of the film's construction which makes one forget everything except the immediacy of the moment.'—*Basil Wright, 1972*

Confidentially Connie
US 1953 71m bw

A Texas rancher starts a price war when he strikes a deal with a local butcher so that the rancher's impecunious son can get half-price meat for his family. Modest comedy which adequately filled the lower half of a bill. Louis Calhern, Janet Leigh, Van Johnson, Walter Slezak, Gene Lockhart, Hayden Rorke. Written by Max Shulman from a story by himself and Herman Wouk; directed by Edward Buzzell; for MGM.

Confirm or Deny*
US 1941 78m bw
TCF (Len Hammond)

An American reporter falls for a wireless operator in wartime London.
Artificial but watchable minor romantic melodrama.

w Jo Swerling, Henry Wales, Samuel Fuller *d* Archie Mayo *ph* Leon Shamroy

Don Ameche, Joan Bennett, Roddy McDowall, Arthur Shields, Raymond Walburn, John Loder

† Fritz Lang directed some scenes.

Conflict*
US 1945 86m bw
Warner (William Jacobs)

A man murders his wife and is apparently haunted by her; but the odd happenings have been arranged by a suspicious psychiatrist.
Leaden and artificial melodrama with both stars miscast; a few effective moments.

w Arthur T. Horman, Dwight Taylor *d* Curtis Bernhardt *ph* Merritt Gerstad *m* Frederick Hollander

Humphrey Bogart, Sydney Greenstreet, Alexis Smith, Rose Hobart, Charles Drake, Grant Mitchell

† The film was completed in August 1943.

Conflict of Wings*
GB 1953 84m Eastmancolor
Group Three (Herbert Mason)
US title: *Fuss over Feathers*

East Anglian villagers fight to save a bird sanctuary from being taken over by the RAF as a rocket range.
Sub-Ealing comedy-drama with a highly predictable outcome; generally pleasant but without much bite.

w Don Sharp, John Pudney *d* John Eldridge *ph* Arthur Grant *m* Philip Green

John Gregson, Muriel Pavlow, Kieron Moore, Niall MacGinnis, Sheila Sweet, Harry Fowler, Barbara Hicks, Charles Lloyd Pack

The Conformist**
Italy / France / West Germany 1969
108m Technicolor
Mars / Marianne / Maran (Giovanni Bertolucci)
original title: *Il Conformista*

In 1938 an inhibited young man tries to conform to the prevailing mood of Fascism, but gets out of his depth when he turns informer.
Psychologically confusing but brilliantly realized recreation of an age.

wd Bernardo Bertolucci, novel Alberto Moravia *ph Vittorio Storaro m* Georges Delerue

Jean-Louis Trintignant, Stefania Sandrelli, Gastone Moschin, Enzo Taroscio, Dominique Sanda, Pierre Clementi

Congo Bill
US 1948 bw serial: 15 eps

A wild animal trainer and jungle expert agrees to deliver a letter to an heiress missing in Africa. Standard serial hokum with witch doctors for villains. Don McGuire, Cleo Moore, Jack Ingram, I. Stanford Jolley. Directed by Spencer Bennet and Thomas Carr; for Columbia.

Congo Crossing
US 1956 85m Technicolor
U-I (Howard Christie)

Assorted fugitives from justice gather at Congotanga, which has no extradition laws.
The poor man's *Casablanca*, quite good looking but dully written and presented.

w Richard Alan Simmons *d* Joseph Pevney *ph* Russell Metty *m* Joseph Gershenson

George Nader, Virginia Mayo, *Peter Lorre*, Michael Pate, Rex Ingram

Congorilla*
US 1932 74m bw

A record of two years spent in the Belgian Congo by Mr and Mrs Martin Johnson.
Excellent exploration documentary of its time. Written and directed by the Johnsons; for Fox.
'Replete with thrills, adventure and laughs, making withal for an excellent entertainment.'—*Variety*

Congress Dances*
Germany 1931 92m bw
UFA (Erich Pommer)
original title: *Der Kongress Tanzt*

At the Congress of Vienna, Metternich attempts to decoy the Tsar with a countess; but the Tsar has a double.
Lubitsch-like treatment of sexual dalliance in high places; no doubt a stunner in its time, but rather faded now.

w Norbert Falk, Robert Liebmann *d Erik Charrell ph* Carl Hoffmann *m Werner Heymann*

Conrad Veidt, Henri Garat / Willy Fritsch, Lilian Harvey
'A revue more than a story . . . grace, taste and a light hand.'—*Variety*

A Connecticut Yankee*
US 1931 96m bw
Fox

A man dreams himself back to the court of King Arthur, and teaches the Middle Ages a thing or two about modern living.
First sound version of Mark Twain's classic fantasy, also filmed in 1921 and 1949. Creaky now, but amiable.

w William Conselman *d* David Butler *ph* Ernest Palmer

Will Rogers, Maureen O'Sullivan, Myrna Loy, Frank Albertson, William Farnum
'Good deluxe comedy . . . should draw substantial grosses.'—*Variety*

'Its laughter will ring through the centuries!'

A Connecticut Yankee in King Arthur's Court*
US 1948 106m Technicolor
Paramount (Robert Fellows)
GB title: *A Yankee in King Arthur's Court*

Gossamer musical version of the above with the emphasis on song and knockabout.
Palatable, with the 'Busy Doin' Nothin' ' sequence the most memorable.

w Edmund Beloin *d* Tay Garnett *ph* Ray Rennahan *md* Victor Young
songs Johnny Burke, Jimmy Van Heusen

Bing Crosby, Rhonda Fleming, William Bendix, *Cedric Hardwicke*, Murvyn Vye
'The tacky pageantry is more suited to the opening of a West Coast supermarket than to an English court in the 6th century.'—*Pauline Kael, 70s*

Connecting Rooms
GB 1969 103m Technicolor
Telstar / Franklin Gollings (Harry Field)

In a seedy Bayswater boarding house, a dismissed schoolmaster befriends a failed cellist whose protégé is a sponging songwriter.
Aggressively dismal melodrama which would be hilarious if it were not so sadly slow and naive.

wd Franklin Gollings, *play* The Cellist by Marion Hart *ph* John Wilcox *m* John Shakespeare

Bette Davis, Michael Redgrave, Alexis Kanner, Kay Walsh, Gabrielle Drake, Leo Genn, Olga Georges-Picot, Richard Wyler, Brian Wilde

The Connection
US 1961 110m bw
Shirley Clarke / Lewis Allen

Junkies hang around waiting for a fix and are filmed by a documentary unit.
Unattractive low-budgeter with occasional impressive moments.

w Jack Gelber *d* Shirley Clarke *ph* Arthur J. Ornitz *m* Freddie Redd *ad* Richard Sylbert

Warren Finnerty, Jerome Raphael, Jim Anderson, Carl Lee, Roscoe Browne

The Conquering Horde
US 1931 73m bw

In Texas after the Civil War, resistance to railroads hampers the movement of cattle.
Strongish western of its period, but of no continuing interest. Richard Arlen, Fay Wray, Claude Gillingwater, Ian MacLaren. Written by Grover Jones, William Slavens McNutt; directed by Edward Sloman; for Paramount.
'Good story, plenty of love interest, action and comedy . . . will do above average.'—*Variety*

'Spectacular as its barbaric passions and savage conquests!'

The Conqueror
US 1955 112m Technicolor
Cinemascope
Howard Hughes (Dick Powell)

A romance of the early life of Genghis Khan, who captures and is enamoured by the daughter of an enemy.
Solemn pantomime with a measure of bloodthirsty action and dancing girls, but featuring too many dull spots between, especially as the star is the most unlikely of eastern warriors and the production values careful but not too steady.

w Oscar Millard *d* Dick Powell *ph* Joseph La Shelle, Leo Tover, Harry J. Wild *m* Victor Young

John Wayne, Susan Hayward, Pedro Armendariz, Agnes Moorehead, Thomas Gomez, John Hoyt, William Conrad, Ted de Corsia, Lee Van Cleef

GENGHIS KHAN: 'This tartar woman is for me, and my blood says, take her!'

'Simply an oriental western.'—*New York Times*

'History has not been well served and nor has the popcorn public.'—*Richard Hatch, Nation*

'It's all that its makers wanted it to be.'—*Manchester Guardian*

'John Wayne as Genghis Khan—history's most improbable piece of casting unless Mickey Rooney were to play Jesus in *King of Kings*.'—*Jack Smith, L.A. Times*

† The location was Utah's Escalante Desert, and three local mountains were renamed Mount Wayne, Mount Hughes and Mount Powell. The desert had been used for atom bomb tests, and twenty-five years after the production, questions were asked when several members of the cast died of cancer.
†† Wayne asked for his role. 'The way the screenplay reads, this is a cowboy picture, and that's how I am going to play Genghis Khan. I see him as a gunfighter.'

The Conquerors
US 1932 88m bw
RKO (David O. Selznick)
TV title: *Pioneer Builders*

Nebraska settlers in the 1870s set the seeds of a banking empire.
Routine family epic with the star playing himself and his own grandson.

w Robert Lord, *story* Howard Estabrook
d William Wellman *ph* Edward Cronjager
m Max Steiner

Richard Dix, Ann Harding, Edna May Oliver, Guy Kibbee, Donald Cook, Julie Haydon, Jed Prouty

'As good as a depression story can be, which isn't much box office.'—*Variety*

Conquest**
US 1937 115m bw
MGM (Bernard Hyman)
GB title: *Marie Walewska*

The life of Napoleon's most enduring mistress. Measured, dignified, and often rather dull historical fiction, lightened by excellent performances and production.

w Samuel Hoffenstein, Salka Viertel, S. N. Behrman, from a Polish play dramatized by Helen Jerome *d* Clarence Brown *ph* Karl Freund *m* Herbert Stothart

Greta Garbo, *Charles Boyer*, Reginald Owen, Alan Marshal, Henry Stephenson, Dame May Whitty, Leif Erickson

'For special first-run openings—and then the clean up.'—*Variety*

'Ornate, unexpectedly tasteful, carefully detailed—and lifeless.'—*Pauline Kael, 70s*

AAN: Charles Boyer

Conquest of Cochise
US 1953 78m Technicolor

An army major is sent to make peace with Cochise, the Apache. Feeble western cheapie. Robert Stack, John Hodiak, Joy Page. Written by Arthur Lewis and De Vallon Scott; directed by William Castle; for Sam Katzman / Columbia.

'See how it will happen—in your lifetime!'
Conquest of Space
US 1955 80m Technicolor
Paramount (George Pal)

In 1980, the Americans have built a space station in the atmosphere, and plan a voyage to the moon but are sent to Mars instead.
So history catches up with science fiction. This sober prophecy looks good but very little happens and the result is as dull as it is bright and shiny.

w James O'Hanlon *d* Byron Haskin *ph* Lionel Lindon *m* Van Cleeve *ad* Hal Pereira, James McMillan Johnson *sp* John P. Fulton, Irmin Roberts, Paul Lerpae, Ivyl Burks, Jan Domella

Eric Fleming, Walter Brooke, Mickey Shaughnessy, William Hopper, Ross Martin

Conquest of the Air
GB 1936 71m bw

A history of man's discovery of the power of flight. Curious schoolbook documentary, of historical interest. Laurence Olivier (as Lunardi), Franklin Dyall, Henry Victor, Hay Petrie, John Turnbull. Written by Hugh Gray and Peter Bezencenet; directed by Zoltan Korda and others; for Alexander Korda.

Conrack*
US 1974 106m De Luxe Panavision
TCF (Martin Ritt, Irving Ravetch)

A young white teacher is assigned to an all-black school in South Carolina, and after some difficulty makes friends with children and parents.
Nostalgically mellow happy-film, lit by bright smiles all round.

w Irving Ravetch, Harriet Frank Jnr, *novel* The Water Is Wide by Pat Conroy *d* Martin Ritt *ph* John Alonzo *m* John Williams

Jon Voight, Paul Winfield, Hume Cronyn, Madge Sinclair, Tina Andrews

'For all its craftsman-like virtues, it seems a conscious turning aside from the complexities of modern cinema to the simpler alternatives of yesteryear. Indeed, with underprivileged white children instead of black and Greer Garson substituting for Jon Voight, the film might have been made all of thirty years ago.'—*John Raisbeck*

Consider Your Verdict
GB 1938 40m bw

A juror proves an accused man not guilty by falsely confessing to the crime himself. Fairly smart little entry into the feature film scene for the Boulting Brothers, from a popular radio play of the time. Marius Goring, Manning Whiley, Olive Sloane, Hay Petrie, George Carney. Written by Francis Miller, from the play by Laurence Housman; directed by Roy Boulting; for Charter.

Consolation Marriage
US 1931 62m bw

A wife keeps a stiff upper lip when her husband strays. Ho-hum domestic drama with attempts at comedy relief. Irene Dunne, Pat O'Brien, John Halliday, Matt Moore, Myrna Loy. Written by Humphrey Pearson; directed by Paul Sloane; for RKO. 'Fair entertainment; will satisfy with good stage support.'—*Variety*

'What conflict in the heart of a nun would make her break her vows?'
Conspiracy of Hearts*
GB 1960 113m bw
Rank (Betty E. Box)

During World War II, Italian nuns smuggle Jewish children across the border from a nearby prison camp.
Highly commercial combination of exploitable sentimental elements: Germans, Jews, nuns, children, war, suspense. Remarkably, it gets by without causing nausea.

w Robert Presnell Jnr *d* Ralph Thomas *ph* Ernest Steward *m* Angelo Lavagnino

Lilli Palmer, Sylvia Syms, Yvonne Mitchell, Albert Lieven, Ronald Lewis, Peter Arne, Nora Swinburne, Michael Goodliffe, Megs Jenkins, David Kossoff, Jenny Laird, George Coulouris, Phyllis Neilson-Terry

Conspirator
GB 1949 87m bw
MGM (Arthur Hornblow Jnr)

A guards officer, unknown to his young wife, is a communist spy.
Singularly awful romantic melodrama which never convinces or entertains for a moment.

w Sally Benson, Gerard Fairlie, *novel* Humphrey Slater *d* Victor Saville *ph* F. A. Young *m* John Wooldridge

Robert Taylor, Elizabeth Taylor, Harold Warrender, Robert Flemyng, Marie Ney

The Conspirators*
US 1944 101m bw
Warner (Jack Chertok)

A Dutch underground leader escapes to Lisbon and clears up international intrigue.
Interestingly cast but often listless wartime melodrama, a doomed attempt to reprise *Casablanca* without Humphrey Bogart.

w Vladimir Pozner, Leo Rosten, *novel* City of Shadows by Frederick Prokosch *d* Jean Negulesco *ph* Arthur Edeson *m* Max Steiner

Hedy Lamarr, Paul Henreid, Sydney Greenstreet, Peter Lorre, *Victor Francen*, Carol Thurston, Vladimir Sokoloff, Joseph Calleia, Edward Ciannelli, Steve Geray, Kurt Katch, George Macready

SYDNEY GREENSTREET (as Quintanilla): 'This may seem to you melodramatic, but indulge me, please. I like melodrama.'

'As exciting as baseball and almost as gentlemanly as cricket.'—*New Statesman*

'I enjoyed it as much as any Warner melodrama since *Casablanca*.'—*Observer*

The Constant Husband*
GB 1955 88m Technicolor print
British Lion / London Films (Frank Launder, Sidney Gilliat)

An amnesiac discovers that he is a multiple bigamist, still wanted by each of his five wives. Flimsy comedy which never really gets going despite an attractive cast.

w Sidney Gilliat, Val Valentine *d* Sidney Gilliat *ph* Ted Scaife *m* Malcolm Arnold

Rex Harrison, Kay Kendall, Margaret Leighton, Cecil Parker, Nicole Maurey, George Cole, Raymond Huntley, Michael Hordern, Eric Pohlmann, Robert Coote

The Constant Nymph*
GB 1933 98m bw
Gaumont (Michael Balcon)

In the Tyrol, a composer leaves his rich wife for a schoolgirl suffering from a heart condition.
Archetypal romantic drama from Margaret Kennedy's book, first filmed in 1928 by the same producer (directed by Adrian Brunel, with Ivor Novello and Mabel Poulton). A standard production of its time, which seems to have vanished with the literary copyright.

w Margaret Kennedy, Basil Dean, from their play based on her novel *d* Basil Dean *ph* Max Greene *m* John Greenwood

Brian Aherne, Victoria Hopper, Leonora Corbett, Lyn Harding, Mary Clare, Jane Baxter

'Beautifully done artistic success from England, of doubtful box office for America.'—*Variety*

'One can say that it has a beginning, a middle and an end, but it lacks something vital.'—*E. V. Lucas, Punch*

The Constant Nymph*
US 1943 112m bw
Warner (Henry Blanke)

Artificially well-produced, overlong Hollywood version of the above.

w Kathryn Scola *d* Edmund Goulding *ph* Tony Gaudio *m* Erich Wolfgang Korngold

Charles Boyer, *Joan Fontaine*, Alexis Smith, Brenda Marshall, Charles Coburn, Dame May Whitty, Peter Lorre, Joyce Reynolds, Jean Muir, Edward Ciannelli, Montagu Love, André Charlot

AAN: Joan Fontaine

Continental Divide
US 1981 103m Technicolor
Universal / Amblin (Bob Larson)

A national columnist finds himself banished to the wilds with a lady ornithologist studying the bald eagle.
Old-fashioned comedy, a cross between *Bringing Up Baby* and *Woman of the Year*. Not actually bad, but somewhat lacking in personality.

w Lawrence Kasdan *d* Michael Apted *ph* John Bailey *m* Michael Small

John Belushi, Blair Brown, Allen Goorwitz, Carlin Glynn

Contraband**
GB 1940 92m bw
British National (John Corfield)
US title: *Blackout*

A Danish merchant captain and a girl in wartime London expose a gang of spies using a cinema as headquarters.
Enjoyable lightweight comedy melodrama on Hitchcock lines, reuniting the unlikely star team from *The Spy in Black*.

w Emeric Pressburger, Michael Powell, Brock Williams *d* Michael Powell *ph* F. A. Young

Conrad Veidt, Valerie Hobson, Esmond Knight, Hay Petrie, Raymond Lovell, Harold Warrender, Charles Victor, Manning Whiley

Contraband Spain
GB 1955 82m Eastmancolor

An American agent in Barcelona investigates the death there of a compatriot involved in drug smuggling. Pretty awful formula thick-ear with bland stars and a boring look. Richard Greene, Anouk Aimée, Michael Denison, John Warwick. Written and directed by Laurence Huntingdon; for Diadem / ABP.

Convention City*
US 1933 78m bw
Warner (Henry Blanke)

Extra-marital fun and games at a Chicago convention.
Amusing and rather risqué comedy which helped to bring down on Hollywood the wrath of the Legion of Decency.

w Robert Lord *d* Archie Mayo *ph* William Rees

Joan Blondell, Guy Kibbee, Adolphe Menjou, Dick Powell, Mary Astor, Frank McHugh, Ruth Donnelly, Hugh Herbert, Hobart Cavanaugh

'Not a dull foot . . . probably the fastest complex comedy of the year and a certain money picture.'—*Variety*

The Conversation**
US 1974 113m Technicolor
Paramount / Francis Ford Coppola

A bugging device expert lives only for his work, but finally develops a conscience.
Absorbing but extremely difficult to follow in detail, this personal, timely (in view of Watergate), Kafkaesque suspense story centres almost entirely on director and leading actor, who have a field day.

wd Francis Ford Coppola *ph* Bill Butler *m* David Shire

Gene Hackman, John Cazale, Allen Garfield, Frederick Forrest

'A private, hallucinatory study in technical expertise and lonely guilt.'—*Sight and Sound*

'A terrifying depiction of a ransacked spirit.'—*New Yorker, 1977*

'Alert, truthful, unarty and absolutely essential viewing.'—*Michael Billington, Illustrated London News*

AAN: best picture; Francis Ford Coppola (as writer)

Conversation Piece
Italy / France 1974 121m Technicolor Todd AO 35
Rusconi / Gaumont (Giovanni Bertolucci)
original title: *Gruppo di Famiglia in un Interno*

When a reclusive professor is persuaded to let his top floor to a young couple he is brought face to face with his latent homosexuality and his approaching death.
Death in Venice revisited, but with much less style and even more obscurity.

w Luchino Visconti, Suso Cecchi d'Amico, Enrico Medioli *d* Luchino Visconti *ph* Pasqualino de Santis *m* Franco Mannino

Burt Lancaster, Helmut Berger, Claudia Marsani, Silvana Mangano

Convict 99*
GB 1938 91m bw
Gainsborough (Edward Black)

A seedy schoolmaster accidentally becomes a prison governor and lets the convicts run the place.
Patchily funny if overlong and in some ways rather serious Will Hay comedy, not quite typical of him.

w Marriott Edgar, Val Guest, Ralph Smart, Jack Davies *d* Marcel Varnel *ph* Arthur Crabtree *md* Louis Levy

Will Hay, Graham Moffatt, Moore Marriott, Googie Withers, Garry Marsh, Peter Gawthorne, Basil Radford, Kathleen Harrison

Convicted*
US 1950 91m bw
Columbia (Jerry Bresler)

When a prison informer is killed, one convict knows who did it.
Routine, over-plotted, strongly cast prison melodrama.

w William Bowers, Fred Niblo Jnr, Seton I. Miller, *play* Martin Flavin *d* Henry Levin *ph* Burnett Guffey *m* George Duning

Glenn Ford, Broderick Crawford, Millard Mitchell, Dorothy Malone, Frank Faylen, Carl Benton Reid, Will Geer

Convicts Four*
US 1962 106m bw
Allied Artists–Lubin–Kaufman (A. Ronald Lubin)
original and GB title: *Reprieve*

A convict reprieved from the electric chair spends eighteen years in prison, becomes a painter, and is rehabilitated.
Odd and unsatisfactory mixture of documentary, melodrama, sentimentality and character study, with stars unexpectedly popping in for cameo appearances. Something worthier was obviously intended.

wd Millard Kaufman, from the autobiography of John Resko *ph* Joseph Biroc *m* Leonard Rosenman

Ben Gazzara, Vincent Price, Rod Steiger, Broderick Crawford, Stuart Whitman, Ray Walston, Jack Kruschen, Sammy Davis Jnr

Convoy*
GB 1940 90m bw
Ealing (Sergei Nolbandov)

A German pocket battleship menaces a British convoy, and a merchant ship sacrifices itself to prevent disaster.
Fluent British war film of the early days, the only substantial work of a much vaunted director who was subsequently killed.

w Pen Tennyson, Patrick Kirwan *d Pen Tennyson* *ph* Gunther Krampf, Roy Kellino *m* Ernest Irving

Clive Brook, John Clements, Edward Chapman, Judy Campbell, Penelope Dudley Ward, Edward Rigby, Allan Jeayes, Albert Lieven

Convoy
US 1978 110m De Luxe Panavision
UA / EMI (Robert M. Sherman)

A folk hero truck driver survives several crashes and his policeman nemesis.
A virtually plotless anthology of wanton destruction. Too noisy to sleep through.

w B. W. L. Norton, based on the song by C. W. McCall *d* Sam Peckinpah *ph* Harry Stradling Jnr *m* Chip Davis

Kris Kristofferson, Ali MacGraw, Ernest Borgnine, Burt Young, Madge Sinclair

'There's a whole lot of nothing going on here . . . strictly a summer popcorn picture for the nondiscriminating.'—*Variety*

'Roughly as much fun as a ride on the New Jersey turnpike with the window open. It not only numbs the brain but pollutes the senses.'—*Richard Schickel, Time*

Coogan's Bluff**
US 1968 94m Technicolor
Universal (Don Siegel)

An Arizona sheriff takes an escaped killer back to New York, and when the man escapes uses western methods to recapture him.
Violent, well-done police story which inspired the TV series *McCloud*.

w Herman Miller, Dean Riesner, Howard Rodman *d Don Siegel* *ph* Bud Thackery *m* Lalo Schifrin

Clint Eastwood, Lee J. Cobb, Susan Clark, Don Stroud, Tisha Sterling, Betty Field, Tom Tully

Cool Breeze
US 1972 102m Metrocolor
MGM / Penelope (Gene Corman)

A miscellaneous gang of crooks is rounded up to commit a robbery, which ultimately fails.
Third, all-black remake of *The Asphalt Jungle* (the others being *The Badlanders* and *Cairo*). Fashionable violence against a Los Angeles backdrop, but not at all memorable.

wd Barry Pollack *ph* Andy Davis *m* Solomon Burke

Thalmus Rasulala, Judy Pace, Jim Watkins, Raymond St Jacques, Lincoln Kilpatrick

'What we've got here is a failure to communicate.'

Cool Hand Luke**
US 1967 126m Technicolor Panavision
Warner / Jalem (Gordon Carroll)

Sentenced to two years' hard labour with the chain gang, a convict becomes a legend of invulnerability but is eventually shot during an escape.
Allegedly a Christ-allegory, this well-made and good-looking film is only partially successful as an entertainment; slow stretches of soul-searching alternate with brutality, and not much acting is possible.

w Donn Pearce, Frank R. Pierson, *novel* Donn Pearce *d Stuart Rosenberg* *ph Conrad Hall* *m* Lalo Schifrin

Paul Newman, George Kennedy, Jo Van Fleet, J. D. Cannon, Lou Antonio, Robert Drivas, Strother Martin, Clifton James

AA: George Kennedy
AAN: Donn Pearce, Frank R. Pierson; Lalo Schifrin; Paul Newman

The Cool Ones
US 1967 96m Technicolor Panavision
Warner (William Conrad)

Former pop singer makes a comeback.
Zazzy showbiz saga with ear-splitting track, quite professionally assembled.

w Joyce Geller *d* Gene Nelson *ph* Floyd Crosby *m* Ernie Freeman

Roddy McDowall, Debbie Watson, Robert Coote, Phil Harris, Nita Talbot

The Co-Optimists*
GB 1929 83m bw
New Era (Gordon Craig)

A revue by a popular pierrot troupe of the time.
Famous as Britain's first musical, this is a dated but valuable record of a stage performance of the kind long vanished.

w Melville Gideon, Laddie Cliff *d* Edwin Greenwood, Laddie Cliff *ph* Basil Emmott, Sidney Blythe

Davy Burnaby, Stanley Holloway, Laddie Cliff, Phyllis Monkman, Melville Gideon, Gilbert Childs, Betty Chester, Elsa MacFarlane, Peggy Petronella, Harry S. Pepper

Copacabana
US 1947 91m bw
(UA) Sam Coslow

A quick-thinking agent forms two acts out of one client, which makes things awkward when both are needed at once.
Thinly produced comedy with both stars doing what is expected of them in surroundings less glamorous than those to which they were previously accustomed.

w Laslo Vadnay, Allen Boretz, Howard Harris *d* Alfred E. Green *ph* Bert Glennon *m* Edward Ward

Groucho Marx, Carmen Miranda, Steve Cochran, Gloria Jean, Andy Russell

Copper Canyon
US 1949 84m Technicolor

After the Civil War, southern veterans trying to rebuild their homes are helped by a gunslinger. Shiny unpersuasive western with stars ill at ease. Ray Milland, Hedy Lamarr, Macdonald Carey, Mona Freeman, Harry Carey Jnr. Written by Jonathan Latimer; directed by John Farrow; for Paramount.

Cops***
US 1922 20m (24 fps) bw silent
First National / Comique Film (Joseph M. Schenck)

An innocent disrupts a parade and is pursued by a horde of policemen.
The perfect Keaton short, a careful assembly of perfectly timed gags.

wd Buster Keaton *ph* Elgin Lessley

Buster Keaton, Virginia Fox

Cops and Robbers*
US 1973 89m De Luxe
UA / EK Corp (Elliott Kastner)

Two New York cops turn crook and pull off a job for the Mafia.
Trendily anti-establishment comedy, quite snappy and smart when you can follow it.

w Donald E. Westlake *d* Aram Avakian *ph* David L. Quaid *m* Michel Legrand

Cliff Gorman, Joe Bologna, Dick Ward, Shepperd Strudwick, Ellen Holly, John P. Ryan

Coquette
US 1929 75m bw

A southern belle has a flirtatious nature.
Disappointing talkie start for a first lady of the silents; she did not recover from it. Mary Pickford, Johnny Mack Brown, Matt Moore, William Janney. Written by John Grey, Allen McNeil, Sam Taylor from a play by George Abbott and Anne Preston; directed by Sam Taylor; for Mary Pickford.

Le Corbeau**
France 1943 92m bw
L'Atelier Français
US title: *The Raven*

Poison pen letters disturb a small provincial town.
Impressively characterized whodunnit with the usual French qualities of detail and discretion. Remade in Hollywood to less effect as *The Thirteenth Letter* (qv).

w Louis Chavance *d Henri-Georges Clouzot* *ph* Nicholas Hayer *m* Tony Aubain

Pierre Fresnay, Pierre Larquey, Ginette Leclerc, Hélène Manson

'By no means as malign or as brilliant as it's cracked up to be, but a sour, clever, amusing job.'—*James Agee*

Corky
US 1971 88m colour

An arrogant auto mechanic becomes a stock car racer. Noisy and unattractive movie about an anti-hero. Robert Blake, Patrick O'Neal, Charlotte Rampling, Christopher Connolly, Laurence Luckinbill, Ben Johnson. Written by Eugene Price; directed by Leonard Horn; for Bruce Geller / MGM.

The Corn is Green*
US 1945 118m bw
Warner (Jack Chertok)

In 1895 Miss Moffat starts a village school for Welsh miners, and after some tribulations sees one of them off to Oxford.
A very theatrical production with unconvincing sets and mannered acting, but the original play has its felicities.

w Casey Robinson, Frank Cavett, *play Emlyn Williams* *d* Irving Rapper *ph* Sol Polito *m* Max Steiner *ad* Carl Jules Weyl

Bette Davis, John Dall, Nigel Bruce, Joan Lorring, Rhys Williams, Rosalind Ivan, Mildred Dunnock, Arthur Shields

'It's very apparent that Hollywood isn't Wales . . . but the film lingers in the memory anyway.'—*New Yorker, 1978*

† Remade as a TV movie in 1978, with Katharine Hepburn.

AAN: John Dall; Joan Lorring

Cornered*
US 1945 102m bw
RKO

After demobilization, a French-Canadian pilot tracks down the collaborationist responsible for the death of his wife. Well-made but humourless revenge thriller.

w John Paxton, *story* John Wexley *d Edward Dmytryk* *ph* Harry J. Wild *m* Roy Webb

Dick Powell, Micheline Cheirel, Walter Slezak, Morris Carnovsky

COOGAN'S BLUFF. Western lawman Clint Eastwood dresses for the part for his foray into the urban jungle of New York. One wonders what he and Tisha Sterling are looking at.

Coronado
US 1935 77m bw

Marital misunderstandings abound at a swanky beach hotel. Thinly plotted but star-spotted comedy musical, notable now for the talent. Jack Haley, Leon Errol, Eddy Duchin and his Orchestra, Johnny Downs, Betty Burgess, Andy Devine, Alice White, Jameson Thomas. Written by Don Hartman, Frank Butler; directed by Norman McLeod; for Paramount.

Coroner Creek
US 1948 89m Cinecolor

A western crusader tracks down the man behind a stagecoach raid. Solid action western between the A and B categories. Randolph Scott, Marguerite Chapman, George Macready, Sally Eilers, Edgar Buchanan, Barbara Reed, Wallace Ford, Forrest Tucker, Douglas Fowley. Written by Kenneth Gamet from novel by Luke Short; directed by Ray Enright; for Harry Joe Brown / Columbia.

Corps Profond*
France 1963 21m Technicolor

A tour inside the human body by courtesy of micro-photography. Spellbinding and educative documentary of a new kind, and just the right length; the later British imitation, *The Body*, outstayed its welcome. Written and directed by Igor Barrière and Etienne Lalou; for Delpire.

The Corpse Came COD
US 1947 87m bw
Columbia (Sam Bischoff)

Rival reporters try to solve the mystery of a wandering body.
Routine crime comedy with too few smart lines.

w George Bricker, Dwight Babcock, *novel* Jimmy Starr *d* Henry Levin *ph* Lucien Andriot *m* George Duning

George Brent, Joan Blondell, Adele Jergens, Jim Bannon, Leslie Brooks, Grant Mitchell, Una O'Connor

'Horror to make your hair stand on end!'
The Corpse Vanishes
US 1942 70m bw

A botanist kidnaps young brides for their body fluids, in the hope of reviving his dead wife. An especially dreary example of Poverty Row horror. Bela Lugosi, Frank Moran, Minerva Urecal, Luana Walters. Written by Harvey Gates; directed by Wallace Fox; for Sam Katzman / Monogram.

Corregidor
US 1943 74m bw

Doctors on Corregidor sort out an eternal triangle while US forces fight the Japs. Feeble wartime quickie, inept in almost every respect. Elissa Landi, Otto Kruger, Donald Woods, Frank Jenks, Rick Vallin, Ian Keith. Written by Doris Malloy, Edgar J. Ulmer; directed by William Nigh; for Dixon R. Harwin-Edward Finney / PRC.

Corridor of Mirrors
GB 1948 105m bw
Cartier–Romney–Apollo (Rudolph Cartier)

An eccentric art collector believes that he and his mistress are reincarnations of 400-year-old lovers in a painting; but they are separated by murder.
Pretentious melodrama of no urgent narrative interest, with all concerned sadly at sea.

w Rudolph Cartier, Edana Romney
from a novel by Chris Massie
d Terence Young *ph* André Thomas
m Georges Auric

Eric Portman, Edana Romney, Barbara Mullen, Hugh Sinclair

'It has aimed at Art. It is, in fact, Effect. Some members of the cast wander in and out of the scenes as if they are not quite sure what has happened to them. Their confusion is not beyond comprehension.'—*MFB*

Corridors of Blood*
GB 1958 86m bw
Producers' Associates (John Croydon)
original title: *Doctor from Seven Dials*

Seeking to discover anaesthetics, a Victorian doctor falls a prey to resurrection men. Unpleasant but well-mounted semi-horror backed by strong cast and art direction.

w Jean Scott Rogers *d Robert Day*
ph Geoffrey Faithfull *m* Buxton Orr
ad Anthony Masters

Boris Karloff, Christopher Lee, Finlay Currie, Frank Pettingell, Betta St John, Francis Matthews, Adrienne Corri, Marian Spencer
† Not released until 1964.

The Corrupt Ones
West Germany 1967 92m colour

An American photographer in the Far East is pursued by a Tong. Rubbishy adventure which just about passes the time. Robert Stack, Elke Sommer, Nancy Kwan, Christian Marquand, Werner Peters. Written by Brian Clemens from a story by Ladislas Fodor; directed by Arthur Brauner; for Warners (Aka: *The Peking Medallion*, *Hell to Macao*)

Corruption
GB 1967 91m Technicolor
Columbia / Titan (Peter Newbrook)

A surgeon kills for pituitary gland fluid to restore his fiancée's beauty.
Highly derivative shocker with no inspiration of its own except an accumulation of gory detail.

w Donald and Derek Ford *d* Robert Hartford Davis *ph* Peter Newbrook *m* Bill McGuffie

Peter Cushing, Sue Lloyd, Noel Trevarthen, Kate O'Mara, David Lodge

Corsair*
US 1931 75m bw

A college football hero turns hi-jacker. Modest gangster saga with signs of style smothered by the script. Chester Morris, Alison Loyd, William Austin, Frank McHugh, Ned Sparks. Written by Josephine Lovett from the novel by Walon Green; directed by Roland West; for his own company. NB: Alison Loyd was a name momentarily adopted by Thelma Todd. 'A bit out-dated . . . will take a lot of nursing to reach average grosses.'—*Variety*

The Corsican Brothers*
US 1942 111m bw
Edward Small

Siamese twins are separated but remain spiritually tied through various adventures. Adequately exciting picturization of the Dumas swashbuckler.

w George Bruce, Howard Estabrook
d Gregory Ratoff *ph* Harry Stradling
m Dmitri Tiomkin

Douglas Fairbanks Jnr, Akim Tamiroff, Ruth Warrick, J. Carrol Naish, H. B. Warner, Henry Wilcoxon

† In 1953 came an undistinguished sequel, *Bandits of Corsica* (GB: *The Return of the Corsican Brothers*), with Richard Greene, Paula Raymond, Raymond Burr and Dona Drake. Written by Richard Schayer; directed by Ray Nazarro; for Global / UA.

AAN: Dmitri Tiomkin

Corvette K 225*
US 1943 97m bw
Universal (Howard Hawks)
GB title: *The Nelson Touch*

A Canadian corvette commander encounters submarines and bombers in mid-Atlantic. Good war film of its period, marred by romantic interest.

w Lt John Sturdy *d* Richard Rosson *ph* Tony Gaudio *m* David Buttolph

Randolph Scott, James Brown, Ella Raines, Barry Fitzgerald, Andy Devine, Richard Lane

AAN: Tony Gaudio

Corvette Summer
US 1979 104m Metrocolor
MGM / Plotto (Hal Barwood)
GB title: *The Hot One*

A Los Angeles student spends the summer looking for his stolen customized car, and has various adventures around Las Vegas.
There are a few choice moments in this disconnected comedy drama, but the appeal is almost entirely to moonstruck teenagers.

w Hal Barwood, Matthew Robbins
d Matthew Robbins *ph* Frank Stanley
m Craig Safan

Mark Hamill, Annie Potts, Eugene Roche, Kim Milford, Richard McKenzie

Cottage on Dartmoor
GB 1929 75m bw
BIP (Bruce Woolfe)
US title: *Escaped from Dartmoor*

A farmer's wife shelters her ex-lover when he breaks jail.
Crude early talkie notable only as an immature work of its director.

wd Anthony Asquith *ph* Stanley Rodwell

Norah Baring, Uno Hemming, Hans Schlettow, Judd Green

Cottage to Let*
GB 1941 90m bw
Gainsborough (Edward Black)
US title: *Bombsight Stolen*

Evacuated to Scotland, a Cockney helps prevent spies from kidnapping his inventor foster-father.
Stagey but often amusing comedy-thriller which after a shaky start becomes agreeably Hitchcockian.

w Anatole de Grunwald, J. O. C. Orton, *play* Geoffrey Kerr *d* Anthony Asquith *ph* Jack Cox *md* Louis Levy

Leslie Banks, *Alastair Sim*, *John Mills*, Jeanne de Casalis, George Cole, Carla Lehmann, Michael Wilding, Frank Cellier, Wally Patch, Muriel Aked, Muriel George, Catherine Lacey, Hay Petrie

'Where crime lords rub elbows with the rich and famous!'
The Cotton Club
US 1984 127m Technicolor Panavision
Zoetrope (Robert Evans)

The story of Harlem's famous night club and the gangsters who frequented it.
A lumpy vehicle, eventually costing fifty million dollars, for some of the talents who made *The Godfather* ten years earlier. Despite a few effective moments, a prime example of the careless extravagance which all but killed the film business.

w William Kennedy, Francis Coppola
d Francis Coppola *ph* Stephen Goldblatt
m John Barry *pd* Richard Sylbert *ed* Barry Malkin, Robert Lovett

Richard Gere, Gregory Hines, Diane Lane, Lonette McKee, Bob Hoskins, James Remar, Nicolas Cage, Allen Garfield, Fred Gwynne, Gwen Verdon

'The narrative is a mess, and keeps interrupting the heartstopping hoofing.'—*Time Out*

AAN: editing, art direction

Cotton Comes to Harlem
US 1970 97m De Luxe

Two black detectives try to beat the police to a bale of cotton containing a fortune in stolen dollars. Rickety vehicle for two amiable black characters presented rather more surely in *Come Back Charleston Blue* (qv). Godfrey Cambridge, Raymond St Jacques, Calvin Lockhart, Judy Pace, Redd Foxx. Written by Arnold Perl and Ossie Davis, from the novel by Chester Himes; directed by Ossie Davis; for Formosa / UA.

Cotton Queen
GB 1937 80m bw

A mill owner's daughter gets work in the mill of her father's rival. Obvious comedy which fails to make use of its talents. Stanley Holloway, Will Fyffe, Mary Lawson, Helen Haye, Jimmy Hanley, C. Denier Warren. Written by Louis Golding, Scott Pembroke; directed by Bernard Vorhaus; for Joe Rock. (US title: *Crying Out Loud*.)

The Couch
US 1962 100m bw

A psychiatrist's patient goes on the rampage with an ice pick. Overstretched suspenser which never really holds the interest. Grant Williams, Shirley Knight, Onslow Stevens. Written by Robert Bloch; directed and produced by Owen Crump; for Warner.

Council of the Gods*
Germany 1950 106m bw
DEFA (Adolf Fischer)

A research chemist working for a big chemical company denounces them after the war when he finds they have been producing poison gas for the concentration camps.
Self-flagellatory expiation of war crimes encased in an absorbing drama.

w Friedrich Wolff, Philipp Gebb *d* Kurt Maetzig *ph* Friedl Behn-Grund *m* Hanns Eisler, Erwin Lehn

Paul Bildt, Agnes Windeck, Yvonne Merin, Fritz Tillman

Counsel for Crime
US 1937 61m bw

A crooked lawyer fixes alibis for his clients before they commit a crime, until he finds his own son on the other side of one of his cases. Adequate programmer. Otto Kruger, Douglass Montgomery, Jacqueline Wells, Thurston Hall, Nana Bryant. Written by Fred Niblo Jnr, Grace Neville, Lee Loeb, Harold Buchman; directed by John Brahm; for Columbia. 'Won't disappoint those who get caught with it on a dual.'—*Variety*

Counsellor at Law*
US 1933 78m bw
Universal (Henry Henigson)

Life in the New York office of a successful Jewish lawyer.
Practised film-making from a Broadway hit.

w Elmer Rice, from his play *d William Wyler* *ph* Norbert Brodine

John Barrymore, Bebe Daniels, Melvyn Douglas, Doris Kenyon, Onslow Stevens, Isabel Jewell, Thelma Todd, Mayo Methot

'Good drama, well produced and with strong b.o. potentialities.'—*Variety*

† Paul Muni was the first choice for the lead, but refused to play a Jewish role.

Counsel's Opinion
GB 1933 76m bw

A widow wins a barrister by pretending to be a flighty socialite. Semi-sophisticated comedy; this rather thin quickie version was done over four years later and became *The Divorce of Lady X* (qv). Henry Kendall, Binnie Barnes, Cyril Maude, Laurence Grossmith. Written by Dorothy Greenhill and Arthur Wimperis, from a play by Gilbert Wakefield; directed by Allan Dwan; for London Films.

Count Five and Die*
GB 1957 92m bw Cinemascope
TCF / Zonic (Ernest Gartside)

British intelligence seeks to give the Nazis false information about the 1944 invasion, but conviction grows that a double agent is among them.
Terse, downbeat war suspenser, gripping in parts but quite forgettable.

w Jack Seddon, David Pursall *d* Victor Vicas *ph* Arthur Grant *m* John Wooldridge

Nigel Patrick, Jeffrey Hunter, Anne-Marie Duringer, David Kossoff

The Count of Monte Cristo***
US 1934 114m bw
Edward Small / Reliance

After spending years in prison, Edmond Dantes escapes and avenges himself on those who framed him.
Classic swashbuckler, extremely well done with due attention to dialogue as well as action; a model of its kind and period.

w Philip Dunne, Dan Totheroh, Rowland V. Lee, *novel* Alexandre Dumas *d Rowland V. Lee* *ph* Peverell Marley *m* Alfred Newman

Robert Donat, Elissa Landi, Louis Calhern, Sidney Blackmer, Raymond Walburn, O. P. Heggie, William Farnum

'A near-perfect blend of thrilling action and grand dialogue.'—*Variety*

Count the Hours
US 1952 74m bw

A man's wife and lawyer fight to save him from the gallows. Stiff and unconvincing suspenser. Teresa Wright, Macdonald Carey, Dolores Moran, Adele Mara, Edgar Barrier, John Craven, Jack Elam. Written by Doane R. Hoag and Karen DeWolf; directed by Don Siegel; for Benedict Bogeaus / RKO. (GB title: *Every Minute Counts.*)

Count Three and Pray
US 1955 92m Technicolor Cinemascope
Columbia / Copa (Ted Richmond)

After the Civil War a roistering Southerner comes home to rebuild his town and become its parson.
Moderate semi-western, fresh and pleasing but not memorable.

w Herb Meadow *d* George Sherman *ph* Burnett Guffey *m* George Duning

Van Heflin, Joanne Woodward (debut), Phil Carey, Raymond Burr, Allison Hayes, Myron Healey, Nancy Kulp, James Griffiths

'Don't dare come alone!'
Count Yorga Vampire
US 1970 90m Movielab
Erica / AIP (Michael Macready)

Inquisitive Los Angeles teenagers are vampirized by a suave foreign visitor.
A semi-professional film that looks it but amid the longueurs provides one or two nasty frissons.

wd Bob Kelljan *ph* Arch Archambault *m* William Marx

Robert Quarry, Roger Perry, Michael Murphy, Michael Macready, Donna Anders, Judith Lang

† *The Return of Count Yorga* followed a year later.

Count Your Blessings
US 1959 102m Metrocolor Cinemascope
MGM (Karl Tunberg)

An English girl marries an aristocratic Frenchman, but the war and other considerations make them virtual strangers until their son is nine years old, when it becomes clear that daddy is a philanderer.
Slight upper-crust comedy, basically rather tedious but kept buoyant by Chevalier as commentator.

w Karl Tunberg, *novel* The Blessing by Nancy Mitford *d* Jean Negulesco *ph* Milton Krasner, George Folsey *m* Franz Waxman

Deborah Kerr, *Maurice Chevalier*, Rossano Brazzi, Martin Stephens, Tom Helmore, Ronald Squire, Patricia Medina, Mona Washbourne

'Negulesco's aspirations to elegance are now familiar . . . this is far too absurd an example of Hollywood's infatuation with Old Europe to arouse much interest.'—*MFB*

Countdown*
US 1967 101m Technicolor Panavision
Warner (William Conrad)

Russian and American spaceships race for the moon.
Earnest, simply-plotted science-fiction in which technology is the centre of interest.

w Loring Mandel *d* Robert Altman *ph* William W. Spencer *m* Leonard Rosenman *ad* Jack Poplin

James Caan, Robert Duvall, Barbara Baxley, Joanna Moore, Charles Aidman, Steve Ihnat

Counterattack
US 1945 89m bw
Columbia
GB title: *One against Seven*

Resistance fighters go behind enemy lines for purposes of sabotage.
Standard World War II actioner, the star appearing above his surroundings.

w John Howard Lawson, *play* Janet and Philip Stevenson *d* Zoltan Korda *ph* James Wong Howe *m* Louis Gruenberg

Paul Muni, Marguerite Chapman, Larry Parks, George Macready, Roman Bohnen

Counterblast
GB 1948 99m bw

An escaped Nazi poses as a British scientist in a research laboratory. Overlong espionage thick ear with some compensations. Robert Beatty, Mervyn Johns, Nova Pilbeam, Margaretta Scott, Marie Lohr, Karel Stepanek, Alan Wheatley. Written by Jack Whittingham, from a story by Guy Morgan; directed by Paul Stein; for British National.

The Counterfeit Traitor*
US 1962 140m Technicolor
Paramount / Perlberg–Seaton

An oil importer, a naturalized Swede born in America, is blackmailed by the Allies into becoming a spy.
Heavy-going espionage drama which divides its time between action and moralizing. Excellent production does not quite make it exciting.

wd George Seaton, *book* Alexander Klein *ph Jean Bourgoin* *m* Alfred Newman

William Holden, Lilli Palmer, Hugh Griffith, Werner Peters, Eva Dahlbeck

'The picture is too long, it is also incessantly exciting, occasionally witty . . . and in its expression of organized sadism comparatively subtle.'—*Time*

Counterpoint*
US 1967 107m Techniscope
Universal (Dick Berg)

In 1944, an American symphony orchestra is captured by the Germans and threatened with execution.
Bizarre war suspenser, quite unconvincing but with effectively suspenseful moments and an old-fashioned portrayal of the Nazis as sadistic music-loving Huns.

w James Lee, Joel Oliansky, *novel* The General by Alan Sillitoe *d* Ralph Nelson *ph* Russell Metty *m* Bronislau Kaper

Charlton Heston, Maximilian Schell, Anton Diffring, Kathryn Hays, Leslie Nielsen

Countess Dracula
GB 1970 93m Eastmancolor
Rank / Hammer (Alexander Paal)

A Hungarian noblewoman restores her youth by bathing in the blood of young virgins.
Risibly sub-Freudian addition to a grotesque Hammer gallery of monsters, indistinguishable from the others once it gets going.

w Jeremy Paul, Alexander Paal, Peter Sasdy, Gabriel Ronay *d* Peter Sasdy *ph* Ken Talbot *m* Harry Robinson

Ingrid Pitt, Nigel Green, Sandor Eles, Maurice Denham, Patience Collier, Peter Jeffrey, Lesley-Anne Down

'At its best the film employs the kind of romantic imagery one associates with Keats; and if it doesn't quite live up to *that* comparison, it is at least a worthy companion to Corman's *Bloody Mama*.'—*David Pirie, MFB*

A Countess from Hong Kong
GB 1967 120m Technicolor
Universal (Jerome Epstein)

An American millionaire diplomat is followed from Hong Kong by his Russian émigrée girl friend, and complications mount when his wife boards the ship at Hawaii.
Flatulent comedy with neither the sparkle of champagne nor even the fizz of lemonade: Chaplin's writing, direction and music are alike soporific, and commiserations are due to the cast.

wd / m Charles Chaplin *ph* Arthur Ibbetson *pd* Don Ashton

Marlon Brando, Sophia Loren, *Patrick Cargill*, Margaret Rutherford, Charles Chaplin, Sydney Chaplin, Oliver Johnston, John Paul

'An unfunny, mindless mess.'—*Robert Windeler*

'So old-fashioned and dull that one can hardly believe it was made now.'—*Philip T. Hartung*

The Countess of Monte Cristo
US 1933 74m bw

A bit player in a musical convinces her friends she is a countess. Mild comedy remade in 1948 as an even milder vehicle for Sonja Henie. Fay Wray, Paul Lukas, Patsy Kelly, Reginald Owen. Written by Karen de Wolf and Gene Lewis; directed by Karl Freund; for Universal.

Country*
US 1984 109m Technicolor Panavision
Touchstone / Far West / Pangaea (William D. Wittliff, Jessica Lange)

Iowa farmers, on the breadline after a tornado, face foreclosure.
Deeply felt modern variation on *The Grapes of Wrath*, not particularly dramatic for those who have not felt the pressure.

w William D. Wittliff *d* Richard Pearce *ph* David M. Walsh *m* Charles Gross *pd* Ron Hobbs *ed* Bill Yahraus

Jessica Lange, Sam Shepard, Wilford Brimley, Matt Clark, Therese Graham

AAN: Jessica Lange

Country Dance
GB 1969 112m Metrocolor
MGM / Keep–Windward (Robert Emmett Ginna)
aka: *Brotherly Love*

An eccentric baronet's incestuous love for his sister finally breaks up her marriage.
Rambling melodrama with O'Toole going mad in squire's tweeds; tediously fashionable but too pallid for general success, it was barely released.

w James Kennaway, from his novel Household Ghosts *d* J. Lee-Thompson *ph* Ted Moore *m* John Addison

Peter O'Toole, Susannah York, Michael Craig, Harry Andrews, Cyril Cusack, Judy Cornwell, Brian Blessed

The Country Doctor*
US 1936 94m bw
TCF (Darryl F. Zanuck)

A rural physician becomes famous when quintuplets are born to one of his patients.
Fictionalization of the birth of the Dionne Quintuplets; pleasantly nostalgic even forty years after its *raison d'être*.

w Sonya Levien *d* Henry King *ph* John F. Seitz, Daniel B. Clark

Jean Hersholt, the Dionne Quins, Dorothy Petersen, June Lang, Slim Summerville, Michael Whalen, Robert Barrat
† Sequels: *Reunion* (1936), *Five of a Kind* (1938).

Country Gentlemen
US 1936 66m bw

A couple of con men help a widow who runs a small-town hotel. Strained comedy in which the gag men misguidedly try to play straight. Ole Olsen, Chic Johnson, Joyce Compton, Lila Lee, Pierre Watkin. Written by Milton Ralson, Jack Harvey, Jo Graham; directed by Ralph Staub; for Republic. 'Missing is the rapidfire buffoonery with which they have been identified in vaudeville.'—*Variety*

'How far should a woman go to redeem the man she loves?'
The Country Girl*
US 1954 104m bw
Paramount (William Perlberg)

The wife of an alcoholic singer blossoms when he is stimulated into a comeback.
Theatrically effective but highly unconvincing, this rather glum stage success made a cold film, miscast with an eye on the box office.

w George Seaton, *play* Clifford Odets *d* George Seaton *ph* John F. Warren *m* Victor Young *songs* Ira Gershwin, Harold Arlen

Bing Crosby, Grace Kelly, William Holden, Anthony Ross, Gene Reynolds

'The dramatic development is not really interesting enough to sustain a film of the intensity for which it strives.'—*Karel Reisz*

'Rather inexplicably, this sado-masochist morass was one of the biggest box office hits of its year.'—*Pauline Kael, 70s*

AA: George Seaton (as writer); Grace Kelly
AAN: best picture; John F. Warren; Bing Crosby

The County Chairman
US 1934 85m bw

A small-town attorney competes with his prospective son-in-law for the post of public prosecutor. Small-town period comedy drama, not among its star's best. Will Rogers, Evelyn Venable, Kent Taylor, Louise Dresser, Mickey Rooney, Stepin Fetchit, Berton Churchill. Written by Sam Hellman, Gladys Lehman, from the novel by George Ade; directed by John Blystone; for Fox.

County Hospital**
US 1932 20m bw

Ollie is in hospital; Stan brings him some hardboiled eggs and some nuts, and nearly wrecks the place. Archetypal star comedy with brilliant character and slapstick sequences, let down by a badly processed car ride home. Laurel and Hardy, Billy Gilbert. Written by H. M. Walker; directed by James Parrott; for Hal Roach.

Coup de Torchon
France 1981 128m colour
Les Films de la Tour / Les Films A2 / Little Bear (Adolphe Viezzi)
GB title: *Clean Slate*

In French West Africa in 1938, an apparently easy-going police officer is inspired to commit a series of murders.
Well-made, heavy-going study of mania.

w Jean Aurenche, Bertrand Tavernier, *novel* POP. 1280 by Jim Thompson *d* Bertrand Tavernier *ph* Pierre William Glenn *m* Philippe Sarde

Philippe Noiret, Isabelle Huppert, Jean-Pierre Marielle, Stéphane Audran, Eddy Mitchell
AAN: best foreign film

Courage
US 1930 65m bw

A widow has a large family of which the one sweet-natured son is left a fortune by the old lady next door. Glutinous mother-love saga from a popular play. Belle Bennett, Marian Nixon, Rex Bell, Leon Janney, Blanche Friderici. Written by Walter Anthony; directed by Archie Mayo; for Warners. 'Should be certain in neighbourhood houses. For abroad, a perfect picture for a glimpse of a real American boy of breeding and the sort of mother who lives in every nation.'—*Variety*

Courage Fuyons*
France 1979 98m Eastmancolor
Gaumont / Gueville (Yves Robert)

A middle-aged man embarks on a series of surprising romantic adventures.
A mainly enjoyable exercise in wish-fulfilment, sharply written and acted.

w Jean-Loup Dabadie, Yves Robert *d* Yves Robert *ph* Yves Lafaye *m* Vladimir Cosma

Jean Rochefort, Catherine Deneuve, Robert Webber, Philippe Leroy-Beaulieu

The Court Jester***
US 1955 101m Technicolor Vistavision
Paramount / Dena (Melvin Frank, Norman Panama)

Opposition to a tyrannical king is provided by the Fox, but it is one of the rebel's meekest men who, posing as a jester, defeats the usurper.
One of the star's most delightful vehicles, this medieval romp has good tunes and lively action, not to mention an exceptional cast and the memorable 'chalice from the palace' routine.

wd Norman Panama, Melvin Frank *ph* Ray June *songs* Sylvia Fine, Sammy Cahn *ad* Hal Pereira, Roland Anderson

Danny Kaye, Glynis Johns, *Basil Rathbone*, Cecil Parker, *Mildred Natwick*, Angela Lansbury, Edward Ashley, Robert Middleton, Michael Pate, Alan Napier

The Court Martial of Billy Mitchell*
US 1955 100m Warnercolor Cinemascope
United States Pictures (Milton Sperling)
GB title: *One Man Mutiny*

In the early twenties, an American general of the Army Air Service is court-martialled for accusing the war department of criminal negligence.
Adequate recreation of a historical incident, with a cast of excellent actors converging for a courtroom scene of some effectiveness.

w Milton Sperling, Emmet Lavery *d* Otto Preminger *ph* Sam Leavitt *m* Dmitri Tiomkin

Gary Cooper, *Rod Steiger*, Ralph Bellamy, Charles Bickford, Elizabeth Montgomery, Fred Clark, Darren McGavin, James Daly

AAN: Milton Sperling, Emmet Lavery

The Courtneys of Curzon Street*
GB 1947 120m bw
Imperadio (Herbert Wilcox)
US title: *The Courtney Affair*

In Victorian times, a baronet's son marries a lady's maid . . . and many years later, their grandson marries a factory worker.
Unbelievable upstairs-downstairs romantic drama spanning three generations; all to be taken with a gigantic pinch of salt, but a huge success when released.

w Nicholas Phipps, *novel* Florence Tranter *d* Herbert Wilcox *ph* Max Greene *m* Anthony Collins

Anna Neagle, Michael Wilding, Gladys Young, Coral Browne, Michael Medwin, Daphne Slater, Jack Watling, Helen Cherry, Bernard Lee

'The dignity of Curzon Street is Hollywoodized, and it is rare in 1945 that people in their sixties look as though they have one foot in the grave.'—*MFB*

'If my livelihood depended on booking the right film into the average cinema, this is one I would not dare to miss.'—*Observer*

The Courtship of Eddie's Father*
US 1962 117m Metrocolor Panavision
MGM / Joe Pasternak

The small son of a widower tries to interest Dad in another woman.
Fairly icky American-style sentimental comedy with most of the stops pulled out; way over-length and too self-indulgently solemn in the last part, but with professional touches.

w John Gay, *novel* Muriel Toby *d* Vincente Minnelli *ph* Milton Krasner *m* George Stoll

Glenn Ford, Ronnie Howard, Shirley Jones, Stella Stevens, Dina Merrill

† A TV series starring Bill Bixby followed in 1971.

Cousin, Cousine**
France 1975 95m Eastmancolor
Pomereu / Gaumont (Bertrand Javal)

Various furtive love affairs centre on a family wedding.
Sprightly satirical comedy full of pleasing touches, mostly jibes at French bourgeois standards.

wd Jean-Charles Tacchella *ph* Georges Lendi *m* Gerard Anfosso

Marie-France Pisier, Marie-Christine Barrault, Victor Lanoux, Guy Marchand, Ginette Garcin

'One of those rare delights you want to see again and again just to share the sheer joy of living, zest for love, genuine affection, all-too-human absurdity, and pure happiness of all those delicious people on screen.'—*Judith Crist, Saturday Review*

AA: best foreign film

Les Cousins*
France 1958 110m bw
AJYM (Claude Chabrol)

A law student stays with his sophisticated cousin in Paris, and his life is altered.
The country cousin fable filled with undramatic detail and given a rather perverse ending without any apparent point.

wd Claude Chabrol *ph* Henri Decaë *m* Paul Misraki

Jean-Claude Brialy, Gérard Blain, Juliette Mayniel, Claude Cerval

A Covenant with Death
US 1966 97m Technicolor
Warner (William Conrad)

A half-Mexican judge in a border town convicts a man who accidentally kills the hangman just as the real murderer confesses.
Dreary moral melodrama with accents, nicely photographed but cold, remote and drawn out.

w Larry Marcus, Saul Levitt, *novel* Stephen Becker *d* Lamont Johnson *ph Robert Burks* *m* Leonard Rosenman

George Maharis, Katy Jurado, Earl Holliman, Sidney Blackmer, Laura Devon, Gene Hackman

'Too thrilling for words, so they set it to music!'

Cover Girl**
US 1944 107m Technicolor
Columbia (Arthur Schwartz)

The road to success for magazine cover models.
Wartime glamour musical with a stronger reputation than it really deserves apart from Kelly's solos; it does however manage a certain *joie de vivre* which should not be despised.

w Virginia Van Upp *d* Charles Vidor *ph* Rudolph Maté *md* Morris Stoloff, Carmen Dragon *songs* Jerome Kern, Ira Gershwin

Rita Hayworth, Gene Kelly, Phil Silvers, Lee Bowman, Jinx Falkenberg, Otto Kruger, Eve Arden, Ed Brophy

'Kelly and Silvers are better than Kelly and Hayworth, though she does look sumptuous, and her big smile could be the emblem of the period.'—*New Yorker, 1977*

'Much of it is not as fresh as it may seem; but its second-handedness and its occasional failures cannot obliterate the pleasure of seeing the work of a production company which obviously knows, cares about and enjoys what it is doing.'—*James Agee*

AA: Morris Stoloff, Carmen Dragon
AAN: Rudolph Maté; song 'Long Ago and Far Away'

Cover Girl Killer
GB 1959 61m bw

A trap is set for the mad murderer of cover models. Good unpretentious second feature with plenty of suspense. Harry H. Corbett, Felicity Young, Spencer Teakle, Victor Brooks. Written and directed by Terry Bishop; for Parroch / Eros.

Cover Up
US 1948 82m bw

An insurance investigator finds senior officials conspiring to obscure the facts of a small-town murder. Modest mystery, initially intriguing but finally unsatisfying. Dennis O'Keefe, William Bendix, Barbara Britton, Art Smith. Written by Jerome Odlum and Jonathan Ritz; directed by Alfred E. Green; for Strand / UA.

The Covered Wagon*
US 1923 103m (24 fps) bw silent
Paramount / Famous Players-Lasky

Pioneer settlers travel west by wagon train.
A classic western which now seems painfully undernourished in terms of plot and character but still retains moments of epic sweep.

w Jack Cunningham, *novel* Emerson Hough *d* James Cruze *ph Karl Brown*

Ernest Torrence, Tully Marshall, J. Warren Kerrigan, Lois Wilson, Alan Hale

'There wasn't a false whisker in the film.'—*James Cruze*

'Forthright, impressive and vigorous, it brought a breath of fresh air into the jazz-ridden film world.'—*Lewis Jacobs*

The Cow and I
France 1959 119m bw
Cyclope / Omnia (Walter Rupp)
original title: *La Vache et le Prisonnier*

A French soldier escapes from a prison camp and takes a farm cow as cover.
Curiously overlong war adventure which hovers uncertainly between comedy and suspense.

w Henri Verneuil, Henri Jeanson, Jean Manse *d* Henri Verneuil *ph Roger Hubert* *m* Paul Durand

Fernandel, René Havard, Albert Remy, Bernard Musson

Cowboy*
US 1957 92m Technicolor
Columbia / Phoenix (Julian Blaustein)

Frank Harris becomes a cattle herder for love of a lady but is quickly disillusioned with the outdoor life.
Fashioned from a lively autobiography, this has interesting moments but is never as fascinating as one would expect.

w Edmund H. North, *book* On the Trail by Frank Harris *d* Delmer Daves *ph* Charles Lawton Jnr *m* George Duning

Jack Lemmon, Glenn Ford, Brian Donlevy, Anna Kashfi, Dick York, Richard Jaeckel, King Donovan

The Cowboy and the Lady
US 1938 91m bw
Samuel Goldwyn

The daughter of a presidential candidate becomes infatuated with a rodeo cowboy.
Insubstantial and witless romantic comedy which suffered many sea changes from script to screen.

w Leo McCarey, S. N. Behrman, Sonya Levien *d* H. C. Potter *ph* Gregg Toland *m* Alfred Newman

Gary Cooper, Merle Oberon, Patsy Kelly, Walter Brennan, Fuzzy Knight, Henry Kolker, Harry Davenport

'By and large only mildly diverting . . . the interest and promise of the early reels is not sustained in the latter half.'—*Variety*

'Just a lot of chestnuts pulled out of other people's dead fires.'—*Otis Ferguson*

AAN: Alfred Newman; title song (*m* Lionel Newman, *ly* Arthur Quenzer)

Cowboy from Brooklyn
US 1938 80m bw

A supposed cowboy crooner is taken out west and proves to be terrified of animals. Genial but witless spoof of a trend of the times. Pat O'Brien, Dick Powell, Priscilla Lane, Dick Foran, Ann Sheridan, Ronald Reagan, Johnnie Davis, James Stephenson. Written by Earl Baldwin from the play Howdy Stranger by Robert Sloane and Louis Pelletier Jnr; directed by Lloyd Bacon; for Warners.

† Remade as *Two Guys from Texas*.

The Cowboys*
US 1972 128m Technicolor
Panavision 70
Sanford / Warner (Mark Rydell)

Deserted by his ranch hands, a cattle drover on a long trail enlists the help of eleven schoolboys, who later avenge his death.
Ambling, climactically violent, extremely unlikely western with good scenes along the way.

w Irving Ravetch, Harriet Frank Jnr, *novel* William Dale Jennings *d* Mark Rydell *ph Robert Surtees* *m* John Williams

John Wayne, Roscoe Lee Browne, Bruce Dern, Colleen Dewhurst, Slim Pickens, Sarah Cunningham

† A TV series followed in 1974 but was shortlived.

Crack in the Mirror
US 1960 97m bw Cinemascope
TCF / Darryl F. Zanuck

A young lawyer and his ageing mentor are at opposite sides of a murder case.
Pointless Paris-set melodrama in which for no obvious reason each of the three stars plays two roles. Relentlessly boring.

w Mark Canfield (Darryl F. Zanuck) *d* Richard Fleischer *ph* William C. Mellor *m Maurice Jarre*

Orson Welles, Bradford Dillman, Juliette Greco, William Lucas, Alexander Knox, Catherine Lacey

'Thank God it's only a motion picture!'
Crack in the World
US 1965 96m Technicolor
Paramount / Security (Philip Yordan, Bernard Glasser, Lester A. Sansom)

A dying scientist fires a missile into the earth's centre, and nearly blows the planet apart.
Jaded science-fiction melodrama, overburdened with initial chat but waking up when the special effects take over.

w Jon Manchip White, Julian Halevy *d* Andrew Marton *ph* Manuel Berenguer *m* John Douglas *ad Eugene Lourié sp John Douglas*

Dana Andrews, Janette Scott, Kieron Moore, Alexander Knox, Peter Damon, Gary Lasdun

Crack Up
US 1936 65m bw

Espionage agents try to corrupt a test pilot. Modestly efficient thriller. Peter Lorre, Brian Donlevy, Helen Wood, Ralph Morgan, Thomas Beck. Written by Charles Kenyon and Sam Mintz; directed by Mal St Clair; for TCF.

Crack Up*
US 1946 93m bw
RKO

A museum curator with an eye for forgery is discredited by crooks who make him appear drunk or half-crazed when he recounts a set of strange events which have happened to him . . .
The intriguing mystery of the opening reels, when solved, is replaced by rather dull detection, but this remains a thriller with a difference, generally well presented.

w John Paxton *d* Irving Reis *ph* Robert de Grasse *m* Leigh Harline

Pat O'Brien, Claire Trevor, Herbert Marshall, Ray Collins

Cracked Nuts
US 1931 65m bw

Two Americans get mixed up in a revolution in a mythical country. Padded farce vehicle for a comedy team. Bert Wheeler, Robert Woolsey, Ben Turpin, Edna May Oliver, Dorothy Lee. Written by Al Boasberg, Ralph Spence; directed by Edward Cline; for RKO. 'As a two-reeler it would be fair entertainment.'—*Variety*

Crackerjack*
GB 1938 79m bw
US title: *The Man with a Hundred Faces*

A gentleman thief poses as butler at a stately home. Fairly smart sardonic star vehicle. *Tom Walls*, Lilli Palmer, Noel Madison, Leon M. Lion, Edmund Breon, Charles Heslop. Written by A. R. Rawlinson, Michael Pertwee and Basil Mason; directed by Albert de Courville; for Gainsborough. 'Carelessly made but fairly engrossing.'—*Variety*

Crackers
US 1984 92m Technicolor
Universal / Edward Lewis

Incompetent crooks run a pawnshop.
Insufficiently rethought, San Francisco set, updating of Monicelli's 1956 comedy *Big Deal on Madonna Street* (*I Soliti Ignoti*). No longer at all funny.

w Jeffrey Fiskin *d* Louis Malle *ph* Laszlo Kovacs *m* Paul Chihara *pd* John L. Lloyd

Donald Sutherland, Jack Warden, Sean Penn, Wallace Shawn, Larry Riley, Trinidad Silva, Charlaine Woodard, Irwin Corey

'One can sense that it would all sound much funnier in Italian.'—*Variety*

The Cracksman
GB 1963 112m Technicolor
Cinemascope

A master locksmith becomes the unwitting dupe of a gang of safecrackers. The most elaborate vehicle devised for this diminutive star; despite bright moments, conventional mounting and over-generous length finally defeat it. Charlie Drake, George Sanders, Dennis Price, Nyree Dawn Porter, Eddie Byrne, Finlay Currie, Percy Herbert. Written by Lew Schwartz and Charlie Drake; directed by Peter Graham Scott; for ABPC.

Cradle Song*
US 1933 78m bw
Paramount (E. Lloyd Sheldon)

A nun adopts a foundling.
Stately transcription of a once-fashionable play, too concerned with its own artistic background and handicapped by a star who didn't travel well, except to those partial to Jewish nuns.

w Marc Connelly, *play* G. M. Martinez Sierra *d Mitchell Leisen* *ph* Charles Lang *m* W. Franke Harling

Dorothea Wieck, Evelyn Venable, Sir Guy Standing, Louise Dresser, Kent Taylor, Gertrude Michael, Nydia Westman, Eleanor Wesselhoeff

'It moves slowly, laboriously . . . as a commercial entry decidedly dubious.'—*Variety*

Craig's Wife*
US 1936 77m bw
Columbia

A middle-class wife lets her house take precedence over her husband.
Capable picturization of a Broadway success, later remade as *Harriet Craig* (qv).

w Mary McCally Jnr, George Kelly, *play* George Kelly *d* Dorothy Arzner *ph* Lucien Ballard *md* Morris Stoloff

Rosalind Russell, John Boles, Billie Burke, Jane Darwell, Dorothy Wilson, Alma Kruger, Thomas Mitchell, Elizabeth Risdon, Raymond Walburn

Crainquebille*
France 1922 70m approx (16 fps) bw silent
Trarieux Films

A street trader is unjustly accused and imprisoned, afterwards finding happiness as a tramp.
Somewhere between Chaplin and Kafka, this fable was long admired for its style.

wd Jacques Feyder, story Anatole France *ph* Léonce Burel

Maurice de Féraudy, Françoise Rosay, Felix Oudart

† Remade 1933 by Jacques de Baroncelli with Maurice Tramel; 1954 by Ralph Habib with Yves Deniaud.

The Cranes Are Flying**
USSR 1957 94m bw
Mosfilm
original title: *Letyat Zhuravli*

When her lover goes to war, a girl refuses to believe later reports of his death even though she has suffered much, including marriage to a bully, in the interim.
Sleek, moving love story with most of the Hollywood production virtues plus an attention to detail and a realism which are wholly Russian.

w Victor Rosov d Mikhail Kalatozov ph Sergei Urusevski

Tatiana Samoilova, Alexei Batalov, Vasili Merkuriev

The Crash
US 1932 59m bw

An unfaithful wife finds her life changed by the stock market crash. Dim high-society goings-on make a poor star vehicle. Ruth Chatterton, George Brent, Paul Cavanagh, Henry Kolker, Barbara Leonard. Written by Earl Baldwin from the novel Children of Pleasure by Larry Barratto; directed by William Dieterle; for Warners. 'A weak sister . . . nothing happens to pique interest or capture sympathy or even provoke hostility.'—*Variety*

Crash Dive*
US 1943 105m Technicolor
TCF (Milton Sperling)

A submarine lieutenant and his commander love the same girl.
Well-staged war thrills in the final reels are prefaced by a long romantic comedy build-up, which probably seemed good propaganda at the time.

w Jo Swerling, *story* W. R. Burnett *d* Archie Mayo *ph* Leon Shamroy *m* David Buttolph *md* Emil Newman *sp Fred Sersen*

Tyrone Power, Anne Baxter, Dana Andrews, James Gleason, Dame May Whitty, Henry Morgan, Frank Conroy, Minor Watson

'One of those films which have no more sense of reality about this war than a popular song.'—*Bosley Crowther*

Crashing Hollywood*
US 1937 60m bw

A studio screenwriter selects a criminal as collaborator, and gets into all kinds of trouble. Lively melodramatic star vehicle with a reasonably vivid background. *Lee Tracy*, Joan Woodbury, Paul Guilfoyle, Lee Patrick, Richard Lane, Jack Carson, Tom Kennedy. Written by Paul Yawitz and Gladys Atwater, from a play by Paul Dickey and Mann Page; directed by Lew Landers; for RKO. 'Completely satisfactory programme picture.'—*Variety*

Crashout
US 1955 83m bw

Six convicts escape from prison, but most of them die en route. Watchable melodrama, fairly savage for its day. William Bendix, Arthur Kennedy, Luther Adler, William Talman, Gene Evans, Marshall Thompson, Beverly Michaels. Written by Hal E. Chester and Lewis R. Foster; directed by Lewis R. Foster; for Hal E. Chester / Standard.

Craze
GB 1973 95m Technicolor
(EMI) Harbour (Herman Cohen)

An African idol accidentally causes a death which brings money to its owner, who kills again and again in the hope of more loot.
Crude shocker from the bottom of even this producer's barrel, notable for the star cast which was surprisingly roped in.

w Aben Kandel, Herman Cohen, *novel* Infernal Idol by Henry Seymour *d* Freddie Francis *ph* John Wilcox *m* John Scott

Jack Palance, Diana Dors, Julie Ege, Edith Evans, Hugh Griffith, Trevor Howard, Michael Jayston, Suzy Kendall, Martin Potter, Percy Herbert, Kathleen Byron

Crazy House
US 1943 80m bw
Universal (Erle C. Kenton)

Olsen and Johnson go to Hollywood to make a film.
Lame sequel to *Hellzapoppin*; after an explosively well edited first reel of panic in the studio, it degenerates into a slew of below-par variety turns.

w Robert Lees, Frederic I. Rinaldo *d* Edward Cline *ph* Charles Van Enger *md* George Hale, Milt Rosen

Ole Olsen, Chic Johnson, Martha O'Driscoll, Patric Knowles, Percy Kilbride, Cass Daley, Thomas Gomez, Edgar Kennedy

† Sherlock Holmes fans may or may not wish to record a two-line comic bit by Basil Rathbone and Nigel Bruce in character.

Crazy Joe
US / Italy 1973 99m Technicolor

The rise and fall of a Mafia hood in New York. Noisy, violent, reasonably proficient gangster movie which seems to have some pretensions to play against stereotype. Peter Boyle, Paula Prentiss, Fred Williamson, Charles Cioffi, Rip Torn, Luther Adler, Eli Wallach, Henry Winkler. Written by Lewis John Carlino; directed by Carlo Lizzani; for Bright-Persky / De Laurentiis.

Crazy Mama
US 1975 80m colour
New World (Julie Corman)

In 1958 Arkansas, mother and daughter set off on a series of robberies and kidnaps which end in violence.
Exploitation crime movie with no apparent basis in fact; as such, occasionally exciting for those who can tolerate this kind of thing.

w Robert Thom *d* Jonathon Demme *ph* Tak Fujimoto *m* Snotty Scotty and the Hankies

Cloris Leachman, Ann Sothern, Stuart Whitman, Jim Backus, Linda Purl, Brian Englund

The Crazy World of Julius Vrooder
US 1974 98m colour

A Vietnam veteran withdraws from the world. Well-meaning but tiresome problem pic which gets nowhere. Timothy Bottoms, Barbara Seagull, Lawrence Pressman, Albert Salmi. Written by Daryl Henry; directed by Arthur Hiller; for TCF.

The Crazy World of Laurel and Hardy**
US 1964 83m bw
Hal Roach / Jay Ward

A compilation of Laurel and Hardy extracts from their classic period.
Although the material is in itself excellent and some of the build-up sequences well done, the clips are all too short to achieve maximum impact, and virtually none is identified.

w Bill Scott *m* Jerry Fielding *narrator* Garry Moore

'Not since the beginning of time has the world beheld terror like this!'

The Creature from the Black Lagoon
US 1954 79m bw 3-D
U-I (William Alland)

Up the Amazon, scientists encounter a fearful fanged creature who is half man, half fish.
Unpersuasive and unsuspenseful horror hokum from the bottom drawer of imagination: it did, however, coin enough pennies to generate two even worse sequels, *Revenge of the Creature* (1955) and *The Creature Walks Among Us* (1956). And the underwater photography is super.

w Harry Essex, Arthur Ross *d* Jack Arnold *ph* William E. Snyder *md* Joseph Gershenson *m* Herman Stein, Hans Salter

Richard Carlson, Julie Adams, Richard Denning, Antonio Moreno, Nestor Paiva, Ricou Browning (in the rubber suit)

The Creature with the Atom Brain
US 1955 80m bw

A scientist creates super-strong robot men, who go on the rampage. Comic strip style chiller, not too bad to sit through. Richard Denning, Angela Stevens, Gregory Gaye, Tristam Coffin. Written by Curt Siodmak; directed by Edward L. Cahn; for Sam Katzman / Columbia.

Creatures the World Forgot
GB 1970 95m Technicolor
Columbia / Hammer (Michael Carreras)

Quarrels break out between rival tribes of Stone Age men.
Feeble follow-up to *One Million Years BC* and *When Dinosaurs Ruled the Earth*: someone forgot to order any monsters.

w Michael Carreras *d* Don Chaffey
ph Vincent Cox *m* Mario Nascimbene

Julie Ege, Brian O'Shaughnessy, Robert John, Marcia Fox, Rosalie Crutchley

The Creeper
US 1948 63m bw

Scientists disagree over a serum which changes humans into cats. Nonsense horror item with stalwart cast. Ralph Morgan, Eduardo Ciannelli, Onslow Stevens, June Vincent, Richard Lane. Written by Maurice Tombragel; directed by Jean Yarbrough; for TCF.

The Creeping Flesh*
GB 1972 91m Eastmancolor
Tigon / World Film Services (Michael Redbourn)

A Victorian scientist discovers that water causes the recomposing of tissue on the skeleton of a Neanderthal man.
Absurd but persuasive horror film, quite well done in all departments.

w Peter Spenceley, Jonathan Rumbold
d Freddie Francis *ph* Norman Warwick
m Paul Ferris

Peter Cushing, Christopher Lee, Lorna Heilbron, George Benson, Kenneth J. Warren, Duncan Lamont, Michael Ripper

'The most fun you'll ever have being scared!'

Creepshow
US 1982 120m colour
United Film Distribution / Laurel Show (Richard P. Rubenstein)

A boy reads five gruesome stories from a horror comic.
Supposedly funny but mainly rather nasty recreation of a famous 'comic' style; far too extended for its own good.

w Stephen King *d* George A. Romero
ph Michael Gornick *m* John Marrison
pd Tom Savini

Carrie Nye, Viveca Lindfors, Stephen King, Leslie Nielsen, Hal Holbrook, Adrienne Barbeau, E. G. Marshall

'Robert Bloch and Freddie Francis did it all so much better in *Torture Garden*.'—*Tom Milne, MFB*

Creepshow 2
US 1987 89m colour

Cheapjack sequel, of no interest whatsoever. Lois Chiles, George Kennedy, Dorothy Lamour, Tom Savini, Domenick John. Written by George A. Romero from stories by Stephen King; directed by Michael Gornick; for Laurel/New World. 'An omnibus snoozefest, utterly lacking in chills or thrills.' *Daily Variety*

'The night the loving ended and the killing began!'

Crescendo*
GB 1969 95m Technicolor
Warner / Hammer (Michael Carreras)

A girl researcher goes to stay with the widow of a famous composer, and finds herself in mortal danger . . .
Lunatic Hammer horror with the courage of its shameless borrowings from *Taste of Fear, Fanatic, Nightmare, Maniac* and all the films about mad twin brothers, to which this chaotic brew adds dollops of sex and heroin addiction.

w Jimmy Sangster, Alfred Shaughnessy
d Alan Gibson *ph* Paul Beeson *m* Malcolm Williamson

Stefanie Powers, James Olson, Margaretta Scott, Jane Lapotaire, Joss Ackland

Cries and Whispers***
Sweden 1972 91m Eastmancolor
Cinematograph (Ingmar Bergman)
original title: *Viskingar och Rop*

A young woman dying of cancer in her family home is tended by her two sisters.
Quiet, chilling, classical chapter of doom which variously reminds one of Chekhov, Tolstoy and Dostoievsky but is also essential Bergman. Tough but important viewing, it lingers afterwards in the mind like a picture vividly painted in shades of red.

wd Ingmar Bergman *ph Sven Nykvist*
m Chopin and Bach

Harriet Andersson, Kari Sylwan, Ingrid Thulin, Liv Ullmann

'Harrowing, spare and perceptive, but lacking the humour that helps to put life and death into perspective.'—*Michael Billington, Illustrated London News*

AA: Sven Nykvist
AAN: best picture; Ingmar Bergman (as writer); Ingmar Bergman (as director)

Crime and Punishment*
US 1935 88m bw
Columbia

A student kills a pawnbroker and is tortured by remorse.
Heavy-going rendering of Dostoievsky with some pictorial interest.

w S. K. Lauren, Joseph Anthony *d Josef Von Sternberg* *ph* Lucien Ballard *m* Arthur Honegger *md* Louis Silvers

Peter Lorre, Edward Arnold, Tala Birell, Marian Marsh, Elizabeth Risdon, Mrs Patrick Campbell

'Will have to be sold, but should average fair takings.'—*Variety*

Crime and Punishment*
France 1935 110m bw

Incisive, well-acted French version.

w Marcel Aymé *d* Pierre Chenal *m* Artur Honegger

Pierre Blanchar, Harry Baur, Marcelle Geniat, Madeleine Ozeray

'There's a real picture in this Dostoievsky book, and the French have proved it.'—*Variety*

Crime and Punishment USA
US 1958 96m bw
Allied Artists / Sanders Associates (Terry Sanders)

A student murders an old pawnbroker and is driven mad by guilt.
Pointless updating of Dostoievsky by two young film-makers who seemed for years to be on the brink of a masterpiece but never actually produced it. Some points of interest, but the low budget is cramping.

w Walter Newman *d* Denis Sanders *ph* Floyd Crosby *m* Herschel Burke Gilbert

George Hamilton, Frank Silvera, Mary Murphy, John Harding, Marian Seldes

'There is about it a strange quality of aimlessness which nullifies much of its effect.'—*MFB*

Crime by Night*
US 1944 72m bw
Warner (William Jacobs)

A private detective reluctantly solves a small-town murder, and finds a spy.
Second feature which was thought at the time to have established a new pair of married detectives in the tradition of *The Thin Man*. However, one poor sequel, *Find the Blackmailer*, put paid to the idea.

w Richard Weil, Joel Malone, *novel* Forty Whacks by Geoffrey Homes *d* William Clemens *ph* Henry Sharpe

Jerome Cowan, Jane Wyman, Faye Emerson, Charles Lang, Eleanor Parker, Cy Kendall, Creighton Hale

Crime Doctor
US 1934 75m bw

A criminologist uses his special knowledge to wreak vengeance on his wife's lover. Smart co-feature which doubtless pleased a good many audiences. Otto Kruger, Karen Morley, Nils Asther, Judith Wood, William Frawley, Donald Crisp. Written by Jane Murfin from a story by Israel Zangwill; directed by John Robertson; for RKO. 'Good in every department, with mounting suspense.'—*Variety*

Crime Doctor*
US 1943 66m bw
Columbia

An amnesiac becomes a successful psychiatrist, then discovers that he was once a wanted gangster.

CRIES AND WHISPERS. Even a still conveys some of the unrelenting power and intensity of Ingmar Bergman at his most bleak and harrowing. Not an easy film to watch but a completely compelling one.

Time-passing second feature from a popular radio series. Ten *Crime Doctor* films were made between 1943 and 1949, all starring Warner Baxter, all except the first being locked room mysteries which seldom played fair with the audience.

w Graham Baker, Louise Lantz *d* Michael Gordon *m* Louis Silvers

Warner Baxter, Margaret Lindsay, John Litel, Ray Collins, Harold Huber, Leon Ames, Don Costello

The sequels:
1943: CRIME DOCTOR'S STRANGEST CASE
1944: SHADOWS IN THE NIGHT, CRIME DOCTOR'S COURAGE
1945: CRIME DOCTOR'S WARNING
1946: CRIME DOCTOR'S MANHUNT, JUST BEFORE DAWN
1947: THE MILLERSON CASE
1948: CRIME DOCTOR'S GAMBLE
1949: CRIME DOCTOR'S DIARY

Crime Does Not Pay

A celebrated series of two-reel shorts made by MGM between 1935 and 1947. In a hard-driving, tensely commentated manner more reminiscent of Warner filmmaking, they gave ample scope to trainee actors and directors in allegedly truthful re-enactments of contemporary crimes, often introduced by the state governor or police commissioner.

The titles were as follows:
BURIED LOOT (1935); *d* George B. Seitz; with Robert Taylor, Robert Livingston.
ALIBI RACKET (1935); *d* George B. Seitz.
DESERT DEATH (1935); *d* George B. Seitz; with Raymond Hatton, Harvey Stephens.
A THRILL FOR THELMA (1935); *d* Edward Cahn; with Irene Hervey, Robert Warwick.
HIT AND RUN DRIVER (1935); *d* Edward Cahn; with Morgan Wallace, Jonathan Hale.
PERFECT SET-UP (1936); *d* Edward Cahn.
FOOLPROOF (1936); *d* Edward Cahn; with Niles Welch, Alonzo Price.
THE PUBLIC PAYS (1936); *d* Errol Taggart; with Paul Stanton, Cy Kendall.
TORTURE MONEY (1936); *d* Harold S. Bucquet; AA.
IT MAY HAPPEN TO YOU (1937); *d* Harold S. Bucquet.
SOAK THE POOR (1937); *d* Harold S. Bucquet.
GIVE TILL IT HURTS (1937); *d* Felix Feist; with Janet Beecher, Howard Hickman.
BEHIND THE CRIMINAL (1937); *d* Harold S. Bucquet; with Edward Emerson, Walter Kingsford.
WHAT PRICE SAFETY (1938); *d* Harold S. Bucquet; with John Wray, George Huston.
MIRACLE MONEY (1938); *d* Leslie Fenton; with John Miljan, Claire DuBrey.
COME ACROSS (1938); *d* Harold S. Bucquet; with Bernard Nedell, Donald Douglas.
A CRIMINAL IS BORN (1938); *d* Leslie Fenton; with George Breakston, David Durand.
THEY'RE ALWAYS CAUGHT (1938); *d* Harold S. Bucquet; with Stanley Ridges, John Eldredge.
THINK IT OVER (1938); *d* Jacques Tourneur; with Lester Matthews, Dwight Frye.
THE WRONG WAY OUT (1938); *d* Gustav Machaty; with Linda Terry, Kenneth Howell.
MONEY TO LOAN (1939); *d* Joe Newman; with Alan Dinehart, Paul Guilfoyle.
WHILE AMERICA SLEEPS (1939); *d* Fred Zinnemann; with Dick Purcell, Roland Varno.
HELP WANTED (1939); *d* Fred Zinnemann; with Tom Neal, Jo Ann Sayers.
THINK FIRST (1939); *d* Roy Rowland; with Laraine Day, Marc Lawrence, Sara Haden.
DRUNK DRIVING (1939); *d* David Miller; with Dick Purcell, Jo Ann Sayers.
POUND FOOLISH (1940); *d* Felix Feist; with Neil Hamilton, Lynne Carver.
KNOW YOUR MONEY (1940); *d* Joe Newman; with Dennis Moore, Noel Madison.
JACKPOT (1940); *d* Roy Rowland; with Tom Neal, Ann Morriss.
WOMEN IN HIDING (1940); *d* Joe Newman; with Marsha Hunt, C. Henry Gordon.
BUYER BEWARE (1940); *d* Joe Newman; with Charles Arnt.
SOAK THE OLD (1940); *d* Sammy Lee; with Ralph Morgan, Kenneth Christy.
YOU THE PEOPLE (1940); *d* Roy Rowland; with C. Henry Gordon, Paul Everton.
RESPECT THE LAW (1941); *d* Joe Newman.
FORBIDDEN PASSAGE (1941); *d* Fred Zinnemann; with Harry Woods; AAN.
COFFINS ON WHEELS (1941); *d* Joe Newman; with Cy Kendall, Darryl Hickman.
SUCKER LIST (1941); *d* Roy Rowland; with Lynne Carver, John Archer.
FOR THE COMMON DEFENSE (1942); *d* Allen Kenward; with Van Johnson, Douglas Fowley.
KEEP 'EM SAILING (1942); *d* Basil Wrangell; with Jim David, Lou Smith.
PLAN FOR DESTRUCTION (1943); *d* Edward Cahn; with Lewis Stone.
PATROLLING THE ETHER (1944); *d* Paul Burnford.
EASY LIFE (1944); *d* Walter Hart; with Bernard Thomas, Steve Geray.
DARK SHADOWS (1944); *d* Paul Burnford; with Arthur Space, Henry O'Neill.
FALL GUY (1945); *d* Paul Burnford; with Leon Ames.
THE LAST INSTALLMENT (1945); *d* Walter Hart; with Cameron Mitchell, Walter Sande.

PHANTOMS INC. (1945); *d* Harold Young; with Frank Reicher, Ann Shoemaker.
A GUN IN HIS HAND (1945); *d* Joseph Losey; with Anthony Caruso, Richard Gaines.
PURITY SQUAD (1945); *d* Harold Kress; with Byron Foulger, Dick Elliott.
LUCKIEST GUY IN THE WORLD (1947); *d* Joe Newman; with Barry Nelson, Eloise Hardt; AAN.

Crime in the Streets*
US 1956 91m bw
Allied Artists (Vincent M. Fenelly)

Rival knife gangs bring havoc to tenement dwellers.
Lively semi-documentary low-life melodrama; routine subject, excellent credits.

w Reginald Rose, from his TV play *d Don Siegel ph* Sam Leavitt *m* Franz Waxman

John Cassavetes, James Whitmore, Sal Mineo, Mark Rydell

The Crime of Dr Crespi
US 1935 64m bw

A surgeon induces suspended animation in a hated rival, and has him buried. Crude and tasteless variation on Poe's 'The Premature Burial'. Erich Von Stroheim, Dwight Frye, Paul Guilfoyle, Harriet Russell. Written by Lewis Graham, Edward Olmstead; directed by John H. Auer; for Republic. 'As a baby scarer it's a weak entry.'—*Variety*

The Crime of Dr Forbes
US 1936 75m bw

A gravely injured scientist asks to be put out of his misery, and a colleague is accused of murder. Competently handled minor item, more a mystery story than a consideration of euthanasia. Robert Kent, J. Edward Bromberg, Gloria Stuart, Henry Armetta, Sara Haden, Alan Dinehart. Written by Frances Hyland and Saul Elkins; directed by George Marshall; for TCF.

The Crime of Dr Hallet
US 1938 68m bw

A doctor working on jungle fever finds it convenient to disappear and take over a dead colleague's identity. Implausible time-passer. Ralph Bellamy, Josephine Hutchinson, William Gargan, Barbara Read. Written by Lester Cole and Brown Holmes; directed by S. Sylvan Simon; for Universal. (Remade in 1946 as *Strange Conquest,* with Lowell Gilmore and Jane Wyatt.)

The Crime of Monsieur Lange**
France 1935 85m bw
Obéron (André Halley des Fontaines)

When the hated boss of a publishing house is believed killed, the workers turn it into a successful co-operative. When he reappears, they kill him.
The political elements of this fable now seem unimportant, but it still shows its original charm and cinematic skill.

w Jacques Prévert d Jean Renoir ph Jean Bachelet *m* Jean Wiener

René Lefèbvre, Jules Berry, Florelle, Sylvie Bataille, Henri Guisol

Crime of Passion
US 1956 86m bw
UA / Bob Goldstein (Herman Cohen)

An executive's wife sleeps his way to the top, but when the boss does not come through with promotion she shoots him.
Old-fashioned star melodrama on a low budget.

w Jo Eisinger *d* Gerd Oswald *ph* Joseph La Shelle *m* Paul Dunlap

Barbara Stanwyck, Sterling Hayden, Raymond Burr, Fay Wray, Royal Dano, Virginia Grey

Crime of the Century
US 1933 74m bw

A doctor commits a robbery by hypnotism, but is himself assaulted and the money disappears. Smart exploitation mystery with an intermission for the audience to check the clues, and a revelation that the police investigator is the guilty man. Jean Hersholt, Robert Elliott, Wynne Gibson, Stuart Erwin, Frances Dee, David Landau. Written by Florence Ryerson and Brian Marlow from the play The Grootman Case by Walter Maria Espe; directed by William Beaudine; for B. P. Schulberg / Paramount. 'Can be built up into a better than average below the de luxe theatres.'—*Variety*

Crime Over London
GB 1936 84m bw

A department store becomes a hide-out for gangsters. Stolid attempt at a British gangster picture; doesn't come off. Margot Grahame, Paul Cavanagh, Joseph Cawthorn, Basil Sydney, Rene Ray. Written by Norman Alexander, Harold French from the novel House of a Thousand Windows by Louis de Wohl; directed by Alfred Zeisler; for Criterion / Douglas Fairbanks.

Crime School*
US 1938 86m bw
Warner (Bryan Foy)

Problems of the warden of a reform school. Predictable vehicle for the Dead End Kids; watchable at the time.

w Crane Wilbur, Vincent Sherman *d* Lewis Seiler *ph* Arthur Todd *m* Max Steiner

Humphrey Bogart, Gale Page, Billy Halop, Huntz Hall, Leo Gorcey, Bobby Jordan, Gabriel Dell, Bernard Punsley, Paul Porcasi, Al Bridge

'A rough entertainment, sometimes brutal . . . should do well where audiences like 'em tough.'—*Variety*

Crime Wave
US 1954 74m bw

An ex-con is prevented from going straight. Basically humdrum programmer with lively detail. Sterling Hayden, Gene Nelson, Phyllis Kirk, Ted De Corsia, Charles Bronson. Written by Crane Wilbur; directed by André de Toth; for Warner. (GB title: *The City Is Dark.*)

'He had tired of her—and for that he was sorry! He was tied to her—and for that he hated her!'

Crime without Passion**
US 1934 82m bw
Paramount (Ben Hecht, Charles MacArthur)

A lawyer is driven to commit murder. Effective melodrama notable for then-new techniques which were blended into the mainstream of movie-making, and for the first appearance in Hollywood of a smart new writer-producer-director team.

wd Ben Hecht, Charles MacArthur, from their story Caballero of the Law *ph Lee Garmes sp* Slavko Vorkapitch *m* Oscar Levant

Claude Rains, Margo, Whitney Bourne, Stanley Ridges

'It turns a lot of established motion picture conventions topsy-turvy . . . shouldn't have much trouble at the box office, and inside the theatre it is safe.'—*Variety*

'The whole venture seems to take a long stride forward for the movies.'—*Otis Ferguson*

'A flamboyant, undisciplined, but compulsively fascinating film classic.'—*Peter John Dyer, 1966*

Crimes at the Dark House
GB 1939 69m bw
Pennant (George King)

A Victorian landowner kills his wife and conceals the fact by using a lunatic as her double.
Cheeky adaptation of a classic to make one of the star's most lip-smacking barnstormers.

w Edward Dryhurst, Frederick Hayward, H. F. Maltby from The Woman in White by Wilkie Collins *d* George King *ph* Hone Glendinning

Tod Slaughter, Hilary Eaves, Sylvia Marriott, Hay Petrie, David Horne

Crimes of Passion
US 1984 104m colour
New World (Barry Sandler)

A prostitute tells her story at a group therapy session.
Predictably from this director, a hysterically overheated stew of sex and murder; one to walk away from.

w Barry Sandler *d* Ken Russell *ph* Dick Bush *m* Rick Wakeman

Kathleen Turner, Anthony Perkins, John Laughlin, Annie Potts

'Film walks an uneasy line at times between comedy and drama, but is entertaining in the manner of a great B picture all about sex.'—*Variety*

'One of the silliest movies in a long time.'—*Roger Ebert*

The Crimes of Stephen Hawke
GB 1936 69m bw

A nineteenth-century moneylender is exposed as the mysterious murderer who had terrorized London. Amusing barnstormer, a vehicle for

Tod Slaughter; with Eric Portman, Marjorie Taylor, Gerald Barry. Written by H. F. Maltby; directed by George King; for George King / MGM.

Crimes of the Heart*
US 1986 105m Technicolor
De Laurentiis / Freddie Fields-Burt Sugarman

Three sisters try to reconcile themselves with their family past. Somewhat overwrought but generally compelling southern comedy-drama.
w Beth Henley from her play *d* Bruce Beresford *ph* Dante Spinotti *m* Georges Delerue *pd* Ken Adam

Diane Keaton, Jessica Lange, Sissy Spacek, Sam Shepard, Tess Harper, David Carpenter, Hurd Hatfield

AAN: Sissy Spacek, Tess Harper

The Criminal*
GB 1960 97m bw
Merton Park (Jack Greenwood)
US title: *The Concrete Jungle*

Sent to jail for a racecourse snatch, a gangster comes out fifteen years later to regain the loot and is followed by other criminals who kill him.
Relentlessly grim saga of prison life, with a few sensational trimmings.
w Alun Owen, Jimmy Sangster *d* Joseph Losey *ph Robert Krasker* *m* Johnny Dankworth

Stanley Baker, Sam Wanamaker, Margit Saad, *Patrick Magee*, Noel Willman, Grégoire Aslan, Jill Bennett, Kenneth J. Warren, Nigel Green, Patrick Wymark, Murray Melvin

'A savage, almost expressionistic picture of English underworld life.'—*NFT, 1973*

The Criminal Code*
US 1930 97m bw
Columbia (Harry Cohn)

A young man kills in self-defence, is railroaded into jail and becomes involved in another murder.
Impressive melodrama with good performances and sharp handling.
w Seton I. Miller, Fred Niblo Jnr, *play* Martin Flavin *d Howard Hawks* *ph* James Wong Howe, William O'Connell

Walter Huston, Phillips Holmes, Constance Cummings, Mary Doran, De Witt Jennings, John Sheehan, Boris Karloff

'It can play to any type of audience: they'll understand it and talk about it. A corking picture.'—*Variety*

† Remade as *Penitentiary* (1938) with Walter Connolly and *Convicted* (1950) with Broderick Crawford.

AAN: Seton I. Miller, Fred Niblo Jnr

Criminal Court
US 1946 63m bw

A lawyer is blackmailed by a crooked club owner. Stock crime and lawcourt yarn, rather stodgily put together but with interesting moments. Tom Conway, Martha O'Driscoll, Robert Armstrong, Addison Richards. Written by Lawrence Kimble; directed by Robert Wise; for RKO.

Criminal Lawyer
US 1936 72m bw

A smart lawyer who has devoted his career to getting criminals off the hook has a change of heart when appointed district attorney.
Standard programmer with a first-rate star performance. *Lee Tracy*, Margot Grahame, Eduardo Ciannelli, Erik Rhodes. Written by G. V. Atwater, Thomas Lennon, from a story by Louis Stevenson; directed by Christy Cabanne; for RKO. 'Strong fronter for a dual, but can go solo where Tracy's name will draw.—*Variety*

The Criminal Life of Archibaldo de la Cruz*
Mexico 1955 91m bw
Alianza Cinematografica (Roberto Figueroa)
original title: *Ensayo de un Crimen*

A fantasist determines to kill all women who cross his path, but fate intervenes.
Cheaply made macabre joke, one of its director's throwaway oddities: not too smooth, but often amusing.
w Luis Bunuel, E. Ugarte *d Luis Bunuel* *ph* Augusto Jimenez *md* Jorge Perez

Ernesto Alonso, Ariadna Welter, Miroslava Stern, Rita Macedo

The Crimson Canary
US 1945 64m bw

A jazz band vocalist is murdered. Routine murder mystery with appearances by Coleman Hawkins, Oscar Pettiford and Josh White. Noah Beery Jnr, Lois Collier, Danny Morton, John Litel, Steve Geray. Written by Henry Blankfort, Peggy Phillips; directed by John Hoffman; for Bob Faber / Universal.

The Crimson Circle
GB 1936 76m bw

Scotland Yard rounds up a blackmail gang. Lively Edgar Wallace adaptation. Hugh Wakefield, Alfred Drayton, Noah Beery, June Duprez, Niall MacGinnis. Written by Howard Irving Young; directed by Reginald Denham; for Wainwright. 'Considerably superior to pictures of its kind coming out of the tight little isle.'—*Variety*

† An earlier version in 1929 (part-talkie) with Stewart Rome was directed by Fred Zelnick for British Talking Pictures.

The Crimson Curtain*
France 1952 43m bw
Argos
original title: *Le Rideau Cramoisi*

An officer billeted with a bourgeois family is visited at night by the beautiful daughter, who finally dies in his arms.
A curious polished fragment with narration replacing spoken dialogue. For those in the mood, it works.
wd Alexandre Astruc, from a story by Barbey d'Aurevilly *ph* Eugene Schufftan *m* Jean-Jacques Grunenwald

Jean-Claude Pascal, Anouk Aimée, Madeleine Garcia, Jim Gerald

'In its limited time, with the greatest economy of means, it evokes an authentic sense of the past, as well as telling a story movingly and dramatically.'—*Richard Roud*

The Crimson Ghost
US 1946 bw serial: 12 eps

Professor Chambers invents a counteratomic device called the Cyclotrode; a criminologist prevents The Crimson Ghost from getting his hands on it. Typical serial of its time, with a deathshead-style villain. Charles Quigley, Linda Stirling, Clayton Moore (later the Lone Ranger, here as a villain), I. Stanford Jolley. Directed by William Witney and Fred Brannon; for Republic.

The Crimson Kimono
US 1959 82m bw
Columbia / Globe (Samuel Fuller)

Detectives seeking the murderer of a stripper in Los Angeles' Little Tokyo both fall in love with a witness.
Self-conscious local colour, though quite freshly observed and well photographed, finally overwhelms an ordinary little murder mystery.
wd Samuel Fuller *ph* Sam Leavitt *m* Harry Sukman

Glenn Corbett, James Shigeta, Victoria Shaw, Anna Lee, Paul Dubov

'Ask me no questions: believe only what you see!'

The Crimson Pirate*
GB 1952 104m Technicolor
Warner / Norma (Harold Hecht)

An 18th-century pirate and an eccentric inventor lead an island's people in rebellion against a tyrant.
One suspects that this started off as a straight adventure and was turned halfway through production into a spoof; at any rate, the effect is patchy but with spirited highlights, and the star's acrobatic training is put to good use.
w Roland Kibbee *d* Robert Siodmak *ph* Otto Heller *m* William Alwyn

Burt Lancaster, Nick Cravat, Eva Bartok, Torin Thatcher, James Hayter, Margot Grahame, Noel Purcell, Frank Pettingell

Crimson Romance
US 1934 70m bw

Two Americans join the German Air Force and one is killed fighting Americans. Very curious action drama which does not make its actual sympathies very clear. Ben Lyon, James Bush, Erich Von Stroheim, Sari Maritza, Bodil Rosing, Herman Bing. Written by Al Martin, Sherman Lowe; directed by David Howard; for Mascot. 'By indie standards a pretentious production . . . but not very promising for localities where resentment is rife.'—*Variety*

Crin Blanc**
France 1953 47m bw
Albert Lamorisse
aka: *Wild Stallion*

A small boy befriends and rides a wild horse in the Camargue.
A favourite short film of great beauty, but a shade overlong for its content.

wd Albert Lamorisse ph Edmond Séchan
m Maurice Le Roux

Alain Emery, Pascal Lamorisse

'For every man who struck gold—a hundred tried to take it away from him!'

Cripple Creek
US 1952 78m colour

A federal agent uncovers smugglers during a gold rush. Adequate co-feature western in murky colour. George Montgomery, Karin Booth, Jerome Courtland, William Bishop, Richard Egan, Don Porter. Written by Richard Schayer; directed by Ray Nazarro; for Edward Small/Columbia.

Crisis*
US 1950 96m bw
MGM (Arthur Freed)

A brain surgeon is forced to operate secretly on a South American dictator, and his wife is kidnapped by revolutionaries.
Dour intellectual suspense piece, in key with the genteel enlightenment of the Dore Schary regime at MGM. Well made but cold.

wd Richard Brooks, *story* George Tabori
ph Ray June *m* Miklos Rozsa

Cary Grant, Jose Ferrer, Signe Hasso, Paula Raymond, Ramon Navarro, Antonio Moreno, Leon Ames, Gilbert Roland

'Original, arresting and considered . . . so far the most striking example of Dore Schary's policy of encouraging the development of new talents.'—*Gavin Lambert*

'A bold piece of movie adventuring.'—*L.A. Mirror*

Criss Cross*
US 1948 87m bw
U-I (Michael Draike)

An armoured car guard and his double-crossing ex-wife get mixed up with vicious gangsters.
Sordid *film noir* with a poor plot but suspenseful sequences.

w Daniel Fuchs, *novel* Don Tracy *d Robert Siodmak ph Franz Planer m* Miklos Rozsa

Burt Lancaster, Yvonne de Carlo, Dan Duryea, Stephen McNally, Richard Long, Tom Pedi, Alan Napier

'Siodmak's talent for brooding violence and the sombre urban setting gives the film a relentlessly mounting tension.'—*Peter John Dyer*

Critical Condition
US 1986 100m Technicolor

Pretending to be mad in order to escape the Mafia, our hero is instead mistaken for a doctor. Zany, hepped-up comedy which fails on all counts. Richard Pryor, Rachel Ticotin, Ruben Blades, Joe Mantegna, Bob Dishy. Written by Denis and John Hamill; directed by Michael Apted; for Ted Field, Robert Cort/Paramount. 'Fans will find little to cheer about.'—*Daily Variety*

Critic's Choice
US 1963 100m Technicolor
Panavision
Warner / Frank P. Rosenberg

A ruthless Broadway critic is forced by his scruples to write a bad review of his wife's play.
Unsuitable vehicle for stars who have shorn a good comedy of wit and strive vainly for sentiment, wisecracks and pratfalls.

w Jack Sher, *play* Ira Levin *d* Don Weis
ph Charles Lang *m* George Duning

Bob Hope, Lucille Ball, Marilyn Maxwell, Rip Torn, Jessie Royce Landis, John Dehner, Jim Backus, Marie Windsor

'For instant stultification.'—*Judith Crist*

Critters
US 1986 86m De Luxe

Hair-ball-like creatures arrive from an asteroid and devastate Kansas. Childish horror spoof which makes *Gremlins* look like *War and Peace*. Dee Wallace Stone, M. Emmet Walsh, Billy Green Bush, Scott Grimes. Written by Stephen Herek, Dominic Muir; directed by Stephen Herek; for Sho Films / Smart Egg / New Line. 'Irritatingly insipid and lightweight.'—*Variety*

Crocodile Dundee*
Australia 1986 102m Kodacolour
Panavision
Paramount / Hoyts / Rimfire (John Cornell)

An outback hero goes to Manhattan and puts New Yorkers in their place.
Easygoing comedy with no real style, which astounded the industry by becoming one of America's most popular films in 1986.

w Paul Hogan, Ken Shadie *d* Peter Faiman
ph Russell Boyd *m* Peter Best

Paul Hogan, Linda Koslowski, John Meillon, Mark Blum

'*Romancing the Stone* combined with *Tarzan's New York Adventure*.'—*Sight and Sound*

† *Crocodile Dundee II*, which followed in 1988, offered very much the mixture as before.

AAN: best original screenplay

Cromwell*
GB 1970 141m Technicolor
Panavision
Columbia / Irving Allen (Andrew Donally)

An account of the rise of Cromwell to power, the execution of Charles I, and the Civil War.
Disappointingly dull schoolbook history, with good production values but glum handling.

wd Ken Hughes *ph Geoffrey Unsworth*
m Frank Cordell *pd John Stoll*

Richard Harris, Alec Guinness, Robert Morley, Dorothy Tutin, Frank Finlay, Timothy Dalton, Patrick Wymark, Patrick Magee, Nigel Stock, Charles Gray, Michael Jayston, Anna Cropper, Michael Goodliffe

'It tries to combine serious intentions with the widest kind of popular appeal and falls unhappily between the two. It will offend the purists and bore the kiddies.'—*Brenda Davies*

'Shakespeare spoiled us for this sort of thing. We wait for great speeches and witty remarks, for rage and poetry, and we get dedicated stodginess.'—*Pauline Kael*

AAN: Frank Cordell

The Crooked Billet
GB 1929 82m bw

Spies and detectives converge on an old inn where documents are hidden. Fairly unwatchable now, this once-entertaining melodrama was shot as a silent and had sound clumsily added. Its cast remains notable: Carlyle Blackwell, Madeleine Carroll, Miles Mander, Gordon Harker. Written by Angus Macphail, from the play by Dion Titherage; directed by Adrian Brunel; for Michael Balcon / Gainsborough.

The Crooked Road
GB / Yugoslavia 1964 92m bw

An American journalist plans to expose as a crook the dictator of a small Balkan state, but finds himself framed for murder. Lugubrious and too-talkative melodrama of political intrigue. Robert Ryan, Stewart Granger, Marius Goring, Nadia Gray, Catherine Woodville, George Coulouris. Written by J. Garrison and Don Chaffey, from the novel *The Big Story* by Morris West; directed by Don Chaffey; for Argo / Triglav.

The Crooked Way
US 1949 87m bw

An amnesiac ex-veteran finds that he was once a minor gangster. Predictable thick ear with film noir aspirations. John Payne, Sonny Tufts, Ellen Drew, Rhys Williams. Written by Richard Landau, from a radio play *No Blade Too Sharp* by Robert Monroe; directed by Robert Florey; photographed by John Alton; for Benedict Bogeaus.

The Crooked Web
US 1955 77m bw

A restaurant owner is lured into a scheme to recover buried Nazi gold from Germany, but finds it is a means of arresting him on an old murder charge. Ingenious but somehow uninteresting puzzle melodrama. Frank Lovejoy, Richard Denning, Mari Blanchard. Written by Lou Breslow; directed by Nathan Juran; for Sam Katzman / Columbia.

Crooks and Coronets
GB 1969 106m Technicolor
Warner Seven Arts / Herman Cohen
US title: *Sophie's Place*

American gangsters plan to rob a stately home but are taken over by the dowager in charge. Overlong and mainly flatulent comedy, with a good climax involving a vintage plane.

wd Jim O'Connelly *ph* Desmond Dickinson *m* Patrick John Scott

Telly Savalas, Edith Evans, Warren Oates, Nicky Henson, Cesar Romero, Harry H. Corbett

Crooks Anonymous*
GB 1962 87m bw
Anglo Amalgamated (Nat Cohen)

A petty thief joins an organization for reforming criminals, but is tempted again . . . and so are they.
Amusingly devised and plotted minor comedy with an exceptional cast.

w Jack Davies, Henry Blyth *d* Ken Annakin *ph* Ernest Steward *m* Muir Mathieson, Henry Martin

Leslie Phillips, Stanley Baxter, Wilfrid Hyde White, Julie Christie, James Robertson Justice, Robertson Hare, Charles Lloyd Pack

Crooks in Cloisters
GB 1963 97m Technicolor Scope

Forgers pose as monks but are reformed by the country life. Busy comedy full of familiar faces; perhaps a small cut above the *Carry Ons*. Ronald Fraser, Barbara Windsor, Grégoire Aslan, Bernard Cribbins, Davy Kaye, Wilfred Brambell. Written by Mike Watts; directed by Jeremy Summers; for ABPC.

Crooks' Tour*
GB 1940 84m bw
British National (John Corfield)

English tourists are mistaken for spies by Nazis in Baghdad.
Amusing vehicle for two comic actors who excelled at portraying the English abroad.

w John Watt, Max Kester, from the radio serial by Sidney Gilliat and Frank Launder *d* John Baxter *ph* James Wilson *m* Kennedy Russell

Basil Radford, Naunton Wayne, Greta Gynt, Abraham Sofaer, Gordon McLeod

'Their bland imperturbability in the face of extraordinary circumstances provides no little fun.'—*Picture Show*

Crooner
US 1932 64m bw

A radio singer who is more than something of a prig gets his come-uppance. Would-be satire with more bore than bite. David Manners, Ann Dvorak, Ken Murray, William Janney, Eddie Nugent, J. Carrol Naish. Written by Charles Kenyon from a story by Rian James; directed by Lloyd Bacon; for Warners. 'A general slap at that ether pest who for a time held popular sway . . . but there is no sympathy for anybody in the cast.'—*Variety*

The Cross and the Switchblade
US 1970 106m colour

A minister sets out to rid his New York streets of delinquents. Arrant but alas unconvincing do-goodery. Pat Boone, Erik Estrada, Jackie Giroux. Written by Don Murray and James Bonnet; directed by Don Murray; for Dick Ross Associates.

Cross Country
Canada 1983 104m colour

The boy friend of a murdered girl finds himself being driven west at gunpoint by a mad nymphomaniac and her protector. No-holds-barred 'adult' thriller whose excesses become risible. Richard Beymer, Nina Axelrod, Michael Ironside, Brent Carver. Written by Logan N. Danforth (John Hunter); directed by Paul Lynch; for Filmline / Yellowbill.

'The true story about the woman who wrote "The Yearling"!'
Cross Creek*
US 1983 122m Technicolor
EMI / Radnitz / Ritt (Robert B. Radnitz)

In 1928 Marjorie Kinnan Rawlings leaves her journalist husband and goes to live in the Florida backwoods, where she hopes to write a Gothic romance.
Elongated study of writer's block (though the subject did eventually write *The Yearling*). Altogether too typical of its producer and director—and too slow—to hold much surprise or interest.

w Dalene Young *memoir* Marjorie Kinnan Rawlings *d* Martin Ritt *ph* John A. Alonzo *m* Leonard Rosenman *pd* Walter Scott Herndon

Mary Steenburgen, Rip Torn, Peter Coyote, Dana Hill, Ike Eisenmann, Alfre Woodard

'The landscapes are attractive, but much too lushly filmed with lyrical inserts in which the wonders of the bayou are contemplated. Good performances fail to mask the fact that the characters are stereotypes from start to finish.'—*Tom Milne, MFB*

'Everything is lighted to look holy, and when the score isn't shimmering and burnishing, nature is twittering.'—*New Yorker*

AAN: Rip Torn, Alfre Woodard, Leonard Rosenman

Cross My Heart*
US 1945 83m bw
Paramount (Harry Tugend)

A romantic girl confesses to murder, is acquitted, and finds the real murderer.
Modest remake of *True Confession* (qv), with frenetic pace but not much style.

w Claude Binyon, Harry Tugend, Charles Schnee *d* John Berry *ph* Charles Lang Jnr *m* Robert Emmett Dolan

Betty Hutton, Sonny Tufts, Michael Chekhov, Rhys Williams, Ruth Donnelly, Al Bridge, Howard Freeman, Iris Adrian

Cross of Iron*
GB / West Germany 1977 133m Technicolor
EMI–Rapid Film / Terra Filmkunst (Wolf C. Hartwig)

Militarily and emotionally at the end of its tether, a German battalion is decimated while fighting the Russians in 1943.
Painful to follow, occasionally beautiful to watch, this quite horrid film offers too much opportunity for its director to wallow in unpleasant physical details, and its main plot of bitter rivalry offers no relief.

w Julius J. Epstein, Herbert Asmodi *d* Sam Peckinpah *ph John Coquillon* *m* Ernest Gold

James Coburn, James Mason, Maximilian Schell, David Warner, Klaus Löwitch, Senta Berger

'Morally dubious but technically brilliant.'—*Michael Billington, Illustrated London News*

The Cross of Lorraine*
US 1944 91m bw
MGM (Edwin Knopf)

In a German camp for French prisoners, an escape leads to a rising by local villagers.
Standard war propaganda piece, made with enthusiasm on unconvincing sets.

w Michael Kanin, Ring Lardner Jnr, Alexander Esway, Robert Andrews *d* Tay Garnett *ph* Sidney Wagner *m* Bronislau Kaper

Gene Kelly, Jean-Pierre Aumont, Cedric Hardwicke, Peter Lorre, Joseph Calleia, Richard Whorf, Hume Cronyn

'Half a football team worked on the story, yet except for a foolish coda it is one of the most edged, well-characterized, and naturally cinematic scripts of the year.'—*James Agee*

Crossed Swords
Italy / USA 1954 83m Pathecolor
Viva Films (J. Barrett Mahon, Vittorio Vassarotti)
original title: *Il Maestro di Don Giovanni*

The son of an Italian duke prevents an uprising.
A thin swashbuckler showing the perils of early co-production.

wd Milton Krims *ph* Jack Cardiff

Errol Flynn, Gina Lollobrigida, Cesare Danova, Nadia Gray, Paola Mori

'Sensational? No, it's dynamite!'
Crossfire****
US 1947 86m bw
RKO (Adrian Scott)

A Jew is murdered in a New York hotel, and three soldiers are suspected.
Tense, talky thriller shot entirely at night with pretty full expressionist use of camera technique; notable for style, acting, experimentation, and for being the first Hollywood film to hit out at racial bigotry.

w John Paxton, novel The Brick Foxhole by Richard Brooks *ph J. Roy Hunt* *d Edward Dmytryk* *m* Roy Webb

Robert Young, Robert Mitchum, *Robert Ryan*, Gloria Grahame, *Paul Kelly*, Sam Levene, Jacqueline White, Steve Brodie

AAN: best picture; John Paxton; Edward Dmytryk; Robert Ryan; Gloria Grahame

The Crossing of the Rhine*
France / Italy / West Germany 1960 125m bw
Franco-London-Gibe-Jonia-UFA (Ralph Baum)
original title: *Le Passage du Rhin*

Two French soldiers escape from the Germans in 1940 and after various adventures meet up again in Paris in 1945.

Two crowded plots and not a great deal of point emerge from this watchable war film full of conventional set pieces.

w André Cayatte, Armand Jammot *d* André Cayatte *ph* Roger Fellous *m* Louiguy

Charles Aznavour, Nicole Courcel, Georges Rivière, Cordula Trantow

Crossplot
GB 1969 97m Eastmancolor
UA / Tribune (Robert S. Baker)

An advertising executive gets involved in a spy ring.
Old-fashioned, London-set amalgam of secret codes, disappearing bodies, helicopter attacks, and a finale frustrating the assassination of a statesman in Hyde Park.

w Leigh Vance *d* Alvin Rakoff *ph* Brendan J. Stafford *m* Stanley Black

Roger Moore, Martha Hyer, Alexis Kanner, Francis Matthews, Bernard Lee

Crossroads**
Japan 1928 80m approx bw silent
Shochiku
original title: *Jujiro*

A woman kills her seducer. Her brother thinks he has killed a man and takes refuge with her, only to die of shock when he sees the man alive.
The only widely distributed Japanese silent film, this curious piece is fragmentarily told and will remind many of *Rashomon* with its mixture of flashbacks and dreams.

wd Teinosuke Kinugasa *ph* Kohei Sugiyama

J. Bandoha, A. Tschihaya, Yujiko Ogawa, I. Sohma

Crossroads*
US 1942 84m bw
MGM (Edwin Knopf)

A French diplomat who once lost his memory is blackmailed by crooks who claim he was once a criminal.
Smooth mystery melodrama adapted from the French film *Carrefour*.

w Howard Emmett Rogers, John Kafka *d* Jack Conway *ph* Joseph Ruttenberg *m* Bronislau Kaper

William Powell, Hedy Lamarr, Basil Rathbone, Claire Trevor, Margaret Wycherly, Felix Bressart, Sig Rumann

'Well directed and acted with polish, delightful romantic moments breaking up the general atmosphere of excitement and suspense.'—*Picturegoer*

Crossroads
US 1986 96m Technicolor

Urged by a young musician, an old jazzman travels the South in search of his legendary companion's lost music. Rather specialized and unsatisfactory road pic which loses its way well before the end. Ralph Macchio, Joe Seneca, Jamie Gertz, Joe Morton. Written by John Fusco; directed by Walter Hill; for Mark Carliner / Delphi IV / Columbia. 'You can tell what's wrong with *Crossroads* when you try to describe it to friends. Half-way through the plot description, their eyes glaze over.'—*People*

Crosswinds
US 1951 93m Technicolor

Treasure-hunting boatmen fall out in New Guinea. Adequate outdoor thick-ear; good value for money as the lower half of a double bill. John Payne, Rhonda Fleming, Forrest Tucker, Robert Lowery, Alan Mowbray, John Abbott. Written and directed by Lewis R. Foster; for Pine / Thomas (Paramount).

The Crouching Beast
GB 1935 80m bw

In Turkey during World War I an American newspaperwoman is menaced by a Turkish agent. Slow and muddled espionage melodrama. Fritz Kortner, Wynne Gibson, Richard Bird, Isabel Jeans, Peter Gawthorne. Written and directed by Victor Hanbury from the novel Clubfoot by Valentine Williams; for John Stafford / RKO.

The Crowd***
US 1928 98m bw silent
MGM (King Vidor)

Episodes in the life of a city clerk.
A deliberately humdrum story, chosen to show that drama can exist in the lowliest surroundings, retains much of its original power, though some of the director's innovations have become clichés.

w King Vidor, John V. A. Weaver, Harry Behn *d King Vidor* *ph* Henry Sharp *ad* Cedric Gibbons, Arnold Gillespie *ed* Hugh Wynn

James Murray, Eleanor Boardman, Bert Roach, Estelle Clark

'No picture is perfect, but this comes as near to reproducing reality as anything you have ever witnessed.'—*Photoplay*

AAN: King Vidor

The Crowd Roars*
US 1932 85m bw
Warner

A star motor-racing driver tries to prevent his young brother from following in his footsteps. Typical early Cagney vehicle, still spectacularly pacy but dated in its dialogue scenes.

w Kubec Glasmon, John Bright, Niven Busch *d* Howard Hawks *ph* Sid Hickox, John Stumar *md* Leo Forbstein

James Cagney, Joan Blondell, Ann Dvorak, Eric Linden, Guy Kibbee, Frank McHugh, Regis Toomey

'A thin and uneventful story, but a majority of the footage is devoted to three stirring contests.'—*Variety*

'As so often Hawks seems bitter at the world men have created but respects those who have to attempt to live it to the full.'—*NFT, 1963*

'The story is not precisely exciting . . . the closing episode is the best, for it reveals a certain originality in having the injured automobile racers eager to continue the race in ambulances on the way to hospital.'—*Mordaunt Hall, New York Times*

† Remade in 1939 as *Indianapolis Speedway*.

The Crowd Roars*
US 1938 90m bw
MGM (Sam Zimbalist)

A young boxer becomes involved with the underworld.
Standard star vehicle with efficient trimmings.

w Thomas Lennon, George Bruce, George Oppenheimer *d* Richard Thorpe *ph* John Seitz *m* Edward Ward

Robert Taylor, Frank Morgan, Edward Arnold, Maureen O'Sullivan, William Gargan, Frank Craven, Jane Wyman, Lionel Stander, Nat Pendleton

'Exciting melodrama with plenty of ring action, some plausible romance and several corking good characterizations.'—*Variety*

† Remade as *Killer McCoy*.

The Crowded Day
GB 1954 82m bw

Problems of five assistants in a department store during the Christmas rush. Naïve little portmanteau which suited its purpose. Joan Rice, John Gregson, Freda Jackson, Patricia Marmont, Josephine Griffin, Sonia Holm, Rachel Roberts, Thora Hird, Dora Bryan, Edward Chapman, Sid James, Richard Wattis. Written by Talbot Rothwell; directed by John Guillermin; for Advance.

The Crowded Sky
US 1960 104m Technicolor
Warner (Michael Garrison)

As two planes fly unwittingly towards each other, the passengers muse on their personal problems. An emergency landing averts total disaster.
The format goes back as far as *Friday the Thirteenth*, and forward to *Airport 75*, but this was in fact a cut-rate rehash of *The High and the Mighty*, with dull characters and insufficiently tense handling, not to mention a second team cast.

w Charles Schnee *d* Joseph Pevney *ph* Harry Stradling *m* Leonard Rosenman

Dana Andrews, Rhonda Fleming, Efrem Zimbalist Jnr, John Kerr, Anne Francis, Keenan Wynn, Troy Donahue, Joe Mantell, Patsy Kelly

The Cruel Sea**
GB 1953 126m bw
Ealing (Leslie Norman)

Life and death on an Atlantic corvette during World War II.
Competent transcription of a bestselling book, cleanly produced and acted; a huge box office success.

w Eric Ambler, *novel* Nicholas Monsarrat *d Charles Frend* *ph* Gordon Dines, Jo Jago, Paul Beeson *m* Alan Rawsthorne

Jack Hawkins, Donald Sinden, Stanley Baker, John Stratton, Denholm Elliott, John Warner, Bruce Seton, Virginia McKenna, Moira Lister, June Thorburn

'This is a story of the battle of the Atlantic, a story of an ocean, two ships and a handful of men. The men are the heroes. The heroines are the ships. The only villain is the sea—the cruel sea—that man has made even more cruel.'—*opening narration*

'One is grateful nowadays for a film which does not depict war as anything but a tragic and bloody experience, and it is this quality which gives the production its final power to move.'—*John Gillett*

'Sensitivity, faithfulness, and almost inevitable tedium.'—*Time Out, 1984*

AAN: Eric Ambler

Cruisin' Down the River
US 1953 79m colour

A nightclub singer inherits a riverboat. Slim excuse for a musical variety bill. Dick Haymes, Audrey Totter, Billy Daniels, Cecil Kellaway, the Bell Sisters, Erze Ivan. Written by Blake Edwards, Richard Quine; directed by Richard Quine; for Columbia.

Cruising
US 1980 106m Technicolor
Lorimar (Jerry Weintraub)

A New York cop becomes degraded in his search among homosexuals for a sadistic killer. Alleged thriller with phoney pretensions and repellent detail.

wd William Friedkin *ph* James Contner *m* Jack Nitzsche

Al Pacino, Paul Sorvino, Karen Allen, Richard Cox, Don Scardino, Joe Spinell

'Like any approach to the bizarre, it's fascinating for about fifteen minutes. After that, it suffers from the same boring repetition that makes porno so uninteresting generally.'—*Variety*

'Wonders to dazzle the human imagination—in a flaming love story set in titanic world conflict!'

The Crusades**
US 1935 127m bw
Paramount / Cecil B. de Mille

Spurred by his wife Berengaria, Richard the Lionheart sets off on his holy wars.
Heavily tapestried medieval epic, spectacular sequences being punctuated by wodges of uninspired dialogue. A true de Mille pageant.

w Harold Lamb, Waldemar Young, Dudley Nichols *d Cecil B. de Mille ph Victor Milner sp* Gordon Jennings *m* Rudolph Kopp

Henry Wilcoxon, Loretta Young, C. Aubrey Smith, Ian Keith, Katherine de Mille, Joseph Schildkraut, Alan Hale, C. Henry Gordon, George Barbier, Montagu Love, Lumsden Hare, William Farnum, Hobart Bosworth, Pedro de Cordoba, Mischa Auer

'Mr de Mille's evangelical films are the nearest equivalent today to the glossy German colour prints which decorated mid-Victorian bibles. There is the same lack of a period sense, the same stuffy horsehair atmosphere of beards and whiskers, and, their best quality, a childlike eye for detail.'—*Otis Ferguson*

'Cinema addicts by now have some idea what to expect in a de Mille version of the Holy Wars. *The Crusades* should fulfil all expectations. As a picture it is historically worthless, didactically treacherous, artistically absurd. None of these defects impairs its entertainment value. It is a hundred-million-dollar sideshow which has at least three features to distinguish it from the long line of previous de Mille extravaganzas. It is the noisiest; it is the biggest; it contains no baths.'—*Time*

'Probably only de Mille could make a picture like this and get away with it. It's long, and slow, and the story is not up to some of his previous films, but the production has sweep and spectacle.'—*Variety*

AAN: Victor Milner

Cry Baby Killer
US 1958 62m bw

A gunman on the run barricades himself and hostages in a storeroom. Modest second feature which served its purpose. Jack Nicholson, Harry Lauter, Carolyn Mitchell, Brett Halsey. Written by Leo Gordon, Melvin Levy; directed by Jus Addiss; for Roger Corman/AA.

Cry Danger*
US 1951 79m bw
RKO / Olympic (Sam Wiesenthal, W. R. Frank)

After serving five years for robbery, a man gets out on parole and clears his name.
Slick little slice of thick ear, very lively all round.

w William Bowers, *story* Jerome Cady *d* Robert Parrish *ph* Joseph F. Biroc *m* Emil Newman, Paul Dunlap *ad* Richard Day

Dick Powell, Rhonda Fleming, Richard Erdman, William Conrad, Regis Toomey, Jay Adler

Cry Freedom**
GB 1987 158m colour Panavision
Marble Arch / Universal (Richard Attenborough)

South African journalist Donald Woods is forced to flee the country after attempting to investigate the death in custody of his friend the black activist Steve Biko.
Part thriller, part social conscience tract, the film has magnificent set pieces typical of the director's work. However it failed to satisfy either opponents or supporters of apartheid.

w John Briley *d* Richard Attenborough *m* George Fenton, Jonas Gwangwa *pd* Stuart Craig

Kevin Kline, Penelope Wilton, Denzel Washington, Alec McCowen, Kevin McNally, Zakes Moke

AAN: Denzel Washington

Cry for Happy
US 1961 110m Eastmancolor Cinemascope
Columbia (William Goetz)

Four navy cameramen in Japan help geishas to found an orphanage.
As bad as it sounds, a repellent mixture of sentiment and knockabout.

w Irving Brecher *d* George Marshall *ph* Burnett Guffey *m* George Duning

Glenn Ford, Donald O'Connor, Miiko Taka, James Shigeta, Mikoshi Umeki, Joe Flynn, Howard St John

'Any film which expends most of its energies on a protracted joke about how far you can go with a geisha could hardly fail to be as charmless and witless as this.'—*MFB*

A Cry from the Streets
GB 1958 100m bw
Film Traders (Ian Dalrymple)

Episodes from the work of child welfare officers.
Mildly pleasing but unconvincing semi-documentary, with children competing with the star at scene-stealing.

w Vernon Harris, *novel* The Friend in Need by Elizabeth Coxhead *d* Lewis Gilbert *ph* Harry Gillan *m* Larry Adler

Max Bygraves, Barbara Murray, Colin Petersen, Dana Wilson, Kathleen Harrison, Eleanor Summerfield, Mona Washbourne

Cry Havoc
US 1943 97m bw
MGM (Edwin Knopf)

War nurses are caught up in the Bataan retreat.
An all-woman cast adequately handles a stagey melodrama about a tragic situation.

w Paul Osborn, *play* Proof thro' the Night by Allen R. Kenward *d* Richard Thorpe *ph* Karl Freund *m* Daniele Amfitheatrof

Margaret Sullavan, Joan Blondell, Ann Sothern, Fay Bainter, Marsha Hunt, Ella Raines, Frances Gifford, Diana Lewis, Heather Angel, Connie Gilchrist

'A sincere fourth-rate film made from a sincere fifth-rate play.'—*James Agee*

'Its popularity will stem less from its probably factual record of nurses starving, sweating and dying in the beleaguered Philippine jungle than from the impressive all-woman cast which MGM has rounded up for the occasion.'—*Newsweek*

A Cry in the Night
US 1956 75m bw
Warner / Jaguar (George C. Bertholon)

A peeping Tom, caught by a teenage couple, abducts the girl and threatens rape.
Odd little domestic thriller, with parents and police working together. Watchable, but a bit over the top.

w David Dortort *d* Frank Tuttle *ph* John Seitz *m* David Buttolph

Edmond O'Brien, Brian Donlevy, Natalie Wood, Raymond Burr, Richard Anderson, Irene Hervey, Anthony Caruso

Cry of the Banshee
GB 1970 87m Movielab
AIP (Gordon Hessler)

A 16th-century magistrate is cursed by a witch, who sends a devil in the form of a young man to destroy him.
Modest horror film which fails to do justice to its interesting plot.

w Tim Kelly, Christopher Wicking *d* Gordon Hessler *ph* John Coquillon *m* Les Baxter

Vincent Price, Elisabeth Bergner, Patrick Mower, Essy Persson, Hugh Griffith, Hilary Dwyer, Sally Geeson

Cry of the City**
US 1948 96m bw
TCF (Sol C. Siegel)

A ruthless gangster on the run is pursued by a policeman who was once his boyhood friend.
Very well produced but relentlessly miserable New York thriller on the lines of *Manhattan Melodrama* and *Angels with Dirty Faces*.

w Richard Murphy, *novel* The Chair for Martin Rome by Henry Helseth *d Robert Siodmak ph Lloyd Aherne m* Alfred Newman

w Richard Murphy *d Robert Siodmak ph Lloyd Aherne m* Alfred Newman

Victor Mature, Richard Conte, Mimi Agulia, Shelley Winters, Tommy Cook, Fred Clark, Debra Paget

'When the city cries in a movie, it's with the desolate wail of police sirens and with rain-streaked sidewalks; but most of all with poetic justification.'—*Paul Taylor, Time Out, 1980*

Cry Terror**
US 1958 96m bw
MGM / Andrew Stone

As security against ransom money being delivered, an airline bomber kidnaps a family.
Unabashed suspenser which screws panic situations as far as they will go and farther.

wd Andrew Stone ph Walter Strenge *m* Howard Jackson

James Mason, Rod Steiger, Inger Stevens, Neville Brand, Angie Dickinson, Kenneth Tobey, Jack Klugman, Jack Kruschen

Cry the Beloved Country*
GB 1951 96m bw
London Films (Alan Paton)
US title: *African Fury*

In South Africa, a white farmer and a black preacher find friendship through linked family tragedies.
Well-intentioned, earnest, rather high-flown racial drama.

w Alan Paton, from his novel *d* Zoltan Korda *ph* Robert Krasker *m* Raymond Gallois-Montbrun

Canada Lee, Sidney Poitier, Charles Carson, Charles McRae, Joyce Carey, Geoffrey Keen, Michael Goodliffe, Edric Connor

Cry Vengeance
US 1954 81m bw
Allied Artists (Lindsley Parsons)

An innocent man is released from jail and seeks vengeance against the man who framed him and killed his wife and child.
Adequate toughie with no particular flair.

w Warren Douglas, George Brinker *d* Mark Stevens *ph* William Sickner *m* Paul Dunlap

Mark Stevens, Martha Hyer, Skip Homeier, Joan Vohs, Douglas Kennedy

Cry Wolf
US 1947 83m bw
Warner (Henry Blanke)

A widow claims her husband's estate and finds his mysterious uncle very difficult to deal with . . .
Rather obvious old dark house mystery with a not very interesting solution, all relying too heavily on star performances.

w Catherine Turney, *novel* Marjorie Carleton *d* Peter Godfrey *ph* Carl Guthrie *m* Franz Waxman

Barbara Stanwyck, Errol Flynn (as the apparent heavy), Geraldine Brooks, Richard Basehart, Helene Thimig

Cry Wolf
GB 1980 31m bw

A scientist accidentally imbibes a canine serum and turns into a werewolf. Flattish comedy which is mainly indistinguishable from the low-budget British shockers it satirizes, but manages a few good moments. Paul Maxwell, Rosalind Ayres, Stephen Greif. Written by Stan Hey; directed by Leszek Burzynski; photographed by Robert Krasker; for Picture Partnership / Paramount.

The Crystal Ball*
US 1943 82m bw
(Richard Blumenthal)

A failed beauty contestant becomes a fortune teller and is involved in a land swindle.
Pleasant comedy with fanciful moments, ending with a pie-throwing contest.

w Virginia Van Upp *d* Elliott Nugent *ph* Leo Tover *m* Victor Young

Paulette Goddard, Ray Milland, Gladys George, Virginia Field, Cecil Kellaway, William Bendix, Ernest Truex

Cuba
US 1979 122m Technicolor
UA / Alex Winitsky, Arlene Sellers

Upper-crust characters are caught in Havana when the Castro revolution starts.
Aimless romantic melodrama which gets absolutely nowhere and might have been better played in the *Casablanca* vein.

w Charles Wood *d* Richard Lester *ph* David Watkin *m* Patrick Williams *pd* Gil Parrando

Sean Connery, Brooke Adams, Jack Weston, Hector Elizondo, Denholm Elliott, Martin Balsam, Chris Sarandon

Cuba Si!*
France 1961 58m bw
Films de la Pléïade

A documentary on the Cuban revolution and Castro's rise to power.
Remarkable and influential at the time for its use of techniques which are now the commonplaces of television, this documentary still has its flashes of interest.

wd, ph Chris Marker m E. G. Mantici, J. Calzada *ed* Eva Zora

'An eloquent, personal record of history in the making.'—*Georges Sadoul*

Cuban Love Song
US 1931 86m bw
MGM (Albert Lewin)

A marine on leave in Cuba falls in love; years later he returns to retrieve his illegitimate child, whose mother has died.
Pathetic musical melodrama which did not advance its singing star's film career.

w John Lynch *d* W. S. Van Dyke *ph* Harold Rosson *songs* various *m* Charles Maxwell

Lawrence Tibbett, Lupe Velez, Jimmy Durante, Ernest Torrence, Karen Morley, Louise Fazenda

'Tibbett may be a sensation on the concert stage, but it's not the same in pictures.'—*Variety*

Cuban Pete
US 1946 61m bw

A Cuban orchestra leader comes to New York. Flatfooted second feature introducing the gentleman who later married Lucille Ball. Desi Arnaz, Joan Fulton, Beverly Simmons, Don Porter. Written by Robert Presnell Snr, M. Coates Webster; directed by Jean Yarbrough; for Will Cowan / Universal. 'Dull pace and few chuckles.'—*Variety*

A Cuckoo in the Nest*
GB 1933 85m bw
Gaumont (Ian Dalrymple, Angus MacPhail)

A newlywed husband is forced to spend a night at an inn with an old flame pretending to be his wife.
Classic Aldwych farce with the stage company in excellent form; directorial style on the stagey side.

w Ben Travers, A. R. Rawlinson, *play Ben Travers d* Tom Walls *ph* Glen MacWilliams

Ralph Lynn, Tom Walls, Yvonne Arnaud, Mary Brough, Veronica Rose, Gordon James, Cecil Parker, Roger Livesey, Robertson Hare

† Remade 1955 as *Fast and Loose.*

The Cuckoos
US 1930 90m bw (Technicolor sequences)

Two tramps become fortune tellers. The most ambitiously staged, and probably the most popular of this team's gag marathons. Bert Wheeler, Robert Woolsey, Jobyna Howland, June Clyde, Hugh Trevor, Dorothy Lee. Written by Cy Woods from the musical comedy The Ramblers by Philip H. Goodman; directed by Paul Sloane; for RKO. 'It holds little between the laughs and doesn't need anything else.'—*Variety*

Cujo
US 1983 91m CFI colour

A St Bernard dog is bitten by a rabies-infected bat, and becomes a vicious killer. Not much of a basis for a horror film, and this is not much of a horror film. Dee Wallace, Daniel-Hugh Kelly, Danny Pintauro, Ed Lauter, Christopher Stone. Written by Don Carlos Dunaway, Lauren Currier, from the novel by Stephen King; directed by Lewis Teague; for Sunn Classic / Taft.

Cul de Sac
GB 1966 111m bw
Compton–Tekli (Gene Gutowski)

Two gangsters on the run take refuge in an old castle on a desolate Northumbrian island, but find their nemesis in the effeminate owner and his voluptuous wife.
Overlong, eccentric black comedy, more perplexing than entertaining.

w Roman Polanski, Gerard Brach *d* Roman Polanski *ph* Gilbert Taylor *m* Komeda

Lionel Stander, Donald Pleasence, Jack MacGowran, Françoise Dorléac, William Franklyn, Robert Dorning, Renée Houston

The Culpeper Cattle Company*
US 1972 92m De Luxe
TCF (Paul A. Helmick)

A 16-year-old would-be cowboy joins a cattle trail but is shocked at the harsh realities of western life.
Excellent moody photography helps to convince us that the old west was really like this, but the story is more brutal than interesting.

w Eric Bercovici, Gregory Prentiss *d* Dick Richards *ph Lawrence Edward Williams, Ralph Woolsey* *m* Tom Scott, Jerry Goldsmith

Gary Grimes, Billy 'Green' Bush, Luke Askew, Bo Hopkins, Geoffrey Lewis, Wayne Sutherlin

Cult of the Cobra
US 1955 79m bw

Six GIs are cursed by the high priest of an Indian cobra cult. Back in New York, a mysterious woman brings about their deaths, and when the survivor kills a cobra, it turns into her. Glossy but wholly unconvincing and unexciting non-horror potboiler. Faith Domergue, Richard Long, Marshall Thompson, Kathleen Hughes, Jack Kelly. Written by Jerry Davis, Cecil Maiden and Richard Collins; directed by Francis D. Lyon; for Universal-International.

A Cup of Kindness
GB 1934 81m bw

Young lovers marry despite parental disapproval on both sides. Farcical updating of *Romeo and Juliet*; it hasn't worn too well, but the stars are at their peak. Tom Walls, Ralph Lynn, Robertson Hare, Claude Hulbert, Dorothy Hyson, Eva Moore. Written by Ben Travers, from his play; directed by Tom Walls; for Michael Balcon / Gaumont.

The Cure****
US 1917 20m approx bw silent
Mutual / Charles Chaplin

A dipsomaniac sent to a spa gets his booze mixed up with the spa water.
One of the funniest of the Chaplin shorts, with no pathos intervening (nor come to that much plot); it is simply a succession of balletic slapstick scenes of the highest order.

wd Charles Chaplin *ph* William C. Foster, Rollie Totheroh

Charles Chaplin, Edna Purviance, Eric Campbell, Henry Bergman

The Cure*
GB 1950 18m bw

A health nut tries every possible remedy for lumbago. Richard Massingham huffs and puffs in his endearing way through a short which is too long by far to be effective in his particular vein; but it does identify his particular persona. Written, directed and produced by Richard and Betty Massingham (with Michael Law).

The Cure for Love
GB 1949 98m bw
London Films (Robert Donat)

An ex-soldier goes home and tries to get married.
Thin Lancashire comedy which seemed an astonishing choice for Robert Donat, whose acting and direction are equally ill at ease.

w Robert Donat, Alexander Shaw, Albert Fennell, *play* Walter Greenwood *d* Robert Donat *ph* Jack Cox *m* William Alwyn

Robert Donat, Renée Asherson, Dora Bryan, Marjorie Rhodes, Charles Victor, Thora Hird, Gladys Henson
'Antediluvian regional farce.'—*MFB*

Curly Top*
US 1935 78m bw
TCF (Darryl F. Zanuck, Winfield Sheehan)

An orphan waif is adopted by a playboy, and not only sets his business right but fixes his romantic interest in her sister.
Archetypal Temple vehicle, a loose remake of *Daddy Longlegs*.

w Patterson McNutt, Arthur Beckhard *d* Irving Cummings *ph* John Seitz *songs* Ray Henderson, Ted Koehler, Edward Heyman, Irving Caesar

Shirley Temple, John Boles, Rochelle Hudson, Jane Darwell, Rafaela Ottiano, Esther Dale, Arthur Treacher, Etienne Girardot
'Cinch b.o. for almost any house.'—*Variety*

'The creature created by man is forgotten by nature!'
The Curse of Frankenstein**
GB 1957 83m Eastmancolor
Warner / Hammer (Anthony Hinds)

A lurid revamping of the 1931 *Frankenstein*, this time with severed eyeballs and a peculiarly unpleasant and uncharacterized creature, all in gory colour. It set the trend in nasty horrors from which we have all suffered since, and launched Hammer Studios on a long and profitable career of charnelry. But it did have a gruesome sense of style.

w Jimmy Sangster *d Terence Fisher* *ph* Jack Asher *m James Bernard* *ad* Ted Marshall

Peter Cushing, Christopher Lee, Hazel Court, Robert Urquhart, Valerie Gaunt, Noel Hood

'A tender tale of terror!'
The Curse of the Cat People*
US 1944 70m bw
RKO (*Val Lewton*)

A child is haunted by the spirit of the cat people.
A gentle film ordered by the studio as a sequel to *Cat People* but turned by Lewton into a fantasy of childhood. Slow to start but finally compelling, it's a pleasing and unusual film in a minor key.

w De Witt Bodeen *d* Robert Wise, Gunther Fritsch *ph* Nicholas Musuraca *m* Roy Webb

Kent Smith, Simone Simon, Jane Randolph, Julia Dean, Ann Carter, Elizabeth Russell
'Full of the poetry and danger of childhood.'—*James Agee*
'A clumsy coming together of unrealized ideas, gothic effects, and stiff, dull acting.'—*New Yorker, 1979*

Curse of the Crimson Altar
GB 1968 89m Eastmancolor
Tigon / AIP (Tony Tenser)
aka: *The Crimson Cult*

Witchcraft, diabolism and mystery in an English country house.
A derivative, muddled scribble of a horror film, making no sense and wasting much talent.

w Mervyn Haisman, Henry Lincoln *d* Vernon Sewell *ph* John Coquillon *m* Peter Knight

Boris Karloff, Christopher Lee, Rupert Davies, Mark Eden, Barbara Steele, Michael Gough

'Entombed for eons—turned to stone—seeking women, women, women!'
Curse of the Faceless Man
US 1958 67m bw

An encrusted man, found in the earth near Pompeii, is revived and goes on the rampage, but is eventually dissolved by water. Absurd chiller with the saving grace of not taking itself seriously. Richard Anderson, Elaine Edwards, Adele Mara, Gary Moore, Felix Locher. Written by Jerome Boxby; directed by Edward L. Cahn; for Vogue / United Artists.

Curse of the Living Corpse
US 1963 78m bw

A millionaire vows to return and kill all his relatives if he is buried alive, which he is . . . Gothic cheapie made in Stamford, Connecticut, where they have little experience of such things. Roy Scheider, Candace Hillgoss. Written, directed and produced by Del Tenney; for TCF.

'Half bone, half bandage . . . all blood-curdling terror!'
Curse of the Mummy's Tomb
GB 1964 80m Technicolor Techniscope
Columbia / Hammer (Michael Carreras)

An Egyptian mummy taken to London goes on the rampage, and meets its own wicked brother who has been cursed to eternal life.
Absurd farrago which takes too long to set up its plot and then finds little to do with its monster.

w Henry Younger (Michael Carreras) *d* Michael Carreras *ph* Otto Heller *m* Carlo Martelli

Ronald Howard, Terence Morgan, *Fred Clark*, Jeanne Roland, George Pastell, Jack Gwyllim, John Paul

Curse of the Pink Panther
GB 1983 110m Technicolor Panavision
MGM-UA / Titan / Jewel (Blake Edwards, Gerald T. Nutting)

Inspector Clouseau has disappeared, and Dreyfus selects the world's worst detective to replace him.
Unspeakably awful attempt at prolonging a series whose star died two episodes ago. Crude, tasteless and unfunny throughout.

w Blake Edwards, Geoffrey Edwards *d* Blake Edwards *ph* Dick Bush *pd* Peter Mullins *m* Henry Mancini

Ted Wass, Joanna Lumley, Herbert Lom, David Niven, Robert Wagner, Capucine, Harvey Korman, Burt Kwouk

'Another bout of film-making as grave robbing.'—*Sight and Sound*

'The ultimate version of deadpan humour . . . the most tedious of the whole series.'—*Richard Combs, MFB*

Curse of the Undead
US 1959 79m bw

A black-clad stranger in a western town turns out to be a vampire of Spanish origin.
Abysmal attempt to substitute Wyoming for Transylvania; more skill and sensitivity were required. Michael Pate, Eric Fleming, Kathleen Crowley, John Hoyt. Written and directed by Edward Dein; for Universal-International.

'He had but one body—yet lived with two souls!'

Curse of the Werewolf
GB 1961 92m Technicolor
U-I / Hammer (Anthony Hinds)

A beggar rapes a servant girl and their offspring grows up to be a werewolf.
Doleful Hammer horror in a Spanish setting, with an absurd but predictable plot and a lack of sympathy for its fancy, hairy hero.

w John Elder (Anthony Hinds) *d* Terence Fisher *ph* Arthur Grant *m* Benjamin Frankel

Oliver Reed, Clifford Evans, Catherine Feller, Yvonne Romain, Anthony Dawson, Richard Wordsworth, Warren Mitchell

The Curse of the Wraydons
GB 1946 94m bw

The Victorian story of Spring-heeled Jack, here depicted as a mad inventor out for revenge. Too long and stagey to be one of its star's better barnstormers, especially as by this time his girth made the notion of his springing about somewhat hilarious. Tod Slaughter, Bruce Seton, Gabriel Toyne. Written by Michael Barringer; directed by Victor M. Gover; for Bushey.

Curtain Call*
US 1940 63m bw
RKO

Two Broadway producers buy an awful play in order to get even with a temperamental star, but she likes it.
Amusing second feature, a kind of flashforward to *The Producers*. A reprise the following year, *Footlight Fever*, did not work.

w Dalton Trumbo *d* Frank Woodruff *ph* Russell Metty *m* Roy Webb

Alan Mowbray, Donald MacBride, Helen Vinson, Barbara Read, John Archer

Curtain Call at Cactus Creek*
US 1949 83m Technicolor
U-I (Robert Arthur)
GB title: *Take the Stage*

A travelling repertory company in the old west exposes a gang of bank robbers.
Cheerful minor comedy with good pace and amusing burlesques of old melodramas.

w Oscar Brodney *d* Charles Lamont *ph* Russell Metty *m* Walter Scharf

Donald O'Connor, Gale Storm, Eve Arden, Vincent Price, Walter Brennan, Chick Chandler

Curtain Up*
GB 1952 85m bw
Rank / Constellation (Robert Garrett)

A seaside repertory company runs into trouble when the producer is at loggerheads with the author of next week's play.
Fairly amusing farce which has now acquired historical value for the light it throws on the old weekly reps.

w Michael Pertwee, Jack Davies, *play* On Monday Next by Philip King *d* Ralph Smart *ph* Stanley Pavey *m* Malcolm Arnold

Margaret Rutherford, Robert Morley, Olive Sloane, Joan Rice, Charlotte Mitchell, Kay Kendall, Liam Gaffney, Michael Medwin

Curucu, Beast of the Amazon
US 1956 76m colour

Amazon explorers set out to find a man masquerading as a monster. Rubbishy hokum, for tolerant kids. John Bromfield, Beverly Garland, Tom Payne. Written and directed by Curt Siodmak; for Universal.

Custer of the West
US 1967 146m Super Technirama 70
Cinerama / Security (Louis Dolivet, Philip Yordan, Irving Lerner)

After the Civil War, Custer is offered a cavalry command, becomes disillusioned, and is massacred with his troops at Little Big Horn.
Gloomily inaccurate spectacular with pauses for Cinerama carnival thrills and dour bits of melodrama.

w Bernard Gordon, Julian Halevy *d* Robert Siodmak *ph* Cecilio Paniagua *m* Bernardo Segall

Robert Shaw, Mary Ure, Robert Ryan, Jeffrey Hunter, Ty Hardin, Lawrence Tierney, Kieron Moore

Custer's Last Stand
US 1936 bw serial: 15 eps

An Indian brave is involved in a search for gold while trying to warn Custer of the danger at Little Big Horn. Fanciful western serial without much excitement. Custer does not appear. Rex Lease, William Farnum, Reed Howes, Jack Mulhall. Directed by Elmer Clifton; for Stage and Screen.

Cutter and Bone
US 1981 109m Technicolor
United Artists / Gurian
GB title: *Cutter's Way*

A California failure witnesses the aftermath of murder, and with a crippled ex-Vietnam veteran turns detective.
Heavy-going melodrama which tries very hard to be something more than a thriller, and manages only to imply that the world stinks; so it might as well have stuck to Philip Marlowe.

w Jeffrey Alan Fiskin, *novel* Newton Thornburg *d* Ivan Passer *ph* Jordan Cronenweth *m* Jack Nitzsche *ed* Caroline Ferriol

Jeff Bridges, John Heard, Lisa Eichhorn, Ann Dusenberry, Stephen Elliott, Nina Van Pallandt

The Cyclops
US 1956 65m bw
B and H (Bert I. Gordon)

Explorers in Mexico find animals turned by radiation into monsters, plus a one-eyed 25-foot-tall human.
Modest monster movie, quite palatable of its kind.

wd Bert I. Gordon *ph* Ira Morgan *m* Albert Glasser

James Craig, Lon Chaney Jnr, Gloria Talbot, Tom Drake

Cynara**
US 1933 78m bw
Samuel Goldwyn

A London barrister has an affair with a young girl who commits suicide when he goes back to his wife.
Solidly carpentered, effective star vehicle of the old school, now dated but preserving its dignity.

w Frances Marion, Lynn Starling, *novel* An Imperfect Lover by Robert Gore Brown *d* King Vidor *ph* Ray June *m* Alfred Newman

Ronald Colman, Kay Francis, Phyllis Barry, *Henry Stephenson*, Paul Porcasi

'The values it involves are wholly unlike those which US audiences are usually called upon to comprehend.'—*Time*

Cynthia
US 1947 98m bw
MGM (Edwin H. Knopf)
GB title: *The Rich Full Life*

An over-protected girl finds an outlet in music and her parents finally allow her to lead her own life.
An overlong domestic drama in which thin writing and acting are backed by unsound psychology.

w Harold Buchman, Charles Kaufman, *play* Vina Delmar *d* Robert Z. Leonard *ph* Charles Schoenbaum *m* Bronislau Kaper

Elizabeth Taylor, George Murphy, Mary Astor, S. Z. Sakall, James Lydon, Gene Lockhart, Spring Byington

Cyrano de Bergerac*
US 1950 112m bw
Stanley Kramer

In the 17th century a long-nosed poet, philosopher and buffoon writes letters enabling a friend to win the lady he loves himself.

The classic romantic verse play does not take kindly to a hole-in-corner black-and-white production, but at the time it was lapped up as a daring cultural breakthrough.

w Brian Hooker, *play* Edmond Rostand *d* Michael Gordon *ph* Franz Planer *m* Dmitri Tiomkin

Jose Ferrer, Mala Powers, William Prince, Morris Carnovsky, Ralph Clanton, Virginia Farmer, Edgar Barrier, Elena Verdugo

AA: Jose Ferrer

D. C. Cab
US 1983 99m Technicolor
Cab drivers for a run-down Washington company capture kidnappers. Brainless extravaganza with aspirations somewhere between *Taxi* and *Carry On*. Mr T, Max Gail, Adam Baldwin, Charlie Barnett, Gary Busey, Gloria Gifford. Written and directed by Joel Schumacher; for Guber-Peters / RKO-Universal. (GB title: *Street Fleet*.) 'Artificial energy used to bolster wretched material.'—*Steve Jenkins, MFB*

D.O.A.**
US 1950 83m bw
(UA) Leo C. Popkin
The victim of a slow poison tracks down his own killer. Semi-classic suspense drama, sufficiently original to be remembered though the plot details become hazy.
w Russel Rouse, Clarence Greene (partly from a 1931 German film *Der Mann der seinen Mörder Sucht*) *d* Rudolph Maté *ph* Ernest Laszlo *m Dmitri Tiomkin*
Edmond O'Brien, Pamela Britton, Luther Adler, Neville Brand, Beverly Campbell
† The title is a police abbreviation for 'dead on arrival'.
†† Remade as *Colour Me Dead* (qv).

Dad Rudd films see On Our Selection

Daddy Longlegs*
US 1931 80m bw
Fox
An orphan girl grows up to fall in love with her mysterious benefactor.
Cinderella-like romance, adequately adapted from a novel which became the classic American version of the January–May romance.
w Sonya Levien, *novel* Jean Webster *d* Alfred Santell *ph* Lucien Andriot
Janet Gaynor, Warner Baxter, Una Merkel, John Arledge, Claude Gillingwater, Louise Closser Hale
'A smash . . . one of those rare talkers with universal appeal.'—*Variety*
† Other versions were made in 1919 with Mary Pickford and Mahlon Hamilton, directed by Marshal Neilan; in 1935 disguised as *Curly Top* (qv) and in 1955 (see below).

Daddy Longlegs*
US 1955 126m Technicolor
Cinemascope
TCF (Samuel G. Engel)
Overlong and unsuitably wide-screened musical version of a popular story (see above). Generally clumsy and dispirited, but Astaire is always worth watching and a couple of the dances are well staged.
w Phoebe and Henry Ephron *d* Jean Negulesco *ph* Leon Shamroy *m* Alfred Newman *songs* Johnny Mercer
Fred Astaire, Leslie Caron, *Fred Clark*, Thelma Ritter, Terry Moore, Charlotte Austin, Larry Keating
AAN: Alfred Newman; song 'Something's Gotta Give' (*m / ly* Johnny Mercer)

Daddy's Gone A-Hunting
US 1969 108m Technicolor
Warner / Red Lion (Mark Robson)
A child and its mother are threatened by her deranged ex-husband.
Unpleasant and protracted suspenser with the emphasis on sex rather than thrills.
w Larry Cohen, Lorenzo Semple Jnr *d* Mark Robson *ph* Ernest Laszlo *m* John Williams
Carol White, Paul Burke, Scott Hylands, Mala Powers, Andrea King

Dad's Army**
GB 1971 95m Technicolor
Columbia / Norcon (John R. Sloan)
Misadventures of a number of elderly gents in Britain's wartime Home Guard.
Expanded big-screen version of the long-running TV series, a pleasant souvenir but rather less effective than was expected because everything is shown—the town, the Nazis, the wives—and thus the air of gentle fantasy disappears, especially in the face of much coarsened humour.
w Jimmy Perry, David Croft *d* Norman Cohen *ph* Terry Maher *m* Wilfred Burns
Arthur Lowe, John Le Mesurier, John Laurie, James Beck, Ian Lavender, *Arnold Ridley*, Liz Fraser, *Clive Dunn*, Bill Pertwee, Frank Williams, Edward Sinclair

Daisy Kenyon
US 1947 99m bw
TCF (Otto Preminger)
A fashion designer has two men in her life. Adequate woman's picture which hardly justifies its cast.
w David Hertz, *novel* Elizabeth Janeway *d* Otto Preminger *ph* Leon Shamroy *m* David Raksin
Joan Crawford, Henry Fonda, Dana Andrews, Ruth Warrick, Martha Stewart, Peggy Ann Garner

Daisy Miller*
US 1974 92m Technicolor
Paramount / Copa de Oro (Peter Bogdanovich)
In the 19th century, an American girl tourist in Europe falls in love but dies of the Roman fever.
Curious attempt to film a very mild and uneventful Henry James story, with careful production but inadequate leads. The first sign that Bogdanovich was getting too big for his boots.
w Frederic Raphael *d* Peter Bogdanovich *ph* Alberto Spagnoli *m* classical themes *ad* Ferdinando Scarfiotti
Cybill Shepherd, Barry Brown, Cloris Leachman, Mildred Natwick, Eileen Brennan, James MacMurtry
'A historical film bereft of any feeling for history, and a literary adaptation which reveals a fine contempt for literary subtlety.'—*Jan Dawson*
'Appallingly crass . . . directed with all the subtlety of a sledgehammer.'—*Michael Billington, Illustrated London News*
'Trying to make that little thing he's with into Daisy Miller was hilarious. God almighty couldn't do that. She's so coy.'—*Henry Hathaway*

Dakota
US 1945 82m bw
Republic (Joseph Kane)
The daughter of a railroad tycoon elopes with a cowboy and becomes involved in a land war. Adequate star western.
w Lawrence Hazard, *story* Carl Foreman *d* Joseph Kane *ph* Jack Marta *m* Walter Scharf
John Wayne, Vera Hruba Ralston, Walter Brennan, Ward Bond, Ona Munson, Hugo Haas, Mike Mazurki, Paul Fix, Grant Withers, Jack La Rue

Dakota Incident
US 1956 88m bw
Strangers take cover when they are attacked by Indians. A formula older than *Stagecoach* is played out to humdrum results. Linda Darnell, Dale Robertson, Regis Toomey, John Lund, Ward Bond, Skip Homeier, Irving Bacon, John Doucette, Whit Bissell. Written by Frederic Louis Fox; directed by Lewis R. Foster; for Republic.

Daleks: Invasion Earth 2150 AD see Dr Who and the Daleks

Dallas*
US 1950 94m Technicolor
Warner (Anthony Veiller)

A renegade ex-Confederate colonel is pardoned for bringing law and order to Dallas. Routinely competent top-of-the-bill western.

w John Twist *d* Stuart Heisler *ph* Ernest Haller *m* Max Steiner

Gary Cooper, Ruth Roman, Raymond Massey, Steve Cochran, Barbara Payton, Leif Erickson, Antonio Moreno, Jerome Cowan

The Daltons Ride Again
US 1945 72m bw

An outlaw gang's last raid is complicated when one of them falls in love. Unhistorical action western with B feature appeal. Alan Curtis, Kent Taylor, Lon Chaney Jnr, Noah Beery Jnr, Martha O'Driscoll, Thomas Gomez, Milburn Stone, John Litel. Written by Roy Chanslor, Paul Ganglin; directed by Ray Taylor; for Howard Welch / Universal.

The Dam Busters**
GB 1954 125m bw
ABPC (Robert Clark)

In 1943 the Ruhr dams are destroyed by Dr Barnes Wallis' bouncing bombs.
Understated British war epic with additional scientific interest and good acting and model work, not to mention a welcome lack of love interest.

w R. C. Sheriff, books by Guy Gibson and Paul Brickhill *d* Michael Anderson *ph* Eric Hillier *m* Leighton Lucas, *Eric Coates* *sp* George Blackwell

Michael Redgrave, Richard Todd, Basil Sydney, Derek Farr, Patrick Barr, Ernest Clark, Raymond Huntley, Ursula Jeans

Damaged Goods
US 1937 56m bw

A young man infects his wife and child with syphilis. An 'awful warning' which seemed naive even at the time; there had been a silent version in 1914. Pedro de Cordoba, Douglas Walton, Arletta Duncan, Esther Dale, Phyllis Barry. Written by Upton Sinclair from the play by Eugene Brieux; directed by Phil Stone; for Grand National.

Damaged Lives
US 1937 61m (plus a 29m lecture) bw

A young man infects his wife with syphilis. One of a rival pair of moral tales (see above); both had trouble with the censors on subject matter alone. Not otherwise notable. Diane Sinclair, Lyman Williams, Cecilia Parker, George Irving, Jason Robards. Written by Donald Davis and Edgar C. Ulmer; directed by Edgar G. Ulmer; for Weldon.

Dames**
US 1934 90m bw
Warner (Robert Lord)

A millionaire purity fanatic tries to stop the opening of a Broadway show.
Typical Warner musical of the period: its real *raison d'être* is to be found in the splendidly imaginative numbers at the finale, but it also gives very full rein to the roster of comic actors under contract at the time.

w Delmer Daves *d* Ray Enright *ch Busby Berkeley ph* Sid Hickox, George Barnes *m* various

Joan Blondell, Hugh Herbert, Guy Kibbee, Zasu Pitts, Dick Powell, Ruby Keeler

'That Warners was able to fashion so zestful an entertainment under post-Haysian restrictions is a credit to the collective ingenuities of the studio artificers. . . . Swell entertainment, no matter how you slice it.'—*Variety*

† Originally intended as *Gold Diggers of 1934*.

Les Dames du Bois de Boulogne*
France 1946 90m bw
Films Raoul Ploquin

Hélène revenges herself on her bored lover by arranging for him to marry a prostitute.
Spare, symbolic melodrama which has occasioned as much irritation as applause.

w Robert Bresson, Jean Cocteau, from Diderot's Jacques Le Fataliste *d Robert Bresson ph* Philippe Agostini *m* Jean-Jacques Grunenwald

Maria Casarès, Elina Labourdette, Lucienne Bogaert, Paul Bernard

'Through abstraction, Bresson has been able to make a film in which the tragedy is implicit not only in the plot but also in the form.'—*Richard Roud, MFB, 1966*

'The first time was only a warning!'
Damien: Omen Two
US 1978 109m De Luxe Panavision
TCF (Harvey Bernhard)

The antichrist who got rid of the entire cast of *The Omen* now, as a teenager, starts in on his foster parents.
Once was enough.

w Stanley Mann, Michael Hodges *d* Don Taylor *ph* Bill Butler *m* Jerry Goldsmith

William Holden, Lee Grant, Jonathan Scott-Taylor, Robert Foxworth, Lucas Donat, Lew Ayres, Sylvia Sidney, Elizabeth Shepherd

Damn Yankees**
US 1958 110m Technicolor
Warner (George Abbott, Stanley Donen)
GB title: *What Lola Wants*

The devil interferes in the fortunes of a failing baseball team.
Smartly-styled but very American musical based on *Faust*; brilliant moments but some tedium.

w George Abbott, *novel* Douglas Wallop *d* George Abbott, Stanley Donen *ph Harold Lipstein m / ly* Richard Adler, Jerry Ross *md* Ray Heindorf

Gwen Verdon, Tab Hunter, Ray Walston, Russ Brown, Shannon Bolin

AAN: Ray Heindorf

Damnation Alley
US 1977 95m De Luxe
TCF / Hal Landers, Bobby Roberts, Jerome M. Zeitman

Four survivors from World War Three try to reach a colony of fellow-survivors in New York.
Feeble attempt at a low-budget blockbuster.

w Alan Sharp, Lukas Heller, *novel* Roger Zelazny *d* Jack Smight *ph* Harry Stradling Jnr *m* Jerry Goldsmith *pd* Preston Ames

Jan-Michael Vincent, George Peppard, Dominique Sanda, Paul Winfield

The Damned*
France 1947 105m bw
Speva Film
original title: *Les Maudits*

In 1945 fanatical Nazis escape in a submarine but make the mistake of stopping to sink a freighter.
Unusual melodrama with a brilliant sense of claustrophobia, good characterization and much suspense.

w Jacques Remy, René Clément, Henri Jeanson *d René Clément ph* Henri Alekan *m* Yves Baudrier

Paul Bernard, Henri Vidal, Marcel Dalio, Michel Auclair, Florence Marly

The Damned*
GB 1961 87m bw Hammerscope
Columbia / Hammer–Swallow (Anthony Hinds)
US title: *These Are the Damned*

A scientist keeps radioactive children in a cliff cave, sealed off from the world's corruption.
Absurdly pompous, downcast and confused sci-fi melodrama set in Weymouth, with a secondary plot about motor-cycling thugs.

w Evan Jones, *novel* The Children of Light by H. L. Lawrence *d* Joseph Losey *ph* Arthur Grant *m* James Bernard

Macdonald Carey, Shirley Ann Field, Alexander Knox, Viveca Lindfors, Oliver Reed, Walter Gotell, James Villiers

'A *folie de grandeur*.'—*Tom Milne*

'Out of this wild mishmash some really magnificent images loom.'—*John Coleman*

The Damned**
West Germany / Italy 1969 164m Eastmancolor
Praesidens / Pegaso
original title: *Götterdämmerung*

A family of German industrialists divides and destroys itself under Nazi influence.
A film which has been called baroque, Wagnerian, and just plain unpleasant; it is also rather a strain to watch, with exaggerated colour and make-up to match the rotting theme.

w Nicola Badalucco, Enrico Medioli, Luchino Visconti *d Luchino Visconti ph* Armando Nannuzzi, Pasquale de Santis *m* Maurice Jarre *ad* Enzo del Prato, Pasquale Romano

Dirk Bogarde, Ingrid Thulin, Helmut Berger, Renaud Verley, Helmut Griem, René Kolldehof, Albrecht Schönhals, Umberto Orsini

'One is left lamenting that such a quondam master of realism as Visconti is making his films look like operas from which the score has been inexplicably removed.'—*MFB*

THE DAMNED. Briton Dirk Bogarde looks ill at ease among the Nazi trappings, although he is playing a German.

'The ludicrous flailings of puny puppets in inscrutable wooden frenzies.'—*John Simon*

AAN: script

'The private lady of a public enemy!'

The Damned Don't Cry
US 1950 103m bw
Warner (Jerry Wald)

A middle-class housewife leaves her husband for a gambler, and becomes involved with gangsters, but eventually reforms.
Rather dreary stimulation for female audiences who like safe dreams of danger.

w Harold Medford, Jerome Weidman, *novel* Case History by Gertrude Walker *d* Vincent Sherman *ph* Ted McCord *m* Daniele Amfitheatrof

Joan Crawford, Kent Smith, David Brian, Steve Cochran, Hugh Sanders, Selena Royle, Morris Ankrum, Richard Egan

'The private lady of a public enemy!'—*publicity*

'Mad adventure! Daring deeds! White hot love with music!'

A Damsel in Distress*
US 1937 101m bw
RKO (Pandro S. Berman)

An American dancing star falls for an aristocratic young Englishwoman.
Astaire without Rogers, but the style is the same and there are some very good numbers.

w P. G. Wodehouse, S. K. Lauren, Ernest Pagano *d* George Stevens *ph* Joseph H. August *m / ly* George and Ira Gershwin *ch* Hermes Pan

Fred Astaire, George Burns, Gracie Allen, Joan Fontaine, Reginald Gardiner, Constance Collier, Ray Noble, Montagu Love

'Plenty for the b.o.—dancing, comedy, marquee values, the usual sumptuous investiture accorded by Pandro Berman, and those Gershwin songs.'—*Variety*

† Rogers had demanded a break from musicals, so she was replaced by the demure Miss Fontaine, who was generally thought disappointing.

Dance Band
GB 1935 75m bw

A band leader who croons falls for the boss of an all-ladies orchestra. Fairly slick light musical fare of its period. Buddy Rogers, June Clyde, Fred Duprez, Richard Hearne, Steve Geray, Magda Kun. Written by Roger Burford; directed by Marcel Varnel; for BIP.
'Popular entertainment from start to finish, cut to a point where there is hardly a draggy moment.'—*Variety*

Dance Fools Dance
US 1931 82m bw
MGM

A lady reporter in Chicago proves her worth.
Bizarrely-titled gangster thriller based on the Jake Lingle killing. Very moderate of its kind.

w Richard Schayer, Aurania Rouverol *d* Harry Beaumont *ph* Charles Rosher

Joan Crawford, Lester Vail, Cliff Edwards, William Bakewell, William Holden (the other one), Clark Gable, Earle Foxe, Joan Marsh

'It will rock the b.o. . . . sex, romance, punch, suspense, and everything a deluxer can sell.'—*Variety*

Dance Girl Dance*
US 1940 88m bw
RKO (Erich Pommer)

Private problems of the members of a nightclub dance troupe.
Competent and sometimes interesting formula drama with a harder edge than usual.

w Tess Slesinger, Frank Davis, *story* Vicki Baum *d Dorothy Arzner ph* Russell Metty *m* Edward Ward

Maureen O'Hara, Louis Hayward, Lucille Ball, Maria Ouspenskaya, Ralph Bellamy, Virginia Field, Mary Carlisle, Walter Abel, Edward Brophy, Harold Huber

Dance Hall
US 1941 73m bw

A ballroom singer is chased by the manager. Slim romantic drama. Carole Landis, Cesar Romero, J. Edward Bromberg, William Henry, June Storey, Charles Halton. Written by Stanley Rauh, Ethel Hill from a novel by W. R. Burnett; directed by Irving Pichel; for Sol M. Wurtzel/TCF.

Dance Hall*
GB 1950 80m bw
Ealing (E. V. H. Emmett)

Four factory girls seek relaxation and various kinds of romance at the local palais.
Untypically flat Ealing slice of life, now watchable only with a smile as musical nostalgia.

w E. V. H. Emmett, Diana Morgan, Alexander Mackendrick *d* Charles Crichton *ph* Douglas Slocombe *md* Ernest Irving

Natasha Parry, Donald Houston, Diana Dors, Bonar Colleano, Jane Hylton, Petula Clark, Gladys Henson, Sydney Tafler; the bands of Geraldo and Ted Heath

Dance Little Lady
GB 1954 87m Eastmancolor

An ambitious man tries to turn his balletomane daughter into a film star. Artless melodrama in poor colour. Terence Morgan, Mai Zetterling, Mandy Miller, Guy Rolfe, Eunice Gayson. Written by Val Guest and Doreen Montgomery; directed by Val Guest; for George Minter / Renown.

The Dance of Death*
GB 1968 149m Technicolor
BHE / National Theatre (John Brabourne)

Edgar and Alice live alone on an island, their marriage having become a constant war.
Too-literal film transcription of an applauded theatrical production, with the camera anchored firmly in the middle of the stalls.

w August Strindberg (*translation* by C. D. Locock) *d* David Giles *ph* Geoffrey Unsworth

Laurence Olivier, Geraldine McEwan, Robert Lang, Carolyn Jones

Dance Pretty Lady
GB 1932 64m bw

Ballerina loves artist but settles unwisely for respectability. Stilted early talkie from Compton Mackenzie's *Carnival*, qv under its own title. Ann Casson, Carl Harbord, Michael Hogan. Written and directed by Anthony Asquith; for H. Bruce Woolfe / British Instructional.

Dance Team
US 1931 80m bw

Struggles of a couple to become top ballroom dancers. Easy-going star fare which needed tightening. James Dunn, Sally Eilers, Minna Gombell, Ralph Morgan. Written by Edwin Burke from the novel by Sarah Addington; directed by Sidney Lanfield; for Fox. 'Its comedy overcomes drawn-out sequences laden with sentimentality.'—*Variety*

Dance with a Stranger*
GB 1985 101m Technicolor
Goldcrest / NFFC / First Picture Co (Roger Randall-Cutler)

Ex-prostitute Ruth Ellis, infatuated with a worthless sponger, shoots him dead rather than lose him.
Muddled account of the last woman to hang in Great Britain: no sympathies are aroused and no clear viewpoint taken.

w Shelagh Delaney *d* Mike Newell *ph* Peter Hannan *m* Richard Hartley *pd* Andrew Mollo *ed* Mick Audsley

Miranda Richardson, Rupert Everett, Ian Holm, Matthew Carroll, Stratford Johns

Dancers in the Dark
US 1932 76m bw

A taxi dancer with a shady past tries to prove that she's really in love. Banal show business melodrama with authentic-seeming nightclub background. Miriam Hopkins, Jack Oakie, George Raft, William Collier Jnr, Lyda Roberti, Eugene Pallette. Written by Herman J. Mankiewicz; directed by David Burton; for Paramount. 'Only fair for Times Square, looks surefire in the hinterland.'—*Variety*

Dancing Co-ed
US 1939 90m bw
MGM (Edgar Selwyn)
GB title: *Every Other Inch a Lady*

A college girl makes it in show business as well as the groves of academe.
Mindless vehicle for a 19-year-old star.

w Albert Mannheimer, *story* Albert Treynor *d* S. Sylvan Simon *ph* Alfred Gilks *m* David Snell, Edward Ward

Lana Turner, Richard Carlson, Artie Shaw, *Leon Errol*, Ann Rutherford, Lee Bowman, Monty Woolley, Roscoe Karns, June Preisser, Walter Kingsford

'Better than average programme entertainment.'—*Variety*

Dancing in the Dark*
US 1949 92m Technicolor
TCF (George Jessel)

A silent movie idol makes a comeback as a talent scout, and spots his own daughter.
Thin but unusual Hollywood drama with music; in the long run too sentimental.

w Mary C. McCall Jnr, *play* The Band Wagon by George F. Kaufman, Howard Dietz, Arthur Schwarz *d* Irving Reis *ph* Harry Jackson *m* Alfred Newman

William Powell, Adolphe Menjou, Mark Stevens, Betsy Drake, Hope Emerson, Lloyd Corrigan, Walter Catlett, Jean Hersholt

Dancing Lady*
US 1933 94m bw
MGM (David O. Selznick)

A successful dancer chooses between a playboy and her stage manager.
Routine backstage semi-musical with interesting talent applied rather haphazardly.

w Allen Rivkin, P. J. Wolfson, *novel* James Warner Bellah *d* Robert Z. Leonard *ph* Oliver T. Marsh *m* various *md* Louis Silvers

Joan Crawford, Clark Gable, *Fred Astaire*, Franchot Tone, May Robson, Ted Healy and his Stooges (the Three Stooges), Winnie Lightner, Robert Benchley, Nelson Eddy

'Very potent b.o. in the screen musical cycle.'—*Variety*

The Dancing Masters
US 1943 63m bw
TCF (Lee Marcus)

Laurel and Hardy run a ballet school, and get involved with gangsters and inventors.
Insubstantial star comedy featuring reworkings of old routines, and a back-projected runaway bus climax.

w Scott Darling, George Bricker *d* Mal St Clair *ph* Norbert Brodine *m* Arthur Lange

Stan Laurel, Oliver Hardy, Trudy Marshall, Bob Bailey, Margaret Dumont, Matt Briggs, Robert Mitchum

Dancing with Crime
GB 1947 83m bw

A dance hall is the front for black marketeers, who are exposed by a resourceful taxi driver. Tolerable post-war melodrama aping Hollywood. Richard Attenborough, Barry K. Barnes, Sheila Sim, Garry Marsh, John Warwick, Barry Jones. Written by Brock Williams; directed by John Paddy Carstairs; for Coronet-Alliance.

The Dancing Years
GB 1949 97m Technicolor
ABPC (Warwick Ward)

A composer loves a singer who leaves him after a misunderstanding but later bears his son . . . all in the Alps pre-1914.
Lamentable transcription of an operetta; precisely the ingredients which worked so well on stage seem embarrassing on film, and the performances and direction do not help.

w Warwick Ward, Jack Whittingham, from Ivor Novello's operetta *d* Harold French *ph* Stephen Dade *m Ivor Novello*

Dennis Price, Gisèle Préville, Patricia Dainton, Anthony Nicholls, Grey Blake, Muriel George, Olive Gilbert

Dandy Dick
GB 1935 72m bw

A country vicar becomes innocently involved with racehorse doping. Flatly-handled farce which helped to introduce Will Hay to the screen, though not in his accustomed role; with Nancy Burne, Esmond Knight, Davy Burnaby. Written by William Beaudine, Frank Miller, Clifford Grey and Will Hay, from the play by Sir Arthur Wing Pinero; directed by William Beaudine; for BIP.

'His mission is murder! His victim—himself!'
A Dandy in Aspic
GB 1968 107m Technicolor Panavision
Columbia (Anthony Mann)

A double agent in Berlin is given orders to kill himself.
Muddled, pretentious spy thriller; flat, nebulous and boring.

w Derek Marlowe, from his novel *d* Anthony Mann *ph* Christopher Challis *m* Quincy Jones

Laurence Harvey, Tom Courtenay, Lionel Stander, Mia Farrow, Harry Andrews, Peter Cook, Per Oscarsson

† Anthony Mann died during shooting, and Laurence Harvey completed the direction.

Dandy the All-American Girl
US 1976 90m Metrocolor Panavision

A much convicted woman car thief determines to become the legitimate owner of a Dino Ferrari. The American dream gone sour again, this time offering in its wake a curious stream of moral values. Stockard Channing, Sam Waterston, Richard Doughty, Franklin Ajaye. Written by B. J. Perla and Marilyn Goldin; directed by Jerry Schatzberg; for MGM. (GB title: *Sweet Revenge*.)

Danger: Diabolik
Italy / France 1967 105m Technicolor
Dino de Laurentiis / Marianne (Bruno Todini)

International police bait a golden trap for a master criminal.
Superior Batman-type adventures with a comic strip hero-villain.

w Dino Maiuri, Adriano Baracco, Mario Bava *d* Mario Bava *ph* Antonio Rinaldi *m* Ennio Morricone

John Phillip Law, Marisa Mell, Michel Piccoli, Adolfo Celi, Terry-Thomas

Danger Island
US 1931 bw serial: 12 eps

A radium deposit on an African island attracts adventurers of all kinds. Modest serial excitements. Kenneth Harlan, Lucile Browne, Tom Rickells. Directed by Ray Taylor; for Universal.

Danger Lights*
US 1930 87m bw

Railroad owners face various problems.
Routine would-be thriller intended to show off a wide screen system called Spoor-Bergen Natural Vision; it failed owing to cost and the thin quality of the film. Louis Wolheim, Robert Armstrong, Jean Arthur, Hugh Herbert. Written by James Ashmore Creelman, Hugh Herbert; directed by George B. Seitz; for RKO.

Danger, Love at Work*
US 1937 84m bw
TCF (Harold Wilson)

A young lawyer needs the signature of a rich crazy family to conclude a land sale.
The title doesn't suggest it, but this is a not inconsiderable comedy in the tradition of *My Man Godfrey* and *You Can't Take It With You.* A highly competent cast does its best.

w James Edward Grant, Ben Markson *d* Otto Preminger *ph* Virgil Miller *md* David Buttolph

Ann Sothern, Jack Haley, Edward Everett Horton, Mary Boland, Walter Catlett, John Carradine, Maurice Cass, Alan Dinehart, E. E. Clive

'Not important enough to be a main feature but a very good dualler.'—*Variety*

Danger Route
GB 1967 92m De Luxe
UA / Amicus (Max J. Rosenberg, Milton Subotsky)

An 'eliminator' for the British secret service finds after a series of adventures that he must dispose of his own girl friend.
Dour sub-Bondian thriller with little to commend it.

w Meade Roberts, *novel* The Eliminator by Andrew York *d* Seth Holt *ph* Harry Waxman *m* John Mayer

Richard Johnson, Diana Dors, Sylvia Syms, Carol Lynley, Barbara Bouchet, Gordon Jackson, Sam Wanamaker, Maurice Denham, Harry Andrews

Danger Signal
US 1945 77m bw

A smooth heel implicated in murder charms a modest stenographer and her mother. Tedious and less than competent melodrama. Faye Emerson, Zachary Scott, Dick Erdman, Rosemary de Camp, Bruce Bennett, Mona Freeman. Written by Adele Comandini and Graham Baker, from novel by Phyllis Bottome; directed by Robert Florey; for William Jacobs / Warner.

'Four hundred plan to escape—one plans to betray!'

Danger Within**
GB 1958 101m bw
British Lion / Colin Lesslie
US title: *Breakout*

Escape plans of officers in a prisoner-of-war camp are threatened by an informer.
Familiar comedy and melodrama with an added whodunnit element, smartly handled and very entertaining.

w Bryan Forbes, Frank Harvey, novel Michael Gilbert *d Don Chaffey ph* Arthur Grant *m* Francis Chagrin

Richard Todd, Bernard Lee, Michael Wilding, Richard Attenborough, Dennis Price, Donald Houston, William Franklyn, Vincent Ball, Peter Arne

Dangerous*
US 1935 78m bw
Warner (Harry Joe Brown)

An alcoholic actress is rehabilitated.
Unconvincing and only adequately handled melodrama which won the star her first Oscar, presumably from sympathy at her losing it the previous year for *Of Human Bondage.*

w Laird Doyle *d* Alfred E. Green *ph* Ernest Haller

Bette Davis, Franchot Tone, Margaret Lindsay, Alison Skipworth, John Eldridge, Dick Foran

'Well-acted and directed drama with *femme* appeal.'—*Variety*

† Remade 1941 as *Singapore Woman.*

AA: Bette Davis

Dangerous Blondes
US 1943 81m bw

A detective story writer and his wife solve a real life murder. More Thin Man imitations, rather tepid this time. Allyn Joslyn, Evelyn Keyes, John Hubbard, Edmund Lowe, Anita Louise, Frank Craven, William Demarest. Written by Richard Flournoy and Jack Henley; directed by Leigh Jason; for Samuel Bischoff / Columbia.

Dangerous Corner*
US 1934 67m bw
RKO

After dinner conversation reveals what might have been if friends had spoken the truth about a long-ago suicide.
A fascinating trick play makes interesting but scarcely sparkling cinema.

w Anne Morrison Chapin, Madeleine Ruthven, *play* J. B. Priestley *d* Phil Rosen *ph* J. Roy Hunt *m* Max Steiner

Melvyn Douglas, Conrad Nagel, Virginia Bruce, Erin O'Brien Moore, Ian Keith, Betty Furness, Henry Wadsworth

'Confusing mixture of a mystery and problem play . . . doubtful as to general fan appeal.'—*Variety*

Dangerous Crossing*
US 1953 75m bw
TCF (Robert Bassler)

At the start of an Atlantic sea voyage a woman's husband disappears, and she is assured that he never existed. He does, and is trying to murder her.
Adequately handled twist on the vanishing lady story: grade A production covers lapses of grade B imagination.

w Leo Townsend, *story* John Dickson Carr *d* Joseph M. Newman *ph* Joseph La Shelle *md* Lionel Newman

Jeanne Crain, Michael Rennie, Carl Betz, Casey Adams, Mary Anderson, Willis Bouchey

Dangerous Curves
US 1929 75m bw
Paramount

A bareback rider loves a high wire artist.
Obvious circus melodrama, a modest star vehicle.

w Donald David, Florence Ryerson *d* Lothar Mendes *ph* Harry Fischbeck

Clara Bow, Richard Arlen, Kay Francis, David Newell, Anders Randolf

Dangerous Exile
GB 1957 90m Eastmancolor Vistavision
Rank (George H. Brown)

After the French Revolution, the young would-be Louis XVII is brought across the Channel and hidden in Pembrokeshire, where enemies attack him.
Historical romance, ineptly plotted but quite well produced.

w Robin Estridge, *novel* Vaughan Wilkins *d* Brian Desmond Hurst *ph Geoffrey Unsworth m* Georges Auric

Louis Jourdan, Belinda Lee, Keith Michell, Richard O'Sullivan, Martita Hunt, Finlay Currie, Anne Heywood, Jacques Brunius

A Dangerous Game
US 1941 61m bw

Various weird characters converge on a lunatic asylum where a fortune is hidden. Failed attempt at black farce: the actors are game, but the material doesn't hold water. Richard Arlen, Andy Devine, Jeanne Kelly, Edward Brophy, Marc Lawrence, Andrew Tombes, Tom Dugan. Written by Larry Rhine, Ben Chapman, Maxwell Shane; directed by John Rawlins; for Universal. 'For all its frantic, deafening slapstick it remains stubbornly humourless . . . if there's such a thing as a Class D picture, this is it.'—*Variety*

Dangerous Millions
US 1946 69m bw

Eight would-be inheritors of a millionaire's estate find themselves at the mercy of a warlord in the Chinese mountains. Odd little second feature confusion of *The Cat and the Canary* and *Shanghai Express*; quite watchable. Kent Taylor, Dona Drake, Tala Birell, Leonard Strong, Konstantin Shayne. Written by Irving Cummings Jnr and Robert G. North; directed by James Tinling; for TCF. (GB title: *The House of Tao Ling*.)

Dangerous Mission
US 1954 75m Technicolor 3-D
RKO (Irwin Allen)

In Montana's Glacier National Park, a policeman tries to protect an innocent girl witness from big city gangsters.
Tolerable routine double-bill thriller with a predictable cable car climax.

w Horace McCoy, W. R. Burnett, Charles Bennett, James Edmiston *d* Louis King *ph* William Snyder *m* Roy Webb

Victor Mature, Piper Laurie, Vincent Price, William Bendix, Betta St John, Dennis Weaver

'The scenery received the best notices.'—*James Robert Parish 1976*

'This is your melody—you gave it to me. I'll never play it again without thinking of you!'

Dangerous Moonlight*
GB 1941 98m bw
RKO (William Sistrom)
US title: *Suicide Squadron*

A Polish pianist escapes from the Nazis and loses his memory after flying in the Battle of Britain.
Immensely popular wartime romance which introduced Richard Addinsell's Warsaw Concerto. Production values and script somewhat below par.

w Shaun Terence Young, Brian Desmond Hurst, Rodney Ackland *d* Brian Desmond Hurst *ph* Georges Périnal, Ronald Neame

Anton Walbrook, Sally Gray, Derrick de Marney, Cecil Parker, Percy Parsons, Kenneth Kent, Guy Middleton, John Laurie, Frederick Valk

Dangerous Moves*
Switzerland 1985 100m colour

The world championship chess showdown is between the Soviet title holder and an exiled dissident challenger. Interesting, rather specialized actor's piece with political overtones. Michel Piccoli, Leslie Caron, Liv Ullmann, Alexandre Arbatt. Written and directed by Richard Dembo; for Arthur Cohn.
AA: best foreign film.

Dangerous Number
US 1937 71m bw

A showgirl is confused by her husband's rich relations. Rather tedious comedy drama which never really gets anywhere. Robert Young, Ann Sothern, Reginald Owen, Cora Witherspoon, Dean Jagger, Barnett Parker. Written by Carey Wilson from a story by Leora Dalrymple; directed by Richard Thorpe; for MGM. 'A compact piece of entertainment, though pretty shallow on the drama end.'—*Variety*

Dangerous Partners
US 1945 74m bw

Nazi agents trying to get out of America are converted to democracy. Bewildering mixture of propaganda and melodrama: nothing seems to mesh. James Craig, Signe Hasso, Edmund Gwenn, Audrey Totter, Mabel Paige. Written by Marion Parsonnet, Edmund L. Hartmann, from story by Oliver Weld Bayer; directed by Edward L. Cahn; for Arthurt J. Field/MGM.

A Dangerous Profession
US 1949 79m bw

An ex-detective tries to help a beautiful woman and becomes involved in murder and the bail bond racket. Undistinguished crime melodrama providing a satisfactory vehicle for its stars: Pat O'Brien, George Raft, Ella Raines, Jim Backus, Bill Williams. Written by Martin Rackin and Warren Duff; directed by Ted Tetzlaff; for RKO.

A Dangerous Summer
Australia 1982 94m colour Panavision

In a Blue Mountain resort, a partner decides to burn down the buildings for the insurance. Modest melodrama with spectacular fire sequences. James Mason, Tom Skerritt, Ian Gilmour, Wendy Hughes, Kim Deacon. Written by David Ambrose and Quentin Masters; directed by Quentin Masters; for McElroy and McElroy.

Dangerous to Know*
US 1938 70m bw
Paramount

A ruthless Chicago gangster comes a cropper when his Chinese mistress discovers he has fallen for a socialite.
Flatly handled but mildly interesting adaptation of a highly successful play, the potential of which seems to have been thrown away.

w William R. Lippmann, Horace McCoy, *play* On the Spot by Edgar Wallace *d* Robert Florey *ph* Theodor Sparkuhl

Akim Tamiroff, Anna May Wong, Gail Patrick, Lloyd Nolan, Harvey Stephens, Anthony Quinn, Porter Hall

Dangerous When Wet**
US 1953 95m Technicolor
MGM (George Wells)

An entire Arkansas family is sponsored to swim the English Channel.
A bright and lively vehicle for an aquatic star, who in one sequence swims with Tom and Jerry. Amusing sequences give opportunities to a strong cast.

w Dorothy Kingsley *d* Charles Walters *ph* Harold Rosson *md* George Stoll *songs* Johnny Mercer, Arthur Schwarz

Esther Williams, Charlotte Greenwood, William Demarest, Fernando Lamas, Jack Carson, Denise Darcel, Barbara Whiting

Dangerously They Live
US 1941 77m bw
Warner (Ben Stoloff)

American Nazi agents try to get a secret memorized by a British girl agent injured in a car crash.
Watchable, routine spy propaganda fare.

w Marion Parsonnet *d* Robert Florey *ph* William O'Connell

John Garfield, Raymond Massey, Nancy Coleman, Moroni Olsen, Lee Patrick, Christian Rub, Frank Reicher

Dangerously Yours
US 1933 74m bw

A gentleman crook falls for a lady detective. Ho-hum society crook drama. Warner Baxter, Miriam Jordan, Herbert Mundin, Florence Eldredge, Florence Roberts, Mischa Auer. Written by Horace Jackson from a story by Paul Hervey Fox; directed by Frank Tuttle; for Fox. 'None too potent.'—*Variety*

Dangerously Yours
US 1937 60m bw

On board ship a detective captures a lady jewel thief but reforms her. Very tolerable programme filler with watchable performances. Cesar Romero, Phyllis Brooks, Jane Darwell, Alan Dinehart, Douglas Wood, Leon Ames. Written by Lou Breslow, John Patrick; directed by Mal St Clair; for TCF. 'Fox is turning out a pretty good quality of B product.'—*Variety*

Dangers of the Canadian Mounted
US 1948 bw serial: 12 eps

Mounties and outlaws clash over the discovery of ancient Chinese treasure. Standard serial heroics with a high proportion of action highlights. Jim Bannon, Virginia Belmont, Anthony Warde, Dorothy Granger. Directed by Fred Brannon and Yakima Canutt; for Republic.

Daniel
US 1983 129m Technicolor
World Film Services (John Van Eyssen)

The children of executed spies are traumatized by the past.
Patchwork vision of thirties America, with Jewishness thrown in for added weight. Not easy to watch.

w E. L. Doctorow from his novel The Book of Daniel *d* Sidney Lumet *ph* Andrzej Bartkowiak *m* Bob James *pd* Philip Rosenberg

Timothy Hutton, Mandy Patinkin, Lindsay Crouse, Ed Asner, Ellen Barkin, Tovah Feldshuh

'Only with the last scene does one realize that it has collapsed into an empty liberal squeak.'—*Tom Milne, MFB*

Danny Boy
GB 1941 80m bw

A singer searches for her estranged husband and small son who have become street entertainers. Sentimental drama with music; not for the critical. Ann Todd, Wilfrid Lawson, Grant Tyler, John Warwick, David

Farrar. Written by Oswald Mitchell and A. Barr-Carson; directed by Oswald Mitchell; for Butcher's.

Dante's Inferno**
US 1935 89m bw
TCF (Sol M. Wurtzel)

A ruthless carnival owner gets too big for his boots, and has a vision of hell induced by one of his own attractions.
Curiously unpersuasive melodrama with a moral, but the inferno sequence is one of the most unexpected, imaginative and striking pieces of cinema in Hollywood's history.

w Philip Klein, Robert Yost *d Harry Lachmann ph Rudolph Maté sp Fred F. Sersen, Ralph Hammeras sets Willy Pogany*, from drawings by Gustav Doré *m* Hugo Friedhofer, Samuel Kaylin, R. H. Bassett, Peter Brunelli
Spencer Tracy, Claire Trevor, Henry B. Walthall, Alan Dinehart, Scotty Beckett, Rita Hayworth (her first appearance, as a dancer)
'A pushover for vigorous exploitation . . . accentuate the inferno sequence and forget the rest, including the story.'—*Variety*
'We depart gratefully, having seen papier maché photographed in more ways than we had thought possible.'—*Robert Herring*
'One of the most unusual and effectively presented films of the thirties.'—*John Baxter, 1968*

'The spectacle is shattering.'—*Sunday Times*
'Immediately following the 10-minute picturization of Hell, the story reverts to its native dullness.'—*Variety*

Danton*
France / Poland 1982 136m colour
Losange / Group X (for Gaumont / TFI)

Robespierre quarrels with his colleague Danton, who hopes for a new spirit of tolerance.
Vivid historical re-creation which finally exhausts the spectator and is a little too concerned to make political points.

w Jean-Claude Carrière from the play The Danton Affair by Stanlislawa Przybyszewska *d Andrzej Wajda ph* Igor Luther *m* Jean Prodromides

Gérard Depardieu, Wojciech Pszoniak, Anne Alvaro, Roland Blanche
'The temptation to see it in terms of Solidarity is unavoidable.'—*Philip Strick, MFB*
'By any reasonable standard, terrible.'—*New Yorker*

BFA: best foreign-language film

Darby O'Gill and the Little People*
US 1959 90m Technicolor
Walt Disney

An Irish caretaker falls down a well and is captured by leprechauns, who allow him three wishes to rearrange his life.
Pleasantly barmy Irish fantasy with brilliant trick work but some tedium in between.

w Lawrence Edward Watkin, *stories* H. T. Kavanagh *d* Robert Stevenson *ph* Winton C. Hoch *m* Oliver Wallace *sp Peter Ellenshaw, Eustace Lycett, Joshua Meador*

Albert Sharpe, *Jimmy O'Dea*, Sean Connery, Janet Munro, Kieron Moore, Estelle Winwood, Walter Fitzgerald, Denis O'Dea, J. G. Devlin, Jack MacGowran
'One of the best fantasies ever put on film.'—*Leonard Maltin*

Darby's Rangers
US 1957 121m bw
Warner (Martin Rackin)
GB title: *The Young Invaders*

A tough American commando unit is trained in Britain before seeing action in Africa and Sicily.
Standard World War II actioner, adequately executed.

w Guy Trosper, *book* Major James Altieri *d* William Wellman *ph* William H. Clothier *m* Max Steiner

James Garner, Etchika Choureau, Jack Warden, Edward Byrnes, Venetia Stevenson, Torin Thatcher, Stuart Whitman, Andrea King, Frieda Inescort, Reginald Owen, Adam Williams

Daredevils of the Red Circle
US 1939 bw serial: 12 eps

Three college athletes foil the dastardly plans of an ex-convict impersonating a powerful businessman. No-holds-barred serial adventures with an unusual array of familiar faces. Charles Quigley, Carole Landis, Herman Brix, David Sharpe, Miles Mander, Charles Middleton, Raymond Bailey. Directed by William Witney and John English; for Republic.

Daredevils of the West
US 1943 bw serial: 12 eps

Duke Cameron foils a plot to ruin the Foster Stage Line. Unremarkable serial exploits. Allan Lane, Kay Aldridge, Eddie Acuff, William Haade, Robert Frazer. Directed by John English; for Republic.

The Daring Game
US 1967 101m Eastmancolor
Paramount / Tors (Gene Levitt)

A commercial group experiments with airborne and underwater inventions, and rescues a scientist from a police state.
Well photographed but haphazardly assembled adventures, aimed at TV.

w Andy White *d* Laslo Benedek *ph* Edmund Gibson *m* George Bruns

Lloyd Bridges, Nico Minardos, Joan Blackman, Michael Ansara

The Dark
US 1979 92m colour

A homicidal alien stalks Los Angeles, ripping off people's heads. Unconsidered shocker with nothing to it but the shocks. William Devane, Cathy Lee Crosby, Richard Jaeckel, Keenan Wynn, Vivian Blaine. Written by Stanford Whitmore; directed by John Cardos; for Film Ventures International.

The Dark Angel*
US 1925 83m (24 fps) bw silent
First National (Samuel Goldwyn)

During World War I, a blinded officer tries to persuade his fiancée to marry another man, without her knowing of his own infirmity.
Vilma Banky's first American film, her first teaming with Colman and a mid-twenties hit of colossal proportions.

w Frances Marion, *play* Guy Bolton *d* George Fitzmaurice *ph* George Barnes

Ronald Colman, Vilma Banky, Wyndham Standing, Frank Elliott, Charles Lane, Florence Turner, Helen Jerome Eddy

The Dark Angel*
US 1935 105m bw
Samuel Goldwyn

Tearstained melodrama from another age (see above), neatly packaged for the romantic 1935 public.

w Lillian Hellman, Mordaunt Shairp *d* Sidney Franklin *ph* Gregg Toland *m* Alfred Newman *ad* Richard Day

Merle Oberon, Fredric March, Herbert Marshall, Janet Beecher, John Halliday, Henrietta Crosman, Frieda Inescort, George Breakston, Claud Allister
'A sockaroo woman's picture.'—*Variety*
'A highly literate screen adaptation, telling the story with feeling and good taste.'—*New York Times*
'It makes a systematic and skilful appeal to those untrustworthy emotions which may suddenly cause the most hardened intellects to dissolve before the most obvious sentimentality.'—*The Times*

AAN: Merle Oberon
AA: Richard Day

The Dark at the Top of the Stairs**
US 1960 124m Technicolor
Warner (Michael Garrison)

Twenties small town drama about a young boy's awakening to the sexual tensions around him.
Archetypal family drama set in that highly familiar American street. The perfect essence of this playwright's work, with high and low spots, several irrelevancies, but a real feeling for the people and the place.

w Harriet Frank Jnr, Irving Ravetch, *play William Inge d* Delbert Mann *ph* Harry Stradling *m* Max Steiner

Robert Preston, Dorothy McGuire, Angela Lansbury, *Eve Arden*, Shirley Knight, Frank Overton, Lee Kinsolving, Robert Eyer
'Every time a woman turns her face away because she's tired or unwilling, there's someone waiting like me . . .'—*publicity*
† The curious title turns out to be a synonym for life, which one should never be afraid of.

AAN: Shirley Knight

The Dark Avenger*
GB 1955 85m Eastmancolor
Cinemascope
Allied Artists (Vaughan N. Dean)
US title: *The Warriors*

The Black Prince quells some French rebels. Good-humoured historical romp with the ageing star in his last swashbuckling role, helped by a good cast and brisk pace.

w Daniel B. Ullman *d* Henry Levin *ph* Guy Green *m* Cedric Thorpe Davie

Errol Flynn, Peter Finch, Joanne Dru, Yvonne Furneaux, Patrick Holt, Michael Hordern, Moultrie Kelsall, Robert Urquhart, Noel Willman

Dark City
US 1950 97m bw
Paramount / Hal B. Wallis

A bookmaker finds himself on the run from a revenge-seeking psychopath.
Unattractive and heavily-handled underworld melodrama, a disappointment from the talents involved.

w John Meredyth Lucas, Larry Marcus *d* William Dieterle *ph* Victor Milner *m* Franz Waxman

Charlton Heston (his first Hollywood appearance), Lizabeth Scott, Viveca Lindfors, Dean Jagger, Don Defore, Jack Webb, Ed Begley, Henry Morgan, Mike Mazurki

'A jaded addition to a type of thriller which has become increasingly tedious and unreal.'—*MFB*

Dark Command*
US 1940 92m bw
Republic (Sol C. Siegel)

In pre-Civil War Kansas, an ambitious ex-schoolteacher named Cantrill organizes guerrilla bands to pillage the countryside.
Semi-historical hokum, quite well done with a good cast.

w Grover Jones, Lionel Houser, F. Hugh Herbert, *novel* W. R. Burnett *d* Raoul Walsh *ph* Jack Marta *m* Victor Young

John Wayne, Claire Trevor, Walter Pidgeon, Roy Rogers, George 'Gabby' Hayes, Porter Hall, Marjorie Main

'It's the highest budgeter for Republic to date, running in neighbourhood of 700,000 dollars in negative cost. In the family and action houses, it's a natural to roll up good grosses.'—*Variety*

AAN: Victor Young

The Dark Corner*
US 1946 98m bw
TCF (Fred Kohlmar)

A private eye with a criminal record thinks he is being menaced by an old adversary, but the latter is found murdered.
Moody, brutish, well-made thriller with a plot put together from bits and pieces of older, better movies, notably Clifton Webb's reprise of his *Laura* performance and William Bendix ditto *The Glass Key*.

w Jay Dratler, Bernard Schoenfeld, *story* Leo Rosten *d Henry Hathaway ph Joe MacDonald m* Cyril Mockridge

Mark Stevens, Clifton Webb, Lucille Ball, William Bendix, Kurt Kreuger, Cathy Downs, Reed Hadley, Constance Collier

JARDINE (Clifton Webb): 'I hate the dawn. The grass always looks as though it's been left out all night.'

BRAD (Mark Stevens): 'There goes my last lead. I feel all dead inside. I'm backed up in a dark corner, and I don't know who's hitting me.'

'Not so much a whodunnit as a whodunnwhat . . . all seem bent on "getting" each other and their internecine plottings add up to an alpha thriller.'—*Daily Mail*

The Dark Crystal**
GB 1982 94m Technicolor Panavision
Universal / AFD / ITC (David Lazer)

Two young people defeat the evil creatures who have taken over the world by replacing a shard which has been taken from the Dark Crystal.
Surprisingly effective piece of mysticism performed entirely by hand puppets from the Muppet stable.

w *David Odell d Jim Henson, Frank Oz conceptual designer Brian Froud ph* Oswald Morris *pd Harry Lange ed* Ralph Kemplen

'A dazzling technological and artistic achievement . . . could teach a lesson in morality to youngsters at the same time as it is entertaining their parents.'—*Variety*

Dark Delusion
US 1947 90m bw

A neurotic girl may have to be committed to an asylum. Last episode of the Dr Gillespie series; not a sensation on its own account. Lionel Barrymore, James Craig, Lucille Bremer, Edward Arnold, Keye Luke. Written by Jack Andrews and Harry Ruskin; directed by Willis Goldbeck; for MGM. (GB title: *Cynthia's Secret*.)

Dark Eyes: see Black Eyes

Dark Eyes of London*
GB 1939 75m bw
Pathe / Argyle (John Argyle)
US title: *The Human Monster*

The proprietor of a home for the blind uses a mute giant to drown insured victims.
Reasonably effective British horror, a rarity at the time.

w John Argyle, Walter Summers, Patrick Kirwan, *novel* Edgar Wallace *d* Walter Summers *ph* Bryan Langley

Bela Lugosi, Hugh Williams, Greta Gynt, Wilfrid Walter, Edmon Ryan

Dark Hazard
US 1934 72m bw

A compulsive gambler loses his wife as well as his money. Modest star drama, remade in 1937 as *Wine, Women and Horses*. Edward G. Robinson, Glenda Farrell, Robert Barrat, Hobart Cavanagh. Written by Ralph Block and Brown Holmes; directed by Alfred E. Green; for Warner.

The Dark Horse
US 1932 75m bw

A nitwit runs for governor and nearly makes it. Mild political satire; closer to farce, really. Guy Kibbee, Bette Davis, Warren William, Frank McHugh. Written by Joseph Jackson and Wilson Mizner; directed by Alfred E. Green; for Warner.

Dark Journey*
GB 1937 82m bw
London Films / Victor Saville

In 1915 Stockholm, a French woman spy masquerading as a traitor falls in love with her German spy contact.
Unconvincing but entertaining romantic adventure with good star performances.

w Lajos Biro, Arthur Wimperis, *play* Lajos Biro *d* Victor Saville *ph* Georges Périnal, Harry Stradling *m* Richard Addinsell

Conrad Veidt, Vivien Leigh, Joan Gardner, Anthony Bushell, Ursula Jeans, Eliot Makeham, Austin Trevor, Edmund Willard

'An exceptional quantity of carefully thought out direction . . . the financial success will depend on whether the general public will understand and keep pace with the plot.'—*Variety*

The Dark Man
GB 1950 91m bw
Rank / Independent Artists (Julian Wintle)

A mysterious murderer haunts a seaside resort.
Limp, disappointing location police thriller, with too much chat and generally mishandled moments of suspense

wd Jeffrey Dell *ph* Eric Cross *m* Hubert Clifford

Maxwell Reed, Edward Underdown, Natasha Parry, Barbara Murray, William Hartnell, Cyril Smith, Geoffrey Sumner

'The contrivances of the script are not helped by stilted dialogue.'—*MFB*

'One twin loves—and one twin loves to kill!'

The Dark Mirror**
US 1946 85m bw
International

A police detective works out which of identical twin girls is a murderer.
Unconvincing but highly absorbing thriller with all credits plus; the best brand of Hollywood moonshine.

w Nunnally Johnson, *original story* Vladimir Posner *d Robert Siodmak ph* Milton Krasner *m* Dmitri Tiomkin

Olivia de Havilland, Lew Ayres, Thomas Mitchell, Garry Owen

'Smooth and agreeable melodrama . . . the detective work involves inkblot and word association tests and an amusingly sinister tandem of oscillating pens which register concealed emotions as one of the sisters talks.'—*James Agee*

AAN: Vladimir Posner

Dark Passage**
US 1947 106m bw
Warner (Jerry Wald)

A convicted murderer escapes from jail and proves his innocence.
Loosely assembled, totally unconvincing star thriller which succeeds because of its professionalism, some good cameos, and a number of narrative tricks including subjective camera for the first half hour.

w Delmer Daves, *novel* David Goodis *d Delmer Daves ph Sid Hickox m* Franz Waxman

Humphrey Bogart, Lauren Bacall, Agnes Moorehead, Bruce Bennett, *Tom D'Andrea, Houseley Stevenson*

'An almost total drag.'—*New Yorker, 1977*

The Dark Past**
US 1948 75m bw
Columbia (Buddy Adler)

A psychiatrist turns the tables on convicts who break into his home.
Tense, economical remake of *Blind Alley* (qv); a fresh look at a familiar situation (*The Small Voice, The Desperate Hours,* etc) helped by excellent performances.

w Philip Macdonald, Malvin Wald, Oscar Saul *d Rudolph Maté ph* Joseph Walker *m* George Duning

William Holden, Lee J. Cobb, Nina Foch, Adele Jergens, Stephen Dunne

'A picture so packed with skill and imagination that every minute is absorbing.'—*Richard Mallett, Punch*

'The mission of the Strangelove generation!'

Dark Star*
US 1974 83m Metrocolor
Jack H. Harris (John Carpenter)

In the 22nd century, the bored crew of a starship on an intergalactic mission become prey to their own phobias and to the alien mascot they are taking back to earth.
A semi-professional film which turned out to be one of the screen's neatest low-budget entries in the pulp science fiction genre. That doesn't make it wholly entertaining, but its credentials are impeccable.

w John Carpenter, Dan O'Bannon *d John Carpenter pd, ed Dan O'Bannon ph* Douglas Knapp *m* John Carpenter

Brian Narelle, Dre Pahich, Cal Kuniholm, Dan O'Bannon

The Dark Tower
GB 1943 93m bw
Warner (Max Milder)

A circus hypnotist possessively controls a girl trapezist.
Heavy-handed but quite effective melodrama.

w Brock Williams, Reginald Purdell, *play* Alexander Woolcott, George S. Kaufman *d* John Harlow *ph* Otto Heller

DARK VICTORY. A moment of light before tears and darkness set in. Humphrey Bogart makes a happy point to Bette Davis while Geraldine Fitzgerald shares the joke.

Ben Lyon, Anne Crawford, David Farrar, Herbert Lom, William Hartnell, Frederick Burtwell, Josephine Wilson

'Never a love so exquisite! She smiled at the cost, and bravely paid the reckoning when her heart's happy dancing was ended!'

Dark Victory**
US 1939 106m bw
Warner (David Lewis)

A good-time society girl discovers she is dying of a brain tumour.
A highly commercial tearjerker of its day, this glutinous star vehicle now works only fitfully.

w Casey Robinson, *play* George Brewer Jnr, Bertram Bloch *d* Edmund Goulding *ph* Ernest Haller *m* Max Steiner

Bette Davis, George Brent, Humphrey Bogart, Ronald Reagan, Geraldine Fitzgerald, Henry Travers, Cora Witherspoon, Dorothy Peterson

JUDITH (Bette Davis): 'Nothing can hurt us now. What we have can't be destroyed. That's our victory—our victory over the dark. It is a victory because we're not afraid.'

'If it were an automobile, it would be a Rolls-Royce with the very best trimmings.'—*Time*

'Will turn in a good account of itself at the box office, though not rating socko proportions.'—*Variety*

'A completely cynical appraisal would dismiss it all as emotional flim-flam . . . but it is impossible to be that cynical about it.'—*Frank S. Nugent*

'A gooey collection of clichés, but Davis slams through them in her nerviest style.'—*New Yorker, 1976*

† Remade 1963 as *Stolen Hours*, with Susan Hayward; 1975 as *Dark Victory* (TV movie) with Elizabeth Montgomery.

AAN: best picture; Bette Davis; Max Steiner

Dark Water*
GB 1980 28m colour

A girl locked in a swimming pool is terrorized by a mad killer. Agreeably watchable thriller full of shadows and shocks. Phil Davis, Gwyneth Strong, David Beames. Written by Andrew Bogle and Tony Grisoni; directed by Andrew Bogle; for Dragonfly / ITC.

Dark Waters**
US 1944 90m bw
Benedict Bogeaus

Recovering from being torpedoed, an orphan girl visits her aunt and uncle in Louisiana and has some terrifying experiences.
Competent frightened-lady melodrama helped by its bayou surroundings. Possibly discarded by Hitchcock, but with sequences well in his manner.

w Joan Harrison, Marian Cockrell *d André de Toth ph John Mescall m* Miklos Rozsa

Merle Oberon, Franchot Tone, *Thomas Mitchell, Fay Bainter, John Qualen*, Elisha Cook Jnr, Rex Ingram

Darker than Amber
US 1970 96m Technicolor
Cinema Center / Major Films (Walter Seltzer)

A Florida private eye rescues a girl who is subsequently murdered and turns out to be part of a confidence racket.
Routine suspenser from the Travis McGee books; not very stimulating.

w Ed Waters, *novel* John D. MacDonald *d* Robert Clouse *ph* Frank Phillips *m* John Parker

Rod Taylor, Suzy Kendall, Theodore Bikel, James Booth, Jane Russell, Janet McLachlan, William Smith

Darkest Africa
US 1936 bw serial: 15 eps

A lion trapper meets a jungle boy and rescues a fair heroine from a lost city. Great stuff, but the budget is a lot less than Steven Spielberg had to play with 45 years later. Clyde Beatty, Manuel King, Elaine Shepherd, Lucien Prival. Directed by B. Reeves Eason and Joseph Kane; for Republic.

'When she was good she was very very good. When she was bad, she was . . .'
Darling**
GB 1965 127m bw
Anglo-Amalgamated / Vic / Appia (Joseph Janni, Victor Lyndon)

An ambitious young woman deserts her journalist mentor for a company director, an effeminate photographer and an Italian prince.
Fashionable mid-sixties concoction of smart swinging people and their amoral doings. Influential, put over with high style, and totally tiresome in retrospect.

w Frederic Raphael *d John Schlesinger ph* Ken Higgins *m* John Dankworth

Julie Christie, Dirk Bogarde, Laurence Harvey, Roland Curram, Alex Scott, Basil Henson, Pauline Yates

BOGARDE to Christie: 'Your idea of being fulfilled is having more than one man in bed at the same time.'

'As empty of meaning and mind as the empty life it's exposing.'—*Pauline Kael*

AA: Frederic Raphael; Julie Christie
AAN: best picture; John Schlesinger

Darling How Could You
US 1951 96m bw
Paramount (Harry Tugend)
GB title: *Rendezvous*

Children long separated from their parents have fantasies about them.
Faded-looking Edwardian comedy which does not quite have the style or the cast for success. (Or the title, come to that.)

w Dodie Smith, Lesser Samuels, *play* Alice Sit by the Fire by J. M. Barrie *d* Mitchell Leisen *ph* Daniel L. Fapp *m* Frederick Hollander

Joan Fontaine, John Lund, Mona Freeman, Peter Hanson, David Stollery, Lowell Gilmore, Robert Barrat, Gertrude Michael

Darling Lili*
US 1970 136m Technicolor Panavision
Paramount / Geoffrey (Owen Crump)

During World War I, an American air ace falls for a German lady spy, and waits till the war is over to marry her.
Farce and romance mix oddly with aerial acrobatics in this expensive and dull extravaganza which bore the sub-title *Where Were You the Night I Shot Down Baron Von Richthofen?* (which probably sums up its aims and its failure). A coffee table film, good to look at and with occasional striking moments.

wd Blake Edwards *co-w* William Peter Blatty *ph Russell Harlan, Harold E. Wellman m* Henry Mancini *pd* Fernando Carrere

Julie Andrews, Rock Hudson, Jeremy Kemp, Lance Percival, Michael Witney, Jacques Marin, André Maranne

AAN: Henry Mancini; song 'Whistling Away the Dark' (*m* Henry Mancini, *ly* Johnny Mercer)

The Darwin Adventure*
GB 1971 91m Eastmancolor
(TCF) Palomar (Joseph Strick, Irving Lerner)

In 1831, Charles Darwin becomes ship's naturalist on the *Beagle* and studies wild life in South America.
Rather naive biopic of Darwin which tries to cover too much with too slender resources but makes a pleasant introduction to the subject.

w William Fairchild *d* Jack Couffer
ph Denys Coop, Jack Couffer *m* Marc Wilkinson

Nicholas Clay, Susan Macready, Ian Richardson, Christopher Martin, Robert Flemyng, Aubrey Woods, Hugh Morton

'The biopic plague, which has ravaged the screen lives of Pasteur, Juarez, Cole Porter and countless others, has now struck down the memory of famed naturalist Charles Darwin. The filmgoing public's own version of Darwin's natural selection theory will immediately weed out this inferior species.'—*Variety*

D.A.R.Y.L.
US 1985 99m TVC colour

A mysterious young man is really a robot, 'data analysing robot youth lifeform'; but he begins to have feelings . . . Muddled sentimental fantasy which doesn't seem to know where it's going. Mary Beth Hurt, Michael McKean, Kathryn Walker, Colleen Camp. Written by David Ambrose, Allan Scott, Jeffrey Ellis; directed by Simon Wincer; for John Heyman/Columbia. 'The kind of project that must have looked great on paper.'—*Variety*

A Date with Judy
US 1948 113m Technicolor
MGM (Joe Pasternak)

A teenager wrongly suspects her friend of an illicit affair.
Ambitious but flat comedy musical which neatly wraps up all kinds of forties people and institutions: teenagers, small towns, families, Carmen Miranda and Miss Taylor, not to mention the producer.

w Dorothy Cooper, Dorothy Kingsley
d Richard Thorpe *ph* Robert Surtees
m / ly various *md* George Stoll

Wallace Beery, Elizabeth Taylor, Jane Powell, Carmen Miranda, Xavier Cugat, Robert Stack, Selena Royle, Scotty Beckett, Leon Ames

Daughter of Darkness
GB 1947 91m bw
Kenilworth–Alliance (Victor Hanbury)

A murderous Irish servant girl has a fatal flair for men.
Absurd melodrama, almost Grand Guignol, louringly set on the Yorkshire moors but lethargically handled all round.

w Max Catto, from his play They Walk Alone
d Lance Comfort *ph* Stanley Pavey

Siobhan McKenna, Anne Crawford, Maxwell Reed, George Thorpe, Barry Morse, Honor Blackman, Liam Redmond, David Greene

Daughter of Dr Jekyll
US 1957 74m bw

An evil doctor tells his ward that she is the daughter of the unfortunate Dr Jekyll and therefore responsible for a series of werewolf killings. Bathetic cheapie with risible views of England and a tendency to mix up several myths in one package. Arthur Shields, John Agar, Gloria Talbott, John Dierkes. Written by Jack Pollexfen; directed by Edgar C. Ulmer; for Allied Artists.

The Daughter of Rosie O'Grady*
US 1950 104m Technicolor
Warner (William Jacobs)

A girl determines to follow in her dead mother's musical comedy footsteps against the wishes of her still-grieving father.
Absolutely standard period musical, quite pleasantly handled but with below-par musical numbers.

w Jack Rose, Mel Shavelson, Peter Milne
d David Butler *ph* Wilfred M. Cline
md David Buttolph

June Haver, Gordon Macrae, *James Barton*, S. Z. Sakall, Gene Nelson, Debbie Reynolds, Sean McClory, Jane Darwell

Daughter of Shanghai*
US 1937 63m bw

The daughter of a wealthy merchant revenges herself on smugglers who kill him. Pacy lower-berth melodrama packed with good talent. Anna May Wong, Charles Bickford, Philip Ahn, Larry Crabbe, Cecil Cunningham, Anthony Quinn, J. Carrol Naish, Evelyn Brent. Written by Gladys Unger and Garnett Weston; directed by Robert Florey; for Paramount. 'Meaningless title to a routine crime meller . . . downstairs dualler, but not half bad.'—*Variety*

Daughter of the Dragon
US 1931 70m bw

Fu Manchu continues to seek revenge on Dr Petrie for the loss of his wife in the Boxer rebellion. Muddled thriller with too much plot and too little action. Warner Oland, Anna May Wong, Sessue Hayakawa, Bramwell Fletcher, Holmes Herbert. Written by Lloyd Corrigan and Monte Katterjohn; directed by Lloyd Corrigan; for Paramount. 'Chinese blunderings, murders, and silly acting. Best for the combos where the kids may get a kick out of it.'—*Variety*

Daughters Courageous*
US 1939 107m bw
Warner (Hal B. Wallis)

A prodigal father returns to his family and sorts out their problems.
Following the success of *Four Daughters* (qv) the cast was reassembled to make this amiable rehash about a different family.

w Julius and Philip Epstein, *play* Fly Away Home by Dorothy Bennett, Irving White *d* Michael Curtiz *ph James Wong Howe* *m* Max Steiner

Claude Rains, John Garfield, Jeffrey Lynn, Fay Bainter, Priscilla Lane, Rosemary Lane, Lola Lane, Gale Page, Donald Crisp, May Robson, Frank McHugh, Dick Foran, Berton Churchill

'Suited to the family trade anywhere . . . but there's something to be said against a running time of an hour and 47 minutes.'—*Variety*

'For its intelligent use of small town locations, its skilled acting, fine camerawork and evenly paced, sympathetic direction, it surpasses everything of its type.'—*John Baxter, 1968*

'Attractive people, good dialogue and camerawork, and skilful direction can work wonders.'—*Richard Mallett, Punch*

'For this woman—he broke God's own commandments! The fire and tempest of their love still flames across 3000 years!'

David and Bathsheba*
US 1951 116m Technicolor
TCF (Darryl F. Zanuck)

King David loves the wife of one of his captains, and ensures that the latter is killed in battle.
Deliberately sober bible-in-pictures, probably intended as a riposte to Cecil B. de Mille. Somewhat lacking in excitement, but you can't call it gaudy.

w Philip Dunne *d* Henry King *ph* Leon Shamroy *m* Alfred Newman

Gregory Peck, Susan Hayward, James Robertson Justice, Raymond Massey, Kieron Moore, Jayne Meadows, John Sutton, Dennis Hoey, Francis X. Bushman, George Zucco

'Hardly a single unintentional laugh.'—*Richard Mallett, Punch*

AAN: Phillip Dunne; Leon Shamroy; Alfred Newman

David and Lisa*
US 1963 94m bw
Continental (Paul M. Heller)

Two disturbed adolescents at a special school fall in love.
Case history drama, earnest and well meaning rather than exciting.

w Eleanor Perry, book Theodore Isaac Rubin *d Frank Perry* *ph* Leonard Hirschfield *m* Mark Lawrence

Keir Dullea, Janet Margolin, Howard da Silva, Neva Patterson, Clifton James, Richard McMurray

AAN: Eleanor Perry; Frank Perry

'One of the greatest stories of love and adventure ever told is brought to the screen as Dickens himself would wish it!'

David Copperfield****
US 1934 132m bw
MGM (David O. Selznick)

Disliked by his cruel stepfather and helped by his eccentric aunt, orphan David grows up to become an author and eventually to marry his childhood sweetheart.
Only slightly faded after forty-five years, this small miracle of compression not only conveys the spirit of Dickens better than the screen has normally managed but is a particularly pleasing example of Hollywood's handling of literature and of the deployment of a great studio's resources. It also overflows with memorable character cameos, and it was a box office giant.

w Hugh Walpole, Howard Estabrook, *novel* Charles Dickens *d George Cukor* *ph* Oliver T. Marsh *m* Herbert Stothart
montages Slavko Vorkapitch *ad Cedric Gibbons*

Freddie Bartholomew (young David), *Frank Lawton* (David as a man), *W. C. Fields* (Micawber), *Roland Young* (Uriah Heep), *Edna May Oliver* (Aunt Betsy), *Lennox Pawle* (Mr Dick), *Basil Rathbone* (Mr Murdstone), Violet Kemble Cooper (Miss Murdstone), Maureen O'Sullivan (Dora), Madge Evans (Agnes), Elizabeth Allan (Mrs Copperfield), *Jessie Ralph* (Peggotty), Lionel Barrymore (Dan Peggotty), Hugh Williams (Steerforth), Lewis Stone (Mr Wickfield), *Herbert Mundin* (Barkis), Elsa Lanchester (Clickett), Jean Cadell (Mrs Micawber), Una O'Connor (Mrs Gummidge), John Buckler (Ham), Hugh Walpole (the Vicar), Arthur Treacher (donkey man)

'One of the best ensembles ever . . . unusually good production which will win general approval.'—*Variety*

'Though half the characters are absent, the whole spectacle of the book, Micawber always excepted, is conveyed.'—*James Agee*

'The most profoundly satisfying screen manipulation of a great novel that the camera has ever given us.'—*André Sennwald*

'Perhaps the finest casting of all time.'—*Basil Wright, 1972*

† Charles Laughton was originally cast as Micawber, but resigned from the role after two days of shooting. It was said at the time that 'he looked as though he were about to molest the child.'

AAN: best picture

David Harum*
US 1934 83m bw
Fox

A wily old rancher plays matchmaker.
Simple, pleasing small-town comedy-drama, ably fashioned for its star.

w Walter Woods, *play* Edward Westcott *d* James Cruze *ph* Hal Mohr *m* Louis de Francesco

Will Rogers, Evelyn Venable, Kent Taylor, Louise Dresser, Stepin Fetchit, Charles Middleton, Noah Beery

'Looks like a sugar picture.'—*Variety*

Davy*
GB 1957 84m Technirama
Ealing (Basil Dearden)

A member of a family music hall act auditions at Covent Garden.
Curiously unsuccessful vehicle for a popular singing comic; the script and continuity are simply poor, and swamped by the wide screen.

w William Rose *d* Michael Relph *ph* Douglas Slocombe *m* various classics

Harry Secombe, Ron Randell, George Relph, Alexander Knox, Susan Shaw, Bill Owen

Davy Crockett*
US 1955 93m Technicolor
Walt Disney

Episodes in the career of the famous Tennessee hunter and Indian scout who died at the Alamo.
Disjointed and naive but somehow very fresh and appealing adventures; made for American television (as 3 × 50m episodes) but elsewhere an enormous hit in cinemas.

w Tom Blackburn *d* Norman Foster *ph* Charles Boyle *m* George Bruns

Fess Parker, Buddy Ebsen, Basil Ruysdael, William Bakewell, Hans Conried, Kenneth Tobey, Nick Cravat

† 1956 sequel on similar lines: *Davy Crockett and the River Pirates.*

Dawn*
GB 1928 90m approx bw silent

In 1914 Brussels, Nurse Edith Cavell helps 210 English soldiers to escape before the Germans catch and execute her. Inspirational piece, totally dated now; remade by the same producer in 1939 as *Nurse Edith Cavell*, with Anna Neagle. Sybil Thorndike, Marie Ault, Mary Brough, Haddon Mason. Written by Herbert Wilcox and Robert J. Cullen, from play by Reginald Berkeley; directed and produced by Herbert Wilcox for British and Dominions.

Dawn at Socorro
US 1954 80m Technicolor

A gunfighter is trapped into one last duel. Moderate western programmer. Rory

Calhoun, David Brian, Alex Nicol, Piper Laurie, Edgar Buchanan. Written by George Zuckerman; directed by George Sherman; for Universal-International.

'When there's no more room in Hell, the dead will walk the earth . . .'

Dawn of the Dead
US 1979 127m Technicolor

America is filled by legions of carnivorous zombies. Seemingly endless horror comic with absurd pretensions to be an allegory of something or other; occasionally laughable, otherwise sickening or boring. David Emge, Ken Foree, Scott H. Reininger, Gaylen Ross. Written and directed by George A. Romero; for Laurel Group. (GB title: *Zombies*.)

'Roaring into the blood-red dawn—fighting for women they had never seen—for love they might never know!'
'Forty youngsters sporting with fate!'

The Dawn Patrol**
US 1930 90m bw
Warner

In France during World War I, flying officers wait their turn to leave on missions which may mean death.
The second version (see below) is more watchable today, but this early talkie was highly effective in its time, and much of its aerial footage was re-used.

w John Monk Saunders *d Howard Hawks*
ph Ernest Haller

Richard Barthelmess, Douglas Fairbanks Jnr, Neil Hamilton, William Hanney, *James Finlayson*, Clyde Cook, Edmund Breon, Frank McHugh

'No women and few laughs, so needs good surrounding comedy shorts.'—*Variety*

'Bare, cleancut, uncluttered technique, a stark story line, terse dialogue . . . and a pervasive atmosphere of hopelessness captured with economy and incisiveness.'—*Andrew Sarris, 1963*

† TV title is *Flight Commander*, which was the title of Saunders' original story.

AAN: John Monk Saunders

'There's no chance for a flight to get through, but one man—flying low, hedgehopping—might make it!'

The Dawn Patrol**
US 1938 103m bw
Warner (Hal B. Wallis)

A remarkably early but trim and competent remake of the above, using much of the same aerial footage.

w Seton I. Miller, Dan Totheroh *d Edmund Goulding* *ph* Tony Gaudio *m* Max Steiner

Errol Flynn, Basil Rathbone, David Niven, Melville Cooper, Donald Crisp, Barry Fitzgerald, Carl Esmond

'A powerful, red-corpuscled drama . . . geared for top grosses.'—*Variety*

'A great deal of self-pity and romanticism have gone into the making of this excellent ham sandwich.'—*Graham Greene*

The Day
GB 1960 26m bw

A young Ibizan travels a long way to collect his relatives for the celebration of the birth of a baby. Vivid and yet rather boring short which could have done with a twist in the tail. Written, directed and produced by Peter Finch.

A Day at the Races****
US 1937 109m bw (blue-tinted ballet sequence)
MGM (Lawrence Weingarten)

The Marxes help a girl who owns a sanatorium and a racehorse.
Fashions in Marxism change, but this top quality production, though lacking their zaniest inspirations, does contain several of their funniest routines and a spectacularly well integrated racecourse climax. The musical and romantic asides are a matter of taste but delightfully typical of their time.

w Robert Pirosh, George Seaton, George Oppenheimer *d Sam Wood* *ph Joseph Ruttenberg* *m* Franz Waxman

Groucho, Chico, Harpo, Margaret Dumont, Maureen O'Sullivan, Allan Jones, *Douglass Dumbrille, Esther Muir, Sig Rumann*

'The money is fairly splashed about; the capitalists have recognized the Marx Brothers; ballet sequences, sentimental songs, amber fountains, young lovers. Easily the best film to be seen in London, but all the same I feel a nostalgia for the old cheap rickety sets.'—*Graham Greene*

Day for Night***
France / Italy 1973 116m Eastmancolor
Films du Carrosse / PECF / PIC (Marcel Bébert)
original title: *La Nuit Américaine*

Frictions and personality clashes beset the making of a romantic film in Nice.
Immensely enjoyable, richly detailed, insider's-eye-view of the goings-on in a film studio. A fun film with melodramatic asides.

w François Truffaut, Jean-Louis Richard, Suzanne Schiffman *d François Truffaut*
ph Pierre-William Glenn *m* Georges Delerue

Jacqueline Bisset, Valentina Cortese, Jean-Pierre Aumont, Jean-Pierre Léaud, Dani, Alexandra Stewart, Jean Champion, François Truffaut, David Markham

'I thought I'd had my last dram of enjoyment out of the Pagliacci theme and studio magic, and Truffaut shows there's life in the old whirl yet.'—*Stanley Kauffmann*

'Made with such dazzling craftsmanship and confidence that you can never quite believe Truffaut's point that directing a movie is a danger-fraught experience.'—*Michael Billington, Illustrated London News*

† Graham Greene, as Henry Graham, played an insurance representative.

AA: best foreign film

AAN: script; François Truffaut (as director); Valentina Cortese

A Day in the Death of Joe Egg**
GB 1971 106m Eastmancolor
Columbia / Domino (David Deutsch)

A teacher and his wife are frustrated by their own inability to cope with the problem of their spastic daughter.
A well-filmed version of a sincerely human play, with humour and fantasy sequences leavening the gloom.

w Peter Nichols, from his play *d Peter Medak*
ph Ken Hodges *m* Elgar

Alan Bates, Janet Suzman, Peter Bowles, Sheila Gish, *Joan Hickson*

'It's unsatisfying, and it's not to be missed.'—*Stanley Kauffmann*

A Day of Fury
US 1956 78m Technicolor

A marshal is reluctant to shoot a wandering gunman who once saved his life. Fair little western with more tension than usual. Dale Robertson, Jock Mahoney, Mara Corday, Carl Benton Reid. Written by James Edmiston, Oscar Brodney; directed by Harmon Jones; for Robert Arthur / Universal.

The Day of the Animals
US 1976 98m De Luxe Todd AO 35
Film Ventures International (Edward L. Montero)

In the Californian High Sierras, animals of all kinds suddenly turn on human beings, but a day later are all found dead.
Irritatingly pointless horror fable borrowing heavily from *The Birds*; basically an exploitation shocker, most efficient when most unpleasant.

w William and Eleanor Norton *d* William Girdler *ph* Tom McHugh *m* Lalo Schifrin

Christopher George, Lynda Day George, Leslie Nielsen, Robert Sorrentino, Richard Jaeckel, Michael Ansara, Ruth Roman, Paul Mantee, Gil Lamb

Day of the Badman
US 1957 82m Eastmancolor
Cinemascope

A circuit judge stands up against threatening outlaws. Uninvolving western which can't fill the wide screen. Fred MacMurray, Joan Weldon, John Ericson, Robert Middleton, Edgar Buchanan. Written by Irving Glassberg; directed by Harry Keller; for Universal-International.

Day of the Dead
US 1985 102m colour

Zombies outnumber normal humans by 400,000 to one, but a doctor is trying to domesticate them. Gory but very talkative successor to *Dawn of the Dead*; not for regular audience consumption. Lori Cardille, Terry Alexander, Jarlath Conroy, Joseph Pilato. Written and directed by George A. Romero; for Laurel / United.

The Day of the Dolphin*
US 1973 104m Technicolor
Panavision
Avco–Embassy / Icarus (Robert E. Relyea)

A marine biologist researching dolphins off the Florida coast discovers they are being used in a plot to blow up the President's yacht.
A strangely unexpected and unsuccessful offering from the talent involved: thin and repetitive as scientific instruction (the dolphins' language in any case topples it into fantasy), and oddly childlike as spy adventure.

w Buck Henry, *novel* Robert Merle *d* Mike Nichols *ph William A. Fraker* *m* Georges Delerue *pd* Richard Sylbert

George C. Scott, Trish Van Devere, Paul Sorvino, Fritz Weaver

'The whole thing seems to have been shoved through the cameras as glibly as possible, so that everyone concerned could grab the money and run.'—*Stanley Kauffmann*

'An eight and a half million dollar Saturday afternoon special for sheltered nine-year-olds.'—*Judith Crist*

'Dolphins may live in a state of ecstasy, but the cast of this film seems lost in a state of confusion, wondering whether they are in an enlightened documentary, juvenile fantasy, or lurid soap opera.'—*Les Keyser, Hollywood in the Seventies*

'The most expensive Rin Tin Tin movie ever made.'—*Judith Crist*

AAN: Georges Delerue

The Day of the Evil Gun*
US 1968 93m Metrocolor Panavision
MGM (Jerry Thorpe)

Returning home after three years, a rancher finds that his wife and child have been carried off by Indians.
Competent standard western which resolves itself into a duel of wits between the hero and his rival.

w Charles Marquis Warren, Eric Bercovici *d* Jerry Thorpe *ph* W. Wallace Kelley *m* Jeff Alexander

Glenn Ford, Arthur Kennedy, Dean Jagger, Paul Fix, John Anderson, Nico Minardos

The Day of the Jackal**
GB / France 1973 142m Technicolor
Universal / Warwick / Universal France (John Woolf, David Deutsch)

British and French police combine to prevent an OAS assassination attempt on de Gaulle by use of a professional killer.
An incisive, observant and professional piece of work based on a rather clinical bestseller. Lack of a channel for sympathy, plus language confusions, are its main drawbacks.

w Kenneth Ross, *novel* Frederick Forsyth *d Fred Zinnemann* *ph Jean Tournier* *m* Georges Delerue

Edward Fox, Michel Lonsdale, Alan Badel, Eric Porter, Cyril Cusack, Delphine Seyrig, Donald Sinden, Tony Britton, Timothy West, Olga Georges-Picot, Barrie Ingham, Maurice Denham, Anton Rodgers

'Before *Jackal* is five minutes old, you know it's just going to be told professionally, with no flavour and no zest.'—*Stanley Kauffmann*

'All plot, with scarcely a character in sight.'—*Michael Billington, Illustrated London News*

'A better than average thriller for those who haven't read the book.'—*Judith Crist*

'A rare lesson in film-making in the good old grand manner.'—*Basil Wright, 1972*

'It happened in Hollywood—but it could have happened in Hell!'

The Day of the Locust**
US 1975 143m Technicolor
Paramount / Long Road (Jerome Hellman, Sheldon Shrager)

In Hollywood in the 1930s, a novice art director is bewildered by the eccentricities of life and an innocent man is martyred by the crowd.
A curious and interesting work from a savagely satirical novel; full of stimulating scenes and characters, it barely succeeds as a whole and was a disaster at the box office.

w Waldo Salt, *novel* Nathanael West *d John Schlesinger* *ph* Conrad Hall *m* John Barry *pd* Richard MacDonald

Donald Sutherland, William Atherton, Karen Black, Burgess Meredith, Geraldine Page, Richard A. Dysart, Bo Hopkins, Lelia Goldoni

AAN: Conrad Hall; Burgess Meredith

The Day of the Outlaw**
US 1958 96m bw
UA / Security Pictures (Sidney Harmon)

Two rival cattlemen forget their differences to fight six outlaws who ride into town.
Bleak and wintry western, well done and sufficiently unusual to stick in the mind.

w Philip Yordan, *novel* Lee Wells *d André de Toth* *ph Russell Harlan* *m* Alexander Courage

Robert Ryan, Burl Ives, Tina Louise, Nehemiah Persoff, David Nelson, Venetia Stevenson, Jack Lambert, Lance Fuller

'In the best William S. Hart tradition.'—*MFB*

The Day of the Triffids*
GB 1962 95m Eastmancolor Cinemascope
Philip Yordan (George Pitcher)

Almost everyone in the world is blinded by meteorites prior to being taken over by intelligent plants.
Rough and ready adaptation of a famous sci-fi novel, sometimes blunderingly effective and with moments of good trick work.

w Philip Yordan, *novel* John Wyndham *d* Steve Sekely *ph* Ted Moore *m* Ron Goodwin

Howard Keel, Nicole Maurey, Kieron Moore, Janette Scott, Alexander Knox

Day of Wrath***
Denmark 1943 105m bw
Palladium
original title: *Vredens Dag*

In a 17th-century village an old woman is burned as a witch and curses the pastor who judged her. He dies and his mother accuses her daughter-in-law, in love with another man, of using witchcraft to kill him.
Harrowing, spellbinding melodrama with a message, moving in a series of Rembrandtesque compositions from one horrifying sequence to another. Depressing, but marvellous.

w Carl Dreyer, Poul Knudsen, Mogens Skot-Hansen, *play* Anne Pedersdotter by Hans Wiers Jenssen *d Carl Dreyer* *ph Carl Andersson* *m* Poul Schierbeck *ad* Erik Ases, Lis Fribert

Thorkild Roose, Lisbeth Movin, Sigrid Neiiendam, Preben Lerdoff Rye, Anna Svierkier

The Day the Earth Caught Fire**
GB 1961 99m bw with filters Dyaliscope
British Lion / Pax (Val Guest)

Nuclear tests knock the world off its axis and send it careering towards the sun.
A smart piece of science fiction told through the eyes of Fleet Street journalists and showing a sharp eye for the London scene. Rather exhaustingly talkative, but genuinely frightening at the time.

w Wolf Mankowitz, Val Guest *d Val Guest* *ph* Harry Waxman *m* Monty Norman

Edward Judd, Janet Munro, Leo McKern, *Arthur Christiansen* (ex-editor of the Daily Express), Michael Goodliffe, Bernard Braden, Reginald Beckwith, Austin Trevor, Renée Asherson, Edward Underdown

'From out of space—a warning and an ultimatum!'

The Day the Earth Stood Still**
US 1951 92m bw
TCF (Julian Blaustein)

A flying saucer arrives in Washington and its alien occupant, aided by a robot, demonstrates his intellectual and physical power, warns the world what will happen if wars continue, and departs.
Cold-war wish-fulfilment fantasy, impressive rather than exciting but very capably put over with the minimum of trick work and the maximum of sober conviction.

w Edmund H. North *d Robert Wise* *ph Leo Tover* *m Bernard Herrmann*

Michael Rennie, Patricia Neal, Hugh Marlowe, Sam Jaffe, Billy Gray

'Quite wry and alarmingly smooth.'—*New Yorker, 1977*

The Day the Fish Came Out
GB / Greece 1967 109m De Luxe
TCF / Michael Cacoyannis

Atomic material contaminates a Mediterranean island.
Addle-pated, would-be satirical mod fantasy with establishment figures cast as world villains.

wd Michael Cacoyannis *ph* Walter Lassally *m* Mikis Theodorakis

Tom Courtenay, Colin Blakely, Sam Wanamaker, Candice Bergen, Ian Ogilvy, Patricia Burke

The Day the Hot Line Got Hot
US 1968 92m Eastmancolor
Russian and American agents are outwitted by their go-between. Feeble espionage comedy teaming two big stars at the end of their careers. Charles Boyer, Robert Taylor, George Chakiris, Marie Dubois. Written by Paul Jarrico, Dominique Fabre and M. Trueblood; directed by Etienne Périer; for Commonwealth United.

The Day They Robbed the Bank of England*
GB 1960 85m bw
MGM / Summit (Jules Buck)
In 1901 Irish patriots plan a coup against the British government . . .
Small-scale, well-detailed period caper story, marred by a slow-starting script and unsympathetic acting.
w Howard Clewes, Richard Maibaum, *novel* John Brophy *d* John Guillermin *ph* Georges Périnal *m* Edwin Astley
Peter O'Toole, Aldo Ray, Elizabeth Sellars, Kieron Moore, Albert Sharpe, Hugh Griffith, John Le Mesurier, Joseph Tomelty, Miles Malleson, Colin Gordon

A Day to Remember
GB 1953 92m bw
A darts team takes a day trip to France. Pleasant compendium of mini-stories with an agreeable cast. Stanley Holloway, Donald Sinden, Joan Rice, Odile Versois, James Hayter, Edward Chapman, Harry Fowler, Peter Jones, Bill Owen. Written by Robin Estridge from the novel The Hand and Flower by Jerrard Tickell; directed by Ralph Thomas; for Box-Thomas/GFD (Rank).

The Day Will Dawn*
GB 1942 98m bw
Niksos (Paul Soskin)
US title: *The Avengers*
Norwegian freedom fighters destroy a U-boat base and are saved by commandos.
Dated propaganda piece with an interesting cast.
w Terence Rattigan, Anatole de Grunwald, Patrick Kirwan *d* Harold French *ph* Bernard Knowles *m* Richard Addinsell
Ralph Richardson, Deborah Kerr, Hugh Williams, Griffith Jones, Francis L. Sullivan, Roland Culver, Niall MacGinnis, Finlay Currie, Bernard Miles, Patricia Medina

Daybreak*
US 1931 85m approx bw
MGM
An Austrian guardsman falls in love out of his class.
Elegant romantic fable comparable with *Letter From an Unknown Woman*; equally unpopular and quite forgotten.
w Ruth Cummings, Zelda Sears, Cyril Hume, *play* Arthur Schnitzler *d Jacques Feyder* *ph* J. Merrit Gerstad
Ramon Novarro, Helen Chandler, C. Aubrey Smith, Karen Morley, Kent Douglass, Jean Hersholt, Glenn Tryon
'One of those pictures that won't draw after opening . . . pretty flat all the way . . . good only insofar as Novarro will draw anywhere.'—*Variety*

Daybreak
GB 1946 81m bw
GFD / Triton (Sydney Box)
A barber and part-time hangman marries a destitute girl, loses her to a Swedish seaman, and kills himself in such a way as to implicate the other man.
Dockside melodrama of extraordinary pretentious gloominess; laughable in most respects. A curious follow-up from the *Seventh Veil* team.
w Muriel and Sydney Box, *play* Monckton Hoffe *d* Compton Bennett *ph* Reg Wyer
Ann Todd, Eric Portman, Maxwell Reed, Edward Rigby, Bill Owen, Jane Hylton, Maurice Denham

Days of Glory
US 1944 86m bw
RKO (Casey Robinson)
Russian peasants fight the invading Nazis.
Lower-berth wartime propaganda piece chiefly notable for introducing Gregory Peck to the screen.
w Casey Robinson, *story* Melchior Lengyel *d* Jacques Tourneur *ph* Tony Gaudio *m* Daniele Amfitheatrof
Tamara Toumanova, Gregory Peck, Alan Reed, Maria Palmer, Lowell Gilmore, Hugo Haas

'Your eyes—your ears—your senses will be overwhelmed!'

Days of Heaven**
US 1978 95m Metrocolor
Paramount / OP (Bert and Harold Schneider)
In the early 20th century, three young immigrants leave Chicago for the wheatfields.
Visually a superb slice of period life, let down by obsessively self-important and symbolic drama; also by imperfect sound recording.
wd Terrence Malick *ph Nestor Almendros* *m* Ennio Morricone
Richard Gere, Brooke Adams, Sam Shepard, Linda Manz
'It's serious, yes, very solemn, but not depressing.'—*Roger Ebert*
AAN: Ennio Morricone

Days of Thrills and Laughter***
US 1961 93m bw
(TCF) *Robert Youngson*
Appealing if rather miscellaneous silent film compilation with the accent on action and thrills as well as comedy. Like the other Youngson histories, a boon to film archivists despite a facetious commentary.
m Jack Shaindlin *narrator* Jay Jackson
Stan Laurel, Oliver Hardy, Snub Pollard, Douglas Fairbanks, Charles Chaplin, Pearl White, Houdini, Harry Langdon, Ben Turpin, Charlie Chase, Boris Karloff, Warner Oland, Fatty Arbuckle, Keystone Kops

Days of Wine and Roses**
US 1962 117m bw
Warner (Martin Manulis)
A PR man becomes an alcoholic; his wife gradually reaches the same state, but he recovers and she does not.
Smart satirical comedy confusingly gives way to melodrama, then sentimentality; quality is evident throughout, but all concerned are happiest with the first hour.
w J. P. Miller *d* Blake Edwards *ph Philip Lathrop* *m Henry Mancini*
Jack Lemmon, Lee Remick, Charles Bickford, Jack Klugman, Alan Hewitt, Debbie Megowan, Jack Albertson
AA: title song (*m* Henry Mancini, *ly* Johnny Mercer)
AAN: Jack Lemmon; Lee Remick

A Day's Pleasure*
US 1919 20m bw silent
First National / Charles Chaplin
Mishaps of a family picnic.
Very mild Chaplin, reaching for but not achieving a kind of lyric quality. Amusing bits rather than scenes.
wd Charles Chaplin *ph* Rollie Totheroh
Charles Chaplin, Edna Purviance, Henry Bergman, Babe Lincoln

Daytime Wife
US 1939 71m bw
A young wife finds that her husband is still dating his secretary, and retaliates by dating his colleague. Hollywood version of a French farce; not terrific, but watchable. Tyrone Power, Linda Darnell, Warren William, Binnie Barnes, Wendy Barrie, Joan Davis, Leonid Kinskey. Written by Art Arthur, Robert Harari; directed by Gregory Ratoff; for TCF. 'Will give a good account of itself in the key runs.'—*Variety*

Dayton's Devils
US 1968 103m Eastmancolor
Madison / Harold Goldman (Robert W. Stabler)
A former USAF colonel assembles a group of misfits and adventurers to steal an army payroll.
Overlong, routine caper film with a surprisingly crisp climax (when it comes).
w Fred de Gorter *d* Jack Shea *ph* Brick Marquard *m* Marlin Skiles
Leslie Nielsen, Rory Calhoun, Lainie Kazan, Hans Gudegast

D-Day the Sixth of June
US 1956 106m Eastmancolor Cinemascope
TCF (Charles Brackett)

On the way to invade France in 1944, a British colonel and an American captain reminisce about their love for the same woman.
Turgid war romance with some good action scenes and the usual hilarious Hollywood view of London. General effect very wooden.

w Ivan Moffat, Harry Brown, *novel* Lionel Shapiro *d* Henry Koster *ph* Lee Garmes *m* Lyn Murray

Robert Taylor, Richard Todd, Dana Wynter, Edmond O'Brien, John Williams, Jerry Paris, Richard Stapley

'Reminiscent of *Mrs Miniver* in style and feeling.'—*MFB*

'He made evil an art, vice a virtue and pain a pleasure!'

De Sade*
US / Germany 1969 113m Movielab
AIP / CCC / Transcontinental (Louis M. Heyward, Artur Brauner)

The unbalanced Marquis de Sade is tormented by his wicked uncle with thoughts of his past.
Mildly interesting attempt by AIP at European debauchery, with a good theatrical framework for the fantasies but too much flailing about by all concerned, especially in the slow motion orgy sequences, which are relentlessly boring, as is the film.

w Richard Matheson *d* Cy Endfield *ph Heinz Pehlke ad Jurgen Kiebach m* Billy Strange

Keir Dullea, *John Huston*, Lilli Palmer, Senta Berger, Anna Massey, Uta Levka

The Dead***
GB 1987 83m FotoKem colour
Vestron / Zenith / Liffey Films (Wieland Schulz-Keil, Chris Sievernich)

Two Irish spinster sisters throw a winter dinner for their relatives and friends.
Its director's last film is a warm and somehow invigorating reminiscence of things past.
w Tony Huston from Dubliners by James Joyce *d John Huston ph* Fred Murphy *m* Alex North *pd* Stephen Grimes, Dennis Washington *costumes* Dorothy Jeakins

Anjelica Huston, Donal McCann, Rachel Dowling, Cathleen Delany, Dan O'Herlihy, Helena Carroll, Donal Donnelly

'A delicate coda in a minor key to an illustrious 46-year career.'—*Daily Variety*

'A small masterpiece, perfectly achieved.'—*Time Out*

AAN: Dorothy Jeakins

'You may not like these people, nor pity them, but you'll never forget this picture!'

Dead End***
US 1937 92m bw
Samuel Goldwyn

A slice of life in New York's east side, where slum kids and gangsters live in a river street next to a luxury apartment block.
Highly theatrical film of a highly theatrical play, more or less preserving the single set and overcoming the limitations of the script and setting by sheer cinematic expertise. It is chiefly remembered, however, for introducing the Dead End Kids to a delighted world.

w Lillian Hellman, *play Sidney Kingsley d William Wyler ph Gregg Toland ad Richard Day m* Alfred Newman

Joel McCrea, Sylvia Sidney, *Humphrey Bogart*, Wendy Barrie, Claire Trevor, Allen Jenkins, *Marjorie Main*, James Burke, Ward Bond, *The Dead End Kids* (Billy Halop, Leo Gorcey, Bernard Punsley, Huntz Hall, Bobby Jordan, Gabriel Dell)

'Tense and accurate transcription, but sordid and depressing . . . in for a disappointing career.'—*Variety*

AAN: best picture; Gregg Toland; Claire Trevor

The Dead End Kids
The films in which the original gang of young 'hooligans' (see above) appeared were as follows:

1937: DEAD END
1938: CRIME SCHOOL, ANGELS WITH DIRTY FACES
1939: THEY MADE ME A CRIMINAL, HELL'S KITCHEN, ANGELS WASH THEIR FACES
1940: THE DEAD END KIDS ON DRESS PARADE

Subsequently they broke up into the LITTLE TOUGH GUYS, the EAST SIDE KIDS, and the BOWERY BOYS (all qv)

Dead Heat on a Merry Go Round
US 1967 108m Technicolor
Columbia (Carter de Haven)

An ex-con breaks parole and plans to rob Los Angeles Airport.
Boringly arty caper comedy-melodrama, concentrating less on the robbery than on its hero's sexual prowess. All very superficially flashy, and what the title means is anybody's guess.

wd Bernard Girard *ph* Lionel Lindon *m* Stu Phillips

James Coburn, Camilla Sparv, Aldo Ray, Nina Wayne, Robert Webber, Rose Marie, Todd Armstrong, Marian Moses, Severn Darden

'Just fills the space between a frisky title and a tricky TV-comedy ending, but doesn't fill it with any revels that require a viewer's complete attention.'—*Time*

Dead Man's Eyes
US 1944 64m bw

In order to trap a murderer, a blind artist pretends to have recovered his sight. Cheerless lower-case thriller from the disappointing *Inner Sanctum* series. Lon Chaney Jnr, Jean Parker, Paul Kelly. Written by Dwight V. Babcock; directed by Reginald LeBorg; for Universal.

Dead Man's Shoes
GB 1939 67m bw

A wealthy Paris manufacturer is accused of being a criminal who once disappeared. Sufficiently absorbing courtroom / amnesia melodrama, with British actors in a French setting. Leslie Banks, Joan Marion, Geoffrey Atkins, Wilfred Lawson, Judy Kelly, Nancy Price, Peter Bull, Walter Hudd, Ludwig Stossel. Written by Hans Kafka, Nina Jarvis; directed by Thomas Bentley; for Associated British. 'Goes straight into tense situations, and there are unexpected twists . . . should do well.'—*Variety*

Dead Men Are Dangerous
GB 1938 69m bw

A down-and-out changes clothes with a corpse and is accused of murder. Lethargic thriller, unconvincing in detail. Robert Newton, Betty Lynne, John Warwick, Peter Gawthorne. Written by Victor Kendall, Harry Hughes and Vernon Clancy; directed by Harold French; for Pathé.

Dead Men Don't Wear Plaid*
US 1982 88m bw
Universal / Aspen Film Society (David V. Picker, William E. McEuen)

A private eye is hired by a beautiful girl to find her father's murderer.
Ingenious but overstretched prank in which the hero apparently (by intercutting) gets involved with famous crime stars of the forties: Bogart, Ladd, Bacall, Stanwyck, etc. The basic script is simply not funny enough to support the superstructure, though the selection of lines from the oldies is often ingenious.

w Carl Reiner, George Gipe, Steve Martin *d* Carl Reiner *ph* Michael Chapman *m* Miklos Rozsa *ed* Bud Molin *pd* John DeCuir

Steve Martin, Rachel Ward, Carl Reiner, Reni Santoni

'The content is undergraduate facetiousness at its worst, but at least the excerpts themselves provide a pleasant *noir* anthology.'—*Sight and Sound*

Dead Men Tell No Tales
GB 1938 80m bw

The matron of a school for boys is murdered after winning a lottery. Reasonably intriguing mystery. Emlyn Williams, Hugh Williams, Marius Goring, Lesley Brook, Sara Seegar. Written by Walter Summers and others, from the novel *The Norwich Victims* by Francis Beeding; directed by David MacDonald; for British National.

Dead Men Walk
US 1943 64m bw

A vampire returns from death to destroy his twin brother. Incompetent chiller partly sustained by its star performance. George Zucco, Mary Carlisle. Written by Fred Myton; directed by Sam Newfeld; for PRC.

Dead of Night****
GB 1945 104m bw
Ealing (Sidney Cole, John Croydon)

An architect is caught up in an endless series of recurring dreams, during which he is told other people's supernatural experiences and finally murders the psychiatrist who is trying to help him.
Chillingly successful and influential compendium of the macabre, especially effective in its low-key handling of the linking sequence with its circular ending.

w John Baines, Angus Macphail, based on stories by themselves, H. G. Wells, E. F. Benson *d Cavalcanti, Charles Crichton, Robert Hamer, Basil Dearden ph* Douglas Slocombe, Stan Pavey *m Georges Auric ad Michael Relph*

Mervyn Johns, Roland Culver, Mary Merrall, Judy Kelly, Anthony Baird, *Sally Ann Howes, Frederick Valk, Googie Withers*, Ralph Michael, Esmé Percy, Basil Radford, Naunton Wayne, Miles Malleson, *Michael Redgrave*, Hartley Power, Elizabeth Welch

'In a nightmare within a nightmare are contained five separate ghost stories . . . they have atmosphere and polish, they are eerie, they are well acted.'—*Richard Winnington*

'One of the most successful blends of laughter, terror and outrage that I can remember.'—*James Agee*

'The five ghost stories accumulate in intensity until the trap closes in the surrealist climax.'—*Pauline Kael, 1968*

Dead of Winter
US 1986 100m Metrocolor

An actress finds herself cast for a role which involves her being trapped in a country house with two villains. Oddball suspenser with talent which seems to have expected something better. May Steenburgen, Roddy McDowall, Jan Rubes. Written by Marc Shmuger, Mark Malone; directed by Arthur Penn; for John Bloomgarden, Marc Shmuger/MGM-UA.

Dead or Alive
Italy / US 1967 89m Eastmancolor
Documento / Selmur (Albert Band)
US title: *A Minute to Pray, a Second to Die*

A gunman with a paralysed right arm helps a state governor rid a town of bandits.
Semi-spaghetti western with a strong cast and violent action scenes.

w Ugo Liberatore, Louis Garfinkle *d* Franco Giraldi *ph* Aiace Parolin *m* Carlo Rustichelli

Robert Ryan, Arthur Kennedy, Alex Cord, Nicoletta Machiavelli

Dead Pigeon on Beethoven Street
West Germany 1972 103m De Luxe

An American private eye is shot dead in Germany by an international extortion gang, and his partner arrives to seek revenge.
Cheapskate thriller of interest only to addicts of the director. Glenn Corbett, Christa Lang, Anton Diffring. Written and directed by Samuel Fuller; for Bavaria Atelier. (NB: Filmed in English.)

Dead Reckoning*
US 1947 100m bw
Columbia (Sidney Biddell)

Two war veterans are on their way to be decorated in Washington when one disappears.
Dour, complexly plotted thriller, a typical Hollywood *film noir* of the post-war years but a long way behind *Gilda* in likeability. The hero confesses the plot to a priest, and all the way it is more glum than fun.

w Oliver H. P. Garrett, Steve Fisher *d John Cromwell ph* Leo Tover *m* Marlin Skiles *md* Morris Stoloff

Humphrey Bogart, Lizabeth Scott, *Morris Carnovsky*, Charles Cane, William Prince, Marvin Miller, Wallace Ford, James Bell

'The atmosphere is fraught with sinister suggestion.'—*Sunday Express*

Dead Ringer*
US 1964 116m bw
Warner (William H. Wright)
GB title: *Dead Image*

A woman shoots her rich twin sister and assumes her identity.
High camp star vehicle, full of memories of long ago but rather drearily assembled and far too long, though Miss Davis as ever is in fighting form.

w Albert Beich, Oscar Millard *d* Paul Henreid *ph* Ernest Haller *m* André Previn

Bette Davis, Karl Malden, Peter Lawford, Philip Carey, Jean Hagen, Estelle Winwood, George Chandler, Cyril Delevanti

The Dead Zone*
US 1983 103m Technicolor
Lorimar / Dino de Laurentiis (Cebra Hill)

The survivor of a road accident discovers that he has psychic powers.
Glum thriller with a fairly predictable outcome but some well-staged episodes

w Jeffrey Boan, *novel* Stephen King *d David Cronenberg ph* Mark Irwin *m* Michael Kamen *pd* Carol Spier

Christopher Walken, Brooke Adams, Tom Skerritt, Herbert Lom, Anthony Zerbe, Colleen Dewhurst

Deadfall
GB 1968 120m De Luxe
TCF / Salamanda (Paul Monash, Jack Rix)

Robbery turns sour when a cat burglar falls in love with the wife of his homosexual partner.
Drearily fashionable romantic melodrama with far too few high spots and generally dull performances.

w Bryan Forbes, *novel* Desmond Cory *d* Bryan Forbes *ph* Gerry Turpin *m* John Barry

Michael Caine, Eric Portman, Giovanna Ralli, Nanette Newman, David Buck

'Exhausted no doubt by their past passions and childhood traumas, the principal protagonists move like so many somnambulists through the turgid labyrinth . . . whatever the intention, *Deadfall* merely falls flat on its somewhat ludicrous face.'—*MFB*

Deadlier Than the Male
GB 1967 101m Techniscope
Rank / Sydney Box (Betty E. Box)

Bulldog Drummond traces the death of oil company executives to a master criminal using glamorous female assassins.
Just about tolerable recreation of Drummond in the modern world, with too little style, too much violence and sex, and an almost total lack of self-mockery. A sequel *Some Girls Do* (qv), was an unmitigated disaster.

w Jimmy Sangster, David Osborn, Liz Charles-Williams *d* Ralph Thomas *ph* Ernest Steward *m* Malcolm Lockyer *ad* Alex Vetchinsky

Richard Johnson, Nigel Green, Elke Sommer, Sylva Koscina, Suzanna Leigh, Zia Mohyeddin, Steve Carlson

'The original Drummond would have found the whole thing rather distasteful.'—*MFB*

Deadline at Dawn
US 1946 82m bw
RKO

A sailor on leave passes out, finds the girl he was with has been murdered, and is helped by a philosophical taxi driver and a girl.
This could have been another *Crossfire*, but is smothered by pretentious writing and uncertain direction. The credits are interesting, though.

w Clifford Odets *d* Harold Clurman *ph* Nicholas Musuraca *m* Hanns Eisler

Paul Lukas, Bill Williams, Susan Hayward, Osa Massen, Lola Lane

Deadline for Murder
US 1946 64m bw

A gambler gets mixed up in the theft of a government document. Reliable supporting fare. Paul Kelly, Kent Taylor, Sheila Ryan, Jerome Cowan, Renee Carson. Written by Irving Cummings Jnr; directed by James Tinling; for Sol M. Wurtzel / TCF.

Deadline USA*
US 1952 87m bw
TCF (Sol C. Siegel)
GB title: *Deadline*

Despite threats and the killing of a witness, a crusading newspaper editor goes ahead with a story about the crimes of a powerful gangster.
Watchable newspaper melodrama with nothing much to say except that America must wake up to the enemy within. Smooth production, but too much semi-pretentious talk.

wd Richard Brooks *ph* Milton Krasner *m* Cyril Mockridge

Humphrey Bogart, Kim Hunter, Ethel Barrymore, Ed Begley, Paul Stewart, Warren Stevens, Martin Gabel, Joe de Santis, Audrey Christie, Jim Backus

The Deadly Affair**
GB 1966 106m Technicolor
Columbia / Sidney Lumet

A Foreign Office man apparently commits suicide; his colleague is unconvinced and finally uncovers a spy ring.
Compulsive if heavy-going thriller from the sour-about-spies era, deliberately glum, photographed against the shabbiest possible London backgrounds in muddy colour. Solidly entertaining for sophisticated grown-ups.

w Paul Dehn, novel Call for the Dead by John Le Carré *d Sidney Lumet ph* Frederick A. Young *m* Quincy Jones

James Mason, Simone Signoret, Harry Andrews, Maximilian Schell, Harriet Andersson, Kenneth Haigh, *Max Adrian*, Robert Flemyng, Roy Kinnear, Lynn Redgrave

The Deadly Bees
GB 1966 83m Technicolor

A pop singer goes on holiday to a remote farm and finds herself menaced by killer bees. Flat little thriller with one very obvious twist and no monster: just those bees. Frank Finlay, Guy Doleman, Suzanna Leigh, Catherine Finn. Written by Robert Bloch and Anthony Marriott; directed by Freddie Francis; for Amicus.

'To the valley of mystery came the shadow of death!'

Deadly Blessing
US 1981 102m Metrocolor
Polygram / Interplanetary (William Gilmore)

A strict Hittite sect in Pennsylvania is disrupted by the murderous activities of an incubus.
Further developments from the school of *Alien, Omen* and *The Exorcist*; basically a succession of well-engineered shocks punctuated by long periods of boredom.

w Glenn M. Benest, Matthew Barr, Wes Craven *d* Wes Craven *ph* Robert Jessup *m* James Horner *sp* Jack Bennett

Maren Jensen, Susan Buckner, Jeff East, Ernest Borgnine, Lisa Hartman, Lois Nettleton

The Deadly Companions*
US 1961 90m Pathecolor Panavision
Warner / Pathe America (Charles B. Fitzsimmons)

An army sergeant, a deserter, a trigger-happy gunman and a saloon hostess join forces to rob a bank.
Disjointed but rather attractive little western let down by corny moments in the script.

w A. S. Fleishman *d Sam Peckinpah ph* William H. Clothier *m* Martin Skiles, Raoul Kraushaar

Brian Keith, Maureen O'Hara, Chill Wills, Steve Cochran

Deadly Friend
US 1986 99m Technicolor

A bright kid robotizes a victimized girl and helps her get her revenge. Silly but nasty horror flick of the Elm Street genre. Matthew Laborteaux, Kristy Swanson, Michael Sharrett, Anne Twomey. Written by Bruce Joel Rubin from the novel Friend by Diana Henstell; directed by Wes Craven; for Pan Arts Layton / Warner.

'See a 1000-ton insect monster hungering for human prey!'

The Deadly Mantis
US 1957 78m bw

A 'prehistoric' mantis escapes from Arctic ice and travels rapidly towards New York. Absurd and poorly crafted monster movie. Craig Stevens, Alix Talton, William Hopper. Written by Martin Berkeley; directed by Nathan Juran; for Universal-International.

Deadly Strangers
GB 1974 93m Eastmancolor
Rank / Silhouette (Peter Miller)

A girl accepts a lift from a motorist at a time when a mad strangler is on the loose.
Sub-Hitchcock melo-thriller with enough red herrings to sink a ship. Smartly enough done, but the grisliness needed balancing by humour.

w Philip Levene *d* Sidney Hayers *ph* Graham Edgar *m* Ron Goodwin

Hayley Mills, Simon Ward, Sterling Hayden, Ken Hutchison, Peter Jeffrey

The Deadly Trackers
US 1973 104m Technicolor
Warner / Cine Film (Ed Rosen, Fouad Said)
A sheriff stalks the bandits who killed his wife and son.
Lurid and ludicrous western started, and abandoned, by Samuel Fuller; the challenge need not have been taken up.

w Lukas Heller *d* Barry Shear *ph* Gabriel Torres *m* various

Rod Taylor, Richard Harris, Al Lettieri, Neville Brand, William Smith

'It is no more than the outline of a shadow.'—*Tony Rayns*

'An incoherent, blood-soaked chase story.'—*New Yorker, 1977*

The Deadly Trap
France / Italy 1971 100m Eastmancolor

The children of an American couple in Paris are kidnapped. Smoothly made thriller which spends rather too much time being chic. Faye Dunaway, Frank Langella, Barbara Parkins. Written by Sidney Buchman and Eleanor Perry, from the novel *The Children are Gone* by Arthur Cavanaugh; directed by René Clément; for Corona / Pomereu / Oceania.

Deadwood Dick
US 1940 bw serial: 15 eps

A crusading editor in disguise takes on a gang of renegades led by The Skull. Mildly hilarious western serial, under the gun of Laurel and Hardy's old director. Don Douglas, Lane Chandler, Harry Harvey. Directed by James W. Horne; for Columbia.

Deal of the Century
US 1983 98m Technicolor

An arms dealer is urged not to sell a new weapon to a warmongering dictator. Complex comedy, descending into farce when the visiting general is bribed by the availability of American women. Not a success. Chevy Chase, Sigourney Weaver, Gregory Hines, Vince Edwards, William Jarvis, William Marquez. Written by Paul Brickman; directed by William Friedkin; for Bud Yorkin / Warner.

Dear Brigitte
US 1965 100m De Luxe Cinemascope
TCF (Henry Koster)

The small son of an American professor writes a love letter to Brigitte Bardot, and when they finally go to Paris she is charming to them. Mild family comedy quaintly set around a decaying Mississippi riverboat home; despite assured performances, it all gets a bit icky at times.

w Hal Kanter, *novel* Erasmus with Freckles by John Haase *d* Henry Koster *ph* Lucien Ballard *m* George Duning

James Stewart, Glynis Johns, Fabian, Cindy Carol, Billy Mumy, John Williams, Jack Kruschen, Brigitte Bardot, Ed Wynn, Alice Pearce

Dear Heart*
US 1964 114m bw
Warner (Martin Manulis)

At a postmasters' convention in New York, two middle-aged delegates fall in love. Charming, understated, overlong romantic drama in the *Marty* tradition; all quite professional and satisfying.

w Tad Mosel d Delbert Mann *ph* Russell Harlan *m* Henry Mancini

Glenn Ford, Geraldine Page, Angela Lansbury, Michael Anderson Jnr, Barbara Nichols, Patricia Barry, Charles Drake, Ruth McDevitt, Neva Patterson, Alice Pearce, Richard Deacon
AAN: title song (*m* Henry Mancini, *ly* Jay Livingston, Ray Evans)

Dear Inspector*
France 1977 105m Eastmancolor
Ariane / Mondex (Alexander Mnouchkine)
Original title: *Tendre Poulet*

A female detective chases a murderer, helped by her professor boyfriend.
Very likeable comedy-thriller with neat performances. Popular in America, it was translated into a series for television, but didn't run.

w Michel Audiard, Philippe de Broca, *novel* Jean-Paul Rouland and Claude Olivier *d Philippe de Broca ph* Jean-Paul Schwartz *m* Georges Delerue

Annie Girardot, Philippe Noiret, Catherine Alric, Hubert Deschamps

Dear John*
Sweden 1964 111m bw
Sandrew (Bo Jonsson)
original title: *Kare John*

An unmarried mother in a seaside village falls for a seaman.
A slight story effectively tricked out with all manner of cinematic devices including a multitude of flashbacks. Very watchable if a little self-conscious.

wd Lars Magnus Lindgren, novel Olle Lansburg *ph* Rune Ericson *m* Bengt-Arne Wallin

Jarl Kulle, Christina Schollin, Helena Nilsson, Morgan Anderson

'It shines with the cool clear light of the Swedish summer, and despite its glossy surface manages also to convey strong sensual pleasure.'—*Brenda Davies*

AA: best foreign film

Dear Mr Prohack
GB 1949 91m bw
GFD / Wessex (Ian Dalrymple, Dennis Van Thal)

A treasury official copes admirably with public money but is helpless when he comes into a private fortune.
Flat little comedy in which the minor amusements are incidental to the story.

w Ian Dalrymple, Donald Bull, *novel* Arnold Bennett *d* Thornton Freeland *ph* H. E. Fowle *m* Temple Abady

Cecil Parker, Hermione Baddeley, Dirk Bogarde, Sheila Sim, Glynis Johns, Heather Thatcher, Henry Edwards, Judith Furse

Dear Murderer
GB 1947 94m bw
GFD / Gainsborough (Betty E. Box)

Plot and counterplot among an adulterous triangle.
Thoroughly artificial pattern play set among the unreal rich, from one of those unaccountable West End successes, here boringly filmed.

w Muriel and Sydney Box, Peter Rogers, *play* St John L. Clowes *d* Arthur Crabtree *ph* Stephen Dade

Eric Portman, Greta Gynt, Dennis Price, Maxwell Reed, Jack Warner, Hazel Court, Andrew Crawford, Jane Hylton

Dear Octopus**
GB 1943 86m bw
GFD / Gainsborough (Edward Black)
US title: *The Randolph Family*

Members of a well-to-do British family reunite for Golden Wedding celebrations.
Traditional upper-class British comedy drama, and very well done too, with opportunities for excellent character acting.

w R. J. Minney, Patrick Kirwan, *play Dodie Smith d* Harold French *ph* Arthur Crabtree

Margaret Lockwood, Michael Wilding, *Helen Haye, Frederick Leister, Celia Johnson, Roland Culver, Athene Seyler*, Basil Radford, Nora Swinburne, Jean Cadell, Kathleen Harrison, Ann Stephens, Muriel George, Antoinette Cellier, Graham Moffatt

'The screen's gayest love story!'

Dear Ruth*
US 1947 95m bw
Paramount (Paul Jones)

A schoolgirl causes confusion when she writes love letters to a soldier using her elder sister's photograph.
Smoothly amusing family comedy from a Broadway success.

w Arthur Sheekman, *play* Norman Krasna *d* William D. Russell *ph* Ernest Laszlo *m* Robert Emmett Dolan

Joan Caulfield, William Holden, Mona Freeman, Billy de Wolfe, Edward Arnold, Mary Philips, Virginia Welles

'It is unlikely that 1947 will bring a more satisfying comedy . . . so many surprising and funny twists.'—*John Thompson, New York Mirror*

† Two less amusing sequels were made using virtually the same cast: *Dear Wife* (1949, 88m, *d* Richard Haydn); *Dear Brat* (1951, 82m, *d* William A. Seiter).

Death at Broadcasting House*
GB 1934 71m bw
ABFD / Phoenix (Hugh Perceval)

A radio actor is murdered during a broadcast.
Intriguing little murder mystery with an unusual background.

w Basil Mason, *novel* Val Gielgud *d* Reginald Denham *ph* Gunther Krampf *md* Geoffrey Goodhardt

Ian Hunter, Austin Trevor, Mary Newland, Henry Kendall, Val Gielgud, Peter Haddon, Betty Ann Davies, Jack Hawkins, Donald Wolfit

Death Before Dishonor
US 1986 95m De Luxe

The Marines fight terrorists in an Arab country. Violent exploitation actioner which will satisfy its audience. Fred Dryer, Brian Keith, Paul Winfield, Joanna Pacula. Written by Frank Capra Jnr, Lawrence Kubik, John Gatliff; directed by Terry J. Leonard; for Kubik/MPI/BIMA/New World.

Death from a Distance
US 1936 73m bw

A murderer is trapped in a planetarium. Modest second feature which benefits from its unusual setting. Russell Hopton, Lola Lane, George Marion Snr, Lee Kohlmar. Written by John Krafft; directed by Frank Strayer; for Maury M. Cohen / Chesterfield.

Death Hunt
US 1981 97m Technicolor
Golden Harvest (Murray Shostak)

In 1931 Yukon, a reclusive trapper turns to violence when goaded by other wanderers and drunken mounties.
An arctic cross between *Straw Dogs* and *Death Wish*, and not even so good as either.

w Michael Grais, Mark Victor *d* Peter Hunt *ph* James Devis *m* Jerrold Immel

Charles Bronson, Lee Marvin, Angie Dickinson, Andrew Stevens, Ed Lauter, Carl Weathers, Henry Beckman

Death in Venice**
Italy 1971 128m Technicolor Panavision
Warner / Alfa (Mario Gallo)
original title: *Morte a Venezia*

In a lush Venetian hotel one summer in the early years of the century, a middle-aged German composer on holiday falls for the charms of a silent young boy, and stays in the city too long to escape the approaching plague.
Incredibly extended and rather pointless fable enriched by moments of great beauty and directorial style; these do not quite atone for the slow pace or the muddled storyline.

w Luchino Visconti, Nicola Bandalucco, *novel* Thomas Mann *d Luchino Visconti ph* Pasquale de Santis *m* Gustav Mahler *md* Franco Mannino *ad Ferdinando Scarfiotti*

Dirk Bogarde, Bjorn Andresen, Silvana Mangano, Marisa Berenson, Mark Burns

'Maybe a story as elusive as *Death in Venice* simply can't be filmed. Visconti has made a brave attempt, always sensitive to the original; but it's finally not quite the same thing.'—*David Wilson, MFB*

'Camp and miscalculated from start to finish . . . a prime contender for the title Most Overrated Film of All Time.'—*Time Out, 1985*

The Death Kiss
US 1932 74m bw

During the making of a film an actor is murdered. Promising murder mystery which becomes more and more muddled as it progresses; it wasn't helped by advertising suggesting that Lugosi was again playing a vampire instead of a red herring. David Manners, Adrienne Ames, Bela Lugosi, John Wray, Vince Barnett, Edward Van Sloan. Written by Barry Barringer and Gordon Kahn from the novel by Madelon St Dennis; directed by Edwin L. Marin; for KBS / World Wide.

Death of a Champion
US 1939 67m bw

A champion show dog is murdered, and a memory expert and a small boy solve the mystery. Medium support with few opportunities for its star. Lynne Overman, Donald O'Connor, Virginia Dale, Joseph Allen Jnr, Harry Davenport, Robert Paige. Written by Stuart Palmer and Cortland Fitzsimmons, from a story by Frank Gruber; directed by Robert Florey; for Paramount. 'Skimpy on plot; fair dualler.'—*Variety*

Death of a Cyclist*
Spain / Italy 1955 85m bw
Guion-Suevia / Trionfalcine
original title: *Muerte de un Ciclista*

An accident – a cyclist is knocked down and killed by an adulterous couple – tragically affects the lives of many people.
Rather like a politically conscious version of *An Inspector Calls*, this mannered and unemotional film was most interesting because of its almost Hollywoodian self-assurance.

wd Juan Antonio Bardem story Luis de Igoa *ph* Alfredo Fraile *m* Isrido Maiztegui

Lucia Bose, Alberto Closas, Otello Toso, Carlos Casaravilla

'Is it love or guilt that's making you marry me after all these years?'

Death of a Gunfighter*
US 1969 100m Technicolor
Universal (Richard E. Lyons)

An unpopular marshal refuses to resign, and the situation leads to gunplay.
Downcast character western set in the early years of the century.

w Joseph Calvelli *d* Robert Totten, Don Siegel *ph* Andrew Jackson *m* Oliver Nelson

Richard Widmark, Lena Horne, John Saxon, Carroll O'Connor, Larry Gates, Kent Smith

'A salesman's got to dream—it comes with the territory!'
'One mistake—seen by his son—unleashes with overwhelming power the great drama of our day!'

Death of a Salesman***
US 1951 112m bw
Columbia (Stanley Kramer)

An ageing travelling salesman recognizes the emptiness of his life and commits suicide.
A very acceptable screen version of a milestone play which has become an American classic; stage conventions and tricks are cleverly adapted to cinematic use, especially when the hero walks from the present into the past and back again.

w Stanley Roberts, *play Arthur Miller d Laslo Benedek ph* Franz Planer *m* Alex North *md* Morris Stoloff

Fredric March, Kevin McCarthy, Cameron Mitchell, Mildred Dunnock, Howard Smith, Royal Beal, Jesse White

MRS LOMAN: 'Attention must finally be paid to such a man. He's not to be allowed to fall into his grave like an old dog.'

WILLY LOMAN: 'A salesman is somebody way up there in the blue, riding on a smile and a shoeshine . . .'

'Its time shifts with light, which were poetic in the theatre, seemed shabby in a medium that can dissolve time and space so easily.'—*Stanley Kauffmann*

AAN: Franz Planer; Alex North; Fredric March; Kevin McCarthy; Mildred Dunnock

Death of a Scoundrel*
US 1956 119m bw
RKO / Charles Martin

A Czech in New York becomes rich by fraud.
Unconvincing but intermittently entertaining melodrama, a vehicle for a male Bette Davis.

wd Charles Martin *ph* James Wong Howe *m* Max Steiner

George Sanders, Yvonne de Carlo, Coleen Gray, Victor Jory, Zsa Zsa Gabor, Nancy Gates, John Hoyt, Tom Conway

'Vague moralizing and some attempts at social comment scarcely enliven this protracted study in megalomania.'—*MFB*

Death of a Soldier
Australia 1986 93m colour Panavision

The story of Edward J. Leonski, a psychopathic GI hanged in 1942 for the murders of three women. Case history, most interesting for its re-creation of a period. James Coburn, Reb Brown, Bill Hunter, Maurie Fields, Michael Pate. Written by William Nagle; directed by Philippe Mora; for Suatu / Scotti.

The Death of Mario Ricci*
Switzerland / France / West Germany 1983 101m Eastmancolor
Pegase / TSR / Swanie / FR3 / Tele München

A Swiss TV journalist arrives in a remote village to record an interview with a malnutrition expert, and finds himself in the middle of a mystery about the death of an Italian immigrant worker.
A rather uncontrolled drama which begins by suggesting *Bad Day at Black Rock* but becomes less interesting as it proceeds.

w Claude Goretta, Georges Haldas *d* Claude Goretta *ph* Hans Liechti *m* Arie Dzierlatka

Gian-Maria Volonte, Magali Noel, Mimsy Farmer, Heinz Bennent, Jean-Michael Dupuis

Death on the Diamond
US 1934 69m bw

Murder during a baseball game. The story isn't much, so the picture's appeal depends on one's addiction to baseball. Robert Young, Madge Evans, Nat Pendleton, Ted Healy, C. Henry Gordon, Paul Kelly, Edward Brophy, Mickey Rooney, David Landau. Written by Harvey Thew, Joseph Sherman and Ralph Spence from the novel by Courtland Fitzsimmons; directed by Edward Sedgwick; for MGM. 'Due to plot, miscasting and some minor league technical preparation, it was two strikes to the bad before the cameras started to grind.'—*Variety*

Death on the Nile*
GB 1978 140m Technicolor
EMI (John Brabourne, Richard Goodwin)

Hercule Poirot solves the mystery of who killed the spoilt heiress on a steamer cruising down the Nile.
A pleasant thirties atmosphere and the travel poster backgrounds are the chief assets of this rather hesitant whodunnit which plays fair enough with the audience but gives its popular cast too little to do, while its constant repetitions of the crime become rather ghoulish. On the whole, though, a very passable representation of an old-fashioned genre, and a few points up on *Murder on the Orient Express*.

w Anthony Shaffer, *novel* Agatha Christie *d* John Guillermin *ph* Jack Cardiff *pd* Peter Murton *m* Nino Rota

Peter Ustinov, Bette Davis, Mia Farrow, Angela Lansbury, Jane Birkin, David Niven, George Kennedy, Jack Warden, Simon MacCorkindale, Lois Chiles, Jon Finch, Maggie Smith, Olivia Hussey, Harry Andrews, *I. S. Johar*

Death Race 2000*
US 1975 79m colour
New World (Roger Corman)

In the year 2000, the world's most popular sport involves motor racers who compete for the highest total of human casualties.
Cheaply made macabre satire, quite well enough made to please addicts of the blackest of black comedy.

w Robert Thom, Charles Griffith, Ib Melchior *d* Paul Bartel *ph* Tak Fujimoto *m* Paul Chihara

David Carradine, Simone Griffeth, Sylvester Stallone, Mary Woronov

'The script is hardly Swiftian and therefore treads a thin delicate line between mockery and exploitation.'—*Michael Billington, Illustrated London News*

Death Ship
Canada 1980 91m CFI color

Survivors of a shipwreck take refuge on a mysterious empty ship which sets about killing them one by one. Yes, that's the synopsis, in the wake of *Killdozer* and *The Car*, and this film is stupider than either. George Kennedy, Richard Crenna, Nick Mancuso, Sally Ann Howes, Kate Reid. Written by John Robins; directed by Alvin Rakoff; for Astral Bellevue Pathé / Bloodstar.

'No woman ever loved such a man! The whole world waited while he made love!'

Death Takes a Holiday*
US 1934 78m bw
Paramount (E. Lloyd Sheldon)

In the form of a mysterious prince, Death visits an Italian noble family to see why men fear him so.
A somewhat pretentious classic from a popular play of the twenties; interesting handling and performances, but a slow pace by modern standards.

w Maxwell Anderson, Gladys Lehman, Walter Ferris based on plays by Maxwell Anderson and Alberto Casella *d Mitchell Leisen ph* Charles Lang *ad* Ernst Fegte *m* Bernhard Kaun, Sigmund Krumgold

Fredric March, Evelyn Venable, Sir Guy Standing, Katherine Alexander, Gail Patrick, Helen Westley, Kathleen Howard, Henry Travers, Kent Taylor

'Highly fantastic, but well done . . . likely to have greater appeal among the intelligentsia.'—*Variety*

Death Trap
US 1976 89m colour
Mars (Mohammed Rustam)

The proprietor of a motel on the edge of a swamp is a maniac who murders his guests and feeds them to his pet crocodile.
Pretty sick rip-off of *Psycho*, with no holds barred; a typical and regrettable example of the so-called Gothic horrors of the independent American cinema in the late seventies.

w Alvin L. Fast, Mardi Rustam *d* Tobe Hooper *ph* Jack Beckett *m* Tobe Hooper, Wayne Bell

Neville Brand, Mel Ferrer, Carolyn Jones, Marilyn Burns, William Finley, Stuart Whitman

DEATH TAKES A HOLIDAY. It's difficult to understand why Evelyn Venable looks quite so serene since Fredric March is Death incarnate.

Death Trap (1982): see Deathtrap

'Not even a scream escapes!'
Death Valley
US 1981 88m Technicolor
Universal (Elliott Kastner)

A boy on vacation in Arizona finds himself being chased by a murderer.
Tedious shocker with little in the way of scenic background to relieve the unpleasant monotony.

w Richard Rothstein *d* Dick Richards
ph Stephen H. Burum *m* Dana Kaproff
ed Joel Cox

Paul Le Mat, Catherine Hicks, Stephen McHattie, A. Wilford Brimley, Edward Herrman

Death Weekend
Canada 1976 94m Eastmancolor

Four louts take revenge on a lady driver by following her to a secluded country house. Hoary shocker chiefly concerned with rape, the threat of rape, and various unpleasant methods of murder. Brenda Vaccaro, Don Stroud, Chuck Shamata. Written and directed by William Fruet; for Quadrant.

'Exploitation of the emptiest and most blatant kind.'—*MFB.*

'Vigilante, city style . . . judge, jury and executioner!'
Death Wish*
US 1974 94m Technicolor
Paramount / Dino de Laurentiis (Hal Landers, Bobby Roberts, Michael Winner)

When his wife dies and his daughter becomes a vegetable after an assault by muggers, a New York businessman takes the law into his own hands.
After a highly unpleasant and sensational opening, this curious and controversial film settles down into what amounts to black comedy, with the audience well on the vigilante's side. It's not very good, but it keeps one watching.

w Wendell Mayes, *novel* Brian Garfield
d Michael Winner *ph* Arthur J. Ornitz
m Herbie Hancock

Charles Bronson, Hope Lange, Vincent Gardenia, Stuart Margolin, Stephen Keats, William Redfield

'This urban version of *Walking Tall* transcends its violence to satisfy every base instinct that "we liberals" are heir to.'—*Judith Crist*

Death Wish 2
US 1981 95m colour
Golan–Globus / Landers–Roberts

His maid gang-raped and killed, his handicapped daughter driven to her death, Paul Kersey resumes his stalking of urban thugs.
A badly made exercise in the exploitation of the most repellent aspects of violence, without the first film's saving grace of slickness and humour.

w David Engelbach *d* Michael Winner
ph Richard L. Kline, Tom Del Ruth
m Jimmy Page

Charles Bronson, Jill Ireland, Vincent Gardenia, J. D. Cannon, Anthony Franciosa

'Bad art is one thing, but *Death Wish II* is ludicrous.'—*Variety*

'The sort of sequel which makes you realize that the original wasn't half so bad as you thought.'—*Margaret Hinxman, Daily Mail*

'It doesn't contain an ounce of life. It slinks onto the screen and squirms for a while, and is over.'—*Roger Ebert*

Death Wish 3
GB 1985 90m colour

Paul Kersey, the urban vigilante, eliminates a gang of thugs terrorizing an apartment block. The killing sprees have become routine, and there's nothing else of interest in this boring sequel to a sequel. Charles Bronson, Deborah Raffin, Ed Lauter, Martin Balsam, Gavan O'Herlihy. Written by Michael Edmonds; directed by Michael Winner; for Cannon.

† *Death Wish 4: The Crackdown* in 1988 added nothing new.

The Deathmaster
US 1973 88m De Luxe

California surfers cheerfully adopt a local mystic, not knowing that he is a vampire. Modestly budgeted teenage screamer, competently made but of interest only to avid bibliographers of Count Dracula. Robert Quarry, Brenda Dickson, Bill Ewing, John Fiedler. Written by R. L. Grove; directed by Ray Danton; for RF World Entertainment / AIP.

Deathsport
US 1978 83m Metrocolor
New World (Roger Corman)

A popular game of the future involves gladiators willing to lose their lives against lethal motorcyclists.
Low-budget shocker for teenagers, by *Rollerball* out of *Death Race.* Of no possible interest except as exploitation.

w Henry Suso, Donald Stewart *d* Henry Suso, Allan Arkush *ph* Gary Graver
m Andrew Stein

David Carradine, Claudia Jennings, Richard Lynch, William Smithers

Deathtrap*
US 1982 116m Technicolor
Warner / LAH (Burtt Harris)

A playwright past his best conceives a plan to murder an upcoming rival and steal his script. This thriller on the lines of *Sleuth* was enjoyable enough on stage, but on the screen, despite pretensions to style, it takes far too long to unravel its very few twists, the last of which is badly fumbled.

w Jay Presson Allen, *play* Ira Levin *d* Sidney Lumet *ph* Andrzej Bartkowiak *m* Johnny Mandel *pd* Tony Walton

Michael Caine, Christopher Reeve, Dyan Cannon, Irene Worth, Henry Jones

'It plays absolutely fair, more or less, and yet fools us every time, more or less.'—*Roger Ebert*

Decameron Nights
GB 1952 94m Technicolor
Film Locations (M. J. Frankovich)

Young Boccaccio entertains a glamorous widow and her three guests with stories.
Feeble costume charade with all the cuckolding off-screen: insipid and artificial.

w George Oppenheimer *d* Hugo Fregonese *ph* Guy Green *m* Antony Hopkins

Louis Jourdan, Joan Fontaine, Binnie Barnes, Joan Collins, Godfrey Tearle, Eliot Makeham, Noel Purcell

'The sort of hybrid international production of which experience has made one mistrustful.'—*Gavin Lambert*

Deception**
US 1946 112m bw
Warner (Henry Blanke)

A European cellist returning to America after the war finds that his former girl friend has a rich and jealous lover.
Downcast melodrama made when its star was beginning to slide; today it seems irresistible bosh with a background of classical music, done with intermittent style especially by Claude Rains as the egomaniac lover.

w John Collier, *play* Monsieur Lamberthier by Louis Verneuil *d* Irving Rapper *ph* Ernest Haller *m* Erich Wolfgang Korngold

Bette Davis, *Claude Rains*, Paul Henreid, John Abbott, Benson Fong

'It's like grand opera, only the people are thinner . . . I wouldn't have missed it for the world.'—*Cecelia Ager*

'Exquisitely foolish: a camp classic.'—*New Yorker, 1977*

† Previously filmed in 1929 as *Jealousy*, with Fredric March and Jeanne Eagels.

Decision at Sundown
US 1957 77m Technicolor

A cowboy tracks down the badman who has seduced his wife. Routine small-town western, efficiently done. Randolph Scott, John Carroll, Karen Steele, Valerie French, Noah Beery Jnr, Andrew Duggan. Written by Charles Lang Jnr; directed by Budd Boetticher; for Harry Joe Brown / Columbia.

Decision before Dawn*
US 1951 119m bw
TCF (Anatole Litvak, Frank McCarthy)

In 1944, anti-Nazi German POWs are parachuted into Germany to obtain information.
Meticulous, well made but unexciting spy story which seldom comes vividly to life.

w Peter Viertel, *novel* Call It Treason by George Howe *d* Anatole Litvak *ph* Franz Planer *m* Franz Waxman

Oskar Werner, Richard Basehart, Gary Merrill, Hildegarde Neff, Dominique Blanchar, Helene Thimig, O. E. Hasse, Hans Christian Blech

AAN: best picture

The Decision of Christopher Blake
US 1948 75m bw
Warner (Ranald MacDougall)

A 12-year-old boy reunites his divorcing parents.
Sentimental slop, surprisingly ill done, but with a few good lines.

w Ranald MacDougall, *play* Moss Hart *d* Peter Godfrey *ph* Karl Freund *m* Max Steiner

Alexis Smith, Robert Douglas, *Cecil Kellaway*, Ted Donaldson, *Harry Davenport*, John Hoyt, Mary Wickes, Art Baker, Lois Maxwell

The Decks Ran Red
US 1958 84m bw
MGM / Andrew and Virginia Stone

Unscrupulous sailors plan to murder the entire crew of a freighter and claim the salvage money.
Solidly crafted but basically uninteresting melodrama.

w Andrew and Virginia Stone *d* Andrew Stone *ph* Meredith M. Nicholson

James Mason, Broderick Crawford, Dorothy Dandridge, Stuart Whitman

Decline and Fall
GB 1968 113m De Luxe
TCF / Ivan Foxwell
aka: *Decline and Fall of a Birdwatcher*

An innocent, accident-prone Oxford undergraduate is expelled and after various adventures in high and low society is convicted as a white slaver.
Flabby, doomed attempt to film a satirical classic which lives only on the printed page. Odd moments amuse.

w Ivan Foxwell, *novel* Evelyn Waugh *d* John Krish *ph* Desmond Dickinson *m* Ron Goodwin

Robin Phillips, Donald Wolfit, Genevieve Page, Robert Harris, Leo McKern, Colin Blakely, Felix Aylmer, Donald Sinden, Griffith Jones

'The British *Graduate*.'—*New Yorker*

'Literate, lavishly furnished, tastefully faithful.'—*Observer*

Decoy
US 1947 76m bw

The girl friend of an executed gangster tries to get her hands on his buried loot. Surprisingly tough little co-feature of its day; even more surprisingly, the leading lady is British. Jean Gillie, Edward Norris, Herbert Rudley, Robert Armstrong. Written by Nedrick Young; directed by Jack Bernhard; for Monogram.

Dédée d'Anvers*
France 1948 95m bw
Sacha Gordine (André Paulvé)
aka: *Woman of Antwerp; Dédée*

A dockside prostitute falls for a sailor and arouses the jealousy of her protector.
Seamy low life melodrama, presented *con brio*, but rather like a tenth copy of *Quai des Brumes*.

w Yves Allégret, Jacques Sigurd *d* Yves Allégret *ph* Jean Bourgoin *m* Jacques Besse

Simone Signoret, Marcel Pagliero, Bernard Blier, Marcel Dalio, Jane Marken

The Deep
US 1977 124m Metrocolor Panavision
Columbia / EMI / Casablanca (Peter Guber)

Underwater treasure seekers off Bermuda clash with black villains seeking a lost consignment of morphine.
An expensive action picture which is singularly lacking in action and even in plot, but oozes with brutality and overdoes the splendours of submarine life, forty per cent of it taking place under water.

w Peter Benchley, Tracy Keenan Wynn, *novel* Peter Benchley *d* Peter Yates *ph* Christopher Challis, Al Giddings, Stan Waterman *m* John Barry *pd* Tony Masters

Jacqueline Bisset, Robert Shaw, Nick Nolte, Lou Gossett, Eli Wallach

'The ultimate disco experience . . . it dances on the spot for two hours, taking voodoo, buried treasure, morphine, violence and sea monsters in its stride.'—*Time Out*

'Peter Yates has knocked himself out doing masterly underwater action sequences in the service of a woefully crummy book.'—*Russell Davies, Observer*

The Deep Blue Sea*
GB 1955 99m Eastmancolor Cinemascope
TCF / London Films (Anatole Litvak)

A judge's wife attempts suicide when jilted by her ex-RAF lover.
Undistinguished adaptation of a very good play, hampered by wide screen and muddy colour, helped by thoughtful performances.

w Terence Rattigan, from his play *d* Anatole Litvak *ph* Jack Hildyard *m* Malcolm Arnold

Vivien Leigh, Kenneth More, Eric Portman, *Emlyn Williams*, Moira Lister, Arthur Hill, Dandy Nichols, Jimmy Hanley, Miriam Karlin

Deep End*
West Germany / USA 1970 88m Eastmancolor
Maran / Kettledrum / Bavaria Atelier (Judd Bernard)

Sexual problems of two young people on the staff of a London municipal bathhouse.
Interestingly made but rather dreary and vaguely symbolic modern fable.

w Jerzy Skolimowski, Jerzy Gruza, Boleslaw Sulik *d* Jerzy Skolimowski *ph* Charly Steinberger *m* Cat Stevens

Jane Asher, John Moulder-Brown, Diana Dors, Karl Michael Vogler, Christopher Sandford

'A study in the growth of obsession that is both funny and frighteningly exact.'—*Nigel Andrews, MFB*

Deep in My Heart*
US 1954 132m Eastmancolor
MGM (Roger Edens)

Sigmund Romberg, a composer-waiter in New York, is helped by writer Dorothy Donnelly and showman Florenz Ziegfeld to become a famous writer of musicals.
Standard fictionalized biopic with plenty of good turns and a sharper script than usual.

w Leonard Spiegelgass *d* Stanley Donen *ph* George Folsey *m* Sigmund Romberg *ad* Cedric Gibbons, Edward Carfagno *ch* Eugene Loring

Jose Ferrer, Merle Oberon, Paul Henreid (as Ziegfeld), Walter Pidgeon, Helen Traubel, Doe Avedon, Tamara Toumanova, Paul Stewart, Isobel Elsom, David Burns, Jim Backus . . . and Gene Kelly, Fred Kelly, Rosemary Clooney, Jane Powell, Ann Miller, Cyd Charisse, James Mitchell, Howard Keel, Tony Martin, Joan Weldon

The Deep Six
US 1958 110m Warnercolor
Jaguar (Martin Rackin)

A Quaker is unhappy at being drafted into the navy, but after initial unpopularity becomes a hero.
An ageing star contends with many hazards: slipshod production, poor colour, a dull script, and an unplayable part.

w John Twist, Martin Rackin, Harry Brown *d* Rudolph Maté *ph* John Seitz *m* David Buttolph

Alan Ladd, William Bendix, Efrem Zimbalist Jnr, Dianne Foster, Keenan Wynn, James Whitmore, Joey Bishop, Jeanette Nolan

Deep Valley
US 1947 104m bw
Warner (Henry Blanke)

The daughter of a poor California farmer falls for a convict on a work gang.
Downright peculiar melodrama, a cross between *Tobacco Road* and *Cold Comfort Farm*, with touches of *High Sierra*. For collectors.

w Salka Viertel, Stephen Morehouse Avery, *novel* Dan Totheroh *d* Jean Negulesco *ph* Ted McCord *m* Max Steiner

Ida Lupino, Dane Clark, Wayne Morris, Henry Hull, Fay Bainter, Willard Robertson

Deep Waters
US 1948 85m bw
TCF

A problem orphan boy is content when adopted by a lobster fisherman.
Forgettable family film, smoothly directed and photographed.

w Richard Murphy *d* Henry King *ph* Joseph La Shelle *m* Cyril Mockridge

Jean Peters, Dana Andrews, Dean Stockwell, Cesar Romero, Anne Revere

The Deer Hunter*
US 1978 182m Technicolor Panavision
Universal / EMI (Barry Spikings, Michael Deeley, Michael Cimino, John Peverall)

Three friends from a small Pennsylvania town go to fight in Vietnam.
The three-hour running time is taken up with crosscutting of a wedding, a deer hunt and a game of Russian roulette. Presumably the audience has to guess the point, if any; meanwhile it may be repelled by this long and savage if frequently engrossing film.

w Deric Washburn, *story* Michael Cimino, Louis Garfinkle, Quinn K. Redeker and Washburn *d Michael Cimino* *ph* Vilmos Zsigmond *m* Stanley Myers

Robert De Niro, John Cazale, John Savage, Christopher Walken, Meryl Streep

'A hollow spectacle, less about war than its effect on a community, full of specious analogies, incoherent sentimentality and belief in its own self-importance.'—*Time Out*

AA: best picture; direction; Christopher Walken
AAN: Deric Washburn; Vilmos Zsigmond; Robert de Niro; Meryl Streep

The Defector
France / West Germany 1966 101m Eastmancolor
PECF / Rhein Main (Raoul Lévy)
original title: *L'Espion*

An American physicist in East Germany gets involved in the spy game.
Disenchanted espionage 'realism', not very well styled and hampered by a star at the end of his tether.

w Robert Guenette, Raoul Lévy, *novel* The Spy by Paul Thomas *d* Raoul Lévy *ph* Raoul Coutard *m* Serge Gainsbourg

Montgomery Clift, Hardy Kruger, Macha Meril, Roddy McDowall, David Opatoshu, Christine Delaroche, Jean-Luc Godard

Defence of the Realm**
GB 1985 96m colour
(Rank) Enigma / NFFC (David Puttnam) (Linda Miles)

A journalist tries to check the relationship between an MP and a Russian agent.
Efficient political melodrama, basically too old-fashioned to start a cult.

w Martin Stellman *d David Drury* *ph* Roger Deakins *m* Richard Hartley *pd* Roger Murray-Leach *ed* Michael Bradsall

Gabriel Byrne, Greta Scacchi, Denholm Elliott, Ian Bannen, Fulton Mackay, Bill Paterson

BFA: best supporting actor, Denholm Elliott

Defiance
US 1980 102m Movielab

A young seaman staying in New York fights back against the power of an urban gang.
Belated and unnecessary addition to the gang cycle; violent nonsense. Jan Michael Vincent, Theresa Saldana, Danny Lopez. Written by Thomas Michael Donnelly; directed by John Flynn; for AIP.

The Defiant Ones**
US 1958 96m bw
UA / Stanley Kramer

A black and a white convict escape from a chain gang, still linked together but hating each other.
Schematic melodrama with a moral, impeccably done and with good performances.

w Nathan E. Douglas, Harold Jacob Smith *d Stanley Kramer* *ph Sam Leavitt* *m* Ernest Gold

Tony Curtis, Sidney Poitier, Theodore Bikel, Charles McGraw, Lon Chaney Jnr, King Donovan, Claude Akins, Lawrence Dobkin, Whit Bissell, Carl 'Alfalfa' Switzer, Cara Williams

'Probably Kramer's best picture. The subject matter is relatively simple, though "powerful"; the action is exciting; the acting is good. But the singleness of purpose behind it all is a little offensive.'—*Pauline Kael*

AA: Nathan E. Douglas, Harold Jacob Smith; Sam Leavitt
AAN: best picture; Stanley Kramer; Tony Curtis; Sidney Poitier; Theodore Bikel; Cara Williams

Le Defroqué*
France 1953 111m bw
SFC / SNEG

A defrocked priest performs a gallant action which persuades an acquaintance to become a priest himself and try to draw his friend back into the fold.
Curious but holding moral melodrama embellished by good acting.

w Leo Joannon, Denys de la Patellière *d Leo Joannon* *ph* Nicolas Torporkoff *m* Jean-Jacques Grunenwald

Pierre Fresnay, Pierre Trabaud, Nicole Stéphane, Marcelle Geniat, Guy Decomble, Leo Joannon, René Blancard

Deja Vu
GB 1985 90m colour

Lovers discover that they are reincarnations of a couple who perished 50 years ago in a fire.
Muddling, over-talkative supernatural thriller with dollops of sex. Jaclyn Smith, Nigel Terry, Claire Bloom, Shelley Winters. Written by Ezra D. Rappoport, Anthony Richmond, from book by Trevor Meldal-Johnsen; directed by Anthony Richmond; for Michael Kagan / Cannon.

The Delavine Affair
GB 1954 64m bw

A reporter is framed for killing an informer.
Routine British second feature. Honor Blackman, Peter Reynolds, Gordon Jackson, Michael Balfour. Written by George Fisher, from the story 'Winter Wears a Shroud' by Robert Chapman; directed by Douglas Pierce; for John Croydon / Monarch. (US title: *Murder Is News*.)

A Delicate Balance*
US 1975 134m colour
American Express / Ely Landau / Cinevision

A quarrelsome Connecticut family is dominated by an ageing matriarch, and tensions mount to a climax of fear and threats.
Honourable but slightly boring film version of an essentially theatrical play: the acting is the thing.

w Edward Albee, from his play *d* Tony Richardson *ph* David Watkin *m* none

Katharine Hepburn, Paul Scofield, Joseph Cotten, Lee Remick, Kate Reid, Betsy Blair

The Delicate Delinquent
US 1956 101m bw Vistavision
Paramount / Jerry Lewis

A New York policeman tries to make friends with an eccentric youth who mixes with thugs; the boy decides to train as a policeman.
Jerry Lewis' first film without Dean Martin: a sobering experience combining zany comedy, sentiment, pathos and social comment. The mixture fails to rise.

wd Don McGuire *ph* Haskell Boggs *m* Buddy Bregman

Jerry Lewis, Darren McGavin, Martha Hyer, Robert Ivers, Horace McMahon

Delicious
US 1931 106m bw
Fox

An Irish girl in New York falls for a rich man.
Early musical, very thin, but an agreeable museum piece for collectors.

w Guy Bolton, Sonya Levien *d* David Butler *ph* Ernest Palmer *songs George and Ira Gershwin*

Janet Gaynor, Charles Farrell, El Brendel, Lawrence O'Sullivan, Virginia Cherrill, Mischa Auer

'Cream puffs, applesauce, and plenty of nuts . . . should do the team's business on its name strength.'—*Variety*

Delightfully Dangerous
US 1945 93m bw

A straitlaced girl discovers that her eldest sister is a burlesque dancer. Mild family comedy with music. Jane Powell, Constance Moore, Ralph Bellamy, Arthur Treacher. Written by Walter De Leon and Arthur Phillips; directed by Arthur Lubin; for Charles R. Rogers/UA.

Deliverance**
US 1972 109m Technicolor Panavision
Warner / Elmer Enterprises (John Boorman)

Four men spend a holiday weekend canoeing down a dangerous river, but find that the real danger to their lives comes from themselves and other humans.
Vigorous, meaningful, almost apocalyptic vision of man's inhumanity, disguised as a thrilling adult adventure.

w James Dickey, from his novel *d John Boorman ph* Vilmos Zsigmond *m* Eric Weissberg

Burt Reynolds, Jon Voight, Ned Beatty, Ronny Cox, James Dickey

'There is fundamentally no view of the material, just a lot of painful grasping and groping.'—*Stanley Kauffmann*

AAN: best picture; John Boorman

Delta Force
US 1986 129m colour
Cannon (Menahem Golan)

A TWA plane is hijacked in Athens and rescued by an elite force.
What starts more or less as a recapitulation of fact turns at the half-way point into macho fantasy. Oddly enough, the paying customers rejected the mix.

w James Bruner, Menahem Golan *d* Menahem Golan *ph* David Gurfinkel *m* Alan Silvestri

Chuck Norris, Lee Marvin, Martin Balsam, Joey Bishop, Shelley Winters, Robert Forster, Lainie Kazan, George Kennedy, Hanna Schygulla, Susan Strasberg, Bo Svenson, Robert Vaughn

'An exercise in wish fulfilment . . . it's easy to get off on all this, as millions surely will, so long as you are willing to put your brain in hibernation for more than two hours.'—*Variety*

Dementia 13*
US / Eire 1963 81m bw
Filmgroup / AIP (Roger Corman)
GB title: *The Haunted and the Hunted*

An axe murderer attacks members of a noble Irish family at their lonely castle.
Nastily effective macabre piece with interesting credits.

wd Francis Ford Coppola ph Charles Hannawalt *m* Ronald Stein

Luana Anders, William Campbell, Bart Patton, Mary Mitchell, Patrick Magee, Eithne Dunn

Demetrius and the Gladiators**
US 1954 101m Technicolor Cinemascope
TCF (Frank Ross)

A Greek slave who keeps Christ's robe after the crucifixion is sentenced to be one of Caligula's gladiators and becomes involved in Messalina's wiles.
Lively, efficient sequel to *The Robe*, with emphasis less on religiosity than on the brutality of the arena and our hero's sexual temptations and near-escapes. Good Hollywood hokum.

w Philip Dunne d Delmer Daves ph Milton Krasner *m* Franz Waxman

Victor Mature, Susan Hayward, Michael Rennie (as Peter), Debra Paget, Anne Bancroft, Jay Robinson, Barry Jones, William Marshall, Richard Egan, Ernest Borgnine

'An energetic attempt to fling the mantle of sanctity over several more millions of the entertainment dollar.'—*The Times*

The Demi-Paradise*
GB 1943 114m bw
Two Cities (Anatole de Grunwald)
US title: *Adventure for Two*

In 1939, a Russian inventor is sent to observe the British way of life.
Pleasant, aimless little satirical comedy in which this blessed plot seems to be peopled entirely by eccentrics.

w Anatole de Grunwald *d* Anthony Asquith *ph* Bernard Knowles *m* Nicholas Brodszky

Laurence Olivier, Penelope Dudley Ward, *Margaret Rutherford*, Leslie Henson, Marjorie Fielding, Felix Aylmer, Guy Middleton, Michael Shepley, George Thorpe, Edie Martin, Muriel Aked, Joyce Grenfell

'A backhanded way of showing us poor juvenile-minded cinemagoers that the England of Mr Punch and Mrs Malaprop lives forever.'—*Richard Winnington*

Demon Seed
US 1977 95m Metrocolor Panavision
MGM (Herb Jaffe)

A scientist invents too perfect a computer: it locks up his wife, rapes her, and incubates a child . . .
Science fiction at the end of its tether, all very smart and self-conscious, but at this length very tasteless. Hitchcock would have got it into a television half-hour.

w Robert Jaffe, Roger O. Hirson, *novel* Dean R. Koontz *d* Donald Cammell *ph* Bill Butler *m* Jerry Fielding *pd* Edward Carfagno

Julie Christie, Fritz Weaver, Gerrit Graham, Berry Kroeger, Lisa Lu

The Dentist**
US 1932 19m bw

Classic star short with W. C. Fields working up briskly to a dentist sketch in which he deals summarily with a variety of patients. Directed by Leslie Pearce; for Paramount / Sennett.

Denver and Rio Grande
US 1952 89m Technicolor

Railroad companies compete to lay track through a narrow gorge. Adequate western thick-ear. Edmond O'Brien, Sterling Hayden, Dean Jagger, Laura Elliot, Zasu Pitts, Lyle Bettger, J. Carrol Naish. Written by Frank Gruber; directed by Byron Haskin; for Nat Holt / Paramount.

Deported
US 1950 88m bw

A gangster is sent back to his native Italy and tries to smuggle in his stolen money, but is finally redeemed. Slightly unusual from this studio at this time, but not very interesting. Jeff Chandler, Marta Toren, Claude Dauphin, Marina Berti, Richard Rober. Written by Robert Buckner; directed by Robert Siodmak; for Universal-International.

The Depraved
GB 1957 63m bw

An American officer helps his beloved kill her unattractive husband. Shades of *Double Indemnity*, but only shades. Anne Heywood, Robert Arden, Carroll Levis, Basil Dignam. Written by Brian Clemens; directed by Paul Dickson; for the Danzigers.

Derby Day
GB 1952 84m bw
British Lion / Wilcox-Neagle (Maurice Cowan)
US title: *Four Against Fate*

Intercut comic and melodramatic stories of four people who go to the Derby.
Quietly efficient, class-conscious entertainment on the lines of *Friday the 13th* and *The Bridge of San Luis Rey*. No surprises, but plenty of familiar faces.

w John Baines, Monckton Hoffe, Alan Melville *d* Herbert Wilcox *ph* Max Greene *m* Anthony Collins

Anna Neagle, Michael Wilding, Googie Withers, Gordon Harker, John McCallum, Peter Graves, Suzanne Cloutier, Gladys Henson, Ralph Reader, Alfie Bass, Edwin Styles, Nigel Stock

'Excessive loyalty to a formula has produced far from happy results.'—*Penelope Houston, MFB*

Derelict
US 1930 73m bw

Two sea dogs battle over a ship and a girl. Well-filmed melodrama, with plenty of location work. George Bancroft, William Boyd, Jessie Royce Landis, Donald Stuart. Written by Max Marcin, William Slavens McNutt, Grover Jones; directed by Rowland V. Lee; for Paramount. 'One of the best sea pictures filmed . . . a cinch for the deluxers.'—*Variety*

Le Dernier Milliardaire*
France 1934 100m bw
Pathé-Natan

The queen of a small principality invites a financial wizard to pay court to her daughter. The girl elopes with a bandleader, the financier is engaged to the queen, and is then revealed as a sham.
Rather too determined to be satirical, this comedy sadly lacks the pace and flair of the director's best work but there are several sequences of interest.

wd René Clair *ph* Rudolph Maté, Louis Née *m* Maurice Jaubert

Max Dearly, Renée Saint-Cyr, Marthe Mellot, Raymond Cordy

'This film is so unpopular here that the crowd is rioting against it nightly—partly because they think it's rotten and partly because they don't like the way it kids the State . . . despite flop here, American specialized houses should do well with it.'—*Variety, Paris*

Le Dernier Tournant*
France 1939 90m bw

A French version of *The Postman Always Rings Twice*, *qv* for plot. Interesting but not remarkable. Fernand Gravet, Corinne Luchaire, Michel Simon, Marcel Vallée, Florence Marly. Written by Charles Spaak and Henry Torres from the novel by James M. Cain; directed by Pierre Chenal; for Lux. 'Class B at best.'—*Variety*

Les Dernières Vacances*
France 1947 95m bw
Pathé

During a country house holiday in the twenties, the last before the house is sold, old friends conduct amorous intrigues and so do their teenage progeny.
A moderately charming little fable making a rather obscure social point.

w R. Breuil, Roger Leenhardt *d* Roger Leenhardt *ph* Philippe Agostini

Berthe Bovy, Renée Devillers, Pierre Dux, Jean d'Yd, Odile Versois, Michel François

Derrière la Façade*
France 1939 90m bw

A judge, his son, a soldier and a prostitute are involved in a night of attempted and actual murders. Complex puzzle drama which made its mark. Lucien Baroux, Jacques Baumer, Jules Berry, Gaby Morlay, Michel Simon, Betty Stockfield, Erich Von Stroheim, Carette, André Lafaur. Directed by Yves Mirade and Georges Lacombe; for Filmsonor.

Dersu Uzala*
USSR / Japan 1975 140m colour

A Russian surveyor mapping Siberian wastes becomes friendly with a wily Mongolian hunter.
Magnificent vistas punctuate an essentially plodding propaganda piece which does not rank with its director's best work. Maxim Munzuk, Juri Solomine. Written by Yuri Nagibin and Akira Kurosawa; directed by Akira Kurosawa; for Mosfilm / Toho.
AA: best foreign film.

Desert Bloom
US 1985 104m Metrocolor
Columbia / Carson / Delphi IV (Michael Hausman)

In 1950 Las Vegas, an ex-GI runs a gas station, illtreats his stepdaughters and falls for his sister-in-law.
Why do paying customers need to know all this? A downbeat enterprise which never got released.

w,d Eugene Corr *story* Linda Remy *ph* Reynaldo Villalobos *m* Brad Fiedel

Jon Voight, JoBeth Williams, Ellen Barkin, Allen Garfield, Annabeth Gish

'Viewers looking for sensitive, discreetly handled fare will be amply rewarded.'—*Variety*

The Desert Fox**
US 1951 88m bw
TCF (Nunnally Johnson)
GB title: *Rommel, Desert Fox*

Rommel returns, disillusioned, to Hitler's Germany after his North African defeat, and is involved in the July plot.
Vivid but scrappy account of the last years of a contemporary hero. At the time it seemed to show a new immediacy in film-making, and was probably the first film to use an action sequence to arrest attention before the credit titles.

w Nunnally Johnson, book Rommel by Desmond Young *d Henry Hathaway* *ph Norbert Brodine* *m* Daniele Amfitheatrof

James Mason, Jessica Tandy, Cedric Hardwicke, Luther Adler (as Hitler), Everett Sloane, *Leo G. Carroll, George Macready*, Richard Boone, Eduard Franz, Desmond Young

'Two men wanted her love—the third wanted her life!'

Desert Fury
US 1947 96m Technicolor
Paramount (Hal B. Wallis)

Against advice, a girl is attracted to a neurotic gambler who may have murdered his first wife.
Muddled melodrama slightly helped by Arizona colour settings; unconvincing characters mouth unspeakable lines in an airless tedium.

w Robert Rossen, *novel* Desert Town by Ramona Stewart *d* Lewis Allen *ph* Charles Lang, Edward Cronjager *m* Miklos Rozsa

Lizabeth Scott, Wendell Corey, Burt Lancaster, John Hodiak, Mary Astor, Kristine Miller

'The only fury I could sense was in my corner of the balcony.'—*C. A. Lejeune*

The Desert Hawk
US 1944 bw serial: 15 eps

Evil Hassan slips back into his native land and plots to overthrow his twin brother. Standard serial heroics with a dual role for the star. Gilbert Roland, Mona Maris, Ben Welden, Kenneth MacDonald, Frank Lackteen, I. Stanford Jolley. Directed by B. Reeves Eason; for Columbia.

The Desert Hawk
US 1950 77m Technicolor

Against an Arabian Nights background, a cheerful outlaw abducts a princess. Tolerable cloak-and-sandal action comedy. Richard Greene, Yvonne de Carlo, Jackie Gleason, George Macready, Rock Hudson, Carl Esmond. Written by Aubrey Wisberg, Jack Pollexfen and Gerald Drayson Adams; directed by Frederick de Cordova; for Universal-International.

Desert Hearts
US 1985 91m colour

A would-be divorcée in Reno becomes a lesbian. A fairly accessible piece of special pleading, nicely made and good to look at. Helen Shaver, Patricia Charbonneau, Audra

Lindley, Andra Akers. Written by Natalie Cooper from novel *Desert of the Heart* by Jane Rule; directed and produced by Donna Deitch; for Desert Heart Productions.

'The Legion's my life. A girl doesn't fit into it. Especially a girl like you!'

Desert Legion
US 1953 86m Technicolor
Universal (Ted Richmond)

A Foreign Legion captain rids a lost city of menacing bandits.
Schoolboy stuff, impudent in its silly story and its unconvincing Shangri-La, but quite entertaining for those prepared to let their hair down.

w Irving Wallace, Lewis Meltzer *d* Joseph Pevney *ph* John Seitz *m* Frank Skinner

Alan Ladd, Richard Conte, Arlene Dahl, Akim Tamiroff, Leon Askin

Desert Mice
GB 1959 83m bw
Artna / Welbeck / Sydney Box (Michael Relph, Basil Dearden)

Adventures of a concert party sent to entertain the troops in North Africa during World War II.
A most promising idea is wasted on a singularly unfunny script which leaves its actors all at sea.

w David Climie *d* Michael Relph *ph* Ken Hodges *m* Philip Green

Alfred Marks, Sid James, Patricia Bredin, Dick Bentley, Dora Bryan, Irene Handl, Kenneth Fortescue, Reginald Beckwith, Joan Benham, Marius Goring

The Desert Rats*
US 1953 88m bw
TCF (Robert L. Jacks)

An English captain commands an Australian detachment in the siege of Tobruk, and survives an encounter with Rommel.
Actioner made to cash in on the success of *The Desert Fox* (qv). Stars and battle scenes survive a studio look.

w Richard Murphy *d* Robert Wise *ph* Lucien Ballard *m* Leigh Harline *md* Nathaniel Finston

James Mason (as Rommel), Richard Burton, Robert Newton, Robert Douglas, Torin Thatcher, Chips Rafferty

AAN: Richard Murphy

The Desert Song
US 1929 106m bw (Technicolor sequences)
Warner

A romantic and mysterious figure leads North African natives against evil Arabs.
Primitive sound version of the highly successful 1926 operetta.

w Harvey Gates, *play* Otto Harbach, Lawrence Schwab, Frank Mandel *d* Roy del Ruth *ph* Barney McGill *m Sigmund Romberg* *ly* Oscar Hammerstein II

John Boles, Carlotta King, Louise Fazenda, Johnny Arthur, Edward Martindel, Jack Pratt

The Desert Song
US 1943 96m Technicolor
Warner (Robert Florey)

Updated version with Nazis as the real villains.

adaptation Robert Buckner *d* Robert Florey *ph* Bert Glennon *m* Heinz Roemheld

Dennis Morgan, Irene Manning, Bruce Cabot, Lynne Overman, Gene Lockhart, Victor Francen, Faye Emerson, Curt Bois, Jack La Rue, Marcel Dalio, Nestor Paiva, Gerald Mohr

The Desert Song
US 1953 110m Technicolor
Warner (Rudi Fehr)

Well staged straight version of the musical, with full score.

adaptation Roland Kibbee *d* Bruce Humberstone *ph* Robert Burks *m adaptation* Max Steiner

Gordon Macrae, Kathryn Grayson, Steve Cochran, Raymond Massey, Dick Wesson, Allyn McLerie, Ray Collins, Paul Picerni, William Conrad

Desert Victory****
GB 1943 60m bw
Ministry of Information / British Army Film Unit

Montgomery's army chases the Nazis through Tripoli.
Classic war documentary.

w (anonymous) *d* David MacDonald *speaker* James Langdale Hodson *m William Alwyn* *ed* A. Best, F. Clarke

'The greatest battle film of the war . . . it puts the audience right in the middle . . . Americans who see this film will be anxiously waiting for the next—and a US equivalent.'—*Variety*

'A first rate work of art.'—*Time*

'The finest factual film ever made.'—*Daily Telegraph*

'Profoundly moving, and fierce in its impact upon imagination, eye and ear.'—*Scotsman*

† A few shots were reconstructed in the studio.

The Deserter
Italy / Yugoslavia / USA 1970 99m Technicolor Panavision
Dino de Laurentiis / Jadran / Heritage (Norman Baer, Ralph Serpe)
original title: *La Spina Dorsale del Diavolo*

In the southwest in 1886, a cavalry captain tracks down the Apaches who tortured his wife to death.
Brutal revenge western, as muddled as its international credits would suggest.

w Clair Huffaker *d* Burt Kennedy *ph* Aldo Tonti *m* Piero Piccione *pd* Mario Chiari

Bekim Fehmiu, John Huston, Richard Crenna, Chuck Connors, Ricardo Montalban, Ian Bannen, Brandon de Wilde, Slim Pickens, Albert Salmi, Woody Strode, Patrick Wayne, Fausto Tozzi

'Three people who loved each other very much!'

Design for Living**
US 1933 88m bw
Paramount (Ernst Lubitsch)

Two friends love and are loved by the same worldly woman, and they set up house together.
Elegant but miscast version of a scintillating play, with all the sex and the sting removed (at the insistence of the Legion of Decency, then coming into power). Ben Hecht claimed to have removed all but one line of Coward's dialogue: 'For the good of our immortal souls!'

w Ben Hecht, *play* Noel Coward *d Ernst Lubitsch* *ph* Victor Milner *m* Nathaniel Finston *ad* Hans Dreier

Gary Cooper, Fredric March, Miriam Hopkins, Edward Everett Horton, Franklin Pangborn, Isabel Jewell

'Can't miss because it holds plenty . . . an improvement on the original.'—*Variety*

'A delightfully smart, crisp piece of entertainment, cleverly conceived and delightfully executed.'—*New York American*

'A partial cleansing for the screen of a stage story notorious for its wealth and variety of moral code infractions.'—*Martin Quigley*

Design for Scandal
US 1941 85m bw

A reporter is assigned by his boss to get a lady judge disbarred. Mechanical star comedy. Rosalind Russell, Walter Pidgeon, Edward Arnold, Guy Kibbee, Lee Bowman. Written by Lionel Houser; directed by Norman Taurog; for MGM.

Designing Woman*
US 1957 118m Metrocolor Cinemascope
MGM (Dore Schary)

A sports reporter marries a dress designer and finds that their common interests are few.
Lumbering comedy which aims for sophistication but settles for farce: tolerable for star watchers who have dined well.

w George Wells *d* Vincente Minnelli *ph* John Alton *m* André Previn

Gregory Peck, Lauren Bacall, Dolores Gray, Sam Levene, Tom Helmore, Mickey Shaughnessy, Jesse White, Chuck Connors, Jack Cole

AA: George Wells

Desirable
US 1934 68m bw

An actress keeps her daughter at school rather than admit she is 19. Mildly amusing comedy-drama of its day. Verree Teasdale, Jean Muir, George Brent, John Halliday. Written by Mary McCall Jnr; directed by Archie Mayo; for Edward Chodorov / Warner. 'The purity seal is remembered throughout.'—*Variety*

Desire**
US 1936 89m bw
Paramount (Ernst Lubitsch)

In Spain, an American car designer falls for a glamorous jewel thief.
Romantic comedy which the producer should have worked on longer: it begins brilliantly and keeps its style, but the pace and wit ebb away.

w Edwin Justus Mayer, Waldemar Young, Samuel Hoffenstein, from a German film Die schönen Tage von Aranjuez and a play by Hans Szekely and R. A. Stemmle *d Frank Borzage ph* Charles Lang, Victor Milner *m* Frederick Hollander *ad* Hans Dreier, Robert Usher

Marlene Dietrich, Gary Cooper, *John Halliday*, William Frawley, Ernest Cossart, Akim Tamiroff, Alan Mowbray, Zeffie Tilbury

'It sparkles and twinkles . . . one of the most engaging pictures of the season.'—*Frank S. Nugent, New York Times*

'A sure, beautifully written piece about the usual Lubitsch trifles, about crooks and fake countesses breathless before the dawn of romance.'—*Alistair Cooke*

'Brilliant treatment, superb staging and inspiring acting. Irresistible entertainment.'—*CEA Film Report*

Desire in the Dust
US 1960 102m bw Cinemascope
TCF / Associated Producers (William F. Claxton)

A wealthy southern aristocrat is involved in a fatal car crash and persuades a young farmhand to take the blame.
Derivative hothouse drama, a little better than its title, with a cast breathing heavily in imitation of refugees from Tennessee Williams or William Faulkner.

w Charles Lang, *novel* Harry Whittington *d* William F. Claxton *ph* Lucien Ballard *m* Paul Dunlap

Raymond Burr, Martha Hyer, Joan Bennett, Ken Scott, Brett Halsey, Anne Helm, Jack Ging, Edward Binns

Desire Me
US 1947 91m bw
MGM (Arthur Hornblow Jnr)

The wife of a Normandy villager hears that he has died in a concentration camp. She marries the bearer of the news, who turns out to be a psychotic who has left her husband for dead . . . but he is not.
Dreary drama, troubled during production and offering little for the actors to chew on.

w Marguerite Roberts, Zoe Akins, Casey Robinson, *novel* Leonhard Frank *d* not credited, but mostly by George Cukor, Mervyn Le Roy, Jack Conway *ph* Joseph Ruttenberg *m* Herbert Stothart

Greer Garson, Robert Mitchum, Richard Hart, George Zucco, Morris Ankrum

'The supporting cast includes a number of characters who give the appearance of having come out of a dusty cupboard marked "French Types—Assorted".'—*MFB*

† Robert Montgomery shot a few scenes before bowing out to be replaced by Richard Hart.

Desire under the Elms
US 1958 111m bw Vistavision
Paramount (Don Hartman)

A New England farmer brings home a young bride and causes friction with his son.
This bid for culture turns out like a hoary and very slow melodrama, not exactly risible but annoying because it teeters between several styles.

w Irwin Shaw, *play* Eugene O'Neill *d* Delbert Mann *ph* Daniel L. Fapp *m* Elmer Bernstein

Sophia Loren, Burl Ives, Anthony Perkins, Frank Overton, Pernell Roberts, Anne Seymour

'The film is consistently and unhappily out of its depth.'—*Penelope Houston*

'A challenging and inspiring picture.'—*News of the World*

AAN: Daniel L. Fapp

'Their story is not in the history books. It has never been seen on the screen—until now!'

Desirée
US 1954 110m De Luxe Cinemascope
TCF (Julian Blaustein)

Fictionalized biopic of one of Napoleon's mistresses.
Heavy-going costume piece, with all contributors distinctly uncomfortable.

w Daniel Taradash, *novel* Annemarie Selinko *d* Henry Koster *ph* Milton Krasner *m* Alex North

Jean Simmons, Marlon Brando, Merle Oberon, Michael Rennie, Cameron Mitchell, Elizabeth Sellars, Cathleen Nesbitt, Isobel Elsom

The Desk Set**
US 1957 103m Eastmancolor Cinemascope
TCF (Henry Ephron)
GB title: *His Other Woman*

Ladies in a broadcasting company's reference section are appalled when an electronics expert is sent to improve their performance.
Thin comedy, altered from a Broadway success; patchy as a whole, but with several splendid dialogue scenes for the principals.

w Phoebe and Henry Ephron, *play* William Marchant *d* Walter Lang *ph* Leon Shamroy *m* Cyril Mockridge

Spencer Tracy, Katharine Hepburn, Joan Blondell, Gig Young, Dina Merrill, Neva Patterson

'They lope through this trifling charade like a couple of oldtimers who enjoy reminiscing with simple routines.'—*Bosley Crowther, New York Times*

Despair*
West Germany / France 1978 119m Eastmancolor
NF Geria / Bavaria / SFP (Peter Märthesheimer)
West German title: *Eine Reise ins Licht*

In 1930 Berlin, a Russian immigrant businessman leads a fantasy life which drives him to murder and insanity.
Filmed in English, this curious cross between *Lolita* and *Repulsion* found surprisingly little critical favour, considering its participants.

w Tom Stoppard, *novel* Vladimir Nabokov *d* Rainer Werner Fassbinder *ph* Michael Ballhaus *m* Peer Raben *pd* Rolf Zehetbauer

Dirk Bogarde, Andrea Ferreol, Volker Spengler, Klaus Löwitsch, Berhard Wicki

'It begins magnificently, remains sporadically brilliant throughout, but grows heavier and heavier until it finally sinks into inertia.'—*Tom Milne, MFB*

Desperadoes
US 1943 85m Technicolor

A gunman rides into town to cause trouble, but finds romance and renews an old friendship. Lively star western of its day.
Randolph Scott, Glenn Ford, Evelyn Keyes, Edgar Buchanan, Claire Trevor, Guinn Williams. Written by Max Brand, Robert Carson; directed by Charles Vidor; for Harry Joe Brown / Columbia.

† This was Columbia's first film in colour.

Desperadoes of the West
US 1950 bw serial: 12 eps

Ranchers drilling for oil are hampered by marauding gangs. Routine serial exploits.
Richard Powers, Judy Clark, Roy Barcroft, I. Stanford Jolley. Directed by Fred C. Brannon; for Republic.

'Hang on to your money, your woman, and your life!'

The Desperados
US 1968 90m Technicolor
Columbia / Meadway (Irving Allen)

After the Civil War, a fanatic 'parson' leads a tribe of violent outlaws including his three sons.
Rough-and-tumble western in the modern savage manner; made in Spain.

w Walter Brough *d* Henry Levin *ph* Sam Leavitt *m* David Whitaker

Vince Edwards, Jack Palance, George Maharis, Neville Brand, Sylvia Syms, Christian Roberts, Kate O'Mara, Kenneth Cope, John Paul

Desperate*
US 1947 73m bw
RKO (Michel Kraike)

A trucker becomes innocently involved in a robbery and goes on the run.
Lively second feature from the studio's best period, with plenty of burgeoning talent.

w Harry Essex *d Anthony Mann ph* George E. Diskant *m* Paul Sawtell

Steve Brodie, Audrey Long, Raymond Burr, Jason Robards Snr, Douglas Fowley, William Challee, Ilka Gruning

'Amazingly watchable within its formulary limits.'—*Tom Milne, MFB, 1982*

Desperate Characters*
US 1971 106m colour
ITC / TDJ (Frank D. Gilroy)

Residents of New York's east side find the rigours of life hard to take.
Curious but interesting suburban drama, a kind of deglamorized and updated *City for Conquest*.

wd Frank D. Gilroy, *novel* Paula Fox *ph* Urs Furrer *m* Lee Konitz, Ron Carter, Jim Hall

Shirley Maclaine, Gerald S. O'Loughlin, Kenneth Mars, Sada Thompson, Jack Somack

'The most blistering indictment of New York City since *Midnight Cowboy*.'—*Rex Reed*

'A film of authenticity, of delicately realized intangibles.'—*Stanley Kauffmann*

The Desperate Hours*
US 1955 112m bw Vistavision
Paramount (William Wyler)

Three escaped convicts take over a suburban house but are finally outwitted by the family.
Ponderous treatment of an over-familiar situation with only the acting and an 'A' picture look to save it.

w Joseph Hayes, from his novel and play *d* William Wyler *ph* Lee Garmes *m* Gail Kubik

Fredric March, Humphrey Bogart, Martha Scott, Arthur Kennedy, Gig Young, Dewey Martin, Mary Murphy, Robert Middleton, Richard Eyer

'A solid, deliberate and long-drawn-out exercise in the mechanics of suspense.'—*Penelope Houston*

† Bogart's role had been played on stage by Paul Newman. March's role had been offered to Spencer Tracy, but he wouldn't take second billing.

Desperate Journey**
US 1942 109m bw
Warner (Hal B. Wallis)

Three POWs in Nazi Germany fight their way back to freedom.
When you pit Errol Flynn against the Nazis, there's no doubt who wins; and the last line is 'Now for Australia and a crack at those Japs!' Exhilarating adventure for the totally uncritical; professional standards high.

w Arthur Horman *d Raoul Walsh* *ph* Bert Glennon *m* Max Steiner

Errol Flynn, Alan Hale, Ronald Reagan, Nancy Coleman, Raymond Massey, Arthur Kennedy, Ronald Sinclair, Albert Basserman, Sig Rumann, Ilka Gruning, Pat O'Moore

'Yarn is an extreme strain on anyone's credulity, and yet it's so exciting that the preposterousness of it all is only something to be thought about on the way home from the theatre.'—*Variety*

'A 1942 treatment of *The Three Musketeers*, packed with action, shorn of romance, and utilizing the Third Reich for terrain. Folks who sacrifice reason for fast action and the joy of seeing Nazis foiled, will find it entirely gratifying.'—*New York Times*

Desperate Moment
GB 1953 88m bw
GFD / Fanfare (George H. Brown)

In Poland, a man imprisoned for murder finds he didn't do it, escapes, and tracks down the real criminal, his best friend.
Cliché-ridden melodrama climaxing in a car chase; poor in all departments.

w Patrick Kirwan, George H. Brown, *novel* Martha Albrand *d* Compton Bennett *ph* C. Pennington-Richards *m* Ronald Binge

Dirk Bogarde, Mai Zetterling, Philip Friend, Albert Lieven, Carl Jaffe, Gerald Heinz

Desperately Seeking Susan*
US 1985 104m De Luxe
Orion / Sarah Pillsbury, Midge Sanford

A bored housewife causes confusion and mayhem when out of curiosity she tracks down what's behind some intriguing ads in the personal column.
Mildly diverting romantic mystery which could have been both funnier and more thrilling.

w Leona Barish *d* Susan Seidelman *ph* Edward Lachman *m* Thomas Newman *pd* Santo Loquasto *ed* Andrew Mondsheim

Rosanna Arquette, Madonna, Aidan Quinn, Mark Blum, Robert Joy

'Simply easy entertainment, with a lively cast caught up in a silly situation.'—*Variety*

BFA: Rosanna Arquette

'Roaring across the land of Marco Polo and Genghis Khan come Uncle Sam's sailors on camels!'

Destination Gobi*
US 1953 90m Technicolor
TCF (Stanley Rubin)

American soldiers get Mongol help against the Japanese in the Gobi desert.
A curious war adventure, a kind of camel opera, apparently based on fact; mildly enjoyable, though the outlandish is gradually replaced by the predictable.

w Everett Freeman *d* Robert Wise *ph* Charles G. Clarke *m* Sol Kaplan

Richard Widmark, Don Taylor, Casey Adams, Murvyn Vye, Darryl Hickman, Martin Milner, Ross Badgasarian, Rodolfo Acosta

Destination Moon*
US 1950 91m Technicolor
Universal / George Pal

An American inventor gets private backing to build a rocket so that the US can reach the moon before the Russians.
Semi-documentary prophecy with impressive gadgetry encased in a tedious and totally unsurprising script.

w Rip Van Ronkel, Robert Heinlein, James O'Hanlon *d* Irving Pichel *ph Lionel Lindon* *m* Leith Stevens

Warner Anderson, John Archer, Tom Powers, Dick Wesson

'Heavy-handed, unimaginative and very badly acted.'—*MFB*

Destination Tokyo*
US 1943 135m bw
Warner (Jerry Wald)

A US submarine is sent into Tokyo harbour.
Solid, well acted war suspenser, but overlong.

w Delmer Daves, Albert Maltz, *original story* Steve Fisher *d* Delmer Daves *ph* Bert Glennon *m* Franz Waxman

Cary Grant, John Garfield, Alan Hale, John Ridgely, Dane Clark, Warner Anderson, William Prince, Robert Hutton, Tom Tully, Peter Whitney, Faye Emerson, John Forsythe

'We don't say it is credible; we don't even suggest that it makes sense. But it does make a pippin of a picture from a purely melodramatic point of view.'—*Bosley Crowther*

'Even moviegoers who have developed a serious allergy for service pictures should find it high among the superior films of the war.'—*Newsweek*

AAN: Steve Fisher

Destination Unknown
US 1933 69m bw

Bootleggers, in a crippled ship with a mutinous crew, are saved by a mysterious stranger. Curious melodrama which turns halfway through into *The Passing of the Third Floor Back*. Pat O'Brien, Ralph Bellamy, Alan Hale, Russell Hopton, Tom Brown, Betty Compson, Noel Madison. Written by Tom Buckingham; directed by Tay Garnett; for Universal. 'Good sea melodrama ruined by change of intent.'—*Variety*

Destiny*
Germany 1921 100m approx bw silent
Decla-Bioscop
original title: *Der Müde Tod*

In the 19th-century a young woman tries to save her lover from the presence of Death, who shows her that whatever she does it is inevitable.
A solemn fantasy on the lines of *Appointment in Samarra*, the framing story being more effective than the 'illustrations'.

w Thea Von Harbou, Fritz Lang *d* Fritz Lang *ph* Fritz Arno Wagner, Erich Nitschmann, Hermann Saalfrank

Lil Dagover, Rudolph Klein-Rogge, Bernhard Götzke, Walter Janssen

Destiny*
US 1944 65m bw
Universal (Roy William Neill)

An escaped convict on the run finds refuge with a blind girl on a lonely farm.
Curious second feature, interesting because it began as a story eliminated from *Flesh and Fantasy* (qv); extra footage was added to bring it up to the required length. The original footage is mainly the nightmare suffered by the girl.

w Roy Chanslor (*F and F* Ernest Pascal) *d* Reginald Le Borg (*F and F* Julien Duvivier) *ph* George Robinson (*F and F* Paul Ivano) *m* Frank Skinner

Gloria Jean, Alan Curtis (who died in the original but here survives), Frank Craven, Grace McDonald

Destiny of a Man**
USSR 1959 98m bw
Sovexportfilm / Mosfilm (G. Kuznetsov)
original title: *Sudba Cheloveka*

During World War II a Russian is captured by Nazis but escapes and returns home only to find his family dead.
Strikingly styled sob story whose very glumness prevented it from being hailed as a masterpiece; in technique however it is in the best Russian tradition.

w Y. Lukin, F. Shakhmagonov, *story* Mikhail Sholokhov *d Sergei Bondarchuk ph* Vladimir Monakhov *m* V. Basnov

Sergei Bondarchuk, Zinaida Kirienko, Pavlik Boriskin

'Of all Soviet post-war films, this will be looked on as the greatest and most original work of the period.'—*MFB*

'What nation will survive?'
Destroy all Monsters
Japan 1969 89m colour

Moon invaders gain control of Godzilla and his friends. Typically inept Japanese monster rally full of men in rubber suits. Akira Kubo, Jun Tazaki, Kyoko Ai. Written by Kaoru Mabuchi; directed by Ishiro Honda; for Toho/AIP.

'Her only rival is his ship!'
Destroyer
US 1943 99m bw
Columbia (Louis F. Edelmann)

An old sea dog talks himself into a job on a World War II destroyer but works his men too hard.
Flat propaganda piece, not too well made.

w Frank Wead, Lewis Meltzer, Borden Chase *d* William A. Seiter ph Franz Planer *m* Anthony Collins

Edward G. Robinson, Glenn Ford, Marguerite Chapman, Edgar Buchanan, Leo Gorcey, Regis Toomey, Ed Brophy

Destry*
US 1954 95m Technicolor
U-I (Stanley Rubin)

Almost scene-for-scene remake of *Destry Rides Again* (qv). Well enough made and tolerably acted, but it doesn't have the sparkle, despite employing the same director.

w Edmund H. North, D. D. Beauchamp *d* George Marshall *ph* George Robinson *m* Joseph Gershenson

Audie Murphy, Mari Blanchard, Lyle Bettger, Thomas Mitchell, Edgar Buchanan, Wallace Ford, Lori Nelson, Alan Hale Jnr, Mary Wickes

'The impression is of a school revival of the original production.'—*MFB*

'They make the fighting sinful west blaze into action before your eyes!'
Destry Rides Again****
US 1939 94m bw
Universal (Joe Pasternak)

A mild-mannered sheriff finally gets mad at local corruption and straps on his guns.
Classic western which manages to encompass suspense, comedy, romance, tenderness, vivid characterization, horseplay, songs and standard western excitements, without moving for more than a moment from a studio main street set. It starts with a sign reading 'Welcome to Bottleneck' and an outburst of gunfire; it ends with tragedy followed by a running joke. Hollywood expertise at its very best.

w Felix Jackson, Gertrude Purcell, Henry Myers, novel Max Brand *d George Marshall ph Hal Mohr songs Frederick Hollander, Frank Loesser m Frank Skinner*

James Stewart, Marlene Dietrich, Brian Donlevy, Charles Winninger, Samuel S. Hinds, Mischa Auer, Irene Hervey, Jack Carson, *Una Merkel*, Allen Jenkins, Warren Hymer, *Billy Gilbert*

'Makes the b.o. grade in a big way . . . just plain, good entertainment.'—*Variety*

'I think it was Lord Beaverbrook who said that Marlene Dietrich standing on a bar in black net stockings, belting out *See What the Boys in the Back Room Will Have,* was a greater work of art than the Venus de Milo.'—*Richard Roud*

† An early sound version in 1932 starred Tom Mix; *Frenchie* (1950) was a slight variation. See also *Destry.*

The Detective**
US 1968 114m De Luxe Panavision
TCF / Arcola / Millfield (Aaron Rosenberg)

A New York police detective fights crime and corruption.
Determinedly sleazy and 'frank' cop stuff, quite arrestingly narrated and with something to say about police methods. Good violent entertainment, with just a shade too many homosexuals and nymphomaniacs for balance.

w Abby Mann, novel Roderick Thorp *d Gordon Douglas ph* Joseph Biroc *m* Jerry Goldsmith

Frank Sinatra, Lee Remick, Jacqueline Bisset, Ralph Meeker, Jack Klugman, Horace MacMahon, Lloyd Bochner, William Windom, Tony Musante, Al Freeman Jnr, Robert Duvall

'It vacillates uncertainly between murder mystery, political allegory, and a psychological study of the hero.'—*Jan Dawson*

Detective*
France 1985 98m colour

Four groups of people find their paths intersecting in a Paris hotel while the hotel detective tries to solve a murder. Eccentric *Grand Hotel*-style compendium with many baffling asides presumably attributable to the director. One suspects that the audience is expected to be a detective too. Claude Brasseur, Nathalie Baye, Johnny Hallyday, Laurent Terzieff, Jean-Pierre Léaud, Alain Cuny. Written by Alain Sarde, Philippe Setbon, Anne-Marie Mieville, Jean-Luc Godard; directed by Jean-Luc Godard; for Sara / JLG.

Detective Lloyd*
GB 1932 bw serial: 12 eps

Lloyd of the Yard combats The Panther for a valuable amulet also coveted by priests of the temple of Amenhotep II. A remarkable novelty: the only serial filmed in England, and not bad of its naïve kind. Jack Lloyd, Wallace Geoffrey, Muriel Angelus, Lewis Dayton, Janice Adair. Directed by Henry McRae; for Universal.

'A man whose wife was more woman than angel!'
Detective Story**
US 1951 103m bw
Paramount (William Wyler)

A day in a New York precinct police station, during which a detective of almost pathological righteousness discovers a stain on his family and himself becomes a victim of violence.
Clever, fluent transcription of a Broadway play with some of the pretensions of Greek tragedy; it could have been the negation of cinema, but professional handling makes it the essence of it.

w Philip Yordan, Robert Wyler, play Sidney Kingsley d William Wyler ph Lee Garmes

Kirk Douglas, Eleanor Parker, William Bendix, Cathy O'Donnell, George Macready, Horace MacMahon, Gladys George, *Joseph Wiseman, Lee Grant*, Gerald Mohr, Frank Faylen, Luis Van Rooten

'The admirably directed interaction of movement and talk all over the big room is what gives the thing its satisfying texture.'—*Richard Mallett, Punch*

† No music was used.

AAN: Philip Yordan, Robert Wyler; William Wyler; Eleanor Parker; Lee Grant

Detour*
US 1945 68m bw
PRC (Leon Fromkess)

On his way to Hollywood to meet a girl friend, a night club pianist assumes the identity of a dead man.
A minor cult movie with as much doomladen dialogue and film noir angles as could be shovelled into a Poverty Row 'B' at the time. On the whole, less than meets the eye.

w Martin Goldsmith *d* Edgar G. Ulmer *ph* Benjamin H. Kline *m* Leo Erdody

Tom Neal, Ann Savage, Claudia Drake, Edmund MacDonald, Tim Ryan

Devi*
India 1960 93m bw
Satyajit Ray Productions
aka: *The Goddess*

While his son is away at university, a farmer persuades his daughter-in-law that she is a goddess, and the events which follow, including the death of her son, are too much for her reason.
A curious, 'foreign' story which does not have the usual Ray tempo or feeling for character, but wins one's attention by its very strangeness.

wd Satyajit Ray, *story* Prabhat Kumar Mukherjee *ph* Subrata Mitra *m* Ali Akbar Khan

Chhabi Biswas, Sharmila Tagore, Soumitra Chatterjee, Karuna Bannerjee

The Devil and Max Devlin
US 1981 95m Technicolor
Walt Disney (Jerome Courtland)

An unscrupulous apartment manager is knocked down by a bus. Finding himself in hell, he is offered freedom if he can buy three young souls within two months.
Frowsty Freudian comedy, a very unhappy indication of the depths to which Disney productions have sunk since Walt's death. To carry this kind of thing off requires a hundred times more style than is evidenced here.

w Mary Rodgers *d* Steven Hilliard Stern *ph* Howard Schwartz *m* Buddy Baker

Elliott Gould, Bill Cosby, Susan Anspach, Adam Rich, Charles Shamata, Ronnie Schell

The Devil and Miss Jones**
US 1941 97m bw
RKO / Frank Ross, Norman Krasna

A millionaire masquerades as a clerk in his own department store to investigate worker complaints.
Attractive comedy with elements of the crazy thirties and the more socially conscious forties.

w Norman Krasna *d* Sam Wood *ph* Harry Stradling *m* Roy Webb

Jean Arthur, *Charles Coburn*, Robert Cummings, Spring Byington, S. Z. Sakall, William Demarest

AAN: Norman Krasna; Charles Coburn

'Her sin—their death?'
Devil and the Deep*
US 1932 73m bw
Paramount (Emmanuel Cohen)

A submarine commander goes mad with jealousy of his faithless wife.
A turgid melodrama notable for its stars.

w Benn Levy *d* Marion Gering *ph* Charles Lang

Tallulah Bankhead, Charles Laughton, Gary Cooper, Cary Grant, Paul Porcasi

'Of femme interest despite lukewarm performance of Tallulah Bankhead . . . a fair commercial release.'—*Variety*

The Devil and the Nun*
Poland 1960 108m bw
Kadr
original title: *Matka Joanna od Aniolow;*
aka: *Mother Joan of the Angels*

In a 17th-century convent nuns are possessed by devils. A priest who tries to help is burned at the stake; another becomes possessed himself.
Reasonably dispassionate and fairly stylized version of the same facts that were treated so hysterically by Ken Russell in *The Devils*.

w Tadeusz Konwicki, Jerzy Kawalerowicz, *novel* Jaroslav Iwaszkiewicz *d* Jerzy Kawalerowicz *ph* Jerzy Wojcik *m* Adam Walacinski

Lucyna Winnicka, Mieczyslaw Voit, Anna Ciepielewska

The Devil at Four o'Clock
US 1961 126m Eastmancolor
Columbia / Leroy / Kohlmar (Fred Kohlmar)

A drunken missionary and three convicts save a colony of leper children from a South Seas volcano.
Muddled adventure melodrama with a downbeat ending long delayed.

w Liam O'Brien, *novel* Max Catto *d* Mervyn Le Roy *ph* Joseph Biroc *m* George Duning

Spencer Tracy, Frank Sinatra, Kerwin Mathews, Jean-Pierre Aumont, Grégoire Aslan, Alexander Scourby, Barbara Luna

The Devil Bat
US 1942 70m bw

A crazed scientist trains bats to kill at the scent of a certain perfume. Horror comic hokum from the bottom of the barrel. Bela Lugosi, Suzanne Kaaren, Dave O'Brien. Written by John Neville; directed by Jean Yarbrough; for PRC. *Devil Bat's Daughter* (1946), with Rosemary La Planche, was an even tamer sequel.

Devil Bat's Daughter
US 1946 67m bw
A girl who thinks she is the daughter of a vampire consults a psychiatrist, who encourages her to murder his wife. Tolerable, potboiling shocker. Rosemary La Planche, John James, Michael Hale, Nolan Leary. Written by Griffin Jay from story by Frank Wisbar and Ernst Jaeger; directed by Frank Wisbar; for PRC.

The Devil Commands*
US 1941 65m bw
Columbia (Wallace MacDonald)

An electrical scientist tries to communicate with his dead wife through a medium.
Modestly effective horror thriller, though rather too deliberately paced.

w Robert D. Andrews, Milton Gunzberg, *story* The Edge of Running Water by William Sloane *d* Edward Dmytryk *ph* Allan G. Siegler *md* Morris Stoloff

Boris Karloff, Richard Fiske, Amanda Duff, Anne Revere, Ralph Penney

Devil Dogs of the Air*
US 1935 86m bw
Warner (Lou Edelman)

Rivalry and romance in the Marine Flying Corps.
Standard, lively vehicle for Cagney and O'Brien, with excellent stunt flying sequences.

w Malcolm Stuart Boylan, Earl Baldwin, *novel* John Monk Saunders *d* Lloyd Bacon *ph* Arthur Edeson *md* Leo F. Forbstein

James Cagney, Pat O'Brien, Margaret Lindsay, Frank McHugh, Helen Lowell, John Arledge, Robert Barrat, Russell Hicks, Ward Bond

'Exhibs should have no squawks and may even cheer if they put a little steam behind their selling.'—*Variety*

'A loud and roughneck screen comedy, both amusing and exciting.'—*André Sennwald*

The Devil Doll**
US 1936 79m bw
MGM (E.J.Mannix)

A refugee from Devil's Island disguises himself as an old lady who sells human dolls which murder those responsible for his imprisonment.
Interesting rather than exciting tall tale with a Paris backdrop; despite impressive moments it does not quite have the right *frisson*.

w Tod Browning, Garrett Fort, Erich Von Stroheim, Guy Endore, *novel* Burn Witch Burn by A. A. Merritt *d Tod Browning* *ph Leonard Smith* *m* Franz Waxman *ad* Cedric Gibbons

Lionel Barrymore, Maureen O'Sullivan, Frank Lawton, Henry B. Walthall, Rafaela Ottiano, Grace Ford, Arthur Hohl

'Grotesque, slightly horrible and consistently interesting.'—*Frank Nugent, New York Times*

'Earth menaced by fantastic powers!'
Devil Girl from Mars
GB 1954 76m bw
Edward J. and Harry Lee Danziger

A female Martian is sent to Earth to bring back a stock of men for breeding purposes.
Absurd attempt to cash in on the then new space fiction craze. The budget matches the imagination.

w John C. Maher, James Eastwood *d* David MacDonald *ph* Jack Cox *m* Edwin Astley

Patricia Laffan, Hugh McDermott, Joseph Tomelty, Adrienne Corri, Peter Reynolds, Hazel Court, John Laurie, Sophie Stewart

'There is really no fault in this film that one would like to see eliminated. Everything, in its way, is quite perfect.'—*Gavin Lambert, Sight and Sound*

Devil Horse
US 1932 bw serial: 12 eps
A wild boy defends wild horses from poachers. Earnest stuff for a serial, and not enough violent incident. Harry Carey, Noah Beery, Frankie Darro. Directed by Otto Brower; for Mascot.

The Devil Is a Sissy
US 1936 92m bw
MGM (Frank Davis)
aka: *The Devil Takes the Count*

The young son of divorcing parents gets into bad company.
Adequate juvenile melodrama

w John Lee Mahin, Richard Schayer, Roland Brown *d* W. S. Van Dyke *ph* Harold Rosson, George Schneidermann *m* Herbert Stothart

Freddie Bartholomew, Jackie Cooper, Mickey Rooney, Ian Hunter, Peggy Conklin, Katherine Alexander, Gene Lockhart, Dorothy Peterson

DEVI. Sharmila Tagore, the woman at the centre of Ray's somewhat atypical drama.

'Men are my slaves—and glad to be!'

The Devil Is a Woman*
US 1935 82m bw
Paramount

In Seville in the 1890s a *femme fatale* has several admirers.
The last Dietrich vehicle to be directed by Von Sternberg, and rather splendid in its highly decorative and uncommercial way; a treat for addicts.

w John Dos Passos, S. K. Winston, *novel* La Femme et le Pantin by Pierre Louÿs *d Josef Von Sternberg ph Josef Von Sternberg, Lucien Ballard ad Hans Dreier m* from Rimsky-Korsakov

Marlene Dietrich, Lionel Atwill, Cesar Romero, Edward Everett Horton, Alison Skipworth, Don Alvarado, Morgan Wallace, Tempe Pigott

'A somewhat monotonous picture . . . sophisticated audiences are its best bet.'—*Variety*

'One of the most sophisticated films ever produced in America.'—*André Sennwald, New York Times*

'Light and shadow are splashed liberally around over the white-painted sets; cafés, tobacco factories, stairs and balconies are decorated with every conceivable device and camera-level.'—*Peter John Dyer, 1964*

'A clever, perversely dehumanized picture said to be one of Von Sternberg's favourites.'—*New Yorker, 1977*

The Devil is Driving
US 1937 69m bw

An attorney protects a friend's son from a drunk driving charge, but finally indicts himself for perjury. Standard moral melodrama with the star in good form.
Richard Dix, Joan Perry, Nana Bryant, Frank C. Wilson, Ian Wolfe, Elisha Cook Jnr, Henry Kolker, Ann Rutherford, Walter Kingsford. Written by Jo Milward, Richard Blake; directed by Harry Lachman; for Columbia.
'Carries a good deal of punch, but not enough to lug it above the moderate biz bracket.'—*Variety*

The Devil Makes Three
US 1952 90m bw
MGM (Richard Goldstone)

An American intelligence officer in post-war Germany becomes involved with neo-Nazis.
A curious break from dancing for Gene Kelly, this obscurely titled thriller has little to commend it but authentic locations.

w Jerry Davis, *story* Lawrence Bachmann
d Andrew Marton *ph* Vaclav Vich
m Rudolph G. Kopp

Gene Kelly, Pier Angeli, Richard Rober, Richard Egan, Claus Clausen

Devil on Horseback
GB 1954 89m bw
Group 3 (John Grierson, Isobel Pargiter)

A teenage jockey gets to the top the hard way.
Highly resistible compendium of racetrack clichés and sentiment, not at all what one expected from Group 3.

w Neil Paterson, Montagu Slater *d* Cyril Frankel *ph* Denny Densham *m* Malcolm Arnold

Googie Withers, John McCallum, Jeremy Spenser, Meredith Edwards, Liam Redmond, Sam Kydd

The Devil, Probably*
France 1977 95m Eastmancolor
Sunchold / GMF (Stéphane Tchalgadchieff)
original title: *Le Diable, Probablement*

A young Parisian goes to the devil and arranges to have himself shot.
A despairing vision of an arid world, seen through unpleasant details of city life. A fascinating but enervated film very typical of its director.

wd Robert Bresson ph Pasqualino de Santis
m Philippe Sarde *pd* Eric Simon

Antoine Monnier, Tina Irissari, Henri de Maublanc

The Devil Rides Out*
GB 1967 95m Technicolor
Hammer (Anthony Nelson Keys)
US title: *The Devil's Bride*

The Duc de Richleau rescues a friend from a group of Satanists.
Rather stodgy adaptation of a frightening novel; moments of suspense.

w Richard Matheson, *novel* Dennis Wheatley
d Terence Fisher *ph* Arthur Grant *m* James Bernard

Christopher Lee, *Charles Gray*, Leon Greene, Patrick Mower, Gwen Ffrangcon Davies

Devil Ship Pirates
GB 1963 96m Technicolor
Hammerscope
ABP / Hammer (Anthony Nelson Keyes)

At the time of the Armada, Spanish privateers terrorize a Cornish seaside village.
Lacklustre pirate yarn with not much action and some elements of Hammer horror.

w Jimmy Sangster *d* Don Sharp *ph* Michael Reed *m* Gary Hughes

Christopher Lee, John Cairney, Barry Warren, Ernest Clark, Andrew Keir, Duncan Lamont

The Devil Thumbs a Ride
US 1947 63m bw

A commercial traveller gives a lift to a man who turns out to be wanted for murder.

Predictable suspenser without much entertainment value. Ted North, Lawrence Tierney, Nan Leslie. Written and directed by Felix Feist; for RKO.

The Devil to Pay*
US 1930 72m bw
Samuel Goldwyn

The prodigal son of a snooty English family returns to cheer them all up.
Agreeably lighthearted star comedy in the drawing-room tradition.

w Frederick Lonsdale *d* George Fitzmaurice *ph* Gregg Toland, George Barnes *m* Alfred Newman

Ronald Colman, Loretta Young, Myrna Loy, Frederick Kerr

'Snappy British comedy that should please everywhere . . . a set-up for femmes.'—*Variety*

'Six reels of Mr Colman being charming . . . a polished, tasteful and entirely likeable screen comedy.'—*New York Herald Tribune*

The Devil with Hitler
US 1942 44m bw

Hell's board of directors want to sack Satan and bring in Hitler. Somewhat infantile war farce, one of this producer's very few successful medium-length 'screenliners'. Alan Mowbray, Bobby Watson, George E. Stone, Joe Devlin. Written by Cortland FitzSimmons, Al Martin; directed by Gordon Douglas, for Hal Roach. NB. The Hays Office gave special permission, in a just cause, for the use of the word 'Hell'.

A Devil with Women
US 1930 76m bw
Fox (George Middleton)

Soldiers of fortune in a banana republic end the regime of a notorious bandit and compete for a fair señorita.
Primitive Flagg-and-Quirt style knockabout.

w Dudley Nichols, Henry M. Johnson, *novel* Dust and Sun by Clements Ripley *d* Irving Cummings *ph* Arthur Todd *m* Peter Brunelli

Victor McLaglen, Humphrey Bogart, Mona Maris, Michael Vavitch

'No real plot or continuity, but has some laughs. Best for neighbourhood grinds.'—*Variety*

'Hell holds no surprises . . . for them!'
The Devils
GB 1970 111m Technicolor Panavision
Warner / Russo (Robert H. Solo, Ken Russell)

An account of the apparent demoniacal possession of the 17th-century nuns of Loudun, climaxing in the burning of their priest as a sorcerer.
Despite undeniable technical proficiency this is its writer-director's most outrageously sick film to date, campy, idiosyncratic and in howling bad taste from beginning to end, full of worm-eaten skulls, masturbating nuns, gibbering courtiers, plague sores, rats and a burning to death before our very eyes . . . plus a sacrilegious dream of Jesus. A pointless pantomime for misogynists.

wd Ken Russell, *play* John Whiting, *book* The Devils of Loudun by Aldous Huxley *ph David Watkin* *m* Peter Maxwell Davies *ad* Robert Cartwright

Vanessa Redgrave, Oliver Reed, Dudley Sutton, Max Adrian, Gemma Jones, Murray Melvin, Michael Gothard, Graham Armitage

'Ken Russell doesn't report hysteria, he markets it.'—*New Yorker, 1976*

'Russell's swirling multi-colored puddle . . . made me glad that both Huxley and Whiting are dead, so that they are spared this farrago of witless exhibitionism.'—*Stanley Kauffmann*

'A garish glossary of sado-masochism . . . a taste for visual sensation that makes scene after scene look like the masturbatory fantasies of a Roman Catholic boyhood.'—*Alexander Walker*

The Devil's Advocate
West Germany 1977 109m colour
Geria (Lutz Hengst)

A dying priest is summoned to Rome to investigate the cult of a dead partisan nominated for sainthood.
Well-meaning but rather tepid and inconclusive adaptation of a bestseller which presumably made its points more firmly.

w Morris West, from his novel *d* Guy Green *ph* Billy Williams *m* Bert Grund

John Mills, Stéphane Audran, Jason Miller, Timothy West, Patrick Mower, Paola Pitagora, Daniel Massey, Leigh Lawson, Raf Vallone, Jack Hedley

The Devil's Agent
GB 1962 77m bw
British Lion / Emmet Dalton

A wine salesman in Germany is duped by Soviet agents.
Scrappy cold war adventures which look as though they were originally intended as episodes in a TV series.

w Robert Westerby *d* John Paddy Carstairs *ph* Gerald Gibbs *m* Philip Green

Peter Van Eyck, Marianne Koch, Macdonald Carey, Christopher Lee, Billie Whitelaw, David Knight, Marius Goring, Helen Cherry, Colin Gordon, Niall MacGinnis, Eric Pohlmann, Peter Vaughan

The Devil's Brigade
US 1968 132m De Luxe Panavision
UA / David L. Wolper

For combat in Norway and Italy during World War II a US officer assembles a platoon of thugs and misfits to work with crack Canadian commandos.
Flagrant but routine imitation of *The Dirty Dozen*, quite undistinguished.

w William Roberts *d* Andrew V. McLaglen *ph* William Clothier *m* Alex North

William Holden, Cliff Robertson, Vince Edwards, Andrew Prine, Claude Akins, Carroll O'Connor, Richard Jaeckel

'After nearly three decades of World War II films, it is hardly surprising that Hollywood is beginning to suffer from combat fatigue.'—*Time*

Devil's Canyon
US 1953 92m Technicolor 3-D
RKO / Edmund Grainger

Life in a notorious Arizona prison in the 1880s; a marshal is unjustly convicted but wins his pardon.
Fairly brutal western, quite unmemorable.

w Frederick Hazlitt Brennan *d* Alfred Werker *ph* Nicholas Musuraca *m* Daniele Amfitheatrof

Dale Robertson, Virginia Mayo, Stephen McNally, Arthur Hunnicutt, Robert Keith, Jay C. Flippen, Whit Bissell

The Devil's Disciple*
GB 1959 82m bw
UA / Hecht–Hill–Lancaster / Brynaprod (Harold Hecht)

In 1777 an American ne'er-do-well almost allows himself to be hanged by the British in mistake for a rebel pastor.
Star-studded but indifferently staged adaptation of a minor Shavian frolic. Patchy, with good moments.

w John Dighton, Roland Kibbee, *play* Bernard Shaw *d* Guy Hamilton *ph* Jack Hildyard *m* Richard Rodney Bennett *ad* Terence Verity, Edward Carere

Burt Lancaster, Kirk Douglas, *Laurence Olivier* (as General Burgoyne), Eva Le Gallienne, Janette Scott, Harry Andrews, Basil Sidney, George Rose, Neil McCallum, David Horne, Mervyn Johns

Devil's Doorway
US 1950 84m bw
MGM (Nicholas Nayfack)

A Shoshone Indian fights valiantly in the Civil War but on his return to Wyoming finds himself hated and threatened by his former colleagues.
Dull pro-Indian western with a most unsuitable star.

w Guy Trosper *d* Anthony Mann *ph* John Alton *m* Daniele Amfitheatrof

Robert Taylor, Louis Calhern, Paula Raymond, Marshall Thompson, James Mitchell, Edgar Buchanan, Rhys Williams, Spring Byington

The Devil's Eight
US 1968 98m Pathecolor
AIP / Burt Topper

A federal agent on the trail of a moonshine gang recruits a gang of hardened convicts and arranges for them to escape.
The Dirty Dozen all over again, and not good.

w James Gordon White, Willard Huyck, John Milius *d* Burt Topper *ph* Richard C. Glouner *m* Mike Curb

Christopher George, Ralph Meeker, Fabian, Tom Nardini, Leslie Parrish, Ross Hagen

The Devil's Eye*
Sweden 1960 90m bw
Svensk Filmindustri

An old proverb says that a woman's chastity is a stye in the devil's eye. So when Satan has a sore eye he comes down to earth to put things right.
Surprisingly shoddily-made comedy with just a few of the sharpnesses of technique and mystifications of plot which one had come to expect from this maestro.

wd Ingmar Bergman *ph* Gunnar Fischer *m* Domenico Scarlatti

Jarl Kulle, Bibi Andersson, Nils Poppe, Stig Järrel, Gunnar Björnstrand

The Devil's General
West Germany 1955 121m bw
Ryal (Gyula Trebitsch)

In 1941 a German air ace becomes estranged from the high command and is tortured by the Gestapo. On release he helps a Jewish couple . . .
Heavy-going melodrama which nevertheless paints a convincing picture of Berlin during the war.

w George Hurdalek, Helmut Kautner, *play* Carl Zuckmayer *d* Helmut Kautner *ph* Albert Benitz

Curt Jurgens, Victor de Kowa, Karl John, Eva-Ingeborg Scholz

The Devil's Hairpin
US 1957 83m Technicolor Vistavision
Paramount / Cornel Wilde

A former motor racing champion makes a comeback, and redeems his past boorish behaviour.
Efficient routine melodramatics with good action sequences.

w James Edmiston, Cornel Wilde *d* Cornel Wilde *ph* Daniel Fapp *m* Van Cleave

Cornel Wilde, Jean Wallace, Arthur Franz, *Mary Astor*, Paul Fix

Devil's Holiday*
US 1930 80m bw

A mercenary lady repents her life on the make. Very dated moral story which at the time was showered with praise. Nancy Carroll, Phillips Holmes, James Kirkwood, Hobart Bosworth, Ned Sparks, Jed Prouty, Paul Lukas, Zasu Pitts. Written and directed by *Edmund Goulding*; for Paramount. 'It is pictures such as this which revive the drooping confidence in the screen as a mirror of things as they really are.'—*Variety*.
AAN: Nancy Carroll.

The Devil's in Love
US 1933 70m bw

At a French Foreign Legion post, an outcast doctor falls in love with the niece of a mission father. Old-fashioned and predictable romantic drama. Victor Jory, Loretta Young, Vivienne Osborne, David Manners, C. Henry Gordon, Herbert Mundin, J. Carrol Naish. Written by Howard Estabrook from a story by Harry Hervey; directed by William Dieterle; for Fox. 'Given any kind of a break returns should be fair.'—*Variety*

Devil's Island*
US 1939 63m bw
Warner (Bryan Foy)

A surgeon is sent to Devil's Island for aiding an escaped convict.
Sharply-made exposé of the notorious French penal colony; commendable pace and vigour all round.

w Kenneth Gamet, Don Ryan *d* William Clemens

Boris Karloff, James Stephenson, Nedda Harrigan, Adia Kuznetzoff, Robert Warwick, Pedro de Cordoba

The Devil's Mask
US 1946 66m bw

An unclaimed parcel containing a shrunken head is found after a plane crash; murder follows. Involved but amusing entry in the *I Love a Mystery* series. Jim Bannon, Anita Louise, Michael Duane, Mona Barrie, Byron Foulger. Written by Charles O'Neal; directed by Henry Levin; for Columbia.

The Devil's Playground*
Australia 1976 107m Eastmancolor
The Feature Film House (Fred Schepsi)

Tensions between masters and boys in a Catholic seminary in the fifties.
Well made but rather dislikeable intrusion into *Mr Perrin and Mr Traill* country with the addition of modern frankness.

wd Fred Schepsi *ph* Ian Baker *m* Bruce Smeaton

Arthur Dignam, Nick Tate, Simon Burke, Charles McCallum, John Frawley

The Devil's Rain
US 1975 86m colour Todd-AO 35
Sandy Howard

Witchcraft in the modern west causes victims to melt; the son of one of them takes arms against the leading Satanist.
Interestingly cast example of the low-budget seventies exploitation picture, with more nastiness than logic.

w Gabe Essoe, James Ashton, Gerald Hopman *d* Robert Fuest *ph* Alex Phillips Jnr *m* Al de Lory

Ernest Borgnine, Ida Lupino, Eddie Albert, William Shatner, Keenan Wynn, Tom Skerritt

Devils of Darkness
GB 1964 90m Eastmancolor

A vampire disguises himself as a French count and preys on young girls. Mainly tatty shocker with a few lively scenes. William Sylvester, Hubert Noel, Tracy Reed, Diana Decker, Rona Anderson. Written by Lyn Fairhurst; directed by Lance Comfort; for Tom Blakeley / Planet.

The Devil's Wanton*
Sweden 1949 80m bw
Terrafilm
original title: *Fängelse*
aka: *Prison*

Film-makers discuss some rather unpleasant projects but put them aside as unsatisfactory. A bit of a Scandinavian wallow, with heavy expressionism and low-life themes.

wd Ingmar Bergman *ph* Göran Strindberg *m* Erland von Koch

Doris Svedlund, Birger Malmsten, Eva Henning, Hasse Ekman

'It employs all the paraphernalia associated with Scandinavian angst.'—*John Gillett, MFB*

Devotion
US 1931 84m bw

A woman falls in love with a barrister and takes a job as governess to his son. Rather winsome tear-jerker entirely dependent on its stars. Ann Harding, Leslie Howard, Robert Williams, O. P. Heggie, Louise Closser Hale, Dudley Digges. Written by Graham John and Horace Jackson, from the novel *A Little Flat in the Temple* by Pamela Wynne; directed by Robert Milton; for RKO-Pathé. 'Much talk and little action. Star's name its best chance of rating more than mild financially.'—*Variety*

'It tells ALL about those Brontë sisters! . . . They didn't dare call it love—they tried to call it devotion!'

Devotion**
US 1943 (released 1946) 107m bw
Warner (Robert Buckner)

A highly romanticized account of the lives of the Brontë sisters and their brother Branwell.
An enjoyably bad example of a big-budget Hollywood production which tampers with things it cannot understand, in this case life in a Yorkshire parsonage in Victorian times. An excuse is found to give the curate an Austrian accent to fit the available actor, but this and other *faux pas* are atoned for by the vividness of Emily's recurrent dream of death as a silhouetted man on horseback. In general, an interesting period piece in more senses than one.

w Keith Winter *d Curtis Bernhardt ph Ernest Haller m* Erich Wolfgang Korngold

Ida Lupino (Emily), Olivia de Havilland (Charlotte), Nancy Coleman (Anne), Arthur Kennedy (Branwell), Montagu Love (Revd Brontë), Paul Henreid (Revd Nicholls), Ethel Griffies (Aunt Branwell), Sidney Greenstreet (Thackeray), Eily Malyon, Forrester Harvey, Victor Francen

'I found it painless. It never got nearer to the subject than names and consequently didn't hurt. But I would like to know who was devoted to whom and why.'—*Richard Winnington*

† More items from the extraordinary publicity campaign devised by Warners for this placid Victorian romance:

Emily: she ruled in that strange quiet house! None could resist the force of her will!

The man in black (i.e. the Revd Nicholls): he fled from her demands into her sister's arms!

Charlotte: the sweetness of love and the meaning of torment—she learned them both together!

The 'friend'—the furious fat man (i.e. William Makepeace Thackeray): they couldn't fool him—they couldn't trust him!

†† Dialogue includes the celebrated exchange between two celebrated London literary figures:

THACKERAY: 'Morning, Dickens.'
DICKENS: 'Morning, Thackeray.'

The DI
US 1957 106m bw
Warner / Mark VII (Jack Webb)

A tough marine drill instructor takes a special interest in a backward member of his platoon.
Noisy recruiting poster heroics in which the producer gives himself a loud but boring part. The drill sequences are well done, but the film is overlong and repetitive.

w James Lee Barrett *d* Jack Webb *ph* Edward Colman *m* David Buttolph

Jack Webb, Don Dubbins, Jackie Loughery, Lin McCarthy, Monica Lewis

Le Diable au Corps*
France 1947 110m bw
Transcontinental
US title: *Devil in the Flesh*

When her husband is away at war, a young married woman falls for a college student and dies bearing his child.
A love story of World War I; a great commercial success, but tending to be slow and dreary.

w Jean Aurenche, Pierre Bost, *novel* Raymond Radiguet *d* Claude Autant-Lara *ph* Michel Kelber *m* René Cloërc

Micheline Presle, Gérard Philipe, Jean Debucourt, Denise Grey, Jacques Tati

Les Diaboliques***
France 1954 114m bw
Filmsonor (Henri-Georges Clouzot)
aka: *Diabolique; The Fiends*

A sadistic headmaster's wife and mistress conspire to murder him; but his body disappears and evidence of his presence haunts them.
Highly influential, suspenseful and scary thriller with a much-copied twist typical of its authors. Slow to start and shabby-looking as befits its grubby school setting, it gathers momentum with the murder and turns the screw with fine professionalism.

w Henri-Georges Clouzot, G. Geronimi, *novel* The Woman Who Was by Pierre Boileau and Thomas Narcejac *d Henri-Georges Clouzot* *ph* Armand Thirard *m* Georges Van Parys

Simone Signoret, Vera Clouzot, Charles Vanel, Paul Meurisse

'Scary, but so calculatedly sensational that it's rather revolting.'—*New Yorker, 1978*

'It depends very much on the intimate details of the seedy fourth-rate school, with its inadequate education and uneatable food, its general smell of unwashed children, hatred and petty perversions.'—*Basil Wright, 1972*

† Remade in 1976 as a TV movie, *Reflections of Murder*.

Diagnosis: Murder
GB 1974 90m Eastmancolor
Silhouette (Patrick Dromgoole, Peter Miller)

A psychiatrist's wife disappears, and the police suspect her husband.
Well-upholstered but sadly old-fashioned domestic crime thriller; one is vaguely surprised to see it in colour, having seen it so often in black-and-white.

w Philip Levene *d* Sidney Hayers *ph* Bob Edwards *m* Laurie Johnson

Jon Finch, Judy Geeson, Christopher Lee, Tony Beckley, Dilys Hamlett, Jane Merrow, Colin Jeavons

'If a woman answers—hang on for dear life!'

Dial M For Murder**
US 1954 105m Warnercolor 3-D
Warner (Alfred Hitchcock)

An ageing tennis champion tries to arrange the death of his wife so that he will inherit, but his complex plan goes wrong.
Hitchcock did not try very hard to adapt this highly commercial play for the cinema, nor did he exploit the possibilities of 3-D. But for a one-room film with a not very exciting cast the film holds its grip pretty well.

w Frederick Knott, from his play *d Alfred Hitchcock* *ph* Robert Burks *m* Dmitri Tiomkin

Ray Milland, John Williams, Grace Kelly, Robert Cummings, Anthony Dawson

'All this is related with Hitchcock's ghoulish chic but everyone in it seems to be walking around with tired blood.'—*Pauline Kael, 1968*

Dial 1119*
US 1950 75m bw
MGM (Richard Goldstone)
GB title: *The Violent Hour*

An assortment of people are held up in a bar by a maniac.
Suspenseful thriller when it sticks to its central theme; dullish when it tries characterization. A good second feature.

w John Monks Jnr *d Gerald Mayer* *ph* Paul Vogel *m* André Previn

Marshall Thompson, Virginia Field, Andrea King, Leon Ames, Keefe Brasselle, Richard Rober, James Bell, William Conrad

Diamond City
GB 1949 90m bw
GFD / Gainsborough (A. Frank Bundy)

Law and order is maintained during the working of a South African diamond field.
British imitation of a Wyatt Earp western; very milk-and-water.

w Roger Bray, Roland Pertwee *d* David MacDonald *ph* Reginald Wyer *m* Clifton Parker

David Farrar, Honor Blackman, Diana Dors, Niall MacGinnis, Andrew Crawford, Mervyn Johns, Bill Owen, Phyllis Monkman

Diamond Frontier
US 1940 72m bw

An honest diamond dealer is framed and sent to prison. Co-feature action stuff, with South Africa standing in for the west. Victor McLaglen, Anne Nagel, John Loder, Philip Dorn, Cecil Kellaway. Written by Edmund L. Hartmann and Stanley Rubin; directed by Harold Schuster; for Universal.

Diamond Head
US 1962 107m Eastmancolor Panavision
Columbia (Jerry Bresler)

A domineering Hawaiian landowner almost ruins the lives of his family.
Predictable, heavy-going transcription of a bestseller.

w Marguerite Roberts, *novel* Peter Gilman *d* Guy Green *ph* Sam Leavitt *m* Johnny Williams

Charlton Heston, Yvette Mimieux, George Chakiris, France Nuyen, James Darren, Aline MacMahon, Elizabeth Allen, Richard Loo

Diamond Horseshoe
US 1945 104m Technicolor
TCF (William Perlberg)
aka: *Billy Rose's Diamond Horseshoe*

A nightclub singer gives up her career for a medical student.
Lavish but humourless star vehicle with standard numbers.

wd George Seaton, *play* The Barker by Kenyon Nicholson *ph* Ernest Palmer *songs* Mack Gordon, Harry Warren

Betty Grable, Dick Haymes, *William Gaxton*, Phil Silvers, Beatrice Kay, Carmen Cavallero, Margaret Dumont

Diamond Jim*
US 1935 93m bw
Universal (Edmund Grainger)

A fantasia on the life of the nineties millionaire who sailed pretty close to the wind in business, adored Lillian Russell, and developed a gargantuan appetite.
Cheerful period comedy drama with plenty of gusto.

w Preston Sturges *d* A. Edward Sutherland *ph* George Robinson *m* Ferde Grofe, Franz Waxman

Edward Arnold, Jean Arthur, Binnie Barnes, Cesar Romero, Eric Blore

'Good picture and title. Lacks real pull names.'—*Variety*

The Diamond Queen
US 1953 80m Supercinecolor
Warner / Melson (Frank Melford, Edward L. Alperson Jnr)

Frenchmen journey to India to bring back a diamond for the crown of Louis XIV.
The adventures are basically lively enough to warrant a better production.

w Otto Englander *d* John Brahm *ph* Stanley Cortez *m* Paul Sawtell

Fernando Lamas, Arlene Dahl, Gilbert Roland, Sheldon Leonard, Michael Ansara

The Diamond
GB 1954 83m bw 3D
Gibraltar Films (Stephen Pallos)
US title: *The Diamond Wizard*

An American agent in London investigates a million-dollar treasury robbery involving a process for making synthetic diamonds.
Leaden cops-and-robbers which went out on the bottom of a bill instead of being shown in three dimensions.

w John C. Higgins, *story* The Bowstring Murders by Maurice Procter *m* Montgomery Tully *m* Matyas Seiber

Dennis O'Keefe, Margaret Sheridan, Philip Friend, Alan Wheatley, Francis de Wolff

Diamonds
US 1975 108m Eastmancolor
Avco Embassy / AmeriEuro (Menahem Golan)

A London diamond merchant sets himself up to be robbed so that he can blackmail the culprits into a raid on the Tel Aviv diamond repository.
Cheerful but unremarkable caper movie with an upbeat ending.

w David Paulsen, Menahem Golan *d* Menahem Golan *ph* Adam Greenberg *m* Roy Budd

Robert Shaw, Richard Roundtree, Barbara Seagull, Shelley Winters

Diamonds Are Forever*
GB 1971 120m Technicolor Panavision
UA / Eon / Danjaq (Harry Saltzman, Albert R. Broccoli)

Seeking a diamond smuggler, James Bond has adventures in Amsterdam, a Los Angeles crematorium, various Las Vegas gambling parlours, and a secret installation in the desert.
Campy, rather vicious addition to a well-worn cycle, with an element of nastiness which big-budget stunts cannot conceal. Panavision does not help, and Connery's return to the role for a final throw is disappointing.

w Richard Maibaum, Tom Mankiewicz, *novel* Ian Fleming *d* Guy Hamilton *ph* Ted Moore *m* John Barry *pd* Ken Adam

Sean Connery, Jill St John, Charles Gray, Lana Wood, Jimmy Dean, Bruce Cabot, Bernard Lee, Lois Maxwell

'It has been claimed that the plot is impossible to describe, but I think I could if I wanted to. I can't think why anyone would want to, though.'—*Roger Ebert*

Diamonds for Breakfast
GB 1968 102m Eastmancolor
Paramount / Bridge Films (Carlo Ponti, Pierre Rouve)

An impoverished Russian aristocrat decides to retrieve from a museum the crown jewels of his ancestors, and seduces seven female accomplices.
Yawning caper yarn embellished with sex and slapstick.

w N. F. Simpson, Pierre Rouve, Ronald Harwood *d* Christopher Morahan *ph* Gerry Turpin *m* Norman Kay

Marcello Mastroianni, Rita Tushingham, Elaine Taylor, Warren Mitchell, Nora Nicholson, Bill Fraser, Leonard Rossiter

Diane
US 1956 110m Eastmancolor Cinemascope
MGM (Edwin H. Knopf)

Diane de Poitier becomes a consultant to the king and falls in love with his son.
Solidly boring slice of Hollywood history, with all concerned out of their depth.

w Christopher Isherwood *d* David Miller *ph* Robert Planck *m* Miklos Rozsa

Lana Turner, Roger Moore, Cedric Hardwicke, Pedro Armendariz, Marisa Pavan

A Diary for Timothy****
GB 1945 40m bw

A baby is born as the war ends, and the narrator ponders its future. Brilliant sentimental documentary, a summing up of the aims and feelings of Britain at the time.
Written by E. M. Forster; speaker Michael Redgrave; directed by Humphrey Jennings; for Basil Wright / Crown Film Unit.

The Diary of a Chambermaid*
US 1946 86m bw
Benedict Bogeaus (Burgess Meredith, Paulette Goddard)

A 19th-century serving girl causes sexual frustration and other troubles in two households.
Hollywood notables were all at sea in this wholly artificial and unpersuasive adaptation of a minor classic.

w Burgess Meredith, *novel* Octave Mirbeau *d Jean Renoir ph* Lucien Andriot *pd* Eugene Lourié *m* Michel Michelet

Paulette Goddard, Burgess Meredith, Hurd Hatfield, Francis Lederer, Judith Anderson, Florence Bates, Irene Ryan, Reginald Owen, Almira Sessions

The Diary of a Chambermaid*
France / Italy 1964 98m bw Franscope
Speva / Ciné Alliance / Filmsonor / Dear (Serge Silberman, Michel Sabra)
original title: *Le Journal d'une Femme de Chambre*

Interesting but not especially successful Bunuel version: the subject is certainly up his street, but the novel seems to restrict him and the visual quality is unattractive.

w Luis Bunuel, Jean-Claude Carrière *d* Luis Bunuel *ph* Roger Fellous *m* none

Jeanne Moreau, Georges Géret, Michel Piccoli, Françoise Lugagne

The Diary of a Country Priest***
France 1950 120m bw
Union Générale Cinématographique (Léon Carré)
original title: *Journal d'un Curé de Campagne*

A lonely young priest fails to make much impression in his first parish; and, falling ill, he dies alone.
Striking, depressing, slow and austere, with little dialogue but considerable visual beauty; a very typical work of its director.

wd Robert Bresson, novel Georges Bernanos *ph* L. Burel *m* Jean-Jacques Grunenwald

Claude Laydu, Jean Riveyre, Armand Guibert, Nicole Ladmiral

Diary of a Lost Girl**
Germany 1929 110m approx bw silent
G. W. Pabst Film
original title: *Tagebuch einer Verlorenen*

A rich man's daughter is seduced, has an illegitimate child, is placed in a house of correction and finds herself later in a brothel.
Heavily Germanic Road to Ruin, superbly mounted in best cinematic style, with several memorable sequences. Heavily mutilated by censors; according to the screenwriter the film ends just after the middle of his script.

w Rudolf Leonhardt, *novel* Margaret Böhme *d G. W. Pabst ph* Sepp Allgeier

Louise Brooks, Fritz Rasp, Josef Ravensky
† A previous version had been made in 1918, written and directed by Richard Oswald.

Diary of a Mad Housewife**
US 1970 95m Technicolor
Universal / Frank Perry

The bored and repressed wife of a lawyer tries an affair, walks out on her husband, and opts for group therapy.
An agreeably mordant view of the contemporary American scene, with good dialogue and performances, but the little bits of satire do not really add up to a satisfactory film.

w Eleanor Perry, novel Sue Kaufman *d Frank Perry ph* Gerald Hirschfeld

Carrie Snodgress, Richard Benjamin, Frank Langella, Lorraine Cullen, Frannie Michel

'A prototypical contemporary American artifact . . . all its assorted talents and technological smartness are turned to the varnishing of mediocrity.'—*Stanley Kauffmann*

AAN: Carrie Snodgress

The Diary of a Madman
US 1962 96m Technicolor
UA / Admiral (Robert E. Kent)

A murderer explains to a magistrate that he was possessed by an evil spirit.
Ponderous transcription of a Maupassant story with a few moments of horror.

w Robert E. Kent *d* Reginald Le Borg *ph* Ellis W. Carter *m* Richard La Salle

Vincent Price, Nancy Kovack, Chris Warfield, Stephen Roberts

The Diary of a Married Woman
Germany 1953 83m bw
Magna
original title: *Tagebuch einer Verliebten*

A wife divorces her adulterous husband, but their small son brings them together again.
One long Hollywood cliché, assembled with some spirit; notable only as one of the rare post-war German films to get distribution in English-speaking countries.

w Emil Burri, Johann Mario Simmel *d* Josef Von Baky *ph* Oskar Snirch *m* Alois Melichar

Maria Schell, O. W. Fischer, Franco Andrei

Diary of a Shinjuku Thief*
Japan 1969 94m bw / Eastmancolor
Sozosha (Masayuki Nakajima)
original title: *Shinjuku Dorobo Nikki*

A minor theft in a bookstore brings a young man in contact with a mysterious girl who leads him into various sexual experiments. Inexplicable but quite fascinating piece of oriental mystification in which sex equates to some extent with revolution.

w Tsutomu Tamura and others *d* Nagisa Oshima *ph* Yasuhiro Yamaguchi *m* none

Tadanori Yokoo, Rie Yokoyama, Moichi Tanabe

The Diary of Anne Frank**
US 1959 170m bw Cinemascope
TCF / George Stevens

In 1942, a family of Dutch Jews hides in an attic from the Nazis; just before the war ends they are found and sent to concentration camps.
Based on the famous diaries of a girl who died at Auschwitz, this solemn adaptation is elephantine in its length, its ponderousness and its use of Cinemascope when the atmosphere is supposed to be claustrophobic.

w Frances Goodrich, Albert Hackett, from their play based on Anne Frank's diaries *d* George Stevens *ph William C. Mellor* *m* Alfred Newman

Millie Perkins, *Joseph Schildkraut, Shelley Winters, Ed Wynn*, Richard Beymer, Gusti Huber, Lou Jacobi, Diane Baker

AA: William C. Mellor; Shelley Winters
AAN: best picture; George Stevens; Alfred Newman; Ed Wynn

The Diary of Major Thompson
France 1955 83m bw
SNE Gaumont / Paul Wagner
original title: *Les Carnets de Major Thompson;* US title: *The French They Are a Funny Race*

An Englishman married to a Frenchwoman keeps notes on the French way of life.
Tatty filming of a mildly amusing book; it falls away into a number of badly-timed and presented gags, and one can't believe that its creator was once the top comedy genius of Hollywood.

wd Preston Sturges *ph* Maurice Barry, Christian Matras *m* Georges Van Parys

Jack Buchanan, Martine Carol, Noel-Noel, Genevieve Brunet

'Even allowing for the appalling editing and the frequently incomprehensible dubbed soundtrack, there is little evidence to suggest that this film could ever have been anything but a shambles.'—*Peter John Dyer, MFB*

Dick Barton

The radio detective was created by Edward J. Mason in the mid-forties, and three rough-and-ready film versions were subsequently made by Hammer / Exclusive. They were *Dick Barton Special Agent* (1948); *Dick Barton Strikes Back* (1949); and *Dick Barton at Bay* (1950); all with Don Stannard. Critical comment would be irrelevant.

Dick Deadeye, or Duty Done
GB 1975 81m Technicolor
Bill Melendez Productions (Leo Rost)

A naval officer is commissioned by Queen Victoria to retrieve the Ultimate Secret from the Wicked Sorcerer.
Fairly joyless animated amalgam of several Gilbert and Sullivan operas, fussily designed by Ronald Searle and with modernized lyrics. Sure to infuriate G and S devotees and to bewilder everyone else.

w Robin Miller, Leo Rost *d* Bill Melendez *animation d* Dick Horn

Dick Tracy
US 1937 bw serial: 15 eps

The fearless detective combats an arch-criminal known as The Spider. Hearty serialized thick-ear. Ralph Byrd, Kay Hughes, Smiley Burnette, Francis X. Bushman. Directed by Ray Taylor and Alan James; for Republic.

Dick Tracy Returns
US 1938 bw serial: 15 eps

Dick Tracy combats a criminal family, the Starks. More hectic and hilarious exploits of the jut-jawed hero, now a G-man. Ralph Byrd, Lynne Roberts, Charles Middleton, Jerry Tucker, David Sharpe. Directed by William Witney and John English; for Republic.

Dick Tracy's G-Men
US 1939 bw serial: 15 eps

Dick Tracy combats Zarnoff, an international spy who has been executed but revived by powerful drugs. Serial cliffhangers par excellence. Ralph Byrd, Irving Pichel, Ted Pearson, Phyllis Isley (Jennifer Jones). Directed by William Witney and John English; for Republic.

Dick Tracy vs Crime Inc.
US 1941 bw serial: 15 eps

Dick Tracy combats a master criminal known as The Ghost. Repetition is now beginning to set in. Ralph Byrd, Michael Owen, Jan Wiley, Ralph Morgan. Directed by William Witney and John English; for Republic.

Dick Tracy
US 1945 61m bw
RKO (Herman Schlom)
GB title: *Splitface*

The jut-jawed detective routs a disfigured criminal named Splitface.
Vigorous second feature from the comic strip.

w Eric Taylor, *strip* Chester Gould *d* William Berke *ph* Frank Redman *m* Roy Webb

Morgan Conway, Jane Greer, Mike Mazurki, Anne Jeffreys, Lyle Latell, Joseph Crehan, Trevor Bardette

† Sequels: *Dick Tracy vs Cueball* (1946) with Morgan Conway, *d* John Rawlins; *Dick Tracy Meets Gruesome* (1947) with Ralph Byrd, Boris Karloff, *d* John Rawlins; *Dick Tracy's Dilemma* (1947), with Ralph Byrd, *d* John Rawlins. There had been several Republic serials featuring Tracy, and in the fifties a cartoon series appeared.

Dick Turpin
GB 1933 79m bw
Stoll-Stafford (Clyde Cook)

In this version the highwayman's ride to York is to prevent an enforced marriage.
Mild British costume piece which sent its star to Hollywood.

w Victor Kendall, *novel* Rookwood by Harrison Ainsworth *d* Victor Hanbury, John Stafford *ph* Desmond Dickinson

Victor McLaglen, Jane Carr, Frank Vosper, James Finlayson, Gillian Lind

The Dictator*
GB 1935 86m bw
Toeplitz
aka: *For Love of a Queen; The Loves of a Dictator*

In 18th-century Denmark, a country doctor falls in love with his queen and overthrows the mad king.
Stiff-backed middle-class romance, an interesting example of English-German co-production at the time.

w Benn Levy, Hans Wilhelm, H. G. Lustig, Michael Hogan *d* Victor Saville, Alfred Santell *ph* Franz Planer

Clive Brook, Madeleine Carroll, Helen Haye, Emlyn Williams, Isabel Jeans, Alfred Drayton, Frank Cellier

'One of the most lavish costume pictures that has yet come out of England: supposed to have cost 500,000 dollars. It's great pictorially, but not moving enough.'—*Variety*

Did You Hear the One about the Travelling Saleslady?
US 1967 96m Techniscope
Universal (Si Rose)

In a Kansas town in 1910 an eccentric saleslady offers pianolas which tend to go berserk.
Cornbelt comedy vehicle for an unappealing star.

w John Fenton Murray *d* Don Weis *ph* Bud Thackery *m* Vic Mizzy

Phyllis Diller, Bob Denver, Joe Flynn, Jeanette Nolan

Die Laughing
US 1980 108m Technicolor

After the murder of a nuclear scientist, a young musician who knows too much is chased by the murderers and the FBI. Witless black comedy rehash of *The 39 Steps*. Robby Benson, Linda Grovenor, Charles Durning, Elsa Lanchester, Bud Cort. Written by Jerry Segal, Robby Benson and Scott Parker; directed by Jeff Werner; for Jon Peters / Orion / Warner.

Dieu A Besoin des Hommes*
France 1950 100m bw
Transcontinental (Paul Graetz)
aka: *Isle of Sinners; God Needs Men*

The priest of a Breton island leaves in horror at the sinfulness of his flock, and the fisherfolk appoint one of their number as priest.
Cold, gloomy, rather pointless fable, often a pleasure to look at.

w Jean Aurenche, Pierre Bost, *novel* Un Recteur de l'Ile de Sein by H. Queffléc *d* Jean Delannoy *ph Robert Le Fèbvre* *m* René Cloërc

Pierre Fresnay, Madeleine Robinson, Daniel Gélin, Andrée Clément, Sylvie, Jean Brochard

A Different Story
US 1978 106m CFI color
Avco / Alan Belkin

A homosexual falls in love with a lesbian. One supposes it had to come, but one doesn't really have to watch it.

w Henry Olek *d* Paul Aaron *ph* Philip Lathrop *m* David Frank

Perry King, Meg Foster, Valerie Curtin, Peter Donat

'There's something in *A Different Story* to turn off audiences of every sexual persuasion—and movie lovers most of all.'—*Richard Schickel, Time*

Digby: the Biggest Dog in the World
GB 1973 88m Technicolor
TCF / Walter Shenson

An old English sheepdog accidentally eats a chemical intended to increase the size of vegetables . . .
Nice to see this kind of gimmick used for comedy instead of horror, but the result is rather tame and old-fashioned, though for several years it made a pleasant television offering for Christmas.

w Michael Pertwee *d* Joseph McGrath *ph* Harry Waxman *sp* Tom Howard *m* Edwin T. Astley

Jim Dale, Spike Milligan, Angela Douglas, Milo O'Shea, Dinsdale Landen, Garfield Morgan, Victor Spinetti, Bob Todd

Dillinger*
US 1945 70m bw
Monogram (Frank and Maurice King)

The life of American public enemy number one who was shot by the police in 1934.
Slick, speedy gangster thriller, possibly the most tolerable movie to come from this low-budget studio.

w Philip Yordan *d Max Nosseck* *ph* Jackson Rose *m* Dmitri Tiomkin

Lawrence Tierney, Edmund Lowe, Anne Jeffreys

AAN: Philip Yordan

Dillinger*
US 1973 107m Movielab
AIP (Buzz Feitshans)

Violence-soaked version, with black comedy touches, of the last year of Dillinger's life. Not badly done, with a style reminiscent of *Bonnie and Clyde.*

wd John Milius *ph* Jules Brenner *m* Barry Devorzon

Warren Oates, Ben Johnson (as Melvin Purvis), Michelle Philips, Cloris Leachman, Harry Dean Stanton, Richard Dreyfuss

Dimension 5
US 1966 88m colour

CIA agents use a time converter to jump ahead three weeks and prevent the Chinese from bombing Los Angeles. Silly spy fantasy with inadequate effects. Jeffrey Hunter, France Nuyen, Harold Sakata, Donald Woods. Written by Arthur C. Pierce; directed by Franklin Adreon; for United Pictures Corporation.

Dimples**
US 1936 82m bw
TCF (Darryl F. Zanuck, Nunnally Johnson)

In the New York Bowery in pre-Civil War days, a child and her reprobate grandfather win the hearts of high society.
Excellent Temple vehicle with good period flavour.

w Arthur Sheekman, Nat Perrin *d* William A. Seiter *ph* Bert Glennon *m* Louis Silvers *songs* Jimmy McHugh, Ted Koehler

Shirley Temple, Frank Morgan, Helen Westley, Berton Churchill, Robert Kent, Delma Byron, Astrid Allwyn

Diner**
US 1982 110m Technicolor
MGM / SLM (Jerry Weintraub)

In 1959 Baltimore, college students congregate at their old meeting place and find themselves more occupied by adult problems than of yore.
Generally amusing group character study, an awkward attempt to divine the meaning of life through the accumulation of detail. A little masterpiece of observation, for those with ears to hear; but not necessarily a great film.

wd Barry Levinson *ph* Peter Sova *m* Bruce Brody, Ivan Kral *pd* Leon Harris *ed* Stu Linder

Steve Guttenberg, Daniel Stern, Mickey Rourke, Kevin Bacon, Timothy Daly, Ellen Barkin, Paul Reiser, Kathryn Dowling, Michael Tucker, Jessica James

AAN: original screenplay

Dingaka
South Africa 1965 97m Technicolor Cinemascope
Embassy (Jamie Uys)

Tribal antagonisms cause a simple native to seek revenge in the city.
Unconvincing and now very dated melodrama with rather too much local colour.

wd Jamie Uys *ph* Manie Botha *m* Bertha Egnos, Eddie Domingo, Basil Gray

Ken Gampu, Stanley Baker, Juliet Prowse, Siegfried Mynhardt, Paul Makgoba

Dinky
US 1935 65m bw

The mother of a military school cadet is framed into a prison term. Sentimental drama of little interest. Jackie Cooper, Mary Astor, Roger Pryor, Henry Armetta, Henry O'Neill, Edith Fellowes. Written by Harry Sauber; directed by D. Ross Lederman and Howard Bretherton; for Warners. 'A rapidly maturing Jackie Cooper is revealed here as lacking the strength to stand alone.'—*Variety*

Dinner at Eight***
US 1933 113m bw
MGM (David O. Selznick)

Guests at a society dinner party all find themselves in dramatic circumstances.
Artificial but compelling pattern play from a Broadway success.

w Frances Marion, Herman J. Mankiewicz, *play* George S. Kaufman, Edna Ferber *d George Cukor* *ph* William Daniels *m* William Axt

Marie Dressler, John Barrymore, Lionel Barrymore, Billie Burke, Wallace Beery, *Jean Harlow*, Lee Tracy, Edmund Lowe, Madge Evans, Jean Hersholt, Karen Morley, Louise Closser Hale, Phillips Holmes, May Robson, Grant Mitchell, Elizabeth Patterson

KITTY (Jean Harlow): 'You know, I read a book the other day. It's all about civilization or something—a nutty kind of a book. Do you know that the guy said machinery is going to take the place of every profession?'

CARLOTTA (Marie Dressler): 'Oh, my dear. That's something *you* need *never* worry about!'

'Marquee speaks for itself. It spells money, and couldn't very well be otherwise.'—*Variety*

Dinner at the Ritz
GB 1937 77m bw
New World (Robert T. Kane)

A French girl exposes swindlers who faked her father's suicide.
Once-diverting comedy melodrama with an international cast.

w Roland Pertwee, Romney Brent *d* Harold Schuster *ph* Philip Tannura

Annabella, Paul Lukas, David Niven, Romney Brent, Stewart Rome, Francis L. Sullivan, Nora Swinburne, Frederick Leister

'Slow and shoddily made British product.'—*Variety*

'It moves with old world decorum and occasional touches of gout.'—*New York Times*

Dino
US 1957 93m bw

A juvenile delinquent released from prison has trouble reforming. Adequately made social drama with good credentials. Sal Mineo, Brian Keith, Susan Kohner, Frank Faylen, Joe DeSantis. Written by Reginald Rose from his tv play; directed by Thomas Carr; for Bernice Block/AA.

Diplomaniacs
US 1933 59m bw

Two halfwits are offered a fortune to go to Geneva and make the peace delegates stop fighting. Fatuous comedy which never gets going. Bert Wheeler, Robert Woolsey, Hugh Herbert, Marjorie White, Phyllis Barry, Louis Calhern. Written by Joseph Mankiewicz and Henry Meyers; directed by William Seiter; for RKO. 'A baddie; rhymed dialogue no help for inane plot.'—*Variety*

Diplomatic Courier*
US 1952 98m bw
TCF (Casey Robinson)

American and Russian agents clash on a train between Salzburg and Trieste; an unexpected master spy is revealed after several chases. Lively cold war intrigue, well produced and played with relish.

w Casey Robinson, Liam O'Brien, *novel* Sinister Errand by Peter Cheyney *d* Henry Hathaway *ph* Lucien Ballard *md* Lionel Newman *m* Sol Kaplan

Tyrone Power, Patricia Neal, Stephen McNally, Hildegarde Neff, Karl Malden, James Millican, Herbert Berghof

'A reversion to the oldest tradition of spy fiction.'—*Penelope Houston*

Dirigible*
US 1931 102m bw
Columbia

The story of an airship disaster. Economical epic with a few Capra touches.

w Jo Swerling, Dorothy Howell, *story* 'Spig' Wead *d* Frank Capra *ph* Joe Wilbur, Elmer Dyer, Joseph Walker

Jack Holt, Fay Wray, Ralph Graves, Hobart Bosworth, Roscoe Karns

'Plenty of everything expected in a flying film spectacle.'—*Variety*

Dirty Dancing*
US 1987 97m colour

In 1963, kids go dance crazy at a borscht belt resort. Mildly agreeable variant on *Saturday Night Fever*, almost equally successful at the box office. Jennifer Grey, Patrick Swayze, Jerry Orbach, Cynthia Rhodes, Jack Weston. Written by Eleanor Bergman; directed by Emile Ardolino; for Linda Gottlieb/Vestron.

AA: song 'I've Had the Time of My Life'

Dirty Dingus Magee
US 1970 91m Metrocolor Panavision
MGM (Burt Kennedy)

A likeable western outlaw crosses swords with an old enemy. Fair burlesque western often stooping to vulgarity.

w Tom Waldman, Frank Waldman, Joseph Heller, *novel* David Markson *d* Burt Kennedy *ph* Harry Stradling *m* Jeff Alexander

Frank Sinatra, George Kennedy, Anne Jackson, Lois Nettleton, Jack Elam, John Dehner, Henry Jones, Harry Carey Jnr, Paul Fix

'Skittish burlesque, scripted in the brash and undisciplined style of a TV show . . . heavily reliant on the *Carry On* brand of humour.'—*David McGillivray*

'Damn them or praise them—you'll never forget them!'

The Dirty Dozen**
US / Spain 1967 150m Metrocolor 70mm
MGM / Kenneth Hyman (Raymond Anzarut)

In 1944, twelve convicts serving life sentences are recruited for a commando suicide mission. Professional, commercial but unlikeable slice of wartime thick ear; pretensions about capital punishment are jettisoned early on in favour of frequent and violent bloodshed. Much imitated, e.g. by *The Devil's Brigade, A Reason to Live, a Reason to Die*, etc.

w Nunnally Johnson, Lukas Heller from novel by E. M. Nathanson *d Robert Aldrich* *ph* Edward Scaife *m* Frank de Vol

Lee Marvin, Ernest Borgnine, Robert Ryan, Charles Bronson, Jim Brown, John Cassavetes, George Kennedy, Richard Jaeckel, Trini Lopez, Telly Savalas, Ralph Meeker, Clint Walker, Robert Webber, Donald Sutherland

AAN: John Cassavetes

'You don't assign him to murder cases—you just turn him loose!'

Dirty Harry**
US 1971 103m Technicolor Panavision
Warner / Malpaso (Don Siegel)

A violently inclined San Francisco police inspector is the only cop who can bring to book a mad sniper. When the man is released through lack of evidence, he takes private revenge.
A savage cop show which became a cult and led to a spate of dirty cop movies, including two sequels, *Magnum Force* (qv) and *The Enforcer*. Well done for those who can take it.

w Harry Julian Fink, Rita M. Fink, Dean Riesner *d Don Siegel* *ph* Bruce Surtees *m* Lalo Schifrin

Clint Eastwood, Harry Guardino, Reni Santoni, John Vernon, Andy Robinson, John Larch, John Mitchum

Dirty Little Billy
US 1972 92m Eastmancolor
Columbia / WRG / Dragoti (Jack L. Warner)

The violent young life of Billy the Kid. Squalid little western with few attractive aspects except that it presents its hero as the mentally retarded delinquent which history says he was.

w Charles Moss, Stan Dragoti *d* Stan Dragoti *ph* Ralph Woolsey *m* Sascha Burland

Michael J. Pollard, Lee Purcell, Richard Evans, Charles Aidman

'The gap between its ostensible aims and its manner of realizing them continually leaves the film bogged down in its own scrupulously realistic mud.'—*Tony Rayns*

Dirty Mary, Crazy Larry
US 1974 92m De Luxe
Academy Pictures Corporation (Norman T. Herman)

Two racing drivers and a kooky groupie rob a supermarket and almost elude their police pursuers.
Elaborately stunted chase film, agreeable enough to watch if the characters were not so disagreeable.

w Leigh Chapman, Antonio Santean, *novel* The Chase by Richard Unekis *d* John Hough *ph* Mike Margulies *m* Jimmie Haskell

Peter Fonda, Susan George, Adam Roarke, Vic Morrow, Kenneth Tobey, Roddy McDowall, Eugene Daniels

'The film's general delight in destruction and despoliation makes one wonder if it is the cinema that reflects the ugliness of modern society or the ugliness of modern society that reflects trends in the cinema.'—*Michael Billington, Illustrated London News*

Dirty Work***
US 1933 20m bw

Chimney sweeps cause havoc in the house of an eccentric scientist. Hilarious star comedy with splendid timing and comedy touches. Laurel and Hardy, Lucien Littlefield, Sam Adams. Written by H. M. Walker; directed by Lloyd French; for Hal Roach.

Dirty Work
GB 1934 78m bw
Gaumont (Michael Balcon)

Shop assistants pose as crooks in order to catch thieves.
Rather thin Ben Travers farce with some authentic moments.

w Ben Travers, from his play *d* Tom Walls *ph* Phil Tannura

Ralph Lynn, Gordon Harker, Robertson Hare, Lillian Bond, Basil Sydney, Cecil Parker, Margaretta Scott, Gordon James, Peter Gawthorne

The Disappearance
GB / Canada 1977 102m Eastmancolor
Trofar / Tiberius (David Hemmings)

An international hit man finds that his wife has disappeared.
Confusing and pretentious thriller which spends more time on introspection than action and ends up not satisfying anybody.

w Paul Mayersberg, *novel* Echoes of Celandine by Derek Marlowe *d* Stuart Cooper *ph* John Alcott *m* Robert Farnon

Donald Sutherland, Francine Racette, David Hemmings, John Hurt, David Warner, Peter Bowles, Virginia McKenna, Christopher Plummer

Disbarred
US 1938 58m bw

A lady lawyer is paid by a crime czar to defend a gangster. Slick mini-melo of the kind at which this studio excelled at the time. Otto Kruger, Gail Patrick, Robert Preston, Sidney Toler, Charles D. Brown. Written by Lillie Hayward and Robert Presnell; directed by Robert Florey; for Paramount. 'Moderately entertaining drama; nicely fills the lower brackets.'—*Variety*

The Discreet Charm of the Bourgeoisie***
France / Spain / Italy 1972 105m Eastmancolor
Greenwich (Serge Silberman)
original title: *Le Charme Discret de la Bourgeoisie*

The efforts of a group of friends to dine together are continually frustrated.
A frequently hilarious, sometimes savage

surrealist fable which makes all its points beautifully and then goes on twenty minutes too long. The performances are a joy.

w Luis Bunuel, Jean-Claude Carrière d Luis Bunuel ph Edmond Richard

Fernando Rey, Delphine Seyrig, Stéphane Audran, Bulle Ogier, Jean-Pierre Cassel, Paul Frankeur, Julien Bertheau

'A perfect synthesis of surreal wit and blistering social assault.'—*Jan Dawson, MFB*

AA: best foreign film

AAN: Luis Bunuel, Jean-Claude Carrière (script)

The Disembodied
US 1957 73m bw

In the tropics, a doctor's wife is really a voodoo queen who is trying to kill him by supernatural means. Verbose rubbish with more yawns than thrills. Allison Hayes, Paul Burke, John Wengraf. Written by Jack Townley; directed by Walter Grauman; for Allied Artists.

Dishonored**
US 1931 91m bw
Paramount

An officer's widow turned streetwalker is hired by the German government as a spy.
Rather gloomy melodrama which helped to establish its star as a top American attraction; but the heavy hand of her Svengali, Von Sternberg, was already evident.

w Daniel H. Rubin *d Josef Von Sternberg ph Lee Garmes m* Karl Hajos

Marlene Dietrich, Victor McLaglen, Lew Cody, Gustav Von Seyffertitz, Warner Oland, Barry Norton, Wilfred Lucas

'Miss Dietrich rises above her director . . . should make the money grade of an A1 draw talker.'—*Variety*

'The most exciting movie I have seen in several months . . . yet I hope I may die young if I ever again have to listen to a manuscript so full of recusant, stilted, outmoded theatrical mouthings.'—*Pare Lorentz*

'The whole film has a kind of magnificent grandeur embellished, of course, by its shining central performance.'—*John Gillett, 1964*

'She insulted her soul!'
Dishonored Lady
US 1947 85m bw
Mars Film (Hedy Lamarr)

A girl with a past is cleared of a murder charge by her psychiatrist.
Melodramatic showpiece designed for herself by a glamorous star; OK for the silly season.

w Edmund H. North, *play* Edward Sheldon, Margaret Ayer Barnes *d* Robert Stevenson *ph* Lucien Andriot *m* Carmen Dragon

Hedy Lamarr, John Loder, Dennis O'Keefe, Paul Cavanagh, William Lundigan, Natalie Schaefer, Morris Carnovsky

Dishonour Bright*
GB 1936 82m bw
GFD / Cecil (Herman Fellner, Max Schach)

An ageing playboy is blackmailed about a past affair.
Interesting semi-smart comedy of the period, tailored for its star.

w Ben Travers *d* Tom Walls *ph* Phil Tannura

Tom Walls, Eugene Pallette, Betty Stockfield, Diana Churchill, Arthur Wontner, Cecil Parker, George Sanders, Henry Oscar, Basil Radford

The Disorderly Orderly
US 1964 89m Technicolor
Paramount / York (Paul Jones)

A hospital orderly creates havoc by his inefficiency and his sympathy for other people's predicaments.
Spasmodic farce with far too much pathos between its highlights.

wd Frank Tashlin *ph* W. Wallace Kelley *m* Joseph Lilley

Jerry Lewis, Glenda Farrell, Everett Sloane, Kathleen Freeman, Karen Sharpe, Susan Oliver, Alice Pearce

Disorderly Conduct
US 1932 82m bw

A cop turns crook after being demoted. Heavy-going melodrama apparently intended as a tribute to the New York police. Spencer Tracy, Sally Eilers, El Brendel, Dickie Moore, Ralph Bellamy, Ralph Morgan, Alan Dinehart. Written by William Anthony McGuire; directed by John W. Considine Jnr; for Fox. 'Good entertainment . . . mother-love sentiment with some kid atmosphere.'—*Variety*

Les Disparus de St Agil*
France 1938 95m bw

Students disappear in a school whose headmaster is a forger and murderer. Curious black comedy: a half-success. Michel Simon, Erich Von Stroheim, Aimé Clariond, Armand Bernard. Written by J. H. Blanchon, from a novel by Pierre Véry; directed by Christian-Jaque; for Vog Films.

A Dispatch from Reuters**
US 1940 90m bw
Warner (Henry Blanke)
GB title: *This Man Reuter*

The story of the man who provided Europe's first news service.
Acceptable if slightly dull addition to Warner's prestige biopics; well made and acted.

w Milton Krims *d William Dieterle ph James Wong Howe m* Max Steiner

Edward G. Robinson, Edna Best, Eddie Albert, Albert Basserman, Gene Lockhart, Otto Kruger, Montagu Love, Nigel Bruce, James Stephenson

Disputed Passage*
US 1939 90m bw
Paramount (Harlan Thompson)

A young scientist who wants to marry meets resistance from his mentor.
Adequate screen version of a bestseller.

w Anthony Veiller, Sheridan Gibney, *novel* Lloyd C. Douglas *d* Frank Borzage *ph* William C. Mellor *m* Frederick Hollander, James Leopold

Dorothy Lamour, John Howard, Akim Tamiroff, Judith Barrett, William Collier Snr, Victor Varconi, Keye Luke, Elizabeth Risdon

'Fine drama of medical science: a top-of-the-bill attraction.'—*Variety*

'I should describe the flavour as a rather nauseating blend of iodine and glucose.'—*Graham Greene*

'It dwarfs the stage!'
Disraeli*
US 1929 89m bw
Warner

Fictionalized episodes in the life of the Victorian statesman, including his activities as a matchmaker.
Very early star talkie, of primarily archival interest; Arliss had appeared in a silent version in 1921.

w Julian Josephson, *play* Louis N. Parker *d* Alfred E. Green *ph* Lee Garmes *md* Louis Silvers

George Arliss, Joan Bennett, Florence Arliss, Anthony Bushell, David Torrence, Ivan Simpson, Doris Lloyd

'Those seeking a fuller assessment of the man and his work would have been better off in a library.'—*Clive Hirschhorn, 1982*

AA: George Arliss
AAN: best picture; Julian Josephson

'The rescue . . . the throbbing jungle drums . . . the man-devouring marsh wilderness aflame with unseen menace!'
Distant Drums
US 1951 101m Technicolor
United States Pictures (Milton Sperling)

In 1840 Florida, an army officer rescues prisoners from an Indian fort and decimates the Seminoles who threaten their return journey.
Overlong action saga, with dull stretches compensated by a dominating star and some lively incident.

w Niven Busch, Martin Rackin *d* Raoul Walsh *ph* Sid Hickox *m* Max Steiner

Gary Cooper, Mari Aldon, Richard Webb, Ray Teal, Arthur Hunnicutt, Robert Barrat

'Don't look for surprises. Mr Cooper is kept steady and laconic throughout, the action is serio-comic, and the pace is conventionally maintained.'—*Bosley Crowther, New York Times*

A Distant Trumpet
US 1964 116m Technicolor Panavision
Warner (William H. Wright)

The new commander of a cavalry outpost tightens up discipline, which serves him well when Indian trouble erupts.
Moderate western, quite well staged but with a second team cast.

w John Twist, *novel* Paul Horgan *d* Raoul Walsh *ph* William Clothier *m* Max Steiner

Troy Donahue, Suzanne Pleshette, James Gregory, Diane McBain, William Reynolds, Claude Akins, Kent Smith, Judson Pratt

Distant Voices, Still Lives*
GB 1988 84m colour
BFI / Film Four International (Colin MacCabe)

Working-class family life in Liverpool in the 40s and 50s.
Low-budget labour of love filmed at intervals over two years, succeeding through close, unsentimental observation and excellent performances by a cast of unknowns.

w,d Terence Davies *ph* William Diver, Patrick Duval *pd* Miki van Zwanenberg

Freda Dowie, Pete Postlethwaite, Angela Walsh

'While its pacing and structure may exasperate some, should envelop receptive audiences with its special magic.'—*Variety*

Ditte, Child of Man*
Denmark 1946 106m bw
Nordisk
original title: *Ditte Menneskebarn*

An unmarried mother abandons her daughter, who grows up to be a servant and to be seduced in her turn.
Impressive, doom-laden Scandinavian saga, highly thought of on its release.

wd Astrid and Bjarne Henning-Jensen, *novel* Martin Andersen *ph* Werner Jenssen *m* Herman Koppel

Tove Maes, Rasmus Ottesen, Karen Poulsen

Diva*
France 1981 117m Eastmancolor
Galaxie / Greenwich / Antenne 2 (Irene Silberman)

A black prima donna in Paris becomes accidentally involved in drug smuggling and murder.
A curious hybrid of violence and surrealism which doesn't seem to know what effect it's aiming at, or at least doesn't let the viewer in on the secret, being content to entertain in a flashy and sometimes shocking way.

w Jean-Jacques Beineix, Jean Van Hamme, *novel* Delacorta *d Jean-Jacques Beineix* *ph* Philippe Rousselot *m* Vladimir Cosma *pd Hilton McConnico*

Frederic Andrei, Roland Bertin, Richard Bohringer, Wilhelmenia Wiggins Fernandez, Jean-Jacques Moreau, Chantal Deruaz

Dive Bomber*
US 1941 133m Technicolor
Warner (Hal B. Wallis)

Aviation scientists work to eliminate pilot blackout.
Somewhat rarefied propaganda piece with too many reels of romantic banter but tense climactic scenes and good star performances.

w Frank 'Spig' Wead, Robert Buckner *d* Michael Curtiz *ph* Bert Glennon, Winton C. Hoch *m* Max Steiner *md* Leo F. Forbstein

Errol Flynn, Fred MacMurray, Ralph Bellamy, Alexis Smith, Regis Toomey, Robert Armstrong, Allen Jenkins, Craig Stevens, Moroni Olsen, Gig Young, William Hopper, Charles Drake, Russell Hicks, Addison Richards, Ann Doran, Herbert Anderson

AAN: Bert Glennon, Winton C. Hoch

The Divided Heart**
GB 1954 89m bw
Ealing (Michael Truman)

A boy believed to be a war orphan is lovingly brought up by foster parents; then his real mother turns up and wants him back.
Effective 'woman's picture' set in Europe and giving a genuine sense of post-war feelings and problems.

w Jack Whittingham d Charles Crichton *ph* Otto Heller *m* Georges Auric

Cornell Borchers, Yvonne Mitchell, Armin Dahlen, Alexander Knox, Geoffrey Keen, Michel Ray, Liam Redmond, Eddie Byrne

The Divine Lady*
US 1929 100m bw
Warner

The adventures of Emma, Lady Hamilton.
Historical charade which titillated at the time.

w Agnes Christine Johnson, Forrest Halsey *d* Frank Lloyd *ph* John Seitz

Corinne Griffith, Victor Varconi, H. B. Warner, Montagu Love, Marie Dressler

AA: Frank Lloyd
AAN: John Seitz

Divine Madness
US 1980 93m Technicolor Panavision

A record of a Bette Midler concert performance. 'Since this is the time capsule version of my show, I may as well do everything I know.' It certainly isn't a movie. Directed by Michael Ritchie; photographed by William A. Fraker; for Ladd Company / Warner.

The Divine Woman*
US 1927 95m approx (24 fps) bw silent
MGM

The loves of Sarah Bernhardt.
Garbo's first star role; a typical Hollywood melodramatization of facts.

w Dorothy Farnum, *play* Starlight by Gladys Unger *d* Victor Sjostrom

Greta Garbo, Lars Hanson, Lowell Sherman, John Mack Brown, Polly Moran

Divorce
US 1945 71m bw

A much-married woman tries to break up another happy family. This somewhat elementary tract was the star's first independent production, and not a success. Kay Francis, Bruce Cabot, Helen Mack, Jonathan Hale, Jerome Cowan. Written by Sidney Sutherland, Harvey Gates; directed by William Nigh; for Jeffrey Bernerd / Kay Francis / Monogram. 'A lacklustre script grooves it for the duals.'—*Variety*

'In America the ring costs two dollars to put on—and a fortune to take off!'

Divorce American Style**
US 1967 109m Technicolor
Columbia / Tandem (Norman Lear)

Well-heeled Los Angeles suburbanites toy with divorce but eventually resume their domestic bickering.
Rather arid and patchy but often sharply sardonic comedy about a society in which people can't afford to divorce.

w Norman Lear d Bud Yorkin *ph* Conrad Hall *m David Grusin pd* Edward Stephenson

Dick Van Dyke, Debbie Reynolds, Jean Simmons, Jason Robards Jnr, Van Johnson, Joe Flynn, Shelley Berman, Martin Gabel, Lee Grant, Tom Bosley, Dick Gautier

AAN: Norman Lear

A Divorce in the Family
US 1932 78m bw

A boy is affected by his parents' divorce. Dated drama, an odd choice of vehicle for a boy star fresh from *The Champ*. Jackie Cooper, Conrad Nagel, Lois Wilson, Lewis Stone, Jean Parker, Lawrence Grant. Written by Delmer Daves, Maurice Rapf; directed by Charles Reisner; for MGM. 'Not more than medium box office; Cooper fans will not be attracted by the title.'—*Variety*

'A delightfully daring plan to give marriage a surprise ending!'

Divorce Italian Style**
Italy 1961 108m bw
Lux / Vides / Galatea (Franco Cristaldi)
original title: *Divorzio all'Italiana*

A Sicilian nobleman explains how, wishing to be rid of his wife, he arranged for her to be seduced and later shot by a jealous lover.
Sardonic, stylized comedy which, rather in the manner of *Kind Hearts and Coronets*, manages while retailing a black comedy plot to satirize Italian manners and institutions.

w Ennio de Concini, Pietro Germi, Alfredo Gianetti d Pietro Germi ph Leonida Barboni *m* Carlo Rustichelli

Marcello Mastroianni, Daniela Rocca, Stefania Sandrelli, Leopoldo Trieste

AA: script
AAN: Pietro Germi; Marcello Mastroianni

The Divorce of Lady X**
GB 1938 92m Technicolor
London Films (Alexander Korda)

A nobleman's daughter wins a barrister by posing as a divorce client.
Pleasing comedy with high production standards of its time, deftly performed by a distinguished cast.

w Lajos Biro, Arthur Wimperis, Ian Dalrymple, *play* Counsel's Opinion by Gilbert Wakefield *d Tim Whelan ph* Harry Stradling *m* Miklos Rozsa

Laurence Olivier, Merle Oberon, Binnie Barnes, Ralph Richardson, Morton Selten, J. H. Roberts

'Her sin was no greater than his, but she was a woman! If the world permits the husband to philander—why not the wife?'

The Divorcee*
US 1930 83m bw
MGM (Robert Z. Leonard)

Would-be liberal young marrieds divorce when she puts up with his affairs but he can't tolerate hers. She falls in love with another married man but sends him back to his wife.
Rather wan illustration of the double standard which was being much discussed in society at the time.

w John Meehan, Nick Grinde, Zelda Sears, *novel* Ex-Wife by Ursula Parrott *d* Robert Z. Leonard *ph* Norbert Brodine *ad* Cedric Gibbons

Norma Shearer, Chester Morris, Conrad Nagel, Robert Montgomery, Florence Eldridge

'Shearer's specialty was sexy suffering in satin gowns by Adrian; here, she almost seems to want to abandon herself to naughtiness, but one line after another stops her.'—*Pauline Kael, 70s*

AA: Norma Shearer
AAN: best picture; Robert Z. Leonard; John Meehan, Nick Grinde, Zelda Sears

Dixiana
US 1930 100m bw (Technicolor sequences)

A Dutchman from Pennsylvania tries to run a plantation in Louisiana. Lavish but utterly witless musical comedy which just lies there and dies there. Bebe Daniels, Bert Wheeler, Robert Woolsey, Everett Marshall, Joseph Cawthorn, Jobyna Howland, Dorothy Lee, Bill Robinson. Written and directed by Luther Reed from a play by Ann Caldwell; for RKO.
'Not much but bigness for exploiting.'—*Variety*

Dixie*
US 1943 90m Technicolor
Paramount (Paul Jones)

The life of old-time minstrel man Dan Emmett.
Lighter-than-air fictionalized biography with pleasing mid-19th-century settings.

w Karl Tunberg, Darrell Ware *d* A. Edward Sutherland *ph* William C. Mellor *m* Robert Emmet Delan *songs* Johnny Burke, Jimmy Van Heusen

Bing Crosby, Dorothy Lamour, Marjorie Reynolds, *Lynne Overman, Eddie Foy Jnr, Billy de Wolfe, Raymond Walburn*, Grant Mitchell

Dixie Dugan
US 1943 63m bw

A secretary with a screwball family gets a government job in Washington. Fairly feeble adaptation from a popular comic strip. Lois Andrews, James Ellison, Charlie Ruggles, Charlotte Greenwood, Raymond Walburn, Eddie Foy Jnr. Written by Lee Loeb and Harold Bruckman; directed by Otto Brower; for Walter Morosco / TCF.

DOA**
US 1949 81m bw
Cardinal Pictures (Leo C. Popkin)

A businessman discovers that he has effectively been murdered by a slow-acting poison. In the few hours left to him he tracks down and kills his murderer, and confesses to the police.
Unusual and effective thriller, well photographed on location in San Francisco and Los Angeles.

w Russell Rouse, Clarence Greene d Rudolph Maté ph Ernest Laszlo m Dmitri Tiomkin

Edmond O'Brien, Luther Adler, Pamela Britton, William Ching
† Remade 1970 as *Colour Me Dead*, with Tom Tryon.

The Do It Yourself Cartoon Kit**
GB 1961 6m Eastmancolor

A commercial for the kit in question, poking fun at all comers in a Monty Pythonish way. Great stuff for those who like zany humour well controlled. Written by *Colin Pearson*; directed by *Bob Godfrey*; for Biographic.

'What should a girl do when opportunity knocks . . . twice?'

Do Not Disturb
US 1965 102m De Luxe Cinemascope
TCF / Melcher / Arcola (Aaron Rosenberg, Martin Melcher)

An American wool executive is posted to London; his dizzy wife makes him jealous by flirting with a French antique dealer.
Silly farce which paints a lunatic picture of English and French life but occasionally raises a wild laugh or two. Thin script and production.

w Milt Rosen, Richard Breen, *play* William Fairchild *d* Ralph Levy *ph* Leon Shamroy *m* Lionel Newman

Doris Day, Rod Taylor, *Sergio Fantoni*, Reginald Gardiner, Hermione Baddeley, Leon Askin

Do You Like Women?
France / Italy 1964 100m bw
Francoriz / Number One / Federiz (Pierre Kalfon)
original title: *Aimez-Vous Les Femmes?*

Secret rival sects of woman-eaters cause an outbreak of murders in Paris.
Bizarre black comedy that doesn't quite work but provides ghoulish fun along the way.

w Roman Polanski, Gérard Brach, *novel* Georges Bardawil *d* Jean Léon *ph* Sacha Vierny *m* Ward Swingle

Sophie Daumier, Guy Bédos, Edwige Feuillère, Grégoire Aslan, Roger Blin

'It has the provoking quality of a carefully-prepared firework display which, due to faulty timing or bad connections, is never actually ignited.'—*MFB*

Do You Love Me?
US 1946 91m Technicolor
TCF (George Jessel)

The lady dean of a music school gets herself glamorized.
Thin, mildly agreeable but forgettable musical.

w Robert Ellis, Helen Logan *d* Gregory Ratoff *ph* Edward Cronjager *songs* various

Maureen O'Hara, Dick Haymes, Harry James and his Orchestra, Reginald Gardiner, Richard Gaines, Stanley Prager

Doc*
US 1971 96m De Luxe
UA / Frank Perry

Doc Holliday goes to Tombstone to die of TB, but is drawn into the feud between the Clantons and his friend Wyatt Earp, whose motives are not of the highest.
A somewhat glum debunking of the west's most heroic myth, backing dour character study with grubby pictures. The result lacks excitement but maintains interest.

w Pete Hamill *d* Frank Perry *ph Gerald Hirschfeld m* Jimmy Webb

Stacy Keach (Doc), Harris Yulin (Earp), Faye Dunaway (Kate Elder), Mike Witney, Denver John Collins, Dan Greenberg

'The physical realism that *Doc* is at pains to establish becomes simply a convention of its own.'—*Richard Combs*

'Have no fear, Doc Savage is here!'

Doc Savage, Man of Bronze
US 1975 100m Technicolor
Warner (George Pal)

A thirties superman and his assistants the Amazing Five fly to South America to avenge the death of Doc's father.
Stolid, humourless adaptation from a comic strip, totally lacking in the necessary panache.

w George Pal, Joe Morhaim, *stories* Kenneth Robeson *d* Michael Anderson *ph* Fred Koenekamp *m* John Philip Sousa

Ron Ely, Paul Gleason, Bill Lucking, Michael Miller, Eldon Quick

'A slick, ultra-self-conscious camp that denies the material its self-respect.'—*Colin Pahlow*

'Nothing in this unfortunate enterprise is likely to please anyone: former Savage fans will be enraged, newcomers bored, and children will probably feel superior to the whole mess . . .'—*New Yorker*

The Dock Brief
GB 1962 88m bw
(MGM) Dimitri de Grunwald
US title: *Trial and Error*

An incompetent barrister defends his client on a murder charge. The client is found guilty but the sentence is quashed on the grounds of inadequate defence.
Flat filming of a TV play which was a minor milestone; the film is twice the length and half as funny, and both stars quickly become tiresome.

w John Mortimer, Pierre Rouve, *play* John Mortimer *d* James Hill *ph* Ted Scaife *m* Ron Grainer

Peter Sellers, Richard Attenborough, Beryl Reid, David Lodge, Frank Pettingell

Docks of New York**
US 1928 80m (24 fps) bw silent
Paramount

A stoker marries a girl he has saved from suicide. Further unfortunate incidents result in his going to prison, but she waits for him.
Glum melodrama chiefly remarkable for its sets and lighting, reminiscent of the later *Quai des Brumes*.

w Jules Furthman, *story* The Dock Walloper by John Monk Saunders *d Josef Von Sternberg ph Harold Rosson ad Hans Dreier*

George Bancroft, Betty Compson, Olga Baclanova, Clyde Cooke, Gustav Von Seyffertitz

'One comes away with the memory of a film impregnated with a life whose essential is in its energy and force.'—*Louis Chavance*

The Doctor and the Devils
GB 1985 93m Rank Colour Panavision
Brooksfilm (Jonathan Sanger)

In the late eighteenth century an Edinburgh surgeon starts to pay for bodies as specimens, and doesn't ask their provenance.
Yet another version (see *The Body Snatcher*, *The Flesh and the Fiends*, *Burke and Hare*) of the tale of Dr Knox, and this time a pretty poor one, justified by the use of Dylan Thomas's script.

w Ronald Harwood, from Dylan Thomas *d* Freddie Francis *ph* Gerry Turpin, Norman Warwick *m* John Morris *pd* Robert Laing

Timothy Dalton, Jonathan Pryce, Twiggy, Julian Sands, Lewis Fiander, Stephen Rea

'Unrelentingly serious treatment of a gruesome subject is unlikely to attract many warm bodies to the box office.'—*Variety*

The Doctor and the Girl
US 1949 98m bw
MGM (Pandro S. Berman)

A young doctor renounces specialization to help the poor.
Antediluvian medical romance full of the nicest people. Technically very competent.

w Theodore Reeves, from 'a literary work' by Maxene Van Der Meersch *d* Curtis Bernhardt *ph* Robert Planck *m* R. G. Kopp

Glenn Ford, Charles Coburn, Gloria de Haven, Janet Leigh, Bruce Bennett, Warner Anderson

Doctor at Large
GB 1957 104m Eastmancolor
Rank (Betty E. Box)

Simon Sparrow tries two country practices, but returns at last to St Swithin's.
Hit-or-miss medical comedy with honours about even.

w Nicholas Phipps, *novel* Richard Gordon *d* Ralph Thomas *ph* Ernest Steward *m* Bruce Montgomery

Dirk Bogarde, Muriel Pavlow, James Robertson Justice, Donald Sinden, Shirley Eaton, Derek Farr, Michael Medwin, Edward Chapman, Barbara Murray, Gladys Henson, Lionel Jeffries, A. E. Matthews, Athene Seyler, George Coulouris

Doctor at Sea*
GB 1955 93m Technicolor VistaVision
Rank / Group Films (Betty E. Box)

Simon Sparrow becomes medical officer on a cargo steamer.
Reasonably lively comedy of errors with nice seascapes and predictable jokes.

w Nicholas Phipps, Jack Davies *d* Ralph Thomas *ph* Ernest Steward *m* Bruce Montgomery

Dirk Bogarde, Brigitte Bardot, Brenda de Banzie, James Robertson Justice, Maurice Denham, Michael Medwin, Hubert Gregg, Raymond Huntley, Geoffrey Keen, George Coulouris, Jill Adams, James Kenney

'Brisk professional humour has given way to the more elementary business of traditional British farce.'—*Penelope Houston, MFB*

Doctor Blood's Coffin
GB 1960 92m Eastmancolor
UA / Caralan (George Fowler)

A disbarred doctor sets up in a Cornish tin mine and begins to emulate Dr Frankenstein.
Lurid horror piece which makes no sort of sense.

w Jerry Juran *d* Sidney J. Furie *ph* Stephen Dade *m* Buxton Orr

Kieron Moore, Hazel Court, Ian Hunter, Gerald C. Lawson, Kenneth J. Warren, Fred Johnson

'It lacks style, suspense and imagination and will scarcely satisfy even the most naive necrophiliac.'—*MFB*

'He's the main stem's specialist in heart trouble—and lead poisoning!'

Dr Broadway
US 1942 75m bw

A young medico gets involved with guns, girls and gangsters. Adequate filler which failed to spawn the intended series. Macdonald Carey, Jean Phillips, J. Carrol Naish, Richard Lane, Eduardo Ciannelli. Written by Art Arthur, from a story by Borden Chase; directed by Anthony Mann; for Paramount.

Dr Bull
US 1933 75m bw

A genial country doctor triumphs over his own lack of medical knowledge. Rather lumpy star vehicle which paid its way. Will Rogers, Vera Allen, Marian Nixon, Berton Churchill, Louise Dresser, Andy Devine, Ralph Morgan. Written by Paul Green from The Last Adam by James Gould Cozzens; directed by John Ford; for Fox. 'Drips with human interest and can scarcely miss.'—*Variety*

Dr Christian
Following the success of THE COUNTRY DOCTOR (qv), a rival studio (RKO) made a series of second features about a fictional country doctor, the rights to Dr Dafoe's life story being unavailable. Jean Hersholt again played the leading role and the films were immensely popular in small towns. A TV series followed in the fifties, starring Macdonald Carey.

1939: MEET DR CHRISTIAN
1940: THE COURAGEOUS DR CHRISTIAN, DR CHRISTIAN MEETS THE WOMEN, REMEDY FOR RICHES
1941: MELODY FOR THREE, THEY MEET AGAIN

Dr Crippen*
GB 1962 98m bw
ABP / John Clein

A quiet doctor murders his wife and elopes with a typist.
Straightforward account of a famous and rather unsurprising Edwardian murder case; well enough made but with no special *raison d'être*.

w Leigh Vance *d* Robert Lynn *ph* Nicolas Roeg *m* Kenneth Jones

Donald Pleasence, Coral Browne, Samantha Eggar, Donald Wolfit

'Diabolical dictator . . . devastating discoverer of the most frightening invention in the history of civilized man!'

Dr Cyclops*
US 1940 76m Technicolor
Paramount (Merian C. Cooper)

Jungle travellers are captured and miniaturized by a mad scientist.
Splendid special effects and an appropriately sombre atmosphere are hampered by a slow-paced narrative in this minor horror classic.

w Tom Kilpatrick *d* Ernest Schoedsack *ph Henry Sharp, Winton Hoch m* Ernst Toch, Gerard Carbonera, Albert Hay Malotte

Albert Dekker, Janice Logan, Victor Kilian, Thomas Coley, Charles Halton

'The picture made behind locked doors!'—*publicity*

Dr Dolittle
US 1967 152m De Luxe Todd-AO
TCF / APJAC (Arthur P. Jacobs)

In a Victorian English village, Dr Dolittle is a veterinary surgeon who talks to his patients; escaping from a lunatic asylum, he travels with friends to the South Seas in search of the Great Pink Sea Snail.
Lumpish family spectacular with no imagination whatever, further handicapped by charmless performances and unsingable songs.

w / songs Leslie Bricusse, *novels* Hugh Lofting *d* Richard Fleischer *ph* Robert Surtees *pd* Mario Chiari *md* Lionel Newman, Alex Courage

Rex Harrison, Anthony Newley, Samantha Eggar, *Richard Attenborough*, William Dix, Peter Bull

AA: song 'Talk to the Animals'
AAN: best picture; Robert Surtees; Lionel Newman, Alex Courage; Leslie Bricusse (*m*)

Dr Ehrlich's Magic Bullet***
US 1940 103m bw
Warner (Wolfgang Reinhardt)
aka: *The Story of Dr Ehrlich's Magic Bullet*

A German scientist develops a cure for venereal disease.
Excellent period biopic: absorbing, convincing and extremely well put together.

DR ERLICH'S MAGIC BULLET. A reminder to anyone who thought that Ruth Gordon was never young as she pours tea for scientific pioneer Edward G. Robinson. Otto Kruger looks on.

w John Huston, Heinz Herald, Norman Burnside *d William Dieterle ph James Wong Howe m* Max Steiner

Edward G. Robinson, Ruth Gordon, Otto Kruger, Donald Crisp, Maria Ouspenskaya, Montagu Love, Sig Rumann, Donald Meek, Henry O'Neill, Albert Basserman, Edward Norris, Harry Davenport, Louis Calhern, Louis Jean Heydt

'A superb motion picture.'—*Pare Lorentz*

AAN: John Huston, Heinz Herald, Norman Burnside

Dr Faustus
GB 1967 93m Technicolor
Columbia / Oxford University Screen Productions / Nassau Films / Venfilms (Richard Burton, Richard McWhorter)

A medieval scholar conjures up Mephistopheles and offers his soul in exchange for a life of voluptuousness.
Marlowe's play has been adapted and 'improved', and there is some good handling of the poetry, but the production is flat, dingy and uninspired, as well as ludicrous when Miss Taylor makes her silent appearances.

w Nevill Coghill, *play* Christopher Marlowe *d* Richard Burton, Nevill Coghill *ph* Gabor Pogany *m* Mario Nascimbene *pd* John de Cuir

Richard Burton, Andreas Teuber, Ian Marter, Elizabeth Donovan, Elizabeth Taylor (as Helen of Troy)

'It is of an awfulness that bends the mind. The whole enterprise has the immense vulgarity of a collaboration in which academe would sell its soul for a taste of the glamour of Hollywood, and the stars are only too happy to appear a while in academe.'—*John Simon*

'It turns out to be the story of a man who sold his soul for Elizabeth Taylor.'—*Judith Crist*

Dr Gillespie's Criminal Case
US 1943 89m bw

The elderly doctor solves a murder for which an innocent man is in prison. Skilled programme filler with beloved characters. Lionel Barrymore, Margaret O'Brien, Donna Reed, Van Johnson, Keye Luke, Marilyn Maxwell. Written by Martin Berkeley, Harry Ruskin and Lawrence Bachmann; directed by Willis Goldbeck; for MGM. (GB title: *Crazy to Kill.*) See also *Dr Kildare*.

Dr Gillespie's New Assistant
US 1942 88m bw

Shorn of young Dr Kildare, Gillespie chooses a new support from three interns, and meanwhile concentrates on an amnesia case. Slick series entry which played widely as top of the bill. Lionel Barrymore, Van Johnson, Keye Luke, Richard Quine, Susan Peters. Written by Willis Goldbeck, Harry Ruskin and Lawrence Bachmann; directed by Willis Goldbeck; for MGM. See also *Dr Kildare*.

Dr Goldfoot and the Bikini Machine
US 1965 90m Pathecolor Panavision
AIP (Anthony Carras)

Dr G. makes girl robots programmed to lure wealthy men into their clutches.
Way-out farce for the jaded end of the teenage market; a few lively touches and a climactic chase partly atone for the general tastelessness.

w Elwood Ullman, Robert Kaufman *d* Norman Taurog *ph* Sam Leavitt *m* Les Baxter *ad* Daniel Haller

Vincent Price, Fred Clark, Frankie Avalon, Dwayne Hickman, Susan Hart, Jack Mullaney

'Meet the girls with the thermo-nuclear navels! The most titillating time bombs you've ever been tempted to trigger!'

Dr Goldfoot and the Girl Bombs
US / Italy 1966 86m colour

The evil mastermind teams up with Red China to cause trouble between Russia and the USA. Inane teenage nonsense, almost enough to make one swear off movies. Vincent Price, Fabian Forte, Franco Franchi, Laura Antonelli. Written by Louis M. Heyward and Robert Kaufmann; directed by Mario Bava; for AIP.

Dr Heckyl and Mr Hype
US 1980 99m Metrocolor

An ugly scientist is transformed into a handsome young sadist. Would-be comic variation on a well-worn theme; the level of comedy is indicated by the title. Oliver Reed, Sunny Johnson, Mel Wells, Maia Danziger. Written and directed by Charles B. Griffith; for Golan-Globus.

Doctor in Clover
GB 1966 101m Eastmancolor
Rank / Betty E. Box–Ralph Thomas

Grimsdyke goes back to his old hospital for a refresher course and finds a rejuvenating drug useful in his philandering.
Depressing mixture of smut and slapstick.

w Jack Davies, *novel* Richard Gordon *d* Ralph Thomas *ph* Ernest Steward *m* John Scott

Leslie Phillips, James Robertson Justice, Shirley Anne Field, Joan Sims, John Fraser, Arthur Haynes, Fenella Fielding, Noel Purcell, Jeremy Lloyd, Eric Barker, Terry Scott, Alfie Bass

Doctor in Distress
GB 1963 102m Eastmancolor
Rank / Betty E. Box–Ralph Thomas

Simon Sparrow goes back to work for Sir Lancelot Spratt and finds his old mentor in love.

Tedious flummery whose characters fail to perform with the old pizazz.

w Nicholas Phipps, Ronald Scott Thorn *d* Ralph Thomas *ph* Ernest Steward *m* Norrie Paramour

Dirk Bogarde, James Robertson Justice, Mylene Demongeot, Samantha Eggar, Barbara Murray, Donald Houston, Jessie Evans, Ann Lynn, Leo McKern, Dennis Price

Doctor in Love
GB 1960 97m Eastmancolor
Rank / Betty E. Box–Ralph Thomas

Dr Burke and Dr Hare have various adventures, mostly amorous, in city and country practices.
Virtually plotless collection of weak sketches based on schoolboy smut.

w Nicholas Phipps, *novel* Richard Gordon *d* Ralph Thomas *ph* Ernest Steward *m* Bruce Montgomery

Michael Craig, Leslie Phillips, James Robertson Justice, Virginia Maskell, Nicholas Phipps, Reginald Beckwith, Joan Sims, Liz Fraser, Ambrosine Philpotts, Irene Handl

Doctor in the House**
GB 1954 91m Eastmancolor
Rank (Betty Box)

Amorous and other misadventures of medical students at St Swithin's Hospital.
A comedy with much to answer for: several sequels and an apparently endless TV series. The original is not bad, as the students, though plainly over age, constitute a formidable mass of British talent at its peak.

w Nicholas Phipps, book Richard Gordon *d* Ralph Thomas *ph* Ernest Steward *m* Bruce Montgomery

Dirk Bogarde, Kenneth More, Donald Sinden, Donald Houston, Kay Kendall, Muriel Pavlow, *James Robertson Justice*, Geoffrey Keen

'Works its way with determined high spirits through the repertoire of medical student jokes.'—*MFB*

† Sequels, of increasing inanity and decreasing connection with the original characters, were: *Doctor at Sea, Doctor at Large, Doctor in Love, Doctor in Distress, Doctor in Clover* and *Doctor in Trouble. Carry on Doctor* and *Carry on Again Doctor* were horses of a different colour.

Doctor in the Village*
Holland 1958 92m bw
Nationale Filmproductie Maatschappij (Bobby Roosenboom)
original title: *Dorp aan de Rivier*

Stories are recalled of an eccentric but respected country doctor at the turn of the century.
Tragi-comic incidents in the vein of Pagnol, a little too rich in farce and melodrama to be convincingly human.

w Hugo Claus, *novel* Antoon Coolen *d* Fons Rademakers *ph* Eduard J. R. van der Enden *m* Jurriaan Andriessen

Max Croiset, Mary Dresselhuys, Bernhard Droog, Jan Teulings

'Scenes which should have had disturbing power crowd one upon another with an almost repellent relish which falls over into parody.'—*Peter John Dyer, MFB*

Doctor in Trouble
GB 1970 90m Technicolor
Rank / Betty Box

Dr Burke inadvertently becomes a stowaway on an Atlantic cruise.
Witless tailpiece to the Doctor saga, like a half-hearted wrapping-up of discarded jokes from the other episodes.

w Jack Davies, *novel* Doctor on Toast by Richard Gordon *d* Ralph Thomas *ph* Ernest Steward *m* Eric Rogers

Leslie Phillips, Harry Secombe, Angela Scoular, Irene Handl, Robert Morley, Simon Dee, Freddie Jones, James Robertson Justice, Joan Sims, John Le Mesurier, Fred Emney

Doctor Jack*
US 1922 72m approx (24 fps) bw silent
Pathé / Rolin

A quack country doctor does more good than the licensed medicos.
Pleasing but not hilariously funny star vehicle.

w Sam Taylor, Jean Havez *d* Fred Newmeyer

Harold Lloyd, Mildred Davis, John Prince, Eric Mayne

'The greatest drama of dual identity ever written!'

Dr Jekyll and Mr Hyde**
US 1921 63m (24 fps) bw silent
Paramount Artcraft

A respected London physician experiments with a drug which separates out the evil part of his soul.
A lively star vehicle which renewed John Barrymore's popularity with film audiences. Some scenes still grip, and Barrymore accomplished some transformations in full view of the camera, by facial contortions.

w Clara S. Beranger, *novel* Robert Louis Stevenson *d* John S. Robertson

John Barrymore, Nita Naldi, Martha Mansfield, Louis Wolheim

'Strange desires! Loves and hates and secret yearnings . . . hidden in the shadows of a man's mind!'

Doctor Jekyll and Mr Hyde****
US 1931 98m bw
Paramount (Rouben Mamoulian)

A Victorian research chemist finds a formula which separates the good and evil in his soul; when the latter predominates, he becomes a rampaging monster.
The most exciting and cinematic version by far of the famous horror story; the make-up is slightly over the top, but the gas-lit London settings, the pace, the performances and clever camera and sound tricks make it a film to enjoy over and over again. Subjective camera is used at the beginning, and for the first transformation the actor wore various layers of make up which were sensitive to different colour filters and thus produced instant change.

w Samuel Hoffenstein, Percy Heath, novel Robert Louis Stevenson d Rouben Mamoulian ph Karl Struss ad Hans Dreier

Fredric March, Miriam Hopkins, Rose Hobart, Holmes Herbert, Halliwell Hobbes, Edgar Norton

'Promises abundant shocks and returns now that the fan public is horror conscious. Probably loses something on popular appeal by highbrow treatment.'—*Variety*

'As a work of cinematic imagination this film is difficult to fault.'—*John Baxter, 1968*

† The screenplay with 1,400 frame blow-ups was published in 1976 in the Film Classics Library (editor Richard J. Anobile).
†† The film was subsequently edited down to 80m, and this is the only version remaining.

AA: Fredric March
AAN: Samuel Hoffenstein, Percy Heath; Karl Struss

Dr Jekyll and Mr Hyde**
US 1941 122m bw
MGM (Victor Saville, Victor Fleming)

Curiously misconceived, stately, badly cast version with elaborate production including Freudian dream sequences. Always worth watching, but not a success.

w John Lee Mahin *d* Victor Fleming *ph* Joseph Ruttenberg *m* Franz Waxman

Spencer Tracy, Ingrid Bergman, Lana Turner, Ian Hunter, C. Aubrey Smith, Donald Crisp, Sara Allgood

'Not so much evil incarnate as ham rampant . . . more ludicrous than dreadful.'—*New York Times*

'A romantic gentleman by day—a love-mad beast at night!'—*publicity*

† Other versions: *The Two Faces of Dr Jekyll* (1960), *I Monster* (1970). Variations: *Daughter of Dr Jekyll* (1957), *Abbott and Costello Meet Dr Jekyll and Mr Hyde* (1954), *Son of Dr Jekyll* (1951), *The Ugly Duckling* (1960), *House of Dracula* (1945), *The Nutty Professor* (1963), *Dr Jekyll and Sister Hyde* (1971).

AAN: Joseph Ruttenberg; Franz Waxman

Dr Jekyll and Sister Hyde*
GB 1971 97m Technicolor
Hammer (Albert Fennell, Brian Clemens)

A twist: Jekyll now turns into a young and beautiful woman, and kills prostitutes so that he can continue his research.
Half-successful attempt to link the legend with Jack the Ripper, killed by gore and overlength.

w Brian Clemens *d* Roy Ward Baker *ph* Norman Warwick *m* David Whitaker

Ralph Bates, Martine Beswick, Gerald Sim, Lewis Fiander, Dorothy Alison

Dr Kildare
This long-running screen hero was a young intern at Blair Hospital, under the cranky tutelage of old Dr Gillespie. Created by Max Brand in a series of novels, he first appeared on the screen in a 1937 Paramount double-biller called INTERNS CAN'T TAKE MONEY, played by Joel McCrea with Barbara Stanwyck, no less, providing the love interest. Kildare came up against gangsters; Gillespie did not appear. MGM then took over the property and went to town with it, making fifteen films in ten years. They were as follows:

1938: YOUNG DR KILDARE
1939: CALLING DR KILDARE, THE SECRET OF DR KILDARE
1940: DR KILDARE'S STRANGE CASE (qv), DR KILDARE GOES HOME (qv), DR KILDARE'S CRISIS (qv)
1941: THE PEOPLE vs DR KILDARE
1942: DR KILDARE'S WEDDING DAY (qv)
1942: DR KILDARE'S VICTORY (qv), CALLING DR GILLESPIE, DR GILLESPIE'S NEW ASSISTANT (qv)
1943: DR GILLESPIE'S CRIMINAL CASE (qv)
1944: THREE MEN IN WHITE, BETWEEN TWO WOMEN
1947: DARK DELUSION

Lew Ayres played Kildare, but in 1942 declared himself a conscientious objector and was dropped. The emphasis shifted to Gillespie, played by Lionel Barrymore from a wheelchair, and he proceeded to deal with a whole series of interns. The films were well enough made on medium budgets; nine were directed by Harold S. Bucquet and the last five by Willis Goldbeck, one by W. S. Van Dyke. In 1961 a TV series began with Richard Chamberlain and Raymond Massey, and ran for seven years.

Dr Kildare Goes Home
US 1940 79m bw
Young Dr Kildare temporarily deserts Blair Hospital to help his father establish a small-town clinic. Rather below par episode with obvious outcome. Lew Ayres, Lionel Barrymore, Laraine Day, Samuel S. Hinds, Gene Lockhart. Written by Willis Goldbeck and Harry Ruskin; directed by Harold S. Bucquet; for MGM.

Dr Kildare's Crisis
US 1940 75m bw
Dr Kildare's fiancée may have epilepsy in the family. The series at its peak. Lew Ayres, Lionel Barrymore, Robert Young, Laraine Day, Nat Pendleton, Marie Blake. Written by Willis Goldbeck and Harry Ruskin; directed by Harold S. Bucquet; for MGM.

Dr Kildare's Strange Case
US 1940 77m bw
The young doctor cures a mental patient by the newest methods. Crisp series episode. Lew Ayres, Lionel Barrymore, Laraine Day, Shepperd Strudwick, Samuel S. Hinds. Written by Willis Goldbeck and Harry Ruskin; directed by Harold S. Bucquet; for MGM.

Dr Kildare's Victory
US 1942 92m bw
GB title: *The Doctor and the Débutante*
Back at Blair, Dr Kildare fights ambulance zoning regulations. Rather heavy-going episode, its star's last before becoming a conscientious objector and leaving Hollywood for the duration. Lew Ayres, Lionel Barrymore, Ann Ayars, Robert Sterling. Written by Harry Ruskin and Willis Goldbeck; directed by W. S. Van Dyke; for MGM.

Dr Kildare's Wedding Day
US 1941 83m bw
Dr Kildare's fiancée is killed in a road accident. Rather deliberately downbeat episode, well enough assembled. Lew Ayres, Lionel Barrymore, Laraine Day, Red Skelton, Nils Asther. Written by Lawrence Bachmann and Ormond Ruthven; directed by Harold S. Bucquet; for MGM. (GB title: *Mary Names the Day*.)

Dr Knock*
France 1936 74m bw
A sly young doctor takes over a country practice and turns the townsfolk into hypochondriacs. Amusing version of a modern French comedy classic. *Louis Jouvet*, Palau, Le Vigan, Moor, Alexandre Rignault. Written by *Jules Romains* from his play; directed by Louis Jouvet and Roger Goupillières; for Pathé-Natan. 'Once under way it scoots along like a Bermuda sloop, and holds right till the surprise fadeout.'—*Variety*

Doctor Mabuse the Gambler***
Germany 1922 101m (24 fps) bw silent
UFA (Erich Pommer)
original title: *Doktor Mabuse, der Spieler*
A criminal mastermind uses hypnotism and blackmail in his efforts to obtain world domination, but when finally cornered is discovered to be a raving maniac.
A real wallow in German post-war depression and melodrama, in the form of a Fu Manchu / Moriarty type thriller. Fascinating scene by scene, but by now a slightly tiresome whole.
w Thea Von Harbou, Fritz Lang, *novel* Norbert Jacques *d Fritz Lang* *ph* Carl Hoffman *ad* Otto Hunte, Stahl-Urach, Erich Kettelhut, Karl Vollbrecht
Rudolph Klein-Rogge, Alfred Abel, Gertrude Welcker, Lil Dagover, Paul Richter
† Originally issued in Germany in two parts, *Der Grosse Spieler* and *Inferno*, adding up to a much longer running time.
†† See sequels, *The Testament of Dr Mabuse* and *The Thousand Eyes of Dr Mabuse*.

Dr Monica
US 1934 80m bw
Warner (Henry Blanke)
A lady doctor allows her husband to fall for another woman.
Heavy-handed 'woman's picture' which did well at the time.
w Charles Kenyon, *play* Marja Morozowicz *d* William Keighley
Kay Francis, Warren William, Jean Muir, Verree Teasdale, Philip Reed, Emma Dunn

Doctor No***
GB 1962 111m Technicolor
UA / Eon (Harry Saltzman, Albert R. Broccoli)
A British secret service agent foils a master criminal operating in the West Indies.
First of the phenomenally successful James Bond movies, mixing sex, violence and campy humour against expensive sets and exotic locales. Toned down from the original novels, they expressed a number of sixties attitudes, and proved unstoppable box office attractions for nearly fifteen years. The first was, if not quite the best, reasonably representative of the series.
w Richard Maibaum, Johanna Harwood, Berkely Mather, *novel* Ian Fleming *d* Terence Young *ph* Ted Moore *m Monty Norman*
Sean Connery, *Ursula Andress*, Jack Lord, Joseph Wiseman, John Kitzmiller, Bernard Lee, Lois Maxwell, Zena Marshall, Eunice Gayson, Anthony Dawson
† The subsequent titles, all qv, were *From Russia with Love* (1963), *Goldfinger* (1964), *Thunderball* (1965), *You Only Live Twice* (1967), *On Her Majesty's Secret Service* (1969), *Diamonds Are Forever* (1971), *Live and Let Die* (1973), *The Man with the Golden Gun* (1974), *The Spy Who Loved Me* (1977), *Moonraker* (1979), *For Your Eyes Only* (1981), *Octopussy* (1983), *Never Say Never Again* (1984).
Casino Royale (1967) was a Bond spoof made by other hands.

Dr O'Dowd
GB 1940 70m bw
A drunken doctor redeems himself. Somewhat wobegone tearjerker with an interesting cast, Shaun Glenville, Peggy Cummins, Mary Merrall, Liam Gaffney, Patricia Roc, Walter Hudd, Irene Handl. Written by Derek Twist and Austin Melford from story by L. A. G. Strong; directed by Herbert Mason; for Warners.

'The sting's in the tale!'
Dr Phibes Rises Again*
GB 1972 89m De Luxe
AIP (Richard Dalton)
The immortal Phibes and his wife rise from the dead to seek an Egyptian elixir of life, and cross swords with a satanic Egyptologist.
Uncertainly paced but generally zippy comic strip for adults, with all concerned entering gleefully into the evil spirit of the thing. See prequel, *The Abominable Dr Phibes*.
w Robert Fuest, Robert Blees *d* Robert Fuest *ph* Alex Thomson *m* John Gale *ad Brian Eatwell*

Vincent Price, Robert Quarry, Valli Kemp, Fiona Lewis, Peter Cushing, Beryl Reid, Terry-Thomas, Hugh Griffith, *Peter Jeffrey*, Gerald Sim, John Thaw, John Cater, Lewis Fiander

'It's refreshing to find a sequel which is better than its prototype.'—*Philip Strick, MFB*

Dr Renault's Secret
US 1942 58m bw

A scientist turns an ape into a semi-human, which runs amok. Fairly well done horror support. George Zucco, J. Carrol Naish, John Shepperd, Lynne Roberts. Written by William Bruckner and Robert F. Metzler; directed by Harry Lachman; for TCF.

Dr Rhythm*
US 1938 80m bw

A veterinary surgeon goes into show business. Easy-going star musical with pleasant songs. Bing Crosby, Beatrice Lillie, Mary Carlisle, Andy Devine, Laura Hope Crews, Rufe Davis. Written by Jo Swerling, Richard Connell, from a story by O. Henry; directed by Frank Tuttle; for Paramount.

'Armed with a doctor's kit, he fought a thousand killers!'
Dr Socrates*
US 1935 70m bw
Warner (Robert Lord)

A small-town doctor is forced to help wounded gangsters, and becomes involved. Good star melodrama.

w Robert Lord, *novel* W. R. Burnett *d* William Dieterle ph Tony Gaudio *md* Leo F. Forbstein

Paul Muni, Ann Dvorak, Barton Maclane, Robert Barrat, John Eldridge, Hobart Cavanaugh, Mayo Methot, Samuel S. Hinds, Henry O'Neill

'Arriving at the tail end of the G-man and gangster cycle, Dr Socrates is a graceful valedictory.'—*Variety*

'Rapid, strong and exciting.'—*Sunday Times*

† Remade as *King of the Underworld* and *Bullet Scars*.

'The hot line suspense comedy!'
Dr Strangelove; or, How I Learned to Stop Worrying and Love the Bomb***
GB 1963 93m bw
Columbia / Stanley Kubrick (Victor Lyndon)

A mad USAF general launches a nuclear attack on Russia, and when recall attempts fail, and retaliation is inevitable, all concerned sit back to await the destruction of the world. Black comedy resolving itself into a series of sketches, with the star playing three parts (for no good reason): the US president, an RAF captain, and a mad German-American scientist. Historically an important film in its timing, its nightmares being those of the early sixties, artistically it clogs its imperishable moments by untidy narrative and unattractively contrasty photography.

w Stanley Kubrick, Terry Southern, Peter George, *novel* Red Alert by Peter George *d* Stanley Kubrick *ph* Gilbert Taylor *m* Laurie Johnson *ad Ken Adam*

Peter Sellers, George C. Scott, Peter Bull, Sterling Hayden, Keenan Wynn, Slim Pickens, James Earl Jones, Tracy Reed

GENERAL (George C. Scott): 'I don't say we wouldn't get our hair mussed, but I do say no more than ten to twenty million people killed.'

'Scarcely a picture of relentless originality; seldom have we seen so much made over so little.'—*Joan Didion*

† *Fail Safe* (qv), which took the same theme more seriously, was released almost simultaneously.

AAN: best picture; script; Stanley Kubrick (as director); Peter Sellers

Dr Syn*
GB 1937 80m bw
Gaumont (Michael Balcon)

The vicar of Dymchurch in 1780 is really a pirate believed dead.
This now obscure, lively pirate yarn was its star's last film.

w Michael Hogan, Roger Burford, *novel* Russell Thorndike *d Roy William Neill* *ph* Jack Cox *md* Louis Levy

George Arliss, Margaret Lockwood, John Loder, Roy Emerton, Graham Moffatt, Frederick Burtwell, Meinhart Maur, George Merritt

'With Arliss in the name part it doesn't ring true.'—*Variety*

Dr Syn Alias the Scarecrow
GB 1962 98m Technicolor
Walt Disney (Bill Anderson)

The vicar of Dymchurch is really a smuggler who manages to outwit a rascally general and save a prisoner from Dover Castle.
Oddly released the same year as another version of the story, *Captain Clegg*, this rather set-bound adventure yarn turns its hero into a Robin Hood figure. It was originally made to be shown in three parts on American TV.

w Robert Westerby, *novel* Christopher Syn by Russell Thorndike, William Buchanan *d* James Neilson *ph* Paul Beeson *m* Gerard Schurmann

Patrick McGoohan, George Cole, Tony Britton, Geoffrey Keen, Kay Walsh, Patrick Wymark, Alan Dobie, Eric Pohlmann

The Doctor Takes a Wife*
US 1940 89m bw
Columbia (William Perlberg)

A young doctor has to pretend to be the husband of a socialite.
Typical high life comedy of its period, quite brisk and diverting.

w George Seaton, Ken Englund *d* Alexander Hall *ph* Sid Hickox *m* Frederick Hollander *md* Morris Stoloff

Loretta Young, Ray Milland, Edmund Gwenn, Reginald Gardiner, Gail Patrick, Frank Sully, George Metaxa, Charles Halton, Chester Clute

Dr Terror's House of Horrors
GB 1965 98m Techniscope
Amicus (Milton Subotsky)

An eccentric, who turns out to be Death himself, tells the fortunes of five men in a railway carriage.
One of the first Amicus horror compendiums and a weak one, not helped by wide screen, a couple of naïve scripts and ho-hum acting. The book-ends are quite pleasant, though.

w Milton Subotsky *d* Freddie Francis *ph* Alan Hume *m* Elisabeth Lutyens

Peter Cushing, Ursula Howells, Max Adrian, Roy Castle, Alan Freeman, Bernard Lee, Jeremy Kemp, Kenny Lynch, Christopher Lee, Michael Gough, Donald Sutherland

† Later collections from the same stable include *Torture Garden, Tales from the Crypt, Vault of Horror* and *Asylum*.

Dr Who and the Daleks
GB 1965 83m Techniscope
British Lion / Regal / Aaru (Milton Subotsky, Max J. Rosenberg)

Three children and their grandfather accidentally start his time machine and are whisked away to a planet where villainous robots rule.
Junior science fiction from the BBC series. Limply put together, and only for indulgent children.

w Milton Subotsky *d* Gordon Flemyng *ph* John Wilcox *m* Malcolm Lockyer

Peter Cushing, Roy Castle, Jennie Linden, Roberta Tovey, Barrie Ingham

† A sequel, no better, emerged in 1966: *Daleks: Invasion Earth 2150 AD*, with similar credits except that Bernard Cribbins instead of Roy Castle provided comic relief.

'A full moon was his signal to kill!'
Dr X**
US 1932 82m Technicolor
Warner (Hal Wallis)

A reporter investigates a series of moon murders and narrows his search to one of several doctors at a medical college.
Fascinating, German-inspired, overblown and generally enjoyable horror mystery whose armless villain commits murders by growing limbs from 'synthetic flesh'.

w Earl Baldwin, Robert Tasker, *play* Howard W. Comstock, Allen C. Miller *d Michael Curtiz* *ph Richard Tower, Ray Rennahan* *md* Leo Forbstein

Lee Tracy, Lionel Atwill, Preston Foster, Fay Wray, George Rosener, Mae Busch, Arthur Edmund Carewe, John Wray

'The settings, lighting and final battle with the man-monster are quite stunning.'—*NFT, 1974*

'It almost makes Frankenstein seem tame and friendly.'—*New York Times*

Doctor You've Got to be Kidding
US 1967 93m Metrocolor Panavision
MGM / Trident (Douglas Laurence)

A girl arrives at a maternity hospital chased by three prospective husbands.

Wild and wacky farce which leaves little impression.

w Phillip Shuken, *novel* Patte Wheat Mahan
d Peter Tewkesbury *ph* Fred Koenekamp
m Kenyon Hopkins

Sandra Dee, George Hamilton, Celeste Holm, Bill Bixby, *Dwayne Hickman*, Dick Kallman, Mort Sahl, Allen Jenkins

'A love caught in the fire of revolution!'

Doctor Zhivago***
US 1965 192m Metrocolor
Panavision 70
MGM / Carlo Ponti

A Moscow doctor is caught up in World War I, exiled for writing poetry, forced into partisan service and separated from his only love.
Beautifully photographed and meticulously directed, this complex epic has been so reduced from the original novel that many parts of the script simply do not make any kind of sense. What remains is a collection of expensive set pieces, great for looking if not listening.

w Robert Bolt, *novel* Boris Pasternak
d David Lean ph Frederick A. Young
m Maurice Jarre

Omar Sharif, Julie Christie, Rod Steiger, Alec Guinness, Rita Tushingham, Ralph Richardson, Tom Courtenay, Geraldine Chaplin, Siobhan McKenna, Noel Willman, Geoffrey Keen, Adrienne Corri

'A long haul along the road of synthetic lyricism.'—*MFB*

'David Lean's *Doctor Zhivago* does for snow what his *Lawrence of Arabia* did for sand.'—*John Simon*

'It isn't shoddy (except for the music); it isn't soap opera; it's stately, respectable, and dead. Neither the contemplative Zhivago nor the flow of events is intelligible, and what is worse, they seem unrelated to each other.'—*Pauline Kael*

AA: Robert Bolt; Frederick A. Young; Maurice Jarre
AAN: best picture; David Lean; Tom Courtenay

A Doctor's Diary
US 1937 77m bw

The resident physician of a privately-endowed hospital is impatient with the niceties of procedure. Unsurprising medical drama which adequately filled half a bill. George Bancroft, John Trent, Helen Burgess, Ruth Coleman, Charles Waldron, Ra Hould, Sidney Blackmer. Written by Sam Ornitz, Joseph Anthony; directed by Charles Vidor; for Paramount. 'Packs enough drama to hold attention.'—*Variety*

The Doctor's Dilemma*
GB 1958 99m Metrocolor
MGM / Anatole de Grunwald

Eminent Harley Street surgeons debate the case of a devoted wife and her tubercular artist husband.

DODGE CITY. Errol Flynn takes a break from swashbucklers and cleans up the Wild West in swashbuckling style.

Well acted but curiously muffled filming of Shaw's Edwardian play about ethics and human values.

w Anatole de Grunwald, *play* Bernard Shaw
d Anthony Asquith *ph* Robert Krasker
m Joseph Kosma *ad* Paul Sheriff

Leslie Caron, Dirk Bogarde, *John Robinson*, Alastair Sim, Felix Aylmer, Robert Morley, Michael Gwynn, Maureen Delany, Alec McCowen

Doctors' Wives
US 1970 102m Eastmancolor
Columbia / M. J. Frankovich

When Dr Dellman shoots his unfaithful wife, his colleagues reconsider their sex lives.
Adult soap opera from talents who at other times have found better things to do. In the sensational circumstances, two sanguinary operation sequences are tastelessly irrelevant.

w Daniel Taradash, *novel* Frank G. Slaughter
d George Schaefer *ph* Charles B. Lang
m Elmer Bernstein

Richard Crenna, Janice Rule, Gene Hackman, John Colicos, Dyan Cannon, Diana Sands, Rachel Roberts, Carroll O'Connor, Cara Williams, Ralph Bellamy, Richard Anderson

'Crisis follows hard on crisis to breathlessly ludicrous effect.'—*Tom Milne*

'West of Chicago there was no law! West of Dodge City there was no God!'

Dodge City***
US 1939 104m Technicolor
Warner (Robert Lord)

An ex-soldier and trail boss helps clean up the west's great railroad terminus.
Standard, satisfying big-scale western with all clichés intact and very enjoyable, as is the soft, rich early colour. The story is plainly inspired by the exploits of Wyatt Earp.

w Robert Buckner *d Michael Curtiz ph Sol Polito, Ray Rennahan* *m* Max Steiner

Errol Flynn, Olivia de Havilland, Ann Sheridan, Bruce Cabot, Alan Hale, Frank McHugh, John Litel, Victor Jory, William Lundigan, Henry Travers, Henry O'Neill, Guinn Williams, Gloria Holden

'A lusty western, packed with action, including some of the dandiest mêlée stuff screened.'—*Variety*

'It looks programmed and underpopulated, though in an elegantly stylized way.'—*New Yorker, 1980*

Dodsworth***
US 1936 101m bw
Samuel Goldwyn

An American businessman takes his wife on a tour of Europe, and their lives are changed. Satisfying, well-acted drama from a bestselling novel; production values high.

w Sidney Howard, novel Sinclair Lewis d William Wyler ph Rudolph Maté *m* Alfred Newman

Walter Huston, Mary Astor, Ruth Chatterton, David Niven, Paul Lukas, Gregory Gaye, *Maria Ouspenskaya*, Odette Myrtil, Spring Byington, John Payne

'No one, I think, will fail to enjoy it, in spite of its too limited and personal plot, the sense it leaves behind of a very expensive, very contemporary, Bond Street vacuum flask.'—*Graham Greene*

'William Wyler has had the skill to execute it in cinematic terms, and a gifted cast has been able to bring the whole alive to our complete satisfaction.'—*New York Times*

'A smoothly flowing narrative of substantial interest, well-defined performances and good talk.'—*New York Times*

'An offering of dignity and compelling power to provide you with a treat you can rarely experience in a picture house.'—*Hollywood Spectator*

AAN: best picture; Sidney Howard; William Wyler; Walter Huston; Maria Ouspenskaya

Dog Day Afternoon**
US 1975 130m Technicolor
Warner / AEC (Martin Bregman, Martin Elfland)

Two incompetent robbers are cornered in a Brooklyn bank.
Recreation of a tragi-comic episode from the newspaper headlines; for half its length a fascinating and acutely observed film which then bogs itself down in a surplus of talk and excessive sentiment about homosexuality.

w Frank Pierson, *book* Patrick Mann *d Sidney Lumet ph* Victor J. Kemper *m* none

Al Pacino, John Cazale, *Charles Durning*, Sully Boyar, James Broderick, *Chris Sarandon*

'There is plenty of Lumet's vital best here in a film that at least glancingly captures the increasingly garish pathology of our urban life.'—*Jack Kroll*

'Scattered moments of wry humour, sudden pathos and correct observation.'—*John Simon*

'The mask of frenetic cliché doesn't spoil moments of pure reporting on people in extremity.'—*New Yorker*

'A long and wearying case history of the beaten, sobbing, despairing and ultimately powerless anti-hero.'—*Karyn Kay, Jump Cut*

'Full of galvanic mirth rooted in human desperation.'—*Michael Billington, Illustrated London News*

'Brisk, humorous and alive with urban energies and angers fretting through the 92 degree heat.'—*Sight and Sound*

AA: Frank Pierson
AAN: best picture; Sidney Lumet; Al Pacino; Chris Sarandon

A Dog of Flanders
US 1959 97m De Luxe Cinemascope
TCF / Associated Producers (Robert B. Radnitz)

A small boy wants to be an artist; when he runs away in frustration, his shaggy dog, formerly a stray, leads his family to him.
Old-fashioned tear-jerker for well-brought-up children, previously filmed as a silent; quite accomplished in presentation.

w Ted Sherdeman, *novel* Ouida *d* James B. Clark *ph* Otto Heller *m* Paul Sawtell, Bert Shefter

David Ladd, Donald Crisp, Theodore Bikel, Max Croiset, Monique Ahrens

A Dog's Life*
US 1918 30m approx bw silent
First National / Charles Chaplin

A tramp and a stray mongrel help each other towards a happy ending.
Threatening sentiment is kept at bay by amusing sight gags in this pleasing star featurette.

wd Charles Chaplin ph Rollie Totheroh

Charles Chaplin, Edna Purviance, Chuck Riesner, Henry Bergman, Albert Austin, Scraps

Dogpound Shuffle
Canada 1974 97m Eastmancolor

An old Irish hobo lives on the earnings of his dancing dog. Dog-eared 'family film' which didn't seem to entertain many families. Ron Moody, David Soul, Ray Stricklyn. Written and directed by Jeffrey Bloom; for Elliott Kastner / Bulldog. (Aka: *Spot.*)

The Dogs of War
GB 1980 118m Technicolor
UA / Silverwold (Norman Jewison, Patrick Palmer)

A disenchanted mercenary becomes involved in a plot to take over an impoverished West African state.
Tough but seemingly dated modern irony, somewhat lacking in action and surprise.

w Gary DeVore, George Malko *novel* Frederick Forsyth *d* John Irvin *ph* Jack Cardiff *m* Geoffrey Burgon

Christopher Walken, Tom Berenger, Colin Blakely, Hugh Millais, Paul Freeman, Robert Urquhart

La Dolce Vita**
Italy / France 1960 173m bw Totalscope
Riama / Pathé Consortium (Giuseppe Amato)
aka: *The Sweet Life*

A journalist mixes in modern Roman high society and is alternately bewitched and sickened by what he sees.
Episodic satirical melodrama, a marathon self-indulgent wallow with a wagging finger never far away. Not a successful whole, but full of choice moments such as a statue of Christ being flown by helicopter over the city.

w Federico Fellini, Tullio Pinelli, Ennio Flaiano, Brunello Rondi *d Federico Fellini ph* Otello Martelli *m* Nino Rota *ad* Piero Gherardi

Marcello Mastroianni, Anita Ekberg, Anouk Aimée, Alain Cuny, Yvonne Furneaux, Magali Noel, Nadia Gray, Lex Barker

'Its personification of various familiar symbols—love, death, purity, sin, reason and so on—never succeeds in reflecting human values or creating intellectual excitement . . . Its actual significance rests in the way its (albeit specious) social attack has stirred the imagination of other Italian film-makers, as well as public interest in their work.'—*Robert Vas, MFB*

AAN: script; Federico Fellini

Doll Face
US 1945 80m bw
TCF (Bryan Foy)
GB title: *Come Back to Me*

A burlesque queen goes to Broadway.
Lower case musical of minimal interest.

w Leonard Praskins *d* Lewis Seiler *ph* Joseph La Shelle *songs* Harold Adamson, Jimmy McHugh

Vivian Blaine, Dennis O'Keefe, Carmen Miranda, Perry Como, Martha Stewart, Michael Dunne, Reed Hadley, George E. Stone, Donald McBride, Edgar Norton

The Dollar Bottom
GB 1981 33m Eastmancolor

A sharp-witted public schoolboy sells his friends insurance against being beaten. Ingenious but thinly acted short, with the added hazard of impenetrable accents. Rikki Fulton, Robert Urquhart, Jonathan McNeil. Written by Shane Connaughton, from the story by James Kennaway; directed by Roger Christian; for Rocking Horse Films / Paramount.

Dollars*
US 1971 120m Technicolor
Columbia / M. J. Frankovich
GB title: *The Heist*

An American security expert installs an electronic system in a Hamburg bank which he plans to rob himself.
Overlong caper comedy-drama which is quite good to watch when it starts moving, though the quick cutting, short takes and deliberately obscure narrative leave one breathless.

wd Richard Brooks *ph* Petrus Schloemp *m* Quincy Jones

Warren Beatty, Goldie Hawn, Gert Frobe, Robert Webber, Scott Brady, Arthur Brauss

'An essay in virtuoso film construction . . . rather as if one were watching a perfect machine in full throttle but with nowhere to go.'—*John Gillet*

A Doll's House*
GB 1973 95m Eastmancolor
Elkins / Freeward (Hillard Elkins)

A wife begins to resist her husband's will. Ibsen's feminist play was always good value; set in Norway in the nineties, it was taken up eighty years later as a precursor of women's lib, which accounts for two film versions in one year. This one is simply staged and well performed, but suffers from a bad translation.

w Christopher Hampton, *play* Henrik Ibsen *d* Patrick Garland *ph* Arthur Ibbetson *m* John Barry

Claire Bloom, Anthony Hopkins, Ralph Richardson, Denholm Elliott, Anna Massey, Edith Evans

A Doll's House

GB / France 1973 106m Eastmancolor
World Film Services / Les Films de la Boétie (Joseph Losey)

Opened out but less effective version of the above, with too much solemnity and the central part miscast.

w David Mercer, *play* Henrik Ibsen *d* Joseph Losey *ph* Gerry Fisher *m* Michel Legrand

Jane Fonda, David Warner, Trevor Howard, Edward Fox, Delphine Seyrig, Anna Wing

The Dolly Sisters**

US 1945 114m Technicolor
TCF (George Jessel)

The lives of a Hungarian sister act in American vaudeville.
Fictionalized biographical musical, only fair in the script department but glittering to look at in superb colour, and enriched by splendid production values. Undoubtedly among the best of its kind.

w John Larkin, Marian Spitzer *d* Irving Cummings *ph Ernest Palmer* *md* Alfred Newman, Charles Henderson *songs* various *ch* Seymour Felix *ad Lyle Wheeler, Leland Fuller*

Betty Grable, June Haver, John Payne, S. Z. Sakall, Reginald Gardiner, Frank Latimore, Gene Sheldon, Sig Rumann, Trudy Marshall

AAN: song 'I Can't Begin to Tell You' (*m* Johnny Monaco, *ly* Mack Gordon)

w Alfred Machard, Leonide Moguy *d* Leonide Moguy *ph* Mario Craveri, Renato del Frate *m* Alessandro Cicognini

Vittorio de Sica, Lois Maxwell, Gabrielle Dorziat, Anna Maria Pierangeli, Gino Leurini

Domani è Troppo Tardi

Italy 1950 101m bw
Rizzoli (Giuseppe Amato)
GB title: *Tomorrow Is Too Late*

Inquisitive pupils and repressive teachers at a co-educational school almost cause a tragedy.
Possibly well intentioned, but in effect an old-fashioned melodrama which works well enough on its level.

w Alfred Machard, Leonide Moguy *d* Leonide Moguy *ph* Mario Craveri, Renato del Frate *m* Alessandro Cicognini

Vittorio de Sica, Lois Maxwell, Gabrielle Dorziat, Anna Maria Pierangeli, Gino Leurini

Domenica d'Agosto**

Italy 1950 75m bw
Colonna (Sergio Amidei)
GB title: *Sunday in August*

Various Romans enjoy Sunday by the sea at Ostia.
Fragmented comedy-drama which succeeds in being charming throughout, every detail being freshly observed through an inquisitive eye.

w Franco Brusati, Luciano Emmer, Giulio Macchi, Cesare Zavattini *d Luciano Emmer* *ph* Domenico Scala, Leonida Barboni, Ubaldo Marelli *m* Roman Vlad *ed* Jolanda Benvenuti

Anna Baldini, Franco Interlenghi, Elvy Lissiak, Massimo Serato, Marcello Mastroianni, Corrado Verga

The Dominant Sex

GB 1937 71m bw

A woman demands the right to her own individuality after marriage. Tepid comedy drama from a popular stage play. Phillips Holmes, Diana Churchill, Carol Goodner, Romney Brent, Hugh Miller, Billy Milton. Written by Vino de Vesci, John Fernald, from the play by Michael Kean; directed by Herbert Brenon; for BIP.

'Dominique will make you shriek!'

Dominique

GB 1978 100m colour
Grand Prize / Melvin Simon (Milton Subotsky, Andrew Donally)

A woman who was convinced that her husband was deliberately driving her mad is found dead, and buried, but seemingly returns . . .
The old *Diabolique* syndrome revamped in a very parsimonious production with little to hold the interest.

w Edward and Valerie Abraham, *novel* What Beckoning Ghost by Harold Lawlor *d* Michael Anderson *ph* Ted Moore *m* David Whitaker

Cliff Robertson, Jean Simmons, Jenny Agutter, Simon Ward, Ron Moody, Judy Geeson, Michael Jayston, Flora Robson, David Tomlinson, Jack Warner.

'Trust no one. No one!'

The Domino Principle

US 1977 100m CFI color
Associated General Films (Lew Grade, Martin Starger) / Stanley Kramer
GB title: *The Domino Killings*

A murderer is offered his freedom if he will assassinate a national figure.
Fashionable, complex and rather boring political thriller.

w Adam Kennedy, from his novel *d* Stanley Kramer *ph* Fred Koenekamp, Ernest Laszlo *m* Billy Goldenberg

Gene Hackman, Richard Widmark, Candice Bergen, Mickey Rooney, Edward Albert, Eli Wallach, Ken Swofford, Neva Patterson

'Terrible movies tend to start with a preposterous premise and then laboriously work their way to an impossible conclusion. This one however starts with an arrant impossibility and works its way to whatever lies beyond and below that.'—*John Simon*

Don Camillo's Last Round*

Italy 1955 98m bw
Rizzoli
original title: *Don Camillo e l'Onorevole Peppone*

The village Catholic priest tries to stop the re-election of the communist mayor.
Pleasant third collection of encounters with familiar characters.

w Giovanni Guareschi and others, from his books *d* Carmine Gallone *ph* Anchise Brizzi *m* Alessandro Cicognini

Fernandel, Gino Cervi, Claude Silvain, Leda Gloria

'The episodic narrative is full of mildly amusing incident.'—*MFB*

Don Daredevil Rides Again

US 1951 bw serial: 12 eps

A young rancher assumes the character of Don Daredevil to fight off marauding badmen. Or, Zorro Rides Again in this adequate western serial. Ken Curtis, Aline Towne, Roy Barcroft, Lane Bradford. Directed by Fred C. Brannon; for Republic.

Don Giovanni

France-Italy-Germany 1979 184m colour
Gaumont-Opera-Camera One (Michel Seydoux)

Grandiose but artistically somewhat hesitant version of Mozart's opera; little here for film buffs.

cinematic conception Rolf Lieberman *d* Joseph Losey *ph* Gerry Fisher *ad* Alexander Trauner

Ruggero Raimondi, John Macurdy, Edda Moser, Kiri Te Kanawa

The Don is Dead

US 1973 117m Technicolor
Universal / Hal B. Wallis (Paul Nathan)

Cross and double cross among Mafia families.
A failed attempt to cash in on *The Godfather*, this endless melodrama is boringly violent and totally predictable.

w Marvin H. Albert, from his novel *d* Richard Fleischer *ph* Richard H. Kline *m* Jerry Goldsmith

Anthony Quinn, Frederic Forrest, Robert Forster, Al Lettieri, Angel Tompkins, Charles Cioffi

Don Juan**

US 1926 126m (synchronized) bw
Warner

Exploits of the famous lover and adventurer at Lucretia Borgia's court.
Lithe swashbuckler in the best silent tradition, but with a synchronized score (by William Axt) which made it a sensation and led directly to the talkie revolution.

w Bess Meredyth *d* Alan Crosland *ph Byron Haskin*

John Barrymore, Mary Astor, Warner Oland, Estelle Taylor, Myrna Loy, Phyllis Haver, Willard Louis, Montagu Love

Don Juan Quilligan
US 1945 76m bw

A would-be romantic bargee becomes engaged to two girls simultaneously, one on each side of the Hudson. Thin comedy of bigamy, similar to *The Captain's Paradise*, which came later. William Bendix, Phil Silvers, Joan Blondell, Mary Treen, Anne Revere, George Macready. Written by Arthur Kober and Frank Gabrielson; directed by Frank Tuttle; for TCF.

'The finest adventure tale ever screened!'

Don Q Son of Zorro*
US 1925 170m (16 fps) bw silent
United Artists

Further adventures in the manner of the star's 1920 hit (see *The Mark of Zorro*).

d Donald Crisp *w* Jack Cunningham *novel* K. and H. Pritchard *ph* Henry Sharp

Douglas Fairbanks, Mary Astor, Donald Crisp, Jack McDonald, Jean Hersholt

Don Quixote*
France 1933 82m bw
Vandor / Nelson / Wester

An adequate potted version starring Fedor Chaliapin and in the English version George Robey (French version: Dorville).

w Paul Morand, Alexandre Arnoux, from Cervantes *d* G. W. Pabst *ph* Nikolas Farkas, Paul Portier *ad* André Andreiev *m* Jacques Ibert

'Strictly for the arty clientele . . . for general consumption tedious and dull. Americans in general may feel that the story scarcely rates retelling.'—*Variety*

Don Quixote**
USSR 1957 105m Agfacolor Sovscope
Lenfilm

An extremely handsome version with a commanding star performance.

w E. Schwarz *d* Grigori Kozintsev *ph* Andrei Moskvin, Apollinari Dudko *ad* Yevgeny Yenei *m* Kara-Karayev

Nikolai Cherkassov, Yuri Tolubeyev

† Other versions came from France in 1902 and 1908, Italy in 1910, France in 1911, USA in 1915, Britain in 1923, Denmark in 1926, Spain in 1927, Britain in 1972, and Britain (ballet version with Nureyev) in 1975.

Don Winslow of the Navy
US 1942 bw serial: 15 eps

A hero of Naval Intelligence combats The Scorpion. Plenty of serial action with a maritime background. Don Terry, Walter Sande, Wade Boteler, John Litel. Directed by Ford Beebe and Ray Taylor; for Universal.

Dona Flor and Her Two Husbands
Brazil 1976 110m Eastmancolor
Carnaval (Luis Carlos Barreto)

A young widow remarries, and has to share her bed with her late husband's ghost.
Semi-pornographic comedy which achieved some fashionable success.

wd Bruno Barreto, *novel* Jorge Amado *ph* Maurito Salles *m* Chico Buarque de Holanda

Sonia Braga, Jose Wilker, Mauro Mendonca

Dondi
US 1960 80m bw

GIs in Italy adopt an orphan boy, who stows away to be with them in America. Glutinous, sentimental comedy-drama. David Janssen, Patti Page, Walter Winchell, Mickey Shaughnessy, Robert Strauss, Arnold Stang, Gale Gordon. Written by Albert Zugsmith and Gus Edson, from a comic strip; directed by Albert Zugsmith; for Allied Artists.

Donovan's Brain*
US 1953 81m bw
UA / Dowling (Tom Gries)

An unscrupulous tycoon is fatally injured, but his brain is kept alive by a surgeon who finds himself dominated by it.
Modest competence marks this version of a much filmed novel, with quiet suspense and a firm central performance.

w Felix Feist, *novel* Curt Siodmak *d* Felix Feist *ph* Joseph Biroc *m* Eddie Dunstedter

Lew Ayres, Gene Evans, Nancy Davis, Steve Brodie, Lisa K. Howard

Donovan's Reef
US 1963 108m Technicolor
Paramount (John Ford)

War veterans settle down on a South Sea island; when the daughter of one of them comes to visit, his reputation must be protected.
Good-humoured but finally enervating mixture of rough-house and slapstick, with the appearance of an old friends' benefit and the director in familiar sub-standard form.

w Frank Nugent, James Edward Grant *d* John Ford *ph* William H. Clothier *m* Cyril Mockridge

John Wayne, Lee Marvin, Jack Warden, Elizabeth Allen, Dorothy Lamour, Cesar Romero, Mike Mazurki

Don's Party*
Australia 1976 90m Eastmancolor

In suburban Sydney, a political celebration party turns into a pretence of wife-swapping. Fairly acute observation of middle-class antipodean mores, interrupted with predictable bouts of antipodean crudeness. Ray Barrett, Clare Binney, Pat Bishop, Graeme Blundell, John Hargreaves. Written by David Williamson, from his own play; directed by Bruce Beresford; for Double Head / AFC.

Don't Bother to Knock*
US 1952 76m bw
TCF (Julian Blaustein)

A deranged girl gets a baby-sitting job in a hotel and terrifies all concerned by threatening to kill her charge.
Curious vehicle for the emergent Monroe, who is not up to it, as who would be? Technical credits par, but entertainment value small.

w Daniel Taradash, *novel* Charlotte Armstrong *d* Roy Baker *ph* Lucien Ballard *m* Lionel Newman

Marilyn Monroe, Richard Widmark, Anne Bancroft, Donna Corcoran, Jeanne Cagney, Lurene Tuttle, Jim Backus, Elisha Cook Jnr

Don't Bother to Knock
GB 1961 89m Technicolor Cinemascope
ABP / Haileywood (Frank Godwin)
US title: *Why Bother to Knock*

A Casanova travel agent gives each of his girl friends a key to his Edinburgh flat.
Poorly developed and self-conscious sex farce.

w Dennis Cannan, Frederick Gotfurt, Frederic Raphael, *novel* Clifford Hanley *d* Cyril Frankel *ph* Geoffrey Unsworth *m* Elisabeth Lutyens

Richard Todd, *Judith Anderson*, Elke Sommer, June Thorburn, Nicole Maurey, Rik Battaglia, Eleanor Summerfield, John Le Mesurier

Don't Ever Leave Me
GB 1949 85m bw

A kidnapped teenager falls for her abductor. *No Orchids for Miss Blandish* played as a family comedy; quite unmemorable. Jimmy Hanley, Petula Clark, Edward Rigby, Hugh Sinclair, Linden Travers, Anthony Newley. Written by Robert Westerby, from Anthony Armstrong's novel *The Wide Guy*; directed by Arthur Crabtree; for Triton / Rank.

Don't Give Up the Ship
US 1959 89m bw

A dim-witted naval lieutenant is accused of stealing a destroyer. Feeble American service farce. Jerry Lewis, Dina Merrill, Diana Spencer, Mickey Shaughnessy, Robert Middleton, Gale Gordon. Written by Herbert Baker, Edmund Beloin and Henry Garson; directed by Norman Taurog; for Hal Wallis (Paramount).

Don't Go Near the Water*
US 1957 107m Metrocolor Cinemascope
MGM / Avon (Lawrence Weingarten)

The US Navy sets up a public relations unit on a South Pacific island.
Loosely cemented service farce full of fumbling lieutenants and bumbling commanders, a more light-hearted *M*A*S*H*. Boring romantic interludes separate some very funny farcical sequences.

w Dorothy Kingsley, George Wells, *novel* William Brinkley *d* Charles Walters *ph* Robert Bronner *m* Bronislau Kaper

Glenn Ford, Fred Clark, Gia Scala, Romney Brent, Mickey Shaughnessy, Earl Holiman, Anne Francis, Keenan Wynn, Eva Gabor, Russ Tamblyn, Jeff Richards, Mary Wickes

'Drop everything! And see the cheekiest comedy of the year!'

Don't Just Lie There, Say Something!
GB 1973 91m Eastmancolor

By a strange chapter of accidents, a politician finds himself in bed with his under-secretary and a lady not his wife. Stupefying from-the-stalls rendering of a successful stage farce; in this form it simply doesn't work. Brian Rix, Leslie Phillips, Joan Sims, Joanna Lumley, Derek Royle, Peter Bland. Written by Michael Pertwee, from his play; directed by Bob Kellett; for Comocroft / Rank.

Don't Just Stand There
US 1967 99m Techniscope
Universal (Stan Margulies)

A mild-mannered watch smuggler gets himself involved with kidnapping, murder, and finishing a sex novel.
Frantic but ineffective farce which keeps on the move but does not arrive anywhere.

w Charles Williams, from his novel The Wrong Venus *d* Ron Winston *ph* Milton Krasner *m* Nick Perito

Mary Tyler Moore, Robert Wagner, *Barbara Rhoades*, Glynis Johns, Harvey Korman
'Paris locations might have helped, but we're stuck with the San Fernando Valley.'—*Robert Windeler*

Don't Look Now***
GB 1973 110m Technicolor
BL / Casey / Eldorado (Peter Katz)

After the death of their small daughter, the Baxters meet in Venice two old sisters who claim mediumistic connection with the dead girl. The husband scorns the idea, but repeatedly sees a little red-coated figure in shadowy passages by the canals. When he confronts it, it proves to be a maniac dwarf who stabs him to death.
A macabre short story has become a pretentious and puzzling piece of high cinema art full of vague suggestions and unexplored avenues. Whatever its overall deficiencies, it is too brilliant in surface detail to be dismissed. Depressingly but fascinatingly set in wintry Venice, it has to be seen to be appreciated.

w Allan Scott, Chris Bryant, *story* Daphne du Maurier *d Nicolas Roeg ph Anthony Richmond m* Pino D'Onnagio *ad* Giovanni Soccol

Donald Sutherland, Julie Christie, Hilary Mason, Clelia Matania, Massimo Serrato
'The fanciest, most carefully assembled enigma yet seen on the screen.'—*New Yorker*
'A powerful and dazzling visual texture.'—*Penelope Houston*

Don't Look Now . . . We're Being Shot At!*
France 1966 130m Eastmancolor Panavision
Les Films Corona (Robert Dorfmann)
original title: *La Grande Vadrouille*

During World War II three members of a British bomber crew bale out over Paris and make a frantic escape to the free zone by means of various wild disguises.
Freewheeling star farce, a shade lacking in control, but with some funny sequences.

wd Gérard Oury *ph* Claude Renoir *m* Georges Auric

Terry-Thomas, Bourvil, Louis de Funès, Claudio Brook, Mike Marshall
'Both the sight gags and the characters evoke pale echoes of Laurel and Hardy, but it is not familiarity that breeds contempt here so much as the debasement of the familiar.'—*MFB*

Don't Make Waves
US 1967 97m Metrocolor Panavision
MGM / Filmways (Julian Bercovici)

A swimming-pool salesman attempts to get his own back on an impulsive young woman who has wrecked his car.
Malibu beach farce for immature adults, made by professionals helpless in the face of a weak script, but boasting a funny climax with a house teetering on the edge of a cliff.

w Ira Wallach, George Kirgo, *novel* Muscle Beach by Ira Wallach *d* Alexander Mackendrick *ph* Philip Lathrop *m* Vic Mizzy

Tony Curtis, Claudia Cardinale, Robert Webber, Joanna Barnes, Sharon Tate, Jim Backus, Mort Sahl

Don't Open till Christmas
GB 1983 86m colour

A maniac goes about killing Father Christmases. Tawdry horror film of marginal interest because of subject and cast. Edmund Purdom, Alan Lake, Gerry Sundquist, Belinda Mayne, Mark Jones. Written by Derek Ford and Al McGoohan; directed by Edmund Purdom; for 21st Century.

Don't Panic, Chaps!
GB 1959 85m bw

British and German units are sent to set up observation posts on the same Adriatic island, and agree to sit out the war in comfort. An ingenious idea is ill-served by a poorly written script and a rather bored cast. Dennis Price, George Cole, Thorley Walters, Harry Fowler, Nicholas Phipps, Percy Herbert, Nadja Regin. Written by Jack Davies; directed by George Pollock; for Hammer / ACT.

'The fun never sets on the British Empire!'

Don't Raise the Bridge, Lower the River
GB 1967 100m Technicolor
Columbia / Walter Shenson

An American turns his English wife's home into a discotheque.
Dreary comedy apparently intent on proving that its star can be just as unfunny abroad as at home.

w Max Wilk *d* Jerry Paris *ph* Otto Heller *m* David Whitaker

Jerry Lewis, Terry-Thomas, Jacqueline Pearce, Bernard Cribbins, Patricia Routledge, Nicholas Parsons, Michael Bates

Don't Take it to Heart*
GB 1944 90m bw
GFD / Two Cities (Sydney Box)

A genial castle ghost is unleashed by a bomb and affects the love affair of a researcher with the daughter of the house.
Amiably lunatic British-upper-class extravaganza with eccentric characters and some felicitous moments.

wd Jeffrey Dell ph Eric Cross *m* Mischa Spoliansky

Richard Greene, *Edward Rigby*, Patricia Medina, Alfred Drayton, Richard Bird, Wylie Watson, Moore Marriott, Brefni O'Rourke, Amy Veness, Claude Dampier, Joan Hickson, Joyce Barbour, Ronald Squire, Ernest Thesiger
'A cheerful and rewarding entertainment.'—*Richard Mallett, Punch*
'Not funny accidental but funny deliberate, and nine times out of ten the joke comes off.'—*Observer*

Don't Trust Your Husband
US 1948 90m bw

An executive conceals from his wife the sex of the client with whom he has to spend a lot of time. Ho-hum comedy with a laborious plotline and a flagging cast. Fred MacMurray, Madeleine Carroll, Charles Rogers. Written by Lou Breslow and Joseph Hoffman; directed by Lloyd Bacon; for James Nasser / United Artists.

The Doolins of Oklahoma
US 1949 90m bw

When his old gang claims his return to lawlessness, Bill Doolin walks into the sheriff's guns rather than cause his wife unhappiness. Moderate western with an unusually less-than-sympathetic role for its star. Randolph Scott, George Macready, Louise Allbritton, John Ireland, Noah Beery Jnr, Dona Drake. Written by Kenneth Gamet; directed by Gordon Douglas; for Harry Joe Brown / Columbia. (GB title: *The Great Manhunt*.)

The Doomed Battalion*
US / Germany 1932 74m bw

Austrians fight Italians high in the Alps. Interesting but not very effective attempt to internationalize a German 'bergfilm'. Luis Trenker, Tala Birell, Victor Varconi, Albert Conti, C. Henry Gordon, Gibson Gowland, Henry Armetta, Gustav Von Seyffertitz. Written by Luis Trenker and Carl Hartl; directed by Cyril Gardner; for Universal.
'Beaucoup snow and ice stuff for hot weather appeal . . . capable of sustaining bally.'—*Variety*

Doomed to Die: see Mr Wong

Doomwatch
GB 1972 92m colour
Tigon (Tony Tenser)

An investigator of coastal pollution discovers a village in which dumped chemicals have given all the inhabitants a distorting disease called acromegaly.

An unsatisfactory horror film is drawn from a moderately serious TV series about ecology.

w Clive Exton *d* Peter Sasdy *ph* Kenneth Talbot *m* John Scott

Ian Bannen, Judy Geeson, John Paul, Simon Oates, George Sanders, Percy Herbert, Geoffrey Keen, Joseph O'Conor

The Door in the Wall*
GB 1956 29m Technicolor Vistavision
AB Pathé / BFI / Lawrie (Howard Thomas)

A man is obsessed by a childhood dream of a green door which leads into a beautiful garden.
The story is chosen to experiment with Dynamic Frame, a system in which the picture changes shape and size according to the subject matter. In this case the results are entertaining enough.

wd Glenn H. Alvey Jnr ph Jo Jago *m* James Bernard

Stephen Murray, Ian Hunter

The Door with Seven Locks
GB 1940 89m bw
Rialto (John Argyle)
US title: *Chamber of Horrors*

A mad doctor abducts an heiress in the hope of gaining her wealth.
Old-fashioned barnstormer, ineptly made.

w Norman Lee, John Argyle, Gilbert Gunn, *novel* Edgar Wallace *d* Norman Lee *ph* Desmond Dickinson

Leslie Banks, Lilli Palmer, Romilly Lunge, Gina Malo, Richard Bird, David Horne, Cathleen Nesbitt

Doorway to Hell
US 1930 79m (approx) bw
Warner
GB title: *A Handful of Clouds*

A young gangster tries to go straight but is driven back into crime.
Vividly written but dramatically evasive crime-does-not-pay story, trying to eat its cake and have it.

w George Rosener, *story* A Handful of Clouds by Rowland Brown *d* Archie Mayo *ph* Barney McGill *md* Leo Forbstein

Lew Ayres, Charles Judels, James Cagney, Dorothy Matthews, Leon Janney, Robert Elliott

'Swell gang picture, handled so as to just slip by the censors.'—*Variety*

AAN: original story

Dosshouse*
GB 1933 53m bw
Sound City (John Baxter)

An escaped convict is captured by a reporter and detective posing as tramps.
Low-budget featurette which deserves a footnote in film history for its social consciousness, rare at the time, especially in the dosshouse scenes.

w Herbert Ayres *d John Baxter*

Frank Cellier, Arnold Bell, Herbert Franklyn, J. Hubert Leslie

Double Bunk
GB 1961 92m bw

Newlyweds live in an old houseboat. Thin comedy which turns out not to be leakproof. Ian Carmichael, Janette Scott, Liz Frazer, Sid James, Dennis Price, Reginald Beckwith, Irene Handl, Noel Purcell, Naunton Wayne. Written and directed by C. M. Pennington-Richards; for George H. Brown/Bryanston/British Lion.

Double Confession
GB 1950 85m bw
ABP / Harry Reynolds

At a seaside resort, a man finds his wife dead and tries to frame her lover, but becomes confused with two real murderers with a different purpose.
Confused and unlikely melodrama which signally lacks the ancient mariner's eye.

w William Templeton, *novel* All on a Summer's Day by John Garden *d* Ken Annakin *ph* Geoffrey Unsworth *m* Benjamin Franklin

Derek Farr, Peter Lorre, William Hartnell, Joan Hopkins, Naunton Wayne, Ronald Howard, Kathleen Harrison, Leslie Dwyer, Edward Rigby

Double Crime in the Maginot Line
France 1939 83m bw

A spy is discovered in the French system of international fortifications. A topical melodrama which quickly became very dated indeed. Victor Francen, Jacques Baumer, Vera Korene, Fernand Fabre. Written by Felix Gandera and Robert Bibal from a novel by Pierre Nord; directed by Felix Gandera for his own company.

Double Crossbones
US 1950 75m Technicolor

Circumstances force our hero to assume the identity of a pirate, in which disguise he rescues a fair lady. Lamebrained burlesque unworthy of its star. Donald O'Connor, Helena Carter, Will Geer, John Emery, Hope Emerson, Charles McGraw, Alan Napier. Written by Oscar Brodney; directed by Charles R. Barton; for Universal-International.

'Frankenstein, Dracula and other screen monsters pale by comparison with this fiendish, decadent woman!'

Double Door
US 1934 75m bw

A selfish, wealthy Fifth Avenue spinster takes a dislike to her brother's girlfriend and locks her up in a vault. Silly, rather boring melodrama which may have worked on the stage but did not take to the screen. Mary Morris (the American one), Evelyn Venable, Kent Taylor, Sir Guy Standing, Anne Revere, Colin Tapley, Halliwell Hobbes. Written by Gladys Lehman, Jack Cunningham from the play by Elizabeth McFadden; directed by Charles Vidor; for Paramount. 'Not likely to get anywhere at the b.o. . . . dull, drab and incredible.'—*Variety*

Double Dynamite
US 1951 (produced 1948) 80m bw
RKO (Irving Cummings)
aka: *It's Only Money*

A bank teller wins a fortune at the race track but is afraid his winnings will be thought the proceeds of a bank robbery.
Insultingly mild comedy, nearly saved by a few quips from Groucho.

w Melville Shavelson, Harry Crane, Leo Rosten *d* Irving Cummings *ph* Robert de Grasse *m* Leigh Harline

Frank Sinatra, Jane Russell, Groucho Marx, Don McGuire, Howard Freeman

Double Harness
US 1933 70m bw

A girl sets out to trick a rich man into marriage. Mildly amusing comedy which in its time was considered risqué. Ann Harding, William Powell, Henry Stephenson, Lillian Bond, Reginald Owen, George Meeker, Kay Hammond. Written by Jane Murfin from the play by Edward Montgomery; directed by John Cromwell; for RKO. 'Managed with such reticence that at no time is there a note of offence . . . this class actress again triumphs over her surroundings, and the picture will please her large following.'—*Variety*

Double Indemnity: see River's End

'You can't kiss away a murder!'

Double Indemnity****
US 1944 107m bw
Paramount (Joseph Sistrom)

An insurance agent connives with the glamorous wife of a client to kill her husband and collect.
Archetypal *film noir* of the forties, brilliantly filmed and incisively written, perfectly capturing the decayed Los Angeles atmosphere of a Chandler novel but using a simpler story and more substantial characters. The hero / villain was almost a new concept.

w Billy Wilder, Raymond Chandler, novel James M. Cain d Billy Wilder ph John Seitz m Miklos Rozsa

Fred MacMurray, Barbara Stanwyck, Edward G. Robinson, Tom Powers, Porter Hall, Jean Heather, Byron Barr, Richard Gaines

Opening narration: Office memorandum. Walter Neff to Barton T. Keyes, Claims Manager, Los Angeles, July 16, 1938. Dear Keyes: I suppose you'll call this a confession when you hear it. Well, I don't like the word confession. I just want to set you right about something you couldn't see because it was smack up against your nose . . . I killed Dietrichson. Me, Walter Neff, insurance salesman, 35 years old, unmarried, no visible scars. Until a while ago, that is . . .

'The sort of film which revives a critic from the depressive effects of bright epics about the big soul of America or the suffering soul of Europe and gives him a new lease of faith.'—*Richard Winnington*

'The most pared-down and purposeful film ever made by Billy Wilder.'—*John Coleman, 1966*

DOUBLE INDEMNITY. Barbara Stanwyck exudes more sex appeal fully clothed than most of today's screen sirens manage with a minimum of cover. No wonder Fred MacMurray is doomed.

'Profoundly, intensely entertaining.'—*Richard Mallett, Punch*

'One of the highest summits of *film noir* . . . without a single trace of pity or love.'—*Charles Higham, 1971*

AAN: best picture; script, direction; John Seitz; Miklos Rozsa; Barbara Stanwyck

'This woman inspired him—this woman feared him!'

A Double Life**
US 1947 103m bw
(Universal) Kanin Productions (Michael Kanin)

An actor playing Othello is obsessed by the role and murders a woman he imagines to be Desdemona.
An old theatrical chestnut (cf *Men Are Not Gods*) is decked out with smartish backstage dialogue but despite a pleasant star performance remains unrewarding if taxing, and the entertainment value of the piece is on the thin side considering the mighty talents involved.

w Ruth Gordon, Garson Kanin *d* George Cukor *ph* Milton Krasner *m* Miklos Rozsa

Ronald Colman, Shelley Winters, Signe Hasso, Edmond O'Brien, Millard Mitchell

AA: Miklos Rozsa; Ronald Colman
AAN: Ruth Gordon, Garson Kanin; George Cukor

The Double McGuffin
US 1979 100m colour

Kids turn into amateur detectives when they find that a visiting foreign leader is to be assassinated. Barely tolerable lightweight mystery for an audience which probably doesn't exist. Ernest Borgnine, George Kennedy, Elke Sommer, Rod Browning. Written, directed and produced by Joe Camp for Mulberry Square.

The Double Man*
GB 1967 105m Technicolor
Warner / Hal E. Chester

A CIA agent investigates the death of his son on a Swiss skiing holiday and finds the murder was a lure to get him there so that an enemy lookalike can substitute for him.
Rather ruthless but good-looking and generally watchable spy melodrama.

w Frank Tarloff, Alfred Hayes, *novel* Henry S. Maxfield *d* Franklin Schaffner *ph Denys Coop m* Ernie Freeman

Yul Brynner, Clive Revill, Anton Diffring, Britt Ekland, Moira Lister

Double Negative
Canada 1980 96m colour

A photo journalist tries to find the murderer of his wife, and discovers he's an amnesiac and did it himself. Ho-hum mystery thriller centring on an ancient wheeze; treatment resolutely plodding. Michael Sarrazin, Susan Clark, Anthony Perkins, Howard Duff, Kate Reid. Written by Thomas Hedley Jnr, Janis Allen and Charles Dennis, from *The Three Roads* by Ross Macdonald; directed by George Bloomfield; for Quadrant.

Double or Nothing
US 1937 90m bw

Inheritors under a trick will must double their bequests or lose them. Flat comedy with music; none of the elements are really up to scratch. Bing Crosby, Martha Raye, Andy Devine, William Frawley, Mary Carlisle, Benny Baker. Written by Charles Lederer and others; directed by Theodore Reed; for Paramount. 'Due for big openings and tapering-off business. Will squeeze through.'—*Variety*

Double Wedding
US 1937 87m bw
MGM (Joseph L. Mankiewicz)

A bohemian artist makes a play for the lady of his choice by romancing her sister.
Zany star comedy which doesn't quite come off.

Jo Swerling, *play* Great Love by Ferenc lolnar *d* Richard Thorpe *ph* William aniels *m* Edward Ward

William Powell, Myrna Loy, John Beal, Florence Rice, Jessie Ralph, Edgar Kennedy, Sidney Toler, Barnett Parker, Katherine Alexander, Donald Meek

'OK for topflight business . . . would be funnier if it were shorter.'—*Variety*

Double Whoopee**
US 1928 20m bw silent

Incompetent doormen at a swank hotel cause havoc. Simple-minded but pleasing star farce. Laurel and Hardy, Jean Harlow, Charlie Hall. Written by Leo McCarey and H. M. Walker; directed by Lewis R. Foster; for Hal Roach.

Doubting Thomas
US 1935 78m bw

Small-town 'society' puts on an amateur show. Slight but attractive star vehicle. Will Rogers, Billie Burke, Alison Skipworth, Sterling Holloway, Andrew Tombes, Gail Patrick. Written by William Conselman and Bartlett Cormack from the play The Torch Bearers by George Kelly; directed by David Butler; for Fox. 'There is one thing that Rogers knows, and that is how to get laughs with any sort of a situation, and he didn't learn that just from reading the papers.'—*Variety*

Douce*
France 1943 106m bw
Société Parisienne de l'Industrie Cinématographique

In 1887 Paris a sheltered young rich girl falls for a steward and encounters family opposition.
A charming old-fashioned story which provides a well-taken opportunity for a portrait of the old bourgeoisie.

w Jean Aurenche, Pierre Bost *d Claude Autant-Lara ph* Gaston Thonnart *m* René Cloërc

Odette Joyeux, Jean Debucourt, Marguerite Moreno, Roger Pigaut, Madeleine Robinson

'Direction and camerawork constantly reveal touches of felicity.'—*MFB*

Doughboys*
US 1930 80m approx bw
MGM / Buster Keaton (Lawrence Weingarten)
GB title: *Forward March*

A young eccentric joins the army.
Simple-minded farce with a few good routines for the star.

w Richard Schayer *d* Edward Sedgwick *ph* Leonard Smith

Buster Keaton, Sally Eilers, Cliff Edwards, Edward Brophy

'Keaton's first talker is comedy with a kick.'—*Variety*

The Doughgirls*
US 1944 102m bw
Warner (Mark Hellinger)

In a crowded wartime Washington hotel, a honeymoon is frustrated by constant interruption, not to mention the discovery that the wedding was not legal.
Frantic farce, generally well adapted, and certainly played with gusto.

w James V. Kern, Sam Hellman, *play* Joseph Fields *d* James V. Kern *ph* Ernest Haller *m* Adolph Deutsch

Alexis Smith, Jane Wyman, Jack Carson, Ann Sheridan, Irene Manning, *Eve Arden*, Charlie Ruggles, John Alexander, John Ridgely, Craig Stevens, Alan Mowbray, Donald MacBride

'There's nothing so good in it that you must attend, just as there is nothing bad enough to keep you away.'—*Archer Winsten*

The Dove*
US 1968 15m bw

Back in the countryside of his childhood, a Nobel prize winner recalls the events of a summer . . . Elaborate Ingmar Bergman spoof complete with sub-titles and pidgin Swedish. Hilarious at the time for those who had just seen *Wild Strawberries*. David Zirlin, George Coe, Pamela Burrell. Written by Sidney Davis; directed by George Coe and Anthony Lover; for Coe / Davis Ltd.

The Dove*
US 1974 104m Technicolor Panavision
St George Productions (Gregory Peck)

Yachtsman Robin Lee Graham makes a five-year voyage around the world.
Bland, rather stolid adventure story for boatniks, based on real incidents; good to look at.

w Peter Beagle, Adam Kennedy from book by Robin Lee Graham, Derek Gill *d* Charles Jarrott *ph Sven Nykvist m* John Barry

Joseph Bottoms, Deborah Raffin, John McLiam, Dabney Coleman

'Postcard views flick by to the strains of a saccharine score.'—*David McGillivray*

Down Among the Sheltering Palms
US 1952 86m Technicolor
TCF (Fred Kohlmar)

An American army unit takes over a south sea island, but fraternization is forbidden.
Tolerable comedy-musical with familiar jokes and situations.

w Claude Binyon, Albert Lewin, Burt Styler *d* Edmund Goulding *ph* Leon Shamroy *m* Leigh Harline *songs* Harold Arlen, Ralph Blane

William Lundigan, Jane Greer, Mitzi Gaynor, David Wayne, Gloria de Haven, Gene Lockhart, Jack Paar, Billy Gilbert

Down and Out in Beverly Hills*
US 1985 97m Technicolor
Touchstone (Paul Mazursky)

A wandering con artist is taken in by an insecure Beverly Hills family.
Somewhat bumbling but sporadically effective rehash of Renoir's *Boudu Sauvé des Eaux* (qv), with a few modern jabs and effectively eccentric performances.

w Paul Mazursky, Leon Capetanos *play* René Fauchois *d* Paul Mazursky *ph* Donald McAlpine *m* Andy Summers *pd* Pato Guzman

Nick Nolte, Richard Dreyfuss, Bette Midler, Little Richard, Tracy Nelson, Elizabeth Pena

Down Argentine Way*
US 1940 94m Technicolor
TCF (Harry Joe Brown)

A wealthy American girl falls in love with an Argentinian horse-breeder.
A very moderate musical which happened to bring both Grable and Miranda to star stature and set Fox off on their successful run of forties extravaganzas, reasonably pleasant to look at but empty-headed.

w Karl Tunberg, Darrell Ware *d* Irving Cummings *ph* Ray Rennahan, Leon Shamroy *songs* Harry Warren, Mack Gordon

Betty Grable, Carmen Miranda, Don Ameche, Charlotte Greenwood, J. Carrol Naish, Henry Stephenson, Leonid Kinskey, The Nicholas Brothers

'I dislike Technicolor in which all pinks resemble raspberry sauce, reds turn to sealing wax, blues shriek of the washtub, and yellows become suet pudding.'—*James Agate*

'So outrageous—that it's hard to believe it isn't at least partly intentional—but why would anybody make this picture on purpose.'—*New Yorker, 1976*

AAN: Ray Rennahan, Leon Shamroy; title song (*m* Harry Warren, *ly* Mack Gordon)

Down Memory Lane*
US 1949 70m bw

A kaleidoscope of Mack Sennett comedy shorts, linked by Steve Allen as a disc jockey. Much Bing Crosby; Fields in *The Dentist*; an appearance by Sennett himself. Directed by Phil Karlson; for Aubrey Schenck.

Down Three Dark Streets*
US 1954 85m bw
UA / Edward Small (Arthur Gardner, Jules V. Levy)

An FBI agent is shot on duty, and his friend avenges him in the course of clearing up three cases in which he was involved.
Competent, enjoyable police film with three cases for the price of one.

w The Gordons, Bernard C. Schoenfeld, *book* Case File FBI by the Gordons *d Arnold Laven ph* Joseph Biroc *m* Paul Sawtell

Broderick Crawford, Ruth Roman, Martha Hyer, Marisa Pavan, Casey Adams, Kenneth Tobey

† One of the first collaborations of the prolific production company Laven-Gardner-Levy.

Down to Earth
US 1932 79m bw

Nouveau riche Americans return from Europe and find themselves misfits at home. Thin sequel to *They Had to See Paris*. Will Rogers, Dorothy Jordan, Irene Rich, Matty Kemp, Mary Carlisle. Written by Edwin Burke, from a story by Homer Croy. 'Will need support . . . the least powerful in draw of all Rogers' pictures.'—*Variety*

Down to Earth*
US 1947 101m Technicolor
Columbia (Don Hartman)

The muse Terpsichore comes down to help a Broadway producer fix a new show in which she is featured.
Pleasant but undistinguished musical fantasy, a sequel to *Here Comes Mr Jordan*. The heavenly sequences promise more amusement than they produce.

w Edwin Blum, Don Hartman *d* Alexander Hall *ph* Rudolph Maté *m* Heinz Roemheld

Rita Hayworth, Larry Parks, Roland Culver (as Mr Jordan), *Edward Everett Horton* (repeating as Messenger 7013), Marc Platt, James Gleason

'Just the film to make the spectator forget the troubles of life.'—*MFB*

'Celestial whimsy musical, with arch acting and a dull score.'—*New Yorker, 1977*

Down to the Sea in Ships*
US 1948 120m bw
TCF (Elmer Clifton)

An old whaling skipper wants his grandson to follow in his footsteps.
Seagoing spectacle with strong characters; all concerned show Hollywood in its most professional form, but the film somehow fails to catch the imagination or live in the memory.

w John Lee Mahin, Sy Bartlett *d* Henry Hathaway *ph Joe MacDonald m* Alfred Newman

Lionel Barrymore, Dean Stockwell, Richard Widmark, *Cecil Kellaway*, Gene Lockhart

Downhill
GB 1927 80m approx (24 fps) bw silent
Gainsborough (Michael Balcon)
US title: *When Boys Leave Home*

A sixth-form schoolboy, accused of theft, is expelled and goes to the bad in Marseilles before being found innocent.
Absurd novelette with only marginal glimpses of the director's emerging talent.

w Eliot Stannard, *play* Ivor Novello and Constance Collier *d* Alfred Hitchcock *ph* Claude McDonnell *ed* Ivor Montagu

Ivor Novello, Ben Webster, Robin Irvine, Sybil Rhoda, Lillian Braithwaite, Isabel Jeans, Ian Hunter

Famous line: 'Does this mean, sir, that I shall not be able to play for the Old Boys?'

Downhill Racer*
US 1969 101m Technicolor
Paramount / Wildwood (Richard Gregson)

An ambitious American skier gains a place on the team competing in Europe.
Virtually plotless, casually assembled study of a man and a sport, good to look at, often exciting, but just as frequently irritating in its throwaway style.

w James Salter, *novel* Oakley Hall *d* Michael Ritchie *ph Brian Probyn* *m* Kenyon Hopkins

Robert Redford, Gene Hackman, Camilla Sparv, Joe Jay Jalbert, Timothy Kirk, Dabney Coleman

Downstairs
US 1932 77m bw

A villainous chauffeur blackmails the other servants. Failed attempt by a falling star to do something different. John Gilbert, Virginia Bruce, Paul Lukas, Hedda Hopper, Reginald Owen, Olga Baclanova. Written by Melville Baker and Lenore Coffee from a story by John Gilbert; directed by Monta Bell; for MGM.

'The strangest love a woman has ever known . . . a livid face bent over her in the ghostly mist!'

Dracula***
US 1931 84m bw
Universal (Carl Laemmle Jnr)

A Transylvanian vampire count gets his come-uppance in Yorkshire.
A film which has much to answer for. It started its star and its studio off on horror careers, and it launched innumerable sequels (see below). In itself, after two eerie reels, it becomes a pedantic and slow transcription of a stage adaptation, and its climax takes place offscreen; but for all kinds of reasons it remains full of interest.

w Garrett Fort, *play* Hamilton Deane, John Balderston, *novel Bram Stoker* *d Tod Browning* *ph Karl Freund* *m* Tchaikovsky

Bela Lugosi, Helen Chandler, David Manners, *Dwight Frye, Edward Van Sloan*

'Must have caused much uncertainty as to the femme fan reaction . . . as it turns out the signs are that the woman's angle is all right and that sets the picture for better than average money . . . it comes out as a sublimated ghost story related with all surface seriousness and above all with a remarkably effective background of creepy atmosphere.'—*Variety*

'A too literal adaptation of the play (*not* the book) results in a plodding, talkative development, with much of the vital action taking place off-screen.'—*William K. Everson*

'The mistiest parts are the best; when the lights go up the interest goes down.'—*Ivan Butler*

'It'll chill you and fill you with fears. You'll find it creepy and cruel and crazed.'—*New York Daily News*

† Later advertising variations concentrated on the horror element:

'In all the annals of living horror one name stands out as the epitome of evil! So evil, so fantastic, so degrading you'll wonder if it isn't all a nightmare! Innocent girls lured to a fate truly worse than death!'

†† Lugosi was not the first choice for the role of the Count. Ian Keith and William Powell were strongly favoured.

††† Sequels include *Dracula's Daughter* (qv), *Son of Dracula* (qv); the later Hammer sequence consists of *Dracula* (see below), *Brides of Dracula* (qv), *Dracula Prince of Darkness* (qv), *Dracula Has Risen From the Grave* (qv), *Taste the Blood of Dracula* (qv), *Scars of Dracula* (qv), *Dracula AD 1972* (qv), *The Satanic Rites of Dracula* (qv). Other associated films in which the Count or a disciple appears include (all qv) *Return of the Vampire* (1944), *House of Frankenstein* (1945), *House of Dracula* (1945), *Abbott and Costello Meet Frankenstein* (1948), *The Return of Dracula* (1958), *Kiss of the Vampire* (1963), *The Fearless Vampire Killers* (1967), *Count Yorga Vampire* (1969), *Countess Dracula* (1970), *Vampire Circus* (1970), *The House of Dark Shadows* (1970), *Vampire Lovers* (1971), *Blacula* (1972). Minor potboilers are legion.

'Who will be his bride tonight?'

Dracula***
GB 1958 82m Technicolor
Hammer (Anthony Hinds)
US title: *Horror of Dracula*

A remake of the 1930 film.
Commendably brief in comparison with the later Hammer films, this was perhaps the best horror piece they turned out as well as the most faithful to its original. Decor and colour were well used, and the leading performances are striking.

w Jimmy Sangster *d Terence Fisher* *ph Jack Asher* *m James Bernard* *ad Bernard Robinson*

Peter Cushing (as Van Helsing), *Christopher Lee* (as Dracula), Melissa Stribling, Carol Marsh, Michael Gough, John Van Eyssen, Valerie Gaunt, Miles Malleson

Dracula
Italy 1974 93m colour
aka: *Andy Warhol's Dracula*

In this sick and gory version, Dracula becomes ill if he feasts on anything but pure virgin's blood. The hero saves the heroine in the predictable way. Not for the squeamish. Udo Kier, Arno Juerging, Vittorio De Sica, Maxime McEmory, Joe Dalessandro. Written and directed by Paul Morrissey; for Andrew Braunsberg.

Dracula*
GB 1979 112m Technicolor Panavision
Universal / Mirisch (Marvin Mirisch / Tom Pevsner)

A lush, expensive and romantic version which presents the count as a matinée idol and spends too much time on the romantic scenes to distract attention from an old old story.

w W. D. Richter *d* John Badham *ph* Gilbert Taylor *pd* Peter Murton *m* John Williams

Frank Langella, Laurence Olivier, Donald Pleasence, Kate Nelligan, Trevor Eve

'A triumphantly lurid creation that seems bound to be either under-valued for its circus effects or over-valued for the stylishness with which it steers between the reefs of camp and theatrical indulgence.'—*Richard Combs, MFB*

'The Count is back, with an eye for London's hot pants, and a taste for everything!'

Dracula AD 1972
GB 1972 95m Eastmancolor
Warner / Hammer (Josephine Douglas)

Dracula reappears among Chelsea teenagers practising black magic.
Depressed attempt to update a myth; the link with modern sin makes it seem not only tarnished but tasteless, and the film itself is lamentably short on excitement.

w Don Houghton *d* Alan Gibson *ph* Richard Bush *m* Michael Vickers

Peter Cushing, Christopher Lee, Stephanie Beacham, Michael Coles, Christopher Neame, William Ellis

'You just can't keep a good man down!'

Dracula Has Risen from the Grave
GB 1968 92m Technicolor
Hammer (Aida Young)

Dracula again terrorizes the village in the shadow of his castle, and is routed by a bishop.
Tedious, confined and repetitive shocker with little conventional action and an unusual emphasis on sex.

w John Elder (Anthony Hinds) *d* Freddie Francis *ph* Arthur Grant *m* James Bernard

Christopher Lee, Rupert Davies, Veronica Carlson, Barbara Ewing, Barry Andrews, Ewan Hooper

'A bloody bore.'—*Judith Crist*

Dracula Prince of Darkness
GB 1965 90m Techniscope
Warner / Hammer (Anthony Nelson Keys)

Stranded travellers are made welcome at the late count's castle by his sinister butler, who proceeds to use the blood of one of them to revivify his master.
Ingenious rehash of incidents from the original story, largely dissipated by poor colour and unsuitable wide screen.

w John Sansom *d* Terence Fisher *ph* Michael Reed *m* James Bernard

Christopher Lee, *Philip Latham*, Barbara Shelley, Thorley Walters, Andrew Keir, Francis Matthews, Suzan Farmer, Charles Tingwell

'Run-of-the-coffin stuff . . . only for ardent fang-and-cross fans.'—*Judith Crist*

'More sensational than her unforgettable father!'

Dracula's Daughter**
US 1936 70m bw
Universal (E. M. Asher)

The daughter of the old count follows his remains to London.
Lively sequel which develops in the manner of a Sherlock Holmes story.

w Garrett Fort *d Lambert Hillyer ph* George Robinson *m* Heinz Roemheld

Otto Kruger, Marguerite Churchill, Edward Van Sloan, Gloria Holden, Irving Pichel, Nan Grey, Hedda Hopper, Gilbert Emery, Claud Allister, E. E. Clive, Halliwell Hobbes, Billy Bevan

'There's more to the legend than meets the throat!'

Dracula's Dog
US 1977 88m De Luxe
Vic (Albert Band, Frank Ray Perelli)
GB title: *Zoltan, Hound of Dracula*

The resurrected servant of Dracula tries to use his vampire dog to create a new master.
Ingenious but unattractive addition to the saga, with dogs as chief villains; the style varies between spoof and rather nasty horror.

w Frank Ray Perelli *d* Albert Band *ph* Bruce Logan *m* Andrew Belling

Jose Ferrer, Reggie Nalder, Michael Pataki, Jan Shutan

Draegerman Courage
US 1937 59m bw

Problems of a Nova Scotian gold mine cave-in. Adequate action fare inspired by a real event. (Draegermen are burrowers.) Jean Muir, Barton MacLane, Henry O'Neill, Robert Barrat, Addison Richards, Gordon Oliver. Written by Anthony Coldeway; directed by Louis King; for Warners. 'Vivid and often thrilling.'—*Variety*

The Dragnet*
US 1928 77m approx (24 fps) bw silent
Paramount

When his buddy is killed, a detective resigns from the force and takes to the bottle.
Obviously interesting sequel to *Underworld*. It can't be evaluated because no print is known to exist.

w Jules and Charles Furthman, *story* Night Stick by Oliver H. P. Garrett *d* Josef von Sternberg *ph* Harold Rosson *ad* Hans Dreier

George Bancroft, Evelyn Brent, William Powell, Fred Kohler, Francis MacDonald, Leslie Fenton

Dragnet*
US 1954 93m Warnercolor
Mark VII (Jack Webb)

Sgt Joe Friday solves the murder of an ex-convict.
Moderately interesting but overlong attempt to transfer television techniques to the big screen; laconic dialogue, question and answer, cheap sets, close-ups and convenient Los Angeles locations.

w Richard Breen *d Jack Webb ph* Edward Colman *m* Walter Schumann

Jack Webb, Ben Alexander, Richard Boone, Stacy Harris, Ann Robinson, Virginia Gregg

Dragnet
US 1987 106m De Luxe
Universal / Applied Action / Bernie Brillstein.

The nephew of Sgt Joe Friday gets involved in a murder case.
Overlong parody with some obvious amusements before the whole thing becomes tiresome.

w Dan Aykroyd, Alan Zweibel, Tom Mankiewicz *d* Tom Mankiewicz *ph* Matthew F. Leonetti *m* Ira Newborn *pd* Robert F. Boyle

Dan Aykroyd, Tom Hanks, Christopher Plummer, Harry Morgan, Alexander Paul, Elizabeth Ashley, Dabney Coleman.

Dragon Seed*
US 1944 144m bw
MGM (Pandro S. Berman)

Chinese peasants fight the Japs.
Ill-advised attempt to follow the success of *The Good Earth*; badly cast actors mouth propaganda lines in a mechanical script which provokes more boredom and unintentional laughter than sympathy.

w Marguerite Roberts, Jane Murfin, *novel* Pearl S. Buck *d* Jack Conway, Harold S. Bucquet *ph* Sidney Wagner *m* Herbert Stothart

Katharine Hepburn, Walter Huston, Turhan Bey, Aline MacMahon, Akim Tamiroff, Hurd Hatfield, Frances Rafferty, Agnes Moorehead, Henry Travers, J. Carrol Naish

'A kind of slant-eyed *North Star*. Often awkward and pretentious, it nevertheless has moments of moral and dramatic grandeur.'—*Time*

'A fine film in anybody's sweepstakes. It'll wow 'em at the box office.'—*Variety* (It didn't.)

AAN: Sidney Wagner; Aline MacMahon

'Only sorcery can destroy it!'

Dragonslayer
US 1981 110m Metrocolor Panavision
Walt Disney / Paramount (Howard W. Koch, Hal Barwood)

A sorcerer's apprentice uses his master's magic amulet to ward off various dangers.
Heavy-going sword-and-sorcery fable, not helped at all by slow plotting and dark photography. The dragons however are genuinely fierce.

w Hal Barwood, Matthew Robbins *d* Matthew Robbins *ph* Derek Vanlint *m* Alex North *pd* Elliot Scott *sp* Thomas Smith

Peter MacNichol, Caitlin Clarke, Ralph Richardson, John Hallam, Peter Eyre, Albert Salmi

'Verges on the nasty for the nippers; sails too close to *déjà vu* for fantasy fans.'—*Time Out*

AAN: Alex North; make-up

Dragonwyck*
US 1946 103m bw
TCF (Darryl F. Zanuck)

In the 1840s a farmer's daughter marries her rich cousin, not knowing that he has poisoned his first wife.
Good-looking but rather tedious romance of the Jane Eyre / Rebecca school: tyrannical recluse, mystery upstairs, spooky house, etc. Heavy going.

w Joseph L. Mankiewicz, *novel* Anya Seton *d* Joseph L. Mankiewicz *ph Arthur Miller* *m* Alfred Newman

Gene Tierney, Vincent Price, Glenn Langan, Walter Huston, Anne Revere, Spring Byington, Henry Morgan, Jessica Tandy

Drake of England
GB 1935 104m bw
BIP (Walter C. Mycroft)
US titles: *Drake the Pirate; Elizabeth of England*

Sir Francis Drake is knighted by Queen Elizabeth for his seafaring exploits, and defeats the Spanish Armada.
Stiffly moving historical pageant; you can smell the mothballs.

w Clifford Grey, Akos Tolney, Marjorie Deans, Norman Watson *d* Arthur Woods *ph* Claude Friese-Greene, Ronald Neame

Matheson Lang, Athene Seyler, Jane Baxter, Donald Wolfit, Henry Mollison, George Merritt, Amy Veness, Sam Livesey, Ben Webster

Dramatic School*
US 1938 80m bw
MGM (Mervyn Le Roy)

Young actresses compete for success.
Another, less lively, *Stage Door*; tolerable but not exciting.

w Ernst Vajda, Mary McCall Jnr, *play* School of Drama by Hans Szekely, Zoltan Egyed *d* Robert B. Sinclair Jnr *ph* William Daniels *m* Franz Waxman

Luise Rainer, Paulette Goddard, Alan Marshal, Lana Turner, Anthony Allan (later John Hubbard), Henry Stephenson, Genevieve Tobin, Gale Sondergaard, Melville

Cooper, Erik Rhodes, Ann Rutherford, Margaret Dumont, Virginia Grey, Hans Conried

'A disappointing effort which arouses little interest in its unfolding.'—*Variety*

Drango
US 1957 92m bw
UA / Hall Bartlett

After the Civil War, a Union Army officer is assigned to bring law and order to a Georgia community.
Eccentric, downbeat semi-western with aspirations to be some kind of *film noir*; does not come off.

wd Hall Bartlett *ph James Wong Howe*
m Elmer Bernstein

Jeff Chandler, Ronald Howard, Joanne Dru, Julie London, Donald Crisp, John Lupton, Morris Ankrum

The Draughtsman's Contract**
GB 1982 108m colour
BFI / Channel Four (David Payne)

In 1694 a young draughtsman receives a curious commission from a country gentlewoman, his rewards to include bed and bawd.
Pleasantly unusual, stylized puzzle film which involves both sex and murder while maintaining a detached attitude to both. The period costumes help to give it an air of fantasy which was presumably intended.

wd Peter Greenaway *ph* Curtis Clark
m Michael Nyman *ed* John Wilson

Anthony Higgins, Janet Suzman, Anne Louise Lambert, Neil Cunningham, Hugh Fraser, Dave Hill

'Mannered and idiosyncratic, the speeches are so arch and twitty that they seem to be pitched higher than a dog whistle.'—*Pauline Kael, New Yorker*

'Perhaps the four-hour version which may one day become available is clearer if not more concise.'—*Guardian*

'Best enjoyed as a sly piece of double bluff, a puzzle without a solution, an *avant garde* hoax in the spirit of Dada and the surrealists.'—*Observer*

Dream Girl
US 1947 86m bw
Paramount (P. J. Wolfson)

A girl revels in her own romantic dreams, one of which nearly comes true.
Potentially pleasant comedy about a female Walter Mitty does not work because the director has run out of ideas, the star is miscast and Hollywood has insisted on making the girl rich to begin with, which robs the dreams of any point.

w Arthur Sheekman, *play* Elmer Rice
d Mitchell Leisen *ph* Daniel L. Fapp
m Victor Young

Betty Hutton, Macdonald Carey, Walter Abel, Patric Knowles, Virginia Field, Peggy Wood, Lowell Gilmore

Dream Lover
US 1986 104m Technicolor
MGM-UA / Alan J. Pakula, Jon Boorstin

A dream researcher is assigned to the case of a girl who has fatally stabbed an intruder.
Flabby and overlong case history with no very interesting conclusion.

w Jon Boorstin *d* Alan J. Pakula *ph* Sven Nykvist *m* Michael Small

Kristy McNichol, Ben Masters, Paul Shenar, John McMartin, Gayle Hunnicutt, Justin Deas

The Dream of a Rarebit Fiend*
US 1906 4m (24 fps) bw silent

Early trick film depicting a nightmare resulting from overeating. Written by Winsor McKay; directed and produced by Edwin S. Porter.

A Dream of Kings
US 1969 110m Technicolor
National General (Jules Schermer)

Episodes in the life of an improvident, lusty, poetical Chicago Greek with a dying son.
The part screamed for Anthony Quinn and got him, with the result that it has all been seen before, too frequently. Well made, with strong appeal to Chicago Greeks.

w Harry Mark Patrakis, Ian Hunter, *novel* Harry Mark Patrakis *d* Daniel Mann
ph Richard H. Kline *m* Alex North

Anthony Quinn, Irene Papas, Inger Stevens, Sam Levene, Val Avery, Tamara Daykarhanova

A Dream of Passion
Greece 1978 110m Eastmancolor
Branfilm / Melinafilm (Jules Dassin)

A woman who, Medea-like, has killed her children is drawn into an eccentric relationship with an actress playing Medea on the stage.
Weird and ineffective character drama which badly needs discipline.

wd Jules Dassin *ph* George Arvanitis
m Ionnis Markopoulos

Melina Mercouri, Ellen Burstyn, Andreas Voutsinas, Despo Diamantidou

Dream Street*
US 1921 89m (at 24 fps) bw silent
D. W. Griffith Inc

Three Limehouse folk, torn between good and evil, act out their dreams.
Trilogy of moral tales, fancifully and often charmingly assembled by the master director who often reminds one of a Victorian lace maker.

wd D. W. Griffith, from stories by Thomas Burke *ph Henrik Sartov*

Carol Dempster, Ralph Graves, Charles Emmett Mack, Edwart Peil, Tyrone Power Snr, W. J. Ferguson

Dream Wife
US 1953 99m bw
MGM (Dore Schary)

An executive leaves his ambitious wife for a sheik's daughter schooled in the art of pleasing men, but naturally finds drawbacks.
Very moderate comedy with strained situations and few laughs. The stars work hard.

w Sidney Sheldon, Herbert Baker, Alfred L. Levitt *d* Sidney Sheldon *ph* Milton Krasner
m Conrad Salinger

Cary Grant, Deborah Kerr, Walter Pidgeon, Betta St John, Eduard Franz, Buddy Baer, Les Temayne

Dreamboat*
US 1952 83m bw
TCF (Sol C. Siegel)

A romantic star of the silent film era is embarrassed when his old movies turn up on television.
Hollywood rather blunderingly makes fun of its arch enemy in this sometimes sprightly but often disappointing comedy which should have been a bulls-eye.

wd Claude Binyon *ph* Milton Krasner
m Cyril Mockridge

Clifton Webb, Ginger Rogers, Anne Francis, Jeffrey Hunter, Elsa Lanchester, Fred Clark, Ray Collins, Paul Harvey

'A merry comedy filled with uproarious laughter from beginning to end.'—*Hollywood Reporter*

Dreamchild
GB 1985 93m Technicolor
Thorn EMI / PFH (Rick McCallum, Kenith Trodd)

An old lady who was Lewis Carroll's original Alice visits New York in 1932 and finds fact and fiction mingling in her memory.
Misbegotten, ill-thought-out and generally pointless exercise in literary muckraking, with ugly 'creatures' displayed in ineffective flashes. It might have worked better if displayed at leisure on BBC2 for a minority audience, but as an item for general consumption it hasn't a hope.

w Dennis Potter *d* Gavin Millar *ph* Billy Williams *m* Stanley Myers *pd* Roger Hall
ed Angus Newton

Coral Browne, Ian Holm, Peter Gallagher, Nicola Cowper, Amelia Shankley

'Ambitious but unsatisfying and gimmicky.' —*Variety*

Dreaming
GB 1944 78m bw

A soldier on leave gets a bump on the head, and dreams . . . Rather elementary series of sketches with a few good laughs and interesting guest appearances. Flanagan and Allen, Hazel Court, Dick Francis, Philip Wade, Teddy Brown, Reginald Foort, Gordon Richards, Alfredo Campoli. Written by Bud Flanagan and Reginald Purdell; directed by John Baxter; for Ealing.

Dreaming Lips*
GB 1936 94m bw
Trafalgar (Paul Czinner)

The wife of an invalid musician has an affair with another man and commits suicide.

Standard star fare, possibly Miss Bergner's most notable film, also available in a German version.

w Margaret Kennedy, Lady Cynthia Asquith, Carl Mayer, *play* Henry Bernstein *d* Paul Czinner, Lee Garmes *ph* Lee Garmes *m* William Walton

Elisabeth Bergner, Romney Brent, Raymond Massey, Joyce Bland, Sydney Fairbrother, Felix Aylmer, Donald Calthrop

'In many respects one of the finest productions ever made in England . . . made in Hollywood, the story would be whitewashed and much of its strength weakened.'—*Variety*

Dreams That Money Can Buy*
US 1946 81m Technicolor
Art of the Century (Hans Richter, Peggy Guggenheim, Kenneth MacPherson)

A young itinerant sells dreams to people who need them.
Semi-underground surrealist film, momentarily of interest, but disjointed and with no real apparent purpose.

wd Hans Richter *ph* Arnold Eagle *md* Louis Applebaum

'Arch, snobbish and sycophantic, about as genuinely experimental as a Chemcraft set.'—*James Agee*

† The individual dreams are directed by Max Ernst, Man Ray, Fernand Leger, Marcel Duchamp and Alexander Calder as well as Richter.

Dreamscape
US 1984 99m CFI color

Experiments prove that it is possible for a dreamer to enter the dreams of others, and a subject finds himself being used for a plot against the president of the US. Complex fantasy melodrama with a cold war basis; neither exciting nor praiseworthy. Dennis Quaid, Max Von Sydow, Christopher Plummer, Eddie Albert, Kate Capshaw. Written by David Loughery, Joseph Ruben, Chuck Russell; directed by Joseph Ruben; for Zupnik-Curtis / Bella.

Drei von der Tankstelle*
Germany 1930 80m bw
UFA

Three penniless young men find happiness as petrol station attendants.
Light-hearted operetta of the Depression era, well received at the time.

w Franz Schultz, Paul Frank *d William Thiele* *ph* Franz Planer *m* Werner Heymann

Willy Fritsch, Lilian Harvey, Oskar Karlweis, Heinz Ruhmann, Olga Tchekhova

'When leaving this charming talker operetta, one feels in good humour, humming the catchy hits of its talented composer . . . constant laughter and enthusiasm.'—*Variety*

† Remade 1955 by Hans Wolff, with a cast still led by Willy Fritsch.

Die Dreigroschenoper**
Germany 1931 114m bw
Warner / Tobis / Nero
US title: *The Threepenny Opera*

In turn-of-the-century London, Mack the Knife marries the daughter of the beggar king and runs into trouble.
Heavy-footed but interesting updating of *The Beggar's Opera*, with splendid sets.

w Bela Balazs, Leo Lania, Ladislas Vajda, from Bertolt Brecht's version *d G. W. Pabst* *ph* Fritz Arno Wagner *m Kurt Weill* *ad Andrei Andreiev*

Lotte Lenya, Rudolf Forster, Fritz Rasp, Caroline Neher, Reinhold Schunzel, Valeska Gert, Vladimir Sokoloff

† Brecht disliked the film and sued the makers, but lost.

†† A French version was also released under the title *L'Opéra de Quat'sous*, with Albert Préjean.

Dressed to Kill (1946): see Sherlock Holmes

'Every nightmare has a beginning. This one never ends!'

Dressed to Kill**
US 1980 105m Technicolor
Filmways / Samuel Z. Arkoff / Cinema 77 (George Litto)

A sexually disturbed matron under analysis is murdered by a transvestite slasher, who then goes after a witness.
Occasionally brilliant, generally nasty suspenser clearly derived from many viewings of *Psycho*. Certainly not for the squeamish.

wd Brian de Palma *ph* Ralf Bode *m* Pino Donaggio *pd* Gary Weist

Michael Caine, Angie Dickinson, Nancy Allen, Keith Gordon, Dennis Franz

'De Palma goes right for the audience jugular . . . it fully milks the boundaries of its "R" rating.'—*Variety*

'By casting a halo of excitement around killing, a glow of degradation around living, and linking the two in a queasy, guilty partnership, de Palma is asking us to celebrate the joys of barbarism in a world already drunk on rape, torture, murder and war.'—*Sunday Times*

'De Palma earns the title of master, all right . . . but Hitch remains the grand master.'—*Roger Ebert*

The Dresser*
GB 1983 118m colour
Columbia / Goldcrest / World Film Services (Peter Yates)

An exhausted Shakespearean actor-manager has a wild last day on tour, comforted and restrained by his homosexual dresser.
A strained film, but a valuable record of a play based on the touring career of Donald Wolfit, whose dresser the author was. The leading performances are too strident for the close-ups.

w Ronald Harwood from his own play *d* Peter Yates *ph* Kelvin Pike *pd* Stephen Grimes *m* James Horner

Albert Finney, Tom Courtenay, Edward Fox, Zena Walker, Eileen Atkins, Michael Gough, Betty Marsden, Lockwood West

'The best sort of drama, fascinating us on the surface with colour and humour and esoteric detail, and then revealing the truth underneath.'—*Roger Ebert*

AAN: best picture; Tom Courtenay; Albert Finney; Peter Yates as director; Ronald Harwood (adaptation)

The Dressmaker*
GB 1988 90m colour
Film Four International / British Screen (Ronnie Shedlo)

Teenage Rita is brought up in wartime Liverpool by her two aunts—one narrow-minded, the other life-loving.
What would otherwise be a low-key chamber piece is redeemed by fine performances from two of Britain's best actresses.

w John McGrath, from novel by Beryl Bainbridge *d* Jim O'Brien *ph* Michael Coulter *m* George Fenton *pd* Carolin Amies

Joan Plowright, Billy Whitelaw, Jane Horrocks, Tim Ransom

Dreyfus*
GB 1931 80m bw
BIP (F. W. Kraemer)
US title: *The Dreyfus Case*

In 1894 France, a Jewish officer is accused of spying.
Primitive version of a much-filmed story (cf *The Life of Emile Zola, I Accuse*).

w Rehfisch Herzog, Reginald Berkeley, Walter C. Mycroft *d* F. W. Kraemer, Milton Rosmer *ph* Willy Minterstein

Cedric Hardwicke, George Merritt (as Zola), Charles Carson, Sam Livesey, Garry Marsh (as Esterhazy), Randle Ayrton, George Zucco

'A picture of the documentary class, well out of the ordinary.'—*Variety*

Drifters*
GB 1929 40m approx bw
Empire Marketing Board (John Grierson)

A documentary of the North Sea fishing fleet.
A highly influential documentary, made at a time when British films were totally unrealistic and studio-bound. Unfortunately it now seems extremely dull.

wd, ed John Grierson *ph* Basil Emmott

Driftwood
US 1947 90m bw

An orphan is adopted by a kindly doctor. Lavender-scented family yarn with pleasant backgrounds and expert performances. Natalie Wood, Ruth Warrick, Walter Brennan, Dean Jagger, Charlotte Greenwood. Written by Mary Loos and Richard Sale; directed by Allan Dwan; for Republic.

'She needed the money—and I needed her!'

Drive a Crooked Road
US 1954 82m bw
Columbia (Jonie Taps)

A garage mechanic falls in with bank robbers. Terse crime melodrama, quite watchable.

w Blake Edwards *d* Richard Quine *ph* Charles Lawton Jnr *md* Ross di Maggio

Mickey Rooney, Kevin McCarthy, Dianne Foster

Drive He Said
US 1970 90m colour
Columbia / Drive Productions / BBS (Steve Blauner)

An easygoing college basketball star is helped by an eccentric rebel to ensure his own unfitness for military service. Both run into trouble.
Flabby celebration of against-the-government attitudes, expressed partly through sex and bad language. Defiantly hard to like.

w Jeremy Larner, Jack Nicholson *d* Jack Nicholson *ph* Bill Butler *m* David Shire

Michael Margotta, William Tepper, Bruce Dern, Karen Black, Robert Towne, Henry Jaglom

Drive-in
US 1976 96m Technicolor
Columbia (George Litto)

In Texas, various illicit activities find their climax at a drive-in movie.
Mild sex-and-destruction comedy which raises few laughs and makes little sense.

w Bob Peete *d* Rod Amateau *ph* Robert Jessup *m* various

Lisa Lemole, Glen Morshower, Gary Cavagnaro, Billy Milliken, Lee Newsome, Regan Kee

The Driver*
US 1978 91m De Luxe
TCF / EMI / Lawrence Gordon

A detective determines to catch an old enemy, a getaway driver.
Noisy melodrama, very proficient in the screeching tyre department but extremely empty as a character.

wd Walter Hill *ph* Philip Lathrop *m* Michael Small

Ryan O'Neal, Bruce Dern, Isabelle Adjani, Ronee Blakeley

Drôle de Drame*
France 1936 100m approx bw
aka: *Bizarre, Bizarre* (84m American version)

A complicated chain of bizarre events is set in motion when a botanist pretends not to be a detective story writer, a bishop tries to be a detective, and a murderer seeks revenge for libel.
A curious satirical comedy which is never quite as funny as it seems about to be, but should be seen for its downright peculiar London sets and its array of actors in top form.

w Jacques Prévert, *novel* The Lunatic at Large by J. Storer Clouston *d* Marcel Carné *ph* Eugen Schufftan *m* Maurice Jaubert

Françoise Rosay, Michel Simon, Louis Jouvet, Jean-Louis Barrault, Jean-Pierre Aumont

'Art theatres and foreign-language houses will do fair business.'—*Variety*

'No one with any taste for nonsense should miss it.'—*Richard Mallett, Punch*

Drop Dead Darling
GB 1966 100m Technicolor Panavision
Seven Arts (Ken Hughes)
US title: *Arrivederci Baby*

A con man who marries and murders rich women meets a con lady with similar intentions.
Loud, restless black comedy which squanders its moments of genuine inventiveness among scenes of shouting, confusion and action for action's sake.

wd Ken Hughes, *story* The Careful Man by Richard Deeming *ph* Denys Coop *m* Dennis Farnon

Tony Curtis, Rosanna Schiaffino, Lionel Jeffries, Zsa Zsa Gabor, Nancy Kwan, Fenella Fielding, Anna Quayle, Warren Mitchell, Mischa Auer

Drowning by Numbers**
GB 1988 119m Kodacolour
Film Four International / Elsevier Vendex

Three women (all with the same name) murder their respective husbands with the collusion of the local coroner.
Cynical black comedy, beautifully played and more accessible than this director's earlier work, although with some obscure formalism.

w,d Peter Greenaway *ph* Sacha Vierny *m* Michael Nyman *pd* Ben Van Os, Jan Roelfs

Bernard Hill, Joan Plowright, Juliet Stevenson, Joely Richardson, Jason Edwards

The Drowning Pool
US 1975 108m Technicolor Panavision
Warner / Coleytown (Lawrence Turman, David Foster)

Private eye Lew Harper goes to New Orleans to investigate an anonymous letter which ends in murder.
Dreary sequel to *Harper* (qv), full of boring characters uninventively deployed.

w Tracy Keenan Wynn, Lorenzo Semple Jnr, Walter Hill, *novel* John Ross MacDonald *d* Stuart Rosenberg *ph* Gordon Willis *m* Michael Small

Paul Newman, Joanne Woodward, Coral Browne, Tony Franciosa, Murray Hamilton, Gail Strickland, Linda Hayes, Richard Jaeckel

'The impenetrable mystery is not particularly gripping; and the general air of pointlessness is only intensified by the sudden rush of clarifications at the end.'—*Tom Milne*

'It recycles every private eye cliché known to civilized man as it crawls through Louisiana talking all the way.'—*Paul D. Zimmermann*

'All the clichés of cheapjack TV private eye capers have been added to MacDonald's book; whatever separates him from the paperback hacks has been deleted.'—*Judith Crist*

The Drum*
GB 1938 96m Technicolor
London Films (Alexander Korda)
US title: *Drums*

The British army helps an Indian prince to resist his usurping uncle.
Reasonably entertaining story of the Raj, with adequate excitement after a meandering start.

w Lajos Biro, Arthur Wimperis, Patrick Kirwan, Hugh Gray, *novel* A. E. W. Mason *d* Zoltan Korda *ph* Georges Périnal *m* John Greenwood, Miklos Rozsa

Sabu, Roger Livesey, Raymond Massey, Valerie Hobson, Desmond Tester, David Tree, Francis L. Sullivan, Roy Emerton, Edward Lexy

'Looks like a 100% commercial bet.'—*Variety*

Drum
US 1976 100m Metrocolor Panavision
Dino de Laurentiis (Ralph Serpe)

In 1860 New Orleans, a bordello house slave faces all manner of sexual predators.
Tediously single-minded sequel to the appalling *Mandingo*.

w Norman Wexler, *novel* Kyle Onstott *d* Steve Carver *ph* Lucien Ballard *m* Charles Smalls

Warren Oates, Ken Norton, Isela Vega, Yaphet Kotto, John Colicos

'Shamelessly it exploits the factors which explain the success of the prototype: a feeble pretence at outraged historical exposé of the abuses of the slave trade provides the excuse for an orgy of wish dreams, of sadism, flagellation, domination, sexuality of all tastes, popular fantasies of negro potency.'—*David Robinson, The Times*

Drumbeat
US 1954 111m Warnercolor CinemaScope
Jaguar (no producer credited)

An Indian fighter sets out to make peace with a renegade.
Long, dull western, stolid all round.

wd Delmer Daves *ph* J. Peverell Marley *m* Victor Young

Alan Ladd, Audrey Dalton, Marisa Pavan, Robert Keith, Rodolpho Acosta, Charles Bronson, Warner Anderson, Elisha Cook Jnr, Anthony Caruso

Drums Across the River
US 1954 78m Technicolor
Universal-International (Melville Tucker)

A young westerner who hates Indians finally helps them to overthrow a white crook.
Slick little western with almost every familiar ingredient.

w John K. Butler, Lawrence Roman *d* Nathan Juran *ph* Harold Lipstein *m* Joseph Gershenson

Audie Murphy, Walter Brennan, Lyle Bettger, Lisa Gaye, Hugh O'Brian, Jay Silverheels, Emile Meyer

THE DRUM. Sabu keeps the beat for the British Raj. The presence of another tympanist might explain why America changed the title to *Drums*.

Drums along the Mohawk**
US 1939 103m Technicolor
TCF (Raymond Griffith)

Colonists survive Indian attacks in upstate New York during the Revolutionary War.
Patchy, likeable period adventure story with domestic and farming interludes; in its way a key film in the director's canon.

w Lamar Trotti, Sonya Levien, *novel* Walter Edmonds *d John Ford ph Bert Glennon, Ray Rennahan m* Alfred Newman

Claudette Colbert, Henry Fonda, *Edna May Oliver*, Eddie Collins, John Carradine, Dorris Bowdon, Jessie Ralph, Arthur Shields, Robert Lowery, Roger Imhof, Ward Bond

'Outdoor spec, a top-bracketer, though not in the smash division.'—*Variety*

'No one appears to know why the picture is being made, or what its point is, exactly.'—*Pauline Kael, 70s*

AAN: Edna May Oliver

Drums in the Deep South
GB 1951 87m Supercinecolor

A Confederate officer finds himself fighting a lonely battle with his best friend from West Point. Barely stimulating semi-western in appalling colour. James Craig, Barbara Payton, Guy Madison, Barton Maclane, Craig Stevens, Tom Fadden, Taylor Holmes. Written by Philip Yordan and Sidney Harmon; directed by William Cameron Menzies (also production designer); for King Brothers / RKO.

Drums of Fu Manchu*
US 1940 bw serial: 15 eps

The Yellow Peril seeks the long-lost sceptre of Genghis Khan, which will allow him to rule the eastern hordes. Spirited rendering of an ideal serial theme. Henry Brandon, William Royle, Robert Kellard, Gloria Franklin, Olaf Hytten, Luana Walters, Dwight Frye. Directed by William Witney and John English; for Republic.

'A volcano erupts! A hurricane strikes! A man . . . a woman . . . discover passion in each other's arms!'

Drums of Tahiti
US 1953 73m Technicolor 3D

In 1877 an American helps the queen of Tahiti, who doesn't want to become a French possession. Cheapskate potboiler with an extended volcanic climax (courtesy of older, better movies). Dennis O'Keefe, Patricia Medina, Francis L. Sullivan, Sylvia Lewis. Written by Douglas Heyes and Robert E. Kent; directed by William Castle; for Sam Katzman / Columbia.

Dry Rot
GB 1956 87m bw
Romulus (Jack Clayton)

Three bookmakers plot to make a fortune by substituting a doped horse for the favourite. Flat filming of a long-running theatrical farce.

w John Chapman, from his play *d* Maurice Elvey *ph* Arthur Grant *m* Peter Akister

Ronald Shiner, Brian Rix, Sid James, Michael Shepley, Joan Haythorne, Joan Sims, Heather Sears, Lee Patterson, Peggy Mount.

Dual Alibi
GB 1947 81m bw
British National (Louis H. Jackson)

Twin trapezists fall out over a lottery ticket and a worthless woman, but later extract a unique revenge.
Sprightly circus melodrama, shot on a shoestring.

w Alfred Travers, Stephen Clarkson *d* Alfred Travers *ph* James Wilson

Herbert Lom, Phyllis Dixey, Ronald Frankau, Terence de Marney, Abraham Sofaer, Eugene Deckers

Du Barry, Woman of Passion
US 1930 88m bw

Incidents in the life of the mistress of Louis XV. Tedious early talkie which marked the virtual end of its star's career. Norma Talmadge, William Farnum, Hobart Bosworth, Conrad Nagel, Alison Skipworth. From the play by David Belasco; directed by Sam Taylor; for Talmadge / United Artists.
'Wholly unimpressive . . . nix for kids and the sticks.'—*Variety*

Dubarry Was a Lady
US 1943 101m Technicolor
MGM (Arthur Freed)

A New Yorker imagines himself back at the court of Louis XIV.
Dull, stiff adaptation of a Broadway musical comedy, with changed songs.

w Irving Brecher, *book* B. G. De Sylva, Herbert Fields *d* Roy del Ruth *ph* Karl Freund *md* George Stoll *songs* Cole Porter

Gene Kelly, Lucille Ball, Red Skelton, Virginia O'Brien, Zero Mostel, Rags Ragland, Tommy Dorsey and his Orchestra

'If the rustlers didn't get you . . . the hustlers did!'
The Duchess and the Dirtwater Fox
US 1976 104m De Luxe Panavision
TCF (Melvin Frank)

A Barbary Coast con man and a saloon singer have various hectic adventures.
Wild and woolly spoof western which fires off aimlessly in a variety of styles and becomes merely tiresome despite good scenes.

w Melvin Frank, Barry Sandler *d* Melvin Frank *ph* Joseph Biroc *m* Charles Fox

George Segal, Goldie Hawn, Conrad Janis, Thayer David, Roy Jenson, Bob Hoy, Bennie Dobbins

'The classic western has now been shot to death by Sam Peckinpah, laughed to death by Mel Brooks and pondered to death by Arthur Penn, and Frank is like a scavenger picking up stray relics from its body.'—*Newsweek*

'The relentless vulgarity of the enterprise suggests that Mr Frank, having been so long constrained by the Hollywood Production Code when churning out vehicles for Bob Hope and Danny Kaye, is still making up for lost time.'—*Philip French, The Times*

The Duchess of Idaho
US 1950 98m Technicolor
MGM (Joe Pasternak)

Romantic misunderstandings among candidates for Miss Idaho Potato.
Lightweight musical, quite pleasant if routine, with guest spots.

w Dorothy Cooper, Jerry Davis *d* Robert Z. Leonard *ph* Charles Schoenbaum *md* Georgie Stoll

Esther Williams, Van Johnson, John Lund, Paula Raymond, Clinton Sundberg; guests Red Skelton, Eleanor Powell, Lena Horne

Duck Soup****
US 1933 68m bw
Paramount

An incompetent becomes President of Fredonia and wages war on its scheming neighbour.
The satirical aspects of this film are fascinating but appear to have been unintentional. Never mind, it's also the most satisfying and undiluted Marx Brothers romp, albeit the one without instrumental interludes. It does include the lemonade stall, the mirror sequence, and an endless array of one-liners and comedy choruses.

w Bert Kalmar, Harry Ruby, Arthur Sheekman, Nat Perrin d Leo McCarey ph Henry Sharp *m / ly Bert Kalmar, Harry Ruby ad Hans Dreier, Wiard Ihnen*

The Four Marx Brothers, Margaret Dumont, Louis Calhern, Edgar Kennedy, Raquel Torres

'Practically everybody wants a good laugh right now, and this should make practically everybody laugh.'—*Variety*

'So much preliminary dialogue is necessary that it seems years before Groucho comes on at all; and waiting for Groucho is agony.'—*E. V. Lucas, Punch*

'The most perfect of all Marxist masterpieces.'—*Time Out, 1984*

Due Soldi di Speranza*
Italy 1952 98m bw
Universalcine (Sandro Ghenzi)
GB title: *Two Pennyworth of Hope*

Demobilized after World War II, Antonio finds life in his native village hard to take.
Neo-realist comedy-melodrama full of gesticulating rustics; good for those who like this sort of thing.

w Renato Castellani, Titina de Filippo *d* Renato Castellani *ph* Arturo Gallea *m* Alessandro Cicognini

Vincenzo Musolino, Maria Fiore, Filumena Russo, Luigi Astarita

Duel: see *Television Companion*

Duel at Diablo*
US 1966 103m De Luxe
UA / Nelson / Engel / Cherokee / Rainbow / Brien

White and black man fight together as Apaches attack.
Well-paced, old-fashioned, shoot-em-up star western.

w Marvin H. Albert, Michel M. Grilikhes *d* Ralph Nelson *ph* Charles F. Wheeler *m* Neal Hefti

Sidney Poitier, James Garner, Bibi Andersson, Bill Travers, William Redfield, John Hoyt, John Hubbard

Duel at Silver Creek
US 1952 77m Technicolor
U-I (Leonard Goldstein)

An honest man is murdered by claim jumpers, and the Silver Kid is suspected.
Modest, efficient western.

w Gerald Drayson Adams, Joseph Hoffman *d* Don Siegel *ph* Irving Glassberg *m* Hans Salter

Audie Murphy, Stephen McNally, Faith Domergue, Susan Cabot, Gerald Mohr, Eugene Iglesias, Lee Marvin, Walter Sande

Duel in the Jungle
GB 1954 101m Technicolor
ABP / Marcel Hellman

An African explorer intends to defraud an insurance company and sets traps for the investigator who pursues him.
Lackadaisical romp in the studio jungle, none of it with much style or film sense.

w Sam Marx, T. J. Morrison *d* George Marshall *ph* Erwin Hillier *m* Mischa Spoliansky

Dana Andrews, Jeanne Crain, David Farrar, Patrick Barr

Duel in the Sun**
US 1946 135 or 138m Technicolor
David O. Selznick

A half-breed girl causes trouble between two brothers.
Massive western, dominated and fragmented by its producer, who bought the best talent and proceeded to interfere with it, so that while individual scenes are marvellous, the narrative has little flow. The final gory shoot-up between two lovers was much discussed at the time.

w David O. Selznick, Oliver H. P. Garrett, *novel* Niven Busch *d King Vidor* (and others) *second unit B. Reeves Eason, Otto Brower ph Lee Garmes, Harold Rosson, Ray Rennahan m Dmitri Tiomkin ad James Basevi pd J. McMillan Johnson*

Jennifer Jones, Joseph Cotten, Gregory Peck, Lionel Barrymore, Lillian Gish, Walter Huston, Herbert Marshall, Charles Bickford, Tilly Losch, Joan Tetzel, Harry Carey, Otto Kruger, Sidney Blackmer

'A knowing blend of oats and aphrodisiac.'—*Time*

'Cornographic is a word that might have been coined for it.'—*Daily Mail*

'As sexual melodrama with a spectacular background it is in its way remarkable.'—*New Statesman*

'A razzmatazz of thunderous naïvety simmering into a kind of majestic dottiness.'—*Basil Wright, 1972*

'A lavish, sensual spectacle, so heightened it becomes a cartoon of passion.'—*Pauline Kael, 70s*

† The uncredited directors included Joseph Von Sternberg, William Dieterle, B. Reeves Eason, and Selznick himself.

AAN: Jennifer Jones; Lillian Gish

Duel on the Mississippi
US 1955 72m Technicolor

A river planter owes money to pirates.
Standard second feature excitements with romantic interludes. Patricia Medina, Lex Barker, Craig Stevens, Warren Stevens. Written by Gerald Drayson Adams; directed by William Castle; for Sam Katzman / Columbia.

The Duellists*
GB 1977 101m colour
Scott Free / NFFC / David Puttnam

In the early 1800s, two Hussar Officers challenge each other to a series of duels; after sixteen years an ironic truce is called. A singularly pointless anecdote; its main virtue is that it is coldly attractive to look at.

w Gerald Vaughan-Hughes, *story* The Point of Honour by Joseph Conrad *d* Ridley Scott *ph* Frank Tidy *m* Howard Blake *pd* Peter J. Hampton

Keith Carradine, Harvey Keitel, Albert Finney, Edward Fox, Cristina Raines, Tom Conti, Robert Stephens, John McEnery

Duet for One
GB 1986 107m Rank colour

A leading lady violinist contracts multiple sclerosis. Lamentable opening out of a two-character play, all gloom and doom and overstatement. Julie Andrews, Alan Bates, Max Von Sydow, Rupert Everett, Margaret Courtenay. Written by Tom Kempinski, Jeremy Lipp and Andrei Konchalovsky from the play by Tom Kempinski; directed by Andrei Konchalovsky; for Cannon.

'Some helpful hints for those who are very rich, very beautiful, very hip, elaborately oversexed, tuned in, turned on and bored to death!'

Duffy
GB 1968 101m Technicolor
Columbia / Martin Manulis

Two half-brothers plan to rob their millionaire father.
Would-be with-it caper film, all flashy fragments and pop art, like sitting through a feature-length commercial. Exasperating.

w Donald Cammell, Harry Joe Brown Jnr *d* Robert Parrish *ph* Otto Heller *m* Ernie Freeman

James Coburn, James Mason, James Fox, Susannah York, John Alderton, Guy Deghy, Tutte Lemkow, Carl Duering, Marne Maitland

Duffy of San Quentin
US 1953 78m bw
Allied Artists (Berman Swarttz, Walter Doniger)
GB title: *Men Behind Bars*

An elderly warden institutes prison reforms which cause him problems.
Semi-true melodrama with standard excitements and too much talk.

wd Walter Doniger *ph* John Alton *m* Paul Dunlap

Paul Kelly, Louis Hayward, Maureen O'Sullivan, Joanne Dru, George Macready, Horace MacMahon

Duffy's Tavern
US 1945 97m bw
Paramount (Danny Dare)

The owner of a bar is helped by Hollywood stars.
Flat comedy based on a radio show and not helped by dismal guest star appearances.

w Melvin Frank, Norman Panama *d* Hal Walker *ph* Lionel Lindon *m* Robert Emmet Dolan

Ed Gardner, Victor Moore, Marjorie Reynolds, Barry Sullivan and guests including Bing Crosby, Bob Hope, Betty Hutton, Alan Ladd, Dorothy Lamour, Veronica Lake, William Bendix, Joan Caulfield

'Two thousand men and a girl!'

The Duke of West Point*
US 1938 112m bw
Edward Small

An extrovert army cadet finds the going tough. Dated romantic flagwaver which pleased at the time.

w George Bruce *d* Alfred E. Green *ph* Robert Planck

Louis Hayward, Joan Fontaine, Tom Brown, Richard Carlson, Alan Curtis, Donald Barry, Gaylord Pendleton, Jed Prouty, Marjorie Gateson

'Fairly good entertainment. Much human interest, but the comedy relief is rather light.'—*Variety*

The Duke Wore Jeans
GB 1958 89m bw

An aristocrat persuades his cockney double to woo a princess on his behalf. Moderately lively comedy with songs, tailored for Britain's new musical star. Tommy Steele, June Laverick, Michael Medwin, Alan Wheatley, Eric Pohlmann. Written by Norman Hudis; directed by Gerald Thomas; for Peter Rogers / Insignia.

Dulcima
GB 1971 98m Technicolor
EMI (Basil Rayburn)

A farmer's daughter reluctantly moves in with a persistent, lecherous old miser.
Weird sex melodrama from *Cold Comfort Farm* country, more risible than interesting.

wd Frank Nesbitt, *story* H. E. Bates *ph* Tony Imi *m* Johnny Douglas

John Mills, Carol White, Stuart Wilson, Bernard Lee, Dudley Foster

Dumb Dicks
US 1986 90m Telecolor

Incompetent private eyes become involved with feuding Italian families. Uninteresting location comedy with a title that suits its style. David Landsberg, Lorin Dreyfuss, Christian De Sica, Valeria Golino. Written by Landsberg and Dreyfuss; directed by Filippo Ottoni; for Cannon.

Dumbo****
US 1941 64m Technicolor
Walt Disney

A baby circus elephant finds that his big ears have a use after all.
Delightful cartoon feature notable for set pieces such as the drunken nightmare and the crows' song.

w various *d* Ben Sharpsteen *m* Frank Churchill, Oliver Wallace

AA: music
AAN: song, 'Baby Mine' (*m* Frank Churchill, *ly* Ned Washington)

The Dummy Talks
GB 1943 85m bw

A ventriloquist turns to blackmail and is murdered backstage. Curious, oddly cast murder mystery, not unentertaining at the time. Jack Warner, Claude Hulbert, Beryl Orde, G. H. Mulcaster, Ivy Benson, Manning Whiley. Written by Michael Barringer; directed by Oswald Mitchell; for British National.

Dune
US 1984 140m Technicolor Todd-AO
Dino de Laurentiis (Raffaella de Laurentiis)

Armies from several planets descend on another which has valuable spice guarded by monster worms.
A basically simple space fiction plot is immensely complicated by a welter of characters who are not properly introduced and who indeed are mostly irrelevant. The result, which cost nearly 50 million dollars, is inaudible, invisible (because of dim lighting) and unentertaining: a disaster of the very first order.

w,d David Lynch, *novel* Frank Herbert *ph* Freddie Francis *m* Toto *pd* Anthony Masters *ed* Antony Gibbs

Francesca Annis, Jose Ferrer, Sian Phillips, Brad Dourif, Dean Stockwell, Freddie Jones, Linda Hunt, Kenneth McMillan, Richard Jordan, Kyle MacLachlan, Silvana Mangano, Jurgen Prochnow, Max Von Sydow, Sting

'Huge, hollow, imaginative and cold.'—*Variety*

'This movie is a real mess, an incomprehensible, ugly, unstructured, pointless excursion into the murkier realms of one of the most confusing screenplays of all time.'—*Roger Ebert*

Dunkirk**
GB 1958 135m bw
MGM / Ealing (Michael Balcon)

In 1940 on the Normandy beaches, a small group gets detached from the main force.
Sober, small-scale approach to an epic subject; interesting but not inspiring, with performances to match.

w W. P. Lipscomb, David Divine *d* Leslie Norman *ph* Paul Beeson *m* Malcolm Arnold

John Mills, Richard Attenborough, Bernard Lee, Robert Urquhart, Ray Jackson

'Men invoke its horror! Women invite its shame!'

The Dunwich Horror*
US 1970 90m Movielab
AIP (Roger Corman, Jack Bohrer)

A young warlock plans to use his girl friend in a fertility rite.
Bookish horror story, quite well done against a village background.

w Curtis Lee Hanson, Henry Rosenbaum, Ronald Silkosky, *story* H. P. Lovecraft *d* *Daniel Haller* *ph* Richard C. Glouner *m* Les Baxter

Dean Stockwell, Sandra Dee, Ed Begley, Sam Jaffe, Lloyd Bochner

Duped Till Doomsday*
East Germany 1957 97m bw
DEFA (Adolf Fischer)
original title: *Betrogen bis zum Jungsten Tag*

Three Nazi NCOs go to the bad.
Propagandist anti-Nazi war melodrama, very well made in parts.

w Kurt Bortfeldt, *novel* Kameraden by Franz Fuhmann *d* Kurt Jung-Alsen *ph* Walter Fehdmer

Wolfgang Kieling, Rudolph Ulrich, Hans-Joachim Martens

During One Night
GB 1961 80m bw

During World War II, a country girl helps a USAAF deserter dispel his fear of impotence. Glum sex drama, a curious and unsuccessful attempt. Don Borisenko, Susan Hampshire, Sean Sullivan, Joy Webster. Written and directed by Sidney J. Furie; for Galaworldfilm.

Dust
Belgium / France 1985 87m Fujicolor

On an isolated South African farm, a girl murders her adulterous father. Doomladen saga redeemed by strong pictorial style. Jane Birkin, Trevor Howard, John Matshikiza. Written and directed by Marion Hansel, from *In the Heart of the Country* by J. M. Coetzee; for Mans / Daska / Flach / FR3.

Dust Be My Destiny*
US 1939 88m bw
Warner (Lou Edelman)

A young misfit tries to find himself in the country.
Dated but well made social melodrama.

w Robert Rossen, *story* Jerome Odlum *d* Lewis Seiler *ph* James Wong Howe *m* Max Steiner

John Garfield, Priscilla Lane, Alan Hale, Frank McHugh, John Litel, Charles Grapewin, Billy Halop, Bobby Jordan, Stanley Ridges

'Strong programmer, though overlong and episodic.'—*Variety*

'You can tell from the title that John Garfield has his usual part—the angry, bitter, tough poor young man with slight persecution mania.'—*Richard Mallett, Punch*

† Remade 1942 as *I Was Framed*, with Michael Ames.

Dusty Ermine
GB 1938 74m bw

Scotland Yard chases counterfeiters to Switzerland, and the hunt ends in a ski chase. Modestly effective melodrama with dated romantic leads. Jane Baxter, Anthony Bushell, Ronald Squire, Margaret Rutherford, Athole Stewart, Katie Johnson, Austin Trevor, Felix Aylmer. Written by Paul Hervey Fox from a play by Neil Grant; directed by Bernard Vorhaus; for Julius Hagen/Twickenham. 'The humour is of the British kind—not too hilarious but still tickling.'—*Variety* (US title: *Hideout in the Alps.*)

Dutchman*
GB 1966 56m bw
Gene Persson

On a New York subway train a woman humiliates a black man and finally knifes him. An allegory for addicts who can ferret out the meaning; on the surface, vaguely Pinterish and mainly boring.

w LeRoi Jones, from his play *d* Anthony Harvey *ph* Gerry Turpin *m* John Barry

Shirley Knight, Al Freeman Jnr

Dynamite**
US 1929 129m bw
MGM (Cecil B. de Mille)

In order to gain an inheritance, a socialite marries a man about to be executed . . . but he is reprieved.
Dated but still dynamic social melodrama of the early talkie period.

w Jeanie Macpherson *d* Cecil B. de Mille *ph* Peverell Marley *m* Herbert Stothart

Kay Johnson, Charles Bickford, Conrad Nagel, Julia Faye, Joel McCrea

'A pot-pourri of all previous de Mille efforts crammed into one picture.'—*Variety*

'Exuberant, wonderfully vigorous, the film skilfully evokes the look and character of the Jazz Age.'—*Charles Higham*

'An astonishing mixture, with artificiality vying with realism and comedy hanging on the heels of grim melodrama.'—*Mordaunt Hall, New York Times*

E.T.***
US 1982 115m De Luxe
Universal (Steven Spielberg, Kathleen Kennedy)

When an alien spacecraft is disturbed in a Los Angeles suburb, one of its crew members is left behind and befriended by a small boy. Stupefyingly successful box office fairy tale by the current wonder kid Spielberg, taken to the world's heart because he dares to make films without sex, violence or bad language. This one could hardly be simpler, but it works; and the ailing cinema would love to know how to repeat the trick several times a year.

w Melissa Mathison d Steven Spielberg ph Allen Daviau *m John Williams pd* James D. Bissell *creator of E.T. Carlo Rimbaldi*

Dee Wallace, Henry Thomas, Peter Coyote, Robert MacNaughton, Drew Barrymore, K. C. Martel
† E.T. = extra-terrestrial.
AA: visual effects; music; sound
AAN: best picture; direction; original screenplay; cinematography; editing
BFA: best score

Each Dawn I Die*
US 1939 84m bw
Warner (David Lewis)

A crusading reporter is framed for manslaughter and becomes a hardened prisoner.
Efficient, vigorous yet slightly disappointing star vehicle; the talents are in the right background, but the script is wobbly.

w Norman Reilly Raine, Warren Duff, Charles Perry, *novel* Jerome Odlum *d* William Keighley *ph* Arthur Edeson *m* Max Steiner *ad* William Cameron Menzies

James Cagney, George Raft, Jane Bryan, George Bancroft, Maxie Rosenbloom, Stanley Ridges, Alan Baxter, Victor Jory

'Rich in horror and brutality.'—*New York Sunday Mirror*

'In addition to its crackling screenplay, it is made memorable by the easy mastery of its two principals.'—*Time*

'Towards the end of the thirties Warners underworld pictures began to get hazy and high-minded, and in this one the pre-Second World War spiritual irradiation blurs the conventions of the prison genre.'—*Pauline Kael, 70s*

† Original title: *Killer Meets Killer*.

Eadie was a Lady
US 1945 80m bw

An upper-crust co-ed leads a double night life as a burlesque dancer. Modestly effective minor musical. Ann Miller, Joe Besser, William Wright, Jeff Donnell. Written by Monte Brice; directed by Arthur Dreifuss; for Michael Kraike / Columbia.

The Eagle**
US 1925 80m approx (24 fps) bw silent
(United Artists) Joseph M. Schenck

A Cossack lieutenant turns masked outlaw when his father's lands are annexed.
Enjoyable romp in the wake of Robin Hood, the Scarlet Pimpernel and Zorro; the eye-flashing star is somewhere near his best.

w Hans Kraly, *story* Dubrowsky by Alexander Pushkin *d Clarence Brown ph George Barnes*

Rudolph Valentino, Vilma Banky, Louise Dresser

The Eagle and the Hawk**
US 1933 72m bw
Paramount

In 1918 France, two American army fliers dislike each other but come together before the death of one of them.
Dawn Patrol melodrama, well done with unusually vivid dialogue and acting.

w Bogart Rogers, Seton I. Miller, *story* John Monk Saunders *d* Stuart Walker *ph* Harry Fischbeck

Fredric March, Cary Grant, Carole Lombard, Sir Guy Standing, Jack Oakie, Forrester Harvey

'Will make good with those it attracts, but is handicapped by the mass of earlier flight pictures.'—*Variety*

The Eagle and the Hawk
US 1949 86m bw
(Paramount) Pine-Thomas

During the Mexican wars, a US government agent tracks down a traitor who is supplying arms to the rebel Juarez.
Stolid adventure yarn, energetically played.

w Geoffrey Homes, Lewis R. Foster *d* Lewis R. Foster *ph* James Wong Howe *m* David Chudnow

John Payne, Dennis O'Keefe, Rhonda Fleming, Thomas Gomez, Fred Clark, Frank Faylen, Eduardo Noriega

The Eagle Has Landed*
GB 1976 135m Eastmancolor Panavision
ITC / Associated General (Jack Wiener, David Niven Jnr)

During World War II, enemy aliens infiltrate an English village in the hope of killing Churchill.
Elaborately plotted but uninvolving spy melodrama, lethargically directed, muddily coloured and too concerned to create some good Germans.

w Tom Mankiewicz, *novel* Jack Higgins *d* John Sturges *ph* Anthony Richmond *m* Lalo Schifrin

Michael Caine, Donald Sutherland, Robert Duvall, Jenny Agutter, Donald Pleasence, Anthony Quayle, Jean Marsh, Sven-Bertil Taube, John Standing, Judy Geeson, Larry Hagman, Maurice Roeves

Eagle in a Cage*
GB 1970 103m Eastmancolor
Group W / Ramona (Millard Lampell, Albert Schwarz)

In 1815, a professional soldier becomes governor of St Helena and jailer to Napoleon. Talkative, anecdotal, heavily serious historical reconstruction with good acting but little control.

w Millard Lampell *d* Fielder Cook *ph* Frano Vodopivec *m* Marc Wilkinson

John Gielgud, Ralph Richardson, Kenneth Haigh, Billie Whitelaw, Moses Gunn, Ferdy Mayne, Lee Montague

Eagle Squadron
US 1942 102m bw
Universal (Walter Wanger)

During World War II, American fliers join the RAF.
Studio-bound air epic, leavened with conventional romance but little humour or sympathy.

w Norman Reilly Raine, *story* C. S. Forester *d* Arthur Lubin *ph* Stanley Cortez *m* Frank Skinner

Robert Stack, Diana Barrymore, John Loder, Eddie Albert, Nigel Bruce, Leif Erickson, Edgar Barrier, Jon Hall, Evelyn Ankers, Isobel Elsom, Alan Hale Jnr, Don Porter, Frederick Worlock, Gladys Cooper

Eagle's Wing
GB 1979 111m Eastmancolor Panavision
Rank / Peter Shaw (Ben Arbeid)

A Comanche chief pursues a white man who has stolen a prize Indian horse.
Would-be poetic western which emerges as very pretty but stultifyingly dull; an odd thing indeed to come from a moribund British studio.

w John Briley *d* Anthony Harvey *ph Billy Williams m* Marc Wilkinson *pd* Herbert Westbrook

Martin Sheen, Sam Waterston, Harvey Keitel, Stephane Audran, John Castle

Earl Carroll Sketchbook
US 1946 90m bw

A songwriter gives up and sells radio jingles. Modest follow-up to *Earl Carroll Vanities*, a background for half-a-dozen songs. Constance Moore, William Marshall, Bill Goodwin, Edward Everett Horton, Vera Vague, Johnny Coy, Hillary Brooke. Written by Frank Gill Jnr and Parke Levy; directed by Albert S. Rogell; for Republic. (GB title: *Hats Off to Rhythm*.)

Earl Carroll Vanities
US 1945 91m bw
Republic (Albert J. Cohen)

A Ruritanian princess in need of a loan becomes the singing star of a New York night club.
Nit-witted musical with no style but an engaging cast.

w Frank Gill Jnr *d* Joseph Santley *ph* Jack Marta *md* Walter Scharf *songs* Walter Kent, Kim Gannon

Constance Moore, Dennis O'Keefe, Alan Mowbray, Eve Arden, Otto Kruger (as Earl Carroll), Pinky Lee, Mary Forbes, Stephanie Bachelor, Parkyakarkus, Leon Belasco, Robert Greig

AAN: song 'Endlessly' (*ly* Kim Gannon, *m* Walter Kent)

The Earl of Chicago*
US 1939 87m bw
MGM (Victor Saville)

An American gangster accedes to an English earldom but is tried for murder.
Unusual but unsatisfactory comedy-drama which rambles to a dismal conclusion but has entertaining passages.

w Lesser Samuels, *novel* Brock Williams *d* Richard Thorpe *ph* Ray June *m* Werner Heymann

Robert Montgomery, Edward Arnold, Reginald Owen, Edmund Gwenn

† This had been planned as a British production, but the war intervened.

The Early Bird
GB 1965 98m Eastmancolor
Rank / Hugh Stewart

A milkman gets involved in an inter-company war.
Star farcical comedy; not the worst of Wisdom, but overlong and mainly uninventive.

w Jack Davies, Norman Wisdom, Eddie Leslie, Henry Blyth *d* Robert Asher *ph* Jack Asher *m* Ron Goodwin

Norman Wisdom, Edward Chapman, Jerry Desmonde, Paddie O'Neil, Bryan Pringle, Richard Vernon, John Le Mesurier, Peter Jeffrey

Early to Bed
US 1928 20m bw silent

Stan becomes Ollie's butler but rebels when his friend's fortune goes to his head. One of the most untypical and seldom seen Laurel and Hardy comedies, with both stars prankishly out of characters. On its own account however it is mainly very funny. Written by H. M. Walker; directed by Emmett Flynn; for Hal Roach.

Earth***
USSR 1930 63m approx (24 fps) bw silent
VUFKU
original title: *Zemlya*

Trouble results in a Ukrainian village when a landowner refuses to hand over his land for a collective farm.
The melodramatic little plot takes second place to lyrical sequences of rustic beauty, illustrating life, love and death in the countryside.

wd, ed Alexander Dovzhenko ph Danylo Demutsky

Semyon Svashenko, Stephan Shkurat, Mikola Nademsky, Yelena Maximova

'Stories in themselves do not interest me. I choose them in order to get the greatest expression of essential social forms.'—*Dovzhenko*

'A picture for filmgoers who are prepared to take their cinema as seriously as Tolstoy took the novel.'—*James Agate*

Earth Versus the Flying Saucers
US 1956 83m bw

Saucermen from another planet try to disintegrate the earth. Elementary science fiction with special effects in a similar if enthusiastic vein. Hugh Marlowe, Joan Taylor, Donald Curtis, Morris Ankrum. Written by George Worthing Yates and Raymond T. Marcus, from a story by Curt Siodmak; directed by Fred F. Sears; special effects by *Ray Harryhausen*; for Charles H. Schneer / Columbia.

Earthbound*
US 1940 67m bw

The ghost of a murdered man helps his widow to bring the murderer to justice. Curious attempt at *Topper* without laughs, nicely done once you get used to the idea. Warner Baxter, Lynn Bari, Andrea Leeds, Charles Grapewin, Henry Wilcoxon, Elizabeth Patterson. Written by John Howard Lawson and Samuel Engel, from a story by Basil King; directed by Irving Pichel; for Sol M. Wurtzel / TCF.

Earthquake*
US 1974 123m Technicolor Panavision
Universal / Jennings Lang / Mark Robson

Various personal stories intertwine in a Los Angeles earthquake.
Dreary drama with very variable special effects, gimmicked up by Sensurround. A box office bonanza.

w George Fox, Mario Puzo *d* Mark Robson *ph* Philip Lathrop *m* John Williams *pd* Alexander Golitzen *sp* Albert Whitlock

Charlton Heston, Ava Gardner, Lorne Greene, Marjoe Gortner, Barry Sullivan, George Kennedy, Richard Roundtree, Geneviève Bujold, Walter Matthau (under the alias of his real name)

'The picture is swell, but it isn't a cheat. It's an entertaining marathon of Grade A destruction effects, with B-picture stock characters spinning through it.'—*Pauline Kael*

AAN: Philip Lathrop

Earthworm Tractors
US 1936 69m bw

A salesman whose fiancée wants him to think big turns to tractors. One of the star's livelier comedies. *Joe E. Brown*, June Travis, Guy Kibbee, Dick Foran. Written by Richard Macauley, Joe Traub and Hugh Cummings; directed by Ray Enright; for Warner. (GB title: *A Natural Born Salesman*.)

'The frank fearless drama of a woman who sinned!'

The Easiest Way
US 1931 86m bw
MGM

A hard-working slum girl falls into the lap of luxury but her easy virtue finally causes her to be rejected.
Familiar moral melodrama which got past the Hays Office only after some heavy deletions.

w Edith Ellis, *play* Eugene Walter *d* Jack Conway *ph* John Mescall

Constance Bennett, Robert Montgomery, Adolphe Menjou, Anita Page, Marjorie Rambeau, J. Farrell MacDonald, Clark Gable, Clara Blandick

'Gilded wickedness played by flawless cast: will entice.'—*Variety*

East Is West
US 1930 72m bw

Half-caste Big Time Charlie Young lords it over San Francisco's Chinatown. Muddled melodrama reminiscent of many silent films. Edward G. Robinson, Lupe Velez, Lew Ayres, Henry Kolker, Mary Forbes, Edgar Norton. Written by Tom Reed from the play by Sam Shipman and John Hymer; directed by Monta Bell; for Universal. 'Good daily change grind meller.'—*Variety*

East Lynne
US 1931 102m bw
Fox

A Victorian lady is unjustly divorced by her husband, and later loses both her lover and her sight.
Much caricatured melodrama, here presented in stolidly acceptable form.

w Bradley King, Tom Barry, *novel* Mrs Henry Wood *d* Frank Lloyd *ph* John Seitz *m* Richard Fall

Ann Harding, Clive Brook, O. P. Heggie, Conrad Nagel, Cecilia Loftus, Beryl Mercer, Flora Sheffield

'A lavish production, some corking direction, and the elemental appeal of all dramatic hokum.'—*Variety*

† Previous versions had been made by Fox, in 1916 with Theda Bara and in 1925 with Alma Rubens.

AAN: best picture

East Lynne on the Western Front
GB 1931 85m bw

War rookies produce *East Lynne* to relieve boredom. Slapstick army farce which tickled a few fancies at the time.
Herbert Mundin, Wilfred Lawson, Mark Daly, Harold French. Written by Donovan Parsons, Mary Parsons; directed by George Pearson; for Gaumont-Welsh-Pearson. 'Recording is not good and the production shoddy, but it's crammed with hoke and will do good business for juvenile matinées and in the neighbourhoods.'–*Variety*

East Meets West
GB 1936 74m bw

A proud sultan learns that his son is having an affair with the wife of a crook. Derivative star vehicle, very stagey even then. George Arliss, Godfrey Tearle, Lucie Mannheim, Romney Brent, Ballard Berkeley, John Laurie. Written by Maude Howell, from Edwin Greenwood's play *The Lake of Life*; directed by Herbert Mason; for Gaumont.

'Of what a boy did . . . what a girl did . . . of ecstasy and revenge!'
'The most shocking revenge a girl ever let one brother take on another!'

East of Eden**
US 1955 115m Warnercolor Cinemascope
Warner (Elia Kazan)

In a California farming valley in 1917 a wild adolescent rebels against his stern father and discovers that his mother, believed dead, runs a nearby brothel.
Turgid elaboration of Genesis with strong character but nowhere to go. Heavily over-directed and rousingly acted.

w Paul Osborn, *novel* John Steinbeck *d Elia Kazan* *ph* Ted McCord *m* Leonard Rosenman *ad* James Basevi, Malcolm Bert

Raymond Massey, James Dean (his first star role), Julie Harris, Dick Davalos, *Jo Van Fleet*, Burl Ives, Albert Dekker

'The first distinguished production in Cinemascope.'—*Eugene Archer*

AA: Jo Van Fleet
AAN: Paul Osborn; Elia Kazan; James Dean

East of Elephant Rock
GB 1976 92m colour
Boyd's Company / Kendon (Don Boyd)

In 1948 Malaya a womanizing civil servant is shot by his jealous mistress.
Style-less and quite uncredited re-hash of *The Letter*, striving vainly to recreate the spirit of Somerset Maugham.

wd Don Boyd *ph* Keith Goddard *m* Peter Skellern

Judi Bowker, Jeremy Kemp, John Hurt, Christopher Cazenove, Anton Rodgers, Vajira, Tariq Yunus

'Punishingly inept in every department.'—*David Badder, MFB*

East of Java
US 1935 72m bw

After a shipwreck, menagerie animals take refuge along with the passengers on a tropic island. The synopsis says it all; the production is sub-standard. Charles Bickford, Elizabeth Young, Frank Albertson, Sig Rumann. Written by James Ashmore, Sam Creelman and Paul Perez, from the story 'Tiger Island' by Goeverneur Morris; directed by George Melford; for Universal. 'Highly thrilling, weak on names.'—*Variety*

East of Piccadilly
GB 1940 79m bw
ABPC (Walter C. Mycroft)
US title: *The Strangler*

A novelist and a girl reporter catch a silk stocking murderer.
Adequate lower case mystery with good atmosphere.

w Lesley Storm, J. Lee-Thomson, *novel* Gordon Beckles *d* Harold Huth *ph* Claude Friese-Greene

Sebastian Shaw, Judy Campbell, Henry Edwards, Niall MacGinnis, George Pughe, Martita Hunt, George Hayes, Cameron Hall, Edana Romney

East of Sudan
GB 1964 94m Techniscope
Columbia / Ameran (Charles H. Schneer)

A trooper, a governess and others escape downriver from one of General Gordon's outposts.
Shameless borrowing of plot from *The African Queen* and footage from *The Four Feathers*. The purest hokum.

w Jud Kinberg *d* Nathan Juran *ph* Wilkie Cooper *m* Laurie Johnson

Anthony Quayle, Sylvia Syms, Jenny Agutter.

'Nathan Juran could direct this kind of thing blindfold, and for once would appear to have done so.'—*MFB*

East of Sumatra*
US 1953 82m Technicolor
U-I (Albert J. Cohen)

A mining engineer has trouble with the ruthless chief of a Pacific island.
A good example of routine Hollywood hokum, efficiently staged and acted.

w Frank Gill Jnr from novel by Louis L'Amour *d Budd Boetticher* *ph* Clifford Stine *md* Joseph Gershenson

Jeff Chandler, Anthony Quinn, Marilyn Maxwell, John Sutton

East of the River
US 1940 73m bw

A young gangster and his respectable brother both love the same girl. Tedious formula melodrama in a studio New York. John Garfield, William Lundigan, Brenda Marshall, Marjorie Rambeau, George Tobias. Written by Fred Niblo Jnr; directed by Alfred E. Green; for Warner.

East Side of Heaven
US 1939 85m bw

A singing taxi driver looks after an abandoned baby. Modestly pleasing comedy with music and sentiment; Baby Sandy subsequently starred in her own series. Bing Crosby, Joan Blondell, Mischa Auer, C. Aubrey Smith, Irene Hervey. Written by William Consetman; directed by David Butler; for Universal. 'A grand package of entertainment that will play a merry tune at the b.o.'—*Variety*

The East Side Kids
US 1940 62m bw

Street kids reform after helping to catch counterfeiters. See entry for *The Dead End Kids*; this is the first attempt at a splinter group, and one that did not suggest longevity. Leon Ames, Dave O'Brien, Joyce Bryant; and Hally Chester (later Hal E. Chester, producer), Harris Burger, Frankie Burke, Donald Haines, David Durand. Written by Robert Lively; directed by Bob Hill; for Sam Katzman / Monogram. 'An absurdly poor picture that will command little interest even from the vast army of Dead End Kids devotees.'—*Variety*

East Side West Side*
US 1949 108m bw
MGM (Voldemar Veltuguin)

A New York businessman is torn between his wife and another woman.
High class soap opera with all the production stops pulled out; generally well acted and reasonably entertaining.

w Isobel Lennart, *novel* Marcia Davenport *d* Mervyn Le Roy *ph* Charles Rosher *m* Miklos Rozsa

James Mason, Barbara Stanwyck, Van Heflin, Ava Gardner, *Gale Sondergaard*, Cyd Charisse, Nancy Davis, William Conrad

'No company is quite so adept as MGM at presenting basically uninteresting material with such style, and such a strong cast, that it cannot fail to entertain.'—*Penelope Houston*

Easter Parade**
US 1948 109m Technicolor
MGM (Arthur Freed)

A song and dance man quarrels with one partner but finds another.
A musical which exists only in its numbers, which are many but variable. All in all, an agreeable lightweight entertainment without the style to put it in the top class.

w Sidney Sheldon, Frances Goodrich, Albert Hackett *d* Charles Walters *ph* Harry Stradling *m / ly Irving Berlin* *md* Roger Edens, Johnny Green

Fred Astaire, Judy Garland, Ann Miller, Peter Lawford, Clinton Sundberg, Jules Munshin

'The important thing is that Fred Astaire is back, with Irving Berlin calling the tunes.'—*Newsweek*

† Fred Astaire was actually second choice, replacing Gene Kelly who damaged an ankle.

AA: Roger Edens, Johnny Green

Easy Come, Easy Go
US 1947 78m bw
Paramount (Kenneth MacGowan)

An old Irishman gambles away the money his daughter earns.
Whimsical sentimental comedy with an unattractive central character.

w Francis Edward Faragoh, John McNulty, Anne Froelich *d* John Farrow *ph* Daniel L. Fapp *m* Roy Webb

Barry Fitzgerald, Diana Lynn, Sonny Tufts, Dick Foran, Frank McHugh, Allen Jenkins, John Litel, Arthur Shields

Easy Come, Easy Go
US 1966 97m Technicolor
(Paramount) Wallis-Hazen

A frogman tries to salvage a treasure from a wreck off the Californian coast.
Empty-headed star vehicle, almost indistinguishable from many of the others.

w Allan Weiss, Anthony Lawrence *d* John Rich *ph* William Margulies *m* Joseph J. Lilley

Elvis Presley, Dodie Marshall, Pat Priest, Pat Harrington, Skip Ward, Frank McHugh, Elsa Lanchester

'Where there's smoke, there must be somebody smoking!'

Easy Living**
US 1937 91m bw
Paramount (Arthur Hornblow Jnr)

A fur coat is thrown out of a window and lands on a typist . . .
Amusing romantic comedy with farcical trimmings; it now stands among the semi-classic crazy comedies of the thirties.

w Preston Sturges d Mitchell Leisen ph Ted Tetzlaff *md* Boris Morros

Jean Arthur, Ray Milland, *Edward Arnold*, Luis Alberni, Mary Nash, Franklin Pangborn, William Demarest, Andrew Tombes

'Slapstick farce which does not fulfil the box office possibilities of its stars.'—*Variety*

'Secretaries, millionaires, jokes, sight gags, furies, attacks of cool sense—there are always three things going on at once.'—*New Yorker, 1977*

Easy Living
US 1949 77m bw
RKO (Robert Sparks)

An ageing football star wants to retire but has to satisfy the living standards of his ambitious wife.
Dim drama.

w Charles Schnee, *story* Irwin Shaw
d Jacques Tourneur *ph* Harry J. Wild *m* Roy Webb

Victor Mature, Lucille Ball, Lizabeth Scott, Sonny Tufts, Lloyd Nolan, Paul Stewart, Jack Paar, Jeff Donnell

Easy Money
GB 1948 93m bw
GFD / Gainsborough (A. Frank Bundy)

Four people win big prizes on the football pools.
Short story compendium; very average.

w Muriel and Sydney Box, *play* Arnold Ridley *d* Bernard Knowles *m* Temple Abady *ph* Jack Asher

Edward Rigby, Greta Gynt, Dennis Price, Jack Warner, Mervyn Johns, Petula Clark, Marjorie Fielding, Bill Owen, Raymond Lovell

Easy Money
US 1983 100m bw

A baby photographer is left a fortune provided that he totally reforms. Overlong and increasingly feeble comedy with a star who quickly outstays his welcome. Rodney Dangerfield, Joe Pesci, Geraldine Fitzgerald, Candy Azzara, Val Avery. Written by Dangerfield, Michael Endler, P. J. O'Rourke, Dennis Blair; directed by James Signorelli; for Orion.

'A man went looking for America and couldn't find it anywhere!'

Easy Rider***
US 1969 94m Technicolor
Columbia / Pando / Raybert (Peter Fonda)

Two drop-outs ride across America on motorcycles.
Happening to please hippies and motor-cycle enthusiasts as well as amateur politicians, this oddball melodrama drew freakishly large audiences throughout the world and was much imitated though never equalled in its casual effectiveness, nor did promising careers ensue for the actors mainly concerned.

w Peter Fonda, Dennis Hopper, Terry Southern *d* Dennis Hopper *ph* Laszlo Kovacs *m* various recordings

Peter Fonda, Dennis Hopper, *Jack Nicholson*

'*Cinéma-vérité* in allegory terms.'—*Peter Fonda*

'Ninety-four minutes of what it is like to swing, to watch, to be fond, to hold opinions and to get killed in America at this moment.'—*Penelope Gilliatt*

AAN: script; Jack Nicholson

Easy Street****
US 1917 22m approx bw silent
Mutual / Charles Chaplin

In a slum street, a tramp is reformed by a dewy-eyed missionary, becomes a policeman, and tames the local bully.
Quintessential Chaplin, combining sentimentality and social comment with hilarious slapstick.

wd Charles Chaplin ph William C. Foster, Rollie Totheroh

Charles Chaplin, Edna Purviance, Albert Austin, Eric Campbell

Easy to Love*
US 1933 62m bw

A pair of couples get into a romantic mix-up. Innocent predecessor of *Bob and Carol and Ted and Alice*; come to think of it, quite sophisticated for its year. Adolphe Menjou, Genevieve Tobin, Mary Astor, Edward Everett Horton, Guy Kibbee, Patricia Ellis, Hugh Herbert. Written by Carl Erickson and Manuel Seff from a play by Thompson Buchanan; directed by William Keighley; for Warners. 'Adaptation, direction and able performances make an old story amusing entertainment.'—*Variety*

Easy to Love
US 1953 96m Technicolor
MGM (Joe Pasternak)

The romances of an aqua-queen in Florida's Cypress Gardens.
Thin, humourless and forgettable musical vehicle sustained by spectacular water ballets.

w Laslo Vadnay, William Roberts *d* Charles Walters *ph* Ray June *md* Lennie Hayton, George Stoll; numbers staged by *Busby Berkeley*

Esther Williams, Tony Martin, Van Johnson

Easy to Wed*
US 1946 110m Technicolor
MGM (Jack Cummings)

A socialite threatens a newspaper editor with libel; he postpones his own wedding and sets a friend to compromise her.
Bright but tasteless remake of *Libelled Lady*, with a second team cast trying hard.

w Dorothy Kingsley, Maurine Watkins, Howard Emmett Rogers, George Oppenheimer *d* Edward Buzzell *ph* Harry Stradling *m* Johnny Green

Van Johnson, Esther Williams, *Lucille Ball*, Keenan Wynn, Cecil Kellaway, Carlos Ramirez, Ben Blue, Ethel Smith

Easy Virtue
GB 1927 73m (24 fps) bw silent
Gainsborough (Michael Balcon)

A drunkard's wife falls for a young man who kills himself. Her past then prevents her attempts to lead a respectable life.
Vapid social melodrama with minimal points of interest despite its credits.

w Eliot Stannard, *play* Noël Coward *d* Alfred Hitchcock *ph* Claude McDonnell *ed* Ivor Montagu

Isabel Jeans, Franklyn Dyall, Eric Bransby Williams, Ian Hunter, Violet Farebrother, Robin Irvine

Eat the Peach*
Eire 1986 95m Technicolor
Strongbow / Film Four International (David Collins)

Out-of-work Irish devise a mad scheme to construct a motorcycle Wall of Death.
Fairly amusing comedy, like an Irish version of Ealing.

w Peter Ormrod, John Kelleher *d* Peter Ormrod *ph Arthur Wooster m* Donal Lummy

Stephen Brennan, Eamon Morrissey, Catherine Byrne, Niall Toibin, Joe Lynch, Tony Doyle

Eating Raoul*
US 1982 83m Pacific Color
Bartel Film (Anne Kimmel)

A restaurateur kills a drunken swinger, and finds that he has a profitable sideline on his hands . . .
Black comedy with insufficient humour to offset tastelessness.

w Richard Blackburn, Paul Bartel *d* Paul Bartel *ph* Gary Thieltges *m* Arlon Ober

Paul Bartel, Mary Woronov, Robert Beltran, Susan Saiger, Richard Blackburn.

'I wanted to make a film about two greedy, uptight people who are at the same time not so unlike you and me and Nancy and Ronnie, to keep it funny and yet communicate something about the psychology and perversity of these values . . . My movie touches on many things: the perversion of middle class values, the resurgence of Nixonism, machismo versus WASP fastidiousness, *film noir* . . .'—*Paul Bartel*

Ebb Tide**
US 1937 92m Technicolor
Paramount (Lucien Hubbard)

Sailors are stranded with a dangerous fanatic on a South Sea island.
Interesting adaptation of Stevenson, notable both for its early colour and its genuinely sour, anti-romantic mood, almost unique for Hollywood in this period.

w Bertram Millhauser, *novel* R. L. Stevenson and Lloyd Osbourne *d* James Hogan *ph* Leo Tover *m* Victor Young

Ray Milland, Frances Farmer, Oscar Homolka, Barry Fitzgerald, Lloyd Nolan

'More pretentious as to production than dramatically. Does not suggest big b.o.'—*Variety*

† Remade 1946 as *Adventure Island*.

The Echo Murders
GB 1945 80m bw

Sexton Blake conquers Nazi spies. Feebly made addition to the short Blake cycle. David Farrar, Dennis Price, Pamela Stirling, Julien Mitchell. Written and directed by John Harlow; for British National. 'About as modern as a reissue of *The Perils of Pauline*.'—*Variety*

Echo of Barbara
GB 1958 58m bw

A stripper poses as the daughter of an ex-con in a plot to retrieve hidden loot. Taut little crime support, not bad at all. Mervyn Johns, Maureen Connel, Paul Stassino, Ronald Hines, Tom Bell. Written by John Kruse, from a novel by Jonathan Burke; directed by Sidney Hayers; for Independent Artists.

Echo Park*
Austria 1985 92m colour
Sasha Wein / Walter Shenson

In a rundown area of Los Angeles, three unsuccessful youngsters await the big break.
Vaguely entertaining slice-of-life drama with good observational touches.

w Michael Ventura *d* Robert Dornhelm *ph* Karl Kofler *m* David Rickets

Susan Dey, Thomas Hulce, Michael Bowen, Christopher Walker

Echoes of a Summer
US / Canada 1975 98m Eastmancolor
Beata / Castle / Astral / Bryanston (Robert L. Joseph)

An 11-year-old girl dying of heart disease spends her last summer with her parents on holiday in a Nova Scotian village.
Excruciating.

w Robert L. Joseph *d* Don Taylor *ph* John Coquillon *m* Terry James

Jodie Foster, Richard Harris, Lois Nettleton, Geraldine Fitzgerald, William Windom, Brad Savage

'The only honest thing about this movie is its desire to make a buck.'—*Frank Rich, New York Post*

The Eclipse*
Italy / France 1962 125m bw
Interopa-Cineriz / Paris Film (Robert and Raymond Hakim)
original title: *L'Eclisse*

A young Roman woman breaks off one affair and begins another.
A portrait in depth, rather tiresomely long and with at least one totally irrelevant stock-market sequence; but superbly done for connoisseurs.

wd Michelangelo Antonioni, Tonino Guerra, Elio Bartolini, Ottiero Ottieri *ph* Gianni di Venanzo *m* Giovanni Fusco

Monica Vitti, Alain Delon, Francisco Rabal

L'Ecole Buissonière*
France 1948 89m bw
UGC / CGCF
US title: *I Have a New Master*

At a provincial village school, a new teacher introduces new methods and takes a while to win over the locals.
Rustic comedy-drama of a kind the French do well.

w Jean-Paul Le Chanois, Elise Freinet *d* Jean-Paul Le Chanois *ph* Marc Fossard, Maurice Pecqueux, André Dumaître *m* Joseph Kosma

Bernard Blier, Juliette Fabre, Edouard Delmont

'It's big and bright as those banjo eyes!'
The Eddie Cantor Story
US 1953 116m Technicolor
Warner (Sidney Skolsky)

After a tough childhood on New York's east side, Israel Iskowitz becomes a famous entertainer.
Deliberately patterned after the success of *The Jolson Story*, this is an unhappy example of how close are success and failure; the elements are the same, but this film suffers from unsure timing, lack of humour, rather apologetic numbers, a really dismal script and a caricature performance in the lead.

w Jerome Weidman, Ted Sherdeman, Sidney Skolsky *d* Alfred E. Green *ph* Edwin DuPar *md* Ray Heindorf *songs* various *ch* Le Roy Prinz

Keefe Brasselle, Marilyn Erskine, Aline MacMahon, Arthur Franz, Alex Gerry, Gerald Mohr, William Forrest (as Ziegfeld), Will Rogers Jnr (as Will Rogers), and Eddie Cantor (who also sings the songs off screen)

Eddie Macon's Run
US 1983 95m Technicolor
Universal / Martin Bregman (Louis A. Stroller)

A man innocently convicted escapes and hotfoots it back home. Old-style chase film marred by passages of sex and crude backwoods violence.

w,d,ed Jeff Kanew, *novel* James McLendon *ph* James A. Contner *m* Norton Buffalo

John Schneider, Kirk Douglas, Lee Purcell, Leah Ayres

The Eddy Duchin Story
US 1956 123m Technicolor Cinemascope
Columbia (Jonie Taps, Jerry Wald)

The success story of a pianist who died of leukemia.
Predictable, glossy, sentimental musical biopic.

w Samuel Taylor, *original story* Leo Katcher *d* George Sidney *ph* Harry Stradling *md* George Duning *piano* Carmen Cavallero

Tyrone Power, Kim Novak, *Victoria Shaw,* James Whitmore, Shepperd Strudwick, Frieda Inescort, Gloria Holden, Larry Keating

AAN: Leo Katcher; Harry Stradling; George Duning

Edgar Wallace

Between 1960 and 1963 no fewer than 47 second features emerged from Jack Greenwood's production unit at the London suburban studios of Merton Park, under the Edgar Wallace banner and prefaced by a sinister revolving bust of the author (though few had very much to do with his original stories). All maintained a better standard than any other crime second features of the period, and a few were seized on with delight by the critics. They were subsequently popular on television, though the Independent Broadcasting Authority banned repeats on the grounds that they were without merit. In this complete list, details are given for the more interesting items:

THE CLUE OF THE TWISTED CANDLE
A MARRIAGE OF CONVENIENCE
THE MALPAS MYSTERY
THE MAN WHO WAS NOBODY

THE CLUE OF THE NEW PIN*
(*w* Philip Mackie, *d* Allan Davis, with Paul Daneman, Bernard Archard)
PARTNERS IN CRIME
THE FOURTH SQUARE
THE MAN AT THE CARLTON TOWER
THE CLUE OF THE SILVER KEY
ATTEMPT TO KILL
THE SINISTER MAN*
(*w* Philip Mackie, *d* Clive Donner, with Patrick Allen, John Bentley)
NEVER BACK LOSERS
MAN DETAINED
RICOCHET
THE DOUBLE
THE RIVALS
TO HAVE AND TO HOLD
THE PARTNER
FIVE TO ONE
ACCIDENTAL DEATH
WE SHALL SEE
DOWNFALL
THE VERDICT
WHO WAS MADDOX?*
(*w* Roger Marshall, *d* Geoffrey Nethercott, with Bernard Lee, Finlay Currie)
ACT OF MURDER*
(*w* Lewis Davidson, *d* Alan Bridges, with John Carson, Anthony Bate)
FACE OF A STRANGER
NEVER MENTION MURDER*
(*w* Robert Banks Stewart, *d* John Nelson Burton, with Maxine Audley, Dudley Foster)
THE MAIN CHANCE
GAME FOR THREE LOSERS
DEAD MAN'S CHEST
CHANGE PARTNERS
STRANGLER'S WEB*
(*w* George Baxt, *d* John Moxey, with Griffith Jones, Gerald Harper)
BACKFIRE
CANDIDATE FOR MURDER*
(*w* Lukas Heller, *d* David Villers, with Michael Gough, John Justin)
FLAT TWO
THE SHARE-OUT
NUMBER SIX
TIME TO REMEMBER
PLAYBACK*
(*w* Robert Banks Stewart, *d* John Nelson Burton, with Maxine Audley, Dudley Foster)
SOLO FOR SPARROW
LOCKER 69
DEATH TRAP
THE SET-UP
ON THE RUN
THE £20,000 KISS
INCIDENT AT MIDNIGHT
RETURN TO SENDER

Edge of Darkness*
US 1943 124m bw
Warner (Henry Blanke)

Norwegian village patriots resist the Nazis.
High-intentioned, ambitiously cast but ultimately bathetic resistance melodrama, high principled down to its tragic finale but compromised by backlot shooting and the presence of Errol Flynn.

w Robert Rossen *d* Lewis Milestone *ph* Sid Hickox *m* Franz Waxman

Errol Flynn, Ann Sheridan, Walker Huston, Judith Anderson, Ruth Gordon, Nancy Coleman, Helmut Dantine, Morris Carnovsky, Charles Dingle, John Beal, Richard Fraser, Helene Thimig

'It is not a tea party. It is an icy shower turned loose on audiences in the hope of driving home what this war is about.'—*Motion Picture Herald*

Edge of Doom
US 1950 97m bw
Samuel Goldwyn
GB title: *Stronger than Fear*

A desperate youth kills a priest and struggles with his conscience.
A sanctimonious weirdie, extremely odd coming from this producer, and unhappily re-edited before release. Someone was interested enough to want to make it, but it seems to have been killed by the cast and the front office.

w Philip Yordan, *novel* Leo Brady *d* Mark Robson *ph* Harry Stradling *m* Hugo Friedhofer

Dana Andrews, Farley Granger, Joan Evans, Robert Keith, Paul Stewart, Mala Powers, Adele Jergens, Harold Vermilyea, Mabel Paige

Edge of Eternity*
US 1959 80m Technicolor Cinemascope
Columbia / Thunderbird (Kendrick Sweet)

A Grand Canyon sheriff traces three murders to an ownership struggle over a disused mine.
Routine but suspenseful thriller with splendid locations.

w Knut Swenson, Richard Collins *d Don Siegel ph Burnett Guffey m* Daniele Amfitheatrof

Cornel Wilde, Victoria Shaw, Edgar Buchanan, Mickey Shaughnessy, Jack Elam

Edge of Hell
US 1956 76m bw

In a slummy rooming house, a beggar who lives by his dog's talents falls for the new lodger. Self-parodying sub-Jannings melodrama with an unlikely star. Hugo Haas, Francesca de Scaffa, Ken Carlton, June Hammerstein. Written, directed and produced by Hugo Haas; for Universal-International.

Edge of the City**
US 1957 85m bw
MGM / Jonathan (David Susskind, Jim di Ganci)
GB title: *A Man is Ten Feet Tall*

Racial tensions lead to tragedy in the railroad yards of New York's waterfront.
Tense, brutal melodrama, which has historical interest as an effective opening-up in cinematic terms of a TV play, in its imitation of *On the Waterfront*, and in its rebel hero and relaxed black friend.

w Robert Alan Arthur, from his play *d Martin Ritt ph* Joseph Brun *m* Leonard Rosenman

Sidney Poitier, John Cassavetes, Jack Warden, Kathleen Maguire, Ruby Dee, Robert Simon, Ruth White

Edge of the World**
GB 1937 80m bw
GFD / Rock (Joe Rock)

Life, love and death on Foula, a remote Shetland island.
Rare for its time, a vigorous location drama in the Flaherty tradition; sometimes naïve, usually exhilarating.

wd Michael Powell ph Ernest Palmer and others *m* Lambert Williamson

Niall MacGinnis, Belle Chrystal, John Laurie, Finlay Currie, Eric Berry

'Scant of plot and unlikely to be hailed by the public at large.'—*Variety*

'The love of a woman . . . the courage of a fighting America . . . lifted him from obscurity to thrilling fame!'

Edison the Man**
US 1940 107m bw
MGM (John W. Considine Jnr)

Edison struggles for years in poverty before becoming famous as the inventor of the electric light bulb.
Standard, well-made biopic following on from *Young Tom Edison*; reasonably absorbing, but slightly suspect in its facts.

w Dore Schary, Talbot Jennings, Bradbury Foote, Hugo Butler *d Clarence Brown ph* Harold Rosson *m* Herbert Stothart

Spencer Tracy, Rita Johnson, Lynne Overman, Charles Coburn, Gene Lockhart, Henry Travers, Felix Bressart

AAN: Dore Schary, Hugo Butler (original story)

Edouard et Caroline**
France 1951 99m bw
UGC / CICC

A young pianist and his wife quarrel while preparing for an important recital.
Gay, slight, charming comedy, a two-hander taking place within the course of a few hours.

w Annette Wademant, Jacques Becker d Jacques Becker ph Robert Le Fèbvre *m* Jean-Jacques Grunenwald

Daniel Gélin, Anne Vernon, Jacques François, William Tubbs, Jean Galland, Elina Labourdette, Betty Stockfield

'It lifts its weighty trivialities into a world of enchantment.'—*Sunday Times*

Educated Evans
GB 1936 86m bw

A racetrack bookie becomes a trainer. Rather unyielding vehicle for a fast-talking star. Max Miller, Nancy O'Neil, Clarice Mayne, Albert Whelan, Hal Walters. Written by Frank Launder and Robert Edmunds, from an Edgar Wallace character; directed by William Beaudine; for Warner. († A sequel followed in 1938—*Thank Evans*.)

Educating Rita*
GB 1983 110m Technicolor
Rank / Acorn (Lewis Gilbert)

A cheerful young hairdresser improves her knowledge of English Literature by enrolling on an Open University course.
Rather dismal, thinly characterized and ill-lit variation on *Pygmalion*, with endless talk leading nowhere (it was originally a two-character play). Due to its Liverpudlian modishness it achieved surprising box office success.

w Willy Russell from his play *d* Lewis Gilbert *ph* Frank Watts *m* David Hentschel

Michael Caine, Julie Walters, Michael Williams, Maureen Lipman

'If only I'd been able to believe they were actually reading the books, everything else would have fallen into place.'—*Roger Ebert*

AA: Michael Caine, Julie Walters
AAN: Willy Russell

Edvard Munch*
Norway / Sweden 1976 215m colour

The life of the 19th-century Norwegian expressionist painter. A yawn for the majority but a delight for connoisseurs of a certain kind; with a wholly non-professional cast. Geir Westby, Gro Fraas, Johan Halsborg, Lotte Teig. Written and directed by *Peter Watkins*; for New Yorker/SR.

Edward My Son
GB 1949 112m bw
MGM (Edwin H. Knopf)

A rich, unscrupulous man remembers the people he has made unhappy, and the son to whom he never behaved as a father should.
Unsatisfactory, rather ugly-looking adaptation of a gripping piece of theatre, with casting and direction remarkably uncertain from such professionals.

w Donald Ogden Stewart, *play* Robert Morley *d* George Cukor *ph* F. A. Young *m* John Woolbridge, Malcolm Sargent

Spencer Tracy, Deborah Kerr, Ian Hunter, James Donald, Leueen McGrath, Mervyn Johns

AAN: Deborah Kerr

The Effect of Gamma Rays on Man-in-the-Moon Marigolds
US 1972 101m De Luxe
Newman–Foreman

A slatternly middle-aged woman dreams of better times for herself and her children.
Well-written but essentially banal and pretentious domestic drama, the kind of film that only gets made when powerful stars see in it a juicy role.

w Alvin Sargent, *play* Paul Zendel *d* Paul Newman *ph* Adam Holender *m* Maurice Jarre

Joanne Woodward, Nell Potts, Roberta Wallach, Judith Lowry

Effi Briest*
West Germany 1974 140m bw
Tango Film (Rainer Werner Fassbinder)
original title: *Fontane Effi Briest*

A teenage girl is married to a rich baron, but fails to understand what is expected of her.
Overlong but often fascinating picture of a vanished society in which not the slightest weakening of structure is permitted.

wd Rainer Werner Fassbinder, *novel* Theodor Fontane *ph* Jürgen Jürges, Dietrich Lohmann *m* from Saint-Saens

Hanna Schygulla, Wolfgang Schenck, Ulli Lommel, Karl-Heinz Böhm, Ursula Strätz

The Egg and I*
US 1947 104m bw
U-I (Chester Erskine)

A city couple try to become gentleman farmers.
Mild, pleasant comedy notable chiefly for introducing a hillbilly couple, Ma and Pa Kettle, who went on, in the personae of Main and Kilbride, to make several later features. (See under *Kettles*.)

w Chester Erskine, Fred Finkelhoffe, *novel* Betty Macdonald *d* Chester Erskine *ph* Milton Krasner *m* Frank Skinner

Claudette Colbert, Fred MacMurray, *Marjorie Main, Percy Kilbride*, Louise Allbritton, Richard Long, Billy House, Ida Moore, Donald MacBride

'Marjorie Main, in an occasional fit of fine, wild comedy, picks the show up and brandishes it as if she were wringing its neck. I wish to God she had.'—*James Agee*

AAN: Marjorie Main

'10,965 pyramids! 5,337 dancing girls! One million swaying bulrushes! 802 sacred bulls!'

The Egyptian*
US 1954 140m De Luxe Cinemascope
TCF (Darryl F. Zanuck)

In ancient Egypt an abandoned baby grows up to be physician to the pharaoh.
More risible than reasonable, sounding more like a parody than the real thing, this pretentious epic from a bestseller flounders helplessly between its highlights but has moments of good humour and makes an excellent example of the pictures they don't make 'em like any more.

w Philip Dunne, Casey Robinson, *novel* Mika Waltari *d* Michael Curtiz *ph* Leon Shamroy *m* Bernard Herrmann, Alfred Newman *ad* Lyle Wheeler, George W. Davis

Edmund Purdom, Victor Mature, *Peter Ustinov*, Bella Darvi, Gene Tierney, Michael Wilding, Jean Simmons, Judith Evelyn, Henry Daniell, John Carradine, Carl Benton Reid

'The novel . . . supplied the reader with enough occurrences and customs of Akhnaton's time . . . to hide some of the more obvious contrivances of the story. The film does not do this.'—*Carolyn Harrow, Films in Review*

AAN: Leon Shamroy

The Eiger Sanction*
US 1975 125m Technicolor Panavision
Universal / Malpaso (Jennings Lang)

An art teacher returns to the CIA as an exterminator, and finds himself in a party climbing the Eiger.
Silly spy melodrama with some breathtaking mountain sequences.

w Warren B. Murphy, Hal Dresner, Rod Whitaker, *novel* Trevanian *d* Clint Eastwood *ph* Frank Stanley, John Cleare, Jeff Schoolfield, Peter Pilafian, Pete White *m* John Williams

Clint Eastwood, George Kennedy, Vonetta McGee, Jack Cassidy, Heidi Bruhl, Thayer David

'All the villains have been constructed from prefabricated Bond models.'—*Richard Combs*

Eight and a Half**
Italy 1963 138m bw
Cineriz (Angelo Rizzoli)
original title: *Otto e Mezzo*

A successful film director on the verge of a nervous breakdown has conflicting fantasies about his life.
A Fellini self-portrait in which anything goes. Some of it is fascinating, some not worth the trouble of sorting out.

w Federico Fellini, Ennio Flaiano, Tullio Pinelli, Brunello Rondi *d Federico Fellini* *ph* Gianni di Venanzo *m* Nino Rota *ad* Piero Gherardi

Marcello Mastroianni, Claudia Cardinale, Anouk Aimée, Sandra Milo, Rossella Falk, Barbara Steele, Madeleine Lebeau

'The whole may add up to a magnificent folly, but it is too singular, too candid, too vividly and insistently alive to be judged as being in any way diminishing.'—*Peter John Dyer, MFB*

'Fellini's intellectualizing is not even like dogs dancing; it is not done well, nor does it surprise us that it is done at all. It merely palls on us, and finally appals us.'—*John Simon*

'A de luxe glorification of creative crisis, visually arresting but in some essential way conventional-minded.'—*Pauline Kael, 70s*

AAN: best foreign film; script; direction

Eight Iron Men
US 1952 80m bw
Columbia / Stanley Kramer

In the ruins of an Italian village, eight American infantrymen wait for relief.
Quickie war film in which everyone talks a lot and they all survive; from the time when Kramer was discovering how fast he could turn 'em out.

w Harry Brown, from his play A Sound of Hunting *d* Edward Dmytryk *ph* Roy Hunt *m* Leith Stevens *pd* Rudolph Sternad

Bonar Colleano, Lee Marvin, Arthur Franz, Richard Kiley, Nick Dennis, James Griffith, Dick Moore, George Cooper

Eight O'Clock Walk
GB 1953 87m bw
British Lion / George King

A young barrister proves a taxi driver innocent of murder.
Minor-league courtroom stuff, an adequate time-passer.

w Katherine Strueby, Guy Morgan, *story* Jack Roffey, Gordon Harbord *d* Lance Comfort *ph* Brendan Stafford *m* George Melachrino

Richard Attenborough, Derek Farr, Cathy O'Donnell, Ian Hunter, Maurice Denham, Bruce Seton, Harry Welchman

Eight on the Lam
US 1966 107m De Luxe
United Artists / Hope Enterprises (Bill Lawrence)
GB title: *Eight on the Run*

A bank teller is suspected of embezzlement and goes on the run with his seven children.
Feeble comedy punctuated by even feebler chases; the star had lost his comic character.

w Albert E. Lewin, Burt Styler, Bob Fisher, Arthur Marx *d* George Marshall *ph* Alan Stensvold *m* George Romanis

Bob Hope, Phyllis Diller, Jonathan Winters, Shirley Eaton, Jill St John

Eighty Thousand Suspects*
GB 1963 113m bw Cinemascope
Rank / Val Guest

A smallpox epidemic terrorizes the city of Bath.
Predictable melodrama which adequately passes the time.

w Val Guest, *novel* Pillars of Midnight by Elleston Trevor *d* Val Guest *ph* Arthur Grant *m* Stanley Black

Claire Bloom, Richard Johnson, Yolande Donlan, Cyril Cusack, Michael Goodliffe, Mervyn Johns, Kay Walsh, Basil Dignam, Ray Barrett

84 Charing Cross Road**
GB 1986 97m Rank colour
Columbia / Brooksfilm (Geoffrey Helman)

A New York woman conducts a long correspondence with an antiquarian bookseller in London.
Pleasant picturization of a now famous book which had already been seen on TV and stage.

w Hugh Whitemore from the book by Helene Hanff *d David Jones* *ph* Brian West *m* George Fenton *pd* Eileen Diss, Edward Pisoni

Anne Bancroft, Anthony Hopkins, Judi Dench, Maurice Denham, Jean de Baer, Eleanor David

El**
Mexico 1952 91m bw
Nacional Film (Oscar Dancigers)
aka: *This Strange Passion; Torments*

A middle-aged aristocrat marries a beautiful young girl and falls victim to insane jealousy.
A tragi-comic case history with chilling and memorable details; not one of its director's great works, but an engaging minor one.

w Luis Bunuel, Luis Alcoriza, *novel* Pensamientos by Mercedes Pinto *d Luis Bunuel* *ph* Gabriel Figueroa *m* Luis Hernandez Breton

Arturo de Cordova, Delia Garces, Luis Beristain, Aurora Walker

El Cid*
US / Spain 1961 184m Super Technirama
Samuel Bronston

A legendary 11th-century hero drives the Moors from Spain.
Endless glum epic with splendid action sequences as befits the high budget.

w Frederic M. Frank, Philip Yordan *d* Anthony Mann *ph* Robert Krasker *m* Miklos Rozsa

Charlton Heston, Sophia Loren, Raf Vallone, Geraldine Page, John Fraser, Gary Raymond, Herbert Lom, Hurd Hatfield, Massimo Serato, Andrew Cruickshank, Michael Hordern, Douglas Wilmer, Frank Thring

AAN: Miklos Rozsa; song 'The Falcon and the Dove' (*m* Miklos Rozsa, *ly* Paul Francis Webster)

El Condor
US 1970 102m Technicolor
National General / Carthay Continental (André de Toth)

An escaped convict and a con man seek a fortune in gold believed to be hidden in a fortress in the Mexican desert.
Blood and guts western with few moments of interest.

w Larry Cohen, Steven Carabatsos *d* John Guillermin *ph* Henri Persin *m* Maurice Jarre

Jim Brown, Lee Van Cleef, Patrick O'Neal, Marianna Hill, Iron Eyes Cody, Elisha Cook Jnr

'The kind of fun you can find at your friendly neighbourhood abattoir.'—*Judith Crist, 1977*

'The big one with the big two!'
El Dorado*
US 1966 126m Technicolor
Paramount / Laurel (Howard Hawks)

A gunfighter and a drunken sheriff tackle a villainous cattle baron.
Easy-going, semi-somnolent, generally likeable but disappointing western . . . an old man's movie all round.

w Leigh Brackett, *novel* The Stars in their Courses by Harry Joe Brown *d* Howard Hawks *ph* Harold Rosson *m* Nelson Riddle

John Wayne, Robert Mitchum, James Caan, Charlene Holt, Michele Carey, Ed Asner, Arthur Hunnicutt, R. G. Armstrong, Paul Fix, Christopher George

'A rumbustious lament for the good days of the bad old west.'—*Tom Milne*

'A claustrophobic, careless and cliché-ridden thing, wavering constantly between campy self-deprecation and pretentious pomposity.'—*Richard Schickel*

'Wayne and Mitchum, parodying themselves while looking exhausted.'—*Pauline Kael, 70s*

El Greco
Italy / France 1964 94m Eastmancolor Cinemascope
(TCF) Artistiche Internazionale / Arco-Films du Siècle (Alfredo Bini, Mel Ferrer)

In the 16th century, a Greek-Italian painter finds favour in Spain and falls in love with an aristocratic girl.
Heavily embellished history with a few good scenes.

w Guy Elmes, Massimo Franciosa, Luigi Magni, Luciano Salce *d* Luciano Salce *ph* Leonida Barboni *m* Ennio Morricone

Mel Ferrer, Rosanna Schiaffino, Adolfo Celi, Angel Aranda

El Paso
US 1949 92m Cinecolor
Paramount / Pine–Thomas

After the civil war, a young lawyer brings a corrupt township to its senses by learning to outshoot the badmen.
Lively, fairly tough western with all the familiar ingredients.

wd Lewis R. Foster *ph* Ellis Carter *m* Darrell Calker

John Payne, Gail Russell, Dick Foran, Sterling Hayden, George 'Gabby' Hayes

El Topo*
Mexico 1971 124m Eastmancolor
Producciones Panic

An evil gunfighter rides through the old west and has various encounters, after which he sets himself on fire.
Curious, perverse, powerful surrealist allegory which takes in the life of Christ and the fate of man among some exceedingly unpleasant violence. A treat for connoisseurs of the unpleasantly absurd.

w, d, m, ad Alexandro Jodorowsky *ph* Raphael Corkidi

Alexandro Jodorowsky, Brontis Jodorowsky, Mara Lorenzio, David Silva

'He's a good cop on a big bike on a bad road!'
Electra Glide in Blue*
US 1973 113m De Luxe Panavision
UA / James William Guercio / Rupert Hitzig

A small-town motor-cycle cop becomes disillusioned.
Agreeable desert melodrama in the wake of *Easy Rider*, freshly observed with mordant humour, marred by a fashionable downbeat ending.

w Robert Boris *d / m* James William Guercio *ph Conrad Hall*

Robert Blake, Billy Green Bush, Mitch Ryan, Jeannine Riley, Elisha Cook Jnr, Royal Dana

Electric Dreams
GB 1984 112m Metrocolor
Virgin / MGM-UA (Rusty Lemorande, Larry de Waay)

A computer becomes jealous of its owner's love affair.
Gruesomely extended revue sketch which totally fails to develop its characters and offers instead a very sparing amount of cleverness.

w Rusty Lemorande *d* Steve Barron *ph* Alex Thomson *m* Giorgio Moroder *pd* Richard MacDonald

Lenny Von Dohlen, Virginia Madsen, Maxwell Caulfield, Bud Cort, Don Fellows

The Electric Horseman*
US 1979 120m Technicolor Panavision
Columbia / Universal (Ray Stark / Wildwood)

A horseman advertising breakfast cereal in Las Vegas suddenly tires of it all and heads for the wilderness.
Pretty but slightly sheepish moral saga with too much technique for its own good.

w Robert Garland *d* Sydney Pollack *ph* Owen Roizman *m* Dave Grusin *pd* Stephen Grimes

Robert Redford, Jane Fonda, Valerie Perrine, Willie Nelson, John Saxon, Nicholas Coster
'Overlong, talky and diffused.'—*Variety*

Eleni
US 1985 117m colour
CBS / Vanoff / Pick / Gage

A journalist back in Greece investigates his mother's death in the civil war of the late 1940s.
Deadeningly boring true life drama with flashbacks which fail to communicate the author's sense of revenge.

w Steve Tesich *book* Nicholas Gage *d* Peter Yates *ph* Billy Williams *m* Bruce Smeaton *pd* Roy Walker *ed* Ray Lovejoy

Kate Nelligan, John Malkovitch, Linda Hunt, Oliver Cotton, Ronald Pickup, Rosalie Crutchley
'As lofty in ambition as it is deficient in accomplishment.'—*Variety*

Elephant Boy**
GB 1937 91m bw
London Films (Alexander Korda)

In India, a boy elephant keeper helps government conservationists.
Documentary drama which seemed fresh and extraordinary at the time, has dated badly since, but did make an international star of Sabu.

w John Collier, Akos Tolnay, Marcia de Sylva, *novel* Toomai of the Elephants by Rudyard Kipling *d Robert Flaherty, Zoltan Korda* *ph* Osmond Borradaile *m* John Greenwood

Sabu, Walter Hudd, Allan Jeayes, W. E. Holloway, Wilfrid Hyde White

'Should draw anywhere in the world.'—*Variety*

'This is a fractured film, its skeleton is awry, its bones stick out through the skin.'—*Richard Griffith, 1941*

'It has gone the way of *Man of Aran*: enormous advance publicity, director out of touch with the press for months, rumours of great epics sealed in tins, and then the disappointing diminutive achievement.'—*Graham Greene*

The Elephant Man**
US 1980 124m bw Panavision
EMI / Brooksfilms (Stuart Cornfield)

In 1884 London, a penniless man deformed by a rare illness is rescued by a doctor from a fairground freak show, and becomes a member of fashionable society.
A curious story which happens to be true; the film sets its scene superbly, has splendid performances and a fascinating make-up. Yet it fails to move quite as it should, perhaps because the central figure is treated as a horrific come-on, like the hunchback of Notre Dame.

w Christopher de Core, Eric Bergren, David Lynch, from various memoirs *d* David Lynch *ph* Freddie Francis *m* John Morris *pd* Stuart Craig

Anthony Hopkins, *John Hurt*, John Gielgud, Anne Bancroft, Freddie Jones, Wendy Hiller, Michael Elphick, Hannah Gordon
'If there's a wrong note in this unique movie—in performance, production design, cinematography or anywhere else—I must have missed it.'—*Paul Taylor, Time Out*
'In an age of horror movies this is a film which takes the material of horror and translates it into loving kindness.'—*Dilys Powell, Punch*

AAN: best film; screenplay; David Lynch; editing (Anne V. Coates); art direction (Stuart Craig, Bob Cartwright, Hugh Scaife); John Morris; costume design (Patricia Norris); John Hurt
BFA: best film; production design; John Hurt

Elephant Walk*
US 1954 103m Technicolor
Paramount (Irving Asher)

The owner of a Ceylon tea plantation takes back an English wife who finds the atmosphere strange and turns to a friendly overseer for comfort.
Echoes of *Jane Eyre* and *Rebecca*, with stampeding elephants instead of a mad or dead wife. Grade A fiction for ladies.

w John Lee Mahin, *novel* Robert Standish *d* William Dieterle *ph* Loyal Griggs *m* Franz Waxman

Elizabeth Taylor, Peter Finch, Dana Andrews, Abraham Sofaer
'The climactic elephant stampede's a rouser—if you're still awake.'—*Judith Crist*

Eleven Harrowhouse*
GB 1974 108m De Luxe Panavision
TCF / Harrowhouse (Elliott Kastner)

An American diamond merchant is robbed of a valuable jewel, and finds himself in the middle of an ingenious plot.
Amusing caper story marred by sudden changes of mood.

w Jeffrey Bloom, *novel* Gerald A. Browne *d* Aram Avakian *ph* Arthur Ibbetson *m* Michael J. Lewis

Charles Grodin, *James Mason*, Trevor Howard, John Gielgud, Candice Bergen, Peter Vaughan, Helen Cherry, Jack Watson, Jack Watling
'This lackadaisical caper comedy is inoffensive, but the comic ideas don't build or erupt, and since the director fails to get any suspense going, it becomes a bumbling and stupid romp.'—*Pauline Kael*

Elinor Norton
US 1935 71m bw

A wife has a jealous husband and a South American lover. Underwritten triangle drama which never comes to boiling point. Claire Trevor, Gilbert Roland, Hugh Williams, Henrietta Crossman, Norman Foster. Written by Rose Franken and Philip Klein from the novel The State versus Elinor Norton by Mary Roberts Rinehart; directed by Hamilton McFadden; for Fox. 'No cast for b.o. and results look mild.'—*Variety*

Eliza Fraser
Australia 1976 127m colour

A shipwrecked couple have to live with Aborigines; later she becomes a fairground attraction. Would-be bawdy historical romp on the lines of *Tom Jones*; it seldom works. Susannah York, Trevor Howard, Noel Ferrier, John Waters, Charles Tingwell. Written by David Williamson; directed and produced by Tim Burstall; for Hexagon.

Elizabeth and Essex: see The Private Lives of Elizabeth and Essex

Elizabeth of Ladymead
GB 1948 97m Technicolor
BL / Imperadio (Herbert Wilcox)

Four husbands of different generations come home from war (1854, 1903, 1919, 1946) to find their wives altered.
Thin star vehicle turns into an amateur-night compendium with a few funny moments.

w Frank Harvey, from his play *d* Herbert Wilcox *ph* Max Greene

Anna Neagle, Hugh Williams, Bernard Lee, Michael Laurence, Nicholas Phipps, Isobel Jeans, Michael Shepley, Jack Allen

Ella Cinders**
US 1926 83m approx bw silent

A servant girl wins a trip to Hollywood. Famous and still pleasing comedy from the comic strip Cinderella in the Movies. Colleen Moore, Lloyd Hughes, Vera Lewis, Doria Baker. Written by Frank Griffin, Mervyn Le Roy; directed by Alfred E. Green; for First National.

Ellery Queen

The debonair detective created by Manfred B. Lee and Frederic Dannay was seen in several unremarkable second features, usually with his secretary Nikki and his police inspector father. The first two were made for Republic, the rest for Columbia.

1935: THE SPANISH CAPE MYSTERY with Donald Cook
1936: THE MANDARIN MYSTERY (Eddie Quillan)
1940: ELLERY QUEEN MASTER DETECTIVE (Ralph Bellamy)
1941: ELLERY QUEEN'S PENTHOUSE MYSTERY, ELLERY QUEEN AND THE PERFECT CRIME, ELLERY QUEEN AND THE MURDER RING (all Bellamy)

1942: A CLOSE CALL FOR ELLERY QUEEN, A DESPERATE CHANCE FOR ELLERY QUEEN, ENEMY AGENTS MEET ELLERY QUEEN (all William Gargan)
In 1971 Peter Lawford starred in a TV pilot, *Don't Look behind You,* and in 1975 a one-season series starred Jim Hutton. The books, pseudonymously authored by Ellery Queen, were far more popular than any of the movies.

Elmer and Elsie
US 1934 65m bw

A wife harbours big ideas for her meek-and-mild husband. Unsuccessful attempt to find a change of pace for a fading star. George Bancroft, Frances Fuller, Roscoe Karns, George Barbier, Nella Walker. Written by Humphrey Pearson from the play To the Ladies by George S. Kaufman and Marc Connelly; directed by Gilbert Pratt; for Paramount. 'Screen version has not only removed most of the verve, pace and bite but has loaded itself down with a couple of maladroit cases of miscasting.'—*Variety*

Elmer Gantry**
US 1960 146m Eastmancolor
UA / Bernard Smith

The exploits of an American evangelist in the twenties.
Mainly gripping but overlong exposé of commercialized small-town religion

wd Richard Brooks, novel Sinclair Lewis *ph John Alton m* André Previn *ad Edward Carrere*

Burt Lancaster, Jean Simmons, Arthur Kennedy, *Shirley Jones*, Dean Jagger, Edward Andrews, Patti Page, John McIntire

AA: Richard Brooks (as writer); Burt Lancaster; Shirley Jones
AAN: best picture; André Previn

Elmer the Great
US 1933 74m bw
Warner (Ray Griffith)

A country hick turns out to be a great baseball hitter.
Best and most farcical version of a play also filmed in 1929 as *Fast Company* and in 1939 as *The Cowboy Quarterback.*

w Tom Geraghty, *play* Ring Lardner, George M. Cohan *d* Mervyn Le Roy

Joe E. Brown, Patricia Ellis, Frank McHugh, Claire Dodd, Sterling Holloway, Emma Dunn, Douglass Dumbrille, Jessie Ralph, J. Carrol Naish

Elopement
US 1951 82m bw
TCF (Fred Kohlmar)

A girl student eloping with her professor is chased by her father.
Unconvincing domestic comedy with some lively chase sequences.

w Bess Taffell *d* Henry Koster *ph* Joseph La Shelle *m* Cyril Mockridge

Clifton Webb, Charles Bickford, Anne Francis, William Lundigan, Margalo Gillmore, Evelyn Varden, Reginald Gardiner

'A picture that goes beyond what men think about . . . because no man ever thought about it in quite this way!'—*publicity*

Elstree Calling*
GB 1930 95m bw and colour
Wardour / BIP (John Maxwell)

A film studio mounts a television show. Slender excuse for an all-star revue which luckily preserves much light entertainment talent of the time.

w Adrian Brunel, Walter C. Mycroft, Val Valentine *d* Adrian Brunel, Alfred Hitchcock, Jack Hulbert, André Charlot, Paul Murray *ph* Claude Friese-Greene

Tommy Handley, Jack Hulbert, Cicely Courtneidge, Will Fyffe, Lily Morris, Teddy Brown, Anna May Wong, Gordon Harker, Donald Calthrop, John Longden, Jameson Thomas, Bobbie Comber

The Elstree Story*
GB 1952 61m bw
ABPC (Gilbert Gunn)

A compilation drawn from 25 years of film-making at Elstree Studios. Highlights include Hitchcock's *Number Seventeen*; *The White Sheik*; *Piccadilly*; *Bulldog Drummond*; *Arms and the Man*; *The Informer*; *Blossom Time*; and *Poison Pen*. Commentary and presentation are adequate.

d Gilbert Gunn *m* Philip Green

The Elusive Pimpernel*
GB 1950 109m Technicolor
BL / London Films (Michael Powell, Emeric Pressburger)
US title: *The Fighting Pimpernel*

A foppish 18th-century London dandy is actually the hero who rescues French aristocrats from the guillotine.
Expensive remake of *The Scarlet Pimpernel* which fails to please, apparently because the talents were not congenial to the subject. Interesting detail, though.

wd Michael Powell, Emeric Pressburger, *novel* Baroness Orczy *ph* Christopher Challis *m* Brian Easdale *ph* Hein Heckroth

David Niven, Margaret Leighton, Cyril Cusack, Jack Hawkins, David Hutcheson, Robert Coote

'The quality of excitement which should carry the film is quite lost. *The Elusive Pimpernel* is highly—often too highly—coloured, and has an artificiality quite different in character from that of the original.'—*Penelope Houston*

'I never thought I should feel inclined to leave a Powell and Pressburger film before the end; but I did here.'—*Richard Mallett, Punch*

'Niven plays the Scarlet Pimpernel with the sheepish lack of enthusiasm of a tone deaf man called upon to sing solo in church. His companions lumber through their parts like schoolboys about to go down with mumps.'—*Daily Express*

Elvira Madigan*
Sweden 1967 95m Eastmancolor
Europa Film (Waldemar Bergendahl)

A married army officer runs off with a tightrope dancer; when they run out of money they live in the woods and finally commit suicide rather than part.
A simple Victorian romantic idyll, based on a true incident; a director's and photographer's piece which entrances the eyes and ears while starving the mind.

wd Bo Widerberg *ph Jorgen Persson m* Mozart

Thommy Berggren, Pia Degermark

Embassy*
US 1972 90m colour
Hemdale / Triad / Weaver (Mel Ferrer)

At the US Embassy in Beirut, a Soviet official seeking asylum is in danger from a KGB killer.
Goodish suspenser with reasonably literate dialogue and several Hitchcockian sequences.

w William Fairchild d Gordon Hessler ph Raoul Coutard *m* Jonathan Hodge

Richard Roundtree, Chuck Connors, Max Von Sydow, Broderick Crawford, Ray Milland

Embraceable You
US 1948 80m bw

A gangster on the run fatally injures a young girl, and stays to nurse her during her last weeks. Incredible heavy-handed romantic melodrama. Dane Clark, Geraldine Brooks, Wallace Ford, S. Z. Sakall, Richard Rober. Written by Edna Anhalt; directed by Felix Jacoves; for Warner.

Embryo
US 1976 104m colour
Cine Artists (Arnold H. Orgolini, Anita Doohan)

A researcher experiments on foetuses with growth hormones, and lives to regret it.
Rather unpleasant mixture of science fiction and old-fashioned horror; slickness can't conceal a total lack of taste.

w Anita Doohan, Jack W. Thomas *d* Ralph Nelson *ph* Fred Koenekamp *m* Gil Melle

Rock Hudson, Diane Ladd, Barbara Carrera, Roddy McDowall

The Emerald Forest**
GB 1985 113m Technicolor Panavision
Embassy / John Boorman

An American engineer sets off to find his lost son in the jungles of Brazil.
Heavy-going, dazzling to look at, finally uncomforting dalliance with themes originally explored in *Tarzan the Ape Man*, e.g. would man do better to return to nature?

w Rospo Pallenberg *d John Boorman ph* Philippe Rousselot *m* Junior Homrich, Brian Gascoyne *pd* Simon Holland

Powers Boothe, Meg Foster, Charley Boorman

'Begins as a breathtaking fable and ends as a routine action movie. Somewhere along the way, there was a failure of the imagination.'—*Roger Ebert*

Emergency Call*
GB 1952 90m bw
Butcher's / Nettlefold (Ernest G. Roy)
US title: *Emergency!*

Inspector Lane tracks down several people who share a rare blood group needed to save a life.
Now a boringly predictable collection of mild anecdotes, but then a rather smart idea, much better executed than one would normally expect of Britain's Poverty Row.

w Vernon Harris, Lewis Gilbert *d* Lewis Gilbert *ph* Wilkie Cooper *m* Wilfred Burns

Jack Warner, Joy Shelton, Anthony Steel, Sidney James, Freddie Mills, Earl Cameron, John Robinson, Thora Hird

The Emigrants*
Sweden 1970 191m Technicolor
Svensk Filmindustri (Bengt Forslund)
original title: *Utvandrarna*

A family of farmers leaves famine-stricken 19th-century Sweden for America, and builds a homestead in Minnesota.
Solemn, forceful, overlong epic which while full of trial and tribulation is sufficiently well made to cast a hypnotic spell and was a major hit among Swedish-Americans.

w Jan Troell, Bengt Forslund, from four novels by Vilhelm Moberg *d, ph, ed Jan Troell* *m* Erik Nordgren

Max Von Sydow, Liv Ullmann, Eddie Axberg, Svenolof Bern

'A Fordian canvas without the Fordian warmth.'—*Sight and Sound*

† A sequel, *The New Land*, shortly appeared, and this was also the title of a short-lived TV series on the subject.

AAN: best picture; Jan Troell (direction and script); Liv Ullmann

Emil and the Detectives*
Germany 1931 80m bw
UFA

City children discover and chase a crook, who is finally arrested.
A pleasing fable for children which has survived several subsequent versions; the original is probably the best.

w Billy Wilder, *novel* Erich Kästner *d* Gerhard Lamprecht *ph* Werner Brandes *m* Allan Grey

Fritz Rasp, Kathe Haack

† Other versions: Britain 1934, directed by Milton Rosmer, with George Hayes; West Germany 1954, directed by R. A. Stemmle, with Kurt Meisel; US 1964 (Walt Disney), directed by Peter Tewkesbury, with Walter Slezak.

Emma*
US 1932 73m bw
MGM

A servant marries into the family.
Predictably cosy family drama tailored for its star.

w Frances Marion, Leonard Praskins, Zelda Sears *d* Clarence Brown *ph* Oliver T. Marsh

Marie Dressler, Richard Cromwell, Jean Hersholt, Myrna Loy, John Miljan, Purnell E. Pratt

'A hoke story saved by the star.'—*Variety*

AAN: Marie Dressler

Emmanuelle*
France 1974 94m Eastmancolor
Trinacra / Orphée (Yves Rousset-Rouard)

The bored bride of a French Embassy official in Siam is initiated by well-meaning friends into various forms of sexual activity.
Not much sexier than a Sunday colour supplement, this fashionable piece of sub-eroticism took off like a bomb and spawned half-a-dozen so-called sequels. Future students may well wonder why.

w Jean-Louis Richard, *novel* Emmanuelle Arsan *d* Just Jaeckin *ph* Richard Suzuki, Marie Saunier *m* Pierre Bachelet

Sylvia Kristel, Marika Green, Daniel Sarky, Alain Cuny

'Much hazy, soft-focus coupling in downtown Bangkok.'—*Michael Billington, Illustrated London News*

The Emperor Jones*
US 1933 72m bw

A train porter becomes king of the Haitian jungle. Stagey transcript of a stagey play, with acting of some interest at the time. *Paul Robeson*, *Dudley Digges*, Frank Wilson. From the play by Eugene O'Neill; directed by Dudley Murphy; for UA. 'For the classes rather than the masses, and questionable commercially.'—*Variety*

Emperor of the North Pole*
US 1973 119m De Luxe
TCF / Inter Hemisphere (Robert Aldrich)
GB title: *Emperor of the North*

In 1933 Oregon, freeloading hobos are brutally attacked by a sadistic train guard.
Unlikely melodrama with vicious but exhilarating high spots separating acres of verbiage.

w Christopher Knopf *d* Robert Aldrich *ph* Joseph Biroc *m* Frank de Vol

Lee Marvin, Ernest Borgnine, Keith Carradine, Charles Tyner, Malcolm Atterbury, Elisha Cook Jnr

'It's hard, contrived, pointless in its thesis, repulsive in its people, and it's singularly joyless and contemptible in its glorification of the bum and freeloader.'—*Judith Crist*

'The biggest thing that ever happened to Bing—or to you!'

The Emperor Waltz
US 1948 106m Technicolor
Paramount (Charles Brackett)

In 1901 Austria, a countess falls for an American phonograph salesman.
Thin to the point of emaciation, this witless comedy with music, dully set-bound, proved its director's strangest and most unsatisfactory choice.

w Charles Brackett, Billy Wilder *d* Billy Wilder *ph* George Barnes *m* Victor Young *songs* Johnny Burke, Jimmy Van Heusen *ad* Hans Dreier, Franz Bachelin

Bing Crosby, Joan Fontaine, Roland Culver, Lucile Watson, Richard Haydn, Harold Vermilyea, Sig Rumann, Julie Dean

AAN: Victor Young

The Emperor's Candlesticks*
US 1937 89m bw
MGM (John Considine Jnr)

In old Russia, spies on opposite sides fall in love.
Lavish romantic comedy drama, generally well handled; superior Hollywood moonshine.

w Monckton Hoffe, Herman J. Mankiewicz, Harold Goldman, *novel* Baroness Orczy *d* George Fitzmaurice *ph* Harold Rosson *m* Franz Waxman

William Powell, Luise Rainer, Maureen O'Sullivan, Robert Young, Frank Morgan, Douglass Dumbrille

'It's about international spies in evening dress during that long ago period when Russia had a Czar, Vienna was the scene of brilliant *valasques*, and the favour of royalty was something to get excited over . . . it's acted with unusual seriousness midst settings of unusual extravagance.'—*Variety*

Empire of the Ants
US 1977 89m Movielab
AIP / Cinema 77 (Bert I. Gordon)

Giant ants menace a stretch of the Florida coast.
A long way behind *Them*, but as exploitation it could be worse.

w Jack Turley, *story* H. G. Wells *d* Bert I. Gordon *ph* Reginald Morris *m* Dana Kaproff

Joan Collins, Robert Lansing, John David Carson, Albert Salmi, Jaqueline Scott

Empire State
GB 1987 104m colour

An American gangster tries to infiltrate London's East End. Over-the-top melodrama with an irritating pictorial style. Cathryn Harrison, Jason Hoganson, Elizabeth Hickling, Jamie Foreman, Martin Landau, Ray McAnally. Written by Ron Peck and Mark Ayres; directed by Ron Peck; for Virgin.

The Empire Strikes Back**
US 1980 124m Eastmancolor
Panavision
TCF / Lucasfilm (Gary Kurtz)

The Rebel Alliance takes refuge from Darth Vader on a frozen planet.
More exhilarating interplanetary adventures, as mindless as *Star Wars* but just as enjoyable for aficionados.

w Leigh Brackett, Lawrence Kasdan, *story* George Lucas *d* Irvin Kershner *ph* Peter Suschitzky *m* John Williams *pd Norman Reynolds*

Mark Hamill, Harrison Ford, Carrie Fisher, Billy Dee Williams

'Slightly encumbered by some mythic and neo-Sophoclean overtones, but its inventiveness, humour and special effects are scarcely less inspired than those of its phenomenally successful predecessor.'—*New Yorker*

AAN: art direction
BFA: music

Empire of the Sun***
US 1987 152m Technicolor
Robert Shapiro / Amblin (Steven Spielberg, Kathleen Kennedy, Frank Marshall)

Semi-autobiographical story of an 11-year-old English boy learning to grow up in a Japanese internment camp during World War Two.

w Tom Stoppard, from novel by J. G. Ballard *d* Steven Spielberg *ph* Allen Daviau *m* John Williams *pd* Norman Reynolds

Christian Bale, John Malkovich, Miranda Richardson, Nigel Havers, Joe Pantoliano

'A masterpiece of popular cinema.'—*MFB*

Employees' Entrance*
US 1933 75m bw

A ruthless department store manager gets his comeuppance. Smart comedy-melodrama with solidly familiar cast. *Warren William*, Loretta Young, Alice White, Wallace Ford, Allen Jenkins, Marjorie Gateson. Written by Robert Presnell, from a play by David Boehm; directed by Roy del Ruth; for Warner.

'Here's one that calls for preferred dating . . . plenty to sell for the mobs.'—*Variety*

The Empty Canvas
Italy / France 1964 118m bw
CC Champion / Concordia (Joseph E. Levine, Carlo Ponti)
original title: *La Noia*

A young painter, obsessed by his own spiritual emptiness, becomes paranoically jealous of his promiscuous young mistress.
An extraordinarily boring film version of a novel which needed Bunuel, if anybody, to handle it.

w Tonino Guerra, Ugo Liberatore, Damiano Damiani, *novel* Alberto Moravia *d* Damiano Damiani *ph* Roberto Gerardi *m* Luis Enriquez Bacalov

Horst Buchholz, Catherine Spaak, Bette Davis, Isa Miranda, Lea Padovani

En Cas de Malheur*
France / Italy 1958 120m bw
Iena / UCIL / Incom
aka: *Love Is My Profession*

A wealthy, middle-aged lawyer leaves his wife for a worthless young wanton whom he is defending on a robbery charge.
Good solid melodrama with excellent credits: it caught all concerned on top form and had international success, but the theme is not in itself very interesting.

w Jean Aurenche, Pierre Bost, *novel* Georges Simenon *d Claude Autant-Lara ph* Jacques Natteau *m* René Cloërc

Jean Gabin, Edwige Feuillère, Brigitte Bardot, Franco Interlenghi

En Rade*
France 1927 60m approx bw silent
Neofilm

A Marseilles docker dreams of escaping his pent-in existence and fleeing with his mistress to the South Seas.
More realistic than Pagnol's *Marius* trilogy, which used the same setting, this remains an interesting slice of romantic realism, with good attention to detail.

w Alberto Cavalcanti, Claude Heymann *d* Alberto Cavalcanti *ph* Jimmy Rogers, A. Fairli, P. Enberg

Catherine Hessling, Philippe Heriat, Georges Charlia

Enchanted April
US 1935 66m bw

A woman becomes lonely when her husband turns into a successful novelist. Thin marital comedy-drama for fans of the star. Ann Harding, Frank Morgan, Katharine Alexander, Reginald Owen, Jane Baxter, Jessie Ralph. Written by Samuel Hoffenstein and Ray Harris, from the novel by 'Elizabeth'; directed by Harry Beaumont; for RKO. 'Very British in background and proceeding at all times with a lifted eyebrow.'—*Variety*

The Enchanted Cottage*
US 1945 92m bw
RKO

A plain girl and a disfigured man are beautiful to each other.
Wartime updating of a sentimental old play; insufficiently well considered to be more than tolerable.

w De Witt Bodeen, Herman J. Mankiewicz, *play* Sir Arthur Wing Pinero *d* John Cromwell *ph* Ted Tetzlaff *m* Roy Webb

Dorothy McGuire, Robert Young, Herbert Marshall, Mildred Natwick

AAN: Roy Webb

† A silent version in 1924 starred Richard Barthelmess and May McAvoy.

The Enchanted Forest*
US 1945 77m Cinecolor
PRC

Old John the Hermit talks to trees and animals, and rescues a lost child.
Surprising piece of Victorian whimsy, remarkably effective in its unambitious way, especially as a product of this studio. The best known example of Cinecolor.

w Robert Lee Johnson, John Le Bar, Lou Brock *d* Lew Landers *ph* Marcel Le Picard *m* Alfred Hay Malotte

Harry Davenport, Edmund Lowe, Brenda Joyce, Billy Severn

Enchanted Island
US 1958 94m Technicolor
Waverly (Benedict Bogeaus)

In the 1840s two sailors jump ship and settle on what they later discover to be a cannibal island.
Tame adaptation of a minor classic, with the actors all at sea.

w James Leicester, Harold Jacob Smith, *novel* Typee by Herman Melville *d* Allan Dwan *ph* George Stahl *m* Raul Lavista

Jane Powell (an unconvincing Polynesian), Dana Andrews, Don Dubbins, Arthur Shields, Ted de Corsia, Friedrich Ledebur

Enchantment*
US 1948 101m bw
Samuel Goldwyn

A London house tells the story of three generations.
Yes, a house tells the story, and the leading characters are called Rollo and Lark, but this is a very appealing piece of period romantic nonsense, with the highest possible gloss upon it.

w John Patrick, novel A Fugue in Time by Rumer Godden *d Irving Reis ph Gregg Toland m* Hugo Friedhofer

David Niven, Teresa Wright, Evelyn Keyes, Farley Granger, Jayne Meadows, Leo G. Carroll

'Deliberate in pace, and artfully contrived as an emotional holiday, yet genuinely moving on its own terms.'—*Newsweek*

'Genuinely moving on its own terms, produced with a careful good taste that should disarm the critics of lachryma and old lace.'—*Newsweek*

Encore*
GB 1951 88m bw
GFD / Two Cities (Antony Darnborough)

Three more Somerset Maugham short stories introduced by the author.
The final follow-up to the success of *Quartet* and *Trio*; television playlets quickly made this kind of short story seem old-fashioned, but the standard here was high.

w T. E. B. Clarke, Arthur Macrae, Eric Ambler, *stories* The Ant and the Grasshopper, Winter Cruise, Gigolo and Gigolette *d* Pat Jackson, Anthony Pelissier, Harold French *ph* Desmond Dickinson *m* Richard Addinsell

Nigel Patrick, Roland Culver, *Kay Walsh*, Noel Purcell, Ronald Squire, John Laurie, Glynis Johns, Terence Morgan, David Hutcheson

'A comedy for you and your next of kin!'

The End
US 1978 100m De Luxe
UA / Lawrence Gordon (Hank Moonjean)

A selfish man finds he is dying and unsuccessfully tries to change what remains of his life.
Presumably intended as an ironic black comedy, this comes over as tasteless ham; nobody involved, least of all the director-star, has any idea how to handle it.

w Jerry Belson *d* Burt Reynolds *ph* Bobby Byrne *m* Paul Williams *pd* Jan Scott

Burt Reynolds, Dom de Luise, Sally Field, Strother Martin, David Steinberg, Joanne Woodward, Norman Fell, Myrna Loy, Pat O'Brien, Robby Benson, Carl Reiner

The End of August*
US 1981 107m Metrocolor
Sewanee (Martin Jurow)

In 1900, a bored young wife takes a lover beneath her station.
Unexpectedly nostalgic wallow in days gone by, the background detail seeming more important than the personal story, and certainly very good to look at.

w Eula Seaton, Leon Heller, *novel* The Awakening by Kate Chopin *d* Bob Graham *ph Robert Elswit m* Shirley Walker *pd* Warren Jacobson, Erin Jo Jurow

Sally Sharp, Lilia Skala, David Marshall Grant, Kathleen Widdoes, Paul Roebling, Paul Shenar

'Reminiscent of nothing so much as the turning of pages in a family album.'—*Jo Imeson, MFB*

The End of St Petersburg**
USSR 1927 110m approx bw silent
Mezhrabpom-Russ
original title: *Konyets Sankt-Peterburga*

A peasant comes to live in St Petersburg in 1914, understands the workers' problems, and joins in the revolution.
Exhilarating propaganda, reprehensible but superbly conceived, with an especially rousing climax.

w Nathan Zarkhi *d V. I. Pudovkin*
ph Anatoli Golovnya, K. Vents
ad S. Kozlovsky

Ivan Chuvelov, Vera Baranovskaya, A. P. Christiakov

† The film was officially commissioned as part of the 10th anniversary celebrations.

The End of the Affair
GB 1954 106m bw
Columbia / Coronado (David Lewis)

In wartime London, a repressed wife has an affair with a writer but develops religious guilt which leads indirectly to her death.
Glum sinning in Greeneland; over-ambitious, miscast, and poor-looking.

w Lenore Coffee, *novel* Graham Greene
d Edward Dmytryk *ph* Wilkie Cooper
m Benjamin Frankel

Deborah Kerr, Van Johnson, Peter Cushing, John Mills, Stephen Murray, Nora Swinburne, Charles Goldner

End of the Game*
US / West Germany 1976 104m colour
TCF / Maximilian Schell

A retiring police inspector intensifies his vendetta against the crooked industrialist who thirty years earlier killed the woman they both loved.
Chess-like revenge melodrama very typical of its author, with no light relief and a few existentialist touches added for general confusion. Well made and sometimes fascinating, but finally annoying.

w Maximilian Schell and Friedrich Durrenmatt, from Durrenmatt's novel *The Judge and his Hangman d* Maximilian Schell *ph* Ennio Guarnieri, Klaus Koenig, Roberto Gerardi

Jon Voight, Robert Shaw, Martin Ritt, Jacqueline Bisset

'A more addled, overreaching, misjudged, ill-made, wasteful, posturizing, uninteresting and tedious little epic has not toddled into town in years.'—*Charles Champlin, Los Angeles Times*

The End of the River*
GB 1947 83m bw
GFD / The Archers (Michael Powell, Emeric Pressburger)

A South American Indian boy flees to the outside world and finds life in the city as dangerous as in the jungle.
Strange but oddly impressive departure for British film-makers at this time. A commercial and critical disaster.

w Wolfgang Wilhelm *d* Derek Twist
ph Christopher Challis m Lambert Williamson

Sabu, Esmond Knight, Bibi Ferreira, Robert Douglas, Antoinette Cellier, Raymond Lovell, Torin Thatcher

The End of the Road
GB 1936 71m bw

A travelling singer loses heart when he hears of the death of his daughter. Stilted star vehicle of archival interest. *Harry Lauder,* Ruth Haven, Ethel Glendinning, Bruce Seton. Written by Edward Dryhurst; directed by Alan Bryce; for Fox British.

The End of the Road*
GB 1954 77m bw
Group Three (Alfred Shaughnessy)

A retired engineer becomes frustrated by idleness, and his family contemplate sending him to an old people's home.
Reasonably absorbing study of old age, suffering from a contrived end.

w James Forsyth, Geoffrey Orme *d* Wolf Rilla *ph* Arthur Grant *m* John Addison

Finlay Currie, Duncan Lamont, Naomi Chance, David Hannaford

End of the World*
France 1930 105m bw
Ecran d'Art (Abel Gance)
Original title: *La Fin du Monde*

Social and economic panic is caused when a comet is about to hit the earth.
Massive attempt by Gance to rival his Napoleon in scope. Made in German, French and English, it cost a phenomenal sum which it never regained; Gance found work hard to get in future, especially since he set himself up as a prophet.

w,d Abel Gance

Abel Gance, Colette Darfeuil, Sylvia Grenade, Victor Francen

'A megalomaniac's effort turned out without consideration for financial results, and containing a strange mixture of crazy stuff, with successfully directed spectacular sequences.'—*Variety*

† The full title is *The End of the World as Seen, Heard and Rendered by Abel Gance*

The End of the World (in our usual bed in a night full of rain)
Italy 1978 104m colour

An American lady photographer has a bumpy romance with an Italian communist journalist with expensive tastes. Pretentious talk-piece which slowly gets nowhere. Candice Bergen, Giancarlo Giannini. Written and directed by Lina Wertmuller; for Gil Shiva/Liberty/Warner.

Endangered Species
US 1982 97m Metrocolor
MGM / Alive Enterprises (Carolyn Pfeiffer)

Citizens of a small Wyoming town discover that their cattle are being systematically murdered.
Curious melodrama which never really explains itself but seems to be carrying a message about chemical warfare. With a proper ending it could have been a good suspenser.

w Alan Rudolph, John Binder, *story* Judson Kinger, Richard Woods *d* Alan Rudolph *ph* Paul Lohmann *m* Gary Wright *pd* Trevor Williams

Robert Urich, Jobeth Williams, Paul Dooley, Hoyt Axton, Peter Coyote

'It's not over . . . it's not over!'
Endless Love
US 1981 110m Technicolor
Polygram (Keith Barish)

A high school student's love for a 15-year-old girl is thwarted by circumstance and accident.
Overheated melodrama with unbelievable and unlikeable characters. Why this director should choose to make it is mysterious.

w Judith Rascoe, *novel* Scott Spencer
d Franco Zeffirelli *ph* David Watkin
m Jonathan Tunick *pd* Ed Wittstein

Brooke Shields, Martin Hewitt, Shirley Knight, Don Murray, Richard Kiley, Beatrice Straight

Endless Night*
GB 1971 99m Eastmancolor
BL / EMI (Leslie Gilliat)

An American girl buys an English stately home and marries a chauffeur, but is later frightened to death.
Bumpy British thriller, structurally weak and peopled by the dullest conceivable characters, but with watchably scary sequences.

wd Sidney Gilliat, *novel* Agatha Christie
ph Harry Waxman *m* Bernard Herrmann

Hayley Mills, Hywel Bennett, George Sanders, Britt Ekland, Per Oscarsson, Lois Maxwell

The Endless Summer
US 1966 95m Technicolor

A study of surfing round the world. A documentary which became a cult for those influenced by this Californian obsession; smashing photography hardly atones for an approach so naïve as to become fatuous. Written, directed, photographed and edited by *Bruce Brown,* for Bruce Brown Films / Columbia.

Enemy Agent
US 1940 64m bw

An aircraft worker is framed as a spy. Nifty little topical support with not much sense but plenty of zest. Richard Cromwell, Philip Dorn, Helen Vinson, Marjorie Reynolds, Robert Armstrong, Vinton Haworth, Abner Biberman, Jack Carson, Jack La Rue. Written by Sam Robbins and Edmund L. Hartmann; directed by Lew Landers; for Universal.

Enemy Agents Meet Ellery Queen
US 1942 64m bw

Sailors and marines help Ellery to rout Nazi spies. Unco-ordinated extravaganza which signalled the end of the Queen series. William Gargan, Margaret Lindsay, Charley Grapewin, Gale Sondergaard, Gilbert Roland, Sig Rumann. Written by Eric Taylor; directed by James Hogan; for Ralph Cohn / Columbia.

The Enemy Below*
US 1957 98m Technicolor Cinemascope
TCF (Dick Powell)

During World War II an American destroyer in the South Atlantic is involved in a cat-and-mouse operation with a U-boat.
Well-staged, unsurprising naval thriller with good pace and a pat let's-not-be-nasty-to-each-other ending.

w Wendell Mayes, *novel* Commander D. A. Rayner *d Dick Powell ph* Harold Rosson *m* Leigh Harline

Robert Mitchum, Curt Jurgens, Theodore Bikel, David Hedison

The Enemy General
US 1960 74m bw
Columbia (Sam Katzman)

An American officer takes revenge on the German general who executed his fiancée.
Routine World War II heroics with a plot deserving a rather better production.

w Dan Pepper, Burt Picard *d* George Sherman *ph* Basil Emmott *md* Mischa Bakaleinikoff

Van Johnson, Jean-Pierre Aumont, John Van Dreelen, Dany Carrel, Françoise Prévost

Enemy Mine
US 1985 108m De Luxe

A space pilot goes down on Dracon and makes friends with his lizard-like captor. All talk and little action, this is a way-out piece of do-goodery which tests the patience. Dennis Quaid, Lou Gossett Jnr. Written by Edward Khmara, from story by Barry Longyear; directed by Wolfgang Petersen; for Kings Road / TCF.

An Enemy of the People*
US 1977 103m Metrocolor
First Artists (George Schaefer)

A small-town doctor discovers that for commercial reasons his colleagues propose to conceal the fact that the local spa is contaminated by tannery waste.
Ibsen's plot is well intentioned but well worn – it more or less served as the starting point for *Jaws* – so in any modern version the acting is all. Here it isn't enough, though the star so badly wanted to do it that arguments and sulks kept him off the screen for three years.

w Alexander Jacobs, from Arthur Miller's version of the play by Henrik Ibsen *d* George Schaefer *ph* Paul Lohmann *m* Leonard Rosenman

Steve McQueen, Charles Durning, Bibi Andersson, Eric Christmas, Richard Bradford, Richard A. Dysart

'The main thing I was shooting for was not to make bucks but to have something I could believe in.'—*Steve McQueen*

L'Enfant Sauvage*
France 1969 84m bw
UA / Films du Carrosse (Marcel Berbert)
US title: *The Wild Child*

In 1797, a scientist tames and studies a young boy who has mysteriously been living wild in the forest.
Slightly flat but generally interesting reconstruction of a true event, the same one which subsequently inspired TV projects such as *Stalk the Wild Child* and *Lucan.*

w François Truffaut, Jean Gruault *d* François Truffaut *ph* Nestor Almendros *m* Vivaldi

Jean-Pierre Cargol, François Truffaut, Jean Dasté, Françoise Seigner

Les Enfants du Paradis****
France 1945 195m bw
Pathé (Fred Orain, Raymond Borderic)
US title: *Children of Paradise*

In the 'theatre street' of Paris in the 1840s, a mime falls in love with the elusive Garance, but her problems with other men keep them apart.
A magnificent evocation of a place and a period, this thoroughly enjoyable epic melodrama is flawed only by its lack of human warmth and of a real theme. It remains nevertheless one of the cinema's most memorable films.

w Jacques Prévert d Marcel Carné ph Roger Hubert m Maurice Thiriet, Joseph Kosma, G. Mouque *ad Alexandre Trauner, Léon Barsacq, Raymond Gabutti*

Arletty, Jean-Louis Barrault, Pierre Brasseur, Marcel Herrand, Maria Casarès, Louis Salon, Pierre Renoir, Gaston Modot, Jane Marken

'A magnificent scenario . . . Prévert is as adept with wit as with poignancy . . . I don't believe a finer group of actors was ever assembled on film'—*John Simon*

AAN: Jacques Prévert

Les Enfants Terribles*
France 1950 100m bw
Jean-Pierre Melville
aka: *The Strange Ones*

The hothouse relationship of an adolescent brother and sister leads to tragedy.
Rough-edged, stage-bound but occasionally quite powerful exploration into familiar Cocteau territory.

wd Jean-Pierre Melville, novel Jean Cocteau *ph* Henri Decaë *m* Bach, Vivaldi

Nicole Stéphane, Edouard Dermithe, Renée Cosima, Jacques Bernard

'The first story of the double-fisted DA who tore apart the evil dynasty that peddled murder for a price!'

The Enforcer***
US 1950 87m bw
United States Pictures (Milton Sperling)
GB title: *Murder, Inc*

A crusading District Attorney tracks down the leader of a gang which murders for profit.
Extremely suspenseful and well-characterized police yarn based on fact. One of the very best of its kind.

w Martin Rackin d Bretaigne Windust ph Robert Burks m David Buttolph

Humphrey Bogart, Everett Sloane, Zero Mostel, Ted de Corsia, Roy Roberts, King Donovan

'A tough, very slickly-made thriller with a host of fine character parts.'—*NFT, 1969*

'Absorbing and exciting, with little of the violence that so often disfigures films of this kind.'—*Richard Mallett, Punch*

'The first fifteen minutes is as powerful and rapid a sketch of tension as I can recall for seasons. The last fifteen might make Hitch weep with envy.'—*Observer*

The Enforcer
US 1976 96m De Luxe Panavision
Warner / Malpaso (Robert Daley)

Brutal Inspector Callahan of the San Francisco police redeems himself by rounding up a group of psychopathic hoodlums.
Dirty Harry, phase three: for hardened veterans only.

w Stirling Silliphant, Dean Riesner *d* James Fargo *ph* Richard Glouner *m* Jerry Fielding

Clint Eastwood, Tyne Daly, Harry Guardino, Bradford Dillman, John Mitchum, DeVeren Brookwalter, John Crawford

'A new low in mindless violence is reached in this film, which is so bad it would be funny if it were not for the gut-thumping killings from beginning to end.'—*William F. Fore, Film Information*

The Engagement*
GB 1970 44m Technicolor
Memorial (David Barber)

A young executive spends a devastating afternoon trying to borrow money to pay for an engagement ring which cost more than he expected.
Brisk little comedy which doesn't wear out its welcome.

w Tom Stoppard *d* Paul Joyce *ph* Tony Spratling *m* John Dankworth

David Warner, Michael Bates, George Innes, Juliet Harmer, Paul Curran, Barbara Couper, Peter Copley

England Made Me**
GB 1972 100m Eastmancolor Panavision
Hemdale / Atlantic (Jack Levin)

In 1935 a sponging Englishman becomes involved through his sister with a German financier.
Somewhat altered from the novel, this unusual film remains a lively, intelligent character melodrama.

w Desmond Cory, Peter Duffell, *novel* Graham Greene *d Peter Duffell* *ph* Ray Parslow *m* John Scott

Peter Finch, Michael York, Hildegarde Neil, *Michael Hordern*, Joss Ackland

English without Tears*
GB 1944 89m bw
GFD / Two Cities (Anatole de Grunwald, Sydney Box)
US title: *Her Man Gilbey*

World War II a rich ATS girl falls for her butler who has become a lieutenant.
Wispy satirical comedy with amusing moments, chiefly interesting for the pre-war League of Nations sequences.

w Terence Rattigan, Anatole de Grunwald *d* Harold French *ph* Bernard Knowles

Lilli Palmer, Michael Wilding, *Margaret Rutherford*, Penelope Dudley Ward, Albert Lieven, Roland Culver, Peggy Cummins

An Englishman's Home
GB 1939 79m bw
US title: *Madmen of Europe*

An English family plays unwitting host to a foreign spy. Hilarious clinker, far too unintentionally funny to make the effective propaganda intended. Edmund Gwenn, Mary Maguire, Paul Von Hernreid, Geoffrey Toone, Richard Ainley, Desmond Tester. Written by (catch them all) Dennis Wheatley, Edward Knoblock, Ian Hay, Robert Edmunds, Dora Nirva, Clifford Grey, Richard Llewellyn and Rodney Ackland; directed by Albert de Courville; for Aldwych. 'There is nothing to be said for this film—though it might prove useful propaganda in enemy countries, purporting to illustrate the decadence of English architecture and taste.'—*Graham Greene.*

Enigma
GB / France 1982 101m colour
Embassy / Filmcrest / Peter Shaw

An East German refugee is recruited by the CIA to return to East Berlin.
Threadbare spy stuff with an indecipherable plot.

w John Briley, *novel* Michael Barak *d* Jeannot Szwarc *ph* Jean-Louis Picavet *m* Marc Wilkinson

Martin Sheen, Brigitte Fossey, Sam Neill, Derek Jacobi, Michel Lonsdale, Frank Finlay, Michael Williams, Warren Clarke

'Well made but insufficiently exciting.'—*Variety*

'The mystery is why they bothered.'—*Guardian*

Ensign Pulver
US 1964 104m Technicolor Panavision
Warner (Joshua Logan)

Further naval misadventures of the character from *Mr Roberts*.
Threadbare naval comedy with every expected cliché.

w Joshua Logan, Peter S. Feibleman, *play* Joshua Logan, Thomas Heggen *d* Joshua Logan *ph* Charles Lawton *m* George Duning

Robert Walker, Burl Ives, Walter Matthau, Tommy Sands, Millie Perkins, Kay Medford, Larry Hagman, James Farentino, James Coco, Al Freeman Jnr

Entente Cordiale*
France 1939 95m bw
Max Glass

A history of relations between England and France from Victorian times to the present day.
Ambitious pageant from the French point of view.

w Steve Passeur, Max Glass, *book* Edward VII and His Times by André Maurois *d Marcel l'Herbier* *ph* Ted Pahle, Marc Fossard *m* Darius Milhaud

Victor Francen (Edward VII), Gaby Morlay (Queen Victoria), André Lefaur, Jean Perier, Jean d'Yd, Jean Worms

'One of the most outstanding productions of its type ever made in France.'—*Variety*

Enter Arsène Lupin
US 1944 72m bw

A master thief protects a beautiful girl's emerald. Stiff little second which failed to bring forth a series. Charles Korvin, Ella Raines, J. Carrol Naish, George Dolenz, Gale Sondergaard, Miles Mander. Written by Bertram Millhauser; directed by Ford Beebe; for Universal.

Enter Inspector Duval
GB 1961 64m bw

A French detective helps Scotland Yard solve the murder of a socialite. Dim mystery with no hope of becoming a series. Anton Diffring, Diane Hart, Mark Singleton. Written by J. Henry Piperno; directed by Max Varnel; for Bill Luckwell.

Enter Laughing*
US 1967 111m Technicolor
Columbia / Acre / Sajo (Carl Reiner, Joseph Stein)

In New York in the thirties, a young man about to train as a pharmacist decides to become an actor instead.
Strident Jewish comedy based on the writer-director's own youthful experiences, which might have been more effectively strained by another hand. The talent is there, though.

w Joseph Stein, Carl Reiner, *play* Carl Reiner *d* Carl Reiner *ph* Joseph Biroc *m* Quincy Jones

Reni Santoni, Jose Ferrer, Shelley Winters, Elaine May, Jack Gilford, Janet Margolin, David Opatoshu, Michael J. Pollard

Enter Madame
US 1934 83m bw

A millionaire is humbled when he marries a glamorous opera singer. Modest comedy operetta, with the star's voice dubbed by Nina Koshetz. Elissa Landi, Cary Grant, Lynne Overman, Sharon Lynne, Paul Porcasi. Written by Charles Brackett and Gladys Lehmann, from the play by Gilda Varesi Archibald and Dorothea Donn-Byrne; directed by Elliott Nugent; for Paramount.

Enter the Dragon*
US / Hong Kong 1973 99m Technicolor Panavision
Warner / Concord (Fred Weintraub, Paul Heller)

A master of martial arts is enlisted by British intelligence to stop opium smuggling.
The first Hollywood-based Kung Fu actioner; not bad, on the lines of a more violent James Bond.

w Michael Allin *d* Robert Clouse *ph* Gilbert Hubbs *m* Lalo Schifrin

Bruce Lee, John Saxon, Shih Kien, Jim Kelly, Bob Wall

'A good-natured example of the pleasures of schlock art.'—*Pauline Kael*

The Entertainer*
GB 1960 96m bw
BL / Bryanston / Woodfall / Holly (John Croydon)

A faded seaside comedian reflects on his failure as an entertainer and as a man.
Even with Olivier repeating his stage triumph, or perhaps because of it, this tragi-comedy remains defiantly theatrical and does not take wing on film.

w John Osborne, Nigel Kneale, *play* John Osborne *d* Tony Richardson *ph* Oswald Morris *m* John Addison

Laurence Olivier, Joan Plowright, Brenda de Banzie, *Roger Livesey*, Alan Bates, Shirley Anne Field, Albert Finney, Thora Hird, Daniel Massey

'No amount of deafening sound effects and speciously busy cutting can remove one's feeling that behind this distracting façade of heightened realism lurks a basic lack of confidence.'—*Peter John Dyer*

† A 1975 version for television starred Jack Lemmon.

AAN: Laurence Olivier

Entertaining Mr Sloane*
GB 1969 94m Technicolor
Pathe / Canterbury (Douglas Kentish)

A lodger attracts the amorous attention of both the middle-aged daughter and older son of the house.
A Gothic *tour de force* of bad taste which worked better on the stage but has its moments.

w Clive Exton, *play* Joe Orton *d* Douglas Hickox *ph* Wolfgang Suschitsky *m* Georgie Fame

Beryl Reid, Harry Andrews, Peter McEnery, Alan Webb

The Entity
US 1981 125m Technicolor Panavision
(TCF) Pelleport Investors / American Cinema (Harold Schneider)

A young mother is attacked and raped by an invisible entity which may come from her own id.
Unpleasant nonsense, way overlong but with the occasional well-staged scene for those who can stay the course.

w Frank DeFelitta, from his novel *d* Sidney J. Furie *ph* Stephen H. Burum *m* Charles Bernstein *pd* Charles Rosen *ed* Frank J. Urioste

Barbara Hershey, Ron Silver, David Labiosa, George Coe, Jacqueline Brookes

Entr'acte**
France 1924 20m approx bw silent
Ballets Suédois

Various eccentric characters become involved in a crazy chase.
Hilarious nonsense short, devised originally to be shown between the acts of a Dadaist ballet. Very clearly the start of a famous directorial career.

w Francis Picabia *d, ed René Clair*
ph J. Berliet

Jean Borlin, Inge Fries, Francis Picabia, Man Ray, Georges Auric, Marcel Achard, Marcel Duchamps

Entre Onze Heures et Minuit*
France 1948 103m bw
Francinex (Jacques Roitfeld)

A police detective solves his case by impersonating one of the victims.
Twisty, elaborate murder mystery, very competently performed but a little overlong.

w Henri Decoin, Marcel Rivet, *novel* Le Sosie de la Morgue by Claude Luxel *d* Henri Decoin *ph* Nicolas Hayer *m* Henri Saguet

Louis Jouvet, Madeleine Robinson, Robert Arnoux, Gisèle Casadeus

Entrée des Artistes*
France 1938 100m bw

Jealousies among the students at the Paris Conservatory lead to murder. Predictable but well-made audience pleaser. Louis Jouvet, Odette Joyeux, Claude Dauphin, Janine Darcey, Carette, Dalio, Sylvie. Written by Henri Jeanson, André Cayatte; directed by Marc Allegret; for Regina.

L'Equipage*
France 1935 107m bw

A World War I flier finds that the love of his wife is the wife of his colleague. Tense romantic drama with aerial sequences, subsequently remade in Hollywood as *The Woman Between. Charles Vanel, Jean-Pierre Aumont*, Annabella. From a story by Joseph Kessel; directed by *Anatole Litvak*; for Pathé-Natan. 'A gripping human story, beautifully told.'—*Variety*

Equus*
GB 1977 137m colour
UA / Winkast (Denis Holt)

A middle-aged psychiatrist tries to find out why a 17-year-old boy blinded six horses.
Overlong film version of a play which was a *succès d'estime*; it makes the fatal mistake of showing the tragic events realistically instead of stylistically as was done on the stage, and as a study in abnormal psychology it is scarcely gripping or revealing.

w Peter Shaffer, from his play *d* Sidney Lumet *ph* Oswald Morris *m* Richard Rodney Bennett *pd* Tony Walton

Richard Burton, Peter Firth, Colin Blakely, Joan Plowright, Harry Andrews, Eileen Atkins, Jenny Agutter, Kate Reid

'It sets Peter Shaffer's worst ideas on a pedestal.'—*Pauline Kael*

AAN: Peter Shaffer; Richard Burton; Peter Firth

Eraserhead
US 1976 89m bw

A nondescript man has a number of increasingly nightmarish experiences including becoming pregnant and being consumed by a planet. Tediously elongated piece of schlock surrealism. At least Bunuel and Dali didn't take so long about their nonsense. John Nance, Charlotte Stewart, Allen Joseph. Written, produced and directed by David Lynch; photographed by David Elmes and Herbert Cardwell; for David Lynch.

'A compulsive hybrid mix of punk surrealism and B picture.'—*Time Out*

Eroica*
Poland 1957 83m bw
Kadr
aka: *Heroism*

Two ironic episodes of war; in the 1944 Warsaw uprising and in a POW camp.
Nicely-judged little stories with a sting.

w Jerzy Stefan Stawinski, from his novels *d* Andrzej Munk *ph* Jerzy Wojcik *m* Jan Krenz

Barbara Polomska, L. Niemszyk, Edward Dziewonski, K. Rudzki, Roman Klosowski, Josef Nowak

Erotikon*
Sweden 1920 85m approx bw silent
Svensk Filmindustri

When a professor discovers that his wife is unfaithful, he consoles himself with his young niece.
Sophisticated comedy drama filled with material which might later have appealed to Lubitsch; a little faded now, but it still has charm.

w Gustav Molander, Mauritz Stiller, *play* Franz Herzeg *d Mauritz Stiller*
ph Henrik Jaenzon

Lars Hanson, Karin Molander, Tora Teje, Anders de Wahl

Erotikon*
Czechoslovakia 1929 85m approx bw silent
Gem Film

A stationmaster's daughter takes a rich lover.
Atmospheric little sex drama which sufficiently justified its title to be a big international success.

wd Gustav Machaty ph Vaclav Vich

Ita Rina, Karel Schleichert, Olaf Fjord, Theo Pistek

The Errand Boy
US 1961 92m bw
Paramount / Jerry Lewis (Ernest D. Glucksman)

A dimwit paperhanger causes havoc in a Hollywood studio but is eventually signed up as a comic to rival Jerry Lewis.
Feeble comedy with the star at his self-satisfied worst.

wd Jerry Lewis *ph* W. Wallace Kelley
m Walter Scharf

Jerry Lewis, Brian Donlevy, Sig Rumann, Fritz Feld, Isobel Elsom, Iris Adrian

Escapade
US 1935 87m bw
MGM (Bernard Hyman)

Affairs of a Viennese artist.
Turgid romantic drama copied from the more successful German film *Maskerade*.

w Herman J. Mankiewicz, *original* Walter Reisch *d* Robert Z. Leonard *ph* Ernest Haller *m* Bronislau Kaper, Walter Jurmann

William Powell, Luise Rainer, Virginia Bruce, Mady Christians, Reginald Owen, Frank Morgan, Laura Hope Crews, Henry Travers

'A triumph of studio slickness.'—*Variety*

Escapade*
GB 1955 87m bw
Pinnacle (Daniel Angel)

Parents row with a headmaster when their three sons steal an aeroplane, but all is well when it turns out that they are on a peace mission.
Whimsical comedy-drama with a rather foolish point; the cast however can hardly fail to provide entertaining moments.

w Gilbert Holland (Donald Ogden Stewart), *play* Roger MacDougall *d* Philip Leacock *ph* Eric Cross *m* Bruce Montgomery

ESCAPE. Romance, suspense and anti-Nazi propaganda expertly blended, MGM-style: Robert Taylor and Norma Shearer in a somewhat stagey pose.

John Mills, Alastair Sim, Yvonne Mitchell, Colin Gordon, Marie Lohr

Escapade in Florence
US 1962 80m Technicolor
Walt Disney (Bill Anderson)

Two American students in Florence uncover art thefts.
Cheerful adventure for children, well enough produced on location, but quite unmemorable.
w Maurice Tombragel from the novel The Golden Doors by Edward Fenton *d* Steve Previn *ph* Kurt Grigoleit *m* Buddy Baker

Ivan Desny, Tommy Kirk, Annette Alliotto, Nino Castelnuovo

Escapade in Japan
US 1957 93m Technirama
RKO (Arthur Lubin)

An American boy survives a plane crash in Tokyo and the crisis reunites his parents.
Nicely photographed travelogue with a thread of plot; pleasant but hardly sustaining.
w Winston Miller *d* Arthur Lubin
ph William Snyder *m* Max Steiner

Cameron Mitchell, Teresa Wright, Jon Prevost, Philip Ober

Escape
GB 1930 69m bw
ATP (Basil Dean)

An escaped convict on Dartmoor is helped and hindered by various chance encounters.
Episodic, unsatisfactory drama from a stilted play.

wd Basil Dean, *play* John Galsworthy
ph Jack Mackenzie

Gerald du Maurier, Edna Best, Madeleine Carroll, Gordon Harker, Horace Hodges, Mabel Poulton, Lewis Casson, Ian Hunter, Felix Aylmer

'A more careful work than most of the British talker product, but as an entertainment proposition it doesn't mean much.'—*Variety*

'There is a love from which no man can escape!'
Escape**
US 1940 104m bw
MGM (Lawrence Weingarten)
reissue title: *When the Door Opened*

An American gets his mother out of a Nazi concentration camp before World War II.
Ingenious but somewhat slow-moving melodrama with an exciting climax and good production values.

w Arch Oboler, Marguerite Roberts, *novel* Ethel Vance *d Mervyn Le Roy ph* Robert Planck *m* Franz Waxman

Norma Shearer, Robert Taylor, *Conrad Veidt, Nazimova*, Felix Bressart, Albert Basserman, Philip Dorn, Bonita Granville

'It takes an hour to get started and makes just another feeble fable from headlines.'—*Otis Ferguson*

'Far and away the most dramatic and hair-raising picture yet made on the sinister subject of persecution in a totalitarian land.'—*Bosley Crowther, New York Times*

'One of the most poignant dramatic films of the year.'—*Modern Screen*

'The director takes forever to set up the manoeuvres, and the villain is so much more attractive than the hero that the whole thing turns into a feeble, overproduced joke.'—*Pauline Kael, 70s*

'Some men are born to imperilled adventure! Some women are drawn to the most dangerous of loves!'
Escape
GB 1948 79m bw
TCF (William Perlberg)

Wholly artificial, predictable and uninteresting remake of the 1930 film.

w Philip Dunne *d* Joseph L. Mankiewicz
ph Frederick A. Young *m* William Alwyn

Rex Harrison, Peggy Cummins, William Hartnell, Norman Wooland, Jill Esmond

The Escape Artist*
US 1982 93m Technicolor
Zoetrope Studios (Doug Claybourne, Buck Houghton)

A young boy justifies his descent from 'the world's greatest escape artist'.
Curiously unfulfilled fable, too vague to satisfy the family audience it seems to aim at, but with pleasant moments.
w Melissa Mathison, Stephen Zito, *novel* David Wagoner *d* Caleb Deschanel *ph* Stephen H. Burum *m* Georges Delerue *pd* Dean Tavoularis

Griffin O'Neal, Raul Julia, Teri Garr, Joan Hackett, Gabriel Dell, Desi Arnaz

Escape by Night
GB 1953 79m bw
Tempean (Robert S. Baker, Monty Berman)

A tough reporter tries to get the inside story on a vice ring.
Formula thick ear with what now seems the world's most unlikely villain—Sid James.
wd John Gilling *ph* Monty Berman
m Stanley Black

Bonar Colleano, Andrew Ray, Sidney James, Ted Ray, Simone Silva, Avice Landone, Patrick Barr

Escape from Alcatraz*
US 1979 112m De Luxe
Paramount / Malpaso (Don Siegel)

The allegedly true story of a 1960 escape from the prison on a rock in San Francisco Bay.
A dour, terse, depressing prison movie which makes an uncomfortable star vehicle and not very much of an entertainment, but does preserve a certain integrity right to its ambiguous ending.

w Richard Tuggle, *book* J. Campbell Bruce *d* Don Siegel *ph* Bruce Surtees *m* Jerry Fielding *pd* Allen Smith

Clint Eastwood, Patrick McGoohan, Roberts Blossom, Jack Thibeau, Larry Hankin

'An almost entirely interior film masquerading as an exterior one.'—*Tom Milne, MFB*

Escape from Dartmoor*
GB 1930 77m bw

A barber murders his wife's lover. Stilted melodrama, of interest only as an early British part-talkie. (The only words heard are from a film in a cinema which the characters visit.) Nora Baring, Uno Henning, Hans Schlettow. Written by Herbert Price; directed by *Anthony Asquith*; for Pro Patria. 'Morbid material, interesting only because of clever direction.'—*Variety*

Escape from East Berlin
Germany / US 1962 94m bw
MGM / Walter Wood / Hans Albin
aka: *Tunnel 28*

An East German chauffeur is persuaded to help an escape attempt by digging and tunnelling under the Berlin Wall.
Cheerless escape melodrama, thinly based on fact but without much suspense.

w Gabrielle Upton, Peter Berneis, Millard Lampell *d* Robert Siodmak *ph* Georg Krause *m* Hans-Martin Majewski

Don Murray, Christine Kaufmann, Werner Klemperer, Ingrid van Bergen

Escape from Fort Bravo*
US 1953 98m Anscocolor
MGM (Nicholas Nayfack)

A girl helps her Confederate lover to escape from a Yankee fort in Arizona; the commander then tries to save them from Indians.
Grade A western, effectively shot in Death Valley.

w Frank Fenton *d* John Sturges *ph* Robert Surtees *m* Jeff Alexander

William Holden, Eleanor Parker, John Forsythe, William Demarest

Escape from New York*
US 1981 99m
Metrocolor Panavision
Avco Embassy / International Film Investors / Goldcrest (Larry Franco, Debra Hill)

In 1997 the whole of Manhattan Island has become a vast security prison; a president has to bale out over it and is taken hostage.
Inventive but too complex melodrama with unattractive detail; its director's biggest production but not his most rewarding.

w John Carpenter, Nick Castle *d John Carpenter* *ph* Jim Lucas *m* John Carpenter *pd* Joe Alves

Kurt Russell, Lee Van Cleef, Ernest Borgnine, Donald Pleasence, Isaac Hayes, Season Hubley, Adrienne Barbeau, Harry Dean Stanton

Escape from the Dark
GB 1976 104m Technicolor
Walt Disney (Ron Miller)

In 1909 Yorkshire, two boys save pit ponies from the slaughterhouse.
Efficient family fare with plenty of suspense and good character cameos.

w Rosemary Anne Sisson *d* Charles Jarrott *ph* Paul Beeson *m* Ron Goodwin

Alastair Sim, Peter Barkworth, Maurice Colbourne, Susan Tebbs, Geraldine McEwan, Prunella Scales, Leslie Sands, Joe Gladwin

Escape from the Planet of the Apes
US 1971 97m De Luxe Panavision
TCF / APJAC (Arthur P. Jacobs, Frank Capra Jnr)

Three educated apes travel back from the disaster-strewn future to warn mankind of what lies ahead. Mankind naturally misunderstands. Predictable third in the series, with infantile humour alternating with a downbeat trend.

w Paul Dehn *d* Don Taylor *ph* Joseph Biroc *m* Jerry Goldsmith

Roddy McDowall, Kim Hunter, Bradford Dillman, Ricardo Montalban, Natalie Trundy, Eric Braeden, William Windom, Sal Mineo

† See also *Planet of the Apes*.

Escape from Zahrain
US 1961 93m Technicolor Panavision
Paramount (Ronald Neame)

Prisoners escape across the desert from an oil sheikdom.
Slow, boring adventure film; good to look at, with James Mason unbilled in a tiny part.

w Robin Estridge *d* Ronald Neame *ph* Ellsworth Fredericks *m* Lyn Murray

Yul Brynner, Sal Mineo, Madlyn Rhue, Jack Warden, Jay Novello

Escape in the Desert
US 1945 81m bw
Warner (Alex Gottlieb)

An American flier outwits renegade Nazis.
Oddball remake of *The Petrified Forest*, with Nazis sitting in for gangsters. Of no interest in itself.

w Thomas Job, *play* Robert E. Sherwood *d* Edward A. Blatt *ph* Robert Burks *m* Adolph Deutsch

Philip Dorn, Helmut Dantine, Alan Hale, Jean Sullivan, Irene Manning, Samuel S. Hinds

Escape in the Fog
US 1945 65m bw

A nurse sees a man attacked in a dream, and helps to save him when the events recur in real life. Muddy little spy story with premonition used as a book-end. Nina Foch, Otto Kruger, William Wright. Written by Aubrey Wisberg; directed by Budd Boetticher; for Columbia.

Escape Me Never*
GB 1935 95m bw
B and D (Herbert Wilcox)

The mother of an illegitimate baby marries a composer who loves someone else.
Archetypal romantic weepie which has probably the star's most memorable and likeable performance.

w Carl Zuckerman, Robert Cullen, *play* Margaret Kennedy *d* Paul Czinner *ph* Georges Périnal

Elisabeth Bergner, Hugh Sinclair, Griffith Jones, Penelope Dudley Ward, Irene Vanbrugh, Leon Quartermaine, Lyn Harding

'Story stirs audience resentment, yet its able presentation commands attention.'—*Variety*

'That it is a thoroughly British film is proved by the fact that among the staff one can see names like Andrejiev, Allgeier and Strassner, that the principal actress is German, and the producer is German too.'—*James Agate*

AAN: Elisabeth Bergner

Escape Me Never
US 1947 104m bw
Warner (Henry Blanke)

Muddled remake of the above with shifted emphasis. So ill-conceived it's like watching through frosted glass.

w Thomas Williamson *d* Peter Godfrey *ph* Sol Polito *m* Erich Wolfgang Korngold

Errol Flynn, Ida Lupino, Eleanor Parker, Gig Young, Reginald Denny, Isobel Elsom, Albert Basserman, Ludwig Stossel, Helene Thimig

Escape Route
GB 1952 79m bw

Man on the run turns out to be FBI agent on the spy trail. A moderate co-feature, as unremarkable as its plot. George Raft, Sally Gray, Clifford Evans, Reginald Tate. Written by John Baines and Nicholas Phipps; directed by Seymour Friedman and Peter Graham Scott; for Banner / Eros. (US title: *I'll Get You*.)

Escape to Athena
GB 1979 117m Eastmancolor Panavision
ITC / Pimlico (David Niven Jnr, Jack Wiener)

Prisoners-of-war on a Greek island during World War II recruit the aid of their sympathetic camp commandant in harassing the SS.
Expensive but not very involving thick-ear, hampered by tediously typecast actors and an uninventive script.

w Edward Anhalt, Richard S. Lochte *d* George Pan Cosmatos *ph* Gil Taylor *m* Lalo Schifrin

Roger Moore, David Niven, Elliott Gould, Sonny Bono, Telly Savalas, Claudia Cardinale, Stefanie Powers, Richard Roundtree, Anthony Valentine

'Performing as though they had met up by chance on holiday . . . the clutch of box office stars do what they can in a situation where they are the stand-ins and the stuntmen (especially the motorcyclists) dominate the screen.'—*Martyn Auty, MFB*

Escape to Burma
US 1955 88m Technicolor Superscope
Benedict Bogeaus

An adventurer suspected of murder hides out on the tea plantation of an indomitable American woman.
Far Eastern hokum in which the heroine has a way with elephants.

w Talbot Jennings, Herbert Donovan *d* Allan Dwan *ph* John Alton *m* Louis Forbes

Barbara Stanwyck, Robert Ryan, David Farrar, Murvyn Vye, Reginald Denny

Escape to Danger
GB 1943 92m bw
RKO (William Sistrom)

A British schoolmistress becomes a spy.
Adequate propaganda hokum.

w Wolfgang Wilhelm, Jack Whittingham *d* Lance Comfort *ph* Max Greene *m* William Alwyn

Eric Portman, Ann Dvorak, Karel Stepanek, Ronald Ward, Ronald Adam, Lily Kann, David Peel, Felix Aylmer, A. E. Matthews

Escape to Glory
US 1940 74m bw
Columbia (Sam Bischoff)
aka: *Submarine Zone*

A merchant ship with a variety of passengers is stalked by a Nazi submarine.
Minor *Grand Hotel* afloat: quite brisk and watchable.

w P. J. Wolfson *d* John Brahm *ph* Franz Planer

Pat O'Brien, Constance Bennett, John Halliday, Alan Baxter, Melville Cooper, Edgar Buchanan, Marjorie Gateson

Escape to Witch Mountain*
US 1974 97m Technicolor
Walt Disney (Jerome Courtland)

Two mysterious orphan children have extraordinary powers, are chased by a scheming millionaire, and prove to come from another planet.
Mildly ingenious story frittered away by poor scripting and special effects. A stimulating change in children's films, however.

w Robert Malcolm Young, *novel* Alexander Key *d* John Hough *ph* Frank Phillips *m* Johnny Mandel *sp* Art Cruickshank, Danny Lee

Ray Milland, Donald Pleasence, Eddie Albert, Kim Richards, Ike Eisenmann, Walter Barnes, Reta Shaw, Denver Pyle

Escort West
US 1958 75m bw Cinemascope

An ex-Confederate soldier helps the survivors of a Union wagon train attack. Watchable lower-berth western. Victor Mature, Elaine Stewart, Faith Domergue, Noah Beery Jnr, Rex Ingram, John Hubbard. Written by Leo Gordon and Fred Hartsook; directed by Francis D. Lyon; for Batjac / Romina / UA.

Eskimo*
US 1933 120m bw

The life of an Eskimo hunter and his family. Curious fated attempt by a major studio to do a northern version of the successful *White Shadows in the South Seas*. Despite a melodramatic plot and gripping documentary sequences, the locale chilled audiences to the marrow. Mala, Peter Freuchen. Written by John Lee Mahin from books by Peter Freuchen; directed by W. S. Van Dyke; for MGM. 'Igloo whoopee variations not sufficiently hotcha to spell b.o.'—*Variety*

Espionage*
US 1937 67m bw
MGM (Harry Rapf)

Spies and counter spies mingle on the Orient Express.
Lively second feature on familiar lines.

w Manuel Seff, Leonard Lee, Ainsworth Morgan, *play* Walter Hackett *d* Kurt Neumann *ph* Ray June *m* William Axt

Edmund Lowe, Madge Evans, Paul Lukas, Ketti Gallian, Skeets Gallagher, Leonid Kinskey, Barnett Parker, Frank Reicher

'Quite some laughs but chiefly for the duals.'—*Variety*

Espionage Agent
US 1939 83m bw
Warner (Louis F. Edelmann)

An American diplomat falls in love with a spy.
Anti-isolationist, semi-documentary exposé, a rather sketchy cross between *Foreign Correspondent* and *Confessions of a Nazi Spy*.

w Warren Duff, Michael Fessier, Frank Donaghue, Robert Buckner *d* Lloyd Bacon *ph* Charles Rosher

Joel McCrea, Brenda Marshall, Jeffrey Lynn, George Bancroft, Stanley Ridges, James Stephenson, Nana Bryant

'War headlines dramatized. Lots of openings for exploitation.'—*Variety*

Les Espions
France 1957 136m bw
Cinedis (L. de Mazure)
aka: *The Spies*

Spies from all sides converge on a psychiatric clinic where an atomic scientist is being hidden.
Unsatisfactory thriller with some aims to be both a whimsy and a parable. Not one of its director's successes.

w Henri-Georges Clouzot, Gerome Geronomi *d* Henri-Georges Clouzot *ph* Christian Matras *m* Georges Auric

Martita Hunt, Peter Ustinov, Sam Jaffe, Vera Clouzot, Gabrielle Dorziat, Curt Jurgens, Gerard Sety, O. E. Hasse

Espoir*
France / Spain 1938–45 73m bw
Cornignion / Moligniec
aka: *Days of Hope; Man's Hope*

Events of the Spanish Civil War, recreated by surviving combatants.
Anti-fascist propaganda which seems a good deal less inspiring than on its first release, but has some vivid cinematic ideas.

wd André Malraux *ph* Louis Page *m* Darius Milhaud

Mejuto, Nicolas Rodriguez, Jose Lado

'And it was written—gather together all the fair young virgins unto the palace—and let the maiden which pleaseth the king be queen.'

Esther and the King
US 1960 109m Technicolor Cinemascope
TCF / Galatea (Raoul Walsh)

A Persian king selects a new bride who helps defend him from his enemies.
Tedious biblical hokum with a muddled script and the usual co-production deficiencies.

w Raoul Walsh, Michael Elkins *d* Raoul Walsh *ph* Mario Bava *m* Francesco Lavagnino, Roberto Nicolosi

Richard Egan, Joan Collins, Dennis O'Dea, Sergei Fantoni, Rik Battaglia

Esther Waters
GB 1947 108m bw
GFD / Wessex (Ian Dalrymple)

In the 1870s, a maid is seduced by a squire but insists on bringing up her child without help.
Faded costumer with tentative performances and little else to recommend it.

w Michael Gordon, William Rose, Gerard Tyrrell, *novel* George Moore *d* Ian Dalrymple, Peter Proud *ph* C. Pennington-Richards, H. E. Fowle *m* Gordon Jacob

Kathleen Ryan, Dirk Bogarde, Cyril Cusack, Ivor Barnard, Fay Compton, Mary Clare, Morland Graham

Eternal Love
US 1929 110m approx bw silent

Swiss lovers find their only option is to commit suicide. Thin Romeo and Juliet stuff for which the star was too old. John Barrymore, Camilla Horn, Victor Varconi, Hobart Bosworth, Bodil Rosing. Written by Hans Kraly from a novel by Jakob Beer; directed by Ernst Lubitsch; for Feature/UA.

The Eternal Sea
US 1955 96m bw
Republic (John H. Auer)

The career of an aircraft carrier captain in World War II and Korea.
Solemn biopic of John Hoskins: competent but quite uninspired.

w Allen Rivkin *d* John H. Auer *ph* John L. Russell Jnr *m* Elmer Bernstein

Sterling Hayden, Alexis Smith, Dean Jagger, Virginia Grey

Eternally Yours*
US 1939 95m bw
Walter Wanger

A magician's wife thinks he is too interested in his tricks.
Slightly scatty romantic comedy, amiable if not quite good enough to stand the test of time, but with a great cast.

w Gene Towne, Graham Baker *d* Tay Garnett *ph* Merritt Gerstad *m* Werner Janssen

Loretta Young, David Niven, Broderick Crawford, Hugh Herbert, Billie Burke, C. Aubrey Smith, Raymond Walburn, Zasu Pitts, Virginia Field, Eve Arden, Herman the Rabbit

'Will have to depend on the name power to get it by.'—*Variety*

'An amusing and irresponsible picture, though on the whole more irresponsible than amusing.'—*New York Times*

AAN: Werner Janssen

L'Etoile du Nord*
France 1982 124m Fujicolor
Sara Films / Antenne 2 (Alain Sarde)

On a transcontinental train, a petty con man finds a new lover but is involved in an argument which leads to murder.
Curious semi-thriller with good credentials, compromised by the fact that having changed most of the original novel it tries to make new statements of its own.

w Jean Aurenche, Michel Grisolia, Pierre Granier-Deferre *novel* Le Locataire by Georges Simenon *d* Pierre Granier-Deferre *ph* Pierre-William Glenn *m* Philippe Sarde

Philippe Noiret, Simone Signoret, Fanny Cottençon, Julie Jezequel

Eureka
GB / USA 1982 129m Technicolor
MGM / UA / RPC / JF (Jeremy Thomas)

An immensely rich gold striker becomes a recluse and is murdered by Mafia hoods.
Unpleasant in detail and obscure in meaning, this is the sort of film of which the fact that it was financed at all is the most interesting thing about it.

w Paul Mayersberg, *book* Who Killed Sir Harry Oakes? by Marshall Houts *d* Nicolas Roeg *ph* Alex Thomson *m* Stanley Myers *pd* Michael Seymour

Gene Hackman, Theresa Russell, Rutger Hauer, Jane Lapotaire, Mickey Rourke, Ed Lauter

'A Roeg elephant film.'—*Variety*

'Between them Roeg and Mayersberg have worked an astonishing alchemy through which an abstraction of the basic patterns of human intercourse is rendered wholly concrete. Embodying Vico's cyclical theory of history, it expounds the despair of humanity's vicious circle from ecstasy to agony, as the impulse to love and possession leads inevitably to loss and destruction.'—*Tom Milne, Monthly Film Bulletin*

'I've a feeling it will become a cult movie, but no one will convince me that it isn't just the poshest kind of tosh.'—*Margaret Hinxman, Daily Mail*

Eureka Stockade
GB 1948 103m bw
Ealing (Leslie Norman)
US title: *Massacre Hill*

In 1854, Australian gold miners revolt against a harsh governor.
Unconvincingly made historical actioner from Ealing's antipodean period.

w Harry Watt, Walter Greenwood, Ralph Smart *d* Harry Watt *ph* Gerald Heath *m* John Greenwood

Chips Rafferty, Jane Barrett, Gordon Jackson, Jack Lambert, Peter Illing, Ralph Truman, Peter Finch

Europa 51*
Italy 1952 110m bw
Ponti / de Laurentiis

An American society woman living in Rome seeks vainly for truth in the chaotic post-war world and is committed to an asylum by her husband.
A despairing, ironic comment on a period which unfortunately does not convince on the personal level.

w Roberto Rossellini and others *d* Roberto Rossellini *ph* Aldo Tonti *m* Renzo Rossellini

Ingrid Bergman, Alexander Knox, Ettore Giannini, Giulietta Masina

The Europeans*
GB 1979 83m colour
Merchant Ivory (Ismail Merchant)

In 1850, a European baroness arrives in Boston in search of a husband.
Charming if rather tentative period mood piece, probably the most professional and judicious of all the overpraised Merchant Ivory offerings.

w Ruth Prawer Jhabvala, *novel* Henry James *d* James Ivory *ph* Larry Pizer *m* Richard Robbins *ad* Jeremiah Rusconi

Lee Remick, Robin Ellis, Tim Woodward, Wesley Addy, Lisa Eichhorn

'A film of astonishing delicacy and richness in which the tiniest gesture or intonation reverberates with a world of meanings.'—*Tom Milne, MFB*

Eva
France / Italy 1962 135m bw
Paris / Interopa (Robert and Raymond Hakim)

A raw Welsh novelist in Venice is humiliated by a money-loving Frenchwoman who erotically ensnares him.
Foolish story of a *femme fatale*; elegantly Freudian at moments, it long outstays its welcome.

w Hugo Butler, Evan Jones, *novel* James Hadley Chase *d* Joseph Losey *ph* Gianni di Venanzo *m* Michel Legrand

Stanley Baker, Jeanne Moreau, Virna Lisi, James Villiers

Eve Knew her Apples
US 1945 64m bw

A radio singer sets off incognito for a vacation. Mild musical support whose plot owes something to *It Happened One Night*.
Ann Miller, William Wright, Robert Williams, Ray Walker. Written by E. Elwin Moran; directed by Will Jason; for Wallace McDonald / Columbia.

The Eve of St Mark
US 1944 95m bw
TCF (William Perlberg)

A small-town boy goes to war and his sweetheart waits for him.
Poetic propaganda based on a sticky play which however had a tragic ending which the film eschews. Smartly made is all one can say.

w George Seaton, *play* Maxwell Anderson *d* John M. Stahl *ph* Joseph La Shelle *m* Cyril Mockridge

William Eythe, Anne Baxter, Michael O'Shea, Vincent Price, Ruth Nelson, Ray Collins, Stanley Prager, Henry Morgan

Eve Wants to Sleep*
Poland 1957 98m bw
Film Polski (Wislaw Mincer)

An innocent country girl arrives in a city overrun by subversives.
Curious yet sympathetic black farce, like a cross between *Hellzapoppin* and *M*. One on its own.

wd Tadeusz Chmielewski ph Stefan Matyjaskiewicz *m* Henryk Czyz

Barbara Kwiatkowska, Stanislaw Mikulski, Ludwik Benoit

Evel Knievel
US 1971 90m Metrocolor
(MGM) Fanfare (George Hamilton)

Episodes from the life of a motor-cycle stuntman.
Mildly entertaining ragbag of action sequences and fragments of philosophy which might have been more tolerable had EK played himself.

w Alan Caillou, John Milius *d* Marvin Chomsky *ph* David Walsh *m* Pat Williams

George Hamilton, Sue Lyon, Bert Freed, Rod Cameron

Evelyn Prentice
US 1934 80m bw
MGM (John W. Considine Jnr)

The wife of a criminal lawyer has an affair with a man who blackmails her.
Moderate domestic-cum-courtroom melodrama, heavily reliant on its popular stars.

w Lenore Coffee, *novel* W. E. Woodward *d* William K. Howard *ph* Charles G. Clarke *md* Oscar Radin

Myrna Loy, William Powell, Una Merkel, Harvey Stephens, Isabel Jewell, Rosalind Russell, Henry Wadsworth, Edward Brophy

'Uneven film but extra heavy cast and strong femme sob yarn will put it in the money class.'—*Variety*

Evenings for Sale
US 1932 68m bw

An impoverished count becomes a dancing master. Scented Viennese romance intended to extend the star's success in *Trouble in Paradise.* Herbert Marshall, Sari Maritza, Mary Boland, Charles Ruggles. Written by S. K. Lauren, Agnes Brand Leahy from a novel by I. A. R Wylie; directed by Stuart Walker; for Paramount. 'Fair entertainment but extremely doubtful on the draw.'—*Variety*

Evensong*
GB 1934 84m bw
Gaumont (Michael Balcon)

At the turn of the century, an Austrian prima donna gives up her career for love.
Well-made romantic drama of its type, notable as the best of its star's few films.

w Edward Knoblock, Dorothy Farnum, *play* Beverly Nichols *d* Victor Saville *ph* Max Greene

Evelyn Laye, Fritz Kortner, Carl Esmond, Alice Delysia, Emlyn Williams, Muriel Aked

'A highly absorbing and intelligently produced musical . . . looks like money.'—*Variety*

Ever in My Heart
US 1933 70m bw

A Daughter of the American Revolution finds that her husband is a German spy. Heavy romantic drama with a tragic finish. One for the ladies. Barbara Stanwyck, Otto Kruger, Ralph Bellamy, Ruth Donnelly, Frank Albertson. Written by Bertram Millhauser from a story by Beulah Marie Dix; directed by Archie Mayo; for Warners. 'A clean picture, more for the nabes than the first runs.'—*Variety*

'She'd say yes, but she no's him too well!'

Ever Since Eve
US 1937 80m bw
Warner (Earl Baldwin)

A publisher falls for a pretty girl, not realizing that she is his own plain secretary in disguise.
Silly romantic comedy which sadly lacks wit, style and believability.

w Lawrence Riley, Earl Baldwin, Lillie Hayward *d* Lloyd Bacon *ph* George Barnes *m* Heinz Roemheld

Marion Davies (her last film), Robert Montgomery, Frank McHugh, Patsy Kelly, Louise Fazenda, Barton MacLane, Mary Treen

'A highly incredible script, and badly handled . . . it just doesn't jell.'—*Variety*

Ever Since Venus
US 1944 74m bw

The inventors of a new lipstick formula can't get production facilities. Modestly effective wartime comedy with good talent not ill-used. Hugh Herbert, Billy Gilbert, Ina Ray Hutton, Glenda Farrell, Ann Savage, Ross Hunter, Alan Mowbray, Fritz Feld, Thurston Hall, Marjorie Gateson. Written by Arthur Dreifuss and McElbert Moore; directed by Arthur Dreifuss; for Columbia.

Evergreen**
GB 1934 90m bw
Gaumont (Michael Balcon)

A star's daughter takes her mother's place, with romantic complications.
Pleasant musical with more wit and style than might be expected.

w Emlyn Williams, Marjorie Gaffney, *play* Benn W. Levy *d Victor Saville ph* Glen Mac Williams *songs* Rodgers and Hart ('Dancing on the Ceiling', 'Dear Dear'); all other songs Harry Woods

Jessie Matthews, Sonnie Hale, Betty Balfour, Barry Mackay, Ivor McLaren, Hartley Power

Every Day's a Holiday*
US 1937 79m bw
Paramount (Emmanuel Cohen)

A confidence girl in the old Bowery sells Brooklyn Bridge to suckers.
The most satisfactory example of post-Legion of Decency Mae West, the smut being replaced by a lively cast of comedians.

w Mae West d A. Edward Sutherland *ph* Karl Struss *songs* various

Mae West, Edmund Lowe, Charles Butterworth, Charles Winninger, Walter Catlett, Lloyd Nolan, Herman Bing, Roger Imhof, Chester Conklin

'A lively, innocuously bawdy, and rowdy entertainment.'—*Variety*

Every Girl Should be Married
US 1948 84m bw
RKO (Don Hartman, Dore Schary)

A determined girl sets her cap at a bachelor pediatrician.
Woefully thin star comedy with few laughs.

w Stephen Morehouse Avery, Don Hartman *d* Don Hartman *ph* George E. Diskant *m* Leigh Harline

Cary Grant, Betsy Drake, Franchot Tone, Diana Lynn, Alan Mowbray, Elizabeth Risdon, Richard Gaines

'In the past, Cary Grant has shown a talent for quietly underplaying comedy. In this picture, he has trouble finding comedy to play.'—*Time*

Every Home Should Have One
GB 1970 94m Eastmancolor
British Lion / Example (Ned Sherrin)

An advertising man goes berserk when he tries to think up an erotic way of selling porridge.
Tiresomely frenetic star comedy with the emphasis on smut.

w Marty Feldman, Barry Took, Denis Norden *d* James Clark *ph* Ken Hodges *m* John Cameron

Marty Feldman, Shelley Berman, Judy Cornwell, Julie Ege, Patrick Cargill, Jack Watson, Patience Collier, Penelope Keith, Dinsdale Landen

Every Little Crook and Nanny
US 1972 92m Metrocolor
MGM (Leonard J. Ackerman)

A Mafia chief finds his child's new nanny has a grudge against him.
Sporadically amusing farce.

w Cy Howard, Jonathan Axelrod, Robert Klane *d* Cy Howard *ph* Philip Lathrop *m* Fred Karlin

Victor Mature, Lynn Redgrave, Paul Sand, Maggie Blye, Austin Pendleton, John Astin, Dom De Luise

Every Night at Eight
US 1935 80m bw
Paramount (Walter Wanger)

Three sisters become a successful radio singing team.
Forgettable comedy musical with a mildly interesting cast.

w Gene Towne, Graham Baker *d* Raoul Walsh *ph* James Van Trees *songs* Dorothy Fields, Jimmy McHugh

George Raft, Alice Faye, Frances Langford, Patsy Kelly, The Radio Rogues, Walter Catlett, Herman Bing

'Looks like another case of missed opportunity . . . a routine show world romance.'—*Variety*

Every Saturday Night: see The Jones Family

Every Time we Say Goodbye
US 1986 95m colour

In 1942 Jerusalem, an American pilot falls for a Sephardic Jewish girl. Patchy and spasmodically developed story of love across the cultures: TV movie stuff. Tom Hanks, Cristina Marsillach, Benedict Taylor, Anat Atzmon. Written by Moshe Mizrahi, Rachel Fabien, Leah Appet; directed by Moshe Mizrahi; for Jacob Kotzky / Tri-Star.

Every Which Way But Loose
US 1978 114m De Luxe
Warner / Malpaso

A Los Angeles trucker wins an orang-utan in a prize fight and becomes involved in sundry brawls and chases.
Easy-going, shambling star vehicle which was liked by nobody but the public.

w Jeremy Joe Kronsberg *d* James Fargo *ph* Rexford Metz *md* Steve Dorff

Clint Eastwood, Sondra Locke, Ruth Gordon, Geoffrey Lewis, Walter Barnes
† The 1980 sequel, almost indistinguishable, was *Any Which Way You Can.*

Everybody Dance
GB 1936 74m bw
Gainsborough

A nightclub singer is forced to pose as a rural do-gooder. Thin comedy vehicle. Cicely Courtneidge, Ernest Truex, Charles Riesner Jnr, Billie de la Volta, Percy Parsons. Written by Stafford Dickens, Ralph Spence and Leslie Arliss; directed by Charles Riesner; for Gaumont.

Everybody Does It
US 1949 98m bw
TCF (Nunnally Johnson)

A stage-struck wife is chagrined to see her dull husband accidentally become an opera singer. Very mild remake of *Wife, Husband and Friend*; everyone tries to be zany, but the result is often just silly.

w Nunnally Johnson *d* Edmund Goulding *ph* Joseph La Shelle *m* Alfred Newman

Paul Douglas, Celeste Holm, Linda Darnell, Charles Coburn, Millard Mitchell, Lucile Watson, John Hoyt, George Tobias, Leon Belasco

'For sheer momentary enjoyment it would be hard to beat.'—*Richard Mallett, Punch*

Everybody Sing*
US 1937 80m bw
MGM (Harry Rapf)

An eccentric theatrical family is upstaged by its servants, who put on a Broadway show. Agreeably zany comedy with music.

w Florence Ryerson, Edgar Allan Woolf *d* Edwin L. Marin *ph* Joseph L. Ruttenberg *m* William Axt

Allan Jones, *Fanny Brice, Judy Garland*, Reginald Owen, Billie Burke, Lynne Carver, Monty Woolley, Reginald Gardiner, Henry Armetta

'Excellent film musical with fresh ideas and a corking cast . . . for the top spots.'—*Variety*

Everything But the Truth
US 1956 83m Technicolor
U-I (Howard Christie)

A small boy embarrasses his family by telling the truth at all times.
Dum-dum formula comedy made with jaded professionalism.

w Herb Meadow *d* Jerry Hopper *ph* Maury Gertsman *m* Milton Rosen

Maureen O'Hara, John Forsythe, Tim Hovey, Frank Faylen, Barry Atwater

Everything Happens at Night
US 1939 77m bw
TCF (Harry Joe Brown)

Two reporters fall for the daughter of a Nobel Peace Prize winner on the run from the Gestapo.
The star's sixth American film plays down the music and skating in favour of rather jaded spy comedy. Modest entertainment.

w Art Arthur, Robert Harari *d* Irving Cummings *ph* Edward Cronjager *m* various

Sonja Henie, Ray Milland, Robert Cummings, Maurice Moscovitch, Leonid Kinskey, Alan Dinehart, Fritz Feld, Victor Varconi

'At no time does very much happen that is of interest.'—*Variety*

Everything I Have Is Yours
US 1952 92m Technicolor
MGM (George Wells)

A song and dance team is disrupted when the wife decides to become a mother.
Uninventive but lively musical vehicle for the Champions.

w George Wells *d* Robert Z. Leonard *ph* William V. Skall *md* David Rose *ch* Nick Castle, Gower Champion

Marge and Gower Champion, Dennis O'Keefe, Eduard Franz

Everything Is Rhythm
GB 1936 73m bw

A dance band leader wins a European princess. Modest programme filler remarkable only for its record of a top band of its time. Harry Roy and his Band, Princess Pearl, Ivor Moreton, Dave Kaye. Written by Syd Courtenay, Jack Byrd and Stanley Haynes; directed by Alfred Goulding; for Joe Rock.

Everything Is Thunder*
GB 1936 76m bw
Gaumont British (S. C. Balcon)

A German girl helps a British prisoner of war to escape.
Tolerable let's-not-be-beastly melodrama, quite unusual in its time.

w Marion Dix, John Orton, *novel* J. B. Hardy *d* Milton Rosmer *ph* Gunther Krampf

Constance Bennett, Douglass Montgomery, Oscar Homolka, Roy Emerton, Frederick Lloyd, George Merritt

Everything You Always Wanted to Know About Sex*
US 1972 87m De Luxe
UA (Charles H. Joffe)

Seven sketches on sexual themes.
Dishevelled revue with a reasonable number of laughs for broadminded audiences.

wd Woody Allen, *book* Dr David Reuben *ph* David M. Walsh *m* Mundell Lowe *pd* Dale Hennesy

Woody Allen, Lynn Redgrave, Anthony Quayle, John Carradine, Lou Jacobi, Louise Lasser, Tony Randall, Burt Reynolds, Gene Wilder

Everything's Ducky
US 1961 81m bw

Two naval ratings adopt a talking duck. Anything-goes service farce, with material below the standard of the talent available. Mickey Rooney, Buddy Hackett, Jackie Cooper, Joanie Summers, Roland Winters. Written by John Fenton Murray and Benedict Freedman; directed by Don Taylor; for Barboo / Columbia.

The Evictors
US 1979 92m Movielab

Axe murders abound when a young couple move into an old house with a history. Old-hat horror, out of *Psycho* and *The Amityville Horror*: strictly for drive-ins. Michael Parks, Jessica Harper, Vic Morrow, Sue Ane Langdon. Written by Charles B. Pierce, Gary Rusoff and Paul Fisk; directed by Charles B. Pierce; for AIP.

The Evil
US 1978 89m Movielab
New World / Rangoon (Ed Carlin)

A psychologist takes a team to investigate a haunted house, and is soon sorry he meddled. Another variation on the theme of *The Haunting* and *The Legend of Hell House*; more this time on the horror comic level, but reasonably effective.

w Donald G. Thompson *d* Gus Trikonis *ph* Mario Di Leo *m* Johnny Harris

Richard Crenna, Joanna Pettet, Andrew Prine, Cassie Yates, Victor Buono, Lynne Moody

The Evil Dead
US 1980 (released 1983) 85m Du Art

Five youngsters in a remote cabin find an old book which helps them summon up dormant demons from a nearby forest. Semi-professional horror rubbish, blown up from 16mm and looking it. When released in England, it was prosecuted as unsuitable for public showing. Bruce Campbell, Ellen Sandweiss, Betsy Baker. Written and directed by Sam M. Raimi; for Renaissance. 'The *ne plus ultra* of low-budget gore and shock effects.'—*Variety*

† *Evil Dead 2* followed in 1987.

'The monster's back and no one can stop him!'

The Evil of Frankenstein
GB 1964 94m Technicolor
U-I / Hammer (Anthony Hinds)

Frankenstein returns to his derelict castle and finds the Monster preserved in a glacier.
For their third Frankenstein film Hammer made a distribution deal with Universal and thus for the first time were able to use fragments of the old plots as well as something approximating to the Karloff make-up. Production and writing, however, are sadly dispirited except when relying on sadism.

w John Elder (Anthony Hinds) *d* Freddie Francis *ph* John Wilcox *m* Don Banks

Peter Cushing, Peter Woodthorpe, Sandor Eles, Kiwi Kingston (as the monster), Duncan Lamont, Katy Wild, David Hutcheson

The Evil that Men Do
US 1984 90m CFI color
ITC / Capricorn / Zuleika Farms (Pancho Kohner)

A professional killer is asked to eliminate a sadistic political torturer in Guatemala.
More than usually turgid and unpleasant vehicle for a star who is now too old for this kind of thing.

w David Lee Henry, John Crowther, *novel* R. Lance Hill *d* J. Lee Thompson *ph* Javier Ruvalcaba Cruz *m* Ken Thorne

Charles Bronson, Theresa Saldana, Joseph Maher, Jose Ferrer, René Enriquez, John Glover, Raymond St Jacques

Evil Under the Sun
GB 1982 117m Technicolor Panavision
EMI / Mersham / Titan (John Brabourne, Richard Goodwin)

Hercule Poirot solves the murder of a film star on an Adriatic holiday island.
Very competent but somehow too bland package in the Agatha Christie series, not quite so lively as *Death on the Nile*.

w Anthony Shaffer, *novel* Agatha Christie *d* Guy Hamilton *ph* Christopher Challis *m* Cole Porter *pd* Elliot Scott

Peter Ustinov, James Mason, Diana Rigg, Maggie Smith, Colin Blakely, Jane Birkin, Nicholas Clay, Roddy McDowall, Sylvia Miles, Dennis Quilley

'They have swapped elegant English menace for a splurge of theatrical camp.'—*Time Out*

'Temperance beverage Noël Coward.'—*Sunday Times*

Ex-Champ
US 1939 72m bw

A retired boxer works as a doorman and has trouble with his ungrateful and semi-criminal son. Father-love weepie, rather hard to take. Victor McLaglen, Tom Brown, Nan Grey, William Frawley, Constance Moore. Written by Alex Gottleib, Edmund L. Hartmann, Gordon Kahn; directed by Phil Rosen; for Universal. 'Pathos and sentiment expertly mixed for satisfactory dualler.'—*Variety*

Ex-Flame
US 1930 68m bw

A modernized version of *East Lynne*. With so many American accents attached to the British peerage, this is mainly for laughs – unintentional ones. Neil Hamilton, Marian Nixon, Norman Kerry, Roland Drew, Snub Pollard. Written and directed by Victor Halperin; for Liberty. 'Old-fashioned mush stuff for the woman.'—*Variety*

'We don't dare tell you how daring it is!'

Ex-Lady*
US 1933 70m bw

A lady artist has ultra-modern views on sex and marriage, but turns conventional when she falls in love. Mildly shocking in its day, this romantic drama was one of the contributing factors to the onslaught of the Legion of Decency which transformed Hollywood output in the following year. Bette Davis (her first starring role), Gene Raymond, Frank McHugh, Monroe Owsley, Clare Dodd. Written by David Boehm from a story by Edith Fitzgerald and Robert Riskin (previously filmed in 1931 as *Illicit*); directed by Robert Florey; for Warner.

The Ex-Mrs Bradford*
US 1936 87m bw
MGM (Edward Kaufman)

A doctor's scatty ex-wife involves him in solving a murder plot.
Amusing crime comedy, just a little way behind *The Thin Man*.

w Anthony Veiller, James Edward Grant *d* Stephen Roberts *ph* J. Roy Hunt *m* Roy Webb

William Powell, Jean Arthur, James Gleason, Eric Blore, Robert Armstrong, Lila Lee, Grant Mitchell, Ralph Morgan

'Forged by a god! Foretold by a wizard! Found by a king!'
'No mortal could possess it! No kingdom could command it!'

Excalibur*
US 1981 140m Technicolor
Warner / Orion (John Boorman)

The story of King Arthur, Merlin, Uther Pendragon, the Holy Grail and the Lady of the Lake.
Curiously pointless retelling of a legend with unexplained flashes of realism and bouts of gore alternating with romance and modern wisecracks. Of mainly visual interest.

w Rospo Pallenberg, John Boorman *d* John Boorman *ph* Alex Thomson *m* Trevor Jones *pd Anthony Pratt*

Nigel Terry, Helen Mirren, Nicol Williamson, Nicholas Clay, Cherie Lunghi, Paul Geoffrey

'Left entirely to his own devices, Boorman seems to run in self-defeating circles.'—*Richard Combs, MFB.*

'It tries overhard to be simultaneously critical and credulous, magical and earthy, inspiring and entertaining.'—*Sunday Times*

'A record of the comings and goings of arbitrary, inconsistent, shadowy figures who are not heroes but simply giants run amok.'—*Roger Ebert*

AAN: Alex Thomson

'Racket rule sweeps midwest city!'

Exclusive
US 1937 76m bw

Journalist sacrifices himself for daughter whose views he despises. Solid newspaper drama jinxed by the excellent tragic performance of a star too long regarded as a comedian. *Charles Ruggles,* Fred MacMurray, Frances Farmer, Lloyd Nolan. Written by John C. Moffitt, Sidney Salkow, Rian James; directed by Alexander Hall; for Paramount. 'Hokey newspaper-gangster yarn of old-fashioned meller calibre.'—*Variety*. 'In the tough race it falls behind—it can't make the 1937 speed in murder, and the result, like lavender, is not unagreeable.'—*Graham Greene*.

Exclusive Story
US 1934 75m bw

A newspaperman has a go at the numbers racket. Tolerable anti-gangster crusade. Franchot Tone, Madge Evans, *Joseph Calleia,* Stuart Erwin, J. Carrol Naish. Written by Michael Fessier and Martin Mooney; directed by George B. Seitz; for MGM. 'Publicity possibilities should put this one over, but it also has plenty of excitement to sell.'—*Variety*

Excuse My Dust*
US 1951 82m Technicolor
MGM (Jack Cummings)

The inventor of a horseless carriage loves the daughter of a livery stable owner.
Innocuous small-town nineties comedy with a race climax. Quite pleasant.

w George Wells *d* Roy Rowland *ph* Alfred Gilks *m* Arthur Schwarz

Red Skelton, Sally Forrest, Macdonald Carey, William Demarest

'Every day he loves, somebody else dies!'

The Executioner*
GB 1970 107m Technicolor Panavision
Columbia / Ameran (Charles H. Schneer)

A British spy suspects a colleague of being a double agent.
Dour espionage thriller with a reasonably holding narrative and predictable performances.

w Jack Pulman *d* Sam Wanamaker *ph* Denys Coop *m* Ron Goodwin

George Peppard, Nigel Patrick, Joan Collins, Judy Geeson, Oscar Homolka, Charles Gray, Keith Michell, George Baker, Alexander Scourby, Peter Bull, Ernest Clark, Peter Dyneley

'Does not escape from the well-worn shallow groove in which the contemporary spy film is in danger of becoming stuck.'—*Russell Campbell*

Executive Action*
US 1973 91m colour
EA Enterprises / Wakefield Orloff (Edward Lewis)

An imaginative version of the facts behind the 1963 assassination of President Kennedy.
Interesting but rather messy mixture of fact and fiction; makes one sit up while it's unreeling.

w Dalton Trumbo, *story* Mark Lane, Donald Freed *d* David Miller *ph* Robert Steadman *m* Randy Edelman

Burt Lancaster, Robert Ryan, Will Geer, Gilbert Green, John Anderson

'A dodo bird of a movie, the winner of the *Tora Tora Tora* prize.'—*Variety*

'High up in the skyscraper beauty and power clash in conflict!'

Executive Suite**
US 1954 104m bw
MGM (John Houseman)

When the president of a big company dies, the boardroom sees a battle for control.
First of the boardroom films of the fifties, a calculatedly commercial mixture of business ethics and domestic asides, with an all-star cast working up effective tensions.

w Ernest Lehman, novel Cameron Hawley *d Robert Wise* *ph* George Folsey *m* none

Fredric March, William Holden, June Allyson, *Barbara Stanwyck*, Walter Pidgeon, Shelley Winters, Paul Douglas, *Louis Calhern*, Dean Jagger, *Nina Foch*, Tim Considine

'Not a classic, not a milestone in movie making, but it does suggest a standard of product that could bring back to the box office those vast audiences long alienated by trivia.'—*Arthur Knight*

'The only trouble with all these people is that they are strictly two-dimensional. They give no substantial illusion of significance, emotion or warmth.'—*Bosley Crowther, New York Times*

† A TV series followed in 1976.

AAN: George Folsey; Nina Foch

The Exile*
US 1948 90m bw
U-I (Douglas Fairbanks Jnr)

The man who is to return to the English throne as Charles II hides in Holland, receives his friends and despatches his enemies.
Curious, talkative swashbuckler with only a few moments of action; the available talents are simply not used, though the director imposes a nice pictorial style.

w Douglas Fairbanks Jnr, *novel* His Majesty the King by Cosmo Hamilton *d Max Ophuls ph Franz Planer m* Frank Skinner

Douglas Fairbanks Jnr, Maria Montez, Paula Corday, Henry Daniell, Nigel Bruce, Robert Coote

† Originally released in sepia.

Exile Express
US 1939 70m bw

A lab assistant is innocently involved in the murder of her boss by a spy gang. Lumpy comedy thriller taking place mainly on a train; very forgettable. Anna Sten, Alan Marshal, Jerome Cowan, Jed Prouty, Stanley Fields, Walter Catlett, Leonid Kinskey, Harry Davenport, Irving Pichel. Written by Edwin Justus Mayer, Ethel La Blanche; directed by Otis Garrett; for Grand National. 'Both story and direction take it up all sorts of dull and impossible alleys.'—*Variety*

Exit Smiling**
US 1926 71m (24 fps) bw silent
MGM (Sam Taylor)

The worst actress in a stock company saves the show.
Amusing comedy for a star who never quite made it in films: this is the best of her vehicles.

w Sam Taylor, Tim Whelan, *play* Marc Connelly *d* Sam Taylor *ph* Andre Barlatier

Beatrice Lillie, Jack Pickford, Harry Myers, Doris Lloyd, DeWitt Jennings, Louise Lorraine, Franklin Pangborn

Exodus*
US 1960 220m Technicolor Super Panavision 70
UA / Carlyle / Alpha (Otto Preminger)

The early years of the state of Israel, seen through various eyes.
Heavy-going modern epic, toned down from a passionate novel.

w Dalton Trumbo, *novel* Leon Uris *d* Otto Preminger *ph* Sam Leavitt *m* Ernest Gold

Paul Newman, Eva Marie Saint, Ralph Richardson, Peter Lawford, Lee J. Cobb, Sal Mineo, John Derek, Hugh Griffith, Gregory Ratoff, Felix Aylmer, David Opatoshu, Jill Haworth, Alexandra Stewart, Martin Benson, Martin Miller

'Professionalism is not enough—after three and a half hours the approach seems more exhausting than exhaustive.'—*Penelope Houston*

† Jewish comedian Mort Sahl, invited by the director to a preview, is said to have stood up after three hours and said: 'Otto—let my people go!'

AA: Ernest Gold

AAN: Sam Leavitt; Sal Mineo

The Exorcist*
US 1973 122m Metrocolor
Warner / Hoya (William Peter Blatty)

A small girl is unaccountably possessed by the devil and turned into a repellent monster who causes several violent deaths before she is cured.
Spectacularly ludicrous mishmash with uncomfortable attention to physical detail and no talent for narrative or verisimilitude. Its sensational aspects, together with a sudden worldwide need for the supernatural, assured its enormous commercial success.

w William Peter Blatty, from his novel *d* William Friedkin *ph* Owen Roizman *m* George Crumb and others *pd* Bill Malloy

Ellen Burstyn, Max Von Sydow, Jason Miller, Linda Blair, Lee J. Cobb, Kitty Winn, Jack McGowran

'No more nor less than a blood and thunder horror movie, foundering heavily on the rocks of pretension.'—*Tom Milne*

'*The Exorcist* makes no sense, [but] if you want to be shaken, it will scare the hell out of you.'—*Stanley Kauffmann*

'It exploits the subject of diabolic possession without telling you anything about it . . . just a stylistic exercise.'—*Michael Billington, Illustrated London News*

'There is a little exposition, some philosophy and theology, a quiet interlude, and then pandemonium reigns: rooms shake, heads turn full circle on bodies, wounds fester, vomit spews forth in bilious clouds besmirching a saintly priest, a possessed adolescent girl masturbates bloodily on a crucifix as she barks blasphemies and obscenities, and hoary demons freeze the soul.'—*Les Keyser, Hollywood in the Seventies*

'I know how to do it. I just throw everything at the audience and give them a real thrill. That's what they want. They don't want to go into a theater and treat it like a book. They don't even read books!'—*William Peter Blatty*

'This one was scheduled for 105 days. It wound up 200 days. We were plagued by strange and sinister things from the beginning.'—*William Peter Blatty*

'. . . raw and painful experience. Are people so numb that they need movies of this intensity in order to feel anything at all?'—*Roger Ebert*

† Published 1974: *The Story Behind the Exorcist* by Peter Travers and Stephanie Reiff.

AA: William Peter Blatty

AAN: best picture; William Friedkin; Owen Roizman; Ellen Burstyn; Jason Miller; Linda Blair

'It's four years later. What does she remember?'

Exorcist II: The Heretic
US 1977 117m Technicolor
Warner (Richard Lederer, John Boorman)

Father Lamont, investigating the case related in *The Exorcist*, finds that the evil in Regan, apparently exorcized, is only dormant.
Highly unsatisfactory psychic melodrama which, far from the commercial route of the shocker followed by its predecessor, falls flat on its face along some wayward path of metaphysical and religious fancy. A commercial disaster, it was released in two versions and is unintelligible in either.

w William Goodhart *d* John Boorman *ph* William A. Fraker *m* Ennio Morricone *pd* Richard MacDonald

Richard Burton, Linda Blair, Louise Fletcher, Kitty Winn, Max Von Sydow, Paul Henreid, James Earl Jones, Ned Beatty

Experiment in Terror**
US 1962 123m bw
Columbia / Geoffrey-Kate Productions (Blake Edwards)
GB title: *The Grip of Fear*

An asthmatic stranger threatens the life of a bank teller and her sister if she does not help him commit a robbery.
Detailed, meticulous police thriller with San Francisco locations. Good stuff, a bit long.

w The Gordons, from their novel Operation Terror *d* Blake Edwards *ph* Philip Lathrop *m* Henry Mancini

Glenn Ford, Lee Remick, Ross Martin

Experiment Perilous*
US 1944 91m bw
RKO (Warren Duff)

A woman's wealthy husband is killed in mysterious circumstances, and she is suspected.
Enjoyable mystery melodrama which takes itself with a pinch of salt.

w Warren Duff, *novel* Margaret Carpenter *d Jacques Tourneur ph* Tony Gaudio *m* Roy Webb

Hedy Lamarr, Paul Lukas, George Brent, Albert Dekker, Margaret Wycherly

The Exploits of Elaine*
US 1914 14 episodes, each 20m approx bw silent
Pathé / Wharton

Detective Craig Kennedy helps his girl friend avenge her father's murder.
Archetypal cliffhanger serial following on the success of *The Perils of Pauline*. It was itself followed within a year by *The New Exploits of Elaine* and *The Romance of Elaine*. Chapter

headings included such now familiar clichés as 'The Clutching Hand', 'The Vanishing Jewels', 'The Poisoned Room', 'The Death Ray' and 'The Devil Worshippers'. The films were much praised by critics for their pace and inventiveness.

w Charles W. Goddard, George B. Seitz, from stories by Arthur B. Reeve *d* Louis Gasnier, George B. Seitz

Pearl White, Creighton Hale, Sheldon Lewis, Arnold Daly

Explorers
US 1985 109m Technicolor
Paramount / Edward S. Feldman / Industrial Light and Magic

Two boys make off in a space craft and encounter an alien race whose culture consists of intercepted American television programmes.
Slightly interesting but overlong fantasy spoof, probably not for popular consumption.

w Eric Luke *d* Joe Dante *ph* John Hora *m* Jerry Goldsmith *pd* Robert F. Boyle

Ethan Hawke, River Phoenix, Jason Presson, Amanda Peterson

'One of the weirdest and most endearingly offbeat alien pix to have surfaced in recent years.'—*Variety*

Exposed
US 1983 99m Metrocolor

A fashion model falls for a concert violinist who turns out to be a notorious terrorist. A glossy absurdity confected from reading too many indigestible headlines, Nastassja Kinski, Rudolf Nureyev, Harvey Keitel, Ian McShane, Bibi Andersson, Ron Randell, Pierre Clementi. Written and directed by James Toback; for MGM-UA. 'It often seems to be working out of a tension between sophisticated ambition and the capabilities of a tyro director, a kind of neo-primitivism (with a hint, perhaps, of Fuller, especially in its cultural name-dropping – Bach, Bosch, Dostoievsky, Heifetz, Perlman, Stern, to name a few).'—*Richard Combs, MFB*

'Johnny never had it so good—or lost it so fast!'

Expresso Bongo*
GB 1959 111m bw Dyaliscope
BL / Britannia / Conquest (Val Guest)

A Soho agent turns a nondescript teenage singer into an international star.
Heavily vulgarized version of a stage skit on the Tommy Steele rock phenomenon, divested of most of its satirical barbs and only intermittently amusing.

w Wolf Mankowitz, from his play *d* Val Guest *ph* John Wilcox *songs* David Heneker, Monty Norman

Laurence Harvey, Sylvia Syms, Yolande Donlan, Cliff Richard, *Meier Tzelniker*, Gilbert Harding, Ambrosine Philpotts, Eric Pohlmann, Wilfrid Lawson, Hermione Baddeley, Reginald Beckwith, Martin Miller

THE EXTERMINATING ANGEL. 'Basically I simply see a group of people who couldn't do what they want to', said Luis Bunuel, entering his Golden Age with one of his most effective parables attacking the bourgeoisie.

The Exquisite Sinner
US 1926 80m approx at 24 fps bw silent

A young French industrialist becomes bored with his society and takes off with a band of gypsies. Curious and unsatisfactory farrago originally directed by Josef von Sternberg, but with extensive retakes by Phil Rosen (who also took credit the following year for an almost exactly similar film with a different title, *Heaven on Earth,* but featuring the same stars: Conrad Nagel and Renee Adoree). Written by Josef von Sternberg and Alice Duer Miller; for MGM.

Extase*
Czechoslovakia 1932 90m bw
Universal Elektra Film
aka: *Ecstasy*

A country girl takes a lover.
Simple love story with Freudian sequences, quite successfully and cinematically done. It caused a sensation at the time and was issued in various censored versions; the star's husband later tried to destroy all the copies.

w Gustav Machaty, story Viteslav Nezval *d* Gustav Machaty *ph* Jan Stallich *m* Giuseppe Becce

Hedy Kiesler (later Hedy Lamarr), Aribert Mog

'The first important film to come out of Czechoslovakia since *Erotikon*, and what a hornet's nest it has stirred up! Critics and public are divided into two camps. Some proclaim it the world's worst, others rank it among the best productions of the year. It would never get by the censor in America.'—*Variety*

The Exterminating Angel***
Mexico 1962 95m bw
Uninci Films 59 (Gustavo Alatriste)
original title: *El Angel Exterminador*

High society dinner guests find themselves unable to leave the room, stay there for days, and go totally to the bad before the strange spell is broken; when they go to church to give thanks, they find themselves unable to leave.
Fascinating surrealist fantasia on themes elaborated with even more panache in *The Discreet Charm of the Bourgeoisie.*
Nevertheless, one of its director's key films.

wd Luis Bunuel (story assistance from Luis Alcoriza) *ph* Gabriel Figueroa *ad* Jesus Bracho

Silvia Pinal, Enrique Rambal, Jacqueline Andere, Jose Baviera

'An unsound and unsightly mixture of spurious allegory and genuine craziness.'—*John Simon*

The Exterminator
US 1980 102m Movielab
Interstar (Mark Buntzman)

An ex-Vietnam vet goes berserk when his friend is killed by a street gang, and vows revenge.
Vigilante movie with aspects of the modern horror-comic tradition; not much doubt that its real purpose is exploitation. It aroused some anger in America when a murder seemed to be based on its methods, but it was quickly succeeded by even more violent films.

wd James Glickenhaus *ph* Robert M. Baldwin *m* Joe Renzetti

Robert Ginty, Christopher George, Samantha Eggar, Steve James

'Glickenhaus has plundered the iconographic treasury of recent American cinema, wrenching the images of war, sexuality and street crime out of their contexts and deploying them portentously so as to lend spurious significance to his film.'—*Martyn Auty, MFB*

Exterminator 2
US 1984 90m TVC colour

An unemployed Vietnam veteran in New York eliminates punks with a flame thrower. Violence fantasy, an extreme form of *Death Wish*; quite reprehensible, and not for the squeamish. Robert Ginty, Deborah Geffner, Mario Van Peebles, Frankie Faison. Written by Mark Buntzman, William Sachs; directed by Mark Buntzman; for Cannon.

The Extra Day
GB 1956 83m Eastmancolor
British Lion / William Fairchild (E. M. Smedley Aston)

The personal problems of five film extras who are recalled when a scene has to be reshot.
Thin excuse for portmanteau drama, only amusing in its depiction of a British movie being made with mostly foreign talent.

wd William Fairchild *ph* Arthur Grant *m* Philip Green

Richard Basehart, Simone Simon, Sid James, Josephine Griffin, George Baker, Colin Gordon, Laurence Naismith, Charles Victor, Olga Lindo, Beryl Reid, Dennis Lotis

The Extra Girl*
US 1923 69m bw silent
Mack Sennett

A small town girl wins a beauty contest and goes to Hollywood.
A comparatively restrained comedy with slapstick interludes, this charming film shows its star at her best and admirably illustrates Hollywood in the early twenties.

d Mack Sennett *m* Jack Ward

Mabel Normand, Max Davidson, Ralph Graves, George Nicholls

The Extraordinary Seaman
US 1968 80m Metrocolor Panavision
MGM / John Frankenheimer / Edward Lewis (John H. Cushingham, Hal Dresner)

Four stranded sailors come upon the ghostly Royal Navy captain of a ghostly World War II ship.
Curious sixties attempt at forties fantasy; obviously, from its short running time and fragmented style, something went sadly adrift during its making, and the wide screen does not help, but there are scattered funny moments.

w Philip Rock, Hal Dresner *d* John Frankenheimer *ph* Lionel Lindon *m* Maurice Jarre

David Niven, Faye Dunaway, Alan Alda, Mickey Rooney, Jack Carter, Juano Hernandez, Barry Kelley

'A cleverly made curiosity, not so much produced as manufactured.'—*Marjorie Bilbow*

Extreme Prejudice
US 1987 104m Technicolor

A Texas Ranger pins down a drug trafficker. Ordinary urban thriller with overplayed violence. Nick Nolte, Powers Boothe, Michael Ironside, Rip Torn, Clancy Brown, Conchita Alonso. Written by Deric Washburn and Harry Kleiner; directed by Walter Hill; for Buzz Feitshans/Carolco/Tri-Star.

Extremities
US 1986 90m colour

A girl takes revenge on the man who raped her. Unpleasant when it's not verbose; anything but entertaining. Farrah Fawcett, James Russo, Diana Scarwid, Alfred Woodard. Written by William Mastrosimone, from his play; directed by Robert M. Young; for Burt Sugarman / Atlantic Releasing.

An Eye for an Eye
France / Italy 1956 93m Technicolor VistaVision
UGC / Jolly (André Cayatte)

A doctor finds himself trekking across the desert with a demented man whose wife has died in his care.
Initially striking melodrama which becomes increasingly unconvincing and has a tendency to harp on unpleasant detail.

wd André Cayatte, *novel* Vahe Katcha *ph* Christian Matras *m* Louiguy

Curt Jurgens, Folco Lulli, Lea Padovani

An Eye for an Eye
US 1981 104m CFI Color

An undercover cop resigns from the force but uncovers a drug ring. Tedious and violent actioner with a martial arts champion for hero. Chuck Norris, Christopher Lee, Richard Roundtree, Matt Clark, Mako. Written by William Gray and James Bruner; directed by Steve Carver; for Wescom.

'Terror that tears the scream right out of your throat!'

Eye of the Cat*
US 1969 102m Technicolor
Universal / Joseph M. Schenck (Bernard Schwarz, Philip Hazelton)

A young man who hates cats goes to stay with his crippled aunt who keeps a house full of them.
Odd, *Psycho*-like thriller (from the same screen writer) with plenty of scary sequences but an inadequate resolution.

w Joseph Stefano *d* David Lowell Rich *ph* *Russell Metty, Ellsworth Fredericks* *m* Lalo Schifrin *cat trainer* Ray Berwick

Eleanor Parker, Michael Sarrazin, Gayle Hunnicutt, Tim Henry, Laurence Naismith

'Not so much a good film as an extravagantly enjoyable one.'—*MFB*

Eye of the Devil*
GB 1967 92m bw
MGM / Filmways (John Calley, Ben Kadish)

A French nobleman is obsessed by a family tradition of pagan self-sacrifice.
Diabolical goings-on in a spooky castle, not really helped by a glittering supporting cast any more than by miscast stars, sluggish direction or a general atmosphere of gloom rather than suspense.

w Robin Estridge, Dennis Murphy, *novel* Day of the Arrow by Philip Loraine *d* J. Lee-Thompson *ph* Erwin Hillier *m* Gary McFarland

David Niven, Deborah Kerr, Emlyn Williams, Flora Robson, Donald Pleasence, Edward Mulhare, David Hemmings, Sharon Tate, John Le Mesurier, Donald Bisset

'It is hard to say why the total effect is so constantly hilarious.'—*MFB*

† The film had a chequered career. The first attempt to make it was abandoned because of Kim Novak's inadequacy; it then went through three titles and a lot of trouble with the censor.

'To love a stranger is easy . . . to kill a lover is not!'

Eye of the Needle
GB 1981 113m Technicolor
UA / Kings Road (Stephen Friedman)

In London in 1940 a German agent murders his landlady but is eventually cornered by a girl on a Scottish island.
Listless espionage narrative with very little drive or interest: the shape of the story defies suspense.

w Stanley Mann, *novel* Ken Follett *d* Richard Marquand *ph* Alan Hume *m* Miklos Rozsa

Donald Sutherland, Kate Nelligan, Christopher Cazenove, Ian Bannen, Alex McCrindle

Eye of the Tiger
US 1986 90m United color

A vigilante avenges his wife's murder. Predictable thriller with video in mind. Gary Busey, Yaphet Kotto, Seymour Cassel, Bert Remsen, William Smith. Written by Michael Montgomery; directed by Richard Sarafian; for Scotti Brothers.

Eye Witness
GB 1956 82m bw
Rank / Sydney Box

A maniacal burglar pursues a witness of his crime into the emergency ward of a local hospital.
Naïve but adequate suspenser with too many character cameos getting in the way of the plot.

w Janet Green *d* Muriel Box ph Reg Wyer *m* Bruce Montgomery

Donald Sinden, Muriel Pavlow, Belinda Lee, Michael Craig, Nigel Stock, Susan Beaumont, David Knight, *Ada Reeve*

Eye Witness
US 1981 108m Technicolor
TCF (Peter Yates)
GB title: *The Janitor*

A bashful janitor with a crush on a TV star finds himself hunted down by a murderer afraid of identification.
Odd little character thriller which despite pleasant touches never really seems to have its mind on its plot.

w Steve Tesich *d* Peter Yates *ph* Matthew F. Leonetti *m* Stanley Silverman *pd* Philip Roseberg

William Hurt, Christopher Plummer, Sigourney Weaver, Irene Worth, James Woods, Kenneth McMillan, Steven Hill

Eyes in the Night*
US 1942 80m bw
MGM (Jack Chertok)

A blind detective sets out to discover whether a mysterious man engaged to an heiress is really a Nazi spy.
Tolerable wartime puzzler.

w Guy Trosper, Howard Emmett Rogers, *novel* Odor of Violets by Bayard Kendrick *d Fred Zinnemann* *ph* Robert Planck, Charles Lawton *m* Lennie Hayton

Edward Arnold, Ann Harding, Donna Reed, Allen Jenkins, John Emery, Stephen McNally, Reginald Denny, Rosemary de Camp, Stanley Ridges

'They have converted a basically humdrum yarn into a tense and tingling little thriller.'—*New York Times*

† Edward Arnold appeared once more as Duncan Maclain, in *The Hidden Eye* (1944).

Eyes of Laura Mars
US 1978 104m Metrocolor
Columbia / Jon Peters (Jack H. Harris)

A fashion photographer has violent premonitions about a series of murders.
Silly and often unpleasant suspenser which despite its chic appearance never bothers to explain itself.

w John Carpenter, David Zelag Goodman *d* Irvin Kershner *ph* Victor J. Kemper *m* Artie Kane

Faye Dunaway, Tommy Lee Jones, Brad Dourif, René Auberjonois, Raul Julia, Frank Adonis

'Long on trendy settings, high-priced actors and vicious murders, but devoid of narrative thrills.'—*Richard Schickel, Time*

'Perhaps the most austerely elegant horror film ever made.'—*New Yorker*

Eyes of the Underworld
US 1941 61m bw

A crusading lawyer exposes an auto theft ring.
Efficient little support which was smart enough to play top on its original release. Richard Dix, Lon Chaney Jnr, Wendy Barrie, Don Porter, Bill Lee, Lloyd Corrigan. Written by Michael L. Simmons and Arthur Strawn; directed by Roy William Neill; for Universal.

Eyes without a Face*
France / Italy 1959 90m bw
Champs Elysées / Lux (Jules Borkon)
original title: *Les Yeux sans Visage*
US title: *The Horror Chamber of Dr Faustus*

When his daughter is mutilated in a car accident, a mad professor murders young girls in the process of grafting their faces onto hers.
Unpleasant horror film which its director seems to have made as a joke; the years have made it a cult.

w Jean Redon, from his novel *d Georges Franju* *ph* Eugen Schufftan *m* Maurice Jarre

Pierre Brasseur, Alida Valli, Edith Scob, François Guérin

Eyewitness*
GB 1970 91m Technicolor
ITC / ABP (Paul Maslansky)

A boy is the sole witness to an assassination, but no one believes him except the assassins.
The Window all over again, the standard clichés being tricked out with fancy photography, sub-Hitchcock set-ups and Mediterranean locations, which make it all very tolerable.

w Ronald Harwood, *novel* Mark Hebden *d* John Hough *ph* David Holmes *m* Fairfield Parlour, David Whitaker

Mark Lester, Lionel Jeffries, Susan George, Tony Bonner, Jeremy Kemp, Peter Vaughan, Peter Bowles, Betty Marsden

F for Fake*
France / Iran / West Germany 1973 85m colour
Astrophore / Saco / Janus (Dominique Antoine, François Reichenbach)
French title: *Vérités et Mensonges*

Orson Welles, at a railway station, lectures the audience in truth and falsehood, in art, in films and in life.
A ragbag of an entertainment, cannibalizing as it does more than one unsold documentary, shredded at the editing table to match the narrator's illusionist style. Despite the raptures of some critics, this is an irritating effusion, and Welles now looks more like a clever charlatan than a master film-maker.

w Orson Welles, Oja Palinkas *d* Orson Welles *ph* Gary Graver, Christian Odasso *m* Michel Legrand

'Welles stretches his material and his legend just about as thin as possible in this tedious treatise on truth and illusion.'—*Kevin Thomas, Los Angeles Times*

† Joseph Cotten, Paul Stewart and Laurence Harvey make fleeting appearances.

The FBI Story*
US 1959 149m Technicolor
Warner (Mervyn Le Roy)

An FBI agent thinks back on his career with the bureau.
Predictable mix of domestic sentimentality (very trying) and competent crime capsules: mad bomber, Ku Klux Klan, thirties hoodlums, Nazi spy rings and the cold war.

w Richard L. Breen, John Twist *d* Mervyn Le Roy *ph* Joseph Biroc *m* Max Steiner *ad* John Beckman

James Stewart, Vera Miles, Larry Pennell, Nick Adams, Murray Hamilton

'Insufferably cosy.'—*MFB*

FBI Code 98
US 1964 94m bw

G-men track down a mad bomber. Thin action thriller originally intended for TV. Jack Kelly, Ray Danton, Andrew Duggan, Philip Carey, William Reynolds. Written and produced by Stanley Niss; directed by Leslie H. Martinson; for Warner.

F.P.1*
GB / Germany 1933 93m bw
Gaumont / UFA (Erich Pommer)

Financiers try to destroy the first floating aerodrome.
'Futuristic' melodrama about an aircraft carrier. Very well done, and shot in two languages, but now dated in most respects.

w Curt Siodmak, Walter Reisch, Robert Stevenson, Peter Macfarlane *d* Karl Hartl *ph* Gunther Rittau, Konstantin Tochet

Conrad Veidt, Leslie Fenton, Jill Esmond, George Merritt, Donald Calthrop, Nicholas Hannen, Francis L. Sullivan

The Fabulous Adventures of Marco Polo
France / Italy / Yugoslavia / Egypt / Afghanistan 1964 115m Eastmancolor Franscope
Ittac / Prodi / Avala / Mounir Rafla / Italaf Kaboul (Raoul Lévy)
aka: *Marco the Magnificent*

In 1271 Marco Polo carries a message of peace to Kubla Khan.
Curious mixture of melodrama and pantomime, with a star cast half playing for laughs.

w Raoul Lévy, Denys de la Patellière *d* Denys de la Patellière, Noel Howard *ph* Armand Thirard *m* George Garvarentz

Horst Buchholz, Anthony Quinn, Orson Welles, Akim Tamiroff, Robert Hossein, Omar Sharif, Elsa Martinelli, Grégoire Aslan, Massimo Girotti, Folco Lulli

The Fabulous Dorseys
US 1947 91m bw
UA (Charles R. Rogers)

Two quarrelling bandleader brothers are reunited on the death of their father.
Slight, comedic biopic with the Dorseys playing well and trying hard.

w Richard English, Art Arthur, Curtis Kenyon *d* Alfred E. Green *ph* James Van Trees *m* Leo Shuken

Tommy Dorsey, Jimmy Dorsey (and their bands), Janet Blair, Paul Whiteman, William Lundigan

The Fabulous Texan
US 1947 97m bw

Confederate officers after the Civil War return home to find Texas overrun by carpetbaggers and despotic state police. Fairly handsome western which gets by without ever being memorable. William Elliott, John Carroll, Catherine McLeod, Andy Devine, Albert Dekker, Ruth Donnelly, Harry Davenport, Douglass Dumbrille. Written by Lawrence Hazard and Horace McCoy; directed by Edward Ludwig; for Republic.

The Face***
Sweden 1958 103m bw
Svensk Filmindustri
original title: *Ansiktet;* US title: *The Magician*

In 19th-century Sweden, a mesmerist and his troupe are halted at a country post to be examined by three officials. Partly exposed as a fraud, he takes a frightening revenge.
A virtually indecipherable parable which may be about the survival of Christianity (and may not), this wholly personal Bergman fancy has to be enjoyed chiefly for its surface frissons, for its acting and its look, which are almost sufficient compensation.

wd Ingmar Bergman ph Gunnar Fischer *m* Erik Nordgren

Max Von Sydow, Ingrid Thulin, *Gunnar Bjornstrand*, Naima Wifstrand, Ake Fridell, Lars Ekborg, Bengt Ekerot

The Face at the Window*
GB 1939 65m bw
Pennant / Ambassador (George King)

In 1880 Paris, a murderer uses his moronic half-brother to distract his victims but is foiled when a dead man apparently incriminates him.
Roistering melodrama which provided Tod Slaughter with one of his juiciest roles and is here effectively presented, which is more than can be said for the screen treatments of most of his other vehicles.

w A. R. Rawlinson, Randall Faye, *play* F. Brooke Warren *d* George King *ph* Hone Glendinning *md* Jack Beaver

Tod Slaughter, Marjorie Taylor, John Warwick, Leonard Henry, Aubrey Mallalieu

'One of the best English pictures I have seen . . . leaves the American horror films far behind.'—*Graham Greene*

The Face behind the Mask*
US 1941 69m bw
Columbia (Wallace MacDonald)

When his face is disfigured in a fire, an immigrant turns to a life of crime.
Effective second feature melodrama with a good star performance.

w Allen Vincent, Paul Jarrico, *play* Thomas O'Connell *d* Robert Florey *ph* Franz Planer *md* Sidney Cutner

Peter Lorre, Evelyn Keyes, *Don Beddoe,* George E. Stone

A Face in the Crowd***
US 1957 126m bw
(Warner) Newton (Elia Kazan)

A small-town hick becomes a megalomaniac when television turns him into a cracker-barrel philosopher.
Brilliantly cinematic melodrama of its time which only flags in the last lap and paints a luridly entertaining picture of modern show business.

w Budd Schulberg, from his story Your Arkansas Traveller *d Elia Kazan ph Harry Stradling, Gayne Rescher m* Tom Glazer

Andy Griffith, Lee Remick, Walter Matthau, Patricia Neal, Anthony Franciosa, Percy Waram, Marshall Neilan

'Savagery, bitterness, cutting humour.'—*Penelope Houston*

'If Kazan and Schulberg had been content to make their case by implication, it might have been a completely sophisticated piece of movie-making. Instead, everything is elaborately spelled out, and the film degenerates into preposterous liberal propaganda.'—*Andrew Sarris*

'Some exciting scenes in the first half, but the later developments are frenetic, and by the end the film is a loud and discordant mess.'—*Pauline Kael, 70s*

A Face in the Rain*
US 1963 80m bw
Filmways / Calvic (John Calley)

During World War II an American spy in Italy bungles his mission, and hides in the apartment of a professor's wife.
Offbeat, talkative melodrama with a few neat touches.

w Hugo Butler, Jean Rouverol *d Irvin Kershner ph Haskell Wexler m* Richard Markowitz

Rory Calhoun, Marina Berti, Niall MacGinnis

Face in the Sky
US 1932 68m bw

A sign painter falls for a farmer's daughter. Curious, whimsical comedy romance which didn't work at any level. Spencer Tracy, Marian Nixon, Stuart Erwin, Sam Hardy, Lila Lee. Written by Humphrey Pearson from a story by Myles Connolly; directed by Harry Lachman; for Fox. 'Why it was considered feature-length picture material is hard to understand.'—*Variety*

Face of a Fugitive*
US 1959 81m Eastmancolor
Columbia / Morningside

A man falsely accused of murder makes a new life in a frontier town.
Lively western melodrama with good atmosphere.

w David T. Chantler *d Paul Wendkos ph* Wilfrid M. Cline *m* Jerry Goldsmith

Fred MacMurray, Lin McCarthy, Alan Baxter, James Coburn

The Face of Fu Manchu**
GB 1965 96m Techniscope
Anglo-EMI / Hallam (Harry Alan Towers)

In the twenties, Nayland Smith of Scotland Yard links an oriental crime wave with evil mastermind Fu Manchu.
A splendidly light touch and attention to detail make this entertaining spoof like a tuppenny blood come to life.

w Peter Welbeck (Harry Alan Towers) *d Don Sharp ph* Ernest Steward *m* Chris Whelan *ad Frank White*

Nigel Green, Christopher Lee, Tsai Chin, Howard Marion Crawford

The Face of Marble
US 1946 70m bw

A scientist revives the dead through voodoo. Grade Z shocker with entertaining moments. John Carradine, Robert Shayne, Claudia Drake, Maris Wrixon. Written by Michael Jacoby; directed by William Beaudine; for Jeffrey Bernard / Monogram.

Face to Face
US 1952 89m bw

Two stories of confrontation, artificially presented by an independent company. *The Secret Sharer* by Joseph Conrad: James Mason, Gene Lockhart, Michael Pate. *The Bride Comes to Yellow Sky* by Stephen Crane: Robert Preston, Marjorie Steele, Minor Watson. Written respectively by Aeneas Mackenzie and James Agee; directed by John Brahm and Bretaigne Windust; for Huntington Hartford/(RKO).

Face to Face**
Sweden 1976 136m colour

A psychiatrist staying with her grandparents finds herself in need of guidance. Fascinating material edited down from a tv series; too long as a film. *Liv Ullman*, Erland Josephson, Gunnar Bjornstrand, Aino Taube-Henrikson. Written, directed and produced by *Ingmar Bergman*; photographed by Sven Nykvist; for De Laurentiis/Sveriges Radio.

Faces*
US 1968 130m bw
Maurice McEndree

A discontented Los Angeles executive tries but fails to go through with a divorce.
A personal, probing study of middle-aged loneliness, made with the director's usual long-winded relentlessness but quite frequently compelling.

wd John Cassavetes *ph* Al Ruban *m* Jack Ackerman

John Marley, Gena Rowlands, Lynn Carlin, Fred Draper, Seymour Cassell

'The cast are all painfully and overpoweringly real.'—*Jan Dawson*

AAN: John Cassavetes (as writer); Lynn Carlin; Seymour Cassell

Faces in the Dark*
GB 1960 85m bw
Rank / Welbeck / Penington Eady (Jon Penington)

A blind man survives a plot against his life.
Unlikely but watchable puzzler, betrayed by lifeless handling. Hitchcock could have worked wonders with such a plot.

w Ephraim Kogan, John Tulley, *novel* Pierre Boileau, Thomas Narcejac *d* David Eady *ph* Ken Hodges *m* Edwin Astley

John Gregson, Mai Zetterling, Michael Denison, John Ireland, Tony Wright, Nanette Newman

The Facts of Life*
US 1960 103m bw
(UA) HLP (Norman Panama)

Two middle-aged married suburbanites have an abortive affair.
Star comedy with muted slapstick and earnest acting, a good try, but less effective than their normal pratfalls.

w Norman Panama, Melvin Frank *d* Melvin Frank *ph* Charles Lang Jnr *m* Leigh Harline

Bob Hope, Lucille Ball, Ruth Hussey, Don Defore, Louis Nye, Philip Ober

'Random shots of mockery aimed effectively at the American middle-class way of life.'—*Peter John Dyer*

AAN: Norman Panama, Melvin Frank (script); Charles Lang Jnr; title song (*m / ly* Johnny Mercer)

Fahrenheit 451*
GB 1966 112m Technicolor
Rank / Anglo Enterprise / Vineyard (Lewis M. Allen)

In a fascist future state, a fireman's job is to burn books.
1984 stuff, a little lacking in plot and rather tentatively directed, but with charming moments.

w François Truffaut, Jean-Louis Richard, *novel* Ray Bradbury *d* François Truffaut *ph* Nicolas Roeg *m* Bernard Herrmann *design consultant* Tony Walton

Oskar Werner, Julie Christie, Cyril Cusack, Anton Diffring, Jeremy Spenser

'He barely dramatizes the material at all, and though there are charming, childlike moments, the performers seem listless, and the whole enterprise is a little drab.'—*Pauline Kael*

† All the credits in this film are spoken.

Fail Safe***
US 1964 111m bw
Columbia / Max E. Youngstein / Sidney Lumet

An American atomic bomber is accidentally set to destroy Moscow, and the president has to destroy New York in retaliation.
Despite a confusing opening, this deadly earnest melodrama gets across the horror of its situation better than the contemporaneous *Dr Strangelove* which treated the same plot as black comedy. Here the details are both terrifying and convincing.

w Walter Bernstein, *novel* Eugene Burdick, Harvey Wheeler *d Sidney Lumet ph* Gerald Hirschfeld *m* none

Henry Fonda, Walter Matthau, Dan O'Herlihy, Frank Overton, Fritz Weaver, Edward Binns, Larry Hagman, Russell Collins

'It will have you sitting on the brink of eternity.'—*publicity*

Fair Warning
US 1937 70m bw
A sheriff solves the murder of a Death Valley miner. Very watchable little second feature. J. Edward Bromberg, Betty Furness, John Howard Payne, Victor Kilian, Gavin Muir, Andrew Tombes. Written and directed by Norman Foster, from a story by Philip Wylie; for TCF. 'Stereotype whodunit comedy.'—*Variety*. 'An hour of genuine entertainment and taut suspense.'—*Film Daily*

Fair Wind to Java
US 1952 92m Trucolor
Republic (Joseph Kane)
A sailor with a mutinous crew seeks a South Sea treasure.
Routine adventure culminating in a volcanic explosion.
w Richard Tregaskis, *novel* Garland Roark *d* Joseph Kane *ph* Jack Marta *m* Victor Young
Fred MacMurray, Vera Hruba Ralston, Robert Douglas, Victor McLaglen

Faithful in My Fashion
US 1946 81m bw
A soldier on leave causes havoc in a department store where his girl friend is manager. Sentimental comedy, forgettable for itself but containing endearing performances by a number of favourite character actors. Tom Drake, Donna Reed, Edward Everett Horton, Spring Byington, Harry Davenport, Sig Rumann, Margaret Hamilton, Hobart Cavanaugh. Written by Lionel Houser; directed by Sidney Salkow; for MGM.

Faithless
US 1932 76m bw
MGM
A spoiled rich girl and her beau both descend to working-class level and almost further.
Would-be sensational drama ruined by censorship and miscasting.
w Carey Wilson, *novel* Tinfoil by Mildred Cram *d* Harry Beaumont *ph* Oliver T. Marsh
Tallulah Bankhead, Robert Montgomery, Hugh Herbert, Maurice Murphy, Louise Closser Hale, Lawrence Grant, Henry Kolker
'They pile the suffering on so thick that any but the most naive theatregoers are going to revolt and scoff.'—*Variety*

The Fake
GB 1953 81m bw
The Tate Gallery hires an American investigator who discovers that one of their da Vincis is a substitute. Very standard co-feature mystery with pleasant touches. Dennis O'Keefe, Coleen Gray, Hugh Williams, John Laurie, Guy Middleton. Written by Patrick Kirwan; directed by Godfrey Grayson; for Steven Pallos / Pax.

The Falcon
A debonair solver of crime puzzles allegedly created by Michael Arlen but owing much to The Saint and resulting from a need by RKO for more of the same. Helped by a tough / comic manservant, he flourished during the forties in sixteen second features (the last three for Film Classics). After three episodes George Sanders tired of the role and was written out by being 'shot' and having his real-life brother Tom Conway take over as his fictional one. The performances of these two actors are pleasant, though the films are now fairly unwatchable, but John Calvert who took over for the last three was not a success.
1941: THE GAY FALCON, A DATE WITH THE FALCON
1942: THE FALCON TAKES OVER (the plot was borrowed from Raymond Chandler's FAREWELL MY LOVELY), THE FALCON'S BROTHER
1943: THE FALCON STRIKES BACK, THE FALCON AND THE CO-EDS, THE FALCON IN DANGER
1944: THE FALCON IN HOLLYWOOD, THE FALCON IN MEXICO, THE FALCON OUT WEST
1945: THE FALCON IN SAN FRANCISCO
1946: THE FALCON'S ALIBI, THE FALCON'S ADVENTURE
1948: THE DEVIL'S CARGO, APPOINTMENT WITH MURDER, SEARCH FOR DANGER

The Falcon and the Snowman
US 1984 123m De Luxe
Orion / Gabriel Katzka, John Schlesinger (John Daly)
A college dropout and a drug pusher sell secrets to the Russians.
A true case is made to seem not merely impossible but uninteresting by flaccid cinematic treatment.
w Steven Zaillian *book* Robert Lindsey *d* John Schlesinger *ph* Allen Daviau *m* Pat Metheny, Lyle Mays *pd* James D. Bissell *ed* Richard Marden
Timothy Hutton, Sean Penn, David Suchet, Lori Singer, Pat Hingle, Dorian Harewood

The Fall*
Argentina 1958 86m bw
Argentine Sono (Leopoldo Torre Nilsson)
original title: *La Caida*
A strictly brought-up college girl lodges with an eccentric family whose strange world comes to mean more to her than the love of a young lawyer.
Odd, claustrophobic melodrama from a very personal film-maker.
w Beatriz Guido, Leopoldo Torre Nilsson, *novel* Beatriz Guido *d Leopoldo Torre Nilsson* *ph* Alberto Etchebehere *m* Juan Carlos Paz
Elsa Daniel, Duilio Marzia, Lydia Lamaison, Carlos Lopez Monet

Fall In
US 1943 48m bw
Two army sergeants resent each other. Very mild farce, another of Hal Roach's middle-length 'screenliners'. William Tracy, Joe Sawyer, Robert Barrat, Jean Porter, Arthur Hunnicutt. Written by Eugene Conrad and Edward E. Seabrook; directed by Kurt Neumann; for Hal Roach.

The Fall of Berlin*
USSR 1949 160m Agfacolor
Mosfilm
A steel worker turns soldier, sees all the major Russian battles of World War II, and has his hand shaken by Stalin.
Out-and-out propaganda, with caricatures of famous people and magnificently staged battles.
w M. Chiaureli, P. A. Pavlenko *d* M. Chiaureli *ph* L. V. Kosmatov *m* Dmitri Shostakovich
B. Andreyev, M. Gelovani (as Stalin), V. Stanitsine (as Churchill), M. Kovaleva

The Fall of the House of Usher
France 1928 48m (24 fps) bw silent
Roderick Usher's sister, prone to catalepsy, is buried alive; her unexpected return to life is instrumental in setting the house ablaze. The original story is not so much stated as inferred in this very impressionistic version, of limited interest only to art movie buffs. Marguerite Gance, Jean Debucourt, Charles Lamy. Written and directed by Jean Epstein and Luis Bunuel; art direction by Pierre Kefer.

The Fall of the House of Usher
GB 1949 70m bw
Dismally inept low-budgeter, a pain to sit through. Gwen Watford, Kay Tendeter, Irving Steen. Written by Kenneth Thompson, Dorothy Catt; directed by Ivan Barnett; for GIB.

The Fall of the House of Usher: for the Vincent Price version, see House of Usher

The Fall of the Roman Empire**
US / Spain 1964 187m Technicolor Ultra Panavision 70
Samuel Bronston
After poisoning the Emperor Marcus Aurelius his mad son Commodus succumbs to dissipation and allows Rome to be ravaged by pestilence and the Barbarians.
Would-be distinguished epic with an intellectual first hour; unfortunately the hero is a priggish bore, the villain a crashing bore, the heroine a saintly bore, and the only interesting character is killed off early. A chariot race, a javelin duel, some military clashes and a mass burning at the stake keep one watching, and the production values are high indeed.
w Ben Barzman, Philip Yordan *d Anthony Mann* *ph* Robert Krasker, John Moore *m* Dmitri Tiomkin *pd* Venerio Colasanti
Alec Guinness, Christopher Plummer, Stephen Boyd, James Mason, Sophia Loren, John Ireland, Eric Porter, Anthony Quayle, Mel Ferrer, Omar Sharif
'The film works from a restricted palette, and the result is weirdly restraining and severe, a dignified curb on absurdities.'—*John Coleman*

† The forum set in this film is said to be the largest ever built.

AAN: Dmitri Tiomkin

'Even now she stood between us—the taunt of her smile like a black curse on our love!'

Fallen Angel*
US 1945 97m bw
TCF (Otto Preminger)

A man plans to get rid of his wife and marry another woman, but it is the latter who is murdered.
Oddly sleazy melodrama, not more successful then because it was unexpected than now because it is miscast. Some good sequences, though.

w Harry Kleiner, *novel* Marty Holland *d Otto Preminger ph Joseph La Shelle m* David Raksin

Dana Andrews, Alice Faye, Linda Darnell, Charles Bickford, Anne Revere, Bruce Cabot, John Carradine, Percy Kilbride

'It holds you by its undertones of small-town life and frustration.'—*Richard Winnington*

'It isn't in the class of *Laura*, but it's tolerable, in a tawdry sort of way.'—*Pauline Kael, 70s*

The Fallen Idol***
GB 1948 94m bw
British Lion / London Films (Carol Reed)
US title: *The Lost Illusion*

An ambassador's small son nearly incriminates his friend the butler in the accidental death of his shrewish wife.
A near-perfect piece of small-scale cinema, built up from clever nuances of acting and cinematic technique.

w Graham Greene, from his story The Basement Room *d Carol Reed ph Georges Périnal m* William Alwyn

Ralph Richardson, Michèle Morgan, *Bobby Henrey*, Sonia Dresdel, Jack Hawkins

'A short story has become a film which is compact without loss of variety in pace and shape.'—*Dilys Powell*

'It's too deliberate and hushed to be much fun . . . you wait an extra beat between the low-key lines of dialogue.'—*Pauline Kael, 70s*

AAN: Graham Greene; Carol Reed

The Fallen Sparrow*
US 1943 93m bw
RKO (Robert Fellows)

An American veteran of the Spanish Civil War finds himself hounded in New York by Nazis seeking the Spanish flag of freedom.
Obscure melodrama, very good to look at but hardly worth unravelling; a precursor of Hollywood's post-war *films noirs*.

w Warren Duff, *novel* Dorothy B. Hughes *d* Richard Wallace *ph Nicholas Musuraca md* Roy Webb, Constantin Bakaleinikoff

John Garfield, Maureen O'Hara, Walter Slezak, Martha O'Driscoll, Patricia Morison, Bruce Edwards, John Banner, John Miljan

AAN: Roy Webb, Constantin Bakaleinikoff

Falling in Love*
US 1984 107m Technicolor
Paramount / Marvin Worth

Meeting as commuters, Frank and Molly, each married to someone else, think about having an affair.
Rather tedious rehash of *Brief Encounter*, with no real interest in the characters or their backgrounds.

w Michael Cristofer *d* Ulu Grosbard *ph* Peter Suschitzky *m* Dave Grusin *pd* Santo Loquasto *ed* Michael Kahn

Robert de Niro, Meryl Streep, Harvey Keitel, Jane Kaczmarek, George Martin

'The effect of this talented pair acting in such a lightweight vehicle is akin to having Horowitz and Rubinstein improvise a duet on the theme of Chopsticks.'—*Variety*

Falling in Love Again*
US 1980 103m colour
International Picture Show of Atlanta (Steven Paul)

A middle-aged New Yorker remembers his young romances and his dreams of success.
Warm little independent production harking back to the days of *H. M. Pulham Esquire* and none the worse for that.

w Steven Paul, Ted Allan, Susannah York *d* Steven Paul *ph* Michael Mileham, Dick Bush, Wolfgang Suschitzky *m* Michel Legrand

Elliott Gould, Susannah York, Stuart Paul, Kaye Ballard

Falling for You*
GB 1933 88m bw
Gainsborough (Michael Balcon)

Fleet Street journalists in Switzerland try to outsmart each other.
Dated comedy very typical of the stars' extremely casual style, with immaculate set pieces.

w Jack Hulbert, Douglas Furber, Robert Stevenson, *story* Sidney Gilliat *d* Jack Hulbert, Robert Stevenson *ph* Bernard Knowles *songs* Vivian Ellis, Douglas Furber

Jack Hulbert, Cicely Courtneidge, Tamara Desni, Garry Marsh, Alfred Drayton, O. B. Clarence, Morton Selten

Fame*
US 1980 133m Metrocolor
MGM (David de Silva, Alan Marshall)

Assorted teenagers attend Manhattan's High School for the Performing Arts.
Cleverly shot and edited slice of life which unfortunately features people whose language and personalities are fairly repellent. The result is like *A Chorus Line* without the music.

w Christopher Gore *d Alan Parker ph* Michael Seresin *m* Michael Gore and others *pd* Geoffrey Kirkland

Irene Cara, Lee Curreri, Laura Dean, Paul McCrane, Barry Miller, Gene Anthony Ray

'Our film, I hope, will be a microcosm of New York . . . a dozen races pitching in and having their own crack at the American dream.'—*Alan Parker*

'Its soft-centred view of human relationships is periodically undercut by what can only be described as the grotesque.'—*John Pym*

AA: screenplay; best original song (Michael Gore, Dean Pitchford); editing (Gerry Hambling)

Fame Is the Spur*
GB 1947 116m bw
GFD / Two Cities / Charter Films (John Boulting)

The rise to political eminence of a working-class socialist.
Disappointingly flat historical drama from a novel allegedly based on the career of Ramsay MacDonald. Interesting moments.

w Nigel Balchin, *novel* Howard Spring *d* Roy Boulting *ph* Gunther Krampf, Harry Waxman

Michael Redgrave, Rosamund John, Bernard Miles, Carla Lehmann, Hugh Burden, Marjorie Fielding, Seymour Hicks

A Family Affair*
US 1937 69m bw
MGM (Lucien Hubbard)

A small-town judge faces a few family problems.
The second feature that started the highly successful Hardy family series (qv under *Hardy*). In this case the judge and his wife were played by actors who did not persevere into the series, but the stage was otherwise set for a long run, and the town of Carvel came to mean home to many Americans abroad.

w Kay Van Riper, *play* Skidding by Aurania Rouverol *d* George B. Seitz *ph* Lester White *m* David Snell

Lionel Barrymore, Spring Byington, *Mickey Rooney*, Eric Linden, Cecilia Parker, Sara Haden, Charles Grapewin, Julie Haydon

'Family trade and tops in dual locations.'—*Variety*

Family Honeymoon
US 1948 90m bw
U-I (John Beck, Z. Wayne Griffin)

A college professor marries a widow whose three children join them on their Grand Canyon honeymoon.
Very ordinary and predictable star comedy.

w Dane Lussier, Homer Croy *d* Claude Binyon *ph* William Daniels *m* Frank Skinner

Claudette Colbert, Fred MacMurray, Rita Johnson, Gigi Perreau, Peter Miles, Jimmy Hunt, Hattie McDaniel, Chill Wills

The Family Jewels
US 1965 100m Technicolor
Paramount / York / Jerry Lewis

A child heiress chooses a new father from among her five uncles.
Unfunny star farce with multiple impersonations.

w Jerry Lewis, Bill Richmond *d* Jerry Lewis *ph* W. Wallace Kelley *m* Pete King

Jerry Lewis, Donna Butterworth, Sebastian Cabot, Robert Strauss

Family Life**
GB 1971 108m Technicolor
EMI / Kestrel (Tony Garnett)

A 19-year-old girl is driven into a mental collapse by emotional and family problems.
A slice of suburban life and an indictment of it, put together with unknown actors and probing TV techniques. Somewhat too harrowing for fiction, but extraordinarily vivid.

w David Mercer, from his play In Two Minds *d Ken Loach ph* Charles Stewart *m* Marc Wilkinson

Sandy Ratcliff, Bill Dean, Grace Cave

'There's no body in the family plot!'
Family Plot**
US 1976 126m Technicolor
Universal (Alfred Hitchcock)

A fake medium tries for easy money by producing a lost heir.
Talkative, complex, patchy, low-key but always interesting Hitchcock suspenser in an unusually friendly vein.

w Ernest Lehman, *novel* The Rainbird Pattern by Victor Canning *d* Alfred Hitchcock *ph* Leonard J. South *m* John Williams *pd* Henry Bumstead

Karen Black, Bruce Dern, Barbara Harris, William Devane, Ed Lauter, Cathleen Nesbitt

'Full of benign mischief, beautiful craftsmanship and that elusive sense of cinematic rhythm that has always been Hitchcock's trump card.'—*Michael Billington, Illustrated London News*

'The picture bogs down in one talky, undramatic sequence after another, and the plot, with all its exposition and loose ends, is involved beyond belief.'—*De Witt Bodeen, Films in Review*

Family Portrait **
GB 1950 24m bw
Festival of Britain / Wessex (Ian Dalrymple)

A study of the English tradition and spirit through history.
The last work of a director–poet; not his most vivid movie, yet an accurate distillation of the themes which concerned him and of a dream-like patriotism which now seems lost.

wd Humphrey Jennings ph Martin Curtis *ed* Stewart MacAllister *comm* Michael Goodliffe

'Perhaps the most polished in style of all Jennings' films . . . continuously fascinating, sharp and evocative.'—*MFB*

The Family Secret
US 1951 85m bw
Columbia / Santana (Robert Lord, Henry S. Kesler)

The son of a suburban family kills his best friend in a brawl, and his mother insists he conceal the truth even when another man is charged.
Television-style pattern play, not even very interesting at the time.

w Francis Cockrell, Andrew Solt *d* Henry Levin *ph* Burnett Guffey *m* George Duning

John Derek, Lee J. Cobb, Erin O'Brien Moore, Jody Lawrance, Henry O'Neill, Carl Benton Reid

'The general atmosphere is one of outward torment unbacked by inner emotion.'—*MFB*

The Family Way*
GB 1966 115m Eastmancolor
BL / Jambox (John Boulting)

There is consternation in a Lancashire family when the son cannot consummate his marriage.
Overstretched domestic farce-drama. Good scenes and performances, but it was all much sharper as a one-hour TV play.

w Bill Naughton, from his play Honeymoon Deferred *d* Roy Boulting *ph* Harry Waxman *m* Paul McCartney

John Mills, *Marjorie Rhodes*, Hywel Bennett, Hayley Mills, *Avril Angers*, Murray Head, Wilfred Pickles, Barry Foster, Liz Fraser

The Famous Ferguson Case
US 1932 80m bw

Reporters on a small town paper expose their own hang-ups as they argue over the outcome of a current murder trial. Generally unsuccessful attempt to do something mildly different. Joan Blondell, Tom Brown, Adrienne Dore, Walter Miller, Leslie Fenton, J. Carrol Naish, Grant Mitchell. Written by Harvey Thew from a story by Courtenay Terrett and Granville Moore; directed by Lloyd Bacon; for Warners. 'Dull, trite, talky exposé of yellow journalism.'—*Variety*

The Fan*
US 1949 79m bw
TCF (Otto Preminger)
GB title: *Lady Windermere's Fan*

Scandal almost results when Lady Windermere loses her fan.
Reasonably polished, rather dull version of an old play, not really helped by modern bookends.

w Walter Reisch, Dorothy Parker, Ross Evans, *play* Lady Windermere's Fan by Oscar Wilde *d* Otto Preminger *ph* Joseph La Shelle *m* Daniele Amfitheatrof

George Sanders, Madeleine Carroll, Jeanne Crain, Richard Greene, Martita Hunt, John Sutton, Hugh Dempster, Richard Ney

The Fan
US 1981 95m Technicolor
Paramount / Robert Stigwood / Filmways

A Broadway actress is threatened by a disturbed admirer.
Ruthless, witless thriller with no suspense cliché unturned.

w Priscilla Chapman, John Hartwell *d* Edward Bianchi *ph* Dick Bush *m* Pino Donaggio *pd* Santo Loquasto

Lauren Bacall, James Garner, Maureen Stapleton, Hector Elizondo, Michael Biehn, Anna Maria Horsford

'Horror comic mechanics . . . the theatrical milieu fails to register, either individually or collectively.'—*Gilbert Adair, MFB*

Fanatic*
GB 1965 96m Technicolor
Hammer / Seven Arts (Anthony Hinds)
US title: *Die! Die! My Darling*

An American girl in England visits the mother of her dead fiancé and finds herself the prisoner of a religious maniac.
Boringly overlong Grand Guignol which even defeats its gallantly unmade-up and deathly-looking star; mildly notable however as a record of one of her last performances.

w Richard Matheson, *novel* Nightmare by Anne Blaisdell *d* Silvio Narizzano *ph* Arthur Ibbetson *m* Wilfrid Josephs *pd* Peter Proud

Tallulah Bankhead, Stefanie Powers, Peter Vaughan, Yootha Joyce, Donald Sutherland

The Fanatics*
France 1957 92m bw
Cinégraphe-Regent (Pierre Lévy)

Patriots quarrel over the assassination by bomb of a South American dictator when he travels by public plane.
Suspense melodrama with many artificial twists, but slick and well acted.

w Alex Joffé, Jean Levitte *d* Alex Joffé *ph* L. H. Burel *m* Paul Misraki

Pierre Fresnay, Michel Auclair, Grégoire Aslan, Betty Schneider

Fancy Pants**
US 1950 92m Technicolor
Paramount (Robert Welch)

A British actor stranded in the far west poses as a butler.
Lively western comedy remake of *Ruggles of Red Gap* (qv), one of the star's better vehicles.

w Edmund Hartman, Robert O'Brien *d George Marshall ph* Charles Lang Jnr *m* Van Cleave

Bob Hope, Lucille Ball, Bruce Cabot, Jack Kirkwood, Lea Penman, Eric Blore, John Alexander, Norma Varden

Fanfan la Tulipe*
France 1951 98m bw
Filmsonor-Ariane-Amato

Recruited into the army of Louis XV by a prophecy that he will marry the king's daughter, a young braggart does everything he can to live up to it.
Rather like a spoof Errol Flynn effort, this likeable swashbuckler can't quite summon up enough buckle or swash to be the minor classic it clearly intends.

w René Wheeler, Jean Fallet *d* Christian-Jaque *ph* Christian Matras *m* Georges Van Parys, Maurice Thiriet

Gérard Philipe, Gina Lollobrigida, Noel Roquevert, Marcel Herrand

'A daring and delightful piece of work.'—*Times*

Fanny (Pagnol) see Marius

'There are three men in her life. The one she married . . . the young adventurer . . . and the baby they all shared!'
Fanny*
US 1960 133m Technicolor
Warner / Mansfield (Joshua Logan)

Life on the Marseilles waterfront, and in particular the story of two old men and two lovers.
Lumbering adaptation of three Pagnol films of the thirties (*Marius, Fanny, César*—see *Marius*) previously seen as a 1938 Hollywood film (*Port of Seven Seas*) and later as a Broadway musical. This is the dullest version despite fine photography and a couple of good performances.

w Julius J. Epstein, *play* S. N. Behrman, Joshua Logan, *films* Marcel Pagnol *d* Joshua Logan *ph Jack Cardiff* *m* Harold Rome *md* Morris Stoloff, Harry Sukman

Charles Boyer, Maurice Chevalier, Leslie Caron, Horst Buchholz, Georgette Anys, Salvatore Baccaloni, Lionel Jeffries, Raymond Bussières, Victor Francen

† The film was proudly advertised as 'Joshua Logan's *Fanny*' until the press pointed out the double meaning.

AAN: best picture; Jack Cardiff; Morris Stoloff, Harry Sukman; Charles Boyer

Fanny and Alexander**
Sweden / France / West Germany 1982 188m Eastmancolor
AB Cinematograph / Swedish Film Institute / Swedish TV One / Gaumont / Persona Film / Tobis (Jorn Donner)

A well-to-do Uppsala family comes together to celebrate Christmas 1907.
An interesting mixture of *Dear Octopus* and *Wild Strawberries* turns into something more akin to *The Face* or *The Night Comers*. A kind of Bergman compendium, and impossible to describe exactly for those who have not seen it.

wd Ingmar Bergman ph Sven Nykvist *m* Daniel Bell *pd Anna Asp*

Gunn Walgren, Ewa Froeling, Jarl Kulle, Erland Josephson, Allan Edwall, Boerje Ahlstedt, Mona Malm, Gunnar Bjornstrand, Jan Malmsjoe

'It's as if Bergman's neuroses had been tormenting him for so long that he cut them off and went sprinting back to Victorian health and domesticity.'—*New Yorker*

AA: cinematography; best foreign-language film; art direction; costume
AAN: direction; screenplay

Fanny by Gaslight**
GB 1944 108m bw
GFD / Gainsborough (Edward Black)
US title: *Man of Evil*

The illegitimate daughter of a cabinet minister is saved from a lustful Lord.
Highly-coloured Victorian romantic melodrama, enjoyably put over with no holds barred and a pretty high budget for the time.

w Doreen Montgomery, Aimée Stuart, *novel* Michael Sadleir *d Anthony Asquith* *ph* Arthur Crabtree *m* Cedric Mallabey

James Mason, Phyllis Calvert, Stewart Granger, Wilfrid Lawson, John Laurie, Margaretta Scott, Stuart Lindsell, Jean Kent

'Seldom have I seen a film more agreeable to watch, from start to finish.'—*William Whitebait*

'Mr Asquith does not seem to have made much effort to freshen it by interesting treatment, so that the rare unusual device seems quite out of key among so much that is simple, obvious, hackneyed.'—*Richard Mallett, Punch*

† One of several costume melodramas patterned after the success of *The Man in Grey* (qv).

Fanny Foley Herself
US 1931 73m Technicolor

A female vaudeville entertainer chooses between her profession and looking after her two daughters. Rather disappointing comedy drama. Edna May Oliver, Hobart Bosworth, Helen Chandler, Rochelle Hudson, John Darrow. Written by Carey Wilson from a story by Juliet Wilbur Tompkins; directed by Melville Brown; for RKO.

Fanny Hill
West Germany 1965 104m bw

Adventures of an 18th-century woman of pleasure. Tacky exploitation piece half-spoofing a suddenly fashionable piece of pornography. Miriam Hopkins, Laetitia Roman, Walter Giller, Alex D'Arcy, Helmut Weiss. Written by Robert Heel; directed by Russ Meyer; for Albert Zugsmith / Pan World.

Fantasia****
US 1940 135m Technicolor
Walt Disney

A concert of classical music is given cartoon interpretations. The pieces are:
Bach: Toccata and Fugue in D Minor
Tchaikovsky: The Nutcracker Suite
Dukas: The Sorcerer's Apprentice
Stravinsky: The Rite of Spring
Beethoven: The Pastoral Symphony
Ponchielli: Dance of the Hours
Moussorgsky: Night on a Bare Mountain
Schubert: Ave Maria
Brilliantly inventive for the most part, the cartoons having become classics in themselves. The least part (the Pastoral Symphony) can be forgiven.

supervisor Ben Sharpsteen *md* Edward H. Plumb

Leopold Stokowski, the Philadelphia Orchestra, Deems Taylor

'Dull as it is towards the end, ridiculous as it is in the bend of the knee before Art, it is one of the strange and beautiful things that have happened in the world.'—*Otis Ferguson*

'It is ambitious, and finely so, and one feels that its vulgarities are at least unintentional.'—*James Agate*

† Multiplane cameras, showing degrees of depth in animation, were used for the first time.

Fantastic Voyage*
US 1966 100m De Luxe Cinemascope
TCF (Saul David)

When a top scientist is shot and suffers brain damage, a team of doctors and a boat are miniaturized and injected into his blood stream . . . but one is a traitor.
Engagingly absurd science fiction which keeps its momentum but is somewhat let down by its decor.

w Harry Kleiner *d Richard Fleischer* *ph* Ernest Laszlo *m* Leonard Rosenman *ad* Dale Hennesy, Jack Martin Smith *sp* L. B. Abbott, Art Cruickshank, Emil Kosa Jnr

Stephen Boyd, Raquel Welch, Edmond O'Brien, Donald Pleasence, Arthur Kennedy, Arthur O'Connell, William Redfield

'The process shots are so clumsily matted . . . that the actors look as if a child has cut them out with blunt scissors.'—*Pauline Kael*

AA: art direction
AAN: Ernest Laszlo

Fantomas*
France / Italy 1966 104m bw

A master crook is also a master of disguise. One of several films made in the sixties in affectionate imitation of a French silent serial. Jean Marais, Louis de Funes, Mylene Demongeot, Jacques Dynam. Written by Jean Halain, Pierre Foucaud; directed by Andre Hunebelle; for SNEG.

The Far Country*
US 1954 97m Technicolor
U-I (Aaron Rosenberg)

Two cowboys on their way to the Alaska goldfields are beset by swindlers.
Sturdy star western with good production values.

w Borden Chase *d* Anthony Mann *ph* William Daniels *m* Hans Salter

James Stewart, Walter Brennan, Ruth Roman, Corinne Calvet, John McIntire

Far East
Australia 1982 100m colour

An Australian bar owner in an Asian city rampant with violence is confronted by a girl from his past. A disappointing attempt to redo *Casablanca* without the wit or style. Bryan Brown, Helen Morse, John Bell, Sinan Leong. Written and directed by John Duigan; for Richard Mason / Alfred Road.

Far from the Madding Crowd*
GB 1967 175m Technicolor Panavision 70
EMI / Vic / Appia (Joseph Janni)

In Victorian Wessex a headstrong girl causes unhappiness and tragedy.
Good-looking but slackly handled version of a melodramatic and depressing novel.

w Frederic Raphael, *novel* Thomas Hardy *d* John Schlesinger *ph Nicolas Roeg* *m* Richard Rodney Bennett *pd* Richard Macdonald

Julie Christie, Peter Finch, Alan Bates, Terence Stamp, Prunella Ransome

'In this rather plodding film the insufficiency of the foreground is partly offset by the

FAR FROM THE MADDING CROWD. Alan Bates and Julie Christie look too clean and too contemporary in John Schlesinger's lavish period piece.

winsomeness of the backgrounds. The very sheep are so engaging as to entice our gaze into some extremely amiable woolgathering.'—*John Simon*

AAN: Richard Rodney Bennett

The Far Horizons
US 1955 108m Technicolor
Vistavision
(Paramount) Pine–Thomas

The story of Lewis and Clark's 1803 expedition west through the Louisiana Purchase territory.
Flabbily-handled historical hokum; potential interest quickly dissipated.

w Winston Miller, Edmund H. North *d* Rudolph Maté *ph* Daniel L. Fapp *m* Hans Salter

Fred MacMurray, Charlton Heston, Donna Reed, Barbara Hale, William Demarest

Farewell Again**
GB 1937 85m bw
Pendennis / London Films (Erich Pommer)
US title: *Troopship*

Soldiers returning from India have six hours' shore leave to sort out their problems.
Dated but sharply made compendium drama, a solid success of its time.

w Clemence Dane, Patrick Kirwan *d Tim Whelan* *ph* James Wong Howe, Hans Schneeberger *m* Richard Addinsell

Flora Robson, Leslie Banks, Robert Newton, René Ray, Patricia Hilliard, Sebastian Shaw, Leonora Corbett, Anthony Bushell, Edward Lexy, Wally Patch, Edmund Willard, Martita Hunt, John Laurie

Farewell My Lovely***
US 1944 95m bw
RKO (Adrian Scott)
aka: *Murder My Sweet*

A private eye searches for an ex-convict's missing girl friend.
A revolutionary crime film in that it was the first to depict the genuinely seedy milieu suggested by its author. One of the first *films noirs* of the mid-forties, a minor masterpiece of expressionist film making, and a total change of direction for a crooner who suddenly became a tough guy.

w John Paxton, novel Raymond Chandler d Edward Dmytryk ph Harry J. Wild m Roy Webb

Dick Powell, Claire Trevor, Anne Shirley, *Mike Mazurki, Otto Kruger*, Miles Mander, Douglas Walton, Ralf Harolde, Don Douglas, Esther Howard

MARLOWE (Dick Powell): ' "Okay Marlowe," I said to myself. "You're a tough guy. You've been sapped twice, choked, beaten silly with a gun, shot in the arm until you're crazy as a couple of waltzing mice. Now let's see you do something really tough—like putting your pants on." '

MARLOWE: 'I caught the blackjack right behind my ear. A black pool opened up at my feet. I dived in. It had no bottom.'

MARLOWE: 'My fingers looked like a bunch of bananas.'

'A nasty, draggled bit of dirty work, accurately observed.'—*C. A. Lejeune*

Farewell My Lovely**
US 1975 95m Technicolor
Avco Embassy / Elliott Kastner / ITC
(George Pappas, Jerry Bruckheimer)

A pretty sharp remake of the above, with the plot slightly rewritten but tightened, and an excellent performance from a rather over-age star.

w David Zelag Goodman d Dick Richards *ph* John A. Alonzo *m* David Shire *pd* Dean Tavouraris

Robert Mitchum, Charlotte Rampling, John Ireland, Sylvia Miles, Anthony Zerbe, Jack O'Halloran, Kate Murtagh

'A moody, bluesy, boozy recreation of Marlowe's tacky, neon-flashed Los Angeles of the early forties.'—*Judith Crist*

'A delicious remake with a nice, smoky 1940s atmosphere.'—*Michael Billington, Illustrated London News*

AAN: Sylvia Miles

A Farewell to Arms**
US 1932 78m bw
(Paramount) Frank Borzage
In World War I, a wounded American ambulance driver falls in love with his nurse.
Now very dated but important in its time, this romantic drama was one of the more successful Hemingway adaptations to be filmed.

w Benjamin Glazer, Oliver H. P. Garrett, *novel Ernest Hemingway d Frank Borzage ph* Charles Lang *m* W. Franke Harling

Gary Cooper, *Helen Hayes*, Adolphe Menjou, Mary Philips, Jack La Rue, Blanche Frederici, Henry Armetta

'Too much sentiment and not enough strength.'—*Mordaunt Hall, New York Times*

'Borzage has invested the war scenes with a strange, brooding expressionist quality . . . indeed, the overall visual style is most impressive.'—*NFT, 1974*

'Corking femme film fare at any angle or price.'—*Variety*

† Remade as *Force of Arms* (qv) and see below.

AA: Charles Lang
AAN: best picture

A Farewell to Arms
US 1957 150m De Luxe Cinemascope
TCF / David O. Selznick
Elaborate ill-fated remake which tried to make an adventure epic out of a low-key war drama. Its failure caused David O. Selznick to produce no more films.

w Ben Hecht *d* Charles Vidor *pd* Alfred Junge *ph* Piero Portalupi, Oswald Morris *m* Mario Nascimbene

Rock Hudson, Jennifer Jones, Vittorio de Sica, Alberto Sordi, Kurt Kasznar, Mercedes McCambridge, Oscar Homolka, Elaine Stritch, Victor Francen

AAN: Vittorio de Sica

Fargo
US 1964 99m Technicolor
Universal / Pennebaker (Al Ruddy)
aka: *Wild Seed*
A teenage girl hitch-hikes from New York to Los Angeles and is befriended by a young tramp.
Peripatetic romance in the modern manner, with no conclusions drawn and not much entertainment value beyond the scenery.

w Les Pine *d* Brian G. Hutton *ph* Conrad Hall *m* Richard Markowitz

Michael Parks, Celia Kaye, Ross Elliott, Woodrow Chambliss, Eva Novak

The Farmer Takes a Wife*
US 1935 91m bw
TCF (Winfield Sheehan)
By the Erie Canal in the 1820s, a wandering girl finds security with a farmer.
Pleasantly 'different' romantic drama, quite ably executed and introducing Henry Fonda to the screen.

w Edwin Burke, *play* Frank B. Elser and Marc Connelly, *novel* Rome Haul by Walter D. Edmonds *d* Victor Fleming *ph* John Seitz *m* Arthur Lange

Janet Gaynor, Henry Fonda, Charles Bickford, Slim Summerville, Andy Devine, Roger Imhof, Jane Withers, Margaret Hamilton, Sig Rumann, John Qualen

'It will pull in the Gaynor fans, and do much to return her to favour.'—*Variety*

The Farmer Takes a Wife*
US 1953 81m Technicolor
TCF (Frank P. Rosenberg)
Musical remake with an agreeably stylized look, hampered by a slowish script and dull cast.

w Walter Bulloch, Sally Benson, Joseph Fields *d* Henry Levin *ph* Arthur E. Arling *m* Cyril Mockridge *ad Lyle Wheeler, Addison Hehr songs* Harold Arlen, Dorothy Fields

Betty Grable, Dale Robertson, Thelma Ritter, Eddie Foy Jnr, John Carroll

The Farmer's Daughter
US 1940 60m bw
Paramount (William C. Thomas)
A stage struck country girl tries to horn in on a Broadway musical rehearsing nearby.
Feeble comedy for the sticks.

w Lewis R. Foster, Delmer Daves *d* James Hogan *ph* Leo Tover

Martha Raye, Charles Ruggles, Richard Denning, Gertrude Michael, William Frawley, William Demarest, Jack Norton

'Now she's raising eyebrows instead of corn!'

The Farmer's Daughter**
US 1947 97m bw
David O. Selznick (Dore Schary)
The Swedish maid of a congressman becomes a political force.
Well-made Cinderella story with a touch of asperity and top notch production values and cast.

w Allen Rivkin, Laura Kerr d H. C. Potter ph Milton Krasner m Leigh Harline

Loretta Young, Joseph Cotten, Ethel Barrymore, Charles Bickford, Rose Hobart, Rhys Williams, Harry Davenport, Tom Powers

'Patricians, politicians, even peasants are portrayed with unusual perception and wit.'—*James Agee*

AA: Loretta Young
AAN: Charles Bickford

The Farmer's Wife
GB 1928 67m approx bw silent
BIP (John Maxwell)
A farmer seeks a wife and after three disappointments settles for his housekeeper.
A simple and not very interesting silent screen version of a stage success which depended largely on dialogue.

wd Alfred Hitchcock, *play* Eden Phillpotts *ph* Jack Cox

James Thomas, Gordon Harker, Lillian Hall-Davis

'Some pleasant photography and a subtle impression of rural life rescued the picture from complete failure.'—*George Perry, 1966*

The Farmer's Wife
GB 1940 82m bw
Talkie remake of the above, a perfectly adequate photographed play. Basil Sydney, Wilfrid Lawson, Nora Swinburne, Patricia Roc, Michael Wilding. Written by Norman Lee, Leslie Arliss and J. E. Hunter; directed by Norman Lee and Leslie Arliss; for Associated British.

Farrebique**
France 1947 85m bw
L'Ecran Français / Les Films Etienne Lallier
Problems of a peasant family in central France.
Superbly-filmed semi-documentary, acted by a real family.

wd Georges Rouquier ph André Dantan m Henri Sauguet

'Definitely a film for posterity.'—*MFB*

Fashions of 1934*
US 1934 78m bw
Warner (Henry Blanke)
A confidence trickster conquers the French fashion world.
Slight musical comedy with a couple of splendid Berkeley numbers.

w F. Hugh Herbert, Carl Brickson *d* William Dieterle *ch Busby Berkeley ph* William Rees *m / ly* Sammy Fain, Irving Kahal *ad* Jack Okey

William Powell, Bette Davis, Verree Teasdale, Frank McHugh, Reginald Owen, Hugh Herbert, Henry O'Neill

Fast and Furious: see Fast Company (1938)

Fast and Loose
US 1930 70m bw
Paramount
A spoiled rich girl falls in love with a car mechanic.
Tiresome melodrama, dully scripted.

w Doris Anderson, Jack Kirkland, Preston Sturges, *play* The Best People by Avery Hopwood, David Gray *d* Fred Newmeyer *ph* William Steiner

Miriam Hopkins, Carole Lombard, Frank Morgan, Charles Starrett, Henry Wadsworth, David Hutcheson, Ilka Chase

Fast and Loose*
US 1939 80m bw
MGM (Frederick Stephani)

Married detectives and rare book experts solve the mystery of a missing Shakespeare manuscript.
Pleasing comedy mystery in the wake of *The Thin Man*.

w Harry Kurnitz *d* Edwin L. Marin *ph* George Folsey

Robert Montgomery, Rosalind Russell, Ralph Morgan, Reginald Owen, Etienne Girardot, Alan Dinehart, Joan Marsh, Sidney Blackmer

Fast and Loose
GB 1954 75m bw

By a series of accidents, a married man has to spend a night at an inn with an old flame. Spiritless and miscast remake of *A Cuckoo in the Nest*; all talents below form. Brian Reece, Stanley Holloway, Kay Kendall, Reginald Beckwith, Charles Victor, June Thorburn. Written by A. R. Rawlinson and Ben Travers, from the latter's play; directed by Gordon Parry; for Group Films / Rank.

Fast Company*
US 1938 75m bw

A couple in the rare book business are implicated in the murder of a rival. First of three whodunnits featuring Joel and Garda Page, whose style was not at all dissimilar from that of Nick and Nora Charles in the *Thin Man* series. A polished time-passer. Melvyn Douglas, Florence Rice, Clare Dodd, Louis Calhern, George Zucco. Written by Marco Page (Harry Kurnitz); directed by Edward Buzzell; for MGM. (NB: The follow-ups had different stars as the pair of sleuths. *Fast and Loose* (qv) featured Robert Montgomery and Rosalind Russell; Sidney Blackmer, Ralph Morgan and Reginald Owen supported. *Fast and Furious,* also released in 1939, starred Franchot Tone and Ann Sothern, with Ruth Hussey, Lee Bowman and Allyn Joslyn.)

Fast Company
US 1953 67m bw

A girl inherits a racing stable and discovers a little chicanery. Ho-hum support wasting a good cast. Howard Keel, Nina Foch, Polly Bergen, Marjorie Main. Written by William Roberts; directed by John Sturges; for MGM.

The Fast Lady**
GB 1962 95m Eastmancolor
Rank / Group Films (Teddy Baird)

A bashful suitor buys an old Bentley, becomes a roadhog, passes his test, captures some crooks and gets the girl.
Spirited if aimless farcical comedy which crams in all the jokes about cars anyone can think of.

w Jack Davies, Henry Blyth *d* Ken Annakin *ph* Reg Wyer *m* Norrie Paramor

Stanley Baxter, James Robertson Justice, Leslie Phillips, Julie Christie, Dick Emery

Fast Talking
Australia 1983 95m Eastmancolor

The youngest son of a shiftless and semi-criminal Sydney family gets into trouble and finally drives off on his motor cycle to an uncertain future. Depressingly downbeat comedy-drama about characters of whom any audience must quickly tire. Rod Zuanic, Toni Allaylis, Christ Truswell, Gail Sweeny, Steve Bisley. Written and directed by Ken Cameron; for Ross Matthews / Oldata.

Fast Times at Ridgemont High
US 1982 92m Technicolor
Universal / Refugee (C. O. Erickson)

Students at a California high school aim to lose their virginity.
The tiresome content of this teen comedy is slightly offset by bright handling. But only slightly.

w Cameron Crowe, from his book *d* Amy Heckerling *ph* Matthew F. Leonetti *m / songs* Rob Fahey

Sean Penn, Jennifer Jason Leigh, Judge Reinhold, Phoebe Cates, Brian Backus, Robert Romanus, Ray Walston

Fast-Walking
US 1981 116m Metrocolor

Racial disharmony and violence prevail at a midwest state prison. Curious black comedy dealing entirely with unpleasant types. James Woods, Tim McIntire, Kay Lenz, Robert Hooks, M. Emmet Walsh. Written and directed by James B. Harris from the novel The Rap by Ernest Brawley; for Lorimar.
'What do people think of when they write a script these days? Don't they have any sense of human values or human decency?'—*Arthur Knight*

Fast Workers
US 1933 68m bw

Rivalries erupt among skyscraper workers. Standard action programmer with which MGM terminated John Gilbert's contract after an illustrious rise and dramatic fall. Also cast: Mae Clarke, Willard Mack, Robert Armstrong. Written by Laurence Stallings; directed by Tod Browning; for MGM.

The Fastest Guitar Alive
US 1966 87m Metrocolor

Inept confederate soldiers are sent on a spy mission. Ham-handed farce with music, unappealing on either count. Roy Orbison, Sammy Jackson, Maggie Pierce, Joan Freeman, Lyle Bettger. Written by Robert E. Kent; directed by Michael Moore; for Sam Katzman / MGM.

The Fastest Gun Alive*
US 1956 89m bw
MGM (Clarence Greene)

A mild-mannered western storekeeper proves to be the son of a famous gunfighter, and is put to the test.
Flimsily contrived mini-western helped by good performances.

w Frank D. Gilroy, Russel Rouse *d* Russel Rouse *ph* George Folsey *m* André Previn

Glenn Ford, Broderick Crawford, Jeanne Crain, Russ Tamblyn, Allyn Joslyn, Leif Erickson, John Dehner

Fat City*
US 1972 96m Eastmancolor
Columbia / Rastar (Ray Stark)

In a small Californian town, a has-been boxer tries to get back to the top, but loses his self respect and becomes a hobo.
Vivid but over-casual exploration of failure, with more interest in the characters than the sport.

w Leonard Gardner, from his novel *d* John Huston *ph* Conrad Hall *md* Marvin Hamlisch *pd* Richard Sylbert

Stacy Keach, Jeff Bridges, Susan Tyrell

AAN: Susan Tyrell

The Fat Man
US 1950 77m bw
U-I (Aubrey Schenck)

The murder of a dentist leads to the circus.
Dense murder mystery featuring a gourmet 17-stone detective; understandably, no series resulted.

w Harry Essex, Leonard Lee *d* William Castle *ph* Irving Glassberg *m* Bernard Green

J. Scott Smart, Rock Hudson, Julie London, Clinton Sundberg, Jerome Cowan, Jayne Meadows

Fatal Attraction**
US 1987 119m Technicolor
Paramount / Jaffe-Lansing (Stanley Jaffe, Sherry Lansing)

A married man finds it difficult to shed his nearly homicidal light of love.
A kind of rehash of *Play Misty for Me*, and a sensational success at the box office: the timing must have been right, even if the details aren't always persuasive.

w James Dearden *d Adrian Lyne* *ph* Howard Atherton *m* Maurice Jarre *pd* Mel Bourne

Michael Douglas, *Glenn Close*, Anne Archer, Fred Gwynne

'A predictable dog's dinner of thriller clichés—will appeal strongly to those who think women should be kept on a short leash.'—*Time Out*

AAN: Glenn Close; Anne Archer; Adrian Lyne; best picture; James Dearden; editors (Michael Kahn, Peter E. Berger)

The Fatal Glass of Beer*
US 1933 18m bw

The prodigal son returns to a snowbound cabin in the Yukon. Absurd star comedy with appeal to addicts only: most of the humour consists of repeats of one line, ' 'Taint a fit night out for man nor beast.' *W. C. Fields*, Rosemary Theby, Rychard Cramer, George Chandler. Written by Fields; directed by Clyde Bruckman; for Paramount / Sennett.

Fatal Lady
US 1936 77m bw

An opera singer has trouble with men and becomes involved with murder. Lively melodrama with songs, very much of its period. Mary Ellis, Walter Pidgeon, John

Halliday, Ruth Donnelly, Alan Mowbray, Edgar Kennedy. Written by Jules Furthman; directed by Edward Ludwig; for Walter Wanger / Paramount.

The Fatal Night*
GB 1948 49m bw
(Anglofilm) Mario Zampi

A joke haunting has unfortunate consequences.
A small, cheaply-made film which really thrilled.

w Gerald Butler, *story* The Gentleman from America by Michael Arlen *d Mario Zampi* *ph* Cedric Williams *m* Stanley Black

Lester Ferguson, Jean Short, Leslie Armstrong, Brenda Hogan, Patrick MacNee

Fate Is the Hunter
US 1964 106m bw Cinemascope
TCF / Arcola (Aaron Rosenberg)

An airline executive investigates the cause of a fatal crash in which his friend the pilot was a victim.
Watchable how-did-it happen melodrama marred by pretentious dialogue.

w Harold Medford, *novel* Ernest K. Gann *d* Ralph Nelson *ph* Milton Krasner *m* Jerry Goldsmith

Glenn Ford, Rod Taylor, Nehemiah Persoff, Nancy Kwan, Suzanne Pleshette, Jane Russell

AAN: Milton Krasner

Father Brown***
GB 1954 91m bw
(Columbia) Facet (Vivian A. Cox)
US title: *The Detective*

A Catholic clergyman retrieves a priceless church cross from master thief Flambeau.
Delightfully eccentric comedy based closely on the famous character, with a sympathetic if rather wandering script, pointed direction and some delicious characterizations. A thoroughly civilized entertainment.

w Thelma Schnee, *story* The Blue Cross by G. K. Chesterton *d Robert Hamer* *ph* Harry Waxman *m* Georges Auric

Alec Guinness, *Joan Greenwood*, *Peter Finch*, Sidney James, *Cecil Parker*, *Bernard Lee*, *Ernest Thesiger*, Marne Maitland

'It has wit, elegance, and kindly humour—all somewhat rare commodities in the 1954 cinema.'—*Star*

Father Brown Detective*
US 1934 67m bw

Flambeau, the thief, decides to steal Father Brown's blue cross. Early attempt at the same story used in the 1954 *Father Brown* with Alec Guinness; quite pleasantly interesting. Walter Connolly, Paul Lukas, Gertrude Michael, Robert Loraine, Halliwell Hobbes, Una O'Connor, E. E. Clive. 'Clean, but not strong enough to stand solo.'—*Variety*

Father Came Too
GB 1963 93m Eastmancolor
Rank / Independent Artists

Honeymooners agree to live with her overbearing actor manager father.
Less funny sequel to *The Fast Lady*, with comic household disasters striking every couple of minutes. Easy-going, and predictably amusing in spots.

w Jack Davies, Henry Blyth *d* Peter Graham Scott *ph* Reg Wyer *m* Norrie Paramor

Stanley Baxter, James Robertson Justice, Leslie Phillips, Sally Smith, Ronnie Barker, Timothy Bateson, Philip Locke

Father Goose*
US 1964 116m Technicolor
U-I / Granox (Robert Arthur)

During World War II a South Seas wanderer is compelled by the Australian navy to act as sky observer on a small island, where he finds himself in charge of six refugee schoolchildren and their schoolmistress.
Eager-to-please but unsatisfactory film which wanders between farce, adventure and sex comedy, taking too long about all of them.

w Peter Stone, Frank Tarloff *d* Ralph Nelson *ph* Charles Lang Jnr *m* Cy Coleman

Cary Grant, Leslie Caron, Trevor Howard

(Cary Grant): 'Let me tell you I am not a father figure. I am not a brother figure or an uncle figure or a cousin figure. In fact, the only figure I intend being is a total stranger figure.'

'Reasoning would indicate a made-to-order Christmas package for the family trade. However, the more sophisticated may be bored and exasperated after some of the initial brightness wears off.'—*Cue*

'Cary Grant wrings what there is to be wrung from the role, but never quite enough to conceal the fact that *Father Goose* is a waste of his talent and the audience's time.'—*Arthur Knight*

AA: Peter Stone, Frank Tarloff

Father Is a Bachelor
US 1950 85m bw
Columbia (S. Sylvan Simon)

A young tramp cares for a family of orphaned children.
Boringly sentimental semi-western.

w Aleen Leslie, James Edward Grant *d* Norman Foster, Abby Berlin *ph* Burnett Guffey *m* Arthur Morton

William Holden, Coleen Gray, Charles Winninger, Stuart Erwin, Sig Rumann

'Saccharine, paper thin. At least one spectator at the Palace yesterday couldn't take it—a tot of about four, wearing a cowboy suit, who aimed a toy pistol at the screen and popped off the cast one by one.'—*New York Times*

Father Is a Prince: see Big Hearted Herbert

'The bride gets the thrills! Father gets the bills!'

Father of the Bride**
US 1950 93m bw
MGM (Pandro S. Berman)

A dismayed but happy father surveys the cost and chaos of his daughter's marriage.
Fragmentary but mainly delightful suburban comedy which finds Hollywood in its best light vein and benefits from a strong central performance.

w Frances Goodrich, *Albert Hackett*, *novel Edward Streeter* *d* Vincente Minnelli *ph* John Alton *m* Adolph Deutsch

Spencer Tracy, Joan Bennett, Elizabeth Taylor, Don Taylor, Billie Burke, Moroni Olsen, Leo G. Carroll, Taylor Holmes, Melville Cooper

'The idealization of a safe sheltered existence, the good life according to MGM: 24 carat complacency.'—*New Yorker*, *1980*

† Jack Benny badly wanted the role but was thought unsuitable.

AAN: best picture; Frances Goodrich, Albert Hackett; Spencer Tracy

Father Takes a Wife*
US 1941 80m bw
RKO (Lee S. Marcus)

A famous actress marries a shipping magnate and runs into resentment from his children.
Disappointing comedy with a script too flat for the stars to make interesting.

w Dorothy and Herbert Fields *d* Jack Hively *ph* Robert de Grasse *m* Roy Webb

Gloria Swanson, Adolphe Menjou, Desi Arnaz, John Howard, Helen Broderick, Florence Rice, Neil Hamilton

Father Was a Fullback
US 1949 84m bw
TCF (Fred Kohlmar)

The coach of a college football team has domestic problems.
Thin star comedy, strictly double bill.

w Aleen Leslie, Casey Robinson, Richard Sale, Mary Loos, *play* Clifford Goldsmith *d* John M. Stahl *ph* Lloyd Ahern *m* Cyril Mockridge

Fred MacMurray, Maureen O'Hara, Betty Lynn, Natalie Wood, Rudy Vallee, Jim Backus

Father's Doing Fine
GB 1952 83m Technicolor

An impoverished lady has trouble with her daughters, one of whom is pregnant.
Agreeable madcap farce from a long-running stage success (so why did they change the title?). Heather Thatcher, Richard Attenborough, Susan Stephen, Noel Purcell, George Thorpe. Written by Anne Burnaby, from the play *Little Lambs Eat Ivy* by Noel Langley; directed by Henry Cass; for Marble Arch / ABP.

Father's Little Dividend
US 1951 81m bw
MGM (Pandro S. Berman)

Sequel to *Father of the Bride*, in which the newlyweds have a baby.
A very flat follow-up, palatable enough at the time but quite unmemorable.

w Frances Goodrich, Albert Hackett *d* Vincente Minnelli *ph* John Alton *m* Albert Sandrey

Spencer Tracy, Joan Bennett, Elizabeth Taylor, Don Taylor, Billie Burke, Moroni Olsen, Frank Faylen, Marietta Canty, Russ Tamblyn

'The world's most uncovered undercover agent!'

Fathom
GB 1967 99m De Luxe Franscope
TCF (John Kohn)

Adventures of a glamorous sky-diving spy. Watchable romp with nothing memorable about it.

w Lorenzo Semple Jnr, *novel* Larry Forrester *d* Leslie Martinson *ph* Douglas Slocombe, Ken Vos *m* Johnny Dankworth

Raquel Welch, Tony Franciosa, Clive Revill, Ronald Fraser, Greta Chi, Richard Briers, Tom Adams

'Belongs not in the category of High Camp but in that of Good Wholesome Fun.'—*MFB*

Fatso
US 1980 93m De Luxe

A fat man fails to make much headway at slimming, and gives up. Unappealing mixture of sentiment, satire, shouting and crude humour. Dom DeLuise, Anne Bancroft, Ron Carey, Candice Azzara. Written and directed by Anne Bancroft; for Brooksfilms / TCF. 'As bumbling and sluggish as its title might suggest, a lamentable affair which ricochets uncontrollably between attempts at hilarity and pathos.'—*Variety*.

Faust**
Germany 1926 100m approx bw silent
UFA

A superbly stylish version of the legend about a man who sells his soul to the devil. The best of many silent versions; see also *All That Money Can Buy*.

w Hans Kyser *d F. W. Murnau* *ph* Carl Hoffman

Emil Jannings, Gosta Ekman, Camilla Horn, Yvette Guilbert, William Dieterle

Favourites of the Moon*
France 1984 102m Eastmancolor

Characters in Paris find that their paths cross as they pursue their obsessions. Bunuel-like surrealism without Bunuel's intensity of vision results in a film which sometimes pleases but eventually becomes tiresome. Katïa Rupe, Hans Peter Cloos, Alix de Montaigu, Francois Michel. Written by Otar Iosseliani, Gerard Brach; directed by *Otar Iosseliani*; for Philippe Dussart / FR3. (Original title: *Les Favoris de la Lune*.)

Fear
US 1946 68m bw
Monogram

A student kills his professor, and a detective taunts him to the point of confession.
Cheeky second feature version of *Crime and Punishment*, with a twist ending. Not too bad in its way.

w Alfred Zeisler, Dennis Cooper *d* Alfred Zeisler *ph* Jackson Rose

Warren William, Peter Cookson, Anne Gwynne, Nestor Paiva

Fear Eats the Soul*
West Germany 1973 92m colour
Tango Film (Christian Hohoff)

A Moroccan immigrant in Munich comes up against social and racial prejudice when he marries a sixty-year-old charwoman.
Unexceptionable moral tale which can hardly have been necessary in view of the infrequency of such cases.

wd Rainer Werner Fassbinder *ph* Jürgen Jürges

Brigitti Mira, El Hedi Ben Salem, Barbara Valentin, Irm Hermann, Rainer Werner Fassbinder

Fear in the Night**
US 1947 72m bw
Maxwell Shane

A man suffering from a strange nightmare discovers he has been hypnotized into committing a murder.
Intriguing small-scale puzzler later remade to less effect as *Nightmare* (qv). Adequate performances and handling, but the plot's the thing.

wd Maxwell Shane *ph* Jack Grennhalgh *m* Rudy Schraeger

Paul Kelly, De Forrest Kelley, Ann Doran, Kay Scott

Fear in the Night*
GB 1972 85m Technicolor
Hammer (Jimmy Sangster)

A girl recovering from a nervous breakdown is deluded into committing a murder.
Yet another variant on *Les Diaboliques*, ingeniously worked out with good touches of detail to produce an air of general competence.

w Jimmy Sangster, Michael Syson *d* Jimmy Sangster *ph* Arthur Grant *m* John McCabe

Peter Cushing, Judy Geeson, Joan Collins, Ralph Bates

Fear Is the Key*
GB 1972 108m Technicolor Panavision
EMI / KLK (Alan Ladd Jnr, Elliott Kastner)

A man conceives an elaborate plot to track down those responsible for killing his wife and family in a plane crash.
Reasonably absorbing, surprise-plotted thriller.

w Robert Carrington, *novel* Alistair MacLean *d* Michael Tuchner *ph* Alex Thomson *m* Roy Budd

Suzy Kendall, Barry Newman, John Vernon, Dolph Sweet, Ben Kingsley, Ray McAnally

Fear Strikes Out
US 1957 100m bw Vistavision
Paramount / Alan Pakula

A father wants his son to become a professional baseball player, and the son in consequence suffers a nervous breakdown.
Rather flat biopic of Jim Piersall; well-intentioned and careful in its psychological insights, but too often just plain dull.

w Ted Berkman, Raphael Blau *d* Robert Mulligan *ph* Haskell Boggs *m* Elmer Bernstein

Anthony Perkins, Karl Malden, Norma Moore, Perry Wilson

Fearless Fagan
US 1952 78m bw

A circus clown is enlisted and takes his pet lion along. Rather silly comedy padded out with sentimentality. Carleton Carpenter, Janet Leigh, Keenan Wynn, Richard Anderson, Ellen Corby. Written by Charles Lederer; directed by Stanley Donen; for MGM.

The Fearless Vampire Killers, or Pardon Me, Your Teeth Are in My Neck*
US 1967 124m Metrocolor Panavision
MGM / Cadre Films / Filmways (Gene Gutowski)
aka: *Dance of the Vampires*

A professor and his assistant stake a Transylvanian vampire.
Heavy, slow spoof of *Dracula*, most of which shows that sense of humour is very personal; a few effective moments hardly compensate for the prevailing stodge.

w Gerard Brach, Roman Polanski *d* Roman Polanski *ph Douglas Slocombe* *m* Krzystof Komeda *pd* Wilfrid Shingleton

Jack McGowran, Roman Polanski, Alfie Bass, Sharon Tate, *Ferdy Mayne*, Iain Quarrier, Terry Downes

'An engaging oddity . . . long stretches might have been lifted intact from any Hammer horror.'—*Tom Milne*

† A credit ran: Fangs by Dr Ludwig von Krankheit.

The Fearmakers
US 1958 85m bw
Pacemaker (Martin H. Lancer)

A brainwashed Korean War veteran returns to Washington and finds that his PR firm has been taken over by communist racketeers.
Unusual but cheaply made anti-Red propaganda, too talkative to be very entertaining.

w Elliot West, Chris Appley, *novel* Darwin Teilhet *d* Jacques Tourneur *ph* Sam Leavitt *m* Irving Gertz

Dana Andrews, Dick Foran, Mel Tormé

A Feather in Her Hat
US 1935 72m bw
Columbia

A London widow with delusions of grandeur tells her son that his real mother was a famous actress.

Outmoded mother-love drama, interestingly cast.

w Lawrence Hazard, *story* I. A. R. Wylie *d* Alfred Santell *ph* Joseph Walker

Pauline Lord, Basil Rathbone, Louis Hayward, Billie Burke, Wendy Barrie, J. M. Kerrigan, Victor Varconi, Nydia Westman, Thurston Hall

'Too British for general appeal, though well acted.'—*Variety*

Feather Your Nest*
GB 1937 86m bw
ATP (Basil Dean)

A gramophone record technician substitutes his own voice for a star and becomes world famous.
The star in less farcical vein than usual; this is the one in which he sings 'Leaning on a Lamp-post'.

w Austin Melford, Robert Edmunds, Anthony Kimmins *d* William Beaudine *ph* Ronald Neame

George Formby, Polly Ward, Enid Stamp Taylor, Val Rosing, Davy Burnaby

Federal Agents vs Underworld Inc
US 1949 bw serial: 12 eps

An archaeologist disappears after discovering the Golden Hands of Kurigal. Routine thick-ear for serial addicts. Kirk Alyn, Rosemary La Planche, Roy Barcroft, Carol Forman. Directed by Fred Brannon; for Republic.

Federal Operator 99
US 1945 bw serial: 12 eps

An underworld leader escapes from a prison train and plans to steal Princess Cornelia's jewels. Nothing surprising, but the pot keeps boiling. Marten Lamont, Helen Talbot, George J. Lewis, Lorna Gray. Directed by Spencer Bennet and Wallace Grissell; for Republic.

Fedora*
West Germany / France 1978 110m Eastmancolor
Geria / SFP (Billy Wilder)

An ageing star who seems miraculously to have kept her beauty comes out of retirement. *Sunset Boulevard* revisited, with a less bitter approach and less effectiveness; but any civilized film is welcome in the late seventies.

w I. A. L. Diamond, Billy Wilder, from a story in Crowned Heads by Tom Tryon *d* Billy Wilder *ph* Gerry Fisher *m* Miklos Rozsa

William Holden, Marthe Keller, Hildgarde Knef, Jose Ferrer, Mario Adorf, Henry Fonda, Michael York

'Rife with Wilderean gallows humour and a sumptuous sense of decay in never-never land.'—*Sight and Sound*

'A thrill a minute! A laugh a second! A comedy cyclone!'

Feet First**
US 1930 88m bw
Harold Lloyd

A shoe salesman gets entangled with crooks and has a narrow escape when hanging from the side of a building.
Very funny early talkie comedy, probably the comedian's last wholly satisfactory film.

w Lex Neal, Felix Adler, Paul Gerard Smith *d Clyde Bruckman* *ph* Walter Ludin, Henry Kohler

Harold Lloyd, Robert McWade, Barbara Kent

'That Lloyd was a bit pressed for laughs may be guessed from the fact that he is again dangling from the front of a skyscraper.'—*Variety*

Fellini Satyricon: see Satyricon

Female*
US 1933 60m bw

A high-powered lady president of a motor car company has a secret night life. Slick star vehicle reminiscent of *Peg's Paper* but absorbing while on screen. *Ruth Chatterton*, George Brent, Johnny Mack Brown, Ruth Donnelly, Douglass Dumbrille, Lois Wilson. Written by Gene Markey and Kathryn Scola, from a story by Donald Henderson Clarke; directed by Michael Curtiz and William Dieterle; for Warner. 'The story is worthy neither of this actress nor of the high-grade production.'—*Variety*

The Female Animal
US 1957 82m bw Cinemascope
U-I (Albert Zugsmith)

A beach bum becomes the lover of a film star, then falls in love with her daughter.
Dreary and humourless melodrama notable only for the comeback appearance of one of the screen's legendary glamour queens.

w Robert Hill *d* Harry Keller *ph* Russell Metty *m* Hans Salter

Hedy Lamarr, Jan Sterling, Jane Powell, George Nader, James Gleason

'Once she was too hungry for love to be afraid—but now—it was too late!'

The Female on the Beach
US 1955 97m bw
U-I (Albert Zugsmith)

A wealthy widow visits her late husband's beach house and falls for the gigolo next door, who later seems intent on murdering her.
Absurd and jaded melodrama, a rehash of *Love from a Stranger*, enlivened by some hilarious love-hate dialogue.

w Robert Hill, Richard Alan Simmons *d* Joseph Pevney *ph* Charles Lang *m* Joseph Gershenson

Joan Crawford, Jeff Chandler, Jan Sterling, Cecil Kellaway, Natalie Schaefer
(Joan Crawford) to Jeff Chandler: 'I would have you if you were hung with diamonds, upside down!'

The Feminine Touch
US 1941 97m bw
MGM (Joseph L. Mankiewicz)

A professor gets into woman trouble when he writes a book about jealousy.
Matrimonial comedy rather less interesting than its credits suggest.

w George Oppenheimer, Edmund L. Hartmann, Ogden Nash *d* W. S. Van Dyke *m* Franz Waxman

Rosalind Russell, Don Ameche, Kay Francis, Van Heflin, Donald Meek, Henry Daniell, Sidney Blackmer

The Feminine Touch
GB 1956 91m Technicolor
Ealing (Jack Rix)
US title: *The Gentle Touch*

Five young student nurses arrive at St Augustine's Hospital.
Portmanteau soap opera of no absorbing interest.

w Ian McCormick from the novel A Lamp is Heavy by Sheila Mackay Russell *d* Pat Jackson *ph* Paul Beeson *m* Clifton Parker

George Baker, Belinda Lee, Delphi Lawrence, Adrienne Corri, Henryetta Edwards, Barbara Archer, Diana Wynyard, Mandy Miller

La Femme de Nulle Part*
France 1922 70m approx bw silent
aka: *The Woman from Nowhere*

A woman who feels that her life has been ruined through love returns home and persuades a young girl not to do the same.

A minor atmospheric piece of some power, comparable with *Partie de Campagne* and cinematically very interesting.

wd Louis Delluc *ph* Lucas Gibory *ad* F. Jourdain

Eve Francis, Roger Karl, Gine Avril

Une Femme Disparait*
France 1944 104m bw
aka: *A Woman Disappeared, Portrait of a Woman*

When a body is found, four people believe it to be that of a loved one who has disappeared; their stories are told in flashback. Virtually a short story portmanteau to accommodate five performances by its star, directed by her husband. *Françoise Rosay*, Henri Guisol, Jean Nohain, Claire Gérard. Written and directed by Jacques Feyder from novel by Jacques Viot; for Mayer-Burstyn.

La Femme du Boulanger**
France 1938 110m bw
Marcel Pagnol
aka: *The Baker's Wife*

Villagers put a stop to the infidelity of the baker's wife because her husband no longer has the heart to make good bread.
Best-known of Pagnol's rustic fables, this rather obvious and long-drawn-out joke is important because international critics hailed it as a work of art (which it isn't) and because it fixed an image of the naughty bucolic French.

wd Marcel Pagnol, novel Jean Le Bleu by Jean Giono *ph* G. Benoit, R. Lendruz, N. Daries *m* Vincent Scotto

FEDORA. Billy Wilder's late, less pointed, bite at the hand that fed him finds film star Michael York playing film star Michael York and Marthe Keller following his lead.

Raimu, Ginette Leclerc, Charles Moulin, Charpin, Maximilienne

'It is a long film with a small subject, but the treatment is so authentic that it seems over far too soon, and the acting is superb.'—*Graham Greene*

La Femme Infidèle**
France / Italy 1968 98m Eastmancolor
La Boétie / Cinégai (André Génovès)
aka: *The Unfaithful Wife*

A middle-aged insurance broker, set in his ways, murders his wife's lover; when she suspects the truth, they are drawn closer together.
Almost a Bunuel-like black comedy, spare and quiet, with immaculate performances.

wd Claude Chabrol ph Jean Rabier *m* Pierre Jansen

Stéphane Audran, Michel Bouquet, Maurice Ronet

'On any level, this bizarre murder framed by whiskies emerges as Chabrol's most flawless work to date.'—*Jan Dawson, MFB*

Une Femme ou Deux
France 1985 97m colour
aka: *One Woman or Two*

An advertising woman uses an archaeologist as basis for a new campaign, then falls in love with him. Lighthearted, not to say light-headed, romantic comedy with silly asides: Doris Day and Rock Hudson, where are you?
Gerard Depardieu, Sigourney Weaver, Michel Aumont, Dr Ruth Westheimer, Zabou, Jean-Pierre Bisson. Written by Daniel Vigne and Elisabeth Rappeneau; directed by Daniel Vigne; for AAA/Hachette/Philippe Dussart/FR3/DD.

Femmes de Paris*
France 1954 85m approx Agfacolor
Optimax-Lux (Edgar Bacquet)
aka: *Ah! Les Belles Bacchantes*

A touring revue is almost run out of town for indecency.
A rather crude but quite valuable record of Dhéry's stage revue, which convulsed London in the fifties.

w Robert Dhéry *d* Jean Loubignac *ph* René Colas *m* Gérard Calvi

Robert Dhéry, Colette Brosset, Louis de Funès, Raymond Bussières, the Bluebell Girls

La Ferme du Pendu*
France 1946 90m bw
Corona
aka: *Hanged Man's Farm*

The lecherous son of a farming family brings tragedy to the lives of himself and his brothers and sister.
Cold Comfort Farm with a vengeance, appropriately played: arrant melodrama, but watchable.

w André-Paul Antoine *d* Jean Dréville
ph André Thomas

Alfred Adam, Charles Vanel, Arlette Merry

Ferris Bueller's Day Off*
US 1986 103m Metrocolor Panavision
Paramount / John Hughes, Tom Jacobson

A teenage student enjoys an aimless day playing truant.
Aimless it is, and juvenile, but people have found pleasing things in it.

w,d John Hughes *ph* Tak Fujimoto *m* Ira Newborn *pd* John W. Corso *ed* Paul Hirsch

Matthew Broderick, Alan Ruck, Mia Sara, Jeffrey Jones, Cindy Pickett, Jennifer Grey

Ferry to Hong Kong
GB 1958 113m Eastmancolor Cinemascope
Rank (George Maynard)

An Austrian layabout can land at neither of the Hong Kong ferry's ports of call, but shows his true worth when a typhoon strikes.
Silly storyline and rampant bad acting ruin the Rank Organization's first attempt at an international epic.

w Vernon Harris, Lewis Gilbert *d* Lewis Gilbert *ph* Otto Heller *m* Kenneth V. Jones

Curt Jurgens, Sylvia Syms, Orson Welles, Jeremy Spenser, Noel Purcell

La Fête à Henriette*
France 1952 113m bw
Regina-Filmsonor
aka: *Holiday for Henrietta*

Two screenwriters disagree whether or not to give their hero and heroine a happy ending.
A rather heavy-handed romantic joke which does have its moments and was later—fatally—Americanized as *Paris When It Sizzles*.

w Julien Duvivier, Henri Jeanson *d Julien Duvivier ph* Roger Hubert *m* Georges Auric

Dany Robin, Michel Auclair, Hildegarde Neff, Michel Roux, Saturnin Fabre, Julien Carette

Le Feu Follet*
France / Italy 1963 110m bw
Nouvelles Editions / Arco
aka: *Will o' the Wisp; A Time to Live and a Time to Die*

The last 24 hours, before his suicide, in the life of an ex-alcoholic playboy.
Not quite as weary as it sounds, and full of admirable touches, this is nevertheless a fairly downbeat film and a pointless one.

wd Louis Malle, novel Pierre Drieu la Rochelle *ph* Ghislain Cloquet *m* Erik Satie

Maurice Ronet, Léna Skerla, Yvonne Clech, Hubert Deschamps, Jeanne Moreau

Feudin', Fussin' and A-fightin'
US 1948 78m bw

A fast-running travelling salesman is kidnapped by a hillbilly town which needs him in its annual sports. Unpretentious lower-berth comedy for middle America. Donald O'Connor, Marjorie Main, Percy Kilbride, Penny Edwards, Joe Besser. Written by D. D. Beauchamp; directed by George Sherman; for Universal-International.

A Fever in the Blood
US 1960 117m bw
Warner (Roy Huggins)

Candidates for governor sharpen their campaigns on a murder trial.
Interestingly-cast, flabbily-written melodrama.

w Roy Huggins, Harry Kleiner, *novel* William Pearson *d* Vincent Sherman *ph* J. Peverell Marley *m* Ernest Gold

Efrem Zimbalist Jnr, Angie Dickinson, Don Ameche, Herbert Marshall, Jack Kelly, Ray Danton, Jesse White, Rhodes Reason, Robert Colbert

Fever Pitch
US 1985 96m Metrocolor
MGM-UA / Freddie Fields

A compulsive Vegas gambler gets in deep with loan sharks. You might think there was more to the plot than that, but no; and the whole thing is just glum.

w,d Richard Brooks *ph* William Fraker *m* Thomas Dolby *pd* Raymond G. Storey

Ryan O'Neal, Catherine Hicks, Giancarlo Giannini, Bridgette Andersen, Chad Everett, John Saxon

'The cards are stacked against it.'—*Variety*

Fiddler on the Roof**
US 1971 180m Technicolor
Panavision 70
UA / Mirisch (Norman Jewison)

In a pre-revolutionary Russian village, Tevye the Jewish milkman survives family and political problems and when the pogroms begin cheerfully emigrates to America.
Self-conscious, grittily realistic adaptation of the stage musical, with slow and heavy patches in its grossly overlong celebration of a vanished way of life. The big moments still come off well though the songs tend to be thrown away and the photography is unnecessarily murky.

w Joseph Stein, from his play and Sholom Aleichem's story Tevye and his Daughters *d* Norman Jewison *ph* Oswald Morris *m Jerry Bock* *md* John Williams *pd* Robert Boyle *ly* Sheldon Harnick

Topol, Norma Crane, Leonard Frey, Molly Picon

'Jewison hasn't so much directed a film as prepared a product for world consumption.'—*Stanley Kauffmann*

AA: Oswald Morris; John Williams
AAN: best picture; Norman Jewison (as director); Topol; Leonard Frey

Fiddlers Three*
GB 1944 87m bw
Ealing (Robert Hamer)

Sailors struck by lightning on Salisbury Plain are transported back to ancient Rome.
Sequel to *Sailors Three*; despite a harsh and unattractive look, every conceivable joke about old Romans is deftly mined and the good humour flows free.

w Diana Morgan, Angus Macphail *d* Harry Watt *ph* Wilkie Cooper *m* Spike Hughes

Tommy Trinder, Sonnie Hale, Frances Day, Francis L. Sullivan, Ernest Milton, Diana Decker, Elizabeth Welch, Mary Clare

'Don't be ashamed to scream! Everyone in the theatre will be screaming with you!'

The Fiend Who Walked the West
US 1958 101m bw Cinemascope
TCF (Herbert B. Swope Jnr)

A sadistic killer released from prison tracks down the associates of a cellmate and terrorizes the district.
Western remake of *Kiss of Death*, with babyface Robert Evans in the Widmark role. Violent and dull.

w Harry Brown, Philip Yordan *d* Gordon Douglas *ph* Joe MacDonald *m* Leon Klatzkin

Hugh O'Brian, Dolores Michaels, Robert Evans, Linda Cristal, Stephen McNally, Edward Andrews

The Fiend without a Face
GB 1957 75m bw
Producers' Associates (John Croydon)

A scientist working on materialized thought produces monsters from his own id.
Tepid shocker with well-organized mobile brains.

w H. J. Leder *d* Arthur Crabtree *ph* Lionel Banes *m* Buxton Orr *sp* Ruppel and Nordhoff

Kynaston Reeves, Terry Kilburn, Marshall Thompson

The Fiendish Plot of Dr Fu Manchu
US 1980 108m Technicolor
Warner / Orion / Playboy (Hugh Hefner)

The 'yellow peril' returns to the western world to mastermind diamond thefts.
Feeble spoof with a history of production troubles; clearly the only thing in anybody's mind was to get it over with.

w Jim Moloney, Rudy Dochtermann *d* Piers Haggard *ph* Jean Tournier *m* Marc Wilkinson *pd* Alexander Trauner

Peter Sellers, Helen Mirren, David Tomlinson, Sid Caesar, Simon Williams, Steve Franken, Stratford Johns, John Le Mesurier, Clive Dunn

The Fiercest Heart
US 1961 90m De Luxe Cinemascope
TCF (George Sherman)

A British army deserter joins a Boer trek into South Africa.
Pioneer 'western', poorly done but with novelty value.

w Edmund H. North, *novel* Stuart Cloete *d* George Sherman *ph* Ellis Carter *m* Irving Gertz

Stuart Whitman, Juliet Prowse, Raymond Massey, Ken Scott, Geraldine Fitzgerald, Rafer Johnson

Fiesta
US 1947 102m Technicolor
MGM (Jack Cummings)

A young Mexican wants to be a musician though his father insists he should be a bullfighter.
An extremely boring idea for a musical which at best is a tedious time-passer.

w George Bruce, Lester Cole *d* Richard Thorpe *ph* Sidney Wagner, Charles Rosner, William Cline *m* Aaron Copland *md* John Green

Esther Williams, Ricardo Montalban, Cyd Charisse, Mary Astor, John Carroll, Akim Tamiroff, Hugo Haas

AAN: music

Fièvre*
France 1921 50m approx bw silent
Alhambre

A brawl in a Marseilles bar ends in murder.
A dramatic sketch, filmed with remarkable detail and artistry.

wd Louis Delluc *ph* A. Gibory *ad* Bécan

Eve Francis, Edmond Van Daele, Gaston Modot

Fifi la Plume
France 1964 80m bw
Les Films Montsouris (Albert Lamorisse)

A burglar becomes a circus bird-man, learns to fly, and is everywhere mistaken for an angel.
A likeable fantasy idea which doesn't quite come off, alternating uneasily between slapstick and sentiment.

wd Albert Lamorisse *ph* Pierre Petit *m* Jean-Michel Defaye

Philippe Avron, Mireille Nègre, Henri Lambert, Raoul Delfosse

Fifth Avenue Girl*
US 1939 83m bw
RKO (Gregory La Cava)

An unemployed girl is persuaded by a millionaire to pose as a gold digger and annoy his avaricious family.
Brightish comedy of the Cinderella kind.

w Allan Scott *d* Gregory La Cava *ph* Robert de Grasse

Ginger Rogers, Walter Connolly, Verree Teasdale, Tim Holt, James Ellison, Franklin Pangborn, Kathryn Adams, Louis Calhern

'Substantial comedy drama for top grosses.'—*Variety*

The Fifth Musketeer
Austria 1978 106m Eastmancolor
Sascha-Wien Film / Ted Richmond
aka: *Behind the Iron Mask*

Louis XIII and his twin brother Philippe vie for the crown of France.
Virtually a remake of *The Man in the Iron Mask*, with patchy style and a few excisable sex scenes added. The 1939 version was better.

w David Ambrose *d* Ken Annakin *ph* Jack Cardiff *m* Riz Ortolani

Beau Bridges, Sylvia Kristel, Ursula Andress, Cornel Wilde (as D'Artagnan), Lloyd Bridges, Alan Hale Jnr, Jose Ferrer (the ageing musketeers), Rex Harrison (Colbert), Olivia de Havilland (Queen Anne), Ian McShane, Helmut Dantine

55 Days at Peking*
US / Spain 1962 154m Super Technirama 70
Samuel Bronston

In 1900 Peking, Boxer fanatics are encouraged by the Empress to take over the city and besiege the international diplomatic quarter; an American major leads the defence.
Spasmodically lively action spectacular weighed down by romantic stretches.

w Philip Yordan, Bernard Gordon *d* Nicholas Ray, Andrew Marton *ph* Jack Hildyard, Manuel Berenguer *m* Dmitri Tiomkin *ad* Venerio Colasanti, John Moore

Charlton Heston, David Niven, Ava Gardner, Flora Robson, Robert Helpmann, Leo Genn, Paul Lukas, John Ireland, Harry Andrews, Elizabeth Sellars, Massimo Serrato, Jacques Sernas, Geoffrey Bayldon

'An open-air western in Chinese.'—*David Niven*

'Pictorially this is a beautiful film, but the characters are conventional siege figures.'—*Sunday Times*

AAN: Dmitri Tiomkin; song 'So Little Time' (*m* Dmitri Tiomkin, *ly* Paul Francis Webster)

Fifty Million Frenchmen
US 1931 68m Technicolor

A rich American in Paris tries to prove that he was able to win a blonde without the aid of his bankroll. Much changed and enfeebled version of a Broadway musical, with the Broadway talent transplanted. Olsen and Johnson, William Gaxton, John Halliday, Helen Broderick, Claudia Dell, Lester Crawford. Written by Al Boasberg, Eddie Welch, Joseph Jackson; directed by Lloyd Bacon; for Warners. 'Will have to depend mostly on its title for b.o. attraction.'—*Variety*

Fifty Roads to Town*
US 1937 80m bw

Mistaken identities abound in a snowbound cabin. Fairly funny minor comedy. Don Ameche, Ann Sothern, Slim Summerville, Jane Darwell, John Qualen, Douglas Fowley, Stepin Fetchit. Written by George Marion Jnr and William Conselman; directed by Norman Taurog; for TCF. 'Just about right for summer audiences . . . pleasant light romantic comedy demanding a minimum of concentration.'—*Variety*

52 Pick-up
US 1986 114m TVC colour
Cannon (Henry T. Weinstein)

A businessman rounds on blackmailers who take films of his sex life.
Uninteresting melodrama based on the same novel as *The Ambassador*, released two years earlier by the same company.

w Elmore Leonard, John Steppling *novel* Elmore Leonard *d* John Frankenheimer *ph* Jost Vacano *m* Gary Chang

Roy Scheider, Ann-Margret, Vanity, John Glover, Robert Trebor, Lonny Chapman

'There is no rush of energy to propel the film past its improbability.'—*Variety*

52nd Street
US 1937 83m bw

A strictly-brought-up young woman shocks her family by falling for a singer. Tame romantic comedy with musical items. Kenny Baker, Ella Logan, Ian Hunter, Zasu Pitts, Leo Carrillo. Written by Grover Jones; directed by Harold Young; for Walter Wanger. 'It may have been a good idea to make a film about the metamorphosing of 52nd Street into a lane of niteries, but the conception doesn't come through . . . filmgoers are likely to wonder what it's all about, and why.'—*Variety*

Fight for Your Lady*
US 1937 67m bw

A jilted tenor is helped by a wrestling trainer. Odd little comedy which contrives to amuse. John Boles, Jack Oakie, Ida Lupino, Margot Grahame, Erik Rhodes, Billy Gilbert. Written by Ernest Pagano, Harry Segall, Harold Kusell; directed by Ben Stoloff; for RKO. 'This picture is going to entertain whether it sells or not.'—*Variety*

The Fighter
US 1952 78m bw
GH (Alex Gottlieb)

A Mexican fisherman whose family is murdered by government troops becomes a prizefighter to earn money for the rebels.
A rather glum attempt to turn a few ringside clichés.

w Aben Kandel, Herbert Kline, *story* The Mexican by Jack London *d* Herbert Kline *ph* James Wong Howe *m* Vincente Gomez

Richard Conte, Vanessa Brown, Lee J. Cobb, Frank Silvera

Fighter Attack
US 1953 80m bw

Exploits of an American air base in Corsica. Routine war action efficiently dispensed. Sterling Hayden, J. Carrol Naish, Joy Page, Kenneth Tobey, Anthony Caruso. Written by Simon Wincelberg; directed by Lesley Selander; for Allied Artists.

Fighter Squadron
US 1948 96m Technicolor
Warner (Seton I. Miller)

In World War II, a dedicated flier risks his friends' lives.
Routine aerial actioner.

w Seton I. Miller *d* Raoul Walsh *ph* Sid Hickox, Wilfrid M. Cline *m* Max Steiner

Edmond O'Brien, Robert Stack, John Rodney, Tom D'Andrea, Henry Hull, Walter Reed, Shepperd Strudwick, Rock Hudson

Fighting Back
US 1982 98m Technicolor
Dino de Laurentiis (D. Constantine Conte)
GB title: *Death Vengeance*

After his wife and mother are both injured in crimes of violence, a delicatessen owner forms a vigilante group and is backed to some extent by police and businessmen.
Smartly made but ethically muddled urban shocker.

w Tom Hedley, David Zelag Goodman *d* Lewis Teague *ph* Franco DiGiacomo *m* Piero Piccioni

Tom Skerritt, Michael Sarrazin, Patti LuPone, Yaphet Kotto, David Rasche

Fighting Back
Australia 1982 100m Eastmancolor

A teenager runs riot at home and at school. Tolerable problem picture with no surprises. Lewis FitzGerald, Kris McQuade, Caroline Gillmer, Paul Smith. Written by Tom Jeffrey, Michael Cove, from the book Tom by John Embling; directed by Michael Caulfield; for Samson.

Fighting Caravans
US 1931 91m bw

A covered wagon party faces various dangers. Slow-moving western. Gary Cooper, Lily Damita, Ernest Torrence, Fred Kohler, Tully Marshall, Eugene Pallette. Written by E. E. Paramore Jnr, Keene Thompson, Agnes Leahy, from the novel by Zane Grey; directed by Otto Brower and David Burton; for Paramount. 'Very mild western, rating de luxe house attention on the cast names . . . lacks a punch.'—*Variety*

Fighting Devil Dogs
US 1938 bw serial: 12 eps

Marine lieutenants in a tropical protectorate fight organized bandits led by The Lightning, who has invented an electric thunderbolt. Excessively juvenile shenanigans for Saturday morning audiences. Lee Powell, Herman Brix, Eleanor Stewart, Montagu Love. Directed by William Witney and John English; for Republic.

Fighting Father Dunne
US 1948 93m bw
RKO (Phil L. Ryan)

A clergyman looks after unfortunate boys.
A slum melodrama which all concerned could have made with their eyes closed, and probably did.

w Martin Rackin, Frank Davis *d* Ted Tetzlaff *ph* George E. Diskant *m* Roy Webb

Pat O'Brien, Darryl Hickman, Charles Kemper, Una O'Connor

The Fighting Guardsman
US 1945 84m bw

Under the tyrannical reign of Louis XVI a young nobleman leads a peasants' revolt. Stiff swashbuckler in which the actors appear to have been only recently introduced to their clothes. Willard Parker, Anita Louise, George Macready, John Loder. Written by Franz Spencer and Edward Dein; directed by Henry Levin; for Columbia.

The Fighting Kentuckian
US 1949 100m bw
Republic (John Wayne)

In 1810 a farmer combats land-grabbing criminals.
Standard star western for the family.

wd George Waggner *ph* Lee Garmes *m* George Antheil

John Wayne, Vera Ralston, Oliver Hardy, Philip Dorn, Marie Windsor, Mae Marsh

Fighting Mad
US 1976 90m De Luxe
TCF / Santa Fe (Roger Corman)

A rancher and his son are murdered by a local industrialist who wants their land, and the rancher's city-bred son takes revenge.
Another vigilante western in modern dress, very laborious and violent without being very exciting.

wd Jonathan Demme *ph* Bill Birch *m* Bruce Langhorne

Peter Fonda, Lynn Lowry, John Doucette, Philip Carey, Scott Glen

'Demme has allowed violence to outweigh ideas to such a degree that the picture becomes a turnoff, little more than a blatantly obvious play to the yahoo mentality.'—*Kevin Thomas, Los Angeles Times*

Fighting Man of the Plains
US 1949 94m Cinecolor

A reformed outlaw becomes marshal but is exposed. Tolerable western with familiar elements. Randolph Scott, Bill Williams, Victor Jory, Jane Nigh, Douglas Kennedy. Written by Frank Gruber; directed by Edwin L. Marin; for Nat Holt / (TCF).

Fighting Marines
US 1935 bw serial: 12 eps

A criminal called The Tiger Shark has an anti-gravity gun . . . Predictable cliffhanging heroics. Grant Withers, Ann Rutherford, Adrian Morris, Robert Warwick. Directed by B. Reeves Eason and Joseph Kane; for Mascot.

The Fighting O'Flynn
US 1949 94m bw
U-I (Douglas Fairbanks Jnr)

In 18th-century Ireland, a penniless young adventurer aborts Napoleon's plan for invasion.
Lively minor-league adventure.

w Douglas Fairbanks Jnr, Robert Thoeren, *novel* Justin Huntly McCarthy *d* Arthur Pierson *ph* Arthur Edeson *m* Frank Skinner

Douglas Fairbanks Jnr, Helena Carter, Richard Greene, Patricia Medina, Arthur Shields, J. M. Kerrigan

'Fairbanks plays the irrepressible O'Flynn with unflagging energy and tongue in cheek good humour; the rest of the cast stolidly refuses to see the joke.'—*MFB*

The Fighting Prince of Donegal
GB 1966 104m Technicolor
Walt Disney (Bill Anderson)

Adventures of an Irish rebel in the reign of Elizabeth I.
Adequate Boys' Own Paper romp.

w Robert Westerby, *novel* Red Hugh, Prince of Donegal by Robert T. Reilly *d* Michael O'Herlihy *ph* Arthur Ibbetson *m* George Bruns

Peter McEnery, Susan Hampshire, Tom Adams, Gordon Jackson, Andrew Keir, Norman Woolland, Richard Leech

The Fighting Seabees
US 1944 100m bw
Republic (Albert J. Cohen)

During World War II in the Pacific, construction workers attack the Japanese.
Routine, studio-staged war melodrama, heavily fleshed out with love interest.

w Borden Chase, Aeneas Mackenzie *d* Edward Ludwig *ph* William Bradford *m* Walter Scharf, Roy Webb

John Wayne, Susan Hayward, Dennis O'Keefe, William Frawley, Duncan Renaldo, Addison Richards, Leonid Kinskey, Paul Fix

AAN: Walter Scharf, Roy Webb

The Fighting 69th*
US 1940 89m bw
Warner (Hal B. Wallis)

During World War I in the trenches, a cocky recruit becomes a hero and loses his life in the process.
Recruiting poster stuff, all well enough done but bewildering in its changes of mood.

w Norman Reilly Raine, Fred Niblo Jnr, Dean Franklin *d* William Keighley *ph* Tony Gaudio *m* Adolph Deutsch

James Cagney, Pat O'Brien, George Brent, Jeffrey Lynn, Alan Hale, Frank McHugh, Dennis Morgan, Dick Foran, William Lundigan, Guinn Williams, John Litel, Henry O'Neill

'The picture is better if you can manage to forget the plot and think of it instead as the human, amusing and frequently gripping record of a regiment marching off to war.'—*Frank Nugent, New York Times*

Fighting Stock
GB 1935 68m bw
Gainsborough

The family gets together to save a girl from a blackmailer. Fair example of the Aldwych farces, with the trio in good form. Tom Walls, Ralph Lynn, Robertson Hare, Marie Lohr, Lesley Waring. Written by Ben Travers; directed by Tom Walls; for Gaumont.

Fighting with Kit Carson
US 1933 bw serial: 12 eps

The famous wagon train scout survives an ambush and rounds up The Mystery Riders. Western serial with all the expected elements. Johnny Mack Brown, Betsy King Ross, Noah Beery, Noah Berry Jnr, Robert Warwick. Directed by Armand Schaefer and Colbert Clark; for Mascot.

The Figurehead*
GB 1952 8m Technicolor

A carved saint is turned into a figurehead and can't respond when a mermaid falls in love with him. Pleasant whimsy, one of the better jobs from this team of animators. Narrated by Robert Beatty; animation and production by John Halas and Joy Batchelor; from a poem by Crosbie Garstin.

Figures in a Landscape
GB 1970 110m Technicolor Panavision
Cinecrest (John Kohn)

Two men on the run are pursued by soldiers and helicopters; only one crosses the frontier.
Portentous Pinterish parable, very long-winded and relentlessly boring though good to look at. Everything is symbolic, nothing is specific, not even the country.

w Robert Shaw, *novel* Barry England *d* Joseph Losey *ph* Henri Alekan *m* Richard Rodney Bennett

Robert Shaw, Malcolm McDowell

The File of the Golden Goose
GB 1969 109m De Luxe
UA / Theme / Caralan / Dador (David E. Rose)

An American agent works with Scotland Yard to track down counterfeiters.
Incredibly predictable spy thriller which almost makes an eccentricity out of collecting so many clichés and so many tourist views of London. Like ten TV episodes cut together.

w John C. Higgins, James B. Gordon *d* Sam Wanamaker *ph* Ken Hodges *m* Harry Robinson

Yul Brynner, Edward Woodward, Charles Gray, John Barrie, Bernard Archard, Ivor Dean, Adrienne Corri, Graham Crowden, Karel Stepanek

'The film plods wearily homewards through an exceptionally uninteresting batch of fights, intrigues and sinister encounters.'—*MFB*

The File on Thelma Jordon*
US 1949 100m bw
Paramount (Hal B. Wallis)
aka: *Thelma Jordon*

A district attorney falls for a murder suspect and has her acquitted by losing the case.
Stylishly made, murkily plotted melodrama and a superior star vehicle of its time.

w Ketti Frings *d* Robert Siodmak *ph* George Barnes *m* Victor Young

Barbara Stanwyck, Wendell Corey, Paul Kelly, Joan Tetzel, Stanley Ridges, Richard Rober, Minor Watson, Barry Kelley

La Fille du Puisatier*
France 1946 131m bw
Marcel Pagnol
aka: *The Well-Digger's Daughter*

A stern old well-digger feels bound to send his daughter away when she becomes pregnant.
More country matters from Pagnol, this time

with an East Lynne type plot getting in the way of some fine acting. Not much comedy.

wd Marcel Pagnol

Raimu, Fernandel, Charpin, Josette Day

'There is a feeling in France that such films are made for the foreigner and exploit the eccentricities of French rural life rather than the realities.'—*MFB*

Film
GB 1979 26m Eastmancolor

No synopsis is possible for this speechless parable about a poor old man fighting (presumably) against personal obscurity, but its credits make it interesting; it was originally written for Buster Keaton. Max Wall, Patricia Hayes. Written by Samuel Beckett; directed by David Rayner Clark; photographed by Mike Tomlinson; designed by Ariane Gastambide; for BFI.

Film ohne Titel*
West Germany 1947 100m bw
Camera Film (Erwin Gitt)
aka: *Film without Title*

Scriptwriters discuss how it is possible to make a comedy film in post-war Germany, and evolve a story with alternative endings.
Elegantly conceived but rather humourlessly executed, this interesting film was one of the first post-war German exports, but failed to start a trend. It has similarities to *La Fête à Henriette* and *Rashomon*.

w Helmut Kautner, Ellen Fechner, Rudolf Jugert d Rudolf Jugert *ph* Igor Oberberg *m* Bernard Eichhorn

Hans Söhnker, Hildegarde Knef, *Irene Von Meyendorff*, Willy Fritsch

La Fin du Jour**
France 1939 106m bw
Filmsonor / Regina

Tensions mount in a home for retired actors.
Fascinating opportunity for three fine actors to play off each other.

w Charles Spaak, Julien Duvivier *d* Julien Duvivier *ph* Christian Matras *m* Maurice Jaubert

Michel Simon, *Louis Jouvet*, *Victor Francen*, Gabrielle Dorziat, Madeleine Ozeray, Sylvie

'Any time, any place, at any game—Samson Shillitoe can outfox them all!'

'The power of evil is no longer in the hands of a child!'

The Final Conflict
US 1981 108m De Luxe Panavision
TCF / Mace Neufeld (Harvey Bernhard)

The Antichrist, now head of Thorn Industries, arranges to become US Ambassador in London.
The devil as an adult proves somehow less chilling than the devil as a child, and all the elaborate mayhem seems decidedly old hat in this sequel to *The Omen* and *Damien: Omen II*.

w Andrew Birkin *d* Graham Baker
ph Robert Paynter, Phil Meheux *m* Jerry Goldsmith *pd* Herbert Westbrook

Sam Neill, Rossano Brazzi, Don Gordon, Lisa Harrow, Mason Adams, Robert Arden

'If Armageddon is as boring as this movie, we'll need a program to tell the players.'—*Roger Ebert*

The Final Countdown*
US 1980 105m TVC colour Panavision
UA / Bryna (Peter Vincent Douglas)

An aircraft carrier on manoeuvres near Hawaii passes through a strange storm and finds itself back at Pearl Harbor.
Quite an enjoyable bit of schoolboy science fiction, but containing no more body than an episode of *Twilight Zone*. The ending, as so often, is impenetrable.

w David Ambrose, Gerry Davis, Thomas Hunter, Peter Powell *d* Don Taylor
ph Victor J. Kemper *m* John Scott
pd Fernando Carrere

Kirk Douglas, Martin Sheen, Katherine Ross, James Farentino, Ron O'Neal, Charles Durning

'The future is cancelled!'

The Final Programme
GB 1973 89m Technicolor
Goodtimes / Gladiole (John Goldstone, Sanford Lieberson)
US title: *The Last Days of Man on Earth*

In the future, when the world is torn by famine and war, a scientist awaits a new messiah.
Intellectualized sci-fi, hard to take as entertainment but very glossy.

wd Robert Fuest, *novel* Michael Moorcock
ph Norman Warwick *m* Paul Beaver, Bernard Krause

Jon Finch, Jenny Runacre, Sterling Hayden, Hugh Griffith

'Clumsy and almost incomprehensible.'—*Sight and Sound*

The Final Test
GB 1953 90m bw
Rank / ACT (R. J. Minney)

A cricketer looks forward to his last game but is out for a duck; he is however cheered by the crowd and comforted by his son.
Flat character study some way below the author's best style, cluttered up with real cricketers and stymied by lack of action.

w Terence Rattigan *d* Anthony Asquith
ph Bill McLeod *m* Benjamin Frankel

Jack Warner, Robert Morley, George Relph

Finally, Sunday*
France 1983 111m bw
Films du Carrosse / Films A2 / Soprofilms (Armand Barbault)
French title: *Vivement Dimanche*

When his friend is murdered, a small-town estate agent becomes a prime suspect.
Agreeable Hitchcock parody which goes on too long and runs out of steam.

w François Truffaut, Suzanne Schiffman, Jean Aurel, *novel* The Long Saturday Night by Charles Williams *d* François Truffaut
ph Nestor Almendros *m* Georges Delerue
pd Hilton McConnico

Fanny Ardant, Jean-Louis Trintignant, Philippe Laudenbach, Caroline Sihol

'Devoid of interest or distinction, a comedy-thriller that is not funny and most emphatically not thrilling. Ardant and Trintignant fancy themselves as Carole Lombard and Fredric March, an illusion not likely to be shared by anyone else . . .'—*Gilbert Adair, MFB*

Find the Blackmailer
US 1943 55m bw

A private eye seeks a talking crow which may have evidence in a murder case. Modest mystery filler. Jerome Cowan, Faye Emerson, Gene Lockhart, Marjorie Hoshelle, Robert Kent. Written by Robert E. Kent from story by G. E. Fleming-Roberts; directed by D. Ross Lederman; for Warner.

Finders Keepers
GB 1966 94m Eastmancolor
UA / Interstate (George H. Brown)

The Americans lose an atomic bomb off the Spanish coast, and it's found by a pop group.
Harmless youth musical without much style.
Tunes poor, comedy rather too easy-going.

w Michael Pertwee *d* Sidney Hayers *ph* Alan Hume *m* The Shadows, Norrie Paramor

Cliff Richard, The Shadows, Robert Morley, Peggy Mount, Viviane Ventura, Graham Stark, John Le Mesurier, Robert Hutton

Finders Keepers
US 1984 96m Technicolor
CBS (Sandra Marsh, Terence Marsh)

On a train from California to New York, various factions try to grab stolen money hidden in a coffin.
Yawnworthy comedy-thriller with a zany streak; all the elements have been better done in other movies.

w Ronny Graham, Charles Dennis, Terence Marsh from Dennis' novel The Next to Last Train Ride *d* Richard Lester *ph* Brian West *m* Ken Thorne *pd* Terence Marsh

Michael O'Keefe, Beverly D'Angelo, Lou Gossett Jnr, Pamela Stephenson, Ed Lauter, David Wayne, Brian Dennehy, John Schuck

A Fine Madness*
US 1966 104m Technicolor
Warner Seven Arts (Jerome Hellman)

A frustrated New York poet has outbursts of violence.
Patchy, interesting, with-it comedy which suffers from too many changes of mood.

w Elliot Baker, from his novel *d* Irvin Kershner *ph Ted McCord m* John Addison

Sean Connery, Jean Seberg, Joanne Woodward, Patrick O'Neal, Colleen Dewhurst, Clive Revill

'Straddling a no man's land somewhere between the *nouvelle vague* and the crazy comedies of Old Hollywood.'—*Tom Milne*

A Fine Mess
US 1985 88m De Luxe Panavision
Columbia / BEE / Delphi V (Tony Adams)

Two private eyes who accidentally know too much are chased by gangsters.

Not enough plot for a feature, and not enough comedy talent for a comedy, despite the dedication to Laurel and Hardy.

w,d Blake Edwards *ph* Harry Stradling *m* Henry Mancini *pd* Rodger Maus *ed* John F. Burnett

Ted Danson, Howie Mandel, Richard Mulligan, Stuart Margolin, Paul Sorvino

'Word of mouth is unlikely to be favourable . . . mechanically contrived funny business, most of which falls pretty flat.'—*Variety*

'The plot needn't be the thing, but then the gags and setpieces aren't much either.'—*Sight and Sound*

A Fine Pair
Italy 1968 115m Technicolor Panavision
Vides (Franco Cristaldi)
original title: *Ruba al Prossimo Tua*

A New York detective falls for an Italian girl jewel thief.
Tedious, meandering comedy-thriller with nothing to offer apart from a good robbery sequence.

w Francesco Maselli, Luisa Montagnana, Larry Gelbart, Virgil C. Leone *d* Francesco Maselli *ph* Alfio Contino *m* Ennio Morricone

Rock Hudson, Claudia Cardinale, Tomas Milian, Leon Askin, Ellen Corby

The Finest Hours*
GB 1964 116m Technicolor

The life of Winston Churchill is built up from newsreels plus a few feature film clips and some original location shooting. Generally excellent documentary, a handy introduction to Churchill's own writing and rather more entertaining than the later *Young Winston*. Written by Victor Wolfson; directed by Peter Baylis; for *Jack Le Vien*.

The Finger Points
US 1931 88m bw

A crime reporter succumbs to pressures from the underworld. Humourless and low-geared exposé-style melodrama. Richard Barthelmess, Clark Gable, Fay Wray, Regis Toomey. Written by John Monk Saunders, W. R. Burnett and Robert Lord; directed by John Francis Dillon; for Warner.

Fingerprints
US 1931 bw serial: 10 eps

Secret service agents catch a gang of smugglers. Oddly-titled serial containing no memorable moments. Kenneth Harlan, Edna Murphy, Gayne Whitman, Gertrude Astor. Directed by Ray Taylor; for Universal.

Fingers*
US 1977 90m Technicolor

A would-be concert pianist gets involved with his father's gangster friends, and violence results. Lively and interesting skirmish with an overworked and essentially downbeat subject. Harvey Keitel, Tisa Farrow, Jim Brown, Marion Seldes. Written and directed by *James Toback*; for Brut.

Fingers at the Window
US 1942 90m bw
MGM (Irving Starr)

A stage magician hypnotizes lunatics into murdering all those who stand between him and an inheritance.
Slow-starting thriller which never achieves top gear.

w Rose Caylor, Lawrence P. Bachmann *d* Charles Lederer *ph* Harry Stradling, Charles Lawton *m* Bronislau Kaper

Basil Rathbone, Lew Ayres, Laraine Day, Walter Kingsford, Miles Mander, Russell Gleason

'The kind of picture actors do when they need work.'—*Lew Ayres*

Finian's Rainbow*
US 1968 140m Technicolor Panavision 70
Warner Seven Arts (Joseph Landon)

A leprechaun tries to retrieve a crock of gold from an old wanderer who has taken it to America.
Musical whimsy-whamsy, a long way after a 1947 Broadway success; in this overlong and overblown screen version the elements and the style do not jell and there is too much sentimental chat, but moments of magic shine through.

w E. Y. Harburg, Fred Saidy, from their play *d* Francis Ford Coppola *ph* Philip Lathrop *m* Burton Lane *ly* E. Y. Harburg *pd* Hilyard M. Brown *md* Ray Heindorf

Fred Astaire, Petula Clark, Tommy Steele, Don Francks, Keenan Wynn, Barbara Hancock, Al Freeman Jnr

AAN: Ray Heindorf

Finis Terrae*
France 1929 90m approx bw silent
Société Générale des Films

A re-enacted account of the lives of fishermen on remote Brittany islands.
A feature documentary which was impressive at the time; very similar to Flaherty's *Man of Aran*.

wd Jean Epstein *ph* Joseph Barth, Joseph Kottula

Finishing School
US 1934 73m bw
RKO (Kenneth MacGowan)

A girl at an exclusive school falls for an intern.
Modest pap for the teenage audience.

w Wanda Tuchock, Laird Doyle *d* George Nicholls Jnr *ph* J. Roy Hunt *m* Max Steiner

Frances Dee, Ginger Rogers, Billie Burke, Bruce Cabot, John Halliday, Beulah Bondi, Sara Haden

The Finishing Touch*
US 1928 20m bw silent

Stan and Ollie accidentally destroy the house they are building. Excellent early star slapstick with predictable but enjoyable gags. Laurel and Hardy, Edgar Kennedy, Dorothy Coburn. Written by H. M Walker; directed by Clyde Bruckman; for Hal Roach.

Finn and Hattie
US 1930 77m bw

A newly rich American takes his family to Paris. Dodsworth-like comedy, fairly well regarded in its time but now looking very thin. Leon Errol, Zasu Pitts, Mitzi Green, Jackie Searl, Regis Toomey, Lilyan Tashman. Written by Sam Mintz, Joseph L. Mankiewicz, from the story by Donald Ogden Stewart; directed by Norman Taurog, Norman McLeod; for Paramount.

Fire and Ice
US 1982 82m colour

Evil Lord Nekron uses black magic to subdue the good King Jarol. Fair cartoon feature in the mould of *Conan the Barbarian*. Written by Roy Thomas, Jerry Conway; directed by Ralph Bakshi; for Polyc International.

'Three of the biggest in one of the best!'
Fire Down Below
GB 1957 116m Technicolor Cinemascope
Columbia / Warwick (Irving Allen, Albert Broccoli)

Partners in a Caribbean fishing and smuggling business fall out over a woman.
Overheated melodrama with thin characters, predictable incident and ill-advised casting.

w Irwin Shaw, *novel* Max Catto *d* Robert Parrish *ph* Desmond Dickinson *m* Arthur Benjamin

Rita Hayworth, Robert Mitchum, Jack Lemmon, Herbert Lom, Bonar Colleano, Bernard Lee, Edric Connor, Peter Illing

A Fire Has Been Arranged
GB 1935 70m bw
Twickenham (Julius Hagen)

Ex-convicts find a building in the field where they buried the loot.
Modest star comedy. Was this the first use of this well-worn plot?

w H. Fowler Mear, Michael Barringer *d* Leslie Hiscott

Bud Flanagan, Chesney Allen, Alastair Sim, Robb Wilton, Mary Lawson, Harold French, C. Denier Warren

'A world of women seeking male partners to carry on their race!'
Fire Maidens from Outer Space
GB 1956 80m bw

Space explorers find that the thirteenth moon of Jupiter is inhabited solely by sixteen beautiful girls and an aged patriarch. A strong contender for the title of worst movie ever made, with diaphanously clad English gals striking embarrassed poses against cardboard sets. Must be seen to be believed. Susan Shaw,

Anthony Dexter, Harry Fowler, Sidney Tafler, Owen Berry, Paul Carpenter. Written and directed by Cy Roth; for Criterion Films / Eros. 'Even the most dedicated connoisseurs of the artless are likely to find this something of a strain on their patience.'—*MFB.*

Fire Over England***
GB 1937 92m bw
London Films / Pendennis (Erich Pommer)

Elizabeth I and her navy overcome the Spanish Armada.
Though the film has a faded air and the action climax was always a bath-tub affair, the splendid cast keeps this pageant afloat and interesting.

w Clemence Dane, Sergei Nolbandov, *novel* A. E. W. Mason *d* William K. Howard *ph* James Wong Howe *m* Richard Addinsell

Flora Robson, Laurence Olivier, Leslie Banks, Vivien Leigh, Raymond Massey, Tamara Desni, Morton Selten, Lyn Harding, James Mason

'Should bring much artistic acclaim but, outside of the urban class spots, business will be stubborn . . . if it had marquee strength it would stand an excellent chance.'—*Variety*

'Pommer and Howard have done one remarkable thing: they have caught the very spirit of an English public schoolmistress's vision of history.'—*Graham Greene*

'Swashbuckling nonsense, but with a fine spirit.'—*Pauline Kael, 70s*

Fire Sale*
US 1977 88m De Luxe
TCF (Marvin Worth)

Misadventures of a frantic, eccentric New York-Jewish family who own a department store.
Frenzied black farce for ethnic audiences.

w Robert Klane, from his novel *d* Alan Arkin *ph* Ralph Woolsey *m* Dave Grusin

Alan Arkin, Rob Reiner, Vincent Gardenia, Anjanette Comer, Kay Medford, Sid Caesar, Alex Rocco

'It moves fast enough to carry the occasional lapses from its own high standards of tastelessness.'—*Jan Dawson, MFB*

The Fireball
US 1950 84m bw

A juvenile delinquent becomes a ruthless roller-skating champion. Predictable and unattractive star character drama with sporting asides. Mickey Rooney, Pat O'Brien, Beverly Tyler, Glenn Corbett. Written by Tay Garnett and Horace McCoy; directed by Tay Garnett; for Thor / TCF.

The Firebird
US 1934 75m bw

An actor with the reputation of a Lothario is murdered. Well cast but rather disappointing murder mystery. Verree Teasdale, Ricardo Cortez, Lionel Atwill, C. Aubrey Smith, Anita Louise, Dorothy Tree, Hobart Cavanaugh. Written by Charles Kenyon from the play by Lajos Zilahy; directed by William Dieterle; for Warners. 'Padding in late reels keeps it from ace rating.'—*Variety*

Firecreek
US 1968 104m Technicolor Panavision
Warner Seven Arts (Philip Leacock)

The people of Firecreek protect themselves from wandering gunmen.
Dour, predictable little western which does not show its stars at their best.

w Calvin Clements *d* Vincent McEveety *ph* William Clothier *m* Alfred Newman

James Stewart, Henry Fonda, Inger Stevens, Gary Lockwood, Dean Jagger, Ed Begley, Jay C. Flippen, Jack Elam, James Best, Barbara Luna

'This cramped and clumsy western grinds to a standstill in its attempts to give Firecreek symbolic status . . . while the gunmen roister like mad and the townsfolk rhubarb glumly in the background.'—*MFB*

Fired Wife
US 1943 75m bw

A radio actress has to keep her marriage a secret in order to preserve her job. Decidedly humdrum comedy. Louise Allbritton, Diana Barrymore, Robert Paige, Walter Abel, George Dolenz, Walter Catlett, Ernest Truex, Rex Ingram, Richard Lane. Written by Michael Fessier and Ernest Pagano; directed by Charles Lamont; for Universal.

'It will make 1937 remembered always as the year of the first romantic dramatic musical film!'

The Firefly*
US 1937 131m bw
MGM (Hunt Stromberg)

Adventures of a Spanish lady spy during the Napoleonic war.
Solid production of a romantic operetta; splendid stuff for connoisseurs.

w Frances Goodrich, Albert Hackett, Ogden Nash *d* Robert Z. Leonard *ph* Oliver Marsh *original book / ly* Otto Harbach *m* Rudolf Friml *md* Herbert Stothart

Jeanette MacDonald, *Allan Jones* (who sings the Donkey Serenade), Warren William, Billy Gilbert, Henry Daniell, George Zucco, Douglass Dumbrille

'The sepia tint is monotonous . . . the length will seriously militate against popularity.'—*Variety*

'A lavish musical monstrosity.'—*New Yorker, 1978*

'The musical film par excellence . . . resplendent and gorgeous.'—*Evening News*

Firefox
US 1982 136m De Luxe Panavision
Warner / Malpaso (Clint Eastwood)

An American pilot is disguised as a businessman and sent to Moscow to steal a new supersonic Soviet fighter.
Dreary melodrama with doleful acting and very little action or suspense.

w Alex Lasker, Wendell Willman, *novel* Craig Thomas *d* Clint Eastwood *ph* Bruce Surtees *m* Maurice Jarre *sp* John Dykstra

Clint Eastwood, Freddie Jones, David Huffman, Warren Clarke, Ronald Lacey, Kenneth Colley, Nigel Hawthorne

'What is most curious about this farrago is that Eastwood, the actor and the director, should have walked through it all with scarcely a thought for each other.'—*Richard Combs, MFB*

'Despite the tense mission being depicted, there's no suspense, excitement or thrills to be had, and lackadaisical pacing gives the viewer plenty of time to ponder the gaping implausibilities that skilful execution could have rendered irrelevant.'—*Variety*

'Immensely long, unfailingly dull, and not even silly enough to be funny.'—*Sunday Times*

Fireman Save My Child
US 1932 67m bw

A fireman is more interested in baseball but becomes a hero all the same. Thin star comedy. Joe E. Brown, Evalyn Knapp, Lillian Bond, Guy Kibbee. Written by Ray Enright, Robert Lord and Arthur Caesar; directed by Lloyd Bacon; for Warner / First National.

Fireman Save My Child
US 1954 80m bw
U-I (Howard Christie)

In 1910 San Francisco, incompetent firemen accidentally catch a gang of crooks.
Slapstick farce intended for Abbott and Costello, taken over by a new team which did not catch on, played like the Keystone Kops. Mildly funny during the chases.

w Lee Loeb, John Grant *d* Leslie Goodwins *ph* Clifford Stine *m* Joseph Gershenson

Buddy Hackett, Spike Jones and the City Slickers, Hugh O'Brian, Adèle Jergens

The Firemen's Ball*
Czechoslovakia / Italy 1967 73m Eastmancolor
Barrandov / Carlo Ponti
original title: *Hori, Ma Panenko*

In a small provincial town, arrangements for the firemen's annual ball go wrong at every turn.
Vaguely amusing Tati-esque comedy with not quite enough funny moments and a prevailing atmosphere of pessimism.

w Milos Forman, Ivan Passer, Jaroslav Papousek *d* Milos Forman *ph* Miroslav Ondricek *m* Karel Mares

Jan Vostrcil, Josef Kolb, Josef Svet, Frantisek Debelka

'A compendium of superb items.'—*Philip Strick*

AAN: best foreign film

Firepower
GB 1979 104m Technicolor
ITC / Michael Winner

A chemist about to expose contaminated drugs is murdered; his widow persuades the US

Justice Department to hire her ex-lover, a gangster, to track down his killers.
Globe-trotting kaleidoscope of the familiar patterns of violence; tolerable for those who haven't been here a hundred times before.

w Gerald Wilson *d* Michael Winner *ph* Robert Paynter, Dick Kratina *md* Jay Cattaway

Sophia Loren, James Coburn, Anthony Franciosa, O. J. Simpson, Eli Wallach, George Grizzard, Vincent Gardenia, Victor Mature

'The nearest thing yet to film-making by numbers, with identikit characters jet-setting across a travel brochure landscape to an orchestration of gunfire, car smashes and colourful explosions.'—*Clyde Jeavons, MFB*

Fires on the Plain**
Japan 1959 108m bw
Daiei (Masaichi Nagata)
original title: *Nobi*

In the Philippines during World War II, a half-demented Japanese private takes to the hills, becomes a cannibal, and is shot by the Americans when he tries to surrender.
Stomach-turning anti-war epic with fine scenes and performances but dubious intent.

w Natto Wada, *novel* Shohei O-oka *d Kon Ichikawa ph* Setsuo Kobayashi *m* Yasushi Akatagawa

Eiji Funakoshi, Osamu Takizawa, Micky Curtis

Fires Were Started**
GB 1943 63m bw
Crown Film Unit (Ian Dalrymple)
aka: *I Was a Fireman*

One day and night in the life of a National Fire Service unit during the London blitz.
Thoughtful, slow-moving, poetic documentary originally intended as a training film but generally released to boost morale. Not its director's finest work, but perhaps his most ambitious.

wd Humphrey Jennings ph C. Pennington-Richards *m* William Alwyn

'An astonishingly intimate portrait of an isolated and besieged Britain . . . an unforgettable piece of human observation, affectionate, touching, and yet ironic.'—*Georges Sadoul*

'It transforms its observation into a personal, epic celebration of the courage and dignity of ordinary people in times of stress.'—*Time Out, 1984*

† The firemen were real firemen, but the scenes were re-enacted.

Firestarter
US 1984 114m Technicolor
Universal (Frank Capra Jnr)

A young girl is capable of starting fires by pyrokinesis, and the government wants to use her as a weapon.
Complicated and dislikeable piece of political science fiction.

w Stanley Mann, from the novel by Stephen King *d* Mark L. Lester *ph* Giuseppe Ruzzolini *m* Tangerine Dream

Drew Barrymore, George C. Scott, David Keith, Martin Sheen, Freddie Jones, Heather Locklear, Art Carney, Louise Fletcher, Moses Gunn

'The most astonishing thing in the movie is how boring it is.'—*Roger Ebert*

Firewalker
US 1986 104m TVC colour
Cannon (Norman Akadjem, Jeffrey M. Rosenbaum)

Adventurers seek gold in an Aztec temple.
Old hat heroics and violence in the wake of *Raiders of the Lost Ark*. Not a happy outcome.
Chuck Norris, Lou Gossett Jnr, Melody Anderson, John Rhys-Davies, Will Sampson

First a Girl
GB 1935 94m bw

A messenger girl attracts attention by posing as a boy, and becomes a star. Moderate light star vehicle. Jessie Matthews, Sonnie Hale, Griffith Jones, Anna Lee, Alfred Drayton, Martita Hunt, Eddie Gray. Written by Marjorie Gaffney, from the play *Viktor und Viktoria* by Reinhold Schunzel; directed by Victor Saville; for Gaumont.

First Blood
US 1982 94m Technicolor Panavision
Carolco (Buzz Feitshans)

A former Green Beret gets into trouble in a small Californian community and sets himself against the forces of law.
Pure blood and thunder with some decent action sequences.

w Michael Kazall, William Sackheim, Sylvester Stallone, *novel* David Marell *d* Ted Kotcheff *ph* Andrew Laszlo *m* Jerry Goldsmith

Sylvester Stallone, Richard Crenna, Brian Dennehy, David Caruso, Jack Starrett

'Socially irresponsible . . . there are enough nuts out there without giving them a hero to cheer for.'—*Variety*

First Comes Courage
US 1943 88m bw
Columbia (Harry Joe Brown)

During World War II, a Norwegian girl appears to be a Quisling but is really a spy getting information from the Nazis by fraternizing with them.
Doleful war drama with little to commend it except propaganda.

w Lewis Meltzer, Melvin Levy, *novel* The Commandos by Elliott Arnold *d* Dorothy Arzner *ph* Joseph Walker *m* Ernst Toch

Merle Oberon, Brian Aherne, Carl Esmond, Fritz Leiber, Erik Rolf, Reinhold Schunzel, Isobel Elsom

The First Deadly Sin
US 1980 112m TVC color
Filmways / Artanis / Cinema Seven (Elliott Kastner)

A police lieutenant tracks down a homicidal lunatic but is unable to save his own wife who is dying in hospital from an obscure ailment.
The two halves of this depressing cop show don't seem to relate, and it offers little in the way of entertainment value beyond the traditional tracking down of the murderer.

w Mann Rubin, *novel* Lawrence Sanders *d* Brian G. Hutton *ph* Jack Priestley *m* Gordon Jenkins

Frank Sinatra, Faye Dunaway, David Dukes, George Coe, Brenda Vaccaro, Martin Gabel, Anthony Zerbe, James Whitmore

'An odd collection of pretensions seem to be rattling round in an overlength TV film.'—*Mark Lefanu, MFB*

'Mystery without meaning, despite a froth of intercutting and religious iconography.'—*Sight and Sound*

The First Gentleman*
GB 1948 111m bw
Columbia (Joseph Friedman)
US title: *Affairs of a Rogue*

The affairs and foibles of the Prince Regent.
Dullish adaptation of a successful West End play about 18th-century court life; script and performances still entertain.

w Nicholas Phipps, Reginald Long, *play Norman Ginsbury d* Cavalcanti *ph* Jack Hildyard

Cecil Parker, Jean-Pierre Aumont, Joan Hopkins, Margaretta Scott, Jack Livesey, Ronald Squire, Athene Seyler, Hugh Griffith

The First Great Train Robbery*
GB 1978 108m Technicolor Panavision
UA / Starling (John Foreman)
US title: *The Great Train Robbery*

In 1855, an elegant but ruthless crook picks out a gang to help him rob the Folkestone express of gold bullion.
Patchy but generally very likeable period crime story, with just a few lapses of pace and taste.

wd Michael Crichton, from his novel *ph Geoffrey Unsworth m* Jerry Goldsmith *ph* Maurice Carter

Sean Connery, Donald Sutherland, Lesley-Anne Down, Alan Webb, Robert Lang, Malcolm Terris

'My dream was that the historical world was going to be lovingly recreated, and then I was going to shoot *The French Connection* inside it.'—*Michael Crichton*

The First Hundred Years
US 1938 75m bw

A self-supporting wife is reluctant to give up her career. Tolerable matrimonial comedy resolved by pregnancy. Robert Montgomery, Virginia Bruce, Warren William, Binnie Barnes, Alan Dinehart, Harry Davenport, Nydia Westman. Written by Melville Baker from a story by Norman Krasna; directed by Richard Thorpe; for MGM.

First Lady*
US 1937 82m bw
Warner (Hal B. Wallis)

The President's wife is a power behind the scenes.
Solidly entertaining Washington comedy.

w Rowland Leigh, *play* George S. Kaufman, Katherine Dayton *d* Stanley Logan *ph* Sid Hickox
m Max Steiner

Kay Francis, Preston Foster, Anita Louise, Walter Connolly, Verree Teasdale, Victor Jory, Marjorie Rambeau, Louise Fazenda

'Smart stuff but generally palatable.'—*Variety*

The First Legion*
US 1951 86m bw
Sedif (Douglas Sirk)

Priests are bewildered when one of their number is the centre of an apparent miracle.
Talkative religious drama of a peculiarly American kind which likes to have its cake and eat it; watchable for the performances.

w Emmet Lavery, from his play *d* Douglas Sirk *ph* Robert de Grasse *m* Hans Sommer

Charles Boyer, William Demarest, Lyle Bettger, Barbara Rush, Leo G. Carroll, Walter Hampden, George Zucco, Taylor Holmes

First Love*
US 1939 84m bw
Universal (Joe Pasternak)

An orphaned teenager goes to live with her uncle and his snobbish family, and falls for a local bigwig's son.
A vehicle carefully conceived to introduce its star to grown-up romance. The compromises show, but it's palatable enough.

w Bruce Manning, Lionel Houser *d* Henry Koster *ph* Joseph Valentine *m* Frank Skinner *md* Charles Previn

Deanna Durbin, Robert Stack, Eugene Pallette, Helen Parrish, Lewis Howard, Leatrice Joy

'A top-bracketer for general audiences in keys and subsequents.'—*Variety*

'The most obvious Cinderella story I ever met with, apart from *Cinderella*.'—*Richard Mallett, Punch*

'There is nothing at all to resent in the picture: it is admirably directed, amusingly written, and acted with immense virtuosity by a fine cast.'—*Graham Greene*

AAN: Charles Previn

First Man into Space
GB 1958 78m bw
Producers' Associates (John Croydon)

An astronaut runs into a cloud of meteor dust and returns to earth a vampirish killer.
Quatermass-like shocker with modest budget but firm control.

w John C. Cooper, Lance Z. Hargreaves
d Robert Day *ph* Geoffrey Faithfull
m Buxton Orr

Marshall Thompson, Marla Landi, Bill Edwards

First Men in the Moon*
GB 1964 103m Technicolor Panavision
Columbia / Ameran (Charles H. Schneer)

A Victorian eccentric makes a voyage to the moon and is forced to stay there.
Rather slack in plot development, but an enjoyable schoolboy romp with a good eye for detail and tongue firmly in cheek.

w Nigel Kneale, Jan Read, *novel* H. G. Wells *d* Nathan Juran *ph* Wilkie Cooper *m* Laurie Johnson *sp* Ray Harryhausen

Lionel Jeffries, Edward Judd, Martha Hyer
† Uncredited, Peter Finch played the bit part of a process server.

'In the Supreme Court, there are only eight of them against all of her!'

First Monday in October
US 1981 99m Metrocolor Panavision
Paramount (Paul Heller, Martha Scott)

Ruth Loomis becomes the first woman to be appointed to the US Supreme Court, and wins over her severest critic.
Fairly yawnworthy comedy which has nowhere to go from its initial situation, and has detail too complex for any but politically minded Americans.

w Jerome Lawrence, Robert E. Lee, from their play *d* Ronald Neame *ph* Fred J. Koenekamp *m* Sousa, Handel, arr. Ian Fraser *pd* Philip M. Jefferies

Jill Clayburgh, Walter Matthau, Barnard Hughes, Jan Sterling, James Stephens, Joshua Bryant

'Any attempts to inject a little healthy subversion or a few dangerous thoughts are soon smothered by the plot demands of middle-aged romantic whimsy.'—*Sunday Times*

The First of the Few**
GB 1942 117m bw
Melbourne / British Aviation (Leslie Howard, George King, Adrian Brunel, John Stafford)
US title: *Spitfire*

The story of R. J. Mitchell who saw World War II coming and devised the Spitfire.
Low-key but impressive biopic with firm acting and good dialogue scenes. Production values slightly shaky.

w Anatole de Grunwald, Miles Malleson, Henry C. James, Katherine Strueby *d* Leslie Howard *ph* Georges Perinal *m* William Walton

Leslie Howard, David Niven, Rosamund John, Roland Culver, David Horne

'Full of action, Schneider Trophy races, test flying and flashes from the Battle of Britain.'—*Sunday Times*

The First Texan
US 1956 82m Technicolor Cinemascope
Allied Artists (Walter Mirisch)

The Governor of Tennessee helps Texas win its independence.
Generally well done biopic of Sam Houston, with the usual western excitements.

w Daniel B. Ullman *d* Byron Haskin
ph Wilfrid Cline *m* Roy Webb

Joel McCrea, Felicia Farr, Jeff Morrow, Wallace Ford, Abraham Sofaer

The First Time
US 1968 90m De Luxe
UA / Mirisch / Rogallan (Roger Smith, Allan Carr)
GB title: *You Don't Need Pajamas at Rosie's*

Three teenage boys who fantasize about sex help a stranded girl under the impression that she is a prostitute.
Embarrassingly sentimental teenage sex comedy, all the more irritating by its restraint. Not a patch on *Summer of '42*.

w Jo Heims, Roger Smith *d* James Nielson
ph Ernest Laszlo *m* Kenyon Hopkins

Jacqueline Bisset, Wes Stern, Rick Kelman, Wink Roberts, Sharon Acker

First to Fight
US 1967 97m Technicolor Panavision
Warner (William Conrad)

A World War II hero is taken home and fêted, but on returning to the front he loses his nerve.
War film in the guise of a psychological study; competently done but very American in its sentiments and a bit shaky on period detail.

w Gene L. Coon *d* Christian Nyby
ph Harold Wellman *m* Fred Steiner

Chad Everett, Gene Hackman, Dean Jagger, Marilyn Devon, Claude Akins

The First Travelling Saleslady
US 1956 92m Technicolor
RKO (Arthur Lubin)

Two women set out to sell barbed wire in the old west.
Strained comedy with very few effective moments.

w Devery Freeman, Stephen Longstreet
d Arthur Lubin *ph* William Snyder *m* Irving Gertz

Ginger Rogers, Carol Channing, Barry Nelson, James Arness, David Brian, Clint Eastwood

First Yank into Tokyo
US 1945 82m bw

An army pilot undergoes plastic surgery so that he can infiltrate the Japanese lines. Highly unconvincing spy fiction ripped off from the headlines as the war ended. Tom Neal, Richard Loo, Marc Cramer, Barbara Hale, Keye Luke. Written and produced by J. Robert Bren; directed by Gordon Douglas; for RKO.

The First Year*
US 1932 80m bw

Problems of a couple in their first year of married life. Pleasant star vehicle. Janet

Gaynor, Charles Farrell, Minna Gombell, Dudley Digges, Leila Bennett. Written by Lynn Starling from the play by Frank Craven; directed by William K. Howard; for Fox. 'Gaynor and Farrell in a story that's as close to perfection for them as any piece of screenwriting could be.'—*Variety*

Firstborn
US 1984 100m Technicolor

A divorced woman's children defend her against her malevolent second husband. Heavy-handed melodrama with no clue to what inspired its making. Teri Garr, Peter Weller, Christopher Collet, Corey Haim, Sarah Jessica Parker. Written by Ron Koslow; directed by Michael Apted, for Paul Junger Witt / Tony Thomas / Paramount.

A Fish Called Wanda
US 1988 108m Technicolor
MGM (Michael Shamberg)

Diamond-heist comedy depending on Anglo-American rivalries for its laughs. Monty Python fans found it disappointing, but it went down well in the US.

w John Cleese *d* Charles Crichton *ph* Alan Hume *m* John Du Prez *pd* Roger Murray-Leach

John Cleese, Jamie Lee-Curtis, Kevin Kline, Michael Palin, Maria Aitken

Fisherman's Wharf
US 1939 72m bw

The relationship of a boy and his foster father is upset by the arrival of relations on their fishing boat. Family fare for addicts of the singing boy star. Bobby Breen, Leo Carrillo, Lee Patrick, Henry Armetta, Tommy Bupp. Written by Bernard Schubert, Ian Hunter, Herbert Clyde Lewis; directed by Bernard Vorhaus; for Sol Lesser / RKO. 'Lightweight entertainment which will find its level in the duals.'—*Variety*

F.I.S.T.*
US 1978 145m Technicolor
UA / Norman Jewison (Gene Corman)

The rise and fall of a union boss.
Reminiscent of *All the King's Men* and *On the Waterfront*, this much overlong melodrama has compelling passages, but the star is not quite equal to it and parts are both repetitive and obscure.

w Joe Eszterhas, Sylvester Stallone *d* Norman Jewison *ph* Laszlo Kovacs *m* Bill Conti *pd* Richard MacDonald

Sylvester Stallone, Rod Steiger, Peter Boyle, Melinda Dillon, David Huffman, Tony L. Bianco, Cassie Yates, Peter Donat, Henry Wilcoxon

'Stallone exerts the same compulsive presence we saw in *Rocky*—and this time there is the added bonus that you can understand what he's saying.—*Variety*

A Fistful of Dollars*
Italy / Germany / Spain 1964 100m Techniscope
UA / Jolly / Constantin / Ocean (Arrigo Colombo, Georgio Papi)
Original title: *Per un Pugno di Dollari*

An avenging stranger, violent and mysterious, cleans up a Mexican border town.
A film with much to answer for: it began the craze for 'spaghetti westerns', took its director to Hollywood, and made a TV cowboy into a world star. In itself it is simple, noisy, brutish and actionful.

w Sergio Leone, Duccio Tessari *d Sergio Leone* *ph* Massimo Dallamano *m* Ennio Morricone

Clint Eastwood, Gian Maria Volonte, Marianne Koch

† Direct sequels by Leone, apart from numerous imitations, are *For a Few Dollars More* and *The Good, the Bad and the Ugly*.

A Fistful of Dynamite
Italy 1971 150m Techniscope
UA / Rafran / San Marco / Miura (Fulvio Morsella)
aka: *Duck, You Sucker*

In 1913 a Mexican bandit and an ex-IRA explosives expert join forces to rob a bank. Overblown action spectacular, far too long to be sustained by its flashes of humour and excitement. A good instance of what happens to a small talent when success goes to its head.

wd Sergio Leone *ph* Giuseppe Ruzzolini *m* Ennio Morricone

Rod Steiger, James Coburn

Fists in the Pocket*
Italy 1965 113m bw
Doria (Ezio Passadore)
original title: *I Pugni in Tasca*

One of a family of epileptics murders most of the others in order to help his normal eldest brother.
Complex black melodrama which makes its points, if it has any, with great style.

wd Marco Bellocchio *ph* Alberto Marrama *m* Ennio Morricone

Lou Castel, Paola Pitagora, Liliona Gerace

'There have been few debuts as exciting as this in recent years.'—*Tom Milne, MFB*

Fit for a King
US 1937 73m bw

A cub reporter falls for a princess. Standard star comedy with action climax. Joe E. Brown, Helen Mack, Halliwell Hobbes, Paul Kelly, Harry Davenport, John Qualen. Written by Richard Flournoy; directed by Edward Sedgwick; for RKO.

Fitzcarraldo***
West Germany 1982 158m colour
Werner Herzog / Project Filmproduktion / Zweite Deutsches Fernsehen / Wildlife Films, Peru (Werner Herzog, Lucki Stipetic)

In Peru at the turn of the century, an eccentric Irishman succeeds against all odds in establishing an opera house in the jungle.
A strange and brilliant film centring on the hero's successful attempt to drag his massive boat from one river to another.

wd Werner Herzog *ph Thomas Mauch* *m Popol Vuh*

Klaus Kinski, Claudia Cardinale, Jose Lewgoy, Paul Hittscher

† 'Fitzcarraldo' is the nearest the natives can get to 'Fitzgerald'.

Fitzwilly*
US 1967 102m De Luxe Panavision
UA / Dramatic Features Inc / Walter Mirisch
GB title: *Fitzwilly Strikes Back*

A New York butler, in order to keep his lady in style, has to organize the staff into a crime syndicate.
Moderately inventive, good-looking comedy with rather too much plot and not enough funny lines.

w Isobel Lennart, *novel* A Garden of Cucumbers by Poyntz Tyler *d* Delbert Mann *ph* Joseph Biroc *m* Johnny Williams

Dick Van Dyke, Edith Evans, Barbara Feldon, John McGiver, Harry Townes, John Fiedler, Norman Fell, Cecil Kellaway, Anne Seymour, Sam Waterston, Billy Halop

Five
US 1951 89m bw
Columbia (Arch Oboler)

There are only five survivors of an atomic holocaust, and their political and racial tensions soon reduce the number to two. Gutless talkfest which becomes interesting only when the camera moves out of doors; otherwise, too pretentious and dull by half.

wd Arch Oboler *ph* Lou Stoumen, Ed Spiegel, Sid Lubow *m* Henry Russell

William Phipps, Susan Douglas, James Anderson, Charles Lampkin, Earl Lee

'The talk leaves one with a strong impression that in this case the fittest did not survive.'—*Penelope Houston*

Five Against the House
US 1955 84m bw
Columbia (Sterling Silliphant, John Barnwell)

College students try to rob a casino. Meandering caper melodrama with too much flabby dialogue.

w Sterling Silliphant, John Barnwell, *novel* Jack Finney *d* Phil Karlson *ph* Leslie White *m* George Duning

Guy Madison, Kim Novak, Brian Keith, Kerwin Mathews, William Conrad

Five and Ten
US 1931 88m bw

A chain store heiress elopes with a married man, but is tamed by family misfortune. Solid star drama which maintains points of interest. Marion Davies, Leslie Howard, Richard Bennett, Irene Rich, Kent Douglass, Halliwell

FITZCARRALDO. Klaus Kinski's intensity comes across powerfully even in a still: Claudia Cardinale looks demure.

Hobbes. Written by A. P. Younger and Edith Fitzgerald, from the novel by Fannie Hurst; directed by Robert Z. Leonard; for MGM. (GB title: *Daughter of Luxury*.)

Five Boys from Barska Street*
Poland 1953 115m Agfacolor
Film Polski
original title: *Piatka z Ulicy Barskiej*

Five city boys are placed on probation and gradually change their attitudes towards life and society.
Rather dated propaganda piece with a plot which surprisingly follows western models.

wd Aleksander Ford, *novel* Kazimierz Kozniewski *ph* Jaroslav Tuzar *m* Kazimierz Serocki

Tadeusz Janczar, Aleksandra Slaska, Andrzej Kozak

Five Branded Women
Italy / US 1960 100m bw
Paramount / Dino de Laurentiis

Five Yugoslav girls have their heads shaved for associating with German soldiers, and after various adventures join the partisans.
Rough, tough war adventure which makes a few boring points about love and war.

w Ivo Perelli, *novel* Ugo Pirro *d* Martin Ritt *ph* Giuseppe Rotunno *m* Francesco Lavagnino

Silvana Mangano, Van Heflin, Vera Miles, Barbara Bel Geddes, Jeanne Moreau, Richard Basehart, Harry Guardino, Steve Forrest, Alex Nicol

'For the most part the film is devoted to unexciting guerrilla action and uninviting partisan life . . . obstinately unreal despite lashings of blood, mutilation, childbirth and death.'—*MFB*

Five Came Back**
US 1939 75m bw
RKO (Robert Sisk)

A passenger plane crashlands in the jungle. It can carry back only five survivors, and headhunters are coming closer . . .

A minor film which gradually achieved cult status and was remade as *Back to Eternity* as well as being the starting point for many variations. Still gripping in its dated way.

w Jerry Cady, Dalton Trumbo, Nathanael West *d John Farrow* *ph* Nicholas Musuraca *m* Roy Webb

Chester Morris, Lucille Ball, C. Aubrey Smith, Elizabeth Risdon, Wendy Barrie, John Carradine, Joseph Calleia, Allen Jenkins, Kent Taylor, Patric Knowles

'Exceptionally well-made adventure yarn, out of the B category and almost rates A . . . looks like a solid click.'—*Variety*

Five Card Stud
US 1968 103m Technicolor
Paramount / Hal. B. Wallis

Members of a lynching party are murdered one by one.
Would-be nonchalant murder mystery western: the stars just about hold it together, but it's an uphill fight.

w Marguerite Roberts, *novel* Ray Gaulden *d* Henry Hathaway *ph* Daniel L. Fapp *m* Maurice Jarre

Dean Martin, Robert Mitchum, Inger Stevens, Roddy McDowall, Katherine Justice, John Anderson, Yaphet Kotto

'Marginally watchable . . . but destined to sink without trace minutes after one leaves the cinema.'—*Gavin Millar*

'So mediocre you can't get mad at it.'—*Judith Crist*

Five Days One Summer*
US 1982 108m Technicolor
Warner / Ladd (Fred Zinnemann)

In 1932 a middle-aged Scots doctor takes his young mistress on an Alpine climbing holiday, and she falls for the guide.
Superbly photographed and crafted mountain movie, akin to the German epics of the early thirties. Alas, the content is very thin.

w Michael Austin, *story* Maiden Maiden by Kay Boyle *d Fred Zinnemann* *ph Giuseppe Rotunno* *m* Elmer Bernstein *pd* Willy Holt *ed* Stuart Baird

Sean Connery, Betsy Brantley, Lambert Wilson, Jennifer Hilary, Isabel Dean, Anna Massey

'Dawdling and eventually silly, though the veteran director's tenacity and craftsmanship provide muted applause.'—*Variety*

Five Easy Pieces**
US 1970 98m Technicolor
Columbia / Bert Schneider (Bob Rafelson, Richard Wechsler)

A middle-class drifter jilts his pregnant mistress for his brother's fiancée, but finally leaves both and hitches a ride to nowhere in particular.
Echoes of *Easy Rider*, *The Graduate* and *Charlie Bubbles* abound in this generally likeable but insubstantial modern anti-drama which at least takes place in pleasant surroundings and is firmly directed.

w Adrien Joyce *d* Bob Rafelson *ph* Laszlo Kovacs *m* various

Jack Nicholson, Karen Black, Susan Anspach, Lois Smith, Billy 'Green' Bush, Fannie Flagg

AAN: best picture; Adrien Joyce; Jack Nicholson; Karen Black

Five Finger Exercise
US 1962 109m bw
Columbia / Sonnis (Frederick Brisson)

A snobbish wife falls in love with a young house guest, with dire effect on her husband and son.
This West End study of a neurotic family is probably not good film material, certainly not adaptable to California, and above all not suitable to this star's whizzbang dramatics. Numbing hysteria arrives early and stays till the end.

w Frances Goodrich, Albert Hackett, *play* Peter Shaffer *d* Daniel Mann *ph* Harry Stradling *m* Jerome Moross

Rosalind Russell, Jack Hawkins, Maximilian Schell, Richard Beymer

'There are many kinds of love, but are there any without guilt?'—*publicity*

Five Fingers**
US 1952 108m bw
TCF (Otto Lang)

The valet of the British ambassador in Ankara sells military secrets to the Germans, who pay him but never use the information.
Absorbing, lightweight film adaptation of a true story of World War II; civilized suspense entertainment with all talents contributing nicely.

w Michael Wilson, *book* Operation Cicero by L. C. Moyzich *d Joseph L. Mankiewicz* *ph* Norbert Brodine *m* Bernard Herrmann *ad* Lyle Wheeler, George W. Davis

James Mason, Danielle Darrieux, Michael Rennie, Walter Hampden, Oscar Karlweis, Herbert Berghof, John Wengraf, Michael Pate

'One of the highest, fastest and most absorbing spy melodramas since Hitchcock crossed the Atlantic.'—*Arthur Knight*

AAN: Michael Wilson; Joseph L. Mankiewicz

Five Gates to Hell
US 1959 98m bw Cinemascope

A Vietcong warlord carries off a nun and seven nurses; the latter escape by brutal means. Unpleasant shocker showing no signs of talent in any department. Dolores Michaels, Patricia Owens, Neville Brand, Kevin Scott, Nobu McCarthy, Nancy Kulp, Shirley Knight, Irish McCalla. Written, directed and produced by James Clavell; for TCF. 'This grimly amateurish war film exploits sex and violence with an emotional arrest bordering on paranoia.'—*MFB.*

Five Golden Dragons
GB 1965 92m Techniscope

An American playboy in Hong Kong becomes involved in the affairs of five master criminals preparing to sell out to the Mafia. Anything-goes comedy-thriller, patchy at best, unintelligible at worst, and filled with ageing stars. Robert Cummings, Rupert Davies, Margaret Lee, Maria Perschy, Klaus Kinski, Dan Duryea, Brian Donlevy, Christopher Lee, George Raft. Written by Harry Alan Towers; directed by Jeremy Summers; for Harry Alan Towers.

Five Golden Hours
GB / Italy 1960 90m bw
(Columbia) Anglofilm / Fabio Jegher (Mario Zampi)

A con man tries to murder three widows who have invested money in one of his schemes. Ill-judged black comedy, sadly lacking style.

w Hans Wilhelm *d* Mario Zampi *ph* Christopher Challis *m* Stanley Black

Ernie Kovacs, Cyd Charisse, Kay Hammond, George Sanders, Dennis Price, Reginald Beckwith, Martin Benson, Ron Moody, Finlay Currie, Avis Landone, Sidney Tafler, John Le Mesurier, Clelia Matania

Five Graves to Cairo***
US 1943 96m bw
Paramount (Charles Brackett)

During the North Africa campaign, British spies try to destroy Rommel's secret supply dumps.
Intriguing spy melodrama set in a desert hotel, a notable example of Hollywood's ability to snatch polished drama from the headlines.

w Charles Brackett, Billy Wilder, *play* Lajos Biro *d Billy Wilder* *m* Miklos Rozsa *ph* John Seitz

Franchot Tone, Anne Baxter, *Erich Von Stroheim* (as Rommel), Akim Tamiroff, Peter Van Eyck, Miles Mander

'Von Stroheim has all the other movie Huns backed completely off the screen.'—*Variety*

'Billy Wilder must have had something a little grander in mind: the cleverness lacks lustre.'—*New Yorker, 1978*

'A fabulous film fable, but it has been executed with enough finesse to make it a rather exciting pipe dream.'—*Howard Barnes, New York Herald Tribune*

† Locations representing the African desert include California's Salton Sea and Yuma, Arizona.

AAN: John Seitz

Five Guns West
US 1955 78m Pathecolor

Five criminals are recruited into the southern army to catch a traitor and some Union gold. Western trial run for *The Dirty Dozen*; cheapjack actioner, quite tolerable of its kind. John Lund, Dorothy Malone, Chuck Connors, Paul Birch. Written by R. Wright Campbell; directed and produced by Roger Corman; for Palo Alto.

Five Little Peppers and How They Grew
US 1939 58m bw

While Mrs Pepper is out working, eldest daughter Polly must take care of the other children. Sentimental second feature which quickly spawned two others, *Five Little Peppers at Home* and *Five Little Peppers in Trouble*. Edith Fellows, Clarence Kolb, Dorothy Peterson, Ronald Sinclair, Tommy Bond. Written by Nathalie Bucknall and Jefferson Parker from the novel by Margaret Sidney; directed by Charles Barton; for Columbia.

Five Miles to Midnight*
France / Italy 1962 110m bw
UA / Filmsonor / Dear Film (Anatole Litvak)

A neurotic believed dead forces his terrified wife to collect his life insurance.
Hysterical melodrama, smoothly made with all the familiar expressionist devices, but far too long for its content.

w Peter Viertel, Hugh Wheeler *d Anatole Litvak ph Henri Alekan m* Mikis Theodorakis

Sophia Loren, Anthony Perkins, Gig Young, Jean-Pierre Aumont, Yolande Turner, Tommy Norden

'From the polished immediacy of the cars, streets, shop windows and café tables to the off-focus vertigo shots of panic, from the overhead view of neighbours on stairs . . . to the close-ups of hands in filing trays touching off the details of fear and guilt, there is a thread of colour to keep you watching.'—*MFB*

'One of those movies without a country that are becoming as fixed a part of the international scene as the Duke and Duchess of Windsor.'—*Arthur Schlesinger Jnr, Show*

Five of a Kind
US 1938 83m bw

Two reporters compete for the best stories about the Dionne Quintuplets. Third effort to exploit the famous quins, then four years old. Not otherwise remarkable. Jean Hersholt, Claire Trevor, Cesar Romero, Slim Summerville, Henry Wilcoxon, John Qualen, Jane Darwell. Written by Lou Breslow, John Patrick; directed by Herbert I. Leeds; for TCF. 'Will find difficulty in generating much audience enthusiasm except in spots where women patronage predominates.'—*Variety*

The Five Pennies*
US 1959 117m Technicolor Vistavision
Paramount / Dena (Jack Rose)

The rags-to-riches success story of cornet player Red Nichols.
The only touch of originality in this biopic is that the subject is given touches of irascibility. Production values reach a good standard.

w Jack Rose, Melville Shavelson *d* Melville Shavelson *ph* Daniel L. Fapp *md* Leith Stevens *ad* Hal Pereira, Tambi Larsen *songs* Sylvia Fine *trumpet solos* Red Nichols

Danny Kaye, Barbara Bel Geddes, *Louis Armstrong*, Bob Crosby, Harry Guardino, Tuesday Weld, Ray Anthony

AAN: Daniel L. Fapp; Leith Stevens; title song (*m / ly* Sylvia Fine)

Five Star Final**
US 1931 89m bw
Warner

A sensation-seeking newspaper editor causes tragedy.
Dated but still powerful melodrama which set the pattern for all the newspaper films of the thirties.

w Robert Lord, Byron Morgan, play Louis Weitzenkorn *d Mervyn Le Roy ph* Sol Polito *md* Leo F. Forbstein

Edward G. Robinson, H. B. Warner, Marian Marsh, Anthony Bushell, George E. Stone, Ona Munson, Aline MacMahon, Boris Karloff

'All the elements to make a hit attraction.'—*Variety*

† Remade in 1936 with Humphrey Bogart, as *Two Against the World*.

AAN: best picture

Five Steps to Danger
US 1956 80m bw
UA / HSK

A girl possessing secret information from her dead scientist brother has a mental breakdown, and is pursued by spies.
Lively if cliché-ridden espionage melodrama, like an old-time serial.

wd Henry S. Kesler, *novel* Donald Hamilton *ph* Kenneth Peach *m* Paul Sawtell, Bert Shefter

Sterling Hayden, Ruth Roman, Werner Klemperer, Richard Gaines

The Five Thousand Fingers of Doctor T*
US 1953 88m Technicolor
Columbia / *Stanley Kramer*

A boy who hates piano lessons dreams of his teacher as an evil genius who keeps five hundred boys imprisoned in a castle of musical instruments.
Badly scripted fantasy with gleaming sophisticated dream sequences which deserve a better frame. A real oddity to come from Hollywood at this time, even though Dr Seuss' books were and are bestsellers.

w Dr Seuss (Theodore Geisel), Alan Scott *d* Roy Rowland *ph Franz Planer m* Frederick Hollander *ly* Dr Seuss *pd Rudolph Sternad ch* Eugene Loring

Hans Conried, Tommy Rettig, Peter Lind Hayes, Mary Healy

AAN: Frederick Hollander

Five Weeks in a Balloon
US 1962 101m De Luxe Cinemascope
TCF (Irwin Allen)

In 1862 a professor is financed on a balloon trip into central Africa.
Would-be humorous semi-fantasy which strives to equal *Journey to the Center of the Earth* but unfortunately falls flat on its face despite the interesting talent available. Limp comedy situations, poor production values.

w Charles Bennett, Irwin Allen, Albert Gail, *novel* Jules Verne *d* Irwin Allen *ph* Winton Hoch *m* Paul Sawtell *ad* Jack Martin Smith, Alfred Ybarra

Cedric Hardwicke, Peter Lorre, Red Buttons, Fabian, Richard Haydn, Billy Gilbert, Herbert Marshall, Reginald Owen, Henry Daniell

Fixed Bayonets
US 1951 93m bw
TCF (Jules Buck)

An American division in Korea fights a rearguard action.
Downbeat war melodrama of a familiar kind, with more characterization than action.

wd Samuel Fuller *ph* Lucien Ballard *m* Roy Webb

Richard Basehart, Gene Evans, Michael O'Shea, Richard Hylton, Craig Hill

The Fixer
US 1968 130m Metròcolor
MGM / Edward Lewis, John Frankenheimer

A Jew in Tsarist Russia denies his race but becomes a scapegoat for various crimes and is imprisoned without trial until he becomes a *cause célèbre*.
Worthy but extremely dreary realist melodrama.

w Dalton Trumbo, *novel* Bernard Malamud *d* John Frankenheimer *ph* Marcel Grignon *m* Maurice Jarre

Alan Bates, Dirk Bogarde, Georgia Brown, Jack Gilford, Hugh Griffith, Elizabeth Hartman, Ian Holm, David Warner, Carol White, Murray Melvin, Peter Jeffrey, Michael Goodliffe

'The kind of film in which one has to admire much of the acting simply because it is all there is to admire.'—*David Pirie*

'A totally false film, devoid of a breath of human life or truth.'—*Arthur Schlesinger Jnr*

'Alan Bates's bare posterior, known to us from *Georgy Girl* and *King of Hearts*, makes another timely appearance here, thus becoming one of the most exposed arses in cinematic annals.'—*John Simon*

AAN: Alan Bates

The Fixer Uppers
US 1935 20m bw

Christmas card salesmen try to help a bored wife, but her jealous husband challenges Ollie to a duel. Rather flat comedy marking a tailing-off from the stars' best period. Laurel and Hardy, Mae Busch, Charles Middleton, Arthur Housman. Writer uncredited; directed by Charles Rogers; for Hal Roach. (NB: A remake of an early silent, *Slipping Wives*.)

The Flag Lieutenant
GB 1933 85m bw
British and Dominions (Herbert Wilcox)

A naval lieutenant, thought to be a coward, shows his true courage when a fort is beleaguered.

Boy's Own Paper stuff from a popular play previously filmed in 1919 (with George Wynn) and 1926 (with Henry Edwards).

w W. P. Drury, Leo Tover, from their play *d* Henry Edwards

Henry Edwards, Anna Neagle, Joyce Bland, Peter Gawthorne, Sam Livesey, O. B. Clarence, Abraham Sofaer

The Flame
US 1947 97m bw
Republic (John H. Auer)

A nurse marries for money, but her ailing spouse recovers and she falls in love with him. Turgid melodrama, ineptly presented.

w Lawrence Kimble *d* John H. Auer *ph* Reggie Lanning *m* Heinz Roemheld

Vera Hruba Ralston, John Carroll, Robert Paige, Broderick Crawford, Henry Travers, Blanche Yurka, Constance Dowling, Hattie McDaniel, Sen Yung

'A good picture to stay away from, with or without a good book.'—*Cue*

The Flame and the Arrow*
US 1950 88m Technicolor
(Warner) Harold Hecht, Frank Ross

In medieval Italy, a rebel leader seeks victory over a tyrant.
Good-humoured Robin Hood stuff with the star at his most acrobatic.

w Waldo Salt *d* Jacques Tourneur *ph* Ernest Haller *m* Max Steiner *ad* Edward Carrere

Burt Lancaster, Virginia Mayo, Robert Douglas, Aline MacMahon, Frank Allenby, Nick Cravat

'I never found a Technicolor costume picture so entertaining.'—*Richard Mallett, Punch*

AAN: Ernest Haller; Max Steiner

The Flame and the Flesh
US 1954 104m Technicolor
MGM (Joe Pasternak)

An unscrupulous American woman in Naples has a fatal fascination for the local menfolk. Dreary remake of *Naples au Baiser du Feu* (France 1937), with the dullest possible handling all round.

w Helen Deutsch, *novel* Auguste Bailly *d* Richard Brooks *ph* Christopher Challis *m* Nicholas Brodszky

Lana Turner, Carlos Thompson, Bonar Colleano, Pier Angeli, Charles Goldner, Peter Illing

Flame in the Streets
GB 1961 93m colour Cinemascope
Rank / Somerset (Roy Baker)

A liberal-minded union man erupts when his daughter proposes to marry a black man. Predictable East End problem picture, unconvincingly set and acted and boring into the bargain.

w Ted Willis, from his TV play Hot Summer Night *d* Roy Baker *ph* Christopher Challis *m* Phil Green

John Mills, Brenda de Banzie, Sylvia Syms, Earl Cameron, Johnny Sekka, Ann Lynn, Wilfred Brambell

'Its methods belong more to the writer's study than to life.'—*John Gillett*

'Adventure blazes across the burning sands!'

Flame of Araby
US 1951 76m Technicolor

An Arabian princess, forced to marry, makes herself the prize in a horse race which she hopes her chosen man will win. Trifling Eastern nonsense. Maureen O'Hara, Jeff Chandler, Richard Egan, Susan Cabot, Lon Chaney Jnr, Buddy Baer, Maxwell Reed. Written by Gerald Drayson Adams; directed by Charles Lamont; for Universal-International.

Flame of Calcutta
US 1953 70m Technicolor

In 18th-century India a mysterious girl leads attacks against a usurper. Saturday matinee historical romp without much flair. Denise Darcel, Patric Knowles, Paul Cavanagh, George Keymas. Written by Robert E. Kent; directed by Seymour Friedman; for Sam Katzman / Columbia.

The Flame of New Orleans*
US 1941 79m bw
Universal (Joe Pasternak)

A European adventuress settles in America. Fluffy comedy romance with the exiled director scarcely in top form.

w Norman Krasna *d* René Clair *ph* Rudolph Maté *m* Frank Skinner

Marlene Dietrich, Roland Young, Bruce Cabot, Mischa Auer, Andy Devine, Frank Jenks, Eddie Quillan, Laura Hope Crews, Franklin Pangborn

† Remade as *Scarlet Angel.*

Flame of the Barbary Coast
US 1945 97m bw
Republic (Joseph Kane)

In old San Francisco, a cowboy becomes involved with a night club queen, and their fortunes are resolved by the earthquake. Tolerable period melodrama, and the one in which Wayne played a character named Duke: the nickname stuck.

w Borden Chase *d* Joseph Kane *ph* Robert de Grasse *m* Dale Butts *sp* Howard and Theodore Lydecker

John Wayne, Ann Dvorak, Joseph Schildkraut, William Frawley, Virginia Grey, Russell Hicks, Jack Norton, Paul Fix, Marc Lawrence

AAN: Dale Butts

Flame of the Islands
US 1955 90m Trucolor
Republic (Edward Ludwig)

A girl invests a bequest in a Bahamas night club, and there becomes involved with four men.
Barely competent time-filler.

w Bruce Manning *d* Edward Ludwig *ph* Bud Thackery *m* Nelson Riddle

Yvonne de Carlo, Howard Duff, Zachary Scott, Kurt Kasznar, Barbara O'Neil, James Arness, Frieda Inescort

The Flame Within
US 1935 73m bw

A lady psychiatrist falls for the husband of one of her patients. Decent star melodrama. Ann Harding, Maureen O'Sullivan, Louis Hayward, Henry Stephenson, Herbert Marshall. Written, directed (and produced) by *Edmund Goulding*; for MGM.

Flaming Feather
US 1951 78m Technicolor

Arizona is harassed by an outlaw called The Sidewinder who leads a troupe of pillaging Indians. Spot-the-villain western; not much to detain one. Sterling Hayden, Forrest Tucker, Barbara Rush, Richard Arlen, Victor Jory, Edgar Buchanan. Written by Gerald Drayson Adams; directed by Ray Enright; for Nat Holt / Paramount.

Flaming Frontiers
US 1938 bw serial: 15 eps

An Indian scout helps his girl friend to rid a town of outlaws. Unremarkable serial fare. Johnny Mack Brown, Eleanor Hansen, Ralph Bowman, Charles Middleton. Directed by Ray Taylor and Alan James; for Universal.

Flaming Star*
US 1960 92m De Luxe Cinemascope
TCF (David Weisbart)

A half-breed family is torn between two loyalties.
Solemn, unusual Civil War western with a downbeat ending.

w Clair Huffaker, Nunnally Johnson *d* Don Siegel *ph* Charles G. Clarke *m* Cyril Mockridge

Elvis Presley, Dolores del Rio, Steve Forrest, Barbara Eden, John McIntire, Rodolpho Acosta

'Despite familiar absurdities, it has more than its share of good moments.'—*MFB*

The Flamingo Kid
US 1984 100m De Luxe

In 1963, a teenager comes of age while working at a beach club. Innocent but unexciting comedy-drama about matters which scarcely concern grown-ups. Matt Dillon, Richard Crenna, Hector Elizondo, Jessica Walter, Fisher Stevens. Written by Neal Marshall and Garry Marshall (no relation); directed by Garry Marshall; for Michael Phillips / Mercury / ABC.

'A wrong girl from the right side of the tracks!'

Flamingo Road*
US 1949 94m bw
Warner (Jerry Wald)

A tough carnival dancer is stranded in a small town and soon affects the lives of the local politicians.
Standard melodrama from a bestseller, absurd but well performed.

w Robert Wilder, from his novel *d* Michael Curtiz *ph* Ted McCord *m* Max Steiner

Joan Crawford, David Brian, Sidney Greenstreet, Zachary Scott, Gladys George, Virginia Huston, Fred Clark

The Flanagan Boy
GB 1953 81m bw
Hammer

A young merchant seaman becomes a boxer and is corrupted by a hard-boiled blonde.
Competent British imitation of an American B movie. Tony Wright, Barbara Payton, Sidney James, John Slater, Frederick Valk, Marie Burke. Written by Guy Elmes; directed by Reginald LeBorg; for Exclusive. US title: *Bad Blonde*.

Flap
US 1970 106m Technicolor Panavision
Warner (Jerry Adler)
GB title: *The Last Warrior*

A drunken Indian on a dilapidated modern reservation starts a public relations war and leads a march on the city.
Unendearing comedy with a tragic end tacked on, not very entertaining as whimsy, farce or social conscience.

w Clair Huffaker, from his novel Nobody Loves a Drunken Indian *d* Carol Reed *ph* Fred Koenekamp *m* Marvin Hamlisch

Anthony Quinn, Claude Atkins, Tony Bill, Victor Jory, Shelley Winters

Flare Up
US 1969 98m Metrocolor
MGM / GMF (Leon Fromkes)

A man kills his wife and threatens her friends who he feels are responsible for the break-up of his marriage.
Sensationally violent melodrama with a plot that goes back to *Sudden Fear* and further. Adequately made.

w Mark Rodgers *d* James Neilson *ph* Andrew J. McIntyre *m* Les Baxter

Raquel Welch, James Stacy, Luke Askew, Don Chastain, Ron Rifkin

Flash Gordon*

The hero of the 25th century was created in comic strip form by Alex Raymond and his chief claims to film fame are three wild and woolly serials made by Universal: *Flash Gordon* (1936), *Flash Gordon's Trip to Mars* (1938), and *Flash Gordon Conquers the Universe* (1940), all starring Buster Crabbe with Charles Middleton as the wily Emperor Ming. Their cheap and cheerful futuristic sets and their non-stop action have kept them popular with film buffs through the years.
In 1974 a semi-porno spoof, *Flesh Gordon*, appeared.

Flash Gordon
GB 1980 115m Technicolor Todd-AO
EMI / Famous / Starling (Dino de Laurentiis)

A football hero, his girl friend, and Dr Zarkov have adventures on the planet Mongo.
Lively comic strip addition to the increasing numbers of such things being restaged at enormous expense fifty years after their prime.

w Lorenzo Semple Jnr, from characters created by Alex Raymond *d* Michael Hodges *ph* Gil Taylor *m* Queen *pd Danilo Donati*

Sam J. Jones, Melody Anderson, Topol, Max Von Sydow, Timothy Dalton, Brian Blessed, Peter Wyngarde

'An expensively irrelevant gloss on its sources.'—*Richard Combs, MFB*

'Don't you understand? When you give up the dream, you die!'

Flashdance*
US 1983 98m Movielab
Paramount / Polygram (Don Simpson, Jerry Bruckheimer)

A female welder in a Pittsburgh factory has ambitions to be a ballet dancer.
Slickly-made, disco-style but dramatically empty entertainment.

w Tom Hedley, Joe Eszterhas *d* Adrian Lyne *ph* Don Peterman *m* Giorgio Moroder *ed* Bud Smith, Walt Mulconery

Jennifer Beals, Michael Nouri, Lilia Skala, Sunny Johnson, Kyle T. Heffner, Belinda Bauer

'It resembles an extended video for a record album.'—*Observer*

'A preposterous success.'—*Guardian*

'Basically, a series of rock videos.'—*New Yorker*

AA: song, 'Flashdance . . . What a Feeling' (*m* Giorgio Moroder, *ly* Keith Forsey, Irene Cara)

AAN: cinematography; editing; song, 'Maniac' (*m* and *ly* Michael Sembello, Dennis Matkosky)

Flashpoint
US 1985 94m Metrocolor
Home Box Office / Silver Screen

Border patrolmen discover treasure and decide to make off with it.
Competent action melodrama which doesn't quite hang together in the later stretches but has plenty of lively moments.

w Dennis Shryack, Michael Butler *novel* George La Fountaine *d* William Tannen *ph* Peter Moss *m* various, performed by Tangerine Dream

Kris Kristofferson, Treat Williams, Rip Torn, Kevin Conway

Flaxy Martin
US 1948 86m bw
Warner (Saul Elkins)

A lawyer falls for a racketeer's girl friend and finds himself framed for murder.
Flatly-handled melodrama with unsympathetic characters.

w David Lang *d* Richard Bare *ph* Carl Guthrie

Zachary Scott, Virginia Mayo, Dorothy Malone, Tom d'Andrea, Elisha Cook Jnr

A Flea in Her Ear*
US / France 1968 94m De Luxe Panavision
TCF (Fred Kohlmar)

Various suspicious wives and husbands converge on the notorious Hotel Coq d'Or.
Disappointing filming of a Feydeau farce, which needs to be much more cleverly handled to come over with its full theatrical force.

w John Mortimer, *play* La Puce à l'Oreille by Georges Feydeau *d* Jacques Charon *ph* Charles Lang *m* Bronislau Kaper *pd Alexander Trauner*

Rex Harrison, Rachel Roberts, Rosemary Harris, Louis Jourdan, John Williams, Grégoire Aslan, Edward Hardwicke, Frank Thornton, Victor Sen Yung

'The plunge into madness never comes, and one is left with the sight of a group of talented players struggling with alien material.'—*Michael Billington, Illustrated London News*

'Gobs of glee! A boatload of beauties! A shipful of songs!'

The Fleet's In*
US 1942 93m bw
Paramount (Paul Jones)

A sailor on leave in San Francisco takes a bet that he can kiss the glamorous singer at a swank nightclub.
Mindless wartime musical which happened to set the seal of success on a number of young talents. Previously a Clara Bow vehicle.

w Walter de Leon, Sid Silvers *d* Victor Schertzinger *ph* William Mellor *m / ly* Victor Schertzinger, Johnny Mercer

Dorothy Lamour, William Holden, *Eddie Bracken, Betty Hutton*, Cass Daley, Gil Lamb, Leif Erickson, Betty Jane Rhodes

Songs: 'I Remember You'; 'When You Hear the Time Signal'; 'The Fleet's In'; 'Tomorrow You Belong to Uncle Sam'; 'Arthur Murray Taught Me Dancing in a Hurray'; 'If Somebody Builds a Better Mousetrap'; 'Somebody Else's Moon'; 'Tangerine'; 'Conga from Honga'

'A slim and obvious comedy with some good tunes. Much of the film is a roughhouse; several reels towards the end are turned over to straight vaudeville.'—*Eileen Creelman, New York Sun*

The Flemish Farm
GB 1943 82m bw
Two Cities (Sydney Box)

An attempt is made to retrieve a buried flag from occupied Belgium.
Tolerable wartime flagwaver.

w Jeffrey Dell, Jill Craigie *d* Jeffrey Dell *ph* Eric Cross

Clive Brook, Clifford Evans, Jane Baxter, Philip Friend, Brefni O'Rourke

'He sacrificed his career for the sake of a woman's lying lips!'

Flesh*
US 1932 95m bw
MGM

A German wrestler in the US falls for a street waif.
Unusual, rather unattractive, but vivid melodrama.

w Leonard Praskins, Edgar Allen Woolf, Moss Hart, *story* Edmund Goulding *d* John Ford *ph* Arthur Edeson

Wallace Beery, Ricardo Cortez, Karen Morley, John Miljan, Jean Hersholt, Herman Bing, Edward Brophy

'Not bad, could have been better . . . that it takes 95 minutes to get home is the big fault.'—*Variety*

Flesh and Blood
GB 1951 102m bw
BL / Harefield (Anatole de Grunwald)

Three generations of a family suffer from the effects of heredity.
Fragmented Scottish period piece which never settles down long enough to make an impact with any group of characters.

w Anatole de Grunwald, *play* A Sleeping Clergyman by James Bridie *d* Anthony Kimmins *ph* Otto Heller *m* Charles Williams

Richard Todd, Glynis Johns, Joan Greenwood, André Morell, Ursula Howells, Freda Jackson, George Cole, James Hayter, Ronald Howard, Muriel Aked

Flesh and Blood
US 1985 126m De Luxe Technovision

In a dark medieval world, a young bride-to-be is kidnapped and raped, but grows to like it. Unpleasant wallow in a decadent world of the imagination. Rutger Hauer, Jennifer Jason Leigh, Tom Burlinson, Jack Thompson. Written by Gerard Soeteman and Paul Verhoeven; directed by Paul Verhoeven; for Gys Versluys / Riverside / Orion.

Flesh and Fantasy*
US 1943 94m bw
Universal (Charles Boyer, Julien Duvivier)

A club bore tells three strange stories.
A portmanteau with ingredients of varying interest, attempting to emulate the success of *Tales of Manhattan*. The fourth episode planned was deleted and turned up as *Destiny* (qv). All quite stylish, the best section being *Lord Arthur Savile's Crime*.

w Ernest Pascal, Samuel Hoffenstein, Ellis St Joseph, *stories* Ellis St Joseph, Oscar Wilde, Laslo Vadnay *d Julien Duvivier ph Paul Ivano, Stanley Cortez m* Alexandre Tansman

Robert Benchley, *Edward G. Robinson*, Barbara Stanwyck, Charles Boyer, Betty Field, Robert Cummings, *Thomas Mitchell*, C. Aubrey Smith, Dame May Whitty, Edgar Barrier, David Hoffman

Flesh and Fury
US 1952 82m bw

A young deaf mute becomes a successful prizefighter. Totally unremarkable programmer with a happy ending. Tony Curtis, Jan Sterling, Mona Freeman, Wallace Ford, Connie Gilchrist. Written by Bernard Gordon; directed by Joseph Pevney; for Leonard Goldstein / Universal-International.

Flesh and the Devil*
US 1926 109m bw silent
MGM

A temptress toys with three men.
Hokey but good-looking star melodrama, climaxing with death on an ice floe. A huge commercial success because of the off-screen Garbo-Gilbert romance.

w Benjamin Glazer, *novel* The Undying Past by Hermann Sudermann *d Clarence Brown*

Greta Garbo, John Gilbert, Lars Hanson, Marc McDermott, Barbara Kent

'A film of more than passing cleverness . . . the theme is sheer undiluted sex, and Brown uses a series of close-ups to get this across with considerable effect.'—*Paul Rotha, The Film Till Now*

The Flesh and the Fiends
GB 1959 97m bw Dyaliscope
Regal / Triad (Robert Baker, Monty Berman)
US title: *Mania*

In 1820 Edinburgh, 'resurrection men' commit murders to keep anatomists supplied.
Dr Robert Knox rides again, in a version more bloody but less entertaining than *The Body Snatcher*.

w John Gilling, Leon Griffiths *d* John Gilling *ph* Monty Berman *m* Stanley Black

Peter Cushing, June Laverick, George Rose, Donald Pleasence, Renée Houston, Billie Whitelaw, Dermot Walsh

The Flesh Is Weak
GB 1957 88m bw

A girl goes from bad to worse when she finds that her boy friend is head of a vice ring. Road to Ruin, fifties style; competently made, but neither shocking nor entertaining, just an exploitation piece. John Derek, Milly Vitale, William Franklyn, Martin Benson, Freda Jackson, Norman Wooland, Harold Lang, Patricia Jessel, John Paul. Written by Leigh Vance; directed by Don Chaffey; for Raymond Stross / Eros.

Fletch*
US 1985 96m Technicolor
Universal / Douglas / Greisman

A newspaper columnist with a penchant for disguise tracks down a nefarious con man.
A lightness of touch unusual for the eighties makes this comedy mystery more welcome than most.

w Andrew Bergman *novel* Gregory McDonald *d Michael Ritchie ph* Fred Schuler *m* Harold Faltermeyer

Chevy Chase, Dana Wheeler-Nicholson, Tim Matheson, Joe Don Baker, Richard Libertini, Kenneth Mars, M. Emmet Walsh

'What would you do if the man you loved wanted you to love his pal?'

Flight
US 1929 110m bw
Columbia (Harry Cohn)

Two rival flyers join a mission to rescue US Marines ambushed in Nicaragua.
Pale stuff now, but in its time an ambitious action movie showing a new suppleness in its young director.

w Frank Capra, Ralph Graves *d* Frank Capra *ph* Joseph Walker *ad* Harrison Wiley

Jack Holt, Lila Lee, Ralph Graves, Alan Roscoe, Harold Goodwin, Jimmy de la Cruze

'The first all-talking drama of the air!'—*publicity*

Flight Angels
US 1940 74m bw

Airline stewardesses compete for the favours of a romantic pilot. An efficient potboiler, now most interesting for its depiction of 1939 air travel. Virginia Bruce, Dennis Morgan, Wayne Morris, Ralph Bellamy, Jane Wyman, John Litel. Written by Maurice Leo; directed by Lewis Seiler; for Edmund Grainger / Warner.

Flight Command
US 1940 116m bw
MGM (J. Walter Ruben)

A cocky recruit makes good in the naval air arm.
Routine flagwaver.

w Wells Root, Cmdr Harvey Haislip *d* Frank Borzage *ph* Harold Rosson *m* Franz Waxman

Robert Taylor, Ruth Hussey, Walter Pidgeon, Paul Kelly, Nat Pendleton, Red Skelton, Shepperd Strudwick, Dick Purcell

Flight Commander see *The Dawn Patrol*, for which this is the TV title (1930 version).

Flight for Freedom
US 1943 101m bw
RKO (David Hempstead)

Biography of an intrepid aviatrix and her husband.
Patchy job based on the life of Amelia Earhart, suggesting that her final disappearance was on a government mission. Dull production.

w Oliver H. P. Garrett, S. K. Lauren *d* Lothar Mendes *ph* Lee Garmes *m* Roy Webb

Rosalind Russell, Fred MacMurray, Herbert Marshall, Eduardo Ciannelli, Walter Kingsford

Flight from Ashiya*
US / Japan 1963 102m Eastmancolor Panavision
UA / Harold Hecht / Daiei

When a cargo vessel sinks off the coast of Japan during a typhoon, the helicopter rescue service springs into action.
Conventional Grade A action thriller with flashbacks to earlier disasters in the lives of its heroes.

w Elliot Arnold, Waldo Salt *d* Michael Anderson *ph* Joe MacDonald, Burnett Guffey *m* Frank Cordell *pd* Eugène Lourié

Yul Brynner, Richard Widmark, George Chakiris, Shirley Knight, Daniele Gaubert, Suzy Parker

Flight from Destiny
US 1941 74m bw

An elderly professor with six months to live determines on one good deed . . . which includes murder. Likeable minor melodrama, well put together. Thomas Mitchell, Geraldine Fitzgerald, Jeffrey Lynn, Mona Maris. Written by Barry Trivers, from a play by Anthony Berkeley; directed by Vincent Sherman; for Warner.

Flight from Folly
GB 1944 93m bw

A chorus girl cures a playwright's amnesia. Leadenly-titled and played variation on *Random Harvest,* with dreary musical numbers. Pat Kirkwood, Hugh Sinclair, Sydney Howard, Marian Spencer, Tamara Desni, Jean Gillie, A. E. Matthews. Written by Basil Woon, Lesley Storm and Katherine Strueby; directed by Herbert Mason; for Warner.

Flight from Glory*
US 1937 66m bw

Tensions mount among fliers who cross the Andes daily between secluded mines and their supply base. Tense 'B' picture which looks like a trial run for *Only Angels Have Wings*. Chester Morris, Whitney Bourne, Onslow Stevens, Van Heflin, Richard Lane, Paul Guilfoyle. Written by David Silverstein, John Twist; directed by Lew Landers; for Robert Sisk / RKO. 'Better than the average programmer and worth strong exhibitor plugging. In tone the picture may be fairly described as semi-sophisticated, which for rank and file purposes is probably just the right amount of sophistication.'—*Variety*

Flight Lieutenant
US 1942 80m bw

A careless pilot crashes a plane, but atones heroically for his former misdeeds. Inept wartime flagwaver. Glenn Ford, Pat O'Brien, Evelyn Keyes, Minor Watson, Jonathan Hale. Written by Michael Blankfort; directed by Sidney Salkow; for B. P. Schulberg / Columbia.

Flight Nurse
US 1953 90m bw

An air force nurse is on the front line during the Korean War. Routine mix of love and action. Joan Leslie, Forrest Tucker, Arthur Franz, Jeff Donnell, Ben Cooper. Written by Alan LeMay; directed by Allan Dwan; for Republic.

Flight of the Doves*
US 1971 101m colour
Columbia / Rainbow (Ralph Nelson)

Two children run away from their bullying stepfather to join their Irish grandmother, but are chased by a wicked uncle who knows they are heirs to a fortune.
Pantomimish whimsy which works in fits and starts, but has little real humour or charm.

wd Ralph Nelson, *novel* Walter Macken *ph* Harry Waxman *m* Roy Budd

Ron Moody, Dorothy McGuire, Helen Raye, Dana, Jack Wild, Stanley Holloway, William Rushton

The Flight of the Phoenix*
US 1965 149m De Luxe
TCF / Associates and Aldrich

A cargo passenger plane crashes in the desert, and the survivors try to avert disaster.
Achingly slow character adventure; an all-star cast works desperately hard but the final flight of the rebuilt plane seems almost an anti-climax after the surfeit of personal melodramatics.

w Lukas Heller, *novel* Elleston Trevor *d* Robert Aldrich *ph* Joseph Biroc *m* Frank de Vol

James Stewart, Richard Attenborough, Hardy Kruger, Peter Finch, Dan Duryea, Ernest Borgnine, Ian Bannen, Ronald Fraser, Christian Marquand, George Kennedy

AAN: Ian Bannen

The Flight that Disappeared
US 1961 73m bw
UA / Harvard (Robert E. Kent)

Atomic scientists on an airliner find themselves in 'heaven' being tried by people of the future.
Eccentric anti-bomb curiosity, a second feature *Outward Bound.*

w Ralph Hart, Judith Hart, Owen Harris *d* Reginald Le Borg *ph* Gilbert Warrenton *m* Richard La Salle

Gregory Morton, Addison Richards, Craig Hill, Paula Raymond, Dayton Lummis

Flight to Hong Kong
US 1956 88m bw

A syndicate boss tried to two-time the mob. Co-feature hokum which barely justifies its length. Rory Calhoun, Barbara Rush, Dolores Donlon, Soo Young, Pat Conway, Werner Klemperer. Written by Leo Townsend, Leo G. O'Callaghan; directed and produced by Joseph M. Newman; for UA.

Flight to Mars
US 1951 75m Cinecolor

After a rocket flight, four scientists discover that the inhabitants of Mars speak perfect American, learned by radio. Pioneering science-fiction entry with nothing going for it but being first: writing, production and acting are alike abysmal. Cameron Mitchell, Marguerite Chapman, Arthur Franz, Virginia Huston, John Litel. Written by Arthur Strawn; directed by Lesley Selander; for Monogram.

Flight to Tangier
US 1953 90m Technicolor 3-D
Paramount (Nat Holt)

A female FBI agent chases a three million dollar letter of credit.
Forced and boring action romance without much of either element.

wd Charles Marquis Warren *ph* Ray Rennahan *m* Paul Sawtell

Joan Fontaine, Jack Palance, Corinne Calvet, Robert Douglas, Marcel Dalio, Jeff Morrow, Murray Matheson, John Doucette

The Flim Flam Man*
US 1967 104m De Luxe Panavision
TCF / Lawrence Turman
GB title: *One Born Every Minute*

An army deserter joins forces with an elderly con man.
Folksy comedy in a small-town setting; none of it really comes to the boil after a couple of early chase sequences.

w William Rose, *novel* Guy Owen *d* Irvin Kershner, *Yakima Canutt* *ph* Charles Lang *m* Jerry Goldsmith

George C. Scott, Michael Sarrazin, Sue Lyon, Harry Morgan, Jack Albertson, Alice Ghostley, Albert Salmi

Flipper
US 1963 87m Metrocolor
(MGM) Ivan Tors

A fisherman's son on the Florida Keys befriends a dolphin.
Harmless boy-and-animal adventure which spawned two sequels and a TV series.

w Arthur Weiss *d* James B. Clark *ph* Lamar Boren, Joseph Brun *m* Henry Vars

Chuck Connors, Luke Halpin, Kathleen Maguire, Connie Scott

† *Flipper's New Adventure* followed in 1964.

Flirtation Walk*
US 1934 97m bw
Warner (Frank Borzage)

Love affairs of West Point cadets.
Light musical very typical of its period, with a few agreeable numbers.

w Delmer Daves *d* Frank Borzage *ch* Bobby Connelly *ph* Sol Polito, George Barnes *m / ly* Allie Wrubel, Mort Dixon

Dick Powell, Ruby Keeler, Pat O'Brien, Ross Alexander, John Arledge, Henry O'Neill, Guinn Williams

'A rousing recruiting poster . . . and a splendid laboratory specimen of the adolescent cinema.'—*André Sennwald, New York Times*

AAN: best picture

The Flirting Widow
US 1930 70m bw

A girl invents a lover, then kills him off . . . but his friend shows up. Whimsical comedy which outstays its welcome. Dorothy Mackaill, Basil Rathbone, Leila Hyams, Claude Gillingwater, William Austin. Written by John F. Goodrich from the story Green Stockings by A. E. W. Mason; directed by William A. Seiter; for First National. 'Slim for the key houses and really built for neighbourhoods.'—*Variety*

Flirting with Fate
US 1938 70m bw

A trailerized vaudeville troupe tours South America. The setting is the only surprising thing about this rather dim comedy. Joe E. Brown, Leo Carrillo, Beverly Roberts, Wynne Gibson, Steffi Duna, Stanley Fields, Leonid Kinskey, Charles Judels. Written by Joseph Moncure March, Ethel La Blanche, Charlie Melson, Harry Clork; directed by Frank McDonald; for David L. Loew.

Flood Tide
US 1958 82m bw scope

A boy is jealous of his widowed mother's interest in a neighbour. Modest melodrama, typical of its studio at the time. George Nader, Cornell Borchers, Michel Ray, Judson Pratt, Joanna Moore. Written by Dorothy Cooper; directed by Abner Biberman; for Universal.

Floods of Fear*
GB 1958 84m bw
Rank / Sydney Box

Two escaped convicts, a warder, and a pretty girl are trapped by floods in a lonely house. Adequate melodrama with impressively gloomy production and performances but not many surprises.

wd Charles Crichton, *novel* Joan and Ward Hawkins *ph* Christopher Challis *m* Alan Rawsthorne

Howard Keel, Anne Heywood, Harry H. Corbett, Cyril Cusack

Floodtide
GB 1949 90m bw

A Clydebank apprentice becomes a ship designer. Boring inspirational drama hindered by the Independent Frame method. Gordon Jackson, Rona Anderson, John Laurie, Jack Lambert, Elizabeth Sellars. Written by Donald B. Wilson and George Blake; directed by Frederick Wilson; for Aquila / Rank.

The Floradora Girl
US 1930 75m bw (Technicolor sequence)

The romance of the last remaining Floradora girl. Not a musical but a period farce which laughs at rather than with the fashions of 1900. It doubtless succeeded with the audiences of its time. Marion Davies, Lawrence Gray, Walter Catlett, Ilka Chase, Vivian Oakland, Jed Prouty. Written by Gene Markey, Ralph Spence, Al Boasberg, Robert Hopkins; directed by Harry Beaumont; for MGM.
'Good hoke entertainment . . . an all-type audience picture with no limitations.'—*Variety*
(GB title: *The Gay Nineties*.)

The Florentine Dagger
US 1935 69m bw

A mysterious Borgia influence is brought to bear on the murder of an art dealer. Vaguely unsatisfactory whodunnit with some intriguing and some pretentious elements. Margaret Lindsay, Donald Woods, C. Aubrey Smith, Robert Barrat, Henry O'Neill. Written by Brown Holmes and Tom Reed, from the novel by Ben Hecht; directed by Robert Florey; for Warner.

Florian
US 1940 91m bw
MGM (Winfield Sheehan)

In 1910 Austria, a poor boy and a rich girl are united by their love of a Lippizaner stallion. Not kinky, but strangely dull.

w Noel Langley, Geza Herczeg, James K. McGuinness *d* Edwin L. Marin *ph* Karl Freund, Richard Rosson *m* Franz Waxman

Robert Young, Helen Gilbert, Charles Coburn, Lee Bowman, Reginald Owen, S. Z. Sakall, Lucile Watson, Irina Baronova

Flower Drum Song*
US 1961 133m Technicolor Panavision
U-I / Rodgers and Hammerstein / Joseph Fields (Ross Hunter)

Romantic problems among the immigrants in San Francisco's Chinatown.
A Broadway musical which on the screen seems old-fashioned, remorselessly cute, and even insulting to the Chinese characters. Within its limits, however, it is well enough staged and performed.

w Joseph Fields *d* Henry Koster *m / ly* Richard Rodgers, Oscar Hammerstein II *md* Alfred Newman, Ken Darby *ph Russell Metty ad* Alexander Golitzen, Joseph Weight *costumes* Irene Sharaff *ch* Hermes Pan

Nancy Kwan, James Shigeta, Juanita Hall, Myoshi Umeki, James Soo, Sen Yung

AAN: Alfred Newman, Ken Darby; Russell Metty

Flowing Gold
US 1940 82m bw

A fugitive from justice finds himself in a western oilfield. Routine melodrama with climactic heroics and nothing to remember next day. John Garfield, Pat O'Brien, Frances Farmer, Raymond Walburn, Cliff Edwards. Written by Kenneth Gamet; directed by Alfred E. Green; for Warner.

Fluffy
US 1964 92m Eastmancolor
U-I / Scarus (Gordon Kay)

A biologist manages to tame a lion. Mindless, cheerful animal comedy.

w Samuel Rocca *d* Earl Bellamy *ph* Clifford Stine *m* Irving Gertz

Tony Randall, Shirley Jones, Edward Andrews, Ernest Truex, Howard Morris, Jim Backus, Frank Faylen

The Flute and the Arrow*
Sweden 1957 75m Technicolor Agascope
Sandrews (Arne Sucksdorff)
original title: *En Djungelsaga*

The story of a remote Indian tribe and a prowling leopard thought to be possessed by a demon.
Superbly photographed but rather dull: Sucksdorff failed to provide enough story for a feature.

wd, ph Arne Sucksdorff *m* Ravi Shankar

'Once it was human . . . even as you and I . . . this monster created by atoms gone wild!'

The Fly
US 1958 94m Eastmancolor Cinemascope
TCF (Kurt Neumann)

A scientist invents a method of transmitting and reassembling atoms. He transmits himself and does not notice a fly in the compartment . . .
Unpleasant horror film which becomes ludicrous but not funny.

w James Clavell *d* Kurt Neumann *ph* Karl Struss *m* Paul Sawtell

David Hedison, Patricia Owens, Herbert Marshall, Vincent Price

† Sequels were *Return of the Fly* (1959) and *Curse of the Fly* (1965), neither worth noting in detail.

The Fly*
US 1986 100m colour
TCF / Brooksfilm (Stuart Cornfeld)

A deliberately gruesome update of the above, with much unpleasant detail carried along by a certain style.

w Charles Edward Pogue, David Cronenberg *d* David Cronenberg *ph* Mark Irwin *m* Howard Shore *pd* Carol Spier *ed* Ronald Sanders

Jeff Goldblum, Geena Davis, John Getz

'One does not have to be totally warped to appreciate this film, but it does take a particular sensibility to embrace it.'—*Variety*

'Stylish acrobatics, cowgum gore.'—*Sight and Sound*

AA: make-up (Chris Wales, Stephen Dupuis)

'Action that makes every pulse beat sound like thunder!'

Fly By Night*
US 1942 74m bw

A doctor, accused of murdering a scientist, goes on the run and uncovers a Nazi spy ring. Hoary *39 Steps* imitation, commendably done on a low budget to furnish wartime propaganda. Richard Carlson, Nancy Kelly, Albert Basserman, Walter Kingsford, Martin Kosleek, Miles Mander. Written by Jay Dratler and F. Hugh Herbert; directed by Robert Siodmak; for Paramount. (GB title: *Secrets of G32*.)

The Flying Deuces*
US 1939 67m bw
Boris Morros

Laurel and Hardy join the Foreign Legion. Patchy comedy from the end of the comedians' period of glory, and showing signs of decline.

w Ralph Spence, Harry Langdon, Charles Rogers, Alfred Schiller *d* Edward Sutherland *ph* Art Lloyd, Elmer Dyer *m* Leo Shuken

Stan Laurel, Oliver Hardy, Jean Parker, James Finlayson, Reginald Gardiner, Charles Middleton

'Mechanical stuff . . . seemed like *Beau Hunks* and *Bonnie Scotland* all over again.'—*William K. Everson*

Flying Devils
US 1933 62m bw

Three war veteran pilots join a flying circus. Smart little programmer which certainly provided money's worth and has no axe to grind. Arline Judge, Bruce Cabot, Ralph Bellamy, Eric Linden, Cliff Edwards. Written by Byron Morgan, Louis Stevens; directed by Russell Birdwell; photographed by Nicholas Musuraca; music by Max Steiner; for RKO. (GB title: *The Flying Circus*.)

Flying Disc Men from Mars
US 1951 bw serial: 12 eps

A young aviator uncovers a plot by Martians to take over Earth. The title sets the level of this silly serial. Walter Reed, Lois Collier, Gregory Gay, James Craven, Harry Lauter. Directed by Fred C. Brannon; for Republic.

Flying Down to Rio**
US 1933 89m bw
RKO (Merian C. Cooper, Lou Brock)

A dance band is a big success in Rio de Janeiro.
A thin musical electrified by the finale in which girls dance on the wings of moving airplanes, and by the teaming of Astaire and Rogers for the first time. Now an irresistible period piece.

w Cyril Hume, H. W. Hannemann, Erwin Gelsey, *play* Anne Caldwell *d* Thornton Freeland *ph* J. Roy Hunt *m* Vincent Youmans *ly* Edward Eliscu, Gus Kahn *ch Dave Gould*

Dolores del Rio, Gene Raymond, Raul Roulien, *Ginger Rogers*, *Fred Astaire*, Blanche Frederici, Walter Walker, Franklin Pangborn, Eric Blore

'Its main point is the screen promise of Fred Astaire . . . the others are all hoofers after him.'—*Variety*

Other songs: 'Music Makes Me'; 'Orchids in the Moonlight'; 'Flying Down to Rio'

AAN: song 'The Carioca'

Flying Elephants
US 1927 20m bw silent

A caveman has the toothache. Fragmentary and generally unsatisfactory comedy starring Laurel and Hardy before they properly teamed, but released after their joint success. Written by Hal Roach and H. M. Walker; directed by Fred Butler and Hal Roach; for Hal Roach.

The Flying Fontaines
US 1959 73m Eastmancolor

Jealousy on the big top trapeze. Old hat circus melodrama, not especially well presented. Michael Callan, Evy Norlund, Joan Evans, Rian Garrick, Joe DeSantis. Written by Donn Mullally and Lee Ewin; directed by George Sherman; for Columbia.

Flying Fortress
GB 1942 110m bw
Warner (Max Milder)

A Canadian becomes a hero of bombing missions over Berlin.
Cardboard propaganda with silly love interest and a hilarious climax in which the hero does his stuff on the wing of a flying plane.

w Brock Williams, Gordon Wellesley, Edward Dryhurst *d* Walter Forde *ph* Gus Drisse, Basil Emmott

Richard Greene, Carla Lehmann, Betty Stockfield, Donald Stewart, Charles Heslop, Sidney King, Basil Radford, John Stuart

Flying G-Men
US 1939 bw serial: 15 eps

Enemy spies strike at the nation's defences—until four stalwart G-men are assigned. Lively nonsense with fast-moving thrill sequences. Robert Paige (alias The Black Falcon), Robert Fiske, James Craig, Lorna Gray. Directed by Ray Taylor and James W. Horne; for Columbia.

Flying High
US 1931 80m bw

A zany inventor breaks a long-distance flight record because he doesn't know how to land. Primitive comedy musical with inept dialogue and a static camera, partially salvaged by two early Busby Berkeley routines. Bert Lahr, Charlotte Greenwood, Pat O'Brien, Charles Winninger, Guy Kibbee, Hedda Hopper. Written by Robert Hopkins, A. P. Younger and Charles Riesner; directed by Charles Riesner; for MGM. (GB title: *Happy Landing*.)

Flying Leathernecks
US 1951 102m Technicolor
RKO (Edmund Grainger)

Two marine officers fight the Japs and each other on Guadalcanal.
Empty, violent war actioner full of phoney heroics.

w James Edward Grant *d* Nicholas Ray *ph* William E. Snyder *m* Roy Webb

John Wayne, Robert Ryan, Janis Carter, Don Taylor, Jay C. Flippen, William Harrigan, James Bell

'Ray's treatment is depressingly second rate and does nothing to alleviate the unpleasant impression of this disturbingly violent production.'—*Penelope Houston*

The Flying Missile
US 1950 92m bw
Columbia (Jerry Bresler)

A submarine commander defies authority to prove that rockets can be launched from the deck of a submarine.
Dated semi-documentary melodrama which was pretty flat on first viewing.

w Richard English, James Gunn *d* Henry Levin *ph* William Snyder *m* George Duning

Glenn Ford, Viveca Lindfors, Henry O'Neill, Carl Benton Reid, Joe Sawyer, John Qualen

The Flying Scotsman
GB 1929 63m bw

An ex-employee tries to wreck a crack train. Fairly presentable example of an early talkie film originally shot silent; one or two climactic thrills. Moore Marriott, Pauline Jameson, Ray Milland, Dino Galvani. Written by Victor Kendal and Garnett Weston; directed by Castleton Knight; for BIP.

The Flying Serpent
US 1945 59m bw

A crazed archaeologist uses a rare bird as a murder instrument. Ineffective low-key horror despite an always interesting star. George Zucco, Ralph Lewis, Hope Kramer, Eddie Acuff. Written by John T. Neville; directed by Sherman Scott; for Sigmund Neufeld / PRC.

'A bomber squadron wouldn't get through . . . but one ship might make it!'

Flying Tigers
US 1942 100m bw
Republic (Edmund Grainger)

American airmen fight the Japs over World War II China.
More mock heroics with noisy but unconvincing action sequences.

w Kenneth Gamet, Barry Trivers *d* David Miller *ph* Jack Marta *m* Victor Young

John Wayne, John Carroll, Anna Lee, Paul Kelly, Mae Clarke

AAN: Victor Young

FM (aka *Citizens' Band)*
US 1978 104m Technicolor

Problems of a commercial radio station whose disc jockeys seek integrity above commerce. Footling cause-pleading is all this 'with-it' movie has to offier apart from its picture of commercial radio in the late seventies, which should be of interest to social historians. Michael Brandon, Eileen Brennan, Alex Karras, Cleavon Little, Martin Mull. Written by Ezra Sacks; directed by John A. Alonzo; for Universal.

Fog
US 1933 70m bw

Three murders occur on an ocean liner enveloped in fog. Promising but increasingly inept mystery with an unconvincing solution. Donald Cook, Mary Brian, Reginald Denny, Robert McQuade, Maude Eburne. Written by Ethel Hill and Dore Schary from a magazine story by Valentine Williams and Dorothy Rice Sims; directed by Albert Rogell; for Columbia. 'Ably directed but deficient on casting and story.'—*Variety*

The Fog*
US 1979 91m Metrocolor Panavision
Avco / Debra Hill

A small Californian town is invaded by the leprous ghosts of mariners wrecked on the coast a hundred years before.

Silly but beguiling horror film with shock effects typical of its director.

w John Carpenter, Debra Hill *d* John Carpenter *ph* Dean Cundey *m* John Carpenter *pd* Tommy Lee Wallace

Adrienne Barbeau, Hal Holbrook, John Houseman, Janet Leigh, Jamie Lee Curtis, Tom Atkins

'An uneasy venture down a blind alley.'—*Tom Milne, MFB*

Fog Island
US 1945 70m bw

A wealthy ex-convict gathers on a foggy island all the people he considers responsible for his downfall. Very tolerable minor mystery lifted without permission from Agatha Christie's *And Then There Were None*. George Zucco, Lionel Atwill, Jerome Cowan, Sharon Douglas, Veda Ann Borg, Ian Keith. Written by Pierre Gendron; directed by Terry Morse; for Leon Fromkess / PRC.

Fog over Frisco***
US 1934 68m bw
Warner (Henry Blanke)

A San Francisco heiress gets herself murdered. Silly whodunnit highly notable for its cinematic style, all dissolves, wipes and quick takes. Probably the fastest moving film ever made, and very entertaining despite its plot inadequacy.

w Robert N. Lee, *novel* George Dyer *d William Dieterle* *ph* Tony Gaudio *md* Leo F. Forbstein *ed Harold McLernon*

Bette Davis, Donald Woods, Margaret Lindsay, Lyle Talbot, Hugh Herbert, Arthur Byron, Robert Barrat, Douglass Dumbrille, Henry O'Neill, Irving Pichel, Alan Hale

'Another racketeering story, mild in entertainment. No marked names of strength.'—*Variety*

'It reveals those qualities of pace and velocity and sharpness which make the Hollywood product acceptable even when the shallow content of ideas makes you want to scream.'—*Robert Forsythe*

'Its speed is artificially created by pacing, wipes, opticals, overlapping sound, camera movement and placing of characters, and by its habit of never having time really to begin or end scenes.'—*William K. Everson*

† Remade 1942 as *Spy Ship*, a second feature.

Folies Bergère***
US 1935 84m bw
Twentieth Century (William Goetz, Raymond Griffith)
GB title: *The Man from the Folies Bergère*

A Parisian banker persuades a music hall artist to impersonate him, but the wife and girl friend become involved in the confusion. Amusing star vehicle with inventive Berkeleyish numbers and some remarkably sexy dialogue.

w Bess Meredyth, Hal Long, *play* The Red Cat by Rudolph Lothar, Hans Adler *d* Roy del Ruth *ph* Barney McGill, Peverell Marley *md* Alfred Newman *ch Dave Gould*

Maurice Chevalier, Merle Oberon, Ann Sothern, Eric Blore

† Remade as *That Night in Rio*, with Don Ameche, and *On the Riviera*, with Danny Kaye (both qv).

Follies Girl
US 1943 71m bw

An Army private visits the forces canteen but falls for the burlesque dancer next door. Feebly developed romance with music, mostly notable for its specialities. Wendy Barrie, Doris Nolan, Gordon Oliver, Anne Barrett, Cora Witherspoon. Written by Marcy Klauber and Charles Robinson; directed and produced by William Rowland; for PRC.

Follow a Star
GB 1959 104m bw
Rank (Hugh Stewart)

A shy amateur singer allows a fading star to mime to his voice.
Star comedy with an antique plot and a superfluity of pathos.

w Jack Davies, Henry Blyth, Norman Wisdom *d* Robert Asher *ph* Jack Asher *m* Philip Green

Norman Wisdom, Jerry Desmonde, June Laverick, Hattie Jacques, Richard Wattis, John Le Mesurier, Fenella Fielding, Ron Moody

'Such comedy as there is is mostly muffed by the lack of any sense of comic timing.'—*MFB*

Follow Me
GB 1971 93m Technicolor Panavision
Universal / Hal B. Wallis (Paul Nathan)
US title: *The Public Eye*

An eccentric private eye is hired to follow an accountant's wife, and she finds him fascinating.
Dullish, whimsical rendering of a dullish, whimsical one-act play; it never springs to life or interest.

w Peter Shaffer, from his play *d* Carol Reed *ph* Christopher Challis *m* John Barry

Topol, Michael Jayston, Mia Farrow

'An uneasy mixture of broad comedy and high romance.'—*Sight and Sound*

Follow Me Boys
US 1966 132m Technicolor
Walt Disney (Winston Hibler)

The domestic trials and tribulations of a small-town schoolmaster.
Sentimental family saga full of patriotic fervour.

w Louis Pelletier, *novel* God and My Country by Mackinlay Kantor *d* Norman Tokar *ph* Clifford Stine *m* George Bruns

Fred MacMurray, Vera Miles, Lillian Gish, Charlie Ruggles, Elliott Reid, Kurt Russell, Luana Patten, Ken Murray

'Demands an extremely strong stomach.'—*MFB*

Follow Me Quietly*
US 1949 60m bw

Police track down a killer who strangles whenever it rains. Effective little urban thriller with nice sense of detail. William Lundigan, Dorothy Patrick, Jeff Corey, Nestor Paiva, Charles D. Brown, Paul Guilfoyle. Written by Lillie Hayward; directed by Richard Fleischer; for Herman Schlom / RKO.

Follow That Camel
GB 1967 95m Eastmancolor

An English gentleman is accused of fraud and joins the Foreign Legion. A Carry On in all but name, and not the best of them despite an American co-star and better-than-average production values. Phil Silvers, Jim Dale, Charles Hawtrey, Kenneth Williams, Anita Harris, Joan Sims, Bernard Bresslaw. Written by Talbot Rothwell; directed by Gerald Thomas; for Peter Rogers / Rank. (Reissue title: *Carry On, Follow That Camel*.)

Follow That Dream
US 1962 110m De Luxe Panavision
UA / Mirisch (David Weisbart)

A wandering family sets up house on a Florida beach.
Tiresomely cute comedy vehicle for a resistible star.

w Charles Lederer, *novel* Pioneer Go Home by Richard Powell *d* Gordon Douglas *ph* Leo Tover *m* Hans Salter

Elvis Presley, Arthur O'Connell, Joanna Moore, Anne Helm, Jack Kruschen

Follow the Band
US 1943 60m bw

A farm worker on his first visit to New York becomes a trombonist in a night club. Minor musical filler which packs in a surprising range of talent. Eddie Quillan, Leon Errol, Mary Beth Hughes, Samuel S. Hinds, Robert Mitchum, Frances Langford, Leo Carrillo, Hilo Hattie, the King Sisters, Skinnay Ennis and his band. Written by Warren Wilson and Dorothy Bennett; directed by Jean Yarbrough; for Paul Malvern / Universal.

Follow the Boys*
US 1944 109m bw
Universal (Charles K. Feldman)

A song and dance man organizes entertainment for the US troops during World War II.
Scrappy, unattractive propaganda tribute by the stars to the stars, enlivened only by a few guest spots.

w Lou Breslow, Gertrude Purcell *d* A. Edward Sutherland *ph* David Abel *m* Leigh Harline and others

George Raft, Vera Zorina, Charley Grapewin, Grace MacDonald, Charles Butterworth, George Macready, Elizabeth Patterson; and Orson Welles, Marlene Dietrich, Jeanette MacDonald, Dinah Shore, Donald O'Connor, Peggy Ryan, W. C. Fields, the Andrews Sisters, Artur Rubenstein, Sophie Tucker, Ted Lewis and his band, etc

AAN: song 'I'll Walk Alone' (*m* Jule Styne, *ly* Sammy Cahn)

Follow the Boys
US 1963 95m Metrocolor Panavision
MGM / Franmet (Laurence P. Bachmann)

An American warship is diverted from Cannes to Santa Margarita, and the waiting wives have to follow by road.
Harmless star comedy musical.

w David T. Chantler, David Osborn
d Richard Thorpe *ph* Ted Scaife

Connie Francis, Paula Prentiss, Dany Robin, Russ Tamblyn, Richard Long

Follow the Fleet**
US 1936 110m bw
RKO (Pandro S. Berman)

Sailors on shore leave romance a couple of girl singers.
Amiable star musical which makes heavy weather of a listless and overlong script, but has good numbers for those who can wait.

w Dwight Taylor, *play* Shore Leave by Hubert Osborne, Allan Scott *d* Mark Sandrich
ph David Abel *m/ly Irving Berlin md* Max Steiner

Fred Astaire, Ginger Rogers, Randolph Scott, Harriet Hilliard, Astrid Allwyn, Harry Beresford, Lucille Ball, Betty Grable, Tony Martin

Songs: 'I'm Putting All My Eggs in One Basket'; 'We Saw the Sea'; 'Let's Face the Music and Dance'; 'Let Yourself Go'; 'But Where Are You?'; 'I'd Rather Lead a Band'; 'Get Thee Behind Me Satan'

'The running time is way overboard . . . dialogue is good and can be depended on for laughs, with the Astaire-Rogers dancing sure to do the rest. But cutting it would have helped a lot more.'—*Variety*

Follow the Leader
US 1930 76m bw

A saucy understudy replaces a kidnapped leading lady. Broadway spoof rather tediously designed as a vehicle for the star's face-pulling. Ed Wynn, Ginger Rogers, Ethel Merman, Lou Holtz, Stanley Smith. Written by Sid Silvers and Gertrude Purcell from the Broadway musical Manhattan Mary; directed by Norman Taurog; for Paramount. 'First-run material and above average.'—*Variety*

Follow the Sun
US 1951 93m bw
TCF (Samuel G. Engel)

Ben Hogan, a professional golfer, recovers slowly and painfully from a car crash and for the first time gains the affection of the crowd.
Modest sporting biopic, generally watchable but rising to no great heights.

w Frederick Hazlitt Brennan *d* Sidney Lanfield *ph* Leo Tover *m* Cyril Mockridge

Glenn Ford, Anne Baxter, Dennis O'Keefe, June Havoc, Larry Keating, Nana Bryant, Roland Winters

Follow Thru
US 1930 93m Technicolor

Two women are after the same pro golfer. Flat film version of a Broadway show. Charles Rogers, Nancy Carroll, Zelma O'Neal, Jack Haley, Eugene Pallette, Thelma Todd. Written from their show by De Sylva, Brown and Henderson; directed by Laurence Schwab and Lloyd Corrigan; for Paramount. 'Paramount has tossed away a heavy money picture.'—*Variety*

Songs: 'Button Up Your Overcoat'; 'You Wouldn't Fool Me Would You'; 'I'm Hard to Please'; 'A Peach of a Pair'; 'It Must be You'.

Folly to be Wise*
GB 1952 91m bw
London Films / Launder and Gilliat

A brains trust at an army unit starts off a battle of the sexes.
Typical James Bridie comedy which starts brightly and whimsically, then peters out and is saved by the acting.

w Frank Launder, John Dighton, *play* It Depends What You Mean by James Bridie
d Frank Launder *ph* Jack Hildyard
m Temple Abady

Alastair Sim, Roland Culver, Elizabeth Allan, Martita Hunt, Colin Gordon

'It seems to get funnier the longer it's spun out.'—*Pauline Kael, 70s*

The Food of the Gods
US 1976 88m Movielab
AIP (Bert I. Gordon)

A curious substance which oozes out of the ground turns common beasts into monsters.
Rather crude horror movie which has little affinity with its literary original.

wd Bert I. Gordon, *story* H. G. Wells
ph Reginald Morris *m* Elliot Kaplan

Marjoe Gortner, Pamela Franklin, Ida Lupino, Ralph Meeker, John McLiam

'Not only sick, but sickening.'—*Arthur Knight*

'I wish I hadn't seen the movie, so I could avoid it like the plague.'—*John Simon*

'More plot holes than any movie in recent memory, and enough dopey lines to make a Saturday night audience howl in all the wrong places.'—*David Sterritt, Christian Science Monitor*

Fool for Love
US 1985 106m Rank Colour Panavision

A wandering cowboy returns hopefully to his old love-hate relationship with May, who runs a broken-down motel. Boring desert drama with unattractive and uninteresting characters who yell at each other all the time. Sam Shepard, Kim Basinger, Harry Dean Stanton, Randy Quaid. Written by Sam Shepard, from his play; directed by Robert Altman; for Canon.

The Fool Killer
US 1965 100m bw

An orphan suspects his friend is an axe murderer. Post-Civil War fable with good performances but not much point. Anthony Perkins, Edward Albert, Dana Elcar, Henry Hull, Salome Jens. Written by David Friedkin and Morton Fine from the novel by Helen Eustis; directed by Servando Gonzalez; for Landau/AA.

A Fool There Was*
US 1914 67m (24 fps) bw silent
William Fox

A financier in Europe forsakes all for a *femme fatale*, and dies in her arms.
Antediluvian moral melodrama which made a star of Bara and added the word 'vamp' to the language.

wd Frank Powell, play Porter Emerson Browne suggested by Rudyard Kipling's poem *The Vampire*

Theda Bara, Edward Jose, Mabel Frenyer, May Allison

Foolin' Around
US 1979 101m De Luxe
Columbia / Arnold Kopelson

A country bumpkin wins a runaway heiress.
Uneasy harkback to the innocence of *It Happened One Night*, with willing performers in search of a script and setting.

w Mike Kane, David Swift *d* Richard T. Heffron *ph* Philip Lathrop *m* Charles Bernstein

Gary Busey, Annette O'Toole, John Calvin, Eddie Albert, Cloris Leachman, Tony Randall

Foolish Wives**
US 1921 85m approx (24 fps); originally much longer bw silent
Universal

In Monte Carlo, a fake count seduces and blackmails rich women.
Weird melodrama with memorable moments and a vast set; Stroheim's most vivid star performance and one of his most lavish productions.

wd Erich Von Stroheim ph Ben Reynolds, William Daniels *ad Erich Von Stroheim, Richard Day*

Erich Von Stroheim, Mae Busch, Maud George, Cesare Gravina

'A very superior piece of photoplay craftsmanship, original in ideas and treatment and deserving of higher rating than *Orphans of the Storm*, *Loves of Pharaoh*, *The Storm* and other second-class material which however brought forth applause and bravos from screen public and scribes.'—*Tamar Lane, What's Wrong with the Movies*

† The film was released in Latin America at a length of 6hrs 48m.

Fools
US 1970 93m Eastmancolor

An unsuccessful actor has an idyllic love affair with a girl he meets in a park; but her jealous millionaire husband shoots her dead. Foolish is the word for those who concocted this tedious parable about the innocence of love and the sickness of society. Jason Robards Jnr, Katharine Ross, Scott Hylands. Written by Robert Rudelson; directed by Tom Gries; for Translor.

Fools for Scandal*
US 1938 81m bw
Warner (Mervyn Le Roy)

A Hollywood movie star falls in love with a French nobleman.
Disappointingly leaden romantic comedy.

w Herbert and Joseph Fields, *play* Return Engagement by Nancy Hamilton, Rosemary Casey, James Shute *d* Mervyn Le Roy *ph* Ted Tetzlaff *m* Richard Rodgers, Lorenz Hart

Carole Lombard, Fernand Gravet, Ralph Bellamy, Allen Jenkins, Isabel Jeans, Marie Wilson, Ottola Nesmith

'Many diverting moments . . . will do average business.'—*Variety*

Fools Parade**
US 1971 98m Eastmancolor
Columbia / Stanmore / Penbar (Andrew V. McLaglen)
GB title: *Dynamite Man from Glory Jail*

An ex-con has trouble cashing a cheque for his prison savings, especially as outlaws are after it.
Curious admixture of comedy, adventure and violence with a thirties setting, from the author of *Night of the Hunter*; generally gripping entertainment.

w James Lee Barrett, novel Davis Grubb d Andrew V. McLaglen *ph* Harry Stradling Jnr *m* Henry Vars

James Stewart, George Kennedy, Strother Martin, Anne Baxter, Kurt Russell, William Windom, Mike Kellin

'A quintessentially American tribute to the quiet heroism of the self-made man.'—*Nigel Andrews*

Fools Rush In
GB 1949 82m bw
Pinewood

A girl changes her mind on her wedding day, and causes repercussions through the family.
Thin, flat film version of a successful play.
Sally Ann Howes, Guy Rolfe, Nora Swinburne, Nigel Buchanan, Raymond Lovell, Thora Hird. Written by Geoffrey Kerr, from the play by Kenneth Horne; directed by John Paddy Carstairs; for Rank.

'Can you even think of missing it?'

Footlight Parade***
US 1933 104m bw
Warner (Robert Lord)

A determined producer of cine-variety numbers gets the show going despite great difficulty.
Classic putting-on-a-show musical distinguished by rapid-fire dialogue, New York setting, star performances and some of the best Busby Berkeley numbers.

w Manuel Seff, James Seymour *d Lloyd Bacon ch Busby Berkeley ph* George Barnes *ad Anton Grot, Jack Okey m / ly* Harry Warren, Al Dubin, Sammy Fain, Irving Fahal

James Cagney, Joan Blondell, Ruby Keeler, Dick Powell, Frank McHugh, Guy Kibbee, Ruth Donnelly, Hugh Herbert, Claire Dodd, Herman Bing

Songs: 'By a Waterfall'; 'Ah, the Moon Is Here'; 'Sitting on a Backyard Fence'; 'Shanghai Lil'; 'Honeymoon Hotel'

'1,000 surprises! 300 beauties! 20 big stars!'—*publicity*

'Bevies of beauty and mere males disport themselves in a Honeymoon Hotel, by (and in) a Waterfall, and over several acres of Shanghai.'—*C. A. Lejeune*

† The Chester Kent studio was a take-off of Fanchon and Marco, who had just such a studio on Sunset Boulevard.

Footlight Serenade
US 1942 80m bw
TCF (William LeBaron)

A boxer romances a showgirl.
Indifferent star musical.

w Robert Ellis, Helen Logan, Lynn Starling *d* Gregory Ratoff *ph* Lee Garmes *md* Charles Henderson *songs* Ralph Rainger, Leo Robin

Betty Grable, John Payne, Victor Mature, James Gleason, Phil Silvers, Jane Wyman, Cobina Wright Jnr, June Lang, Mantan Moreland

Footloose
US 1984 107m Movielab
Paramount / Indieprod (Lewis J. Rachmil, Craig Zadan)

The domination of an old-fashioned local preacher is slackened by a young newcomer who insists on arranging a dance.
Odd fable which seeks to combine *Flashdance* with *Rebel without a Cause*, and misses out on both.

w Dean Pitchford *d* Herbert Ross *ph* Ric Waite *pd* Ron Hobbs *m* various

Kevin Bacon, Lori Singer, John Lithgow, Dianne Wiest, Christopher Penn

'The celebration of teenage frustration as dance reduces the issues to the level of platitude.'—*Donald Greig, MFB*

AAN: title song (*m* and *ly* Kenny Loggins, Dean Pitchford; song 'Let's Hear It for the Boy' (*m* and *ly* Dean Pitchford, Tom Snow)

Footsteps in the Dark
US 1941 96m bw
Warner (Robert Lord)

A would-be detective novelist on the lookout for story material finds himself solving a murder.
Lethargic modern vehicle for Flynn between his swashbucklers, a poor imitation of the *Thin Man* style.

w Lester Cole, John Wexley, *play* Blondie White by Ladislas Fodor *d* Lloyd Bacon *ph* Ernest Haller *m* Frederick Hollander

Errol Flynn, Brenda Marshall, Ralph Bellamy, Alan Hale, Lucile Watson, Allen Jenkins, Lee Patrick, William Frawley, Roscoe Karns, Grant Mitchell

'The footsteps were those of restless patrons on their way out to buy popcorn.'—*Clive Hirschhorn*

'When he comes to her room at midnight, is it to kiss or kill?'

Footsteps in the Fog*
GB 1955 90m Technicolor
Film Locations / Mike Frankovich (Maxwell Setton)

A Victorian murderer plans to eliminate a blackmailing maid.
This variation on *Gaslight* turns into a black comedy without laughs, but it has effective moments and is efficiently if charmlessly made.

w Dorothy Reid, Lenore Coffee, *story* The Interruption by W. W. Jacobs *d* Arthur Lubin *ph* Christopher Challis *m* Benjamin Frankel *ad* Wilfrid Shingleton

Stewart Granger, Jean Simmons, Bill Travers, Ronald Squire, Finlay Currie, Peter Bull

For a Few Dollars More
Italy / Spain / West Germany 1965 130m Techniscope
PEA / Gonzales / Constantin (Alberto Grimaldi)
Original title: *Per Qualche Dollari in Più*

Bounty hunters in El Paso agree to work together.
Vague, inflated, sometimes good-looking sequel to *A Fistful of Dollars*, with customary violence and predictably mean performances.

wd Sergio Leone *ph* Massimo Dallamano *m* Ennio Morricone

Clint Eastwood, Lee Van Cleef, Gian Maria Volonte, Klaus Kinski

For Better For Worse
GB 1954 84m Eastmancolor

Tribulations of a young married couple.
Undernourished comedy with an agreeable cast but no surprises. Dirk Bogarde, Susan Stephen, Cecil Parker, Dennis Price, Athene Seyler, Eileen Herlie, Thora Hird, James Hayter, Pia Terri, Sid James, Charles Victor. Written and directed by J. Lee-Thompson, from the play by Arthur Watkyn; for Kenneth Harper/Kenwood. (US title: *Cocktails in the Kitchen*).

For Freedom
GB 1940 88m bw
GFD / Gainsborough (Edward Black, Castleton Knight)

Events surrounding the Battle of the River Plate and the sinking of the Graf Spee.
Economical wartime potboiler with much use of newsreel.

w Miles Malleson, Leslie Arliss *d* Maurice Elvey, Castleton Knight *ph* Arthur Crabtree

Will Fyffe, Anthony Hulme, E. V. H. Emmett, Guy Middleton, Albert Lieven

For Heaven's Sake
US 1950 92m bw
TCF (William Perlberg)

Two angels are sent to earth to mend a Broadway producer's marriage.
Silly, flat whimsy of the *Here Comes Mr Jordan* school, and originating from the same author. Stale beer, but historically interesting.

w George Seaton, *play* Harry Segall *d* George Seaton *ph* Lloyd Ahern *m* Alfred Newman

Clifton Webb, Edmund Gwenn, Robert Cummings, Joan Bennett, Joan Blondell, Gigi Perreau, Jack La Rue

For Love of Ivy
US 1968 100m Perfectcolor
Cinerama / Palomar (Edgar J. Scherick, Jay Weston)

An invaluable coloured maid gives notice, and the family blackmails a likeable black ne'er-do-well to make love to her so that she will stay.
Unhappy whimsy with an extremely laboured script and no jokes, notable only as Hollywood's first bow towards a black love affair.

w Robert Alan Aurthur, *story* Sidney Poitier *d* Daniel Mann *ph* Joseph Coffey *m* Quincy Jones

Sidney Poitier, Abby Lincoln, Beau Bridges, Carroll O'Connor, Nan Martin, Lauri Peters

AAN: title song (*m* Quincy Jones, *ly* Bob Russell)

For Love or Money
US 1963 108m Technicolor
U-I (Robert Arthur)

A rich widow hires a lawyer to look after the affairs of her three wayward daughters; he picks the eldest for himself.
Slow, thin, overlong comedy with a surfeit of witless chat.

w Larry Marks, Michael Morris *d* Michael Gordon *ph* Clifford Stine *m* Frank de Vol

Kirk Douglas, Mitzi Gaynor, Thelma Ritter, William Bendix, Gig Young

For Me and My Gal***
US 1942 104m bw
MGM (Arthur Freed)

Just before World War I, a girl vaudevillian chooses between two partners.
A routine musical romance at the time of its production, this film now stands out because of its professional execution, its star value, and the fact that they don't make 'em like that any more.

w Richard Sherman, Sid Silvers, Fred Finkelhoffe *d Busby Berkeley ph William Daniels md* Georgie Stoll, Roger Edens

Judy Garland, Gene Kelly, George Murphy, Marta Eggerth, Ben Blue, Richard Quine, Stephen McNally

'A touch of imagination and a deal more than a touch of energy.'—*The Times*

AAN: Georgie Stoll, Roger Edens

For Men Only
US 1952 95m bw

A college professor is shocked when a death ensues from a freshman 'hazing' ceremony. Weird exploitation study of supposed college rites. Paul Henreid, Robert Sherman, Russell Johnson, Margaret Field, Vera Miles. Written by Lou Morheim and Herbert Margolies; directed and produced by Paul Henreid; for Lippert. 'Henreid allots himself an over-generous proportion of screen time—walking in and out of doors, smiling at the camera, being charming.'—*MFB*.

For Pete's Sake*
US 1974 90m Eastmancolor
Columbia / Rastar / Persky–Bright–Barclay (Martin Erlichmann, Stanley Shapiro)

A New York taxi driver's wife borrows money and finds herself heavily committed to work off the debt.
Involved farcical comedy with amusing passages.

w Stanley Shapiro, Martin Richlin *d* Peter Yates *ph* Laszlo Kovacs *m* Artie Butler

Barbra Streisand, Michael Sarrazin, Estelle Parsons, William Redfield, Molly Picon

'Revives memories of how much more inventively they used to do it thirty years ago.'—*Sight and Sound*

For Queen and Country*
GB/US 1988 106m Eastmancolor
Zenith / Atlantic (Working Title)

Black paratrooper returns home after demob to a run-down council estate, where he tangles with the police, racism and inner-city riots.
Well-intentioned topical tale, with solid social detail, undermined by casting an American star as a streetwise South Londoner.

w Martin Stellman, Trix Worrell *d* Martin Stellman *ph* Richard Greatrex *m* Michael Kamen *pd* Andrew McAlpine

Denzel Washington, Dorian Healey, Amanda Redman, Sean Chapman

For the Defense*
US 1930 62m bw

Exploits of a New York criminal lawyer. Slick programme picture of its day; it gave a lift to its star's career. William Powell, Kay Francis, Scott Kolk, Thomas E. Jackson, William H. Davidson. Written by Oliver H. P. Garrett (based on the career of William J. Fallon); directed by John Cromwell; for Paramount. 'Certain to hold its head up on grosses.'—*Variety*

For the First Time
US 1959 97m Technirama
MGM / Corona / Orion (Alexander Gruter)

A famous tenor slips off incognito to Capri and falls in love with a deaf girl.
Slipshod co-production (with West Germany) with a hoary sentimental plot, a fat star, and some agreeable picture postcard views.

w Andrew Solt *d* Rudolph Maté *ph* Aldo Tonti *md* Georgie Stoll

Mario Lanza, Johanna von Koczian, Kurt Kasznar, Zsa Zsa Gabor, Hans Sohnker

For the Love of Benji
US 1977 84m colour

A small dog gets lost in the Greek islands. Adequate follow-up to *Benji*; what more can one say? Patsy Garrett, Cynthia Smith, Peter Bowles, Ed Nelson. Written by Ben Vaughn and Joe Camp; directed by Joe Camp; for Mulberry Square.

For the Love of Mary
US 1948 90m bw
Universal (Robert Arthur)

A White House switchboard operator gets tangled up in politics when the president helps cure her hiccups.
Tedious comedy with music, a hasty vehicle for a star past her peak.

w Oscar Brodney *d* Frederick de Cordova *ph* William Daniels *m* Frank Skinner

Deanna Durbin, Edmond O'Brien, Harry Davenport, Don Taylor, Jeffrey Lynn, Ray Collins, Hugo Haas

'A warning to all interfering presidents.'—*MFB*

For the Love of Mike
US 1927 74m (24 fps) bw silent

Three bachelors adopt an abandoned baby boy, who nearly (but not quite) lets them down when he grows up. Sentimental comedy most notable now as the leading lady's first movie. Claudette Colbert, Ben Lyon, George Sidney, Ford Sterling, Hugh Cameron, Skeets Gallagher. Written by Leland Hayward and J. Clarkson Miller, from the story 'Hell's Kitchen' by John Moroso; directed by Frank Capra; photographed by Ernest Haller; for First National.

For the Love of Mike*
US 1960 84m De Luxe Cinemascope
TCF / Shergari (George Sherman)
GB title: *None But the Brave*

An Indian boy in New Mexico is helped by a priest to care for sick animals.
Sentimental outdoor film for young people with a pleasantly light touch.

w D. D. Beauchamp *d* George Sherman *ph* Alex Phillips *m* Raul La Vista

Richard Basehart, Stuart Erwin, Arthur Shields, Armando Silvestre

For Them That Trespass
GB 1948 93m bw
ABP (Victor Skutezky)

A man proves himself innocent of the crime for which he has served fifteen years in prison.
Tedious melodrama which served to introduce Richard Todd to the screen.

w J. Lee-Thompson *d* Alberto Cavalcanti *ph* Derick Williams *m* Philip Green

Richard Todd, Stephen Murray, Joan Dowling, Patricia Plunkett, Michael Laurence, Rosalyn Boulter

For Those in Peril
GB 1943 67m bw

Exploits of the air / sea rescue service. Standard semi-documentary morale-raiser. David Farrar, Ralph Michael, Robert Wyndham, John Slater. Written by Harry Watt, J. O. C. Orton and T. E. B. Clarke; directed by Charles Crichton; for Ealing.

For Those Who Think Young
US 1964 96m Techniscope
UA / Aubrey Schenck-Howard W. Koch (Hugh Benson)

College students save their favourite club from closure.

FOR PETE'S SAKE. Barbra Streisand is unmistakable, despite the dark glasses and blond wig.

Tedious beach party frolic, very typical of its day, with some odd cameo appearances.

w James and George O'Hanlon, Dan Beaumont *d* Leslie H. Martinson *ph* Harold E. Stine *m* Jerry Fielding

James Darren, Pamela Tiffin, Woody Woodbury, Nancy Sinatra, Tina Louise, Paul Lynde, Bob Denver, Jack La Rue, George Raft, Allen Jenkins, Robert Armstrong, Roger Smith

For Valour*
GB 1937 95m bw
GFD / Capitol (Max Schach)

Adventures in two wars of a major, his shady friend, and their sons.
Agreeable adult farce with the stars each playing father and son.

w Ben Travers *d* Tom Walls *ph* Phil Tanner *md* Van Phillips

Tom Walls, Ralph Lynn, Veronica Rose, Joan Marion, Hubert Harben

'A very pleasant antidote to the Coronation, though a little marred by its inability to remain wholly flippant.'—*Graham Greene*

'168 minutes of breathless thrills and romance!'

For Whom the Bell Tolls**
US 1943 168m Technicolor
Paramount (Sam Wood)

An American joins partisan fighters in the Spanish Civil War and falls in love with a refugee girl before going on a suicide mission.
Portentous, solemn adventure story based on a modern classic but without much cinematic impetus despite careful handling and useful performances. It looks expensive, though.

w Dudley Nichols, *novel* Ernest Hemingway *d* Sam Wood *ph* Ray Rennahan *m* Victor Young *pd* William Cameron Menzies

Gary Cooper, Ingrid Bergman, Akim Tamiroff, Arturo de Cordova, *Katina Paxinou*, Vladimir Sokoloff, Mikhail Rasumny, Victor Varconi, Joseph Calleia, Alexander Granach

MARIA (Ingrid Bergman): 'I do not know how to kiss, or I would kiss you. Where do the noses go?'

'Everybody must have thought they were making a classic . . . but what with the typical Hollywood compromises, plus the political pressures from Spain and from Catholics—or the fears of such pressures—the whole thing became amorphous and confused.'—*Pauline Kael, 70s*

'The rhythm of this film is the most defective I have ever seen in a super-production . . . colour is very nice for costume pieces and musical comedies, and has a great aesthetic future in films, but it still gets fatally in the way of any serious imitation of reality.'—*James Agee*

AA: Katina Paxinou
AAN: best picture; Ray Rennahan; Victor Young; Gary Cooper; Ingrid Bergman; Akim Tamiroff

For You Alone
GB 1944 98m bw

Romance of a naval officer and a vicar's daughter. Sentimental drama with music; you can smell the lavender a mile off, but it was probably the most ambitious production of this indefatigable Poverty Row production company. Lesley Brook, Jimmy Hanley, Dinah Sheridan, G. H. Mulcaster, Manning Whiley. Written by Montgomery Tully; directed by Geoffrey Faithfull; for Butcher's.

For Your Eyes Only*
GB 1981 127m Technicolor Panavision
UA / Eon (Albert R. Broccoli)

James Bond traces a top secret device sunk in a surveillance vehicle off the Greek coast. Lively set pieces can't quite redeem this wholly uninventive addition to the Bond canon. Fun while it's on, but next morning there's nothing left to remember.

w Richard Maibaum, Michael G. Wilson *d* John Glen *ph* Alan Hume *m* Bill Conti *pd* Peter Lamont

Roger Moore, Carole Bouquet, Topol, Lynn-Holly Johnson, Julian Glover, Jill Bennett, Jack Hedley, Lois Maxwell, Desmond Llewellyn, Geoffrey Keen

'Roger Moore fronts for a succession of stunt men with all the relaxed, lifelike charm of a foyer poster of himself.'—*Sunday Times*

'Pretty boring between the stunts, as if the director isn't interested in actors, and Broccoli forgot to commission a screenplay.'—*Guardian*

† The first Bond in which original author Ian Fleming doesn't even rate a credit.
AAN: title song (*m* Bill Conti, *ly* Mick Leeson)

Forbidden
US 1931 83m bw

Our heroine loves the DA, but to save his marriage she marries someone else. Turgid renunciation drama with some interest added by stars and director. Barbara Stanwyck, Adolphe Menjou, Ralph Bellamy. Written by Frank Capra and Jo Swerling; directed by Frank Capra; for Columbia. 'A cry picture for the girls, and on that presumption stands a good chance of going out and getting itself and the theatre some coin.'—*Variety*

Forbidden
GB 1949 87m bw

A man in love with another woman tries to poison his extravagant wife. Turgid melodrama with funfair background. Douglass Montgomery, Hazel Court, Patricia Burke, Garry Marsh, Ronald Shiner, Kenneth Griffith. Written by Katherine Strueby; directed by George King; for Pennant / British Lion.

Forbidden
US 1953 85m bw

A detective falls in love with the woman a mobster has hired him to find. Would-be intense *film noir*; talent does not enable it to register. Tony Curtis, Joanne Dru, Lyle Bettger, Marvin Miller, Sen Yung. Written by William Sackheim and Gil Doud; directed by Rudolph Maté; for Universal-International.

Forbidden Cargo
GB 1954 85m bw
Rank / London Independent Productions (Sydney Box)

A customs investigator prevents a large consignment of drugs from reaching its English outlets.
Routine British thick ear.

w Sydney Box *d* Harold French *ph* C. Pennington-Richards *m* Lambert Williamson

Nigel Patrick, Elizabeth Sellars, Terence Morgan, Jack Warner

Forbidden Fruit*
France 1952 103m bw
Gray Film
original title: *Le Fruit Défendu*

A widowered doctor marries again, then falls for a prostitute.
One of the rather solemn romantic melodramas in which the star insisted from time to time in becoming involved.

w Jacques Companeez, Henri Verneuil, Jean Manse, *novel* Lettre à Mon Juge by Georges Simenon *d* Henri Verneuil *ph* Henri Alekan *m* Paul Durand

Fernandel, Claude Nollier, Françoise Arnoul, Sylvie

Forbidden Games: see Jeux Interdits

Forbidden Paradise
US 1924 60m (24 fps) bw silent
Paramount

The amorous intrigues of Catherine the Great of Russia.
Seldom seen these days, this was judged at the time a scintillating satire, with its sly innuendo and modern references such as motor cars and bobbed hair. Remade, more or less, as *Czarina.*

w Hans Kraly, Agnes Christine Johnson, *play* The Czarina by Melchior Lengyel, Lajos Biro *d Ernst Lubitsch* *ph* Charles Van Enger *ad* Hans Dreier

Pola Negri, Adolphe Menjou, Rod La Rocque, Pauline Starke, Fred Malatesta

'Lubitsch's most brilliant film'—*Paul Rotha, 1949*

'More than a year in production!'
Forbidden Planet**
US 1956 98m Eastmancolor Cinemascope
MGM (Nicholas Nayfack)

In AD 2200 a space cruiser visits the planet Altair Four to discover the fate of a previous mission.
Intriguing sci-fi with a plot derived from *The Tempest* and a Prospero who unwittingly creates monsters from his own id. High spirits and suspense sequences partially cancelled out by wooden playing from the younger actors and some leaden dialogue.

w Cyril Hume *d Fred M. Wilcox* *ph* George Folsey *m* Louis and Bebe Barron *ad* Cedric Gibbons, Arthur Lonergan

Walter Pidgeon, Anne Francis, Leslie Nielsen, Warren Stevens, Jack Kelly, Richard Anderson, Earl Holliman

'It's a pity they didn't lift some of Shakespeare's language.'—*New Yorker, 1977*

The Forbin Project**
US 1969 100m Technicolor Panavision
Universal (Stanley Chase)
GB title: *Colossus, The Forbin Project*

An enormous computer takes over the defence of the western world; but it goes into collaboration with the Russian one.
Good-looking sci-fi for intellectual addicts.

w James Bridges, *novel* Colossus by D. F. Jones *d* Joseph Sargent *ph* Gene Polito *m* Michel Columbier

Eric Braeden, Gordon Pinsent, Susan Clark, William Schallert

Force of Arms*
US 1951 100m bw
Warner (Anthony Veiller)

A soldier in the Italian campaign falls in love with his nurse.
Routine variation on *A Farewell to Arms*, adequately but unexcitingly mounted.

w Orin Jannings, *story* Richard Tregaskis *d* Michael Curtiz *ph* Ted McCord *m* Max Steiner

William Holden, Nancy Olson, Frank Lovejoy, Gene Evans, Dick Wesson, Paul Picerni

'The romance rings true and the battle scenes are dangerously alive.'—*Variety*

Force of Evil***
US 1948 78m bw
MGM / Enterprise (Bob Roberts)

A racketeer's lawyer finds that his boss has killed the lawyer's brother.
Involved, atmospheric melodrama about the numbers racket, moodily and brilliantly photographed in New York streets, gloweringly well acted and generally almost as hypnotic as *Citizen Kane*.

w Abraham Polonsky, Ira Wolfert, *novel* Tucker's People by Ira Wolfert *d Abraham Polonsky* *ph George Barnes* *m David Raksin*

John Garfield, *Thomas Gomez*, Beatrice Pearson, Marie Windsor

'It credits an audience with intelligence in its ears as well as its eyes.'—*Dilys Powell*

Force Ten from Navarone
GB 1978 118m Technicolor Panavision
Columbia / AIP / Guy Hamilton (Oliver A. Unger)

During World War II, commandos are detailed to blow up a vital bridge separating the Germans and partisans in Yugoslavia.
Routine war hokum with plenty of explosions and sudden death, but not much sense. Nothing, really, to do with *The Guns of Navarone.*

w Robin Chapman, *novel* Alistair MacLean *d* Guy Hamilton *ph* Chris Challis *m* Ron Goodwin *pd* Geoffrey Drake

Robert Shaw, Edward Fox, Franco Nero, Harrison Ford, Barbara Bach, Richard Kiel

A Foreign Affair**
US 1948 116m bw
Paramount (Charles Brackett)

A deputation of American politicians goes to visit post-war Berlin and a congresswoman finds herself in an emotional triangle with a captain and his German mistress.
Bleakly sophisticated comedy from this team's headline-grabbing period; full of interest and amusement, it never quite sparkles enough to remove the doubtful taste.

w Charles Brackett, Billy Wilder, Richard Breen *d Billy Wilder* *ph* Charles Lang Jnr *m* Frederick Hollander

Jean Arthur, Marlene Dietrich, John Lund, Millard Mitchell, Peter Von Zerneck, Stanley Prager

'This deliberately cynical political farce . . . often seems on the verge of being funny, but the humour is too clumsily forced.'—*New Yorker, 1980*

AAN: script; Charles Lang Jnr

Foreign Affaires
GB 1935 71m bw
Gainsborough (Michael Balcon)

A gambler and a car salesman get mixed up with a phoney casino.
Mild star farce.

w Ben Travers *d* Tom Walls *ph* Roy Kellino

Tom Walls, Ralph Lynn, Robertson Hare, Norma Varden, Marie Lohr, Diana Churchill, Cecil Parker

Foreign Correspondent****
US 1940 120m bw
Walter Wanger

An American journalist is sent to Europe in 1938 and becomes involved with spies.
Thoroughly typical and enjoyable Hitchcock adventure with a rambling script which builds up into brilliantly managed suspense sequences: an assassination, a windmill, an attempted murder in Westminster Cathedral, a plane crash at sea. The final speech was an attempt to encourage America into the war.

w Charles Bennett, Joan Harrison, James Hilton, Robert Benchley, from Personal History by Vincent Sheean *d Alfred Hitchcock* *ph Rudolph Maté* *m* Alfred Newman *sp* Lee Zavitz *ad* Alexander Golitzen *pd* William Cameron Menzies

Joel McCrea, Laraine Day, *Herbert Marshall, Albert Basserman, Edmund Gwenn, George Sanders, Eduardo Ciannelli, Robert Benchley, Harry Davenport*, Martin Kosleck

HAVERSTOCK (Joel McCrea): 'I've been watching a part of the world blown to pieces! I can't read the rest of the speech I had because the lights have gone out. It is as if the lights were out everywhere, except in America. Keep those lights burning there! Cover them with steel! Ring them with guns! Build a canopy of battleships and bombing planes around them! Hello, America! Hang on to your lights, they're the only lights left in the world!'

'If you have any interest in the true motion and sweep of pictures, watching that man work is like listening to music . . . If you would like a seminar in how to make a movie travel the lightest and fastest way, in a kind of beauty that is peculiar to movies alone, you can see this once, and then again to see what you missed, and then study it twice.'—*Otis Ferguson*

'The most excitingly shot and edited picture of the year.'—*Basil Wright*

'A masterpiece of propaganda, a first class production which no doubt will make a certain impression upon the broad masses of the people in enemy countries.'—*Joseph Goebbels*

'This juxtaposition of outright melodramatics with deadly serious propaganda is eminently satisfactory . . . Hitchcock uses camera tricks, cinematic rhythm and crescendo to make his points.'—*Howard Barnes, New York Herald Tribune*

'Easily one of the year's finest pictures.'—*Time*

AAN: best picture; script; Rudolph Maté; Albert Basserman

Foreign Intrigue*
US 1956 100m Eastmancolor
UA / Sheldon Reynolds

A press agent investigates the death of a man who had been blackmailing potential traitors.
Location espionage melodrama of the cold war fifties, quite well done in a rather dismal vein, but a long way from *Foreign Correspondent*.

wd Sheldon Reynolds *ph* Bertil Palmgrem *m* Paul Durand

Robert Mitchum, Genevieve Page, Ingrid Thulin, Eugene Deckers

The Foreman Went to France**
GB 1941 87m bw
Ealing (Alberto Cavalcanti)
US title: *Somewhere in France*

Before Dunkirk, a Welsh foreman is sent on a mission to salvage secret French machinery.
Fresh, appealing comedy drama based on a true incident of World War II.

w John Dighton, Angus Macphail, Leslie Arliss, Roger Macdougall, Diana Morgan, *story* J. B. Priestley *d* Charles Frend *ph* Wilkie Cooper *m* William Walton

Tommy Trinder, Constance Cummings, Clifford Evans, Robert Morley, Gordon Jackson, Ernest Milton

'The thrilling story of women who play with fire, and men who fight it!'

The Forest Rangers*
US 1942 85m Technicolor
Paramount (Robert Sisk)

A socialite marries a district ranger and rescues her disgruntled rival during a forest blaze.
Routine, competent, box office actioner of its time, with popular stars, adequate plot, but precious little inventiveness.

w Harold Shumate *d* George Marshall *ph* Charles Lang *m* Victor Young

Fred MacMurray, Paulette Goddard, Susan Hayward, Lynne Overman, Albert Dekker, Eugene Pallette, Regis Toomey, Rod Cameron

'Another tale of the tall timbers, complete with conflagrations, he-men, and women like cats.'—*New York Times*

Forever Amber*
US 1947 137m Technicolor
TCF (William Perlberg)

Adventures of a desirable young lady during the reign of Charles II.
Much-bowdlerized version of a sensational novel of the forties; pretty but rather thin, with a colourless cast, saved by lively action sequences.

w Philip Dunne, Ring Lardner Jnr, *novel* Kathleen Winsor *d* Otto Preminger *ph Leon Shamroy* *m* David Raksin *ad Lyle Wheeler*

Linda Darnell, Cornel Wilde, *George Sanders* (as Charles II), Richard Greene, Glenn Langan, Richard Haydn, Jessica Tandy, Anne Revere, Robert Coote, John Russell, Leo G. Carroll

AAN: David Raksin

Forever and a Day**
US 1943 104m bw
RKO (Herbert Wilcox, Victor Saville)

The history of a London house from 1804 to the blitz of World War II.
Made for war charities by a combination of the European talents in Hollywood, this series of sketches was unavoidably patchy but gave good opportunities to several familiar performers and stands as a likeable quick reference to their work at this period.

w Charles Bennett, C. S. Forester, Lawrence Hazard, Michael Hogan, W. P. Lipscomb, Alice Duer Miller, John Van Druten, Alan Campbell, Peter Godfrey, S. M. Herzig, Christopher Isherwood, Gene Lockhart, R. C. Sherriff, Claudine West, Norman Corwin, Jack Hartfield, James Hilton, Emmet Lavery, Frederick Lonsdale, Donald Ogden Stewart, Keith Winter *ph* Robert de Grasse, Lee Garmes, Russell Metty, Nicholas Musuraca *m* Anthony Collins *d* René Clair, Edmund Goulding, Cedric Hardwicke, Frank Lloyd, Victor Saville, Robert Stevenson, Herbert Wilcox *ad* Albert D'Agostino, Lawrence Williams, Al Herman

Anna Neagle, Ray Milland, *Claude Rains*, *C. Aubrey Smith*, Dame May Whitty, Gene Lockhart, Edmund Gwenn, Ian Hunter, *Jessie Matthews*, *Charles Laughton*, Montagu Love, *Cedric Hardwicke*, Reginald Owen, *Buster Keaton*, Wendy Barrie, Ida Lupino, *Brian Aherne*, Edward Everett Horton, June Duprez, Eric Blore, Merle Oberon, Una O'Connor, Nigel Bruce, *Roland Young*, *Gladys Cooper*, Robert Cummings, Richard Haydn, Elsa Lanchester, Sara Allgood, Robert Coote, Donald Crisp, Ruth Warrick, Kent Smith, Herbert Marshall, Victor McLaglen, many others in bit parts

'One of the most brilliant casts of modern times has been assembled to bolster up one of the poorest pictures.'—*James Agate*

'It is holding and entertaining . . . a production of outstanding quality.'—*CEA Film Report*

† The film is notable for having the longest-ever list of credited co-writers.

Forever Darling
US 1956 91m Eastmancolor
MGM / Zanra (Desi Arnaz)

A couple's matrimonial difficulties are solved by her guardian angel.
Cutesy-pie comedy with all concerned embarrassed by their material.

w Helen Deutsch *d* Alexander Hall *ph* Harold Lipstein *m* Bronislau Kaper

Lucille Ball, Desi Arnaz, James Mason (as the angel), John Emery, Louis Calhern, John Hoyt, Natalie Schaefer

Forever England see Brown on Resolution

Forever Female
US 1953 93m bw
Paramount (Pat Duggan)

A young writer sells his play to a Broadway producer who wants to transform it into a vehicle for his ex-wife; she falls for the writer but eventually discourages him.
Talky romantic comedy without much style or sense of Broadway; a long way from *All About Eve*.

w Julius J. Epstein, Philip G. Epstein, *play* Rosalind by J. M. Barrie *d* Irving Rapper *ph* Harry Stradling *m* Victor Young

Ginger Rogers, William Holden, Paul Douglas, James Gleason, Pat Crowley

Forever Young
GB 1984 84m colour
Goldcrest (Chris Griffin)

Father Michael finds himself influenced by sexual tensions among his flock.
Rather slight drama chiefly concerning a twelve-year-old boy who idolizes his fallible priest.

w Ray Connolly *d* David Drury *ph* Norman Langley *md* Anthony King

James Aubrey, Nicholas Gecks, Alec McCowen, Karen Archer

Forfaiture see The Cheat

Forget Me Not
GB 1936 72m bw
London Films (Alexander Korda)
US title: *Forever Yours*

On board ship, a young girl falls for a widowed tenor.
Bland romance, notable only for the star's singing.

w Hugh Gray, Arthur Wimperis *d* Zoltan Korda, Stanley Irving *ph* Hans Schneeberger *m* Mischa Spoliansky

Beniamino Gigli, Joan Gardner, Ivan Brandt, Hugh Wakefield

'As a larynx exercise it possesses an appeal for those audiences which go for singing.'—*Variety*

Forgotten Commandments*
US 1932 75m bw

In a Russia which has renounced Christianity, a scientist who considers himself above emotion is led by jealousy into the murder of his mistress. Vague, feeble and absurd modern parable which takes in its stride a 20-minute excerpt from de Mille's 1923 *The Ten*

Commandments. Gene Raymond, Sari Maritza, Irving Pichel, Marguerite Churchill, Edward Van Sloan, Harry Beresford. Written by J. B. Fagan, Agnes Brand Leahy; directed by Louis Gasnier and William Schoor; for Paramount. 'Hardly a single dramatic sequence and not over three laughs at the New York opening – and one of them at, not with, the picture.'—*Variety*

Forgotten Faces
US 1936 70m bw

Jailed for killing his wife's lover, a man escapes to thwart his wife's further plans. Slightly unusual melodrama which was remade as *A Gentleman After Dark*. Herbert Marshall, Gertrude Michael, James Burke, Robert Cummings. Written by Marguerite Roberts, Robert Yost, Brian Marlow; directed by E. A. Dupont; for Paramount.

Forgotten Girls
US 1943 68m bw

A girl is convicted for a murder committed by her stepmother. Minor saga of prison life, with an absurd method of proving the heroine's innocence. Louise Platt, Donald Woods, Wynne Gibson, Robert Armstrong, Eduardo Ciannelli, Jack La Rue. Written by Joseph March, F. Hugh Herbert, Frank McDonald; directed by Phil Rosen; for Robert North / Republic.

Forgotten Woman
US 1939 68m bw

A woman wrongfully imprisoned has a baby in prison and emerges embittered. Heavygoing tearjerker. Sigrid Gurie, Eve Arden, Donald Briggs, William Lundigan, Elizabeth Risdon. Written by Lionel Houser, Harold Buchman, John Kobler; directed by Harold Young; for Edmund Grainger / Universal.

The Formula
US 1980 117m Metrocolor
MGM / CIP (Steve Shagan)

A cop follows a murder trail to West Germany and finds that it all hinges on a secret formula for turning coal into petrol.
Convoluted thriller which is all McGuffin and no interest.

w Steven Shagan, from his novel *d* John G. Avildsen *ph* James Crabe *m* Bill Conti

George C. Scott, Marlon Brando, Marthe Keller, John Gielgud, Beatrice Straight, Richard Lynch

AAN: James Crabe

Forsaking All Others*
US 1934 84m bw
MGM (Bernard H. Hyman)

A wife nearly breaks up her rather dull marriage, but thinks better of it.
Star power carries this thin comedy drama.

w Joseph L. Mankiewicz, *play* Edward Barry Roberts, Frank Morgan Cavett *d* W. S. Van Dyke *ph* Gregg Toland, George Folsey *m* William Axt

Clark Gable, Joan Crawford, Robert Montgomery, *Charles Butterworth*, Billie Burke, Frances Drake, Rosalind Russell, Arthur Treacher

'Sock romantic comedy despite some messy hokum.'—*Variety*

'Contrary to expectation, sophistication is at a minimum.'—*Time*

'Where a woman meant more to a man than anywhere else in the world!'

Fort Algiers
US 1952 85m bw

A female French agent loves a fellow spy who turns up as a Foreign Legionnaire, working against an evil Emir. Quite lively old-fashioned hokum, satisfactory on its level. Yvonne de Carlo, Carlos Thompson, Raymond Burr, Leif Erickson, Anthony Caruso. Written by Theodore St John; directed by Lesley Selander; for Erco / UA.

Fort Apache**
US 1948 127m bw
RKO (John Ford, Merian C. Cooper)

In the old west, a military martinet has trouble with his family as well as the Indians.
Rather stiff and unsatisfactory epic western which yet contains sequences in its director's best manner.

w Frank S. Nugent, *story* Massacre by James Warner Bellah *d John Ford* *ph* Archie Stout *m* Richard Hageman

Henry Fonda, John Wayne, Shirley Temple, Pedro Armendariz, Ward Bond, Irene Rich, George O'Brien, John Agar, Victor McLaglen, Anna Lee, Dick Foran, Guy Kibbee

'A visually absorbing celebration of violent deeds.'—*Howard Barnes*

'The whole picture is bathed in a special form of patriotic sentimentality: scenes are held so that we cannot fail to appreciate the beauty of the American past.'—*New Yorker, 1976*

'Shirley Temple and her husband handle the love interest as though they were sharing a soda fountain special, and there is enough Irish comedy to make me wish Cromwell had done a more thorough job.'—*James Agee*

Fort Apache, the Bronx
US 1980 123m De Luxe
Time Life / Producer Circle (David Susskind)

A veteran policeman deals with various violent crimes in New York.
This instantly forgettable movie unspools like an ultra-violent *Dixon of Dock Green*, but Newman is no Jack Warner.

w Heywood Gould *d* Daniel Petrie *ph* John Alcott *m* Jonathan Tunick *pd* Ben Edwards

Paul Newman, Ed Asner, Ken Wahl, Danny Aiello, Rachel Ticotin, Pam Grier, Kathleen Beller

Fort Defiance
US 1951 81m Cinecolor

Ben Shelby comes back from the Civil War to avenge his brother's death. Complicated lower-berth western, crudely executed. Dane Clark, Ben Johnson, Peter Graves, Tracey Roberts, George Cleveland. Written by Louis Lantz; directed by John Rawlins; for Ventura / UA.

Fort Dobbs
US 1957 90m bw

Man on the run rescues widow from Comanches and clears his name. Very routine medium-scale western showcasing a TV star. Clint Walker, Virginia Mayo, Brian Keith, Richard Eyer. Written by George W. George and Burt Kennedy; directed by Gordon Douglas; for Warner.

Fort Massacre
US 1958 80m De Luxe Cinemascope

A cavalry sergeant becomes reckless when he has to lead to safety the survivors of an Indian attack. Psychological western without the skill necessary to realize its pretensions. Joel McCrea, Forrest Tucker, Susan Cabot, John Russell. Written by Martin N. Goldsmith; directed by Joseph Newman; for Mirisch / UA.

Fort Ti
US 1953 73m Technicolor 3-D
Columbia (Sam Katzman)

In 1759 a platoon of Rogers' Rangers marches north to defend their territory against Indians. Cheap and feeble western memorable only for the amount of miscellaneous objects thrown at the audience via 3-D photography.

w Robert E. Kent *d* William Castle
ph Lester E. White, Lathrop B. Worth
md Ross di Maggio

George Montgomery, Joan Vohs, Irving Bacon, James Seay

'The lack of restraint is remarkable. To the injury of tomahawks, rifle shots, cannon balls, flaming arrows, broken bottles and blazing torches is added the insult of grubby redskins hurled judo style into one's lap.'—*David Robinson*

Fort Utah
US 1967 84m Technicolor Techniscope

Crazed killers take over a cavalry fort. Muddled western with the producer's usual roster of familiar old faces. John Ireland, Virginia Mayo, Scott Brady, John Russell, Robert Strauss, James Craig, Richard Arlen, Jim Davis, Donald Barry. Written by Steve Fisher, Andrew Craddock; directed by Lesley Selander; for A. C. Lyles/Paramount.

Fort Vengeance
US 1953 75m Cinecolor

A new Mountie recruit is an Indian killer. Uninteresting western with stock cast and situations. James Craig, Rita Moreno, Keith Larsen, Reginald Denny, Morris Ankrum. Written by Dan Ullman; directed by Lesley Selander; for Walter Wanger / Allied Artists.

Fort Worth
US 1951 80m Technicolor

A newspaper editor combats a would-be dictator. Satisfying star western. Randolph Scott, Phyllis Thaxter, David Brian, Dick Jones, Paul Picerni. Written by John Twist; directed by Edwin L. Marin; for Warner.

Fort Yuma
US 1955 78m colour

Indians steal army uniforms and attack a fort. Minor but efficient co-feature western. Peter Graves, Joan Vohs, John Hudson, Joan Taylor, Addison Richards. Written by Danny Arnold; directed by Lesley Selander; for Howard W. Koch / UA.

The Fortune
US 1975 88m Technicolor Panavision
Columbia (Hank Moonjean)

A twenties heiress elopes with her lover and his dim-witted friend but discovers that they mean to murder her for her money.
Bungled black comedy with top talent over-confident of carrying it.

w Adrien Joyce (Carol Eastman) *d* Mike Nichols *ph* John A. Alonzo *m* various songs *pd* Richard Sylbert

Jack Nicholson, Warren Beatty, Stockard Channing, Florence Stanley, Richard B. Shull, John Fiedler

'Like the ill-assorted styles of the film generally, the stars themselves frequently seem to belong in different movies.'—*Richard Combs*

'A silly, shallow, occasionally enjoyable comedy trifle . . . classy 20's production values often merit more attention than the plot.'—*Variety*

Fortune and Men's Eyes
Canada / US 1971 102m Metrocolor
MGM / Cinemex / CFD (Lester Persky, Lewis M. Allen)

Life among homosexuals in a Canadian jail. A welter of sensational incident outweighs any point the author may have had; this prison seems to be beyond reform.

w John Herbert, from his play *d* Harvey Hart *ph* Georges Dufaux *m* Galt McDermot

Wendell Burton, Michael Greer

The Fortune Cookie*
US 1966 125m bw Panavision
UA / Mirisch / Phalanx / Jalem (Billy Wilder)
GB title: *Meet Whiplash Willie*

A crooked lawyer forces his slightly injured client to sue for a million dollars.
Flat, stretched-out, only occasionally effective comedy which relies too much on mordant attitudes and a single star performance.

w Billy Wilder, I. A. L. Diamond *d* Billy Wilder *ph* Joseph La Shelle *m* André Previn

Walter Matthau, Jack Lemmon, Ron Rich, Cliff Osmond, Lurene Tuttle

'A jackhammer of a film savagely applied to those concrete areas of human spirit where cupidity and stupidity have been so long entrenched.'—*Richard Schickel*

AA: Walter Matthau
AAN: Billy Wilder, I. A. L. Diamond (script); Joseph La Shelle

Fortune Is a Woman*
GB 1956 95m bw
Columbia / Frank Launder, Sidney Gilliat
US title: *She Played with Fire*

An insurance assessor investigates a fire, finds a murder, marries the victim's widow, and is blackmailed . . .
Slackly-handled mystery thriller, a disappointment from the talents involved.

w Frank Launder, Sidney Gilliat, *novel* Winston Graham *d* Sidney Gilliat *ph* Gerald Gibbs *m* William Alwyn

Jack Hawkins, Arlene Dahl, Dennis Price, Geoffrey Keen, Violet Farebrother, John Robinson, Bernard Miles, Greta Gynt

Fortunes of Captain Blood
US 1950 91m bw

The famous Caribbean pirate eludes his pursuers by taking over their own ship. Lethargic adventures on a low budget; the cast was there for something better. Louis Hayward, Patricia Medina, George Macready, Dona Drake, Alfonso Bedoya. Written by Michael Hogan, Robert Libbott and Frank Burt; directed by Gordon Douglas; for Harry Joe Brown / Columbia.

Forty Carats*
US 1973 109m Metrocolor
Columbia / M. J. Frankovich

A 40-year-old divorcee on holiday in Greece has a brief affair with a 22-year-old man. Curiously miscast and mishandled comedy for the smart set; scores a laugh or two but never really takes off.

w Leonard Gershe, *play* Pierre Barillet, Jean-Pierre Gredy *d* Milton Katselas *ph* Charles Lang Jnr *m* Michel Legrand

Liv Ullmann, Edward Albert, Gene Kelly, Billy 'Green' Bush, Binnie Barnes, Nancy Walker, Deborah Raffin, Don Porter, Natalie Schaefer, Rosemary Murphy

Forty Eight Hours
US 1982 96m Movielab
Paramount / Lawrence Gordon

A cop and a criminal on parole combine to track down the latter's former associates.
Reasonable action melodrama with comedy asides and San Francisco locations; but too violent for its own good.

w Roger Spottiswoode and Walter Hill & Larry Gross and Steven E. de Souza *d* Walter Hill *ph* Ric Waite *m* James Horner *pd* John Vallone

Nick Nolte, Eddie Murphy, Annette O'Toole, Frank McRae

'It's like *The French Connection*, *Dirty Harry* and *Butch Cassidy* all put in a compactor and pressed into cartoon form.'—*New Yorker*

The Forty First*
USSR 1927 80m approx bw silent
Mezhrabpom
original title: *Sorok Pervyi*

During the Civil War in Turkestan, a girl sniper for the Reds becomes the companion in adventure of a White lieutenant. But in the end he becomes her 41st victim.
Strong action melodrama which found an international audience.

w Boris Lavryenov, from his novel *d* Yakov Protazanov *ph* Pyotr Yermolov

Ada Voitsik, Ivan Kovan-Samborsky
† Remade in 1956 by Grigori Chukrai, in colour.

Forty-Five Fathers
US 1937 71m bw

A show business orphan becomes the personal ward of the Gun and Spear Club. Palatable vehicle for a growing child star. Jane Withers, Paul and Grace Hartman, Thomas Beck, Louise Henry, Richard Carle, Nella Walker, Andrew Tombes. Written by Frances Hyland, Albert Ray, Mary Bickel; directed by James Tinling; for John Stone / TCF.

Forty Guns
US 1957 80m bw Cinemascope
TCF / Globe (Samuel Fuller)

A powerful ranchwoman protects her hoodlum brother.
Heavily melodramatic and slow-moving western with a few effective moments.

wd Samuel Fuller *ph* Joseph Biroc *m* Harry Sukman

Barbara Stanwyck, Barry Sullivan, Dean Jagger, Gene Barry, John Ericson

Forty Guns to Apache Pass
US 1967 95m Technicolor

A cavalry captain protects homesteaders when Cochise attacks. Flat and overlong star western compounded of excessively familiar elements. Audie Murphy, Michael Burns, Kenneth Tobey, Laraine Stephens. Written by Willard and Mary Willingham; directed by William Witney; for Admiral / Columbia.

Forty Little Mothers
US 1940 90m bw
MGM (Harry Rapf)

A teacher in a girls' school finds himself in charge of a baby.
Ill-advised star vehicle composed largely of whimsy . . . and no musical numbers.

w Dorothy Yost, Ernest Pagano *d* Busby Berkeley *ph* Charles A. Lawton Jnr

Eddie Cantor, Judith Anderson, Bonita Granville, Rita Johnson, Diana Lewis, Nydia Westman, Martha O'Driscoll

Forty Naughty Girls
US 1937 68m bw

Hildegarde Withers solves a murder backstage. Weak addition to a faltering series. Zasu Pitts, James Gleason, Marjorie Lord, George Shelley, Joan Woodbury. Written by John Grey, Stuart Palmer; directed by Edward Cline; for William Sistrom / RKO. 'Decidedly tame, and won't cause much ripple on nether side of duals, where it'll undoubtedly land.'—*Variety*

The Forty Niners
US 1954 70m bw

A marshal tracks down three men who were accomplices to a murder. Very tolerable minor western. Wild Bill Elliott, Virginia Grey, Henry Morgan, John Doucette, Lane Bradford. Written by Dan Ullman; directed by Thomas Carr; for Allied Artists.

Forty Ninth Parallel***
GB 1941 123m bw
GFD / Ortus (John Sutro, Michael Powell)
US title: *The Invaders*

In Canada, five stranded U-boat men try to escape into the US.
Episodic, effective propaganda piece which develops some nice Hitchcockian touches and allows a range of star actors to make impact.

w Emeric Pressburger, Rodney Ackland d Michael Powell ph F. A. Young *m* Ralph Vaughan Williams

Eric Portman, Laurence Olivier, *Anton Walbrook, Leslie Howard, Raymond Massey*, Glynis Johns, Niall MacGinnis, Finlay Currie, Raymond Lovell, John Chandos

'Some of the plotting and characterization look rather rusty at this remove, but the sense of landscape and figures passing through it remains authoritatively dynamic.'—*Tony Rayns, Time Out, 1979*

'An admirable piece of work from every point of view.'—*MFB*

AA: original story (Emeric Pressburger)
AAN: best picture; script

Forty Pounds of Trouble*
US 1963 105m Eastmancolor Panavision
U-I / Curtis Enterprises (Stan Margulies)

A casino manager is chased by his ex-wife's detective for alimony payments, and also has to look after an abandoned six-year-old girl.
Standard sentimental comedy with some verve and a lively climactic chase through Disneyland.

w Marion Hargrove *d* Norman Jewison *ph* Joe MacDonald *m* Mort Lindsey

Tony Curtis, Phil Silvers, Suzanne Pleshette, Edward Andrews

The Forty-Ninth Man
US 1953 73m bw

Spies try to infiltrate a big bomb into the US. Tolerable low-berth security thriller on semi-documentary lines. John Ireland, Richard Denning, Suzanne Dalbert, Touch Connors. Written by Harry Essex from a story by Ivan Tors; directed by Fred F. Sears; for Sam Katzman/Columbia.

'Mightier than Broadway ever beheld.'
Forty-Second Street****
US 1933 89m bw
Warner (Hal B. Wallis)

A Broadway musical producer has troubles during rehearsal but reaches a successful opening night.
Archetypal Hollywood putting-on-a-show musical in which the leading lady is indisposed and a chorus girl is told to get out there and come back a star. The clichés are written and performed with great zest, the atmosphere is convincing, and the numbers when they come are dazzlers.

w James Seymour, Rian James, novel Bradford Ropes *d Lloyd Bacon ch Busby Berkeley ph Sol Polito m / ly Al Dubin, Harry Warren*

Warner Baxter, Ruby Keeler, Bebe Daniels, George Brent, Una Merkel, Guy Kibbee, Dick Powell, *Ginger Rogers* (as Anytime Annie), *Ned Sparks*, George E. Stone, Allen Jenkins

Songs: 'Forty-Second Street'; 'Shuffle Off to Buffalo'; 'Young and Healthy'; 'You're Getting to Be a Habit with Me'

(Warner Baxter): 'Sawyer, you listen to me, and you listen hard. Two hundred people, two hundred jobs, two hundred thousand dollars, five weeks of grind and blood and sweat depend upon you. It's the lives of all these people who've worked with you. You've got to go on, and you've got to give and give and give. They've got to like you. Got to. Do you understand? You can't fall down. You can't because your future's in it, my future and everything all of us have is staked on you. All right, now I'm through, but you keep your feet on the ground and your head on those shoulders of yours and go out, and Sawyer, you're going out a youngster but you've got to come back a star!'

'The story has been copied a hundred times since, but never has the backstage atmosphere been so honestly and felicitously caught.'—*John Huntley, 1966*

'It gave new life to the clichés that have kept parodists happy.'—*New Yorker, 1977*

AAN: best picture

Forty Thousand Horsemen
Australia 1940 100m bw

The story of the Australian Light Horse in Palestine during World War I. One of the first Australian bids for the world market; in itself, just a competent little war movie, and too long. Chips Rafferty, Betty Bryant, Grant Taylor. Written by Mrs Charles Chauvel; directed by Charles Chauvel; also produced by him.

Foul Play*
US 1978 116m Movielab
Paramount / Thomas L. Miller, Edward K. Milkis

Two innocents in San Francisco get involved in a plot to assassinate the visiting pope.
Sometimes sprightly, sometimes tired rehash of Hitchcock elements, rather on the level of the similar *Silver Streak*.

wd Colin Higgins *ph* David M. Walsh *m* Charles Fox

Goldie Hawn, Chevy Chase, Burges Meredith, Rachel Roberts, Eugene Roche, Dudley Moore, Billy Barty

AAN: song, 'Ready to Take a Chance Again'

The Fountain
US 1934 84m bw
RKO (Pandro S. Berman)

During World War I a British woman is tempted to forsake her mangled German air ace husband for her childhood sweetheart.
A slice of impenetrable gloom from an intractable novel.

w Jane Murfin, Samuel Hoffenstein, *novel* Charles Morgan *d* John Cromwell *ph* Henry W. Gerrard *m* Max Steiner

Ann Harding, Brian Aherne, Paul Lukas, Jean Hersholt, Ralph Forbes, Violet Kemble-Cooper, Sara Haden

'One of the talkiest talkies yet.'—*Variety*

'Long and solemn and wonderfully empty.'—*Otis Ferguson*

The Fountainhead**
US 1949 114m bw
Warner (Henry Blanke)

An idealistic architect clashes with big business.
Overripe adaptation of a rather silly novel, full of Freudian symbols and expressionist techniques with which the star really can't cope; but an enjoyable field day for the director and the rest of the cast.

w Ayn Rand, from her novel *d King Vidor ph Robert Burks m* Max Steiner

Gary Cooper, *Patricia Neal, Raymond Massey*, Kent Smith, Robert Douglas, Henry Hull, Ray Collins, Moroni Olson, Jerome Cowan

'If you like deep thinking, hidden meanings, plus pure modern architecture, then this is something for which you have been waiting a long time.'—*Screenland*

'The most bizarre movie in both Vidor's and Cooper's filmographies, this adaptation mutes Ms Rand's neo-Nietzschian philosophy of "objectivism" but lays on the expressionist symbolism with a "free enterprise" trowel.'—*Time Out, 1980*

Four Clowns**
US 1970 96m bw
Robert Youngson Productions (Herb Gelbspan)

Studies of four silent comedians. Laurel and Hardy in excerpts from *Putting Pants on Philip, The Second Hundred Years, Their Purple Moment, Big Business, Two Tars* and *Double Whoopee*; Charley Chase in *Us, What Price Goofy, Fluttering Hearts, The Family Group* and *Limousine Love*; Buster Keaton in *Seven Chances*.
An essential compendium, especially for the Charley Chase revaluation which was long overdue.

w Robert Youngson *m* Manny Alban *narr* Jay Jackson

Four Daughters***
US 1938 90m bw
Warner (Henry Blanke)

Domestic and romantic adventures of a small-town family.
Standard small-town hearth-fire hokum, impeccably done and really quite irresistible.

w Julius Epstein, Lenore Coffee, *novel* Sister Act by Fannie Hurst *d Michael Curtiz ph* Ernest Haller *m* Max Steiner

Claude Rains, *John Garfield* (a sensation in his first role), Priscilla Lane, Rosemary Lane, Lola Lane, Gale Page, Jeffrey Lynn, Frank McHugh, *May Robson*, Dick Foran

'It may be sentimental, but it's grand cinema.'—*New York Times*

'It simply, yet powerfully, brings into focus a panorama of natural but startling events.'—*Motion Picture Herald*

† An immediate sequel was required, but the Garfield character had been killed off, so to accommodate him a variation was written under the title *Daughters Courageous*; then came two proper sequels without him, *Four Wives* and *Four Mothers*. In 1955 the original was remade as *Young at Heart* (qv).

AAN: best picture; script; Michael Curtiz; John Garfield

The Four Days of Naples*
Italy 1962 119m bw
Titanus-Metro (Goffredo Lombardo)

A reconstruction of the 1943 city battle in which the Nazis were driven out by civilian fury.
A kind of update of *Open City*: much admired, but a little ill-timed.

w Nanni Loy and others *d Nanni Loy* *ph* Marcello Gatti *m* Carlo Rustichelli

Lea Massari, Frank Wolff, Domenico Formato, Raffaele Barbato

AA: best foreign film

AAN: script

Four Faces West
US 1948 90m bw
Enterprise (David Loewe, Charles Einfeld)
aka: *They Passed This Way*

A young man turns bandit to save his father's ranch. Thoughtful minor western, nicely made.

w Graham Baker, Teddie Sherman from novel Paso por aqui by Eugene Rhodes *d* Alfred E. Green *ph* Russell Harlan *m* Paul Sawtell

Joel McCrea, Frances Dee, Charles Bickford, Joseph Calleia

The Four Feathers**
US 1929 83m bw
Paramount (David O. Selznick)

During the Sudan campaign of the nineties, a stay-at-home receives four white feathers as a symbol of cowardice; but he goes undercover, becomes a hero, and rescues his best friend.
Ambitious early talkie based on a famous adventure novel, partly filmed in Africa; interesting but now very stilted.

w Howard Estabrook, *novel* A. E. W. Mason *d* Lothar Mendes, Merian C. Cooper, Ernest Schoedsack *ph* Robert Kurlle, Merian C. Cooper, Ernest Schoedsack *m* William F. Peters

Richard Arlen, Fay Wray, Clive Brook, William Powell, George Fawcett, Theodore Von Eltz, Noah Beery

The Four Feathers****
GB 1939 130m Technicolor
London (Alexander Korda, Irving Asher)

The standard version of the above, perfectly cast and presented, with battle scenes which have since turned up in a score of other films from *Zarak* to *Master of the World*; also a triumph of early colour.

w R. C. Sheriff, Lajos Biro, Arthur Wimperis *d Zoltan Korda* *ph* Georges Périnal, Osmond Borradaile, Jack Cardiff *m* Miklos Rozsa

John Clements, Ralph Richardson, C. Aubrey Smith, June Duprez, Allan Jeayes, Jack Allen, Donald Gray, Henry Oscar, John Laurie

'It cannot fail to be one of the best films of the year . . . even the richest of the ham goes smoothly down, savoured with humour and satire.'—*Graham Greene*

† Remade 1956 as *Storm over the Nile* (qv).

The Four Feathers: see *Television Companion* for the TV movie

Four for Texas
US 1963 124m Technicolor
Warner / Sam Company (Robert Aldrich)

Two survivors of a stagecoach raid doublecross each other for the loot and become rival saloon owners.
Flabby western comedy, tediously directed and casually performed.

w Teddi Sherman, Robert Aldrich *d* Robert Aldrich *ph* Ernest Laszlo *m* Nelson Riddle

Dean Martin, Frank Sinatra, Anita Ekberg, Ursula Andress, Charles Bronson, Victor Buono, the Three Stooges

'The major laughs come from the Three Stooges doing an ancient routine and an old lady falling out of her wheelchair. Zowie.'—*Judith Crist*

'One suspects that the most amusing antics were those that went on off-screen.'—*Films and Filming*

Four Friends
US 1981 115m Technicolor
Filmways / Cinema 77 / Geria (Arthur Penn, Gene Lasko)
GB title: *Georgia's Friends*

A Yugoslavian boy grows up in Indiana and is influenced by the adult behaviour of his three friends.
Mildly interesting semi-autobiographical nostalgia movie, a vein which has been mined twice too often.

w Steve Tesich *d* Arthur Penn *ph* Ghislain Cloquet *m* Elizabeth Swados *pd* David Chapman

Craig Wasson, Jodi Thelen, Michael Huddleston, Jim Metzler

'They threw away conventions with their tattered clothes!'
Four Frightened People*
US 1934 78m bw
Paramount / Cecil B. de Mille

A bubonic plague outbreak on board ship causes four survivors to escape via a lifeboat and trek through dangerous jungle.
Studio-bound but interesting action melodrama, of a type unusual from this director.

w Bartlett Cormack, Lenore Coffee, *novel* E. Arnot Robertson *d Cecil B. de Mille* *ph* Karl Struss *m* Karl Hajos and others

Claudette Colbert, Herbert Marshall, William Gargan, Mary Boland, Leo Carrillo, Nella Walker, Tetsu Komai, Ethel Griffies

'The adventures are episodic and disjointed, running the gamut from stark tragedy to unbelievable farce.'—*Variety*

'A cumbersome sort of melodrama . . . despite some mildly entertaining jungle scenes.'—*Literary Digest*

Four Girls in Town
US 1956 85m Technicolor Cinemascope
U-I (Aaron Rosenberg)

Girls from various countries are chosen for Hollywood screen tests.
Formula romantic comedy adequately exposing young talent.

wd Jack Sher *ph* Irving Glassberg *m* Alex North

George Nader, Julie Adams, Marianne Cook, Elsa Martinelli, Gia Scala, Sidney Chaplin, Grant Williams, John Gavin

Four Girls in White
US 1938 88m bw
MGM (Nat Levine)

Drama among the student nurses.
Standard hospital fare designed as a try-out for budding talent.

w Nathalie Bucknall, Endre Boehm *d* S. Sylvan Simon

Florence Rice, Alan Marshal, Ann Rutherford, Una Merkel, Buddy Ebsen, Mary Howard, Kent Taylor, Jessie Ralph, Sara Haden, Philip Terry, Tom Neal

Four Guns to the Border
US 1954 83m Technicolor

Things go wrong for four bank robbers after a raid. Rather downbeat western with insufficient excitement. Rory Calhoun, Walter Brennan, Coleen Miller, George Nader, Nina Foch, John McIntire, Charles Drake. Written by George Van Marter and Franklin Coen; directed by Richard Carlson; for Universal-International.

The Four Horsemen of the Apocalypse**
US 1921 150m approx bw silent
Metro

A young Argentinian fights for his father's country, France, in World War I.
Highly derivative dramatic spectacle, almost a pageant, from a fairly unreadable novel. Despite its variable if exotic style, it made a star of Rudolph Valentino.

w June Mathis, *novel* Vicente Blasco-Ibanez *d Rex Ingram* *ph John F. Seitz*

Rudolph Valentino, Alice Terry, Nigel de Brulier, Alan Hale, Jean Hersholt, Wallace Beery

'A blend of exotic settings, striking composition, dramatic lighting, and colourful if sordid atmosphere.'—*Lewis Jacobs*

'Not only was it marvellously effective in its appeal to the eye, but the logical and dramatic unfolding of the basic story was a striking revelation of the valuable service that an expert scenario-writer may render to the professional writer of novels.'—*Edward S. Van Zile, That Marvel the Movie*

The Four Horsemen of the Apocalypse*
US 1961 153m Metrocolor Cinemascope
MGM (Julian Blaustein)

In this ill-fated modernization, the idle grandson of an Argentinian beef tycoon finds his manhood at last as a member of the French resistance during World War II. The visionary skyriding figures of death and pestilence simply do not fit in with bombs and concentration camps. Glum acting by a too elderly company, ugly colour and the usual hindrances of Cinemascope.

w Robert Ardrey, John Gay *d* Vincente Minnelli *ph* Milton Krasner *m* André Previn

Glenn Ford, Ingrid Thulin, Charles Boyer, Paul Henreid, Lee J. Cobb, Paul Lukas, Karl Boehm, Yvette Mimieux

'An elephantine helping of hysteria and hokum.'—*Judith Crist, 1973*

Four Hours to Kill**
US 1935 74m bw
Paramount (Arthur Hornblow Jnr)

A psychopathic gangster gets loose during an evening at the theatre.
Tense, well-handled melodrama making full use of its setting.

w Norman Krasna, from his play Small Miracle *d Mitchell Leisen ph* Theodor Sparkuhl

Richard Barthelmess, Ray Milland, Gertrude Michael, Joe Morrison, Helen Mack, Dorothy Tree, Roscoe Karns, Henry Travers

'It fails to grip and isn't long on laughs.'—*Variety*

The Four Hundred Blows**
France 1958 94m bw Dyaliscope
Films du Carrosse / SEDIF
original title: *Les Quatre Cents Coups*

A 12-year-old boy, unhappy at home, finds himself in a detention centre but finally escapes and keeps running.
Little more in plot terms than a piece of character observation, this engaging film is so controlled and lyrical as to be totally refreshing, and it gives a very vivid picture of the Paris streets.

wd François Truffaut ph Henri Decaë m Jean Constantin

Jean-Pierre Léaud, Claire Maurier, Albert Rémy

† The film is said to be based on Truffaut's own childhood.

AAN: script

Four in a Jeep*
Switzerland 1951 96m bw
Praesensfilm (Lazar Wechsler)

In the post-war international zone of Vienna, the four nationals of a police patrol come to blows over the cases they encounter.
Historically interesting but rather bland illustration of an untenable and even tragic political situation which was treated more melodramatically in *The Third Man*.

w Richard Schweizer *d Leopold Lindtberg ph* Emil Barna *m* Robert Blum

Viveca Lindfors, Ralph Meeker, Yoseph Yadin, Michael Medwin

Four in the Morning*
GB 1965 94m bw

Four personal stories are intercut during one London night. Attractive minor effort which takes the eye without engaging the mind. Ann Lynn, Judi Dench, Norman Rodway, Brian Phelan, Joe Melia. Written and directed by *Anthony Simmons*; for John Morris / West One.

Four Jacks and a Jill
US 1941 68m bw
RKO (John Twist)

Four struggling musicians adopt a down-and-out girl.
Flimsy remake of *That Girl from Paris*; the talent is given little opportunity to rise.

w John Twist *d* Jack Hively *ph* Russell Metty *songs* Mort Greene, Harry Revel

Anne Shirley, Ray Bolger, Desi Arnaz, Jack Durant, June Havoc, Eddie Foy Jnr, Fritz Feld

Four Jills in a Jeep
US 1944 89m bw
TCF (Irving Starr)

Four Hollywood glamour girls entertain the troops.
Condescending, dispirited 'semi-documentary' war musical.

w Robert Ellis, Helen Logan, Snag Werris *d* William A. Seiter *ph* Peverell Marley *md* Emil Newman

Kay Francis, Martha Raye, Carole Landis, Mitzi Mayfair, Jimmy Dorsey and his band, John Harvey, Phil Silvers, Dick Haymes; guest stars Alice Faye, Betty Grable, Carmen Miranda, George Jessel

'It gives the painful impression of having been tossed together in a couple of hours.'—*Bosley Crowther*

The Four Just Men*
GB 1939 85m bw
Ealing–Capad (S. C. Balcon)
US title: *The Secret Four*

To save the Empire, four stalwart Britishers agree to murder a villainous MP.
Bright, unusual but dated thriller from a popular novel.

w Roland Pertwee, Angus Macphail, Sergei Nolbandov, *novel* Edgar Wallace *d* Walter Forde *ph* Ronald Neame *m* Ernest Irving

Hugh Sinclair, Francis L. Sullivan, Frank Lawton, Griffith Jones, Anna Lee, Basil Sidney, Alan Napier, Athole Stewart, Edward Chapman, Garry Marsh, Ellaline Terriss, Lydia Sherwood, George Merritt

† The TV series of the late fifties restrained its heroes from criminal acts; the men were Jack Hawkins, Richard Conte, Dan Dailey, Vittorio de Sica.

Four Men and a Prayer*
US 1938 85m bw
TCF (Kenneth MacGowan)

Four young Englishmen set out to clear the name of their dishonoured father.
Pleasantly performed mystery which improves after a slowish start.

w Richard Sherman, Sonya Levien, Walter Ferris, *novel* David Garth *d John Ford ph* Ernest Palmer *md* Louis Silvers

Loretta Young, Richard Greene, George Sanders, David Niven, William Henry, C. Aubrey Smith, J. Edward Bromberg, John Carradine, Alan Hale, Reginald Denny, Barry Fitzgerald, Berton Churchill, John Sutton

'Better cast than story . . . the pace is so uneven that the general effect at times is bewildering.'—*Variety*

'Energetically told, compactly presented.'—*New York Times*

Four Mothers
US 1940 86m bw
Warner (Henry Blanke)

The four Lemp sisters, all happily married, have financial problems.
Third and last in the *Four Daughters* trilogy; quite attractively made but very routine.

w Stephen Morehouse Avery *d* William Keighley *m* Heinz Roemheld

Priscilla Lane, Rosemary Lane, Lola Lane, Gale Page, Claude Rains, Dick Foran, Frank McHugh, Jeffrey Lynn, Eddie Albert, Vera Lewis

'What has eight legs, feathers, and is usually seen coming to the rescue?'

The Four Musketeers (The Revenge of Milady)*
Panama 1974 103m Technicolor
TCF / Film Trust / Este (Alexander Salkind, Michael Salkind)

Athos, Porthos, Aramis and D'Artagnan have a final battle with Rochefort.
Perfunctory sequel to the same team's *The Three Musketeers*; allegedly the two films were intended as one, but if so the first ten reels were by far the best, though this section has its regulation quota of high spirits and lusty action.

w George MacDonald Fraser *d* Richard Lester *ph* David Watkin *m* Lalo Schifrin *pd* Brian Eatwell

Michael York, Oliver Reed, Frank Finlay, Richard Chamberlain, Raquel Welch, Faye Dunaway, Charlton Heston, Christopher Lee, Simon Ward, Geraldine Chaplin, Jean-Pierre Cassel, Roy Kinnear

'The whole sleek formula has rolled over to reveal a very soft, very flabby underside.'—*Tony Rayns*

The Four-Poster
US 1952 103m bw
Columbia / Stanley Kramer

The history of a marriage told in a series of bedroom scenes.

Hastily shot and rather tatty looking version of a stage play; unfortunately film can't contrast the comedy of the opening and the tragedy of the close within one small set, and the UPA cartoon bridges, though smart in themselves, are merely an irritation.

w Allan Scott, *play* Jan de Hartog *d* Irving Reis *ph* Hal Mohr *m* Dmitri Tiomkin

Rex Harrison, Lilli Palmer

AAN: Hal Mohr

'Here's to our friends—and the strength to put up with them!'

The Four Seasons**
US 1981 108m Technicolor
Universal (Martin Bregman)

Three married couples take seasonal holidays together, and remain united despite various tensions.
Rueful sexual comedy which maintains considerable momentum and actually makes us laugh at its sympathetic characters.

wd Alan Alda *ph* Victor J. Kemper *m* Antonio Vivaldi

Alan Alda, Carol Burnett, Len Cariou, Sandy Dennis, Rita Moreno, Jack Weston, Bess Armstrong

'An odd mingling of perspicuity and histrionics . . . a real middle-of-the-road film.'—*Geoff Brown, MFB*

'Unfailingly amusing, touchingly honest, and in the end refreshingly decent.'—*Margaret Hinxman, Daily Mail*

'See! a strange and beautiful woman created before your eyes!'

Four Sided Triangle
GB 1952 81m bw
Hammer (Michael Carreras, Alexander Paal)

When a scientist's girl friend marries another, he creates a clone but finds that it has the same preferences.
A very early entry in this field; not too well done, but faithful to its silly theme.

w Paul Tabori, Terence Fisher, *novel* William F. Temple *d* Terence Fisher *ph* Reg Wyer *m* Malcolm Arnold

Stephen Murray, Barbara Payton, James Hayter, John Van Eyssen, Percy Marmont, Kynaston Reeves

The Four Skulls of Jonathan Drake
US 1959 70m bw
UA / Vogue (Robert E. Kent)

A family is cursed by a head-hunting Equadorian medicine man.
Cheaply made but full-blooded occult horror, rather effectively done by a cast that knows how.

w Orville H. Hampton *d* Edward L. Cahn *ph* Maury Gertsman *m* Paul Dunlap

Henry Daniell, Eduard Franz, Valerie French, Grant Richards, Paul Cavanagh

'Amazonian Indians may find the plot a shade far-fetched.'—*MFB*

Four Sons*
US 1940 89m bw
TCF (Darryl F. Zanuck)

A Czech family is divided when the Nazis take over.
Predictable po-faced anti-Hitler melodrama released to an indifferent public well before America entered the war. A remake of a silent film set during World War I.

w John Howard Lawson *d* Archie Mayo *ph* Leon Shamroy *m* David Buttolph

Don Ameche, Eugenie Leontovich, Mary Beth Hughes, Alan Curtis, George Ernest, Robert Lowery, Sig Rumann, Lionel Royce, Ludwig Stossel

'It partakes more of sentimental melodrama than of tragedy. . . . Neither in its performance nor its writing does the film ever rise to any passion.'—*New York Times*

Four Steps in the Clouds*
Italy 1942 90m bw
Cines Amato
original title: *Quattro Passi fra le Nuvole*

A travelling salesman on a bus gets involved with the problems of a pregnant girl, but misunderstandings are finally cleared up to general satisfaction.
A comedy on the American model which was a great success in wartorn Italy. Not particularly remarkable in itself, it was remade in 1957, as *The Virtuous Bigamist*, with Fernandel. It does show the lighter side of Italian neo-realism.

w Cesare Zavattini, Giuseppe Amato, Piero Tellini, Aldo de Benedetti *d* Alessandro Blasetti *ph* Vaclav Vich *m* Alessandro Cicognini

Gino Cervi, Adriana Benetti, Giuditta Rissone

Four Wives*
US 1939 110m bw
Warner (Henry Blanke)

Three of the Lemp girls find a new husband for their widowed sister.
Lively and thickly textured sequel to *Four Daughters*; predecessor of the less interesting *Four Mothers*.

w Julius J. and Philip G. Epstein, Maurice Hanline, *novel* Sister Act by Fannie Hurst *d* Michael Curtiz *ph* Sol Polito *m* Max Steiner

Claude Rains, Priscilla Lane, Rosemary Lane, Lola Lane, Gale Page, Jeffrey Lynn, Eddie Albert, May Robson, Frank McHugh, Dick Foran, John Garfield (briefly)

'Will ride along on momentum to excellent box office.'—*Variety*

Four's a Crowd
US 1938 91m bw
Warner (Hal B. Wallis / David Lewis)

A public relations man has the job of promoting a mean-spirited millionaire, and falls in love with his daughter.
Floppy comedy, neither very witty nor as crazy as might have been expected. However, it ambles along quite engagingly.

w Casey Robinson, Sig Herzig *d* Michael Curtiz *ph* Ernest Haller *m* Heinz Roemheld, Ray Heindorf

Errol Flynn, Rosalind Russell, Olivia de Havilland, Patric Knowles, Walter Connolly, Hugh Herbert, Melville Cooper, Franklin Pangborn, Herman Bing, Margaret Hamilton

'Goofy click comedy that moves along to a whirlwind laugh finish.'—*Variety*

Fourteen Hours***
US 1951 92m bw
TCF (Sol C. Siegel)

A man stands on the ledge of a tall building and threatens to jump.
Well-made documentary drama based on a true occurrence but given a happy ending. First class detail gives an impression of realism.

w John Paxton, article Joel Sayre *d Henry Hathaway* *ph* Joe MacDonald *m* Alfred Newman

Richard Basehart, Paul Douglas, Barbara Bel Geddes, Grace Kelly, Debra Paget, Agnes Moorehead, Robert Keith, Howard da Silva, Jeffrey Hunter, Martin Gabel, Jeff Corey

'A model of craftsmanship in all departments.'—*Penelope Houston*

'A highly enjoyable small scale picture, with a strength immensely greater than its size would suggest.'—*Richard Mallett, Punch*

The Fourth Protocol*
GB 1987 119m Rank colour
Rank (Timothy Burrill)

Vying masterspies narrowly avert nuclear disaster.
Very competent but somehow old hat espionage thriller, from a best seller.

w Frederick Forsyth from his novel *d* John Mackenzie *ph* Phil Meheux *m* Lalo Schifrin *pd* Alan Cameron

Michael Caine, Pierce Brosnan, Joanna Cassidy, Ned Beatty, Betsy Brantley, Ray McAnally, Ian Richardson, Anton Rodgers

'There is an uneasy feeling that the whole affair could have been better made into an excellent miniseries.'—*Daily Variety*

'Between Ellen and Jill came Paul . . .'

The Fox*
US / Canada 1967 110m De Luxe
Warner / Raymond Stross / Motion Pictures International (Howard Koch)

On an isolated farm, two lesbians are disturbed by the arrival of a wandering seaman.
Rather obvious sexual high jinks full of symbolism and heavy breathing.

w Lewis John Carlino, Howard Koch, *novel* D. H. Lawrence *d* Mark Rydell *ph* Bill Fraker *m* Lalo Schifrin

Anne Heywood, Sandy Dennis, Keir Dullea

AAN: Lalo Schifrin

Fox*
West Germany 1975 123m Eastmancolor
Tango Film (Rainer Werner Fassbinder)
aka: *Fox and His Friends*
original title: *Faustrecht der Freiheit*

The decline of a homosexual sideshow performer.

Ironic, semi-autobiographical melodrama in the *Blue Angel* tradition, with sidelong glances at Hollywood glamour. In its way very memorable, but overlong.

w Rainer Werner Fassbinder, Christian Hohoff *d Rainer Werner Fassbinder* *ph* Michael Ballhaus *m* Peer Raben

Rainer Werner Fassbinder, Karl-Heinz Boehm, Peter Chatel, Harry Bär, Adrian Hoven, Ulla Jacobsen

The Fox and the Hound*
US 1981 83m Technicolor
Walt Disney (Wolfgang Reitherman, Art Stevens)

A fox cub makes friends with a hound puppy, but their friendship is tested when they grow up.
Not unpleasant but somewhat heavy-going for a feature cartoon, made with some of the old Disney style but none of the old inventiveness.

w various, *novel* Daniel P. Mannix *d* Art Stevens, Ted Berman, Richard Rich

voices: Mickey Rooney, Kurt Russell, Pearl Bailey, Jack Albertson, Sandy Duncan, Jeanette Nolan

'Laughs are few and far between . . . the whole enterprise lacks vitality.'—*Brenda Davies, MFB*

Fox Movietone Follies of 1929
US 1929 82m bw (sequence in colour)
Fox
GB title: *Movietone Follies of 1929*

An all-star review.
Every studio had its early talkie musical using up its contract stars; this was perhaps the least interesting.

wd David Butler, William K. Wells

ph Charles Van Enger *m* Con Conrad, Sidney Mitchell, Archie Gottlieb *md* Arthur Kay

Sue Carol, Lola Lane, Dixie Lee, Sharon Lynn, Stepin Fetchit

Foxes
US 1980 106m Technicolor

Four teenage girls battle with sex, drugs and life in general. Well-meaning but entirely resistible melodrama from behind the headlines. Jodie Foster, Scott Baio, Sally Kellerman, Randy Quaid, Adam Faith. Written by Gerald Ayres; directed by Adrian Lyne; for Casablanca / UA. 'Almost nil adult appeal.'—*Variety.*

The Foxes of Harrow
US 1947 117m bw
TCF (William A. Bacher)

In 1820 New Orleans, a philanderer seeks advancement by breaking up his marriage.
Tolerable but rather flat adaptation of a bestseller, stultified by central miscasting.

w Wanda Tuchock, *novel* Frank Yerby *d* John M. Stahl *ph* Joseph La Shelle *m* Alfred Newman

Rex Harrison, Maureen O'Hara, Richard Haydn, Victor McLaglen, Vanessa Brown, Patricia Medina, Gene Lockhart, Hugo Haas

† Rex Harrison's role had been turned down by Tyrone Power.

'I don't care what they call you! I only care that you are all man—and all mine!'

Foxfire
US 1955 92m Technicolor
U-I (Aaron Rosenberg)

A rich New York girl on holiday in Arizona is attracted to a half-Apache miner.
Romantic melodrama with action asides; watchable for women who like that sort of thing.

w Ketti Frings, *novel* Anya Seton *d* Joseph Pevney *ph* William Daniels *m* Frank Skinner

Jane Russell, Jeff Chandler, Frieda Inescort, Dan Duryea

Foxhole in Cairo
GB 1960 80m bw
Omnia (Steven Pallos, Donald Taylor)

A German agent in Libya is allowed to get back to Rommel with false information.
Interesting true spy story deflated by muddled handling.

w Leonard Mosley, from his book The Cat and the Mice *d* John Moxey *ph* Desmond Dickinson *m* Wolfram Rohrig, Douglas Gamley, Ken Jones

James Robertson Justice, Adrian Hoven, Albert Lieven (as Rommel), Niall MacGinnis, Peter Van Eyck, Robert Urquhart, Fenella Fielding

Foxtrot
Mexico / Switzerland 1977 91m Technicolor

Rich people retreat to a desert island to avoid World War II, but their servants revolt. A more or less direct attempt to remake *La Règle du Jeu*; it sinks into boredom. Peter O'Toole, Charlotte Rampling, Max Von Sydow, Jorge Luke, Helena Rojo, Claudio Brook. Written by Arturo Ripstein, José Emilio Pacheco, H. A. L. Craig; directed by Arturo Ripstein; for Gerald Green / New World.

Fra Diavolo**
US 1933 90m bw
MGM / Hal Roach
aka: *The Devil's Brother*

Two incompetent bandits are hired as manservants by a real bandit.
Auber's 1830 operetta becomes a vehicle for Laurel and Hardy, setting a pattern they followed with *Babes in Toyland* and *The Bohemian Girl.* They have excellent sequences, but overall the film lacks pace.

w Jeanie McPherson *d* Hal Roach, Charles Rogers *ph* Art Lloyd, Hap Depew *md* Le Roy Shield

Stan Laurel, Oliver Hardy, Dennis King, *James Finlayson*, Thelma Todd

'An early 19th-century comic opera doesn't make for particularly good film fare despite its hoking.'—*Variety*

Fragment of an Empire*
USSR 1929 100m approx bw silent
Sovkino

A young man who lost his memory in World War I regains it in 1928 and surveys the changed social order.
Mildly satirical propaganda piece with a vivid impression of Leningrad at the time.

w Friedrich Ermier, Katerina Vinogradskaya *d* Friedrich Ermler *ph* Yevgeni Schneider

Fyoder Nikitin, Yakov Gudkin, Ludmila Semyonova

Fragment of Fear*
GB 1970 95m Technicolor
Columbia (John R. Sloan)

A young writer investigates the murder of his aunt, but finds that he may himself be mad.
What appears to be a whodunnit turns into a flashy, fashionable, sub-Antonioni puzzle with no ending, but despite the considerable irritation this causes, the details and character cameos are excellent.

w Paul Dehn, *novel* John Bingham *d* Richard C. Sarafian *ph* Oswald Morris *m* Johnny Harris

David Hemmings, Gayle Hunnicutt, Roland Culver, Daniel Massey, Flora Robson, Wilfrid Hyde White, Adolfo Celi, Mona Washbourne

Framed
US 1947 82m bw

A drunken out-of-work engineer is used as fall guy by two thieves planning an elaborate coup. Lugubrious mixture of puzzle, character drama and gloomy philosophizing, complete with femme fatale who is handed over to the cops at the end. Glenn Ford, Janis Carter, Barry Sullivan. Written by Ben Maddow; directed by Richard Wallace; for Columbia. (GB title: *Paula.*)

Framed
US 1974 106m Metrocolor

A Tennessee gambler inadvertently kills a sheriff, is sent to prison, gets out on parole and wreaks revenge on those who framed him. Violent thick-ear update of *The Count of Monte Cristo,* of interest only to connoisseurs of gratuitous nastiness. Joe Don Baker, Conny Van Dyke, Gabriel Dell, Brock Peters, John Marley, John Larch. Written by Mort Briskin; directed by Phil Karlson; for Paramount.

Frances
US 1982 140m Technicolor
EMI / Brooksfilm (Jonathan Sanger)

The downhill career of 30s actress Frances Farmer.
Long, glum, and not particularly convincing in its inferences, this exhaustive study of a person who didn't deserve all this fuss is illuminated only by a strong star performance.

w Eric Bergren, Christopher Devore, Nicholas Kazan *d* Graeme Clifford *ph* Laszlo Kovacs *m* John Barry *pd* Richard Sylbert

Jessica Lange, Kim Stanley, Sam Shepard, Bart Burns, Jeffrey de Munn
AAN: Jessica Lange; Kim Stanley

The Franchise Affair*
GB 1950 88m bw
ABP (Robert Hall)

A young girl accuses two gentlewomen of kidnapping and ill-treating her.
Unusual and absorbing mystery based on a true 18th-century case; the treatment however is rather too mild.

w Robert Hall, Lawrence Huntington, *novel* Josephine Tey *d* Lawrence Huntington *ph* Gunther Krampf *m* Philip Green

Michael Denison, Dulcie Gray, Anthony Nicholls, Marjorie Fielding, Athene Seyler, Ann Stephens, Hy Hazell, John Bailey, Kenneth More

Francis*
US 1950 90m bw
U-I (Robert Arthur)

An army private makes friends with a talking mule who causes him some embarrassment.
Simple-minded, quite agreeable if rather slow-moving fantasy farce which was popular enough to spawn several sequels and later a TV series called *Mister Ed.*

w David Stern, from his novel *d* Arthur Lubin *ph* Irving Glassberg *m* Frank Skinner

Donald O'Connor, Patricia Medina, Zasu Pitts, Ray Collins, John McIntyre, Eduard Franz, Robert Warwick, and Chill Wills as Francis' voice.

Sequels (the first six with Donald O'Connor):
1951: FRANCIS GOES TO THE RACES
1952: FRANCIS GOES TO WEST POINT
1953: FRANCIS COVERS BIG TOWN
1954: FRANCIS JOINS THE WACS
1955: FRANCIS IN THE NAVY
1956: FRANCIS IN THE HAUNTED HOUSE (with Mickey Rooney)

Francis of Assisi
US 1961 107m De Luxe Cinemascope
TCF / Perseus (Plato A. Skouras)

The son of a medieval cloth merchant takes a vow of poverty, cares for animals and dies a hermit.
Tedious biopic.

w Eugene Vale, Jack Thomas, James Forsyth *d* Michael Curtiz *ph* Piero Portalupi *m* Mario Nascimbene

Bradford Dillman, Dolores Hart, Stuart Whitman, Eduard Franz, Pedro Armendariz, Cecil Kellaway, Finlay Currie, Mervyn Johns, Athene Seyler

'To have seen it is to wear a badge of courage!'
'A monster science created but could not destroy!'

Frankenstein****
US 1931 71m bw
Universal (Carl Laemmle Jnr)

A research scientist creates a living monster from corpses, but it runs amok.
Whole books have been written about this film and its sequels. Apart from being a fascinating if primitive cinematic work in its own right, it set its director and star on interesting paths and established a Hollywood attitude towards horror (mostly borrowed from German silents such as *The Golem*). A seminal film indeed, which at each repeated viewing belies its age.

w Garrett Fort, Francis Edward Faragoh, John L. Balderston, from the play by Peggy Webling and the novel by Mary Wollstonecraft Shelley *d James Whale, ph Arthur Edeson m* David Broekman *ad Charles D. Hall*

Boris Karloff, Colin Clive, Mae Clarke, John Boles, *Edward Van Sloan, Frederick Kerr, Dwight Frye*

'Still the most famous of all horror films, and deservedly so.'—*John Baxter, 1968*

'The horror is cold, chilling the marrow but never arousing malaise.'—*Carlos Clarens*

† Direct sequels by the same studio (all qv) include *The Bride of Frankenstein, Son of Frankenstein, Ghost of Frankenstein, Frankenstein Meets the Wolf Man, House of Frankenstein, House of Dracula, Abbott and Costello Meet Frankenstein.* The later Hammer series, which told the story all over again in gorier vein, includes (all qv) *The Curse of Frankenstein, The Revenge of Frankenstein, The Evil of Frankenstein, Frankenstein Created Woman, Frankenstein Must be Destroyed, Horror of Frankenstein, Frankenstein and the Monster from Hell.* Other Frankenstein films date from as early as 1908, and scores have been made in various languages. *Young Frankenstein* (qv) is a partly effective spoof on the Hollywood series; *The Munsters* was a sixties comedy series for TV which used the monster as its leading character in a domestic setting.

†† Robert Florey is said to have contributed to the script, having been the first choice for director.

Frankenstein and the Monster from Hell
GB 1973 99m Technicolor

The Baron turns an injured lunatic into a hairy ape man. Cheaply made and very ghoulish horror comic in the unattractive setting of an asylum; very little entertainment is provided. Peter Cushing, Shane Briant, Madeleine Smith, John Stratton, Bernard Lee, Dave Prowse. Written by John Elder (Anthony Hinds); directed by Terence Fisher; for Hammer / Avco.

'A beautiful woman with the soul of a devil!'

Frankenstein Created Woman
GB 1966 86m Technicolor

The Baron invests the body of a dead girl with the soul of her dead lover, and a murder spree results. Crude and gory farrago, with the central laboratory sequence apparently excised at the last moment. Peter Cushing, Thorley Walters, Susan Denberg, Robert Morris, Duncan Lamont. Written by John Elder (Anthony Hinds); directed by Terence Fisher; for Hammer / Warner.

'Titans of terror, clashing in mortal combat!'

Frankenstein Meets the Wolf Man**
US 1943 73m bw
Universal (George Waggner)

Lawrence Talbot, the wolf man, travels to Vasaria in the hope of a cure, and finds the Frankenstein monster being reactivated.
Once one recovered from the bargain basement combination of two monsters in one picture, this was a horror comic with stylish sequences, weakened by cuts in the script and a miscast Bela Lugosi.

w Curt Siodmak *d Roy William Neill ph* George Robinson *m* Hans Salter

Lon Chaney Jnr, Ilona Massey, Bela Lugosi (as the monster), Patric Knowles, *Maria Ouspenskaya*

Frankenstein Must Be Destroyed
GB 1969 96m Technicolor

The Baron transplants the brain of one colleague into the body of another. Spirited but decidedly unpleasant addition to the cycle, made more so by a genuine note of pathos. Peter Cushing, Freddie Jones, Veronica Carlson, Simon Ward, Thorley Walters, Maxine Audley. Written by Bert Batt; directed by Terence Fisher; for Hammer / Warner-Pathé.

Frankenstein '70
US 1958 83m bw Cinemascope
Allied Artists (Aubrey Schenck)

Television film-makers descend on Castle Frankenstein; the current Count needs the money to finance some monster making of his own.
Boringly talkative and very silly 'futuristic' blot on an honourable name, apart from a rather frightening pre-credits sequence.

w Richard Landau, G. Worthing Yates *d* Howard W. Koch *ph* Carl Guthrie *m* Paul Dunlap

Boris Karloff, Tom Duggan, Jana Lund

Frankie and Johnny*
US 1966 87m Technicolor
UA / F and J (Edward Small)

On a Mississippi riverboat, a gambling singer is the despair of his lady partner.
Mildly amusing pastiche both of the old song and of the various riverboat dramas.

w Alex Gottlieb *d* Frederick de Cordova *ph* John Marquette *m* Fred Karger

Elvis Presley, Donna Douglas, Sue Ane Langdon, Harry Morgan, Nancy Kovack, Audrey Christie, Jerome Cowan

Frantic*
US 1988 120m colour
Warner / Mount

An American cardiologist in Paris hunting for his kidnapped wife becomes embroiled with Arab terrorists.
Amiable thriller with Hitchcockian touches, quite untypical of this director.

w Roman Polanski, Gérard Brach *d* Roman Polanski *ph* Witold Sobocinski *m* Ennio Morricone *pd* Pierre Guffroy

Harrison Ford, Betty Buckley, Emmanuelle Seigner, Alexandra Stewart

'Disappointingly conventional mystery.'—*Variety*

Fräulein
US 1958 100m Eastmancolor Cinemascope
TCF (Walter Reisch)

During World War II an American prisoner of war escapes and is helped by the daughter of a German professor.
Studio-bound war heroics with little conviction achieved or aimed at.

w Lee Townsend, *novel* James McGowan *d* Henry Koster *ph* Leo Tover *m* Daniele Amfitheatrof

Dana Wynter, Mel Ferrer, Margaret Hayes, Dolores Michaels, Theodore Bikel, Helmut Dantine

Fräulein Doktor
Italy / Yugoslavia 1968 104m Technicolor
(Paramount) Dino de Laurentiis / Avala

In World War I, a German lady spy outwits British intelligence.
Rather glum international action melodrama.

w Diulio Coletti, H. A. L. Craig, Stanley Mann, Vittoriano Petrilli, Alberto Lattuada *d* Alberto Lattuada *ph* Luigi Kuveiller *m* Ennio Morricone

Suzy Kendall, Kenneth More, James Booth, Capucine, Alexander Knox, Nigel Green, Roberto Bisacco
† A similar story was filmed in 1936 as *Mademoiselle Docteur*.

Freaks**
US 1932 64m bw
MGM (Tod Browning)

A lady trapeze artist marries a midget, then poisons him for his money; his abnormal friends take revenge by turning her into a freak.
Made but disowned by MGM after accusations of tastelessness, this strident and silly melodrama has dated badly but has sequences of great power, especially the final massing of the freaks, slithering to their revenge in a rainstorm. It would have been better as a silent; the dialogue kills it.

w Willis Goldbeck, Leon Gordon, *novel* Spurs by Tod Robbins *d Tod Browning ph* Merrit B. Gerstad

Wallace Ford, Olga Baclanova, Leila Hyams, Roscoe Ates

'Either too horrible or not sufficiently so.'—*Variety*

'It is a skilfully presented production but of a character which in consideration of the susceptibilities of mass audiences should be avoided.'—*Martin Quigley*

'For pure sensationalism it tops any picture yet produced.'—*Louella Parsons*

'I want something that out-horrors Frankenstein.'—*Irving Thalberg*

'Touching and funny and made with a miraculous delicacy.'—*Evening Standard, 1964*

Freaky Friday
US 1976 100m Technicolor
Walt Disney (Ron Miller)

A 13-year-old and her mother, each discontented with their lot, express a wish to change places—and do.
A trendy update of *Vice Versa*, padded out with Disney irrelevancies and long outstaying its welcome.

w Mary Rodgers, from her novel *d* Gary Nelson *ph* Charles F. Wheeler *m* Johnny Mandel

Jodie Foster, Barbara Harris, John Astin, Patsy Kelly, Dick Van Patten, Sorrell Booke, Marie Windsor

Freckles
US 1935 69m bw

A mild teenager gets a job as a timber guard.
Unsensational version of a rustic classic. Written by Dorothy Yost from the novel by Gene Stratton-Porter; directed by Edward Killy and William Hamilton; for Pandro S. Berman / RKO. 'The novel, published in 1875, is shown to have sold 2,000,000 copies. It will have a tough time making the same grade as a picture . . . its appeal is of a past generation.'—*Variety*
† A 1960 remake for Fox starred Martin West.

Free and Easy
US 1930 75m bw
MGM (Edward Sedgwick)

A beauty contest winner is taken to Hollywood by her accident-prone manager.
Primitive talkie showing a great silent comedian all at sea with the new techniques, and the MGM studio offering entertainment on the level of a very bad school concert.

w Al Boasberg, Richard Schayer *d* Edward Sedgwick *ph* Leonard Smith

Buster Keaton, Anita Page, Robert Montgomery, Trixie Freganza

Free and Easy
US 1941 56m bw

In British high society, father and son both seek rich wives. A remarkable cast is all at sea in a potted version of Ivor Novello's *The Truth Game*. Nigel Bruce, Robert Cummings, Ruth Hussey, Judith Anderson, C. Aubrey Smith, Reginald Owen, Tom Conway, Forrester Harvey. Written by Marvin Borowsky; directed by George Sidney; for MGM. 'This one must have slipped through the Metro wringer while the brains department was out to lunch.'—*Variety*

Free for All
US 1949 83m bw
U-I (Robert Buckner)

A young inventor finds a way of turning water into petrol.
Scatty comedy with mildly amusing moments.

w Robert Buckner *d* Charles T. Barton *ph* George Robinson *m* Frank Skinner

Robert Cummings, Ann Blyth, Percy Kilbride, Ray Collins, Donald Woods, Mikhail Rasumny

A Free Soul*
US 1931 91m bw
MGM

An unconventional lawyer regrets allowing his daughter to consort with a gangster.
Heavy melodrama with outdated attitudes, but an impressive example of the studio's style in the early thirties.

w John Meehan, *novel* Adela Rogers St John *d* Clarence Brown *ph* William Daniels *m* William Axt

Lionel Barrymore, Norma Shearer, Leslie Howard, Clark Gable, Lucy Beaumont, James Gleason

'An ungainly, rambling and preposterous theme, awkwardly brought to the screen.'—*Variety*
† Remade 1953 as *The Girl Who Had Everything*.
AA: Lionel Barrymore (who had a 14-minute speech)
AAN: Clarence Brown; Norma Shearer

'Today they demolished 23 cars, four motor cycles and one apartment building. But don't call the cops. They *are* the cops!'

Freebie and the Bean*
US 1974 113m Technicolor Panavision
Warner (Richard Rush)

Two vaguely incompetent cops try to link a mobster with the numbers racket.
Violent comedy melodrama with a high mortality rate, amoral outlook, and the usual seventies reliance on incoherent plot, bumbled dialogue and excessive background noise. Occasionally funny all the same.

w Richard Kaufman *d* Richard Rush *ph* Laszlo Kovacs *m* Dominic Frontière

Alan Arkin, James Caan, Loretta Swit, Jack Kruschen, Mike Kellin

'It summarizes Hollywood's favourite thematic elements of the early seventies: platonic male love affair, police corruption, comic violence, cynicism in high places, San Francisco, gay villains, the car chase. A return to the Keystone Kops, with character trimmings and lashings of sado-masochistic mayhem.'—*Clyde Jeavons*

'A tasteless film from a spitball script.'—*Variety*

'There is a beating or a killing, or at least a yelling scene, every couple of minutes.'—*New Yorker, 1980*

Freedom Radio
GB 1941 95m bw
Columbia / Two Cities (Mario Zampi)
US title: *A Voice in the Night*

In Vienna during World War II, the husband of a Nazi actress runs a secret radio transmitter for Allied propaganda.
Moderate wartime flagwaver.

w Basil Wood, Gordon Wellesley, Louis Golding, Anatole de Grunwald, Jeffrey Dell, Bridget Boland, Roland Pertwee *d* Anthony Asquith *ph* Bernard Knowles

Diana Wynyard, Clive Brook, Raymond Huntley, Joyce Howard, Derek Farr, Howard Marion Crawford, Morland Graham

French Can-Can**
France / Italy 1955 105m Technicolor
Franco-London / Jolly (Louis Wipf)

How the can-can was launched in Paris night clubs.
A dramatically thin vehicle splendidly evoking a vision of vanished Paris: a feast for the eyes.

w André-Paul Antoine *d* Jean Renoir *ph Michel Kelber m* Georges Van Parys

Jean Gabin, Françoise Arnoul, Maria Félix, Jean-Roger Caussimon, Edith Piaf, Patachou

'Doyle is bad news . . . but a good cop!'
The French Connection***
US 1971 104m De Luxe
TCF / Philip D'Antoni

New York police track down a consignment of drugs entering the country in a car.
Lively semi-documentary based on the true exploits of a tough cop named Eddie Egan who liked to break a few rules. Most memorable for a car chase scene involving an elevated railway, for showing the seamy side of New York more or less as it is, and for the most mumbled dialogue and the poorest sound track in years.

w Ernest Tidyman, *book* Robin Moore *d William Friedkin* *ph* Owen Roizman *m* Don Ellis

Gene Hackman, Roy Scheider, *Fernando Rey*, Tony Lo Bianco

AA: best picture; Ernest Tidyman; William Friedkin; Gene Hackman
AAN: Owen Roizman; Roy Scheider

French Connection II
US 1975 119m De Luxe
TCF (Robert L. Rosen)

The New York cop who in *The French Connection* smashed most of a drug ring arrives in Marseilles to track down its elusive leader.
Sleazy, virtually plotless and unattractive sequel which rises to a few good action moments but is bogged down by bad language, unconvincing characterization and an interminable and irrelevant 'cold turkey' sequence.

w Robert Dillon, Laurie Dillon, Alexander Jacobs *d* John Frankenheimer *ph* Claude Renoir *m* Don Ellis

Gene Hackman, Fernando Rey, Bernard Fresson, Jean-Pierre Castaldi

'Visually as well as morally the film makes you uncertain where its feet are.'—*New Yorker*

French Dressing
GB 1963 86m bw
ABP / Kenwood (Kenneth Harper)

A deckchair attendant and a local reporter believe that what Bardot can do for St Tropez they can do for Gormleigh-on-Sea.
Cinema's *enfant terrible* directs this his first theatrical film at breakneck speed with echoes of Tati, Keaton and the Keystone Kops. Alas, lack of star comedians and firm control make its exuberance merely irritating.

w Peter Myers, Ronald Cass, Peter Britt *d Ken Russell* *ph* Ken Higgins *m* Georges Delerue

James Booth, Roy Kinnear, Marisa Mell, Bryan Pringle

The French Key
US 1946 67m bw

Private eyes, locked out of their hotel room for non-payment of rent, use the fire escape and find a body inside. Minor mystery which seemed passable at the time. Albert Dekker, Mike Mazurki, Evelyn Ankers, John Eldredge, Frank Fenton. Written by Frank Gruber, from his novel; directed by Walter Colmes; for Republic.

French Leave
GB 1930 100m bw

In order to be near her husband, a British girl pretends to be French and goes behind the trenches. Flat picturization of a popular stage farce of the twenties. Madeleine Carroll, Sydney Howard, Arthur Chesney, Haddon Mason, Henry Kendall. Written by W. P. Lipscomb, Reginald Berkeley from the latter's play; directed by Jack Raymond; for D and H.
† Remade in 1937 with Betty Lynne, directed by Norman Lee, for Welwyn.

'She was lost from the moment she saw him . . . '
The French Lieutenant's Woman*
GB 1981 123m Technicolor
UA / Juniper (Leon Clore)

In 1867 Lyme Regis, a gentleman forsakes his fiancée for the abandoned mistress of a French seaman.
Vaguely unsatisfactory and muddily coloured adaptation of a novel which set its thin story against the entire social background of the Victorian age as related to our own. The attempt to replace this by an equally thin modern story about actors playing the Victorian roles fails rather dismally; but the enterprise supplies points of interest along the way.

w Harold Pinter, *novel* John Fowles *d* Karel Reisz *ph* Freddie Francis *m* Carl Davis *pd Assheton Gorton*

Jeremy Irons, *Meryl Streep*, Leo McKern, Patience Collier, Peter Vaughan, Hilton McRae

'Pinter's reduction not only shears away the sliding historical perspective, but robs the narrative of its Victorian charisma.'—*Tom Milne, MFB*

'There are some lovely moments, and a few have magical undertones, but most of the picture might be taking place in a glass case.'—*Pauline Kael*

'If you see the movie, the book will still surprise you, and that's as it should be.'—*Roger Ebert*

AAN: Harold Pinter; editing (John Bloom); Meryl Streep
BFA: best sound; Carl Davis; Meryl Streep

The French Line
US 1953 102m Technicolor 3-D
RKO (Edmund Grainger)

A cheery Texas oil heiress finds a husband while travelling to France.
Very thinly plotted but quite attractive light musical with a good-humoured star wearing costumes once thought censorable.

w Mary Loos, Richard Sale *d* Lloyd Bacon *ph* Harry J. Wild *m* Walter Scharf *md* Lionel Newman *ch* Jack Cole

Jane Russell, Gilbert Roland, Arthur Hunnicutt, Mary McCarty

'A slouching Amazon, her clothes appear to stay put just as long as she agrees not to burst out of them; essentially a good sort, she has an ever-annihilating sneer for the false, the pretentious and the fresh.'—*MFB*

A French Mistress
GB 1960 98m bw
British Lion / Charter (John Boulting)

An attractive new mistress causes havoc at a boys' school.
Sloppy, predictable comedy with practised performers getting a few easy laughs. The producers tried to excuse its imperfections by promoting it as 'a romp'.

w Roy Boulting, Jeffrey Dell, *play* Robert Monro (Sonnie Hale) *d* Roy Boulting *ph* Max Greene *m* John Addison

James Robertson Justice, Cecil Parker, Raymond Huntley, Ian Bannen, Agnes Laurent, Thorley Walters, Edith Sharpe, Athene Seyler, Kenneth Griffith

French without Tears**
GB 1939 85m bw
Paramount / Two Cities (Mario Zampi)

Young Britons at a French crammers fall for the young sister of one of their number.
Pleasant light comedy from a successful West End play.

w Terence Rattigan, Anatole de Grunwald, Ian Dalrymple, *play Terence Rattigan* *d* Anthony Asquith *ph* Bernard Knowles *m* Nicholas Brodszky

Ray Milland, Ellen Drew, *Guy Middleton*, *Ronald Culver*, David Tree, Jim Gerald, Janine Darcy, Kenneth Morgan

'There is always something a little shocking about English levity. The greedy exhilaration of these blithe young men when they learn that another fellow's girl is to join them at the establishment where they are learning French, the scramble over her luggage, the light-hearted badinage, the watery and libidinous eye—that national mixture of prudery and excitement—would be unbearable if it were not for Mr Asquith's civilized direction.'—*Graham Greene*

† Incredibly, Paramount had purchased the property as a vehicle for Marlene Dietrich.

Frenchie
US 1950 80m Technicolor
U-I (Michael Kraike)

A saloon queen sets up shop in Bottleneck, her real aim being to track down her father's murderers.
Modest western of the *Destry Rides Again* school.

w Oscar Brodney *d* Louis King *ph* Maury Gertsman *m* Hans Salter

Shelley Winters, Joel McCrea, Paul Kelly, Elsa Lanchester, Marie Windsor, John Emery, George Cleveland, John Russell

'For 24 reckless hours the arms of adventure embraced her—and she knew the thrill of true love!'

Frenchman's Creek*
US 1944 112m Technicolor
Paramount (B. G. De Sylva)

In Restoration England, a lady flees from a lascivious nobleman to her family home in Cornwall, where she falls in love with a French pirate.
Enjoyable Girls' Own Paper romance, dressed to kill and entertaining despite its many palpable absurdities.

w Talbot Jennings, *novel* Daphne du Maurier *d Mitchell Leisen ph George Barnes m* Victor Young *ad Hans Dreier, Ernest Fegte*

Joan Fontaine, Arturo de Cordova, Basil Rathbone, Nigel Bruce, *Cecil Kellaway*, Ralph Forbes, Moyna McGill

'Masturbation fantasy triple distilled.'—*James Agee*

Frenzy*
Sweden 1944 101m bw
Svensk Filmindustri
original title: *Hets;* aka: *Torment*

A sadistic Latin teacher and his sensitive pupil find themselves competing for the same girl.
Hothouse melodrama of the *Blue Angel* school: it seemed pretty powerful at the time.

w Ingmar Bergman *d Alf Sjöberg ph* Martin Bodin *m* Hilding Rosenberg

Stig Jarrel, Alf Kjellin, Mai Zetterling

'From the master of shock, a shocking masterpiece!'

Frenzy*
GB 1972 116m Technicolor
Universal / Alfred Hitchcock

A disillusioned and aggressive ex-RAF officer is suspected through circumstantial evidence of being London's 'necktie murderer'.
Has-been, unconvincing, cliché-ridden thriller, an old man's sex suspenser, which would have been derided if anyone but Hitchcock had made it. As it is, a few comic and suspenseful touches partly atone for the implausibilities and lapses of taste.

w Anthony Shaffer, *novel* Goodbye Piccadilly, Farewell Leicester Square by Arthur La Bern *d* Alfred Hitchcock *ph* Gilbert Taylor *m* Ron Goodwin

Jon Finch, *Alec McCowen, Barry Foster*, Vivien Merchant, Anna Massey

'Hitchcock's most stodgy piece since *Dial M for Murder* and possibly his least interesting film from any period.'—*William S. Pechter*

'There is suspense, and local colour, and always, Hitchcock smacking his lips and rubbing his hands and delighting in his naughtiness.'—*Roger Ebert*

The Freshman**
US 1925 75m (24 fps) bw silent
Harold Lloyd

An awkward college student accidentally becomes a star football player.
A rather slow but striking star vehicle with assured set-pieces. The football game climax was later used as the first reel of *Mad Wednesday*.

w Sam Taylor, Ted Wilde, Time Whelan, John Grey *d* Fred Newmeyer, Sam Taylor *ph* Walter Lundin, Henry Kohler

Harold Lloyd, Jobyna Ralston, Brooks Benedict

Freud**
GB 1962 140m bw
U-I (Wolfgang Reinhardt)

Vienna 1885; Dr Sigmund Freud, a neurologist, uses hypnotism to treat hysteria, and finds new interest in the case of a boy whose hatred of his father springs from incestuous love of his mother, a failing which Freud finds in himself.
Earnest and competent biopic harking back to Warners' similar films of the thirties, with the addition of franker language. Generally absorbing, but undeniably hard tack.

w Charles Kaufman, Wolfgang Reinhardt *d John Huston ph* Douglas Slocombe *m* Jerry Goldsmith

Montgomery Clift, Larry Parks, Susannah York, Eileen Herlie, Susan Kohner, David McCallum

'The dream sequences, photographed mostly in negative or overexposure, belong not on the couch of Dr Freud but in the Cabinet of Dr Caligari.'—*John Simon*

'It is impossible, I would think, for any educated person to sit through *Freud* without bursting into laughter at least once.'—*Ernest Callenbach, Film Quarterly*

AAN: script; Jerry Goldsmith

Fric Frac*
France 1939 95m bw

A provincial jeweller's assistant falls in with underworld characters. Well-prized French comedy with dialogue entirely in thieves' slang. Michel Simon, Fernandel, Arletty, Helene Robert. Written by Michel Duran from the play by Edouard Bourdet; directed by Maurice Lehmann; for his own company.

Friday the Thirteenth***
GB 1933 84m bw
Gainsborough (Michael Balcon)

Several people are involved in a bus crash, and we turn back the clock to see how they came to be there.
Highly competent compendium of comedies and dramas looking back to *The Bridge of San Luis Rey* and forward to the innumerable all-star films of the forties.

w G. H. Moresby-White, Sidney Gilliat, Emlyn Williams d Victor Saville ph Charles Van Enger

Sonnie Hale, Cyril Smith, *Eliot Makeham*, Ursula Jeans, *Emlyn Williams*, Frank Lawton, Belle Chrystal, *Max Miller*, Alfred Drayton, Edmund Gwenn, Mary Jerrold, Gordon Harker, *Robertson Hare*, Martita Hunt, Leonora Corbett, Jessie Matthews, Ralph Richardson

Friday the Thirteenth
US 1980 95m colour
Georgetown (Sean S. Cunningham)

When a summer camp is reopened after many years, the grisly murders which closed it down begin again.
Horror suspense story with no *raison d'être* but a series of inventively gory shock moments, which were enough however for it to ring the box office bell.

w Victor Miller *d* Sean S. Cunningham *ph* Barry Abrams

Betsy Palmer, Adrienne King, Jeannine Taylor, Robbi Morgan

'An oversexed couple makes love in the bottom bunk, there's a dead body in the top bunk and the rest of the bunk is in the television commercials.'—*Variety*

Friday the Thirteenth Part Two
US 1981 87m De Luxe

The sole survivor of the massacre at Camp Crystal Lake is murdered, and five years later the mayhem begins again, the villain being the son of the woman who committed the former killings. Virtually a remake of the first film, starting with a long flashback to it; short sharp shocks punctuate slabs of tedium. Amy Steel, John Furey, Adrienne King, Kirsten Baker. Written by Ron Kurz; directed by Steve Miner; for Georgetown Productions.

Friday the Thirteenth Part Three
US 1982 95m Movielab 3D

Crazy Jason is still murdering kids up at Crystal Lake. No better than its predecessors for being in three dimensions; in fact, half as bad again. Dana Kimmell, Richard Brooker, Catherine Parks, Paul Kratka. Written by Martin Kitrosser and Carol Watson; directed by Steve Miner; for Georgetown productions. 'The first was dreadful and took seventeen million. The second was just as bad and took more than ten million. No doubt the distributor will be happy to learn that the third is terrible too.'—*Variety*.

Friday the Thirteenth: Final Chapter
US 1984 91m Movielab

Supposedly dead Jason escapes from cold storage at the morgue and goes on another rampage. The awful mixture as before: would the title meant what it says. E. Erich Anderson, Judie Aronson, Peter Barton, Kimberly Beck. Written by Barney Cohen; directed by Joseph Zito; for Paramount. 'Yet another catalogue of mindless slaughter which doesn't even offer the courtesy of a story.'—*Daily Mail*. 'The censor says you have to be 18 to see it. I would suggest you merely have to be daft.'—*Sunday Times*

† The sequels kept coming despite the title of this one: by 1986 we had passed *A New Beginning* and were up to *Part Six*. By 1988 we were up to *Part Seven—The New Blood*.

Frieda*
GB 1947 97m bw
Ealing (Michael Relph)

An RAF officer marries and takes home a girl who helped him escape from a POW camp. Stuffy and dated drama about how one English family learned to love one particular German. Timely when it appeared, however, and well made within its conventions.

w Angus Macphail, Ronald Millar, *play* Ronald Millar *d* Basil Dearden *ph* Gordon Dines *m* John Greenwood

Mai Zetterling, David Farrar, Glynis Johns, Flora Robson, Albert Lieven

Friendly Enemies
US 1925 70m (24 fps) bw silent

Two German immigrants are divided when the United States enters the war. Curious comedy-drama for two vaudevillians, based on a topical play of the time. Joe Weber, Lew Fields, Virginia Brown Faire, Jack Mulhall. Written by Alfred A. Cohn, from the play by Samuel Shipman and Aaron Hoffman; directed by George Melford; for PDC. (Remade in 1942 with Charles Winninger.)

Friendly Persuasion**
US 1956 139m De Luxe
AA (William Wyler)

At the outbreak of the Civil War, a family of Quakers has to consider its position. Sentimental, homespun western fare, well done without being especially engrossing.

w Michael Wilson, *novel* Jessamyn West *d* *William Wyler* *ph* Ellsworth Fredericks *m* Dmitri Tiomkin

Gary Cooper, Dorothy McGuire, Anthony Perkins, Marjorie Main, Richard Eyer, Robert Middleton, Walter Catlett

'The material is a little tenuous . . . but Wyler's sure-handed direction constantly illuminates it with a humour, a gentle charm and a feeling for fundamental values that are rare indeed.'—*Moira Walsh, America*

† For TV movie remake, see *Television Companion.*

AAN: best picture; Michael Wilson; William Wyler; Anthony Perkins; song 'Thee I Love' (*m* Dmitri Tiomkin, *ly* Paul Francis Webster)

'Who needs the world when you own the moon and stars?'

Friends
GB 1971 102m Technicolor
Paramount (Lewis Gilbert)

Teenage lovers run away to a country cottage and have a child.
Peculiar idyll given corny 'poetic' treatment: a real non-starter.

w Jack Russell, Vernon Harris *d* Lewis Gilbert *ph* Andrew Winding *m* Elton John

Sean Bury, Anicee Alvina, Toby Robbins, Ronald Lewis

Friends and Lovers
US 1931 67m bw
RKO (William Le Baron)

A society wife causes several hearts to flutter illicitly. Unsatisfactory comedy-drama which lurches along from one mood to another and may have been intended as satire.

w Wallace Smith, *novel* The Sphinx Has Spoken by Maurice Dekobra *d* Victor Schertzinger *ph* J. Roy Hunt *m* Victor Schertzinger, Max Steiner

Adolphe Menjou, Laurence Olivier, Lily Damita, Erich Von Stroheim, Hugh Herbert, Frederick Kerr, Blanche Friderici

'Dumb sentimental romance . . . the people never once display motives that are understandable or reasonable.'—*Variety*

The Friends of Eddie Coyle*
US 1973 102m Technicolor
Paramount (Paul Monash)

An ageing hoodlum agrees to become a police informer and is hunted down by his former associates.
Dour gangster melodrama held together by its central performance.

w Paul Monash, *novel* George V. Higgins *d* Peter Yates *ph* Vernon J. Kemper *m* Dave Grusin

Robert Mitchum, Peter Boyle, Richard Jordan, Steven Keats, Mitch Ryan, Alex Rocco

Friends of Mr Sweeney*
US 1934 68m bw

A brow-beaten reporter gets drunk, faces life, and changes his personality. Amusing minor comedy of a kind no longer made. *Charles Ruggles,* Eugene Pallette, Berton Churchill, Robert Barrat, Ann Dvorak. Written by Warren Duff and Sidney Sutherland, from the novel by Elmer Davis; directed by Edward Ludwig; for Warner. 'Old situations given a new comedy coating . . . positive all-round fun for every family.'—*Variety*

Fright
GB 1971 87m Eastmancolor

A babysitter is menaced by a psychotic. Unattractive screamer which starts on a hysterical note and never lets up. Susan George, Ian Bannen, Dennis Waterman, Honor Blackman, John Gregson, Maurice Kaufman. Written by Tudor Gates; directed by Peter Collinson; for Fantale / British Lion.

Fright Night
US 1985 105m Metrocolor

A vampire moves in next door to a teenage horror film buff. Fairly agreeable mixture of modest comedy and genuine scares; but no classic. Chris Sarandon, William Ragsdale, Amanda Bearse, Roddy McDowall. Written and directed by Tom Holland; for Herb Jaffe / Columbia.

Frightened City
GB 1961 98m bw
Anglo Amalgamated / Zodiac (John Lemont)

Gangsters fall out over a protection racket. Reasonably terse racketeer melodrama rather surprisingly set in London.

w Leigh Vance *d* John Lemont *ph* Desmond Dickinson *m* Norrie Paramour

Herbert Lom, Sean Connery, John Gregson, Alfred Marks, Yvonne Romain, Kenneth Griffith

The Frightened Lady
GB 1932 87m bw

A mad young lord is protected by his mother. Modest chiller remade later as *The Case of the Frightened Lady* (qv). Norman McKinnel, Cathleen Nesbitt, Emlyn Williams, Gordon Harker, Belle Chrystall, Finlay Currie. Written by Angus McPhail and Bryan Edgar Wallace, from the play by Edgar Wallace; directed by T. Hayes Hunter; for Gainsborough.

(US title: *Criminal at Large.*)

Frisco Jenny
US 1933 73m bw

A Barbary Coast lady is prosecuted for murder by her own son. Antediluvian melodramatic plot, borrowed from *Madame X*, provides an adequate star vehicle. Ruth Chatterton, Donald Cook, Louis Calhern, J. Carrol Naish, James Murray. Written by Wilson Mizner and Robert Lord; directed by William A. Wellman; for Warner.

The Frisco Kid*
US 1935 77m bw
Warner (Samuel Bischoff)

A Shanghaied sailor rises to power among the riff raff of the Barbary Coast in the 1860s. Fair melodrama with the star in action and (less interestingly) in love.

w Warren Duff, Seton I. Miller *d* Lloyd Bacon *ph* Sol Polito *md* Leo F. Forbstein

James Cagney, Margaret Lindsay, Ricardo Cortez, Lili Damita, Donald Woods, Barton MacLane, George E. Stone, Addison Richards

'So similar to *Barbary Coast* as almost to be its twin . . . nevertheless, good entertainment.'—*Variety*

The Frisco Kid
US 1979 108m Technicolor
Warner (Howard W. Koch Jnr)

In the old west, a rabbi heading for San Francisco makes friends with an outlaw. Unsuccessful episodic comedy, unreasonably alternating farce with sentimentality.

w Michael Elias, Frank Shaw *d* Robert Aldrich *ph* Robert B. Hauser *m* Frank De Vol

Gene Wilder, Harrison Ford, Ramon Bieri, Leo Fuchs, Penny Peyser

'A very forced comedy, made all the worse by the fact that Aldrich seems to time and edit comedy as though it were a melodrama only played a little slower.'—*Richard Combs, MFB*

Frisco Lil
US 1942 62m bw

A girl law student traps a killer and clears her dad. Formula second feature, quite adequate in its way. Irene Hervey, Kent Taylor, Minor

THE FRISCO KID (1935). Some reviewers seemed to be bothered by seeing Cagney in a stiff collar and waistcoat: Margaret Lindsay, however, clearly approves.

Watson, Jerome Cowan. Written by George Bricker and Michael Jacoby; directed by Erle C. Kenton; for Universal.

Frisco Sal
US 1945 63m bw

A New England girl goes to California to avenge her brother's murder. Minor musical vehicle for a star being groomed as a rival to Deanna Durbin. Susanna Foster, Turhan Bey, Alan Curtis, Andy Devine, Thomas Gomez, Samuel S. Hinds. Written by Curt Siodmak and Gerald Geraghty; directed by George Waggner; for Universal.

Fritz the Cat**
US 1971 78m De Luxe
Fritz Productions / Aurica (Steve Krantz)

An alleycat student in New York seeks new and varied experience.
Cartoon feature which applies the old anthropomorphism to the contemporary scene, and whips up more obscenity and violence than Disney ever dreamed of. A fast-moving orgy of outrage which could never have got by in live form.

wd / animator Ralph Bakshi, comic strip R. H. Crumb *m* Ed Bogas, Ray Shanklin

'A bitter and snarling satire that refuses to curl up in anyone's lap.'—*Bruce Williamson*

The Frog*
GB 1937 75m bw
Herbert Wilcox

The mysterious leader of a criminal organization is unmasked.
Lively old-fashioned mystery melodrama.

w Ian Hay, Gerald Elliott, *novel* The Fellowship of the Frog by Edgar Wallace *d* Jack Raymond *ph* Frederick A. Young

Gordon Harker, Carol Goodner, Noah Beery, Jack Hawkins, Richard Ainley, Esmé Percy, Felix Aylmer

'Badly directed, badly acted, it is like one of those plays produced in country towns by stranded actors. It has an old-world charm: Scotland Yard is laid up in lavender.'—*Graham Greene*

† Sequel 1938: *The Return of the Frog.*

The Frogmen
US 1951 96m bw
TCF (Samuel G. Engel)

Underwater demolition experts pave the way for the invasion of a Japanese-held island.
Standard, efficient war fare.

w John Tucker Battle *d* Lloyd Bacon *ph* Norbert Brodine *m* Cyril Mockridge

Richard Widmark, Dana Andrews, Gary Merrill, Jeffrey Hunter, Warren Stevens, Robert Wagner, Harvey Lembeck

'Competent, unpretentious and free from jingoism.'—*MFB*

AAN: original story (Oscar Millard); Norbert Brodine

'Frogs lay millions and millions of eggs each year! What if they all hatched? Today the pond—tomorrow the world!'

Frogs*
US 1972 91m Movielab
AIP (George Edwards, Peter Thomas)

A remote, inhabited island in the southern States is overtaken by reptiles.
As Hitchcock might have said, the frogs is coming; instead of monsters, ordinary creepy-crawlies in their thousands devour most of the cast. Well enough done for those with strong stomachs.

w Robert Hutchison, Robert Blees *d* George McCowan *ph* Mario Tosi *m* Les Baxter

Ray Milland, Joan Van Ark, Sam Elliott, Adam Roarke, Judy Pace

'One of the most remarkable and impressive onslaughts since *King Kong*.'—*David Pirie*

From Beyond the Grave*
GB 1973 98m Technicolor
Warner / Amicus (Milton Subotsky)

The proprietor of an East End antique shop involves his customers in horrific situations.
Reasonably lively portmanteau of tall tales from a familiar stable.

w Robin Clarke, Raymond Christodoulou *d* Kevin Connor *ph* Alan Hume *m* David Gamley *pd* Maurice Carter

David Warner, Donald Pleasence, Ian Bannen, Diana Dors, Margaret Leighton, Ian Carmichael, Nyree Dawn Porter, Ian Ogilvy

From Headquarters
US 1933 63m bw
Warner (Sam Bischoff)

The police solve a murder by scientific methods.
Efficient, rather boring programmer.

w Robert N. Lee, Peter Milne *d* William Dieterle *ph* William Reese

George Brent, Margaret Lindsay, Eugene Pallette, Hugh Herbert, Hobart Cavanaugh, Robert Barrat, Henry O'Neill, Edward Ellis

From Hell It Came
US 1957 71m bw

An executed native of Kalai returns to life in the form of a vengeful tree stump. Absolute rubbish, just about worth sitting through for the unintentional laughs. Tod Andrews, Tina Carver, Linda Watkins. Written by Richard Bernstein; directed by Dan Milner; for Milner Brothers / Allied Artists.

From Hell to Heaven
US 1933 67m bw

Stories of a racetrack hotel. Very minor *Grand Hotel*, neatly made for its time. Carole Lombard, Jack Oakie, Sidney Blackmer, Adrienne Ames, David Manners. Written by

Percy Heath and Sidney Buchman from a story by Lawrence Hazard; directed by Erle C. Kenton; for Paramount.

From Hell to Texas
US 1958 100m Eastmancolor Cinemascope
TCF (Robert Buckner)
GB title: *Manhunt*

After accidentally killing a man, a cowboy is vengefully pursued by the victim's father.
Competent chase western with a stand against violence.

w Robert Buckner, Wendell Mayes *d* Henry Hathaway *ph* Wilfrid Cline *m* Daniele Amfitheatrof

Don Murray, Diane Varsi, Chill Wills, Dennis Hopper, R. G. Armstrong, Margo, Jay C. Flippen

From Here to Eternity***
US 1953 118m bw
Columbia (Buddy Adler)

Life in a Honolulu barracks at the time of Pearl Harbor.
Cleaned up and streamlined version of a bestseller in which the mainly sexual frustrations of a number of unattractive characters are laid bare. As a production, it is Hollywood in good form, and certainly took the public fancy as well as establishing Sinatra as an acting force.

w Daniel Taradash, *novel* James Jones *d Fred Zinnemann* *ph* Burnett Guffey *m* George Duning

Burt Lancaster, Deborah Kerr, *Frank Sinatra*, Donna Reed, Ernest Borgnine, Montgomery Clift, Philip Ober, Mickey Shaughnessy

'This is not a theme which one would expect Zinnemann to approach in the hopeful, sympathetic mood of his earlier films; but neither could one expect the negative shrug of indifference with which he seems to have surrendered to its hysteria.'—*Karel Reisz, Sight and Sound*

† The story was remade for TV in 1979 as a six-hour mini-series.

†† Frank Sinatra got his key role after Eli Wallach dropped out.

AA: best picture; Daniel Taradash; Fred Zinnemann; Burnett Guffey; Frank Sinatra; Donna Reed
AAN: George Duning; Burt Lancaster; Deborah Kerr; Montgomery Clift

From Noon Till Three
US 1976 99m De Luxe
UA / Frankovich-Self

A bank robber becomes a local legend when he interrupts a raid to dally with an attractive widow. Later, when someone else is shot in mistake for him, he is reduced to penury, unable to prove his identity or live up to his own legend.
Curious, shapeless, lumpy western satire, difficult to synopsize or analyse. Despite effort all round, it's just plain unsatisfactory.

wd Frank D. Gilroy, from his novel *ph* Lucien Ballard *m* Elmer Bernstein

Charles Bronson, Jill Ireland, Douglas Fowley, Stan Haze, Damon Douglas

'It squanders its early sparkle for a pot of message.'—*Michael Billington, Illustrated London News*

'The main thing—hell, the only thing—worth noting about *From Noon Till Three* is that it is profoundly weird, which is not quite the same thing as being good.'—*Frank Rich, New York Post*

From Russia with Love***
GB 1963 118m Technicolor
UA / Eon (Harry Saltzman, Albert Broccoli)

A Russian spy joins an international crime organization and develops a plan to kill James Bond and steal a coding machine.
The second Bond adventure and possibly the best, with Istanbul and Venice for backdrops and climaxes involving a speeding train and a helicopter. Arrant nonsense with tongue in cheek, on a big budget.

w Richard Maibaum, Johanna Harwood, novel Ian Fleming *d* Terence Young *ph Ted Moore* *m* John Barry *titles Robert Brownjohn*

Sean Connery, Robert Shaw, Pedro Armendariz, Daniela Bianchi, *Lotte Lenya*, Bernard Lee, Eunice Gayson, Lois Maxwell

From Soup to Nuts*
US 1928 20m bw silent

Two temporary waiters wreck a dinner party.
Very funny slapstick which the stars subsequently reworked into *A Chump at Oxford*. Laurel and Hardy, Anita Garvin, Tiny Sandford. Written by H. M. Walker; directed by Edgar Kennedy; for Hal Roach.

From the Earth to the Moon
US 1958 100m Technicolor
Waverley (Benedict Bogeaus)

In the 1880s an armaments millionaire finances a trip to the moon in a projectile fired by his own invention.
Cardboard science fiction, with an imposing cast at sea in an unspeakable script and an unseaworthy production.

w Robert Blees, James Leicester, *novel* Jules Verne *d* Byron Haskin *ph* Edwin DuPar *m* Louis Forbes *ad* Hal Wilson Cox

Joseph Cotten, George Sanders, Henry Daniell, Carl Esmond, Melville Cooper, Don Dubbins, Debra Paget, Patric Knowles

From the Life of the Marionettes*
West Germany 1980 104m colour / bw
ITC / Martin Starger

An inquiry into the killing of a prostitute by a rich businessman.
A film somehow very typical of its director, but far from his most interesting work.

wd Ingmar Bergman *ph Sven Nykvist* *m* Rols Wilhelm *pd* Rolf Zechetbauer

Robert Atzorn, Christine Buchegger, Martin Benrath

From the Mixed-Up Files of Mrs Basil E. Frankweiler
US 1973 105m colour

Two children hide out in New York's Metropolitan Museum of Art and befriend a rich woman. An unusual idea makes ho-hum entertainment for well-brought-up children. Ingrid Bergman, Sally Prager, Johnny Doran, George Rose, Richard Mulligan. Written by Blanche Hanalis from the novel by E. L. Konigsberg; directed by Fielder Cook; for Cinema 5.

From the Terrace
US 1960 144m De Luxe Cinemascope
TCF / Linebrook (Mark Robson)

Life among Pennsylvania's idle rich.
Heavy-going family melodrama from a bestseller peopled with boorish characters.

w Ernest Lehman, *novel* John O'Hara *d* Mark Robson *ph* Leo Tover *m* Elmer Bernstein

Paul Newman, Joanne Woodward, Myrna Loy, Ina Balin, Leon Ames, Felix Aylmer, George Grizzard, Patrick O'Neal, Elizabeth Allen

From This Day Forward***
US 1946 95m bw
RKO (William L. Pereira)

After World War II, a New York couple think back to their early years in the poverty-stricken thirties.
Effective sentimental realism coupled with Hollywood professionalism made this film more memorable than it may sound.

w Hugo Butler, Garson Kanin, *novel* All Brides Are Beautiful by Thomas Bell *d John Berry* *ph George Barnes* *m* Leigh Harline

Joan Fontaine, Mark Stevens, Rosemary de Camp, Henry Morgan, Wally Brown, Arline Judge, Bobby Driscoll, Mary Treen

'Distinguished from the usual film about Young Love and Young Marriage by irony, poetry and realism.'—*Richard Winnington*

The Front*
US 1976 95m Metrocolor
Columbia / Persky-Bright, Devon (Martin Ritt, Charles H. Joffe)

For a small commission, a bookmaker puts his name to scripts by blacklisted writers.
Rather bland satire on the communist witch hunts of the fifties; interesting, but neither funny nor incisive enough.

w Walter Bernstein *d* Martin Ritt *ph* Michael Chapman *m* Dave Grusin

Woody Allen, Zero Mostel, Herschel Bernardi, Michael Murphy, Andrea Marcovicci, Lloyd Gough

'The pacing is off, the sequences don't flow, and the film seems sterile, unpopulated and flat.'—*New Yorker*

'A light comedy forged out of dark and authentic pain.'—*Frank Rich, New York Post*

'It catches the anguish of America's creative community with wit and feeling.'—*Sunday Express*

AAN: Walter Bernstein

The Front Page***
US 1931 101m bw
Howard Hughes

A Chicago reporter wants to retire and marry, but is tricked by his scheming editor into covering one last case.
Brilliant early talkie perfectly transferring into screen terms a stage classic of the twenties. Superficially a shade primitive now, its essential power remains.

w Bartlett Cormack, Charles Lederer, *play Charles MacArthur, Ben Hecht* *d Lewis Milestone* *ph* Glen MacWilliams

Adolphe Menjou (Walter Burns), *Pat O'Brien* (Hildy Johnson), Mary Brian (Peggy), Edward Everett Horton (Bensinger), Walter Catlett (Murphy), George E. Stone (Earl Williams), Mae Clarke (Molly), Slim Summerville (Pincus), Matt Moore (Kruger), Frank McHugh (McCue)

'Sure money-getter . . . it will universally entertain and please.'—*Variety*

'The most riproaring movie that ever came out of Hollywood.'—*Pare Lorentz*

'It excelled most of the films of its day by sheer treatment. The speedy delivery of lines and business and the re-emphasis upon cutting as a prime structural element made the film a model of mobility for confused directors who did not know yet how to handle sound.'—*Lewis Jacobs, The Rise of the American Film*

† Remade 1940 as *His Girl Friday* (qv).

AAN: best picture; Lewis Milestone; Adolphe Menjou

The Front Page**
US 1974 105m Technicolor Panavision
U-I (Paul Monash)

Disappointing Billy Wilder remake, relying overmuch on bad language and farcical intrusions, while tending to jettison the plot in the latter half. Some laughs nevertheless.

w Billy Wilder, I. A. L. Diamond *d* Billy Wilder *ph* Jordan S. Cronenweth *m* Billy May

Walter Matthau, Jack Lemmon, Susan Sarandon, *David Wayne*, Carol Burnett, Vincent Gardenia, Allen Garfield, Herb Edelmann, Charles Durning, *Austin Pendleton*

'The signs of coarsening in Wilder's comedy technique are unmistakable.'—*MFB*

'I can't think of a better tonic for the winter glooms.'—*Michael Billington, Illustrated London News*

Front Page Story*
GB 1953 99m bw
British Lion / Jay Lewis

A day in the life of a Fleet Street newspaper, when the editor is torn between several big stories and nearly loses his wife.
Dogged 'slice of life' drama with few excitements but some incidental entertainment and a production of routine competence.

w Jay Lewis, Jack Howells *d* Gordon Parry *ph* Gilbert Taylor *m* Jackie Brown

Jack Hawkins, Elizabeth Allan, Derek Farr, Michael Goodliffe, Martin Miller

Front Page Woman**
US 1935 82m bw
Warner (Samuel Bischoff)

Rival reporters try to outshine each other. Lively comedy-melodrama very typical of its style and time.

w Laird Doyle, Lillie Hayward, Roy Chanslor *d* Michael Curtiz *ph* Tony Gaudio *m* Heinz Roemheld *md* Leo Forbstein

Bette Davis, George Brent, Roscoe Karns, Wini Shaw, J. Carroll Naish, Walter Walker

'Completely screwy but will get fair b.o.'—*Variety*

'A swift-moving, unsensational, unsentimental, honest piece of cynicism which is really good value for money.'—*Monthly Film Bulletin*

Frontier Badmen
US 1943 74m bw

Texas ranchers try to break a cattle-buying monopoly. The good guys and the bad guys at it again, with fair results. Robert Paige, Anne Gwynne, Lon Chaney Jnr, Noah Beery Jnr, Diana Barrymore, Leo Carrillo, Andy Devine, Thomas Gomez, William Farnum. Written by Gerald Geraghty and Morgan B. Cox; directed by William McGann; for Ford Beebe Universal.

Frontier Gal
US 1945 84m Technicolor
Universal (Michael Fessier, Ernest Pagano)
GB title: *The Bride Wasn't Willing*

An outlaw weds a saloon girl at pistol point; emerging five years later from prison, he finds he has a daughter.
Rambling western with some pretensions to humour and sentiment; not a success, but it established de Carlo as a star.

w Michael Fessier, Ernest Pagano *d* Charles Lamont *ph* George Robinson, Charles Boyle *m* Frank Skinner

Yvonne de Carlo, Rod Cameron, Sheldon Leonard, Andy Devine, Fuzzy Knight, Andrew Tombes, Clara Blandick

Frontier Marshal*
US 1933 66m bw

A marshal cleans up Tombstone. Interesting trial run for the 1939 film, which was subsequently done over as *My Darling Clementine*. George O'Brien, Irene Bentley, George E. Stone, Ruth Gillette. Written by William Conselman and Stuart Anthony, from the book by Stuart N. Lake; directed by Lew Seiler; for Fox. (NB: For legal reasons in this version the marshal is called Michael Wyatt instead of Wyatt Earp.)

Frontier Marshal*
US 1939 70m bw
TCF (Sol M. Wurtzel)

Wyatt Earp cleans up Tombstone. Simple-minded, pleasing western, later worked over by Ford as *My Darling Clementine*.

w Sam Hellman *book* Stuart N. Lake *d* Allan Dwan *ph* Charles Clarke *m* Samuel Kaylin

Randolph Scott, Nancy Kelly, Cesar Romero (as Doc Holliday), Binnie Barnes, John Carradine, Joe Sawyer, Lon Chaney Jnr, Ward Bond, Edward Norris, Eddie Foy Jnr

'Strong programme western, in-betweener for key duals, but a top biller in subsequents.'—*Variety*

† Eddie Foy Jnr appeared as his father, who historically did perform in Tombstone at the time. The equivalent in *My Darling Clementine* was the Shakespearean actor played by Alan Mowbray.

The Frozen Dead
GB 1966 95m Eastmancolor

In an English laboratory, a scientist is trying to revive the frozen corpses of Nazi leaders. Flatfooted horror piece providing very little of interest to pass the time. Dana Andrews, Anna Palk, Philip Gilbert, Karel Stepanek, Kathleen Breck. Written, directed and produced by Herbert J. Leder; for Goldstar / Seven Arts.

The Frozen Ghost
US 1945 61m bw

When a drunk dies while under his influence, a hypnotist fears he has the will and power to kill. Absurdly titled and insufficiently vigorous entry in the *Inner Sanctum* series. Lon Chaney Jnr, Evelyn Ankers, Martin Kosleck, Milburn Stone, Tala Birell, Douglass Dumbrille. Written by Bernard Schubert and Luci Ward; directed by Harold Young; for Universal.

The Frozen Limits*
GB 1939 84m bw
Gainsborough (Edward Black)

Six impecunious comedians hear of the Yukon gold rush, and join it . . . forty years too late. The Crazy Gang not quite at its best, but working hard, with a few hilarious moments and a special assist from Moore Marriott.

w Marriott Edgar, Val Guest, J. O. C. Orton *d Marcel Varnel* *ph* Arthur Crabtree

Flanagan and Allen, Nervo and Knox, Naughton and Gold, *Moore Marriott*, Eileen Bell, Anthony Hulme, Bernard Lee, Eric Clavering

'The funniest English picture yet produced . . . it can bear comparison with *Safety Last* and *The General*.'—*Graham Greene*

Fu Manchu
The Yellow Peril, or evil Oriental master criminal, was created by Sax Rohmer in a 1911 novel, which led to 13 more plus some short stories. A long series of British two-reelers was made in the twenties, and talking films are as follows:

1929: THE MYSTERIOUS DR FU MANCHU, with Warner Oland (Paramount)
1930: THE RETURN OF DR FU MANCHU (ditto)
1931: DAUGHTER OF THE DRAGON (ditto)

1932: THE MASK OF FU MANCHU (qv) with Boris Karloff (MGM)
1939: DRUMS OF FU MANCHU, with Henry Brandon (Republic serial).

The remainder are British productions by Harry Alan Towers, with Christopher Lee:
1965: THE FACE OF FU MANCHU (qv)
1966: BRIDES OF FU MANCHU
1968: THE VENGEANCE OF FU MANCHU
1969: THE BLOOD OF FU MANCHU
1970: THE CASTLE OF FU MANCHU

Fuddy Duddy Buddy**
US 1952 7m Technicolor

Mr Magoo mistakes a walrus for his friend the colonel. Top drawer Magoo adventure climaxing with the celebrated line: 'I don't care if he *is* a walrus. I like him. I like him!' Written and directed by *John Hubley*; music by *William Lava*; for UPA.

The Fugitive*
US 1947 104m bw
Argosy (Merian C. Cooper, John Ford)

In an anti-clerical country, a priest is on the run.
Ford's attempt to do a Mexican *Informer* is slow and rather boring, but the pictures are nice to look at even though the original novel has been totally emasculated.

w Dudley Nichols, *novel* The Power and the Glory by Graham Greene *d John Ford* *ph Gabriel Figueroa* *m* Richard Hageman

Henry Fonda, Dolores del Rio, Pedro Armendariz, J. Carrol Naish, Leo Carrillo, Ward Bond, Robert Armstrong, John Qualen

'A symphony of light and shade, of deafening din and silence, of sweeping movement and repose.'—*Bosley Crowther*

'The most pretentious travesty of a literary work since *For Whom the Bell Tolls*.'—*Richard Winnington*

The Fugitive Kind
US 1960 121m bw
UA / Martin Jurow / Richard A. Shepherd / Pennebaker

A Mississippi drifter in a small strange town runs into trouble with women.
Doom-laden melodrama, almost a parody of the author's works, full of cancer patients, nympho-dipsos, and cemetery seductions; we are however spared the final castration.

w Tennessee Williams, Meade Roberts, *play* Orpheus Descending by Tennessee Williams *d* Sidney Lumet *ph* Boris Kaufman *m* Kenyon Hopkins *pd* Richard Sylbert

Marlon Brando, Anna Magnani, Joanne Woodward, Victor Jory, Maureen Stapleton, R. G. Armstrong

'A series of mythological engravings, determined by a literary text and a lurid concept of hell on earth.'—*Peter John Dyer*

'Sidney Lumet is usually clever at least part of the time—an acquisitive magpie who has picked up, along with the selly trash, a few small gems. This time he brings us nothing but bits of coloured glass.'—*Stanley Kauffmann*

Fugitive Lovers
US 1933 74m bw

A convict escapes on a transcontinental bus. Unsatisfactory comedy drama with a miscast star; chiefly interesting for showing the form of travel, but *It Happened One Night* did it better in the following year. Robert Montgomery, Madge Evans, Ted Healy and the 3 Stooges, Nat Pendleton, C. Henry Gordon. Written by Ferdinand Reyher, Frank Wead; directed by Richard Boleslawski; for MGM. 'Acceptable for lesser houses but not de luxe quality.'—*Variety*

Fugitive Road
US 1934 69m bw

A would-be immigrant into Austria has trouble with the patrol captain of a border garrison. Curious, aimless, cheaply made drama which doesn't even provide a coherent role for its fallen star. Erich Von Stroheim, Vera Evgeles, Leslie Fenton, George Humbert. Written by Charles S. Belden, Robert Ellis; directed by Frank Strayer; for Chesterfield. 'Picture won't rate solo in many places.'—*Variety*

Full Circle
GB / Canada 1976 97m Eastmancolor
Paramount / Fetter-Classic (Peter Fetterman, Alfred Parisier)

After the death of her small daughter, a woman leaves home to live in an old house which is haunted by the malevolent spirit of another dead child.
Unpleasant and incompetent supernatural nonsense, seeking a niche somewhere between *Don't Look Now* and *The Exorcist*.

w Dave Humphries, *novel* Julia by Peter Straub *d* Richard Loncraine *ph* Peter Hannan *m* Colin Towns

Mia Farrow, Keir Dullea, Tom Conti, Jill Bennett, Robin Gammell, Cathleen Nesbitt, Mary Morris, Edward Hardwicke

Full Confession
US 1939 73m bw

A priest bound by the sanctity of confession urges a murderer to give himself up. Neat little melodrama with a plot much copied subsequently. Victor McLaglen, Barry Fitzgerald, Sally Eilers. Written and directed by John Farrow; for RKO. 'Rather interesting, but not strong enough for the upper bracket.'—*Variety*

Full Metal Jacket**
GB 1987 116m Rank colour
Warner / Stanley Kubrick

After rigorous training, US marines land in Vietnam.
Smartly ordered but rather ordinary and predictable war film to come from one of the cinema's acknowledged masters after seven years of silence.

w Stanley Kubrick, Michael Herr, Gustav Hasford from the novel The Short Timers by Hasford *d Stanley Kubrick* *ph* Douglas Milsome *m* Abigail Mead *pd* Anton Furst

Matthew Modine, Adam Baldwin, Vincent D'Onofrio, Lee Ermey, Dorian Harewood, Arliss Howard.

AAN: best adapted screenplay

Full of Life*
US 1956 91m bw
Columbia (Fred Kohlmar)

A poor New York / Italian couple expect a baby.
Domestic comedy drama with good scenes but fatally uncertain mood.

w John Fante, from his novel *d* Richard Quine *ph* Charles Lawton Jnr *m* George Duning

Judy Holliday, Richard Conte, Esther Minciotti, Salvatore Baccaloni

'A new experience in screen suspense!'
The Full Treatment
GB 1960 109m bw Megascope
Columbia / Hilary / Falcon (Val Guest)
US title: *Stop Me Before I Kill*

A racing driver crashes and subsequently tries to murder his wife; psychiatric help leads to further gruesome goings-on.
Variation on *Les Diaboliques*, with very little mystery and too much talk from boring characters.

w Val Guest, Ronald Scott Thorn, *novel* Ronald Scott Thorn *d* Val Guest *ph* Gilbert Taylor *m* Stanley Black

Ronald Lewis, Diane Cilento, Claude Dauphin, Françoise Rosay, Bernard Braden

The Fuller Brush Girl*
US 1950 85m bw
Columbia (S. Sylvan Simon)
GB title: *Affairs of Sally*

A cosmetics saleslady gets involved in murder.
Fairly amusing slapstick mystery with the star in good form.

w Frank Tashlin *d* Lloyd Bacon *ph* Charles Lawton *m* Heinz Roemheld

Lucille Ball, Eddie Albert, Carl Benton Reid, Gale Robbins, Jeff Connell, John Litel, Jerome Cowan, Lee Patrick

The Fuller Brush Man*
US 1948 93m bw
Columbia (S. Sylvan Simon)
GB title: *That Mad Mr Jones*

A door-to-door salesman gets involved in homicide.
Bright star comedy with slow patches.

w Frank Tashlin, Devery Freeman *d* S. Sylvan Simon *ph* Leslie White *m* Heinz Roemheld

Red Skelton, Janet Blair, Don McGuire, Adele Jergens

Fun and Fancy Free*
US 1947 73m Technicolor
Walt Disney (Ben Sharpsteen)

Cartoon stories told by and to Jiminy Cricket and Edgar Bergen.
Variable Disney ragbag including *Bongo* the

Bear, and a lengthy version of *Jack and the Beanstalk*.

w various *d* various

Fun in Acapulco
US 1963 97m Technicolor
Paramount / Hal B. Wallis

A trapeze artist becomes a lifeguard and is pursued by a lady bullfighter.
Dim comedy musical.

w Allan Weiss *d* Richard Thorpe *ph* Daniel Fapp *m* Joseph J. Lilley

Elvis Presley, Ursula Andress, Paul Lukas

Fun on a Weekend
US 1947 93m bw

A girl with self-confidence persuades a penniless man to pose as a millionaire.
Weakish comedy with good moments. Eddie Bracken, Priscilla Lane, Tom Conway, Allen Jenkins, Arthur Treacher, Clarence Kolb. Written, directed and produced by Andrew Stone; for United Artists.

Fun with Dick and Jane
US 1976 100m Metrocolor
Columbia / Peter Bart, Max Pelevsky

When an aerospace executive is fired, in order to keep up with the Joneses he and his wife embark on a life of crime.
This being a 1970s satire, they actually get away with it, providing some, but not enough, fun on the way.

w David Giler, Jerry Belson, Mordecai Richler, *story* Gerald Gaiser *d Ted Kotcheff* *ph* Fred J. Koenekamp *m* Ernest Gold

George Segal, Jane Fonda, Ed McMahon, Dick Gautier, Alan Miller

'A nitwit mixture of counterculture politics, madcap comedy and toilet humour.'—*New Yorker*

† The sequence in which the heroine discusses the family predicament while sitting on a toilet was later deleted, reducing the running time by two minutes.

Funeral in Berlin*
GB 1967 102m Technicolor
Paramount / Harry Saltzman (Charles Kasher)

Harry Palmer is sent to Berlin to check a story that a Russian colonel wants to defect.
Initially intriguing, finally confusing, always depressing spy yarn in the sixties manner, i.e. with every character devious and no one a hero. Good production.

w Evan Jones, *novel* The Berlin Memorandum by Len Deighton *d* Guy Hamilton *ph* Otto Heller *m* Konrad Elfers *pd* Ken Adam

Michael Caine, *Oscar Homolka*, Eva Renzi, Paul Hubschmid, *Hugh Burden*, Guy Doleman, Rachel Gurney

'So many twists that even Sherlock Holmes might have been baffled . . . before long it becomes difficult to remember who is watching whom and why, or indeed whether anybody *was* watching anybody at any given moment.'—*Tom Milne*

† Second in the Harry Palmer series, of which the first was *The Ipcress File* and the third *Billion Dollar Brain* (both qv).

The Funniest Man in the World*
US 1967 102m bw

Moderately intelligent compilation of sequences from the films of Charlie Chaplin, including *Making a Living*, *Kid Auto Races at Venice*, *Tillie's Punctured Romance*, *The Tramp*, *A Night Out*, *The Rink*, *The Immigrant* and *Easy Street*. The later shorts and features, on which Chaplin himself claimed full copyright, are not included. Written and directed by Vernon P. Becker; for Funnyman Inc.

Funny Face**
US 1956 103m Technicolor Vistavision
Paramount (Roger Edens)

A fashion editor and photographer choose a shy bookstore attendant as their 'quality woman'.
Stylish, wistful musical with good numbers but drawn-out dialogue; finally a shade too sophisticated and a whole lot too fey.

w Leonard Gershe *d Stanley Donen* *ph Ray June* *m / ly George and Ira Gershwin*

Fred Astaire, Audrey Hepburn, Kay Thompson, Michel Auclair, Robert Flemyng

AAN: Leonard Gershe; Ray June

Funny Girl**
US 1968 169m Technicolor Panavision 70
Columbia / Rastar (Ray Stark)

Fanny Brice, an ugly Jewish girl from New York's east side, becomes a big Broadway star but loses her husband in the process.
Interminable cliché-ridden musical drama relieved by a few good numbers, high production gloss and the unveiling of a new powerhouse star.

w Isobel Lennart, from her play *d* William Wyler *ph* Harry Stradling *md* Walter Scharf *m Jule Styne* *ly* Bob Merrill *pd* Gene Callahan

Barbra Streisand, Omar Sharif, Walter Pidgeon, Kay Medford, Anne Francis, Lee Allen, Gerald Mohr, Frank Faylen

AA: Barbra Streisand
AAN: best picture; Harry Stradling; Walter Scharf; Kay Medford; title song

Funny Lady*
US 1975 138m Eastmancolor Panavision
Columbia / Rastar / Persky–Bright / Vista (Ray Stark)

Fanny Brice marries Billy Rose.
Unnecessary sequel to the above, entirely predictable and far from the truth, but with the occasional pleasures that a high budget brings.

w Jay Presson Allen, Arnold Schulman *d* Herbert Ross *ph James Wong Howe* *m / ly* various *md* Peter Matz *pd* George Jenkins

Barbra Streisand, James Caan, *Ben Vereen*, Omar Sharif, Roddy McDowall, Larry Gates

'The plot line is as slackly handled as the milieu.'—*Geoff Brown*

'As Fanny Brice, Streisand is no longer human; she's like a bitchy female impersonator imitating Barbra Streisand.'—*New Yorker*

AAN: James Wong Howe; Peter Matz; song 'How Lucky Can You Get' (*m / ly* Fred Ebb, John Kander)

A Funny Thing Happened on the Way to the Forum**
GB 1966 99m De Luxe
UA / Quadrangle (Melvin Frank)

In ancient Rome, a conniving slave schemes to win his freedom.
Bawdy farce from a Broadway musical inspired by Plautus but with a New York Jewish atmosphere. The film pays scant attention to the comic numbers that made the show a hit, but adds some style of its own, including a free-for-all slapstick climax.

w Melvin Frank, Michael Pertwee, *musical comedy* Burt Shevelove, Larry Gelbart *m / ly Stephen Sondheim* *md* Ken Thorne *d Richard Lester* *ph Nicolas Roeg* *pd* Tony Walton *titles* Richard Williams

Zero Mostel, Phil Silvers, Michael Crawford, Jack Gilford, *Michael Hordern*, Buster Keaton, Patricia Jessel, Leon Greene, Beatrix Lehmann

'Actors have to be very fast and very sly to make themselves felt amid the flash and glitter of a characteristic piece of Lester film-mosaic.'—*John Russell Taylor*

'He proceeds by fits and starts and leaves jokes suspended in mid-air . . . like coitus interruptus going on forever.'—*Pauline Kael*

AA: Ken Thorne

Funnyman
US 1967 100m bw and colour
Korty Films (Hugh McGraw, Stephen Schmidt)

A satirical comedian seeks some better occupation in life, but finally agrees he's best as a comic.
One suspects Korty has seen *Sullivan's Travels* several times; but even though his film tries hard, it finally provides more yawns than appreciative chuckles.

w John Korty, Peter Bonerz *d John Korty* *ph* John Korty *m* Peter Schickele

Peter Bonerz, Sandra Archer, Carol Androsky, Gerald Hiken

'It has its dull patches, but it made me laugh louder and more often than any other film this year.'—*Michael Billington, Illustrated London News*

The Furies*
US 1950 109m bw
Paramount / Hal B. Wallis

A cattle baron feuds with his tempestuous daughter.
Interesting but heavy-going western, more solemn than stimulating despite its Freudian excesses.

w Charles Schnee, *novel* Niven Busch *d* Anthony Mann *ph* Victor Milner *m* Franz Waxman

Barbara Stanwyck, *Walter Huston*, Wendell Corey, Judith Anderson, Gilbert Roland, Thomas Gomez, Beulah Bondi, Wallace Ford, Albert Dekker, Blanche Yurka

'An immoral saga, capably mounted, with some pretentious psychological trimmings.'—*MFB*

AAN: Victor Milner

The Further Perils of Laurel and Hardy***
US 1967 99m bw
TCF / *Robert Youngson*

A compilation of longish extracts from the stars' silent comedies, including *Early to Bed, The Second Hundred Years, Should Married Men Go Home, You're Darn Tootin', Habeas Corpus, That's My Wife*, and *Leave 'Em Laughing*. The producer is to be congratulated on refurbishing so many deteriorating negatives, though the commentary leaves much to be desired.

w, ed Robert Youngson *m* John Parker

Fury***
US 1936 94m bw
MGM (Joseph L. Mankiewicz)

A traveller in a small town is mistaken for a murderer and apparently lynched; he escapes in a fire but determines to have his persecutors hanged for his murder.
Powerful drama which becomes artificial in its latter stages but remains its director's best American film.

w Bartlett Cormack, Fritz Lang, *story* Norman Krasna *d Fritz Lang ph Joseph Ruttenberg m* Franz Waxman

Spencer Tracy, Sylvia Sidney, Bruce Cabot, Walter Abel, Edward Ellis, Walter Brennan, Frank Albertson

'The surface of American life has been rubbed away: *Fury* gets down to the bones of the thing and shows them for what they are.'—*C. A. Lejeune*

'Since the screen began to talk, no other serious film except *The Front Page* has so clearly shown that here is a new art and what this new art can do.'—*John Marks*

'Everyday events and people suddenly took on tremendous and horrifying proportion; even the most insignificant details had a pointed meaning.'—*Lewis Jacobs*

'For half its length a powerful and documented piece of fiction about a lynching, and for the remaining half a desperate attempt to make love, lynching and the Hays Office come out even.'—*Otis Ferguson*

'Astonishing, the only film I know to which I have wanted to attach the epithet of *great*.'—*Graham Greene*

AAN: Norman Krasna

The Fury*
US 1978 117m De Luxe
TCF / Frank Yablans (Ron Preissman)

The head of a government institute for psychic research finds that his own son is wanted by terrorists who wish to use his lethal psychic powers.
Flashy, kaleidoscopic nonsense which never even begins to make sense but is used as the basis for the director's showing-off, which is occasionally worth a glance for those with hardened stomachs.

w John Farris, from his novel *d* Brian de Palma *ph* Richard H. Kline *m* John Williams

Kirk Douglas, John Cassavetes, Carrie Snodgress, Charles Durning, Andrew Stevens, Amy Irving, Fiona Lewis

'A conception of cinema that is closer to Ken Russell than Alfred Hitchcock.'—*Richard Combs, MFB*

Fury at Furnace Creek*
US 1948 88m bw
TCF

A westerner clears the name of his father, a general accused of diverting a wagon train into hostile Indian territory.
Adequate old-fashioned western with a good story line and standard excitements.

w Charles G. Booth *d* H. Bruce Humberstone *ph* Harry Jackson *m* David Raksin *md* Alfred Newman

Victor Mature, Coleen Gray, Glenn Langan, Reginald Gardiner

Fury at Smugglers' Bay
GB 1960 96m Eastmancolor Panascope
(Regal) Mijo (Michael Green, Joe Vegoda)

The squire of a Cornish village is being blackmailed by the vicious leader of a gang of wreckers.
Watchable, then forgettable variation on *Jamaica Inn*.

wd John Gilling *ph* Harry Waxman *m* Harold Geller

Peter Cushing, John Fraser, Bernard Lee, William Franklyn, June Thorburn, Miles Malleson, Michele Mercier, George Coulouris

Futtock's End*
GB 1969 49m Eastmancolor

Adventures of a weekend in an English country mansion. A collection of visual gags, rather thinly spread, with dialogue replaced by squeaks and mumblings. Like all Barker's subsequent comedies on similar lines (*The Picnic, By the Sea*, etc) one chuckles in constant anticipation of guffaws which never come. Ronnie Barker, Michael Hordern, Roger Livesey, Julian Orchard, Kika Markham, Mary Merrall, Richard O'Sullivan. Written by Ronnie Barker; directed by Bob Kellett; for Paradine / Gannet / British Lion.

Futureworld*
US 1976 107m Metrocolor
AIP (James T. Aubrey Jnr, Paul Lazarus III)

The robot factory seen in *Westworld* (qv) now aims at world domination by duplicating influential figures.
Amusing and fairly suspenseful fantasy with a bigger budget than its predecessor.

w Mayo Simon, George Schenck *d* Richard T. Heffron *ph* Howard Schwarz, Gene Polito *m* Fred Karlin

Peter Fonda, Blythe Danner, Arthur Hill, Yul Brynner, John Ryan, Stuart Margolin, Jim Antonio

Fuzz*
US 1972 93m De Luxe
UA / Filmways / Javelin (Jack Farren)

Detectives of Boston's 87th precinct try to catch a rapist.
A black farce devoted to police incompetence, though taken from a straight 'Ed McBain' story. Brisk and sometimes funny.

w Evan Hunter ('Ed McBain') *d* Richard A. Colla *ph* Jacques Marquette *m* Dave Grusin

Burt Reynolds, Raquel Welch, Jack Weston, Yul Brynner, Tom Skerritt, James McEachin

The Fuzzy Pink Nightgown
US 1957 88m bw
UA / Russ–Field (Robert Waterfield)

A glamorous film star falls in love with her kidnapper.
Unendurable cheap romantic farce.

w Richard Alan Simmons, *novel* Sylvia Tate *d* Norman Taurog *ph* Joseph La Shelle *m* Billy May

Jane Russell, Ralph Meeker, Keenan Wynn, Fred Clark, Adolphe Menjou, Una Merkel

F/X
US 1985 106m Technicolor

A special effects man is paid to stage a phony assassination, then finds himself the target of hit men. Initially mysterious premise settles down into a long chase, which of its kind isn't badly done but goes on forever. Bryan Brown, Brian Dennehy, Diane Venora, Cliff Young, Mason Adams, Jerry Orbach. Written by Robert T. Megginson, Gregory Fleeman; directed by Robert Mandel; for Orion. (GB title: *Murder by Illusion*.)

GI Blues
US 1960 104m Technicolor
Paramount / Hal B. Wallis (Paul Nathan)

A guitar-playing gunner with the American army in West Germany falls for a cabaret dancer.
Routine star vehicle marking Presley's return from military service.

w Edmund Beloin, Henry Garson *d* Norman Taurog *ph* Loyal Griggs *m* Joseph J. Lilley

Elvis Presley, Juliet Prowse, Robert Ivers, Leticia Roman, Arch Johnson

G Men***
US 1935 85m bw
Warner (Lou Edelman)

A young lawyer becomes a G-man to avenge the murder of his best friend, and finds himself tracking down another old friend who is a gangster.
In the face of mounting criticism of their melodramas making heroes of gangsters, Warners pulled a clever switch by showing the same crimes from a different angle, that of the law enforcer. As an action show it became pretty good after a slow start.

w Seton I. Miller d William Keighley *ph* Sol Polito *md* Leo F. Forbstein

James Cagney, Ann Dvorak, Margaret Lindsay, Robert Armstrong, Barton MacLane, Lloyd Nolan, William Harrigan

'Cagney joins the government and cleans up the gangsters. Just loads of action, knocked off in bing-bang manner. Strong b.o.'—*Variety*

'The gangster is back, racing madly through one of the fastest melodramas ever made.'—*New York Sun*

'The headiest dose of gunplay that Hollywood has unleashed in recent months.'—*André Sennwald, New York Times*

'It is not violence alone which is in the air: there is also a skilfully contrived and well-maintained suspense, and throughout a feeling of respect for the men who are paid to die in the execution of necessary work.'—*The Times*

'A swell show: the construction is swift and staccato.'—*New York World Telegraph*

'Not for the kiddies, but see it if your nerves are good.'—*Photoplay*

G-Men Never Forget
US 1948 bw serial: 12 eps

A criminal changes his face by plastic surgery and takes the place of the police commissioner. Energetic serial thick-ear. Clayton Moore, Roy Barcroft, Ramsay Ames, Tom Steele, Dave Van Sickel. Directed by Fred Brannon and Yakima Canutt; for Republic.

G-Men vs The Black Dragon
US 1943 bw serial: 15 eps

British, American and Chinese secret agents wipe out a Japanese sabotage ring. Tolerable wartime propaganda serial. Rod Cameron, Roland Got, Constance Worth, Nino Pipitone. Directed by William Witney; for Republic.

'They had more than love . . . they had fame!'

Gable and Lombard
US 1976 131m Technicolor
Universal (Harry Korshak)

After Carole Lombard's death in a 1942 air crash, Clark Gable recalls their years together. Vulgar and inaccurate representation of two Hollywood stars of the thirties; it fails even as titillation.

w Barry Sandler *d* Sidney J. Furie *ph* Jordan S. Cronenweth *m* Michel Legrand
pd Edward Carfagno

James Brolin, Jill Clayburgh, Allen Garfield (as Louis B. Mayer), Red Buttons, Joanne Linville

'A limply raunchy, meaningless movie with nothing to say about the movies, about love, or about stardom.'—*New Yorker*

'An uneven combination of smut and sentimentality.'—*Les Keyser, Hollywood in the Seventies*

'It comes like a marching army to thrill the nation!'
'The picture that will make 1933 famous!'

Gabriel over the White House*
US 1933 87m bw
MGM / Walter Wanger

A crook becomes president and mysteriously reforms.
Pleasing, dated New Deal fantasy.

w Carey Wilson, Bertram Bloch, *novel* Rinehard by T. F. Tweed *d* Gregory La Cava *ph* Bert Glennon *m* William Axt

Walter Huston, Karen Morley, Franchot Tone, C. Henry Gordon, Samuel S. Hinds, Jean Parker, Dickie Moore

'Flag-waving flapdoodle, shrewdly dished up for the man in the street and his best girl. Beautifully produced, cannily hoked, and looks like money all round.'—*Variety*

Gabriela
Brazil 1983 99m colour

In a coastal town in 1925, the sensual Gabriela marries a bar owner but becomes involved again with her old gangster cronies. Ethnic melodrama of familiar type, a spin-off from an immensely popular Brazilian TV series. Sonia Braga, Marcello Mastroianni, Antonio Cantafora. Written by Leopoldo Sarran, Bruno Barreto, from the novel by Jorge Amada; directed by Bruno Barreto; for Sultana.

Gaby
US 1956 97m Eastmancolor
Cinemascope
MGM (Edwin H. Knopf)

Flabby remake of *Waterloo Bridge* (qv); saccharine, fussy and outmoded, despite updated settings and a happy ending.

w Albert Hackett, Frances Goodrich, Charles Lederer *d* Curtis Bernhardt *ph* Robert Planck *m* Conrad Salinger

Leslie Caron, John Kerr, Cedric Hardwicke, Taina Elg, Margalo Gillmore

Gaiety George
GB 1946 98m bw
Embassy (George King)
US title: *Showtime*

The career in the London theatre of Irish impresario George Howard in the early part of the century.
Tepid musical biopic.

w Katherine Strueby *d* George King *ph* Otto Heller

Richard Greene, Ann Todd, Peter Graves, Hazel Court, Leni Lynn, Ursula Jeans, Morland Graham, Frank Pettingell

Gaily, Gaily**
US 1969 117m De Luxe
UA / Mirisch / Cartier
GB title: *Chicago, Chicago*

The early life on a Chicago newspaper of Ben Hecht.
Busy, farcical, melodramatic, always interesting biopic of the formative years of a celebrated literary figure.

w Abram S. Ginnes, book Ben Hecht
d Norman Jewison ph Richard Kline
m Henry Mancini *pd* Robert Boyle

Beau Bridges, Melina Mercouri, *Brian Keith*, George Kennedy, Hume Cronyn, Margot Kidder, Wilfrid Hyde White, Melodie Johnson, John Randolph

GABLE AND LOMBARD. While James Brolin and Jill Clayburgh doubtless tried hard they still look like James Brolin and Jill Clayburgh.

The Gal Who Took the West
US 1949 84m Technicolor

In 1890, an opera singer travels west and is the object of romantic rivalry. Lame attempt to equal the splendid idiocy of *Salome Where She Danced.* Yvonne de Carlo, Charles Coburn, Scott Brady, John Russell, James Millican. Written by William Bowers and Oscar Brodney; directed by Frederick de Cordova; for Universal-International.

Galileo*
GB 1975 145m Eastmancolor
Ely Landau / Cinevision

In the 17th century, a poor Italian mathematics teacher has trouble establishing his 'heretical' astronomical theories.
Overlong play-on-celluloid for the American Film Theatre: very decently made and acted, it lacks inspiration.

w Barbara Bray, Joseph Losey, *play* Bertolt Brecht *d* Joseph Losey *ph* Michael Reed *m* Hanns Eisler

Topol, Edward Fox, Michel Lonsdale, Richard O'Callaghan, Tom Conti, Judy Parfitt, Patrick Magee, Michael Gough, John Gielgud, Colin Blakely, Margaret Leighton, Clive Revill

Gallant Bess
US 1946 99m Cinecolor

A soldier's horse saves his life and becomes his peacetime friend. Boy-and-horse story with a wartime setting; good for small towns. Marshall Thompson, George Tobias, Clem Bevans, Donald Curtis. Written by Jeanne Bartlett; directed by Andrew Marton; for MGM.

The Gallant Blade
US 1948 81m Cinecolor

In France in 1648, a dashing young lieutenant rescues his general from the plot of a would-be revolutionary. Pinchpenny swashbuckler which maintains a commendable verve. Larry Parks, Marguerite Chapman, Victor Jory, George Macready. Written by Walter Ferris and Morton Grant; directed by Henry Levin; for Columbia.

The Gallant Hours*
US 1959 115m bw
UA / James Cagney / Robert Montgomery

Episodes in the career of Admiral William F. Halsey.
Adulatory but physically restrained biopic which covers World War II with barely a scene outside control room sets: interesting but finally too talky.

w Beirne Lay Jnr, Frank D. Gilroy *d* Robert Montgomery *ph* Joe MacDonald *m* Roger Wagner

James Cagney, Dennis Weaver, Richard Jaeckel, Ward Costello, Carl Benton Reid

'Imaginatively conceived but erroneously realized.'—*Robert Vas*

Gallant Journey
US 1946 86m bw
Columbia (William A. Wellman)

The life of an early American aviation pioneer.
Curious biopic, very tentatively done, about an inventor so obscure as to be virtually fictitious. Sentimental, artificial, but harmless.

w Byron Morgan, William A. Wellman *d* William A. Wellman *ph* Burnett Guffey *m* Marlin Skiles

Glenn Ford, Janet Blair, Charles Ruggles, Henry Travers, Arthur Shields

Gallant Lady
US 1933 84m bw
(UA) Twentieth Century (Darryl F. Zanuck)

A woman allows her illegitimate son to be adopted, but years later marries his stepfather. A tearjerker very typical of its time, moderately well assembled; later remade as *Always Goodbye* (qv).

w Sam Mintz, *story* Gilbert Emery, Doug Doty *d* Gregory La Cava *ph* Peverell Marley *m* Alfred Newman

Ann Harding, Clive Brook, Otto Kruger, Tullio Carminati, Dickie Moore, Janet Beecher

The Gallant Legion
US 1948 86m bw

The Texas Rangers are formed but have to prove themselves. Acceptable second-string western with plenty of action and a strong cast. William Elliott, Adrian Booth, Joseph Schildkraut, Bruce Cabot, Andy Devine, Jack Holt, Grant Withers, Adele Mara. Written by Gerald Drayson Adams; directed by Joseph Kane; for Republic.

Gallant Sons
US 1940 71m bw

Schoolboys club together to get the father of one of them off a murder charge. Unlikely and undemanding but pleasant filler. Jackie Cooper, Bonita Granville, Gene Reynolds, Gail Patrick, Ian Hunter, June Preisser, Leo Gorcey, William Tracy, El Brendel. Written by William R. Lipman and Marion Parsonnet; directed by George B. Seitz; for MGM.

'From a place you may never have heard of, a story you'll never forget!'

Gallipoli*
Australia 1981 111m Eastmancolor Panavision
Associated R and R (Martin Cooper, Ben Gannon)

In 1915, two friends trek from Perth across the desert to join up, and one dies in the Dardanelles.
Consistently interesting aspects of the 1914–18 war, but rather broken-backed as a story.

w David Williamson *d Peter Weir* *ph* Russell Boyd *md* Brian May

Mark Lee, Mel Gibson, Bill Hunter, Robert Grubb, Tim McKenzie, Bill Kerr

'Like so many of Weir's films it promises more than it delivers.'—*Time Out, 1984*

The Galloping Ghost
US 1931 bw serial: 12 eps

A school football hero begins a campaign to clear his name after an accusation of fixing. Tedious and dated serial. Harold Grange, Dorothy Gulliver, Walter Miller, Francis X. Bushman. Directed by B. Reeves Eason; for Mascot.

The Galloping Major*
GB 1951 82m bw
British Lion / Romulus (Monja Danischewsky)

A group of suburbanites form a syndicate to buy a racehorse.
Rather contrived and imitative sub-Ealing comedy which fails to generate much steam.

w Monja Danischewsky, Henry Cornelius *d* Henry Cornelius *ph* Stan Pavey *m* Georges Auric

Basil Radford, Janette Scott, Hugh Griffith, Jimmy Hanley, René Ray, Joyce Grenfell, Sidney Tafler, Charles Victor, A. E. Matthews

Gambit**
US 1966 109m Techniscope
Universal (Leo L. Fuchs)

A cockney thief conspires with a Eurasian girl to rob a multi-millionaire of a prize statue.
An enjoyably light pattern of cross and double cross is well sustained to the end.

w Jack Davies, Alvin Sargent *d* Ronald Neame *ph* Clifford Stine *m* Maurice Jarre

Michael Caine, Shirley Maclaine, Herbert Lom, John Abbott, Roger C. Carmel, Arnold Moss

'He's been bruised, blackmailed, sliced and slammed. But nothing can stop him from going after the big money!'

The Gambler*
US 1975 111m Eastmancolor
Paramount (Irwin Winkler, Robert Chartoff)

A compulsive gambler has a will to lose.
Flashily made but basically uninteresting sub-Freudian study, vaguely based on Dostoievsky.

w James Tomack *d* Karel Reisz *ph* Victor J. Kemper *m* Mahler *md* Jerry Fielding

James Caan, Paul Sorvino, Lauren Hutton, Morris Carnovsky, Jacqueline Brookes, Burt Young

Gambler from Natchez
US 1954 88m Technicolor
TCF (Leonard Goldstein)

A professional gambler returns to New Orleans to avenge his father's murder, and disposes of his enemies one by one.
Mildly watchable semi-western with a plot borrowed from *The Count of Monte Cristo.*

w Gerald Drayson Adams, Irving Wallace *d* Henry Levin *ph* Lloyd Ahern *md* Lionel Newman

Dale Robertson, Debra Paget, Thomas Gomez, Kevin McCarthy

Gambling*
US 1934 82m bw

A professional gambler ferrets out the killer of his ward. Transcript of a George M. Cohan play, with the star in good form; but the presentation is uncinematic and tedious. *George M. Cohan*, Wynne Gibson, Dorothy Burgess, Theodore Newton. Written by Garrett Graham, from Cohan's play; directed by Rowland V. Lee; for Fox/Harold B. Franklin. 'It moves too slowly towards an intelligent but almost wholly mental climax.'—*Variety*

Gambling House
US 1950 80m bw

An immigrant gambler is threatened with deportation when involved in a murder. Heavy melodrama with assumed social conscience. Victor Mature, Terry Moore, William Bendix, Basil Ruysdael. Written by Marvin Borowsky and Allen Rivkin; directed by Ted Tetzlaff; for RKO.

Gambling Lady*
US 1934 66m bw
Warner (Henry Blanke)

The daughter of a gambling suicide follows in father's footsteps and becomes involved in murder.
Fast-paced melodrama with a happy ending: smart entertainment of its time.

w Ralph Block, Doris Malloy *d* Archie Mayo *ph* George Barnes

Barbara Stanwyck, Joel McCrea, Pat O'Brien, Claire Dodd, C. Aubrey Smith, Robert Barrat, Philip Reed

Gambling on the High Seas
US 1940 56m bw

A reporter proves that a gambling ship owner is a murderer. Unsurprising filler. Wayne Morris, Jane Wyman, Gilbert Roland, William Pawley, John Litel. Written by Robert E. Kent; directed by George Amy; for Warner.

Gambling Ship
US 1933 70m bw

A big shot gambler annoys rivals by opening a gambling ship off Long Beach. Any freshness this once had wore off long ago. Cary Grant, Benita Hume, Roscoe Karns, Glenda Farrell, Jack La Rue. Written by Marcia and Seton I. Miller; directed by Max Marcin; for Paramount. 'A fair flicker . . . but in toto it's a familiar formula of mob vs mob.'—*Variety*

A Game for Vultures
GB 1979 106m colour

In Rhodesia, a sanctions-buster comes to understand a black freedom fighter. After a lot of violence and attitudinizing, that is, in this unattractively pretentious piece of bloodthirsty hokum. Richard Harris, Richard Roundtree, Ray Milland, Joan Collins, Sven Bertil Taube, Denholm Elliott. Written by Phillip Baird, from a novel by Michael Hartmann; directed by James Fargo; for Columbia.

A Game of Death
US 1945 72m bw
RKO

Cheap remake of *The Most Dangerous Game* (qv); excitement dissipated by poor handling.

w Norman Houston *d* Robert Wise *ph* J. Roy Hunt *m* Paul Sawtell

John Loder, Audrey Long, Edgar Barrier, Russell Wade, Russell Hicks

Games*
US 1967 100m Techniscope
Universal (George Edwards)

A sophisticated New York couple play complex games, one of which turns out to have a deadly effect.
Tedious variation on *Les Diaboliques*, with interesting moments.

w Gene Kearney *d Curtis Harrington* *ph* William A. Fraker *m* Samuel Matlovsky

Simone Signoret, James Caan, Katharine Ross, Don Stroud, Kent Smith, Estelle Winwood, Marjorie Bennett

The Games*
GB 1970 97m De Luxe Panavision
TCF (Lester Linsk)

Four men in various parts of the world prepare to take part in the marathon at the Rome Olympics.
Tepid multi-drama with good locations and a well-shot and exciting climactic race.

w Erich Segal, *novel* Hugh Atkinson *d* Michael Winner *ph Robert Paynter* *m* Francis Lai

Stanley Baker, Michael Crawford, Ryan O'Neal, Charles Aznavour, Jeremy Kemp, Elaine Taylor, Kent Smith, Mona Washbourne

The Gamma People
GB 1955 79m bw

Journalists in a Balkan state uncover a plot by a mad scientist to control the minds of children by gamma rays. Artless serial-like thriller with little suspense. Paul Douglas, Leslie Phillips, Eva Bartok, Walter Rilla, Philip Leaver. Written by John Gilling and John Gossage; directed by John Gilling; for Warwick / Columbia.

'His goal was freedom . . . his strategy was peace . . . his weapon was his humanity!'

Gandhi***
GB 1982 188m Technicolor Panavision
Columbia / Goldcrest / Indo-British / International Film Investors / National Film Development Corporation of India (*Richard Attenborough*)

The life of the young Indian advocate who became a revolutionary, a saint and a martyr.
A straightforward treatment with the odd twists and turns expected of this director; but the remarkable things about the film are first, that it was made at all in an age which regards inspirational epics as very old hat; and secondly, that it has brought into life so splendid a leading performance. Beside these factors the sluggish pace and the air of schoolbook history seem comparatively unimportant.

w John Briley *d* Richard Attenborough *ph* Billy Williams, Ronnie Taylor *m* George Fenton *pd* Stuart Craig *ed* John Bloom

Ben Kingsley, Candice Bergen, Edward Fox, John Mills, John Gielgud, Trevor Howard, Martin Sheen, Ian Charleson, Athol Fugard, Saeed Jaffrey

'It reminds us that we are, after all, human, and thus capable of the most extraordinary and wonderful achievements, simply through the use of our imagination, our will, and our sense of right.'—*Roger Ebert*

† Opening dedication: 'No man's life can be encompassed in one telling . . . what can be done is to be faithful in spirit to the record and try to find one's way to the heart of the man.'

AA: best picture; Ben Kingsley; Richard Attenborough as director; John Briley; cinematography; costume design (John Mollo, Bhanu Athalya); art direction (Stuart Craig, Bob Laing); editing (John Bloom)
AAN: music
BFA: best film; best direction; best actor; best supporting actress (Rohini Hattangady); outstanding newcomer (Ben Kingsley)

Gang Buster*
US 1931 65m bw

A small-town sap defeats gangsters by accident. Lively comedy which scored in the middle of the first gangster cycle. Jack Oakie, Jean Arthur, William Boyd, Wynne Gibson, Tom Kennedy. Written by Joseph L. Mankiewicz from a story by Percy Heath; directed by A. Edward Sutherland; for Paramount. 'First-rate week-stander . . . inlaid with surefire comic devices.'—*Variety*

Gang Busters
US 1942 bw serial: 12 eps

Police run down a gang of city terrorists. Lively serial antics which also survived as a 'potted' feature. Kent Taylor, Irene Hervey, Ralph Morgan, Robert Armstrong, Joseph Crehan, Ralf Harolde. Directed by Ray Taylor and Noel Smith; for Universal.

The Gang That Couldn't Shoot Straight
US 1971 96m Metrocolor
MGM (Robert Chartoff, Irwin Winkler)

Members of the New York Mafia organize a cycle race and start antagonisms that end in mass murder.
Unfunny black comedy with all concerned gesticulating wildly.

w Waldo Salt, *novel* Jimmy Breslin *d* James Goldstone *ph* Owen Roizman *m* Dave Grusin

Jerry Orbach, Leigh Taylor-Young, Jo Van Fleet, Lionel Stander, Robert de Niro, Herve Villechaize, Joe Santos

Gang War*
US 1958 75m bw

When his wife is killed by gangsters a reluctant witness seeks revenge. Minor prototype for *Death Wish* and the star's other vehicles in similar vein. Charles Bronson, Kent Taylor, Jennifer Holden, John Doucette, Gloria

Henry. Written by Louis Vittes from the novel The Hoods Take Over by Ovid Demaris; directed by Gene Fowler Jnr; in RegalScope; for Harold E. Knox/Fox.

The Gang's All Here*
GB 1939 77m bw
ABP (Walter C. Mycroft, Jack Buchanan)
US title: *The Amazing Mr Forrest*

An insurance investigator goes undercover among gangsters.
Lively comedy-melodrama.

w Ralph Spence *d* Thornton Freeland *ph* Claude Friese-Greene

Jack Buchanan, Googie Withers, Edward Everett Horton, Syd Walker, Otto Kruger, Jack La Rue, Walter Rilla

† Buchanan played the same character in *Smash and Grab*

The Gang's All Here**
US 1943 103m Technicolor
TCF (William Le Baron)
GB title: *The Girls He Left Behind*

A serviceman is caught between a fiery entertainer and a Park Avenue socialite.
Frenetic wartime musical with some of Busby Berkeley's most outré choreography (e.g. The Lady in the Tutti Frutti Hat) and gleamingly effective Technicolor.

w Walter Bullock *d / ch Busby Berkeley ph Edward Cronjager md* Alfred Newman *songs* Leo Robin, Harry Warren

Alice Faye, Carmen Miranda, James Ellison, Phil Baker, Benny Goodman, Charlotte Greenwood, Eugene Pallette, Edward Everett Horton

'Those who consider Berkeley a master consider this film his masterpiece.'—*New Yorker, 1976*

'Mainly made up of Busby Berkeley's paroxysmic production numbers, which amuse me a good deal.'—*James Agee*

Gangs of New York*
US 1938 67m bw

A cop infiltrates the mob and impersonates a tough gangster. Highly unlikely but entertaining programmer, a good shot for a B studio. Charles Bickford, Ann Dvorak, Alan Baxter, Wynne Gibson, Harold Huber, Willard Robertson, Maxie Rosenbloom, John Wray. Written by Wellyn Totman, Sam Fuller, Charles Francis Royal; directed by James Cruze; for Republic. 'Rapid-fire gangster meller . . . sure to be a strong entry.'—*Variety*

Gangs of the Waterfront
US 1945 55m bw

When his brother is killed, a taxidermist who looks like a gang leader assumes the leader's place and rounds up the mob. Serial-like action antics; a reliable second feature. Robert Armstrong, Stephanie Batchelor, Martin Kosleck, Marion Martin. Written by Albert Beich; directed and produced by George Blair; for Republic.

The Gangster
US 1947 84m bw

Rival gangs rub each other out. Shoddy-looking Poverty Row melodrama with little rhyme, reason or interest. Barry Sullivan, Akim Tamiroff, Belita, John Ireland. Written by Daniel Fuchs; directed by Gordon Wiles; for Monogram / King Bros.

Gangway*
GB 1937 89m bw
GFD / Gaumont (Michael Balcon)

A girl reporter poses as a star's maid and is accused of theft.
Mildly pleasing star vehicle.

w Lesser Samuels, Sonnie Hale *d* Sonnie Hale *ph* Glen MacWilliams

Jessie Matthews, Barry Mackay, Nat Pendleton, Noel Madison, Alastair Sim

Gangway for Tomorrow
US 1943 69m bw

Five defence workers with problematical pasts unite in the cause of war. Naïve but oddly stirring little propaganda piece. Robert Ryan, Margo, John Carradine. Written by Arch Oboler; directed by John H. Auer; for RKO.

Garbo Talks*
US 1984 103m Technicolor
MGM–UA / Elliott Kastner (Burtt Harris)

A dying woman's last obsession is to meet her idol Greta Garbo.
New Yorkish wry comedy which doesn't seem entirely clear of its point but is smartly acted and produced.

w Larry Grusin *d* Sidney Lumet *ph* Andrzej Bartkowiak *m* Cy Coleman *pd* Philip Rosenberg *ed* Andrew Mondshein

Anne Bancroft, Ron Silver, Carrie Fisher, Catherine Hicks, Steven Hill, Howard Da Silva, Harvey Fierstein, Dorothy Loudon, Hermione Gingold

'A sweet and sour film clearly not for all tastes.'—*Variety*

Garde a Vue*
France 1981 88m Eastmancolor
Ariane / TF1 (Georges Dancigers, Alexandre Mnouchkine)
GB title: *The Inquisitor*

In a French provincial town a wealthy lawyer is interrogated by police, who think he may be implicated in a rape case.
Basically a talk-piece, though with a twist ending, this is a smart little film which would undoubtedly have its best effect when not understood through sub-titles.

w Claude Miller, Jean Herman, *novel* Brainwash by John Wainwright *d Claude Miller ph* Bruno Nuytten *m* Georges Delerue

Lino Ventura, Michel Serrault, Guy Marchand, Romy Schneider

'Not unlike a *Twelve Angry Men* from which all comfortable certainties have been withdrawn.'—*Tom Milne, MFB*

'Dangerous love in a desert paradise!'
The Garden of Allah**
US 1936 80m Technicolor
David O. Selznick

A disenchanted socialite falls in love with a renegade monk in the Algerian desert.
Arty old-fashioned romantic star vehicle; great to look at, and marking a genuine advance in colour photography, but dramatically a bit of a drag.

w W. P. Lipscomb, Lynn Riggs, *novel* Robert Hichens *d* Richard Boleslawski *ph W. Howard Greene, Harold Rosson m Max Steiner ad* Sturges Carne, Lyle Wheeler, Edward Boyle

Marlene Dietrich, Charles Boyer, Basil Rathbone, Tilly Losch

'The last word in colour production, but a pretty dull affair.'—*Variety*

'Hopelessly dated folderol.'—*J. R. Parish*

'The juiciest tale of woe ever, produced in poshly lurid colour, with a Max Steiner score poured on top.'—*Judith Crist*

'Alas! my poor church, so picturesque, so noble, so superhumanly pious, so intensely dramatic. I really prefer the *New Statesman* view, shabby priests counting pesetas on their dingy fingers before blessing tanks.'—*Graham Greene*

† Previous, silent, versions had been made in 1917, with Tom Santschi and Helen Ware, and in 1927 with Ivan Petrovich and Alice Terry.

AA: photography
AAN: Max Steiner

Garden of Evil*
US 1954 100m Technicolor Cinemascope
TCF (Charles Brackett)

En route to the Californian goldfields an ex-sheriff and a gambler help a woman to rescue her husband from a mine, but are trapped by Indians.
High-flying western melodrama with the principals glowering at each other. Stock situations quite skilfully compiled.

w Frank Fenton *d* Henry Hathaway *ph* Milton Krasner *m Bernard Herrmann*

Susan Hayward, Gary Cooper, Richard Widmark, Hugh Marlowe, Cameron Mitchell

The Garden of the Finzi-Continis**
Italy / West Germany 1970 95m Eastmancolor
Documento Film / CCC Filmkunst (Gianni Hecht Lucari, Arthur Cohn)

In 1938, a family of wealthy Italian Jews sees its world collapse, with a concentration camp as the next destination.
A dreamlike, poignant, and very beautiful film.

w Tullio Pinelli, Valerio Zurlini, Franco Brusati, Ugo Pirro, Vittorio Bonicelli, Alain Katz, *novel* Giorgio Bassani *d Vittorio de Sica ph Ennio Guarnieri m* Manuel de Sica

Dominique Sanda, Lino Capolicchio, Helmut Berger, Romolo Valli, Fabio Testi

'I lived through the period. The same feelings I experienced in life I transposed to the picture: that is the definition of the artist.'—*Vittorio de Sica*

AAN: script

Garden of the Moon
US 1938 94m bw
Warner (Lou Edelman)

A night club owner vies with his bandleader for the affections of his leading singer. Pleasant talent can't turn this script into anything but a tedious small-scale musical, especially since both director and songwriters are operating below par.

w Jerry Wald, Richard Macauley *d* Busby Berkeley *songs* Al Dubin, Harry Warren

Pat O'Brien, Margaret Lindsay, John Payne, Melville Cooper, Isabel Jeans

Gardens of Stone
US 1987 111m De Luxe

A soldier trains youngsters for the Vietnam War despite his conviction that the war is wrong. Muddled talk-piece which fails to make any point. James Caan, Anjelica Huston, James Earl Jones, D. B. Sweeney, Dean Stockwell, Dick Anthony Williams. Written by Ronald Bass from the novel by Nicholas Proffitt; directed by Francis Coppola; for Levy-Coppola/Tri-Star.

The Garment Jungle*
US 1957 88m bw
Columbia (Harry Kleiner)

Union and gangster problems abound for a family in the New York clothing business. Reasonably powerful melodrama fashioned from familiar material in the wake of *On the Waterfront.*

w Harry Kleiner *d* Robert Aldrich, Vincent Sherman *ph* Joseph Biroc *m* Leith Stevens

Lee J. Cobb, Kerwin Mathews, Gia Scala, Richard Boone, Valerie French, Robert Loggia, Joseph Wiseman

Gas House Kids
US 1946 71m bw

Young New Yorkers help a crippled veteran buy a chicken ranch. First of three forgotten attempts to stretch out the Dead End Kids genre; not good. Billy Halop, Alfalfa Switzer, Robert Lowery, Teala Loring, Rex Downing, David Reed. Written by Raymond Schrock, George and Elsie Bricker; directed by Sam Newfield; for PRC. (The other titles, both in 1947, were *Gas House Kids Go West* and *Gas House Kids in Hollywood*.)

Gas! or It Became Necessary to Destroy the World in Order to Save It
US 1970 79m Movielab
AIP / San Jacinto (Roger Corman)

A gas which speeds up the ageing process is accidentally released and kills everyone over twenty-five.
Psychedelic sci-fi for the Easy Rider set. Very mildly diverting.

w Graham Armitage *d* Roger Corman *ph* Ron Dexter *m* Country Joe and the Fish

Robert Corff, Elaine Giftos, Pat Patterson, Graham Armitage, Alex Wilson, Ben Vereen, Bud Cort

Gasbags*
GB 1940 77m bw
Gainsborough (Edward Black)

Airmen stranded in Germany by a barrage balloon return in a captured secret weapon. Fast-moving knockabout from the Crazy Gang; often inventive despite reach-me-down script and production.

w Val Guest, Marriott Edgar *d* Marcel Varnel *ph* Arthur Crabtree

Flanagan and Allen, Nervo and Knox, Naughton and Gold, Moore Marriott, Wally Patch, Peter Gawthorne, Frederick Valf

Gaslight****
GB 1939 88m bw
British National (John Corfield)
US title: *Angel Street*

A Victorian schizophrenic drives his wife insane when she seems likely to stumble on his guilty secret of an old murder and hidden rubies.
Modest but absolutely effective film version of a superb piece of suspense theatre.

w A. R. Rawlinson, Bridget Boland, *play Patrick Hamilton d Thorold Dickinson* *ph* Bernard Knowles *m Richard Addinsell*

Anton Walbrook, Diana Wynyard, Frank Pettingell, Cathleen Cordell, Robert Newton, Jimmy Hanley

'The electric sense of tension and mid-Victorian atmosphere are entirely cinematic.'—*Sequence, 1950*

'A melodrama of a strange love!'
Gaslight**
US 1944 114m bw
MGM (Arthur Hornblow Jnr)
GB title: *The Murder in Thornton Square*

Grossly overblown and less effective version of the above, but with moments of power, effective performances and superior production.

w John Van Druten, Walter Reisch, John L. Balderston *d George Cukor ph Joseph Ruttenberg m* Bronislau Kaper *ad Cedric Gibbons*

Charles Boyer, Ingrid Bergman, Joseph Cotten, Dame May Whitty, Barbara Everest, *Angela Lansbury*. Edmund Breon, Halliwell Hobbes

'This is love . . . clouded by evil . . . darkened by a secret no one dared to guess! The strange drama of a captive sweetheart!'—*publicity*

† Irene Dunne and Hedy Lamarr were previously offered the Ingrid Bergman part, and turned it down.
AA: Ingrid Bergman
AAN: best picture; script; Joseph Ruttenberg; Charles Boyer; Angela Lansbury

Gasoline Alley
US 1951 76m bw

Young marrieds open a diner. Placid comedy-drama from a 30-year-old comic strip; the intended series did not materialize. Scotty Beckett, Jimmy Lydon, Susan Morrow, Don Beddoe, Dick Wessel, Gus Schilling. Written and directed by Edward Bernds from the strip by Frank O. King; for Milton Feldman/Columbia.

Gate of Hell*
Japan 1953 90m Eastmancolor
original title: *Jigokumon*

After a 12th-century war, a soldier demands as his prize a woman who has helped him; but she is married.
Curious traditional Japanese saga, its emphases strange to western eyes and ears. Its colour, however, is devastatingly beautiful.

wd Teinosuke Kinugasa, *novel* Kan Kikuchi *ph Kohei Sugiyama m* Yasushi Akutagawa

Machiko Kyo, Kazuo Hasegawa, Isao Yamagata

AA: best foreign film

Gateway*
US 1938 75m bw
TCF (Darryl F. Zanuck)

An Irish girl emigrating to the US is helped on board ship by a war correspondent.
Brisk romantic drama which provides an interesting recreation of the Ellis Island procedures still effective in the thirties.

w Lamar Trotti *d* Alfred Werker *ph* Edward Cronjager *m* Arthur Lange, Charles Maxwell

Don Ameche, Arleen Whelan, Gregory Ratoff, Raymond Walburn, Binnie Barnes, Gilbert Roland, John Carradine, Harry Carey

'*Grand Hotel* treatment applied to Ellis Island . . . should look to fair b.o.'—*Variety*

A Gathering of Eagles
US 1962 115m Eastmancolor
U-I (Sy Bartlett)

A colonel becomes unpopular when he strives to improve the efficiency of a Strategic Air Command base.
Tame revamp of *Twelve O'clock High* without the justification of war; all strictly routine and perfectly dull.

w Robert Pirosh *d* Delbert Mann *ph* Russell Harlan *m* Jerry Goldsmith

Rock Hudson, Mary Peach, Rod Taylor, Barry Sullivan, Kevin McCarthy

'Come and get him!'
Gator
US 1976 116m De Luxe Todd AO 35
UA / Levy-Gardner-Laven

A convicted moonshiner is blackmailed into becoming a government undercover man in the organization of a hoodlum.
Shambling mixture of action, violence, and raw humour.

w William Norton *d* Burt Reynolds *ph* William A. Fraker *m* Charles Bernstein

Burt Reynolds, Jack Weston, Lauren Hutton, Jerry Reed, Alice Ghostley, Dub Taylor, Mike Douglas

'The relentless violence, the sentimentality, the raucous stag party humour, the inability to cut off a scene once it has made its point, attest to the influence of Robert Aldrich.'—*Philip French, The Times*

The Gaucho*
US 1928 115m approx bw silent

An outlaw reforms when he falls for the Girl of the Shrine. Subdued star swashbuckler leading up to a fine climax. Douglas Fairbanks, Lupe Velez, Geraine Greear, Gustav von Seyffertitz. Written by Lotto Woods from a story by Fairbanks; directed by F. Richard Jones; for Douglas Fairbanks.

The Gaunt Stranger*
GB 1938 73m bw
Northwood / Capad (Ealing) (S. C. Balcon)
US title: *The Phantom Strikes*

A criminal master of disguise threatens to kill a much more despicable criminal at an appointed hour . . . and does so despite police protection.
A highly reliable suspenser of which this is perhaps the best film version.

w Sidney Gilliat, *novel and play* The Ringer by Edgar Wallace *d* Walter Forde *ph* Ronald Neame

Sonnie Hale, Wilfrid Lawson, Alexander Knox, Louise Henry, Patricia Roc, Patrick Barr, John Longden, George Merritt

'Dialogue, humour and suspense are effectively alternated . . . the film is in fact capital crime fiction.'—*Kine Weekly*

† Other versions, as *The Ringer*, appeared in 1931 and 1953.

The Gauntlet*
US 1977 109m De Luxe Panavision
Warner / Malpaso (Robert Daly)

A disreputable cop is assigned to escort a foul-mouthed prostitute to a courtroom across country, through the gauntlet of baddies who want them both dead.
The epitome of seventies violence, with no excuse except to stage one detailed shoot-up or explosion after another. Well done for those who like this sort of thing.

w Michael Butler, Dennis Shryack *d* Clint Eastwood *ph* Rexford Metz *m* Jerry Fielding

Clint Eastwood, Sondra Locke, Pat Hingle, William Prince

'At times the whole world seems to be firing at them. Buildings and cars are turned to lace. You look at the screen even though there's nothing to occupy your mind . . .'—*Pauline Kael*

† This was the first film to give a credit for first aid.

Gawain and the Green Knight*
GB 1973 93m Technicolor Panavision
UA / Sancrest (Philip Breen)

The medieval legend of a supernatural knight who challenges the king's men to kill him.
Enterprising if unsuccessful low-budget attempt to create a medieval world; too long by half.

w Philip Green, Stephen Weeks *d* Stephen Weeks *ph* Ian Wilson *m* Ron Goodwin *ad Anthony Woollard*

Murray Head, Ciaran Madden, Nigel Green, Anthony Sharp, Robert Hardy, Murray Melvin

The Gay Bride
US 1934 80m bw
MGM (John Considine Jnr)

A gold-digging chorus girl marries a racketeer but soon becomes a widow.
Misfiring satirical melodrama which quickly becomes tedious.

w Bella and Samuel Spewack, *story* Repeal by Charles Francis Coe *d* Jack Conway *ph* Ray June

Carole Lombard, Chester Morris, Zasu Pitts, Nat Pendleton, Leo Carrillo

'Gangster pictures are gone, and this won't do anything to bring them back.'—*Variety*

The Gay Deception*
US 1935 79m bw
TCF (Jesse L. Lasky)

A Ruritanian prince becomes a doorman at a swank New York hotel, and marries a secretary.
Lightly-handled Cinderella story showing most of its director's accomplishment.

w Stephen Morehouse Avery, Don Hartman *d William Wyler* *ph* Joseph Valentine *m* Louis de Francesco

Francis Lederer, Frances Dee, Benita Hume, Alan Mowbray, Akim Tamiroff, Lennox Pawle, Richard Carle, Lionel Stander

'Doesn't lean too much to sophistication to miss appreciation in the hamlet houses.'—*Variety*

AAN: script

The Gay Desperado**
US 1936 85m bw
Mary Pickford

An heiress is held for ransom by a romantic bandit.
Very light, quite amusing, sometimes irritatingly skittish musical spoof sparked by the director's ideas.

w Wallace Smith, *story* Leo Birinski *d Rouben Mamoulian* *m* Alfred Newman *ph* Lucien Andriot

Ida Lupino, Nino Martini, Leo Carrillo, Harold Huber, Mischa Auer

'Fairly diverting Mexican western . . . it'll do spotty trade, depending on locale.'—*Variety*

'One of the best light comedies of the year . . . Mr Mamoulian's camera is very persuasive.'—*Graham Greene*

'While some of the show is fetching, the ideas mostly misfire and the spell is fitful and unsure.'—*Otis Ferguson*

'It has the lightness of touch which goes into the making of the perfect meringue.'—*Basil Wright*

The Gay Diplomat
US 1931 66m bw

A Russian officer is sent to Bucharest to combat a woman superspy. Thoroughly confused and inane mixture of romance, presumed sophistication and dark doings. Ivan Lebedeff, Genevieve Tobin, Ilka Chase, Betty Compson. Written by Doris Anderson from a story by Benn W. Levy; directed by Richard Boleslawski; for RKO. 'A picture almost without a merit.'—*Variety*

'The gayest of mad musicals!'
'The dance-mad musical triumph of two continents!'

The Gay Divorcee****
US 1934 107m bw
RKO (Pandro S. Berman)
GB title: *The Gay Divorce*

A would-be divorcee in a Brighton hotel mistakes an author who loves her for a professional co-respondent.
Wildly and hilariously dated comedy musical with splendidly archaic comedy routines supporting Hollywood's great new dance team in their first big success. Not much dancing, but 'The Continental' is a show-stopper.

w George Marion Jnr, Dorothy Yost, Edward Kaufman, *musical comedy* Dwight Taylor *d Mark Sandrich* *ph* David Abel *md* Max Steiner *songs* various *sp Vernon Walker* *ad* Van Nest Polglase, Carroll Clark

Fred Astaire, Ginger Rogers, Edward Everett Horton, Alice Brady, Erik Rhodes, Eric Blore, Lillian Miles, Betty Grable

'Cinch box office anywhere and certain of big foreign grosses.'—*Variety*

'The plot is trivial French farce, but the dances are among the wittiest and most lyrical expressions of American romanticism on the screen.'—*New Yorker, 1977*

AA: song 'The Continental' (*m* Con Conrad, *ly* Herb Magidson)
AAN: best picture; musical adaptation (Ken Webb, Samuel Hoffenstein)

The Gay Dog
GB 1954 87m bw

A miner trains a pet greyhound to win races. Modest, set-bound regional comedy. Wilfred Pickles, Petula Clark, Megs Jenkins, John Blythe. Written by Peter Rogers, from the play by Joseph Colton; directed by Maurice Elvey; for Coronet / Eros.

The Gay Intruders
US 1948 68m bw

Quarrelling stage marrieds consult psychiatrists, who end up more confused than the patients. Unusual second feature comedy with a few good laughs; allegedly based on Tallulah Bankhead. Tamara Geva, John Emery, Leif Erickson, Virginia Gregg. Written by Francis Swann; directed by Ray McCarey; for TCF.

Gay Purree*
US 1962 85m Technicolor
UPA (Henry Saperstein)

A country cat goes to Paris and is Shanghaied. Feature cartoon similar to Disney's later *The Aristocats* and about as good, i.e. not quite up to the best standards.

w Dorothy and Chuck Jones *d* Abe Levitow *md* Mort Lindsey *m/l* Harold Arlen, E. Y. Harburg

voices Judy Garland, Robert Goulet, Hermione Gingold

The Gay Sisters*
US 1942 110m bw
Warner (Henry Blanke)

Three sisters refuse to sell their aristocratic New York mansion to make way for development.
Slowish but quite interesting family drama with Chekhovian touches.

w Lenore Coffee, *novel* Stephen Longstreet *d* Irving Rapper *ph* Sol Polito *m* Max Steiner

Barbara Stanwyck, George Brent, Geraldine Fitzgerald, Donald Crisp, *Gig Young* (so named after his part in this film; formerly Byron Barr), Nancy Coleman, Gene Lockhart, Larry Simms, Donald Woods, Grant Mitchell

The Gazebo*
US 1959 102m bw
MGM / Avon (Lawrence Weingarten)

A TV writer kills a blackmailer (he thinks) and hides his body in the garden.
Frenetic black comedy which must have worked better on the stage but produces a few laughs.

w George Wells, *play* Alec Coppel *d* George Marshall *ph* Paul C. Vogel *m* Jeff Alexander

Glenn Ford, Debbie Reynolds, Carl Reiner, John McGiver, Mabel Albertson, Doro Merande, Zasu Pitts, Martin Landau

The Geisha Boy
US 1958 98m Technicolor Vistavision
Paramount (Jerry Lewis)

A third-rate magician joins a USO entertainment tour in Japan.
Disconnected farce which amuses only fitfully, and actively displeases when it becomes sentimental with the star drooling over a baby.

wd Frank Tashlin *ph* Haskell Boggs *m* Walter Scharf

Jerry Lewis, Marie MacDonald, Barton MacLane, Sessue Hayakawa, Suzanne Pleshette

The Gene Krupa Story
US 1959 101m bw
Columbia (Philip A. Waxman)
GB title: *Drum Crazy*

A successful jazz drummer is convicted on a drugs charge and falls from grace.
Dreary biopic with the expected music track.

w Orin Jannings *d* Don Weis *ph* Charles Lawton Jnr *m* Leith Stevens

Sal Mineo, Susan Kohner, James Darren, Susan Oliver, Yvonne Craig, Lawrence Dobkin, Celia Lovsky; and Red Nichols, Shelly Manne, Buddy Lester

'Everybody laughs but Buster!'

The General******
US 1926 80m approx (24 fps) bw silent
UA / Buster Keaton (Joseph M. Schenck)

A confederate train driver gets his train and his girl back when they are stolen by Union soldiers.
Slow-starting, then hilarious action comedy, often voted one of the best ever made. Its sequence of sight gags, each topping the one before, is an incredible joy to behold.

w Al Boasberg, Charles Smith d Buster Keaton, Clyde Bruckman ph J. Devereux Jennings, Bert Haines

Buster Keaton, Marion Mack, Glen Cavander

'It has all the sweet earnestness in the world. It is about trains, frontier America, flower-faced girls.'—*New Yorker, 1977*

'The production itself is singularly well mounted, but the fun is not exactly plentiful . . . here he is more the acrobat than the clown, and his vehicle might be described as a mixture of cast iron and jelly.'—*Mordaunt Hall, New York Times*

† The story is based on an actual incident of the Civil War, treated more seriously in *The Great Locomotive Chase*.

†† The screenplay with 1,400 freeze frames was issued in 1976 in the Film Classics Library (editor, Richard Anobile).

'He strides recklessly into the vortex of cyclonic romantic adventure, sweeping monarchs from their thrones to suit a gypsy's whim!'

General Crack
US 1930 100m approx bw (colour sequences)

Exploits of an eighteenth-century brigand prince. Elaborate swashbuckler which provided the star with his first talkie but boringly demonstrates the technical problems of films of this period, however highly budgeted. John Barrymore, Marian Nixon, Hobart Bosworth, Armida, Lowell Sherman. Written by J. Grubb Alexander and others; directed by Alan Crosland; for Warner.

'Gary goes to town for the best-looking gal in China!'

The General Died at Dawn**
US 1936 93m bw
Paramount (William le Baron)

A mercenary in China overcomes an evil warlord and falls in love with a spy.
Heavy-going but very decorative studio-bound intrigue which seems to take place on the old *Shanghai Express* sets with an extra infusion of dry ice. An intellectual's picture of its day.

w Clifford Odets, *novel* Charles Booth *d Lewis Milestone ph Victor Milner m* Werner Janssen, Gerard Carbonara

Gary Cooper, Madeleine Carroll, *Akim Tamiroff, Dudley Digges*, Porter Hall, *William Frawley*

'If it were not for a rather ludicrous ending, this would be one of the best thrillers for some years.'—*Graham Greene*

'In terms of cinematic invention, a fascinating technical exercise.'—*John Baxter, 1968*

'A curious study in exoticism.'—*NFT, 1974*

'In direction and photography it has undeniable class . . . but like most movies, it is empty of any ideas or characters that stay with you longer than it takes to reach the nearest subway entrance.'—*Brooklyn Daily Eagle*

AAN: Victor Milner; Werner Janssen; Akim Tamiroff

The General Line**
USSR 1929 90m (24 fps) bw silent
Sovkino
original title: *Staroye i Novoye;* aka: *Old and New*

A country woman helps to start a village co-operative.
A slight piece of propaganda, put together with all of Eisenstein's magnificent cinematic resources: the cream separator demonstration is one of the most famous montage sequences in cinema history.

wd Sergei Eisenstein co-d Grigori Alexandrov *ph Edouard Tissé.*

Marta Lapkina and a cast of non-professionals

General Spanky
US 1936 73m approx bw

A small boy is instrumental in a famous Civil War victory. Uneasy sentimental melodrama vehicle for one of the moppet stars of 'Our Gang'. Spanky McFarland, Phillips Holmes, Hobart Bosworth, Ralph Morgan, Irving Pichel. Written by Richard Flournoy, Hal Yates and John Guedal; directed by Gordon Douglas and Fred Newmeyer; for Hal Roach / MGM. 'Desultory, overlong . . . built for the lesser family trade.'—*Variety*

General Suvorov
USSR 1941 90m bw

The career of the general who turned back Napoleon at the gates of Moscow. Competent propaganda piece, but not one of the Russian classics. N. P. Cherkasov, A. Yachnitscki, S. Kiligin. Written by G. Grebner; directed by V. I. Pudovkin; for Mosfilm.

Il Generale della Rovere
Italy / France 1959 137m bw
Zebra / Gaumont (Morris Ergas)

During World War II, a con man is persuaded to impersonate a dead general, and becomes so imbued with the latter's code of honour that he goes before a firing squad rather than expose a partisan.
An unlikely piece of tragic whimsy with some good acting, but imperfectly assembled and at too great length.

w Sergio Amidei, Diego Fabbri, Indro Montanelli, Roberto Rossellini *d* Roberto Rossellini *ph* Carlo Carlini *m* Renzo Rossellini

Vittorio de Sica, Hannes Messemer, Sandra Milo, Giovanna Ralli, Anne Vernon

AAN: script

Generation*
Poland 1954 90m bw
Film Polski
original title: *Pokolenie*

In occupied Warsaw in 1942 a teenager becomes hardened by life and joins the resistance.
Heavy-going but quite striking propaganda piece, amply demonstrating its director's talents.

w Bohdan Czeszko, from his novel *d Andrzej Wajda ph* Jerzy Lipman *m* Andrzej Markowski

Tadeusz Lomnicki, Urszula Modrzynska, Roman Polanski, Zbigniew Cybulski

Generation
US 1969 104m Technicolor
Avco Embassy / Frederick Brisson
GB title: *A Time for Giving*

A Denver advertising executive is horrified by his daughter's ideas of modern marriage.
Lame generation-gap comedy centring on a couple who intend to deliver their own baby.

w William Goodheart, from his play
d George Schaefer *ph* Lionel Lindon
m Dave Grusin

David Janssen, Kim Darby, Carl Reiner, Pete Duel, Andrew Prine, James Coco, Sam Waterston, Don Beddoe

'Slightly too sticky for comfort.'—*MFB*

Genevieve****
GB 1953 86m Technicolor
GFD / Sirius (Henry Cornelius)

Two friendly rivals engage in a race on the way back from the Brighton veteran car rally.
One of those happy films in which for no very good or expected reason a number of modest elements merge smoothly to create an aura of high style and memorable moments. A charmingly witty script, carefully pointed direction, attractive actors and locations, an atmosphere of light-hearted British sex and a lively harmonica theme turned it, after a slowish start, into one of Britain's biggest commercial hits and most fondly remembered comedies.

w William Rose d Henry Cornelius
ph Christopher Challis *m Larry Adler* (who also played it) *md* Muir Mathieson
ad Michael Stringer

Dinah Sheridan, John Gregson, Kay Kendall, Kenneth More, Geoffrey Keen, Joyce Grenfell, Reginald Beckwith, Arthur Wontner

'One of the best things to have happened to British films over the last five years.'—*Gavin Lambert*

AAN: William Rose; Muir Mathieson

'In the eight centuries since he ruled the world, no man has matched the magnificence of his adventure!'

Genghis Khan*
US 1964 126m Technicolor Panavision
Columbia / Irving Allen / CCC / Avala

Temujin raises a Mongol army and revenges himself on his old enemy Jamuga.
Meandering epic in which brutality alternates with pantomimish comedy and bouts of sex.
Necessarily patchy but reasonably watchable.

w Clarke Reynolds, Beverly Cross *d* Henry Levin *ph* Geoffrey Unsworth *m* Ducan Radic

Omar Sharif, Stephen Boyd, Françoise Dorléac, *James Mason*, Robert Morley, Telly Savalas, Woody Strode, Eli Wallach, Yvonne Mitchell

Genius at Work
US 1946 61m bw

Radio detectives expose a killer. Rackety vehicle for a comedy team which never even approached Abbott and Costello. Wally Brown, Alan Carney, Anne Jeffries, Bela Lugosi, Lionel Atwill. Written by Robert E. Kent, Monte Brice; directed by Leslie Goodwins; for RKO.

Les Gens du Voyage*
France 1938 123m bw

Trials and tribulations of circus people on the road. Interesting but overlong multi-drama. Françoise Rosay, André Brule, Fabien Loris, Marie Glory, Sylvia Bataille. Written by Jacques Feyder and Jacques Viol; directed by Jacques Feyder; for Tobis. 'Boredom is unavoidably the impression.'—*Variety*

Gentle Annie
US 1944 80m bw

A marshal deals with a lady rancher who sees no harm in an occasional bank robbery to augment her income. Tidy MGM second-string western, originally intended for Robert Taylor. James Craig, Marjorie Main, Donna Reed, Henry Morgan, Paul Langton, Barton MacLane. Written by Lawrence Hazard, from the novel by Mackinlay Kantor; directed by Andrew Marton; for MGM.

The Gentle Giant
US 1967 93m Eastmancolor

A small boy in Florida befriends a bear, which later saves his disapproving father's life. Lumbering family movie which provided the impetus for a TV series. Dennis Weaver, Clint Howard, Vera Miles, Ralph Meeker, Huntz Hall. Written by Edward J. Lakso and Andy White, from the novel *Gentle Ben* by Walt Morey; directed by James Neilson; for Ivan Tors / Paramount.

The Gentle Gunman
GB 1952 88m bw
GFD / Ealing (Michael Relph)

Tensions mount in an IRA family where one brother believes in peace.
Stilted and unconvincing pattern play which wouldn't have done at all once the Troubles restarted.

w Roger MacDougall, from his play *d* Basil Dearden *ph* Gordon Dines *m* John Greenwood *ed* Peter Tanner

John Mills, Dirk Bogarde, Elizabeth Sellars, Barbara Mullen, Robert Beatty, Eddie Byrne, Joseph Tomelty, Gilbert Harding, Liam Redmond, Jack MacGowran

The Gentle Sex**
GB 1943 93m bw
Rank / Two Cities / Concanen (Leslie Howard, Derrick de Marney)

Seven girls from different backgrounds are conscripted into the ATS.
Unassuming war propaganda, quite pleasantly done and historically very interesting.

w Moie Charles, Aimée Stuart, Phyllis Rose, Roland Pertwee *d* Leslie Howard, Maurice Elvey *ph* Robert Krasker *m* John Greenwood

Rosamund John, Joan Greenwood, Joan Gates, Jean Gillie, Lilli Palmer, Joyce Howard, Barbara Waring, John Justin, Frederick Leister, Mary Jerrold, Everley Gregg

† Leslie Howard is heard as narrator and recognizably glimpsed in two scenes photographed from behind.

A Gentleman after Dark
US 1942 74m bw
Edward Small

A jewel thief comes out of prison to pay back his vindictive wife for shopping him.
Efficient melodrama of a dated kind.

w Patterson McNutt, George Bruce, *story* A Whiff of Heliotrope by Richard Washburn Child *d* Edwin L. Marin *ph* Milton Krasner *m* Dmitri Tiomkin

Brian Donlevy, Miriam Hopkins, Preston Foster, Harold Huber, Philip Reed, Gloria Holden, Douglass Dumbrille, Ralph Morgan

† Previously filmed in 1920 as *Heliotrope* with Fred Burton; in 1928 as *Forgotten Faces* with Clive Brook; and in 1936 as *Forgotten Faces* with Herbert Marshall.

A Gentleman at Heart
US 1942 66m bw

A racetrack bookie has aspirations to the art business but finds there are crooks there too. Fairly lively second feature. Cesar Romero, Carole Landis, Milton Berle, J. Carrol Naish, Rose Hobart, Jerome Cowan, Elisha Cook Jnr, Steve Geray. Written by Lee Loeb and Harold Buchman, from a story by Paul Hervey Fox; directed by Ray Macarey; for Walter Morosco / TCF.

The Gentleman in Room Six*
US 1951 11m bw

In a seedy room in South America, a man we can't see gives orders to old associates. As he finally goes to shave, we see in the mirror that he is—Adolf Hitler! A fairly sensational novelty at the time, and historically interesting thirty years later. Written by Sidney Carroll; directed by Alexander Hammid; produced by George Brest for Meteor Films.

Gentleman Jim**
US 1942 104m bw
Warner (Robert Buckner)

The rise to fame of boxer Jim Corbett.
Cheerful biopic of a nineties show-off, mostly played for comedy.

w Vincent Lawrence, Horace McCoy, *book* The Roar of the Crowd by James J. Corbett *d Raoul Walsh ph* Sid Hickox *m* Heinz Roemheld

Errol Flynn, Alan Hale, Alexis Smith, John Loder, Jack Carson, *Ward Bond*, William Frawley, Rhys Williams, Arthur Shields

'Good-natured enough, but it lacks flavour.'—*New Yorker, 1976*

A Gentleman of Paris
GB 1931 76m bw

A philandering French judge knows that the girl before him is innocent of murder, but dare not say so. Tolerable melodrama of its time. Arthur Wontner, Hugh Williams, Vanda Greville, Phyllis Konstam, Sybil Thorndike. Written by Sydney Gilliat, Sewell Collins, from the novel *His Honour the Judge* by Niranjan Pal; directed by Sinclair Hill; for Stoll / Gaumont.

'Now! It comes to the screen with nothing left unsaid and no emotion unstressed!'

Gentleman's Agreement**
US 1947 118m bw
TCF (Darryl F. Zanuck)

A journalist poses as a Jew in order to write about anti-semitism.
Worthy melodrama which caused a sensation at the time but as a film is alas rather dull and self-satisfied.

w Moss Hart, *novel* Laura Z. Hobson *d* Elia Kazan *ph* Arthur Miller *m* Alfred Newman

Gregory Peck, Dorothy McGuire, *John Garfield*, Celeste Holm, *Anne Revere*, June Havoc, Albert Dekker, Jane Wyatt, Dean Stockwell

AA: best picture; Elia Kazan; Celeste Holm
AAN: Moss Hart; Gregory Peck; Dorothy McGuire; Anne Revere

Gentleman's Fate
US 1930 90m bw

A man goes to the bad after his wife walks out on him. Dismal early talkie, one of several which killed off its star's career. John Gilbert, Louis Wolheim, Leila Hyams, Anita Page, John Miljan, Marie Prevost. Written from a story by Ursula Parrott; directed by Mervyn Le Roy; for MGM. 'It got a laugh at the Strand Saturday afternoon, where all of the audience probably thought the same thing, that Gilbert died too late as the picture had been dying since its start.'—*Variety*

A Gentleman's Gentleman
GB 1939 70m bw

A valet thinks his master is a murderer, and tries a little blackmail. Uneasy serio-comic vehicle for a London stage character who had made his name in Hollywood. Eric Blore, Peter Coke, Marie Lohr, David Hutcheson. Written by Austin Melford and Elizabeth Meehan, from the play by Philip MacDonald; directed by Roy William Neill; for Warner.

Gentlemen Are Born
US 1934 74m bw

College graduates find it hard to get jobs. Tedious and uninventive quartet of linked stories. Franchot Tone, Ross Alexander, Dick Foran, Robert Light, Jean Muir, Margaret Lindsay, Ann Dvorak, Charles Starrett. Written by Eugene Solow and Robert Lee Johnson; directed by Alfred E. Green; for Warner.

Gentlemen Marry Brunettes
US 1955 95m Technicolor Cinemascope
UA / Russ–Field (Richard Sale, Robert Waterfield)

Two American shopgirls seek rich husbands in Paris, and find that their aunts were notorious there.
Jaded sequel to *Gentlemen Prefer Blondes*; it barely raises a smile and the numbers are dismal.

w Mary Loos, Richard Sale *d* Richard Sale *ph* Desmond Dickinson *m* Robert Farnon *ad* Paul Sheriff *ch* Jack Cole

Jane Russell, Jeanne Crain, Alan Young, Scott Brady, Rudy Vallee

Gentlemen Prefer Blondes*
US 1953 91m Technicolor
TCF (Sol. C. Siegel)

A dumb blonde and a showgirl go to Paris in search of rich husbands.
Musicalized and updated version of the twenties satire; no real vigour, but not too bad.

w Charles Lederer, *novel* Anita Loos *d* Howard Hawks *ph* Harry J. Wild *md* Lionel Newman *songs* Jule Styne, Leo Robin *ch* Jack Cole

Jane Russell, Marilyn Monroe, Charles Coburn, Tommy Noonan, Norma Varden, Elliott Reid, George Winslow

Geordie*
GB 1955 99m Technicolor
British Lion / Argonaut (Sidney Gilliat, Frank Launder)
US title: *Wee Geordie*

A weakly Scottish boy takes a physical culture course and becomes an Olympic hammer-thrower.
Slight comic fable, good to look at but without the necessary style to follow it through.

w Sidney Gilliat, Frank Launder, *novel* David Walker *d* Frank Launder *ph* Wilkie Cooper *m* William Alwyn

Bill Travers, Alastair Sim, Norah Gorsen, Raymond Huntley, Brian Reece, Miles Malleson, Stanley Baxter

George and Margaret
GB 1940 77m bw

The frictions of a suburban family come to boiling point. Fairly spruce film version of a stage comedy in which the title pair were much talked of but never seen. Judy Kelly, Marie Lohr, Oliver Wakefield, Noel Howlett, Ann Casson, Arthur Macrae. Written by Brock Williams and Rodney Ackland, from the play by Gerald Savory; directed by George King; for Warner.

George and Mildred
GB 1980 93m colour

A suburban husband on a weekend package holiday is mistaken for a hired killer. Abysmal TV spinoff, seeming even more lugubrious since it was released after the death of the female star. Yootha Joyce, Brian Murphy, Stratford Johns, Norman Eshley, Sheila Fearn, Kenneth Cope. Written by Dick Sharples; directed by Peter Frazer Jones; for Chips / ITC. 'Flaccid entertainment even by routine sit-com standards.'—*Martyn Auty, MFB.*

George in Civvy Street
GB 1946 79m bw
Columbia (Marcel Varnel, Ben Henry)

A soldier returns to his country pub and finds himself in the middle of a beer war.
The star's last film was oddly lacklustre and compared very badly with his earlier successes.

w Peter Fraser, Ted Kavanaugh, Max Kester, Gale Pedrick *d* Marcel Varnel *ph* Phil Grindrod

George Formby, Rosalyn Boulter, Ronald Shiner, Ian Fleming, Wally Patch

The George Raft Story
US 1961 105m bw
Allied Artists (Ben Schwab)
GB title: *Spin of a Coin*

In twenties New York, a dancer falls in with gangsters, but eludes them when he goes to Hollywood, where his acting career is harmed by temperament.
Tepid, unconvincing biopic, rather shoddily made but with flashes of interest.

w Crane Wilbur *d* Joseph M. Newman *ph* Carl Guthrie *m* Jeff Alexander

Ray Danton, Julie London, Jayne Mansfield, Frank Gorshin, Neville Brand (as Al Capone)

George Washington Slept Here
US 1942 93m bw
Warner (Jerry Wald)

A New York couple move to a dilapidated country house.
Disappointingly stiff and ill-timed version of a play that should have been a natural.

w Everett Freeman, *play* George Kaufman, Moss Hart *d* William Keighley *ph* Ernest Haller *m* Adolph Deutsch

Jack Benny, Ann Sheridan, Percy Kilbride, Charles Coburn, Hattie McDaniel, William Tracy, Lee Patrick, John Emery, Charles Dingle

George White's Scandals*
US 1934 79m bw
Fox (Winfield Sheehan)

Romance blossoms backstage during the production of a big musical.
Revue with minimum plot and some impressive numbers.

w Jack Yellen, from the Broadway show directed by George White *d* Thornton Freeland, Harry Lachman, George White *ph* Lee Garmes, George Schneiderman *songs* various

George White, Rudy Vallee, Alice Faye, Jimmy Durante, Dixie Dunbar, Adrienne Ames, Cliff Edwards, Gertrude Michael, Gregory Ratoff

George White's 1935 Scandals*
US 1935 83m bw
Fox (Winfield Sheehan)

A small-town star is discovered by a Broadway producer.
Again, basic plot serves to introduce some pretty good acts.

w Jack Yellen, Patterson McNutt *d* George White *ph* George Schneiderman *songs* various

George White, Alice Faye, James Dunn, Eleanor Powell, Ned Sparks, Lyda Roberti, Cliff Edwards, Arline Judge

George White's Scandals*
US 1945 95m bw
RKO (Jack J. Gross, Nat Holt, George White)

Ex-Scandals girls get together, and one disappears.
Lively comedy-musical with vaudeville orientations.

w Hugh Wedlock, Parker Levy, Howard Green *d* Felix E. Feist *m* Leigh Harline *ph* Robert de Grasse *songs* various

Joan Davis, Jack Haley, Philip Terry, Martha Holliday, Ethel Smith, Margaret Hamilton, Glenn Tryon, Jane Greer, Fritz Feld, Rufe Davis

Georgy Girl*
GB 1966 100m bw
Columbia / Everglades (Otto Plaschkes, Robert A. Goldston)

An unattractive girl is fancied by her middle-aged employer but escapes to look after the illegitimate baby of her ungrateful friend.
Frantic black farce which seems determined to shock, but has a few good scenes once you get attuned to the mood. A censorship milestone.

w Margaret Forster, Peter Nichols, *novel* Margaret Forster *d Silvio Narizzano ph* Ken Higgins *m* Alexander Faris

James Mason, Lynn Redgrave, Charlotte Rampling, Alan Bates, Bill Owen, Clare Kelly, Rachel Kempson

'Another swinging London story filled with people running through London late at night, dancing madly in the rain, and visiting deserted children's playgrounds to ride on the roundabouts.'—*MFB*

'So glib, so clever, so determinedly kinky that everything seems to be devalued.'—*Pauline Kael*

'Its barrage of fashionable tricks proves exhausting.'—*Sight and Sound*

AAN: Ken Higgins; James Mason; Lynn Redgrave; title song (*m* Tom Springfield, *ly* Jim Dale)

Gerald McBoing Boing***
US 1951 7m Technicolor

A small boy becomes famous because he can't speak words: 'he goes boing-boing instead'. Highly influential cartoon in what was then a new style; told with a light touch which is still extremely funny. Followed less successfully by *Gerald McBoing Boing's Symphony* and *Gerald McBoing Boing On Planet Moo*. Written by *Dr Seuss* (Theodore Geisel); directed by *Robert Cannon*; designed by *John Hubley*; music by *Gail Kubik*; for UPA.

The German Sisters*
West Germany 1981 107m Fujicolor
Bioskop Film / (Eberhard Junkersdorf)
original title: *Die Bleierne Zeit*

Based on a real-life case, this is a suppositional account of how two well-brought-up girls can develop so differently.

wd Margarethe von Trotta ph Franz Rath m Nicolas Economou *ed* Dagmar Hirtz

Jutte Lampe, Barbara Sukowa, Rudiger Vogler, Doris Schade, Verenice Rudolph

'Beautifully acted and strikingly shot, it all has a calculated, crowd-pleasing fervour.'—*Tom Milne, MFB*

Germany Year Zero*
France / Italy 1947 78m bw
Union Générale Cinématographique / DEFA

Life in post-war Germany is so appalling that a boy kills his father and then himself.
Both realistic and pessimistic, this depressing film has a savage power of its own but totally fails to be constructive.

wd Roberto Rossellini *ph* Robert Juillard *m* Renzo Rossellini

Franz Gruger and a cast of non-professionals

'Ten thousand red raiders roar into battle!'
Geronimo!
US 1939 89m bw
Paramount

The seventh cavalry gives the Indians a run for their money.
Muddled western of no discernible merit.

wd Paul H. Sloane *ph* Henry Sharp *m* Gerald Carbonara

Ellen Drew, Preston Foster, Andy Devine, Gene Lockhart, Ralph Morgan, William Henry

'Lusty and actionful melodrama geared to hit popular appeal.'—*Variety*

Geronimo
US 1962 101m Technicolor Panavision
UA / Laven–Gardner–Levy

In 1883 Geronimo and his remaining Apaches seek peace but are betrayed.
Moderate western held back by script and performances.

w Pat Fielder *d* Arnold Laven *ph* Alex Phillips *m* Hugo Friedhofer

Chuck Connors, Ross Martin, Kamala Devi

Gertrud*
Denmark 1966 115m bw

A lawyer's wife leaves him for an unhappy affair with a young musician. Austere psychological drama, better to look at than to listen to. Nina Pens Rode, Bendt Rothe, Ebbe Rode, Axel Strobye. Written and directed by Carl Theodor Dreyer from the play by Hjalmar Soderberg; for Palladium/Pathe Contemporary.

Gervaise*
France 1956 116m bw
Agnès Delahaye–Silver Films–CLCC

In 19th-century Paris, a laundrymaid is deserted by her lover, settles with another man and is able to open her own laundry, but they both take to drink.
The French equivalent of David Lean's Dickens films, superbly detailed and wonderful to look at, but with a plot which finally seems worthless and depressing.

w Jean Aurenche, Pierre Bost, *novel* L'Assommoir by Emile Zola *d René Clément ph René Juillard m* Georges Auric *decor Paul Bertrand*

Maria Schell, François Périer, Suzy Delair, Mathilde Casadeus

'A tremendous *tour de force* of literal realism . . . a piece for the admiration of technicians, or for those whose consciences are purged and hands kept clean by the vicarious contemplation of how the other half lived—once upon a time.'—*David Robinson, MFB*

† Other French versions were made in 1902, 1909, 1911 and 1933.

AA: best foreign film

Get Carter*
GB 1971 112m Metrocolor
MGM / Mike Klinger

A racketeer goes to Newcastle to avenge his brother's death at the hands of gangsters. He kills those responsible but is himself shot by a sniper.
Brutal British crime melodrama with faint echoes of Raymond Chandler. Sex and thuggery unlimited, narrative disjointed, rewards few.

wd Mike Hodges, *novel* Jack's Return Home by Ted Lewis *ph* Wolfgang Suschitsky *m* Roy Budd

Michael Caine, John Osborne, Ian Hendry, Britt Ekland

'TV on the big screen—more sex, more violence, but no more attention to motivation or plot logic.'—*Arthur Knight*

'So calculatedly cool and soulless and nastily erotic that it seems to belong to a new era of virtuoso viciousness.'—*Pauline Kael*

Get Cracking*
GB 1942 96m bw
Columbia (Ben Henry)

George joins the home guard.
Adequate star comedy.

w L. DuGarde Peach *d* Marcel Varnel *ph* Stephen Dade *md* Harry Bidgood

George Formby, Edward Rigby, Frank Pettingell, Dinah Sheridan, Ronald Shiner, Wally Patch, Irene Handl

Get Hep to Love
US 1942 79m bw

A child concert prodigy is overworked by a mercenary aunt and goes off alone for a vacation. Uninspired musical vehicle for young studio talents. Gloria Jean, Donald O'Connor, Peggy Ryan, Jane Frazee, Robert Paige, Nana Bryant, Edith Barrett, Cora Sue Collins. Written by Jay Dratler, M. M. Musselman; directed by Charles Lamont; for Universal. (GB title: *She's My Lovely*.)

Get Off My Foot
GB 1935 83m bw
Warner (Irving Asher)

A Smithfield porter becomes a butler, and later finds himself heir to a fortune.
The nearest Max Miller came to being a genuine film star was in this first of eight Warner comedies, but the screen simply couldn't contain him.

w Frank Launder, Robert Edmunds, *play* Money By Wire by Edward Paulton *d* William Beaudine *ph* Basil Emmott

Max Miller, Chili Bouchier, Morland Graham, Jane Carr, Norma Varden, Reginald Purdell, Wally Patch

Get to Know Your Rabbit
US 1972 91m Technicolor

A bored businessman enrols in a school of magic. Whimsical satire which never takes off. Tom Smothers, John Astin, Suzanne Zenor, Orson Welles, Samantha Jones, Allen Garfield, Katharine Ross. Written by Jordon Crittenden; directed by Brian DePalma; for Bernhardt-Gaer/Warners.

The Getaway
US 1941 89m bw

A lawman goes to jail, gets to know an imprisoned mob leader, and breaks out with him. Routine rehash of 1935's *Public Hero Number One*. Robert Sterling, Dan Dailey, Donna Reed, Charles Winninger, Henry O'Neill. Written by Wells Root and W. R. Burnett; directed by Edward Buzzell; for MGM.

'It takes two to make it. The big two!'

The Getaway**
US 1972 122m Technicolor Todd-AO 35
Solar / First Artists (David Foster, Mitchell Brower)

A convict leaves jail and promptly joins his wife in a bank robbery.
Violent, amoral, terse and fast-moving action melodrama which generally holds the interest despite its excesses.

w Walter Hill, *novel* Jim Thompson *d Sam Peckinpah ph* Lucien Ballard *m* Quincy Jones

Steve McQueen, Ali MacGraw, Ben Johnson, Sally Struthers, Al Lettieri, Slim Pickens

'This pair have no mission or "meaning". As in all romances, *The Getaway* simply extracts one element of reality and dwells on it. Nor is the violence "American". Pictures like this don't fail overseas.'—*Stanley Kauffmann*

Getting Gertie's Garter
US 1945 73m bw

A businessman tries all manner of wiles to retrieve an incriminating garter. Silly variation on *Up in Mabel's Room*, with similar team and cast. A few laughs are inevitable. Dennis O'Keefe, Marie McDonald, Mischa Auer, Binnie Barnes, Barry Sullivan, J. Carrol Naish. Written by Allan Dwan and Karen de Wilf, from the play by Wilson Collinson and Avery Hopwood; directed by Allan Dwan; for Edward Small / UA.

The Getting of Wisdom**
Australia 1977 101m Eastmancolor
Southern Cross / AFC / Victorian Film Corporation / 9 Television Network (Phillip Adams)

In 1897 a backwoods girl is sent to an exclusive Melbourne ladies' college and eventually wins a music scholarship.
Praiseworthy period piece which thankfully seems to have no axe to grind and is all the better for it.

w Eleanor Witcombe, *novel* Henry Handel Richardson (Ethel Richardson) *d Bruce Beresford ph* Donald McAlpine *m* various *pd* John Stoddart

Susannah Fowle, Sheila Helpman, Patricia Kennedy, John Waters, Barry Humphries, Kerry Armstrong

Getting Straight*
US 1970 125m Eastmancolor
Columbia / The Organization (Richard Rush)

A political activist returns to college in order to teach and discovers the foolishness of most contemporary attitudes.
Modish comedy, too long, far too pleased with itself, and now irrevocably dated.

w Robert Kaufman *novel* Ken Kolb *d* Richard Rush *ph* Laszlo Kovacs *m* Ronald Stein

Elliott Gould, Candice Bergen, Robert F. Lyons, Jeff Corey, Max Julien, Cecil Kellaway

The Ghost and Mr Chicken
US 1965 90m Techniscope
Universal (Edward J. Montagne)

An incompetent small-town reporter finds ghosts in a local murder mansion.
Old-fashioned scare comedy starring a highly resistible comic. A big hit in American small towns.

w James Fritzell, Everett Greenbaum *d* Alan Rafkin *ph* William Margulies *m* Vic Mizzy

Don Knotts, Skip Homeier, Joan Staley, Liam Redmond, Dick Sargent, Reta Shaw

'Doin' what comes supernaturally . . . it's the man-woman affair that's like nothing on earth!'

The Ghost and Mrs Muir*
US 1947 104m bw
TCF (Fred Kohlmar)

A widow refuses to be frightened away from her seaside home by the ghost of a sea captain, with whom she falls in love.
Charming sentimental fable in Hollywood's best style.

w Philip Dunne, *novel* R. A. Dick *d* Joseph L. Mankiewicz *ph Charles Lang m Bernard Herrmann ad* Richard Day and George Davis

Gene Tierney, Rex Harrison, George Sanders, Edna Best, Vanessa Brown, Anna Lee, Robert Coote, Natalie Wood, Isobel Elsom

'A not at all disagreeable piece of whimsy.'—*News Chronicle*

'A jolly caper, gently humorous and often sparkling.'—*New York Times*

† A half-hour TV series followed in 1968.

AAN: Charles Lang

The Ghost and the Guest
US 1943 59m bw

A honeymooning couple find no peace in an eerie country house with hidden ghosts and gangsters. Predictable, mildly amusing second feature comedy-thriller. James Dunn, Florence Rice, Mabel Todd, Sam McDaniel, Robert Dudley. Written by Morey Amsterdam from story by Milt Gross; directed by William Nigh; for Arthur Alexander / PRC.

The Ghost Breakers***
US 1940 85m bw
Paramount (Arthur Hornblow Jnr)

A girl inherits a West Indian castle and finds herself up to her neck in ghosts, zombies and buried treasure.
Archetypal comedy horror, very well done; a follow-up to the success of *The Cat and the Canary*, and just about as entertaining.

w Paul Dickey, Walter de Leon, play Paul Dickey, *Charles W. Goddard d George Marshall ph Charles Lang m Ernst Toch ad Hans Dreier*

Bob Hope, Paulette Goddard, Paul Lukas, *Willie Best*, Richard Carlson, *Lloyd Corrigan*, Anthony Quinn, Noble Johnson, Pedro de Cordova

'Bob Hope can joke, apparently, even with a risen corpse.'—*Monthly Film Bulletin*

'Paramount has found the fabled formula for making audiences shriek with laughter and fright at one and the same time.'—*New York Times*

† Previously filmed in 1914 with H. B. Warner; in 1922 with Wallace Reid; and remade in 1953 as *Scared Stiff*.

Ghost Catchers
US 1944 68m bw

A southern colonel and his beautiful daughters have spooks in their mansion—or bats in the belfry. Lower-case farce made when the stars' contract was being allowed to run out. Ole Olsen, Chic Johnson, Gloria Jean, Leo Carrillo, Martha O'Driscoll, Andy Devine, Lon Chaney Jnr, Walter Catlett, Henry Armetta. Written by Edmund L. Hartmann, from a story by Milt Gross and Edward Cline; directed by Edward Cline; for Universal.

The Ghost Comes Home
US 1940 79m bw

The return of a long-lost father causes embarrassment to his family. Hoary hide-in-the-closet farce with all concerned straining at the leash. Frank Morgan, Billie Burke, Ann Rutherford, John Shelton, Reginald Owen, Donald Meek, Nat Pendleton. Written by Richard Maibaum and Harry Ruskin; directed by William Thiele; for MGM.

The Ghost Goes West***
GB 1935 85m bw
London Films (Alexander Korda)

When a millionaire buys a Scottish castle and transports it stone by stone to America, the castle ghost goes too.

THE GETTING OF WISDOM. Susannah Fowle in a class of her own.

Amusing whimsy which is always pleasant but never quite realizes its full potential; fondly remembered for its star performance.

w Robert E. Sherwood, Geoffrey Kerr, *story* Eric Keown *d René Clair ph* Harold Rosson *m* Mischa Spoliansky

Robert Donat, Jean Parker, Eugene Pallette, Elsa Lanchester, Ralph Bunker, Patricia Hilliard, Morton Selten

'Fine business likely in the keys, but not for the tanks.'—*Variety*

'Although the film is not cast in the fluid, rapidly paced style of Clair's typical work, it has a sly wit and an adroitness of manner that make it delightful.'—*André Sennwald, New York Times*

'It is typical of the British film industry that M. René Clair should be brought to this country to direct a Scottish film full of what must to him be rather incomprehensible jokes about whisky and bagpipes, humorous fantasy without any social significance, realistic observation, or genuine satire.'—*Graham Greene*

The Ghost in the Invisible Bikini
US 1966 82m Pathecolor

A motor cycle gang gets mixed up with a rejuvenated corpse in a haunted mansion.

Mindless beach party stuff suffering under one of Hollywood's most inane titles. Boris Karloff, Basil Rathbone, Patsy Kelly, Tommy Kirk, Deborah Walley, Aron Kincaid, Quinn O'Hara, Jesse White. Written by Louis M. Heyward and Elwood Ullman; directed by Don Weis; for American International.

'You can't keep a good monster down!'

The Ghost of Frankenstein
US 1942 67m bw
Universal (George Waggner)

Frankenstein's second son implants evil shepherd Igor's brain into the monster.

The rot set in with this flatly-handled potboiler, which had none of the literary mood or cinematic interest of *Bride* or *Son* which preceded it, and suffered from a particularly idiotic script.

w W. Scott Darling, *story* Eric Taylor *d* Erle C. Kenton *ph* Milton Krasner, Woody Bredell *m* Charles Previn *md* Hans J. Salter

Cedric Hardwicke, Lon Chaney Jnr (as the monster), Bela Lugosi, Lionel Atwill, Evelyn Ankers, Ralph Bellamy

† See *Frankenstein* for other episodes in series

The Ghost of St Michael's**
GB 1941 82m bw
Ealing (Basil Dearden)

A school is evacuated to the Isle of Skye, and the local ghost turns out to be an enemy agent. The star's schoolmaster character is here at its seedy best, and he is well supported in a comedy-thriller plot.

w Angus Macphail, John Dighton d Marcel Varnel ph Derek Williams

Will Hay, Claude Hulbert, Felix Aylmer, Raymond Huntley, Elliot Mason, Charles Hawtrey, John Laurie, Hay Petrie, Roddy Hughes, Manning Whiley

Ghost of Zorro*
US 1949 bw serial: 12 eps

A survey engineer out west dons a mask in order to crusade against an outlaw empire. Well-mounted serial typical of the genre's later days. Clayton Moore, Pamela Blake, Roy Barcroft, George J. Lewis, Gene Roth. Directed by Fred C. Brannon; for Republic.

The Ghost Ship
US 1943 69m bw
RKO (Val Lewton)

The captain of a merchant ship is driven mad by isolation.

Long unavailable because of legal problems, this very minor Val Lewton thriller inevitably disappoints because it has no supernatural elements and must compare unfavourably with both *The Caine Mutiny* and *The Sea Wolf*, which plotwise it closely resembles.

w Donald Henderson Clarke *d* Mark Robson *ph* Nicholas Musuraca *m* Roy Webb

Richard Dix, Russell Wade, Edith Barrett, Ben Bard, Edmund Glover, Skelton Knaggs

The Ghost Ship
GB 1952 74m bw

A motor yacht proves to be haunted by the previous owner's murdered wife. Mildly unusual second feature. Dermot Walsh, Hazel Court, Hugh Burden, John Robinson. Written and directed by Vernon Sewell; for Anglo Amalgamated.

'She'll never rest till her tale is told!'

Ghost Story*
GB 1974 89m Fujicolor
Stephen Weeks

Former college acquaintances spend a weekend at a country house, and one of them is drawn into tragic events of forty years before.

Overlong chiller, ingeniously shot in India but very variably acted; aims for the M. R. James style and sometimes achieves it, but badly needs cutting.

w Rosemary Sutcliff, Stephen Weeks *d* Stephen Weeks *ph* Peter Hurst *m* Ron Geesin

Murray Melvin, Larry Dann, Vivian Mackerall, Marianne Faithfull, Anthony Bate, Leigh Lawson, Barbara Shelley

Ghost Story
US 1981 110m Technicolor
Universal (Ronald G. Smith)

Four old men tell each other ghost stories, but are haunted by a guilty secret of their own. Bizarre vehicle for four welcome old actors, ruined by the director's insistence on frequent shock cuts to the rotting spectre. A subtler treatment akin to that of *The Uninvited* might have produced a little masterpiece.

w Lawrence D. Cohen, *novel* Peter Straub *d* John Irvin *ph* Jack Cardiff *m* Philippe Sarde

Fred Astaire, Melvyn Douglas, John Houseman, Douglas Fairbanks Jnr, Craig Wasson, Patricia Neal, Alice Krige, Jacqueline Brookes

The Ghost That Never Returns*
USSR 1929 80m approx (24 fps) bw silent
Sovkino
original title: *Prividenie, Kotoroe ne Vozvrashchaetsya*

After ten years' imprisonment for leading a strike, a South American worker is given a day's leave which may result in his death. Unsatisfactory communist propaganda of its time, probably rescued from obscurity by its title. A few strikingly visual moments stand out, but the narrative is needlessly obscure.

w Valentin Turkin, *story* Henri Barbusse *d* Abram Room *ph* Dmitri Feldman

B. Ferdinandov, Olga Zhizneva, Maxime Straukh

The Ghost That Walks Alone
US 1943 63m bw

Honeymooners find a dead radio producer in their suite. Ho-hum second feature mystery. Arthur Lake, Janis Carter, Frank Sully, Lynne Roberts. Written by Doris Shattuck and Clarence Upson Young; directed by Lew Landers; for Columbia.

Ghost Town
US 1956 72m bw

Stagecoach passengers are forced to spend the night in a ghost town beset by Indians. Thin western second with a few effectively restrained moments. Kent Taylor, John Smith, Marian Carr, John Doucette. Written by Jameson Brewer; directed by Allen Miner; for Bel Air / UA.

The Ghost Train**
GB 1931 72m bw
Gainsborough (Michael Balcon)

Passengers stranded at a haunted station in Cornwall include a detective posing as a silly ass in order to trap smugglers.
Excellent early sound version of a comedy-thriller play which has not only been among the most commercially successful ever written but also provided the basic plot for many another comedy: *Oh Mr Porter*, *The Ghost of St Michael's*, *Back Room Boy*, *Hold That Ghost*, etc. Previously filmed as a silent in 1927, with Guy Newall.

w Angus Macphail, Lajos Biro, play Arnold Ridley d Walter Forde ph Leslie Rowson

Jack Hulbert, Cicely Courtneidge, Donald Calthrop, Ann Todd, Cyril Raymond, Angela Baddeley, Allan Jeayes

The Ghost Train*
GB 1941 85m bw
Gainsborough (Edward Black)

Adequate remake with the lead split into two characters, which doesn't work quite so well.

w Marriott Edgar, Val Guest, J. O. C. Orton *d* Walter Forde *ph* Jack Cox

Arthur Askey, Richard Murdoch, Kathleen Harrison, Morland Graham, Linden Travers, Peter Murray Hill, *Herbert Lomas*

The Ghost Walks
US 1934 70m bw

A hired 'ghost' engaged for a party is scared off by a real one. Cheeseparing spooky house comedy-thriller. John Miljan, June Collyer, Richard Carle. Written by Edward T. Lowe; directed by Frank Strayer; for Chesterfield.
'Above the indie norm all round.'—*Variety*

Ghostbusters*
US 1984 105m Metrocolor Panavision
Columbia / Delphi (Ivan Reitman)

Unemployed academic parapsychologists set themselves up as ghostbusters and destroy several monstrous apparitions on the streets of New York.
Crude farce with expensive special effects. It took more money—millions more—than *Indiana Jones and the Temple of Doom*, which must say something about the age we live in.

w Dan Aykroyd, Harold Ramis *d* Ivan Reitman *ph* Laszlo Kovacs, Herb Wagreitch *m* Elmer Bernstein *pd* John De Cuir *ed* Sheldon Kahn, David Blewitt

Bill Murray, Dan Aykroyd, Harold Ramis, Sigourney Weaver, Rick Moranis, Annie Potts, William Atherton
AAN: title song (*m,ly* Ray Parker)

The Ghosts of Berkeley Square*
GB 1947 89m bw
British National (Louis H. Jackson)

Two 18th-century ghosts are doomed to haunt a London house until royalty visits.
Thin, skittish whimsy with pleasant moments.

w James Seymour, *novel* No Nightingales by S. J. Simon, Caryl Brahms *d* Vernon Sewell *ph* Ernest Palmer

Robert Morley, Claude Hulbert, Felix Aylmer, Yvonne Arnaud, Abraham Sofaer, Ernest Thesiger, Marie Lohr, Martita Hunt, A. E. Matthews, John Longden, Ronald Frankau, Wilfrid Hyde White, Esmé Percy, Mary Jerrold, Wally Patch, Martin Miller

The Ghoul**
GB 1933 79m bw
Gaumont (Michael Balcon)

An Egyptologist returns from the tomb to uncover stolen jewels and a murderer. Fascinating minor horror piece reminiscent of *The Old Dark House*, with many effective moments and a ripe cast.

w Frank King, Leonard Hines, L. DuGarde Peach, Roland Pertwee, John Hastings Turner, Rupert Downing, *novel* Frank King *d T. Hayes Hunter ph* Gunther Krampf *make-up* Heinrich Heitfeld

Boris Karloff, Cedric Hardwicke, Ralph Richardson, Kathleen Harrison, Ernest Thesiger, Dorothy Hyson, Anthony Bushell, D. A. Clarke-Smith
'Lacks general US appeal because of bad plot mechanics, mostly bad acting, and colourless camerawork.'—*Variety*
† Remade after a fashion as *What A Carve Up* (1962).

The Ghoul
GB 1975 87m Eastmancolor
Tyburn (Kevin Francis)

In the twenties, a group of stranded travellers is reduced in number when they take shelter in the house of a former clergyman.
The build-up is too slow, the revelation too nasty, and the whole thing is a shameless rip-off of the structure of *Psycho*.

w John Elder *d* Freddie Francis *ph* John Wilcox *m* Harry Robinson

Peter Cushing, Alexandra Bastedo, John Hurt, Gwen Watford, Veronica Carlson, Don Henderson
'Peter Cushing brings out his violin for a soothing spot of the classics, the local copper mutters veiled warnings before trundling off on his bike, and thick fog swirls round the exterior sets at the drop of a canister.'—*Geoff Brown*

Giant**
US 1956 197m Warnercolor
Warner (George Stevens, Henry Ginsburg)

The life of a Texas cattle rancher through two generations.
Sprawling, overlong family saga with unconvincing acting but good visual style.

w Fred Guiol, Ivan Moffat, *novel* Edna Ferber *d George Stevens ph* William C. Mellor, Edwin DuPar *m Dmitri Tiomkin*

Rock Hudson, Elizabeth Taylor, James Dean, Mercedes McCambridge, Carroll Baker, Chill Wills, Jane Withers, Dennis Hooper, Sal Mineo, Rod Taylor, Judith Evelyn, Earl Holliman, Alexander Scourby, Paul Fix

AA: George Stevens
AAN: best picture; script; Dmitri Tiomkin; Rock Hudson; James Dean; Mercedes McCambridge

The Giant Behemoth
GB 1959 70m bw

A radioactive palaeosaurus menaces London. Underfed monster, undercast melodramatics. Gene Evans, André Morell, Leigh Madison, John Turner, Jack MacGowran. Written by Eugene Lourie; directed by Eugene Lourie and Douglas Hickox; for Artistes Alliance / Stratford. (Aka: *Behemoth the Sea Monster*.)

The Giant Claw
US 1957 71m bw

A monstrous bird threatens New York. Incompetent horror item: the bird is mostly talons and sound track. Jeff Morrow, Mara Corday, Morris Ankrum. Written by Samuel Newman and Paul Gargelin; directed by Fred F. Sears; for Sam Katzman / Clover.

The Giant Spider Invasion
US 1975 76m Eastmancolor

Nuclear fall-out causes giant spiders to breed and go on the rampage. Thinly scripted reprise of one of those small-town horror thrillers of the fifties. Barbara Hale, Steve Brodie, Leslie Parrish, Alan Hale. Written by Richard L. Huff and Robert Easton; directed by Bill Rebane; for Transcentury Pictures.

Gideon's Day*
GB 1958 91m Technicolor
Columbia / John Ford (Michael Killanin)
US title: *Gideon of Scotland Yard*

A Scotland Yard Inspector has an eventful but frustrating day.
Pleasant, ordinary little TV style police yarn showing no evidence of its director's particular talents.

w T. E. B. Clarke, *novel* John Creasey *d* John Ford *ph* Frederick A. Young *m* Douglas Gamley *ad* Ken Adam

Jack Hawkins, Dianne Foster, Anna Lee, Andrew Ray, Anna Massey, Frank Lawton, John Loder, Cyril Cusack

Gidget
US 1959 95m Eastmancolor Cinemascope
Columbia (Lewis J. Rachmil)

A 16-year-old girl falls for a surfer; her parents disapprove until he turns out to be the son of their best friend.
Commercial mixture of domestic comedy and beach athletics, for nice teenagers and their moms and pops.

w Gabrielle Upton, *novel* Frederick Kohner *d* Paul Wendkos *ph* Burnett Guffey *m* George Duning *md* Morris Stoloff

Sandra Dee, Cliff Robertson, James Darren, Arthur O'Connell
† Sequels include *Gidget Goes Hawaiian* (1961) with Deborah Walley; *Gidget Goes to Rome* (1962) with Cindy Carol; and two TV movies.

The Gift Horse*
GB 1952 100m bw
British Lion / Molton (George Pitcher)
US title: *Glory at Sea*

In 1940 an old US destroyer is given to Britain, and an officer reluctantly takes charge of it.
Conventional, popular seafaring war adventure.

w William Fairchild, Hugh Hastings, William Rose *d* Compton Bennett *ph* Harry Waxman *m* Clifton Parker

Trevor Howard, Richard Attenborough, Sonny Tufts, James Donald, Joan Rice, Bernard Lee, Dora Bryan, Hugh Williams, Robin Bailey

The Gift of Gab
US 1934 71m bw
Universal

A conceited radio announcer gets his comeuppance.
Odd little comedy drama notable only for its long list of stars making cameo appearances.

w Rian James, Lou Breslow *d* Karl Freund *m* Albert Von Tilzer, Con Conrad, Charles Tobias

Edmund Lowe, Gloria Stuart, Ruth Etting, Phil Baker, Alexander Woollcott, Ethel Waters, Victor Moore, Boris Karloff, Bela Lugosi, Paul Lukas, Chester Morris, Binnie Barnes, Douglass Montgomery, Wini Shaw

'A hodge-podge, an elongated short.'—*Variety*

The Gift of Love
US 1958 105m Eastmancolor Cinemascope
TCF (Charles Brackett)

A dying wife adopts an orphan girl so that her husband will not be lonely.
Incredibly cloying and miscast remake of *Sentimental Journey* (qv).

w Luther Davis *d* Jean Negulesco *ph* Milton Krasner *m* Cyril Mockridge

Lauren Bacall, Robert Stack, Evelyn Rudie, Lorne Greene

Gigi*
France 1948 109m bw
Codo Cinema (Claude Dolbert)

In Paris in the nineties, a young girl is trained by her aunt to be a cocotte, but when married off to a rake she reforms him.
Charming, overlong, non-musical version of a famous story, chiefly memorable for its local colour.

w Pierre Laroche, *novel* Colette *d Jacqueline Audry ph* Gérard Perrin *m* Marcel Landowski

Daniele Delorme, *Gaby Morlay, Yvonne de Bray*, Frank Villard, Jean Tissier, Madeleine Rousset

Gigi***
US 1958 119m Metrocolor Cinemascope
MGM (Arthur Freed)

Laundered and musicalized version; delightfully set, costumed and performed, but oddly lacking dance numbers.

w / ly Alan Jay Lerner m Frederick Loewe d Vincente Minnelli ph Joseph Ruttenberg md André Previn *pd / cost Cecil Beaton*

Leslie Caron, Louis Jourdan, Maurice Chevalier, Hermione Gingold, Isabel Jeans, Jacques Bergerac, Eva Gabor, John Abbott

'It has the sureness expected when a group of the most sophisticated talents are able to work together on material entirely suited to them.'—*Penelope Houston*

AA: best picture; Alan Jay Lerner; Vincente Minnelli; Joseph Ruttenberg; André Previn; Cecil Beaton; Adrienne Fazan (editing); Preston Ames and Keogh Gleason (art directors); title song (*m* Frederick Loewe, *ly* Alan Jay Lerner); Maurice Chevalier (special award)

Gigot
US 1962 104m De Luxe
TCF / Seven Arts (Kenneth Hyman)

The mute caretaker of a Montmartre boarding house looks after an ailing prostitute and her child.
From Paris, Hollywood, comes a grotesque piece of self-indulgence, the arch example of the clown who wanted to play Hamlet. Plotless, mawkish and wholly unfunny.

w John Patrick, Jackie Gleason *d* Gene Kelly *ph* Jean Bourgoin *m* Jackie Gleason *md* Michael Magne *ad* Auguste Capelier

Jackie Gleason, Katherine Kath, Gabrielle Dorziat, Jean Lefebvre, Jacques Marin

'Chaplinesque pretensions have proved fatal before to artists who will not accept their own limitations.'—*Gavin Lambert*

AAN: Michael Magne

Gilda***
US 1946 110m bw
Columbia (Virginia Van Upp)

A gambler in a South American city resumes a love-hate relationship with an old flame . . . but she is now married to his dangerous new boss.
Archetypal Hollywood *film noir*, wholly studio-bound and the better for it, with dialogue that would seem risible if it did not happen to be dealt with in this style and with these actors, who keep the mood balanced between suspense and absurdity.

w Marion Parsonnet, story E. A. Ellington *d Charles Vidor ph Rudolph Maté m* Hugo Friedhofer *md* Morris Stoloff, Marlin Skiles

Rita Hayworth, Glenn Ford, George Macready, Steve Geray, Joseph Calleia, Joe Sawyer, Gerald Mohr, Ludwig Donath

'There never was a woman like Gilda!'—*publicity*

'From a quietly promising opening the film settles into an intractable obscurity of narrative through which as in a fog three characters bite off at each other words of hate.'—*Richard Winnington*

'He fed her popcorn and kisses on a park bench!'

The Gilded Lily*
US 1935 85m bw
Paramount (Albert Lewis)

A poor stenographer who meets her reporter boy friend on a park bench is wooed by a British peer.
Good depression era romantic comedy with the heroine inevitably choosing poverty.

w Claude Binyon *d* Wesley Ruggles *ph* Victor Milner

Claudette Colbert, Fred MacMurray, Ray Milland, C. Aubrey Smith, Luis Alberni, Donald Meek

'Breezy romance . . . should carry box-office draught.'—*Variety*

Ginger and Fred***
Italy / France / West Germany 1985 colour 126m
REA / Revcom / Stella / RAI (Alberto Grimaldi)

An ageing pair of dancers is brought out of retirement to appear on a TV show.
Melancholy comedy with resonances, chiefly taking the side of age against youth, with 'Fred' as an image of Fellini himself.

w Federico Fellini, Tonino Guerra, Tullio Pinelli d Federico Fellini ph Tonino Delli Colli, Ennio Guarnieri m Nicola Piovani *ad* Dante Ferretti

Giulietta Masina, Marcello Mastroianni, Franco Fabrizi, Frederick Von Ledenberg

A Girl, a Guy and a Gob
US 1941 91m bw
RKO / Harold Lloyd
GB title: *The Navy Steps Out*

A secretary and her sailor boy friend teach her stuffy boss how to enjoy life.
Did producer Lloyd intend himself for the role played by O'Brien? If so, he would have needed a stronger script to prevent this Capraesque comedy from falling flat.

w Frank Ryan, Bert Granet *d* Richard Wallace *ph* Russell Metty *m* Roy Webb

Lucille Ball, Edmond O'Brien, George Murphy, George Cleveland, Henry Travers, Franklin Pangborn, Marguerite Churchill, Lloyd Corrigan

The Girl and the General
Italy / France 1967 113m Technicolor
MGM / Champion / Corcordia (Carlo Ponti)

During World War I, a captured Austrian general escapes with a girl partisan.
Turgid war epic veering from melodrama to comedy.

w Luigi Malerba, Pasquale Festa Campanile *d* Pasquale Festa Campanile *ph* Ennio Guarnieri *m* Ennio Morricone

Rod Steiger, Virna Lisi, Umberto Orsini

The Girl Can't Help It*
US 1956 97m Eastmancolor Cinemascope
TCF (Frank Tashlin)

A theatrical agent grooms a gangster's dumb girl friend for stardom.
Scatty, garish pop scene spoof with a plot borrowed from *Born Yesterday* and a lot of jokes about its new star's superstructure. Some scenes are funny, and it puts the first rock and roll stars in pickle for all time.

w Frank Tashlin, Herbert Baker, *story* Do Re Mi by Garson Kanin *d Frank Tashlin ph* Leon Shamroy *md* Lionel Newman

Jayne Mansfield, Tom Ewell, Edmond O'Brien, Henry Jones, John Emery; and Julie London, Ray Anthony, Fats Domino, Little Richard, the Platters

Girl Crazy
US 1932 75m bw

Romance at a desert college. Early talkie version of the musical comedy (see below), here redesigned as a weak vehicle for two comedy stars. Bert Wheeler, Robert Woolsey, Eddie Quillan, Dorothy Lee, Mitzi Green, Arline Judge. Written by Tim Whelan, Herman J. Mankiewicz; directed by William A. Seiter; for RKO. 'A weak sister . . . after a while it all becomes too silly.'—*Variety*

Girl Crazy*
US 1943 99m bw
MGM (Arthur Freed)
aka: *When the Girls Meet the Boys*

Romance at a desert college.
Predictable star musical with good tunes.

w Fred F. Finkelhoffe, *play* Guy Bolton, Jack McGowan *d* Norman Taurog *ph* William Daniels, Robert Planck *md* Georgie Stoll *songs George and Ira Gershwin*

Judy Garland, Mickey Rooney, Guy Kibbee, Gil Stratton, Robert E. Strickland, Rags Ragland, June Allyson, Nancy Walker, Tommy Dorsey and his band

† Remade 1965 as *When the Boys Meet the Girls.*

The Girl Downstairs
US 1938 77m bw

A rich bachelor in Europe chooses the maid instead of the mistress. Feeble rewrite of *Cinderella.* Franchot Tone, Franciska Gaal, Walter Connolly, Rita Johnson, Reginald Owen, Reginald Gardiner, Franklin Pangborn, Robert Coote. Written by Harold Goldman, Felix Jackson and Karl Noti; directed by Norman Taurog; for MGM.

'Keen direction and fine performances highlight moderate programmer.'—*Variety*

The Girl Friend
US 1935 67m bw

An actor and two songwriters become rural con men. Thin comedy with music. Ann Sothern, Jack Haley, Roger Pryor, Thurston Hall, Victor Kilian. Written by Gertrude Purcell, Benny Rubin; directed by Eddie Buzzell; for Columbia. 'Enough hoke to make it a welcome laugh picture for lesser towns.'—*Variety*

The Girl from Avenue A
US 1940 73m bw

A slum brat is picked up by an author, who takes her home to use for reference. *Pygmalion* did this far better, but the star was adolescent and the studio didn't know what else to do with her. Jane Withers, Kent Taylor, Katharine Aldridge, Elyse Knox, Laura Hope Crews, Jessie Ralph, Harry Shannon, Ann Shoemaker. Written by Frances Hyland, from Maude Fulton's play *The Brat*; directed by Otto Brower; for Sol M. Wurtzel / TCF.

The Girl from Jones Beach
US 1949 78m bw

A commercial artist meets a schoolteacher who is the real-life counterpart of his 'perfect girl'. Predictable comedy with only the dimmest professional sparkle. Ronald Reagan, Virginia Mayo, Eddie Bracken, Dona Drake, Henry Travers, Florence Bates. Written by I. A. L. Diamond; directed by Peter Godfrey; for Warner.

The Girl from Manhattan
US 1948 81m bw
UA / Benedict Bogeaus

A model returns home to help her uncle with his mortgaged boarding house.
Mouldy comedy-drama full of kind thoughts, charming failures and worldly priests. Interesting for cast.

w Howard Estabrook *d* Alfred E. Green *ph* Ernest Laszlo *md* David Chudnow *m* Heinz Roemheld

Dorothy Lamour, Charles Laughton, George Montgomery, Ernest Truex, Hugh Herbert, Constance Collier, Sara Allgood, Frank Orth, Howard Freeman, Adeline de Walt Reynolds, George Chandler, Maurice Cass

The Girl from Maxim's
GB 1933 79m bw

Circumstances force a doctor to pass off a singer as his wife. Tolerable period farce from a Feydeau original. Leslie Henson, Francis Day, George Grossmith, Lady Tree, Stanley Holloway. Written by Arthur Wimperis and Harry Graham; directed by Alexander Korda; for London Films.

The Girl from Mexico see Mexican Spitfire

The Girl from Missouri*
US 1934 75m bw
MGM (Bernard H. Hyman)
aka: *100% Pure*
original titles: *Born to be Kissed, Eadie was a Lady*

A chorus girl determines to remain virtuous until the right millionaire comes along.
Smart, amusing comedy very typical of its period.

w Anita Loos, John Emerson d Jack Conway *ph* Ray June *m* William Axt

Jean Harlow, Franchot Tone, Lionel Barrymore, Lewis Stone, Patsy Kelly, Alan Mowbray, Clara Blandick, Henry Kolker

'It's going to be in the money . . . one that plenty of purity crusaders will see and like.'—*Variety*

'Noisily defiant, rip-roaring and raucous in spots . . . fast and furious adult fare.'—*Photoplay*

The Girl from Petrovka
US 1974 103m Technicolor
Universal / Richard Zanuck, David Brown

An American correspondent in Moscow falls for a Russian girl.
Lugubrious and lethargic romantic comedy-drama.

w Allan Scott, Chris Bryant *d* Robert Ellis Miller *m* Henry Mancini

Goldie Hawn, Hal Holbrook. Anthony Hopkins, Grégoire Aslan, Anton Dolin

The Girl from Scotland Yard
US 1937 61m bw

A female agent tracks down the cause of mysterious explosions. Lacklustre second feature. Karen Morley, Robert Baldwin, Katherine Alexander, Eduardo Ciannelli. Written by Doris Anderson, Dore Schary; directed by Robert Vignola; for Paramount. 'Weak thriller . . . only for the back seat in duals.'—*Variety*

The Girl from Tenth Avenue
US 1935 69m bw
Warner (Robert Lord)
GB title: *Men on Her Mind*

A jilted attorney drowns his sorrows and marries on the rebound.
Watchable 'woman's picture'.

w Charles Kenyon, *play* Hubert Henry Davies *d* Alfred E. Green *ph* James Van Trees

Bette Davis, Ian Hunter, Colin Clive, Alison Skipworth, Katherine Alexander, John Eldredge, Philip Reed

'Bette Davis' first starring venture . . . she should pull the picture through to good returns.'—*Variety*

The Girl Habit
US 1931 77m bw

A mild Lothario tries to get arrested as protection from the gangster husband who has threatened him. Easy-going farce which established Ruggles in Hollywood. Charles Ruggles, Tamara Geva, Margaret Dumont, Allen Jenkins, Donald Meek, Sue Conroy. Written by Owen Davis and Gertrude Purcell from a play by A. E. Thomas and Clayton Hamilton; directed by Eddie Cline; for Paramount. 'Hardly a dynamic b.o. prospect, but nice entertainment.'—*Variety*

Girl Happy
US 1965 96m Metrocolor Panavision
MGM / Euterpe (Joe Pasternak)

A pop singer in Florida is forced to chaperone a group of college girls including a gangster's daughter.
Standard star vehicle, quite professionally made and totally forgettable.

w Harvey Bullock, R. S. Allen *d* Boris Sagal *ph* Philip Lathrop *m* George Stoll

Elvis Presley, Harold J. Stone, Shelley Fabares, Gary Crosby, Nita Talbot

The Girl He Left Behind
US 1956 103m bw
Warner (Frank P. Rosenberg)

The army makes a man of a spoiled youth. Platitudinous recruiting comedy for dim American teenagers.

w Guy Trosper, *book* Marion Hargrove *d* David Butler *ph* Ted McCord *m* Roy Webb

Tab Hunter, Natalie Wood, Jessie Royce Landis, Jim Backus, Henry Jones, Murray Hamilton, Alan King, James Garner, David Janssen

The Girl Hunters
GB 1963 100m bw Panavision
Present Day (Robert Fellows)

Private eye Mike Hammer solves a few murders plus the disappearance of his own ex-secretary.
Comic strip thuggery with the author playing his own slouchy hero; the general incompetence gives this cheap production an air of Kafkaesque menace.

w Mickey Spillane, Roy Rowland, Robert Fellows *d* Roy Rowland *ph* Ken Talbot *m* Phil Green

Mickey Spillane, Shirley Eaton, Lloyd Nolan

A Girl in a Million
GB 1946 90m bw

Having divorced a nagging wife, a chemist marries a dumb girl, but when he cures her . . . Thin comedy which must have seemed funnier on the page than it does on the screen. Joan Greenwood, Hugh Williams, Basil Radford, Naunton Wayne, Wylie Watson, Yvonne Owen. Written by Muriel and Sydney Box; directed by Francis Searle; for Boca / British Lion.

The Girl in Black
Greece 1955 93m bw
Hermes
original title: *To Koritsi me ta Mavra*

A writer holidaying on a remote fishing island causes tension and tragedy when he falls for a local maiden.
Watchable mood piece benefiting from its star female performance.

wd Michael Cacoyannis *ph* Walter Lassally *m* Argyris Kounadis, Manos Hadji Bredkis

Elle Lambetti, George Foundas, Dimitri Horna

The Girl in Black Stockings
US 1957 71m bw

Suspects abound when a young woman is killed in a Utah hotel. Tolerable murder mystery. Anne Bancroft, Lex Barker, Mamie Van Doren, John Dehner, Ron Randell, Marie Windsor. Written by Richard Landau, from the story 'Wanton Murder' by Peter Godfrey; directed by Howard W. Koch; for Bel Air / UA.

A Girl in Every Port*
US 1928 62m (24 fps) bw silent
Fox

Two sailors brawl over women.
Adventure comedy with themes typical of its director.

w Seton Miller, James K. McGuinness *d* Howard Hawks *ph* R. J. Bergquist, L. W. O'Connel *m* William Perry

Victor McLaglen, Natalie Joyce, Dorothy Matthews, Maria Casajuana, Louise Brooks, Francis McDonald

'Brief and essentially anecdotal, it now looks more than anything else like a preliminary sketch for concerns which Hawks would later elaborate.'—*Tim Pulleine, MFB*

A Girl in Every Port
US 1951 87m bw
RKO (Irwin Allen, Irving Cummings Jnr)

Two accident-prone sailors have trouble with a racehorse.
Dismally mechanical farce.

wd Chester Erskine *ph* Nicholas Musuraca *m* Roy Webb

Groucho Marx, William Bendix, Marie Wilson, Don Defore, Gene Lockhart

The Girl in the Headlines*
GB 1963 93m bw
Bryanston / Viewfinder (John Davis)
US title: *The Model Murder Case*

Scotland Yard investigates the murder of a model.
Standard police mystery, well enough done.

w Vivienne Knight, Patrick Campbell, *novel* The Nose on My Face by Laurence Payne *d* Michael Truman *ph* Stan Pavey *m* John Addison

Ian Hendry, Ronald Fraser, Margaret Johnston, Natasha Parry

The Girl in the Kremlin
US 1957 81m bw

An OSS agent infiltrates the Iron Curtain to assist a plot to overthrow Stalin. Boring cold war nonsense with the leading lady for some reason playing three parts. Lex Barker, Zsa Zsa Gabor, Jeffrey Stone, Maurice Manson, William Schallert. Written by Gene L. Coon and Robert Hill; directed by Russell Birdwell; for Universal.

The Girl in the News*
GB 1940 78m bw
TCF (Edward Black)

A nurse is framed for the death of her employer.
Easy-going British mystery of the Agatha Christie school.

w Sidney Gilliat, *novel* Roy Vickers *d* Carol Reed *ph* Otto Kanturek *md* Louis Levy

Margaret Lockwood, Barry K. Barnes, Emlyn Williams, Margaretta Scott, Roger Livesey, Basil Radford, Wyndham Goldie, Irene Handl, Mervyn Johns, Kathleen Harrison, Richard Bird, Michael Hordern, Roland Culver, Edward Rigby

The Girl in the Red Velvet Swing*
US 1955 109m De Luxe Cinemascope
TCF (Charles Brackett)

In New York at the turn of the century, a rich unstable man shoots his mistress's former lover.
Plushy but not very interesting recounting of a celebrated murder case in which the victim was a famous architect, Stanford White.

w Walter Reisch, Charles Brackett *d* Richard Fleischer *ph* Milton Krasner *m* Leigh Harline *ad* Lyle R. Wheeler, Maurice Ransford

Ray Milland, Farley Granger, Joan Collins, Glenda Farrell, Luther Adler, Cornelia Otis Skinner, Philip Reed, John Hoyt

'A needlessly long-winded piece of lush sensationalism.'—*Penelope Houston*

The Girl in the Taxi
GB 1937 72m bw

The head of the purity league is drawn into an adulterous flirtation. Moderately piquant comedy shot in English and French versions. Frances Day, Henri Garat, Lawrence Grossmith, Jean Gillie, Mackenzie Ward, Helen Haye, Albert Whelan. Written by Austin Melford, Val Valentine and Fritz Gottfurcht, from the play by George Okonowski; directed by André Berthomieu; for British Unity.

The Girl in White*
US 1952 93m bw
MGM (Armand Deutsch)
GB title: *So Bright the Flame*

The story of Dr Emily Dunning, the first woman to become an intern in one of New York's hospitals.
Bland biopic, modestly produced, with predictable plot crises.

w Irmgard Von Cube, Allen Vincent, *book* Bowery to Bellevue by Emily Dunning Barringer *d* John Sturges *ph* Paul C. Vogel *m* David Raksin

June Allyson, Arthur Kennedy, Gary Merrill, Mildred Dunnock, Jesse White, Marilyn Erskine

The Girl Most Likely
US 1958 98m Technicolor RKOscope
RKO (Stanley Rubin)

A girl finds herself engaged to three men at the same time, and envisions marriage with each.
Dully cast, quite brightly handled remake of *Tom, Dick and Harry*, with modest songs and dances.

w Devery Freeman *d* Mitchell Leisen *ph* Robert Planck *m* Nelson Riddle *songs* Ralph Blane, Hugh Martin

Jane Powell, Cliff Robertson, Keith Andes, Tommy Noonan, Kaye Ballard, Una Merkel
† For Mitchell Leisen and RKO studios, their last film.

A Girl Must Live**
GB 1939 92m bw
Gainsborough (Edward Black)

A runaway schoolgirl falls among chorus girls planning to marry into the nobility.
Light, peppery comedy with a strong cast.

w Frank Launder, Michael Pertwee, *novel* Emery Bonnet *d Carol Reed* *ph* Jack Cox *md* Louis Levy

Margaret Lockwood, Renée Houston, Lilli Palmer, George Robey, Hugh Sinclair, Naunton Wayne, Moore Marriott, Mary Clare, David Burns, Kathleen Harrison, Martita Hunt, Helen Haye

'An unabashed display of undressed femininity, double-meaning dialogue alternating between piquancy and vulgarity, and hearty knockabout involving scantily attired young viragos who fight furiously in a whirligig of legs and lingerie.'—*Kine Weekly*

'He was half-oriental . . . but he used the women of two continents without shame or guilt!'

A Girl Named Tamiko
US 1962 119m Technicolor Panavision
Paramount / Hal B. Wallis (Paul Nathan)

A Eurasian photographer uses his women in an attempt to get American nationality.
Humdrum romantic melodrama with dim performances.

w Edward Anhalt, *novel* Ronald Kirkbride *d* John Sturges *ph* Charles Lang Jnr *m* Elmer Bernstein

Laurence Harvey, France Nuyen, Martha Hyer, Michael Wilding, Miyoshi Umeki

The Girl Next Door
US 1953 92m Technicolor
TCF (Robert Bassler)

A Broadway musical star falls for her suburban neighbour.
Mild musical linked by UPA cartoon sequences.

w Isobel Lennart *d* Richard Sale *ph* Leon Shamroy *md* Lionel Newman *songs* Josef Myrow, Mack Gordon *ch* Richard Barstow

Dan Dailey, June Haver, Natalie Schaefer, Dennis Day, Cara Williams

The Girl of the Golden West
US 1930 81m bw
Warner (Robert North)

A gun-toting, saloon-owning girl marries an outlaw and saves him from the sheriff.
Straight version of a dusty old Broadway success, later musicalized under the same title (see below).

w Waldemar Young, *play* David Belasco *d* John Francis Dillon *ph* Sol Polito

Ann Harding, James Rennie, Harry Bannister, Ben Hendricks Jnr, J. Farrell MacDonald
† A silent version was made in 1923 by First National, with Sylvia Breamer and J. Warren Kerrigan, directed by Edwin Carewe.

The Girl of the Golden West
US 1938 121m bw (sepia release)
MGM (William Anthony McGuire)

In backwoods Canada, a girl loves a bandit who is being chased by the Mounties.
Solemn musical melodrama in which the stars seem miscast and a bit of pep is badly needed. Taken from a hoary David Belasco spectacular, and looks it.

w Isobel Dawn, Boyce DeGaw *d* Robert Z. Leonard *ph* Oliver Marsh *songs* Sigmund Romberg, Gus Kahn

Jeanette MacDonald, Nelson Eddy, Walter Pidgeon, Leo Carrillo, Buddy Ebsen, Olin Howland

'This musical mustanger finds the stars not only out of their element, but hemmed in by a two-hour mélange of the great outdoors, Mexican bandits, early Spanish-Californian atmosphere and musical boredom . . . a spotty entry.'—*Variety*

Girl of the Limberlost
US 1934 86m bw

A girl of the swamps becomes a high school graduate. Tearful rehash of an old sentimental warhorse. Louise Dresser, Ralph Morgan, Marian Marsh, Henry B. Walthall, Helen Jerome Eddy, Betty Blythe. Written by Adele Comandini from the novel by Gene Stratton Porter; directed by Christy Cabanne; for Monogram. 'Wholesome to a fault. A family film good enough for anybody to see, but the fault lies in that not everybody will want to see it.'—*Variety*

Girl of the Night
US 1960 93m bw

A streetwalker confesses all to her psychiatrist. Stalwart exploitation picture of its time. Anne Francis, Lloyd Nolan, Kay Medford, John Kerr, Arthur Storch, James Broderick. Written by Ted Berkman, Raphael Blau, from the book The Call Girl by Dr Harold Greenwald; directed by Joseph Cates; for Vanguard/Warners.

Girl on a Motorcycle
GB / France 1968 91m Technicolor
Mid Atlantic / Ares (William Sassoon)
US title: *Naked under Leather;* French title: *La Motocyclette*

A married woman leaves her husband, zooms off on her motorcycle to see her lover, and crashes to her death while indulging in sexual reverie.
An incredibly plotless and ill-conceived piece of sub-porn claptrap, existing only as a long series of colour supplement photographs.

w Ronald Duncan, *novel* La Motocyclette by André Pieyre de Mandiargues *d* Jack Cardiff *ph* Jack Cardiff, René Guissart *m* Les Reed

Marianne Faithfull, Alain Delon, Roger Mutton

The Girl on the Boat
GB 1962 91m bw
UA / Knightsbridge (John Bryan)

On a transatlantic liner in the twenties, two Englishmen fall in love.
Curious attempt to do something different with a star comic, who is clearly outclassed by the lighter talents at hand.

w Reuben Ship, *story* P. G. Wodehouse *d* Henry Kaplan *ph* Denys Coop *m* Kenneth V. Jones

Norman Wisdom, *Richard Briers*, Millicent Martin, Athene Seyler, Sheila Hancock, Philip Locke

The Girl on the Front Page
US 1936 74m bw

The lady owner of a newspaper gets a job on it under an assumed name, and helps the editor solve a mystery. Fairly pleasing programmer. Edmund Lowe, Gloria Stuart, Spring Byington, Reginald Owen. Written by Austin Parker, Albert R. Perkins and Alice Duer Miller; directed by Harry Beaumont; for Universal.

The Girl Rosemarie
West Germany 1958 100m bw
Roxy
original title: *Das Mädchen Rosemarie*

Corrupt industrialists and investigators alike are relieved when a girl who had been the mistress of all of them is murdered .
Slick melodrama based on an actual case; almost a documentary exposé.

w Erich Kuby, Rolf Thiele, Joe Herbst, Rolf Urich *d* Rolf Thiele *ph* Klaus von Rautenfeld *m* Norbert Schultze

Nadja Tiller, Peter Van Eyck, Carl Raddatz, Gert Frobe, Mario Adorf, Horst Frank

The Girl Rush
US 1955 85m Technicolor Vistavision
Paramount (Frederick Brisson, Robert Alton)

A gambler's daughter inherits a half share in a Las Vegas hotel.
Dull charmless semi-musical vehicle for a star who can't quite carry it.

w Phoebe and Henry Ephron *d* Robert Pirosh *ph* William Daniels *m* Herbert Spencer, Earle Hagen *ch* Robert Alton

Rosalind Russell, Eddie Albert, Fernando Lamas, James Gleason, Gloria de Haven, *Marion Lorne*

Girl Stroke Boy
GB 1971 88m Eastmancolor
Hemdale / Virgin (Ned Sherrin, Terry Glinwood)

A well-to-do couple try to find out whether their son's house guest is male or female.
Initially funny but appallingly extended one-joke comedy which many will find merely embarrassing.

w Caryl Brahms, Ned Sherrin, *play* Girlfriend by David Percival *d* Bob Kellett *ph* Ian Wilson *m* John Scott

Joan Greenwood, Michael Hordern, Clive Francis, Patricia Routledge, Peter Bull, Rudolph Walker, Elizabeth Welch

Girl Trouble
US 1942 82m bw

A South American in New York rents the apartment of a socialite who pretends to be his maid. Thin romantic comedy with half-hearted screwball touches. Don Ameche, Joan Bennett, Billie Burke, Frank Craven, Alan Dinehart. Written by Ladislas Fodor and Robert Riley Crutcher; directed by Harold Schuster; for Robert Bassler / TCF.

The Girl Who Couldn't Quite
GB 1950 85m bw

Smile, that is. A tramp cures a teenager's amnesia and she fails to recognize him afterwards. Sentimental bosh from a mildly popular play of its time. Bill Owen, Iris Hoey, Elizabeth Henson, Betty Stockfield. Written by Norman Lee and Marjorie Deans, from the play by Leo Marks; directed by Norman Lee; for Argyle.

The Girl Who Couldn't Say No
Italy 1968 104m Techniscope

A medical assistant has an on-off relationship with an eccentric girl. Downright peculiar romantic comedy with an American star all at sea in the Mediterranean. George Segal, Virna Lisi, Lila Kedrova. Written by Franco Brusati and Ennio de Concini; directed by Franco Brusati; for INC / PC / Fulcro. (Original title: *Il Suo Modo di Fari.*)

The Girl Who Had Everything
US 1953 69m bw
MGM (Armand Deutsch)

The daughter of a wealthy criminal lawyer falls in love with one of her father's crooked clients.
Glossy melodrama of purely superficial interest.

w Art Cohn, *novel* Adela Rogers St John *d* Richard Thorpe *ph* Paul Vogel *m* André Previn

Elizabeth Taylor, William Powell, Fernando Lamas, Gig Young
† Remake of *A Free Soul.*

Girl with Green Eyes**
GB 1963 91m bw
UA / Woodfall (Oscar Lewenstein)

An artless young Dublin girl falls for a middle-aged writer.
Lyrical romance which just about preserves its charm by good location sense.

w Edna O'Brien, from her novel The Lonely Girl *d Desmond Davis ph Manny Wynn* *m* John Addison

Peter Finch, Rita Tushingham, Lynn Redgrave

A Girl with Ideas
US 1937 70m bw

A rich girl takes control of a daily paper which libelled her. Lively comedy on familiar lines. Wendy Barrie, Walter Pidgeon, Kent Taylor, George Barbier, Dorothea Kent, Samuel S. Hinds. Written by Bruce Manning, Robert T. Shannon; directed by S. Sylvan Simon; for Universal. 'Bright and original comedy, suitable for the more important first runs.'—*Variety*

Girlfriends*
US 1978 86m Du Art
Cyclops (Claudia Weill, Jan Saunders)

A Jewish girl photographer in New York is ditched by her girl friend and considers men.
Mild, amusing, well-observed little comedy-drama which goes nowhere in particular and slightly outstays its welcome.

w Vicki Polon *d* Claudia Weill *ph* Fred Murphy *m* Michael Small

Melanie Mayron, Eli Wallach, Anita Skinner, Bob Balaban

Les Girls*
US 1957 114m Metrocolor Cinemascope
MGM (Sol. C. Siegel)

Two members of a girl dancing troupe sue over a memoir written by the third.
Disappointing, talent-laden comedy-musical with a *Rashomon*-like flashback plot and a curious absence of the expected wit and style.

w John Patrick, *novel* Vera Caspary *d* George Cukor *ph* Robert Surtees *m / ly* Cole Porter *ch* Jack Cole

Gene Kelly, *Kay Kendall*, Mitzi Gaynor, Taina Elg, Jacques Bergerac, Leslie Phillips, Henry Daniell, Patrick MacNee

Girls about Town
US 1931 80m bw

Gold diggers find true love. A laugh, a tear and a wisecrack in the big city: very dated, but may have seemed fresh at the time. Kay Francis, Joel McCrea, Lilyan Tashman, Eugene Pallette, Alan Dinehart, George Barbier. Written by Raymond Griffith, Brian Marlow from a story by Zoe Akins; directed by George Cukor; for Paramount. 'Generally only fair b.o. as ultra sophistication may be small-town setback.'—*Variety*

Girls at Sea
GB 1958 80m Technicolor

After a shipboard party, three girls are left aboard a battleship. Vulgarized remake of *The Middle Watch* (qv). Guy Rolfe, Ronald Shiner, Alan White, Michael Hordern, Anne Kimbell, Fabia Drake. Written by T. J. Morrison, Gilbert Gunn, Walter C. Mycroft; directed by Gilbert Gunn; for ABP.

Girls' Dormitory*
US 1936 66m bw
TCF

A college girl falls for her headmaster.
Old-fashioned romance for nice young people, smoothly produced in the Fox mid-thirties manner.

w Gene Markey, *story* Ladislaus Fodor *d* Irving Cummings *m* Arthur Lange *ph* J. Merrit Gerstad

Herbert Marshall, *Simone Simon*, Ruth Chatterton, Constance Collier, J. Edward Bromberg, Dixie Dunbar, Tyrone Power

Girls, Girls, Girls
US 1962 106m Technicolor
Wallis–Hazen (Hal B. Wallis)

A nightclub singer runs a fishing boat as a hobby.
Empty-headed, lighter than air vehicle for star fans.

w Edward Anhalt, Allan Weiss *d* Norman Taurog *ph* Loyal Griggs *m* Joseph J. Lilley

Elvis Presley, Stella Stevens, Laurel Goodwin, Jeremy Slate

Girls in the Night
US 1953 82m bw

The son of a New York tenement family falls under suspicion of murder. Very mildly sensational low-life melodrama, like a citified *Tobacco Road*. Glenda Farrell, Harvey Lembeck, Joyce Holden, Glen Roberts, Don Gordon. Written by Ray Buffum; directed by Jack Arnold; for Universal. (GB title: *Life After Dark.*)

The Girls of Pleasure Island
US 1953 96m Technicolor
Paramount (Paul Jones)

In 1945 the Marines land on a tiny Pacific island, disturbing the life of an English gentleman and his three inexperienced but beautiful daughters.
Tedious and wholly artificial comedy with a leaden touch, devised as a try-out for young talent.

w F. Hugh Herbert *d* F. Hugh Herbert, Alvin Ganzer *ph* Daniel Fapp *m* Lyn Murray

Leo Genn, Gene Barry, Don Taylor, Elsa Lanchester, Dorothy Bromiley, Audrey Dalton, Joan Elan

Girls on Probation
US 1937 62m bw

The child of wealthy parents is neglected. Formula social conscience piece, a programme filler. Dolores Costello, Bonita Granville, Natalie Moorehead, Donald Crisp, Emmett Vogan. Written by Lawrence Kimble from a story by Jean Negulesco; directed by Arthur Lubin; for Warners. 'A creditable job.'—*Variety*

Giro City*
GB 1982 102m colour
Silvarealm / Rediffusion / Channel 4 (Sophie Balhetchet, David Payne)

A television documentary team tries to present honest programmes about Ireland and about local government corruption.
Smartly made if somewhat predictably and stridently left-wing slice of so-called realism.

wd Karl Francis *ph* Curtis Clark *m* Alun Francis *ed* Kent Pan

Glenda Jackson, Jon Finch, Kenneth Colley, James Donnelly, Emrys James, Simon Jones

Giuseppina*
GB 1960 32m Technicolor

The daughter of an Italian petrol station proprietor has an amusing afternoon watching customers. Pleasing little Tatiesque sponsored comedy. Written, directed and produced by James Hill; for British Petroleum.

Give a Girl a Break*
US 1953 84m Technicolor
MGM (Jack Cummings)

A Broadway star walks out on a show and three girls audition as replacements.
Minor musical vehicle for the Champions; an agreeable time-passer.

w Frances Goodrich, Albert Hackett
d Stanley Donen *ph* William Mellor
md André Previn *songs* Ira Gershwin, Burton Lane *ch* Stanley Donen, Gower Champion

Marge and Gower Champion, Debbie Reynolds, Bob Fosse, Kurt Kasznar

Give Her a Ring
GB 1934 79m bw

A telephonist falls for her employer. Curious romantic comedy attempting to woo continental audiences. Clifford Mollison, Wendy Barrie, Zelma O'Neal, Erik Rhodes, Bertha Belmore, Stewart Granger (in a bit). Written by Clifford Grey, Ernst Wolff, Marjorie Deans and Wolfgang Wilhelm, from a play by H. Rosenfeld; directed by Arthur Woods; for BIP. 'Delightful and unassuming'—*National Film Theatre, 1970.*

Give Me a Sailor
US 1938 80m bw
Paramount (Jeff Lazarus)

An ugly girl envies her sister her beaux, but ends up winning a competition for beautiful legs.
One of the double bill comedies which got Bob Hope's career off to a shaky start.

w Doris Anderson, Frank Butler, *play* Anne Nichols *d* Elliott Nugent *ph* Victor Milner *md* Boris Morros *songs* Leo Robin, Ralph Rainger

Martha Raye, Bob Hope, Betty Grable, Jack Whiting, Clarence Kolb

'Not so funny farce.'—*Variety*

Give Me the Stars
GB 1944 90m bw

An American girl takes charge of her Scottish grandfather. Half-hearted comedy of the music halls. Will Fyffe, Leni Lynn, Jackie Hunter, Olga Lindo, Stanelli, Ronald Chesney. Written by Maclean Rogers and Austin Melford; directed by Maclean Rogers; for British National.

'Daringly intimate—it's strictly adult entertainment! The picture every woman will want some man to see!'

Give Me Your Heart
US 1936 88m bw

A socialite has a child by a married man. Dated tearjerker. Kay Francis, George Brent, Patric Knowles, Roland Young, Henry Stephenson, Frieda Inescort. Written by Casey Robinson, from the play *Sweet Aloes* by Joyce Gary; directed by Archie Mayo; for Warner. (GB title: *Sweet Aloes.*)

Give My Regards to Broad Street*
GB 1984 108m colour
TCF / MPL (Andros Epimanondas)

An international rock star fears that the priceless tapes of his new album have been stolen, and searches London for them.
An absurdly thin premise even for a musical which is essentially an ego trip for Paul McCartney, who at least squandered his own money on it and not the bank's. Some of the numbers have merit but the mood never connects.

w Paul McCartney *d* Peter Webb *ph* Ian McMillan *m* Paul McCartney *pd* Anthony Pratt

Paul McCartney, Bryan Brown, Ringo Starr, Barbara Bach, Tracey Ullman, Ralph Richardson, George Martin, John Bennett

Give My Regards to Broadway*
US 1948 89m Technicolor
TCF (Walter Morosco)

An old-time vaudevillian yearns to get back into show business.
Pleasantly performed, sentimental family comedy with familiar tunes.

w Samuel Hoffenstein, Elizabeth Reinhardt *d* Lloyd Bacon *ph* Harry Jackson

Dan Dailey, *Charles Winninger*, Fay Bainter, Charles Ruggles, Nancy Guild

'Vaudeville is dead. I wish to God someone would bury it.'—*James Agee*

Give Out, Sisters
US 1942 65m bw

For reasons of pure plot, the Andrews Sisters pose as wealthy old maids. One of scores of musical seconds produced by Universal at this time; this one has an unusually strong cast. The Andrews Sisters, Grace McDonald, Dan Dailey, Charles Butterworth, Walter Catlett, William Frawley, Donald O'Connor, Peggy Ryan. Written by Paul Gerard Smith and Warren Wilson; directed by Edward F. Cline; for Universal.

Give Us the Moon
GB 1944 95m bw
GFD / Gainsborough (Edward Black)

In post-war London a club is opened for idle members only.
Whimsical comedy which fell with a dull thud.

wd Val Guest, *novel* The Elephant is White by Caryl Brahms, S. J. Simon

Margaret Lockwood, Vic Oliver, Peter Graves, Max Bacon, Roland Culver, Frank Cellier, Jean Simmons

Give Us This Day
GB 1949 120m bw
Plantagenet (Rod E. Geiger, N. A. Bronsten)
US title: *Salt to the Devil*

Depression struggles of an Italian immigrant family in New York.
An unconvincing, self-pitying wallow, a very curious enterprise for a British studio.

w Ben Barzman, *story* Christ in Concrete by Pietro di Donato *d* Edward Dmytryk *ph* C. Pennington Richards *m* Benjamin Frankel

Sam Wanamaker, Lea Padovani, Kathleen Ryan, Charles Goldner, Bonar Colleano, William Sylvester, Karel Stepanek, Sidney James

'Dmytryk insisted on cutting the film himself and he has left in at least three spare reels.'—*Richard Winnington*

'Worth making and worth seeing, but cramped by its symbolism and its language.'—*Richard Mallett, Punch*

Give Us Wings
US 1940 60m bw

City boys become pilots in the Army Air Corps. Undistinguished combining of the Dead End Kids with the East Side Kids. Billy Halop, Huntz Hall, Gabriel Dell, Bernard Punsley, Bobby Jordan, Wallace Ford, Anne Gwynne, Victor Jory, Shemp Howard. Written by Arthur T. Horman, Robert Lee Johnson; directed by Charles Lamont; for Universal.

The Gladiator
US 1938 70m bw

A poor boy wins a prize and becomes a college football hero. Elementary star farce. Joe E. Brown, Man Mountain Dean, June Travis, Dickie Moore, Lucien Littlefield. Written by Charles Melson, Arthur Sheekman, from the novel by Philip Wylie; directed by Edward Sedgwick; for Columbia. 'Goofy but a lot of fun.'—*Variety*

Glamour
US 1934 74m bw
Universal

A day in the life of a Broadway star.
Competent minor entertainment.

w Doris Anderson, *story* Edna Ferber *d* William Wyler *ph* George Robinson

Constance Cummings, Paul Lukas, Philip Reed, Joseph Cawthorne, Doris Lloyd, Olaf Hytten

'A good b.o. number with special pull for the femmes.'—*Variety*

Glamour Boy*
US 1941 79m bw

An ex-child star finds himself tutoring his successor. Quite an appealing peep inside Hollywood, and especially wry at the time because the star was still a household word. Jackie Cooper, Susanna Foster, Walter Abel, Darryl Hickman, Ann Gillis, William Demarest. Written by Bradford Ropes, Val Burton; directed by Ralph Murphy; for Colbert Clark / Paramount. 'One of the happiest "idea" pictures turned out by Hollywood in a long time.'—*Variety* (GB title: *Hearts in Springtime*.)

Glamorous Night
GB 1937 81m bw
ABP (Walter C. Mycroft)

An opera singer and her gypsy friends save a Ruritanian king from his scheming prime minister.
Modest transcription of a popular stage musical.

w Dudley Leslie, Hugh Brooke, William Freshman, *play* Ivor Novello *d* Brian Desmond Hurst *ph* Fritz Arno Wagner *m* Ivor Novello *ly* Christopher Hassall

Mary Ellis, Otto Kruger, Victor Jory, Barry Mackay, Trefor Jones, Finlay Currie, Felix Aylmer

† Although several of the original songs are either sung or heard, much of the background music is not Novello's.

'Underwater . . . undercover . . . under any circumstances . . . you must see the wildest, funniest new comedy!'

The Glass Bottom Boat
US 1966 110m Metrocolor Panavision
MGM / Arwin–Reame (Martin Melcher)

A young widow gets involved with spies.
Frantic spy spoof, pleasantly set on the Californian coast, but overflowing with pratfalls, messy slapstick and pointless guest appearances.

w Everett Freeman *d* Frank Tashlin *ph* Leon Shamroy *m* Frank de Vol

Doris Day, Rod Taylor, Arthur Godfrey, Paul Lynde, John McGiver, Edward Andrews, Eric Fleming, Dom De Luise

'He carries his love in his iron fists!'

The Glass Key**
US 1935 87m bw
Paramount (E. Lloyd Sheldon)

A slightly corrupt but good-natured politician is saved by his henchman from being implicated in a murder.
Lively transcription of a zesty crime novel.

w Kathryn Scola, Kubec Glasmon, Harry Ruskin, *novel Dashiell Hammett* *d* Frank Tuttle *ph* Henry Sharp

Edward Arnold, George Raft, Claire Dodd, Rosalind Keith, Guinn Williams, Ray Milland

'Will have to struggle to strike above-average grosses.'—*Variety*

The Glass Key**
US 1942 85m bw
Paramount (Fred Kohlmar)

Nifty remake of the above which finds some limited talents in their best form, helped by a plot which keeps one watching.

w Jonathan Latimer *d Stuart Heisler* *ph Theodor Sparkuhl* *m* Victor Young

Brian Donlevy, Alan Ladd, Veronica Lake, Bonita Granville, *William Bendix*, Richard Denning, Joseph Calleia, Moroni Olsen

MADVIG (Brian Donlevy): 'I'm going to society. He's practically given me the key to his house.'

BEAUMONT (Alan Ladd): 'Yeah, a glass key. Be sure it doesn't break up in your hand.'

The Glass Menagerie**
US 1950 107m bw
Warner / Charles K. Feldman (Jerry Wald)

A shy crippled girl seeks escape from the shabby reality of life in St Louis and from her mother's fantasies.
Pleasantly moody version of one of its author's lighter and more optimistic plays; fluent and good-looking production, memorable performances.

w Tennessee Williams (with Peter Berneis) from his play *d Irving Rapper* *ph Robert Burks* *m* Max Steiner

Gertrude Lawrence, Jane Wyman, Kirk Douglas, Arthur Kennedy

† For the TV movie starring Katharine Hepburn, see *Television Companion*.

The Glass Menagerie
US 1987 130m Du Art Color

Rather flat version without any of the magic, acted in the modern manner. *Joanne Woodward*, John Malkovich, Karen Allen, James Naughton. Directed by Paul Newman, for Burt Harris/Cineplex.

The Glass Mountain
GB 1949 98m bw
Victoria (John Sutro, Joseph Janni, Fred Zelnik)

In the Dolomites, a married composer loves an Italian girl who saved his life during the war.
Tedious sudser, ineptly produced; an enormous British box office success because of its theme music.

w Joseph Janni, John Hunter, Emery Bonnet, Henry Cass, John Cousins *d* Henry Cass *ph* Otello Martelli, William McLeod *m* Nino Rota

Michael Denison, Dulcie Gray, Valentina Cortese, Tito Gobbi, Sebastian Shaw

The Glass Slipper
US 1954 94m Eastmancolor
MGM (Edwin H. Knopf)

The story of Cinderella.
To those used to the pantomime version this is dull, dreary, high-flown stuff: limbo sets, ballets, psychological rationalization and virtually no comedy.

w / ly Helen Deutsch *d* Charles Walters *ph* Arthur E. Arling *m* Bronislau Kaper *ch* Roland Petit

Leslie Caron, Michael Wilding, Elsa Lanchester, Barry Jones, *Estelle Winwood* (as Fairy Godmother)

The Glass Sphinx
Spain / Italy 1968 98m colour

An archaeologist is in danger because of his discoveries. Multi-national mish-mash only notable as one of the last films of its star. Robert Taylor, Anita Ekberg, Gianna Sera, Jack Stuart. Written by Adriano Bolzoni and Louis M. Heyward; directed by Fulvio Lucisano; for AIP.

The Glass Web
US 1953 81m bw 3-D
U-I (A. J. Cohen)

A TV executive kills a blackmailing actress and allows a young scriptwriter to be accused.
Boring thriller set in a TV studio.

w Robert Blees, Leonard Lee *d* Jack Arnold *ph* Maury Gertsman *m* Joseph Gershenson

Edward G. Robinson, John Forsythe, Marcia Henderson, Richard Denning

Glen or Glenda
US 1953 / 61m bw

A doctor relates stories about transvestites and sex-change operations. Notorious grade Z exploitation piece, often counted among the worst films ever made. See for yourself. Lyle Talbot, Timothy Farrell, Bela Lugosi. Written, directed and produced by Edward D. Wood Jnr. (Also known as *I Changed My Sex, He or She, The Transvestite, I Led Two Lives*.)

The Glenn Miller Story**
US 1953 116m Technicolor
U-I (Aaron Rosenberg)

The life of the unassuming trombonist and bandleader whose plane disappeared during World War II.
Competent musical heartwarmer with a well-cast star and successful reproduction of the Miller sound. A big box office hit.

w Valentine Davies, Oscar Brodney
d Anthony Mann ph William Daniels
md Henry Mancini, Joseph Gershenson

James Stewart, June Allyson, Harry Morgan, Charles Drake, Frances Langford, Louis Armstrong, Gene Krupa

AAN: script; music direction

A Global Affair
US 1963 84m bw
Seven Arts / Hall Bartlett

A United Nations official has to look after an abandoned baby.
Flat sentimental farce which embarrassingly tries to say something about the UN.

w Arthur Marx, Bob Fisher, Charles Lederer
d Jack Arnold *ph* Joseph Ruttenberg
m Dominic Frontière

Bob Hope, Lilo Pulver, Michèle Mercier, Yvonne de Carlo

'Squaresville incarnate, with a side trip into Leersville.'—*Judith Crist, 1973*

Gloria*
US 1980 121m Technicolor
Columbia (Sam Shaw)

In the Bronx, an innocent woman finds she has to meet violence with violence in order to protect a small boy from the mob.
Overlong but lively and oddly entertaining; however, one is never quite sure what if anything it is getting at.

wd John Cassavetes *ph* Fred Schuler *m* Bill Conti

Gena Rowlands, John Adames, Bucky Henry

AAN: Gena Rowlands

Glorifying the American Girl*
US 1929 87m bw, colour sequence
Paramount (Florenz Ziegfeld)

A chorus girl rejects her boy friend for the sake of stardom.
Archetypal show-must-go-on musical.

w J. P. McEvoy, Millard Webb *d* Millard Webb, John Harkrider *ph* George Folsey
md Frank Tours

Mary Eaton, Edward Crandall; and as guests Eddie Cantor, Helen Morgan, Rudy Vallee, Florenz Ziegfeld, Adolph Zukor, Otto Kahn, Texas Guinan, Mayor Jimmy Walker, Ring Lardner, Noah Beery, Johnny Weissmuller

The Glorious Adventure*
GB 1921 100m (approx) Prizmacolor silent
Stoll / J. Stuart Blackton

Various lives are affected by the Great Fire of London in 1666.
Stagey costume drama, notable only as the first British film in colour.

w Felix Orman *d* J. Stuart Blackton
ph William T. Crespinal

Lady Diana Manners, Victor McLaglen, Gerald Lawrence, Cecil Humphreys, Alex Crawford, Lennox Pawle (as Pepys)

Glorious Betsy
US 1928 90m approx bw silent

Napoleon's younger brother loves an American girl. Popular period romance of its day. Conrad Nagel, Dolores Costello, John Miljan, Betty Blythe. Written by Anthony Coldeway, from the play by Rida Johnson Young; directed by Alan Crosland; for Warner. (NB: Remade as *Hearts Divided.*)

† The happy ending is not historical.

AAN: Anthony Coldeway

Glory
US 1955 100m Technicolor Superscope
RKO (David Butler)

Girl loves horse more than boy.
Conventional young love / Kentucky Derby marshmallow.

w Peter Milne *d* David Butler *ph* Wilfrid Cline *m* Frank Perkins

Margaret O'Brien, Walter Brennan, Charlotte Greenwood, John Lupton

Glory Alley
US 1952 79m bw
MGM (Nicholas Nayfack)

A sullen young boxer has trouble with his girl, her father and the demon rum.
Flat, boring second feature with musical interludes.

w Art Cohn *d* Raoul Walsh *ph* William Daniels *md* Georgie Stoll

Leslie Caron, Ralph Meeker, Kurt Kasznar, Gilbert Roland, John McIntire, Louis Armstrong, Jack Teagarden

'This is the kind of film that contains bits of everything. New Orleans night life and an episode of the Korean war; an arty French ballet sequence and jazz from Louis Armstrong; a boxer who acquired a neurosis in childhood when his father hit him over the head and a blind old father with a French accent, who knows all about everything.'—*MFB*

The Glory Brigade
US 1953 82m bw
TCF (William Bloom)

Greek soldiers fight in Korea alongside the Americans.
Modest war adventure with predictable racial tensions.

w Franklin Coen *d* Robert D. Webb
ph Lucien Andriot *md* Lionel Newman

Victor Mature, Alexander Scourby, Lee Marvin, Richard Egan

The Glory Guys*
US 1965 112m De Luxe Panavision
UA / Levy–Gardner–Laven

Officers of the US cavalry disagree about dealing with the Indians.
Standard big-budget western.

w Sam Peckinpah, *novel* The Dice of God by Hoffman Birney *d* Arnold Laven *ph* James Wong Howe *m* Riz Ortolani

Tom Tryon, Harve Presnell, Senta Berger, Andrew Duggan, James Caan, Slim Pickens, Michael Anderson Jnr

The Gnome-Mobile*
US 1967 90m Technicolor
Walt Disney (James Algar)

A millionaire and his family go for a forest picnic and help a colony of gnomes.
Cheerful adventures for small children, with good trick work.

w Ellis Kadison, *novel* Upton Sinclair
d Robert Stevenson *ph* Edward Colman
m Buddy Baker

Walter Brennan, Matthew Garber, Karen Dotrice, Richard Deacon, Sean McClory, Ed Wynn, Jerome Cowan, Charles Lane

The Go-Between**
GB 1970 116m Technicolor
EMI / World Film Services (John Heyman, Norman Priggen)

Staying at a stately home around the turn of the century, 12-year-old Leo carries love letters from a farmer to his friend's sister.
A rather tiresome plot sustains a rich picture of the Edwardian gentry, a milieu with which however the director is not at home and treats far too slowly and tricksily.

w Harold Pinter, *novel* L. P. Hartley
d Joseph Losey *ph Geoffrey Fisher m* Michel Legrand *ad Carmen Dillon*

Alan Bates, Julie Christie, Michael Redgrave, Dominic Guard, Michael Gough, Margaret Leighton, Edward Fox

'It's an almost palpable recreation of a past environment, and that environment is the film's real achievement, not the drama enacted within it.'—*Stanley Kauffmann*

AAN: Margaret Leighton

Go Chase Yourself
US 1938 70m bw

A bank clerk gets involved with gangsters. Mild Comedy for a radio star. Joe Penner, Lucille Ball, June Travis, Richard Lane, Fritz Feld, Tom Kennedy. Written by Paul Yawitz, Bert Granet; directed by Edward F. Cline; for Robert Sisk/RKO.

Go for a Take
GB 1972 90m colour
Rank / Century Films (Roy Simpson)

Two waiters in debt to a gangster take refuge in a film studio.
Painful British farce.

w Alan Hackney *d* Harry Booth *ph* Mark McDonald *m* Glen Mason

Reg Varney, Norman Rossington, Sue Lloyd, Dennis Price, Julie Ege, Patrick Newell, David Lodge

Go for Broke
US 1951 93m bw
MGM (Dore Schary)

World War II exploits of Japanese-American soldiers.
Absolutely unsurprising war film with all the anti-Japs converted by the end. Production quite good.

wd Robert Pirosh *ph* Paul C. Vogel
m Alberto Columbo

Van Johnson, Lane Nakano, George Miki, Akira Fukunaga, Warner Anderson, Don Haggerty

AAN: Robert Pirosh (as writer)

Go into Your Dance**
US 1935 89m bw
Warner (Sam Bischoff)
GB title: *Casino de Paree*

A big-headed star gets his come-uppance and finds happiness.
Moderate backstage musical notable for the only teaming of Jolson and Keeler, who were then married.

w Earl Baldwin *d* Archie Mayo *ph* Tony Gaudio, Sol Polito *songs* Harry Warren, Al Dubin

Al Jolson, Ruby Keeler, Glenda Farrell, Benny Rubin, Phil Regan, Barton MacLane, Sharon Lynne, Akim Tamiroff, Helen Morgan, Patsy Kelly

'It has everything for the box office.'—*Variety*

Go Man Go
US 1954 82m bw
Alfred Palca (Anton M. Leader)

How Abe Saperstein moulded and trained the Harlem Globetrotters basketball team.
Not so much a film as an athletic demonstration with some actors round the edges.

w Arnold Becker *d James Wong Howe* *ph* Bill Steiner *m* Alex North

Dane Clark, Sidney Poitier, Pat Breslin, Edmond Ryan

Go Naked in the World
US 1960 103m Metrocolor Cinemascope
MGM / Arcola (Aaron Rosenberg)

A prostitute causes a rift between son and millionaire father.
Antediluvian melodrama with overblown performances.

wd Ranald MacDougall, *novel* Tom Chanales *ph* Milton Krasner *m* Adolph Deutsch

Gina Lollobrigida, Tony Franciosa, Ernest Borgnine, Luana Patten, Will Kuluva, Philip Ober

'A good example of how the increased liberation of Hollywood can be misused.'—*MFB*

Go Tell the Spartans
US 1978 114m CFI color
Spartan Company (Allan F. Badah, Mitchell Cannold)

In Vietnam, a seasoned commander tries to get a platoon of raw soldiers out of a Vietcong ambush.
We have been here before, in other wars, and since there is little heroism to be had from Vietnam it is difficult to see why we are invited again.

w Wendell Mayes, *story* Daniel Ford *d* Ted Post *ph* Harry Stradling Jnr *m* Dick Halligan

Burt Lancaster, Craig Wasson, Jonathan Goldsmith, Marc Singer

Go to Blazes
GB 1961 84m Technicolor Cinemascope
ABP (Kenneth Harper)

Ex-convicts become firemen, intending to use the engine for smash and grab raids.
Mild comedy ruined by wide screen.

w Patrick Campbell, Vivienne Knight *d* Michael Truman *ph* Erwin Hillier *m* John Addison

Dave King, Daniel Massey, Norman Rossington, Wilfrid Lawson, Maggie Smith, Robert Morley, Coral Browne

'Laughter is what it has nothing else but!'

Go West*
US 1925 70m (24 fps) bw silent
Metro-Goldwyn / Buster Keaton (Joseph M. Schenck)

A tenderfoot makes friends with a cow and takes it everywhere.
Disappointingly slow star comedy with splendid moments.

w Raymond Cannon *d* Buster Keaton *ph* Bert Haines, E. Lessley

Buster Keaton, Howard Truesdall, Kathleen Myers

Go West**
US 1940 82m bw
MGM (Jack Cummings)

Three zanies tackle a western villain.
Minor Marx comedy with a good start (the ticket office sketch) and a rousing finale as they take a moving train to bits, but some pretty soggy stuff in between.

w Irving Brecher *d* Edward Buzzell *ph* Leonard Smith *m* Bronislau Kaper *md* Georgie Stoll

Groucho, Harpo, Chico, John Carroll, Diana Lewis, Robert Barrat

Go West Young Lady
US 1940 70m bw

A lawless western town expects a sheriff who turns out to be a girl. Mildly pleasing variation on *Destry Rides Again.* Glenn Ford, Penny Singleton, Charles Ruggles. Written by Karen de Wolf and Richard Flournoy; directed by Frank Strayer; for Columbia.

'How you gonna keep 'em down on the farm, after they've seen Mae West?'

Go West Young Man
US 1936 80m bw
Paramount (Emanuel R. Cohen)

A movie star has a car breakdown in Pennsylvania and falls for a local lad.
Cleaned-up Mae West vehicle, all rather boring.

w Mae West, *play* Personal Appearance by Lawrence Riley *d* Henry Hathaway *ph* Karl Struss *m* George Stoll

Mae West, Randolph Scott, Warren William, Lyle Talbot, Alice Brady, Isabel Jewell, Elizabeth Patterson

'On the way to snug profits.'—*Variety*

'Quite incredibly tedious, as slow and wobbling in its pace as Miss West's famous walk. The wisecracks lack the old impudence, and seldom have so many feet of film been expended on a mere dirty look.'—*Graham Greene*

God Is My Co-Pilot
US 1945 89m bw
Warner (Robert Buckner)

Pacific air adventures during World War II.
Adequate flagwaver.

w Peter Milne, Abem Finkel, *book* Col. Robert Lee Scott Jnr *d* Robert Florey *ph* Sid Hickox *m* Franz Waxman

Dennis Morgan, Dane Clark, Raymond Massey, Alan Hale, Andrea King, John Ridgely, Stanley Ridges, Craig Stevens

'A slapped-together attraction . . . all the flashbacks, supposedly emotional scenes, and fragments of philosophy which punctuate the aerial action vitiate a tale which might have been a notable addition to the screen's extensive considerations of the far-flung theatres of the war.'—*Howard Barnes, New York Herald Tribune*

God Is My Partner
US 1957 82m bw Regalscope

A surgeon retires and begins to give his money away to religious causes; members of his family file suit against him. Rather obvious fable in the *Mr Deeds* tradition. Walter Brennan, John Hoyt, Marion Ross, Jesse White. Written by Charles Francis Royal; directed by William F. Claxton; for Sam Hersh / TCF.

God Told Me To
US 1976 89m colour

A detective investigates the death of a mad sniper and finds it to be a case of demonic possession. Unsavoury mix of several genres, insufficiently well written to compel. Tony Lo Bianco, Deborah Raffin, Sandy Dennis, Sylvia Sidney, Sam Levene, Robert Drivas, Richard Lynch, Harry Bellaver. Written, directed and produced by Larry Cohen; for Larco. (GB title: *Demon.)*

The Goddess*
US 1958 105m bw
Columbia (Milton Perlman)

A small-town girl becomes a Hollywood sex symbol and lives to regret it.
Savage attack on the Marilyn Monroe cult, a bit lachrymose and compromised by miscasting, but with interesting detail.

w Paddy Chayevsky *d* John Cromwell *ph* Arthur J. Ornitz *m* Virgil Thompson

Kim Stanley, Lloyd Bridges, Steven Hill, Betty Lou Holland

AAN: Paddy Chayevsky

The Godfather***
US 1972 175m Technicolor
Paramount / Alfran (Albert S. Ruddy)

When, after ruling for two generations, the Mafia's New York head dies of old age, his son takes over reluctantly but later learns how to kill.
A brilliantly-made film with all the fascination of a snake pit: a warm-hearted family saga except that the members are thieves and murderers. Cutting would help, but the duller conversational sections do heighten the cunningly judged moments of suspense and violence.

w Francis Ford Coppola, Mario Puzo, *novel* Mario Puzo *d Francis Ford Coppola* *ph* Gordon Willis *m* Nino Rota *pd* Dean Tavoularis

Marlon Brando (unintentionally comic in an absurd make-up), *Al Pacino*, Robert Duvall, James Caan, Richard Castellano, Diane Keaton, Talia Shire, Richard Conte, John Marley

'The immorality lies in his presentation of murderers as delightful family men—the criminal is the salt of the earth—and to our shame we rub it into the wounds of our Watergate-world morality and even ask for more.'—*Judith Crist, 1974*

'They have put pudding in Brando's cheeks and dirtied his teeth, he speaks hoarsely and moves stiffly, and these combined mechanics are hailed as great acting . . . Like star, like film, the keynote is inflation. *The Godfather* was made from a big bestseller, a lot of money was spent on it, and it runs over three hours. Therefore it's important.'—*Stanley Kauffmann*

AA: best picture; script; Marlon Brando
AAN: Francis Ford Coppola (as director); Al Pacino; Robert Duvall; James Caan

THE GODFATHER. One for the family album: Al Pacino, Marlon Brando, James Caan and John Cazale and, possibly, their getaway car.

The Godfather, Part Two***
US 1974 200m Technicolor
Paramount / the Coppola Company (Francis Ford Coppola)

In 1958, Michael Corleone reflects on the problems of himself and his father before him.
Curious rehash of part of the original with new scenes, a shade difficult to follow but full of good scenes and performances.

w Francis Ford Coppola, Mario Puzo *d Francis Ford Coppola* *ph* Gordon Willis *m* Nino Rota *pd* Dean Tavoularis

Al Pacino, *Robert de Niro*, Diane Keaton, Robert Duvall, John Cazale, Lee Strasberg, Michael V. Gazzo, Talia Shire, Troy Donahue

'The complete work is an epic vision of the corruption of America.'—*New Yorker*

† The two films were eventually combined and extended for television into a ten-hour serial, *The Godfather Saga*.

AA: best picture; script; Francis Ford Coppola (as director); Nino Rota; Robert de Niro
AAN: Al Pacino; Lee Strasberg; Michael V. Gazzo; Talia Shire

God's Country and the Woman
US 1936 80m Technicolor
Warner (Lou Edelman)

The junior partner of a lumber company goes to work undercover in an opponent's camp, causes trouble, and falls in love.
Adequate outdoor melodrama in early colour.

w Norman Reilly Raine, *novel* James Oliver Curwood *d* William Keighley *ph* Tony Gaudio *m* Max Steiner

George Brent, Beverly Roberts, Barton MacLane, Robert Barrat, Alan Hale, Addison Richards, El Brendel, Roscoe Ates, Billy Bevan

'Great outdoors in Technicolor, but not likely for much b.o.'—*Variety*

God's Gift to Women
US 1931 72m bw

In Paris, a descendant of Don Juan is pursued by numerous women but falls for an American girl. Tedious comedy with a star out of his element. Frank Fay, Joan Blondell, Laura la Plante, Charles Winninger, Louise Brooks. Written by Joseph Jackson and Raymond Griffith from the play The Devil Was Sick by Jane Hinton; directed by Michael Curtiz; for Warners. 'No gift to audiences.'—*Variety*

'The story that no one dared film till now becomes the most adult motion picture ever made!'
God's Little Acre*
US 1958 110m bw
Security (Sidney Harmon)

A poor white farmer in Georgia neglects his land in a fruitless search for gold.
Tobacco Road under another name, and not so lively: bowdlerized and eventually tedious despite a welter of sensational incident and depraved characters.

w Philip Yordan, *novel* Erskine Caldwell *d* Anthony Mann *ph* Ernest Haller *m Elmer Bernstein*

Robert Ryan, Aldo Ray, Tina Louise, Buddy Hackett, Jack Lord, Vic Morrow, Rex Ingram

The Gods Must Be Crazy
South Africa 1980 109m colour Panavision

A Coca Cola bottle falls from a plane and becomes a religious object to Kalahari bushmen. Unexpected throwback farce with the blacks behaving almost as stupidly as Mantan Moreland in an old Charlie Chan movie. One for the Race Relations Board. N'Xau, Marius Weyers, Sandra Prinsloo. Written, directed and produced by Jamie Uys; for Mimosa / CAT.

'The gospel according to today!'
Godspell*
US 1973 102m TVC color
Columbia / Lansbury / Duncan / Beruh (Edgar Lansbury)

The Gospel according to St Matthew played out musically by hippies in the streets of New York.
Wild and woolly film version of the successful theatrical fantasy, surviving chiefly by virtue of its gleaming photography.

w David Greene, John Michael Tebelak, *play* John Michael Tebelak *d David Greene* *ph Richard G. Heimann* *m / ly Stephen Schwarz*

Victor Garber, David Haskell, Jerry Sroka, Lynne Thigpen, Robin Lamont

'A patch of terra incognita somewhere between *Sesame Street* and the gospel according to *Laugh-In*.'—*Bruce Williamson*

Godzilla
Japan 1955 80m (dubbed version) bw
Toho (Tomoyuki Tanaka)
original title: *Gojira*

A prehistoric monster is awakened by H-bomb tests and menaces Tokyo.
Tepid forerunner of scores of Japanese monster movies peopled by men in rubber suits.

w Takeo Murato, Inoshiro Honda *d* Inoshiro Honda

Raymond Burr, Takashi Shimura, Momoko Kochi

† Sequels included *Godzilla vs the Thing*, *King Kong vs Godzilla*, *Godzilla vs the Sea Monster*, *Godzilla vs the Smog Monster*, *Destroy All Monsters*. Other monstrous creations included *Rodan*, *Manda* and *Mothra*.

Gog*
US 1954 85m Color Corporation 3D
Ivan Tors

In an underground laboratory in New Mexico, a giant computer controls two robots, and a spy programmes it to kill.
Brisk, imaginative low-budget sci-fi in gleaming colour, well staged and developed.

w Tom Taggart *d* Herbert B. Strock
ph Lothrop B. Worth *m* Harry Sukman

Richard Egan, Constance Dowling, Herbert Marshall

The Go-Getter
US 1937 90m bw
Warner (Sam Bischoff)

A one-legged navy veteran is determined that his injury will not prevent him from becoming a success.
Moderate comedy-drama, agreeably played.

w Delmer Daves, Peter B. Kyne *d* Busby Berkeley *ph* Arthur Edeson *md* Leo F. Forbstein

George Brent, Charles Winninger, Anita Louise, John Eldredge, Henry O'Neill, Willard Robertson, Eddie Acuff

'A fair amount of comedy within a story bordering on the ridiculous.'—*Variety*

Goha
France / Tunisia 1957 90m Agfacolor
Films Franco-Africains

A young Arab helps a blind musician and falls in love with a wise man's young bride.
Curiously winning, good-looking little romance which, apart from an unexpected sad ending, plays like an update of the Arabian Nights.

w Georges Schéhadé, *novel* Le Livre de Goha le Simple by A. Ades, A. Jospiovici
d Jacques Baratier *ph* Jean Bourgoin
m Maurice Ohana

Omar Chérif (later Sharif), Zina Bouzaiane, Lauro Gazzolo

Going Bye Bye**
US 1934 20m bw

A violent convict escapes to take vengeance on the two innocents whose evidence sent him up. Splendid star comedy displaying most of the team's most endearing aspects. Laurel and Hardy, Walter Long, Mae Busch. Written by Anon; directed by Charles Rogers; for Hal Roach.

Going Highbrow
US 1935 68m bw

Two *nouveaux riches* people try to trick their way into society. Agreeably cast farce that outstays its welcome. Edward Everett Horton, Guy Kibbee, Zasu Pitts, Ross Alexander, Judy Canova. Written by Edward Kaufmann, Sy Bartlett, Ralph Spence; directed by Robert Florey; for Warners. 'So-so flicker for the lesser spots.'—*Variety*

Going Hollywood*
US 1933 80m bw

A crooner is pursued by a girl who poses as a French maid. Lively comedy with a studio setting; anything goes. Bing Crosby, Marion Davies, Patsy Kelly, Stuart Erwin. Written by Donald Ogden Stewart; directed by Raoul Walsh; for MGM. 'Lavishly produced musical with everything but a story.'—*Variety*

Going Home
US 1971 98m colour

An ex-convict who killed his wife while drunk assumes an ambivalent relationship with his son. Thoroughly uninteresting melodrama which was barely released. Robert Mitchum, Jan-Michael Vincent, Brenda Vaccaro. Written by Lawrence Marcus; directed by Herbert B. Leonard; for MGM.

Going in Style
US 1979 97m Technicolor
Warner / Tony Bill

Three bored elderly men decide to plan a bank robbery.
Curiously aimless sentimental comedy-drama which is simply neither funny enough, thrilling enough or moving enough to hold the interest.

wd Martin Brest *ph* Billy Williams
m Michael Small

George Burns, Art Carney, Lee Strasberg

Going My Way**
US 1944 126m bw
Paramount (Leo McCarey)

A young priest comes to a New York slum parish and after initial friction charms the old pastor he is to succeed.
Sentimental comedy which got away with it wonderfully at the time, largely through careful casting, though it seems thin and obvious now.

w Frank Butler, Frank Cavett, Leo McCarey *d* Leo McCarey *ph* Lionel Lindon *m* Robert Emmett Dolan *songs Johnny Burke, James Van Heusen, J. R. Shannon*

Bing Crosby, Barry Fitzgerald, Rise Stevens, Frank McHugh, James Brown, Gene Lockhart, Jean Heather, Porter Hall

'I should not feel safe in recommending it to anyone but a simple-hearted sentimentalist with a taste for light music.'—*Richard Mallett, Punch*

'The lessons, if I read them right, are that leisureliness can be excellent, that if you take a genuine delight in character the universe is opened to you, and perhaps above all that a movie, like any other genuine work of art, must be made for love. But I am willing to bet that the chief discernible result of *Going My Way* will be an anxiety-ridden set of vaudeville sketches about Pat and Mike in cassocks.'—*James Agee*

† Father O'Malley reappeared in *The Bells of St Mary's* and *Say One for Me* (both qv).

AA: best picture; script; original story (Leo McCarey); Leo McCarey (direction); Bing Crosby; Barry Fitzgerald; song, 'Swinging on a Star' (*m* James Van Heusen, *ly* Johnny Burke)
AAN: Lionel Lindon

Going Places
US 1939 84m bw

A sporting goods salesman poses as a jockey and has to ride a horse to victory. Thin musical spurred by the hit song 'Jeepers Creepers'. Dick Powell, Anita Louise, Ronald Reagan, Louis Armstrong, Allen Jenkins, Walter Catlett. Written by Jerry Wald, Sig Herzig and Maurice Leo, from the play *The Hottentot* (filmed thrice previously) by Victor Mapes and William Collier; directed by Ray Enright; for Warner. 'Satisfactory but not smash.'—*Variety*.

AAN: song 'Jeepers Creepers', by Al Dubin and Harry Warren.

'Saved from the hangman for a fate worse than death!'

Goin' South
US 1978 101m Metrocolor
Paramount (Henry Gittes, Harold Schneider)

An unwashed outlaw is saved from the rope when a young girl promises to marry and reform him . . .
. . . for no very good reason. Curious semi-comic western which might have made a good two-reeler.

w John Herman Shaner, Al Ramrus, Charles Shyer, Alan Mandel *d* Jack Nicholson
ph Nestor Almendros *m* Van Dyke Parks, Perry Botkin Jnr

Jack Nicholson, Mary Steenburgen, Christopher Lloyd, John Belushi, Veronica Cartwright, Richard Bradford

'Mae's a lady now and she'll lick anyone in the house who says she ain't!'

Goin' to Town*
US 1935 74m bw
Paramount (William Le Baron)

A western oil heiress moves into society.
Reasonably satisfactory Mae West vehicle, but not in the old bawdy style.

w Mae West *d* Alexander Hall *ph* Karl Struss *songs* Sammy Fain, Irving Kahal
md Andrea Setaro

Mae West, Paul Cavanagh, Ivan Lebedeff, Tito Coral, Marjorie Gateson, Fred Kohler Snr, Monroe Owsley

'No amount of epigrammatic hypoing can offset the silly story.'—*Variety*

Gold*
Germany 1934 105m bw

Scientists invent a machine that will make synthetic gold. Overlong melodrama made in German and French, boring when the equipment is off the screen. Hans Albers, Brigg Helm, Lien Deyers, Michael Bohnen. Written by Rolf E. Vanloo; directed by Karl Hartl; for UFA.

NB: The central sequences were reused years later for the climax of *The Magnetic Monster* (*qv*).

Gold*
GB 1974 124m Technicolor Panavision
Hemdale / Avton (Michael Klinger)

A South African mining engineer falls for the boss's granddaughter and exposes a conspiracy.
Old-fashioned thick ear with spectacular underground sequences and a rousing finale.

w Wilbur Smith, Stanley Price, *novel* Goldmine by Wilbur Smith *d Peter Hunt ph Ousama Rawi m* Elmer Bernstein

Roger Moore, Susannah York, Ray Milland, Bradford Dillman, John Gielgud, Tony Beckley

AAN: song 'Wherever Love Takes Me' (*m* Elmer Bernstein, *ly* Don Black)

Gold Diggers of Broadway*
US 1929 98m Technicolor
Warner

Three Broadway chorus girls seek rich husbands.
Fascinating primitive musical.

w Robert Lord, *play* The Gold Diggers by Avery Hopwood *d* Roy del Ruth *ph* Barney McGill, Ray Rennahan *songs* Al Dubin, Joe Burke

Nancy Welford, Conway Tearle, Winnie Lightner, Ann Pennington, Lilyan Tashman, William Bakewell, Nick Lucas

'Exceeds in pretentiousness and beauty anything which has yet appeared on the screen!'—*publicity*

† Other versions of the play include *The Gold Diggers* (1923), *Gold Diggers of 1933* (qv), *Painting the Clouds with Sunshine* (qv).

Gold Diggers of 1933***
US 1933 96m bw
Warner (Robert Lord)

Cheerful, competent, well-cast remake of the above; numbers include 'My Forgotten Man', 'We're in the Money' and 'Pettin' in the Park'.

w Erwin Gelsey, James Seymour, David Boehm, Ben Markson *d Mervyn Le Roy ch Busby Berkeley songs Harry Warren, Al Dubin ph Sol Polito*

Warren William, Joan Blondell, *Aline MacMahon*, Ruby Keeler, Dick Powell, Guy Kibbee, Ned Sparks, Ginger Rogers, Clarence Nordstrom

'It sums up what is meant by the phrase "pure thirties": electrically wired chorus girls singing "In the Shadows Let Me Come and Sing to You" merge to form a big illuminated violin.'—*New Yorker, 1979*

'It is memorable chiefly because Busby Berkeley created a mad geometry of patterned chorines. . . . The innocent vulgarity of the big numbers is charming and uproarious, and aesthetically preferable to the pretentious ballet finales of fifties musicals like *An American in Paris*. Even those of us who were children at the time did not mistake *Gold Diggers* for art—and certainly no one took it for life.'—*Pauline Kael, 1968*

'Your dream of perfect beauty come true!'—*publicity*

Gold Diggers of 1935**
US 1935 95m bw
Warner (Robert Lord)

A socialite puts on a Broadway show at her country home, and is taken in by a swindler. Heavy-handed but laugh-provoking comedy with familiar faces of the day, climaxed by big numbers including 'Lullaby of Broadway'.

w Manuel Seff, Peter Milne, Robert Lord *d / ch Busby Berkeley ph* George Barnes *songs Al Dubin, Harry Warren*

Dick Powell, Adolphe Menjou, Gloria Stuart, Alice Brady, Hugh Herbert, Glenda Farrell, Frank McHugh, Grant Mitchell, Wini Shaw

'Busby Berkeley, the master of scenic prestidigitation, continues to dazzle the eye and stun the imagination.'—*André Sennwald, New York Times*

'A decidedly heady mixture.'—*Pare Lorentz*

AA: song 'Lullaby of Broadway'

Gold Diggers of 1937*
US 1936 100m bw
Warner (Hal B. Wallis)

A group of insurance salesmen back a show. Mild tailing-off of the Gold Diggers series, though with the accustomed production polish.

w Warren Duff, *play* Richard Maibaum, Michael Wallach, George Haight *d* Lloyd Bacon *ch Busby Berkeley ph* Arthur Edeson *songs* Harry Warren, Al Dubin, E. Y. Harburg, Harold Arlen

Dick Powell, Joan Blondell, Glenda Farrell, Victor Moore, Lee Dixon, Osgood Perkins, Charles D. Brown

Gold Diggers in Paris*
US 1938 95m bw
Warner (Sam Bischoff)
GB title: *The Gay Imposters*

Three girls chase rich husbands abroad.
A thin end to the series, saved by an agreeable cast.

w Earl Baldwin, Warren Duff *d* Ray Enright *ph* Sol Polito, George Barnes *ch Busby Berkeley songs* Harry Warren, Al Dubin, Johnny Mercer

Rudy Vallee, Rosemary Lane, Hugh Herbert, Allen Jenkins, Gloria Dickson, Melville Cooper, Fritz Feld, Ed Brophy, Curt Bois

Gold Dust Gertie
US 1931 66m bw

A tough divorcee tries to sponge on her former spouses. Silly and unattractive comedy. Winnie Lightner, Chic Johnson, Ole Olsen, Dorothy Carlisle, Claude Gillingwater. Written by W. K. Wells and Ray Enright; from the play The Life of the Party by Len D. Hollister; directed by Lloyd Bacon; for Warners. (GB Title: *Why Change Your Husband?*)

'Roughest kind of comedy dialogue; in need of careful surgery.'—*Variety*

Gold Is Where You Find It*
US 1938 90m Technicolor
Warner (Sam Bischoff)

Gold rush miners settle as California farmers. Agreeable western in excellent early colour.

w Warren Duff, Clements Ripley, Robert Buckner *d* Michael Curtiz ph Sol Polito m Max Steiner

George Brent, Olivia de Havilland, Claude Rains, Margaret Lindsay, John Litel, Marcia Ralston, Barton MacLane, Tim Holt, Sidney Toler

Gold of Naples
Italy 1955 135m bw
Ponti-de Laurentiis
original title: *L'Oro di Napoli*

Six sketches, comic and tragic, give an impression of Naples today.
A variable collection, mainly shown around the world in abridged versions.

w Cesare Zavattini, Vittorio de Sica, Giuseppe Marotta *d* Vittorio de Sica *ph* Otello Martelli *m* Alessandro Cicognini

Vittorio de Sica, Eduardo de Filippo, Toto, Sophia Loren, Paolo Stoppa, Silvana Mangano

Gold of the Seven Saints
US 1961 89m bw Warnerscope
Warner (Leonard Freeman)

Cowboys compete in a search for lost gold. Adequate minor western using TV stars.

w Leigh Brackett, Leonard Freeman *d* Gordon Douglas *ph* Joseph Biroc *m* Howard Jackson

Clint Walker, Roger Moore, Leticia Roman, Robert Middleton, Chill Wills, Gene Evans

The Gold Rush***
US 1925 72m (sound version 1942) bw
Charles Chaplin

A lone prospector in the Yukon becomes rich after various adventures.
Essentially a succession of slowly but carefully built visual gags, this is Chaplin's finest example of comedy drawn from utter privation; as such it appealed vastly to the poor of the world. As a clown, Chaplin himself is near his best, though as usual there is rather too much straining for pathos.

w, d, p, m Charles Chaplin ph Rollie Totheroh, Jack Wilson

Charles Chaplin, Georgia Hale, Mack Swain, Tom Murray

The Golden Age of Buster Keaton**
US 1975 97m bw
Jay Ward (Raymond Rohauer)

A useful introductory package to the shorts and features of Buster Keaton, with most of the great silent scenes present.

commentary Bill Scott

The Golden Age of Comedy****
US 1957 78m bw
Robert Youngson Productions

First of the scholarly compilations of silent comedy which saved many negatives from destruction, this is a fast-paced general survey which despite a facetious sound track does provide a laugh a minute. It particularly brought Laurel and Hardy back into public notice, and includes sections from *Two Tars* and *The Battle of the Century*.

wd Robert Youngson narrators Dweight Weist, Ward Wilson *m* George Steiner

Stan Laurel, Oliver Hardy, Harry Langdon, Ben Turpin, Will Rogers, Billy Bevan, Charlie Chase, Andy Clyde

Golden Arrow
US 1936 68m bw

An heiress tricks a newspaper reporter into a marriage of convenience. Dull, schematic romantic comedy. Bette Davis, George Brent, Eugene Pallette, Dick Foran. Written by Charles Kenyon, from the play by Michael Arlen; directed by Alfred E. Green; for Warner.

Golden Arrow
GB 1949 82m bw

On a transcontinental train, three men have different daydreams about the same girl. Transparent portmanteau comedy which didn't click. Jean Pierre Aumont, Paula Valenska, Burgess Meredith, Richard Murdoch, Kathleen Harrison, Karel Stepanek, Edward Lexy. Written by Paul Darcy and Sid Colin; directed by Gordon Parry; for Anatole de Grunwald. (US title: *The Gay Adventure*.)

'His blade of gold, a legend in battle—her kiss of surrender, the prize of victory!'

The Golden Blade
US 1953 80m Technicolor
U-I (Richard Wilson)

With the help of a magic sword, Harun saves a princess and captures a rebel.
Standard cut-rate Arabian Nights adventure, very typical of its studio during the fifties.

w John Rich *d* Nathan Juran *ph* Maury Gertsman *m* Joseph Gershenson

Rock Hudson, Piper Laurie, George Macready, Gene Evans, Kathleen Hughes

Golden Boy*
US 1939 101m bw
Columbia (William Perlberg)

A poor boy is torn between two absorbing interests: prizefighting and the violin.
Personalized version of a socially conscious play; moderately effective with smooth production and good cast.

w Lewis Meltzer, Daniel Taradash, Sarah Y. Mason, Victor Heerman, *play* Clifford Odets *d Rouben Mamoulian ph* Nicholas Musuraca, Karl Freund *m* Victor Young *md* Morris Stoloff

Barbara Stanwyck, *William Holden*, Adolphe Menjou, Joseph Calleia, *Lee J. Cobb*, Sam Levene, Edward Brophy, Don Beddoe

'Strong entertainment with general audience appeal.'—*Variety*

'A slick, swift, exciting but insensitive movie.'—*Gordon Sager*

'Interesting, entertaining, dramatic, but scarcely first-rate.'—*Frank Nugent, New York Times*

AAN: Victor Young

The Golden Child
US 1986 93m Metrocolor
Paramount / Feldman-Meeker / Eddie Murphy

A social worker is assigned to look for a mystic child who will bring peace to the earth.
Astonishingly inept fantasy.

w Dennis Feldman *d* Michael Ritchie *ph* Donald E. Thorin *m* Michael Colimbier

Eddie Murphy, Charles Dance, Charlotte Lewis, Victor Wong

The Golden Coach
Italy / France 1953 100m Technicolor
Hoche / Panaria (Valentine Brosio, Giuseppe Bordognoi)
original title: *Le Carrosse d'Or*

In Spanish South America in the 18th century, the leading lady of a band of strolling players turns all heads including that of the viceroy, who scandalizes all by making her a present of his official golden coach.
The director seems to have been chiefly interested in the colour and the backgrounds: the story is a bore and the leading lady ill-chosen.

w Jean Renoir, Jack Kirkland, Renzo Avanzo, Giulio Macchi, *play* Prosper Merimée *d* Jean Renoir *ph Claude Renoir m* Vivaldi

Anna Magnani, Duncan Lamont, Paul Campbell, Ricardo Rioli, William Tubbs

Golden Dawn
US 1930 81m Technicolor

An English regiment holds the blacks at bay. An operetta outmoded even in 1930, stagily brought to the screen. Walter Woolf, Vivienne Segal, Noah Beery, Alice Gentle, Lupino Lane. Adapted by Walter Anthony; songs by Emmerich Kalman and Herbert Stothart; directed by Ray Enright; for Warners.
'Everybody seems to sing, even Noah Beery in blackface.'—*Variety*

'Now you know the way a gypsy loves!'

Golden Earrings*
US 1947 95m bw
Paramount (Harry Tugend)

A British Intelligence officer is helped by a gypsy to sneak a poison gas formula out of Nazi Germany.
One of the silliest stories of all time, despite the presence of Quentin Reynolds asserting that he believed it; also lacking in the humour which might have saved it, but produced with polish and interesting for the two stars at this stage in their careers.

w Abraham Polonsky, Frank Butler, Helen Deutsch, *novel* Yolanda Foldes *d Mitchell Leisen ph* Daniel L. Fapp *m* Victor Young

Ray Milland, Marlene Dietrich, Murvyn Vye, Bruce Lester, Dennis Hoey, Reinhold Schuntzel, Ivan Triesault

'A good deal of torso work goes on which I can't help feeling they're a bit old for.'—*Richard Winnington*

The Golden Fleecing
US 1940 68m bw

A timid insurance salesman becomes embroiled with gangsters. Modestly effective double-bill comedy. Lew Ayres, Lloyd Nolan, Virginia Grey, Leon Errol, Rita Johnson, Nat Pendleton, William Demarest, Marc Lawrence. Written by S. J. and Laura Perelman; directed by Leslie Fenton; for Edgar Selwyn/MGM.

Golden Girl*
US 1951 108m Technicolor
TCF (George Jessel)

The story of Lotta Crabtree, who after the Civil War determined to become a great musical star.
Harmless semi-western biopic with good tunes.

w Walter Bullock, Charles O'Neal, Gladys Lehman *d* Lloyd Bacon *ph* Charles G. Clarke *md* Lionel Newman *ch* Seymour Felix

Mitzi Gaynor, Dale Robertson, Dennis Day, James Barton, Una Merkel, Raymond Walburn, Gene Sheldon

AAN: song 'Never' (*m* Lionel Newman, *ly* Eliot Daniel)

Golden Gloves
US 1939 69m bw

A sports reporter cleans up a boxing racket. Competent second feature. Richard Denning, Jeanne Cagney, William Frawley, Robert Ryan. Written by Maxwell Shane and Lewis R. Foster; directed by Edward Dmytryk; for Paramount.

The Golden Hawk
US 1952 83m Technicolor

A pirate determines to avenge his mother's death at the hands of the governor of Cartagena. Clean-cut period romp for boys who don't demand realism. Sterling Hayden, Rhonda Fleming, John Sutton, Helena Carter, Paul Cavanagh. Written by Robert E. Kent, from the novel by Frank Yerby; directed by Sidney Salkow; for Columbia.

The Golden Head
US / Hungary 1964 115m Technirama 70
Cinerama / Hungarofilm (Alexander Paal)

Passengers on a Danube pleasure boat become involved in the theft of the golden head of St Laszlo.
Travelogue with a thin plot, somewhat slow moving but suitable for children.

w Stanley Boulder, Ivan Boldizsar *d* Richard Thorpe *ph* Istvan Hildebrand *m* Peter Fenyes

George Sanders, Buddy Hackett, Douglas Wilmer, Jess Conrad, Robert Coote

The Golden Horde
US 1951 76m Technicolor
U-I (Howard Christie)
aka: *The Golden Horde of Genghis Khan*

Crusaders meet Mongols in Samarkand, and Sir Guy wins a princess.
Rather priceless idiocies are perpetrated in this variation on the studio's favourite Arabian Nights theme, but somehow they fail to make one laugh, which should be the only possible response to such a farrago.

w Gerald Drayson Adams *d* George Sherman *ph* Russell Metty *m* Hans Salter

David Farrar, Ann Blyth, George Macready, Henry Brandon, Richard Egan, Marvin Miller

The Golden Madonna
GB 1949 88m bw
IFP / Pendennis (John Stafford)

Two young people search Italy for a religious painting stolen by thieves.
Stilted but eager to please, this romantic comedy-drama seemed a bit lacking in drive.

w Akos Tolnay *d* Ladislas Vajda *ph* Anchise Brizzi

Phyllis Calvert, Michael Rennie, Tullio Carminati, David Greene, Aldo Silvani

The Golden Mistress*
US 1954 80m Technicolor
UA / RK (Richard Kay, Harry Rybnick)

An American and his girl friend search the sea bed for the forbidden treasure of a Haitian tribe.
Curious independent production, an adventure in the style of silent serials; amateur in many ways, yet with a freshness of photography and location plus some powerful voodoo scenes.

wd Fred Judge *ph William C. Thompson* *m* Raoul Kraushaar

John Agar, Rosemarie Bowe, Abner Biberman

'Whoever owns them can rule the world!'
Golden Needles
US 1974 92m Movielab Panavision
AIP / Sequoia (Fred Weintraub, Paul Heller)

Various factions seek a Hong Kong statue showing seven miraculous acupuncture points.
Youth / sex / Kung Fu / James Bond action amalgam.

w S. Lee Pogostin, Sylvia Schneble *d* Robert Clouse *ph* Gilbert Hubbs *m* Lalo Schifrin

Joe Don Baker, Elizabeth Ashley, Jim Kelly, Burgess Meredith, Ann Sothern

Golden Rendezvous
US 1977 109m colour
Film Trust / Milton Okun (Andre Pieterse)

Murderous mercenaries take over a freighter, but reckon without the courageous first officer.
Blood-and-thunder hokum with many casualties but not much sense.

w Stanley Price, *novel* Alistair MacLean *d* Ashley Lazarus *ph* Ken Higgins *m* Jeff Wayne

Richard Harris, Ann Turkel, David Janssen, Burgess Meredith, John Vernon, Gordon Jackson, Keith Baxter, Dorothy Malone, John Carradine, Robert Flemyng, Leigh Lawson, Robert Beatty

The Golden Salamander
GB 1949 87m bw
GFD / Pinewood (Ronald Neame, Alexander Galperson)

An Englishman in Tunis defeats gun runners.
Boring and unconvincing action hokum.

w Lesley Storm, Victor Canning, Ronald Neame, *novel* Victor Canning *d* Ronald Neame *ph* Oswald Morris *m* William Alwyn

Trevor Howard, Anouk Aimée, Herbert Lom, Miles Malleson, Walter Rilla, Jacques Sernas, Wilfrid Hyde White, Peter Copley

The Golden Seal*
US 1983 94m Metrocolor
Samuel Goldwyn Jnr (Russell Thatcher)

On a bleak Aleutian island a boy stops hunters from killing a seal once thought mythical.
Rather chilling and thinly plotted moral fable for children, who may, however, be bored. The seals, the scenery and the music just about save it.

w John Groves, *novel* A River Ran Out of Eden by James Vance Marshall *d* Frank Zuniga *ph* Eric Saarinen *m* Dana Kaproff, John Barry

Steve Railsback, Michael Beck, Penelope Milford, Torquil Campbell

The Golden Voyage of Sinbad*
GB 1973 105m Eastmancolor
Columbia / Morningside (Charles H. Schneer)

Sinbad finds a strange map and crosses swords with a great magician.
Routine, rather uninspired fantasy enlivened by grotesque trick effects.

w Brian Clemens, Ray Harryhausen *d* Gordon Hessler *ph* Ted Moore *m* Miklos Rozsa *sp Ray Harryhausen* *pd* John Stoll

John Philip Law, Caroline Munro, Tom Baker, Douglas Wilmer, Grégoire Aslan

Goldfinger***
GB 1964 112m Technicolor
UA / Eon (Harry Saltzman, Albert R. Broccoli)

James Bond prevents an international gold smuggler from robbing Fort Knox.
Probably the liveliest and most amusing of the Bond spy spoofs, with a fairly taut plot between the numerous highlights. The big budget is well used.

w Richard Maibaum, Paul Dehn, novel Ian Fleming *d Guy Hamilton ph Ted Moore m John Barry pd Ken Adam titles Robert Brownjohn*

Sean Connery, Honor Blackman, Gert Frobe, Harold Sakata, Shirley Eaton, Bernard Lee, Lois Maxwell, Desmond Llewellyn

'A dazzling object lesson in the principle that nothing succeeds like excess.'—*Penelope Gilliatt*

'A diverting comic strip for grown-ups.'—*Judith Crist*

Goldie
US 1931 58m bw

A carnival girl causes a rift between two sailors.
Curious comedy-drama notable only for its stars. Spencer Tracy, Jean Harlow, Warren Hymer, Lina Basquette, Maria Alba. Written by Gene Towne, Paul Perez; directed by Ben Stoloff; for Fox.

The Goldwyn Follies**
US 1938 115m Technicolor
Samuel Goldwyn

A Hollywood producer seeks the average girl to test his scripts.
Goldwyn's failure to become Ziegfeld, chiefly due to a lack of humour in the script, still has a soupçon of effective Hollywood satire and some excellent numbers.

w Ben Hecht *d* George Marshall *ph* Gregg Toland *m* Alfred Newman *ch* George Balanchine *ad* Richard Day

Kenny Baker, Vera Zorina, *the Ritz Brothers, Adolphe Menjou*, Edgar Bergen and Charlie McCarthy, Helen Jepson, Phil Baker, Ella Logan, Bobby Clark, Jerome Cowan, Nydia Westman, Andrea Leeds

'An advance glimpse at next Sunday's amusement section from any metropolitan newspaper.'—*Variety*

'The bizarre in musical pretentiousness.'—*Commonweal*

'Many features to suit all tastes and not enough of them to suit anybody's.'—*Time*

AAN: Alfred Newman

The Golem***
Germany 1920 75m approx bw silent
UFA

In 16th-century Prague a Jewish Rabbi constructs a man of clay to defend his people against a pogrom.
There were several versions of this story (Germany 1913, sequel 1917; Czechoslovakia 1935 and 1951), but this is almost certainly the best, its splendid sets, performances and certain scenes all being clearly influential on later Hollywood films, especially *Frankenstein*.

w Paul Wegener, Henrik Galeen *d Paul Wegener, Carl Boese ph Karl Freund, Guido Seeber ad Hans Poelzig*

Paul Wegener, Albert Steinruck, Ernst Deutsch

The Golem*
Czechoslovakia 1936 95m bw

Rather disappointing remake with entirely French crew. Harry Baur, Roger Karl, Ferdinand Hart, Charles Dorat. Written by André Paul Antoine and Julien Duvivier; directed by Julien Duvivier; for AB. (GB title: *The Legend of Prague*.)

'Sequences are scattered; there's no build-up, and no human interest is created.'—*Variety*

The Golf Specialist**
US 1930 18m bw

A film version of *W. C. Fields* in his classic vaudeville golfing sketch (also reprised in *You're Telling Me*). Directed by Monte Brice; for RKO.

Golgotha*
France 1935 100m bw

The trial and passion of Jesus Christ. Impressive version made at a time when the portrayal of Christ was still virtually taboo. Harry Baur (Herod), Jean Gabin (Pilate), Robert le Vigan (Jesus), Charles Granval (Caiaphas), Edwige Feuillère (Claudia). Written and directed by Julien Duvivier; music by Jacques Ibert; for D'Agular. 'An accomplishment that should bring world-wide prestige to the French film industry.'—*Variety*

Gone to Earth
GB 1950 110m Technicolor
London Films / David O. Selznick
US title: *The Wild Heart*

In the 1890s, a wild Shropshire girl is desired by the local squire.
Unintentionally funny film version of an intractable novel.

w / p / d Michael Powell and Emeric Pressburger, *novel* Mary Webb
ph Christopher Challis *m* Brian Easdale
pd Hein Heckroth

Jennifer Jones, David Farrar, Cyril Cusack, Esmond Knight, Sybil Thorndike, Edward Chapman, George Cole, Hugh Griffith, Beatrice Varley

'It tries hard to be a powerful work of art, but it is intrinsically artificial and pretentious.'—*Richard Mallett, Punch*

† For the version shown in US, additional scenes were directed by Rouben Mamoulian.

Gone with the Wind****
US 1939 220m Technicolor
MGM / *David O. Selznick*

An egotistic Southern girl survives the Civil War but finally loses the only man she cares for.
The only film in history which could be profitably revived for forty years: 'still pure gold', said the *Daily Mirror* in 1975. Whole books have been written about it; its essential appeal is that of a romantic story with strong characters and an impeccable production. The widescreen version produced in the late sixties ruined its composition and colour, but it is to be hoped that the original negative still survives.

w Sidney Howard (and others), *novel Margaret Mitchell d Victor Fleming* (and George Cukor, Sam Wood) *ph Ernest Haller, Ray Rennahan m Max Steiner pd William Cameron Menzies ad Lyle Wheeler*

Clark Gable, Vivien Leigh, Olivia de Havilland, Leslie Howard, Thomas Mitchell, Barbara O'Neil, *Hattie McDaniel, Butterfly McQueen*, Victor Jory, Evelyn Keyes, Ann Rutherford, Laura Hope Crews, Harry Davenport, Jane Darwell, Ona Munson, Ward Bond

'A major event in the history of the industry but only a minor event in motion picture art. There are moments when the two categories meet on good terms, but the long stretches between are filled with mere spectacular efficiency.'—*Franz Hoellering, The Nation*

'Shakespeare's *The Taming of the Shrew* seems to have got mixed up with one of the novels of Ethel M. Dell.'—*James Agate*

'Perhaps the key plantation movie.'—*Time Out, 1980*

'Forget it, Louis, no Civil War picture ever made a nickel.'—*Irving Thalberg to Louis B. Mayer, 1936*

† The best account of the film's making is in Gavin Lambert's 1975 book, *GWTW*.
†† In the early seventies a stage musical version toured the world; music by Harold Rome.

AA: best picture; Sidney Howard; Victor Fleming; Ernest Haller, Ray Rennahan; Lyle Wheeler; Vivien Leigh; Hattie McDaniel; Hal C. Kern and James E. Newcom (editors)
AAN: Max Steiner; Clark Gable; Olivia de Havilland

The Good Companions**
GB 1932 113m bw
Gaumont / Welsh–Pearson (T. A. Welsh, George Pearson)

Three ill-assorted people take to the road and in various capacities join the Dinky Doos pierrot troupe.
Gallant, mini-budgeted version of Priestley's popular picaresque novel. A little faded now, it retains some of its vigour, and the performances please.

w W. P. Lipscomb, Angus Macphail, Ian Dalrymple *novel J. B. Priestley d* Victor Saville *ph* Bernard Knowles *songs* George Posford (*m*), Douglas Furber (*ly*) *md* Louis Levy

Edmund Gwenn, Mary Glynne, John Gielgud, *Jessie Matthews*, Percy Parsons, A. W. Baskomb, Dennis Hoey, Richard Dolman, Frank Pettingell, Finlay Currie, *Max Miller*, Jack Hawkins, George Zucco

The Good Companions*
GB 1956 104m Technicolor Cinemascope
ABP (Hamilton Inglis, J. Lee-Thompson)

Faint-hearted remake of the above, unwisely Cinemascoped and leaving no impression.

w T. J. Morrison *d* J. Lee-Thompson
ph Gilbert Taylor *m* Laurie Johnson

Eric Portman, Celia Johnson, John Fraser, Janette Scott, Hugh Griffith, Bobby Howes, Rachel Roberts, John Salew, Thora Hird

† A stage musical version (music by André Previn) had moderate success in London in 1974.

Good Dame
US 1934 77m bw

A penniless chorus girl falls for a cardsharp. Unsurprising pattern play for two miscast stars. Sylvia Sidney, Fredric March, Jack La Rue, Noel Francis, Russell Hopton. Written by William K. Lipman, Vincent Lawrence, Frank Partos and Sam Hellman; directed by Marion Gering; for Paramount. (GB title: *Good Girl*.)

Good Day for a Hanging
US 1959 85m Columbia Color

A young outlaw is arrested and seems destined to be lynched; the marshal tries to see fair play. Moody western in which the protected hero turns out to be very guilty after all. Fred MacMurray, Robert Vaughn, Maggie Hayes, Joan Blackman, James Drury. Written by Daniel B. Ullman and Maurice Zimm; directed by Nathan Juran; for Columbia.

The Good Die Young*
GB 1954 98m bw
Remus (Jack Clayton)

Four crooks, all with private problems, set out to rob a mail van.
Glum all-star melodrama which set a pattern for such things; worth waiting for is the climactic chase through underground stations.

w Vernon Harris, Lewis Gilbert *d* Lewis Gilbert *ph* Jack Asher *m* Georges Auric

Laurence Harvey, Margaret Leighton, Gloria Grahame, Richard Basehart, Joan Collins, John Ireland, René Ray, Stanley Baker, Robert Morley

'To the memory of Irving Grant Thalberg we dedicate this picture—his last great achievement!'

The Good Earth***
US 1937 138m bw
MGM (*Irving Thalberg*)

A Chinese peasant grows rich but loses his beloved wife.
A massive, well-meaning and fondly remembered production which is nevertheless artificial, unconvincing and pretty undramatic in the second half. The star performances impress to begin with, then wear thin, but the final locust attack is as well done as it originally seemed. Historically valuable as a Hollywood prestige production of the thirties.

w Talbot Jennings, Tess Schlesinger, Claudine West, *play* Owen and Donald Davis, *novel* Pearl S. Buck *d Sidney Franklin ph Karl Freund m* Herbert Stothart *montage* Slavko Vorkapitch *ad* Cedric Gibbons

Paul Muni, Luise Rainer, Walter Connolly, Tilly Losch, Jessie Ralph, Charley Grapewin, Keye Luke, Harold Huber

GONE WITH THE WIND. Half a century on, David O. Selznick's epic still commands attention. Vivien Leigh seems to have offended Hattie McDaniel.

'A true technical achievement with names enough to send it across. But it's not going to be easy to get the three-million-dollar investment back. And if it does come back it's going to take a long time.'—*Variety*

'Performances, direction and photography are of a uniform excellence, and have been fused perfectly into a dignified, beautiful, but soberly dramatic production.'—*New York Times*

'One of the superb visual adventures of the period.'—*John Baxter, 1968*

'Prestigious boredom, and it goes on for a very long time.'—*New Yorker, 1977*

AA: Karl Freund; Luise Rainer
AAN: best picture; Sidney Franklin

The Good Fairy*
US 1935 90m bw
Universal (Henry Henigson)

A beautiful but naïve cinema usherette ensnares three rich men.
Unusual, rather lumpy romantic comedy using top talent.

w Preston Sturges, play Ferenc Molnar *d William Wyler* *ph* Norbert Brodine

Margaret Sullavan, Herbert Marshall, Frank Morgan, Reginald Owen, Alan Hale, Beulah Bondi, Cesar Romero, Eric Blore, Al Bridge

'It's rather slapsticking a master but it's for the box office. Will not please those who cherish memories of the play but it will please a more important audience.'—*Variety*

† Remade as *Because of Him* (qv).

The Good Fellows
US 1943 70m bw

A family man spends too much time with his fraternal order. Mild, pleasant family comedy. Cecil Kellaway, Helen Walker, James Brown, Mabel Paige. Written by Hugh Wedlock Jnr and Howard Snyder, from a play by George S. Kaufman and Herman Mankiewicz; directed by Jo Graham; for Paramount.

Good Girls Go To Paris*
US 1939 75m bw
Columbia (William Perlberg)

After several zany adventures, a Greek professor marries a gold digger.
Amusingly crazy comedy, one of the last of its type.

w Gladys Lehman, Ken Englund *d* Alexander Hall *ph* Henry Freulich *md* Morris Stoloff

Melvyn Douglas, Joan Blondell, Walter Connolly, Alan Curtis, Joan Perry, Isabel Jeans, Alexander D'Arcy, Clarence Kolb

'It can't stand analysis much, but it pleases while you're there.'—*Variety*

The Good Guys and the Bad Guys*
US 1969 90m Technicolor Panavision
Warner (Robert M. Goldstein)

An ageing sheriff and a train robber have one last showdown.
Good-humoured, black-flavoured western set in the early days of automobiles.

w Ronald M. Cohen, Dennis Shyrack *d* Burt Kennedy *ph* Harry Stradling Jnr *m* William Lava

Robert Mitchum, George Kennedy, David Carradine, Tina Louise, Douglas Fowley, Martin Balsam, Lois Nettleton, John Davis Chandler, John Carradine, Marie Windsor

Good Morning Babylon*
Italy / France 1987 115m colour
Filmtre / MK2 / Pressman / RAI / Films A2

Italian film-makers set out for Hollywood to restore the family fortunes.
Likeable but sometimes inept fantasia on Hollywood's early silent days.

w,d Paolo and Vittorio Taviani *ph* Giuseppe Lanci *m* Nicola Piovani *ad* Gianni Shara

Vincent Spano, Joaquim de Almeida, Greta Scacchi, Desiree Becker, Charles Dance (as D. W. Griffith)

'They have made a molehill of a picture out of a mountain of an idea.'—*Daily Variety*

Good Morning Boys**
GB 1937 79m bw
GFD / Gainsborough (Edward Black)

A schoolmaster takes his troublesome pupils to Paris and becomes involved with an art theft.
Sprightly vehicle for the star's seedy schoolmaster persona: it established him as a major draw in British films.

w Marriott Edgar, Val Guest, Anthony Kimmins d Marcel Varnel *ph* Arthur Crabtree

Will Hay, Graham Moffatt, Lilli Palmer, Mark Daly, Peter Gawthorne, Martita Hunt, Charles Hawtrey, Will Hay Jnr

† Remade with Ronald Shiner as *Top of the Form.*

Good Morning, Judge
US 1943 66m bw

A music publisher falls for the lady lawyer suing him for plagiarism. Light, predictable comedy for double billing. Dennis O'Keefe, Louise Allbritton, J. Carrol Naish, Mary Beth Hughes, Louise Beavers, Samuel S. Hinds. Written by Maurice Geraghty and Warren Wilson; directed by Jean Yarbrough; for Paul Malvern / Universal.

Good Morning Miss Dove
US 1955 107m Eastmancolor Cinemascope
TCF (Samuel G. Engel)

While recovering from an operation, a small-town schoolmistress looks back on her career. A fairly spirited weepie with a happy ending and a strong sense of cynicism behind the scenes.

w Eleanore Griffin, *novel* Frances Gray Patton *d* Henry Koster *ph* Leon Shamroy *m* Leigh Harline

Jennifer Jones, Robert Stack, Robert Douglas, Kipp Hamilton, Peggy Knudsen, Marshall Thompson, Chuck Connors, Mary Wickes

'Mr Chips has changed sex and habitat while preserving intact his ability to provoke epidemics of sentimentality.'—*MFB*

Good Morning, Vietnam*
US 1987 120m DeLuxe
Touchstone (Mark Johnson, Larry Brezner)

Exploits of an Armed Forces Radio disc-jockey in Saigon at the height of the Vietnam War. Largely a vehicle for the frenetic irreverence of Robin Williams, enjoyed by many for the 60s hits used copiously on the soundtrack.

w Mitch Markowitz *d* Barry Levinson *ph* Peter Sova *m* Alex North *pd* Roy Walker

Robin Williams, Forest Whitaker, Tung Thanh Tran, Chintara Sukapatana, Bruno Kirby

Good Neighbour Sam
US 1964 130m Eastmancolor
Columbia / David Swift

A prissy suburban advertising man becomes innocently involved in a pretence to be the husband of the divorcee next door.
A promising comic idea is here ruined by lengthiness, lack of funny lines, and no apparent idea of how to film a farce. The actors are driven to repeating every trick a dozen times.

w James Fritzell, Everett Greenbaum, David Swift, *novel* Jack Finney *d* David Swift *ph* Burnett Guffey *m* Frank de Vol

Jack Lemmon, Romy Schneider, Dorothy Provine, Senta Berger, Edward G. Robinson, Mike Connors, Edward Andrews, Louis Nye

Good News
US 1930 85m approx bw
MGM

Fraternity tensions are sorted out in time for the big football game.
Spirited early talkie musical.

w Frances Marion, Joe Farnham *d* Nick Grinde, Edgar McGregor *ph* Percy Hilburn *songs* De Sylva, Brown and Henderson

Bessie Love, Stanley Smith, Gus Shy, Mary Lawlor, Lola Lane, Dorothy McNulty, Cliff Edwards
Songs: 'He's a Ladies' Man'; 'The Best Things in Life Are Free'; 'Varsity Drag'; 'Good News'; 'Tait Song'; 'Students Are We'; 'If You're Not Kissing Me'; 'Football'; 'I Feel Pessimistic'; 'I'd Like to Make You Happy'

'Not the smash hit the show was. Too fast, too peppy, too entertaining to flop, though.'—*Variety*

Good News*
US 1947 83m Technicolor
MGM (Arthur Freed)

Bright, good-humoured remake of the above.

w Betty Comden, Adolph Green *d* Charles Walters *ph* Charles Schoenbaum *md* Lennie Hayton

June Allyson, Peter Lawford, Patricia Marshall, *Joan McCracken*, Mel Tormé

AAN: song 'Pass that Peace Pipe' (*m / ly* Ralph Blane, Hugh Martin, Roger Edens)

The Good Old Days
GB 1939 79m bw
Warner (Jerome Jackson)

A noble child is kidnapped by a chimney sweep and saved by strolling players.
Curious Victorian vehicle for a snappy 20th-century star.

w Austin Melford, John Dighton *d* Roy William Neill *ph* Basil Emmott

Max Miller, Hal Walters, Kathleen Gibson, H. F. Maltby, Martita Hunt, Allan Jeayes, Roy Emerton

Good Old Soak
US 1937 67m bw

A small-town drunk beats a teetotal banker guilty of a shady transaction. Amiable star comedy. *Wallace Beery*, Una Merkel, Eric Linden, Judith Barrett, Betty Furness, Janet Beecher, Robert McWade, Margaret Hamilton. Written by A. E. Thomas from the play The Old Soak by Don Marquis; directed by J. Walter Ruben; for MGM. 'A melodramatic sentimentality that will probably do okay.'—*Variety*

Good Sam
US 1948 114m bw
Rainbow (Leo McCarey)

A small-town business man is so charitable that he finds himself bankrupt.
Poor, disjointed, overlong and obvious comedy in the Capra style.

w Ken Englund *d* Leo McCarey *ph* George Barnes *m* Robert Emmett Dolan

Gary Cooper, Ann Sheridan, Ray Collins, Edmund Lowe, Joan Lorring, Ruth Roman, Clinton Sundberg

'A bit too long, but in its incidentals often very enjoyable.'—*Richard Mallett, Punch*

The Good, the Bad and the Ugly*
Italy 1966 180m Techniscope
PEA (Alberto Grimaldi)
original title: *Il Buono, il Bruto, il Cattivo*

During the American Civil War, three men seek hidden loot.
Intermittently lively, very violent, and interminably drawn out western with a number of rather hilarious stylistic touches.

w Age Scarpelli, Luciano Vincenzoni, Sergio Leone *d* Sergio Leone *ph* Tonino delli Colli *m* Ennio Morricone

Clint Eastwood, Eli Wallach, Lee Van Cleef

Good Time Girl
GB 1948 93m bw

A girl escapes from a remand home and starts on the road to ruin.
Risible vehicle for a rising star; at the time it set the box offices clicking. Jean Kent, Dennis Price, Flora Robson, Griffith Jones, Herbert Lom, Bonar Colleano. Written by Muriel and Sidney Box and Ted Willis, from the novel *Night Darkens the Street* by Arthur La Bern; directed by David MacDonald; for Triton / Rank.

Good Times
US 1967 92m De Luxe

A singing duo in Hollywood imagines starring in films of various types. Mildly agreeable light fantasy. Sonny and Cher, George Sanders, Norman Alden, Larry Duran. Written by Tony Barrett; directed by William Friedkin; for Motion Picture International.

The Good Wife
Australia 1987 92m Eastmancolor

In 1939, a wife is bored with her backwater life, and takes a lover. Heavy-going domestic drama with an interesting setting. Rachel Ward, Bryan Brown, Sam Neill, Steven Vidler. Written by Peter Kenna; directed by Ken Cameron; for Laughing Kookaburra.

Goodbye Again
US 1933 66m bw

An author's secretary is jealous of his rekindled interest in an old flame. Unassuming star comedy which entertained at the time. Warren William, Joan Blondell, Genevieve Tobin, Hugh Herbert, Helen Chandler, Ruth Donnelly. Written by Ben Markson, from the play by George Haight and Allan Scott; directed by Michael Curtiz; for Warner. (NB: *Honeymoon for Three* in 1941 [qv] was a leaden remake.)

Goodbye Again*
US 1961 120m bw
UA / Mercury / Argus / Anatole Litvak

A woman of forty swaps her rich lover for a young law student.
Melancholy romantic drama, well produced and staged on Paris locations.

w Samuel Taylor, *novel* Aimez-vous Brahms by Françoise Sagan *d* Anatole Litvak *ph Armand Thirard* *m* Georges Auric

Ingrid Bergman, Anthony Perkins, Yves Montand, Jessie Royce Landis, Jackie Lane

'A grey-toned Sagan novella, spread wide and lush over two hours of screen time.'—*MFB*

'The kind of "woman's picture" that gives women a bad name.'—*Judith Crist, 1973*

Goodbye Charlie*
US 1964 116m De Luxe Cinemascope
TCF / Venice (David Weisbart)

A philandering gangster, shot dead by an irate husband, is reincarnated in his friend's house as a dishy blonde.

Overlong but amusing Broadway comedy for wisecrackers, uninventively adapted.

w Harry Kurnitz, *play* George Axelrod *d* Vincente Minnelli *ph* Milton Krasner *m* André Previn

Debbie Reynolds, Pat Boone, Walter Matthau, Tony Curtis

'Every father's daughter is a virgin!'

Goodbye Columbus**

US 1969 105m Technicolor
Paramount / Willow Tree (Stanley Jaffe)

A young Jewish librarian has an affair with the wilful daughter of a *nouveau riche* family.
An amusing and well-observed delineation of two kinds of Jewish life in New York; the story, despite its frank talk of penises and diaphragms, leaves much to be desired, and the style is post-*Graduate*.

w Arnold Schulman, *novel* Philip Roth *d Larry Peerce* *ph* Gerald Hirschfeld *m* Charles Fox

Richard Benjamin, Ali MacGraw, Jack Klugman, Nan Martin, Michael Meyers, Lori Shelle

AAN: Arnold Schulman

Goodbye Gemini

GB 1970 89m colour
Cinerama / Josef Shaftel (Peter Snell)

A 20-year-old brother and sister share a world of petulant fantasy which leads to murder.
Abysmally over-the-top melodrama with a swinging London backdrop. Its immaculate appearance only makes matters worse.

w Edmund Ward, *novel* Ask Agamemnon by Jenni Hall *d* Alan Gibson *ph* Geoffrey Unsworth *m* Christopher Gunning *pd* Wilfrid Shingleton

Judy Geeson, Martin Potter, Michael Redgrave, Alexis Kanner, Mike Pratt, Freddie Jones, Peter Jeffrey

'Every man she ever loved thought a permanent relationship was a three-day weekend!'

The Goodbye Girl*

US 1977 110m Metrocolor
Warner / Rastar (Ray Stark)

A misunderstanding about the lease of an apartment results in a girl dancer agreeing to share it with a would-be actor.
A very moderate script assisted by excellent acting and the usual array of Neil Simon one-liners. Nothing at all new, but enjoyable.

w Neil Simon *d* Herbert Ross *ph* David M. Walsh *m* Dave Grusin

Richard Dreyfuss, Marsha Mason, Quinn Cummings, Paul Benedict, Barbara Rhoades

AA: Richard Dreyfuss
AAN: best picture; Neil Simon; Marsha Mason; Quinn Cummings

Goodbye Mr Chips***

GB 1939 114m bw
MGM (Victor Saville)

The life of a shy schoolmaster from his first job to his death.
Sentimental romance in MGM's best style, a long-standing favourite for its performances and humour; but the production seems slightly unsatisfactory these days.

w R. C. Sherriff, Claudine West, Eric Maschwitz, *novel* James Hilton *d Sam Wood* *ph* Frederick A. Young *m* Richard Addinsell

Robert Donat, Greer Garson, Paul Henreid, Lyn Harding, Austin Trevor, Terry Kilburn, John Mills, Milton Rosmer, Judith Furse

'Charming, quaintly sophisticated . . . more for the big situations than the smaller towns.'—*Variety*

'The whole picture has an assurance, bears a glow of popularity like the face of a successful candidate on election day. And it is wrong to despise popularity in the cinema.'—*Graham Greene*

'The picture has no difficulty in using two hours to retell a story that was scarcely above short story length. *Mr Chips* is worth its time.'—*New York Times*

'The novel became an American best seller when that old sentimentalist Alexander Woollcott touted it on the radio . . . the movie clogs the nose more than necessary.'—*Pauline Kael, 70s*

AA: Robert Donat
AAN: best picture; script; Sam Wood; Greer Garson

'He is a shy schoolmaster. She is a music hall star. They marry and immediately have 283 children—all boys!'

Goodbye Mr Chips*

GB 1969 147m Metrocolor Panavision 70
MGM / APJAC (Arthur P. Jacobs)

Elaborate musical remake of the above. Slow and slushy, with no improvement visible whatever; but a few of the trimmings please.

w Terence Rattigan *d* Herbert Ross *ph* Oswald Morris *m* Leslie Bricusse *pd* Ken Adam *ad* John Williams

Peter O'Toole, Petula Clark, Michael Bryant, Michael Redgrave, George Baker, Jack Hedley, Sian Phillips, Alison Leggatt

'The sum total is considerably less than the parts.'—*Variety*

'An overblown version with songs where they are not needed (and Leslie Bricusse's songs are never needed).'—*Pauline Kael, New Yorker*

† Originally sought for the title role, in order of preference, were Richard Burton and Rex Harrison; for the female lead, Samantha Eggar and Lee Remick.

AAN: Leslie Bricusse; John Williams; Peter O'Toole

Goodbye My Fancy

US 1951 107m bw
Warner (Henry Blanke)

A congresswoman returns to her old college for an honorary degree, and falls in love.
Tolerable romantic flim-flam.

w Ivan Goff, Ben Roberts, *play* Fay Kanin *d* Vincent Sherman *ph* Ted McCord *m* Daniele Amfitheatrof

Joan Crawford, Robert Young, Frank Lovejoy, Eve Arden, Janice Rule

Goodbye My Lady*

US 1956 95m bw
Batjac

A Mississippi swamp boy finds a valuable dog but eventually returns it to its owner.
Reliable, slightly unusual family film.

w Sid Fleischman, *novel* James Street *d* William Wellman *ph* William H. Clothier, Archie Stout *m* Laurindo Almeida, George Field

Brandon de Wilde, Walter Brennan, Phil Harris, Sidney Poitier, William Hopper, Louise Beavers

The Goodbye People

US 1984 104m De Luxe

Middle-aged eccentrics meet on a beach.
Saroyanesque talk piece which never quite comes off, and will probably be seen only at festivals. Martin Balsam, Judd Hirsch, Pamela Reed, Ron Silver, Michael Tucker, Gene Saks. Written and directed by Herb Gardner, from his stage play; for Coney Island Productions.

Goodbye Pork Pie*

New Zealand 1980 105m Eastmancolor
NZ Film Commission / NZ United Corporation / Nigel Hutchinson, Geoff Murphy

Three young people go on an illegal road spree and are arrested one by one.
Familiar high jinks with a moral conclusion. Fun up to a point, and good to look at.

w Geoff Murphy, Ian Mune *d* Geoff Murphy *ph* Alun Bollinger *m* John Charles

Tony Barry, Kelly Johnson, Claire Oberman

'Displays encouraging physical flair in its cross-country sweep of action.'—*Tim Pulleine, MFB*

Goodnight Vienna

GB 1932 76m bw
British and Dominions (Herbert Wilcox)
US title: *Magic Night*

In 1913 Vienna, a general's son falls for a shopgirl.
Already dated when it was made, this thin musical romance nevertheless made a star of Anna Neagle and re-established Jack Buchanan on the screen.

w Holt Marvel, George Posford, from their radio play *d* Herbert Wilcox *ph* F. A. Young

Jack Buchanan, Anna Neagle, Gina Malo, Clive Currie, William Kendall

The Goonies

US 1985 111m Technicolor Panavision
Warner / Steven Spielberg

Kids discover a pirate map and set out on a fantasy treasure hunt.
The bottomless pit of the Spielberg genre, a silly tale which takes forever to get going and

is acted by children who have not studied elocution. The trick effects when they come are OK, but it's a long annoying haul to that point.

w Chris Columbus *story* Steven Spielberg *d* Richard Donner *ph* Nick McLean *m* Dave Grusin *pd* J. Michael Riva *ed* Michael Kahn

Sean Astin, Josh Brolin, Jeff Cohen, Corey Feldman, Kerri Green, Martha Plimpton, Ke Huy Kwan

The Goose and the Gander
US 1935 65m bw

A divorcee can't leave her ex-husband's life alone. Tolerable farcical goings-on which just fail to come to the boil. Kay Francis, George Brent, Genevieve Tobin, John Eldredge, Claire Dodd. Written by George Kenyon; directed by Alfred E. Green; for Warners.
'Well-played little farce with too much story for its own good.'—*Variety*

The Goose Steps Out*
GB 1942 79m bw
Ealing (S. C. Balcon)

To steal a secret weapon, an incompetent teacher is sent into Germany in place of his Nazi double.
Quite amusing star vehicle, not up to his best standards.

w Angus Macphail, John Dighton *d* Will Hay, Basil Dearden *ph* Ernest Palmer *m* Bretton Byrd

Will Hay, Charles Hawtrey, Frank Pettingell, Julien Mitchell, Peter Croft, Jeremy Hawk, Peter Ustinov, Raymond Lovell, Barry Morse

The Goose Woman
US 1925 90m approx bw silent
Universal

A young actress falls for the son of an embittered old one.
Interesting character melodrama of which prints have survived.

w Melville Brown, *story* Rex Beach *d* Clarence Brown *ph* Milton Moore

Louise Dresser, Jack Pickford, Constance Bennett, James Barrows

Gordon of Ghost City
US 1933 bw serial: 12 eps

A cowboy hunts down cattle rustlers. Simple-minded serial with a stalwart hero. Buck Jones, Madge Bellamy, Walter Miller, Hugh Enfield, William Desmond. Directed by Ray Taylor; for Universal.

Gordon's War
US 1973 90m TVC color
TCF / Palomar (Robert L. Schaffel)

A black Vietnam veteran returns to Harlem and avenges the death of his wife.
Violent vigilante melodrama with vivid locations.

w Howard Friedlander, Ed Spielman *d* Ossie Davis *ph* Victor J. Kemper *m* Andy Bodale, Al Ellis

Paul Winfield, Carl Lee, David Downing

'An unbeatable cast in an unequalled drama! Metro's successor to The Great Ziegfeld!'

The Gorgeous Hussy*
US 1936 105m bw
MGM (Joseph L. Mankiewicz)

The love life of Peggy O'Neal, protégée of President Andrew Jackson.
Bowdlerized all-star historical drama; the production values are better than the script.

w Ainsworth Morgan, Stephen Morehouse Avery, *novel* Samuel Hopkins Adams *d Clarence Brown ph* George Folsey *m* Herbert Stothart

Joan Crawford, Lionel Barrymore, Franchot Tone, Melvyn Douglas, Robert Taylor, James Stewart, Alison Skipworth, Louis Calhern, Beulah Bondi, Melville Cooper, Sidney Toler, Gene Lockhart

† A Foreword read: 'This story of Peggy Eaton and her times is not presented as a precise account of either, rather as fiction founded upon historical fact.'

AAN: George Folsey; Beulah Bondi

'This is the big one! Two years in the making!'

Gorgo
GB 1960 78m Technicolor
King Brothers (Wilfrid Eades)

A prehistoric monster is caught in Irish waters and brought to London, but rescued by its mother.
Amiable monster hokum with a happy ending but not much technical resource.

w John Loring, Daniel Hyatt *d* Eugene Lourié *ph* Frederick A. Young *m* Angelo Lavagnino *sp* Tom Howard

Bill Travers, William Sylvester, Vincent Winter, Christopher Rhodes, Joseph O'Conor, Bruce Seton, Martin Benson

The Gorgon*
GB 1964 83m Technicolor
Hammer (Anthony Nelson Keys)

A castle ruin near a German village is infested by Megaera, the gorgon of ancient myth, whose gaze turns people to stone and who can take over the form of an unknowing villager.
Writhing snakes in the hair-do being too great a challenge to the make-up man, the monster is barely glimpsed and the film becomes a who-is-it, all quite suspenseful despite the central idea being too silly for words.

w John Gilling *d* Terence Fisher *ph* Michael Reed *m* James Bernard

Peter Cushing, Christopher Lee, Barbara Shelley, Richard Pasco, Patrick Troughton

The Gorilla*
US 1939 66m bw
TCF

A murderer blames an escaped gorilla for his crimes.
Spooky house mystery comedy revamped as a Ritz Brothers vehicle; not much suspense, but it all looks good and the cast is highly satisfactory.

w Rian James, Sid Silvers, *play* Ralph Spence *d Allan Dwan ph Edward Cronjager md* David Buttolph

The Ritz Brothers, Bela Lugosi, Lionel Atwill, Patsy Kelly, Joseph Calleia, Anita Louise, Edward Norris, Wally Vernon

'A good programmer that will get by for normal biz where the Ritzes can attract.'—*Variety*

† There were two previous versions, in 1927 with Charlie Murray and 1931 with Joe Frisco.

'Get out of the way—before it's too late!'

Gorilla at Large
US 1954 93m Technicolor 3-D
TCF / Panoramic (Robert L. Jacks)

A circus gorilla is used as a cover for murder. Silly thriller with the gorilla as unconvincing as the story.

w Leonard Praskins, Barney Slater *d* Harmon Jones *ph* Lloyd Ahernc *m* Lionel Newman

Anne Bancroft, Lee J. Cobb, Cameron Mitchell, Lee Marvin, Raymond Burr, Charlotte Austin, Peter Whitney, Warren Stevens

The Gorilla Man
US 1942 63m bw

A wounded commando discovers that his hospital is run by Nazis, who then try to prove him insane so that he won't be believed. There must have been less laborious ways, one assumes, but at least this farrago is good for a few unintentional laughs. John Loder, Ruth Ford, Richard Fraser, Paul Cavanagh, John Abbott. Written by Anthony Coldeway; directed by D. Ross Lederman; for Warner.

Gorillas in the Mist**
US 1988 129m Technicolor
Guber / Peters (Arnold Glimcher)

Story of anthropologist Diane Fossey and her fight to preserve the mountain gorillas of Central Africa.
Although the character may have been somewhat romanticized, Weaver's intense, angry performance won praise; and the scenes with the gorillas (some quite brilliantly faked) were universally acclaimed.

w Anna Hamilton Phelan *d* Michael Apted *ph* John Seale *m* Maurice Jarre *pd* John Graysmark *sp makeup eff* Rick Baker

Sigourney Weaver, Bryan Brown, Julie Harris, John Omirah Miluwi, Iain Cuthbertson

Gorky Park*
US 1983 128m Technicolor
Orion / Eagle (Gene Kirkwood, Howard W. Koch Jnr)

The Moscow police link murders with a sable-smuggling operation.
Bleak thriller which doggedly makes its way through a conventional plot but fails to convey the book's detail of life in Moscow today. (The film was shot in Helsinki.)

w Dennis Potter, *novel* Martin Cruz Smith *d* Michael Apted *ph* Ralf D. Bode *m* James Horner *pd* Paul Sylbert

Lee Marvin, William Hurt, Brian Dennehy, Ian Bannen, Joanna Pacula, Michael Elphick, Richard Griffiths, Alexander Knox

The Gospel According to St Matthew*
Italy / France 1964 142m bw
Arco / Lux (Alfredo Bini)
original title: *Il Vangelo Secondo Matteo*

The life of Christ seen almost as a ciné-vérité documentary: the tone is realist but not notably iconoclastic.

wd Pier Paolo Pasolini *ph* Tonino delli Colli *m* Bach, Mozart, Prokofiev *md* Luis Enrique Bacalov

Enrique Irazoqui, Susanna Pasolini, Mario Socrate

AAN: Luis Enrique Bacalov

Gothic
GB 1986 90m Eastmancolor
Virgin Visions (Penny Corke)

Byron, the Shelleys and Dr Polidori spend a weekend thinking up ghost stories.
Somewhat unhinged version of a famous occurrence in 1816, full of nauseous detail typical of its director.
w Stephen Volk *d* Ken Russell *ph* Mike Southon *m* Thomas Dolby *pd* Christopher Hobbs
Gabriel Byrne, Julian Sands, Natasha Richardson, Miriam Cyr, Timothy Spall

'The thinking man's *Nightmare on Elm Street.*'—*Daily Variety*

Goupi Mains Rouges*
France 1943 95m bw
Minerva
US title: *It Happened at the Inn*

A French village is largely populated by members of the same family, and one of them murders another.
An odd little black comedy which strengthened its director's reputation.
w Pierre Véry, Jacques Becker, *novel* Pierre Véry *d* Jacques Becker *ph* Pierre Montazel, Jean Bourgoin *m* Jean Alfaro

Fernand Ledoux, Georges Rollin, Blanchette Brunoy, Robert Le Vigan

Government Agents vs The Phantom Legion
US 1951 bw serial: 12 eps

A G-man goes undercover as a truck driver in order to expose hijackers. Routine serial thick-ear showing a touch of desperation in the title department. Walter Reed, Mary Ellen Kay, Dick Curtis, John Pickard, Fred Coby. Directed by Fred C. Brannon; for Republic.

Government Girl
US 1943 94m bw

War Department secretaries find their love lives confused in wartime Washington, where rooms have to be shared. Thin variation on a theme curiously dear to Hollywood at the time. Olivia de Havilland, Sonny Tufts, Anne Shirley, James Dunn, Paul Stewart, Agnes Moorehead, Harry Davenport, Una O'Connor, Sig Rumann, Jane Darwell. Written and directed by Dudley Nichols; from an adaptation by Budd Schulberg of a story by Adela Rogers St John; for RKO.

Grace Quigley
US 1984 95m colour
Cannon / Northbrook (Christopher Pearce)
aka: *The Ultimate Solution of Grace Quigley*

An aged widow blackmails a hit man into performing his services for all her elderly and miserable friends.
Yukky black comedy which ill befits its star and is an embarrassment from start to finish.
w A. Martin Zweiback *d* Anthony Harvey *ph* Larry Pizer *m* John Addison

Katharine Hepburn, Nick Nolte, Elizabeth Wilson, Walter Abel, Kit Le Fever, Chip Zuen

† The *Grace Quigley* version has a contrived happy ending. In the original, Grace walks into the sea and the hit man is drowned trying to save her.

The Gracie Allen Murder Case*
US 1939 74m bw

Gracie Allen helps Philo Vance solve the murder of an escaping convict. At the time of Gracie Allen's radio eminence, this was a cute comedy idea. Gracie Allen, Warren William, Ellen Drew, Kent Taylor, Jed Prouty, Jerome Cowan, Donald McBride, H. B. Warner, William Demarest. Written by Nat Perrin from a novel by S. S. Van Dine; directed by Alfred E. Green; for George K. Arthur / Paramount. 'Smacko for general audiences . . . one of the top comedies of the season.'—*Variety*

'This is Benjamin . . . he's a little worried about his future!'

The Graduate***
US 1967 105m Technicolor Panavision
UA / Embassy (Lawrence Turman)

A rich Californian ex-student is led into an affair with the wife of his father's friend, then falls in love with her daughter.
Richly reflecting the anything-goes mood of the late sixties, this lushly-filmed sex comedy opened a few new doors, looked ravishing, was well acted and had a popular music score, so that few people noticed that only the first half was any good.
w Calder Willingham, Buck Henry, *novel Charles Webb d Mike Nichols ph Robert Surtees songs Paul Simon singers Simon and Garfunkel* *m* Dave Grusin *pd Richard Sylbert*

Dustin Hoffman, Anne Bancroft, Katharine Ross, Murray Hamilton, William Daniels, Elizabeth Wilson

BENJAMIN: 'Mrs Robinson, if you don't mind my saying so, this conversation is getting a little strange.'

'Seeing *The Graduate* is a bit like having one's most brilliant friend to dinner, watching him become more witty and animated with every moment, and then becoming aware that what one may really be witnessing is the onset of a nervous breakdown.'—*Renata Adler*

'Yes, there are weaknesses . . . But in cinematic skill, in intent, in sheer connection with us, *The Graduate* is a milestone in American film history.'—*Stanley Kauffmann*

AA: Mike Nichols
AAN: best picture; script; Robert Surtees; Dustin Hoffman; Anne Bancroft; Katharine Ross

Grand Canary
US 1934 76m bw

In the Canary Islands, a missionary girl tries to reform a derelict doctor, who finds true love elsewhere. Curiously slack adaptation; one feels that something grandly philosophical was attempted and failed. Warner Baxter, H. B. Warner, Madge Evans, Marjorie Rambeau, Juliette Compton, Zita Johann. Written by Ernest Pascal from the novel by A. J. Cronin; directed by Irving Cummings; for Jesse Lasky / Fox. 'Essentially dull and slow . . . nothing very much happens.'—*Variety*

Grand Central Murder
US 1942 72m bw
MGM (B. F. Zeidman)

A murder is solved in New York's giant railway station.
Very moderate time-filler with a rather lethargic script.
w Peter Ruric, *novel* Sue McVeigh *d* S. Sylvan Simon *ph* George F. Folsey *m* David Snell

Van Heflin, Cecilia Parker, Sam Levene, Connie Gilchrist, Millard Mitchell, Tom Conway, Virginia Grey, Samuel S. Hinds

The Grand Duchess and the Waiter*
US 1926 90m approx bw silent

A millionaire becomes a servant in order to win the heart of a titled lady. Sophisticated silent comedy with a good reputation. Adolphe Menjou, Florence Vidor, Lawrence Grant, Andre Beranger. Written by Pierre Collings and John Lynch from a play by Alfred Savoir; directed by Malcolm St Clair; photographed by Lee Garmes; for Famous Players.

Grand Exit
US 1935 68m bw

An insurance company sleuth traps an arson fiend. Lively co-feature mystery. Edmund Lowe, Ann Sothern, Onslow Stevens, Robert Middlemass, Selmer Jackson, Edward Van Sloan. Written by Gene Towne, Graham Baker, Bruce Manning, Lionel Houser; directed by Erle C. Kenton; for Columbia. 'Novel story, crisp dialogue, distinguished direction.'—*Variety*

'The greatest cast in stage or screen history!'

Grand Hotel**
US 1932 115m bw
MGM (Irving Thalberg)

The lives of various hotel guests become intertwined and reach their climaxes.

It's a little faded now, but much of the magic still works in this first of the portmanteau movies; the production is opulent yet somehow stiff, and the performances have survived with varying success.

w William A. Drake, *novel* Vicki Baum *d Edmund Goulding ph* William Daniels *ad* Cedric Gibbons

Greta Garbo, *John Barrymore*, Lionel Barrymore, Joan Crawford, Wallace Beery, Jean Hersholt, Lewis Stone

DOCTOR (Lewis Stone): 'Grand Hotel. Always the same. People come, people go. Nothing ever happens.'

GRUSINSKAYA (Greta Garbo): 'I want to be alone . . . I think I have never been so tired in my life.'

† Remade as *Weekend at the Waldorf* (qv).

AA: best picture

Le Grand Jeu*
France 1934 115m bw

A young man joins the Foreign Legion to forget a woman, meets another who reminds him of her, and is condemned to death for murdering the second woman's lover.
Hokey melodrama whose great interest lay in its picture of life in the Legion.

w Charles Spaak, Jacques Feyder *d* Jacques Feyder *ph* Harry Stradling, Maurice Forster *m* Hanns Eisler

Pierre-Richard Wilm, Marie Bell (in a dual role), Françoise Rosay, Charles Vanel

'At last a good French film.'—*Variety*

† A remake appeared in 1953, directed by Robert Siodmak and starring Jean-Claude Pascal, Gina Lollobrigida and Arletty. Sometimes known as *Card of Fate*, it is of little interest.

Le Grand Méliès*
France 1952 30m bw

Georges Méliès, conjuror and pioneer film maker, is played by his own son André in a series of vignettes separated by clips from the films. An interesting documentary reconstruction. Written and directed by Georges Franju; for Fred Orain / Armor Films.

Grand National Night
GB 1953 80m bw
Talisman (George Minter)
US title: *The Wicked Wife*

A stable owner accidentally kills his drunken wife, but fate and a complex series of events clear him.
Slightly dubious morally, but otherwise an adequate detective story with the outcome hinging on train timetables and the like.

w Dorothy and Campbell Christie, from their play *d* Bob McNaught *ph* Jack Asher *m* John Greenwood

Nigel Patrick, Moira Lister, Beatrice Campbell, Betty Ann Davies, Michael Hordern, Noel Purcell, Leslie Mitchell, Barry Mackay, Colin Gordon

Grand Prix*
US 1966 179m Metrocolor
Super Panavision
MGM / Douglas and Lewis (Edward Lewis)

Motor racers converge on Monte Carlo and other European centres.
Seemingly endless montage, mostly in multi-split screens, of motor races, with some very jaded personal footage between. It looks a dream but quickly becomes a bore.

w Robert Alan Arthur *d John Frankenheimer ph Lionel Lindon m* Maurice Jarre *pd Richard Sylbert*

James Garner, Eva Marie Saint, Brian Bedford, Yves Montand, Toshiro Mifune, Jessica Walter, Françoise Hardy, Adolfo Celi, Claude Dauphin, Genevieve Page

'The same old story with the same types we've seen flying planes and riding horses in dozens of fast, cheap, hour-and-a-quarter movies.'—*Pauline Kael*

'Nothing more nor less than a paean to the racing car . . . off the track, though, the film is firmly stuck in bottom gear.'—*MFB*

Grand Slam
US 1933 65m bw

A Russian waiter is called in to make a fourth at bridge and proves to be an expert. Able spoof of the bridge craze then sweeping America; precise knowledge unnecessary. Paul Lukas, Loretta Young, Frank McHugh, Glenda Farrell, Helen Vinson, Walter Byron, Ferdinand Gottschalk. Written by David Boehm and Ernest Gelsey from the novel by B. Russell Herts; directed by William Dieterle; for Warners. 'It just about makes three spades doubled, which isn't bad when you're vulnerable, and that should be enough to show a profit.'—*Variety*

Grand Slam
Italy / Spain / West Germany 1967 120m
Techniscope
(Paramount) Jolly-Coral-Constantin (Harry Columbo, George Papi)
original title: *Ad Ogni Costo*

A retired professor has a plan for a diamond robbery, but recruits his aides unwisely.
Long-drawn-out caper melodrama with good sequences but nothing at all new; a very poor man's *Rififi*.

w Mino Roli, Caminito, Marcello Fondato, Antonio de la Loma *d* Giuliano Montaldo *ph* Antonio Macasoli *m* Ennio Morricone

Janet Leigh, Edward G. Robinson, Klaus Kinski, Robert Hoffman, Georges Rigaud, Adolfo Celi

La Grande Illusion***
France 1937 117m bw
RAC (Frank Rollmer, Albert Pinkovitch)

During World War I, three captured French pilots have an uneasy relationship with their German commandant.
Celebrated mood piece with much to say about war and mankind; more precisely, it is impeccably acted and directed and has real tragic force.

w Jean Renoir, Charles Spaak d Jean Renoir ph Christian Matras, Claude Renoir, Bourgoin, Bourreaud *m* Joseph Kosma

Pierre Fresnay, Erich Von Stroheim, Jean Gabin, Julien Carette, Marcel Dalio, Gaston Modot, Jean Dasté, Dita Parlo

'Artistically masterful.'—*Variety*

'The story is true. It was told to me by my friends in the war . . . notably by Pinsard who flew fighter planes. I was in the reconnaissance squadron. He saved my life many times when the German fighters became too persistent. He himself was shot down seven times. His escapes are the basis for the story.'—*Jean Renoir*

'One of the true masterpieces of the screen.'—*Pauline Kael, 70s*

AAN: best picture

Les Grandes Manoeuvres*
France / Italy 1955 106m Eastmancolor
Filmsonor / Rizzoli
aka: *Summer Manoeuvres*

In 1913, an army lieutenant takes a bet that he can win any woman in the town in which his regiment is quartered during manoeuvres.
An elegant, but surprisingly unwitty film from this director, saddled with a well-worn and very predictable plot.

wd René Clair *ph* Robert Le Fèbvre, Robert Juillard *m* Georges Van Parys

Gérard Philipe, Michèle Morgan, Brigitte Bardot, Yves Robert, Jean Desailly, Pierre Dux

Grandma's Boy*
US 1922 50m approx (24 fps) bw
silent

Inspired by the heroism of his own grandpa, a meek and mild young fellow subdues a terrifying tramp. Modest second-feature-length comedy of a burgeoning star, no great shakes by his later standards. Harold Lloyd, Dick Sutherland, Anna Townsend. Directed by Fred Newmeyer; for Associated Exhibitors.

Granny Get Your Gun
US 1939 56m bw

An indomitable old lady turns sheriff to get her granddaughter off the hook for murder. Energetic second feature comedy mystery from a Perry Mason story; pleasant performances. May Robson, Harry Davenport, Margot Stevenson, Hardie Albright. Written by Kenneth Gamet; directed by George Amy; for Warner.

'The thousands who have read the book will know why WE WILL NOT SELL ANY CHILDREN TICKETS to see this picture!'

The Grapes of Wrath****
US 1940 128m bw
TCF (Nunnally Johnson)

After the dust-bowl disaster of the thirties, Oklahoma farmers trek to California in the hope of a better life.
A superb film which could scarcely be improved upon. Though the ending is softened from the book, there was too much here for

filmgoers to chew on. Acting, photography, direction combine to make this an unforgettable experience, a poem of a film.

w Nunnally Johnson, novel John Steinbeck *d John Ford ph Gregg Toland m* Alfred Newman

Henry Fonda, Jane Darwell, John Carradine, Charley Grapewin, Dorris Bowdon, Russell Simpson, Zeffie Tilbury, O. Z. Whitehead, John Qualen, Eddie Quillan, Grant Mitchell

TOM (Henry Fonda) reading grave marker: 'This here's William James Joad, died of a stroke, old, old man. His fokes bured him because they got no money to pay for funerls. Nobody kilt him. Just a stroke and he died.'

MA (Jane Darwell): 'Rich fellas come up, an' they die, an' their kids ain't no good, an' they die out. But we keep a-comin'. We're the people that live. Can't lick us. We'll go on forever, Pa, because we're the people.'

MA: 'Well, Pa, woman can change bettern a man. Man lives—well, in jerks. Baby born or somebody dies, that's a jerk. Gets a farm or loses one, an' that's a jerk. With a woman, it's all one flow, like a stream—little eddies, little waterfalls—but the river, it goes right on. Woman looks at it that way.'

'A genuinely great motion picture which makes one proud to have even a small share in the affairs of the cinema.'—*Howard Barnes*

'The most mature motion picture that has ever been made, in feeling, in purpose, and in the use of the medium.'—*Otis Ferguson*

'A sincere and searing indictment of man's cruel indifference to his fellows.'—*Basil Wright*

AA: John Ford; Jane Darwell
AAN: best picture; Nunnally Johnson; Henry Fonda

Grass*
US 1925 50m approx bw silent
Famous Players-Lasky

Nomadic Iranian tribes make an annual migration in search of fresh pasture.
Striking early documentary marred by facetious sub-titles.

w, d, ph Merian C. Cooper, Ernest Schoedsack *titles* Terry Ramsaye

The Grass Is Greener*
GB 1960 104m Technirama
Grandon (Stanley Donen)

The wife of an English earl falls for an American millionaire tourist.
Heavy-going and unsuitably widescreened version of an agreeable piece of West End fluff. Performances just about save it.

w Hugh and Margaret Williams, from their play *d* Stanley Donen *ph* Christopher Challis *m / ly* Noel Coward *md* Muir Mathieson

Cary Grant, Deborah Kerr, Robert Mitchum, *Jean Simmons, Moray Watson*

'It's too bad Coward couldn't have written the wisecracks too.'—*Philip T. Hartung*

'The stars do not glitter or even glow. Instead of being liberated and propelled by the screenplay, they are chained and sunk. It is one of the year's most disappointing films.'—*James Powers, Hollywood Reporter*

The Grasshopper
US 1969 98m Technicolor
NGP (Jerry Belson, Barry Marshall)

A small-town girl goes from man to man in Los Angeles and Las Vegas, finally becoming a call girl.
The road to ruin in modern dress; nicely made and quite entertaining in its gaudy way.

w Jerry Belson, *novel* The Passing of Evil by Mark MacShane *d* Jerry Paris *ph* Sam Leavitt *m* Billy Goldenberg

Jacqueline Bisset, Jim Brown, Joseph Cotten, Corbett Monica

Gray Lady Down
US 1978 111m Technicolor Panavision
Universal / Mirisch (Walter Mirisch)

After a collision, an American submarine lodges in the neck of an underwater canyon.
A rather boring update of *Morning Departure* with added technology.

w James Whittaker, Howard Sackler, *novel* Event 1000 by David Levallee *d* David Greene *ph* Stevan Larner *m* Jerry Fielding

Charlton Heston, David Carradine, Stacy Keach, Ned Beatty, Stephen McHattie, Ronny Cox, Dorian Harewood, Rosemary Forsyth

'The crew eventually reach the surface, but the film deserves to sink without trace.'—*Nicholas Wapshott, The Times*

Grease**
US 1978 110m Metrocolor Panavision
Paramount / Robert Stigwood, Allan Carr

The path of true love in a fifties high school does not run smoothly.
Amiable 'period' musical for teenagers: a highly fashionable exploitation of the new star John Travolta, its commercialism was undeniable, and it carefully built in appeal to older age groups.

w Bronte Woodard, *stage musical play* Jim Jacobs, Warren Casey *d* Randal Kleiser *ph* Bill Butler *pd* Phil Jefries *titles* John Wilson

John Travolta, Olivia Newton-John, Stockard Channing, Eve Arden, Frankie Avalon, Joan Blondell, Edd Byrnes, Sid Caesar, Alice Ghostley, Sha Na Na, Jeff Conaway, Barry Pearl, Michael Tucci

'A bogus, clumsily jointed pastiche of late fifties high school musicals, studded with leftovers from *West Side Story* and *Rebel Without A Cause*.'—*New Yorker*

AAN: song, 'Hopelessly Devoted to You'

Grease 2
US 1982 114m Metrocolor Panavision
Paramount (Robert Stigwood, Allan Carr)

In 1961 an English boy causes emotional problems when he joins the senior class of Rydell High School.
Despite the mixture as before, this sequel was a resounding flop in all departments, perhaps proving that the success of the original was only a fluke of timing.

w Ken Finkleman *d* Patricia Birch *ph* Frank Stanley *m* Louis St Louis *songs* various

Maxwell Caulfield, Michele Pfeiffer, Adrian Zmed, Lorna Luft, Eve Arden, Sid Caesar, Tab Hunter, Connie Stevens

'It's like being cooped up for two hours inside a combination of juke box and pinball machine, with you as the ball.'—*Daily Mail*

Greased Lightning
US 1977 96m Movielab
Third World (Hannah Weinstein)

A black Virginian moonshiner becomes a famous stock car racer.
Fashionable action hokum based on a real character.

w Kenneth Vose, Lawrence DuKore, Melvin Van Peebles, Leon Capetanos *d* Michel Schultz *ph* George Bouillet *m* Fred Karlin

Richard Pryor, Beau Bridges, Pam Grier, Cleavon Little, Vincent Gardenia

The Great Adventure**
Sweden 1953 73m bw
Arne Sucksdorff

Two boys on a farm rescue an otter and keep it as a pet.
Superbly photographed wild life film featuring a variety of small animals.

w,d,ph,ed Arne Sucksdorff m Lars Erik Larsson

Anders Norberg, Kjell Sucksdorff, Arne Sucksdorff

The Great Adventures of Captain Kidd
US 1953 bw serial: 15 eps

Naval officers assigned to track down Captain Kidd the pirate realize that he is really a patriot. Unhistorical serial charade, not really in the most entertaining tradition. Richard Crane, David Bruce, John Crawford, George Wallace. Directed by Derwin Abbe and Charles Gould; for Columbia.

The Great Adventures of Wild Bill Hickok
US 1938 bw serial: 15 eps

The marshal of Abilene opposes the Phantom Raiders. Standard serial exploits. Gordon Elliott, Monte Blue, Carole Wynne, Frankie Darro. Directed by Mack V. Wright and Sam Nelson; for Columbia.

The Great Alaskan Mystery*
US 1944 bw serial: 13 eps

Dr Miller invents a defence weapon called the Peratron, and goes to Alaska, followed by evil fascists, in search of the one element which will make it work. Good serial stuff with a remarkably recognizable cast, and Ralph Morgan for once not the villain. Milburn Stone, Marjorie Weaver, Edgar Kennedy, Ralph Morgan, Samuel S. Hinds, Martin Kosleck, Joseph Crehan, Fuzzy Knight, Harry Cording. Directed by Ray Taylor and Lewis D. Collins; for Universal.

The Great American Broadcast*
US 1941 90m bw
TCF (Kenneth MacGowan)

A romantic triangle set against the burgeoning years of the radio industry.
Pleasant musical, amusing if historically inaccurate.

w Don Ettlinger, Edwin Blum, Robert Ellis, Helen Logan *d* Archie Mayo *ph* Leon Shamroy, Peverell Marley *songs* Mack Gordon, Harry Warren

Alice Faye, John Payne, Jack Oakie, Cesar Romero, The Ink Spots, The Nicholas Brothers, The Wiere Brothers

The Great American Pastime
US 1956 89m bw
MGM (Henry Berman)

A mild lawyer takes over a junior baseball team but incurs parental jealousy.
Thin lower-bracket comedy.

w Nathaniel Benchley *d* Herman Hoffman *ph* Arthur E. Arling *m* Jeff Alexander

Tom Ewell, Anne Francis, Ann Miller, Dean Jones, Raymond Bailey

The Great Bank Robbery*
US 1969 98m colour Panavision
Warner (Malcolm Stuart)

Would-be bank robbers turn up in a western town disguised as priests.
Western spoof without the courage of its convictions, but easy enough to watch.

w William Peter Blatty, novel Frank O'Rourke *d* Hy Averback *ph* Fred J. Koenekamp *m* Nelson Riddle

Kim Novak, Zero Mostel, Clint Walker, Claude Akins, Akim Tamiroff, Larry Storch, John Anderson, Sam Jaffe, Ruth Warrick, Elisha Cook Jnr

The Great Barrier
GB 1937 85m bw
A professional cardplayer gets involved in the building of the Canadian Pacific Railway. Forgotten epic which has scenes of some grandeur. Richard Arlen, Antoinette Cellier, Lilli Palmer, Barry Mackay, Roy Emerton. Written by Michael Barringer, Milton Rosmer, from the novel The Great Divide by Alan Sullivan; directed by Milton Rosmer; for Gaumont British. (US Title: *Silent Barriers.*)
'Authentic history done sensitively . . . ranks with the best made anywhere . . . will certainly achieve commercial and artistic success throughout the world.'—*Variety*

The Great Caruso**
US 1950 109m Technicolor
MGM (Joe Pasternak)

Semi-fictional biography of the Italian tenor. Dramatically flat but opulently staged biopic, turned into a star vehicle and a huge commercial success.

w Sonya Levien, William Ludwig *d* Richard Thorpe *ph* Joseph Ruttenberg *md* Johnny Green, Peter Herman Adler

Mario Lanza, Ann Blyth, Dorothy Kirsten, Jarmila Novotna, Carl Benton Reid, Eduard Franz, Richard Hageman, Ludwig Donath, Alan Napier

AAN: Johnny Green, Peter Herman Adler

Great Catherine
GB 1968 98m Technicolor
Warner / Keep Films (Jules Buck)

An English captain visits the court of Catherine the Great.
Chaos results from the attempt to inflate an ill-considered Shavian whimsy into a feature film: the material is simply insufficient and the performances flounder in irrelevant production values.

w Hugh Leonard, *play* Bernard Shaw *d* Gordon Flemyng *ph* Oswald Morris *m* Dmitri Tiomkin *pd* John Bryan

Jeanne Moreau, Peter O'Toole, Zero Mostel, Jack Hawkins, Marie Lohr, Akim Tamiroff, Marie Kean, Kenneth Griffith
'All Shaw's jokes work very well, but the film has been padded out with Cossack dances, frantic chases, and unfunny slapstick.'—*Michael Billington, Illustrated London News*

The Great Chase
US 1963 82m bw

A compendium of chase sequences from silent films, including William S. Hart, Douglas Fairbanks Snr, and Buster Keaton (in *The General*). Written by Harvey Kort, Paul Killiam and Saul Turrell; for Continental.

The Great Commandment
US 1940 bw 78m

In AD 30, with Judaea still under Roman rule, a village scholar preaches the teachings of Jesus. Thin little religious fable, independently produced and without much going for it. John Beal, Albert Dekker, Maurice Moscovitch, Marjorie Cooley, Lloyd Corrigan. Written by Dana Burnet; directed by Irving Pichel; for John T. Coyle.

The Great Dan Patch
US 1949 92m bw

The career of a famous racehorse at the turn of the century. Modest small-town crowd-pleaser. Dennis O'Keefe, Gail Russell, Ruth Warrick, Charlotte Greenwood, Henry Hull, John Hoyt, Arthur Hunnicutt. Written and produced by John Taintor Foote; directed by Joseph Newman; for W. R. Frank / United Artists.

Great Day
GB 1945 79m bw
RKO British (Victor Hanbury)

A village Women's Institute prepares for a visit by Mrs Roosevelt.
Modestly pleasing little drama from a successful play.

w Wolfgang Wilhelm, John Davenport, *play* Lesley Storm *d* Lance Comfort *ph* Erwin Hillier

Eric Portman, Flora Robson, Sheila Sim, Isabel Jeans, Walter Fitzgerald, Philip Friend, Marjorie Rhodes, Maire O'Neill, Beatrice Varley

Great Day in the Morning
US 1955 92m Technicolor Superscope
RKO (Edmund Grainger)

At the outbreak of the Civil War, Denver has divided loyalties.
Solemn semi-western without much excitement.

w Lesser Samuels, *novel* Robert Hardy Andrews *d* Jacques Tourneur *ph* William Snyder *m* Leith Stevens

Robert Stack, Virginia Mayo, Ruth Roman, Alex Nicol, Raymond Burr, Regis Toomey

The Great Diamond Robbery
US 1954 69m bw

Crooks convince a dumb jewellery apprentice to help them. Tedious second feature comedy, the star's last for the studio. Red Skelton, Cara Williams, James Whitmore, Kurt Kasznar, Reginald Owen. Written by Laslo Vadnay; directed by Robert Z. Leonard; for MGM.

The Great Dictator**
US 1940 129m bw
Charles Chaplin

A Jewish barber is mistaken for dictator Adenoid Hynkel.
Chaplin's satire on Hitler has a few funny moments, but the rest is heavy going, the production is cheeseparing, and the final speech to the world is a grave mistake.

wd Charles Chaplin *ph* Karl Struss, Rollie Totheroh *md* Meredith Willson *ad* J. Russell Spencer

Charles Chaplin, Paulette Goddard, *Jack Oakie* (as Napaloni), Reginald Gardiner, Henry Daniell, Billy Gilbert, Maurice Moscovitch
'For this film he takes on more than a mimed representation of common humanity; he states, and accepts, the responsibility of being one of humanity's best and most widely-known representatives.'—*Basil Wright*
'The last impassioned speech about peace and serenity still wrecks everything that has gone before: Chaplin mawkish can always overrule Chaplin the innocent mime.'—*New Yorker, 1978*
'You must go back to *Intolerance* for another motion picture that is so completely one man's personal expression of his attitude on something about which he feels deeply and passionately.'—*James Shelley Hamilton, National Board of Review*
'No time for comedy? Yes, I say, time for comedy. Time for Chaplin comedy. No time ever for Chaplin to preach as he does in those last six minutes, no matter how deeply he may feel what he wrote and says. He is not a good preacher. Indeed, he is frighteningly bad.'—*John O'Hara*
'Some moments actually work, but they are very few and far between.'—*Time Out, 1984*

AAN: best picture; Charles Chaplin (as writer and actor); Meredith Willson; Jack Oakie

The Great Escape**
US 1963 173m De Luxe Panavision
UA / Mirisch / Alpha (John Sturges)

Allied prisoners plan to escape from a German prison camp.
Pretty good but overlong POW adventure with a tragic ending.

w James Clavell, W. R. Burnett, *book* Paul Brickhill *d* John Sturges *ph Daniel Fapp* *m* Elmer Bernstein

James Garner, *Steve McQueen*, Richard Attenborough, James Donald, Charles Bronson, Donald Pleasence, James Coburn, David McCallum, Gordon Jackson, John Leyton, Nigel Stock

Great Expectations
US 1934 100m bw
Universal

A poor boy becomes unexpectedly rich and mistakes the source of his good fortune.
Solidly carpentered but never inspired version of a sprawling novel later tackled with much more style by David Lean. See below.

w Gladys Unger *novel* Charles Dickens *d* Stuart Walker

Phillips Holmes (Pip), Jane Wyatt (Estella), Henry Hull (Magwitch), Florence Reed (Miss Havisham), Alan Hale (Joe Gargery), Rafaela Ottiano (Mrs Joe), Francis L. Sullivan (Jaggers)

'First half represents a fine achievement . . . and then it all falls apart.'—*Variety*

Great Expectations****
GB 1946 118m bw
Rank / Cineguild (Anthony Havelock-Allan)

A boy meets an escaped convict on the Romney Marshes, with strange consequences for both of them.
Despite the inevitable simplifications, this is a superbly pictorial rendering of a much-loved novel, with all the famous characters in safe hands and masterly judgement in every department.

w Ronald Neame, David Lean, Kay Walsh, Cecil McGivern, Anthony Havelock-Allan *d David Lean* *ph Guy Green* *ad John Bryan*

John Mills, Bernard Miles, *Finlay Currie*, *Martita Hunt*, Valerie Hobson, *Jean Simmons*, Alec Guinness, Francis L. Sullivan, Anthony Wager, Ivor Barnard, Freda Jackson, Hay Petrie, O. B. Clarence, George Hayes, Torin Thatcher, Eileen Erskine

'The first big British film to have been made, a film that sweeps our cloistered virtues out into the open.'—*Richard Winnington*

'The best Dickens adaptation, and arguably David Lean's finest film.'—*NFT, 1969*

'*It does for Dickens what Henry V* did for Shakespeare. That is, it indicates a sound method for translating him from print to film . . . almost never less than graceful, tasteful and intelligent, and some of it better than that.'—*James Agee*

† See *Television Companion* for the later TV version with Michael York.

AA: Guy Green; John Bryan
AAN: best picture; script; David Lean (as director)

The Great Flamarion
US 1945 78m bw

A jealous vaudeville sharpshooter hunts down and kills the woman he loves because she prefers another. Heavy-handed melodrama reminiscent of German silents but without their flair. Erich Von Stroheim, Dan Duryea, Mary Beth Hughes. Written by Heinz Harald, Ann Widton and Richard Weil; directed by Anthony Mann; for Republic.

The Great Flirtation
US 1934 71m bw

An actor is jealous of his wife's stardom. Would-be sophisticated comedy with far too many loose ends. Adolphe Menjou, Elissa Landi, David Manners, Lynne Overman, Raymond Walburn, Paul Porcasi, Akim Tamiroff. Written by Humphrey Pearson from a story by Gregory Ratoff; directed by Ralph Murphy; for Paramount. 'Hardly a picture of strong audience appeal.'—*Variety*

The Great Gabbo
US 1929 88m bw

A ventriloquist's personality is taken over by that of his dummy. Yes, that old chestnut, here in tedious and primitive early talkie form. Erich Von Stroheim, Betty Compson, Margie Kane. Written by F. Hugh Herbert from a story by Ben Hecht; directed by James Cruze; for Sono Art.

The Great Gambini
US 1937 70m bw

A mindreader's efforts to solve a murder only point to his own guilt. Talkative twister which doesn't quite work. Akim Tamiroff, John Trent, Marian Marsh, Genevieve Tobin, Reginald Denny, William Demarest, Edward Brophy. Written by Frederick Jackson, Frank Partos, Howard Irving Young; directed by Charles Vidor; for Paramount. 'Not enough punch to produce better than ordinary entertainment.'—*Variety*

The Great Game
GB 1952 80m bw

A football club chairman gets involved in crooked deals. Dismal comedy drama which gives few opportunities to anybody. James Hayter, Diana Dors, Thora Hird, Sheila Shand Gibbs, John Laurie, Glyn Houston. Written by Wolfgang Wilhelm, from the play *Shooting Star* by Basil Thomas; directed by Maurice Elvey; for Advance.

The Great Garrick**
US 1937 91m bw
Warner (Mervyn Le Roy)

When Garrick goes to act in Paris, members of the Comédie Française take over a wayside inn and try to teach him a lesson, but the plan goes awry.
A pleasant unhistorical conceit makes a rather literary film to have come from Hollywood, but it is all very winning and cast and director keep the fun simmering happily.

w Ernest Vajda *d James Whale* *ph* Ernest Haller *m* Adolph Deutsch

Brian Aherne, Edward Everett Horton, Olivia de Havilland, Lionel Atwill, *Melville Cooper*, *Luis Alberni*, *Étienne Girardot*, Marie Wilson, Lana Turner, Albert Dekker, Fritz Leiber, Dorothy Tree, Chester Clute

'Finely made period romantic comedy, but its reception at the paygate is extremely problematical.'—*Variety*

'As elegantly witty as anything Whale ever did.'—*Tom Milne*

'A jestful and romantic piece.'—*Frank S. Nugent, New York Times*

The Great Gatsby*
US 1949 90m bw
Paramount (Richard Maibaum)

Events leading to the death of a retired gangster and mysterious Long Island plutocrat.
Rather bland and uninteresting attempt to accommodate a unique author to a formula star.

w Richard Maibaum, *novel* F. Scott Fitzgerald *d* Elliott Nugent *ph* John Seitz *m* Robert Emmett Dolan

Alan Ladd, Macdonald Carey, Betty Field, Barry Sullivan, Howard da Silva

† A silent version in 1926 had starred Warner Baxter.

The Great Gatsby**
US 1974 146m Eastmancolor
Paramount / Newdon (David Merrick)

Plush version with lavish production values and pleasing period sense but not much grip on the story or characters. Overlong footage is not made to seem shorter by snail's pace and dull performances.

w Francis Ford Coppola *d* Jack Clayton *ph Douglas Slocombe* *m* Nelson Riddle *pd* John Box

Robert Redford, Mia Farrow, Karen Black, Scott Wilson, *Sam Waterston*, Lois Chiles

'Pays its creator the regrettable tribute of erecting a mausoleum over his work.'—*Richard Combs*

'Leaves us more involved with six-and-a-half-million dollars' worth of trappings than with human tragedy.'—*Judith Crist*

'A total failure of every requisite sensibility.'—*Stanley Kauffmann*

'Profoundly unfilmable: a poetic and ultimately pessimistic comment on the American dream is transformed by cinematic realism into pure prose.'—*Michael Billington, Illustrated London News*

AA: Nelson Riddle

The Great Gildersleeve
US 1942 61m bw

A small town loudmouth is always in hot water. Film debut for a radio character from Fibber McGee and Molly; unremarkable. Three more second features followed. Harold Peary, Jane Darwell, Nancy Gates, Charles Arnt, Thurston Hall. Written by Jack Townley, Joseph Josephson; directed by Gordon Douglas; for Herman Schlom / RKO.

Great Guns*
US 1941 74m bw
TCF (Sol M. Wurtzel)

A young millionaire's retainers join the army with him.
Disappointing Laurel and Hardy comedy, their first for Fox and the beginning of their decline. A few good jokes, but no overall control or inventiveness.

w Lou Breslow *d* Monty Banks *ph* Glen MacWilliams *m* Emil Newman

Stan Laurel, Oliver Hardy, Sheila Ryan, Dick Nelson, Edmund Macdonald, Charles Trowbridge, Ludwig Stossel, Mae Marsh

Great Guy*
US 1936 73m bw
Grand National (Douglas Maclean)
GB title: *Pluck of the Irish*

An ex-prizefighter joins the bureau of weights and measures and fights corruption.
Rather tame racket film, Cagney's first independent venture away from Warners. He atones for rather thin production values.

w Henry McCarthy, Henry Johnson, James Edward Grant, Harry Ruskin *d* John G. Blystone *ph* Jack McKenzie *m* Marlin Skiles

James Cagney, Mae Clarke, James Burke, Edward Brophy, Henry Kolker

'It's all typical Cagney stuff, and that's the trouble with it. Cagney apparently is doing the things he likes best, but they're repetitious and apt to disappoint a public anticipating something finer from this star after his quite lengthy absence.'—*Variety*

The Great Hospital Mystery
US 1937 59m bw

The lady superintendent of a hospital has a busy night including impersonation and murder. Confused but watchable second feature. Jane Darwell, Joan Davis, Sig Rumann, Sally Blane, Thomas Beck, William Demarest. Written by Bess Meredyth, William Conselman and Jerry Cady, from a novel by Mignon G. Eberhardt; directed by James Tinling; for TCF.

The Great Hotel Murder
US 1934 70m bw

Rival sleuths find the truth about a murder less important than being first to find it out. Lively programme filler of its day, with the stars still doing their Flagg and Quirt act. Edmund Lowe, Victor McLaglen, Rosemary Ames, Mary Carlisle. Written by Arthur Kober from a story by Vincent Starrett; directed by Eugene Forde; for TCF.

The Great Impersonation*
US 1935 81m bw
Universal (Edmund Grainger)

During World War I, a German murders an English nobleman and, being his double, takes over.
Reliable espionage melodrama with atmospheric country house asides, from a sturdily compelling novel, previously filmed in 1921 with James Kirkwood.

w Frank Wead, Eve Greene, *novel* E. Phillips Oppenheim *d* Alan Crosland *ph* Milton Krasner *m* Franz Waxman

Edmund Lowe, Valerie Hobson, Vera Engels, Henry Mollison, Lumsden Hare, Spring Byington, Charles Waldron, Dwight Frye

'They giggled a bit when Lowe went to bed with candles, and an hour later a sliding panel attempt on his life has him pushing an electric light switch . . . probably doesn't matter that the 1914 characters are dressed throughout in 1935 modishness and drive around in streamlined automobiles.'—*Variety*

The Great Impersonation*
US 1942 71m bw
Universal (Paul Malvern)

Okay quickie updating of the above, serviceable rather than inventive.

w W. Scott Darling *d* John Rawlins *ph* George Robinson *m* Hans Salter

Ralph Bellamy, Evelyn Ankers, Aubrey Mather, Edward Norris, Karen Verne, Henry Daniell, Ludwig Stossel

The Great Imposter*
US 1961 112m bw
U-I (Robert Arthur)

The career of Ferdinand Waldo Demara, a marine and Trappist monk who also impersonated a Harvard research fellow, a prison warden, a naval doctor and a schoolteacher.
Uncertain mood hampers this biopic of a likeable fantasist.

w Liam O'Brien, *book* Robert Crichton *d* Robert Mulligan *ph* Robert Burks *m* Henry Mancini

Tony Curtis, Raymond Massey, Karl Malden, Edmond O'Brien, Arthur O'Connell, Gary Merrill, Frank Gorshin, Joan Blackman, Robert Middleton

Great—Isambard Kingdom Brunel*
GB 1975 28m Eastmancolor

A musical biography of the great Victorian engineer. Quite unexpected, and therefore the more delightful. Conceived and directed by *Bob Godfrey*; for British Lion.

The Great Jasper
US 1933 83m bw

An Irish motorman becomes a fortune teller, and has his way with lots of women. Curious comedy-melodrama which never quite hits the right style. Richard Dix, Wera Engels, Edna May Oliver, Florence Eldredge, Bruce Cabot. Written by Sam Ornitz and H. W. Hanemann, from the novel by Fulton Oursler; directed by J. Walter Ruben; for RKO. 'Okay as a critics' film but looks like an in-and-outer.'—*Variety*

The Great Jesse James Raid
US 1953 70m Ansco Color

Jesse James comes out of retirement for one last haul. Boring two-bit western, all preparation and no action. Willard Parker, Barbara Payton, Tom Neal, Wallace Ford, Jim Bannon. Written by Richard Landau; directed by Reginald Le Borg; for Lippert.

The Great Jewel Robber
US 1950 91m bw

The exploits of real-life society thief Gerald Graham Dennis. Surprisingly acceptable and entertaining reconstruction. David Brian, Marjorie Reynolds, John Archer, Jacqueline de Wit. Written by Borden Chase; directed by Peter Godfrey; for Warner.

The Great John L.
US 1945 96m bw
(UA) Bing Crosby Productions (Frank Mastroly, James Edward Grant)
GB title: *A Man Called Sullivan*

Women in the life of prizefighter John L. Sullivan.
Very mild period biopic without the zest of *Gentleman Jim*.

w James Edward Grant *d* Frank Tuttle *ph* James Van Trees *m* Victor Young

Greg McClure, Linda Darnell, Barbara Britton, Lee Sullivan, Otto Kruger, Wallace Ford, Robert Barrat

'Sometimes there's a terrible penalty for telling the truth . . .'

The Great Lie***
US 1941 107m bw
Warner (Hal B. Wallis, Henry Blanke)

A determined girl loses the man she loves, believes him dead in a plane crash, and takes over the baby which his selfish wife does not want.
Absurd melodrama becomes top-flight entertainment with all concerned in cracking form and special attention on the two bitchy female leads, splendidly played. Classical music trimmings, too.

w Leonore Coffee, *novel* January Heights by Polan Banks *d* *Edmund Goulding* *ph* *Tony Gaudio* *m* *Max Steiner*

Bette Davis, *Mary Astor*, *George Brent*, Lucile Watson, Hattie McDaniel, Grant Mitchell, Jerome Cowan

AA: Mary Astor

The Great Locomotive Chase*
US 1956 76m Technicolor Cinemascope
Walt Disney (Lawrence Edward Watkin)

During the Civil War, Union spies steal a train and destroy track and bridges behind them.
A serious version of Buster Keaton's *The General*, based on a true incident; good sequences but no overall pace.

w Lawrence Edward Watkin *d* Francis D. Lyon *ph* Charles Boyle *m* Paul Smith

Fess Parker, Jeffrey Hunter, Jeff York, John Lupton, Kenneth Tobey

The Great Lover
US 1931 77m bw

Capers of a philandering opera star. Satisfactory drama-comedy vehicle for a durable star. Adolphe Menjou, Irene Dunne, Neil Hamilton, Olga Baclanova. Written by Gene Markey; directed by Harry Beaumont; for MGM. 'Appeal limited to the mature fan.'—*Variety*

The Great Lover*
US 1949 80m bw
(Paramount) Hope Enterprises (Edmund Beloin)

On a transatlantic liner, a timid scoutmaster catches a strangler.
Amusing suspense comedy, a good star vehicle.

w Edmund Beloin, Melville Shavelson, Jack Rose *d* Alexander Hall *ph* Charles Lang *m* Joseph J. Lilley

Bob Hope, Rhonda Fleming, *Roland Young*, Jim Backus, Roland Culver, George Reeves

'He'll give you the biggest heart sock, laugh shock you ever thrilled to!'

The Great McGinty**
US 1940 83m bw
Paramount
GB title: *Down Went McGinty*

A hobo and a crook have a hectic political career.
Lively comedy-drama which signalled the arrival as director of a new and stimulating Hollywood talent.

wd Preston Sturges ph William C. Mellor *m* Frederick Hollander

Brian Donlevy, Akim Tamiroff, Muriel Angelus, Louis Jean Heydt, Arthur Hoyt

PROLOGUE: 'This is the story of two men who met in a banana republic. One of them never did anything dishonest in his life except for one crazy minute. The other never did anything honest in his life except for one crazy minute. They both had to leave the country.'

'This is his first directing job and where has he been all our lives? He has that sense of the incongruous which makes some of the best gaiety.'—*Otis Ferguson*

'The tough dialogue is matched by short, snappy scenes; the picture seems to have wasted no time, no money.'—*Gilbert Seldes*

'A director as adroit and inventive as any in the business . . . it starts like a five-alarm fire and never slackens pace for one moment until its unexpected conclusion.'—*Pare Lorentz*

'Sturges takes the success ethic and throws it in the face of the audience.'—*James Orsini*

'Capra with the gloves off.'—*Raymond Durgnat*

AA: script

The Great McGonagall
GB 1974 89m Eastmancolor

An unemployed Scot aims to become Queen Victoria's Poet Laureate. Appalling tribute to a minor figure of sub-literature. Spike Milligan, Peter Sellers, Julia Foster, Julian Chagrin, John Bluthal, Valentine Dyall, Victor Spinetti. Written by Joe McGrath, Spike Milligan; directed by Joe McGrath; for Darlton.

The Great Man**
US 1956 92m bw
U-I (Aaron Rosenberg)

A memorial programme to a much-loved TV personality turns into an exposé.
Patchy melodrama with a *Citizen Kane* framework; the best bits are very effective.

w Jose Ferrer, Al Morgan, novel Al Morgan *d* Jose Ferrer *ph* Harold Lipstein *m* Herman Stein

Jose Ferrer, Dean Jagger, Keenan Wynn, *Julie London*, Joanne Gilbert, *Ed Wynn*, Jim Backus

'Its distinction is in its unwavering tone—one of blunt and frequently savage irony and cynicism.'—*MFB*

'The movie is almost over before one realizes what a slick, fast sell it is (resembling nothing so much as what it is attacking).'—*Pauline Kael, 1968*

The Great Man Votes*
US 1938 72m bw
RKO

A drunken professor turns out to have the casting vote in a local election.
Slow-starting but progressively funny political comedy with some favourite talents in good form.

w John Twist, *story* Gordon Malherbe Hillman *d Garson Kanin ph* Russell Metty *m* Roy Webb

John Barrymore, Virginia Weidler, Peter Holden, *William Demarest, Donald MacBride*

'It will be hailed by class audiences as a fine example of the film art, yet carrying sock appeal for mass patronage.'—*Variety*

The Great Man's Lady*
US 1941 90m bw
Paramount (William A. Wellman)

A western pioneer is inspired and encouraged by his wife.
Adequate but unsurprising flashback family drama starting with its star as a lady of 109.

w W. L. Rivers, *story* Vina Delmar *d* William L. Wellman *ph* William C. Mellor *m* Victor Young

Barbara Stanwyck, Joel McCrea, Brian Donlevy, Katharine Stevens, Thurston Hall, Lloyd Corrigan

The Great Meadow
US 1931 80m bw

Early settlers from Virginia walk to Kentucky. Dim pioneering fable, without even a covered wagon. John Mack Brown, Eleanor Boardman, Lucille La Verne, Anita Louise, Gavin Gordon, Guinn Williams. Written by Edith Ellis, Charles Brabin, from the novel by Elizabeth Madox Roberts; directed by Charles Brabin; for MGM. 'Rather a sorry mess . . . cannot be depended on for an average gross.'—*Variety*

The Great Missouri Raid
US 1950 81m Technicolor

Jesse and Frank James are seen as Civil War guerrillas, subsequently forced into crime by a vengeful officer. Unsuccessful whitewash job, tediously told. Macdonald Carey, Wendell Corey, Ward Bond, Ellen Drew, Bruce Bennett, Bill Williams, Anne Revere, Edgar Buchanan. Written by Frank Gruber; directed by Gordon Douglas; for Nat Holt / Paramount.

The Great Mr Handel*
GB 1942 103m Technicolor
Rank / GHW (James B. Sloan)

How the 18th-century composer came to write the Messiah.
Earnest, unlikely biopic, naïve but rather commendable.

w Gerald Elliott, Victor MacClure, *play* L. DuGarde Peach *d* Norman Walker *ph* Claude Friese-Greene

Wilfrid Lawson, Elizabeth Allan, Malcolm Keen, Michael Shepley, Hay Petrie, A. E. Matthews

'A graceful addition to the ranks of prestige pictures.'—*Kine Weekly*

The Great Mr Nobody
US 1941 71m bw

A classified ad salesman is too prone to let colleagues take the credit for his ideas. Thin character comedy which did nobody concerned any good. Eddie Albert, Joan Leslie, Alan Hale, William Lundigan, John Litel. Written by Ben Markson, Kenneth Gamet; directed by Ben Stoloff; for Warner.

'They booed him to greatness!'

The Great Moment**
US 1944 83m bw
Paramount

How anaesthetics may have been invented. Curious biopic of Dr W. T. G. Morgan, poised somewhere between utter seriousness and pratfall farce. The beginning of its director's decline, but always interesting in itself.

wd Preston Sturges, book Triumph over Pain by René Fulop-Miller *ph* Victor Milner *m* Victor Young

Joel McCrea, Betty Field, William Demarest, Harry Carey, Franklin Pangborn, Porter Hall, Grady Sutton

'Mr Sturges has triumphed over stiffness in screen biography.'—*New York Times*

'The careless, careful authority is there . . . the contrivance is smart enough.'—*Sunday Times*

The Great Mouse Detective*
US 1986 80m Technicolor
Walt Disney / Silver Screen Partners II (Burny Mattinson)
GB title: *Basil, The Great Mouse Detective*

A mouse who has studied Sherlock Holmes solves the mystery of a missing mouse toymaker and outwits the evil Professor Rattigan.
One of the better recent Disney cartoon features, but the texture will probably never again be so rich as in the days of *Pinocchio* and *Bambi*.

directors: John Musker, Ron Clements, Dave Michener and Burry Mattinson, who also assisted with the storyline, taken from *Basil of Baker Street* by Eve Titus; music: Henry Mancini
voices: Barrie Ingham, Vincent Price, Val Bettin, Alan Young

The Great Muppet Caper**
GB 1981 97m Technicolor
ITC (David Lazer, Frank Oz)

Kermit and Fozzie are reporters sent to solve a jewel robbery.
Considerably livelier than *The Muppet Movie* but a badly timed flop at the box office, this genial caper has a pleasant collection of guest stars as well as showing the familiar puppets at their most typical.

w Tom Patchett, Jay Tarses, Jerry Juhl, Jack Rose *d Jim Henson ph* Oswald Morris *m Joe Raposo pd Harry Lange*

Diana Rigg, Charles Grodin, John Cleese, Robert Morley, Trevor Howard, Peter Ustinov, Jack Warden

'Large chunks are pleasingly daft.'—*Sight and Sound*

The Great Northfield Minnesota Raid*
US 1971 91m Technicolor
Universal / Robertson and Associates / Jennings Lang

In 1876 a gang of bandits, technically pardoned, plan a bank robbery.
'Realistic' western in which the settings and photography have an impressively rough look but the script leaves much to be desired.

wd Philip Kaufman *ph Bruce Surtees m* Dave Grusin

Cliff Robertson, Robert Duvall, Luke Askew, Elisha Cook Jnr

The Great O'Malley
US 1937 77m bw
Warner (Harry Joe Brown)

An overzealous cop cares for the wife and child of a petty criminal whom he has sent to prison.
Considering the talent involved, an astonishingly routine programmer.

w Milton Krims, Tom Reed, *story* The Making of O'Malley by Gerald Beaumont *d* William Dieterle *ph* Ernest Haller *m* Heinz Roemheld

Pat O'Brien, Humphrey Bogart, Ann Sheridan, Sybil Jason, Frieda Inescort, Donald Crisp, Henry O'Neill, Hobart Cavanagh, Mary Gordon

'Familiar sentimental police theme: little action or appeal.'—*Variety*

† Previously filmed in 1923 with Milton Sills, as *The Making of O'Malley*.

The Great Profile*
US 1940 82m bw
TCF (Raymond Griffith)

A dissipated actor disgraces his family and becomes an acrobat.
Shapeless farce in which a great talent on his last legs parodies himself.

w Milton Sperling, Hilary Lynn *d* Walter Lang *ph* Ernest Palmer *m* Cyril Mockridge

John Barrymore, Mary Beth Hughes, Gregory Ratoff, Anne Baxter, John Payne, Lionel Atwill, Edward Brophy, Willie Fung

'The greatest comedy ever made!'

The Great Race***
US 1965 163m Technicolor Super Panavision
Warner / Patricia / Jalem / Reynard (Martin Jurow)

In 1908, the Great Leslie and Professor Fate are leading contenders in the first New York to Paris car race.
Elaborate comedy spectacular with many good moments, notably the early disasters, a western saloon brawl, and a custard pie fight. Elsewhere, there is more evidence of an oversize budget than of wit or finesse, and the entire Prisoner of Zenda spoof could have been omitted. Excellent production detail and general good humour.

w Arthur Ross *d* Blake Edwards *ph Russell Harlan m Henry Mancini pd Fernando Carrere*

Jack Lemmon, Tony Curtis, Peter Falk, Natalie Wood, George Macready, Ross Martin, Vivian Vance, Dorothy Provine

AAN: Russell Harlan; song 'The Sweetheart Tree' (*m* Henry Mancini, *ly* Johnny Mercer)

The Great Rupert
US 1950 87m bw

A family of impoverished acrobats are assisted by a pet squirrel which proves lucky in more ways than one. Modest whimsical comedy which outstays its welcome. Jimmy Durante, Terry Moore, Tom Drake, Sara Haden, Frank Orth. Written by Laslo Vadnay; directed by Irving Pichel; for George Pal / Eagle Lion. (NB: The squirrel was part puppet.)

The Great St Trinian's Train Robbery
GB 1966 94m Eastmancolor
British Lion / Braywild (Leslie Gilliat)

The staff of St Trinian's is infiltrated by would-be train robbers.
Flat-footed farce with a sense of strain evident from first to last shot.

w Frank Launder, Ivor Herbert *d* Frank Launder, Sidney Gilliat *ph* Ken Hodges *m* Malcolm Arnold

Frankie Howerd, Dora Bryan, Reg Varney, Desmond Walter-Ellis, Raymond Huntley, Richard Wattis, George Benson, Eric Barker, Godfrey Winn, George Cole, Colin Gordon, Barbara Couper, Elspeth Duxbury

The Great Santini*
US 1979 115m Technicolor
Warner / Orion / Bing Crosby Productions

A crack fighter pilot has difficulty adjusting to peacetime domestic life.
Overlong but generally absorbing star character drama.

wd Lewis John Carlino, *novel* Pat Conway *ph* Ralph Woolsey *m* Elmer Bernstein *pd* Jack Poplin

Robert Duvall, Blythe Danner, Michael O'Keefe, Lisa Jane Perskey, Julie Anne Haddock

AAN: Robert Duvall; Michael O'Keefe (supporting actor)

'They were not forgotten by history—they were left out on purpose!'

The Great Scout and Cathouse Thursday
US 1976 102m Technicolor
AIP (Jules Buck and David Korda)
reissue title: *Wildcat*

While trying to revenge himself on an absconding partner, an old cowboy falls for a young prostitute.
Downright peculiar comedy western which never seems to make up its mind what it's trying to be, and too often is merely embarrassing.

w Richard Shapiro *d* Don Taylor *ph* Alex Phillips Jnr *m* John Cameron *pd* Jack Martin Smith

Lee Marvin, Oliver Reed, Kay Lenz, Robert Culp, Elizabeth Ashley, Strother Martin, Sylvia Miles

'It takes more than a dollop or two of sentiment and acres of dirty talk to make a movie.'—*Michael Billington, Illustrated London News*

'It sounds like the latest in the cute twosome series launched by *Butch Cassidy and the Sundance Kid.* In fact it features not two but seven wacky westerners who all seem addicted to stealing, hee-hawing, falling into puddles and punching each other in the privates.'—*Janet Maslin, Newsweek*

The Great Sinner*
US 1949 110m bw
MGM (Gottfried Reinhardt)

A serious young writer becomes a compulsive gambler.
Rather pointless and heavy-handed but extremely good-looking and splendidly cast period drama vaguely based on Dostoievsky.

w Ladislas Fodor, Christopher Isherwood *d* Robert Siodmak *ph George Folsey m* Bronislau Kaper *ad Cedric Gibbons, Hans Peck*

Gregory Peck, *Walter Huston*, Ava Gardner, Agnes Moorehead, Ethel Barrymore, Melvyn Douglas, Frank Morgan

The Great Sioux Massacre
US 1965 93m Eastmancolor Cinemascope
Columbia / FF (Leon Fromkess)

Two officers are court-martialled after Custer's last stand.
Fragmentary flashback western let down by production and performances.

w Fred C. Dobbs *d* Sidney Salkow *ph* Irving Lippman *m* Emil Newman, Edward B. Powell

Joseph Cotten, Darren McGavin, Phil Carey, Nancy Kovack, Julie Sommars, Michael Pate

The Great Sioux Uprising
US 1953 80m Technicolor
U-I (Albert J. Cohen)

Indians rebel when their horses are stolen for sale to the commander of Fort Laramie.
Moderate western programmer.

w Richard Breen, Gladys Atwater *d* Lloyd Bacon *ph* Maury Gertsman *m* Joseph Gershenson

Jeff Chandler, Faith Domergue, Lyle Bettger

The Great Smokey Roadblock
US 1976 106m colour
Marvista (Allan F. Bodon)

A truckdriver avoiding the finance company picks up an assortment of eccentrics and starts on a wild chase.
What possessed Henry Fonda to appear in this hick action melodrama will be forever unclear.

w,d John Leone *ph* Ed Brown Snr *m* Craig Safan

Henry Fonda, Eileen Brennan, John Byner, Dub Taylor, Susan Sarandon, Dana House, Robert Englund, Melanie Mayron, Valerie Curtin

The Great Stone Face*
US 1968 93m bw

A very acceptable biography of Buster Keaton, with unusual emphasis on the very early films. Written and directed by Vernon P. Becker; for Funnyman Productions.

The Great Train Robbery***
US 1903 10m approx bw silent
Edison

Bandits tie up a telegraph operator and rob a train, but are arrested.
In its day this was a real pioneer. It was among the longest films then made, it had the most complicated story line, it was the first western and it used new technical tricks such as the pan and the close-up. Needless to say, it must now be viewed with sympathy.

wd Edwin S. Porter

Marie Murray, Broncho Billy Anderson, George Barnes

The Great Train Robbery (1978, Sean Connery): see The First Great Train Robbery

'The grandest of love stories told to the tunes of the grandest musical score ever written!'

The Great Victor Herbert*
US 1939 91m bw
Paramount (Andrew L. Stone)

At the turn of the century a famous composer plays cupid to two young singers.
Pleasant minor musical with excellent songs and an infectious cheerfulness.

w Russel Crouse, Robert Lively *d Andrew L. Stone* *ph* Victor Milner *md* Phil Boutelje, Arthur Lange

Walter Connolly, Allan Jones, Mary Martin, Susanna Foster, Lee Bowman

'Elaborately produced, visually effective . . . but audiences will learn from it very little about Victor Herbert.'—*Variety*

'Not highbrow, not lowbrow, but strictly on the beam for both mass and class audiences.'—*Motion Picture Herald*

AAN: Phil Boutelje, Arthur Lange

'What do you do when the war is over and you're the second best pilot in the world?'

The Great Waldo Pepper*
US 1975 108m Technicolor Todd-AO 35
Universal (George Roy Hill)

In the twenties, a World War I flier becomes an aerial stuntman.
Whimsical spectacular which concentrates less on the mystique of flying than on a series of splendid stunts.

w William Goldman *d George Roy Hill* *ph Robert Surtees* *m* Henry Mancini

Robert Redford, Bo Svenson, Bo Brundin, Susan Sarandon, Geoffrey Lewis

'Charged with enthralling balletic precision.'—*Tom Milne*

'One hundred per cent pure plastic adolescent male fantasy.'—*New Yorker*

'Miliza Korjus—rhymes with gorgeous!'

The Great Waltz***
US 1938 103m bw
MGM (Bernard Hyman)

Young Johann Strauss becomes Vienna's waltz king.
Exhilarating old-fashioned studio-set musical located in Hollywood's endearing vision of Old Vienna, assisted by streamlined production and excellent cast. Musical schmaltz.

w Walter Reisch, Samuel Hoffenstein, *story* Gottfried Reinhardt *d Julien Duvivier* *ph* Joseph Ruttenberg *m* Dmitri Tiomkin

Fernand Gravet, Luise Rainer, Miliza Korjus, Lionel Atwill, Hugh Herbert, Herman Bing, Curt Bois

'Should click nicely, but in these swingaroo days the waltz part may slow down anticipated b.o. enthusiasm.'—*Variety*

'A film to set the feet itching, and to make you want to grab a partner and join in.'—*Film Weekly*

AA: Joseph Ruttenberg
AAN: Miliza Korjus

The Great Waltz*
US 1972 134m Metrocolor Panavision 70
MGM (Andrew L. Stone)

Heavy-going remake set on real locations and hampered by them, styled in the manner of the same director's *Song of Norway*, i.e. with no real style at all. The music survives.

wd Andrew L. Stone *ph* David Boulton *ad* William Albert Havenmeyer *m* the Strauss family, adapted by Robert Wright, Chet Forrest *ch* Onna White

Horst Buchholz, Nigel Patrick, Mary Costa, Rossano Brazzi, Yvonne Mitchell

'Take a box of chocolates—soft-centred, of course.'—*Michael Billington, Illustrated London News*

'He could beat any white man in the world. He just couldn't beat all of them!'

The Great White Hope**
US 1970 103m De Luxe Panavision
TCF (Lawrence Turman)

In 1910, a black boxer becomes world heavyweight champ but has trouble through his affair with a white girl.
Vivid, slightly whitewashed biopic of Jack Johnson (called Jefferson). Dramatic deficiencies outweighed by excellent period detail and a spellbinding central performance.

w Howard Sackler, from his play *d Martin Ritt* *ph Burnett Guffey* *m* negro traditionals *md* Lionel Newman *pd John de Cuir*

James Earl Jones, Jane Alexander, Lou Gilbert, Joel Fluellen, Chester Morris, Robert Webber, Hal Holbrook

AAN: James Earl Jones; Jane Alexander

The Great Ziegfeld**
US 1936 179m bw
MGM (Hunt Stromberg)

The growth and Broadway fame of impresario Florenz Ziegfeld.
Mammoth biopic which despite a few show-stopping numbers never takes off dramatically and becomes something of an endurance test; interesting, however, as a spectacular of its time.

w William Anthony McGuire *d* Robert Z. Leonard *ph* Oliver T. Marsh, Ray June, George Folsey *md* Arthur Lange *ad* Cedric Gibbons

William Powell, Luise Rainer (as Anna Held), Myrna Loy (as Billie Burke), Frank Morgan, Reginald Owen, Nat Pendleton, Virginia Bruce, *Ray Bolger*, Harriett Hoctor, Ernest Cossart, *Fanny Brice*, Robert Greig, Gilda Gray, Leon Errol, Stanley Morner (Dennis Morgan)

'This huge inflated gas-blown object bobs into the critical view as irrelevantly as an airship advertising somebody's toothpaste at a south coast resort. It lasts three hours. That is its only claim to special attention.'—*Graham Greene*

'Everything should have been tightened—not in the team job of cutting those miles of negative, but in boiling down the script, saving a line here, combining two scenes into one.'—*Otis Ferguson*

AA: best picture; Luise Rainer
AAN: William Anthony McGuire; Robert Z. Leonard

The Greatest
US / GB 1977 101m Metrocolor
Columbia / EMI (John Marshall)

The life and times of Muhammed Ali.
Bland confection of rags to riches in the boxing ring, its only plus being that Ali plays himself and offers a predictable array of enjoyable one-liners.

w Ring Lardner Jnr, from Ali's autobiography The Greatest *d* Tom Gries *ph* Harry Stradling *m* Michael Masser

Muhammed Ali, Ernest Borgnine, Roger E. Mosley, Lloyd Haynes, Malachi Throne, John Marley, Robert Duvall, David Huddleston, Ben Johnson, James Earl Jones, Dina Merrill, Paul Winfield

The Greatest Show on Earth*
US 1952 153m Technicolor
Paramount / Cecil B. de Mille (Henry Wilcoxon)

Various dramas come to a head under the big top.
Moribund circus drama with bad acting, stilted production, an irrelevant train crash climax and a few genuinely spectacular and enjoyable moments.

w Fredric M. Frank, Theodore St John, Frank Cavett, Barre Lyndon *d* Cecil B. de Mille *ph* George Barnes, Peverell Marley, Wallace Kelley *m Victor Young ad* Hal Pereira, Walter Tyler

Betty Hutton, Cornel Wilde, James Stewart, Charlton Heston, Dorothy Lamour, Gloria Grahame, Lyle Bettger, Henry Wilcoxon, Emmett Kelly, Lawrence Tierney, John Kellogg, John Ringling North

AA: best picture
AAN: original story (Fredric M. Frank, Theodore St John, Frank Cavett); Cecil B. de Mille (as director)

The Greatest Story Ever Told**
US 1965 225m Technicolor Ultra Panavision 70
UA / George Stevens

Solemn spectacular with an elephantine pace, shot in Utah because allegedly it looked more like Palestine than Palestine did. All frightfully elegant and reverent, but totally unmoving, partly because of the fatal casting of stars in bit parts. (John Wayne looks in merely to say 'Truly this man was the son of God.')

w James Lee Barrett, George Stevens, from various sources *d* George Stevens *ph William C. Mellor, Loyal Griggs m* Alfred Newman *ad Richard Day, William Creber*

Max Von Sydow, Dorothy McGuire, Claude Rains, Jose Ferrer, David McCallum, Charlton Heston, Sidney Poitier, Donald Pleasence, Roddy McDowall, Gary Raymond, Carroll Baker, Pat Boone, Van Heflin, Sal Mineo, Shelley Winters, Ed Wynn, John Wayne, Telly Savalas, Angela Lansbury, Joseph Schildkraut, Victor Buono, Nehemiah Persoff

'George Stevens was once described as a water buffalo of film art. What this film more precisely suggests is a dinosaur.'—*MFB*

'God is unlucky in *The Greatest Story Ever Told.* His only begotten son turns out to be a bore . . . the photography is inspired mainly by Hallmark Cards . . . as the Hallelujah Chorus explodes around us stereophonically and stereotypically it becomes clear that Lazarus was not so much raised from the tomb as blasted out of it. As for pacing, the picture does not let you forget a single second of its four hours.'—*John Simon*

'No more than three minutes have elapsed before we suspect that Stevens' name and fame have been purchased by the Hallmark Greeting Card Company, and that what we are looking at is really a lengthy catalogue of greeting cards for 1965—for Those Who Care Enough to Send the Very Best.'—*Stanley Kauffmann*

'Who but an audience of diplomats could sit through this thing? As the picture ponderously unrolled, it was mainly irritation that kept me awake.'—*Shana Alexander, Life*

'If the subject-matter weren't sacred, we would be responding to the picture in the most charitable way by laughing at it from start to finish.'—*Brendan Gill, New Yorker*

'A big windy bore.'—*Bruce Williamson, Playboy*

† The film was originally released at 4 hours 20 minutes. Subsequent versions were at 3 hours 58 minutes, 3 hours 17 minutes, 2 hours 27 minutes and 2 hours 7 minutes.

AAN: William C. Mellor, Loyal Griggs; Alfred Newman

Greed***
US 1923 110m (24 fps) bw silent
Metro-Goldwyn (Erich Von Stroheim, Irving Thalberg)

An ex-miner dentist kills his avaricious wife. Later in Death Valley he also kills her lover, but is bound to him by handcuffs.
This much-discussed film is often cited as its director's greatest folly: the original version ran eight hours. Re-edited by June Mathis, it retains considerable power sequence by sequence, but is necessarily disjointed in development. However, it must be seen to be appreciated.

wd Erich Von Stroheim, novel McTeague by Frank Norris *ph* Ben Reynolds, William Daniels, Ernest B. Schoedsack *ad* Richard Day, Cedric Gibbons, Erich Von Stroheim

Gibson Gowland, Zasu Pitts, *Jean Hersholt*, Chester Conklin, Dale Fuller

'The end leaves one with an appalling sense of human waste, of futility, of the drabness and cruelty of lives stifled by genteel poverty. Every character in the film is overwhelmed by it.'—*Gavin Lambert*

'Von Stroheim is a genius—*Greed* established that beyond all doubt—but he is badly in need of a stopwatch.'—*Robert E. Sherwood*

† In 1972 Herman G. Weinberg published a complete screenplay with 400 stills.
†† The original length at the première is said to have been 420m.

The Greed of William Hart
GB 1948 78m bw
Bushey (Gilbert Church)

In old Edinburgh, grave robbers procure corpses for an anatomist.
Cheapie version of a much filmed subject. This scenario was refurbished eleven years later by the same writer as *The Flesh and the Fiends*; see also *The Body Snatcher, Burke and Hare.*

w John Gilling *d* Oswald Mitchell *ph* S. D. Onions

Tod Slaughter, Henry Oscar, Aubrey Woods, Arnold Bell

The Greek Tycoon
US 1978 106m Technicolor Panavision
Universal / ABKCO (Allan Klein, Ely Landau)

A billionaire shipping tycoon marries the widow of an American president.
Rather messy 'faction' based on Onassis and Jacqueline Kennedy; entirely uninteresting save for glossy backgrounds and the relentlessness with which the characters swear at each other.

w Mort Fine *d* J. Lee Thompson *ph* Tony Richmond *m* Stanley Myers *pd* Michael Stringer

Anthony Quinn, Jacqueline Bisset, Raf Vallone, Edward Albert, James Franciscus, Camilla Sparv

† Among its other idiocies, this is the first film to credit 'Assistant to the assistant to the Unit Publicist'.

The Greeks Had a Word for Them*
US 1932 77m bw
UA (Samuel Goldwyn)

Adventures of three New York gold diggers.
Smart early talkie which helped launch the *Gold Diggers* series and TCF's parallel *Three Little Mice / Moon over Miami / How to Marry a Millionaire* series.

w Sidney Howard, *play* Zoe Akins *d* Lowell Sherman *ph* George Barnes *m* Alfred Newman

Joan Blondell, Madge Evans, Ina Claire, David Manners, Lowell Sherman, Phillips Smalley, Betty Grable

'Grand rowdy comedy . . . a revel in femme clothes and a picture calculated to fascinate women. Backwater clienteles questionable.'—*Variety*

The Green Archer
US 1940 bw serial: 15 eps

A villain unjustly imprisons his brother and takes over the family castle, only to be stalked by a mysterious green archer. Richly absurd serial which doesn't quite exploit its possibilities. Victor Jory (a hero for once), Iris Meredith, James Craven, Robert Fiske. Directed by James W. Horne; for Columbia.

'Their badge of honour was a green beret, and it said they had lived it all . . . the night jumps, the ambushes, the hand-to-hand combat, and the long nights of terror they filled with courage!'

The Green Berets
US 1968 141m Technicolor Panavision
Warner / Batjac (Michael Wayne)

After extensive training, two tough army detachments see service in Vietnam.
Overlong actioner criticized for unquestioningly accepting the Vietnam cause; in itself, violent, exhausting and dull.

w James Lee Barrett, *novel* Robin Moore *d* John Wayne, Ray Kellogg *ph* Winton C. Hoch *m* Miklos Rozsa

John Wayne, David Janssen, Jim Hutton, Aldo Ray, Raymond St Jacques, Jack Soo, Bruce Cabot, Patrick Wayne, Irene Tsu, Jason Evers, Luke Askew

'Propaganda as crude as this can only do damage to its cause.'—*David Wilson*

'A film best handled from a distance and with a pair of tongs.'—*Penelope Gilliatt*

The Green Buddha
GB 1954 62m bw

A charter pilot finds his clients are thieves and rounds them up. Fair second feature thick-ear. Wayne Morris, Mary Germaine, Walter Rilla, Arnold Marle. Written by Paul Erickson; directed by John Lemont; for Republic.

The Green Cockatoo
GB 1937 65m bw
TCF / New World (Robert T. Kane)
aka: *Four Dark Hours; Race Gang*

A man seeks revenge on the gangsters who killed his brother.
Sleazy little Soho-set thriller, mainly remarkable for cast and credits.

w Edward O. Berkman, Arthur Wimperis, *story* Graham Greene *d* William Cameron Menzies *ph* Mutz Greenbaum (Max Greene) *m* Miklos Rozsa

John Mills, Robert Newton, Rene Ray, Bruce Seton, Charles Oliver

'A fiery girl dares the dangers of the sea and a strange land—fighting for the love of a bold adventurer!'

Green Dolphin Street
US 1947 141m bw
MGM (Carey Wilson)

A Channel Islander emigrates to New Zealand and sends home for the wrong bride.
Silly 19th-century romance climaxed by rather a good earthquake. Expensively but falsely produced.

w Samson Raphaelson, *novel* Elizabeth Goudge *d* Victor Saville *ph* George Folsey *m* Bronislau Kaper

Lana Turner, Richard Hart, Edmund Gwenn, Van Heflin, Donna Reed

'The actors in this stupefyingly flimsy epic seem to be in competition for booby prizes.'—*Pauline Kael, 70s*

AAN: George Folsey

Green Fingers
GB 1946 83m bw

An unqualified osteopath tries to achieve respectability. Unsurprising and flatly made drama of eventual success against all odds. Robert Beatty, Carol Raye, Nova Pilbeam, Felix Aylmer, Moore Marriott, Edward Rigby. Written by Jack Whittingham, from the novel *Persistent Warrior* by Edith Arundel; directed by John Harlow; for British National.

Green Fire
US 1954 100m Eastmancolor Cinemascope
MGM (Armand Deutsch)

Two engineers disagree over their mining of Colombia emeralds.
Routine adventure story with good action highlights including landslide, flood and storm, all deadened by dull dialogue and romantic complications.

w Ivan Goff, Ben Roberts *d* Andrew Marton *ph* Paul Vogel *m* Miklos Rozsa

Stewart Granger, Paul Douglas, Grace Kelly

Green for Danger***
GB 1946 93m bw
Rank / Individual (Frank Launder, Sidney Gilliat)

A mysterious murderer strikes on the operating table at a wartime emergency hospital.
Classic comedy-thriller, with serious detection balanced by excellent jokes and performances, also by moments of fright.

w Sidney Gilliat, Claud Gurney, novel Christianna Brand *d Sidney Gilliat ph Wilkie Cooper m* William Alwyn

Alastair Sim, Sally Gray, Rosamund John, Trevor Howard, Leo Genn, Megs Jenkins, Judy Campbell, Ronald Ward, Moore Marriott

'Slick, witty and consistently entertaining.'—*Daily Telegraph*

'Launder and Gilliat have told an exciting story excitingly.'—*Times*

The Green Glove
US / France 1952 89m bw
UA / Benagoss (George Maurer)

A paratrooper against all odds returns a jewelled relic to its proper place in a French church.
An unsatisfactory concoction by people who have clearly seen *The Maltese Falcon* as well as lots of Hitchcock films, this interestingly cast and credited independent production never really takes off.

w Charles Bennett *d* Rudolph Maté *ph* Claude Renoir *m* Joseph Kosma

Glenn Ford, Cedric Hardwicke, Geraldine Brooks, George Macready, Gaby André, Roger Treville

The Green Goddess*
US 1930 80m bw
Warner

An Indian potentate holds Britishers prisoner.
Early talkie star vehicle which was also successful on the stage and as a silent but has little appeal now.

w Julian Josephson, *play* William Archer *d* Alfred E. Green *ph* James Van Trees

George Arliss, Alice Joyce, H. B. Warner, Ralph Forbes, David Tearle

'Nice programme fare, but it suggests too many synthetic thrillers that have gone before.'—*Variety*

† Remade 1942 as *Adventure in Iraq.*

AAN: George Arliss

Green Grass of Wyoming
US 1948 88m Technicolor
TCF

A rancher captures his runaway white stallion and wins the local trotting races.
Predictable, good-looking family film shot on location; a second sequel to *My Friend Flicka.*

w Martin Berkeley, *novel* Mary O'Hara *d* Louis King *ph* Charles G. Clarke *m* Cyril Mockridge

Peggy Cummins, Charles Coburn, Robert Arthur, Lloyd Nolan

AAN: Charles G. Clarke

Green Grow the Rushes
GB 1951 77m bw
ACT Films (John Gossage)

Civil servants discover that a Kentish village is devoted to smuggling.
Amiable but disappointingly feeble imitation of Ealing comedy by a company formed from the technicians' union; it simply hasn't got the right snap in any department.

w Derek Twist, Howard Clewes, *novel* Howard Clewes *d* Derek Twist *ph* Harry Waxman *m* Lambert Williamson

Roger Livesey, Richard Burton, Honor Blackman, Frederick Leister, John Salew, Colin Gordon, Geoffrey Keen, Harcourt Williams, Vida Hope

Green Hell*
US 1940 87m bw
Universal (Harry Edgington)

Explorers seek Inca treasure in the South American Jungle.
Studio-bound potboiler unworthy of its director but mainly enjoyable as a romp.

w Frances Marion *d* James Whale *ph* Karl Freund

Douglas Fairbanks Jnr, Joan Bennett, George Sanders, Vincent Price, Alan Hale, Gene Garrick, George Bancroft, John Howard

'It's the old nickelodeon mellerdrammer, at higher prices.'—*Picture Play*

† The temple set was re-used the same year in *The Mummy's Hand.*

The Green Helmet
GB 1961 88m bw
MGM (Charles Francis Vetter)

A race driver with shattered nerves makes his last job the introduction of an American car of new design.
Totally conventional motor racing thriller. Most of the work could just as effectively have been phoned in.

w Jon Cleary, from his novel *d* Michael Forlong *ph* Geoffrey Faithfull *m* Ken Jones

Bill Travers, Ed Begley, Sidney James, Nancy Walters, Ursula Jeans, Megs Jenkins

The Green Hornet
US 1940 bw serial: 13 eps

A crusading publisher in disguise fights various rackets. Archetypal serial in the Batman and Robin mould; the assistant here is a judo expert. Gordon Jones, Wade Boteler, Keye Luke, Anne Nagel, Philip Trent. Directed by Ford Beebe and Ray Taylor; for Universal.

The Green Hornet Strikes Again
US 1940 bw serial: 13 eps

See above, but with Warren Hull in the lead. Directed by Ford Beebe and John Rawlins; for Universal.

Green Ice
GB 1981 116m colour
ITC / Lew Grade (Jack Wiener)

An aimless American in Mexico becomes involved with emerald thieves.
Dismally routine punch-ups and car chases are enlivened by a mildly original theft by balloon, but the overall effect is soporific.

w Edward Anhalt, Ray Hassett, Anthony Simmons, Robert de Laurentis, *novel* Gerald Browne *d* Ernest Day *ph* Gilbert Taylor *m* Bill Wyman

Ryan O'Neal, Anne Archer, Omar Sharif, Philip Stone

'It should not tempt anyone away from doubtlessly superior versions of the same material on television.'—*Geoff Brown, MFB*

The Green Light*
US 1937 85m bw
Warner (Henry Blanke)

A dedicated doctor gives up his practice when a patient dies.
Adequate star melodrama.

w Milton Krims, *novel* Lloyd C. Douglas *d* Frank Borzage *ph* Byron Haskin *m* Max Steiner

Errol Flynn, Anita Louise, Margaret Lindsay, Cedric Hardwicke, Henry O'Neill, Spring Byington

'Customer lure in the title and the player names . . . it will carry a weak sister nicely.'—*Variety*

The Green Man*
GB 1956 80m bw
BL / Grenadier (Frank Launder, Sidney Gilliat)

A professional assassin stalks a pompous politician.
Cheerful but not very subtle black comedy, suffering from the attempt to make a star part out of a very minor character.

w Sidney Gilliat, Frank Launder, from their play Meet a Body *d* Robert Day *ph* Gerald Gibbs *m* Cedric Thorpe Davie

Alastair Sim, George Cole, Jill Adams, Terry-Thomas, Avril Angers, John Chandos, Dora Bryan, Colin Gordon, Raymond Huntley

Green Mansions
US 1959 104m Metrocolor Cinemascope
MGM / Avon (Edmund Grainger)

In a remote Amazon forest an adventurer encounters Rima, a child of nature who takes him on a quest for truth.
Absurd studio-bound Shangri-La story based on an Edwardian fantasy that may well have suited the printed page, but not the wide screen. Dismally photographed in shades of green, with all concerned looking acutely uncomfortable.

w Dorothy Kingsley, *novel* W. H. Hudson *d* Mel Ferrer *ph* Joseph Ruttenberg *m* Bronislau Kaper, Hector Villa-Lobos

Anthony Perkins, Audrey Hepburn, Lee J. Cobb, Henry Silva

The Green Pastures***
US 1936 93m bw
Warner (Henry Blanke)

Old Testament stories as seen through simple-minded negro eyes.
Though recently attacked as setting back the cause of black emancipation, this is a brilliantly sympathetic and humorous film, very cunningly adapted for the screen in a series of dramatic scenes which make the material work even better than it did on the stage.

w Marc Connelly, from his play and stories by Roark Bradford *d William Keighley, Marc Connelly ph Hal Mohr m Erich Wolfgang Korngold*

Rex Ingram, Oscar Polk, Eddie Anderson, Frank Wilson, George Reed

'I imagine God has a sense of humour, and I imagine that He is delighted with *The Green Pastures*.'—*Don Herold*

'That disturbance around the Music Hall yesterday was the noise of shuffling queues in Sixth Avenue and the sound of motion picture critics dancing in the street.'—*Bosley Crowther, New York Times*

'This is as good a religious play as one is likely to get in this age from a practised New York writer.'—*Graham Greene*

Green Promise
US 1949 88m bw
RKO / Glenn McCarthy (Robert Paige, Monty F. Collins)
GB title: *Raging Waters*

A farmer refuses to move from the dust bowl area, and a landslide causes a flood.
Curiously stilted independent production which doesn't really bear comparison with *The Grapes of Wrath*.

w Monty F. Collins *d* William D. Russell *ph* John Russell *m* David Chudnow

Marguerite Chapman, Walter Brennan, Robert Paige, Natalie Wood, Ted Donaldson, Connie Marshall

The Green Scarf
GB 1954 96m bw
B and A (Bertram Ostrer, Albert Fennell)

An elderly French lawyer takes on the defence of a blind, deaf and dumb murder suspect.
Plodding courtroom drama with familiar faces in unconvincing French guise.

w Gordon Wellesley, *novel* The Brute by Guy des Cars *d* George More O'Ferrall *ph* Jack Hildyard *m* Brian Easdale

Michael Redgrave, Ann Todd, Leo Genn, Kieron Moore

The Green Years*
US 1946 127m bw
MGM (Leon Gordon)

A young boy brought up strictly in Ireland makes friends with his mischievous grandfather.
Period family film in familiar style, sparked only by its scene-stealing star performance.

w Robert Ardrey, Sonya Levien, *novel* A. J. Cronin *d* Victor Saville *ph* George Folsey *m* Herbert Stothart *ad* Cedric Gibbons, Hans Peters

Charles Coburn, Dean Stockwell, Tom Drake, Beverly Tyler, Hume Cronyn, Gladys Cooper, Selena Royle, Jessica Tandy, Richard Haydn, Andy Clyde

'It has been described in the ads as "wonderful" by everyone within Louis B. Mayer's purchasing power except his horses, so I hesitate to ask you to take my word for it: the picture is awful.'—*James Agee*

AAN: George Folsey; Charles Coburn

The Greengage Summer*
GB 1961 99m Technicolor
Columbia / PKL (Victor Saville, Edward Small)
US title: *Loss of Innocence*

A young girl staying at a hotel falls in love with a jewel thief but is accidentally responsible for his capture.
Old-fashioned and not very interesting story with an appeal, one supposes, to well-brought-up young women. Decently made.

w Howard Koch, *novel* Rumer Godden *d* Lewis Gilbert *ph* Frederick A. Young *m* Richard Addinsell

Kenneth More, Danielle Darrieux, Susannah York, Claude Nollier, Jane Asher, Elizabeth Dear, Maurice Denham

Greenwich Village*
US 1944 82m Technicolor
TCF (William Le Baron)

In the twenties, a hick composer in New York allows his concerto to be used in a jazz musical.
Lightweight musical romp.

w Michael Fessier, Ernest Pagano *d* Walter Lang *ph* Leon Shamroy, Harry Jackson *songs* Leo Robin, Nacio Herb Brown

Carmen Miranda, Don Ameche, William Bendix, Vivian Blaine, Felix Bressart, Tony and Sally De Marco, Adolph Green, Betty Comden, Alvin Hammer, Judy Holliday

Greetings*
US 1968 88m Eastmancolor

A draftee tries every which way to be exempted, then subjects himself to a whirl of physical experience. Kaleidoscopic stringing together of fleeting satirical bits; talent undeniable but equally uncontrolled. Jonathan Warden, Robert de Niro, Gerrit Graham, Megan McCormick. Written by Charles Hirsch and Brian de Palma; directed and edited by Brian de Palma; for West End Films.

Gregory's Girl**
GB 1980 91m colour
Lake / NFFC / STV (Davina Belling, Clive Parsons)

In a Scottish new town, a school footballer becomes aware of sex.
Curiously diverting comedy peopled by dreamers but handicapped by impenetrable accents. An unexpected world-wide success.

wd Bill Forsyth ph Michael Coulter *m* Colin Tully

Gordon John Sinclair, Dee Hepburn, Jake D'Arcy, Claire Grogan

BFA: best script

Gremlins*
US 1984 106m Technicolor
Warner / Amblin (Michael Finnell)

Small furry creatures called mogwais prove to be immensely prolific and dangerous when wet.
Juvenile horror comic, a kind of deliberate inversion of *E.T.* Slow to start, and a little too knowingly nasty, with variable special effects; but a pretty hot commercial success.

w Chris Columbus *d* Joe Dante (with Steven Spielberg as a presumably involved producer) *ph* John Hora *m* Jerry Goldsmith *gremlin designer* Chris Walas *ed* Tina Hirsch

Zach Galligan, Phoebe Cates, Hoyt Axton, Polly Holliday, Keye Luke, Scott Brady, Edward Andrews

'Don't go if you still believe in Santa Claus.'—*Roger Ebert*

The Grey Fox*
Canada 1982 91m Eastmancolor
Mercury (Peter O'Brian)

The more or less true story of a turn-of-the-century stagecoach bandit who in 1901 was released from a long prison term, genially committed more crimes, and disappeared.
Likeable semi-western with an excellent sense of place and time.

w John Hunter *d Philip Borsos ph Frank Tidy m* Michael Conway

Richard Farnsworth, Jackie Burroughs, Ken Pogue, Wayne Robson

Greyfriars Bobby*
GB 1960 91m Technicolor
Walt Disney (Hugh Attwooll)

A Skye terrier keeps persistent vigil over his master's grave and is made a freeman of the city of Edinburgh.
Adequately produced film of a charming old Victorian story.

w Robert Westerby *d* Don Chaffey *ph* Paul Beeson *m* Francis Chagrin

Donald Crisp, Laurence Naismith, Alexander Mackenzie, Kay Walsh, Andrew Cruickshank, Vincent Winter, Moultrie Kelsall, Duncan Macrae

'The better Disney qualities of exact period detail and childlike directness are apparent.'—*MFB*

† The story was previously filmed as *Challenge to Lassie*.

Greystoke: The Legend of Tarzan, Lord of the Apes
GB 1984 130m Eastmancolor Panavision
Warner / WEA Records (Hugh Hudson, Stanley S. Canter)

In the 1880s, an English lord and lady are killed in Africa, and their son is brought up by apes.
An absurd attempt to treat the story seriously after 70 years of hokum, this meandering chronicle, cut down from something much longer and even less endurable, has men in ape suits, an eye for unpleasant detail, and Ralph Richardson sliding down the stairs on a tray. The attempt to moralize at the end is emetic.

w P. H. Vazak (Robert Towne), Michael Austin, *novel* Tarzan of the Apes by Edgar Rice Burroughs *d* Hugh Hudson *ph* John Alcott *m* John Scott *pd* Stuart Craig

Ralph Richardson, Ian Holm, James Fox, Christopher Lambert, Andie MacDowell, Cheryl Campbell, Paul Geoffrey, John Wells, Nigel Davenport, Ian Charleson, Richard Griffiths

'A unique mixture of pomposity and ineptitude . . . in the second half the movie simply loses its mind, and dribbles to a pathetically indecisive conclusion.'—*Pauline Kael, New Yorker*

AAN: Ralph Richardson (supporting actor), adapted screenplay

Il Grido*
Italy 1957 102m bw
SPA Cinematografica / Robert Alexander
aka: *The Cry*

A man whose wife has left him travels across the Po Valley with his daughter in search of new happiness, but fails to find it and commits suicide.
Watchable but rather aimlessly depressing character drama.

w Michelangelo Antonioni, Elio Bartolini, Ennio de Concini *d* Michelangelo Antonioni *ph* Gianni di Venanzo *m* Giovanni Fusco

Steve Cochran, Alida Valli, Dorian Gray, Betsy Blair, Lynn Shaw

Grip of the Strangler*
GB 1958 78m bw
Producers' Associates (John Croydon)
US title: *The Haunted Strangler*

A novelist investigating an old murder case finds that he was himself the murderer.
Moderate thriller with a predictable but efficient plot.

w Jan Read *d* Robert Day *ph* Lionel Banes *m* Buxton Orr

Boris Karloff, Elizabeth Allan, Jean Kent, Vera Day, Anthony Dawson

Grissly's Millions
US 1945 71m bw

An heiress is in danger from less successful relations. Watchable co-feature. Paul Kelly, Virginia Grey, Don Douglas, Elisabeth Risdon, Robert Barrat, Clem Bevans. Written by Muriel Roy Bolton; directed by John English; for Republic.

The Grissom Gang
US 1971 128m Metrocolor
Associates and Aldrich / ABC

In 1931, a New York heiress is kidnapped by gangsters and comes to like it.
Unpleasant remake of *No Orchids for Miss Blandish* (previously filmed under that title, incredibly badly, in GB in 1948), with too much footage of lush blonde being slobbered over by psychotic thug, and an inevitable emphasis on violence.

w Leon Griffiths, *novel* James Hadley Chase *d* Robert Aldrich *ph* Joseph Biroc *m* Gerald Fried *ad* James Dowell Vance

Scott Wilson, Kim Darby, Tony Musante, Robert Lansing, Irene Dailey, Connie Stevens, Wesley Addy

'Offensive, immoral and perhaps even lascivious.'—*Vincent Canby*

'18 feet of towering fury! The most dangerous jaws on land!'

Grizzly
US 1976 91m Movielab Todd AO 35
Film Ventures International (David Sheldon, Harvey Flaxman)
aka: *Killer Grizzly*

A mammoth bear preys upon campers in a national park.
Inept and boring shocker in the wake of *Jaws*.

w Harvey Flaxman, David Sheldon *d* William Girdler *ph* William Asman *m* Robert O. Ragland

Christopher George, Andrew Prine, Richard Jaeckel, Joan McCall

The Groom Wore Spurs
US 1951 81m bw

A supposed tough cowboy star gets into trouble in Las Vegas. Tedious star comedy. Ginger Rogers, Jack Carson, Joan Davis, Stanley Ridges, James Brown. Written by Robert Carson from his novel Legal Bride; directed by Richard Whorf; for Howard Welsch / Universal.

Ground Zero*
Australia 1987 109m Eastmancolor Panavasion

A cinematographer stumbles on dangerous secrets when investigating his father's death 30 years previously. Smart contemporary thriller with a political theme. Colin Friels, Jack Thompson, Donald Pleasence, Natalie Bate. Written by Jan Sardi, Mac Gudgeon; directed by Michael Pattinson, Bruce Myles; for BDB / Pattinson-Burrowes.

Grounds for Marriage
US 1950 90m bw

A divorced couple meet again and find they have strange effects on each other. Stolid romantic comedy with second team talent.

Van Johnson, Kathryn Grayson, Paula Raymond, Lewis Stone, Reginald Owen, Barry Sullivan. Written by Allen Rivkin and Laura Kerr; directed by Robert Z. Leonard; for MGM.

'We challenge you to guess the ending!'

The Groundstar Conspiracy*
US 1972 96m Technicolor Panavision
Universal / Hal Roach International (Trevor Wallace)

An explosion rips apart a top secret space project, and the surviving scientist loses his memory.
Gimmicky but generally compulsive sci-fi mystery yarn, with an effective though predictable climax.

w Matthew Howard, *novel* The Alien by L. P. Davies *d* Lamont Johnson *ph* Michael Reed *m* Paul Hoffert

George Peppard, Michael Sarrazin, James Olson, Christine Belford, Tim O'Connor, James McEachin

The Group***
US 1966 152m De Luxe
UA / Famous Artists (Sidney Buchman)

The subsequent love lives of a group of girls who graduate from Vassar in 1933.
Patchy but generally fascinating series of interwoven sketches and character studies, with mainly tragic overtones; good attention to period detail, and dazzling array of new talent.

w Sidney Buchman, novel Mary McCarthy d Sidney Lumet ph Boris Kaufman *m* Charles Gross *pd Gene Callahan*

Joanna Pettet, Candice Bergen, *Jessica Walter*, *Joan Hackett*, Elizabeth Hartman, Mary Robin-Redd, *Kathleen Widdoes*, Shirley Knight, Larry Hagman, *Hal Holbrook*, *Robert Emhardt*, Robert Mulligan, James Congdon, James Broderick

'Although it is a strange, inclusive, no-holds-barred movie that runs the gamut from scenes that are almost soap-operaish, to amusing scenes that are almost satire, to outrageously frank scenes that are almost voyeuristic, it is still greatly exhilarating while it provokes thought and pushes the viewer into examining his own conscience.'—*Philip T. Hartung, Commonweal*

THE GROUP. Sidney Lumet gave Mary McCarthy's novel typically careful attention. But whatever happened to some of the actresses who were part of the group?

Grumpy
US 1930 74m bw

A very elderly gentleman is still in control of his family. Interesting but not exciting transcript of a production which was having surprising success on Broadway with English players, though a very musty vehicle even then. Cyril Maude, Phillips Holmes, Paul Cavanagh, Frances Dade, Halliwell Hobbes, Paul Lukas. Written by Doris Anderson from a play by Horace Hodges and Thomas Wigney Percyval; directed by George Cukor and Cyril Gardner; for Paramount. 'Its box office fate is in the balance.'—*Variety*

Guadalcanal Diary*
US 1943 93m bw
TCF (Bryan Foy)

Marines fight for a vital Pacific base.
Standard war propaganda, with good action scenes.

w Lamar Trotti, *book* Richard Tregaskis *d* Lewis Seiler *ph* Charles G. Clarke *m* David Buttolph

Preston Foster, Lloyd Nolan, William Bendix, Richard Conte, Anthony Quinn, Richard Jaeckel, Roy Roberts, Minor Watson, Ralph Byrd, Lionel Stander, Miles Mander, Reed Hadley

The Guardsman*
US 1931 83m bw
MGM (Albert Lewin)

A jealous actor tests his wife's fidelity.
Theatrically effective comedy filmed for the sake of its stars; later remade as a musical, *The Chocolate Soldier* (qv).

w Ernest Vajda, Claudine West, *play* Ferenc Molnar *d* Sidney Franklin *ph* Norbert Brodine

Alfred Lunt, Lynn Fontanne, Roland Young, Zasu Pitts, Maude Eburne, Herman Bing, Ann Dvorak

'Looks like a smash engagement on Broadway and less than moderate returns on general release.'—*Variety*

AAN: Alfred Lunt; Lynn Fontanne

La Guerre Est Finie
France / Sweden 1966 122m bw
Sofracima / Europa Film
aka: *The War Is Over*

A Spanish revolutionary maintains his ideals even though he is warned that he will be sold out.
Dreary drama with romantic interludes and a fussy technique involving what appears to be the first use of flashforwards.

w Jorge Semprun *d* Alain Resnais *ph* Sacha Vierny *m* Giovanni Fusco

Yves Montand, Ingrid Thulin, Geneviève Bujold, Michel Piccoli

AAN: Jorge Semprun

Guess Who's Coming to Dinner**
US 1967 112m Technicolor
Columbia / Stanley Kramer

A well-to-do San Francisco girl announces that she is going to marry a black man, and her parents find they are less broad-minded than they thought.
The problem picture that isn't really, since everyone is so nice and the prospective bridegroom is so eligible. It looks like a photographed play, but isn't based on one; the set is unconvincing; but the acting is a dream.

w William Rose *d* Stanley Kramer *ph* Sam Leavitt *md* Frank de Vol *pd* Robert Clatworthy

Spencer Tracy, Katharine Hepburn, Katharine Houghton (Hepburn's niece), *Sidney Poitier*, Cecil Kellaway, Roy E. Glenn Snr, Beah Richards, Isabell Sanford, Virginia Christine

'Suddenly everybody's caught up in a kind of integrated drawing-room comedy, and unable to decide whether there's anything funny in it or not.'—*Ann Birstein, Vogue*

'A load of embarrassing rubbish. In the circumstances there is little that director Stanley Kramer can do but see that his camera plod from room to room and make the most of people sitting down and getting up again.'—*Penelope Mortimer*

'What Rose and Kramer have done is to create a number of elaborate Aunt Sallies, arrange them in attractive patterns, and dispose of them with the flick of a feather.'—*Basil Wright, 1972*

'Mendacious and sanctimonious drivel.'—*John Simon*

AA: William Rose; Katharine Hepburn
AAN: best picture; Stanley Kramer; Frank de Vol; Spencer Tracy; Cecil Kellaway; Beah Richards

Guest in the House*
US 1944 121m bw
Hunt Stromberg

A seemingly pleasant young woman is invited to stay with a family and brings tragedy and hatred to them.
Theatrical and rather unconvincing melodrama.

w Ketti Frings, *play* Dear Evelyn by Dale Eunson, Hagar Wilde *d* John Brahm *ph* Lee Garmes *m* Werner Janssen *pd* Nicolai Remisoff

Anne Baxter, Ralph Bellamy, Aline MacMahon, Ruth Warrick, Scott McKay, Jerome Cowan, Marie McDonald, Percy Kilbride, Margaret Hamilton

AAN: Werner Janssen

Guest Wife
US 1945 90m bw
(UA) Jack H. Skirball

For business purposes a man allows his wife to pretend to be the wife of another.
Stereotyped star farce which seemed tolerable at the time.

w Bruce Manning, John Klorer *d* Sam Wood *ph* Joseph Valentine *md* Daniele Amfitheatrof

Claudette Colbert, Don Ameche, Dick Foran, Charles Dingle, Grant Mitchell

'Mr Wood is a big gun to be trained on so trivial a target, but the result justifies the choice.'—*Richard Mallett, Punch*

AAN: Daniele Amfitheatrof

'For the married man who's thinking single—or the single man who's just thinking!'

A Guide for the Married Man**
US 1967 91m De Luxe Panavision
TCF (Frank McCarthy)

A practised wolf explains to a perfect husband how to be unfaithful.
Generally funny revue with as many hilarious moments as flat spots.

w Frank Tarloff *d* Gene Kelly *ph* Joe Macdonald *m* Johnny Williams

Walter Matthau, Inger Stevens, *Robert Morse*, Sue Anne Langdon, Lucille Ball, Art Carney, Jack Benny, Polly Bergen, Joey Bishop, Sid Caesar, Wally Cox, Jayne Mansfield, Carl Reiner, Phil Silvers, Jeffrey Hunter, Terry-Thomas, Ben Blue

'One of the funniest films of the last several seasons . . . it has sense enough to sit down when it's through.'—*Robert Windeler*

Guilt Is My Shadow
GB 1950 86m bw

A girl kills her villainous husband and is helped by a farmer. Tedious melodrama, stiffly told and not helped by rural surroundings. Patrick Holt, Elizabeth Sellars, Peter Reynolds, Lana Morris, Avice Landone. Written by Ivan Foxwell, Roy Kellino and John Gilling, from the novel *You're Best Alone* by Peter Curtis; directed by Roy Kellino; for Ivan Foxwell.

The Guilt of Janet Ames
US 1947 83m bw
Columbia

A paralysed war widow seeks to discover whether her husband's sacrifice was worthwhile.
Embarrassing attempt by a comedienne to play Hamlet.

w Louella Macfarlane, Allen Rivkin, Devery Freeman, *story* Lenore Coffee *d* Henry Levin *ph* Joseph Walker *m* Morris Stoloff

Rosalind Russell, Melvyn Douglas, Sid Caesar, Betsy Blair, Nina Foch, Harry Von Zell, Arthur Space

Guilty?
GB 1956 93m bw
Grand National / Gibraltar (Charles A. Leeds)

An ex-resistance heroine is on trial for murder at the Old Bailey; her young solicitor goes to Avignon to prove her innocence.
Solidly cast old-fashioned mystery with a courtroom climax.

w Maurice J. Wilson, *novel* Death Has Deep Roots by Michael Gilbert *d* Edmond Greville *ph* Stan Pavey *m* Bruce Montgomery

John Justin, Barbara Laage, Donald Wolfit, Stephen Murray, Norman Wooland, Frank Villard, Sydney Tafler, Betty Stockfield

Guilty as Hell*
US 1932 82m bw

A doctor commits what he hopes is the perfect murder. Smart murder story with two points of interest: the audience knows who done it from the start, and the detective and reporter roles are worked over to fit the actors who played Flagg and Quirt. It certainly pleased at the time, and was remade in 1937 as *Night Club Scandal*, with John Barrymore in the lead as the doctor. Edmund Lowe, Victor McLaglen, Richard Arlen, Ralph Ince, Adrienne Ames, Henry Stephenson, Elizabeth Patterson. Written by Arthur Kober and Frank Partos, from the play Riddle Me This by Daniel Rubin; directed by Erle C. Kenton; for Paramount. 'Excellent entertainment and should do a good business where the title does not hurt.'—*Variety*

The Guilty Generation
US 1931 82m bw

A gangster has social ambitions for his daughter's sake. Rather heavy melodrama which didn't catch on. Leo Carrillo, Constance Cummings, Robert Young, Boris Karloff, Emma Dunn. From the play by Jo Milward and J. Kerby Hawkes; directed by Rowland V. Lee; for Columbia. 'Merits a fair showing . . . will do average or better.'—*Variety*

Guilty Hands
US 1931 60m bw

A district attorney commits murder and tries to frame a girl, but is killed when rigor mortis makes the gun go off in his victim's hand.

Risible melodrama which might with better writing have been effective. Lionel Barrymore, Kay Francis, Madge Evans, William Bakewell, C. Aubrey Smith, Polly Moran, Alan Mowbray. Written by Bayard Veiller; directed by W. S. Van Dyke; for MGM. 'Someone missed here, and plenty.'—*Variety*

Guilty of Treason
US 1950 86m bw

An account of the trial by the Russians of the Hungarian primate Cardinal Mindzenty. Gutter press version of real events, with cheap production and fictional frills. Charles Bickford, Paul Kelly, Bonita Granville, Richard Derr, Barry Kroeger, Elisabeth Risdon. Written by Emmet Lavery; directed by Felix Feist; for Eagle Lion. (GB title: *Treason.*)

The Guinea Pig**
GB 1948 97m bw
Pilgrim (John Boulting)
US title: *The Outsider*

The first poor boy to win a scholarship to a famous public school has a hard time. Enjoyable though unrealistic school drama with chief interest centring on the staff. A rude word ('kick up the arse') ensured its popularity.

w Bernard Miles, Warren Chetham Strode, from the latter's play *d* Roy Boulting *ph* Gilbert Taylor *m* John Wooldridge

Richard Attenborough, *Robert Flemyng, Cecil Trouncer*, Sheila Sim, Bernard Miles, Joan Hickson

Gulliver's Travels**
US 1939 74m Technicolor
(Paramount) Max Fleischer

Animated cartoon version which invents a Romeo-Juliet romance between Lilliput and Blefuscu and has the usual trouble with romantic humans. At the time it represented a genuine challenge to Disney, but has not worn well in terms of pace or inventiveness. Fleischer made one more feature cartoon, *Mr Bug Goes to Town.*

d Dave Fleischer *m* Victor Young *songs* Ralph Rainger, Leo Robin

'Effective entertainment, but may not reach the grosses of *Snow White.*'—*Variety*

AAN: song 'Faithful Forever'; Victor Young

Gulliver's Travels
GB 1976 81m Eastmancolor
EMI / Valeness-Belvision (Josef Shaftel)

An ineffective treatment, again aimed at children, in which Gulliver is the only human element and all the Lilliputians are cartooned.

w Don Black *d* Peter Hunt *ph* Alan Hume *pd* Michael Stringer *m* Michel Legrand

Richard Harris, Catherine Schell, Norman Shelley

'Bonelessly inoffensive.'—*Sight and Sound*

The Gumball Rally
US 1976 107m Technicolor
Warner / First Artists (Chuck Bail)

A variety of vehicles take part in a crazy race from New York to Long Beach.
The stuntmen are the real stars of this good-looking but dramatically deficient chase and destruction extravaganza.

w Leon Capetanos *d* Chuck Bail *ph Richard Glouner* *m* Dominic Frontière *stunt co-ordinator* Eddie Donno

Michael Sarrazin, Normann Burton, Gary Busey, John Durren, Susan Flannery

Gumshoe**
GB 1971 85m Eastmancolor
Columbia / Memorial (David Barber)

A Liverpool bingo caller dreams of becoming a Bogart-like private eye and finds himself in the middle of a murder case.
A likeable spoof which is never quite as funny as it means to be. Billy Liar did it better, but there's plenty of amusing detail.

w Neville Smith *d* Stephen Frears *ph* Chris Menges *m* Andrew Lloyd Webber

Albert Finney, Billie Whitelaw, Fulton Mackay, Frank Finlay, Janice Rule

Gun Crazy*
US 1950 87m bw
King Brothers
reissue title: *Deadly is the Female*

A boy and girl set off on a trail of armed robbery and murder.
Modernized Bonnie and Clyde story which has become a minor cult film.

w Dalton Trumbo, *story* Mackinlay Kantor *d Joseph H. Lewis* *ph* Russell Harlan *m* Victor Young

John Dall, Peggy Cummins, Morris Carnovsky, Barry Kroger, Annabel Shaw, Harry Lewis

Gun for a Coward
US 1956 88m Technicolor Cinemascope

Three brothers join forces on a cattle drive, but one is killed. Slightly pretentious western co-feature. Fred MacMurray, Jeffrey Hunter, Dean Stockwell, Chill Wills, Janice Rule. Written by R. Wright Campbell; directed by Abner Biberman; for Universal-International.

Gun Fury
US 1953 80m Technicolor 3-D
Columbia (Lewis J. Rachmil)

Outlaws rob a stagecoach and abduct a girl; her fiancé follows and takes revenge.
Adequate western programmer.

w Irving Wallace, Roy Huggins *d* Raoul Walsh *ph* Lester H. White *md* Mischa Bakaleinikoff

Rock Hudson, Donna Reed, Phil Carey, Lee Marvin, Neville Brand

Gun Glory
US 1957 89m Metrocolor Cinemascope
MGM (Nicholas Nayfack)

A gunfighter returns home to settle down, but finds his wife dead and his son resentful.
Dull, unexciting star western.

w William Ludwig, *novel* Man of the West by Philip Yordan *d* Roy Rowland *ph* Harold J. Marzorati *m* Jeff Alexander

Stewart Granger, Rhonda Fleming, Chill Wills, Steve Rowland, James Gregory

The Gun Runners*
US 1958 82m bw
UA / Seven Arts (Clarence Greene)

The owner of a Florida motor cruiser innocently rents it to a gun merchant.
Modestly effective action melodrama, the third version of *To Have and Have Not* (qv).

w Daniel Mainwaring, Paul Monash *d Don Siegel* *ph Hal Mohr* *m* Leith Stevens

Audie Murphy, Eddie Albert, Patricia Owens, Everett Sloane

'In the bullring at Bajo Rio, Mexico, on Saturday at 4 pm, they'll pay to see two men kill each other!'

A Gunfight*
US 1970 94m Technicolor
Harvest / Thoroughbred / Bryna (Ronnie Lubin, Harold Jack Bloom)

Two famous gunfighters on their uppers stage a duel for money.
Austere and anti-climactic western supposedly against popular blood lust.

w Harold Jack Bloom *d* Lamont Johnson *ph* David M. Walsh *m* Laurence Rosenthal

Kirk Douglas, Johnny Cash, Karen Black, Raf Vallone, Jane Alexander

Gunfight at Comanche Creek
US 1963 90m De Luxe Panavision

In 1875 a detective goes undercover to unmask the brains behind a robber gang with complex methods. Ingenious but over-emphatic western programmer. Audie Murphy, Ben Cooper, Coleen Miller, John Hubbard, DeForrest Kelley. Written by Edward Bernds; directed by Frank McDonald; for Allied Artists.

Gunfight at Dodge City
US 1958 81m De Luxe Cinemascope
UA / Mirisch

After various problems, Bat Masterson is elected sheriff of Dodge City.
Fair standard western with emphasis on plot and character.

w Daniel B. Ullman, Martin M. Goldsmith *d* Joseph M. Newman *ph* Carl Guthrie *m* Hans Salter

Joel McCrea, Julie Adams, John McIntire, Richard Anderson, Nancy Gates

Gunfight at the OK Corral**
US 1957 122m Technicolor Vistavision
Paramount / Hal Wallis

Wyatt Earp and Doc Holliday defeat the Clanton Gang.
Watchable, ambitious, but vaguely disappointing super-western.

w Leon Uris *d* John Sturges *ph* Charles B. Lang *m* Dmitri Tiomkin

Burt Lancaster, Kirk Douglas, Jo Van Fleet, Rhonda Fleming, John Ireland, Frank Faylen, Kenneth Tobey, Earl Holliman

'Carefully and lavishly mounted, but overlong and overwrought.'—*John Cutts*

Gunfight in Abilene
US 1967 86m Technicolor

After the Civil War, an officer goes home to find strife between farmers and cattlemen. Fairly sensible and pleasing lower-berth western. Bobby Darin, Emily Banks, Leslie Nielsen, Donnelly Rhodes, Don Galloway, Michael Sarrazin. Written by Berne Giler and John D. F. Black; directed by William Hale; for Universal.

'His only friend was his gun—his only refuge, a woman's heart!'

The Gunfighter**
US 1950 84m bw
TCF (Nunnally Johnson)

A gunfighter fails to shake off his past. Downbeat, small-scale but very careful adult western set in a believable community.

w William Bowers, William Sellers *d Henry King ph Arthur Miller m* Alfred Newman

Gregory Peck, Helen Westcott, Millard Mitchell, Jean Parker, Karl Malden, Skip Homeier, Mae Marsh

'Preserves throughout a respectable level of intelligence and invention.'—*Lindsay Anderson*

'Not merely a good western, a good film.'—*Richard Mallett, Punch*

'The movie is done in cold, quiet tones of gray, and every object in it—faces, clothing, a table, the hero's heavy moustache—is given an air of uncompromising authenticity, suggesting those dim photographs of the nineteenth-century west. . .'—*Robert Warshow, The Immediate Experience*

AAN: original story (William Bowers)

Gunfighters
US 1947 87m Cinecolor

A retired gunfighter is suspected of the murder of his best friend. Presentable star western. Randolph Scott, Barbara Britton, Dorothy Hart, Bruce Cabot, Forrest Tucker. Written by Alan Le May, from the novel *Twin Sombreros* by Zane Grey; directed by George Waggner; for Columbia. (GB title: *The Assassin.*)

Gunfighters of the Northwest
US 1954 bw serial: 15 eps

The Royal Canadian Mounties ride into action. Just what you'd expect of a serial with this title. Jack Mahoney (later Jock), Clayton Moore, Phyllis Coates, Marshall Reed, Lyle Talbot. Directed by Spencer Bennet; for Columbia.

Gung Ho!
US 1943 88m bw
Universal / Walter Wanger

Adventures of the Marines in the Pacific War. Trite flagwaver, popular at the time.

w Lucien Hubbard, based on the experiences of Captain W. S. LeFrancois USMC *d* Ray Enright *ph* Milton H. Krasner *m* Frank Skinner, Hans Salter

Randolph Scott, Grace MacDonald, Alan Curtis, Noah Beery Jnr, J. Carrol Naish, David Bruce, Peter Coe, Robert Mitchum

Gung Ho
US 1986 111m Continental colour

Japanese management takes over an American small town. Basically old-fashioned hands-across-the-sea stuff, without any very clear attitude except gentle fun. It rapidly led to a TV series, which folded, and that's about its level. Michael Keaton, Gedde Watanabe, George Wendt, Mimi Rogers. Written by Lowell Ganz, Babaloo Mandel; directed and produced by Ron Howard; for Tony Ganz, Deborah Blum / Paramount. 'A film that's not much of anything except two hours long.'—*People*

'Thrills for a thousand movies plundered for one mighty show!'
'Romance aflame through dangerous days and nights of terror! In a land where anything can happen—most of all to a beautiful girl alone!'

Gunga Din***
US 1939 117m bw
RKO (George Stevens)

Three cheerful army veterans meet adventure on the North-West Frontier.
Rousing period actioner with comedy asides, one of the most entertaining of its kind ever made.

w Joel Sayre, Fred Guiol, Ben Hecht, Charles MacArthur, *poem* Rudyard Kipling *d George Stevens ph Joseph H. August m* Alfred Newman *ad* Van Nest Polglase

Cary Grant, Victor McLaglen, Douglas Fairbanks Jnr, Sam Jaffe, Eduardo Ciannelli, Joan Fontaine, Montagu Love, Robert Coote, Cecil Kellaway, Abner Biberman, Lumsden Hare

'One of the big money pictures this year . . . will recoup plenty at the box office window.'—*Variety*

'One of the most enjoyable nonsense-adventure movies of all time.'—*Pauline Kael, 1968*

'Bravura is the exact word for the performances, and Stevens' composition and cutting of the fight sequences is particularly stunning.'—*NFT, 1973*

Gunman's Walk*
US 1958 97m Technicolor Cinemascope
Columbia (Fred Kohlmar)

A tough westerner has two sons, one of whom follows too literally in his footsteps.
Competent action melodrama with good characterization.

w Frank Nugent *d* Phil Karlson *ph* Charles Lawton *m* George Duning

Van Heflin, Tab Hunter, James Darren, Kathryn Grant

Gunn*
US 1967 95m Technicolor
Paramount / Geoffrey (Owen Crump)

A private eye is hired to find a gangster's killer.
Tongue-in-cheek violence from the television series, with Craig Stevens doing a Cary Grant imitation.

w Blake Edwards, William Peter Blatty *d* Blake Edwards *ph* Philip Lathrop *m* Henry Mancini

Craig Stevens, Laura Devon, Ed Asner, Sherry Jackson, Helen Traubel, J. Pat O'Malley, Regis Toomey

'Falters between parody and straight action.'—*MFB*

Gunpoint
US 1966 86m Technicolor

A Colorado sheriff goes after train robbers. Simple-minded but quite professional and good-looking western programmer. Audie Murphy, Joan Staley, Warren Stevens, Edgar Buchanan, Denver Pyle. Written by Mary and Willard Willingham; directed by Earl Bellamy; for Universal.

Guns at Batasi*
GB 1964 103m bw Cinemascope
TCF / George H. Brown

The headquarters of an Anglo-African regiment is threatened by rebels.
Basically the old chestnut about a group of disparate types trapped in a dangerous situation, this is given shape and stature by the star's lively performance as the martinet of an RSM.

w Robert Hollis, from his novel The Siege of Battersea *d* John Guillermin *ph* Douglas Slocombe *m* John Addison

Richard Attenborough, Flora Robson, Mia Farrow, Jack Hawkins, Cecil Parker, Percy Herbert, Errol John, John Leyton, Earl Cameron

Guns for San Sebastian
France / Mexico / Italy 1967 111m Metrocolor Franscope
MGM / Cipra / Filmes / Ernesto Enriques (Jacques Bar)

In Mexico in 1746, a rebel on the run stays to defend a besieged village.
Multi-national actioner, violent but quite undistinguished.

w Serge Ganz, Miguel Morayta, Ennio de Concini from book A Wall for San Sebastian by William B. Flaherty *d* Henri Verneuil *ph* Armand Thirard *m* Ennio Morricone

Anthony Quinn, Charles Bronson, Sam Jaffe, Anjanette Comer, Silvia Pinal

Guns in the Heather
US 1968 90m Technicolor

An American schoolboy in Ireland finds that his elder brother is a CIA agent. Tolerable kiddie-fodder from the Disney treadmill; later desiccated for TV. Glenn Corbett, Alfred Burke, Kurt Russell, Patrick Barr. Written by Herman Groves; directed by Robert Butler; for Walt Disney.

Guns of Darkness
GB 1962 102m bw
ABP / Cavalcade (Thomas Clyde)

A British plantation boss in Latin America escapes with his wife when rebels strike. Chase / escape film with a few tiny comments about violence.

w John Mortimer, *novel* Act of Mercy by Francis Clifford *d* Anthony Asquith *ph* Robert Krasker *m* Benjamin Frankel

David Niven, Leslie Caron, James Robertson Justice, David Opatoshu

The Guns of Fort Petticoat
US 1957 79m Technicolor
Columbia / Brown-Murphy (Harry Joe Brown)

During the Civil War, a wandering Texan trains townswomen into a fighting force. Unlikely western which passes the time.

w Walter Doniger *d* George Marshall *ph* Ray Rennahan *m* Mischa Bakaleinikoff

Audie Murphy, Kathryn Grant, Hope Emerson, Jeff Donnell, Isobel Elsom

The Guns of Loos*
GB 1927 89m (24 fps) bw silent
Stoll / New Era

A blinded hero of the war returns home to run an industrial empire and is confronted by a strike.
One of the better British silents, with a strong plot and an interesting cast.

w L. H. Gordon, Reginald Fogwell, Sinclair Hill *d* Sinclair Hill *ph* Desmond Dickinson

Henry Victor, Madeleine Carroll, Bobby Howes, Hermione Baddeley

The Guns of Navarone**
GB 1961 157m Technicolor Cinemascope
Columbia / Carl Foreman (Cecil F. Ford)

In 1943 a sabotage team is sent to destroy two giant guns on a Turkish Island.
Ambitiously produced Boy's Own Paper heroics, with lots of noise and self-sacrifice; intermittently exciting but bogged down by philosophical chat.

w Carl Foreman, *novel* Alistair Maclean *d* J. Lee-Thomson *ph* Oswald Morris *m* Dmitri Tiomkin *ad* Geoffrey Drake

Gregory Peck, David Niven, Stanley Baker, Anthony Quinn, Anthony Quayle, James Darren, Gia Scala, James Robertson Justice, Richard Harris, Irene Papas, Bryan Forbes

'A desperate imbalance: the moral arguments cut into the action without extending it.'—*Penelope Houston*

AAN: best picture; Carl Foreman; J. Lee-Thompson; Dmitri Tiomkin

Guns of the Magnificent Seven
US 1969 106m De Luxe Panavision
UA / Mirisch (Vincent M. Fennelly)

Seven mercenaries rescue a Mexican Robin Hood.
Stale, flat and unprofitable third serving of this particular hash.

w Herman Hoffman *d* Paul Wendkos *ph* Antonio Macasoli *m* Elmer Bernstein

George Kennedy, Monte Markham, Joe Don Baker, James Whitmore, Bernie Casey, Scott Thomas, Reni Santoni, Michael Ansara, Wende Wagner, Fernando Rey, Frank Silvera

Guns of the Timberland
US 1960 91m Technicolor
Jaguar (Aaron Spelling)

Loggers are opposed by cattle interests.
Routine star western with tolerable production values.

w Joseph Petracca, Aaron Spelling from novel by Louis L'Amour *d* Robert D. Webb *ph* John Seitz *m* David Buttolph

Alan Ladd, Jeanne Crain, Gilbert Roland, Frankie Avalon, Lyle Bettger, Noah Beery Jnr

Gunsmoke
US 1953 79m Technicolor

A cowboy befriends the rancher he has been hired to kill. Moderate western with too many pauses for sentiment. Audie Murphy, Paul Kelly, Susan Cabot, Mary Castle, Charles Drake. Written by D. D. Beauchamp; directed by Nathan Juran; for Universal.

The Guru
US / India 1969 112m De Luxe
TCF / Arcadia (Ismail Merchant)

In India, an English pop singer succumbs to the local atmosphere.
Pleasant, affectionate but forgettable anecdote of modern India.

w Ruth Prawer Jhabvala, James Ivory *d* James Ivory *ph* Subrata Mitra *m* Ustad Vilayat Khan

Michael York, Rita Tushingham, Utpal Dutt, Aparna Sen, Barry Foster

Gus
US 1976 96m Technicolor
Walt Disney (Ron Miller)

A football team co-opts a mule which can kick a hundred yard ball.
Predictable Disney fantasy comedy with a direct line back to *The Absent Minded Professor*.

w Arthur Alsberg, Don Nelson *d* Vincent McEveety *ph* Frank Phillips *m* Robert F. Brunner

Ed Asner, Don Knotts, Gary Grimes, Tim Conway, Liberty Williams, Bob Crane, Harold Gould, Tom Bosley, Dick Van Patten

'In the current comedy climate, when humour so often hinges on a four-letter word or its lengthier variant, a light-hearted football game spoof is a breath of fresh air.'—*Tatiana Balkoff Lipscomb, Films in Review*

The Guvnor
GB 1935 88m bw
Gaumont (Michael Balcon)
US title: *Mr Hobo*

By chance a tramp becomes a bank director. Predictable star vehicle with Arliss a most unlikely tramp.

w Maude Howell, Guy Bolton *d* Milton Rosmer *ph* Max Greene

George Arliss, Gene Gerrard, Viola Keats, Patric Knowles, Frank Cellier, Mary Clare, George Hayes

'His admirers need not fear that he has lost any of his usual refinement or sentiment, his cultured English accent, his Universal certificate.'—*Graham Greene*

A Guy Named Joe
US 1944 120m bw
MGM (Everett Riskin)

A flier is killed but comes back as a ghost to supervise his ex-girl's new romance.
Icky romantic comedy-drama with strong propaganda intent; the stars make it tolerable.

w Dalton Trumbo *d* Victor Fleming *ph* George Folsey, Karl Freund *m* Herbert Stothart

Spencer Tracy, Irene Dunne, Ward Bond, Van Johnson, James Gleason, Lionel Barrymore, Barry Nelson, Don Defore, Henry O'Neill

'As far as I could judge, the audience loved it: melodrama, farce, fake philosophy, swimming eyes and all.'—*Richard Mallett, Punch*

'It neatly obtunds death's sting as ordinary people suffer it by not only assuming but photographing a good, busy, hearty hereafter.'—*James Agee*

† The title was explained by one of the characters who observed that 'in the Army Air Corps, any fellow who is a right fellow is called Joe'.

AAN: original story (David Buchan, Chandler Sprague)

The Guy Who Came Back
US 1951 92m bw

A pro football player hates the thought of retiring. Sentimental sporting drama without much life in it. Paul Douglas, Joan Bennett, Linda Darnell, Don Defore, Zero Mostel. Written by Allan Scott; directed by Joseph Newman; for TCF.

Guys and Dolls*
US 1955 149m Eastmancolor Cinemascope
Samuel Goldwyn

A New York gangster takes a bet that he can romance a Salvation Army lady.
The artifices of Runyonland are made more so by a defiantly studio-bound production and thoroughly flat handling; but the songs and sometimes the performances survive.

wd Joseph L. Mankiewicz, *musical* Jo Swerling and Abe Burrows *ph* Harry Stradling, *songs Frank Loesser* *md* Cyril Mockridge, Jay Blackton *ch* Michael Kidd *ad* Joseph Wright *pd* Oliver Smith

Frank Sinatra, Marlon Brando, Jean Simmons, *Vivian Blaine, Stubby Kaye*, B. S. Pully, Robert Keith, Sheldon Leonard, George E. Stone

'Quantity has been achieved only at the cost of quality.'—*Penelope Houston*

AAN: Harry Stradling; Cyril Mockridge, Jay Blackton

Gypsy
GB 1936 78m bw

An ageing playboy marries a gypsy but gives her back to her true love. Hard-to-swallow drama with insufficient comedy relief for its star. Roland Young, Chili Bouchier, Hugh Williams, Frederick Burtwell. Written by Brock Williams and Terence Rattigan, from the novel *Tsigane* by Lady Eleanor Smith; directed by Roy William Neill; for Warner.

'The girl who became the greatest show in show business!'

Gypsy*
US 1962 149m Technirama
Warner (Mervyn Le Roy)

The early days of stripteaser Gypsy Rose Lee, and the exploits of her ambitious mother.
A vaudeville musical that is nowhere near raucous enough, or brisk enough, for its subject, and is miscast into the bargain. The songs are great, but not here: Miss Russell is as boring as an electric drill in a role that should have been reserved for Ethel Merman.

w Leonard Spiegelgass, *book* Arthur Laurents *d* Mervyn Le Roy *m Jule Styne ly Stephen Sondheim ph* Harry Stradling *md* Frank Perkins *ad* John Beckman

Rosalind Russell, Natalie Wood, *Karl Malden*, James Milhollin

AAN: Harry Stradling; Frank Perkins

The Gypsy and the Gentleman
GB 1957 107m Eastmancolor
Rank (Maurice Cowan)

A penniless Regency rake marries a tempestuous gypsy, with melodramatic and tragic results.
Expensive and typically mistimed Rank attempt to re-do *The Man in Grey*; a barnstormer notable only for waste of talent.

w Janet Greene, *novel* Darkness I Leave You by Nina Warner Hooke *d* Joseph Losey *ph* Jack Hildyard *m* Hans May *ad* Ralph Brinton

Melina Mercouri, Keith Michell, Patrick McGoohan, June Laverick, Flora Robson, Helen Haye

Gypsy Colt
US 1954 72m Ansco Color

A cherished colt has to be sold, but makes its way back home. Disguised second feature remake of *Lassie Come Home*; good for children. Donna Corcoran, Ward Bond, Frances Dee, Larry Keating, Lee Van Cleef. Written by Martin Berkeley; directed by Andrew Marton; for MGM.

The Gypsy Moths*
US 1969 110m Metrocolor
MGM / Frankenheimer-Lewis (Hal Landers, Bobby Roberts)

Sky-diving stuntmen find love and death on a small-town tour.
Brilliantly breathtaking actioner which too frequently gets grounded, and does not find a reason for being so glum.

w William Hanley, *novel* James Drought *d* John Frankenheimer *ph* Philip Lathrop *aerial ph Carl Boenisch m* Elmer Bernstein

Burt Lancaster, Deborah Kerr, Gene Hackman, Scott Wilson, William Windom, Bonnie Bedelia, Sheree North

'A Bergmanesque world of inner emotions and ambiguous means. . . . As in many of Frankenheimer's films it rains, and the wind in the trees in the park and the sound of traffic all contribute to the realism that makes his work so satisfying.'—*Gerald Pratley*

Gypsy Wildcat
US 1944 77m Technicolor
Universal (George Waggner)

A Transylvanian gypsy girl is really a long lost countess.
Universal's Frankenstein sets are put to lighter use in a quite incredible piece of downright hokum.

w James Hogan, Gene Lewis, James M. Cain *d* Roy William Neill *ph* George Robinson, W. Howard Greene *m* Edward Ward

Maria Montez, Jon Hall, Leo Carrillo, Gale Sondergaard, Douglass Dumbrille, Nigel Bruce, Peter Coe, Curt Bois

'The picture's so bad, it's bound to make money.'—*Cue*

'Never rises to the wild camp of *Cobra Woman*; it's just *opéra bouffe* without music.'—*Pauline Kael, 70s*

H. M. Pulham Esquire**
US 1940 120m bw
MGM (King Vidor)

A moderately successful Bostonian businessman looks back over his rather stuffy life and has a fling.
Solidly upholstered drama which does not quite do justice to the book on which it is based.

w King Vidor, Elizabeth Hill, *novel* John P. Marquand *d* King Vidor *ph* Ray June *m* Bronislau Kaper

Robert Young, Ruth Hussey, Hedy Lamarr, Charles Coburn, Van Heflin, Fay Holden, Bonita Granville

Habeas Corpus*
US 1928 20m bw silent

A mad professor sends two vagabonds out to look for a body. Unusual star comedy, more grotesque and pantomimish than any of the others. Laurel and Hardy, Richard Carle. Written by H. M. Walker; directed by James Parrott; for Hal Roach.

Hail the Conquering Hero***
US 1944 101m bw
Paramount (Preston Sturges)

An army reject is accidentally thought a hero when he returns to his small-town home.
Skilfully orchestrated Preston Sturges romp, slightly marred by an overdose of sentiment but featuring his repertory of comic actors at full pitch.

wd Preston Sturges *ph* John Seitz *m* Werner Heymann

Eddie Bracken, William Demarest, Ella Raines, *Franklin Pangborn*, Elizabeth Patterson, *Raymond Walburn, Alan Bridge*, Georgia Caine, Freddie Steele, Jimmy Conlin, Torben Meyer

'Mob scenes, rough-houses and sharply serious passages are played for all the pantomime they are worth . . . one of the happiest, heartiest comedies in a twelvemonth.'—*Otis L. Guernsey Jnr*

'First rate entertainment, a pattern of film making, not to be missed.'—*Richard Mallett, Punch*

'The energy, the verbal density, the rush of Americana and the congestion seen periodically in *The Miracle of Morgan's Creek* stagger the senses in this newest film.'—*James Ursini*

'It tells a story so touching, so chock-full of human frailties and so rich in homely detail that it achieves a reality transcending the limitations of its familiar slapstick.'—*James Agee*

'He uses verbal as well as visual slapstick, and his comic timing is so quirkily effective that the dialogue keeps popping off like a string of firecrackers.'—*New Yorker, 1977*

AAN: Preston Sturges (as writer)

Hair*
US 1979 121m Technicolor Panavision
UA / CIP (Lester Persky, Michael Butler)

An Oklahoman on his way to enlist for Vietnam service stops off in New York and becomes embroiled with the flower people.
Slick, vigorous but eventually unsatisfying version of a quickly dated musical frolic with some obvious points to make.

w Michael Weller, *musical play* Galt MacDermot (music) and Gerome Ragni / James Rado (book) *d* Milos Forman *ph* Miroslav Ondricek, Richard Kratina, Jean Talvin

John Savage, Treat Williams, Beverly D'Angelo, Annie Golden, Dorsey Wright

The Hairy Ape
US 1944 91m bw
Jules Levy

A ship's stoker aims to kill a socialite who has insulted him.
Patchy treatment of an intractable and dated play.

w Jules Levy, *play* Eugene O'Neill *d* Alfred Santell *ph* Lucien Andriot *m* Michel Michelet, Edward Paul

William Bendix, Susan Hayward, John Loder, Dorothy Comingore, Roman Bohnen, Alan Napier

AAN: Michel Michelet, Edward Paul

Half a Hero
US 1953 71m bw

A timid journalist has problems with wife, baby, boss and new house. Aimless comedy quite unsuited to its star. Red Skelton, Jean Hagen, Charles Dingle, Mary Wickes, Polly Bergen. Written by Max Shulman; directed by Don Weis; for MGM.

Half a Sinner
US 1934 70m bw

A cheerful elderly cardsharp masquerades as a deacon. Midwestern pleaser not too well made here, but later remade under its original title as a Bob Burns vehicle. Berton Churchill, Joel McCrea, Sally Blane, Mickey Rooney, Spencer Charters. Written by Earle Snell, Clarence Marks, from the play Alias the Deacon by John B. Hymer and LeRoy Clemens; directed by Kurt Neumann; for Universal. 'Little marquee strength, but sufficient punch to please 'em once they're in.'—*Variety*

'It's everything a motion picture can be!'

Half a Sixpence*
GB 1967 148m Technicolor Panavision
Paramount / Ameran (Charles H. Schneer, George Sidney)

A draper's assistant inherits a fortune and moves into society.
Mildly likeable but limp and overlong musical which would have benefited from more intimate, sharper treatment than the wide screen can give. The period decor and lively numbers seem insufficient compensation for the longueurs.

w Beverly Cross, from his play based on Kipps by H. G. Wells *d* George Sidney *ph* Geoffrey Unsworth *m / ly* David Heneker *pd* Ted Haworth *ch Gillian Lynne*

Tommy Steele, Julia Foster, Cyril Ritchard, Penelope Horner, Elaine Taylor, Hilton Edwards, Pamela Brown, James Villiers

'The confessions of a female sleepwalker!'

Half Angel
US 1951 80m Technicolor

A prim and proper nurse has a more forthright personality when she sleepwalks. Silly romantic comedy with amusing moments. Loretta Young, Joseph Cotten, Cecil Kellaway, Basil Ruysdael, Jim Backus, Irene Ryan. Written by Robert Riskin; directed by Richard Sale; for TCF.

The Half-Breed
US 1952 81m Technicolor

A gambler helps a half-breed and wins the respect of the Apaches. Half-hearted western which could never be more than the bottom half of a double bill. Robert Young, Jack Buetel, Janis Carter, Barton MacLane, Reed Hadley, Porter Hall, Connie Gilchrist.

Written by Harold Shumate and Richard Wormser; directed by Stuart Gilmore; for RKO.

Half Moon Street
US 1986 90m Technicolor

A lady PhD turns to prostitution to augment her income, and becomes involved in Middle Eastern schemes. Totally muddled compromise between thriller and exploitation piece; its message seems to have got left on the cutting room floor. Sigourney Weaver, Michael Caine, Patrick Kavanaugh, Keith Buckley. Written by Bob Swaim and Edward Behr; directed by Bob Swaim; for Geoff Reeve Enterprises. 'A half-baked excuse for a film.'—*Variety*

The Half Naked Truth*
US 1932 67m bw
RKO (David O. Selznick)

A publicity agent has trouble with a temperamental actress whose schemes are always over the top.
Amusing wisecracking comedy.

w Bartlett Cormack, Corey Ford *d* Gregory La Cava *ph* Bert Glennon *m* Max Steiner

Lee Tracy, Lupe Velez, Eugene Pallette, Frank Morgan, Bob McKenzie

Half Shot at Sunrise*
US 1930 78m bw

Allegedly one of the best representations of a star comedy duo who went into a decline after 1932. Bert Wheeler, Robert Woolsey, Edna May Oliver, Dorothy Lee, John Rutherford. Written by James Ashmore Creelman; directed by Paul Sloane; for RKO. 'Laugh programmer beyond ordinary . . . it will do business, including de luxers.'—*Variety*

Half Way to Shanghai
US 1942 61m bw

Spies are included among the passengers on a Burma night train before the Japanese invasion. Watchable if muddled mystery with a good cast; Shanghai is neither relevant nor mentioned. Kent Taylor, Irene Hervey, Henry Stephenson, J. Edward Bromberg, George Zucco, Alexander Granach, Lionel Royce. Written by Stuart Palmer; directed by John Rawlins; for Paul Malvern / Universal.

The Halfway House*
GB 1944 99m bw
Ealing (Cavalcanti)

Overnight guests at an inn find it was bombed a year before and they have all been given a supernatural chance to reconsider their lives.
Interesting pattern play which would have benefited from lighter handling.

w Angus Macphail, Diana Morgan, *play* Denis Ogden *d* Basil Dearden *ph* Wilkie Cooper *m* Lord Berners

Françoise Rosay, Tom Walls, Alfred Drayton, Sally Ann Howes, Mervyn Johns, Glynis Johns, Esmond Knight, Richard Bird, Guy Middleton

Hallelujah!**
US 1929 106m bw
MGM (King Vidor)

A black cotton worker accidentally kills a man and decides to become a preacher.
Hollywood's unique black melodrama now seems stilted because of its early talkie technique, but at the time its picture of negro life had a freshness and truth which was not reached again for thirty years.

w Wanda Tuchock, King Vidor *d King Vidor* *ph* Gordon Avil *md Eva Jessye*

Daniel Haynes, Nina Mae McKinney, William Fountaine, Fannie Belle De Knight, Harry Gray

'The central theme became swamped by the forty or so singing sequences of folk songs, spirituals, baptism wails, love songs and blues.'—*Peter Noble, The Negro in Films*

AAN: King Vidor

Hallelujah, I'm a Bum**
US 1933 80m bw
Lewis Milestone
GB titles: *Hallelujah I'm a Tramp; Lazy Bones*

The leader of a group of Central Park tramps smartens himself up for love of a lady who lost her memory. When she recovers it, he becomes a tramp again.
Curious whimsy expressed mainly in recitative, with embarrassing stretches relieved by moments of visual and verbal inspiration.
Very typical of the Depression, with the tramps knowing best how life should be lived.

w S. N. Behrman, Ben Hecht d Lewis Milestone ph Lucien Andriot ad Richard Day *rhymes / m / ly Richard Rodgers, Lorenz Hart*

Al Jolson, Harry Langdon, Madge Evans, Frank Morgan, Chester Conklin

Songs: 'Hallelujah I'm a Bum'; 'You Are Too Beautiful'; 'I'll Do It Again'; 'What Do You Want with Money?'; 'I've Got to Get Back to New York'

'It must rise or fall by Al Jolson's rep . . . it won't bore, once in, but it's not a mass play picture.'—*Variety*

'Given a scene or two of high sentiment, he still has you wrapped round his little finger.'—*The Times, 1973*

The Hallelujah Trail
US 1965 167m Technicolor Ultra Panavision 70
UA / Mirisch / Kappa (John Sturges)

In 1867 a wagonload of whisky bound for Denver is waylaid by Indians, temperance crusaders and the civilian militia.
Absurdly inflated, prolonged, uninventive comedy western with poor narrative grip; all dressed up and nowhere to go.

w John Gay, *novel* Bill Gulick *d* John Sturges *ph Robert Surtees* *m* Elmer Bernstein

Burt Lancaster, Lee Remick, Brian Keith, Jim Hutton, Donald Pleasence, Martin Landau

The Halliday Brand*
US 1956 78m bw
UA / Collier Young

A tough farmer / sheriff conflicts with his son over his attitude to Indians.
Dour, reliable western melodrama with a good cast.

w George W. George, George S. Slavin *d* Joseph H. Lewis *ph* Ray Rennahan *m* Stanley Wilson

Joseph Cotten, Viveca Lindfors, Ward Bond, Betsy Blair, Bill Williams, Jay C. Flippen

Halloween*
US 1978 91m Metrocolor Panavision
Falcon International (Irwin Yablans)

In a small Illinois town, a mad killer escapes from the asylum.
Single-minded shocker with virtually no plot, just a succession of bloody attacks in semi-darkness. Very well done if you like that kind of thing, though the final suggestion of the supernatural is rather baffling.

w John Carpenter, Debra Hill *d John Carpenter* *ph* Dean Cundy *m* John Carpenter *pd* Tommy Wallace

Donald Pleasence, Jamie Lee Curtis, Nancy Loomis, P. J. Soles

'One of the cinema's most perfectly engineered devices for saying Boo!'—*Richard Combs, MFB*

Halloween Two
US 1981 92m Metrocolor Panavision
Dino de Laurentiis (Debra Hill, John Carpenter)

The motiveless murderer from *Halloween* escapes from the asylum fifteen years later.
A totally unnecessary sequel which seems merely an excuse for assorted mayhem at close quarters.

w John Carpenter, Debra Hill *d* Rick Rosenthal *ph* Dean Cundey *m* John Carpenter, Alan Howarth

Donald Pleasence, Jamie Lee Curtis, Charles Cyphers, Jeffrey Kramer

Halloween Three: Season of the Witch
US 1983 98m Technicolor Panavision
Dino de Laurentiis (Debra Hill, John Carpenter)

A malicious toy maker intends to restore Halloween to its witch cult origins through magic masks made at his Santa Mira factory.
The Halloween zombie-killer makes no appearance: this is a fresh story inspired by *Invasion of the Body Snatchers*. Alas, its good intentions flounder in a bath of gore.

w,d Tommy Lee Wallace *ph* Dean Cundey *m* John Carpenter, Alan Howarth *pd* Peter Jamison

Tom Atkins, Stacey Nelkin, Dan O'Herlihy, Ralph Strait, Michael Currie

†Nigel Kneale wrote the original script but asked to have his name removed from the credits.

Halls of Anger
US 1969 99m De Luxe
UA / Mirisch (Herbert Hirschman)

A black basketball star goes to teach in his home town and faces segregation problems. Schematic melodrama, as well meaning as it is boring.

w John Shaner, Al Ramrus *d* Paul Bogart *ph* Burnett Guffey *m* Dave Grusin

Calvin Lockhart, Janet McLachlan, Jeff Bridges

Halls of Montezuma*
US 1950 113m Technicolor
TCF (Robert Bassler)

Marines fight World War II in the Pacific. Well-mounted, simple-minded actioner.

w Michael Blankfort *d* Lewis Milestone *ph* Winton C. Hoch, Harry Jackson *m* Sol Kaplan *md* Lionel Newman

Richard Widmark, Jack Palance, Reginald Gardiner, Robert Wagner, Karl Malden, Richard Hylton, Richard Boone, Skip Homeier, Jack Webb, Bert Freed, Neville Brand, Don Hicks, Martin Milner

'By far the noisiest war film I ever encountered.'—*Richard Mallett, Punch*

Ham and Eggs at the Front
US 1927 70m approx at 24 fps bw silent

Two black soldiers have adventures in the trenches. Irresistibly-titled war farce with our heroes played by whites in blackface. Tom Wilson, Charlie Conklin, Myrna Loy. Written by Darryl F. Zanuck; directed by Roy Del Ruth; for Warner.

Hambone and Hillie
US 1983 90m colour Panavision
Sandy Howard / Adams Apple (Gary Gillingham)

A small dog is lost at New York airport and tracks his aged mistress on foot to California. Basically a revamp of *Lassie Come Home*, with a cute dog and some attractive exteriors, but made unsuitable for its presumably intended family audience by the death of a second dog and a horrific pitchfork sequence in which a heavily pregnant woman is attacked by marauders.

w Sandra K. Bailey, Michael Murphey, Joel Soisson *d* Roy Watts *ph* Jon Kranhouse *m* George Garvarentz

Lillian Gish, Timothy Bottoms, Candy Clark, Robert Walker, O. J. Simpson, Jack Carter, Alan Hale

Hamburger Hill*
US 1987 110m Technicolor

An untried squad goes into action in Vietnam. One of several Vietnam pics released almost simultaneously; neither the worst nor the best. Anthony Barrie, Michael Patrick Boatman, Don Cheadle, Michael Dolan, Don James. Written by Jim Carabatsos; directed by John Irvin; for Paramount / RKO.

Hamlet**
GB 1948 142m bw
Rank / Two Cities (Laurence Olivier)

Prince Hamlet takes too long making up his mind to revenge his father's death.
The play is sharply cut, then time is wasted having the camera prowl pointlessly along gloomy corridors . . . but much of the acting is fine, some scenes compel, and the production has a splendid brooding power.

w William Shakespeare *d* Laurence Olivier *ph Desmond Dickinson* *pd Roger Furse* *m* William Walton *ad Carmen Dillon*

Laurence Olivier, Eileen Herlie, Basil Sydney, Jean Simmons, Felix Aylmer, Norman Wooland, Terence Morgan, *Stanley Holloway*, Peter Cushing, Esmond Knight, Anthony Quayle, Harcourt Williams, John Laurie, Niall MacGinnis, Patrick Troughton

'Be you 9 or 90, a PhD or just plain Joe, *Hamlet* is the movie of the year.'—*Washington Times*

AA: best picture; Laurence Olivier (as actor)
AAN: Laurence Olivier (as director); William Walton; Jean Simmons

Hamlet*
USSR 1964 150m bw Sovscope
Lenfilm

A Russian version of the play, with lowering sets, brooding photography and strong acting.

translation Boris Pasternak *d* Grigori Kozintsev *ph* I. Gritzys *m* Dmitri Shostakovich

Innokenti Smoktunovsky, Mikhail Nazvanov, Elsa Radzin, Anastasia Vertinskaya

'An opportunity almost deliberately missed.'—*Basil Wright, 1972*

Hamlet*
GB 1969 119m colour

A version which has its moments but fails to impress as a whole. Nicol Williamson, Anthony Hopkins, Gordon Jackson, Judy Parfitt, Marianne Faithfull, Mark Dignam, Roger Livesey. Directed by Tony Richardson; for Woodfall / Filmways / Columbia.

Hammerhead
GB 1968 99m Technicolor
Columbia / Irving Allen

An American secret agent captures a master criminal.
Jaded James Bond imitation, full of would-be fashionable detail.

w William Bast, Herbert Baker, *novel* James Mayo *d* David Miller *ph* Kenneth Talbot, Wilkie Cooper *m* David Whitaker

Vince Edwards, Peter Vaughan, Judy Geeson, Diana Dors, Michael Bates, Beverly Adams, Patrick Cargill, Patrick Holt

Hammersmith Is Out*
US 1972 114m Du Art Color
Cinerama / J. Cornelius Cream (Alex Lucas)

With the help of a male nurse, a homicidal mental inmate escapes and becomes the most influential man in the country.
Pretentious updating of Faust into a kind of black farce that seldom amuses but is interesting in fits and starts.

w Stanford Whitmore *d* Peter Ustinov *ph* Richard Kline *m* Dominic Frontière

Richard Burton, Elizabeth Taylor, Peter Ustinov, Beau Bridges, Leon Ames, John Schuck, George Raft

Hammett*
US 1982 97m Technicolor
Orion / Zoetrope (Francis Coppola)

San Francisco 1928: Dashiell Hammett is asked to locate a missing Chinese girl and gets involved in sinister goings-on which provide the basis for another mystery book.
Careful and interesting crime thriller in which, however, the rather pretentious framework is largely irrelevant, leaving a detective story slightly off-beat in treatment but otherwise indistinguishable from many others.

w Ross Thomas, Dennis O'Flaherty, *novel* Joe Gores *d Wim Wenders* *ph* Philip Lathrop, Joseph Biroc *m* John Barry *pd Dean Tavoularis, Eugene Lee* *ed* Barry Malkin, Marc Laub, Robert Q. Lovett, Randy Roberts

Frederic Forrest, Peter Boyle, Marilu Henner, Roy Kinnear, Elisha Cook Jnr, R. G. Armstrong, Richard Bradford, Sylvia Sidney, Royal Dano, Samuel Fuller

'A symbolic liquidation by Wenders of the massive, but ambivalent patrimony of the American cinematic and cultural tradition that has increasingly dominated his work.'—*Sheila Johnston, MFB*

† The film was actually in pre-production from 1975, though shooting did not begin until 1980. This version was abandoned in rough cut and two-thirds of it was shot again in 1981 with a different crew. Sylvia Miles and Brian Keith were in the first version and not the second.

The Hand
GB 1960 60m bw

When an old man has his hand severed and is subsequently murdered, the trail leads to a doctor who subsequently commits suicide. Confused second feature which seems to have been badly edited but might otherwise have been quite entertaining. Derek Bond, Ronald Leigh-Hunt, Reed de Rouen, Ray Cooney, Harold Scott. Written by Ray Cooney and Tony Hilton; directed by Henry Cass; for Bill and Michael Luckwell / Butcher's.

The Hand
US 1981 104m Technicolor
Warner / Orion (Edward R. Pressman)

A cartoonist loses his hand, which takes on a life of its own to wreak vengeance on his enemies.
Pale imitation of *The Beast with Five Fingers*, which wasn't all that good to begin with.

wd Oliver Stone, from his novel The Lizard's Tail *ph* King Baggot *m* James Horner *pd* John Michael Riva *sp* Carlo Rambaldi *ed* Richard Marks

Michael Caine, Andrea Marcovicci, Viveca Lindfors, Rosemary Murphy, Bruce McGill

Hand in Hand*
GB 1960 80m bw
ABP / Helen Winston

The friendship of two 7-year-olds is affected by racial prejudice because one is Catholic and the other Jewish; but after misunderstandings their friendship is confirmed by priest and rabbi.
Pleasant, well-meaning drama apparently intended for older children.

w Diana Morgan *d* Philip Leacock *ph* Frederick A. Young *m* Stanley Black

Lorette Parry, Phillip Needs, Sybil Thorndike, John Gregson, Finlay Currie

Handgun
US 1982 101m Du Art
EMI / Kestrel (Tony Garnett)

A schoolmistress, raped at gunpoint, takes her revenge.
Overlong, unpleasant, uninteresting exploitation melodrama.

w,d Tony Garnett *ph* Charles Stewart *m* Mike Post *pd* Lilly Kilvert

Karen Young, Clayton Day, Suzie Humphreys, Helena Humann

Handle with Care*
US 1958 82m bw
MGM (Morton Fine)

Small-town college students stage a mock trial and come up with some embarrassing answers.
Interesting melodrama with a disappointing ending; a well done second feature.

w Morton Fine, David Friedkin d David Friedkin ph Harold J. Marzorati *m* Alexander Courage

Dean Jones, Joan O'Brien, Thomas Mitchell, Walter Abel, John Smith

Hands across the Table*
US 1935 81m bw
Paramount (E. Lloyd Sheldon)

A manicurist determines to marry a rich man.
Lively romantic comedy, smoothly made and typical of its time.

w Norman Krasna, Vincent Lawrence, Herbert Fields *d Mitchell Leisen ph* Ted Tetzlaff *m* Sam Coslow, Frederick Hollander

Carole Lombard, Fred MacMurray, Ralph Bellamy, Astrid Allwyn, Ruth Donnelly, Marie Prévost, William Demarest, Ed Gargan

'Snappy comedy that should satisfy all over.'—*Variety*

'A happy mixture of brainwork and horseplay and a reminder that when intelligence goes for a walk among even the oldest props, the props may come to life.'—*Otis Ferguson*

† Ray Milland was originally cast, but bowed out saying that he couldn't play comedy.

The Hands of Orlac
GB / France 1960 105m bw
Riviera / Pendennis (Steven Pallos, Don Taylor)

A concert pianist's hands are crushed in an accident, and a mad surgeon grafts on those of an executed murderer.
Flatulent remake of the 1926 German silent and the 1935 American *Mad Love*. Stilted, hammy, threadbare and overlong.

w John Baines, Edmond T. Gréville, *novel* Maurice Renard *d* Edmond T. Gréville *ph* Desmond Dickinson *m* Claude Bolling

Mel Ferrer, Donald Wolfit, Christopher Lee

Hands of the Ripper
GB 1971 85m Technicolor
Hammer (Aida Young)

Jack the Ripper stabs his wife to death in view of his small daughter, who grows up a sexually repressed murderess.
Gory Hammer horror with well done scenes.

w L. W. Davidson *d* Peter Sasdy *ph* Kenneth Talbot *m* Christopher Gunning *ad Roy Stannard*

Angharad Rees, Eric Porter, Dora Bryan, Jane Merrow, Derek Godfrey

Hands over the City
Italy 1963 105m bw
Galatea
original title: *Le Mani sulla Città*

A property tycoon wangles local politicians so that he gets development on the property he controls.
An angry political film which is too strident to have much entertainment value.

w Enzo Provencale, Enzo Forcella, Raffaele La Capria, Francesco Rosi *d* Francesco Rosi *m* Piero Piccioni *ph* Gianni di Venanzo

Rod Steiger, Salvo Randone, and non-professionals

Hands Up*
US 1926 65m (24 fps) bw silent

General Lee assigns a spy to prevent a Union man from getting his hands on a gold cache.
Pleasant Civil War comedy with a curious Mormon happy ending. *Raymond Griffith*, Marion Nixon, Virginia Lee Corbin, Mack Swain, Montagu Love. Written by Monty Brice, Lloyd Corrigan; directed by Clarence Badger; for Paramount.

Handy Andy
US 1934 82m bw
Fox

A midwestern druggist is married to a snob.
Competent star vehicle overflowing with crackerbarrel philosophy.

w William Counselman, Henry Johnson, *play* Merry Andrew by Lewis Beach *d* David Butler *ph* Arthur Miller

Will Rogers, Peggy Wood, Conchita Montenegro, Mary Carlisle, Roger Imhof, Robert Taylor (his first film), Paul Harvey

'They made two mistakes—they hanged the wrong man, and they didn't finish the job!'

Hang 'em High
US 1967 114m De Luxe
UA / Malpaso / Leonard Freeman

A cowboy is rescued from lynching and takes revenge on his persecutors.
Hollywood's first attempt to imitate the gore and brutality of spaghetti westerns and to take back its own errant star. Emetic and interminable.

w Leonard Freeman, Mel Goldberg *d* Ted Post *ph* Leonard South, Richard Kline *m* Dominic Frontière

Clint Eastwood, Inger Stevens, Ed Begley, Pat Hingle, James MacArthur, Arlene Golonka, Charles McGraw, Ben Johnson, L. Q. Jones

Hangar 18
US 1980 97m Technicolor

A UFO crashlands and is cared for in secret by the American government. A cinematic equivalent to the yellow press, supposing villainous behaviour by all concerned but eager only to provide low grade thriller entertainment. Darren McGavin, Robert Vaughn, Gary Collins, Philip Abbott. Written by Steven Thornley; directed by James L. Conway; for Sunn Classic.

The Hanging Tree*
US 1958 106m Technicolor
Warner / Baroda (Martin Jurow, Richard Shepherd)

Life is tough in a Montana gold-mining camp, especially for a doctor who has killed his unfaithful wife.
Lowering western with a feeling for place and period, plus a welter of melodramatic incident.

w Wendell Mayes, Halstead Welles, *novel* Dorothy M. Johnson *d* Delmer Daves *ph* Ted McCord *m* Max Steiner

Gary Cooper, Maria Schell, Karl Malden, Ben Piazza, George C. Scott

AAN: title song (*m* Jay Livingston, *ly* Ray Evans)

The Hangman
US 1959 86m bw
Paramount (Frank Freeman Jnr)

A marshal with a reputation for getting his man deliberately allows one to escape.
Dour, low-key western, competent but rather flat and uninteresting.

w Dudley Nichols *d* Michael Curtiz *ph* Loyal Griggs *m* Harry Sukman

Robert Taylor, Jack Lord, Fess Parker, Tina Louise, Mickey Shaughnessy

Hangman's House
US 1928 72m (24 fps) bw silent
Fox

To please her dying father, an Irish girl marries a wastrel instead of the man she loves, but her husband is killed in a duel.
Blarney-filled melodrama, like a sober *Quiet Man*. John Wayne can be glimpsed as an extra.

w Marion Orth, *story* Don Byrne *d* John Ford *ph* George Schneiderman

June Collyer, Larry Kent, Earle Foxe, Victor McLaglen, Hobart Bosworth

Hangman's Knot
US 1952 81m Technicolor

Confederate soldiers returning home with Union booty are waylaid at a way station by renegades. Adequate suspense western.

Randolph Scott, Donna Reed, Claude Jarman Jnr, Frank Faylen, Glenn Langan, Richard Denning, Lee Marvin, Jeanette Nolan.
Written and directed by Roy Huggins; for Harry Joe Brown / Columbia.

Hangmen Also Die*
US 1943 131m bw
Arnold Pressburger / Fritz Lang (T. W. Baumfield)
Reissue title: *Lest We Forget*

The Nazis take revenge for the killing of Heydrich.
Disappointingly heavy-handed, though deeply felt war propaganda set in Hollywood's idea of Czechoslovakia. Only moments of interest remain.

w John Wexley, *story* Fritz Lang, Bertolt Brecht *d Fritz Lang ph James Wong Howe* *m* Hanns Eisler

Brian Donlevy, Anna Lee, Walter Brennan, Gene Lockhart, Dennis O'Keefe, Alexander Granach, Margaret Wycherly, Nana Bryant, Hans von Twardowski (as Heydrich), Jonathan Hale, Lionel Stander

'Lang, working with American actors on an American theme, has produced *Fury*. Lang trying to recreate his own Central Europe on a Hollywood set is completely at sea.'—*Paul Rotha, 1949*

'Directed with a skill which excites and delights . . . brilliant use of the tiny, shocking detail.'—*Dilys Powell*

'They have chosen to use brutality, American gangster idiom, and middle high German cinematic style to get it across, and it is rich with clever melodrama, over-*maestoso* directional touches, and the sort of Querschnitt sophistication for detail which Lang always has.'—*James Agee*

† Working titles included *The Silent City* and *Never Surrender*.

AAN: Hanns Eisler

Hangover Square*
US 1944 77m bw
TCF (Robert Bassler)

In 1903 London, a psychopathic composer murders pretty women.
This rather empty melodrama has almost nothing to do with the book from which it is allegedly taken, but the Hollywoodian evocation of gaslit London is richly entertaining and good to look at.

w Barre Lyndon, *novel* Patrick Hamilton *d John Brahm ph Joseph La Shelle* *m Bernard Herrmann ad Lyle Wheeler, Maurice Ransford*

Laird Cregar, Linda Darnell, George Sanders, Glenn Langan, Faye Marlowe, Alan Napier, Frederick Worlock

'Cregar lumbers around with a Karloffian glare in the spacious mists which happily blur the architectural decor.'—*Richard Winnington*

'Distinguished photography gets the last glint of fancy fright out of the pomps and vanities of the turn of the century.'—*Time*

'A half-chewed collection of reminiscences of *Dr Jekyll and Mr Hyde* and *The Lodger*.'—*Richard Mallett, Punch*

'The worst betrayal of a first class novel that I can remember.'—*James Agate*

'A better than average horror picture up to, but not including, its wildly overloaded climax.'—*James Agee*

† Tragically, Laird Cregar died after slimming for this role, to which he was in any case unsuited.

Hanky Panky
US 1982 107m Metrocolor
Columbia (Martin Ransohoff)

A girl on a spy mission is pursued by assassins and enlists the reluctant aid of an architect she meets in a taxi.
Frantic spoof of *North by Northwest*, which was itself as spoofy as all get out. This strained effort lacks wit, substituting shouting, violence and an exasperating hero.

w Henry Rosenbaum, David Taylor *d* Sidney Poitier *ph* Arthur Ornitz *m* Tom Scott *pd* Ben Edwards *ed* Harry Keller

Gene Wilder, Gilda Radner, Kathleen Quinlan, Richard Widmark

'The plot, rather like Mr Wilder, rushes hither and yon at the slightest excuse without ever adding up to very much. Even McGuffins are supposed to make more sense than this'.—*Richard Combs, MFB*

'A comedy thriller designed solely as a vehicle for Wilder's uninhibited hysteria is bad enough; one that so thoroughly submerges everyone else is so much worse.'—*Sight and Sound*

'One long screech.'—*Ibid.*

Hannah and her Sisters***
US 1985 106m Technicolor
Orion / Charles R. Joffe, Jack Rollins (Robert Greenhut)

Relationships intermingle for a New York family over a two-year period between Thanksgiving dinners.
Even though it has nowhere in particular to go, and certain scenes are over the top, this is a brilliantly assembled and thoroughly enjoyable mélange of fine acting and New Yorkish one-liners, with particularly sharp editing and a nostalgic music score.

w,d Woody Allen ph Carlo di Palma *m* popular and classical extracts *pd* Stuart Wurtzel *ed Susan E. Morse*

Woody Allen, Mia Farrow, Dianne Wiest, Michael Caine, Carrie Fisher, Barbara Hershey, Maureen O'Sullivan, Lloyd Nolan, Max von Sydow, Daniel Stern, Sam Waterston, Tony Roberts

'A loosely knit canvas of Manhattan interiors and exteriors.'—*Sight and Sound*

'One of Woody Allen's great films.'—*Variety*

AA: best original screenplay; Michael Caine; Dianne Wiest
AAN: best picture; Woody Allen as director; Susan E. Morse; set decoration (Carol Joffe)

Hannibal
Italy 1959 103m Technicolor Supercinescope
Liber Film (Ottavio Poggi)

Hannibal crosses the Alps and falls for the daughter of a Roman senator.
Unhistorical farrago which totally fails to entertain on any level.

w Mortimer Braus *d* Carlo Ludovico Bragaglia, Edgar G. Ulmer *ph* Raffaele Masciocchi *m* Carlo Rustichelli

Victor Mature, Rita Gam, Gabriele Ferzetti, Milly Vitale, Rik Battaglia

'Not even the elephants emerge with dignity.'—*MFB*

Hannibal Brooks
GB 1968 102m De Luxe
UA / Scimitar (Michael Winner)

A British POW in Germany escapes over the Alps with an elephant.
Curious action adventure which seems undecided whether to take itself seriously. Some passable sequences.

w Dick Clement, Ian La Frenais *d* Michael Winner *ph* Robert Paynter *m* Francis Lai

Oliver Reed, Michael J. Pollard, Wolfgang Preiss, Karen Baal

Hannie Caulder
GB 1971 85m colour Panavision
Tigon / Curtwel (Tony Tenser)

Raped by three outlaws who murdered her husband, a western woman takes revenge.
Unintentionally comical action melodrama with the star defeating all comers.

w Z. X. Jones (Burt Kennedy, David Haft) *d* Burt Kennedy *ph* Ted Scaife *m* Ken Thorne

Raquel Welch, Robert Culp, Ernest Borgnine, Strother Martin, Jack Elam, Christopher Lee, Diana Dors

Hanover Street
GB 1979 108m Technicolor Panavision
Columbia (Paul N. Lazarus III)

In 1943, an American bomber pilot meets a Red Cross nurse in a bus queue.
Wartime romance of a rather sticky sort, which turns with little warning into escape adventure, with our hero rescuing his loved one's husband from certain death.

wd Peter Hyams *ph* David Watkin *m* John Barry *pd* Philip Harrison

Harrison Ford, Lesley-Anne Down, Christopher Plummer, Alec McCowen, Richard Masure, Michael Sacks, Max Wall

Hans Christian Andersen*
US 1952 112m Technicolor
Samuel Goldwyn

A storytelling cobbler leaves his village to make shoes for the prima ballerina in Copenhagen.
Artificial, sugary confection with little humour and far too little magic of any kind; the star carries it nicely, but he is on his own apart from the songs.

w Moss Hart *d* Charles Vidor *ph* Harry Stradling *md* Walter Scharf *songs Frank Loesser ad Richard Day ch* Roland Petit

Danny Kaye, Zizi Jeanmaire, Farley Granger, John Qualen, Joey Walsh

† 16 screenplays were written before this one was chosen. Moira Shearer was signed for the

role of ballerina but became pregnant. Gary Cooper was thought of for the lead, with William Wyler as director.

AAN: Harry Stradling; Walter Scharf; song 'Thumbelina' (*m / ly* Frank Loesser)

The Happening
US 1967 101m Technicolor
Columbia / Horizon / Dover (Jud Kinberg)

Four young hippies kidnap a wealthy businessman and don't know what to do with him; he turns the tables.
Freewheeling irresponsible comedy which even at the time of swinging cities seemed very irritating.

w Frank R. Pierson, James D. Buchanan, Ronald Austin *d* Eliot Silverstein *ph* Philip Lathrop *m* Frank de Vol *pd* Richard Day

Anthony Quinn, George Maharis, Michael Parks, Faye Dunaway, Robert Walker, Oscar Homolka, Martha Hyer, Milton Berle, Jack Kruschen

'A wacky comedy à la mode, oddly mixed and only spasmodically effective.'—*Variety*

Happidrome
GB 1943 87m bw

A play intended seriously becomes a comedy hit. A theme later used by *The Producers* forms the background for this naive screen version of a wartime radio series. Harry Korris, Robbie Vincent, Cecil Frederick, Bunty Meadows, Lisa Lee, 'Hutch', the Cairoli Brothers. Written by Tom Arnold, James Seymour; directed by Phil Brandon; for Aldwych.

The Happiest Days of Your Life***
GB 1950 81m bw
British Lion / Individual (Frank Launder)

A ministry mistake billets a girls' school on a boys' school.
Briskly handled version of a semi-classic post-war farce, with many familiar talents in excellent form.

w Frank Launder, John Dighton, *play John Dighton* *d Frank Launder* *ph* Stan Pavey *m* Mischa Spoliansky

Alastair Sim, Margaret Rutherford, Joyce Grenfell, Richard Wattis, Edward Rigby, Guy Middleton, Muriel Aked, John Bentley, Bernadette O'Farrell

'Absolutely first rate fun.'—*Richard Mallett, Punch*

'Launder couldn't have knocked another laugh out of the situation if he'd used a hockey stick.'—*Sunday Express*

'The best mixed comedy pairing since Groucho Marx and Margaret Dumont.'—*Sunday Chronicle*

The Happiest Millionaire
US 1967 159m Technicolor
Walt Disney (Bill Anderson)

In 1916, a sporting millionaire has several surprising interests but finds time to sort out family problems.
Drearily inept family entertainment with a couple of good songs and an amusing alligator sequence but acres of yawning boredom in between.

w A. J. Carothers, *play* Kyle Crichton, *book* My Philadelphia Father by Cornelia Drexel Biddle *d* Norman Tokar *ph* Edward Colman *m / ly* Richard M. and Robert B. Sherman

Fred MacMurray, *Tommy Steele*, Greer Garson, John Davidson, Gladys Cooper, Lesley Anne Warren, Geraldine Page, Hermione Baddeley

Happiness Ahead
US 1934 80m bw

A rich girl finds her true love in a singing window cleaner. Not anybody's idea of a big attraction, but it passed the time for small towns. Dick Powell, Josephine Hutchinson, John Halliday, Dorothy Dare, Frank McHugh, Allen Jenkins, Ruth Donnelly. Written by Ralph Spence, Philip Dunne; directed by Mervyn le Roy; for First National.
'Pleasant comedy, bound to amuse.'—*Variety*

The Happiness of Three Women
GB 1954 78m bw

A village postman and busybody adopts various subterfuges to improve the future happiness of his clients. Minor Welsh waffle which pleased naïve audiences at the time. Brenda de Banzie, Eynon Evans, Petula Clark, Donald Houston, Patricia Burke, Patricia Cutts. Written by Eynon Evans, from his play *Wishing Well*; directed by Maurice Elvey; for Advance.

Happy Anniversary
US 1959 83m bw
UA / Ralph Fields

A television set causes family trouble.
Marital farce designed to take a few sideswipes at TV.

w Joseph Fields, Jerome Chodorov, from their play Anniversary Waltz *d* David Miller *ph* Lee Garmes *m* Sol Kaplan, Robert Allan

David Niven, Mitzi Gaynor, Carl Reiner, Loring Smith, Patty Duke, Phyllis Povah

Happy Anniversary*
France 1961 13m bw

A husband is late for his anniversary dinner because of a traffic jam. Amusing gag comedy, virtually silent and all the better for it. *Pierre Etaix*, Loriot, Nono Zammit. Written and directed by *Pierre Etaix*; for Capac.

Happy Birthday to Me
Canada 1980 111m Metrocolor
Birthday / CFDC / Famous Players (John Dunning, Andre Link)

Members of the senior class at Crawford Academy are killed off one at a time by one of their number.
Abysmal teenage shocker which grinds on relentlessly for nearly two hours.

w Timothy Bond, Peter Jobin, John Saxton *d* J. Lee Thompson *ph* Miklos Lente *m* Bo Harwood, Lance Rubin

Melissa Sue Anderson, Glenn Ford, Laurence Dane, Sharon Acker, Frances Hyland

Happy Birthday Wanda June*
US 1971 105m Technicolor
Columbia (Lester Goldsmith)

An adventurer believed dead returns just as his wife is about to choose one of two suitors.
A farcical situation becomes in this writer's hands an investigation of the hero cult, with many zany jokes, episodes in heaven, and bad language. Interesting in spots, but it would have worked better with a more fluent cinematic technique.

w Kurt Vonnegut Jnr, from his play *d* Mark Robson *ph* Fred J. Koenekamp

Rod Steiger, Susannah York, George Grizzard, Don Murray

'We can only assume that Mr Robson deserted the filmic instincts that brought him commercial success because here he was, finally, in the presence of Art.'—*Hollis Alpert*

'Nothing more than a miscast film record of the dialogue and plot outline of the stage work.'—*Judith Crist*

Happy Days
US 1930 86m bw Grandeur
Fox

A showboat singer is a hit in New York and helps her old friends.
Virtually a revue, with spectacular effects on the giant screen.

w Sidney Lanfield, Edwin Burke *d* Benjamin Stoloff *ph* Lucien Andriot and others *music* various

Marjorie White; and Janet Gaynor, Charles Farrell, Victor McLaglen, Edmund Lowe, El Brendel, Walter Catlett, James J. Corbett, Tom Patricola, Dixie Lee, Sharon Lynn, Whispering Jack Smith

'We don't love. We just make love. And damn little of that!'

The Happy Ending*
US 1969 112m Technicolor Panavision
UA / Pax Films (Richard Brooks)

A middle-aged woman reflects over sixteen years of unhappy marriage.
Sometimes glib, sometimes trenchant sophisticated drama with enough interesting scenes to make it more than merely a 'woman's picture'.

wd Richard Brooks *ph* Conrad Hall *m* Michel Legrand

Jean Simmons, John Forsythe, Shirley Jones, Lloyd Bridges, Teresa Wright, Dick Shawn, Nanette Fabray, Bobby Darin, Tina Louise

'Packed with punchy little epigrams floating in a vacuum of glossy superficiality.'—*David Wilson*

'The truth about the process of ageing is what binds this film together like cement.'—*Alexander Walker*

AAN: Jean Simmons; song 'What Are You Doing the Rest of Your Life' (*m* Michel Legrand, *ly* Alan and Marilyn Bergman)

Happy Ever After
GB / Germany 1932 86m bw
UFA (Erich Pommer)

Window-cleaners put a young actress on the way to stardom.
Cheerful comedy, set and made in Germany by mainly British talent.

w Jack Hulbert, Douglas Furber, from a story

by Walter Reisch and Billy Wilder *d* Paul Martin, Robert Stevenson

Lilian Harvey, Jack Hulbert, Cicely Courtneidge, Sonnie Hale, Edward Chapman

Happy Ever After*
GB 1954 87m Technicolor
ABP / Mario Zampi
US title: *Tonight's the Night*

Irish villagers draw lots for the privilege of murdering their rascally squire.
Fairly hilarious black comedy with a good cast entering into the spirit of the thing.
w Jack Davies, Michael Pertwee, L. A. G. Strong *d* Mario Zampi *ph* Stan Pavey *m* Stanley Black

David Niven, Yvonne de Carlo, A. E. Matthews, Michael Shepley, George Cole, Barry Fitzgerald

The Happy Family
GB 1952 86m bw

A shopkeeper refuses to move and provide a site for the Festival of Britain. Pale Ealing imitation with amiable cast. Stanley Holloway, Kathleen Harrison, Naunton Wayne, George Cole, Dandy Nichols, Miles Malleson. Written by Muriel and Sydney Box, from a play by Michael Clayton Hutton; directed by Muriel Box; for London Independent. (US title: *Mr Lord Says No.*)

Happy Go Lovely
GB 1950 97m Technicolor
Excelsior (Marcel Hellman)

A chorus girl meets a millionaire during the Edinburgh Festival.
For a semi-official contribution to the Festival of Britain this is a lamentably unspontaneous musical with no use of cinema techniques or natural locales. Even allowing for the flat handling, it is tedious.
w Val Guest *d* Bruce Humberstone *ph* Erwin Hillier *m* Mischa Spoliansky

David Niven, Vera-Ellen, Cesar Romero, Bobby Howes, Diane Hart, Gordon Jackson, Barbara Couper, Gladys Henson, Joyce Carey

† A remake of *Paradise for Two.*

Happy Go Lucky
US 1937 69m bw

A musical comedy singer is mistaken for an aviator and kidnapped. Thin vehicle for a star who didn't last. Phil Regan, Evelyn Venable, Jed Prouty, William Newell. Written by Raymond Schrock, Olive Cooper and others; directed by Aubrey Scotto; for Nat Levine / Republic.

Happy Go Lucky
US 1942 81m Technicolor
Paramount (Harold Wilson)

A cigarette girl chases a millionaire to a Caribbean island.
Flimsy musical for those who like the stars.
w Walter de Leon, Melvin Frank, Norman Panama *d* Curtis Bernhardt *ph* Karl Struss, Wilfrid Cline *songs* Frank Loesser, Jimmy McHugh

Mary Martin, Dick Powell, Betty Hutton (singing 'Murder He Says'), Rudy Vallee, Eddie Bracken, Mabel Paige, Eric Blore, Clem Bevans

Happy Gypsies*
Yugoslavia 1967 90m Eastmancolor
Avala
aka: *I Even Knew Happy Gypsies*

A handsome, cruel-natured gypsy and his wife have violent adventures and find themselves on the run from the police.
The first film in the gypsy language does not make one too sympathetic to their cause, but some scenes are well managed and the colour is fine.
wd Alexander Petrovic *ph* Tomislav Pinter *m* gypsy melodies

Bekim Fehmiu, Olivera Vuco, Bata Zivojinovic

AA: best foreign film

The Happy Hooker
US 1975 98m Movielab
Double H / Cannon-Happy (Fred Caruso)

A Dutch girl in New York starts a career as a prostitute and finds she enjoys it.
Glum sex comedy based on the supposed exploits of a real madam; crude and not very funny. If this is emancipation, Shirley Temple seems more attractive by the minute.
w William Richert, *book* Xaviera Hollander *d* Nicholas Sgarro *ph* Dick Kratina *m* Don Elliott

Lynn Redgrave (hilariously miscast), Jean-Pierre Aumont, Lovelady Powell, Nicholas Pryor, Elizabeth Wilson, Tom Poston, Conrad Janis, Richard Lynch

† Follow-ups: *The Happy Hooker Goes to Washington* (1977), *The Happy Hooker Goes to Hollywood* (1980)

Happy Is the Bride*
GB 1957 84m bw
Panther / Paul Soskin

A couple planning a quiet summer wedding reckon without the intervention of her parents.
Tame remake of *Quiet Wedding*; the right spirit but not much sparkle.
w Jeffrey Dell, Roy Boulting, *play* Esther McCracken *d* Roy Boulting *ph* Ted Scaife *m* Benjamin Frankel

Ian Carmichael, Janette Scott, Cecil Parker, Joyce Grenfell, Terry-Thomas, John Le Mesurier, Eric Barker, Edith Sharpe, Athene Seyler

Happy Land*
US 1943 75m bw
TCF (Kenneth MacGowan)

Grandfather's ghost comes back to comfort a family which has lost its son at war.
Sentimental flagwaver very typical of its time; well made, it ensured not a dry eye in the house.
w Kathryn Scola, Julien Josephson, *novel* Mackinlay Kantor *d* Irving Pichel *ph* Joseph La Shelle *m* Cyril Mockridge

Don Ameche, Frances Dee, Harry Carey, Ann Rutherford, Cara Williams, Henry Morgan, Richard Crane, Dickie Moore

Happy Landing*
US 1938 102m bw
TCF (David Hempstead)

A Norwegian girl falls for an American flier who crashes near her home.
Lightweight skating musical, well put together.
w Milton Sperling, Boris Ingster *d* Roy del Ruth *ph* John Mescall *md* Louis Silvers

Sonja Henie, Don Ameche, Cesar Romero, Ethel Merman, Jean Hersholt, Billy Gilbert, Wally Vernon, El Brendel

'Just about everything to ensure entertainment value, shrewdly blended.'—*Variety*

Happy New Year*
France / Italy 1973 115m Eastmancolor
Films 13 / Rizzoli (Claude Lelouch)
original title: *La Bonne Année*

A thief is paroled on New Year's Eve in the hope that he will lead police to his confederates. In fact he learns a lot about the world and himself.
Bitter comedy apparently intended to distance the director from the romantic fervour of *A Man and a Woman*, a clip from which is screened for the convicts at the beginning.
w, d, ph Claude Lelouch *m* Francis Lai

Lino Ventura, Françoise Fabian, Charles Gérard, André Falcon

Happy New Year*
US 1987 85m Continental Color

Two middle-aged jewel thieves head for a big score in Florida. Loose remake of Lelouch's *La Bonne Année*, quite watchable in its familiar way. Peter Falk, Charles Durning, Wendy Hughes, Tom Courtenay, John Copeland. Written by Warren Lane; directed by John G. Avildsen; for Delphi IV / Columbia.

The Happy Road*
US / France 1956 100m bw
MGM / Thor (Gene Kelly)

Two children run away from a Swiss school and are pursued by the American father of one of them.
Whimsical peripatetic comedy which fails to come off despite charming passages.
w Arthur Julian, Joseph Morhain, Harry Kurnitz *d* Gene Kelly *ph* Robert Juillard *m* Georges Van Parys

Gene Kelly, Barbara Laage, Michael Redgrave, Bobby Clark, Brigitte Fossey

The Happy Thieves
US 1962 88m bw
UA / Hillworth (James Hill, Rita Hayworth)

A gentleman thief and his accomplice become unwittingly involved in murder.
Dreary comedy which turns into equally dreary drama and makes its European backgrounds look ugly.
w John Gay, *novel* The Oldest Confession by Richard Condon *d* George Marshall *ph* Paul Beeson *m* Mario Nascimbene

Rex Harrison, Rita Hayworth, Grégoire Aslan, Joseph Wiseman, Alida Valli

The Happy Time***
US 1952 94m bw
Columbia / Stanley Kramer (Earl Felton)

Domestic misadventures of a family of French Canadians during the twenties.
Basically concerned with adolescent sexual stirrings, this very agreeable film has a light touch and is most deftly directed and acted.

w Earl Felton, play Samuel A. Taylor *d Richard Fleischer ph Charles Lawton Jnr m* Dmitri Tiomkin *pd Rudolph Sternad*

Charles Boyer, Louis Jourdan, Bobby Driscoll, Marsha Hunt, Marcel Dalio, Kurt Kasznar, Linda Christian, Jeanette Nolan, Jack Raine, Richard Erdman

The Happy Years
US 1950 86m bw
MGM (Carey Wilson)

The taming of an unruly pupil at a turn-of-the-century American school.
A curiously unrealized piece of Americana, with only moments to suggest what was being aimed at.

w Harry Ruskin, from 'The Lawrenceville School Stories' by Owen Johnson *d* William Wellman *ph* Paul C. Vogel *m* Leigh Harline

Dean Stockwell, Leo G. Carroll, Darryl Hickman, Scotty Beckett, Leon Ames, Margalo Gillmore

Hara Kiri*
Japan 1962 135m bw Grandscope
Shochiku
original title: *Seppuku*

17th-century samurai often pretend to commit hara kiri so that a grand lord will have sympathy and take them on. One of them is forced to go through with it.
Strange, traditional, slow and explicitly brutal costume piece, for specialized western eyes only.

w Shinodu Hashimoto *d* Masaki Kobayashi *ph* Yoshio Miyajima *m* Toru Takemitsu *ad* Junichi Ozumi

Tatsuya Nakadai, Shimai Iwashita, Akira Isahama

The Hard Boiled Canary
US 1941 80m bw

A young burlesque singer is softened at a summer music school. Another Pygmalion enterprise, but the story is only a slim vehicle for the songs. Susanna Foster, Allan Jones, Margaret Lindsay, Lynne Overman, William Collier Snr. Written by Frederick Jackson, from story by Andrew L. Stone and Robert Lively and idea by Ann Ronell; directed and produced by Andrew Stone; for Paramount. (GB title: *There's Magic in Music.*)

Hard Contract
US 1969 106m De Luxe Panavision
TCF (Marvin Schwarz)

A professional killer has sexual hang-ups.
Heavy-going modern thriller with lively scenes separated by too much self-analytical chat, not to mention a tour of Europe.

wd S. Lee Pogostin *ph* Jack Hildyard *m* Alex North

James Coburn, Lilli Palmer, Lee Remick, Burgess Meredith, Patrick Magee, Sterling Hayden, Helen Cherry, Karen Black, Claude Dauphin

'Behind it one glimpses a much better film than its surface suggests.'—*MFB*

'Like a flat-footed James Bond story that soaked its feet in a hot bath of existentialism.'—*John Simon*

Hard Country
US 1981 104m CFI Color
AFD (David Greene, Mack Bing)

An urban cowboy has no ambitions until he falls in love.
Simple modern western with music, not at all bad but with a scant potential audience.

w Michael Kane *d* David Greene *ph* Dennis Dalzell *m* Michael Martin Murphey, Jimmie Haskell *ed* John A. Martinelli *pd* Edward Richardson

Jan-Michael Vincent, Kim Basinger, Michael Parks, Tanya Tucker, Gailard Sartain

A Hard Day's Night****
GB 1964 85m bw
(UA) Proscenium (Walter Shenson)

Harassed by their manager and Paul's grandpa, the Beatles embark from Liverpool by train for a London TV show.
Comic fantasia with music; an enormous commercial success with the director trying every cinematic gag in the book, it led directly to all the kaleidoscopic swinging London spy thrillers and comedies of the later sixties, and so has a lot to answer for; but at the time it was a sweet breath of fresh air, and the Beatles even seemed willing and likeable.

w Alun Owen d Richard Lester ph Gilbert Taylor songs The Beatles md George Martin

The Beatles, Wilfrid Brambell, Norman Rossington, *Victor Spinetti*

'A fine conglomeration of madcap clowning . . . with such a dazzling use of camera that it tickles the intellect and electrifies the nerves.'—*Bosley Crowther*

'All technology was enlisted in the service of the gag, and a kind of nuclear gagmanship exploded.'—*John Simon*

AAN: Alun Owen; George Martin

Hard, Fast and Beautiful
US 1951 76m bw
RKO / The Filmmakers (Collier Young)

A girl tennis player is influenced by her ambitious mother.
Unusual but not very effective melodrama.

w Martha Wilkerson, *novel* John R. Tunis *d* Ida Lupino *ph* Archie Stout *m* Roy Webb

Claire Trevor, Sally Forrest, Carleton Young, Robert Clarke, Kenneth Patterson, Joseph Kearns

Hard Steel
GB 1942 86m bw
GFD / GHW (James B. Sloan)
reissue title: *What Shall It Profit*

A steel worker is promoted and loses his humanity, but comes to his senses when his wife leaves him.
Modest moral drama from the uplift side of the Rank empire.

w Lydia Hayward, *novel* Steel Saraband by Roger Dataller *d* Norman Walker *ph* Claude Friese-Greene

Wilfrid Lawson, Betty Stockfield, John Stuart, George Carney, Joan Kemp-Welch, Hay Petrie

Hard Times*
US 1975 93m Metrocolor Panavision
Columbia (Lawrence Gordon)
GB title: *The Streetfighter*

In New Orleans in the Depression-hit thirties, a prizefighter and a promoter help each other.
Interesting, atmospheric melodrama on the lone stranger theme.

w Walter Hill, Bryan Gindorff, Bruce Henstell *d* Walter Hill *ph* Philip Lathrop *m* Barry DeVorzon

Charles Bronson, James Coburn, Jill Ireland, Strother Martin, Maggie Blye

Hard to Get
US 1938 80m bw

An architect is reduced to working at a gas station; here he meets and falls in love with a millionairess. Arch romantic comedy which failed to enhance its stars. Dick Powell, Olivia de Havilland, Charles Winninger, Thurston Hall, Isabel Jeans, Penny Singleton, Allen Jenkins. Written by Jerry Wald, Maurice Leo and Richard Macauley; directed by Ray Enright; for Warner. 'Will carry in top brackets mainly due to selling names.'—*Variety*

Hard to Handle**
US 1933 75m bw
Warner (Robert Lord)

The success story of a cheerful public relations man.
Punchy star comedy with interesting sidelights on the social fads of the early thirties including marathon dancing, get-rich-quick schemes and grapefruit diets.

w Wilson Mizner, Robert Lord *d* Mervyn Le Roy *ph* Barney McGill

James Cagney, Ruth Donnelly, Mary Brian, Allen Jenkins, Claire Dodd

'Hokum this time instead of the realism that boosted him to stardom.'—*Variety*

'A violent, slangy, down-to-the-pavement affair which has many a mirthful moment.'—*Mordaunt Hall*

'There are two sides to every story—and every woman!'

The Hard Way*
US 1942 109m bw
Warner (Jerry Wald)

A strong-willed girl pushes her reluctant sister to the heights of show business.
Unconvincing but well-mounted drama.

w Daniel Fuchs, Peter Viertel *d* Vincent Sherman *ph* James Wong Howe *m* Heinz Roemheld *md* Leo F. Forbstein

Ida Lupino, Joan Leslie, Dennis Morgan, Jack Carson, Gladys George, Faye Emerson, Paul Cavanagh, Roman Bohnen

Hardcore*
US 1978 108m Metrocolor
Columbia / A-Team (John Milius)
GB title: *The Hardcore Life*

A religious man from Michigan journeys to Los Angeles in search of his daughter, who has taken to acting in porno films.
Intense and solemn treatment of a situation that could have gone over the top, and very nearly does; the acting saves it.

wd Paul Schraeder *ph* Michael Chapman *m* Jack Nitzsche

George C. Scott, Peter Boyle, Season Hubley, Dick Sargent, Leonard Gaines

'Flawed and uneven, it contains moments of pure revelation.'—*Roger Ebert*

The Harder They Fall*
US 1956 109m bw
Columbia (Philip Yordan)

A press agent exposes the crooked fight game. Wearily efficient sporting melodrama.

w Philip Yordan, *novel* Budd Schulberg *d* Mark Robson *ph* Burnett Guffey *m* Hugo Friedhofer

Humphrey Bogart (his last performance), Rod Steiger, Jan Sterling, Mike Lane, Max Baer, Edward Andrews, Harold J. Stone

AAN: Burnett Guffey

The Hardy Family
America's favourite fictional characters just before and during World War II were the family of a small-town judge, who seemed to personify all that everyone was fighting for, especially as the young son was always getting into amusing scrapes. Designed by a delighted MGM as low-budgeters, they paid for many an expensive failure, and introduced, as young Andy's girl friends, a series of starlets who went on to much bigger things. The basic family was Lewis Stone, Fay Holden, Mickey Rooney, Cecilia Parker and Sara Haden (as the spinster aunt); but in the very first episode Lionel Barrymore and Spring Byington played the judge and his wife.

A FAMILY AFFAIR (1936); 69m; *d* George B. Seitz; *w* Kay Van Riper, *play* Aurania Rouverol
YOU'RE ONLY YOUNG ONCE (1938); 78m; *d* George B. Seitz; *w* Kay Van Riper; introducing Ann Rutherford (who became a regular)
JUDGE HARDY'S CHILDREN (1938); 78m; *d* George B. Seitz; *w* Kay Van Riper; *with* Ruth Hussey
LOVE FINDS ANDY HARDY (1938); 90m; *d* George B. Seitz; *w* William Ludwig; *with* Judy Garland, Lana Turner
OUT WEST WITH THE HARDYS (1938); 90m; *d* George B. Seitz; *w* Kay Van Riper, Agnes Christine Johnson, William Ludwig
THE HARDYS RIDE HIGH (1939); 81m; *d* George B. Seitz; *w* as above
ANDY HARDY GETS SPRING FEVER (1939); 85m; *d* W. S. Van Dyke II; *w* Kay Van Riper
JUDGE HARDY AND SON (1939); 90m; *d* George B. Seitz; *w* Carey Wilson; *with* June Preisser, Maria Ouspenskaya
ANDY HARDY MEETS A DEBUTANTE (1940); 89m; *d* George B. Seitz; *w* Annalee Whitmore, Thomas Seller; *with* Judy Garland
ANDY HARDY'S PRIVATE SECRETARY (1941); 101m; *d* George B. Seitz; *w* Jane Murfin, Harry Ruskin; *with* Kathryn Grayson, Ian Hunter
LIFE BEGINS FOR ANDY HARDY (1941); 100m; *d* George B. Seitz; *w* Agnes Christine Johnson; *with* Judy Garland
THE COURTSHIP OF ANDY HARDY (1942); 93m; *d* George B. Seitz; *w* Agnes Christine Johnson; *with* Donna Reed
ANDY HARDY'S DOUBLE LIFE (1942); 92m; *d* George B. Seitz; *w* Agnes Christine Johnson; *with* Esther Williams, Susan Peters
ANDY HARDY'S BLONDE TROUBLE (1944); 107m; *d* George B. Seitz; *w* Harry Ruskin, William Ludwig, Agnes Christine Johnson; *with* Bonita Granville, Jean Porter, Herbert Marshall, the Wilde twins
LOVE LAUGHS AT ANDY HARDY (1946); 94m; *d* Willis Goldbeck; *w* Harry Ruskin, William Ludwig; *with* Bonita Granville
ANDY HARDY COMES HOME (1958); 80m; *d* Howard Koch; *w* Edward Everett Hutshing, Robert Morris Donley; *without* Lewis Stone

Harem
US / France 1985 113m colour

A New York girl is abducted and taken to an Arabian prince's harem. Weird and unsatisfactory romantic fantasy; the sheikh, it turns out, is only making a romantic gesture and foists no demands on the girl. Any significance is submerged in yawns. Nastassja Kinski, Ben Kingsley, Dennis Goldson, Zohra Segal. Written by Arthur Joffe, Tom Rayfiel, Richard Prieur; directed by Arthur Joffe; for Alain Sarde / UGC / Sara.

Harem Girl
US 1952 70m bw

The secretary to a princess vanquishes her employer's Arab ill-wishers. Dispirited pratfall farce, its star's last movie. Joan Davis, Peggie Castle, Arthur Blake, Paul Marion. Written by Edward Bernds and Ellwood Ullman; directed by Edward Bernds; for Columbia.

Harlequin
Australia 1980 93m Eastmancolor Panavision

A faith healer cures a politician's son, seduces his wife, and proves to be of supernatural origin. Muddled and unsatisfactory fantasy in the manner of *The Passing of the Third Floor Back*; in this case far too much is left unexplained, and the film is scarcely entertaining despite effort all round. Robert Powell, David Hemmings, Carmen Duncan, Broderick Crawford. Written by Everett de Roche; directed by Simon Wincer; for FG Films.

'She was famous for light dresses, loose living, and trips to the bottom between pictures!'

Harlow
US 1965 125m Technicolor Panavision
Paramount / Embassy / Prometheus (Joseph E. Levine)

In 1929, starlet Jean Harlow is shot to fame by her agent Arthur Landau.
Absurdly whitewashed and excruciatingly boring rags-to-riches yarn with most of the characters fictitious and little to do with the real Jean Harlow. Only the studio scenes are mildly interesting.

w John Michael Hayes *d* Gordon Douglas *ph* Joseph Ruttenberg *m* Neal Hefti *ad* Hal Pereira, Roland Anderson *costumes Edith Head*

Carroll Baker, Peter Lawford, Mike Connors, Red Buttons, Raf Vallone, Angela Lansbury, *Martin Balsam*

'Hollywood once again succeeds in reducing one of its few fascinating realities to the sleazy turgid level of its more sordid fictions.'—*Judith Crist*

† A rather better television tape drama of the same title, starring Carol Lynley and Ginger Rogers, was made almost simultaneously. It was converted to film ('Electronovision') but had few bookings.

Harmony Heaven*
GB 1930 61m colour
BIP

A composer becomes famous with the help of his girl friend.
Unbelievably naïve musical, notable only as British and in colour. Not tolerable today as entertainment.

w Arthur Wimperis, Randall Faye *d* Thomas Bentley *ph* Theodor Sparkuhl *songs* Edward Brandt, Eddie Pola

Polly Ward, Stuart Hall, Trilby Clark, Jack Raine

Harmony Lane
US 1935 85m bw

The life of Stephen Foster. Heavygoing biopic from an independent studio; for rural audiences only. Douglass Montgomery, Evelyn Venable, Adrienne Ames, Joseph Cawthorn, William Frawley, Clarence Muse. Story Milton Krims, adapted by Joseph Santley; directed by Joseph Santley; for Colbert Clark/Mascot

Harold and Maude*
US 1971 92m Technicolor
Paramount / Mildred Lewis / Colin Higgins

A repressed young man, fixated on death and funerals, has an affair with an 80-year-old woman.
Often hilarious black comedy for those who can stand it; the epitome of bad taste, splashed around with wit and vigour, it became a minor cult.

w Colin Higgins d Hal Ashby ph John A. Alonzo *m* Cat Stevens

Bud Cort, Ruth Gordon, Vivian Pickles, Cyril Cusack

Harold Lloyd's Funny Side of Life***
US 1963 99m bw
Harold Lloyd (Duncan Mansfield)

Excerpts from twenties comedies plus a shortened version of *The Freshman* (1925).
Excellent compilation, though the mini-feature makes it a little unbalanced.

w Arthur Ross *m* Walter Scharf

Harold Lloyd

Harold Lloyd's World of Comedy****
US 1962 97m bw
Harold Lloyd

Generous clips from the comic climaxes of Lloyd's best silent and sound comedies including *Safety Last, The Freshman, Hot Water, Why Worry, Girl Shy, Professor Beware, Movie Crazy* and *Feet First*.
As Lloyd's work lends itself well to extract, this can hardly fail to be a superb anthology capsuling the appeal of one of America's greatest silent comedians. The timing is just perfect.

m Walter Scharf *commentary* Art Ross

Harold Teen
US 1934 66m bw

A young reporter saves a small-town bank from collapse. Teenage romantic comedy previously filmed in 1928 (with Arthur Lake and Mary Brian, directed by Mervyn Le Roy) and here reduced to second feature status. Hal Le Roy, Rochelle Hudson, Patricia Ellis, Guy Kibbee, Hobart Cavanagh. Written by Paul Gerard Smith and Al Cohn, from the comic strip by Carl Ed; directed by Murray Roth; for Warner. (GB title: *Dancing Fool.*)

Harper*
US 1966 121m Technicolor Panavision
Warner / Gershwin–Kastner
GB title: *The Moving Target*

A Los Angeles private eye is hired by a rich woman to find her missing husband.
Formula Californian detection distinguished by its cast rather than by any special talent in the writing or presentation. It seemed likely to produce a new Chandleresque school, but imitations proved very sporadic; the star repeated the role less successfully in *The Drowning Pool* (qv).

w William Goldman, *novel* The Moving Target by John Ross Macdonald *d* Jack Smight *ph* Conrad Hall *m* Johnny Mandel

Paul Newman, Lauren Bacall, Shelley Winters, Arthur Hill, Julie Harris, Janet Leigh, Pamela Tiffin, Robert Wagner, Robert Webber, Strother Martin

'It isn't a bad try, but it never really slips into overdrive.'—*Penelope Houston*

'Nothing needs justification less than entertainment; but when something planned only to entertain fails, it has no justification. A private-eye movie without sophistication and style is ignominious.'—*Pauline Kael, 1968*

The Harrad Experiment
US 1973 97m Eastmancolor
Cinerama / Cinema Arts (Dennis F. Stevens)

A college professor conducts a series of tests on sexual relationships.
Low-keyed Kinsey Report for the seventies, pleasantly made but not very stimulating.

w Michael Werner, Ted Cassidy, *novel* Robert H. Rimmer *d* Ted Post *ph* Richard Kline *m* Artie Butler

James Whitmore, Tippi Hedren, Don Johnson, Laurie Walters, Robert Middleton

'Ludicrously sober-sided amalgam of nude yoga and extra-curricular groping, which should set sex educational theory back ten years.'—*Sight and Sound*

Harriet Craig
US 1950 94m bw
Columbia (William Dozier)

A wife's only real love is her meticulously kept and richly appointed house.
Ho-hum remake of a sturdy thirties film *Craig's Wife* (qv).

w Anne Froelick, James Gunn, *play* Craig's Wife by George Kelly *d* Vincent Sherman *ph* Joseph Walker *m* George Duning *md* Morris Stoloff

Joan Crawford, Wendell Corey, Allyn Joslyn, Lucile Watson, William Bishop, K. T. Stevens, Raymond Greenleaf

'They're two men with nothing in common—they're father and son!'

Harry and Son
US 1984 117m Technicolor
Orion / Paul Newman

An ageing construction worker is at odds with his twenty-one-year-old son, who lives with him.
One can't imagine why Paul Newman wanted to make this boring shouting match between people no one can care for.

w Ronald L. Buck, Paul Newman, suggested by the novel A Lost King by Raymond DeCapite *d* Paul Newman *ph* Donald McAlpine *m* Henry Mancini

Paul Newman, Robby Benson, Ellen Barkin, Wilford Brimley

Harry and the Hendersons
US 1987 110m De Luxe

A camping family meets a docile Big Foot. Elementary kiddie/family pic in the wake of *E.T.* John Lithgow, Melinda Dillon, David Suchet, Don Ameche, Margaret Langrick, Joshua Rudoy. Written by William Dear and others; directed by Dear; for Amblin Entertainment. (GB title: *Big Foot and the Hendersons.*)

Harry and Tonto*
US 1974 115m De Luxe
TCF (Paul Mazursky)

An elderly New York widower and his cat are evicted and trek to Chicago.
Amiable character study, very watchable but rather pointless.

w Paul Mazursky, Josh Greenfield *d* Paul Mazursky *ph* Michael Butler *m* Bill Conti

Art Carney, Ellen Burstyn, Chief Dan George, Geraldine Fitzgerald, Larry Hagman, Arthur Hunnicutt, Herbert Berghof

'A vivacious and affectionate folk tale.'—*New Yorker*

'It has a life-affirming quality as welcome contrast to the destructive delirium of most modern movies.'—*Michael Billington, Illustrated London News*

AA: Art Carney
AAN: Paul Mazursky (as writer)

Harry and Walter go to New York
US 1976 120m Metrocolor Panavision
Columbia (Don Devlin, Harry Gittes)

In oldtime New York, two carnival entertainers get involved with suffragettes and a safecracker.
Extended period romp in which the high humour soon palls and a general lack of talent makes itself felt.

w John Byrum, Robert Kaufman *d* Mark Rydell *ph* Laszlo Kovacs *m* David Shire *pd Harry Horner*

James Caan, Elliott Gould, Michael Caine, Diane Keaton, Charles Durning, Lesley Ann Warren, Jack Gilford

'A charmless mishmash.'—*Sight and Sound*

'This film fails to work as a light comedy, as a period piece, as a jigsaw puzzle . . . mainly, it just sits there and dies.'—*Frank Rich, New York Post*

'Strictly for those who'll laugh at anything.'—*Kevin Thomas, Los Angeles Times*

'The woman or the tiger? He can't have them both!'

Harry Black and the Tiger
GB 1958 117m Technicolor Cinemascope
Mersham (John Brabourne)
US title: *Harry Black*

A famous tiger hunter allows his best friend to prove himself a hero, and falls in love with the friend's wife.
Lethargic melodrama with good Indian backgrounds.

w Sydney Boehm, *novel* David Walker *d* Hugo Fregonese *ph* John Wilcox *m* Clifton Parker

Stewart Granger, Anthony Steel, Barbara Rush, *I. S. Johar*

Harry in Your Pocket
US 1973 103m De Luxe Panavision
UA / Cinema Video (Bruce Geller)

Adventures of a young, a middle-aged and an old pickpocket.
Partly pleasant but rather aimless comedy drama, agreeably set in Seattle and Salt Lake City.

w Ron Austin, James Buchanan *d* Bruce Geller *ph* Fred Koenekamp *m* Lalo Schifrin

James Coburn, *Walter Pidgeon*, Michael Sarrazin, Trish Van Devere

Harum Scarum
US 1965 95m Metrocolor

An American star on the way to the middle eastern première of his latest film is kidnapped by assassins. Flavourless comedy with music;

before dull backgrounds the star performs adequately. Elvis Presley, Mary Ann Mobley, Fran Jeffries, Michael Ansara, Theo Marcuse, Jay Novello, Billy Barty. Written by Gerald Drayson Adams; directed by Gene Nelson; for Sam Katzman / MGM. (GB title: *Harem Holiday*.)

Harvest
France 1937 122m bw
Marcel Pagnol
original title: *Regain*

A poacher and an itinerant girl set up house in a deserted village and bring it back to life.
Somewhat charming but interminably slow rustic parable.

wd Marcel Pagnol, *novel* Jean Giono
ph Willy *m* Arthur Honegger

Gabriel Gabrio, Fernandel, Orane Demazis, E. Delmont

Harvey***
US 1950 104m bw
U-I (John Beck)

A middle-aged drunk has an imaginary white rabbit as his friend, and his sister tries to have him certified.
An amiably batty play with splendid lines is here transferred virtually intact to the screen and survives superbly thanks to understanding by all concerned, though the star is as yet too young for a role which he later made his own.

w Mary Chase (with Oscar Brodney) from her play *d Henry Koster ph* William Daniels
m Frank Skinner

James Stewart, Josephine Hull, Victoria Horne, Peggy Dow, *Cecil Kellaway*, Charles Drake, *Jesse White*, Nana Bryant, Wallace Ford

VETA LOUISE (Josephine Hull): 'Myrtle Mae, you have a lot to learn, and I hope you never learn it.'

ELWOOD (James Stewart): 'I've wrestled with reality for 35 years, and I'm happy, doctor. I finally won out over it.'

ELWOOD: 'Harvey and I have things to do . . . we sit in the bars . . . have a drink or two . . . and play the juke box. Very soon the faces of the other people turn towards me and they smile. They say: "We don't know your name, mister, but you're all right, all right." Harvey and I warm ourselves in these golden moments. We came as strangers—soon we have friends. They come over. They sit with us. They drink with us. They talk to us. They tell us about the great big terrible things they've done and the great big wonderful things they're going to do. Their hopes, their regrets. Their loves, their hates. All very large, because nobody ever brings anything small into a bar. Then I introduce them to Harvey, and he's bigger and grander than anything they can offer me. When they leave, they leave impressed. The same people seldom come back.'

ELWOOD (describing his first meeting with Harvey): 'I'd just helped Ed Hickey into a taxi. Ed had been mixing his drinks, and I felt he needed conveying. I started to walk down the street when I heard a voice saying: "Good evening, Mr Dowd". I turned, and there was this big white rabbit leaning against a lamp-post. Well, I thought nothing of that! Because when you've lived in a town as long as I've lived in this one, you get used to the fact that everybody knows your name . . .'

AA: Josephine Hull
AAN: James Stewart

The Harvey Girls**
US 1946 101m Technicolor
MGM (Arthur Freed)

A chain of 19th-century restaurants hires young ladies to go out west as waitresses.
Sprightly if overlong musical based on fact; a good example of an MGM middle-budget extravaganza.

w Edmund Beloin, Nathaniel Curtis
d George Sidney *ph* George Folsey
md Lennie Hayton *songs* Johnny Mercer, Harry Warren

Judy Garland, Ray Bolger, John Hodiak, Preston Foster, Virginia O'Brien, Angela Lansbury, Marjorie Main, Chill Wills, Kenny Baker, Selena Royle

'Anybody who did anything at all in America up to 1900 is liable to be made into a film by MGM.'—*Richard Winnington*

'An abundance of chromatic spectacle and an uncommonly good score.'—*New York Times*

'A perfect example of what Hollywood can do with its vast resources when it wants to be really showy.'—*New York Herald Tribune*

AA: song 'On the Atcheson, Topeka and the Santa Fe'
AAN: Lennie Hayton

Harvey Middleman Fireman*
US 1965 76m Eastmancolor
Columbia (Robert L. Lawrence)

A frustrated middle-aged fireman begins an affair; the resulting guilt complex drives him to a psychiatrist.
Grotesque satirical comedy from one of the sixties' most fashionable cartoonists. Mild, quite pleasing, occasionally crude.

wd / m Ernest Pintoff ph Karl Malkames

Gene Troobnick, Hermione Gingold, Pat Harty

Has Anybody Seen My Gal?**
US 1952 89m Technicolor
U-I (Ted Richmond)

A multi-millionaire pretends to be poor and moves in with distant relatives to test their worthiness.
Very agreeable comedy set in the twenties and centring on a satisfying star performance.

w Joseph Hoffman *d Douglas Sirk*
ph Clifford Stine *m* Joseph Gershenson
ad Bernard Herzbrun, Hilyard Brown

Charles Coburn, Piper Laurie, Rock Hudson, Gigi Perreau, Lynn Bari, Larry Gates, William Reynolds, Skip Homeier, James Dean

The Hasty Heart*
GB 1949 104m bw
ABP (Vincent Sherman)

At an army hospital in Burma, attitudes to an arrogant young Scot change when it is learned that he has only a few weeks to live.
Flat, adequate filming of a successful sentimental stage play.

w Ronald MacDougall, *play* John Patrick
d Vincent Sherman *ph* Wilkie Cooper
m Jack Beaver

Richard Todd, Patricia Neal, Ronald Reagan, Orlando Martins, Howard Marion-Crawford

AAN: Richard Todd

Hat Check Honey
US 1944 66m bw

A veteran comic wants his son to click, but is not so sure when the boy gets a Hollywood contract. Lightweight musical filler with more numbers than plot. Leon Errol, Grace McDonald, Richard Davis, Walter Catlett, Milburn Stone. Written by Maurice Leo, Stanley Davis, Al Martin; directed by Edward F. Cline; for Will Cowan / Universal.

Hat, Coat and Glove
US 1934 64m bw

A New York lawyer accidentally kills an old flame. Tiresome courtroom melodrama, told in a rather stilted manner. Ricardo Cortez, Barbara Robbins, John Beal, Margaret Hamilton, Sara Haden, Samuel S. Hinds. Written by Francis Faragoh, from a play by Wilhelm Speyer; directed by Worthington Miner; for RKO.

Hatari!*
US 1962 158m Technicolor
Paramount / Malabar (Howard Hawks)

International hunters in Tanganyika catch game to send to zoos.
Plotless adventure film with good animal sequences but no shape or suspense; a typical folly of its director, whose chief interest is seeing smart men and women in tough action. The elephants steal this overlong show.

w Leigh Brackett *d* Howard Hawks
ph Russell Harlan m Henry Mancini

John Wayne, Elsa Martinelli, Red Buttons, Hardy Kruger

'Hawks was taking his friends and cast and crew on a trip he wanted to make personally, and the film is both the incidental excuse for and the record of that experience.'—*Joseph Gelmis, 1970*

AAN: Russell Harlan

'A beautiful butterfly broken on the wheel of life!'

The Hatchet Man
US 1932 74m bw
Warner
GB title: *The Honourable Mr Wong*

The executioner of a San Francisco tong dutifully kills his best friend but promises to care for his daughter.
Unconvincing Chinese-American melodrama.

w J. Grubb Alexander, *play* Achmed Abdullah, David Belasco *d* William A. Wellman *ph* Sid Hickox

Edward G. Robinson, Loretta Young, Dudley Digges, Leslie Fenton, Edmund Breese, Tully Marshall, J. Carrol Naish, Noel Madison, Blanche Frederici

'Mild gang stuff in oriental trappings . . . dynamic action or high voltage drama is missing.'—*Variety*

A Hatful of Rain*
US 1957 108m bw Cinemascope
TCF / (Buddy Adler)

A war veteran becomes a drug addict and upsets his wife and family.
One of the first drug dramas: straightforward, well acted, and quite powerful.

w Michael V. Gazzo (with Alfred Hayes), from his play *d Fred Zinnemann ph* Joe Macdonald *m* Bernard Herrmann

Eva Marie Saint, Don Murray, Anthony Franciosa, Lloyd Nolan, Henry Silva

AAN: Anthony Franciosa

'Are you shockproof? Then you will dare to see this famous drama of violence—of hate—of men who teach women the terror of cruelty and mad obsession!'

Hatter's Castle**
GB 1941 102m bw
Paramount British (Isadore Goldsmith)

In the nineties, a megalomaniac Scottish hatter ruins the lives of his wife and daughter.
Enjoyable period melodrama with a rampant star performance and pretty good detail.

w Rodney Ackland, *novel* A. J. Cronin *d* Lance Comfort *ph* Max Greene *m* Horace Shepherd

Robert Newton, Deborah Kerr, James Mason, Beatrice Varley, Emlyn Williams, Henry Oscar, Enid Stamp-Taylor, Brefni O'Rourke

Haunted Harbor
US 1944 bw serial: 15 eps

Heroes and villains sort out the truth of sea monster stories near an ocean trading post.
Muddled serial with a poor monster. Kane Richmond, Kay Aldridge, Roy Barcroft. Directed by Spencer Bennet and Wallace Grissell; for Republic.

Haunted Honeymoon
US 1986 82m Rank Colour
Orion / Susan Ruskin

A radio actor takes his fiancée to the family's gloomy country estate, where werewolves and transvestites are some of the creatures which abound.
Mainly unfunny spoof: all concerned should have taken a closer look at *The Cat and the Canary*.

w Gene Wilder, Terence Marsh *d* Gene Wilder *ph* Fred Schuler *m* John Morris *pd* Terence Marsh *ed* Christopher Greenbury

Gene Wilder, Gilda Radner, Dom DeLuise, Jonathan Pryce, Peter Vaughan, Bryan Pringle

'Faintly amusing but singularly uncompelling.'—*Variety*

The Haunted Palace
US 1963 85m Pathecolor Panavision
AIP / Alta Vista (Roger Corman)

In 1875 a New Englander claims an old mansion as his inheritance and is haunted by his vicious ancestor.
Plodding horror comic, too slow to give opportunities to its stalwart cast.

w Charles Beaumont, from material by H. P. Lovecraft and Edgar Allan Poe *d* Roger Corman *ph* Floyd Crosby *m* Ronald Stein

Vincent Price, Lon Chaney Jnr, Debra Paget, Frank Maxwell, Leo Gordon, Elisha Cook Jnr, John Dierkes

'For those of ghoulish bent, or lovers of the perfectly awful.'—*Judith Crist*

The Haunting*
GB 1963 112m bw Panavision
MGM / Argyle (Robert Wise)

An anthropologist, a sceptic and two mediums spend the weekend in a haunted Boston mansion.
Quite frightening but exhausting and humourless melodrama with a lot of suspense, no visible spooks, and not enough plot for its length. The wide screen is a disadvantage.

w Nelson Gidding, *novel* The Haunting of Hill House by Shirley Jackson *d* Robert Wise *ph David Boulton m* Humphrey Searle *pd* Elliot Scott

Richard Johnson, Claire Bloom, Russ Tamblyn, Julie Harris, Lois Maxwell, Valentine Dyall

'You may not believe in ghosts, but you cannot deny terror!'—*publicity*

Havana Widows*
US 1933 63m bw

Gold diggers seek millionaires in Havana. Lively second feature with the Warner repertory company. Joan Blondell, Glenda Farrell, Guy Kibbee, Lyle Talbot, Allen Jenkins, Frank McHugh, Ruth Donnelly, Hobart Cavanagh. Written by Stanley Logan, Earl Badwin; directed by Ray Enright; for First National. 'Hasn't been a picture in weeks with the same content of rapid-fire laughs, all legitimately gained and inescapable.'—*Variety*

Have a Heart
US 1934 75m bw

A dancing instructress becomes a cripple and is deserted by her boy friend. Family drama with comedy asides, plus a dog and a mystery element. Jean Parker, James Dunn, Una Merkel, Stuart Erwin, Willard Robertson. Written by Florence Ryerson and Edgar Allen Woolf; directed by David Butler; for MGM. 'Such a barrage of sobbing hokum is a novelty in itself in this supposedly sophisticated age.'—*Variety*

Having a Wonderful Crime
US 1945 70m bw

Three amateur detectives solve the mystery of a disappearing magician. Easy-going comedy thriller. Pat O'Brien, Carole Landis, George Murphy. Written by Howard J. Green, Stewart Sterling and Parke Levy; directed by Eddie Sutherland; for RKO.

Having Wonderful Time
US 1938 70m bw
RKO (Pandro S. Berman)

A New York girl falls in love at a summer camp.
Mild comedy which, robbed of its original Jewish milieu, falls resoundingly flat.

w Arthur Kober, from his play *d* Alfred Santell *ph* Robert de Grasse *m* Roy Webb

Ginger Rogers, Douglas Fairbanks Jnr, Peggy Conklin, Lucille Ball, Lee Bowman, Eve Arden, Red Skelton, Donald Meek, Jack Carson

Hawaii*
US 1966 186m De Luxe Panavision
UA / Mirisch (Lewis J. Rachmil)

In 1820 a pious Yale divinity student becomes a missionary to the Hawaiian islands.
Ambitious attempt to contrast naïve dogma with native innocence, ruined by badly handled sub-plots, storms, a childbirth sequence and other distractions, all fragments of an immense novel. Heavy going.

w Daniel Taradash, Dalton Trumbo, *novel* James A. Michener *d* George Roy Hill *ph* Russell Harlan *m* Elmer Bernstein *2nd unit Richard Talmadge pd* Cary Odell

Max Von Sydow, Julie Andrews, Richard Harris, *Jocelyn la Garde*, Carroll O'Connor, Torin Thatcher, Gene Hackman

'Consistently intelligent humanism gives it a certain stature among the wide screen spectacles.'—*Brenda Davies*

AA: Elmer Bernstein
AAN: cinematography; Jocelyn La Garde

Hawaii Calls
US 1938 73m bw

Boy stowaways catch a steamer from San Francisco to Hawaii. Slight vehicle for a singing star. Bobby Breen, Ned Sparks, Irvin S. Cobb, Warren Hull, Gloria Holden, Pua Lani. Written by Wanda Tuchock, from the novel Stowaways in Paradise by Don Blanding; directed by Edward F. Cline; for Sol Lesser / RKO. 'Okay musically but light on romance.'—*Variety*

The Hawaiians
US 1970 132m De Luxe Panavision
UA / Mirisch (Walter Mirisch)
GB title: *Master of the Islands*

A young scion of a shipping business leaves after an argument and strikes oil in terrain supposedly barren.
More fragments from Michener, covering 1870 to 1900 and comprising an absolutely uninteresting family chronicle with moments of spectacle.

w James R. Webb *d* Tom Gries *ph* Philip Lathrop *m* Henry Mancini *pd* Cary Odell

Charlton Heston, Tina Chen, Geraldine Chaplin, John Philip Law, Alec McCowen, Mako, Ann Knight, Lyle Bettger, Keye Luke

'A quickfire succession of corruption, revolution, plague, fire and questions of moral responsibility.'—*MFB*

'Total relaxation—preferably of the brain—is recommended.'—*Judith Crist*

Hawk of the Wilderness
US 1938 bw serial: 12 eps

A shipwreck on an unknown island kills two scientists: their baby grows up with a lost tribe. He's called Kioga, not Tarzan, but this serial follows predictable paths. Herman Brix, Mala, Monte Blue, Noble Johnson. Directed by William Witney and John English; for Republic.

Hawk the Slayer
GB 1980 93m colour
ITC / Chips (Harry Robertson)

Good and evil brothers compete for possession of a magical flying sword.
Curiously unexciting and rather gloomy sword-and-sorcery epic.

w Terry Marcel, Harry Robertson *d* Terry Marcel *ph* Paul Beeson *m* Harry Robertson

Jack Palance, John Terry, Bernard Bresslaw, Ray Charleson, Annette Crosbie, Cheryl Campbell, Peter O'Farrell

Hawmps
US 1976 127m colour

The Texas cavalry experiments with the use of camels in the southwestern desert. Incredibly overstretched and tedious period comedy with some bright patches. James Hampton, Christopher Connelly, Slim Pickens, Denver Pyle, Jennifer Hawkins, Jack Elam. Written by William Bickley and Michael Warren; directed by Joe Camp; for Mulberry Square.

Hazard
US 1948 95m bw
Paramount (Mel Epstein)

A compulsive lady gambler agrees to marry the winner of a dice game, but runs away and is chased by a private detective.
Silly, unamusing romantic comedy-drama.

w Arthur Sheekman, Roy Chanslor *d* George Marshall *ph* Daniel L. Fapp *m* Frank Skinner

Paulette Goddard, Macdonald Carey, Fred Clark, Stanley Clemens, Maxie Rosenbloom, Charles McGraw

A good bit this side of inspired.'—*New York Times*

He Found a Star
GB 1941 88m bw

A theatrical agent loses his star singer and thinks again about his secretary. A strong contender for the Golden Turkey Award (British Division); the ineptitude has to be sampled to be believed. Vic Oliver, Sarah Churchill, Joan Greenwood, Evelyn Dall, Robert Atkins. Written by Austin Melford and Bridget Boland; directed by John Paddy Carstairs; for John Corfield.

He Knows You're Alone
US 1980 92m Metrocolor

A sex-starved maniac attacks teenage girls. Cheapjack horror comic full of fashionable slashing and screaming; of no cinematic interest whatever. Don Scardino, Elizabeth Kemp. Written by Scott Parker; directed by Armand Mastroianni; for Lansbury-Beruh / MGM. 'At this point in the killer-with-a-knife sweepstakes, every company in Hollywood is getting into the act . . . more ingenuity is going into the titles and campaigns than into the films.'—*Variety*.

He Laughed Last*
US 1956 77m Technicolor
Columbia (Jonie Taps)

In the twenties, New York gangsters battle for control of a night club.
Small-scale gangster burlesque which comes off rather better than its credits suggest.

wd Blake Edwards *ph* Henry Freulich *m* Arthur Morton

Frankie Laine, Lucy Marlow, Anthony Dexter, *Jesse White*

He Married his Wife
US 1939 82m bw

A divorced wife falls back in love with her husband. Pleasant minor comedy with screwball touches. Joel McCrea, Nancy Kelly, Roland Young, Mary Boland, Cesar Romero, Lyle Talbot, Elisha Cook Jnr. Written by Sam Hellman, Darrell Ware, Lynn Starling, John O'Hara, Frank Lazarus, Scott Darling; directed by Roy Del Ruth; for Raymond Griffith / TCF.

'Dynamite fills the screen with their kind of love!'

He Ran All the Way*
US 1951 78m bw
UA / Bob Roberts

A hoodlum on the run from the police virtually picks up a girl and hides in her family's apartment.
Uninteresting situation melodrama helped by intelligent acting and handling.

w Guy Endore, Hugo Butler, *novel* Sam Ross *d John Berry* *ph James Wong Howe* *m* Franz Waxman

John Garfield, Shelley Winters, Wallace Ford, Selena Royle, Gladys George, Norman Lloyd, Bobby Hyatt

He Rides Tall
US 1964 84m bw

A marshal postpones his marriage after being forced to kill his stepbrother. Semi-adult western, of no particular consequence. Tony Young, Dan Duryea, Madlyn Rhue, Jo Morrow, R. G. Armstrong. Written by Charles W. Irwin and Robert Creighton; directed by R. G. Springsteen; for Universal.

He Snoops to Conquer
GB 1944 103m bw
Columbia (Ben Henry, Marcel Varnel)

A local handyman exposes a corrupt council. Spotty star comedy with insufficient zest for its great length.

w Stephen Black, Howard Irving Young, Norman Lee, Michael Vaughan, Langford Reed *d* Marcel Varnel *ph* Roy Fogwell

George Formby, Robertson Hare, Elizabeth Allan, Aubrey Mallalieu

He Stayed for Breakfast
US 1940 89m bw
Columbia (B. P. Schulberg)

A Parisian communist waiter hides out in the apartment of American capitalists, and learns from them.
Post-*Ninotchka* comedy, not bad but somehow rather uninteresting and mechanical.

w P. J. Wolfson, Michael Fessier, Ernest Vajda, *play* Liberté Provisoire by Michel Duran *d* Alexander Hall *ph* Joseph Walker *m* Werner Heymann

Melvyn Douglas, Loretta Young, Alan Marshal, Eugene Pallette, Una O'Connor, Curt Bois, Leonid Kinskey

He Walked by Night*
US 1948 80m bw
Eagle–Lion / Bryan Foy

A burglar becomes a cop-killer and is hunted down by the police.
Interesting if rather flatly handled documentary melodrama in clear imitation of *Naked City*.

w John C. Higgins, Crane Wilbur *d* Alfred Werker *ph John Alton* *m* Leonid Raab

Richard Basehart, Scott Brady, Roy Roberts, Whit Bissell

He Was Her Man
US 1934 70m bw

A safecracker goes straight in order to get even with old rivals. Sassy comedy-drama, not quite smart enough to match its star. James Cagney, Joan Blondell, Victor Jory, Frank Craven, Harold Huber. Written by Niven Busch and Tom Buckingham; directed by Lloyd Bacon; for Warner. 'No help will be President Roosevelt's pronunciamento of last Saturday (May 19) in which he decried the public penchant for romanticizing crime.'—*Variety*

He Who Gets Slapped*
US 1924 80m approx (24 fps) bw silent
MGM

A scientist starts a new life as a circus clown.
Odd poetic tragedy, Metro-Goldwyn-Mayer's very first production; the public took to it surprisingly well.

w Victor Sjostrom, Carey Wilson, *play* Leonid Andreyev *d* Victor Sjostrom

Lon Chaney, Norma Shearer, John Gilbert, Tully Marshall, Ford Sterling

'For dramatic value and a faultless adaptation of a play, this is the finest production we have yet seen.'—*New York Times*

He Who Must Die*
France / Italy 1957 126m bw
Cinemascope
Indusfilms
original title: *Celui Qui Doit Mourir*

In a Greek village in 1921, preparations for a passion play are interrupted by the arrival of refugees from the mountains.
Occasionally striking, but mainly arty and pretentious parable; however well meant, a bore to watch.

w Ben Barzman, Jules Dassin, *novel* Nikos Kazantzakis *d* Jules Dassin *ph* Jacques Natteau *m* Georges Auric

Jean Servais, Carl Mohner, Pierre Vaneck, Melina Mercouri, Fernand Ledoux

He Who Rides a Tiger
GB 1965 103m bw
British Lion / David Newman

A feckless burglar comes out of prison and returns to the old life.
Cliché crime yarn which tries rather desperately after fresh detail but bogs down in romantic asides.
w Trevor Peacock *d* Charles Crichton *ph* John Von Kotze *m* Alexander Faris

Tom Bell, Judi Dench, Paul Rogers, Kay Walsh, Ray McAnally, Jeremy Spenser

Head*
US 1968 85m Technicolor
Columbia (Bert Schneider)

Fantasia on the life of a sixties pop group.
A psychedelic trip of a movie which does for the Monkees what *A Hard Day's Night* and *Yellow Submarine* did for the Beatles, and what *Monty Python* did for us all. Sometimes funny, slick and clever; often just plain silly.

w Jack Nicholson, Bob Rafaelson *d* Bob Rafaelson *ph* Michael Hugo *m* Ken Thorne *sp* Chuck Gaspar

The Monkees, Victor Mature, Annette Funicello, Timothy Carey

'Random particles tossed around in some demented jester's wind machine.'—*Richard Combs, MFB, 1978*

'A mind-blowing collage of mixed media, a free-for-all freakout of rock music and psychedelic splashes of colour.'—*Daily Variety*

Head Over Heels*
GB 1937 81m bw
Gaumont (S. C. Balcon)
US title: *Head Over Heels in Love*

A singing star can't make up her mind between two men.
Interestingly dated light star vehicle.

w Dwight Taylor, Fred Thompson, Marjorie Gaffney, *play* Francois de Croisset *d* Sonnie Hale *ph* Glen McWilliams

Jessie Matthews, Robert Flemyng, Louis Borell, Romney Brent, Helen Whitney Bourne, Eliot Makeham

Head Over Heels
US 1980 97m Technicolor
aka: *Chilly Scenes of Winter*

A government office worker thinks back on his on-again off-again relationship with the woman he loves. Quirky comedy drama without the zest of *Annie Hall*, which it much resembles; too much like a television play for box office success. John Heard, Mary Beth Hurt, Peter Riegert, Kenneth McMillan, Gloria Grahame. Written and directed by Joan Macklin Silver, from the novel *Chilly Scenes of Winter* by Ann Beattie; for Triple Play / UA.

Heads Up
US 1930 76m bw

A coastguard ensign is assigned to a private yacht under suspicion of rum-running.
Tedious, flat musical, only interesting for starring the 'boop boop a doop girl', who soon outstays her welcome. Charles Rogers, Helen Kane, Victor Moore, Margaret Breen. Written from the musical play by Jack McGowan and Jack Kirkland; directed by Victor Schertzinger; for Paramount. 'Holds nothing to pull above average grosses and will slide many a house below that mark.'—*Variety*

Health*
US 1979 102m De Luxe
TCF / Robert Altman

Complications result when a health foods convention is staged in a Florida hotel.
Zany satirical all-star romp on the lines of *A Wedding* but by no means as likeable or laughable, considering its cast, as it should be.

w Robert Altman, Paul Dooley, Frank Barhydt *d* Robert Altman *ph* Edmond L. Koons *m* Joseph Byrd

Lauren Bacall, Glenda Jackson, James Garner, Dick Cavett, Carol Burnett, Paul Dooley, Henry Gibson, Donald Moffat

Hear Me Good
US 1957 82m bw VistaVision

Adventures of a confidence trickster in the beauty contest racket. Sub-Damon Runyon goings on, featuring a brash new comedian who was subsequently little heard from. Hal March, Jean Willes, Joe E. Ross, Merry Anders, Milton Frome. Written and directed by Don McGuire; for Paramount.

Heart Beat
US 1979 109m Technicolor

The literary career of Jack Kerouac is paralleled with his curious sex life. Hesitant and generally unsatisfactory analysis of the so-called beat generation. John Heard, Nick Nolte, Sissy Spacek, Ray Sharkey, Tony Bill. Written and directed by John Byrun; for Orion / Warner.

The Heart is a Lonely Hunter*
US 1968 123m Technicolor
Warner Seven Arts (Joel Freeman)

Incidents in the life of a gentle deaf mute in a small southern town.
Wispy film of a wistful novel; quite well done but overlong and hard to cheer at.

w Thomas C. Ryan, *novel* Carson McCullers *d* Robert Ellis Miller *ph James Wong Howe* *m* Dave Grusin

Alan Arkin, Sondra Locke, Stacy Keach, Laurinda Barrett, Chuck McCann, Biff McGuire, Percy Rodriguez, Cicely Tyson

AAN: Alan Arkin; Sondra Locke

Heart like a Wheel*
US 1983 113m CFI colour
Aurora (Charles Rovin)

The wife of a service station owner stops at nothing to become a racing driver.
Well-made study of an obsession, with the usual racing thrills.

w Ken Friedman *d* Jonathan Kaplan *ph* Tak Fujimoto *m* Laurence Rosenthal *pd* James William Newport

Bonnie Bedelia, Beau Bridges, Leo Rossi, Hoyt Axton, Bill McKinney

'An Americanized *Chariots of Fire* for the drive-in market.'—*Observer*

Heart of a Nation**
original title: *Untel Père et Fils*
France 1940 111m bw
Paul Graetz

The story of a Paris family from the Franco–Prussian war to 1939.
Uneven and episodic but consistently interesting piece completed just as the Nazis moved into Paris and suppressed by them, but later released from America with linking narrative by Charles Boyer.

w Charles Spaak *d* Julien Duvivier *ph* Jules Kruger *m* Jean Wiener

Louis Jouvet, Raimu, Suzy Prim, Lucien Nat, Michèle Morgan

Heart of Glass*
West Germany 1976 94m Eastmancolor
Werner Herzog

A wandering herdsman with special powers supplies a factory owner with the secret of making a very precious glass.
Apocalyptic visionary parable which may mean everything, or nothing, but amuses fitfully while it's on the screen.

wd Werner Herzog, *text* Herbert Achternbusch *ph* Jorg Schmidt-Reitwin *m* Popol Vuh

Josef Bierbichler, Stefan Guttler, Clemens Scheitz, Sepp Müller

Heart of New York*
US 1932 74m bw

A plumber invents a washing machine and becomes a millionaire. Ethnic farce set in New York's Jewish quarter; of considerable curiosity value. Smith and Dale, George Sidney, Anna Apfel, Aline MacMahon, Donald Cook. Written by Arthur Caesar and Houston Branch from the play *Mendel Inc* by David Freedman; directed by Mervyn Le Roy; for Warners. 'Gabby to an extreme . . . too much dialect and too little animation.'—*Variety*

The Heart of the Matter*
GB 1953 105m bw
British Lion / London Films (Ian Dalrymple)

In 1942 in an African colony a police officer has an affair while his wife is away, is blackmailed, and plans suicide despite his staunch Catholic belief.
Rather stodgy attempt to film Graham Greene; perhaps everyone tries a little too hard, and in any case the ending is compromised.

w Ian Dalrymple, Lesley Storm, *novel* Graham Greene *d* George More O'Ferrall *ph* Jack Hildyard *m* Brian Easdale

Trevor Howard, Maria Schell, Elizabeth Allan, Denholm Elliott, Peter Finch, Gérard Oury, George Coulouris, Earl Cameron, Michael Hordern, Colin Gordon, Cyril Raymond, Orlando Martins

'A curious choice for commercial filming.'—*Lindsay Anderson*

Heart of the North
US 1938 74m Technicolor

The Canadian Mounties chase after gold and fur thieves. Routine adventure utilizing early developments in colour processing. Dick Foran, Gloria Dickson, Gale Page, Allen Jenkins, Patric Knowles, James Stephenson. Written by Lee Katz, Vincent Sherman, from novel by William Byron Mowery; directed by Lew Seiler; for Bryan Foy / Warner.

Heartbeat
US 1946 102m bw
RKO / Robert and Raymond Hakim

A French gamin released from reform school becomes a professional pickpocket.
Unamusing remake of *Battement de Coeur*, with script and most performances very strained.

w Hans Wilhelm, Max Kolpe, Michel Druan, Morrie Ryskind *d* Sam Wood *ph* Joe Valentine *m* Paul Misraki

Ginger Rogers, Jean-Pierre Aumont, Adolphe Menjou, *Basil Rathbone*, Mikhail Rasumny, Melville Cooper, Mona Maris, Henry Stephenson

'The heartbeat is irregular and sadly ailing.'—*Photoplay*

The Heartbreak Kid*
US 1972 106m De Luxe
(TCF) Palomar (Edgar J. Scherick)

Disappointed with his honeymoon, a sporting goods salesman promptly sets his cap at a richer, prettier prospective spouse.
Heartless modern comedy reminiscent of *The Graduate*; quite well done but unsympathetic and somehow too American to export satisfactorily.

w Neil Simon, *story* A Change of Plan by Bruce Jay Friedman *d* Elaine May *ph* Owen Roizman *m* Garry Sherman

Charles Grodin, Cybill Shepherd, Jeannie Berlin, Eddie Albert, Audra Lindley, William Prince, Art Metrano

'The latest in a relatively new kind of American film—glittery trash.'—*Stanley Kauffmann*

AAN: Jeannie Berlin; Eddie Albert

Heartbreak Ridge
US 1986 130m Technicolor
Warner / Malpaso / Jay Weston (Clint Eastwood)

An ageing gunnery sergeant transforms raw recruits into fighting men who become heroes in Grenada.
Dismayingly predictable potboiler with nothing but foul language to pass the time.

w James Carabatsos *d* Clint Eastwood *ph* Jack N. Green *m* Lennie Niehaus

Clint Eastwood, Marsha Mason, Everett McGill, Moses Gunn, Eileen Heckart, Bo Svenson

'Now looking increasingly like an Easter Island statue, he has a voice pickled in Bourbon, a tongue like razor wire and a body so full of shrapnel he can't walk through airport metal detectors.'—*Time Out*

Heartburn*
US 1986 108m Technicolor
Paramount / Mike Nichols, Robert Greenhut

Romantic problems of a busy professional couple.
Rather ordinary and overstretched scripting is enlivened by star playing, but the overall feeling is one of disappointment.

w Nora Ephron, from her novel *d* Mike Nichols *ph* Nestor Almendros *m* Carly Simon *pd* Tony Walton *ed* Sam O'Steen

Meryl Streep, *Jack Nicholson*, Jeff Daniels, Maureen Stapleton, Stockard Channing, Richard Masur, Steven Hill, Milos Forman, Catherine O'Hara

'A movie of colossal inconsequence. Heartburn? No, just a bad attack of wind.'—*Time Out*

Heartland*
US 1979 96m Du Art
Wilderness Women Productions / Filmhaus (Annick Smith)

In 1910 Wyoming, a woman with a small daughter takes up her arduous duties as housekeeper to a dour rancher.
Impressive if not very likeable semi-documentary which certainly rubs one's nose in the unfairness of life.

w Beth Ferris, from the papers of Elmore Randall Stewart *d Richard Pearce ph Fred Murphy* *m* Charles Gross

Conchata Ferrell, Rip Torn, Barry Primus, Lila Skala

Heart's Desire
GB 1935 82m bw

In old Vienna, a tenor finds that a glamorous socialite wants him for his voice rather than himself. Dated operetta, but the star still reigns supreme. *Richard Tauber,* Leonora Corbett, Diana Napier, Frank Vosper. Written by Clifford Grey, L. DuGarde Peach, Jack Davies, Roger Burford and Bruno Frank; directed by Paul Stein; for BIP.

Hearts Divided
US 1936 76m bw

Napoleon's brother weds a Baltimore beauty. Uneasy remake of *Glorious Betsy* (qv) with a couple of musical numbers added; a splendid cast retires defeated. Marion Davies, Dick Powell, Edward Everett Horton, Claude Rains, Charles Ruggles, Arthur Treacher, Henry Stephenson. Written by Laird Doyle and Casey Robinson; directed by Frank Borzage; for Warner.

Hearts of the West*
US 1975 103m Metrocolor
MGM / Bill–Zieff (Tony Bill)
GB title: *Hollywood Cowboy*

In the early thirties a naïve mid-westerner almost accidentally becomes a Hollywood star.
Overstretched comedy poking gentle fun at old Hollywood: likeable but finally disappointing, as it obviously needed a Buster Keaton.

w Rob Thompson *d* Howard Zieff *ph* Mario Tosi *m* Ken Lauber

Jeff Bridges, Alan Arkin, Andy Griffith, Blythe Danner, Donald Pleasence, Richard B. Shull, Herb Edelman

Hearts of the World*
US 1918 80m (24 fps) bw silent
Artcraft (David Wark Griffith)

Of various people involved in World War I, the patriotic and dutiful ones come out best.
Rather dim patriotic propaganda made by Griffith at the request of the British government and using a good deal of newsreel as well as reconstruction. The personal stories are on the predictable side.

wd David Wark Griffith *ph* Billy Bitzer *ed* James Smith

Lillian Gish, Dorothy Gish, Robert Harron, Josephine Crowell, Erich Von Stroheim, Noel Coward

'Here we have an art of pure emotion which can go beneath thought, beneath belief, beneath ideals, down to the brute fact of emotional psychology, and make a man or a woman who has hated war, all war, even this war, feel the surge of group emotion, group loyalty and group hate.'—*Kenneth MacGowan, The New Republic (1918)*

† For the screenplay credit Griffith used the pseudonym of Gaston de Tolignac.

Heat
US 1987 101m Technicolor

A Las Vegas gambler gets into trouble with gangsters. Unremarkable toughie with the star at his most predictable. Burt Reynolds, Karen Young, Peter MacNicol, Howard Hesseman, Diana Scarwid. Written by William Goldman from his novel; directed by R. M. Richards; for Rotman-Pappas/Vista/New Century.

Heat and Dust**
GB 1982 130m colour
Merchant Ivory Productions (Ismail Merchant)

A woman discovers India's past through her great-aunt's letters.
Much praised by those who admire the work of this team, but found (as usual) mildly bewildering by others, this has at least a large

enough budget to produce interest in its historically re-created backgrounds if not its complex plot structure.

w Ruth Prawer Jhabvala from her novel *d* James Ivory *ph* Walter Lassally *m* Richard Robbins

Julie Christie, Christopher Cazenove, Shashi Kapoor, Greta Scacchi, Nickolas Grace, Jennifer Kendal, Julian Glover, Susan Fleetwood

'A likeable patchwork of concepts and cameos.'—*Philip Strick, MFB*

BFA: screenplay

Heat Lightning
US 1934 63m bw

A lady gas station attendant in the hot southwest becomes involved with two murderers on the run. Cautionary tale which does not quite jell despite effort all round. Aline MacMahon, Ann Dvorak, Preston Foster, Lyle Talbot, Glenda Farrell, Frank McHugh, Ruth Donnelly. Written by Brown Holmes and Warren Duff, from the play by George Abbott and Leon Abrams; directed by Mervyn Le Roy; for Warner. (NB: remade in 1941 as *Highway West*.) 'Drab background, little sex appeal and not enough tension. It's a sluffo for deluxers, but can get by elsewhere.'—*Variety*

The Heat's On
US 1943 79m bw
Columbia (Milton Carter)
GB title: *Tropicana*

A star seeks financial backing from an elderly angel whose sister runs the Legion of Purity. Dim musical vehicle for a fading star; her last film for twenty-seven years.

w Fitzroy Davis, George S. George, Fred Schiller *d* Gregory Ratoff *ph* Franz Planer *md* Yasha Bunchuk *m* John Leipold

Mae West, Victor Moore, William Gaxton, Almira Sessions, Lester Allan, Mary Roche, Hazel Scott, Alan Dinehart, Lloyd Bridges, Xavier Cugat and his Orchestra

'A stale-ale musical in which a lot of good people apathetically support the almost equally apathetic Mae West.'—*James Agee*

Heatwave*
Australia 1982 95m Eastmancolor
M and L Enterprises / Preston Crothers (Hilary Linstead)

Community activists move to prevent the schemes of a Sydney developer.
Rather like an Ealing drama descending into melodrama; a polished piece of committed film journalism masquerading as fiction.

w Marc Rosenberg, Phillip Noyce *d* Phillip Noyce *ph* Vincent Monton *m* Cameron Allan *pd* Ross Major

Judy Davis, Richard Moir, Chris Haywood, Bill Hunter, John Meillon, John Gregg
† A similarly themed Australian film, *The Killing of Angel Street*, came out almost simultaneously.

Heaven Can Wait***
US 1943 112m Technicolor
TCF (Ernst Lubitsch)

On arrival in Hades, an elderly playboy reports his peccadilloes to Satan, who sends him Upstairs.
Charming period piece with fantasy bookends; the essence of the piece is its evocation of American society in the nineties, and in its director's waspish way with a funny scene.

w Samson Raphaelson, play Birthday by Lazlo Bus-Fekete *d Ernst Lubitsch ph Edward Cronjager m* Alfred Newman *ad James Basevi, Leland Fuller*

Don Ameche, Gene Tierney, *Laird Cregar, Charles Coburn, Marjorie Main*, Eugene Pallette, *Allyn Joslyn*, Spring Byington, Signe Hasso, Louis Calhern

'It was so good I half believed Lubitsch could still do as well as he ever did, given half a chance.'—*James Agee*

AAN: best picture; Ernst Lubitsch; Edward Cronjager

Heaven Can Wait*
US 1978 100m Movielab
Paramount / Warren Beatty (Howard W. Koch Jnr, Charles H. McGuire)

A football star finds himself accidentally in heaven after a car accident; when he is allowed to return, his body has been cremated, so he has to find another.
Unexpectedly commercially successful (the late seventies clearly needed religion) remake of 1941's *Here Comes Mr Jordan*. It lacks the sharpness and style of its predecessor, and despite amusing moments is often merely tacky.

w Warren Beatty, Elaine May, *play* Harry Segall *d* Warren Beatty, Buck Henry *ph* William A. Fraker *m* Dave Grusin *pd* Paul Sylbert

Warren Beatty, Julie Christie, James Mason (as Mr Jordan), Jack Warden, Charles Grodin, *Dyan Cannon*, Buck Henry, Vincent Gardenia, Joseph Maher

AAN: best picture; script; direction; photography; music; Warren Beatty (as actor); Jack Warden; Dyan Cannon

Heaven Fell That Night
France / Italy 1958 90m Eastmancolor Cinemascope
IENA / CEIAP (Raoul Levy)
original title: *Les Bijoutiers du Clair de Lune*

A young girl becomes involved in a revenge plot and finds herself on the run with a killer. Heavy going sex-and-violence hokum.

w Roger Vadim, Peter Viertel, *novel* Albert Vidalie *d* Roger Vadim *ph* Armand Thirard *m* Georges Auric

Brigitte Bardot, Alida Valli, Stephen Boyd, Pepe Nieto

Heaven Help Us
US 1985 104m Metrocolor
Tri-Star / HBO / Silver Screen (Dan Wigutow, Mark Carliner)

In mid-sixties Brooklyn, a new priest has trouble with teenagers at a Catholic boys' school.
Lively if rather wearing exploration of teenage sex pranks and Catholic guilt, treated rather uncertainly as comedy.

w Charles Purpura *d* Michael Dinner *ph* Miroslav Ondricek *m* James Horner *pd* Michael Molly *ed* Stephen A. Rotter

Donald Sutherland, John Heard, Andrew McCarthy, Mary Stuart Masterson, Kevin Dillon, Kate Reid

Heaven Is Round the Corner
GB 1943 94m bw

A war veteran is helped to find his long-lost love. Sentimental tosh with music, a second team effort which went down well enough in wartime. Will Fyffe, Leni Lynn, Austin Trevor, Magda Kun, Peter Glenville. Written by Austin Melford; directed by Maclean Rogers; for British National/Fred Zelnick.

Heaven Knows Mr Allison*
US 1957 105m Technicolor Cinemascope
TCF (Buddy Adler, Eugene Franks)

Marooned on a small Pacific island during World War II, a marine and a nun, antagonistic to each other, combine to outwit the Japs.
Silly adventure story with predictably well-handled action sequences separated by even more predictable dialogue, lots of it.

w John Lee Mahin, John Huston, *novel* Charles Shaw *d* John Huston *ph* Oswald Morris *m* Georges Auric

Robert Mitchum, Deborah Kerr

AAN: script; Deborah Kerr

Heaven on Earth
US 1931 78m bw

Mississippi steamship owners feud with the shanty houseboaters who line the riverbank. Oddly titled melodrama with a conscience; it doesn't really work. Lew Ayres, Anita Louise, Harry Beresford, Elizabeth Patterson, Slim Summerville. Written by Ray Doyle from the novel Mississippi by Ben Lucian Burman; directed by Russel Mack; for Universal. 'Needs strong stage support wherever chanced.'—*Variety*

Heaven on Earth: see The Exquisite Sinner

Heaven Only Knows
US 1947 98m bw
(UA) Seymour Nebenzal

An angel is sent to the old west to reform a bad man.
Whimsical comedy-drama which doesn't work at all, even as a distant cousin of *Here Comes Mr Jordan*.

w Art Arthur, Rowland Leigh *d* Albert S. Rogell *ph* Karl Struss *m* Heinz Roemheld

Robert Cummings, Brian Donlevy, Marjorie Reynolds, Bill Goodwin, John Litel, Stuart Erwin

Heaven with a Barbed Wire Fence
US 1939 61m bw

A New York clerk hitch-hikes his way to Arizona, where he has bought a piece of land. Subdued flagwaver with everybody behaving just swell in God's own country. Glenn Ford (his first film), Jean Rogers, Richard Conte, Marjorie Rambeau, Raymond Walburn, Eddie Collins, Ward Bond. Written by Dalton Trumbo, Leonard Hoffman and Ben Grauman Kohn; directed by Ricardo Cortez; for TCF.
'A slightly clouded title, with little possibility of propelling many customers through the front door.'—*Variety*

Heaven with a Gun
US 1969 101m Metrocolor Panavision

The determined new preacher of a small western town is an ex-gunfighter. Solidly carpentered half-a-bill western. Glenn Ford, Carolyn Jones, David Carradine, J. D. Cannon, Barbara Hershey, Noah Beery Jnr. Written by Richard Carr; directed by Lee Katzin; for King Brothers / MGM.

The Heavenly Body
US 1943 93m bw
MGM (Arthur Hornblow Jnr)

An astronomer is too busy to notice his wife, so she takes up astrology and meets a dark handsome stranger as predicted.
Thin romantic comedy which despite crazy touches never actually makes one laugh.

w Michael Arlen, Walter Reisch *d* Alexander Hall *ph* Robert Planck *m* Bronislau Kaper

William Powell, Hedy Lamarr, James Craig, Fay Bainter, Henry O'Neill, Spring Byington, Morris Ankrum, Connie Gilchrist

Heavenly Days
US 1944 72m bw

Fibber McGee and Molly go to Washington. Extension of a radio comedy series about a man who simply can't tell the truth; amusing at the time, but with topical references which mean little today. Jim Jordan, Marion Jordan, Eugene Pallette, Gordon Oliver, Raymond Walburn, Barbara Hale, Don Douglas, Frieda Inescort. Written and directed by Howard Estabrook; for Robert Fellows / RKO.

Heavens Above*
GB 1963 118m bw
British Lion / Charter (Roy Boulting)

A northern parson with proletarian sympathies is accidentally appointed to a snobby village where he converts the dowager aristocrat to works of absurd charity. Eventually he has the whole country in an uproar and takes the place of an astronaut.
Patchy satirical comedy which takes unsteady aim at too many targets but scores some predictable laughs.

w Frank Harvey, John Boulting *d* John Boulting *ph* Max Greene *m* Richard Rodney Bennett

Peter Sellers, Isabel Jeans, Cecil Parker, Brock Peters, Ian Carmichael, Irene Handl, Eric Sykes, Bernard Miles

'What one loves about life are the things that fade . . .'
'The most talked-about film of the decade!'
'The only thing greater than their passion for America . . . was their passion for each other!'

Heaven's Gate
US 1980 219m Technicolor
UA / Michael Cimino

1890 Wyoming: established cattlemen fight immigrants.
Totally incoherent, showy western which was lambasted by the critics and quickly withdrawn. A vital turning point in Hollywood policy, hopefully marking the last time a whiz kid with one success behind him is given a blank cheque to indulge in self-abuse.

wd Michael Cimino *ph* Vilmos Zsigmond *m* David Mansfield

Kris Kristofferson, Christopher Walken, John Hurt, Sam Waterston, Brad Dourif, Isabelle Huppert, Joseph Cotten, Jeff Bridges

'The trade must marvel that directors now have such power that no one, in the endless months since work on the picture began, was able to impose some structure and sense.'—*Variety*

'All too much and not enough.'—*Sunday Times*

'A film which John Ford would have brought in on time and on budget with quite as much social, critical and political comment—and much more entertainment value.'—*Margaret Hinxman, Daily Mail*

'It fails so completely that you might suspect Mr Cimino sold his soul to the devil to obtain the success of *The Deer Hunter*, and the devil has just come around to collect.'—*Vincent Canby, New York Times*

'A step beyond science fiction!'

Heavy Metal*
US 1981 90m Metrocolor
Columbia / Ivan Reitman, Leonard Vogel

A complicated comic strip / science fiction story, with soft core jokes in the modern manner, is told by international teams of animators each working on an episode.
The experiment is interesting rather than successful.

w Dan Goldberg, Len Blum *d* Gerald Potterton

'Something of a hodge-podge . . . the script is a skeletal, whimsically mystical affair . . .'—*John Pym, MFB*

Hedda*
GB 1975 102m Technicolor
Brut (Robert Enders)

A selfish pregnant woman is bored by her husband and revolted at the idea of carrying his child. She takes an opportunity to revenge herself on an old lover, but the scheme rebounds on herself.
Rather flat rendering of a play which has received more than its due share of attention.

wd Trevor Nunn, *play* Henrik Ibsen *ph* Douglas Slocombe *m* Laurie Johnson

Glenda Jackson, Peter Eyre, Timothy West, Jennie Linden, Patrick Stewart

AAN: Glenda Jackson

Heidi*
US 1937 88m bw
TCF (Raymond Griffith)

An orphan is sent to stay with her crusty grandfather in a mountain village.
Star-tailored version of a favourite children's story; just what the box office ordered at the time.

w Walter Ferris, Julian Josephson, *novel* Johanna Spyri *d* Allan Dwan *ph* Arthur Miller *md* Louis Silvers

Shirley Temple, Jean Hersholt, Arthur Treacher, Helen Westley, Pauline Moore, Mary Nash, Thomas Beck, Sidney Blackmer, Mady Christians, Sig Rumann, Marcia Mae Jones, Christian Rub

'Good for the average Temple draw or better.'—*Variety*

Heimat**
aka *Homeland*
West Germany 1984 924m part colour
Edgar Reitz / WDR / SFB

An epically conceived story of life in a German village between 1919 and 1982.
Essentially a superior soap opera with pretensions of grandeur, this beautifully photographed serial has moments of magic amid much that is merely pretentious and unexplained. Despite the symbolism and the irony (a village idiot is ever present), an eager if arty audience found that it had much to say, though no one could explain its lapses from colour to black-and-white and back again.

w Edgar Reitz, Peter Steinbach *d Edgar Reitz ph Gernot Roll m* Nikos Mamangakis

Marita Breuer, Michael Lesch, Dieter Schaad, Karin Kienzler, Eva Maria Bayerswaltes, Rüdiger Weigang, Karin Rasenach

'She was taught to love and hate—by masters!'

The Heiress**
US 1949 115m bw
Paramount (William Wyler)

A plain but rich young woman takes revenge on her fortune-seeking lover.
Richly-decorated and generally pleasing version of a stage success based on a Henry James story set in the nineties.

w Ruth and Augustus Goetz, from their play and Henry James's Washington Square *d William Wyler ph* Leo Tover *m* Aaron Copland *ad John Meehan*

Olivia de Havilland, Ralph Richardson, Montgomery Clift, Miriam Hopkins, Vanessa Brown, Mona Freeman, Ray Collins

'Wyler is that rarest of craftsmen who can take such a drama, already completely fulfilled in theatre terms, and convert it to film without ever permitting the play-form to dominate the screen.'—*Hermione Isaacs, Films in Review*

AA: Aaron Copland; Olivia de Havilland
AAN: best picture; William Wyler; Leo Tover; Ralph Richardson

'No star ever climbed higher—no woman ever fell lower!'

The Helen Morgan Story
US 1957 118m bw Cinemascope
Warner (Martin Rackin)
GB title: *Both Ends of the Candle*

A young singer rises from vaudeville to Broadway but becomes an alcoholic.
Moderately truthful biopic with effective twenties trimmings.

w Oscar Saul, Dean Riesner, Stephen Longstreet, Nelson Gidding *d* Michael Curtiz *ph* Ted McCord *m* various *ad* John Beckman

Ann Blyth, Paul Newman, Richard Carlson, Gene Evans, Alan King, Cara Williams, Walter Woolf King (as Ziegfeld)

'All the tumultuous wonder and tremendous drama in the story of history's most famous runaway lovers! Soon the whole world will know of its greatness!'

Helen of Troy
US / Italy 1955 118m Warnercolor Cinemascope
Warner (Robert Wise)

Helen is kidnapped by Paris and regained by use of the Trojan Horse.
Dingy historical spectacular, stultifyingly boring until the final spectacle, with the actors obviously wishing themselves doing anything but mouthing the doggerel dialogue.

w John Twist, Hugh Gray *d* Robert Wise *ph* Harry Stradling *m* Max Steiner

Rosanna Podesta, Jacques Sernas, Cedric Hardwicke, Niall MacGinnis, Stanley Baker, Nora Swinburne, Robert Douglas, Torin Thatcher, Harry Andrews, Janette Scott, Ronald Lewis, Brigitte Bardot

Hell and High Water
US 1954 103m Technicolor Cinemascope
TCF (Raymond A. Klune)

A privately-financed anti-Red scientific expedition sets off for Alaska to prevent a Chinese anti-American plot.
Early scoper which mixes deviously plotted schoolboy fiction with submarine spectacle and cold war heroics.

wd Samuel Fuller *ph* Joe MacDonald *m* Alfred Newman

Richard Widmark, Bella Darvi, Victor Francen, David Wayne, Cameron Mitchell, Gene Evans

'Out of the warm arms of women—into the cold grip of the sea!'

Hell Below
US 1933 105m bw
MGM

Tensions mount at a Mediterranean submarine base during World War I.

THE HEIRESS. Montgomery Clift looks understandably tortured and clearly something is worrying Olivia de Havilland.

Adequate war actioner with appropriate trimmings of heroism, tragedy, comedy and romance.

w John Lee Mahin, John Meehan, Laird Doyle, Raymond Schrock, *novel* Pigboats by Commander Edward Ellsberg *d* Jack Conway *ph* Harold Rosson

Robert Montgomery, Walter Huston, Madge Evans, Jimmy Durante, Eugene Pallette, Robert Young, Edwin Styles, John Lee Mahin, Sterling Holloway

'Not a two dollar picture, but will be more than oke in the grinds.'—*Variety*

Hell Below Zero
GB 1954 91m Technicolor
Columbia / Warwick (Irving Allen, Albert Broccoli)

An American adventurer accompanies the daughter of a whaling captain to the Antarctic to discover who killed her father.
Adequate outdoor thick ear with an unusual setting and lively cast.

w Alec Coppel, Max Trell, *novel* The White South by Hammond Innes *d* Mark Robson *ph* John Wilcox *m* Clifton Parker

Alan Ladd, Joan Tetzel, Basil Sydney, Stanley Baker, Jill Bennett, Niall MacGinnis

Hell Boats
GB 1970 95m Technicolor

An American commander with the British navy is assigned to blockade Malta. Decently made small-scale war epic. James Franciscus, Elizabeth Shepherd, Ronald Allen, Inigo Jackson. Written by Anthony Spinner, Donald and Derek Ford; directed by Paul Wendkos; for Oakmont/UA.

Hell Divers*
US 1931 113m bw
MGM

Friendly rivalry exists between two officers in the Naval Air Force.
Routine romantic melodrama with action highlights; a crowdpuller of its day.

w Harvey Gates, Malcolm Stuart Boylan, *story* Spig Wead *d* George Hill *ph* Harold Wenstrom

Wallace Beery, Clark Gable, Conrad Nagel, Dorothy Jordan, Marjorie Rambeau, Marie Prévost, Cliff Edwards

'Fine technical naval aviation display, and no story . . . unusually long on footage and short on entertainment.'—*Variety*

'It's a matter of squadron after squadron of planes, the mechanics attached thereto, the cutting in and around newsreel material, which Metro does so well, and Beery's excellent personal performance.'—*Hollywood Reporter*

Hell Drivers*
GB 1957 108m bw Vistavision
Rank / Aqua (Ben Fisz)

Fast driving on death-trap roads is required of rival lorry drivers for a cheapjack haulage firm.
Absurd, violent, hilarious and constantly surprising melodrama with the silliest of premises backed by a good cast and well handled thrill sequences.

w John Kruse, C. Raker Endfield *d* C. Raker Endfield *ph Geoffrey Unsworth* *m* Hubert Clifford

Stanley Baker, Patrick McGoohan, Herbert Lom, Peggy Cummins, William Hartnell, Wilfrid Lawson, Sidney James, Jill Ireland, Alfie Bass, Gordon Jackson

'This extraordinary film may interest future historians for its description of road haulage and masculine social behaviour in the mid-20th century . . . though produced with efficiency and assurance it is disagreeable and occasionally vicious.'—*MFB*

Hell Harbour
US 1930 90m bw

Derelicts congregate in a Caribbean harbour. Low-life dramatics and scenery, but not much story interest. Lupe Velez, Jean Hersholt, Gibson Gowland, John Holland, Al St John. Written by Clarke Silvernall from a story by Rida Johnson Young; directed by Henry King; for United Artists. 'Production of great beauty retarded by a story which fails to retain interest.'—*Variety*

Hell in the Heavens
US 1934 79m bw

In the 1918 air war, an American helps a French unit to get an ace German flier. Routine *Dawn Patrol* stuff which somehow fails to make an impact. Warner Baxter, Conchita Montenegro, Herbert Mundin, Russell Hardie, Andy Devine, Ralph Morgan. Written by Byron Morgan and Ted Parsons, from the play The Ace by Herman Rossmann; directed by John G. Blystone; for Fox. 'Interesting but probably too familiar at this date.'—*Variety*

Hell in the Pacific*
US 1969 104m Technicolor Panavision
Cinerama / Selmur (Reuben Bercovitch)

During World War II, an American pilot and a Japanese naval officer who are stranded on the same tiny Pacific island almost become friends.
Highly artificial and pretentious allegorical two-parter which is occasionally well acted and good to look at.

w Alexander Jacobs, Eric Bercovici *d* John Boorman *ph Conrad Hall* *m* Lalo Schifrin

Lee Marvin, Toshiro Mifune

'No real reverberation and no real excitement, intellectual or physical.'—*Tom Milne*

Hell Is a City*
GB 1959 93m bw Hammerscope
ABP / Hammer (Michael Carreras)

A jewel thief breaks jail and is hunted by the Manchester police.
Lively semi-documentary, cameo-filled cop thriller filmed on location.

wd Val Guest, novel Maurice Proctor *ph Arthur Grant* *m* Stanley Black

Stanley Baker, John Crawford, Donald Pleasence, Maxine Audley, Billie Whitelaw, Joseph Tomelty, George A. Cooper, Vanda Godsell

'A hectic pace, with frequent scene changes, mobility of camera and performers, and much rapid, loud, intense dialogue.'—*MFB*

Hell Is for Heroes*
US 1962 90m bw
Paramount (Henry Blanke)

In 1944, embittered GIs fight and die while taking a German pillbox near the Siegfried line.
Fairly routine anti-war film with a strong cast and effectively-directed moments battling a generally artificial look.

w Robert Pirosh, Richard Carr *d* Don Siegel *ph* Harold Lipstein *m* Leonard Rosenman

Steve McQueen, Bobby Darin, Fess Parker, James Coburn, Bob Newhart, Harry Guardino

Hell Is Sold Out
GB 1951 84m bw

A novelist returns from the supposed dead to find that a glamorous woman is posing as his widow and issuing best-sellers under his name. Downright peculiar comedy-drama which never jells for long enough to be enjoyable. ('Hell Is Sold Out' is the title of a book in the story.) Herbert Lom, Mai Zetterling, Richard Attenborough. Written by Guy Morgan and Moie Charles; directed by Michael Anderson; for Raymond Stross/Zelstro.

Hell on Frisco Bay
US 1955 98m Warnercolor Cinemascope
Jaguar (George Berthelon)

An ex-cop sets out to find the man who framed him for manslaughter.
Tedious actioner enlivened by the character parts and a violent climax.

w Sidney Boehm, Martin Rackin, *novel* William P. McGivern *d* Frank Tuttle *ph* John Seitz *m* Max Steiner

Alan Ladd, Edward G. Robinson, Joanne Dru, *Paul Stewart*, William Demarest, Fay Wray

Hell to Eternity
US 1960 132m bw
Allied Artists / Atlantic (Irving H. Levin)

Marine Guy Gabaldon, brought up by Japanese foster parents, has divided loyalties after Pearl Harbor.
Battle-strewn biopic which after two hours seems to lose its point, if it ever had one, but is efficiently made.

w Ted Sherdeman, Walter Roeber Schmidt *d* Phil Karlson *ph* Burnett Guffey *m* Leith Stevens

Jeffrey Hunter, David Janssen, Vic Damone, Patricia Owens, Richard Eyer, Sessue Hayakawa

'They all had something to sell—courage—sex—corruption!'

The Hell with Heroes
US 1968 102m Techniscope
Universal (Stanley Chase)

Air cargo experts find themselves unwittingly smuggling cigarettes into France, and American counter-intelligence steps in.
Unremarkable, totally predictable action melodrama.

w Halsted Welles, Harold Livingston *d* Joseph Sargent *ph* Bud Thackery *m* Quincy Jones

Rod Taylor, Claudia Cardinale, Harry Guardino, Kevin McCarthy, Pete Deuel, William Marshall

Hellcats of the Navy
US 1957 82m bw

Exploits of a daring submarine commander in the war against Japan. Flimsy jingoistic potboiler. Ronald Reagan, Nancy Davis, Arthur Franz, Robert Arthur. Written by David Lang; directed by Nathan Juran; for Charles H. Schneer / Columbia.

Helldorado
US 1934 75m bw

A penniless hitchhiker finds a ghost town with a gold mine. Feeble fable unpersuasively presented. Richard Arlen, Madge Evans, Henry B. Walthall, Ralph Bellamy, James Gleason, Helen Jerome Eddy. Written by Frances Hyland, Rex Taylor, from a story by Frank M. Dazey; directed by James Cruze; for Jesse L. Lasky / Fox. 'Incredible story poorly cast and not at all likely at the b.o.'—*Variety*

Heller in Pink Tights*
US 1960 100m Technicolor Vistavision
Paramount / Ponti–Girosi

Adventures of a dramatic company touring the west in the 1880s.
Genteel spoof western which does not quite come off.

w Dudley Nichols, Walter Bernstein, *novel* Louis L'Amour *d* George Cukor *ph* Harold Lipstein *m* Daniele Amfitheatrof *ad* Hal Pereira, Eugene Allen

Sophia Loren, Anthony Quinn, Steve Forrest, Eileen Heckart, Edmund Lowe, Margaret O'Brien, Ramon Novarro

'It has a welcome individuality which is never quite smothered by its lapses into convention.'—*Penelope Houston*

Hellfighters
US 1969 120m Technicolor Panavision
Universal (Robert Arthur)

Oil well fire-fighting specialists have problems among themselves and with their womenfolk. Ham-fisted story line and performances are slightly, but only slightly, compensated by excellent special effects.

w Clair Huffaker *d* Andrew V. McLaglen *ph* William H. Clothier *m* Leonard Rosenman

John Wayne, Jim Hutton, Katharine Ross, Vera Miles, Jay C. Flippen, Bruce Cabot, Barbara Stuart

'The overall effect is unpardonably tedious.'—*MFB*

The Hellfire Club*
GB 1960 93m Eastmancolor Dyaliscope
Regal / New World (Robert S. Baker, Monty Berman)

In the 18th century, a nobleman's child escapes from his degenerate father, joins a travelling circus, and later returns to claim his inheritance.
Sprightly historical romantic melodrama lightly based on the nefarious activities of the real Hellfire Club; energetic and entertaining if slightly too jokey.

w Leon Griffiths, Jimmy Sangster
d / ph Robert S. Baker, Monty Berman
m Clifton Parker

Keith Michell, Peter Arne, Adrienne Corri, Kai Fischer, Bill Owen, Peter Cushing, David Lodge, Francis Matthews

Hellgate
US 1952 87m bw

In the 1860s a veterinary surgeon is wrongly convicted and sent to a savage prison.
Competent exploitation melodrama, not apparently based on truth. Sterling Hayden, Ward Bond, Joan Leslie, Jim Arness, Peter Coe. Written and directed by Charles Marquis Warren; for Commander Films / Lippert.

The Hellions
GB 1961 80m Technirama
Columbia / Irving Allen, Jamie Uys (Harold Huth)

In the 1860s, a family of South African outlaws starts a reign of terror in a small village.
A British attempt to restage the OK Corral; it goes sadly awry.

w Harold Swanton, Patrick Kirwan, Harold Huth *d* Ken Annakin *ph* Ted Moore
m Larry Adler

Richard Todd, Lionel Jeffries, James Booth, Jamie Uys, Ronald Fraser, Anne Aubrey, Zena Walker, Marty Wilde, Colin Blakely

'Unconvincingly staged and plotted, tediously violent, uncertainly directed and very badly acted.'—*MFB*

Hello Dolly**
US 1969 129m De Luxe Todd-AO
TCF / Chenault (Ernest Lehman)

In 1890 New York, a widowed matchmaker has designs on a wealthy grain merchant.
Generally agreeable but overblown musical based on a slight but much worked-over farce, fatally compromised by the miscasting of a too-young star. Some exhilarating moments.

w Ernest Lehman, *musical Jerry Herman (m / ly)* and Michael Stewart (*book*), from *Thornton Wilder's* play The Matchmaker
d Gene Kelly ph Harry Stradling md Lennie Hayton, Lionel Newman *pd John de Cuir ch Michael Kidd*

Barbra Streisand, Walter Matthau, *Michael Crawford, Marianne McAndrew*, E. J. Peaker, Tommy Tune, David Hurst

'The film leaves an oddly negative impression; a good deal of synthetic effervescence . . . but very little real vitality.'—*David Wilson*

† Carol Channing, Ginger Rogers and Betty Grable all fought to get the title role.

AA: music direction; art direction; set decoration
AAN: best picture; photography

Hello Down There
US 1969 98m Eastmancolor

The designer of an underwater house volunteers to live in it for a month. Curious comedy with predictable obstacles to the happy ending. Tony Randall, Janet Leigh, Jim Backus, Roddy McDowall, Merv Griffin, Ken Berry, Richard Dreyfuss. Written by Frank Telford and John McGreevey; directed by Jack Arnold; for Ivan Tors / MGM.

'A lady bountiful with a ready song on her lips to hide the ache of emptiness in her own heart!'

Hello Everybody
US 1932 69m bw

An overweight girl becomes a national radio celebrity. Slim vehicle in which its star sings nine times. *Kate Smith*, Randolph Scott, Sally Blane, Jerry Tucker, George Barbier. Written by Dorothy Yost, Lawrence Hazard, from a story by Fannie Hurst; directed by William Seiter; for Paramount. 'Should do okay outside big cities.'—*Variety*

Hello Frisco Hello*
US 1943 98m Technicolor
TCF (Milton Sperling)

On the Barbary Coast, a girl singer becomes a star.
Moderately pleasing period musical with plenty going on but nothing very striking.

w Robert Ellis, Helen Logan, Richard Macauley *d* Bruce Humberstone *ph* Charles Clarke, Allen Davey *songs* various *ad James Basevi, Boris Leven*

Alice Faye, John Payne, Jack Oakie, Lynn Bari, Laird Cregar, June Havoc, Ward Bond, Aubrey Mather, George Barbier, Frank Orth

AA: song 'You'll Never Know' (*m* Harry Warren, *ly* Mack Gordon)
AAN: Charles Clarke, Allen Davey

Hello Goodbye
US 1970 101m De Luxe
TCF (André Hakim)

A cheerful young Englishman falls for a mysterious Frenchwoman who turns out to be the wife of a Baron.
Modest, aimless, forgettable romantic comedy, full of old-fashioned clichés imperfectly remembered.

w Roger Marshall *d* Jean Negulesco
ph Henri Decaë m Francis Lai *pd* John Howell *ad* Auguste Capelier

Michael Crawford, Geneviève Gilles, Curt Jurgens, Ira Furstenberg

Hello Sister*
US 1933 62m bw
Fox (Winfield Sheehan)
aka: *Walking down Broadway*

Boy meets girl in New York.
A mild little romance, only notable because it was edited down from an original by Erich Von Stroheim, and touches of his work remain.

w Erich Von Stroheim, Leonard Spiegelgass, *novel* Dawn Powell *d* Erich Von Stroheim, Alfred Werker *ph* James Wong Howe

James Dunn, Boots Mallory, Zasu Pitts, Minna Gombell

Hell's Angels****
US 1930 135m bw (some scenes in colour)
Howard Hughes

Two Americans become fliers in World War I. Celebrated early talkie spectacular, with zeppelin and flying sequences that still thrill. The dialogue is another matter, but all told this expensive production, first planned as a silent, is a milestone of cinema history.

w Howard Estabrook, Harry Behn *d Howard Hughes ph Tony Gaudio, Harry Perry, E. Burton Steene m* Hugo Reisenfeld

Ben Lyon, James Hall, Jean Harlow, John Darrow, Lucien Prival

'That it will ever pay off for its producer is doubtful . . . he's in so deep it can't really matter to him now. Minus blue nose interference, it can't miss, but it's up to the brim with sex.'—*Variety*

'It is not great, but it is as lavish as an eight-ring circus, and when you leave the theatre you will know you have seen a movie and not a tinny reproduction of a stage show.'—*Pare Lorentz*

† The film was reissued in 1940 in a 96m version which has not survived.

AAN: Tony Gaudio, Harry Perry, E. Burton Steene

Hell's Five Hours
US 1958 75m bw

A psychopath takes hostages and threatens to blow up a rocket fuel plant. Standard suspense programmer, tolerable but entirely forgettable. Stephen McNally, Vic Morrow, Coleen Gray. Written and directed by Jack L. Copeland; for Allied Artists.

Hell's Half Acre
US 1953 91m bw

A soldier missing after Pearl Harbor turns up years later in Hawaii under a different identity. Complex melodrama ending in self-sacrifice; amusing bits don't make it hang together. Wendell Corey, Evelyn Keyes, Elsa

Lanchester, Nancy Gates, Philip Ahn, Keye Luke. Written by Steve Fisher; directed by John H. Auer; for Republic.

Hell's Heroes
US 1930 65m bw
Universal

Three cowboys find an abandoned baby. Yet another version of *Three Godfathers*; maybe not the best but the shortest.

w Tom Reed, *novel* Peter Kyne *d* William Wyler *ph* George Robinson

Charles Bickford, Raymond Hatton, Fred Kohler, Fritzi Ridgeway

† Photographed in the Mojave and Panamint Deserts.

Hell's Highway*
US 1932 62m bw

A convict plans escape from a forced labour gang, under the threat of the lash and the sweatbox. Well-made but heavy-going melodrama without light relief. Richard Dix, Rochelle Hudson, Tom Brown, C. Henry Gordon, Louise Carter. Written by Samuel Ornitz, Robert Tasker, Rowland Brown; directed by Rowland Brown; for RKO. 'The story is too sodden to carry a general appeal.'—*Variety*

Hell's House
US 1932 72m bw

A boy is wrongly sentenced to a corrupt reform school. Primitive cheapie notable only for the early appearance of Bette Davis; with Pat O'Brien, Junior Durkin, Junior Coghlan, Emma Dunn, Charley Grapewin. Written by Paul Gangelin and B. Harrison Orkow; directed by Howard Higgins; for Capital Films.

Hell's Island*
US 1955 84m Technicolor Vistavision
Paramount / Pine–Thomas

Crooks congregate on a Caribbean island in search of a famous ruby.
Cheeky rehash of *The Maltese Falcon*, not bad in its own routine way.

w Maxwell Shane *d* Phil Karlson *ph* Lionel Lindon *md* Irvin Talbot

John Payne, Mary Murphy, *Francis L. Sullivan*, Arnold Moss

Hell's Kitchen
US 1939 82m bw

Boys revolt under the cruel headmaster of a reformatory. Dreary vehicle for the Dead End Kids. Billy Halop, Leo Gorcey, Bobby Jordan, Huntz Hall, Gabriel Dell, Bernard Punsley, Ronald Reagan, Margaret Lindsay, Stanley Fields, Grant Mitchell. Written by Crane Wilbur, Fred Niblo Jnr; directed by Lewis Seiler and E. A. Dupont; for Warners. 'A quagmire of misplaced sentimentality, hokum and general incredulousness.'—*Variety*

The Hellstrom Chronicle
US 1971 90m CFI colour

A scientist explains the range and variety of insect life. Odd documentary in fictional bookends; smart and quite sensational for those with strong stomachs. Laurence Pressman as Nils Hellstrom. Written by David Seltzer; directed by Walon Green; for David Wolper.

Hellzapoppin***
US 1942 84m bw
Universal / Mayfair (Glenn Tryon, Alex Gottlieb)

Two incompetent comics make a picture. Zany modification of a smash burlesque revue; the crazy jokes are toned down and a romantic interest is added (and tentatively sent up). The result is patchy but often hilarious, and the whole is a handy consensus of forties humour and pop music.

w Nat Perrin, Warren Wilson *d H. C. Potter* *ph* Woody Bredell *md* Charles Previn *m* Frank Skinner

Ole Olsen, Chic Johnson, Hugh Herbert, Martha Raye, Mischa Auer, Robert Paige, Jane Frazee, Shemp Howard, Elisha Cook Jnr, Richard Lane

'Alive with good gags, mechanical surprise effects, and novelty touches.'—*CEA Report*
† The Frankenstein monster and Man Who Falls into Pool were played by Dale Van Sickel.

Help!*
GB 1965 92m Eastmancolor
(UA) Walter Shenson / Suba Films

An oriental high priest chases the Beatles around the world because one of them has a sacred ring.
Exhausting attempt to outdo *A Hard Day's Night* in lunatic frenzy, which goes to prove that some talents work better on low budgets. The humour is a frantic cross between *Hellzapoppin*, the Goons, Bugs Bunny and the shade of Monty Python to come. It looks good but becomes too tiresome to entertain.

w Charles Wood, Marc Behm *d* Dick Lester *ph David Watkin* *m The Beatles* *ad Ray Simm*

The Beatles, Leo McKern, Eleanor Bron, Victor Spinetti

Helpmates***
US 1932 20m bw

Stan helps Ollie clean up after a wild party while the wife was away. A brilliant succession of catastrophe gags in the stars' best tradition. Laurel and Hardy. Written by H. M. Walker; directed by James Parrott; for Hal Roach.

Helter Skelter
GB 1949 75m bw
GFD / Gainsborough (Anthony Darnborough)

An heiress with hiccups is helped by the staff of the BBC.
Scatty comedy which tries everything, from custard pies and guest stars to a clip from a silent Walter Forde comedy. It isn't the British *Hellzapoppin* it sets out to be, but hardened buffs will find it worth a look.

w Patrick Campbell *d* Ralph Thomas *ph* Jack Asher *m* Francis Chagrin

Carol Marsh, David Tomlinson, Mervyn Johns, Peter Hammond, Jimmy Edwards, Richard Hearne, Jon Pertwee, Terry-Thomas

Hemingway's Adventures of a Young Man*
US 1962 145m De Luxe Cinemascope
TCF (Jerry Wald)
aka: *Adventures of a Young Man*

The son of a weak doctor and a religious mother breaks away from his family circle on a voyage of discovery.
Curious mélange of ill-assimilated Hemingway stories based on his Nick Adams character. The film has good intentions but no shape or style, and the guest stars don't help.

w A. E. Hotchner, *stories* Ernest Hemingway *d* Martin Ritt *ph* Lee Garmes *m* Franz Waxman

Richard Beymer, Diane Baker, Corinne Calvet, Fred Clark, Dan Dailey, James Dunn, Juano Hernandez, Arthur Kennedy, Ricardo Montalban, Susan Strasberg, Paul Newman, Jessica Tandy, Eli Wallach

'They had killed a woman and destroyed his life. Now he will kill a woman and destroy their nation!'

Hennessy
GB 1975 104m colour
AIP / Marseilles (Peter Snell)

Angered at the death of his family in the Belfast troubles, an Irish revolutionary hurries to London to blow up the Houses of Parliament.
Unattractive, uninventive thriller with a silly script and not an ounce of real suspense.

w John Gay, *story* Richard Johnson *d* Don Sharp *ph* Ernest Steward *m* John Scott *pd* Ray Simm

Rod Steiger, Richard Johnson, Lee Remick, Trevor Howard, Eric Porter, Peter Egan, David Collings

Henry Aldrich
Henry was originally a radio character created by Ezra Stone, an awkward small-town youth who like Andy Hardy was always getting into scrapes. Clifford Goldsmith wrote the original play which hit Broadway as well as the radio waves before starting a Hollywood series of amiable Paramount second features, most of them starring Jimmy Lydon with Charles Smith as his friend Dizzy.

1939: WHAT A LIFE (with Jackie Cooper)
1941: LIFE WITH HENRY (with Jackie Cooper), HENRY ALDRICH FOR PRESIDENT
1942: HENRY AND DIZZY, HENRY ALDRICH EDITOR
1943: HENRY ALDRICH GETS GLAMOUR, HENRY ALDRICH SWINGS IT, HENRY ALDRICH HAUNTS A HOUSE
1944: HENRY ALDRICH BOY SCOUT, HENRY ALDRICH PLAYS CUPID, HENRY ALDRICH'S LITTLE SECRET

Henry Nine Till Five*
GB 1970 6m colour

A commuter spends his working days fantasizing about sex. Typical and very lively cartoon by *Bob Godfrey*; written by Stan Heyward; for British Lion.

Henry V****
GB 1944 137m Technicolor
Rank / Two Cities (Laurence Olivier)

Shakespeare's historical play is seen in performance at the Globe Theatre in 1603; as it develops, the scenery becomes more realistic.
Immensely stirring, experimental and almost wholly successful production of Shakespeare on film, sturdy both in its stylization and its command of more conventional cinematic resources for the battle.

w Laurence Olivier, Alan Dent, *play* William Shakespeare *d Laurence Olivier ph Robert Krasker m William Walton ad Paul Sheriff*

Laurence Olivier, *Robert Newton, Leslie Banks, Esmond Knight*, Renée Asherson, George Robey, *Leo Genn*, Ernest Thesiger, Ivy St Helier, Ralph Truman, Harcourt Williams, Max Adrian, Valentine Dyall, Felix Aylmer, John Laurie, Roy Emerton

'His production—it was his first time out as a director—is a triumph of colour, music, spectacle, and soaring heroic poetry, and, as actor, he brings lungs, exultation, and a bashful wit to the role.'—*Pauline Kael, 70s*

AAN: best picture; William Walton; Laurence Olivier (as actor)

Henry VIII and His Six Wives*
GB 1972 125m Technicolor
EMI (Roy Baird)

Dullish historical account of the king's reign, staged as recollections from his deathbed but lacking any of the sparkle of *The Private Life of Henry VIII* made forty years previously. Accurate sets and costumes fail to compensate for lack of film flair.

w Ian Thorne *d* Waris Hussein *ph* Peter Suschitsky *m* David Munro

Keith Michell, Frances Cuka (Aragon), Charlotte Rampling (Boleyn), Jane Asher (Seymour), Jenny Bos (Cleves), Lynne Frederick (Howard), Barbara Leigh-Hunt (Parr), Donald Pleasence (Thomas Cromwell)
† The production was stimulated by a highly successful BBC TV series, *The Six Wives of Henry VIII*

Henry the Rainmaker
US 1948 64m bw

A concerned citizen runs for mayor and calls in a rainmaker to solve a drought. Pleasant homely comedy which ran to a brief series. Raymond Walburn, Walter Catlett, William Tracy, Mary Stuart, Barbara Brown. Written by Lane Beauchamp; directed by Jean Yarbrough; for Peter Scully / Monogram.

Her Adventurous Night
US 1946 75m bw

An imaginative boy spreads a story which lands his headmaster in jail, but absolves himself by solving a murder mystery.
Agreeable minor comedy for the hinterlands. Dennis O'Keefe, Helen Walker, Tom Powers, Fuzzy Knight, Scotty Beckett. Written by Jerry Warner; directed by John Rawlins; for Marshall Grant / Universal.

Her Cardboard Lover*
US 1942 93m bw
MGM (J. Walter Ruben)

A flirtatious lady hires a lover to make her fiancé jealous.
Paper-thin comedy previously filmed in silent days as *The Passionate Plumber* (with Buster Keaton). It did nobody any good, but preserves some style despite a witless script.

w Jacques Deval, John Collier, Anthony Veiller, William H. Wright, *play* Jacques Deval *d* George Cukor *ph* Harry Stradling, Robert Planck *m* Franz Waxman

Norma Shearer, Robert Taylor, George Sanders, Frank McHugh, Elizabeth Patterson, Chill Wills

Her Favourite Husband
GB 1950 79m bw

A wife finds that her husband has been replaced by a gangster who aims to rob a bank. Rather tiresome Italian-set comedy with funny moments. Jean Kent, Robert Beatty, Gordon Harker, Margaret Rutherford, Rona Anderson, Max Adrian. Written by Noel Langley and W. F. Templeton, from a play by Pepine de Felipe; directed by Mario Soldati; for Orlux / Renown.
(US title: *The Taming of Dorothy*.)

Her First Beau
US 1941 76m bw

A teenage girl finds her childhood sweetheart is taking her for granted. Mild family comedy, but the star did not easily take to semi-adult roles. Jane Withers, Jackie Cooper, Edith Fellows, Josephine Hutchinson, William Tracy, Una O'Connor, Edgar Buchanan. Written by Gladys Lehman, Karen DeWolf; directed by Theodore Reed; for B. B. Kahane / Columbia.

Her First Romance
US 1951 73m bw

A schoolgirl pursues an older boy to a summer camp. Flat little adolescent comedy which did no good for a star in her awkward age. Margaret O'Brien, Allen Martin Jnr, Jimmy Hunt, Sharyn Moffett. Written by Albert Mannheimer; directed by Seymour Friedman; for Columbia. (GB title: *Girls Never Tell*.)

Her Highness and the Bellboy
US 1945 112m bw
MGM (Joe Pasternak)

A hotel bellboy forsakes his crippled sweetheart to woo a visiting princess.
Glutinous sentimental mishmash; one waits for musical numbers which never happen.

w Richard Connell, Gladys Lehmann *d* Richard Thorpe *ph* Harry Stradling *m* Georgie Stoll

Hedy Lamarr, Robert Walker, June Allyson, Rags Ragland, Agnes Moorehead, Carl Esmond, Warner Anderson, Ludwig Stossel

Her Husband Lies
US 1937 74m bw

A New York gambler tries to ensure that his kid brother is not contaminated. Adequate remake of *Street of Chance*. Ricardo Cortez, Gail Patrick, Akim Tamiroff, Tom Brown, Louis Calhern. Written by Wallace Smith, Eve Brown, from a story by O. H. P. Garrett; directed by Edward Ludwig; for Paramount. 'Superb direction and expert acting.'—*Variety*

Her Husband's Affairs*
US 1947 83m bw
Columbia (Raphael Hakim)

A husband and wife team of advertising agents promote a depilatory which turns out to grow hair instead.
Mildly amiable crazy comedy.

w Ben Hecht *d* S. Sylvan Simon *ph* Charles Lawton Jnr *m* George Duning

Lucille Ball, Franchot Tone, Edward Everett Horton, Mikhail Rasumny, Gene Lockhart, Nana Bryant, Jonathan Hale, Mabel Paige

'See the mystical hypnotic rites of the white goddess of the jungle! See the plane crash in the tragic typhoon! See the ravening charge of the hundred sacred crocodiles!'

Her Jungle Love*
US 1938 81m Technicolor
Paramount (George M. Arthur)

An aviator crashlands in the jungle, where he is comforted by a lovely lady, a chimp and a lion but distressed by an earthquake, a volcano and assorted villains.
Second of Dorothy Lamour's jungle hokum shows, and the first in colour; despite its fair technical proficiency, the fact that it once packed 'em in is tribute to the changing tastes of mankind.

w Joseph M. March, Lillie Hayward, Eddie Welch *d* George Archainbaud *ph* Ray Rennahan *m* Gregory Stone

Dorothy Lamour, Ray Milland, Lynne Overman, J. Carrol Naish, Dorothy Howe

'Splendid colour job, but there's little more . . . only slightly varied from the type of a bygone era.'—*Variety*
† The Lynne Overman character wisecracks: 'Those *Esquire* cartoons must be right: there's always just one girl on a desert island.'
†† The lion cub in this case is called Meewa, the chimp Gaga.

Her Kind of Man
US 1946 78m bw

A singer finds a gangster irresistible but eventually settles for a newspaper columnist. Shiny, nondescript forties copy of a thirties style; more yawns than thrills. Dane Clark, Zachary Scott, Janis Paige, Faye Emerson, George Tobias, Sheldon Leonard. Written by Gordon Kahn and Leopold Atlas; directed by Frederick de Cordova; for Warner.

Her Majesty Love
US 1931 76m bw

A well-born Berliner finds it easier to court the barmaid he loves after she has married a baron. Heavy-handed musical comedy worth excavating for the odd talents involved. Marilyn Miller, Ben Lyon, W. C. Fields, Leon Errol, Chester Conklin, Ford Sterling. Written by Robert Lord and Arthur Caesar; directed by William Dieterle; for Warner. 'An exceptionally dismal musical.'—*Clive Hirschhorn 1983*

Her Man*
US 1930 85m bw

The story of Frankie and Johnnie is transposed to a French apache setting. Comedy melodrama which has its adherents. Helen Twelvetrees, Ricardo Cortez, Marjorie Rambeau, James Gleason, Franklin Pangborn, Phillips Holmes, Thelma Todd. Written by Howard Higgins and Tay Garnett; directed by Tay Garnett; for Pathé. 'Looks like box office . . . full of action.'—*Variety*

Her Master's Voice
US 1936 75m bw

Henpecked by his wife and her mother, a man makes a name for himself as a radio troubadour. Mild comedy from a stage success. Edward Everett Horton, Peggy Conklin, Laura Hope Crews, Elizabeth Patterson, Grant Mitchell. Written by Dore Schary, Harry Sauber from the play by Clare Kummer; directed by Joseph Santley; for Walter Wanger / Paramount. 'Suitable because of frothy humour for family and nabe audiences solo.'—*Variety*

Her Primitive Man
US 1944 87m bw

An author disguises himself as a savage in order to denounce a woman trying to prove his theories a fraud. Very silly comedy partly salvaged by a few good lines. Robert Paige, Louise Allbritton, Robert Benchley, Edward Everett Horton, Helen Broderick, Ernest Truex, Walter Catlett, Nydia Westman. Written by Michael Fessier and Ernest Pagano; directed by Charles Lamont; for Universal.

Her Sister's Secret
US 1946 86m bw

A pregnant girl hands over her child to her sister; but what will the sister's husband say? *Peg's Paper* in modern dress, but an ambitious project for this Poverty Row company. Nancy Coleman, Margaret Lindsay, Philip Reed, Felix Bressart, Regis Toomey, Henry Stephenson, Fritz Feld. Written by Anne Green, from novel *Dark Angel* by Gina Kaus; directed by Edgar G. Ulmer; for Henry Brash / PRC.

Her Twelve Men
US 1954 91m Anscocolor
MGM (John Houseman)

A woman teacher in a boys' school reforms a difficult class.
Predictable, sugary and artificial school story with the star exuding sweetness and light.

w William Roberts, Laura Z. Hobson *d* Robert Z. Leonard *ph* Joseph Ruttenberg *m* Bronislau Kaper

Greer Garson, Robert Ryan, Richard Haydn, Barry Sullivan

Her Wedding Night
US 1930 78m bw

On the Italian riviera a man marries his friend's wife under the impression that they are only booking rooms for the night. Spicy bedroom farce which crested the wave of its star's notoriety. Clara Bow, *Charles Ruggles*, Ralph Forbes, Skeets Gallagher. Written by Henry Myers from the play by Avery Hopwood; directed by Frank Tuttle; for Paramount. 'Deftly handled for smartness and taste . . . ought to make women talk.'—*Variety*

Herbie Goes Bananas
US 1980 100m Technicolor

Two Americans take their magical Volkswagen on a South American holiday. Listless addition to a series which has already gone on too long. Charles Martin Smith, Stephan W. Burns, Cloris Leachman, John Vernon. Written by Don Tait; directed by Vincent McEveety; for Walt Disney.

Herbie Goes to Monte Carlo
US 1977 105m Technicolor
Walt Disney (Ron Miller)

The Volkswagen with a mind of its own enters the Monte Carlo rally and routs a gang of thieves.
Utterly predictable, patchily made family comedy.

w Arthur Alsberg, Don Nelson *d* Vincent McEveety *ph* Leonard J. South *m* Frank de Vol

Dean Jones, Don Knotts, Julie Sommars, Jacques Marin, Roy Kinnear, Bernard Fox
† Second sequel to *The Love Bug.*

Herbie Rides Again
US 1974 88m Technicolor

A Volkswagen with a mind of its own helps an old lady to rout a property developer. Acceptable sequel to *The Love Bug*. Helen Hayes, Ken Berry, Stefanie Powers, John McIntyre, Keenan Wynn, Huntz Hall. Written and produced by Bill Walsh; directed by Robert Stevenson; for Walt Disney.

Hercules
Italy 1957 105m Eastmancolor Dyaliscope
Oscar / Galatea (Federico Teti)
original title: *Le Fatiche di Ercole*

Hercules helps Jason find the golden fleece. The strong man epic which started a genre; of little interest in itself.

w Pietro Francisci, Ennio de Concini, Gaio Frattini *d* Pietro Francisci *ph* Mario Bava *m* Enzo Masetti

Steve Reeves, Sylva Koscina, Gianna Maria Canale, Fabrizio Mione

Hercules Unchained
Italy / France 1959 105m Eastmancolor Dyaliscope
Lux / Galatea (Bruno Vailati)
original title: *Ercole e la Regina di Lidia*

Hercules has problems with the king of Thebes and the queen of Lidia.
More comic-strip versions of old legends. This item had more spent on it in publicity than in production cost, and consequently was seen by vast audiences around the world. It isn't very good.

w Pietro Francisci, Ennio di Concini *d* Pietro Francisci *ph* Mario Bava *m* Enzo Masetti

Steve Reeves, Sylva Koscina, Sylvia Lopez, Primo Carnera
† Many sequels followed, the hero sometimes being known as Ursus or Goliath.

Here Come the Coeds
US 1945 88m bw
Universal (John Grant)

Janitors help to forestall a mortgage foreclosure on a college for women.
Routine star vehicle with few highlights.

w Arthur T. Horman, John Grant *d* Jean Yarbrough *ph* George Robinson *songs* Jack Brooks, Edgar Fairchild

Bud Abbott, Lou Costello, Lon Chaney Jnr, Peggy Ryan, Martha O'Driscoll, Donald Cook, June Vincent, Charles Dingle

Here Come the Girls*
US 1953 78m Technicolor
Paramount / Hope Enterprises (Paul Jones)
original title: *Champagne for Everybody*

In the nineties an ageing chorus boy traps a mysterious murderer.
Spotty, ineptly titled star comedy with music; in fact among the last of his passable vehicles, with excellent production backing.

w Edmund Hartmann, Hal Kanter *d* Claude Binyon *ph* Lionel Lindon *md* Lyn Murray *ad Hal Pereira, Roland Anderson*

Bob Hope, Rosemary Clooney, Tony Martin, Arlene Dahl, Millard Mitchell, Fred Clark, William Demarest, Robert Strauss

Here Come the Huggetts*
GB 1948 93m bw
Rank / Gainsborough (Betty Box)

A suburban family has its ups and downs.
Cosy domestic comedy drama, a presage of TV soap operas to come, or Britain's answer to the Hardys, depending how you look at it. Tolerable at the time.

w Mabel and Denis Constanduros, Muriel and Sydney Box, Peter Rogers *d* Ken Annakin *ph* Reg Wyer *m* Anthony Hopkins

Jack Warner, Kathleen Harrison, Jane Hylton, Susan Shaw, Petula Clark, Jimmy Hanley, David Tomlinson, Diana Dors, Peter Hammond, John Blythe
† The Huggetts had actually originated in *Holiday Camp* the previous year, and appeared again in *Vote for Huggett* and *The Huggetts Abroad*; Warner and Harrison became an inseparable duo for many years.

Here Come the Nelsons
US 1951 76m bw
The sons of an advertising agent get involved with gangsters. Empty-headed family comedy based on the long-running TV show *The Adventures of Ozzie and Harriet*. Ozzie Nelson, Harriet Hilliard, David and Ricky Nelson, Rock Hudson, Barbara Lawrence, Ann Doran, Jim Backus. Written by Ozzie Nelson, Donald Nelson and William Davenport; directed by Frederick de Cordova; for Universal.

Here Come the Waves
US 1944 98m bw
Paramount (Mark Sandrich)
A sailor falls in love with identical twin Waves.
Empty-headed, professionally executed musical recruiting poster.
w Allen Scott, Ken Englund, Zion Myers *d* Mark Sandrich *ph* Charles Lang *md* Robert Emmett Dolan *songs* Harold Arlen, Johnny Mercer
Bing Crosby, Betty Hutton, Sonny Tufts, Ann Doran, Gwen Crawford
'An almost totally negligible musical.'—*James Agee*
AAN: song 'Accentuate the Positive' (*m* Harold Arlen, *ly* Johnny Mercer)

Here Comes Cookie
US 1935 65m bw
Gracie comes into money and opens a theatre-cum-hotel for vaudevillians. Slight star comedy with its share of laughs. George Burns, Gracie Allen, George Barbier, Betty Furness, Andrew Tombes. Written by Sam Mintz and Don Hartman; directed by Norman Z. McLeod; for William le Baron / Paramount. 'Situation and gag pounding without an ounce of seriousness or sense.'—*Variety*

Here Comes Mr Jordan***
US 1941 93m bw
Columbia (Everett Riskin)
A prizefighter who is also an amateur saxophonist crashes in his private plane and goes to heaven by mistake: he was supposed to survive and live another forty years. Unfortunately when he goes back for his body it has been cremated, so he has to find another one, recently deceased . . .
Weird heavenly fantasy which succeeded because of its novelty and because heaven in wartime was a comforting vision. As a movie taken on its own merits, it suffers from illogicalities, a miscast star and a wandering plot, but scene for scene there is enough firmness and control to make it memorable. It certainly had many imitations, including *Angel on My Shoulder, Down to Earth, A Guy Named Joe, Heaven Only Knows, The Horn Blows at Midnight* and *That's the Spirit*.
w Seton I. Miller, Sidney Buchman, play Halfway to Heaven by Harry Segall *d Alexander Hall ph* Joseph Walker *m* Frederick Hollander *md* Morris Stoloff
Robert Montgomery, Evelyn Keyes, Rita Johnson, *Claude Rains, James Gleason, Edward Everett Horton*, John Emery, *Donald MacBride*, Halliwell Hobbes, Don Costello
'There is something about this original so sweet-spirited and earnest that it transcends its plot devices and shines through its comedic asides to beome a true morality play without once becoming either preachy or mawkish.'—*Kit Parker catalogue, 1980*
'Audiences loved this chunk of whimsy . . . the slickly hammy Rains gives Mr Jordan a sinister gloss, as if he were involved in some heavenly racket, like smuggling Chinese.'—*Pauline Kael, 70s*
† Remade 1978 as *Heaven Can Wait*.
AA: original story (Harry Segall); script
AAN: best picture; Seton I. Miller, Sidney Buchman; Alexander Hall; Joseph Walker; Robert Montgomery; James Gleason

Here Comes the Band
US 1935 82m bw
Buddies from an army band are stuck in the taxi business. Shapeless comedy with interesting numbers. But not very. *Ted Lewis* and his Band, Ted Healy, Nat Pendleton, Virginia Bruce, Harry Stockwell, Donald Cook, Spanky McFarland. Written by Paul Sloane, Ralph Spence, Victor Mansfield; directed by Paul Sloane; for MGM. 'Not punchy enough for the de luxe trade . . . best as second stringer.'—*Variety*

Here Comes the Groom*
US 1951 114m bw
Paramount (Frank Capra)
A journalist adopts war orphans and reforms his selfish fiancée.
Tired attempt by Capra to recapture his pre-war mood; despite intermittent pleasures it has neither the right style nor the topical substance.
w Virginia Van Upp, Myles Connelly, Liam O'Brien, *story* Robert Riskin *d Frank Capra ph* George Barnes *md* Joseph Lilley *songs* Jay Livingston, Ray Evans
Bing Crosby, Jane Wyman, Franchot Tone, Alexis Smith, James Barton, Connie Gilchrist, Robert Keith, Anna Maria Alberghetti
'The general impression is of a loud, strident, rather vulgar comedy in which technique is used to disappointingly mechanical ends, and which a few bright lines of dialogue cannot rescue from tedium.'—*Penelope Houston*
AA: song 'In the Cool Cool Cool of the Evening' (*m* Hoagy Carmichael, *ly* Johnny Mercer)
AAN: Robert Riskin

Here Comes the Navy*
US 1934 86m bw
Warner
An aggressive young naval rating fights with his former friend, now Petty Officer.
Breezy comedy melodrama teaming Cagney and O'Brien for the first time and offering star heroics as a sop to the Legion of Decency.
w Ben Markson, Earl Baldwin *d* Lloyd Bacon *ph* Arthur Edeson *m* Leo F. Forbstein
James Cagney, Pat O'Brien, Dorothy Tree, Gloria Stuart, Frank McHugh, Robert Barrat
'It's a bit too masculine for matinée appeal and it'll have to be a case of the kids and men dragging the womenfolk along.'—*Variety*
'Rapid and reasonably authentic, a satisfactory addition to a series of cinema cartoons which, because their colour and mood are indigenous and timely, may be more interesting twenty years from now.'—*Time*
AAN: best picture

Here Comes the Sun
GB 1945 91m bw
Racetrack touts help to breathe fresh life into a provincial newspaper. Amiable comedy with a touch of do-goodery, very typical of this producer. Bud Flanagan, Chesney Allen, Joss Ambler, Dick Francis. Written by Geoffrey Orme; directed and produced by John Baxter.

Here I Am a Stranger
US 1939 81m bw
A rich woman tries to prevent her son being influenced by her once-drunken ex-husband. Predictable family drama which was catnip to 1939 audiences. Gladys George, Richard Dix, Richard Greene, Brenda Joyce, Roland Young, Russell Gleason, George Zucco. Written by Sam Hellman and Milton Sperling from a story by Gordon Malherbe Hillman; directed by Roy del Ruth; for Harry Joe Brown / TCF. 'Strong programme drama will catch many top key spots.'—*Variety*

Here Is My Heart
US 1934 73m bw
An American radio crooner on the riviera pretends to be a waiter in order to court a princess. Musical remake of *The Grand Duchess and the Waiter*; not bad of its type. Bing Crosby, Kitty Carlisle, Roland Young, Alison Skipworth, Reginald Owen, Akim Tamiroff. Written by Edwin Justus Mayer and Harlan Thompson; directed by Frank Tuttle; for Paramount. 'First-class entertainment . . . though it seems they adapted it by running it through the electric fan.'—*Variety*. Songs by Leo Robin and Ralph Rainger: 'Love Is Just Around the Corner'; 'With Every Breath I Take'; 'June in January'; 'Here Is my Heart'; 'You Can't Make a Monkey of the Moon'.

Here We Go Again
US 1942 75m bw
Various radio celebrities congregate at Silvertip Lodge. Random excuse for a variety show, with top talent of its day; a sequel to

Look Who's Laughing. Jim Jordan, Marion Jordan (Fibber McGee and Molly), Edgar Bergen, Charlie McCarthy, Harold Peary (The Great Gildersleeve), Ginny Simms, Gale Gordon, Ray Noble and his orchestra. Written by Paul Gerard Smith and Joe Bigelow; directed and produced by Allan Dwan; for RKO.

Here We Go round the Mulberry Bush*
GB 1967 96m Technicolor
UA / Giant (Larry Kramer, Clive Donner)

A school-leaver is obsessed by sex and determines to lose his virginity.
Repetitive comedy which certainly opened new avenues in British humour and seemed pretty permissive at the time (pre-*Graduate*). In itself, however, more modish than sympathetic.

w Hunter Davies (with Larry Kramer), from his novel *d Clive Donner* *ph* Alex Thomson *m* various groups

Barry Evans, Judy Geeson, Angela Scoular, Adrienne Posta, Sheila White, Vanessa Howard, Denholm Elliott, Maxine Audley, Moyra Fraser, Michael Bates

'The only incongruity is that it should have been made by adults, so completely does it enter into the teenager's view of himself.'—*MFB*

Here's to Romance
US 1935 82m bw

A young tenor who finds a patron in Paris is pursued by the wealthy wife. Amiable piece of musical froth which somehow failed to make a big singing star of Martini. Nino Martini, Genevieve Tobin, Reginald Denny, Anita Louise, Mme Schumann-Heink, Maria Gambarelli. Written by Ernest Pascal and Arthur Richman; directed by Alfred E. Green; for Jesse L. Lasky / TCF. 'Given a sturdier story he might have emerged as a Grace Moore for talkers.'—*Variety*

A Hero Ain't Nothing but a Sandwich
US 1977 107m CFI color
New World / Radnitz-Mattel (Robert B. Radnitz)

Problems for an urban family in the black ghetto.
Well-intentioned but ultimately wearisome and cliché-strewn melodrama.

w Alice Childress, from her novel *d* Ralph Nelson *ph* Frank Stanley *m* Tom McIntosh

Cicely Tyson, Paul Winfield, Larry B. Scott, Helen Martin, Glynn Turman

'The sort of dreaded wholesome film that cultural and societal groups heavily endorse but nobody pays money to go see.'—*Variety*

Hero at Large
US 1980 98m Metrocolor

An actor playing Captain Avenger accidentally becomes a real-life hero, but his fans turn against him when they find he's just an ordinary guy. Muddled satirical comedy-melodrama with too many pauses for love interest. John Ritter, Anne Archer, Bert Convy, Kevin McCarthy, Harry Bellaver. Written by A. J. Carothers; directed by Martin Davidson; for Stephen Freedman / MGM.

Heroes
US 1977 113m Technicolor
Universal (David Foster, Lawrence Turman)

A Vietnam veteran, made slightly kooky by his experiences, settles down after several adventures when he falls in love.
Just plain awful: a would-be star vehicle that doesn't work.

w James Carabatsos (and, uncredited, David Freeman) *d Jeremy Paul Kagan* *ph* Frank Stanley *m* Jack Nitzche, Richard Hazard

Henry Winkler, Sally Field, Harrison Ford, Val Avery

The Heroes Are Tired
France 1955 101m bw
Cila-Terra
original title: *Les Héros Sont Fatigués*

Two ex-wartime pilots, one Free French and the other German, set up an air charter service in Liberia but come to grief over stolen diamonds.
Gloomy post-war *film noir* set in a peculiarly depressing atmosphere, and not really sharp enough to overcome its squalid plot.

w Yves Ciampi, Jacques-Laurent Bost, *novel* Christine Garnier *d* Yves Ciampi *ph* Henri Alekan *m* Louiguy

Yves Montand, Maria Félix, Jean Servais, Curt Jurgens, Gérard Oury

Heroes for Sale
US 1933 73m bw

A war veteran becomes in turn a drug addict, a millionaire and the central figure in a labour dispute. Minor social-conscience melodrama with watchable elements. Richard Barthelmess, Aline MacMahon, Loretta Young, Berton Churchill, Robert Barrat. Written by Robert Lord and Wilson Mizner; directed by William A. Wellman; for Warner.

'This attempted satire on unemployment conditions just prior to the Roosevelt election is not well told . . . b.o. doubtful.'—*Variety*

The Heroes of Telemark*
GB 1965 131m Technicolor Panavision
Rank / Benton (Ben Fisz)

Norwegian resistance workers in World War II help the Allies to smash a heavy water plant.
Ambling narrative with big action sequences which often seem irrelevant, so that the story as a whole fails to excite.

w Ivan Moffat, Ben Barzman *d* Anthony Mann *ph Robert Krasker* *m* Malcolm Arnold

Kirk Douglas, Richard Harris, Ulla Jacobsson, Roy Dotrice, Anton Diffring, Michael Redgrave

Heroes of the West
US 1932 bw serial: 12 eps

Young Noah Blaine helps his father to build the transcontinental railroad. Fairly ambitious serial of its time. Noah Beery Jnr, Diane Duval, Onslow Stevens, William Desmond. Directed by Ray Taylor; for Universal.

Hero's Island*
US 1962 94m Technicolor Panavision
UA / Daystar / Portland (James Mason, Leslie Stevens)

In 1718 bondslaves settle on a Carolina island, are attacked by fishermen and protected by one of the aides of Blackbeard the Pirate.
An oddly personal, patchy, rather mysterious film with a rhetorical script and rather good action sequences.

wd Leslie Stevens *ph* Ted McCord *m* Dominic Frontière

James Mason, Kate Manx, Neville Brand, Rip Torn

Herr Puntila and his Servant Matti*
Austria 1955 95m Agfacolor
Bauerfilm

A rich landowner, usually drunk, is rescued from scrapes by his patient valet.
A cogent comedy which its author is said to have approved in this version.

w Alberto Cavalcanti, Vladimir Pozner, Ruth Wieden, *play* Bertolt Brecht *d* Alberto Cavalcanti *ph* André Bac, Arthur Hämmerer *m* Hanns Eisler

Curt Bois, Hans Engelmann, Maria Emo, Edith Prager

Hers to Hold
US 1943 94m bw
Universal (Felix Jackson)

A girl decides whether or not to marry a serviceman.
Limp star vehicle, a sequel to *Three Smart Girls* (qv).

w Lewis R. Foster *d* Frank Ryan *ph* Elwood Bredell *md* Charles Previn *m* Frank Skinner

Deanna Durbin, Joseph Cotten, Charles Winninger, Nella Walker, Gus Schilling, Ludwig Stossel

AAN: song 'Say a Prayer for the Boys Over There' (*m* Jimmy McHugh, *ly* Herb Magidson)

He's a Cockeyed Wonder
US 1950 77m bw

An orange sorter goes into the magic business. Energetic low-budget comedy vehicle for unsophisticated audiences. Mickey Rooney, Terry Moore, William Demarest, Charles Arnt, Mike Mazurki. Written by Jack Henley; directed by Peter Godfrey; for Columbia.

Hester Street*
US 1974 89m bw
Midwest Films (Raphael D. Silver)

How Jewish immigrants settled in East Side New York in the nineties.

Modest, humorous, but not always smooth or dramatically emphatic chronicle of a familiar background; the detail however is excellent.

wd Joan Macklin Silver, *story* Yeki by Abraham Cahan *ph* Kenneth Van Sickle *m* William Bolcom

Steven Keats, Carol Kane, Mel Howard, Dorrie Kavanaugh, Doris Roberts

'A small, beautifully detailed, slightly shaggy independent film of charm and substance.'—*Judith Crist*

'For old diehards who still go to the cinema seeking humanity, tenderness and insight.'—*Michael Billington, Illustrated London News*

AAN: Joan Macklin Silver (as writer); Carol Kane

Hey, Good-Lookin'
US 1982 76m Technicolor

Life in 1953 Brooklyn centres round two young womanizers. Enterprising attempt to use animation to tell a youth melodrama; interesting but not successful. Written, directed and produced by Ralph Bakshi; for Warners.

Hey! Hey! USA
GB 1938 92m bw

An education expert sails to America, falls in with gangsters, and saves a boy from being kidnapped by them. Misconceived star vehicle which provides some laughs, but not of the expected kind. Will Hay, Edgar Kennedy, David Burns, Fred Duprez. Written by J. O. C. Orton; directed by Marcel Varnel; for Gainsborough.

Hey Rookie
US 1944 71m bw

A musical comedy producer in the army puts on a show. Virtually a non-stop revue, with Ann Miller, Joe Besser, Larry Parks, Joe Sawyer, the Condos Brothers, Jack Gilford, the Hal McIntyre Orchestra. Written by Henry Myers, Edward Ellsen, Jay Gurney, from play by K. B. and Doris Culvan; directed by Charles Barton; for Irving Briskin / Columbia. 'Brief, to the point, and will do.'—*Variety*

Hi Buddy
US 1943 66m bw

Soldiers stage a benefit show at a boys' club. Luckily the sentiment does not get in the way of the numbers; ordinary modest musical filler. Dick Foran, Harriet Hilliard, Robert Paige, Marjorie Lord, the King's Men, the Four Sweethearts, Dolores Diane. Written by Warren Wilson; directed by Harold Young; for Paul Malvern / Universal.

Hi Diddle Diddle*
US 1943 72m bw
UA / Andrew Stone
aka: *Try and Find It*

Young lovers are hampered by con artist parents.
Scatty comedy with amusing patches and some zest in the telling.

w Edmund L. Hartmann *d* Andrew L. Stone *ph* Charles Van Enger *m* Phil Boutelje

Adolphe Menjou, Pola Negri, Dennis O'Keefe, Billie Burke, Martha Scott, June Havoc

AAN: Phil Boutelje

Hi Gang
GB 1941 100m bw
Rank / Gainsborough (Edward Black)

American expatriates in London get involved in a case of mistaken identity.
Icky farce based faintly on a wartime radio variety series, notable only for preserving the three stars involved.

w Val Guest, Marriott Edgar, J. O. C. Orton, Howard Irving Young *d* Marcel Varnel *ph* Jack Cox

Bebe Daniels, Ben Lyon, Vic Oliver, Graham Moffatt, Moore Marriott, Felix Aylmer, Sam Browne

Hi, Mom!*
US 1969 86m Movielab

Adventures of a young porno film maker and of the eccentrics who live in the same building. Busy comedy of the drop-out life, full of random satirical jabs and *hommages* to other film makers. Robert de Niro, Allen Garfield, Gerrit Graham, Jennifer Salt. Written and directed by *Brian de Palma;* for West End films.

Hi Nellie*
US 1934 79m bw
Warner (Robert Presnell)

An ex-editor is demoted to advice to the lovelorn and gets involved in city rackets.
Minor, effective star comedy-melodrama.

w Abem Finkel, Sidney Sutherland *d* Mervyn Le Roy *ph* Sol Polito

Paul Muni, Glenda Farrell, Ned Sparks, Robert Barrat, Hobart Cavanaugh, Berton Churchill, Donald Meek, Douglass Dumbrille, Edward Ellis

'Barely gets by as fair entertainment . . . it's a better Muni performance than a picture.'—*Variety*

† Remade in 1935 as *Front Page Woman*; 1937 as *Love Is on the Air*; 1942 as *You Can't Escape Forever*; 1949 as *The House across the Street.*

Hi Ya Chum
US 1943 61m bw

On their way to Hollywood, variety performers are stranded in a small town. Thin star comedy support. The Ritz Brothers, Jane Frazee, Robert Paige, June Clyde. Written by Edmund L. Hartmann; directed by Harold Young; for Universal. (GB title: *Everything Happens to Us*.)

Hiawatha
US 1952 80m Cinecolor

A young brave prevents war between three Indian tribes. Muddled actioner which has little to do with Longfellow's poem. Vincent Edwards, Yvette Dugay, Keith Larsen, Morris Ankrum, Ian MacDonald. Written by Arthur Strawn and Dan Ullman; directed by Kurt Neumann; for Allied Artists.

Hickey and Boggs
US 1972 111m De Luxe
UA / Film Guarantors Ltd (Fouad Said)

Two down and out private eyes, hired to find a girl, keep falling over dead bodies.
Extraordinarily confused thriller with moments of humour and well staged action sequences.

w Walter Hill *d* Robert Culp *ph* Wilmer Butler *m* Ted Ashford

Robert Culp, Bill Cosby, Rosalind Cash

The Hidden Eye
US 1945 69m bw

A blind detective gets on the trail of a murderer who deliberately leaves confusing clues. Thin successor to *Eyes in the Night*: no style at all. Edward Arnold, Frances Rafferty, William Phillips, Ray Collins, Thomas Jackson. Written by George Harmon Coxe and Harry Ruskin; directed by Richard Whorf; for MGM.

Hidden Fear
US 1957 83m bw

An American cop in Copenhagen clears his sister of a murder charge. Patchy, tough thriller with some pretensions to style sabotaged by a muddled script. John Payne, Anne Neyland, Alexander Knox, Conrad Nagel, Elsy Albiin. Written by André de Toth and John Ward Hawkins; directed by André de Toth; for St Aubrey-Kohn / UA.

The Hidden Fortress*
Japan 1958 123m bw Tohoscope
Toho (Masumi Fujimoto)
original title: *Kakushi Toride No San-Akunin*

In medieval Japan, the heiress of a feudal lord is saved from a bandit by a samurai.
Roistering eastern western.

w Ryuzo Kikushima, Hideo Oguni, Shinobu Hashimoto, Akira Kurosawa *d* Akira Kurosawa *ph* Ichio Yamazaki *m* Masaru Sato

Toshiro Mifune, Misa Uehara, Minoru Chiaki

The Hidden Hand
US 1942 67m bw

Murders proliferate in the house of a wealthy old spinster. Heavy-going spoof of the thunderstorm mystery; sometimes amusing for connoisseurs of the genre. Craig Stevens, Elizabeth Fraser, Julie Bishop, Willie Best, Milton Parsons. Written by Anthony Coldeway; directed by Ben Stoloff; for Warner.

Hide and Seek
GB 1963 90m bw
British Lion / Albion / Spectrum (Hal E. Chester)

A research scientist is the centre of a kidnap plan designed to make it appear that he has defected.
Too many mysterious happenings with too little explanation sink this comedy-thriller from the start.

w David Stone *d* Cy Endfield *ph* Gilbert Taylor *m* Muir Mathieson, Gary Campbell

Ian Carmichael, Janet Munro, Curt Jurgens, Hugh Griffith, George Pravda, Kieron Moore, Edward Chapman

Hide in Plain Sight
US 1980 92m Metrocolor
MGM (Robert Christiansen, Rick Rosenberg)

A factory worker searches for his children when his former wife is hidden by the government to protect her husband, an informer.
Unpersuasive melodrama with little more than its unusual plot to commend it.

w Spencer Eastman *book* Leslie Waller *d* James Caan *ph* Paul Lohmann *m* Leonard Rosenman

James Caan, Jill Eikenberry, Robert Viharo

Hideaway Girl
US 1936 71m bw

A girl suspected of stealing a necklace goes on the run. Humdrum comedy melodrama with songs: a hotchpotch. Martha Raye, Shirley Ross, Robert Cummings, Monroe Owsley. Written by Joseph Moncure March; directed by George Archainbaud; for A. M. Botsford / Paramount. 'Rowdy, nonsensical lightweight, geared for doubles.'—*Variety*

Hideout
US 1934 83m bw

An injured racketeer takes refuge with a farm family and is reformed by the simple life and true love. Schematic eat-your-cake-and-have-it melodrama which pleased audiences at the time. Robert Montgomery, Maureen O'Sullivan, Mickey Rooney, Edward Arnold, C. Henry Gordon, Elizabeth Patterson, Edward Brophy, Herman Bing. Written by Frances Goodrich and Albert Hackett; directed by W. S. Van Dyke; for MGM.

The Higgins Family
US 1938 65m bw

An advertising man is driven almost to divorce when his wife becomes a radio personality. Modest family comedy which ran to a short series. James Gleason, Lucile Gleason, Russell Gleason, Lynne Roberts, Harry Davenport. Written by Paul Gerard Smith, Jack Townley, Richard English; directed by Gus Meins; for Republic. 'Shows fine promise.'—*Variety*

High and Low*
Japan 1963 142m bw Tohoscope
Toho (Tomoyuki Tanaka)

A wealthy shoe manufacturer's chauffeur's son is kidnapped in mistake for his own, and he faces a moral dilemma.
Interesting, rather gloomy Japanese version of a light American thriller with all the style expected of the director.

w Hideo Oguni, Ryuzo Kikushima, Eijiro Hisaito, Akira Kurosawa, *novel* The King's Ransom by Ed McBain *d* Akira Kurosawa *ph* Asakazu Makai, Takao Saito *m* Masaru Sato

Toshiro Mifune, Kyoko Kagawa, Tatsuya Nakadai

The High and the Mighty*
US 1954 147m Warnercolor Cinemascope
Wayne–Fellows

A big passenger plane is in trouble over the Pacific, and its occupants react in various ways to the prospect of a crash landing.
Compendium fiction with even the pilot having a personal problem which could cloud his judgment. Tolerable, well made hokum.

w Ernest K. Gann, from his novel *d* William Wellman *ph* William Clothier *m* Dmitri Tiomkin

John Wayne, Robert Newton, Robert Stack, Doe Avedon, Claire Trevor, Laraine Day, Jan Sterling, Phil Harris, Sidney Blackmer, John Howard

AA: Dmitri Tiomkin
AAN: William Wellman; Claire Trevor; Jan Sterling; title song (*m* Dmitri Tiomkin, *ly* Ned Washington)

High Anxiety*
US 1977 94m De Luxe
TCF / Crossbow (Mel Brooks)

A psychologist taking up a new appointment suspects that his predecessor may have been murdered.
Elementary but somewhat entertaining spoof of various Hitchcock movies (*Spellbound, North by Northwest, The Birds*), with the level of humour as unsubtle and lavatorial as one has come to expect.

w Mel Brooks, Ron Clark, Rudy DeLuca, Barry Levinson *d* Mel Brooks *ph* Paul Lohmann *m* John Morris

Mel Brooks, Madeline Kahn, Cloris Leachman, Harvey Korman, Ron Carey, Howard Morris, Dick Van Patten

'It basically just shambles along, in search of the next big set-piece to send up.'—*Richard Combs, MFB*

'Brooks has no idea of how to build a sequence, how to tell a story, when to leave well enough (or ill enough) alone.'—*Philip French, Observer*

'A child's idea of satire—imitations, with a comic hat and a leer.'—*New Yorker*

High-Ballin'
US 1978 100m Movielab
AIP / Stanley Chase / Pando (Jan Slan)

An independent trucker battles hijackers as well as pressures from a giant trucking firm.
Routine action hokum, a long way behind 1948's *Thieves' Highway* and even less entertaining than TV's *Movin' On*.

w Paul Edwards *d* Peter Carter *ph* René Verzier *m* Paul Hoffert

Peter Fonda, Jerry Reed, Helen Shaver, Chris Wiggins

High Barbaree
US 1947 91m bw
MGM (Everett Riskin)

A pilot crashlands in the Pacific and finds himself drifting towards a Utopian island fancifully described by his favourite uncle.
Thin Hollywood mysticism on Shangri-La lines but without the solid virtues of plot, dialogue and imagination.

w Anne Morrison Chapin, Whitfield Cook, Cyril Hume *d* Jack Conway *ph* Sidney Wagner *m* Herbert Stothart

Van Johnson, June Allyson, Thomas Mitchell, Marilyn Maxwell

The High Bright Sun
GB 1965 114m Technicolor
Rank (Betty Box)
US title: *McGuire Go Home*

In 1957 Cyprus the British army is beleaguered by partisans, and an officer tries to contact a leading rebel.
Confused and boring attempt to make romantic drama out of an intractably sad situation.

w Ian Stuart Black, from his novel *d* Ralph Thomas *ph* Ernest Steward *m* Angelo Lavagnino

Dirk Bogarde, Susan Strasberg, George Chakiris, Denholm Elliott

The High Command*
GB 1936 88m bw
ABFD / Fanfare / Wellesley (Gordon Wellesley)

The general of a West African garrison has a guilty secret known to his young medical officer.
Dated melodrama, rather interestingly performed and directed.

w Katherine Strueby, *novel* The General Goes Too Far by Lewis Robinson *d Thorold Dickinson* *ph* Otto Heller *m* Ernest Irving

James Mason, Lionel Atwill, Lucie Mannheim, Steve Geray, Leslie Perrins

High Conquest
US 1947 79m bw

A young man tries to climb the Matterhorn, on which his father was killed. Unsatisfactory and ill-edited drama filmed partly in Switzerland and Austria. A good cast is largely wasted. Anna Lee, Gilbert Roland, Warren Douglas, Beulah Bondi, C. Aubrey Smith, John Qualen, Helene Thimig. Written by Max Troll and Eben Kandel; directed and produced by Irving Allen; for Monogram.

The High Cost of Loving*
US 1958 87m bw Cinemascope
MGM (Milo O. Frank Jnr)

HIGH ANXIETY. Actor as *auteur*. Mel Brooks pays homage to Hitchcock but does it his way.

A happily married middle class couple have doubts about their future.
Pleasant, mildly satirical romantic comedy which doesn't really get anywhere.

w Rip Van Ronkel *d* Jose Ferrer *ph* George J. Folsey *m* Jeff Alexander

Jose Ferrer, Gena Rowlands, Joanne Gilbert, Jim Backus, Bobby Troup, Philip Ober, Edward Platt, Werner Klemperer

High Flight
GB 1957 102m Technicolor Cinemascope
Columbia / Warwick (Phil C. Samuel)

Cadets train at the Royal Air Force College.
Simple-minded peacetime flagwaver.

w Joseph Landon, Ken Hughes *d* John Gilling *ph* Ted Moore *md* Muir Mathieson *m* Kenneth V. Jones, Douglas Gamley *title march* Eric Coates

Ray Milland, Bernard Lee, Kenneth Haigh, Anthony Newley, Kenneth Fortescue, Sean Kelly, Helen Cherry

High Flyers
US 1937 70m bw
RKO (Lee Marcus)

Two incompetents are duped into smuggling contraband gems.
Feeble finale to the career of two comedians.

w Benny Rubin, Bert Granet, *play* Victor Mapes *d* Edward Cline *ph* Jack Mackenzie *m* Roy Webb *songs* Herman Ruby, Dave Dreyer

Bert Wheeler, Robert Woolsey, Lupe Velez, Marjorie Lord, Margaret Dumont, Jack Carson, Paul Harvey

High Lonesome
US 1950 80m Technicolor

A young man believed to be crazed and homicidal flees into the desert and returns to establish his innocence. Thinly-stretched western not helped by an exhibitionist star performance. John Barrymore Jnr, Chill Wills, Kristine Miller, Lois Butler. Written and directed by Alan Le May; for Eagle Lion.

'When the hands point up . . . the excitement starts!'

High Noon****
US 1952 85m bw
Stanley Kramer

A marshal gets no help when he determines to defend his town against revengeful badmen. A minor western with a soft-pedalled message for the world, this turned out to be a classic simply because it was well done, with every scene and performance clearly worked out. Cinematically it was pared to the bone, and the theme tune helped.

w Carl Foreman, story The Tin Star by John W. Cunningham *d Fred Zinnemann ph Floyd Crosby m Dmitri Tiomkin singer* Tex Ritter

Gary Cooper, Grace Kelly, Thomas Mitchell, Lloyd Bridges, Katy Jurado, Otto Kruger, Lon Chaney, Henry Morgan

'The western form is used for a sneak civics lesson.'—*Pauline Kael, 70s*

'Like nearly all the Kramer productions, this is a neat, well-finished and literate piece of work, though its limitations are more conventional than most.'—*Gavin Lambert*

'A western to challenge *Stagecoach* for the all-time championship.'—*Bosley Crowther*

'A series of crisp and purposeful scenes that interpret each other like the pins on a strategist's war map.'—*Robert L. Hatch*

'It is astonishing how much of the simple western story is told visually by rapid cross-cutting.'—*Films in Review*

'Few recent westerns have gotten so much tension and excitement into the classic struggle between good and evil.'—*Life*

AA: Dmitri Tiomkin; Gary Cooper; title song (*m* Dmitri Tiomkin, *ly* Ned Washington)
AAN: best picture; Carl Foreman; Fred Zinnemann

'They'll never forget the day he drifted into town!'

High Plains Drifter*
US 1972 105m Technicolor Panavision
Universal / Malpaso (Robert Daley)

A mysterious stranger rides into town and terrifies the inhabitants.
Semi-supernatural, mystical revenge western with an overplus of violence. Very watchable, but irritating.

w Ernest Tidyman *d* Clint Eastwood *ph* Bruce Surtees *m* Dee Barton *ad* Henry Bumstead

Clint Eastwood, Verna Bloom, Marianna Hill, Mitch Ryan, Jack Ging

'Ritualized violence and plodding symbolism make for heavy going.'—*Sight and Sound*

'A nervously humorous, self-conscious near-satire on the prototype Eastwood formula.'—*Variety*

High Pressure*
US 1932 74m bw

A would-be tycoon believes there's a fortune to be made in artificial rubber. Amusing con man comedy with good work all round. *William Powell*, Evelyn Brent, George Sidney, Guy Kibbee, Frank McHugh. Written by Joseph Jackson, from Abem Kandel's play *Hot Money*; directed by Mervyn Le Roy; for Warner. 'Well acted, but lacks strength to attract much business.'—*Variety*

High Risk
US 1981 94m colour
American Cinema (Joe Raffill, Gerard Green)

A documentary film-maker enlists three buddies to steal a million dollars from a South American drugs dealer.
Moderately entertaining caper movie which stops too often for action and occasionally for comedy.

wd Stewart Raffill *ph* Alex Phillips Jnr *m* not credited *ed* Tom Walls Jnr

James Brolin, Cleavon Little, Lindsay Wagner, Ernest Borgnine, Bruce Davison, Chick Vennera, Anthony Quinn, James Coburn

High Road to China
US 1983 105m Technicolor
Golden Harvest / Pan Pacific (Fred Weintraub)

In the twenties, an American heiress in Afghanistan has adventures with a drunken flier.
Abysmal attempt to mate James Bond with a cut-price *Raiders of the Lost Ark*. It comes up with nothing at all, and is on the lowest level for continuity, dialogue and direction.

w Sandra Weintraub Roland, S. Lee Pogostin, *novel* Jon Cleary *d* Brian G. Hutton *ph* Ronnie Taylor *m* John Barry *pd* Robert Laing

Tom Selleck, Bess Armstrong, Jack Weston, Robert Morley, Wilford Brimley, Brian Blessed

'An attempt to revive the sort of comedy-adventure romance in which Clark Gable and Jean Harlow would squabble furiously but you knew they were really in love. But as scripted and abominably directed, the thing is as flat as a pancake.'—*Guardian*

High Season
GB 1987 92m colour

A female photographer meets strange friends in Rhodes. Spies, thieves and tourists make an odd lightweight mixture in a movie best suited for tv. Jacqueline Bisset, James Fox, Irene Papas, Sebastian Shaw, Kenneth Branagh, Robert Stephens. Written by Mark and Clare Peploe; directed by Clare Peploe; for British screen, Film Four, Curzon, Michael White, Hemdale.

'The blazing mountain manhunt for Killer Mad-Dog Earle!'

High Sierra*
US 1941 96m bw
Warner (Hal. B. Wallis, Mark Hellinger)

An ex-con gangster plans one last heist in the Californian mountains, but is mortally wounded through his involvement with two women.
Rather dreary action melodrama which gave Bogart his first real star part (after George Raft turned it down). Remade 1955 as *I Died a Thousand Times* (qv); also in 1949 as a western, *Colorado Territory*.

w John Huston, W. R. Burnett, *novel* W. R. Burnett *d Raoul Walsh ph* Tony Gaudio *m* Adolph Deutsch

Humphrey Bogart, Ida Lupino, Joan Leslie, Alan Curtis, Arthur Kennedy, Henry Hull, Henry Travers, Jerome Cowan

'The last swallow, perhaps, of the gangsters' summer.'—*William Whitebait*

'Like it or not, I'll be damned if you leave before the end, or go to sleep.'—*Otis Ferguson*

'As gangster pictures go, this one has everything—speed, excitement, suspense, and that ennobling suggestion of futility which makes for irony and poetry.'—*New York Times*

High Society
US 1956 107m Technicolor Vistavision
MGM (Sol C. Siegel)

A haughty rich girl chooses between several suitors.
Cold, flat, dull musical reworking of *The Philadelphia Story* (qv), with ill-cast performers and just a few bright moments.

w John Patrick *d* Charles Walters *ph* Paul C. Vogel *m / ly* Cole Porter *md* Johnny Green, Saul Chaplin *ad* Cedric Gibbons, Hans Peters

Bing Crosby, Grace Kelly, Frank Sinatra, Celeste Holm, Louis Armstrong, Sidney Blackmer, Margalo Gillmore, Louis Calhern, Lydia Reed, John Lund

Songs include 'Swell Party'; 'High Society'; 'Who Wants to be a Millionaire?'
AAN: Johnny Green, Saul Chaplin; song 'True Love'

High Society Blues
US 1930 102m bw
Fox

A girl ditches a French count in favour of an all-American hero.
Frothy musical romance which did nothing for its stars and is now unwatchable.

w Howard J. Green *d* David Butler *ph* Charles Van Enger *songs* Joe McCarthy, James Hanley

Janet Gaynor, Charles Farrell, William Collier Snr, Hedda Hopper, Louise Fazenda, Lucien Littlefield, Joyce Compton

'Certain to please the average fan . . . commercial product of the first programme grade.'—*Variety*

High Tension
US 1936 63m bw

Exploits of a cable layer in Hawaii. Routine brawling comedy. Brian Donlevy, Norman Foster, Glenda Farrell, Helen Wood, Robert McWade. Written by Lou Breslow, Edward Eliscu and John Patrick; directed by Allan Dwan; for TCF.

The High Terrace
GB 1956 82m bw

A theatrical producer is murdered, and members of the cast protect their leading lady; but she is guilty. Rather solemn, enclosed little mystery which evokes no compulsion to go on watching. Lois Maxwell, Dale Robertson, Derek Bond, Eric Pohlmann, Mary Laura Wood, Lionel Jeffries. Written by Alfred Shaughnessy and Norman Hudis; directed by Henry Cass; for CIPA / Robert S. Baker.

High Tide*
Australia 1987 104m colour

A drunken support pop singer is helped by an adolescent girl and her grandmother. Strongish drama which holds the interest. Judy Davis, Jan Adele, Claudia Karvan, Colin Friels. Written by Laura Jones; directed by *Gillian Armstrong*; for FGH/SJL/Filmpac.

High Tide at Noon
GB 1957 111m bw
Rank (Julian Wintle)

Passions run high among lobster fishermen in Nova Scotia.
Neat, clean romantic melodrama in agreeable surroundings.

w Neil Paterson *d* Philip Leacock *ph* Eric Cross *m* John Veale

Betta St John, Michael Craig, Patrick McGoohan, William Sylvester, Flora Robson, Alexander Knox, Peter Arne, Patrick Allen, Susan Beaumont

High Time
US 1960 103m De Luxe Cinemascope
TCF / Bing Crosby (Charles Brackett)

A middle-aged widower goes back to college.
Flaccid comedy-musical with some undergraduatish jokes.

w Tom and Frank Waldman *d* Blake Edwards *ph* Ellsworth Fredericks *m* Henry Mancini *songs* Sammy Cahn, Jimmy Van Heusen

Bing Crosby, Tuesday Weld, Fabian, Richard Beymer, Nicole Maurey

AAN: song 'The Second Time Around' (*m* Jimmy Van Heusen, *ly* Sammy Cahn)

High Treason
GB 1929 90m bw

In 1940, women unite to prevent a second world war. Tired little prophetic fable with primitive techniques. Jameson Thomas, Benita Hume, Basil Gill, Humberston Wright. Written by L'Estrange Fawcett, from the play by Noel Pemberton-Billing; directed by Maurice Elvey; for Gaumont.

High Treason*
GB 1951 93m bw
GFD / Conqueror (Paul Soskin)

Saboteurs are routed by the London police.
Unconvincing documentary melodrama which moves fast enough to be entertaining.

w Frank Harvey, Roy Boulting *d* Roy Boulting *ph* Gilbert Taylor *m* John Addison

Liam Redmond, André Morell, Anthony Bushell, Kenneth Griffith, Patric Doonan, Joan Hickson, Anthony Nicholls, Mary Morris, Geoffrey Keen, Dora Bryan

High Wall
US 1947 99m bw
MGM (Robert Lord)

A war veteran is put in an asylum after confessing to killing his wife, but later events prove that he was drugged into saying so.
Adequately entertaining, supremely unconvincing mystery melodrama.

w Sydney Boehm *d* Curtis Bernhardt *ph* Paul C. Vogel *m* Bronislau Kaper

Robert Taylor, Herbert Marshall, Audrey Totter, Dorothy Patrick, H. B. Warner, Warner Anderson

High, Wide and Handsome*
US 1937 110m bw
Paramount (Arthur Hornblow Jnr)

Pennsylvania 1859: a travelling showgirl falls in love with a farmer.
Disappointingly stilted period musical with most of the talent ill at ease until the final reel.

w Oscar Hammerstein II *d* Rouben Mamoulian *ph* Victor Milner, Theodore Sparkuhl *ch* LeRoy Prinz *songs* Jerome Kern, Oscar Hammerstein II *md* Boris Morros *ad* Hans Dreier, John Goodman

Irene Dunne, Randolph Scott, Dorothy Lamour, Raymond Walburn, Alan Hale, Elizabeth Patterson, Charles Bickford, William Frawley, Akim Tamiroff, Ben Blue, Irving Pichel, Lucien Littlefield

'Not a road show, but a big picture, and should get nice returns.'—*Variety*

'There are two hours of this long, dumb and dreary picture . . . one is left with a few dim distressing memories.'—*Graham Greene*

'Irene Dunne at her cornball primmest, singing alongside a farmhorse when Randolph Scott isn't around.'—*Pauline Kael, 70s*

A High Wind in Jamaica*
GB 1965 104m De Luxe Cinemascope
TCF (John Croydon)

In Victorian days, English children en route home from Jamaica are captured by pirates and influence their lives.
Semi-serious adventure story with a highly unlikely ending in which the chief pirate allows himself to be executed for a murder committed by a child. There are however pleasures along the way.

w Stanley Mann, Ronald Harwood, Denis Cannan, *novel* Richard Hughes *d* Alexander Mackendrick *ph* Douglas Slocombe *m* Larry Adler

Deborah Baxter, Anthony Quinn, James Coburn, Isabel Dean, Nigel Davenport, Gert Frobe, Lila Kedrova

Higher and Higher*
US 1943 90m bw
RKO (Tim Whelan)

Servants have an elaborate plan to restore the family fortune.
Unamusing musical which undernourishes several talents.

w Jay Dratler, Ralph Spence, *play* Gladys Hurlbut, Joshua Logan *d* Tim Whelan *ph* Robert de Grasse *md* Constantin Bakaleinikoff *songs* Jimmy McHugh, Harold Adamson

Michele Morgan, Jack Haley, *Frank Sinatra*, Leon Errol, Marcy McGuire, *Victor Borge*, Mary Wickes, Barbara Hale, Elizabeth Risdon

AAN: Constantin Bakaleinikoff; song 'I Couldn't Sleep a Wink Last Night (*m* Jimmy McHugh, *ly* Harold Adamson)

'There may be some folks who can't figure out the reasons for Sinatra's meteoric rise, or might be wondering whether he's here to stay or not, but in his first screen starring role he at least gets in no one's way.'—*Variety*

The Highest Honour
Australia 1982 143m colour
aka: *Southern Cross*

In 1942, an Australian spy befriends his captor and finally executioner. Sombre true story, far too long in the telling. John Howard, Atsuo Nakamura, Stuart Wilson, Steve Bisley. Written by Lee Robinson; directed by Peter Maxwell; for Southern International Films.
'Largely fails to ignite.'—*Julian Petley, MFB*

Highlander
GB / US 1986 111m Technicolor
EMI / Highlander (Peter S. Davis, William N. Panzer)

A 14th-century Scotsman apparently dies in battle but finds he is an immortal, and is still crossing swords with his enemy the Kurgan in 20th-century Manhattan.
Muddled, violent and noisy fantasy: the explanation doesn't come until most people will have given up.

w Gregory Widden, Peter Bellwood, Larry Ferguson *d* Russell Mucahy *ph* Gerry Fisher *m* Michael Kamen *pd* Allan Cameron *ed* Peter Honess

Christopher Lambert, Roxanne Hart, Clancy Brown, Sean Connery

'While there are entertaining moments, total work is a mess.'—*Variety*

'A moody combination of *Blade Runner*, *The Terminator* and your last really good nightmare.'—*People*

Highly Dangerous
GB 1950 88m bw
Rank / Two Cities (Anthony Darnborough)

A lady entomologist in a Balkan country is suspected of spying but manages to outwit her enemies.
Odd blend of straight adventure and spoof; it doesn't quite come off.

w Eric Ambler *d* Roy Baker *ph* Reg Wyer *m* Richard Addinsell

Margaret Lockwood, Dane Clark, Marius Goring, Naunton Wayne, Eugene Deckers, Wilfrid Hyde White, Michael Hordern, Gladys Henson

Highpoint
Canada 1984 (filmed 1979) 88m Eastmancolor

An industrialist is on the run from both the Mafia and the CIA. Routine thriller with a finale atop Toronto's CN Tower. Richard Harris, Christopher Plummer, Beverly D'Angelo, Kate Reid, Peter Donat. Written by Richard Guttman, Ian Sutherland; directed by Peter Carter; for Highpoint / New World.

Highway Dragnet
US 1954 71m bw

A lady photographer gives a lift to an ex-marine who may or may not be a murderer. Twisty lower-berth thriller in which all is not as it seems. Joan Bennett, Richard Conte, Wanda Hendrix, Reed Hadley, Mary Beth Hughes, Iris Adrian. Written by Herb Meadow and Jerome Odlum; directed by Nathan Juran; for William F. Broidy / Allied Artists.

Highway 301*
US 1950 83m bw
Warner (Bryan Foy)

The Tri-State Gang is apprehended by police. Actionful gangster melodrama of the *Bonnie and Clyde* type, with plenty of suspenseful situations and slick camerawork.

wd Andrew Stone ph Carl Guthrie
m William Lava

Steve Cochran, Virginia Grey, Gaby Andre, Edmon Ryan, Richard Egan, Robert Webber

'Several good suspense sequences, some good comic observation, and many pleasing visual moments of the wet-streets-at-night category.'—*Richard Mallett, Punch*

The Highwayman
US 1951 82m Cinecolor
Allied Artists / Jack Dietz (Hal. E. Chester)

A 17th-century nobleman disguises himself as a Quaker and becomes a highwayman to right wrongs.
Curious Poverty Row period actioner with ideas generally above its station, not to mention an unexpected tragic ending.

w Jan Jeffries, *poem* Alfred Noyes *d* Lesley Selander *ph* Harry Neumann *m* Herschel Burke Gilbert

Philip Friend, Charles Coburn, Victor Jory, Wanda Hendrix, Cecil Kellaway, Scott Forbes, Virginia Huston, Dan O'Herlihy

Highways by Night
US 1942 62m bw

A millionaire drafts legal resources to round up hi-jackers. Formula thick-ear with romance. Richard Carlson, Jane Randolph, Jane Darwell, Barton Maclane, Ray Collins. Written by Lynn Root and Frank Fenton, from a story by Clarence Budington Kelland; directed by Peter Godfrey; for RKO.

'I want to live like a man—and still be a woman!'

Hilda Crane
US 1956 87m Technicolor
Cinemascope
TCF (Herbert B. Swope Jnr)

An unhappy woman marries for the third time and convinces herself it won't work.
Emotional melodrama of the old school: very moderate in all departments.

wd Philip Dunne, *play* Samson Raphaelson
ph Joe MacDonald *m* David Raksin

Jean Simmons, Guy Madison, Jean-Pierre Aumont, *Evelyn Varden*, Judith Evelyn, Peggy Knudsen

'They went up like men! They came down like animals!'

The Hill**
GB 1965 122m bw
MGM / Seven Arts (Kenneth Hyman)

Prisoners rebel against the harsh discipline of a British military detention centre in North Africa during World War II.
Lurid melodrama which descends fairly quickly into black farce with a number of sweaty actors outshouting each other.
Enjoyable on this level when you can hear the dialogue through the poor sound recording.

w Ray Rigby, from his TV play *d* Sidney Lumet *ph* Oswald Morris *m* none

Sean Connery, Harry Andrews, Michael Redgrave, Ian Bannen, Alfred Lynch, *Ossie Davis*, Roy Kinnear, Jack Watson, Ian Hendry

A Hill in Korea
GB 1956 81m bw
British Lion / Wessex (Anthony Squire)
US title: *Hell in Korea*

During the Korean war, a small patrol guards a hill.
Minor war talk-piece, shot in Surrey and looking it.

w Ian Dalrymple, Anthony Squire, Ronald Spencer, *novel* Max Catto *d* Julian Amyes *ph* Freddie Francis *m* Malcolm Arnold

George Baker, Harry Andrews, Stanley Baker, Michael Medwin, Ronald Lewis, Stephen Boyd, Victor Maddern, Harry Landis

'Character is adequately sketched into a suitably laconic script.'—*MFB*

Hill 24 Doesn't Answer
Israel 1954 101m bw
Sikor (Thorold Dickinson, Peter Frye)

Four friends defend Hill 24 against the Arabs on the eve of the cease-fire, and are all killed. Israel's first feature film, a curious amalgam of the slick and the amateur, with long flashbacks which make it resemble *The Bridge of San Luis Rey*.

w Zvi Kolitz, Peter Frye, Joanna and Thorold Dickinson *d* Thorold Dickinson *ph* Gerald Gibbs *m* Paul Ben-Haim

Michael Wager, Edward Mulhare, Haya Hararit, Arie Lavi, Michael Shilo

The Hills Have Eyes
US 1977 90m Movielab

Holidaymakers are waylaid and killed by a family of desert cannibals. Low-grade shocker which mysteriously achieved some cult status. John Steadman, Janus Blythe, Arthur King, Russ Grieve. Written and directed by Wes Craven; for Blood Relations. 'Simultaneously risible and nauseating.'—*Tim Pulleine, MFB.*

The Hills of Home
US 1948 95m Technicolor

A doctor returns to his Scottish village to practise medicine, and brings his faithful collie. Adequate addition to the Lassie saga, with competent work all round. Edmund Gwenn, Tom Drake, Donald Crisp, Rhys Williams, Reginald Owen. Written by William Ludwig; directed by Fred Wilcox; for MGM. (GB title: *Master of Lassie*.)

The Hindenburg*
US 1975 125m Technicolor
Panavision
Universal / Filmmakers (Robert Wise)

In 1937, sabotage causes the airship Hindenburg to crash on arrival at New York. An extremely uninteresting guess at the cause of this famous disaster. The plot and dialogue are leaden, and such actors as have more than a couple of lines look extremely glum. The special effects, however, are fine despite curious blue-rinse photographic processing.

w Nelson Gidding, *novel* Michael M. Mooney
d Robert Wise *ph* Robert Surtees
pd Edward Carfagno *sp Albert Whitlock*
m David Shire

George C. Scott, Anne Bancroft, Burgess Meredith, William Atherton, Roy Thinnes, Gig Young, Charles Durning, Robert Clary, René Auberjonois

'The tackiest disaster movie yet—a cheap and chaotic collage of painted drops, wooden actors and not-so-special effects that manages to make one of this century's most sensational real-life catastrophes seem roughly as terrifying as a badly stubbed toe.'—*Frank Rich*

AAN: Robert Surtees

Hindle Wakes
GB 1952 82m bw

A Lancashire millgirl spends a week at Blackpool with the master's son but causes a scandal when she refuses to marry him. Modestly competent version of a semi-classic play about class distinctions. Lisa Daniely, Leslie Dwyer, Brian Worth, Sandra Dorne, Ronald Adam. Written by John Baines, from the play by Stanley Houghton; directed by Arthur Crabtree; for Monarch. (US title: *Holiday Week*.) (NB: A probably better, but unavailable version was made in 1931 by Victor Saville for Gaumont, with Belle Chrystall, Edmund Gwenn, John Stuart, Ruth Peterson, Norman McKinnel and Sybil Thorndike.)

Hips Hips Hooray
US 1934 68m bw

Two salesmen pitch flavoured lipstick to a beauty parlour chain. Tired star comedy. Bert Wheeler, Robert Woolsey, Ruth Etting, Thelma Todd, Dorothy Lee, George Meeker. Written by Harry Ruby and Bert Kalmar; directed by Mark Sandrich; for RKO. 'Femme display chief asset.'—*Variety*

The Hired Hand
US 1971 93m Technicolor
Universal / Pando (William Hayward)

Two western drifters avenge the killing of their friend and settle down to work on a farm; but violence follows them.

A potentially enjoyable small-scale western is spoiled by pretentious direction and effects which bore the spectator to death.

w Alan Sharp *d* Peter Fonda *ph* Vilmos Zsigmond *m* Bruce Langhorne

Peter Fonda, Warren Oates, Verna Bloom, Severn Darden

'The first slow-motion western, with endless artsy photography not quite succeeding in obscuring the rambling plot.'—*Judith Crist, 1973*

'When a film begins with a "lyrical" shot, your heart has a right to sink.'—*Stanley Kauffmann*

Hired Wife
US 1940 96m bw

A secretary who loves her boss saves his company by marrying him so that it can be transferred to her name. After which the plot has absolutely nowhere to go. Rosalind Russell, Brian Aherne, Virgina Bruce, Robert Benchley, John Carroll, Hobart Cavanagh. Written by Richard Connell and Gladys Lehman; directed by William A. Seiter; for Universal.

The Hireling*
GB 1973 108m colour
Columbia / World Film Services (Ben Arbeid)

In the twenties, a lady's chauffeur falls in love with her.
Talkative drama, elegant but not much fun.

w Wolf Mankowitz, *novel* L. P. Hartley *d Alan Bridges* *ph* Michael Reed *m* Marc Wilkinson *pd Natasha Kroll*

Sarah Miles, Robert Shaw, Peter Egan, Elizabeth Sellars, Caroline Mortimer

Hiroshima Mon Amour*
France / Japan 1959 91m bw
Argos / Comei / Pathé / Daiei

A French actress working in Hiroshima falls for a Japanese architect and remembers her tragic love for a German soldier during the occupation.
Jumbled mixture of flashbacks and flashforwards which can now be recognized as typical of this director and on its first appearance was hailed as a work of art in an innovative new style.

w Marguerite Duras *d Alain Resnais* *ph* Sacha Vierny, Takahashi Michio *m* Giovanni Fusco, Georges Delerue

Emmanuele Riva, Eiji Okada

AAN: Marguerite Duras

His and Hers
GB 1960 90m bw

An author gets lost with the Bedouin while on a research trip, and by the time he gets home his personality is transformed. The thinnest of comedy ideas becomes a film of almost no substance at all. Terry-Thomas, Janette Scott, Wilfrid Hyde White, Nicole Maurey, Joan Sims, Kenneth Connor, Kenneth Williams, Meier Tzelniker, Joan Hickson, Colin Gordon, Oliver Reed, Francesca Annis. Written by Stanley Mann and Jan and Mark Lowell; directed by Brian Desmond Hurst; for Hal E. Chester / Eros.

His Brother's Wife
US 1936 91m bw
MGM (Lawrence Weingarten)

A young scientist is helped out of trouble by his brother, on condition he disappears; the brother then weds the scientist's girl friend.
Heavy romantic melodrama containing everything including jungle fever, flung together to take advantage of the stars' real-life romance.

w Leon Gordon, John Meehan, *story* George Auerbach *d* W. S. Van Dyke II *ph* Oliver T. Marsh *m* Franz Waxman

Robert Taylor, Barbara Stanwyck, Joseph Calleia, John Eldredge, Jean Hersholt, Samuel S. Hinds, Leonard Mudie, Jed Prouty

His Butler's Sister*
US 1943 94m bw
Universal (Felix Jackson)

A temporary maid falls for her sophisticated boss.
Pleasant comedy musical: no great shakes, but the principals give the air of enjoying themselves.

w Samuel Hoffenstein, Betty Reinhardt *d* Frank Borzage *ph* Elwood Bredell *m* Hans Salter

Deanna Durbin, Franchot Tone, Pat O'Brien, Evelyn Ankers, Walter Catlett, Alan Mowbray, Akim Tamiroff, Else Janssen, Iris Adrian

His Double Life*
US 1933 63m bw

A famous painter, when his valet dies, takes his identity. Adequate transcription of an Arnold Bennett novel later redone as *Holy Matrimony*. Roland Young, Lillian Gish, Lumsden Hare, Lucy Beaumont. Written by Arthur Ellis; directed by Arthur Hopkins; for Eddie Dowling / Paramount. 'Pleasant little film; big grosses unlikely.'—*Variety*

His Excellency
GB 1951 84m bw
Ealing (Michael Truman)

The Labour government sends a trade union official to govern a Mediterranean colony.
Disappointingly tacky-looking and stagebound version of an unpersuasive West End comedy.

w Robert Hamer, W. P. Lipscomb, *play* Dorothy and Campbell Christie *d* Robert Hamer *ph* Douglas Slocombe *m* selections from Handel *md* Ernest Irving

Eric Portman, Cecil Parker, Helen Cherry, Susan Stephen, Edward Chapman, Clive Morton, Robin Bailey, Geoffrey Keen

His Family Tree
US 1935 59m bw

An Irishman migrates to America and gets involved in politics. Lively second feature for the Irish halls. James Barton, Margaret Callahan, Maureen Delany, Addison Randall, William Harrigan. Written by Joel Sayre and John Twist from the play Old Man Murphy by Patrick Kearney and Henry Wagstaff Gribble; directed by Charles Vidor; for RKO. 'With more care, this might have been much better.'—*Variety*

His Girl Friday****
US 1940 92m bw
Columbia (Howard Hawks)

A remake of *The Front Page* (qv), with Hildy Johnson turned into a woman.
Frantic, hilarious black farce with all participants at their best; possibly the fastest comedy ever filmed, and one of the funniest.

w Charles Lederer, play The Front Page by Charles MacArthur, Ben Hecht *d Howard Hawks* *ph* Joseph Walker *m* Sydney Cutner *md* Morris Stoloff

Rosalind Russell, Cary Grant, Ralph Bellamy, Gene Lockhart, Porter Hall, *Ernest Truex,* Cliff Edwards, *Clarence Kolb, Roscoe Karns, Frank Jenks,* Abner Biberman, Frank Orth, John Qualen, Helen Mack, *Billy Gilbert,* Alma Kruger

'The kind of terrific verbal slam-bang that has vanished from current film-making.'—*New Yorker, 1975*

'One of the fastest of all movies, from line to line and from gag to gag.'—*Manny Farber, 1971*

'Overlapping dialogue carries the movie along at breakneck speed; word gags take the place of the sight gags of silent comedy, as this vanished race of brittle, cynical, childish people rush around on corrupt errands.'—*Pauline Kael, 1968*

'The main trouble is that when they made *The Front Page* the first time, it stayed made.'—*Otis Ferguson*

† The Rosalind Russell role had first been turned down by Jean Arthur, Ginger Rogers, Claudette Colbert and Irene Dunne.

His Glorious Night
US 1929 85m bw
MGM
GB title: *Breath of Scandal*

A princess falls in love with a commoner.
Soporific early talkie, remade in 1960 as *A Breath of Scandal.* The movie which first exposed its star's high-pitched voice, it is credited with killing his career.

w Willard Mack, *play* Olimpia by Ferenc Molnar *d* Lionel Barrymore *ph* Percy Hilburn

John Gilbert, Catherine Dale Owen, Hedda Hopper, Gustav von Seyffertitz, Nance O'Neil

His Kind of Woman*
US 1951 120m bw
RKO (Howard Hughes, Robert Sparks)

At a remote Mexican ranch resort, a gangster on the run holds up residents including a fortune-hunting girl and a fading matinee idol.
Agreeable tongue-in-cheek melodrama which slightly outstays its welcome but is generally good fun.

w Frank Fenton, *d* John Farrow *ph* Harry J. Wild *m* Leigh Harline *md* Constantin Bakaleinikoff

Robert Mitchum, Jane Russell, *Vincent Price,* Raymond Burr, Tim Holt, Charles McGraw, Marjorie Reynolds, Jim Backus

His Lordship*
GB 1936 71m bw
Gaumont (S. C. Balcon)
US title: *Man of Affairs*

A politician's twin takes his place to expose an old murder.
Comfortable star comedy-drama.

w Maude Howell, Edwin Greenwood, L. DuGarde Peach, *play* The Nelson Touch by Neil Grant *d* Herbert Mason *ph* Gunther Krampf

George Arliss, Rene Ray, Romilly Lunge, Jessie Winter, Allan Jeayes

His Majesty O'Keefe
GB 1954 90m Technicolor
Warner / Norma (Harold Hecht)

Native islanders are taught by an easygoing mariner how to exploit their natural resources and defend themselves against pirates.
Thin adventure romance with too little for its star to do.

w Borden Chase, James Hill, *novel* Lawrence Kingman and Gerald Green *d* Byron Haskin *ph* Otto Heller *m* Robert Farnon

Burt Lancaster, Joan Rice, André Morell, Abraham Sofaer, Benson Fong, Archie Savage

His Night Out
US 1935 74m bw

A henpecked office help saves the bonds from gangsters. Typical star farce, a remake of *The Mollycoddle.* Edward Everett Horton, Irene Hervey, Robert McWade, Jack La Rue, Willard Robertson. Written by Doris Malloy, Harry Cock; directed by William Nigh; for Universal.

'From the ends of the earth . . . a darling baby brings them together!'
His Woman
US 1931 80m bw
Paramount

The captain of a tramp freighter finds himself in charge of an abandoned baby and a runaway girl.
Slow, indifferent comedy drama, previously filmed in 1929 as *Sal of Singapore.*

w Adelaide Heilbron, Melville Baker, *novel* The Sentimentalist by Dale Collins *d* Edward Sloman *ph* William Steiner, Arthur Ellis

Gary Cooper, Claudette Colbert, Averill Harris, Richard Spiro, Douglass Dumbrille, Joseph Calleia, Harry Davenport

'Actionless picture . . . too many barnacles cling to the script.'—*Variety*

Une Histoire D'Amour*
France 1951 95m bw
Jacques Roitfeld / Cité Films
GB title: *Love Story*

A police inspector discovers that a young couple killed themselves because of parental opposition.
A rather soggy little drama made watchable by its careful detail and immaculate leading performance.

w Michel Audiard *d* Robert Clavel *ph* Louis Page *m* Paul Misraki

Louis Jouvet, Daniel Gélin, Dany Robin

History Is Made at Night*
US 1937 97m bw
Walter Wanger

A divorcee and her new love have trouble from her ex-husband.
Atmospheric, artificial, generally entertaining romantic comedy-drama of a kind which went out of fashion long ago.

w Gene Towne, Graham Baker *d* Frank Borzage *ph* Gregg Toland *m* Alfred Newman

Charles Boyer, Jean Arthur, *Leo Carrillo*, Colin Clive

'A weird and unbelievable melodrama . . . mildly entertaining with good scenes.'—*Variety*

'So souped up with demonic passions and tender glances and elegant photography that it's rather fun.'—*New Yorker, 1978*

'Frank Borzage, who could turn *Frankenstein Meets the Wolf Man* into a romantic reverie, is quite undeterred by the venality rampant in the script and interjects his vision of what Andrew Sarris called love over probability. Oh, there's an iceberg disaster too.'—*Kit Parker catalogue*

The History of Mr Polly*
GB 1949 94m bw
GFD / Two Cities (John Mills)

A draper's assistant buys a small shop but tires of his nagging wife and decides the time has come for a change.
Patchy but generally amusing version of a popular comic novel, very English and rather appealingly done.

w Anthony Pelissier, *novel* H. G. Wells *d Anthony Pelissier ph Desmond Dickinson* *m* William Alwyn

John Mills, Sally Ann Howes, Megs Jenkins, Finlay Currie, Betty Ann Davies, Edward Chapman

History of the World Part One
US 1981 92m De Luxe Panavision
Brooksfilms (Mel Brooks)

Episodes from world history are presented with the author's usual lack of taste or wit: a woeful collection of schoolboy scatology.

wd Mel Brooks *ph* Woody Omens, Paul Wilson *m* John Morris

Mel Brooks, Dom De Luise, Madeleine Kahn, Cloris Leachman, Harvey Korman, Ron Carey, Sid Caesar, Pamela Stephenson, Henny Youngman

'Most of the time it's just expensive sets sitting around waiting for Brooks to do something funny in front of them.'—*Roger Ebert*

Hit!
US 1973 134m Technicolor Panavision
Paramount (Harry Korshak)

A federal agent takes personal action against a drug ring which caused his daughter's death.
Black vigilante melodrama, very violent and interminably padded out with irrelevancies.

w Alan Trustman, David M. Wolf *d* Sidney J. Furie *ph* John A. Alonzo *m* Lalo Schifrin

Billy Dee Williams, Richard Pryor, Paul Hampton, Gwen Welles

'No more under-the-armpit shots, but obscurity is still the keynote of this Sidney Furie effort in the urban vigilante genre.'—*Sight and Sound*

The Hit
GB 1984 98m Technicolor
Zenith / Central / The Recorded Picture Company (Jeremy Thomas)

A supergrass hiding in Spain is sought by two gang executioners.
Old hat thuggery shown in new-style detail. Violently suspenseful but not otherwise interesting.

w Peter Prince *d* Stephen Frears *ph* Mike Molloy *m* Paco de Lucia *pd* Andrew Sanders

John Hurt, Terence Stamp, Tim Roth, Laura del Sol, Fernando Rey, Bill Hunter

'Sensitive editing and seductive camerawork can't disguise that the exercise is heading nowhere, a road movie without fuel.'—*Philip Strick, MFB*

The Hit Parade
US 1937 77m bw

An agent tries to get a new star into radio. An excuse for a line-up of acts, some quite tolerable. Frances Langford, Phil Regan, Louise Henry, Pert Kelton, Al Pearce, Ed Brophy, William Demarest, Duke Ellington and his Band, Eddy Duchin and his Band, Max Terhune, Monroe Owsley, Inez Courtney, the Tic Toc Girls. Written by Bradford Ropes and Sam Ornitz; directed by Gus Meins; for Nat Levin / Republic. 'Should gather plenty of de luxe dates . . . the tempo guarantees that the average fan will find it diverting.'—*Variety*

Hit Parade of 1941
US 1940 83m bw

The young owner of a radio station subs his singer girlfriend for the sponsor's daughter. Moderate musical in need of a better script. Kenny Baker, Frances Langford, Hugh Herbert, Mary Boland, Ann Miller, Patsy Kelly, Phil Silvers, Sterling Holloway, Donald MacBride, Barnett Parker, Franklin Pangborn, Six Hits and a Miss, Borrah Minevitch and his Harmonica Rascals. Written by Bradford Ropes, F. Hugh Herbert (no relation) and Maurice Leo; directed by John H. Auer; for Sol C. Siegel / Republic.
AAN: Cy Feuer (music); song 'Who Am I?' (*m* Jule Styne, *ly* Walter Bullock)

Hit Parade of 1943
US 1943 90m bw

A plagiaristic songwriter becomes a model swain. Lively comedy musical, third and best of the series. John Carroll, Susan Hayward, Gail Patrick, Eve Arden, Melville Cooper, Walter Catlett, Mary Treen, Tom Kennedy, Dorothy Dandridge, the Golden Gate Quartet, Count Basie and his orchestra. Written by Frank Gill Jnr; directed by Albert S. Rogell; for Albert J. Cohen / Republic.
AAN: Walter Scharf (music)

Hit Parade of 1947
US 1947 90m bw
A struggling songwriter tries in vain to become sophisticated. Tolerable musical jamboree with too thin a storyline. Eddie Albert, Constance Moore, Joan Edwards, Gil Lamb, Bill Goodwin, William Frawley, Richard Lane, Roy Rogers and Trigger, Woody Herman and his orchestra. Written by Mary Loos and Parke Levy; directed and produced by Frank McDonald; for Republic.

Hit the Deck
US 1930 93m bw (colour sequences)
Navy recruits have girl trouble. Lumpy production of a stage musical already well worn. Jack Oakie, Polly Walker, Roger Gray, Harry Sweet. No writer credit; directed by Luther Reed; for RKO. 'No reason why this one should run into trouble on week stands or less.'—*Variety*

Hit the Deck
US 1954 112m Eastmancolor Cinemascope
MGM (Joe Pasternak)
Romantic adventures of three sailors on shore leave in San Francisco.
Boring situations and performances reduce the temperature of this youth musical which is not another *On the Town.*
w Sonya Levien, William Ludwig, *musical play* Herbert Fields, *novel* Shore Leave by Hubert Osborn *ph* George Folsey *m* Vincent Youmans *ly* Leo Robin *ch* Hermes Pan
Tony Martin, Jane Powell, Ann Miller, Debbie Reynolds, Walter Pidgeon, Vic Damone, Gene Raymond

Hitch-hike Lady
US 1935 77m bw
An English housekeeper saves enough money to visit her son in the US, not aware that he is in San Quentin. Easy-going sentimental comedy, shot on the road. Alison Skipworth, Arthur Treacher, Mae Clarke, James Ellison, Warren Hymer, Beryl Mercer. Written by Gordon Rigby and Lester Cole from a story by Wallace MacDonald; directed by Aubrey Scotto; for Republic. 'Happy intermingling of humour and heart tugs.'—*Variety*

Hitler
US 1961 107m bw
Three Crown / E. Charles Straus
A sex-oriented, semi-fictional biopic of the German dictator, from the murder of his niece to his final madness and suicide.
Enterprising sensationalism which deserves a nod for sheer audacity.
w Sam Neuman *d* Stuart Heisler *ph* Joseph Biroc *m* Hans Salter
Richard Basehart, Maria Emo, Martin Kosleck, John Banner

Hitler—Beast of Berlin
US 1939 87m bw
A spy among Hitler's storm troopers escapes to Switzerland. Feeble exploitation item which succeeded only as propaganda. Hitler is not seen. Roland Drew, Steffi Duna, Alan Ladd, Greta Granstedt, Lucien Prival. Written by Shepard Traube from his story Goose Step; directed by Sherman Scott; for PRC. 'There are doubtless powerful pictures to be made on the anti-Nazi theme, but this isn't one.'—*Variety* (aka: *Beasts of Berlin.*)

Hitler—Dead or Alive
US 1942 72m bw
Three Alcatraz graduates try to collect a prize for the capture of Hitler. Silly mix of farce and propaganda. Ward Bond, Dorothy Tree, Warren Hymer, Paul Fix, Russell Hicks, Bobby Watson. Written by Sam Neumann and Karl Brown; directed by Nick Grinde; for Ben Judell / Charles House.

'More morphine for Herr Goering! The greatest gangster picture of all!'
'Did Hitler kill the one woman he loved? What was Hess to Hitler?'

The Hitler Gang**
US 1944 101m bw
Paramount (B. G. De Sylva)
The rise to power of Hitler and his henchmen. Though at the time it seemed rather like a serious cabaret turn, this fictionalization of historical fact has some good impersonations and dramatically effective scenes.
w Frances Goodrich, Albert Hackett *d John Farrow* *ph* Ernest Laszlo *m* David Buttolph
Robert Watson, Martin Kosleck (Goebbels), Victor Varconi (Hess), Luis Van Rooten (Himmler), Alexander Pope (Goering), Roman Bohnen, Ivan Triesault, Helene Thimig, Reinhold Schunzel, Sig Rumann, Alexander Granach

Hitler—The Last Ten Days
GB / Italy 1973 104m Technicolor
MGM / Wolfgang Reinhardt / Westfilm
With Adolf and Eva in the bunker.
Claustrophobic historical reconstruction with an uncomfortable star.
w Ennio de Concini, Maria Pia Fusco, Wolfgang Reinhardt, Ivan Moffat *d* Ennio de Concini *ph* Ennio Guarnieri *m* Mischa Spoliansky
Alec Guinness, Simon Ward, Doris Kunstmann, Adolfo Celi, Diane Cilento, Eric Porter, Joss Ackland

Hitler's Children*
US 1943 83m bw
RKO (Edward A. Golden)
A family reacts to Hitler and the Hitler Youth. Artificial melodrama set in an unlikely Germany but successful at the time because of its topicality and its refusal to play the Nazis as idiots, which was the usual Hollywood line.
w Emmet Lavery, *book* Education for Death by Gregor Ziemer *d* Edward Dmytryk *ph* Russell Metty *m* Roy Webb
Tim Holt, Bonita Granville, Otto Kruger, Kent Smith, H. B. Warner, Lloyd Corrigan, Erford Gage, Gavin Muir, Hans Conried
'A curiously compromised production . . . strong anti-Nazi propaganda, it has not been woven into a defined and moving show.'—*Howard Barnes, New York Herald Tribune*
'The truth about the Nazis from the cradle to the battlefront!'—*publicity*

Hitler's Madman*
US 1943 84m bw
(MGM) PRC / Seymour Nebenzal
aka: *Hitler's Hangman*
Heydrich is assassinated in Czechoslovakia and the Nazis take revenge on the village of Lidice.
Cheapjack sensationalism based on a horrifying incident of World War II; despite its imperfections it generates a certain raw power.
w Peretz Hirshbein, Melvin Levy, Doris Malloy *d* Douglas Sirk *m* Karl Hajos
Patricia Morison, *John Carradine,* Alan Curtis, Ralph Morgan, Ludwig Stossel, Edgar Kennedy, Al Shean, Jimmy Conlin, Blanche Yurka, Victor Kilian
'Newspaper accounts of the bombing of German cities will be pleasant antidotes for the unhappy feeling brought on by the final grim scenes of *Hitler's Madman.'—New York Herald Tribune*
'Even in its poorly depicted scenes of brutality, it inflames a common anger.'—*Theodore Strauss, New York Times*

HMS Defiant*
GB 1962 101m Technicolor Cinemascope
Columbia / GW (John Brabourne)
US title: *Damn the Defiant*
Mutiny erupts on an 18th-century British sailing ship.
Rather unpleasant and unenterprising sea fare reminiscent of the goings-on aboard the *Bounty*. Well enough staged and acted but not very remarkable or memorable.
w Nigel Kneale, Edmund H. North, *novel* Mutiny by Frank Tilsley *d* Lewis Gilbert *ph* Christopher Challis *m* Clifton Parker
Alec Guinness, Dirk Bogarde, Anthony Quayle, Tom Bell, Nigel Stock, Murray Melvin, Victor Maddern, Maurice Denham, Walter Fitzgerald
'It authentically if superficially recreates the days of press gangs, maggots and the cat.'—*Peter John Dyer*

Hobson's Choice***
GB 1953 107m bw
British Lion / London (Norman Spencer)
In the 1890s a tyrannical Lancashire bootmaker is brought to heel by his plain-speaking daughter and her simple-minded husband.
Brilliantly played version of a famous working-class comedy, memorably set and photographed; one regrets only the slight decline of the predictable third act.

w Norman Spencer, Wynard Browne, *play* Harold Brighouse *d David Lean ph Jack Hildyard m Malcolm Arnold ad Wilfrid Shingleton*

Charles Laughton, Brenda de Banzie, John Mills, Richard Wattis, Helen Haye, Daphne Anderson, Prunella Scales

† Previously filmed in 1931 by Thomas Bentley for BIP from a screenplay by Frank Launder, with James Harcourt, Viola Lyel and Frank Pettingell.

'Hope never dies for a man with a good dirty mind.'

Hoffman

GB 1970 113m Technicolor
ABP / Longstone (Ben Arbeid)

A middle-aged misfit blackmails a typist into spending a week with him.
Interminable sex comedy padded out from a short TV play; it quickly becomes claustrophobic, tasteless, and boring.

w Ernest Gebler, from his novel and play *d* Alvin Rakoff *ph* Gerry Turpin *m* Ron Grainer

Peter Sellers, Sinead Cusack, Jeremy Bulloch, Ruth Dunning

Hog Wild***

US 1930 20m bw

Stan helps Ollie to put a radio aerial on the roof of his house. Brilliantly sustained slapstick makes this one of the best star comedies of Laurel and Hardy. Written by H. M. Walker and Leo McCarey; directed by James Parrott; for Hal Roach.

The Holcroft Covenant

GB 1985 112m colour
EMI / Ely and Edie Landau

One of the architects of Hitler's Third Reich leaves a bequest which may fall into the wrong hands.
Muddled political thriller which tends to provoke unintended laughs.

w George Axelrod, Edward Anhalt, John Hopkins *novel* Robert Ludlum *d* John Frankenheimer *ph* Gerry Fisher *m* Stanislas *pd* Peter Mullins

Michael Caine, Anthony Andrews, Victoria Tennant, Lilli Palmer, Mario Adorf, Michael Lonsdale, Bernard Hepton

'A narrative deficient in thrills or plausibility.'—*Variety*

'Master of love! He is to all women what each desires him to be!'

Hold Back the Dawn*

US 1941 115m bw
Paramount (Arthur Hornblow Jnr)

A would-be immigrant into the US via Mexico marries a schoolteacher he does not love.
Surprisingly effective romantic melodrama with a nice style and some mordant lines in the script.

w Charles Brackett, Billy Wilder d Mitchell Leisen ph Leo Tover m Victor Young

Charles Boyer, Olivia de Havilland, Paulette Goddard, Victor Francen, Walter Abel, Curt Bois, Rosemary de Camp, Nestor Paiva, Mitchell Leisen

'All those years with all the others I closed my eyes and thought of you.'—*sample dialogue spoken by Paulette Goddard*

'It has all the vitamins for mass popular appeal.'—*Variety*

† The story is told by Boyer to Mitchell Leisen on a film set where he has just shot a scene from *I Wanted Wings*.

AAN: best picture; Charles Brackett, Billy Wilder; Leo Tover; Victor Young; Olivia de Havilland

Hold Back the Night

US 1956 80m bw

From World War II to Korea, a marine commander carries with him a lucky whisky bottle. Pointlessly titled war heroics, competently mounted. John Payne, Mona Freeman, Peter Graves, Chuck Connors, Audrey Dalton. Written by John C. Higgins and Walter Doniger, from the novel by Pat Frank; directed by Allan Dwan; for Allied Artists.

Hold Back Tomorrow

US 1956 75m bw

A convicted killer's last request is for a woman to spend his last night with him. They fall in love before he is executed. A ripe example of the higher tosh, indifferently made and acted. Cleo Moore, John Agar, Frank de Kova, Dallas Boyd. Written, directed and produced by Hugo Haas; for Universal-International.

Hold 'em Yale

US 1935 61m bw

Four con men find themselves looking after a disinherited heiress. Thin filming of a Damon Runyon story; strictly supporting material. Patricia Ellis, Cesar Romero, Larry Crabbe, William Frawley, Andy Devine, George E. Stone, Warren Hymer. Written by Paul Gerard Smith, Eddie Welch; directed by Sidney Lanfield; for Paramount.

Hold Everything

US 1930 78m Technicolor

A comedian becomes a prizefighter. Pleasant comedy musical which established Joe E. Brown in Hollywood, as it had established Bert Lahr on stage. Joe E. Brown, Winnie Lightner, Georges Carpentier, Sally O'Neill, Bert Roach. From the play by B. G. De Sylva and John McGowan, adapted by Robert Lord; directed by Roy del Ruth; for Warners. 'Pip laugh picture, the best comedy Warners has turned out since talkers came in.'—*Variety*

Hold That Blonde

US 1945 75m bw
Paramount (Paul Jones)

A psychiatrist suggests that romance may cure a kleptomaniac, but the patient unfortunately chooses a jewel thief.
Thin comedy which erupts into frantic farce, with some energetic slapstick and a Harold Lloyd style finale.

w Walter de Leon, Earl Baldwin, E. Edwin Moran *d* George Marshall *ph* Daniel L. Fapp *m* Werner Heymann

Eddie Bracken, Veronica Lake, Albert Dekker, Frank Fenton, George Zucco, Donald MacBride, Norma Varden, Willie Best

Hold That Co-Ed*

US 1938 80m bw
TCF (David Hempstead)
GB title: *Hold That Girl*

A girl dressed as a boy wins a university football match and thereby helps a governor get re-elected.
Intriguingly-cast crazy comedy which works up into a fine frenzy.

w Karl Tunberg, Don Ettinger, Jack Yellen *d* George Marshall *ph* Robert Planck *md* Arthur Lange

John Barrymore, Joan Davis, George Murphy, Marjorie Weaver, Jack Haley, George Barbier, Donald Meek, Johnny Downs, Guinn Williams

'On the wacky side and fairly amusing, but not quite making the big league.'—*Variety*

Hold That Ghost*

US 1941 86m bw
Universal (Burt Kelly, Glenn Tryon)

A group of strangers are stranded in an apparently haunted house.
Long thought of as Abbott and Costello's best comedy, this now seems pretty strained and slow to start, but it has its classic moments.

w Robert Lees, Fred Rinaldo, John Grant *d* Arthur Lubin *ph* Elwood Bredell, Joe Valentine *m* Hans Salter

Bud Abbott, Lou Costello, Joan Davis, the Andrews Sisters, Richard Carlson, *Ted Lewis* and his band, Evelyn Ankers, Marc Lawrence, Mischa Auer

Hold That Kiss

US 1938 75m bw

A man and woman each believe the other to be wealthy. Elementary comedy of misunderstandings, of no abiding interest. Maureen O'Sullivan, Dennis O'Keefe, Mickey Rooney, George Barbier, Jessie Ralph, Ed Brophy. Written by Stanley Rauh; directed by Edwin S. Marin; for MGM. 'Pleasant but undistinguished.'—*Variety*

Hold Your Man*

US 1933 89m bw
MGM (Sam Wood)

A hard-boiled young woman falls for a confidence man, has his baby, and waits for him to emerge from prison.
Briskly-fashioned star comedy-drama with entertaining moments.

w Anita Loos, Howard Emmett Rogers *d* Sam Wood *ph* Harold Rosson *songs* Nacio Herb Brown (*m*), Arthur Freed (*ly*)

Jean Harlow, Clark Gable, Stuart Erwin, Dorothy Burgess, Muriel Kirkland, Paul Hurst

'A real money picture . . . most promising box office prospect in months.'—*Variety*

'The sudden transition from wise-cracking romance to sentimental penitence provides a jolt.'—*Frank S. Nugent*

The Hole*
France / Italy 1959 123m bw
Play-Art / Filmsonor / Titanus (Serge Silberman)
original title: *Le Trou*

Four convicts in a Paris prison dig a tunnel to freedom and almost make it.
Meticulous escape drama nicely shot in very limited sets: hypnotic for those with the patience to adjust to its pace.

w Jacques Becker, José Giovanni, Jean Aurel, *novel* José Giovanni *d* Jacques Becker *ph* Ghislain Cloquet

Philippe Leroy, Mark Michel, Jean Kéraudy, Michel Constantine

A Hole in the Head*
US 1959 120m De Luxe Cinemascope
UA / Sincap (Frank Sinatra)

A Miami hotelier is threatened with foreclosure and tries to raise the money from his provident elder brother.
Easy-going comedy without much point, but various amusing facets artfully deployed.

w Arnold Shulman, from his TV and stage play *d* Frank Capra *ph* William H. Daniels *m* Nelson Riddle

Frank Sinatra, Edward G. Robinson, Eleanor Parker, Eddie Hodges, Carolyn Jones, Thelma Ritter, Keenan Wynn, Joi Lansing

AA: song 'High Hopes' (*m* Jimmy Van Heusen, *ly* Sammy Cahn)

The Hole in the Wall
US 1929 73m bw
Paramount

A gangster falls for a phony fortune teller on a revenge scheme.
Involved melodrama, a primitive talkie notable chiefly for its stars.

w Pierre Collings, *play* Fred Jackson *d* Robert Florey *ph* George Folsey

Edward G. Robinson, Claudette Colbert, David Newell, Nelly Savage, Donald Meek, Louise Closser Hale

Holiday*
US 1930 99m bw
Pathe (E. B. Derr)

A bright-minded rich girl steals her sister's fiancé, a struggling young lawyer.
Competent early talkie version of a hit play.

w Horace Jackson, *play* Philip Barry *d* Edward H. Griffith *ph* Norbert Brodine *m* Josiah Zuro

Ann Harding, Robert Ames, Mary Astor, Edward Everett Horton, Hedda Hopper, Monroe Owsley, William Holden

'A comedy of wide appeal in a finished style.'—*Variety*

AAN: Horace Jackson; Ann Harding

'So daring—so tender—so human—so true—that everyone in love will want to see it!'

Holiday***
US 1938 93m bw
Columbia (Everett Riskin)
GB titles: *Free to Live; Unconventional Linda*

Elegant, highly successful remake of the above; still a stage play on film, but subtly devised to make the very most of the lines and performances.

w Donald Ogden Stewart d George Cukor ph Franz Planer *m* Sidney Cutner

Katharine Hepburn, Cary Grant, Doris Nolan, *Edward Everett Horton* (same role), *Ruth Donnelly, Lew Ayres*, Henry Kolker, Binnie Barnes

'Corking comedy . . . exhibitors will pencil in some extra days.'—*Variety*

'The comedy is full of the best of humour, edged with pathos never allowed to drop into sentimentality. It is played with the greatest cheerfulness and a winning skill.'—*Arthur Pollock, Brooklyn Daily Eagle*

'I suppose actually it is a neat and sometimes elegant job, but under its surface of too much brightness and too many words it seems so deadly bored and weary. Hell, save your money and yawn at home.'—*Otis Ferguson*

'Played with the greatest cheerfulness and a winning skill.'—*Brooklyn Daily Eagle*

Holiday Affair
US 1949 87m bw
RKO (Don Hartman)

A young widow falls for an easy-going boat builder.
Flimsy star-shaped romantic comedy with nice touches.

w Isobel Lennart *d* Don Hartman *ph* Milton Krasner *m* Roy Webb

Robert Mitchum, Janet Leigh, Wendell Corey, Griff Barnett, Esther Dale, Gordon Gebert, Henry O'Neill, Harry Morgan

Holiday Camp*
GB 1947 97m bw
GFD / Gainsborough (Sydney Box)

At a summer holiday camp, a murderer on the prowl affects people's enjoyment in various ways.
Seminal compendium comedy drama, a bore in itself but establishing several post-war norms of the British cinema, including the Huggetts.

w Muriel and Sidney Box, Ted Willis, Peter Rogers, Mabel and Denis Constanduros *d* Ken Annakin *ph* Jack Cox

Jack Warner, Kathleen Harrison, Flora Robson, Dennis Price, Hazel Court, Emrys Jones, Yvonne Owen, Esmond Knight, Jimmy Hanley, Peter Hammond, Esma Cannon, John Blythe, Susan Shaw

'It is real—and true—and it will be a smash at the box office.'—*Sunday Chronicle*

Holiday for Lovers
US 1959 103m De Luxe Cinemascope
TCF (David Weisbart)

To distract his teenage daughter from boys, a Boston psychiatrist organizes a family holiday in South America.
Frail old-fashioned family comedy with entirely predictable situations culminating in a drunk scene for stuffy father.

w Luther Davis *d* Henry Levin *ph* Charles G. Clarke *m* Leigh Harline

Clifton Webb, Jane Wyman, Paul Henreid, Carol Lynley, Jill St John, Gary Crosby, José Greco

Holiday for Sinners
US 1952 72m bw
MGM (John Houseman)

In New Orleans during the Mardi Gras three old friends meet crises in their lives.
Slightly curious but not very interesting portmanteau drama.

w A. I. Bezzerides, *novel* Hamilton Basso *d* Gerald Mayer *ph* Paul Vogel *md* Alberto Columbo

Gig Young, Keenan Wynn, Janice Rule, Richard Anderson, William Campbell, Michael Chekhov, Sandro Giglio, Edith Barrett, Porter Hall

'It gives an impression of blurred, rather heavy-going sincerity.'—*MFB*

Holiday in Mexico
US 1946 127m Technicolor
MGM (Joe Pasternak)

The daughter of the American Ambassador to Mexico falls for Jose Iturbi.
Travel brochure musical in which the occasional plums do not redeem the sogginess of the pudding.

w Isobel Lennart *d* George Sidney *ph* Harry Stradling

Walter Pidgeon, Ilona Massey, Jane Powell, Jose Iturbi, Roddy McDowall

Holiday Inn**
US 1942 101m bw
Paramount (Mark Sandrich)

The joint proprietors of a roadhouse hotel love the same girl.
Plain, simple-minded musical which provided a peg for pleasant performances and good numbers. It hit the box office spot, especially as it introduced 'White Christmas'.

w Claude Binyon, Elmer Rice *d Mark Sandrich ph* David Abel *m / ly Irving Berlin md* Robert Emmett Dolan

Bing Crosby, Fred Astaire, Walter Abel, Marjorie Reynolds, Virginia Dale, Louise Beavers, Irving Bacon, James Bell

'The best musical drama of the year.'—*New York Post*

† Marjorie Reynolds was dubbed by Martha Mears.

AA: song 'White Christmas'
AAN: original story (Irving Berlin); Robert Emmett Dolan

The Holly and the Ivy*
GB 1952 83m bw
British Lion / London (Anatole de Grunwald)

Christmas brings family revelations in a remote Norfolk rectory.
A badly-filmed stage success which succeeds because of its performances.

w Anatole de Grunwald, *play* Wynard Browne *d* George More O'Ferrall *ph* Ted Scaife *m* Malcolm Arnold

Ralph Richardson, Celia Johnson, Margaret Leighton, Denholm Elliott, John Gregson, Hugh Williams, Margaret Halstan, Maureen Delany, William Hartnell, Robert Flemyng, Roland Culver

'This type of direct translation to the screen, using none of the cinema's resources, can only do harm to the play itself.'—*Penelope Houston*

Hollywood and Vine
US 1945 59m bw

A New York writer is ordered to Hollywood to script a film for a dog. Mild satire which works in fits and starts. James Ellison, Wanda McKay, June Clyde, Ralph Morgan, Emmett Lynn, Franklin Pangborn, Leon Belasco. Written by Edith Watkins and Charles Williams; directed by Alexis Thurn-Taxis; for Leon Fromkess/PRC. (GB title: *Daisy Goes to Hollywood.*)

Hollywood Boulevard*
US 1936 75m bw
Paramount (A. M. Botsford)

A washed-up Hollywood actor writes a sensational memoir for publication, but lives to regret it.
Entertaining melodrama with famous names in bit parts.

w Marguerite Roberts *d* Robert Florey *ph* Karl Struss *m* Gregory Stone

John Halliday, Marsha Hunt, Robert Cummings, C. Henry Gordon, Frieda Inescort, Esther Dale; and Gary Cooper, Francis X. Bushman, Maurice Costello, Mae Marsh, Charles Ray, Jane Novak, Bryant Washburn, Jack Mulhall, Creighton Hale, Bert Roach

'A pretty hoary melodrama and a slight enough excuse for a whole series of homilies upon the uncertainty of fame and fortune in the glamour city.'—*New York Times*

Hollywood Canteen*
US 1944 123m bw
Warner (Alex Gottlieb)

The stars give their evenings to entertaining soldiers.
Shoddily made but sociologically fascinating record of Hollywood doing its bit in World War II.

wd Delmer Daves *ph* Bert Glennon *m* Ray Heindorf *md* Leo F. Forbstein

Joan Leslie, Robert Hutton, Dane Clark, Janis Paige; and The Andrews Sisters, Jack Benny, Joe E. Brown, Eddie Cantor, Joan Crawford, Bette Davis, John Garfield, Sidney Greenstreet, Paul Henreid, Peter Lorre, Ida Lupino, Dennis Morgan, Roy Rogers, S. Z. Sakall, Alexis Smith, Barbara Stanwyck, Jane Wyman, etc etc

'The corporal steps slowly backwards, in his eyes that look of glazed ecstasy which Jennifer Jones wore all through *The Song of Bernadette*. He has just been kissed by Joan Leslie.'—*Richard Winnington*

AAN: Ray Heindorf; song 'Sweet Dreams, Sweetheart' (*m* M. K. Jerome, *ly* Ted Koehler)

'It does for the motion picture what Alexander's Ragtime Band did for popular music!'

Hollywood Cavalcade*
US 1939 96m Technicolor
TCF (Harry Joe Brown)

The career of an old-time Hollywood producer.
A lively first half with amusing re-staging of early slapstick comedies gives way depressingly to personal melodrama, but there is enough historical interest to preserve the balance.

w Ernest Pascal *d* Irving Cummings *ph* Allen M. Davey, Ernest Palmer *ad* Richard Day, Wiard B. Ihnen *md* Louis Silvers *m* David Raksin, David Buttolph, Cyril Mockridge

Don Ameche, Alice Faye, *J. Edward Bromberg*, Alan Curtis, Stuart Erwin, Jed Prouty, Buster Keaton, Donald Meek, and the original Keystone Kops

'Surefire . . . should score heavily in theatres of every type.'—*Variety*

† Alice Faye did not sing. The Keystone Kops sequence was directed by Mal St Clair. The Ameche / Faye characters were supposedly based on Mack Sennett and Mabel Normand; Mack Sennett's appearance under his own name seemed to be an effort to throw people off the scent.

Hollywood Hotel
US 1937 109m bw
Warner (Sam Bischoff)

A Hollywood radio show has its problems.
Half-hearted, overlong Warner musical with little of the expected zip.

w Jerry Wald, Maurice Leo, Richard Macauley *d* Busby Berkeley *ph* Charles Rosher, George Barnes *m / ly* Johnny Mercer, Richard Whiting

Dick Powell, Rosemary Lane, Lola Lane, Hugh Herbert, Ted Healy, Glenda Farrell, Louella Parsons, Alan Mowbray, Frances Langford, Allyn Joslyn, Benny Goodman, Edgar Kennedy

Hollywood or Bust
US 1956 95m Technicolor Vistavision
(Paramount) Hal Wallis

Two halfwits win a car and drive across country to Hollywood.
Dopey comedy with more misses than hits; the last film of Martin and Lewis as a team.

w Erna Lazarus *d* Frank Tashlin *ph* Daniel Fapp *m* Walter Scharf

Dean Martin, Jerry Lewis, Pat Crowley, Maxie Rosenbloom, Anita Ekberg

Hollywood Party
US 1934 68m bw (Technicolor sequence)
MGM (Harry Rapf)

A mad Russian throws a party which ends in disaster.
Dismal 'all-star' comedy relieved by guest appearances.

w Howard Dietz, Arthur Kober
d (uncredited) Richard Boleslawski, Allan Dwan, Roy Rowland *ph* James Wong Howe

Laurel and Hardy, Jimmy Durante, Lupe Velez, Charles Butterworth, Eddie Quillan, Ted Healy and the Stooges, Polly Moran

'A big short . . . averagely passable screen divertissement.'—*Variety*

The Hollywood Revue of 1929**
US 1929 116m part-Technicolor
MGM (Harry Rapf)

A variety show featuring most of MGM's talent in slightly surprising acts, this is something of a bore to sit through but an archival must; and just occasionally it boasts surprising vitality.

w Al Boasberg, Robert E. Hopkins *d* Charles F. Reisner *ph* John Arnold, Irving Ries, Maximillian Fabian *ch* Sammy Lee
m / ly various

Jack Benny, Buster Keaton, Joan Crawford, John Gilbert, Norma Shearer, Laurel and Hardy, Marion Davies, Marie Dressler, William Haines, Lionel Barrymore, Conrad Nagel, Bessie Love, Cliff Edwards, Nils Asther

AAN: best picture

Hollywood Speaks
US 1932 71m bw

A Los Angeles columnist exposes Hollywood corruption. Superficial exploitation piece of no interest apart from glimpses of studios. Pat O'Brien, Genevieve Tobin, Lucien Prival, Rita Leroy. Written by Norman Krasna with Jo Swerling; directed by Eddie Buzzell; for Columbia. 'Its field is really the split weeks . . . good bet for the less educated clientele.'—*Variety*

Hollywood Story*
US 1951 76m bw
U-I (Leonard Goldstein)

A young producer solves a 20-year-old studio murder mystery.
Adequate potboiler with a reasonably absorbing plot and glimpses of silent stars.

w Frederick Kohner, Fred Brady *d* William Castle *ph* Carl Guthrie *m* Joseph Gershenson

Richard Conte, Julia Adams, Richard Egan, Henry Hull, Fred Clark, Jim Backus, Paul Cavanagh; and Francis X. Bushman, William Farnum, Betty Blythe, Helen Gibson, Joel McCrea

Holocaust 2000
GB / Italy 1977 102m Technicolor Technovision
(Rank) Aston / Embassy (Edmondo Amati)
aka: *The Chosen*

The executive in charge of a thermonuclear plant in the Middle East is drawn into a legend about the rebirth of the anti-Christ, and discovers that the evil one is his own son.
Extraordinary mishmash of horror, religiosity and social conscience which scarcely works on any level.

w Sergio Donati, Alberto de Martino, Michael Robson *d* Alberto de Martino *ph* Erico Menczer *m* Ennio Morricone

Kirk Douglas, Simon Ward, Agostina Belli, Anthony Quayle, Virginia McKenna, Spiros Focas, Alexander Knox, Adolfo Celi

'The wildest farrago yet to have come out of the demonology genre.'—*Richard Combs, MFB*

Holt of the Secret Service
US 1941 bw serial: 15 eps

The FBI tracks down counterfeiters. Handy serial thick-ear. Jack Holt, Evelyn Brent, Montague Shaw, Tristram Coffin. Directed by James W. Horne; for Columbia.

Holy Matrimony*
US 1943 87m bw
TCF (Nunnally Johnson)

A famous painter comes back from exile for a knighthood; but when his valet dies of pneumonia, has him buried as himself in Westminster Abbey.
Slightly stilted but generally warmly amusing version of a favourite novel, with excellent star performances.

w Nunnally Johnson, *novel* Buried Alive by Arnold Bennett *d* John Stahl *ph* Lucien Ballard *m* Cyril Mockridge

Monty Woolley, Gracie Fields, Laird Cregar, Eric Blore, Una O'Connor

'A pleasant hour and a half, very well produced and acted.'—*James Agate*

AAN: Nunnally Johnson

The Holy Terror
US 1936 66m bw

A child is a mischief-maker at a naval air station. Lightweight star vehicle for Shirley Temple's only competitor. Jane Withers, Tony Martin, Leah Ray, Joan Davis, El Brendel, John Eldredge. Written by Lou Breslow and John Patrick; directed by James Tinling; for TCF. 'Nicely paced for laughs . . . strong dual bill attraction.'—*Variety*

Hombre**
US 1967 111m De Luxe Panavision
TCF / Hombre Productions (Martin Ritt, Irving Ravetch)

Stagecoach passengers at the mercy of a robber are helped by a despised half-caste.
Slow but suspenseful western melodrama which works up to a couple of good climaxes but falls away in an unnecessary tragic ending.

w Irving Ravetch, Harriet Frank, *novel* Elmore Leonard *d Martin Ritt ph James Wong Howe* *m* David Rose

Paul Newman, *Diane Cilento, Fredric March*, Richard Boone, Martin Balsam, Barbara Rush, Cameron Mitchell

'A fine array of quirkish characters . . . and some unusually literate dialogue.'—*Tom Milne*

Home at Seven
GB 1952 85m bw
British Lion / London (Maurice Cowan)
US title: *Murder on Monday*

A clerk suffers a 24-hour loss of memory and may have been involved in a murder.
Intriguing suburban mystery, well acted but all too flatly transferred from the stage, and with a weak solution.

w Anatole de Grunwald, *play* R. C. Sherriff *d* Ralph Richardson *ph* Jack Hildyard, Edward Scaife *m* Malcolm Arnold

Ralph Richardson, Margaret Leighton, Jack Hawkins, Campbell Singer, Michael Shepley, Margaret Withers, Meriel Forbes, Frederick Piper

'A film with a notable absence of imagination in conception, direction and acting is not vindicated because it was made very cheaply in fifteen days . . . it seems ominous that the technique closely resembles that of television.'—*MFB*

Home before Dark
US 1958 137m bw
Warner (Mervyn Le Roy)

A college professor brings his wife home after a year in a mental hospital, but trouble starts again as the circumstances are unchanged.
Overlong, heavygoing, well-made soap opera, quite unconvincing despite firm performances and a suitably gloomy *mise-en-scène*.

w Eileen and Robert Bassing *d* Mervyn Le Roy *ph* Joseph Biroc *m* Franz Waxman *md* Ray Heindorf

Jean Simmons, Efrem Zimbalist Jnr, Dan O'Herlihy, Rhonda Fleming, Mabel Albertson

Home from the Hill
US 1959 150m Metrocolor Cinemascope
MGM / Sol C. Siegel (Edmund Grainger)

A southern landowner with a voracious sexual appetite has trouble with his two sons, legitimate and illegitimate.
Shades of *Cold Comfort Farm* and *Tobacco Road* . . . and this solemn family saga does go on a bit.

w Irving Ravetch, Harriet Frank, *novel* William Humphrey *d* Vincente Minnelli *ph* Milton Krasner *m* Bronislau Kaper

Robert Mitchum, George Hamilton, George Peppard, Eleanor Parker, Luana Patten, Everett Sloane, Constance Ford, Ray Teal

Home in Indiana
US 1944 103m Technicolor
TCF (André Daven)

Farmers compete in trotting races and their progeny fall in love.
Archetypal homespun Americana, well enough made according to its lights, but now like something from another world . . . an innocent one.

w Winston Miller, *novel* The Phantom Filly by George Agnew Chamberlain *d* Henry Hathaway *ph* Edward Cronjager *m* Hugo Friedhofer *md* Emil Newman

Jeanne Crain, June Haver, Lon McCallister, Walter Brennan, Charlotte Greenwood, Ward Bond, Charles Dingle, Willie Best

† Remade as *April Love*.

AAN: Edward Cronjager

Home of the Brave*
US 1949 86m bw
Stanley Kramer

During World War II, a black man finds himself the butt of racist behaviour from the rest of his platoon.
One of the first films to touch the subject of anti-black bias, this now seems pretty tame and dated, and in fact never was much more than a filmed play (in which the butt was originally a Jew).

w Carl Foreman, *play* Arthur Laurents *d* Mark Robson *ph* Robert de Grasse *m* Dmitri Tiomkin

Frank Lovejoy, Lloyd Bridges, Douglas Dick, James Edwards, Steve Brodie, Jeff Corey, Cliff Clark

A Home of Your Own*
GB 1965 44m bw

Calamities pile up on a building site.
Genuinely funny silent comedy, with bits from a variety of familiar faces. Ronnie Barker, George Benson, Richard Briers, Janet Brown, Peter Butterworth, Bernard Cribbins, Fred Emney, Bill Fraser, Ronnie Stevens. Written by Jay Lewis and John Whyte; directed by Bob Kellett; for Dormar / British Lion.

Home Sweet Homicide
US 1946 90m bw
TCF

Children solve a murder mystery with the help of their mother, a detective novelist.
Mild family fare.

w F. Hugh Herbert, *novel* Craig Rice *d* Lloyd Bacon *ph* John Seitz *m* David Buttolph

Lynn Bari, Randolph Scott, Peggy Ann Garner, Connie Marshall, Dean Stockwell, Barbara Whiting

Home to Danger
GB 1951 66m bw

An heiress returns after her father's death and finds herself pursued by a murderer.
Tuppenny shocker, quite amusing in its way. Rona Anderson, Guy Rolfe, Stanley Baker, Francis Lister, Alan Wheatley. Written by Francis Edge and Guy Temple-Smith; directed by Terence Fisher; for Lance Comfort / New World.

The Home Towners
US 1928 84m bw

A wealthy man falls for a girl half his age and is warned by a hometown friend that she may be a gold digger. Fairly fluent early talkie which pleased at the time. Richard Bennett, Robert McWade, Doris Kenyon, Stanley Taylor. Written by Addison Burkhart, from the play by George M. Cohan; directed by Bryan Foy; for Warner. (Remakes include *Times Square Playboy* [1936] with Warren William, Gene Lockhart and June Travis, directed by William McGann; and *Ladies Must Live* [1940] with Wayne Morris, Priscilla Lane and Roscoe Karns; both for Warner.)

Homecoming
US 1948 113m bw
MGM (Sidney Franklin)

A ruthless society doctor is called up in World War II and has his life changed by a brief affair with a nurse who is killed in action.
Ho-hum romantic melodrama which stumbles most badly when it aims to be serious.

w Paul Osborn *d* Mervyn Le Roy *ph* Harold Rosson *md* Charles Previn *m* Bronislau Kaper

Clark Gable, Lana Turner, Anne Baxter, John Hodiak, Ray Collins, Gladys Cooper, Cameron Mitchell, Marshall Thompson

'Its basic substance, like the base of a perfume, has a terrible smell; but to many moviegoers the end-product will seem quite pleasant.'—*Time*

The Homecoming*
GB 1973 114m colour
American Express / Ely Landau

Tensions mount and sexual revelations abound in the house of a retired London butcher.
Plain treatment of an anything-but-plain Pinter play. The result is a record of a performance rather than a film.

w Harold Pinter, from his play *d* Peter Hall *ph* David Watkin *m* Thelonious Monk *pd* John Bury

Paul Rogers, Cyril Cusack, Michael Jayston, Ian Holm, Vivien Merchant, Terence Rigby

'Shocking in its own lucidity, and fascinating as an arrangement of mutually reflecting prisms . . . the remarkable control of Pinter's language guarantees that the dramatic situations are revealed to be even *more* abstract and diagrammatic as they steadily accumulate psychological density.'—*Jonathan Rosenbaum*

The Homestretch
US 1947 97m Technicolor

A racing enthusiast neglects his wife. Thin romantic drama, handsomely photographed on various racecourses. Cornel Wilde, Maureen O'Hara, Glenn Langan, Helen Walker, James Gleason, Henry Stephenson. Written by Wanda Tuchock; directed by H. Bruce Humberstone; for TCF.

'Can your heart stand the challenge when the clock starts the countdown?'
'All those too timid to take the climax will be welcomed to the cowards' corner!'

Homicidal
US 1961 87m bw
Columbia / William Castle

A murderous blonde and a very strange young man both live in the house of a paralysed old lady.
Transvestite horror comic allegedly based on a true case; made on a low budget and played for cheap shocks.

w Robb White *d* William Castle *ph* Burnett Guffey *m* Hugo Friedhofer

Jean Arless, Glenn Corbett, Patricia Breslin, Eugenie Leontovitch, Alan Bunce, Richard Rust

† The film was played with a 'fright break' during which faint-hearted members of the audience might leave before the final onslaught.

Homicide
US 1949 76m bw

A murder witness is intimidated by the killers. Stiff little crime yarn which slowly recovers after a dull beginning. Robert Douglas, Robert Alda, Helen Westcott. Written by William Sackheim; directed by Felix Jacoves; for Warner.

Homicide Bureau
US 1938 56m bw

A tough small-town cop deals with racketeers. Routine programme filler. Bruce Cabot, Rita Hayworth, Marc Lawrence, Moroni Olsen. Written by Earle Snell; directed by C. C. Coleman Jnr; for Columbia. 'Hits new low . . . every department of production way below par.'—*Variety*

L'Homme au Chapeau Rond*
France 1946 91m bw
Alcina

When his wife dies, a man becomes obsessed with causing the downfall of her two lovers. Heavy-going melodrama without much in the way of light relief; chiefly memorable for its central performance.

w Charles Spaak, Jean Loubignic, *novel* The Eternal Husband by Dostoevsky *d* Pierre Billon *ph* Nicolas Torporkoff *m* Maurice Thiriet

Raimu, Aimé Clariond, Lucy Valnor

Hondo*
US 1954 93m Warnercolor 3-D
Wayne–Fellows

In 1874 New Mexico a cavalry despatch rider stops to defend a lonely widow and her son against Indians.
Overwritten but pleasant-looking western, clearly patterned after *Shane*.

w James Edward Grant from novel by Louis L'Amour *d* John Farrow *ph* Robert Burks, Archie Stout *m* Emil Newman, Hugo Friedhofer

w James Edward Grant *d* John Farrow *ph* Robert Burks, Archie Stout *m* Emil Newman, Hugo Friedhofer

John Wayne, Geraldine Page, Ward Bond, Michael Pate

AAN: Geraldine Page

Honey
US 1930 75m bw

A brother and sister rent out their southern mansion and decide to become the butler and cook. Comedy with music, a little heavier than it should have been. Nancy Carroll, Skeets Gallagher, Stanley Smith, Lillian Roth, Harry Green, Mitzi Green, Zasu Pitts. Written by Herman J. Mankiewicz from the play Come Out of the Kitchen by Alice Duer Miller and A. E. Thomas; directed by Wesley Ruggles; for Paramount. 'Not worthy of a big rave but should satisfy the mob.'—*Variety*

'You are cordially invited to a perfectly elegant case of murder!'

The Honey Pot*
US 1966 150m Technicolor
UA / Famous Artists (Charles K. Feldman) (Joseph L. Mankiewicz)

A millionaire pretends to be dying in order to trick three former mistresses; but one of them is murdered.
Uneasy variation, via two other variations, on Ben Jonson's *Volpone*; despite bright moments, the mood is fatally inconsistent, and a cloud of pseudo-sophisticated dialogue hangs over the whole thing like a pall.

wd Joseph L. Mankiewicz, *play* Mr Fox of Venice by Frederick Knott, *novel* The Evil of the Day by Thomas Sterling *ph* Gianni di Venanzo *m* John Addison *pd* John De Cuir

Rex Harrison, Susan Hayward, *Maggie Smith*, Cliff Robertson, Capucine, Edie Adams, Adolfo Celi, Herschel Bernardi

'One of the talkiest pictures ever made.'—*Stephen Farber*

Honeychile
US 1951 89m Trucolor

A music publisher tries to cheat a country composer. Hayseed shenanigans for small-town consumption. Judy Canova, Eddie Foy Jnr, Alan Hale Jnr, Walter Catlett, Claire Carleton, Leonid Kinskey. Written by R. G. Springsteen; for Republic.

'Miss Glamorous and Mr Amorous in a gay elopement adventure that makes Mexico City blush!'

Honeymoon
US 1947 74m bw
RKO (Warren Duff)
GB title: *Two Men and a Girl*

An 18-year-old elopes to Mexico City with an army corporal but meets a sophisticated older man.
Emaciated comedy, one of the reasons for Shirley Temple's early retirement.

w Michael Kanin, *story* Vicki Baum *d* William Keighley *ph* Edward Cronjager *m* Leigh Harline

Shirley Temple, Franchot Tone, Guy Madison, Lina Romay, Gene Lockhart, Grant Mitchell

Honeymoon
Spain / GB 1959 109m Technicolor Technirama / Dimension 180
Suevia / Everdene (Cesario Gonzalez, Michael Powell)
Spanish title: *Luna de Miel*

An ex-ballerina in Spain with her new husband is tempted to return to the boards.

Incredibly shapeless travel poster with some dancing and two interpolated ballets to provide moments of musical interest. An unbelievable disaster from the co-creator of *The Red Shoes*.

w Michael Powell, Luis Escobar *d* Michael Powell *ph* Georges Périnal, Gerry Turpin *m* Mikis Theodorakis

Anthony Steel, Ludmilla Tcherina, Antonio, Leonide Massine

Honeymoon Deferred
US 1940 84m bw

An insurance investigator is called away from honeymoon when his boss is murdered. Unremarkable star programmer. Edmund Lowe, Margaret Lindsay, Elizabeth Risdon, Joyce Compton, Chick Chandler. Written by Roy Chanslor and Eliot Gibbons; directed by Lew Landers; for Universal.

Honeymoon Deferred
GB 1951 79m bw

A war veteran returns for his honeymoon to the Italian village he helped to liberate, but finds himself accused of ruining the crops. Curious hybrid comedy which fails to jell on all levels. Griffith Jones, Sally Ann Howes, Kieron Moore, Lea Padovani. Written by Suso d'Amico and A. Pietrangeli; directed by Mario Camerini; for Vic Films.

Honeymoon for Three
US 1941 77m bw

An author is protected from adoring females by his secretary. Fairly flaccid romantic comedy, a remake of *Goodbye Again* (1933). George Brent, Ann Sheridan, Osa Massen, Charles Ruggles, Jane Wyman, Lee Patrick. Written by Julius J. Epstein, Philip G. Epstein and Earl Baldwin; directed by Lloyd Bacon; for Warner.

Honeymoon Hotel
US 1964 98m Metrocolor Cinemascope
MGM / Avon (Lawrence Weingarten)

A jilted swain goes off with a philandering friend on what was to have been his honeymoon trip . . . only to be followed by his repentant fiancée.
Rather unattractive farce with insufficient funny moments.

w R. S. Allen, Harvey Bulloch *d* Henry Levin *ph* Harold Lipstein *m* Walter Scharf

Nancy Kwan, Robert Goulet, Robert Morse, Jill St John, Elsa Lanchester, Keenan Wynn

Honeymoon in Bali
US 1939 95m bw
(GB title: *Husbands or Lovers?*)

A department store head intends to pursue her career without marriage, but two swains try to prove her wrong. Thin romantic comedy which got by on its stars. Madeleine Carroll, Fred MacMurray, Allan Jones, Akim Tamiroff, Helen Broderick, Osa Massen. Written by Virginia Van Upp; directed by Edward H. Griffith; for Jeff Lazarus / Paramount.
'Infectiously sparkling . . . will click substantially in the regular runs.'—*Variety*
NB. The original title, *Are Husbands Necessary?*, was discarded when Miss Carroll became involved in a divorce suit.

The Honeymoon Machine
US 1961 91m Metrocolor Cinemascope
MGM / Avon (Lawrence Weingarten)

A naval lieutenant uses the ship's computer to break the bank at the Venice casino.
Stolid, expensive-looking comedy which barely raises a laugh.

w George Wells, *play* The Golden Fleecing by Lorenzo Semple Jnr *d* Richard Thorpe *ph* Joseph La Shelle *m* Leigh Harline

Steve McQueen, Brigid Bazlen, Jim Hutton, Paula Prentiss, Dean Jagger, Jack Weston, Jack Mullaney

Honeysuckle Rose
US 1980 119m Technicolor

A happily married country and western star takes to the bottle whenever he goes on the road. Glum modern drama with music, a semi-autobiographical star vehicle; for fans only. Willie Nelson, Dyan Cannon, Amy Irving, Slim Pickens. Written by Carol Sobieski, William D. Wittliff and John Binder; directed by Jerry Schatzberg; for Sydney Pollack / Warner.

Hong Kong
US 1951 91m Technicolor
Paramount / Pine–Thomas

An ex-GI has various adventures with a Chinese orphan and a golden idol.
And a plot that seems to make itself up as they go along. Corn-fed hokum.

w Winston Miller *d* Lewis R. Foster *ph* Lionel Lindon *m* Lucien Cailliet

Ronald Reagan, Rhonda Fleming, Nigel Bruce, Marvin Miller, Lowell Gilmore

The Honkers*
US 1971 102m De Luxe
UA / Levy–Gardner–Laven

An ageing rodeo rider has trouble with his wife.
Quiet, carefully accomplished study of a man and his milieu.

w Steve Ihnat, Stephen Lodge *d* Steve Ihnat *ph* John Crabe *m* Jimmie Haskell

James Coburn, Lois Nettleton, Slim Pickens, Richard Anderson

Honky Tonk
US 1929 80m bw

A nightclub entertainer sacrifices everything for her daughter's education. Primitive cross between *Applause* and *Imitation of Life,* with spirited moments from Sophie Tucker the only plus; also Lila Lee, Audrey Ferris, George Duryea, Mahlon Hamilton. Written by C. Graham Baker and Jack Yellen; directed by Lloyd Bacon; for Warner.
'Every kiss a thrill!'

Honky Tonk*
US 1941 104m bw
MGM (Pandro S. Berman)

A western con man meets his match in the daughter of a fake judge.
Generally amusing comedy melodrama that ambles along between two styles but leaves a pleasant after-effect.

w Marguerite Roberts, John Sandford *d* Jack Conway *ph* Harold Rosson *m* Franz Waxman

Clark Gable, Lana Turner, Frank Morgan, Claire Trevor, Marjorie Main, Albert Dekker, Henry O'Neill, Chill Wills, Betty Blythe
'A lively, lusty western that makes you wish you had been there.'—*Variety*

Honky Tonk Freeway
US 1981 107m Technicolor
EMI / Kendon / HTF Company (Don Boyd, Howard W. Koch Jnr)

The mayor of a small Florida resort town has it painted pink to attract tourists . . . but too many of the wrong kind come in.
Zany farce, rather like *It's a Mad Mad Mad Mad World* without a proper hook to the story. Not an audience-pleaser, and very expensive.

w Edward Clinton *d* John Schlesinger *ph* John Bailey *m* George Martin, Elmer Bernstein

William Devane, Beau Bridges, Teri Garr, Beverly D'Angelo, Hume Cronyn, Jessica Tandy, Howard Hesseman, Geraldine Page, George Dzundza
'A shambles, and a more convincing one than the half-hearted affair which brings it to a close.'—*Richard Combs, MFB*
'A film for "now" which seems almost endearingly bereft of any real ideas about the messed-up contemporary world it inhabits.'—*Guardian*

Honkytonk Man
US 1982 122m Technicolor
Warner / Malpaso (Clint Eastwood)

In the thirties, an ageing and alcoholic country singer turns to his rural family for help.
Yet another occasion when the star should have asked for help instead of doing all the chores himself. Not much real entertainment here, just a very few moments that amuse.

w Clancy Carlile, from his novel *d* Clint Eastwood *ph* Bruce Surtees *m* Steve Dorff *pd* Edward Carfagno

Clint Eastwood, Kyle Eastwood, John McIntire, Verna Bloom, Alexa Kenin, Matt Clark

Honolulu
US 1938 83m bw
MGM (Jack Cummings)

A movie star is mistaken for his double.
Sloppy comedy with a few musical numbers.

w Herbert Fields, Frank Partos *d* Edward Buzzell *ph* Ray June *m* Franz Waxman

Robert Young, Eleanor Powell, George Burns, Gracie Allen, Rita Johnson, Ruth Hussey, Clarence Kolb, Sig Rumann, Eddie Anderson

'Fairly amusing comedy for top brackets in duals.'—*Variety*

'The whole thing seems to have been thrown together so that Eleanor Powell can do a frenetic hula.'—*New Yorker, 1977*

Honor Among Lovers
US 1931 76m bw

A young businessman complicates his life when he decides to marry his secretary. Smart comedy unfolding a complex plot, but slow by modern standards. Claudette Colbert, Fredric March, Monroe Owsley, Charlie Ruggles, Ginger Rogers. Written by Austin Parker and Gertrude Purcell; directed by Dorothy Arzner; for Paramount. 'A sweet piece of work hiding behind a faulty title.'—*Variety*

Honor of the Family
US 1931 66m bw

The young mistress of an aged Budapest resident is after his money. Tiresome comedy drama. Bebe Daniels, Warren William, Frederick Kerr, Alan Mowbray, Blanche Friderici. Written from a play by Emil Fabre and a story by Balzac; directed by Lloyd Bacon; for First National.

The Honorary Consul
GB 1983 104m Movielab
World Film Services (Norma Heyman)
US title: *Beyond the Limit*

In northern Argentina, a doctor is drawn into the kidnapping by activists of a drunken British consul.
Self-parodic visit to Greeneland, with everybody drunk or depressed. Bouts of explicit sex don't help much, if at all.

w Christopher Hampton, *novel* Graham Greene *d* John MacKenzie *ph* Phil Meheux *m* Stanley Myers *pd* Allan Cameron

Michael Caine, Richard Gere, Bob Hoskins, Elpidia Carrillo, Joaquim de Almeida

'Some very old friends: exhausted passion, moral betrayal and relics of religious faith.'—*Sight and Sound*

'All it takes is the character to decide he is a burnt-out case, sleeping with all women but capable of loving none, for all the familiar icons to be ranged in battle array.'—*Tom Milne, MFB*

An Honourable Murder*
GB 1959 70m bw
Danziger

Boardroom executives scheme to be rid of their chairman.
Oddball, interesting attempt to play *Julius Caesar* in modern dress. Not entirely successful, but full marks for trying.

w Brian Clemens, Eldon Howard *d* Godfrey Grayson *ph* James Wilson

Norman Wooland, Margaretta Scott, Lisa Daniely, Douglas Wilmer, Philip Saville, John Longden

The Hoodlum
US 1951 63m bw

A convict is paroled but continues his criminal career. Toughish crime support with interesting moments. Lawrence Tierney, Liza Golm, Edward Tierney, Allene Roberts. Written by Sam Neumann and Nat Tanchuck; directed by Max Nosseck; for Jack Schwarz Productions.

Hoodlum Empire
US 1952 98m bw
Republic (Joseph Kane)

A Congressional committee investigates a racketeer.
Moderate semi-documentary potboiler inspired by the Kefauver investigations.

w Bruce Manning, Bob Considine *d* Joseph Kane *ph* Reggie Lanning *m* Nathan Scott

Brian Donlevy, Forrest Tucker, Claire Trevor, Vera Ralston, Luther Adler, John Russell, Gene Lockhart, Grant Withers, Taylor Holmes

'Familiar gangster melodramatics and repentances, played out in a rigmarole of flashbacks.'—*MFB*

The Hoodlum Priest*
US 1961 100m bw
UA / Don Murray–Walter Wood

A Jesuit teacher tries to help young criminals, especially a condemned murderer.
Moderately well done, very depressing and downbeat chunk of social conscience based on the life of Charles Dismas Clark.

w Don Mankiewicz, Joseph Landon, 'Don Deer' (i.e. Don Murray) *d* Irvin Kershner *ph* Haskell Wexler *m* Richard Markowitz

Don Murray, Keir Dullea, Larry Gates, Cindi Wood, Logan Ramsey

The Hoodlum Saint
US 1946 93m bw
MGM (Cliff Reid)

A cynical newspaperman turns to religion and succours thieves.
Hard-boiled sentimentality, a downright peculiar and doleful comedy drama in deflated post-war mood.

w Frank Wead, James Hill *d* Norman Taurog *ph* Ray June *m* Nathaniel Shilkret

William Powell, Esther Williams, Angela Lansbury, James Gleason, Lewis Stone, Rags Ragland, Frank McHugh, Slim Summerville, Roman Bohnen, Louis Jean Heydt, Charles Arnt, Charles Trowbridge, Henry O'Neill

The Hook
US 1962 98m bw Panavision
MGM / Perlberg–Seaton

Three GIs escaping from Korea are ordered to execute a prisoner but cannot bring themselves to do it.
Predictable, claustrophobic drama which becomes a slick exercise in morality.

w Henry Denker, *novel* The Hameçon by Vahe Katcha *d* George Seaton *ph* Joe Ruttenberg *m* Larry Adler

Kirk Douglas, Robert Walker, Nick Adams, Nehemiah Persoff

Hook Line and Sinker
US 1930 72m bw

Two insurance agents run a derelict hotel. Feeble comedy vehicle. Bert Wheeler, Robert Woolsey, Hugh Herbert, Dorothy Lee, Jobyna Howland, Ralf Harolde. Written by Tim Whelan, Ralph Spence; directed by Eddie Cline; for RKO. 'Will tickle most in those spots where the price is least.'—*Variety*

Hook, Line and Sinker
US 1968 92m Technicolor
Columbia / Jerry Lewis

A salesman who thinks he is dying goes on a spending spree; when he learns the truth, he has to disappear because of his huge debts.
Miserable comedy with frantic slapstick interludes. The plot might have served Preston Sturges.

w Rod Amateau *d* George Marshall *ph* W. Wallace Kelley *m* Dick Stabile

Jerry Lewis, Peter Lawford, Anne Francis, Pedro Gonzales Gonzales

Hooper*
US 1978 99m Metrocolor
Warner / Burt Reynolds, Lawrence Gordon (Hank Moonjean)

An ageing stunt man decides on one last sensational stunt before retiring.
There are some agreeably striking moments, but you can't make a movie out of stunts and loud camaraderie. This one palls half way through.

w Thomas Rickman, Bill Kerby *d* Hal Needham *ph* Bobby Byrne *m* Bill Justis

Burt Reynolds, Sally Field, Brian Keith, Jan-Michael Vincent, John Marley, Robert Klein, James Best, Adam West

'Burt Reynolds's annual Kleenex of a movie: something to use and throw away without any thought beyond a certain gratitude for the convenience of the thing.'—*Richard Schickel, Time*

'Clara Bow . . . red-headed warm-blooded dynamite . . . again releases the torrent of her genius in the most colorful performance of her life.'

Hoopla
US 1933 85m bw

A hardboiled carnival dancer agrees to seduce the son of the show's manager, but ends by marrying him. Strained melodrama with the star, in her last film, at the end of her tether. Clara Bow, Richard Cromwell, Preston Foster, Herbert Mundin, James Gleason, Minna Gombell, Roger Imhof. Written by

Bradley King and J. M. March, from the play *The Barker* by Kenyon Nicholson; directed by Frank Lloyd; for Fox. 'Miss Bow seems ripe to come back strongly.'—*Variety*

Hooray for Love
US 1935 75m bw

A rich college boy plays angel to a musical comedy. Thin pot-pourri of familiar elements. Ann Sothern, Gene Raymond, *Bill Robinson*, Thurston Hall, Pert Kelton, Lionel Stander, *Fats Waller*. Written by Lawrence Hazard, Ray Harris; directed by Walter Lang; for RKO. 'Trouble is entirely traceable to its terribly lethargic tempo and lack of any real production numbers.'—*Variety*

The Hoosegow**
US 1929 20m bw

Stan and Ollie, in prison, contrive to fell a tree on the cook's tent and to smother the governor in boiled rice. Splendid slapstick leading up to one of their best tit-for-tat routines. Laurel and Hardy, James Finlayson, Tiny Sandford. Written by Leo McCarey and H. M. Walker; directed by James Parrott; for Hal Roach.

Hoosier Schoolboy
US 1937 62m bw

A rural boy defends his drunken father, shell-shocked in the war. Simple tale for rural audiences. Mickey Rooney, Anne Nagel, Frank Shields, Edward Pawley. Written by Robert Lee Johnson from the novel by Edward Eggleston; directed by William Nigh; for Ken Goldsmith / Monogram. 'A compelling film which word of mouth might turn into a sleeper.'—*Variety*

Hoosiers
US 1986 114m CFI colour
Orion / Hemdale / Carter De Haven
GB title: *Best Shot*

The training and triumph of an Indiana high school basketball team.
Expertise expended on a subject of very limited interest.

w Angelo Pizzo *d* David Anspaugh *ph* Fred Murphy *m* Jerry Goldsmith

Gene Hackman, Barbara Hershey, Dennis Hopper, Sheb Wooley, Fern Persons

'Both rousing and too conventional.'—*Variety*

AAN: Jerry Goldsmith; Dennis Hopper

Hoots Mon*
GB 1939 77m bw

A cockney comedian starts a popularity contest with a female impressionist. Tolerable comedy whose value is that it preserves, albeit in cleaned-up form, portions of *Max Miller*'s variety act. *Florence Desmond* isn't bad either. With Hal Walters, Davina Craig, Garry Marsh. Written by Roy William Neill, Jack Henley and John Dighton; directed by Roy William Neill; for Warner.

Hop Harrigan
US 1946 bw serial: 15 eps

Civil aviators fight a death-ray-wielding villain called The Chief Pilot. More than faintly absurd action shenanigans, with more yawns than thrills. William Blakewell, Jennifer Holt, Robert 'Buzz' Henry. Directed by Derwin Abrahams; for Columbia.

Hopalong Cassidy
Cassidy, a creation of Clarence E. Mulford, was a fictitious gentleman cowboy who oddly enough wore black; 26 books about him were published between 1912 and 1956 when Mulford died. 66 films were made starring William Boyd as Hoppy, with either George Gabby Hayes or Andy Clyde as comic sidekick: Harry Sherman produced them, first for Paramount and then for UA, and they were later edited down for TV, in which medium Boyd became a folk hero and eventually made a further series. The films were easy-going, slow-moving second features which always pointed an admirable moral for children; their main directors were Howard Bretherton, Nate Watt, Lesley Selander and George Archainbaud.

1935: HOPALONG CASSIDY, THE EAGLE'S BROOD, BAR 20 RIDES AGAIN
1936: CALL OF THE PRAIRIE, THREE ON THE TRAIL, HEART OF THE WEST, HOPALONG CASSIDY RETURNS, TRAIL DUST
1937: BORDERLAND, HILLS OF OLD WYOMING, NORTH OF THE RIO GRANDE, RUSTLERS' VALLEY, HOPALONG RIDES AGAIN, TEXAS TRAIL
1938: HEART OF ARIZONA, BAR 20 JUSTICE, PRIDE OF THE WEST, IN OLD MEXICO, SUNSET TRAIL, THE FRONTIERSMAN, PARTNERS OF THE PLAINS, CASSIDY OF BAR 20
1939: RANGE WAR, LAW OF THE PAMPAS, SILVER ON THE SAGE, RENEGADE TRAIL
1940: SANTA FE MARSHAL, THE SHOWDOWN, HIDDEN GOLD, STAGECOACH WAR, THREE MEN FROM TEXAS
1941: DOOMED CARAVAN, IN OLD COLORADO, BORDER VIGILANTES, PIRATES ON HORSEBACK, WIDE OPEN TOWN, OUTLAWS OF THE DESERT, RIDERS OF THE TIMBERLINE, SECRETS OF THE WASTELAND, STICK TO YOUR GUNS, TWILIGHT ON THE TRAIL
1942: UNDERCOVER MAN
1943: COLT COMRADES, BAR 20, LOST CANYON, HOPPY SERVES A WRIT, BORDER PATROL, THE LEATHER BURNERS, FALSE COLOURS, RIDERS OF THE DEADLINE
1944: MYSTERY MAN, FORTY THIEVES, TEXAS MASQUERADE, LUMBERJACK
1946: THE DEVIL'S PLAYGROUND
1947: FOOL'S GOLD, HOPPY'S HOLIDAY, MARAUDERS, UNEXPECTED GUEST, DANGEROUS VENTURE
1948: SINISTER JOURNEY, SILENT CONFLICT, STRANGE GAMBLE, BORROWED TROUBLE, THE DEAD DON'T DREAM, FALSE PARADISE

Hope and Glory**
GB 1987 113m Technicolor
Columbia/Goldcrest/Nelson (John Boorman)

Adventures of a small boy and his family during World War II in suburban London.
Generally appealing but not too accurate reminiscences of an exciting and emotional time.

w,d John Boorman ph Philippe Rousselot
m Peter Martin *pd* Anthony Pratt

Sarah Miles, Susan Wooldridge, Ian Bannen, David Hayman, Derrick O'Connor, Sebastian Rice-Edwards

AAN: Philippe Rousselot; art direction (Don Dossett); John Boorman as director; best picture; best original screenplay

Hopscotch*
US 1980 104m Movielab
Avco / Edie and Ely Landau (Otto Plaschkes)

An ex-CIA man writes a revealing book and foils the consequent attempts on his life.
Genial but patchy spy comedy caper; a filler for all concerned.

w Brian Garfield, Bryan Forbes, from Garfield's novel *d* Ronald Neame *ph* Arthur Ibbetson *m* Ian Fraser

Walter Matthau, Glenda Jackson, Ned Beatty, Sam Waterston, Herbert Lom, George Baker

Horizons West
US 1952 81m Technicolor
U-I (Albert J. Cohen)

After the Civil War, a rancher builds an empire on greed and ruthlessness, and his brother has to bring him to trial.
Rather lugubrious western with the usual quota of effective action scenes.

w Louis Stevens *d* Budd Boetticher
ph Charles P. Boyle *md* Joseph Gershenson

Rock Hudson, Robert Ryan, Julia Adams, John McIntire, Raymond Burr, Dennis Weaver, Judith Braun

The Horizontal Lieutenant
US 1962 90m Metrocolor Cinemascope
MGM / Euterpe (Joe Pasternak)

World War II Hawaii; an amorous intelligence officer accidentally captures a Japanese guerrilla.
Very moderate army farce of no great skill or memorability.

w George Wells *d* Richard Thorpe
ph Robert Bronner *m* George Stoll

Jim Hutton, Paula Prentiss, Jim Backus, Miyoshi Umeki, Jack Carter

The Horn Blows at Midnight*
US 1945 80m bw
Warner (Mark Hellinger)

An angel is sent to earth to destroy the planet with Gabriel's horn.
Wacky comedy inspired by *Here Comes Mr Jordan*, but on a broader slapstick level; much better than its star always pretended.

w Sam Hellman, James V. Kern *d* Raoul Walsh *ph* Sid Hickox *m* Franz Waxman

Jack Benny, Alexis Smith, Dolores Moran, Allyn Joslyn, Guy Kibbee, Reginald Gardiner, *Franklin Pangborn*, John Alexander, Margaret Dumont

Hornet's Nest
US 1969 109m De Luxe
UA / Triangle (Stanley S. Kanter)

In World War II Italy, a wounded US army demolitions expert is nursed back to health by child partisans, who help him destroy a German-held dam.
Overlong war exploits with the children used as a tiresome gimmick.

w S. S. Schweitzer *d* Phil Karlson *ph* Gabor Pogani *m* Ennio Morricone

Rock Hudson, Sergio Fantoni, Sylva Koscina, Jacques Sernas

Horror Express
Spain / GB 1972 90m Technicolor

In 1906 China a fossilized missing link comes to violent life on a train. Rather nasty horror film which manages to keep one watching despite some obvious fakery. Peter Cushing, Christopher Lee, Telly Savalas, Jorge Rigaud. Written by Arnaud D'Usseau and Julian Halevy; directed by Eugenio Martin; for Granada Madrid / Benmar. (Spanish title: *Pánico en el Transiberiano*.)

Horror Island
US 1941 60m bw

Various people travel to an island where buried treasure might be hidden. Feeble little mystery with very little interest in who done what to whom. Dick Foran, Leo Carrillo, Peggy Moran, Fuzzy Knight, John Eldredge, Walter Catlett, Hobart Cavanaugh. Written by Maurice Tombragel and Victor McLeod; directed by George Waggner; for Universal.

The Horror of Frankenstein
GB 1970 95m Technicolor

Victor Frankenstein is not above murdering his acquaintances for the sake of his experiments in bringing the dead back to life. Ill-advised attempt to remake the original story as a black comedy, with Frankenstein frankly villainous from the start. The last in the Hammer series. Ralph Bates, Kate O'Mara, Graham James, Veronica Carlson, Bernard Archard, Dennis Price, Joan Rice, Dave Prowse. Written and directed by Jimmy Sangster; for Hammer / EMI.

Horrors of the Black Museum
GB 1959 81m Eastmancolor Cinemascope

A crime writer is fascinated by murder, and works out his own plots by practice beforehand. Crude shocker. Michael Gough, Graham Curnow, Shirley Ann Field, Geoffrey Keen. Written by Aben Kandel and Herman Cohen; directed by Arthur Crabtree; for Herman Cohen.

'A scandalous record of low Marx at college—or life among the thirsty co-eds!'

Horse Feathers***
US 1932 69m bw
Paramount (Herman J. Mankiewicz)

A college needs to win at football, and its corrupt new president knows just how to do it. Possibly the Marxes' wildest yet most streamlined kaleidoscope of high jinks and irreverence, with at least one bright gag or line to the minute and lively musical interludes to boot. A classic of zany comedy.

w Bert Kalmar, Harry Ruby, S. J. Perelman, Will B. Johnstone d Norman Z. McLeod *ph* Ray June *m / ly Bert Kalmar, Harry Ruby*

Groucho, Chico, Harpo, Zeppo, *Thelma Todd*, Robert Greig

GROUCHO: 'You have the brain of a four-year-old child, and I'll bet he was glad to get rid of it.'

CHICO: 'There's a man outside with a big black moustache.'

GROUCHO: 'Tell him I've got one.'

GROUCHO (to Zeppo): 'You're a disgrace to our family name of Wagstaff, if such a thing is possible.'

GROUCHO: 'For years before my son was born
I used to yell from night till morn
Whatever it is—I'm against it!
And I've been yelling since I first commenced it—I'm against it!'

'The current Marx comedy is the funniest talkie since the last Marx comedy, and the record it establishes is not likely to be disturbed until the next Marx comedy comes along. As for comparisons, I was too busy having a good time to make any.'—*Philip K. Scheuer*

The Horse in the Grey Flannel Suit
US 1969 112m Technicolor

A teenager's horse beomes the central figure in an advertising campaign for a stomach pill. Interminable kiddie movie which in its virtual absence of plot or excitement is likely to bore kiddies to death. Dean Jones, Fred Clark, Diane Baker, Lloyd Bochner, Morey , Amsterdam. Written by Louis Pelletier, from the novel *The Year of the Horse* by Eric Hatch; directed by Norman Tokar; for Walt Disney.

The Horse Soldiers*
US 1959 119m De Luxe
UA / Mirisch (John Lee Mahin, Martin Rackin)

In 1863 a Union cavalry officer is sent three hundred miles into Confederate territory to demolish a railroad junction.
Typically sprawling John Ford cavalry western with not too many high spots and more sombre ingredients than usual.

w John Lee Mahin, Martin Rackin *d* John Ford *ph* William Clothier *m* David Buttolph

John Wayne, William Holden, Constance Towers, Hoot Gibson

HOLDEN: 'Look here, colonel, I didn't ask to be assigned to this mission . . .'

The Horse without a Head**
GB 1963 89m Technicolor
Walt Disney (Hugh Attwooll)

Stolen money is hidden in an old toy horse, and crooks trying to get it back clash with police and children.
Excellent children's adventure with scenes on trains and in a toy factory.

w T. E. B. Clarke d Don Chaffey ph Paul Beeson *m* Eric Rogers

Leo McKern, Jean-Pierre Aumont, Herbert Lom, Pamela Franklin, Vincent Winter

The Horsemen
US 1970 109m colour Super Panavision
Columbia / John Frankenheimer–Edward Lewis

An Afghan tribesman is determined to rival his father at horsemanship.
Rather tedious variant on *Taras Bulba*; plenty of action but not much characterization, or taste, or interest.

w Dalton Trumbo, *novel* Joseph Kessel *d* John Frankenheimer *ph* Claude Renoir *m* Georges Delerue

Omar Sharif, Jack Palance, Leigh Taylor-Young, Peter Jeffrey, Eric Pohlmann, Despo, David De Keyser

The Horse's Mouth*
GB 1958 93m Technicolor
UA / Knightsbridge (John Bryan)

An obsessive painter is a liability to his friends.
Thin but fitfully amusing light study of a social outcast, with a background of London river and streets. Too slight for real success.

w Alec Guinness, *novel* Joyce Cary *d* Ronald Neame *ph Arthur Ibbetson m* K. V. Jones from Prokofiev *paintings* John Bratby

Alec Guinness, Kay Walsh, Renée Houston, Robert Coote, Arthur Macrae, Michael Gough, Ernest Thesiger

'Immensely and joyously successful at what it sets out to do.'—*Evening Standard*

'A work of genius.'—*News of the World*

AAN: Alec Guinness (as writer)

The Hospital**
US 1971 101m De Luxe Panavision
UA / Simcha (Howard Gottfried)

A city hospital is beset by weird mishaps, and it transpires that a killer is on the loose.
Black comedy with the emphasis on sex and medical ethics; in the same genre as *M*A*S*H*, and very funny if you can take it.

w Paddy Chayevsky d Arthur Hiller *ph* Victor Kemper *m* Morris Surdin

George C. Scott, Diana Rigg, Barnard Hughes, Nancy Marchand, Richard Dysart

AA: Paddy Chayevsky
AAN: George C. Scott

The Hostage
GB 1956 86m bw

A South American president condemns a revolutionary to death; in London, sympathizers kidnap the president's daughter. Tolerable support. Ron Randell, Mary Parker, Carl Jaffe, Margaret Diamond, Cyril Luckham. Written by Alfred Shaughnessy; directed by Harold Huth; for Westridge / Eros.

'They're blasting the Nazis—from inside!'
Hostages
US 1943 88m bw
Paramount (Sol C. Siegel)

In occupied Prague, the Nazis seize a variety of hostages and threaten them with death as a reprisal for underground activities.
Modest morale-builder, unfortunately padded out with melodramatics and overacting.

w Lester Cole, Frank Butler, *novel* Stefan Heym *d* Frank Tuttle *ph* Victor Milner *m* Victor Young

Luise Rainer, Paul Lukas, William Bendix, Oscar Homolka, Arturo de Cordova, Katina Paxinou, Roland Varno

Hostile Guns
US 1967 91m Techniscope

A marshal has to deliver four dangerous convicts to the penitentiary. Rather crude addition to the A. C. Lyles series distinguished only by nostalgic casting. George Montgomery, Tab Hunter, Yvonne de Carlo, Brian Donlevy, Fuzzy Knight, John Russell, Leo Gordon, Robert Emhardt, Richard Arlen. Written by Steve Fisher and Sloan Nibley; directed by R. G. Springsteen; for A. C. Lyles / Paramount.

Hostile Witness
GB 1968 101m De Luxe
UA / Caralan / Dador (David E. Rose)

A barrister suffers a nervous breakdown after the death of his daughter and finds himself accused of murder.
Complex courtroom thriller, filmed in a flatly boring way with stagey sets and performances. The plot is the only interest.

w Jack Roffey, from his play *d* Ray Milland *ph* Gerry Gibbs

Ray Milland, Sylvia Sims, Felix Aylmer, Raymond Huntley, Geoffrey Lumsden, Norman Barrs, Percy Marmont, Ewan Roberts

'If you'd hit me and given me orders on our wedding night, I would have kissed your hand!'
Hot Blood
US 1955 85m Technicolor Cinemascope
Columbia (Howard Welsch)

A dying gypsy king wants his young brother to get married and succeed him.
What promises to be a boring musical proves to be a boring melodrama. Artificial Romany hokum.

w Jesse Lasky Jnr *d* Nicholas Ray *ph* Ray June *m* Les Baxter

Cornel Wilde, Jane Russell, Joseph Calleia, Helen Westcott, Mikhail Rasumny
'Be there when Jane Russell shakes her tambourines!'—*publicity*

Hot Enough for June
GB 1963 98m Eastmancolor
Rank (Betty E. Box)
US title: *Agent 8¾*

A penniless writer is sent to Czechoslovakia on a goodwill mission and finds himself being used as a spy.
Very moderate spoof, neither very funny nor very thrilling.

w Lukas Heller, *novel* The Night before Wenceslas by Lionel Davidson *d* Ralph Thomas *ph* Ernest Steward *m* Angelo Lavagnino

Dirk Bogarde, Sylva Koscina, Robert Morley, Leo McKern, John Le Mesurier

Hot Millions*
US 1968 106m colour
MGM / Mildred Freed Alberg

A confidence trickster makes a fortune out of fictitious companies.
Elaborate, talky, overlong comedy with irresistible star performances.

w Ira Wallach, Peter Ustinov *d* Eric Till *m* Laurie Johnson

Peter Ustinov, Maggie Smith, Bob Newhart, Karl Malden, Robert Morley, Cesar Romero

AAN: Ira Wallach, Peter Ustinov (script)

Hot Pepper
US 1933 76m bw
Fox

Ex-Marines Flagg and Quirt become bootleggers and quarrel over a fiery South American entertainer.
Fourth and last in the comedy-melodrama series stemming from *What Price Glory?* Mild, stereotyped entertainment.

w Barry Connors, Philip Klein, Dudley Nichols *d* John G. Blystone *ph* Charles G. Clarke

Edmund Lowe, Victor McLaglen, Lupe Velez, El Brendel, Lillian Bond

The Hot Rock***
US 1972 105m De Luxe Panavision
TCF (Hal Landers, Bobby Roberts)
GB title: *How to Steal a Diamond in Four Uneasy Lessons*

Four crooks plan to rob the Brooklyn Museum of a priceless diamond.
Enjoyable variation on the caper theme, with relaxed comic performances and highly skilled technical back-up. It's refreshing to come across a film which hits its targets so precisely.

w William Goldman, novel Donald E. Westlake *d Peter Yates ph* Ed Brown *m* Quincy Jones

Robert Redford, George Segal, Zero Mostel, Paul Sand, Ron Leibman, Moses Gunn, William Redfield
'A funny, fast-paced, mventive and infinitely clever crime comedy, almost as if *The French Connection* had been remade as a piece of urban humour.'—*Michael Korda*

'Her lips offered what her heart denied!'
Hot Saturday
US 1932 73m bw

Malicious gossip in a small town causes a girl to lose her job. Small town, small potatoes; interesting chiefly for its two budding male stars. Nancy Carroll, Cary Grant, Randolph Scott, Edward Woods, Lillian Bond, Jane Darwell, William Collier Snr. Written by Seton I. Miller from the novel by Harvey Ferguson; directed by William A. Seiter; for Paramount. 'Fairly agreeable as entertainment, but will not get preferred playing time.'—*Variety*

Hot Spell*
US 1958 86m bw Vistavision
Paramount / Hal Wallis

In a small southern town, a husband seeks to leave his wife and family for a 20-year-old girl.
Overwrought domestic drama slipping perilously close to farce at times, but a good theatrical vehicle for its stars.

w James Poe, *play* Next of Kin by Lonnie Coleman *d* Daniel Mann *ph* Loyal Griggs *m* Alex North

Anthony Quinn, Shirley Booth, Shirley Maclaine, Earl Holliman, Eileen Heckart

Hot Stuff
US 1979 91m Metrocolor
Columbia / Rastar / Mort Engleberg

Members of a Burglary Task Force need convictions, so they set up fences in order to lure criminals, and are embarrassed by the results.
Slightly unusual but rather frantically assembled comedy which wears out its welcome long before the end.

w Michael Kane, Donald E. Westlake *d* Dom DeLuise *ph* James Pergola *m* Patrick Williams

Dom DeLuise, Suzanne Pleshette, Ossie Davis, Jerry Reed, Luis Avalos, Marc Lawrence
'Heavy farce in which a bright comedy is struggling to escape.'—*Tom Milne, MFB*

Hot Summer Night*
US 1957 85m bw
MGM (Morton S. Fine)

A foolhardy reporter determines on an interview with a notorious outlaw, and has to be rescued.
Interesting but disappointing low-budget experiment.

w Morton S. Fine, David Friedkin *d* David Friedkin *ph* Harold S. Marcorati *m* André Previn

Leslie Nielsen, Colleen Miller, Edward Andrews, Jay C. Flippen, James Best, Paul Richards, Robert Wilke, Claude Akins

Hot Water*
US 1924 50m approx (24 fps) bw silent

A young husband has trouble with a turkey, a new car and his in-laws. Casually structured star comedy with brilliant sequences. *Harold Lloyd*, Jobyna Ralston, Josephine Crowell. Written by Harold Lloyd and Sam Taylor; directed by Fred Newmeyer and Sam Taylor; for Harold Lloyd.

Hotel*
US 1967 124m Technicolor
Warner (Wendell Mayes)

Guests at a luxurious New Orleans hotel have various problems.
Old-fashioned omnibus drama from a bestseller, quite brightly done.

w Wendell Mayes, *novel* Arthur Hailey
d Richard Quine *ph* Charles Lang *m* Johnny Keating

Rod Taylor, Catherine Spaak, Karl Malden, Melvyn Douglas, Merle Oberon, Richard Conte, Michael Rennie, Kevin McCarthy, Alfred Ryder

Hotel Berlin*
US 1945 98m bw
Warner (Louis F. Edelman)

Various lives intertwine in a Berlin hotel towards the end of the war.
After five years of total war this view of life on the other side can hardly fail to be unconvincing, but the actors gleefully seize on moments of melodrama.

w Thomas Job, *novel* Vicki Baum *d* Peter Godfrey *ph* Carl Guthrie *m* Franz Waxman

Raymond Massey, Peter Lorre, Faye Emerson, Helmut Dantine, Andrea King, Alan Hale, George Coulouris, Henry Daniell, Helene Thimig, Kurt Kreuger, Steve Geray, Frank Reicher

'The most heavily routine of Warners' political melodramas, stuffed with sympathetic veterans.'—*James Agee*

Hotel du Nord**
France 1938 110m bw
Sedif / Imperial

People with problems congregate at a small hotel.
Melancholy, studio-confined character drama which has its adherents but technically seemed a throwback to earlier standards. The acting rescues it.

Annabella, *Louis Jouvet*, Jean-Pierre Aumont, *Arletty*, Jeanne Marken, Bernard Blier

w Henri Jeanson, Eugene Dabit *d Marcel Carné* *ph* Armand Thirard *m* Maurice Jaubert

'An outstander in this country and possesses good chance abroad.'—*Variety (Paris)*

Hotel for Women
US 1939 83m bw
TCF (Raymond Griffith)

Young city gold diggers are encouraged by a matron.
Slight comedy drama notable for the acting debut of hostess Elsa Maxwell.

w Katherine Scola, Darrell Ware *d* Gregory Ratoff *ph* Peverell Marley *m* David Buttolph

Elsa Maxwell, Linda Darnell, Ann Sothern, James Ellison, John Halliday, Lynn Bari, Alan Dinehart

'Synthetic Cinderella story . . . fluffed up with a generous display of latest fashions.'—*Variety*

Hotel Haywire
US 1937 66m bw
Paramount (Harold Hurley)

An astrologer makes eyes at a dentist's wife, and causes much confusion in a hotel.
Frantic farce which might have been funnier if it had stuck to the original script and cast (it was intended for Burns and Allen).

w Preston Sturges (before studio revision)
d George Archainbaud *ph* Henry Sharp

Leo Carrillo, Lynne Overman, Mary Carlisle, Benny Baker, Spring Byington, George Barbier, Porter Hall, Lucien Littlefield, John Patterson

'Broad comedy applied with sufficient skill and effect to make the journey on the dual route fairly safe.'—*Variety*

'Flaming love drama of the war-torn Balkans!'
'Her beauty sent men marching to their death with a smile!'

Hotel Imperial
US 1939 78m bw
Paramount

Balkans, 1916: a Polish dancer suspects a Hungarian officer of being responsible for her sister's death.
Dim romantic melodrama with espionage trimmings.

w Gilbert Gabriel, Robert Thoeren, *play* Lajos Biro *d* Robert Florey *ph* William Mellor *md* Boris Morros

Ray Milland, Isa Miranda, Reginald Owen, Gene Lockhart, J. Carrol Naish, Curt Bois, Henry Victor, Albert Dekker

'Nothing much to be done about this one . . . a weak sister, dated and inconclusive . . . never seems to generate any interest.'—*Variety*

'A very competent rehash . . . for the unexacting the picture has its moments.'—*Graham Greene*

† Previously made in 1926 by Erich Pommer, with Pola Negri. This version was originally announced in 1936 as *I Loved a Soldier*, to star Marlene Dietrich (or Margaret Sullavan) and Charles Boyer.

The Hotel New Hampshire
US 1984 108m Technicolor
Orion / Woodfall (Neil Hartley, Pieter Kroonenburg, David Patterson)

A schoolmaster and his family are obsessed by the fantasy of living in a hotel, and this fantasy is performed with variations.
A parable of life in the manner of Thornton Wilder's *The Skin of Our Teeth*, and sometimes even more obscure, but generally quite entertaining along the way.

w,d Tony Richardson, *novel* John Irving
ph David Watkin *m* Jacques Offenbach
pd Jocelyn Herbert *ed* Robert K. Lambert

Rob Lowe, Jodie Foster, Paul McCrane, Beau Bridges, Nastassja Kinski, Wallace Shawn, Wilford Brimley

Hotel Paradiso*
US 1966 99m Metrocolor Panavision
MGM (Peter Glenville)

Various romantic affairs come to a head one evening at a seedy hotel.
A famous boulevard farce seems jellied in aspic in this good-looking but very flatly handled film version, in which famous artists are left to caper about on an unsuitable wide screen with no help from the director.

w Peter Glenville, Jean-Claude Carrière, *play* Georges Feydeau *d* Peter Glenville *ph Henri Decaë* *m* Laurence Rosenthal *pd François de Lamothe*

Alec Guinness, Gina Lollobrigida, Robert Morley, Peggy Mount, Douglas Byng, Akim Tamiroff, Robertson Hare

Hotel Reserve
GB 1944 89m bw
RKO (Victor Hanbury)

An Austrian refugee in the south of France is asked by the police to track down a spy among his fellow hotel guests.
Slow, obvious and poorly made suspenser from a good novel.

w John Davenport, *novel* Epitaph for a Spy by Eric Ambler *d* Victor Hanbury, Lance Comfort, Max Greene *ph* Max Greene

James Mason, Lucie Mannheim, Raymond Lovell, Julien Mitchell, Martin Miller, Herbert Lom, Frederick Valk, Valentine Dyall

Hotel Sahara*
GB 1951 96m bw
GFD / Tower (George H. Brown)

In North Africa during World War II, a small hotel changes its loyalties to suit its occupiers.
Overstretched, studio-bound, fitfully amusing comedy.

w George H. Brown, Patrick Kirwan *d* Ken Annakin *ph* David Harcourt *m* Benjamin Franklin

Peter Ustinov, Yvonne de Carlo, David Tomlinson, Roland Culver, Albert Lieven, Bill Owen, Sidney Tafler, Ferdy Mayne

'Cheerful, uncomplicated empty stuff . . . no more subtle than a music hall sketch.'—*Richard Mallett, Punch*

The Hottentot
US 1929 77m bw

A horse lover is forced to masquerade as a champion jockey. Early talkie version of a well-worn theme which had previously appeared as a silent in 1923 with Douglas MacLean; it later turned up as a Joe E. Brown vehicle and in 1938 became *Going Places*, a Dick Powell musical. The 1929 version also starred Patsy Ruth Miller and Douglas Gerrard; written by Harvey Thew, from the play by Victor Mapes and Willie Collier; directed by Roy del Ruth; for Warner.

Houdini*
US 1953 106m Technicolor
Paramount (George Pal)

In the 1890s a fairground magician shows a passionate talent for escapology and finally

HOT MILLIONS. Peter Ustinov and Maggie Smith were better than their material.

kills himself by undertaking increasingly impossible tricks.
Superficial biopic with more attention to romance than to interesting detail. Some zest in the playing is killed by claustrophobic studio sets.

w Philip Yordan *d* George Marshall *ph* Ernest Laszlo *m* Roy Webb

Tony Curtis, Janet Leigh, Torin Thatcher, Sig Rumann, Angela Clarke

The Hound Dog Man
US 1959 87m colour Cinemascope
TCF / Company of Artists (Jerry Wald)

An irresponsible country boy gets his come-uppance.
Mild, competent backwoods comedy drama introducing a teenage rave.

w Fred Gipson, Winston Miller *d* Don Siegel *ph* Charles G. Clarke *m* Cyril Mockridge

Fabian, Stuart Whitman, Carol Lynley, Arthur O'Connell, Betty Field, Royal Dano, Jane Darwell, Edgar Buchanan, Claude Akins

The Hound of the Baskervilles**
US 1939 80m bw
(TCF) Gene Markey

Sherlock Holmes solves the mystery of a supernatural hound threatening the life of a Dartmoor baronet.
Basil Rathbone's first appearance as Sherlock Holmes is in a painstaking studio production which achieves good atmosphere and preserves the flavour if not the letter of the book but is let down by a curious lack of pace.

w Ernest Pascal, *novel* Arthur Conan Doyle *d* Sidney Lanfield *ph* Peverell Marley *m* Cyril Mockridge *ad* Thomas Little

Basil Rathbone, Nigel Bruce, Richard Greene, Wendy Barrie, Lionel Atwill, Morton Lowry, John Carradine, Barlowe Borland, Beryl Mercer, Ralph Forbes, E. E. Clive, Eily Malyon, Mary Gordon

'A startling mystery-chiller . . . will find many bookings on top spots of key duallers.'—*Variety*

'Lush dialogue, stagey sets and vintage supporting cast make it a delectable Hollywood period piece.'—*Judith Crist, 1980*

† For Rathbone's other appearances as Holmes see under *Sherlock Holmes*.

The Hound of the Baskervilles*
GB 1959 86m Technicolor
UA / Hammer (Anthony Hinds)

Spirited remake let down by dogged Hammer insistence on promises of horror and sex; good atmosphere also let down by poor colour.

w Peter Bryan *d* Terence Fisher *ph* Jack Asher *m* James Bernard

Peter Cushing, André Morell, Christopher Lee, Marla Landi, Ewen Solon, Francis de Wolff

The Hound of the Baskervilles
GB 1977 85m Technicolor
Hemdale / Michael White Ltd (John Goldstone)

A pointless, pitiful and vulgar spoof of an enjoyable original.

w Dudley Moore, Peter Cook, Paul Morrissey *d* Paul Morrissey *ph* Dick Bush, John Wilcox *m* Dudley Moore

Peter Cook (Sherlock Holmes), Dudley Moore (Watson), Denholm Elliot (Stapleton), Terry-Thomas (Mortimer), Joan Greenwood, Max Wall. Irene Handl, Kenneth Williams, Hugh Griffith, Roy Kinnear, Penelope Keith, Dana Gillespie, Prunella Scales, Jessie Matthews, Spike Milligan

'As I held her in my arms, how could I know that she was as vicious as she was beautiful?'

The Hour before the Dawn
US 1944 75m bw
Paramount (William Dozier)

When a pacifist English nobleman discovers during World War II that he has married a Nazi spy, he strangles her and joins the forces.
Stultifyingly absurd, badly made and acted melodrama which its author clearly wished he had never written, as it was later withdrawn from his canon.

w Michael Hogan, Lester Samuels, *novel* W. Somerset Maugham *d* Frank Tuttle *ph* John F. Seitz *m* Miklos Rozsa

Franchot Tone, Veronica Lake, John Sutton, Binnie Barnes, Henry Stephenson, Philip Merivale, Nils Asther, Edmund Breon

'Tedious and generally uneventful . . . a weak entry for the duals.'—*Variety*

The Hour of Decision
GB 1957 81m bw

A reporter is assigned to investigate the death of a columnist. A familiar type of second feature whodunit, with little about it to spark enthusiasm. Jeff Morrow, Hazel Court, Lionel Jeffries, Anthony Dawson, Mary Laura Wood. Written by Norman Hudis; directed by C. Pennington-Richards; for Tempean / Eros.

'Wyatt Earp—hero with a badge, or cold-blooded killer?'

Hour of the Gun**
US 1967 101m De Luxe Panavision
UA / Mirisch / Kappa (John Sturges)

After the gunfight at the OK corral, Wyatt Earp tracks down the rest of the Clanton gang.
Vividly set, slowly developed western which makes an ambiguous but forceful figure of Earp. Generally confident and interesting.

w Edward Anhalt d John Sturges ph Lucien Ballard m Jerry Goldsmith

James Garner, Jason Robards Jnr, Robert Ryan, Steve Ihnat, Michael Tolan, Frank Converse, Sam Melville, Monte Markham, Albert Salmi, Jon Voight, William Windom, Charles Aidman

The Hour of the Wolf*
Sweden 1967 89m bw
Svensk Filmindustri (Lars-Owe Carlberg)
original title: *Vargtimmen*

A painter, at his summer island home with his wife, is terrorized by monstrous nightmares and by memories of his own adulterous past.
Rather like the gloomy side of *Smiles of a Summer Night*, this very typical Bergman melodrama doesn't quite flow as intended, and whatever its meaning may be, its surface is less entertaining than usual.

wd Ingmar Bergman *ph* Sven Nykvist *m* Mars Johan Werle

Max Von Sydow, Liv Ullmann, Ingrid Thulin, Erland Josephson

The Hour of Thirteen
GB 1952 78m bw
MGM (Hayes Goetz)

Edwardian London is shocked when policemen are stabbed one by one.
Jaded Hollywood-English thriller, a remake of *The Mystery of Mr X* (qv).

w Leon Gordon, Howard Emmett Rogers, *novel* X vs Rex by Philip MacDonald *d* Harold French *ph* Guy Green *m* John Addison

Peter Lawford, Dawn Addams, Roland Culver, Derek Bond, Leslie Dwyer, Michael Hordern, Colin Gordon, Heather Thatcher

† Originally to be called *T for Terror*.

House
US 1986 93m colour
New World / Sean Cunningham

An old lady is found dead in her spooky house; her nephew moves in and endures various apparitions.
Silly film in which the creatures look ridiculous and the psychology makes no sense, especially when the whole thing attempts to be a protest about Vietnam.

w Ethan Wiley *d* Steve Miner *ph* Mac Ahlberg *m* Harry Manfredini *pd* Gregg Fonseca

William Katt, George Wendt, Richard Moll, Kay Lenz

† *House 2: The Second Story* followed in 1987 and was even worse.

The House across the Bay
US 1940 88m bw
(UA) Walter Wanger

To protect her racketeer husband from his enemies, his wife has him convicted of income tax evasion.
Unpersuasive melodrama, a star potboiler.

w Kathryn Scola *d* Archie Mayo *ph* Merritt Gerstad *m* Werner Janssen

Joan Bennett, George Raft, Lloyd Nolan, Walter Pidgeon, Gladys George, June Knight

The House Across the Street
US 1949 69m bw

A racketeer brings pressure on a newspaper, and a crusading reporter is relegated to giving advice to the lovelorn. Wayne Morris, Janis Paige, James Mitchell, Alan Hale, Bruce Bennett. Tepid remake of *Hi Nellie*. Written by Russell Hughes, from story by Roy Chanslor; directed by Richard Bare; for Saul Elkins / Warner.

House Calls*
US 1978 98m Technicolor
Universal / Jennings Lang (Alex Winitsky, Arlene Sellers)

A middle-aged doctor finds himself widowed and seeks a new mate.
Spotty comedy which tries to combine conventional romantic spats with medical satire, and comes off only in fits and starts.

w Max Shulman, Julius J. Epstein, Alan Mandel, Charles Shyer *d* Howard Zieff *ph* David M. Walsh *m* Henry Mancini

Walter Matthau, Glenda Jackson, Art Carney, Richard Benjamin, Candice Azzara, Thayer David, Dick O'Neill

A House Divided*
US 1931 70m bw
Universal (Paul Kohner)

A tough widowed fisherman seeks a new wife, but she falls in love with his son.
Glum variation on *Desire under the Elms*, interesting for early Wyler touches.

w John P. Clymer, Dale Van Every, John Huston, *story* Heart and Hand by Olive Edens *d William Wyler* *ph* Charles Stumar

Walter Huston, Kent Douglass, Helen Chandler, Vivian Oakland, Frank Hagney, Mary Foy

The House in Nightmare Park*
GB 1973 95m Technicolor
EMI / Associated London / Extonation (Clive Exton, Terry Nation)

In 1907, a ham actor is asked to perform at an old dark house in the country where an axe murderer prowls during the night.
Standard creepy house comedy thriller, well enough done though it would have been better with Bob Hope.

w Clive Exton, Terry Nation *d* Peter Sykes *ph* Ian Wilson *m* Harry Robinson

Frankie Howerd, Ray Milland, Hugh Burden, Kenneth Griffith, John Bennett, Rosalie Crutchley, Ruth Dunning

The House in the Square*
GB 1951 91m Technicolor (b / w endpieces)
TCF (Sol C. Siegel)
US title: *I'll Never Forget You*

An American atomic chemist living in London becomes his own ancestor of two hundred years ago, and falls in love.
Slow-starting but thereafter quite acceptable remake of *Berkeley Square* (qv), with some interesting dialogue and a genuinely affecting fade-out.

w Ranald MacDougall, play John L. Balderston *d* Roy Baker *ph* Georges Périnal *m* William Alwyn *ad* C. P. Norman

Tyrone Power, Ann Blyth, Michael Rennie, Beatrice Campbell, Dennis Price, Raymond Huntley, Irene Browne, Robert Atkins (as Dr Johnson)

A House Is Not a Home
US 1964 98m bw
(Paramount) Embassy (Clarence Greene)

The life story of New York's most famous madam, Polly Adler.
Dismal, unappealing, laundered biopic, cheaply made in an unconvincing period setting.

w Russel Rouse, Clarence Greene *d* Russel Rouse *ph* Harold Stine *m* Joseph Weiss

Shelley Winters, Robert Taylor, Cesar Romero, Ralph Taeger, Broderick Crawford

The House of a Thousand Candles
US 1936 54m bw

A young man must live in an unfinished mansion to inherit under the terms of his grandfather's will. Odd but basically unremarkable little mystery; the title is more interesting than the movie. Phillips Holmes, Mae Clarke, Irving Pichel, Rosita Moreno. Written by H. W. Hanemann and Endre Boehm from the novel by Meredith Nicholson; directed by Arthur Lubin; for Republic.

'The story Tokyo couldn't hide, and Washington couldn't hold back!'

House of Bamboo
US 1955 102m De Luxe Cinemascope
TCF (Buddy Adler)

Japanese and American authorities move into undercover action against Tokyo gangsters.
Routine big-budget crime drama with only the location in its favour; a time passer, vaguely adapted from *The Street with No Name* (qv).

w Harry Kleiner *d* Samuel Fuller *ph* Joe MacDonald *m* Leigh Harline

Robert Stack, Robert Ryan, Shirley Yagamuchi, Cameron Mitchell, Sessue Hayakawa

House of Cards
US 1968 100m Techniscope
Universal / Westward (Dick Berg)

An American becomes tutor in the Paris household of a French general's widow, and finds himself a pawn in a high-powered game of international intrigue.
Good-looking location thriller which after an intricate opening settles into a *39 Steps*-style chase, but makes little of it.

w James P. Bonner, *novel* Stanley Ellin *d* John Guillermin *ph* Piero Portalupi *m* Francis Lai

George Peppard, Inger Stevens, Orson Welles, Keith Michell, William Job, Maxine Audley, Peter Bayliss

House of Dracula*
US 1945 67m bw
U–I (Paul Malvern)

As a result of being visited in one evening by Count Dracula, the Wolf Man and the Frankenstein monster, a sympathetic doctor goes on the rampage.

Mind-boggling finale to the first Universal monster cycle, with a happy ending for the Wolf Man. Cheaply made and not really inventive, but has to be seen to be believed.

w Edward T. Lowe *d* Erle C. Kenton *ph* George Robinson *m* Edgar Fairchild

Onslow Stevens, John Carradine, Lon Chaney Jnr, Glenn Strange, Lionel Atwill, Martha O'Driscoll, Jane Adams

The House of Fear see The Last Warning (1929)

The House of Fear
US 1939 65m bw

Murder in a haunted theatre: an actor dies and the corpse disappears. Lively Crime Club whodunit, a remake of *The Last Warning* (1929). William Gargan, Irene Hervey, Dorothy Arnold, Alan Dinehart, Harvey Stephens, Walter Woolf King, Robert Coote, El Brendel, Tom Dugan. 'Sufficient edge-of-seat suspense to catch lower-bracket bookings in the nabe duallers.'—*Variety*

The House of Fear*
US 1945 68m bw

Members of a club are murdered one by one. A knotty problem for Sherlock Holmes, but rather tediously unravelled. Despite the orange pips it owes virtually nothing to Conan Doyle. Basil Rathbone, Nigel Bruce, Dennis Hoey, Aubrey Mather, Paul Cavanagh, Holmes Herbert, Gavin Muir. Written by Roy Chanslor; directed by Roy William Neill; for Universal.

'Mighty monsters, locked in mortal combat!'

House of Frankenstein*
US 1944 71m bw
U–I (Paul Malvern)

A mad doctor thaws out the monster and the Wolf Man (frozen at the end of *Frankenstein Meets the Wolf Man*) but comes to a sticky end.
Originally called *Chamber of Horrors*, this was the studio's first attempt to package its monsters (the first two reels are about Dracula). It could have been pacier in view of the possibilities, but it has its interest.

w Edward T. Lowe, Curt Siodmak *d* Erle C. Kenton *ph* George Robinson *m* Hans Salter

Boris Karloff, John Carradine, Lon Chaney Jnr, George Zucco, J. Carrol Naish, Anne Gwynne, Elena Verdugo, Lionel Atwill, Sig Rumann, Glenn Strange

'A chiller-diller meller.'—*Variety*

House of Horrors
US 1946 65m bw

An incompetent sculptor tricks a psychopathic killer into murdering his critics. Grade Z thriller with a monster element; crude beyond belief. Martin Kosleck, Rondo Hatton, Robert Lowery, Virginia Grey, Bill Goodwin. Written by George Bricker; directed by Jean Yarbrough; for Universal. (GB title: *Joan Medford Is Missing*.)

House of Games
US 1987 102m Du Art Color
Filmhaus / Orion (Michael Hausman)

A psychiatrist becomes involved in her patient's crooked dealings.
Stylish directorial debut by respected Broadway playwright.

w,d David Mamet *ph* Juan Ruiz Anchia *m* Alaric Jans

Lindsay Crouse, Joe Mantegna, Mike Nussbaum, Lilia Skala

House of Long Shadows: see House of the Long Shadows

House of Numbers
US 1957 92m bw Cinemascope
MGM (Charles Schnee)

A man helps his thuggish twin brother escape from prison.
An original melodramatic idea is frittered away through slow pacing.

w Russel Rouse, Don M. Mankiewicz, *novel* Jack Finney *d* Russel Rouse *ph* George J. Folsey *m* André Previn

Jack Palance, Barbara Lang, Harold J. Stone, Edward Platt

The House of Rothschild**
US 1934 87m bw (Technicolor sequence)
Twentieth Century (William Goetz, Raymond Griffith)

The chronicles of the famous banking family at the time of the Napoleonic Wars.
Lavish historical pageant with interesting scenes and performances.

w Nunnally Johnson, *play* George Hembert Westley *d* Alfred Werker *ph* Peverell Marley *m* Alfred Newman

George Arliss, Loretta Young, Boris Karloff, Robert Young, C. Aubrey Smith, Arthur Byron, Helen Westley, Reginald Owen, Florence Arliss, Alan Mowbray, Holmes Herbert

'A fine picture on all counts . . . one of those occasional 100% smashes which Hollywood achieves.'—*Variety*

'A good dramatic photoplay, finely presented, packed with ripe incident and quite beautiful photography.'—*C. A. Lejeune*

AAN: best picture

House of Secrets
GB 1956 97m Technicolor Vistavision
Rank / Julian Wintle (Vivian A. Cox)
US title: *Triple Deception*

A naval officer is asked to impersonate a lookalike counterfeiter and work undercover to expose the gang.
Old-hat Boys' Own Paper adventure story, mindlessly watchable.

w Robert Buckner, Bryan Forbes *d* Guy Green *ph* Harry Waxman *m* Hubert Clifford

Michael Craig, Julia Arnall, Brenda de Banzie, David Kossoff, Barbara Bates, Gerard Oury, Geoffrey Keen, Anton Diffring

The House of Seven Gables
US 1940 89m bw
Universal (Burt Kelly)

In 17th-century New England, a jealous brother sends his sister's fiancé to prison.
Flat adaptation of a grim, brooding novel; it never grips.

w Lester Cole, *novel* Nathaniel Hawthorne *d* Joe May *ph* Milton Krasner *m* Frank Skinner

George Sanders, Margaret Lindsay, Vincent Price, Alan Napier, Nan Grey, Cecil Kellaway, Dick Foran, Miles Mander

AAN: Frank Skinner

House of Strangers**
US 1949 101m bw
TCF (Sol C. Siegel)

An Italian-American banker who rigidly controls his three sons is arrested for illegal practices, and the family ties slacken.
Interesting ethnic melodrama with good script and performances; much remade, e.g. as *Broken Lance*.

w Philip Yordan, novel Jerome Weidman *d* Joseph L. Mankiewicz *ph* Milton Krasner *m* Daniele Amfitheatrof

Edward G. Robinson, Richard Conte, Susan Hayward, *Luther Adler*, Paul Valentine, Efrem Zimbalist Jnr, Debra Paget, Hope Emerson, Esther Minciotti, Diana Douglas

The House of the Angel**
Argentina 1957 73m bw
Argentina Sono Film (Leopoldo Torre Nilsson)
original title: *La Casa del Angel*

A repressed girl is obsessed for life by the shame of her first love affair.
Fascinating minor classic in a heavily Wellesian style.

w Beatriz Guido, Leopoldo Torre Nilsson, Martin Rodriguez Mentasti, *novel* Beatriz Guido *d Leopoldo Torre Nilsson ph* Anibal Gonzalez Paz *m* Juan Carlos Paz

Elsa Daniel, Lautaro Murua, Guillermo Battaglia

'The first major work of a director of individual vision and strongly national style.'—*Robert Vas, MFB*

The House of the Arrow
GB 1940 66m bw
(US title: *Castle of Crimes*)

A wealthy Frenchwoman is murdered and her English companion is under suspicion. A case for Inspector Hanaud; very tolerable whodunnit. Keneth Kent, Diana Churchill, Belle Chrystall, Peter Murray Hill, Clifford Evans, Catherine Lacey. Written by Doreen Montgomery, from the novel by A. E. W. Mason; directed by Harold French; for ABPC. (A previous version in 1930 starred Dennis Neilson Terry and was directed by Leslie Hiscott. A further version in 1953 with Oscar Homolka as Hanaud was directed by Michael Anderson for Associated British.)

House of the Damned*
US 1963 63m bw
TCF / Associated Producers (Maury Dexter)

An architect is asked to make a survey of an old empty castle, but he and his wife find that someone or something is in hiding there.
Corny but mildly effective second feature with a few neat touches.

w Harry Spalding *d Maury Dexter ph* John Nickolaus Jnr *m* Henry Vars

Ronald Foster, Merry Anders

House of the Long Shadows
GB 1983 101m colour
Cannon (Jenny Craven)

An author takes a bet to isolate himself in a dilapidated house and write a Gothic novel within 24 hours . . .
Semi-spoof variation on an old chestnut, with aged horror practitioners interrupting the silence. Too restricted in script and production to be really effective.

w Michael Armstrong, *play* Seven Keys to Baldpate by George M. Cohan and *novel* by Earl Derr Biggers *d* Pete Walker *ph* Norman Langley *m* Richard Harvey

Christopher Lee, Peter Cushing, Vincent Price, Desi Arnaz Jnr, John Carradine, Sheila Keith, Julie Peasgood, Richard Todd

'Golan and Globus seem to have inherited Lord Grade's habit of assembling advertising packages with movies appended as an afterthought.'—*Kim Newman, MFB*

'A horror flick which basks in the Hammer tradition without in any way understanding it.'—*Guardian*

House of the Seven Hawks
GB 1959 92m bw
MGM / David E. Rose

An American adventurer becomes involved in a search by criminals for buried Nazi loot.
Cliché-ridden thick ear, adequately produced but of no interest.

w Jo Eisinger, *novel* The House of Seven Flies by Victor Canning *d* Richard Thorpe *ph* Ted Scaife *m* Clifton Parker

Robert Taylor, Nicole Maurey, Linda Christian, Donald Wolfit, David Kossoff, Eric Pohlmann, Gerard Heinz

House of Usher*
US 1960 85m Eastmancolor Cinemascope
AIP / Alta Vista (Roger Corman)
GB title: *The Fall of the House of Usher*

The last of the Usher line, prone to catalepsy, is buried alive by her brother and returns to wreak vengeance.
Stylish but grottily-coloured low-budget horror which started the Poe cycle of the sixties. A bit slow, it would have worked better in the standard screen ratio, but there is a tense and spectacular finale.

w Richard Matheson, *story* Edgar Allan Poe *d* Roger Corman *ph* Floyd Crosby *m* Les Baxter *ad* Daniel Haller

Vincent Price, Myrna Fahey, Mark Damon, Harry Ellerbe

'The most astounding motion picture since motion pictures began! Man turned monster stalking show-world beauties! The ultimate dimension in terror!'
'You've never been scared until you've been scared in 3-D!'

House of Wax**
US 1953 88m Warnercolor 3-D
Warner (Bryan Foy)

Mutilated in a fire at his wax museum, a demented sculptor arranges a supply of dead bodies to be covered in wax for exhibition at his new showplace.
Spirited remake of *The Mystery of the Wax Museum* (qv); as a piece of screen narrative it leaves much to be desired, but the sudden shocks are well managed, perhaps because this is the first Grade-A 3-D film, packed with gimmicks irrelevant to the story and originally shown with stereophonic sound.

w Crane Wilbur *d* André de Toth *ph* Bert Glennon *m* David Buttolph

Vincent Price (whose horror career began here), Carolyn Jones, Paul Picerni, Phyllis Kirk, Frank Lovejoy
† The director could not see the 3-D effect, being blind in one eye.

House of Women
US 1962 85m bw

A pregnant woman is sent to prison for a robbery she didn't commit. Loose remake of *Caged*, with very little sense or vigour. Shirley Knight, Andrew Duggan, Constance Ford, Barbara Nichols, Margaret Hayes. Written by Crane Wilbur; directed by Walter Doniger; for Warner.

House on Haunted Hill
US 1958 75m bw
Allied Artists / William Castle

An old house which has seen several murders is the setting for a millionaire's party.
Gimmick ghost story with some (unexplained) gruesome moments; the most outlandish of its producer's cheapjack trick films (*Thirteen Ghosts, The Tingler, Macabre,* etc), it was originally billed as being in Emergo, which meant that at an appropriately horrific moment an illuminated skeleton on wires was suddenly trundled over the heads of the audience.

w Robb White *d* William Castle *ph* Carl Guthrie *m* Von Dexter

Vincent Price, Richard Long, Carol Ohmart, Alan Marshal, Elisha Cook Jnr

The House on 92nd Street***
US 1945 88m bw
TCF (*Louis de Rochemont)*

During World War II in New York, the FBI routs Nazi spies after the atomic bomb formula.
Highly influential documentary-style 'now it can be told' spy drama, which borrowed the feel of its producer's *March of Time* series and applied them to a fairly true story set on genuine locations though with a modicum of fictional mystery and suspense. Highly effective in its own right, it looked forward to *The Naked City* three years later; the later film unaccountably got most of the credit for taking Hollywood out into the open air.

w Barre Lyndon, Charles G. Booth, John Monks Jnr d Henry Hathaway *ph* Norbert Brodine *m* David Buttolph

William Eythe, Lloyd Nolan, Signe Hasso, *Leo G. Carroll*, Gene Lockhart, Lydia St Clair, Harry Bellaver

'Recommended entertainment for those who believe that naïve Americans are no match for wily Europeans in the spy trade, and for those who just like their movies to move.'—*Time*

'Imagine an issue of *The March of Time*. The hard agglomeration of fact; the road drill style; the voice. Prolong it to four times its usual length, throw in a fictional climax, and there you have *The House on 92nd Street*.'—*William Whitebait, New Statesman*

AA: original story (Charles G. Booth)

The House on Telegraph Hill
US 1951 93m bw
TCF (Robert Bassler)

A woman in a concentration camp assumes her dead friend's identity so that on release she can be sent to America; but murder threatens there.
Modernized amalgam of *Gaslight* and *Suspicion*, not as good as either, but the complexities of the story hold adequate interest.

w Elick Moll, Frank Partos, *novel* Dana Lyon *d* Robert Wise *ph* Lucien Ballard *m* Sol Kaplan

Richard Basehart, Valentina Cortesa, William Lundigan, Fay Baker, Gordon Gebert, Steve Geray

The House that Dripped Blood*
GB 1970 102m Eastmancolor
Amicus (Milton Subotsky)

A Scotland Yard man investigating a disappearance is led to a house with a murderous history.
Quartet of stories in *Dead of Night* style, neatly made and generally pleasing despite a low level of originality in the writing.

w Robert Bloch *d Peter John Duffell ph* Robert Parslow *m* Michael Dress

John Bennett, Christopher Lee, Peter Cushing, Denholm Elliott, Joanna Dunham, Nyree Dawn Porter, Jon Pertwee, Ingrid Pitt

Houseboat
US 1958 110m Technicolor Vistavision
Paramount / Scribe (Jack Rose)

A widower with three children engages a maid who is really a socialite, and they all set up house on a boat.
Artificial sentimental comedy with A-1 credits but little style or bite.

w Melville Shavelson, Jack Rose *d* Melville Shavelson *ph* Ray June *m* George Duning

Cary Grant, Sophia Loren, Martha Hyer, Eduardo Ciannelli, Harry Guardino

'The kind of picture to which you can take your stuffy maiden aunt, your wicked sophisticated uncle and your ten-year-old child, and they will all have a wonderful time.'—*Ruth Waterbury, Los Angeles Examiner*

AAN: script; song 'Almost In Your Arms' (*m / ly* Jay Livingston, Ray Evans)

The Housekeeper's Daughter*
US 1939 71m bw
Hal Roach

A gangster's moll returns to mama for a visit and falls in love with the stuffy son of the household.
Zany crime farce which too often lets its zip fade, but atones in a crazy firework finale.

w Rian James, Gordon Douglas, *novel* Donald Henderson Clarke *d* Hal Roach *ph* Norbert Brodine *m* Amedeo de Filippi

Joan Bennett, John Hubbard, Adolphe Menjou, William Gargan, George E. Stone, Peggy Wood, Donald Meek, Marc Lawrence, Lilian Bond, Victor Mature, Luis Alberni

'A smacko laugh generator due for profitable biz up and down the line.'—*Variety*

Housemaster*
GB 1938 95m bw
ABPC (Walter C. Mycroft)

A schoolmaster sides with his boys against the new headmaster's dictatorial methods.
Pleasing photographed play with all concerned in good form.

w Dudley Leslie, Elizabeth Meehan, *play* Bachelor Born by Ian Hay *d* Herbert Brenon *ph* Otto Kanturek

Otto Kruger, Diana Churchill, Phillips Holmes, Joyce Barbour, Kynaston Reeves, Rene Ray, Walter Hudd, John Wood, Cecil Parker, Michael Shepley, Jimmy Hanley

Housewife
US 1934 69m bw
Warner (Robert Lord)

For an advertising copywriter, success almost brings divorce.
Modestly efficient romantic programmer of its day.

w Manuel Seff, Lillie Hayward *d* Alfred E. Green *ph* William Rees *m* Leo F. Forbstein

Bette Davis, George Brent, Ann Dvorak, John Halliday, Ruth Donnelly, Hobart Cavanaugh, Robert Barrat, Phil Regan

'The dramatic punches are not merely telegraphed, but radioed.'—*Frank S. Nugent*

The Houston Story
US 1956 80m bw

An oil worker has a plan for stealing oil, and is employed by the syndicate. Racketeering melodrama of the least interesting kind. Gene Barry, Barbara Hale, Edward Arnold, Paul Richards, Frank Jenks. Written by James B. Gordon; directed by William Castle; for Sam Katzman / Columbia.

How Do I Love Thee
US 1970 109m Metrocolor
ABC (Robert Enders, Everett Freeman)

A philosophy professor recalls the odd career of his atheist father.
Curious comedy about an eccentric and his family relationships, a kind of *Cheaper by the Dozen* with religion added. Not on in 1970.

w Everett Freeman, *novel* Let Me Count the Ways by Peter De Vries *d* Michael Gordon *ph* Russell Metty *m* Randy Sparks

Jackie Gleason, Maureen O'Hara, Shelley Winters, Rick Lenz, Rosemary Forsyth

'Nauseated embarrassment for participants and onlookers alike.'—*Judith Crist*

' "What are you? A man or a saint? I don't want him, I want you!" Her desire scorched both their lives with the vicious breath of scandal!'

How Green Was My Valley***
US 1941 118m bw
TCF (Darryl F. Zanuck)

Memories of childhood in a Welsh mining village.
Prettified and unconvincing but dramatically very effective tearjerker in the style which lasted from Cukor's *David Copperfield* to *The Green Years*. High production values here add a touch of extra class, turning the result into a Hollywood milestone despite its intrinsic inadequacies.

w Philip Dunne, *novel* Richard Llewellyn *d John Ford ph Arthur Miller m* Alfred Newman

Walter Pidgeon, Maureen O'Hara, Roddy McDowall, Donald Crisp, Sara Allgood, Anna Lee, John Loder, Barry Fitzgerald, Patric Knowles, Morton Lowry, Arthur Shields, Frederic Worlock

'Perfection of cinematic narrative . . . pure visual action, pictures powerfully composed, dramatically photographed, smoothly and eloquently put together.'—*James Shelley Hamilton*

† The unseen narrator was Irving Pichel.

AA: best picture; John Ford; Arthur Miller; Donald Crisp
AAN: Philip Dunne; Alfred Newman; Sara Allgood

How He Lied to Her Husband
GB 1930 33m bw

An early film version of Bernard Shaw's playlet about a minor flirtation. Of historical interest only. Edmund Gwenn, Robert Harris, Vera Lennox. Written by Frank Launder; directed by Cecil Lewis; for BIP.

How I Won the War
GB 1967 110m Eastmancolor
UA / Petersham (Richard Lester)

During World War II an earnest young man becomes an officer and survives many tribulations including the death of his comrades.
Appalling kaleidoscope of black comedy and the director's own brand of uncontrolled cinematic zaniness, with echoes of *Candide* and *Oh What a Lovely War!* Just the way to alienate a paying audience.

w Charles Wood, *novel* Patrick Ryan *d* Richard Lester *ph* David Watkin *m* Ken Thorne

Michael Crawford, John Lennon, Roy Kinnear, Lee Montague, Jack McGowran, Michael Hordern, Jack Hedley, Karl Michael Vogler, Ronald Lacey, James Cossins, Alexander Knox

'Pretentious tomfoolery.'—*John Simon*

'One feels that Lester has bitten off more than he can chew . . . the ideas misfire, lost somewhere between the paper on which they were conceived and the celluloid on which they finally appear.'—*MFB*

How Sweet It Is*
US 1968 98m Technicolor Panavision
Warner / Cherokee / National General (Garry Marshall, Jerry Belson)

Suspicious of their son's intentions towards his girl friend on a European holiday, a middle-aged American couple decide to follow.
Good-looking, rather silly comedy, plain spoken in the modern manner but without much entertainment value except when farce gets the upper hand.

w Garry Marshall, Jerry Belson, *novel* The Girl in the Turquoise Bikini by Muriel Resnik *d* Jerry Paris *ph* Lucien Ballard *m* Pat Williams

James Garner, Debbie Reynolds, Maurice Ronet, Paul Lynde, Marcel Dalio, Terry-Thomas, Donald Losby, Hilarie Thompson

'One of those slender marital farces in which the behaviour of the adults is consistently more juvenile than that of the teenagers.'—*MFB*

How the West Was Won*
US 1962 162m Technicolor Cinerama
MGM / Cinerama (Bernard Smith)

Panoramic western following the daughter of a pioneering family from youth (1830) to old age, with several half-relevant stories along the way.
Muddled spectacular with splendid set-pieces but abysmal dullness in between, especially if not seen in three-strip Cinerama (the Cinemascope prints are muddy and still show the dividing lines). An all-star fairground show of its time.

w James R. Webb *d* Henry Hathaway (first half), John Ford (Civil War), George Marshall (train) *ph* William Daniels, Milton Krasner, Charles Lang Jnr, Joseph La Shelle *m* Alfred Newman *ad* George W. Davis, William Ferrari, Addison Hehr

Debbie Reynolds, Carroll Baker, Lee J. Cobb, Henry Fonda, Carolyn Jones, Karl Malden, Gregory Peck, George Peppard, Robert Preston, James Stewart, Eli Wallach, John Wayne, Richard Widmark, Brigid Bazlen, Walter Brennan, David Brian, Andy Devine, Raymond Massey, Agnes Moorehead, Henry Morgan, Thelma Ritter, Russ Tamblyn, Spencer Tracy (narrator)

'That goddamned Cinerama . . . do you know a waist shot is as close as you could get with that thing?'—*Henry Hathaway*

AA: James R. Webb
AAN: best picture; photography; music

How to Be Very Very Popular
US 1955 89m De Luxe Cinemascope
TCF (Nunnally Johnson)

Two belly dancers on the run from gangsters hide out in a co-ed college.
Wacky remake of *She Loves Me Not* (qv); tries hard for a vein of freewheeling lunacy but only occasionally achieves it. A few numbers might have helped.

wd Nunnally Johnson *ph* Milton Krasner *m* Cyril Mockridge

Betty Grable, Sheree North, *Charles Coburn*, Robert Cummings, Orson Bean, Fred Clark, Tommy Noonan

How to Beat the High Cost of Living
US 1980 110m Movielab

Three middle-class women take to robbery when they can't make the housekeeping balance. Undercast, reprehensible and almost totally unfunny alleged comedy. Susan Saint James, Jane Curtin, Jessica Lange, Richard Benjamin, Fred Willard, Eddie Albert. Written by Robert Kaufman; directed by Robert Scheerer; for Filmways.

How to Commit Marriage
US 1969 98m Technicolor
Cinerama / Naho (Bill Larence)

A couple decide to divorce, with repercussions on their family and in-laws.
Tiresome generation-gap comedy.

w Ben Starr, Michael Kanin *d* Norman Panama *ph* Charles Lang *m* Joseph J. Lilley

Bob Hope, Jackie Gleason, Jane Wyman, Leslie Nielsen, Maureen Arthur, Paul Stewart, Tina Louise

How to Marry a Millionaire**
US 1953 96m Technicolor Cinemascope
TCF (Nunnally Johnson)

Three girls rent an expensive New York apartment and set out to trap millionaires.
Cinemascope's first attempt at modern comedy was not quite as disastrous as might have been expected, largely because of the expensiveness of everything and the several stars still brightly twinkling, but the handling of this variation on the old *Golddiggers* theme, while entirely amiable, is dramatically very slack.

w Nunnally Johnson *d* Jean Negulesco *ph* Joe MacDonald *md* Alfred Newman *m* Cyril Mockridge

Lauren Bacall, Marilyn Monroe, Betty Grable, *William Powell*, Cameron Mitchell, David Wayne, Rory Calhoun, Alex D'Arcy, Fred Clark

'Not only educational, but great fun.'—*Star*

† The film has an eight-minute pre-credits concert sequence, which is pretty unnerving when it unspools on TV.

'The last word in do-it-yourself!'
How to Murder a Rich Uncle
GB 1957 80m bw Cinemascope
Columbia / Warwick (Ronald Kinnoch)

An impoverished nobleman decides to murder his rich old uncle.
Feebly-handled black comedy which does not come off at all despite a highly talented cast.

w John Paxton, *play* Il faut tuer Julie by Dider Daix *d* Nigel Patrick *ph* Ted Moore

Nigel Patrick, Charles Coburn, *Katie Johnson*, Wendy Hiller, Anthony Newley, Athene Seyler, Michael Caine, Noel Hood, Kenneth Fortescue

How to Murder Your Wife*
US 1964 118m Technicolor
UA / Murder Inc (George Axelrod)

A strip cartoonist tests out his violent scenes in real life; when his wife disappears he finds himself accused of murder.
Amusing preliminaries give way to dreary plot complications and an overlong courtroom scene. Leave after the first hour.

w George Axelrod *d* Richard Quine *ph* Harry Stradling *m* Neal Hefti *pd Richard Sylbert*

Jack Lemmon, Virna Lisi, *Terry-Thomas, Eddie Mayehoff*, Sidney Blackmer, Claire Trevor

How to Save a Marriage and Ruin Your Life
US 1968 102m Technicolor Panavision
Columbia / Nob Hill (Stanley Shapiro)

An attorney takes it upon himself to convince his friend of the infidelity of the friend's mistress . . .
Tedious sex antics without any sex; a few smiles are not enough to endear it.

w Stanley Shapiro, Nate Monaster *d* Fielder Cook *ph* Lee Garmes *m* Michel Legrand

Dean Martin, Eli Wallach, Stella Stevens, Anne Jackson, Betty Field, Jack Albertson, Katharine Bard

'Another variation on Hollywood's patent version of the Restoration comedy, which as usual abandons the lustiness of its 17th-century prototype in favour of guilt-ridden lechery and a fundamental respect for the married state.'—*MFB*

How to Steal a Million*
US 1966 127m De Luxe Panavision
TCF / World Wide (Fred Kohlmar)

The daughter of an art forger mistakenly involves a private detective in a robbery.
High-class but rather boring romantic comedy; the credits promise much but interest wanes quickly owing to uncertain handling.

w Harry Kurnitz *d* William Wyler *ph* Charles Lang *m* Johnny Williams

Audrey Hepburn, Peter O'Toole, Charles Boyer, Hugh Griffith, Eli Wallach, Fernand Gravet, Marcel Dalio

'Terribly wordy and slow . . . Wyler hasn't got the touch nowadays.'—*Sight and Sound*

'The picture isn't offensive, and it's handsome enough, but it's just blah.'—*Pauline Kael, New Yorker*

How to Succeed in Business without Really Trying**
US 1967 121m De Luxe Panavision
UA / Mirisch (David Swift)

A window cleaner cajoles his way to the top of a New York company.
Cinematically uninventive but otherwise brisk and glowing adaptation of a sharp, slick Broadway musical.

w David Swift, *musical book* Abe Burrows, Jack Weinstock, Willie Gilbert, *book* Shepherd Mead *d* David Swift *ph* Burnett Guffey *m / ly Frank Loesser ch* Dale Moreda after Bob Fosse

Robert Morse, Rudy Vallee, Michele Lee, Anthony Teague, Maureen Arthur, Murray Matheson

'Shows how taste and talent can succeed in bringing a stage musical to the screen with its virtues intact.'—*John Cutts*

Howard the Duck
US 1986 111m De Luxe
Universal / Gloria Katz / George Lucas
GB title: *Howard, a New Breed of Hero*

A duck from outer space comes to earth and has various uncomfortable adventures.
Toned down from an adult comic strip, this peculiar film has nowhere to go because it's too sexy for kids and too stupid for adults.

w Willard Huyck, Gloria Katz from Steve Gerber's character *d* Willard Huyck *ph* Richard H. Kline *m* John Barry *pd* Peter Jamison

Lee Thompson, Jeffrey Jones, Paul Guilfoyle.

The Howards of Virginia
US 1940 117m bw
Columbia (Frank Lloyd)
GB title: *The Tree of Liberty*

A Virginian surveyor finds himself involved in the Revolutionary War.
Historical cavalcade in which central miscasting seems to cast a shadow of artifice over the whole. Interesting but seldom stimulating.

w Sidney Buchman, *novel* The Tree of Liberty by Elizabeth Page *d* Frank Lloyd *ph* Bert Glennon *m* Richard Hageman

Cary Grant, Martha Scott, Cedric Hardwicke, Alan Marshal, Richard Carlson, Paul Kelly, Irving Bacon, Elizabeth Risdon

AAN: Richard Hageman

'Imagine your worst fear a reality!'
The Howling*
US 1980 90m CFI Color
Avco Embassy / International Film Investors / Wescom (Ron Bottin)

A lady newscaster discovers that the medical retreat at which she stays to recover from a nervous breakdown is likely to give her another.
A plethora of werewolves and a glut of in-jokes pale beside a gallery of convincing and horrifying special effects.

w John Sayles, Terence H. Winkless, *novel* Gary Brander *d* Joe Dante *ph* John Hora *m* Pino Donaggio *make-up Rick Baker*

Dee Wallace, Patrick MacNee, Dennis Dugan, Christopher Stone, Kevin McCarthy, John Carradine, Slim Pickens

† Some of the character names: George Waggner, R. William Neill, Sam Newfield, Fred Francis, Terry Fisher, Erle Kenton, Charlie Barton, Lew Landers . . .

Howling II . . . Your Sister is a Werewolf
US 1985 90m colour

An expert goes to Transylvania to track down the werewolf queen. Thin attempt at comedy-horror, which barely got released. Christopher Lee, Annie McEnroe, Reb Brown, Ferdy Mayne. Written by Robert Sarno, Gary Brandner; directed by Philippe Mora; for Steven Lane / Granite / Hemdale / Thorn–EMI. NB. The film, which was shot in Czechoslovakia, has no relation whatsoever to *The Howling*.

Huckleberry Finn
US 1931 71m bw
Paramount

The river adventures of Mark Twain's scapegrace hero.
Adequate early talkie family film.

w Grover Jones, William Slavens McNutt *d* Norman Taurog *ph* David Abel

Jackie Coogan, Junior Durkin, Mitzi Green, Jackie Searl, Eugene Pallette

Huckleberry Finn**
US 1939 90m bw
MGM (Joseph L. Mankiewicz)

Solidly competent remake with excellent production values and several entertaining sequences.

w Hugo Butler *d* Richard Thorpe *ph* John Seitz *m* Franz Waxman

Mickey Rooney, Walter Connolly, William Frawley, Rex Ingram

Huckleberry Finn*
US 1960 107m Metrocolor
MGM (Samuel Goldwyn Jnr)
aka: *The Adventures of Huckleberry Finn*

Another patchy remake.

w James Lee *d* Michael Curtiz *ph* Ted McCord *m* Jerome Moross

Eddie Hodges, Tony Randall, Archie Moore, Neville Brand, Judy Canova, Buster Keaton, Andy Devine

Huckleberry Finn
US 1974 118m De Luxe Panavision
UA / Apjac / Readers Digest (Robert Greenhut)

Ambitious but lustreless version of the famous story, with songs.

w / ly / m Richard M. Sherman, Robert B. Sherman *d* J. Lee-Thompson *ph* Laszlo Kovacs *pd* Philip Jeffries

Jeff East, Paul Winfield, David Wayne, Harvey Korman, Arthur O'Connell, Gary Merrill, Natalie Trundy

'It expires in a morass of treacle.'—*Tom Milne*

'It transforms a great work of fiction into something bland, boring and tasteless.'—*Michael Billington, Illustrated London News*

The Hucksters**
US 1947 115m bw
MGM (Arthur Hornblow Jnr)

Back from the war, an advertising executive finds it difficult to put up with his clients' tantrums.
Good topical entertainment which still entertains and gives a good impression of its period.

w Luther Davis, *novel* Frederic Wakeman *d Jack Conway ph* Harold Rosson *m* Lennie Hayton

Clark Gable, Deborah Kerr, Ava Gardner, *Sidney Greenstreet*, Adolphe Menjou, Keenan Wynn, Edward Arnold, Aubrey Mather

'A good picture, quick and to the point.'—*Photoplay*

Hud***
US 1963 112m bw Panavision
Paramount / Salem / Dover (Martin Ritt, Irving Ravetch)

Life is hard on a Texas ranch, and the veteran owner is not helped by his sexually arrogant ne'er-do-well son, who is a bad influence on the household.
Superbly set in an arid landscape, this incisive character drama is extremely well directed and acted but somehow lacks the touch of greatness.

w Irving Ravetch, Harriet Frank, novel Horseman Pass By by Larry McMurty *d Martin Ritt ph James Wong Howe m* Elmer Bernstein

Paul Newman, Patricia Neal, Melvyn Douglas, Brandon de Wilde

AA: James Wong Howe; Patricia Neal; Melvyn Douglas
AAN: script; Martin Ritt; Paul Newman

Huddle
US 1932 104m bw
GB title: *The Impossible Lover*

A steel worker's son makes good at Harvard, and wants to marry out of his class. Would-be serious class drama which fell over its own feet. Ramon Novarro, Madge Evans, Una Merkel, Conrad Nagel, Arthur Byron, Cliff Edwards. Written by Robert Johnson, C. Gardner Sullivan, Arthur Hyman and Walton Smith; directed by Sam Wood; for MGM.

'Football film doing much to defeat its own purpose by extreme length . . . the Metro foreign production end is substituting soccer for the football portions for European screenings.'—*Variety*

Hudson's Bay**
US 1940 95m bw
TCF (Kenneth MacGowan)

Pierre Radisson, a French Canadian trapper, opens up millions of acres of northern wilderness for England.
Well-made historical saga with good production and performances.

w Lamar Trotti d Irving Pichel ph Peverell Marley, George Barnes *m* Alfred Newman *ad* Richard Day, Wiard B. Ihnen

Paul Muni, Laird Cregar, Gene Tierney, John Sutton, Virginia Field, Vincent Price (as King Charles II), Nigel Bruce, Morton Lowry, Robert Greig, Frederic Worlock, Montagu Love

Hue and Cry***
GB 1946 82m bw
Ealing (Henry Cornelius)

East End boys discover that their favourite boys' paper is being used by crooks to pass information.
The first 'Ealing comedy' uses vivid London locations as background for a sturdy comic plot with a climax in which the criminals are rounded up by thousands of boys swarming over dockland.

w T. E. B. Clarke d Charles Crichton ph Douglas Slocombe, John Seaholme *m* Georges Auric

Alastair Sim, Jack Warner, Harry Fowler, Valerie White, Frederick Piper

'Refreshing, bloodtingling and disarming.'—*Richard Winnington*

Hugo the Hippo
US 1975 78m colour
Brut (Robert Halmi)

An independently-minded hippo combats a Zanzibar magician.
Uninventive cartoon feature, endearing neither in characterization nor in draughtsmanship.

w Thomas Baum *d* William Feigenbaum *md* Bert Keyes

Hugs and Kisses*
Sweden 1966 96m bw
Sandrews (Göran Lindgren)
original title: *Puss och Kram*

A destitute bohemian takes over the house and the wife of the old executive friend who shelters him out of pity.
Rather like a comedy version of the Dirk Stroeve section of *The Moon and Sixpence*, this sophisticated film came under censorship fire for depicting the first full frontal female.

wd Jonas Cornell *ph* Lars Swanberg *m* Bengt Ernryd

Sven-Bertil Taube, Agneta Ekmanner, Hakan Serner

'The brilliance of the film lies in the way humour and sadness are kept in perfect equilibrium.'—*MFB*

Huis Clos*
France 1954 99m bw
Films Marceau

Two women and a man die, go to hell, and are locked up for ever in an elegant room.
Rather flat intellectual fantasy from a play which made great waves when first performed.

w Pierre Laroche, *play* Jean-Paul Sartre *d* Jacqueline Audry *ph* Robert Juillard *m* Joseph Kosma

Arletty, Frank Villard, Gaby Sylvia

'Without the ecstasy, terror and poetic imagination of a Cocteau, the subject becomes a fatally stationary one.'—*Peter John Dyer, MFB*

Huk!
US 1956 83m Eastmancolor

In 1951, an American fights Philippine guerrillas who murdered his father. Crude action melodrama which served a purpose. George Montgomery, Mona Freeman, John Baer, James Bell. Written by Stirling Silliphant, from his novel; directed by John Barnwell; for Collier Young / UA.

Hullabaloo
US 1940 77m bw

A veteran actor goes into radio and causes a furore with a broadcast about men from Mars. Slim framework for a variety show encasing some young MGM talents. Frank Morgan, Virginia Grey, Dan Dailey Jnr, Billie Burke, Nydia Westman, Donald Meek, Reginald Owen, Leni Lynn, Virginia O'Brien, Sara Haden. Written by Nat Perrin; directed by Edwin L. Marin; for Louis K. Sidney / MGM.

The Human Comedy*
US 1943 117m bw
MGM (Clarence Brown)

In a small town during the war, a telegram boy brings tragedy to others and is touched by it himself.
Gooey, sentimental morale booster in the best MGM tradition, a variant on the Hardy family series but with all the pretensions of its author.

w Howard Estabrook, *novel* William Saroyan
d Clarence Brown *ph* Harry Stradling
m Herbert Stothart

Mickey Rooney, Frank Morgan, James Craig, Marsha Hunt, Jackie Jenkins, Fay Bainter, Ray Collins, Van Johnson, Donna Reed

Opening narration by Ray Collins: 'I am Matthew Macauley. I have been dead for two years. So much of me is still living that I know now the end is only the beginning. As I look down on my homeland of Ithaca, California, with its cactus, vineyards and orchards, I see that so much of me is still living there—in the places I've been, in the fields and streets and church and most of all in my home, where my hopes, my dreams, my ambitions still live in the daily life of my loved ones.'

'The dignity and simplicity of the ideas shade off into cheap pretentiousness.'—*Bosley Crowther*

'The best one can say of it . . . is that it tries on the whole to be "faithful" to Saroyan; not invariably a good idea.'—*James Agee*

'The Saroyan touch leaves nothing ordinary: the film is electric with the joy of life.'—*Time*

AA: original story
AAN: best picture; Clarence Brown; Harry Stradling; Mickey Rooney

Human Desire
US 1954 90m bw
Columbia (Lewis J. Rachmil)

A jealous railway official forces his wife to help him murder her suspected lover.
Drab and unattractive remake of *La Bête Humaine.*

w Alfred Hayes *d* Fritz Lang *ph* Burnett Guffey *m* Daniele Amfitheatrof

Gloria Grahame, Glenn Ford, Broderick Crawford, Edgar Buchanan

HUD. Paul Newman with Oscar-winner Patricia Neal.

The Human Factor
GB 1975 95m Technicolor

The family of a NATO war planner in Italy is slaughtered by terrorists. Violent revenge drama, of little interest. George Kennedy, John Mills, Raf Vallone, Arthur Franz, Rita Tushingham, Frank Avianca, Barry Sullivan. Written by Tom Hunter, Peter Powell; directed by Edward Dmytryk; for Frank Avianca.

The Human Factor
GB 1979 114m Technicolor
Panavision
(Rank) Wheel / Sigma / Otto Preminger

An innocent man is suspected of being the 'mole' in the Foreign Office.
Quietly sardonic scenes of diplomatic chess are played far too broadly and literally in this ill-advised and poorly executed foray into the serious spy scene, which despite its stars becomes merely risible before the end.

w Tom Stoppard, *novel* Graham Greene
d Otto Preminger *ph* Mike Malloy
m Richard and Gary Logan

Nicol Williamson, Richard Attenborough, Derek Jacobi, Robert Morley, John Gielgud, Ann Todd, Richard Vernon, Joop Doderer, Iman

'Unfortunately, Preminger stages it all as if he was just trying to get all the actors through their line readings in under two hours, allowing no breathing room or time for character nuance in a tale which resolutely calls for quiet moments.'—*Variety*

The Human Jungle
US 1954 82m bw

A new police captain cleans up a gangster-ridden slum district. Adequate low-life actioner of the kind later taken over by TV. Gary Merrill, Jan Sterling, Paula Raymond, Emile Meyer, Regis Toomey, Lamont Johnson, Chuck Connors. Written by William Sackheim and Daniel Fuchs; directed by Joseph M. Newman; for Allied Artists.

The Human Side
US 1934 60m bw

A philandering theatrical producer returns to his family. Pleasant light comedy, instantly forgettable. Adolphe Menjou, Doris Kenyon, Charlotte Kenyon, Dickie Moore, Reginald Owen, Joseph Cawthorn. Written by Frank Craven and Ernest Pascal, from the play by Christine Ames; directed by Eddie Buzzell; for Universal. 'Homely, wholesome domestic comedy that should find beaucoup favour with the family trade.'—*Variety*

Humanoids of the Deep
US 1980 81m Metrocolor
New World (Martin B. Cohen)
GB title: *Monster*

Gruesome amphibious creatures rise from the ocean to stalk and destroy the most nubile women in sight.
Lurid, nonsensical but very violent horror flick, with much rape and nudity; like a Corman quickie of the fifties but with added gore.

w Frederick James *d* Barbara Peeters (*sic*) *ph* Daniele Lacambre *m* James Horner *costumes* Rob Bottin

Vic Morrow, Doug McClure, Ann Turkel

Humoresque**
US 1947 125m bw
Warner (Jerry Wald)

An ambitious violinist gets emotionally involved with his wealthy patroness.
Lush soaper about suffering in high society, complete with tragic end and lashings of classical music (Isaac Stern on the sound track).

w Clifford Odets, Zachary Gold, *novel* Fannie Hurst *d Jean Negulesco ph Ernest Haller* *md* Franz Waxman

Joan Crawford, John Garfield, Oscar Levant, J. Carrol Naish, Joan Chandler, Tom D'Andrea, Craig Stevens, Ruth Nelson

AAN: Franz Waxman

The Hunchback of Notre Dame**
US 1923 120m approx (24 fps) bw silent
Universal

The deformed Notre Dame bellringer rescues a gypsy girl from the evil intentions of her guardian.
Victorian gothic version with a riveting star performance.

w Percy Poore Sheehan, Edward T. Lowe Jnr, *novel* Notre Dame de Paris by Victor Hugo *d* Wallace Worsley *ph* Robert S. Newhard, Tony Kornman

Lon Chaney, Patsy Ruth Miller, Norman Kerry, Ernest Torrence, Gladys Brockwell, Kate Lester, Brandon Hurst, Tully Marshall

The Hunchback of Notre Dame****
US 1939 117m bw
RKO (Pandro S. Berman)

This superb remake is one of the best examples of Hollywood expertise at work: art direction, set construction, costumes, camera, lighting and above all direction brilliantly support an irresistible story and bravura acting.

w Sonya Levien, Bruno Frank d William Dieterle ph Joseph H. August m Alfred Newman ad Van Nest Polglase

Charles Laughton, Cedric Hardwicke, Maureen O'Hara, Edmond O'Brien, Thomas Mitchell, Harry Davenport, Walter Hampden, Alan Marshal, George Zucco, Katherine Alexander, Fritz Leiber, Rod la Rocque

'A super thriller-chiller. Will roll up healthy grosses at the ticket windows.'—*Variety*

'Has seldom been bettered as an evocation of medieval life.'—*John Baxter, 1968*

'It exceeds in sheer magnificence any similar film in history. Sets are vast and rich in detail, crowds are immense, and camera uses of both are versatile, varied and veracious.'—*Motion Picture Herald*

† Other versions: *Esmeralda* (1906, French); *Notre Dame de Paris* (1911, French); *The Darling of Paris* (1917, US, with Theda Bara); and see above and below.

AAN: Alfred Newman

The Hunchback of Notre Dame
France / Italy 1956 107m Eastmancolor Cinemascope
Paris Films / Panitalia (Robert and Raymond Hakim)

Crude international rehash with nothing to commend it, though the script before dubbing may have been interesting.

w Jacques Prévert, Jean Aurenche *d* Jean Delannoy *ph* Michel Kelber *m* Georges Auric

Anthony Quinn, Gina Lollobrigida, Jean Danet, Alain Cuny, Robert Hirsch

The Hundred Pound Window
GB 1943 84m bw
Warner (Max Milder)

A racecourse clerk becomes involved with gamblers who bribe him to rig the totalizator, but he finally exposes them.
Routine programmer notable only for giving a leading role to an old character actor.

w Abem Finkel, Brock Williams, Rodney Ackland *d* Brian Desmond Hurst *ph* Otto Heller *m* Hans May

Frederick Leister, Mary Clare, Anne Crawford, Richard Attenborough, David Farrar, Niall MacGinnis, David Hutcheson

The Hunger is a mood, a look, an ambience created by Tony Scott. It is the lighting of Stephen Goldblatt, it is the production design of Brian Morris, it is the clothes created by Milena Canonero.'

The Hunger
US 1983 99m Metrocolor Panavision
MGM-UA / Richard Shepherd

A couple of ageless vampires are desperate for blood.
Absurd attempt to update Dracula with lashings of sex, rock music and flashy photography. An ordeal.

w Ivan Davis, Michael Thomas, *novel* Whitley Strieber *d* Tony Scott *ph* Stephen Goldblatt, Tom Mangravite *m* Michael Rubini, Denny Jaeger *pd* Brian Morris

Catherine Deneuve, Susan Sarandon, David Bowie, Cliff de Young

'One of the most incoherent and foolish pictures of recent months.'—*Observer*

Hungry Hill
GB 1946 92m bw
GFD / Two Cities (William Sistrom)

An Irish family feud spans three generations.
Rather uninteresting costume melodrama.

w Daphne du Maurier, Terence Young, Francis Crowdy *d* Brian Desmond Hurst *ph* Desmond Dickinson

Margaret Lockwood, Dennis Price, Cecil Parker, Michael Denison, F. J. McCormick, Dermot Walsh, Jean Simmons, Eileen Herlie, Siobhan McKenna, Eileen Crowe, Dan O'Herlihy

Hunted*
GB 1952 84m bw
GFD / Independent Artists (Julian Wintle)
US title: *The Stranger in Between*

A runaway boy joins forces with a runaway murderer, and the latter sacrifices himself for the boy's safety.
Predictable pattern melodrama, nicely made and acted.

w Jack Whittingham *d Charles Crichton ph Eric Cross m* Hubert Clifford

Dirk Bogarde, Jon Whiteley, Kay Walsh, Elizabeth Sellars, Frederick Piper, Geoffrey Keen, Julian Somers

Hunted Men*
US 1938 67m bw
Paramount

A killer on the run moves into a private home and is outwitted by the head of the house.
Competent second feature which sticks in the memory.

w Horace McCoy, William R. Lipman *d* Louis King *ph* Victor Milner

Lloyd Nolan, Lynne Overman, Mary Carlisle, J. Carrol Naish, Anthony Quinn, Dorothy Peterson

The Hunter
US 1980 117m Metrocolor
Paramount / Rastar / Mort Engelberg

Episodes in the violent career of an urban bounty hunter.

THE HUNCHBACK OF NOTRE DAME. RKO refused to distribute stills showing Charles Laughton's make-up as Quasimodo. Cedric Hardwicke is on the horse and the stunning art direction is by Van Nest Polglase.

The action scenes salvage a mysteriously banal screenplay full of continuity lapses and unexplained characters.

w Ted Leighton, Peter Hyams
book Christopher Keane, and the life of Ralph Thorson *d* Buzz Kulik *ph* Fred J. Koenekamp *m* Michel Legrand

Steve McQueen (his last film), Eli Wallach, Kathryn Harrold, LeVar Burton, Ben Johnson

'The final impression is of an extended TV pilot for yet another police-boosting serial with more action than sense.'—*Sunday Times*

The Hunters
US 1958 108m De Luxe Cinemascope
TCF (Dick Powell)

A fearless American pilot is sent to Korea on a special mission.
Standard war thriller, good to look at when airborne but pretty boring on the ground; propaganda element very strong.

w Wendell Mayes *d* Dick Powell *ph* Charles G. Clarke *m* Paul Sawtell

Robert Mitchum, Robert Wagner, Richard Egan, Mai Britt

The Hunting Party
US 1971 108m De Luxe
UA / Brighton / Levy–Gardner–Levy

A sadistic Texas baron sets out to shoot one by one the outlaws who have kidnapped his wife.
Crude, brutish and repellent melodrama: the epitome of permissiveness, replete with gore, rape and sadism.

w William Norton, Gilbert Alexander, Lou Morheim *d* Don Medford *ph* Cecilio Paniagua *m* Riz Ortolani

Gene Hackman, Candice Bergen, Oliver Reed

'Through miles of raging ocean he defied man's law!'

The Hurricane**
US 1937 110m bw
Samuel Goldwyn (Merritt Hulburd)

The simple life on a South Pacific island is disrupted, not only by a vindictive governor but by a typhoon.

Tolerable island melodrama with a spectacular climax and a generally good cast.

w Dudley Nichols, Oliver H. P. Garrett, *novel* Charles Nordhof, James Norman Hall *d John Ford, Stuart Heisler ph Bert Glennon* *m* Alfred Newman

Dorothy Lamour, Jon Hall, *C. Aubrey Smith, Mary Astor, Raymond Massey, Thomas Mitchell,* John Carradine, Jerome Cowan

'A big money picture . . . a production masterpiece.'—*Variety*

† Remade in 1979.

AAN: Alfred Newman; Thomas Mitchell

Hurricane
US 1979 120m Technicolor Todd AO 70
Dino de Laurentiis / Famous Films (Lorenzo Semple Jnr)

A remake of the 1937 film, lacking the style, the innocence, and even the technical splendour.

w Lorenzo Semple Jnr *d* Jan Troell *ph* Sven Nykvist *m* Nino Rota *pd* Danilo Donati

Jason Robards, Mia Farrow, Trevor Howard, Max Von Sydow, Dayton Ka'ne, Timothy Bottoms, James Keach

Hurricane Island
US 1951 71m Supercinecolor

Spaniards colonizing Florida are beset by evil spirits. Saturday matinee hokum in poor colour. Jon Hall, Edgar Barrier, Marie Windsor, Marc Lawrence. Written by David Matthews; directed by Lew Landers; for Sam Katzman / Columbia.

Hurricane Smith
US 1952 90m Technicolor
Paramount / Nat Holt

An adventurer charters a boat to find a South Sea treasure but the boat owner turns the tables on him.
Standard thick ear with plenty of action.

w Frank Gruber *d* Jerry Hopper *ph* Ray Rennahan *m* Paul Sawtell

John Ireland, Yvonne de Carlo, James Craig, Forrest Tucker

'Will the south overcome the bigotry of the hate-laden white aristocrats?'

Hurry Sundown
US 1967 146m Technicolor Panavision
Paramount / Sigma (Otto Preminger)

Post-war racial problems in Georgia farmland, with degenerate whites and noble blacks. Incredibly cliché-ridden epic melodrama with action and sex asides, from a rock bottom bestseller. It long outstays its welcome even for unintentional hilarity.

w Thomas C. Ryan, Horton Foote, *novel* K. B. Gilden *d* Otto Preminger *ph* Loyal Griggs, Milton Krasner *m* Hugo Montenegro

Jane Fonda, Michael Caine, Rex Ingram, Diahann Carroll, Burgess Meredith, John Philip Law, Robert Hooks, Faye Dunaway, Beah Richards, George Kennedy, Madeleine Sherwood

'Critic Wilfrid Sheed wrote recently that no film is ever so bad that you can't find some virtue in it. He must not have seen *Hurry Sundown*.'—*Rex Reed*

'To criticize it would be like tripping a dwarf.'—*Wilfrid Sheed*

'A pantomime version of Greek tragedy.'—*MFB*

'Preminger's taste is atrocious. His idea of erotic symbolism is Jane Fonda caressing Michael Caine's saxophone.'—*Cue*

'A comedy about love, death, and freedom!'

Husbands*
US 1970 154m De Luxe
Columbia / Faces Music Inc (Al Ruban)

Three married men, shocked by the death of their friend, impulsively get drunk, fly to London and set out on a weekend of dissipation.
Irritatingly rough hewn and insanely overlong, this half-improvised tragi-comedy forces three good actors to overplay embarrassingly; but its best moments are memorable.

wd John Cassavetes ph Victor Kemper *m* none

Peter Falk, John Cassavetes, Ben Gazzara

Husband's Holiday
US 1931 70m bw

A wife takes a passive attitude to her husband's affair. Tepid sophisticated comedy which doesn't register. Clive Brook, Vivienne Osborne, Charles Ruggles, Juliette Compton, Charles Winninger, Elizabeth Patterson. Written by Ernest Pascal from his play The Marriage Bed; directed by Robert Milton; for Paramount. 'Mild drawing-room problem play made even milder by repressed acting.'—*Variety*

'It starts with the most shocking scene of all time – and that's only the beginning!'

Hush Hush Sweet Charlotte*
US 1964 133m bw
TCF / Associates and Aldrich

A southern belle lives thirty-seven years in a lonely mansion tormented by nightmarish memories of her fiancé's murder. Suddenly, after a series of apparent hauntings and other strange events, she finds she didn't do it.
Padded but generally enjoyable replay of elements from *Whatever Happened to Baby Jane*, with a large helping of *Les Diaboliques*. The stars help more than the director.

w Henry Farrell, Lukas Heller *d* Robert Aldrich *ph Joseph Biroc m* Frank de Vol *ad* William Glasgow

Bette Davis, Olivia de Havilland, Joseph Cotten, Cecil Kellaway, Victor Buono, William Campbell, Mary Astor, Agnes Moorehead

'The blood is on the cleaver, the madwoman is on the loose, the headless corpse is on the prowl and the Guignol is about as grand as it can get.'—*Judith Crist*

'Aldrich only just manages to keep this side of being disgusting and that side of being ridiculous.'—*Films and Filming*

AAN: Joseph Biroc; Frank de Vol; Agnes Moorehead; title song (*m* Frank de Vol, *ly* Mack David)

Hush Money
US 1931 68m bw

A girl serves a jail term, but afterwards gets involved with a racketeer. Underworld comedy-drama which paid its way. Joan Bennett, Owen Moore, Hardie Albright, Myrna Loy, C. Henry Gordon, George Raft. Written by Dudley Nichols and Courtney Terret; directed by Sidney Lanfield; for Fox. 'A light programmer for fair grosses.'—*Variety*

Hussy
GB 1979 94m Eastmancolor

A high-class prostitute becomes involved with gangsters but eventually finds a new life for herself and her offspring. Tedious exploitation melodrama, shot like a ninety-minute commercial. Helen Mirren, John Shea, Daniel Chasin, Jenny Runacre. Written and directed by Matthew Chapman; for Boyd's Company.

Hustle
US 1975 118m Eastmancolor
Paramount / RoBurt (Robert Aldrich)

A police lieutenant lives with a call girl and is drawn into her corrupt life.
Doleful crime melodrama with both eyes in the gutter.

w Steve Shagan *d* Robert Aldrich *ph* Joseph Biroc *m* Frank de Vol

Burt Reynolds, Catherine Deneuve, Ben Johnson, Paul Winfield, Eileen Brennan, Eddie Albert, Ernest Borgnine, Catherine Bach, Jack Carter

'A fine companion piece to *Kiss Me Deadly* in its vision of a journey to the end of the night in quest of a myth.'—*Tim Milne*

'Even with such a meandering script as this, one expects more than the paltry fare Aldrich offers.'—*Paul Coleman*

The Hustler**
US 1961 135m bw Cinemascope
TCF / Robert Rossen

A pool room con man comes to grief when he falls in love.
Downbeat melodrama with brilliantly handled and atmospheric pool table scenes; the love interest is redundant.

w Robert Rossen, Sidney Carroll, *novel* Walter Tevis *d Robert Rossen ph Eugen Schufftan m* Kenyon Hopkins

Paul Newman, Jackie Gleason, George C. Scott, Piper Laurie, Myron McCormick, Murray Hamilton, Michael Constantine

'There is an overall impression of intense violence, and the air of spiritual decadence has rarely been conveyed so vividly.'—*David Robinson*

'The supreme classic of that great American genre, the low-life movie.'—*Observer*

AA: Eugen Schufftan

AAN: best picture; script; Robert Rossen (as director); Paul Newman; Jackie Gleason; George C. Scott; Piper Laurie

Hyde Park Corner
GB 1935 84m bw

Events of 1780 at Hyde Park Corner seem to happen again in modern times. Half-hearted reincarnation romance with good moments. Gordon Harker, Binnie Hale, Gibb McLaughlin, Harry Tate, Eric Portman, Donald Wolfit. Written by D. B. Wyndham-Lewis, from the play by Walter Hackett; directed by Sinclair Hill; for Grosvenor.

The Hypnotic Eye
US 1960 79m bw

A mad killer hypnotizes pretty girls into defacing themselves. Unattractive thriller including much mumbo-jumbo about hypnotism. Jacques Bergerac, Allison Hayes, Merry Anders, Marcia Henderson. Written by Gitta and William Read Woodfield; directed by George Blair; for Allied Artists.

Hysteria
GB 1964 85m bw
MGM / Hammer (Jimmy Sangster)

An American suffering from amnesia is discharged from a London clinic and walks into a murder plot.
Complicated and rather unsympathetic Hammer twister.

w Jimmy Sangster *d* Freddie Francis *ph* John Wilcox *m* Don Banks

Robert Webber, Lelia Goldoni, Anthony Newlands, Jennifer Jayne, *Maurice Denham*, Peter Woodthorpe

I Accuse*
GB 1958 99m bw Cinemascope
MGM (Sam Zimbalist)

In 1894 Paris, Alfred Dreyfus is tried for treason and later defended by Emile Zola.
A well tried historical incident is stolidly retold and unsuitably wide-screened; the star cast tends to flounder for lack of assistance.

w Gore Vidal *d* Jose Ferrer *ph* Frederick A. Young *m* William Alwyn

Jose Ferrer (Dreyfus), *Anton Walbrook* (Esterhazy), Emlyn Williams (Zola), Viveca Lindfors, David Farrar, Leo Genn, Herbert Lom, Harry Andrews, Felix Aylmer, George Coulouris, Donald Wolfit

I Aim at the Stars
US 1960 107m bw
Columbia / Morningside / Fama (Charles H. Schneer)

The story of German rocket expert Wernher Von Braun and his later work on American space vehicles.
Shaky biopic of a controversial scientist who changed sides.

w Jay Dratler *d* J. Lee-Thompson *ph* Wilkie Cooper *m* Laurie Johnson

Curt Jurgens, Herbert Lom, James Daly, Gia Scala, Victoria Shaw, Adrian Hoven, Karel Stepanek

'Mannered panning shots and crafty cutting abound, leading to a stylistic St Vitus' Dance.'—*John Gillett*

'The biggest double exposure since Adam and Eve!'

I Am a Camera
GB 1955 99m bw
Romulus (Jack Clayton)

A young English writer observes life in Berlin in the early thirties, and has a platonic relationship with an amoral and reckless young English girl.
A rather flat and flabby treatment of the stories by Christopher Isherwood and the play by John Van Druten, all better known these days in the form of *Cabaret*. Disappointingly unstylish.

w John Collier *d* Henry Cornelius *ph* Guy Green *m* Malcolm Arnold

Julie Harris, Laurence Harvey, Shelley Winters, Ron Randell, Anton Diffring

'Six sticks of dynamite that blasted his way to freedom . . . and awoke America's conscience!'

I Am a Fugitive from a Chain Gang****
US 1932 90m bw
Warner (Hal B. Wallis)

An innocent man is convicted and after brutal treatment with the chain gang becomes a vicious criminal on the run.
Horrifying story in the semi-documentary manner; a milestone in Hollywood history and still a fairly compelling piece of shock entertainment.

w Sheridan Gibney, Brown Holmes, Robert E. Burns d Mervyn Le Roy ph Sol Polito m Bernhard Kaun

Paul Muni, Glenda Farrell, Helen Vinson, Preston Foster, Allen Jenkins, Edward J. Macnamara, Berton Churchill, Edward Ellis

'A picture with guts . . . everything about it is technically 100% . . . shy on romantic angles, but should get nice money all over.'—*Variety*

'To be enthusiastically commended for its courage, artistic sincerity, dramatic vigour, high entertainment concept and social message.'—*Wilton A. Barrett*

'I quarrel with the production not because it is savage and horrible, but because each step in an inevitable tragedy is taken clumsily, and because each character responsible for the hero's doom is shown more as a caricature than as a person.'—*Pare Lorentz*

AAN: best picture; Paul Muni

I Am a Thief
US 1934 64m bw

Robbery and murder on the Orient Express. Involved programmer which becomes as tiresome as its library footage. Mary Astor, Ricardo Cortez, Dudley Digges, Robert Barrat, Irving Pichel. Written by Ralph Block and Doris Malloy; directed by Robert Florey; for Warners. 'Should be able to top on a double bill but will have a tough time singling.'—*Variety*

I Am Not Afraid
US 1939 59m bw

An old man testifies against political terrorists. Tepid remake of *Star Witness*. Charley Grapewin, Jane Bryan, Henry O'Neill, Elizabeth Risdon. Written by Lee Katz; directed by Crane Wilbur; For Warners. (GB title: *The Man Who Dared*.) 'Filler for the duals.'—*Variety*

I Am Suzanne*
US 1933 99m bw

A dancer in love with a puppeteer comes under the influence of gangsters. Curious but vaguely endearing mixture of music and mayhem, with the puppets used as symbolic furtherers of the plot. Lilian Harvey, Gene Raymond, Leslie Banks, Georgia Caine, Halliwell Hobbes. Written by Edwin Justus Mayer and Rowland V. Lee; directed by Rowland V. Lee; for Jesse L. Lasky / Fox. 'Not a wow, but rates fairly well.'—*Variety*

I Am the Law*
US 1938 83m bw
Columbia (Everett Riskin)

A law professor is asked by a civic leader to become a special prosecutor cleaning up rackets.
Adequate star potboiler, quite enjoyable.

w Jo Swerling *d* Alexander Hall *ph* Henry Freulich *md* Morris Stoloff

Edward G. Robinson, Otto Kruger, John Beal, Barbara O'Neil, Wendy Barrie, Arthur Loft, Marc Lawrence

'A slam-bang, rip-roaring meller that has all the elements of previous films inspired by District Attorney Thomas E. Dewey's career.'—*Variety*

'The liveliest melodrama in town.'—*New York Times*

I Believe in You*
GB 1952 95m bw
Ealing (Michael Relph)

Interwoven stories of probation officers; watchable and reasonable but not very compelling.

w Michael Relph, Basil Dearden, Jack Whittingham, Nicholas Phipps *d* Basil Dearden *ph* Gordon Dines *m* Ernest Irving

Celia Johnson, Cecil Parker, Godfrey Tearle, Harry Fowler, George Relph, Joan Collins, Laurence Harvey, Ernest Jay, Ursula Howells, Sidney James, Katie Johnson, Ada Reeve, Brenda de Banzie

I Believed in You
US 1934 69m bw

A wife is driven to leave her radical agitator husband. Initially interesting but unsatisfactory romantic melodrama. Rosemary Ames, Victor Jory, John Boles, Gertrude Michael, George Meeker. Written by William Conselman; directed by Irving Cummings; for Fox. 'Some idea, but lacking punch in plot and direction.'—*Variety*

'The most spinechilling cry that can freeeze the blood!'

I Bury the Living
US 1957 77m bw

The honorary chairman of a cemetery seems to have the power to mark people for death. Unusual enough to be encouraging, sloppy enough to disappoint even mystery lovers. Richard Boone, Theodore Bikel, Herbert Anderson, Peggy Maurer. Written by Louis Garfinkle; directed by Albert Band; for Maxim / UA.

I Can Get It for You Wholesale*
US 1951 89m bw
TCF (Sol C. Siegel)
GB title: *This Is My Affair*
American TV title: Only the Best

An ambitious young mannequin starts her own dressmaking firm and sets her sights high.
Watchable comedy-drama which quickly sheds the edge of satire which might have made it the dressmaker's *All About Eve*.

w Abraham Polonsky, *novel* Jerome Weidman *d* Michael Gordon *ph* Milton Krasner *m* Sol Kaplan *md* Lionel Newman

Susan Hayward, Dan Dailey, George Sanders, Sam Jaffe, Randy Stuart, Marvin Kaplan, Harry Von Zell

I Cheated the Law
US 1948 71m bw

An attorney wins a murder case but finds he has been tricked into providing an alibi.
Meandering crime story which fails to hold the attention. Tom Conway, Steve Brodie, Robert Osterloh, Barbara Billingsley, Russell Hicks. Written by Richard G. Hubler; directed by Edward L. Cahn; for Sam Baerwitz / TCF.

'Crushed lips don't talk!'
I Confess**
US 1953 94m bw
Warner / Alfred Hitchcock

A priest hears the confession of a murderer and cannot divulge it to the police even though he is himself suspected.
Hitchcock is always worth watching, and although this old chestnut gives him very restricted scope he imbues the story with a strong feeling for its setting (Quebec) and an overpowering sense of doom.

w George Tabori, William Archibald, *play* Paul Anthelme *d Alfred Hitchcock* *ph* Robert Burks *m* Dmitri Tiomkin

Montgomery Clift, Anne Baxter, Brian Aherne, Karl Malden, Dolly Haas, O. E. Hasse

'Whatever its shortcomings, it has the professional concentration of effect, the narrative control, of a story teller who can still make most of his rivals look like amateurs.'—*MFB*

I Could Go on Singing*
GB 1963 99m Eastmancolor
Panavision
UA / Barbican (Lawrence Turman)

An American singing star in Britain looks up an old lover and tries to take over their illegitimate son, but the call of the footlights proves stronger.
The star enjoys her last specially-tailored role; a banal, old-fashioned agreeable one-woman show.

w Mayo Simon *d* Ronald Neame *ph* Arthur Ibbetson *m* Mort Lindsey

Judy Garland, Dirk Bogarde, Aline MacMahon, Jack Klugman

'Merely standard fare in an age without standards.'—*John Simon*

I Cover the Waterfront*
US 1933 75m bw
Reliance (Edward Small)

A reporter uses a girl's friendship to expose her father's smuggling activities.
In its time a tough, even daring melodrama, this plot has now become the stuff of every other TV series episode.

w Wells Root, Jack Jevne, Max Miller *d James Cruze* *ph* Ray June *m* Alfred Newman

Claudette Colbert, Ben Lyon, Ernest Torrence, Hobart Cavanaugh

'Combination of title, picturesque background and three good performances should offset inferior story for favourable business.'—*Variety*

'A bit raw and a bit sentimental and a bit routine, the film does let life in through the cracks.'—*Graham Greene*

† Credited with being the origin of the phrase, 'Not tonight, Josephine!'

I Didn't Do It
GB 1945 97m bw
Columbia (Ben Henry, Marcel Varnel)

Murder in a theatrical boarding house, with suspicion pointing at Our George.
One of the star's last vehicles: not too bad at all, but without the sweet smell of success.

w Howard Irving Young, Stephen Black, Norman Lee, Peter Fraser, Michael Vaughan *d* Marcel Varnel *ph* Roy Fogwell

George Formby, Billy Caryll, Hilda Mundy, Gaston Palmer, Jack Daly, Carl Jaffe, Marjorie Browne, Wally Patch

I Died a Thousand Times
US 1955 109m Warnercolor
Cinemascope
Warner (Willis Goldbeck)

An ex-convict plans a big hotel robbery, but things go wrong within his gang.
Overlong, heavygoing, tedious gangster melodrama with too much talk.

w W. R. Burnett *d* Stuart Heisler *ph* Ted McCord *m* David Buttolph

Jack Palance, Shelley Winters, Lori Nelson, Lon Chaney Jnr, Lee Marvin, Gonzales Gonzales, Earl Holliman, Perry Lopez

'This remake of *High Sierra* is scarcely more inspired than its title.'—*MFB*

'It is an insult to the intelligence to pull this old mythological hero out of the archives and set him on a mountaintop again.'—*New York Times*

The I Don't Care Girl*
US 1953 78m Technicolor
TCF (George Jessel)

The life of musical entertainer Eva Tanguay, at her height during World War I, as told by three men in her life.
Breezy, conventional backstage musical biopic.

w Walter Bullock *d* Lloyd Bacon *ph* Arthur Arling *md* Lionel Newman *ch* Jack Cole, Seymour Felix

Mitzi Gaynor, David Wayne, Oscar Levant, *George Jessel*, Warren Stevens

I Don't Want to be Born
GB 1975 94m Eastmancolor
(Rank) Unicapital (Norma Corney)
US title: *The Devil within Her*

An ex-stripper gives birth to a monstrous baby which goes on a murderous rampage.
Sick horror stuff with a high death rate and no notable credits.

w Stanley Price *d* Peter Sasdy *ph* Ken Talbot *m* Ron Grainer

Joan Collins, Ralph Bates, Donald Pleasence, Eileen Atkins, George Claydon

I Dood It!
US 1943 102m bw
MGM (Jack Cummings)
GB title: *By Hook or by Crook*

A tailor falls for a Hollywood star.
Boring star comedy with interpolated musical numbers.

w Sig Herzig, Fred Saidy *d* Vincente Minnelli *ph* Ray June *md* Georgie Stoll

Red Skelton, Eleanor Powell, John Hodiak, Lena Horne, Jimmy Dorsey and his Orchestra, Hazel Scott, Richard Ainley

I Dream of Jeannie
US 1952 90m Trucolor

The loves and financial problems of songwriter Stephen Foster. Low-key musical biopic covering exactly the same ground as *Swanee River*. Ray Middleton (as E. P. Christy), Bill Shirley, Muriel Lawrence, Rex Allen. Written by Alan Le May; directed by Allan Dwan; for Republic.

I Dream Too Much
US 1935 95m bw
RKO (Pandro S. Berman)

A French girl singer marries an American composer.
Forgettable vehicle for an operatic star.

w Edmund North, James Gow *d* John Cromwell *ph* David Abel *songs* Jerome Kern, Dorothy Fields *md* Max Steiner

Lily Pons, Henry Fonda, Eric Blore, Osgood Perkins, Lucien Littlefield, Lucille Ball, Esther Dale, Mischa Auer, Paul Porcasi

'It will be a winner at the box office without breaking any records.'—*Variety*

I Escaped from Devil's Island
US 1973 81m De Luxe
UA Roger Corman, Gene Corman

In 1918, a black convict makes his plans for escape.
Rough, brutish melodrama which plainly aimed to beat *Papillon* to the box office.

w Richard L. Adams *d* William Witney *ph* Rosalio Solano *m* Les Baxter

Jim Brown, Christopher George, Rick Ely, James Luisi, Richard Rust

'Exploitation's own *Papillon*, mercifully free from big brother's pretentiousness.'—*Sight and Sound*

I Escaped from the Gestapo
US 1943 74m bw

An expert counterfeiter is sprung from jail by American Nazis, but he turns the tables on them. Mediocre second feature dramatics; the propaganda is incidental. Dean Jagger, John Carradine, Sidney Blackmer, Mary Brian. Written by Henry Blankfort and Wallace Sullivan; directed by Harold Young; for King Brothers / Monogram.

I Found Stella Parish
US 1935 85m bw

An actress tries to keep her naughty past from her child, but a blackmailer strikes. One for the ladies, who flocked to it in its day. Kay Francis, Paul Lukas, Ian Hunter, Sybil Jason, Jessie Ralph, Barton Maclane. Written by Casey Robinson; directed by Mervyn Le Roy; for Warners. 'Will receive widespread support at the box office all the way from the best runs down to the subsequents, in the big keys and in the smallest towns.'—*Variety*

I Give My Love
US 1934 68m bw

A mother goes to prison for killing her no-good husband. Tedious mother-love story with a happy ending. Paul Lukas, Wynne Gibson, Eric Linden, Anita Louise. Written by Doris Anderson from a novel by Vicki Baum; directed by Karl Freund; for Universal. 'Good, clean, wholesome, although wholly unoriginal entertainment.'—*Variety*

I, Jane Doe
US 1948 85m bw

A French girl comes to America in search of the flyer she married during the war. When she finds he was already married, she shoots him. Melodrama for women, culminating in an unconvincing trial scene. Ruth Hussey, John Carroll, Vera Ralston, Gene Lockhart, John Howard. Written by Lawrence Kimble; directed by John H. Auer; for Republic. (GB title: *Diary of a Bride*).

I Killed Rasputin
France / Italy 1967 100m
Eastmancolor Franscope
Copernic / CGC (Raymond Danon)

The evil monk of the Russian court is killed by Prince Yusopov.
Dull version of a much told story. One of the big international films that never seems to get shown anywhere.

w Alain Decaux, Claude Desailly, Robert Hossein *d* Robert Hossein *ph* Henri Persin *m* André Hossein

Gert Frobe, Peter McEnery, Robert Hossein, Geraldine Chaplin, Ira Furstenberg, Patrick Balkany

'A tedious illustrated history lesson which actually manages to obscure the motivation behind the murder.'—*MFB*

† The script was authorized by Prince Yusopov

I Killed the Count
GB 1939 89m bw
Grafton (Isadore Goldschmidt)
US title: *Who is Guilty?*

Four people confess to the murder of a philanderer.
Inept version of a West End success.

w Alec Coppel, Lawrence Huntington, *play* Alec Coppel *d* Fred Zelnik *ph* Bryan Langley

Syd Walker, Ben Lyon, Terence de Marney, Barbara Blair, Antoinette Cellier, Kathleen Harrison, Athole Stewart, Leslie Perrins, Ronald Shiner

I Know Where I'm Going**
GB 1945 91m bw
GFD / The Archers (Michael Powell, Emeric Pressburger)

A determined girl travels to the Hebrides to marry a wealthy old man, but is stranded on Mull and marries a young naval officer instead.
A strange assembling of attractive but disparate elements: romance, comedy, bleak scenery, a trained hawk and a dangerous whirlpool. At the time it seemed to represent the Elizabethan age of the British cinema, and remains entertaining for its parts though a bit of a puzzle as a whole.

wd Michael Powell, Emeric Pressburger
ph Erwin Hillier

Wendy Hiller, Roger Livesey, Pamela Brown, Nancy Price, Finlay Currie, John Laurie, George Carney, Walter Hudd

'Continuously fresh and interesting, intelligently written and played, and full of beautiful photography.'—*Richard Mallett, Punch*

'The sensitive photography and the intelligent if not very imaginative use of sound do more than enough to make eloquent the influence of place on people; and the whole thing is undertaken with taste and modesty.'—*James Agee*

I Like Your Nerve
US 1931 70m bw

A bookworm goes to Central America and becomes a romantic adventurer. Junior aspiring to Senior's seven league boots; he doesn't quite make it, and that's the script's fault. Douglas Fairbanks Jnr, Loretta Young, Claude Allister, Henry Kolker, Edmund Breon, Boris Karloff. Written by Houston Branch from a story by Roland Pertwee; directed by William McGann; for First National. 'Mediocre, unimpressive and implausible story . . . strictly an off-day booking.'—*Variety*

I Live for Love
US 1935 83m bw
Warner (Bryan Foy)
GB title: *I Live For You*

A socialite has show business leanings.
Minor musical.

w Jerry Wald, Julius Epstein, Robert Andrews *d / ch* Busby Berkeley *ph* George Barnes *md* Leo F. Forbstein

Dolores del Rio, Everett Marshall, Allen Jenkins, Eddie Conrad, Guy Kibbee, Berton Churchill

I Live in Grosvenor Square
GB 1945 113m bw
ABP (Herbert Wilcox)
US title: *A Yank in London*

A duke's daughter falls in love with an American air force sergeant.
Sloppily-made topical romance which was hot box office at the time and started the producer's 'London' romances: *Piccadilly Incident, Spring in Park Lane, Maytime in Mayfair,* etc.

w Nicholas Phipps, William D. Bayles, Maurice Cowan *d* Herbert Wilcox *ph* Max Greene *m* Anthony Collins

Anna Neagle, *Dean Jagger*, Rex Harrison, Robert Morley, Jane Darwell, Nancy Price, Irene Vanbrugh, Edward Rigby, Walter Hudd

I Live My Life
US 1935 85m bw
MGM (Bernard H. Hyman)

A bored society girl falls for a working class archaeologist.
Standard star romance.

w Joseph L. Mankiewicz, *story* Claustrophobia by A. Carter Goodloe *d* W. S. Van Dyke II *ph* George Folsey *m* Dmitri Tiomkin

Joan Crawford, Brian Aherne, Frank Morgan, Aline MacMahon, Eric Blore, Jessie Ralph, Arthur Treacher, Hedda Hopper, Etienne Girardot, Ed Brophy

'An amusing romance is backgrounded by clothes, cocktails and butlers.'—*Variety*

I Lived with You
GB 1933 100m bw

A cockney family find that their lodger is an exiled Russian prince. Overlong whimsy from a successful West End play. Ivor Novello, Ursula Jeans, Ida Lupino, Minnie Rayner, Eliot Makeham, Jack Hawkins. Written by H. Fowler Mear, from the play by Ivor Novello; directed by Maurice Elvey; for Twickenham.

I Love a Mystery*
US 1945 68m bw
Columbia

An eastern secret society offers a businessman a large sum for his head when he dies, as he resembles their founder whose embalmed head is deteriorating.
Start of a short series of mysteries from a radio series; the production was never up to the ingenious plots.

w Charles O'Neal *d* Henry Levin *ph* Burnett Guffey *m* Mario Castelnuovo-Tedesco

George Macready, Jim Bannon, Nina Foch

'She kissed the boys goodbye—until Sonny said hello!'

I Love a Soldier
US 1944 106m bw
Paramount (Mark Sandrich)

A San Francisco girl thinks hard before embarking on a wartime marriage.
Glossy, insubstantial sudser chiefly memorable for casting its leading lady as a welder.

w Allan Scott *d* Mark Sandrich *ph Charles Lang* *m* Robert Emmett Dolan

Paulette Goddard, Sonny Tufts, Beulah Bondi, Walter Sande, Mary Treen, Ann Doran, Barry Fitzgerald

I Love Melvin*
US 1953 77m Technicolor
MGM (George Wells)

A photographer's assistant falls for a high-born chorus girl.
Zippy little musical with all concerned working hard with thin material.

w George Wells *d* Don Weis *ph* Harold Rosson *m / ly* Josef Myrow, Mack Gordon *md* George Stoll *ch* Robert Alton

Donald O'Connor, Debbie Reynolds, Una Merkel, Allyn Joslyn

I Love My Wife
US 1970 95m Technicolor
Universal (Robert Kaufman)

The affairs of a successful doctor with a guilt complex about sex.
Frantic, fashionable comedy drama with wildly erratic treatment and performances.

w Robert Kaufman *d* Mel Stuart *ph* Vilis Lapenieks *m* Lalo Schifrin

Elliott Gould, Brenda Vaccaro, Angel Tompkins

'A leer-laden, anti-feminist tract disguised as a comedy.'—*Judith Crist*

I Love Trouble
US 1947 93m bw

A private eye tries to trace the background of a politician's wife. Standard urban mystery with loose ends, a few notches below Raymond Chandler. Franchot Tone, Janet Blair, Janis Carter, Adele Jergens, Glenda Farrell, Steve Geray, Tom Powers. Written by Roy Huggins, from his novel *The Double Take*; directed by S. Sylvan Simon; produced by him for Columbia.

I Love You Again*
US 1940 99m bw
MGM (Lawrence Weingarten)

A much married man gets amnesia and turns into a gay Lothario.
Sprightly romantic comedy with all concerned letting rip until the pace slows.

w Charles Lederer, George Oppenheimer, Harry Kurnitz *d* W. S. Van Dyke II *ph* Oliver T. Marsh *m* Franz Waxman

William Powell, Myrna Loy, Frank McHugh, Edmund Lowe, Donald Douglas, Nella Walker, Pierre Watkin

I Love You, Alice B. Toklas*
US 1968 93m Technicolor
Warner Seven Arts / Paul Mazursky, Larry Tucker

An asthmatic Los Angeles lawyer escapes his bullying fiancée by joining the flower people. Quite amusing satirical farce about the dangers of marijuana, Gertrude Stein and Jewish mothers, thrown together with no great sense of style but achieving hilarious moments among the longueurs.

w Paul Mazursky, Larry Tucker d Hy Averback *ph* Philip Lathrop *m* Elmer Bernstein *pd* Pato Guzman

Peter Sellers, Jo Van Fleet, Joyce Van Patten, Leigh Taylor-Young, David Arkin, Herb Edelman

'Lips of thunder on lips of fire!'

I Loved a Woman*
US 1933 90m bw
Warner (Henry Blanke)

The career of a Chicago meat packer is hampered by his social-climbing wife.
Potboiling star melodrama which still holds some interest.

w Charles Kenyon, Sidney Sutherland *d* Alfred E. Green *ph* James Van Trees

Edward G. Robinson, Kay Francis, Genevieve Tobin, J. Farrell MacDonald, Henry Kolker, Robert Barrat

'E.G.R. out of his class; may cut biz.'—*Variety*

I Loved You Wednesday
US 1933 77m bw

A man vies with a married friend for a lady's favour. Mildly amusing comedy of the second rank. Warner Baxter, Elissa Landi, Victor Jory, Miriam Jordan, Laura Hope Crews. Written by Philip Klein and Horace Jackson from the play by Molly Ricardei and William Dubois; directed by Henry King and William Cameron Menzies; for Fox. 'A romantic comedy-drama of first-rate possibilities, beautifully made and abundantly provided with class.'—*Variety*

I Married a Doctor
US 1936 87m bw

An idealistic city girl marries a small-town doctor. Solidly carpentered version of Sinclair Lewis's *Main Street* (filmed under its own title in 1923, with Florence Vidor, directed by Harry Beaumont). Josephine Hutchinson, Pat O'Brien, Ross Alexander, Guy Kibbee, Louise Fazenda. Written by Casey Robinson, Harriet Ford and Harvey O'Higgin; directed by Archie Mayo; for Warner.

I Married a Monster from Outer Space*
US 1958 78m bw
Paramount / Gene Fowler Jnr

A young man is taken over by alien invaders but his wife helps to destroy them and bring him back to normal.
Decent, plodding, reasonably effective low-budget science fiction on a well-trampled theme; its minor virtues have been effaced by its silly title.

w Louis Vittes *d* Gene Fowler Jnr *ph* Haskell Boggs *sp* John P. Fulton

Tom Tryon, Gloria Talbott, Robert Ivers

'Carries imaginative plottage which makes it strong fare.'—*Variety*

'Its underlying messages about society and, more specifically, women, are important ones that are particularly relevant today.'—*Cinefantastique, 1974*

'She knows all about love potions . . . and lovely motions!'

I Married a Witch***
US 1942 82m bw
(UA) Cinema Guild / René Clair

A Salem witch and her sorcerer father come back to haunt the descendant of the Puritan who had them burned.
Delightful romantic comedy fantasy which shows all concerned at the top of their form. Hollywood moonshine, impeccably distilled.

w Robert Pirosh, Marc Connelly, novel The Passionate Witch by Thorne Smith *d René Clair ph* Ted Tetzlaff *m* Roy Webb

Fredric March, Veronica Lake, Cecil Kellaway, Robert Benchley, Susan Hayward, Elizabeth Patterson, Robert Warwick

'A delightful sense of oddity and enchantment.'—*New York World Telegram*

AAN: Roy Webb

I Married a Woman
US 1956 85m bw (colour sequence) RKOscope
RKO

A nervous young advertising executive neglects his wife, who determines to make him jealous.
Simple-minded comedy tailored to unsympathetic stars.

w Goodman Ace *d* Hal Kanter *ph* Lucien Ballard *m* Cyril Mockridge

George Gobel, Diana Dors, Adolphe Menjou, Jessie Royce Landis, Nita Talbot

'It brings laughter and song to the screen as this pair from paradise is joyously reunited!'

I Married an Angel
US 1942 84m bw
MGM (Hunt Stromberg)

An attractive angel lures a playboy from his earthly girl friends.
Silly musical fantasy which spelled the end of a great musical star partnership.

w Anita Loos, *play* Vilismary Janos *d* W. S. Van Dyke *ph* Ray June *m / ly* Richard Rodgers, Lorenz Hart

Jeanette MacDonald, Nelson Eddy, Edward Everett Horton, Binnie Barnes, Reginald Owen, Douglass Dumbrille

'As bland as operetta but without its energy.'—*New Yorker, 1978*

I Met a Murderer*
GB 1939 78m bw
Grand National / Gamma (Roy Kellino, Pamela Kellino, James Mason)

A murderer on the run meets a girl novelist who is touring in her motor caravan.
Semi-professional location melodrama which won commendation at the time but now seems very faded.

w Pamela Kellino, James Mason *d* Roy Kellino *ph* Roy Kellino *m* Eric Ansell

James Mason, Pamela Kellino, Sylvia Coleridge, William Devlin, Peter Coke

'Graceful, gallant, resourceful . . . better and more enjoyable than most studio pictures.'—*James Agee*

'That it has a number of defects does not mean that it is not worthy of serious consideration.'—*Basil Wright*

I Met Him in Paris*
US 1937 86m bw
Paramount (Wesley Ruggles)

A fashion designer spends five years' savings on a fling in Paris and finds herself pursued to Switzerland by two philanderers.
Not very witty but likeable romantic comedy with polished performers near their best.

w Claude Binyon *d* Wesley Ruggles *ph* Leo Tover *m* John Leopold *md* Boris Morros

Claudette Colbert, Melvyn Douglas, Robert Young, Lee Bowman, Mona Barrie

'A money picture . . . laughs are piled on laughs.'—*Variety*

'At least half the footage is a perfect scream, and if you miss it you are an old sobersides, and who cares.'—*Otis Ferguson*

I Met My Love Again
US 1937 77m bw
Walter Wanger

A small-town girl marries a drunken writer, but on his death returns to her first love, a biology professor.
Mildly pleasing, rather dated romantic drama with good local colour.

w David Hertz, *novel* Summer Lightning by Aileen Corliss *d* Joshua Logan, Arthur Ripley *ph* Hal Mohr *m* Heinz Roemheld

Henry Fonda, Joan Bennett, Alan Marshal, Dorothy Stickney, Dame May Whitty, Alan Baxter, Louise Platt, Tim Holt, Florence Lake

'Sentimentally as sticky as a gum drop, this sugar-coated romance will have to find its favour with the femmes.'—*Variety*

I, Mobster
US 1958 80m bw Cinemascope
Edward L. Alperson

A slum teenager becomes a top gangster.
Routine gangland thriller.

w Steve Fisher, *novel* Joseph Hilton Smith *d* Roger Corman *ph* Floyd Crosby *m* Gerald Fried

Steve Cochran, Lita Milan, Robert Strauss, Celia Lovsky, Grant Withers

I, Monster*
GB 1970 75m Eastmancolor
Amicus (Milton Subotsky)

A straight remake of *Dr Jekyll and Mr Hyde*, holding closely to the original novel but mysteriously using different names.
Interesting minor work.

w Milton Subotsky *d* Stephen Weeks *ph* Moray Grant *m* Carl Davis *ad* Tony Curtis

Christopher Lee, Peter Cushing, Richard Hurndall, George Merritt

I Never Promised You a Rose Garden
US 1977 96m colour
New World / Imorh / Fadsin (Roger Corman)

A suicidal teenage girl is treated in a psychiatric hospital.
Careful, thoughtful case history which can't help, after so many TV movies of the kind, seeming rather too simple for a theatrical feature, as well as too heavy-going despite the upbeat ending.

w Gavin Lambert, Lewis John Carlino, *novel* Hannah Green *d* Anthony Page *ph* Bruce Logan *m* Paul Chihara *pd* Toby Rafelson

Kathleen Quinlan, Bibi Andersson, Sylvia Sidney, Ben Piazza, Lorraine Gary, Reni Santoni, Signe Hasso

AAN: best adapted screenplay

I Never Sang for My Father*
US 1969 92m Technicolor
Columbia / Jamel (Gilbert Cates)

When his mother dies, a middle-aged widower is saddled with his cantankerous father, who tries to prevent him from remarrying.
Literal transcription of a Eugene O'Neillish play, a fascinating if depressing character study.

w Robert Anderson, from his play *d Gilbert Cates* *ph* Morris Hartzband, George Stoetzel *m* Al Gorgoni, Barry Mann

Melvyn Douglas, Gene Hackman, Dorothy Stickney, Estelle Parsons

AAN: Robert Anderson; Melvyn Douglas; Gene Hackman

I Ought to Be in Pictures*
US 1982 107m De Luxe
TCF (Herbert Ross, Neil Simon)

A young actress hitch-hikes to Hollywood to break into pictures and also to see her estranged scriptwriter father.
Fairly agreeable comedy-drama in the Neil Simon manner, with the studio background an extra plus.

w Neil Simon, from his play *d* Herbert Ross *ph* David M. Walsh *m* Marvin Hamlisch *pd* Albert Brenner

Walter Matthau, Ann-Margret, Dinah Manoff, Lance Guest, Lewis Smith

I Passed for White
US 1960 92m bw
Allied Artists (Fred M. Wilcox)

A light-skinned Negress comes to New York but fails to achieve happiness by pretending to be white.
Earnest, rather dreary social drama which doesn't get anywhere.

d Fred M. Wilcox *ph* George J. Folsey *m* Johnny Williams

Sonya Wilde, James Franciscus, Pat Michon, Elizabeth Council

I Promise to Pay
US 1937 68m bw

An office worker finds himself at the wrong end of the loan shark racket. Competent programmer from the headlines. Chester Morris, Leo Carrillo, Helen Mack, Thomas Mitchell, Thurston Hall. Written by Mary McCall Jnr and Lionel Houser; directed by D. Ross Lederman; for Columbia. 'Just average . . . if placed on a dual bill, it'll be found more than enough to float its end.'—*Variety*

'The sweetest movie anyone would ever wish to see!'
I Remember Mama**
US 1948 134m bw
RKO (Harriet Parsons)

A novelist remembers some of the adventures of growing up with her Norwegian–American family.
Overlong, but well-upholstered nostalgia: warm-hearted, sentimental, nicely detailed, richly acted but just a little boring in spots.

w De Witt Bodeen, *play* John Van Druten, *book* Mama's Bank Account by Kathryn Forbes *d George Stevens* *ph* Nicholas Musuraca *m* Roy Webb

Irene Dunne, Barbara Bel Geddes, Oscar Homolka, Edgar Bergen, Philip Dorn, Ellen Corby, Florence Bates, Cedric Hardwicke, Barbara O'Neil, Rudy Vallee

AAN: Nicholas Musuraca; Irene Dunne; Barbara Bel Geddes; Oscar Homolka; Ellen Corby

I Saw What You Did
US 1965 82m bw
Universal / William Castle

A murderer thinks that two playful teenagers have witnessed his deed, and sets out to kill them too.
Predictable and long-winded suspenser, very short of inventive detail.

w William McGivern, *novel* Ursula Curtiss *d* William Castle *ph* Joseph Biroc *m* Van Alexander

John Ireland, Joan Crawford, Leif Erickson

I See a Dark Stranger**
GB 1945 112m bw
GFD / Individual (Frank Launder, Sidney Gilliat)
US title: *The Adventuress*

An Irish colleen who hates the English comes to England to spy for the Germans but falls in love with a young English officer.
Slipshod plotting does not quite destroy the jolly atmosphere of this comedy-thriller which has the cheek to take an IRA member as its heroine. Good fun, very well staged.

w Frank Launder, Sidney Gilliat, Wolfgang Wilhelm *d Frank Launder* *ph* Wilkie Cooper *m* William Alwyn

Deborah Kerr, Trevor Howard, Raymond Huntley, Norman Shelley, Michael Howard, Brenda Bruce, Liam Redmond, Brefni O'Rourke

'It is the cinematic equivalent of Irish blarney which inspires most of this picture.'—*MFB*

'There is some intelligence, grace and fun here, but essentially this seems to me a supercilious drama, as if it had been made by bright young men who had decided to package and toss a bone to the groundlings.'—*James Agee*

I See Ice
GB 1938 81m bw

The property man in an ice ballet company is a keen amateur photographer who accidentally snaps crooks at work. Fair star comedy with good production. George Formby, Kay Walsh, Betty Stockfield, Cyril Ritchard, Garry Marsh. Written by Anthony Kimmins and Austin Melford; directed by Anthony Kimmins; for ATP.

I Sell Anything
US 1935 70m bw

An auctioneer rises in the business. Mildly interesting comedy-drama with character progress but not much plot. Pat O'Brien, Ann Dvorak, Claire Dodd, Roscoe Karns, Hobart Cavanaugh. Written by Brown Holmes, Sidney Sutherland; directed by Robert Florey; for First National. 'Nicely made and played, but all in one key.'—*Variety*

I Shot Jesse James
US 1948 81m bw

The story of Bob Ford, who gunned down the famous outlaw. Doubtfully historical but quite lively western melodrama. Preston Foster, John Ireland, Barbara Britton, Reed Hadley, J. Edward Bromberg, Victor Kilian, Tom Tyler. Written and directed by Samuel Fuller; for Carl K. Hittleman / Lippert / Screen Guild.

I Start Counting
GB 1969 105m De Luxe
UA / Triumvirate (David Greene)

A young girl thinks her foster-brother may be the sex murderer known to be rampant in the locality. But after a great many red herrings, of course, he is not. Strained psychological suspenser with good moments between the *longueurs*.

w Richard Harris, *novel* Audrey Erskine Lindop *d* David Greene *ph* Alex Thomson *m* Basil Kirchin *pd* Brian Eatwell

Jenny Agutter, Bryan Marshall, Clare Sutcliffe, Simon Ward, Lana Morris, Billy Russell, Fay Compton, Lally Bowers

I Stole a Million
US 1939 89m bw
Universal (Burt Kelly)

A cab driver cheated by a finance company becomes a criminal to support his family. Ho-hum star melodrama.

w Nathanael West, *story* Lester Cole *d* Frank Tuttle *ph* Milton Krasner

George Raft, Claire Trevor, Dick Foran, Henry Armetta, Victor Jory, Joe Sawyer, Stanley Ridges

'Crime drama neatly packaged . . . topper for key duals at normal b.o.'—*Variety*

I Take This Woman
US 1931 74m bw
Paramount

A reckless society girl falls for a cowhand and agrees to live in his ramshackle house. Patchy romantic comedy–drama of little remaining interest.

w Vincent Lawrence, *novel* Lost Ecstasy by Mary Roberts Rinehart *d* Marion Gering, Slavko Vorkapitch *ph* Victor Milner

Gary Cooper, Carole Lombard, Helen Ware, Lester Vail, Charles Trowbridge, Clara Blandick

I Take This Woman
US 1939 97m bw
MGM (Louis B. Mayer)

A doctor marries a beautiful European and decides too late that he does not love her. Thin comedy–drama which Louis B. Mayer unaccountably took it into his head to produce personally. The results had to be re-shot so much and so often that Hollywood dubbed the film *I Re-Take This Woman.* It offers little in the way of entertainment.

w James Kevin McGuinness, *story* Charles MacArthur *d* W. S. Van Dyke *ph* Harold Rosson *m* Bronislau Kaper

Spencer Tracy, Hedy Lamarr, Verree Teasdale, Kent Taylor, Laraine Day, Mona Barrie, Jack Carson, Paul Cavanagh, Marjorie Main

I Thank a Fool
GB 1962 100m Metrocolor Cinemascope
MGM (Anatole de Grunwald)

A woman found guilty of the murder of her lover is offered a fresh start in the home of the prosecutor's family . . . but another nightmare situation builds up. Jane Eyre melodrama of the loonier type, with good actors struggling through a wild but unrewarding script.

w Karl Tunberg, *novel* Audrey Erskine Lindop *d* Robert Stevens *ph* Harry Waxman *m* Ron Goodwin

Peter Finch, Susan Hayward, Diane Cilento, Cyril Cusack, Kieron Moore, Athene Seyler

I Thank You
GB 1941 81m bw

Actors seeking a backer become servants to a titled ex-star. Acceptable comedy vehicle. Arthur Askey, Richard Murdoch, Lily Morris, Moore Marriott, Graham Moffatt, Kathleen Harrison. Written by Howard Irving Young, Val Guest and Marriott Edgar; directed by Marcel Varnel; for Gainsborough.

I the Jury
US 1953 87m bw 3-D
Parklane (Victor Saville)

Private eye Mike Hammer avenges the murder of his friend.
Charmless toughie, roughly made and devoid of plot or character interest.

wd Harry Essex *ph* John Alton *m* Franz Waxman

Biff Elliott, Peggie Castle, Preston Foster, Elisha Cook Jnr, John Qualen

I the Jury
US 1982 109m colour
American Cinema / Larco / Solofilm (Robert Solo)

An amoral private eye avenges the murder of his Vietnam buddy.
Hard, brutal thriller more in line than the previous version with the tone of the novel.

w Larry Cohen *d* Richard T. Heffron *ph* Andrew Laszlo *m* Bill Conti *pd* Robert Gundlach

Armand Assante, Barbara Carrera, Luarene London, Alan King, Geoffrey Lewis, Paul Sorvino

'The repellent formula as usual, with the gun and the penis as interchangeable instruments of quick-fire tough-guy virility.'—*Sunday Times*

I Wake Up Screaming**
US 1941 79m bw
TCF (Milton Sperling)
GB and alternative title: *Hot Spot*

A model is murdered and her sister joins forces with the chief suspect to find the real killer.
Moody thriller with plenty going for it including one memorable performance.

w Dwight Taylor, *novel* Steve Fisher *d H. Bruce Humberstone* *ph Edward Cronjager* *m* Cyril Mockridge

Betty Grable, Victor Mature, Carole Landis, *Laird Cregar*, William Gargan, Alan Mowbray, Allyn Joslyn, Elisha Cook Jnr
† Remade as *Vicki* (qv).

I Walk Alone*
US 1947 98m bw
Paramount (Hal B. Wallis)

An ex-smuggler comes out seeking vengeance after fourteen years in prison.
Dreary gangster drama unworthy of its stars.

w Charles Schnee, *play* Beggars Are Coming to Town by Theodore Reeves *d* Byron Haskin *ph* Leo Tover *m* Victor Young

Burt Lancaster, Kirk Douglas, Lizabeth Scott, Wendell Corey, Kristine Miller, George Rigaud, Marc Lawrence, Mike Mazurki

'The picture deserves, like four out of five other movies, to walk alone, tinkle a little bell, and cry Unclean, unclean.'—*James Agee*

I Walk the Line*
US 1970 97m Eastmancolor Panavision
Columbia / Frankenheimer / Lewis / Halcyon / Atticus (Harold D. Cohen)

A Tennessee sheriff protects moonshiners for the favours of their daughter; when an investigator arrives, bloodshed results. Competent but uninteresting hothouse melodrama in which only the plot twists compel attention.

w Alvin Sargent, *novel* An Exile by Madison Jones *d* John Frankenheimer *ph David M. Walsh* *md* Robert Johnson

Gregory Peck, Tuesday Weld, Estelle Parsons, Ralph Meeker

I Walked with a Zombie*
US 1943 68m bw
RKO (*Val Lewton*)

A nurse is retained by a Caribbean planter to care for his voodoo-sick wife.
Mild horror from the famous Lewton package; some style, but generally thin stuff, the plot having been mirthfully borrowed from *Jane Eyre.*

w Curt Siodmak, Ardel Wray *d Jacques Tourneur* *ph* J. Roy Hunt *m* Roy Webb

Frances Dee, James Ellison, Tom Conway, Christine Gordon, Edith Barrett, James Bell, Sir Lancelot

I Wanna Hold Your Hand
US 1978 104m Technicolor
Universal / Steven Spielberg (Tamara Asseyev, Alex Rose)

A day in 1964 finds assorted New Jersey teenagers eagerly awaiting the Beatles' appearance on the Ed Sullivan Show. Modest period comedy utilizing fresh young talent.

w Robert Zemeckis, Bob Gale *d* Robert Zemeckis *ph* Donald M. Morgan *m* Meredith Wilson

Nancy Allen, Bobby diCicco, Marc McClure, Susan Kendall Newman

I Want a Divorce
US 1940 74m bw
Paramount

A young law student marries rashly, but is prevented from doing anything about it by examples of the unhappiness brought by divorce.
Peculiar comedy-drama which never seems to make up its mind to any particular course.

w Frank Butler, *story* Adela Rogers St John *d* Ralph Murphy *ph* Ted Tetzlaff *m* Victor Young

I WALK THE LINE. Generation gap. Gregory Peck and Tuesday Weld.

Dick Powell, Joan Blondell, Frank Fay, Gloria Dickson, Jessie Ralph, Conrad Nagel, Harry Davenport, Sidney Blackmer, Louise Beavers

I Want to Live*
US 1958 120m bw
(UA) Walter Wanger

A vagrant prostitute is executed in the gas chamber despite growing doubt as to her guilt.
Sober, harrowing treatment of the Barbara Graham case, uneasily adapted to provide a star role amid the tirade against capital punishment.

w Nelson Gidding, Don Mankiewicz *d* Robert Wise *ph* Lionel Lindon *m* John Mandel

Susan Hayward, Simon Oakland, Virginia Vincent, Theodore Bikel, Wesley Lau, Philip Coolidge

'An inconclusive amalgam of variously unexplored themes.'—*Peter John Dyer*

AA: Susan Hayward
AAN: Nelson Gidding, Don Mankiewicz; Robert Wise; Lionel Lindon

I Want What I Want
GB 1971 105m Eastmancolor
Marayan (Raymond Stross)

Roy has a sex change operation and becomes Wendy.
Although based on an actual trans-sexual experience, this film confuses more than it informs, and provokes unintentional mirth when its glamorous star is playing a boy.

w Gillian Freeman, *novel* Geoff Brown *d* John Dexter *ph* Gerry Turpin *m* Johnny Harris

Anne Heywood, Paul Rogers, Harry Andrews, Jill Bennett

I Want You
US 1951 101m bw
Samuel Goldwyn

A family reacts to the Korean war.
Glossy small-town flagwaver; no *Best Years of Our Lives*.

w Irwin Shaw *d* Mark Robson *ph* Harry Stradling *m* Leigh Harline *ad Richard Day*

Dorothy McGuire, Dana Andrews, Farley Granger, Peggy Dow, Robert Keith, Ray Collins, Mildred Dunnock, Martin Milner, Jim Backus

'A recruiting picture which seems to accept a third world war almost as a present reality.'—*Penelope Houston*

'Below the entertaining surface it has very little of value to offer.'—*Richard Mallett, Punch*

'Blonde bomber—she flew them into the ground!'

I Wanted Wings*
US 1941 131m bw
Paramount (Arthur Hornblow Jnr)

The fortunes of three recruits to the American Air Force.
Cheerful, overlong recruiting poster with concessions to melodrama.

w Richard Maibaum, Beirne Lay Jnr, Sig Herzig *d* Mitchell Leisen *ph* Leo Tover, Elmer Dyer *m* Victor Young

Ray Milland, William Holden, Brian Donlevy, Wayne Morris, Veronica Lake, Constance Moore, Harry Davenport, Phil Brown

'Far more a poster than a drama.'—*Howard Barnes, New York Herald Tribune*

'All the life and death moments a man can know!'

I Was a Communist for the FBI
US 1951 83m bw
Warner (Bryan Foy)

Matt Cvetic, a Pittsburgh steel worker, is actually an FBI agent working undercover to trap communists.
Crude and shoddy Red-baiting melodrama, a kind of updating of *Confessions of a Nazi Spy* but using a sadly deteriorated technique.

w Crane Wilbur, Matt Cvetic *d* Gordon Douglas *ph* Edwin DuPar *m* Max Steiner

Frank Lovejoy, Dorothy Hart, Phil Carey, James Millican, Richard Webb, Paul Picerni, Konstantin Shayne

'It seems that this is a subject which Hollywood is incapable of tackling even at its customary level of journalistic efficiency.'—*Penelope Houston*

I Was a Male War Bride**
US 1949 105m bw
TCF (Sol C. Siegel)
GB title: *You Can't Sleep Here*

A WAC in Europe marries a French officer and can't get him home.
High-spirited farce against realistic backgrounds of war-torn Europe, which scarcely accord with Cary Grant's pretending to be a Frenchman (and later a Frenchwoman). Funny, though.

w Charles Lederer, Hagar Wilde, Leonard Spiegelgass *d Howard Hawks* *ph* Norbert Brodine, Osmond Borradaile *m* Cyril Mockridge *md* Lionel Newman

Cary Grant, *Ann Sheridan*, Marion Marshall, Randy Stuart

'It is excellent light entertainment but it is not likely to appeal to the prudish and some discretion should be exercised in booking it.'—*CEA Film Report*

I Was a Prisoner on Devil's Island
US 1941 71m bw

A young American seaman is involved in a brawl in which his captain dies; result, three years on Devil's Island. Hokey but boring melodrama with production values at low level. Donald Woods, Sally Eilers, Edward Ciannelli, Victor Kilian, Charles Halton. Written by Karl Brown; directed by Lew Landers; for Wallace MacDonald / Columbia.

I Was a Spy**
GB 1933 89m bw
Gaumont (Michael Balcon)

In Belgium 1914, a nurse is trained as a spy. Good standard war espionage melodrama.

w W. P. Lipscomb, Ian Hay, *book* Marthe McKenna *d* Victor Saville *ph* Charles Van Enger

Madeleine Carroll, Conrad Veidt, Herbert Marshall, Gerald du Maurier, Edmund Gwenn, Donald Calthrop, Nigel Bruce, Anthony Bushell, Martita Hunt

'Body of a boy! Mind of a monster! Soul of an unearthly thing!'
I Was a Teenage Frankenstein
US 1957 72m bw
American International (Herman Cohen)
GB title: *Teenage Frankenstein*

Professor Frankenstein fashions a creature from selected morsels of old corpses, and kills a teenager to give it a more handsome head. It seemed gruesome enough at the time, but by 1980 standards this is tame, cheap stuff, only notable for its occasional bravura.

w Kenneth Langtry *d* Herbert J. Strock *ph* Lothrop Worth *m* Paul Dunlap

Whit Bissell, Phyllis Coates, Gary Conway, Robert Burton

PROFESSOR TO MONSTER: 'Answer me! I know you have a civil tongue in your head, because I sewed it in there!'

† In-joke: when the professor crates up the monster to send it to London, the address is 113 Wardour Street, which is Hammer House . . .

'The most amazing motion picture of our time!'
I Was a Teenage Werewolf
US 1957 76m bw
AIP / Sunset (Herman Cohen)

A scientist experiments on an aggressive student and turns him into a werewolf. Hilarious farrago with a title which achieved a splendour of its own.

w Ralph Thornton *d* Gene Fowler Jnr *ph* Joseph La Shelle *m* Paul Dunlap

Michael Landon, Whit Bissell, Yvonne Lime

I Was An Adventuress*
US 1940 81m bw
TCF (Darryl F. Zanuck)

A ballerina works as decoy for a pair of confidence tricksters.
Pleasing comedy drama with striking cast.

w Karl Tunberg, Don Ettlinger, John O'Hare *d* Gregory Ratoff *ph* Leon Shamroy, Edward Cronjager *md* David Buttolph

Vera Zorina, Erich Von Stroheim, Peter Lorre, Richard Greene, Sig Rumann, Fritz Feld, Cora Witherspoon

I Was an American Spy
US 1951 84m bw

Stranded in Manila after occupation, an American girl assumes Italian identity and charms Japanese officers. Fairly gripping co-feature, remotely based on fact. Ann Dvorak, Gene Evans, Douglas Kennedy, Richard Loo, Philip Ahn. Written by Sam Rocca, from articles in *Reader's Digest*; directed by Lesley Selander; for David Diamond / Allied Artists.

I Was Happy Here*
GB 1965 91m bw
Partisan (Roy Millichip)
US title: *Time Lost and Time Remembered*

A girl leaves her husband in London and returns to the little Irish port of her childhood. Nicely made, over-mannered study in nostalgia and lost illusions.

w Edna O'Brien, Desmond Davis *d Desmond Davis ph Manny Wynn m* John Addison

Sarah Miles, Cyril Cusack, Julian Glover, Sean Caffrey, Marie Kean

I Was Monty's Double**
GB 1958 100m bw
Film Traders / Maxwell Setton
US title: *Hell, Heaven and Hoboken*

To distract the Nazis in Africa, an actor is hired to pose as General Montgomery.
An amusing and intriguing first hour gives way to spy chases, but the overall provides solid entertainment.

w Bryan Forbes, book M. E. Clifton-James *d John Guillermin ph* Basil Emmott *m* John Addison

John Mills, Cecil Parker, M. E. Clifton-James, Patrick Allen, Leslie Phillips, Michael Hordern, Marius Goring

I Will . . . I Will . . . for Now
US 1975 108m Technicolor
Brut (C. O. Erickson)

Divorcees with sex problems eventually get together again.
Witless soft core farrago of coy jokes, as clumsy and unappealing as its title.

w Norman Panama, Albert E. Lewin *d* Norman Panama *ph* John A. Alonzo *m* John Cameron *pd* Fernando Carrere

Elliott Gould, Diane Keaton, Paul Sorvino, Victoria Principal, Warren Berlinger, Candy Clark, Robert Alda

I Wonder Who's Kissing Her Now*
US 1947 104m Technicolor
TCF (George Jessel)

The career of nineties songwriter Joseph E. Howard.
Routine biopic, quite pleasantly handled.

w Lewis R. Foster *d* Lloyd Bacon *ph* Ernest Palmer *md* Alfred Newman *ad* Richard Day, Boris Leven *ch* Hermes Pan

Mark Stevens, June Haver, Martha Stewart, Reginald Gardiner, Lenore Aubert, William Frawley, Gene Nelson

Ice-Capades Revue
US 1942 79m bw

A New England farm girl inherits a bankrupt ice show. Thin excuse for an ice revue, which is tolerable. Ellen Drew, Richard Denning, Jerry Colonna, Barbara Jo Allen, Harold Huber, Vera Hruba, Joe Jackson Jnr. Written by Bradford Ropes and Gertrude Purcell; directed by Bernard Vorhaus; for Robert North / Republic.

Ice Castles
US 1978 109m Metrocolor
Columbia / International Cinemedia Center (John Kemeny)

Nick and Lexie meet and fall in love at the ice rink. He goes into professional ice hockey; she becomes an Olympic champion but an accident leaves her blind.
Slick, empty, three-handkerchief wallow in the modern manner; well made but instantly forgettable.

w Donald Wrye, Gary L. Baim *d* Donald Wrye *ph* Bill Butler *m* Marvin Hamlisch *pd* Joel Schiller

Robby Benson, Lynn-Holly Johnson, Colleen Dewhurst, Tom Skerritt, Jennifer Warren, David Huffman

Ice Cold in Alex**
GB 1958 132m bw
ABP (W. A. Whittaker)
US title: *Desert Attack*

In 1942 Libya, the commander of a motor ambulance gets his vehicle and passengers to safety despite the hazards of minefields and a German spy.
Engrossing desert adventure with plenty of suspense sequences borrowed from *The Wages of Fear*; long, but very well presented.

w T. J. Morrison, Christopher Landon *d J. Lee-Thompson ph Gilbert Taylor m* Leighton Lucas

John Mills, Sylvia Sims, Anthony Quayle, Harry Andrews

Ice Follies of 1939
US 1939 82m bw (Technicolor sequence)
MGM (Harry Rapf)

A Hollywood star goes east to help her old ice-skating friends put on a show.
The downright peculiar sight of these particular stars on ice is backed by good turns and practically no story.

w Florence Ryerson, Edgar Allan Woolf *d* Reinhold Schunzel *ph* Joseph Ruttenberg, Oliver T. Marsh *m* Franz Waxman

Joan Crawford, James Stewart, Lew Ayres, Lewis Stone, Lionel Stander, Bess Ehrhardt, Charles D. Brown, the International Ice Follies

Ice Palace
US 1960 143m Warnercolor
Warner (Henry Blanke)

After World War I, two men set up a fishery business in Alaska, and their subsequent lives are tied up with the political development of the state.
Tedious saga from a bestseller, with entertaining incidents but no real grip.

w Harry Kleiner, *novel* Edna Ferber *d* Vincent Sherman *ph* Joseph Biroc *m* Max Steiner *ad* Malcolm Bert

Richard Burton, Robert Ryan, Martha Hyer, Carolyn Jones, Jim Backus, Ray Danton, Diane McBain, Karl Swenson

The Ice Pirates
US 1984 94m Metrocolor

On a distant planet in the future, water has become precious, and the evil Templars have cornered it. Extraordinarily talkative and unpersuasive space opera: pretentious hokum. Robert Urich, Mary Crosby, Michael D. Roberts, Anjelica Huston, Ron Perlman, John Carradine. Written by Stewart Raffill, Stanford Sherman; directed by Stewart Raffill; for John Foreman / MGM–UA.

Ice Station Zebra
US 1968 148m Metrocolor Super Panavision
MGM / Filmways (James C. Pratt)

Russian and American agents speed towards the North Pole to recover a lost capsule containing vital military information.
Talky and unconvincingly staged spy adventure with a disappointing lack of action and a great many cold war platitudes.

w Douglas Heyes, Harry Julian Fink, *novel* Alistair MacLean *d* John Sturges *ph* Daniel L. Fapp *m* Michel Legrand

Rock Hudson, Patrick McGoohan, Ernest Borgnine, Jim Brown, Tony Bill, Lloyd Nolan, Gerald S. O'Loughlin, Alf Kjellin

'It's terrible in such a familiar way that at some level it's pleasant. We learn to settle for so little, we moviegoers.'—*Pauline Kael*

AAN: Daniel L. Fapp

Ice-Capades
US 1941 88m bw

A newsreel cameraman fakes an ice show in Central Park. Tepid musical entertainment. James Ellison, Phil Silvers, Jerry Colonna, Dorothy Lewis, Barbara Jo Allen, Alan Mowbray. Written by Jack Townley and others; directed by Joseph Sanley; for Republic.

Iceland
US 1942 79m bw

A marine in Reykjavik falls for a local belle. Superficial musical with a stage farce plot and unreal musical numbers. Sonja Henie, John Payne, Jack Oakie, Felix Bressart, Osa Massen. Written by Robert Ellis, Helen Logan; directed by Bruce Humberstone; for William LeBaron / TCF. (GB title: *Katina*.)

Iceman
US 1984 99m Technicolor

An oil-drilling team in the Arctic discovers the perfectly preserved body of a Neanderthal man, who having been returned to civilization wakes up and creates havoc. All civilization's fault, of course: initial suspense gives way to boredom when morals are preached. Timothy Hutton, Lindsay Crouse, John Lone, Josef Sommer. Written by Chip Proser, John Drimmer; directed by Fred Schepisi; for Patrick Palmer, Norman Jewison / Universal.

Ichabod and Mr Toad**
US 1949 68m Technicolor
Walt Disney

Cartoon versions of stories by Washington Irving and Kenneth Grahame.
An uncomfortable double bill; the story of Ichabod, though well narrated by Basil Rathbone, is macabre without being very interesting; *The Wind in the Willows*, however, is charmingly pictured, and Mr Toad is splendidly voiced by Eric Blore.

d Jack Kinney, Clyde Geronimi, James Algar *supervisor* Ben Sharpsteen

I'd Climb the Highest Mountain*
US 1951 88m Technicolor
TCF (Lamar Trotti)

A Methodist preacher and his wife face the problems of life in a remote part of North Georgia.
Pleasant, rambling, adequately serious and old-fashioned family entertainment, well presented in Hollywood's medium style.

w Lamar Trotti, *novel* Corra Harris *d Henry King* *ph* Edward Cronjager *m* Sol Kaplan *md* Lionel Newman

Susan Hayward, William Lundigan, Rory Calhoun, Barbara Bates, Gene Lockhart, Lynn Bari, Ruth Donnelly, Alexander Knox

I'd Rather Be Rich*
US 1964 96m Eastmancolor
U-I / Ross Hunter

To comfort her dying grandfather, an heiress introduces an eligible stranger as her fiancé . . . but the old man recovers and begins matchmaking.
Reasonably zesty remake of *It Started with Eve*, kept afloat by Chevalier's performance.

w Oscar Brodney, Leo Townsend, Norman Krasna *d* Jack Smight *ph* Russell Metty *m* Percy Faith

Maurice Chevalier, Sandra Dee, Robert Goulet, Andy Williams, Gene Raymond, Hermione Gingold, Charles Ruggles

An Ideal Husband*
GB 1947 96m Technicolor
British Lion / London Films (Alexander Korda)

In the nineties, the career of a London diplomat is threatened by the reappearance of an old flame.
A slight, stiff play is swamped by the cast, the decor, and very garish colour, but there are moments of enjoyment along the way.

w Lajos Biro, *play* Oscar Wilde *d* Alexander Korda *ph* Georges Périnal *m* Arthur Benjamin *ad Vincent Korda* *cost Cecil Beaton*

Paulette Goddard, Hugh Williams, Michael Wilding, Diana Wynyard, *C. Aubrey Smith*, *Constance Collier*, Glynis Johns, Christine Norden

'The composing and cutting of this fine raw material is seldom above medium grade.'—*James Agee*

Identity Unknown
US 1945 71m bw

An amnesiac soldier comes back from the war. Curious propaganda piece with everything but roses round the door. Richard Arlen, Cheryl Walker, Roger Pryor, Bobby Driscoll, Lola Lane, Ian Keith. Written by Richard Weil, Robert Newman; directed by Walter Colmes; produced by him for Republic.

Idiot's Delight*
US 1939 105m bw
MGM (Hunt Stromberg)

At the outbreak of World War II, in a hotel on the Swiss border, a hoofer with an all-girl troupe meets an old flame masquerading as a Russian countess.
Interesting but quite unsuccessful film version of a highly artificial play which had been carried off superbly by the Lunts but was now somewhat less well cast, though it did represent an early Hollywood challenge to Hitler. The flagwaving in fact made it more than a little boring.

w Robert E. Sherwood, from his play *d* Clarence Brown *ph* William Daniels *m* Herbert Stothart

Clark Gable, Norma Shearer, Edward Arnold, Charles Coburn, Burgess Meredith, Joseph Schildkraut, Laura Hope Crews, Skeets Gallagher, Pat Patterson, Fritz Feld

'Exceptionally entertaining comedy, a b.o. sock.'—*Variety*

'The fun and excitement are still there, however filtered it may be.'—*Film Daily*

'The mood of the whole thing is forced and cheap—the coming world war staged by Maurice Chevalier.'—*Otis Ferguson*

'Exactly the same pseudo-qualities as *The Petrified Forest*: a moral pretentiousness, a kind of cellophaned intellectuality.'—*Graham Greene*

The Idle Class*
US 1922 30m approx bw silent
First National / Charles Chaplin

A tramp dreams of the rich life and is mistaken for the husband of a lady.
Rather slight later Chaplin without the full-blooded farcical elements which made him so popular around 1917.

wd Charles Chaplin *ph* Rollie Totheroh

Charles Chaplin, Edna Purviance, Mack Swain

The Idol
GB 1966 111m bw
Embassy (Leonard Lightstone)

A divorced woman falls in love with her son's friend.
Stupefyingly boring generation-gap sex drama.

w Millard Lampell *d* Daniel Petrie *ph* Ken Higgins *m* Johnny Dankworth

Jennifer Jones, Michael Parks, John Leyton, Jennifer Hilary, Guy Doleman, Natasha Pyne

Idol of Paris
GB 1948 105m bw
Premier (R. J. Minney)

In old Paris, a ragman's daughter becomes queen of the demi-mondaines.
Unintentionally hilarious copy of the Gainsborough period romances which had been so popular; much criticized because the leading ladies fight a duel with whips, but that's the least of its faults.

w Norman Lee, Stafford Dickens, Henry Ostrer, *novel* Paiva Queen of Love by Alfred Shirkauer *d* Leslie Arliss *ph* Jack Cox *m* Mischa Spoliansky

Beryl Baxter, Christine Norden, Michael Rennie, Margaretta Scott, Keneth Kent, Henry Oscar, Miles Malleson, Andrew Osborn, Andrew Cruickshank

The Idolmaker
US 1980 119m Technicolor
United Artists / Gene Kirkwood, Howard W. Koch

A songwriter accurately sums up his own limited talent and turns agent and starmarker.
Sharp but padded look behind the scenes of the pop industry; in the end of interest only to initiates.

w Edward Di Lorenzo *d* Taylor Hackford *ph* Adam Holender *m* Jeff Barry

Ray Sharkey, Tovah Feldshuh, Peter Gallagher, Paul Land

If . . .***
GB 1968 111m Eastmancolor
Paramount / Memorial (Lindsay Anderson, Michael Medwin)

Discontent at a boys' public school breaks out into rebellion.
Allegorical treatment of school life with much fashionable emphasis on obscure narrative, clever cutting, variety of pace, even an unaccountable changing from colour to monochrome and vice versa. Intelligence is clearly at work, but it seems to have suffered from undigested gobs of Pinter, and the film as a whole makes no discernible point.

w David Sherwin d Lindsay Anderson ph Miroslav Ondricek *m* Marc Wilkinson *pd* Jocelyn Herbert

Malcolm McDowell, David Wood, Richard Warwick, Robert Swann, Christine Noonan, Peter Jeffrey, Arthur Lowe, Anthony Nicholls

'The school . . . is the perfect metaphor for the established system all but a few of us continue to accept.'—*David Wilson*

'It's something like the Writing on the Wall.'—*Lindsay Anderson*

'Combines a cold and queasy view of youth with a romantic view of violence.'—*New Yorker*

If a Man Answers
US 1962 102m Technicolor
Universal / Ross Hunter

A wife decides to make her husband jealous.
Derivative second-team matrimonial comedy, all dressed up but with nowhere to go.

w Richard Morris, *novel* Winifred Wolfe *d* Henry Levin *ph* Russell Metty *m* Hans Salter

Sandra Dee, Bobby Darin, Micheline Presle, John Lund, Cesar Romero, Stephanie Powers

If I Had a Million**
US 1932 88m bw
Paramount (Benjamin Glazer, Louis D. Lighton)

Various people each receive a million dollars from an eccentric who wants to test their reactions.
Interesting, dated multi-part comedy drama remembered chiefly for the brief sequence in which Laughton blows a raspberry to his boss and Fields chases road hogs. As an entertainment it's patchy, lacking an overall style.

w Claude Binyon, Whitney Bolton, Malcolm Stuart Boylan, John Bright, Sidney Buchman, Lester Cole, Isabel Dawn, Boyce DeGaw, Walter de Leon, Oliver H. P. Garrett, Harvey Gates, Grover Jones, Ernst Lubitsch, Lawton Mackaill, Joseph L. Mankiewicz, William Slavens McNutt, Seton I. Miller, Tiffany Thayer, *story* Robert D. Andrews *d* Ernst Lubitsch, Norman Taurog, Stephen Roberts, Norman Z. McLeod, James Cruze, William A. Seiter, H. Bruce Humberstone

W. C. Fields, *Charles Laughton, May Robson*, Richard Bennett, Alison Skipworth, Gary Cooper, Wynne Gibson, George Raft, Jack Oakie, Frances Dee, Charles Ruggles, Mary Boland, Roscoe Karns, Gene Raymond, Lucien Littlefield

'Not uninteresting, but spotty in retrospect . . . the cinematic porridge is naturally replete with a diversity of seasonings.'—*Variety*

'It develops an obvious idea in an obvious way.'—*Time*

If I Had My Way*
US 1940 82m bw
Universal (David Butler)

Two vaudevillians help an orphan girl and open a new night club.
Quite likeable and very typical star vehicle of its period.

w William Conselman, James V. Kern *d* David Butler *ph* George Robinson *m* Frank Skinner

Bing Crosby, Charles Winninger, Gloria Jean, El Brendel, Allyn Joslyn, Donald Woods, Eddie Leonard, Claire Dodd, Blanche Ring

If I Were Free
US 1933 65m bw

A man and woman, each unhappily married, try to get together. Rather soppy drama which fails to develop. Irene Dunne, Clive Brook, Nils Asther, Henry Stephenson, Laura Hope Crews. Written by Dwight Taylor from the play Behold We Live by John Van Druten; directed by Elliott Nugent; for RKO. 'Thin in texture, it never reaches a pace that really counts.'—*Variety*

'His love-making was as dangerous as his swordplay!'

If I Were King*
US 1938 101m bw
Paramount (Frank Lloyd)

The 14th-century poet and rascal François Villon matches wits with Louis XI and leads an uprising of the people.
A story which we have grown used to seeing with music as *The Vagabond King* is here well presented but somehow rings hollow, with insufficient derring-do; it is the wrong kind of swashbuckling for its star, who is for once outacted by Rathbone in an unusual wily characterization.

w Preston Sturges *d* Frank Lloyd *m* Richard Hageman *ph* Theodor Sparkuhl

Ronald Colman, *Basil Rathbone*, Frances Dee, Ellen Drew, C. V. France, Heather Thatcher, Henry Wilcoxon, Sidney Toler

'Healthy box office that will hit extended runs right down the line.'—*Variety*

'A well mounted and splendid production that carries along at a fascinating pace.'—*Daily Variety*

AAN: Richard Hageman; Basil Rathbone

If I'm Lucky
US 1945 79m bw
TCF (Brian Foy)

A singer runs for state governor and exposes corruption.
Lacklustre remake of *Thanks a Million*, with decidedly dispirited elements.

w Snag Werris, Robert Ellis, Helen Logan, George Bricker *d* Lewis Seiler *ph* Glen MacWilliams *songs* Edgar de Lange, Joseph Myrow *md* Emil Newman

Vivian Blaine, Perry Como, Carmen Miranda, Harry James, Phil Silvers, Edgar Buchanan, Reed Hadley

If It's Tuesday, This Must Be Belgium*
US 1969 98m De Luxe
UA / Wolper (Stan Margulies)

A group of American tourists have various adventures during a lightning tour of Europe.
Amusing comedy which does pretty well by a good idea.

w David Shaw *d* Mel Stuart *ph* Vilis Lapenieks *m* Walter Scharf

Suzanne Pleshette, Ian McShane, Mildred Natwick, Murray Hamilton, Michael Constantine, Sandy Baron, Norman Fell, Peggy Cass, Marty Ingels, Pamela Britton, Luke Halpin, Aubrey Morris

If Winter Comes
US 1948 97m bw
MGM (Victor Saville)

A sentimental idealist, unhappily married, finds himself at the mercy of village gossip when he takes in a pregnant girl.
Artificial romantic nonsense, unconvincingly staged and modernized from a very dated bestseller.

w Marguerite Roberts, Arthur Wimperis, *novel* A. S. M. Hutchinson *d* Victor Saville *ph* George Folsey *m* Herbert Stothart

Walter Pidgeon, Deborah Kerr, Janet Leigh, Angela Lansbury, Binnie Barnes, Dame May Whitty, Reginald Owen

If You Could Only Cook
US 1935 72m bw
Columbia

A young millionaire meets a poor girl and they get jobs as cook and butler.
Whimsical comedy-romance; thin but moderately beguiling.

w F. Hugh Herbert, Gertrude Purcell, Howard J. Green *d* William A. Seiter

Jean Arthur, Herbert Marshall, Leo Carrillo, Lionel Stander, Frieda Inescort

'Plenty of chuckles . . . offers particularly strong promise for the nabes.'—*Variety*

† This was the film which enabled Frank Capra to get out of his Columbia contract, because they accidentally promoted it in Europe as being directed by him.

If You Knew Susie*
US 1948 90m bw
RKO (Eddie Cantor)

A vaudeville couple retire to his ancestral home in New England.
Mild family comedy capitalizing on the team established in *Show Business*.

w Warren Wilson, Oscar Brodney *d* Gordon Douglas *ph* Frank Redman

Eddie Cantor, Joan Davis, Allyn Joslyn, Bobby Driscoll, Charles Dingle

Ikiru*
Japan 1952 143m bw
Toho
aka: *Living; Doomed*

A clerk learns that he is dying and spends his last months creating a children's playground.
A moving and beautifully made personal drama which also gives an interesting background of modern Japan.

w Hideo Oguni, Shinobu Hashimoto, Akira Kurosawa *d Akira Kurosawa* *ph* Asaishi Nakai *m* Fumio Hayasaka

Takashi Shimura, Nobuo Kaneko, Kyoko Seki

'Both living a secret—each afraid to tell!'
I'll Be Seeing You**
US 1944 85m bw
David O. Selznick (Dore Schary)

A lady convict at home on parole for Christmas meets and falls for a shell-shocked soldier.
Schmaltzy, middle-American romantic drama with some nicely handled moments and plenty of talent on hand. In the Hollywood mainstream.

w Marion Parsonnet, *novel* Charles Martin *d William Dieterle* *ph Tony Gaudio* *m* Daniele Amfitheatrof

Ginger Rogers, Joseph Cotten, Shirley Temple, Spring Byington, Tom Tully, Chill Wills

'A sentimental, improbable picture, but unexpectedly rewarding in detail.'—*Richard Mallett, Punch*

I'll Be Your Sweetheart
GB 1945 104m bw
Gainsborough (Louis Levy)

In 1900, songwriters fight with copyright pirates.
Studio-bound musical romance without the necessary resonance.

w Val Guest, Val Valentine *d* Val Guest *ph* Phil Grindrod *md* Louis Levy

Margaret Lockwood, Michael Rennie, Vic Oliver, Peter Graves, Moore Marriott, Frederick Burtwell, Maudie Edwards, Garry Marsh

I'll Be Yours
US 1947 90m bw
Universal (Felix Jackson)

A small-town girl tries to make good in the big city.
Slackly handled remake of *The Good Fairy*. A doubtful 'A' production which did nothing for its star's ailing career.

w Preston Sturges (adapted anonymously from his previous screenplay based on the Molnar original) *d* William A. Seiter *ph* Hal Mohr

Deanna Durbin, Tom Drake, William Bendix, Adolphe Menjou, Walter Catlett, Franklin Pangborn

I'll Cry Tomorrow*
US 1955 119m bw
MGM (Lawrence Weingarten)

Lillian Roth, a Broadway / Hollywood star of the early thirties, becomes an alcoholic.
Fictionalized biopic, pretty well done of the True Confessions kind.

w Helen Deutsch, Jay Richard Kennedy, *book* Lillian Roth, Gerold Frank *d* Daniel Mann *ph* Arthur E. Arling *m* Alex North

Susan Hayward, Richard Conte, Eddie Albert, Jo Van Fleet, Don Taylor, Ray Danton, Margo

'By emphasizing physical degradation in almost every frame, the film makes her less an object of acutely personal concern than a street casualty seen remotely from the top of a bar.'—*Alexander Walker*

AAN: Arthur E. Arling; Susan Hayward

I'll Get By
US 1950 86m Technicolor
TCF (William Perlberg)

Two song writers meet success, then join the marines and are reunited with their former girl friends.
Fair standard musical, a modernization of *Tin Pan Alley*.

w Mary Loos, Richard Sale *d* Richard Sale *ph* Charles G. Clarke *md* Lionel Newman

June Haver, Gloria de Haven, William Lundigan, Dennis Day, Harry James, Thelma Ritter

AAN: Lionel Newman

I'll Get You for This
GB 1950 83m bw

An American gambler in Italy goes after the gangsters who framed him. Second-grade star thick-ear. George Raft, Coleen Gray, Charles Goldner, Walter Rilla, Greta Gynt, Enzo Staiola. Written by George Callahan and William Rose, from the novel *High Stakes* by James Hadley Chase; directed by Joseph M. Newman; for Romulus. (US title: *Lucky Nick Cain*.)

I'll Give a Million*
US 1938 70m bw
TCF (Darryl F. Zanuck)

A millionaire becomes a tramp and disappears, letting it be known that he will give a fortune for genuine acts of kindness. Tramps are then royally entertained all over town.
Amusing depression comedy with satirical touches.

w Boris Ingster, Milton Sperling *d* Walter Lang *ph* Lucien Andriot *md* Louis Silvers

Warner Baxter, Peter Lorre, Marjorie Weaver, Jean Hersholt, John Carradine, J. Edward Bromberg, Lynn Bari, Fritz Feld, Sig Rumann

'Not worth that much . . . the plot sags at the halfway mark and the wind-up is disappointing.'—*Variety*

Ill Met by Moonlight
GB 1956 104m bw Vistavision
Rank / Vega (Michael Powell, Emeric Pressburger)
US title: *Night Ambush*

In Crete during the German occupation, British agents work with partisans to capture a German general.
Disappointingly dreary war adventure with too many night locations, too little suspense and characterization, and photography which seems to be deliberately unattractive.

wd Michael Powell, Emeric Pressburger, *book* W. Stanley Moss *ph* Christopher Challis *m* Mikis Theodorakis

Dirk Bogarde, Marius Goring, David Oxley, Cyril Cusack, John Cairney, Laurence Payne, Wolfe Morris, Michael Gough

I'll Never Forget Whatshisname*
GB 1967 96m Technicolor
Universal / Scimitar (Michael Winner)

An advertising executive gives up power and money for integrity on a small literary magazine, but is won back by a mogul.
Vivid yet muddled tragi-comedy of the sixties, with splashes of sex and violence in trendy settings, a hero one really doesn't believe in, and a title which seems to have no meaning whatsoever.

w Peter Draper *d Michael Winner* *ph* Otto Heller *m* Francis Lai

Oliver Reed, Orson Welles, Carol White, Harry Andrews, Michael Hordern, Wendy Craig, Marianne Faithfull

I'll See You in My Dreams*
US 1952 112m bw
Warner (Louis F. Edelman)

The domestic and professional life of songwriter Gus Kahn.
Quiet-toned, well made, quite forgettable musical.

w Melville Shavelson, Jack Rose *d* Michael Curtiz *ph* Ted McCord *md* Ray Heindorf *ch* Le Roy Prinz

Doris Day, Danny Thomas, Frank Lovejoy, Patrice Wymore, James Gleason

I'll Take Romance
US 1937 85m bw
Columbia (Everett Riskin)

When an opera singer refuses to fulfil a South American contract, her impresario kidnaps her.
Moderate star vehicle.

w George Oppenheimer, Jane Murfin *d* Edward H. Griffith *ph* Lucien Andriot *songs* various

Grace Moore, Melvyn Douglas, Helen Westley, Stuart Erwin, Margaret Hamilton, Walter Kingsford, Esther Muir

I'll Take Sweden
US 1965 96m Technicolor
UA / Edward Small

A widowed oil company executive accepts a Stockholm posting to remove his teenage daughter from an unsuitable attachment.
Feeble comedy which unwisely attempts to be with it, but is bogged down by amateurish handling and wit-wise is sadly without it.

w Nat Perrin, Bob Fisher, Arthur Marx *d* Frederick de Cordova *ph* Daniel L. Fapp *m* Jimmy Haskell

Bob Hope, Tuesday Weld, Frankie Avalon, Dina Merrill, Jeremy Slate, John Qualen, Walter Sande

I'll Tell the World
US 1945 76m bw

A small-town sports announcer starts a lonely hearts programme. Amiable second feature, a reworking of the star's earlier *Advice to the Lovelorn.* Lee Tracy, Brenda Joyce, Raymond Walburn, June Preisser, Thomas Gomez. Written by Henry Blankfort; directed by Leslie Goodwins; for Universal. 'Feasible b.o., but not a strong drafter where the Tracy name can't help.'—*Variety*

Illegal*
US 1955 88m bw
Warner (Frank P. Rosenberg)

A disillusioned District Attorney becomes a racketeer's lawyer but finally denounces him at the cost of his own life.
Competent remake of *The Mouthpiece* (qv), a good star melodrama.

w W. R. Burnett, James R. Webb, *story* Frank J. Collins *d* Lewis Allen *ph* Peverell Marley *m* Max Steiner

Edward G. Robinson, Nina Foch, Albert Dekker, Hugh Marlowe, Jayne Mansfield, Howard St John, Ellen Corby

'Hard-hitting stuff in the old gangster tradition.'—*MFB*

Illegal Entry
US 1949 84m bw

Undercover agents investigate a smuggling racket. Routine, quite entertaining alleged exposé. Howard Duff, George Brent, Marta Toren, Tom Tully, Paul Stewart, Gar Moore. Written by Joel Malone; directed by Frederick de Cordova; for Universal-International.

Illegal Traffic
US 1938 67m bw

The FBI tracks down an organization devoted to smuggling criminals away from danger. Smart second feature based on J. Edgar Hoover's *Persons in Hiding.* J. Carrol Naish, Mary Carlisle, Robert Preston. Written by Robert Yost, Lewis Foster and Stuart Anthony; directed by Louis King; for Paramount. 'Good racketeer film . . . should do better than average business.'—*Variety*

Illicit
US 1931 81m bw

A disillusioned wife walks out on her husband and seeks solace elsewhere. Undistinguished weepie, which later became *Ex-Lady.* Barbara Stanwyck, Ricardo Cortez, Joan Blondell, Charles Butterworth. Written by Harvey Thew; directed by Archie Mayo; for Warner. 'Lacks a wallop and action.'—*Variety*

'Don't dare stare at . . .'

The Illustrated Man*
US 1969 103m Technicolor Panavision
Warner / SKM (Howard B. Kreitsek, Ted Mann)

A strange wanderer tells weird stories based on the tattooed pictures which cover him from tip to toe.
Oddball compendium based rather insecurely on Ray Bradbury stories; in this form they don't amount to much but the presentation is assured.

w Howard B. Kreitsek *d* Jack Smight *ph* Philip Lathrop *m* Jerry Goldsmith *ad* Joel Schiller

Rod Steiger, Claire Bloom, Robert Drivas, Don Dubbins, Jason Evers

'A curiously passionless affair – efficient enough, meaty enough, but without poetry, without charm, without beauty.'—*Philip Strick*

'A pretentious comic strip of maudlin and muddled fantasies.'—*Judith Crist*

Illustrious Corpses*
Italy / France 1975 120m Technicolor
PEA / UA (Alberto Grimaldi)
original title: *Cadaveri Eccellenti*

A right-wing conspiracy to arouse feelings against dissidents is found to be behind the murders of public figures.
Elegant police melodrama on an unlikely political thesis.

w Francesco Rosi, Tonino Guerra, Lino Jannuzzi, *novel* Il Contesto by Leonardo Sciascia *d Francesco Rosi* *ph* Pasqualino de Santis *m* Piero Piccioni

Lino Ventura, Alain Cuny, Maolo Bonacelli, Marcel Bozzuffi, Max Von Sydow, Fernando Rey, Charles Vanel, Tina Aumont

'Like watching layer after layer peeled off some diseased flower until the poisoned root is reached.'—*Michael Billington, Illustrated London News*

I'm All Right Jack***
GB 1959 104m bw
British Lion / Charter (Roy Boulting)

A world-innocent graduate takes a job in industry; by starting at the bottom he provokes a national strike.
Satirical farce which manages to hit most of its widespread targets and finds corruption in high, low and middle places. A not inaccurate picture of aspects of British life in the fifties, and a presage of the satire boom to come with *Beyond the Fringe* and *That Was the Week That Was.*

w Frank Harvey, John Boulting, novel Private Life by *Alan Hackney* *d* John Boulting *ph* Max Greene *m* Ken Hare

Ian Carmichael, Peter Sellers, Irene Handl, Richard Attenborough, *Terry-Thomas,* Dennis Price, Margaret Rutherford, Liz Fraser, *John Le Mesurier,* Sam Kydd

I'm Dancing as Fast as I Can
US 1982 106m Movielab
Paramount / Edgar J. Scherick / Scott Rudin

A documentary film-maker is rehabilitated after dependence on drugs.
Unabsorbing case history more suitable as a TV movie except that the acting for TV would not have been so far over the top.

w David Robe, *book* Barbara Gordon *d* Jack Hofsiss *ph* Jan de Bont *m* Stanley Silverman

Jill Clayburgh, Nicol Williamson, Dianne Wiest, Joe Pesci, Geraldine Page, James Sutorius, Richard Masur, Kathleen Widdoes

I'm from Missouri
US 1939 77m bw

The wife of a Missouri farmer and mule breeder has social aspirations. Rural comedy patterned after the Will Rogers successes. Bob Burns, Gladys George, Gene Lockhart, Judith Barrett, William Henry, Patricia Morrison, E. E. Clive, Melville Cooper. Written by John C. Moffitt and Duke Atterbury; directed by Theodore Reed; for Paramount. 'Moderate grosser for family trade.'—*Variety*

'Just a sensitive gal who climbed the ladder of success . . . wrong by wrong! A story about a gal who lost her reputation—and never missed it!'

I'm No Angel***
US 1933 88m bw
Paramount (William Le Baron)

A carnival dancer gets off a murder charge, moves into society and sues a man for breach of promise.
The star's most successful vehicle, credited with saving the fortunes of Paramount, remains a highly diverting side show with almost a laugh a minute. Released before the Legion of Decency was formed, it also contains some of Mae's fruitiest lines.

w Mae West d Wesley Ruggles *ph* Leo Tover *songs* Harvey Brooks (m), Gladys Dubois (ly)

Mae West, Edward Arnold, Cary Grant, Gregory Ratoff, Ralf Harolde, Kent Taylor, Gertrude Michael

'The most freewheeling of all Mae's screen vehicles, and the most satisfying of the lot.'—*James Robert Parish*

'A quality of balance and proportion which only the finest films attain.'—*Views and Reviews*

Images
Eire 1972 101m Technicolor Panavision
Lions Gate / Hemdale (Tommy Thompson)

A semi-hysterical woman is confronted by the images of her former lovers.
Pretentious psycho-drama which might have made a good half-hour.

wd Robert Altman *ph* Vilmos Zsigismond *m* John Williams

Susannah York, René Auberjonois, Marcel Bozzuffi

AAN: John Williams

Imitation General
US 1958 88m bw
MGM (William Hawks)

France 1944: when a general is killed, a sergeant takes his place to preserve morale.
Odd, rather unpalatable war comedy-drama.

w William Bowers *d* George Marshall *ph* George Folsey

Glenn Ford, Red Buttons, Taina Elg, Dean Jones, Kent Smith

Imitation of Life**
US 1934 109m bw
Universal (John M. Stahl)

A woman becomes rich through the pancake recipe of her black servant, but the latter has a tragic life because her daughter passes for white.
Monumentally efficient tearjerker, generally well done.

w William Hurlbut, *novel* Fannie Hurst *d John Stahl ph* Merritt Gerstad *m* Heinz Roemheld

Claudette Colbert, Warren William, *Louise Beavers*, Ned Sparks, Rochelle Hudson, Fredi Washington, Alan Hale, Henry Armetta

'Grim and harsh stuff . . . its reception in the south cannot be judged or guessed by a northerner.'—*Variety*

'Classic, compulsively watchable rags-to-riches-and-heartbreak weeper.'—*New Yorker, 1977*

AAN: best picture

Imitation of Life*
US 1959 124m Eastmancolor
U-I (Ross Hunter)

Glossy remake of the above with its heroine now an actress; stunningly produced but dully acted, making its racially sensitive plot seem insincere.

w Eleanore Griffin, Allan Scott *d Douglas Sirk ph* Russell Metty *m* Frank Skinner

Lana Turner, Juanita Moore, John Gavin, Susan Kohner, Dan O'Herlihy, Sandra Dee, Robert Alda

AAN: Juanita Moore; Susan Kohner

The Immigrant**
US 1917 20m approx bw silent
Mutual

A penniless immigrant befriends a girl on the boat and later helps her in a café.
One of the most inventive early Chaplins, with touches of sentiment and social comment which for once only strengthen and do not antagonize.

wd Charles Chaplin ph William C. Foster, Rollie Totheroh

Charles Chaplin, Edna Purviance, Albert Austin, Henry Bergman, Eric Campbell

'In its roughness and apparent simplicity it is as much a jewel as a story by O. Henry.'—*Photoplay*

Immoral Tales
France 1974 103m Eastmancolor
Argos (Anatole Dauman)

Four bawdy stories, ranging from 1498 to 1970.
The usual sex portmanteau with a little more strength in the detail and interest in human behaviour than usual.

wd Walerian Borowczyk *ph* Bernard Daillencourt, Guy Durban, Michel Zolat, Noel Véry *m* Maurice Le Roux

Lise Danvers, Charlotte Alexandra, Paloma Picasso, Florence Bellamy

'You come out having learned something about the waywardness of life and love and having been taken on a mystery tour into the present, the past, and the enigmatic strangeness of womanhood.'—*Michael Billington, Illustrated London News*

The Immortal Sergeant*
US 1943 90m bw
TCF (Lamar Trotti)

In the North African campaign, a battle-toughened sergeant is killed after inspiring the raw recruits under his command.
'Inspirational' war adventure, quite neatly done but a shade embarrassed by its own poetic leanings.

w Lamar Trotti, *novel* John Brophy *d* John Stahl *ph* Arthur Miller *m* David Buttolph

Henry Fonda, Thomas Mitchell, Maureen O'Hara, Allyn Joslyn, Reginald Gardiner, Melville Cooper, Branwell Fletcher, Morton Lowry

'By the time the first soldier has bit the sand, the film identifies itself: it is none other than Hollywood's old friend the Foreign Legion of Beau Geste vintage, jerked from the shelf and clothed in a new uniform.'—*Time*

The Immortal Story
France 1968 60m Eastmancolor
Albina / ORTF (Micheline Rozan)

In 19th-century Macao, a rich merchant tries to make an old seaman's story come true.
Muddled and stiltedly told fable which would have excited no attention if it had not been associated with the elusive Mr Welles.

wd Orson Welles, *story* Isak Dinesen *ph* Willy Kurant *m* Erik Satie

Orson Welles, Jeanne Moreau, Roger Coggio, Norman Eshley

Impact
US 1949 111m bw
(UA) Harry M. Popkin

A woman and her lover plan the murder of her rich industrialist husband, but things go wrong and the husband survives under another name . . .
Curiously elongated but watchable melodrama, with the impression of a second team doing its best.

w Dorothy Reid *d* Arthur Lubin *ph* Ernest Laszlo

Brian Donlevy, Ella Raines, Charles Coburn, Helen Walker

The Impatient Maiden
US 1932 78m bw

A romantic maidservant learns the difference between life and fantasy. Solidly made comedy-drama which doesn't seem to have inspired its director. Mae Clarke, Lew Ayres, Una Merkel, John Halliday, Andy Devine, Berton Churchill. Written by Richard Schayer and Winifred Dunn, from the novel *The Impatient Virgin* by Donald Henderson Clarke; directed by James Whale; for Universal. 'Trashy stuff . . . aims at smartness and sophistication, and achieves but crudity.'—*Variety*

The Impatient Years
US 1944 91m bw
Columbia (Virginia Van Upp)

A soldier finds difficulty in adjusting to his civilian matrimonial state.
Thin star comedy.

w Virginia Van Upp *d* Irving Cummings *ph* Hal Mohr *m* Marlin Skiles

Jean Arthur, Lee Bowman, Charles Coburn, Edgar Buchanan, Harry Davenport, Grant Mitchell, Jane Darwell

'Scandal seeks her out—even on her wedding night!'

The Imperfect Lady
US 1946 97m bw
Paramount (Karl Tunberg)
GB title: *Mrs Loring's Secret*

In nineties London, an MP marries a lady with a past.
Dusty melodrama, adequately produced.

w Karl Tunberg, *story* Ladislas Fodor *d* Lewis Allen *ph* John F. Seitz *m* Victor Young

Ray Milland, Teresa Wright, Cedric Hardwicke, Virginia Field, Anthony Quinn, Reginald Owen, Melville Cooper, George Zucco, Rhys Williams, Charles Coleman, Miles Mander, Edmund Breon, Frederick Worlock

The Impersonator*
GB 1961 64m bw
Bryanston / Herald (Anthony Perry)

Americans at a British air base are suspected when a murderous prowler strikes.
Well made second-feature thriller with effective locations, suspense sequences and village atmosphere.

wd Alfred Shaughnessy ph John Coquillon *m* de Wolfe

John Crawford, Jane Griffith, Patricia Burke, John Salew

The Importance of Being Earnest**
GB 1952 95m Technicolor
Rank / Javelin / Two Cities (Teddy Baird)

Two wealthy and eligible bachelors of the nineties have problems with their marriage prospects.
Disappointingly stagey rendering (when compared, say, with *Occupe-toi d'Amélie*) of Britain's most wondrously witty lighter-than-air comedy of manners. As a record of a theatrical performance, however, it is valuable.

w Anthony Asquith, *play* Oscar Wilde *d* Anthony Asquith *ph* Desmond Dickinson *m* Benjamin Frankel *ad Carmen Dillon*

Michael Redgrave, Michael Denison, Edith Evans, Margaret Rutherford, Joan Greenwood, Miles Malleson, Dorothy Tutin, Walter Hudd

'A more positive decision on style should have been taken. A film of this kind must be either an adaptation or a piece of filmed theatre. This one, being partially both, is not wholly either.'—*Gavin Lambert*

The Impossible Years
US 1968 98m Metrocolor Panavision
MGM / Marten (Lawrence Weingarten)

A university psychiatrist has trouble controlling his nubile 17-year-old daughter.
Wacky farce which veers between the tasteless and the ludicrous, and is never more than momentarily entertaining.

w George Wells, *play* Bob Fisher, Arthur Marx *d* Michael Gordon *ph* William H. Daniels *m* Don Costa

David Niven, Lola Albright, Chad Everett, Ozzie Nelson, Cristina Ferrare, Don Beddoe

'A comedy of the generation gap which didn't bridge it but fell right into it.'—*Gerald Garrett*

The Impostor
US 1944 92m bw

A French convict escapes during a Nazi bombing raid, and in the guise of a dead man fights bravely for France. Propagandist melodrama, more stiffly made than its talent would suggest. Jean Gabin, Ellen Drew, Richard Whorf, Allyn Joslyn, Peter Van Eyck, Ralph Morgan. Written and directed by Julien Duvivier; for Universal. (TV title: *Strange Confession*.)

Improper Channels
Canada 1979 91m colour

A father runs into administrative trouble when he takes his injured daughter to hospital.
Salutary but not very commanding tale for our times, with a leading performance that suffers from overfamiliarity.

w Morrie Rubinsky, Ian Sutherland, Adam Arkin *d* Eric Till *ph* Anthony Richmond *m* Maribeth Solomon, Micky Erbe

Alan Arkin, Mariette Hartley, Monica Parker, Harry Ditson

Impulse
US 1984 99m De Luxe

After an earthquake, a small farming community is menaced by a mysterious subterranean substance which makes people self-destructive. Modest, mildly humorous sci-fi which has its fun without explaining anything at all. Tim Matheson, Meg Tilly, Hume Cronyn, John Karlen, Amy Stryker. Written by Bart Davis, Don Carlos Dunaway; directed by Graham Baker; for Tim Zinnemann / ABC Motion Pictures.

In a Lonely Place*
US 1950 93m bw
Columbia / Santana (Robert Lord)

An embittered Hollywood scriptwriter escapes a murder charge but loses his girl friend through his violent temperament.
Curious character melodrama which intrigues without satisfying.

w Andrew Solt, *novel* Dorothy B. Hughes *d* Nicholas Ray *ph* Burnett Guffey *m* George Antheil

Humphrey Bogart, Gloria Grahame, Frank Lovejoy, Carl Benton Reid, Art Smith, Jeff Donnell

'It remains better than average, but lacks the penetration which would make it really interesting.'—*Gavin Lambert*

In a Year with 13 Moons
West Germany 1978 129m colour

Ordeals of a man who undergoes a sex change. Unattractive case history with expressionist decoration. Volker Spengler, Ingrid Caven, Gottfried John. Written and directed by Rainer Werner Fassbinder; for Tango / Project / Filverlag der Autoren.

In Caliente
US 1935 85m bw
Warner

In a Mexican horse racing resort, a dancer falls for the magazine editor who criticized her act. Very slim storyline fails to make this a major musical despite attractive numbers including 'The Lady in Red'.

w Jerry Wald, Julius Epstein *d* Lloyd Bacon *ph* Sol Polito, George Barnes *ch Busby Berkeley songs* various

Dolores del Rio, Pat O'Brien, Edward Everett Horton, Leo Carrillo, Glenda Farrell, Judy Canova, Phil Regan, Wini Shaw, Herman Bing

In Celebration
GB 1974 131m Eastmancolor
Ely Landau / Cinevision

Three sons travel north for their miner father's fortieth wedding anniversary.
Sharply observant but fairly predictable dramatics, plainly filmed.

w David Storey, from his play *d* Lindsay Anderson *ph* Dick Bush *m* Christopher Gunning

Alan Bates, James Bolam, Brian Cox, Constance Chapman, Bill Owen

In Cold Blood*
US 1967 134m bw Panavision
Columbia / Richard Brooks

An account of a real life crime in which an entire family was brutally murdered by wandering gunmen.
Unnecessarily complicated as narrative, and uncompromisingly brutal in treatment, this well-meaning film is hard to take in many ways.

wd Richard Brooks, *book* Truman Capote *ph* Conrad Hall *m* Quincy Jones

Robert Blake, Scott Wilson, John Forsythe, Paul Stewart, Gerald S. O'Loughlin, Jeff Corey

'It marks a slight step up for its director, best remembered for reducing *Lord Jim* to pablum and *The Brothers Karamazov* to pulp.'—*John Simon*

AAN: Richard Brooks (as writer); Richard Brooks (as director); Conrad Hall; Quincy Jones

In Enemy Country
US 1968 107m Techniscope
Universal (Harry Keller)

In 1939 Paris, the French secret service evolves an elaborate four-year undercover plan.
Standard, overlong espionage melodrama with no surprises.

w Edward Anhalt, *story* Sy Bartlett *d* Harry Keller *ph* Loyal Griggs *m* William Lava

Tony Franciosa, Anjanette Comer, Guy Stockwell, Paul Hubschmid, Tom Bell, Harry Townes, Michael Constantine, John Marley

In Gay Madrid
US 1930 78m bw

A Spanish blade is torn between two women. Feeble star vehicle, presumably aimed at the Spanish market. Ramon Novarro, Dorothy Jordan, Lettice Howell, Claude King, Eugenie Besserer. Written by Bess Meredyth, Edwin Justus Mayer and Salisbury Field from a novel by Alejandro Perez Lugin; directed by Robert Z. Leonard; for MGM. 'Unreal story, poor acting, ditto direction and general lack of popular appeal.'—*Variety*

In God We Trust
US 1980 97m Technicolor

A monk leaves his monastery to raise some ready cash. Dismal and tasteless attempt at religious satire. Marty Feldman, Peter Boyle, Louise Lasser, Richard Pryor, Wilfrid Hyde White. Written by Marty Feldman and Chris

Allen; directed by Marty Feldman; for Universal. 'A rare achievement—a comedy with no laughs. Its energy is prodigious. But only rarely is it matched by invention.'—*Variety*

In Harm's Way*
US 1965 167m bw Panavision
Paramount / Sigma (Otto Preminger)

The American navy retaliates after Pearl Harbor.
Odd mix of all-star action, spectacle (mostly models) and personal romances, with a few interesting scenes; shorn of colour it seems rather half-hearted.

w Wendell Mayes, *novel* James Bassett *d* Otto Preminger *ph* Loyal Griggs *m* Jerry Goldsmith *titles* Saul Bass

John Wayne, Kirk Douglas, Patricia Neal, Tom Tryon, Paula Prentiss, Brandon de Wilde, Stanley Holloway, Burgess Meredith, Henry Fonda, Dana Andrews, Franchot Tone, Jill Haworth, George Kennedy, Hugh O'Brian, Carroll O'Connor, Patrick O'Neal, Slim Pickens, Bruce Cabot, Larry Hagman, James Mitchum

'Lacks even a touch of the touch.'—*Stanley Kauffmann*

AAN: Loyal Griggs

In Like Flint
US 1967 107m De Luxe Cinemascope
TCF (Saul David)

Top agent Derek Flint unmasks a subversive female spy ring which has kidnapped the President.
This sequel to *Our Man Flint* (qv) is silly rather than funny, a spy spoof which becomes irritatingly hard to take.

w Hal Fimberg *d* Gordon Douglas *ph* William Daniels *m* Jerry Goldsmith

James Coburn, Lee J. Cobb, Jean Hall, Andrew Duggan, Anna Lee

'It gently founders in yards of flat dialogue, lavishly uninteresting sets, fuzzy colour processing, and a supporting cast in which all the girls look alarmingly mass produced.'—*MFB*

In Love and War
US 1958 111m Eastmancolor Cinemascope
TCF (Jerry Wald)

Three men from different backgrounds join the US Marines and see service in the Pacific.
Self-conscious propaganda concoction of bare routine interest.

w Edward Anhalt, *novel* Anton Myrer *d* Philip Dunne *ph* Leo Tover *m* Hugo Friedhofer

Jeffrey Hunter, Robert Wagner, Bradford Dillman, Dana Wynter, Hope Lange, Sheree North, France Nuyen

In Name Only*
US 1939 94m bw
RKO (Pandro S. Berman)

A rich man falls in love but his wife refuses a divorce.The stars seem unhappy in this sombre matrimonial drama, but of its kind it's surprisingly well made.

w Richard Sherman, *novel* Memory of Love by Bessie Brewer *d John Cromwell* *ph* J. Roy Hunt *m* Roy Webb

Cary Grant, Carole Lombard, Kay Francis, Charles Coburn, Helen Vinson

'Sock romantic drama . . . will get maximum playing time and the best dating the country offers.'—*Variety*

'Shot with a refined taste for interior decoration . . . it is oversweetened with the material for tears.'—*Graham Greene*

'The talking picture reaches perfection!'
In Old Arizona**
US 1929 95m bw
Fox

Adventures of the Cisco Kid.
Primitive sound western, a sensation in its day but now of purely historical interest.

w Tom Barry, *stories* O. Henry *d* Raoul Walsh, Irving Cummings *ph* Arthur Edeson

Warner Baxter, Edmund Lowe, Dorothy Burgess, J. Farrell MacDonald
† See also *The Cisco Kid.*

AA: Warner Baxter
AAN: best picture; Tom Barry; Raoul Walsh, Irving Cummings; Arthur Edeson

In Old California
US 1942 89m bw

A Boston pharmacist heads west towards gold rush California. Moderate star western with parsimonious budget. John Wayne, Binnie Barnes, Albert Dekker, Helen Parrish, Patsy Kelly, Edgar Kennedy, Dick Purcell, Charles Halton. Written by Gertrude Purcell and Frances Hyland; directed by William McGann; for Republic.

In Old Chicago***
US 1937 115m bw
TCF (Kenneth MacGowan)

Events leading up to the great Chicago fire include a torrid romance between a gambler and a café singer.
Spectacular melodrama which with its two-million-dollar budget was a deliberate attempt to outdo *San Francisco*, and only failed because the cast was less interesting. A splendid studio super-production.

w Lamar Trotti, Sonya Levien, *novel* We the O'Learys by Niven Busch *d Henry King, ph Peverell Marley* *m* Louis Silvers *sp H. Bruce Humberstone, Daniel B. Clark, Fred Sersen, Louis J. Witte ad William Darling*

Tyrone Power, Alice Faye, Don Ameche, *Alice Brady,* Andy Devine, Brian Donlevy, Phyllis Brooks, Tom Brown, Sidney Blackmer, Berton Churchill, Paul Hurst, Rondo Hatton, Eddie Collins

'Sock spectacle film . . . an elaborate and liberally budgeted entertainment.'—*Variety*

AA: Alice Brady
AAN: best picture; Niven Busch (original story); Louis Silvers

In Old Kentucky
US 1935 85m bw

A family feud is settled by a horse race. Warm-hearted, old-fashioned stuff, and the star's last film. Will Rogers, Bill Robinson, Dorothy Wilson, Russell Hardie. Written by Sam Hellman, Gladys Lehmann, from play by Charles T. Daxey; directed by George Marshall; for Edward Butcher / TCF.

In Our Time*
US 1944 110m bw
Warner (Jerry Wald)

English girl marries Polish count and helps defy the Nazis.
Ambitious, would-be meaningful melodrama that doesn't quite come off.

w Ellis St Joseph, Howard Koch *d* Vincent Sherman *ph* Carl Guthrie *m* Franz Waxman

Ida Lupino, Paul Henreid, Nancy Coleman, *Nazimova*, Mary Boland, Victor Francen, Michael Chekhov

'The story starts a good many hares but prudently refrains from following them.'—*Richard Mallett, Punch*

In Person
US 1935 85m bw
RKO (Pandro S. Berman)

A glamorous but exhausted film star tries to escape her public by fleeing incognito to the country.
Mild star comedy.

w Allan Scott, *novel* Samuel Hopkins Adams *d* William A. Seiter *ph* Edward Cronjager *m* Roy Webb *songs* Oscar Levant, Dorothy Fields

Ginger Rogers, George Brent, Alan Mowbray, Grant Mitchell, Samuel S. Hinds, Spencer Charters

'Inept starring debut for Ginger Rogers . . . a very weak affair.'—*Variety*

In Search of Gregory
GB 1969 90m Technicolor
Universal / Vic Films / Vera Films (Joe Janni, Daniele Senatore)

A girl attends her father's wedding to meet a mysterious guest named Gregory, whom she never quite contacts.
Irritatingly pretentious Pinterish puzzle-drama with apparently no hidden depths except the urge to be clever.

w Tonino Guerra, Lucile Laks *d* Peter Wood *ph* Otto Heller, Giorgio Tonti *m* Ron Grainer

Julie Christie, Michael Sarrazin, John Hurt, Adolfo Celi, Roland Culver, Tony Selby

'Moments in a vacuum: however lively the surface, the centre remains depressingly inert.'—*MFB*

'A thousand thrills . . . and Hayley Mills'
In Search of the Castaways***
GB 1961 100m Technicolor
Walt Disney (Hugh Attwooll)

With the aid of an eccentric professor, three children seek their lost explorer father in some

IN OLD CHICAGO. One of Hollywood's most expensive ($1,800,000) films of the time. The gentleman in the bathing suit in the background seems to be spellbound by what Thomas Mitchell is telling Tyrone Power.

geographically fantastic regions of South America.
Engaging Victorian fantasy which starts realistically but builds up to sequences in the manner of *The Wizard of Oz* and concludes in *Treasure Island* vein. Jaunty juvenile fare.

w Lowell S. Hawley, *novel* Captain Grant's Children by Jules Verne *d* Robert Stevenson *ph* Paul Beeson *m* William Alwyn *ad* Michael Stringer

Maurice Chevalier, Hayley Mills, George Sanders, Wilfrid Hyde White, *Wilfrid Brambell*

In Society*
US 1944 74m bw
Universal (Edmund Hartmann)

Two incompetent plumbers ruin a mansion.
One of the better A & C romps, with little padding between the comedy highlights, though the trimmings are fearsomely dated.

w John Grant, Hal Finberg, Edmund L. Hartmann *d* Jean Yarbrough *ph* Jerome Ash *m* Edgar Fairchild

Bud Abbott, Lou Costello, Kirby Grant, Ann Gillis, Arthur Treacher, Steve Geray, George Dolenz, Marion Hutton

In the Cool of the Day
US 1962 91m Metrocolor Panavision
MGM (John Houseman)

The frail wife of a New York publisher dies in Greece after an affair with his colleague.
Travelogue with romantic asides; a pretty glum business.

w Meade Roberts, *novel* Susan Ertz *d* Robert Stevens *ph* Peter Newbrook *m* Francis Chagrin *ad* Ken Adam

Jane Fonda, Peter Finch, Arthur Hill, Angela Lansbury, Constance Cummings

In the Doghouse
GB 1961 93m bw
Rank (Hugh Stewart)

Misadventures of a newly qualified vet.
Easy-going farce with animal interest and a great many familiar faces.

w Michael Pertwee, *novel* It's a Vet's Life by Alex Duncan *d* Darcy Conyers *ph* Alan Hume *m* Philip Green

Leslie Phillips, Peggy Cummins, Hattie Jacques, James Booth, Dick Bentley, Colin Gordon, Joan Heal, Fenella Fielding, Esma Cannon, Richard Goolden, Joan Hickson, Vida Hope, Harry Locke, Kynaston Reeves

'Anywhere but Paris it would have been a scandal!'

In the French Style*
US / France 1962 105m bw
Columbia / Casanna / Orsay (Robert Parrish, Irwin Shaw)

An American girl in Paris has affairs with a young boy and with a divorced newspaperman.
Smooth, episodic, romantic character study, well made but with no perceptible dramatic point.

w Irwin Shaw *d* Robert Parrish *ph Michel Kelber* *m* Josef Kosma

Jean Seberg, Stanley Baker, Philippe Fouquet

In the Good Old Summertime*
US 1949 102m Technicolor
MGM (Joe Pasternak)

In a Chicago music store in 1906, a salesgirl corresponds through a dating service with a man who turns out to be the manager she detests.
Cheerful remake of *The Shop around the Corner* (qv), with agreeable music, garish colour and not much style.

w Albert Hackett, Frances Goodrich, Ivan Tors, *play* Miklos Laszlo *d* Robert Z. Leonard *ph* Harry Stradling *md* George Stoll *ad* Randell Duell *ch* Robert Alton

Judy Garland, Van Johnson, S. Z. Sakall, Spring Byington, Clinton Sundberg, Buster Keaton, Lilian Bronson

In the Heat of the Night**
US 1967 109m De Luxe
UA / Mirisch (Walter Mirisch)

In a small southern town, the bigoted and bombastic sheriff on a murder hunt grudgingly accepts the help of a black detective.
Overrated policier in which the personality clash is amusing (and was timely) but the murder puzzle is a complete throwaway.

w Sterling Silliphant *d Norman Jewison* *ph Haskell Wexler* *m* Quincy Jones

Sidney Poitier, Rod Steiger, Warren Oates, Quentin Dean, William Schallert

'A very nice film and a very good film and yes, I think it's good to see a black man and a white man working together . . . but it's not going to take the tension out of New York City; it's not going to stop the riots in Chicago.'—*Rod Steiger*

† Poitier subsequently starred in a couple of very inferior sequels, *They Call Me Mister Tibbs* and *The Organization* (both qv).

AA: best picture; Sterling Silliphant; Rod Steiger
AAN: Norman Jewison

In the Meantime, Darling
US 1944 72m bw
TCF (Otto Preminger)

A wealthy bride lives in an overcrowded boarding house to be near her husband's army camp.
Unassuming wartime soaper of very little interest.

w Arthur Kober, Michael Uris *d* Otto Preminger *ph* Joe MacDonald *m* Emil Newman

Jeanne Crain, Frank Latimore, Mary Nash, Eugene Pallette, Stanley Prager, Gale Robbins, Jane Randolph

In the Navy*
US 1941 86m bw
Universal (Alex Gottlieb)

Two incompetents and a singing heart-throb are naval recruits.
A basically feeble follow-up to *Buck Privates* which outgrossed its predecessor and now stands as an interesting pointer to how mass entertainment has changed since 1941.

w John Grant, Arthur T. Horman *d* Arthur Lubin *ph* Joseph Valentine *songs* Gene de Paul, Don Raye

Bud Abbott, Lou Costello, Dick Powell, The Andrews Sisters, Claire Dodd, Dick Foran, Shemp Howard

In the Soup
GB 1936 72m bw

A solicitor and his wife are forced to pose as their own servants. Undernourished star comedy. Ralph Lynn, Judy Gunn, Morton Selten, Nelson Keyes, Bertha Belmore. Written by H. Fowler Mear, from a play by Ralph Lumley; directed by Henry Edwards; for Twickenham.

'No one is as good as Bette when she's bad!'
In This Our Life**
US 1942 101m bw
Warner (David Lewis)

A neurotic girl steals her sister's husband, leaves him in the lurch, dominates her hapless family and is killed while on the run from the police.
Splendid star melodrama with good supporting acting and background detail.

w Howard Koch, novel Ellen Glasgow *d John Huston ph* Ernest Haller *m* Max Steiner

Bette Davis, Charles Coburn, Olivia de Havilland, Frank Craven, George Brent, Dennis Morgan, Billie Burke, Hattie McDaniel, Lee Patrick, Walter Huston (uncredited)

In Which We Serve****
GB 1942 114m bw
Rank / Two Cities (Noel Coward)

Survivors from a torpedoed destroyer recall their life at sea and on leave.
Dated but splendid flagwaver; an archetypal British war film of almost limitless propaganda value.

w Noel Coward d Noel Coward, David Lean ph Ronald Neame *m* Noel Coward

Noel Coward, Bernard Miles, *John Mills,* Richard Attenborough, *Celia Johnson,* Kay Walsh, Joyce Carey, Michael Wilding, Penelope Dudley Ward, Kathleen Harrison, Philip Friend, George Carney, Geoffrey Hibbert, James Donald

COMMANDER (Noel Coward): 'The *Torrin* has been in one scrap after another, but even when we've had men killed, the majority survived and brought the old ship back. Now she lies in 1500 fathoms and with her more than half our shipmates. If they had to die, what a grand way to go! And now they lie all together with the ship we loved, and they're in very good company. We've lost her, but they're still with her. There may be less than half the *Torrin* left, but I feel that we'll all take up the battle with even stronger heart. Each of us knows twice as much about fighting, and each of us has twice as good a reason to fight. You will all be sent to replace men who've been killed in other ships, and the next time you're in action, remember the *Torrin*! I should like to add that there isn't one of you that I wouldn't be proud and honoured to serve with again.'

'One of the screen's proudest achievements at any time and in any country.'—*Newsweek*

'Never at any time has there been a reconstruction of human experience which could touch the savage grandeur and compassion of this production.'—*Howard Barnes, New York Herald Tribune*

† The story and the Coward character were based on the experiences of Louis Mountbatten, whose ship, HMS *Kelly*, was sunk under him.

AAN: best picture; Noel Coward (as writer)

Inadmissible Evidence**
GB 1968 96m bw
Paramount / Woodfall (Ronald Kinnoch)

A frustrated 40-year-old solicitor is on the verge of a nervous breakdown.
Interesting and surprisingly successful transcription of a difficult play which was virtually an anti-humanity soliloquy.

w John Osborne, from his play *d Anthony Page ph* Kenneth Hodges *m* Dudley Moore *ad* Seamus Flannery

Nicol Williamson, Eleanor Fazan, Jill Bennett, Peter Sallis, Eileen Atkins, Isobel Dean

'A play that was conceived as an increasingly bad dream has been made into a grittily detailed, naturalistic film.'—*Stanley Kauffmann*

'She was the biggest sucker of them all!'
Incendiary Blonde*
US 1945 112m Technicolor
Paramount (Joseph Sistrom)

The life of twenties nightclub queen Texas Guinan.
Laundered biopic with guns, girls and gangsters as well as songs.

w Claude Binyon, Frank Butler *d* George Marshall *ph Ray Rennahan m* Robert Emmett Dolan

Betty Hutton, Arturo de Cordova, Charles Ruggles, Albert Dekker, Barry Fitzgerald, Mary Phillips, Bill Goodwin, Eduardo Ciannelli, Maurice Rocco

'It runs its noisy but high-minded course through steamy emotion, painful misunderstanding and dramatic self-sacrifice, winding up in the snow among the blood of dead gangsters. Have we ever seen gangsters in Technicolor before?'—*Richard Mallett, Punch*

'A brassy synthesis of colour, song and dance, spattered with laughs.'—*Daily Herald*

AAN: Robert Emmett Dolan

Inchon
US 1981 140m colour
One Way Productions (Mitsuharu Ishii)

General MacArthur is affected by divine guidance during a major battle of the Korean war.
A very curious enterprise apparently financed by the Moonies. The religious angle sits oddly with the war scenes, and the result is an unsatisfactory mess.

w Robin Moore, Laird Koenig *d* Terence Young *ph* Bruce Surtees *m* Jerry Goldsmith

Laurence Olivier (as MacArthur), Jacqueline Bisset, David Janssen, Ben Gazzara, Toshiro Mifune, Richard Roundtree, Gabriele Ferzetti, Rex Reed

'A near total loss as well as a laugh.'—*Bruce Williamson, Playboy*

'The worst movie ever made, a turkey the size of Godzilla.'—*Jack Kroll, Newsweek*

'Quite possibly the worst movie ever made . . . stupefyingly incompetent.'—*Peter Rainer, Los Angeles Herald Examiner*

'As military spectacles go, one of the sorriest in military history.'—*Richard Schickel, Time*

Incident at Owl Creek*
France 1961 27m bw
Marcel Ichac / Films de Centaure / Paul de Roubaix
original title: *La Rivière du Hibou*

During the American Civil War a man is about to be hanged, and imagines how he might escape.
Intriguing but somewhat overpraised short with a rather obvious solution.

wd Robert Enrico, *story* Ambrose Bierce *ph* Jean Boffety *m* Henri Lanoë

Roger Jacquet, Anne Cornaly, Anker Larsen

'A powerful and remarkable film.'—*MFB*

Incident at Phantom Hill
US 1966 88m Technicolor

Two men face desperate odds to reach one million dollars in gold. Full-blooded western programmer with useful performances. Robert Fuller, Dan Duryea, Jocelyn Lane, Claude Akins, Noah Beery Jnr. Written by Frank Nugent; directed by Earl Bellamy; for Universal.

Les Inconnus dans la Maison*
France 1941 94m bw
Continental

An embittered ex-barrister saves his teenage daughter from a murder charge.
Unlikely melodrama remade as *Stranger in the House*; this version has more compelling writing and acting.

w Henri-Georges Clouzot, novel Georges Simenon d Henri Decoin *ph* Jules Kruger *m* Roland Manuel

Raimu, Juliette Faber, Jacques Baumer, Jean Tissier

The Incredible Journey**
US 1963 80m Technicolor
Walt Disney (James Algar)

Two dogs and a cat, separated from their owners, escape and travel 250 miles home.
A novelty attraction which keeps going purely on its animal interest, which is considerable.

w James Algar, *book* Sheila Burnford *d* Fletcher Markle *ph* Kenneth Peach, Jack Couffer, Lloyd Beebe *m* Oliver Wallace

The Incredible Melting Man
US 1977 84m Movielab
AIP / Quartet (Max J. Rosenberg)

The survivor of a space flight is rushed to hospital with radiation burns and an infection which causes his flesh to melt.
Unpleasant and nonsensical horror film with a few unintentional laughs and a plot borrowed from *The Quatermass Experiment.*

wd William Sachs *ph* Willy Curtis *m* Arlon Ober

Alex Rebar, Burr DeBenning, Myron Healey, Myron Aldredge

The Incredible Mr Limpet
US 1964 102m Technicolor
Warner (John C. Rose)

A meek but patriotic clerk is turned down by the navy and turns into a fish. In this form he becomes a radar assistant to a warship.
Sentimental sub-Disney goo, part animated.

w Jameson Bewer, John C. Rose, *novel* Theodore Pratt *d* Arthur Lubin *ph* Harold Stine *m* Frank Perkins

Don Knotts, Andrew Duggan, Larry Keating, Jack Weston

The Incredible Sarah*
GB 1976 105m Technicolor
Readers Digest (Helen M. Strauss)

The career of French actress Sarah Bernhardt up to the age of thirty-five.
Mildly pleasing old-fashioned biopic with remarkably unreliable detail and a regrettably bland approach to its fascinating subject.

w Ruth Wolff *d* Richard Fleischer
ph Christopher Challis *m* Elmer Bernstein
pd Elliot Scott

Glenda Jackson, Daniel Massey, Yvonne Mitchell, Douglas Wilmer, David Langton, Simon Williams, John Castle, Edward Judd, Peter Sallis

'An incredibly old-fashioned movie full of the most unforgettable moments you have ever tried to forget.'—*Andrew Sarris, Village Voice*

'A job lot of obligatory Hollywood platitudes strung together with all the skill of Captain Hook trying to thread a needle.'—*Benny Green, Punch*

'In the stupefying tradition of *Song of Norway*.'—*Pauline Kael.*

'So incredible you'll talk about it for years to come!'

The Incredible Shrinking Man*
US 1957 81m bw
U-I (Albert Zugsmith)

After being caught in a radioactive mist, a man shrinks inexorably to micro-size.
Horrifyingly inevitable sci-fi with imaginative touches gracing a cheap production.

w Richard Matheson d Jack Arnold *ph* Ellis W. Carter *m* Joseph Gershenson *sp Clifford Stine, Roswell A. Hoffman, Everett H. Bronssard m* Hans Salter

Grant Williams, Randy Stuart, April Kent, Paul Langton

'It opens up new vistas of cosmic terror.'—*Peter John Dyer*

'One hails a science fiction film which is both inventive and humane.'—*Sunday Times*

'Simple, ingenious, effective.'—*The Times*

The Incredible Shrinking Woman
US 1981 88m Technicolor
Universal / Lija (Hank Moonjean)

A housewife finds herself shrinking after using a new perfume . . .
Hamfisted spoof on *The Incredible Shrinking Man*, with flat jokes and rather poor trick photography.

w Jane Wagner *d* Joel Schumacher *ph* Bruce Logan *m* Suzanne Ciani

Lily Tomlin, Charles Grodin, Ned Beatty, Henry Gibson, Elizabeth Wilson

'Leaden satire on consumerism . . . even the special effects are barely passable.'—*Time Out, 1984*

The Incredible Two-Headed Transplant
US 1970 88m De Luxe
Mutual General / Trident / American International (John Lawrence)

A mad doctor grafts an extra head onto a homicidal maniac.
Full-blooded nonsense on a low budget; utterly repellent to some, but done with sufficient verve to be a minor cult title to others.

w James Gordon White, John Lawrence *d* Anthony M. Lanza *ph* John Steely, Glen Gano, Paul Hipp *m* John Barber

Bruce Dern, Pat Priest, Casey Kasem, Berry Kroeger

The Incredibly Strange Creatures who stopped Living and Became Mixed-up Zombies
US 1963 82m colour

A gypsy fortune-teller keeps monsters of her own making at the back of her tent. Murder and mayhem at the carnival: cheap exploitation item which for long was thought to be a fragment of someone's imagination, but turns out really to exist. Cash Flagg, Carolyn Brandt, Brett O'Hara. Written by Gene Pollock, Robert Silliphant; directed by Cash Flagg (Ray Dennis Steckler); for Morgan Steckler Productions.

Incubus
Canada 1981 92m colour

Women are raped by a rampant demon. Utterly distasteful horror film. John Cassavetes, Kerrie Keane, Helen Hughes, Erin Flannery, John Ireland. Written by George Franklin, from the novel by Ray Russell; directed by John Hough; for Guardian Trust Company.

'300,000 volts of horror!'

Indestructible Man
US 1956 70m bw

The dead body of a vicious killer is given new life by a mad doctor. Low-budget horror mayhem with no style at all. Lon Chaney Jnr, Robert Shayne, Casey Adams, Marian Carr. Written by Vy Russell and Sue Bradford; directed by Jack Pollexfen; for Allied Artists.

The Indian Fighter
US 1955 88m Technicolor Cinemascope
UA / Bryna (William Schorr)

An Indian fighter protects a wagon train from the Sioux.
Simple-minded western with touches of philosophy and not much drive.

w Frank Davis, Ben Hecht *d* André de Toth *ph* Wilfrid M. Cline *m* Franz Waxman

Kirk Douglas, Elsa Martinelli, Walter Abel, Walter Matthau, Diana Douglas, Eduard Franz, Lon Chaney Jnr, Alan Hale Jnr, Elisha Cook Jnr

Indian Scout
US 1949 70m bw

Episodes in the life of Davy Crockett. Minor western which hit the spot with small-town audiences, and in the late fifties, after the success of the Disney film, was reissued as *Davy Crockett, Indian Scout.* George Montgomery, Ellen Drew, Philip Reed, Noah Beery Jnr. Written by Richard Schayes; directed by Ford Beebe; for Edward Small.

'The hero is back!'

Indiana Jones and the Temple of Doom*
US 1984 118m Rank / De Luxe Panavision
Paramount / Lucasfilm (Robert Watts)

A prequel to *Raiders of the Lost Ark*: Jones in 1935 finds the sacred Sankara stone.
Slow-starting adventure romp with much ingenuity and too much brutality and horror. In the US it caused the creation of a new censor certificate: PG(13).

w Willard Huyck, Gloria Katz, *story* George Lucas *d Steven Spielberg ph* Douglas Slocombe, Allan Daviau *m* John Williams *pd Elliot Scott*

Harrison Ford, Kate Capshaw, Ke Huy Kwan, Philip Stone

'One of the most sheerly pleasurable physical comedies ever made.'—*Pauline Kael, New Yorker*

'A thin, arch, graceless affair.'—*Observer*
'A two-hour series of none too carefully linked chase sequences . . . sitting on the edge of your seat gives you a sore bum but also a numb brain.'—*Guardian*
AAN: music

Indianapolis Speedway
US 1939 82m bw
A racetrack driver wants his kid brother to continue in college, but he has the racing fever. Editor's-bench mélange of *The Crowd Roars* (1932) and *Here Comes the Navy*; this doesn't star Cagney. Pat O'Brien, Ann Sheridan, John Payne, Gale Page, Frank McHugh, Regis Toomey. Written by Sig Herzig and Wally Klein; directed by Lloyd Bacon; for Warners. 'It contains just about every cliché such type melodrama can have.'—*Variety*
†Frank McHugh played the same role in the 1932 version.

The Indians Are Coming
US 1930 bw serial: 12 eps
A cowboy escorts two friends to a wagon train, deflecting attacks from villains and outlaws en route. Unremarkable western chapters. Tim McCoy, Allene Ray, Charles Royal, Francis Ford. Directed by Henry McRae; for Universal.

'Through one indiscretion . . . a woman with a future became a woman with a past!'
Indiscreet
US 1931 92m bw
Art Cinema Corporation (Joseph M. Schenck)
A socialite endangers her own romance when she tries to protect her younger sister.
Embarrassing and slow-moving farce which helped to kill its star's career.
w / songs Brown, de Sylva and Henderson *d* Leo McCarey *ph* Ray June, Gregg Toland *m* Alfred Newman
Gloria Swanson, Ben Lyon, Monroe Owsley, Barbara Kent, Arthur Lake, Maude Eburne, Henry Kolker

'How dare he make love to me—and not be a married man!'
Indiscreet**
GB 1958 100m Technicolor
Grandon (Stanley Donen)
An American diplomat in London falls in love with an actress but protects himself by saying he is married.
Affairs among the ultra rich, amusing when played by these stars but with imperfect production values which the alarmingly thin plot allows one too much time to consider.
w Norman Krasna, from his play Kind Sir *d* Stanley Donen *ph* Frederick A. Young *m* Richard Bennett, Ken Jones
Cary Grant, Ingrid Bergman, Phyllis Calvert, Cecil Parker, David Kossoff, Megs Jenkins
'One is often on the point of being bored, but one never is, quite.'—*Richard Roud*
'A film to which you would not hesitate to take your jeweller, your architect, your home decorator, your dressmaker and your domestic staff.'—*Alexander Walker*

Indiscretion of an American Wife*
Italy / US 1954 75m bw
David O. Selznick (Vittorio de Sica)
Alternative titles: *Terminus Station, Indiscretion*
An American woman and an Italian professor say goodbye in Rome's terminal station.
Strained attempt to re-do *Brief Encounter* against the busy background of a great railway station; moments of interest, but artificiality prevails, and the plot never gets up enough steam.
w Cesare Zavattini, Truman Capote, etc *d* Vittorio de Sica *ph* G. R. Aldo *m* Aldo Cicognini
Jennifer Jones, Montgomery Clift, Gino Cervi, Richard Beymer

Inferno**
US 1953 83m Technicolor 3-D
TCF (William Bloom)
When a millionaire breaks his leg in the desert, his wife and her lover leave him to die; but he contrives to catch up with them.
An outdoor melodrama which made better use of 3-D than any other film, suggesting the lone handicapped figure in the vast spaces; but the lovers are dull and the fire climax perfunctory.
w Francis Cockrell *d* Roy Baker *ph Lucien Ballard* *m* Paul Sawtell
Robert Ryan, William Lundigan, Rhonda Fleming

Inferno
Italy 1980 107m Technicolor
A New York apartment house is occupied by satanists who murder those who learn their secret. Absurdly overplotted and mainly incomprehensible shocker with some small pretensions to style. Leigh McCloskey, Irene Miracle, Eleonora Giorgi. Written and directed by Dario Argento; for TCF.

The Informer***
US 1935 91m bw
RKO (Cliff Reid)
An IRA leader is betrayed by a simple-minded hanger-on who wants money to emigrate; he is hounded by fellow rebels and his own conscience.
A tedious plot is turned into brilliant cinema by full-blooded acting and a highly stylized yet brilliantly effective *mise en scène* which never attempts reality.
w Dudley Nichols, *novel* Liam O'Flaherty *d John Ford* *ph Joseph H. August* *m Max Steiner* *ad Van Nest Polglase*
Victor McLaglen, Heather Angel, Margot Grahame, Una O'Connor, Wallace Ford, Preston Foster, J. M. Kerrigan, Joe Sawyer, Donald Meek
'A tough subject, a sure critic's picture, but dubious box office.'—*Variety*
'As impressive as *Scarface*, or anything in the whole powerful literature redolent of fog and grime and dreariness which the Germans gave to the Americans.'—*Bardèche and Brasillach*
'Among the best five pictures since the coming of sound.'—*Baltimore Sun*
† An early British sound version was made in 1929 by Arthur Robison for BIP, with Lars Hansen and Lya de Putti.
AA: Dudley Nichols; John Ford; Max Steiner; Victor McLaglen
AAN: best picture

The Informers
GB 1963 104m bw
Rank (William MacQuitty)
US title: *Underworld Informers*
A police informer is murdered and his brother takes revenge.
Basic police melodrama, with clumsy script and jaded direction.
w Alun Falconer, *novel* Death of a Snout by Douglas Warner *d* Ken Annakin *ph* Reg Wyer *m* Clifton Parker
Nigel Patrick, Colin Blakely, Derren Nesbitt

L'Ingénue Libertine
France 1950 88m approx bw
Codo-Cinéma (Jean Velter)
A romantic girl lives in an imaginary world of affairs, but can't bring herself to consummate her marriage.
Minor period sex comedy which has the distinction of being Britain's first 'X' film, though the naughtiness is more implied than stated.
w P. Laroche, *novel* Colette *d* Jacqueline Audry *ph* Grignon *m* Vincent Scotto
Daniele Delorme, Frank Villard, Jean Tissier

Inherit the Wind**
US 1960 127m bw
UA / Lomitas (Stanley Kramer)
A fictionalized account of the 1925 Scopes 'monkey trial', when a schoolmaster was accused of teaching the theory of evolution.
Splendid theatrics with fine performances, marred by boring subplots but enhanced by a realistic portrait of a sweltering southern town.
w Nathan E. Douglas, Harold Jacob Smith, *play* Jerome Lawrence, Robert E. Lee *d Stanley Kramer* *ph Ernest Laszlo* *m* Ernest Gold
Spencer Tracy, Fredric March, Florence Eldridge, Gene Kelly, Dick York, Donna Anderson, Harry Morgan, Elliott Reid, Claude Akins
AAN: script; Ernest Laszlo; Spencer Tracy

The In-Laws
US 1979 103m Technicolor
Warner (Alan Arkin)
A timorous dentist and a CIA spy, whose children are to marry, find themselves unwillingly linked together in gunplay in a South American republic.

Two charismatic actors can't fail to get some laughs, but the extended script makes it a bumpy ride.

w Andrew Bergman *d* Arthur Hiller *ph* David M. Walsh *m* John Morris *pd* Pato Guzman

Peter Falk, Alan Arkin, Richard Libertini, Penny Peyser, Nancy Dussault

'It seems incapable either of adhering to the conventions of a comedy-thriller plot or of mustering sufficient invention to abandon plot altogether for a farcical free-for-all.'—*Tim Pulleine, MFB*

Inn for Trouble
GB 1960 90m bw

A suburban couple become country publicans. Amiable extension of a popular tv series, The Larkins. Peggy Mount, David Kossoff, Leslie Phillips, Bill Owen, Charles Hawtrey, A. E. Matthews, Yvonne Monlaur. Written by Fred Robinson; directed by C. M. Pennington-Richards; for Film Locations/Eros.

The Inn of the Sixth Happiness**
GB 1958 158m De Luxe Cinemascope
TCF (Mark Robson)

An English servant girl becomes a missionary and spends many arduous years in China.
Romanticized biopic of Gladys Aylward, with lots of children, a happy ending, and everyone sensationally miscast. Somehow it all works, even North Wales standing in for China.

w Isobel Lennart, *book* The Small Woman by Alan Burgess *d* Mark Robson *ph* Frederick A. Young *m* Malcolm Arnold

Ingrid Bergman, Curt Jurgens, Robert Donat, Athene Seyler, Ronald Squire, Richard Wattis, Moultrie Kelsall

AAN: Mark Robson

Inner Sanctum

The title was taken from a radio show featuring mystery stories with a last minute twist. The films were introduced rather oddly by a misshapen head in a crystal ball on the empty table of a boardroom. The head belonged to David Hoffman, and he introduced each film: 'This . . . is the inner sanctum . . .' (The original reference was presumably to the innermost working of the human mind.) The films, made for Universal, all starred Lon Chaney Jnr (who alternated as hero and villain); they were among the most boring and badly made second feature thrillers of the forties.
1943: CALLING DR DEATH
1944: WEIRD WOMAN, DEAD MAN'S EYES
1945: STRANGE CONFESSION (remake of THE MAN WHO RECLAIMED HIS HEAD), THE FROZEN GHOST
1946: PILLOW OF DEATH

Innerspace*
US 1987 120m Technicolor
Warner/Amblin/Steven Spielberg/Guber-Peters (Michael Finnell)

A miniaturized air force flyer is injected into the body of a grocery clerk.
Derivative comedy with clever twists; very tolerable of its kind, but no *Back to the Future*.

w Jeffrey Boam, Chip Proser *d* Joe Dante *ph* Andrew Laszlo *m* Jerry Goldsmith *pd* James H. Spencer

Dennis Quaid, Martin Short, Meg Ryan, Kevin McCarthy, Fiona Lewis

AA: special visual effects (Dennis Mauren)

Innocent Bystanders*
GB 1972 110m Eastmancolor
Sagittarius (George H. Brown)

The British secret service sends three agents to trace a Russian traitor.
Confused and violent espionage thriller; rather a waste of good production.

w James Mitchell *d* Peter Collinson *ph* Brian Probyn *m* John Keating

Stanley Baker, Geraldine Chaplin, Dana Andrews, Donald Pleasence

Innocent Sinners**
GB 1957 95m bw
Rank (Hugh Stewart)

A 13-year-old London girl builds a garden in the rubble of a bombed church, and gets into trouble with the police.
Likeable, slightly unfinished, mildy astringent little human drama full of well-observed character sketches.

w Neil Paterson, novel An Episode of Sparrows by Rumer Godden *d Philip Leacock ph* Harry Waxman *m* Philip Green

Flora Robson, Catherine Lacey, David Kossoff, Barbara Mullen, June Archer

The Innocents**
GB 1961 99m bw Cinemascope
TCF / Achilles (Jack Clayton)

In Victorian times, a spinster governess in a lonely house finds her young charges possessed by evil demons of servants now dead.
Elaborate revamping of Henry James' *The Turn of the Screw*, the ghosts being now (possibly) the figments of a frustrated woman's imagination. The frissons would have worked better on a normal-shaped screen, but the decor, lighting and general handling are exceptional.

w William Archibald, Truman Capote *d Jack Clayton ph Freddie Francis m* Georges Auric *ad Wilfrid Shingleton*

Deborah Kerr, Megs Jenkins, Pamela Franklin, Martin Stephens, Michael Redgrave, Peter Wyngarde

Innocents in Paris
GB 1953 102m bw
Romulus (Anatole de Grunwald)

British tourists spend a weekend in the gay city.
Strained compendium of anecdotes which misses an easy target.

w Anatole de Grunwald *d* Gordon Parry *ph* Gordon Lang *m* Josef Kosma

Alastair Sim, Margaret Rutherford, Jimmy Edwards, Claire Bloom, Laurence Harvey, Ronald Shiner

Innocents of Paris
US 1929 69m bw
Paramount / Jesse L. Lasky

A Parisian junk dealer saves a boy's life and falls for his aunt.
Heavygoing and dated musical comedy which introduced Chevalier to world audiences.

w Ethel Doherty, Ernest Vajda, *play* Flea Market by Charles Andrews *d* Richard Wallace *ph* Charles Lang *songs* Leo Robin, Richard A. Whiting

Maurice Chevalier, Sylvia Beecher, Russell Simpson, George Fawcett

Inquest*
GB 1939 60m bw
Charter (John Boulting)

A coroner has his suspicions as to who murdered the deceased.
Modest courtroom suspenser which marked the Boultings' first attempt (the second was *Suspect*) to raise the standard of second features.

w Francis Miller, *play* Michael Barringer *d* Roy Boulting *ph* D. P. Cooper

Elizabeth Allan, Herbert Lomas, Hay Petrie, Barbara Everest, Olive Sloane

'A degenerate film with dignity!'
Inserts
GB 1975 117m De Luxe
UA / Film and General (Davina Belling, Clive Parsons)

In 1930 Hollywood, a fading silent queen and a has-been director take to drugs.
Curious, interesting semi-porno melodrama with Pinterish asides and an inaccurate but stimulating feel of the film city at its height.

wd John Byrum ph Denys Coop *md* Jessica Harper

Richard Dreyfuss, Jessica Harper, Veronica Cartwright, Bob Hoskins, Stephen Davies

'The ludicrous plot and the painfully obvious symbolism make it tempting to interpret *Inserts* as a comedy. Yet to assume that a bad movie about the making of a bad movie is somehow good by virtue of its badness is to be guilty of a kind of mimetic fallacy.'—*Robert Asahina, New Leader*

Inside Daisy Clover*
US 1965 128m Technicolor Panavision
Warner / Pakula–Mulligan (Alan J. Pakula)

Tribulations of an adolescent movie star in thirties Hollywood.
Amusing, rather hysterical variant on *A Star Is Born*; agreeably wacky in spots, glum in others. Would have benefited from the greater permissiveness possible a few years later.

w Gavin Lambert, from his novel *d* Robert Mulligan *ph* Charles Lang Jnr *m* André Previn *ch* Herbert Ross *ad* Robert Clatworthy

Natalie Wood, Robert Redford, Ruth Gordon, Christopher Plummer, Roddy MacDowall

'The movie is short on characters, detail, activity, dialogue, even music; it's as if it's so determined to be stylish and sophisticated that rather than risk vulgarity or banality, it eliminates almost everything.'—*Pauline Kael, 1968*

AAN: Ruth Gordon

Inside Detroit
US 1955 82m bw

A racketeer comes out of prison and tries to regain control of the car workers' union. Tedious support, like a grossly extended *Crime Does Not Pay*. Pat O'Brien, Dennis O'Keefe, Tina Carver, Mark Damon. Written by Robert E. Kent and James B. Gordon; directed by Fred F. Sears; for Sam Katzman / Columbia.

Inside Moves
US 1980 113m colour
Goodmark (Mark M. Tanz, R. W. Goodwin)

A failed suicide makes friends in Max's bar with other handicapped people.
Curious tragi-comedy which generally settles for sentimentality but provides a few funny moments along the way.

w Valerie Curtin, Barry Levinson, *novel* Todd Walton *d* Richard Donner *ph* Laszlo Kovacs *m* John Barry

John Savage, David Morse, Diana Scarwid, Amy Wright, Tony Burton, Harold Russell

'A dismal contribution in the Year of the Disabled Person.'—*John Pym, MFB*

'If you imagine *The Iceman Cometh* rewritten by William Saroyan as a tribute to Frank Capra, that's about it.'—*Sunday Times*

AAN: Diana Scarwid (supporting actress)

Inside Out*
GB / West Germany 1975 97m Technicolor
Warner / Kettledrum (Judd Bernard)
TV title: *The Golden Heist*
aka: *Hitler's Gold*

A German ex-commandant of a POW camp enlists the aid of Americans in a daring plan to kidnap a Nazi war criminal from East Germany and find buried Nazi loot.
Entertaining but very silly actioner with too many changes of mood, though some sequences please.

w Judd Bernard, Stephen Schneck *d* Peter Duffell *ph* John Coquillon *m* Konrad Elfers

Telly Savalas, James Mason, Robert Culp, Aldo Ray, Gunter Meisner, Adrian Hoven, Charles Korvin, Richard Warner

Inside Straight
US 1951 89m bw
MGM (Richard Goldstone)

The life of a 19th-century tycoon is revealed in flashbacks during a poker game.
Solid melodrama which doesn't quite have the required spark.

w Guy Trosper *d* Gerald Mayer *ph* Ray June *m* Lennie Hayton

David Brian, Arlene Dahl, Barry Sullivan, Mercedes McCambridge, Paula Raymond, Claude Jarman Jnr, Lon Chaney Jnr, John Hoyt

Inside the Walls of Folsom Prison
US 1951 87m bw

A prison riot results in the death of the governor; when a replacement with more humane ideas is appointed, this does not stop violence from breaking out again. Old-fashioned prison movie on highly predictable lines. Steve Cochran, David Brian, Phil Carey, Ted de Corsia, Scott Forbes. Written and directed by Crane Wilbur; for Bryan Foy / Warner.

Insignificance
GB 1985 108m colour
Zenith / Recorded Picture Company (Jeremy Thomas)

On a hot night in 1953, a professor, an actress, a senator and a ballplayer meet in a New York hotel room.
Presumably meaningful but very boring talk piece in which the audience is supposed to recognize not merely well-known figures but a cross-section of America at the time.

w Terry Johnson, from his play *d* Nicholas Roeg *ph* Peter Hannan *m* Stanley Myers

Gary Busey, Tony Curtis, Theresa Russell, Michael Emil

The Inspector*
GB 1961 111m De Luxe Cinemascope
TCF (Mark Robson)
US title: *Lisa*

In 1946 a Dutch policeman rescues a Jewish girl from an ex-Nazi and helps smuggle her to Palestine.
Peripatetic melodrama with surface suspense and subdued thoughts of ideology and race. Moments of interest, but generally dully developed and acted.

w Nelson Gidding, *novel* Jan de Hartog *d* Philip Dunne *ph* Arthur Ibbetson *m* Malcolm Arnold

Stephen Boyd, Dolores Hart, Leo McKern, *Hugh Griffith*, Donald Pleasence, Harry Andrews, Robert Stephens, Marius Goring

'A sluggish mélange of melodrama, romance, mystery and what the inactive might call action.'—*Judith Crist*

An Inspector Calls**
GB 1954 79m bw
British Lion / Watergate (A. D. Peters)

In 1912 a prosperous Yorkshire family is visited by a mysterious inspector who proves that each of them was partly responsible for the death of a young girl.
Tactful, enjoyable record of a celebrated play in its author's most typical manner.

w Desmond Davis, *play J. B. Priestley d Guy Hamilton ph Ted Scaife m* Francis Chagrin *ad* Joseph Bato

Alastair Sim, Jane Wenham, Arthur Young, Olga Lindo, Brian Worth, Eileen Moore, Bryan Forbes

Inspector Clouseau
GB 1968 105m Eastmancolor Panavision
UA / Mirisch (Lewis J. Rachmil)

An incompetent French policeman is brought to London to investigate the aftermath of the Great Train Robbery.
Tiresome charade with all the jokes well telegraphed, and a background of swinging London.

w Tom and Frank Waldman *d* Bud Yorkin *ph* Arthur Ibbetson *m* Ken Thorne

Alan Arkin, Delia Boccardo, Frank Finlay, Patrick Cargill, Beryl Reid, Barry Foster

The Inspector General**
US 1949 101m Technicolor
Warner (Jerry Wald)
aka: *Happy Times*

An assistant elixir salesman with a travelling fair is mistaken by villagers for the dreaded inspector general.
Well wrought but basically boring version of a basically boring classic farce full of rhubarbing Old Russians. Nice production and hilarious moments do not quite atone for the dull stretches.

w Philip Rapp, Harry Kurnitz, *play* Nikolai Gogol *d* Henry Koster *ph* Elwood Bredell *songs* Sylvia Fine *m* John Green *ad* Robert Haas

Danny Kaye, Walter Slezak, Barbara Bates, Elsa Lanchester, Gene Lockhart, Alan Hale, Benny Baker, Walter Catlett

Inspector Hornleigh*
GB 1938 87m bw
TCF (Robert T. Kane)

The Chancellor of the Exchequer's bag is stolen.
First of three police comedy-dramas based on a character created for the radio series Monday Night at Eight by Hans Priwin. Not bad, but the thinnest of the trio.

w Bryan Wallace, Gerald Elliott, Richard Llewellyn *d* Eugene Forde *ph* Derrick Williams, Phil Tannura *md* Bretton Byrd

Gordon Harker, Alastair Sim, Miki Hood, Hugh Williams, Steve Geray, Wally Patch, Edward Underdown, Gibb McLaughlin, Ronald Adam

'The opening shots—the murder in the squalid lodging and the stamp auction with the rows of poker faces and the elaborately mute bids—are not only good cinema, they are good English cinema, as national as a shot, say, from a Feyder, a de Mille or a Pommer.'—*Graham Greene*

'Interest is well sustained from the exciting opening shots to the crescendo at the close.'—*Monthly Film Bulletin*

Inspector Hornleigh Goes to It*
GB 1940 87m bw
TCF (Edward Black)
US title: *Mail Train*

Hornleigh and Bingham track down a fifth columnist.
Zestful comedy thriller climaxing on an express train: good fun for addicts of the genre.

w Val Guest, J. O. C. Orton, Frank Launder *d* Walter Forde *ph* John Cox *md* Louis Levy

Gordon Harker, Alastair Sim, Phyllis Calvert, Edward Chapman, Charles Oliver, Raymond Huntley, Percy Walsh, David Horne, Peter Gawthorne

Inspector Hornleigh on Holiday*
GB 1939 87m bw
TCF (Edward Black)

The inspector and his sergeant solve the death of a fellow boarder at a seaside hotel.
Lively Hitchcockian comedy-thriller romp with an excellent script and plenty of variety of location.

w Frank Launder, Sidney Gilliat, J. O. C. Orton *d* Walter Forde *ph* John Cox *md* Louis Levy

Gordon Harker, Alastair Sim, Linden Travers, Wally Patch, Edward Chapman, Philip Leaver, Kynaston Reeves

Inspiration
US 1930 74m bw
MGM

A French artists' model renounces her lover in case she harms his career.
Inane romantic melodrama.

w Gene Markey *d* Clarence Brown *ph* William Daniels

Greta Garbo, Robert Montgomery, Lewis Stone, Marjorie Rambeau, Beryl Mercer, John Miljan

'As an adult problem it holds and never offends . . . box office certainly, and a cinch for women.'—*Variety*

'Camille without the cough.'—*Motion Picture*

The Intelligence Men
GB 1965 104m Eastmancolor
Rank / Hugh Stewart
US title: *Spylarks*

Two incompetent spies blunder through a series of adventures.
Inept and rather embarrassing big-screen debut for two excellent television comedians.

w S. C. Green, R. M. Hills *d* Robert Asher *ph* Jack Asher *m* Phillip Green

Eric Morecambe, Ernie Wise, William Franklyn, April Olrich, Richard Vernon, David Lodge, Warren Mitchell, Francis Matthews

Intent to Kill*
GB 1958 89m bw Cinemascope
TCF / Zonic (Adrian Worker)

In a Montreal hospital, attempts are made on the life of a South American dictator recovering from a brain operation.
Solidly entertaining suspenser.

w Jimmy Sangster *d* Jack Cardiff *ph* Desmond Dickinson *m* Kenneth V. Jones

Richard Todd, Betsy Drake, Herbert Lom, Warren Stevens, Alexander Knox

Interference
US 1929 75m bw

To prevent his wife from being blackmailed, a dying man commits murder and turns himself in. Dreary drama with the distinction of being Paramount's first talking picture. William Powell, Evelyn Brent, Clive Brook, Doris Kenyon. Written by Ernest Pascal and Hope Loring, from the play by Roland Pertwee and Harold Dearden; directed by Lothar Mendes and Roy Pomeroy; for Paramount.

Interiors*
US 1978 95m Technicolor
UA / Jack Rollins-Charles H. Joffe

Everybody in a well-heeled American family has problems.
Curious attempt by Woody Allen to make his own version of the Bergmanesque psycho-dramas he usually satirizes. Apparently this is the real Woody, and the comedian was a mask. Oh, well.

wd Woody Allen *ph* Gordon Willis *m* none

Kristin Griffith, Marybeth Hurt, Richard Jordan, Diane Keaton, E. G. Marshall, Geraldine Page, Maureen Stapleton, Sam Waterston

AAN: script; direction; Geraldine Page; Maureen Stapleton

'As dull as toothache and as predictable as a metronome.'—*Barry Took, Punch*

Interlude
US 1957 89m Technicolor Cinemascope
U-I (Ross Hunter)

An American girl in Munich falls in love with an orchestral conductor but leaves him because of his insane wife.
Dull remake of *When Tomorrow Comes* (qv), with poor script and performances.

w Daniel Fuchs, Franklin Coen *d* Douglas Sirk *ph* R. F. Schoengarth *m* Frank Skinner

Rossano Brazzi, June Allyson, Françoise Rosay, Marianne Cook, Keith Andes, Jane Wyatt

'Contains every cliché known to romantic fiction.'—*MFB*

Interlude*
GB 1968 113m Technicolor
Columbia / Domino (David Deutsch, Jack Hanbury)

A girl reporter falls for a celebrated orchestral conductor; they have an affair but he finally goes back to his wife.
Intermezzo remade for the swinging London set, quite agreeable in parts because of the acting but generally rather soggy.

w Lee Langley, Hugh Leonard *d* Kevin Billington *ph Gerry Fisher* *m* Georges Delerue *pd* Tony Woolard

Oskar Werner, Barbara Ferris, *Virginia Maskell, John Cleese*, Donald Sutherland, Nora Swinburne, Alan Webb

'If you laughed at *Brief Encounter* you will roar over this one.'—*Wilfrid Sheed*

'It's got all the schmaltz and none of the style of the tearjerkers of yesteryear.'—*Judith Crist, 1973*

'Wild longings . . . fierce desires he could not name . . . for an interlude of stolen love! To one woman he gave his memories—to another he gave his dreams!'

Intermezzo***
US 1939 69m bw
David O. Selznick
GB title: *Escape to Happiness*

A renowned, married violinist has an affair with his musical protégée.
Archetypal cinema love story, Hollywoodized from a Swedish original but quite perfect in its brief, sentimental way.

w George O'Neil, *original scenario* Gosta Stevens, Gustav Molander *d Gregory Ratoff* *ph* Gregg Toland *m Robert Henning, Heinz Provost* *m (score)* Lou Forbes

Leslie Howard, Ingrid Bergman, John Halliday, Edna Best, Cecil Kellaway

† William Wyler is said to have assisted in the direction.

AAN: Lou Forbes

'Stars of stage, screen radio and boudoir throw a party for your entertainment!'

International House*
US 1933 73m bw
Paramount

A weird variety of travellers are quarantined in a Shanghai hotel where a local doctor has perfected television.
Madcap farce which succeeds in hits and misses.

w Francis Martin, Walter de Leon, Lou Heifetz, Neil Brant *d* Edward Sutherland *ph* Ernest Haller *songs* Ralph Rainger, Leo Robin

W. C. Fields, George Burns, Gracie Allen, Peggy Hopkins Joyce, Stuart Erwin, Sari Matitza, Bela Lugosi, Edmund Breese, Lumsden Hare, Rose Marie, Rudy Vallee, Sterling Holloway, Cab Calloway and his band, Colonel Stoopnagle and Budd

'Cast includes enough names to offset the effects of an otherwise second-rate picture.'—*Variety*

'Constructed along the lines of a mammoth vaudeville show, the motivating story often is sidetracked entirely to permit a lot of unrelated hokum comedy.'—*Motion Picture Herald*

'A thousand thrills as two men battle across a continent!'

International Lady*
US 1941 102m bw
Edward Small

An FBI man falls for the lady Axis agent he is chasing.
Cliché-ridden melodrama partially saved by light comedy touches.

w Howard Estabrook *d* Tim Whelan *ph* Hal Mohr *m* Lucien Moraweck

George Brent, Basil Rathbone, Ilona Massey, Gene Lockhart, George Zucco, Francis Pierlot, Martin Kosleck, Marjorie Gateson

International Settlement
US 1938 75m bw
TCF (Darryl F. Zanuck)

An adventurer becomes involved in Shanghai gun-running during the war between China and Japan.
Brisk action romance with good technical credits.

w Lou Breslow, John Patrick *d* Eugene Forde *ph* Lucien Andriot *md* Samuel Kaylin

George Sanders, Dolores del Rio, June Lang, Dick Baldwin, Ruth Terry, John Carradine, Keye Luke, Harold Huber, Pedro de Cordoba

'Strong supporting picture for double bills.'—*Variety*

International Squadron*
US 1941 87m bw
Warner (Edmund Grainger)

A playboy becomes a fighting air ace.
Standard war story, quite well done; remake of *Ceiling Zero* (qv).

w Barry Trivers, *story* Frank Wead *d* Lewis Seiler *ph* Arthur Edeson

Ronald Reagan, James Stephenson, Julie Bishop, Cliff Edwards, Reginald Denny, Olympe Bradna, William Lundigan, John Ridgely

International Velvet
GB 1978 125m Metrocolor
MGM (Bryan Forbes)

A hostile orphan becomes an international horsewoman. Disappointing attempt to produce a sequel to 1944's *National Velvet*; none of it coheres, one is not clear to whom it is intended to appeal, and some of the dialogue is fearsome.

wd Bryan Forbes *ph* Tony Imi *m* Francis Lai *pd* Keith Wilson

Nanette Newman, Tatum O'Neal, Anthony Hopkins, Christopher Plummer, Peter Barkworth, Dinsdale Landen

The Internecine Project*
GB 1974 89m Eastmancolor
Maclean and Co / Lion International / Hemisphere (Barry Levinson, Andrew Donally)

A Harvard professor arranges the mutual extermination of four people who could spoil a politician's presidential chances.
Coldly murderous romp with plenty of style.

w Barry Levinson, Jonathan Lynn, *novel* Mort W. Elkind *d* *Ken Hughes* *ph* Geoffrey Unsworth *m* Roy Budd

James Coburn, Lee Grant, Harry Andrews, Ian Hendry, Michael Jayston, Keenan Wynn

'He risked his life to save a rat—and what did he get for it?'

Internes Can't Take Money*
US 1937 75m bw
Paramount (Benjamin Glazer)
GB title: *You Can't Take Money*

A hospital doctor persuades a gangster friend to help a woman find her missing child.
Quite interesting minor melodrama, first of the Dr Kildare series which was subsequently recast and restyled by MGM.

w Rian James, Theodore Reed, *story* Max Brand *d* *Alfred Santell* *ph* Theodor Sparkuhl *m* Gregory Stone

Joel McCrea, Barbara Stanwyck, Lloyd Nolan, Stanley Ridges, Lee Bowman, Irving Bacon

'Satisfactory melodrama with a tear . . . better than average standing at the box office.'—*Variety*

'Their nights are as fast and frantic as their days! Don't miss the wildest party ever filmed!'

The Interns*
US 1962 130m bw
Columbia / Interns Co. / Robert Cohn

In an American hospital, newly qualified doctors have personal and career problems. Birth, abortion, sudden death, drugs and women's lib all figure in this melodramatic compendium which succeeds well enough on its own level and spawned a sequel (*The New Interns*) and an unsuccessful TV series.

w Walter Newman, David Swift, *novel* Richard Frede *d* David Swift *ph* Russell Metty *m* Leith Stevens

Cliff Robertson, Michael Callan, James MacArthur, Nick Adams, Suzy Parker, Buddy Ebsen, Telly Savalas

Interpol
GB 1957 92m bw Cinemascope
Columbia / Warwick (Irving Allen, Albert R. Broccoli)
US title: *Pickup Alley*

The US Anti-Narcotics Squad trails across Europe the insane and ruthless leader of a drug ring.
Drearily routine thick ear electrified by one performance but not helped by wide screen.

w John Paxton *d* John Gilling *ph* Ted Moore *m* Richard Bennett

Victor Mature, Anita Ekberg, *Trevor Howard,* Bonar Colleano, Marne Maitland, Eric Pohlmann, Alec Mango, Peter Illing, Sidney Tafler

The Interrupted Journey
GB 1949 80m bw
Valiant (Anthony Havelock-Allan)

An author leaves his wife for another woman, changes his mind on the journey, pulls the communication cord and causes a train crash. Or does he?
Minor melodrama with expressionist tendencies and a dream explanation. Interesting for its parts rather than its whole.

w Michael Pertwee *d* Daniel Birt *ph* Erwin Hillier

Richard Todd, Valerie Hobson, Christine Norden, Tom Walls, Ralph Truman, Vida Hope

Interrupted Melody
US 1955 106m Eastmancolor Cinemascope
MGM (Jack Cummings)

The story of Marjorie Lawrence, an Australian opera singer who fell victim to polio.
Standard biopic which jells less well than some.

w William Ludwig, Sonya Levien *d* Curtis Bernhardt *ph* Joe Ruttenberg, Paul Vogel *music supervisor* Saul Chaplin

Eleanor Parker, Glenn Ford, Roger Moore, Cecil Kellaway, Stephen Bekassy

AA: script
AAN: Eleanor Parker

Intimacy*
US 1965 87m bw
Goldstone (David Heilwell)

A businessman in need of a government contract tries to compromise the official concerned.
Unusual minor melodrama, interesting but not quite successful.

w Eva Wolas *d* Victor Stoloff *ph* Ted Saizis *m* Geordie Hormel

Barry Sullivan, Nancy Malone, Jack Ging, Joan Blackman, Jackie Shannon

Intimate Relations see Les Parents Terribles

The Intimate Stranger*
GB 1956 95m bw
Anglo–Guild (Alec Snowden)
US title: *Finger of Guilt*

An American film producer in England is plagued by a strange girl who claims to have been his mistress.
Acceptable mystery thriller which holds the interest and has good detail.

w Peter Howard from his novel Pay the Piper *d* Joseph Walton (Joseph Losey) *m* Trevor Duncan *ph* Gerald Gibbs

Richard Basehart, Mary Murphy, Mervyn Johns, Constance Cummings, Roger Livesey, Faith Brook

Into the Blue
GB 1950 83m bw
(US title: *Man in the Dinghy*)

A cheerful stowaway on a yacht helps the owners catch smugglers. Emaciated comedy which never gets going. Michael Wilding, Odile Versois, Jack Hulbert, Constance Cummings, Edward Rigby. Written by Pamela Wilcox Bower, Donald Taylor and Nicholas Phipps; directed by Herbert Wilcox; for Imperadio.

Into the Night
US 1985 115m Technicolor
Universal / George Folsey Jnr, Ron Koslow

A harassed husband becomes even more so when one night at the airport he meets a dizzy girl with six smuggled emeralds.
A kind of nocturnal road film into which for some reason the director has crammed a number of his colleagues. None of it really works, even as an in-joke.

w Ron Koslow *d* John Landis *ph* Robert Paynter *m* Ira Newborn *pd* John Lloyd

Jeff Goldblum, Michelle Pfeiffer, Richard Farnsworth, Irene Papas, Paul Mazursky, Roger Vadim, David Bowie

Intolerance****
US 1916 115m approx (24 fps) bw silent
D. W. Griffith

Four stories—including Belshazzar's feast and the massacre of St Bartholomew—of intolerance through the ages are intercut and linked by the image of a mother and her baby: 'out of the cradle, endlessly rocking'.
A massive enterprise of which audiences at the time and after were quite intolerant. Hard to take in parts, it rises to a fine climax as all the stories come to a head, including a modern one with a race between a car and train, and has been called 'the only film fugue'. At the time, by far the most expensive film ever made.

wd D. W. Griffith ph Billy Bitzer, Karl Brown

Mae Marsh, Lillian Gish, Constance Talmadge, Robert Harron, Elmo Lincoln, Eugene Pallette

'A mad, brilliant, silly extravaganza. Perhaps the greatest movie ever made. In it one can see the source of most of the major traditions of the screen: the methods of Eisenstein and Von Stroheim, the Germans and the Scandinavians, and, when it's bad, de Mille.'—*New Yorker, 1980*

Intrigue
US 1947 90m bw
UA / Star (Sam Bischoff)

In Shanghai after the war, a civilian pilot becomes unwittingly involved in drug smuggling.
Tedious and flashy pot-boiler.

w Barry Trivers, George Slavin *d* Edwin L. Marin *ph* Lucien Andriot *m* Louis Forbes

George Raft, June Havoc, Tom Tully, Helena Carter

The Intruder*
GB 1953 84m bw
British Lion / Ivan Foxwell

An ex-army officer surprises a burglar and recognizes his old comrade who has been ill-served by society.
Watchable but rather mechanical compendium drama in which a series of cameos supposedly sum up the problems of life in post-war Britain.

w Robin Maugham, John Hunter, *novel* Line on Ginger by Robin Maugham *d* Guy Hamilton *ph* Ted Scaife *m* Francis Chagrin

Jack Hawkins, Michael Medwin, Hugh Williams, George Cole, Dennis Price, Dora Bryan

The Intruder*
US 1961 84m bw
Filmgroup (Roger Corman)
GB title: *The Stranger*

A mild-mannered stranger arrives in a southern town and stirs up racist trouble.
Cheaply-made social melodrama with many effective moments.

w Charles Beaumont, from his novel *d Roger Corman ph* Taylor Byars *m* Herman Stein

William Shatner, Frank Maxwell, Beverly Lunsford, Robert Emhardt, Jeanne Cooper, Leo Gordon, Charles Beaumont

Intruder in the Dust***
US 1949 87m bw
MGM (Clarence Brown)

In a southern town, a boy and an old lady solve a mystery and prevent a black man from being lynched.
Excellent character drama which also offers vivid local colour, a murder puzzle and social comment. A semi-classic.

w Ben Maddow, novel William Faulkner *d Clarence Brown ph Robert Surtees m* Adolph Deutsch

Juano Hernandez, Elizabeth Patterson, David Brian, Claude Jarman Jnr, *Porter Hall*, Will Geer

'It is surely the years of range and experience which have given him a control of the medium so calm, sure and—apparently—easy that he can make a complex story seem simple and straightforward.'—*Pauline Kael*

'A really good movie that is also and incidentally the first honestly worked out "racial" film I have seen.'—*Richard Winnington*

'An example of gripping film craftsmanship.'—*News of the World*

'From out of space—came hordes of green monsters!'

Invaders from Mars
US 1953 82m Cinecolor 3D
Edward L. Alperson

Martian invaders use hypnotized humans as saboteurs.
Poverty Row sci-fi partly redeemed by its erratic but talented designer who provides flashes of visual imagination.

INTRUDER IN THE DUST. MGM made few concessions to box office popularity with their powerful indictment of racial bigotry, here typified by Porter Hall, gun in hand.

w Richard Blake *d / pd William Cameron Menzies* *ph* John Seitz *m* Raoul Kraushaar

Helena Carter, Arthur Franz, Leif Erickson, Hillary Brooke

Invaders from Mars
US 1986 100m TVC colour Panavision
Cannon (Menahem Golan, Yoram Globus)

A boy one night sees a space ship land in his back yard.
Astonishingly witless remake of a show that was a cheap second feature in 1953.

w Dan O'Bannon, Don Jakoby *d* Tobe Hooper *ph* Daniel Pearl *m* Christopher Young

Karen Black, Hunter Carson, Timothy Bottoms, Louise Fletcher, Bud Cort

Invasion*
GB 1966 82m bw
AA / Merton Park (Jack Greenwood)

An English village is beset one night by invaders from outer space.
Understated, effective little suspenser, well done in all departments.

w Roger Marshall *d Alan Bridges* *ph* James Wilson *m* Bernard Ebbinghouse

Edward Judd, Valerie Gearon, Lyndon Brook, Yoko Tani, Tsai Chin, Barrie Ingham, Arthur Sharp

'A modest but highly intelligent science fiction thriller.'—*Financial Times*

'The world as they knew it was slipping away from them. Time was running out for the human race. And there was nothing to hold on to—except each other!'

Invasion of the Body Snatchers****
US 1956 80m bw Superscope
Allied Artists / Walter Wanger

A small American town is imperceptibly taken over by an alien force.
Persuasive, thoroughly satisfying, low-budget science fiction, put across with subtlety and intelligence in every department.

w Daniel Mainwaring, *novel Jack Finney* *d Don Siegel* *ph* Ellsworth Fredericks *m* Carmen Dragon

Kevin McCarthy, Dana Wynter, Larry Gates, *King Donovan*, Carolyn Jones, Virginia Christine, Sam Peckinpah

Invasion of the Body Snatchers*
US 1978 115m Technicolor
UA / Robert H. Solo

Flashy updating of the 1956 classic, mistakenly set in a big city (San Francisco) and confusingly unravelled, with nobody for the audience to empathize with. Its nicest effect is to have Kevin McCarthy repeat his old role in a cameo.

w W. D. Richter *d* Philip Kaufman *ph* Michael Chapman *m* Denny Zeitlin *pd* Charles Rosen

Donald Sutherland, Brooke Adams, Leonard Nimoy, Veronica Cartwright, Jeff Goldblum, Art Hindle, Lelia Goldoni, Kevin McCarthy, Don Siegel

Invasion Quartet
GB 1961 87m bw
MGM (Ronald Kinnoch)

An ill-assorted foursome of officers and a boffin take on the dangerous mission of silencing a Nazi gun trained on Dover.
A plot which could have been handled any way is played unsatisfactorily for farce, and all concerned are understandably uneasy.

w Jack Trevor Story, John Briley, *story* Norman Collins *d* Jay Lewis *ph* Geoffrey Faithfull, Gerald Moss *m* Ron Goodwin

Bill Travers, Spike Milligan, Grégoire Aslan, John Le Mesurier, Thorley Walters, Maurice Denham, Millicent Martin, Cyril Luckham

'America wasn't ready—but he was!'

Invasion USA
US 1952 70m bw
Columbia (Albert Zugsmith)

A hypnotist in a New York bar gives a group of people a foretaste of what might happen to them under atomic attack.
Ludicrous, dangerous, hilarious low-budget exploitationer composed mainly of rubber rocks and old newsreels.

w Robert Smith *d* Alfred E. Green *ph* John L. Russell *m* Albert Glasser

Dan O'Herlihy, Gerald Mohr, Peggie Castle

Invasion USA
US 1985 107m TVC colour
Cannon (Menahem Golan, Yoram Globus)

Ruthless foreign mercenaries invade the southern US.
Brainless farrago of violence which goes out of its way to be unpleasant but ends up being rather funny.

w James Bruner, Chuck Norris *d* Joseph Zito *ph* Joao Fernandes *m* Jay Chattaway

Chuck Norris, Richard Lynch, Melissa Prophet, Alaxander Zale

Investigation of a Citizen above Suspicion*
Italy 1970 115m Technicolor
Vera (Daniele Senatore)

A successful police inspector kills his mistress and, paranoically considering himself above suspicion, plants clues leading to himself and even confesses the crime.
Fairly engrossing character study with political undertones; cinematically quite striking, too.

w Ugo Pirro, Elio Petri *d Elio Petri* *ph* Luigi Kuveiller *m* Ennio Morricone

Gian Maria Volonte, Florinda Bolkan, Salvo Randone, Gianni Santuccio

AAN: best foreign film; script

Invisible Agent*
US 1942 84m bw
Universal (George Waggner)

Nazi and Japanese spies seek the secret of invisibility from its inventor.
Lively fantasy thriller with a cast more distinguished than it deserves.

w Curt Siodmak *d* Edwin L. Marin *sp John P. Fulton* *m* Hans Salter

Cedric Hardwicke, Peter Lorre, Ilona Massey, Jon Hall, Albert Basserman, J. Edward Bromberg, John Litel

Invisible Boy
US 1957 89m bw
MGM / Pan (Nicholas Nayfack)

A scientist allows his 10-year-old son to repair a robot, which comes under the control of an alien force.
Minor sci-fi utilizing the robot from *Forbidden Planet*.

w Cyril Hume *d* Herman Hoffman *ph* Harold Wellman *m* Les Baxter

Richard Eyer, Philip Abbott, Harold J. Stone, Diane Brewster

'Even the moon is frightened of me—frightened to death!'

The Invisible Man****
US 1933 71m bw
Universal (Carl Laemmle Jnr)

A scientist discovers a means of making himself invisible, but in the process becomes a megalomaniac.
Superb blend of eccentric character comedy, melodrama and trick photography in a Hollywood English setting; remarkably faithful to the spirit of the book. It made a star of Claude Rains in his first film, even though he is seen for only a couple of seconds.

w R. C. Sheriff, Philip Wylie, novel H. G. Wells *d James Whale* *ph Arthur Edeson* *sp John P. Fulton* *m* W. Frank Harling

Claude Rains, Gloria Stuart† William Harrigan, Henry Travers, *E. E. Clive, Una O'Connor*, Forrester Harvey, Dudley Digges, Holmes Herbert

GRIFFIN (Claude Rains): 'We'll start with a few murders. Big men, little men—just to show we make no distinction.'

'Well made and full of intentional and unintentional laughs. Should do well.'—*Variety*

'Taken either as a technical exercise or as a sometimes profoundly moving retelling of the Frankenstein fable, it is one of the most rewarding of recent films.'—*William Troy*

† Sequels, successively less interesting, were (all qv) *The Invisible Man Returns* (1940), *Invisible Woman* (1941), *Invisible Agent* (1942), *The Invisible Man's Revenge* (1944) and *Abbott and Costello Meet the Invisible Man* (1951). A TV series with an anonymous hero was made by ATV in 1955; a Universal one with David McCallum followed in 1975, and was restructured as *The Gemini Man* in 1976.

†† Boris Karloff had been first choice for the role, but he turned it down.

The Invisible Man Returns
US 1940 81m bw
Universal (Ken Goldsmith)

A man convicted of killing his brother uses the secret of invisibility to find the real culprit.

Second in the series takes itself too seriously: a slow starter which works its way to a strong climax.

w Curt Siodmak, Lester Cole, Cedric Belfrage *d* Joe May *ph* Milton Krasner *m* Hans Salter, Frank Skinner *sp John P. Fulton*

Vincent Price, Cedric Hardwicke, John Sutton, Nan Grey, Cecil Kellaway, Alan Napier, Forrester Harvey

'Though the film has its bright moments, and some weird ones too, the first freshness is gone. Even the effects seem repetitive.'—*Pauline Kael, 70s*

The Invisible Man's Revenge
US 1944 77m bw
Universal (Ford Beebe)

A psychopathic killer on the run takes refuge with a doctor who has discovered the secret of invisibility.
Curious reversion to the original story in that the invisible man is now again the villain; but otherwise there's no flavour at all to this horror comic set in a phoney England.

w Bertram Millhauser *d* Ford Beebe *m* Hans Salter *sp John P. Fulton*

Jon Hall, Leon Errol, John Carradine, Alan Curtis, Evelyn Ankers, Gale Sondergaard, Halliwell Hobbes

The Invisible Menace
US 1938 55m bw

Murder at an army base brings strange revelations of the past. Standard mystery in which the star seems misplaced. Boris Karloff, Regis Toomey, Marie Wilson, Henry Kolker. Written by Crane Wilbur, from a play by Ralph S. Zink; directed by John Farrow; for Warner. (NB: Remade in 1943 as *Murder at the Waterfront*.) 'Undistinguished mystery meller, for bottom-lining the duals.'—*Variety*

The Invisible Monster
US 1950 bw serial: 12 eps

Alien smuggling is the new pastime of a scientific criminal who calls himself The Phantom Ruler. Cheerful serial nonsense. Richard Webb, Aline Towne, Lane Bradford, Stanley Price, John Crawford. Directed by Fred C. Brannon; for Republic.

The Invisible Ray*
US 1935 79m bw
Universal (Edmund Grainger)

A scientist discovers a superpowerful element which makes him homicidal.
Slow-moving science fiction with a touch of horror, and the pattern for its star's many later roles as a sympathetic man who turns into a monster. Interesting rather than stimulating.

w John Colton, *story* Howard Higgin, Douglas Hodges *d* Lambert Hillyer *ph* George Robinson *m* Franz Waxman *sp John P. Fulton*

Boris Karloff, Bela Lugosi, Frances Drake, Frank Lawton, Walter Kingsford, Beulah Bondi, Violet Kemble Cooper, Nydia Westman

'An easy number to sell, it should do pretty good business.'—*Variety*

Invisible Stripes
US 1939 82m bw
Warner (Hal B. Wallis)

An ex-con finds it difficult to go straight.
By 1940 Warners must have been able to make rip-offs of *Angels with Dirty Faces* in their sleep, and this one, despite its cast, suggests that they did.

w Warren Duff, *book* Warden Lewis E. Lawes *d* Lloyd Bacon *ph* Ernest Haller *m* Heinz Roemheld

George Raft, Humphrey Bogart, William Holden, Flora Robson, Jane Bryan, Paul Kelly, Lee Patrick, Henry O'Neill, Moroni Olson

'It's a familiar cinematic yarn but strengthened by a zippy pace, excellent performances and direction.'—*Variety*

The Invisible Woman
US 1941 72m bw
Universal (Burt Kelly)

A mad scientist turns a model invisible.
Screwball comedy with a deteriorating star at his hammiest: generally very laboured, but with some funny moments.

w Robert Lees, Fred Rinaldo, Gertrude Purcell *d* A. Edward Sutherland *ph* Elwood Bredell *md* Charles Previn

John Barrymore, Charles Ruggles, Virginia Bruce, John Howard, Oscar Homolka, Donald MacBride, Edward Brophy, Shemp Howard, Margaret Hamilton, Maria Montez

Invitation
US 1952 81m bw
MGM (Lawrence Weingarten)

When a millionaire's daughter believes she is dying, revelations ensue about her beloved husband's original intentions.
Competently idiotic weepie with a happy ending.

w Paul Osborn, *story* Jerome Weidman *d* Gottfried Reinhardt *ph* Ray June *m* Bronislau Kaper

Dorothy McGuire, Van Johnson, Ruth Roman, Louis Calhern, Ray Collins, Michael Chekhov

'The dialogue is stagey and the treatment indeterminate, with overmuch reliance on the dubious emotional reinforcement of loud background music.'—*Penelope Houston*

Invitation to a Gunfighter*
US 1964 92m De Luxe
UA / Stanley Kramer (Richard Wilson)

A small-town tyrant hires a smooth gunfighter to keep down the farmers he has cheated.
Predictable, rather self-satisfied little western with a studio look. Smart script and performances.

w Elizabeth and Richard Wilson *d* Richard Wilson *ph* Joseph MacDonald *m* David Raksin

Yul Brynner, George Segal, Janice Rule, Pat Hingle

Invitation to Happiness
US 1939 95m bw
Paramount (Wesley Ruggles)

A society girl marries a prizefighter.
Routine star romantic drama.

w Claude Binyon *d* Wesley Ruggles *ph* Leo Tover *m* Frederick Hollander

Irene Dunne, Fred MacMurray, Charles Ruggles, Billy Cook, William Collier Snr, Marion Martin

'Heartthrob drama, geared for good biz.'—*Variety*

Invitation to the Dance**
GB 1954 92m Technicolor
MGM (Arthur Freed)

Three stories in dance and mime.
Unsuccessful ballet film which closed its star's great period and virtually ended the heyday of the Hollywood musical. The simple fact emerged that European ballet styles were not Kelly's forte; yet there was much to enjoy in *Circus, Ring around the Rosy* and *The Magic Lamp*.

w, ch, d Gene Kelly *ph* Frederick A. Young *m* Jacques Ibert, André Previn, Rimsky-Korsakov *ad* Alfred Junge

Gene Kelly, Igor Youskevitch, Tommy Rall, Belita, Tamara Toumanova

Invitation to the Wedding
GB 1985 90m colour widescreen

An aristocratic wedding causes trouble when the bride's uncle, the bishop, marries her to the wrong man at rehearsal. A situation which could have been mildly amusing in the *Quiet Wedding* vein is botched by an unfunny script and wildly eccentric casting. Ralph Richardson, John Gielgud (as an American evangelist), Paul Nicholas, Elizabeth Shepherd, Ronald Lacey (as two people for some reason), John Standing, Susan Brooks. Written by William Fairchild; photographed by Freddie Young; composed, directed and produced by Joseph Brooks; for Chancery Lane.

The Ipcress File**
GB 1965 109m Techniscope
Rank / Steven / Lowndes (Harry Saltzman)

An intelligence man traces a missing scientist and finds that one of his own superiors is a spy.
The attempt to present a low-key James Bond (glasses, good at cookery, supermarket shopper) is frustrated by flashy direction and a confused plot. It did herald a new genre though the whole ambiance is now sadly dated, like an old copy of *The Sunday Times* Colour Supplement.

w Bill Canaway, James Doran, *novel* Len Deighton *d* Sidney J. Furie *ph* Otto Heller *m* John Barry *ad* Ken Adam

Michael Caine, Nigel Green, Guy Doleman, Sue Lloyd, Gordon Jackson

† Two sequels appeared starring 'Harry Palmer' (never named in the books): *Funeral in Berlin* and *Billion Dollar Brain* (both qv).

Irene
US 1940 101m bw (colour sequence)
RKO / Imperator (Herbert Wilcox)

A New York Irish shopgirl moves into society. Fairly dim picturization of the old musical: the cast does its best.

w Alice Duer Miller, *play* James H. Montgomery *d* Herbert Wilcox *ph* Russell Metty *md* Anthony Collins *songs* Harry Tierney, Joseph McCarthy

Anna Neagle, Ray Milland, Roland Young, Alan Marshal, May Robson, Billie Burke, Arthur Treacher, Marsha Hunt, Isabel Jewell, Ethel Griffies

'This pre-camp version tries to be innocuously charming, and the effort is all too evident.'—*New Yorker, 1976*

† Previously filmed in 1926 with Colleen Moore.

AAN: Anthony Collins

Irish Eyes Are Smiling**
US 1944 90m Technicolor
TCF (Damon Runyon)

The life and times of a nineties songwriter, Ernest R. Ball.
Standard musical biopic, handsomely mounted.

w Earl Baldwin, John Tucker Battle *d* Gregory Ratoff *ph* Harry Jackson *md* Alfred Newman, Charles Henderson

Dick Haymes, June Haver, Monty Woolley, Anthony Quinn, Beverly Whitney, Maxie Rosenbloom, Veda Ann Borg, Clarence Kolb

AAN: Alfred Newman, Charles Henderson

The Irish in Us
US 1935 84m bw
Warner (Samuel Bischoff)

Adventures of three New York brothers.
Routine, good-natured star action frolic.

w Earl Baldwin *d* Lloyd Bacon *ph* George Barnes *md* Leo F. Forbstein

James Cagney, Pat O'Brien, Olivia de Havilland, Mary Gordon, Frank McHugh, Allen Jenkins, J. Farrell MacDonald, Thomas Jackson

'A hokey laugh ensemble that will be oke.'—*Variety*

'A story of bloodshed, passion, desire and death . . . everything in fact that makes life worth living!'

Irma La Douce*
US 1963 146m Technicolor Panavision
UA / Phalanx / Mirisch / Edward L. Alperson (Billy Wilder)

A Paris policeman falls for a prostitute and becomes her pimp.
A saucy yarn originally presented inventively as a small-scale stage musical becomes a tasteless yawn on the big screen, especially when presented at such length and without the songs. Minor compensations abound but are insufficient.

w Billy Wilder, I. A. L. Diamond *d* Billy Wilder *ph* Joseph La Shelle *md* André Previn *musical themes* Marguerite Monnot *ad* Alexander Trauner

Shirley Maclaine, Jack Lemmon, Lou Jacobi, Herschel Bernardi, Joan Shawlee, Bruce Yarnell

AA: André Previn
AAN: Joseph La Shelle; Shirley Maclaine

Ironweed
US 1987 143m Technicolor
Taft Entertainment / Keith Barish / Home Box Office

An alcoholic down-and-out returns to his home town, where he is haunted by his violent past. Although forgiven by his family, he takes to the road again.
Relentlessly gloomy and ploddingly faithful re-creation of a Pulitzer prizewinner.

w William Kennedy, from his novel *d* Hector Babenco *ph* Lauro Escorel *m* John Morris *pd* Jeannine C. Oppewall

Jack Nicholson, Meryl Streep, Carroll Baker, Michael O'Keefe, Diane Venora, Tom Waits

Iron Claw
US 1941 bw serial: 15 eps

A newspaper reporter reveals the identity of the infamous Iron Claw. Serial hi-jinks in the *Clutching Hand* tradition. Charles Quigley, Walter Sande, Joyce Bryant, Forrest Taylor. Directed by James W. Horne; for Columbia.

The Iron Curtain
US 1948 87m bw
TCF (Sol C. Siegel)

A Russian official in Ottawa becomes disillusioned and reveals to the US authorities details of a spy ring.
Cold war biopic of Igor Gouzenko; not badly done in the semi-documentary mould.

w Milton Krims *d* William Wellman *ph* Charles G. Clarke *md* Alfred Newman, using Russian themes

Dana Andrews, Gene Tierney, Berry Kroeger, Edna Best

The Iron Duke*
GB 1934 88m bw
Gaumont (Michael Balcon)

After Waterloo, the Duke of Wellington defeats a French scheme to discredit him.
A popular historical star vehicle of its time and a good example of British pre-war production in the Korda mould.

w Bess Meredith, play H. M. Harwood *d* Victor Saville *ph* Curt Courant

George Arliss, Gladys Cooper, Emlyn Williams, Ellaline Terriss, A. E. Matthews, Edmund Willard, Felix Aylmer

Iron Eagle
US 1986 119m Metrocolor
Tri-Star (Ron Samuels, Joe Wizan)

A young man rescues his hostage father from a Middle Eastern country.
Increasingly suspenseful adventure drama which suited America's mood.

w Kevin Elders, Sidney J. Furie *d* Sidney J. Furie *ph* Adam Greenberg *m* Basil Poledouris *pd* Robb Wilson King *ed* George Grenville

Louis Gossett Jnr, Jason Gedrick, David Suchet, Tim Thomerson, Larry B. Scott

'Theaters may have to stay open from high noon to red dawn to handle the crowd.'—*Variety*

The Iron Glove
US 1954 77m Technicolor

A staunch supporter of the Old Pretender meets friends and enemies in London at the court of George I. Stilted costume piece, unsuitably cast and flatly written. Robert Stack, Ursula Thiess, Richard Stapley, Alan Hale Jnr. Written by Jesse L. Lasky Jnr, De Vallon Scott and Douglas Heyes; directed by William Castle; for Columbia.

The Iron Horse*
US 1924 119m (24 fps) bw silent
Fox

A man seeking to avenge his father's murder works on the first transcontinental railroad.
Archetypal western, very slow to start but with an authentic cast of thousands.

w Charles Kenyon, John Russell *d* John Ford *ph* George Schneidermann

George O'Brien, Madge Bellamy, Cyril Chadwick, Fred Kohler

The Iron Maiden
GB 1962 98m Eastmancolor
Anglo Amalgamated / GHW (Peter Rogers)
US title: *The Swinging Maiden*

An aircraft designer gets into trouble because of his affection for traction engines.
Feeble attempt to duplicate the success of *Genevieve*, this time starring a steamroller. Very English.

w Vivian Cox, Leslie Bricusse *d* Gerald Thomas *ph* Alan Hume *m* Eric Rogers

Michael Craig, Alan Hale Jnr, Jeff Donnell, Cecil Parker, Noel Purcell, Roland Culver, the Duke of Bedford, Anne Helm

The Iron Major
US 1943 85m bw

The life of Frank Cavanaugh, football coach and hero of World War I. Sub-standard biopic. Pat O'Brien, Ruth Warrick, Robert Ryan, Leon Ames. Written by Aben Kandel and Warren Duff; directed by Ray Enright; for RKO. 'A respectful, rather dull picture . . . all the talk is in words of less than one syllable.'—*James Agee.*

The Iron Man
US 1931 73m bw
Universal (Carl Laemmle Jnr)

A prizefighter is spurred on by his money-hungry wife.
Competent, routine, ringside melodrama.

w Francis Edward Faragoh, *novel* W. R. Burnett *d* Tod Browning *ph* Percy Hilburn

Lew Ayres, Jean Harlow, Robert Armstrong, John Miljan, Eddie Dillon, Ned Sparks

† Remade in 1937 as *Some Blondes Are Dangerous* and in 1951 under the original title.

Iron Man
US 1951 81m bw

A coal miner is persuaded to become a prizefighter, but success changes his character. A somewhat changed version of the 1931 film; no better. Jeff Chandler, Evelyn Keyes, Stephen McNally, Joyce Holden, Rock Hudson, Jim Backus, James Arness. Written by George Zuckerman and Borden Chase; directed by Joseph Pevney; for Universal-International.

The Iron Mask*
US 1929 97m bw talking sequences, sound and music score
(UA) Douglas Fairbanks

The true prince of France is kidnapped and imprisoned, but the villains reckon without D'Artagnan and the three musketeers.
Spirited star rendition of Dumas, the last big silent costume drama of the twenties.

w W. Elton Thomas (Douglas Fairbanks), *novel* Ten Years After by Alexandre Dumas *d* Allan Dwan *ph* Henry Sharp *pd* Maurice Leloir *m* Hugo Riesenfeld

Douglas Fairbanks, Nigel de Brulier, Belle Bennett, Marguerite de la Motte

The Iron Mistress
US 1952 107m Technicolor
Warner (Henry Blanke)

The life of westerner Jim Bowie and his famous knife.
Stolid actioner with uninspired script and performances.

w James R. Webb, *novel* Paul I. Wellman *d* Gordon Douglas *ph* John Seitz *m* Max Steiner

Alan Ladd, Virginia Mayo, Joseph Calleia, Phyllis Kirk, Alf Kjellin, Douglas Dick, Tony Caruso, George Voskovec

The Iron Petticoat
GB 1956 96m Technicolor Vistavision
Remus / Harry Saltzman (Betty E. Box)

An American air force officer persuades a Russian lady flier of the advantages of the western way of life.
Feeble imitation of *Ninotchka* with a saucy star team which simply doesn't jell.

w Ben Hecht *d* Ralph Thomas *ph* Ernest Steward *m* Benjamin Frankel

Bob Hope, Katharine Hepburn, James Robertson Justice, Robert Helpmann, David Kossoff, Alan Gifford, Paul Carpenter, Noelle Middleton

'They seem amazed to find themselves in a comedy that has no humour, and they go through the motions grimly, like children at dancing school, hoping it will all be over soon.'—*William K. Zinsser*

Irreconcilable Differences
US 1984 113m Technicolor

Nine-year-old Casey interferes in her parents' planned divorce. An ancient wheeze for a romantic comedy, here decked out with modern trimmings but no better intrinsically than it was in the thirties. Ryan O'Neal, Shelley Long, Drew Barrymore, Sam Wanamaker, Allen Garfield, Sharon Stone. Written by Nancy Meyers, Charles Shyer; directed by Charles Shyer; for Lantana / Warner.

Is Everybody Happy?
US 1929 80m bw

The life of a clarinettist who rises from poverty. Or, The Ted Lewis Story, a primitive musical. Ted Lewis, Alice Day, Ann Pennington, Lawrence Grant. Written by Joseph Jackson and James A. Starr; directed by Archie Mayo; for Warner.

Is Everybody Happy?
US 1943 73m bw

A virtual remake of the above, with the star fourteen years older; low-budget filler with a few good numbers. Ted Lewis, Larry Parks, Michael Duane, Nan Gwyn. Written by Monte Brice; directed by Charles Barton; for Columbia.

Is Paris Burning?
France / US 1965 165m Panavision bw (colour sequence)
Paramount / Transcontinental / Marianne (Paul Graetz)

A multi-storied account of the 1944 liberation of Paris.
Muddled, scribbled, tedious and confusing attempt at a thinking man's all-star war epic.

w Francis Ford Coppola, Gore Vidal from book Paris, brûle-t-il? by Larry Collins and Dominique Lapierre *d* René Clément *ph* Marcel Grignon *m* Maurice Jarre

Leslie Caron, Gert Frobe, Charles Boyer, Yves Montand, Orson Welles, Alain Delon, Jean-Pierre Cassel, Jean-Paul Belmondo, Kirk Douglas, Glenn Ford, Claude Dauphin, Daniel Gélin, Anthony Perkins, Simone Signoret, Robert Stack, George Chakiris

AAN: Marcel Grignon

Isadora*
GB 1968 138m Eastmancolor
Universal (Robert and Raymond Hakim)
US title: *The Loves of Isadora*

Eccentric character dancer Isadora Duncan reflects on her crowded and unconventional life.
Ambitious and expensive but finally unsatisfactory biopic of a controversial figure of the twenties.

w Melvyn Bragg, Clive Exton *d Karel Reisz* *ph* Larry Pizer *m* Maurice Jarre *pd* Jocelyn Herbert *ad* Michael Seymour, Ralph Brinton

Vanessa Redgrave, Jason Robards Jnr, James Fox, Ivan Tchenko, John Fraser, Bessie Love

'A brave attempt at a daunting task.'—*Tom Milne*

AAN: Vanessa Redgrave

Ishtar
US 1987 107m Technicolor
Columbia / Delphi V (Warren Beatty)

Two untalented songwriters get involved with Middle Eastern turmoil.
Bitty rehash of old jokes and situations, vaguely resembling a Hope-Crosby Road picture of long ago, but far less funny despite costing 50 million dollars.

w,d Elaine May *ph* Vittorio Storaro *pd* Paul Sylbert

Dustin Hoffman, Warren Beatty, Isabelle Adjani, Charles Grodin, Jack Weston, Tess Harper

'One can't help but wonder whether the camel was the only blind creature who had something to do with this picture.'—*Daily Variety*

The Island*
Japan 1961 92m bw
Kindai Eiga Kyokai (Kaneto Shindo)
original title: *Hadaka no Shima*

The quiet tenor of life for the only family inhabiting a tiny island is eventually broken by illness and death.
Slow, controlled, beautiful film in which not a single word of dialogue is spoken. The artificiality of this concept eventually diminishes its stature.

wd Kaneto Shindo *ph* Kiyoshi Kuroda *m* Hikaru Hayashi

Nobuko Otowa, Taiji Tonoyama, Shinji Tanaka, Masanori Horimoto

'A visual poem which mirrors tedium without ever inducing it.'—*MFB*

'For 300 years a terrifying secret has been kept from the outside world!'

The Island
US 1980 114m Technicolor
Universal (Richard Zanuck and David Brown)

A journalist is in fear of his life on a Caribbean island inhabited by the bloodthirsty descendants of seventeenth-century buccaneers.
Ridiculous shocker from the *Jaws* people; stupidly plotted and gruesome in detail.

w Peter Benchley, from his novel *d* Michael Ritchie *ph* Henri Decaë *m* Ennio Morricone

Michael Caine, David Warner, Angela Punch McGregor, Frank Middlemass, Dudley Sutton, Clyde Jeavons

'Suspense gives way to gut-level sadism aimed at the lowest common audience denominator.'—*Variety*

The Island at the Top of the World**
US 1974 93m Technicolor
Walt Disney (Winston Hibler)

In 1907, a rich Englishman commissions an airship to take him to a mythical arctic Shangri-La in search of his lost son.
Generally brisk and effective adventure fantasy whose trick effects are sufficiently splendid to redeem a sag in the middle and an overplus of Viking chatter which has to be laboriously translated.

w John Whedon, *novel* The Lost Ones by Ian Cameron *d* Robert Stevenson *ph* Frank

Phillips *m* Maurice Jarre *pd Peter Ellenshaw sp Art Cruickshank, Danny Lee*

Donald Sinden, David Hartman, Jacques Marin, Mako

Island in the Sky*
US 1953 109m bw
Wayne–Fellows (Robert Fellows)

A transport plane makes a forced landing north of Greenland, and the crew must survive till help comes.
Well made outdoor suspenser shot in the California Sierras.

w Ernest K. Gann, from his novel *d* William Wellman *ph* Archie Stout *m* Hugo Friedhofer *md* Emil Newman

John Wayne, Lloyd Nolan, Walter Abel, Allyn Joslyn, Andy Devine, James Arness

Island in the Sun*
GB 1957 119m Technicolor Cinemascope
TCF (Darryl F. Zanuck)

Sexual and racial problems erupt on a West Indian island.
Portmanteau romantic melodrama which generally misfires, especially in an attempt to parallel *Crime and Punishment*; but the cast is interesting.

w Alfred Hayes, *novel* Alec Waugh *d* Robert Rossen *ph* Frederick A. Young *m* Malcolm Arnold

James Mason, Joan Fontaine, Harry Belafonte, John Williams, Dorothy Dandridge, Joan Collins, Michael Rennie, Patricia Owens, Stephen Boyd, Basil Sydney, Diana Wynyard, Ronald Squire, John Justin

The Island of Dr Moreau*
US 1977 98m Movielab
AIP / Cinema 77 (Skip Steloff, John Temple-Smith)

In 1911, shipwrecked sailors land on a Pacific island where a mad doctor experiments with animal mutations.
A sprightly version of an old story; unfortunately it lacks any sense of the sinister, and the star is no match for Charles Laughton in *Island of Lost Souls*.

w John Herman Shaner, Al Ramrus, *story* H. G. Wells *d* Don Taylor *ph* Gerry Fisher *m* Laurence Rosenthal

Burt Lancaster, Michael York, Nigel Davenport, Barbara Carrera, Richard Basehart, Nick Cravat

'Cursed with lush colour photography instead of black and white atmospherics, and Lancaster's stolid mania instead of Laughton's manic zeal.'—*Sight and Sound*

Island of Lost Men
US 1939 64m bw

An Oriental girl seeks her lost father in waterfront dives and finds him on a prison island. Adequate action programmer. Anna May Wong, Broderick Crawford, Anthony Quinn, J. Carrol Naish. Written by William R. Lipman and Horace McCoy; directed by Kurt Neumann; for Paramount.
† A remake of *White Woman*.

'Out of the dark fantastic madness of his science he created her—the panther woman—throbbing to the hot flush of new-found love!'

Island of Lost Souls*
US 1932 74m bw
Paramount

On a remote South Sea island, mad Dr Moreau transforms animals into humans by vivisection.
Unchilling but interesting thriller with a rolling-eyed star performance.

w Waldemar Young, Philip Wylie, *story* The Island of Dr Moreau by H. G. Wells *d* Erle C. Kenton *ph* Karl Struss

Charles Laughton, Bela Lugosi, Richard Arlen, Kathleen Burke, Leila Hyams

Island of Lost Women
US 1958 72m bw

A newspaperman lands on a remote island where a scientist has retired from the world with his daughters. Unexciting hokum with more talk than action. Jeff Richards, Venetia Stevenson, John Smith, Alan Napier. Written by Ray Buffum; directed by Frank Tuttle; for Jaguar / Warner.

Island of Love
US 1963 101m Technicolor Panavision
Warner / Belgrave (Morton da Costa)

A gangster finances a film providing his girl friend stars, but when it flops he chases the producers to a Greek island.
Dismally unfunny comedy wasting a talented cast.

w David R. Schwarz *d* Morton da Costa *ph* Harry Stradling *m* George Duning

Robert Preston, Tony Randall, Walter Matthau, Giorgia Moll

Island of Terror
GB 1966 89m Eastmancolor
Planet (Tom Blakeley)

On an Irish island, a scientist makes monsters who thrive on bone.
Horror hokum, moderately done.

w Edward Andrew Mann, Alan Ramsen *d* Terence Fisher *ph* Reg Wyer *m* Malcolm Lockyer *sp* John St John Earl

Peter Cushing, Edward Judd, Carole Gray, Eddie Byrne, Sam Kydd, Niall MacGinnis

Island of the Blue Dolphins
US 1964 93m Eastmancolor
U-I / Robert B. Radnitz

Two orphaned children grow up alone on a Californian island, protected by wild dogs.
Pleasant if unconvincing family film based on a true story.

w Ted Sherdeman, Jane Klove, *novel* Scott O'Dell *d* James B. Clark *ph* Leo Tover *m* Paul Sawtell

Celia Kaye, Larry Dornasin, George Kennedy

Island of the Lost
US 1968 92m colour

An anthropologist sets sail for an uncharted island and is shipwrecked on it. Good-looking but singularly plotless action adventure. Richard Greene, Luke Halpin, Mark Hulswit. Written by Richard Carlson and Ivan Tors; directed by Richard Carlson; for Ivan Tors.

Islands in the Stream
US 1976 105m Metrocolor Panavision
Paramount (Peter Bart, Max Palevsky)

On a Bahamian island in 1940, an expatriate American artist welcomes his three sons and reflects on the futility of life.
Shapeless semi-autobiographical fragments culminating unpersuasively in an action climax of heroic self-sacrifice. A film on which no expense has been spared and which doesn't work at all.

w Denne Bart Petitclerc, *novel* Ernest Hemingway *d* Franklin Schaffner *ph* Fred J. Koenekamp *m* Jerry Goldsmith

George C. Scott, David Hemmings, Gilbert Roland, Susan Tyrell, Richard Evans, Claire Bloom, Hart Bochner, Julius Harris

'It is all too awful for words.'—*Benny Green, Punch*

AAN: photography

Isle of Forgotten Sins
US 1943 82m bw

In the south seas, villains congregate in search of sunken treasure. Patchy tropical melodrama with a cast more interesting than the script. John Carradine, Gale Sondergaard, Sidney Toler, Frank Fenton, Rita Quigley, Veda Ann Borg. Written by Raymond L. Schrock, from story by Edgar G. Ulmer; directed by Edgar G. Ulmer; for Peter R. Van Duinen / PRC.

Isle of Fury
US 1936 60m bw

A fugitive from justice finds temporary peace on a South Sea island. Limp remake of *The Narrow Corner* (qv); its star later pretended he hadn't made it. Humphrey Bogart, Margaret Lindsay, Donald Woods. Written by Robert Andrews and William Jacobs; directed by Frank McDonald; for Warner.

Isle of Missing Men
US 1942 67m bw

Convicts on a prison island try to make a break. The very poor man's *Papillon*. Gilbert Roland, Helen Gilbert, John Howard. Written by Richard Oswald and Robert Chapin; directed by Richard Oswald; for Monogram.

Isle of the Dead**
US 1945 72m bw
RKO (*Val Lewton*)

On a Balkan island in 1912 a group of people shelter from the plague and fear that one of their number is a vampire.
Glum, ghoulish melodrama with some neatly handled shocks; quite different from any other horror film.

w Ardel Wray, Josef Mischel *d Mark Robson ph Jack Mackenzie m* Leigh Harline

Boris Karloff, Ellen Drew, Helene Thimig, Marc Cramer, Katherine Emery, Alan Napier, Jason Robards

Isn't It Romantic*
US 1948 87m bw
Paramount (Daniel Dare)

Romance hits the household of an ex-Civil War colonel in Indiana.
Pleasant but forgettable period semi-musical.

w Theodore Strauss, Josef Mischel, Richard Breen *d* Norman Z. McLeod *ph* Lionel Lindon *m* Joseph J. Lilley

Veronica Lake, Mona Freeman, Mary Hatcher, Roland Culver, Billy de Wolfe, Patric Knowles, Richard Webb, Kathryn Givney, Pearl Bailey

Isn't Life Wonderful?*
US 1924 99m (24 fps) bw silent
(UA) David Wark Griffith

The life of a family in post-war Germany.
An unpopular subject, and a grey-looking film, but the director shows a lot of his strength in it.

wd D. W. Griffith, *story* Geoffrey Moss

Carol Dempster, Neil Hamilton, Helen Lowell, Frank Puglia, Marcia Harris, Lupino Lane

Isn't Life Wonderful?*
GB 1952 83m Technicolor
ABP (Warwick Ward)

In 1902, drunken Uncle Willie runs a bicycle shop and manages to reconcile a lovers' quarrel.
Engaging, well cast family comedy.

w Brock Williams from novel Uncle Willie and the Bicycle Shop by Brock Williams *d* Harold French *ph* Erwin Hillier *m* Philip Green *ad* Terence Verity

Donald Wolfit, Eileen Herlie, Cecil Parker, Eleanor Summerfield, Robert Urquhart, Cecil Trouncer

Istanbul
US 1956 84m Technicolor Cinemascope
U-I (Albert J. Cohen)

Various adventurers and an amnesiac girl seek stolen diamonds in Istanbul.
Dim remake of a flat-footed piece of thick ear called *Singapore*.

w Seton I. Miller, Barbara Gray, Richard Alan Simmons *d* Joseph Pevney *ph* William Daniels *m* Joseph Gershenson

Errol Flynn, Cornell Borchers, John Bentley, Torin Thatcher, Leif Erickson, Martin Benson, Vladimir Sokoloff, Werner Klemperer, Nat King Cole, Peggy Knudsen

It*
US 1927 72m (24 fps) bw silent
Famous Players-Lasky / Paramount (B. P. Schulberg)

A shopgirl tries to live by the tenets of Elinor Glyn's book, and finally marries her boss.
In its day a fast and funny spoof, and the years have not dealt too unkindly with it.

w Hope Loring, Louis D. Lighton, *adaptation* Elinor Glyn *d* Clarence Badger *ph* H. Kinley Martin

Clara Bow, Antonio Moreno, William Austin, Jacqueline Gadson, Gary Cooper, Elinor Glyn

It Ain't Hay
US 1943 79m bw
Universal (Alex Gottlieb)
GB title: *Money for Jam*

When a racehorse dies, a New York cabbie and his friend try to find a new one for the impecunious owners.
Formula Abbott and Costello with a small injection of sentiment and Runyonese. Not their best by a mile.

w Allen Boretz, John Grant, *story* Princess O'Hara by Damon Runyon *d* Erle C. Kenton *ph* Charles Von Enger *songs* Harry Revel, Paul Francis Webster

Bud Abbott, Lou Costello, Grace McDonald, Cecil Kellaway, Patsy O'Connor, Eugene Pallette, Shemp Howard, Eddie Quillan

It All Came True*
US 1940 97m bw
Warner (Mark Hellinger)

A gangster hides out in a boarding house and puts it back on its feet.
Competent New York fairy story full of sweetness and light.

w Michael Fessier, Lawrence Kimble, *story* Better Than Life by Louis Bromfield *d* Lewis Seiler *ph* Ernest Haller *m* Heinz Roemheld

Humphrey Bogart, Ann Sheridan, Jeffrey Lynn, Zasu Pitts, Una O'Connor, Jessie Busley, John Litel, Grant Mitchell, Felix Bressart

It Always Rains on Sunday***
GB 1947 92m bw
Ealing (Henry Cornelius)

An escaped convict takes refuge in his married mistress's house in East London.
Influential slumland melodrama, now dated—the stuff of every other television play—but at the time electrifyingly vivid and very well done.

w Angus Macphail, Robert Hamer, Henry Cornelius, novel Arthur La Bern d Robert Hamer ph Douglas Slocombe m Georges Auric

Googie Withers, John McCallum, Jack Warner, Edward Chapman, Susan Shaw, Sidney Tafler

'Let me pay it the simplest of compliments and say that it has the persuasiveness of an exciting story professionally told.'—*Sunday Times*

It Came from beneath the Sea
US 1955 80m bw
Columbia / Sam Katzman (Charles Schneer)

A giant octopus half destroys San Francisco.
Tepid monster movie; special effects only fair.

w George Worthing Yates, Hal Smith *d* Robert Gordon *ph* Henry Freulich *md* Mischa Bakaleinikoff

Kenneth Tobey, Faith Domergue, Donald Curtis, Ian Keith

It Came from Outer Space**
US 1953 80m bw 3-D
U-I (William Alland)

A young astronomer sees a space ship land in the Arizona desert and tracks down the occupants who can adopt human appearance at will.
Quite bright science fiction, the first to use this theme of borrowing bodies and the first to utilize the western desert locations. 3-D adds a shock moment or two.

w Harry Essex, story Ray Bradbury *d Jack Arnold ph* Clifford Stine *m* Herman Stein *md* Joseph Gershenson

Richard Carlson, Barbara Rush, Charles Drake, Kathleen Hughes

'A solid piece of eerie entertainment, replete with wild screams and bug-eyed monsters guaranteed to send scared customers out of this world.'—*Hollywood Reporter*

'Desert was Arnold's favourite location, and he used it consistently to create a sense of strangeness and menace otherwise much restricted by his budgets.'—*Time Out, 1982*

It Comes Up Love
US 1942 64m bw

A businessman tries to bring up two motherless daughters. A slim plotline serves as an excuse for a brief but snappy 'B' musical. Gloria Jean, Donald O'Connor, Ian Hunter, Frieda Inescort, Louise Allbritton, Charles Coleman. Written by Dorothy Bennett, Charles Kenyon; directed by Charles Lamont; for Ken Goldsmith / Universal.

(GB title: *A Date With an Angel.*)

It Conquered the World
US 1956 68m bw

Something from another planet is sheltered by a well-meaning scientist who discovers too late that its intentions are evil. Tolerable horror comic on a risibly low budget. Peter Graves, Beverly Garland, Lee Van Cleef, Sally Fraser, Charles B. Griffith. Written by Lou Rusoff; directed and produced by Roger Corman; for AIP.

It Could Happen to You
US 1939 73m bw

After a stag party, an advertising man finds a body in his car. Neat second-feature mystery. Stuart Erwin, Gloria Stuart, Raymond Walburn, Douglas Fowley. Written by Allen Rivkin and Lou Breslow; directed by Alfred Werker; for TCF.

It Grows on Trees
US 1952 84m bw
U-I (Leonard Goldstein)

A housewife finds a money tree in her backyard.
Protracted fantasy comedy.

w Leonard Praskins, Barney Slater *d* Arthur Lubin *ph* Maury Gertsman *m* Frank Skinner

Irene Dunne (her last film), Dean Jagger, Joan Evans, Richard Crenna, Edith Meiser, Dee Pollock

It Had To Be You
US 1947 98m bw
Columbia / Don Hartman

A dizzy dame runs out on three prospective husbands and is pursued by an Indian.
Weak sex farce without the courage of its lack of convictions.

w Norman Panama, Melvin Frank *d* Don Hartman, Rudolph Maté *ph* Rudolph Maté *m* Heinz Roemheld *md* Morris Stoloff

Ginger Rogers, Cornel Wilde, Percy Waram, Spring Byington, Thurston Hall, Ron Randell

It Had to Happen
US 1936 80m bw

An Italian immigrant becomes the political boss of New York City. Unconvincing melodrama with star appeal. George Raft, Rosalind Russell, Leo Carrillo, Arline Judge, Alan Dinehart, Andrew Tombes. Written by Howard Ellis Smith, Kathryn Scola, Rupert Hughes; directed by Roy del Ruth; for Raymond Griffith / Fox. 'Incredible story precludes its b.o. chances.'—*Variety*

It Happened at the World's Fair
US 1962 104m Metrocolor Panavision
MGM / Ted Richmond

At the Seattle World's Fair, two crop-dusting pilots have romantic intrigues.
Routine star vehicles.

w Si Rose, Seaman Jacobs *d* Norman Taurog *ph* Joseph Ruttenberg *m* Leith Stevens

Elvis Presley, Gary Lockwood, Joan O'Brien, Yvonne Craig, Ginny Tiu

It Happened Here**
GB 1963 99m bw
UA / Kevin Brownlow, Andrew Mollo

What might have happened if the Germans had invaded England in 1940.
A remarkable semi-professional reconstruction which took seven years to film and is totally convincing in detail, but unfortunately rather confused and padded as drama.

wd Kevin Brownlow, Andrew Mollo *ph* Peter Suschitsky *m* Jack Beaver

Sebastian Shaw, Pauline Murray, Fiona Lekland, Honor Fehrson

'For a grain of artistic truth, we can forgive even the grainy photography and wavering sound with which part of it is afflicted.'—*John Simon*

It Happened in Athens
US 1961 100m De Luxe Cinemascope
TCF (James S. Elliott)

At the first revival of the Olympic Games in 1896 a publicity-seeking actress announces that she will marry whoever wins the Marathon.
Witless extravagant romp, well mounted but adding up to zero.

w Laszlo Vadnay *d* Andrew Marton *ph* Curt Courant *m* Manos Hadjidakis

Jayne Mansfield, Trax Colton, Bob Mathias

It Happened in Brooklyn*
US 1947 103m bw
MGM (Jack Cummings)

Young New Yorkers with musical talents find their way to fame.
Well-handled routine musical of its time.

w Isobel Lennart *d* Richard Whorf *ph* Robert Planck *m* Johnny Green *songs* Jule Styne, Sammy Cahn

Frank Sinatra, Jimmy Durante, Kathryn Grayson, Peter Lawford, Gloria Grahame

'Aside from Sinatra and Durante the show amounts to practically nothing, but there is a general kindliness about it which I enjoyed.'—*James Agee*

It Happened in Hollywood
US 1937 67m bw

A silent cowboy star is washed up when talkies come in. Indifferent studio story. Richard Dix, Fay Wray, Victor Kilian, Franklin Pangborn, Charles Arnt, Granville Bates. Written by Ethel Hill, Harvey Ferguson, Sam Fuller, Myles Connolly; directed by Harry Lachman; for Columbia. 'It will have difficulty fitting in . . . won't particularly satisfy 'em in the duals.'—*Variety*

It Happened on Fifth Avenue*
US 1947 115m bw
Allied Artists (Roy del Ruth)

A child of divorce finds amiable squatters in her millionaire father's house.
Curious, overlong, cheerful Capraesque comedy with the mildest of social pretensions.

w Everett Freeman, Frederick Stephani, Herbert Clyde Lewis *d* Roy del Ruth *ph* Henry Sharp

Gale Storm, Ann Harding, Victor Moore, Charles Ruggles, Don Defore

AAN: script

It Happened One Night***
US 1934 105m bw
Columbia (Frank Capra)

A runaway heiress falls in love with the reporter who is chasing her across America.
Highly successful and influential romantic comedy, the first to use buses and motels as background and still come up sparkling; it remains superlative in patches, but overall has a faded, dated air.

w Robert Riskin, story Night Bus by Samuel Hopkins Adams *d Frank Capra* *ph* Joseph Walker *md* Louis Silvers

Clark Gable, Claudette Colbert, Walter Connolly, Roscoe Karns, Alan Hale, Ward Bond, Jameson Thomas, Arthur Hoyt

'A laughing hit that will mean important coin.'—*Variety*

'It will be a long day before we see so little made into so much.'—*Otis Ferguson*

'Something to revive your faith in a medium which could belong among the great arts.'—*Robert Forsythe*

'We may look askance at Capra's sententious notions about the miserable rich and the happy poor, but there's no doubting the chord he struck in depression audiences.'—*Time Out, 1980*

'It made audiences happy in a way that only a few films in each era do. In the mid-30s, the Colbert and Gable of this film became Americans' idealized view of themselves—breezy, likeable, sexy, gallant, and maybe just a little harebrained. It was the *Annie Hall* of its day—before the invention of anxiety.'—*Pauline Kael, 70s*

† Remade 1956 (badly) as *You Can't Run away From It.*

†† Robert Montgomery was the first choice for the Gable role, but he refused it because he had been on a bus in *Fugitive Lovers*. The Colbert role was first offered to Myrna Loy, Margaret Sullavan and Constance Bennett. Colbert was lured by a 40,000-dollar fee.

'One of the most entertaining films that has ever been offered to the public.'—*Observer*

AA: best picture; Robert Riskin; Frank Capra; Clark Gable; Claudette Colbert

It Happened One Sunday
GB 1943 99m bw

In Liverpool, a Canadian seaman falls for an Irish maid. Overlong romantic comedy with nowhere to go. Robert Beatty, Barbara White, Marjorie Rhodes, Ernest Butcher, Judy Kelly, Irene Vanbrugh. Written by Victor Skuzetsky, Friedrich Gotfurt and Stephen Black; directed by Karel Lamac; for ABPC.

It Happened to Jane
US 1959 98m Technicolor Cinemascope
Columbia / Arwin (Richard Quine)

A lady lobster dealer becomes involved in a battle with the railroad whose inefficiency affects her business.
Witless, wholesome farce which promises more than it delivers.

w Norman Karkov *d* Richard Quine *ph* Charles Lawton Jnr *m* George Duning

Doris Day, Jack Lemmon, *Ernie Kovacs*, Steve Forrest

It Happened Tomorrow***
US 1944 84m bw
(UA) Arnold Pressburger

A reporter meets an old man with the power to show him tomorrow's newspaper headlines, so that he always gets scoops—including his own death . . .
Engaging fantasy, flawlessly made and quietly very entertaining.

w Dudley Nichols, René Clair *d René Clair* *ph Archie Stout* *m* Robert Stolz

Dick Powell, Linda Darnell, Jack Oakie, *John Philliber*, Edgar Kennedy, Ed Brophy, George Cleveland, Sig Rumann

'Students of cinematic style will find many shrewdly polished bits to admire and enjoy.'—*James Agee*

'Diverting escapist entertainment for all audiences.'—*Variety*

AAN: Robert Stolz

It Happens Every Spring
US 1949 80m bw
TCF (William Perlberg)

A chemistry teacher discovers a formula that makes baseballs repellent to wood.
Smartly produced but rather desperate fantasy comedy.

w Valentine Davies *d* Lloyd Bacon *ph* Joe MacDonald *m* Leigh Harline

Ray Milland, Jean Peters, Paul Douglas, Ed Begley, Ted de Corsia, Ray Collins, Jessie Royce Landis, Alan Hale Jnr

AAN: original story (Shirley W. Smith, Valentine Davies)

It Happens Every Thursday*
US 1953 80m bw
U-I (Anton Leader)

The new owner of a small-town newspaper becomes unpopular through his attempts to boost the circulation.
Pleasant comedy with amusing scenes.

w Dane Lussier *d* Joseph Pevney *ph* Russell Metty *m* Joseph Gershenson

Loretta Young, John Forsythe, Jimmy Conlin, Frank McHugh, Edgar Buchanan, Jane Darwell

It Pays to Advertise
US 1931 66m bw

A mild youth is turned by his girl into a business success. Fair film version of a popular stage comedy. Norman Foster, Carole Lombard, Skeets Gallagher, Eugene Pallette, Louise Brooks, Lucien Littlefield. Written by Arthur Kober from the play by Walter Hackett; directed by Frank Tuttle; for Paramount. 'Good enough programme material.'—*Variety*

It Should Happen to You**
US 1954 87m bw
Columbia (Fred Kohlmar)

A slightly daffy New York model with an urge to be famous rents a huge billboard and puts her name on it.
Likeable comedy which starts brightly and slowly falls apart, disappointing considering the credentials of the talents involved and the satiric possibilities of the plot.

w Ruth Gordon, Garson Kanin d George Cukor ph Charles Lang *m* Frederick Hollander

Judy Holliday, Jack Lemmon, Peter Lawford, Michael O'Shea

It Shouldn't Happen to a Dog
US 1946 70m bw

A lady detective, her dog and a reporter solve a murder case more by good luck than good management. Acceptable comedy support. Allyn Joslyn, Carole Landis, Margo Woode, Henry Morgan, Reed Hadley, John Alexander. Written by Eugene Ling and Frank Gabrielson; directed by Herbert I. Leeds; for TCF.

It Shouldn't Happen to a Vet
GB 1976 93m Technicolor
EMI / Talent Associates / Readers Digest
US title: *All Things Bright and Beautiful*

Adventures of a Yorkshire vet just before World War II.
Competent sequel to *All Creatures Great and Small* (qv).

w Alan Plater, *books* James Herriot *d* Eric Till *ph* Arthur Ibbetson *m* Laurie Johnson

John Alderton, Colin Blakely, Lisa Harrow, Bill Maynard, Richard Pearson, Raymond Francis, John Barrett, Paul Shelley

It Started in Naples*
US 1960 100m Technicolor
Vistavision
Paramount / Capri (Jack Rose)

A Philadelphia lawyer goes to Naples to settle his dead brother's affairs, and falls for his nephew's aunt.
Nicely made, formula romantic comedy which started life as a vehicle for Gracie Fields.

w Melville Shavelson, Jack Rose, Susi Cecchi d'Amico *d* Melville Shavelson *ph* Robert Surtees *m* Alessandro Cicognini

Clark Gable, Sophia Loren, Vittorio de Sica, Marietto, Paulo Carlini

It Started in Paradise
GB 1952 94m Technicolor
GFD / British Film Makers (Leslie Parkyn, Sergei Nolbandov)

The career of an ambitious dress designer.
Stilted and garishly coloured but often amusing backstage melodrama of the fashion world: a Hollywood-style star vehicle which seems faintly surprising as a British product.

w Marghanita Laski *d* Compton Bennett *ph* Jack Cardiff *m* Malcolm Arnold *ad* Edward Carrick

Jane Hylton, Ian Hunter, Terence Morgan, Muriel Pavlow, Brian Worth, *Martita Hunt, Ronald Squire, Harold Lang*, Joyce Barbour, Kay Kendall

It Started with a Kiss
US 1959 104m Metrocolor
Cinemascope
MGM / Arcola (Aaron Rosenberg)

An army sergeant posted to Spain is embarrassed when his wife follows him.
Flabby comedy with the emphasis on sex and pratfalls.

w Charles Lederer *d* George Marshall *ph* Robert Bronner *m* Jeff Alexander

Glenn Ford, Debbie Reynolds, Fred Clark, Edgar Buchanan, Eva Gabor

It Started with Eve**
US 1941 93m bw
Universal (Joe Pasternak)

A dying millionaire wants to see his grandson engaged, so a waitress obliges for an hour . . . but the old man recovers.
Charming comedy which was probably the star's best film; remade as *I'd Rather be Rich* (qv).

w Norman Krasna, Leo Townsend *d* Henry Koster *ph* Rudolph Maté *md* Charles Previn, Hans Salter

Deanna Durbin, Charles Laughton, Robert Cummings, Margaret Tallichet, Guy Kibbee, Walter Catlett, Catherine Doucet

'The perfect 8 to 80 picture.'—*Variety*

AAN: Charles Previn, Hans Salter

It! The Terror from Beyond Space
US 1958 69m bw

A space ship returning from Mars is invaded by a worm-like monster. Laughable but lively precursor of *Alien*; rather more fun on the whole. Marshall Thompson, Shawn Smith, Kim Spaulding, Ann Doran, Dabbs Greer. Written by Jerome Bixby; directed by Edward L. Cahn; for Vogue/United Artists.

The Italian Job**
GB 1969 100m Eastmancolor
Panavision
Paramount / Oakhurst (Michael Deeley)

Crooks stage a traffic jam in Turin in order to pull off a bullion robbery.
Lively caper comedy which provides a good measure of entertainment.

w Troy Kennedy Martin *d* Peter Collinson *ph* Douglas Slocombe, Norman Warwick *m* Quincy Jones

Michael Caine, Noel Coward, Benny Hill, Raf Vallone, Tony Beckley, Rossano Brazzi, Maggie Blye, Irene Handl, John Le Mesurier, Fred Emney

An Italian Straw Hat***
France 1927 74m (24 fps) bw silent
Albatross
original title: *Un Chapeau de Paille d'Italie*

The hero is prevented from getting to a wedding when his horse chews up a lady's straw hat and her escort demands that it be replaced.
Lively but gentle comedy of errors, a stage farce expanded for the screen and filled with visual gags. A very influential and still amusing piece.

wd René Clair, play Eugène Labiche *ph* Maurice Desfassiaux, Nicolas Roudakoff *ad Lazare Meerson*

Albert Préjean, Olga Tschekowa, Marise Maia, Alice Tissot

'The very springtime of screen comedy.'—*Tatler*

'One of the funniest films ever made.'—*Tribune, 1945*

'Still one of the funniest films in the world.'—*Sunday Times, 1948*

It's a Big Country
US 1952 89m bw
MGM (Robert Sisk)

Seven stories show the diversity of the US and the glory of being one of its citizens.
Stultifying flagwaver memorable chiefly as a waste of good actors.

w William Ludwig, Helen Deutsch, George Wells, Allen Rivkin, Dorothy Kingsley, Isobel

Lennart *d* Richard Thorpe, Don Weis, John Sturges, Don Hartman, William Wellman, Charles Vidor, Clarence Brown *ph* John Alton, Ray June, William Mellor, Joseph Ruttenberg *m* Bronislau Kaper, Rudolph G. Kopp, David Raksin, David Rose

Ethel Barrymore, Keefe Brasselle, Nancy Davis, Van Johnson, Gene Kelly, Janet Leigh, Marjorie Main, Fredric March, George Murphy, William Powell, S. Z. Sakall, Lewis Stone, James Whitmore

It's a Boy
GB 1933 80m bw

A blackmailer claims to be a bridegroom's long-lost illegitimate son. Heavy-footed version of popular stage farce. Leslie Henson, Edward Everett Horton, Heather Thatcher, Alfred Drayton, Albert Burdon, Robertson Hare, Wendy Barrie. Written by Austin Melford, John Paddy Carstairs and L. H. Gordon, from the play by Franz Arnold, Ernst Bach and Austin Melford; directed by Tim Whelan; for Gainsborough.

It's a Date*
US 1940 100m bw
Universal / Joe Pasternak

The daughter of a Broadway musical heroine has stage ambitions of her own, and chases an older man who is more interested in her mother.
Fairly pleasant but unduly elongated star comedy.

w Norman Krasna *d* William Seiter *ph* Joe Valentine *m* Charles Previn

Deanna Durbin, Walter Pidgeon, Kay Francis, Eugene Pallette, Henry Stephenson, Cecilia Loftus, Samuel S. Hinds, S. Z. Sakall

'A natural which will roll grosses of upper bracket proportions.'—*Variety*

It's a Gift**
US 1934 73m bw
Paramount (William Le Baron)

A general store proprietor buys an orange ranch by mail and transports his family to California.
Roughly assembled comedy of disasters which happens to show the star more or less at his best, though the expected climax is lacking.

w Jack Cunningham, *story* W. C. Fields, J. P. McEvoy *d* Norman Z. McLeod *ph* Henry Sharp

W. C. Fields, Kathleen Howard, Jean Rouverol, Julian Madison, Tommy Bupp, Baby LeRoy

'An enormously amusing succession of rough and ready gags.'—*Literary Digest*

It's a Grand Life
GB 1953 102m bw

A nitwit army private plays Cupid. Senseless and under-rehearsed farce which has interest for fans of the usually drunken star. Frank Randle, Diana Dors, Dan Young, Michael Brennan, Jennifer Jayne, John Blythe. Written by H. F. Maltby, Frank Randle; directed and produced by John E. Blakeley; for Mancunian.

It's a Great Feeling*
US 1949 85m Technicolor
Warner (Alex Gottlieb)

No one will direct a Jack Carson movie, so he has to do it himself.
Amiable studio farce with plenty of guest appearances.

w Jack Rose, Mel Shavelson *d* David Butler *ph* Wilfrid M. Cline *m / ly* Jule Styne, Sammy Cahn *m* Ray Heindorf

Jack Carson, Doris Day, Dennis Morgan, Bill Goodwin, Gary Cooper, Joan Crawford, Errol Flynn, Sidney Greenstreet, Danny Kaye, Patricia Neal, Edward G. Robinson, Jane Wyman, Eleanor Parker, Ronald Reagan

AAN: title song

It's a Mad Mad Mad Mad World**
US 1963 192m Technicolor Ultra Panavision 70
UA / Stanley Kramer

An assortment of people including a frustrated cop are overcome by greed when they hear of buried loot.
Three hours of frantic chasing and violent slapstick is too much even when done on this scale and with this cast, but one must observe that scene for scene it is extremely well done and most of the players are in unusually good form though they all outstay their welcome and are upstaged by the stunt men.

w William and Tania Rose *d Stanley Kramer ph Ernest Laszlo m Ernest Gold stunts Carey Loftin titles Saul Bass*

Spencer Tracy, Jimmy Durante, *Milton Berle*, Sid Caesar, Ethel Merman, Buddy Hackett, Mickey Rooney, Dick Shawn, *Phil Silvers, Terry-Thomas*, Jonathan Winters, Edie Adams, Dorothy Provine, Eddie Anderson, Jim Backus, William Demarest, Peter Falk, Paul Ford, Leo Gorcey, Ben Blue, Edward Everett Horton, Buster Keaton, Joe E. Brown, Carl Reiner, the Three Stooges, Zasu Pitts, Sterling Holloway, Jack Benny, Jerry Lewis

'To watch on a Cinerama screen in full colour a small army of actors inflict mayhem on each other with cars, planes, explosives and other devices for more than three hours with stereophonic sound effects is simply too much for the human eye and ear to respond to, let alone the funny bone.'—*Dwight MacDonald*

AAN: Ernest Laszlo; Ernest Gold; title song (*m* Ernest Gold, *ly* Mack David)

It's a Pleasure
US 1945 90m Technicolor

The career of an ice-skating couple is interrupted when he takes to drink.
Unimpressive vehicle from the star's waning years: the numbers are good but the rest very soggy. Sonja Henie, Michael O'Shea, Marie McDonald. Written by Lynn Starling and Eliot Paul; directed by William A. Seiter; for International / RKO.

It's a Small World
US 1935 72m bw

A man and woman fall in love after being stranded by a car crash in a small Louisiana town. Mildly amusing comedy. Spencer Tracy, Wendy Barrie, Raymond Walburn, Virginia Sale, Irving Bacon. Written by Sam Hellman and Gladys Lehman; directed by Irving Cummins; for Fox. 'Very weak entertainment, strictly for double bills.'—*Variety*

It's a 2'6" above the Ground World
GB 1972 96m Eastmancolor
British Lion / Welbeck / Betty E. Box–Ralph Thomas
Also known as: *The Love Ban*

A Roman Catholic couple go on the pill. Smutty, not very funny sex comedy.

w Kevin Laffan, from his play *d* Ralph Thomas *ph* Tony Imi *m* Stanley Myers

Nanette Newman, Hywel Bennett, Russell Lewis, Simon Henderson, Milo O'Shea

It's a Wise Child
US 1931 73m bw

When a girl is thought to be pregnant, her family hunts the father. Tasteless comedy with too few laughs. Marion Davies, Sidney Blackmer, James Gleason, Polly Moran, Marie Prevost, Lester Vail. Written by Laurence E. Johnson from his play; directed by Robert Z. Leonard; for Cosmopolitan / MGM. 'No subject matter here for family audiences . . . it must prove embarrassing to young unmarried couples attending the theatre together.'—*Variety*

It's a Wonderful Life****
US 1946 129m bw
RKO / Liberty Films (Frank Capra)

A man is prevented from committing suicide by an elderly angel, who takes him back through his life to show him what good he has done.
Superbly assembled small-town comedy drama in a fantasy framework; arguably Capra's best and most typical work.

w Frances Goodrich, Albert Hackett, Frank Capra d Frank Capra ph Joseph Walker, Joseph Biroc m Dmitri Tiomkin

James Stewart, Henry Travers, Donna Reed, Lionel Barrymore, Thomas Mitchell, Beulah Bondi, Frank Faylen, Ward Bond, Gloria Grahame, H. B. Warner, Frank Albertson, Samuel S. Hinds, Mary Treen

CLARENCE (Henry Travers): 'Every time you hear a bell ring, it means that some angel's just got his wings.'

'One of the most efficient sentimental pieces since *A Christmas Carol*.'—*James Agee*

'The most brilliantly made motion picture of the 1940s, so assured, so dazzling in its use of screen narrative.'—*Charles Higham*

'In its own icky, bittersweet way, it's terribly effective.'—*New Yorker, 1977*

AAN: best picture; Frank Capra; James Stewart

It's a Wonderful World*
US 1939 86m bw
MGM (Frank Davis)

IT'S A GIFT. W. C. Fields takes one more disaster philosophically and hangs on to his cigar, if not his dignity. The film was a reworking of Fields's 1926 silent *It's the Old Army Game.*

Kidnapped by a suspected murderer, a girl helps him track down the real criminal.
Madcap comedy mystery which now seems much fresher and funnier than it did at the time. A highlight of the crazy comedy cycle.

w Ben Hecht, Herman J. Mankiewicz *d* W. S. Van Dyke II *ph* Oliver Marsh *m* Edward Ward

Claudette Colbert, James Stewart, Guy Kibbee, Nat Pendleton, Frances Drake, Edgar Kennedy, Ernest Truex, Richard Carle, Sidney Blackmer, Andy Clyde, Cliff Clark, Hans Conried

'It's right down the alley for general audiences.'—*Variety*

'One of the few genuinely comic pictures in a dog's age.'—*Otis Ferguson*

'Save your screams till you see its face!'

It's Alive
US 1974 91m Technicolor
Warner / Larco (Larry Cohen)

A new-born baby turns out to be a vicious monster.
Exploitation horror flick in the worst of taste, with a good central performance.

wd Larry Cohen *ph* Fenton Hamilton *m* Bernard Herrmann

John Ryan, Sharon Farrell, Andrew Duggan, Guy Stockwell, James Dixon, Michael Ansara

† *It's Alive 2* and *It's Alive 3* regrettably followed, in 1978 and 1987 respectively. *It's Alive 2* was sometimes known as *It Lives Again*.

It's All Happening
GB 1963 101m Eastmancolor
British Lion / Magna / KNP (Norman Williams)
US title: *The Dream Maker*

A talent scout for a recording agency helps to save an orphanage and makes himself a star in the process.
Unassuming, jolly little comedy with music; a better title would have made it more memorable.

w Leigh Vance *d* Don Sharp *ph* Ken Hodges *m* Philip Green

Tommy Steele, Angela Douglas, Michael Medwin, Bernard Bresslaw, Walter Hudd, Jean Harvey, Richard Goolden

It's All Yours
US 1937 80m bw

A millionaire leaves a fortune to his favourite secretary, hoping that it will make his nephew take notice of her. Unpersuasive romantic comedy with slightly crazy touches. Madeleine Carroll, Francis Lederer, Mischa Auer, Grace Bradley. Written by Mary C. McCall Jnr; directed by Elliott Nugent; for Columbia.

'Of the whimsy, gay school currently in vogue . . . too light to figure importantly at solo b.o.'—*Variety*

It's Always Fair Weather**
US 1955 101m Eastmancolor Cinemascope
MGM (Arthur Freed)

In 1945 three army veterans vow to meet ten years on, but they find each other dull failures until they go on a wild spree.
Rather dejected New Yorkish comedy with musical sequences; some of it works very well, but the colour is crude and the wide screen doesn't help.

w / ly / m Betty Comden, Adolph Green *d* Gene Kelly, Stanley Donen *ph* Robert Bronner *md* André Previn

Gene Kelly, Dan Dailey, Michael Kidd, Dolores Gray, Cyd Charisse

AAN: Betty Comden, Adolph Green (as writers); André Previn

It's Great to Be Young*
GB 1956 93m Technicolor
AB–Pathé / Marble Arch (Victor Skutezky)

A popular teacher falls foul of the new headmaster who tries to disband the school orchestra.
Very acceptable but totally forgettable star comedy.

w Ted Willis *d* Cyril Frankel *ph* Gilbert Taylor *m* Ray Martin, Lester Powell, John Addison

John Mills, Cecil Parker, Jeremy Spenser, Dorothy Bromiley, John Salew, Derek Blomfield, Eleanor Summerfield, Bryan Forbes

It's Hard to Be Good
GB 1948 93m bw
GFD / Two Cities (Jeffrey Dell)

A demobbed war hero determines to spread peace and goodwill, but comes one cropper after another.
Well intended but somehow unprofessional comedy which irritates more than it amuses.

wd Jeffrey Dell *ph* Laurie Friedman *m* Antony Hopkins

Jimmy Hanley, Anne Crawford, Raymond Huntley

It's in the Air*
GB 1938 86m bw
ATP (Basil Dean)
US title: *George Takes the Air*

Adventures of an accident-prone RAF recruit.
Amiable star comedy with good situations and songs.

wd Anthony Kimmins *ph* Gordon Dines, Ronald Neame

George Formby, Garry Marsh, Polly Ward, Julien Mitchell, Jack Hobbs, Hal Gordon

It's in the Bag**
US 1945 87m bw
(UA) Manhattan Productions
GB title: *The Fifth Chair*

The owner of a flea circus seeks a legacy hidden in one of five chairs which have been sold to a variety of people.
Patchily amusing, star-studded comedy which was also filmed as *Keep Your Seats Please* and *The Twelve Chairs*. Full enjoyment requires some knowledge of American radio characters.

w Jay Dratler, Alma Reville *d* Richard Wallace *ph* Russell Metty *m* Werner Heymann

Fred Allen, Binnie Barnes, *Jack Benny*, Robert Benchley, Don Ameche, Victor Moore, Rudy Vallee, William Bendix, Jerry Colonna

'An untidy piece that doesn't make the most of itself but is full of fun.'—*Richard Mallett, Punch*

It's Love Again*
GB 1936 83m bw
Gaumont (Michael Balcon)

A chorus girl poses as a socialite who has hit the headlines without ever existing.
Delightfully dated comedy musical.

w Lesser Samuels, Marian Dix, Austin Melford *d Victor Saville ph* Glen MacWilliams *songs* Harry Woods (*m*), Sam Coslow (*ly*)

Jessie Matthews, Robert Young, Sonnie Hale, Ernest Milton, Robb Wilton, Sara Allgood, Athene Seyler, Cyril Raymond.

'Mr Saville has directed it with speed, efficiency and a real sense of the absurd.'—*Graham Greene*

'The tops in topsy-turvy romance!'

It's Love I'm After*
US 1937 90m bw
Warner (Harry Joe Brown)

A beloved stage star couple fight like cat and dog behind the scenes.
Amusing romantic farce which has worn rather less well than might have been expected but does present two stars at their peak.

w Casey Robinson *d* Archie Mayo *ph* James Van Trees *m* Heinz Roemheld

Bette Davis, Leslie Howard, Olivia de Havilland, Patric Knowles, Eric Blore, George Barbier, Spring Byington, Bonita Granville, E. E. Clive

'Smash comedy hit. Arrange extra playing time for this one.'—*Variety*

'One of the most delightful and diverting comedies the madcap cinema has yet turned out.'—*New York World Telegram*

'Proceeds like a somewhat deranged *Taming of the Shrew* . . . [BD and LH] are surrounded by that set of millionaires, valets and heiresses that were at one time as much of a convention in American comedy as the fops of Restoration theatre.'—*American Film Institute*

It's My Turn
US 1980 90m Metrocolor
Columbia / Rastar / Martin Elfand

A lady mathematics professor decides to seize her chances when she falls for the son of her father's new wife.
Unattractive and rather uninteresting comedy-drama with strong overtones of women's lib.

w Eleanor Bergstein *d* Claudia Weill *ph* Bill Butler *m* Patrick Williams

Jill Clayburgh, Michael Douglas, Charles Grodin, Beverly Garland, Steven Hill

It's Never Too Late
GB 1956 95m Eastmancolor

A mother considered dull by her family starts a new career as a scriptwriter. Acceptable but quite unexciting matinée comedy. Phyllis Calvert, Guy Rolfe, Susan Stephen, Patrick Barr, Delphi Lawrence, Sarah Lawson, Peter Hammond. Written by Edward Dryhurst, from the play by Felicity Douglas; directed by Michael McCarthy; for Park Lane / ABP.

It's Never Too Late to Mend
GB 1937 67m bw

An evil squire schemes for the hand of the farmer's beautiful daughter. Archetypal melodrama of the 'Fie, Sir Jasper' school, mainly interesting in this version for the antics of its heavy-breathing star. *Tod Slaughter*, Marjorie Taylor, Jack Livesey, Lawrence Hanray. Written by H. F. Maltby, from the play by Charles Reade and Arthur Shirley; directed by David MacDonald; for George King.

It's Not Cricket
GB 1948 77m bw
GFD / Gainsborough (Betty Box)

Bowler-hatted officers catch a Nazi spy.
Over-spoofed comedy which barely allows the stars a real chance.

w Lyn Lockwood, Bernard MacNab *d* Alfred Roome *ph* Gordon Lang *m* Arthur Wilkinson

Basil Radford, Naunton Wayne, Maurice Denham, Susan Shaw, Nigel Buchanan

It's Only Money
US 1962 84m bw
Paramount / York / Jerry Lewis Productions (Paul Jones)

A TV repair mechanic hampers his detective friend in a search for a missing heir, which turns out to be himself.
Patchy mystery spoof with the star in rather better form than usual, and a memorable scene in which he is chased by an army of lawnmowers.

w John Fenton Murray *d* Frank Tashlin *ph* W. Wallace Kelley *m* Walter Scharf

Jerry Lewis, Zachary Scott, Joan O'Brien, Jesse White, Jack Weston

It's That Man Again**
GB 1942 84m bw
GFD / Gainsborough (Edward Black)

The Mayor of Foaming-at-the-Mouth puts on a show to save a bombed theatre.
Smart, fast-moving comedy which no longer seems particularly funny in itself but is an invaluable record of the characters and wisecracks of a radio show which proved a prime morale booster during World War II.

w Howard Irving Young, *Ted Kavanagh d Walter Forde*

Tommy Handley, Jack Train, Greta Gynt, Dino Galvani, Dorothy Summers, Horace Percival, Sidney Keith, Clarence Wright

It's Tough to be Famous
US 1932 81m bw

A young naval hero finds that fame destroys his private life. Unco-ordinated comedy-drama. Douglas Fairbanks Jnr, Mary Brian, Walter Catlett, J. Carrol Naish. Written by Robert Lord, Mary McCall Jnr; directed by Alfred E. Green; for first National. 'Lightweight feature possessing sufficient entertainment value to give theatres a moderate week.'—*Variety*

Ivan the Terrible**
USSR 1942–6 100m (part one), 88m (part two) bw (some Agfacolor in part two)
Mosfilm
original title: *Ivan Groznyi*

The life of a 16th-century tsar.
A heavy-going film overflowing with grim, gloomy and superbly composed images: the plot is by the way, and part two (also known as *The Boyars' Plot*) is not up to the standard of part one, in which the coronation sequence alone is a masterpiece of cinema.

wd, ed Sergei Eisenstein ph Edouard Tissé (exteriors), Andrei Moskvin (interiors) *m Sergei Prokoviev ad Isaac Shpinel, L. Naumova*

Nikolai Cherkassov, Ludmilla Tselikovskaya, Serafima Birman

'A visual opera, with all of opera's proper disregard of prose-level reality . . . an extraordinarily bold experiment, fascinating and beautiful to look at.'—*James Agee*

Ivanhoe*
GB 1952 106m Technicolor
MGM (Pandro S. Berman)

Derring-do among the knights of medieval England.
Tolerable, big-budget spectacular based on Sir Walter Scott's novel.

w Noel Langley, Aeneas Mackenzie *d* Richard Thorpe *ph* F. A. Young *m* Miklos Rozsa

Robert Taylor, Joan Fontaine, Elizabeth Taylor, Emlyn Williams, George Sanders, Robert Douglas, Finlay Currie, Felix Aylmer, Francis de Wolff, Guy Rolfe, Norman Wooland, Basil Sydney

AAN: best picture; F. A. Young; Miklos Rozsa

I've Always Loved You
US 1946 116m Technicolor
Republic
GB title: *Concerto*

A brilliant pianist becomes jealous of his girl pupil, despite his love for her.
High-flown romantic tosh with music, an unusual departure for this studio; most notable for Artur Rubenstein on the sound track.

w Borden Chase *d* Frank Borzage *ph* Tony Gaudio *m* Walter Scharf

Philip Dorn, Catherine McLeod, Felix Bressart, Maria Ouspenskaya, William Carter

I've Got Your Number
US 1934 68m bw

Telephone service engineers help prove a girl innocent of burglary. Cheerful, fast-moving programmer typical of its studio at the time.
Joan Blondell, Pat O'Brien, Allen Jenkins, Glenda Farrell, Eugene Pallette. Written by Warren Duff and Sidney Sutherland; directed by Ray Enright; for Warner.

I've Lived Before
US 1956 82m bw
U–I (Howard Christie)

After a plane crash, the pilot recovers but believes himself to be another airman who died in 1918.
Dullish, talky drama which wastes its interesting reincarnation theme.
w Norman Jolley, William Talman *d* Richard Bartlett *ph* Maury Gertsman *m* Herman Stein

Jock Mahoney, Leigh Snowden, Ann Harding, John McIntire, Raymond Bailey, Jerry Paris

Ivy*
US 1947 99m bw
Universal (William Cameron Menzies)

In Edwardian society England, a lady poisoner gets her come-uppance.
Curiously ineffective period thriller in which the star is the elegant but artificial production design: the script is deadly dull.
w Charles Bennett, *novel* Mrs Belloc Lowndes *d Sam Wood ph Russell Metty m* Daniele Amfitheatrof *pd William Cameron Menzies*

Joan Fontaine, Herbert Marshall, Patric Knowles, Richard Ney, Cedric Hardwicke, Lucile Watson, Sara Allgood, Henry Stephenson, Rosalind Ivan, Lilian Fontaine, Una O'Connor, Isobel Elsom, Alan Napier, Paul Cavanagh, Gavin Muir, Norma Varden

'The real star is whoever was responsible for the dressing, setting, lighting and shooting, and that, I infer from past performance, is the producer, William Cameron Menzies.'—*James Agee*

J. W. Coop*
US 1971 112m Eastmancolor
Columbia / Robertson and Associates (Cliff Robertson)

After ten years in prison, a rodeo rider returns to his home town.
Well-made but rather inconsequential drama with attractive locations.

w Cliff Robertson, Gary Cartwright, Bud Shrake *d* Cliff Robertson *ph* Frank Stanley *m* Don Randi, Louie Shelton

Cliff Robertson, Cristina Ferrare, Geraldine Page, R. G. Armstrong

Jabberwocky
GB 1977 101m Technicolor
Umbrella (John Goldstone, Sandy Lieberson)

A medieval cooper's apprentice is mistaken for a prince and slays the dragon which is terrorizing the neighbourhood.
An intellectual Carry On film, with very little more taste and a great deal more unpleasant imagery. Despite much re-editing, the laughs are very intermittent.

w Charles Alverson, Terry Gilliam *d* Terry Gilliam *ph* Terry Bedford *m* De Wolfe *pd* Roy Smith

Michael Palin, Max Wall, Deborah Fallender, Warren Mitchell, John Le Mesurier, Harry H. Corbett, Rodney Bewes, Bernard Bresslaw
'The constant emphasis on blood, excrement, dismemberment and filth ultimately becomes rather wearing.'—*Michael Billington, Illustrated London News*

J'Accuse*
France 1939 95m bw

A scientist intends his invention to end war; when it is put to a contrary purpose, he calls the war dead to rise from their graves and accuse humanity. Stern, well acted, but (as it proved) ineffective propaganda. Victor Francen, Jean Max, Renée Devilliers. Written and directed by Abel Gance; for Forrester-Parant.

Jack Ahoy
GB 1934 82m bw

An accident-prone naval rating routs bandits and wins the girl. Tailor-made star comedy with skilful moments. Jack Hulbert, Nancy O'Neil, Alfred Drayton, Tamara Desni. Written by Jack Hulbert, Leslie Arliss, Gerald Fairlie and Austin Melford; directed by Walter Forde; for Gaumont. 'Mr Hulbert is equal to all his occasions . . . his abounding energy and high spirits are never monotonous or wearisome.'—*E. V. Lucas, Punch.*

Jack and the Beanstalk
US 1952 78m Supercinecolor
Warner / Alex Gottlieb

A babysitter dreams the story he is reading aloud.
Rather feeble star comedy aimed entirely at the kiddie set, and with none of the familiar routines. The 'bookends', as is customary, are in black and white.

w Nat Curtis *d* Jean Yarbrough *ph* George Robinson *m* Heinz Roemheld

Bud Abbott, Lou Costello, Buddy Baer, Dorothy Ford, William Farnum

Jack Armstrong
US 1947 bw serial: 15 eps

An aviation company developing atom-powered motors is threatened by enemy agents. Rousing serial stuff for the kids. John Hart, Rosemary La Planche, Charles Middleton, Claire James, Pierre Watkin. Directed by Wallace Fox; for Columbia.

Jack London
US 1943 93m bw

Jack London seeks various kinds of adventure, writes a book about the Klondike, and warns the world of the Japanese menace.
Occasionally bright but generally faltering biopic, obviously made on the cheap. Michael O'Shea, Susan Hayward, Osa Massen, Harry Davenport, Virginia Mayo, Jonathan Hale. Written by Ernest Pascal; directed by Alfred Santell; for Samuel Bronston / United Artists.

AAN: Frederick E. Rich (music)

Jack McCall Desperado
US 1952 75m Technicolor

A Union officer is forced into outlawry but redeems himself. Tolerable minor western. George Montgomery, Angela Stevens, Douglas Kennedy, James Seay, Jay Silverheels. Written by John O'Dea; directed by Sidney Salkow; for Sam Katzman / Columbia.

Jack of All Trades*
GB 1936 76m bw

A cheerful con man talks his way into a top job in an international firm. Odd amalgam of star comedy, musical numbers of the Astaire / Rogers type, shafts of satire from the original play, and finally some flat-footed farce. Certainly worth a look. Jack Hulbert, Gina Malo, Robertson Hare, Athole Stewart, Felix Aylmer, H. F. Maltby. Written by Jack Hulbert, Austin Melford and J. O. C. Orton, from the play *Youth at the Helm* by Paul Vulpuis; directed by Jack Hulbert and Robert Stevenson; for Gainsborough.

Jack of Diamonds
US / West Germany 1967 105m Metrocolor

A retired jewel thief introduces a brilliant pupil into society. Repetitive and rather glum comedy-drama which perks up occasionally. George Hamilton, Joseph Cotten, Marie Laforet, Maurice Evans, Wolfgang Preiss, Lilli Palmer, Carroll Baker, Zsa Zsa Gabor. Written by Jack de Witt and Sandy Howard; directed by Don Taylor; for Harris / Bavaria Atelier / MGM.

Jack Slade
US 1953 90m bw

A western gunman becomes a psychopathic killer. Cliché-ridden but rather brutish western, thought sensationally violent at the time. Mark Stevens, Dorothy Malone, Barton Maclane, John Litel, Paul Langton, Harry Shannon. Written by Warren Douglas; directed by Harold Schuster; for Allied Artists. (GB title: *Slade.*)

Jack the Giant Killer**
US 1961 94m Technicolor
Zenith / Edward Small (Robert E. Kent)

Demon Pendragon kidnaps the princess of Cornwall but she is rescued by a farmer's son.
Very creditable fairy tale, with the right style and atmosphere assisted by vigorous acting, good pace and excellent trick effects. Unfortunately it turned out rather scary for a child audience and so fell between two stools.

w Orville Hampton, Nathan Juran d Nathan Juran ph David S. Horsley m Paul Sawtell, Bert Shefter *sp Howard Anderson ad Fernando Carere, Frank McCoy*

Kerwin Mathews, Judi Meredith, *Torin Thatcher, Don Beddoe*, Walter Burke, Barry Kelley

'He baffled the great Scotland Yard, the celebrated Arthur Conan Doyle, and Robert Louis Stevenson!'

Jack the Ripper
GB 1958 84m bw
Mid Century (Baker and Berman)

In Victorian London the Ripper murders are finally attributed to a demented surgeon.
Flat and rather flabby treatment of a *cause célèbre,* saved by a reasonably convincing period look.

w Jimmy Sangster *d / ph* Robert S. Baker, Monty Berman *m* Stanley Black

Ewen Solon, Lee Patterson, Eddie Byrne, Betty McDowell, John Le Mesurier

Jackass Mail
US 1942 80m bw
MGM (John Considine Jnr)

A horse thief marries the proprietress of a gambling saloon in the hope of hijacking her mail line, but she reforms him.
Boisterously conceived but anaemically scripted western comedy with the stars in full throttle.

w Lawrence Hazard *d* Norman Z. McLeod *ph* Clyde de Vinna *m* David Snell, Earl Brent

Wallace Beery, Marjorie Main, J. Carrol Naish, Darryl Hickman, William Haade, Hobart Cavanaugh

'This time at least they are repeating their variation on the Min-and-Bill routine among companions whose resemblance to burlesque is as unabashed as their own.'—*Bosley Crowther, New York Times*

Jackboot Mutiny
Germany 1955 77m bw
Arca-Ariston
original title: *Es Geschah am 20 Juli*

An account of the army officers' plot to assassinate Hitler.
Documentary-like treatment without much att mpt at characterization. An important historical document nevertheless.

w W. P. Zibaso, Gustav Machaty *d* G. W. Pabst *ph* Kurt Hasse *m* Johannes Weissenbach

Bernhard Wicki, Karl Ludwig Diehl, Carl Wery

The Jackpot**
US 1950 85m bw
TCF (Samuel G. Engel)

A suburban husband finds that life becomes complicated when winning the jackpot on a radio quiz makes him a celebrity.
Modest, skilful comedy in Hollywood's best manner.

w Phoebe and Henry Ephron d Walter Lang ph Joseph La Shelle *md* Lionel Newman

James Stewart, Barbara Hale, James Gleason, Fred Clark, Alan Mowbray, Patricia Medina, Natalie Wood, Tommy Rettig, Robert Gist, Lyle Talbot

Jack's the Boy*
GB 1932 91m bw
Gainsborough (Michael Balcon)
US title: *Night and Day*

The police commissioner's son proves his worth in rounding up a smash-and-grab gang.
Dated but lively farce which established its star as a British box office attraction of the thirties.

w W. P. Lipscomb *d* Walter Forde *ph* Leslie Rowson

Jack Hulbert, Cicely Courtneidge, Francis Lister, Winifred Shotter, Peter Gawthorne, Ben Field

'A riotously funny, good, clean, honest British picture.'—*Sydney Carroll, Sunday Times*

† The film in which Hulbert sang 'The Flies Crawled Up the Window' (*m* Vivian Ellis, *ly* Douglas Furber).

Jackson County Jail
US 1976 84m Metrocolor
(UA) New World (Roger Corman)

A lady driver is hijacked, attacked, disbelieved by the local police, thrown into jail and raped by the jailer, whom she brains with a stool.
An exploitation piece with social pretensions which it in no way justifies: it is however quite competently entertaining in its mindlessly violent way.

w Donald Stewart *d* Michael Miller *ph* Bruce Logan *m* Loren Newkirk

Yvette Mimieux, Tommy Lee Jones, Robert Carradine, Frederic Cook, Severn Darden, Howard Hesseman

Jacqueline*
GB 1956 93m bw
Rank (George H. Brown)

A Belfast shipyard worker cannot stand heights, takes to drink, and is helped by his small daughter.
Convincing, well-made, realistically set domestic comedy-drama.

w Patric Kirwan, Liam O'Flaherty *d* Roy Baker *ph Geoffrey Unsworth m* Cedric Thorpe Davie

John Gregson, Kathleen Ryan, Jacqueline Ryan, Noel Purcell, Cyril Cusack, Marie Kean, Liam Redmond, Maureen Delany

The Jade Box
US 1930 bw serial: 10 eps

Members of an Eastern cult determine to recover a mystical stolen box. Primitive talkie serial. Louise Morraine, Jack Perrin, Francis Ford. Directed by Ray Taylor; for Universal.

Jagged Edge**
US 1985 108m Metrocolor
Columbia / Marvin Ransohoff

A lady lawyer defends a newspaper publisher who may or may not be guilty of murder.
Well-crafted courtroom mystery with fashionable violence and a few unexpected twists.

w Joe Eszterhas *d* Richard Marquand *ph* Matthew F. Leonetti *m* John Barry *pd* Gene Callahan *ed* Sean Barton, Conrad Buff

Jeff Bridges, Glenn Close, Peter Coyote, Robert Loggia, Leigh Taylor-Young, John Dehner

AAN: Robert Loggia (supporting actor)

Jaguar Lives
US 1979 90m Eastmancolor

Exploits of an international secret agent with skill in the martial arts. Flashy, violent, James Bond rip-off, years behind its time. Joe Lewis, Christopher Lee, Donald Pleasence, Capucine, Barbara Bach, Joseph Wiseman, Woody Strode, John Huston. Written by Yabo Yablonsky; directed by Ernest Pintoff; for Sandy Howard / Jaguar.

Jailhouse Rock*
US 1957 96m bw Cinemascope
MGM (Pandro S. Berman)

An ex-convict becomes a pop star.
Reasonably competent star vehicle, sourer in tone than most.

w Guy Trosper *d* Richard Thorpe *ph* Robert Bronner *md* Jeff Alexander

Elvis Presley, Judy Tyler, Mickey Shaughnessy, Vaughn Taylor, Dean Jones

Jake Speed
US 1986 100m Technicolor

A famous hero tracks down an American girl abducted in Paris. Adventure hokum with spoof elements which don't come off. Wayne Crawford, John Hurt, Donnis Christopher, Karen Kopins, Leon Ames. Written by Wayne Crawford and Andrew Lane; directed by Andrew Lane; for Crawford / Lane / Foster / Balcor.

Jalna
US 1935 75m bw

Episodes in the life of the Whiteoaks family. Flat adaptation of a Canadian bestseller. Kay Johnson, Ian Hunter, C. Aubrey Smith, Jessie Ralph, Nigel Bruce, David Manners, Peggy Wood, Halliwell Hobbes. Written by Anthony Veiller, Garrett Fort, Larry Bachmann, from the novel by Mazo de la Roche; directed by John Cromwell; for RKO. 'Nice production of a not very good adaptation.'—*Variety*

Jamaica Inn*
GB 1939 107m bw
Mayflower (Erich Pommer)

In old Cornwall, an orphan girl becomes involved with smugglers.
Stagey, stilted adventure story which never loses its studio feel or takes fire as a Hitchcock picture. The cast keeps it interesting.

w Sidney Gilliat, Joan Harrison, J. B. Priestley, *novel* Daphne du Maurier *d Alfred Hitchcock ph* Harry Stradling, Bernard Knowles *m* Eric Fenby

Charles Laughton, Maureen O'Hara, Leslie Banks, Robert Newton, Emlyn Williams, Wylie Watson, Marie Ney, Morland Graham

'Should get good but not outstanding b.o. Superb direction, excellent casting, expressive playing and fine production offset an uneven screenplay.'—*Variety*

'I was irresistibly reminded of an all-star charity matinee.'—*Graham Greene*

Jamaica Run
US 1953 92m Technicolor
Paramount Pine–Thomas

A search for documents, which may apportion a great house to another branch of the family, leads to murder.
Plot-bound romantic mystery in period, with elements of a Caribbean *Rebecca*. Watchable medium-budget hokum.

wd Lewis R. Foster, *novel* Max Murray *ph* Lionel Lindon *m* Lucien Cailliet

Ray Milland, Arlene Dahl, Wendell Corey, Patric Knowles

The James Brothers of Missouri
US 1950 bw serial: 12 eps

Jesse and Frank determine to re-establish themselves as members of society. Another serial contravention of history. Keith Richards, Robert Bice, Noel Neill, Roy Barcroft. Directed by Fred C. Brannon; for Republic.

Jane Eyre
US 1934 62m bw

A Poverty Row transcription of the Charlotte Brontë novel: see below. Virginia Bruce, Colin Clive, Beryl Mercer, Jameson Thomas, Aileen Pringle. Written by Adele Comandini; directed by Christy Cabanne; for Monogram.
'The cast appear to have considered their tasks with considerable melancholy.'—*Variety*

'A love story every woman would die a thousand deaths to live!'

Jane Eyre***
US 1943 96m bw
TCF (William Goetz)

In Victorian times, a harshly treated orphan girl becomes governess in a mysterious Yorkshire mansion with a brooding master.
Sharply paced, reasonably faithful and superbly staged Hollywood version of Charlotte Brontë's archetypal romantic novel which stimulated so many imitations, including *Rebecca*.

w Aldous Huxley, Robert Stevenson, John Houseman d Robert Stevenson ph George Barnes m Bernard Herrmann sp Fred Sersen ad Wiard B. Ihnen, James Basevi

Joan Fontaine, Orson Welles, Margaret O'Brien, *Henry Daniell*, John Sutton, Agnes Moorehead, Elizabeth Taylor, Peggy Ann Garner, Sara Allgood, Aubrey Mather, Hillary Brooke, Edith Barrett, Ethel Griffies, Barbara Everest, *John Abbott*

'A careful and tame production, a sadly vanilla-flavoured Joan Fontaine, and Orson Welles treating himself to road operatic sculpturings of body, cloak and diction, his eyes glinting in the Rembrandt gloom, at every chance, like side orders of jelly.'—*James Agee*

'The essentials are still there; and the non-essentials, such as the gloom, the shadows, the ground mist, the rain and the storms, have been expanded and redoubled and magnified to fill up the gaps.'—*Richard Mallett, Punch*

Janice Meredith
US 1924 153m bw silent
Metro-Goldwyn / Cosmopolitan
GB title: *The Beautiful Rebel*

Vicissitudes of the coquettish daughter of a New Jersey family through the War of Independence.
Marathon melodrama not unlike *Gone with the Wind* in subject matter, but of no remaining interest.

w Lilly Hayward, *novel* Paul Leicester Ford *d* E. Mason Hopper *ad* Joseph Urban *music score* Deems Taylor

Marion Davies, Harrison Ford, Macklyn Arbuckle, Joseph Kilgour, George Nash, Tyrone Power Snr, May Vokes, W. C. Fields, Olin Howland

Janie
US 1944 106m bw
Warner (Brock Pemberton)

The teenage daughter of a middle-class American household gets into innocent scrapes with the army.
Deafening tomboy farce.

w Agnes Christine Johnson, Charles Hoffman, *play* Josephine Bentham, Herschel V. Williams Jnr *d* Michael Curtiz *ph* Carl Guthrie *songs* Lee David, Sammy Cahn, Jule Styne

Joyce Reynolds, Robert Hutton, Ann Harding, Edward Arnold, Robert Benchley, Claire Foley, Hattie McDaniel
† *Janie Gets Married*, made the following year and running 89m, had almost identical credits except that Joan Leslie replaced Joyce Reynolds and Dorothy Malone joined the cast.

Japanese War Bride*
US 1952 94m bw
TCF / Bernhard (Joseph Bernhard)

An officer wounded in Korea marries his Japanese nurse and takes her home to California.
Predictable domestic drama very similar to the British *Frieda*, marginally interesting for sociological reasons.

w Catherine Turney *d* King Vidor *ph* Lionel Lindon *m* Arthur Lange *md* Emil Newman

Shirley Yamaguchi, Don Taylor, Cameron Mitchell, Marie Windsor, James Bell, Louise Lorimer

Jason and the Argonauts***
GB 1963 104m Technicolor
Columbia / Charles H. Schneer

With help and hindrance from the gods, Jason voyages in search of the Golden Fleece and meets all kinds of monsters.
Rambling semi-classic mythological fantasy which keeps its tongue firmly in its cheek and provides a framework for some splendid stop-frame animation.

w Jan Read, Beverly Cross *d Don Chaffey ph* Wilkie Cooper *m Bernard Herrmann sp Ray Harryhausen*

Todd Armstrong, Honor Blackman, Niall MacGinnis, Andrew Faulds, Nancy Kovack

Jassy
GB 1947 102m Technicolor
GFD / Gainsborough (Sydney Box)

A gypsy servant girl falls in love with her master but is accused of murder.
Period romantic melodrama of the *Man in Grey* school; poor of its kind despite high production values.

w Dorothy and Campbell Christie, Geoffrey Kerr, *novel* Norah Lofts *d* Bernard Knowles *ph* Jack Asher

Margaret Lockwood, Patricia Roc, Dennis Price, Basil Sydney, Dermot Walsh, Nora Swinburne, Linden Travers, Ernest Thesiger, Cathleen Nesbitt, John Laurie, Jean Cadell, Clive Morton

'As a piece of unabashed romantic hokum, I found it more and more diverting as the plot thickened.'—*Evening Standard*

Java Head*
GB 1934 85m bw
ATP (Basil Dean)

In 1850 Bristol, a shipbuilder forsakes his Manchu wife for an English girl.
Rather obvious period melodrama with full-blooded acting.

w Martin Brown, Gordon Wellesley *d* J. Walter Ruben *ph* Bert Glennon

Anna May Wong, John Loder, Ralph Richardson, Elizabeth Allan, Edmund Gwenn, Herbert Lomas, George Curzon, Roy Emerton

Jaws**
US 1975 125m Technicolor Panavision
Universal / Zanuck–Brown (William S. Gilmore Jnr)

A man-eating shark causes havoc off the Long Island coast.
In the exploitation-hungry seventies this film took more money than any other. In itself, despite genuinely suspenseful and frightening sequences, it is a slackly narrated and sometimes flatly handled thriller with an over-abundance of dialogue and, when it finally appears, a pretty unconvincing monster.

w Peter Benchley, Carl Gottlieb, *novel* Peter Benchley *d Steven Spielberg ph* Bill Butler *m John Williams*

Robert Shaw, Roy Scheider, Richard Dreyfuss, Lorraine Gary, Murray Hamilton, Carl Gottlieb

'A mind-numbing repast for sense-sated gluttons. Shark stew for the stupefied.'—*William S. Pechter*

'The opening sequences have few parallels in modern cinema; like the shower scene in *Psycho* they will haunt a whole generation.'—*Les Keyser, Hollywood in the Seventies*
AA: John Williams
AAN: best picture

Jaws: The Revenge
US 1987 100m colour
Superfluous fourth story in the Jaws series, almost indistinguishable from the others once you accept that the sharks are after Brody's widow. Lorraine Gary, Lance Guest, Mario Von Peebles, Karen Young, Michael Caine. Written by Michael de Guzman; directed by Joseph Sargent; for Universal.

Jaws 2
US 1978 117m Technicolor Panavision
Universal / Richard Zanuck, David Brown (Joe Alves)
Another man-eating shark menaces teenagers in the Long Island resort of Amity. Repetitive and feeble sequel aimed directly at the popcorn market.
w Carl Gottlieb, Howard Sackler, Dorothy Tristan *d* Jeannot Szwarc *ph* Michael Butler, David Butler, Michael McGowan *m* John Williams
Roy Scheider, Lorraine Gary, Murray Hamilton, Joseph Mascolo, Colin Wilcox
'A manipulation of the audience, in the best sense of the term '—*Jeannot Szwarc, director*

'The third dimension is terror!'
Jaws 3-D
US 1983 99m Technicolor Arrivision 3-D
A man-eating shark turns up in a Florida theme park. Noisy final chapter to this string of shocks. Dennis Quaid, Bess Armstrong, Simon MacCorkindale, Louis Gossett Jnr, John Putch, Lea Thompson. Written by Richard Matheson, Carl Gottlieb; directed by Joe Alves; for Alan Landsburg / Universal.

The Jayhawkers
US 1959 110m Technicolor Vistavision
Paramount / Panama and Frank
Before the Civil War, a farmer defeats a militant posse of private raiders. Unconvincing but rather unusual western, flat patches alternating with striking ones.
w Melvin Frank, Joseph Petracca, Frank Fenton, A. I. Bezzerides *d* Melvin Frank *ph* Loyal Griggs *m* Jerome Moross
Fess Parker, Jeff Chandler, Nicole Maurey, Henry Silva, Herbert Rudley

Jazz Comedy*
USSR 1934 93m bw
Mosfilm
original title: *Vesolye Rebyata*
A shepherd is frequently mistaken for a famous conductor.

THE JAZZ SINGER. 'You ain't heard nothing yet!' Mother love *par excellence*—Al Jolson and Eugenie Besserer.

Peripatetic comedy with many sight gags and western slapstick: Russian comedy being still a rare thing, it seems something of a revelation.
w Grigori Alexandrov, Nikolai Erdman, V. Mass *d Grigori Alexandrov* *ph* Vladimir Nilsen *m* Isaac Dunayevsky
Lubov Orlova, Leonid Utyosov, Maria Strelkova

'New songs and old favourites sung by Mr Jolson during the action of the story on the Vitaphone!'
The Jazz Singer****
US 1927 89m bw
Warner
A cantor's son makes it big in show business. Archetypal Jewish weepie which became of absorbing interest as the first talkie film (songs and a few fragments of speech) and in its way, surprisingly, is not half bad.
w Alfred A. Cohn, *play* Samson Raphaelson *d Alan Crosland* *ph* Hal Mohr
Al Jolson, May McAvoy, Warner Oland, Eugenie Besserer, Otto Lederer
'A beautiful period piece, extravagantly sentimental . . . yet entirely compelling in its own conviction.'—*NFT, 1969*
'*The Jazz Singer* definitely establishes the fact that talking pictures are imminent. Everyone in Hollywood can rise up and declare that they are not, and it will not alter the fact. If I were an actor with a squeaky voice I would worry.'—*Welford Beaton, The Film Spectator*
AAN: Alfred A. Cohn

The Jazz Singer
US 1953 107m Technicolor
Warner (Louis F. Edelman)
Ill-considered, schmaltzy remake of the above.
w Frank Davis, Leonard Stern, Lewis Meltzer *d* Michael Curtiz *ph* Carl Guthrie *md* Ray Heindorf *m* Max Steiner
Danny Thomas, Peggy Lee, Mildred Dunnock, Eduard Franz
AAN: Ray Heindorf; Max Steiner

The Jazz Singer
US 1980 115m De Luxe
EMI / Jerry Leider
Oddly-timed reprise of the above, with doting mum replaced by patient wife. A good basis for a best-selling album, otherwise a pointless enterprise.
w Herbert Baker, Stephen H. Foreman *d* Richard Fleischer *ph* Isidore Mankofsky *m* Leonard Rosenman *pd* Harry Horner

Neil Diamond, Laurence Olivier, Lucie Arnaz, Catlin Adams, Sully Boyar

'What is jazz to Neil Diamond and what is Neil Diamond to jazz? Old title has nothing to do with music on display here and would seem meaningless to modern audiences.'—*Variety*

Jazzboat
GB 1959 96m bw Cinemascope

A jazz musician pretends to be a crook and leads the police to an important gang. Flimsy comedy with a background of pop acts. Very dated. Anthony Newley, Anne Aubrey, David Lodge, Lionel Jeffries, Bernie Winters, James Booth, Al Mulock, Joyce Blair, Leo McKern, Ted Heath and his Music. Written by Ken Hughes and John Antrobus; directed by Ken Hughes; for Warwick / Columbia.

Jealousy
US 1929 66m bw

A young artist is jealous of his wife's older friend, and kills him. Turgid adaptation of a two-character play; interesting only for its cast, though the star died before it was released. Jeanne Eagels, Fredric March, Halliwell Hobbes, Henry Daniell. Written by Garrett Fort and John D. Williams, from the play by Louis Verneuil; directed by Jean De Limur; for Paramount.

Jealousy
US 1934 66m bw

A boxer is knocked out and dreams that his jealousy has landed him in the electric chair. Disagreeable melodrama not saved by its tricks. Nancy Carroll, George Murphy, Donald Cook, Raymond Walburn. Written by Kubec Glasmon, Joseph Moncure March; directed by Roy William Neill; for Columbia.

Jealousy*
US 1945 70m bw

A failed writer, jealous of his wife's friendship with another man, is found murdered. Curious but interesting melodrama with much talent breaking through. Nils Asther, John Joder, Jane Randolph, Karen Morley. Written by Arnold Phillips, Gustav Machaty and Dalton Trumbo; directed by Gustav Machaty; music by Hans Eisler; for Republic. 'It is a sympathetic film, and in spite of its overall failure, contains enough sincerity and enough artistry to make most of the other films mentioned here look sick.'—*James Agee.*

Jean de Florette**
France 1986 121m Eastmancolor Technovision
Renn / Films A2 / RAI2 / DD

Elemental story of feuding over water supplies in rural France in the 20s.
Stunning performances and detailed depiction of Provençal farming life made it a wild success in France, repeated to a remarkable extent abroad.

w Claude Berri, Gérard Brach, from novel by Marcel Pagnol *d* Claude Berri *ph* Bruno Nuytten *m* Jean-Claude Petit *pd* Bernard Vezat

Yves Montand, Gérard Depardieu, Daniel Auteuil, Elisabeth Depardieu

† The saga continued in *Manon des Sources* of the same year (114m, from Pagnol's sequel L'eau de collines) with Emmanuelle Béart in the title role.

Jeanne Eagels*
US 1957 114m bw
Columbia (George Sidney)

A sideshow dancer becomes a Broadway star of the twenties but dies of drugs.
Well-upholstered but basically too conventional showbiz biopic.

w Daniel Fuchs, Sonya Levien, John Fante *d George Sidney ph Robert Planck m* George Duning

Kim Novak, Jeff Chandler, Agnes Moorehead, Charles Drake, Larry Gates, *Virginia Grey*

Jeannie*
GB 1941 101m bw
GFD / Tansa (Marcel Hellman)
US title: *Girl in Distress*

A Scots girl comes into money and takes a European holiday.
Mildly astringent, generally amusing comedy which overcomes shaky production. Remade as *Let's Be Happy* in 1952.

w Anatole de Grunwald, Roland Pertwee, *play* Aimée Stuart *d* Harold French *ph* Bernard Knowles *m* Mischa Spoliansky

Barbara Mullen, Michael Redgrave, *Albert Lieven*, Wilfrid Lawson, Kay Hammond, Edward Chapman, Googie Withers, Gus MacNaughton

'One of the easiest, sweetest of light comedies.'—*James Agee*

'As enchanting a bit of rue and nonsense as we've succumbed to in many a month.'—*New York Times*

'The drama of all women who meet the demands of love!'

Jennie Gerhardt
US 1933 85m bw
Paramount (B. P. Schulberg)

An unmarried mother is hard done by but gets the man she loves in the end.
Archetypal weepie, adequately put across.

w Josephine Lovett, Joseph M. March, S. K. Lauren, Frank Portos, *novel* Theodore Dreiser *d* Marion Gering *ph* Leon Shamroy

Sylvia Sidney, Donald Cook, Mary Astor, Edward Arnold, H. B. Warner, Theodor Von Eltz

'Doesn't look to become a general b.o. favourite because it is a story without action.'—*Variety*

Jennifer
US 1953 73m bw
AA (Berman Swartz)

The lady housekeeper of a California mansion broods on the mysterious disappearance of her predecessor.
Slight, quietly effective suspenser with a let-down ending.

w Virginia Myers *d* Joel Newton *ph James Wong Howe m* Ernest Gold

Ida Lupino, Howard Duff, Robert Nicholas, Mary Shipp

Jeopardy
US 1952 69m bw
MGM (Sol Baer Fielding)

A man on a camping holiday falls off a jetty and gets stuck in the timbers while the water rises; his wife frantically seeks help from an escaped convict.
Panic melodrama enjoyable for its clichés.

w Mel Dinelli *d* John Sturges *ph* Victor Milner *m* Dmitri Tiomkin

Barbara Stanwyck, Barry Sullivan, Ralph Meeker

'Some say he's dead . . . some say he never will be!'

Jeremiah Johnson**
US 1972 107m Technicolor Panavision
Warner (Joe Wizan)

In the 1850s an ex-soldier becomes a mountain trapper.
Splendidly made if rather desultorily plotted adventure story with the feel of raw reality.

w John Milius, Edward Anhalt *d Sydney Pollack ph* Andrew Callaghan *m* John Rubinstein, Tim McIntire

Robert Redford, Will Geer, Allyn McLerie

Jeremy
US 1973 90m De Luxe
UA / Kenasset (George Pappas)

A music student falls in love with a ballet dancer.
Sentimental love story with nothing positive to commend it, chiefly interesting because for commercial release it was blown up from 16mm.

wd Arthur Barron *ph* Paul Goldsmith *m* Lee Holdridge

Robby Benson, Glynnis O'Connor, Len Bari, Leonardo Cimino

Jericho
GB 1937 77m bw
Buckingham (Walter Futter, Max Schach)
US title: *Dark Sands*

A court-martialled officer pursues a murderous deserter across Africa.
Lively star vehicle of its day.

w Frances Marion, George Barraud, Peter Ruric, Robert N. Lee *d* Thornton Freeland *ph* John W. Boyle

Paul Robeson, Henry Wilcoxon, Wallace Ford, John Laurie, James Carew

'Can't fail to interest audiences throughout the world.'—*Variety*

The Jerk
US 1979 94m Technicolor
Universal / Aspen (Peter MacGregor-Scott)

An innocent white man brought up by black sharecroppers goes out into the world and first makes, then loses a fortune.

Hit-or-miss star vehicle with flashes of satire and fallen aspirations to be a modern *Candide*.

w Steve Martin, Carl Gottlieb, Michael Elias *d* Carl Reiner *ph* Victor J. Kemper *m* Jack Elliott

Steve Martin, Bernadette Peters, Catlin Adams, Bill Macy, Maurice Evans

'Goofy, dumb, innocent, loud, uncoordinated, bashful and quite dirty.'—*Variety*

The Jerusalem File
US / Israel 1971 96m Metrocolor
MGM / Sparta (Ram Ben Efraim)

American archaeologists in Jerusalem become involved in Arab / Israeli espionage.
Muddled mixture of action and politics.

w Troy Kennedy Martin *d* John Flynn *ph* Raoul Coutard *m* John Scott

Bruce Davison, Nicol Williamson, Donald Pleasence, Ian Hendry

Jesse James**
US 1938 106m Technicolor
TCF (Nunnally Johnson)

After the Civil War, two brothers take to train robbing when railroad employees harass their family.
The life of an outlaw turns into family entertainment when Hollywood bathes it in sentiment, soft colour, family background and warm humour. It works dangerously well, and the action sequences are splendid.

w Nunnally Johnson d Henry King ph George Barnes md Louis Silvers *ad William Darling, George Dudley*

Tyrone Power, Henry Fonda, Nancy Kelly, Jane Darwell, Randolph Scott, Henry Hull, Slim Summerville, Brian Donlevy, J. Edward Bromberg, John Carradine, Donald Meek

'Sock outdoors meller, vigorous and intensely dramatic in its unfolding . . . box office smacko.'—*Variety*

'An authentic American panorama.'—*New York Times*

† Sequel 1940: *The Return of Frank James*. Remake 1957: *The True Story of Jesse James*.

Jesse James Rides Again
US 1947 bw serial: 13 eps

A reformed Jesse James tries to go straight. Unlikely serial heroics. Clayton Moore, Linda Stirling, Roy Barcroft, Tristram Coffin. Directed by Fred C. Brannon and Thomas Carr; for Republic.

Jessica
France / Italy / US 1962 105m Technicolor Panavision
UA / Ariane / Dear Film (Jean Negulesco)

The attractive midwife in a Sicilian village causes the women to go on a sex strike.
Synthetic rustic naughtiness showing several influences imperfectly assimilated.

w Edith Sommer, *novel* The Midwife of Pont Clery by Flora Sundstrom *d* Jean Negulesco *ph* Piero Portalupi *m* Mario Nascimbene

Angie Dickinson, Maurice Chevalier, Noel Noel, Gabriele Ferzetti, Sylva Koscina, Agnes Moorehead, Marcel Dalio

Jesus Christ Superstar*
US 1973 107m Technicolor Todd-AO 35
Universal (Norman Jewison, Robert Stigwood)

Young tourists in Israel re-enact episodes of the life of Christ.
Location-set fantasia based on the phenomenally successful rock opera; some of it works, but the original concept was a theatrical one.

w Melvyn Bragg, Norman Jewison, *book* Tim Rice *d* Norman Jewison *m Andrew Lloyd Webber ph Douglas Slocombe md* André Previn

Ted Neeley, Carl Anderson, Yvonne Elliman, Barry Dennen

'One of the true fiascos of modern cinema.'—*Paul D. Zimmerman*

AAN: André Previn

Jet over the Atlantic
US 1958 95m bw
Warner / Inter Continental (Benedict Bogeaus)

A noble British passenger on a plane from Madrid to New York has planted a gas bomb in the luggage compartment.
Mechanical airborne suspenser with the usual assortment of unconvincing types making unconvincing gestures.

w Irving H. Cooper *d* Byron Haskin *ph* George Stahl *m* Lou Forbes

Guy Madison, Virginia Mayo, George Raft, George Macready, Ilona Massey, Anna Lee, Margaret Lindsay, Venetia Stevenson, Mary Anderson, Brett Halsey, Frederic Worlock

Jet Pilot
US 1950–57 112m Technicolor
Howard Hughes (Jules Furthman)

A Russian lady spy falls for an American pilot.
Lamentably dull and stupid romantic actioner of which all concerned should be thoroughly ashamed, especially as it took seven years to complete and is not even technically competent.

w Jules Furthman *d* Josef Von Sternberg (and others) *ph* Winton C. Hoch *m* Bronislau Kaper

John Wayne, Janet Leigh, Jay C. Flippen, Paul Fix, Richard Rober, Roland Winters, Ivan Triesault, Hans Conried

'One of the most childish, tedious and futile cold war spy dramas yet concocted by a Hollywood screenwriter.'—*John Gillett*

Jet Storm*
GB 1959 99m bw
British Lion / Britannia / Pendennis (Steven Pallos)

An airliner in flight from London to New York is discovered to have a bomb on board.
All-star slice-of-life suspenser with competently handled dialogue and situations.

w Cy Endfield, Sigmund Miller *d* Cy Endfield *ph* Jack Hildyard *m* Thomas Rajna

Richard Attenborough, George Rose, Hermione Baddeley, Mai Zetterling, Diane Cilento, Stanley Baker, Harry Secombe, Virginia Maskell, Elizabeth Sellars, Sybil Thorndike, Bernard Braden, Cec Linder, David Kossoff

Jeux Interdits***
France 1952 84m bw
Robert Dorfmann (Paul Joly)
aka: *Forbidden Games; The Secret Game*

In 1940, the little daughter of refugee parents sees her parents killed, and takes refuge with a peasant family, the small son of which helps her bury her dead puppy. They make a game of building a cemetery, which leads to a village feud . . .
Poignant anti-war tract which seemed a masterpiece at the time and is full of marvellous moments, but no longer holds up as a whole.

w Jean Aurenche, Pierre Bost, novel François Boyer *d René Clément ph* Robert Julliard *m* Narciso Yepes

Brigitte Fossey, Georges Poujouly, Amédée, Laurence Badie, Jacques Marin, Suzanne Courtal, Lucien Hubert

'A truly imposing achievement of blending several seemingly unrelated elements into a totally meaningful whole.'—*John Simon, 1967*

AA: best foreign film
AAN: François Boyer (original story)

Les Jeux Sont Faits*
France 1947 91m bw
Films Gibe

Falling in love in Purgatory, two murdered people get a second chance to return to earth, but spend their time quarrelling.
Somewhat despondent romantic fantasy with morsels of wit.

w Jean-Paul Sartre *d* Jean Delannoy *ph* Christian Matras *m* Georges Auric

Micheline Presle, Marcel Pagliero, Marguerite Moreno, Charles Dullin

Jew Suss**
GB 1934 109m bw
Gaumont (Michael Balcon)
US title: *Power*

In old Württemberg, a Jew gains power to help his people, then finds he is Gentile.
Interesting, heavy-handed historical satire on the pointlessness of race distinctions, made partly in answer to Nazi oppression in Germany.

w Dorothy Farnum, A. R. Rawlinson, *novel* Leon Feuchtwangler *d* Lothar Mendes

Conrad Veidt, Benita Hume, Frank Vosper, Cedric Hardwicke, Gerald du Maurier, Pamela Ostrer

'Powerful as an artistic film achievement . . . but may have to struggle for commercial contentment.'—*Variety*

JESSE JAMES. Tyrone Power takes a break from robbing trains and evading the law to gaze soulfully at Nancy Kelly.

Jew Suss*
Germany 1940 85m bw
Terra

Celebrated travesty of the above, in which the Jew is wholly evil and rapes Aryan girls.

w Ludwig Metzger, Veit Harlan, Eberhard Wolfgang Möller *d* Veit Harlan *ph* Bruno Mondi *m* Wolfgang Zeller

Ferdinand Marian, Werner Krauss, Heinrich George, Kristina Söderbaum

'The epitome of anti-semitic propaganda . . . the most notorious film of the Third Reich and one which brought disgrace on almost everyone connected with it.'—*Georges Sadoul*

'Highly recommended for its artistic value and, to serve the politics of the State, recommended for young people.'—*Josef Goebbels*

'When the going gets tough, the tough get going!'

Jewel of the Nile*
US 1985 104m Technicolor
TCF / Michael Douglas

A lady novelist gets into trouble when she accepts an invitation from a Middle Eastern potentate.
Moderate sequel to *Romancing the Stone*; plenty of action, but dull spots in between.

w Mark Rosenthal, Lawrence Konner *d* Lewis Teague *ph* Jan DeBont *m* Jack Nitzsche *pd* Richard Dawking, Terry Knight

Michael Douglas, Kathleen Turner, Danny DeVito, Spiros Focas

'Mass destruction, endless gunfire and a fiery finish . . . the only box office question is whether the film comes late in the cycle for Saturday matinee revivals.'—*Variety*

Jewel Robbery*
US 1932 68m bw
Warner

A jewel thief and a millionaire's wife fall in love in Vienna.
Good sparkling fun in the shadow of *Trouble in Paradise* (qv).

w Erwin Gelsey, *play* Ladislaus Fodor *d William Dieterle* *ph* Robert Kurrle

William Powell, Kay Francis, Hardie Albright, André Luguet, Henry Kolker, Spencer Charters, Alan Mowbray, Helen Vinson, Lawrence Grant

Jezebel***
US 1938 104m bw
Warner (Henry Blanke)

Before the Civil War, a southern belle stirs up trouble among the menfolk by her wilfulness and spite, but atones when a plague strikes.
Superb star melodrama, tossed to her in compensation for losing *Gone with the Wind*, and dealt with in high style by all concerned.

w Clements Ripley, Abem Finkel, John Huston, *play* Owen Davis Snr *d William Wyler* *ph Ernest Haller* *m Max Steiner*

Bette Davis, Henry Fonda, George Brent, Margaret Lindsay, Fay Bainter, Richard Cromwell, Donald Crisp, Henry O'Neill, John Litel, Spring Byington, Eddie Anderson, Gordon Oliver, Irving Pichel

'Good femme film, assured of okay results.'—*Variety*

'Its excellences come from many sources—good plotting and writing, a director and photographer who know how to make the thing flow along with dramatic pictorial effect, and a cast that makes its story a record of living people.'—*James Shelley Hamilton, National Board of Review*

'Without the zing Davis gave it, it would have looked very mossy indeed.'—*Pauline Kael, 1968*

AA: Bette Davis; Fay Bainter
AAN: best picture; Ernest Haller; Max Steiner

Jigsaw
US 1949 72m bw
(UA) Tower (The Danzigers)

An assistant District Attorney uncovers a mob stirring up racial hatred.
Undistinguished piece of do-goodery, curiously decorated by guest stars doing bit parts as a gesture of goodwill.

w Fletcher Markle, Vincent McConnor *d* Fletcher Markle *ph* Don Malkames *m* Robert Stringer

Franchot Tone, Jean Wallace, Myron McCormick, Marc Lawrence, Marlene Dietrich, Henry Fonda, John Garfield, Marsha Hunt, Leonard Lyons, Burgess Meredith

Jigsaw**
GB 1962 107m bw Cinemascope
British Lion / Britannia / Figaro (Val Guest)

Brighton policemen track down the murderer of a woman found in a lonely house on the beach.
Absorbing and entertaining little murder mystery which sustains its considerable length with interesting detail and plays as fair as can be with the audience. Excellent unassuming entertainment.

wd Val Guest, play Sleep Long My Love by Hilary Waugh *ph* Arthur Grant *m* none

Jack Warner, Ronald Lewis, *Michael Goodliffe*, Yolande Donlan, John Barron

The Jigsaw Man
GB 1985 98m colour
J and M

A British traitor in Moscow is given a new face and sent back home, where he becomes a double agent.

Somewhat elementary cold war chicanery with an abundance of talk before a routine action finish. Production was interrupted by financial crises, and the final result is patchy to say the least.

w Jo Eisinger *d* Terence Young *ph* Freddie Francis *m* John Cameron

Michael Caine, Laurence Olivier, Robert Powell, Susan George, Michael Medwin, Vladek Sheybal

Jim Thorpe, All-American
US 1951 105m bw
Warner (Everett Freeman)
GB title: *Man of Bronze*

A Red Indian becomes a star footballer, but later succumbs to drink.
Adequate sporting biopic.

w Douglas Morrow, Everett Freeman *d* Michael Curtiz *ph* Ernest Haller *m* Max Steiner

Burt Lancaster, Charles Bickford, Steve Cochran, Phyllis Thaxter, Dick Wesson

Jimmy the Gent*
US 1934 67m bw
Warner (Robert Lord)

A racketeer supplies heirs for unclaimed estates.
Adequate star crime comedy.

w Bertram Millhauser *d* Michael Curtiz *ph* Ira Morgan *md* Leo F. Forbstein

Jimmy Cagney, Bette Davis, Alice White, Allen Jenkins, Arthur Hohl, Mayo Methot, Alan Dinehart, Hobart Cavanaugh, Ralf Harolde, Philip Reed, Joe Sawyer

'Fast and flip, rough and rowdy.'—*New York American*

Jinxed!
US 1982 103m Technicolor
MGM-UA / Herb Jaffe

A frustrated blackjack dealer seduces the girl of a frequent winner.
Unfunny gambling comedy which never begins to cohere.

w Bert Blessing, David Newman *d* Don Siegel *ph* Vilmos Zsigmond *m* Bruce Roberts, Miles Goodman

Bette Midler, Ken Wahl, Rip Torn, Val Avery, Jack Elam, Benson Fong, Jacqueline Scott

Jitterbugs*
US 1943 75m bw
TCF (Sol M. Wurtzel)

Laurel and Hardy help a nightclub singer to fight off gangsters.
The last Laurel and Hardy film to contain any good scenes, and almost the only one of their TCF films that did.

w Scott Darling *d* Mal St Clair *ph* Lucien Andriot *songs* Charles Newman (*m*), Lew Pollack (*ly*) *md* Emil Newman

Stan Laurel, Oliver Hardy, Vivian Blaine, Bob Bailey, Douglas Fowley, Noel Madison, Lee Patrick

Jivaro
US 1953 91m Technicolor 3D
Paramount / William H. Pine, William C.Thomas
GB title: *Lost Treasure of the Amazon*

A mixed party of Americans follows a drunken treasure seeker into the jungle.
Elementary treasure hunt adventure, hampered by studio foliage, bad script and half-hearted acting.

w Winston Miller, *story* David Duncan *d* Edward Ludwig *ph* Lionel Lindon *m* Gregory Stone

Fernando Lamas, Rhonda Fleming, Brian Keith, Lon Chaney Jnr, Marvin Miller, Richard Denning

Joan of Arc
US 1948 145m Technicolor
(RKO) Sierra / Walter Wanger

The last campaign of the Maid of Orleans.
Strictly from Dullsville; one studio-set piece follows another, and a group of talented people clearly thought that prestige would sell itself without the hard work that goes into more commercial productions.

w Maxwell Anderson, Andrew Solt, *play* Joan of Lorraine by Maxwell Anderson *d* Victor Fleming *ph* Joe Valentine *m* Hugo Friedhofer *md* Emil Newman *ad* Richard Day

Ingrid Bergman, Jose Ferrer, George Coulouris, Francis L. Sullivan, Gene Lockhart, Ward Bond, John Ireland, Hurd Hatfield, Cecil Kellaway, George Zucco, J. Carrol Naish

'A bad film with one or two good things. It is childishly oversimplified, its battles *papier mâché*, its heroine far too worldly, its spiritual content that of a chromo art calendar.'—*Herman G. Weinberg*

AA: Joe Valentine
AAN: Hugo Friedhofer; Ingrid Bergman; Jose Ferrer

Joan of Ozark
US 1942 82m bw

A hillbilly sharpshooter becomes a national spy heroine. Scatty comedy of moderate liveliness. Judy Canova, Joe E. Brown, Eddie Foy Jnr, Jerome Cowan, Alexander Granach. Written by Robert Harari, Eve Greene and Jack Townley; directed by Joseph Santley; for Republic. (GB title: *The Queen of Spies*.)

Joan of Paris
US 1942 95m bw
TCF (David Hempstead)

A French resistance leader sacrifices herself so that Allied pilots can escape.
Well-made propaganda adventure dignified by excellent cast.

w Charles Bennett, Ellis St. Joseph, *story* Jacques Thery, Georges Kessel *d* Robert Stevenson *ph* Russell Metty *m* Roy Webb

Michele Morgan, Paul Henreid, Thomas Mitchell, Laird Cregar, May Robson, Alexander Granach, Alan Ladd

AAN: Roy Webb

Joan the Woman**
US 1916 125m approx bw silent

The story of Joan of Arc: an epic spectacle typical of its director. Geraldine Farrar, Raymond Hatton, Wallace Reid, Hobart Bosworth, Theodore Roberts. Written by Jeanie Macpherson; directed by Cecil B. DeMille; for Cardinal.

Joanna
GB 1968 122m De Luxe Panavision
TCF / Laughlin (Michael S. Laughlin)

A girl art student comes to London and quickly finds the road to ruin.
Antediluvian rubbish tarted up with swinging London settings.

wd Michael Sarne *ph* Walter Lassally *m* Rod McKuen

Genevieve Waite, Christian Doermer, Calvin Lockhart, Donald Sutherland

'An unnecessarily protracted punishing of a very dead quadruped.'—*MFB*

The Job**
Italy 1961 90m bw
24 Horses Films (Alberto Soffientini)
original tile: *Il Posto*

A teenage boy gets his first job, and progresses from office boy to clerk when a senior man dies.
Appealingly observant social comedy, very simple and extremely effective.

wd Ermanno Olmi *ph* Lamberto Caimi

Sandro Panzeri, Loredana Detto

'Rueful and funny and honest . . . the players have been encouraged not so much to act as to behave. Olmi stalks them like a naturalist, and the result is a small, unique and perfect achievement in film-making.'—*Penelope Houston, MFB*

Joe*
US 1970 107m De Luxe
Cannon (David Gil)

A construction worker in a bar meets a businessman who has just killed his daughter's drug addicted lover; they become buddies in their hatred of hippies.
Highly successful in America as a backlash against permissiveness, this rough-hewn opportunistic melodrama is vivid enough but moves in fits and starts.

w Norman Wexler *d / ph* John G. Avildsen *m* Bobby Scott

Peter Boyle, Dennis Patrick, Audrey Caire, Susan Sarandon

'A bad film disfigured by brute strokes of tendentiousness.'—*Penelope Gilliatt*

AAN: Norman Wexler

Joe Butterfly
US 1957 90m Technicolor Cinemascope
U-I (Aaron Rosenberg)

Shortly after World War II, American occupying troops are conned by a Japanese interpreter.
Dull comedy intent on healing old wounds.

w Sy Gomberg, Jack Sher, Marion Hargrove *d* Jesse Hibbs *ph* Irving Glassberg *m* Joseph Gershenson

Burgess Meredith, Audie Murphy, George Nader, Keenan Wynn, Fred Clark, John Agar, Charles McGraw

Joe Dakota
US 1957 90m Technicolor Cinemascope
U-I (Howard Christie)

A stranger appears in a western town in search of his Indian friend, who turns out to have been murdered by the townspeople so that they can share the profits from his oil well.
Feeble rip-off of *Bad Day at Black Rock*.

w William Talman, Norman Jolley *d* Richard Bartlett *ph* George Robinson *md* Joseph Gershenson *m* Hans Salter

Jock Mahoney, Luana Patten, Charles McGraw, Barbara Lawrence, Claude Akins, Lee Van Cleef

Joe Kidd
US 1972 87m Technicolor Panavision
Universal / Malpaso (Sidney Beckerman)

A disreputable bounty hunter tracks down the leader of a tribe of Mexican bandits.
Rough and tumble star western with untenable moral attitudes.

w Elmore Leonard *d* John Sturges *ph* Bruce Surtees *m* Lalo Schifrin

Clint Eastwood, Robert Duvall, John Saxon, Don Stroud, James Wainwright

Joe Macbeth
GB 1955 90m bw
Film Locations / Frankovich (George Maynard)

A gangster is urged by his wife to rub out his boss.
Almost too bad to be funny, this effort to update Shakespeare has actors behaving as though they were stuck in treacle, and its gimmick quality is quickly dissipated by an indifferent production.

w Philip Yordan *d* Ken Hughes *ph* Basil Emmott *m* Trevor Duncan

Paul Douglas, Ruth Roman, Grégoire Aslan, Bonar Colleano, Sidney James

Joe Palooka, Champ
US 1946 72m bw

A boxing promoter grooms a young dope for the ring. Modest series opener with plenty to be modest about. Leon Errol, Joe Kirkwood, Elyse Knox, Eduardo Ciannelli, Joe Sawyer, Elisha Cook Jnr. Written by George Moskov and Albert de Pina; directed by Reginald Le Borg; for Hal E. Chester / Monogram.

Joe Smith American*
US 1942 63m bw
MGM (Jack Chertok)
GB title: *Highway to Freedom*

An aircraft factory worker with special knowledge is kidnapped by Nazis but leads the FBI to his captors.
Watchable propaganda thriller credited with easing Americans into a war mood.

w Allen Rivkin, *story* Paul Gallico *d* Richard Thorpe *ph* Charles Lawton Jnr

Robert Young, Marsha Hunt, Darryl Hickman, Harvey Stephens, Jonathan Hale, Noel Madison, Joseph Anthony

'Not a high-powered movie, it is a first rate die for the new propaganda models which Hollywood is readying for mass production.'—*Time*

Joey Boy
GB 1965 91m bw
British Lion / Launder–Gilliat

In 1941, a group of petty crooks join the army.
Abysmal service comedy, incredibly cheap and tatty and the nadir of several of the talents involved.

wd Frank Launder *ph* Arthur Lavis *m* Philip Green

Harry H. Corbett, Stanley Baxter, Bill Fraser, Reg Varney, Percy Herbert, Lance Percival

'As visually shoddy as it is unfunny . . . the final shot (Corbett pulling a lavatory chain) is all too crudely apt.'—*MFB*

Johann Mouse***
US 1952 8m Technicolor

Strauss' mouse dances to his master's music; the cat, to lure him out, learns to play the piano. Splendid Tom and Jerry cartoon from the great period of this neglected art.
Produced by Fred Quimby; for MGM. AA: best cartoon.

John and Julie
GB 1955 82m Eastmancolor
Group Three (Herbert Mason)

Two children run away to see the coronation.
Genial little family comedy full of stock comic characters.

wd William Fairchild *ph* Arthur Grant *m* Philip Green

Colin Gibson, Leslie Dudley, Peter Sellers, Moira Lister, Wilfrid Hyde White, Sidney James, Andrew Cruickshank

John and Mary*
US 1969 92m De Luxe Panavision
TCF / Debrod (Ben Kadish)

Two New Yorkers have a one-night affair and cannot decide whether to continue.
Slight, disappointing sex comedy vehicle for two stars who were very hot at the time.

w John Mortimer, *novel* Mervyn Jones *d* Peter Yates *ph* Gayne Rescher *m* Quincy Jones *pd* John Robert Lloyd

Dustin Hoffman, Mia Farrow, Michael Tolan, Sunny Griffin, Tyne Daly

'The emphasis is not on action but on acting, which although skilful and subtly nuanced does not in this case amount to the same thing as character.'—*Jan Dawson*

'Despite all the "now" sets and surfaces, it's like an old comedy of the thirties—minus the comedy.'—*Judith Crist*

John Goldfarb Please Come Home
US 1965 96m De Luxe Cinemascope
TCF / Steve Parker / J. Lee-Thompson

An American spy pilot crashlands near the palace of a Middle Eastern potentate at the same time as a girl reporter arrives for an interview.
Would-be satire on the cold war, anti-feminism, American football, American / Arab relations, etc. None of it works for a minute, and the actors' desperation can be plainly seen.

w William Peter Blatty *d* J. Lee-Thompson *ph* Leon Shamroy *m* Johnny Williams

Shirley Maclaine, Richard Crenna, Peter Ustinov, Fred Clark, Wilfrid Hyde White, Jim Backus

John Loves Mary
US 1948 87m bw
Warner (Jerry Wald)

A GI returns home to get married, but unfortunately, to help a friend, he has already entered into a marriage of convenience.
Moderately amusing comedy with an excess of complications.

w Phoebe and Henry Ephron, *play* Norman Krasna *d* David Butler *ph* Peverell Marley *m* David Buttolph

Ronald Reagan, Patricia Neal, Jack Carson, Virginia Field

John Meade's Woman
US 1937 82m bw

A timber industrialist marries a farm girl.
Solemn star drama. Edward Arnold, Francine Larrimore, Gail Patrick, George Bancroft.
Written by Vincent Lawrence and Herman J. Mankiewicz; directed by Richard Wallace; for Paramount. 'One more picture with a message. Edward Arnold's pictures are beginning to look alike.'—*Variety*

John Paul Jones
US 1959 126m Technirama
Warner / Samuel Bronston

At the time of the American revolution a young Scotsman rises to great heights in the American navy.
Fragmented biopic with a succession of guest stars which turn it into a charade almost as silly as *The Story of Mankind*. On that level it is not unentertaining.

wd John Farrow *ph* Michel Kelber *m* Max Steiner

Robert Stack, Charles Coburn (as Benjamin Franklin), Bette Davis (as Catherine the Great), Marisa Pavan, Jean-Pierre Aumont, Peter Cushing, Bruce Cabot, Macdonald Carey

Johnny Allegro*
US 1949 81m bw
Columbia (Irving Starr)
GB title: *Hounded*

A private eye eliminates a counterfeiter and marries his wife.
Cheeky variation on the plot of *Gilda*, with

Macready repeating his role; later stages borrow from *The Most Dangerous Game*. All mildly diverting.

w Karen de Wolf, Guy Endore, James Edward Grant *d* Ted Tetzlaff *ph* Joseph Biroc *m* George Duning

George Raft, George Macready, Nina Foch, Will Geer, Ivan Triesault

'Without any particular distinction, but certainly not boring.'—*Richard Mallett, Punch*

Johnny Angel*
US 1945 79m bw
RKO (William L. Pereira)

A seaman solves the mystery of his father's ship, found empty and adrift in the Gulf of Mexico.
Very watchable mystery with plenty of plot twists and efficient presentation.

w Steve Fisher *d* Edwin L. Marin *ph* Harry J. Wild *m* Leigh Harline

George Raft, Claire Trevor, Signe Hasso, Lowell Gilmore, Hoagy Carmichael, Marvin Miller

Johnny Apollo
US 1940 93m bw
TCF (Harry Joe Brown)

A well-heeled young man turns crook.
Moderate crime melo, impeccably turned out.

w Philip Dunne, Rowland Brown *d* Henry Hathaway *ph* Arthur Miller *m* Cyril Mockridge *md* Alfred Newman

Tyrone Power, Dorothy Lamour, Edward Arnold, Lloyd Nolan, Charles Grapewin, Lionel Atwill, Marc Lawrence, Jonathan Hale

'There was temptation in her helpless silence—and then torment!'

Johnny Belinda**
US 1948 103m bw
Warner (Jerry Wald)

In a remote fishing community, a deaf mute girl is raped and the sympathetic local doctor is suspected of being the father of her baby.
Melodrama of the old school which in 1948 seemed oddly to mark a new permissiveness and made a big star of Jane Wyman; the production and locations were also persuasive.

w Irmgard Von Cube, Allen Vincent, *play* Elmer Harris *d Jean Negulesco ph Ted McCord m* Max Steiner *md* Leo F. Forbstein

Jane Wyman, Lew Ayres, Charles Bickford, Agnes Moorehead, Stephen McNally, Jan Sterling, Rosalind Ivan, Mabel Paige

'Hollywood has tried something dangerously different here, and succeeded in making a powerful and sensitive job of it.'—*Observer*

'An atmosphere in which the hokey, tearjerking elements are used for more than mere pathos—an example of technique over subject matter.'—*Pauline Kael, 70s*

AA: Jane Wyman
AAN: best picture; script; Jean Negulesco; Ted McCord; Max Steiner; Lew Ayres; Charles Bickford; Agnes Moorehead

Johnny Come Lately*
US 1943 97m bw
Cagney Productions (William Cagney)
GB title: *Johnny Vagabond*

A travelling newspaperman is jailed for vagrancy in a small town and stays to expose corrupt politicians.
A turn-of-the-century folksy drama seemed an odd choice for a Cagney independent production, and it was not very persuasively made, but the star produced moments of his old charisma.

w John Van Druten, *novel* McLeod's Folly by Louis Bromfield *d* William K. Howard *ph* Theodor Sparkuhl *m* Leigh Harline

James Cagney, *Grace George*, Marjorie Main, Marjorie Lord, Hattie McDaniel, Edward McNamara, Bill Henry, Robert Barrat, George Cleveland, Margaret Hamilton, Lucien Littlefield, Irving Bacon

'The kind of business that might result if Jimmy Cagney, the immortal Hollywood movie star, had returned to play the lead in the annual production of his old high school's Masque and Film Club.'—*John T. McManus*

'The film does show a fatal commercial uneasiness and, I half suspect, radical loss or atrophy of cinematic judgment. But . . . there is a general ambience of hope and pleasure about the production which, regrettably, loses its glow.'—*James Agee*

AAN: Leigh Harline

Johnny Comes Flying Home
US 1946 65m bw

Three discharged flyers build an air freight company. *The Best Years of Our Lives* it isn't, not on this budget, but it clumsily expresses some of the same concerns. Richard Crane, Faye Marlowe, Martha Stewart, Roy Roberts, Henry Morgan. Written by Jack Andrews and George Bricker; directed by Ben Stoloff; for Aubrey Schenck / TCF.

Johnny Concho
US 1956 84m bw
UA / Kent (Frank Sinatra)

A coward runs Cripple Creek because he has a gunfighter brother, but when the latter is shot another gunman takes over.
Unexpected small-scale western, pleasantly made but no *High Noon*.

w David P. Harmon, Don McGuire *d* Don McGuire *ph* William Mellor *m* Nelson Riddle

Frank Sinatra, *William Conrad*, Phyllis Kirk, Wallace Ford, John Qualen

Johnny Cool*
US 1963 101m bw
UA / Chrislaw (William Asher)

A Sicilian bandit is sent to the US on a mission of vengeance.
Chilling gangster thriller, the callousness of which is apparently meant to be counterpointed by the humorous cameo appearances of several well-known faces. This does not work.

w Joseph Landon, *novel* John McPartland *d* William Asher *ph* Sam Leavitt *m* Billy May

Henry Silva, Elizabeth Montgomery, Jim Backus, Marc Lawrence, John McGiver, Sammy Davis Jnr, Mort Sahl, Telly Savalas, Joseph Calleia, Robert Armstrong, Douglass Dumbrille, Elisha Cook Jnr

'Organized crime has never been so disorganized!'

Johnny Dangerously
US 1984 90m De Luxe
TCF / Edgewood (Michael Hertzberg)

A boy takes up crime to pay for an operation for his ailing mother.
1930s gangster send-up which fails to register, and is filled with unnecessary excesses.

w Norman Steinberg, Bernie Kukoff, Harry Colomby, Jeff Harris *d* Amy Heckerling *ph* David M. Walsh *m* John Morris *pd* Joseph R. Jennings *ed* Pembroke J. Herring

Michael Keaton, Joe Piscopo, Marilu Henner, Maureen Stapleton, Peter Boyle, Griffin Dunne, Richard Dmitri, Glynnis O'Connor, Dom DeLuise, Ray Walston

'The material given all of them just gets worse and worse.'—*Variety*

Johnny Dark
US 1954 85m Technicolor
U-I (William Alland)

A motor company produces a new sports car designed by an employee, who drives it in a race.
Competent, unremarkable action melodrama tailor-made for its star.

w Franklin Coen *d* George Sherman *ph* Carl Guthrie *m* Hans Salter

Tony Curtis, Piper Laurie, Don Taylor, Paul Kelly, Ilka Chase, Sidney Blackmer

Johnny Doesn't Live Here Any More
US 1944 bw 77m

A girl using her army boy friend's Washington flat finds that he has loaned keys to several friends. Tepid farce which presumably amused at the time. Simone Simon, James Ellison, William Terry, Minna Gombell, Chick Chandler, Alan Dinehart, Robert Mitchum. Written by Philip Yordan, John H. Kafka; directed by Joe May; for Maurice and Frank King / Monogram.

Johnny Doughboy
US 1943 bw 64m

A teenage girl star runs away, falls for a middle-aged playwright, and joins an acting troupe called The Hollywood Victory Caravan. Curious attempt to make a child star grow up, with a supporting cast laced with others of her ilk. Jane Withers, Henry Wilcoxon, William Demarest, Ruth Donnelly; and Bobby Breen, Baby Sandy, Butch and Buddy, Spanky McFarland, etc. Written by Lawrence Kimble; directed and produced by John H. Auer; for Republic. AAN: Walter Scharf (music).

Johnny Eager*
US 1942 107m bw
MGM (John W. Considine)

A gangster makes a play for a society girl. Well-made, rather unattractive gangster melodrama.

w John Lee Mahin, James Edward Grant *d* Mervyn Le Roy *ph* Harold Rosson *m* Bronislau Kaper

Robert Taylor, *Van Heflin*, Lana Turner, Edward Arnold, Robert Sterling, Patricia Dane, Glenda Farrell, Henry O'Neill

'The flaming drama of a high-born beauty who blindly loved the most icy-hearted big shot gangland ever knew!'—*publicity*

AA: Van Heflin

Johnny Frenchman
GB 1945 111m bw
Ealing (S. C. Balcon)

Rivalry between the fishermen of Cornwall and Brittany prevents the course of true love from running smooth.
Rhubarbing extras and studio sets make this an unreal and disappointing Ealing melodrama, and all the actors look helpless.

w T. E. B. Clarke *d* Charles Frend *ph* Roy Kellino *m* Clifton Parker

Françoise Rosay, Tom Walls, Patricia Roc, Paul Dupuis, Ralph Michael, Frederick Piper, Arthur Hambling

Johnny Got His Gun
US 1971 111m colour
World Entertainments Ltd (Bruce Campbell)

In 1918 a soldier is so badly wounded as to lose arms, legs, eyes, ears, mouth and nose, and begs his doctors to kill him.
A horrifying and fascinating premise turns out to have nowhere to go, at least not in this talky treatment which the author has nurtured too long.

wd Dalton Trumbo *ph* Jules Brenner *m* Jerry Fielding

Timothy Bottoms, Jason Robards Jnr, Marsha Hunt, Donald Sutherland, Kathy Fields, Diane Varsi

Johnny Guitar*
US 1953 110m Trucolor
Republic (Nicholas Ray)

In old Arizona, the proprietress of a gambling saloon stakes a claim to valuable land and incurs the enmity of a lady banker.
Weird Freudian western notable for a running catfight between its lady protagonists; the title character is decidedly secondary. Not exactly a good movie, but memorable because it's almost always over the top.

w Philip Yordan, *novel* Roy Chanslor *d* Nicholas Ray *ph* Harry Stradling *m* Victor Young

Joan Crawford, Mercedes McCambridge, Sterling Hayden, Ernest Borgnine, Ward Bond, John Carradine, Scott Brady

'A very rum western, with cockeyed feminist attitudes.'—*New Yorker, 1975*

Johnny Holiday
US 1949 92m bw

A reform school boy becomes a goodie through devotion to his sergeant. Sentimental mush. William Bendix, Stanley Clements, Allen Martin Jnr, Herbert Newcomb, Hoagy Carmichael. Written by Jack Andrews, Willis Goldbeck and Frederick Stephani; directed by Willis Goldbeck; for R. W. Alcorn / United Artists.

Johnny Nobody
GB 1960 88m bw Warwickscope
Columbia / Viceroy (Irving Allen, Albert Broccoli)

A drunken Irish author challenges God to strike him dead for blasphemy. When an amnesiac shoots him, a nationwide religious controversy begins, but the deed is found to have a mercenary motive.
A mysterious rigmarole which irritates more than it entertains.

w Patrick Kirwan, *story* The Trial of Johnny Nobody by Albert Z. Carr *d* Nigel Patrick *ph* Ted Moore *m* Ron Goodwin

Nigel Patrick, Aldo Ray, Yvonne Mitchell, William Bendix, Cyril Cusack, Niall MacGinnis, Bernie Winters, Noel Purcell, Jimmy O'Dea

'The more one thinks of it, the more one is amazed that anyone should have thought a plot and players as uniformly unlikely as these could have worked out satisfactorily.'—*Peter John Dyer, MFB*

Johnny O'Clock
US 1946 95m bw

A gambler appears to be involved in the death of a crooked policeman, but a girl helps to clear him. Tawdry material made palatable by surface slickness. Dick Powell, Ellen Drew, Lee J. Cobb, Evelyn Keyes. Written and directed by Robert Rossen; photographed by Burnett Guffey; for Columbia.

Johnny One-Eye
US 1950 80m bw

Two gangsters out to get each other are led together by a small girl and a dog.
Unpalatable mixture of violence and sentiment. Pat O'Brien, Wayne Morris, Dolores Moran, Gayle Reed. Written by Richard E. Landau, from a story by Damon Runyon; directed by Robert Florey; for Benedict Bogeaus / United Artists.

Johnny Rocco
US 1958 83m bw

The small son of a gangster is affected by his father's notoriety. Awful sentimental melodrama with tear-stained ending; for connoisseurs of cliché. Richard Eyer, Stephen McNally, Coleen Gray, Russ Conway. Written by James O'Hanlon and Samuel F. Roeca; directed by Paul Landres; for Allied Artists.

'Their bullets talked where law stopped!'

Johnny Stool Pigeon
US 1949 75m bw
U-I (Aaron Rosenberg)

A detective releases a convict on condition that he leads him to a drug smuggling gang.
Competent low budget addition to the documentary police cycle.

w Robert L. Richards *d* William Castle *ph* Maury Gertsman *m* Milton Schwarzwald

Howard Duff, Shelley Winters, Dan Duryea, Gary Moore, Tony Curtis, John McIntire, Barry Kelley, Leif Erickson

Johnny Tremain
US 1957 81m Technicolor
Walt Disney

In 1773 Boston an apprentice silversmith joins the Sons of Liberty and helps start the War of Independence.
Schoolbook history with little vitality.

w Tom Blackburn, *novel* Esther Forbes *d* Robert Stevenson *ph* Charles B. Boyle *m* George Bruns

Hal Stalmaster, Luana Patten, Jeff York, Sebastian Cabot, Richard Beymer, Walter Sande

Johnny Trouble
US 1956 88m bw
Clarion (John H. Auer)

An elderly widow becomes involved with a boys' college and thinks she has found her lost grandson.
Sentimental, whimsical star vehicle.

w Charles O'Neal, David Lord *d* John H. Auer *ph* Peverell Marley *m* Frank de Vol

Ethel Barrymore, Stuart Whitman, Cecil Kellaway, Carolyn Jones, Jesse White

The Johnstown Flood*
US 1926 70m approx (24 fps) bw silent
Fox

A construction worker is warned by his girl friend of an approaching flood, in which she dies.
Curious melodrama with mild spectacle.

w Efrid Bingham, Robert Lord *d* Irving Cummings

George O'Brien, Janet Gaynor (her first film), Paul Panzer, George Harris

The Joker Is Wild*
US 1957 126m bw Vistavision
Paramount / Charles Vidor

Joe E. Lewis, a twenties nightclub singer, loses his voice after an attack by gangsters, and becomes a comedian.
Reasonably lively showbiz biopic in jaundiced vein; good atmosphere but far too long.

w Oscar Saul, *book* Art Cohn *d* Charles Vidor *ph* Daniel L. Fapp *m* Walter Scharf

Frank Sinatra, Mitzi Gaynor, Eddie Albert, Jeanne Crain, Beverly Garland, Jackie Coogan, Ted de Corsia

AA: song 'All the Way' (*m* Jimmy Van Heusen, *ly* Sammy Cahn)

The Jokers**
GB 1967 126m Technicolor
Universal / Adastra / Gildor / Scimitar (Maurice Foster, Ben Arbeid)

Two young brothers in London society plan to create a sensation by borrowing (and replacing) the crown jewels.
Bright suspense comedy which sums up the swinging London era pretty well and is generally amusing though it finally lacks aplomb.

w Dick Clement, Ian La Frenais d Michael Winner ph Ken Hodges *m* Johnny Pearson

Michael Crawford, Oliver Reed, Harry Andrews, *James Donald*, Daniel Massey, Michael Hordern, Gabriella Licudi, Frank Finlay, Warren Mitchell, Rachel Kempson, Peter Graves

A Jolly Bad Fellow*
GB 1964 95m bw
British Lion / Pax / Tower / Michael Balcon (Donald Taylor)
US title: *They All Died Laughing*

A brash chemistry don tries a new poison on his enemies.
Interesting but finally irritating comedy of murders with a punnish rather than a donnish script and only moments of genuine sub-Ealing hilarity.

w Robert Hamer, Donald Taylor, *novel* Don Among the Dead Men by C. E. Vulliamy *d* Robert Hamer *ph* Gerald Gibbs *m* John Barry

Leo McKern, Janet Munro, Maxine Audley, Duncan Macrae, Dennis Price, Miles Malleson, Leonard Rossiter

Jolson Sings Again**
US 1949 96m Technicolor
Columbia (Sidney Buchman)

Al Jolson's later career and second marriage to a nurse he met while entertaining troops in World War II.
Breezy, routine, rather empty sequel to the following.

w Sidney Buchman *d* Henry Levin *ph* William Snyder *md* Morris Stoloff, George Duning

Larry Parks, Barbara Hale, William Demarest, Ludwig Donath, Bill Goodwin, Tamara Shayne, Myron McCormick

'Just relax and enjoy yourself.'—*Daily Express*

'I love it now—every last sentimental showbiz cliché, every oversung song.'—*Daily Telegraph, 1969*

† 3rd biggest moneyspinner of 1946, after *The Best Years of Our Lives* and *Duel in the Sun*

AAN: Sidney Buchman; William Snyder; Morris Stoloff, George Duning

The Jolson Story****
US 1946 129m Technicolor
Columbia (Sidney Skolsky)

Asa Yoelson, son of a cantor, becomes Al Jolson, the great entertainer of the twenties; but showbiz success brings marital difficulties.
Whitewashed biopic in impeccable Hollywood style, with everything working shamelessly right, a new star in the leading role, perfect if unambitious production values, and a deluge of the best songs ever written.

w Stephen Longstreet d Alfred E. Green, Joseph H. Lewis ph Joseph Walker *md* Morris Stoloff

Larry Parks (using Jolson's own voice), *William Demarest, Evelyn Keyes, Ludwig Donath, Tamara Shayne*, Bill Goodwin, *Scotty Beckett*, John Alexander

'I have nothing in the world against this picture except that at least half of it seemed to me enormously tiresome.'—*James Agee*

AA: Morris Stoloff
AAN: Joseph Walker; Larry Parks; William Demarest

'Everyone's book is now everyone's motion picture!'

Jonathan Livingston Seagull
US 1973 114m De Luxe Panavision
Paramount / JLS Partnership / Hall Bartlett

The life of a seagull who aims to fly faster than any of his peers and eventually arrives in a perfect world.
Weird 'family' fantasy based on a phenomenally successful book which clearly could not translate easily to the screen. The bird photography is much more successful than the mysticism.

w Richard Bach, from his book *d* Hall Bartlett *ph Jack Couffer m* Neil Diamond, Lee Holdridge *ph* Boris Leven

'A parable couched in the form of a nature film of overpowering beauty and strength in which, perhaps to our horror, we are forced to recognize ourselves in a seagull obsessed with the heights.'—*Michael Korda*

'It may be that the creature best qualified to review it is another seagull.'—*Benny Green, Punch*

'If one must spend two hours following the adventures of a bird, far better that the hero be Donald Duck.'—*Jay Cocks, Time*

'The sort of garbage that only a seagull could love.'—*Judith Crist*

AAN: Jack Couffer

The Jones Family
Less human, more farcical than the Hardy films (qv), this series was TCF's second feature answer to MGM's money-makers, and pleased a lot of people at the time. Pop was Jed Prouty, Mom was Spring Byington, Grandma was Florence Roberts, and the youngsters included Kenneth Howell, George Ernest, Billy Mahan, June Carlson and June Lang. The first script was from a play by Katharine Cavanaugh, and the principal director was Frank Strayer.
1936: EVERY SATURDAY NIGHT, EDUCATING FATHER, BACK TO NATURE
1937: OFF TO THE RACES, BORROWING TROUBLE, HOT WATER
1938: LOVE ON A BUDGET, TRIP TO PARIS, SAFETY IN NUMBERS, DOWN ON THE FARM
1939: EVERYBODY'S BABY, QUICK MILLIONS, THE JONES FAMILY IN HOLLYWOOD, TOO BUSY TO WORK
1940: ON THEIR OWN

† An earlier series with different actors was abandoned after two episodes: *Young as You Feel* (1931), *Business and Pleasure* (1932).

Joseph Andrews
GB 1977 104m Eastmancolor
UA / Woodfall (Neil Hartley)

Adventures of a naïve 18th-century footman.
Woebegone attempt to restage *Tom Jones*.

w Allan Scott, Chris Bryant *d* Tony Richardson *ph* David Watkin *m* John Addison *pd* Michael Annals

Peter Firth, Ann-Margret, Michael Hordern, Beryl Reid, Jim Dale, Peter Bull, John Gielgud, Hugh Griffith, Timothy West, Wendy Craig, Peggy Ashcroft, James Villiers, Karen Dotrice, Ronald Pickup

'Even the incidental pleasures cannot offset the sense of *déjà vu* which pervades this musty enterprise.'—*John Pym, MFB*

'The epic love story in which everybody has a great role and a big part.'—*publicity*

Josephine and Men
GB 1955 98m Eastmancolor
Charter (John and Roy Boulting)

The three romances of a determined young woman.
Alarmingly thin, old-fashioned romantic comedy with all resolved in a country cottage. Nothing quite works, especially the colour.

w Nigel Balchin, Roy Boulting, Frank Harvey *d* Roy Boulting *ph* Gilbert Taylor *m* John Addison

Glynis Johns, *Jack Buchanan*, Donald Sinden, Peter Finch, Heather Thatcher, Ronald Squire

Josette
US 1938 73m bw
TCF (Gene Markey)

A New Orleans coquette teases two men.
Very minor musical, well enough presented but adding up to almost nothing.

w James Edward Grant *d* Allan Dwan *ph* John Mescall *songs* Harry Revel, Mack Gordon

Simone Simon, Don Ameche, Robert Young, Joan Davis, Bert Lahr, Paul Hurst, William Collier Snr, Lynn Bari, William Demarest

'Rollicking farce with music . . . a corking good entertainment.'—*Variety*

Jour de Fête***
France 1948 87m bw
Francinex (Fred Orain)

A village postman sees a film about the efficiency of the American postal service and decides to smarten himself up.
First, and some say best, of Tati's comedy vehicles: two-thirds superb local colour, one-third hilarious slapstick.

w Jacques Tati, Henri Marquet *d Jacques Tati ph* Jacques Mercanton *m* Jean Yatove

Jacques Tati, Guy Decomble, Paul Fankeur, Santa Relli

'You could watch it with a bout of toothache and it would make you laugh.'—*Daily Express*

† A reissue version had colour items hand-painted in each frame, and proved quite effective.

Le Jour Se Lève***
France 1939 95m bw
Sigma
aka: *Daybreak*

A murderer is besieged by police in his attic room, remembers his past through the night, and shoots himself.
A model of French poetic realism, and a much-praised film which was almost destroyed when it was bought for an American remake (*The Long Night*).

w Jacques Viot, Jacques Prévert d Marcel Carné ph Curt Courant, Philippe Agostini, André Bac *m* Maurice Jaubert *ad* Alexander Trauner

Jean Gabin, Jules Berry, Arletty, Jacqueline Laurent

'The man walks about his room, moves a few things, lies on his bed, looks out of the window, chain-smokes . . . and one is genuinely interested in him all the time (remembering afterwards that there exist directors who contrive to be boring even when they use fifteen characters in a motor car chase crackling with revolver shots).'—*Richard Mallett, Punch*

Journal of a Crime
US 1934 65m bw

A woman shoots her husband's mistress and gets amnesia before she can confess.
Melodramatic farrago which entertains by its very excesses. Ruth Chatterton, Adolphe Menjou, Claire Dodd, Douglass Dumbrille, George Barbier. Written by F. Hugh Herbert and Charles Kenyon from the play by Jacques Deval; directed by William Keighley; for Warner. 'High in sympathetic interest and force.'—*Variety*

The Journey
US 1959 125m Technicolor
MGM / Alby (Anatole Litvak)

During the 1956 Hungarian uprising, a busload of international passengers is detained overnight by a Russian major.
Pretentious, predictable and dull multi-melodrama peopled by uninteresting characters; different handling might have made a *Casablanca* of it.

w George Tabori *d* Anatole Litvak *ph* Jack Hildyard *m* Georges Auric

Yul Brynner, Deborah Kerr, Jason Robards Jnr, Anouk Aimée, Robert Morley, E. G. Marshall, Anne Jackson, David Kossoff, Kurt Kasznar, Gerard Oury

'Ten minutes of this and we know where we are: we are back in the 1930s with Alfred Hitchcock and that glamorous band of international characters trapped in Mitteleuropa.'—*Steven Marcus*

Journey Back to Oz*
US 1964 (released 1974) 90m colour

Dorothy makes a return journey over the rainbow to fight the wicked witch's sister.
Competent cartoon version of Frank Baum themes from *The Wizard of Oz*. Voices: Liza Minnelli, Milton Berle, Ethel Merman, Margaret Hamilton, Mickey Rooney, Paul Ford, etc. Conceived and produced by Norm Prescott and Lou Scheimer; directed by Hal Sutherland; for Filmation.

Journey for Margaret*
US 1942 81m bw
MGM (B. P. Fineman)

An American correspondent brings home an orphan from the London blitz.
Efficient tearful propaganda which coincidentally made a star of little Margaret O'Brien.

w David Hertz, William Ludwig, *book* William L. White *d* W. S. Van Dyke *ph* Ray June *m* Franz Waxman

Robert Young, Laraine Day, *Margaret O'Brien*, Billy Severn, Fay Bainter, Signe Hasso, Nigel Bruce, Halliwell Hobbes

Journey into Autumn*
Sweden 1954 86m bw
Sandrews (Rune Waldekrantz)
original title: *Kvinnodrom*

Two business women visiting Gothenburg have difficult relationships to settle.
Moody, impressionist sex drama which succeeds by fits and starts.

wd Ingmar Bergman *ph* Hilding Bladh

Eva Dahlbeck, Harriet Andersson, Gunnar Bjornstrand, Ulf Palme, Inga Landgre, Naima Wifstrand

'Scenes of austere anti-romanticism and painful irony.'—*Peter John Dyer, MFB*

Journey into Fear***
US 1942 71m bw
RKO (Orson Welles)

A munitions expert finds himself in danger from assassins in Istanbul, and has to be smuggled home.
Highly enjoyable impressionist melodrama supervised by Orson Welles and full of his touches and excesses.

w Joseph Cotten, Orson Welles, novel Eric Ambler d Norman Foster (and *Orson Welles*) *ph Karl Struss m* Roy Webb *md* Constantin Bakaleinikoff

Joseph Cotten, Dolores del Rio, Jack Moss, Orson Welles, Ruth Warrick, Agnes Moorehead

'Brilliant atmosphere, the nightmare of pursuit, eccentric encounters on the way, and when the shock comes it leaps at eye and ear.'—*William Whitebait*

† A 1976 remake, much heralded, was for obscure legal reasons hardly seen. Directed by Daniel Mann for New World, it starred Zero Mostel, Shelley Winters, Stanley Holloway, Vincent Price, Donald Pleasence, Sam Waterston, Joseph Wiseman, Scott Marlowe and Yvette Mimieux.

Journey into Light
US 1951 87m bw
TCF / Joseph Bernhard

A minister loses his faith, becomes a derelict, and is reformed by a blind girl.
An old-fashioned tract in pictures. Has to be seen to be believed, but quite nicely made.

w Stephanie Nordli, Irving Schulman *d* Stuart Heisler

Sterling Hayden, Viveca Lindfors, Thomas Mitchell, H. B. Warner, Ludwig Donath, Jane Darwell, Charles Evans

'Slow, inept, and often extremely embarrassing.'—*MFB*

The Journey of Natty Gann
US 1985 105m colour
Walt Disney (Michael Lobell)

During the Chicago depression, a girl follows her father west and hitch-hikes across America.
A kind of human *Lassie Come Home*: doggedly watchable but not inspiring, especially since it was shot in Canada.

w Jeanne Rosenberg *d* Jeremy Kagan *ph* Richard Bush *m* James Horner

Meredith Salenger, John Cusack, Ray Wise, Scatman Crothers

'Cut to an hour, it would make a fine Disney telepic.'—*Variety*

Journey to Shiloh
US 1966 101m Techniscope

Seven young Texans leave home to fight in the Civil War. Episodic western which failed in its ambition to reach epic stature. James Caan, Michael Sarrazin, Brenda Scott, Paul Petersen, Don Stroud, Michael Burns, Michael Vincent, Harrison Ford, John Doucette, Noah Beery Jnr. Written by Gene Coon, from the novel *Fields of Honour* by Will Henry; directed by William Hale; for Universal.

Journey to the Center of the Earth***
US 1959 132m De Luxe Cinemascope
TCF (Charles Brackett)

An Edinburgh professor and assorted colleagues follow an explorer's trail down an extinct Icelandic volcano to the earth's centre.
Enjoyable hokum which gets more and more fantastic but only occasionally misses its footing; it ends splendidly with the team being catapulted out of Stromboli on a tide of lava.

w Walter Reisch, Charles Brackett, novel Jules Verne *d Henry Levin ph* Leo Tover *m Bernard Herrmann ad* Lyle R. Wheeler, Franz Bachelin, Herman A. Blumenthal

James Mason, Arlene Dahl, Pat Boone, Peter Ronson, Diane Baker, Thayer David

'The attraction of a Jules Verne fantasy . . . is in the endearing contrast between the wildest adventures and the staidest Victorian propriety on the part of those undergoing them . . . There is about the whole film a good-natured enjoyment of its own excesses.'—*Penelope Houston*

Journey to the Far Side of the Sun*
GB 1969 99m De Luxe Cinemascope
Universal / Century 21 Productions (Gerry Anderson)
Alternative title: *Doppelgänger*

An astronaut on a mission to a hitherto undetected planet discovers it to be an exact duplicate of Earth, and his own double returns in his place.

Intriguing, impeccably produced, but rather dull science fiction.

w Gerry and Sylvia Anderson, Donald James *d* Robert Parrish *ph* John Read *m* Barry Gray *sp* Harry Oakes *models* Derek Meddings

Ian Hendry, Roy Thinnes, Patrick Wymark, Lynn Loring, Herbert Lom, George Sewell, Ed Bishop

Journey Together*

GB 1944 95m bw
RAF Film Unit (John Boulting)

Trainee pilots receive instruction in England and America before going on their first bombing mission.
Modest wartime semi-documentary, pleasingly done.

w Terence Rattigan *d* John Boulting *ph* Harry Waxman *m* Gordon Jacob *pd* John Howell

Richard Attenborough, Jack Watling, David Tomlinson, Edward G. Robinson, Hugh Wakefield, Sebastian Shaw, Ronald Adam, Bessie Love

'It has a natural dignity as well as a natural fun.'—*Listener*

'One of the most realistic and brilliant films of the war in the air.'—*News Chronicle*

Journey's End*

GB-US 1930 120m bw
Gainsborough / Welsh-Pearson / Tiffany-Stahl (George Pearson)

France 1917: personal tensions mount as men die in the trenches.
Primitive early sound version (made in Hollywood because of better equipment) of a justly celebrated play first performed a year earlier. Cinematically uninteresting, with acting generally over the top, but it kept Whale and Clive in Hollywood where they shortly collaborated on *Frankenstein*.

w Joseph Moncure March, Gareth Gundrey, *play R. C. Sheriff* *d* James Whale *ph* Benjamin Kline *m* none

Colin Clive, Ian MacLaren, David Manners, Billy Bevan, Anthony Bushell, Robert Adair

'No crystal gazing required to forecast a big measure of success.'—*Variety*

'It has been transferred to the screen with the greatest possible tact and discretion.'—*James Agate*

'Hollywood has produced its first sex-appeal-less film. Mr George Pearson is to be congratulated on his restraint.'—*Punch*

'Almost painfully English . . . I cannot believe that the strangulated emotions which resulted can have meant much to audiences outside the English-speaking world.'—*Basil Wright, 1972*

† NB: The first Anglo-American co-production.

Joy House

US 1964 98m colour Franscope

The husband of a wealthy American woman in France tries to kill her boy friend. Weird hothouse drama, an unsuccessful attempt to combine French and American styles. Jane Fonda, Alain Delon, Lola Albright. Written by René Clément, Pascal Jardin and Charles Williams; directed by René Clément; for Jacques Bar / MGM. (Aka: *The Love Cage*.)

Joy in the Morning

US 1965 103m Metrocolor
MGM (Henry T. Weinstein)

Early episodes in the marriage of a poor teenage student.
Glutinous romantic drama, quite well made.

w Sally Benson, Alfred Hayes, Norman Lessing, *novel* Betty Smith *d* Alex Segal *ph* Ellsworth Fredericks *m* Bernard Herrmann

Richard Chamberlain, Yvette Mimieux, Arthur Kennedy, Oscar Homolka, Joan Tetzel, Sidney Blackmer

Joy of Living*

US 1938 90m bw
RKO (Felix Young)

A practical-minded Broadway songstress succumbs to the charms of an aristocratic freewheeler.
Zany romantic comedy, not quite zippy enough to make one forget its irritating archness, but socio-historically very interesting, in the mould of *You Can't Take It with You*.

w Gene Towne, Allan Scott, Graham Baker *d* Tay Garnett *ph* Joseph Walker *md* Frank Tours *songs* Jerome Kern, Dorothy Fields

Irene Dunne, Douglas Fairbanks Jnr, Alice Brady, Guy Kibbee, Lucille Ball, Eric Blore, Jean Dixon, Warren Hymer, Billy Gilbert

'Fair farce . . . bereft of sufficient novelty or comedy plot to sustain itself through an hour and a half of gags.'—*Variety*

Joyless Street*

Germany 1925 139m (24 fps) bw silent
Sofar Film
original title: *Die Freudlose Gasse*

Problems of the inhabitants of a street in Vienna after World War I.
Realistic but studio-set melodrama which brought its director and Greta Garbo to international fame. In itself the film begins by stimulating and ends by boring.

w Willy Haas, *novel* Hugo Bettauer *d G. W. Pabst* *ph* Guido Seeber, Curt Oertel, Robert Lach

Asta Nielsen, Werner Krauss, *Greta Garbo*, Valeska Gert, Agnes Esterhazy

'Moments of searing pain, of mental anguish, of sheer unblemished beauty.'—*Paul Rotha, The Film Till Now*

'See it now! Remember it always!'
'A story so momentous it required six Academy Award stars and a cast of 1,186 players!'

Juarez**

US 1939 132m bw
Warner (Hal. B. Wallis, Henry Blanke)

A revolutionary leader causes the downfall of Emperor Maximilian of Mexico.
Spectacular historical drama with many fine moments which do not quite coalesce into a dramatic whole, chiefly owing to the lack of a single viewpoint.

w John Huston, Wolfgang Reinhardt, Aeneas Mackenzie *d William Dieterle* *ph Tony Gaudio* *m Erich Wolfgang Korngold*

Brian Aherne, Bette Davis, Paul Muni, Claude Rains, John Garfield, Donald Crisp, Gale Sondergaard, Joseph Calleia, Gilbert Roland, Henry O'Neill, Pedro de Cordoba, Montagu Love, Harry Davenport

'With such potent box office values, its success at theatres seems assured.'—*Variety*

'A million dollars' worth of ballroom sets, regimentals, gauze shots and whiskers.'—*Otis Ferguson*

'Dramatically by far the most effective of Warners' biographical films of the thirties.'—*Graham Greene*

'Muni's big-star solemn righteousness is like a dose of medicine.'—*New Yorker, 1977*

† Based vaguely on two novels: *The Phantom Crown* by Bertita Harding, and *Maximilian and Carlotta* by Franz Werfel.

†† According to Brian Aherne the film was to have been called *The Phantom Crown*, but Muni's contract enabled him to insist that the name of his character should appear in the title.

AAN: Brian Aherne

Jubal

US 1955 101m Technicolor Cinemascope
Columbia (William Fadiman)

A rancher's wife causes trouble when she falls in love with a wandering cowhand.
Solid sex western, moderately interestingly done.

w Russell S. Hughes, Delmer Daves, *novel* Jubal Troop by Paul Wellman *d* Delmer Daves *ph* Charles Lawton *m* David Raksin

Glenn Ford, Ernest Borgnine, Felicia Farr, Rod Steiger, Valerie French, Charles Bronson, Noah Beery Jnr

Jubilee*

GB 1978 104m colour
Whaley-Malin / Megalovision

Queen Elizabeth I is transported by her astrologer into the latter part of the 20th century, and is appalled by what she sees.
Outrageous dissection of modern urban life, full of black jokes: it has the right attitudes but is not free of a determination to shock at all costs.

w Derek Jarman and others *d* Derek Jarman *ph* Peter Middleton *m* Brian Eno

Jenny Runacre, Little Nell, Toyah Willcox, Jordan, Hermine Demoriane

'One of the most intelligent and interesting films to be made in Britain in a long time.'—*Scott Meek, MFB*

JUAREZ. Warner Brothers mount a lavish display for their dignified biopic, and bemedalled Donald Crisp demonstrates that he knows just how to treat dignified Bette Davis.

Jubilee Trail*
US 1954 103m Trucolor
Republic (Joseph Kane)

Jealousy and murder by covered wagon en route from New Orleans to the California gold fields.
Bumpy adventure melodrama, generally quite entertaining.

w Bruce Manning, *novel* Gwen Bristow *d* Joseph Kane *ph* Jack Marta *m* Victor Young

Vera Hruba Ralston, Forrest Tucker, Joan Leslie, Pat O'Brien, John Russell, Ray Middleton

Judex**
France 1916 12 episodes totalling 5 hours approx bw silent
Gaumont

A Robin Hood type crimefighter destroys the empire of an evil banker.
Stylishly enjoyable serial from the maker of *Les Vampires* and *Fantômas*.

w Arthur Bernade, Louis Feuillade *d Louis Feuillade*

René Creste, Musidora, Yvette Andreyor, Louis Leubas

† Another *Judex* serial was made in 1917, and in 1933 came a feature version directed by Maurice Champreux, with René Ferte. In 1963 Georges Franju directed another feature remake with Channing Pollock, and this was extremely well received.

Judge Priest*
US 1934 79m bw

A political judge sees fair play through a criminal case. Mainly effective star vehicle.
Will Rogers, Tom Brown, Anita Louise, *Henry B. Walthall*, David Landau, Rochelle Hudson. Written by Dudley Nichols, Lamar Trotti, from the stories by Irvin S. Cobb; directed by John Ford; for Fox. 'A great part for Will Rogers and a box office bet.'—*Variety*

The Judge Steps Out*
US 1947 91m bw
RKO
GB title: *Indian Summer*

A middle-aged judge leaves his wife and sets off on an aimless journey in the course of which he falls in love with a café proprietress.
A pleasing human story, simply told in a manner which at the time seemed more French than American.

w Boris Ingster, Alexander Knox *d* Boris Ingster *ph* Robert de Grasse *m* Constantin Bakaleinikoff

Alexander Knox, Ann Sothern, George Tobias, Sharyn Moffett

'The things you'll see and the things you'll feel are the things that will be part of you as long as you live!'
Judgment at Nuremberg**
US 1961 190m bw
UA / Roxlom (Stanley Kramer)

A fictionalized version of the 1948 trial of the Nazi leaders for crimes against humanity.
Interminable, heavy-going dramatic documentary expanded from a succinct TV play into a courtroom marathon with philosophical asides. All good stuff, but too much of it.

w Abby Mann, from his play *d* Stanley Kramer *ph* Ernest Laszlo *m* Ernest Gold *pd* Rudolph Sternad

Spencer Tracy, Marlene Dietrich, Burt Lancaster, Richard Widmark, *Maximilian Schell*, Judy Garland, Montgomery Clift, William Shatner, Edward Binns, Werner Klemperer, Torben Meyer, Alan Baxter, Ray Teal

'Some believe that by tackling such themes Kramer earns at least partial remission from criticism. How much? 20 per cent off for effort?'—*Stanley Kauffmann*

† Burt Lancaster replaced Laurence Olivier, who was originally cast.

AA: Abby Mann; Maximilian Schell
AAN: best picture; Stanley Kramer; Ernest Laszlo; Spencer Tracy; Judy Garland; Montgomery Clift

Judgment Deferred
GB 1951 88m bw
Group Three (John Baxter)

A collection of Dorset eccentrics brings to book the head of a dope smuggling ring who has framed one of their associates.
An unusual story can't compensate for stagey handling in this first disappointing production of a company set up by the National Film Finance Corporation to make low budget films with top talent.

w Geoffrey Orme, Barbara Emary, Walter Meade *d* John Baxter *ph* Arthur Grant *m* Kennedy Russell

Hugh Sinclair, Helen Shingler, Abraham Sofaer, Leslie Dwyer, Joan Collins, Harry Locke, Elwyn Brook Jones, Bransby Williams, Maire O'Neill, Harry Welchman

† This was an expanded remake of *Dosshouse*.

Judith
US 1965 109m Technicolor Panavision
Paramount / Cumulus / Command (Kurt Unger)

In 1947 Israel, loyalists rescue the wife of an escaped war criminal and ask her to identify him, but she takes her own revenge.
Glowering kibbutz adventures, well enough made but adding up to neither one thing nor the other, and rather confusing to non-Jews.

w Jon Michael Hayes, *story* Lawrence Durrell *d* Daniel Mann *ph* John Wilcox *m* Sol Kaplan *pd* Wilfrid Shingleton

Sophia Loren, Peter Finch, Jack Hawkins, Hans Verner, André Morell

Judith of Bethulia
US 1913 42m (24 fps) bw silent
D. W. Griffith for Biograph

A widow in a city attacked by the Assyrians courts their leader and beheads him.
Semi-biblical melodrama in Griffith's most Victorian style.

w Frank Woods *d* D. W. Griffith *ph* Billy Bitzer

Blanche Sweet, Henry B. Walthall, Lillian Gish, Dorothy Gish, Lionel Barrymore, Mae Marsh, Robert Harron

Juggernaut
GB 1937 64m bw
Ambassador (Julius Hagen)

A scientist lacking funds for his experiments agrees to commit murder.
Tedious melodrama which wastes Karloff's time.

w Cyril Campion, H. Fowler Mear, H. Fraenkel *d* Henry Edwards *ph* Sidney Blythe

Boris Karloff, Mona Goya, Joan Wyndham, Arthur Margetson, Anthony Ireland, Morton Selten

'It gets into motion slowly and reaches the meat of the plot after numerous distractions.'—*Variety*

Juggernaut**
GB 1974 110m De Luxe Panavision
United Artists / David E. Picker (Richard Alan Simmons)

A transatlantic liner is threatened by a mad bomber.
Elaborate suspense spectacular, most of which works pretty well.

w Richard Alan Simmons *d* Richard Lester *ph* Gerry Fisher *m* Ken Thorne *pd* Terence Marsh

Richard Harris, David Hemmings, Omar Sharif, Anthony Hopkins, Ian Holm, Shirley Knight, Roy Kinnear, Cyril Cusack, Freddie Jones

'However unoriginal its basic ingredients, it hardly ever slackens its pace or diverts attention from its central premise.'—*Jonathan Rosenbaum*

'Jaunty, cynical slapstick.'—*New Yorker*

The Juggler
US 1953 88m bw
Columbia / Stanley Kramer

A Jewish refugee in Palestine has a horror of being imprisoned, and runs away from a transit camp with a small wandering boy.
Well-meaning cheapie, a curiously aimless topical drama which fails to make any of its several points.

w Michael Blankfort, from his novel *d* Edward Dmytryk *ph* Roy Hunt *m* Georges Antheil

Kirk Douglas, Milly Vitale, Paul Stewart, Joey Walsh

Juke Girl
US 1942 90m bw
Warner (Jack Saper, Jerry Wald)

Fruit workers in Florida get involved in murder.
Hokum melodrama with all concerned treading water.

w A. I. Bezzerides, *novel* Theodore Pratt *d* Curtis Bernhardt *ph* Bert Glennon *m* Adolph Deutsch

Ann Sheridan, Ronald Reagan, Richard Whorf, Gene Lockhart, Faye Emerson, George Tobias, Alan Hale, Howard da Silva, Donald McBride, Fuzzy Knight, Willie Best

Jules et Jim**
France 1962 105m bw Franscope
Films du Carrosse / SEDIF (Marcel Berbert)

Before World War I, in Paris, a girl alternates between a French and a German student, and after the war they meet again to form a constantly shifting triangle.
The plot bores before the end, but the treatment is consistently interesting and the acting almost equally so.

w François Truffaut, Jean Gruault, novel Henri-Pierre Roche *d François Truffaut* *ph* Raoul Coutard *m* Georges Delerue

Oskar Werner, Jeanne Moreau, Henri Serre

'The sense is of a director intoxicated with the pleasure of making films.'—*Penelope Houston, MFB*

'A story of turmoil, of courage, of love!'
Julia**
US 1977 117m Technicolor
TCF (Julien Derode)

Lillian Hellman reflects on the fortunes of her friend Julia, filled with enthusiasm for European causes and finally killed by the Nazis.
Thoughtful, elegant patchwork of thirties memories, a vehicle for actors and a subtle, self-effacing director.

w Alvin Sargent, *book* Pentimento by Lillian Hellman *d Fred Zinnemann* *ph* Douglas Slocombe *m* Georges Delerue *ph* Carmen Dillon, Gene Callahan, Willy Holt

Jane Fonda, Vanessa Redgrave, Jason Robards Jnr, Maximilian Schell, Hal Holbrook, Rosemary Murphy, Cathleen Nesbitt, Maurice Denham

'After a while it becomes apparent that Zinnemann and Sargent are trafficking in too many quotations and flashbacks because they can't find the core of the material.'—*Pauline Kael*

AA: script; Vanessa Redgrave; Jason Robards Jnr

AAN: best picture; Fred Zinnemann; Douglas Slocombe; Georges Delerue; Jane Fonda; Maximilian Schell

Julia Misbehaves
US 1948 99m bw
MGM (Everett Riskin)

An actress returns to her stuffy husband when her daughter is about to marry.
Desperate attempt to find a vehicle for a fading star team.

w William Ludwig, Arthur Wimperis, Harry Ruskin, *novel* The Nutmeg Tree by Margery Sharp *d* Jack Conway *ph* Joseph Ruttenberg *m* Adolph Deutsch

Greer Garson, Walter Pidgeon, Elizabeth Taylor, Peter Lawford, Cesar Romero, Lucile Watson, Nigel Bruce, Mary Boland, Reginald Owen, Ian Wolfe, Edmund Breon, Fritz Feld, Aubrey Mather, Henry Stephenson

Julie*
US 1956 97m bw
MGM / Arwin (Marty Melcher)

A concert pianist plans to murder his wife.
Wildly improbable but entertaining suspenser in which the lady finally has to assume control of an airplane.

wd Andrew Stone *ph* Fred Jackman Jnr *m* Leith Stevens

Doris Day, Louis Jourdan, Barry Sullivan, Frank Lovejoy, John Gallaudet

'Some of the dialogue reaches a fine pitch of banality.'—*MFB*

AAN: Andrew Stone (as writer); title song (*m* Leith Stevens, *ly* Tom Adair)

Juliet of the Spirits*
Italy / France 1965 145m Technicolor
Federiz / Francoriz (Clemente Fracassi)
original title: *Giulietta degli Spiriti*

A bored middle-aged woman finds she can conjure up spirits who lead her into a life of sensual gratification.
A fascinating patchwork of autobiographical flashbacks, the distaff side of *Eight and a Half*.

w Federico Fellini, Tullio Pinnelli, Brunello Rondi, Ennio Flaiano *d Federico Fellini* *ph Gianni di Venanzo* *m* Nino Rota

Giulietta Masina, Mario Pisu, Sandra Milo, Valentina Cortese, Sylva Koscina

'A kaleidoscope of fantasy, a series of cerebral inventions, of which only a few are artistically justified . . . an extravagant illusion, a huge confidence trick, with little new to say and an often pedantic way of saying it.'—*David Wilson, MFB*

'Greater than *Ivanhoe*!'
Julius Caesar**
US 1953 121m bw
MGM (John Houseman)

Cassius and Brutus lead the conspirators who murder Caesar, but are themselves routed by Mark Antony.
Straightforward, rather leaden presentation of Shakespeare's play, lit by effective moments in the acting, but the sudden change from talk to battle is not smoothed over.

wd Joseph L. Mankiewicz *ph* Joseph Ruttenberg *m* Miklos Rozsa *ad* Cedric Gibbons, Edward Carfagno

John Gielgud, James Mason, Marlon Brando, Greer Garson, Deborah Kerr, Louis Calhern, Edmond O'Brien, George Macready, Michael Pate, John Hoyt, Alan Napier

'Thrill to ruthless men and their goddess-like women in a sin-swept age!'—*publicity*

'Thrill to traitors and heroes, killings and conspiracies, passions and violence in Rome's most exciting age!'—*publicity*

AAN: best picture; Joseph Ruttenberg; Miklos Rozsa; Marlon Brando

Julius Caesar
GB 1969 116m Technicolor Panavision
Commonwealth United (Peter Snell)

Elementary production with a surprising number of faults and very few merits.

w Robert Furnival *d* Stuart Burge *ph* Ken Higgins *m* Michael Lewis *pd* Julia Trevelyan Oman

Richard Johnson, Jason Robards Jnr, *John Gielgud*, Charlton Heston, Robert Vaughn, Richard Chamberlain, Diana Rigg, Jill Bennett, Christopher Lee, Alan Browning, Andrew Crawford

AAN: Michael Lewis

Jumbo*
US 1962 124m Metrocolor Panavision
MGM (Joe Pasternak, Martin Melcher)
aka: *Billy Rose's Jumbo*

In 1910, the daughter of the owner of a shaky circus prevents a take-over bid.
Hoary circus story with music. General effect disappointing: the elephant steals the show.

w Sidney Sheldon, *play* Ben Hecht, Charles MacArthur *d* Charles Walters *ph* William H. Daniels *m / ly* Richard Rodgers, Lorenz Hart *md* George Stoll *ch Busby Berkeley*

Doris Day, Jimmy Durante, Stephen Boyd, Martha Raye, Dean Jagger

AAN: George Stoll

Jump for Glory
GB 1937 89m bw
Criterion (Douglas Fairbanks Jnr, Marcel Hellman)
US title: *When Thief Meets Thief*

Adventures of a cat burglar who accidentally kills his ex-partner.
Curious star comedy drama with pleasing scenes.

w John Meehan Jnr, Harold French, *novel* Gordon MacDonnell *d* Raoul Walsh *ph* Cedric Williams

Douglas Fairbanks Jnr, Valerie Hobson, Alan Hale, Edward Rigby, Barbara Everest, Jack Melford, Anthony Ireland

'Starts off at a commendable pace but doesn't carry through.'—*Variety*

Jump into Hell
US 1955 93m bw
Warner (David Weisbart)

Paratroops relieve a fort in Indo-China.
Mediocre semi-documentary war heroics.

w Irving Wallace *d* David Butler *ph* Peverell Marley *m* David Buttolph

Jacques Sernas, Kurt Kasznar, Arnold Moss, Peter Van Eyck, Pat Blake

Jumpin' Jack Flash
US 1986 100m De Luxe

A black office worker finds herself plunged into espionage. Tiresome, dirty-talking, would-be wild and woolly comedy which fails to establish itself. Whoopi Goldberg, Stephen Collins, John Wood, Carol Kane, Annie Potts, Roscoe Lee Browne. Written by David H. Franzoni and others; directed by Penny Marshall; for Lawrence Gordon-Joel Silver/TCF.

Jumping for Joy
GB 1955 88m bw
Rank / Raymond Stross

A track attendant acquires a winning greyhound and exposes a group of crooks.
Totally predictable star comedy which needs livening up.

w Jack Davies, Henry E. Blyth *d* John Paddy Carstairs *ph* Jack Cox *m* Larry Adler

Frankie Howerd, Stanley Holloway, A. E. Matthews, Tony Wright, Alfie Bass, Joan Hickson, Lionel Jeffries

Jumping Jacks*
US 1952 96m bw
Paramount / Hal B. Wallis

Two cabaret comedians join the paratroops.
Standard star farce, one of Martin and Lewis' best.

w Robert Lees, Fred Rinaldo, Herbert Baker *d* Norman Taurog *ph* Daniel L. Fapp *m* Joseph J. Lilley

Dean Martin, *Jerry Lewis*, Mona Freeman, Robert Strauss, Don Defore

June Bride
US 1948 97m bw
Warner (Henry Blanke)

Two bickering reporters are sent to cover a small-town wedding.
Sloppily structured romantic farce in which nothing ever comes together.

w Ranald MacDougall, *play* Feature for June by Eileen Tighe, Graeme Lorimer *d* Bretaigne Windust *ph* Ted McCord *m* David Buttolph

Bette Davis, Robert Montgomery, Fay Bainter, Tom Tully, Betty Lynn, Barbara Bates, Jerome Cowan, Mary Wickes, Debbie Reynolds

The Jungle Book*
US 1942 109m Technicolor
Alexander Korda (W. Howard Greene)
aka: *Rudyard Kipling's Jungle Book*

Growing up with animals in an Indian forest, a boy forestalls the getaway of three thieves. High-budgeted but rather boring live action version with stiff-jointed model animals.

w Laurence Stallings, *stories* Rudyard Kipling *d* Zoltan Korda, André de Toth *ph* Lee Garmes, W. Howard Greene *m* Miklos Rozsa

Sabu, Joseph Calleia, John Qualen, Frank Puglia, Rosemary de Camp

'More thrilling than the deeds of man . . . more beautiful than the love of woman . . . more wonderful than the dreams of children!'—*publicity*

AAN: cinematography; Miklos Rozsa

Jungle Book*
US 1967 78m Technicolor
Walt Disney

Cartoon version relying less on action than on songs and voices; patchily successful but no classic.

d Wolfgang Reitherman *m / ly* Richard and Robert Sherman, Terry Gilkyson
voices George Sanders, Phil Harris, Louis Prima, Sebastian Cabot, Sterling Holloway

AAN: song 'The Bare Necessities' (*m / ly* Terry Gilkyson)

Jungle Captive
US 1945 63m bw

A mad doctor steals the body of Paula the ape woman and restores it to life. Arrant rubbish, a sequel to *Captive Wild Woman* and *Jungle Woman*. Otto Kruger, Phil Brown, Rondo Hatton, Jerome Cowan, Amelita Ward. Written by M. Coates Webster and Dwight V. Babcock; directed by Harold Young; for Universal.

Jungle Drums of Africa
US 1953 bw serial: 12 eps

A mining engineer puts paid to a villainous hunter who is on the trail of uranium deposits. Routine serial exploits with a wild life background (by courtesy of the stock shot library). Clayton Moore, Phyllis Coates, Johnny Spencer, Roy Glenn. Directed by Fred C. Brannon; for Republic.

Jungle Girl
US 1941 bw serial: 15 eps

A scientist's daughter grows up with natives and outwits her wicked uncle. Exploits of a female Tarzan. Frances Gifford, Tom Neal, Trevor Bardette, Gerald Mohr, Eddie Acuff. Directed by William Witney and John English; for Republic.

Jungle Jim
US 1937 bw serial: 12 eps

A white hunter leads a safari in search of an American heiress raised in the jungle. Naïve adventures with a villain called The Cobra. Grant Withers, Betty Jane Rhodes, Raymond Hatton, Henry Brandon, Evelyn Brent, Al Bridge. Directed by Ford Beebe and Cliff Smith; for Universal.

Jungle Jim

When Johnny Weissmuller began to show his middle-age spread, Columbia put him in a jacket and more or less redid his Tarzan thing in a series of second features which appeared to be shot in producer Sam Katzman's back garden and gradually indulged in wilder and wilder plots. None of them has more than curiosity value. Main scriptwriters were Carroll Young, Dwight Babcock, Sam Newman; main directors William Berke, Lee Sholem, Spencer G. Bennet.

1948: JUNGLE JIM
1949: THE LOST TRIBE
1950: CAPTIVE GIRL, MARK OF THE GORILLA, PYGMY ISLAND
1951: FURY OF THE CONGO, JUNGLE MANHUNT
1952: JUNGLE JIM IN THE FORBIDDEN LAND, VOODOO TIGER
1953: SAVAGE MUTINY, VALLEY OF THE HEADHUNTERS, KILLER APE
1954: JUNGLE MANEATERS, CANNIBAL ATTACK
1955: JUNGLE MOON MEN, DEVIL GODDESS

Jungle Menace
US 1937 bw serial: 15 eps

A Malayan rubber-planter's crop is attacked by rover pirates, and an adventurer hastens to help. Unusual setting for routine adventures. Frank Buck, John St Polis, Charlotte Henry, William Bakewell. Directed by George Melford and Harry Fraser; for Columbia.

The Jungle Mystery
US 1932 bw serial: 12 eps

Americans in Africa combat ivory hunters. Early talkie serial with footage which now seems hilarious. Tom Tyler, Cecilia Parker, William Desmond, Noah Beery Jnr. Directed by Ray Taylor; for Universal.

'Men staked their lives for just one look at the thrilling beauty of this tiger woman!'

The Jungle Princess*
US 1936 84m bw
Paramount (E. Lloyd Sheldon)

A British hunter is injured on a tropical island and rescued by a native girl and her animal retinue.
Dorothy Lamour's first film role cast her as the female Tarzan she was to play (in a sarong, of course) a dozen times again. This is strictly a programmer, but after its success it was all done again, rather better, as *Her Jungle Love*.

w Cyril Hume, Gerald Geraghty, Gouverneur Morris *d* William Thiele *ph* Harry Fischbeck *md* Boris Morros

Dorothy Lamour, Ray Milland, Akim Tamiroff, Lynne Overman, Molly Lamont, Hugh Buckler

'Fairly palatable entertainment most of the way.'—*Variety*

'Poor Mr Lynne Overman is expected to lend humorous relief to a film already richly comic.'—*Graham Greene*

† On this trip the tiger was Liamu and the chimp Bogo.

Jungle Queen
US 1945 bw serial: 13 eps

Nazis stir up African tribes against the Allies, who have a friend in a mysterious queen. Echoes of *She* abound in this tried-and-tested serial. Ruth Roman, Eddie Quillan, Edward Norris, Douglass Dumbrille, Lois Collier, Tala Birell. Directed by Ray Taylor and Lewis D. Collins; for Universal.

Jungle Raiders
US 1945 bw serial: 15 eps

An evil trader holds captive a doctor who knows the whereabouts of secret treasure. Standard jungle hazards, including crocodile swamps, volcanoes and landslides, lend colour to this listless serial. Kane Richmond, Eddie Quillan, Veda Ann Borg, Carol Hughes, Charles King, I. Stanford Jolley. Directed by Lesley Selander; for Columbia.

Jungle Woman
US 1944 54m bw

A mad doctor restores an ape to life. It turns into a beautiful woman. Middle section of a talentless trio of which the first is *Captive Wild Woman* and the third *Jungle Captive*. Written by Bernard Schubert, Henry Sucher and Edward Dein; directed by Reginald LeBorg; for Universal.

Junior Army
US 1943 70m bw

An English boy goes to an American military academy. Routine propaganda item which might almost have been titled David Copperfield meets the Dead End Kids. Freddie Bartholomew, Billy Halop, Huntz Hall, Bobby Jordan, Don Beddoe, Peter Lawford, Boyd Davis. Written by Albert Bein, Paul Gangelin; directed by Lew Landers; for Colbert Clark / Columbia.

Junior Bonner*
US 1972 105m Movielab Todd-AO 35
ABC / Booth–Gardner / Joe Wizan / Solar

An ageing rodeo star returns to his home town and finds his family in trouble.
Well-made, rather downcast and not very interesting drama, remarkably gentle from this director.

w Jeb Rosebrook *d* Sam Peckinpah
ph Lucien Ballard *m* Jerry Fielding

Steve McQueen, Ida Lupino, Robert Preston, Joe Don Baker, Ben Johnson

Junior G-Men
US 1940 bw serial: 12 eps

The son of a G-man enlists street friends to track down a vanished military leader. Serial situations retailored for reformed Dead End Kids. Billy Halop, Huntz Hall, Gabriel Dell, Bernard Punsley, Philip Terry, Russell Hicks. Directed by Ford Beebe and John Rawlins; for Universal.

Junior G-Men of the Air
US 1942 bw serial: 13 eps

The son of an airplane junkyard owner recruits friends to unmask a fifth-column organization. Fairly lively wartime serial. Billy Halop, Gene Reynolds, Lionel Atwill, Frank Albertson, Richard Lane, Huntz Hall, Gabriel Dell, Bernard Punsley, Frankie Darro, Turhan Bey. Directed by Ray Taylor and Lewis D. Collins; for Universal.

Junior Miss*
US 1945 94m bw
TCF (William Perlberg)

A teenager causes trouble by meddling in the lives of her family.
Amusing family comedy from a hit play.

w George Seaton, *play* Jerome Chodorov and Joseph Fields, *and stories* Sally Benson *d* George Seaton *ph* Charles Clarke *m* David Buttolph

Peggy Ann Garner, Allyn Joslyn, Faye Marlowe, Mona Freeman, Michael Dunne, John Alexander

Juno and the Paycock
GB 1930 85m bw
British International (John Maxwell)
US title: *The Shame of Mary Boyle*

During the Irish troubles of the early twenties, tragedy comes to a poor Dublin family.
A plainly done film version of a modern classic whose changes of mood would not in any case have worked well on the screen.

w Alfred Hitchcock, Alma Reville, *play* Sean O'Casey *d* Alfred Hitchcock *ph* Jack Cox

Sara Allgood, Edward Chapman, Maire O'Neill, Sidney Morgan, John Laurie
'A film which completely justifies the talkies.'—*James Agate*

'Just a photograph of a stage play.'—*Alfred Hitchcock*

Jupiter's Darling*
US 1954 96m Eastmancolor Cinemascope
MGM (George Wells)

Advancing on Rome, Hannibal falls in love with the dictator's fiancée.
A splendid example of the higher lunacy, with coloured elephants decorating an MGM musical about the fall of the Roman Empire. Small elements can be salvaged, and the gall is enough to be divided into three parts.

w Dorothy Kingsley, *play* The Road to Rome by Robert E. Sherwood *d* George Sidney *ph* Paul C. Vogel, Charles Rosher *m* Burton Lane *ly* Harold Adamson *ch* Hermes Pan *ad* Cedric Gibbons, Uric McCleary

Esther Williams, Howard Keel, George Sanders, Marge and Gower Champion, Richard Haydn, William Demarest

Jury's Evidence
GB 1935 71m bw

The jury in a murder trial disagrees. Courtroom drama with an unsatisfactory finish. Hartley Power, Margaret Lockwood, Nora Swinburne, Sebastian Shaw. Written by Ian Dalrymple, Jack de Leon; directed by Ralph Ince; for British Lion.

The Jury's Secret
US 1937 64m bw

The guilty man in a murder case is on the jury. Slow-moving courtroom drama with an unsatisfactory twist. Kent Taylor, Fay Wray, Jane Darwell, Nan Grey, Larry Blake, Fritz Leiber. Written by Lester Cole, Newman Levy; directed by Edward Sloman; for Universal. 'Doomed for no honours such as b.o.'—*Variety*

Just a Gigolo
US 1931 71m bw

A young lord masquerades as a gigolo to avoid being the prey of gold diggers. Slackly handled comedy which doesn't come off. William Haines, Irene Purcell, C. Aubrey Smith, Lillian Bond. Written by Hans Kraly, Richard Schayer, Claudine West; directed by Jack Conway; for MGM. 'Too much talk, too little action.'—*Variety*

Just a Gigolo
West Germany 1978 147m colour
Leguan (Rolf Thiele)

A young Prussian veteran of World War I intends to succeed, but stumbles through the Berlin underworld and is accidentally shot in a street skirmish.
An international misadventure whose English version is not only interminable and badly dubbed but extremely clumsily made.

w Ennio de Concini, Joshua Sinclair *d* David Hemmings *ph* Charly Steinberger *m* Gunther Fischer *pd* Peter Rothe

David Bowie, Sydne Rome, Kim Novak, Marlene Dietrich, David Hemmings, Maria Schell, Curt Jurgens, Erika Pluhar
'It often goes for laughs it hasn't a hope of getting; sometimes it aspires to tragic dignity and looks truly inept. It would be kinder to yourself and to everybody involved to overlook it.'—*Time Out*

Just Across the Street
US 1952 78m bw

Complications arise when a plumber's secretary pretends to be rich. Silly and pointless comedy which provides its talent with nothing to do. Ann Sheridan, John Lund, Robert Keith, Cecil Kellaway, Harvey Lembeck, Natalie Schaefer, Alan Mowbray. Written by Rosell Rogers and Joel Malone; directed by Joseph Pevney; for Leonard Goldstein / Universal–International.

Just Around the Corner
US 1938 70m bw
TCF (David Hempstead)

A little girl helps her dad to get on in business. Tedious Little Miss Fixit tale from the period when Shirley's star was sliding.

w Ethel Hill, J. P. McEvoy, Darrel Ware *d* Irving Cummings *ph* Henry Sharp *md* Louis Silvers

Shirley Temple, Charles Farrell, Bert Lahr, Joan Davis, Amanda Duff, Bill Robinson, Franklin Pangborn, Cora Witherspoon
'Top flight for general all-round entertainment.'—*Variety*

Just Before Dawn
US 1980 90m Movielab

Visitors to a mountain area are terrorized by a cleaver-wielding killer. Teenage shocker with just a little more style than most. George Kennedy, Mike Kellin, Chris Lemmon, Gregg Henry, Deborah Benson. Written by Mark Arywitz and Gregg Irving; directed by Jeff Lieberman; for Oakland.

Just Between Friends
US 1986 120m De Luxe
Orion / MTM (Edward Teets, Allan Burns)

A middle-aged woman finds little excitement in her household, and fancies a lesbian relationship; but her husband dies and she finds herself pregnant.
Ho-hum melodrama of our time.

w,d Allan Burns *ph* Jordan Cronenweth *m* Patrick Williams *pd* Sydney Z. Litwack

Mary Tyler Moore, Ted Danson, Christine Lahti, Sam Waterston, Salome Jens
'The main difference between this and a TV movie is that this doesn't have commercials.'—*Variety*

Just for You
US 1952 104m Technicolor
Paramount (Pat Duggan)

A successful songwriter finds that his troublesome teenage son is in love with his own fiancée.
Tiresomely scripted, pleasantly played romantic comedy with music.

w Robert Carson, *novel* Famous by Stephen Vincent Benet *d* Elliott Nugent *ph* George Barnes *m* Hugo Friedhofer *md* Emil Newman *songs* Harry Warren, Leo Robin

Bing Crosby, Jane Wyman, Bob Arthur, Ethel Barrymore, Natalie Wood, Cora Witherspoon, Regis Toomey

AAN: song 'Zing a Little Zong'

Just Imagine
US 1930 102m bw
Fox

A man who dies in 1930 is revived in 1980 and can't get used to the pace of life.
Famous fantasy which doesn't live up to its reputation and can now be seen as hampered by poor sets, script and acting. Futuristic sets are few but choice.

d David Butler *w, songs* De Sylva, Brown, Henderson *ch* Seymour Felix *ph* Ernest Palmer

El Brendel, Maureen O'Sullivan, John Garrick, Frank Albertson, Marjorie White, Hobart Bosworth, Mischa Auer, Wilfred Lucas
'Needs to be sold in advance on its novelty angle . . . it seems essential that something be done to make them say "Go down and take a look at that crazy picture".'—*Variety*

Just Like a Woman
GB 1966 89m Eastmancolor
Dormar (Bob Kellett)

A TV director's wife leaves him and gets ideas above her station.
Curious comedy which aims at sophistication but starts flagging in the first five minutes. Familiar performers just about keep it afloat.

wd Bob Fuest *ph* Billy Williams *m* Ken Napper

Wendy Craig, Francis Matthews, John Wood, Dennis Price, Miriam Karlin, Peter Jones, Clive Dunn, Ray Barrett

Just My Luck
GB 1957 86m bw
Rank (Hugh Stewart)

A jeweller's assistant becomes involved in horse racing.
Flat star vehicle.

w Alfred Shaughnessy *d* John Paddy Carstairs *ph* Jack Cox *m* Philip Green

Norman Wisdom, Jill Dixon, Leslie Phillips, Margaret Rutherford, Delphi Lawrence

Just Off Broadway
US 1942 66m bw

Michael Shayne investigates a court case on which he is sitting as a juror. Standard second feature mystery, reasonably well made. Lloyd Nolan, Marjorie Weaver, Phil Silvers, Janis Carter, Richard Derr, Chester Clute. Written by Armand D'Usseau; directed by Herbert I. Leeds; for Sol M. Wurtzel / TCF.

Just Tell Me What You Want
US 1980 112m Technicolor
Warner / Jay Presson Allen, Sidney Lumet

A powerful tycoon starts to weave plots when one of his harem wants to go independent.
Thoroughly silly melodrama with a few incidental humours.

w Jay Presson Allen, from her novel *d* Sidney Lumet
ph Oswald Morris *m* Charles Strouse
pd Tony Walton

Ali MacGraw, Alan King, Myrna Loy, Keenan Wynn, Tony Roberts, Dina Merrill, Peter Weller

'Jay Presson Allen has adapted her trashy novel into a trashy picture . . . Myrna Loy looks as if she's constantly amazed at the kinds of films getting made these days, and she's absolutely right.'—*Variety*

Just the Way You Are
US 1984 95m Metrocolor

A young fluteplayer tries to carve a career for herself while overcoming a physical disability. Odd little comedy-drama with little plot beyond the central character's crippled leg; not likely to make much headway. Kristy McNichol, Michael Ontkean, Kaki Hunter, André Dussolier, Robert Carradine. Written by Allan Burns; directed by Edouard Molinaro; for Leo L. Fuchs / MGM-UA.

Just You and Me, Kid
US 1979 93m Metrocolor
Columbia / Irving Fein-Jerome M. Zeitman

An elderly comedian reluctantly takes care of a naked teenager on the run from a dope pusher.
Virtually a one-set comedy which quickly tires the eye and ear; not a good idea despite the veteran star.

w Oliver Hailey, Leonard Stern *d* Leonard Stern *ph* David Walsh *m* Jack Elliott

George Burns, Brooke Shields, Burl Ives, Lorraine Gary, John Schuck, Keye Luke, Leon Ames, Ray Bolger, Carl Ballantine

Justice Est Faite*
France 1950 105m bw
Silver Films

The personal lives of jurors in a mercy killing case affect their verdict.
Absorbing courtroom drama with a message.

w Charles Spaak, André Cayatte d André Cayatte ph Jean Bourgoin *m* Raymond Legrand

Valentine Tessier, Claude Nollier, Jacques Castelot, Michel Auclair

Justine
US 1969 116m De Luxe Panavision
TCF / Pandro S. Berman

In Alexandria in the thirties, the beautiful wife of a wealthy banker influences the lives of all who meet her.
Disastrous condensed version of a very unusual set of novels whose atmosphere has not translated at all well. The result is like a bad rehearsal for a film, which is not surprising in view of the number of producers variously involved. The author feared 'a sort of *Peyton Place* with camels', and got it.

w Lawrence B. Marcus, *novels* The Alexandria Quartet by Lawrence Durrell
d George Cukor *ph* Leon Shamroy *m* Jerry Goldsmith

Anouk Aimée, Michael York, Dirk Bogarde, Anna Karina, John Vernon, George Baker, Philippe Noiret, Robert Forster, Jack Albertson, Michael Dunn, Barry Morse, Cliff Gorman, Severn Darden

'Could well stand as a model of what can happen when Hollywood gets to grips with a celebrated literary property.'—*David Wilson*

'Despite leaden forays into homosexuality, transvestitism, incest, and child prostitution, it remains as naively old-fashioned in its emotional and intellectual vocabulary as in its actual verbiage and cinematic technique.'—*John Simon*

Kagemusha**
Japan 1980 179m Eastmancolor
TCF / Toho (Akira Kurosawa)
aka: *The Double*; *Shadow Warrior*

On the death of a clan chief his place is taken by the lookalike hired to overlook battlefields while the chief is really busy elsewhere.
Fascinating Japanese epic centring on stately ritual and court intrigue, with the occasional battle for spectacular action; one of the director's most impressive works.

w Akira Kurosawa, Masato Ide *d Akira Kurosawa*
ph Kazuo Miyagawa, Asaiachi Nakai
m Shinichiro Ikebe

Tatsura Nakadai, Tsutomu Yamazaki, Kenichi Hagiwara

AAN: best foreign film; art direction
BFA: direction; costume design

Kaleidoscope*
GB 1966 103m Technicolor
Warner / Winkast (Elliott Kastner)
Reissue title: *The Bank Breaker*

An American playboy breaks into a playing card factory and marks the designs so that he can win in every European casino.
Would-be swinging comedy-thriller which in fact is entertaining only when it stops trying to dazzle.

w Robert and Jane Howard-Carrington
d Jack Smight *ph Christopher Challis*
m Stanley Myers *ad* Maurice Carter

Warren Beatty, Susannah York, Clive Revill, Eric Porter, Murray Melvin

'A "groovie movie" it certainly is, with a battery of fashionable camera tricks, kaleidoscopic dissolves, and virtually every scene introduced from behind an irrelevant piece of furniture.'—*David Wilson*

Kameradschaft*
Germany 1931 92m bw
Nerofilm
aka: *Comradeship*

On the Franco-German border French miners are imprisoned below ground and Germans burrow to free them.
Salutary message film with good dramatic pointing.

w Laszlo Vajda, Karl Otten, Peter Martin Lampel *d G. W. Pabst ph* Fritz Arno Wagner, Robert Baberski

Ernst Busch, Alexander Granach, Fritz Kampers, Gustav Puttjer

Kanal*
Poland 1956 97m bw
Film Polski (Stanislaw Adler)
aka: *They Loved Life*

In 1944, an anti-Nazi resistance group is trapped in a sewer.
A suffocatingly unpleasant film to watch; its message and technical excellence are undoubted.

w Jerzy Stawinski, from his novel Kloakerne *d Andrzej Wajda ph* Jerzy Lipman *m* Jan Krenz

Teresa Izewska, Tadeusz Janczar, Emil Kariewicz, Wienczylaw Glinski

Kangaroo
US 1952 84m Technicolor
TCF (Robert Bassler)

In old Australia, a con man pretends to be a rancher's long lost heir, then complicates things by falling in love with the rancher's daughter.
Standard romantic action hokum.

w Harry Kleiner *d* Lewis Milestone
ph Charles G. Clarke *m* Sol Kaplan

Maureen O'Hara, Peter Lawford, Finlay Currie, Richard Boone, Chips Rafferty, Charles Tingwell

'I'll make this town keep the peace—if I have to blow it to pieces!'

The Kansan
US 1943 79m bw

A wandering marksman stops off to become marshal of a frontier town. Solid routine western with good performances. Richard Dix, Albert Dekker, Jane Wyatt, Eugene Pallette, Victor Jory, Robert Armstrong, Clem Bevans, Hobart Cavanaugh, Willie Best. Written by Harold Shumate, from book by Frank Gruber; directed by George Archainbaud; for Harry Sherman/UA. AAN: Gerard Carbonara (music).

Kansas City Bomber
US 1972 99m Metrocolor
MGM / Levy–Gardner–Laven / Raquel Welch (Marty Elfand)

A roller skating star finds time between affairs to beat her rival in a big match.
Vulgar melodrama with good action scenes.

w Thomas Rickman, Calvin Clements
d Jerrold Freedman *ph* Fred Koenekamp
m Don Ellis

Raquel Welch, Kevin McCarthy, Norman Alden, Jeanne Cooper

Kansas City Confidential
US 1952 98m bw
United Artists / Edward Small
GB title: *The Secret Four*

An ex-detective plans a perfect crime, and recruits three confederates who all remain unknown to each other by wearing masks.
Moderately lively if violent thriller which gets less inventive as it goes along but satisfies the action buffs.

w George Bruce, Harry Essex *d* Phil Karlson
ph George Diskant *m* Paul Sawtell

Preston Foster, John Payne, Coleen Gray, Lee Van Cleef, Neville Brand, Jack Elam, Dona Drake

Kansas City Princess
US 1934 64m bw

Gold diggers go to Paris. Light farce comedy, somewhat lacking in punch. Joan Blondell, Glenda Farrell, Hugh Herbert, Robert Armstrong, Osgood Perkins, Hobart Cavanaugh. Written by Sy Bartlett and Manuel Seff; directed by William Keighley; for Warners. 'Just a comedy, good for better than moderate biz.'—*Variety*

Kansas Raiders
US 1951 80m Technicolor

During the Civil War, Jesse James joins Quantrill's Raiders. Fast-moving, fairly violent western only remotely based on fact. Audie Murphy, Brian Donlevy, Marguerite Chapman, Scott Brady, Tony Curtis, Richard Arlen, James Best, Richard Long. Written by Robert L. Richards; directed by Ray Enright; for Universal-International.

Kaos**
Italy 1984 188m Eastmancolor
RAI-TV / Filmtre (Giuliano de Negri)

Five stories by Pirandello are combined in settings near his birthplace.
Generally fascinating mixture of tales which range from comedy to horror, styled by master film-makers.

KAGEMUSHA. Akira Kurosawa's epic was the most expensive Japanese film ever made but it also had its quieter moments, here with Tatsura Nakadai.

w,d Paolo and Vittorio Taviani ph Giuseppe Lanci m Nicola Piovanni *ed* Roberto Perignani

Margarita Lozano, Claudio Bigagli, Enrica Maria Modugno, Ciccio Ingrassia, Franco Franchi, Biagio Barone, Omero Antonutti

Kapo
Italy / France 1960 115m bw
Vides / Zebra / Francinex

A French Jewess survives the horrors of a Nazi concentration camp and becomes camp guard.
Curious exploitation piece which turns tragedy into melodrama, and doesn't even do that with much flair.

w Franco Solinas, Gillo Pontecorvo *d* Gillo Pontecorvo *ph* Goffredo Bellisario, Alexander Sekulovic *m* Carlo Rustichelli

Susan Strasberg, Laurent Terzieff, Emmanuelle Riva
AA: best foreign film

The Karate Kid*
US 1984 127m Metrocolor
Columbia / Delphi II (Jerry Weintraub)

A teenage boy, new to California, joins a karate club and defeats the local bullies.
A kind of amateur *Rocky*, not bad in its way, but its huge commercial success in the US remains mystifying.

w Robert Mark Kamen *d* John G. Avildsen *ph* James Crabe *m* Bill Conti *pd* William J. Cassidy *ed* Bud Smith, Walt Mulconery

Ralph Macchio, Noriyuki 'Pat' Morita, Elizabeth Shue, Martin Kove, Randee Heller, William Zabka
AAN: Pat Morita (supporting actor)

The Karate Kid Part Two
US 1986 113m De Luxe

Daniel's teacher heads back to Okinawa where his father is gravely ill. Tedious attempt to spin out a surprise hit; no surprises this time.
Pat Morita, Ralph Macchio, Nobu McCarthy. Written by Robert Mark Kamen; directed by John G. Avildsen; for Jerry Weintraub / Columbia Delphi II.
AAN: song 'Glory of Love'

Kate Plus Ten
GB 1938 81m bw
Wainwright (Richard Wainwright)

A police inspector falls for the attractive female leader of a bullion gang.
Curious comedy thriller with insufficient of either commodity.

w Jack Hulbert, Jeffrey Dell, *novel* Edgar Wallace *d* Reginald Denham *ph* Roy Kellino

Jack Hulbert, Genevieve Tobin, Noel Madison, Francis L. Sullivan, Arthur Wontner, Frank Cellier, Googie Withers, Peter Haddon, Felix Aylmer, Leo Genn, Edward Lexy

Kathleen
US 1941 88m bw
MGM (George Haight)

A neglected daughter finds a new wife for her widowed father.
One of the reasons for Shirley Temple's early retirement.

w Mary McCall Jnr, *story* Kay Van Riper *d* Harold S. Bucquet *ph* Sidney Wagner *m* Franz Waxman

Shirley Temple, Herbert Marshall, Laraine Day, Gail Patrick, Felix Bressart, Nella Walker, Lloyd Corrigan

Kathy O
US 1958 99m Eastmancolor Cinemascope
U-I (Sy Gomberg)

A temperamental child star befriends a lonely columnist.
Overlong Hollywood comedy drama with amusing moments.

w Jack Sher, Sy Gomberg *d* Jack Sher *ph* Arthur E. Arling *m* Frank Skinner *songs* Charles Tobias, Ray Joseph

Patty McCormack, Dan Duryea, Jan Sterling, Sam Levene

Katie Did It
US 1951 81m bw
Universal–International (Leonard Goldstein)

A small town is shocked when young Katie comes back having posed in scanty attire for a commercial artist.
Feeble comedy which totters to a lame conclusion.

w Jack Henley *d* Frederick de Cordova Russell Metty *m* Frank Skinner

Ann Blyth, Mark Stevens, Cecil Kellaway, Elizabeth Patterson, Jesse White, Harold Vermilyea, Craig Stevens

The Keep
US 1983 93m Metrocolor Scope
Paramount (Gene Kirkwood, Howard W. Koch Jnr)

German troops in 1941 occupy a castle in the Carpathian Alps, and discover that it contains an evil force.
Extraordinary combination of war and fantasy fiction, not entirely dissimilar from *Castle Keep* which had a similar exposition.

w,d Michael Mann *novel* F. Paul Wilson *ph* Alex Thomson *m* Tangerine Dream

Scott Glenn, Alberta Watson, Jurgen Prochnow, Robert Prosky, Gabriel Byrne, Ian McKellen

Keep 'Em Flying
US 1941 86m bw
Universal (Glenn Tryon)

Two incompetents in the Army Air Corps get mixed up with identical twin girls.
A big moneymaker of its day, this comedy now seems especially resistible.

w True Boardman, Nat Perrin, John Grant *d* Arthur Lubin *ph* Joseph Valentine *m* Frank Skinner

Bud Abbott, Lou Costello, Martha Raye, Carol Bruce, William Gargan, Dick Foran, Charles Lang

AAN: song 'Pig Foot Pete' (*m* Gene de Paul, *ly* Don Raye)

Keep Fit*
GB 1937 82m bw
ATP (Basil Dean)

A barber mistaken for an athlete finally excels at sport and also catches a thief.
Good star vehicle with snappy songs and fast comedy scenes.

w Anthony Kimmins, Austin Melford *d Anthony Kimmins* *ph* Ronald Neame, Gordon Dines

George Formby, Kay Walsh, Guy Middleton, Gus McNaughton, Edmund Breon, George Benson, C. Denier Warren, Hal Gordon, Hal Walters, Leo Franklyn

Keep Smiling*
GB 1938 91m bw
TCF (Robert T. Kane)
US title: *Smiling Along*

Problems of a touring concert party.
Pretty good star vehicle, though with unfortunate signs of an attempt to glamorize Our Gracie.

w Val Valentine, Rodney Ackland *d* Monty Banks *ph* Max Greene

Gracie Fields, Roger Livesey, Mary Maguire, Peter Coke, Jack Donohue, Tommy Fields, Eddie Gray, Edward Rigby, Hay Petrie

Keep Smiling
US 1938 77m bw

The niece of a Hollywood director finds him on the skids. More than usually substantial star comedy-drama. Jane Withers, Henry Wilcoxon, Gloria Stuart, Helen Westley, Jed Prouty, Pedro de Cordoba, Douglas Fowley. Written by Frances Hyland, Albert Ray; directed by Herbert I. Leeds; for John Stone / TCF. 'A kids' picture with an adult punch.'—*Variety*

Keep Your Powder Dry
US 1945 93m bw
MGM (George Haight)

Three girls from different backgrounds join the WACS.
Totally uninteresting and unconvincing female flagwaver.

w Mary C. McCall Jnr, George Bruce *d* Edward Buzzell *ph* Ray June *m* David Snell

Lana Turner, Laraine Day, Susan Peters, Agnes Moorehead, Bill Johnson, Natalie Schaefer, June Lockhart, Lee Patrick

Keep Your Seats Please*
GB 1936 82m bw
ATP (Basil Dean)

A prospective heir seeks a fortune hidden in one of six chairs.
Good star comedy on a theme later reworked in *It's in the Bag* (qv) and *The Twelve Chairs* (qv).

w Tom Geraghty, Ian Hay, Anthony Kimmins, *play* Twelve Chairs by Elie Ilf, Eugene Petrov *d* Monty Banks *ph* John W. Boyle

George Formby, Florence Desmond, Alastair Sim, Gus McNaughton, Harry Tate

Keeper of the Bees
US 1935 76m bw

A country boy makes good. Victorian-style fable for rural audiences. Neil Hamilton, Betty Furness, Emma Dunn, Edith Fellows, Hobart Bosworth. Written by Adele Buggington from the novel by Gene Stratton Porter; directed by Christy Cabanne; for Trem Carr / Monogram. 'For discriminating patronage, a washout . . . a calico narrative for the crossroads.'—*Variety*

Keeper of the Flame*
US 1942 100m bw
MGM (Victor Saville)

A reporter befriends the widow of a politician and forces her to disclose her husband's guilty secret.
Well-acted but over-solemn melodrama which badly needs a sting in the tail.

w Donald Ogden Stewart, *novel* I. A. R. Wylie *d* George Cukor *ph* William Daniels *m* Bronislau Kaper

Spencer Tracy, Katharine Hepburn, Richard Whorf, Margaret Wycherly, Donald Meek, Stephen McNally, Audrey Christie, Frank Craven

'An expensive testimonial to Hollywood's inability to face a significant theme.'—*Time*

'Unorthodox and on the whole absorbing drama. Ominous portents and overtones take the place of physical action.'—*Christian Science Monitor*

'A gothic wet blanket of a movie.'—*Pauline Kael, 70s*

Keepers of Youth
GB 1931 70m bw
BIP (John Maxwell)

A young schoolmaster finds his fresh ideas make him unpopular, especially when he is found in a compromising position with the assistant matron.
Old-fashioned drama with a few lively scenes.

w Frank Launder, *play* Arnold Ridley *d* Thomas Bentley *ph* James Wilson, Bert Ford

Garry Marsh, Ann Todd, Robin Irvine, John Turnbull, O. B. Clarence, Mary Clare

Keeping Company
US 1940 80m bw

A young man announces his engagement but has trouble when his ex-girlfriend returns to town. Amiable family comedy which was announced to be the first of a series, but stayed lonely. Frank Morgan, Irene Rich, John Shelton, Ann Rutherford, Virginia Weidler, Dan Dailey, Gene Lockhart, Virginia Grey. Written by James Hill, Harry Ruskin and Adrian Scott; directed by S. Sylvan Simon; for MGM.

Kelly and Me
US 1956 86m Technicolor Cinemascope
U-I (Robert Arthur)

The ups and downs of a song and dance man and the dog who shares his act.
Mild vaudeville saga with totally predictable twists.

w Everett Freeman *d* Robert Z. Leonard *ph* Maury Gertsman *m* Joseph Gershenson

Van Johnson, Piper Laurie, Martha Hyer, Onslow Stevens

Kelly the Second
US 1936 71m bw

A determined lady trains a dimwitted prizefighter. Easy-going farce from a studio which knew how to make them; but this wasn't one of the best. Patsy Kelly, Guinn Williams, Charley Chase, Pert Kelton, Harold Huber. Written by Jack Jevne and Gordon Douglas; directed by Hal Roach; for MGM.

Kelly's Heroes
US / Yugoslavia 1970 143m Metrocolor Panavision
MGM / The Warriors / Avala (Irving Leonard)

During World War II, an American platoon abducts a German general and accidentally discovers the whereabouts of a fortune in gold.
Crude slam-bang actioner for the obvious market.

w Troy Kennedy Martin *d* Brian G. Hutton *ph* Gabriel Figueroa *m* Lalo Schifrin *2nd unit* Andrew Marton

Clint Eastwood, Telly Savalas, Don Rickles, Donald Sutherland, Carroll O'Connor, Stuart Margolin, Dick Davalos

'Over two hours of consistently devastating explosions, pyrotechnics and demolition.'—*MFB*

'Made for no possible reason other than a chance to use the Yugoslav army at cut rates.'—*Judith Crist, 1973*

The Kennel Murder Case**
US 1933 73m bw
Warner (Robert Presnell)

Philo Vance proves that an apparent suicide is really murder.
Complex murder mystery, very smartly handled and often cited as a classic of the genre; later remade as *Calling Philo Vance*.

w Robert N. Lee, Peter Milner, *novel* S. S. Van Dine *d Michael Curtiz* *ph* William Reese

William Powell, Mary Astor, Eugene Pallette, Ralph Morgan, Helen Vinson, Jack La Rue, Paul Cavanagh, Robert Barrat

'Entertaining all the way.'—*Variety*

'Players are cast so inevitably to type that the film is like a demonstration of the principles of running a stock company.'—*New Yorker, 1978*

'Stylistically a little gem.'—*Clive Hirschhorn*

† See also *Philo Vance*.

The Kentuckian
US 1955 104m Technicolor Cinemascope
UA / Hecht–Lancaster

A Kentucky backwoodsman takes his small son to settle in Texas.
Ambling mid-western with moments of interest.

w A. B. Guthrie Jnr, *novel* The Gabriel Horn by Felix Holt *d* Burt Lancaster *ph* Ernest Laszlo *m* Bernard Herrmann

Burt Lancaster, Dianne Foster, Diana Lynn, *Walter Matthau*, John McIntire, Una Merkel, John Carradine

Kentucky*
US 1938 95m Technicolor
TCF (Gene Markey)

Horse-breeding rivalry prevents the smooth running of true love.
Harmless family entertainment, more professionally handled than its innumerable later imitations. Remade as *April Love*.

w Lamar Trotti, *novel* The Look of Eagles by John Taintor Foote *d* David Butler *ph* Ernest Palmer *md* Louis Silvers

Loretta Young, Richard Greene, Walter Brennan, Douglass Dumbrille, Karen Morley, Moroni Olsen, Russell Hicks

'An outstanding effort, geared for top money.'—*Variety*

AA: Walter Brennan

The Kentucky Fried Movie
US 1977 90m colour

Comedy sketches from the University of Wisconsin; the writers later gave us *Airplane*. Enough said? Marilyn Joi, Saul Kahan, Marcy Goldman, Joe Medalis. Written by David and Jerry Zucker, Jim Abrahams; directed by John Landis; for United Film.

Kentucky Kernels
US 1934 74m bw

An orphan left with two musicians proves to be the heir to a fortune, but the way to it is through feuding hillbilly country. Fairly funny Wheeler and Woolsey comedy, in other words one of their better efforts. Bert Wheeler, Robert Woolsey, Mary Carlisle, Spanky McFarland, Noah Beery, Willie Best. Written by Bert Kalmar, Harry Ruby and Fred Guiol; directed by George Stevens; for RKO. (GB title: *Triple Trouble*.)

Kentucky Moonshine*
US 1938 87m bw

In the hope of a radio contract, the Ritz Brothers masquerade as hillbillies and find themselves in the middle of a feud. One of the trio's best solo vehicles. *The Ritz Brothers*, Tony Martin, Marjorie Weaver, Slim Summerville, John Carradine, Wally Vernon, Berton Churchill, Eddie Collins. Written by Art Arthur and M. M. Musselman; directed by David Butler; for TCF. 'It's crazy and it's wild, but it's funny and grand entertainment.'—*Variety*

La Kermesse Héroïque**
France 1935 115m bw
Tobis
aka: *Carnival in Flanders*

When Spaniards invade a Flemish town in 1616, the men make themselves scarce and the women find other ways of conquering.
Sprightly though overlong comedy which seemed risqué at the time and therefore enjoyed international success.

w Charles Spaak, Jacques Feyder, novel Charles Spaak *d Jacques Feyder ph* Harry Stradling *m* Louis Beydts *ad* Lazare Meerson

Françoise Rosay, Louis Jouvet, Jean Murat, Alfred Adam, André Alerme

'A mixture of gay absurdity and shrewd comment, selecting its own pitch and holding it—comedy, you might say, self-contained.'—*Otis Ferguson*

'Everything fits perfectly into the pattern of cultured and sophisticated entertainment. Nowhere is there a false touch.'—*The Times, 1952*

Kes*
GB 1969 109m Technicolor
UA / Woodfall (Tony Garnett)

In a northern industrial town, a boy learns about life from the fate of his pet bird.
'Realistic' family drama, full of the kind of merit that does not equate with entertainment: hard to take and harder to hear.

w Barry Hines, Ken Loach, Tony Garnet, *novel* A Kestrel for a Knave by Barry Hines *d Ken Loach ph* Chris Menges *m* John Cameron

David Bradley, Lynne Perrie, Colin Welland, Freddie Fletcher, Brian Glover

'There emerges a most discouraging picture of life in the industrial north . . . infinitely sad in its total implications, it is also immensely funny in much of its detail.'—*Brenda Davies*

The Kettles
The rustic couple evolved from characters in *The Egg and I* (qv); Marjorie Main and Percy Kilbride went on to play them in a cheap but very popular series for Universal, variously scripted and directed.

1949: MA AND PA KETTLE
1950: MA AND PA KETTLE GO TO TOWN
1951: MA AND PA KETTLE BACK ON THE FARM
1952: MA AND PA KETTLE AT THE FAIR
1953: MA AND PA KETTLE ON VACATION
1954: MA AND PA KETTLE AT HOME
1955: MA AND PA KETTLE AT WAIKIKI
1956: THE KETTLES IN THE OZARKS (Arthur Hunnicutt instead of Kilbride)
1957: THE KETTLES ON OLD MACDONALD'S FARM (Parker Fennelly instead of Kilbride)

The Key*
US 1934 71m bw

In Ireland in the twenties, a British army captain falls for the wife of an intelligence officer. Heroics among the black and tans; interesting but dated drama. William Powell, Edna Best, Colin Clive, Hobart Cavanaugh, Halliwell Hobbes, Henry O'Neill, Arthur Treacher, Donald Crisp. Written by Laird Doyle, from the play by R. Gore-Brown and J. L. Hardy; directed by Michael Curtiz; for Warner.

'The door opened into a haven from hell . . . and the girl came with the key!'

The Key*
GB 1958 134m bw Cinemascope
Columbia / Open Road (Carl Foreman)

World War II tugboat skippers, about to embark on dangerous missions, pass on the key to an apartment and a girl to go with it.
Rather foolish symbolic melodrama which never makes its purpose clear but along the way provides fragments of love story, chunks of the supernatural and dollops of war action, rather languidly assembled with great technical competence but little real feeling. The talent occasionally shows through.

w Carl Foreman, *novel* Stella by Jan de Hartog *d* Carol Reed *ph* Oswald Morris *m* Malcolm Arnold

William Holden, Sophia Loren, *Trevor Howard*, Oscar Homolka, Kieron Moore

'A storm of fear and fury in the sizzling Florida keys!'

Key Largo***
US 1948 101m bw
Warner (Jerry Wald)

A returning war veteran fights gangsters on the Florida keys.
Moody melodrama on similar lines to *To Have and Have Not*: it sums up the post-war mood of despair, allows several good acting performances, and builds up to a pretty good action climax.

w Richard Brooks, John Huston, play Maxwell Anderson *d John Huston ph Karl Freund m* Max Steiner

Humphrey Bogart, Lauren Bacall, *Claire Trevor, Edward G. Robinson, Lionel Barrymore*, Thomas Gomez, Marc Lawrence

'It's a confidently directed, handsomely shot movie, and the cast go at it as if the nonsense about gangsters and human dignity were high drama.'—*New Yorker, 1977*

'A completely empty, synthetic work.'—*Gavin Lambert*

AA: Claire Trevor

Key to the City
US 1950 101m bw
MGM (Z. Wayne Griffin)

At a San Francisco convention, two mayors get involved in several escapades and fall in love.
Routine romantic comedy.

w Robert Riley Crutcher *d* George Sidney *ph* Harold Rosson *m* Bronislau Kaper

Clark Gable, Loretta Young, Frank Morgan, James Gleason, Marilyn Maxwell, Raymond Burr, Lewis Stone, Raymond Walburn, Pamela Britton

'A comedy made to measure . . . the script concerns itself with wringing every possible laugh from a number of stock situations.'—*Variety*

The Keyhole*
US 1933 70m bw

A divorce investigator falls for the wife he is commissioned to frame. Unsavoury little drama, unusual enough to be interesting. Kay Francis, George Brent, Glenda Farrell, Allen Jenkins, Monroe Owsley. Written by Robert Presnell from Adventures by Alice Duer Miller; directed by Michael Curtiz; for Warners.

The Keys of the Kingdom*
US 1944 137m bw
TCF (Joseph L. Mankiewicz)

The life of a 19th-century Scottish priest in China.
Studio-made missionary melodrama, a big hit for its new star but otherwise an undistinguished piece of work with a shuffling pace and not much by way of climax.

w Joseph L. Mankiewicz, Nunnally Johnson, *novel* A. J. Cronin *d* John M. Stahl *ph* Arthur Miller *m* Alfred Newman *ad* James Basevi, William Darling

Gregory Peck, Thomas Mitchell, Vincent Price, Rose Stradner, Roddy McDowall, Edmund Gwenn, Cedric Hardwicke, Peggy Ann Garner, James Gleason, Anne Revere

'Long, earnest, long, worthy, interesting and long.'—*Richard Mallett, Punch*

AAN: Arthur Miller; Alfred Newman; Gregory Peck

'Where the Nile divides, their mighty conflict begins!'
Khartoum*
GB 1966 134m Technicolor Ultra Panavision
UA / Julian Blaustein

The last years of General Gordon.
Dullish history book stuff which fails to explain Gordon the man but occasionally erupts into glowing action.

w Robert Ardrey *d* Basil Dearden *ph Edward Scaife, Harry Waxman* *m* Frank Cordell

Charlton Heston, Laurence Olivier, Ralph Richardson, Richard Johnson, Hugh Williams, Alexander Knox, Johnny Sekka, Nigel Green, Michael Hordern

'Academic accuracy and spectacular battles are unhappy partners.'—*MFB*

'Beautifully photographed, lavishly mounted, intelligently acted, but ultimately dull.'—*Sight and Sound*

AAN: Robert Ardrey

Kicking the Moon Around
GB 1938 78m bw
Vogue (Howard Welsch)
US titles: *The Playboy; Millionaire Merry Go Round*

A millionaire goes into show business to establish a career for his singing protégée. Mild, frothy comedy, dated but quite fluent.

w Angus McPhail, Roland Pertwee, Michael Hogan, Harry Fowler Mear *d* Walter Forde *ph* Francis Carver

Ambrose and his Orchestra, Evelyn Dall, Hal Thompson, Florence Desmond, Harry Richman, C. Denier Warren, Max Bacon

The Kid***
US 1921 52m approx (24 fps) bw silent
First National / Charles Chaplin

A tramp brings up an abandoned baby, and later loses him to his mother; but there is a happy ending.
Sentimental comedy set in the slums. The comedy is very sparingly laid on, but the effect of the whole is much less painful than the synopsis would suggest, the production is comparatively smooth, the child actor is sensational, and the film contains much of the quintessential Chaplin.

wd Charles Chaplin ph Rollie Totheroh

Charles Chaplin, Jackie Coogan, Edna Purviance

Kid Auto Races at Venice
US 1914 6m approx bw silent
Keystone / Mack Sennett

This much mentioned film is no more than a few candid camera shots of a children's car race on the California beach. It so happened that the young Charles Chaplin was called upon to liven up proceedings by causing a nuisance, and hastily conceived his tramp costume to do so. His fragments of comedy, primitive though they now seem, made him a star.

wd Henry Lehrman *ph* Frank D. Williams

Kid Blue
US 1973 100m De Luxe Panavision
TCF / Marvin Schwarz Productions

In 1902 Texas a young outlaw tries to go straight.
Deliberately myth-deflating western with agreeably rich detail.

w Edwin Shrake *d* James Frawley *ph* Billy Williams *m* Tim McIntyre, John Rubenstein *pd* Joel Schiller

Dennis Hopper, Warren Oates, Peter Boyle, Ben Johnson, Lee Purcell, Janice Rule, Clifton James

The Kid Comes Back
US 1937 61m bw

A tenderfoot from Texas is trained by an ex-champion prizefighter. Not really a sequel to *Kid Galahad*, but a second feature in its wake; as such, fair. Wayne Morris, Barton MacLane, June Travis, Maxie Rosenbloom. Written by George Bricker, E. J. Flanagan; directed by B. Reeves Eason; for Warners. 'Brisk, fast, strong dualler.'—*Variety*

A Kid for Two Farthings*
GB 1955 96m Eastmancolor
London Films (Carol Reed)

Among the colourful characters of London's Petticoat Lane market moves a boy whose pet goat seems to have the magical power of a unicorn.
Whimsical character comedy-drama made with some style but too insubstantial and unconvincing to be affectionately remembered.

w Wolf Mankowitz *d* Carol Reed *ph* Ted Scaife *m* Benjamin Frankel

Celia Johnson, Diana Dors, David Kossoff, Brenda de Banzie, Sidney Tafler, Primo Carnera, Joe Robinson, Jonathan Ashmore

The Kid from Brooklyn
US 1946 114m Technicolor
Samuel Goldwyn

A timid milkman becomes a prizefighter.
Yawn-provoking comedy, a remake of Harold Lloyd's *The Milky Way*; the first indication that Danny Kaye could be a bore.

w Grover Jones, Frank Butler, Richard Connell *d* Norman Z. McLeod *ph* Gregg Toland *md* Carmen Dragon *songs* Jule Styne, Sammy Cahn

Danny Kaye, Virginia Mayo, Vera-Ellen, Steve Cochran, Eve Arden, Walter Abel, Lionel Stander, Fay Bainter, Clarence Kolb

† NB: Lionel Stander played the same role in *The Milky Way*.

The Kid from Kokomo
US 1939 92m bw

A farm boy's fight manager decides that for publicity purposes he must acquire a family. Yet another follow-up to *Kid Galahad*, this time on the farcical side. Not bad, but too long. Pat O'Brien, Wayne Morris, Joan Blondell, May Robson, Jane Wyman, Stanley Fields, Maxie Rosenbloom, Sidney Toler, Ed Brophy. Written by Jerry Wald, Richard Macauley, Dalton Trumbo; directed by Lewis Seiler; for Warners. 'Full of laughs, and a very probable money-getter.'—*Variety*

The Kid from Left Field
US 1953 80m bw

A big league basketball player is reduced to selling peanuts at the games, but passes on advice through his small son, who is appointed team manager. Half-hearted whimsy for addicts. Dan Dailey, Billy Chapin, Anne Bancroft, Lloyd Bridges, Ray Collins, Richard Egan. Written by Jack Sher; directed by Harmon Jones; for TCF.

The Kid from Spain**
US 1932 90m bw
Samuel Goldwyn

A simpleton is mistaken for a celebrated bullfighter.
Charmingly dated star musical which, though primitive in some respects, is a splendid reminder of its period.

w William Anthony McGuire, Bert Kalmar, Harry Ruby *d* Leo McCarey *ph* Gregg Toland *ch Busby Berkeley*

Eddie Cantor, Lyda Roberti, Robert Young, Ruth Hall, John Miljan, Noah Beery, J. Carrol Naish, Stanley Fields, Betty Grable, Paulette Goddard

'A corking comedy . . . it'll get a lot of money.'—*Variety*

The Kid from Texas
US 1950 85m Technicolor

The last rampage of Billy the Kid. Surprisingly violent western for its time; otherwise unremarkable. Audie Murphy, Gale Storm, Albert Dekker, Shepperd Strudwick, Will Geer, William Talman. Written by Robert Hardy Andrews and Karl Kamb; directed by Kurt Neumann; for Universal–International. (GB title: *Texas Kid, Outlaw*.)

Kid Galahad*
US 1937 101m bw
Warner (Samuel Bischoff)
TV title: *Battling Bellhop*

A bellhop is groomed as a prizefighter, and his trainer grows jealous.
Good standard prizefight melodrama, remade as *The Wagons Roll at Night* and later as *Kid Galahad* with Elvis Presley (see below).

w Seton I. Miller, *novel* Francis Wallace *d* Michael Curtiz *ph* Tony Gaudio *m* Heinz Roemheld, Max Steiner

Edward G. Robinson, Bette Davis, Wayne Morris, Jane Bryan, Humphrey Bogart, Harry Carey

'Good prizefight picture with action, melodrama and names. Unusual in that women will like it.'—*Variety*

Kid Galahad
US 1962 96m De Luxe Panavision
UA / Mirisch (David Weisbart)

Tolerable light-hearted musical remake of the above.

w William Fay *d* Phil Karlson *ph* Burnett Guffey *m* Jeff Alexander

Elvis Presley, Lola Albright, Gig Young, Joan Blackman, Charles Bronson, Ned Glass, David Lewis, Robert Emhardt

Kid Glove Killer*
US 1942 73m bw
MGM (Jack Chertok)

A police laboratory scientist tracks down the murderer of the mayor and finds his best friend is the culprit.
Professional police suspenser of the kind now tackled by television.

w John Higgins, Allen Rivkin *d* Fred Zinnemann *ph* Paul C. Vogel *m* David Snell

Van Heflin, Lee Bowman, Marsha Hunt, Samuel S. Hinds, Eddie Quillan

Kid Millions*
US 1935 90m bw (Technicolor sequence)
Samuel Goldwyn

An East Side kid inherits a fortune and has the time of his life.
Dated star musical with moments which still please.

w George Oppenheimer, William Anthony McGuire, Nunnally Johnson *d* Roy del Ruth *ph* Gregg Toland *m/ly* various *md* Alfred Newman *ad* Richard Day

Eddie Cantor, Ethel Merman, Ann Sothern, George Murphy, Warren Hymer

'Goldwyn-Cantor girl-and-gag socko.'—*Variety*

Kid Nightingale
US 1939 56m bw

A waiter is promoted into a prizefighter, and sings as he knocks out each opponent. Self-spoofing comedy with some laughs. John Payne, Jane Wyman, Walter Catlett, Ed Brophy, Charles D. Brown. Written by Charles Belden, Raymond Schrock, Lee Katz; directed by George Amy; for Warners. 'It's so absolutely silly it's almost good.'—*Variety*

'One man had been like any other to Nora. Then she met the kid.'

Kid Rodelo
US / Spain 1966 91m bw

An outlaw fresh from prison races his former partners for the hidden loot. Dull western. Don Murray, Janet Leigh, Richard Carlson, Broderick Crawford, Jose Nieto. Written by Jack Natteford from a story by Louis L'Amour; directed by Richard Carlson; for Trident/ Fenix/Paramount.

Kidnapped*
US 1938 93m bw
TCF (Kenneth MacGowan)

During the Jacobite rebellion a young boy is sold by his wicked uncle as a slave, and is helped by an outlaw.
Much altered version of a classic adventure story, exciting enough in its own right, and well made in the thirties tradition.

w Sonya Levien, Richard Sherman, Walter Ferris, *novel* Robert Louis Stevenson *d* Alfred L. Werker *ph* Bert Glennon *m* Arthur Lange

Warner Baxter, Freddie Bartholemew, Arleen Whelan, John Carradine, C. Aubrey Smith, Nigel Bruce, Reginald Owen

'Strange modifications have been wrought . . . ambitious effort which misses top rating.'—*Variety*

Kidnapped*
GB 1959 95m Technicolor
Walt Disney (Hugh Attwooll)

A remake fairly faithful to the book, which results in a few *longueurs*; but in general the action is spirited.

wd Robert Stevenson *ph* Paul Beeson *m* Cedric Thorpe Davie

Peter Finch, James MacArthur, Bernard Lee, John Laurie, Finlay Currie, Niall MacGinnis, Peter O'Toole, Miles Malleson, Oliver Johnston, Duncan Macrae, Andrew Cruickshank

Kidnapped*
GB 1971 107m Movielab Panavision
Omnibus (Frederick H. Brogger)

Remake incorporating sections of *Catriona*. Not particularly exciting, but the acting helps.

w Jack Pulman *d* Delbert Mann *ph* Paul Beeson *m* Roy Budd

Michael Caine, Lawrence Douglas, Trevor Howard, Jack Hawkins, Donald Pleasence, Gordon Jackson, Freddie Jones, Jack Watson

The Kidnappers*
GB 1953 95m bw
Rank / Nolbandov–Parkyn
US title: *The Little Kidnappers*

In a Nova Scotian village at the turn of the century a stern old man denies his young grandchildren a pet, so they borrow a baby and hide it in the woods.
Fairly pleasing and popular whimsy for family audiences.

w Neil Paterson *d* Philip Leacock *ph* Eric Cross *m* Bruce Montgomery

Duncan Macrae, Vincent Winter, Jon Whiteley, Theodore Bikel, Jean Anderson

The Kidnapping of the President*
Canada 1980 113m De Luxe
Sefel (George Mendeluk, John Ryan)

Third-world terrorists devise a plot to bring America to its knees by kidnapping the president.
Spirited political thriller which suffers chiefly from overlength.

w Richard Murphy, *novel* Charles Templeton *d* George Mendeluk *ph* Mike Malloy *m* Paul J. Zaza

Hal Holbrook, William Shatner, Van Johnson, Ava Gardner, Miguel Fernandez, Cindy Girling, Elizabeth Shepherd

Kiki
US 1931 96m bw
UA / Mary Pickford (Joseph M. Schenck)

Long unseen star musical.
A tomboyish chorus girl sets her cap at her divorced producer.

w Sam Taylor, *play* David Belasco *d* Sam Taylor *ph* Karl Struss

Mary Pickford, Reginald Denny, Joseph Cawthorne, Margaret Livingston

'Too long and too light . . . what was to have been a cocktail has turned out to have been a soda.'—*Variety*

Kill Her Gently
GB 1958 75m bw

A madman hires two convicts to murder his wife. Very mild and unmemorable thriller. Griffith Jones, Maureen Connell, Marc Lawrence, George Mikell. Written by Paul Erickson; directed by Charles Saunders; for Fortress / Columbia.

Kill Me Tomorrow
GB 1957 80m bw

A down-and-out reporter confesses to murder in order to obtain cash for his son's operation.

Tepid melodrama without much chemistry. Pat O'Brien, Lois Maxwell, George Coulouris, Wensley Pithey, Tommy Steele. Written by Robert Falconer and Manning O'Brine; directed by Terence Fisher; for Delta.

Kill or Cure
GB 1962 88m bw
MGM (George H. Brown)

A series of murders at a nature clinic are solved by a bumbling private detective. Flatfooted and unprofessional murder farce whose only pace is slow.

w David Pursall, Jack Seddon *d* George Pollock *ph* Geoffrey Faithfull *m* Ron Goodwin

Terry-Thomas, Eric Sykes, Dennis Price, Lionel Jeffries, Moira Redmond, David Lodge, Ronnie Barker

Kill the Umpire
US 1950 78m bw

An over-age baseball player can't get the game out of his mind, and returns as an argumentative umpire. Minor comedy of presumed pleasure to sports addicts. William Bendix, Una Merkel, Ray Collins, Gloria Henry, William Frawley. Written by Frank Tashlin; directed by Lloyd Bacon; for Columbia.

The Killer Elite
US 1975 120m De Luxe Panavision
UA / Exeter–Persky Bright (Martin Baum, Arthur Lewis)

A private crime fighting organization handles cases which the CIA prefers not to.
Smooth, fashionable violence which seems to proclaim the end of a cycle.

w Marc Norman, Stirling Silliphant, *novel* Monkey in the Middle by Robert Rostand *d* Sam Peckinpah *ph* Philip Lathrop *m* Jerry Fielding

James Caan, Robert Duvall, Arthur Hill, Gig Young, Mako, Bo Hopkins, Burt Young, Tom Clancy

'Merely a commercial chore.'—*Tom Milne*

'A mysterious, elliptical, visually triumphant film about personal survival in a world of mean-minded machination.'—*Michael Billington, Illustrated London News*

Killer Fish
France / Brazil 1978 101m colour

The leader of a burglary gang hides their haul in a dammed reservoir which he stocks with piranha fish. Heavy-going underwater shocker, with no fun while the fish are off-screen. Lee Majors, Karen Black, Margaux Hemingway, Marisa Berenson, James Franciscus. Written by Michael Rogers; directed by Antonio Margheriti; for Fawcett-Majors / Victoria / Filmar do Brazil. 'A slapdash actioner which casts its rod in water so overfished of late that it's amazing there's still anything down there biting.'—*Variety*.

The Killer is Loose
US 1956 73m bw

A bank robber swears revenge on a policeman who accidentally killed his wife. Star potboiler, just about tolerable. Joseph Cotten, Wendell Corey, Rhonda Fleming, Alan Hale Jnr, Michael Pate. Written by Harold Medford; directed by Budd Boetticher; for Crown / United Artists.

Killer McCoy
US 1947 104m bw
MGM (Sam Zimbalist)

A prizefighter becomes involved in a murder. Grade A production applied to a grade B script.

w Frederick Hazlitt Brennan, Thomas Lennon, George Bruce, George Oppenheimer *d* Roy Rowland *ph* Joseph Ruttenberg *m* David Snell

Mickey Rooney, Ann Blyth, Brian Donlevy, James Dunn, Tom Tully, Sam Levene, James Bell, Gloria Holden

The Killer That Stalked New York
US 1950 75m bw
Columbia (Robert Cohn)
GB title: *Frightened City*

New York is on the alert for a girl smallpox carrier.
Absurdly-titled minor thriller, quite competent but wholly unsurprising.

w Harry Essex *d* Earl McEvoy *ph* Joseph Biroc *m* Hans Salter

Charles Korvin, Evelyn Keyes, William Bishop, Dorothy Malone, Lola Albright, Barry Kelley, Carl Benton Reid, Ludwig Donath

The Killers***
US 1946 105m bw
U-I (Mark Hellinger)
TV title: *A Man Alone*

In a small sleazy town a gangster waits for two assassins to kill him, and we later find out why.
Elaborate tale of cross and double-cross, stunningly executed.

w Anthony Veiller, story Ernest Hemingway *d Robert Siodmak ph Elwood Bredell m* Miklos Rozsa

Burt Lancaster, Edmond O'Brien, Ava Gardner, Albert Dekker, Sam Levene, John Miljan, Virginia Christine, Vince Barnett, Charles D. Brown, Donald MacBride, Phil Brown, Charles McGraw, William Conrad

'About one tenth is Hemingway's, the rest is Universal-International's.'—*Richard Winnington*

'Seldom does a melodrama maintain the high tension that distinguishes this one.'—*Variety*

'There is nothing unique or even valuable about the picture, but energy combined with attention to form and detail doesn't turn up every day; neither does good entertainment.'—*James Agee*

† John Huston contributed to the script but is not credited.

AAN: Anthony Veiller; Robert Siodmak; Miklos Rozsa

The Killers*
US 1964 95m Pathecolor
U-I (Don Siegel)

Zesty, brutal remake intended for TV, but released theatrically because of its violence.

w Gene L. Coon *d* Don Siegel *ph* Richard L. Rawlings *m* Johnny Williams

John Cassavetes, Lee Marvin, Clu Gulager, Angie Dickinson, Ronald Reagan, Claude Akins

'Her soft mouth was the road to sin-smeared violence!'

Killer's Kiss
US 1955 64m bw
UA / Stanley Kubrick

A prizefighter rescues a girl from her gangster lover, and is marked for death.
Tedious low-budget indie which first brought its director into notice.

w / d / ph Stanley Kubrick *m* Gerald Fried

Frank Silvera, Irene Kane, Jamie Smith

The Killers of Kilimanjaro
GB 1959 91m Technicolor Cinemascope
Columbia / Warwick (John R. Sloan)
US title: *Adamson of Africa*

A railroad engineer helps a girl find her lost father and fiancé.
Old-fashioned safari adventure full of action and animals.

w Richard Maibaum, Cyril Hume *d* Richard Thorpe *ph* Ted Moore *m* William Alwyn

Robert Taylor, Anne Aubrey, Grégoire Aslan, Anthony Newley

The Killing**
US 1956 83m bw
UA / Harris–Kubrick (J. B. Harris)

An ex-convict recruits helpers to steal two million dollars from a racetrack.
Incisive, entertaining, downbeat caper movie clearly influenced by *The Asphalt Jungle* and *Rififi*.

wd Stanley Kubrick, novel Clean Break by Lionel White *ph* Lucien Ballard *m* Gerald Fried

Sterling Hayden, Marie Windsor, Jay C. Flippen, Elisha Cook Jnr, Coleen Gray, Vince Edwards, Ted de Corsia, Joe Sawyer, Tim Carey

'The visual authority constantly dominates a flawed script.'—*Arlene Croce*

'The camera watches the whole shoddy show with the keen eye of a terrier stalking a pack of rats.'—*Time*

The Killing Fields***
GB 1984 141m colour
Goldcrest / Enigma (*David Puttnam*)

An American journalist is engulfed in the horror of Cambodia, and his native adviser disappears and is thought to be dead.
Brilliantly filmed, but probably too strong for a commercial audience to stomach, this true adventure tosses one into the horror of modern war and leaves one reeling despite its comparatively happy ending.

w Bruce Robinson, from the article 'The Death and Life of Dith Pran' by Sidney Schanberg *d Roland Joffe ph Chris Menges m* Mike Oldfield *pd* Roy Walker *ed* Jim Clark

Sam Waterston (as Sidney Schanberg), *Haing S. Ngor* (as Dith Pran), John Malkovitch, Julian Sands, Craig T. Nelson

AA: Haing S. Ngor (supporting actor), photography, editing

AAN: best picture, Sam Waterston, adapted screenplay, Roland Joffe

BFA: best picture, adapted screenplay, Haing S. Ngor (supporting actor)

The Killing of a Chinese Bookie
US 1976 113m colour

A Los Angeles nightclub owner is prevailed upon by gangsters to pay off his debt by eliminating a troublesome Chinese. Another unendurable slab of Cassavetes pretentiousness; why he goes on trying, in the face of twenty years of public indifference, is beyond imagining. Ben Gazzara, Timothy Carey, Seymour Cassel, Morgan Woodward. Written and directed by John Cassavetes, for his own company.

The Killing of Angel Street
Australia 1981 100m colour

Residents fight to save old terraced houses from demolition. Rather routine light drama, like an Ealing comedy without laughs. Elizabeth Alexander, John Hargreaves, Reg Lye, David Downer. Written by Michael Craig, Cecil Holmes, Evan Jones; directed by Donald Crombie; for Forest Home Films.

The Killing of Sister George*
US 1969 138m Metrocolor
Associates and Aldrich / Palomar

An ageing lesbian actress is fired from a TV serial and her life collapses around her.
Heavily handled film version of an amusing and moving play; everything is clumsily spelt out, including the love scenes, and the actresses are forced to repeat themselves.

w Lukas Heller, *play Frank Marcus d* Robert Aldrich *ph* Joseph Biroc *m* Gerald Fried

Beryl Reid, Susannah York, *Coral Browne*, Roland Fraser, Patricia Medina, Hugh Paddick, Cyril Delevanti

'The play was second-rate, but with its nice blend of the homely and the chilling, the absurdist and the perverse, it had the quality of a Kraft-Ebbing comic book. Aldrich and Heller have turned this material into a crawling tear-jerker, the lines spoken at a speed adjusted to non-English or non-language-speaking audiences.'—*John Simon*

'A clumpingly archaic piece of film-making.'—*New Yorker, 1982*

Kilroy Was Here
US 1947 68m bw

A hellraiser of the Pacific war goes to college. Mild comedy reuniting two former child stars, but without many other ideas. Jackie Cooper, Jackie Coogan, Wanda McKay, Frank Jenks. Written by Dick Irving Hyland; directed by Phil Karlson; for Sid Luft / Monogram.

Kim*
US 1950 112m Technicolor
MGM (Leon Gordon)

The orphaned son of a British soldier in India has adventures with his horseman friend who belongs to the British secret service.
Colourful Boys' Own Paper high jinks, quite lively but never convincing.

w Leon Gordon, Helen Deutsch, Richard Schayer, *novel* Rudyard Kipling *d* Victor Saville *ph* William Skall *m* André Previn

Errol Flynn, Dean Stockwell, Paul Lukas, Robert Douglas, Thomas Gomez, Cecil Kellaway, Arnold Moss, Reginald Owen

'Ornate, lavish, but curiously lacking in genuine atmosphere, vitality or period sense.'—*Penelope Houston*

Kind Hearts and Coronets***
GB 1949 106m bw
Ealing (Michael Relph)

An impecunious heir eliminates eight D'Ascoynes who stand between him and the family fortune.
Witty, genteel black comedy well set in the stately Edwardian era and quite deserving of its reputation for wit and style; yet the effect is curiously muffled and several opportunities missed.

w Robert Hamer, John Dighton, novel Noblesse Oblige by Roy Horniman *d Robert Hamer ph* Douglas Slocombe

Dennis Price, Alec Guinness (in eight roles), *Valerie Hobson, Joan Greenwood*, Miles Malleson, Arthur Lowe

'A brilliant misfire for the reason that its plentiful wit is literary and practically never pictorial.'—*Richard Winnington*

'Enlivened with cynicism, loaded with dramatic irony and shot through with a suspicion of social satire.'—*Daily Telegraph*

'A film which can be seen and seen again with undiminished pleasure.'—*Basil Wright, 1972*

Kind Lady*
US 1935 76m bw
MGM / Lucien Hubbard
aka: *House of Menace*

A confidence trickster insinuates himself and his criminal friends into the house of an invalid lady.
Unusual but unconvincing melodrama with overwrought leading performances.

w Bernard Schubert, *play* Edward Chodorov, *story* Hugh Walpole *d* George B. Seitz *ph* George Folsey *m* Edward Ward

Basil Rathbone, Aline MacMahon, Mary Carlisle, Frank Albertson, Dudley Digges, Doris Lloyd

'Leisurely pace cramps effectiveness.'—*Variety*

Kind Lady*
US 1951 78m bw
MGM (Armand Deutsch)

Edwardian-set remake of the above, rather more subtly acted but failing to extract all possible frissons.

w Jerry Davis, Edward Chodorov, Charles Bennett *d* John Sturges *ph* Joseph Ruttenberg *m* David Raksin

Maurice Evans, Ethel Barrymore, Angela Lansbury, Keenan Wynn, Betsy Blair, John Williams

'A curiously tame melodrama whose shocks, when they do come, are muffled and ineffectual.'—*Penelope Houston*

A Kind of Loving***
GB 1962 112m bw
Anglo-Amalgamated / Waterhall / Vic Films (Joe Janni)

A young north country draughtsman is forced into marriage, has to live with his dragon-like mother in law, and finally sorts out a relationship with his unhappy wife.
Blunt melodrama with strong kinship to *Saturday Night and Sunday Morning*, strikingly directed and photographed amid urban grime and suburban conformity.

w Keith Waterhouse, Willis Hall, novel Stan Barstow d John Schlesinger ph Denys Coop m Ron Grainer

Alan Bates, June Ritchie, Thora Hird, Bert Palmer, Gwen Nelson

'You will be shocked by this highly moral film only if you are shocked by life.'—*Evening News*

King and Country*
GB 1964 86m bw
BHE (Norman Priggen, Joseph Losey)

In the trenches during World War I, a private is courtmartialled and shot for desertion.
Neat cinematic treatment of a very downbeat play.

w Evan Jones, *play* Hamp by John Wilson *d* Joseph Losey *ph Denys Coop m* Larry Adler *pd* Richard Macdonald

Tom Courtenay, *Dirk Bogarde*, Leo McKern, Barry Foster, James Villiers, Peter Copley

The King and Four Queens
US 1956 86m De Luxe Cinemascope
UA / Russ / Field / Gabco (David Hempstead)

A cowboy braves the wrath of a lady sharpshooter to gain gold and the hand of one of her four daughters.
Tawdry sex western sporadically enlivened by good-humoured playing.

w Margaret Fitts, Richard Alan Simmons *d* Raoul Walsh *ph* Lucien Ballard *m* Alex North

Clark Gable, Eleanor Parker, Jo Van Fleet, Jean Willes, Barbara Nichols, Sara Shane, Roy Roberts

'A superficially cynical exercise in the rival attractions of sex and money.'—*MFB*

The King and I*
US 1956 133m Eastmancolor Cinemascope 55
TCF (Charles Brackett)

Musical remake of *Anna and the King of Siam* (qv), from the highly successful stage production. The film is opulent in lush detail but quite lacking in style.

w Ernest Lehman *d* Walter Lang *ph* Leon Shamroy *m Richard Rodgers book / ly Oscar Hammerstein II* *md* Alfred Newman, Ken Darby *ad* Lyle Wheeler, John de Cuir

Deborah Kerr, Yul Brynner, Rita Moreno, Martin Benson, Alan Mowbray, Geoffrey Toone, Terry Saunders

'Gaiety has something of a struggle to survive.'—*Penelope Houston*

AA: Yul Brynner; Alfred Newman, Ken Darby
AAN: best picture; Walter Lang; Leon Shamroy; Deborah Kerr

The King and the Chorus Girl
US 1937 94m bw
Warner (Mervyn Le Roy)
GB title: *Romance Is Sacred*

A European prince on the spree falls for a New York chorine.
Reasonably lively romantic comedy.

w Norman Krasna, Groucho Marx, from their story Grand Passion *d* Mervyn Le Roy *ph* Tony Gaudio *m* Werner Heymann

Joan Blondell, Fernand Gravet, Edward Everett Horton, Jane Wyman, Alan Mowbray, Mary Nash, Kenny Baker

'Sure word of mouth and a shoo-in for dough.'—*Variety*

King Arthur Was a Gentleman
GB 1942 99m bw
GFD / Gainsborough (Edward Black)

A soldier becomes a hero when he believes he has King Arthur's sword.
Not-too-successful attempt to turn a music hall comedian into a figure of Chaplinesque pathos.

w Val Guest, Marriott Edgar *d* Marcel Varnel *ph* Arthur Crabtree

Arthur Askey, Evelyn Dall, Anne Shelton, Max Bacon, Jack Train, Peter Graves, Vera Frances, Ronald Shiner, Brefni O'Rourke

King Creole
US 1958 116m bw Vistavision
(Paramount) Hal B. Wallis

A failed graduate becomes a singer in a New Orleans night club, and gets involved with gangsters.
Disagreeable crook melodrama turned into a musical star vehicle.

w Herbert Baker, Michael V. Gazzo, *novel* A Stone for Danny Fisher by Harold Robbins *d* Michael Curtiz *ph* Russell Harlan *m* Walter Scharf

Elvis Presley, Carolyn Jones, Dean Jagger, Walter Matthau, Dolores Hart, Paul Stewart

King David
GB / US 1985 114m Rank colour Panavision
Paramount / Martin Elfand

The biblical story of David's involvements with Saul, Goliath and Bathsheba.
Astonishingly tedious, confused and inept retelling of familiar tales, especially so for an audience which needs to be lured back to them.

w Andrew Birkin, James Costigan *d* Bruce Beresford *ph* Donald McAlpine *m* Carl Davis *pd* Ken Adam *ed* William Anderson

Richard Gere, Edward Woodward, Denis Quilley, Jack Klaff, Cherie Lunghi, Alice Krige, Hurd Hatfield, John Castle, Niall Buggy

King for a Night
US 1933 78m bw

A minister's son becomes a boxer and goes to the electric chair for a murder committed by his sister. Glum and incredible moral saga. Chester Morris, Helen Twelvetrees, Grant Mitchell, Alice White, John Miljan, George E. Stone. Written by W. A. McGuire and others; directed by Kurt Neumann; for Universal.

A King in New York*
GB 1957 109m bw
Attica (Charles Chaplin)

A penniless European king finds himself at odds with the American way of life.
Feeble Chaplin comedy from his anti-American period; tedious dialogue and poor physical production allow only momentary flashes of the satire intended.

wd / m Charles Chaplin *ph* Georges Périnal

Charles Chaplin, Michael Chaplin, *Oliver Johnson*, Dawn Addams, Jerry Desmonde, Harry Green, Maxine Audley, Sid James

'Unhappily he is a sadder and an older man; the real punch is gone. His dethroned king is an ironically apt image.'—*Marvin Felheim*

'Maybe the worst film ever made by a celebrated film artist.'—*New Yorker, 1977*

'It shows how the coming of sound was a curse to Chaplin; how its freedoms dissipated his strengths; how his attempts to exploit it intellectually and ideologically played to his weaknesses; how, in short, he was much more grievously hurt by history in art than by history in politics.'—*Stanley Kauffmann*

'An overblown, self-piteous excursion into autobiography.'—*Time Out, 1984*

King Kong********
US 1933 100m bw
RKO (Merian C. Cooper)

A film producer on safari brings back a giant ape which terrorizes New York.
The greatest monster movie of all, a miracle of trick work and suspense, with some of the most memorable moments in film history.

w James Creelman, Ruth Rose, *story* Edgar Wallace *d Merian C. Cooper, Ernest Schoedsack* *ph* Edward Linden, Verne Walker, J. O. Taylor *sound effects* Murray Spivak *chief technician Willis J. O'Brien* *m Max Steiner*

Robert Armstrong, Fay Wray, Bruce Cabot, Frank Reicher

CARL DENHAM (Robert Armstrong): 'It wasn't the airplanes. It was beauty killed the beast.'

'If properly handled, should gather good grosses in a walk . . . and may open up a new medium for scaring babies via the screen.'—*Variety*

'Just amusing nonsense punctuated by such reflections as why, if the natives wanted to keep the monster on the other side of the wall, they should have built a door big enough to let him through.'—*James Agate*

AAN: photography

'The most exciting motion picture event of all time!'

King Kong
US 1976 135m Metrocolor Panavision
Dino de Laurentiis

Semi-spoof remake with added sexual overtones; though launched on a massive wave of publicity, it lacks both the charm and the technical resources of its predecessor.

w Lorenzo Semple Jnr *d* John Guillermin *ph* Richard H. Kline *m* John Barry *pd* Dale Hennesy, Mario Chiari

Jeff Bridges, Charles Grodin, Jessica Lange, John Randolph, René Auberjonois, Julius Harris, Ed Lauter

'The one and original lovable monster is lost amid all the hydraulic manipulations in what now emerges as the story of a dumb blonde who falls for a huge plastic finger.'—*Judith Crist, Saturday Review*

'Even with colour, the settings of Kong II are no match for the rich black-and-white chiaroscuro of Kong I, with its echoes of artists like Gustave Doré and Max Ernst and its sensitivity to the emotional values of tone and texture.'—*Jack Kroll, Newsweek*

AAN: Richard H. Kline

† *King Kong Lives* crept out minimally in 1986.

King Lear*
GB / Denmark 1970 137m bw
Columbia / Filmways–Laterna (Michael Birkett)

Tragedy ensues when an old king prematurely divides his kingdom between his daughters.
Miserably photographed in freezing Jutland, this is a deliberately downbeat version which despite its varied points of interest is extremely hard to sit through.

w William Shakespeare (a cut text) *d* Peter Brook *ph* Henning Kristiansen *m* none *pd* Georges Wakhevitch

Paul Scofield, Irene Worth, Alan Webb, Tom Fleming, Susan Engel, Cyril Cusack, Patrick Magee, Jack MacGowran

King Lear
US 1987 90m colour

A culture expert travelling in France thinks of a mad old man and his daughter as subjects for a film. Sheer nonsense doodled by the director with someone else's money. Burgess Meredith, Peter Sellars, Molly Ringwald, Jean-Luc Godard. Written and directed by Jean-Luc Godard; for Cannon.

King of Alcatraz*
US 1938 56m bw
Paramount (William C. Thomas)

Convicts escape on a freighter, but one needs surgery. Pacy programmer with a stalwart cast.

w Irving Reis *d* Robert Florey *ph* Harry Fischbeck *md* Boris Morros

Gail Patrick, J. Carrol Naish, Lloyd Nolan, Harry Carey, Robert Preston, Anthony Quinn, Dennis Morgan, Porter Hall

'Good gangster actioner . . . will please those liking crime cinematics.'—*Variety*

King of Burlesque*
US 1935 88m bw
TCF (Kenneth MacGowan)

A vaudeville impresario overcomes his troubles.
Well-written musical with plenty of variety talent.

w James Seymour, Gene Markey, Harry Tugend *d* Sidney Lanfield *ph* Peverell Marley *songs* various

Warner Baxter, Alice Faye, Jack Oakie, Mona Barrie, Arline Judge, Dixie Dunbar, Gregory Ratoff, Herbert Mundin, *Fats Waller*, Kenny Baker
Songs: 'I've Got My Fingers Crossed'; 'Lovely Lady'; 'Spreadin' Rhythm Around'; 'Who's Big Baby Are You?'; 'I'm Shooting High'; 'I Love to Ride the Horses'

'Big-time musical, with production, material and cast making up for story shortcomings.'—*Variety*

† Remade as *Hello Frisco Hello.*

King of Chinatown
US 1939 56m bw

A top racketeer is double-crossed by his henchman. Smartly paced underworld melodrama. Anna May Wong, Akim Tamiroff, Sidney Toler, J. Carrol Naish, Philip Ahn, Anthony Quinn. Written by Lillie Hayward, Irving Reis, Herbert Biberman; directed by Nick Grinde; for Stuart Walker / Paramount. 'Good support for key duals.'—*Variety*

King of Comedy***
US 1982 109m Technicolor
TCF / Embassy International (Arnon Milchan)

Obsessed with becoming a chat show host, an aspiring comedian kidnaps his idol and ransoms him for a spot in the show.
Amusing, underplayed farce with a tragic lining: a very convincing picture of the media today.

w Paul D. Zimmermann d Martin Scorsese ph Fred Schuler *m* various *pd* Boris Leven

Robert de Niro, Jerry Lewis, Diahnne Abbott, Sandra Bernard

'This is a very frightening film, and in retrospect nothing about it seems funny at all.'—*Variety*

'Unquestionably one of the films of the year.'—*Guardian*

'A most eerie and memorable picture.'—*Spectator*

BFA: best original screenplay

King of Gamblers
US 1937 79m bw
Paramount
aka: *Czar of the Slot Machines*

A ruthless gangster loves a singer who loves a reporter who is out to expose him.
A muddled script mars this pacy lower-birth item.

w Doris Anderson *d* Robert Florey *ph* Harry Fischbeck *md* Boris Morros

Akim Tamiroff, Claire Trevor, Lloyd Nolan, Buster Crabbe, Porter Hall

'Well enough done to rate okay in the smaller spots solo.'—*Variety*

King of Hearts
France / Italy 1966 110m Eastmancolor
UA / Fildebroc / Montoro (Philippe de Broca)
original title: *Le Roi de Coeur*

In World War I, a Scottish soldier finds a war-torn town occupied only by lunatics who have escaped from the asylum and who want to make him their king.
Heavy-handed whimsy which never catches fire despite the talents involved.

w Daniel Boulanger *d* Philippe de Broca *ph* Pierre Lhomme *m* Georges Delerue

Alan Bates, Geneviève Bujold, Jean-Claude Brialy, Françoise Christophe, Pierre Brasseur, Micheline Presle, Adolfo Celi, Julien Guiomar

King of Jazz***
US 1930 101m Technicolor
Universal (Carl Laemmle Jnr)

Musical revue.
Stylish, spectacular, revelatory early musical: a treasure trove.

devised / d John Murray Anderson w Harry Ruskin, Charles MacArthur *pd* Hal Mohr, Ray Rennahan, Jerome Ash *ad Herman Rose*

Paul Whiteman and his orchestra, John Boles, Bing Crosby (with the Rhythm Boys), Laura la Plante, Glenn Tryon, Slim Summerville, Walter Brennan
Songs: 'Happy Feet'; 'A Bench in the Park'; 'My Bridal Veil'; 'Song of the Dawn'; 'I Like to Do Things for You'; 'Music Has Charms'; 'My Lover'; 'It Happened in Monterey'; 'Ragamuffin Romeo'; 'So the Bluebirds and the Blackbirds Got Together'

'A box office picture anywhere for one week.'—*Variety*

'Under a master director and the reverent genius of great players, the story of Christ has taken human form and greater understanding!'
'Dramatic magnificence, spectacular splendour, riotous joy, tigerish rage, undying love, terrifying tempests, appalling earthquakes!'

King of Kings**
US 1927 155m approx (24 fps) (various versions) bw silent
(Pathé) Cecil B. de Mille
Famous subtitle: *Harness my zebras, gift of the Nubian king!*

The life of Jesus, seen more or less from the viewpoint of Mary Magdalene.
A patchy but frequently moving and pictorially effective work, ranging from the sublime (the first view of Jesus as a blind man regains his sight) to the ridiculous ('Harness my zebras, gift of the Nubian king!' says the Queen of Sheba in a sub-title).

w Jeanie Macpherson *d Cecil B. de Mille ph J. Peverell Marley*

H. B. Warner, Jacqueline Logan, Joseph Schildkraut (Judas), Ernest Torrence (Peter), Victor Varconi (Pilate), Dorothy Cumming (Mary, mother of Jesus), Rudolph Schildkraut (Caiaphas)

'The most impressive of all motion pictures.'—*Mordaunt Hall, New York Times*

'A picture which will tend to standardize the world's conception of the New Testament . . . de Mille has one of the best business minds in pictures and making *King of Kings* was the most brilliant stroke of his successful business career.'—*Welford Beaton, The Film Spectator*

'A story of the Christ! The glory of his spoken words!'

King of Kings*
US 1961 161m Super Technirama
MGM / Samuel Bronston

The life of Jesus Christ.
Known in the trade as *I Was a Teenage Jesus*, this good-looking but rather tedious film is neither vulgar nor very interesting; a solemn, decent, bible-in-pictures pageant.

w Philip Yordan *d* Nicholas Ray *ph* Franz Planer, Manuel Berenger *m* Miklos Rozsa *ad* Georges Wakhevitch

Jeffrey Hunter, Robert Ryan, Siobhan McKenna, Frank Thring, Hurd Hatfield, Rip Torn, Harry Guardino, Viveca Lindfors, Rita Gam

The King of Marvin Gardens*
US 1972 104m Eastmancolor
Columbia / BBS (Bob Rafaelson)

The host of a late night radio talk show gets embroiled in his brother's schemes.
Thoughtful tragi-comedy overweighted by talk, but with good performances.

w Jacob Brackman *d* Bob Rafaelson *ph* Laszlo Kovacs

Jack Nicholson, Bruce Dern, Ellen Burstyn, Julia Anne Robinson

'Indecipherable dark nonsense about brothers and goals and the American dream. An unqualified disaster.'—*New Yorker*

'Glum news from the people who made *Five Easy Pieces*, which had a lot of good work in it along with some pretentious flab. In their new picture the flab has taken over.'—*Stanley Kauffmann*

King of Paris
GB 1935 75m bw

The story of a French stage impresario, supposedly based on Sacha Guitry. Interesting try for a minority audience. Cedric Hardwicke, Marie Glory, Ralph Richardson,

THE KING OF MARVIN GARDENS. Art film, American style—Bruce Dern embraces an embarrased-looking Jack Nicholson.

Phillis Monkman. Written by W. P. Lipscomb, John Drinkwater, Paul Gangelin from play La Voie Lactée by Alfred Savoir, John van Druten; directed by Jack Raymond; for Herbert Wilcox/British and Dominions. 'Nothing much to be desired in this picture, excepting a story.'—*Variety*

King of the Carnival
US 1955 bw serial: 12 eps

Circus acrobats help the treasury department to track down counterfeiters. A lively background prevents this serial from becoming tedious. Harry Lauter, Fran Bennett, Keith Richards, Robert Shayne. Directed by Franklin Adreon; for Republic.

King of the Congo
US 1952 bw serial: 15 eps

An air force captain assumes the identity of a dead pilot taking secret microfilm to a subversive group in Africa; but he is captured by The Rock People. Rather splendid serial with all the trimmings. Buster Crabbe, Gloria Dee, Leonard Penn, Jack Ingram. Directed by Spencer Bennet and Wallace Grissell; for Columbia.

King of the Damned*
GB 1935 76m bw
Gaumont (Michael Balcon)

On a South Seas convict settlement, harsh treatment leads to mutiny.
A downright peculiar project for a British studio at this time, but technically very competent for those who like this kind of thing.

w Charles Bennett, Sidney Gilliat, Noel Langley, *play* John Chancellor *d* Walter Forde *ph* Bernard Knowles *md* Louis Levy

Conrad Veidt, Helen Vinson, Noah Beery, Cecil Ramage, Edmund Willard, Raymond Lovell, Allan Jeayes, Percy Parsons

'Goes so far overboard on gloom that it defeats its own end.'—*Variety*

King of the Forest Rangers
US 1946 bw serial: 12 eps

Strange prehistoric towers hold the key to vast wealth, and the Forest Rangers prevent villains from getting it. He-man stuff, adequately mounted. Larry Thompson, Helen Talbot, Stuart Hamblen, Anthony Warde. Directed by Spencer Bennet and Fred Brannon; for Republic.

King of the Gypsies
US 1978 112m Technicolor
Paramount / Dino de Laurentiis (Anna Gross)

A gypsy leader is denied the hand in marriage of the daughter of a rival, so he kidnaps her.
Ethnic melodrama which despite its vigorous insistence on tradition—or perhaps because of it—plays like a mad musical without any songs.

w Frank Pierson, *novel* Peter Maas *d* Frank Pierson *ph* Sven Nykvist, Edward Lachman *m* David Grisman *pd* Gene Callahan

Sterling Hayden, Brooke Shields, Shelley Winters, Susan Sarandon, Judd Hirsch, Eric Roberts

'Body of a Greek god! Strength of a Hercules!'
King of the Jungle
US 1933 73m bw

A small boy grows up with lions; he is captured with them and sold to an American circus. Sub-Tarzan hokum which cheered up the kids. Buster Crabbe, Frances Dee, Douglass Dumbrille, Robert Adair, Robert Barrat. Written by Philip Wylie, Fred Niblo Jnr, C. T. Stoneham; directed by H. Bruce Humberstone and Max Marcin; for Paramount. 'Minus any help from the marquee it will have to attract on merit alone, and on merit it rates fair business.'—*Variety*

King of the Khyber Rifles
US 1954 100m Technicolor Cinemascope
TCF (Frank Rosenberg)

In 1857 a British garrison in India is threatened by the forces of Kuuram Khan but saved by a half-caste officer.
Standard North-West Frontier adventure, old-fashioned and rather dull.

w Ivan Goff, Ben Roberts *d* Henry King *ph* Leon Shamroy *m* Bernard Herrmann

Tyrone Power, Terry Moore, Michael Rennie, Guy Rolfe, John Justin

King of the Mounties
US 1942 bw serial: 12 eps

Activities of the Canadian Fifth Column result in that country being mercilessly bombed by a new craft called The Falcon. The Mounties once more get their man. Allan Lane, Gilbert Emery, Russell Hicks, Douglass Dumbrille, Peggy Drake, Abner Biberman, Duncan Renaldo. Directed by William Witney; for Republic.

King of the Roaring Twenties
US 1961 106m bw
Warner / AA / Bischoff–Diamond
GB title: *The Big Bankroll*

A gambler, Arnold Rothstein, becomes powerful among twenties gangsters.
Routine crime drama, shoddily made.

w Jo Swerling *d* Joseph M. Newman *ph* Carl Guthrie *m* Franz Waxman

David Janssen, Dianne Foster, Mickey Rooney, Mickey Shaughnessy, Diana Dors, Dan O'Herlihy, Jack Carson, Keenan Wynn, William Demarest, Joseph Schildkraut, Regis Toomey, Murvyn Vye

'Superficial, shopworn biography of an infamous bookie.'—*MFB*

King of the Rocket Men
US 1949 bw serial: 12 eps

Diabolical Dr Vulcan menaces a desert research project, but is foiled by The Rocket Man. Irresistible serial nonsense with all the ingredients. Tristram Coffin, Mae Clarke, Don Haggerty, House Peters Jnr, I. Stanford Jolley. Directed by Fred Brannon; for Republic.

King of the Royal Mounted
US 1940 bw serial: 12 eps

A new discovery called Compound X is sought by enemy agents. Just what you expect from a serial about the Mounties. Allan Lane, Robert Strange, Robert Kellard, Lita Conway, Harry Cording, Bryant Washburn. Directed by William Witney and John English; for Republic.

King of the Texas Rangers
US 1941 bw serial: 12 eps

The son of a Texas Ranger avenges his father's death by routing a gang of saboteurs. Fair average serial. Sammy Baugh, Neil Hamilton, Pauline Moore, Duncan Renaldo, Charles Trowbridge, Monte Blue. Directed by William Witney and John English; for Republic.

King of the Turf
US 1939 88m bw

A gambler out of luck befriends a small boy who turns out to be his own son. Hard to take even at the time, this sentimental tarididdle does not bear later scrutiny. Adolphe Menjou, Dolores Costello, Walter Abel, Roger Daniel. Written and directed by George Bruce; for Edward Small.

'Dandy racetrack yarn . . . it has a refreshing appeal and the dialogue is excellent.'—*Variety*

King of the Underworld
US 1938 69m bw

When her husband is killed by gangsters, a doctor takes her own steps to round them up. Sex-change remake of *Dr Socrates*; certainly no better. Kay Francis, Humphrey Bogart, James Stephenson, John Eldredge. Written by George Bricker, Vincent Sherman; directed by Lewis Seiler; for Warners. 'It will have trouble even in the duals.'—*Variety*

King of the Wild
US 1931 bw serial: 12 eps

Several adventurers search for a diamond mine. Early talkie serial with little of the later style. Walter Miller, Nora Lane, Boris Karloff, Dorothy Christy, Tom Santschi. Directed by Richard Thorpe; for Mascot.

King, Queen, Knave*
US / West Germany 1972 92m Eastmancolor
Wolper / Maran (Lutz Hengst)

The wife of a Munich bookseller falls for his adolescent nephew.
Amusing, capriciously directed sex comedy.

w David Shaw, David Seltzer, *novel* Vladimir Nabokov *d* Jerzy Skolomowski *ph* Charly Steinberger *m* Stanley Myers

Gina Lollobrigida, David Niven, John Moulder-Brown, Mario Adorf, Carl Fox-Duering

'Even Hell had to have a monarch!'
King Rat**
US 1965 134m bw
Columbia / Coleytown (James Woolf)

In Singapore's Changi Gaol during World War II an American corporal lives more comfortably than the other prisoners by shabby dealings with the camp guards.
Overlong but generally gripping character melodrama—'not a story of escape but a story of survival'.

wd Bryan Forbes, novel James Clavell *ph* Burnett Guffey *m* John Barry

George Segal, Tom Courtenay, John Mills, James Fox, Denholm Elliott, Todd Armstrong, Patrick O'Neal, James Donald, Alan Webb, Leonard Rossiter, Geoffrey Bayldon

AAN: Burnett Guffey

King Richard and the Crusaders
US 1954 113m Warnercolor Cinemascope
Warner (Henry Blanke)

During the Crusades, the dreaded Saladin arrives in England in disguise and falls in love with Lady Edith . . .
Crudely confected comic strip version of Sir Walter Scott's *The Talisman*, ineptly written and cast, with poor production values.

w John Twist *d* David Butler *ph* Peverell Marley *m* Max Steiner

Rex Harrison (as Saladin), Virginia Mayo, George Sanders, Laurence Harvey, Robert Douglas

LADY EDITH (Virginia Mayo): 'Fight, fight, fight! That's all you think of, Dick Plantagenet!'

'Do not adjust your set—the sound you hear is Sir Walter Scott turning in his grave.'—*Sunday Express*

'It shows why the Crusades never really amounted to much.'—*Time*

King Solomon of Broadway
US 1935 72m bw

A night-club owner gambles away money he has borrowed from the mob. Stale underworld melodrama. Edmund Lowe, Dorothy Page, Pinky Tomlin, Louise Henry, Charles Grapewin. Written by Harry Clork, Doris Malloy; directed by Alan Crosland; for Universal. 'Won't go very far; mostly for doubles.'—*Variety*

King Solomon's Mines*
GB 1937 80m bw
Gainsborough (Geoffrey Barkas)

Explorers in Africa persuade an exiled chief to help them find a diamond mine.
Rather somnolent though well-cast version of a favourite adventure novel, with a splendid final reel.

w Michael Hogan, A. R. Rawlinson, Roland Pertwee, Ralph Spence, Charles Bennett, *novel* H. Rider Haggard *d Robert Stevenson* *ph* Glen MacWilliams *m* Mischa Spoliansky

Cedric Hardwicke, *Paul Robeson*, Roland Young, John Loder, Anna Lee, Sydney Fairbrother, Robert Adams

'If the pop houses can accept its half-throttle speed, they'll get all the thrills and entertainment they want.'—*Variety*

'They kept the eye of the camera open for every form of wild and savage life and crammed it all into the picture, so one gets the impression that Allan Quartermain is delivering a lecture with illustrations rather than taking part in an adventure.'—*Richard Mallett, Punch*

King Solomon's Mines*
US 1950 102m Technicolor
MGM (Sam Zimbalist)

A remake which is largely travelogue with the merest trimmings of story.

w Helen Deutsch *d* Compton Bennett *ph* Robert Surtees

Stewart Granger, Deborah Kerr, Richard Carlson, Hugo Haas, Lowell Gilmore

† Andrew Marton directed the second unit sequences.

AA: Robert Surtees
AAN: best picture

King Solomon's Mines
US 1985 100m colour CinemaScope
Quartermain is hired by a girl who wants to find her kidnapped father. Adaptation in the vein of *Indiana Jones* and then some: the leading characters are almost boiled in a pot. Enjoyment depends on your sense of humour. Richard Chamberlain, Sharon Stone, Herbert Lom, John Rhys-Davies, Ken Gampu. Written by Gene Quintano, James R. Silke; directed by J. Lee Thompson; for Cannon.
'The cinema's equivalent to junk food.'—*Sunday Mail*

The King Steps Out*
US 1936 85m bw
Columbia (William Perlberg)
Emperor Franz Josef falls in love with the sister of the princess to whom he is betrothed.
Rather heavy-handed romance with music, not in its director's best style but showing flashes of his decorative talent.
w Sidney Buchman, *operetta* Cissy by Herbert and Ernst Marischka *d* Josef Von Sternberg *ph* Lucien Ballard *songs* Fritz Kreisler, Dorothy Fields *ad* Stephen Goossen
Grace Moore, Franchot Tone, Walter Connolly, Raymond Walburn, Herman Bing, Victor Jory, Elizabeth Risdon, Nana Bryant, Frieda Inescort, Thurston Hall
'Josef Von Sternberg asked that it not be included in retrospectives of his work, but he really did make the damned thing.'—*New Yorker, 1977*

Kingdom of the Spiders
US 1977 95m colour
Arachnid / Dimension (Henry Fownes)
In an Arizona valley the death rate soars when tarantulas begin preying in groups on humans instead of singly on each other.
The spiders is coming, as Hitch might have remarked, and not even giant-size. Standard shudders, efficiently presented.
w Richard Robinson, Alan Caillou *d* John Cardos *ph* John Morrill, John Wheeler *md* Igo Kantor
William Shatner, Tiffany Bolling, Woody Strode, David MacLean

Kings Go Forth
US 1958 109m bw
UA / Ross–Eton (Frank Ross)
August 1944: two American soldiers fall out over a black French woman who is torn between them.
Heavy-going war melodrama, well enough done for those who can take it.
w Merle Miller, *novel* Joe David Brown *d* Delmer Daves *ph* Daniel Fapp *m* Elmer Bernstein
Frank Sinatra, Tony Curtis, Natalie Wood, Leora Dana, Karl Swenson

Kings of the Road
Germany 1975 176m bw
Two men on a bus talk of their past lives, their problems, their hopes and their fears.
Impossibly tedious two-hander which doubtless says something about life for those with the patience to sit it out. Ruediger Vogler, Hanns Zischler. Written and directed by Wim Wenders; for Wim Wenders Productions. (Original title: *Im Lauf der Zeit.*)

Kings of the Sun
US 1963 108m De Luxe Panavision
UA / Mirisch (Lewis J. Rachmil)
A Mayan tribe emigrates from Mexico to Texas and makes peace with the local Indian chief.
Ponderous dark age epic replete with human sacrifice, high-mindedness and solemn pauses. The actors and sets carry it as far as it will go.
w Elliot Arnold, James R. Webb *d* J. Lee-Thompson *ph* Joe MacDonald *m* Elmer Bernstein *ad* Alfred Ybarra
Yul Brynner, George Chakiris, Shirley Anne Field, Richard Basehart, Brad Dexter, Barry Morse

'The king's ships . . . the king's gold . . . the king's girls . . . were the treasure!'
The King's Pirate
US 1967 100m Technicolor
Universal (Robert Arthur)
An American in the 18th-century British navy infiltrates a pirate stronghold in Madagascar.
Tatty remake of *Against All Flags*, rising to a few minor heights of swashbuckling.
w Paul Wayne *d* Don Weis *ph* Clifford Stine *m* Ralph Ferraro
Doug McClure, Jill St John, Guy Stockwell, Kurt Kasznar, Torin Thatcher, Richard Deacon, Sean McClory

King's Rhapsody
GB 1955 93m Eastmancolor Cinemascope
Everest (Herbert Wilcox)
An exiled Ruritanian king leaves his mistress to return home to a political marriage.
Love versus duty in a ludicrously inept film of Ivor Novello's highly theatrical musical drama, cheaply made and killed stone dead by casting and wide screen.
w Pamela Bower, Christopher Hassall, A. P. Herbert *d* Herbert Wilcox *ph* Max Greene
Errol Flynn, Anna Neagle, Patrice Wymore, Martita Hunt, Finlay Currie

'The town they talk of in whispers!'
King's Row****
US 1941 127m bw
Warner (David Lewis)
In a small American town during the early years of the century, three children grow up into a world of cruelty and madness.
Superb Hollywood melodrama, a Peyton Place with great visual strength, haunting music and a wholly absorbing if incredible plot.
w Casey Robinson, novel Henry Bellamann *d Sam Wood ph James Wong Howe m Erich Wolfgang Korngold pd William Cameron Menzies*
Ann Sheridan, Robert Cummings, Ronald Reagan, *Claude Rains*, Betty Field, Charles Coburn, Nancy Coleman, *Maria Ouspenskaya*, Harry Davenport, Judith Anderson, Karen Verne
DRAKE (Ronald Reagan): 'Where's the rest of me?'
'Half masterpiece and half junk.'—*James Agate*
'Out of the hushed strangeness of these lives, and out of the shadows that hid their shame, filmdom has fashioned a drama most unusual, most touching and most wonderful!'—*publicity*
'Tranquilly accepting many varieties of psychopathic behaviour as the simple facts of life, this film has its own kind of sentimental glow, yet the melodramatic incidents are surprisingly compelling.'—*New Yorker, 1982*
'One of the great melodramas, a veritable Mount Rushmore of physical and emotional cripples.'—*Time Out, 1981*
AAN: best picture; Sam Wood; James Wong Howe

A King's Story*
GB 1965 102m Technicolor
Le Vien Films (Jack Le Vien)
Interviews with the Duke and Duchess of Windsor are interspersed with newsreels of the abdication crisis.
Earnest popular documentary with many points in its favour, including a resounding commentary by Orson Welles.
w Glyn Jones *d* Harry Booth *m* Ivor Slaney

The King's Thief
US 1955 79m Eastmancolor Cinemascope
MGM (Edwin H. Knopf)
The Duke of Brampton plots treason against Charles II but a highwayman robs him of an incriminating notebook.
Dismal swashbuckler with neither zest nor style, just a cast of unhappy-looking actors.
w Charles Knopf *d* Robert Z. Leonard *ph* Robert Planck *m* Miklos Rozsa
David Niven, Edmund Purdom, Ann Blyth, George Sanders, Roger Moore

The King's Vacation
US 1933 62m bw
A king abdicates to seek the simple life.
Pleasing fable with a few theatrical ironies. George Arliss, Florence Arliss, Dick Powell, Marjorie Gateson, Dudley Digges. Written by Ernest Pascal and Maude T. Howell; directed by John Adolfi; for Warner.

Kipps***
GB 1941 112m bw
TCF (Edward Black)
US title: *The Remarkable Mr Kipps*
In 1906, a draper's assistant comes into money and tries to crash society.
Charming, unassuming film of a well-loved novel, later musicalized as *Half a Sixpence*.
w Sidney Gilliat, *novel* H. G. Wells *d Carol Reed ph* Arthur Crabtree *m* Charles Williams

Michael Redgrave, Phyllis Calvert, Diana Wynyard, *Arthur Riscoe*, Max Adrian, Helen Haye, Michael Wilding, Lloyd Pearson, Edward Rigby, Hermione Baddeley, Frank Pettingell, Beatrice Varley, Kathleen Harrison, Felix Aylmer

'It has the old fashioned charm of wax roses under a glass bell.'—*New York Times*

Kismet
US 1930 90m bw 65mm Vitascope
Warner

An Oriental magician overcomes a wicked vizier.
Rather tame filming of a spectacular which belongs on the stage.

w Howard Estabrook, *play* Edward Knoblock *d* John Francis Dillon *ph* John Seitz

Otis Skinner, Loretta Young, David Manners, Mary Duncan, Sidney Blackmer, Fred Sterling, Edmund Breese, Montagu Love

Kismet*
US 1944 100m Technicolor
MGM (Everett Riskin)
TV title: *Oriental Dream*

Hollow and humourless but striking-looking remake of the above.

w John Meehan, *d William Dieterle ph Charles Rosher m* Herbert Stothart *ad* Cedric Gibbons, Daniel B. Cathcart

Ronald Colman, Marlene Dietrich, James Craig, Edward Arnold, Hugh Herbert, Joy Ann Page, Florence Bates, Harry Davenport, Hobart Cavanaugh, Robert Warwick

'Enormous sets and crowding players are handled with such a clarity of line and colour that their gorgeousness never becomes untidy.'—*Monthly Film Bulletin*

AAN: Charles Rosher; Herbert Stothart

Kismet
US 1955 113m Eastmancolor Cinemascope
MGM (Arthur Freed)

Unlucky musical remake from the stage show with Borodin music.

w Charles Lederer, Luther Davis, from their musical play *d* Vincente Minnelli *ph* Joseph Ruttenberg *ch* Jack Cole *ad* Cedric Gibbons, Preston Ames

Howard Keel, Ann Blyth, Dolores Gray, Vic Damone, Monty Woolley, Sebastian Cabot, Jay C. Flippen, Mike Mazurki, Jack Elam

The Kiss*
US 1929 64m approx (24 fps) bw silent
MGM (Albert Lewin)

A woman is accused of the murder of her jealous husband.
A wisp of a melodrama, enlivened by its star; otherwise only notable as MGM's last silent picture.

w Hans Kraly *d* Jacques Feyder *ph* William Daniels

Greta Garbo, Lew Ayres, Conrad Nagel, Holmes Herbert, Anders Randolf

'Women were putty in his hands!'
Kiss and Make Up
US 1934 80m bw
Paramount (B. P. Schulberg)

A Parisian beauty specialist forsakes a rich client for his loyal secretary.
Forgettable romantic comedy.

w Harlan Thompson, George Marion Jnr, *play* Stephen Bekeffi *d* Harlan Thompson *ph* Leon Shamroy

Cary Grant, Genevieve Tobin, Helen Mack, Edward Everett Horton, Lucien Littlefield, Mona Maris

'More gags than romance . . . a nice picture lacking sufficient strength to wow, but should do all right.'—*Variety*

Kiss and Tell*
US 1945 92m bw
Columbia (Sol C. Siegel)

To protect another girl, an irrepressible teenager pretends to be pregnant.
Good-humoured farcical comedy which at the time was thought pretty shocking, especially with the infant darling of the thirties in the lead.

w F. Hugh Herbert, from his play *d* Richard Wallace *ph* Charles Lawton *m* Werner Heymann

Shirley Temple, Robert Benchley, Walter Abel, Jerome Courtland, Katherine Alexander, Porter Hall, Tom Tully

'All brilliantly characteristic of the worst anyone could think of American life.'—*James Agee*

A Kiss before Dying*
US 1956 94m De Luxe Cinemascope
UA / Crown (Robert Jacks)

A college boy kills women who get in his way.
Reasonably absorbing exercise in psychopathology which would have been more effective on a smaller screen.

w Lawrence Roman, *novel* Ira Levin *d* Gerd Oswald *ph* Lucien Ballard *m* Lionel Newman

Jeffrey Hunter, Joanne Woodward, Robert Wagner, Virginia Leith, *Mary Astor*, George Macready

The Kiss before the Mirror
US 1933 66m bw

A lawyer defends a man who killed his wife from jealousy, then finds that the same thing is happening to him. Stilted drama which was thought stylish at the time but is now a disappointment from this director; miscast, too. Frank Morgan, Nancy Carroll, Gloria Stuart, Paul Lukas, Charles Grapewin. Written by William Anthony McGuire, from the play by Lazslo Fodor; directed by James Whale; for Universal. (NB: remade in 1938 as *Wives Under Suspicion*.) 'Direction and adaptation lift this one into passable entertainment.'—*Variety*

A Kiss for Corliss
US 1949 88m bw
UA / Strand / James Nasser (Colin Miller)
aka: *Almost a Bride*

A teenager develops a crush on a middle-aged *roué*.
Dismal sequel to *Kiss and Tell* in the shadow of *The Bachelor and the Bobby Soxer*.

w Howard Dimsdale *d* Richard Wallace *ph* Robert de Grasse *m* Werner Heymann

David Niven, Shirley Temple, Tom Tully, Darryl Hickman, Virginia Welles

'A disastrous teenage potboiler.'—*David Niven*

'I sometimes think that David Niven
Should not take all the parts he's given;
While of the art of Shirley Temple
I, for the moment, have had ample.'—*C. A. Lejeune*

A Kiss in the Dark
US 1949 87m bw
Warner (Harry Kurnitz)

A concert pianist finds romance in a boarding house peopled with zany characters.
Paper-thin romantic comedy.

w Harry Kurnitz *d* Delmer Daves *ph* Robert Burks *m* Max Steiner

David Niven, Jane Wyman, Broderick Crawford, Maria Ouspenskaya, Victor Moore, Wayne Morris, Joseph Buloff, Curt Bois

Kiss Me Again**
US 1925 77m approx (24 fps) bw silent
Warner

A bored wife is tempted to stray, but doesn't.
Excellent silent comedy from an old boulevard farce, remade to less effect in the forties as *That Uncertain Feeling*.

w Hans Kraly, *play* Divorcons by Victorien Sardou, Emile de Najac *d Ernst Lubitsch ph* Charles Von Enger

Marie Prévost, Monte Blue, John Roche, Willard Louis, Clara Bow

'Another sex masterpiece from the Attila of Hollywood . . . Continental high comedy done in the central European manner with Germanic harshness and irony of attack.'—*Ted Shane, New Yorker*

'Perhaps the most exquisite light screen comedy ever made on the subject of l'amour.'—*Herman G. Weinberg*

Kiss Me Again
US 1931 74m Technicolor

A French lieutenant and a cabaret singer chase each other half across the world. Modest musical from Victor Herbert's *Mademoiselle Modiste*; popular at the time as a vehicle for two-colour Technicolor. Walter Pidgeon, Bernice Claire, Frank McHugh, Edward Everett Horton. Written by Julien Josephson and Paul Perez; directed by William A. Seiter; for Warner. (GB title: *Toast of the Legion*.) 'Doubtful as strong b.o. but clean, deserving, and may get a break.'—*Variety*

'I don't care what you do to me, Mike—just do it fast!'
Kiss Me Deadly*
US 1955 105m bw
UA / Parklane (Robert Aldrich)

By helping a girl who is nevertheless murdered, Mike Hammer prevents crooks from stealing a case of radio-active material.
Curiously arty and excruciatingly boring private eye thriller, a ripe piece of cinematic cheese full of tilt shots and symbols: even the titles read from down to up.

w A. I. Bezzerides *d* Robert Aldrich *ph* Ernest Laszlo *m* Frank de Vol

Ralph Meeker, Albert Dekker, Cloris Leachman, Paul Stewart, Juano Hernandez, Wesley Addy, Maxene Cooper

'This meeting of "art" and pulp literature is, to say the least, curious.'—*Monthly Film Bulletin*

Kiss Me Goodbye
US 1982 101m De Luxe
TCF / Boardwalk / Burt Sugarman / Keith Barish (Robert Mulligan)

A widow planning to marry again is harassed by the ghost of her first husband.
It worked in *Blithe Spirit*, but this is on a different level, a toned-down rendering of the heavy-breathing Brazilian farce *Donna Flor and Her Two Husbands*, and it doesn't work on any level.

w Charlie Peters w Robert Mulligan *ph* Donald Peterman *m* Ralph Burns *pd* Philip M. Jefferies *ed* Sheldon Kahn

James Caan, Sally Field, Jeff Bridges, Paul Dooley, Claire Trevor, Mildred Natwick, William Prince

Kiss Me Kate**
US 1953 111m Anscocolor 3-D
MGM (Jack Cummings)

The married leading players of a musical version of *The Taming of the Shrew* lead an equally tempestuous life backstage.
Brisk, bright screen version of the Broadway musical hit.

w Dorothy Kingsley, *play* Samuel and Bella Spewack *d George Sidney* *ph* Charles Rosher *m / ly Cole Porter* *md* André Previn, Saul Chaplin *ch Hermes Pan*

Howard Keel, Kathryn Grayson, Ann Miller, Keenan Wynn, Bobby Van, Tommy Rall, James Whitmore, Bob Fosse, Kurt Kasznar

AAN: André Previn, Saul Chaplin

Kiss Me Stupid*
US 1964 124m bw Panavision
UA / Mirisch / Phalanx / (Billy Wilder)

A womanizing pop singer stops overnight in a small California desert town and shows interest in an unsuccessful songwriter in order to get at his wife.
Draggy, tasteless, surprisingly unamusing smoking room story, with the actors behaving as though driven against their will (apart from Dean Martin, ideally cast as the idol who gets a headache if he doesn't have sex every night). Some good wisecracks, but it should have been much faster and funnier.

w Billy Wilder, I. A. L. Diamond, *play* L'oro della fantasia by Anna Bonacci *d* Billy Wilder *ph* Joseph La Shelle *m* André Previn *pd* Alexander Trauner *songs* George and Ira Gershwin

Dean Martin, Kim Novak, Ray Walston, Cliff Osmond

'A work of ferocious tastelessness . . . Swiftian in its relentless disgust.'—*Peter Barnes*

'You know what I do to squealers? I let them have it in the belly. So they can roll around for a long time thinking it over!'

Kiss of Death**
US 1947 98m bw
TCF (Fred Kohlmar)

A captured thief informs on his own gang, and a psychopathic killer is sent to extract vengeance.
Gloomy, well-made semi-location thriller which descends into heavy melodrama.
Remade as *The Fiend Who Walked the West*.

w Ben Hecht, Charles Lederer *d* Henry Hathaway *ph* Norbert Brodine *m* David Buttolph

Victor Mature, Richard Widmark, Brian Donlevy, Coleen Gray, Karl Malden, Taylor Holmes

'A tense, terrifying crime melodrama with an unusually authentic seamy atmosphere.'—*New Yorker, 1980*

'Economy of narration enhances the compactness and tautness of the whole and achieves that rarity, a picture minus unnecessary footage.'—*National Board of Review*

'It illustrates a new and vigorous trend in US moviemaking. One of the best things that is happening in Hollywood is the tendency to move out of the studio—to base fictional pictures on fact, and to shoot them not in painted studio sets but in actual places.'—*James Agee*

AAN: original story (E. Lipsky); Richard Widmark

Kiss of Fire
US 1955 86m Technicolor
Universal–International (Samuel Marx)

An ex-soldier escorts an exiled princess on a dangerous journey through Mexico.
Slightly unusual but rather clumsy swashbuckler of no especial merit.

w Franklin Coen, Richard Collins, *novel* The Rose and the Flame by Jonreed Luaritzen *d* Joseph M. Newman *ph* Carl Guthrie *md* Joseph Gershenson *m* Hans Salter

Jack Palance, Barbara Rush, Martha Hyer

Kiss of the Spider Woman**
US / Brazil 1985 119m MGM Color
HB / Sugarloaf (David Weisman)

Fantasies of two prisoners in a South American jail.
One of those lucky flukes, an opening up of a fringe novel about the relationship between a flagrant homosexual and a political prisoner; the former entertains the latter with accounts of his favourite pulp movies. Not for Aunt Edna.

w Leonard Schrader *novel* Manuel Puig *d* Hector Babenco *ph* Radolfo Sanchez *m* John Neschling *pd* Clovis Bueno

William Hurt, Raul Julia

AA: William Hurt

AAN: best picture, direction, adapted screenplay

BFA: William Hurt

Kiss of the Vampire*
GB 1962 88m Eastmancolor
U-I / Hammer (Anthony Hinds)
US title: *Kiss of Evil*

In 1910 a Bavarian disciple of Dracula lures a British honeymoon couple.
This unsubtle variation on *Dracula* is handled in lively fashion, with a splendid climax in which assorted white-robed vampires are destroyed by bats.

w John Elder *d Don Sharp* *ph* Alan Hume *m* James Bernard

Noel Willman, Clifford Evans, Edward De Souza, Jennifer Daniel, Isobel Black

PROF. ZIMMER (Noel Willman): 'You must not expect your Queensberry rules here, Mr Harcourt.'

'They won't stop us—nobody can stop us!'

Kiss the Blood Off My Hands
US 1948 80m bw
Universal / Hecht-Norma (Harold Hecht)
GB title: *Blood on My Hands*

A nurse helps a seaman on the run for murder.
Risible romantic melodrama in never-was London docks setting, with Newton large as life and twice as villainous.

w Leonardo Bercovici, *novel* Gerald Butler *d* Norman Foster *ph* Russell Metty *m* Miklos Rozsa

Joan Fontaine, Burt Lancaster, Robert Newton, Lewis Russell, Aminta Dyne

Kiss the Boys Goodbye*
US 1941 85m bw
Paramount

A Broadway producer falls for one of his chorines.
Moderately smart musical entertainment of its time.

w Harry Tugend, Dwight Taylor, *play* Clare Boothe *d* Victor Schertzinger *m / ly* Victor Schertzinger, Frank Loesser *ph* Ted Tetzlaff

Don Ameche, Mary Martin, Oscar Levant, Rochester, Raymond Walburn, Connie Boswell, Virginia Dale, Barbara Jo Allen, Elizabeth Patterson

Kiss the Bride Goodbye
GB 1944 89m bw

A runaway couple are unwittingly abetted by her uncle. Unsubtle family farce. Patricia Medina, Jimmy Hanley, Frederick Leister, Marie Lohr, Claud Allister, Ellen Pollock, Wylie Watson. Written by Jack Whittingham; directed by Paul Stein; for Butcher.

Kiss the Girls and Make Them Die
Italy 1966 106m Technicolor
Dino de Laurentiis
original title: *Si Tutte le Donne del Mondo . . .*

A rich industrialist has a plan to sterilize the whole male population of the world and restock it with his own mistresses, whom he keeps in suspended animation.
Patchy James Bond spoof.

w Jack Pulman, Dino Maiuri *d* Henry Levin, Dino Maiuri *ph* Aldo Tonti *m* Mario Nascimbene

Michael Connors, Dorothy Provine, Raf Vallone, Terry-Thomas

Kiss Them for Me
US 1957 105m Eastmancolor Cinemascope
TCF (Jerry Wald)

Three navy pilots spend a weekend's unofficial leave in San Francisco, and get into various kinds of trouble.
Based on a novel which also served as source for the musical *Hit the Deck*, this very heavy-footed comedy with serious asides is most unsuitably cast and generally ill-timed and unattractive.

w Julius Epstein, *novel* Shore Leave by Frederick Wakeman *d* Stanley Donen *ph* Milton Krasner *m* Lionel Newman

Cary Grant, Jayne Mansfield, Suzy Parker, Ray Walston, Larry Blyden, Leif Erickson, Werner Klemperer

Kiss Tomorrow Goodbye
US 1950 102m bw
Cagney Productions (William Cagney)

A violent criminal breaks jail and plans several daring robberies.
Surprisingly brutal star melodrama which failed to repeat the success of *White Heat*.

w Harry Brown, *novel* Horace McCoy *d* Gordon Douglas *ph* Peverell Marley *m* Carmen Dragon

James Cagney, Barbara Payton, Ward Bond, Luther Adler, Helena Carter, Steve Brodie, Rhys Williams, Barton MacLane, Frank Reicher, John Litel

'The mixture as before without an ingredient changed.'—*Otis Guernsey Jnr*

Kisses for Breakfast
US 1941 81m bw

A man just married loses his memory and marries again. Poorly developed farce comedy with stars who can't help. Dennis Morgan, Jane Wyatt, Shirley Ross, Lee Patrick, Jerome Cowan, Una O'Connor, Barnett Parker, Cornel Wilde. Written by Kenneth Gamet, from play by Seymour Hicks; directed by Lewis Seiler; for Warner.

Kisses for My President
US 1964 113m bw
Warner / Pearlayne (Curtis Bernhardt)

America's first woman president causes problems for her husband.
Solidly-carpentered comedy with too few ideas for its length.

w Claude Binyon, Robert G. Kane *d* Curtis Bernhardt *ph* Robert Surtees *m* Bronislau Kaper

Polly Bergen, Fred MacMurray, Arlene Dahl, Eli Wallach, Edward Andrews

Kissin' Cousins
US 1963 96m Metrocolor Panavision
MGM / Four Leaf (Sam Katzman)

The USAF wants to build a missile base on Smokey Mountain, and their PR man discovers that one of the hillbillies is his double.
A feeble production in every sense, even below its star's usual standard.

w Gerald Drayson Adams, Gene Nelson *d* Gene Nelson *ph* Ellis W. Carter *md* Fred Karger

Elvis Presley, Arthur O'Connell, Glenda Farrell, Jack Albertson

The Kissing Bandit
US 1948 102m Technicolor
MGM (Joe Pasternak)

In old California, a young businessman finds he is expected to keep up his bandit father's criminal and romantic reputation.
Silly, witless musical which never settles into gear; mocked by its star as Benny mocked *The Horn Blows at Midnight*.

w Isabel Lennart, John Briard Harding *d* Laslo Benedek *ph* Robert Surtees *m* Georgie Stoll *songs* Nacio Herb Brown, Earl Brent, Edward Heyman

Frank Sinatra, Kathryn Grayson, J. Carrol Naish, Mildred Natwick, Mikhail Rasumny, Billy Gilbert, Clinton Sundberg

Kit Carson
US 1940 95m bw

Adventures of the pioneer Indian scout. Thinly-scripted western imaginings with a sturdy but not alluring cast. Jon Hall, Lynn Bari, Dana Andrews, Harold Huber, Ward Bond, Renee Riano, Raymond Hatton. Written by George Bruce; directed by George B. Seitz; for Edward Small.

The Kitchen Toto*
GB 1987 95m colour

1950: in Kenya, a police officer agrees to take in the son of a black priest murdered by the Mau Mau. Rather lumpy but well-meaning drama with a tragic ending. Bob Peck, Phyllis Logan, Edwin Mahinda, Robert Urquhart. Written and directed by Harry Hook; for Skreba/British Screen/Film Four.

Kitten with a Whip
US 1964 83m bw

A girl escaped from reform school takes refuge with a politician whose wife is away. Over-the-top melodrama thought bannable at the time. Ann-Margret, John Forsythe, Patricia Barry, Ann Doran, Audrey Dalton. Written and directed by Douglas Heyes, from a book by Wade Miller; for Universal.

Kitty
GB 1928 90m (24 fps) bw silent
BIP / Burlington (Victor Saville)

A shopgirl loves a paralysed amnesiac, but his mother interferes.
Uninteresting romantic melodrama, notable only as Britain's first sound film: a few dialogue sequences were quickly added (in New York).

w Violet Powell, Benn W. Levy, *novel* Warwick Deeping *d* Victor Saville *ph* Karl Puth

John Stuart, Estelle Brody, Dorothy Cumming, Marie Ault, Olaf Hytten

'She had all London on a MARRY-go-round!'

Kitty***
US 1945 103m bw
Paramount (Karl Tunberg)

In 18th-century London, an aristocrat makes a duchess of a guttersnipe.
Well-detailed period *Pygmalion* which works much better than one would expect.

w Darrell Ware, Karl Tunberg, *novel* Rosamund Marshall *d Mitchell Leisen* *ph Daniel L. Fapp* *m* Victor Young

Paulette Goddard, Ray Milland, Cecil Kellaway, Constance Collier, Reginald Owen, Patric Knowles, Dennis Hoey, Sara Allgood, Eric Blore, Gordon Richards, Michael Dyne

'Enough sex, wit and urbane cynicism to make one forget a footling ending.'—*Peter John Dyer, MFB*

'It is excellently cast, delightfully acted, and the rather sordid story is told with subtlety and skill.'—*Picture Show*

'The most glamorous study of unrelieved sordidness that the screen has presented.'—*Motion Picture Herald*

'The most daring novel every written by a man about a woman!'

Kitty Foyle**
US 1940 108m bw
RKO (Harry E. Edgington, David Hempstead)

A white-collar girl has a troubled love life.
Solid entertainment of its time, especially aimed at ambitious young ladies.

w Dalton Trumbo, Donald Ogden Stewart, *novel* Christopher Morley *d* Sam Wood *ph* Robert de Grasse *m* Roy Webb

Ginger Rogers, Dennis Morgan, James Craig, *Eduardo Ciannelli*, Ernest Cossart, Gladys Cooper, Mary Treen

AA: Ginger Rogers
AAN: best picture; Dalton Trumbo, Donald Ogden Stewart; Sam Wood

The Klansman
US 1974 112m Technicolor
Paramount / Atlanta (William Alexander)

An Alabama sheriff confronts the Ku Klux Klan.
Violent melodrama, all noise, brutality and bad acting.

w Millard Kaufman, Samuel Fuller, *novel* William Bradford Huie *d* Terence Young *ph* Lloyd Ahern, Aldo Tonti *m* Stax Organisation

Lee Marvin, Richard Burton, Cameron Mitchell, O. J. Simpson, Lola Falana, David Huddleston, Luciana Paluzzi, Linda Evans

'There's not a shred of quality, dignity, relevance or impact in this yahoo-oriented bunk.'—*Variety*

'Mae goes north and Alaska goes west!'
Klondike Annie
US 1936 83m bw
Paramount (William Le Baron)

A torch singer on the run disguises herself as a missionary and revivifies a Klondike mission.
Laundered Mae West vehicle, from her fading period but not too bad.

w Mae West, Marion Morgan, George B. Dowell *d* Raoul Walsh *ph* George Clemens

Mae West, Victor McLaglen, Philip Reed, Helen Jerome Eddy, Harry Beresford, Harold Huber, Esther Howard

Klute***
US 1971 114m Technicolor Panavision
Warner (Alan J. Pakula)

A policeman leaves the force to investigate the disappearance of a research scientist, and takes up with a call girl who is involved.
Excellent adult thriller with attention to detail and emphasis on character.

w Andy K. Lewis, Dave Lewis d Alan J. Pakula ph Gordon Willis *m* Michael Small

Jane Fonda, Donald Sutherland, Charles Cioffi, Roy Scheider, Rita Gam

AA: Jane Fonda
AAN: Andy K. Lewis, Dave Lewis

The Knack***
GB 1965 84m bw
UA / Woodfall (Oscar Lewenstein)

A sex-starved young teacher lets one room of his house to a successful womanizer, another to an innocent girl from the north.
An excuse for an anarchic series of visual gags, a kaleidoscope of swinging London in which anything goes. Brilliantly done in the style of *A Hard Day's Night*.

w Charles Wood, *play* Ann Jellicoe *d Richard Lester ph David Watkin m* John Barry

Michael Crawford, Ray Brooks, Rita Tushingham, Donal Donnelly

Knave of Hearts*
GB 1954 103m bw
Transcontinental (Paul Graetz)
aka: *Monsieur Ripois et Son Nemesis*
US title: *Lover Boy*

A born philanderer confesses all his affairs to his wife.
Well-observed though strangely flat and disappointing sex comedy, something of a pioneer in its time and therefore perhaps too diffident in its approach.

w René Clément, Hugh Mills *d* René Clément *ph* Oswald Morris *m* Roman Vlad

Gérard Philipe, Margaret Johnston, Joan Greenwood, Natasha Parry, Valerie Hobson

Knickerbocker Holiday*
US 1944 84m bw
UA / Harry Joe Brown / PCA

In old New Amsterdam, a one-legged tyrant finally sees the light.
Artificial musical from a famous stage original, with engaging moments including Charles Coburn singing 'September Song'.

w Thomas Lennon, from the 1938 stage musical (*m* Kurt Weill, *ly* Maxwell Anderson) based on Father Knickerbocker's History of New York by Washington Irving *d* Harry Joe Brown *ph* Phil Tammura *m* Werner Heymann

Charles Coburn, Nelson Eddy, Constance Dowling, Ernest Cossart, Shelley Winters, Otto Kruger

AAN: Werner Heymann

Knife in the Water*
Poland 1962 94m bw
ZRF Kamera (Stanislaw Zylewicz)
original title: *Noz w Wodzie*

A young couple ask a hitchhiker to spend a weekend on their yacht, and regret it.
Detached little melodrama in which the sex and violence hover beneath the surface. All very watchable, but in a minor key.

w Jerzy Skolimowski, Roman Polanski, Jakub Goldberg *d Roman Polanski ph* Jerzy Lipman *m* Krzystof Komeda

Leon Niemczyk, Jolanta Umecka, Zygmunt Malanowicz

AAN: best foreign film

Knight without Armour**
GB 1937 107m bw
London Films (Alexander Korda)

During the Russian Revolution of 1917, a widowed countess is helped to safety by a British translator.
Underrated romantic adventure with big production values and some splendid moments.

w Lajos Biro, Arthur Wimperis, Frances Marion, *novel* James Hilton *ph Harry Stradling d Jacques Feyder m* Miklos Rozsa

Robert Donat, Marlene Dietrich, Irene Vanbrugh, Herbert Lomas, Austin Trevor, Basil Gill, David Tree, John Clements, Lawrence Hanray

'Another feather in the cap of Alexander Korda for his series of artistic film productions. There is relatively little to find fault with and much to praise.'—*Variety*

'A first class thriller, beautifully directed, with spare and convincing dialogue and a nearly watertight scenario.'—*Graham Greene*

Knights of the Round Table*
GB 1953 115m Eastmancolor Cinemascope
MGM (Pandro S. Berman)

Lancelot, banished from King Arthur's court for loving Guinevere, returns to defeat the evil Modred.
Disappointingly flat, pageant-like adaptation of the legends, with a few lively strands insufficiently firmly drawn together.

w Talbot Jennings, Jan Lustig, Noel Langley *d* Richard Thorpe *ph* Frederick A. Young, Stephen Dade *m* Miklos Rozsa *ad* Alfred Junge, Hans Peters

Robert Taylor, Mel Ferrer, Ava Gardner, Anne Crawford, Stanley Baker, Felix Aylmer, Robert Urquhart, Niall MacGinnis

Knights of the Teutonic Order*
Poland 1960 180m Eastmancolor Dyaliscope
Studio Unit (Zygmunt Krol)

Teutonic knights pillage Poland on the pretext of converting the inhabitants to Christianity; when they kill a noblewoman, her daughter swears revenge.
Medieval epic differing little from those of Hollywood, but splendid to look at.

w Jerzy Stafan Stawinski, Aleksander Ford, *novel* Henryk Sienkiewicz *d* Aleksander Ford *ph* Mieczyslaw Jahoda *m* Kazimierz Serocki

Urszula Modrzynska, Grazyna Staniszewska, Andrzej Szalawski

Knock on Any Door*
US 1949 100m bw
Columbia / Santana (Robert Lord)

A defence lawyer pleads with the jury for the life of a slum boy on a murder charge.
Smartly-made but empty melodrama making facile social points.

w Daniel Taradash, John Monks Jnr, *novel* Willard Motley *d* Nicholas Ray *ph* Burnett Guffey *m* George Antheil

Humphrey Bogart, John Derek, George Macready, Allene Roberts

Knock on Wood**
US 1954 103m Technicolor
Paramount (Norman Panama, Melvin Frank)

Stolen plans are hidden inside the dummy of an unsuspecting ventriloquist.
Excellent star comedy with good script and production (but some strange ideas of London's geography).

wd Norman Panama, Melvin Frank ph Daniel Fapp *songs* Sylvia Fine *m* Leith Stevens *ch* Michael Kidd

Danny Kaye, Mai Zetterling, David Burns, Torin Thatcher, Leon Askin, Abner Biberman, Steve Geray

AAN: Norman Panama, Melvin Frank (script)

Knute Rockne, All American
US 1940 98m bw
Warner (Robert Fellows)
GB titles: *Knockout*; *A Modern Hero*

The career of a famous Notre Dame football coach.
Standard sporting biopic.

w Robert Buckner *d* Lloyd Bacon *ph* Tony Gaudio *m* Ferde Grofé

Pat O'Brien, Ronald Reagan, Gale Page, Donald Crisp, Albert Basserman, John Qualen, John Sheffield

Koenigsmark
France 1935 114m bw

A princess falls for a commoner. Rather elementary royal romance in a Ruritanian background, filmed simultaneously in French and English by the same principals. Elissa Landi, Pierre Fresnay, John Lodge. From a novel by Pierre Benoit; directed by Maurice Tourneur; for Roger Richebé/Capitol.

Kongo
US 1932 86m bw
MGM

An embittered African recluse takes revenge on the daughter of his former enemy.
No-holds-barred melodrama which never really exerts the right grip; a remake of the Lon Chaney silent *West of Zanzibar*.

w Leon Gordon, *play* Chester de Vonde, Kilbourn Gordon *d* William Cowen *ph* Harold Rosson

Walter Huston, Lupe Velez, Virginia Bruce, Conrad Nagel, C. Henry Gordon

'Horror and tropical stuff combined . . . chiefly for the daily grinds.'—*Variety*

Kotch*
US 1971 114m Metrocolor
ABC / Kotch Company (Richard Carter)

An eccentric 72-year-old widower is at odds with his family and helps a pregnant babysitter.
Variously amusing, moving and sentimental, this generally likeable film about a crotchety grandpa is sustained by its star performance.

w John Paxton, *novel* Katherine Topkins *d* Jack Lemmon *ph* Richard H. Kline *m* Marvin Hamlisch

Walter Matthau, Deborah Winter, Felicia Farr, Charles Aidman

AAN: Walter Matthau; song 'Life Is What You Make It' (*m* Marvin Hamlisch, *ly* Johnny Mercer)

Koyaanisqatsi*
US 1983 86m De Luxe

A panoramic view of contemporary America without commentary or narrative, using time-lapse photography. The title is an Indian word meaning 'a state of life that calls for another way of living'. A rather pointless, very beautiful, and finally rather boring experience. Written by Ron Fricke, Godfrey Reggio, Michael Hoenig, Alton Walpole; directed by Godfrey Reggio; for the Institute for Regional Education. 'Arrogant bombast, provoking no response except "wow".'—*Sight & Sound*

Krakatoa, East of Java
US 1968 136m Technicolor Cinerama
ABC / Cinerama (Lester A. Sansom)

In 1883 the SS *Batavia Queen* leaves Singapore and is engulfed by the Krakatoa eruption.
Mindless spectacular, technically quite impressive but with no dramatic interest whatsoever.

w Clifford Newton Gould, Bernard Gordon *d* Bernard Kowalski *ph* Manuel Berenguer *m* Frank de Vol *pd / sp Eugene Lourié*

Maximilian Schell, Diane Baker, Brian Keith, Rossano Brazzi, Barbara Werle, John Leyton, Sal Mineo, J. D. Cannon, Marc Lawrence

'Apparently designed to disprove the old adage, "they don't make them like that any more". At a conservative count it includes such sure-fire cinematic ingredients as hidden treasure, deep-sea divers with shattered lungs and claustrophobia, mutiny *and* fire on board ship, nuns, convicts, a lost orphan boy, girl divers and even a little striptease, climaxing in the biggest explosion and the greatest tidal wave known to history.'—*MFB*

'There are three sides to this love story!'
Kramer versus Kramer***
US 1979 105m Technicolor
Columbia / Stanley Jaffe (Richard C. Fischoff)

A divorced advertising executive gets temporary custody of his seven-year-old son.
New-fashioned tearjerker, as slick as a colour supplement and catnip to the emotion-starved masses.

wd Robert Benton, *novel* Avery Corman *ph* Nestor Almendros *md* Erma E. Levin *pd* Paul Sylbert

Dustin Hoffman, Justin Henry, Meryl Streep, Jane Alexander, Howard Duff

'Pastel colours, a cute kid and a good script made this one of the most undeserved successes of the year: wall-to-wall sentiment.'—*Time Out*

AA: best picture; Robert Benton (as director); Dustin Hoffman; Meryl Streep; screen play adapted from another medium

AAN: Justin Henry, Jane Alexander

'If you miss the first five minutes you miss one suicide, two executions, one seduction and the key to the plot!'
The Kremlin Letter
US 1970 122m De Luxe Panavision
TCF (Carter de Haven, Sam Wiesenthal)

An American intelligence team is sent undercover to Moscow to retrieve an arms treaty mistakenly signed.
Tediously violent cold war mystifier: a few good performances do not make it worth unravelling.

w John Huston, Gladys Hill, *novel* Noel Behn *d* John Huston *ph* Ted Scaife *m* Robert Drasnin *pd* Ted Haworth

Richard Boone, Orson Welles, Bibi Andersson, Max Von Sydow, Patrick O'Neal, Ronald Radd, George Sanders, Dean Jagger, Nigel Green, Barbara Parkins, Lila Kedrova, Michael MacLiammoir, Sandor Eles, Niall MacGinnis, John Huston

'One of those all-star international spy sagas that trick out an indecipherably tortuous plot with a series of vignettes in which the pleasures of star-spotting are expected to compensate for any narrative longueurs.'—*Nigel Andrews*

Krull
GB 1983 121m Metrocolor
Columbia / Ted Mann–Ron Silverman

Prince Colwyn's bride-to-be is abducted by the Beast of the Black Fortress.
Old-fashioned derring-do taking place on a somewhat unattractive planet; nevertheless fairly lively in its action and trick effects.

w Stanford Sherman *d* Peter Yates *ph* Peter Suschitzky *m* James Horner *pd* Stephen Grimes

Ken Marshall, Lysette Anthony, Freddie Jones, Francesca Annis, Alun Armstrong, David Battley, Bernard Bresslaw, John Welsh, Tony Church, Bernard Archard

'Nearly everything in it has been done before, in some cases rather better, but rarely quite so likeably.'—*Nick Roddick, MFB*

'Not really thrilling enough to be a blockbuster and not light enough to be anything else.'—*Sight and Sound*

Kwaidan*
Japan 1964 164m Eastmancolor Tohoscope
Ninjin Club / Bungei

Four elegant ghost stories by Lafcadio Hearn.
Visually a superb production; all the stories have merit, but *en masse* prove a bit much at one sitting.

w Yoko Mizuki *d Masaki Kobayashi* *ph Yoshio Miyajima* *m* Toru Takemitsu *ad Shigemasa Toda*

Rentaro Mikuni, Ganjiro Nakamura, Katsuo Nakamura

AA: best foreign film

The L-Shaped Room*
GB 1962 142m bw
British Lion / Romulus (James Woolf, Richard Attenborough)

A girl intending to have an abortion takes a room in a London suburban house which is none too clean but full of characters.
Watchable, mildly sensational low-life-melodrama of the pre-swinging London era when well-to-dos thought it amusing to live in garrets. Hellishly overlong but enjoyable in patches because of the professionalism with which it is made.

w Bryan Forbes, *novel* Lynne Reid Banks *d Bryan Forbes ph* Douglas Slocombe *m* Brahms, John Barry

Leslie Caron, Tom Bell, *Brock Peters, Cicely Courtneidge*, Bernard Lee, *Avis Bunnage, Patricia Phoenix, Emlyn Williams*

'It would be hard to imagine a more unlikely, or commercially more sure-fire group of lodgers living under a single roof than this pregnant French girl, maladjusted negro, lesbian actress, couple of prostitutes, and unpublished writer who finally commits it all to paper—shades of *I Am a Camera* as well as *A Taste of Honey*.'—*MFB*

AAN: Leslie Caron

La Conga Nights
US 1940 59m bw

An elderly music moron helps to found a night club. Flimsy excuse for a musical, with the star playing himself, four sisters and his mother. Hugh Herbert, Dennis O'Keefe, Constance Moore, Eddie Quillan. Written by Jay Dratler, Harry Clork, Paul Smith; directed by Lew Landers; for Universal.

Laburnum Grove**
GB 1936 73m bw
ATP (Basil Dean)

A suburban father reveals he is a forger.
Agreeable worm-turns comedy melodrama, much copied since.

w Gordon Wellesley, Anthony Kimmins, *play J. B. Priestley d Carol Reed ph* John W. Boyle

Cedric Hardwicke, Edmund Gwenn, Victoria Hopper, Ethel Coleridge, Katie Johnson, Francis James

'Here at last is an English film one can unreservedly praise.'—*Graham Greene*

Labyrinth
US 1986 101m colour
Tri-Star / Eric Rattray, George Lucas

A young girl embarks on a fantasy adventure to save her stepbrother from the clutches of the Goblin King.
Bizarre but tedious attempt to create a new *Alice in Wonderland*, with the inventor of the Muppets in charge. Unfortunately his creatures become less attractive with each attempt, and the script is emaciated.

w Terry Jones, from script by Dennis Less and Jim Henson *d* Jim Henson *ph* Alex Thomson *m* Trevor Jones *pd* Elliot Scott *conceptual design* Brian Froud

David Bowie, Jennifer Connelly, Toby Froud, Shelley Thompson

'A crashing bore . . . no real charm or texture to capture the imagination.'—*Variety*

The Lacemaker
France / Switzerland / West Germany 1977 107m Eastmancolor
Action / FR3 / Citel / Janus (Yves Gasser)
original title: *La Dentellière*

An 18-year-old girl becomes ill and withdrawn when her first affair breaks up.
Careful social character study, witty and observant but in memory insufficiently differentiated from numerous exploitation pieces with similar plots.

w Pascal Lainé, Claude Goretta, *novel* Pascal Lainé *d* Claude Goretta *ph* Jean Boffety *m* Pierre Jansen

Isabelle Huppert, Yves Beneyton, Florence Giorgetti, Anne Marie Düringer

Lacombe, Lucien**
France 1974 141m Eastmancolor
TCF

A boy is rejected for the French resistance and joins the Gestapo instead.
Tragic fable, a mite overlong, which caused its creator to migrate to America because of criticism received in France.

w Louis Malle, Patrick Modiano *d Louis Malle ph* Tonino Delli Colli *m Django Reinhardt*

Pierre Blaise, Aurore Clement, Holger Lowenadler, Thérèse Gieshe

Laddie
US 1935 70m bw

A young farmer loves the squire's daughter, but the squire says no. Rather dim old-fashioned rural romance. John Beal, Gloria Stuart, Virginia Weidler, Charlotte Henry, Donald Crisp. Written by Ray Harris, Dorothy Yost, from novel and play by Gene Stratton Porter; directed by George Stevens; for Pandro S. Berman / RKO.

† Remade in 1940 by Cliff Reid for RKO, with Tim Holt, Virginia Gilmore.

Ladies Courageous
US 1944 88m bw
Universal (Walter Wanger)

Girls ferry war planes from base to base for the USAF. Absolutely predictable propaganda potboiler.

w Norman Reilly Raine, Doris Gilbert *d* John Rawlins *ph* Hal Mohr *m* Dmitri Tiomkin

Loretta Young, Geraldine Fitzgerald, Diana Barrymore, Evelyn Ankers, Anne Gwynne, Philip Terry, David Bruce, Lois Collier, Samuel S. Hinds

'Needs exploitation hype to catch nominal biz . . . wandering continuity fails to generate much punch.'—*Variety*

Ladies' Day
US 1943 62m bw

A baseball pitcher loses his touch when he falls in love, so has to be kept away from his latest girl. Mildly wacky comedy with a fairly nimble touch. Lupe Velez, Eddie Albert, Patsy Kelly, Max Baer, Jerome Cowan, Iris Adrian. Written by Charles E. Roberts and Dale Lussier, from play by Robert Considine, Edward C. Lilley and Bertrand Robinson; directed by Leslie Goodwins; for Bert Gilroy / RKO.

Ladies in Love*
US 1936 97m bw
TCF (B. G. De Sylva)

Man-hunting girls in Budapest form a joint plan.
Amusing romantic nonsense.

w Melville Baker, *play* Ladislaus Bus-Fekete *d* Edward H. Griffith *ph* Hal Mohr *md* Louis Silvers

Janet Gaynor, Loretta Young, Constance Bennett, Simone Simon, Don Ameche, Paul Lukas, Tyrone Power, Alan Mowbray, Wilfred Lawson, J. Edward Bromberg, Virginia Field

Ladies in Retirement**
US 1941 92m bw
Columbia (Lester Cowan)

A housekeeper murders her employer for the sake of her two mentally disturbed sisters. Splendidly effective Grand Guignol, from a well-written play but filmically quite interesting. Remade with lots of gore as *The Mad Room* (qv).

w Reginald Denham, Edward Percy, Garrett Fort, *play* Reginald Denham, Edward Percy *d Charles Vidor* *ph* George Barnes *m* Ernst Toch

Ida Lupino, Louis Hayward, Isobel Elsom, Edith Barrett, Elsa Lanchester, Emma Dunn

'General excellence of script, direction, acting and mounting . . . but too strong to catch general audience reaction on favourable plane.'—*Variety*

AAN: Ernst Toch

Ladies Love Brutes
US 1930 83m bw
Paramount

A gangster tries to improve himself to marry a socialite.
Uneasy comedy-drama with good moments.

w Waldemar Young, Herman J. Mankiewicz, *play* Pardon My Glove by Zoe Akins *d* Rowland V. Lee *ph* Harry Fischbeck

George Bancroft, Mary Astor, Fredric March, Margaret Quimby, Stanley Fields

Ladies Love Danger
US 1935 69m bw

A playwright and amateur sleuth solves a series of murders. Light, bright whodunit. Gilbert Roland, Mona Barrie, Donald Cook, Adrienne Ames, Hardie Albright, Herbert Mundin. Written by Samson Raphaelson from a story by Ilya Zorn; directed by H. Bruce Humberstone; for Fox. 'Stronger marquee strength would have sent it into ace spots. As is, looks best for secondaries.'—*Variety*

Ladies' Man*
US 1931 70m bw
Paramount

A man of the world preys successfully on rich women until one grows jealous when her daughter falls for him.
Vivid, hard melodrama showing the blacker side of early thirties high society living.

w Herman J. Mankiewicz *d* Lothar Mendes *ph* Victor Milner

William Powell, Kay Francis, Carole Lombard, Gilbert Emery, Olive Tell

'He's a hit with the misses, they go for his kisses!'

Ladies' Man
US 1947 90m bw

A poor farmer strikes oil, becomes a millionaire, and finds himself a prize for the ladies. Below-par comedy which wastes an agreeable cast. Eddie Bracken, Cass Daley, Virginia Welles, Spike Jones and his City Slickers. Written by Edmund Beloin, Jack Rose and Lewis Meltzer; directed by William D. Russell; for Paramount.

Ladies' Man
US 1961 106m Technicolor
Paramount / York (Jerry Lewis)

The adventures of an accident-prone houseboy at a Hollywood hotel for aspiring actresses. Hit-or-miss collection of comic scraps which might have benefited from being put together on a less grandiose scale.

w Jerry Lewis, Bill Richmond *d* Jerry Lewis *ph* W. Wallace Kelley *m* Walter Scharf

Jerry Lewis, Helen Traubel, Jack Kruschen, Doodles Weaver, Gloria Jean

'Regression into infantilism cannot be carried much further than this.'—*MFB*

Ladies Must Live: see The Home Towners

Ladies of Leisure
US 1930 98m bw

A gold digger gets an attack of conscience and gives up her rich fiancé. Only fitfully interesting early Capra, with little sparkle in any department. Barbara Stanwyck, Lowell Sherman, Ralph Graves, Marie Prevost. Written by Milton Herbert Gropper and Jo Swerling; directed by Frank Capra; for Columbia.

Ladies of the Big House
US 1931 77m bw
Paramount

A married couple are framed on a murder charge and sent to prison.
Melodramatic nonsense in the wake of *The Big House.*

w Louis Weitzenkorn *d* Marion Gering *ph* David Abel

Sylvia Sidney, Gene Raymond, Wynne Gibson, Rockcliffe Fellows, Earle Foxe

'Powerful in heart appeal and should do very well.'—*Variety*

Ladies of the Chorus
US 1949 61m bw

A Broadway burlesque queen falls for a socialite. Threadbare backstage support, notable only for the first leading performance of Marilyn Monroe. Adele Jergens, Rand Brooks. Written by Harry Sauber and Joseph Carole; directed by Phil Karlson; for Columbia.

Ladies of the Jury
US 1932 64m bw

A lady changes the minds of a murder jury to 'not guilty'. Light-hearted early variation on *Twelve Angry Men. Edna May Oliver*, Ken Murray, Roscoe Ates, Kitty Kelly, Guinn Williams, Cora Witherspoon. From the play by Frederick Ballard; directed by Lowell Sherman; for RKO. 'A highly satisfying B house release.'—*Variety*

Ladies Should Listen
US 1934 63m bw
Paramount (Douglas MacLean)

A knowledgeable switchboard operator helps a financier with his problems.
Moderately beguiling, instantly forgettable romantic frou-frou.

w Claude Binyon, Frank Butler, Guy Bolton *d* Frank Tuttle *ph* Harry Sharp

Cary Grant, Frances Drake, Edward Everett Horton, Rosita Morena, George Barbier, Nydia Westman, Charles Ray

'Synthetic farce that strains too hard for laughs.'—*Variety*

Ladies They Talk About*
US 1933 69m bw
Warner

Trouble in a women's prison.
Entertaining comedy-melodrama which had some brushes with the Hays Office because of its frankly man-hungry characters.

w Sidney Sutherland, Brown Holmes, *play* Women in Prison by Dorothy Mackaye, Carlton Miles *d* Howard Bretherton, William Keighley *ph* John Seitz

Barbara Stanwyck, Lyle Talbot, Preston Foster, Dorothy Burgess, Lillian Roth, Maude Eburne, Ruth Donnelly, Harold Huber

'Will get average business if sold to the hilt.'—*Variety*

Ladies Who Do
GB 1963 85m bw
British Lion / Bryanston / Fanfare (George H. Brown)

Charladies form a successful company from tips they salvage from wastepaper baskets.
Mild farce sustained by familiar actors.

w Michael Pertwee *d* C. M. Pennington-Richards *ph* Geoffrey Faithfull *m* Ron Goodwin

Peggy Mount, Miriam Karlin, Robert Morley, Harry H. Corbett, Dandy Nichols

The Lady and the Bandit
US 1951 78m bw

A highwayman sacrifices his own life to avenge his father and protect his wife. Fairly pathetic example of historical whitewashing to provide minor excitements. Louis Hayward, Patricia Medina, Suzanne Dalbert, Tom Tully, John Williams, Alan Mowbray. Written by Robert Libbott and Frank Burt; directed by Ralph Murphy; for Harry Joe Brown / Columbia. (GB title: *Dick Turpin's Ride.*)

The Lady and the Mob
US 1939 65m bw
Columbia (Fred Kohlmar)

A lady bank owner menaced by gangsters forms her own mob.
Weak comedy.

w Richard Maibaum, Gertrude Purcell *d* Ben Stoloff *ph* John Stumar

Fay Bainter, Ida Lupino, Lee Bowman, Henry Armetta, Warren Hymer, Harold Huber

'Neat, entertaining farce; rates exploitation.'—*Variety*

The Lady and the Monster
US 1944 86m bw
Republic (George Sherman)
aka: *Tiger Man*
GB title: *The Lady and the Doctor*

A scientist keeps alive the brain of a mortally injured financier, and it comes to dominate him.
Fair, over-padded version of a much filmed thriller (see also *Donovan's Brain, Vengeance*).

w Dane Lussier, Frederick Kohner, *novel* Donovan's Brain by Curt Siodmak *d* George Sherman *ph* John Alton *m* Walter Scharf

Erich Von Stroheim, Richard Arlen, Vera Hruba Ralston, Mary Nash, Sidney Blackmer, Helen Vinson

Lady and the Tramp**
US 1955 76m Technicolor Cinemascope
Walt Disney (Erdmann Penner)

A pedigree spaniel falls foul of two Siamese cats and has a romantic adventure with a mongrel who helps her.
Pleasant cartoon feature in Disney's cutest and most anthropomorphic vein.

d Hamilton Luske, Clyde Geronomi, Wilfred Jackson *m* Oliver Wallace

Lady Be Good
US 1941 111m bw
MGM (Arthur Freed)

Married songwriters produce a musical.
Thin musical with good talent and tunes; very little connection with the 1924 musical show.

w Jack McGowan, Kay Van Riper, John McClain *d* Norman Z. McLeod *ph* George J. Folsey, Oliver T. Marsh *md* George Stoll *songs* various

Eleanor Powell, Robert Young, Ann Sothern, Red Skelton, Dan Dailey, Virginia O'Brien, Reginald Owen, John Carroll, Lionel Barrymore, Jimmy Dorsey and his Orchestra

'A molasses-paced picture that extravagantly wastes talent and time . . . poor direction, unimaginative story-telling and slipshod photography.'—*Variety*

AA: song 'The Last Time I Saw Paris' (*m* Jerome Kern, *ly* Oscar Hammerstein II)
Other songs: 'Hang on to Me'; 'Fascinating Rhythm'; 'Lady Be Good'; 'You'll Never Know'; 'Your Words and My Music'

Lady By Choice*
US 1934 78m bw
Columbia

A publicity-mad dancer adopts an old rummy as a Mother's Day stunt.
Amusing sentimental comedy in the wake of *Lady for A Day*.

w Jo Swerling, Dwight Taylor *d* David Burton *ph* Ted Tetzlaff

Carole Lombard, May Robson, Walter Connolly, Roger Pryor, Arthur Hohl, Raymond Walburn, James Burke, Henry Kolker

'Can very well stand on its own outside the deluxers if properly sold.'—*Variety*

Lady Caroline Lamb*
GB 1972 123m Eastmancolor Panavision
EMI / GEC / Pulsar / Video Cinematographica (Fernando Ghia)

In 1805, impulsive Lady Caroline Ponsonby marries William Lamb, later Lord Melbourne, and then disgraces him by her wildness.
Pale, disappointing historical fiction with good spots but no reverence for fact; slackly written and handled, and not helped by the wide screen.

wd Robert Bolt *ph* Oswald Morris *m* Richard Rodney Bennett *ad* Carmen Dillon

Sarah Miles, Jon Finch, Richard Chamberlain (as Byron), Margaret Leighton, John Mills (as Canning), *Ralph Richardson* (as George III), *Laurence Olivier* (as Wellington)

Lady Chatterley's Lover
France 1955 101m / 84m (English version) bw
Regie du Film / Orsay Film (Gilbert Cohen-Séat)

The wife of a crippled and impotent mine-owner has an affair with a coarse gamekeeper and enjoys it.
Hilariously po-faced transcription of a notorious novel, of no cinematic interest whatever.

w Gaston Bonheur, Philippe de Rothschild, Marc Allégret, *novel* D. H. Lawrence *d* Marc Allégret *ph* Georges Périnal *m* Joseph Kosma

Danielle Darrieux, Leo Genn, Erno Crisa

'The classic of erotic literature!'
Lady Chatterley's Lover
GB / France 1981 104m colour
Cannon / Producteurs Associés

A 'period' remake, lovingly photographed but with some risible soft porn episodes and no great interest in the acting.

w Christopher Wicking, Just Jaeckin *d* Just Jaeckin *ph* Robert Fraisse *m* Stanley Myers, Richard Harvey

Sylvia Kristel, Nicholas Clay, Shane Briant, Ann Mitchell, Elizabeth Spriggs

The Lady Consents
US 1936 76m bw
RKO (Edward Kaufman)

When a doctor's wife sees that he is in love with another woman, she makes it easy for him to get a divorce; but he finally comes back to her.
Unbelievable matinée drama for star fans.

w P. J. Wolfson, Anthony Veiller, *play* The Indestructible Mrs Talbot by P. J. Wolfson *d* Stephen Roberts *ph* J. Roy Hunt *m* Roy Webb

Ann Harding, Herbert Marshall, Margaret Lindsay, Walter Abel, Edward Ellis, Hobart Cavanaugh, Ilka Chase

'Pretty fair entertainment; good woman's picture.'—*Variety*

The Lady Eve***
US 1941 97m bw
Paramount (Paul Jones)

A lady cardsharper and her father are outsmarted on a transatlantic liner by a millionaire simpleton; she plans an elaborate revenge.
Hectic romantic farce, the first to show its director's penchant for mixing up sexual innuendo, funny men and pratfalls. There are moments when the pace drops, but in general it's scintillating entertainment, especially after viewing its weak remake *The Birds and the Bees* (qv).

wd Preston Sturges, play Monckton Hoffe *ph* Victor Milner *m* Leo Shuken, Charles Bradshaw

Barbara Stanwyck, Henry Fonda, Charles Coburn, Eugène Pallette, William Demarest, Eric Blore, Melville Cooper, Martha O'Driscoll, Janet Beecher, Robert Greig, Luis Alberni, Jimmy Conlin

'The whole theme, with all its variations of keys, is played to one end, to get laughs, and at several different levels it gets them.'—*National Board of Review*

'Preston Sturges, they tell me, is known in Hollywood as "the streamlined Lubitsch". This needn't put you off, because if he goes on producing films as lively as this one he will one day come to be known as Preston Sturges.'—*William Whitebait*

'This time Preston Sturges has wrapped you up another package that is neither very big nor very flashy, but the best fun in months.'—*Otis Ferguson*

'A mixture of visual and verbal slapstick, of high artifice and pratfalls . . . it represents the dizzy high point of Sturges' writing.'—*New Yorker, 1977*

'The brightest sort of nonsense, on which Preston Sturges' signature is written large. The result has a sustained comic flavour and an individual treatment that are rarely found in Hollywood's antic concoctions.'—*New York Herald Tribune*

'A more charming or distinguished gem of nonsense has not occurred since *It Happened One Night*.'—*New York Times*

AAN: Monckton Hoffe (original story)

Lady for a Day***
US 1933 95m bw
Columbia (Frank Capra)

Gangsters help an old apple seller to pose as a rich woman when her daughter visits.
Splendid sentimental comedy full of cinematic resource; the best translation of Runyon to the screen.

w Robert Riskin, story Madame La Gimp by Damon Runyon *d Frank Capra ph* Joseph Walker

May Robson, Warren William, Guy Kibbee, Glenda Farrell, Ned Sparks, Jean Parker, Walter Connolly, Nat Pendleton

'Exceptionally adroit direction and scenario . . . sell it with plenty of adjectives as it will please everybody.'—*Variety*

AAN: best picture; Robert Riskin; Frank Capra; May Robson

LADY CAROLINE LAMB. Jon Finch looks rather uncomfortable with Sarah Miles in his arms. Perhaps it's because the director, Robert Bolt, was her real-life husband.

Lady for a Night
US 1941 87m bw
Republic (Albert J. Cohen)

The lady owner of a gambling boat determines to break into society.
Moderate period comedy with a belated murder plot.

w Isabel Dawn, Boyce DeGaw *d* Leigh Jason *ph* Norbert Brodine *m* David Buttolph

Joan Blondell, John Wayne, Ray Middleton, Philip Merivale, Blanche Yurka, Edith Barrett, Leonid Kinskey, Montagu Love

The Lady from Cheyenne
US 1941 87m bw
Universal (Frank Lloyd)

In 1860 Wyoming, a schoolmistress fights for women's rights.
Mild western star romance.

w Kathryn Scola, Warren Duff *d* Frank Lloyd *ph* Milton Krasner *m* Frank Skinner

Loretta Young, Robert Preston, Gladys George, Edward Arnold, Frank Craven, Jessie Ralph, Spencer Charters, Alan Bridge

Lady from Lisbon
GB 1942 75m bw

A millionaire spies for the Nazis in return for the promise of art treasures. Modest potboiling comedy-melodrama. Jane Carr, Francis L. Sullivan, Martita Hunt, Charles Victor, Antony Holles. Written by Michael Barringer; directed by Leslie Hiscott; for Shaftesbury/British National.

Lady from Louisiana
US 1941 84m bw
Republic (Bernard Vorhaus)

In old Mississippi, a lottery-owner's daughter falls in love with a lawyer employed to make her father's business illegal.
Curious pot-boiler containing everything but the kitchen stove, including murder and a raging storm.

w Vera Caspary, Guy Endore, Michael Hogan *d* Bernard Vorhaus *ph* Jack Marta *m* Cy Feuer

John Wayne, Ona Munson, Ray Middleton, Henry Stephenson, Helen Westley, Dorothy Dandridge, Jack Pennick

The Lady from Nowhere
US 1936 60m bw

A manicurist tries to lose her identity after witnessing a gangland killing. A silly plot robs this second feature of the interest it might otherwise deserve. Mary Astor, Charles Quigley, Thurston Hall, Victor Kilian, Spencer Charters. Written by Fred Niblo Jnr, Ben G. Kohn, Arthur Strawn, Joseph Krumgold; directed by Gordon Wiles; for Columbia. 'Mild entertainment.'—*Variety*

The Lady from Shanghai**
US 1948 87m bw
Columbia (Richard Wilson, William Castle)

A seaman becomes involved in the maritime wanderings of a crippled lawyer and his homicidal frustrated wife.
Absurd, unintelligible, plainly much cut and rearranged, this thriller was obviously left too much in Welles' hands and then just as unfairly taken out of them; but whole sequences of sheer brilliance remain, notably the final shoot-out in the hall of mirrors.

wd Orson Welles, novel If I Die Before I Wake by Sherwood King *ph Charles Lawton Jnr* *m* Heinz Roemheld

Orson Welles, Rita Hayworth, *Everett Sloane, Glenn Anders*, Ted de Corsia, Erskine Sanford, Gus Schilling

'The slurred social conscience of the hero leads him to some murky philosophizing, all of which with many individualities of diction clog the issue and the sound track. Sub-titles, I fear, would have helped.'—*Richard Winnington*

The Lady from Texas
US 1951 78m Technicolor

A Civil War widow is thought to be committable. Mild comedy of insanity, a pale shadow of *Harvey* whose star it borrows. Josephine Hull, Mona Freeman, Howard Duff, Gene Lockhart, Craig Stevens, Ed Begley. Written by Gerald Drayson Adams and Connie Lee Bennett; directed by Joseph Pevney; for Universal-International.

The Lady Gambles
US 1949 99m bw
U-I (Michael Kraike)

A happy woman destroys her marriage when she becomes addicted to gambling.
Boring, overwrought, underplotted fiction for women.

w Lewis Meltzer, Oscar Saul *d* Michael Gordon *ph* Russell Metty *m* Frank Skinner

Barbara Stanwyck, Robert Preston, Stephen McNally, Edith Barrett, John Hoyt

'A kind of *Lost Weekend* of the gaming tables.'—*Ella Smith*

'The relentless drama of a woman driven to the depths of emotion by a craving beyond control!'—*publicity*

Lady Godiva
US 1955 89m Technicolor
U-I (Robert Arthur)
GB title: *Lady Godiva of Coventry*

Lord Leofric tames a Saxon shrew but she suspects his motives and rides naked through the streets of Coventry to prove the loyalty of the Saxons.
Comic strip historical legend, reliably turned out for midwestern family audiences.

w Oscar Brodney, Harry Ruskin *d* Arthur Lubin *ph* Carl Guthrie *m* Hans Salter

George Nader, Maureen O'Hara, Vic Morrow, Eduard Franz, Torin Thatcher

Lady Godiva Rides Again
GB 1951 90m bw
British Lion / London Films / Sidney Gilliat, Frank Launder

A waitress wins a local beauty contest and becomes a charm school starlet and later a stripteaser.
Disappointing satirical comedy with good credentials.

w Frank Launder, Val Valentine *d* Frank Launder *ph* Wilkie Cooper *m* William Alwyn

Pauline Stroud, Stanley Holloway, Diana Dors, Alastair Sim, George Cole, Dennis Price, John McCallum, Bernadette O'Farrell, Kay Kendall, Dora Bryan

The Lady Has Plans
US 1942 77m bw
Paramount (Fred Kohlmar)

A lady reporter in Lisbon is mistaken for a Nazi spy.
Competent fluff which veers between comedy and melodrama.

w Harry Tugend *d* Sidney Lanfield *ph* Charles Lang *m* Leo Shuken, Leigh Harline

Paulette Goddard, Ray Milland, Albert Dekker, Roland Young, Margaret Hayes, Cecil Kellaway, Addison Richards, Edward Norris

Lady Ice
US 1973 92m Technicolor Panavision
Tomorrow Entertainment (Harrison Starr)

An insurance investigator steals a diamond and goes into partnership with a gangster's daughter.
Unamusing Miami-based thriller.

w Alan Trustman, Harold Clemins *d* Tom Gries *ph* Lucien Ballard *m* Perry Botkin Jnr

Donald Sutherland, Jennifer O'Neil, Robert Duvall, Patrick Magee

'Because of its frank nature, we urge you—do not see it alone!'

Lady in a Cage
US 1964 97m bw
American Entertainments Corp. (Luther Davis)

A rich widow is trapped by roving marauders in her private elevator.
Unpleasant and boring suspenser with nasty details.

w Luther Davis *d* Walter Grauman *ph* Lee Garmes *m* Paul Glass *pd* Rudolf Sternad

Olivia de Havilland, James Caan, Ann Sothern, Jeff Corey

'The film parades its pretensions on a note of high-pitched hysteria.'—*MFB*

Lady in a Jam
US 1942 78m bw
Universal (Gregory La Cava)

A scatterbrained socialite loses her money and inherits an Arizona farm.
A very thin vehicle for a star who deserved better.

w Eugene Thackey, Frank Cockrell, Otho Lovering *d* Gregory La Cava *ph* Hal Mohr *m* Frank Skinner

Irene Dunne, Patric Knowles, Ralph Bellamy, Eugene Pallette, Robert Homans, Samuel S. Hinds

Lady in Cement
US 1968 93m De Luxe Panavision
TCF / Arcola / Millfield (Aaron Rosenberg)

A Florida private eye on his morning swim finds a dead blonde.
Routine private eye stuff with fashionable sex and violence added.

w Marvin H. Albert, Jack Guss *d* Gordon Douglas *ph* Joseph Biroc *m* Hugo Montenegro

Frank Sinatra, Raquel Welch, Richard Conte, Martin Gabel, Lainie Kazan, Pat Henry, Steve Peck

'While *Tony Rome* seemed to herald a return to the forties thriller, *Lady in Cement* marks nothing more exciting than a return to *Tony Rome*.'—*MFB*

The Lady in Question*
US 1940 81m bw
Columbia

A Parisian shopkeeper on a jury is responsible for getting a girl acquitted of a murder charge, but begins to worry when his son falls in love with her.
Stagey but quite satisfying Hollywood remake of the French drama *Gribouille,* with Raimy and Michele Morgan.

w Lewis Meltzer, *story* Marcel Achard *d* Charles Vidor *ph* Lucien Andriot *m* Lucien Moraweck

Brian Aherne, Rita Hayworth, Glenn Ford, Irene Rich, George Coulouris, Lloyd Corrigan, Evelyn Keyes, Edward Norris, Curt Bois, Frank Reicher

The Lady in Red
US 1979 93m Metrocolor

The story of Dillinger's mistress. Okay but uninspired gangster drama from a fresh angle. Pamela Sue Martin, Robert Conrad, Louise Fletcher, Robert Hogan, Rod Gist. Written by John Sayles; directed by Lewis Teague; for New World.

The Lady in the Car with Glasses and a Gun
France / US 1969 105m Eastmancolor Panavision
Lira Film / Columbia (Anatole Litvak)

An English secretary in Paris decides to drive to the coast but has various adventures which make her believe she is either mad or amnesiac.
Muddled, tedious suspenser with a totally implausible 'explanation'.

w Richard Harris, Eleanor Perry, *novel* Sebastien Japrisot *d* Anatole Litvak *ph* Claude Renoir *m* Michel Legrand

Samantha Eggar, Oliver Reed, John McEnery, Stéphane Audran

'The minx in mink with a yen for men!'

Lady in the Dark**
US 1944 100m Technicolor
Paramount (Richard Blumenthal)

The editress of a fashion magazine is torn between three men, has worrying dreams, and takes herself to a psychoanalyst.
Lush, stylish and frequently amusing version of a Broadway musical, lacking most of the songs; despite its faults, an excellent example of studio spectacle and a very typical forties romantic comedy.

w Frances Goodrich, Albert Hackett, *play* Moss Hart *d Mitchell Leisen ph Ray Rennahan m Kurt Weill ly* Ira Gershwin *md* Robert Emmett Dolan *sp* Gordon Jennings *ad Hans Dreier*

Ginger Rogers, Warner Baxter, Ray Milland, Jon Hall, *Mischa Auer,* Mary Phillips, Barry Sullivan

† The film was completed in 1942 but held up because of overstock.
†† Paramount chief Buddy de Sylva is credited with ruining the film by cutting the theme song, 'My Ship', which is the key to the psychoanalysis.

AAN: Ray Rennahan; Robert Emmett Dolan

Lady in the Iron Mask
US 1952 78m Natural Colour

Princess Anne's twin sister is kept in an iron mask to prevent dispute about the succession. Naïve twist on a well-worn legend; production values below par. Louis Hayward, Patricia Medina, Alan Hale Jnr, Judd Holden, Steve Brodie, John Sutton. Written by Jack Pollexfen and Aubrey Wisberg; directed by Ralph Murphy; for Wanger–Frenke / TCF.

The Lady in the Lake*
US 1946 103m bw
MGM (George Haight)

A private eye is assigned to find a missing wife . . .
Complex private eye yarn which makes the original Chandler dialogue sound childish by over-reliance on the subjective camera method: we see the hero's face only when he looks in a mirror. An experiment that failed because it was not really understood.

w Steve Fisher, *novel* Raymond Chandler *d* Robert Montgomery *ph* Paul C. Vogel *m* David Snell

Robert Montgomery, Audrey Totter, Lloyd Nolan, Tom Tully, Leon Ames

Lady in the Morgue*
US 1938 70m bw
(GB title: *The Case of the Missing Blonde)*

A private eye investigates a suicide and uncovers three murders. Smart 'B' feature frequently cited as a model of its kind. Preston Foster, Frank Jenks, Patricia Ellis, Thomas Jackson. Written by Eric Taylor and Robertson White from the novel by Jonathan Latimer; directed by Otis Garrett; for Universal. (A previous film with the same characters, actors and director was *The Westland Case*.)

The Lady Is a Square
GB 1958 99m bw
ABP / Wilcox–Neagle

An impoverished socialite widow tries to keep her husband's symphony orchestra going and is helped by a pop singer.
Strained attempt to carry on the *Spring in Park Lane* tradition, with a few inspirations from Joe Pasternak and *One Hundred Men and a Girl*. Earnest performances, obvious jokes.

w Harold Purcell, Pamela Bower, Nicholas Phipps *d* Herbert Wilcox *ph* Gordon Dines *md* Wally Stott

Anna Neagle, Frankie Vaughan, Anthony Newley, Janette Scott, Wilfrid Hyde White

The Lady is Willing
GB 1933 74m bw

An ex-officer becomes a detective and takes his revenge on the financier who ruined him. Interesting comedy-melodrama with strong cast. Leslie Howard, Cedric Hardwicke, Binnie Barnes, Nigel Playfair, Nigel Bruce. Written by Guy Bolton, from the play by Louis Verneuil; directed by Gilbert Miller; for Columbia British.

The Lady Is Willing
US 1942 91m bw
Columbia (Mitchell Leisen)

A musical comedy star adopts a baby and falls in love with its pediatrician.
Dull mixture of light drama and heavy comedy, with all concerned ill at ease.

w James Edward Grant, Albert McCleery *d* Mitchell Leisen *ph* Ted Tetzlaff *m* W. Frank Harling

Marlene Dietrich, Fred MacMurray, Aline MacMahon, Stanley Ridges, Arline Judge, Marietta Canty

Lady Jane
GB 1986 142m Technicolor
Paramount / Peter Snell

After the death in 1553 of Edward VI, a faction pushes into power his second cousin Lady Jane Grey.
The puzzle is why this dreary and overlong historical piece was made in an unsympathetic age; and why such an unsuitable leading lady was cast.

w David Edgar, Chris Bryant *d* Trevor Nunn *ph* Douglas Slocombe *m* Stephen Oliver *pd* Allan Cameron *ed* Anne V. Coates

Helena Bonham Carter, Cary Elwes, John Wood, Michael Hordern, Jill Bennett, Jane Lapotaire, Sara Kestelman, Joss Ackland, Patrick Stewart, Richard Vernon

† The story was previously told in 1936 as *Tudor Rose.*

Lady Killer***
US 1933 76m bw
Warner (Henry Blanke)

A cinema usher turns to crime, flees to Hollywood, and becomes a movie star.
Hectic slam-bang action comedy with melodramatic moments. Great fun.

w Ben Markson, *novel* The Finger Man by Rosalind Keating Shaffer *d Roy del Ruth* *ph* Tony Gaudio *md* Leo F. Forbstein

James Cagney, Mae Clarke, Leslie Fenton, Margaret Lindsay, Henry O'Neill, Willard Robertson, Raymond Hatton, Russell Hopton

'An all-time high in roughneck character work even for this rough-and-tumble star.'—*Variety*

'A kind of résumé of everything he has done to date in the movies.'—*New York Evening Post*

'Sprightly, more or less daring, thoroughly entertaining.'—*New York World Telegram*

The Lady Killers: see The Ladykillers

Lady L
France / Italy / US 1965 124m Eastmancolor Panavision
Concordia / Champion / MGM (Carlo Ponti)

An 80-year-old lady recalls her romantic life from her youth as a Paris laundress.
Unhappy, lumbering, styleless attempt to recapture several old forms, indifferently though expensively made and acted.

wd Peter Ustinov, *novel* Romain Gary *ph* Henri Alekan *m* Jean Françaix *ad* Jean D'Eaubonne, Auguste Capelier

Sophia Loren, David Niven, Paul Newman, Peter Ustinov, Claude Dauphin, Philippe Noiret, Michel Piccoli, Marcel Dalio, Cecil Parker, Eugène Deckers

Lady, Let's Dance
US 1943 86m bw

An entertainment director for a California resort needs a new star. Thin musical with production values ambitious for its source. Belita, James Ellison, Frick and Frack, Walter Catlett, Lucien Littlefield. Written by Peter Milne and Paul Gerard Smith; directed by Frank Woodruff; for Scott R. Dunlap / Monogram.
AAN: Edward Kay (music); song 'Silver Shadows and Golden Dreams' (*m* Lew Pollack, *ly* Charles Newman)

The Lady Lies
US 1929 75m bw

A wealthy widowed attorney courts a working-class girl and offends his children. Dated melodrama in primitive talkie technique. Walter Huston, Claudette Colbert, Charles Ruggles, Tom Brown. Written by John Meehan and Garrett Fort; directed by Hobart Henley; for Paramount.

Lady Luck
US 1946 97m bw
RKO (Warren Duff)

The daughter of a long line of ill-fated gamblers marries one and tries to reform him, but the reverse happens.
Tedious comedy drama.

w Lynn Root, Frank Fenton *d* Edwin L. Marin *ph* Lucien Andriot *m* Leigh Harline

Robert Young, Barbara Hale, Frank Morgan, James Gleason, Don Rice, Harry Davenport, Lloyd Corrigan

Lady of Burlesque*
US 1943 91m bw
Hunt Stromberg
GB title: *Striptease Lady*

A burlesque dancer solves a number of backstage murders.
Agreeable murder mystery with strong injections of comedy.

w James Gunn, *novel* The G-String Murders by Gypsy Rose Lee *d* William A. Wellman *ph* Robert de Grasse *m* Arthur Lange

Barbara Stanwyck, Michael O'Shea, J. Edward Bromberg, Iris Adrian, Gloria Dickson, Charles Dingle

AAN: Arthur Lange

Lady of Scandal
US 1930 67m bw

The son of a noble house wants to marry an actress, but the family is nasty to her. Dated melodrama with sophisticated comedy asides. Ruth Chatterton, Basil Rathbone, Ralph Forbes, Nance O'Neill, Frederick Kerr, Herbert Bunston. Written by Hans Kraly from the play The High Road by Frederick Lonsdale; directed by Sidney Franklin; for MGM. 'Should register well in any but the lowest grind.'—*Variety*

Lady of Secrets
US 1936 73m bw

A rich girl's father prevents her marriage without knowing that she is pregnant. Complicated and very boring mother-love yarn with the faint perfume of a bygone age. Ruth Chatterton, Otto Kruger, Lionel Atwill, Lloyd Nolan, Marion Marsh, Elizabeth Risdon. Written by Joseph Anthony, Zoe Akins, Katherine Brush; directed by Marion Gering; for B. P. Schulberg / Columbia. 'Chatterton, back to the screen after a long absence, is still having trouble with her offspring. This time she is also having trouble with the play, the direction, and the photography.'—*Variety*

Lady of the Tropics
US 1939 92m bw
MGM (Sam Zimbalist)

An American playboy in Saigon marries a half-caste girl but her former admirer prevents her from getting a passport.
Interminable romantic melodrama with stars apparently straight from the taxidermist.

w Ben Hecht *d* Jack Conway *ph* George Folsey *m* Franz Waxman

Robert Taylor, Hedy Lamarr, Joseph Schildkraut, Gloria Franklin, Ernest Cossart

'Mediocre and stagey romance, but stars should pull it through.'—*Variety*

Lady on a Train*
US 1945 84m bw
Universal (Felix Jackson)

A girl arriving in New York by train sees a murder committed and can't make anyone believe her.
Cheerful mystery which starts in the right spirit but does not progress too satisfactorily.

w Edmund Beloin, Robert O'Brien, *novel* Leslie Charteris *d* Charles David *ph* Elwood Bredell *m* Miklos Rozsa

Deanna Durbin, Ralph Bellamy, David Bruce, Edward Everett Horton, George Coulouris, Allen Jenkins, Dan Duryea, Patricia Morison

The Lady Pays Off
US 1951 80m bw

A gambling schoolteacher agrees to pay off her debts by tutoring the casino owner's daughter. Flat and unprofitable romantic comedy-drama. Linda Darnell, Stephen McNally, Gigi Perreau, Virginia Field, Ann Codee. Written by Frank Gill Jnr and Albert J. Cohen; directed by Douglas Sirk; for Universal-International.

Lady Possessed
US 1952 86m bw
Republic / Portland (James Mason)

An unbalanced woman imagines she is destined to take the place of a pianist's dead wife.
Weary melodramatic nonsense dating from Hollywood's first obsession with psychiatry.

w Pamela Kellino, James Mason, *novel* Del Palma by Pamela Kellino *d* William Spier, Roy Kellino *ph* Karl Struss *m* Nathan Scott

James Mason, June Havoc, Stephen Dunne, Fay Compton, Pamela Kellino, Steven Geray

The Lady Says No
US 1951 83m bw
UA / Stillman (Frank Ross, John Stillman Jnr)

A magazine photographer tames a female chauvinist author.
Very silly comedy with neither wit nor style.

w Robert Russell *d* Frank Ross *ph* James Wong Howe *m* Emil Newman

Joan Caulfield, David Niven, James Robertson Justice, Lenore Lonergan, Henry Jones

Lady Scarface
US 1941 69m bw
RKO (Cliff Reid)

A police lieutenant captures a dangerous female gangster.
Weird gangster second feature with too many domestic comedy asides; notable only for the appearance in it of its dignified lead, fresh from *Rebecca*.

w Armand D'Usseau, Richard Collins
d Frank Woodruff *ph* Nicholas Musuraca

Judith Anderson, Dennis O'Keefe, Frances Neal, Mildred Coles, Eric Blore, Marc Lawrence

Lady Sings the Blues*
US 1972 144m Eastmancolor Panavision
Paramount / Motown / Weston / Furie (Jay Weston, James S. White)

The disastrous private life of blues singer Billie Holliday.
Old-fashioned showbiz biopic with new-fashioned drugs, sex and squalor.

w Terence McCloy, Chris Clark, Suzanne de Passe *d* Sidney J. Furie *ph* John Alonzo *m* Michel Legrand *md* Gil Askey

Diana Ross, Billy Dee Williams, Richard Pryor, James Callahan, Sid Melton

AAN: script; Gil Askey; Diana Ross

A Lady Surrenders
US 1930 95m bw

A misunderstanding turns an innocent husband into a bigamist after his wife has supposedly divorced him. Totally effete romantic drama with no comedy relief. Conrad Nagel, Genevieve Tobin, Basil Rathbone, Rose Hobart, Carmel Myers. Written by Gladys Lehman from the novel Sincerity by John Erskine; directed by John Stahl; for Universal. 'It fails from all angles: too stilted, slow, talky and punchless.'—*Variety*

A Lady Takes a Chance
US 1943 86m bw
RKO (Frank Ross)
aka: *The Cowboy and the Girl*

A New York office girl on holiday in Oregon falls for a rodeo rider.
Slender star action romance.

w Robert Ardrey *d* William A. Seiter *ph* Frank Redman *m* Roy Webb

Jean Arthur, John Wayne, Charles Winninger, Phil Silvers, Mary Field, Don Costello, John Philliber, Grady Sutton, Hans Conried

The Lady Takes a Flyer
US 1958 95m Eastmancolor Cinemascope

A pilot's wife finds that life at home is not easy, especially with a baby. Heavy comedy or light drama; on either count a bore. Lana Turner, Jeff Chandler, Richard Denning, Chuck Connors, Andra Martin. Written by Danny Arnold; directed by William Alland; for Universal-International.

The Lady Takes a Sailor*
US 1949 99m bw

A girl devoted to telling the truth insists on proving her story of a mysterious submarine which saved her after a sailing accident. Curious romantic farce with echoes of the old slapstick tradition. Jane Wyman, Dennis Morgan, Eve Arden, Allyn Joslyn, Robert Douglas, William Frawley. Written by Everett Freeman; directed by Michael Curtiz; for Warner.

A Lady to Love
US 1930 92m bw
MGM

An ageing grape grower spots an attractive waitress, sends her a marriage proposal by mail, but encloses a photo of his handsome foreman.
Rather primitive but well acted version of a subject later filmed more fluently under the title of the original play.

w Sidney Howard, from his play They Knew What They Wanted *d* Victor Seastrom *ph* Merritt B. Gerstad

Edward G. Robinson, Vilma Banky, Robert Ames, Richard Carle

'A hit as a talker: well directed, acted and treated.'—*Variety*

Lady Tubbs
US 1935 69m bw

An ex-cook crashes society and shows up the pretenders. Mildly agreeable sentimental farce. Alice Brady, Douglass Montgomery, Anita Louise, Alan Mowbray, Minor Watson, Russell Hicks, Hedda Hopper. Written by Barry Trivers from the novel by Homer Croy; directed by Alan Crosland; for Universal. 'Solid laugh fare for the nabes.'—*Variety*

The Lady Vanishes**
GB 1938 97m bw
Gaumont British / Gainsborough (Edward Black)

En route back to England by train from Switzerland, an old lady disappears and two young people investigate.
The disappearing lady trick brilliantly refurbished by Hitchcock and his screenwriters, who even get away with a horrid model shot at the beginning. Superb, suspenseful, brilliantly funny, meticulously detailed entertainment.

w Sidney Gilliat, Frank Launder, novel The Wheel Spins by Ethel Lina White *d Alfred Hitchcock* *ph* Jack Cox *md* Louis Levy

Margaret Lockwood, Michael Redgrave, Dame May Whitty, Paul Lukas, Basil Radford, Naunton Wayne, Catherine Lacey, Cecil Parker, Linden Travers, Googie Withers, *Mary Clare*, Philip Leaver

'If it were not so brilliant a melodrama, we should class it as a brilliant comedy.'—*Frank S. Nugent*

'No one can study the deceptive effortlessness with which one thing leads to another without learning where the true beauty of this medium is to be mined.'—*Otis Ferguson*

'Directed with such skill and velocity that it has come to represent the very quintessence of screen suspense.'—*Pauline Kael, 70s*

† Hitchcock was actually second choice as director. The production was ready to roll as *Lost Lady*, directed by Roy William Neill, with Charters and Caldicott already in place, when Neill became unavailable and Hitch stepped in.

The Lady Vanishes
GB 1979 97m Eastmancolor Panavision
Rank / Hammer (Michael Carreras, Tom Sachs)

A remake of the above in which everything goes wrong: wrong shape, wrong actors, wrong style (or lack of it). Reasonable adherence to the original script can't save it.

w George Axelrod *d* Anthony Page
ph Douglas Slocombe *m* Richard Hartley
pd Wilfred Shingleton

Cybill Shepherd, Elliott Gould, Angela Lansbury, Herbert Lom, Arthur Lowe, Ian Carmichael, Gerald Harper, Jenny Runacre, Jean Anderson

Lady Windermere's Fan*
US 1925 80m (24 fps) bw silent
Warner

The mysterious Mrs Erlynne almost causes a scandal in London society.
Oscar Wilde's play transposed to the twenties, with the Lubitsch touch daringly displacing Wildean epigrams. Still more amusing than the sound remake, *The Fan.*

w Julien Josephson d Ernst Lubitsch
ph Charles Van Enger

Ronald Colman, May McAvoy, Irene Rich, Bert Lytell, Edward Martindel

'Lubitsch's best silent film, full of incisive details, discreet touches, nuances of gestures, where behaviour betrays the character and discloses the sentiment of the personages.'—*Georges Sadoul*

The Lady with a Lamp*
GB 1951 110m bw
British Lion / Imperadio (Herbert Wilcox)

The life of Florence Nightingale and her work in reforming the nursing service in 19th-century England.
Solid biopic, not quite in accord with history.

w Warren Chetham Strode, *play* Reginald Berkeley *d* Herbert Wilcox *ph* Max Greene *m* Anthony Collins *ad* William C. Andrews

Anna Neagle, Michael Wilding, Gladys Young, Felix Aylmer, Julian D'Albie, Arthur Young, Edwin Styles, Barbara Couper, Cecil Trouncer, Rosalie Crutchley

'A slow, sedate, refined chronicle . . . Herbert Wilcox is a good deal more at ease with the balls and dinners, than with anything that happens later.'—*Penelope Houston*

'It may please fans of Anna Neagle and Michael Wilding, but not fans of Florence Nightingale.'—*Richard Mallett, Punch*

Lady with a Past*
US 1932 80m bw
RKO (Charles R. Rogers)
GB title: *Reputation*

A wealthy but shy girl almost accidentally finds herself with a reputation as a scarlet woman, and the men flock around her.
Moderately enjoyable star comedy drama.

w Horace Jackson, *novel* Harriet Henry
d Edward H. Griffith *ph* Hal Mohr *m* Max Steiner

Constance Bennett, Ben Lyon, David Manners, Astrid Allwyn, Merna Kennedy, Blanche Frederici, Nella Walker

'Light and satisfying material for the women.'—*Variety*

Lady with Red Hair*
US 1940 78m bw
Warner (Edmund Grainger)

The life of actress Mrs Leslie Carter and her association with impresario David Belasco.
Mildly interesting but unsatisfying biopic of a lady scarcely remembered.

w Charles Kenyon, Milton Krims, N. Brewster Morse, Norbert Faulkner *d* Curtis Bernhardt
ph Arthur Edeson *m* Heinz Roemheld

Miriam Hopkins, Claude Rains, Richard Ainley, John Litel, Laura Hope Crews, Helen Wesley, Mona Barrie, Victor Jory, Cecil Kellaway, Fritz Leiber, Halliwell Hobbes

The Lady with the Little Dog*
USSR 1959 90m bw
Lenfilm
original title: *Dama s Sobachkoi*

In Yalta at the turn of the century, an unhappily married woman and a married man start an affair which lasts secretly over the years.
Modestly pleasing, subtly acted anecdote.

wd Josef Heifits, story Anton Chekhov
ph Andrei Moskvin *ed* D. Meschiev *m* Jiri Sternwald

Ya Savvina, Alexei Batalov, Ala Chostakova

A Lady without Passport*
US 1950 84m bw
MGM (Samuel Marx)

A secret service undercover man tracks down aliens being smuggled into the US, and falls in love with one of them.
Routine material, very well handled.

w Howard Dimsdale *d Joseph H. Lewis*
ph Paul C. Vogel *m* David Raksin

Hedy Lamarr, John Hodiak, James Craig, George Macready, Steve Geray

'Cursed for eternity! No force in heaven will release them . . . no power on earth can save them!'

Ladyhawke
US 1985 124m Technicolor
Warner / Richard Donner, Lauren Schuler

Medieval boy and girl lovers have been changed respectively into a wolf and a hawk, never simultaneously to resume their true forms.
Unpersuasive legend, dolefully told at excessive length.

w Edward Khmara, Michael Thomas, Tom Mankiewicz *d* Richard Donner *ph* Vittorio Storaro *m* Andrew Powell *pd* Wolf Kroeger *ed* Stuart Baird

Matthew Broderick, Rutger Hauer, Michelle Pfeiffer, Leo McKern, John Wood

The Ladykillers*
GB 1955 97m Technicolor
Ealing (Seth Holt)

An old lady takes in a sinister lodger, who with his four friends commits a robbery. When she finds out, they plot to kill her, but are hoist with their own petards.
Overrated comedy in poor colour; those who made it quite clearly think it funnier than it is.

w William Rose *d* Alexander Mackendrick
ph Otto Heller *m* Tristam Cary

Alec Guinness, *Katie Johnson*, Peter Sellers, Cecil Parker, Herbert Lom, Danny Green, Jack Warner, Frankie Howerd, Kenneth Connor

'To be frivolous about frivolous matters, that's merely boring. To be frivolous about something that's in some way deadly serious, that's true comedy.'—*Alexander Mackendrick*

AAN: William Rose

The Lady's from Kentucky
US 1939 75m bw

A crooked bookie is reformed by a lady horse breeder. Yawnworthy drama with an unattractive hero. George Raft, Ellen Drew, Hugh Herbert, Zasu Pitts, Louise Beavers, Forrester Harvey. Written by Malcolm Stuart Boylan; directed by Alexander Hall; for Jeff Lazarus / Paramount. 'It starts with promise, stumbles in the middle section, and drags itself across the line for the finish.'—*Variety*

A Lady's Morals
US 1930 86m bw
MGM
GB titles: *Jenny Lind*; *The Soul Kiss*

The 'Swedish nightingale' learns that love is more important than a singing career.
Cliché-strewn romance with music.

w Hans Kraly, Claudine West, John Meehan, Arthur Richman *d* Sidney Franklin
m Herbert Stothart

Grace Moore, Reginald Denny, Wallace Beery, Jobyna Howland

'Class production of money potentialities.'—*Variety*

† Wallace Beery played P. T. Barnum, a role he was to repeat four years later in *The Mighty Barnum*.

A Lady's Profession
US 1933 65m bw

A British nobleman comes to America to retrieve his lost fortune, and starts a speakeasy. Rather silly farce which generally disappoints. Alison Skipworth, Roland Young, Sari Maritza, Kent Taylor, Roscoe Karns. Written by Walter de Leon and Malcolm Stuart Boylan; directed by Norman McLeod; for Paramount. 'Slow. Some bright spots, but too widely spaced.'—*Variety*

Lafayette
France / Italy 1961 158m Super Technirama 70
Copernic / Cosmos (Maurice Jacquin)

French officers help America in the revolutionary war of 1776.
Nerveless international epic, interesting only for its star cameos.

w Jean-Bernard Luc, Suzanne Arduini, Jacques Sigurd, François Ponthier, Jean

Dréville, Maurice Jacquin *d* Jean Dréville *ph* Claude Renoir, Roger Hubert *m* Steve Laurent, Pierre Duclos

Michel Le Royer, Jack Hawkins, Orson Welles, Howard St John, Vittorio de Sica, Edmund Purdom, Jacques Castelot, Folco Lulli

'It looks, sounds and smells like nothing so much as the same old indigestible, ill-dubbed, co-produced continental spectaculars which have already turned the stomach in a whole range of lesser screen ratios.'—*MFB*

Lafayette Escadrille
US 1957 93m bw
Warner (William Wellman)
GB title: *Hell Bent for Glory*

Early in World War I, a young American joins the French air force.
The director's valedictory film, on a subject close to his heart, is a curiously disappointing, flat and disjointed affair, partly salvaged by a good period feel.

w A. S. Fleischmann *d* William A. Wellman *ph William Clothier* *m* Leonard Rosenman

Tab Hunter, David Janssen, Clint Eastwood, Will Hutchins, Paul Fix

Lake Placid Serenade
US 1944 85m bw

A Czech girl skater is sent to America to represent her country. Simple-minded entertainment overloaded with musical numbers. Vera Hruba Ralston, Robert Livingston, Eugene Pallette, Vera Vague, Walter Catlett, Lloyd Corrigan, William Frawley. Written by Dick Irving Hyland and Doris Gilbert; directed by Steve Sekely; for Harry Grey / Republic.

Lamb
GB 1986 110m Eastmancolor
Cannon / Flickers / Limehouse / Channel Four (Neil Zeiger)

The principal of a boys' remand home on the Irish west coast goes on the run with a new inmate who has not long to live.
Rather wearisome transcription of religious thesis into makeshift drama: disturbing but not satisfying.

w Bernard MacLaverty, from his novel *d* Colin Gregg *ph* Mike Garfath *m* Van Morrison

Liam Neeson, Hugh O'Conor, Harry Towb, Frances Tomelty, Ian Bannen

The Lambeth Walk
GB 1939 84m bw
CAPAD / Pinebrook (Anthony Havelock-Allan)

A cockney bloke inherits a dukedom.
Mild screen version of a popular musical play and a song which became a nationwide hit.

w Clifford Grey, John Paddy Carstairs, Robert Edmunds, *play* Me and My Girl by Louis Rose, Douglas Furber, Noel Gay *d* Albert de Courville *ph* Francis Carver

Lupino Lane, Sally Gray, Seymour Hicks, Enid Stamp Taylor, Wilfrid Hyde White, Charles Heslop, Norah Howard

The Lamp Still Burns
GB 1943 90m bw
GFD / Two Cities (Leslie Howard)

Adventures of wartime probationary nurses. Understated wartime morale-builder, no longer very interesting.

w Elizabeth Baron, Roland Pertwee, *novel* One Pair of Feet by Monica Dickens *d* Maurice Elvey *ph* Robert Krasker

Rosamund John, Stewart Granger, Godfrey Tearle, Sophie Stewart, John Laurie, Margaret Vyner, Cathleen Nesbitt, Joyce Grenfell

Lancashire Luck
GB 1937 74m bw

A poor girl's life is changed when her father wins the pools. Modest comedy which started its star's career. Wendy Hiller, George Carney, Muriel George, Nigel Stock, George Galleon. Written by A. R. Rawlinson, from a story by Ronald Gow; directed by Henry Cass; for Paramount British.

Lancelot and Guinevere*
GB 1962 117m Eastmancolor Panavision
Emblem (Cornel Wilde)
US title: *Sword of Lancelot*

Sir Lancelot covets the wife of his beloved King Arthur, but after Arthur's death she takes the veil.
Decently made, rather tame transcription of the legends, with all concerned doing quite creditably but not brilliantly.

w Richard Schayer, Jefferson Pascal *d* Cornel Wilde *ph* Harry Waxman *m* Ron Goodwin

Cornel Wilde, Jean Wallace, Brian Aherne, George Baker, John Barrie

Lancer Spy*
US 1937 80m bw
TCF

A German spy is captured and his English double is sent back to replace him.
World War I yarn on the lines of *The Great Impersonation* (qv). Excellent production and a good beginning and end, but a slow middle.

w Philip Dunne, *novel* Marthe McKenna *d* Gregory Ratoff *ph* Barney McGill *m* Arthur Lange

George Sanders, Dolores del Rio, Peter Lorre, Joseph Schildkraut, Virginia Field, Sig Rumann, Fritz Feld

'Sometimes exciting, always absorbing, and played with serious intensity.'—*Variety*

Land of Liberty*
US 1939 137m bw

A compilation of footage from American historical films, amounting hopefully to a history of America as seen by Hollywood. A pretty impressive job of selection and editing, compiled for the New York World's Fair. Written by Jeannie McPherson, Jesse Lasky Jnr; edited by Cecil B. de Mille and others; for Motion Picture Producers and Distributors of America.

'Her treachery stained every stone of the pyramid!'

Land of the Pharaohs*
US 1955 105m Warnercolor Cinemascope
Warner / Continental (Howard Hawks)

Pharaoh is obsessed with life after death and builds a great pyramid for himself and his treasures . . . but his wife is ambitious . . .
Unexpected, interesting excursion into Ancient Egypt, distended by Cinemascope; basically a macabre melodrama with a final spectacular twist. The engineering details would make a fascinating documentary.

w William Faulkner, Harry Kurnitz, H. Jack Bloom *d* Howard Hawks *ph Lee Garmes, Russell Harlan* *m Dmitri Tiomkin* *ad Alexander Trauner*

Jack Hawkins, Joan Collins, Alexis Minotis, James Robertson Justice, Sidney Chaplin

'20,000 workers and technicians! 1,600 camels! 104 specially built barges! 9,753 players in one scene alone!'—*publicity*

The Land That Time Forgot*
GB 1974 91m Technicolor
Amicus (John Dark)

In 1916, survivors from a torpedoed supply ship find themselves on a legendary island full of prehistoric monsters.
Lively old-fashioned adventure fantasy with good technical credits.

w James Cawthorne, Michael Moorcock, *novel* Edgar Rice Burroughs *d* Kevin Connor *ph* Alan Hume *m* Douglas Gamley *pd Maurice Carter* *sp* Derek Meddings, Roger Dicken

Doug McClure, John McEnery, Susan Penhaligon, Keith Barron, Anthony Ainley

The Land Unknown*
US 1957 78m bw Cinemascope
U-I (William Alland)

A plane is forced down into a strange Antarctic valley where dinosaurs still roam.
Efficient adventure fantasy on *King Kong* lines but without any of that film's panache.

w Laslo Gorog *d* Virgil Vogel *ph* Ellis Carter *m* Hans Salter *sp* Roswell Hoffman, Fred Knoth, Orien Ernest, Jack Kevan

Jock Mahoney, Shawn Smith, William Reynolds, Henry Brandon

Land without Bread*
Spain 1932 27m bw
Ramon Acin
aka: *Las Hurdes*

A famous documentary showing the poorest region of northern Spain, notable for some stunningly unpleasant images impeccably staged.

wd, ed Luis Bunuel *ph* Eli Lotar

Land without Music*
GB 1936 80m bw
Capitol Films (Max Schach)
US title: *Forbidden Music*

The ruler of a Ruritanian country bans music because her subjects are too busy singing to make money. A revolutionary singer however

wins the duchess's hand and reverses her decision.
Artless but attractively played operetta with the star in excellent form.

w Marian Dix, L. Du Garde Peach *d* Walter Forde *ph* John Boyle *m* Oscar Straus

Richard Tauber, Jimmy Durante, Diana Napier, June Clyde, Derrick de Marney, Esme Percy, George Hayes, Edward Rigby

Landfall
GB 1949 88m bw
ABPC (Victor Skuzetzky)

A test pilot mistakenly believes that he accidentally sank a British submarine.
Second rate transcription of a popular novel.

w Talbot Jennings, Gilbert Gunn, Anne Burnaby, *novel* Nevil Shute *d* Ken Annakin *ph* Wilkie Cooper

Michael Denison, Patricia Plunkett, Kathleen Harrison, David Tomlinson, Joan Dowling, Maurice Denham, A. E. Matthews, Margaretta Scott, Sebastian Shaw, Laurence Harvey

The Landlord*
US 1970 110m De Luxe
United Artists / Mirisch / Carter (Norman Jewison)

A tycoon's son buys a tenement in Brooklyn's black ghetto, and conscience diverts him into improving the lot of his tenants.
Overlong satirical comedy, good on detail but short on structure.

w Bill Gunn, *novel* Kristin Hunter *d Hal Ashby* *ph* Gordon Willis *m* Al Kooper *pd* Robert Boyle

Beau Bridges, Lee Grant, Pearl Bailey, Diana Sands

'Bad taste from start to finish . . . not an avenue of offensiveness to any race is left unexplored.'—*Judith Crist*

AAN: Lee Grant

Landru
France / Italy 1962 115m Eastmancolor
Rome-Paris / CC Champion (Carlo Ponti, Georges de Beauregard)
aka: *Bluebeard*

The true story of a furniture dealer who murdered women for financial gain, also treated by Chaplin in *Monsieur Verdoux*.

A curious artificial style has been adopted, making a tragi-comedy look like a farce which isn't very funny, and falls on very stony ground indeed despite the all star cast.

w Françoise Sagan *d* Claude Chabrol *ph* Jean Rabier *m* Pierre Jansen

Charles Denner, Michèle Morgan, Danielle Darrieux, Hildegarde Knef, Stéphane Audran, Catherine Rouvel

Larceny
US 1948 89m bw
Universal (Aaron Rosenberg)

A con man fleeces a war widow into paying for a memorial to her husband, but falls in love with her.
Drearily predictable melodrama.

w Herbert F. Margolis, Louis Markein, William Bowers *novel* The Velvet Fleece by Lois Ely, John Fleming *d* George Sherman *ph* Irving Glassberg *m* Leith Stevens

Joan Caulfield, John Payne, Dan Duryea, Shelley Winters, Dorothy Hart, Richard Rober, Dan O'Herlihy

Larceny Inc.
US 1942 95m bw
Warner (Jack Saper, Jerry Wald)

An ex-convict tries to rob a bank but finds that honesty pays best.
Tepid comedy-drama from the period when Warners were taming their gangster image.

w Everett Freeman, Edwin Gilbert, *play* The Night before Christmas by Laura and S. J. Perelman *d* Lloyd Bacon *ph* Tony Gaudio

Edward G. Robinson, Jane Wyman, Broderick Crawford, Anthony Quinn, Jack Carson, Edward Brophy, Harry Davenport, John Qualen, Barbara Jo Allen, Jackie Gleason, Grant Mitchell, Andrew Tombes

The Las Vegas Story
US 1952 88m bw
RKO (Robert Sparks)

When an investment broker and his new wife stop at Las Vegas, her shady past begins to emerge.
So-so programmer with some eccentric talents in average form, capped by a desert helicopter chase.

w Earl Felton, Harry Essex *d* Robert Stevenson *ph* Harry J. Wild *m* Leigh Harline *md* Constantin Bakaleinikoff

Jane Russell, Victor Mature, Vincent Price, Hoagy Carmichael, Colleen Miller, Brad Dexter, Jay C. Flippen

The Lash
US 1930 76m bw

Adventures of a Spanish-Californian Robin Hood. Or, *The Mark of Zorro* in all but name: a stalwart early talkie. Richard Barthelmess, Mary Astor, James Rennie, Marian Nixon. Written by Bradley King from the story Adios by Lanier Virginia Bartlett; directed by Frank Lloyd; for First National. 'A good action talker in the western romantic strain.'—*Variety*

NB: Filmed in VitaScope (65mm).

Lassie
The official Lassie series, made by MGM, was as follows:

1943: LASSIE COME HOME (qv)
1945: SON OF LASSIE (*d* S. Sylvan Simon *with* Peter Lawford, Donald Crisp, Nigel Bruce)
1946: COURAGE OF LASSIE (*d* Fred M. Wilcox *with* Elizabeth Taylor, Frank Morgan, Tom Drake)
1948: THE HILLS OF HOME[1] (*d* Fred M. Wilcox *with* Edmund Gwenn, Donald Crisp, Tom Drake)
1949: THE SUN COMES UP (*d* Richard Thorpe *with* Jeanette MacDonald, Lloyd Nolan)
1949: CHALLENGE TO LASSIE (*d* Richard Thorpe *with* Edmund Gwenn, Donald Crisp)
1951: THE PAINTED HILLS (*d* Harold F. Kress *with* Paul Kelly, Bruce Cowling)

† Later 'Lassie' features were taken from episodes of the long-running TV series.

[1](GB title: *Master of Lassie*)

Lassie Come Home*
US 1943 88m Technicolor
MGM (Samuel Marx)

A poor family is forced to sell its beloved dog, but she makes a remarkable journey to return to them.
First of the Lassie films and certainly the best: an old-fashioned heartwarmer.

w Hugo Butler, *novel* Eric Knight *d* Fred M. Wilcox *ph* Leonard Smith *m* Daniele Amfitheatrof

Roddy McDowall, Elizabeth Taylor, Donald Crisp, Edmund Gwenn, Dame May Whitty, Nigel Bruce, Elsa Lanchester, J. Pat O'Malley

'The late Eric Knight wrote this immortal essay in Doggery-Woggery. MGM finished it off.'—*Richard Winnington*

AAN: Leonard Smith

Lassiter
US 1984 100m Technicolor
Pan Pacific / Golden Harvest (Albert S. Ruddy)

An American detective in pre-war London is forced by Scotland Yard to steal papers from the German Embassy.
Flat to the point of stultification, this marks yet another failure to make a big screen star of Tom Selleck.

w David Taylor *d* Roger Young *ph* Gil Taylor *m* Ken Thorne *pd* Peter Mullins *ed* Benjamin Weissman, Richard Hiscott

Tom Selleck, Jane Seymour, Lauren Hutton, Bob Hoskins, Joe Regalbuto, Ed Lauter, Warren Clarke

The Last Adventurers
GB 1937 77m bw

Adventures on board a fishing trawler. Acceptable low-budget outdoor drama. Niall MacGinnis, Linden Travers, Roy Emerton, Kay Walsh, Peter Gawthorne, Katie Johnson. Written by Denison Clift; directed by Roy Kellino; for Conway.

The Last American Hero*
US 1973 95m De Luxe Panavision
TCF / Wizan / Rojo (John Cutts, William Roberts)

The adventures of an illicit whisky distiller with a passion for fast cars.
Observant, amusing hillbilly comedy drama based on the early life of racing driver Junior Johnson.

w William Roberts *d Lamont Johnson* *ph* George Silano *m* Charles Fox

Jeff Bridges, Valerie Perrine, Geraldine Fitzgerald, Ned Beatty, Art Lund, Gary Busey

† Reissue title: *Hard Driver.*

The Last Angry Man*
US 1959 100m bw
Columbia (Fred Kohlmar)

An old doctor in a Brooklyn slum is made the subject of a TV documentary.
Self-confidently sentimental wallow which just about works.

w Gerald Green *d* Daniel Mann *ph* James Wong Howe *m* George Duning

Paul Muni, David Wayne, Betsy Palmer, Luther Adler, Dan Tobin, Robert F. Simon

AAN: Paul Muni

The Last Blitzkrieg
US 1959 84m bw
Columbia / Sam Katzman

During the Battle of the Bulge a German leads a squad of American saboteurs.
Weakly pacifist, technically incompetent war adventure.

w Lou Morheim *d* Arthur Dreifuss *ph* Ted Scaife *m* Hugo de Groot

Van Johnson, Kerwin Mathews, Dick York, Larry Storch

The Last Bridge
Austria / Yugoslavia 1953 95m bw
Cosmopol / UFUS (Carl Szokoll)

During World War II, a German nurse in Yugoslavia is captured by partisans and turns to their point of view.
Message melodrama, very ably put together with a bleakly tragic climax; but nothing at all new.

w Helmut Kautner, Norbert Kunze *d* Helmut Kautner *ph* Elio Carniel *m* Carl de Groof

Maria Schell, Bernhard Wicki, Barbara Rütting, Carl Möhner

The Last Chance*
Switzerland 1945 105m bw
Praesens Film

In 1943 an Englishman and an American escape from a fascist camp in northern Italy and with the help of refugees cross the mountains into Switzerland.
Earnest propaganda piece which struck the spot at the time: cinematically rather plodding, but with some exciting scenes.

w Richard Schweitzer *d* Leopold Lindtberg *ph* Emil Berna *m* Robert Blum

E. G. Morrison, Ray Reagan, John Hoy, Luisa Rossi

The Last Command**
US 1928 100m approx (24 fps) bw silent
Paramount

An exiled Russian general goes berserk when given a role in a movie which virtually involves playing himself.
Fascinating ironic comedy tailored for an international star who was not to survive the talkies.

w John S. Goodrich, *story* Lajos Biro *d Josef Von Sternberg* *ph* Bert Glennon *ad* Hans Dreier

Emil Jannings, William Powell, Evelyn Brent, Nicholas Soussanin

AA: Emil Jannings
AAN: best picture; Lajos Biro

The Last Command*
US 1955 110m Trucolor
Republic (Frank Lloyd)

Jim Bowie returns to Texas in the 1830s and dies at the Alamo alongside other famous men.
Reasonably interesting western on a subject which has often figured but seldom worked.

w Warren Duff *d* Frank Lloyd *ph* Jack Marta *m* Max Steiner

Ernest Borgnine, Sterling Hayden, Anna Maria Alberghetti, Arthur Hunnicutt, Richard Carlson, J. Carrol Naish

The Last Days of Dolwyn*
GB 1949 95m bw
London / BLPA (Anatole de Grunwald)
US title: *Woman of Dolwyn*

A Welsh valley is flooded to make a reservoir and a village has to be evacuated.
Interesting but rather stagey drama based on an actual 19th-century event, with personal melodrama added.

wd Emlyn Williams *ph* Otto Heller *m* John Greenwood

Edith Evans, Emlyn Williams, Richard Burton, Hugh Griffith, Barbara Couper, Allan Aynesworth

'The conventionally picturesque Welsh flavour and mounting probabilities apart, the treatment is stiff and episodic.'—*MFB*

'Pompeii . . . drunk with wealth and power . . . rotten with pagan pleasures . . . doomed to fiery death from the skies!'

The Last Days of Pompeii*
US 1935 96m bw
RKO (Merian C. Cooper)

In ancient Pompeii, various personal dramas are submerged in the eruption of Vesuvius.
Starchy melodrama capped by a reel of spectacular disaster.

w Ruth Rose, Boris Ingster, *novel* Lord Lytton *d* Merian C. Cooper, Ernest Schoedsack *ph* Eddie Linden Jnr, J. Roy Hunt *m* Roy Webb *sp Vernon Walker, Harry Redmond*

Preston Foster, Basil Rathbone, Alan Hale, Dorothy Cooper

'Well-done spectacle minus romance and cast names. Should do all right generally.'—*Variety*

The Last Detail**
US 1973 104m Metrocolor
Columbia / Acrobat / Persky–Bright (Gerald Ayres)

Two hardened naval petty officers escort a young recruit, sentenced for thieving, from Virginia to a New Hampshire jail, and give him a wild last night.
Foul-mouthed weekend odyssey, with a few well-observed moments for non-prudes.
Technically the epitome of Hollywood's most irritating seventies fashion, with fuzzy sound recording, dim against-the-light photography, and a general determination to show up the ugliness of everything around us.

w Robert Towne, *novel* Darryl Ponicsan *d* Hal Ashby *ph* Michael Chapman *m* Johnny Mandel

Jack Nicholson, Otis Young, Randy Quaid, Clifton James, Carol Kane

'Visually it is relentlessly lower-depths gloomy, and the material, though often very funny, is programmed to wrench your heart.'—*New Yorker*

AAN: Robert Towne; Jack Nicholson; Randy Quaid

The Last Dinosaur
US 1977 100m colour
Rankin-Bass Productions

An oil-drilling team discovers a *tyrannosaurus rex* while probing the polar oil-cap.
Inept monster saga with poorish special effects from a Japanese team.

w William Overgard *d* Alex Grasshof, Tom Kotani *ph* Shoshi Ueda *m* Maury Laws

Richard Boone, Joan Van Ark, Steven Keats

'He thinks someone is trying to kill him. He's dead right!'

Last Embrace
US 1979 101m Technicolor
UA (Michael Taylor, Dan Wigutow)

An investigator survives a number of attacks on his life, though his wife is killed in the first of them.
Hitchcockian mystery without the master's zest or humour, though it leads to a pretty exciting climax at Niagara Falls.

w David Shaber, *novel* The 13th Man by Murray Teigh Bloom *d* Jonathan Demme *ph* Tak Fujimoto *m* Miklos Rozsa

Roy Scheider, Janet Margolin, Sam Levene, John Glover, Charles Napier, Christopher Walken, Jacqueline Brookes

'A case study of late seventies movie-making which does everything in its power to avoid taking risks.'—*John Pym, MFB*

The Last Emperor**
Italy / Hong Kong 160m approx. Technicolor Technovision
Jeremy Thomas

The life of China's last imperial ruler, from ascending the throne as a puppet-like 3-year-old, to serene old age as a gardener in Mao's People's Republic.
A lavish spectacle which caught the imagination of audiences, though many found the compression of 60 years of Chinese politics baffling.

w Mark Peploe, Bernardo Bertolucci *d Bernardo Bertolucci* *ph* Vittorio Storaro *m* Ryuichi Sakamoto, David Byrne, Cong Su *pd* Ferdinando Scarfiotti

John Lone, Joan Chen, Peter O'Toole, Ying Ruocheng

The Last Escape
GB 1970 90m De Luxe

An American officer in Munich tries to rescue a German scientist from the Nazis. Standard World War II actioner. Stuart Whitman, John Collin, Martin Jarvis, Pinkas Braun. Written by Herman Hoffman; directed by Walter Grauman; for Oakmont/UA.

The Last Flight***
US 1931 80m bw
Warner

In 1919, four veteran American fliers stay on in Paris in the hope of calming their shattered physical and emotional states.
Fascinatingly offhand study on post-war cynicism and the faint hope of a better world, beautifully written and directed in a manner more effective than *The Sun Also Rises*.

w John Monk Saunders, from his novel Single Lady *d William Dieterle ph* Sid Hickox

Richard Barthelmess, Helen Chandler, David Manners, John Mack Brown, *Elliott Nugent*, Walter Byron

'If the crowd can understand that girl character in this picture the film is an undoubted grosser.'—*Variety*

'A narrative as tight and spare as a Racine tragedy . . . unique in Hollywood of that time in its persistent, calculated understatement.'—*Tom Milne, 1975*

† In magazine form the story was known as 'Nikki and her War Birds'.

The Last Flight of Noah's Ark
US 1980 98m Technicolor
Walt Disney

An impecunious pilot reluctantly flies an orphanage worker and a cargo of animals across the Pacific, only to be stranded with them on a desert island.
It must have sounded like a good idea, but if it was to work at all it needed much sharper handling.

w Steven W. Carabatsos, Sandy Glass, George Arthur Bloom, *story* The Gremlin's Castle by Ernest K. Gann *d* Charles Jarrott *ph* Charles F. Wheeler *m* Maurice Jarre

Elliott Gould, Geneviève Bujold, Ricky Schroder, Tammy Lauren, Vincent Gardenia

The Last Frontier
US 1932 bw serial: 12 eps

A western newspaper editor battles a gang of outlaws. Routine serial, a rare commodity from this studio. Creighton Chaney (Lon Chaney Jnr), Dorothy Gulliver, Mary Jo Desmond. Directed by Spencer Bennet; for RKO.

'The big fellow is out of Alcatraz—ready to show them no mercy!'

The Last Gangster*
US 1937 81m bw
MGM (J. J. Cohn)

A gangster is released from Alcatraz and plans vengeance on his wife for deserting him.
Clean-cut star melodrama which suddenly turns sentimental.

w John Lee Mahin *d* Edward Ludwig *ph* William Daniels *montage Slavko Vorkapitch m* Edward Ward

Edward G. Robinson, Rose Stradner, James Stewart, Lionel Stander, Douglas Scott, John Carradine, Sidney Blackmer, Edward Brophy

'May indeed be the last gangster movie . . . a good film which will blossom at the b.o.'—*Variety*

'A lot of water has flowed under the bridge since *Little Caesar*, but Mr Robinson has breasted the tides to make his impersonation of a 1937 thug as persuasive as was his portrait of a killer in that earlier classic of rats and rackets.'—*Frank Nugent*

The Last Gentleman
US 1934 80m bw

The career of a New England millionaire. Pleasing star family drama. George Arliss, Edna May Oliver, Ralph Morgan, Janet Beecher, Charlotte Henry. Written by Leonard Praskins; directed by Sidney Lanfield; for Fox. 'A prolonged monologue . . . mediocre film which must depend on the star's rep.'—*Variety*

The Last Grenade
GB 1969 93m Eastmancolor Panavision
Cinerama / Dimitri de Grunwald / Josef Shaftel

An army mercenary is betrayed by an ex-friend in the Congo and pursues him to Hong Kong.
Violent action melodrama with few redeeming qualities.

w Kenneth Ware, *novel* The Ordeal of Major Grigsby by John Sherlock *d* Gordon Flemyng *ph* Alan Hume *m* Johnny Dankworth

Stanley Baker, Alex Cord, Honor Blackman, Richard Attenborough, Rafer Johnson, Andrew Keir, Ray Brooks, Julian Glover, John Thaw

The Last Hard Men
US 1976 97m De Luxe Panavision
TCF / Belasco–Seltzer–Thatcher

A train robber breaks jail and sets out to revenge himself on the now-retired lawman who committed him.
Tough action adventure without much sense except to paint the end of the golden days of the west.

w Guerdon Trueblood, *novel* Gun Down by Brian Garfield *d* Andrew V. McLaglen *ph* Duke Callaghan *m* Jerry Goldsmith

Charlton Heston, James Coburn, Barbara Hershey, Christopher Mitchum, Michael Parks, Jorge Rivero, Thalmus Rasulala

'Script and direction seem equally tired.'—*Sight and Sound*

'The action proceeds slackly from one setpiece shoot-up to the next, barely providing the voltage for the two leads to expand their stereotyped roles into displays of star power.'—*Richard Combs, MFB*

Last Holiday*
GB 1950 88m bw
ABPC / Watergate (Stephen Mitchell, A. D. Peters, J. B. Priestley)

A man with a short time to live has a thoroughly enjoyable and useful final fling.
Slight, amusing and moving comedy drama spoiled by an unnecessary double twist.

w J. B. Priestley *d* Henry Cass *ph* Ray Elton *m* Francis Chagrin

Alec Guinness, Kay Walsh, Beatrice Campbell, Grégoire Aslan, Bernard Lee, Wilfrid Hyde White, Helen Cherry, Sidney James, Muriel George

The Last Hunt*
US 1955 103m Eastmancolor Cinemascope
MGM (Dore Schary)

Buffalo hunters fall out with each other.
Terse, brutish outdoor western with something to say about old western myths and a famous ending in which the bad guy freezes to death while waiting to gun down the hero.

wd Richard Brooks ph Russell Harlan *m* Daniele Amfitheatrof

Stewart Granger, Robert Taylor, Debra Paget, Lloyd Nolan, Russ Tamblyn, Constance Ford

The Last Hurrah**
US 1958 125m bw
Columbia (John Ford)

The political boss of a New England town fights his last campaign.
Enjoyable if disjointed melodrama, an old man's film crammed with cameo performances from familiar faces: important as one of Hollywood's great sentimental reunions.

w Frank Nugent, novel Edwin O'Connor *d John Ford ph* Charles Lawton Jnr

Spencer Tracy, Jeffrey Hunter, Dianne Foster, *Pat O'Brien, Basil Rathbone, Edward Brophy, Donald Crisp, James Gleason, John Carradine, Ricardo Cortez, Wallace Ford, Frank McHugh*, Frank Albertson, Anna Lee, Jane Darwell, Willis Bouchey, Basil Ruysdael

† A TV version was subsequently made with Carroll O'Connor.

The Last Journey*
GB 1935 66m bw
Twickenham (Julius Hagen)

The driver of an express train, driven mad with jealousy, goes berserk.
Workmanlike little train suspenser with an exciting climax.

w John Soutar, H. Fowler Mear, *story* J. Jefferson Farjeon *d* Bernard Vorhaus

Godfrey Tearle, Hugh Williams, Julien Mitchell, Judy Gunn, Nelson Keys, Frank Pettingell, Olga Lindo, Sydney Fairbrother

The Last Laugh***
Germany 1924 73m approx (24 fps) bw silent
UFA
original title: *Der Letzte Mann*

The old doorman of a luxury hotel is given the job of lavatory attendant but comes into a fortune and gets his revenge.
Ironic anecdote made important by its virtual abandonment of dialogue and whole-hearted adoption of the camera eye technique which gives some thrilling dramatic effects.

w Carl Mayer d F. W. Murnau ph Karl Freund

Emil Jannings, Max Hiller, Maly Delschaft, Hans Unterkirchen

'A marvellous picture—marvellous in its simplicity, its economy of effect, its expressiveness, and its dramatic power.'—*Life*

† A German remake of 1955 had Hans Albers in the lead and was of no interest.

The Last Man to Hang?
GB 1956 75m bw

Sir Roderick Strood is on trial for the murder of his neurotic wife. Reasonably interesting co-feature based on Gerald Bullett's The Jury; the title refers to the no-hanging bill then passing through Parliament. Tom Conway, Elizabeth Sellars, Eunice Gayson, Freda Jackson, Hugh Latimer, Anthony Newley, Margaretta Scott. Written by Gerald Bullett and others; directed by Terence Fisher; for ACT Films/Columbia.

The Last Married Couple in America
US 1979 102m Technicolor
Universal / Cates Brothers (John Shaner)

A Los Angeles couple resist the efforts of their friends to involve them in the swinging life.
Tolerable sex comedy of modern mores, a shade too long delayed after *Bob and Carol and Ted and Alice*.

w John Herman Shaner *d* Gilbert Cates *ph* Ralph Woolsey *m* Charles Fox *pd* Gene Callahan

Natalie Wood, George Segal, Richard Benjamin, Arlene Golonka, Arlan Arbus, Marilyn Sokol, Dom DeLuise, Valerie Harper

The Last Metro*
France 1980 131m Fujicolor
Les Films du Carrosse / Andrea / SEDIF / TF1 / SFP (Jean-José Richer)

In occupied Paris, the Jewish manager of a theatre hides in the cellar of the building.
Tightly enclosed symbolic melodrama which doesn't work nearly so well as *Les Visiteurs du Soir*, which had something very similar to say about the spirit of la belle France.

w François Truffaut, Suzanne Schiffman *d* François Truffaut *ph* Nestor Almendros *m* Georges Delerue

Catherine Deneuve, Gérard Depardieu, Jean Poiret, Heinz Bennent

AAN: best foreign film

THE LAST METRO. Truffaut brilliantly evoked the climate of the Occupation and backstage life and gave Catherine Deneuve (centre) a role which, for once, really stretched her talents.

The Last Mile*
US 1932 84m bw
World Wide (E. W. Hammons)

Tensions mount in jail as the execution of Killer Mears approaches.
Strident melodrama which works up quite a head of hysteria.

w Seton I. Miller, *play* John Wexley *d* Sam Bischoff *ph* Arthur Edeson

Preston Foster, Howard Phillips, George E. Stone, Noel Madison

'Subject's lure is confined to the morbid-minded sensation seeker . . . without feminine interest.'—*Variety*

The Last Mile
US 1959 81m bw
UA / Vanguard (Milton Subotsky)

Even more hysterical remake, retaining the original period. A cheerless, though literally electrifying, entertainment.

w Milton Subotsky, Seton I. Miller *d* Howard W. Koch *ph* Joseph Brun *m* Van Alexander

Mickey Rooney, Clifford David, Frank Conroy, Frank Overton, Leon Janney

The Last Movie
US 1971 108m Technicolor

Moviemakers go to Peru to film a western. Muddled and pretentious melodrama following the success of *Easy Rider*. Dennis Hopper, Julie Adams, Rod Cameron, Daniel Ades, Michael Anderson Jnr. Written by Stewart Stern; directed by Dennis Hopper; for Universal.

The Last of Mrs Cheyney
US 1929 94m bw
MGM

A confidence woman in British high society falls in love.
Old theatrical warhorse, much filmed but never very satisfactorily. (See below.)

w Hans Kraly, Claudine West, *play* Frederick Lonsdale *d* Sidney Franklin *ph* William Daniels

Norma Shearer, Basil Rathbone, George Barraud, Hedda Hopper, Maude Turner Gordon, Herbert Bunston

The Last of Mrs Cheyney
US 1937 98m bw
MGM (Lawrence Weingarten)

Adequate, unexciting remake.

w Leon Gordon, Samson Raphaelson, Monckton Hoffe *d* Richard Boleslawski *ph* George Folsey *m* William Axt

Joan Crawford, Robert Montgomery, William Powell, Frank Morgan, Jessie Ralph, Nigel Bruce, Benita Hume, Melville Cooper, Sara Haden

'Good film fodder, although not particularly socko.'—*Variety*

† A further remake was *The Law and the Lady* (qv).

'Any number can play; any number can die!'

The Last of Sheila*
US 1973 123m Technicolor
Warner (Herbert Ross)

A Hollywood star is killed by a hit-and-run driver; a year later her husband invites six friends to his yacht, and murders begin.
Confused, in-jokey showbiz whodunnit with flashes of interest.

w Stephen Sondheim, Anthony Perkins *d* Herbert Ross *ph* Gerry Turpin *m* Billy Goldenberg *ad* Ken Adam

Richard Benjamin, Dyan Cannon, James Coburn, James Mason, Joan Hackett, Ian MacShane, Raquel Welch

'The most teasing riddles for an audience are likely to be the real identities of the personalities being satirized.'—*MFB*

The Last of the Buccaneers
US 1950 79m Technicolor

The story of Jean Lafitte, French privateer in the war of 1812. Cheerful low-budget swashbuckler. Paul Henreid, Jack Oakie, Karin Booth, Edgar Barrier, Mary Anderson, John Dehner. Written by Robert E. Kent; directed by Lew Landers; for Columbia.

The Last of the Comanches*
US 1953 85m Technicolor
Columbia (Buddy Adler)
GB title: *The Sabre and the Arrow*

Survivors of an Indian raid take refuge in an abandoned mission until help arrives.
Competent western remake of *Sahara* (which was a remake of *The Lost Patrol*).

w Kenneth Gamet *d* André de Toth *ph* Charles Lawton Jnr *m* George Duning

Broderick Crawford, Barbara Hale, Lloyd Bridges, Martin Milner

Last of the Fast Guns
US 1959 82m Eastmancolor Cinemascope

Rival gunfighters form a friendship but fall out over their mission. Mildly unusual western programmer. Gilbert Roland, Jock Mahoney, Linda Cristal, Eduard Franz, Lorne Greene, Carl Benton Reid. Written by David P. Harmon; directed by George Sherman; for Universal-International.

The Last of the Mohicans
US 1936 91m bw
Edward Small

Incidents during colonial America's French–Indian war.
Vigorous if rough-and-ready western, later remade (poorly) as *Last of the Redmen* and as a Canadian TV series.

w Philip Dunne, John Balderston, Paul Perez, Daniel Moore, *novel* James Fenimore Cooper *d* George B. Seitz *ph* Robert Planck *m* Roy Webb

Randolph Scott, Binnie Barnes, Bruce Cabot, Henry Wilcoxon, Heather Angel, Hugh Buckler

Last of the Red Hot Lovers*
US 1972 98m Technicolor
Paramount (Howard W. Koch)

A middle-aged fish restaurateur feels the need for an extra-marital spree.
Modest, plainly-filmed sex comedy from a reliable stable.

w Neil Simon, from his play *d* Gene Saks *ph* Victor J. Kemper *m* Neal Hefti

Alan Arkin, Paula Prentiss, Sally Kellerman, Renée Taylor

Last of the Redmen
US 1947 78m Vitacolor

British soldiers escort a general's children through Indian country. Tinpot rendition of *The Last of the Mohicans*. Jon Hall, Michael O'Shea, Evelyn Ankers, Julie Bishop, Buster Crabbe. Written by Herbert Dalmas, George H. Plympton; directed by George Sherman; for Sam Katzman/Columbia. (GB title: *Last of the Redskins*.)

Last of the Secret Agents
US 1966 90m Technicolor

Two odd job men are recruited as spies. Pratfall comedy featuring a briefly existing comedy double act. Marty Allen, Steve Rossi, John Williams, Nancy Sinatra, Lou Jacobi, Theo Marcuse, Sig Rumann. Written by Mel Tolkin; directed by Norman Abbott; for Paramount.

'Open war between a handful of English and swarming tribesmen! Hidden war between fellow-officers who love the same woman!'

The Last Outpost*
US 1935 75m bw
Paramount (E. Lloyd Sheldon)

A British officer is captured by the Kurds and freed by an adventurer whose wife he covets.
Patchy, unusual adventure story with good moments.

w Philip MacDonald, *story* F. Britten Austin *d* Charles Barton, Louis Gasnier *ph* Theodor Sparkuhl

Cary Grant, Claude Rains, Gertrude Michael, Kathleen Burke, Colin Tapley, Akim Tamiroff, Billy Bevan, Jameson Thomas

'Loosely-woven melodramatic mélange.'—*Variety*

'Half of it is remarkably good and half of it quite abysmally bad. One can even put one's finger on the joins.'—*Graham Greene*

The Last Outpost
US 1951 89m Technicolor
Paramount / Pine–Thomas

A Civil War colonel finds his brother fighting on the other side.
Routine historical action romance.

w Geoffrey Homes, G. Worthing Yates, Winston Miller *d* Lewis R. Foster *ph* Loyal Griggs *m* Lucien Cailliet

Ronald Reagan, Bruce Bennett, Rhonda Fleming, Noah Beery Jnr

The Last Page
GB 1952 84m bw

A bookseller is framed for the death of a blackmailer. Curious English mystery with American stars. George Brent, Marguerite Chapman, Diana Dors, Raymond Huntley, Peter Reynolds, Eleanor Summerfield. Written by Frederick Knott, from a play by James Hadley Chase; directed by Terence Fisher; for Hammer-Lippert. (US title: *Manbait*.)

The Last Parade
US 1931 82m bw

A detective and a racketeer are buddies in the war, but not afterwards. Predictable character melodrama with no remaining interest. Jack Holt, Constance Cummings, Tom Moore, Gaylord Pendleton. Written by Dorothy Howell, Casey Robinson; directed by Erle C. Kenton; for Columbia. 'In for money, but not that strong for a holdover.'—*Variety*

The Last Picture Show***
US 1971 118m bw
Columbia / LPS / BBS (Stephen J. Friedman)

Teenage affairs in a small Texas town in 1951, ending with the hero's embarkation for Korea and the closing of the tatty cinema.
Penetrating nostalgia with over-emphasis on sex; the detail is the attraction.

w Larry McMurtry, Peter Bogdanovich *d Peter Bogdanovich ph Robert Surtees m* original recordings *pd Polly Platt*

Timothy Bottoms, Jeff Bridges, Cybill Shepherd, *Ben Johnson, Cloris Leachman,* Ellen Burstyn

'The most important work by a young American director since *Citizen Kane*.'—*Paul D. Zimmerman*

'So many things in it are so good that I wish I liked it more.'—*Stanley Kauffmann*

'Colour always had a tendency to prettify, and I didn't want that. I didn't want it to be a nostalgic piece.'—*Peter Bogdanovich*

AA: Ben Johnson; Cloris Leachman
AAN: best picture; script; Peter Bogdanovich (as director); Robert Surtees; Jeff Bridges; Ellen Burstyn

The Last Posse
US 1953 73m bw

Members of a thief-catching posse fall out on the way and return in disgrace. Stumbling little western, a poor return to the star after *All the King's Men*. Broderick Crawford, John Derek, Wanda Hendrix, Charles Bickford. Written by Seymour and Connie Lee, Bennett and Kenneth Gamet; directed by Alfred Werker; for Columbia.

'A different kind of love story!'

The Last Remake of Beau Geste
US 1977 85m Technicolor
Universal (William S. Gilmore Jnr)

The Geste brothers find themselves in the Foreign Legion after the theft of the Blue Water sapphire.
Woebegone spoof of a romantic original, with most of the jokes totally irrelevant to the purpose and seldom at all funny.

w Marty Feldman, Chris J. Allen *d* Marty Feldman *ph* Gerry Fisher *m* John Morris

Marty Feldman, Michael York, Ann-Margret, Peter Ustinov, Trevor Howard, James Earl Jones, Henry Gibson, Terry-Thomas, Roy Kinnear, Spike Milligan, Hugh Griffith, Irene Handl

'A ragbag of a film which looks like nothing so much as a Monty Python extravaganza in which inspiration has run dry and the comic timing gone sadly awry.'—*Tom Milne, MFB*

The Last Run*
US 1971 92m Metrocolor Panavision
MGM (Carter de Haven)

An ex-Chicago gangster retired to a Portuguese fishing village undertakes one last fatal job.
Well-made, rather uninteresting downbeat melodrama.

w Alan Sharp *d* Richard Fleischer *ph* Sven Nykvist *m* Jerry Goldsmith

George C. Scott, Tony Musante, Trish Van Devere

The Last Safari
GB 1967 110m Technicolor
Paramount (Henry Hathaway)

A disillusioned white hunter takes on one last safari.
Dullsville adventure story with good animal photography redeeming some of the clichés.

w John Gay, *novel* Gilligan's Last Elephant by Gerald Hanley *d* Henry Hathaway *ph* Ted Moore *m* Johnny Dankworth

Stewart Granger, Kaz Garas, Gabriella Licudi, Johnny Sekka, Liam Redmond, Eugene Deckers

The Last Shot You Hear
GB 1970 90m bw

Lovers plot murder, but the scheme backfires. Unassuming mystery programmer from a West End success. Hugh Marlowe, Zena Walker, Patricia Haines, William Dysart, Thorley Walters. Written by Tim Shields, from the play *The Sound of Murder* by William Fairchild; directed by Gordon Hessler; for Lippert-TCF.

The Last Stage*
Poland 1947 110m bw
Film Polski
original title: *Ostatni Etap*

Women suffer but one is finally rescued from the Nazi concentration camp at Auschwitz.
A dour, obsessive, horrifying record of human inhumanity, set in the actual camp and made by two former inmates.

w Wanda Jakubowska, Gerda Schneider *d* Wanda Jakubowska *ph* Borys Monastyrski *m* R. Palester

Huguette Faget, W. Bartowna, T. Gorecka

The Last Starfighter*
US 1984 101m Technicolor Panavision
Lorimar / Universal (Gary Adelson, Edward O. Denault)

A teenage whiz at video games is abducted by the survivors of a distant planet who need his skills if they are to outwit their enemies.
A surprisingly pleasant variation on the *Star Wars* boom, with sharp and witty performances from two reliable character actors and some elegant gadgetry to offset the teenage mooning.

w Jonathan Betuel *d* Nick Castle *ph* King Baggot *m* Craig Safan *pd* Ron Cobb *ed* C. Timothy O'Meara

Lance Guest, *Robert Preston*, *Dan O'Herlihy*, Catherine Mary Stewart, Barbara Bosson, Norman Snow

Last Summer*
US 1969 97m Eastmancolor
Alsid / Francis (Alfred Crown, Sidney Beckerman)

Well-to-do teenagers have sexual adventures on a summer seaside holiday.
Striking off-beat melodrama with vividly sketched characters.

w Eleanor Perry, novel Evan Hunter *d Frank Perry* *ph* Gerald Hirschfeld *m* John Simon

Barbara Hershey, Richard Thomas, Bruce Davison, Cathy Burns, Ernesto Gonzales, Ralph Waite

AAN: Cathy Burns

The Last Sunset
US 1961 112m Eastmancolor
U-I (Brynaprod) (Eugene Frenke, Edward Lewis)

A killer and his hunter learn a lot about each other before the final showdown.
Slow psycho-western with pretensions to tragedy.

w Dalton Trumbo, *novel* Showdown at Crazy Horse by Howard Rigsby *d* Robert Aldrich *ph* Ernest Laszlo *m* Ernest Gold

Rock Hudson, Kirk Douglas, Dorothy Malone, Carol Lynley, Joseph Cotten, Regis Toomey, Neville Brand

Last Tango in Paris*
France / Italy / US 1972 129m Technicolor
Les Artistes Associés / PEA / UA (Alberto Grimaldi)

A middle-aged man and a young French girl have a doomed love affair.
Pretentious sex melodrama mainly notable for being banned.

w Bernardo Bertolucci, Franco Arcalli *d* Bernardo Bertolucci *ph* Vittorio Storaro *m* Gato Barbieri

Marlon Brando, Maria Schneider, Jean-Pierre Léaud

'An intense meditation on the realization of mortality.'—*Sight and Sound*

AAN: Bernardo Bertolucci (as director); Marlon Brando

The Last Temptation of Christ*
US / Canada 163m Technicolor
Universal / Cineplex Odeon (Harry Ufland)

On the cross, Jesus dreams of escaping his destiny and living the life of an ordinary man.
Beautifully shot and strikingly acted, but wordy and too long; pre-release notoriety muffled consideration of the film's intentions.

w Paul Schrader, from novel by Nikos Kazantzakis *d* Martin Scorsese *ph* Michael Ballhaus *m* Peter Gabriel *pd* John Beard

Willem Dafoe, Harvey Keitel, Barbara Hershey, Harry Dean Stanton, David Bowie

'A film of challenging ideas and not salacious provocations.'—*Variety*

The Last Time I Saw Archie
US 1961 98m bw
UA / Mark VII / Manzanita / Talbot (Jack Webb)

Adventures of a con man amid overage civilian pilots at an army / air force base.
Patchy service comedy.

w William Bowers *d* Jack Webb *ph* Joe MacDonald *m* Frank Comstock

Jack Webb, Robert Mitchum, Martha Hyer, France Nuyen, Louis Nye, Jimmy Lydon, Richard Arlen, Don Knotts, Robert Strauss, Joe Flynn

The Last Time I Saw Paris
US 1954 116m Technicolor
MGM (Jack Cummings)

A writer recalls his romance with a wealthy American girl in Paris.
Dull romantic drama which very deadeningly and predictably updates F. Scott Fitzgerald's *Babylon Revisited.*

w Julius J. and Philip G. Epstein, Richard Brooks *d* Richard Brooks *ph* Joseph Ruttenberg *m* Conrad Salinger

Elizabeth Taylor, Van Johnson, Walter Pidgeon, Donna Reed, Eva Gabor

Last Train from Bombay
US 1952 72m bw

A diplomat in Bombay is falsely accused of the murder of an old friend. Stilted melodrama culminating in a hectic train ride. Jon Hall, Christine Larson, Lisa Ferraday, Douglas Kennedy. Written by Robert Yale Libbott; directed by Fred F. Sears; for Sam Katzman / Columbia.

Last Train from Gun Hill*
US 1959 98m Technicolor Vistavision
(Paramount) Hal B. Wallis / Bryna

A marshal tracks down the man who raped and murdered his wife; it turns out to be the son of an old friend.
Good suspense and action western culminating in a *High Noon* situation.

w James Poe *d John Sturges* *ph* Charles Lang Jnr *m* Dmitri Tiomkin

Kirk Douglas, Anthony Quinn, Earl Holliman, Carolyn Jones, Brian Hutton

'Flaming love drama set against the background of Spain's Civil War!'

The Last Train from Madrid
US 1937 85m bw
Paramount (George M. Arthur)

A variety of people escape the fighting in the Spanish Civil War.
Tawdry topical melodrama with cliché characters and situations.

w Louis Stevens, Robert Wyler *d* James Hogan *ph* Harry Fischbeck *md* Boris Morros

Dorothy Lamour, Lew Ayres, Gilbert Roland, Karen Morley, Lionel Atwill, Helen Mack, Robert Cummings, Olympe Bradna, Anthony Quinn, Lee Bowman, George Lloyd

'It is probably the worst film of the decade and should have been the funniest.'—*Graham Greene*

'Simply a topical and different background for a glib little fiction.'—*Frank S. Nugent*

The Last Tycoon
US 1976 124m Technicolor
Paramount / Academy / Sam Spiegel

The production head of a Hollywood studio in the thirties has his troubles complicated when he falls in love with a girl who reminds him of his dead wife.
Astonishingly inept and boring big budget all-star melodrama which doesn't even begin promisingly (the scenes from supposed thirties films are woefully inaccurate in style); it then bogs down in interminable dialogue scenes, leaving its famous cast all at sea.

w Harold Pinter, *novel* F. Scott Fitzgerald *d* Elia Kazan *ph* Victor Kemper *m* Maurice Jarre *pd* Eugene F. Callahan

Robert de Niro, Robert Mitchum, Tony Curtis, Jeanne Moreau, Jack Nicholson, Ingrid Boulting, Donald Pleasence, Ray Milland, Dana Andrews, John Carradine

'So enervated it's like a vampire movie after the vampires have left.'—*New Yorker*

'That the result is incoherent is no surprise; that it is so hollow and visually graceless adds a kind of wonder to the disappointment.'—*Sight and Sound*

'The breathless reverence that informs the movie kills it stone dead.'—*Michael Billington, Illustrated London News*

'It seems to me that Kazan and Pinter have failed disastrously, but then perhaps the task is impossible anyway.'—*Benny Green, Punch*

The Last Valley
GB 1970 128m Eastmancolor Todd-AO
ABC / Season / Seamaster (James Clavell)

In 1641 during the Thirty Years War a scholar tries to defend a remote and prosperous Swiss valley against a horde of mercenaries.
Big-scale historical action picture crammed with pillage, torture, rape, death at the stake, throat cutting and general carnage; reasonably literate for all that, and convincingly set.

wd James Clavell, *novel* J. B. Pick *ph* Norman Warwick *m* John Barry *ad* Peter Mullins

Michael Caine, Omar Sharif, Florinda Bolkan, Nigel Davenport, Per Oscarsson, Arthur O'Connell, Brian Blessed

The Last Voyage*
US 1960 91m Metrocolor
MGM / Andrew and Virginia Stone

A boiler room explosion causes an old passenger liner to sink.
Spectacular if dramatically deficient actioner for which a genuine liner (awaiting scrapping) was sunk.

wd Andrew L. Stone ph Hal Mohr *m* Rudy Schrager

Robert Stack, Dorothy Malone, Edmond O'Brien, George Sanders, Woody Strode, Jack Kruschen

'A prolonged nerve stretcher.'—*MFB*

'They pitted the fire of their youth against the flame of the frontier—when America was moving west!'

The Last Wagon
US 1956 99m Eastmancolor Cinemascope
TCF (William B. Hawks)

A half breed wanted for murder joins an 1875 wagon train.
Heavy-going big-scale western.

w James Edward Grant, Delmer Daves, Gwen Bagni *d* Delmer Daves *ph* Wilfrid Cline *m* Lionel Newman

Richard Widmark, Felicia Farr, Tommy Rettig, Susan Kohner, Ray Stricklyn, Nick Adams, Carl Benton Reid

The Last Waltz
US 1978 115m De Luxe
UA / Martin Scorsese, Jonathan Taplin

Rock documentary featuring the last concert of The Band.
An occasion for specialists, very adequately packaged.

d Martin Scorsese *pd* Boris Leven *ph* Michael Chapman

The Last Warning*
US 1929 88m bw
Universal

Murder backstage.
Shot as a silent film, with sound hurriedly added, this remains a stylish comedy-thriller with all the familiar ingredients of the whodunnit.

w Alfred A. Cohn *d Paul Leni ph* Hal Mohr

Laura La Plante, Montagu Love, Roy D'Arcy, John Boles, Mack Swain, Slim Summerville, Margaret Livingston
† Remade in 1938 as *The House of Fear*, a William Gargan second feature.

The Last Warning
US 1938 62m bw
Universal (Irving Starr)

A private eye mystery.
Better-than-average second feature.

w Edmund L. Hartmann, *novel* The Dead Don't Care by Jonathan Latimer *d* Albert S. Rogell

Preston Foster, Joyce Compton, Frank Jenks

The Last Wave*
Australia 1977 106m Atlab
(UA) Ayer / MacElroy / Derek Power

During a spell of freak weather, a lawyer has recurrent dreams which give him the key to an Aborigine prophecy about the world being destroyed by flood . . .
Curious supernatural drama successfully played as a mystery, with excellent atmosphere and special effects.

w Peter Weir, Tony Morphett, Petru Popescu *d* Peter Weir *ph* Russell Boyd *m* Charles Wain *pd* Goran Warff

Richard Chamberlain, Olivia Hamnet, Frederick Parslow

'A Hitchcockian sense of minatory dislocation.'—*Tim Pulleine, MFB*

The Last Word
US 1979 105m colour

An Irish inventor by wily stratagems prevents the demolition of the apartment block he occupies. Oddly old-fashioned comedy drama of little obvious appeal. Richard Harris, Karen Black, Martin Landau, Biff McGuire. Written by Michael Varhol, Greg Smith and Kit Carson; directed by Roy Boulting; for Variety International Pictures.

Last Year in Marienbad**
France / Italy 1961 94m bw Dyaliscope
Terra / Tamara / Cormoran / Precitel / Como / Argos / Cinetel / Silver / Cineriz (Raymond Froment)

In a vast old-fashioned hotel, a man meets a woman who may or may not have had an affair with him the previous year in Marienbad—or was it Frederiksbad?
A dreamy, elegant film which presents a puzzle with no solution. It has its attractions for film buffs and cryptogram addicts, but is not for anyone who simply wants to be told a story.

w Alain Robbe-Grillet d Alain Resnais ph Sacha Vierny *m* Francis Seyrig *ad* Jacques Saulnier

Delphine Seyrig, Giorgio Albertazzi, Sacha Pitoeff

'Elaborate, ponderous and meaningless.'—*Newsweek*

'Clearly the film's creators know exactly what they want to do and have done it with complete success. Whether one responds to the result is entirely a matter of temperament.'—*John Russell Taylor, MFB*

AAN: Alain Robbe-Grillet

The Late Edwina Black*
GB 1951 78m bw
IFD / Elvey–Gartside (Ernest Gartside)
US title: *Obsessed*

When a schoolteacher's wife is found dead, the police have three suspects.
Adequately suspenseful Victorian thriller from a successful play.

w Charles Frank, David Evans, *play* William Dinner, William Morum *d* Maurice Elvey *ph* Stephen Dade *m* Allan Gray

Geraldine Fitzgerald, David Farrar, *Roland Culver*, Jean Cadell, Mary Merrall, Harcourt Williams, Charles Heslop, Ronald Adam

The Late George Apley*
US 1946 96m bw
TCF (Fred Kohlmar)

The uneventful family life of a Boston blueblood.
Pleasant but tame family comedy-drama, solidly carpentered.

w Philip Dunne, *novel* John P. Marquand *d* Joseph L. Mankiewicz *ph* Joseph La Shelle *m* Cyril Mockridge

Ronald Colman, Edna Best, Vanessa Brown, Richard Haydn, Peggy Cummins, Charles Russell

The Late Show*
US 1977 93m Metrocolor
Warner (Robert Altman)

An ageing private eye in Los Angeles finds that his ex-partner's death and a lost cat have a complex connection.
A more-or-less engaging spoof of, or perhaps a valediction to, the private eye genre, with engaging scenes marred by poor colour and occasional excesses of violent action.

wd Robert Benton *ph* Chuck Rosher *m* Ken Wannberg

Art Carney, Lily Tomlin, Bill Macy, Ruth Nelson, Howard Duff, Joanna Cassidy, Eugene Roche

'On its own terms, it's perfectly executed. The squalid settings stink of decay; the spare pacing captures the tough style of Hammett prose; and the stylized use of blood puts some sting into murder.'—*Frank Rich, New York Post*

AAN: Robert Benton

Latin Lovers
US 1953 104m Technicolor
MGM (Joe Pasternak)

An heiress on holiday in Brazil looks for a man who will love her for herself alone.
Barren romantic drama, flatfooted and drawn out.

w Isobel Lennart *d* Mervyn Le Roy *ph* Joseph Ruttenberg *m* George Stoll

Lana Turner, Ricardo Montalban, John Lund, Louis Calhern, Jean Hagen

Latin Quarter*
GB 1945 80m bw
British National (Louis H. Jackson, Derrick De Marney)
US title: *Frenzy*

In nineties Paris a mad sculptor murders his fiancée and hides her inside his latest exhibit.
Artificial-looking but melodramatically effective thriller with a chilling climax and a detailed Dégas-period background.

wd Vernon Sewell ph Gunther Krampf, *play* l'Angoisse by Pierre Mills, Charles Vylars

Derrick de Marney, Joan Greenwood, Beresford Egan, Frederick Valk, Lily Kann, Martin Miller

Laugh and Get Rich
US 1931 72m bw

A man invests his wife's money in a tyre with a whistling valve. Inconsequential comedy with ancient jokes. Hugh Herbert, Edna May Oliver, Dorothy Lee, Robert Emmett Keane. Written by Ralph Spence, Gregory La Cava; directed by Gregory La Cava; for RKO. 'Entertainment for the willing.'—*Variety*

Laugh with Max Linder**
France 1963 88m bw
Films Max Linder
original title: *En Compagnie de Max Linder*

Excerpts from three of the dapper comedian's most famous American comedies: *Be My Wife* (1921), *The Three Must Get Theres* (1922), *Seven Years' Bad Luck* (1923)
A compilation which must serve as a consensus of this almost forgotten comedian's work. The gag with a broken mirror in particular was borrowed by innumerable other comedians, notably the Marx Brothers in *Duck Soup*. Audiences new to Linder's work will find him not especially sympathetic but capable of many felicities. He wrote, produced and directed all three films.

compiler Maud Max Linder

Laugh Your Blues Away
US 1943 65m bw

Jobless actors pose as guests at a society party. Feeble filler. Jinx Falkenberg, Bert Gordon (radio's 'mad Russian'), Isobel Elsom, Douglass Drake. Written by Harry Sauber; directed by Charles Barton; for Jack Fier / Columbia.

Laughing Anne
GB 1953 90m Technicolor
Republic / Wilcox–Neagle

French Anne and her boxing lover are characters of the Javanese waterfront; he kills her after she has fallen for a sea captain.
Cheap and turgid adaptation of a Joseph Conrad story; the author would not recognize it. Studio settings put the lid on hilariously bad work all round.

w Pamela Bower *d* Herbert Wilcox *ph* Max Greene *m* Anthony Collins

Margaret Lockwood, Forrest Tucker, Ronald Shiner, Wendell Corey, Robert Harris

Laughing at Trouble
US 1937 60m bw

A small town newspaper editress untangles personal problems. Acceptable second feature which almost became a series. Jane Darwell, Sara Haden, Lois Wilson, Margaret Hamilton, Allan Lane, John Carradine. Written by Robert Ellis and Helen Logan; directed by Frank R. Strayer; for Max Golden / TCF.

Laughing Boy
US 1934 80m bw

A young Navajo brave marries an outcast maiden. Misguided and absurd melodrama for unsuitable stars. Ramon Novarro, Lupe Velez, Chief Thunderbird, William Davidson. Written by John Colton and John Lee Mahin, from a novel by Oliver La Farge; directed by W. S. Van Dyke; for MGM. 'Touchy theme and plot . . . below par as entertainment.'—*Variety*

Laughing Gravy***
US 1931 20m bw

Stan and Ollie retrieve their dog when the landlord throws it out into the snow. One of the most endearing comedies of these stars, and one of the simplest. Laurel and Hardy, Charlie Hall. Written by H. M. Walker; directed by James W. Horne; for Hal Roach.

The Laughing Lady
GB 1946 93m Technicolor

During the French revolution, an artist under sentence is required to steal an English lady's pearls. Heavy-going operetta with the sense that all concerned have bitten off more than they can chew. Anne Ziegler, Webster Booth, Peter Graves, Felix Aylmer, Francis L. Sullivan, Paul Dupuis, Ralph Truman. Written by Jack Whittingham from play by Ingram d'Abbes; directed by Paul Stein; for Louis H. Jackson / British National.

'Eight people know who the killer is—and they're all dead!'

The Laughing Policeman*
US 1973 112m De Luxe
TCF (Stuart Rosenberg)
GB title: *An Investigation of Murder*

A mad machine-gunner eludes the San Francisco police.
Downbeat, semi-documentary police thriller with pretensions. Too complex by half, with an overplus of characterization, but the location work is excellent.

w Thomas Rickman, *novel* Maj Sjowall, Per Wahloo *d* Stuart Rosenberg *ph* David Walsh *m* Charles Fox

Walter Matthau, Bruce Dern, Lou Gossett, Albert Paulsen, Anthony Zerbe

Laughing Sinners
US 1931 71m bw

A girl with a past joins the Salvation Army. Glum romance which however started an effective star combination. Joan Crawford, Clark Gable, Neil Hamilton, Marjorie Rambeau, Guy Kibbee. Written by Bess Meredyth and Martin Flavin; directed by Harry Beaumont; for MGM.

Laughter**
US 1930 99m bw
Paramount (Herman J. Mankiewicz)

An ex-Follies girl marries a millionaire but later goes on a spree with the composer she once loved.
Sharply observed, before its time romantic comedy reminiscent now of the later *Philadelphia Story* in its attitudes to wealth and love. A precursor of the smart crazy comedies of the mid-thirties.

w Donald Ogden Stewart d Harry d'Abbabie d'Arrast ph George Folsey

Fredric March, Nancy Carroll, Frank Morgan, Glen Anders, Diane Ellis

'One of the best talking pictures I have ever seen.'—*James Agate*

'A talkie with so fast a pace that it crowds the comprehension of half the customers . . . marked at intervals by superb dialogue and the quick hand of a smart director.'—*Pare Lorentz*

'A lovely sophisticated comedy.'—*New Yorker, 1977*

AAN: Donald Ogden Stewart

Laughter in Paradise*
GB 1951 93m bw
Transocean (Mario Zampi)

An eccentric leaves in his will a fortune for each of his relations providing they will perform certain embarrassing or criminal acts.
A funny idea gets half-hearted treatment, but the good bits are hilarious.

w Michael Pertwee, Jack Davies *d* Mario Zampi *ph* William McLeod *m* Stanley Black

Alastair Sim, Joyce Grenfell, Hugh Griffith, Fay Compton, John Laurie, George Cole, Guy Middleton, Ronald Adam, Leslie Dwyer, A. E. Matthews, Beatrice Campbell

† Remade 1972 as *Some Will, Some Won't.*

Laughter in the Dark*
GB / France 1969 104m De Luxe
UA / Woodfall / Winkast / Marceau (Neil Hartley)

A wealthy art dealer is taken in by an ambitious usherette and her lover, and after being blinded in a car accident tries to kill them.
Unsatisfactory adaptation of a novel with a very specialized appeal: conventional swinging London and Riviera settings only confuse the spectator. Moments do work, though.

w Edward Bond, *novel* Vladimir Nabokov *d* Tony Richardson *ph* Dick Bush *m* Raymond Leppard *ad* Julia Trevelyan Oman

Nicol Williamson, Anna Karina, Jean-Claude Drouot, Peter Bowles, Sian Phillips

'It fails to create the slightest interest in its trio of repulsive characters.'—*Philip Strick*

Laughterhouse*
GB 1984 93m colour
Greenpoint / Film Four International

A Norfolk farmer decides to walk his fattened geese to market.
An attempt to revive the tradition of Ealing comedy lands up somewhere on the wrong side of Group Three. Not enough plot, almost no jokes, and the geese are almost the only pleasant creatures.

w Brian Glover *d* Richard Eyre *ph* Clive Tickner *m* Dominic Muldowney

Ian Holm, Penelope Wilton, Bill Owen, Richard Hope, Stephen Moore, Rosemary Martin

Laura***
US 1944 85m bw
TCF (Otto Preminger)

A beautiful girl is murdered . . . or is she? A cynical detective investigates.
A quiet, streamlined little murder mystery that brought a new adult approach to the genre and heralded the mature *film noir* of the later forties. A small cast responds perfectly to a classically spare script, and in Clifton Webb a new star is born.

w Jay Dratler, Samuel Hoffenstein, Betty Reinhardt, novel Vera Caspary *d Otto Preminger ph Joseph La Shelle m David Raksin*

Dana Andrews, Clifton Webb, Gene Tierney, Judith Anderson, *Vincent Price*, Dorothy Adams, James Flavin

WALDO LYDECKER (Clifton Webb): 'It's lavish, but I call it home.'

WALDO: 'I shall never forget the weekend Laura died. A silver sun burned through the sky like a huge magnifying glass. It was the hottest Sunday in my recollection. I felt as if I were the only human being left in New York . . . I had just begun Laura's story when another of those detectives came to see me. I had him wait.'

WALDO: 'In my case, self-absorption is completely justified. I have never discovered any other subject quite so worthy of my attention.'

'Everybody's favourite chic murder mystery.'—*New Yorker, 1977*

† Rouben Mamoulian directed some scenes before handing over to Preminger.

AA: Joseph La Shelle
AAN: script; Otto Preminger; Clifton Webb

The Laurel and Hardy Murder Case
US 1930 30m bw

Heirs to a fortune are menaced by a mad murderer. Empty spoof on *The Cat and the Canary* which affords little scope to Laurel and Hardy. Written by H. M. Walker; directed by James Parrott; for Hal Roach.

Laurel and Hardy's Laughing Twenties**
US 1965 90m bw
MGM / Robert Youngson

Excerpts from lesser comedians of the period—Max Davidson, Charlie Chase—are interspersed with highlights from Laurel and Hardy's silent two reelers.
A hilarious and craftsmanlike compilation, perhaps a little too long for its own good.

w, ed Robert Youngson commentator Jay Jackson *m* Skeets Alquist

† Films extracted include *Putting Pants on Philip, From Soup to Nuts, Wrong Again, The Finishing Touch, Liberty, Double Whoopee, Leave 'Em Laughing, You're Darn Tooting* and the custard pie climax from *The Battle of the Century.*

The Lavender Hill Mob****
GB 1951 78m bw
Ealing (Michael Truman)

A timid bank clerk conceives and executes a bullion robbery.
Superbly characterized and inventively detailed comedy, one of the best ever made at Ealing or in Britain.

w T. E. B. Clarke d Charles Crichton ph Douglas Slocombe m Georges Auric

Alec Guinness, Stanley Holloway, Sidney James, Alfie Bass, Marjorie Fielding, Edie Martin, John Gregson, Gibb McLaughlin

'Amusing situations and dialogue are well paced and sustained throughout: the climax is delightful.'—*MFB*

AA: T. E. B. Clarke
AAN: Alec Guinness

Law and Disorder
GB 1940 73m bw

A solicitor's partner unmasks saboteurs. Light topical comedy thriller, capably performed, Barry K. Barnes, Diana Churchill, Alastair Sim, Edward Chapman, Austin Trevor, Leo Genn. Written by Roger MacDonald; directed by David MacDonald; for K. C. Alexander / British Consolidated.

Law and Disorder*
GB 1958 76m bw
British Lion / Hotspur (Paul Soskin)

Crooks rally round a confederate about to be arrested, to prevent his son from learning of his father's real career.
Amusing, well-pointed caper on sub-Ealing lines.

w T. E. B. Clarke, *novel* Smuggler's Circuit by Denys Roberts *d* Charles Crichton *ph* Ted Scaife *m* Humphrey Searle

Michael Redgrave, Robert Morley, Joan Hickson, Lionel Jeffries, Ronald Squire, Elizabeth Sellars

Law and Disorder*
US 1974 102m Technicolor Panavision
Memorial / Leroy Street / Ugo Fadsin (William Richert)

New York suburbanites aghast at escalating violence form themselves into a vigilante patrol.
Bewilderingly uneven comedy drama which starts as satirical comedy and ends with one of the heroes dead and the other moralizing. Sporadically interesting, and certainly topical.

w Ivan Passer, William Richert, Kenneth Harris Fishman *d* Ivan Passer *ph* Arthur J. Ornitz *m* Andy Badale

Ernest Borgnine, Carroll O'Connor, Karen Black, Ann Wedgeworth, Leslie Ackerman, David Spielberg

The Law and Jake Wade*
US 1958 86m Metrocolor Cinemascope
MGM (William Hawks)

A marshal helps an old outlaw friend to escape from jail, and lives to regret it.
Good standard western, enjoyable throughout but with no outstanding merits.

w William Bowers *d* John Sturges *ph* Robert Surtees

Robert Taylor, Richard Widmark, Patricia Owens, Robert Middleton, Henry Silva

Law and Order*
US 1932 80m bw

A cowboy becomes marshal and cleans up Tombstone. Drily effective fictionalization of Wyatt Earp's exploits, with a good star performance. *Walter Huston,* Harry Carey, Raymond Hatton, Russell Simpson, Russell Hopton. Written by *John Huston,* from the novel *Saint Johnson* by W. R. Burnett; directed by Edward L. Cahn; for Universal.

Law and Order
US 1953 80m Technicolor

Curious belated sequel to the above with Johnson moving on to tame Cottonwood; actual presentation rather dull. Ronald Reagan, Dorothy Malone, Preston Foster, Alex Nicol, Russell Johnson. Written by John and Gwen Bagni and D. D. Beauchamp; directed by Nathan Juran; for Universal-International.

The Law and the Lady
US 1951 104m bw
MGM (Edwin H. Knopf)

A couple of confidence tricksters inveigle themselves into the house of a vulgar millionairess, but one of them has an attack of conscience.
Dreary remake of *The Last of Mrs Cheyney* (qv) with the locale altered, the plot simplified, and the level of wit diluted.

w Leonard Spiegelgass, Karl Tunberg *d* Edwin H. Knopf *ph* George Folsey *m* Carmen Dragon

Greer Garson, Michael Wilding, Fernando Lamas, Marjorie Main, Hayden Rorke, Margalo Gillmore, Ralph Dumke

Law of the Lawless
US 1963 87m Techniscope
Paramount / A. C. Lyles

A judge arrives in a small western town to conduct the murder trial of a former friend.
Jaded western of interest only for the producer's custom of packing the bit roles with former stars.

w Steve Fisher *d* William F. Claxton *ph* Lester Shorr

Dale Robertson, Yvonne de Carlo, William Bendix, Bruce Cabot, Barton MacLane, John Agar, Richard Arlen, Kent Taylor, Lon Chaney Jnr

Law of the Tropics
US 1941 76m bw
Warner (Ben Stoloff)

A café singer on the run from a murder charge marries a South American rubber plantation owner.
Hackneyed melodrama born from a mating of *Oil for the Lamps of China* and *Tropic Zone.*

w Charles Grayson *d* Ray Enright *ph* Sid Hickox *m* Howard Jackson

Constance Bennett, Jeffrey Lynn, Regis Toomey, Mona Maris, Frank Puglia, Thomas Jackson, Craig Stevens

The Law of the Wild
US 1934 bw serial: 12 eps

A young rancher tames the king of the wild horses. Modest serial with strong animal interest. Rex, Rin Tin Tin Jnr, Bob Custer, Ben Turpin. Directed by Armand Schaefer and B. Reeves Eason; for Mascot.

'Out of the most exciting pages of frontier history!'

The Law Versus Billy the Kid
US 1954 73m Technicolor

Billy the Kid is driven into crime to avenge a friend. Technicolor seems wasted on this two-bit western which can't even manage to tell a clear story. Scott Brady, Betta St John, James Griffith, Alan Hale Jnr, Paul Cavanagh. Written by John T. Williams; directed by William Castle; for Sam Katzman / Columbia.

The Lawless
US 1949 83m bw
Paramount / Pine–Thomas
GB title: *The Dividing Line*

The editor of a California small-town newspaper defends a Spanish boy who is being victimized by the racist element.
Well-meaning 'realistic' melodrama, unfortunately among the dullest of the socially conscious movies of this period.

w Geoffrey Homes *d* Joseph Losey *ph* Roy Hunt *m* Mahlon Merrick

Macdonald Carey, Gail Russell, John Sands, John Hoyt, Lee Patrick, Lalo Rios

The Lawless Breed
US 1952 83m Technicolor
U-I (William Alland)

The adventures and repentance of badman John Wesley Hardin.
Standard western programmer with the star in an unlikely role.

w Bernard Gordon *d* Raoul Walsh *ph* Irving Glassberg *m* Joseph Gershenson

Rock Hudson, Julie Adams, John McIntire, Dennis Weaver, Hugh O'Brian

A Lawless Street
US 1955 78m Technicolor
Columbia (Harry Joe Brown)

A marshal marries a dance hall entertainer, and loses interest in his job when she leaves him.
Enjoyable minor western.

w Kenneth Gamet, *novel* Marshal of Medicine Bend by Brad Ward *d* Joseph H. Lewis *ph* Ray Rennahan *m* Paul Sawtell

Randolph Scott, Angela Lansbury, Warner Anderson, Jean Parker, Wallace Ford, John Emery, James Bell, Ruth Donnelly, Michael Pate, Jeanette Nolan, Don Megowan

Lawman*
US 1970 99m Technicolor
UA / Scimitar (Michael Winner)

When a marshal tracks down drunken cowboys who have killed an old man, the townsfolk's resistance leads to a bloodbath.
Terse, violent western with a good cast.

w Gerald Wilson *d* Michael Winner *ph* Bob Paynter *m* Jerry Fielding

Burt Lancaster, Robert Ryan, Lee J. Cobb, Sheree North, Robert Duvall, Joseph Wiseman, John McGiver, Albert Salmi, J. D. Cannon

Lawrence of Arabia***
GB 1962 221m Technicolor Super Panavision 70
Columbia / Horizon (Sam Spiegel)

An adventurer's life with the Arabs, told in flashbacks after his accidental death in the thirties.
Sprawling epic which manages after four hours to give no insight whatever into the complexities of character of this mysterious historic figure, but is often spectacularly beautiful and exciting along the way.

w Robert Bolt *d David Lean* *ph Frederick A. Young* *m Maurice Jarre* *pd John Box* *ad John Stoll*

Peter O'Toole, Omar Sharif, Arthur Kennedy, Jack Hawkins, Donald Wolfit, Claude Rains, Anthony Quayle, *Alec Guinness*, Anthony Quinn, Jose Ferrer, Michel Ray, Zia Mohyeddin

'Grandeur of conception is not up to grandeur of setting.'—*Penelope Houston*

'Lean has managed to market epics as serious entertainment rather than as the spectacles they are.'—*Time Out, 1980*

† Albert Finney turned down the role before O'Toole was offered it.

AA: best picture; David Lean; Frederick A. Young; Maurice Jarre
AAN: Robert Bolt; Peter O'Toole; Omar Sharif

The Lawyer*
US 1970 120m Technicolor
Paramount (Brad Dexter)

An ambitious young Italian-American defence lawyer takes on a murder case.
Smartly-scripted, perfectly ordinary courtroom drama in a well-detailed western setting. The star subsequently played the same character in a TV series, *Petrocelli.*

w Sidney J. Furie, Harold Buchman *d Sidney J. Furie* *ph* Ralph Woolsey *m* Malcolm Dodds

Barry Newman, Harold Gould, Diana Muldaur, Robert Colbert, Kathleen Crowley, Booth Colman

Lawyer Man
US 1932 68m bw
Warner

An honest lawyer becomes corrupted by success.
Smart, cynical melodrama, dated but sufficiently fast-paced to remain interesting.

w Rian James, James Seymour, *novel* Max Trell *d* William Dieterle *ph* Robert Kurrle

William Powell, Joan Blondell, Helen Vinson, Alan Dinehart, Allen Jenkins, David Landau, Claire Dodd

'Good picture in the lawyer cycle.'—*Variety*

Laxdale Hall
GB 1952 77m bw
Group Three (Alfred Shaughnessy)
US title: *Scotch on the Rocks*

MPs are sent to investigate a tiny Hebridean island which refuses to pay road tax.
Thin rehash of *Whisky Galore* put together without the Ealing style. Minor compensations can be found.

w John Eldridge, Alfred Shaughnessy *d* John Eldridge *ph* Arthur Grant *m* Frank Spencer

Raymond Huntley, Ronald Squire, Sebastian Shaw, Fulton Mackay, Kathleen Ryan, Kynaston Reeves

'Constantly amusing in its quiet and wry fashion.'—*Cinema*

Lazy River
US 1934 75m bw

Ex-convicts go to work in a shrimp cannery and defeat a Chinese smuggler. Curious comedy drama which defeats all participants. Jean Parker, Robert Young, Ted Healy, C. Henry Gordon, Nat Pendleton. Written by Lucien Hubbard, from play *Ruby* by Lea David Freeman; directed by George B. Seitz; for MGM.

Le Mans*
US 1971 108m De Luxe Panavision
Solar / Cinema Center (Jack N. Reddish)

A sullen American enters for the 24-hour race.
Almost no plot and little documentary examination; what's left is a multitude of racing shots with Steve McQueen at the wheel. For some this may be enough.

w Harry Kleiner *d* Lee H. Katzin *ph* Robert B. Hauser, René Gruissart Jnr *m* Michel Legrand

Steve McQueen, Siegfried Rauch, Elga Andersen, Ronald Leigh-Hunt

League of Frightened Men
US 1937 71m bw

Nero Wolfe solves another murder case from his armchair. Fair detective story, but a negation of film. Walter Connolly, Lionel Stander, Eduardo Ciannelli, Irene Hervey, Victor Kilian, Nana Bryant. Written by Eugene Solow, Guy Endore, from the novel by Rex Stout; directed by Alfred E. Green; for Columbia. 'Hardly any audience likes to watch a character who just sits and thinks.'—*Variety*

The League of Gentlemen***
GB 1960 112m bw
Rank / Allied Film Makers (Michael Relph)

An ex-army officer recruits high-class misfits with guilty secrets to help him in a bank robbery.
Delightfully handled comedy adventure, from the days (alas) when crime did not pay; a lighter ending would have made it a classic.

w Bryan Forbes, novel John Boland *d Basil Dearden ph* Arthur Ibbetson *m* Philip Green

Jack Hawkins, Richard Attenborough, *Roger Livesey, Nigel Patrick*, Bryan Forbes, Kieron Moore, Terence Alexander, *Norman Bird*, Robert Coote, Melissa Stribling, Nanette Newman, Gerald Harper, Patrick Wymark, David Lodge, Doris Hare, Lydia Sherwood

Lease of Life*
GB 1954 94m Eastmancolor
Ealing (Jack Rix)

A poor clergyman is given a year to live, and puts it to good use.
Somewhat depressing but well-acted drama with excellent village atmosphere.

w Eric Ambler *d* Charles Frend *ph* Douglas Slocombe *m* Alan Rawsthorne

Robert Donat, Kay Walsh, Adrienne Corri, Denholm Elliott

The Leather Boys*
GB 1963 108m bw Cinemascope
British Lion / Garrick (Raymond Stross)

Two working-class teenagers marry for sex; she becomes a drudge and he develops a relationship with a homosexual motorcyclist.
Sharply-observed slice of low life which now seems quite dated, the central figures no longer being of the 'heroic' interest given them at the time. Technically the film is tediously and fashionably flashy.

w Gillian Freeman, *novel* Elliot George *d* Sidney J. Furie *ph* Gerald Gibbs *m* Bill McGuffie

Rita Tushingham, Dudley Sutton, Colin Campbell, Gladys Henson

The Leather Saint
US 1955 86m bw Vistavision
Paramount (Norman Retchin)

To provide his parish hospital with medical equipment, a Catholic priest becomes a commercial prizefighter.
Unlikely piece of religiosity, not too badly done.

w Norman Retchin, Alvin Ganzer *d* Alvin Ganzer *ph* Haskell Boggs *md* Irvin Talbot

Paul Douglas, John Derek, Cesar Romero, *Ernest Truex*, Jody Lawrance

Leathernecking
US 1930 80m bw (colour sequence)
RKO (Louis Sarecky)
GB title: *Present Arms*

A Honolulu socialite falls for a marine, but grows cool when she discovers that he is a private and not an officer as he pretended.
Curiously cast, spasmodically funny non-musical version of a Rodgers and Hart Broadway hit.

w Alfred Jackson, Jane Murfin, *play* Present Arms by Herbert Fields, Rodgers and Hart *d* Edward Cline *ph* J. Roy Hunt *m* Oscar Levant

Irene Dunne (her first role), Ken Murray, Eddie Foy Jnr, Louise Fazenda, Ned Sparks, Lilyan Tashman

'Weak medley of horseplay and romantic musical, and both poor.'—*Variety*

Leave 'Em Laughing*
US 1928 20m bw silent

Stan has toothache, visits the dentist, and accidentally causes all concerned to inhale an overdose of laughing gas. The earlier sequences are only mildly funny, but the laughing finale is irresistible. Laurel and Hardy, Edgar Kennedy, Charlie Hall. Written by Hal Roach and Reed Heustis; directed by Clyde Bruckman; for Hal Roach.

Leave Her to Heaven
US 1945 111m Technicolor
TCF (William A. Bacher)

A selfish, jealous woman causes unhappiness for those around her, even in her suicide.
No-holds-barred melodrama of the old school; what seemed lush production at the time now looks tatty.

w Jo Swerling, *novel* Ben Ames Williams *d* John M. Stahl *ph* Leon Shamroy *m* Alfred Newman

Gene Tierney, Cornel Wilde, Jeanne Crain, Vincent Price, Mary Phillips, Ray Collins, Gene Lockhart, Reed Hadley, Chill Wills

'The story's central idea might be plausible enough in a dramatically lighted black and white picture . . . but in the rich glare of Technicolor, all its rental library characteristics are doubly glaring.'—*James Agee*

'The sum total of all human emotion!'—*publicity*

AA: Leon Shamroy
AAN: Gene Tierney

The Leavenworth Case
US 1935 66m bw

Police investigate the murder of a wealthy man. Sluggish transcription of what claims to be the first American detective story. Donald Cook, Jean Rouverol, Norman Foster, Erin O'Brien-Moore, Maude Eburne, Warren Hymer. Written by Albert DeMond, Sidney Sutherland, from the novel by Anna Katherine Green; for Republic. 'Just another detective meller.'—*Variety*

Leaves from Satan's Book*
Denmark 1919 80m approx (24 fps) bw silent
Nordisk

Episodes from the activities of Satan through the ages: with Christ, the Inquisition, the French Revolution and the Russian Revolution.
Vaguely propagandist short-story compilation with effective moments.

w Edgar Hoyer, Carl Dreyer, *novel* The Sorrows of Satan by Marie Corelli *d* Carl Dreyer *ph* George Schneevoigt

'You can count the truly daring concepts in the making of motion pictures on the fingers of your right hand. Now add . . .'

The Left Hand of God
US 1955 87m De Luxe Cinemascope
TCF (Buddy Adler)

China, 1947: a Catholic priest newly arrived in a small village proves to be an American flier on the run from a warlord; but he contrives to work a small 'miracle'.
Hollywood religiosity at its most contrived, put together without distinction; the players have a wary look.

w Alfred Hayes, *novel* William E. Barrett *d* Edward Dmytryk *ph* Franz Planer *m* Victor Young

Humphrey Bogart, Gene Tierney, Lee J. Cobb, E. G. Marshall, Agnes Moorehead

The Left Handed Gun*
US 1958 102m bw
Warner / Haroll (Fred Coe)

Billy the Kid sets out to shoot four men who have killed his friend.
'Method'-oriented western, efficiently made but somewhat downcast.

w Leslie Stevens, *TV play* Gore Vidal *d* Arthur Penn *ph* Peverell Marley *m* Alexander Courage

Paul Newman, John Dehner, Lita Milan, Hurd Hatfield

'Top of the poll for laughs!'

Left Right and Centre*
GB 1959 95m bw
Vale / Launder and Gilliat

A TV personality becomes Tory candidate at a by-election.
Scrappy political comedy with the saving grace of a large number of comic talents.

w Sidney Gilliat, Val Valentine *d* Sidney Gilliat *ph* Gerald Gibbs *m* Humphrey Searle

Ian Carmichael, Alastair Sim, Patricia Bredin, Richard Wattis, Eric Barker, Gordon Harker, George Benson, Frederick Leister

The Legacy
GB 1978 102m colour
Columbia / Pethurst / Turman-Foster (David Foster)

An American designer goes to stay with her employer and finds herself in the middle of an occult murder plot.
Cliché-ridden screamer which will please the easily pleased.

w Jimmy Sangster, Patrick Tilley, Paul Wheeler *d* Richard Marquand *ph* Dick Bush, Alan Hume *m* Michael J. Lewis

Katharine Ross, Sam Elliot, John Standing, Ian Hogg, Margaret Tyzack, Charles Gray, Lee Montague, Hildegard Neil

Legal Eagles
US 1986 114m Technicolor Panavision
Universal / Northern Lights (Ivan Reitman)

An assistant DA becomes involved for the defence in an arson case.
Sophisticated but messy comedy with odd unrelated asides, reminiscent of the TV series *Moonlighting* but with top production values.

w Jim Cash, Jack Epps Jnr *d* Ivan Reitman *ph* Laszlo Kovacs *m* Elmer Bernstein

Robert Redford, Debra Winger, Daryl Hannah, Brian Dennehy, Terence Stamp, Steven Hill

Legend*
GB 1985 94m Fujicolour Panavision
(TCF / Universal) Legend Productions (Arnon Milchan)

Young peasant Jack takes his sweetheart on a quest to see the last surviving unicorns, but Satan uses them as pawns in his own game.
Elegant fairy tale for the few grown-ups who have use for such a thing. More to look at than to listen to.

w William Hjortsberg *d* Ridley Scott *ph* Alex Thomson *m* Jerry Goldsmith *pd Assheton Gorton* *ed* Terry Rawlings

Tim Curry, Mia Sara, Tom Cruise, David Bennent

'The dying gasp of the sword and sorcery cycle.'—*Philip French, Observer*

'The enchanted forests constantly threaten to sell us something—most frequently soft toilet paper.'—*Ibid.*

AAN: make-up (Rob Bottin, Peter Robb-King)

The Legend of Billie Jean
US 1985 96m Metrocolor
Tri-Star / Rob Cohen (Jon Peters, Peter Guber)

While protecting her brother, a girl becomes an outlaw by accident.
Unattractive and even distasteful farrago which is presumably intended to teach kids, so far as the law is concerned, how to eat their cake and have it.

w Mark Rosenthal, Lawrence Konner *d* Matthew Robbins *ph* Jeffrey L. Kimball *m* Craig Safan *pd* Ted Haworth *ed* Cynthia Schneider

Helen Slater, Keith Gordon, Christian Slater, Richard Bradford, Peter Coyote

'The germ of an idea, but hardly a reason for a film.'—*Variety*

'For the sake of your sanity, pray it isn't true!'

The Legend of Hell House*
GB 1973 94m De Luxe
TCF / Academy (Albert Fennell, Norman T. Herman)

Four people arrive at a haunted house in which several psychic investigators have been killed.
Harrowing thriller, a less solemn but more frightening version of *The Haunting*.

w Richard Matheson, from his novel *d John Hough* *ph* Alan Hume *m* Brian Hodgson, Delia Derbyshire

Pamela Franklin, Roddy McDowall, Clive Revill, Gayle Hunnicutt, Roland Culver, Peter Bowles, Michael Gough

'One of the most absorbing, goose-fleshing and mind-pleasing ghost breaker yarns on film.'—*Judith Crist, 1977*

The Legend of Lobo*
US 1962 67m Technicolor
Walt Disney (James Algar)

The life of a forest wolf.
Anthropomorphic entertainment in which a dreaded animal becomes something of a hero and finally saves his mate from bounty hunters. Impeccably contrived, like a live-action *Bambi*.

w Dwight Hauser, James Algar, *story* Ernest Thompson Seton *d* James Algar *ph* Jack Couffer, Lloyd Beebe *m* Oliver Wallace

The Legend of Lylah Clare*
US 1968 130m Metrocolor Panavision
MGM / Robert Aldrich

A mad director brings an unknown actress to Hollywood because of her resemblance to a former star, his creation, who had died mysteriously.
Unintentionally risible melodrama with echoes of *Svengali* and *Sunset Boulevard*; not to the public's taste, or anyone else's, in the late sixties.

w Hugo Butler, Jean Rouverol, *TV play* Robert Thom, Edward de Blasio *d* Robert Aldrich *ph* Joseph Biroc *m* Frank de Vol

Peter Finch, Kim Novak, Ernest Borgnine, Coral Browne, Milton Seltzer, Rossella Falk, Gabriele Tinti, Valentina Cortesa, George Kennedy

'The film where you hiss the villain and cheer the hero!'

The Legend of the Lone Ranger
US 1981 98m Technicolor Panavision
ITC / Jack Wrather (Walter Coblenz)

A much-betrayed young Texan, almost killed in an ambush, is nursed back to health by an Indian and becomes a masked avenger.
Extremely ill-constructed and moody western, apparently photographed through brown windsor soup, which doesn't slip into the right gear until twenty minutes before the end.

w Ivan Goff, Ben Roberts, Michael Kane, William Roberts *d* William A. Fraker *ph* Laszlo Kovacs *m* John Barry

Klinton Spilsbury, Michael Horse, Christopher Lloyd, Matt Clark

'Wallows in endless sentiment before switching to what may possibly have been intended as parody.'—*Sight and Sound*

'Tedious hokum . . . the kind of film that closes cinemas.'—*Sunday Times*

LE MANS. Real-life racing fanatic Steve McQueen was delighted to be driving on screen: audiences, however, would have preferred more plot.

Legend of the Lost
US 1957 107m Technirama
UA / Batjac / Robert Haggiag / Dear (Henry Hathaway)

Two adventurers and a slave girl seek a lost city in the Sahara.
Tediously vague and underplotted desert adventure with a few attractive moments.

w Robert Presnell Jnr, Ben Hecht *d* Henry Hathaway *ph* Jack Cardiff *m* A. F. Lavagnino

John Wayne, Sophia Loren, Rossano Brazzi

The Legend of the Seven Golden Vampires
GB / Hong Kong 1974 89m Eastmancolor Panavision
Hammer–Shaw (Don Houghton, Vee King Shaw)

In 1904 Chungking, Professor Van Helsing finds his old enemy Dracula behind a Chinese vampire cult.
Hectic, outlandish mix of Hammer horror and Kung Fu; plenty of gusto but not much sense.

w Don Houghton *d* Roy Ward Baker *ph* John Wilcox, Roy Ford *m* James Bernard

Peter Cushing, David Chiang, Julie Ege, Robin Stewart, John Forbes Robertson

The Legend of Tom Dooley
US 1959 77m bw
Columbia / Shpetner

At the end of the Civil War, Confederate youths take the law into their own hands and attack Unionists.
Youthful rebellion in historical mould, decently but rather dully delivered, based on a folk ballad.

w Stan Shpetner *d* Ted Post *ph* Gilbert Warrenton *m* Ronald Stein

Michael Landon, Richard Rust, Jo Morrow

The Lemon Drop Kid*
US 1951 91m bw
Paramount (Robert A. Welch)

A gangster forces a bookie to find the money which he has lost on a horse through the bookie's incompetence.
Amusing Bob Hope / Runyon vehicle despite heavy sentiment about an old folks' home. The Santa Claus sequences are memorable.

w Edmund Hartman, Frank Tashlin, Robert O'Brien, *story* Damon Runyon *d* Sidney Lanfield *ph* Daniel L. Fapp *m* Victor Young

Bob Hope, Marilyn Maxwell, Lloyd Nolan, Jane Darwell, Andrea King, Fred Clark, Jay C. Flippen, William Frawley, Harry Bellaver

† The previous 1934 version starred Lee Tracy, Helen Mack and William Frawley; ran 60m; and was directed by Marshall Neilan for Paramount.

Lenin in October*
USSR 1937 111m bw
Mosfilm
original title: *Lenin v Octiabrye*

The activities of Lenin during the revolution.
Stalwart propaganda piece, of solid but not outstanding cinematic interest.

w Alexei Kapler *d* *Mikhail Romm* *ph* Boris Volchok *m* Anatoli Alexandrov
Boris Shchukin

† The success of this film provoked *Lenin in 1918*, made in the following year (132m) by the same talents, with Cherkassov as Gorky. Many other Russian films on Lenin have followed.

Lenny**
US 1974 111m bw
UA (Marvin Worth)

The career of obscene comedian Lenny Bruce and his struggles with the law.
Old-fashioned rags-to-riches-to-rags story, rampant with the new permissiveness. Filmically extremely clever, emotionally hollow.

w Julian Barry, from his play *d* *Bob Fosse* *ph* Bruce Surtees *md* Ralph Burns *pd* Joel Schiller

Dustin Hoffman, Valerie Perrine, Jan Miner, Stanley Beck, Gary Morton

'For audiences who want to believe that Lenny Bruce was a saintly gadfly who was martyred for having lived before his time.'—*New Yorker*

AAN: best picture; Julian Barry; Bob Fosse; Bruce Surtees; Dustin Hoffman; Valerie Perrine

Leo the Last
GB 1969 104m De Luxe
UA / Char / Wink / Boor (Irwin Winkler, Robert Chartoff)

An alienated aristocrat brings his retinue to a London slum and has an effect on most of the inhabitants.
Infuriating symbolic fantasy; only the writer-director (presumably) has any idea what it is about.

w William Stair, John Boorman *d* John Boorman *ph* Peter Suschitsky *m* Fred Myrow *pd* Tony Woollard

Marcello Mastroianni, Billie Whitelaw, Calvin Lockhart, Glenna Forster Jones, Graham Crowden, Gwen Ffrangcon Davies, David de Keyser, Vladek Sheybal, Kenneth J. Warren

Léon Morin, Priest*
France / Italy 1961 117m bw
Rome-Paris Films (Georges de Beauregard)

During the German occupation of France a young widow finds herself falling in love with the young priest who is converting her to religion.
An intellectual romance, sharp and witty for the most part, with vivid wartime backgrounds.

wd Jean-Pierre Melville, *novel* Béatrix Beck *ph* Henri Decaë *m* Martial Solal, Albert Raisner

Jean-Paul Belmondo, Emmanuele Riva, Irène Tunc, Marielle Gozzi

The Leopard***
US / Italy 1963 205m Technirama
TCF / Titanus / SNPC / GPC (Goffredo Lombardo)
original title: *Il Gattopardo*

The family life of an Italian nobleman at the time of Garibaldi.
Elaborate, complex family saga, painted like an old master with great care and attention to detail, but with not much chance outside Italy of delivering its original dramatic force. Visconti had asked for Lancaster, so TCF picked up the international release but couldn't make head or tail of it commercially; they even ruined its high quality by releasing a dubbed, shortened version in Cinemascope and De Luxe colour of poor standard.

wd Luchino Visconti, novel Giuseppe de Lampedusa *ph Giuseppe Rotunno m* Nino Rota *ad Mario Garbuglia*

Burt Lancaster, Claudia Cardinale, Alain Delon, Paolo Stoppa, Serge Reggiani, Leslie French

Leopard in the Snow
GB / Canada 1977 94m Technicolor
Seastone / Leopard in the Snow (W. Laurence Heisey)

A girl caught in a Cumberland blizzard is rescued by a mysterious stranger with a pet leopard. He turns out to be a disfigured racing driver, and she falls in love with him.
A deliberate cross between *Jane Eyre* and a shopgirl's romance, adequately produced for its intended audience.

w Anne Mather, Jill Hyem, *novel* Anne Mather *d* Gerry O'Hara *ph* Alfie Hicks *m* Kenneth V. Jones

Keir Dullea, Susan Penhaligon, Jeremy Kemp, Kenneth More, Billie Whitelaw

The Leopard Man**
US 1943 59m bw
RKO (*Val Lewton*)

Murders in a Mexican border town are attributed to an escaped leopard.
Effective minor piece in the Lewton horror gallery; poor plot countered by highly effective suspense sequences.

w Ardel Wray, Edward Dein, *novel* Black Alibi by Cornell Woolrich *d Jacques Tourneur ph* Robert de Grasse *m* Roy Webb

Dennis O'Keefe, Jean Brooks, Margo, James Bell, Isabel Jewell

'It's all confusion, too much for an audience to follow.'—*Variety*

Lepke
US 1974 110m De Luxe Panavision
Warner / AmeriEuro Pictures (Menahem Golan)

After World War I a small-time crook becomes head of Murder Incorporated.
Violent but totally uninteresting gangster melodrama; fidelity to fact is not enough.

w Wesley Hau, Tamor Hoffs *d* Menahem Golan *ph* Andrew Davis *m* Ken Wannberg *pd* Jack Degovia

Tony Curtis, Anjanette Comer, Michael Callan, Warren Berlinger, Milton Berle, Gianni Russo

'A kosher version of *The Godfather*.'—*Verina Glaessner*

Les Girls: see under Girls

Les Miserables: see under Miserables

A Lesson in Love
Sweden 1953 95m bw
Svensk Filmindustri

A gynaecologist and his wife grow bored and turn to other partners, but are reconciled.
Slight comedy, surprisingly unsubtle for its creator, but passable.

wd Ingmar Bergman *ph* Martin Bodin, Bengt Nordwal *m* Dag Wiren

Gunnar Bjornstrand, Eva Dahlbeck, Harriet Andersson, Yvonne Lombard, Ake Grönberg

Let 'Em Have It*
US 1935 90m bw
Edward Small
GB title: *False Faces*

The FBI go after criminals on a terror spree.
Lively cops and robbers with some starkly effective moments.

w Joseph Moncure March, Elmer Harris *d* Sam Wood *ph* J. Peverell Marley, Robert Planck

Richard Arlen, Virginia Bruce, Alice Brady, Bruce Cabot, Harvey Stephens, Eric Linden, Joyce Compton, J. Farrell MacDonald

Let Freedom Ring
US 1939 100m sepia
MGM (Harry Rapf)

A westerner returns to his home town and clears it of corruption.
Elementary Hollywood actioner with curious credits, climaxed by Eddy singing *The Star Spangled Banner.*

w Ben Hecht *d* Jack Conway *ph* Sidney Wagner *m* Arthur Lange

Nelson Eddy, Victor McLaglen, Virginia Bruce, Lionel Barrymore, H. B. Warner, Raymond Walburn, Edward Arnold, Guy Kibbee, Charles Butterworth, Billy Bevan

'Big box office . . . lusty patriotic meller. Cinch for exploitation.'—*Variety*

Let George Do It**
GB 1940 82m bw
Ealing (Basil Dearden)

A ukelele player accidentally goes to Bergen instead of Blackpool and is mistaken for a spy.
Generally thought to be the best George Formby vehicle, with plenty of pace, good situations and catchy tunes.

w John Dighton, Austin Melford, Angus MacPhail, Basil Dearden *d* Marcel Varnel *ph* Gordon Dines, Ronald Neame

George Formby, Phyllis Calvert, Garry Marsh, Romney Brent, Bernard Lee, Coral Browne, Torin Thatcher, Hal Gordon

Let No Man Write My Epitaph
US 1960 106m bw
Columbia / Boris D. Kaplan

A slum boy wants to become a concert pianist but falls in with gangsters.
Squalid, predictable melodrama without many redeeming features.

w Robert Presnell Jnr, *novel* Willard Motley *d* Philip Leacock *ph* Burnett Guffey *m* George Duning

James Darren, Shelley Winters, Burl Ives, Jean Seberg, Jeanne Cooper, Ricardo Montalban, Ella Fitzgerald

Let the People Sing*
GB 1942 105m bw
British National (John Baxter)

An out-of-work comedian persuades a drunken nobleman to join a protest against the closing of a village hall.
A development of *The Good Companions* which compares quite nicely with the Capra

films from across the water: naïve but entertaining, with good star performances.

w John Baxter, Barbara K. Emery, Geoffrey Orme, *Novel J. B. Priestley d John Baxter ph* James Wilson

Alastair Sim, Fred Emney, Edward Rigby, Patricia Roc, Oliver Wakefield, Marian Spencer, Olive Sloane, Gus McNaughton, Charles Hawtrey

Let Them Live
US 1937 71m bw

A young man matches wits with a crooked town boss. Tepid second-feature drama. John Howard, Nan Grey, Edward Ellis, Judith Barrett. Written by Bruce Manning and Lionel House; directed by Harold Young; for Universal. 'Better than many of its kind . . . should please in nabes.'—*Variety*

Let Us Be Gay
US 1930 79m bw

Divorcees meet again, many years later, in Paris. Predictable star romance, now very dated, like its title. Norma Shearer, Rod La Rocque, Marie Dressler, Sally Eilers, Raymond Hackett, Hedda Hopper. Written by Frances Marion, from the play by Rachel Crothers; directed by Robert Z. Leonard; for MGM. 'Strong on all counts, romance, comedy, human sympathy and gorgeous clothes against a glamorous setting.'—*Variety*

Let Us Live
US 1937 67m bw

An innocent taxi driver is convicted of murder. Intense little melodrama which served its purpose. Maureen O'Sullivan, Henry Fonda, Ralph Bellamy. Written by Joseph F. Dineen, Anthony Veiller and Allen Rivkin; directed by John Brahm; for Columbia. 'Heavy dramatic preachment with limited appeal.'—*Variety*

Lethal Weapon*
US 1987 110m Technicolor
Warner / Richard Donner, Joel Silver

A slightly unhinged cop uncovers a drug smuggling operation.
Extremely violent *policier* which caters to the Rambo crowd but has enough pizazz to recommend it to most classes.

w Shane Black *d* Richard Donner *ph* Stephen Goldblatt *m* Michael Kamen, Eric Clapton

Mel Gibson, Danny Glover, Gary Busey, Mitchell Ryan, Tom Atkins, Darlene Love

'Style masquerading as content.'—*Daily Variety*

Let's Be Famous
GB 1939 83m bw
Ealing (Michael Balcon)

A stage struck Irish lad and Lancashire lass have various adventures in London.
Easy-going comedy introducing radio personalities of the day.

w Roger MacDougall, Allan MacKinnon *d* Walter Forde *ph* Ronald Neame, Gordon Dines *md* Ernest Irving

Jimmy O'Dea, Betty Driver, Sonnie Hale, Patrick Barr, Basil Radford, Milton Rosmer, Garry Marsh

Let's Be Happy
GB 1957 107m Technicolor Cinemascope
ABP / Marcel Hellman

Footling musical remake of *Jeannie* (qv).

w Diana Morgan *d* Henry Levin *ph* Erwin Hillier *m* Nicholas Brodszky *md* Louis Levy *songs* Nicholas Brodszky, Paul Francis Webster

Vera-Ellen, Tony Martin, Robert Flemyng, Zena Marshall, Guy Middleton, Katherine Kath, Jean Cadell, Gordon Jackson

'Success still eludes the Anglo-American musical.'—*MFB*

Let's Dance
US 1950 112m Technicolor
Paramount (Robert Fellows)

Show business partners reunite after five years of private life.
Tediously plotted musical with a couple of good numbers.

w Allan Scott, *story* Maurice Zolotow *d* Norman Z. McLeod *ph* George Barnes *m* Robert Emmett Dolan *songs* Frank Loesser

Fred Astaire, Betty Hutton, Roland Young, Ruth Warrick, Lucile Watson, Barton MacLane, Shepperd Strudwick, Melville Cooper, Harold Huber, George Zucco

Let's Do It Again
US 1953 95m Technicolor
Columbia (Oscar Saul)

A songwriter and his wife plan a divorce but call it off in the nick of time.
Tame musical remake of *The Awful Truth* (qv), pleasant enough but lacking style and punch.

w Mary Loos, Richard Sale *d* Alexander Hall *ph* Charles Lawton Jnr *m* George Duning *md* Morris Stoloff *songs* Lester Lee, Ned Washington

Jane Wyman, Ray Milland, Aldo Ray, Leon Ames

Let's Do It Again
US 1975 113m Technicolor
Warner / First Artists / Verdon (Melville Tucker, Pembroke J. Herring)

Three Atlanta workers conceive a zany plan to raise money for their church by hypnotizing a boxer into winning a big fight.
Lively but overlong farce reassembling the black talents of *Uptown Saturday Night.*

w Richard Wesley *d* Sidney Poitier *ph* Donald M. Morgan *m* Curtis Mayfield

Sidney Poitier, Bill Cosby, Calvin Lockhart, John Amos, Denise Nicholas, Ossie Davis, Jimmy Walker

Let's Face It
US 1943 76m bw
Paramount (Fred Kohlmar)

A smart-alec soldier has a plot involving a ladies' health camp, but finds himself up to his neck in spies.
Tepid star comedy which unaccountably ditches almost all the numbers from the musical on which it was based.

w Harry Tugend, from the musical play by Dorothy and Herbert Fields and Cole Porter, based on the play Cradle Snatchers by Norma Mitchell and Russell Medcraft *d* Sidney Lanfield *ph* Lionel Lindon *songs* Cole Porter

Bob Hope, Betty Hutton, Eve Arden, Phyllis Povah, Dona Drake, Zasu Pitts, Marjorie Weaver, Raymond Walburn, Joe Sawyer

Let's Fall in Love
US 1934 67m bw

A film director passes off a circus attendant as a glamorous foreign star. Lightweight comedy with music which did okay. Edmund Lowe, Ann Sothern, Miriam Jordan, Gregory Ratoff. Written by Herbert Fields; directed by David Burton; for Columbia. 'No chorus, no legs, no undressing for a change . . . moderately geared for moderate income.'—*Variety*

Let's Get Married
US 1937 68m bw

A politician's daughter falls for the weather bureau chief. Aimless romantic comedy which gets by on its performers. Ida Lupino, Walter Connolly, Ralph Bellamy, Reginald Denny, Raymond Walburn. Written by Ethel Hill from a story by A. H. Z. Carr; directed by Alfred E. Green; for Columbia. 'Mediocre dualler.'—*Variety*

Let's Go Native
US 1930 75m bw

Various people are shipwrecked on a South Sea island. Easy-going farce comedy with music. Jack Oakie, Jeanette MacDonald, Skeets Gallagher, James Hall, Kay Francis. Written by George Marion Jnr, Percy Heath; directed by Leo MacCarey; for Paramount. 'Hokum laughs with songs and dances.'—*Variety*

Let's Go Places
US 1930 70m bw

A young tenor goes to Hollywood, is mistaken for someone more famous and becomes a star. Lightweight comedy with mildly interesting studio scenes. Joseph Wagstaff, Lola Lane, Sharon Lynn, Ilka Chase, Walter Catlett, Dixie Lee. Written by William K. Wells; directed by Frank Strayer; for Fox. 'Plenty of music, no drawing names. Rates moderate for the big houses.'—*Variety*

Let's Kill Uncle
US 1966 92m colour
Universal / William Castle

A boy is threatened by his wicked uncle, and retaliates.
Mildly intriguing black comedy, leadenly handled.

w Mark Rodger, *novel* Rohan O'Grady *d* William Castle *ph* Harold Lipstein *m* Herman Stein

Nigel Green, Mary Badham, Pat Cardi, Robert Pickering

Let's Live a Little
US 1948 85m bw
Eagle-Lion / United California Productions

An advertising agent falls for his lady psychiatrist, and after many vicissitudes they and their former partners make it to the altar. Mild comedy which just about bubbles along despite a rather uncomfortable cast.

w Albert J. Cohen, Jack Harvey *d* Richard Wallace *ph* Ernest Laszlo *m* Werner Heymann

Hedy Lamarr, Robert Cummings, Anna Sten, Robert Shayne, Mary Treen

Let's Live Tonight
US 1935 75m bw

Two millionaire brothers in Monte Carlo love the same girl. Flimsy romantic comedy which gets by on its music. Lilian Harvey, Tullio Carminati, Hugh Williams, Janet Beecher, Tala Birell, Luis Alberni. Written by Gene Markey, Bradley King; directed by Victor Schertzinger; for Columbia. 'A parrot gets most of the laughs, which tips off the script.'—*Variety*

Let's Make a Night of It
GB 1937 92m bw

In Nice, a husband and wife own rival night clubs. Slim musical with rather too many interpolated turns. Buddy Rogers, June Clyde, Claire Luce, Fred Emney, Iris Hoey, Steve Geray, and Syd Walker, Afrique, Oliver Wakefield, Brian Michie, Joe Loss and his Band, Sidney Lipton and his Band. Written by Hugh Brooke, from the radio play The Silver Spoon by Henrik Ege; directed by Graham Cutts; for Associated British. 'Definitely no appeal for the US.'—*Variety*

Let's Make It Legal
US 1951 77m bw

An attractive grandmother divorces her gambler husband and takes up with an old boy friend. Unremarkable but competent star comedy. Claudette Colbert, Zachary Scott, Macdonald Carey, Barbara Bates, Robert Wagner, Marilyn Monroe. Written by F. Hugh Herbert and I. A. L. Diamond; directed by Richard Sale; for TCF.

Let's Make Love*
US 1960 118m De Luxe Cinemascope
TCF (Jerry Wald)

A multi-millionaire, learning that he is to be burlesqued in a Broadway show, joins the cast as an actor.
Complex, moderately sophisticated, occasionally funny musical inspired by *On the Avenue* (qv); lively characterizations but poor numbers.

w Norman Krasna *d* George Cukor *ph* Daniel L. Fapp *ch* Jack Cole *md* Lionel Newman, Earl H. Hagen *songs* Sammy Cahn, Jimmy Van Heusen

Yves Montand, Marilyn Monroe, Tony Randall, Wilfrid Hyde White, Frankie Vaughan, David Burns, and guests Bing Crosby, Gene Kelly, Milton Berle

AAN: Lionel Newman, Earl H. Hagen

Let's Scare Jessica to Death
US 1971 89m colour
Paramount / Jessica Co (Charles B. Mars Jnr)

Back home after a nervous breakdown, our heroine is troubled by voices and visions, not to mention an ambulant corpse and a vampire or two.
Competent screamie.

w Norman Jonas, Ralph Rose *d* John Hancock *ph* Bob Baldwin *m* Orville Stoeber

Zohra Lampert, Barton Heyman

Let's Try Again
US 1934 64m bw

A doctor and his wife drift apart, then get back together again. Formula high-life drama without much conviction. Diana Wynyard, Clive Brook, Irene Hervey, Helen Vinson. Written by Worthington Miner and Allen Scott from the play by Vincent Lawrence; directed by Worthington Miner; for RKO. 'Talky, tedious and far from original: where the cast doesn't mean anything the picture will have plenty of worries.'—*Variety*

The Letter*
US 1929 61m bw
Paramount

Early talkie version of a solid piece of theatre. See below.

story and play W. Somerset Maugham *d* Jean de Limur

Jeanne Eagels, O. P. Heggie, Reginald Owen, Herbert Marshall, Irene Browne

AAN: Jeanne Eagels

'With all my heart, I still love the man I killed!'

The Letter****
US 1940 95m bw
Warner (Robert Lord)

A rubber plantation owner's wife kills a man in what seems to have been self-defence; but a letter from her proves it to have been a crime of passion, and becomes an instrument of blackmail.
Excellent performances and presentation make this the closest approximation on film to reading a Maugham story of the Far East, though censorship forced the addition of an infuriating moral ending.

w Howard Koch, story W. Somerset Maugham d William Wyler ph Tony Gaudio m Max Steiner

Bette Davis, Herbert Marshall, James Stephenson, Sen Yung, Frieda Inescort, Gale Sondergaard, Bruce Lester, Tetsu Komai

'The writing is taut and spare throughout . . . the unravelling of Maugham's story is masterly and the presentation visual and cinematic . . . the audience at the trade show did not move a finger.'—*James Agate*

† Herbert Marshall played the lover in the first version and the husband in the second.

AAN: best picture; William Wyler; Tony Gaudio; Max Steiner; Bette Davis; James Stephenson

A Letter for Evie
US 1945 88m bw

A girl starts confusion when she writes a letter to an unknown soldier; a wimp writes back but sends his he-man buddy's photograph. Predictable comedy with longueurs. Marsha Hunt, John Carroll, Hume Cronyn, Spring Byington, Pamela Britton, Norman Lloyd. Written by De Vallon Scott and Alan Fiedman; directed by Jules Dassin; for William H. Wright / MGM.

'The story that will live . . . as long as there is love!'

Letter from an Unknown Woman****
US 1948 89m bw
Universal / Rampart (John Houseman)

A woman wastes her life in unrequited love for a rakish pianist.
Superior 'woman's picture' which gave its director his best chance in America to recreate his beloved Vienna of long ago. Hollywood production magic at its best.

w Howard Koch, novel Stefan Zweig *d Max Ophuls ph Franz Planer m* Daniele Amfitheatrof *ad Alexander Golitzen*

Joan Fontaine, Louis Jourdan, Mady Christians, Art Smith, Marcel Journet

'A film full of snow, sleigh bells, lights gleaming in ornamental gardens and trysts at night.'—*Charles Higham, 1972*

'It is fascinating to watch the sure deft means by which Ophuls sidetracks seemingly inevitable clichés and holds on to a shadowy, tender mood, half buried in the past. Here is a fragile filmic charm that is not often or easily accomplished.'—*Richard Winnington*

'Film narrative of a most skilled order.'—*William Whitebait*

'Probably the toniest "woman's picture" ever made.'—*Pauline Kael, 70s*

Letter of Introduction*
US 1938 100m bw
Universal (John M. Stahl)

A young actress is encouraged by an ageing star whom she does not know is her father. Commercial melodrama with luxury trimmings, all very neatly packaged.

w Sheridan Gibney, Leonard Spiegelgass *d* John M. Stahl *ph* Karl Freund *m* Charles Previn

Adolphe Menjou, Andrea Leeds, Edgar Bergen (and Charlie McCarthy), George Murphy, Eve Arden, Rita Johnson, Ernest Cossart, Ann Sheridan

'Headed for big business everywhere.'—*Variety*

A Letter to Brezhnev**
GB 1985 95m colour
Yeardream / Film Four International / Palace Productions (Janet Goddard)

Two girls from Liverpool spend a busy night with Russian sailors; when one of them receives no subsequent letters, she writes to Brezhnev and is invited to Moscow.
Vivid it is, but also raucous and seedy until true love enters as a redeeming factor. The critics loved it, thinking it about unemployment and urban decline; it certainly paints a low picture of Liverpool.

w Frank Clarke *d* Chris Bernard *ph* Bruce McGowan *m* Alan Gill *ed* Lesley Walker

Alfred Molina, Peter Firth, Margi Clarke, Tracy Lea, Alexandra Pigg

'Fast-moving, funny, entertaining and poignant . . . in short how to make a British film.'—*Jill Forbes, Monthly Film Bulletin*

'A peek into the other woman's male!'
A Letter to Three Wives**
US 1949 102m bw
TCF (Sol C. Siegel)

Three wives on a picnic receive word from a friend that she has run off with one of their husbands.
Amusing short-story compendium which seemed more revelatory at the time than it does now, and paved the way for its writer-director's heyday.

wd Joseph L. Mankiewicz, novel John Klempner *ph* Arthur Miller *m* Alfred Newman

Jeanne Crain, Ann Sothern, Linda Darnell, Jeffrey Lynn, Kirk Douglas, *Paul Douglas*, Barbara Lawrence, Connie Gilchrist, Florence Bates, Hobart Cavanaugh, and the voice of Celeste Holm

'A mere shadow of those acid Hollywood comedies of the thirties . . . over-written and under-directed . . . but it has a supply of ironies and makes a certain alkaline comment on present-day American customs and manners.'—*Richard Winnington*

'Replete with sharp dialogue. He aims barbed darts at the country's favourite institutions, and makes them score with telling effect.'—*Variety*

AA: Joseph L. Mankiewicz (as writer); Joseph L. Mankiewicz (as director)
AAN: best picture

Letty Lynton
US 1932 84m bw

When one lover is murdered, Letty turns to another to prove her innocent. Bad girl drama which established the star's box office appeal. Joan Crawford, Robert Montgomery, Nils Asther, May Robson, Lewis Stone. Written by John Meehan and Wanda Tuchock; directed by Clarence Brown; for MGM. 'Big grosses are written all over this one.'—*Variety*

Les Liaisons Dangereuses*
France 1959 106m bw
Films Marceau

Valmont and his wife compare notes on each other's affairs.
Showy modernization of a notorious minor classic.

w Roger Vailland, Roger Vadim, Claude Brûlé, *novel* Choderlos de Laclos *d* Roger Vadim *ph* Marcel Grignon *m* Jack Murray, Thelonius Monk

Gérard Philipe, Jeanne Moreau, Annette Vadim, Jeanne Valerie, Simone Renant, Jean-Louis Trintignant

'A woman's picture par excellence.'—*John Russell Taylor, MFB*

Lianna
US 1983 112m Du Art

A wife and mother becomes a lesbian. That's all there is, folks, not much in the way of plot, and barely enough for a TV movie; but some good observation and acting come through. Linda Griffiths, Jane Hallaren, Jon de Vries, Jo Henderson. Written and directed by John Sayles; for Winwood.

Libel*
GB 1959 100m bw
MGM / Comet (Anatole de Grunwald)

An ex-POW baronet is accused of being an impostor.
Old-fashioned courtroom spellbinder, quite adequately done though occasionally creaky.

w Anatole de Grunwald, Karl Tunberg, *play* Edward Wooll *d* Anthony Asquith *ph* Robert Krasker *m* Benjamin Frankel

Dirk Bogarde, Olivia de Havilland, Paul Massie, Wilfrid Hyde White, Robert Morley, Anthony Dawson, Richard Wattis, Martin Miller, Millicent Martin

Libeled Lady**
US 1936 98m bw
MGM (Lawrence Weingarten)

An heiress sues a newspaper, and the editor hires a friend to compromise her.
Lively four-star romantic comedy which sums up its era as well as any.

w Maurine Watkins, Howard Emmett Rogers, George Oppenheimer d Jack Conway ph Norbert Brodine *m* William Axt

Jean Harlow, Myrna Loy, Spencer Tracy, William Powell, Walter Connolly, Charley Grapewin, Cora Witherspoon, E. E. Clive, Charles Trowbridge

'Handsomely mounted and produced, lavishly costumed, cleverly written and artfully directed, *Libeled Lady* is entirely worthy of the noble comedians who head its cast.'—*Bland Johaneson, New York Daily Mirror*

† Remade as *Easy to Wed* (qv); central situation borrowed for *Man's Favorite Sport* (qv).

AAN: best picture

'All she wanted was her black man's money and her white man's love!'
The Liberation of L. B. Jones*
US 1970 102m Technicolor
Columbia / Liberation Co (Ronald Lubin)

Racial murder is the result when a black undertaker wants a divorce in a small Tennessee town.
Violent, pointless but well-made melodrama which really does not take matters much further than *Intruder in the Dust.*

w Stirling Silliphant, Jesse Hill Ford, from Ford's novel *d William Wyler ph* Robert Surtees *m* Elmer Bernstein

Lee J. Cobb, Anthony Zerbe, Roscoe Lee Browne, Lola Falana, Lee Majors, Barbara Hershey, Yaphet Kotto, Arch Johnson, Chill Wills

'With its genuinely ferocious climax it adds up to probably the most powerful, if not the most sophisticated, race-war film the commercial studios have yet produced.'—*Nigel Andrews*

Liberty**
US 1929 20m bw silent

Two convicts escape and have adventures high on a construction site. Amusing gags are succeeded by breathtaking thrills in the Harold Lloyd style. Laurel and Hardy, James Finlayson. Written by Leo McCarey and H. M. Walker; directed by Leo McCary; for Hal Roach.

Licensed to Kill
GB 1965 97m Eastmancolor
Alistair Films (Estelle E. Richmond)
US title: *The Second Best Secret Agent in the Whole Wide World*

The Foreign Office calls in agent Charles Vine to protect a top international scientist.
Cheap copy of James Bond which wins no laurels but produces a few efficient routine thrills.

w Howard Griffiths, Lindsay Shonteff *d* Lindsay Shonteff *ph* Terry Maher *m* Bertram Chappell

Tom Adams, Veronica Hurst, Karel Stepanek, Felix Felton, Peter Bull

Liebelei*
Austria 1932 85m bw
Fred Lissa

A young army officer falls in love; but he is killed in a duel and his girl commits suicide.
Semi-classic romantic novelette, like a warm-up for *Letter from an Unknown Woman.*

w Hans Wilhelm, Kurt Alexander, *story* Arthur Schnitzler *d Max Ophuls ph* Franz Planer *m* Theo Macheber

Magda Schneider, Wolfgang Liebeneiner, Luise Ullrich, Willy Eichberger, Gustaf Gruendgens, Paul Hoerbiger

† A revised French version played as *Une Histoire d'Amour.* The story had previously been shot under the same title in Germany in 1927; and in the sixties Romy Schneider and Alain Delon appeared in a French remake called *Christine.*

Lies My Father Told Me
Canada 1975 102m colour
Columbia / Pentimento / Pentacle (Anthony Bedrich, Harry Gulkin)

Adventures of a poor Jewish boy and his grandfather in Montreal in the twenties. Effectively if rather dishonestly sentimental, this is the kind of family picture for which critics are always clamouring but which few people in the seventies will pay to see.

w Ted Allan, from his book *d* Jan Kadar *ph* Paul Van der Linden *m* Sol Kaplan

Yossi Yadin, Len Birman, Marilyn Lightstone, Jeffrey Lynas

'Sentiment by numbers . . . a lovable child awakening to discovery of the world; a lovable, whimsical old grandfather; a lovable, ne'er-do-well father; a lovable, long-suffering mother; a lovable, broken-down horse; lovable neighbours; a lovable whore across the way. It all strives so hard to be lovable that you want to scream.'—*David Robinson, The Times*

† A British low-budgeter was made from the same story in 1940, changing the venue to Ireland and the race to Irish.

AAN: Ted Allan

Lt Robin Crusoe USN
US 1966 114m Technicolor
Walt Disney (Bill Walsh, Ron Miller)

A navy pilot parachutes on to a Pacific island and gets involved in the local women's lib movement.
Slow-paced family comedy with very few laughs.

w Bill Walsh, Don da Gradi *d* Byron Paul *ph* William Snyder *m* Bob Brunner

Dick Van Dyke, Nancy Kwan, Akim Tamiroff

The Lieutenant Wore Skirts
US 1955 99m Eastmancolor Cinemascope
TCF (Buddy Adler)

When a TV writer joins the service, his wife enlists to be near him; but he is rejected on medical grounds.
Raucous, tasteless farce which tries far too hard to raise laughs.

w Albert Beich, Frank Tashlin *d* Frank Tashlin *ph* Leo Tover *m* Cyril Mockridge

Tom Ewell, Sheree North, Rita Moreno, Rick Jason, Les Tremayne

The Life and Death of a Hollywood Extra*
US 1927 11m (24 fps) bw silent

A nonentity arrives in Hollywood and dreams of becoming a star. Avant-garde short, still interesting if less revolutionary than it seemed at the time. Jules Raucort, Georges Voya. Written, produced and directed by *Robert Florey* and *Slavko Vorkapich*; photographed by Slavko Vorkapich and Gregg Toland; editor and art director, *Slavko Vorkapich*.

The Life and Death of Colonel Blimp***
GB 1943 163m Technicolor
GFD / Archers (Michael Powell, Emeric Pressburger)
US title: *Colonel Blimp*

A British soldier survives three wars and falls in love with three women.
Not the Blimp of the cartoon strip, but a sympathetic figure in a warm, consistently interesting if idiosyncratic love story against a background of war. The Archers as usual provide a sympathetic German lead (friend of the hero); quite a coup in wartime.

wd Michael Powell, Emeric Pressburger *ph* Jack Cardiff *m* Allan Gray *ad* Alfred Junge

Roger Livesey, Anton Walbrook, Deborah Kerr, Roland Culver, James McKechnie, Albert Lieven, Arthur Wontner, A. E. Matthews, David Hutcheson, Ursula Jeans, John Laurie, Harry Welchman

'There is nothing brilliant about the picture, but it is perceptive, witty and sweet-tempered.'—*James Agee*

'No one else has so well captured English romanticism banked down beneath emotional reticence.'—*Time Out, 1985*

'I want peace—and I don't care who I kill to get it!'

The Life and Times of Judge Roy Bean*
US 1972 124m Technicolor Panavision
National General / Famous Artists (John Foreman)

A fantasia on the famous outlaw judge of the old west.
Sporadically entertaining but schematically messy mixture of burlesqued folklore and violent action, not in the same league as *Butch Cassidy*.

w John Milius *d* John Huston *ph* Richard Moore *m* Maurice Jarre

Paul Newman, Ava Gardner, Jacqueline Bisset, Tab Hunter, Stacy Keach, Roddy McDowall, Anthony Perkins, John Huston

AAN: song 'Marmalade, Molasses and Honey' (*m* Maurice Jarre, *ly* A. and M. Bergman)

Life at the Top*
GB 1965 117m bw
Columbia / Romulus (James Woolf)

Ten years after marrying into money, Joe Lampton is dissatisfied, and he and his wife both have affairs.
Rough-talking but basically predictable and old-fashioned sequel to *Room at the Top*, a bit compromised by having to reflect the sixties London scene; the early Yorkshire sequences are the best.

w Mordecai Richler *d* Ted Kotcheff *ph* Oswald Morris *m* Richard Addinsell

Laurence Harvey, Jean Simmons, Honor Blackman, Michael Craig, Donald Wolfit, *Margaret Johnston*, Allan Cuthbertson, Ambrosine Philpotts, Robert Morley, Nigel Davenport, George A. Cooper

'Another thoroughly mean-spirited film of a kind which has been taking root in the British cinema.'—*Tom Milne*

† The character of Joe Lampton was later used in a long running TV series called *Man at the Top*, which sprouted a film of its own under that title.

Life Begins
US 1932 72m bw
Warner (Ray Griffith)
GB title: *Dream of Life*

A night in a maternity hospital.
Multi-melodrama later remade as *A Child Is Born*. Passable.

w Earl Baldwin, *play* Mary McDougal Axelson *d* James Flood *ph* James Van Trees

Loretta Young, Eric Linden, Aline MacMahon, Preston Foster, Glenda Farrell, Frank McHugh, Clara Blandick, Elizabeth Patterson, Gilbert Roland

'Splendid women's picture promising at least solid matinée business.'—*Variety*

Life Begins at Eight Thirty*
US 1942 85m bw
TCF (Nunnally Johnson)
GB title: *The Light of Heart*

A distinguished actor is reduced through drink to being a street corner Santa Claus.
Diluted and sentimentalized version of an agreeable play.

w Nunnally Johnson, *play* The Light of Heart by Emlyn Williams *d* Irving Pichel *ph* Edward Cronjager *m* Alfred Newman

Monty Woolley, Ida Lupino, Cornel Wilde, Sara Allgood, Melville Cooper, J. Edward Bromberg

Life Begins in College*
US 1937 80m bw

Three zanies save the honour of the college football team. Another of the myriad college football stories of the thirties, but this time enlivened by comedians in the leads. The Ritz Brothers, Joan Davis, Tony Martin, Gloria Stuart, Fred Stone, Nat Pendleton. Written by Karl Tunberg and Don Ettlinger; directed by William A. Seiter; for TCF. (GB title: *The Joy Parade*.) 'The Ritzes soar to stardom; a box office touchdown.'—*Variety*

Life for Ruth*
GB 1962 91m bw
Rank / Allied Film Makers (Michael Relph, Basil Dearden)
US title: *Condemned to Life*

A little girl dies because her parents' religion forbids blood transfusions.
Dramatized from the headlines, this little case history is small beer as film-making, and not exactly entertainment, but absorbing as a comment on human behaviour.

w Janet Green, John McCormick *d* Basil Dearden *ph* Otto Heller *m* William Alwyn *md* Muir Mathieson

Michael Craig, Patrick McGoohan, Janet Munro, Paul Rogers, Megs Jenkins, Frank Finlay, Maureen Pryor

Life Force
GB 1985 101m Rank colour Dunton vision
Cannon (Menahem Golan, Yoram Globus)

THE LIFE OF EMILE ZOLA. Art director Anton Grot's Warner Brothers version of Paris with Paul Muni, the studio's king of the biopics, looking studious behind a beard in this stilted still.

Zombies from outer space wreak havoc in London town.
Tacky vampire saga which takes ages to get going, then expires in a welter of bad acting and absurd visuals.

w Dan O'Bannon, Don Jakoby *novel* The Space Vampires by Colin Wilson *d* Tobe Hooper *ph* Alan Hume *m* Henry Mancini *pd* John Graysmark *ed* John Grover

Steve Railsback, Peter Firth, Frank Finlay, Patrick Stewart, Nicholas Ball, Mathilda May

'The unintentional laff-fest of the season.'—*Variety*

A Life in the Balance*
US 1954 75m bw
TCF / Panoramic (Leonard Goldstein)

A Mexican widower springs into action when his young son is kidnapped by a murderer.
Taut little melodrama taking place during one night in Mexico City; made with vigour on a low budget.

w Robert Presnell Jnr, Leo Townsend *d Harry Horner* *ph* J. Gomez Urquiza *m* Raul Lavista

Ricardo Montalban, Anne Bancroft, Lee Marvin

Life Is a Bed of Roses*
France 1983 111m Eastmancolor
Philippe Dusart / Soprofilms / Films A2 / Fideline / Ariane / Filmedis / Ministry of Culture (Philippe Dusart)
Original title: *La Vie est un Roman*

A count opens a temple of happiness and starts to re-educate his friends.
Dense fantasy which never really explains itself but provides pleasant moments along the way.

w Jean Gruault *d* Alain Resnais *ph* Bruno Nuytten *m* M. Philippe-Gerard

Vittorio Gassman, Ruggero Raimondi, Geraldine Chaplin, Fanny Ardant, Pierre Arditi

The Life of Adolf Hitler*
West Germany 1961 102m bw

A documentary culled from newsreel material; somehow less arresting than one would have hoped, though undoubtedly worthy. Written by Helga Koppel; directed and edited by Paul Rotha; for Real Film.

'He plucked from the gutter a faded rose and made an immortal masterpiece!'

The Life of Emile Zola***
US 1937 116m bw
Warner (Henry Blanke)

The French writer intervenes in the case of Alfred Dreyfus, condemned unjustly to Devil's Island.
The box office success of this solidly-carpentered piece of Hollywood history was compounded in equal parts of star power and the sheer novelty of having such a thing turn up at the local Odeon.

w Norman Reilly Raine *story* Heinz Herald and Geza Herczeg *d William Dieterle* *ph Tony Gaudio* *m* Max Steiner *ad Anton Grot*

Paul Muni, Joseph Schildkraut, Gale Sondergaard, Gloria Holden, Donald Crisp, Erin O'Brien Moore, John Litel, Henry O'Neill, Morris Carnovsky, Ralph Morgan, Louis Calhern, Robert Barrat, Vladimir Sokoloff, Harry Davenport, Robert Warwick, Walter Kingsford

'Destined to box office approval of the most substantial character. It is finely made and merits high rating as cinema art and significant recognition as major showmanship.'—*Variety*

'Along with *Louis Pasteur*, it ought to start a new category—the Warner crusading films, costume division.'—*Otis Ferguson*

'A grave story told with great dignity and superbly played and produced.'—*Pare Lorentz*

'One of the fine ones which begin as a film and end as an experience.'—*John Grierson*

'Rich, dignified, honest and strong, it is at once the finest historical film ever made and the greatest screen biography.'—*New York Times*

AA: best picture; script; Joseph Schildkraut
AAN: original story; William Dieterle; Max Steiner; Paul Muni

A Life of Her Own
US 1950 108m bw
MGM (Voldemar Vetluguin)

An innocent girl from Kansas becomes one of New York's top models.
Road to ruin, American style, from the pages of a women's magazine.

w Isabel Lennart *d* George Cukor *ph* George Folsey *m* Bronislau Kaper

Lana Turner, Ray Milland, Tom Ewell, Louis Calhern, Ann Dvorak, Barry Sullivan, Jean Hagen

'This story belongs to the realms of soap opera—extremely artificial, highly moral in tone, and deliberately concocted to combine luxurious settings with an elementary assault on the audience's emotions.'—*MFB*

The Life of Jimmy Dolan
US 1933 85m bw
Warner (Hal B. Wallis)
GB title: *The Kid's Last Fight*

An amiable wanderer is mistaken for a prize-fighter wanted for murder.
Modest character romance, later remade as *They Made Me a Criminal.*

w David Boehm, Erwin Gelsey, *play* Bertram Millhauser, Beulah Marie Dix *d* Archie Mayo *ph* Arthur Edeson

Douglas Fairbanks Jnr, Loretta Young, Aline MacMahon, Guy Kibbee, Lyle Talbot, Fifi D'Orsay, Harold Huber, George Meeker

The Life of Riley
US 1948 87m bw

The trials of a family man in a low-paid job. Adequate transcription from a radio series. William Bendix, James Gleason, Rosemary de Camp, Bill Goodwin, Beulah Bondi, Richard Long. Written, directed and produced by Irving Brecher; for Universal-International.

Life of the Party
US 1930 78m Technicolor

Two gold-digging shop girls operate from a modiste's. Half-hearted vulgar comedy, rather oddly given colour status. Winnie Lightner, Irene Delroy, Charles Butterworth, Jack Whiting. Written by Arthur Caesar from a story by Melville Crossman (Darryl F. Zanuck); directed by Roy del Ruth; for Warners. 'Spotty for laughs and business.'—*Variety*

Life of the Party
US 1937 86m bw

A girl tries to evade suitors arranged by her mother. Very thin comedy with several second-bracket names; not at all memorable. Joe Penner, Harriet Hilliard, Gene Raymond, Parkyakarkus, Victor Moore, Helen Broderick, Billy Gilbert, Ann Miller. Written by Bert Kalmar, Harry Ruby, Viola Brothers Shore; directed by William A. Seiter; for RKO. 'Should prove fairish entertainment and do fairly at the b.o.'—*Variety*

The Life of Vergie Winters
US 1934 82m bw
RKO (Pandro S. Berman)

A rising politician marries for position but keeps watch over his mistress and their child.
Archetypal soap opera, a cross between *Stella Dallas* and *Back Street.*

w Jane Murfin, *novel* Louis Bromfield *d* Alfred Santell *ph* Lucien Andriot *m* Max Steiner

Ann Harding, John Boles, Helen Vinson, Frank Albertson, Lon Chaney Jnr, Sara Haden, Ben Alexander, Donald Crisp

Life Returns
US 1938 62m bw

A fictional story leads up to the actual experiment performed in 1934 by Dr Robert E. Cornish when he brought a dead dog back to life. Weird mélange of fact and fiction; despite the achievement, the presentation never catches fire. The film was banned in Britain. Onslow Stevens, George Breakston, Valerie Hobson, Lois Wilson. Written by Arthur Horman, John F. Goodrich; directed by Eugen Frenke; for Scienart. 'A picture much longer to the audience than its accredited running time would indicate.'—*Variety*

Life Upside Down*
France 1964 92m bw
A.J. Films
original title: *La Vie à l'Envers*

A pleasant, ordinary young man discovers the joy of being absolutely alone, and begins to detach himself from his surroundings, ending up in a barren flat and a private hospital ward.
Engaging semi-comic case history which generates much sympathy for its eccentric hero.

wd Alain Jessua *ph* Jacques Robin *m* Jacques Loussier

Charles Denner, Anna Gaylor, Guy Saint-Jean, Nicole Gueden

'The tone is civilized, quiet, infinitely peaceful and often brilliantly funny.'—*Brenda Davies, MFB*

'Amusing or disturbing depending on whether it is viewed from the outside or the inside, but perceptive and artistic whichever way one views it.'—*John Simon*

'Take your cookie to see the picture that takes the cake for laughs!'

Life with Father*
US 1947 118m Technicolor
Warner (Robert Buckner)

Turn-of-the-century anecdotes of an irascible well-to-do paterfamilias who won't be baptized.
Well-upholstered screen version of a long running play; oddly tedious considering the talent involved.

w Donald Ogden Stewart, *play* Howard Lindsay, Russel Crouse *d* Michael Curtiz *ph* Peverell Marley, William V. Skall *m* Max Steiner *ad* Robert Hass

William Powell, Irene Dunne, Edmund Gwenn, Zasu Pitts, Elizabeth Taylor, Martin Milner, Jimmy Lydon, Emma Dunn, Moroni Olsen, Elizabeth Risdon

'Everybody seems to be trying too hard . . . the director is totally out of his element in this careful, deadly version.'—*New Yorker, 1978*

† Censorship of the day absurdly clipped Father's famous last line: 'I'm going to be baptized, damn it!'

AAN: Peverell Marley, William V. Skall; Max Steiner; William Powell

Lifeboat**
US 1944 96m bw
TCF (Kenneth MacGowan)

Survivors from a torpedoed passenger ship include the U-Boat commander responsible.
Propaganda gimmick melodrama interesting for the casting and for Hitchcock's response to the challenge of filming in one cramped set.

w Jo Swerling, *story* John Steinbeck *d Alfred Hitchcock* *ph* Glen MacWilliams *m* Hugo Friedhofer

Tallulah Bankhead, Walter Slezak, Henry Hull, John Hodiak, Canada Lee, William Bendix, Mary Anderson, Heather Angel, Hume Cronyn

'The initial idea—a derelict boat and its passengers as microcosm—is itself so artificial that . . . it sets the whole pride and brain too sharply to work on a tour de force for its own sake.'—*James Agee*

AAN: John Steinbeck; Alfred Hitchcock; Glen MacWilliams

Lifeguard
US 1976 96m CFI colour

A beach guard at 30 reviews his life and his future. Odd but not unlikeable little personal drama which barely got released. Sam Elliott, Anne Archer, Stephen Young, Parker Stevenson, Kathleen Quinlan. Written by Ron Koslow; directed by Daniel Petrie; for Paramount.

The Lift
Netherlands 1983 99m Eastmancolor

An office block elevator seems to assume deadly powers. After a murderous car, a murderous lift. Slick but rather empty semi-horror. Huub Stapel, Willeke Van Ammelrooy, Josine Van Dalsum. Written and directed by Dick Maas; for Sigma Films.

Lift to the Scaffold*
France 1957 89m bw
Nouvelles Editions de Films (Jean Thuillier)
original title: *Ascenseur pour l'Echafaud*

An executive murders his employer but is trapped in the building all night; meanwhile his car is stolen and he is arrested for a murder committed by the thief.
Complex, watchable suspenser with pretensions.

w Roger Nimier, Louis Malle, *novel* Noel Calef *d* Louis Malle *ph* Henri Decaë *m* Miles Davis

Maurice Ronet, Jeanne Moreau, Georges Poujouly, Yori Bertin, Lino Ventura

'Cold, clever and rather elegant.'—*Penelope Houston, MFB*

The Light across the Street
France 1955 99m bw
EGC / Fernand Rivers (Jacques Gauthier)
original title: *La Lumière d'en Face*

A lorry driver, injured in an accident, becomes insanely jealous of his young wife.
Low-life melodrama tailored for the sultry attractions of its new star.

w Louis Cahavance, René Masson, René Lefèvre *d* Georges Lacombe *ph* Louis Page *m* Norbert Glanzberg

Brigitte Bardot, Raymond Pellégrin, Roger Pigaut, Claude Romain

The Light at the Edge of the World
US / Spain / Liechtenstein 1971 120m Eastmancolor Panavision
Bryna / Jet / Triumfilm (Kirk Douglas, Ilya Salkind)

A lighthouse keeper near Cape Horn resists a band of wreckers.
Pretentious, disaster-prone version of a simple adventure story; one wonders not so much what went wrong as whether anything went right in this international venture.

w Tom Rowe, *novel* Jules Verne *d* Kevin Billington *ph* Henri Decaë *m* Piero Piccioni

Kirk Douglas, Yul Brynner, Samantha Eggar, Jean-Claude Drouot, Fernando Rey, Renato Salvatori

The Light in the Forest
US 1958 92m Technicolor
Walt Disney

Kidnapped by Indians as an infant, a teenager is returned to his parents but finds the white man's ways disturbing.
Modest frontier drama with a moral.

w Lawrence Edward Watkin, *novel* Conrad Richter *d* Herschel Daugherty *ph* Ellsworth Fredericks *m* Paul Smith

James MacArthur, Carol Lynley, Jessica Tandy, Wendell Corey, Fess Parker, Joanne Dru, Joseph Calleia

The Light in the Piazza
GB 1962 101m Metrocolor Cinemascope
MGM (Arthur Freed)

An American matron in Florence tries to marry off her mentally retarded daughter to a wealthy Italian.
Puzzling romantic drama in which one is never quite sure why the characters behave as they do; in the end all one appreciates is the tour of northern Italy.

w Julius J. Epstein, *novel* Elizabeth Spencer *d* Guy Green *ph* Otto Heller *m* Mario Nascimbene

Olivia de Havilland, Yvette Mimieux, George Hamilton, Rossano Brazzi, Barry Sullivan

Light of Day
US 1987 107m Astro Color

A Cleveland family is upset by illness and rock 'n roll. Drab musical wallow which seems to have little point. Michael J. Fox, Joan Jett, Gena Rowlands, Michael McKean. Written and directed by Paul Schrader; for Taft/Keith Barish/Tri-Star.

'Laugh, you little fool, laugh . . . for I'm giving you something you never had before—a soul . . . on canvas!'

The Light that Failed*
US 1939 97m bw
Paramount (William A. Wellman)

A London artist is going blind as the result of a war wound, and must finish the portrait of the little cockney whom he loves.
Nicely-made but rather boring star romance; no surprises in plot or performance.

w Robert Carson, *story* Rudyard Kipling *d* William Wellman *ph* Theodor Sparkuhl *m* Victor Young

Ronald Colman, Walter Huston, Ida Lupino, Dudley Digges, Muriel Angelus, Fay Helm

'Production fine for moderate b.o. Will catch attention of the carriage trade, the literati crowd and the critics.'—*Variety*

† Previously filmed in 1916 and 1923.

The Light Touch
US 1951 107m bw
MGM (Pandro S. Berman)

An elegant art thief tries to doublecross the gangster who employs him.
Elongated and witless romantic charade on European locations.

wd Richard Brooks, *story* Jed Harris, Tom Reed *ph* Robert Surtees *m* Miklos Rozsa

Stewart Granger, George Sanders, Pier Angeli, Kurt Kasznar, Larry Keating, Rhys Williams, Norman Lloyd, Mike Mazurki

'A comedy thriller which moves far too slowly for its imperfections to be overlooked.'—*Penelope Houston, MFB*

Light Up the Sky
GB 1960 90m bw
British Lion / Bryanston (Lewis Gilbert)

Life on a searchlight battery during World War II.
Wartime comedy-drama with accent on the laughs but adding dollops of tragedy and sentiment. A very patchy entertainment.

w Vernon Harris, *play* Touch It Light by Robert Storey *d* Lewis Gilbert *ph* John Wilcox *m* Douglas Gamley

Ian Carmichael, Tommy Steele, Benny Hill, Sydney Tafler, Victor Maddern, Harry Locke, Johnny Briggs, Dick Emery

Lightnin'*
US 1930 94m bw

A country fellow is wiser than he seems, and in between setting other folks' lives right, persuades his own wife not to divorce him.
Archetypal Will Rogers star part which he played on the stage; now his first big talkie hit. *Will Rogers*, Louise Dresser, Joel McCrea, Sharon Lynn, J. M. Kerrigan. From the play by Frank Bacon and Winchell Smith; directed by Henry King; for Fox. 'A production of the highest quality in all its phases.'—*Variety*

The Lightning Express
US 1930 bw serial: 10 eps

A railroad owner's son guards the crack express against saboteurs. Primitive adventure exploits. Lane Chandler, Louise Lorraine, Al Ferguson. Directed by Henry McRae; for Universal.

Lightning Over Water
West Germany / Sweden 1980 91m Movielab

A record of the last months of Nicholas Ray's life, when he was hoping to revive his career while visibly dying from cancer. Unique and uneasy, something for film buffs to chew over. Written and directed by Nicholas Ray and Wim Wenders; for Road Movies / Viking Film. (Aka: *Nick's Movie.*)

Lightning Strikes Twice
US 1951 91m bw
Warner (Henry Blanke)

A woman decides to clear her lover of suspicion of murder, but later has her own doubts.
Silly melodrama with no credibility, little suspense, and too much talk.

w Lenore Coffee, *novel* Margaret Echard *d* King Vidor *ph* Sid Hickox *m* Max Steiner

Richard Todd, Ruth Roman, Mercedes McCambridge, Zachary Scott, Darryl Hickman, Frank Conroy, Kathryn Givney

The Lightning Warrior
US 1931 bw serial: 12 eps

A dog unmasks The Wolf Man, who is terrorizing pioneer settlers. One of the last Rin Tin Tin serials: it satisfied at the time. Frankie Darro, Georgia Hale, George Brent, Pat O'Malley. Directed by Armand Schaefer and Ben Kline; for Mascot.

Lights of New York***
US 1928 57m bw
Warner

A chorus girl becomes involved with gangsters.
The first '100 per cent all-talking' film, dramatically primitive but historically important.

w F. Hugh Herbert, Murray Roth *d* Bryan Foy *ph* E. B. DuPar

Helene Costello, Cullen Landis, Wheeler Oakman, Eugene Pallette, Tom Dugan, Gladys Brockwell, Mary Carr

'100 per cent crude.'—*Variety*

Lights of Old Broadway
US 1925 80m approx at 24 fps bw silent

Twin orphan girls find very different routes to happiness. One of the star's most popular vehicles. Marion Davies, Conrad Nagel, George K. Arthur, Julia Swayne Gordon. Written by Carey Wilson; directed by Monta Bell; for MGM.

Lights of Variety*
Italy 1950 94m bw
Film Capitolium (Alberto Lattuada)

A stage-struck young girl forsakes the manager of the troupe in which she found stardom for the bright lights of the city. Tragi-comical backstage story in which the bits of detail are more entertaining than the plot.

w Federico Fellini *d* Alberto Lattuada *ph* Otello Martelli *m* Felice Lattuada

Peppino de Filippo, Carla del Poggio, Giulietta Masina, John Kitzmiller, Folco Lulli

The Lightship
US 1985 89m colour

A lightship is taken over by a gang of psychopathic crooks on the run. Echoes of *Key Largo* abound in this dreary suspense melodrama which aspires to more meaning than is evident. Robert Duvall, Klaus Maria Brandauer, Tom Bower, Robert Constanzo. Written by William Mai, David Taylor, from novel by Siegfried Lenz; directed by Jerzy Skolimowski; for CBS.

Like Father Like Son
US 1987 98m Technicolor

A surgeon and his son find themselves in each other's bodies. Role-reversal comedy at the beginning of a trend; in itself a bore. Dudley Moore, Kirk Cameron, Sean Astin, Patrick O'Neal, Margaret Colin. Written by Lorne Cameron, Steven L. Bloom; directed by Rod Daniel; for Grazer-Valdes/Tri-Star.

The Likely Lads*
GB 1976 90m bw
EMI (Aida Young)

Two Geordie friends, with wife and mistress, go on a touring holiday.
Valuable as a record of an excellent and long-running TV series, this big screen version finds most of the humour regrettably broadened.

w Dick Clement, Ian La Frenais *d* Michael Tuchner *ph* Tony Imi *m* Mike Hugg

Rodney Bewes, James Bolam, Brigit Forsyth, Mary Tamm, Sheila Fearn, Zena Walker

A Likely Story
US 1947 88m bw
RKO (Richard H. Berger)

A man thinks he has only a short time to live, and in trying to do his best for a girl friend gets mixed up with gangsters.
Even a star cast could not have made much of this zany comedy script.

w Bess Taffel *d* H. C. Potter *ph* Roy Hunt *m* Leigh Harline *md* Constantin Bakaleinikoff

Barbara Hale, Bill Williams, Lanny Rees, Sam Levene, Dan Tobin, Nestor Paiva

Li'l Abner*
US 1959 113m Technicolor Vistavision
Paramount / Panama–Frank (Norman Panama)

The hillbilly town of Dogpatch, tagged the most useless community in America, fights being used as a test site for A-bombs.
Set-bound, intrinsically American, but bright and cheerful film of a stage show about Al Capp's famous comic strip characters.

wd Norman Panama, Melvin Frank from the musical show (*ly Johnny Mercer, words* Gene de Paul) *ph* Daniel L. Fapp *m* Gene de Paul *md* Joseph Lilley, Nelson Riddle *ch Dee Dee Wood, Michael Kidd*

Peter Palmer, Leslie Parrish, Billie Hayes, Howard St John, Stubby Kaye, Stella Stevens, Julie Newmar, Robert Strauss

'As joyous, screwy, dancin' and jokin' a musical show as Hollywood has sent us for a long time.'—*Sunday Dispatch*

AAN: Joseph Lilley, Nelson Riddle

The Lilac Domino
GB 1937 79m bw

A Hungarian count is attracted at the gambling tables by a masked girl. Surprisingly undercast version of a popular operetta. June Knight, Michael Bartlett, Athene Seyler, Richard Dolman, S. Z. Sakall, Fred Emney, Jane Carr. Written by Basil Mason, Neil Gow, R. Hutter and Derek Neame, from the play by Rudolf Bernauer, E. Gatti and B. Jenbach; directed by Fred Zelnik; for Grafton-Capitol-Cecil.

Lilac Time*
US 1928 90m approx bw silent with sound effects
First National
GB title: *Love Never Dies*

A French girl promises to wait for an American flyer, but his stern father tells her he is dead.
Popular war romance which retains moments of interest.

w Carey Wilson, *play* Jane Cowl, Jane Murfin *d / p* George Fitzmaurice *ph* Sid Hickox *m* Nathaniel Shilkret

Colleen Moore, Gary Cooper, Eugenie Besserer, Burr McIntosh, Arthur Lake

Lilacs in the Spring
GB 1954 94m Trucolor
Republic / Everest (Herbert Wilcox)
US title: *Let's Make Up*

During the London blitz a young actress is knocked unconscious and dreams of herself as Nell Gwyn, Queen Victoria and her own mother before waking up to deal with her personal problems.
Good-humoured theatrical charade deadened by poorish production and colour, strengthened by the star's game run-through of her staple characters. How Mr Flynn came to be involved is anybody's guess.

w Miles Malleson (uncredited) from play The Glorious Days by Harold Purcell *d* Herbert Wilcox *ph* Max Greene *m* Robert Farnon

Anna Neagle, Errol Flynn, Peter Graves, David Farrar, Kathleen Harrison

Lili*
US 1952 81m Technicolor
MGM (Edwin H. Knopf)

A 16-year-old orphan girl joins a carnival and falls in love with the magician.
Romantic whimsy dependent entirely on treatment, which is sometimes heavy-handed. Charm, ballet and puppets are provided, but a little cheerful song and dance would not have been amiss.

w Helen Deutsch, *novel* Paul Gallico *d, ch* Charles Walters *ph* Robert Planck *m* Bronislau Kaper *ad* Cedric Gibbons, Paul Stroesse

Leslie Caron, Jean-Pierre Aumont, Mel Ferrer, Kurt Kasznar

'A lovely and beguiling little film, touched with the magic of romance.'—*Bosley Crowther*

AA: Bronislau Kaper
AAN: Helen Deutsch; Charles Walters; Robert Planck; Leslie Caron

Lili Marleen*
West Germany 1980 116m colour
Roxy / CIP / Rialto / Bayerische Rundfunk (Luggi Waldleitner)

A German girl singer becomes famous and notorious during World War II by her rendition of an old song.
Curious mixture of melodrama and satire which doesn't really work but is always lively to watch.

w Manfred Purzer, Joshua Sinclair, Rainer Werner Fassbinder, *novel* The Sky Has Many Colours by Lale Andersen *d* Rainer Werner Fassbinder *ph* Xaver Schwarzenberger *m* Peer Raben

Hanna Schygulla, Giancarlo Giannini, Mel Ferrer, Karl Heinz

Lilies of the Field
US 1930 60m bw

A chorus girl has been robbed of her child by framed divorce court evidence. Backstage melodrama with music, very dated now but with interesting credits. Corinne Griffith, Ralph Forbes, John Loder, Patsy Paige, Freeman Wood, Virginia Bruce. Written by John Goodrich from the play by William Hurlbut; directed by Alexander Korda; for First National. 'Big revue sequences in backstage locale. Better than average programmer.'—*Variety*

Lilies of the Field*
US 1963 94m bw
UA / Rainbow / Ralph Nelson

An itinerant black workman in New Mexico helps a group of German nuns to build a chapel.
Liberal, sentimental, under-dramatized little comedy with everyone coming to understand each other's point of view, so that the audience feels improved if not especially entertained.

w James Poe, *novel* William E. Barrett *d* Ralph Nelson *ph* Ernest Haller *m* Jerry Goldsmith

Sidney Poitier, Lilia Skala

AA: Sidney Poitier
AAN: best picture; James Poe; Ernest Haller; Lilia Skala

Liliom*
US 1930 94m bw
Fox

A Budapest carnival man is killed in a fight but later comes back from heaven to see how his family is doing.
Ingeniously-staged fantasy, very dated but a lot more interesting than its musical remake *Carousel* (qv).

w S. N. Behrman, *play* Ferenc Molnar
d Frank Borzage *ph* Chester Lyons
m Richard Fall

Charles Farrell, Rose Hobart, Estelle Taylor, Lee Tracy, Walter Abel, Guinn Williams, H. B. Warner, Dawn O'Day (Anne Shirley)

'Beyond the depth of Farrell's dramatic ability . . . shapes up as passable for a week-stand in the keys.'—*Variety*

Lilith*
US 1964 126m bw
Columbia / Centaur (Robert Rossen)

A trainee therapist at an asylum falls in love with a patient.
Strange, wistful, poetic and rather soporific character melodrama.

wd Robert Rossen, *novel* J. R. Salamanca
ph Eugen Schufftan *m* Kenyon Hopkins
pd Richard Sylbert

Warren Beatty, Jean Seberg, Peter Fonda, Kim Hunter, Anne Meacham, James Patterson, Jessica Walter, Gene Hackman

'A remarkable attempt to dig a little deeper in an almost untilled field, and to throw some light on the relationship between madness and the creative imagination.'—*Tom Milne*

Lillian Russell*
US 1940 130m bw
TCF (Gene Markey)

The life and loves of the famous nineties entertainer.
Flabby and inaccurate biopic, worth seeing for its highlights but flatly and incompetently written.

w William Anthony McGuire *d* Irving Cummings *ph* Leon Shamroy *md* Alfred Newman

Alice Faye, Don Ameche, Edward Arnold, Warren William, Henry Fonda, Leo Carrillo, Helen Westley, Dorothy Peterson, Ernest Truex, Nigel Bruce, Claud Allister, Lynn Bari, Weber and Fields, Eddie Foy Jnr, Una O'Connor

Lilly Turner
US 1933 65m bw

A girl unwittingly marries a bigamist, then a drunk who will give her baby a name. Turgid mother-love saga. Ruth Chatterton, George Brent, Frank McHugh, Ruth Donnelly, Guy Kibbee, Robert Barrat. Written by Gene Markey and Kathryn Scola from the play by Philip Dunning and George Abbott; directed by William A. Wellman; for Warners. 'Spotty returns most probable.'—*Variety*

Limbo*
US 1972 111m Technicolor
Universal (Linda Gottlieb)
aka: *Chained to Yesterday*

Women wait for their husbands to return from Vietnam.
Worthy but dramatically uninteresting multi-storied semi-propaganda piece with an untried cast.

w Joan Silver, James Bridges *d* Mark Robson *ph* Charles Wheeler *m* Anita Kerr

Kate Jackson, Katherine Justice, Stuart Margolin, Hazel Medina, Kathleen Nolan

'Romantic ruler of London's half-world!'
Limehouse Blues*
US 1934 65m bw
Paramount
aka: *East End Chant*

In London's shady quarter, an oriental roustabout tries to leave his jealous mistress for a girl with a shady past.
Artificial, atmospheric melodrama set in a never-never Limehouse redolent of *Broken Blossoms*. Interesting for its very excesses.

w Arthur Phillips, Cyril Hume, Grover Jones
d Alexander Hall *ph* Harry Fischbeck

George Raft, Anna May Wong, Jean Parker, Kent Taylor, Billy Bevan

'Weak and slow-moving . . . won't satisfy the average fan.'—*Variety*

Limelight
GB 1935 80m bw
GFD / Herbert Wilcox
US title: *Backstage*

A chorus girl helps a street singer to become a star.
Highly predictable backstage musical drama which made a nine days wonder of 'The Street Singer'.

w Laura Whettier *d* Herbert Wilcox
ph Henry Harris

Anna Neagle, *Arthur Tracy*, Jane Winton, Ellis Jeffreys, Muriel George

'A syrupy concatenation to win all British hearts.'—*James Agate*

Limelight***
US 1952 144m bw
Charles Chaplin

A broken-down music hall comedian is stimulated by a young ballerina to a final hour of triumph.
Sentimental drama in a highly theatrical London East End setting. In other hands it would be very hokey, but Chaplin's best qualities, as well as his worst, are in evidence, and in a way the film sums up his own career.

w,d,m Charles Chaplin ph Karl Struss
ad Eugene Lourié photographic consultant Rollie Totheroh

Charles Chaplin, Claire Bloom, Buster Keaton, Sydney Chaplin, Nigel Bruce, Norman Lloyd

'From the first reel it is clear that he now wants to talk, that he *loves* to talk . . . where a development in the story line might easily be conveyed by a small visual effect, he prefers to make a speech about it . . . it is a disturbing rejection of the nature of the medium itself.'—*Walter Kerr*

'Surely the richest hunk of self-gratification since Huck and Tom attended their own funeral.'—*New Yorker, 1982*

'His exhortations about life, courage, consciousness and "truth" are set in a self-pitying, self-glorifying story.'—*Pauline Kael, 70s*

AA: Charles Chaplin (for music)

The Limping Man
GB 1953 74m bw

An American leaving his plane at Heathrow sees another passenger shot by a limping man. Initially intriguing thriller which gives up the ghost and tacks on a dream ending. Lloyd Bridges, Moira Lister, Helene Cordet, Bruce Beeby, Alan Wheatley, Leslie Phillips. Written by Ian Stuart and Reginald Long; directed by Charles de Lautour; for Banner / Eros.

Linda*
GB 1960 61m bw

A teenage girl falls for a member of a street gang. Nicely atmospheric low-life romance; no real content but plenty of raw style. Carol White, Alan Rothwell, Cavan Malone, Lois Dane, Edward Cast. Written by Bill MacIlwraith; directed by Don Sharp; for Independent Artists.

The Lineup*
US 1958 86m bw
Columbia (Frank Cooper)

San Francisco police trap a gunman who is also a drug contact.
Energetic, polished movie version of a popular TV series, *San Francisco Beat*.

w Stirling Silliphant *d Don Siegel ph* Hal Mohr *m* Mischa Bakaleinikoff

Warren Anderson, Robert Keith, Eli Wallach

Link
GB 1986 103m Technicolor
Cannon / EMI (Richard Franklin)

A scientist in a lonely house educates chimpanzees, but one proves malevolent.
Not much plot for a long film, and no suspense either.

w Everett DeRoche *d* Richard Franklin
ph Mike Malloy *m* Jerry Goldsmith

Terence Stamp, Elisabeth Shue, Steven Pinner, Richard Garnett

'What is missing from *Link* is a reason to see it.'—*Variety*

The Lion
GB 1962 96m De Luxe Cinemascope
TCF (Samuel G. Engel)

An American lawyer goes to Africa to visit his ex-wife and their child.

Unabsorbing marital drama with child and animal interest.

w Irene and Louis Kamp, *novel* Joseph Kessel *d* Jack Cardiff *ph* Ted Scaife *m* Malcolm Arnold

William Holden, Trevor Howard, Capucine, Pamela Franklin

'The main fault must be attributed to the spiritless direction of Jack Cardiff, whose recent change of métier has resulted in the industry losing a great lighting cameraman.'—*John Gillett*

The Lion Has Wings*
GB 1939 76m bw
London Films (Alexander Korda)

A documentary drama tracing the steps leading up to the outbreak of war.
Once-inspiring propaganda piece, now regrettably hilarious. Valuable social history, though.

w Adrian Brunel, E. V. H. Emmett *d* Michael Powell, Brian Desmond Hurst, Adrian Brunel *ph* Harry Stradling *m* Richard Addinsell

Merle Oberon, Ralph Richardson, June Duprez, Robert Douglas, Anthony Bushell, Derrick de Marney, Brian Worth, Austin Trevor

'As a statement of war aims, one feels, this leaves the world beyond Roedean still expectant.'—*Graham Greene*

The Lion in Winter*
GB 1968 134m Eastmancolor Panavision
Avco Embassy / Haworth (Martin Poll)

Henry II and Eleanor of Aquitaine celebrate Christmas together and have a family row.
An acting feast for two principals and assorted supports, a talking marathon in which not all the talk is good, a smart comedy with sudden lapses into melodrama; stimulating in parts but all rather tiresome by the end, especially as there is not much medieval splendour.

w James Goldman, from his play *d* Anthony Harvey *ph* Douglas Slocombe *m* John Barry

Katharine Hepburn, Peter O'Toole, Jane Merrow, John Castle, Anthony Hopkins, Nigel Terry, Timothy Dalton

'He is not writing a factual movie about the Plantagenets but an interpretation in which he combines their language and ours.'—*Philip T. Hartung*

AA: James Goldman; John Barry; Katharine Hepburn
AAN: best picture; Anthony Harvey; Peter O'Toole

A Lion Is in the Streets*
US 1953 88m Technicolor
Warner / Cagney Productions (William Cagney)

An itinerant confidence trickster becomes a defender of the people, is nominated for governor, and becomes corrupt.
Busy melodrama which came a bit soon after *All the King's Men.*

w Luther Davis, *novel* Adria Locke Langley *d* Raoul Walsh *ph* Harry Stradling *m* Franz Waxman *pd* Wiard Ihnen

James Cagney, Barbara Hale, Anne Francis, Warner Anderson, John McIntire, Jeanne Cagney, Lon Chaney Jnr, Frank McHugh, Larry Keating, Onslow Stevens, James Millican, Sara Haden

'A headlong and dynamic drama which offers Mr Cagney one of his most colourful and meaningful roles.'—*Bosley Crowther*

Lion of the Desert
US 1980 163m Eastmancolor Panavision
Falcon International (Moustapha Akkad)

In 1929 an Italian general in Libya withstands the attacks of rebel leader Omar Mukhtar.
Whitewashed account of the activities of a patriarchal partisan who was hanged in 1931. Of interest primarily to Arab zealots.

w H. A. L. Craig *d* Moustapha Akkad *ph* Jack Hildyard *m* Maurice Jarre *pd* Mario Garbuglia, Syd Cain

Anthony Quinn, Oliver Reed, Irene Papas, Raf Vallone, Rod Steiger, John Gielgud, Andrew Keir

'Rape was only the beginning!'
Lipstick
US 1976 90m Technicolor
Paramount / Dino de Laurentiis (Freddie Fields)

A girl is raped but gets nowhere in court until her sister lures the man to rape her too.
Franker but not very interesting extension of a fifties co-feature, with all the developments well telegraphed.

w David Rayfiel *d* Lamont Johnson *ph* Bill Butler *m* Michel Polnareff

Margaux Hemingway, Perry King, Anne Bancroft, Chris Sarandon, Mariel Hemingway, Robin Gammell

'One of *Lipstick*'s points is that voyeurism encourages senseless crime, but it unfortunately ignores its own lesson.'—*Marsha McCreadie, Films in Review*

The Liquidator*
GB 1965 104m Metrocolor Panavision
MGM / Leslie Elliott (Jon Pennington)

An ex-war hero is recruited by the secret service as an eliminator of security risks.
Fairly lively James Bond spoof which is never quite as funny as it imagines.

w Peter Yeldham, *novel* John Gardner *d* Jack Cardiff *ph* Ted Scaife *m* Lalo Schifrin

Rod Taylor, Trevor Howard, *David Tomlinson*, Jill St John, Wilfrid Hyde White, Derek Nimmo, Eric Sykes, Akim Tamiroff

Lisbon
US 1956 90m Trucolor Naturama
Republic (Ray Milland)

An international crook negotiates an Iron Curtain prisoner's release, but the man's wife has other ideas.
Glossy international intriguer with smart performances.

w John Tucker Battle *d* Ray Milland *ph* Jack Marta *m* Nelson Riddle

Ray Milland, *Claude Rains*, Maureen O'Hara, Yvonne Furneaux, Francis Lederer, Percy Marmont, Edward Chapman

The Lisbon Story
GB 1946 103m bw

Spies in 1940 Lisbon rescue a French atom scientist. Flat filming of a musical show which kept Britons humming 'Pedro the Fisherman' throughout World War II. Patricia Burke, David Farrar, Walter Rilla, *Richard Tauber,* Austin Trevor, Harry Welchman. Written by Jack Whittingham, from the play by Harold Purcell and Harry Parr-Davies; directed by Paul Stein; for British National.

The List of Adrian Messenger**
US 1963 98m bw
U-I / Joel (Edward Lewis)

An intelligence officer traps a mass murderer with a penchant for disguise.
Old-fashioned mystery thriller, as though Holmes and Watson were combating a modern Moriarty (and a rough-hewn production). The whole thing is camped up like an end-of-term treat, and as a further gimmick four guest stars allegedly appear under heavy disguise in cameo parts.

w Anthony Veiller, *novel* Philip MacDonald *d* John Huston *ph* Joe MacDonald *m* Jerry Goldsmith

George C. Scott, Kirk Douglas, Clive Brook, Dana Wynter, Jacques Roux, Walter Tony Huston, Herbert Marshall, Bernard Archard, Gladys Cooper; and Robert Mitchum, Frank Sinatra, Burt Lancaster, Tony Curtis

'A leisurely, underplayed thriller with some good performances and a gimmick which turns it into a guessing contest.'—*L.A. Times*

Listen Darling
US 1938 70m bw
MGM (Jack Cummings)

Children try to find their widowed mother a new husband.
Slight domestic comedy chiefly notable for its young talent.

w Elaine Ryan, Anne Morrison Chapin, *story* Katherine Brush *d* Edwin L. Marin *ph* Charles Lawton Jnr *m* George Axt *md* George Stoll

Mary Astor, Judy Garland, Freddie Bartholomew, Walter Pidgeon, Alan Hale, Scotty Beckett, Charley Grapewin, Barnett Parker, Gene Lockhart

'Inauspicious start for the Garland-Bartholomew team . . . mediocre story hurts.'—*Variety*

Listen to Britain****
GB 1943 20m bw

Images of Britain at war. A brilliant compilation of almost poetic sights and sounds which distil the essence of a year. Directed by *Humphrey Jennings*; for Ministry of Information (Crown Film Unit).

Lisztomania
GB 1975 104m colour Panavision
Warner / VPS / Goodtimes (Roy Baird, David Puttnam)

The life of Liszt seen in terms of a modern pop performer.
The most excessive and obscene of all this director's controversial works, incapable of criticism on normal terms except that it seems unusually poor in production values.

wd Ken Russell *ph* Peter Suschitsky *md* John Forsyth

Roger Daltrey, Sara Kestelman, Paul Nicholas, Fiona Lewis, John Justin, Ringo Starr

Sample dialogue: 'Piss off, Brahms!'

'Ken Russell's first completely unmitigated catastrophe in several years . . . a welter of arbitrary gags, manic self-references and frantic exploitation-movie clichés.'—*Tony Rayns*

'Oscar Wilde once said "Each man kills the thing he loves", and the remark perfectly suits Ken Russell's film treatments of classical composers . . . he has bludgeoned into pulp some of the finest music civilization has produced.'—*Patrick Snyder*

'This gaudy compendium of camp, second-hand Freud and third-rate pastiche is like a bad song without end.'—*Sight and Sound*

Little Accident
US 1930 82m bw

A man is about to marry again when he finds that his first wife is having his baby. Stretched-out comedy which fumbles its way along. Douglas Fairbanks Jnr, Anita Page, Sally Blane, Zasu Pitts, Joan Marsh, Roscoe Karns, Slim Summerville. Written by Gladys Lehman from the play by Floyd Dell and Thomas Mitchell; directed by William James Craft; for Universal. 'If anybody thinks 82 minutes is the proper time for this film, they should be made to sit through it twice.'—*Variety*

Little Accident
US 1939 65m bw

A baby is passed from hand to hand after her father abandons her. Simple-minded comedy bearing little relation to the above: it's now a vehicle for the baby. Baby Sandy, Hugh Herbert, Richard Carlson, Florence Rice, Ernest Truex, Fritz Feld, Edgar Kennedy. Written by Paul Yawitz and Eve Greene; directed by Charles Lamont; for Universal. 'Elemental comedy for supporting attraction in nabes.'—*Variety*

Little Annie Rooney*
US 1925 99m (24 fps) bw silent
United Artists / Mary Pickford

A 12-year-old tomboy in a New York slum rounds up the killer of her policeman father. Sentimental melodrama tailored for a 32-year-old star who liked playing kids. Of minor historical interest.

w Hope Loring, Louis D. Lighton *d* William Beaudine *ph* Charles Rosher, Hal Mohr *m* Joseph Plunkett

Mary Pickford, William Haines, Walter James, Gordon Griffith

The Little Ark
US 1971 86m De Luxe Panavision
Cinema Center / Robert B. Radnitz

Two war orphans and their pets, trapped in a flood, sail to safety in a houseboat.
Well-meaning, somewhat allegorical family film, too desultory to maintain interest and rather too frightening for children.

w Joanna Crawford, *novel* Jan de Hartog *d* James B. Clark *ph* Austin Dempster, Denys Coop *m* Fred Karlin

Theodore Bikel, Philip Frame, Genevieve Ambas

AAN: song, 'Come Follow Follow Me' (*m* Fred Karlin, *ly* Marsha Karlin)

Little Big Horn*
US 1951 86m bw
Lippert (Carl K. Hittleman)
GB title: *The Fighting Seventh*

A cavalry squad sets out to warn Custer about Little Big Horn, but all the men are massacred before Custer arrives.
Dour, impressive low-budget western.

wd Charles Marquis Warren *ph* Ernest Miller *m* Paul Dunlap

Lloyd Bridges, John Ireland, Marie Windsor, Reed Hadley, Hugh O'Brian, Wally Cassell, King Donovan

Little Big Man*
US 1970 147m Technicolor Panavision
Stockbridge / Hiller / Cinema Center (Stuart Millar)

An aged veteran of the old west recounts his life story—with elaborations.
A number of episodes varying from stark tragedy to satirical farce are framed for no good reason by the star in heavy disguise; the intention is hard to guess but there are goodies along the way.

w Calder Willingham, *novel* Thomas Berger *d* Arthur Penn *ph Harry Stradling* *m* John Hammond *pd* Dean Tavoularis

Dustin Hoffman, Martin Balsam, Faye Dunaway, *Chief Dan George*, Richard Mulligan, Jeff Corey

'A hip epic, with an amiable first hour. Then the massacres and messages take over.'—*New Yorker, 1976*

'A tangy and, I think, unique film with American verve, about some of the things American verve has done.'—*Stanley Kauffmann*

Little Big Shot
US 1935 80m bw

A gangster's child is orphaned and cared for by two con men. Reasonably lively vehicle for a new child star who didn't last. Sybil Jason, Glenda Farrell, Robert Armstrong, Edward Everett Horton, Jack La Rue, J. Carrol Naish, Edgar Kennedy. Written by Jerry Wald, Julius J. Epstein, Robert Andrews; directed by Michael Curtiz; for Warners. 'Should pave the way handily for young Miss Jason's future.'—*Variety*

A Little Bit of Heaven
US 1940 87m bw
Universal (Joe Pasternak)

A 12-year-old girl becomes a singing sensation but runs into family opposition.
Predictable vehicle for a young star being built up as a stop-gap Deanna Durbin.

w Daniel Taradash, Gertrude Purcell, Harold Goldman, *story* Grover Jones *d* Andrew Marton *ph* John Seitz *m* Charles Previn

Gloria Jean, Robert Stack, Hugh Herbert, C. Aubrey Smith, Stuart Erwin, Nan Grey, Eugene Pallette, Billy Gilbert, Butch and Buddy

Little Boy Lost
US 1953 95m bw
Paramount (William Perlberg)

An American returns to Paris after the war to find his wife dead and his small son missing.
Rather dull tearjerker.

wd George Seaton, *novel* Marghanita Laski *ph* George Barnes *m* Victor Young

Bing Crosby, Claude Dauphin, Christian Fourcade, Gabrielle Dorziat, Nicole Maurey

Little Caesar****
US 1930 77m bw
Warner

The rise and fall of a vicious gangster.
Its central character clearly modelled on Al Capone, this also has historical interest as vanguard of a spate of noisy gangster films. The star was forever identified with his role, and the film, though technically dated, moves fast enough to maintain interest over fifty years later.

w Francis Faragoh, Robert E. Lee, *novel* W. R. Burnett *d Mervyn Le Roy* *ph* Tony Gaudio *m* Erno Rapee

Edward G. Robinson, Douglas Fairbanks Jnr, Glenda Farrell, William Collier Jnr, Ralph Ince, George E. Stone, Thomas Jackson, Stanley Fields, Sidney Blackmer

'It has irony and grim humour and a real sense of excitement and its significance does not get in the way of the melodrama.'—*Richard Dana Skinner*

'One of the best gangster talkers yet turned out . . . a swell picture.'—*Variety*

AAN: Francis Faragoh, Robert E. Lee

The Little Colonel**
US 1935 80m bw (colour sequence)
TCF (B. G. De Sylva)

In a southern household after the Civil War, a little girl ends a family feud, plays Cupid to her sister, routs a few villains and mollifies her cantankerous grandfather.
First-class Temple vehicle, the first to boast an expensive production.

w William Conselman, *novel* Annie Fellows Johnson *d* David Butler *ph* Arthur Miller *md* Arthur Lange

Shirley Temple, Lionel Barrymore, Evelyn Venable, John Lodge, Bill Robinson, Hattie McDaniel, Sidney Blackmer

THE LITTLE COLONEL. Hattie McDaniel and Bill Robinson exchange glances of mutual sympathy. They know that Shirley Temple is going to act them off the screen.

The Little Damozel
GB 1933 73m bw

A gambler marries a young singer for a bribe, but falls in love with her. Lavender-tinted romance with music; notable as its star's first major role. Anna Neagle, James Rennie, Benita Hume, Athole Stewart, Alfred Drayton. Written by Donovan Pedelty, from the play by Monckton Hoffe; directed by Herbert Wilcox; for British and Dominions.

Little Darlings
US 1980 92m Metrocolor

Teenage girls at a summer camp take bets on who will lose her virginity first. Crass and tasteless comedy with only prurient appeal. Tatum O'Neal, Kristy McNichol, Krista Errickson, Armande Assante. Written by Kimi Peck and Dalene Young; directed by Ronald F. Maxwell; for Stephen J. Friedman / Paramount.

Little Dorrit**
GB 1987 Part 1 176m / Part 2 181m
Technicolor
Sands / Cannon (*John Brabourne*)

Faithful adaptation of classic novel.
Lovingly made by a large team, economically and authentically re-creating Dickens's London, with a starry cast giving their all. Adored by audiences who could take the length.

w,d Christine Edzard, from novel by Charles Dickens *ph* Bruno De Keyzer *m* Giuseppe Verdi

Derek Jacobi, Joan Greenwood, Max Wall, *Alec Guinness*, Cyril Cusack, Sarah Pickering, Eleanor Bron, Robert Morley

The Little Drummer Girl*
US 1984 130m Technicolor
Warner / Pan Arts (Robert L. Crawford)

An American actress in Britain is persuaded by Israeli agents to lose her Arab sympathies and spy for them.
Tediously protracted and unexciting version of a novel which was generally agreed to have been based on Vanessa Redgrave. Interesting for its quality look and surface style only: the intricate plotting of the Le Carré manner is surely no longer fashionable.

w Loring Mandel, *novel* John Le Carré
d George Roy Hill *ph* Wolfgang Treu
m Dave Grusin *pd* Henry Bumstead
ed William Reynolds

Diane Keaton, Yorgo Voyagis, Klaus Kinski, Sami Frey, Michael Cristofer, David Suchet, Eli Danker, Thorley Walters, Anna Massey

Little Egypt
US 1951 81m Technicolor
Universal–International (Jack Gross)
GB title: *Chicago Masquerade*

An American girl poses as an Egyptian princess at the Chicago World's Fair. Sluggish turn-of-the-century romantic melodrama based on a factual swindle involving a phoney Nile reclamation project.

w Oscar Brodney, Doris Gilbert *d* Frederick de Cordova *ph* Russell Metty *md* Joseph Gershenson

Rhonda Fleming, Mark Stevens, Nancy Guild, Charles Drake, Tom D'Andrea, Minor Watson, Steve Geray

Little Fauss and Big Halsy
US 1970 99m Movielab Panavision
Paramount / Alfran / Furie (Albert S. Ruddy)

Two motor cycle track racers team up and have violent adventures round the country. Rather pointless capers in the wake of *Easy Rider*, neither interesting nor well done.

w Charles Eastman *d* Sidney J. Furie
ph Ralph Woolsey *m* Johnny Cash, Bob Dylan, Carl Perkins Robert Redford, Michael J. Pollard, *Noah Beery Jnr*, Lauren Hutton

'A sort of *Batman and Robin* on wheels.'—*Rex Reed*

The Little Foxes***
US 1941 116m bw
Samuel Goldwyn

A family of schemers in post-Civil War days will stop at nothing to outwit each other. Superb film of a brilliant play; excellent to look at and listen to, with a compelling narrative line and memorable characters.

w Lillian Hellman, from her play *d William Wyler ph Gregg Toland m* Meredith Willson

Bette Davis, Herbert Marshall, Teresa Wright, Richard Carlson, *Charles Dingle, Dan Duryea, Carl Benton Reid, Patricia Collinge*, Jessica Grayson, Russell Hicks

HORACE GIDDENS (Herbert Marshall) 'Maybe it's easy for the dying to be honest. I'm sick of you, sick of this house, sick of my unhappy life with you. I'm sick of your brothers and their dirty tricks to make a dime. There must be better ways of getting rich than building sweatshops and pounding the bones of the town to make dividends for you to spend. You'll wreck the town, you and your brothers. You'll wreck the country, you and your kind, if they let you. But not me. I'll die my own way, and I'll do it without making the world any worse. I leave that to you.'

'One of the really beautiful jobs in the whole range of movie making.'—*Otis Ferguson*

'No one knows better than Wyler when to shift the camera's point of view, when to cut, or how to relate the characters in one shot to those in the next . . . you never have to wonder where you are in a Wyler picture.'—*Arthur Knight*

AAN: best picture; Lillian Hellman; William Wyler; Meredith Willson; Bette Davis; Teresa Wright; Patricia Collinge

Little Friend
GB 1934 85m bw

A girl is driven to attempt suicide by her parents' proposed divorce. Fairly well written but rather stilted domestic drama which maintained a small reputation. Nova Pilbeam, Matheson Lang, Lydia Sherwood, Arthur Margetson, Allan Aynesworth, Jean Cadell, Jimmy Hanley. Written by Margaret Kennedy, Christopher Isherwood and Berthold Viertel, from the novel by Ernst Lothar; directed by Berthold Viertel; for Gaumont.

The Little Giant
US 1933 74m bw
Warner

At the end of Prohibition, a beer baron moves to California and tries to break into society. Disappointingly unfunny gangster comedy which never really gets going.

w Robert Lord, Wilson Mizner *d* Roy del Ruth *ph* Sid Hickox *md* Leo F. Forbstein

Edward G. Robinson, Mary Astor, Helen Vinson, Kenneth Thompson, Russell Hopton, Donald Dillaway

'It makes Robinson a comedy character surrounded by semi-travesty and the fans are likely to resent it.'—*Variety*

'From homicide to house parties—from dames to debutantes!'

Little Giant
US 1946 91m bw
Universal (Joseph Gershenson)
GB title: *On the Carpet*

Misadventures of a vacuum cleaner salesman. Curious, unsatisfactory Abbott and Costello comedy in which the boys play separate characters instead of working as a team. They should have waited for a better script before experimenting.

w Paul Jarrico, Richard Collins, Walter de Leon *d* William A. Seiter *ph* Charles van Enger *m* Edgar Fairchild

Bud Abbott, Lou Costello, Brenda Joyce, George Cleveland, Elena Verdugo

The Little Girl Who Lives Down the Lane
US / Canada / France 1976 94m colour
Zev Braun / ICL / Filmedis-Filmel (Zev Braun)

A 13-year-old girl, when her father dies, is discovered to be keeping her mother's corpse in the cellar, and doesn't stop at more murders to keep her secret.
Tasteless piece of grand guignol, badly directed and over-acted.

w Laird Koenig, from his novel *d* Nicolas Gessner *ph* Pene Verzier *m* Christian Gaubert

Jodie Foster, Alexis Smith, Martin Sheen, Scott Jacoby
† Originally intended as a TV movie.

The Little Hut
US 1957 90m Eastmancolor
MGM / Herbson S A (F. Hugh Herbert, Mark Robson)

A man, his wife and her lover are shipwrecked on a desert island.
Sophisticated French farce which falls resoundingly flat in this bowdlerized Hollywood version in bilious colour, fatally compromising itself at the beginning with a 'realistic' London prologue.

w F. Hugh Herbert, *play* André Roussin and Nancy Mitford *d* Mark Robson *ph* Frederick A. Young *m* Robert Farnon *ad* Elliot Scott

Stewart Granger, David Niven, Ava Gardner, Walter Chiari, Finlay Currie, Jean Cadell

Little Johnny Jones
US 1930 73m bw

An American jockey wins the Derby. Mild comedy with music from the old George M. Cohan play. Eddie Buzzell, Alice Day, Edna Murphy, Robert Edeson. Written by Adelaide Heilbron and Eddie Buzzell; directed by Mervyn Le Roy; for First National. 'Familiar formula but done nicely.'—*Variety*

Little Lord Fauntleroy*
US 1921 11m (24 fps) bw silent
United Artists / Mary Pickford

An American boy who lives with his widowed mother discovers he is heir to an English dukedom.
Over-upholstered sentimental extravaganza tailored for a star in her twenties playing both young Cedric and his mother, a curious double. One can now only wonder at the immense appeal this film had in its own time; but that is not to diminish the vitality of its star.

w Bernard McConville, *novel* Frances Hodgson Burnett *d* Jack Pickford, Alfred E. Green *ph* Charles Rosher *m* Louis F. Gottschalk

Mary Pickford, Claude Gillingwater, Kate Price, James A. Marcus, Emmet King

Little Lord Fauntleroy*
US 1936 98m bw
David O. Selznick

A sound remake which did surprisingly well at the box office and is still very watchable.

w Richard Schayer, Hugh Walpole, David O. Selznick *d* John Cromwell *ph* Charles Rosher *m* Max Steiner

Freddie Bartholomew, *C. Aubrey Smith*, Mickey Rooney, Dolores Costello, Jessie Ralph, Guy Kibbee
† A TV movie version appeared in 1980, with Ricky Schroder and Alec Guinness.

Little Man, What Now?*
US 1934 95m bw
Universal

Problems of Germany in the grip of unemployment.
One of the studio's several 'sequels' to *All Quiet on the Western Front*, poignant at the time but now very dated.

w William Anthony McGuire, *novel* Hans Fallada *d* Frank Borzage *ph* Norbert Brodine

Margaret Sullavan, Douglass Montgomery, Alan Hale, Muriel Kirkland, Alan Mowbray, Mae Marsh

'Human, homely and romantic . . . should get ample b.o. attention.'—*Variety*

Little Men
US 1935 77m bw

Joe and her professor run a school for boys. Slapdash sequel to *Little Women*; not an ambitious production. Ralph Morgan, Erin O'Brien-Moore, Junior Durkin, Cora Sue Collins, Frankie Darro, Dickie Moore. Written by Gertrude Orr from the novel by Louisa M. Alcott; directed by Phil Rosen; for Mascot. 'Goes overboard on pathos . . . tears flow over the most insignificant matters.'—*Variety*
† A remake emerged from RKO in 1940, but was ill received. Running 84 minutes, it starred Kay Francis, Jack Oakie, James Lydon, and Ann Gillis, not to mention Elsie the cow. Mark Kelly and Arthur Caesar wrote it, Norman Z. McLeod directed; for Graham Towne and Gene Baker.

The Little Minister
US 1934 110m bw
RKO (Pandro S. Berman)

In 1840 Scotland, the gypsy girl with whom the new pastor falls unsuitably in love is really the local earl's wayward daughter.
Tedious film version of a cloyingly whimsical play.

w Jane Murfin, Sarah Y. Mason, Victor Heerman, *play* J. M. Barrie *d* Richard Wallace *ph* Henry Gerrard *m* Max Steiner

Katharine Hepburn, John Beal, Alan Hale, Donald Crisp, Lumsden Hare, Andy Clyde, Beryl Mercer, Dorothy Stickney, Frank Conroy, Reginald Denny

'Fine production of an old favourite.'—*Variety*

'Although dear Babbie's elfin whimsies are likely to cause teeth-gnashing among unsympathetic moderns, Miss Hepburn plays the part with likeable sprightliness and charm.'—*André Sennwald, New York Times*

Little Miss Broadway
US 1938 70m bw
TCF (David Hempstead)

A small girl is adopted by the owner of a hotel for vaudeville artistes.
One of the child star's more casual vehicles, but quite pleasing.

w Harry Tugend, Jack Yellen *d* Irving Cummings *ph* Arthur Miller *md* Louis Silvers

Shirley Temple, George Murphy, Jimmy Durante, Edna May Oliver, Phyllis Brooks, George Barbier, Edward Ellis, Jane Darwell, El Brendel, Donald Meek, Claude Gillingwater, Russell Hicks

'It can't be old age, but it does look like weariness.'—*New York Times*

'Shirley is better than her new vehicle, which in turn is better than her last one.'—*Variety*

Little Miss Marker**
US 1934 80m bw
Paramount (B. P. Schulberg)
GB title: *The Girl in Pawn*

A cynical racetrack gambler is forced to adopt a little girl, who not only softens him but saves him from his enemies.
The twin appeals of Temple (a new hot property) and Runyon made this a big hit of its time.

w William R. Lipman, Sam Hellman, Gladys Lehman, *story* Damon Runyon *d* Alexander Hall *ph* Alfred Gilks *songs* Leo Robin, Ralph Rainger

Shirley Temple, Adolphe Menjou, Dorothy Dell, Charles Bickford, Lynne Overman, Frank McGlynn Snr, Willie Best

'A good response to that element which claims there is nothing good in pictures. Clean, funny, with thrills and heart appeal all nicely blended.'—*Variety*

'No one can deny that the infant was a trouper: she delivers her lines with a killer instinct.'—*Pauline Kael, 70s*

† Remade as *Sorrowful Jones* (qv).

Little Miss Marker
US 1980 103m Technicolor
Universal (Jennings Lang)

Mainly glutinous remake of the above, with acerbic asides from the star.

wd Walter Bernstein *ph* Philip Lathrop *m* Henry Mancini

Walter Matthau, Julie Andrews, Tony Curtis, Bob Newhart, Sara Stimson, Lee Grant, Brian Dennehy

Little Mr Jim
US 1946 92m bw

The plight of a youngster when mother dies and father takes to drink. Unabashed tearjerker with a fairly resistible child star. Jackie 'Butch' Jenkins, James Craig, Frances Gifford, Luana Patten, Spring Byington. Written by George Bruce, from novel *Army Brat* by Tommy Wadelton; directed by Fred Zinnemann; for Orville O. Dull / MGM.

Little Murders
US 1971 108m De Luxe
TCF / Brodsky–Gould (Jack Brodsky)

A young photographer rises above all the urban horror of New York life, but when his wife is killed by a sniper he takes to violence.
This adaptation of an ultrablack comedy would have worked better as a comic strip, for its characters are satirical puppets, and when played by human beings the whole thing seems violently silly.

w Jules Feiffer, from his play *d* Alan Arkin *ph* Gordon Willis *m* Fred Kaz

Elliot Gould, Marcia Rodd, Elizabeth Wilson, Vincent Gardenia, Alan Arkin

Little Nellie Kelly*
US 1940 100m bw
MGM (Arthur Freed)

The daughter of a New York Irish cop makes good on the stage.
Sentimental nostalgic vehicle for young Judy Garland, who plays both wife and daughter and sings plenty of standard melodies.

w Jack McGowan, *play* George M. Cohan *d* Norman Taurog *songs* George M. Cohan, Roger Edens, Nacio Herb Brown, Arthur Freed *ph* Ray June

Judy Garland, George Murphy, Charles Winninger, Douglas McPhail, Arthur Shields, Forrester Harvey

A Little Night Music*
Austria / West Germany 1977 125m Eastmancolor
Sascha Film / S & T (Elliott Kastner)

In Vienna at the turn of the century, a middle-aged lawyer, frustrated by the virginity of his young wife, turns to an old actress flame.
Fumbled version of a rather splendid Broadway musical based on Ingmar Bergman's *Smiles of a Summer Night*. The locale is changed, several of the songs are cut, and the leads are miscast.

m Hugh Wheeler, from his stage play *d* Harold Prince *ph* Arthur Ibbetson *m / ly Stephen Sondheim*

Elizabeth Taylor, Diana Rigg, Len Cariou, Lesley-Anne Down, Hermione Gingold, Christopher Guard, Laurence Guittard

Little Old New York
US 1940 100m bw
TCF (Raymond Griffith)

The story of Robert Fulton and his invention of the steamboat.
Romantic hokum with a veneer of fact; good production.

w Harry Tugend, *play* Rida Johnson Young *d* Henry King *ph* Leon Shamroy *m* Alfred Newman

Alice Faye, Richard Greene, Fred MacMurray, Henry Stephenson, Brenda Joyce, Andy Devine, Fritz Feld, Ward Bond

Little Orphan Annie
US 1932 60m bw

A girl orphan charms a millionaire. Ineffective early version of the comic strip used many years later (equally ineffectively) as the basis for *Annie*. Mitzi Green, Edgar Kennedy, May Robson, Buster Phelps. Written by Wanda Tuchock and Tom McNamara; directed by John Robertson; for RKO.

The Little Prince
US 1974 89m Technicolor
Paramount / Stanley Donen

A small boy leaves the asteroid he rules to learn of life on earth.
A whimsical bestseller turns into an arch musical which falls over itself early on and never recovers; in any case it fatally lacks the common touch, though it has pleasing moments.

w Alan Jay Lerner, *novel* Antoine de St-Exupery *d* Stanley Donen *ph Christopher Challis* *m / ly* Frederick Loewe, Alan Jay Lerner *pd* John Barry

Richard Kiley, Steven Warner, *Bob Fosse*, Gene Wilder, Joss Ackland, Clive Revill, Victor Spinetti, Graham Crowden

'Handsome production cannot obscure limited artistic achievement.'—*Variety*

† Kiley replaced Frank Sinatra, who backed out.

AAN: title song; musical adaptation (Angela Morley, Douglas Gamley)

The Little Princess**
US 1939 93m Technicolor
TCF (Gene Markey)

In Victorian London a little girl is left at a harsh school when her father goes abroad.
One of the child star's plushest vehicles, a charming early colour film complete with dream sequence and happy ending.

w Ethel Hill, Walter Ferris, *novel* Frances Hodgson Burnett *d* Walter Lang *ph Arthur Miller, William Skall* *md* Louis Silvers

Shirley Temple, Richard Greene, Anita Louise, Ian Hunter, Cesar Romero, Arthur Treacher, Mary Nash, Sybil Jason, Miles Mander, Marcia Mae Jones, Beryl Mercer, E. E. Clive

A Little Romance
US 1979 108m Technicolor
Warner / Orion (Patrick Kelley)

A French teenager elopes with an American girl, encouraged by a garrulous old pickpocket.
Treacly juvenile romance enriched by in-jokes and an enjoyably over-the-top star performance.

w Allan Burns, *novel* Patrick Cauvin *d* George Roy Hill *ph* Pierre William Glenn *m* Georges Delerue *pd* Henry Bumstead

Laurence Olivier, Diane Lane, Thelonious Bernard, Arthur Hill, Sally Kellerman, Broderick Crawford, David Dukes

A Little Sex
US 1982 94m Technicolor
Universal / MTM (Robert de Laurentiis, Bruce Paltrow)

A young husband has a wandering eye.
Very thin comedy drama more suitable for TV if it were a little less outspoken.

w Robert de Laurentiis *d* Bruce Paltrow *ph* Ralf D. Bode *m* Georges Delerue

Tim Matheson, Kate Capshaw, Edward Herrmann, John Glover

Little Shop of Horrors*
US 1986 88m Technicolor

Workers in a flower shop are menaced by a plant with sinister intent.
Transcript of the off-Broadway musical curiously inspired by a 1961 Roger Corman horror flick which few people saw. A strange item with occasional effective moments.

w Howard Ashman, from his play *m* Alan Menken *d* Frank Oz *ph* Robert Paynter *pd Roy Walker*

Rick Moranis, Ellen Greene, Vincent Gardenia, Steve Martin

'The best movie ever made about a man-eating plant.'—*People*

AAN: song, 'Mean Green Mother from Outer Space'

Little Tokyo USA
US 1942 64m bw

A cop ferrets out Japanese espionage agents in Los Angeles. Tolerable wartime second feature. Preston Foster, Brenda Joyce, June Duprez, Harold Huber, Don Douglas, George E. Stone, Abner Biberman. Written by George Bricker; directed by Otto Brower; for Bryan Foy / TCF.

Little Tough Guy
US 1938 83m bw

A New York slum boy gets involved with a gang and is sent to reform school. A development of the Dead End Kids, with attitudes not yet crystallized, the overall tone being heavy. Billy Halop, Helen Parrish, Marjorie Main, Huntz Hall, Gabriel Dell, Bernard Punsley, Frankie Searl, Hally Chester. Written by Gilson Brown and Brenda Weisburg; directed by Harold Young; for Universal.

Little Tough Guys in Society
US 1938 75m bw

A society matron invites slum boys to her mansion as a corrective for her stuffy son. The cast makes it plain that the Dead End Kids / Little Tough Guys are now headed for comedy, the reason being that their 'serious' films were thought to set a bad example. Mary Boland, Mischa Auer, Edward Everett Horton, Helen Parrish, Jackie Searl, Frankie Thomas, Billy Benedict, Hally Chester, David Gorcey. Written by Edward Eliscu and Mortimer Offner; directed by Erle C. Kenton; for Universal.

'They leap from the book and live!'
Little Women***
US 1933 115m bw
RKO (David O. Selznick, Merian C. Cooper, Kenneth MacGowan)

The growing up of four sisters in pre-Civil War America.
Charming 'big picture' of its day, with excellent production and performances.

w Sarah Y. Mason, Victor Heerman, *novel* Louisa May Alcott *d George Cukor* *ph* Henry Gerrard *m* Max Steiner

Katharine Hepburn, Paul Lukas, Joan Bennett, Frances Dee, Jean Parker, *Spring Byington*, Edna May Oliver, Douglass Montgomery, Henry Stephenson, Samuel S. Hinds, John Lodge, Nydia Westman

'If to put a book on the screen with all the effectiveness that sympathy and good taste and careful artifice can devise is to make a fine motion picture, then *Little Women* is a fine picture.'—*James Shelley Hamilton*

'One of the most satisfactory pictures I have ever seen.'—*E. V. Lucas, Punch*

'A reminder that emotions and vitality and truth can be evoked from lavender and lace as well as from machine guns and precision dances.'—*Thornton Delehanty, New York Post*

AA: script
AAN: best picture; George Cukor

Little Women*
US 1949 122m Technicolor
MGM (Mervyn Le Roy)

Syrupy Christmas-card remake, notably lacking the light touch.

w Andrew Solt, Sarah Y. Mason, Victor Heerman *d* Mervyn Le Roy *ph* Robert Planck, Charles Schoenbaum *m* Adolph Deutsch (after Max Steiner)

June Allyson, Elizabeth Taylor, Peter Lawford, Margaret O'Brien, Janet Leigh, Mary Astor

'It will raise a smile and draw a tear from the sentimental.'—*MFB*

AAN: cinematography

The Little World of Don Camillo*
France / Italy 1952 106m bw
Rizzoli-Amato-Francinex (Giuseppe Amato)

In a small Italian village the parish priest and the communist mayor are in a constant state of amiable feud.
Slightly lethargic character comedy with a mild message for its times, popular enough to warrant several sequels.

w Julien Duvivier, René Barjavel, *novel* Giovanni Guareschi *d* Julien Duvivier *ph* Nicolas Hayer *m* Alessandro Cicognini

Fernandel, Gino Cervi, Sylvie, Manara, Vera Talqui, Franco Interlenghi

'Cute and cosy.'—*MFB*

The Littlest Rebel*
US 1935 70m bw
TCF (B. G. De Sylva)

A small southern girl persuades President Lincoln to release her father.
Charming, archetypal early Temple vehicle, very well produced.

w Edwin Burke, *play* Edward Peple *d* David Butler *ph* John Seitz *m* Cyril Mockridge

Shirley Temple, John Boles, Jack Holt, Karen Morley, *Bill Robinson*, Guinn Williams, Willie Best, Frank McGlynn Snr

'Shirley Temple as the public likes her . . . which means money.'—*Variety*

Live a Little, Steal a Lot
US 1974 102m CFI
American International (Dominick Galate)

Jewel thieves go from success to success, but the police finally force them to strike a bargain and return the gems.
Elaborate but rather unattractive caper story based on the exploits of two real criminals.

w E. Arthur Kuhn *d* Marvin Chomsky *ph* Michael Hugo *m* Philip Lambro

Robert Conrad, Don Stroud, Donna Mills, Robyn Miller, Luther Adler, Paul Stewart

Live and Let Die*
GB 1973 121m Eastmancolor
UA / Eon (Harry Saltzman)

James Bond chases a black master criminal and becomes involved in West Indian Voodoo. Standard tongue-in-cheek spy adventure with a new lightweight star and an air of *déjà vu.* Professional standards high.

w Tom Mankiewicz, *novel* Ian Fleming *d* Guy Hamilton *ph* Ted Moore *m* George Martin *titles* Maurice Binder

Roger Moore, Yaphet Kotto, Jane Seymour, Clifton James, David Hedison, Bernard Lee, Lois Maxwell

'Plot lines have descended further to the level of the old Saturday afternoon serial, and the treatment is more than ever like a cartoon.'—*Variety*

'A Bond movie is not made. It is packaged. Like an Almond Joy. So much coconut to this much chocolate and a dash of raisins.'—*Joseph Gelmis*

AAN: title song (*m / ly* Paul and Linda McCartney)

Live for Life*
France / Italy 1967 130m Eastmancolor
UA / Ariane / Vides
original title: *Vivre pour Vivre*

A news reporter forsakes his wife for a fashion model.
Interminable and unoriginal romantic drama against Sunday supplement backgounds.

w Pierre Uytterhoeven, Claude Lelouch *d, ph* Claude Lelouch *m* Francis Lai

Yves Montand, Candice Bergen, Annie Girardot, Irene Tunc

'The overall effect is of *Gone with the Wind* remade by Jacopetti.'—*New Yorker*

AAN: best foreign film

The Live Ghost
US 1934 20m bw

Two reluctant sailors think they have murdered one of their mates. Somewhat unyielding material for Stan and Ollie, but still funnier than any of their rivals at the time. Laurel and Hardy, Walter Long, Arthur Housman. Written by H. M. Walker; directed by Charles Rogers; for Hal Roach.

Live, Love and Learn
US 1937 78m bw
MGM (Harry Rapf)

A bohemian painter is tamed by marriage.
Tiresome romantic trifle.

w Charles Brackett, Cyril Hume, Richard Maibaum *d* George Fitzmaurice *ph* Ray June *m* Edward Ward

Robert Montgomery, Rosalind Russell, Robert Benchley, Helen Vinson, Mickey Rooney, Monty Woolley, E. E. Clive, Maude Eburne

'Mildly entertaining mixture of slapstick and drama around the theme of art vs material success.'—*Variety*

Live Now, Pay Later
GB 1962 104m bw
(Regal) Woodlands / Jay Lewis (Jack Hanbury)

A credit store salesman is himself heavily in debt, and his private life is in ruins; but even after a chapter of unexpected and tragic events he remains irrepressibly optimistic.
A satirical farce melodrama which lets fly in too many directions at once and has a cumulatively cheerless effect despite funny moments.

w Jack Trevor Story *d* Jay Lewis *ph* Jack Hildyard *m* Ron Grainer

Ian Hendry, John Gregson, June Ritchie, Geoffrey Keen, Liz Fraser

'1750 to 1! Always outnumbered! Never outfought!'

Lives of a Bengal Lancer**
US 1934 119m bw
Paramount (Louis D. Lighton)

Adventures on the North-West Frontier.
British army heroics are here taken rather solemnly, but the film is efficient and fondly remembered.

w Waldemar Young, John F. Balderston, Achmed Abdullah, Grover Jones, William Slavens McNut, *book* Francis Yeats-Brown *d* Henry Hathaway *ph* Charles Lang *m* Milan Roder

Gary Cooper, *Franchot Tone, Richard Cromwell, Sir Guy Standing*, C. Aubrey Smith, Monte Blue, Kathleen Burke, Colin Tapley, *Douglass Dumbrille*, Akim Tamiroff, Noble Johnson

'The best army picture ever made.'—*Daily Telegraph*

AAN: best picture; script; Henry Hathaway

The Living Corpse*
Germany / USSR / 1928 108m (24 fps) bw silent
Prometheus / Mezhrabpomfilm
original title: *Zhivoi Trup*

An unhappy husband, whose wife loves another, tries all manner of means to give her a divorce. Refused by both church and state, he kills himself.
Heavy-going dramatic tract, photographed and directed with stirring style.

w B. Gusman, Anatoly Marienhof, *play* Leo Tolstoy *d Fedor Ozep ph Anatoly Golovnya*

Vsevolod Pudovkin, Maria Jacobini, V. Garden, Gustav Diessl

'One of the really few achievements of the Russian industry: a picture so gripping that it will hold any audience.'—*Variety*

The Living Daylights**
GB 1987 130m Technicolor Panavision
MGM-UA / Eon (Albert R. Broccoli, Michael G. Wilson)

James Bond helps the Soviets chase a KGB defector with sinister intent.
25th-anniversary Bond heroics with more adult style than usual, and all technical aspects up to par.

w Richard Maibaum, Michael G. Wilson *d* John Glen *ph* Alec Mills *m* John Barry *pd* Peter Lamont

Timothy Dalton, Maryam d'Abo, Jeroen Krabbe, Joe Don Baker, John Rhys-Davies, Art Malik, Robert Brown

The Living Desert***
US 1953 72m Technicolor
Walt Disney (James Algar)

A light-hearted documentary showing the animals and insects which live in American desert areas. The aim is entertainment and Disney is not above faking, i.e. the famous sequence in which scorpions appear to do a square dance, but on its level the thing is brilliantly done.

w James Algar, Winston Hibler, Ted Sears *d James Algar ph* N. Paul Kenworthy Jnr, Robert H. Grandall *m* Paul Smith *special processes* Ub Iwerks

'The film has the same cosy anthropomorphism as a Disney cartoon and its facetious commentary and vulgar music score are typical of others in the series.'—*Georges Sadoul*

† The other 'True Life Adventures' were: *Seal Island* 49 (3 reels), *Beaver Valley* 50 (3 reels), *Nature's Half Acre* 51 (3 reels), *Water Birds* 52 (3 reels), *Prowlers of the Everglades* 53 (3 reels), *The Vanishing Prairie* 54, *The African Lion* 55, *Secrets of Life* 56, *White Wilderness* 58, *Jungle Cat* 60.

Living Free
GB 1972 92m colour
Columbia / Open Road / High Road (Paul Radin)

On the death of Elsa the lioness, George and Joy Adamson capture her three cubs and transfer them for their own safety to Serengeti.
Sloppy sequel to *Born Free*, depending very heavily on the appeal of the cubs.

w Maurice Kaufman *d* Jack Couffer *ph* Wolfgang Suschitzky *m* Sol Kaplan

Susan Hampshire, Nigel Davenport, Geoffrey Keen

'Amazing adventures beneath the curse of the jaguar god!'

The Living Idol
Mexico / US 1956 100m Eastmancolor Cinemascope
MGM (Albert Lewin)

A Mexican girl becomes possessed by the spirit of the jaguar to whom local maidens were once sacrificed.
Pretentious but rather enjoyable highbrow hokum of the heady kind expected from this producer.

wd Albert Lewin ph Jack Hildyard *m* Rodolpho Halffter

James Robertson Justice, Steve Forrest, Liliane Montevecchi

Living in a Big Way
US 1947 103m bw
MGM (Pandro S. Berman)

A demobbed GI finds he can't get on with his rich selfish wife and opens up a charity home for the families of war casualties.
Odd mixture of comedy, drama and a few songs and dances, not forgetting a message or two. It mostly falls flat on its face.

w Gregory La Cava, Irving Ravetch *d* Gregory La Cava *ph* Harold Rosson *m* Lennie Hayton

Gene Kelly, Marie McDonald, Charles Winninger, Phyllis Thaxter, Spring Byington, Clinton Sundberg

Living It Up*
US 1954 95m Technicolor
Paramount / Hal B. Wallis (Paul Jones)

A suspected victim of radium poisoning is played up by the press into a national hero.
Remake of *Nothing Sacred* with Lewis as Carole Lombard; deserves a mark for cheek.

w Jack Rose, Mel Shavelson *d* Norman Taurog *ph* Daniel Fapp *m* Walter Scharf

Dean Martin, Jerry Lewis, Janet Leigh, Edward Arnold, Fred Clark, Sheree North, Sig Rumann

Living on Velvet*
US 1935 77m bw
Warner (Edward Chodorov)

A happy-go-lucky aviator changes his life style when he narrowly escapes death in a crash.
Reasonably interesting 'serious' drama of its period.

w Jerry Wald, Julius Epstein *d* Frank Borzage *ph* Sid Hickox *md* Leo F. Forbstein

George Brent, Kay Francis, Warren William, Helen Lowell, Henry O'Neill, Samuel S. Hinds, Russell Hicks, Edgar Kennedy

'Three good names but doubtful of pulling above ordinary business.'—*Variety*

Lizzie
US 1957 81m bw
MGM / Bryna (Jerry Bresler)

Murder and rape turn a girl into a triple personality.
Preposterous cash-in on *The Three Faces of Eve*, too silly to be even funny.

w Mel Dinelli, *novel* The Bird's Nest by Shirley Jackson *d* Hugo Haas *ph* Paul Ivano *m* Leith Stevens

Eleanor Parker, Richard Boone, Joan Blondell, Hugo Haas

'Ruddy peculiar.'—*MFB*

Lloyd's of London**
US 1936 115m bw
TCF (Kenneth MacGowan)

A young messenger boy in the 18th century grows up to found a great insurance company.

Thoroughly well mounted, if unconvincing and slightly boring, historical charade in which the Prince of Wales, Lord Nelson, Dr Johnson and other personages make guest appearances. An archetypal prestige film of its time which also turned out to be box office.

w Ernest Pascal, Walter Ferris, *book* Curtis Kenyon *d Henry King ph Bert Glennon md* Louis Silvers

Tyrone Power, Madeleine Carroll, George Sanders, Freddie Bartholomew, C. Aubrey Smith, Guy Standing, Virginia Field, Montagu Love, Gavin Muir, Miles Mander, Una O'Connor, E. E. Clive

'Fictional history with fine production but weak from marquee standpoint . . . basically it's the story of the beginning and rise of an insurance company, and how can average audiences be asked to get excited about that?'—*Variety*

'The name of England is so freely on the characters' lips that we recognize at once an American picture. These people live, make love, bear children all from the most patriotic motives, and it's all rather like London in coronation week.'—*Graham Greene*

Loan Shark*
US 1952 79m bw

A detective goes undercover as a tyre worker in order to undermine a loan shark operation. Competent co-feature with technical aspects in good shape. George Raft, Dorothy Hart, Paul Stewart, Helen Westcott, John Hoyt. Written by Martin Rackin, Eugene Ling; directed by Seymour Friedman; for Lippert.

Local Hero**
GB 1983 111m colour
Enigma / Goldcrest (David Puttnam)

A young American executive meets various difficulties when he is sent to a Scottish coastal village to arrange for the building of a new refinery.
Reminiscent of various Ealing comedies, especially *Whisky Galore* and *The Maggie*, this ambitious comedy is really not funny enough for its great length.

w,d Bill Forsyth ph Chris Menges *m* Mark Knopfler

Burt Lancaster, Peter Riegert, *Denis Lawson*, Peter Capaldi, Fulton Mackay, Jenny Seagrove

'Little in the way of obvious commercial hooks . . . dominated by a constantly surprising sense of whimsicality.'—*Variety*

BFA: direction

'The restoration comedy about what cannot be restored!'
Lock Up Your Daughters
GB 1969 103m Technicolor
Columbia / Domino (David Deutsch)

In 18th-century London an aristocratic rake and various lower orders are all in search of female companionship and get their wires crossed.
Noisy, vulgar, ill-acted version (without music) of a successful musical based on two old theatrical warhorses.

w Keith Waterhouse, Willis Hall, *play* Bernard Miles based on Rape upon Rape by Henry Fielding and The Relapse by John Vanbrugh *d* Peter Coe *ph* Peter Suschitsky *m* Ron Grainer *pd* Tony Woollard

Christopher Plummer, Roy Kinnear, Georgia Brown, Susannah York, Glynis Johns, Ian Bannen, Tom Bell, Elaine Taylor, Jim Dale, Kathleen Harrison, Roy Dotrice, Vanessa Howard, Fenella Fielding, Peter Bayliss, *Richard Wordsworth,* Peter Bull, Fred Emney

'Subtlety is neither required nor displayed.'—*Jack Ibberson*

The Locked Door
US 1929 70m bw

Husband and wife try to save each other by assuming guilt for a murder. Rather static filmed play. Barbara Stanwyck, Rod la Rocque, William Boyd, Betty Bronson, Zasu Pitts, Mack Swain. Written by C. Gardner Sullivan from the play The Sign on the Door by Channing Pollock; directed by George Fitzmaurice; for United Artists.

The Locket
US 1946 85m bw
RKO (Bert Granet)

A *femme fatale* is bent on destroying men, and eventually we discover why.
Dark, confusing melodrama very typical of the immediate post-war years; it has little to say but says it dourly, even achieving flashbacks within flashbacks within flashbacks.

w Sheridan Gibney *d* John Brahm *ph* Nicholas Musuraca *m* Roy Webb

Laraine Day, Robert Mitchum, Brian Aherne, Gene Raymond, Ricardo Cortez

The Lodger***
GB 1926 84m approx (24 fps) bw silent
Gainsborough (Michael Balcon)
Subtitle: *A Story of the London Fog*

A modern version of the novel about a stranger who is (in this case) wrongly thought to be Jack the Ripper.
The first true Hitchcock film, full of his familiar dramatic visual touches. Oddly enough it was followed by three years during which he seemed to forget them.

w Eliot Stannard, Alfred Hitchcock, *novel* Mrs Belloc Lowndes *d Alfred Hitchcock ph* Baron Ventimiglia *ed* Ivor Montagu

Ivor Novello, June, Marie Ault, Arthur Chesney, Malcolm Keen

'It was the first time I exercised my style . . . you might almost say it was my first picture.'—*Alfred Hitchcock, 1966*

The Lodger*
GB 1932 85m bw
Twickenham (Julius Hagen)
US title: *The Phantom Fiend*

The upstairs lodger is suspected of being Jack the Ripper . . .
Modernized version of a story already tackled by Hitchcock as a silent and to be done again in costume in 1944. Not bad, for a minor British film of the time.

w Ivor Novello, Miles Mander, Paul Rotha, H. Fowler Mear, *novel* Mrs Belloc Lowndes *d* Maurice Elvey *ph* Stanley Blythe, Basil Emmott

Ivor Novello, Elizabeth Allan, A. W. Baskcomb, Jack Hawkins, Barbara Everest, Peter Gawthorne, Kynaston Reeves

'They can make pictures in England . . . the only point for discussion is why they do not make them oftener.'—*Variety*

The Lodger*
US 1944 84m bw
TCF (Robert Bassler)

1880s version of the above in which the lodger *is* Jack the Ripper.
Nicely mounted apart from some anachronisms, but a little dull.

w Barre Lyndon *d John Brahm ph Lucien Ballard m* Hugo Friedhofer

Laird Cregar, Merle Oberon, George Sanders, Cedric Hardwicke, Sara Allgood, Aubrey Mather, Queenie Leonard, Helena Pickard, Lumsden Hare, Frederick Worlock

Logan's Run*
US 1976 118m Metrocolor Todd-AO
MGM (Saul David)

In the future, people try to escape from a society which dooms everyone to death at thirty.
Interesting and quite exciting fantasy melodrama which mercifully moves instead of preaching.

w David Zelag Goodman, novel William F. Nolan *d* Michael Anderson *ph* Ernest Laszlo *m* Jerry Goldsmith *pd* Dale Hennesy

Michael York, Richard Jordan, Jenny Agutter, Roscoe Lee Browne, Farrah Fawcett-Majors, Peter Ustinov, Michael Anderson Jnr

'A science fiction film made by people who don't understand science fiction for the amusement of people who don't care one way or the other.'—*S. Frank, L. A. Panorama*

'It puts the future back two thousand years.'—*Benny Green, Punch*

AAN: Ernest Laszlo

Lola*
France / Italy 1960 91m bw Franscope
Rome-Paris / Euro-International

A cabaret dancer in Nantes chooses between three men.
A slight romance which was much admired for its decoration and visual style, which reminded many of Max Ophuls.

wd Jacques Demy ph Raoul Coutard *m* Michel Legrand

Anouk Aimée, Jacques Harden, Marc Michel, Elina Labourdette

'Like an adolescent's dream of romance, formed from old movies.'—*Pauline Kael, 70s*

Lola*
West Germany 1982 113m colour

A cabaret singer leads a double life. Blue Angel country is the setting for this over-predictable fable from a director whose films always have interest. Barbara Sukowa, Mario Adorf, Armin Mueller-Stahl, Matthias Fuchs. Written by Peter Martesheimer, Pea Froelich, Rainer Maria Fassbinder; directed by Rainer Maria Fassbinder; for Rialto-Trio.

Lola Montes*
France / Germany 1955 140m
Eastmancolor Cinemascope
Gamma / Florida / Oska

The life of the famous courtesan and her romance with the King of Bavaria, told in diverting fragments by a circus ringmaster.
An elaborate, expensive and trickily presented historical charade which confused the public and bankrupted its production company; but the various shorter versions released didn't help.

w Max Ophuls, Annette Wademant, Franz Geiger, *novel* Cécil Saint-Laurent *d Max Ophuls* *ph* Christian Matras *m* Georges Auric *ad* Jean d'Aubonne, Willy Schatz

Martine Carol, Anton Walbrook, Peter Ustinov, Ivan Desny, Oskar Werner, Will Quadflieg

'If you want to know what form can really do for content, rush along.'—*Derek Malcolm, The Guardian, 1978*

Lolita**
GB 1962 152m bw
MGM / Seven Arts / AA / Anya / Transworld (James B. Harris)

A middle-aged lecturer falls for a 14-year-old girl and marries her mother to be near her.
Fitfully amusing but slightly plotted and very lengthy screen version of a sensational novel in which the heroine is only twelve, which makes a difference. The flashback introduction and various comic asides are pretentious and alienating.

w Vladimir Nabokov, from his novel *d* Stanley Kubrick *ph* Oswald Morris *m* Nelson Riddle

James Mason, Shelley Winters, Sue Lyon, Peter Sellers

'The director's heart is apparently elsewhere. Consequently, we face the problem without the passion, the badness without the beauty, the agony without the ecstasy.'—*Andrew Sarris*

'A diluted *Blue Angel* with a teenage temptress instead of a tart.'—*Stanley Kauffmann*

'So clumsily structured that you begin to wonder whether what was shot and then cut out, whether the beginning was intended to be the end; and it is edited in so dilatory a fashion that after the first hour, almost every scene seems to go on too long.'—*Pauline Kael*

† Before Mason was cast, Noel Coward and Laurence Olivier were sought for the role of Humbert Humbert.
AAN: Vladimir Nabokov

Lolly Madonna XXX
US 1973 105m Metrocolor
MGM (Rodney Carr-Smith)
GB title: *The Lolly Madonna War*

Tennessee hillbilly farmers fight over a meadow.
Violent feudin' melodrama, technically accomplished but of limited interest to non-hillbillies.

w Rodney Carr-Smith, Sue Grafton, from her novel *d* Richard C. Sarafian *ph* Philip Lathrop *m* Fred Myrow

Rod Steiger, Robert Ryan, Scott Wilson, Jeff Bridges, Season Hubley

London After Midnight*
US 1927 approx 75m bw silent
MGM (Tod Browning)
GB title: *The Hypnotist*

A creepy house murder is solved by hypnotism, and a grinning monster proves to be a red herring.
Famous star thriller of which lamentably no prints survive; remade as *Mark of the Vampire*.

w Tod Browning, Waldemar Young *d* Tod Browning *ph* Merritt Gerstad

Lon Chaney, Marceline Day, Conrad Nagel, Henry B. Walthall, Polly Moran

London Belongs to Me**
GB 1948 112m bw
GFD / Individual (Frank Launder, Sidney Gilliat)
US title: *Dulcimer Street*

A young boy is arrested on a murder charge and his boarding-house friends rally to his defence.
Unconvincing but highly entertaining sub-Dickensian comedy-drama with a rousing finish and an abundance of character roles.

w Sidney Gilliat, J. B. Williams, *novel* Norman Collins *d Sidney Gilliat* *ph* Wilkie Cooper *m* Benjamin Frankel

Alastair Sim, Stephen Murray, Richard Attenborough, Fay Compton, Wylie Watson, Susan Shaw, Ivy St Helier, Joyce Carey, Andrew Crawford, Eleanor Summerfield, Hugh Griffith, Gladys Henson

The London Blackout Murders
US 1942 58m bw

A mild tobacconist murders people who are sabotaging the war effort. Curious, set-bound little melodrama with an interesting lead performance. *John Abbott*, Mary McLeod, Lloyd Corrigan, Lester Matthews, Anita Bolster, Billy Bevan, Frederick Worlock. Written by Curt Siodmak; directed by George Sherman; for Republic. (GB title: *Secret Motive*.)

London by Night*
US 1937 70m bw

Apparent murders are really part of a blackmail scheme. Reasonably intriguing mystery with good cast and atmosphere. George Murphy, Rita Johnson, Leo G. Carroll, George Zucco, Virginia Field, Montagu Love, Eddie Quillan, Leonard Mudie. Written by George Oppenheimer from the play The Umbrella Man by Will Scott; directed by William Thiele; for MGM.
'Quality is there, but drawing power isn't.'—*Variety*

London Can Take It****
GB 1940 9m bw

Quentin Reynolds, an American war correspondent, shows Americans what the London blitz was like. Historically significant short, credited with inclining Americans towards participation. In its own right, a brilliant job of editing and presentation. Written by Quentin Reynolds; directed by Harry Watt; for the Ministry of Information.

London Melody
GB 1937 75m bw
GFD / Herbert Wilcox
US title: *Girls in the Street*

A diplomat falls for a dancer.
Light but rather humourless musical drama.

w Florence Tranter, Monckton Hoffe *d* Herbert Wilcox *ph* F. A. Young

Anna Neagle, Tullio Carminati, Robert Douglas, Horace Hodges

'Excellent compilation of bromidial mush, beautifully produced and directed, which should satisfy.'—*Variety*

The London Nobody Knows*
GB 1967 53m Eastmancolor

James Mason wanders round the capital's by-ways in search of relics from former ages. Unhurried but generally delightful documentary. Written by Geoffrey Fletcher, from his book; directed by Norman Cohen; for Norcon / British Lion.

London Town*
GB 1946 126m Technicolor
GFD / Wesley Ruggles
US title: *My Heart Goes Crazy*

An understudy finally achieves stardom thanks to his daughter's schemes.
Disastrous and expensive attempt to make a major British musical without a single new idea. Tasteless, tawdry and sluggish, but it does record for posterity four of the star's sketches.

w Elliot Paul, Siegfried Herzig, Val Guest *d* Wesley Ruggles *ph* Erwin Hiller

Sid Field, Greta Gynt, Kay Kendall, Tessie O'Shea, Claude Hulbert, Sonnie Hale, Mary Clare, Petula Clark, Jerry Desmonde

'I can't see the point of importing an American director and giving him all the time and money in the world to play with when we can make bad musicals on our own, and quicker.'—*Richard Winnington*

The Lone Defender
US 1930 bw serial: 12 eps

A dog avenges the death of his prospector owner. More hard work for Rin Tin Tin, nearing the end of his career. Walter Miller, June Marlowe, Buzz Barton. Directed by Richard Thorpe; for Mascot.

The Lone Hand
US 1953 80m Technicolor

A quiet western farmer is really a Pinkerton detective. Slightly unusual western in which the happy ending is not however in doubt. Joel McCrea, Barbara Hale, Alex Nicol, Charles Drake, James Arness. Written by Joseph Hoffman; directed by George Sherman; for Universal-International.

The Lone Ranger

This high-minded western character, with his black mask, his horse Silver and his Indian friend Tonto, originated (complete with 'William Tell' overture) as a 1933 radio serial in which he was played by Bruce Bemmer. In 1938 he came to film via a Republic serial with a sequel in 1939 (see below). In 1949 Clayton Moore brought him to TV in innumerable half-hour adventures. These eventually encouraged two feature versions; see below. Also, *The Legend of the Lone Ranger* (qv).

The Lone Ranger
US 1938 bw serial: 15 eps

A mysterious masked rider turns out to be one of five lawmen combating a ruthless outlaw gang. The original Lone Ranger serial, with Lee Powell (and Chief Thundercloud as Tonto). Herman Brix, Lynne Roberts, Stanley Andrews, William Farnum. Directed by William Witney and John English; for Republic.

The Lone Ranger
US 1955 85m Warnercolor

The masked do-gooder foils a ranchers' plot to destroy an Indian reservation. Tolerably watchable adventures. Clayton Moore, Jay Silverheels, Lyle Bettger, Bonita Granville, Perry Lopez. Written by Herb Meadow; directed by Stuart Heisler; for Jack Wrather.

The Lone Ranger and the Lost City of Gold
US 1958 81m colour

The masked rider solves murders which have been committed for a mysterious medallion. Lively western for kids. Clayton Moore, Jay Silverheels, Douglas Kennedy, Charles Watts. Written by Robert Schaefer and Eric Freiwald; directed by Lesley Selander; for Jack Wrather.

The Lone Ranger Rides Again
US 1939 bw serial: 15 eps

A powerful cattleman wages a campaign of violence against innocent settlers. Sequel serial with a new star. Robert Livingston, Chief Thundercloud, Duncan Renaldo, Jinx Falken, Ralph Dunn, J. Farrell McDonald. Directed by William Witney and John English; for Republic.

Lone Star
US 1952 90m bw
MGM (Z. Wayne Griffin)

Andrew Jackson enlists the aid of a Texas adventurer to persuade Sam Houston to change his mind about an agreement with Mexico.
Slow-moving semi-western, hard to follow for non-Americans. Production values quite high.

w Borden Chase, Howard Estabrook *d* Vincent Sherman *ph* Harold Rosson *m* David Buttolph

Clark Gable, Ava Gardner, Lionel Barrymore, Broderick Crawford, Ed Begley, Beulah Bondi, James Burke, William Farnum, Lowell Gilmore, Moroni Olsen, Russell Simpson, William Conrad

The Lone Wolf

The jewel thief turned sleuth was created by Louis Joseph Vance and turned up in several silent films. During the talkie period several actors played Michael Lanyard; the role of his valet passed from Raymond Walburn to Eric Blore to Alan Mowbray. All the films were made for Columbia, but only the first was anything like a main feature.

1935: THE LONE WOLF RETURNS (*d* Roy William Neill with Melvyn Douglas)
1938: THE LONE WOLF IN PARIS (*d* Albert S. Rogell with Francis Lederer)
1939: THE LONE WOLF SPY HUNT (*d* Peter Godfrey with Warren William)
1940: THE LONE WOLF STRIKES (*d* Sidney Salkow with Warren William)
1941: THE LONE WOLF MEETS A LADY, THE LONE WOLF TAKES A CHANCE, THE LONE WOLF KEEPS A DATE (all as above), SECRETS OF THE LONE WOLF (*d* Edward Dmytryk; WW)
1943: ONE DANGEROUS NIGHT (*d* Michael Gordon: WW), PASSPORT TO SUEZ (*d* André de Toth: WW)
1946: THE NOTORIOUS LONE WOLF (*d* D. Ross Lederman; with Gerald Mohr)
1947: THE LONE WOLF IN LONDON (*d* Leslie Goodwins: GM), THE LONE WOLF IN MEXICO (*d* D. Ross Lederman: GM)
1949: THE LONE WOLF AND HIS LADY (*d* John Hoffman: GM)

Lone Wolf McQuade
US 1983 107m De Luxe

A tough Texas Ranger takes on horse rustlers and hijackers. Adults-only action rubbish, disarmingly competently made. Chuck Norris, David Carradine, Barbara Carrera, Leon Isaac Kennedy. Written by B. J. Nelson; directed by Steve Carver; for 1818 / Top Kick / Orion. 'A winningly ludicrous mish-mash of mayhem-movie rudiments and action-man reputations.'—*Paul Taylor, MFB*

The Loneliness of the Long Distance Runner*
GB 1962 104m bw
British Lion / Bryanston / Woodfall (Tony Richardson)

The only thing a Borstal boy does well is run, and as he trains he thinks back to his depressing life.
Rather pale study of a social outcast; interesting scenes do not quite form a compelling whole.

w Alan Sillitoe, from his short story *d* Tony Richardson *ph* Walter Lassally *m* John Addison

Tom Courtenay, Michael Redgrave, James Bolam, Avis Bunnage, Alec McCowen, Joe Robinson, Julia Foster

Lonely Are the Brave*
US 1962 107m bw Panavision
U-I / Joel (Edward Lewis)

The last of the cowboy rebels is no match for pursuit by jeep and helicopter.
A strange, sad, rather moving fable, with very good performances and action scenes, but a shade too unrelenting in its downbeat tone to become a popular classic.

w Dalton Trumbo, *novel* Brave Cowboy by Edward Abbey *d* David Miller *ph* Philip Lathrop *m* Jerry Goldsmith

Kirk Douglas, Walter Matthau, Gena Rowlands, Michael Kane, Carroll O'Connor, Karl Swenson, George Kennedy, Bill Raisch

Lonely Hearts*
Australia 1981 95m Eastmancolor
Adams Packer Films (John B. Murray)

When his mother dies, a 50-year-old attempts to go on a belated romantic spree.
Unexpectedly amusing comedy reminiscent of a New Yorker cartoon.

w Paul Cox, John Clarke d Paul Cox
ph Yuri Sokol *m* Norman Kaye

Wendy Hughes, *Norman Kaye*, John Finlayson, Julia Blake, Jonathan Hardy

The Lonely Lady
US 1982 92m Technicolor

A girl graduate in Los Angeles suffers various setbacks and assaults on her way to being a film star. Risible concoction designed to show off the non-talents of a non-star in a film financed by her husband. Pia Zadora, Lloyd Bochner, Bibi Besch, Joseph Cali, Anthony Holland, Jared Martin. Written by John Kershaw, Shawn Randall, from the novel by Harold Robbins; directed by Peter Sasdy; for KGA Industries / Harold Robbins International.

The Lonely Man
US 1957 87m bw Vistavision
Paramount (Pat Duggan)

An outlaw hopes to regain social recognition and contacts the son who abhors him.
Dullish psycho western.

w Harry Essex, Robert Smith *d* Henry Levin *ph* Lionel Lindon *m* Van Cleave

Jack Palance, Anthony Perkins, Elaine Aiken, Neville Brand, Lee Van Cleef, Elisha Cook Jnr, Robert Middleton

The Lonely Passion of Judith Hearne**
GB 1987 116m Fuji Color
HandMade (George Harrison, Denis O'Brien)

A middle-aged piano teacher's hopeless life in Dublin boarding houses.
Inevitably gloomy tale, intelligently crafted and with wonderfully detailed performances.

w Peter Nelson, from novel by Brian Moore *d* Jack Clayton *ph* Peter Hannan *m* Georges Delerue *pd* Michael Pickwoad

Maggie Smith, Bob Hoskins, Wendy Hiller, Marie Kean, Prunella Scales

Lonelyhearts*
US 1958 103m bw
UA / Dore Schary

A young journalist finds himself engrossed, appalled and sickened by his work on the agony column.
Episodic, occasionally interesting but generally too vaguely liberal; an intellectual reshaping of a despairing novel. The producer as usual is well meaning but doesn't quite make it.

w Dore Schary, *novel* Nathanael West *d* Vincent J. Donehue *ph* John Alton *m* Conrad Salinger

Montgomery Clift, Robert Ryan, Myrna Loy, Dolores Hart, Maureen Stapleton

AAN: Maureen Stapleton

Lonesome*
US 1928 69m (24 fps) bw silent
Universal (Carl Laemmle Jnr)

Young lovers lose each other at Luna Park but later discover that they are neighbours.
Amiable exploration of the life of city workers, comparable with *The Crowd* but showing a lighter touch.

w Edmund T. Lowe *d* Paul Fejos *ph* Gilbert Warrenton

Glenn Tryon, Barbara Kent

† Had sound effects and some talking sequences.

The Long and the Short and the Tall*
GB 1960 105m bw
ABP / Michael Balcon
US title: *Jungle Fighters*

In Malaya during World War II a Japanese scout is captured by a British patrol.
Stark war melodrama with the emphasis on character. Vivid at the time, it now seems very routine.

w Wolf Mankowitz, *play* Willis Hall *d* Leslie Norman *ph* Erwin Hillier *m* Stanley Black

Laurence Harvey, Richard Todd, David McCallum, Richard Harris, Ronald Fraser, John Meillon, John Rees, Kenji Takaki

The Long Arm**
GB 1956 96m bw
Ealing (Tom Morahan)
US title: *The Third Key*

A Scotland Yard superintendent solves a series of robberies.
Good straightforward police thriller with careful detail.

w Janet Green, Robert Barr d Charles Frend ph Gordon Dines *m* Gerbrand Schurmann

Jack Hawkins, Dorothy Alison, John Stratton, Michael Brooke, Geoffrey Keen, Sidney Tafler, Meredith Edwards, Ralph Truman, Ursula Howells

'A generally efficient example of popular British film-making.'—*MFB*

The Long Dark Hall
GB 1951 86m bw
British Lion / Five Oceans (Anthony Bushell)

A chorus girl is murdered and her married lover is accused.
Miserable mystery with a trick ending, most inappropriately cast.

w Nunnally Johnson, W. E. C. Fairchild *d* Anthony Bushell, Reginald Beck *ph* Wilkie Cooper *m* Benjamin Frankel

Rex Harrison, Lilli Palmer, Raymond Huntley, Denis O'Dea, Anthony Bushell, Henry Longhurst, Patricia Wayne, Meriel Forbes, Brenda de Banzie, Anthony Dawson

The Long Day's Dying
GB 1968 95m Techniscope
Paramount / Junction Films (Harry Fine)

Three British paratroopers in Europe are cut off from their unit and die pointlessly.
Violent, irritating anti-war film which resurrects all the clichés and makes itself unpleasant into the bargain.

w Charles Wood, *novel* Alan White *d* Peter Collinson *ph* Brian Probyn *m* Malcolm Lockyer *pd* Disley Jones

David Hemmings, Tom Bell, Tony Beckley, Alan Dobie

'It is typical of all that is wrong with the film that it should end on a frozen frame of a soldier in the act of dying while heavily ironic patriotic music swells on the sound track.'—*David Wilson*

Long Day's Journey into Night**
US 1961 174m bw
Ely Landau

Connecticut 1912: days in the life of an ageing actor, his drug addicted wife and their sons, one of whom is an alcoholic and the other Eugene O'Neill.
Heavy going, nicely handled, superbly acted version of a play which can be a player's triumph and certainly is here; but it still has more effect in the theatre.

w Eugene O'Neill *d Sidney Lumet ph Boris Kaufman m* André Previn *pd Richard Sylbert*

Ralph Richardson, Katharine Hepburn, Jason Robards Jnr, *Dean Stockwell*

'Letting his players have their head, lighted miraculously so that every flicker of emotion is preserved, and pursuing them with Kaufman's unobtrusive camera, Lumet illuminates the play, line by line, and gives it all the impact of a live performance.'—*Brenda Davies*

'A very great play has been not translated to the screen but reverently put behind glass.'—*John Simon*

AAN: Katharine Hepburn

The Long Duel
GB 1967 115m Technicolor Panavision
Rank (Ken Annakin)

On the North-West Frontier in the twenties, British officers disagree about handling the natives, and one of them forms a strong regard for the native leader.
Unconvincing cut-price Indian adventure with little cohesion and less entertainment value.

w Peter Yeldham *d* Ken Annakin *ph* Jack Hildyard *m* Patrick John Scott

Trevor Howard, Yul Brynner, Harry Andrews, Charlotte Rampling, Virginia North, Andrew Keir, Laurence Naismith, Maurice Denham

'The dialogue seems to have been written by a computer fed a programme of execrable films on the same theme.'—*MFB*

The Long Good Friday*
GB 1980 105m colour
Black Lion / Calendar (Barry Hanson)

A gangland boss faces violent reprisals from the competition.
Heavily melodramatic stylish updating of *Scarface* in a London East End setting. A critical success despite vicious detail and IRA plot involvement.

w Barrie Keefe d John Mackenzie *ph* Phil Meheux *m* Francis Monkman

Bob Hoskins, Helen Mirren, Dave King, Bryan Marshall, Eddie Constantine, Stephen Davis

'Nothing says goodbye like a bullet!'
The Long Goodbye
US 1973 111m Technicolor Panavision
UA / Lions Gate (Jerry Bick)

Philip Marlowe helps an eccentric friend who is suspected of murdering his wife.
Ugly, boring travesty of a well-respected detective novel, the apparent intention being to reverse the author's attitudes completely and to substitute dullness and incomprehensibility.

w Leigh Brackett, *novel* Raymond Chandler *d* Robert Altman *ph* Vilmos Zsigmond *m* John T. Williams

Elliott Gould, Nina Van Pallandt, Sterling Hayden, Mark Rydell, Henry Gibson

'Altman's fragmentation bomb blows up itself rather than the myths he has said he wants to lay to rest.'—*Sight and Sound*

'The trouble is that this Marlowe is an untidy, unshaven, semi-literate dimwit slob who could not locate a missing skyscraper and who would be refused service at a hot dog stand.'—*Charles Champlin*

'A spit in the eye to a great writer.'—*Michael Billington, Illustrated London News*

The Long Gray Line*
US 1955 138m Technicolor Cinemascope
Columbia (Robert Arthur)

The career of an athletics trainer at West Point.

Dim biopic, the kind of true life yarn that Americans like, produced in the cheerful, sentimental, sparring way that John Ford likes.

w Edward Hope, *book* Bring Up the Brass by Merty Maher *d* John Ford *ph* Charles Lawton Jnr *m* George Duning *md* Morris Stoloff

Tyrone Power, Maureen O'Hara, Donald Crisp, Ward Bond, Robert Francis, Betsy Palmer, Phil Carey, Harry Carey Jnr, Patrick Wayne, Sean McClory

'Its celebration of the codes and ideals of West Point vexatiously combines sentimental cosiness and a kind of religious awe.'—*Gavin Lambert*

The Long Hot Summer*
US 1958 118m Eastmancolor Cinemascope
TCF (Jerry Wald)

Conflict arises between a Mississippi town boss and a tenant farmer.
Busy Peyton Place-style family brawling saga with sex on the side, flabby as narrative but compulsive as character study.

w Irving Ravetch, Harriet Frank, *stories* William Faulkner *d* Martin Ritt *ph* Joseph La Shelle *m* Alex North

Orson Welles, Paul Newman, Joanne Woodward, Tony Franciosa, Lee Remick, Angela Lansbury

Long John Silver
Australia 1953 106m Eastmancolor Cinemascope
TI Pictures (Joseph Kaufman)

Back from Treasure Island, Silver and Hawkins plan a return visit with fresh clues to the treasure.
Cheaply produced, bitsy-piecy adventure fragments with no one to restrain the star from eye-rolling.

w Martin Rackin *d* Byron Haskin *ph* Carl Guthrie *m* David Buttolph

Robert Newton, Connie Gilchrist, Kit Taylor, Rod Taylor

The Long Long Trailer*
US 1954 96m Anscocolor
MGM (Pandro S. Berman)

A construction engineer and his bride buy a trailer for their honeymoon, and wish they hadn't.
Disaster comedy with long bright periods and the inevitable saggy bits.

w Frances Goodrich, Albert Hackett, *novel* Clinton Twiss *d* Vincente Minnelli *ph* Robert Surtees *m* Adolph Deutsch

Lucille Ball, Desi Arnaz, Marjorie Main, Keenan Wynn, Moroni Olsen

Long Lost Father
US 1934 63m bw
RKO

A restaurant owner saves his daughter from a theft charge.
Competent minor star drama.

w Dwight Taylor, *novel* G. B. Stern *d* Ernest B. Schoedsack *ph* Nicholas Musuraca *m* Max Steiner

John Barrymore, Helen Chandler, Donald Cook, Alan Mowbray, Claude King

'A mild piece with an unbelievable story . . . British background and dialogue, mostly dull.'—*Variety*

The Long Memory
GB 1952 96m bw
Rank / Europa (Hugh Stewart)

An ex-con, framed for a murder he did not commit, plots revenge but instead uncovers a fresh crime.
Slow and dreary melodrama set largely on a barge, never rising to anything like excitement.

w Robert Hamer, Frank Harvey, *novel* Winston Clewes *d* Robert Hamer *ph* Harry Waxman *m* William Alwyn

John Mills, John McCallum, Elizabeth Sellars, Geoffrey Keen

'Love that promised the world—and paid off in bullets!'

The Long Night*
US 1947 97m bw
(RKO) Anatole Litvak

A young man shoots the seducer of his sweetheart and barricades himself in a room against the police.
Good-looking but empty remake of *Le Jour se Lève*.

w John Wexley, *story* Jacques Viot *d* Anatole Litvak *ph* Sol Polito *m* Dmitri Tiomkin

Henry Fonda, Barbara Bel Geddes, Vincent Price, Ann Dvorak, Queenie Smith

'This film faithfully reproduces the letter while altering the spirit of the original almost beyond recognition.'—*MFB*

'It would be interesting to see it on a double bill with its French original. Both films clearly rate themselves as tragedies; they are merely intelligent trash. But the old one is much more discreet with its self-pity and much more sharply edged.'—*James Agee*

'A classic of the bashful age!'

Long Pants*
US 1927 58m (24 fps) bw silent
First National / Harry Langdon

A country bumpkin has trouble in the city.
Far from the best Langdon comedy, but funny in flashes.

w Arthur Ripley *d* Frank Capra *ph* Elgin Lessley

Harry Langdon, Gladys Brockwell, Alan Roscoe, Alma Bennett

'All the world loves an outlaw. For some damn reason they remember 'em!'

The Long Riders
US 1980 99m Technicolor
UA / Huka (Tim Zinnemann)

The story of western outlaw brothers named Younger, Miller and James.
Well-worn territory with new-fangled violent detail. Not much of an attraction despite the gimmick of having the various anti-heroes played by real brothers.

w Bill Bryden, Steven Phillip Smith, Stacy Keach, James Keach *d* Walter Hill *ph* Ric Waite *m* Ry Cooder *pd* Jack T. Collis

Stacy Keach, James Keach, David Carradine, Keith Carradine, Robert Carradine, Dennis Quaid, Randy Quaid

The Long Ships
GB / Yugoslavia 1963 126m Technirama
Columbia / Warwick / Avila (Irving Allen)

A Viking adventurer and a Moorish prince fall out over a golden bell.
Stilted medieval epic with some visual compensations but more chat than action.

w Berkely Mather, Beverly Cross, *novel* Frank G. Bengtsson *d* Jack Cardiff *ph* Christopher Challis *m* Dusan Radic

Richard Widmark, Sidney Poitier, Russ Tamblyn, Rosanna Schiaffino, Oscar Homolka, Colin Blakely

'To say it was disastrous is a compliment.'—*Sidney Poitier*

The Long, the Short and the Tall: see The Long and the Short and the Tall

'The love of woman in their eyes—the salt of the sea in their blood!'

The Long Voyage Home**
US 1940 104m bw
Walter Wanger

Merchant seamen on shore leave get drunk, philosophize and have adventures.
Stagey-looking but dramatically interesting amalgam of four one-act plays by Eugene O'Neill, with talent abounding.

w Dudley Nichols *d John Ford* *ph* Gregg Toland *m* Richard Hageman

John Wayne, Thomas Mitchell, Ian Hunter, Ward Bond, Barry Fitzgerald, Wilfrid Lawson, *Mildred Natwick*, John Qualen, Arthur Shields, Joe Sawyer

'One of the finest of all movies that deal with life at sea.'—*Pauline Kael, 70s*

AAN: best picture; Dudley Nichols; Gregg Toland; Richard Hageman

The Long Wait
US 1954 93m bw
UA / Parklane (Lesser Samuels)

An amnesia victim returns home to solve a murder in which he was involved.
Flatulent version of a Mickey Spillane novel, over-plotted and inadequately motivated.

w Alan Green, Lesser Samuels *d* Victor Saville *ph* Franz Planer *m* Mario Castelnuovo Tedesco

Anthony Quinn, Charles Coburn, Gene Evans, Peggie Castle, Dolores Donlan

The Longest Day**
US 1962 169m bw Cinemascope
TCF (*Darryl F. Zanuck, Elmo Williams*)

A multi-faceted account of the landings in Normandy in June 1944.
Extraordinarily noisy war spectacular, enjoyable as a violent entertainment once one has caught all the threads, but emotionally unaffecting because every part is played by a star.

w Cornelius Ryan, Romain Gary, James Jones, David Pursall, Jack Seddon, *book* Cornelius Ryan *d* Andrew Marton, Ken Annakin, Bernhard Wicki *ph* Henri Persin, Walter Wottitz, Pierre Levent, Jean Bourgoin *m* Maurice Jarre, Paul Anka

John Wayne, Robert Mitchum, Henry Fonda, Robert Ryan, Rod Steiger, Robert Wagner, Paul Anka, Fabian, Tommy Sands, Richard Beymer, Mel Ferrer, Jeffrey Hunter, Sal Mineo, Roddy McDowall, Stuart Whitman, Steve Forrest, Eddie Albert, Edmond O'Brien, Red Buttons, Tom Tryon, Alexander Knox, Ray Danton, Ron Randell, Richard Burton, Donald Houston, Kenneth More, Peter Lawford, Richard Todd, Leo Genn, John Gregson, Sean Connery, Michael Medwin, Leslie Phillips, Irina Demich, Bourvil, Jean-Louis Barrault, Christian Marquand, Arletty, Curt Jurgens, Paul Hartmann, Gert Frobe, Wolfgang Preiss, Peter Van Eyck, Christopher Lee, Eugene Deckers, Richard Wattis

AA: photography
AAN: best picture

The Longest Yard
US 1974 122m Technicolor
Paramount / Long Road (Albert S. Ruddy)
GB title: *The Mean Machine*

Imprisoned for drunkenness and car theft, a football star is blackmailed into training a prison football team of hulking misfits.
Violent, meandering comedy-drama with murderous jokes but no narrative grip.

w Tracy Keenan Wynn *d* Robert Aldrich *ph* Joseph Biroc *m* Frank de Vol

Burt Reynolds, Eddie Albert, Ed Lauter, Michael Conrad, Jim Hampton

Look Back in Anger*
GB 1959 99m bw
ABP / Woodfall (Gordon L. T. Scott)

A bad-tempered young man with a grudge against life and the government runs a market stall, lives in a squalid flat, and has an affair with his wife's best friend.
Well-made version of a play whose sheer dreariness was theatrically stimulating but in terms of film realism becomes only depressing and stupid despite competence all round. It also set shoddy standards for its many less proficient imitators.

w Nigel Kneale, *play John Osborne d* Tony Richardson *ph Oswald Morris m* Chris Barber

Richard Burton, Mary Ure, Claire Bloom, Edith Evans, Gary Raymond, Glen Byam Shaw, Phyllis Neilson-Terry, Donald Pleasence, George Devine

Look Before You Love
GB 1948 96m bw

Romance in Rio for a girl of the embassy staff. Abysmal romantic comedy with little of either commodity in evidence. Margaret Lockwood, Griffith Jones, Norman Wooland, Phyllis Stanley, Michael Medwin, Maurice Denham. Written by Reginald Long; directed by Harold Huth; for Burnham / Rank.

'The sunshine story of Broadway's glory girl!'

Look for the Silver Lining*
US 1949 106m Technicolor
Warner (William Jacobs)

The life story of twenties stage star Marilyn Miller.
Harmless musical biopic with a sense of humour.

w Phoebe and Henry Ephron, Marian Spitzer, Bert Kalmar, Harry Ruby *d* David Butler *ph* Peverell Marley *md* Ray Heindorf

June Haver, *Ray Bolger, Charles Ruggles*, Gordon Macrae, Rosemary de Camp, S. Z. Sakall, Walter Catlett

AAN: Ray Heindorf

Look in Any Window
US 1961 87m bw

A rich but psychotic youth despises his friends and relations and is arrested as a peeping tom. Psychiatric case history which also wags a social finger. Not particularly convincing. Paul Anka, Ruth Roman, Alex Nicol, Gigi Perreau, George Dolenz, Jack Cassidy. Written by Laurence E. Mascott; directed by William Alland; for Allied Artists.

Look Up and Laugh*
GB 1935 82m bw
ATP (Basil Dean)

Market stallholders defy a big chain store. Good star comedy with music.

w Gordon Wellesley, *story* J. B. Priestley *d* Basil Dean *ph* Robert G. Martin *md* Ernest Irving

Gracie Fields, Douglas Wakefield, Harry Tate, Alfred Drayton, Morris Harvey, Vivien Leigh, Robb Wilton

Look Who's Laughing
US 1941 75m bw

Fibber McGee and Molly act as unexpected hosts to Edgar Bergen and Charlie McCarthy. Exploitation of radio sitcoms, acceptable at the time. With Lucille Ball. Written by James V. Kern and others; directed and produced by Allan Dwan; for RKO. (See also: *Here We Go Again.*)

Looker
US 1981 94m Technicolor Panavision
Warner / Ladd Company (Howard Jeffrey)

Models are being murdered because their hologram replacements are more perfect.
Confused and confusing variation on *The Stepford Wives*, played unsatisfactorily between comedy and melodrama.

w,d Michael Crichton *ph* Paul Lohmann *m* Barry DeVorzon

Albert Finney, James Coburn, Susan Dey, Leigh Taylor-Young, Dorian Harewood, Darryl Hickman

Lookin' to Get Out
US 1982 105m colour
Lorimar / North Star / Voight-Schaffel (Robert Schaffel)

A couple of inveterate gamblers take on the Las Vegas establishment.
Fairly pleasant, mindless, quite forgettable comedy.

w Al Schwartz, Jon Voight *d* Hal Ashby *ph* Haskell Wexler *m* Johnny Mandel *pd* Robert Boyle

Jon Voight, Ann-Margret, Burt Young, Bert Remsen, Jude Farese, Richard Bradford

Looking for Love
US 1964 83m Metrocolor Panavision

A talented girl can't decide between show business and marriage. Limp, would-be-cute romantic nonsense with poor musical numbers. Connie Francis, Jim Hutton, Susan Oliver, Joby Baker, Barbara Nichols, Jay C. Flippen, Jesse White, Charles Lane. Written by Ruth Brooks Flippen; directed by Don Weis; for Joe Pasternak / MGM.

Looking for Mr Goodbar
US 1977 136m Metrocolor Panavision
Paramount (Freddie Fields)

A teacher of deaf children leads a sordid secret night life.
Exploitative and very boring sex melodrama which doesn't even make one believe in its central character.

wd Richard Brooks, *novel* Judith Rossner *ph* William A. Fraker *m* Artie Kane *ad* Edward Carfagno

Diane Keaton, Tuesday Weld, William Atherton, Richard Kiley

'Brooks has laid a windy jeremiad about permissive sex on top of fractured film syntax.'—*Judith Crist*

AAN: William A. Fraker; Tuesday Weld

Looking for Trouble
US 1933 77m bw

Two telephone engineers brawl over a girl. Early star vehicle, quite watchable. Spencer Tracy, Jack Oakie, Constance Cummings, Morgan Conway, Arline Judge. Written by Leonard Praskins and Elmer Harris; directed by William Wellman; for Darryl F. Zanuck / UA. 'Too much of a plug for the phone company . . . plus an overpacked plot and certain dialogue failings.'—*Variety*

Looking Forward
US 1933 76m bw

A shop owner finds he must sell his property and fire valued staff. Depression fable from Dodie Smith's play Service, adequately mounted. Lewis Stone, Lionel Barrymore, Benita Hume, Elizabeth Allan, Phillips

Holmes, Colin Clive. Written by Bess Meredyth, H. M. Harwood; directed by Clarence Brown; for MGM.

The Looking Glass War
GB 1969 107m Technicolor Panavision
Columbia / M. J. Frankovich (John Box)

The British secret service sends a young Pole into East Germany to find a top secret film.
Jaundiced spy story which aims for irony and tragedy but becomes merely verbose and irritating.

wd Frank R. Pierson, *novel* John Le Carré *ph* Austin Dempster *m* Wally Scott

Christopher Jones, Pia Degermark, Ralph Richardson, Anthony Hopkins, Paul Rogers, Susan George, Ray McAnally, Robert Urquhart, Maxine Audley, Anna Massey

'There are a lot of incidental pleasures, but in the final analysis they only add up to half a film.'—*Nigel Andrews*

Looking on the Bright Side*
GB 1931 81m bw
ATP (Basil Dean)

A songwriter gets ideas above his station but eventually returns to the manicurist who loves him.
Dated but lively musical which helped confirm Gracie's stardom.

w Basil Dean, Archie Pitt, Brock Williams *d* Basil Dean *ph* Robert G. Martin *md* Carroll Gibbons

Gracie Fields, Richard Dolman, Julian Rose, Wyn Richmond

Loophole
GB 1980 105m colour
Brent Walker (Julian Holloway, David Korda)

A safecracker plans to rob the vault of a London bank.
Dim caper yarn which can't make its mind up how serious it means to be. As it stands, it is all very old hat and has a cop-out finish.

w Jonathan Hales, *novel* Robert Pollock *d* John Quested *ph* Michael Reed *m* Lalo Schifrin

Albert Finney, Martin Sheen, Susannah York, Colin Blakeley, Jonathan Pryce, Robert Morley, Alfred Lynch

Loose Ankles
US 1930 66m bw

A girl's inheritance will be cancelled if she is involved in scandal. Rival claimants try to ensure that she is. Thin, amiable comedy based on a Broadway success. Loretta Young, Douglas Fairbanks Jnr, Louise Fazenda, Otis Harlan, Daphne Pollard, Inez Courtney. Written by Gene Towne from the play by Sam Janney; directed by Ted Wilde; for First National. 'Will bring a chuckle to the most hard-boiled metropolite.'—*Variety*

Loose Connections*
GB 1983 96m colour
Umbrella / Greenpoint (Simon Perry)

Adventures on a drive to Munich.
Thin, easy-going road comedy. Pleasant enough, but no *Genevieve*.

w Maggie Brooks *d* Richard Eyre *ph* Clive Tickner *m* Dominic Muldowney

Lindsay Duncan, Stephen Rea, Carole Harrison, Frances Low

Loot*
GB 1970 101m Eastmancolor
Performing Arts Ltd (Arthur Lewis)

A crook hides his mother's body and uses the coffin to carry the proceeds of a robbery.
Breakneck black farce which still can't move quite fast enough to cover up its bad taste, though well done by all concerned.

w Ray Galton, Alan Simpson, *play* Joe Orton *d* Silvio Narizzano *ph* Austin Dempster *m* Keith Mansfield, Richard Willing-Denton *ad* Anthony Pratt

Richard Attenborough, Lee Remick, Hywel Bennett, Milo O'Shea, Dick Emery

The Looters
US 1955 87m bw

A plane crashes on Pike's Peak, and rescuers fall out about whether to loot the wreckage.
Competent co-feature of its period and style. Rory Calhoun, Ray Danton, Thomas Gomez, Julie Adams, Frank Faylen, Rod Williams. Written by Richard Alan Simmons; directed by Abner Biberman; for Universal.

Lord Camber's Ladies
GB 1932 80m bw

A nobleman tries to murder his way out of a romantic tangle. Rather dull suspenser notable only for its stagey cast and the fact that Alfred Hitchcock produced it. Gerald du Maurier, Gertrude Lawrence, Benita Hume, Nigel Bruce, Clare Greet, A. Bromley Davenport. Written by Benn W. Levy, Edwin Greenwood and Gilbert Wakefield, from the novel *The Case of Lady Camber* by Horace Annesley Vachell; directed by Benn W. Levy; for BIP.

Lord Edgware Dies
GB 1934 81m bw

Hercule Poirot proves that an elderly nobleman was not killed by his young wife.
Modest whodunnit: the intended series did not catch on. Austin Trevor, Jane Carr, Richard Cooper, John Turnbull, Michael Shepley. Written by H. Fowler Mear, from the novel by Agatha Christie; directed by Henry Edwards; for Real Art.

Lord Jeff
US 1938 78m bw
MGM (Frank Davis)
GB title: *The Boy from Barnardo's*

A well-brought-up boy gets into trouble and is sent under supervision to a naval school.
Adequate family film with absolutely no surprises.

w Bradford Roper, Val Burton, André Boehm *d* Sam Wood *ph* John Seitz *m* Edward Ward

Freddie Bartholemew, Mickey Rooney, Charles Coburn, Herbert Mundin, Terry Kilburn, Gale Sondergaard, Peter Lawford

Lord Jim*
GB 1964 154m Technicolor Super Panavision
Columbia / Keep (René Dupont)

Adventures of a sailor who prowls the Far East looking for truth; he helps enslaved natives, is raped by a tribal chief, and finally sacrifices his life.
Lush and very boring farrago of miscellaneous incident, with a central character about whose fate no one can care. However, an expensive production must have its points of interest, and the belated introduction of a gentleman villain gives a little edge.

wd Richard Brooks, *novel* Joseph Conrad *ph* *Frederick A. Young* *m* Bronislau Kaper *pd* Geoffrey Drake

Peter O'Toole, *James Mason*, Eli Wallach, Paul Lukas, Jack Hawkins, Daliah Lavi, Curt Jurgens, Akim Tamiroff

Lord Love a Duck*
US 1966 105m bw
UA / Charleston (George Axelrod)

A senior Los Angeles student practises hypnotism on his girl friend.
Rather sloppy satire on American culture and fancies, dressed up as crazy comedy; occasional laughs.

w Larry H. Johnson, George Axelrod, *novel* Al Hine *d* George Axelrod *ph* Daniel Fapp *m* Neal Hefti

Roddy McDowall, Tuesday Weld, Lola Albright, Ruth Gordon, Harvey Korman, Max Showalter

Lord of the Flies
GB 1963 91m bw
Allen–Hogdon Productions / Two Arts (Lewis M. Allen)

After a plane crash, a party of English schoolboys are stranded on an uncharted tropical island and gradually turn savage.
Semi-professional production of a semi-poetic novel which worked well on the printed page but on screen seems crude and unconvincing.

wd Peter Brook, *novel* William Golding *ph* Tom Hollyman, Gerald Feil *m* Raymond Leppard

James Aubrey, Tom Chapin, Hugh Edwards, Roger Elwin, Tom Gaman

Lord of the Rings*
US 1978 133m De Luxe
UA / Fantasy (Saul Zaentz)

In Middle Earth the Dark Lord loses a powerful ring, and a Hobbit tries to prevent him from getting it back.
Disappointingly stolid, overlong and confused cartoon version of a modern classic which may well deserve all those adjectives. Parts of it are charming, and the method of making cartoons from film of actors photographed in the ordinary way is certainly ingenious though it denies the cartoon characters their own full richness.

w Chris Conkling, Peter S. Beagle, *books* J. R. R. Tolkien *d* Ralph Bakshi *ph* Timothy Galfas *m* Leonard Rosenman

voices: Christopher Guard, John Hurt, William Squire, Michael Scholes

The Lords of Discipline
US 1982 103m Eastmancolor

Murky goings-on at the Carolina Military Institute. Strictly for those interested in army cadets being unpleasant to each other. David Keith, Robert Prosky, G. D. Spradlin, Barbara Babcock, Michael Biehn, Rick Rossovich. Written by Thomas Pope, Lloyd Fonvielle, from the novel by Pat Conroy; directed by Franc Roddam; for Paramount.

The Lords of Flatbush*
US 1974 86m Technicolor

Adventures of Brooklyn street gangs. Not quite the violent movie one might think, and interesting for its cast as well as some thoughtful passages. Perry King, Henry Winkler, Sylvester Stallone, Paul Mace, Susan Blakely, Maria Smith. Written by Stephen F. Verona, Martin Davidson, Gayle Glecker, Sylvester Stallone; directed by Verona and Davidson; for Verona/Columbia.

Lorna Doone**
GB 1934 90m bw
ATP (Basil Dean)

In 1625 on Exmoor, a farmer comes to love an outlaw's daughter who proves to be in reality a kidnapped heiress.
Simple, straightforward, effective version of the famous romance, with refreshing use of exteriors.

w Dorothy Farnum, Miles Malleson, Gordon Wellesley, *novel* R. D. Blackmore *d Basil Dean* *ph* Robert Martin

Victoria Hopper, John Loder, Margaret Lockwood, *Roy Emerton,* Edward Rigby, Mary Clare, Roger Livesey, George Curzon, D. A. Clarke-Smith, Lawrence Hanray, Amy Veness, Eliot Makeham

'It has polish, but it lacks drama and grip.'—*Variety*

Lorna Doone
US 1951 89m Technicolor
Columbia (Edward Small)

Grotesque remake which treats the story like a cheap western.

w Jesse L. Lasky Jnr, Richard Schayer *d* Phil Karlson *ph* Charles Van Enger *m* George Duning

Barbara Hale, Richard Greene, Anne Howard, William Bishop, Carl Benton Reid, Ron Randell, Sean McClory, Onslow Stevens, Lester Matthews, John Dehner

Loser Takes All
GB 1956 88m Eastmancolor Cinemascope
British Lion / John Stafford

An accountant and his wife are invited to Monte Carlo but the high life estranges them.
Tedious taradiddle from an unexpected quarter; not a success by any standard.

w Graham Greene, from his novel *d* Ken Annakin *ph* Georges Périnal *m* Alessandro Cicognini

Glynis Johns, Rossano Brazzi, Robert Morley, Joyce Carey, A. E. Matthews, Tony Britton, Felix Aylmer, Albert Lieven, Geoffrey Keen

Lost*
GB 1955 89m Technicolor
Rank (Vivian A. Cox)
US title: *Tears for Simon*

The police go on the trail of a stolen child. Mildly effective semi-documentary police story, with good use of locations.

w Janet Green *d* Guy Green *ph* Harry Waxman *m* Benjamin Frankel

David Farrar, David Knight, Julia Arnall, Anthony Oliver, Thora Hird, Eleanor Summerfield, Marjorie Rhodes, Joan Sims

Lost and Found
US 1979 105m Technicolor Panavision
Columbia / Gordon (Melvin Frank)

A widowed American professor meets an English divorcee on a skiing holiday, but after marriage they prove to be incompatible.
Unattractive romantic comedy-drama which despite capable stars degenerates into a series of wounding slanging matches.

w Melvin Frank, Jack Rose *d* Melvin Frank *ph* Douglas Slocombe *m* John Cameron *pd* Trevor Williams

Glenda Jackson, George Segal, Maureen Stapleton, Paul Sorvino, John Cunningham, Hollis McLaren

Lost Angel*
US 1943 91m bw
MGM (Robert Sisk)

A lost little girl is adopted by a reporter.
Good star vehicle for the sentimentally-inclined, with solid production and casting back-up.

w Isabel Lennart *d* Roy Rowland *ph* Robert Surtees *m* Daniele Amfitheatrof

Margaret O'Brien, James Craig, Marsha Hunt, Philip Merivale, Henry O'Neill, Donald Meek, Keenan Wynn

'A beautiful opportunity for true satire is offered and, I regret to say, thrown away. For our little Gulliver is rapidly decivilized by all the familiar bromidic palliatives: love, crooning, fairies and night clubs.'—*Richard Winnington*

Lost Boundaries*
US 1949 105m bw
Film Classics (Louis de Rochemont)

In a New Hampshire town in the forties, a beloved doctor and his wife are found to have negro blood.
Well-meaning but dramatically ineffective racial drama which meanders along allowing an occasional burst of genuine feeling to come through.

w Virginia Shaler, Eugene Ling *d* Alfred Werker *ph* William J. Miller *m* Louis Applebaum

Mel Ferrer, Beatrice Pearson, Richard Hylton, Susan Douglas, Canada Lee, Grace Coppin

'It cannot be said to betray its subject, but is, rather, unequal to it.'—*Gavin Lambert*

The Lost Boys
US 1987 92m Technicolor Panavision

Vampiric bikers corrupt innocent teenagers. Wild nonsense which affronts all classes by its sheer excesses. Jason Patric, Corey Haim, Dianne Wiest, Barnard Hughes, Kiefer Sutherland. Written by Janice Fischer, James Jeremias, Jeffrey Boam; directed by Joel Schumacher; for Richard Donner/Warners.

The Lost City
US 1935 bw serial: 12 eps

Electrical storms disrupt the world, and an engineer tracks the source to Central Africa, where a wizard named Zolok runs a city with the Magnetic Mountain. Agreeably lunatic free-for-all in serial form. Kane Richmond, William 'Stage' Boyd, Claudia Dell. Directed by Harry Revier; for Krellberg.

Lost City of the Jungle
US 1946 bw serial: 13 eps

A warmonger finds an antidote to the atom bomb inside the African tomb of The Glowing Goddess. Absurdities pile on each other in a serial which was clearly the starting point for *Raiders of the Lost Ark*: when the chest is opened, the evil element inside disintegrates those present. Russell Hayden, Jane Adams, Lionel Atwill, Keye Luke, Helen Bennett, John Eldredge, John Miljan. Directed by Ray Taylor and Lewis D. Collins; for Universal.

'Wherever their feet touched ground, a new adventure was born!'

Lost Command
US 1966 128m Technicolor Panavision
Columbia / Red Lion (Mark Robson)

Adventures of a French paratroop regiment in Indo-China and Algeria.
Anti-war war adventure; noisy but scarcely inspired.

w Nelson Gidding, *novel* The Centurions by Jean Larteguy *d* Mark Robson *ph* Robert Surtees *m* Franz Waxman

Anthony Quinn, Alain Delon, George Segal, Michèle Morgan, Maurice Ronet, Claudia Cardinale, Grégoire Aslan, Jean Servais

The Lost Continent*
GB 1968 98m Technicolor
Hammer (Michael Carreras)

The captain of a tramp steamer illegally carries dynamite, and he and his passengers are stranded in a weird Sargasso Sea colony run by the Spanish Inquisition.
Hilariously imaginative hokum with splendid art direction and some of the grottiest monsters on film; but memorable moments do not quite add up to a classic of the genre.

w Michael Nash, *novel* Uncharted Seas by Dennis Wheatley *d* Michael Carreras *ph* Paul Beeson *m* Gerard Schurmann *sp* Robert A. Mattey, Cliff Richardson *ad Arthur Lawson*

Eric Porter, Hildegarde Neff, Suzanna Leigh, Tony Beckley, Nigel Stock, Neil McCallum, Jimmy Hanley, James Cossins, Victor Maddern

'One of the most ludicrously enjoyable bad films since *Salome Where She Danced.*'—*MFB*

Lost Honeymoon
US 1947 70m bw

An amnesiac GI fails to remember either his wife or his young family. Artificial comedy which the actors can't carry off. Franchot Tone, Ann Richards, Tom Conway. Written by Joseph Fields; directed by Leigh Jason; for Eagle-Lion.

Lost Horizon****
US 1937 130m (released at 118m) bw
Columbia (Frank Capra)

Escaping from an Indian revolution, four people are kidnapped by plane and taken to an idyllic civilization in a Tibetan valley, where the weather is always kind and men are not only gentle to each other but live to a very advanced age.
Much re-cut romantic adventure which leaves out some of the emphasis of a favourite Utopian novel but stands up pretty well on its own, at least as a supreme example of Hollywood moonshine, with perfect casting, direction and music. If the design has a touch of Ziegfeld, that's Hollywood.

w Robert Riskin, novel James Hilton d Frank Capra ph Joseph Walker *m Dmitri Tiomkin ad* Stephen Goosson

Ronald Colman, H. B. Warner, Thomas Mitchell, Edward Everett Horton, Sam Jaffe, Isabel Jewell, Jane Wyatt, Margo, John Howard

'One of the most impressive of all thirties films, a splendid fantasy which, physically and emotionally, lets out all the stops.'—*John Baxter, 1968*

'One is reminded of a British critic's comment on *Mary of Scotland,* "the inaccuracies must have involved tremendous research".'—*Robert Stebbins*

'The best film I've seen for ages, but will somebody please tell me how they got the grand piano along a footpath on which only one person can walk at a time with rope and pickaxe and with a sheer drop of three thousand feet or so?'—*James Agate*

'If the long dull ethical sequences had been cut to the bone there would have been plenty of room for the real story: the shock of western crudity and injustice on a man returned from a more gentle and beautiful way of life.'—*Graham Greene*

† A 1943 reissue trimmed down the negative still further, to 109 minutes; but in 1979 the American Film Institute was busily restoring a print of the original length.

AAN: best picture; Dmitri Tiomkin; H. B. Warner

'The adventure that will live forever has been transformed into spectacular musical drama!'
'Come to Shangri-La and a new world of love!'

Lost Horizon*
US 1972 143m Panavision Technicolor
Columbia / Ross Hunter

Torpid remake with a good opening followed by slabs of philosophizing dialogue and an unbroken series of tedious songs.

w Larry Kramer *d* Charles Jarrott *ph Robert Surtees m* Burt Bacharach *songs* Burt Bacharach, Hal David *ad* Preston Ames

Peter Finch, Liv Ullmann, Sally Kellerman, *Bobby Van,* George Kennedy, Michael York, Olivia Hussey, James Shigeta, John Gielgud, Charles Boyer

'It will never play again outside of Shangri-La.'—*Les Keyser, Hollywood in the Seventies*

'Only Ross Hunter would remake a 1937 movie into a 1932 one.'—*Judith Crist*

'It can't even be enjoyed as camp.'—*Newsweek*

'The narrative has no energy, and the pauses for the pedagogic songs are so awkward that you feel the director's wheelchair needs oiling.'—*Pauline Kael*

Lost in a Harem**
US 1944 89m bw
MGM (George Haight)

Two travelling entertainers in the Middle East get mixed up with a conniving sultan, who hypnotizes them.
Lively, well-staged romp which shows the comedians at their best and uses astute borrowings from burlesque, pantomime, and Hollywood traditions of fantasy and running jokes.

w Harry Ruskin, John Grant, Harry Crane d Charles Reisner ph Lester White *m* David Snell

Bud Abbott, Lou Costello, Douglass Dumbrille, Marilyn Maxwell, John Conte, Jimmy Dorsey and his Orchestra

Lost in Alaska: see Abbott and Costello Lost in Alaska

The Lost Jungle
US 1934 bw serial: 12 eps

An animal trainer rescues his girlfriend's father from the jungle. Slightly anaemic serial adventures. Clyde Beatty, Cecilia Parker, Syd Saylor, Mickey Rooney. Directed by Armand Schaefer and David Howard; for Mascot.

A Lost Lady
US 1934 71m bw

A girl falls in love with a much older man. Empty-headed and over-familiar romantic melodrama. Barbara Stanwyck, Frank Morgan, Ricardo Cortez, Lyle Talbot, Philip Reed, Hobart Cavanaugh, Henry Kolker. Written by Gene Markey, Kathryn Scola, from the novel by Willa Cather; directed by Alfred E. Green; for Warners. 'Lightweight in story and interesting only as a femme style display.'—*Variety*

'He crowded a lifetime into 37 suspenseful hours!'

The Lost Man
US 1969 113m Technicolor Panavision
Universal (Ernest B. Wehmeyer)

After a robbery, a crook is pursued by the police and goes into hiding.
Odd Man Out made over as a vehicle for polemics about civil rights for blacks: too shiny, too long, too talky to have any grip.

wd Robert Alan Aurthur *ph* Jerry Finnerman *m* Quincy Jones

Sidney Poitier, Joanna Shimkus, Al Freeman Jnr, Michael Tolan, Leon Bibb, Richard Dysart, David Steinberg, Paul Winfield

'In a strange house of hate—they loved where love had never dared to live before!'

The Lost Moment*
US 1947 89m bw
Universal / Walter Wanger (Martin Gabel)

An American publisher goes to Venice to recover love letters written by a famous poet to a lady now aged 105.
Slightly absurd but memorable period drama with a guilty secret eventually coming to light, all put across with apparently deliberate artificiality.

w Leonardo Bercovici, *novel* The Aspern Papers by Henry James *d* Martin Gabel *ph Hal Mohr m* Daniele Amfitheatrof

Robert Cummings, Susan Hayward, *Agnes Moorehead,* Joan Lorring, Eduardo Ciannelli

'A compelling piece, highly stylized and very personal, with a beautifully photographed studio recreation of Venice.'—*NFT, 1973*

'Boiling passions in the burning sands!'

The Lost Patrol*
US 1934 74m bw
RKO (Cliff Reid)

A small British army group is lost in the Mesopotamian desert under Arab attack.
Much-copied adventure story of a small patrol under attack (compare *Sahara, Bataan* and *The Last of the Comanches* for a start). The original now seems pretty starchy but retains moments of power.

w Dudley Nichols, story Patrol by Philip MacDonald *d John Ford ph Harold Wenstrom m* Max Steiner

Victor McLaglen, Boris Karloff, Wallace Ford, Reginald Denny, J. M. Kerrigan, Billy Bevan, Alan Hale

'Although the running time is long, there's nothing draggy about it.'—*Variety*

† A silent British version was released in 1929, written and directed by Walter Summers for British Instructional, with Cyril McLaglen, Sam Wilkinson and Terence Collier.

AAN: Max Steiner

The Lost People
GB 1949 89m bw
GFD / Gainsborough (Gordon Wellesley)

Displaced persons gather for comfort in a disused German theatre.

THE LOST WEEKEND. The intensity of Ray Milland's oscar-winning performance comes across even in a publicity photograph.

Once again a very flat film has been unsuitably made from an effective piece of theatre, with all possible types present and all views represented. Not on.

w Bridget Boland, from her play Cockpit *d* Bernard Knowles *ph* Jack Asher *m* John Greenwood

Richard Attenborough, Mai Zetterling, Siobhan McKenna, Dennis Price, Maxwell Reed, William Hartnell, Gerard Heinz, Harcourt Williams, Marcel Poncin

The Lost Planet
US 1953 bw serial: 15 eps

Reporters are captured by aliens and taken to the planet Ergro. Plenty going on in this silly serial fantasy, but it could have been more effective if played for laughs. Judd Holdren, Vivian Mason, Ted Thorpe, Forrest Taylor, Gene Roth, I. Stanford Jolley. Directed by Spencer Bennet; for Columbia.

The Lost Special
US 1932 bw serial: 12 eps

A train filled with gold disappears. Amiable serial remotely based on a Conan Doyle story. Frank Albertson, Cecilia Parker, Francis Ford, Ernie Nevers. Directed by Henry McRae; for Universal.

'Shot at only by cameras—yet falling in flames!'

The Lost Squadron*
US 1932 79m bw
RKO (David O. Selznick)

World War I pilots find work stunting for a movie studio.
Unusual comedy-drama with several points of interest.

w Herman J. Mankiewicz, Wallace Smith *d* George Archainbaud *ph* Leo Tover, Edward Cronjager *m* Max Steiner

Richard Dix, Mary Astor, Erich Von Stroheim, Joel McCrea, Dorothy Jordan, Hugh Herbert, Robert Armstrong

'A pretty good show . . . whether it will get back what it cost is something else again.'—*Variety*

'From the best-seller that was talked about in whispers!'
'The picture that dares to bare a man's soul!'

The Lost Weekend****
US 1945 101m bw
Paramount *(Charles Brackett)*

Two days in the life of a young dipsomaniac writer.
Startlingly original on its release, this stark little drama keeps its power, especially in the scenes on New York streets and in a dipso ward. It could scarcely have been more effectively filmed.

w Charles Brackett, Billy Wilder, novel Charles Jackson *d Billy Wilder ph John F. Seitz m* Miklos Rozsa

Ray Milland, Jane Wyman, Philip Terry, *Howard da Silva, Frank Faylen*

DON BIRNAM (Ray Milland): 'It shrinks my liver, doesn't it, Nat? It pickles my kidneys, yeah. But what does it do to my mind? It tosses the sandbags overboard so the balloon can soar. Suddenly I'm above the ordinary. I'm competent, supremely competent. I'm walking a tightrope over Niagara Falls. I'm one of the great ones. I'm Michelangelo, moulding the beard of Moses. I'm Van Gogh, painting pure sunlight. I'm Horowitz, playing the Emperor Concerto. I'm John Barrymore before the movies got him by the throat. I'm Jesse James and his two brothers—all three of 'em. I'm W. Shakespeare. And out there it's not Third Avenue any longer—it's the Nile, Nat, the Nile—and down it moves the barge of Cleopatra.'

'A reminder of what celluloid is capable of achieving when used by a good director.'—*Spectator*

'I undershtand that liquor interesh; innerish; intereshtsh are rather worried about thish film. Thatsh tough.'—*James Agee*

'Most to be admired are its impressions of bare dreadful truth: the real crowds in the real streets as the hero-victim lugs his typewriter to the pawnshop, the trains screaming overhead, the awful night as he makes his escape from the alcoholics' ward.'—*Dilys Powell*

'A distinguished film, rich in cinematic ingenuity.'—*The Times*

AA: best picture; script; Billy Wilder (as director); Ray Milland
AAN: John F. Seitz; Miklos Rozsa

'In the middle of the twentieth century you fall off the brink of time!'

The Lost World
US 1960 98m De Luxe Cinemascope
TCF / Saratoga (Irwin Allen)

Professor Challenger is financed by a newspaper to confirm the report of prehistoric life on a South African plateau.
Pitiful attempt to continue the success of *Journey to the Center of the Earth*, with the story idiotically modernized, unconvincing monsters, a script which inserts conventional romance and villainy, and fatal miscasting of the central part.

w Irwin Allen, Charles Bennett, *novel* Sir Arthur Conan Doyle *d* Irwin Allen *ph* Winton C. Hoch *m* Bert Shefter, Paul Sawtell

Claude Rains, *Michael Rennie*, David Hedison, *Richard Haydn*, Fernando Lamas, Jill St John, Ray Stricklyn

'Resembles nothing so much as a ride on a rundown fairground Ghost Train.'—*MFB*

† There had been a silent version in 1924, with Wallace Beery as Challenger and primitive models by Willis O'Brien.

The Lottery Bride
US 1930 85m bw

A girl goes on the run when she finds herself first prize in a lottery. Dismal operetta from the period when silent techniques were still giving way to sound. Jeanette MacDonald, Joe E. Brown, John Garrick, Zasu Pitts. Written by Horace Jackson, Howard Emmett Rogers, from a story by Herbert Stothart; directed by Paul Stein; for Arthur Hammerstein / United Artists. 'One of the worst of the really very bad features released since sound.'—*Variety*

Lottery Lover
US 1935 80m bw

A shy sailor wins a lottery prize, an introduction to a Folies Bergère star, but falls in love with the public relations girl organizing the stunt. Faded romantic comedy of little surviving interest. Lew Ayres, Reginald Denny, Pat Paterson, Sterling Holloway. Written by Sig Herzic; directed by William Thiele; for Fox.

Louisa*
US 1950 90m bw

A much-married man finds that both his daughter and his mother have boy friend trouble. Friendly generation gap comedy with practised talent. Ronald Reagan, Spring Byington, Charles Coburn, Ruth Hussey, Edmund Gwenn, Piper Laurie, Scotty Beckett. Written by Stanley Roberts; directed by Alexander Hall; for Universal-International.

Louise
France 1939 99m bw

A seamstress is rescued from a life of shame. Ill-advised venture into film opera for an American star. Grace Moore, Georges Thill, André Pernet. Written by Steve Passeur from the opera by Gustave Charpentier; directed by Abel Gance; for European Film Distributors. 'Tedious and unconvincing.'—*Variety*

Louisiana
US 1947 82m bw

A poor singing farmer becomes governor. Musical biopic of only historical interest. Jimmie Davis, Margaret Lindsay, John Gallaudet, Freddie Stewart. Written by Jack de Witt; directed by Phil Karlson; for Lindsley Parsons / Monogram.

Louisiana Purchase*
US 1941 98m Technicolor
Paramount (Harold Wilson)

Efforts are made to compromise a politician. Quite lively transcription of a Broadway musical success with elements of political satire including a climactic filibuster scene.

w Jerome Chodorov, Joseph Fields, *play* Morrie Ryskind *songs* Irving Berlin *d* Irving Cummings *ph* Harry Hallenberger, Ray Rennahan

Bob Hope, Vera Zorina, *Victor Moore*, Irene Bordoni, Dona Drake, Raymond Walburn, Maxie Rosenbloom, Frank Albertson, Donald MacBride, Andrew Tombes

AAN: Harry Hallenberger, Ray Rennahan

Louisiana Story*
US 1948 77m bw
Standard Oil Company (Robert Flaherty)

In the Louisiana bayous a young native boy watches as oil drillers make a strike.
Quite beautiful but over-extended semi-documentary.

w Robert and Frances Flaherty *d* Robert Flaherty *ph* Richard Leacock *m* Virgil Thompson

Joseph Boudreaux, Lionel Leblanc, Frank Hardy

AAN: original story

Loulou
France 1980 105m Eastmancolor
Gaumont / Action Films

A smart young business woman sets up an uneasy menage with a working-class layabout. Curious but not particularly interesting character study, watchable mainly for its detail.

w Arlette Langmann *d* Maurice Pialat *ph* Pierre-William Glenn, Jacques Loiseleux *md* Philippe Sarde

Isabelle Huppert, Gérard Depardieu, Guy Marchand, Humbert Balsan

'Caught in the swirl of passions and sacrifice!'
Love*
US 1927 82m (24 fps) bw silent
MGM (Edmund Goulding)

Anna Karenina leaves her husband and child for Count Vronsky.
Marginally interesting first shot at a famous subject by a star who came back to it in 1935.

w Frances Marion, Lorna Moon, *novel* Leo Tolstoy *d* Edmund Goulding *ph* William Daniels *m* Ernst Luz *ad* Cedric Gibbons, Alexander Toluboff

Greta Garbo, John Gilbert, Brandon Hurst, Philippe de Lacy, George Fawcett, Emily Fitzroy

† An alternative happy ending was provided for exhibitors who wanted it.

Love Affair
US 1932 68m bw
Columbia

An heiress falls for a flying instructor. Mild romantic comedy drama.

w Jo Swerling, *story* Ursula Parrott *d* Thornton Freeland *ph* Ted Tetzlaff

Dorothy Mackaill, Humphrey Bogart, Jack Kennedy, Astrid Allwyn, Halliwell Hobbes, Barbara Leonard

'A neighbourhood operation, that's about its worth.'—*Variety*

Love Affair***
US 1939 89m bw
RKO (Leo McCarey)

On a transatlantic crossing, a European man of the world meets a New York girl, but their romance is flawed by misunderstanding and physical accident.
The essence of Hollywood romance, and one of the most fondly remembered films of the thirties, perhaps because of the easy comedy sense of the first half.

w Delmer Daves, Donald Ogden Stewart, story Mildred Cram, Leo McCarey *d Leo McCarey ph* Rudolph Maté *m* Roy Webb

Charles Boyer, Irene Dunne, Maria Ouspenskaya, Lee Bowman, Astrid Allwyn, Maurice Moscovitch

'Production is of grade A quality . . . its b.o. chances look good.'—*Variety*

'Those excited over the mastery of form already achieved in pictures, will like to follow this demonstration of the qualities of technique and imagination the films must always have and keep on recruiting to their service . . . Clichés of situation and attitude are lifted almost beyond recognition by a morning freshness of eye for each small thing around.'—*Otis Ferguson*

'McCarey brought off one of the most difficult things you can attempt with film. He created a mood, rather than a story; he kept it alive by expert interpolations; he provided comedy when he needed comedy and poignancy when he needed substance; and he did it with the minimum of effort.'—*Pare Lorentz*

† Remade as *An Affair to Remember* (qv).

AAN: best picture; original story; Irene Dunne; Maria Ouspenskaya; song 'Wishing' (*m / ly* Buddy de Sylva)

Love among the Millionaires
US 1930 70m bw

A waitress falls for the son of a railroad president. Ho-hum star vehicle without much get-up-and-go. Clara Bow, Stanley Smith, Mitzi Green, Skeets Gallagher, Stuart Erwin. Written by Grover Jones, William Conselman, Joseph L. Mankiewicz; directed by Frank Tuttle; for Paramount. 'It will call for a lot of faith from the Clara Bow admirers to accept her in this kind of a part, the sweet wishy-washy thing, after the bum publicity she's been getting.'—*Variety*

Love and Bullets
US 1978 103m Metrocolor
ITC (Pancho Kohner)

A gangster's mistress is brought back from Switzerland by a revengeful Phoenix cop. Downbeat bang-bang with a high death rate and a glum finale; generally low-grade stuff.

w Wendell Mayes, John Melson *d* Stuart Rosenberg *ph* Fred Koenekamp *m* Lalo Schifrin *pd* John de Cuir

Charles Bronson, Jill Ireland, Rod Steiger, Henry Silva, Strother Martin, Bradford Dillman, Michael V. Gazzo

'A relatively dismaying example of the Lew Grade entertainment formula: as locations, production values and clichéd set-pieces proliferate, scripts increasingly look like shaggy dog stories desperately in search of a point, and actors are left to do their own thing as characters disintegrate.'—*Richard Combs, MFB*

'Love and bullets my eye: embarrassment and tedium would be more like it.'—*Time Out*

Love and Death*
US 1975 85m De Luxe
UA / Jack Rollins, Charles H. Joffe

In 1812 Russia, a man condemned reviews the follies of his life.
Personalized comedy fantasia inspired by *War and Peace*, Ingmar Bergman and S. J. Perelman. Basically only for star fans.

wd Woody Allen *ph* Ghislain Cloquet
m Prokofiev

Woody Allen, Diane Keaton, Georges Adel, Despo, Frank Adu

'I have a feeling that one of these days Allen will get it most dreadfully together and make a film which is more than a string of funny one-liners and set-pieces. He hasn't quite done it here.'—*Benny Green, Punch*

Love and Hisses*
US 1937 84m bw
TCF (Kenneth MacGowan)

A gossip columnist and a bandleader continue their feud.
Moderate sequel to *Wake Up and Live* (qv); it got by.

w Art Arthur, Curtis Kenyon *d* Sidney Lanfield *ph* Robert Planck *m* Louis Silvers

Walter Winchell, Ben Bernie and his orchestra, Joan Davis, Bert Lahr, Simone Simon, Ruth Terry

Love and Learn
US 1947 83m bw

Two impoverished songwriters are secretly helped by a rich girl. Tame comedy with few laughs. Jack Carson, Robert Hutton, Martha Vickers, Janis Paige, Otto Kruger. Written by Eugene Conrad, Francis Swann and I. A. L. Diamond; directed by Frederick de Cordova; for Warner.

Love and Money
US 1980 95m Metrocolor

A banker kidnaps a financier's wife, and finds himself in dead trouble. Incoherent light melodrama which barely got released. Ray Sharkey, Ornella Muti, Klaus Kinski, Armand Assante, King Vidor (as the hero's senile grandfather), William Prince. Written and directed by James Toback; for Lorimar.

Love and Pain and the Whole Damn Thing
US 1972 113m Eastmancolor
Columbia / Gus (Alan J. Pakula)

An asthmatic young American on holiday in Spain has an affair with an older woman suffering from an incurable disease.
Dreary doomed romance studiously treated as tourist comedy.

w Alvin Sargent *d* Alan J. Pakula
ph Geoffrey Unsworth *m* Michael Small

Maggie Smith, Timothy Bottoms

Love at First Bite*
US 1979 96m colour
Simon (Joel Freeman)

Count Dracula flees from the communists and settles in New York.
Energetic spoof, with jokes on the sexy side; good work all round.

w Robert Kaufman *d* Stan Dragoti
ph Edward Rosson *m* Charles Bernstein
pd Serge Krizman

George Hamilton, Susan St James, Richard Benjamin, Dick Shawn, Arte Johnson

Love Before Breakfast
US 1936 90m bw

Two Park Avenue beaux vie for a socialite. Thinly plotted but quite amusing romantic comedy. Carole Lombard, Preston Foster, Cesar Romero, Janet Beecher, Bert Roach. Written by Herbert Fields, from the novel *Spinster Dinner* by Faith Baldwin; directed by Walter Lang; for Universal.

The Love Bug**
US 1968 107m Technicolor
Walt Disney (Bill Walsh)

An unsuccessful racing driver finds that his small private Volkswagen has a mind of its own.
Amusing, pacy period fantasy in the best Disney style.

w Bill Walsh, Don da Gradi *d Robert Stevenson* *ph* Edward Colman *m* George Bruns *sp Eustace Lycett*

David Tomlinson, Dean Jones, Michele Lee, Buddy Hackett, Joe Flynn, Benson Fong, Joe E. Ross

Love Crazy*
US 1941 100m bw
MGM (Pandro S. Berman)

When his wife threatens to divorce him, a businessman hatches all manner of crazy schemes, including disguising himself as his own sister.
Zany romantic comedy, over-stretched but with a fair share of hilarity.

w William Ludwig, Charles Lederer, David Hertz *d* Jack Cummings *ph* Ray June
m David Snell

William Powell, Myrna Loy, Gail Patrick, Jack Carson, Florence Bates, Sidney Blackmer, Vladimir Sokoloff, Donald MacBride, Sig Rumann, Sara Haden, Elisha Cook Jnr, Kathleen Lockhart

Love Eternal*
France 1943 111m bw
André Paulvé
original title: *L'Eternel Retour*

The love story of Tristan and Isolde.
This modernized version had a Teutonic look and was respected rather than admired.

w Jean Cocteau *d* Jean Delannoy *ph* Roger Hubert *m* Georges Auric *ad* Wakhevitch

Jean Marais, Madeleine Sologne, Jean Murat, Yvonne de Bray

Love from a Stranger*
GB 1936 90m bw
Trafalgar (Max Schach)

A young woman realizes she may have married a maniac.
Stalwart suspenser from a popular novel and play.

w Frances Marion, *play* Frank Vosper, *story* Philomel Cottage by Agatha Christie
d Rowland V. Lee *ph* Philip Tannura
m Benjamin Britten

Ann Harding, Basil Rathbone, Binnie Hale, Bruce Seton, Jean Cadell, Bryan Powley, Joan Hickson, Donald Calthrop

'Gorgeously photographed and splendidly cut . . . takes front rank with the long list of gruesome films produced in recent years.'—*Variety*

Love from a Stranger
US 1947 81m bw
Eagle Lion (James J. Geller)
GB title: *A Stranger Walked In*

Stilted period remake.

w Philip MacDonald *d* Richard Whorf
ph Tony Gaudio *m* Hans Salter

Sylvia Sidney, John Hodiak, Ann Richards, John Howard, Isobel Elsom, Frederick Worlock

The Love God?
US 1969 103m Techniscope
Universal (Edward J. Montagne)

A meek ornithologist is thought to be the brains behind a girlie magazine, and becomes a national sex symbol.
Dispiriting and very talkative star farce which would have been long at half the time.

wd Nat Hiken *ph* William Marguilies *m* Vic Mizzy

Don Knotts, Edmond O'Brien, Anne Francis, James Gregory, Maureen Arthur.

'Strictly for admirers of Don Knotts. Can there really be many?'—*MFB*

The Love Goddesses**
US 1965 87m bw
Paramount / Walter Reade / Sterling

A light-hearted account of female sexuality on the Hollywood screen.
Sharp-eyed compilation film which is worth a dozen books on the subject.

pd Saul J. Turell, Graeme Ferguson *m* Percy Faith *narrator* Carl King

'A compilation of shrapnel from old sex-bomb movies, full of deliciously improbable moments.'—*Newsweek*

† Clips include *Blonde Venus, Morocco, True Heart Susie, Cleopatra* (1934), *Intolerance, The Cheat, The Sheik, Blood and Sand, The Sorrows of Satan, The Loves of Sunya, Diary of a Lost Girl, Ecstasy, L'Atlantide, Peter the Tramp, Cabin in the Cotton, Platinum Blonde, Gold Diggers of 1933, No Man of Her Own, Professional Sweetheart, Love Me Tonight, I'm No Angel, Baby Face, They Won't Forget, College Swing, Her Jungle Love, Gilda, A Place in the Sun, Some Like it Hot.*

Love Happy*
US 1949 85m bw
Lester Cowan / Mary Pickford

A group of impoverished actors accidentally gets possession of the Romanov diamonds. The last dismaying Marx Brothers film, with Harpo taking the limelight and Groucho loping in for a couple of brief, tired appearances. A roof chase works, but Harpo tries too hard for sentiment, and the production looks shoddy.

w Ben Hecht, Frank Tashlin, Mac Benoff *d* David Miller *ph* William Mellor *m* Ann Ronell

Groucho, Harpo, Chico, Eric Blore, Ilona Massey, Marilyn Monroe, Vera-Ellen

Love Has Many Faces
US 1964 104m Eastmancolor
Columbia / Jerry Bresler

A rich woman marries a beach boy and has an affair with another, who is murdered.
Hilarious but unentertaining sex melodrama built around an overage star.

w Marguerite Roberts *d* Alexander Singer *ph* Joseph Ruttenberg *m* David Raksin

Lana Turner, Cliff Robertson, Hugh O'Brian, Stefanie Powers, Ruth Roman, Virginia Grey
'For connoisseurs of perfectly awful movies.'—*Judith Crist*

Love in a Goldfish Bowl
US 1961 88m Technicolor Panavision

On holiday in Honolulu, two teenagers get into mischief. Tiresome youth-oriented family comedy with pleasant backgrounds. Tommy Sands, Fabian, Jan Sterling, Toby Michaels, Edward Andrews, John McGiver. Written and directed by Jack Sher; for Paramount / Jurow-Shepherd.

Love in Bloom
US 1935 76m bw

A carnival owner's daughter marries a songwriter. Lame little romance broken up by crosstalk from Burns and Allen; an ill-considered entertainment. George Burns, Gracie Allen, Dixie Lee, Joe Morrison. Written by J. P. McEvoy, Keene Thompson; directed by Elliott Nugent; for Paramount. 'Radio pair may save their latest celluloid effort, but it won't help their future on the screen.'—*Variety*

Love in Exile
GB 1936 78m bw

A Ruritanian king is induced to abdicate but fights back. Airy comedy with little general appeal. Clive Brook, Helen Vinson, Mary Carlisle, Will Fyffe, Ronald Squire, Tamara Desni, Henry Oscar. Written by Herman Mankiewicz, Roger Burford and Ernest Betts, from the novel *His Majesty's Pajamas* by Gene Markey; directed by Alfred L. Werker; for Capitol.

Love in the Afternoon
US 1957 126m bw
AA (Billy Wilder)

The daughter of a private detective warns an American philanderer in Paris that an enraged husband is en route to shoot him.
Tired and dreary romantic sex comedy, miscast and far too long. With the talent around, there are of course a few compensations.

w Billy Wilder, I. A. L. Diamond, *novel* Claude Arianet *d* Billy Wilder *ph* William Mellor *m* Franz Waxman *ad* Alexander Trauner

Gary Cooper, Audrey Hepburn, Maurice Chevalier, John McGiver

Love Is a Ball
US 1962 112m Technicolor Panavision
UA / Oxford / Gold Medal (Martin H. Poll)
GB title: *All This and Money Too*

A Riviera matchmaker recruits instructors to train his star pupil, but one of them walks away with the lady.
Forgettable comedy in which more effort goes into the glamorous background than the script.

w David Swift, Tom and Frank Waldman, *novel* The Grand Duke and Mr Pimm by Lindsay Hardy *d* David Swift *ph* Edmond Séchan *m* Michel Legrand

Glenn Ford, Charles Boyer, Hope Lange, Ricardo Montalban, Telly Savalas, Ruth McDevitt, Ulla Jacobsson

Love is a Headache
US 1938 73m bw

An actress on hard times gets a break through freak publicity. Wholly artificial comedy, hammed up to little avail. Franchot Tone, Gladys George, Mickey Rooney, Ralph Morgan, Jessie Ralph, Ted Healy, Barnett Parker, Frank Jenks, Virginia Weidler, Fay Holden. Written by Marion Parsonnet, Harry Ruskin, William Lipman, Lou Heifetz, Herbert Klein; directed by Richard Thorpe; for MGM. 'Dialogue is pungent, but fails to cover up slap-happy situations.'—*Variety*

'A love that defied five thousand years of tradition!'
Love Is a Many Splendored Thing*
US 1955 102m De Luxe Cinemascope
TCF (Buddy Adler)

During the Korean War, a Eurasian lady doctor in Hong Kong falls in love with a war correspondent.
Self-admittedly sentimental soaper with a tragic ending; the theme tune kept it popular for years.

w John Patrick, *novel* Han Suyin *d* Henry King *ph* Leon Shamroy *m* Alfred Newman

Jennifer Jones, William Holden, Torin Thatcher, Isobel Elsom, Murray Matheson, Virginia Gregg, Richard Loo

AA: Alfred Newman; title song (*m* Sammy Fain, *ly* Paul Francis Webster)
AAN: best picture; Leon Shamroy; Jennifer Jones

Love Is a Racket
US 1932 72m bw

A newspaperman covers up for a girl suspected of murder, but she lets him down. Jaundiced comedy-drama of Broadway night life; quite effective. Douglas Fairbanks Jnr, Frances Dee, Ann Dvorak, Lee Tracy, Lyle Talbot, Warren Hymer. Written by Courtney Terrett; directed by William Wellman; for Warner.
(GB title: *Such Things Happen*)

Love Is Better Than Ever
US 1951 81m bw
MGM (William H. Wright)
GB title: *The Light Fantastic*

A small-town girl falls for a New York theatrical agent.
Only moderate production values are brought to bear on this wispy plot which shows no signs of development.

w Ruth Brooks Flippen *d* Stanley Donen *ph* Harold Rosson *md* Lennie Hayton

Larry Parks, Elizabeth Taylor, Josephine Hutchinson, Tom Tully, Ann Doran

Love Is News*
US 1937 78m bw
TCF (Earl Carroll, Harold Wilson)

An heiress marries a scoop-hunting reporter just to show him how embarrassing publicity can be.
Silly romantic comedy with plenty of laughs.

w Harry Tugend, Jack Yellen *d* Tay Garnett *ph* Ernest Palmer

Tyrone Power, Loretta Young, Don Ameche, Slim Summerville, Dudley Digges, Walter Catlett, Jane Darwell, Stepin Fetchit, George Sanders, Frank Conroy, Elisha Cook Jnr
'Fast-moving comedy and good star names. Surefire.'—*Variety*

† Remade as *Sweet Rosie O'Grady* and *That Wonderful Urge*.

'Blood on her hands . . . love in her heart!'
Love Letters*
US 1945 101m bw
Paramount (Hal B. Wallis)

A girl who has lost her memory through war shock is threatened by more physical danger.
Oddly unexciting romantic melodrama directed and designed in heavy but satisfying style. Typical post-war depressive fare.

w Ayn Rand, *novel* Pity My Simplicity by Chris Massie *d William Dieterle* *ph* Lee Garmes *m Victor Young* *ad* Hans Dreier, Roland Anderson

Jennifer Jones, Joseph Cotten, Ann Richards, Gladys Cooper, Anita Louise, Cecil Kellaway, Robert Sully, Byron Barr, Reginald Denny, Lumsden Hare

AAN: Jennifer Jones; title song (*m* Victor Young, *ly* Edward Heyman); Victor Young

Love Letters*
US 1983 89m De Luxe

Affected by her mother's old letters revealing an unconsummated love, a twenty-two-year-old girl begins an affair with an older man. Low-budget drama which might have worked better as a television play; but it has its memorable aspects. Jamie Lee Curtis, James Keach, Matt Clark, Bonnie Bartlett, Bud Cort, Amy Madigan. Written and directed by *Amy Jones*; for Roger Corman / Milennium.

Love Letters of a Star
US 1936 66m bw

A blackmailed rich girl takes poison.
Complicated but efficient murder mystery. Henry Hunter, Polly Rowles, C. Henry Gordon, Walter Coy, Hobart Cavanaugh, Mary Alice Rice. Written by Lewis R. Foster, Milton Carruth, James Mulhauser, from the novel The Case of the Constant God by Rufus King; directed by Lewis R. Foster and Milton Carruth; for Universal. 'Good family entertainment . . . ought to do all right.'—*Variety*

Love, Life and Laughter*
GB 1934 83m bw
ATP (Basil Dean)

A film actress catches the eye of a Ruritanian prince.
Lively star vehicle ranging from sentiment to slapstick.

w Robert Edmunds *d* Maurice Elvey

Gracie Fields, John Loder, Norah Howard, Allan Aynesworth, Esme Percy, Robb Wilton, Fred Duprez, Horace Kenney, Veronica Brady

The Love Lottery
GB 1953 83m Technicolor
Ealing (Monja Danischewsky)

A British film star is persuaded to offer himself as first prize in a lottery.
Satirical farce which doesn't come off, mainly owing to paucity of comedy ideas.

w Harry Kurnitz *d* Charles Crichton *ph* Douglas Slocombe *m* Benjamin Frankel *pd* Tom Morahan

David Niven, Herbert Lom, Peggy Cummins, Anne Vernon, Charles Victor, Gordon Jackson, Felix Aylmer, Hugh McDermott

The Love Machine
US 1971 110m Eastmancolor
Columbia / Mike Frankovich

Megalomaniac TV reporter progresses to network programme controller but is finally undone by his vivid sex life.
Stodgy, silly melodrama from a bestseller whose inspiration was well known in TV circles.

w Samuel Taylor, *novel* Jacqueline Susann *d* Jack Haley Jnr *ph* Charles Lang Jnr *m* Artie Butler

John Philip Law, Dyan Cannon, Robert Ryan, Jackie Cooper, David Hemmings, Shecky Greene

Love Me Forever
US 1935 92m bw
Columbia
GB title: *On Wings of Song*

A down and out singer makes good.
Fair star vehicle.

w Jo Swerling, Sidney Buchman *d* Victor Schertzinger *ph* Joe Walker *md* Louis Silvers

Grace Moore, Leo Carillo, Robert Allen, Spring Byington, Michael Bartlett, Thurston Hall, Douglas Dumbrille, Luis Alberni

'Gangsters and grand opera are tough to mix, but . . . should be all right in major towns.'—*Variety*

Love Me or Leave Me**
US 1955 122m Eastmancolor Cinemascope
MGM (Joe Pasternak)

Twenties singer Ruth Etting is befriended by a racketeer who pushes her to the top but drives her to drink and despair in the process.
Agreeably bitter showbiz biopic which gives the impression of being not too far from the truth.

w Daniel Fuchs, Isabel Lennart *d Charles Vidor* *ph* Arthur E. Arling *md* George Stoll *ad* Cedric Gibbons, Urie McCleary

Doris Day, James Cagney, Cameron Mitchell, Robert Keith, Tom Tully, Harry Bellaver, Richard Gaines

AA: original story (Daniel Fuchs)
AAN: script; George Stoll; James Cagney; song 'I'll Never Stop Loving You' (*m* Nicholas Brodszky, *ly* Sammy Cahn)

Love Me Tender
US 1956 95m bw Cinemascope
TCF (David Weisbart)

Three brothers fall out over loot they have brought home from the Civil War.
Odd western designed (perhaps after shooting began) as Presley's introductory vehicle; he sings four songs before getting shot, and reappears in ghostly form at the end.

w Robert Buckner *d* Robert D. Webb *ph* Leo Tover *m* Lionel Newman

Richard Egan, Debra Paget, Elvis Presley, Robert Middleton, William Campbell, Neville Brand, Mildred Dunnock, Bruce Bennett, James Drury, Ken Clark, Barry Coe

Love Me Tonight****
US 1932 104m bw
Paramount (Rouben Mamoulian)

A Parisian tailor accidentally moves into the aristocracy.
The most fluently cinematic comedy musical ever made, with sounds and words, lyrics and music, deftly blended into a compulsively and consistently laughable mosaic of sophisticated nonsense; one better than the best of Lubitsch and Clair.

w Samuel Hoffenstein, Waldemar Young, George Marion Jnr, *play* Tailor in the Château by Leopold Marchand and Paul Armont *d Rouben Mamoulian* *ph Victor Milner* *songs Rodgers and Hart*

Maurice Chevalier, Jeanette MacDonald, Charles Butterworth, Charles Ruggles, Myrna Loy, C. Aubrey Smith, Elizabeth Patterson, Ethel Griffies, Blanche Frederici, Robert Greig

'A musical frolic, whimsical in its aim and delicately carried out in its pattern.'—*Variety*

'Gay, charming, witty, it is everything that the Lubitsch musicals should have been but never were.'—*John Baxter, 1968*

'With the aid of a pleasant story, a good musician, a talented cast and about a million dollars, he has done what someone in Hollywood should have done long ago—he has illustrated a musical score.'—*Pare Lorentz*

'It has that infectious spontaneity which distinguishes the American musical at its best.'—*Peter Cowie, 1970*

'A rich amalgam of filmic invention, witty decoration and wonderful songs.'—*NFT, 1974*

'What a picture! First you have Chevalier, and last you have Chevalier!'—*Photoplay*

The Love Nest
US 1923 22m (24 fps) bw silent

Buster dreams of a solitary voyage in a small boat. Long lost but ultimately disappointing Keaton short. Buster Keaton, Joe Roberts, Virginia Fox. Written and directed by Buster Keaton and Eddie Cline; for Buster Keaton Productions.

Love Nest
US 1951 84m bw

A writer and his wife invest in an apartment building but find their tenants time-consuming. Fairly lively comedy with varied talent. William Lundigan, June Haver, Frank Fay, Marilyn Monroe, Jack Paar, Leatrice Joy. Written by I. A. L. Diamond, from a novel by Scott Corbett; directed by Joseph Newman; for TCF.

The Love of Jeanne Ney*
Germany 1927 98m (24 fps) bw silent
UFA

In the Crimea during the Russian Revolution, a political observer is accidentally killed by his daughter's lover.
Inconsistently-styled contemporary melodrama. The abiding interest is in the detailed treatment rather than the story or acting.

w Ladislas Vajda, Rudolph Leonhardt, Ilya Ehrenberg *d G. W. Pabst* *ph* Fritz Arno Wagner, Walter Robert Lach

Edith Jehane, Uno Henning, Fritz Rasp, Brigitte Helm

The Love of Sunya
US 1927 80m (24 fps) bw silent
Swanson Producing Corporation

A yogi recognizes two young lovers as people he wronged in a previous existence, and warns them of impending disaster.
Star tosh of its period, unthinkable now as a screen attraction.

w Earle Brown, *play* The Eyes of Youth by Max Marcin, Charles Guernon *d* Albert Parker *ph* Dudley Murphy *ad* Hugo Ballin

Gloria Swanson, John Boles, Anders Randolph, Hush Miller, Florbelle Fairbanks, Raymond Hackett

† Previously filmed as *Eyes of Youth* with Clara Kimball Young.

Love on the Dole***
GB 1941 100m bw
British National (John Baxter)

Life among unemployed cotton workers in industrial Lancashire between the wars.
Vividly characterized, old-fashioned social melodrama, well made on a low budget; a rare problem picture for Britain at this time.

w Walter Greenwood, Barbara K. Emery, Rollo Gamble, *novel Walter Greenwood* *d John Baxter* *ph* James Wilson *m* Richard Addinsell

Deborah Kerr, Clifford Evans, *George Carney*, Joyce Howard, Frank Cellier, Geoffrey Hibbert, *Mary Merrall*, Maire O'Neill, *Marjorie Rhodes*, A. Bromley Davenport, Marie Ault, Iris Vandeleur, Kenneth Griffith

'Kissing and kidding their way from Mayfair to the Mediterranean in a transcontinental caravan of jollity!'

Love on the Run*
US 1936 81m bw
MGM (Joseph L. Mankiewicz)

Rival newspapermen help an heiress to escape an unwanted wedding and in the process uncover a ring of spies.
Harebrained star farce, smoothly assembled and still fairly funny.

w John Lee Mahin, Manuel Seff, Gladys Hurlbut *d* W. S. Van Dyke *ph* Oliver T. Marsh *m* Franz Waxman

Clark Gable, Joan Crawford, Franchot Tone, Reginald Owen, Mona Barrie, Ivan Lebedeff, William Demarest

'Should collect its share at the gate through the sheer momentum of the Gable-Crawford combo.'—*Variety*

'A slightly daffy cinematic item of absolutely no importance.'—*New York Times*

Love on the Run*
France 1978 95m Eastmancolor

Antoine Doinel, separated from his family, is still having girl trouble. Amorous adventure of the character first glimpsed in *Les Quatre Cent Coups* and presumably based on the director; fair sophisticated fun for those who appreciate the joke. Jean-Pierre Leaud, Marie-France Pisier, Claude Jade, Rosy Varte. Written by François Truffaut and others; directed by François Truffaut; for Les Films du Carrosse.

Love on Wheels
GB 1932 87m bw

A department store assistant becomes publicity-conscious. Zippy little comedy of its day. Jack Hulbert, Edmund Gwenn, Leonora Corbett, Gordon Harker, Percy Parsons, Roland Culver, Miles Malleson. Written by Victor Saville, Angus Macphail, Robert Stevenson and Douglas Furber; directed by Victor Saville; for Gainsborough.

The Love Parade**
US 1929 112m. bw
Paramount (Ernst Lubitsch)

The prince of Sylvania marries.
Primitive sound operetta set among the idle European rich, with clear but faded instances of the Lubitsch touch.

w Ernest Vajda, Guy Bolton, *play* The Prince Consort by Leon Xanrof and Jules Chancel *d Ernst Lubitsch* *ph* Victor Milner *songs* Victor Schertzinger, Clifford Grey

Maurice Chevalier, Jeanette MacDonald, Lupino Lane, Lillian Roth, Edgar Norton, Lionel Belmore, Eugene Pallette

'The first truly cinematic screen musical in America.'—*Theodore Huff*

AAN: best picture; Ernst Lubitsch; Victor Milner; Maurice Chevalier

Love, Soldiers and Women
France / Italy 1953 96m bw
Franco-London / Continental
original title: *Destinées*; US title: *Daughters of Destiny*

Three stories of women in war: Joan of Arc, Lysistrata, and a modern American war widow visiting her husband's grave.
Uninteresting patchwork with Lysistrata predictably stealing the show.

'Jeanne': *w* Jean Aurenche, Pierre Bost *d* Jean Delannoy *with* Michèle Morgan
'Elizabeth': *w* Sergio Amedei *d* Marcel Pagliero *with* Claudette Colbert, Eleanora Rossi Drago
'Lysistrata': *w* Jean Ferry, Henri Jeanson, Carlo Rim, *play* Aristophanes *d* Christian-Jaque *with* Martine Carol, Raf Vallone, Paolo Stoppa

Love Story
GB 1944 112m bw
GFD / Gainsborough (Harold Huth)
US title: *A Lady Surrenders*

In Cornwall during World War II, a half-blind airman falls for a pianist with a weak heart.
Novelettish love story which became popular because of its Cornish Rhapsody.

w Leslie Arliss, Doreen Montgomery, Rodney Ackland, *novel* J. W. Drawbell *d* Leslie Arliss *ph* Bernard Knowles *m Hubert Bath*

Margaret Lockwood, Stewart Granger, Patricia Roc, Tom Walls, Reginald Purdell, Moira Lister

'A splendid, noble and fatuous piece.'—*C. A. Lejeune*

'In psychology and dialogue this is straight out of *Mabel's Weekly*.'—*Richard Winnington*

Love Story*
US 1970 100m Movielab
Paramount (David Golden)

Two students marry; she dies.
A barrage of ripe old Hollywood clichés spiced with new-fangled bad language. In the circumstances, well enough made, and certainly astonishingly popular.

w Erich Segal, from his novelette *d* Arthur Hiller *ph* Dick Kratina *m* Bach, Mozart, Handel *md* Francis Lai

Ali MacGraw, Ryan O'Neal, Ray Milland, John Marley

'Camille with bullshit.'—*Alexander Walker*

AAN: best picture; Erich Segal; Arthur Hiller; Francis Lai; Ali MacGraw; Ryan O'Neal; John Marley

Love Streams
US 1984 141m Metrocolor

A distraught woman whose marriage has gone sour moves in with her philandering brother. Elongated study of two life styles, not so shapeless as most Cassavetes films, but not exactly dramatic or endearing either. Gene Rowlands, John Cassavetes, Diahnne Abbott, Seymour Cassel, Margaret Abbott. Written by Ted Allan and John Cassavetes, from Allan's play; directed by John Cassavetes; for Cannon.

Love That Brute
US 1950 85m bw
TCF (Fred Kohlmar)

A ruthless Chicago gangleader is actually a softy, leaving his supposedly rubbed-out enemies in a comfortable cellar; a young governess persuades him to reform.
Rickety, dully-scripted gangster farce.

w Darrell Ware, John Lee Mahin, Karl Tunberg *d* Alexander Hall *ph* Lloyd Ahern *m* Cyril Mockridge

Paul Douglas, Jean Peters, Cesar Romero, Joan Davis, Arthur Treacher

Love Thy Neighbour*
US 1940 81m bw

Two radio comics fall out. Curious mixture of fact and fiction, basing its plot on the publicity feud between Benny and Allen, who appear 'in character' as themselves. Jack Benny, Fred Allen, Mary Martin, Eddie Anderson, Verree Teasdale, Virginia Dale, Richard Denning. Written by William Morrow, Edmund Beloin, Ernest Pagano, Z. Myers; directed and produced by Mark Sandrich; for Paramount.

Love Thy Neighbour
GB 1973 85m Technicolor
EMI / Hammer (Roy Skeggs)

A prejudiced white worker has coloured neighbours.
Elongated screen version of the popular TV series in which the West Indians smile through all the insults and come out top in the end. It might have been worse, but not much.

w Vince Powell, Harry Driver *d* John Robins *ph* Moray Grant *m* Albert Elms

Jack Smethurst, Kate Williams, Rudolph Walker, Nina Baden-Semper, Bill Fraser, Charles Hyatt, Keith Marsh, Patricia Hayes, Arthur English

Love Time
US 1934 72m bw

Franz Schubert falls for a duke's daughter. Curious, off-putting costumer with music. Pat Paterson, Nils Asther Herbert Mundin, Harry Green, Henry B. Walthall, Lucien Littlefield. Written by William Conselman, Henry Johnson; directed by James Tinling; for Fox.
'Thin story, and slim chances.'—*Variety*

Love under Fire
US 1937 75m bw
TCF (Nunnally Johnson)

A detective catches up with a lady jewel thief in Madrid during the Spanish Civil War.
Adequately entertaining but rather tasteless adventure comedy.

w Gene Fowler, Allen Rivkin, Ernest Pascal, *play* Walter Hackett *d* George Marshall *ph* Ernest Palmer *m* Arthur Lange

Loretta Young, Don Ameche, Frances Drake, Walter Catlett, John Carradine, Borrah Minevitch and his Rascals, Sig Rumann, Harold Huber, E. E. Clive, Katherine de Mille

'Melodrama with music cooked up for the duals.'—*Variety*

'There is a moment . . . a long moment . . . when everything is risked with the proper stranger!'

Love with the Proper Stranger**
US 1964 100m bw
Paramount / Boardwalk (Alan J. Pakula)

A musician tries to help his pregnant shopgirl friend get an abortion, but they decide to get married instead.
Oddly likeable comedy drama set on New York's Italian East Side, with an excellent location sense.

w Arnold Schulman *d Robert Mulligan* *ph* Milton Krasner *m* Elmer Bernstein

Steve McQueen, Natalie Wood, Tom Bosley, Edie Adams, Herschel Bernardi

AAN: Arnold Schulman; Milton Krasner; Natalie Wood

The Loved One*
US 1965 118m bw
MGM / Filmways (Neil Hartley)

A young English poet in California gets a job at a very select burial ground.
A pointed satire on the American way of death has been allowed to get out of hand, with writer and actors alike laying it on too thick; but there are pleasantly waspish moments in a movie advertised as 'the motion picture with something to offend everybody'.

w Terry Southern, Christopher Isherwood, *novel* Evelyn Waugh *d* Tony Richardson *ph Haskell Wexler* *m* John Addison *pd* Rouben Ter-Arutunian

Robert Morse, John Gielgud, Rod Steiger, *Liberace*, Anjanette Comer, Jonathan Winters, Dana Andrews, Milton Berle, James Coburn, Tab Hunter, Margaret Leighton, Roddy McDowall, Robert Morley, Lionel Stander

'Even a chaotic satire like this is cleansing, and it's embarrassing to pan even a bad movie that comes out against God, mother and country.'—*Pauline Kael, 1968*

'A spineless farrago of collegiate gags.'—*Stanley Kauffmann*

'A sinking ship that makes it to port because everyone on board is too giddy to panic.'—*New Yorker, 1978*

Lovely to Look At*
US 1952 102m Technicolor
MGM (Jack Cummings)

Three Broadway producers inherit a Paris fashion house.
Lavish but dullish remake of *Roberta* (qv), in itself no great shakes as a storyline; again the fashions and the numbers are the thing.

w George Wells, Harry Ruby *d* Mervyn Le Roy *ph* George J. Folsey *m* Jerome Kern *ad* Cedric Gibbons, Gabriel Scognamillo

Howard Keel, Kathryn Grayson, Ann Miller, Red Skelton, Marge and Gower Champion, Zsa Zsa Gabor, Kurt Kasznar

A Lovely Way to Die
US 1968 98m Techniscope
Universal (Richard Lewis)
GB title: *A Lovely Way to Go*

An ex-cop becomes bodyguard to a suspected murderess, but proves her innocent.
Offbeat mélange of caper comedy, black farce, private eye detection, courtroom drama, spectacular action and routine thick ear. Doesn't work.

w A. J. Russell *d* David Lowell Rich *ph* Morris Hartzband *m* Kenyon Hopkins

Kirk Douglas, Sylva Koscina, Eli Wallach, *Martyn Green*, Kenneth Haigh, Sharon Farrell

'The net result is rather as though Philip Marlowe had met Doris Day on his not very inspiring way to the forum.'—*MFB*

Lover Come Back
US 1946 90m bw
Universal (Howard Benedict)

When a war correspondent returns, his wife discovers that he hasn't been so lonely overseas as he might have been.
Very tolerable star comedy which at the time seemed quite fresh.

w Michael Fessier, Ernest Pagano *d* William A. Seiter *ph* Joseph Valentine *m* Hans J. Salter

George Brent, Lucille Ball, Vera Zorina, Charles Winninger, Carl Esmond, Raymond Walburn, Franklin Pangborn, Louise Beavers

'Should chalk up good grosses in most situations.'—*Variety*

Lover Come Back**
US 1961 107m Eastmancolor
U-I / Seven Pictures / Nob Hill / Arwin (Stanley Shapiro, Marty Melcher)

Rival executives find themselves advertising a non-existent product.
Fairly sharp advertising satire disguised as a romantic comedy; the most entertaining of the Day-Hudson charmers.

w Stanley Shapiro, Paul Henning *d* Delbert Mann *ph* Arthur E. Arling *m* Frank de Vol

Doris Day, Rock Hudson, *Tony Randall*, Jack Oakie, Edie Adams

AAN: Stanley Shapiro, Paul Henning

The Lovers
GB 1972 89m Eastmancolor
British Lion / Gildor (Maurice Foster)

A Manchester bank clerk with a prim girl friend finds it difficult to lose his virginity.
Well-written but rather arch comedy which seemed much funnier and fresher as a TV series.

w Jack Rosenthal *d* Herbert Wise *ph* Bob Huke *m* Carl Davis

Richard Beckinsale, Paula Wilcox, Joan Scott, Susan Littler, John Comer, Stella Moray, Nikolas Simmonds

Lovers and Other Strangers***
US 1970 104m Metrocolor
ABC / David Susskind

After living together for eighteen months, Susan and Mike decide to get married, and find their parents have sex problems of their own.
Wise, witty and well acted sex farce, with many actors making the most of ample chances under firm directoral control.

w Renée Taylor, Joseph Bologna, David Zelag Goodman *d Cy Howard* *ph Andrew Laszlo* *m* Fred Karlin

Gig Young, Anne Jackson, Richard Castellano, Bonnie Bedelia, Michael Brandon, *Beatrice Arthur*, Robert Dishy, Harry Guardino, Diane Keaton, Cloris Leachman, Anne Meara, *Marian Hailey*

'An extremely engaging comedy.'—*Gillian Hartnoll*

AA: song 'For All We Know' (*m* Fred Karlin, *ly* Robb Wilson, Arthur James)
AAN: script; Richard Castellano

Lovers Courageous
US 1932 78m bw

An unsuccessful playwright covets the admiral's daughter. Heavily-titled comedy with good performances of the period. Robert Montgomery, Madge Evans, Roland Young, Frederick Kerr, Reginald Owen, Halliwell Hobbes, Alan Mowbray. Written by Frederick Lonsdale; directed by Robert Z. Leonard; for MGM.

The Lovers of Lisbon*
France 1954 112m bw
EGC / Hoche / Fides (Jacques Gauthier)
original title: *Les Amants du Tage*

A man who has killed his unfaithful wife is acquitted of murder, gets a job as a taxi driver in Lisbon, and falls for a rich Englishwoman who has killed her husband and is being pursued by a police inspector.
Pretentious tosh with a few compensations.

w Marcel Rivet, *novel* Joseph Kessel *d* Henri Verneuil *ph* Roger Hubert *m* Lucien Legrand

Daniel Gélin, Françoise Arnoul, Trevor Howard, Ginette Leclerc, Marcel Dalio

The Lovers of Toledo
Italy / France / Spain 1952 82m bw
EGE / Lux / Athenea (Raymond Eger)

In 1825 a cruel police chief releases a political prisoner in return for the hand in marriage of his mistress.
Curiously unpersuasive period melodrama with good credits but too many international cooks.

w Claude Vermorel, *story* Le Coffre et le Revenant by Stendhal *d* Henri Decoin *ph* Michel Kelber *m* Jean-Jacques Grunenwald

Pedro Armendariz, Alida Valli, Gérard Landry, Françoise Arnoul

Loves of a Blonde*
Czechoslovakia 1965 82m bw
Barrandov Studios
original title: *Lasky Jedne Plavovlasky*
aka: *A Blonde in Love*

A factory girl falls for a visiting musician but meets suspicion from his family when she pursues him.

Mild anecdote with excellent humorous detail which endeared it to international critics.

w Milos Forman, Jaroslav Papousek, Ivan Passer *d Milos Forman ph* Miroslav Ondricek *m* Evzen Illin

Hanna Brejchova, Vladimir Pucholt

'It depends on an instinctive sense of timing and a consistent vision of life and people.'—*Georges Sadoul*

AAN: best foreign film

The Loves of Carmen
US 1948 99m Technicolor
Columbia (Charles Vidor)

In 1820s Seville, a dragoon corporal is enslaved by a gypsy, kills her husband and becomes an outlaw.
Unrewarding version of the original much-filmed story, with both stars plainly wishing they were elsewhere.

w Helen Deutsch, *novel* Prosper Mérimée *d* Charles Vidor *ph* William Snyder *m* Mario Castelnuovo-Tedesco

Rita Hayworth, Glenn Ford, Victor Jory, Ron Randell, Luther Adler, Arnold Moss, Margaret Wycherly, Bernard Nedell

AAN: William Snyder

The Loves of Edgar Allan Poe
US 1942 67m bw
TCF (Bryan Foy)

The famous writer marries his childhood sweetheart but becomes an alcoholic.
A curiosity which fails to bring out the bizarre truth and emerges as a stilted charade.

w Samuel Hoffenstein, Tom Reed *d* Harry Lachman *ph* Lucien Andriot *m* Emil Newman

John Shepperd, Linda Darnell, Virginia Gilmore, Jane Darwell, Frank Conroy, Henry Morgan

The Loves of Joanna Godden
GB 1947 89m bw
Ealing (Sidney Cole)

On Romney Marsh at the turn of the century, a woman farmer has three suitors.
Dullish 'woman's picture'.

w H. E. Bates, Angus Macphail, *novel* Sheila Kaye-Smith *d* Charles Frend *ph* Douglas Slocombe *m* Ralph Vaughan Williams

Googie Withers, John McCallum, Jean Kent, Derek Bond, Chips Rafferty, Henry Mollison, Sonia Holm, Edward Rigby, Josephine Stuart
† Robert Hamer directed some scenes.

Lovesick
US 1983 96m Technicolor
Warner / Ladd (Charles Okun)

A New York psychiatrist in love with a patient is guided by the ghost of Sigmund Freud.
Depressing comedy with a non-star and supporting players who must have been embarrassed.

w,d Marshall Brickman *ph* Gerry Fisher *m* Philippe Sarde *pd* Philip Rosenberg

Dudley Moore, Elizabeth McGovern, Alec Guinness (as Freud), John Huston, Larry Rivers, Gene Saks, Renee Taylor, Alan King

'Flat, lamebrained and indigestible.'—*Geoff Brown, MFB*

Lovin' Molly*
US 1973 98m Movielab
Stephen Friedman (David Golden)

In Texas between 1925 and 1945, two men friends and an accommodating lady have a shifting relationship.
Odd little drama compendium, with fragments told by each in turn; too slight in structure and substance for complete success, but interesting most of the way.

w Stephen Friedman, *novel* Leaving Cheyenne by Larry McMurtry *d Sidney Lumet ph* Edward Brown *m* Fred Hellerman

Blythe Danner, Anthony Perkins, Beau Bridges, Edward Binns, Susan Sarandon

Loving**
US 1970 90m Eastmancolor
Columbia / Brooks Ltd (Don Devlin)

A commercial artist reaches crisis point with both his wife and his mistress.
Smart New Yorkish sex comedy, typical of many but better than most.

w Don Devlin, novel Brooks Wilson Ltd by J. M. Ryan *d Irvin Kershner ph* Gordon Willis *m* Bernardo Segall *pd* Walter Scott Herndon

George Segal, Eva Marie Saint, Sterling Hayden, Keenan Wynn, Nancie Phillips, Janis Young, David Doyle

Loving Couples
US 1980 98m Metrocolor
Time Life (Renee Valente)

Man-and-wife doctors decide to liven up their lives by having affairs.
Embarrassingly with-it romantic charade.

w Martin Donovan *d* Jack Smight *ph* Philip Lathrop *m* Fred Karlin

Shirley Maclaine, James Coburn, Susan Sarandon, Stephen Collins, Sally Kellerman

Loving Couples*
Sweden 1964 118m bw
Sandrew (Rune Waldekranz)
original title: *Alskande Par*

Three expectant mothers think back over their sex lives.
Superbly made, rather hollow diatribe against sex, presented as a series of intricate flashbacks. Along the way, there is much to enjoy, but the result is not really a film of importance.

w Mai Zetterling, David Hughes, *novel* Froknarna von Pahlen by Agnes von Krusenstjerna *d Mai Zetterling ph* Sven Nykvist *m* Rodger Wallis

Harriet Andersson, Gunnel Lindblom, Anita Bjork, Gunnar Bjornstrand, Eva Dahlbeck, Frank Sundstrom, Inga Landgre

'. . . that air of packaged neurosis so peculiar to the Swedish cinema.'—*Tom Milne, MFB*

Loving You
US 1957 101m Technicolor Vistavision
Paramount / Hal B. Wallis

A press agent signs a young hillbilly singer to give zest to her husband's band.
Empty-headed, glossy star vehicle.

w Herbert Baker, Hal Kanter *d* Hal Kanter *ph* Charles Lang Jnr *m* Walter Scharf

Elvis Presley, Lizabeth Scott, Wendell Corey, Dolores Hart, James Gleason

Loyalties
GB 1934 74m bw

A vengeful Jew turns the tables when his wallet is stolen at a society party. Badly made film version of a significant play. Basil Rathbone, Miles Mander, Heather Thatcher, Joan Wyndham, Philip Strange. Written by W. P. Lipscomb from John Galsworthy's play; directed by Basil Dean; for Associated British.

The Luck of Ginger Coffey*
Canada / US 1964 100m bw
Crawley / Roth–Kershner (Leon Roth)

An Irish layabout in Canada finds it difficult to keep a job or protect his family.
Mildly interesting character study with good background detail of Montreal.

w Brian Moore, from his novel *d* Irvin Kershner *ph* Manny Wynn *m* Bernardo Segall

Robert Shaw, Mary Ure, Liam Redmond

The Luck of the Irish*
US 1947 99m bw
TCF (Fred Kohlmar)

A New York newsman's love life is complicated by a helpful leprechaun he meets in Ireland.
Hollywood moonshine, second class: the will and the players are there, but the script is not funny enough.

w Philip Dunne, *novel* There Was a Little Man by Constance and Guy Jones *d* Henry Koster *ph* Joseph La Shelle *m* Cyril Mockridge

Tyrone Power, *Cecil Kellaway*, Anne Baxter, Lee J. Cobb, James Todd, Jayne Meadows, J. M. Kerrigan, Phil Brown

AAN: Cecil Kellaway

The Luckiest Girl in the World
US 1936 75m bw

A rich girl bets her father that she can live in New York for a month on 150 dollars.
Lighthearted comedy with farcical trimmings. Jane Wyatt (who really was from the social register), Louis Hayward, Eugene Pallette, Nat Pendleton, Catherine Doucet, Philip Reed. Written by Herbert Fields, Henry Myers, Anne Jordon; directed by Eddie Buzzell; for Charles R. Rogers / Universal.
'Speed and gags offset story absurdity.'—*Variety*

THE LUCK OF GINGER COFFEY. Here Robert Shaw concentrated on acting but in his later movies he was inclined to take the money and run.

Lucky Boy
US 1929 97m bw part silent

A young Jewish boy makes it big on Broadway. Simple-minded fable inspired by *The Jazz Singer* (which Jessel is said to have turned down). George Jessel, Rosa Rosanova, William K. Strauss, Margaret Quimby. Written by George Jessel; directed by Norman Taurog and others; for Tiffany-Stahl.

Lucky Devils
US 1933 63m bw

Hollywood stuntmen rescue an actress from a suicide attempt. Tolerable action special with interesting sidelights. William Boyd, Dorothy Wilson, William Gargan, Robert Rose, Roscoe Ates, Bruce Cabot. Written by Agnes Christine Johnson, Ben Markson, Casey Robinson, Bob Rose; directed by Ralph Ince; for David O. Selznick / RKO.

Lucky Jim**
GB 1957 95m bw
British Lion / Charter (Roy Boulting)

At a provincial university, an accident-prone junior lecturer has a disastrous weekend with his girl friend and his professor.
Quite funny in its own right, this is a vulgarization of a famous comic novel which got its effects more subtly, with more sense of place, time and character.

w Jeffrey Dell, Patrick Campbell, *novel* Kingsley Amis *d* John Boulting *ph* Max Greene *m* John Addison

Ian Carmichael, Hugh Griffith, Terry-Thomas, Sharon Acker, Jean Anderson, Maureen Connell, Clive Morton, John Welsh, Reginald Beckwith, Kenneth Griffith

'An almost endless ripple of comfortable laughter.'—*News Chronicle*

'When he smiles, it's not because he likes you—it's because he likes what he's going to do to you!'

Lucky Jordan
US 1942 83m bw
Paramount (Fred Kohlmar)

A con man is drafted and overcomes Nazi agents.
Forgettable star cheapie.

w Darrell Ware, Karl Tunberg *d* Frank Tuttle *ph* John F. Seitz *m* Adolph Deutsch

Alan Ladd, Helen Walker, Sheldon Leonard, Marie McDonald, Mabel Paige, Lloyd Corrigan, Dave Willock, Miles Mander

'It's still cops and robbers, no matter how you slice it . . . Mr Ware and Mr Tunberg are not above dragging in mother love as the reason the gangster changes from a selfish killer to a patriot.'—*Joseph Pihodna, New York Herald Tribune*

Lucky Lady
US 1975 118m De Luxe
TCF / Gruskoff / Venture (Michael Gruskoff)

A cabaret girl in 1930 Tijuana joins two adventurers in smuggling liquor into the US by boat.
Whatever can be done wrong with such a story has been done, including irritatingly washed out photography, kinky sex, and sudden switches from farce to gore. None of it holds the interest for a single moment.

w Willard Huyck, Gloria Katz *d* Stanley Donen *ph* Geoffrey Unsworth *m* Ralph Burns *pd* John Barry

Liza Minnelli, Gene Hackman, Burt Reynolds, Michael Hordern, Geoffrey Lewis, Robby Benson

'A manic mess that tries to be all things to all people and ends up offering nothing to anyone.'—*Frank Rich*

'It sports its calculations on its sleeve like rhinestones.'—*Sight and Sound*

'They're all rumrunners in the early 30s, and they're meant to be adorable. This is a big expensive movie for people who don't mind being treated like hicks: the audience is expected to shudder with delight every time it hears an obscenity or sees a big movie star grin.'—*Pauline Kael, New Yorker*

Lucky Me*
US 1954 100m Warnercolor Cinemascope
Warner (Henry Blanke)

Theatrical entertainers stranded in Florida get a lucky break.
Watchable, forgettable musical.

w James O'Hanlon, Robert O'Brien, Irving Elinson *d* Jack Donohue *ph* Wilfrid M. Cline *md* Ray Heindorf

Doris Day, Robert Cummings, Phil Silvers, Eddie Foy Jnr, Nancy Walker, Martha Hyer, Bill Goodwin, Marcel Dalio

'The first Cinemascope musical . . . pleasant, light-hearted, frothy entertainment.'—*MFB*

Lucky Night
US 1939 90m bw
MGM (Louis D. Lighton)

An heiress goes out into the world to make a life for herself, and falls for a man she finds on a park bench.
Tedious pattern romance which did neither of its stars any good.

w Vincent Laurence, Grover Jones *d* Norman Taurog *ph* Ray June *m* Franz Waxman

Myrna Loy, Robert Taylor, Joseph Allen, Henry O'Neill, Douglas Fowley, Marjorie Main, Charles Lane, Bernard Nedell

'Light romantic comedy, okay for box office . . . but certain sections might object to so much liquor-imbibing.'—*Variety*

Lucky Partners*
US 1940 101m bw
RKO (George Haight)

Two strangers share a sweepstake ticket and fall in love.
A very thin comedy kept afloat by its stars.

w Allan Scott, John Van Druten, *story* Bonne Chance by Sacha Guitry *d* Lewis Milestone *ph* Robert de Grasse *m* Dmitri Tiomkin

Ronald Colman, Ginger Rogers, Jack Carson, Spring Byington, Cecilia Loftus, Harry Davenport

The Lucky Star*
Canada 1980 110m colour
Tele Metropole International / Claude Leger

During World War II a Dutch Jewish boy studies wild west films and captures a German colonel.
Unusual and likeable family adventure story with an unnecessary downbeat ending.

w Max Fischer, Jack Rosenthal *d* Max Fischer *ph* Frank Tody *m* Art Philipps

Rod Steiger, Louise Fletcher, Brett Marx, Lou Jacobi, Helen Hughes

The Lucky Stiff
US 1948 101m bw

A cabaret singer sentenced to death for murder is secretly reprieved but comes back as a 'ghost' to scare the real culprit into confession. Weird comedy-melodrama which seems to embarrass all concerned. Dorothy Lamour, Brian Donlevy, Claire Trevor, Irene Hervey. Written and directed by Lewis R. Foster, from a novel by Craig Rice; for Amusement Enterprises / UA.

Lucretia Borgia
France / Italy 1952 105m approx Technicolor
Ariane / Filmsonor / Rizzoli

Cesare Borgia uses his beautiful sister as a political pawn.
Well-mounted but rather boring period barnstormer.

w Cécil Saint-Laurent, Jacques Sigurd, Christian-Jaque *d* Christian-Jaque *ph* Christian Matras *m* Maurice Thiriet

Martine Carol, Pedro Armendariz, Massimo Serato, Ventine Tessier

Lucy Gallant*
US 1955 104m Technicolor Vistavision
Paramount / Pine–Thomas

The success story of a dressmaker who comes to run a group of fashion shops but neglects her love life.
Efficient, smartly-handled woman's picture.

w John Lee Mahin, Winston Miller, *novel* The Life of Lucy Gallant by Margaret Cousins *d* Robert Parrish *ph* Lionel Lindon *m* Van Cleave

Jane Wyman, Charlton Heston, Claire Trevor, Thelma Ritter, William Demarest, Wallace Ford, Tom Helmore, Mary Field

Ludwig*
Italy / France / West Germany 1972 186m Technicolor Panavision
Mega / Cinetel / Dieter Gessler / Divina (Robert Gordon Edwards)

The 19th-century King of Bavaria becomes involved in scandal and goes mad.
A stylish but historically questionable and highly coloured view of events; it drags its heels long before history did.

w Luchino Visconti, Enrico Medioli *d* Luchino Visconti *ph* Armando Nannuzzi *md* Franco Nannino

Helmut Berger, Romy Schneider, Trevor Howard, Silvana Mangano, Helmut Griem, Nora Ricci, Gert Frobe, John Moulder Brown

'Happiness is busting out all over!'
Lullaby of Broadway*
US 1951 92m Technicolor
Warner (William Jacobs)

The daughter of a faded Broadway star becomes the new toast of the town.
Reasonably lively musical with solid production values but little style or wit.

w Earl Baldwin *d* David Butler *ph* Wilfrid Cline *md* Ray Heindorf

Doris Day, Billy de Wolfe, Gene Nelson, Gladys George, Florence Bates, S. Z. Sakall

Lulu Belle
US 1948 87m bw

A selfish singer has a bad effect on one man after another. Dreary melodrama with a miscast star. Dorothy Lamour, George Montgomery, Otto Kruger, Albert Dekker, Glenda Farrell. Written by Everett Freeman, from the play by Charles MacArthur and Edward Shelton; directed by Leslie Fenton; for Benedict Bogeaus / Columbia.

Lumière D'Eté*
France 1943 112m bw
Discina (André Paulvé)

The idle and decadent rich in a mountain hotel are affected in various ways by workmen in the valley below.
Unusual and generally interesting character melodrama.

w Jacques Prévert, Pierre Laroche *d Jean Grémillion* *ph* Louis Page *m* Roland Manuel

Madeleine Renaud, Pierre Brasseur, Madeleine Robinson, Paul Bernard, Jane Marken, Georges Marchal

La Luna
Italy 1979 142m Eastmancolor
TCF / Fiction Cinematografica (Giovanni Bertolucci)

A singer has an incestuous relationship with her teenage son.
Interminable catalogue of events few people wanted to experience; the kindest description would be 'pretentious claptrap'.

w Giuseppe and Bernardo Bertolucci, Clare Peploe *d* Bernardo Bertolucci *ph* Vittorio Storaro *m* operatic excerpts

Jill Clayburgh, Matthew Barry, Laura Betti, Renato Salvatori, Fred Gwynne

Lunch on the Grass**
France 1959 91m Eastmancolor
Compagnie Jean Renoir
original title: *Déjeuner sur l'Herbe*

An international scientist hears the pipes of pan, embarks on a country idyll and impregnates a housemaid whom he later marries.
Charming if overlong frolic with ideas, a harking back to earlier Renoir themes such as in *Boudu Sauvé des Eaux*.

wd Jean Renoir *ph* Georges Leclerc *m* Joseph Kosma

Paul Meurisse, Catherine Rouvel, Fernand Sardou, Ingrid Nordine

'A warm, loving, garrulous, undisciplined film.'—*Penelope Houston, MFB*

Lure of the Wilderness
US 1952 92m Technicolor
TCF (Robert L. Jacks)

A man falsely accused of murder hides for eight years in Georgia's Okefenokee swamp.
Remake of *Swamp Water*, with Walter Brennan playing the same part. The plot works fairly well still, but colour doesn't suit the scenery.

w Louis Lantz, *story* Vereen Bell *d* Jean Negulesco *ph* Edward Cronjager *m* Franz Waxman

Jeffrey Hunter, Jean Peters, Walter Brennan, Constance Smith, Jack Elam

Lured*
US 1947 102m bw
(UA) Hunt Stromberg (James Nasser)
GB title: *Personal Column*

An American dancer stranded in London helps Scotland Yard catch a killer.
Minor murder mystery with a pleasing cast.

w Leo Rosten, from the French film *Pièges* *d* Douglas Sirk *ph* William Daniels *m* Michel Michelet *pd* Nicolai Remisoff

Lucille Ball, George Sanders, Charles Coburn, Boris Karloff, Cedric Hardwicke, Alan Mowbray, George Zucco, Joseph Calleia, Robert Coote, Alan Napier

Lust for a Vampire
GB 1970 95m Technicolor
Hammer (Harry Fine, Michael Style)

In 1830 an English writer discerns that a pupil in an exclusive mid-European girls' school is a reincarnated vampire.
Moderate Hammer horror.

w Tudor Gates, based on J. Sheridan Le Fanu's Carmilla *d* Jimmy Sangster *ph* David Muir *m* Harry Robinson

Ralph Bates, Michael Johnson, Barbara Jefford, Suzanna Leigh, Yutte Stensgaard, Mike Raven, Helen Christie

Lust for Gold
US 1949 90m bw
Columbia (S. Sylvan Simon)

A young man goes to Arizona to search for a lost gold mine discovered by his grandfather.
Moderate western drama consisting largely of flashback.

w Ted Sherdeman, Richard English, *novel* Thunder God's Gold by Barry Storm *d* S. Sylvan Simon *ph* Archie Stout *m* George Duning

Ida Lupino, Glenn Ford, Gig Young, William Prince, Edgar Buchanan, Will Geer, Paul Ford

Lust for Life**
US 1956 122m Metrocolor
Cinemascope
MGM (John Houseman)

The life of Vincent Van Gogh.
Fairly absorbing, not inaccurate, but somehow uninspiring biopic, probably marred by poor colour and wide screen; despite good work all round, it simply doesn't fall into a classic category.

w Norman Corwin, *book* Irving Stone *d* Vincente Minnelli *ph* F. A. Young, Russell Harlan *m* Miklos Rozsa *ad* Cedric Gibbons, Hans Peters, Preston Ames

Kirk Douglas, Anthony Quinn (as Gauguin), James Donald, Pamela Brown, Everett Sloane, Niall MacGinnis, Noel Purcell, Henry Daniell, Lionel Jeffries, Madge Kennedy, Jill Bennett, Laurence Naismith

'Two hours of quite shattering and exciting entertainment.'—*Alan Dent, Illustrated London News*

AA: Anthony Quinn
AAN: Norman Corwin; Kirk Douglas

Lust in the Dust
US 1984 87m CFI colour
Fox Run (Allan Glaser, Tab Hunter)

In the old west, a strong silent man and a drag queen beat the baddies to the gold.
Fitfully funny spoof for adults.

w Philip Taylor *d* Paul Bartel *ph* Paul Lohmann *m* Peter Matz *ed* Alan Toomayan

Tab Hunter, Divine, Lainie Kazan, Geoffrey Lewis, Henry Silva, Cesar Romero, Woody Strode

The Lusty Men*
US 1952 113m bw
RKO / Wald–Krasna (Jerry Wald)

Tensions lead to the death of one of a pair of rider friends on a rodeo tour.
Standard melodrama with semi-documentary detail and star performances.

w Horace McCoy, David Dortort *d* Nicholas Ray *ph Lee Garmes* *m* Roy Webb

Robert Mitchum, Arthur Kennedy, Susan Hayward, Arthur Hunnicutt

Luther*
GB 1973 112m Eastmancolor
American Express / Ely Landau / Cinevision

In 1525, the teachings of Luther culminate in the Peasants' Revolt.
Hard-to-watch filming by the American Film Theatre of a singularly theatrical play, and not a very good one at that. Some good acting.

w Edward Anhalt, *play* John Osborne *d* Guy Green *ph* Freddie Young *m* John Addison *pd* Peter Mullins

Stacy Keach, Patrick Magee, Hugh Griffith, Robert Stephens, Alan Badel, Julian Glover, Judi Dench, Leonard Rossiter, Maurice Denham

Luv
US 1967 95m Technicolor Panavision
Columbia / Jalem (Martin Manulis)

When a man prevents an old friend from jumping off the Brooklyn Bridge and brings him home, a sexual square dance develops.
A modern comedy that should have stayed in the theatre.

w Elliott Baker, *play* Murray Shisgal *d* Clive Donner *ph* Ernest Laszlo *m* Gerry Mulligan

Jack Lemmon, Peter Falk, Elaine May, Nina Wayne, Eddie Mayehoff, Paul Hartman, Severn Darden

'A light but incisive comedy about the patterns and language of love in a Freud-ridden society has become an inept and lethally unamusing film farce.'—*MFB*

Luxury Liner
US 1933 72m bw
Paramount

Stories of various passengers on a liner bound from New York to Bremerhaven.
Interesting minor multi-drama, like a rough sketch for *Ship of Fools* (qv).

w Gene Markey, Kathryn Scola, *novel,* Gina Kaus *d* Lothar Mendes *ph* Victor Milner

George Brent, Zita Johann, Vivienne Osborne, Alice White, Verree Teasdale, C. Aubrey Smith, Frank Morgan, Henry Wadsworth, Billy Bevan

'Not even the frank hook-up with *Grand Hotel* will help this entry much . . . a loose and thin catch-as-catch-can affair.'—*Variety*

Luxury Liner
US 1948 98m Technicolor
MGM (Joe Pasternak)

The captain of a liner has trouble with his teenage daughter.
Minor shipboard musical with pleasing talents applied.

w Gladys Lehmann, Richard Connell *d* Richard Whorf *ph* Ernest Laszlo *md* George Stoll

George Brent, Jane Powell, Lauritz Melchior, Frances Gifford, Marina Koshetz, Xavier Cugat, Richard Derr, Connie Gilchrist

'The girl who thought she knew all about love!'
Lydia*
US 1941 104m bw
Alexander Korda (Lee Garmes)

An ageing lady recalls her former beaux.
Pleasing remake of *Carnet du Bal*, with excellent production values.

w Ben Hecht, Samuel Hoffenstein, *story* Julien Duvivier, Laszlo Bus-Fekete *d Julien Duvivier* *ph Lee Garmes* *m* Miklos Rozsa *pd Vincent Korda*

Merle Oberon, Joseph Cotten, Alan Marshal, Edna May Oliver, Hans Yaray, George Reeves, John Halliday, Sara Allgood

AAN: Miklos Rozsa

Lydia Bailey
US 1952 89m Technicolor
TCF (Jules Schermer)

In 1802 a Boston lawyer visits Haiti to obtain the signature of a wayward heiress, and becomes involved in the negro fight against the French.
Standard adventure romance with plenty of excitements.

w Michael Blankfort, Philip Dunne, *novel* Kenneth Roberts *d* Jean Negulesco *ph* Harry Jackson *m* Hugo Friedhofer

Dale Robertson, Anne Francis, Charles Korvin, William Marshall, Adeline de Walt Reynolds

M***
Germany 1931 118m bw
Nero Film (Seymour Nebenzal)

A psychopathic murderer of children evades the police but is caught by the city's criminals who find his activities getting them a bad name.
An unmistakable classic whose oddities are hardly worth criticizing, this is part social melodrama and part satire, but entirely unforgettable, with most of its sequences brilliantly staged.

w Thea Von Harbou, Paul Falkenberg, Adolf Jansen, Karl Vash d Fritz Lang ph Fritz Arno Wagner m Adolf Jansen *ad* Karl Vollbrecht, Emil Hasler

Peter Lorre, Otto Wernicke, Gustav Grundgens

'Visual excitement, pace, brilliance of surface and feeling for detail.'—*New Yorker, 1977*
† Of Lang's later work, *Fury* comes closest to the feeling and style of *M*.

M*
US 1951 82m bw
Columbia (Seymour Nebenzal)

Faithful but fated remake; without the heavy expressionist techniques, the story seems merely silly and the atmosphere is all wrong.

w Norman Reilly Raine, Leo Katcher *d* Joseph Losey *ph* Ernest Laszlo *m* Michel Michelet

David Wayne, Howard da Silva, Luther Adler, Martin Gabel, Glenn Anders, Karen Morley, Norman Lloyd, Walter Burke

'I consciously repeated only one shot . . . essentially Lang's villain was my hero.'—*Joseph Losey*

Ma and Pa Kettle*
US 1949 75m bw
U-I (Leonard Goldstein)

Pa Kettle wins a house in a contest and is accused of cheating.
First of a series of low-budget comedies which, based on characters from *The Egg and I* (qv), had astonishing commercial success in America. The standard varied from adequate to painful.

w Herbert Margolis, Louis Morheim, Al Lewis *d* Charles Lamont *ph* Maury Gertsman *m* Milton Schwarzwald

Marjorie Main, Percy Kilbride, Richard Long, Meg Randall

'Not exactly Noel Coward.'—*Leonard Maltin*
† For others in the series, see under *The Kettles*.

Ma Nuit chez Maud*
France 1969 110m bw
Films du Losange
aka: *My Night at Maud's*

A Catholic clerk in a small town falls in love with an elegant divorcee but can't bring himself to court her openly and marries someone else.
Subdued, literate talk-piece which finally exhausts rather than stimulates.

wd Eric Rohmer *ph* Nestor Almendros

Jean-Louis Trintignant, Françoise Fabian, Marie-Christine Barault

AAN: best foreign film; Eric Rohmer (as writer)

'See it with someone who can carry you home!'
'So terrifying we have to insure your life!'

Macabre
US 1958 73m bw
AA (William Castle)

When a small-town doctor's daughter is kidnapped, he fears she may have been buried alive in the cemetery.
Genuine but unsuccessful attempt to film a horror comic; incredibly stodgy writing, acting and direction put the lid on it.

w Robb White *d* William Castle *ph* Carl Guthrie *m* Les Baxter

William Prince, Jim Backus, Jacqueline Scott, Philip Tonge, Ellen Corby

'A ghoulish but totally ineffective horror piece, set mainly in undertakers' offices and an atmosphere of graveyards and swirling fog.'—*MFB*
† When first released, admission carried insurance against death by fright. Some said it should have been death by boredom.

Macao
US 1952 81m bw
RKO (Alex Gottlieb)

A wandering American in the Far East helps a detective catch a gangster.
A few flashy decorative touches show the director's hand, otherwise this is routine, murky thick ear.

w Bernard C. Schoenfeld, Stanley Rubin *d* Josef Von Sternberg (and Nicholas Ray) *ph* Harry J. Wild *m* Anthony Collins

Robert Mitchum, Jane Russell, William Bendix, Gloria Grahame, Thomas Gomez

MacArthur the Rebel General*
US 1977 130m Technicolor
Universal / Richard D. Zanuck, David Brown (Frank McCarthy)

The exploits of General MacArthur during the Pacific wars and his strained relationships with two presidents.
Sober, earnest political biography with war sequences; very well done but somehow unsympathetic.

w Hal Barwood, Matthew Robbins *d* Joseph Sargent *ph* Mario Tosi *m* Jerry Goldsmith

Gregory Peck, Dan O'Herlihy (as Roosevelt), Ed Flanders (as Truman), Ward Costello, Marj Dusay, Ivan Bonar

'A biopic that begins when its subject is sixty lacks roots—and in this case revelation.'—*Judith Crist*

Macbeth*
US 1948 89m bw
Republic (Orson Welles)

A famous—or infamous—attempt to film Shakespeare in twenty-one days in papier mâché settings running with damp; further hampered by the use of a form of unintelligible bastard Scots. A few striking moments at the beginning remain; the rest should be silence.

d Orson Welles *ph John L. Russell*
m Jacques Ibert *ad* Fred Ritter

Orson Welles, Jeanette Nolan, Dan O'Herlihy, Roddy McDowall, Edgar Barrier, Robert Coote

Macbeth*
GB 1971 140m Technicolor Todd-AO 35
Playboy / Caliban (Andrew Braunsberg)

A sharpened and brutalized version; the blood swamps most of the cleverness and most of the poetry.

d Roman Polanski *ph* Gilbert Taylor *m* the Third Ear Band *pd* Wilfrid Shingleton

Jon Finch, Francesca Annis, Martin Shaw, Nicholas Selby, John Stride

McCabe and Mrs Miller
US 1971 120m Technicolor Panavision
Warner (David Foster, Mitchell Brower)

At the turn of the century a gambling gunfighter comes to a northwest mining town and uses his money to set up lavish brothels. Obscurely scripted, muddy-coloured and harshly recorded western melodrama whose squalid 'realism' comes as close to fantasy as does *The Wizard of Oz*.

w Robert Altman, Brian Mackay, *novel* McCabe by Edmund Naughton *d* Robert Altman *ph* Vilmos Zsigmond *pd* Leon Ericksen

Warren Beatty, Julie Christie, René Auberjonois, Shelley Duvall, John Schuck

'A fleeting, diaphanous vision of what frontier life might have been.'—*Pauline Kael*

'Altman directed *M*A*S*H*, which wandered and was often funny; then *Brewster McCloud*, which wandered and was not funny; now this, which wanders and is repulsive. The thesis seems to be that if you take a corny story, fuzz up the exposition, vitiate the action, use a childishly ironic ending, and put in lots of profanity and nudity, you have Marched On with Time.'—*Stanley Kauffmann*

AAN: Julie Christie

The McConnell Story
US 1955 107m Warnercolor Cinemascope
Warner (Henry Blanke)
GB title: *Tiger in the Sky*

The career and accidental death of a jet ace of the Korean war.
Crude, obvious and saccharine biopic.

w Ted Sherdeman, Sam Rolfe *d* Gordon Douglas *ph* John Seitz, Ted McCord *m* Max Steiner

Alan Ladd, June Allyson, James Whitmore, Frank Faylen, Willis Bouchey

McFadden's Flats
US 1935 65m bw

The quarrel between a bricklayer and a barber affects their children. Modest working-class comedy from a well-worn play. Walter C. Kelly, Andy Clyde, Richard Cromwell, Jane Darwell, Betty Furness, George Barbier. Written by Arthur Caesar, Edward Kaufman, Casey Robinson, Andy Rice, from play by Gus Hill; directed by Ralph Murphy; for Paramount. 'Better-than-average family picture.'—*Variety*

'Even the Mafia calls him Mister!'
Machine Gun McCain
Italy 1970 94m Techniscope

The Mafia springs a hardened criminal from jail and puts him to use. Dull but violent Las Vegas-set mobster story with some echoes of *Bonnie and Clyde*. John Cassavetes, Peter Falk, Britt Ekland, Gabriele Ferzetti. Written by Giuliano Montaldo, Mino Roli; directed by Giuliano Montaldo; for Euroatlantica/ Columbia.

Macho Callahan
US 1970 100m Movielab Panavision
Avco / Felicidad (Bernard Kowalski, Martin C. Schute)

A vengeful cowboy annihilates all who stand in his way.
Squalid Mexican-made western with unremitting emphasis on violence.

w Clifford Newton Gould *d* Bernard Kowalski *ph* Gerry Fisher *m* Pat Williams

David Janssen, Lee J. Cobb, David Carradine, James Booth, Jean Seberg

MacKenna's Gold*
US 1969 136m Technicolor Super Panavision
Columbia / Highroad (Carl Foreman, Dmitri Tiomkin)

A dying Indian entrusts a sheriff with a map of the legendary Valley of Gold, and when the news breaks the map is in demand.
Curious serial-like western melodrama packed with stars and pretensions above its station. On a lower level, it is quite enjoyable.

w Carl Foreman, *novel* Will Henry *d* J. Lee-Thompson *ph* Joseph MacDonald, Harold Wellman *m* Quincy Jones *pd* Geoffrey Drake

Gregory Peck, Omar Sharif, Telly Savalas, Camilla Sparv, Keenan Wynn, Julie Newmar, Ted Cassidy, Eduardo Ciannelli, Eli Wallach, Edward G. Robinson, Raymond Massey, Burgess Meredith, Anthony Quayle, Lee J. Cobb

'Preposterous hotch-potch of every cliché known to the gold lust book.'—*MFB*

'Twelve-year-olds of all ages might tolerate it.'—*Judith Crist*

'A western of truly stunning absurdity, a thriving example of the old Hollywood maxim about how to succeed by failing big.'—*Vincent Canby*

The McKenzie Break*
GB 1970 106m De Luxe
UA / Levy–Gardner–Laven

During World War II, German prisoners at a Scottish camp stage an escape.
Effective little action suspenser.

w William Norton *d* Lamont Johnson *ph* Michael Reed *m* Riz Ortolani

Brian Keith, Helmut Griem, Ian Hendry, Jack Watson, Patrick O'Connell, Horst Janson

'Only Mackintosh can save them now—and Mackintosh is dead!'
The Mackintosh Man*
GB 1973 99m Technicolor
Warner / Newman–Foreman / John Huston

A government agent is sent to prison to contact a criminal gang.
Convoluted but entertaining spy thriller with good performances and action sequences.

w Walter Hill, *novel* The Freedom Trap by Desmond Bagley *d* John Huston *ph* Oswald Morris *m* Maurice Jarre

Paul Newman, James Mason, Dominique Sanda, Nigel Patrick, Harry Andrews, Michael Hordern, Ian Bannen, Peter Vaughan, Roland Culver, Percy Herbert, Robert Lang, Leo Genn

McLintock*
US 1963 127m Technicolor Panavision
UA / Batjac (Michael Wayne)

A cattle baron can control a whole town but not his termagant wife.
Sub-Ford western farce borrowed from *The Taming of the Shrew*, with much fist-fighting and mud-splattering, and rather too much chat in between.

w James Edward Grant *d* Andrew V. McLaglen *ph* William H. Clothier *m* Frank de Vol

John Wayne, Maureen O'Hara, Yvonne de Carlo, Patrick Wayne, Stefanie Powers, Chill Wills, Bruce Cabot, Jack Kruschen

The McMasters
US 1969 90m Technicolor
JayJen (Dimitri de Grunwald)

A black man returning home from the Civil War gets unexpected help from a tough landowner.
Racial western with black, white and red points of view, all very violently expressed.

w Harold Jacob Smith *d* Alf Kjellin *ph* Lester Shorr *m* Coleridge-Taylor Parkinson

Brock Peters, Burl Ives, David Carradine, Nancy Kwan, Jack Palance, Dane Clark, John Carradine, I. Q. Jones, R. G. Armstrong

The Macomber Affair*
US 1947 89m bw
(UA) Benedict Bogeaus (Casey Robinson)

The wife of a bullying big game hunter falls for their guide.
Safari melodrama with a plot which has become a cliché but seemed fresh enough at the time. Goodish writing and acting.

w Casey Robinson, *story* The Short Happy Life of Francis Macomber by Ernest Hemingway *d* Zoltan Korda *ph* Karl Struss *m* Miklos Rozsa

Gregory Peck, Joan Bennett, Robert Preston, Reginald Denny, Carl Harbord, Jean Gillie

'The best movie job on Hemingway to date.'—*James Agee*

'It has survived the hazardous crossing from brilliant short story to film with practically no casualties.'—*Daily Mail*

Macon County Line
US 1973 89m Eastmancolor
Sam Arkoff / Max Baer

In mid-fifties Louisiana, a couple of hell-raisers are harassed by a local sheriff, and much bloodshed results.
Shapeless melodrama more or less in the wake of *Easy Rider*; an unattractive film which unaccountably had great box-office success.

w Max Baer, Richard Compton *d* Richard Compton *ph* Daniel Lacambre *m* Stu Phillips

Alan Vint, Cheryl Waters, Geoffrey Lewis, Joan Blackman, Jesse Vint, Max Baer

'He's a busted cop, his gun is unlicensed, his methods unlawful, his story incredible!'
McQ
US 1974 111m Technicolor Panavision
Warner / Batjac / Levy–Gardner

A Seattle police detective goes after the gangster who killed his friend.

Rambling, violent thriller with good sequences but no cohesion.

w Lawrence Roman *d* John Sturges *ph* Harry Stradling Jnr *m* Elmer Bernstein

John Wayne, Eddie Albert, Diana Muldaur, Colleen Dewhurst, Clu Gulager, David Huddleston, Julie Adams

McVicar
GB 1980 112m Eastmancolor

The true story of the escapes from prison of a violent criminal who was subsequently reformed and rehabilitated. Some smart sequences don't prevent this from being an exploitation item. Roger Daltrey, Adam Faith, Cheryl Campbell, Billy Murray, Georgina Hale. Written by John McVicar and Tom Clegg; directed by Tom Clegg; for The Who Films.

Mad About Men
GB 1954 90m Technicolor
GFD / Group Films (Betty Box)

By mutual agreement, a sports mistress and a mermaid change places for a while.
Laborious rehash of *Miranda* with familiar jokes.

w Peter Blackmore *d* Ralph Thomas *ph* Ernest Steward *m* Benjamin Frankel

Glynis Johns, Donald Sinden, Anne Crawford, Margaret Rutherford, Dora Bryan, Nicholas Phipps, Irene Handl

Mad about Music*
US 1938 98m bw
Universal (Joe Pasternak)

A girl at a Swiss school adopts a personable visitor as her father.
Pleasing star vehicle with charm and humour; badly remade as *Toy Tiger* (qv).

w Bruce Manning, Felix Jackson *d* Norman Taurog *ph* Joseph Valentine *m / ly* Harold Adamson, Jimmie McHugh *m* Frank Skinner, Charles Previn

Deanna Durbin, Herbert Marshall, Gail Patrick, Arthur Treacher, Helen Parrish, Marcia Mae Jones, William Frawley

'Another Durbin smash . . . will mop up at the b.o.'—*Variety*

AAN: original story (Marcella Burke, Frank Kohner); Joseph Valentine; Frank Skinner, Charles Previn

'She knew the ecstasy and terror of loving him!'

The Mad Doctor
US 1940 90m bw
Paramount (George Arthur)
GB title: *A Date with Destiny*

A doctor marries wealthy women and then murders them.
Naïve melodrama of little interest except as a vehicle for its star.

w Howard J. Green *d* Tim Whelan *ph* Ted Tetzlaff *m* Victor Young

Basil Rathbone, Ellen Drew, John Howard, Barbara Allen, Ralph Morgan, Martin Kosleck

The Mad Doctor of Market Street
US 1942 61m bw

Shipwrecked people on a tropical island find that one of their number is a dangerous paranoiac. Dull and misleadingly titled second-feature melodrama. Lionel Atwill, Nat Pendleton, Una Merkel, Claire Dodd. Written by Al Martin; directed by Joseph H. Lewis; for Universal.

The Mad Game
US 1933 73m bw

A gangster turns stool pigeon to round up kidnappers. Fairly lively crime melodrama. Spencer Tracy, Claire Trevor, Ralph Morgan, J. Carrol Naish, John Miljan. Written by William Conselman, Henry Johnson; directed by Irving Cummings; for Fox. 'Enough romance and action to satisfy.'—*Variety*

'Adults Only! Censor's orders!'

The Mad Genius
US 1931 81m bw
Warner

A crippled puppeteer adopts a boy and makes him into a great dancer.
Curious variation on *Trilby*, filmed as *Svengali* the previous year with much the same cast. Not a great success: the script is dreadful.

w J. Grubb Alexander, Harvey Thew, *play* The Idol by Martin Brown *d* Michael Curtiz *ph* Barney McGill *ad Anton Grot*

John Barrymore, Marian Marsh, Donald Cook, Luis Alberni, Carmel Myers, Charles Butterworth, Boris Karloff, Frankie Darro

'Magnificent acting, but not the sort of thing that will panic the fans.'—*Variety*

† Many of the sets in this production had ceilings, ten years before the idea was supposed to have been invented for *Citizen Kane*.

The Mad Ghoul
US 1943 65m bw
Universal (Ben Pivar)

A mad scientist needs fresh hearts to keep alive the victims of his experiments with a poison vapour.
Stagey, tasteless horror melodrama.

w Brenda Weisberg, Paul Gangelin, *story* Hans Kraly *d* James Higan *ph* Milton Krasner *md* Hans Salter

George Zucco, David Bruce, Evelyn Ankers, Turhan Bey, Robert Armstrong, Charles McGraw, Milburn Stone

Mad Holiday
US 1936 72m bw

A rebellious film actor goes on a cruise and gets involved in a murder. Spotty mystery comedy in which the elements don't really jell. Edmund Lowe, Elissa Landi, Edmund Gwenn, Zasu Pitts, Ted Healy, Edgar Kennedy. Written by Florence Ryerson and Edgar Allen Woolf from the story Murder in a Chinese Theatre by Joseph Santley; directed by George B. Seitz; for MGM. 'Very draggy . . . largely a bore.'—*Variety*

Mad Love**
US 1935 83m bw
MGM (John Considine Jnr)
GB title: *The Hands of Orlac*

A pianist loses his hands in an accident; a mad surgeon, in love with the pianist's wife, grafts on the hands of a murderer.
Absurd Grand Guignol done with great style which somehow does not communicate itself in viewer interest, only in cold admiration.

w Guy Endore, P. J. Wolfson, John Balderston, *novel* The Hands of Orlac by Maurice Renard *d Karl Freund* *ph* Chester Lyons, Gregg Toland *m* Dmitri Tiomkin

Colin Clive, Peter Lorre, Frances Drake, Ted Healy, Edward Brophy, Isabel Jewell, Sara Haden

'The results in screen potency are disappointing . . . will probably do fair biz.'—*Variety*

'Mr Lorre cuts deeply into the darkness of the morbid brain.'—*New York Times*

The Mad Magician
US 1954 72m bw
Columbia (Bryan Foy)

A magician's star-struck inventor murders his employer and several others who stand between him and the big time.
Hokey horror flick set in the eighties and originally shown in 3-D.

w Crane Wilbur *d* John Brahm *ph* Bert Glennon *m* Emil Newman

Vincent Price, Mary Murphy, Eva Gabor, John Emery, Patrick O'Neal

The Mad Martindales
US 1942 55m bw

In 1900 San Francisco, an eccentric family gets out of debt. The star's last film for a major studio is a filler of unrelieved tedium. Jane Withers, Alan Mowbray, Marjorie Weaver, Jimmy Lydon, Byron Barr, George Reeves. Written by Francis Edward Faragoh; directed by Alfred Werker; for Walter Morosco / TCF.

Mad Max
Australia 1979 100m Eastmancolor Todd-AO 35
Mad Max Pty (Byron Kennedy)

In the future, motor cycle gangs combat the police.
Violent extravaganza with no real merit save its enthusiasm for destruction of both bikes and bodies.

w James McCausland, George Miller *d* George Miller *ph* David Eggby *m* Brian May

Mel Gibson, Joanne Samuel, Hugh Keays-Byrne, Steve Bisley

Mad Max 2
Australia 1981 96m colour Panavision
Kennedy Miller Entertainment (Byron Kennedy)
US title: *The Road Warrior*

A shortage of petrol causes all-out war between police and bikers.

Not much more than a retread of the above, but a more expensive, spectacular and violent one.

w Terry Hayes, George Miller, Brian Hannant *d* George Miller *ph* Dean Semler *m* Brian May

Mel Gibson, Bruce Spence, Vernon Wells, Emil Minty

'Essentially just another display of vehicles smashing into each other.'—*David McGillivray, MFB*

Mad Max Beyond Thunderdome
Australia 1985 106m colour Panavision

More violent futuristic rubbish in similar vein to its predecessors. Mel Gibson, Tina Turner, Angelo Rossitto, Helen Buday. Written by Terry Hayes, George Miller; directed by George Miller and George Ogilvie; for Kennedy Miller.

The Mad Miss Manton*
US 1938 80m bw
RKO (Pandro S. Berman)

A zany socialite involves her friends in a murder mystery.
Mildly funny comedy-thriller without too much of either, but a good example of the style of thirties craziness at its zenith.

w Philip G. Epstein *d* Leigh Jason *ph* Nicholas Musuraca *m* Roy Webb

Barbara Stanwyck, Henry Fonda, Sam Levene, Frances Mercer, Stanley Ridges, Whitney Bourne, Hattie McDaniel, Miles Mander

'Something ground out by people in a desperate mood.'—*Pauline Kael, 70s*

The Mad Monster
US 1942 77m bw

A mad scientist injects wolf blood into a man, who goes around at night killing people. Inept and uncontrolled shocker, the kind of thing that gives horror films a bad name. George Zucco, Johnny Downs, Glenn Strange, Anne Nagel. Written by Fred Myton; directed by Sam Newfield; for Sigmund Neufeld / PRC.

The Mad Parade
US 1931 62m bw

A story told by women about the effect of the war on their sex. Not really strong enough to be taken seriously, this was played as a novelty. Evelyn Brent, Irene Rich, Louise Fazenda, Lilyan Tashman, Marceline Day. Written by Henry McCarthy and Frank R. Conklin from a story by Gertrude Orr and Doris Malloy; directed by William Beaudine; for Liberty / Paramount. 'Chances for disappointing business greater than the opposite.'—*Variety*

The Mad Room
US 1969 92m Berkey Pathecolor
Columbia / Norman Mauer

A companion kills her wealthy employer so that her mentally retarded brother and sister will have a home.
Tasteless remake of *Ladies in Retirement*, in the brutalized vein which audiences are supposed by producers to want. In modern dress and sharp locations, it succeeds only in being nauseating.

w Bernard Girard, A. Z. Martin *d* Bernard Girard *ph* Harry Stradling Jnr *m* Dave Grusin

Stella Stevens, Shelley Winters, Skip Ward, Carol Cole, Severn Darden

Mad Wednesday*
US 1947 77m bw
Howard Hughes

A middle-aged book-keeper is sacked and goes on the town.
Woolly and unattractive farce which proved something of a disaster for all the talents concerned but historically is of considerable interest. It begins with an excerpt from *The Freshman* and continues to comic adventures with a lion.

wd / pd Preston Sturges (re-edited by others) *ph* Robert Pittack *m* Werner Richard Heymann

Harold Lloyd, Jimmy Conlin, Raymond Walburn, Franklin Pangborn, Al Bridge, Margaret Hamilton, Edgar Kennedy

'Whatever it is that French women have—Madame Bovary had more of it!'
Madame Bovary
US 1949 114m bw
MGM (Pandro S. Berman)

A passionate girl marries a dull husband, takes a lover, and commits suicide.
Dull, emasculated version of a classic.

w Robert Ardrey, *novel* Gustave Flaubert *d* Vincente Minnelli *ph* Robert Planck *m* Miklos Rozsa

Jennifer Jones, Van Heflin, James Mason, Louis Jourdan, Christopher Kent, Gene Lockhart, Gladys Cooper, John Abbott, George Zucco

'If you hadn't read the book, you wouldn't guess what it was about from this film.'—*Pauline Kael, 70s*

† Previously filmed in 1932 as *Unholy Love*.

'One of the world's magnificent romances of great, unselfish love!'
Madame Butterfly
US 1932 88m bw
Paramount (B. P. Schulberg)

A Japanese geisha commits hara kiri when an American lieutenant passes her up for a western girl.
Drearily modernized version of the opera without its music; an odd idea to say the least.

w Josephine Lovett, Joseph M. March, *play* David Belasco, John Luther Long *d* Marion Gering *ph* David Abel *md* W. Franke Harling

Sylvia Sidney, Cary Grant, Charlie Ruggles, Sandor Kallay, Irving Pichel, Helen Jerome Eddy

'The long-drawn tragedy might be bearable if it were expressed in music or poetry, without any such embellishment it is apt to be painfully pathetic.'—*The Times*

'Travels slow and makes for only fair entertainment.'—*Variety*

'Mr and Mrs Miniver together again!'
Madame Curie*
US 1944 124m bw
MGM (Sidney Franklin)

The life and marriage of the woman who discovered radium.
Dignified and rather dull biopic which well exemplifies MGM's best production style of the forties.

w Paul Osborn, Paul H. Rameau, *book* Eve Curie *d* Mervyn Le Roy *ph* Joseph Ruttenberg *m* Herbert Stothart *ad* Cedric Gibbons, Paul Groesse

Greer Garson, Walter Pidgeon, Henry Travers, Albert Basserman, Robert Walker, C. Aubrey Smith, Dame May Whitty, Victor Francen, Elsa Basserman, Reginald Owen, Van Johnson

'It achieves a notable triumph in making the discovery of a new element seem almost as glamorous as an encounter with Hedy Lamarr.'—*C. A. Lejeune*

AAN: best picture; Joseph Ruttenberg; Herbert Stothart; Greer Garson; Walter Pidgeon

Madame De*
France / Italy 1953 102m bw
Franco-London / Indus / Rizzoli
US title: *The Earrings of Madame de*

Tragic misunderstandings arise when a society wife sells her earrings and tells her husband she has lost them.
Elegant, rather heavy-handed but superbly glossy extension of a fashionable novelette.

w Marcel Achard, Max Ophuls, Annette Wademant, *novel* Louise de Vilmorin *d Max Ophuls* *ph* Christian Matras *m* Oscar Straus, Georges Van Parys *ad* Jean d'Eaubonne

Charles Boyer, Danielle Darrieux, Vittorio de Sica, Lea di Lea, Jean Debucourt

Madame Dubarry**
Germany 1919 85m (24 fps) bw silent
Union-UFA
US title: *Passion*

The life and times of the glamorous courtesan of Louis XV.
Milestone silent film which introduced to the cinemas of America and Britain not only the subtleties of the European cinema but the more adaptable subtleties of a key director, here dealing rather heavy-handedly with material which he should later have re-used.

w Fred Orbing, Hans Kraly *d* Ernst Lubitsch *ph* Theodor Sparkuhl

Pola Negri, Emil Jannings, Harry Liedtke, Reinhold Schunzel

Madame Dubarry
US 1934 77m bw

MADAME DE. Danielle Darrieux displays the jewellery that led to the film being titled *The Earrings of Madame de* in the United States.

The life of the legendary courtesan at Versailles. Utterly unpersuasive but sometimes decorative historical charade. Dolores del Rio, Reginald Owen, Victor Jory, Anita Louise, Osgood Perkins, Verree Teasdale. Written by Edward Chodorov; directed by William Dieterle; for Warner. 'A lavish but not particularly distinguished production.'—*Variety*

Madame Racketeer
US 1932 68m bw

Tactics of a middle-aged lady larcenist. Light crime comedy drama, not bad but overlookable. Alison Skipworth, Richard Bennett, Evalyn Knapp, George Raft, Robert McWade. Written by Malcolm Stuart Boylan and Harvey Gates; directed by Alexander Hall and Harry Wagstaff Gribble; for Paramount. 'The subtle high comedy that flows so gently through the script is likely to pass over the hats of the peasantry.'—*Variety*

Madame Rosa
France 1977 120m Eastmancolor

An elderly Jewish prostitute runs an unofficial nursery school and cares especially for a fourteen-year-old Arab. Splendidly acted but basically dreary fable twisted from a novel which took the child's point of view. *Simone Signoret,* Claude Dauphin, Samy Ben Youb. Written and directed by Moshe Mizrahi, from the novel by Emile Ajar; for Lira Films. (Original title: *La Vie Devant Soi.*)

Madame Sans-Gêne
US 1925 110m (24 fps) bw silent

During the French Revolution, Napoleon plays Cupid to a laundry-maid and her lover. The story formed the basis of one of Gloria Swanson's last successes; but it was made in France and did not have the zip of her Hollywood productions. With Charles De Roche, Emile Drain. Written by Forrest Halsey; directed by Leonce Perret; for Paramount.

Madame Sans-Gêne
France / Italy / Spain 1962 100m Technirama
TCF / Cine Alliance / Gesi / Champion / Agata (Maleno Malenotti)
GB and US title: *Madame*

Historical romp based on an old theatrical warhorse. Pretty stilted in this version, especially when dubbed.

w Henri Jeanson and others, *play* Victorien Sardou *d* Christian-Jaque *ph* Roberto Gerardi *m* Francesco Lavagnino

Sophia Loren, Robert Hossein, Julien Bertheau, Marina Berti

Madame Satan*
US 1930 105m bw
MGM (C. B. de Mille)

When her husband strays, a socialite disguises herself as a mysterious *femme fatale* and wins him back.
Abysmal comedy in which both director and principals appear frozen until the closing reels present a crazy, spectacular party on a dirigible which crashes but allows a happy ending.

w Jeanie Macpherson *d* C. B. de Mille
ph Harold Rosson *m* Herbert Stothart

Kay Johnson, Reginald Denny, Lillian Roth, Roland Young

'A strange conglomeration of unreal incidents that are sometimes set forth with no little technical skill.'—*Mordaunt Hall, New York Times*

Madame Spy
US 1934 70m bw

Russian and Austrian spies are married to each other. Absurd melodrama which never gets a grip. Fay Wray, Nils Asther, Edward Arnold, John Miljan, David Torrence. Written by William Hurlbut from a German film, Under False Flags; directed by Karl Freund; for Universal. 'Story too hopeless to mean money anywhere.'—*Variety*

Madame Spy
US 1942 63m bw

A glamorous Nazi spy turns out to be an American secret agent. Elementary espionage stuff without much in the way of plot development. Constance Bennett, Don Porter, John Litel, Edward Brophy, John Eldredge. Written by Lynn Riggs and Clarence Upson Young; directed by Roy William Neill; for Universal.

Madame X*
US 1929 95m bw
MGM
TV title: *Absinthe*

After an accidental death, a wealthy woman disappears and goes down in the world; at a subsequent murder trial she is defended by her unrecognizing son.
Two silent versions (with Dorothy Donnelly and Pauline Frederick) had been made of this old theatrical warhorse; two sound versions followed this one. The thing defies criticism.

w Willard Mack, *play* Alexandre Bisson *d* Lionel Barrymore

Ruth Chatterton, Raymond Hackett, Mitchell Lewis, Sidney Toler, Carroll Nye, Lewis Stone, Richard Carle

'Works like this confound the reformers, elevate the name of pictures, and tell the world that there is an art in film making.'—*Variety*

AAN: Lionel Barrymore; Ruth Chatterton

Madame X*
US 1937 72m bw
MGM (James K. McGuinness)

Competent remake with an excellent cast.

w John Meehan *d* Sam Wood *ph* John B. Seitz *m* David Snell

Gladys George, John Beal, Warren William, Reginald Owen, Lynne Carver, Henry Daniell, Emma Dunn, Ruth Hussey, George Zucco

'An upper bracketer when played with a strong companion.'—*Variety*

'A fine old play, dated and outmoded. Audiences will leave the theatre expecting to find the coachman with horse and buggy.'—*Variety*

'One man drove her to it—one man tempted her—one man degraded her—one man defended her!'

Madame X
US 1965 100m Technicolor
Universal / Ross Hunter / Eltee

An elaborately dressed remake which suffered from a wooden lead; the more expensive the production, the more obvious the holes in the plot and the psychology.

w Jean Holloway *d* David Lowell Rich *ph* Russell Metty *m* Frank Skinner

Lana Turner, John Forsythe, Ricardo Montalban, *Constance Bennett*, Burgess Meredith, Keir Dullea, Virginia Grey, Warren Stevens

'One is free to enjoy a luxurious wallow in emotions that are all the more enjoyable for having no connection whatever with reality.'—*Brenda Davies*

Made for Each Other*
US 1938 90m bw
David O. Selznick

Problems of a lawyer and his new wife culminate in the near-death of their infant son. Smooth star tearjerker.

w Jo Swerling *d* John Cromwell *ph* Leon Shamroy *m* Hugo Friedhofer, David Buttolph, *theme* Oscar Levant *pd* William Cameron Menzies

Carole Lombard, James Stewart, Charles Coburn, Lucile Watson, Harry Davenport, Eddie Quillan, Esther Dale, Louise Beavers

'Made to order for strong box office.'—*Variety*

Made for Each Other*
US 1971 107m De Luxe
TCF / Wylde Films (Roy Townshend)

Romance between two New Yorkers with inferiority complexes.
Elongated cabaret sketch, a Brooklynesque comedy of flashy brilliance but limited general interest.

w Renée Taylor, Joe Bologna *d* Robert B. Bean *ph* William Storz

Renée Taylor, Joe Bologna

Made in Heaven
GB 1952 81m Technicolor

Married couples compete for the Dunmow Flitch. Easy-going family comedy which aims to be liked. David Tomlinson, Petula Clark, Sonja Ziemann, A. E. Matthews, Charles Victor, Sophie Stewart, Richard Wattis, Athene Seyler. Written by William Douglas Home; directed by John Paddy Carstairs; for Fanfare / Rank.

Made in Heaven
US 1987 103m colour

A boy is sent back from heaven to find his lost love. Droopy fantasy on the lines of *Here Comes Mr Jordan* but without the wit. Timothy Hutton, Kelly McGillis, Maureen Stapleton, Don Murray, Marj Dusay, Debra Winger (as Emmett, incognito). Written by Bruce A. Evans, Raynold Gideon; directed by Alan Rudolph; for Rudolph-Blocker/Lorimar.

Made on Broadway
US 1933 65m bw

A public relations man deals with the mayor's dirty linen. Flat and unconvincing political comedy drama. Robert Montgomery, Sally Eilers, Madge Evans, Eugene Pallette, C. Henry Gordon, Jean Parker. Written by Gene Markey from book Public Relations by Courtney Terrett; directed by Harry Beaumont; for MGM.
(GB title: *The Girl I Made*.)

Madeleine*
GB 1949 114m bw
GFD / David Lean / Cineguild (Stanley Haynes)

In Victorian Glasgow a well-to-do young woman is accused of murdering her lover, but the verdict is 'not proven'.
Dramatically dead because of its ambiguous ending, this lavish and good-looking treatment of a *cause célèbre* was a mistake for all concerned, but its incidental pleasures are considerable.

w Nicholas Phipps, Stanley Haynes *d David Lean* *ph Guy Green* *w* William Alwyn *pd John Bryan* *costumes* Margaret Furse

Ann Todd, Leslie Banks, Elizabeth Sellars, Ivor Barnard, Ivan Desny, Norman Wooland, Edward Chapman, Barbara Everest, André Morell, Barry Jones, Jean Cadell, John Laurie, Eugene Deckers

Mademoiselle Docteur*
GB 1937 84m bw
Grafton / Trafalgar (Max Schach)

A German lady spy falls for a British agent. War melodrama vaguely based on fact and later remade as *Fräulein Doktor*.

w Jacques Natanson, Marcel Achard, Ernest Betts *d* Edmond Greville *ph* Otto Heller

Dita Parlo, John Loder, Erich Von Stroheim, Claire Luce, Gyles Isham, Clifford Evans, John Abbott

Mademoiselle Fifi*
US 1944 69m bw
RKO (Val Lewton)

During the Franco-Prussian war a stagecoach is held up because a prostitute, despite the urging of her fellow passengers, refuses to sleep with a Prussian officer. When she gives in, they shun her, and she kills him.
Interesting low budget version of a story which inspired many films.

w Josef Mischel, Peter Ruric, *stories* Boule de Suif / Mademoiselle Fifi by Guy de Maupassant *d* Robert Wise *ph* Harry Wild *m* Werner Heymann

Simone Simon, Kurt Kreuger, John Emery, Alan Napier, Jason Robards Sr, Norma Varden, Helen Freeman, Fay Helm

'There is a gallant, fervent quality about the whole picture, faults and all, which gives it a peculiar kind of life and likeableness, and which signifies that there is one group of men working in Hollywood who have neither lost nor taken care to conceal the purity of their hope and intention.'—*James Agee*

Madhouse*
GB 1974 92m Eastmancolor
AIP / Amicus (Milton Subotsky)

A reluctant horror actor makes a comeback and finds himself involved in a series of grisly murders.
In-jokey horror piece with clips from old AIP chillers; quite likeable.

w Greg Morrison, *novel* Devilday by Angus Hall *d Jim Clark* *ph* Ray Parslow *m* Douglas Gamley

Vincent Price, Peter Cushing, Robert Quarry, Adrienne Corri, Natasha Pyne, Linda Hayden, Barry Dennen

Madigan*
US 1968 100m Techniscope
Universal (Frank P. Rosenberg)

A Brooklyn police detective brings in a dangerous escaped criminal at the cost of his own life.
Lively, well-characterized police thriller with excellent locations.

w Henri Simoun, Abraham Polonsky, *novel* The Commissioner by Richard Dougherty *d Don Siegel* *ph* Russell Metty *m* Don Costa

Richard Widmark, Henry Fonda, Michael Dunn, Inger Stevens, Harry Guardino, James Whitmore, Susan Clark, Steve Ihnat, Don Stroud, Sheree North, Warren Stevens, Raymond St Jacques

† The character was later resurrected for a TV series also starring Richard Widmark.

Madison Avenue
US 1961 94m bw Cinemascope
TCF (Bruce Humberstone)

An advertising executive plans to revenge himself on his treacherous boss.
Predictable melodrama with an adequate plot but dismal acting and presentation.

w Norman Corwin, *novel* The Build-Up Boys by Jeremy Kirk *d* Bruce Humberstone *ph* Charles G. Clarke *m* Harry Sukman

Dana Andrews, Jeanne Crain, Eleanor Parker, Eddie Albert, Howard St John, Henry Daniell, Kathleen Freeman

'Simply nowhere near grand enough.'—*MFB*

Madness of the Heart
GB 1949 105m bw
GFD / Two Cities (Richard Wainwright)

A blind girl marries a French aristocrat and has to cope with a jealous neighbour.
Heavily disguised version of the *Rebecca* theme, with a happy ending after many alarums and excursions, most of them irrelevant. As film-making, very thin.

wd Charles Bennett, *novel* Flora Sandstrom *ph* Desmond Dickinson *m* Allan Gray

Margaret Lockwood, Paul Dupuis, Kathleen Byron, Maxwell Reed

Madonna of the Seven Moons
GB 1944 110m bw
GFD / Gainsborough (R. J. Minney)

Affected by childhood rape, a demure lady has a second life as a daring gypsy.
Novelettish balderdash killed stone dead by stilted presentation; but highly successful in its day.

w Roland Pertwee, Brock Williams, *novel* Margery Lawrence *d* Arthur Crabtree *ph* Jack Cox

Phyllis Calvert, Stewart Granger, Patricia Roc, Peter Glenville, John Stuart, Jean Kent, Nancy Price, Peter Murray Hill, Reginald Tate

'One of the most diverting British films of the forties.'—*Richard Roud*

'The purplest production English cinema has yet achieved.'—*Time and Tide*

The Madonna's Secret
US 1946 79m bw

Women attracted to a Parisian painter are all found dead. Slow-moving mystery which manages to remain suspenseful. Francis Lederer, Gail Patrick, Ann Rutherford, Edward Ashley, Linda Stirling, John Litel. Written by Bradbury Foote and William Thiele; directed by William Thiele; for Stephen Auer / Republic.

The Madwoman of Chaillot*
GB 1969 142m Technicolor
Warner / Commonwealth United (Ely Landau)

An eccentric Parisian lady has equally eccentric friends, but her real life is in the past.
A highly theatrical whimsy which somewhat lacks humour, this should never have been considered as a film, certainly not as an all-star extravaganza; but it was, and it falls flat on its face in the first reel of tedious conversation.

w Edward Anhalt, *play* Jean Giraudoux *d* Bryan Forbes *ph* Claude Renoir, Burnett Guffey *m* Michael J. Lewis *pd* Ray Simm

Katharine Hepburn, Yul Brynner, Danny Kaye, Edith Evans, Charles Boyer, Claude Dauphin, John Gavin, Paul Henreid, Nanette Newman, Oscar Homolka, Margaret Leighton, Giulietta Masina, Richard Chamberlain, Donald Pleasence, Fernand Gravet

'One finds oneself too often longing for the drop of the curtain.'—*Brenda Davies*

'The intentions are honourable—defeat is inevitable.'—*Rex Reed*

'One of Giraudoux's less good and most fragile plays has been rewritten, bloated with inept contemporary references, drawn out to gigantic proportions of humourless vacuity, and peopled with a barrelful of nonacting stars.'—*John Simon*

'The remnants of Giraudoux' slight, whimsical play can still be perceived in Edward Anhalt's vile modernization, and a lot of famous actors can be recognized even in the performances they give here.'—*Pauline Kael, New Yorker*

Maedchen in Uniform*
Germany 1931 90m bw
Deutsche Film-Gemeinschaft
aka: *Girls in Uniform*

A girl at a strict boarding school falls in love with one of the teachers and commits suicide.
Famous early stab at lesbianism, remade in 1958 with Romy Schneider and Lilli Palmer. Interesting for content, not style.

w F. D. Andam, Christa Winsloe, *play* Gestern und Heute by Christa Winsloe *d* Leontine Sagan *ph* Reimar Kuntze *m* Hansen Milde-Meissner

Dorothea Wieck, Ellen Schwannecke, Hertha Thiele, Emilie Lunde

'At once a strident warning against the consequences of Hitler's regime and the first truly radical lesbian film.'—*Time Out, 1981*

The Maggie**
GB 1953 93m bw
Ealing (Michael Truman)
US title: *High and Dry*

An American businessman is tricked into sending his private cargo to a Scottish island on an old puffer in need of repair.
Mildly amusing comedy about the wily Scots; not the studio at its best, but pretty fair.

w William Rose *d Alexander Mackendrick* *ph* Gordon Dines *m* John Addison

Paul Douglas, *Alex Mackenzie*, James Copeland, Abe Barker, Dorothy Alison, Hubert Gregg, Geoffrey Keen, Andrew Keir, Tommy Kearins

Magic
US 1978 107m Technicolor
TCF / Joseph E. Levine

A ventriloquist obsessed by his dummy is impelled to murder.
Pretentious and occasionally unpleasant version of an oft-told tale.

w William Goldman, from his novel *d* Richard Attenborough *ph* Victor J. Kemper *m* Jerry Goldsmith *pd* Terence Marsh

Anthony Hopkins, Ann-Margret, Burgess Meredith, Ed Lauter, E. J. Andre, David Ogden Stiers

'The gloomily withdrawn Hopkins has no vulgarity in his soul—nothing that suggests any connection with the world of entertainment—and the picture grinds along.'—*New Yorker*

The Magic Bow
GB 1946 106m bw
GFD / Gainsborough (R. J. Minney)

Episodes in the life of the violin virtuoso Paganini.
Poor costumer, dramatically and historically unpersuasive.

w Norman Ginsbury, Roland Pertwee *d* Bernard Knowles *ph* Jack Cox *violin solos Yehudi Menuhin*

Stewart Granger, Jean Kent, Phyllis Calvert, Dennis Price, Cecil Parker, Felix Aylmer, Frank Cellier, Marie Lohr, Henry Edwards

The Magic Box*
GB 1951 118m Technicolor
Festival Films (Ronald Neame)

The life of William Friese-Greene, a British cinema pioneer who died in poverty.
A joint British film industry venture to celebrate the Festival of Britain, this rather downbeat and uneventful story takes on the nature of a pageant or a series of charades, with well-known people appearing to no good purpose. But it means well.

w Eric Ambler *d* John Boulting *ph Jack Cardiff* *m* William Alwyn *pd* John Bryan

Robert Donat, Margaret Johnson, Maria Schell, John Howard Davies, Renée Asherson, Richard Attenborough, Robert Beatty, Michael Denison, Leo Genn, Marius Goring, Joyce Grenfell, Robertson Hare, Kathleen Harrison, Jack Hulbert, Stanley Holloway, Glynis Johns, Mervyn Johns, Barry Jones, Miles Malleson, Muir Mathieson, A. E. Matthews, John McCallum, Bernard Miles, Laurence Olivier, Cecil Parker, Eric Portman, Dennis Price, Michael Redgrave, Margaret

Rutherford, Ronald Shiner, Sybil Thorndike, David Tomlinson, Cecil Trouncer, Peter Ustinov, Kay Walsh, Emlyn Williams, Harcourt Williams, Googie Withers

'An honest and often a very moving film.'—*Daily Express*

'Patriotic, sentimental, overlong and faintly embarrassing.'—*Time Out, 1984*

The Magic Carpet
US 1951 84m Supercinecolor

The caliph's son returns as the Scarlet Falcon to rout the usurper. Hopeless kid's matinee rubbish, not even performed with verve. Lucille Ball, Raymond Burr, John Agar, Patricia Medina, George Tobias. Written by David Matthews; directed by Lew Landers; for Sam Katzman / Columbia.

The Magic Christian
GB 1970 95m Technicolor
Commonwealth United / Grand Films (Dennis O'Dell)

An eccentric millionaire spends his wealth deflating those who pursue money or power.
A series of variably funny but always unpleasant sketches, climaxing with citizens delving for spoils in a vat of blood and manure. In its aim to be satirical, very typical of its time.

w Terry Southern, Joseph McGrath, Peter Sellers, *novel* Terry Southern *d* Joseph McGrath *ph* Geoffrey Unsworth *m* Ken Thorne *pd* Assheton Gorton

Peter Sellers, Ringo Starr, Richard Attenborough, Laurence Harvey, Christopher Lee, Spike Milligan, Yul Brynner, Roman Polanski, Raquel Welch, Wilfrid Hyde White, Fred Emney, John Le Mesurier, Dennis Price, Patrick Cargill, John Cleese, Graham Chapman

The Magic Face
US 1951 90m bw
Columbia (Mort Briskin, Robert Smith)

A brilliant German impersonator kills Hitler, takes his place, and leads Germany deliberately into defeat.
Hilariously unlikely anecdote 'as told to William Shirer', performed with vigour but handicapped by a shoddy production.

w Mort Briskin, Robert Smith *d* Frank Tuttle *ph* Tony Braun *m* Herschel Burke Gilbert

Luther Adler, Patricia Knight, Ilka Windish, William L. Shirer

'If Shirer believed this story, then he must be the only person in the world to do so.'—*Gavin Lambert*

Magic Fire
US 1954 94m Trucolor
Republic (William Dieterle)

The life and loves of Richard Wagner.
Remarkably boring biopic with much music but little story or characterization. Ugly colour minimizes German locations.

w Bertita Harding, E. A. Dupont, David Chantler *d* William Dieterle *ph* Ernest Haller *md* Erich Wolfgang Korngold

Alan Badel, Yvonne de Carlo, Peter Cushing, Frederick Valk, Carlos Thompson, Valentina Cortesa

The Magic of Lassie
US 1978 99m colour
Lassie Productions (Bonita Granville)

A collie dog is sold but makes its way back home.
Downright peculiar revamp of *Lassie Come Home* with music and an ageing all-star cast.

w Jean Holloway, Richard B. Sherman, Robert M. Sherman *d* Don Chaffey *m* Irwin Kostal *songs* Richard and Robert Sherman

James Stewart, Alice Faye, Mickey Rooney, Pernell Roberts, Stephanie Zimbalist, Gene Evans

AAN: song, 'When You're Loved'

The Magic Sword
US 1962 80m Eastmancolor
UA / Bert I. Gordon

The son of a well-meaning witch rescues a princess from the clutches of an evil sorcerer.
Shaky medieval fantasy on too low a budget.

w Bernard Schoenfeld *d* Bert I. Gordon *ph* Paul Vogel *m* Richard Markowitz *sp* Milt Rice

Basil Rathbone, Estelle Winwood, Gary Lockwood, Anne Helm

'The guy with the dynamite heart meets the girl with the firecracker eyes!'

Magic Town
US 1947 103m bw
Robert Riskin Productions

An opinion pollster discovers a small town which exactly mirrors the views of the USA at large.
A bright Capraesque idea is extraordinarily dully scripted, the production looks dim, and all concerned are operating one degree under.

w Robert Riskin *d* William A. Wellman *ph* Joseph Biroc *m* Roy Webb

James Stewart, Jane Wyman, Kent Smith, Regis Toomey, Donald Meek, Ned Sparks, Wallace Ford

The Magic Toyshop*
GB 1986 107m colour
Granada (Steve Morrison)

Three children are left in the care of their uncle, a puppet-maker.
Weird, sometimes grotesque fantasy focusing on an adolescent girl's sexual awakening.

w Angela Carter, from her novel *d* David Wheatley *ph* Peter Ibberson *m* Bill Connor *pd* Stephen Fineren

Tom Bell, Caroline Milmoe, Kilian McKenna

The Magician*
US 1926 approx 80m bw silent
MGM

A dabbler in the occult comes to grief when he tries to influence a young girl.
A melodrama with interesting credits; unfortunately no prints remain.

from the novel by Somerset Maugham *d* Rex Ingram

Paul Wegener, Ivan Petrovitch, Alice Terry

The Magician of Lublin
West Germany / Israel 1979 114m colour
Geria-Golan-Globus (Harry N. Blum)

In 1901 an itinerant magician with an active sex life dreams of being able really to fly.
Curious muddled fable with apparent correspondences to the Christ story, like Bergman's *The Face.* In the end it does not confidently address itself to any audience, despite clever moments.

w Irving S. White, Menahem Golan *novel* Isaac Bashevis Singer *d* Menahem Golan *ph* David Gurfinkel *m* Maurice Jarre *pd* Jurgen Kiebach

Alan Arkin, Louise Fletcher, Valerie Perrine, Shelley Winters, Lou Jacobi, Warren Berlinger

'California Polish accents grapple with ham-fisted direction and a script of surpassing banality.'—*Sight and Sound*

The Magnet
GB 1950 79m bw
Ealing (Sidney Cole)

A small boy steals a magnet and accidentally becomes a hero.
Very mild Ealing comedy, not really up to snuff.

w T. E. B. Clarke *d* Charles Frend *ph* Lionel Banes *m* William Alwyn

Stephen Murray, Kay Walsh, William Fox, Meredith Edwards, Gladys Henson, Thora Hird, Wylie Watson

The Magnetic Monster*
US 1953 75m bw
UA / Ivan Tors

A new radio-active element causes 'implosions' of increasing size by drawing energy from the area around it.
Well-told low-budget sci-fi with the audience kept abreast of all developments; the undersea lab scenes are borrowed from an old German film, *Gold.*

w Curt Siodmak, Ivan Tors d Curt Siodmak *ph* Charles Van Enger *pd* George Van Marter *m* Blaine Sanford

Richard Carlson, King Donovan, Jean Byron, Byron Foulger

'A crackling mixture of science and fiction.'—*Time*

'Real life screened more daringly than it's ever been before!'

The Magnificent Ambersons****
US 1942 88m bw
RKO (Orson Welles)

A proud family loses its wealth and its control of the neighbourhood, and its youngest male member gets his come-uppance.
Fascinating period drama told in brilliant

cinematic snippets; owing to studio interference the last reels are weak, but the whole is a treat for connoisseurs, and a delight in its fast-moving control of cinematic narrative.

wd Orson Welles, novel Booth Tarkington *ph Stanley Cortez m Bernard Herrmann ad Mark-Lee Kirr*

Joseph Cotten, Dolores Costello, Agnes Moorehead, Tim Holt, Anne Baxter, Ray Collins, Richard Bennett, Erskine Sanford, Donald Dillaway

NARRATOR (Welles): 'And now Major Amberson was engaged in the profoundest thinking of his life, and he realized that everything which had worried him or delighted him during his lifetime—all his buying and building and trading and banking—that it was all a trifle and a waste beside what concerned him now, for the Major knew now that he had to plan how to enter an unknown country where he was not even sure of being recognized as an Amberson.'

NARRATOR: 'Something had happened. A thing which years ago had been the eagerest hope of many, many good citizens of the town. And now it had come at last: George Amberson Minafer had got his come-uppance. He got it three times filled and running over. But those who had so longed for it were not there to see it, and they never knew it. Those who were still living had forgotten all about it and all about him.'

'Rich in ideas that many will want to copy, combined in the service of a story that few will care to imitate.'—*C. A. Lejeune*

'Nearly every scene is played with a casual perfection which could only come from endless painstaking planning and rehearsals, and from a wonderful sense of timing.'—*Basil Wright, 1972*

'Even in this truncated form it's amazing and memorable.'—*Pauline Kael, 70s*

† Previously filmed in 1925 as *Pampered Youth.*

†† The credits are all at the end and all spoken, ending with: 'I wrote and directed the picture. My name is Orson Welles.'

AAN: best picture; Stanley Cortez; Agnes Moorehead

The Magnificent Brute
US 1936 77m bw

A blast furnace boss becomes involved with stolen money. Star character drama; very predictable. Victor McLaglen, Binnie Barnes, Billy Burrud, William Hall, Jean Dixon. Written by Owen Francis, Lewis J. Foster and Bertram Millhauser; directed by John G. Blystone; for Universal.

'The whisper of every woman—the toast of every man!'

Magnificent Doll
US 1946 95m bw
Universal / Hallmark (Jack H. Skirball, Bruce Manning)

Dolly Madison, wife of the President, finds that traitor Aaron Burr is a memory from her own past.

Uneasy historical semi-fiction, badly cast and rather boring, yet with some sense of period style.

w Irving Stone *d* Frank Borzage *ph* Joseph Valentine *m* Hans Salter

Ginger Rogers, David Niven, Burgess Meredith, Stephen McNally, Peggy Wood, Robert Barrat

'No duller case has ever been made out for liberty.'—*Daily Mail*

'Some day the moviemakers will discover that they can make history wonderfully believable and exciting by just sticking roughly to the facts.'—*The Times*

The Magnificent Dope
US 1942 83m bw
TCF (William Perlberg)

As a publicity stunt a success school brings the nation's most complete failure to New York, and he outsmarts them all.
Dim sub-Capra comedy.

w George Seaton *d* Walter Lang *ph* Peverell Marley *md* Emil Newman *m* David Raksin and others

Henry Fonda, Lynn Bari, Don Ameche, Edward Everett Horton, George Barbier, Frank Orth, Hobart Cavanaugh

The Magnificent Fraud
US 1939 78m bw

The president of a Latin American republic is murdered, and an impersonator takes his place. Sharply played dramatic hokum. Akim Tamiroff, Lynne Overman, Patricia Morison, Mary Boland. Written by Gilbert Gabriel and Walter Ferris; directed by Robert Florey; for Paramount. 'Dull drama; no marquee names; filler fodder for duals.'—*Variety*

The Magnificent Matador
US 1955 94m Eastmancolor Cinemascope
Edward L. Alperson
GB title: *The Brave and the Beautiful*

A matador trains his illegitimate son to follow in his footsteps but has a premonition of his death in the ring.
Dreary bullfighting drama with romantic interludes.

w Charles Lang *d* Budd Boetticher *ph* Lucien Ballard *m* Raoul Kraushaar

Anthony Quinn, Maureen O'Hara, Manuel Rojas, Richard Denning, Thomas Gomez, Lola Albright

Magnificent Obsession**
US 1935 112m bw
Universal (John M. Stahl)

The playboy who is half-responsible for the death of a woman's husband and for her own blindness becomes a surgeon and cures her. Absurd soaper which was phenomenally popular and is certainly well done.

w George O'Neil, Sarah Y. Mason, Victor Heerman, *novel Lloyd C. Douglas d John M. Stahl ph* John Mescall *m* Franz Waxman

Irene Dunne, Robert Taylor, Ralph Morgan, Sara Haden, Charles Butterworth, Betty Furness, Arthur Hoyt, Gilbert Emery, Arthur Treacher

'Capital romance, a cinch for the femme trade.'—*Variety*

Magnificent Obsession**
US 1954 108m Technicolor
Universal (*Ross Hunter*)

Glossy remake which sent Ross Hunter to the commercial heights as a remaker of thirties weepies. This one worked best.

w Robert Blees *d Douglas Sirk ph* Russell Metty *m* Frank Skinner

Jane Wyman, Rock Hudson, Agnes Moorehead, Barbara Rush, Otto Kruger, Gregg Palmer, Paul Cavanagh, Sara Shane

AAN: Jane Wyman

The Magnificent Rebel
US 1960 94m Technicolor
Walt Disney (Peter V. Herald)

Episodes in the life of the young Beethoven. Solid Disney biopic, shot in Vienna with good period detail.

w Joanne Court *d* Georg Tressler *ph* Goran Strindberg *md* Frederick Stark

Karl Boehm, Ernst Nadhering, Ivan Desny, Gabriele Porks

'They were seven—and they fought like seven hundred!'

The Magnificent Seven**
US 1960 138m De Luxe Panavision
UA / Mirisch–Alpha (John Sturges)

A Mexican village hires seven American gunmen for protection against bandits. Popular western based on the Japanese *Seven Samurai*; good action scenes, but the rest is verbose and often pretentious.

w William Roberts *d* John Sturges *ph* Charles Lang Jnr *m Elmer Bernstein*

Yul Brynner, Steve McQueen, Robert Vaughn, *James Coburn, Charles Bronson,* Horst Buchholz, Eli Wallach, Brad Dexter, Vladimir Sokoloff, Rosenda Monteros

AAN: Elmer Bernstein

The Magnificent Seven Deadly Sins
GB 1971 107m colour
Tigon (Graham Stark)

Compendium of comedy sketches, a very variable ragbag of old jokes.

w Bob Larbey, John Esmonde, Dave Freeman, Barry Cryer, Graham Chapman, Graham Stark, Marty Feldman, Alan Simpson, Ray Galton, Spike Milligan *d* Graham Stark *ph* Harvey Harrison Jnr *m* Roy Budd

Bruce Forsyth, Joan Sims, Roy Hudd, Harry Secombe, Leslie Phillips, Julie Ege, Harry H. Corbett, Ian Carmichael, Alfie Bass, Spike Milligan, Ronald Fraser

The Magnificent Seven Ride
US 1972 100m De Luxe
UA / Mirisch (William A. Calihan)

Tired finale to a patchy series (*Return of the Seven, Guns of the Magnificent Seven*) in which the original leader returns to save a Mexican village once again from bandits. Very modest.

w Arthur Rowe *d* George McCowan *ph* Fred Koenekamp *m* Elmer Bernstein

Lee Van Cleef, Stefanie Powers, Mariette Hartley, Pedro Armendariz Jnr, Luke Askew

The Magnificent Two
GB 1967 100m Eastmancolor
Rank (Hugh Stewart)

One of two incompetent travelling salesmen in a Latin American banana republic is persuaded to pose as a dead rebel leader.
More or less a Bob Hope vehicle, adapted for the less realistic Morecambe and Wise with unhappy results: too few sight gags and a curious emphasis on violence. The third and last of their attempts to find film vehicles.

w S. C. Green, R. M. Hills, Michael Pertwee, Peter Blackmore *d* Cliff Owen *ph* Ernest Steward *m* Ron Goodwin

Eric Morecambe, Ernie Wise, Margit Saad, Cecil Parker, Virgilio Teixeira, Isobel Black, Martin Benson

The Magnificent Yankee*
US 1951 88m bw
MGM (Armand Deutsch)
GB title: *The Man with Thirty Sons*

Episodes in the later life of Judge Oliver Wendell Holmes.
Vaguely well-meaning biopic without much dramatic sense.

w Emmet Lavery, from his play *d* John Sturges *ph* Joseph Ruttenberg *m* David Raksin

Louis Calhern, Ann Harding, Eduard Franz, Philip Ober, Richard Anderson, Edith Evanson

AAN: Louis Calhern

Magnum Force
US 1973 124m Technicolor Panavision
Warner / Malpaso (Robert Daley)

Inspector Harry Callahan has to track down his partner who is slaughtering gangsters in cold blood.
Toned-down sequel to *Dirty Harry*; the violence is still there but the hero no longer commits it.

w John Milius *d* Ted Post *ph* Frank Stanley *m* Lalo Schifrin

Clint Eastwood, Hal Holbrook, Mitch Ryan, Felton Perry, David Soul

'A ragbag of western mythology and head-on thuggery.'—*Sight and Sound*

The Magus
GB 1968 116m De Luxe Panavision
TCF / Blazer (John Kohn, Jud Kinberg)

An English schoolmaster on a Greek island is influenced by the local magician.
Fashionable philosophical nonsense, an elaborate mystery with no solution; the kind of film that all concerned begin to wish they had never thought of, especially as the presentation has nothing like the panache required, so that not even the critics liked it.

w John Fowles, from his novel *d* Guy Green *ph* Billy Williams *m* Johnny Dankworth *pd* Don Ashton

Michael Caine, Anthony Quinn, Candice Bergen, Anna Karina, Paul Stassino, Julian Glover, George Pastell

'Faintly ludicrous some of the time and painfully unexciting all of the time.'—*MFB*

'This may not be the most misguided movie ever made, but it's in there pitching.'—*Rex Reed*

'There's enough incoherence pretending to be enigma, sex play and chat about existentialism and self-discovery to make teenagers think they're having an experience; for grown-ups it's an ordeal.'—*Judith Crist*

'It has much of the fascination of a Chinese puzzle, but it would have been infinitely more enthralling if it hadn't been quite so flatly acted and directed.'—*Michael Billington, Illustrated London News*

'Probably the only movie in which one will ever sec a copy of Empson's *Seven Types of Ambiguity*.'—*Pauline Kael, New Yorker*

Mahler*
GB 1974 115m Technicolor
Goodtimes Enterprises (Roy Baird)

Fantasia on the life and times of the Jewish composer.
Fairly successful Ken Russell musical biopic on the lines of his early BBC specials.

wd Ken Russell *ph* Dick Bush

Robert Powell, Georgiana Hale, Richard Morant, Lee Montague, Rosalie Crutchley, Benny Lee, David Collings

'A piece of movie making that sets my pulses racing.'—*Michael Billington, Illustrated London News*

'Whether the title of the opus happens to be *Strauss* or *Tchaikovsky* or *Elgar* or *Brubeck*, the real title is always *Russell*.'—*Benny Green, Punch*

Mahogany
US 1975 109m colour Panavision
Paramount / Nikor (Rob Cohen, Jack Ballard)

The love life of a model and fashion designer.
Virtually a Joan Crawford vehicle redesigned for a black heroine who creates her own clothes. Fairly hilarious.

w John Byrum *d* Berry Gordy *ph* David Watkin *m* Michael Masser

Diana Ross, Billy Dee Williams, Anthony Perkins, Jean-Pierre Aumont, Nina Foch, Beah Richards, Marisa Mell

'The level of silliness rises steadily.'—*Geoff Brown*

'Movies as frantically bad as *Mahogany* can be enjoyed on at least one level; the spectacle of a lot of people making fools of themselves.'—*Time*

'What *Mahogany* does so fascinatingly and sometimes hilariously is to pilfer certain stock clichés of 50's Hollywood and adapt them to a black milieu.'—*Molly Haskell*

AAN: song 'Do You Know Where You're Going To?' (*m* Michael Masser, *ly* Gerry Goffin)

'Love so glorious it was denounced as sin!'
Maid of Salem*
US 1937 86m bw
Paramount (Frank Lloyd)

In 1692 Salem, a young girl is accused of witchcraft but saved by her lover.
Remarkably solemn period melodrama, unfortunately betrayed by amiable but miscast leads.

w Bradley King, Walter Ferris, Durward Grinstead *d* Frank Lloyd *ph* Leo Tover *m* Victor Young

Claudette Colbert, Fred MacMurray, Harvey Stephens, Gale Sondergaard, Louise Dresser, Edward Ellis, Beulah Bondi, Bonita Granville

'Weak and slow saga of witchcraft: stars the only hope.'—*Variety*

'Once the panic of witchcraft starts you are carried along on a vicious crescendo of madness and terror.'—*Stage*

Maid to Order
US 1987 96m De Luxe

A spoiled rich girl takes work as a maid but finds she has a fairy godmother. Weird semi-fantasy which wasn't wanted in the eighties, Cinderella being out of fashion. Ally Sheedy, Michael Ontkean, Beverly D'Angelo, Valerie Perrine, Dick Shawn, Tom Skerritt. Written and directed by Amy Jones (co-writers Perry and Randy Howze); for Vista/New Century.

The Maids
GB 1974 95m Technicolor
Ely Landau / Cinevision

Two Paris maids evolve a sado-masochistic ritual involving the death of their employer, but never go through with it.
Unbalanced and dreary film version of an essentially theatrical play.

w Robert Enders, Christopher Miles, *play* Jean Genet *d* Christopher Miles *ph* Douglas Slocombe *m* Laurie Johnson

Glenda Jackson, Susannah York, Vivien Merchant, Mark Burns

Maid's Night Out
US 1937 65m bw

A wealthy girl falls for the milkman, who is really a rich man who thinks she's the maid. Skittish second-feature comedy which helped to build a new star. Joan Fontaine, Allan Lane, Billy Gilbert, Cecil Kellaway, Hedda Hopper. Written by Bert Granet; directed by Ben Holmes; for RKO.

Maigret Sets a Trap*
France / Italy 1957 119m bw
Intermondia / J. P. Guibert / Jolly Film

Maigret sets a policewoman as decoy for a knife murderer . . .
Probably the best Maigret film, with excellent Parisian atmosphere and excellent acting.

w Michel Audiard, novel Georges Simenon *d Jean Delannoy ph* Louis Page *m* Paul Misraki *ad René Renoux*

Jean Gabin, Annie Girardot, Jean Desailly, Oliver Hussenot, Alfred Adam, Lino Ventura

Mail Order Bride
US 1963 83m Metrocolor Panavision
MGM (Richard E. Lyons)
GB title: *West of Montana*

An old westerner tries to find a bride for a wild young man in his charge.
Mild western comedy drama; quite tolerable.

wd Burt Kennedy *ph* Paul C. Vogel *m* George Bassman

Buddy Ebsen, Lois Nettleton, Keir Dullea, Warren Oates, Marie Windsor

The Main Attraction
GB 1962 90m Metrocolor
Seven Arts (John Patrick)

A wandering singer causes emotional problems backstage at a circus.
Limp melodrama with the star miscast as a fatal charmer.

w John Patrick *d* Daniel Petrie *ph* Geoffrey Unsworth *m* Andrew Adorian

Pat Boone, Mai Zetterling, Nancy Kwan, Yvonne Mitchell, John Le Mesurier

The Main Event
US 1979 112m Technicolor
Warner / First Artists / Barwood (Jon Peters, Barbra Streisand)

A lady entrepreneur takes on a prizefighter.
Thin and very patchy comedy for confirmed addicts of its star.

w Gail Parent, Andrew Smith *d* Howard Zieff *ph* Mario Tosi *m* Michael Melvoin *pd* Charles Rosen

Barbra Streisand, Ryan O'Neal, Paul Sand, Whitman Mayo, James Gregory

Main Street: see I Married a Doctor

Main Street After Dark
US 1944 57m bw

The police launch an assault on con men and petty thieves preying on returning ex-servicemen. Watchable crime filler. Edward Arnold, Selena Royle, Tom Trout, Audrey Totter, Dan Duryea, Hume Cronyn. Written by Karl Kamb and John C. Higgins; directed by Edward L. Cahn; for Jerry Bresler / MGM.

Main Street to Broadway*
US 1953 102m bw
Lester Cowan Productions

After several reverses a young playwright sees his work through to a Broadway opening night; it fails, but he has learned several lessons.
Curious, flat attempt to show the public how Broadway works, with big stars playing themselves in cameo roles.

w Samson Raphaelson *d* Tay Garnett *ph* James Wong Howe

Tom Morton, Mary Murphy, Ethel Barrymore, Lionel Barrymore, Shirley Booth, Rex Harrison, Lilli Palmer, Helen Hayes, Henry Fonda, Tallulah Bankhead, Mary Martin, Louis Calhern, John Van Druten, Cornel Wilde, Joshua Logan, Agnes Moorehead, Gertrude Berg

Les Mains Sales
France 1951 103m bw
Fernand Rivers
aka: *Dirty Hands*

A young communist intellectual, required to kill a traitor, finds he can do so only when he suspects the man of making love to his wife.
Verbose and dull version of a play which had some international success as *Crime Passionel.*

wd Fernand Rivers, *play* Jean-Paul Sartre *ph* Jean Bachelet

Pierre Brasseur, Daniel Gélin, Claude Nollier

Maisie
US 1939 74m bw
MGM (J. Walter Ruben)

Adventures of a Brooklyn showgirl.
Acceptable programmer which led to a series, all quite watchable and absolutely forgettable.

w Mary McCall Jnr, *novel* Dark Dame by Wilson Collinson *d* Edwin L. Marin *ph* Leonard Smith

Ann Sothern, Robert Young, Ian Hunter, Ruth Hussey, Anthony Allan (John Hubbard), Cliff Edwards

The succeeding titles, mostly written by Mary McCall and directed by Marin or Harry Beaumont or Roy del Ruth, were:

1940: CONGO MAISIE (with John Carroll; a remake of RED DUST), GOLD RUSH MAISIE (with Lee Bowman), MAISIE WAS A LADY (with Lew Ayres, Maureen O'Sullivan)
1941: RINGSIDE MAISIE (with George Murphy; GB title CASH AND CARRY)
1942: MAISIE GETS HER MAN (with Red Skelton; GB title SHE GOT HER MAN)
1943: SWING SHIFT MAISIE (with James Craig; GB title THE GIRL IN OVERALLS)
1944: MAISIE GOES TO RENO (with John Hodiak; GB title YOU CAN'T DO THAT TO ME)
1946: UP GOES MAISIE (with George Murphy; GB title UP SHE GOES)
1947: UNDERCOVER MAISIE (with Barry Nelson; GB title UNDERCOVER GIRL)

'Is she a kid—or is she kidding?'

The Major and the Minor**
US 1942 100m bw
Paramount (Arthur Hornblow Jnr)

A girl poses as a child in order to travel half fare on a train, and is helped by an officer who falls for her.
Moderately smart comedy showing the writer-director's emergent style. Remade as *You're Never Too Young* (qv).

w Charles Brackett, Billy Wilder *d Billy Wilder ph* Leo Tover *m* Robert Emmett Dolan

Ginger Rogers, Ray Milland, Rita Johnson, Robert Benchley, Diana Lynn, Edward Fielding, Frankie Thomas, Charles Smith

OSBORNE (Robert Benchley): 'Why don't you get out of that wet coat and into a dry martini?'

'The script seems to have been concocted after the title.'—*New Yorker, 1977*

Major Barbara***
GB 1941 121m bw
Gabriel Pascal

The daughter of an armaments millionaire joins the Salvation Army but resigns when it accepts her father's donation.
Stagey but compulsive version of a play in which the author takes typical side swipes at anything and everything within reach, allowing for some gorgeous acting (and overacting) by an impeccable cast.

w Anatole de Grunwald, Gabriel Pascal, *play Bernard Shaw d* Gabriel Pascal, Harold French, David Lean *ph* Ronald Neame *m* William Walton *ed* Charles Friend *costumes* Cecil Beaton *ad* Vincent Korda, John Bryan

Wendy Hiller, Rex Harrison, Robert Morley, Robert Newton, Marie Lohr, Emlyn Williams, Sybil Thorndike, Deborah Kerr, David Tree, Felix Aylmer, Penelope Dudley Ward, Walter Hudd, Marie Ault, Donald Calthrop

'Shaw's ebullience provides an unslackening fount of energy . . . his all-star cast of characters are outspoken as no one else is in films except the Marx Brothers.'—*William Whitebait*

'To call it a manifest triumph would be an arrant stinginess with words.'—*New York Times*

Major Dundee*
US 1965 134m Eastmancolor Panavision
Columbia (Jerry Bresler)

A small group of men from a US cavalry post sets out to annihilate marauding Indians.
Large-scale, rough and ready western which rambles along in humourless vein but rises to some spectacularly bloodthirsty climaxes.

w Harry Julian Fink, Oscar Saul, Sam Peckinpah *d* Sam Peckinpah *ph* Sam Leavitt *m* Daniele Amfitheatrof

Charlton Heston, Richard Harris, Jim Hutton, James Coburn, Michael Anderson Jnr, Warren Oates, Senta Berger, Slim Pickens

A Majority of One
US 1961 156m Technicolor
Warner (Mervyn Le Roy)

A Jewish widow has a shipboard romance with a Japanese businessman.
Interminable stage-bound comedy-drama, boringly assembled and fatally compromised by the casting of stars who are neither Jewish nor Japanese.

w Leonard Spiegelgass, from his play
d Mervyn Le Roy *ph* Harry Stradling *m* Max Steiner

Rosalind Russell, Alec Guinness, Ray Danton, Madlyn Rhue

AAN: Harry Stradling

Make a Wish
US 1937 75m bw
(RKO) Sol Lesser

A composer discovers a boy singer at a summer camp.
Acceptable family entertainment.

w Gertrude Berg, Bernard Schubert, Earle Snell *d* Kurt Neumann *ph* John Mescall *songs* Oscar Strauss *m* Hugo Riesnfeld

Basil Rathbone, Bobby Breen, Marion Claire, Leon Errol, Henry Armetta, Ralph Forbes, Donald Meek

AAN: Hugo Riesenfeld

Make Haste to Live
US 1954 89m bw
Republic (William A. Seiter)

A lady newspaper owner is embarrassed, to say the least, by the reappearance of her murderer husband, long thought dead.
Competent but rather dull programmer.

w Warren Duff, *novel* The Gordons
d William A. Seiter *ph* John L. Russell
m Elmer Bernstein

Dorothy McGuire, Stephen McNally, Mary Murphy, Edgar Buchanan, John Howard

Make Me a Star
US 1932 80m bw
Paramount (Lloyd Sheldon)

A grocery clerk goes to Hollywood and becomes a film star.
Modest remake of a silent success; see also *Merton of the Movies*.

w Sam Wintz, Walter de Leon, Arthur Kober, *novel* Merton of the Movies by Harry Leon Wilson *d* William Beaudine *ph* Allen Siegler

Stuart Erwin, Joan Blondell, Zasu Pitts, Ben Turpin, Florence Roberts; and Tallulah Bankhead, Clive Brook, Gary Cooper, Maurice Chevalier, Claudette Colbert, Fredric March, Jack Oakie, Charlie Ruggles, Sylvia Sidney

'Packed with laughs which offsets the longish running time.'—*Variety*

Make Me an Offer*
GB 1954 88m Eastmancolor
Group Three (W. P. Lipscomb)

An antique dealer has an ambition to own a famous vase.
Mildly pleasant Jewish comedy with interesting sidelights on the antique business.

w W. P. Lipscomb, *novel* Wolf Mankowitz
d Cyril Frankel *ph* Denny Densham *m* John Addison

Peter Finch, Adrienne Corri, *Meier Tzelniker*, Rosalie Crutchley, Finlay Currie, *Ernest Thesiger*, Wilfrid Lawson, Alfie Bass

Make Mine Music**
US 1946 74m Technicolor
Walt Disney (Joe Grant)

A programme of cartoon shorts: JOHNNY FEDORA, ALL THE CATS JOIN IN, WITHOUT YOU, TWO SILHOUETTES, CASEY AT THE BAT, THE MARTINS AND THE COYS, BLUE BAYOU, AFTER YOU'VE GONE, WILLIE THE SINGING WHALE, PETER AND THE WOLF.

An insubstantial banquet, sometimes arty and sometimes chocolate boxy, which occasionally rises to the expected heights.

w various *d* various

'There is enough genuine charm and imagination and humour to make up perhaps one good average Disney short.'—*James Agee*

Make Way for a Lady
US 1936 63m bw

A girl determines to find a mate for her widowed father. Rather irritating comedy of embarrassment. Herbert Marshall, Anne Shirley, Gertrude Michael, Margot Grahame, Clara Blandick, Taylor Holmes, Willie Best. Written by Gertrude Purcell from the novel Daddy and I by Elizabeth Jordan; directed by David Burton; for Zion Myers / RKO. 'It lacks suspense, surprise, and plausibility.'—*Variety*

'Grandpa moves in! Daughter moves out! And the riot starts!'

Make Way for Tomorrow**
US 1937 94m bw
Paramount (Leo McCarey)

An elderly couple are in financial difficulty and have to be parted because their children will not help.
Sentimental drama which had a devastating effect at the time but now seems oversimplified and exaggerated.

w Vina Delmar, *novel* The Years Are So Long by Josephine Lawrence *d Leo McCarey*
ph William C. Mellor *m* George Antheil

Victor Moore, Beulah Bondi, Thomas Mitchell, Fay Bainter, Porter Hall, Barbara Read, Maurice Moscovitch, Elizabeth Risdon, Gene Lockhart

'Needs special exploitation: even so, business is apt to be spotty where played solo.'—*Variety*

'The most brilliantly directed and acted film of the year.'—*John Grierson*

'A sense of misery and inhumanity is left vibrating in the nerves.'—*Graham Greene*

Make Your Own Bed
US 1944 82m bw

A detective and his girl friend pretend to be servants in order to protect an inventor from Nazis. Mirthless pratfall farce. Jack Carson, Jane Wyman, Irene Manning, Ricardo Cortez, Alan Hale, George Tobias. Written by Francis Swann and Edmund Joseph; directed by Peter Godfrey; for Warner.

Making Love
US 1982 111m De Luxe
TCF / IndieProd (Allen Adler, Danny Melnick)

A young married doctor declares that he is gay and moves in with a friend.
Would-be daring melodrama whose producers quickly found that nobody was interested.

w Barry Sandler, *story* A. Scott Berg
d Arthur Hiller *ph* David M. Walsh
m Leonard Rosenman *pd* James D. Vance
ed William H. Reynolds

Michael Ontkean, Kate Jackson, Harry Hamlin, Wendy Hiller, Arthur Hill, Nancy Olson

Malachi's Cove
GB 1973 75m Technicolor
Penrith / Impact Quadrant Films (Andrew Sinclair, Kent Walwin)
aka: *The Seaweed Children*

In 1880 Cornwall, a 14-year-old girl lives by selling seaweed.
Slimly-plotted film for the family, pleasant without being very interesting.

wd Henry Herbert, *story* Anthony Trollope
ph Walter Lassally *m* Brian Gascoigne

Donald Pleasence, Dai Bradley, Veronica Quilligan, Arthur English, David Howe

Malaga
GB 1954 84m Technicolor

An American woman agent catches drug smugglers in Tangier. Routine international thick ear. Maureen O'Hara, Macdonald Carey, Binnie Barnes, Guy Middleton, Leonard Sachs. Written by Robert Westerby; directed by Richard Sale; for M. J. Frankovich / Film Locations. (US title: *Fire Over Africa*.)

Malaya*
US 1949 95m bw
MGM (Edwin H. Knopf)
GB title: *East of the Rising Sun*

An adventurer attempts to smuggle rubber out of Japanese-occupied Malaya.
Dour action melodrama, unworthy of its considerable cast but watchable.

w Frank Fenton *d* Richard Thorpe
ph George Folsey *m* Bronislau Kaper

Spencer Tracy, James Stewart, Sidney Greenstreet, John Hodiak, Valentina Cortesa, Lionel Barrymore, Gilbert Roland

Malcolm
Australia 1986 86m bw

A retarded but mechanically talented youth lives alone in a Melbourne suburb and takes in a petty criminal and his girl friend. Initially interesting but mishandled character study which never settles into a comfortable groove. Colin Friels, John Hargreaves, Lindy Davies, Chris Haywood, Charles Tingwell. Written and photographed by David Parker; directed by Nadia Tass; for Cascade.

The Male Animal*
US 1942 101m bw
Warner (Wolfgang Reinhardt)

A dry college professor emancipates himself when his wife becomes attracted to a football star.

Stagebound but amusing college comedy with pleasant humour and good performances. Remade as *She's Working Her Way through College* (qv).

w Julius J. and Philip G. Epstein, Stephen Morehouse Avery, *play* James Thurber and Elliott Nugent *d* Elliott Nugent *ph* Arthur Edeson *m* Heinz Roemheld

Henry Fonda, Olivia de Havilland, Jack Carson, Joan Leslie, Eugene Pallette, Don Defore, Herbert Anderson, Hattie McDaniel

Malone

US 1987 92m De Luxe

A disillusioned CIA hit man is not allowed to go 'straight'. Moody but not unwatchable thriller largely set in Oregon. Burt Reynolds, Cliff Robertson, Kenneth McMillan, Cynthia Gibb, Scott Wilson, Lauren Hutton. Written by Christopher Frank from the novel Shotgun by William Wingate; directed by Harley Cokliss; for Leo L. Fuchs/Orion.

The Malta Story

GB 1953 103m bw
GFD / British Film Makers (Peter de Sarigny)

An English flier is involved in the defence of Malta during World War II.
Glib propaganda piece which is not very excitingly written or characterized, and fails to convince on any but the most elementary level.

w William Fairchild, Nigel Balchin *d* Brian Desmond Hurst *ph* Robert Krasker *m* William Alwyn

Alec Guinness, Anthony Steel, Muriel Pavlow, Jack Hawkins, Flora Robson, Renée Asherson, Ralph Truman, Reginald Tate, Hugh Burden

The Maltese Bippy

US 1969 92m Metrocolor Panavision

A skin flick star thinks he is turning into a werewolf. Failed attempt to construct a crazy comedy for the stars of Laugh-In; even the spooky house sequences don't go. Dan Rowan, Dick Martin, Carol Lynley, Julie Newmar, Mildred Natwick, Fritz Weaver, Robert Reed. Written by Everett Freeman, Ray Singer; directed by Norman Panama; for MGM.

The Maltese Falcon**

US 1931 80m bw
Warner
TV title: *Dangerous Female*

After the death of his partner, private eye Sam Spade is dragged into a quest for a priceless statuette.
Excellent crime melodrama with smart pace and performances. Remade as *Satan Met a Lady* (1936); and see below.

w Maude Fulton, Lucien Hubbard, Brown Holmes, *novel Dashiell Hammett d Roy del Ruth ph* William Rees

Ricardo Cortez, Bebe Daniels, *Dudley Digges,* Dwight Frye, Robert Elliott, Thelma Todd, Oscar Apfel

'Any type of audience will enjoy it.'—*Variety*

'The best mystery thriller of the year.'—*New York Times*

'A nice blend of humour, intelligence and suspense.'—*Clive Hirschhorn, 1979*

'A guy without a conscience! A dame without a heart!'
'He's as fast on the draw as he is in the drawing room!'

The Maltese Falcon****

US 1941 101m bw
Warner (Henry Blanke)

A remake which shows the difference between excellence and brilliance; here every nuance is subtly stressed, and the cast is perfection.

wd John Huston ph Arthur Edeson m Adolph Deutsch

Humphrey Bogart, Mary Astor, Sidney Greenstreet, Elisha Cook Jnr, Barton MacLane, Lee Patrick, Peter Lorre, Gladys George, *Ward Bond, Jerome Cowan*

GUTMAN (Sidney Greenstreet): 'I distrust a close-mouthed man. He generally picks the wrong time to talk and says the wrong things. Talking's something you can't do judiciously, unless you keep in practice. Now, sir, we'll talk if you like. I'll tell you right out, I'm a man who likes talking to a man who likes to talk.'

SPADE (Humphrey Bogart) to Cairo (Peter Lorre): 'When you're slapped, you'll take it and like it!'

SPADE to Brigid (Mary Astor): 'Don't be too sure I'm as crooked as I'm supposed to be.'

GUTMAN: 'I distrust a man who says when. If he's got to be careful not to drink too much, it's because he's not to be trusted when he does.'

'The first crime melodrama with finish, speed and bang to come along in what seems like ages.'—*Otis Ferguson*

'A work of entertainment that is yet so skilfully constructed that after many years and many viewings, it has the same brittle explosiveness—and some of the same surprise—that it had in 1941.'—*Pauline Kael, 1968*

'The trick which Mr Huston has pulled is a combination of American ruggedness with the suavity of the English crime school—a blend of mind and muscle—plus a slight touch of pathos.'—*Bosley Crowther, New York Times*

'Admirable photography of the sort in which black and white gives full value to every detail, every flicker of panic.'—*Francis Wyndham*

AAN: best picture; John Huston (as writer); Sidney Greenstreet

Mama Loves Papa*

US 1933 70m bw

A middle-class wife decides to do some social climbing. Slight but amusing comedy which put together a useful team. *Charles Ruggles, Mary Boland*, Lilyan Tashman, George Barbier, Morgan Wallace. Written by Arthur Kober, Nunnally Johnson, Douglas MacLean, Keene Thompson; directed by Norman Z. McLeod; for Paramount. 'Exceptionally funny comedy . . . a cinch builder.'—*Variety*

† A second film under this title was a Leon Errol vehicle of 1945.

Mamba

US 1930 76m Technicolor

Germans in East Africa go to the bad during World War I. Absurd melodrama climaxing with a Zulu uprising. Jean Hersholt, Eleanor Boardman, Ralph Forbes, Josef Swickard. Written by Tom Miranda, Winifred Dunn, from a story by F. Schumann-Heink and John Reinhardt; directed by Al Rogell; for Tiffany. 'It has its lowlights and highlights; in between it's not a bad programmer.'—*Variety*

Mambo

Italy / USA 1954 92m (English version), 107m (Italian version) bw
Paramount / Ponti / De Laurentiis

A Venetian shopgirl loves a worthless gambler, is romanced by a haemophiliac count, and joins a dance troupe.
Patchy melodrama with plenty going on but no grip.

w Guido Piovene, Ivo Perelli, Ennio de Concini, Robert Rossen *d* Robert Rossen *ph* Harold Rosson *m* Nino Rota, Francesco Lavagnino *sets* Andrei Andrejew *ch* Katherine Dunham

Silvana Mangano, Michael Rennie, Shelley Winters, Vittorio Gassman, Eduardo Cianelli, Mary Clare, Katherine Dunham and her troupe

Mame*

US 1974 131m Technicolor Panavision
Warner / ABC (Robert Fryer, James Cresson)

In 1928, a 10-year-old boy goes to live with his eccentric, sophisticated aunt.
Old-fashioned and rather bad film of a much overrated Broadway musical, inept in most departments but with occasional show-stopping moments.

w Paul Zandel, *play* Jerome Lawrence, Robert E. Lee, *book* Patrick Dennis *d* Gene Saks *ph* Philip Lathrop *m / ly* Jerry Herman *pd* Robert F. Boyle

Lucille Ball, Beatrice Arthur, Robert Preston, Bruce Davison, Jane Connell, Joyce Van Patten, John McGiver

'It makes one realize afresh the parlous state of the Hollywood musical, fighting to survive against misplaced superstars and elephantine budgets matched with minuscule imagination.'—*Geoff Brown*

'The cast seem to have been handpicked for their tone-deafness, and Lucille Ball's close-ups are shot blatantly out of focus.'—*Sight and Sound*

'So terrible it isn't boring; you can get fixated staring at it and wondering what Lucille Ball thought she was doing.'—*New Yorker, 1977*

Mammy*
US 1930 84m bw
Warner (Walter Morosco)

Murder backstage at a minstrel show.
One of the star's better musicals.

w L. G. Rigby, Joseph Jackson *d* Michael Curtiz *ph* Barney McGill *m* Irving Berlin

Al Jolson, Lowell Sherman, Hobart Bosworth, Louise Dresser, Lee Moran

'Looks like money . . . a lively picture playing fast.'—*Variety*

A Man, a Woman and a Bank
Canada 1979 101m CFI color

A civil engineer and a computer expert devise a foolproof way of robbing a bank. We have been here before, except that these days the criminals are allowed to get away with it. Ho-hum. Donald Sutherland, Brooke Adams, Paul Mazursky. Written by Raynold Gideon, Bruce A. Evans and Stuart Margolin; directed by Noel Black; for Bennett / McNichol.

A Man About the House
GB 1947 95m bw
British Lion (Edward Black)

Two English ladies inherit an Italian villa and fall under the spell of the handsome handyman, who marries one of them and proceeds slowly to poison her.
Now clearly dull, at the time this seemed a fairly enterprising rehash of *Gaslight, Kind Lady* and *Rebecca*.

w J. B. Williams, Leslie Arliss, *novel* Francis Brett Young and *play* John Perry *d* Leslie Arliss *ph* Georges Perinal *m* Nicholas Brodsky

Margaret Johnston, Dulcie Gray, Kieron Moore, Felix Aylmer, Lilian Braithwaite

A Man About the House
GB 1974 90m colour
EMI / Hammer (Roy Skeggs)

Two young women, their male flatmate and their landlords combine forces to prevent the terrace from being razed for redevelopment.
Mild and rather exhausting sex comedy from the TV series, as relentlessly single-minded as a 'Carry On'.

w Johnnie Mortimer, Brian Cooke *d* John Robins *ph* Jimmy Allen *m* Christopher Gunning

Richard O'Sullivan, Paula Wilcox, Sally Thomsett, Yootha Joyce, Brian Murphy, Peter Cellier, Patrick Newell, Spike Milligan, Arthur Lowe

Man about Town
US 1932 75m bw

A society gambler is really a secret service man. Flabby melodrama which practically dislocates the long arm of coincidence. Warner Baxter, Karen Morley, Conway Tearle, Lawrence Grant, Leni Stengel, Alan Mowbray, Lillian Bond, Halliwell Hobbes. Written by Leon Gordon from the novel by Denison Clift; directed by John Francis Dillon; for Fox. 'Plenty of hodge-podge, and doubtful b.o. Will need strong support almost everywhere.'—*Variety*

Man About Town*
US 1939 85m bw
Paramount (Arthur Hornblow Jnr)

A Broadway producer in London makes his girlfriend jealous.
Fairly amusing comedy-musical programmer.

w Morrie Ryskind *d* Mark Sandrich *ph* Ted Tetzlaff *md* Victor Young

Jack Benny, Dorothy Lamour, Edward Arnold, Binnie Barnes, Phil Harris, Eddie Anderson, Monty Woolley, Isabel Jeans, Betty Grable, E. E. Clive

'Good comedy, rates okay biz.'—*Variety*

Man Afraid
US 1957 84m bw Cinemascope

A priest is forced to kill a hoodlum in self-defence, and is then threatened by the dead man's psychopathic father. Heavy-going melodrama not helped at all by the very wide screen. George Nader, Phyllis Thaxter, Harold J. Stone, Tim Hovey, Eduard Franz. Written by Herb Meadow; directed by Harry Keller; for Universal-International.

Man Alive
US 1945 70m bw

A husband thought to be dead comes back as a 'ghost' and frightens away his wife's new suitor. Curious and rather tasteless comedy. Pat O'Brien, Ellen Drew, Adolphe Menjou, Rudy Vallee, Jack Norton. Written by Edwin Harvey Blum; directed by Ray Enright; for RKO.

A Man Alone*
US 1955 96m Trucolor
Republic

A wandering gunman is framed by other badmen.
Solemn, slow-moving but generally interesting western, the star's first attempt at direction.

w John Tucker Battle *d Ray Milland* *ph* Lionel Lindon *m* Victor Young

Ray Milland, Mary Murphy, Ward Bond, Raymond Burr, Arthur Space, Lee Van Cleef, Alan Hale Jnr

A Man and a Woman**
France 1966 102m Eastmancolor
Les Films 13
aka: *Un Homme et une Femme*

A racing driver and a script girl, both of whose spouses are dead, meet while visiting their children, and an affair leads to marriage.
Slight romantic drama so tricked out with smart images that it looks like a series of expensive commercials. A great box office success, but its director never again succeeded in this vein which he made his own.

w Claude Lelouch, Pierre Uytterhoven *d Claude Lelouch* *ph* Jean Columb, Patrice Pouget *m Francis Lai*

Anouk Aimée, Jean-Louis Trintignant

'When in doubt, Lelouch's motto seems to be, use a colour filter or insert lyrical shots of dogs and horses; when in real doubt, use both.'—*Tom Milne, MFB*

'A slick item with all the Hollywood ingredients.'—*John Simon*

AA: Claude Lelouch, Pierre Uytterhoven
AAN: Claude Lelouch (as director); Anouk Aimée

A Man and a Woman: Twenty Years Later
France 1986 120m Eastmancolor

Slightly macabre attempt to extend the appeal with the same actors, the same technique, and even shots from Lelouch's other movies. A bit of a wallow. Anouk Aimée, Jean-Louis Trintignant, Evelyne Bouix, Marie-Sophie Pochat. Written by Claude Lelouch and others; directed and produced by Lelouch for Films 13 / Warner.

The Man at the Gate
GB 1941 48m bw

The war takes its toll of Cornish fishermen. Modest family drama which strives to be inspirational via a speech made by King George VI. Wilfred Lawson, Mary Jerrold, Kathleen O'Regan. Written by Lydia Hayward and Harold Simpson, from a story by Manning Haynes and a poem by Louise Haskin; directed by Norman Walker; for GHW.

Man at the Top*
GB 1973 87m Technicolor
Hammer / Dufton (Peter Charlesworth)

A pharmaceutical executive finds that his firm is marketing an unsafe drug.
Further adventures of the belligerent hero of *Room at the Top* (qv), this time following a popular television series. All very fashionable and predictable.

w Hugh Whitemore *d* Mike Vardy *ph* Bryan Probyn *m* Roy Budd

Kenneth Haigh, Nanette Newman, Harry Andrews, John Quentin, Charlie Williams

The Man Behind the Gun
US 1952 82m Technicolor

A cavalry officer is sent to quell a rebellion and helps to found Los Angeles. Cheerful western programmer. Randolph Scott, Patrice Wymore, Dick Wesson, Phil Carey. Written by John Twist; directed by Felix Feist; for Warner.

The Man Behind the Mask
GB 1936 79m bw

A mad scientist kidnaps a nobleman's daughter. Serial-like hokum with interesting credits. Hugh Williams, Maurice Schwarz, Jane Baxter, Donald Calthrop, Henry Oscar. Written by Ian Hay, Syd Courtenay, Jack Byrd and Stanley Haynes; directed by Michael Powell; for Joe Rock.

A Man Betrayed
US 1941 82m bw

A hick lawyer in the big city smashes corruption. Somewhat inconsequential melodrama which fails to come through with the powerful entertainment it promises. John Wayne, Frances Dee, Edward Ellis, Wallace Ford, Ward Bond, Harold Huber, Alexander Granach, Barnett Parker. Written by Isabel Dawn; directed by John Auer; for Armand Schaefer / Republic.

(GB title: *Citadel of Crime*.)

The Man Between*
GB 1953 101m bw
British Lion / London Films (Carol Reed)

Ivo Kern operates successfully as a West Berlin racketeer; love causes a softening of his attitudes and leads to his death.
Imitation *Third Man* with an uninteresting mystery and a solemn ending. Good acting and production can't save it.

w Harry Kurnitz *d Carol Reed ph Desmond Dickinson m* John Addison *ad* André Andreiev

James Mason, Hildegarde Neff, Claire Bloom, Geoffrey Toone, Ernst Schroeder

'Reed's love of photogenic corruption, his technical finesse, and his feeling for atmospheric intrigue almost make something really good out of a synthetic script.'—*Variety*

'A cold-hearted film about people with cold feet.'—*Daily Express*

A Man Called Gannon
US 1969 105m Technicolor

A wandering cowboy helps a widow rancher in her fight against encroaching cattlemen.
Adequate remake of *The Man Without a Star*, which somehow had much more stature. Tony Franciosa, Michael Sarrazin, Judi West, Susan Oliver, John Anderson. Written by Gene Kearney, D. D. Beauchamp and Borden Chase; directed by James Goldstone; for Universal.

A Man Called Horse*
US 1970 114m Technicolor Panavision
Cinema Center / Sanford Howard

In 1825 an English aristocrat is captured by Indians, lives with them and eventually becomes their leader.
Harrowing account of tribal life and customs, with much bloodshed and torture and most of the dialogue in Indian. Occasionally impressive but not exactly entertaining.

w Jack di Witt, *story* Dorothy M. Johnson *d* Elliot Silverstein *ph* Robert Hauser *m* Leonard Rosenman

Richard Harris, Judith Anderson, Jean Gascon, Manu Tupou

† Sequels 1976: *The Return of a Man Called Horse*. 1984: *Triumphs of a Man Called Horse*.

The Man Called Noon
GB / Spain / Italy 1973 95m Technicolor
Frontier / Montana / Finarco (Euan Lloyd)

A western gunslinger loses his memory.
Childish western melodrama in the violent manner.

w Scot Finch, *novel* Louis L'Amour *d* Peter Collinson *ph* John Cabrera *m* Luis Bacalov

Richard Crenna, Stephen Boyd, Rosanna Schiaffino, Farley Granger

A Man Called Peter*
US 1955 119m De Luxe Cinemascope
TCF (Samuel G. Engel)

The life of Peter Marshall, a Scottish clergyman who became chaplain to the US Senate.
Careful but rather dreary biopic.

w Eleanore Griffin, *book* Catherine Marshall *d* Henry Koster *ph* Harold Lipstein *m* Alfred Newman

Richard Todd, Jean Peters, Marjorie Rambeau, Jill Esmond, Les Tremayne, Robert Burton

AAN: Harold Lipstein

A Man Called Sledge
Italy 1970 92m Techniscope
Dino de Laurentiis (Carl Olsen)

A bandit tries in vain to mastermind a bank robbery.
Curious change of pace for a genial star. A spaghetti western without style but with plenty of violence, the result doesn't linger in the memory.

w Vic Morrow, Frank Kowalsky *d* Vic Morrow *ph* Luigi Kuveiller *m* not credited

James Garner, Dennis Weaver, Claude Akins, John Marley

A Man Could Get Killed*
US 1966 98m Technicolor Panavision
Universal / Cherokee (Ernest Wehmeyer)

An American businessman in Lisbon is mistaken for a secret agent.
Minor thrill comedy with a confused plot and a willing cast.

w T. E. B. Clarke, Richard Breen, *novel* Diamonds Are Danger by David Walker *d* Ronald Neame, Cliff Owen *ph* Gabor Pogany *m* Bert Kaemfert

James Garner, Melina Mercouri, Sandra Dee, Tony Franciosa, Robert Coote, Roland Culver, Cecil Parker, Grégoire Aslan, Dulcie Gray, Martin Benson, Niall MacGinnis

A Man for All Seasons****
GB 1966 120m Technicolor
Columbia / Highland (Fred Zinnemann)

Sir Thomas More opposes Henry VIII's divorce, and events lead inexorably to his execution.
Irreproachable film version of a play which has had its narrative tricks removed but stands up remarkably well. Acting, direction, sets, locations and costumes all have precisely the right touch.

w Robert Bolt, from his play *d Fred Zinnemann ph Ted Moore m Georges Delerue pd John Box*

Paul Scofield, Wendy Hiller, Susannah York, *Robert Shaw*, Orson Welles, Leo McKern, Nigel Davenport, John Hurt, Corin Redgrave, Cyril Luckham, Jack Gwyllim

'Mr Zinnemann has crystallized the essence of this drama in such pictorial terms as to render even its abstractions vibrant.'—*New York Times*

† Reports indicate that Charlton Heston badly wanted the role of Sir Thomas More.

AA: best picture; Robert Bolt; Fred Zinnemann; Ted Moore; Paul Scofield
AAN: Wendy Hiller; Robert Shaw

'If you've read the book, forget it!'

Man Friday
GB 1975 115m Eastmancolor Panavision
Avco-Embassy / ITC / ABC / Keep Films (Jules Buck)

The story of Robinson Crusoe told so that Friday appears the more intelligent.
A pointless and not very entertaining exercise which wears out its welcome very early.

w Adrian Mitchell *d* Jack Gold *ph* Alex Phillips *m* Carl Davis

Peter O'Toole, Richard Roundtree

'Liberal intentions trail sadly through every sequence and cause absurd fluctuations of tone, since no one seems to have decided whether laborious slapstick, heavy portentousness or method acting is the best vehicle for the message.'—*Jill Forbes*

The Man from Bitter Ridge
US 1955 80m Technicolor

A special agent goes undercover to nail stagecoach bandits, but himself comes under suspicion. Adequate western programmer. Lex Barker, Mara Corday, Stephen McNally, Trevor Bardette, John Dehner. Written by Lawrence Roman; directed by Jack Arnold; for Universal-International.

The Man from Blankley's
US 1930 67m bw
Warner

A drunken aristocrat goes to the wrong party and teaches those present, and himself, a thing or two.
Amusing star trifle, previously filmed as a silent.

w Harvey Thew, Joseph Jackson, *story* F. Anstey *d* Alfred E. Green *ph* James Van Trees

John Barrymore, Loretta Young, William Austin, Albert Gran, Emily Fitzroy

'Dickens comedy, in the Sennett vein, with the Barrymore finesse.'—*Variety*

The Man from Colorado
US 1949 99m Technicolor
Columbia (Jules Schermer)

A maladjusted Civil War veteran becomes a western judge and rules by the gun.
Slightly unusual, watchable star western.

w Robert D. Andrews, Ben Maddow, Borden Chase *d* Henry Levin *ph* William Snyder *m* George Duning

Glenn Ford, William Holden, Ellen Drew, Ray Collins, Edgar Buchanan, Jerome Courtland, James Millican, Jim Bannon

'No more humour than a lawyer's shingle, but it has suspense and some exciting shots of fist fights and burning houses.'—*Time*

The Man from Dakota*
US 1940 75m bw

A Yankee soldier is taken prisoner by the south and becomes a spy. Good period action piece. Wallace Beery, Dolores Del Rio, John Howard, Donald Meek, H. B. Warner, Victor Varconi. Written by Laurence Stallings, from the novel by Mackinlay Kantor; directed by Leslie Fenton; for MGM. (GB title: *Arouse and Beware*.)

Man from Del Rio
US 1956 82m bw
UA / Robert L. Jacks

A Mexican hobo becomes sheriff and forces the local badman to leave town.
Modest, efficient, rather brutal little western.

w Richard Carr *d* Harry Horner *ph* Stanley Cortez *m* Fred Steiner

Anthony Quinn, Katy Jurado, Peter Whitney, Douglas Fowley

The Man from Down Under
US 1943 103m bw

A veteran of World War I smuggles two orphans back into Australia. Appallingly indulgent sentimental star vehicle, a mistake for all concerned. Charles Laughton, Binnie Barnes, Donna Reed, Richard Carlson, Horace McNally, Arthur Shields. Written by Wells Root and Thomas Seller; directed by Robert Z. Leonard; for MGM.

'He came a thousand miles to kill someone he'd never seen!'

The Man from Laramie**
US 1955 104m Technicolor Cinemascope
Columbia (William Goetz)

A wandering cowman seeks revenge on those who killed his brother.
Grade A western with new-fangled touches of brutality touching off the wide screen spectacle.

w Philip Yordan, Frank Burt *d Anthony Mann* *ph* Charles Lang Jnr *m* George Duning *md* Morris Stoloff

James Stewart, Arthur Kennedy, Donald Crisp, Cathy O'Donnell, Alex Nicol, Aline MacMahon, Wallace Ford, Jack Elam

The Man from Morocco
GB 1944 116m bw
ABP (Warwick Ward)

Members of the international brigade are captured and later sent by Vichy to build a Sahara railway for the Germans; one escapes to London with vital information.
Stilted, meandering and extremely unconvincing melodrama with a star ill at ease.

w Warwick Ward, Edward Dryhurst, Marguerite Steen, *story* Rudolph Cartier *d* Max Greene *ph* Basil Emmott

Anton Walbrook, Margaretta Scott, Mary Morris, Reginald Tate, Peter Sinclair, David Horne

The Man from Planet X
US 1951 70m bw

On a remote Scottish island a spacecraft deposits a strange creature with a large head and mesmeric powers. Early, minor, moderately pleasing fragment in the *Close Encounters* cycle. Margaret Field, Raymond Bond, William Schallert. Written and produced by Aubrey Wisberg and Jack Pollexfen; directed by Edgar G. Ulmer; for Sherrill Corwin / United Artists.

The Man from Snowy River
Australia 1982 104m Eastmancolor Panavision
Cambridge Films / Michael Edgley International (Geoff Burrowes)

In 1888, an orphan boy grows up with an obsession about wild horses.
Essentially no more than an Audie-Murphy-style Western given full down-under treatment. An Australian smash, a programmer elsewhere.

w John Dixon, Fred Cullen, from the poem by A. B. Paterson *d* George Miller *ph* Keith Wagstaff *m* Bruce Rowland

Kirk Douglas, Jack Thompson, Sigrid Thornton, Tom Burlinson, Terence Donovan, Lorraine Bayly

The Man from the Alamo*
US 1953 79m Technicolor
U-I (Aaron Rosenberg)

A survivor of the Alamo is thought to be a deserter but proves his story and exposes a villain.
Satisfying western programmer.

w Steve Fisher, D. D. Beauchamp *d* Budd Boetticher *ph* Russell Metty *m* Frank Skinner

Glenn Ford, Victor Jory, Julia Adams, Hugh O'Brian

The Man from the Diners' Club*
US 1963 96m bw
Columbia / Dena / Ampersand (Bill Bloom)

A clerk accidentally lets a credit card go to a notorious gangster, and makes desperate efforts to retrieve it.
Minor star comedy with funny moments surviving a slapdash script.

w Bill Blatty *d* Frank Tashlin *ph* Hal Mohr *m* Stu Philips

Danny Kaye, Telly Savalas, Martha Hyer, Cara Williams, Everett Sloane, George Kennedy

The Man from Uncle

This long-running one-hour TV series (1964-8) began as a spoof of James Bond, which was itself a spoof. Not much more serious or convincing than *Batman*, they caused a lot of people to suspend their disbelief. Robert Vaughn played Napoleon Solo, David McCallum Ilya Kuryakin, and Leo G. Carroll Mr Waverly. Several feature films were made up from various episodes, and did well in cinemas in some countries. They were: TO TRAP A SPY, THE SPY WITH MY FACE, THE KARATE KILLERS, THE SPY IN THE GREEN HAT, ONE OF OUR SPIES IS MISSING, THE HELICOPTER SPIES, HOW TO STEAL THE WORLD and ONE SPY TOO MANY.

A Man from Wyoming
US 1930 70m bw

A slow-speaking engineer joins the army, serves overseas and marries an ambulance driver. Uncertain star vehicle which helped to mould his screen character. Gary Cooper, June Collyer, Regis Toomey, E. H. Calvert, Morgan Farley. Written by John Weaver and Albert Shelby Le Vino; directed by Rowland V. Lee; for Paramount. 'Bad enough to be good entertainment if taken as farce.'—*New York Evening Post.*

'Her body ached for the man she loved!'

The Man from Yesterday
US 1932 71m bw
Paramount

A man is reported missing in World War I, but years later his wife and her new fiancé find him in Switzerland, dying of gas poisoning.
Enoch Arden rides again, and very boringly.

w Oliver H. P. Garrett *d* Berthold Viertel *ph* Karl Struss

Claudette Colbert, Clive Brook, Charles Boyer, Andy Devine, Alan Mowbray, Christian Rub

'Rather too late in the day to expect war scenes, and when the war peters out, there is only scenery and conversation.'—*Variety*

Man Hunt
US 1932 65m bw

A cub reporter hunts a bank robber. Standard support action fare of its time. William Gargan, Ricardo Cortez, Marguerite Chapman, Chic Sale, Maude Eburne. Written by Roy Chanslor, Earl Felton; directed by William Clemens; for Warners. 'Script never lives up to the title's promise.'—*Variety*

Man Hunt**
US 1941 98m bw
TCF (Kenneth MacGowan)

A big game hunter misses a shot at Hitler and is chased back to England by the Gestapo.
Despite hilariously inaccurate English backgrounds, this is perhaps its director's most vivid Hollywood thriller, though watered down in tone from the original novel.

w Dudley Nichols, *novel* Rogue Male by Geoffrey Household *d Fritz Lang* *ph* Arthur Miller *m* Alfred Newman

Walter Pidgeon, Joan Bennett, *George Sanders*, John Carradine, Roddy McDowall, Ludwig Stossel, Heather Thatcher, Frederick Worlock

'A tense and intriguing thriller that is both propaganda and exciting entertainment.'—*Paul M. Jensen, 1969*

'In its manipulation of these dark and intent forces on a checkerboard, it manages to take your breath away.'—*Otis Ferguson*
† Remade for TV in 1976 as *Rogue Male.*

The Man I Love
US 1946 76m bw
Warner (Arnold Albert)

A nightclub singer is involved with a mobster.
Dreary little melodrama which never really gets going.

w Catherine Turney *d* Raoul Walsh *ph* Sid Hickox *m* Max Steiner

Ida Lupino, Robert Alda, Andrea King, Martha Vickers, Bruce Bennett, Alan Hale, Dolores Moran, John Ridgely

The Man I Married*
US 1940 79m bw
TCF (Raymond Griffith)
aka: *I Married a Nazi*

When an American couple take a European vacation, the wife is horrified to find her husband, who is of German parentage, agreeing with the Nazis.
Naïve but striking melodrama exploring attitudes of its time.

w Oliver H. P. Garrett, *novel* Swastika by Oscar Shisgall *d* Irving Pichel *ph* Peverell Marley *m* David Buttolph

Joan Bennett, Francis Lederer, Lloyd Nolan, Anna Sten, Otto Kruger, Maria Ouspenskaya, Ludwig Stossel, Johnny Russell

The Man in Grey**
GB 1943 116m bw
GFD / Gainsborough (Edward Black)

In Regency times, an aristocratic girl's love for her less fortunate friend is repaid by jealousy, treachery and murder.
Rather dully performed flashback costume melodrama which caught the public imagination in the middle of a dreary world war, especially as its evil leading characters were played by stars who rapidly went right to the top. The several imitations which followed, including *The Wicked Lady, Jassy* and *Hungry Hill*, became known as the Gainsborough school.

w Margaret Kennedy, Leslie Arliss, Doreen Montgomery, *novel* Lady Eleanor Smith *d* Leslie Arliss *ph* Arthur Crabtree *m* Cedric Mallabey *ad* Walter Murton

James Mason, Margaret Lockwood, Phyllis Calvert, Stewart Granger, Helen Haye, Nora Swinburne, Raymond Lovell, Martita Hunt

'There was not a moment when I would not gladly have dived for my hat.'—*James Agate*

'All the time-tested materials: gypsy fortune-teller; scowling, black-browed villain; gushy diary kept by a doe-eyed girl who munches candied violets; fire-breathing adventuress who dotes on discord and low-cut gowns . . .'—*Time*

'Even the one girl who loved enough to ask no questions—had to face the fearful truth!'

The Man in Half Moon Street
US 1944 91m bw
Paramount (Walter MacEwen)

A mysteriously handsome young scientist is actually a 90-year-old who has discovered a surgical method of preserving youth.
Boring screen version of a play which was conceived in an almost romantic vein; Hollywood has taken it too literally.

w Charles Kenyon, *play* Barre Lyndon *d* Ralph Murphy *ph* Henry Sharp *m* Miklos Rozsa

Nils Asther, Helen Walker, Brandon Hurst, *Reinhold Schunzel*
† Remade in straight horror vein as *The Man Who Could Cheat Death* (qv).

The Man in Possession
US 1931 81m bw

A lady falls in love with the bailiff's man in temporary charge of her establishment. Light comedy subsequently remade as *Personal Property*; quite tolerable. Robert Montgomery, Irene Purcell, Charlotte Greenwood, C. Aubrey Smith, Beryl Mercer, Reginald Owen, Alan Mowbray. Written by Sarah Y. Mason from the play by H. M. Harwood; directed by Sam Wood; for MGM.
'Should have no trouble where the censors don't interfere . . . where it gets by with the dirt, the dirt should get it over.'—*Variety*

The Man in the Attic
US 1953 82m bw

Remake of the much-remade *The Lodger,* this time with parsimonious production values and no style. Jack Palance, Constance Smith, Byron Palmer, Frances Bavier, Rhys Williams. Written by Robert Presnell Jnr and Barre Lyndon; directed by Hugo Fregonese; for TCF.

The Man in the Back Seat*
GB 1961 57m bw
Independent Artists (Julian Wintle, Leslie Parkyn)

Two robbers fail to separate a bookie from the locked bag chained to his wrist; at first taking him with them they finally kill him and are apparently haunted by him.
Taut, downbeat little crime thriller which won a few critical plaudits.

w Malcolm Hulke, Eric Paice *d Vernon Sewell* *ph* Reg Wyer *m* Stanley Black

Derren Nesbitt, Keith Faulkner, Carol White, Harry Locke

'Death at the carnival—as a killer takes over the switchback!'

Man in the Dark*
US 1953 70m bw 3-D
Columbia (Wallace Macdonald)

A convict submits to a brain operation which will remove his criminal tendencies. Unfortunately it also removes his memory, and on his release he is bewildered when gangsters expect him to know where the loot is hidden.
Silly low-budgeter which is only notable as the 3-D film which most exploited the short-lived medium. Apart from a roller coaster ride, objects hurled at the audience include scissors, spiders, knives, forceps, fists and falling bodies.

w George Bricker, Jack Leonard *d* Lew Landers *ph* Floyd Crosby *md* Ross de Maggio

Edmond O'Brien, Audrey Totter, Ted de Corsia, Horace MacMahon

The Man in the Gray Flannel Suit*
US 1956 152m Eastmancolor Cinemascope
TCF (Darryl F. Zanuck)

A young New York executive is offered a demanding job but decides that his first loyalty is to his wife and children.
An amusingly accurate novel of Madison Avenue mores becomes a marathon emotional melodrama in which the mordant bits quickly give way to domestic problems and a guilt complex about a wartime affair, shown in lengthy flashback. It's all too much.

w Nunnally Johnson, *novel* Sloan Wilson *d* Nunnally Johnson *ph* Charles G. Clarke *m* Bernard Herrmann

Gregory Peck, Fredric March, Jennifer Jones, Ann Harding, *Arthur O'Connell, Henry Daniell*, Marisa Pavan, Lee J. Cobb, Keenan Wynn, Gene Lockhart, Gigi Perreau, Connie Gilchrist, Joseph Sweeney

The Man in the Iron Mask**
US 1939 110m bw
Edward Small

King Louis XIV keeps his twin brother prisoner.
Exhilarating swashbuckler based on a classic novel, with a complex plot, good acting and the three musketeers in full cry.

w George Bruce, novel Alexandre Dumas *d James Whale* *ph* Robert Planck *m* Lucien Moraweck

Louis Hayward, Warren William (as D'Artagnan), Alan Hale, Bert Roach, Miles Mander, Joan Bennett, *Joseph Schildkraut*, Walter Kingsford, Marion Martin, Montagu Love, Albert Dekker

'Substantial entertainment for general appeal and satisfaction.'—*Variety*

'A sort of combination of *The Prisoner of Zenda* and *The Three Musketeers*, with a few wild west chases thrown in . . . not unentertaining.'—*Richard Mallett, Punch*
† Remade 1976 as a TV movie with Richard Chamberlain, and 1978 as *The Fifth Musketeer* (qv).

AAN: Lucien Moraweck

The Man in the Middle*
GB 1964 94m bw Cinemascope
TCF / Pennebaker / Belmont (Walter Seltzer)

In India during World War II, an American lieutenant is indicted for murder and the defence counsel is instructed to lose the case. Courtroom melodrama with unusual angles; quite intriguing, though the wide screen doesn't help.

w Keith Waterhouse, Willis Hall, *novel* The Winston Affair by Howard Fast *d* Guy Hamilton *ph* Wilkie Cooper *m* John Barry

Robert Mitchum, Trevor Howard, Keenan Wynn, Barry Sullivan, France Nuyen, Alexander Knox

'For once Mitchum seems to have an excuse for keeping his eyes at half mast.'—*Judith Crist*

The Man in the Mirror
GB 1936 82m bw
JH Productions (Julius Hagen)

A timid man's reflection steps out of the mirror and organizes him.
Modest comedy with a pleasing star.

w F. McGrew Willis, Hugh Mills, *novel* William Garrett *d* Maurice Elvey *ph* Curt Courant

Edward Everett Horton, Geneviève Tobin, Garry Marsh, Ursula Jeans, Alastair Sim, Aubrey Mather, Felix Aylmer

'High speed sequences of comic incident put over in fine style.'—*Cinema*

Man in the Moon
GB 1960 99m bw
Allied Film Makers / Excalibur (Michael Relph)

A man who earns his living as Mr Normal, a human guinea pig for scientific research, is chosen as the first astronaut.
Dated comedy which rather dismayingly turns from mild satire to outright farce and fantasy.

w Michael Relph, Bryan Forbes *d* Basil Dearden *ph* Harry Waxman *m* Philip Green

Kenneth More, Shirley Anne Field, Michael Hordern, John Phillips, John Glyn-Jones, Charles Gray, Norman Bird

The Man in the Net
US 1958 96m bw
UA / Mirisch-Jaguar (Walter Mirisch)

When a painter is accused of murdering his wife, he goes into hiding and is helped by children.
Extremely tedious and inept mystery, doubly disappointing in view of the credits.

w Reginald Rose, *novel* Patrick Quentin *d* Michael Curtiz *ph* John Seitz *m* Hans Salter

Alan Ladd, Carolyn Jones, Diane Brewster, John Lupton, Charles McGraw, Tom Helmore, John Alexander

The Man in the Road
GB 1957 83m bw

An amnesiac scientist is deceived by communists. Mildly diverting spy caper with a good cast. Derek Farr, Ella Raines, Donald Wolfit, Lisa Daniely, Karel Stepanek, Cyril Cusack. Written by Guy Morgan from the novel He Was Found in the Road by Anthony Armstrong; directed by Lance Comfort; for Gibraltar.

Man in the Saddle
US 1951 87m Technicolor

A small rancher is victimized by his wealthy neighbour. Fairly lively western which develops into a series of gunfights. Randolph Scott, Alexander Knox, Joan Leslie, Ellen Drew, Richard Rober. Written by Kenneth Gamet; directed by André de Toth; for Harry Joe Brown / Columbia. (GB title: *The Outcast.*)

Man in the Shadow*
US 1957 80m bw Cinemascope
U-I (Albert Zugsmith)
GB title: *Pay the Devil*

The sheriff of a small western town investigates a murder against the wishes of a powerful local rancher.
Mini-social drama in which the honest man wins out at last . . . and who would expect anything different. A brooding melodrama which delivers less than it promises.

w Gene L. Coon *d* Jack Arnold *ph* Arthur E. Arling *m* Hans Salter

Jeff Chandler, Orson Welles, Colleen Miller, John Larch, Joe Schneider, Leo Gordon

The Man in the Sky*
GB 1956 87m bw
Ealing (Seth Holt)
US title: *Decision against Time*

A test pilot refuses to bale out when an engine catches fire; his plight is interwoven with scenes of his family, friends and associates.
Thin suspense drama with some effective moments but too many irrelevant asides.

w William Rose, John Eldridge *d* Charles Crichton *ph* Douglas Slocombe *m* Gerbrand Schurmann

Jack Hawkins, Elizabeth Sellars, Walter Fitzgerald, Eddie Byrne, John Stratton, Victor Maddern, Lionel Jeffries, Donald Pleasence

The Man in the Trunk
US 1942 70m bw

The ghost of a murder victim helps a young attorney to nail the culprit. Slightly uneasy spook comedy with a good star performance. *Raymond Walburn*, Lynne Roberts, George Holmes, J. Carrol Naish, Dorothy Peterson. Written by John Larkin; directed by Malcolm St Clair; for TCF.

The Man in the White Suit****
GB 1951 81m bw
Ealing (Sidney Cole)

A scientist produces a fabric that never gets dirty and never wears out. Unions and management are equally aghast.
Brilliant satirical comedy played as farce and put together with meticulous cinematic counterpoint, so that every moment counts and all concerned give of their very best.

w Roger Macdougall, John Dighton, Alexander Mackendrick d Alexander Mackendrick ph Douglas Slocombe m Benjamin Frankel

Alec Guinness, Joan Greenwood, Cecil Parker, Vida Hope, *Ernest Thesiger,* Michael Gough, Howard Marion Crawford, Miles Malleson, *George Benson, Edie Martin*

'The combination of an ingenious idea, a bright, funny and imaginative script, skilful playing and perceptive brisk direction has resulted once more in a really satisfying Ealing comedy.'—*Richard Mallett, Punch*

AAN: script

Man in the Wilderness*
US 1971 105m Technicolor Panavision
Warner / Wilderness (Sanford Howard)

In 1820 in the Canadian northwest, a fur trapper is mauled by a grizzly and left for dead, but he learns to survive and sets out for revenge.
Endurance melodrama modelled after *A Man Called Horse*; a bit stretched and only for the hardened, but taking an agreeably unromantic view of nature.

w Jack di Witt *d* Richard Sarafian *ph* Gerry Fisher *m* Johnny Harris

Richard Harris, John Huston, John Bindon, Prunella Ransome, Henry Wilcoxon, Ben Carruthers

The Man Inside
GB 1958 97m bw Cinemascope
Columbia / Warwick (Harold Huth)

A jeweller's book-keeper steals a priceless diamond and is trailed by various factions half across Europe.
Fairly modest and unenterprising British thriller which hadn't much hope of the world market it was aiming at.

w John Gilling, David Shaw, *novel* M. E. Graber *d* John Gilling *ph* Ted Moore *m* Richard Bennett

Nigel Patrick, Jack Palance, Anita Ekberg, Anthony Newley, Bonar Colleano, Sid James, Donald Pleasence

Man Made Monster*
US 1940 57m bw
Universal (Jack Bernard)
GB title: *The Electric Man*

A scientist experiments with a man who is impervious to electric shock, and turns him into a walking robot.
A smart little semi-horror originally planned for Karloff and Lugosi.

w Joseph West *d* George Waggner *ph* Elwood Bredell *m* Hans Salter *md* Charles Previn *sp John P. Fulton*

Lon Chaney Jnr, Lionel Atwill, Anne Nagel, Frank Albertson, Samuel S. Hinds

'Who were the women who twisted his life and love—gutting the flame of his incredible genius?'

Man of a Thousand Faces**
US 1957 122m bw Cinemascope
U-I (Robert Arthur)

The rise to fame of silent screen character actor Lon Chaney.
Moderately commendable biopic with a strong sense of period Hollywood, an excellent star performance, but too much sudsy emoting about deaf mute parents and an ungrateful wife.

w R. Wright Campbell, Ivan Goff, Ben Roberts *d* Joseph Pevney *ph* Russell Metty *m* Frank Skinner *ad Alexander Golitzen*

James Cagney, Dorothy Malone, Robert Evans (as Irving Thalberg), Roger Smith, *Marjorie Rambeau*, Jane Greer, Jim Backus

'The script and conception are so maudlin and degrading that Cagney's high dedication becomes somewhat oppressive.'—*Pauline Kael, 70s*

AAN: script

Man of Affairs
GB 1937 70m bw

When the foreign secretary is kidnapped, his twin brother impersonates him. Lighthearted star vehicle which satisfied. George Arliss, Romilly Lunge, Rene Ray, Jessie Winter, Allan Jeayes. Written by Maude Howell and L. Du Garde Peach from the play The Nelson Touch by Neil Grant; directed by Herbert Mason; for Gaumont British. 'Business possibilities only moderate.'—*Variety*

Man of Aran**
GB 1934 75m bw
Gainsborough (Michael Balcon)

The primitive life of crofting and fishing folk in the west of Ireland.
A lowering documentary very typical of its maker: highly impressive scene for scene, but tedious as a whole; still, highly remarkable that it was made at all for the commercial cinema.

w Robert and Frances Flaherty *d Robert Flaherty*

Colman King, Maggie Dirane (amateurs)

'In so far as it is a rendering of the efforts of the Atlantic to overwhelm and demolish a wall of rock, it is magnificent; but the human note is inadequate and unnecessary.'—*E. V. Lucas, Punch*

'However real, it would have made better truth if it had been handled with more of the art of fiction.'—*Otis Ferguson*

'Six thousand feet of such fine and purposeful pictorial composition have seldom been seen on the screen.'—*Observer*

Man of Conquest
US 1939 99m bw
Republic (Sol C. Siegel)

The life of western hero Sam Houston, who became president of Texas.
Competent action / domestic biopic.

w Wells Root, E. E. Paramore Jnr *d* George Nicholls Jnr *ph* Joseph H. August *m* Victor Young

Richard Dix, Joan Fontaine, Gail Patrick, Edward Ellis, Victor Jory, Robert Barrat, George Hayes, Ralph Morgan, Robert Armstrong, C. Henry Gordon, Janet Beecher

'A grown-up hoss opera, based on authentic and colourful history, with fairly believable characters, ample action and reasonable suspense.'—*Variety*

AAN: Victor Young

Man of Iron
US 1935 62m bw

A steel works foreman rises to the boardroom, but doesn't like it. Rather obvious moral tale without much excitement. Barton MacLane, Mary Astor, John Eldredge, Dorothy Peterson, Joseph Crehan. Written by William Wister Haines, Dawn Powell; directed by William McGann; for Warners. 'Unimportant programme material.'—*Variety*

Man of Iron*
Poland 1981 152m colour and bw
PRF / Filowy X

The events of 1980 in Poland are seen through the eyes of a strike leader.
A stirring companion piece to *Man of Marble*; hard tack for the entertainment seeker but as honest a piece of history as one is likely to get from a so-called fiction film.

w Aleksander Scibor-Rylski d Andrzej Wajda ph Edward Klosinski *m* Andrzej Korzynski

Jerzy Radziwilowicz, Krystyna Janda, Marian Opania

AAN: best foreign film

Man of La Mancha*
US 1972 132m De Luxe
UA / PEA (Arthur Hiller)

Arrested by the Inquisition and thrown into prison, Miguel de Cervantes relates the story of Don Quixote.
Unimaginative but generally good-looking attempt to recreate on the screen an essentially theatrical experience.

w Dale Wasserman, from his play *d* Arthur Hiller *ph Goffredo Rotunno m Mitch Leigh ly* Joe Darion *md* Laurence Rosenthal *ad* Luciano Damiani

Peter O'Toole, Sophia Loren, James Coco, Harry Andrews, John Castle, Brian Blessed

'Needful of all the imagination the spectator can muster.'—*Variety*

AAN: Laurence Rosenthal

Man of Marble*
Poland 1978 165m colour
PRF / Zespol X (Andrzej Wajda)

Young film makers gather material on a political hero of the fifties.
An extended drama on the style of *Citizen Kane* but with much more relevance to contemporary history. A key film to students of Poland, but too specialized for general entertainment.

w Aleksander Scibor-Rylski *d* Andrzej Wajda *ph* Edward Klosinski *m* Andrzej Korzinski

Jerzy Radziwilowicz, Krystyna Janda, Michael Tarkowski, Tadeusz Lomnicki

Man of the Moment
GB 1935 82m bw

An engaged young man saves a girl from suicide and falls in love with her. Minor romantic comedy of predictable development. Douglas Fairbanks Jnr, Laura La Plante, Claude Hulbert, Margaret Lockwood, Donald Calthrop, Monty Banks. Written by Roland Pertwee, Guy Bolton and A. R. Rawlinson, from a play by Yves Mirande; directed by Monty Banks; for Warner.

Man of the People
US 1937 80m bw

An Italian immigrant works for a law degree but is forced in with crooks. Political power play without much zest despite good acting. Joseph Calleia, Thomas Mitchell, Florence Rice, Ted Healy, Catherine Doucet. Written by Frank Dolan; directed by Edwin L. Marin; for Lucien Hubbard / MGM. 'Patently primed for duals, where it can hold its own.'—*Variety*

Man of the West
US 1958 100m De Luxe Cinemascope
UA / Ashton (Walter M. Mirisch)

In 1874 Arizona, a reformed gunman is cajoled by his old buddies to help them rob a bank.
Talkative, set-bound, cliché-ridden star western with minor compensations.

w Reginald Rose, *novel* Will C. Brown *d* Anthony Mann *ph* Ernest Haller *m* Leigh Harline

Gary Cooper, Lee J. Cobb, Julie London, Arthur O'Connell, Jack Lord, John Dehner, Royal Dano, Robert Wilke

Man of the World
US 1931 71m bw

A gentleman racketeer operates on American playboys in Paris. Predictable but smooth star vehicle. William Powell, Carole Lombard, Wynne Gibson, Guy Kibbee, Lawrence Gray. Written by Herman J. Mankiewicz; directed by Richard Wallace; for Paramount. 'Anything better than moderate for gross must come through the star's personal pull.'—*Variety*

Man of Two Worlds
US 1933 92m bw

An Eskimo is temporarily civilized, but returns to the Arctic wild. Uneventful and somewhat chilly drama which fails to convince. Francis Lederer, Elissa Landi, Henry Stephenson, J. Farrell MacDonald, Walter Byron. Written by Howard and Ainsworth Morgan, from Ainsworth Morgan's novel; directed by J. Walter Ruben; for RKO.

Man on a String
US 1960 92m bw
Columbia / Louis de Rochemont
GB title: *Confessions of a Counterspy*

A Russian-born Hollywood producer is asked by the Russians to work as a spy but becomes a double agent.

Slightly unbelievable biopic about Boris Morros, rather childlike in its simplicity and not too entertaining either.

w John Kafka, Virginia Shaler, *book* Ten Years a Counterspy by Boris Morros *d* André de Toth *ph* Charles Lawton Jnr and others *m* George Duning

Ernest Borgnine, Kerwin Mathews, Colleen Dewhurst, Alexander Scourby, Glenn Corbett, Vladimir Sokoloff

Man on a Swing
US 1975 108m Technicolor
Paramount (Howard B. Jaffe)

Investigations into a murder are helped by a would-be medium.
Overlong and confused psycho-mystery with one stand-out performance.

w David Zelag Goodman *d* Frank Perry *ph* Adam Holender *m* Lalo Schifrin

Cliff Robertson, *Joel Grey*, Dorothy Tristan, Peter Masterson

'Runs out of interest long before it runs out of film.'—*Variety*

Man on a Tightrope*
US 1953 105m bw
TCF (Robert L. Jacks)

A Czech circus owner has trouble with the communist authorities and tries to escape.
Adventure story with cold war pretensions which virtually kill it.

w Robert Sherwood *d* Elia Kazan *ph* Georg Krause *m* Franz Waxman

Fredric March, Cameron Mitchell, Adolphe Menjou, Gloria Grahame, Terry Moore, Richard Boone, John Dehner, Dorothea Wieck

Man on Fire
US 1957 95m bw
MGM (Sol C. Siegel)

When his wife divorces him, a middle-aged man refuses to hand over their son.
Low-key personal drama of very moderate interest and modest budget.

wd Ranald MacDougall *ph* Joseph Ruttenberg *m* David Raksin

Bing Crosby, Inger Stevens, Mary Fickett, E. G. Marshall

A Man on the Beach
GB 1956 29m Eastmancolor

A man on the run is cared for and handed over to the police by a blind recluse. Modest featurette which scarcely justifies its credits. Donald Wolfit, Michael Medwin, Michael Ripper. From a story by Victor Canning; directed by Joseph Losey; for Anthony Hinds / Exclusive.

The Man on the Eiffel Tower*
US 1948 82m Anscocolor
A & T (Irving Allen)

A crazy killer defies Inspector Maigret to discover his identity.
Early independent production, an unsatisfactory crime melodrama with international talent and Paris locations. Some quirky acting carries it through.

w Harry Brown, *novel* A Battle of Nerves by Simenon *d* Burgess Meredith *ph* Stanley Cortez *m* Michel Michelet

Charles Laughton, Burgess Meredith, Franchot Tone, Robert Hutton, Jean Wallace, Patricia Roc, Wilfrid Hyde White, Belita

† Some scenes were directed by Charles Laughton and some by Franchot Tone.

The Man on the Flying Trapeze*
US 1935 65m bw
Paramount (William Le Baron)
GB title: *The Memory Expert*

Adventures of an oppressed family man who is useful to his boss because of his prodigious memory.
Plotless rigmarole of shapeless comedy sketches, for star fans.

w Ray Harris, Sam Hardy, Jack Cunningham, Bobby Vernon, *story* Charles Bogle (W. C. Fields) *d* Clyde Bruckman *ph* Al Gilks

W. C. Fields, Kathleen Howard, Mary Brian, Grady Sutton, Vera Lewis, Lucien Littlefield, Oscar Apfel

'A series of gags unrelated to the title. Under average.'—*Variety*

The Man on the Roof*
Sweden 1976 109m Eastmancolor
Svensk Filmindustri (Per Berglund)
original title: *Mannen pa Taket*

A brutal policeman is murdered, and a rooftop sniper turns out to be the culprit.
Alternately vivid and lumbering police thriller with a regrettable tendency to moralize.

wd Bo Widerberg, *novel* The Abominable Man by Max Sjöwall, Max Wahlöös *ph* Odd Geir Saether, Per Kallberg, others *m* Björn Lindh

Carl Gustav Lindstedt, Gunnel Wadner, Hakan Serner, Sven Wollter

Man on the Run
GB 1949 82m bw

A deserter becomes innocently involved in a jewel robbery. Competent crime programmer. Derek Farr, Joan Hopkins, Edward Chapman, Laurence Harvey, John Stuart. Written and directed by Lawrence Huntingdon; for ABPC.

Man Proof
US 1937 74m bw
MGM (Louis D. Lighton)

In trying to win back her man a woman discovers she really loves someone else.
Modest romantic comedy which leaves its stars at sea.

w Vincent Lawrence, Waldemar Young, George Oppenheimer, *novel* The Four Marys by Fanny Heaslip Lea *d* Richard Thorpe *ph* Karl Freund *m* Franz Waxman

Myrna Loy, Franchot Tone, Walter Pidgeon, Rosalind Russell, Nana Bryant, Ruth Hussey

'A smartly produced, well-directed and excellently acted society comedy drama.'—*Variety*

The Man They Could Not Hang
US 1939 65m bw
Columbia

A scientist working on a mechanical heart causes the death of a volunteer student. He is executed, but his assistant restores him to life and he determines to murder those who convicted him.
Predictable horror hokum which set Karloff on his mad doctor cycle.

w Karl Brown *d* Nick Grinde *ph* Benjamin Kline *md* Morris Stoloff

Boris Karloff, Lorna Gray, Robert Wilcox, Roger Pryor, Don Beddoe, Byron Foulger

A Man to Remember*
US 1938 80m bw
RKO (Robert Sisk)

At a small-town doctor's funeral, his life is remembered by mourners.
Modestly effective family film.

w Dalton Trumbo, *novel* Failure by Katharine Haviland-Taylor *d Garson Kanin* *ph* J. Roy Hunt *m* Roy Webb

Edward Ellis, Anne Shirley, Lee Bowman, William Henry, Granville Bates

'No sock for the marquee but a fine, well-made little picture.'—*Variety*

The Man Upstairs*
GB 1958 88m bw
British Lion / ACT (Robert Dunbar)

A mild-mannered lodger becomes violent, injures a policeman, and barricades himself in his room.
Character melodrama reminiscent of both *Fourteen Hours* and *Le Jour se Lève*, but not so interesting as either.

w Alun Falconer *d* Don Chaffey *ph* Gerald Gibbs

Richard Attenborough, Bernard Lee, Donald Houston, Dorothy Alison, Maureen Connell, Kenneth Griffith, Virginia Maskell, Patricia Jessel

Man Wanted
US 1932 60m bw

A business woman takes on a male secretary. Yawnworthy comedy drama with no surprises. Kay Francis, David Manners, Andy Devine, Una Merkel, Kenneth Thompson. Written by Robert Lord; directed by William Dieterle; for Warners. 'Threadbare plot weakens this for the big theatres and makes it extremely light and familiar entertainment for the others.'—*Variety*

The Man Who Broke the Bank at Monte Carlo*
US 1935 67m bw
Twentieth Century (Nunnally Johnson)

A Russian émigré becomes a taxi driver, wins a fortune at roulette, loses it all again, and returns happily to his cab.

Very mild, unconvincing and not very entertaining malarkey which rested squarely on its star, who carried it with aplomb.

w Nunnally Johnson *d* Stephen Roberts *ph* Ernest Palmer *md* Oliver Bradley

Ronald Colman, Joan Bennett, Colin Clive, Nigel Bruce, Montagu Love, Frank Reicher, Ferdinand Gottschalk

'Nice production though lacks dash . . . Colman at times seems to be playing under wraps. Should do fairly well.'—*Variety*

'The richest roles of romance and redemption they ever played!'

The Man Who Came Back

US 1930 74m bw
Fox

A reckless young man is reformed when he finds his erstwhile sweetheart now a drug addict in Hong Kong.
Earnest melodrama which not surprisingly damaged the talkie success of a celebrated screen team, and must now seem risible in the extreme.

w Edwin J. Burke, *story and novel* John Fleming Wilson, *play* Jules Eckert Goodman *d* Raoul Walsh *ph* Arthur Edeson *pd* Joseph Urban

Janet Gaynor, Charles Farrell, Kenneth MacKenna, William Holden, Mary Forbes, Peter Gawthorne

'Gripping old melodrama of drugs and degradation tamed down and made into a cheerful sentimental piece. Co-star names make it a strong bid.'—*Variety*

'Sophisticates will give it one big horse laugh.'—*Photoplay*

The Man Who Came to Dinner***

US 1941 112m bw
Warner (Jack Saper, Jerry Wald)

An acid-tongued radio celebrity breaks his hip while on a lecture tour, and terrorizes the inhabitants of the suburban home where he must stay for several weeks.
Delightfully malicious caricature of Alexander Woolcott which, though virtually confined to one set, moves so fast that one barely notices the lack of cinematic variety, and certainly provides more than a laugh a minute, especially for those old enough to understand all the references.

w Julius J. and Philip G. Epstein, *play George S. Kaufman, Moss Hart* *d* William Keighley *ph* Tony Gaudio *m* Frederick Hollander

Monty Woolley, Bette Davis, Ann Sheridan, *Jimmy Durante* (spoofing Harpo Marx), *Reginald Gardiner* (spoofing Noel Coward), Richard Travis, *Billie Burke, Grant Mitchell, Ruth Vivian, Mary Wickes*, George Barbier, Elisabeth Fraser

WHITESIDE (Monty Woolley) to his nurse, who won't let him eat chocolates: 'I had an aunt who ate a box of chocolates every day of her life. She lived to be a hundred and two, and when she had been dead three days, she looked healthier than you do now!'

NURSE (Mary Wickes): 'I am not only walking out on this case, Mr Whiteside, I am leaving the nursing profession. I became a nurse because all my life, ever since I was a little girl, I was filled with the idea of serving a suffering humanity. After one month with you, Mr Whiteside, I am going to work in a munitions factory. From now on, anything I can do to help exterminate the human race will fill me with the greatest of pleasure. If Florence Nightingale had ever nursed YOU, Mr Whiteside, she would have married Jack the Ripper instead of founding the Red Cross!'

WHITESIDE (introducing his secretary): 'This ageing debutante, Mr Jefferson, I retain in my employ only because she is the sole support of her two-headed brother.'

BANJO (Jimmy Durante): 'Did you ever get the feeling that you wanted to stay, and still get the feeling that you wanted to go?'

BEVERLY CARLTON (Reginald Gardiner impersonating Noel Coward): 'Don't tell me how you are, Sherry, I want none of the tiresome details. I've very little time, and so the conversation will be entirely about me, and I shall love it. Shall I tell you how I glittered through the South Seas like a silver scimitar, or would you rather hear how I finished a three-act play with one hand and made love to a maharaja's daughter with the other?'

The Man Who Changed His Mind

GB 1936 66m bw

A scientist dabbles in brain transplants. Mild British-style horror piece; not a success. Boris Karloff, Anna Lee, Donald Calthrop, John Loder, Frank Cellier, Cecil Parker. Written by John L. Balderston, L. DuGarde Peach and Sidney Gilliat; directed by Robert Stevenson; for Gainsborough. (US title: *The Man Who Lived Again*.) 'A spine-freezer of routine construction. The accents are very limey and the way laboratory is pronounced may have American schoolchildren wondering.'—*Variety*

The Man Who Cheated Himself

US 1950 81m bw
TCF (Jack M. Warner)

A woman shoots her husband and her homicide detective lover covers up for her. Efficient crime melodrama.

w Seton I. Miller, Philip MacDonald *d* Felix Feist *ph* Russell Harlan *m* Louis Forbes

Lee J. Cobb, Jane Wyatt, John Dall, Terry Frost

The Man Who Could Cheat Death

GB 1959 83m Technicolor
Paramount / Hammer (Anthony Nelson-Keys)

A surgeon looks 35 but is really 104, having had a series of gland operations performed on himself.
Vulgar, gory, gruesomely coloured Hammer version of a rather attractive play, previously filmed under its original title *The Man in Half Moon Street* (qv). The shocks are routine, and entertainment value is minimal.

w Jimmy Sangster, *play* Barre Lyndon *d* Terence Fisher *ph* Jack Asher *m* Richard Rodney Bennett

Anton Diffring, Hazel Court, Christopher Lee, Arnold Marle, Delphi Lawrence, Francis de Wolff

The Man Who Could Work Miracles***

GB 1936 82m bw
London (Alexander Korda)

A city clerk discovers he has the power to work miracles (given him by sportive gods) and nearly causes the end of the earth.
Slow-moving but rather pleasing variation on a simple theme.

w Lajos Biro, *story* H. G. Wells *d* Lothar Mendes *ph* Harold Rosson *m* Mischa Spoliansky

Roland Young, Ralph Richardson, Ernest Thesiger, Edward Chapman, Joan Gardner, Sophie Stewart, Robert Cochrane, George Zucco, Lawrence Hanray, George Sanders

'Supposedly a comedy. A weakling: little draw power on this side.'—*Variety*

'Sometimes fake poetry, sometimes unsuccessful comedy, sometimes farce, sometimes sociological discussion, without a spark of creative talent or a trace of film ability.'—*Graham Greene*

The Man Who Cried Wolf

US 1937 67m bw

An actor continually confesses to crimes he didn't commit in the hope that when he does commit one he won't be believed. An attractive idea rather poorly handled. Lewis Stone, Tom Brown, Barbara Read, Marjorie Main, Forrester Harvey. Written by Charles Grayson and Sy Bartlett; directed by Lewis R. Foster; for Universal. 'Will get by as the number two feature on dual bills.'—*Variety*

The Man Who Dared

US 1933 72m bw

The life of a local politician, based on Mayor Cermak of Chicago. Episodic but not unpleasant biopic; it adds up to very little, though. Preston Foster, Zita Johann, Joan Marsh, Irene Biller, Leon Waycoff. Written by Dudley Nichols, Lamar Trotti; directed by Hamilton McFadden; for Fox. 'The most flattering account ever written of any man's life . . . but as a commercial talker it's not likely to get very far. Even in Chicago they didn't care for it.'—*Variety*

The Man Who Fell to Earth*

GB 1976 138m colour Panavision
British Lion (Michael Deeley, Barry Spikings)

A visitor from another planet tries to colonize Earth, but his powers are destroyed and he ends an alcoholic cripple.
A weird piece of intellectual science fiction made weirder by longueurs of all varieties: obscure narrative, voyeuristic sex, pop music and metaphysics. Not an easy film or a likeable one, despite its great technical skill.

w Paul Mayersburg, *novel* Walter Tevis *d* Nicolas Roeg *ph* Anthony Richmond *md* John Phillips

David Bowie, Rip Torn, Candy Clark, Buck Henry

'Once you have pierced through its glittering veneer, you find only another glittering veneer underneath.'—*Michael Billington, Illustrated London News*

'There is a punch line, but it takes forever, and great expectations slump away.'—*Charles Champlin, L.A. News*

'You feel finally that all that has been achieved has been to impose an aura of mystery and enigma where essentially there is none; to turn a simple tale into the sort of accumulation of sensations that has become fashionable.'—*David Robinson, The Times*

The Man Who Finally Died
GB 1962 100m bw Cinemascope
British Lion / Magna / White Cross (Norman Williams)

A German-born Englishman returns to Bavaria for news of his father, and becomes involved in a spy plot.
Busy adaptation of a TV serial with a convoluted plot which might have been more pacily developed and better explained.

w Lewis Greifer, Louis Marks *d* Quentin Lawrence *ph* Stephen Dade *m* Philip Green

Stanley Baker, Peter Cushing, Mai Zetterling, Eric Portman, Niall MacGinnis, Nigel Green, Barbara Everest, Harold Scott

The Man Who Found Himself
US 1937 67m bw
RKO (Cliff Reid)

A nurse helps a downcast doctor face his problems and renew his enthusiasm for life.
Simple-minded programmer.

w J. Robert Bren, Edmund Hartman, G. V. Atwater *d* Lew Landers *ph* Roy Hunt

John Beal, Joan Fontaine, Philip Huston, Jane Walsh, George Irving

'No names in this hokey B session . . . flapdoodle with a capital F.'—*Variety*

The Man Who Had His Hair Cut Short*
Belgium 1966 94m bw
Belgian Cultural Ministry

A frustrated law clerk has an aberration after attending an autopsy and meeting again an old love.
Pessimistic case history with unpleasant details often brilliantly recorded.

w Anna de Pagter, André Delvaux *d* André Delvaux *ph* Ghislain Cloquet *m* Freddy Devreese

Seene Rouffaer, Beata Tyszkiewicz, Hector Camerlynck

The Man Who Had Power over Women
GB 1970 89m Eastmancolor

A successful public relations man comes to hate himself, his job and what it has done to his marriage. Fashionable wallow in guilt and luxury, not very convincingly done. Rod Taylor, Carol White, James Booth, Penelope Horner, Charles Korvin, Alexandra Stewart, Keith Barron. Written by Alan Scott and Chris Bryant, from the novel by Gordon Williams; directed by John Krish; for Kettledrum / Avco.

The Man Who Haunted Himself
GB 1970 94m Technicolor
ABP / Excalibur (Michael Relph)

After recovering from a road accident, a staid businessman finds that he has an evil doppelganger who steals his wife and his job. Mildly effective if inexplicable story idea which served more suitably as a Hitchcock TV half hour and here, despite adequate production, outstays its welcome.

w Basil Dearden, Michael Relph, *story* The Case of Mr Pelham by Anthony Armstrong *d* Basil Dearden *ph* Tony Spratling *m* Michael Lewis

Roger Moore, Hildegarde Neil, Olga-Georges Picot, Anton Rodgers, Freddie Jones, Thorley Walters, John Carson, John Welsh

The Man Who Knew Too Much***
GB 1934 84m bw
GFD / Gaumont British (Ivor Montagu)

A child is kidnapped by spies to ensure her father's silence, but he springs into action. Splendid early Hitchcock which after a faded start moves into memorable sequences involving a dentist, an East End mission and the Albert Hall. All very stagey by today's standards, but much more fun than the expensive remake.

w A. R. Rawlinson, Charles Bennett, D. B. Wyndham Lewis, Edwin Greenwood, Emlyn Williams *d Alfred Hitchcock ph* Curt Courant *m* Arthur Benjamin

Leslie Banks, Edna Best, *Peter Lorre*, Nova Pilbeam, Frank Vosper, Hugh Wakefield, Pierre Fresnay

'A natural and easy production that runs smoothly and has the hallmark of sincerity.'—*Variety*

'The film's mainstay is its refined sense of the incongruous.'—*Peter John Dyer, 1964*

'A single clash of cymbals that will rock the lives of an American family!'

The Man Who Knew Too Much*
US 1956 120m Technicolor Vistavision
(Paramount) Alfred Hitchcock

Flaccid remake of the above, twice as long and half as entertaining, though it does improve after a very slow start.

w John Michael Hayes, Angus MacPhail *d* Alfred Hitchcock *ph* Robert Burks *m* Bernard Herrmann

James Stewart, Doris Day, Bernard Miles, Brenda de Banzie, Daniel Gelin, Ralph Truman, Mogens Wieth, Alan Mowbray, Hillary Brooke

'The balance between character and incident in the earlier film makes a far better thriller.'—*Observer*

'The remake is heavy and oppressive, the suspense often risible, and the moments of comic relief fall flat.'—*Sunday Times*

'Let's say the first version is the work of a talented amateur and the second was made by a professional.'—*Alfred Hitchcock*

AA: song 'Que Sera Sera' (*m* / *ly* Jay Livingston, Ray Evans)

The Man Who Lost Himself
US 1941 71m bw

A man back from the tropics finds himself playing the part of a lookalike millionaire. Pleasantly nimble farce; not original but agreeable to watch. Brian Aherne, Kay Francis, S. Z. Sakall, Henry Stephenson, Nils Asther, Sig Ruman. Written by Eddie Moran from a novel by H. DeVere Stacpoole; directed by Edward Ludwig; for Universal.

The Man Who Loved Cat Dancing
US 1973 114m Metrocolor Panavision
MGM (Martin Poll, Eleanor Perry)

A runaway wife is kidnapped by train thieves and comes to love one of them.
Outdoor variation on *No Orchids for Miss Blandish*, remarkably lacking in any kind of entertainment value.

w Eleanor Perry, *novel* Marilyn Dunham *d* Richard Sarafian *ph* Harry Stradling Jnr *m* John Williams

Sarah Miles, Burt Reynolds, Lee J. Cobb, Jack Warden, George Hamilton, Bo Hopkins, Robert Donner, Jay Silverheels

'Any number of things have gone wrong with this peculiarly dreary western.'—*Tom Milne*

'Sarah Miles undergoes more perils than Pauline.'—*Variety*

The Man Who Loved Redheads
GB 1954 90m Eastmancolor
British Lion / London Films (Josef Somlo)

Throughout his career, a diplomat seeks women who resemble the redhead with whom in youth he had had an idyllic affair.
West End theatrical moonshine, poorly filmed in ugly colour but saved by the cast.

w Terence Rattigan, from his play Who Is Sylvia? *d* Harold French *ph* Georges Périnal *m* Benjamin Frankel

John Justin, Moira Shearer, *Roland Culver*, Gladys Cooper, Denholm Elliott, Harry Andrews, Patricia Cutts, Moira Fraser, *Joan Benham*, Jeremy Spenser

'Deciding which woman in the world he loved most is driving him out of his mind!'

The Man Who Loved Women
France 1977 119m Eastmancolor
Les Films du Carrosse / PAA (Marcel Bebert)

A man spends his life in pursuit of women and dies in the chase.
Sour comedy which doesn't quite come off.

THE MAN WHO FELL TO EARTH. A moment recognizable to fans of science fiction in Nicolas Roeg's convoluted genre piece.

w François Truffaut, Michel Fermaud, Suzanne Schiffman *d* François Truffaut *ph* Nestor Almendros *m* Maurice Jaubert

Charles Denner, Brigitte Fossey, Leslie Caron, Nelly Borgeaud, Nathalie Baye

The Man Who Loved Women
US 1983 110m Metrocolor
Columbia / Delphi / Blake Edwards (Blake Edwards, Tony Adams)

An American remake of the above, with even less success.

w Blake Edwards, Milton Wexler, Geoffrey Edwards *d* Blake Edwards *ph* Haskell Wexler *m* Henry Mancini

Burt Reynolds, Julie Andrews, Kim Basinger, Marilu Henner, Cynthia Sikes, Jennifer Edwards

'The strangest story in the annals of naval espionage!'
The Man Who Never Was**
GB 1955 102m De Luxe Cinemascope
Sumar / André Hakim

In 1943, the British secret service confuses the Germans by dropping a dead man into the sea with false documents.
Mainly enjoyable true life war story marred by an emotional romantic sub-plot with a double twist but helped by an equally fictitious spy hunt which cheers up the last half hour.

w Nigel Balchin, *book* Ewen Montagu *d* Ronald Neame *ph* Oswald Morris *m* Alan Rawsthorne

Clifton Webb, Robert Flemyng, Gloria Grahame, *Stephen Boyd*, Laurence Naismith, Josephine Griffin

The Man Who Played God*
US 1932 81m bw
Warner
GB title: *The Silent Voice*

A musician goes deaf but finds satisfaction in helping a young student.
Stagey but effective star vehicle which Arliss also played as a silent film. Remade as *Sincerely Yours* (qv).

w Julian Josephson, Maude Howell, *play* The Silent Voice by Jules Eckert Goodman *d* John G. Adolfi *ph* James Van Trees

George Arliss, Violet Heming, Ivan Simpson, *Bette Davis*, Louise Closser Hale, Donald Cook, Ray Milland

'Will need all the Arliss name strength to pull average returns.'—*Variety*

The Man Who Reclaimed His Head*
US 1934 81m bw
Universal (Henry Henigson)

A writer who feels he has been betrayed and his brain sapped by his publisher takes a gruesome revenge.
Oddball period melodrama tailored rather unsuccessfully for a new star. Remade as *Strange Confession* (see *Inner Sanctum*).

w Jean Bart, Samuel Ornitz, *play* Jean Bart *d* Edward Ludwig *ph* Merrit Gerstad *m* Heinz Roemheld

Claude Rains, Joan Bennett, Lionel Atwill, Juanita Quigley, Henry O'Neill, Lawrence Grant

'Interesting screen diversion . . . Far from a smash, but good enough to keep to the average level or above.'—*Variety*

The Man Who Shot Liberty Valance*
US 1962 122m bw
Paramount / John Ford (Willis Goldbeck)

A tenderfoot becomes a hero for shooting a bad man, but the shot was really fired by his friend and protector.
Clumsy, obvious western with the director over-indulging himself but providing some good scenes in comedy vein.

w James Warner Bellah, Willis Goldbeck *d* John Ford *ph* William H. Clothier *m* Cyril Mockridge

James Stewart, John Wayne, Vera Miles, Lee Marvin, Edmond O'Brien, Andy Devine, Jeanette Nolan, John Qualen, Ken Murray, Woody Strode, Lee Van Cleef, Strother Martin, John Carradine

'Like Queen Victoria, John Wayne has become lovable because he stayed in the saddle into a new era.'—*Judith Crist*

'A heavy-spirited piece of nostalgia.'—*Pauline Kael, 1975*

'A film whose fascination lies less in what it is itself than in what it reveals about the art of its maker.'—*William S. Pechter*

The Man Who Talked Too Much
US 1940 75m bw
Warner (Edmund Grainger)

A smart defence attorney gets the goods on a gangster and decides to turn him in.
Below-par remake of *The Mouthpiece* (qv), later filmed again as *Illegal* (qv).

w Walter de Leon, Tom Reed, *play* The Mouthpiece by Frank J. Collins *d* Vincent Sherman *ph* Sid Hickox

George Brent, Brenda Marshall, Richard Barthelmess, Virginia Bruce, William Lundigan, John Litel, George Tobias, Henry Armetta, Alan Baxter

'Human or inhuman, no woman is safe!'
The Man Who Turned to Stone
US 1957 71m bw

A girls' reformatory is taken over by a group of zombie scientists born in the eighteenth century. Cheap horror item with a few choice moments for connoisseurs of the absurd.
Victor Jory, Ann Doran, Charlotte Austin, William Hudson, Paul Cavanagh. Written by Raymond T. Marcus; directed by Leslie Kardos; for Clover / Columbia.

The Man Who Understood Women
US 1959 105m Eastmancolor Cinemascope
TCF (Nunnally Johnson)

An arrogant, exhibitionist film producer finally alienates his long-suffering wife.
Something of an aberration, with good scenes submerged in an unholy mixture of sharp comedy and sentimental melodrama.

wd Nunnally Johnson, *novel* Colours of the Day by Romain Gary *ph* Milton Krasner *m* Robert Emmett Dolan

Henry Fonda, Leslie Caron, Myron McCormick, Cesare Danova, Marcel Dalio, Conrad Nagel, Harry Ellerbe

'A pretentious extravaganza on a romantic theme.'—*MFB*

The Man Who Watched Trains Go By
GB 1952 80m Technicolor
Raymond Stross
aka: *Paris Express*

A clerk steals money in order to fulfil his wish of world travel, and this leads to murder.
Miscast minor Simenon, not exactly badly made but with no spark of excitement or suspense.

wd Harold French, *novel* Georges Simenon *ph* Otto Heller *m* Benjamin Frankel

Claude Rains, Marius Goring, Marta Toren, Anouk Aimée, Herbert Lom, Ferdy Mayne

The Man Who Would Be King*
US 1975 129m colour Panavision
Columbia / Allied Artists / Persky-Bright / Devon (John Foreman)

In India in the 1880s, two adventurers find themselves accepted as kings by a remote tribe, but greed betrays them.
After an ingratiating start this ambitious fable becomes more predictable, and comedy gives way to unpleasantness. Despite its sporadic high quality, one does not remember it with enthusiasm.

w John Huston, Gladys Hill, *story* Rudyard Kipling *d* John Huston *ph* Oswald Morris *m* Maurice Jarre *pd* Alexander Trauner

Sean Connery, Michael Caine, Christopher Plummer (as Kipling), Saeed Jaffrey, Jack May, Shakira Caine

AAN: script

The Man Who Wouldn't Talk
US 1940 72m bw

A man on trial for murder has such a mysterious background that he may even be the victim. Efficient remake of Paul Muni's *The Valiant*. Lloyd Nolan, Jean Rogers, Richard Clarke, Eric Blore, Mae Marsh. Written by Robert Ellis, Helen Logan, Lester Ziffren and Edward Ettinger; directed by David Burton; for Sol M. Wurtzel / TCF.

The Man Who Wouldn't Talk
GB 1957 97m bw
British Lion / Everest (Herbert Wilcox)

A lady QC gets an acquittal for a man who can't defend himself on a murder charge because of loyalty to a scientist on the run.
Efficient courtroom melodrama based on a somewhat incredible and even uninteresting situation.

w Edgar Lustgarten, *story* Stanley Jackson *d* Herbert Wilcox *ph* Gordon Dines *m* Stanley Black

Anna Neagle, Anthony Quayle, Zsa Zsa Gabor, Katherine Kath, Dora Bryan, Patrick Allen

The Man with a Cloak*
US 1951 81m bw
MGM (Stephen Ames)

In 1848 New York, a mysterious stranger (who turns out to be Edgar Allan Poe) helps a young French girl to keep her inheritance.
Curious domestic melodrama set on MGM's choicest sets; its playful literary allusion causes it to fall between suspense thriller and character drama, but the acting keeps one watching.

w Frank Fenton, *story* John Dickson Carr *d Fletcher Markle ph George Folsey m* David Raksin

Joseph Cotten, Barbara Stanwyck, Leslie Caron, Louis Calhern, Joe de Santis, Jim Backus, Margaret Wycherly

The Man with Bogart's Face
US 1980 106m CFI color
TCF / Melvin Simon (Andrew J. Fenady)

An unremarkable private eye gets lots of assignments because he looks like Humphrey Bogart.
Amiably nostalgic romp, not too spoofy to be enjoyable for its own sake, but notably underproduced.

w Andrew J. Fenady, from his novel *d* Robert Day *ph* Richard C. Glouner *m* George Duning

Robert Sacchi, Misty Rowe, Michelle Phillips, Franco Nero, Olivia Hussey, Victor Buono, Herbert Lom, George Raft, Yvonne de Carlo, Jay Robinson, Mike Mazurki, Henry Wilcoxon, Victor Sen Yung

The Man with My Face
US 1951 77m bw

A successful young man finds a double in his place at both home and office, and himself branded as an imposter. Intriguing yarn which deserved a better production. Barry Nelson, Lynn Ainley, John Harvey, Carole Matthews, Jack Warden. Written by Samuel W. Taylor, Edward J. Montagne, T. J. McGowan and Vincent Bogart, from a novel by Samuel W. Taylor; directed by Edward J. Montagne; for Edward F. Gardner / UA.

The Man with Nine Lives*
US 1940 73m bw
Columbia
GB title: *Behind the Door*

A scientist believes he can cure cancer by freezing, but accidentally locks himself and his patients in an underground ice chamber for seven years, and goes berserk when thawed out.
Interesting, rather prophetic science fiction thriller which rather lacks the style required to put it over.

w Karl Brown, story Harold Shumate *d* Nick Grinde *ph* Benjamin Kline

Boris Karloff, Byron Foulger, Roger Pryor, Jo Ann Sayers

The Man with the Deadly Lens: see Wrong is Right

The Man with the Golden Arm*
US 1956 119m bw
Otto Preminger

A Chicago poker dealer finally kicks the drug habit.
Sensational on its first release, with its cold turkey scenes, this now seems a muddled impressionist melodrama with echoes of the silent German cinema and much over-acting and miscasting all round. But Sinatra is good; and it *is* different . . .

w Walter Newman, Lewis Meltzer, *novel* Nelson Algren *d* Otto Preminger *ph Sam Leavitt m Elmer Bernstein pd* Joe Wright *titles Saul Bass*

Frank Sinatra, Kim Novak, Eleanor Parker, Darren McGavin, Arnold Stang, Robert Strauss, John Conte, Doro Merande, George E. Stone

'Nothing very surprising or exciting . . . a pretty plain and unimaginative look-see at a lower depths character.'—*Bosley Crowther*

'A very inferior film . . . the script is inexcusably clumsy, the sets are unbelievable and the casting is ridiculous.'—*Diana Willing, Films in Review*

'It has the same running time as *Citizen Kane* but it seems a whole lot longer.'—*Robert James*

AAN: Elmer Bernstein; Frank Sinatra

The Man with the Golden Gun*
GB 1974 125m Eastmancolor
UA / Eon (Harry Saltzman, Albert R. Broccoli)

James Bond goes to the Far East to liquidate a professional assassin named Scaramanga.
Thin and obvious Bond extravaganza with conventional expensive excitements.

w Richard Maibaum, Tom Mankiewicz, *novel* Ian Fleming *d* Guy Hamilton *ph* Ted Moore, Oswald Morris *m* John Barry *pd* Peter Murton

Roger Moore, Christopher Lee, Britt Ekland, Maud Adams, Hervé Villechaize, Clifton James, Richard Loo, Marc Lawrence

'The script lacks satiric insolence and the picture grinds on humourlessly.'—*New Yorker*

'His gun was for sale—and so was his life!'
The Man with the Gun*
US 1955 84m bw
UA / Formosa (Sam Goldwyn Jnr)
GB title: *The Trouble Shooter*

A gunfighter in search of his estranged wife becomes lawman of a lawless town.
Modest, watchable western.

w N. B. Stone Jnr, Richard Wilson *d* Richard Wilson *ph* Lee Garmes *m* Alex North

Robert Mitchum, Jan Sterling, Karen Sharpe, Henry Hull, Emile Meyer, John Luplon

The Man with the Movie Camera**
USSR 1928 60m approx bw silent
VUFKU
original title: *Chelovek s Kinoapparatom*

A 'camera eye' documentary without any plot, showing, through a succession of street and interior scenes, all the tricks of which the instrument is capable; it takes a bow at the end.
Unique documentary which was understandably a sensation when it first appeared but now often seems merely quaint.

wd, ed Dziga Vertov *ph* Mikhail Kaufman

The Man with the Steel Whip
US 1954 bw serial: 12 eps

A young rancher opposing troublemakers disguises himself as El Latigo, a legendary masked rider. Routine serial in imitation of *The Mark of Zorro*. Richard Simmons, Barbara Bestar, Dale Van Sickel, Lane Bradford. Directed by Franklin Adreon; for Republic.

The Man with Two Faces*
US 1934 72m bw
Warner

An actor takes revenge on a scoundrel who had preyed on his sister.
Pleasing melodrama hinging on disguise; the Hays Office surprisingly allowed the hero to get away with it.

w Tom Reed, Niven Busch, *play* The Dark Tower by George S. Kaufman, Alexander Woolcott *d* Archie Mayo *ph* Tony Gaudio

Edward G. Robinson, Mary Astor, Ricardo Cortez, Louis Calhern, Mae Clarke, John Eldredge

'Fair fodder, but undistinguished in the main, and in spots very confusing.'—*Variety*

The Man Within*
GB 1947 88m Technicolor
GFD / Production Film Service (Muriel and Sydney Box)
US title: *The Smugglers*

An orphan boy discovers that his mysterious new guardian is a smuggler.
Unconvincing period yarn which has managed to drain every vestige of subtlety from the novel, but at least looks good.

w Muriel and Sydney Box, *novel* Graham Greene *d* Bernard Knowles *ph* Geoffrey Unsworth *m* Clifton Parker

Michael Redgrave, Richard Attenborough, Jean Kent, Joan Greenwood

'With more style this might have been rather good. Outside of life more private than I am normally party to I can't recall hearing so many men so often say, to other men, *I hate him!* or *I hate you!*'—*James Agee*

The Man Without a Body
GB 1957 80m bw
Filmplays

A tycoon with a brain tumour steals the head of Nostradamus and has it kept alive to replace his own. Hilarious horror comic, inept in every department. George Coulouris, Robert Hutton, Nadja Regin, Julia Arnall. Written by William Grote; directed by W. Lee Wilder and Charles Saunders; for Guido Coen / Eros.

The Man without a Star*
US 1955 89m Technicolor
U-I (Aaron Rosenberg)

A wandering cowboy helps settlers to put up barbed wire against an owner of vast cattle herds.
Conventional but entertaining star western.

w Borden Chase, D. D. Beauchamp, *novel* Dee Linford *d* King Vidor *ph* Russell Metty *m* Hans Salter

Kirk Douglas, Jeanne Crain, Claire Trevor, William Campbell, Jay C. Flippen, Mara Corday, Richard Boone

† Remade for TV as *A Man Called Gannon.*

Man, Woman and Child
US 1982 100m De Luxe

A married professor discovers that he has a son by his only infidelity. *Angst* among the well-to-do, from the author of *Love Story*. Martin Sheen, Blythe Danner, Craig T. Nelson, David Hemmings, Nathalie Nell. Written by Erich Segal, David Selag Goodman, from the novel by Erich Segal; directed by Dick Richards; for Gaylord.

Man, Woman and Sin
US 1927 85m approx at 24 fps bw silent

A reporter has an affair with his boss's mistress. Glossy romantic drama marking the first screen appearance of a sensational stage star; her effect on screen was more muted. Jeanne Eagels, John Gilbert, Marc McDermott. Written by Alice Duer Miller; directed by Monta Bell; for MGM.

The Manchurian Candidate***
US 1962 126m bw
UA / MC (Howard W. Koch)

A Korean war 'hero' comes back a brainwashed zombie triggered to kill a liberal politician, his control being his own monstrously ambitious mother.
Insanely plotted but brilliantly handled spy thriller, a mixture of Hitchcock, Welles and *All the King's Men.*

w George Axelrod, *novel* Richard Condon *d John Frankenheimer* *ph Lionel Lindon* *m* David Amram *pd Richard Sylbert*

Frank Sinatra, Laurence Harvey, Janet Leigh, James Gregory, Angela Lansbury, Henry Silva, John McGiver

'The unAmerican film of the year.'—*Penelope Houston*

'An intelligent, funny, superbly written, beautifully played, and brilliantly directed study of the all-embracing fantasy in everyday social, emotional and political existence.'—*Philip Strick, 1973*

'Although it's a thriller, it may be the most sophisticated political satire ever to come out of Hollywood.'—*Pauline Kael, 70s*

AAN: Angela Lansbury

Mandalay
US 1934 65m bw

A lady of the tropics murders her lover and pushes his body through a porthole. Steamy melodrama which the masses found absorbing. Kay Francis, Ricardo Cortez, Lyle Talbot, Ruth Donnelly, Shirley Temple, Warner Oland, Lucien Littlefield, Reginald Owen. Written by Austin Parker and Charles Kenyon; directed by Michael Curtiz; for Warner.

Mandingo
US 1975 126m Technicolor
Dino de Laurentiis (Peter Herald)

On a slave breeding plantation in 1840 Louisiana, passions ride high.
Like *Gone with the Wind* with all the characters on heat, this exuberant and unpleasant melodrama goes several points over the top from start to finish but proved to have wide appeal for the groundlings, in the *Tobacco Road* tradition of a wallow in other people's depravities.

w Norman Wexler, *play* Jack Kirkland, *novel* Kyle Onstott *d* Richard Fleischer *ph* Richard H. Kline *m* Maurice Jarre *pd* Boris Leven

James Mason, Susan George, Perry King, Richard Ward, Brenda Sykes, Ken Norton

Mandrake the Magician
US 1939 bw serial: 12 eps

A world-famous magician trails an underworld leader called The Wasp. Rather stylish serial exploits with the added effect of illusions. Warren Hull, Doris Weston, Al Kikume, Rex Downing, Don Beddoe. Directed by Sam Nelson and Norman Denning; for Columbia.

'She'll find a home in every heart! She'll reach the heart of every home!'

Mandy***
GB 1952 93m bw
Ealing (Leslie Norman)
US title: *The Crash of Silence*

A little girl, born deaf, is sent to a special school.
Carefully wrought and very sympathetic little semi-documentary film in which all the adults underplay in concession to a new child star who alas did not last long at the top.

w Nigel Balchin, Jack Whittingham, *novel* This Day Is Ours by Hilda Lewis *d Alexander Mackendrick* *ph* Douglas Slocombe *m* William Alwyn

Jack Hawkins, Terence Morgan, Phyllis Calvert, *Mandy Miller*, Godfrey Tearle, Dorothy Alison

Maneater of Kumaon
US 1948 78m bw

A doctor in the Himalayas helps track down a man-eating tiger. Slightly unusual adventure story based on a currently popular book. Sabu, Wendell Corey, Joanne Page, Morris Carnovsky. Written by Jeanne Bartlett and Lewis Meltzer from book by Jim Corbett; directed by Byron Haskin; for Monty Shaff-Frank Rosenberg / Universal.

MANHATTAN. Woody Allen caught in a typically worried pose (with Diane Keaton). But New York Jewish *angst* proved to be a critical and commercial success.

Manèges*
France 1950 90m bw
Films Modernes-Discina (Emil Natan)
GB title: *The Wanton*

A scheming girl marries the middle-aged owner of a riding school and, with her greedy mother, milks him of his money.
A neat little melodrama with flashbacks so arranged that the girl, paralysed in an accident, seems for the first half to have an angelic character.

w Jacques Sigurd *d* Yves Allégret *ph* Jean Bourgoin

Simone Signoret, Bernard Blier, *Frank Villard*, Jane Marken

Manhandled
US 1949 97m bw
Paramount / Pine–Thomas

The secretary of a bogus psychiatrist becomes involved in a murder and finds herself in danger from all comers.
Modest, overlong suspenser with adequate production values.

w Lewis R. Foster, Whitman Chambers, *novel* The Man Who Stole a Dream by L. S. Goldsmith *d* Lewis R. Foster *ph* Ernest Laszlo *m* David Chudnow

Dorothy Lamour, Dan Duryea, Sterling Hayden, Irene Hervey, Harold Vermilyea, Philip Reed, Alan Napier, Art Smith, Irving Bacon

Manhattan***
US 1979 96m bw Panavision
UA / Jack Rollins / Charles H. Joffe

Episodes in the sex life of a TV comedy writer with an obsession about New York.
As close to a summation of Woody Allen's views and *oeuvre* as anybody needs; some smart jabs about the lives we lead are sometimes bogged down in earnestness and half-comic despair.

w Woody Allen, Marshall Brickman *d* Woody Allen *ph* Gordon Willis *md* Tom Pierson

Woody Allen, Diane Keaton, Meryl Streep, Mariel Hemingway, Michael Murphy

'Given that the identity of his films has increasingly been determined by his compulsion to talk about the things he finds important, but also by his fear of having them come out as anything but a joke, it is not surprising that he has scarcely been able to decide on a form for his "art": from the anything-for-a-laugh skittering of his early films, to the broad parodies and pastiches of his middle period, to the recent confessional / psychoanalytical mode.'—*Richard Combs, MFB*

'A masterpiece that has become a film for the ages by not seeking to be a film of the moment.'—*Andrew Sarris*

AAN: script; Mariel Hemingway

Manhattan Heartbeat
US 1940 71m bw

A husband is reluctant to assume the responsibilities of fatherhood. Oddly-titled support, a remake of *Bad Girl*; no great shakes from any angle. Robert Sterling, Virginia Gilmore, Joan Davis, Edmund MacDonald, Don Beddoe. Written by Harold Buchman, Clark Andrews, Jack Jungmeyer Jnr, Edith Skouras; directed by David Burton; for Sol M. Wurtzel / TCF.

Manhattan Melodrama**
US 1934 93m bw
MGM (David O. Selznick)

Two slum boys grow up friends, one as district attorney and the other as a gangster.
Archetypal American situation drama (cf *Angels with Dirty Faces, Cry of the City*, etc), with the bad guy inevitably indulging in self-sacrifice at the end. An all-star cast makes it palatable in this case, though the film is inevitably dated.

w Oliver H. P. Garrett, Joseph L. Mankiewicz, *story* Arthur Caesar *d* W. S. Van Dyke *ph* James Wong Howe *m* William Axt

William Powell, Clark Gable, Myrna Loy, Leo Carrillo, Nat Pendleton, George Sidney, Isabel Jewell, Thomas E. Jackson

'Action meller of the big town . . . replete with punchy, popularly-appealing ingredients.'—*Variety*

† *Manhattan Melodrama* gained some irrelevant fame as the movie John Dillinger was watching when he was cornered and shot.

AA: Arthur Caesar

Manhattan Merry-go-round*
US 1937 82m bw

A sound recording studio is taken over by a band of racketeers. Sufficient comedy plot to sustain a revue of historical interest. Phil Regan, Leo Carrillo, Ann Dvorak, Tamara Geva, James Gleason, Ted Lewis and his Orchestra, Cab Calloway and his Orchestra, the Kay Thompson Ensemble, Louis Prima and his Band, Gene Autry, Joe Di Maggio. Written by Harry Sauber, Frank Hummert; directed by Charles F. Reisner; for Republic. 'So much talent and novelty has been compressed within the limits of the film that customers dare not sneeze for fear of missing something . . . for the territorial distributors and independent theatres it is something to get excited about.'—*Variety*

Manhattan Parade
US 1931 77m Technicolor

Behind the scenes as a theatrical costumier tries to get into the revue business. Aimless backstage comedy with turns. Smith and Dale, Winnie Lightner, Charles Butterworth, Walter Miller, Luis Alberni. Written by Robert Lord and Houston Branch from a play by Sam Shipman; directed by Lloyd Bacon; for Warners. 'A few laughs dot the scenery, and they're all this musical possesses in value.'—*Variety*

Manhunt of Mystery Island
US 1945 bw serial: 15 eps

A criminologist searches the tropics for a missing scientist, and comes up against a supernatural Captain Mephisto. Serial mumbo-jumbo, all quite tolerable. Richard Bailey, Linda Stirling, Roy Barcroft. Directed by Spencer Bennet, Wallace Grissell, Yakima Canutt; for Republic.

Manhunter
US 1986 119m colour

An FBI agent is summoned from retirement to work on the case of a mass murderer. Steamy melodramatics which become actively unpleasant, partly because of the producer's obsession with musical overkill. William L. Petersen, Kim Greist, Joan Allen, Brian Cox. Written, directed and produced by Michael Mann, from the novel *Red Dragon* by Thomas Harris; for Dino de Laurentiis.

Maniac
GB 1963 86m bw Hammerscope
Columbia / Hammer (Jimmy Sangster)

Murders by oxyacetylene torch in the Camargue, with the wrong lunatic going to the asylum.
Hammer's mark two plot, the shuddery murder mystery in which someone is not quite what he seems; feebly done in this case, with a fatally slow start.

w Jimmy Sangster *d* Michael Carreras
ph Wilkie Cooper

Kerwin Mathews, Donald Houston, Nadia Gray, Justine Lord

Manila Calling
US 1942 82m bw

Americans in the Philippines try to install a short-wave radio transmitter before the Japs take over. Acceptable thick ear with professional trimmings. Lloyd Nolan, Carole Landis, Cornel Wilde, James Gleason, Martin Kosleck, Ralph Byrd. Written by John Larkin; directed by Herbert I. Leeds; for Sol M. Wurtzel / TCF.

The Manitou
US 1978 104m CFI Color
Herman Weist / Melvin Simon (William Girdler)

A fake spiritualist finds his girl friend is possessed by the demon of a 400-year-old Indian.
Boring retread of *The Exorcist*.

w William Girdler, Jon Cedar, Tom Pope, *novel* Graham Masterton *d* William Girdler
ph Michel Hugo *m* Lalo Schifrin

Tony Curtis, Susan Strasberg, Michael Ansara, Stella Stevens, Jon Cedar, Ann Sothern, Burgess Meredith, Paul Mantee

Mannequin
US 1937 95m bw
MGM (Joseph L. Mankiewicz)

The wife of a small-time crook gets a modelling job and falls for a shipping magnate.
Competent star melodrama about a working girl's harassments.

w Lawrence Hazard *d* Frank Borzage
ph George Folsey *m* Edward Ward

Joan Crawford, Spencer Tracy, Alan Curtis, Ralph Morgan, Mary Philips, Elizabeth Risdon, Leo Gorcey

AAN: song 'Always and Always' (*m* Edward Ward, *ly* Chet Forrest, Bob Wright)

'A star vehicle in which the star is so solemnly noble that you want to strangle her.'—*New Yorker*

Manon*
France 1949 96m bw
Alcina (P. E. Decharme)

After the liberation, a girl who has been a collaborator becomes involved in the black market, passes from man to man, and ends up being shot by Arabs in the Sahara desert.
Oddball modernized version of *Manon Lescaut*, with post-war pessimism and the glamour of sin going hand in hand. Worth comparing with *Gilda*.

w H. G. Clouzot, J. Ferry, *novel* L'Abbé Prévost *d* H. G. Clouzot *ph* Armand Thirard *m* Paul Misraki

Michel Auclair, Cécile Aubry, Serge Reggiani, Gabrille Dorziat

'A clever idea, handled cleverly, but without depth of feeling.'—*Penelope Houston*

Manon des Sources
France 1952 190m bw
Films Marcel Pagnol

A Provençal girl who lives in the hills with her goats is thought to be a witch, and takes her revenge on the populace by stopping the water supply.
Insanely long idyll of the countryside with the writer-director unintentionally caricaturing himself.

wd Marcel Pagnol *ph* Willy *m* Raymond Legrand

Jacqueline Pagnol, Raymond Péllégrin, Henri Vibert

'Something of an endurance test for all but the most enthusiastic Pagnol admirers.'—*John Gillett, MFB*

† Pagnol later expanded the story into two novels which were the basis for a two-part film, *Jean de Florette* (qv) and *Manon des Sources*.

Manpower*
US 1941 103m bw
Warner (Mark Hellinger)

Power linesmen fall out over a nightclub hostess.
Yet another variation on *Tiger Shark*, with vivid fisticuff and storm sequences supporting the star performers.

w Richard Macaulay, Jerry Wald *d* Raoul Walsh *ph* Ernest Haller *m* Adolph Deutsch

Edward G. Robinson, George Raft, Marlene Dietrich, Alan Hale, Frank McHugh, Eve Arden, Barton MacLane, Walter Catlett, Joyce Compton, Ward Bond

'The pace and cutting are those of the best gangster films . . . the climax outdoes anything the Lyceum may have known.'—*William Whitebait*

Man's Castle*
US 1933 70m bw
Columbia (Frank Borzage)

Romance blooms among the unemployed who live in a shanty town on the banks of the East River.
Depression moonshine which at the time was taken for realism; sociologically very interesting but very faded as entertainment.

w Jo Swerling, *play* Lawrence Hazard
d Frank Borzage *ph* Joseph August
m W. Franke Harling

Spencer Tracy, Loretta Young, Glenda Farrell, Walter Connolly, Arthur Hohl, Marjorie Rambeau, Dickie Moore

'A picture that goes contrary to normal entertainment appetites and tastes, its possibilities of going places look slender at best.'—*Variety*

'Heavily sentimental yet magically romantic.'—*New Yorker, 1977*

Man's Favourite Sport?*
US 1963 120m Technicolor
Universal / Gibraltar / Laurel (Howard Hawks)

A star salesman of fishing tackle finds his bluff called when he has to enter a fishing competition.
Over-extended romantic farce drawn by the director from memories of older and better films, such as *Libeled Lady* and his own *Bringing Up Baby*.

w John Fenton Murray *d* Howard Hawks
ph Russell Harlan *m* Henry Mancini

Rock Hudson, Paula Prentiss, Maria Perschy, Charlene Holt, John McGiver, Roscoe Karns

'Hawks' deadpan documentation of a physical gag is as effective as ever, but the overall pace of his direction is curiously contemplative, as though he were savoring all his past jokes for the last time.'—*Andrew Sarris*

Manslaughter*
US 1922 80m approx (24 fps) bw silent
Paramount / Famous Players (Cecil B. de Mille)

An idle rich girl accidentally kills a man while driving, and is sent to prison, but falls for the district attorney who convicted her.
De Mille was here testing out his *Ten Commandments* format, with a long flashback during the DA's speech to the idle rich of ancient Rome. It worked like a charm at the box office.

w Jeanie McPherson, *novel* Alice Duer Miller *d* Cecil B. de Mille *ph* Alvin Wyckoff

Leatrice Joy, Thomas Meighan, Lois Wilson, John Miltern

† A 1930 sound remake for Paramount was directed by George Abbott, who also tried in vain to modernize the screenplay (by omitting the flashback). Claudette Colbert and Fredric March starred.

Mantrap
US 1943 57m bw

A retired Scotland Yard man helps the DA's office in a murder case. Entertaining second feature with a geriatric hero; alas, the clues don't play quite fair. Henry Stephenson, Lloyd Corrigan, Joseph Allen Jnr, Dorothy Lovett. Written by Curt Siodmak; directed and produced by George Sherman; for Republic.

Mantrap
US 1961 93m bw Panavision
Paramount / Tiger (Edmond O'Brien, Stanley Frazen)

An honest man is lured by an old Marine friend into a hi-jack attempt which leads to the death of his wife.
Rather uninteresting melodrama, played and directed for more than it's worth.

w Ed Waters, *novel* Taint of the Tiger by John D. Macdonald *d* Edmond O'Brien *ph* Loyal Griggs *m* Leith Stevens

Jeffrey Hunter, David Janssen, Stella Stevens, Hugh Sanders

Manuela*
GB 1957 95m bw
British Lion / Ivan Foxwell
US title: *Stowaway Girl*

In a South American port, the engineer of a tramp steamer smuggles aboard a half caste girl, but it is the disillusioned captain who falls in love with her.
Downbeat seafaring melodrama, fine for those seeking a mood piece.

w William Woods, from his novel *d* Guy Hamilton *ph* Otto Heller *m* William Alwyn

Trevor Howard, Elsa Martinelli, Pedro Armendariz, Donald Pleasence

The Manxman
GB 1929 90m (24 fps) bw silent
British International (John Maxwell)

A fisherman thought drowned comes back to find that his girl is expecting his best friend's baby.
Stern romantic melodrama of virtually no interest despite its director.

w Eliot Stannard, *novel* Hall Caine *d* Alfred Hitchcock *ph* Jack Cox

Carl Brisson, Malcolm Keen, Anny Ondra, Randle Ayrton, Clare Greet
† Previously filmed in 1916 with Henry Ainley and Elizabeth Risdon.

Many Happy Returns
US 1934 62m bw

A scatty girl jinxes her father's department store and a Hollywood studio. Silly comedy with stops for vaudeville. George Burns, Gracie Allen, Guy Lombardo and his Band, Veloz and Yolanda, Ray Milland, George Barbier, Joan Marsh, Franklin Pangborn, William Demarest, Larry Adler. Written by J. P. McEvoy, Claude Binyon, Keene Thompson, Ray Harris, Lady Mary Cameron(!); directed by Norman Z. McLeod; for Paramount. 'Often very funny, at other moments it lags.'—*Variety*

Many Rivers to Cross*
US 1955 94m Eastmancolor Cinemascope
MGM (Jack Cummings)

A trapper bound for Canada is helped by a sharp-shooting girl, and in return he saves her from marauding Indians.
Simple-minded, cheerful, quite refreshing western compounded of equal parts comedy and action.

w Harry Brown, Guy Trosper *d* Roy Rowland *ph* John Seitz *m* Cyril Mockridge

Robert Taylor, Eleanor Parker, Victor McLaglen, Josephine Hutchinson, Jeff Richards, Russ Tamblyn, James Arness, Alan Hale Jnr

Mara Maru
US 1952 98m bw
Warner (David Weisbart)

A Manila salvage expert locates a sunken treasure and defeats crooks who are also in pursuit of it.
Lethargic but pleasant-looking star vehicle with a plot borrowed from *The Maltese Falcon.*

w N. Richard Nash, Philip Yordan, Sidney Harmon, Hollister Noble *d* Gordon Douglas *ph Robert Burks* *m* Max Steiner

Errol Flynn, Ruth Roman, Raymond Burr, Paul Picerni, Richard Webb

Maracaibo
US 1958 88m Technicolor Vistavision
Paramount / Theodora (Cornel Wilde)

A Texan oil fire expert finds himself unexpectedly busy when on holiday in Venezuela.
Meandering action melodrama with too much local colour.

w Ted Sherdeman, *novel* Stirling Silliphant *d* Cornel Wilde *ph* Ellsworth Fredericks *m* Laurindo Almeida

Cornel Wilde, Jean Wallace, Abbe Lane, Francis Lederer, Joe E. Ross, Michael Landon

The Marat / Sade*
GB 1966 116m De Luxe
UA / Marat Sade (Michael Birkett)
aka: *The Persecution and Assassination of Jean-Paul Marat as performed by the inmates of the Asylum of Charenton under the direction of the Marquis de Sade*

The title tells all, except that at the end the inmates go berserk.
Fairly plain filming of an Old Vic *succès d'estime* which it became fashionable to announce that one had seen and understood. The film makes no effort to attract the unbeliever.

w Adrian Mitchell, *play* Peter Weiss *d* Peter Brook *ph* David Watkin *m* Richard Peaslee

Glenda Jackson, Patrick Magee, Ian Richardson, Michael Williams, Robert Lloyd, Clifford Rose, Freddie Jones

'I loathed and detested doing the play. I couldn't wait for it to end. Then we all did the film and it was a shattering experience. People twitching, slobber running down their chins, everyone screaming from nerves and exhaustion.'—*Glenda Jackson*

Marathon Man**
US 1976 126m Metrocolor
Paramount (Robert Evans, Sidney Beckerman)

A vicious Nazi returns from Uruguay to New York in search of diamonds which had been kept for him by his now-dead brother, and is outwitted by the young brother of an American agent he has killed.
Complex mystery thriller which seems to have things to mutter about freedom and McCarthyism and Nazism, but finally settles down to being a simple shocker with a nick-of-time climax. The presentation is dazzling.

w William Goldman, from his novel *d John Schlesinger* *ph Conrad Hall* *m* Michael Small *pd* Richard MacDonald

Dustin Hoffman, *Laurence Olivier,* Roy Scheider, William Devane, Marthe Keller, Fritz Weaver, Marc Lawrence

'A film of such rich texture and density in its construction, so fascinatingly complex in its unfolding, so engrossing in its personalities, and so powerful in its performance and pace that the seduction of the senses has physical force.'—*Judith Crist, Saturday Review*

'Fashionably violent . . . distinctly self-conscious . . . conventionally moralistic . . . and absolutely devoid of resonance.'—*Tom Milne, MFB*

'If at the film's end, you have followed the series of double and triple crosses, braved the torture scenes, and still don't know what it was about, you're bound to have company.'—*Paul Coleman, Film Information*

'A Jewish revenge fantasy.'—*Pauline Kael*

'He has made a most elegant, bizarre, rococo melodrama out of material which, when you think about it, makes hardly any sense at all.'—*Vincent Canby, New York Times*

AAN: Laurence Olivier

The Marauders
US 1955 81m Eastmancolor
MGM (Arthur M. Loew Jnr)

A rancher hires gunmen to drive away squatters, but the gunmen kill him and take over.
Slightly sinister western with a plot probably worth trying again.

w Jack Leonard, Earl Fenton, *novel* Alan Marcus *d* Gerald Mayer *ph* Harold Marzorati *m* Paul Sawtell

Dan Duryea, Jeff Richards, Keenan Wynn, Jarma Lewis, Harry Shannon

March or Die
GB 1977 107m Technicolor
ITC / Associated General (Dick Richards, Jerry Bruckheimer)

In 1918, tensions rise at a Foreign Legion outpost threatened by Arabs.
Incredibly old-hat romantic melodrama of the kind that was being spoofed forty years ago. The considerable talent involved seems

unfortunately under instruction to take it seriously.

w David Zelag Goodman *d* Dick Richards *ph* John Alcott *m* Maurice Jarre

Gene Hackman, Terence Hill, Catherine Deneuve, Max Von Sydow, Ian Holm, Marcel Bozzuffi

† The writer and director more successfully revived a different set of clichés in *Farewell My Lovely*.

Mardi Gras
US 1958 107m De Luxe Cinemascope
TCF (Jerry Wald)

In New Orleans at holiday time, a film star falls for a cadet.
Mindless musical using up available talent.

w Winston Miller, Hal Kanter *d* Edmund Goulding *ph* Wilfrid M. Cline *md* Lionel Newman

Pat Boone, Christine Carere, Sheree North, Tommy Sands, Gary Crosby, Fred Clark, Richard Sargent, Barrie Chase

AAN: Lionel Newman

Mare Nostrum*
US 1925 approx 110m bw silent
MGM

A Spanish captain loves a German spy.
Tragic romantic melodrama, a major attraction of its time.

w Willis Goldbeck, *novel* Vicente Blasco Ibanez *d* Rex Ingram *ph* John Seitz

Antonio Moreno, Alice Terry

'The girl of the moment in the picture of America's hey! hey! day!'
Margie***
US 1946 94m Technicolor
TCF (Walter Morosco)

A married woman reminisces about her college days, when she married the French teacher despite her tendency to lose her bloomers at the most embarrassing moments.
Wholly pleasing nostalgia, very smartly and brightly handled.

w F. Hugh Herbert, *stories* Ruth McKinney, Richard Bransten *d Henry King* *ph* Charles Clarke *md* Alfred Newman

Jeanne Crain, Glenn Langan, *Alan Young*, Lynn Bari, Barbara Lawrence, Conrad Janis, Esther Dale

'Direction, script and settings skilfully interpret the fashions and crazes of the twenties.'—*MFB*

Margin for Error*
US 1943 74m bw
TCF (Ralph Dietrich)

Just before World War II, the Nazi consul in New York is murdered in his own office.
Mildly intriguing whodunnit with the case solved by a Jewish cop.

w Lillie Hayward, *play* Clare Boothe Luce *d* Otto Preminger *ph* Edward Cronjager *m* Leigh Harline

Milton Berle, Joan Bennett, Otto Preminger, Carl Esmond, Howard Freeman, Poldy Dur, Hans Von Twardowski

Marguerite de la Nuit*
France / Italy 1955 126m Technicolor
SNEG / Gaumont Actualités / Cino del Duca (Léon Carré)

An octogenarian signs a pact with the devil in return for his lost youth; but when he has it he causes the death of the woman he loves.
Expensive, sporadically interesting, but unpersuasive updating of *Faust*.

w Ghislaine Autant-Lara, Gabriel Arout *d* Claude Autant-Lara *ph* Jacques Natteau *m* René Cloërc

Michèle Morgan, Yves Montand, Jean-François Calvé, Massimo Girotti

Maria Chapdelaine*
France 1935 73m bw

In a hard Quebec winter Maria loses her mother and her lover, but resists temptation by a man from the city. Artistically telling drama, later flatly remade as *The Naked Heart*. Madeleine Renaud, Jean Gabin, Suzanne Despres, Jean-Pierre Aumont. From the novel by Louis Hemon; directed by Julien Duvivier; for Société Nouvelle. 'A fine achievement, it gives the feeling of a sort of epic poem.'—*Variety*

Maria Marten, or The Murder in the Red Barn
GB 1935 67m bw
George King

A wicked Victorian squire kills his pregnant mistress and is haunted.
Stilted melodrama, ripely played, from a real-life case. (The villain's scalp is still exhibited in a museum at Bury St Edmunds.)

w Randall Faye *d* George King *ph* George Stretton

Tod Slaughter, Sophie Stewart, Eric Portman, Clare Greet

† Several versions had been made in silent days.

Marie
US 1985 112m Technicolor Dunton vision

A battered wife leaves her husband and becomes chairman of the Tennessee parole board. An edifying biopic to which the only answer is, so what? Sissy Spacek, Jeff Daniels, Morgan Freeman. Written by John Briley from book by Peter Maas; directed by Roger Donaldson; for Dino de Laurentiis. 'Blessed are the pure in heart but also deadly dull.'—*Time Out*

Marie Antoinette*
US 1938 160m bw
MGM (Hunt Stromberg)

The last days of the French court before the revolution.
Too slow by half, and so glamorized and fictionalized as to lack all interest, this long delayed production stands only as an example of MGM's expensive prestige movies of the thirties.

w Claudine West, Donald Ogden Stewart, Ernest Vajda *d* W. S. Van Dyke *ph* William Daniels *montage* Slavko Vorkapitch *m* Herbert Stothart *ad* Cedric Gibbons

Norma Shearer, Tyrone Power, John Barrymore, Robert Morley, Gladys George, Anita Louise, Joseph Schildkraut, Henry Stephenson, Reginald Gardiner, Peter Bull, Albert Dekker, Cora Witherspoon, Barnett Parker, Joseph Calleia, Henry Kolker, George Zucco, Henry Daniell, Harry Davenport, Barry Fitzgerald, Mae Busch, Robert Barrat

'Produced on a scale of incomparable splendour and extravagance, it approaches real greatness as cinematic historical literature.'—*Variety*

'A resplendent bore.'—*New Yorker, 1977*

AAN: Herbert Stothart; Norma Shearer; Robert Morley

La Marie du Port
France 1949 95m bw
Sacha Gordine

A Cherbourg restaurateur takes his mistress home for her father's funeral, and falls in love with her younger sister.
Slight romantic drama, well enough put over but not very memorable except for its slightly cynical mood.

w Louis Chavance, Marcel Carné, *novel* Georges Simenon *d* Marcel Carné *ph* Henri Alekan *m* Joseph Kosma

Jean Gabin, Blanchette Brunoy, Nicole Courcel, Claude Romain, Louis Cseigner, Jeanne Marken, Carette

Marie Galante
US 1934 90m bw

A French girl stranded in the Canal Zone becomes involved in international intrigue.
Slightly unusual spy romance. Spencer Tracy, Ketti Gallian, Ned Sparks, Helen Morgan, Sig Rumann, Leslie Fenton, Stepin Fetchit. Written by Reginald Berkeley, from the novel by Jacques Deval; directed by Henry King; for Fox. 'Production and handling should carry it to moderate grosses.'—*Variety*

Marie Octobre
France 1958 102m bw
Orex / SF / Abbey / Doxa (Lucien Viard)
US title: *Secret Meeting*

At a reunion dinner of a wartime resistance group, a traitor is exposed and killed.
Stultifying one-set talkfest employing Hitchcock's long-discarded ten-minute take.

w Julien Duvivier, Jacques Robert, *novel* Jacques Robert *d* Julien Duvivier *ph* Robert Le Fèbvre *m* Jean Yatove *ad* Georges Wakhevitch

Danielle Darrieux, Serge Reggiani, Bernard Blier, Paul Meurisse, Noel Roquevert, Lino Ventura, Paul Guers, Paul Frankeur

Marine Raiders
US 1944 90m bw

The marines do battle in Guadalcanal.
Standard romantic flagwaver. Pat O'Brien,

Robert Ryan, Ruth Hussey, Frank McHugh, Barton Maclane. Written by Warren Duff; directed by Harold Schuster; for Robert Fellows / RKO.

The Marines Fly High
US 1940 68m bw

Two leathernecks combat a mysterious South American villain. Formula action fare, intended as a Flagg and Quirt adventure but made with a second team. Richard Dix, Chester Morris, Lucille Ball, John Eldredge, Steffi Duna. Written by Jerry Cady and A. J. Bolton; directed by George Nicholls Jnr and Ben Stoloff; for Robert Sisk / RKO.

'Up to their necks in fights and loving!'
Marines Let's Go
US 1961 103m De Luxe Cinemascope
TCF (Raoul Walsh)

Marines fighting in Korea are granted leave in Japan.
Brawling tragi-farce with predictable characters, a long way after *What Price Glory*.

w John Twist, *story* Raoul Walsh *d* Raoul Walsh *ph* Lucien Ballard *m* Irving Gertz

Tom Tryon, David Hedison, Tom Reese, Linda Hutchins, William Tyler

'A typically noisy, insensitive and maudlin tribute to the American Marines.'—*MFB*

Marius**
France 1931 125m bw
Marcel Pagnol / Paramount

The son of a Marseilles waterfront café owner gives up his sweetheart to go to sea.
Celebrated character drama which succeeds through the realism and vitality of its people and their dialogue.

w Marcel Pagnol, from his play *d* Alexander Korda *ph* Ted Pahle *m* Francis Grammon

Raimu, Pierre Fresnay, Charpin, Orane Demazis

† Two sequels with the same players and from the same pen made this a famous trilogy. In *Fanny* (1932, 128m, *d* Marc Allégret) the heroine marries an old widower to give her baby a father. In *César* (1936, 117m, *d* Marcel Pagnol) Marius comes back twenty years later and is reunited with his family.
†† *Port of Seven Seas* (MGM 1938) was a hammy and stagey Hollywood compression of the trilogy. See also *Fanny* (1960) a dull version of the stage musical, with the songs removed.

Marjorie Morningstar
US 1958 123m Warnercolor
(Warner) United States Pictures (Milton Sperling)

A New York Jewish girl has great ambitions for herself but ends up a suburban housewife.
Stodgy 'woman's picture' with all talents somewhat uneasy in their assignments, mainly because the Jewish quality is imperfectly conveyed.

w Everett Freeman, *novel* Herman Wouk *d* Irving Rapper *ph* Harry Stradling *m* Max Steiner

Natalie Wood, Gene Kelly, Claire Trevor, Everett Sloane, Ed Wynn, Martin Milner, Carolyn Jones, George Tobias, Jesse White, Martin Balsam

† The first film in which perfume was credited.

AAN: song 'A Very Precious Love' (*m* Sammy Fain, *ly* Paul Francis Webster)

'Lock me up! Please lock me up!'
The Mark*
GB 1961 127m bw Cinemascope
TCF / Raymond Stross / Sidney Buchman

A sexual psychopath finds on emerging from prison that his past still haunts him despite the help of his psychiatrist.
Worthy but evasive social drama which outstays its welcome but provides good performances.

w Sidney Buchman, Stanley Mann *d* Guy Green *ph* Douglas Slocombe *m* Richard Rodney Bennett

Stuart Whitman, Maria Schell, *Rod Steiger*, Brenda de Banzie, Maurice Denham, Donald Wolfit, Paul Rogers, Donald Houston

'There is seriousness and care, but neither boldness nor passion . . . no hint of the truly sordid is allowed to seep through.'—*MFB*

AAN: Stuart Whitman

The Mark of Cain
GB 1947 88m bw
GFD / Two Cities (W. P. Lipscomb)

The attractive housekeeper of a Manchester businessman is blamed when his brother accidentally poisons him.
Turgid period melodrama in which few opportunities are offered and none taken.

w Francis Crowdy, Christianna Brand, W. P. Lipscomb, *novel* Airing in a Closed Carriage by Joseph Shearing *d* Brian Desmond Hurst *ph* Erwin Hillier *m* Bernard Stevens

Sally Gray, Eric Portman, Patrick Holt, Dermot Walsh, Denis O'Dea, Edward Lexy, Miles Malleson

The Mark of the Hawk
US 1958 84m Technicolor Superscope

An educated African fights for the emergence of his people by peaceful means. Well-intentioned but muddled topical drama. Sidney Poitier, Juano Hernandez, Eartha Kitt, John McIntire. Marne Maitland, Patrick Allen. Written by H. Kenn Carmichael; directed by Michael Audley; for Universal-International.

Mark of the Renegade
US 1951 81m Technicolor

In 1824, a Mexican agent in California pretends to be a rotter in order to unmask villains. Shakily constructed action piece which quickly wears out its welcome. Ricardo Montalban, Gilbert Roland, Cyd Charisse, J. Carrol Naish, Andrea King, George Tobias, Antonio Moreno. Written by Louis Solomon and Robert Hardy Andrews, from a story by Johnston McCulley; directed by Hugo Fregonese; for Jack Gross / Universal-International.

Mark of the Vampire*
US 1935 61m bw
MGM (E. J. Mannix)

A policeman tries to solve an old murder in an eerie house by hiring vaudeville performers to pose as vampires.
Semi-spoof horror which is flawed by lack of pace and a patchy script, but contains splendid visual moments. A remake of the Lon Chaney silent, *London After Midnight*.

w Guy Endore, Bernard Schubert *d Tod Browning ph James Wong Howe*

Lionel Barrymore, Jean Hersholt, Elizabeth Allan, Bela Lugosi, Carol Borland, Lionel Atwill, Henry Wadsworth, Donald Meek, Jessie Ralph, Ivan Simpson, Holmes Herbert

'Deftly combines murder mystery, chiller and novelty elements for pretty good entertainment results.'—*Variety*

'Even the adults in the audience may feel a bit skittery at the sight of two or three vampires, a bevy of bats, a drove of rodents, a herd of spiders and a cluster of cobwebs, not forgetting the swarm of fog.'—*New York Times*

The Mark of Zorro*
US 1920 90m (24 fps) bw silent
Douglas Fairbanks

A Mexican Robin Hood carves his initial wherever he turns up to harass the Spanish invaders.
A little faded now, but this swashbuckler opened up a whole new career for its star; the 1940 version clearly has more style.

w from the novel The Curse of Capistrano by Johnston McCulley *d* Fred Niblo *ph* William McGann *m* William Perry

Douglas Fairbanks, Marguerite de la Motte, Noah Beery

The Mark of Zorro***
US 1940 94m bw
TCF (Raymond Griffith)

After being educated in Spain, Diego de Vega returns to California and finds the country enslaved and his father half-corrupted by tyrants. Disguising himself as a masked bandit, he leads the country to expel the usurpers.
Splendid adventure stuff for boys of all ages, an amalgam of *The Scarlet Pimpernel* and *Robin Hood* to which in this version the director adds an overwhelming pictorial sense which makes it stand out as the finest of all.

w John Tainton Foote, Garrett Fort, Bess Meredyth *d Rouben Mamoulian ph Arthur Miller m Alfred Newman ad* Richard Day, Joseph C. Wright

Tyrone Power, Basil Rathbone, J. Edward Bromberg, Linda Darnell, Eugene Pallette, Montagu Love, Janet Beecher, Robert Lowery

AAN: Alfred Newman

Marked Woman*
US 1937 96m bw
Warner (Lou Edelman)

A nightclub girl is persuaded to testify against an underworld boss.
A twist on the usual run of gangster melodramas, performed with the star's accustomed intensity and presented with the studio's usual panache.

w Robert Rossen, Abem Finkel *d* Lloyd Bacon *ph* George Barnes *m* Heinz Roemheld *md* Leo F. Forbstein

Bette Davis, Humphrey Bogart, Jane Bryan, Eduardo Ciannelli, Isabel Jewell, Allen Jenkins, Mayo Methot, Lola Lane, Henry O'Neill

'Spotty draw depending on feminine reaction . . . there is nothing that is light, and very little that is funny.'—*Variety*

† Remade as *Lady Gangster*.

†† Humphrey Bogart's character was based on Thomas E. Dewey, and Eduardo Ciannelli's on Lucky Luciano.

Marlowe*
US 1969 95m Metrocolor
MGM / Katzka–Berne–Cherokee / Beckerman (Sergei Petchnikoff)

Private eye Philip Marlowe is hired by a nervous girl to find her missing brother.
The authentic Chandler atmosphere is caught by this busy thriller, but there seems to be a deliberate attempt to make a confusing plot even more obscure, so that the end result is more tiresome than amusing.

w Stirling Silliphant, *novel* The Little Sister by Raymond Chandler *d* Paul Bogart *ph* William H. Daniels *m* Peter Matz

James Garner, Rita Moreno, Sharon Farrell, Bruce Lee, Gayle Hunnicutt, Carroll O'Connor, William Daniels, Jackie Coogan

'One does wonder whether the simple human squalor of the Bogart–Chandler era can ever be recaptured by an increasingly meretricious Hollywood.'—*MFB*

Marnie*
US 1964 130m Technicolor
Universal / Geoffrey Stanley Inc (Alfred Hitchcock)

A rich man marries a kleptomaniac and cures her, but a nightmare in her past makes her still sexually frigid.
Psychodrama with background crime and suspense, lethargically handled by the old master, who alone knows what he saw in it in the first place, as this heroine does not even have fire under her ice. The production is curiously artificial in many ways, from dummy horses to backcloths to back projection.

w Jay Presson Allen, *novel* Winston Graham *d* Alfred Hitchcock *ph* Robert Burks *m* Bernard Herrmann *pd* Robert Boyle

Tippi Hedren, Sean Connery, Martin Gabel, Diane Baker, Louise Latham

Maroc 7
GB 1967 91m Eastmancolor Panavision

The lady editor of a top fashion magazine doubles as a jewel thief and becomes involved in Moroccan intrigue. Complex sub-Bond tale of cross and double cross; hardly worth following, really. Gene Barry, Elsa Martinelli, Cyd Charisse, Leslie Phillips, Denholm Elliott, Alexandra Stewart, Eric Barker, Angela Douglas. Written by David Osborn; directed by Gerry O'Hara; for Cyclone / Rank.

Marooned*
US 1969 134m Technicolor Panavision 70
Columbia / Frankovich–Sturges (Frank Capra Jnr)

Three astronauts are stranded in space, and a rescue mission gets under way.
Very heavy-going space suspenser with all possible technical accomplishment but little life of its own.

w Mayo Simon, *novel* Martin Caidin *d* John Sturges *ph* Daniel Fapp *pd* Lyle R. Wheeler

Gregory Peck, Richard Crenna, David Janssen, James Franciscus, Gene Hackman, Lee Grant, Nancy Kovack, Mariette Hartley, Scott Brady

'In something like the plight of Ironman One, Sturges' work seems on the point of slowing to a standstill as it drifts further into projects of ever-increasing, self-effacing size and anonymous technical dexterity.'—*Richard Combs*

'It has all the zip, zest and zing of a moon walk, and I suspect a computer fed a dictionary could come up with better dialogue.'—*Judith Crist, 1973*

'A space epic with a horse-and-buggy script.'—*Pauline Kael*

AAN: Daniel Fapp

The Marquise of O*
West Germany / France 1976 107m Eastmancolor
Janus / Films du Losange

At the end of the eighteenth century, during the Russian invasion of an Italian town, a noblewoman finds herself pregnant . . .
Careful novella with many ambiguities, more concerned with what might have happened than with what did. Interesting but exasperating.

wd Eric Rohmer, story Heinrich von Kleist *ph* Nestor Almendros *m* Roger Delmotte

Edith Clever, Bruno Ganz, Peter Luhr, Edda Seippel

'Some may find it slow, sentimental, naïve and old-fashioned; others leisurely, beautiful, controlled and illuminating. I found it both often at the same time.'—*Alan Brien, Sunday Times*

'A bold, funny story becomes a formal, tame film, like a historical work recreated for educational TV.'—*New Yorker, 1980*

The Marriage Circle**
US 1924 78m (24 fps) bw silent
Warner

A bachelor on the loose becomes amorously involved in two marriages.
Feather-light comedy of manners which began a whole new American school, heavily influenced by various European masters.

w Paul Bern, *play* Only a Dream by Lothar Schmidt *d Ernst Lubitsch ph* Charles Van Enger

Monte Blue, Florence Vidor, Marie Prevost, Adolphe Menjou, Creighton Hale

'A vanished world of roses, kisses and embraces, of whispers and sighs, of a woman's shadowed arm encased in georgette beckoning across a moonlit garden . . . and hand-kissing all over the place.'—*Herman G. Weinberg*

'At once perfect cinematography and perfect conventional drama.'—*Iris Barry, The Spectator*

'So slim a plot, so hackneyed if you will, is told with gaiety and a wit that lift it into the very first rank of screen comedy.'—*National Board of Review*

† Remade as *One Hour with You*, also by Lubitsch.

'It's the most hilarious proposition a wife ever had!'

The Marriage Go Round
US 1961 98m De Luxe Cinemascope
TCF (Leslie Stevens)

A Swedish girl suggests to a married American professor that she borrow his body for mating purposes, believing they would produce the perfect child.
Silly, unfunny sex comedy.

w Leslie Stevens from his play *d* Walter Lang *ph* Leo Tover *m* Dominic Frontière

James Mason, Susan Hayward, Julie Newmar, Robert Paige, June Clayworth

'As tedious as it is tasteless.'—*Evening Standard*

'It offers James Mason, an actor who couldn't crack a joke if it was a lichee nut, and Susan Hayward, a bargain basement Bette Davis whose lightest touch as a comedienne would stun a horse.'—*Time*

Marriage Is a Private Affair
US 1943 116m bw
MGM (Pandro S. Berman)

A spoilt rich girl becomes a petulant wife.
Abysmally slow, uninvolving and poorly acted star fodder.

w David Hertz, Lenore Coffee, *novel* Judith Kelly *d* Robert Z. Leonard *ph* Ray June *m* Bronislau Kaper

Lana Turner, James Craig, John Hodiak, Frances Gifford, Keenan Wynn, Natalie Schaefer, Hugh Marlowe, Paul Cavanagh

The Marriage of a Young Stockbroker**
US 1971 95m De Luxe
TCF / Laurence Turman

A stockbroker who finds his life and his marriage dull tries voyeurism and extra-marital sex.
Sardonic adult comedy of the battle between the sexes, pretty lively from start to finish.

w Lorenzo Semple Jnr, novel Charles Webb *d* Laurence Turman *ph* Laszlo Kovacs *m* Fred Karlin

Richard Benjamin, Joanna Shimkus, Elizabeth Ashley, Adam West, Patricia Barry

The Marriage of Corbal
GB 1936 93m bw

Before the French revolution, an aristocratic lady tries to escape disaster by the right marriage. Stilted adventure story with too much talk. Nils Asther, Hugh Sinclair, Hazel Terry, Noah Beery, Davy Burnaby. Written by S. Fullman, from the novel *The Nuptials of Corbal* by Rafael Sabatini; directed by Karl Grune; for Capitol.
(US title: *Prisoner of Corbal.*)

The Marriage of Maria Braun*
West Germany 1978 119m Fujicolor
Albatros / Trio / WDR / FdA (Michael Fengler)

Vicissitudes of a post-war bride who is eventually blown up in a gas explosion.
A mixture of solemnity and irony which keeps its basic points well concealed but, despite a sometimes flagging pace, more or less consistently entertains the eye.

w Peter Märthesheimer, Pea Fröhloch *d* Rainer Werner Fassbinder *ph* Michael Ballhaus *m* Peer Raben

Hanna Schygulla, Klaus Lowitsch, Ivan Desny, Gottfried John

Marriage on the Rocks
US 1965 109m Technicolor Panavision
Warner / A-C / Sinatra (William H. Daniels)

An ad man and his wife decide to go to Mexico for a divorce but once there change their minds; she ends up accidentally married to his best friend.
All this talent retreats fearfully from a witless, tasteless script and slow handling. A dismal comedy.

w Cy Howard *d* Jack Donohue *ph* William H. Daniels *m* Nelson Riddle

Frank Sinatra, Dean Martin, Deborah Kerr, Cesar Romero, Hermione Baddeley, Tony Bill, Nancy Sinatra, John McGiver

'A long, coarse, and nearly always unfunny comedy, hammered together for no apparent reason except to make money.'—*New Yorker*

The Marriage Playground
US 1929 70m bw
Paramount

Children of divorced rich parents wander round Europe in a group.
Slightly unusual drama of its day; sound technique very thin.

w J. Walter Rubin, Doris Anderson, *novel* The Children by Edith Wharton *d* Lothar Mendes *ph* Victor Milner

Fredric March, Kay Francis, Mary Brian, Lilyan Tashman, Huntley Gordon, Anita Louise

Married before Breakfast
US 1937 70m bw

An impecunious inventor has a razorless shaving cream. Scatty comedy which seldom amuses. Robert Young, Florence Rice, June Clayworth, Barnett Parker, Warren Hymer. Written by George Oppenheimer, Everett Freeman, Harry Ruskin; directed by Edwin L. Marin; for MGM. 'It has practically nothing in its favour.'—*Variety*

A Married Woman*
France 1964 98m bw
Anouchka / Orsay (Philippe Dusart)
original title: *Une Femme Mariée*

A pilot's wife has an actor lover.
Fragments of character observation, in various cinematic techniques, build up into an intense personal study if not a plot.

wd Jean-Luc Godard ph Raoul Coutard *m* Claude Nougaro

Macha Meril, Bernard Noel, Roger Leenhardt

'A minefield of paradoxes . . . the essence of cinema 1965.'—*Peter John Dyer, MFB*

Marry Me
GB 1949 97m bw
GFD / Gainsborough (Betty Box)

Four stories of a marriage bureau.
A styleless portmanteau of anecdotes put over by a clear second team.

w Lewis Gilbert, Denis Waldock *d* Terence Fisher *ph* Ray Elton *d* Clifton Parker

Derek Bond, Susan Shaw, Patrick Holt, Carol Marsh, David Tomlinson, Zena Marshall, Guy Middleton, Nora Swinburne, Jean Cadell, Mary Jerrold

Marry Me Again
US 1953 73m bw

A man returns from war to find that his fiancée has inherited a million dollars. Zany comedy with tilts at psychiatry: not too bad. Robert Cummings, Marie Wilson, Ray Walker, Mary Costa, Jess Barker. Written and directed by Frank Tashlin; produced by Alex Gottlieb; for RKO.

The Marrying Kind*
US 1952 93m bw
Columbia (Bert Granet)

A couple seeking divorce tell their troubles to a judge, and change their minds.
Smart, New Yorkish, tragi-comic star vehicle which works pretty well.

w Ruth Gordon, Garson Kanin *d* George Cukor *ph* Joseph Walker *m* Hugo Friedhofer

Judy Holliday, Aldo Ray, Madge Kennedy, Mickey Shaughnessy

Marry the Girl
US 1937 66m bw

A crazy family owns a newspaper syndicate. Fashionable comedy which goes far too far. Mary Boland, Frank McHugh, Hugh Herbert, Mischa Auer, Carol Hughes, Allen Jenkins, Alan Mowbray, Hugh O'Connell. Written by Sig Herzig, Pat C. Flick, Tom Reed, from the novel by Edward Hope; directed by William McGann; for Warners. 'Pic will probably get by on duals in the nabes and should be a panic with juve audiences. But it will probably lay an egg in first runs.'—*Variety*

La Marseillaise*
France 1938 145m bw
Films La Marseillaise (Andre Zwoboda)

The story of the French revolution of 1789. A rather disconnected epic which, despite a few splendid scenes, never moved its audiences to enthusiasm.

wd Jean Renoir *ph* Jean Bourgoin and others *md* Joseph Kosma

Pierre Renoir, Lise Delemare, Louis Jouvet, Leon Larive, Georges Spanelly, Elisa Ruis, William Aguet

'France's super-super film production is a near flopperoo.'—*Variety*

The Marseille Contract
GB / France 1974 89m Eastmancolor
Warner / AIP / Kettledrum / PECF (Judd Bernard)
US title: *The Destructors*

An American narcotics agent in Paris hires an assassin to dispose of a drug smuggler.
Routine action melodrama with a jokey atmosphere not sustained by a downbeat script.

w Judd Bernard *d* Robert Parrish *ph* Douglas Slocombe *m* Roy Budd

Michael Caine, Anthony Quinn, James Mason, Alexandra Stewart, Marcel Bozzufi, Maurice Ronet

Martin Luther*
US / Germany 1953 114m bw
Louis De Rochemont / Lutheran Church Productions (Lothar Wolff)

The career and doubts of Martin Luther.
Frequently vivid, occasionally boring, small-scale account of the first Protestant.

w Allan Sloane, Lothar Wolff, others *d* Irving Pichel *ph* Joseph C. Brun *m* Mark Lothar

Niall MacGinnis, John Ruddock, Pierre Lefèvre, Guy Verney, David Horne, Philip Leaver, Irving Pichel, Alexander Gauge

AAN: Joseph C. Brun

Martin Roumagnac
France 1946 99m bw
Alcina (Marc Le Pelletier)

The trial, with flashbacks, of a small-town businessman who has murdered his mistress.
Wholly unabsorbing and ordinary story of a *crime passionnel*, totally wasting its stars.

wd Georges Lacombe *ph* Roger Hubert *m* Marcel Mirouze

Jean Gabin, Marlene Dietrich, Margo Lion, Marcel Hérrand

Martin's Day
Canada 1985 98m Medallion colour

An escaped convict and the young boy he kidnaps become friends. Predictable melodrama which gets nowhere. Richard Harris, Lindsay Wagner, James Coburn, Justin Henry, Karen Black, John Ireland. Written by Allan Scott, Chris Bryant; directed by Alan Gibson; for World Film Services / MGM-UA.

Marty****
US 1955 91m bw
UA / Hecht–Hill–Lancaster (Harold Hecht)

A 34-year-old Bronx butcher fears he will never get a girl because he is unattractive, but at a Saturday night dance he meets a girl with similar fears. Unfortunately she is not Italian . . .
The first of the filmed teleplays which in the mid-fifties seemed like a breath of spring to Hollywood (they were cheap) and also brought in a new wave of talent. This is one of the best, its new naturalistic dialogue falling happily on the ear; but it has been so frequently imitated since that its revolutionary appearance is hard to imagine.

w Paddy Chayevsky, from his play *d Delbert Mann ph Joseph La Shelle m* Roy Webb

Ernest Borgnine, Betsy Blair, Esther Minciotti, Joe Mantell, Karen Steele, Jerry Paris

'Something rare in the American cinema today: a subtle, ironic and compassionate study of ordinary human relationships.'—*Gavin Lambert*

AA: best picture; Paddy Chayevsky; Delbert Mann; Ernest Borgnine
AAN: Joseph La Shelle; Betsy Blair; Joe Mantell

Mary Burns Fugitive*
US 1935 84m bw
Paramount (Walter Wanger)

The innocent girl friend of a gangster is convicted through circumstantial evidence, escapes from prison and finds true love.
Competent meshing of well-tried thirties elements, a good typical wish-fulfilment melodrama of its time.

w Gene Towne, Graham Baker, Louis Stevens *d* William K. Howard *ph* Leon Shamroy

Sylvia Sidney, Melvyn Douglas, Alan Baxter, Pert Kelton, Wallace Ford, Brian Donlevy, Esther Dale

'As a piece of synthetic studio slickness it has enough on the ball to qualify.'—*Variety*

Mary Jane's Pa
US 1935 70m bw

A husband goes wandering for ten years. On his return, his wife has magnified what he left into a newspaper empire. Adequate stagey comedy, well acted. Aline MacMahon, Guy Kibbee, Tom Brown, Robert McWade, Minor Watson, Nan Gray. Written by Tom Reed, Peter Milne, from the play by Edith Ellis Furness and the novel by Norman Way; directed by William Keighley; for Warners. (GB title: *Wanderlust*)
'Okay for secondary bills.'—*Variety*

Mary Mary
US 1963 126m Technicolor
Warner (Mervyn Le Roy)

A publisher falls in love again with his ex-wife but finds she is being pursued by a film star. Feeble film version of a lighter-than-air Broadway success, with the actors paralysed behind the footlights and the camera asleep in the stalls.

w Richard L. Breen, *play* Jean Kerr
d Mervyn Le Roy *ph* Harry Stradling
m Frank Perkins

Debbie Reynolds, Barry Nelson, Michael Rennie, Diane McBain

Mary of Scotland*
US 1936 123m bw
RKO (Pandro S. Berman)

Mary Stuart refuses to give up her claim to the English throne, and is eventually executed. Sombre historical charade with splendid sets and atmosphere but suffering from script and performances that don't quite make it despite effort all round.

w Dudley Nichols, *play* Maxwell Anderson
d John Ford *ph Joseph H. August*
m Nathaniel Shilkret *ad Van Nest Polglase, Carroll Clark*

Katharine Hepburn, Fredric March, Donald Crisp, Florence Eldridge, Douglas Walton, John Carradine, Robert Barrat, Monte Blue, Moroni Olsen, Frieda Inescort, Alan Mowbray

'An unpromising and stagey play is fleshed out into a rich and confident exercise in filmcraft.'—*John Baxter, 1968*

'Events are walked through as though they were rooms in a museum, and closing time at three.'—*Otis Ferguson*

Mary Poppins***
US 1964 139m Technicolor
Walt Disney (Bill Walsh)

In Edwardian London a magical nanny teaches two slightly naughty children to make life enjoyable for themselves and others.
Sporadically a very pleasant and effective entertainment for children of all ages, with plenty of brightness and charm including magic tricks, the mixing of live with cartoon adventures, and just plain fun. It suffers, however, from a wandering narrative in the second half (when Miss Poppins scarcely appears) and from Mr Van Dyke's really lamentable attempt at Cockney.

w Bill Walsh, Don da Gradi, *novel* P. L. Travers *d* Robert Stevenson *ph* Edward Colman *m / ly Richard M. and Robert B. Sherman pd* Tony Walton *sp Eustace Lycett, Peter Ellenshaw, Robert A. Mattey*

Julie Andrews, David Tomlinson, Glynis Johns, Dick Van Dyke, Reginald Owen, Ed Wynn, Matthew Garber, Karen Dotrice, Hermione Baddeley, Elsa Lanchester, Arthur Treacher, Jane Darwell

AA: Richard M. and Robert B. Sherman; Julie Andrews; song 'Chim Chim Cheree'
AAN: best picture; script; Robert Stevenson; Edward Colman

'They used every passion in their incredible duel, and every man in their savage games of intrigue!'

Mary Queen of Scots
GB 1971 128m Technicolor Panavision
Universal / Hal B. Wallis

The story of Mary Stuart's opposition to Elizabeth I, her imprisonment and execution.
Schoolbook history in which none of the characters comes to life; dramatic movement is almost entirely lacking despite the liberties taken with fact.

w John Hale *ph* Christopher Challis
d Charles Jarrott *m* John Barry

Vanessa Redgrave, Glenda Jackson, Trevor Howard, Patrick McGoohan, Nigel Davenport

'Without a better script, Hercules couldn't lift this story off the ground.'—*Pauline Kael, New Yorker*

AAN: John Barry; Vanessa Redgrave

Mary Stevens M.D.
US 1933 71m bw

A lady doctor decides to have a baby before getting married. Saucy drama which engrossed audiences in its day. Kay Francis, Lyle Talbot, Glenda Farrell, Thelma Todd, Una O'Connor, Hobart Cavanaugh, Harold Huber. Written by Rian James, from the novel by Virginia Kellogg; directed by Lloyd Bacon; for Warners. 'Exceptionally good adult entertainment, with a pronounced feminine appeal.'—*Variety*

M*A*S*H***
US 1970 116m De Luxe Panavision
TCF / Aspen (Ingo Preminger, Leon Ericksen)

Surgeons at a mobile hospital in Korea spend what spare time they have chasing women and bucking authority.
Savage comedy of man's rebellion in the face of death, alternating sex farce with gory operation scenes; hailed as the great anti-everything film, and certainly very funny for those who can take it. It led to a television series which for once did not disgrace its original.

w Ring Lardner Jnr, novel Richard Hooker
d Robert Altman ph Harold E. Stine
m Johnny Mandel

Donald Sutherland, Elliott Gould, Tom Skerritt, Sally Kellerman, Robert Duvall, Jo Ann Pflug, René Auberjonois, Gary Burghof

'Bloody funny. A hyper-acute wiretap on mankind's death wish.'—*Joseph Morgenstern*

'The laughter is blood-soaked and the comedy cloaks a bitter and terrible truth.'—*Judith Crist*

'A foul-mouthed, raucous, anti-establishment comedy, combining gallows humour, sexual slapstick and outrageous satire.'—*Les Keyser, Hollywood in the Seventies*

AA: Ring Lardner Jnr
AAN: best picture; Robert Altman; Sally Kellerman

Mask**
US 1985 120m Technicolor
Universal / Martin Starger

A boy of 16 has a rare and disfiguring bone disease, but his mother fights for his rights. More of a character study than a movie, this also has the problem of being emotionally hard to take; but one ends up respecting it.

w Anna Hamilton Phelan, from her true story of Rocky Dennis *d Peter Bogdanovich* *ph* Laszlo Kovacs *m* Dennis Ricotta *ed* Barbara Ford

Cher, Sam Elliott, Eric Stoltz, Estelle Getty

'Anyone looking for a good uplifting cry should be well satisfied.'—*Variety*

The Mask of Dijon
US 1946 73m bw

A conjuror becomes obsessed by hypnotism and takes to murder to prove his superiority. Heavy-going thriller with little discernible point. Erich Von Stroheim, Jeanne Bates, William Wright. Written by Arthur St Claire and Griffin Jay; directed by Lew Landers; for PRC.

The Mask of Dimitrios**
US 1944 99m bw
Warner (Henry Blanke)

A timid Dutch novelist is drawn into a Middle-Eastern intrigue with money at the centre of it.
Generally successful international intriguer, moodily shot in evocative sets, and remarkable for its time in that the story is not distorted to fit romantic stars: character actors bear the entire burden.

w Frank Gruber, novel Eric Ambler *d Jean Negulesco ph Arthur Edeson m* Adolph Deutsch

Peter Lorre, Sidney Greenstreet, Zachary Scott, Faye Emerson, *Victor Francen, Steven Geray, Florence Bates, Eduardo Ciannelli, Kurt Katch*, John Abbott, Monte Blue

'The picture has more mood than excitement.'—*Pauline Kael, 70s*

The Mask of Fu Manchu**
US 1932 70m bw
MGM

Nayland Smith and his party are caught and threatened with torture by the yellow terror.
Highly satisfactory episode in the nefarious adventures of the master criminal, fast moving, humorous and very good to look at.

w John Willard, Edgar Woolf, Irene Kuhn, *stories* Sax Rohmer *d Charles Brabin, Charles Vidor ph Tony Gaudio*

Boris Karloff, Myrna Loy, Lewis Stone, Karen Morley, Charles Starrett, Jean Hersholt, Lawrence Grant

'The diabolical stuff is piled on so thick at the finish, audiences are liable to laugh where they oughtn't.'—*Variety*

'A tolerable, campy entertainment.'—*Pauline Kael, 70s*

Mask of the Avenger
US 1951 83m Technicolor

During the Austro-Italian War, a count's son avenges his father's death and exposes a traitor. Very moderate swashbuckler on the lines of *The Mark of Zorro*. John Derek, Anthony Quinn, Jody Lawrence, Arnold Moss, Eugene Iglesias. Written by Jesse Lasky Jnr; directed by Phil Karlson; for Hunt Stromberg / Columbia.

The Masked Marvel
US 1943 bw serial: 12 eps

An insurance company hires The Masked Marvel to prove that Japanese agents are sabotaging war industries. Highly derivative serial adventures. David Bacon, William Forrest, Louise Currie, Johnny Arthur. Directed by Spencer Bennet; for Republic.

Maskerade*
Austria 1935 87m bw

An inveterate ladies' man finds himself trapped. Charming romantic comedy. Anton Walbrook, Paula Wesseley, Olga Tscheshowa. Written and directed by Willi Forst; for Tobis / Sascha. 'Not a real masterpiece like *Liebelei*, but it has the same b.o. elements.'—*Variety*

The Masque of the Red Death**
GB 1964 89m Pathecolor 'Scope
AIP / Alta Vista (George Willoughby)

A medieval Italian prince practises devil worship while the plague rages outside, but when he holds a ball, death is an uninvited guest.
Languorous, overstretched, often visually striking horror piece with some extremely effective touches among its longueurs.

w Charles Beaumont, R. Wright Campbell, *story* Edgar Allan Poe *d Roger Corman ph Nicolas Roeg m* David Lee *ad Robert Jones costumes Laura Nightingale*

Vincent Price, Hazel Court, Jane Asher, Patrick Magee, John Westbrook

Masquerade*
GB 1965 101m Eastmancolor
UA / Novus (Michael Relph)

To avert friction between Arab states the young heir to one of them is abducted by a British secret service agent; but one of the plotters has other fish to fry.
Quite a lively spy romp with a spectacular action climax, but the plot is simply too complicated.

w Michael Relph, William Goldman, *novel* Castle Minerva by Victor Canning *d* Basil Dearden *ph* Otto Heller *m* Philip Green *pd* Don Ashton

Cliff Robertson, Jack Hawkins, Charles Gray, Bill Fraser, Marisa Mell, Michel Piccoli, John Le Mesurier

'A gay and gorgeous whirl of romance, adventure and rhythm . . . in the billion-dollar pan-American postwar playground!'

Masquerade in Mexico
US 1945 96m bw
Paramount (Karl Tunberg)

A stranded showgirl is hired by a Mexican banker to entice a gigolo away from his wife. Talent-starved remake of *Midnight* (qv), which seems second-hand even if you don't know why.

w Karl Tunberg *d* Mitchell Leisen *ph* Lionel Lindon *m* Victor Young

Dorothy Lamour, Arturo de Cordova, Patric Knowles, Ann Dvorak, George Rigaud, Natalie Schafer, Mikhail Rasumny, Billy Daniels

The Masquerader*
US 1933 75m bw
Samuel Goldwyn

A drug-addicted politician is replaced by his lookalike cousin.
Pleasing dual role star vehicle with good production and support. Very much of its period.

w Howard Estabrook, Moss Hart, *play* John Hunter Booth, *novel* Katherine Cecil Thurston *d* Richard Wallace *ph* Gregg Toland *m* Alfred Newman

Ronald Colman, Elissa Landi, *Halliwell Hobbes*, Juliette Compton, David Torrence

'A fine production with too much story handicap . . . Colman's best is not enough.'—*Variety*

'The first amusing and believable tale of English politics and society . . . made of all places in Hollywood.'—*Newsweek*

Mass Appeal*
US 1984 100m Technicolor
Universal / Turman-Foster

An idealistic student matches wits with a compromising priest.
Amusing, opened-out version of a two-character play: good for minority audiences.

w Bill C. David from his play *d* Glenn Jordan *ph* Don Peterman *m* Bill Conti *pd* Philip Jeffries

Jack Lemmon, Zeljko Ivanek, Charles Durning, Louise Latham

The Master Gunfighter
US 1975 120m Metrocolor Panavision

In gold rush California, a mysterious avenger rights a variety of wrongs. Pretentious western which failed to advance the career of its somewhat over-confident creator. Tom Laughlin, Ron O'Neal, Lincoln Kilpatrick, Barbara Carrera. Written by Harold Lapland, from a Japanese film *Goyokin* written by Kei Tasaka and Hideo Gosha; directed by Tom Laughlin; for Avondale / Warner.

The Master Key
US 1945 bw serial: 13 eps

Nazi agents led by The Master Key plan to spread panic in the US. Wartime serial with the usual cliffhangers. Milburn Stone, Jan Wiley, Dennis Moore, Addison Richards. Directed by Ray Taylor and Lewis D. Collins; for Universal.

The Master of Ballantrae
GB 1953 89m Technicolor
Warner

Two brothers toss to decide which shall join Bonnie Prince Charlie's 1745 rebellion. Half-hearted version of a classic adventure novel.

w Herb Meadow, *novel* R. L. Stevenson *d* William Keighley *ph* Jack Cardiff *m* William Alwyn

Errol Flynn, Anthony Steel, Roger Livesey, Beatrice Campbell, Felix Aylmer, Mervyn Johns, Jacques Berthier, Yvonne Furneaux, Ralph Truman

'All that can be salvaged from this rather unforgivable Anglo-American junket are some pleasant exteriors.'—*Gavin Lambert*

Master of Bankdam*
GB 1947 105m bw
GFD / Holbein (Nat Bronsten, Walter Forde, Edward Dryhurst)

19th-century chronicles of a mill-owning Yorkshire family.
Archetypal 'trouble at t'mill' saga with moderate production, good acting and undeniably compulsive story.

w Edward Dryhurst, Moie Charles, *novel* The Crowthers of Bankdam by Thomas Armstrong *d* Walter Forde *ph Basil Emmott*

Tom Walls, Anne Crawford, Dennis Price, Stephen Murray, Linden Travers, Jimmy Hanley, Nancy Price, David Tomlinson, Herbert Lomas

Master of the World
US 1961 104m Magnacolor
AIP / Alta Vista (James H. Nicholson, Anthony Carras)

In 1848 a mad inventor takes to the air in his magnificent flying machine in the hope of persuading men to stop war.
Aerial version of *Twenty Thousand Leagues under the Sea*, with cheap sets and much use of stock footage; some scenes however have a certain vigour.

w Richard Matheson, *novels* Jules Verne *d* William Witney *ph* Gil Warrenton *m* Les Baxter

Vincent Price, Charles Bronson, Henry Hull, Mary Webster, David Frankham

The Master Plan
GB 1954 78m bw

An American agent, concealing the fact that he suffers from blackouts, is sent to investigate information leakages in England. Quite lively second feature spylarks. Wayne Morris, Tilda Thamar, Norman Wooland, Mary Mackenzie, Arnold Bell. Written and directed by Hugh Raker (i.e. Cy Endfield); for Gibraltar.

The Master Race
US 1944 96m bw

German generals realize that the war is lost, and plan counter-measures. Timely propaganda melodrama warning against premature rejoicing, from the producer of *Hitler's Children*. George Coulouris, Osa Massen, Stanley Ridges, Nancy Gates, Carl Esmond, Morris Carnovsky, Lloyd Bridges. Written and directed by Herbert J. Biberman; for Edward A. Golden / RKO.

Masters of the Universe
US 1987 106m Metrocolor

He-Man defends the planet Eternia from the evil Skeletor. Live action version of the tv cartoons of the toys of the comic strip. Pretty weak stuff, even for 5-year-olds. Dolph Lundgren, Frank Langella, Meg Foster, Billy Barty. Written by David Odell; directed by Gary Goddard; for Edward R. Pressman / Cannon.

Masterson of Kansas
US 1955 73m Technicolor

The sheriff of Dodge City prevents an Indian uprising by saving an innocent man from the gallows. Unhistorical two-bit western. George Montgomery, Nancy Gates, James Griffith, Jean Willes. Written by Douglas Heyes; directed by William Castle; for Sam Katzman / Columbia.

'Men worshipped her like a goddess, only to be betrayed by a kiss!'

Mata Hari**
US 1931 92m bw
MGM

The career of the famous lady spy of World War I.
Elaborate melodrama, pictorially satisfying and generally more entertaining than might be supposed, with both star and supporting cast in rich thespian form.

w Benjamin Glazer, Leo Birinski, Doris Anderson, Gilbert Emery *d George Fitzmaurice* *ph* William Daniels

Greta Garbo, Ramon Novarro, Lionel Barrymore, Lewis Stone, C. Henry Gordon, Karen Morley, Blanche Frederici

'Picture's strength is all in the players; an important grosser on that account.'—*Variety*

Mata Hari
US 1985 108m Eastmancolor

The career of the famous lady spy of World War I. Absurd melodrama which in places seems to be spoofing itself. Sylvia Kristel, Christopher Cazenove, Oliver Tobias, Gaye Brown, William Fox. Written by Joel Ziskin; directed by Curtis Harrington; for Rony Yacov / Cannon.

Mata Hari, Agent H21*
France / Italy 1964 99m bw
Filmel / Les Films du Carrosse / Simar / Fida Cinematografica (Eugene Lepicier)

A rather unnecessary revamp of the same story, with interesting details but not much resonance.

w Jean-Louis Richard, François Truffaut *d* Jean-Louis Richard *ph* Michel Kelber *m* Georges Delerue *ad* Claude Pignot

Jeanne Moreau, Jean-Louis Trintignant, Claude Rich, Frank Villard

'All that we are left with is a generous dollop of period charm, and the fascinating spontaneity of an actress.'—*Peter John Dyer, MFB*

The Match King
US 1932 80m bw

A world-famous match manufacturer gets into spectacular money difficulties. Thinly veiled biopic of Ivar Kreuger; not at all bad. *Warren William,* Lili Damita, Glenda Farrell, Harold Huber. Written by Houston Branch and Sidney Sutherland; directed by Howard Bretherton; for Warner. 'Good entertainment, uncommonly well acted . . . in Swedish-populated sections should be top moneymaker.'—*Variety*

The Matchmaker*
US 1958 101m bw Vistavision
Paramount (Don Hartman)

In New York at the turn of the century, a rich merchant decides to marry again but the matchmaker he consults has her own eye on him.
Cold and lifeless version of an amusing play which also served as the basis for the musical *Hello Dolly* (qv).

w John Michael Hayes, *play* Thornton Wilder *d* Joseph Anthony *ph* Charles Lang *m* Adolph Deutsch

Shirley Booth, Paul Ford, Anthony Perkins, Shirley Maclaine, Wallace Ford, Robert Morse, Perry Wilson

DOLLY LEVI (Shirley Booth) to the audience: 'Life's never quite interesting enough, somehow. You people who come to the movies know that.'

'Long static dialogue exchanges are further extended by frequent confidences expressed directly to the audience . . . but in spite of the general lack of pace, lightness and dimension there is still a great deal to enjoy.'—*Peter John Dyer*

La Maternelle*
France 1932 89m bw
Photosonor

A maid in a nursery school becomes devoted to the children and in particular to one who causes trouble when her friend decides to marry.
A touching drama of its day which now seems rather primitive.

w Jean Benoit-Lévy *d* Jean Benoit-Lévy, Marie Epstein *ph* Georges Asselin *m* Edouard Flament

Madeleine Renaud, Paulette Elambert, Alice Tissot, Mady Berry

'By any standard the finest foreign-language talker shown in the US in a couple of years.'—*Variety*

Matewan*
US 1987 130m DuArt Color

Unions organize in West Virginia coal mines in the 1930s. Serious stuff which seems to have no place in the American cinema of its time. Chris Cooper, Will Oldham, Mary McDonnell, Bob Gunton, James Earl Jones. Written and directed by *John Sayles*; for Cinecom International.

AAN: cinematography (Haskell Wexler)

Matilda
US 1978 105m Movielab
AIP / Albert S. Ruddy

A down-at-heel theatrical agent finds success with a boxing kangaroo.
Damon Runyon meets Walt Disney in an old-fashioned family audience picture for which there may no longer be an audience.

w Albert S. Ruddy, Timothy Galfas, *novel* Paul Gallico *d* Daniel Mann *ph* Jack Woolf *pd* Boris Leven *m* Jerrold Immel

Elliott Gould, Robert Mitchum, Harry Guardino, Clive Revill, Karen Carlson, Lionel Stander, Art Metrano, Roy Clark

The Mating Game
US 1959 96m Metrocolor Cinemascope
MGM (Philip Barry Jnr)

An income-tax inspector becomes involved in the affairs of an unorthodox farming family.
Dismally unfunny adaptation for Americans of a very English novel; everyone works hard to no avail.

w William Roberts, *novel* The Darling Buds of May by H. E. Bates *d* George Marshall *ph* Robert Bronner *m* Jeff Alexander

Debbie Reynolds, Tony Randall, Paul Douglas, Fred Clark, Una Merkel, Philip Ober, Charles Lane, Philip Coolidge

'Every joke is driven past the point of exhaustion.'—*MFB*

The Mating of Millie
US 1948 87m bw

A self-confident young woman wants to adopt a small boy and tries to propel a bus driver into a marriage of convenience. Amiable if protracted romantic comedy with dashes of sentiment and an obvious outcome. Glenn Ford, Evelyn Keyes, Willard Parker, Jimmy Hunt, Ron Randell. Written by Louella MacFarlane and St Clair McKelway; directed by Henry Levin; for Columbia.

The Mating Season
US 1951 101m bw
Paramount (Charles Brackett)

A factory draughtsman marries an ambassador's daughter; his mother loses her job and comes incognito to work for them as a cook.
Uninteresting mechanical domestic comedy in which the young folk are dull and the older ones overplay.

w Walter Reisch, Charles Brackett, Richard Breen *d* Mitchell Leisen *ph* Charles Lang

Gene Tierney, John Lund, Miriam Hopkins, Thelma Ritter, Jan Sterling

AAN: Thelma Ritter

A Matter of Dignity*
Greece 1957 104m bw
Finos (Anis Nohra)
original title: *To Telefteo Psemma*

The daughter of a bankrupt family reluctantly agrees to marry a millionaire, and the family's false values lead to tragedy.
Rather offbeat melodrama with the director in good form.

wd Michael Cacoyannis *ph* Walter Lassally *m* Manos Hadjidakis

Ellie Lambetti, Georges Pappas, Athena Michaelidou

A Matter of Life and Death****
GB 1946 104m Technicolor
GFD / Archers (Michael Powell, Emeric Pressburger)
US title: *Stairway to Heaven*

A pilot with brain damage after bailing out is torn between this world and the next, but an operation puts things to rights.
Outrageous fantasy which seemed more in keeping after the huge death toll of a world war, and in any case learned the Hollywood lesson of eating its cake and still having it, the supernatural elements being capable of explanation. A mammoth technical job in the heavenly sequences, it deserves full marks for its sheer arrogance, wit, style and film flair.

wd Michael Powell, Emeric Pressburger ph Jack Cardiff m Allan Gray pd Hein Heckroth

David Niven, Roger Livesey, Kim Hunter, Marius Goring, Raymond Massey, Abraham Sofaer

'Powell and Pressburger seem to have reached their heaven at last . . . an illimitable Wembley stadium, surrounded by tinkly music and mists, from which all men of insight, if they were ever careless enough to get there, would quickly blaspheme their way out.'—*Richard Winnington*

'A dazzling mesh of visionary satire, post-war politics and the mystical side of English romanticism.'—*Tony Rayns, Time Out, 1979*

'Beautifully written, beautifully acted, beautifully executed . . . you would think such formidable merits would add up to quite a film—and darned if they don't.'—*Time Out*

'This film, whether or not you find its philosophy half-baked, is downright good cinema, doing things that couldn't be done in any other medium'—*Tribune*

'It compelled attention and created emotion.'—*Basil Wright, 1972*

'Some women are born to have a glorious affair with life . . . !'

A Matter of Time
US / Italy 1976 97m (originally 165m) Technicolor
(AIP) Jack H. Skirball, J. Edmund Grainger

An Italian country chambermaid is taught about life by a faded countess.
Interminable even in its abbreviated form, this woebegone fantasy is a tribute to his miscast daughter by a director who never had much sense of plot to begin with. It has to be seen to be believed.

w John Gay, *novel* The Film of Memory by Maurice Druon *d* Vincente Minnelli *ph* Geoffrey Unsworth *m* Nino Oliviero

Liza Minnelli, Ingrid Bergman, Charles Boyer, Tina Aumont, Gabriele Ferzetti, Spiros Andros

'So hackneyed, inept and stupid as to be almost amusing.'—*John Simon, New York*

'So spectacularly crazy that if Minnelli could only persuade Mel Brooks to put his name on it, *A Matter of Time* might yet be the comedy sleeper of the year.'—*Frank Rich, New York Post*

A Matter of Who
GB 1961 92m bw
MGM / Foray (Walter Shenson, Milton Holmes)

The World Health Organization tracks down a smallpox outbreak.
Curious blend of semi-documentary with suspense and comedy; not really a starter.

w Milton Holmes *d* Don Chaffey *ph* Erwin Hillier *m* Edwin Astley

Terry-Thomas, Sonja Ziemann, Alex Nicol, Guy Deghy, Richard Briers, Clive Morton, Geoffrey Keen, Martin Benson, Honor Blackman, Carol White

Les Maudits
France 1947 103m bw

A U-boat with an assorted human cargo escapes the allied blockade as the war ends. Striking but aimless melodrama which plays like an early *Ship of Fools*. Dalio, Henri Vidal, Michel Auclair, Florence Marly, Paul Bernard. Written by J. Companeez, V. Alexandrov; directed by René Clement; for Speva / Discina. (UK title: *The Damned*.)

Maurice*
GB 1987 140m Technicolor
Cinecom / Merchant Ivory (Ismail Merchant)

The life of a Cambridge homosexual.
Hothouse study of E. M. Forster's posthumously published and semi-autobiographical novel. An acquired taste, but many scenes have general appeal.

w Kit Hesketh-Harvey, James Ivory *d James Ivory ph* Pierre Lhomme *m* Richard Robbins *pd* Brian Ackland-Snow *ed* Katherine Wenning

James Wilby, Hugh Grant, Rupert Graves, Denholm Elliott, Simon Callow, Billie Whitelaw, Ben Kingsley, Judy Parfitt

AAN: costume design (Jenny Beavan, John Bright)

Maxie
US 1985 98m De Luxe

The ghost of a twenties starlet revisits her old apartment and takes over the body of the wife of the tenant. Heavenly comedy which would have been funnier in the forties. Glenn Close, Mandy Patinkin, Ruth Gordon, Barnard Hughes, Valerie Curtin. Written by Patricia Resnick from novel *Marion's Wall* by Jack Finney; directed by Paul Aaron; for Carter De Haven / Ellsboy / Aurora / Orion.

The Maverick Queen
US 1955 90m Trucolor Naturama

A lady rustler falls for a Pinkerton detective sent to arrest her. Tedious western in bilious colour. Barbara Stanwyck, Barry Sullivan, Scott Brady, Mary Murphy, Wallace Ford, Jim Davis. Written by Kenneth Gamet and DeVallon Scott, from the novel by Zane Grey; directed by Joe Kane; for Republic.

Maximum Overdrive
US 1986 97m Technicolor

In a corner of North Carolina, all mechanical devices go haywire, and trucks menace a group of humans caught in a filling station. Idiotic premise for sensational action sequences, which are well staged but go on too long. Emilio Estevez, Pat Hingle, Laura Harrington, Yeardley Smith. Written and directed by Stephen King; for Martha Schumacher / Dino de Laurentiis.

Maya
US 1966 91m Technicolor Panavision
MGM / King Brothers (Mary P. Murray, Herman King)

A teenage American boy arrives in India to visit his disillusioned father, who finally comes to understand him only after he has run away. Good-looking but otherwise uninteresting animal drama which served as the pilot for a TV series.

w John Fante *d* John Berry *ph* Gunter Senftleben *m* Riz Ortolani

Clint Walker, Jay North, I. S. Johar, Sajid Kahn

Mayerling**
France 1935 90m bw

In 1889, imperial lovers are found dead in a country house. Classic French version of a somewhat chilly subject. Charles Boyer, *Danielle Darrieux*, Marthe Regnier, Yolande Laffon, Suzy Prim. Written by Joseph Kessel and V. Cube, from the novel by Claude Anet; directed by *Anatole Litvak*; for Seymour Nebenzal / Nero Film. 'As good a picture as Hollywood could produce, plus some local touches that are inaccessible to Hollywood.'—*Variety*

Mayerling
France / GB 1968 141m Eastmancolor Panavision
Corona / Winchester (Robert Dorfmann)

In 1888 the heir to the Habsburg Empire is forced into a suicide pact with his mistress. Tedious dramatization of historical events which in 1936 had made a delicate French film but in these hands seems an endless and boring manipulation of doubtful events into turgid romance.

wd Terence Young, *novel* Claude Anet *ph* Henri Alekan *m* Francis Lai *pd* Georges Wakhevitch

Omar Sharif, Catherine Deneuve, James Mason, Ava Gardner, James Robertson Justice, Genevieve Page, Ivan Desny, Maurice Teynac

The Mayor of 44th Street
US 1942 86m bw
RKO (Cliff Reid)

Dance bands are threatened by hooligans demanding protection money.
Boring melodrama with music.

w Lewis R. Foster *d* Alfred E. Green *ph* Robert de Grasse *songs* Mort Greene, Harry Revel

George Murphy, Anne Shirley, Richard Barthelmess, William Gargan, Joan Merrill, Millard Mitchell, Mary Wickes, Freddie Martin and band

AAN: song 'There's a Breeze on Lake Louise'

The Mayor of Hell*
US 1933 90m bw
Warner

A racketeer becomes superintendent of a reform school, and it changes his life.
Moderate star vehicle with a plot that did yeoman service thereafter in Dead End Kids films.

w Edward Chodorov *d* Archie Mayo *ph* Barney McGill *m* Leo F. Forbstein

James Cagney, Madge Evans, Allen Jenkins, Dudley Digges, Frankie Darro

'Has the outline of a junior *Big House*. Offers exploitation easily.'—*Variety*

'Propaganda for nothing: like most of what comes out of Hollywood, it is entertaining trash.'—*Time*

† Remade in 1938 as *Crime School* with Humphrey Bogart, 1939 as *Hell's Kitchen* with Ronald Reagan.

Maytime**
US 1937 132m bw (sepia sequence)
MGM (Hunt Stromberg)

An opera star falls in love with a penniless singer but her jealous impresario shoots him. Lush romantic musical which turns gradually into melodrama and ends in a ghostly reunion for the lovers. If that's what you like, it could scarcely be better done.

w Noel Langley, *operetta* Rida Johnson Young *d Robert Z. Leonard ph Oliver T. Marsh m Sigmund Romberg md* Herbert Stothart

Jeanette MacDonald, Nelson Eddy, John Barrymore, Herman Bing, Lynne Carver, Rafaela Ottiano, Paul Porcasi, Sig Rumann

'Click operetta . . . cinch for the foreign market also.'—*Variety*

'Enjoyable for more than camp reasons . . . the atmosphere of thwarted passion is compelling.'—*Pauline Kael, 70s*

† Shooting had begun in colour with Frank Morgan in Bing's part and Paul Lukas in Barrymore's; this footage, directed by Edmund Goulding, was abandoned on Irving Thalberg's death.

AAN: Herbert Stothart

Maytime in Mayfair
GB 1949 95m Technicolor
British Lion / Imperadio (Herbert Wilcox)

A playboy inherits a dress salon and falls for the lady manager.
Witless comedy fit to set one's teeth on edge, with over-acting and poor musical numbers. Not in the same street as its predecessor *Spring in Park Lane*.

w Nicholas Phipps *d* Herbert Wilcox *ph* Max Greene *md* Robert Farnon

Anna Neagle, Michael Wilding, Nicholas Phipps, Peter Graves, Tom Walls

'Painstakingly refined.'—*MFB*

The Maze
US 1953 81m bw 3-D
Allied Artists (Richard Heermance)

The heir to a title also inherits a family curse and turns into a giant frog.
Rather splendidly idiotic horror film which raises plenty of laughs but no frissons.

w Dan Ullman, *story* Maurice Sandoz *d* William Cameron Menzies *ph* Harry Neumann *m* Marlin Skiles

Richard Carlson, Veronica Hurst, Katherine Emery, Michael Pate, Lillian Bond, Hillary Brooke, Owen McGiveney

Me and Marlborough*
GB 1935 84m bw
GFD / Gainsborough (Michael Balcon)

In Marlborough's army, a woman takes the place of her soldier husband to prove his innocence of spying.
Curious period service farce, not quite a success but an interesting attempt at something different.

w Ian Hay, Marjorie Gaffney, *story* W. P. Lipscomb, Reginald Pound *d* Victor Saville *ph* Charles Van Enger

Cicely Courtneidge, Tom Walls, Barry McKay, Alfred Drayton

'In most cases the comedy is totally uncalled for and destroys the period atmosphere.'—*Variety*

Me and My Gal*
US 1932 79m bw
Fox
GB title: *Pier 13*

A cop on the beat romances a hashslinger and catches a crook.
Pleasant little programmer, very evocative of its period.

w Arthur Kober *d Raoul Walsh ph* Arthur Miller

Spencer Tracy, Joan Bennett, George Walsh, Marion Burns, J. Farrell MacDonald, Noel Madison, Henry B. Walthall

'Lacking in nearly everything that makes box office.'—*Variety*

† Remade in 1949 as *Pier 13*.

Me and My Pal*
US 1933 20m bw

Ollie becomes engrossed in a jigsaw puzzle and forgets to get married. Oddball star comedy which nearly comes off but simply doesn't provide enough jokes. Laurel and Hardy, James Finlayson, Eddie Dunn. Written by Stan Laurel; directed by Charles Rogers and Lloyd French; for Hal Roach.

MEAN STREETS. Scorsese's film was acclaimed at the 1973 New York film festival and his career was off and running.

Me and the Colonel
US 1958 110m bw
Columbia / Court–Goetz (William Goetz)

In 1940 an anti-semitic Polish colonel is obliged to flee from France in the company of a Jewish refugee.
Rather obvious war comedy with predictable but not very entertaining situations, sentiment, action and pathos. The stars cope well enough but the picture never picks up steam.

w S. N. Behrman, George Froeschel, *play* Franz Werfel *d* Peter Glenville *ph* Burnett Guffey *m* George Duning

Danny Kaye, Curt Jurgens, Nicole Maurey, Françoise Rosay, Akim Tamiroff, Martita Hunt, Alexander Scourby, Liliane Montevecchi, Ludwig Stossel

Me, Natalie*
US 1969 111m De Luxe
Cinema Center (Stanley Shapiro)

An unattractive 18-year-old girl moves into Greenwich Village and learns to accept herself as she is.
Basically very predictable but rather well done character study with excellent detail.

w A. Martin Zweiback *d Fred Coe*
ph Arthur J. Ornitz *m* Henry Mancini

Patty Duke, James Farentino, Martin Balsam, Elsa Lanchester, Salome Jens, Nancy Marchand, Al Pacino

The Mean Season
US 1985 103m De Luxe Panavision
Orion / Turman-Foster

A Miami police reporter becomes the personal spokesman for a murderous psychopath. Tolerable murder thriller with asides on politics and the media.

w Leon Piedmont *novel* In The Heat of the Summer by John Katzenbach *d* Philip Borsos *ph* Frank Tidy *m* Lalo Schifrin *pd* Philip Jefferies

Kurt Russell, Mariel Hemingway, Richard Jordan, Richard Masur, Richard Bradford, Joe Pantoliano

Mean Streets**
US 1973 110m Technicolor
Taplin–Perry–Scorsese (Jonathan T. Taplin)

Four young Italian-Americans use Tony's Bar as a base for drinking, brawling and hustling. Relentlessly sordid melodrama with a good eye for realistic detail.

w Martin Scorsese, Mardik Martin *d* Martin Scorsese *ph* Norman Gerard

Harvey Keitel, Robert de Niro, David Proval, Amy Robinson, Richard Romanus

'Lacks a sense of story and structure . . . unless a film-maker respects the needs of his audience, he can't complain if that audience fails to show up.'—*Variety*

'A thicker-textured rot than we have ever had in an American movie, and a deeper sense of evil.'—*New Yorker*

'Extraordinarily rich and distinguished on many levels.'—*Joseph Gelmis*

The Meanest Man in the World
US 1943 57m bw

An easy-going small-town lawyer finds that business picks up when he becomes tough and mean. Very minor star comedy with a muddled opening followed by strictly rationed laughs. Jack Benny, Priscilla Lane, Rochester, Edmund Gwenn, Anne Revere. Written by George Seaton and Allan House, from a play by George M. Cohan; directed by Sidney Lanfield; for TCF.

Meatballs
Canada 1979 92m Sonolab Color

Adventures at an ineptly run summer camp. Adolescent fun and games for the easily pleased adolescent. (By 1987, *Meatballs 3* had been reached.) Bill Murray, Harvey Atkin, Russ Banham, Ron Barry. Written by Len Blum, Dan Goldberg, Harold Ramis, Janis Allen; directed by Ivan Reitman; for Paramount.

The Mechanic
US 1972 100m Technicolor
UA / Chartoff / Winkler / Carlino
reissue title: *Killer of Killers*

A professional assassin under contract to the Mafia makes his missions look like accidents. Violent thriller with a few pretensions, but too flashily made to be taken seriously.

w Lewis John Carlino *d* Michael Winner *ph* Richard Kline, Robert Paynter *m* Jerry Fielding

Charles Bronson, Jan-Michael Vincent, Keenan Wynn, Jill Ireland

A Medal for Benny*
US 1945 77m bw
Paramount (Paul Jones)

An old rustic is the centre of small town celebrations in honour of his dead war hero son.
Satirical-sentimental location drama, effective but not memorable.

w Frank Butler, *original story* John Steinbeck, Jack Wagner *d* Irving Pichel *ph* Lionel Lindon *m* Victor Young

Dorothy Lamour, Arturo de Cordova, *J. Carrol Naish*, Mikhail Rasumny, Charles Dingle, Frank McHugh, Grant Mitchell

AAN: original story; J. Carrol Naish

Medal for the General
GB 1944 99m bw

An old general takes in evacuees and finds a new interest in life. Uneventful character drama which seemed mildly pleasing at the time. Godfrey Tearle, Jeanne de Casalis, Morland Graham, Mabel Constanduros, John Laurie, Petula Clark. Written by Elizabeth Baron, from the novel by James Ronald; directed by Maurice Elvey; for British National.

Medea*
Italy / France / West Germany 1970
118m Eastmancolor
San Marco / Number One / Janus (Franco Rossellini, Marina Cicogna)

Jason brings back as his wife the high priestess of the Golden Fleece, but her adjustment is to say the least uncomfortable.
In modern terms the case history of a psychopath, this weird production plays like an opera without music, and seems to have been designed as a vehicle for its charismatic star.

wd Pier Paolo Pasolini, *play* Euripides
ph Ennio Guarnieri

Maria Callas, Giuseppe Gentile, Laurent Terzieff, Massimo Girotti

The Medium*
Italy 1951 80m bw
Transfilm (Walter Lowendahl)

A fake medium feels a genuine manifestation, shoots at it and kills her assistant, but is still not sure whether he was responsible.
A filmic but not entirely satisfactory treatment of a modest but popular modern opera.

wd, m Gian-Carlo Menotti, his opera
co-d Alexander Hammid *ph* Enzo Serafin

Marie Powers, Anna Maria Alberghetti, Leo Coleman

AAN: Gian-Carlo Menotti (for music)

Medium Cool**
US 1969 111m Technicolor
Paramount / H & J Pictures (Tully Friedman)

A TV news cameraman is made apathetic by the events around him.
Stimulating if overlong comment on the quality of life in the sixties, immaculately made and with a rather effective though obvious twist ending.

wd, ph Haskell Wexler m Mike Bloomfield
ad Leon Ericksen

Robert Forster, Verna Bloom, Peter Bonerz, Marianna Hill, Sid McCoy

'A deeply moving questioning of America's violence and voyeurism.'—*Jan Dawson*

'I can't think of any film that tells one more about the texture of American life today.'—*Michael Billington, Illustrated London News*

'By the time he was eleven he had killed nine people!'

The Medusa Touch*
GB / France 1978 109m Technicolor
ITC / Bulldog / Citeca (Arnon Milchan, Elliott Kastner)

A novelist is haunted by the belief that he can cause disaster.
And he does, very predictably, while any intellectual excitement in the script is rapidly replaced by mere mayhem.
Different, but not exciting.

w John Briley, *novel* Peter Van Greenway
d Jack Gold *ph* Arthur Ibbetson *m* Michael J. Lewis *sp* Doug Ferris

Richard Burton, Lee Remick, Lino Ventura, Harry Andrews, Alan Badel, Jeremy Brett, Michael Hordern, Gordon Jackson

Meet Danny Wilson
US 1951 83m bw
U-I (Leonard Goldstein)

An overbearing crooner gets to the top with the help of gangsters.
Fairly abrasive star vehicle, almost amounting to self-parody.

w Don McGuire *d* Joseph Pevney *ph* Maury Gertsman *md* Joseph Gershenson

Frank Sinatra, Shelley Winters, Alex Nicol, Raymond Burr

Meet Dr Christian
US 1939 68m bw

A dedicated small-town doctor has no concern for financial reward. Adequate pot-boiler based on a radio character, and following Hersholt's popularity as Dr Dafoe. Jean Hersholt, Dorothy Lovett, Robert Baldwin, Enid Bennett, Paul Harvey, Marcia Mae Jones. Written by Ian McLellan Hunter, Harvey Gates, Ring Lardner Jnr; directed by Bernard Vorhaus; for William Stephens / RKO. 'First of a series . . . profitable programme material for the family trade.'—*Variety*

Meet John Doe***
US 1941 123m bw
Liberty Films (Frank Capra)

A tramp is hired to embody the common man in a phony political drive, and almost commits suicide.
Vividly staged but over-sentimental Capra extravaganza with high spots outnumbering low.

w Robert Riskin d Frank Capra ph George Barnes *m* Dmitri Tiomkin

Gary Cooper, *Barbara Stanwyck*, Edward Arnold, Walter Brennan, James Gleason, Spring Byington, Gene Lockhart, Rod la Rocque, Irving Bacon, Regis Toomey, Ann Doran, Warren Hymer, Andrew Tombes

'For the sake of a happy ending that would keep Gary Cooper alive, the meanings were so distorted that the original authors sued.'—*New Yorker, 1978*

'Capra is as skilled as ever in keeping things moving along briskly and dramatically.'—*National Board of Review*

'The meanings were so distorted that the original authors sued . . . It starts out in the confident Capra manner, but with a darker tone; by the end, you feel puzzled and cheated.'—*Pauline Kael, 70s*

AAN: original story (Richard Connell, Robert Presnell)

Meet Me after the Show*
US 1951 88m Technicolor
TCF (George Jessel)

A musical star thinks she has discovered an affair between her husband and his glamorous backer.
Surprisingly bright routine musical.

w Mary Loos, Richard Sale *d Richard Sale ph Arthur E. Arling md* Lionel Newman *songs* Jule Styne, Leo Robin

Betty Grable, Macdonald Carey, Rory Calhoun, Eddie Albert, Irene Ryan

Meet Me at Dawn
GB 1946 99m bw
Excelsior / Marcel Hellman
US title: *The Gay Duellist*

A professional duellist is commissioned to provoke a duel with a senator, but unwittingly hires the senator's daughter to play the injured party.
A totally laborious and artificial period comedy which never seems even to aspire to the style required.

w Lesley Storm, James Seymour, Maurice Cowan, *story* Le Tueur by Anatole Litvak, Marcel Achard *d* Thornton Freeland
ph Gunther Krampf *m* Mischa Spoliansky

Hazel Court, William Eythe, Stanley Holloway, Margaret Rutherford, Basil Sydney, Irene Browne

Meet Me at the Fair
US 1952 87m Technicolor
U-I (Albert J. Cohen)

In 1900, an orphan joins a travelling medicine show.
Mildly pleasing open-air comedy drama.

w Irving Wallace, *novel* The Great Companions by Gene Markey *d* Douglas Sirk *ph* Maury Gertsman *md* Joseph Gershenson

Diana Lynn, Dan Dailey, Hugh O'Brian, Chet Allen, Rhys Williams

Meet Me in Las Vegas
US 1956 112m Eastmancolor Cinemascope
MGM (Joe Pasternak)
GB title: *Viva Las Vegas!*

A gambler's luck changes when he grabs the hand of a passing ballerina.
Listless song-and dance extravaganza which wastes a great deal of talent.

w Isabel Lennart *d* Roy Rowland *ph* Robert Bronner *m* Georgie Stoll, Johnny Green
ly Sammy Cahn *ch* Eugène Loring, Hermes Pan

Dan Dailey, Cyd Charisse, Agnes Moorehead, Lili Darvas, Paul Henreid, Oscar Karlweis, Lena Horne, Jerry Colonna, Frankie Laine

'A large-scale musical of almost stupefying banality.'—*MFB*

AAN: Georgie Stoll, Johnny Green

Meet Me in St Louis***
US 1944 113m Technicolor
MGM (Arthur Freed)

Scenes in the life of an affectionate family at the turn of the century.
Patchy but generally highly agreeable musical nostalgia with an effective sense of the passing years and seasons.

w Irving Brecher, Fred F. Finklehoffe, *novel* Sally Benson *d Vincente Minnelli ph* George Folsey *md* Georgie Stoll

Judy Garland, Margaret O'Brien, Tom Drake, Leon Ames, Mary Astor, Lucille Bremer, June Lockhart, *Harry Davenport*, Marjorie Main, Joan Carroll, Hugh Marlowe, Robert Sully, Chill Wills

'A family group framed in velvet and tinsel . . . it has everything a romantic musical should have.'—*Dilys Powell, 1955*

AAN: script; George Folsey; Georgie Stoll; song 'The Trolley Song' (*m / ly* Ralph Blane, Hugh Martin)

Meet Me On Broadway
US 1946 77m bw

A young musical director determines to hit Broadway. Mild revue with a skimpy plot. Marjorie Reynolds, Fred Brady, Jinx Falkenberg, Spring Byington, Gene Lockhart, Allen Jenkins. Written by George Bricker, Jack Henley; directed by Leigh Jason; for Burt Kelly / Columbia.

Meet Me Tonight
GB 1952 85m Technicolor
British Film Makers / Anthony Havelock Allan

Three short Noel Coward plays: *Red Peppers, Fumed Oak, Ways and Means.*
Regrettably bald treatment of three playlets which have not lasted well. A thoroughly artificial evening.

w / m Noel Coward *d* Anthony Pelissier *ph* Desmond Dickinson

Ted Ray, Kay Walsh, Stanley Holloway, Betty Ann Davies, Nigel Patrick, Valerie Hobson

Meet Mr Callaghan
GB 1954 88m bw

A private detective unmasks a rich man's killer. Routine thick ear on American lines; moderately popular at the time, it spawned no sequels. Derrick de Marney, Harriet Johns, Peter Neil, Adrienne Corri, Delphi Lawrence, Belinda Lee. Written by Brock Williams, from the play by Gerald Verner based on Peter Cheyney's novel *The Urgent Hangman*; directed by Charles Saunders; for Pinnacle.

Meet Mr Lucifer*
GB 1953 81m bw
Ealing (Monja Danischewsky)

The Demon King in a tatty provincial pantomime dreams he is the devil preventing people from wasting time watching television. Clean and occasionally amusing piece of topical satire on tellymania; but the prologue is funnier than the sketches.

w Monja Danischewsky, *play* Beggar My Neighbour by Arnold Ridley *d* Anthony Pelissier *ph* Desmond Dickinson *m* Eric Rogers

Stanley Holloway, Peggy Cummins, Jack Watling, Barbara Murray, Joseph Tomelty, Gordon Jackson, Jean Cadell, Kay Kendall, Ian Carmichael, Gilbert Harding, Charles Victor, Humphrey Lestocq

Meet Mr Penny
GB 1938 70m bw

A meek clerk leads a revolt against a speculator who wants to build on allotments. Early Ealing-style social comedy based on a radio character; of no abiding interest. Richard Goolden, Vic Oliver, Fabia Drake, Kay Walsh, Patrick Barr, Hermione Gingold, Wilfrid Hyde-White. Written by Victor Kendall and Doreen Montgomery, from the character created by Maurice Moisiewicz; directed by David MacDonald; for British National.

Meet Nero Wolfe*
US 1936 73m bw
Columbia

A corpulent stay-at-home sleuth solves a disappearance and a murder.
The film debut of an engaging crime character, who oddly never made it to a series.

w Howard J. Green, Bruce Manning, Joseph Anthony, *novel* Fer de Lance by Rex Stout *d* Herbert Biberman *ph* Henry Freulich

Edward Arnold, Lionel Stander, Joan Perry, Rita Hayworth, Victor Jory, Nana Bryant, Walter Kingsford, John Qualen

Meet Simon Cherry
GB 1949 67m bw

A clergyman on holiday proves that a rich recluse was not murdered. Elementary programme filler from a radio series. Hugh Moxey, Zena Marshall, John Bailey, Anthony Forwood, Ernest Butcher, Courtney Hope. Written by Gale Pedrick, A. R. Rawlinson and Godfrey Grayson, from Gale Pedrick's radio series *Meet the Rev*; directed by Godfrey Grayson; for Hammer.

Meet the Baron
US 1933 79m bw

A nincompoop is fêted as the real Baron Munchhausen. An incoherent script provides an opportunity for several comics to do their stuff. Jack Pearl, Jimmy Durante, Zasu Pitts, Ted Healy and his Stooges, Edna May Oliver, Henry Kolker. Written by Herman J. Mankiewicz, Norman Krasna, Allen Rivkin, P. J. Wolfson, Arthur Kober, William K. Wells; directed by Walter Lang; for MGM. 'Not so forte in the material division, but saved by its capable crew of comics.'—*Variety*

Meet the Mayor
US 1938 63m bw

A veteran small-town elevator operator becomes involved in politics. Curious semi-comedy in which the star uses up most of his old vaudeville routines. Frank Fay, Ruth Hall, Hale Hamilton, George Meeker, Berton Churchill, Franklin Pangborn. Written by Walter DeLeon, Charles Belden, Frank Fay; directed by Ralph Ceder; for Frank Fay / Times. 'Flimsy meller for secondary duallers.'—*Variety*

Meet the Missus
US 1937 65m bw

A worm turns when his wife constantly involves him in newspaper contests. Very slight farce for the rurals. Victor Moore, Helen Broderick, Anne Shirley, Alan Bruce, Willie Best. Written by Jack Townley, Bert Granet, Joel Sayre, from the story Lady Average by Jack Goodman and Albert Rice; directed by Joseph Santley; for Albert Lewis / RKO. 'Destined for the lower half of duals.'—*Variety*

Meet the Navy
GB 1946 85m bw (Technicolor sequence)

The story of a revue featuring amateurs from the allied navies. Patchy but generally good-natured wartime entertainment. Lionel Murton, John Pratt, Oscar Naske, Alan Lund. Written by Lester Cooper, James Seymore; directed by Alfred Travers; for British National.

Meet the People
US 1944 100m bw
MGM (E. Y. Harburg)

A Broadway musical star proves she isn't snooty by taking a job in a shipyard.
Thin propaganda musical which wastes a fair amount of talent.

w S. M. Herzig, Fred Saidy, *play* Louis Lantz, Sol and Ben Barzman *d* Charles Reisner *ph* Robert Surtees *songs* various

Lucille Ball, Dick Powell, Virginia O'Brien, Bert Lahr, Rags Ragland, June Allyson, Steve Geray, Phil Regan, Spike Jones and his City Slickers, Vaughn Monroe and his Orchestra

Meet the Stewarts
US 1942 74m bw

Newlyweds have trouble when he's poor and she's used to rich living. Modest marital comedy with young talent. William Holden, Frances Dee, Grant Mitchell. Written by Elizabeth Dunn and Karen de Wolf; directed by Alfred E. Green; for Columbia.

Mein Kampf*
Sweden 1961 118m bw

A newsreel compilation tracing the rise and fall of Nazi Germany. A simple but highly effective and reliable selection of actualities leaves conclusions to the viewer, letting the events speak for themselves. A powerful documentary. Written, directed and edited by *Erwin Leiser*; for Töre Sjöberg / Minerva International. (Original title: *Den Blodiga Tiden.*)

Melba
GB 1953 113m Technicolor
Horizon (Sam Spiegel)

The life of the internationally famous Australian opera singer of Victorian days. Moderately interesting recreation of a woman and an era, though dramatically rather stodgy.

w Harry Kurnitz *d* Lewis Milestone *ph* Ted Scaife *md* Muir Mathieson *ad* André Andreiev

Patrice Munsel, Robert Morley, Alec Clunes, Martita Hunt, Sybil Thorndike, John McCallum

Melody
GB 1971 106m Eastmancolor
Hemdale / Sagittarius / Goodtimes (David Puttnam)
aka: *S.W.A.L.K.*

Calf love at school causes jealousy between two boys.
Tough-sentimental teenage comedy-drama of little interest to adults.

w Alan Parker *d* Waris Hussein *ph* Peter Suschitsky *m* Richard Hewson

Jack Wild, Mark Lester, Tracy Hyde

Melody Cruise
US 1933 74m bw

A lady killer gets his come-uppance on board ship, but wins the girl he really wants. Very messy mixture of comedy, romance and music. Phil Harris, Charles Ruggles, Greta Nissen, Helen Mack, Chick Chandler. Written by Mark Sandrich, Ben Holmes; directed by Mark Sandrich; for Merian C. Cooper / RKO. 'Ought to be a moderate grosser . . . the meat just isn't there for the principals, and they seem to feel it in their work.'—*Variety*

Melody for Two
US 1937 60m bw

A singing bandleader argues with his team and picks up with an all-girl crew. Simple-minded peg for a few songs; rather a yawn. James Melton, Patricia Ellis, Wini Shaw, Marie Wilson, Fred Keating, Dick Purcell. Written by George Bricker, Luci Ward, Joseph K. Watson; directed by Louis King; for Warners. 'Okay twin-bill fodder.'—*Variety*

Melody in Spring
US 1934 75m bw

An ambitious radio singer follows the sponsor's daughter on a European holiday. Mild vehicle for a tenor who didn't sustain. Lanny Ross, Charles Ruggles, Mary Boland, Ann Sothern, George Meeker, Herman Bing. Written by Benn W. Levy; directed by Norman Z. McLeod; for Douglas MacLean / Paramount. 'Farfetched, somewhat boresome, and generally airy.'—*Variety*

The Melody Lingers On
US 1935 65m bw

During World War I, an Italian soldier is killed after fathering an illegitimate baby, which grows up with no knowledge of mother, who watches from afar. Old-fashioned tearjerker with musical background. Josephine Hutchinson, George Houston, John Halliday, Mona Barrie, Helen Westley, Laura Hope Crews. Written by Ralph Spence, Philip Dunne, from the novel by Lowell Brentano; directed by David Burton; for Edward Small. 'Will probably wind up topping the duals.'—*Variety*

Melody Time*
US 1948 75m Technicolor
Walt Disney (Ben Sharpsteen)

An unlinked variety show of cartoon segments.
A mainly mediocre selection with the usual moments of high style: *Once upon a Wintertime, Bumble Boogie, Johnny Appleseed, Little Toot, Trees, Blame it on the Samba, Pecos Bill.*

w various *d* various

'There seems to be an obvious connection between the Disney artists' increasing insipidity and their increasing talent for fright, but I will leave it to accredited sado-masochists to make the discovery.'—*James Agee*

Melvin and Howard*
US 1980 95m Technicolor
Universal (Terry Nelson)

The life of a factory worker is changed when a man he picks up in the Nevada desert claims to be Howard Hughes.
Eccentric comedy which has been compared to the work of Preston Sturges, but has an agreeable style of its own.

w Bo Goldman d Jonathan Demme ph Tak Fujimoto *m* Bruce Langhorne

Paul Le Mat, Jason Robards Jnr, Mary Steenburgen, Elizabeth Cheshire, Michael J. Pollard, Gloria Grahame

'An almost flawless act of sympathetic imagination . . . it's what might have happened if Jean Renoir had directed a comedy script by Preston Sturges.'—*New Yorker*

AA: Bo Goldman; Mary Steenburgen
AAN: Jason Robards Jnr (supporting actor)

The Member of the Wedding*
US 1952 91m bw
Columbia / Stanley Kramer

A 12-year-old girl learns something about life when her sister gets married and a young boy dies.
Boringly contained in a kitchen set, this filmed play has interesting characters but is really not good enough for the talent involved.

w Edna and Edward Anhalt, *play* and *novel* Carson McCullers *d* Fred Zinnemann *ph* Hal Mohr *m* Alex North

Julie Harris, *Ethel Waters*, Brandon de Wilde, Arthur Franz, Nancy Gates, James Edwards

AAN: Julie Harris

Memed My Hawk
GB 1984 110m colour

In 1923 Turkey, an inept tyrant chases one of his young villagers, who flees to the rebels. Weird but not wonderful mix of comedy and melodrama in an unfamiliar and unattractive setting. Peter Ustinov, Herbert Lom, Denis Quilley, Michael Elphick, Simon Dutton. Written and directed by Peter Ustinov, from the novel by Yashar Kemal; for Fuad Kavur / Peter Ustinov Productions.

Memoirs of a Survivor
GB 1981 115m Technicolor
EMI / Memorial (Michael Medwin, Penny Clark)

In the future, a single woman finds that urban civilization has decayed, and after many horrors finds refuge in an old Victorian house.
Unappetizing mixture of *1984* and *Alice in Wonderland*, too despairing and plotless to find many takers.

w Kerry Crabbe, David Gladwell, *novel* Doris Lessing *d* David Gladwell *ph* Walter Lassally *m* Mike Thorn *pd* Keith Wilson *ed* William Shapter

Julie Christie, Christopher Guard, Debbie Hutchings, Leonie Mellinger, Nigel Hawthorne, Pat Keen

'A film of wild ambition, sadly and hopelessly bungled.'—*Geoff Brown, MFB*

The Memphis Belle*
US / GB 1943 43m Technicolor

The last mission over Germany of a Flying Fortress. Impressive on-the-spot documentary which provided a lot of library footage for later movies. Directed by William Wyler; for the War Activities Commission.

'A completely new experience between men and women!'

The Men***
US 1950 85m bw
Stanley Kramer
reissue title: *Battle Stripe*

Paraplegic war veterans are prepared for civilian life; the fiancée of one of them helps overcome his problems.
Vivid semi-documentary melodrama, at the time rather shocking in its no-holds-barred treatment of sexual problems.

w Carl Foreman d Fred Zinnemann ph Robert de Grasse *m* Dmitri Tiomkin

Marlon Brando, Teresa Wright, Everett Sloane, Jack Webb, Howard St John

'Don't be misled into feeling that to see this film is merely a duty; it is, simply, an experience worth having.'—*Richard Mallett, Punch*

'I was afraid I was gonna die . . . now I'm afraid I'm gonna live!'—*more publicity*

AAN: Carl Foreman

Men Against the Sky
US 1940 73m bw

A stunt pilot advises on a new plane design instrumental to the war effort. Routine heroics mixed with romance. Richard Dix, Kent Taylor, Edmund Lowe, Wendy Barrie, Grant Withers. Written by Nathanael West; directed by Leslie Goodwins; for Howard Benedict / RKO.

Men Are Not Gods
GB 1936 92m bw
London (Alexander Korda)

An actor playing Othello nearly strangles his wife.
Tepid melodramatic attempt at a theme later used in *A Double Life.*

w G. B. Stern, Iris Wright *d* Walter Reisch *ph* Charles Rosher

Miriam Hopkins, Sebastian Shaw, Rex Harrison, Gertrude Lawrence, A. E. Matthews, Val Gielgud, Laura Smithson

'A nearer approximation to box office quality than some recent London productions.'—*Variety*

Men Are Such Fools
US 1938 69m bw

The worm turns when his wife threatens to leave him for a singing career. Mediocre is the word for this threadbare drama. Wayne Morris, Humphrey Bogart, Priscilla Lane, Hugh Herbert, Penny Singleton. Written by Norman Reilly Raine and Horace Jackson; directed by Busby Berkeley; for Warner.

Men in Her Diary
US 1945 73m bw

A jealous woman tries to hire an unattractive girl as her husband's secretary. Very mild lower-berth comedy. Peggy Ryan, Jon Hall, Louise Allbritton, William Terry, Virginia Grey, Ernest Truex, Alan Mowbray, Eric Blore, Sig Rumann. Written by F. Hugh Herbert and Elwood Ullman, from a story by Kerry Shaw; directed by Charles Barton; for Universal.

The Men in Her Life
US 1941 90m bw
Columbia (Gregory Ratoff)

A former circus rider becomes a ballerina. Well-worn rags-to-riches romance of little interest.

w Frederick Kohner, Michael Wilson, Paul Trivers, *novel* Ballerina by Lady Eleanor Smith *d* Gregory Ratoff *ph* Harry Stradling, Arthur Miller *md* David Raksin

Loretta Young, Conrad Veidt, Dean Jagger, Eugenie Leontovich, Shepperd Strudwick, Otto Kruger, Paul Baratoff

Men in War
US 1957 104m bw
Security (Sidney Harmon)

Korea 1950: an infantry platoon is cut off from HQ and tries to take an enemy-occupied hill. Stereotyped small-scale war heroics; the film makes its points but fails to entertain.

w Philip Yordan *d* Anthony Mann *ph* Ernest Haller *m* Elmer Bernstein

Robert Ryan, Robert Keith, Aldo Ray, Vic Morrow, James Edwardes, Sen Yung

Men in White*
US 1934 80m bw
MGM (Monta Bell)

An ambitious intern is in love with an attractive socialite who resents his devotion to duty.
Popular but obvious star drama.

w Waldemar Young, *play* Sidney Kingsley *d* Richard Boleslawski *ph* George Folsey

Clark Gable, Myrna Loy, Jean Hersholt, Elizabeth Allan, Otto Kruger, C. Henry Gordon, Wallace Ford

'Belongs in the strictly adult class of pictures . . . show spells money from plenty of angles.'—*Variety*

Men Must Fight
US 1933 73m bw

War comes to New York in 1940. A forgotten pacifist tract which trod the same paths as did H. G. Wells; of historical interest only apart from a spectacular air raid climax. Robert Young, Diana Wynyard, May Robson, Phillips Holmes, Lewis Stone. Written by S. K. Lauren, Reginald Lawrence and C. Gardner Sullivan; directed by Edgar Selwyn; for MGM.

Men of Boys' Town
US 1941 106m bw
MGM (John W. Considine Jnr)

Further adventures of Father Flanagan. Mushy sequel to *Boys' Town* (qv).

w James Kevin McGuinness *d* Norman Taurog *ph* Harold Rosson *m* Herbert Stothart

Spencer Tracy, Mickey Rooney, Bobs Watson, Larry Nunn, Lee J. Cobb, Mary Nash, Henry O'Neill, Darryl Hickman, Anne Revere

Men of Sherwood Forest
GB 1957 77m Eastmancolor

Robin Hood frees King Richard from bondage. Fairly lively adventure romp on a low level. Don Taylor, Reginald Beckwith, Eileen Moore, David King-Wood, Patrick Holt, John Van Eyssen. Written by Allan McKinnon; directed by Val Guest; for Hammer.

Men of Texas
US 1942 71m bw

After the Civil War, a Yankee reporter is sent to investigate rumours of a further uprising. Routine western, not unentertaining in its modest way. Robert Stack, Anne Gwynne, Broderick Crawford, Jackie Cooper, Ralph Bellamy, Jane Darwell, Leo Carrillo, John Litel. Written by Harold Shumate; directed by Ray Enright; for Universal. (GB title: *Men of Destiny*.)

Men of the Fighting Lady
US 1954 80m Anscocolor
MGM (Henry Berman)

Adventures of an aircraft carrier during the Korean War.
Tepid war actioner with a few effective semi-documentary sequences of naval tactics.

w Art Cohn *d* Andrew Marton *ph* George Folsey *m* Miklos Rozsa

Van Johnson, Walter Pidgeon, Louis Calhern, Dewey Martin, Keenan Wynn, Frank Lovejoy, Robert Horton

Men of Tomorrow
GB 1932 88m bw
Paramount (Alexander Korda)

Oxford students have more than academic work on their minds.
Dim comedy-drama with an interesting cast.

w Arthur Wimperis, Anthony Gibbs, *play* Young Apollo by Anthony Gibbs *d* Leontine Sagan *ph* Bernard Browne

Maurice Braddell, Joan Gardner, Emlyn Williams, Merle Oberon, Robert Donat

Men of Two Worlds
GB 1946 109m Technicolor
GFD / Two Cities (John Sutro)
US title: *Witch Doctor*
aka: *Kisenga, Man of Africa*

In Tanganyika, an educated native helps white men to counter the force of witch doctors and persuade tribes to leave an infected area. Earnest but totally unpersuasive semi-documentary shot in unconvincing sets and garish colour.

w Thorold Dickinson, Joyce Cary, E. Arnot Robertson, Herbert Victor *d* Thorold Dickinson *ph* Geoffrey Unsworth, Desmond Dickinson *m* Arthur Bliss

Eric Portman, Phyllis Calvert, Robert Adams, Orlando Martins, Arnold Marle, Cathleen Nesbitt, David Horne, Cyril Raymond

Men o' War*
US 1929 20m bw

Two sailors and two girls have adventures in a park. Simple-minded early talkie star comedy featuring their famous soda fountain routine. Laurel and Hardy, James Finlayson. Written by H. M. Walker; directed by Lewis R. Foster; for Hal Roach.

Men of Yesterday
GB 1936 82m bw

Old army rivalries die down at a reunion. Dated but interesting drama with interpolated variety talent. Stewart Rome, Sam Livesey, Hay Petrie, Cecil Parker, with George Robey, Ella Shields, Will Fyffe, Dick Henderson. Written by Gerald Elliott and Jack Francis; directed by John Baxter; for UK Films.

Men with Wings
US 1938 106m Technicolor
Paramount (William Wellman)

Civil aviation pioneers fall out over a girl. Disappointing epic from the maker of *Wings*, with highly predictable story line, modest acting and ho-hum spectacle.

w Robert Carson *d* William Wellman *ph* W. Howard Greene *m* W. Franke Harling, Gerald Carbonara

Fred MacMurray, Ray Milland, Louise Campbell, Andy Devine, Lynne Overman, Porter Hall, Walter Abel, Virginia Weidler, Donald O'Connor

'To all women who love and admire the fearless heroes of the air, and who, with brave hearts, encourage them, hope, and pray for them.'—*director's dedication*

'Lavish air spectacle in Technicolor that means big business . . . it will triumph through rain, sleet or snow.'—*Variety*

'Give the rats a taste of their own medicine!'

Men without Names
US 1935 67m bw

Bank robbers are cornered in a small town and picked off by the FBI. Routine crime feature, less exciting than it sounds. Fred MacMurray, Madge Evans, Lynne Overman, David Holt, John Wray, Dean Jagger. Written by Marguerite Roberts, Kubec Glasmon, Dale Van Every; directed by Ralph Murphy; for Paramount. 'Another of the new gangster films, and too flimsy. Grooved for the pops.'—*Variety*

Men without Women
US 1930 77m bw
Fox

Men in a submarine are trapped on the ocean bed.
Early talkie action drama noted more for its credits than its accomplishment.

w Dudley Nichols *d* John Ford *ph* Joseph H. August

Kenneth MacKenna, Frank Albertson, Paul Page, Pat Somerset, Stuart Erwin, Warren Hymer, John Wayne

'Stunning, realistic picture that will make talk.'—*Variety*

'A club few will want to join . . . a distasteful piece of work that displays the worst in men.'—*Variety*

The Menace
US 1932 64m bw

A convict escapes, gets a new face through plastic surgery, and plans his revenge.
Muddled melodrama from a story by Edgar Wallace. Walter Byron, H. B. Warner, Bette Davis, Natalie Moorehead, William Davidson, Halliwell Hobbes. Written by Dorothy Howell, Charles Logue, Roy Chanslor; directed by Roy William Neill; for Columbia. 'A halting and frequently clumsy development leads to a weak climax.'—*Variety*

Menace
US 1934 58m bw

Murders follow the suicide of a mining engineer. Compact little dark house thriller with good stagey performances. Gertrude Michael, Paul Cavanagh, Henrietta Crosman, John Lodge, Ray Milland, Berton Churchill, Halliwell Hobbes. Written by Chandler Sprague and Anthony Veiller, from a story by Philip MacDonald; directed by Ralph Murphy; for Paramount. 'A pat specimen of the mystery film, expertly manipulated.'—*Variety*

Menilmontant*
France 1924 50m (24 fps) bw silent

Respected but fairly impenetrable piece of avant-garde which appears to be about two sisters haunted by memories of the murder of their parents, for which they may or may not have been responsible. Written, directed, edited and produced by *Dimitri Kirsanov*; for his own company. 'A flurry of hand-held camera shots, incisive montages and elliptical progressions.'—*Geoff Brown, MFB, 1981.*

The Men's Club
US 1986 100m colour
Atlantic Releasing / Howard Gottfried

Friends nearing forty get together and bemoan their lot.
Curious, talky, rather dreary piece which gets almost nowhere.

w Leonard Michaels, from his novel *d* Peter Medak *ph* John Fleckenstein *m* Lee Holdridge *pd* Ken Davis *ed* Cynthia Scheider, David Dresser, Bill Butler

Roy Scheider, Frank Langella, Harvey Keitel, Treat Williams, Richard Jordan, David Dukes, Craig Wasson, Stockard Channing, Jennifer Jason Leigh

Mephisto**
Hungary 1981 144m Eastmancolor
Mafilm / Manfred Durniok

In Germany in the twenties, an actor committed to the idea of a workers' theatre becomes a puppet of the Nazis.
Heavy-going but stylishly made political melodrama.

w Peter Dobai, Istvan Szabo, *novel* Klaus Mann *d Istvan Szabo* *ph* Lajos Koltai *m* Zdenko Tamassy

Klaus Maria Brandauer, Ildiko Bansagi, Krystyna Janda

AA: best foreign film

The Mephisto Waltz*
US 1971 109m De Luxe
TCF / QM Productions

A satanic concert pianist on the point of death wills his soul into the body of a journalist.
Complex diabolical mumbo-jumbo with plenty of style.

w Ben Maddow, *novel* Fred Mustard Stewart *d Paul Wendkos* *ph* William W. Spencer *m* Jerry Goldsmith

Alan Alda, Jacqueline Bisset, Curt Jurgens, Barbara Parkins

The Mercenaries
GB 1968 100m Metrocolor Panavision
MGM / George Englund
US title: *Dark of the Sun*

In the Belgian Congo in 1960 a mercenary officer is ordered to bring back a fortune in diamonds by armoured train.
Basically an old-fashioned thriller about the hazards of a journey beset by brutish villains and damsels in distress, this unpleasant film is notable for the amount of sadistic action it crams into its running time.

w Quentin Werty, Adrian Spies, *novel* Dark of the Sun by Wilbur Smith *d* Jack Cardiff *ph* Edward Scaife *m* Jacques Loussier

Rod Taylor, Yvette Mimieux, Kenneth More, Jim Brown, Peter Carsten, André Morell, Guy Deghy, Calvin Lockhart, Alan Gifford

'The violence done to the human body is matched by violence done to the intelligence by a stock adventure story given a gloss of topicality and social insult.'—*Judith Crist*

Merely Mary Ann
US 1931 74m bw

The maid of all work falls for the gentleman lodger. Cinderella stuff redesigned for two popular stars, but of no lasting appeal. Janet Gaynor, Charles Farrell, Beryl Mercer, J. M. Kerrigan, G. P. Huntley Jnr. Written by Jules Furthman from the story by Israel Zangwill; directed by Henry King; for Fox. 'Bound to pull after a summer of gang violence, mystery shockers, and much sex urge study.'—*Variety*

Merrill's Marauders
US 1962 98m Technicolor Cinemascope
Warner / US Pictures (Milton Sperling)

Adventures of a crack US army unit in 1942 Burma.
Physically exhausting war adventure with emphasis on hand-to-hand fighting and much bloodshed.

w Samuel Fuller, Milton Sperling *d* Samuel Fuller *ph* William Clothier *m* Howard Jackson

Jeff Chandler, Ty Hardin, Andrew Duggan, Peter Brown, Will Hutchins, Claude Akins

Merrily We Go to Hell
US 1932 78m bw
Paramount
GB title: *Merrily We Go to ——*

A socialite marries a dipsomaniac journalist.
Glum problem drama.

w Edwin Justin Mayer, *novel* I Jerry Take Thee Joan by Cleo Lucas *d* Dorothy Arzner *ph* David Abel

Sylvia Sidney, Fredric March, Adrienne Allen, Richard Gallagher, Florence Burton, Esther Howard, Kent Taylor

Merrily We Live*
US 1938 90m bw
Hal Roach

A zany family hires a chauffeur who is actually a famous writer posing as a tramp.
Quite likeable compound of *My Man Godfrey* and *You Can't Take It with You.*

w Eddie Moran, Jack Jevne *d* Norman Z. McLeod *ph* Norbert Brodine *md* Marvin Hatley

Constance Bennett, Brian Aherne, Billie Burke, Alan Mowbray, Patsy Kelly, Ann Dvorak, Tom Brown, Bonita Granville, Marjorie Rambeau, Clarence Kolb

'In the high cost bracket and rates top billing when dualled, with a chance it is strong enough to carry first runs as a single.'—*Variety*

AAN: Norbert Brodine; Billie Burke; title song (*m* Phil Craig, *ly* Arthur Quenzer)

Merry Andrew
US 1958 103m Metrocolor Cinemascope
MGM / Sol C. Siegel

A stuffy teacher in search of an ancient statue joins a travelling circus.
Deliberately charming star comedy which plumps too firmly for whimsy and, despite its professionalism, provokes barely a smile, let alone a laugh.

w Isabel Lennart, I. A. L. Diamond, *story* Paul Gallico *d / ch* Michael Kidd *ph* Robert Surtees *m* Saul Chaplin *ly* Johnny Mercer

Danny Kaye, Pier Angeli, Baccaloni, Noel Purcell, Robert Coote, Patricia Cutts, Rex Evans, Walter Kingsford, Tommy Rall, Rhys Williams

Merry Christmas, Mr Lawrence*
GB 1982 124m Eastmancolor

In a Japanese prisoner-of-war camp in Java in 1942, an English captive strikes up a strange relationship with the commandant.
Uncomfortably titled and unavoidably downbeat character drama with some unpleasant moments; despite good work all round it seems to head straight for every cliché perpetuated by *The Bridge on the River Kwai*.

w Nagisa Oshima with Paul Mayersberg, *novel* The Seed and the Sower by Laurens van der Post *d* Nagisa Oshima *ph* Toichiro Narushima *m* Ryuichi Sakamoto

'It always seems like a cocktail of saleable ingredients rather than genuine cinema.'—*Sunday Times*

Merry Comes to Town
GB 1937 79m bw

A professor's family is disappointed when a relative visiting from America turns out to be as poor as they are. Thin, predictable comedy with the visitor finally hailed as a saviour. Zasu Pitts, Guy Newall, Betty Ann Davies, Muriel George, Basil Langton. Written by Evadne Price; directed by George King; for Embassy/Sound City. (US title: *Merry Comes to Stay*.) 'A pleasant comedy which will improve with cutting.'—*Variety*

The Merry Frinks
US 1934 68m bw

A sportswriter down on his luck has a crazy family. And didn't everybody in the mid-thirties? But this one is crazy without being very funny. Aline MacMahon, Guy Kibbee, Allen Jenkins, Hugh Herbert, Frankie Darro. Written by Gene Markey, Kathryn Scola; directed by Alfred E. Green; for First National. (GB title: *Happy Family*.) 'The most disagreeable family group since *Three-Cornered Moon*. Poor comedy and lacks names.'—*Variety*

Merry Go Round of 1938
US 1937 87m bw

Four vaudevillians adopt a small girl, and later head for Hollywood. Sentimental farce with zany moments and an encouraging cast. Jimmy Savo, Bert Lahr, Mischa Auer, Billy House, Alice Brady, Louise Fazenda. Written by Monte Brice and A. Dorian Atvos; directed by Irving Cummings; for Universal. 'First rate filmusical packed with laughs.'—*Variety*

The Merry Monahans
US 1944 90m bw
Universal (Michael Fessier, Ernest Pagano)

Adventures of a family of vaudeville performers.
Acceptable backstage comedy drama with good atmosphere.

w Michael Fessier, Ernest Pagano *d* Charles Lamont *ph* Charles Van Enger *m* Hans Salter

Donald O'Connor, Jack Oakie, Rosemary de Camp, Peggy Ryan, Ann Blyth, Isabel Jewell, John Miljan

AAN: Hans Salter

The Merry Widow*
US 1925 111m (24 fps) bw silent
MGM (Irving Thalberg)

A bankrupt king orders a nobleman to woo a wealthy American widow.
An operetta without music (or dialogue) is usually a poor thing, but the director added a few unpredictable touches.

w Erich Von Stroheim, Benjamin Glazer, *operetta* Victor Leon, Leo Stein *d Erich Von Stroheim ph* Oliver Marsh, Ben Reynolds, William Daniels *m* William Axt, D. Mendoza

Mae Murray, John Gilbert, Roy D'Arcy, Tully Marshall

† The story goes that when reproved by Thalberg for wasting film stock on, for instance, endless shots of a wardrobe full of shoes, Von Stroheim remarked: 'The character has a foot fetish.' 'And you,' said Thalberg, 'have a footage fetish!'

'Surrender to the happy seduction of Ernst Lubitsch's most glorious picture holiday!'

The Merry Widow**
US 1934 99m bw
MGM

Patchy, but sometimes sparkling version.

w Samson Raphaelson, Ernest Vajda *d Ernst Lubitsch ph* Oliver T. Marsh *m Franz Lehar*

Maurice Chevalier, Jeanette MacDonald, Edward Everett Horton, Una Merkel, George Barbier, Donald Meek, Sterling Holloway, Shirley Ross

'Fine all-around job and an entertainment natural.'—*Variety*

'It is Lubitsch; it is also Hollywood; it is the cream of the American bourgeois film. It is a charlotte russe.'—*Peter Ellis, New Masses*

The Merry Widow
US 1952 105m Technicolor
MGM (Joe Pasternak)

Chill, empty remake.

w Sonya Levien, William Ludwig *d* Curtis Bernhardt *ph* Robert Surtees

Fernando Lamas, Lana Turner, Richard Haydn, Una Merkel, Thomas Gomez, John Abbott

'Nothing has been omitted (except the spirit of the original).'—*MFB*

The Merry Wives of Reno*
US 1934 61m bw

Three couples go to a Reno hotel to get a divorce. Amusing but scrappy comedy in the vein of the successful *Convention City*. Margaret Lindsay, Donald Woods, Guy Kibbee, Glenda Farrell, Ruth Donnelly, Hugh Herbert, Frank McHugh, Roscoe Ates, Hobart Cavanaugh. Written by Robert Lord; directed by H. Bruce Humberstone; for Warners. 'Stylized farce with excellent cast and considerable humour.'—*Variety*

Merton of the Movies*
US 1947 82m bw
MGM

An innocent young man in Hollywood becomes a star.
The plot and characterizations of this old chestnut are resistible, but the Hollywood background is well managed and convincing.

w George Wells, Lou Breslow, *novel* Henry Leon Wilson *d* Robert Alton *ph* Paul C. Vogel *m* David Snell

Red Skelton, Virginia O'Brien, Alan Mowbray

† There were previous versions in 1924 and (as *Make Me a Star*) in 1932.

A Message to Garcia*
US 1936 86m bw
TCF (Raymond Griffith)

During the Spanish–American war a Cuban girl helps an American agent get through to the rebel leader with a diplomatic message.
Agreeable embroidery of a historical incident: good production values and entertaining star performances.

w W. P. Lipscomb, Gene Fowler, *book* Andrew S. Rohan *d* George Marshall *ph* Rudolph Maté *m* Louis Silvers

Wallace Beery, Barbara Stanwyck, John Boles, Alan Hale, Herbert Mundin, Mona Barrie

Meteor
US 1979 107m Movielab Panavision
Palladium (Sandy Howard, Gabriel Katzka)

A huge meteor, preceded by dangerous fragments, heads relentlessly towards Earth . . .
Talkative disaster movie with occasional moments of interest.

w Stanley Mann, Edmund H. North *d* Ronald Neame *ph* Paul Lohmann *m* Laurence Rosenthal *visual effects* Margo Anderson, William Cruse

Sean Connery, Natalie Wood, Karl Malden, Brian Keith, Martin Landau, Trevor Howard, Henry Fonda, Joseph Campanella

'There are moments that make *Godzilla* look like a masterpiece.'—*Boxoffice*

Metropolis***
Germany 1926 120m approx (24 fps) bw silent
UFA (Erich Pommer)

In the year 2000, the workers in a modernistic city live underground and unrest is quelled by the persuasion of a saintly girl, Maria; but a mad inventor creates an evil Maria to incite them to revolt.
Always somewhat overlong, and certainly heavy-going in places, this futuristic fantasy not only has many brilliant sequences which created genuine excitement and terror, but it inspired a great many Hollywood clichés to come, notably the Frankenstein theme. The BBC's version of the seventies, with an electronic music sound track, is the most satisfactory.

w Thea Von Harbou d Fritz Lang ph Karl Freund, Günther Rittau sp Eugen Schufftan *ad Otto Hunte, Erich Kettelhut, Karl Vollbrecht*

Brigitte Helm, Alfred Abel, Gustav Fröhlich, Rudolf Klein-Rogge, Fritz Rasp

'It goes too far and always gets away with it.'—*New Yorker, 1978*

'A wonderful, stupefying folly.'—*New Yorker, 1982*

† In 1984 Giorgio Moroder put out his own new version, with tinted sequences and a re-edited running time of 83 minutes. It was received with a mixture of distaste, respect and caution.

Metropolitan*
US 1935 79m bw
TCF (Darryl F. Zanuck)

A capricious prima donna walks out of the Metropolitan Opera and forms her own company.
Earnest and well-made melodrama with song; it earned critical plaudits but was a disappointment at the box office.

w Bess Meredyth, George Marion Jnr
d Richard Boleslawski *ph* Rudolph Maté
md Alfred Newman

Lawrence Tibbett, Alice Brady, Virginia Bruce, Cesar Romero, Thurston Hall, Luis Alberni

'Tibbett and exploitation should carry so-so operatic story into fair money.'—*Variety*

Meurtres*
France 1950 91m bw

A doctor's wife suffering from an incurable illness begs him to give her an overdose of morphia; he does so and proposes to give himself up for murder; his family, afraid of scandal, try to have him certified. A distinct change of pace for a star comedian, and not an unsuccessful one, though the satire is rather crudely handled. *Fernandel*, Raymond Souplex, Jacques Varennes, Jeanne Moreau. Written by Charles Plisnier and Maurice Barry; directed by Richard Pottier; for Cité Film / Fides.

Mexican Hayride
US 1948 77m bw
Universal (Robert Arthur)

Various swindlers come together at a Mexican bullfight.
A Cole Porter Broadway musical without the music makes an odd sort of vehicle for Abbott and Costello, but they inject a few good vaudeville gags.

w Oscar Brodney, John Grant, *play* Herbert and Dorothy Fields *d* Charles Barton
ph Charles Van Enger

Bud Abbott, Lou Costello, Virginia Grey, John Hubbard, Pedro de Cordoba, Fritz Feld, Luba Malina

Mexican Manhunt
US 1953 73m bw

A detective helps solve an old crime. Routine support which coasts along on the strength of its star. George Brent, Hillary Brooke, Morris Ankrum, Karen Sharpe, Marjorie Lord. Written by George Bricker; directed by Rex Bailey; for Lindsley Parsons / AA.

Mexican Spitfire
A series of second feature comedies nominally about a young businessman and his temperamental Mexican wife (Donald Woods and Lupe Velez), whose interest shifted firmly to the young man's accident-prone uncle Matt and his aristocratic boss Lord Epping, both of whom were played by the rubber-legged Ziegfeld comic Leon Errol at something near the top of his form. The plots made little sense, but the hectic situations provoked hearty roars of laughter. The films were all made by RKO, and all directed by Leslie Goodwins.

1939: THE GIRL FROM MEXICO, MEXICAN SPITFIRE
1940: MEXICAN SPITFIRE OUT WEST
1941: MEXICAN SPITFIRE'S BABY, MEXICAN SPITFIRE AT SEA
1942: MEXICAN SPITFIRE SEES A GHOST, MEXICAN SPITFIRE'S ELEPHANT
1943: MEXICAN SPITFIRE'S BLESSED EVENT

Mexicana
US 1945 83m bw

The Frank Sinatra of Mexico is beset by bobbysoxers. Thin excuse for a moderate musical. Tito Guizar, Constance Moore, Leo Carrillo, Howard Freeman, Steve Geray, Estelita Rodriguez. Written by Frank Gill Jnr; directed and produced by Alfred Santell; for Republic.

'America's playground becomes gang war battleground!'

Miami Exposé
US 1956 74m bw

An undercover policeman cracks down on a vice operation. Routine thick ear with more suspense than sense. Lee J. Cobb, Patricia Medina, Edward Arnold. Written by James B. Gordon; directed by Fred F. Sears; for Sam Katzman / Columbia.

The Miami Story
US 1954 75m bw

The syndicate is cracked by a reformed gangster. Routine gangster alarms and excursions, like an extended Crime Does Not Pay. Barry Sullivan, Luther Adler, John Baer, Adele Jergens, Beverly Garland. Written by Robert E. Kent; directed by Fred F. Sears; for Sam Katzman / Columbia.

Michael and Mary
GB 1931 85m bw

A husband thought dead for many years returns to disturb his wife's second marriage. Acceptable comedy from a popular stage play; it headed its stars towards Hollywood. Herbert Marshall, Edna Best, Elizabeth Allan, Frank Lawton, D. A. Clarke-Smith. Written by Angus MacPhail, Robert Stevenson and Lajos Biro, from the play by A. A. Milne; directed by Victor Saville; for Gaumont.

Michael Shayne
The private eye created by Brett Halliday was featured in several second features starring Lloyd Nolan, mostly directed by Eugene Forde for Fox. They were adequate time-passers without too much sparkle.

1940: MICHAEL SHAYNE PRIVATE DETECTIVE
1941: DRESSED TO KILL, JUST OFF BROADWAY, THE MAN WHO WOULDN'T DIE
1942: TIME TO KILL (a version of Chandler's FAREWELL MY LOVELY), BLUE WHITE AND PERFECT

The Michigan Kid
US 1947 70m Cinecolor

Several people hunt for treasure stolen from a stagecoach. Lower berth western. Jon Hall, Victor McLaglen, Rita Johnson, Andy Devine, Byron Foulger, Milburn Stone. Written by Roy Chanslor, from a novel by Rex Beach; directed by Ray Taylor; for Universal.

Mickey One*
US 1965 93m bw
Columbia / Florin / Tatira (Arthur Penn, Harrison Starr)

A nightclub entertainer runs away after an orgy to find some meaning in his life.
Obscure symbolic melodrama whose flashes of talent and interest needed firmer control.

w Alan Surgal *d* Arthur Penn *ph* Ghislain Cloquet *m* Eddie Sauter *pd* George Jenkins

Warren Beatty, Hurd Hatfield, Alexandra Stewart, Franchot Tone, Teddy Hart, Jeff Corey

'Arresting at first, it becomes more and more bogged down by its own pretensions, until one's main interest is simply in seeing it through.'—*MFB*

Mickey's Christmas Carol***
US 1983 26m Technicolor

A cartoon version of Dickens with the parts played by familiar Disney characters; and a supreme re-establishment of the old Disney production values. Produced and directed by Burney Mattinson; for Disney. 'For anyone over 35, this little jewel of a film is truly the Ghost of Christmas Past.'—*Gilbert Adair, MFB*

Micki and Maude*
US 1984 118m Metrocolor Panavision
Columbia / Delphi III / B.E.E. (Tony Adams)

A TV show host accidentally gets his wife and his mistress pregnant at the same time.
Wild and overlong farce with some undeniably funnier scenes than have been noted in the participants' work for some years.

w Jonathan Reynolds *d* Blake Edwards
ph Harry Stradling *m* Lee Holdridge
pd Roger Maus *ed* Ralph E. Winters

Dudley Moore, Amy Irving, Ann Reinking, Richard Mulligan, George Gaynes, Wallace Shawn, John Pleshette

Midas Run
US 1969 104m Technicolor
Raymond Stross / MPI (Leon Chooluck)
GB title: *A Run on Gold*

An ageing secret service chief plans to hi-jack a bullion shipment.
Incompetently handled caper story with interest unwisely shifted for romantic purposes to the plotter's recruits.

w James D. Buchanan, Ronald Austin, Berne Giler *d* Alf Kjellin *ph* Ken Higgins *m* Elmer Bernstein

Fred Astaire, Richard Crenna, Anne Heywood, Ralph Richardson, Roddy McDowall, Adolfo Celi, Maurice Denham, Cesar Romero

Middle Age Crazy
Canada 1980 91m De Luxe

A 40-year-old husband begins to feel his age. Mildly satirical sex comedy, all too easily forgotten among the rest. Bruce Dern, Ann-Margret, Graham Jarvis, Eric Christmas. Written by Carl Kleinschmitt; directed by John Trent; for Sid and Marty Krofft / Tormont.

Middle of the Night**
US 1959 118m bw
Columbia (George Justin)

An elderly garment manufacturer falls in love with a young girl.
Serious and moving examination of a human predicament, shot against beautifully observed New York backgrounds.

w Paddy Chayevsky, from his TV play *d* Delbert Mann *ph Joseph Brun* *m* George Bassman

Fredric March, Kim Novak, Glenda Farrell, Jan Norris, Lee Grant

'A work of greater cogency than his New York play script and of deeper maturity than his *Marty*.'—*Time*

'The best of the TV transformations into film.'—*Stanley Kauffmann*

The Middle Watch
GB 1930 112m bw

Female guests on board ship have to be hidden from the captain. Naval froth in primitive talkie form; absurdly long but popular. Owen Nares, Jacqueline Logan, Jack Raine, Dodo Watts, Reginald Purdell. Written by Norman Walker and Frank Launder, from the play by Ian Hay and Stephen King-Hall; directed by Norman Walker; for BIP. (NB: In 1940 ABPC made a smoother version with Jack Buchanan, Greta Gynt, David Hutcheson, Kay Walsh, Fred Emney and Reginald Purdell [in the same role]; directed by Thomas Bentley.)

Midnight
US 1934 80m bw
Universal / All Star (Chester Erskine)
aka: *Call It Murder*

A jury foreman in a murder trial tips the scales in favour of guilty, but is haunted when his own daughter kills her lover.
Tepid family melodrama, very stagebound.

wd Chester Erskine, *play* Paul and Claire Sifton *ph* William Steiner

Sidney Fox, O. P. Heggie, Henry Hull, Humphrey Bogart, Margaret Wycherly, Lynne Overman, Richard Whorf, Cora Witherspoon

'It's pretty strong stuff and will hold audiences once they're in . . . but it's not a good adaptation and is badly dialogued.'—*Variety*

Midnight***
US 1939 95m bw
Paramount (Arthur Hornblow Jnr)

A girl stranded in Paris is hired by an aristocrat to seduce the gigolo paying unwelcome attention to his wife.
Sparkling sophisticated comedy which barely flags until a slightly disappointing ending; all the talents involved are in excellent form.

w Billy Wilder, Charles Brackett, story Edwin Justus Mayer, Franz Schultz *d Mitchell Leisen* *ph* Charles Lang *m* Frederick Hollander

Claudette Colbert, Don Ameche, *John Barrymore*, Francis Lederer, Mary Astor, Elaine Barrie, Hedda Hopper, Rex O'Malley

'Leisen's masterpiece, one of the best comedies of the thirties.'—*John Baxter, 1968*

'One of the authentic delights of the thirties.'—*New Yorker, 1976*

'It has the elements of an American *La Règle du Jeu*.'—*John Gillett*

'Just about the best light comedy ever caught by the camera.'—*Motion Picture Daily*

Midnight Club
US 1933 65m bw

An American detective in London nabs a jewel gang. Very tolerable smart-set crime melodrama. Clive Brook, George Raft, Helen Vinson, Alison Skipworth, Sir Guy Standing, Alan Mowbray. Written by Seton I. Miller and Leslie Charteris, from a story by E. Phillips Oppenheim; directed by Alexander Hall; for Paramount. 'Its London manners and locale lend it a polish which should renew interest in this school of celluloid melodramatics.'—*Variety*

'To tell you the truth, I ain't a real cowboy. But I'm one helluva stud!'
Midnight Cowboy***
US 1969 113m De Luxe
UA / Jerome Hellman

A slightly dim-witted Texan comes to New York to offer his services as a stud for rich ladies, but spends a hard winter helping a tubercular con man.
Life in the New York gutter, brilliantly if not too accurately observed by a master showman with no heart.

w Waldo Salt, *novel* James Leo Herlihy *d John Schlesinger* *ph Adam Holender* *md* John Barry *pd* John Robert Lloyd

Jon Voight, Dustin Hoffman, Brenda Vaccaro, Sylvia Miles, John McGiver

'If only Schlesinger's directorial self-discipline had matched his luminous sense of scene and his extraordinary skill in handling actors, this would have been a far more considerable film.'—*Arthur Schlesinger Jnr (no relation)*

'A great deal besides cleverness, a great deal of good feeling and perception and purposeful dexterity.'—*Stanley Kauffmann*

AA: best picture; Waldo Salt; John Schlesinger
AAN: Dustin Hoffman; Jon Voight; Sylvia Miles

Midnight Episode
GB 1950 78m bw
Columbia / Triangle (Thomas Lageard)

An old busker stumbles over a dead body and a lot of money.
Tame British version of Raimu's French success *Monsieur La Souris*, saved only by its star performance.

w Rita Barisse, Reeve Taylor, Paul Vincent Carroll, David Evans, William Templeton *d* Gordon Parry *ph* Hone Glendining

Stanley Holloway, Natasha Parry, Leslie Dwyer, Reginald Tate, Meredith Edwards, Wilfrid Hyde White, Joy Shelton

Midnight Express*
GB 1978 121m Eastmancolor
Columbia / Casablanca (Alan Marshall, David Puttnam)

Tribulations of an American student arrested in Turkey for carrying hashish.
Misleadingly-titled wallow in prison atrocities, extremely well made but certainly not entertaining and with little discernible point.

w Oliver Stone, *memoir* Billy Hayes *d* Alan Parker *ph* Michael Seresin *m* Giorgio Moroder

Brad Davis, Randy Quaid, John Hurt, Irene Miracle, Bo Hopkins

'One of the ugliest sado-masochistic trips, with heavy homosexual overtones, that our thoroughly nasty movie age has yet produced.'—*Richard Schickel, Time*

'The film details all [the horrors] so relentlessly on one screaming note that it is rather like being hit in the gut until you no longer feel a thing.'—*Derek Malcolm, The Guardian*

'Muted squalor with a disco beat in the background, all packaged as social protest.'—*New Yorker, 1982*

AA: script; music
AAN: best picture; Alan Parker; John Hurt

Midnight Lace*
US 1960 108m Eastmancolor
Universal (Ross Hunter, Martin Melcher)

The wife of a rich Londoner is terrorized by threatening phone calls and voices in the fog.
Thoroughly silly rehash of *Gaslight* and *The Boy Who Cried Wolf*; its glamorous accoutrements can't fight a lack of humour or predictable plot development.

w Ivan Goff, Ben Roberts, *play* Matilda Shouted Fire by Janet Green *d* David Miller *ph* Russell Metty *m* Frank Skinner

Doris Day, Rex Harrison, John Gavin, Myrna Loy, Roddy McDowall, Herbert Marshall, Natasha Parry, John Williams, Anthony Dawson, Hermione Baddeley, Richard Ney, Rhys Williams, Doris Lloyd

Midnight Madonna
US 1937 56m bw

There is a legal fight for custody of a child who has inherited a fortune. Efficient programmer built around a new child actress, Kitty Clancy, who didn't take. Warren William, Mady Corell, Edward Ellis, Robert Baldwin, Jonathan Hale. Written by Doris Malloy, Gladys Lehman; directed by James Flood; for Paramount. 'It will be found fairly entertaining by the family trade.'—*Variety*

The Midnight Man
US 1974 117m Technicolor
Universal / Norlan (Roland Kibbee, Burt Lancaster)

An ex-cop, paroled after killing his wife's lover, takes a job as security guard and runs into a murder case.
Muddled mystery with pretentious characterization and bouts of violence.

wd Roland Kibbee, Burt Lancaster, *novel* The Midnight Lady and the Mourning Man by David Anthony *ph* Jack Priestley *m* Dave Grusin

Burt Lancaster, Susan Clark, Cameron Mitchell, Morgan Woodward, Harris Yulin, Robert Quarry, Joan Lorring, Lawrence Dobin, Ed Lauter

'A thriller that has the impenetrability of Chandler but none of the flavour.'—*Tom Milne*

'Efficient enough but lifeless, and burdened with portentous sentiments about solitude, violence and the nature of the beast.'—*Sight and Sound*

Midnight Mary
US 1933 76m bw

A gangster's moll on trial for her life thinks back to her past. Intolerable now, but a hit of its year despite star miscasting. Loretta Young, Ricardo Cortez, Franchot Tone, Una Merkel, Andy Devine, Harold Huber. Written by Gene Markey and Anita Loos; directed by William Wellman; for MGM.

Midnight Patrol*
US 1933 20m bw

Incompetent policemen arrest their own chief as a burglar. Good standard star slapstick. Laurel and Hardy, Charlie Hall, Walter Plinge. Writer uncredited; directed by Lloyd French; for Hal Roach.

Midnight Taxi
US 1937 73m bw

A G-man becomes a taxi driver to rout a gang of counterfeiters. Competent, predictable crime programmer. Brian Donlevy, Frances Drake, Alan Dinehart, Sig Rumann, Gilbert Roland, Harold Huber, Lon Chaney Jnr. Written by Lou Breslow and John Patrick; directed by Eugene Forde; for TCF.

The Midshipmaid
GB 1932 84m bw

A naval commander loves the daughter of a politician out to effect navy cuts. Very modest comedy with music, a key step in the star's success story. Jessie Matthews, Frederick Kerr, Basil Sydney, Nigel Bruce, Claud Allister, John Mills, George Zucco. Written by Ian Hay and Stephen King-Hall, from their play; directed by Albert de Courville; for Gaumont. (US title: *Midshipmaid Gob*.)

Midshipman Easy
GB 1935 77m bw
ATP (Basil Dean, Thorold Dickinson)
US title: *Men of the Sea*

In 1790, young naval officers rescue a girl from Spanish bandits.
Stilted adventure story with interesting credits.

w Anthony Kimmins, *novel* Frederick Marryat *d* Carol Reed *ph* John W. Boyle

Hughie Green, Margaret Lockwood, Harry Tate, Robert Adams, Roger Livesey, Lewis Casson

'Three centuries in the making!'

A Midsummer Night's Dream***
US 1935 133m bw
Warner (Max Reinhardt)

Two pairs of lovers sort out their problems with fairy help at midnight in the woods of Athens.
Shakespeare's play is treated with remarkable respect in this super-glamorous Hollywood adaptation based on the Broadway production by Max Reinhardt. Much of it comes off, and visually it's a treat.

w Charles Kenyon, Mary McCall Jnr, *play* William Shakespeare *d Max Reinhardt, William Dieterle ph Hal Mohr, Fred Jackman, Byron Haskin, H. F. Koenekamp*
m Mendelssohn *md Erich Wolfgang Korngold ch Bronislawa Nijinska ad Anton Grot*

James Cagney, Dick Powell, Jean Muir, Ross Alexander, Olivia de Havilland, Joe E. Brown, Hugh Herbert, Arthur Treacher, Frank McHugh, Otis Harlan, Dewey Robinson, *Victor Jory*, Verree Teasdale, *Mickey Rooney*, Anita Louise, Grant Mitchell, Ian Hunter, Hobart Cavanaugh

'General b.o. chances could be improved by judicious pruning and appreciative selling . . . a fine prestige picture not only for Warners but for the industry as a whole.'—*Variety*

'You must see it if you want to be in a position to argue about the future of the film!'—*Picturegoer*

'The publicity push behind the film is tremendous—it is going to be a success or everyone at Warner Brothers is going to get fired.'—*Robert Forsythe*

'Its assurance as a work of film technique is undoubted.'—*John Baxter, 1968*

'Its worst contradiction lies in the way Warners first ordered up a whole batch of foreign and high-sounding names to handle music, dances, general production—and then turned around and handed them empty vessels for actors.'—*Otis Ferguson*

AA: photography
AAN: best picture

A Midsummer Night's Sex Comedy*
US 1982 88m Technicolor
Warner / Orion / Rollins-Joffe (Robert Greenhut)

Around the turn of the century, a Wall Street broker expects various weekend guests at his country retreat.
Subdued, melancholy and rather uninventive Woody Allen variation on *Smiles of a Summer Night*.

wd Woody Allen *ph* Gordon Willis *m* from Mendelssohn *pd* Mel Bourne *ed* Susan E. Morse

Woody Allen, Mia Farrow, Jose Ferrer, Julie Hagerty, Tony Roberts, Mary Steenburgen

Midway*
US 1976 131m Technicolor Panavision Sensurround
Universal / Mirisch Corporation (Walter Mirisch)
GB title: *The Battle of Midway*

The tide turns for the Americans when the Japanese attack the Pacific island of Midway in 1942.
Noisy flagwaver with confused strategy and too many stars in small parts.

w Donald S. Sanford *d* Jack Smight
ph Harry Stradling Jnr *m* John Williams

Charlton Heston, Henry Fonda, Robert Mitchum, Glenn Ford, Edward Albert, James Coburn, Hal Holbrook, Toshiro Mifune, Robert Wagner, Robert Webber, Ed Nelson, James Shigeta, Monte Markham, Chris George, Glenn Corbett

'We are over-informed about the movements of every ship and plane, under-informed about how the battle was finally won, and positively swamped with tedious human interest.'—*Sight and Sound*

The Mighty Barnum*
US 1934 87m bw
Twentieth Century (Darryl F. Zanuck)

A fictionalized biopic of the great showman of the nineties.
Lively without being very memorable.

w Gene Fowler, Bess Meredyth from their play *d* Walter Lang *ph* Peverell Marley
m Alfred Newman

Wallace Beery, Virginia Bruce, Adolphe Menjou, Janet Beecher, Rochelle Hudson

'The ten most terrific thrills ever pictured!'

Mighty Joe Young*
US 1949 94m bw
RKO (Merian C. Cooper)

A little girl brings back from Africa a pet gorilla which grows to enormous size and causes a city to panic.

MIDNIGHT. Mitchell Leisen was in peak form and clearly Don Ameche and Claudette Colbert responded in kind. John Barrymore looks on.

Rather tired comic-sentimental follow-up to *King Kong*, with a tedious plot and variable animation but a few endearing highlights.

w Ruth Rose *d* Ernest Schoedsack *ph* J. Roy Hunt *m* Roy Webb *sp* Willis O'Brien, Ray Harryhausen

Terry Moore, Ben Johnson, Robert Armstrong, Frank McHugh, Douglas Fowley

The Mighty McGurk
US 1946 bw 83m

In the Bowery in the 1890s, a bragging ex-fighter takes in a small boy. Sentimental melodrama which unspools like a joint remake of *The Champ* and *The Bowery*. Wallace Beery, Dean Stockwell, Edward Arnold, Aline MacMahon, Cameron Mitchell, Aubrey Mather. Written by William H. Lipman, Grant Garrett, Harry Clork; directed by John Waters; for Nat Perrin / MGM.

The Mikado*
GB 1939 91m Technicolor
GFD / G and S (Geoffrey Toye, Joseph Somlo)

In Japan, a timid official is appointed Lord High Executioner and finds that his first intended victim is the Emperor's son, travelling incognito.
Agreeable film version of the classic Gilbert and Sullivan comic opera, with some of the D'Oyly Carte Company's most celebrated members in excellent form.

w Geoffrey Toye, *opera* W. S. Gilbert *m* Arthur Sullivan *d* Victor Schertzinger *ph* Bernard Knowles

Martyn Green, John Barclay, Sydney Granville, Kenny Baker, Jean Colin, Constance Willis

† The 1966 version by British Home Entertainment featured a later D'Oyly Carte company including John Reed but suffered from a frozen camera and flat lighting, so that little of the original vivacity and charm came over.

Mikey and Nicky
US 1976 118m colour
Paramount (Michael Hausman)

Two crooks are old friends, but one has been hired to kill the other . . .
Intolerable improvisatory sentimental melodrama. Who on earth shells out the money for pictures like this?

wd Elaine May *ph* Victor Kemper *m* John Strauss

Peter Falk, John Cassavetes, Ned Beatty, Sanford Meisner, Rose Arrick, Joyce Van Patten

'An impenetrable, ugly and almost unendurable mess.'—*Frank Rich, New York Post*

'A pretext for Falk and Cassavetes to indulge in one of those long, lugubrious Actors' Studio exercises that wore out its welcome with the last frame of *Husbands* and the first frame of *The Killing of a Chinese Bookie*.'—*Molly Haskell, Village Voice*

The Milagro Beanfield War
US 1988 118m MGM color Universal (Robert Redford)

Impoverished farmers in New Mexico defy developers who try to take over their land.
Serious issues treated with quirky humour and visual lyricism.

w David Ward, John Nichols, from book by Nichols *d* Robert Redford *ph* Robbie Greenberg *m* Dave Grusin *ad* Joe Aubel

Ruben Blades, Richard Bradford, Sonia Braga, Julie Carmen, James Gammon, John Heard, M. Emmet Walsh

'A very peculiar mixture of warmed-over movie conventions.'—*MFB*

'The kind of woman most men want . . . and shouldn't have!'
Mildred Pierce**
US 1945 113m bw
Warner (Jerry Wald)

A dowdy housewife breaks with her husband, becomes the owner (through hard work) of a restaurant chain, and survives a murder case before true love comes her way.
A woman's picture par excellence, glossily and moodily photographed, with a star suffering in luxury on behalf of the most ungrateful daughter of all time.

w Ranald MacDougall, Catherine Turney, *novel* James M. Cain *d Michael Curtiz ph Ernest Haller m Max Steiner ad Anton Grot*

Joan Crawford, Jack Carson, Zachary Scott, *Eve Arden, Ann Blyth,* Bruce Bennett, George Tobias, Lee Patrick, Moroni Olsen

'Constant, lambent, virulent attention to money and its effects, and more authentic suggestions of sex than one hopes to see in American films.'—*James Agee*

AA: Joan Crawford
AAN: best picture; script; Ernest Haller; Eve Arden; Ann Blyth

The Milkman
US 1950 87m bw
Universal-International (Ted Richmond)

Two milkmen tangle with gangsters.
Odd little comedy which gets the benefit of the doubt more by bringing its stars together than by giving them anything to do.

w Albert Beich, James O'Hanlon, Martin Ragaway, Leonard Stern *d* Charles Barton *ph* Clifford Stine *m* Milton Rosen

Donald O'Connor, Jimmy Durante, Joyce Holden, Piper Laurie, William Conrad, Paul Harvey, Henry O'Neill

The Milky Way*
US 1936 88m bw
Paramount / Harold Lloyd (Edward Sheldon)

A milkman becomes a prizefighter and overcomes a gang of crooks.
Modest Harold Lloyd comedy towards the end of his career; remade as *The Kid from Brooklyn* (qv).

w Grover Jones, Frank Butler, Richard Connell, *play* Lynn Root, Harry Clark *ph* Alfred Gilks *d* Leo McCarey

Harold Lloyd, Adolphe Menjou, Verree Teasdale, Helen Mack, William Gargan, George Barbier, Lionel Stander

'The work of many hands, all laid on expertly.'—*Otis Ferguson*

'One is more amazed than ever at the good fortune of this youngish man whose chief talent is not to act at all, to do nothing, to serve as a blank wall for other people to scrawl their ideas on.'—*Graham Greene*

The Milky Way*
France / Italy 1968 102m Eastmancolor
Greenwich / Medusa (Serge Silberman)
original title: *La Voie Lactée*

Two tramps set off on pilgrimage from Paris to a Spanish shrine, and have various surprising encounters.
A picaresque examination of Catholic doctrine, full of surface interest but requiring special knowledge for full appreciation.

w Luis Bunuel, Jean-Claude Carrière *d Luis Bunuel ph* Christian Matras *m* Luis Bunuel

Laurent Terzieff, Paul Frankeur, Delphine Seyrig, Edith Scon

'A mere trifle wrapped in a triple cloak of befuddling obscurantism.'—*John Simon*

The Mill on the Floss
GB 1937 94m bw

A Victorian mill owner and the lord of the manor start a family feud which ends in tragedy. Romeo and Juliet in crinolines; a stilted and unpersuasive film of the book. Geraldine Fitzgerald, Frank Lawton, James Mason, Victoria Hopper, Fay Compton, Griffith Jones, Mary Clare, Athene Seyler, Felix Aylmer. Written by John Drinkwater, Garnett Weston, Austin Melford and Tim Whelan, from the novel by George Eliot; directed by Tim Whelan; for Morgan / National Provincial. 'A series of stiff little sequences, decorously posed.'—*New York Times.*

Le Million****
France 1931 89m bw
Tobis (Frank Clifford)

An artist and an ingratiating crook search Paris for a lost lottery ticket.
With its delicate touch, perfect sense of comedy timing and infectious use of recitative and song, this is superb screen entertainment using most of the medium's resources.

wd René Clair, musical comedy Georges Berr, M. Guillemaud *ph* Georges Périnal *m Georges Van Parys, Armand Bernard, Philippe Parès ad* Lazare Meerson

Annabella, René Lefèvre, *Paul Olivier*, Louis Allibert, Vanda Gréville, Raymond Cordy

'A good musical farce that ought to do well everywhere . . . it has speed, laughs, splendid photography and a good cast.'—*Variety*

'René Clair at his exquisite best; no one else has ever been able to make a comedy move with such delicate inevitability.'—*New Yorker, 1978*

'I wanted an atmosphere of foolishness . . . we put gauze between the actors and the sets, which created an illusion of unreality.'—*René Clair*

† The style of this film was developed and expanded in Hollywood by Lubitsch in *One Hour with You* and by Mamoulian in *Love Me Tonight.*

Million Dollar Baby
US 1941 100m bw
Warner (Hal B. Wallis, David Lewis)

A girl inherits a fortune and a lot of problems.
Very predictable but sometimes sprightly comedy with a hard-working cast.

w Richard Macaulay, Jerry Wald, Casey Robinson, *story* Miss Wheelwright Discovers America by Leonard Spiegelgass *d* Curtis Bernhardt *ph* Charles Rosher *m* Max Steiner

Priscilla Lane, Jeffrey Lynn, Ronald Reagan, May Robson, Lee Patrick, Helen Westley, George Barbier, John Qualen, Walter Catlett, Nan Wynn

Million Dollar Duck
US 1971 92m Technicolor
Walt Disney (Bill Anderson)

A duck lays eggs with solid gold yolks, which provoke interest from gangsters as well as the government.
Minor Disney fantasy borrowed without permission from *Mr Drake's Duck* (qv).

w Roswell Rogers *d* Vincent McEveety *ph* William Snyder *m* Buddy Baker

Dean Jones, Sandy Dennis, Joe Flynn

'Roaring laughs in a story built of goofer dust and frog fur!'
Million Dollar Legs*
US 1932 64m bw
Paramount

A mythical sport-ridden country decides to enter the Olympic Games.
The good gags in this film are weighted down by plodding treatment, and the general effect is more doleful than funny.

w Harry Myers, Nick Barrows, Joseph L. Mankiewicz *d* Edward Cline *ph* Arthur Todd

W. C. Fields, Jack Oakie, Andy Clyde, Lyda Roberti, Ben Turpin, Hugh Herbert, Billy Gilbert, George Barbier, Susan Fleming

'One of the silliest and funniest pictures ever made.'—*New Yorker, 1977*

Million Dollar Legs
US 1939 59m bw
Paramount

College students back a favourite horse. Very modest collegiate comedy.

w Lewis Foster, Richard English *d* Nick Grinde *ph* Harry Fischbeck

Betty Grable, John Hartley, Donald O'Connor, Jackie Coogan, Buster Crabbe, Thurston Hall

Million Dollar Mermaid*
US 1952 115m Technicolor
MGM (Arthur Hornblow Jnr)
GB title: *The One Piece Bathing Suit*

The story of Australian swimmer Annette Kellerman.
Inaccurate biopic with a *raison d'être* in its spectacular aquashow scenes, but nothing at all new in its script.

w Everett Freeman *d* Mervyn Le Roy *ph* George J. Folsey *md* Adolph Deutsch *ch Busby Berkeley*

Esther Williams, Victor Mature, Walter Pidgeon, David Brian, Jesse White, Maria Tallchief, Howard Freeman

AAN: George J. Folsey

Million Dollar Ransom
US 1934 67m bw

A racketeer consolidates his family affairs before being bumped off by his gang. Slightly odd underworld melodrama, interesting but not very satisfying. Edward Arnold, Phillips Holmes, Mary Carlisle, Wini Shaw, Andy Devine. Written by William R. Lipman, Ben Ryan, from a story by Damon Runyon; directed by Murray Roth; for Universal. 'Lacks names but offers fair possibilities.'—*Variety*

The Million Pound Note*
GB 1954 91m Technicolor
GFD / Group Films (John Bryan)
US title: *Man with a Million*

A man inherits a million dollars in the form of a single banknote and finds it difficult to spend.
Fairly pleasing period comedy which wears its one joke pretty thin but is nicely decorated and acted.

w Jill Craigie, *story* Mark Twain *d* Ronald Neame *ph* Geoffrey Unsworth *m* William Alwyn

Gregory Peck, Jane Griffiths, Ronald Squire, Joyce Grenfell, A. E. Matthews, Reginald Beckwith, Hartley Power, Wilfrid Hyde White

The Millionaire*
US 1931 80m bw

A bored millionaire retires and secretly buys a garage. Fairly deft star comedy which well satisfied depression audiences. *George Arliss*, Florence Arliss, Evalyn Knapp, David Manners, Noah Beery, J. Farrell MacDonald, James Cagney. Written by Julien Josephson and Booth Tarkington, from a story by Earl Derr Biggers; directed by John Adolfi; for Warner. (NB: Remade in 1947 as *That Way with Women* [qv].) 'Should bring Arliss within mental reach of all theatres. . . Should enjoy a substantial career.'—*Variety*

A Millionaire for Christy
US 1951 91m bw
TCF (Bert Friedlob)

A lawyer's secretary is sent to Los Angeles to inform an heir of his good fortune, and decides to marry him.
Modest romantic comedy with plenty to be modest about.

w Ken Englund *d* George Marshall *ph* Harry Stradling *m* Victor Young

Eleanor Parker, Fred MacMurray, Richard Carlson, Douglass Dumbrille

'From naughty, notorious George Bernard Shaw, the sultry story of the beautiful babe in the Balmain gowns who pants for romance . . . !'

The Millionairess*
GB 1960 90m De Luxe Cinemascope
TCF / Dimitri de Grunwald (Pierre Rouve)

The richest woman in the world falls for a poor Indian doctor.
Messy travesty of a Shavian comedy that was never more than a star vehicle to begin with. Hardly any of it works despite the star cast, who are mostly miscast.

w Wolf Mankowitz, *play* Bernard Shaw *d* Anthony Asquith *ph* Jack Hildyard *m* Georges Van Parys

Sophia Loren, Peter Sellers, Alastair Sim, Vittorio de Sica, Dennis Price, Gary Raymond, Alfie Bass, Miriam Karlin, Noel Purcell

'The result, lacking any sort of dramatic cohesion or continuity and seemingly planned less as a film than as a series of haphazard effects, is merely tiring.'—*Peter John Dyer*

Millions
GB 1936 70m bw

A struggling composer is really the son of a millionaire. Fairly lively comedy of rival self-made men. Gordon Harker, Frank Pettingell, Richard Hearne, Jane Carr. Written by Michael Barringer; directed by Leslie Hiscott; for Herbert Wilcox.

Millions in the Air
US 1935 72m bw

Complications of a radio amateur contest. Scrappy comedy with more historical interest than entertainment value. Willie Howard, John Howard, Robert Cummings, Inez Courtney, Benny Baker, Dave Chasen, Wendy Barrie, Samuel S. Hinds. Written by Sig Herzig, Jane Storm; directed by Ray McCarey; for Harold Hurley / Paramount. 'Without a substantial monicker in the cast, it hasn't much to offer at the box office.'—*Variety*

Millions like Us**
GB 1943 103m bw
GFD / Gainsborough (Edward Black)

The tribulations of a family in wartime, especially of the meek daughter who goes into war work and marries an airman, who is killed.
Fragmentary but reasonably accurate picture of the Home Front during World War II; a little more humour would not have been out of place, but as propaganda it proved an effective weapon.

wd Frank Launder, Sidney Gilliat ph Jack Cox *md* Louis Levy

Patricia Roc, Gordon Jackson, Moore Marriott, Eric Portman, Anne Crawford, Basil Radford, Naunton Wayne, Joy Shelton, Megs Jenkins

'There is an unsentimental warmheartedness which I hope we shall cling to and extend in filmed representations of the British scene.'—*Richard Winnington*

† The only picture Launder and Gilliat directed side by side on the floor.

Mills of the Gods
US 1934 66m bw

An elderly businesswoman, unimpressed by her family, turns her business over to a committee of executives. Interesting plot which would have justified better production. May Robson, Fay Wray, Victor Jory, Raymond Walburn, Mayo Methot. Written by Garrett Fort, John S. Kirkland, Melville Baker; directed by Roy William Neill; for Columbia. 'Stilted story with some good trouping. A double-upper.'—*Variety*

Mimi
GB 1935 94m bw

In a Paris garret, a poor girl dies after encouraging a playwright. *La Bohème* without the music; not a good idea. Douglas Fairbanks Jnr, Gertrude Lawrence, Diana Napier, Harold Warrender, Carol Goodner, Richard Bird. Written by Clifford Grey, Paul Merzbach, Jack Davies and Denis Waldock, from the novel *La Vie Bohème* by Henri Murger; directed by Paul Stein; for BIP.

'A cyclone of human emotion roars across the screen!'

Min and Bill**
US 1930 69m bw
MGM

A boozy old waterfront character and his wife try to keep her daughter from being placed in care.
Well-remembered and much-loved character comedy which led to the even more successful *Tugboat Annie* with the same team.

w Frances Marion, Marion Jackson, *play* Dark Star by Lorna Moon *d* George Hill *ph* Harold Wenstrom

Marie Dressler, Wallace Beery, Dorothy Jordan, Marjorie Rambeau, Donald Dillaway, Russell Hopton

'Comedy-drama of distinction. All ingredients for all theatres, from keys down.'—*Variety*

AA: Marie Dressler

The Mind Benders*
GB 1963 113m bw
Anglo–Amalgamated / Novus (Michael Relph)

A scientist undergoes an experiment aimed at depriving him of all sensation. It works too well; he becomes a sadist; and his colleagues can't reverse the process.
Matter-of-factly played hocus-pocus with spy asides; quite gripping while it's on, but in no way memorable.

w James Kennaway *d* Basil Dearden *ph* Denys Coop *m* Georges Auric

Dirk Bogarde, John Clements, Mary Ure, Michael Bryant

The Mind of Mr Reeder*
GB 1939 75m bw

An elderly government employee unmasks a forger and murderer. Entertaining crime comedy-drama which never quite realizes its potential. Will Fyffe, Kay Walsh, George Curzon, Chili Bouchier, John Warwick. Written by Bryan Edgar Wallace, Marjorie Gaffney and Michael Hogan, from the novel by Edgar Wallace; directed and produced by Jack Raymond.

The Mind of Mr Soames
GB 1970 98m Technicolor
Columbia / Amicus (Teresa Bolland)

A man who has lived in a coma for thirty years is cured but faces the world as a new-born infant.
Ill-advised attempt at science fiction with meaning; its earnestness becomes a bore.

w John Hale, Edward Simpson, *novel* Charles Eric Maine *d* Alan Cooke *ph* Billy Williams *m* Michael Dress

Terence Stamp, Robert Vaughn, Nigel Davenport, Donal Donnelly, Christian Roberts, Vickery Turner, Scott Forbes

The Mind Reader*
US 1933 69m bw

A phoney mind reader tries to go straight for his wife's sake, and ends up in jail. Reasonably mordant satirical drama with good performances. *Warren William*, Constance Cummings, Allen Jenkins, Donald Dillaway, Mayo Methot, Clarence Muse. Written by Wilson Mizner and Robert Lord, from the play by Vivian Cosby; directed by Roy del Ruth; for Warners. 'Star performance plus laugh dialogue enough to send this into okay programmer class.'—*Variety*

Mind Your Own Business
US 1937 75m bw

Boy scouts help to capture gangsters. Slightly rocky comedy which finally comes across as unsatisfactory. Charles Ruggles, Alice Brady, Lyle Talbot, Benny Baker, Jack La Rue, William Demarest, Frankie Darro. Written by Dore Schary from a story by John Francis Larkin; directed by Norman Z. McLeod; for Emmanuel Cohen / Paramount. 'It will have a tough time standing alone.'—*Variety*

Mine Own Executioner***
GB 1947 108m bw
London Films

A lay psychiatrist undertakes the care of a mentally disturbed war veteran, but fails to prevent him from murdering his wife.
When this film first appeared it seemed like the first adult drama featuring sophisticated people to emerge from a British studio. Time and television have blunted its impact, but it remains a well told suspense melodrama with memorable characters.

w Nigel Balchin, from his novel *d Anthony Kimmins ph* Wilkie Cooper *m* Benjamin Frankel

Burgess Meredith, Kieron Moore, Dulcie Gray, Barbara White, Christine Norden

'The first psychoanalytical film that a grown-up can sit through without squirming.'—*Richard Winnington*

'One feels invigorated by having seen and understood other people's lives.'—*Daily Worker*

'His secret meant death to one man if he didn't talk . . . to countless thousands if he did!'

Ministry of Fear**
US 1944 85m bw
Paramount (Seton I. Miller)

During World War II in England, a man just out of a mental hospital wins a cake at a village fair and finds himself caught up in bewildering intrigues.
Little to do with the novel, but a watchable, well-detailed little thriller on Hitchcock lines, once you forgive the usual phoney Hollywood England.

w Seton I. Miller, *novel* Graham Greene *d Fritz Lang ph Henry Sharp m* Victor Young

Ray Milland, Marjorie Reynolds, Carl Esmond, Hillary Brooke, Dan Duryea, Percy Waram, Alan Napier, Erskine Sanford

'A crisp and efficiently made thriller with no pretension to intellectual content.'—*Paul Jensen*

The Miniver Story
GB 1950 104m bw
MGM (Sidney Franklin)

Mrs Miniver faces the tribulations of post-war Britain.
Glum sequel to *Mrs Miniver*, with the dauntless heroine finally succumbing to a glossy but fatal disease. Well enough made, but very hard to take.

w Ronald Millar, George Froeschel *d* H. C. Potter *ph* Joseph Ruttenberg *m* Miklos Rozsa

Greer Garson, Walter Pidgeon, Cathy O'Donnell, John Hodiak, Leo Genn, Reginald Owen, Henry Wilcoxon, William Fox, Anthony Bushell

Minnie and Moskowitz*
US 1971 115m Technicolor
Universal (Al Rubin)

Two lonely Los Angeles misfits have a bumpy courtship.
Enjoyably aimless character comedy.

wd John Cassavetes *ph* Arthur J. Ornitz *m* Bob Harwood

Gena Rowlands, Seymour Cassel

Minstrel Man*
US 1944 70m bw

A minstrel star seeks his long-lost daughter. Interesting sidelights on old-time minstrel shows in a production somewhat less tatty than is usual from this company. Benny Fields, Gladys George, Roscoe Karns. Written by Irwin Franklin and Pierre Gendron; directed by Joseph H. Lewis; for PRC.

AAN: song, 'Remember Me to Carolina'.

The Miracle
Italy 1948 40m bw
Tania Film (Roberto Rossellini)

A simple-minded peasant woman is seduced by a shepherd but believes her baby has been immaculately conceived.
Curious, rather unsatisfactory parable originally intended as part of a two-item tribute to the power of a star actress. (The other section, Cocteau's *The Human Voice*, was withdrawn for copyright reasons.)

w Tullio Pinelli, Roberto Rossellini, Federico Fellini *d* Roberto Rossellini *ph* Aldo Tonti *m* Renzo Rossellini

Anna Magnani, Federico Fellini

'Acting on a plane scarcely known to the cinema.'—*Sunday Times*

'The mightiest story of fame and the flesh known to our time!'

The Miracle
US 1959 121m Technirama
Warner (Henry Blanke)

In Spain during the Peninsular War, a nun breaks her vows in order to follow a British soldier, and a statue of the Virgin Mary steps down to take her place.
And that's only the beginning in this very tall tale, full of heavy breathing, violent action and religiosity, from the old Max Reinhardt pageant. Quite incredible, and sloppily done.

w Frank Butler, *play* Karl Vollmoeller *d* Irving Rapper *ph* Ernest Haller *m* Elmer Bernstein

Carroll Baker, Roger Moore, Walter Slezak, Vittorio Gassman, Katina Paxinou, Dennis King, Isobel Elsom, Torin Thatcher

Miracle in Milan**
Italy 1951 101m bw
PDS / ENIC (Vittorio De Sica)

A foundling goes to live with the poor on the outskirts of Milan, and his erstwhile guardian returns from heaven to help them repel capitalists and fly away on broomsticks to a better land.
An unlikely fable which manages to avoid all the obvious pitfalls and sends one out of the cinema in a warm glow.

w Cesare Zavattini, Vittorio de Sica, *novel* Toto il Buono by Cesare Zavattini *d Vittorio de Sica* *ph* G. R. Aldo *m* Alessandro Cicognini

Francesco Golisano, Brunella Bovo, Emma Gramatica, Paolo Stoppa

Miracle in Soho
GB 1957 93m Eastmancolor
Rank (Emeric Pressburger)

A Soho roadworker falls for a barmaid.
Rudimentary romantic whimsy in an unconvincing street set, with characters either too voluble or just plain dull.

w Emeric Pressburger *d* Julian Amyes *ph* Christopher Challis *m* Brian Easdale

John Gregson, Belinda Lee, Cyril Cusack

'A street corner pick-up that worked a miracle of love! A picture of very special greatness!'

Miracle in the Rain**
US 1954 107m bw
Warner (Frank P. Rosenberg)

A plain New York girl falls for a soldier; when he is killed in action, he keeps their appointment on the church steps as a ghost.
Archetypal Hollywood schmaltz, half acute observation of amusing types, half sentimental whimsy, with a final supernatural touch of eating your cake and having it.

w Ben Hecht d Rudolph Maté ph Russell Metty m Franz Waxman

Jane Wyman, Van Johnson, Fred Clark, Eileen Heckart, William Gargan

The Miracle Man
US 1932 85m bw
Paramount

A gang of crooks is reformed by a faith healer they have exploited.
Adequate remake of the silent Lon Chaney vehicle; no sparks this time.

w Waldemar Young, Samuel Hoffenstein, *play* Frank L. Packard, George M. Cohan *d* Norman Z. McLeod *ph* David Abel *m* W. Franke Marling

Sylvia Sidney, Chester Morris, Irving Pichel, John Wray, Robert Coogan, Hobart Bosworth, Boris Karloff, Ned Sparks, Virginia Bruce

The Miracle of Morgan's Creek***
US 1943 99m bw
Paramount (Preston Sturges)

Chaos results when a stuttering hayseed tries to help a girl accidentally pregnant by a soldier she met hazily at a dance.
Weird and wonderful one-man assault on the Hays Office and sundry other American institutions such as motherhood and politics; an indescribable, tasteless, roaringly funny mêlée, as unexpected at the time as it was effective, like a kick in the pants to all other film comedies.

wd Preston Sturges *ph* John Seitz *m* Leo Shuken, Charles Bradshaw

Betty Hutton, Eddie Bracken, William Demarest, Diana Lynn, Porter Hall, Akim Tamiroff, Brian Donlevy, Alan Bridge

OFFICER KOCKENLOCKER (William Demarest): 'Daughters. They're a mess no matter how you look at 'em. A headache till they get married—*if* they get married—and after that they get worse . . . Either they leave their husbands and come back with four kids and move into your guest room or the husband loses his job and the whole caboodle comes back. Or else they're so homely that you can't get rid of them at all and they sit around like Spanish moss and shame you into an early grave.'

EMILY KOCKENLOCKER (Diana Lynn): 'If you don't mind my mentioning it, father, I think you have a mind like a swamp.'

'Like taking a nun on a roller coaster.'—*James Agee*

'This film moves in a fantastic and irreverent whirl of slapstick, nonsense, farce, sentiment, satire, romance, melodrama—is there any ingredient of dramatic entertainment except maybe tragedy and grand opera that hasn't been tossed into it?'—*National Board of Review*

'Bad taste or no bad taste, I thoroughly enjoyed it.'—*Richard Mallett, Punch*

AAN: Preston Sturges (as writer)

The Miracle of Our Lady of Fatima
US 1952 102m Warnercolor
Warner (Bryan Foy)
GB title: *The Miracle of Fatima*

An account of the 1917 appearance of the Virgin Mary to three Portuguese peasant children.
Poorly staged religious film which manages to be less pro-Catholic than anti-communist, and was clearly seen by Jack L. Warner as a means of atoning for *Mission to Moscow.* A real cold war piece.

w Crane Wilbur, James O'Hanlon *d* John Brahm *ph* Edwin DuPar *m* Max Steiner *ad* Edward Carrere

Gilbert Roland, Frank Silvera, Angela Clarke, Jay Novello

AAN: Max Steiner

The Miracle of the Bells
US 1948 120m bw
Jesse L. Lasky

The death of a glamorous film star causes a small-town miracle and a nationwide publicity stunt.
One hopes that this oddity was intended as a satire; as a straight entertainment it's more than a little icky, and good production values scarcely help.

w Ben Hecht, *novel* Russell Janney *d* Irving Rapper *ph* Robert de Grasse *m* Leigh Harline

Fred MacMurray, Alida Valli, Frank Sinatra, Lee J. Cobb

'An offensive exhibition of vulgar insensitivity.'—*MFB*

'I hereby declare myself the founding father of the Society for the Prevention of Cruelty to God.'—*James Agee*

The Miracle of the White Stallions*
US 1962 118m Technicolor
Walt Disney (Peter V. Herald)
GB title: *The Flight of the White Stallions*

During World War II the Nazis occupy Vienna and the owner of the Spanish Riding School guides his stallions to safety.
Adequate family adventure fare with a dull hero but interesting backgrounds.

w A. J. Carothers *d* Arthur Hiller *ph* Gunther Anders *m* Paul Smith

Robert Taylor, Lilli Palmer, Eddie Albert, Curt Jurgens

Miracle on Main Street*
US 1940 76m bw
RKO / Jack Skirball

A cabaret dancer finds an abandoned baby but her plans are thwarted by the return of her husband.
Odd, interesting but flatly handled melodrama.

w Sam Ornitz, Boris Ingster, *story* Felix Jackson *d* Steve Sekely *ph* Charles Van Enger *m* Walter Jurmann, Hans Salter

Walter Abel, Margo, William Collier, Jane Darwell, Lyle Talbot, Wynne Gibson

Miracle on 34th Street***
US 1947 94m bw
TCF (William Perlberg)
GB title: *The Big Heart*

A department store Santa Claus claims to be the real thing.
Mainly charming comedy fantasy which quickly became an American classic but does suffer from a few dull romantic stretches.

wd George Seaton, story Valentine Davies *ph* Charles Clarke, Lloyd Ahern *m* Cyril Mockridge

Edmund Gwenn, Maureen O'Hara, John Payne, Natalie Wood, Gene Lockhart, Porter Hall, William Frawley, Jerome Cowan, Thelma Ritter

'Altogether wholesome, stimulating and enjoyable.'—*Motion Picture Herald*

AA: George Seaton (as writer); Valentine Davies; Edmund Gwenn
AAN: best picture

The Miracle Rider
US 1935 bw serial: 15 eps

A captain in the Texas Rangers is made a blood brother of the Ravenhead tribe, but the activities of a villain named Zaroff strain the friendship. Unpretentious serial exploits. Tom Mix, Charles Middleton, Jean Gale, Jason Robards. Directed by Armand Schaefer and B. Reeves Eason; for Mascot.

'Never give away what you can sell!'

The Miracle Woman*
US 1932 90m bw
Columbia (Harry Cohn)

A lady evangelist turns confidence trickster. Mild satirical drama inspired by the career of Aimée Semple Macpherson.

w Jo Swerling, *play* Bless You Sister by Robert Riskin, John Meehan *d Frank Capra* *ph* Joseph Walker *m* uncredited

Barbara Stanwyck, Sam Hardy, David Manners, Beryl Mercer, Russell Hopton

'Splendid programme leader, a big and strong film opening up numerous channels of publicity.'—*Variety*

'Such a beauty, well staged and handsomely lighted.'—*New Yorker, 1977*

The Miracle Worker*
US 1962 106m bw
UA / Playfilms (Fred Coe)

The childhood of Helen Keller, taught by Annie Sullivan after being left blind, deaf and dumb in an illness.
A moving real-life story is given hysterical treatment and the good scenes have a hard task winning through; in any case a documentary might have been more persuasive.

w William Gibson, from his play *d* Arthur Penn *ph* Ernest Caparros *m* Laurence Rosenthal *ad* George Jenkins

Anne Bancroft, Patty Duke, Victor Jory, Inga Swenson, Andrew Prine, Beah Richards

AA: Anne Bancroft; Patty Duke
AAN: William Gibson; Arthur Penn

Miracles
US 1985 87m Technicolor Super Techniscope
Orion / Steve Roth, Bernard Williams

A chase begins when bank robbers kidnap an innocent couple.
Exhausting action comedy with no real finesse.

w,d Jim Kouf *ph* John Alcott *m* Peter Bernstein *pd* Terence Marsh

Tom Conti, Teri Garr, Paul Rodriguez, Christopher Lloyd

Miracles for Sale
US 1939 71m bw

An illusionist catches a murderer. What could have been a smart mystery piece is sabotaged by stilted writing and direction, a muddled narrative style, and illusions which are patently faked by the camera. Robert Young, Florence Rice, Henry Hull, Frank Craven, Lee Bowman, William Demarest. Written by James Edward Grant, Marion Parsonnet and Harry Ruskin, from the novel *Death in a Top Hat* by Clayton Rawson; directed by Tod Browning; for MGM. 'Unexciting whodunit . . . the plot stumbles over itself most of the time.'—*Variety*

Mirage**
US 1965 109m bw
U-I (Harry Keller)

During a New York power blackout, an executive falls to his death from a skyscraper and a cost accountant loses his memory.
Striking puzzler, rather slowly developed but generally effective and with a strong sense of place and timing.

w Peter Stone, novel Walter Ericson
d Edward Dmytryk *ph* Joe MacDonald
m Quincy Jones

Gregory Peck, Diane Baker, Walter Abel, *Walter Matthau*, Leif Erickson, Kevin McCarthy

'Worthy of Hitchcock at his vintage best.'—*Daily Express*

Miranda*
GB 1947 80m bw
GFD / Gainsborough / Sydney Box (Betty Box)

A doctor on holiday in Cornwall catches a mermaid and takes her to London disguised as an invalid.
Simple-minded comedy which scores a few easy laughs on obvious targets.

w Peter Blackmore, from his play *d* Ken Annakin *ph* Ray Elton *m* Temple Abady

Glynis Johns, Griffith Jones, Googie Withers, *Margaret Rutherford*, David Tomlinson, Sonia Holm, John McCallum
† Sequel 1949, *Mad about Men.*

'Mirror, mirror, on the wall, who's the killer among them all?'

The Mirror Crack'd
GB 1980 105m Technicolor
EMI / John Brabourne, Richard Goodwin

Murders result from the making of an all-star film in an English village.
After adventures on the Orient Express and the Nile, this follow-up in the Agatha Christie stakes seems woefully restricted with stilted dialogue and playing.

w Jonathan Hales, Barry Sandler
novel Agatha Christie *d* Guy Hamilton
ph Christopher Challis *m* John Cameron
pd Michael Stringer

Angela Lansbury, Geraldine Chaplin, Elizabeth Taylor, Rock Hudson, Tony Curtis, Edward Fox, Kim Novak, Marella Oppenheim, Charles Gray

Mischief*
US 1985 93m De Luxe

Teenage anxieties in smalltown America in 1956. Clearly not for export, but a smooth piece of its kind. Doug McKeon, Catherine Mary Stewart, Kelly Preston, Chris Nash. Written by Noel Black; directed by Mel Damski; for Jere Henshaw-Michael Nolin / TCF.

Les Misérables****
US 1935 109m bw
Twentieth Century (Darryl F. Zanuck)

Unjustly convicted and sentenced to years in the galleys, Jean Valjean emerges to build up his life again but is hounded by a cruel and relentless police officer.
Solid, telling, intelligent version of a much-filmed classic novel; in adaptation and performance it is hard to see how this film could be bettered.

w W. P. Lipscomb, novel Victor Hugo
d Richard Boleslawski *ph Gregg Toland*
m Alfred Newman

Fredric March, Charles Laughton, Cedric Hardwicke, Rochelle Hudson, Frances Drake, John Beal, Jessie Ralph, Florence Eldridge

'Brilliant filmization, sure fire for heavy money.'—*Variety*

'Unbelievably thrilling in all the departments of its manufacture . . . a memorable experience in the cinema.'—*New York Times*

'A superlative effort, a thrilling, powerful, poignant picture.'—*New York Evening Post*

'Deserving of rank among the cinema's finest achievements.'—*New York World Telegram*

† Other versions of the story: 1909, 1913 (French); 1917 (William Farnum); 1923 (French: Gabriel Gabrio); 1929 as *The Bishop's Candlesticks* (Walter Huston); 1934 (French: Harry Baur); 1946 (Italian: Gino Cervi); 1952 (see below); 1956 (French: Jean Gabin); 1978 (British: Richard Jordan).

AAN: best picture; Gregg Toland

Les Misérables**
US 1952 106m bw
TCF (Fred Kohlmar)

Solemn remake, well done but lacking the spark of inspiration.

w Richard Murphy *d* Lewis Milestone
ph Joseph La Shelle *m* Alex North

Michael Rennie, Robert Newton, Edmund Gwenn, Debra Paget, Cameron Mitchell, Sylvia Sidney, Elsa Lanchester, James Robertson Justice, Joseph Wiseman, Rhys Williams

The Misfits*
US 1961 124m bw
United Artists / Seven Arts (Frank E. Taylor)

Cowboys gather in the Nevada desert to rope wild mustangs, and a divorcee becomes involved with one of them.
Ill-fated melodrama whose stars both died shortly afterwards; a solemn, unattractive, pretentious film which seldom stops wallowing in self-pity.

w Arthur Miller *d* John Huston *ph* Russell Metty *m* Alex North

Clark Gable, Marilyn Monroe, Montgomery Clift, Eli Wallach, Thelma Ritter, James Barton, Estelle Winwood, Kevin McCarthy

Mishima*
US 1985 120m Technicolor Panavision

Fragments of autobiography by the self-destructing Japanese writer. A complete switch-off for all but the initiated, this indulgent, delicate, violent kaleidoscope is half a work of art and half an utter waste of other people's money. Ken Ogata, Kanji Sawada, Yasosuke Bando. Written by Paul and Leonard Schrader; directed by Paul Schrader; for Coppola-Lucas / Warner.

The Misleading Lady
US 1932 75m bw

A social butterfly aspires to be an actress. Ho-hum romantic comedy, quite unmemorable. Claudette Colbert, Edmund Lowe, Stuart Erwin, Robert Strange, George Meeker. Written by Adelaide Heilbron, Caroline Francke, from the play by Charles W. Goddard and Paul Dickey; directed by Stuart Walker; for Paramount. 'Lightweight stuff of conventional pattern.'—*Variety*

Miss Annie Rooney
US 1942 86m bw
Edward Small

Poor Irish girl loves rich boy.
A totally routine offering for a teenage star; no wonder she didn't make it.

w George Bruce *d* Edwin L. Marin
ph Lester White *md* Edward Paul

Shirley Temple, William Gargan, Guy Kibbee, Dickie Moore, Peggy Ryan, Gloria Holden, Jonathan Hale, Mary Field

Miss Fane's Baby Is Stolen
US 1933 67m bw

A film star's baby is kidnapped. Fairly straightforward crime yarn with comic asides. Dorothea Wieck, Alice Brady, Baby LeRoy, William Frawley, George Barbier, Alan Hale, Jack La Rue. Written by Adela Rogers St John, Rupert Hughes; directed by Alexander Hall; for Paramount. 'Box office as well as entertainment . . . the first picture of its kind since the Lindbergh kidnapping.'—*Variety* (GB title: *Kidnapped.*)

Miss Grant Takes Richmond*
US 1949 87m bw
Columbia (S. Sylvan Simon)
GB title: *Innocence Is Bliss*

A dumb secretary helps defeat crooks and improve the local housing situation.
Mildly amusing star comedy.

w Nat Perrin, Devery Freeman, Frank Tashlin *d* Lloyd Bacon *ph* Charles Lawton Jnr *m* Heinz Roemheld *md* Morris Stoloff

Lucille Ball, William Holden, Janis Carter, James Gleason, Gloria Henry, Frank McHugh, George Cleveland

'One of the more delightful comedies of the season.'—*Lawrence J. Quirk*

Miss Julie*
Sweden 1950 87m bw
Sandrew (Rene Waldekranz)

In a lonely house, the count's daughter kills herself after being seduced by a valet.
Intense melodramatic fragment, just a little long for comfort.

wd Alf Sjoberg, play August Strindberg
ph Goran Strindberg *m* Dag Wiren

Anita Bjork, Ulf Palme, Anders Henrison

'The outstanding achievement of the Swedish cinema in recent years.'—*Gavin Lambert, Sight and Sound*

Miss London Ltd
GB 1943 99m bw
GFD / Gainsborough (Edward Black)

An escort agency is formed to assist soldiers on leave.
Flagwaving light entertainment with popular performers of the time.

w Val Guest, Marriott Edgar *d* Val Guest
ph Basil Emmott *md* Louis Levy
songs Manning Sherwin (*m*), Val Guest (*ly*)

Arthur Askey, Anne Shelton, Evelyn Dall, Richard Hearne, Max Bacon, Jack Train, Peter Graves, Jean Kent

Miss Marple
Agatha Christie's inquisitive spinster detective was brought to the screen by director George Pollock and star Margaret Rutherford in four increasingly disappointing films for MGM.

1962: MURDER SHE SAID (qv)
1963: MURDER AT THE GALLOP
1964: MURDER MOST FOUL, MURDER AHOY

See also *The Mirror Crack'd.*

Miss Pacific Fleet
US 1935 76m bw

Two stranded show girls enter a popularity contest to win the fare back home. A comedy with little to laugh at. Glenda Farrell, Joan Blondell, Hugh Herbert, Allen Jenkins, Warren Hull, Guinn Williams. Written by Lucille Newmark, Peter Milne and Patsy Flick; directed by Ray Enright; for Warner.

'Maybe oke for double feature bills, but that's the best it can hope for.'—*Variety*

Miss Pilgrim's Progress
GB 1949 82m bw

An American working girl in Britain helps to save a village from development. Wholly artificial and unendearing comedy. Yolande Donlan, Michael Rennie, Garry Marsh, Emrys Jones, Reginald Beckwith, Helena Pickard, Jon Pertwee. Written and directed by Val Guest; for Daniel M. Angel.

Miss Pinkerton*
US 1932 66m bw
Warner

A private nurse helps a police detective to solve a murder case.
Pleasing little mystery comedy.

w Lilyan Hayward, Niven Busch, *story* Mary Roberts Rinehart *d* Lloyd Bacon *ph* Barney McGill

Joan Blondell, George Brent, Mae Madison, John Wray, Ruth Hall, C. Henry Gordon, Elizabeth Patterson

'Formula mystery story . . . picture is outdated and has nothing to draw.'—*Variety*

† Remade as *The Nurse's Secret* (1946).

Miss Robin Hood
GB 1952 78m bw

A lady author pits her wits against crooks and saves an old lady's fortune. Disappointing star comedy with no build-up. Margaret Rutherford, Richard Hearne, Michael Medwin, Peter Jones, James Robertson Justice, Sidney James, Dora Bryan. Written by Val Valentine, Patrick Campbell and Geoffrey Orme; directed by John Guillermin; for Group 3.

Miss Sadie Thompson*
US 1953 91m Technicolor 3-D
Columbia (Lewis J. Rachmil)

Vigorous semi-musical remake of *Rain* (qv); a good star vehicle, but not otherwise notable.

w Harry Kleiner *d* Curtis Bernhardt
ph Charles Lawton *md* George Duning

Rita Hayworth, Jose Ferrer, Aldo Ray, Russell Collins, Harry Bellaver

AAN: song 'Blue Pacific Blues' (*m* Lester Lee, *ly* Ned Washington)

'A story for lovers . . . past, present and perfect!'

Miss Susie Slagle's
US 1946 88m bw
Paramount (John Houseman)

Romances of nursing students in 1910 Baltimore.
Modest melodramatic potboiler.

w Anne Froelich, Hugo Butler, *novel* Augusta Tucker *d* John Berry *ph* Charles Lang Jnr *m* Daniele Amfitheatrof

Veronica Lake, Joan Caulfield, Sonny Tufts, Lillian Gish, Ray Collins, Billy de Wolfe, Bill Edwards, Roman Bohnen, Morris Carnovsky, Lloyd Bridges

Miss Tatlock's Millions*
US 1948 101m bw
Paramount (Charles Brackett)

A stunt man impersonates the idiot heir to a fortune.
Tasteless but quite funny comedy with a cast of eccentrics indulging in enjoyable fooling.

w Charles Brackett, Richard L. Breen
d Richard Haydn *ph* Charles Lang Jnr
m Victor Young

John Lund, Wanda Hendrix, Monty Woolley, Barry Fitzgerald, Robert Stack, Ilka Chase, Dorothy Stickney

Miss V from Moscow
US 1943 70m bw

A Russian spy impersonates a German spy in Paris. Hilariously inept propaganda piece; since the Cold War it has been retitled *Intrigue in Paris.* Lola Lane, Noel Madison, Howard

Banks. Written by Arthur St Claire and Sherman Lowe; directed by Albert Herman; for PRC.

Missing*
US 1982 122m Technicolor
Universal / Polygram / Peter Guber, Jon Peters (Edward and Mildred Lewis)

An American seeks his young son who has disappeared in Chile.
A further link in the chain of political thrillers from this director; well-wrought and compulsive but finally disappointing in its mixture of fact and fiction.

w Costa-Gavras, Donald Stewart, *book* Thomas Hauser *d Costa-Gavras* *ph* Ricardo Aronovich *m* Vangelis *pd* Peter Jamieson *ed* Françoise Bonnot

Jack Lemmon, Sissy Spacek, Melanie Mayron, John Shea, Charles Cioffi, Richard Bradford
'Provocation and entertainment prove to be uneasy allies.'—*Tom Milne, MFB*

AA: Screenplay (adaptation)

AAN: Jack Lemmon; best picture; Sissy Spacek

The Missing Corpse
US 1945 54m bw

A publisher tries to hide a corpse he is suspected of murdering. Adequate filler for indulgent audiences. J. Edward Bromberg, Ben Welden, Frank Jenks, Isabel Randolph. Written by Ray Schrock; directed by Albert Herman; for Leon Fromkess / PRC.

Missing in Action
US 1984 101m Metrocolor

An American colonel, having been taken prisoner and escaped, returns to Vietnam to find other 'missing' men. Naïve, violent, jingoistic romp which caused quite a lot of box office business around the world. Chuck Norris, M. Emmet Walsh, Lenore Kasdorf, James Hong. Written by James Bruner; directed by Joseph Zito; for Cannon.

Missing in Action 2—The Beginning
US 1985 95m TVC colour

A prequel to the above, showing the colonel's first escape. More cheaply made, it runs like a series of offcuts, with emphasis on unpleasant violence. Chuck Norris, Soon Teck-Oh, Cosie Costa, Steven Williams. Written by Arthur Silver, Larry Levinson, Steve Bing; directed by Lance Hool; for Cannon.

The Missing Juror
US 1944 71m bw

Members of a murder jury are killed off one by one. Minor puzzle piece from the *I Love a Mystery* series. Jim Bannon, Janis Carter, George Macready. Written by Charles O'Neal; directed by Budd Boetticher; for Columbia.

The Missing Rembrandt
GB 1932 82m bw

Sherlock Holmes saves a lady's honour and nails a blackmailer. Not the best of this particular series, but Wontner is a Holmes to relish. Arthur Wontner, Ian Fleming, Jane Welsh, Miles Mander, Francis L. Sullivan. Written by Cyril Twyford and H. Fowler Mear, from the story *Charles Augustus Milverton* by Arthur Conan Doyle; directed by Leslie Hiscott; for Twickenham.

The Mission**
GB 1986 128m Rank colour JDC wide screen
Goldcrest / Kingsmere / Enigma / Fernando Ghia (David Puttnam)

In mid-18th-century South America, Jesuit priests fall foul of avaricious colonialists.
Sincere to the point of boredom, this 22-million-dollar would-be epic is short on plot development, long on superb photography of remote actualities.

w Robert Bolt *d Roland Joffe* *ph Chris Menges* *m* Ennio Morricone *pd* Norma Dorme, Francesco Broznik, George Richardson, John King *ed* Jim Clark

Robert De Niro, Jeremy Irons, Ray McAnally, Liam Neeson, Aidan Quinn, Ronald Pickup, Cherie Lunghi

AA: Chris Menges

AAN: best picture; Roland Joffe; Ennio Morricone; Jim Clark; art direction (Stuart Craig); sound (Jack Stephens); costumes (Enrico Sabbatini)

Mission to Moscow**
US 1943 112m bw
Warner (Robert Buckner)

The Russian career of US Ambassador Joseph E. Davies.
Stodgy but fascinating wartime propaganda piece viewing the Russians as warm-hearted allies; in the later days of the McCarthy witch hunt, Jack L. Warner regretted he had ever allowed it to be made.

w Howard Koch, *book* Joseph E. Davies *d* Michael Curtiz *ph* Bert Glennon *m* Max Steiner

Walter Huston, Ann Harding, Oscar Homolka, George Tobias, Gene Lockhart, Eleanor Parker, Richard Travis, Helmut Dantine, Victor Francen, Henry Daniell, Barbara Everest, Dudley Field Malone, Roman Bohnen, Maria Palmer, Moroni Olsen, Minor Watson
'A mishmash: of Stalinism with New Dealism with Hollywoodism with opportunism with shaky experimentalism with mesmerism with onanism, all mosaicked into a remarkable portrait of what the makers of the film think the Soviet Union is like—a great glad two-million-dollar bowl of canned borscht, eminently approvable by the Institute of Good Housekeeping.'—*James Agee*

The Missionary*
GB 1983 86m colour Panavision
HandMade Films (Michael Palin)

In 1906, a clergyman returns from darkest Africa and sets up a Mission to Fallen Women in the East End of London.
Sporadically amusing comedy of a reformer being tempted; the decoration is funnier than the central theme.

w Michael Palin *d* Richard Loncraine *ph* Peter Hannan *m* Mike Moran *ad* Norman Garwood

Michael Palin, Maggie Smith, Michael Hordern, Trevor Howard, Denholm Elliott, Graham Crowden, Phoebe Nichols, Roland Culver
'It leaves one with a half-frozen smile, in anticipation of a comic fulfilment which never quite happens.'—*Nick Roddick, MFB*
'A deliciously straight-faced acceptance of the palpably absurd.'—*Daily Mail*

Mississippi*
US 1935 75m bw
Paramount (Arthur Hornblow Jnr)

A showboat singer has a cloud on his reputation.
Mild period musical with occasional stops for comedy.

w Herbert Fields, Claude Binyon, *story* Booth Tarkington *d* Edward A. Sutherland *ph* Charles Lang *m / ly* Rodgers and Hart

Bing Crosby, W. C. Fields, Joan Bennett, Gail Patrick, Claude Gillingwater, John Miljan, Queenie Smith
'A dull film, rambling and hokey.'—*Variety*

Mississippi Gambler
US 1953 98m Technicolor
U-I (Ted Richmond)

A showboat gambler has trouble with a bad loser, but finally marries his sister.
Picturesque star melodrama with period settings and not much meat in the story.

w Seton I. Miller *d* Rudolph Maté *ph* Irving Glassberg *m* Frank Skinner

Tyrone Power, Piper Laurie, John McIntyre, Julia Adams, Dennis Weaver

The Mississippi Mermaid*
France / Italy 1969 123m Eastmancolor Dyaliscope
Films du Carrosse / PAA / Delphos (Marcel Berbert)
Original title: *La Sirène du Mississippi*

After a courtship by mail, a factory owner on a remote African island finds that the girl who arrives by steamer does not fit his preconceptions . . .
Oddly obsessive romantic murder mystery: the hero continues to love the girl who tries to kill him, and at the end they are still together. Interesting when it is not uncomfortable.

w,d Francois Truffaut *novel* Waltz into Darkness by William Irish *ph* Denys Clerval *m* Antoine Duhamel

Jean-Paul Belmondo, Catherine Deneuve, Michel Bouquet, Nelly Borgeaud, Marcel Berbert

The Missouri Breaks
US 1976 126m De Luxe
UA / Elliott Kastner / Robert B. Sherman

Montana ranchers and rustlers fight over land and livestock, and a hired killer shoots it out with a horse thief.
Savage, dislikeable western with both stars over the top.

w Thomas McGuane *d* Arthur Penn *ph* Michael Butler *m* John Williams

Marlon Brando, Jack Nicholson, Randy Quaid, Kathleen Lloyd, Frederic Forrest, Harry Dean Stanton

'It is typical of the film's richness and ambiguity that the title has about five possible punning meanings.'—*Michael Billington, Illustrated London News*

'Although listed as the director, Mr Penn finds himself perched on Brando's knee and manipulated as shamelessly as Edgar Bergen used to waggle Charlie McCarthy.'—*Benny Green, Punch*

'Nothing more than the self-conscious cleverness of some merry prankster with a blanket of scorn for all who don't share his flippancy.'—*William S. Pechter*

'A pair of million dollar babies in a five and ten cent flick.'—*Charles Champlin, Los Angeles Times*

'A picture of which it might be said they shouldn't make 'em like that any more . . . a picture that explains very little, including why anyone thought it a work that demanded to be made.'—*Robert Hatch, Nation*

Mr Ace
US 1946 84m bw
Benedict Bogeaus

A rich, spoiled congresswoman is backed by a gangster but gets religion.
Odd star drama, perfunctorily made.

w Fred Finklehoffe *d* Edwin L. Marin *ph* Karl Struss *m* Heinz Roemheld

Sylvia Sidney, George Raft, Stanley Ridges, Sara Haden, Jerome Cowan

Mr and Mrs North
US 1941 68m bw

Mr and Mrs find a corpse in their closet. Reasonably lively transcription of a Broadway success. Gracie Allen, William Post Jnr, Paul Kelly, Rose Hobart, Virginia Grey, Tom Conway, Felix Bressart, Porter Hall, Millard Mitchell, Keye Luke, Jerome Cowan. Written by S. K. Lauren from play by Owen Davis; directed by Robert B. Sinclair; for Irving Asher / MGM.

Mr and Mrs Smith*
US 1941 95m bw
RKO (Harry E. Edington)

A much-married couple discover that their marriage wasn't legal.
Smartish matrimonial comedy, surprisingly but not obviously directed by the master of suspense.

w Norman Krasna *d* Alfred Hitchcock *ph* Harry Stradling *m* Edward Ward

Carole Lombard, Robert Montgomery, Gene Raymond, Jack Carson, Philip Merivale, Lucile Watson, William Tracy

'I doubt that your interest or amusement will last as long as the picture.'—*Otis Ferguson*

Mr Belvedere Goes to College*
US 1949 88m bw
TCF (Samuel G. Engel)

A self-styled genius goes back to school and helps a college widow.
Flat follow up to *Sitting Pretty* (qv), with only a few laughs.

w Richard Sale, Mary Loos, Mary McCall Jnr *d* Elliott Nugent *ph* Lloyd Ahern *m* Alfred Newman

Clifton Webb, Shirley Temple, Alan Young, Tom Drake, Jessie Royce Landis, Kathleen Hughes, Taylor Holmes

Mr Belvedere Rings the Bell*
US 1951 87m bw
TCF (André Hakim)

Imperturbable Mr Belvedere enters an old folks' home under false pretences to test his theories of ageing.
A not unagreeable star vehicle for those who can stand the sentiment.

w Ranald MacDougall, *play* The Silver Whistle by Robert E. McEnroe *d* Henry Koster *ph* Joseph La Shelle *m* Cyril Mockridge

Clifton Webb, Joanne Dru, Hugh Marlowe, Zero Mostel, Doro Merande

Mr Big
US 1943 73m bw

Drama school students concoct a musical show. Tolerable minor showcase for a new young star. *Donald O'Connor*, Gloria Jean, Peggy Ryan, Robert Paige, Elyse Knox, Samuel S. Hinds, Florence Bates. Written by Jack Pollexfen and Dorothy Bennett; directed by Charles Lamont; for Ken Goldsmith / Universal.

Mr Billion*
US 1977 93m De Luxe
TCF / Pantheon (Gabriel Katzka, Steve Bach, Ken Friedman)

An Italian garage mechanic becomes heir to a vast estate, providing he can get to San Francisco in time for the signing ceremony and outwit the villains trying to stop him.
Moderately engaging old-fashioned comedy-adventure.

w Ken Friedman, Jonathan Kaplan *d* Jonathan Kaplan *ph* Matthew F. Leonetti *m* Dave Grusin

Terence Hill, Valerie Perrine, Jackie Gleason, Slim Pickens, William Redfield, Chill Wills

Mr Blandings Builds His Dream House***
US 1948 84m bw
RKO (Norman Panama, Melvin Frank)

A New York advertising man longs to live in the Connecticut countryside, but finds the way to rural satisfaction is hard.
It hasn't the lightness and brightness of the book, but this is a fun film for the middle-aged who like to watch three agreeable stars doing their thing.

w Norman Panama, Melvin Frank, novel Eric Hodgkin d H. C. Potter ph James Wong Howe *m* Leigh Harline *md* Constantin Bakaleinikoff

Cary Grant, Myrna Loy, Melvyn Douglas, Reginald Denny, Louise Beavers, Ian Wolfe, Harry Shannon, Nestor Paiva, Jason Robards

'A bulls-eye for middle-class middlebrows.' —*James Agee*

'I loved it. That was really a pleasure to make.'—*H. C. Potter, 1973*

Mister Buddwing
US 1966 99m bw
MGM / DDD / Cherokee (Douglas Laurence, Delbert Mann)
GB title: *Woman without a Face*

An amnesiac wakes up in Central Park and goes in search of his identity.
Rather muddled melodrama in which the characters are so dull that by the time the flashbacks fall into place we scarcely care.

w Dale Wassermann, *novel* Buddwing by Evan Hunter *d* Delbert Mann *ph* Ellsworth Fredericks *m* Kenyon Hopkins

James Garner, Jean Simmons, Angela Lansbury, Suzanne Pleshette, Katharine Ross, George Voskovec, Jack Gilford, Joe Mantell, Raymond St Jacques

Mr Bug Goes to Town*
US 1941 78m Technicolor
Max Fleischer
aka: *Hoppity Goes to Town*

An urban community of insects is in danger from developers.
A cartoon feature which failed to make its mark despite clever detail; perhaps because insects make poor heroes, or because there simply wasn't enough plot.
d Dave Fleischer *m* Leigh Harline

Mr Chedworth Steps Out
Australia 1939 92m bw

In a period of redundancy a clerk has to take a job as a caretaker, but discovers a cache of counterfeit money. Mild comedy-drama. Cecil Kellaway, Jean Hatton, James Raglan, Rita Pauncefort, Peter Finch. Written by Frank Harvey; directed and produced by Ken G. Hall; for Cinesound.

Mister Cinderella
US 1936 75m bw

A meek-and-mild youth aspires to crash high society. Milk-and-water comedy with insufficient get-up-and-go. Jack Haley, Betty Furness, Arthur Treacher, Raymond Walburn, Rosina Lawrence, Monroe Owsley. Written by Arthur Vernon Jones, Richard Flournoy, Jack Jevne; directed by Edward Sedgwick; for Hal Roach / MGM. 'Too crammed with slaptrap hokum to stand alone.'—*Variety*

Mister Cory
US 1957 92m Eastmancolor Cinemascope
U-I (Robert Arthur)

A small-time gangster leaves the Chicago slums to seek fame and fortune among the country-club set.
Modest star comedy drama.

wd Blake Edwards *ph* Russell Metty *m* Joseph Gershenson

Tony Curtis, Martha Hyer, Charles Bickford, Kathryn Grant

Mr Deeds Goes to Town***
US 1936 118m bw
Columbia (Frank Capra)

A small-town poet inherits a vast fortune and sets New York on its heels by his honesty.
What once was fresh and charming now seems rather laboured in spots, and the production is parsimonious indeed, but the courtroom scene still works, and the good intentions conquer all.

w Robert Riskin, story Opera Hat by Clarence Budington Kelland *d Frank Capra ph* Joseph Walker *m* Adolph Deutsch *md* Howard Jackson

Gary Cooper, Jean Arthur, Raymond Walburn, Lionel Stander, Walter Catlett, George Bancroft, Douglass Dumbrille, H. B. Warner, Ruth Donnelly, *Margaret Seddon, Margaret McWade*

'I have an uneasy feeling he's on his way out. He's started to make pictures about themes instead of people.'—*Alistair Cooke*

'Everywhere the picture goes, from the endearing to the absurd, the accompanying business is carried through with perfect zip and relish.'—*Otis Ferguson*

'A comedy quite unmatched on the screen.'—*Graham Greene*

'The film culminates in a courtroom sequence that introduced the word "pixilated" to just about every American home, and set people to examining each other's casual scribbles or sketches—their "doddles".'—*Pauline Kael, 70s*

AA: Frank Capra
AAN: best picture; Robert Riskin; Gary Cooper

Mr Denning Drives North
GB 1951 93m bw
London Films (Anthony Kimmins, Stephen Mitchell)

A wealthy man accidentally kills a criminal in love with his daughter; he hides the body, which then disappears.
Initially suspenseful but finally disappointing melodrama which seems to lack a twist or two.

w Alec Coppel *d* Anthony Kimmins *ph* John Wilcox *m* Benjamin Frankel

John Mills, Phyllis Calvert, Sam Wanamaker, Freda Jackson

Mr District Attorney
US 1941 69m bw

A lady reporter helps a young assistant DA to ferret out crooks. Dim movie version of a radio series. Dennis O'Keefe, Florence Rice, Peter Lorre, Stanley Ridges, Minor Watson. Written by Karl Brown, Malcolm Stuart Boylan; directed by William Morgan; for Leonard Fields / Republic.

Mr Dodd Takes the Air
US 1937 78m bw
Warner (Mervyn Le Roy)

A country cousin becomes a hit as a crooner.
Modest comedy for small towns.

w William Wister Haines, Elaine Ryan, *story* Clarence Budington Kelland *d* Alfred E. Green *ph* Arthur Edeson *songs* Al Dubin, Harry Warren *md* Adolph Deutsch

Kenny Baker, Jane Wyman, Alice Brady, Gertrude Michael, Frank McHugh, Luis Alberni, Henry O'Neill, Harry Davenport

AAN: Al Dubin and Harry Warren for 'Remember Me'

Mr Drake's Duck**
GB 1950 85m bw
Daniel M. Angel / Douglas Fairbanks

A duck lays a uranium egg, and a gentleman farmer finds himself at the centre of international military disagreement.
Brisk and amusing minor comedy deploying British comic types to good purpose.

wd Val Guest, radio play Ian Messiter *ph* Jack Cox *m* Philip Martell

Douglas Fairbanks Jnr, Yolande Donlan, Wilfrid Hyde White, A. E. Matthews, Jon Pertwee, Reginald Beckwith, Howard Marion-Crawford, Peter Butterworth, Tom Gill

'One of the funniest films I have ever seen.'—*News of the World*

Mr Dynamite
US 1935 75m bw

An unconventional private detective outsmarts the police. Amusing, wisecracking crime caper. Edmund Lowe, Jean Dixon, Esther Ralston, Victor Varconi, Minor Watson, Robert Gleckler. Written by Doris Malloy, Harry Clork, from a story by Dashiell Hammett; directed by Alan Crosland; for Universal. 'Nice entertainment.'—*Variety*

Mister 880**
US 1950 90m bw
TCF (Julian Blaustein)

An elderly counterfeiter perplexes the US Secret Service.
Whimsical star comedy which moves along cheerfully enough to be a good example of the Hollywood programmer at its prime.

w Robert Riskin *d* Edmund Goulding *ph* Joseph La Shelle *m* Sol Kaplan

Edmund Gwenn, Burt Lancaster, Dorothy McGuire, Millard Mitchell

AAN: Edmund Gwenn

Mr Emmanuel*
GB 1944 97m bw
Two Cities (William Sistrom)

In 1936 an elderly Jew visits Germany in search of the mother of an orphan boy.
Simply made but quite effective and unusual story giving Aylmer his only star part.

w Gordon Wellesley, Norman Ginsburg, *novel* Louis Golding *d* Harold French *ph* Otto Heller

Felix Aylmer, Greta Gynt, Walter Rilla, Peter Mullins, Ursula Jeans, Elspeth March, Meier Tzelniker

Mr Forbush and the Penguins*
GB 1971 101m Technicolor
EMI / PGI / Henry Trettin

A biologist is sent to the Antarctic to study penguins, and gets a new understanding of life.
Rather broken-backed animal film with a moral; pleasant enough, its two halves don't fit together.

w Anthony Shaffer, *novel* Graham Billey *d* Roy Boulting, *Arne Sucksdorff ph* Harry Waxman, Ted Scaife *m* John Addison

John Hurt, Hayley Mills, Tony Britton, Thorley Walters, Judy Campbell, Joss Ackland, Sally Geeson, Cyril Luckham

Mr Hobbs Takes a Vacation*
US 1962 116m De Luxe Cinemascope
TCF (Jerry Wald)

A city dweller takes a seaside house for a family holiday, but it turns out to be a crumbling ruin.
Overlong, sloppy comedy which devotes too much time to teenage romance but manages occasional smiles.

w Nunnally Johnson, *novel* Edward Streeter *d* Henry Koster *ph* W. C. Mellor *m* Henry Mancini

James Stewart, Maureen O'Hara, Fabian, John Saxon, Marie Wilson, Reginald Gardiner, *John McGiver*

Mr Imperium
US 1951 87m Technicolor
MGM (Edwin H. Knopf)
GB title: *You Belong to My Heart*

An exiled king in Hollywood meets a famous film star with whom he once had a romance.
Minor romantic drama with songs.

w Edwin Knopf, Don Hartman *d* Don Hartman *ph* George J. Folsey *songs* Harold Arlen (*m*), Dorothy Fields (*ly*) *m* Bronislau Kaper

Lana Turner, Ezio Pinza, Marjorie Main, Barry Sullivan, Cedric Hardwicke, Debbie Reynolds

Mr Klein*
France / Italy 1976 123m Eastmancolor
Lira / Adel / Nova / Mondial Te-Fi (Raymond Danon, Alain Delon)

In 1942 Paris, a prosperous antique dealer is mistaken for a mysterious Jew of the same name, and despite the danger gradually assumes his identity.

MR MOTO. Rising anti-Japanese feeling prior to the start of World War Two made Twentieth Century-Fox abandon their *Mr Moto* series. Peter Lorre looks suitably inscrutable, Leon Ames wears his bowler with aplomb.

Complex Kafkaesque character study: occasionally arresting but generally rather glum.

w Franco Solinas *d* Joseph Losey *ph* Gerry Fisher *m* Egisto Macchi, Pierre Porte

Alain Delon, Jeanne Moreau, Suzanne Flon, Michael Lonsdale, Louis Seigner, Juliet Berto

Mr Love
GB 1986 91m colour
Warner / Goldcrest / Enigma (Susan Richards, Robin Douet)

A mild-mannered cinema projectionist develops an erroneous reputation as a Don Juan.
Ineffective character comedy with too few laughs and a minimum of accurate observation.

w Kenneth Eastaugh *d* Roy Battersby *ph* Clive Tickner *m* Willy Russell

Barry Jackson, Maurice Denham, Margaret Tyzack, Linda Marlowe, Cristina Collier
'It renders would-be regional fantasy into something merely parochial.'—*Tim Pulleine, Monthly Film Bulletin*

Mr Lucky*
US 1943 98m bw
RKO (David Hempstead)

During World War II a gambling ship owner goes straight and instigates Bundles for Britain.
Unconvincing mixture of comedy and drama with the actors looking somewhat bewildered.

w Milton Holmes, Adrian Scott *d* H. C. Potter *ph* George Barnes *m* Roy Webb

Cary Grant, Laraine Day, Charles Bickford, Gladys Cooper, Alan Carney, Henry Stephenson, Paul Stewart, Walter Kingsford
'If it weren't for Cary Grant's persuasive personality the whole thing would melt away to nothing at all.'—*Philip G. Hartung*
† Remade 1950 as *Gambling House.*

Mr Majestyk*
US 1974 103m De Luxe
UA / Mirisch (Walter Mirisch)

A Colorado melon grower crosses swords with the local Mafia.
Violent but unexpectedly enjoyable action melodrama.

w Elmore Leonard *d* Richard Fleischer *ph* Richard Kline *m* Charles Bernstein

Charles Bronson, Al Lettieri, Linda Cristal, Lee Purcell, Paul Keslo

Mr Mom
US 1983 91m Metrocolor

Dad loses his executive job and stays home to mind the kids while his wife works. Obvious farce with too much messy slapstick and no real development. Michael Keaton, Teri Garr, Frederick Koehler, Martin Mull, Ann Jillian. Written by John Hughes; directed by Stan Dragoti; for Aaron Spelling / Sherwood. (GB title: *Mr Mum.*) 'The jokes almost sink without trace in a hazy domestic setting straight from the hoariest sitcom.'—*Geoff Brown, MFB*

Mister Moses*
GB 1965 103m Technicolor Panavision
UA / Frank Ross / Talbot

A quack doctor is the only person who can persuade an African tribe to move before their land is flooded, and he leads them to their promised land.
Adventure spectacle with naïve biblical parallels; quite agreeable.

w Charles Beaumont, Monja Danischewsky, *novel* Max Catto *d* Ronald Neame *ph* Oswald Morris *m* John Barry

Robert Mitchum, Carroll Baker, Ian Bannen, Alexander Knox, Reginald Beckwith, Raymond St Jacques

Mr Moto
The Japanese detective created by John P. Marquand and played by Peter Lorre figured in several above-average second features of the late thirties, but the outbreak of war caused him to vanish. The casts were interesting, the TCF production excellent, and the director usually Norman Foster. The 1965 attempt to revive the character with Henry Silva was painfully boring.

1937: THINK FAST MR MOTO (with Virginia Field, Sig Rumann), THANK YOU MR MOTO (with Pauline Frederick, Sidney Blackmer)
1938: MR MOTO'S GAMBLE (with Keye Luke, Lynn Bari), MR MOTO TAKES A CHANCE (with Rochelle Hudson, J. Edward Bromberg), MYSTERIOUS MR MOTO (with Henry Wilcoxon, Erik Rhodes)
1939: MR MOTO'S LAST WARNING (with Ricardo Cortez, George Sanders, Robert Coote, John Carradine), MR MOTO IN DANGER ISLAND (with Jean Hersholt, Warren Hymer), MR MOTO TAKES A VACATION (with Joseph Schildkraut, Lionel Atwill)
1965: THE RETURN OF MR MOTO

Mr Music*
US 1950 113m bw
Paramount (Robert L. Welch)

A college girl is employed to keep an idle middle-aged songwriter's nose to the grindstone.
Bland musical remake of *Accent on Youth* (qv); pleasant performances, moments of comedy, guest stars.

w Arthur Sheekman *d* Richard Haydn *ph* George Barnes *songs* Johnny Burke, James Van Heusen *ad* Hans Dreier, Earl Hedrick

Bing Crosby, Nancy Olson, Charles Coburn, Ruth Hussey, Marge and Gower Champion, Peggy Lee, Groucho Marx

Mr Peabody and the Mermaid
US 1948 89m bw
U-I (Nunnally Johnson)

A middle-aged husband imagines an affair with a mermaid.
Bone-headed quick-cash-in on *Miranda* (qv); it never begins to work.

w Nunnally Johnson, *novel* Guy and Constance Jones *d* Irving Pichel *ph* Russell Metty *m* Robert Emmett Dolan

William Powell, Ann Blyth, Irene Hervey, Andrea King, Clinton Sundberg

Mr Perrin and Mr Traill*
GB 1948 92m bw
GFD / Two Cities (Alexander Galperson)

A handsome young master at a boys' school incurs the jealousy of an embittered colleague.
Flat, over-acted but mildly watchable picturization of a well-known story.

w L. A. G. Strong, *novel* Hugh Walpole *d* Lawrence Huntington *ph* Erwin Hillier *m* Alan Gray

Marius Goring, David Farrar, Greta Gynt, Edward Chapman, Raymond Huntley, Mary Jerrold, Finlay Currie, Ralph Truman

Mister Quilp
GB 1975 119m Technicolor Panavision
Reader's Digest (Helen M. Straus)
aka: *The Old Curiosity Shop*

In 1840 London, an antique-shop owner is in debt to a hunchback moneylender who has designs on his business.
The novel, with its villainous lead, is a curious choice for musicalizing, and in this treatment falls desperately flat, with no sparkle of imagination visible anywhere.

w Louis Kamp, Irene Kamp, *novel* The Old Curiosity Shop by Charles Dickens *d* Michael Tuchner *ph* Christopher Challis *m* Anthony Newley *pd* Elliot Scott *md* Elmer Bernstein *ch* Gillian Lynne

Anthony Newley, Michael Hordern, David Hemmings, Sarah-Jane Varley, David Warner, Paul Rogers, Jill Bennett

'Another soggy piece of family entertainment from Reader's Digest, who produced the toothless screen musicals of *Tom Sawyer* and *Huckleberry Finn*.'—*Philip French*

'Dickens shorn of sentiment, melodrama or love . . . Mr Newley's Quilp, a galvanized Quasimodo on a permanent high, is something of a strain to watch.'—*Michael Billington, Illustrated London News*

Mr Ricco
US 1975 98m Panavision colour
MGM (Douglas Netter)

A defence counsel risks his life to prove his black client innocent.
Complex urban action thriller with a tired, ageing hero and impenetrable plot.

w Robert Hoban *d* Paul Bogart *ph* Frank Stanley *m* Chico Hamilton

Dean Martin, Eugene Roche, Thalmus Rasulala, Denise Nicholas, Cindy Williams, *Geraldine Brooks*, Frank Puglia

Mister Roberts**
US 1955 123m Warnercolor Cinemascope
Warner / Leland Hayward

Life aboard a World War II cargo ship yearning for action.
A mixture of comedy and sentimentality which has become an American minor classic as a play; this film version is a shambling affair but gets most of the effects over.

w Frank Nugent, Joshua Logan, *play* Thomas Heggen and Joshua Logan, *novel Thomas Heggen* *d* John Ford, Mervyn Le Roy *ph* Winton Hoch *m* Franz Waxman

Henry Fonda, James Cagney, William Powell, Jack Lemmon, Betsy Palmer, Ward Bond, Phil Carey, Ken Curtis, Harry Carey Jnr

AA: Jack Lemmon
AAN: best picture

Mr Robinson Crusoe
US 1932 76m bw
Douglas Fairbanks

A playboy takes a bet that he could live alone on a desert island . . . but a girl turns up.
Mild adventure comedy with the star in subdued form.

w Douglas Fairbanks *d* Edward Sutherland *ph* Max Dupont *m* Alfred Newman

Douglas Fairbanks, William Farnum, Earle Browne, Maria Alba

'A man so evil—his face could stop a heart!'
Mr Sardonicus
US 1961 90m bw
Columbia / William Castle

A surgeon is lured to an ex-girl friend's remote home to cure her sadistic husband's crippled face.
Flatly handled, boring semi-horror.

w Robb White *d* William Castle *ph* Burnett Guffey *m* Von Dexter

Ronald Lewis, Guy Rolfe, Audrey Dalton, Oscar Homolka

Mr Scoutmaster
US 1953 87m bw
TCF

A TV personality wants to understand children and is persuaded to take over a scout troop.
A star vehicle which starts promisingly enough in the *Sitting Pretty* vein but quickly falls headlong into an abyss of sentimentality.

w Leonard Praskins, Barney Slater *d* Henry Levin *ph* Joseph La Shelle *m* Cyril Mockridge *md* Lionel Newman

Clifton Webb, Edmund Gwenn, George Winslow, Frances Dee, Veda Ann Borg

Mr Skeffington***
US 1944 127m bw
Warner (Julius J. and Philip G. Epstein)

A selfish beauty finally turns to her discarded dull husband; when he is blind, he doesn't mind her faded looks.
Long, patchily made, but thoroughly enjoyable star melodrama.

w Julius J. and Philip G. Epstein, *novel* 'Elizabeth' *d* Vincent Sherman *ph* Ernest Haller *m* Franz Waxman

Bette Davis, Claude Rains, Walter Abel, Richard Waring, George Coulouris, John Alexander, Jerome Cowan

'An endless woman's page dissertation on What To Do When Beauty Fades.'—*James Agee*

'To call the film a good one would be to exaggerate; but entertaining and interesting, I insist, it is.'—*Richard Mallett, Punch*

AAN: Bette Davis; Claude Rains

Mr Skitch
US 1933 70m bw

A Missouri family heads for California. Very passable star family entertainment. Will Rogers, Zasu Pitts, Florence Desmond, Rochelle Hudson. Written by Anne Cameron from her novel *Green Dice*; directed by James Cruze; for Fox. 'Enough laughs to please in general.'—*Variety*

'Stirring—in the seeing! Precious—in the remembering!'
Mr Smith Goes to Washington****
US 1939 130m bw
Columbia (Frank Capra)

Washington's youngest senator exposes corruption in high places, almost at the cost of his own career.
Archetypal high-flying Capra vehicle, with the little man coming out top as he seldom does in life. Supreme gloss hides the corn, helter-skelter direction keeps one watching, and all concerned give memorable performances. A cinema classic.

w Sidney Buchman, story Lewis R. Foster *d Frank Capra* *ph Joseph Walker* *m Dmitri Tiomkin* *montage Slavko Vorkapich*

James Stewart, Claude Rains, Jean Arthur, Thomas Mitchell, Edward Arnold, Guy Kibbee, Eugene Pallette, Beulah Bondi, *Harry Carey*, H. B. Warner, Astrid Allwyn, Ruth Donnelly, Charles Lane, Porter Hall

SMITH (James Stewart): 'I wouldn't give you two cents for all your fancy rules if, behind them, they didn't have a little bit of plain, ordinary kindness—and a little looking out for the other fella, too.'

'Timely and absorbing drama presented in best Capra craftsmanship.'—*Variety*

'More fun, even, than the Senate itself . . . not merely a brilliant jest, but a stirring and even inspiring testament to liberty and freedom.'—*Frank S. Nugent, New York Times*

'It says all the things about America that have been crying out to be said again—and says them beautifully.'—*Los Angeles Times*

'The great American picture.'—*Billboard*

'I feel that to show this film in foreign

countries will do inestimable harm to American prestige all over the world.'—*Joseph P. Kennedy, then American ambassador to Great Britain*

'A totally compelling piece of movie-making, upholding the virtues of traditional American ideals.'—*NFT, 1973*

'Very good, beautifully done and extremely entertaining; long, but worth the time it takes.'—*Richard Mallett, Punch*

'More of the heartfelt than is good for the stomach.'—*New Yorker, 1977*

AA: Lewis R. Foster
AAN: best picture; Sidney Buchman; Frank Capra; Dmitri Tiomkin; James Stewart; Claude Rains; Harry Carey

Mr Soft Touch
US 1949 93m bw

A gangster is reformed at Christmas by a social worker. Dewy-eyed romance with Damon Runyonish asides; only for soft touches. Glenn Ford, Evelyn Keyes, John Ireland, Beulah Bondi, Percy Kilbride, Roman Bohnen. Written by Orin Jannings; directed by Henry Levin and Gordon Douglas; for Columbia. (GB title: *House of Settlement*.)

Mr Topaze
GB 1961 84m Eastmancolor Cinemascope
TCF / Dimitri de Grunwald (Pierre Rouve)
US title: *I Like Money*

An honest ex-schoolmaster becomes prosperous when he joins some shady businessmen.
Predictable, sluggish character comedy, with a good actor unable to make it as a star. Or as a director.

w Pierre Rouve, *play* Topaze by Marcel Pagnol *d* Peter Sellers *ph* John Wilcox *m* Georges Van Parys

Peter Sellers, Herbert Lom, Leo McKern, Nadia Gray, Martita Hunt, John Neville, Billie Whitelaw, Michael Gough, Joan Sims, John Le Mesurier, Michael Sellers

'A film of minor pleasures and major inadequacies.'—*Penelope Houston, MFB*

† See also *Topaze* (1933).

Mr Universe
US 1951 79m bw

Con men promote a new wrestler. Fair low-class comedy with some laughs. Bert Lahr, Jack Carson, Vincent Edwards, Janis Paige, Robert Alda. Written by Earle Kramer; directed by Joseph Lerner; for Laurel/Eagle Lion.

Mr Winkle Goes to War
US 1944 80m bw
Columbia (Jack Moss)
GB title: *Arms and the Woman*

A middle-aged bank clerk joins the army and becomes a hero.
Agreeable, forgettable propaganda comedy-drama.

w Waldo Salt, George Corey, Louis Solomon, *novel* Theodore Pratt *d* Alfred E. Green *ph* Joseph Walker *m* Carmen Dragon, Paul Sawtell

Edward G. Robinson, Ruth Warrick, Ted Donaldson, Bob Haymes, Richard Lane, Robert Armstrong, Walter Baldwin

Mr Wong

A cheeseparing set of second features from Monogram, based on stories by Hugh Wiley. Boris Karloff was unsuitably cast as a Chinese detective, and in the last film he was replaced by Keye Luke. The films were directed by William Nigh.
1938: MR WONG DETECTIVE
1939: THE MYSTERY OF MR WONG, MR WONG IN CHINATOWN
1940: THE FATAL HOUR, DOOMED TO DIE (GB title: THE MYSTERY OF THE WENTWORTH CASTLE)
1941: PHANTOM OF CHINATOWN

Mr Wu*
US 1927 80m approx (24 fps) bw silent
MGM

A Chinese villain kills his daughter when she wants to marry an Englishman.
Turgid outmoded melodrama from a stage success: purely a star vehicle.

w Lorna Moon, *play* Maurice Vernon, Harold Owen *d* William Nigh *ph* John Arnold

Lon Chaney, Louise Dresser, Anna May Wong, Ralph Forbes, Renee Adoree, Holmes Herbert

Mrs Brown, You've Got a Lovely Daughter
GB 1968 95m Metrocolor Panavision

A young singer inherits a prize greyhound. Inoffensive comedy musical with a swinging London background. Peter Noone and Herman's Hermits, Stanley Holloway, Mona Washbourne, Lance Percival, Marjorie Rhodes. Written by Thaddeus Vane; directed by Saul Swimmer; for MGM.

Mrs Fitzherbert
GB 1947 99m bw
British National (Louis H. Jackson)

The Prince Regent secretly marries a Catholic widow.
Stilted, ill-cast historical charade.

w Montgomery Tully, *novel* Winifred Carter *d* Montgomery Tully *ph* James Wilson *m* Hans May

Peter Graves, Joyce Howard, Leslie Banks, Margaretta Scott

Mrs Gibbons' Boys
GB 1962 82m bw Byronscope

A widow plans to marry respectably for the sake of her three convict sons. Unattractive farce with clodhopping characters and too much slapstick. Kathleen Harrison, Lionel Jeffries, Diana Dors, John Le Mesurier, Frederick Bartman, David Lodge, Dick Emery, Eric Pohlmann, Milo O'Shea. Written by Peter Blackmore and Max Varnel, from the play by Joseph Stein and Will Glickman; directed by Max Varnel; for Byron / British Lion.

Mrs Mike
US 1949 99m bw
Nassour / Huntingdon Hartford (Edward Gross)

A Mountie takes his new wife to live in the frozen northwest.
Predictable sentimental drama, well enough done to keep interest, but only just.

w Lewis Levitt, De Witt Bodeen *d* Louis King *ph* Joseph Biroc *m* Max Steiner

Dick Powell, Evelyn Keyes, J. M. Kerrigan, Angela Clarke

Mrs Miniver**
US 1942 134m bw
MGM (Sidney Franklin)

An English housewife survives World War II. This is the rose-strewn English village, Hollywood variety, but when released it proved a beacon of morale despite its false sentiment, absurd rural types and melodramatic situations. It is therefore beyond criticism, except that some of the people involved should have known better.

w Arthur Wimperis, George Froeschel, James Hilton, Claudine West, *novel* Jan Struther *d* William Wyler *ph* Joseph Ruttenberg *m* Herbert Stothart

Greer Garson, Walter Pidgeon, Teresa Wright, Richard Ney, Dame May Whitty, Henry Travers, Reginald Owen, Henry Wilcoxon, Helmut Dantine, Rhys Williams, Aubrey Mather

VICAR (Henry Wilcoxon) preaching final sermon in bombed church: 'This is not only a war of soldiers in uniforms. It is a war of the people—of all the people—and it must be fought not only on the battlefield but in the cities and in the villages, in the factories and on the farms, in the home and in the heart of every man, woman and child who loves freedom. Well, we have buried our dead, but we shall not forget them. Instead, they will inspire us with an unbreakable determination to free ourselves and those who come after us from the tyranny and terror that threaten to strike us down. This is the people's war. It is our war. We are the fighters. Fight it, then. Fight it with all that is in us. And may God defend the right.'

'That almost impossible feat, a war picture that photographs the inner meaning, instead of the outward realism of World War II.'—*Time*

AA: best picture; script; William Wyler; Joseph Ruttenberg; Greer Garson; Teresa Wright
AAN: Walter Pidgeon; Dame May Whitty; Henry Travers

Mrs O'Malley and Mr Malone*
US 1950 69m bw
MGM (William H. Wright)

On a train to New York, a radio contest winner and a lawyer help solve a murder.
Lively second feature farce.

w William Bowers *d* Norman Taurog *ph* Adolph Deutsch

Marjorie Main, James Whitmore, Ann Dvorak, Fred Clark, Dorothy Malone, Phyllis Kirk

Mrs Parkington
US 1944 124m bw
MGM (Leon Gordon)

A lady's maid marries a miner who becomes wealthy, and pushes her way into society.
Thoroughly unconvincing three-generation drama, with a bewigged and powdered star giving the boot to her conniving relations. It has production values and nothing else.

w Robert Thoeren, Polly James, *novel* Louis Bromfield *d* Tay Garnett *ph* Joseph Ruttenberg *m* Bronislau Kaper

Greer Garson, Walter Pidgeon, Edward Arnold, Agnes Moorehead, Cecil Kellaway, Gladys Cooper, Frances Rafferty, Tom Drake, Peter Lawford, Dan Duryea, Hugh Marlowe, Selena Royle
† The heroine is shown having a romance with Edward VII when Prince of Wales; special scenes were shot for the European version substituting Cecil Kellaway, who played Edward, by Hugo Haas who played a European king of indeterminate origin.

AAN: Greer Garson; Agnes Moorehead

Mrs Pollifax—Spy
US 1970 110m De Luxe
UA / Mellor (Frederick Brisson)

A respectable American matron offers her services to the CIA and sees active service in Albania.
Incredible comedy-dramatic vehicle for a star who won't give up. An obvious failure from the word go.

w C. A. McKnight, *novel* Dorothy Gilman *d* Leslie Martinson *ph* Joseph Biroc *m* Lalo Schifrin

Rosalind Russell, Darren McGavin
† C. A. McKnight was Rosalind Russell.

Mrs Pym of Scotland Yard
GB 1939 65m bw

A lady detective exposes a fake spiritualist. A would-be series character bites the dust through plot malnutrition. Mary Clare, Edward Lexy, Nigel Patrick, Anthony Ireland, Irene Handl. Written by Fred Elles, Peggy Barwell and Nigel Morland, from the novel by Nigel Morland; directed by Fred Elles; for Hurley / Grand National.

Mrs Soffel
US 1984 110m Metrocolor
MGM-UA / Edgar Scherick / Scott Rudin

In 1901 Pittsburgh, a warder's wife falls for a prisoner and helps him escape.
A basis in truth does not prevent this from being both glum and dull from beginning to end, and pretentious treatment doesn't help.

w Ron Nyswaner *d* Gillian Armstrong *ph* Russell Boyd *m* Mark Isham *pd* Luciana Arrighi *ed* Nicholas Beauman

Diane Keaton, Mel Gibson, Matthew Modine, Edward Herrman

Mrs Wiggs of the Cabbage Patch*
US 1934 80m bw
Paramount (Douglas MacLean)

Adventures of a poor family who live on the wrong side of the tracks in a broken down old shack.
A Depression fantasy of respectability and optimism, almost incredible to see now, although it plumbed the same never-never milieu as did Chaplin. Moments of comedy still please, but one does long for Mr Fields' delayed entry.

w William Slavens McNutt, Jane Storm, *novel* Alice Hegan Rice *d* Norman Taurog *ph* Charles Lang

Pauline Lord, *Zasu Pitts, W. C. Fields*, Evelyn Venable, Kent Taylor, Charles Middleton, Donald Meek, Edith Fellows, Virginia Weidler, George Breakston

'A nasty all's-right-with-the-world burlesque of poverty, with emotions to tug at such heartstrings as are worn dangling from the mouth.'—*Otis Ferguson*

Mrs Wiggs of the Cabbage Patch
US 1942 80m bw
Paramount

Curiously quick remake, almost word for word, but without the moments of inspiration.

w Doris Anderson, Jane Storm, William Slavens McNutt *d* Ralph Murphy *ph* Leo Tover

Fay Bainter, Hugh Herbert, Vera Vague, Barbara Britton, Carl Switzer, Moroni Olsen, Billy Lee

Mix Me a Person
GB 1961 116m bw
Wessex (Sergei Nolbandov)

A barrister's psychiatrist wife takes on one of his failures, a client condemned to death for murder.
Once it gets started, a routine suspense thriller with the wrong man convicted and an espresso bar background. Not a very good one, though.

w Ian Dalrymple, *novel* Jack Trevor Story *d* Leslie Norman *ph* Ted Moore *songs* Johnny Worth *md* Muir Mathieson

Anne Baxter, Donald Sinden, Adam Faith, Walter Brown, Glyn Houston

Mixed Company
US 1974 109m De Luxe
UA / Cornell (Melville Shavelson)

A basketball coach and his wife adopt several children of different races.
Room for One More and then some, but not very interesting.

w Melville Shavelson, Mort Lachman *d* Melville Shavelson *ph* Stan Lazan *m* Fred Karlin *pd* Stan Jolley

Barbara Harris, Joseph Bologna, Lisa Gerritson, Arianne Heller

M'liss
US 1936 66m bw

A drunkard's daughter washes dishes in a western saloon. Laundered and fairly inept family version of a roistering tale. Anne Shirley, Guy Kibbee, John Beal, Douglass Dumbrille, Moroni Olsen, Arthur Hoyt. Written by Dorothy Yost, from the story by Bret Harte; directed by George Nicholls Jnr; for RKO.

The Mob*
US 1951 87m bw
Columbia (Jerry Bresler)
GB title: *Remember That Face*

A policeman works undercover to catch a dockside racketeer.
Tough, lively thriller with effectively sustained mystery and a serial-like finale.

w William Bowers d Robert Parrish
ph Joseph Walker *m* George Duning

Broderick Crawford, Richard Kiley, Ernest Borgnine, Neville Brand, Charles Bronson

Mob Town
US 1941 61m bw

A policeman tries to rehabilitate the young brother of an executed gangster. Another spin-off from the Dead End Kids, quite unremarkable. Dick Foran, Anne Gwynne, Billy Halop, Huntz Hall, Bernard Punsley, Gabriel Dell, Samuel S. Hinds. Written by Brenda Weisberg; directed by William Nigh; for Universal.

'America's greatest actor—as you like him!'
Moby Dick*
US 1930 75m bw
Warner

Captain Ahab returns minus a leg from fighting the white whale, and finds that his fiancée is too shocked to love him.
Mangled remake of a fine novel filmed in silent form as *The Sea Beast*.

w J. Grubb Alexander, *novel* Herman Melville *d* Lloyd Bacon *ph* Robert Kurrie

John Barrymore, Joan Bennett, Lloyd Hughes, May Boley, Walter Long

'Money picture, guaranteed by its action and by Barrymore.'—*Variety*

Moby Dick**
GB 1956 116m Technicolor
Warner / Moulin (John Huston)

A whaling skipper is determined to harpoon the white whale which robbed him of a leg.
Pretentious period adventure, rather too obsessed with symbolism and certainly too slowly developed, but full of interesting detail which almost outweighs the central miscasting.

w Ray Bradbury, John Huston, *novel* Herman Melville *d* John Huston *ph Oswald Morris*
m Philip Stainton

Gregory Peck, Richard Basehart, Friedrich Ledebur, Leo Genn, Orson Welles, James Robertson Justice, Harry Andrews, Bernard Miles, Noel Purcell, Edric Connor, Joseph Tomelty, Mervyn Johns

'Interesting more often than exciting.'—*Variety*

Mockery
US 1927 75m approx at 24 fps bw silent

A noble peasant saves a countess from the Russian revolution. Overly serious vehicle for a star more at ease in melodrama. Lon Chaney, Barbara Belford, Ricardo Cortez, Emily Fitzroy. Written and directed by Benjamin Christensen; for MGM.

The Model and the Marriage Broker
US 1951 103m bw
TCF (Charles Brackett)

A broker conceals her profession from a friend but gets the friend fixed up.
Moderate, unsurprising comedy somewhat overweighted by talent which can't express itself.

w Charles Brackett, Walter Reisch, Richard Breen *d* George Cukor *ph* Milton Krasner *m* Cyril Mockridge

Thelma Ritter, Jeanne Crain, Scott Brady, Zero Mostel, Michael O'Shea, Nancy Kulp

Model Wife
US 1941 78m bw

Young marrieds must pretend to be single in order to keep their jobs. Tedious comedy. Joan Blondell, Dick Powell, Charles Ruggles, Lee Bowman, Lucile Watson. Written by Charles Kaufman, Horace Jackson and Grant Garrett; directed by Leigh Jason; for Universal.

A Modern Hero*
US 1934 70m bw

A young circus rider becomes an automobile tycoon but overreaches himself. Unconvincing moral tale, performed and presented with nice touches. Richard Barthelmess, Jean Muir, Marjorie Ranbeau, Verree Teasdale, Florence Eldredge. Written by Gene Markey and Kathryn Scola, from the novel by Louis Bromfield; directed by *G. W. Pabst*; for Warners. 'Essentially weak on plot and characterization.'—*Variety*

'You'll never laugh as long and as loud again as long as you live! The laughs come so fast and so furious you'll wish it would end before you collapse!'

Modern Times***
US 1936 87m bw
Charles Chaplin

An assembly-line worker goes berserk but can't get another job.
Silent star comedy produced in the middle of the sound period; flashes of genius alternate with sentimental sequences and jokes without punch.

wd / m Charles Chaplin *ph* Rollie Totheroh, Ira Morgan

Charles Chaplin, Paulette Goddard, Henry Bergman, Chester Conklin, Tiny Sandford

'A natural for the world market . . . box office with a capital B.'—*Variety*

'A feature picture made out of several one- and two-reel shorts, proposed titles being *The Shop, The Jailbird, The Singing Waiter*.'—*Otis Ferguson*

Modesty Blaise
GB 1966 119m Technicolor
TCF / Modesty Blaise Ltd (Joseph Janni)

Female arch-agent Modesty Blaise defends a shipload of diamonds against a sadistic master criminal.
Comic-strip adventures made by people with no sense of humour; Fu Manchu was much more fun.

w Evan Jones, *comic strip* Peter O'Donnell, Jim Holdaway *d* Joseph Losey *ph* Jack Hildyard *m* Johnny Dankworth

Monica Vitti, Dirk Bogarde, Terence Stamp, Harry Andrews, Michael Craig, Scilla Gabel, Clive Revill, Rossella Falk, Joe Melia

'Flaming love found in the savage heart of the jungle!'

Mogambo*
GB 1953 116m Technicolor
MGM (Sam Zimbalist)

The headquarters of a Kenyan white hunter is invaded by an American showgirl and a British archaeologist and his wife, and they all go off on a gorilla hunt.
Amiable, flabby remake of *Red Dust*, with direction scarcely in evidence and the gorillas out-acting a genial cast.

w John Lee Mahin *d* John Ford *ph* Robert Surtees, F. A. Young

Clark Gable, Ava Gardner, Grace Kelly, Donald Sinden, Laurence Naismith, Philip Stainton

† The story was also made as *Congo Maisie* in 1940.

AAN: Ava Gardner; Grace Kelly

Mohammed, Messenger of God
Lebanon 1976 182m Eastmancolor Panavision
Filmco International (Moustapha Akkad)
aka: *The Message*

The life of the seventh-century religious leader.
Predictably reverential and exceedingly tedious religious epic, rather like a lesser de Mille item and fatally handicapped by the decision never to show Mohammed at all.

w H. A. L. Craig (with Arab advice) *d* Moustapha Akkad *ph* Jack Hildyard *m* Maurice Jarre *pd* Tambi Larsen, Maurice Fowler

Anthony Quinn, Irene Papas, Michael Ansara, Johnny Sekka, Michael Forest, André Morell

'For well over three hours this film stumbles, staggers, lurches and bumbles ahead, without any true rhythm, construction, vision, or even bare minimum of craft.'—*John Simon, New York*

AAN: Maurice Jarre

'Horror crawls from the depths of the earth!'

The Mole People
US 1956 78m bw

Archaeologists fall down a shaft and find themselves in a subterranean civilization where mole people are ruled by albinos.
Thoroughly boring nonsense which would insult a Saturday matinee. John Agar, Cynthia Patrick, Hugh Beaumont, Alan Napier. Written by Lazlo Gorog; directed by Virgil Vogel; for Universal–International.

Molly and Me
US 1945 76m bw
TCF

A cantankerous old man is tamed by his new housekeeper.
Sentimental little star vehicle.

w Leonard Praskins *d* Lewis Seiler *ph* Charles G. Clarke *m* Cyril Mockridge

Gracie Fields, Monty Woolley, Reginald Gardiner, Roddy McDowall, Natalie Schaefer, Edith Barrett

† This followed the more successful teaming of the stars in *Holy Matrimony*.

The Molly Maguires
US 1970 123m Technicolor Panavision
Paramount / Tamm (Martin Ritt, Walter Bernstein)

In the Pennsylvania coalmining district in the 1870s, an undercover detective exposes the leaders of a secret society.
Sober-sided and slow-moving account of actual events which also formed the basis for Conan Doyle's rather more entertaining *The Valley of Fear*. Expensive, nicely photographed, but unpersuasive and empty.

w Walter Bernstein *d* Martin Ritt *ph James Wong Howe* *m* Henry Mancini

Richard Harris, Sean Connery, Samantha Eggar, Frank Finlay, Anthony Zerbe, Bethel Leslie, Art Lund

'The film's vague sense of grievance and harrowing circumstances hangs in the air like the smoky pall cast up by the anthracite workings.'—*Richard Combs*

'A cold, dry and rather perfunctory film.'—*Arthur Schlesinger Jnr*

Moment by Moment
US 1979 105m Technicolor Panavision
Universal (Robert Stigwood)

A bored Beverly Hills wife has an affair with a young drifter.
Tedious proof that even the biggest new stars of the seventies can't carry a no-good picture.

wd Jane Wagner *ph* Philip Lathrop *m* Lee Holdridge *pd* Harry Horner

John Travolta, Lily Tomlin, Andra Akers, Bert Kramer, Debra Feuer

'Little more than an animated snapshot of its leading man, baring body and soul to various effect . . . truly terrible.'—*Gilbert Adair, MFB*

Moment of Danger
GB 1960 87m bw

Thieves fall out and pursue each other to Malaga. Falling between the stools of thriller and character drama, this is a poor effort in either category. Trevor Howard, Dorothy Dandridge, Edmund Purdom, Michael Hordern, Paul Stassino. Written by David Osborn and Donald Ogden Stewart, from a novel by Donald MacKenzie; directed by Laslo Benedek; for ABPC / Douglas Fairbanks Jnr. (US title: *Malaga*.)

Moment to Moment
US 1966 108m Technicolor
Universal (Mervyn Le Roy)

A housewife finds herself with a body on her hands.
Incredibly old-fashioned romantic / melodramatic malarkey set on the French Riviera but scarcely moving a step out of Hollywood. Lush settings made it marketable to women.

w John Lee Mahin, Alec Coppel *d* Mervyn Le Roy *ph* Harry Stradling *m* Henry Mancini

Jean Seberg, *Honor Blackman*, Sean Garrison, Arthur Hill, Grégoire Aslan

Mommie Dearest
US 1981 129m Metrocolor
Paramount / Frank Yablans

An account of the private life of Joan Crawford, from the biography by her adopted daughter Christina, who claimed spectacular ill-treatment.
On the screen it all seemed too silly for words, and nobody cared anyway.

w Frank Yablans, Frank Perry, Tracy Hotchner, Robert Getchell *d* Frank Perry *ph* Paul Lohmann *m* Henry Mancini *pd* Bill Malley

Faye Dunaway, Diana Scarwid, Steve Forrest, Howard da Silva (as Louis B. Mayer)

'The only thing that is not transparent about this film is why it was ever made.'—*Jo Imeson, MFB*

Mon Oncle*
France 1956 116m Eastmancolor
Specta / Gray / Alterdel–Centaure (Louis Dolivet)

A small boy has less affection for his parents than for his vague, clumsy uncle.
Tiresomely long star vehicle, with Tati harping on his theory of detachment, ie keeping his comic character on the fringes of the action. It really doesn't work in a film of this length, and the jokes are thin.

w Jacques Tati, Jacques Lagrange *d* Jacques Tati *ph* Jean Bourgoin *m* Alain Romains, Franck Barcellini

Jacques Tati, Jean-Pierre Zola, Adrienne Servatie, Alain Becourt, Yvonne Arnaud

'Deft, elusive, full of heart.'—*Brenda Davies, MFB*

'Cinema humour at its brilliant best.'—*Daily Worker*

AA: best foreign film

Mona Lisa**
GB 1986 104m Technicolor
HandMade / Palace (Stephen Woolley, Patrick Cassavetti)

An ex-con becomes chauffeur for a prostitute and becomes involved in the kinkier areas of the vice trade.
Only this actor could make a hit of this unsavoury yarn, with its highlights of sex and violence. But he did.

w Neil Jordan, David Leland *d Neil Jordan* *ph* Roger Pratt *m* Michael Kamen *pd* Jamie Leonard *ed* Lesley Walker

Bob Hoskins, Cathy Tyson, Michael Caine

'A film to see again, with the certainty that each viewing will add something new.'—*Monthly Film Bulletin*

Mondo Cane*
Italy 1961 105m Technicolor
Cineriz
aka: *A Dog's Life*

A documentary of thirty sequences of violently eccentric human behaviour, including cannibalism, pig killing, a dog meal restaurant, etc.
Emetic exploitation piece, quite glibly assembled. Its huge commercial success made one worry for the world.

wd Gualtiero Jacopetti *ph* Antonio Climati, Benito Frattari

AAN: song 'More' (*m* Riz Ortolani, Nino Oliviero, *ly* Norman Newell)

Money and the Woman
US 1940 80m bw

A bank executive falls for the wife of a thieving teller. Muddled drama which never gets its storyline straight. Jeffrey Lynn, Brenda Marshall, John Litel, Lee Patrick, Henry O'Neill, Roger Pryor, Henry Kolker. Written by Robert Presnell from a story by James M. Cain; directed by William K. Howard; for First National / Warner.

Money from Home
US 1954 100m Technicolor 3-D
Paramount / Hal Wallis

A racing tipster and an assistant veterinary surgeon find themselves in charge of a horse.
A comedy with two strokes against it: the stars, and that never-never gangster land which was already a terrible cliché in the early fifties.

w Hal Kanter, *story* Damon Runyon *d* George Marshall *ph* Daniel L. Fapp *m* Leigh Harline

Dean Martin, Jerry Lewis, Marjie Millar, Pat Crowley, Richard Haydn, Robert Strauss, Gerald Mohr, Sheldon Leonard

The Money Pit
US 1986 91m Du Art Color
Universal / Steven Spielberg (Frank Marshall, Kathleen Kennedy, Art Levinson)

New Yorkers take on an old suburban house, and find it was no bargain.
Witless semi-remake of *Mr Blandings Builds His Dream House*, with screams instead of subtlety and no real humour at all.

w David Giler *d* Richard Benjamin *ph* Gordon Willis *m* Michel Colombier *pd* Patrizia von Brandenstein *ed* Jacqueline Cambas

Tom Hanks, Shelley Long, Alexander Godunov, Maureen Stapleton, Joe Mantegna, Philip Bosco, Josh Mostel

'It begins unpromisingly and slides irrevocably downward from there.'—*Variety*

The Money Trap
US 1966 92m bw Panavision
MGM (Max E. Youngstein, David Karr)

A hard-up policeman turns to crime.
A cheap thriller decorated with waning stars; competent at the lowest level.

w Walter Bernstein, *novel* Lionel White *d* Burt Kennedy *ph* Paul C. Vogel *m* Hal Schaefer

Glenn Ford, Rita Hayworth, Elke Sommer, Ricardo Montalban, Joseph Cotten, Tom Reese, James Mitchum

Money, Women and Guns
US 1959 80m Eastmancolor Cinemascope

A murdered prospector scrawls a will before dying; a detective investigates the beneficiaries. What could have been an effective western whodunnit is jinxed by erratic writing and direction. Jock Mahoney, Kim Hunter, Tim Hovey, Gene Evans, William Campbell, Lon Chaney Jnr, Tom Drake, James Gleason. Written by Montgomery Pittman; directed by Richard H. Bartlett; for Universal-International.

'The 1931 nut crop is ready!'
Monkey Business***
US 1931 81m bw
Paramount (Herman J. Mankiewicz)

Four ship's stowaways crash a society party and catch a few crooks.
The shipboard part of this extravaganza is one of the best stretches of Marxian lunacy, but after the Chevalier impersonations it runs out of steam. Who's grumbling?

w S. J. Perelman, Will B. Johnstone, Arthur Sheekman *d* Norman Z. McLeod *ph* Arthur L. Todd

Groucho, Chico, Harpo, Zeppo, Thelma Todd, Rockcliffe Fellowes, Ruth Hall, Harry Woods

'Surefire for laughs despite working along familiar lines . . . picture has started off by doing sweeping business all over, and no reason why it shouldn't continue to tickle wherever it plays.'—*Variety*

Monkey Business*
US 1952 97m bw
TCF (Sol C. Siegel)
original title: *Darling I Am Growing Younger*

A chimpanzee in a research lab accidentally concocts an elixir of youth.
Remarkably laboured comedy by and with top people; it can't fail to have funny moments, but they are few and far between.

w Ben Hecht, Charles Lederer, I. A. L. Diamond *d* Howard Hawks *ph* Milton Krasner *m* Leigh Harline

Cary Grant, Ginger Rogers, *Charles Coburn*, *Marilyn Monroe*, Hugh Marlowe

CHARLES COBURN to Marilyn Monroe (playing his secretary): 'Find someone to type this.'

A Monkey in Winter*
France 1962 103m bw Totalvision
CIPRA / Cité (Jacques Bar)
aka: *Une Singe en Hiver; It's Hot in Hell*

In a small Normandy resort, a hotel owner and a literary guest get drunk together and plan great fantasies, but finally return to their responsibilities.
Amiable, meandering star character comedy.
w François Boyer, *novel* Antoine Blondin *d* Henri Verneuil *ph* Louis Page *m* Michel Magne
Jean Gabin, Jean-Paul Belmondo, Suzanne Flon, Noel Roquevert, Paul Frankeur, Gabrielle Dorziat

Monkey on My Back
US 1957 93m bw
UA / Imperial / Edward Small
A Guadalcanal hero is given morphine to relieve malaria and becomes addicted.
Dreary case history sold as exploitation.
w Crane Wilbur, Anthony Veiller, Peter Dudley, from the experiences of Barney Ross *d* André de Toth *ph* Maury Gertsman *m* Paul Sawtell, Bert Shafter
Cameron Mitchell, Dianne Foster, Jack Albertson, Paul Richards

Monkeys Go Home
US 1966 101m Technicolor
Walt Disney (Ron Miller)
An American inherits a French olive farm and trains chimpanzees to harvest the crop.
Footling comedy with not much of an idea, let alone a plot.
w Maurice Tombragel, *novel* The Monkeys by G. K. Wilkinson *d* Andrew V. McLaglen *ph* William Snyder *m* Robert F. Brunner
Maurice Chevalier, Dean Jones, Yvette Mimieux, Bernard Woringer, Jules Munshin, Alan Carney
'Innocuous, extrovertly cheerful and good-humoured—and very dull.'—*MFB*

The Monolith Monsters
US 1957 77m bw
U–I (Howard Christie)
A meteorite lands in the desert and causes rocks to rise and expand, becoming toppling pillars which threaten a local community.
Dully-written science fiction with moderate special effects.
w Norman Jolley, Robert M. Fresco *d* John Sherwood *ph* Ellis Carter *md* Joseph Gershenson
Lola Albright, Grant Williams, Les Tremayne, Phil Harvey

Monsieur Beaucaire*
US 1946 93m bw
Paramount (Paul Jones)
King Louis XV's bumbling barber impersonates a court dandy.
What seemed a lively period burlesque has faded somewhat with age, but it still has its moments. Any relation between this and the silent Valentino film is quite accidental.
w Melvin Frank, Norman Panama *d* George Marshall *ph* Lionel Lindon *md* Robert Emmett Dolan
Bob Hope, Joan Caulfield, Patric Knowles, Marjorie Reynolds, Cecil Kellaway, Joseph Schildkraut, Reginald Owen, Constance Collier, Hillary Brooke, Douglass Dumbrille, Mary Nash
'Whether you yawn or rather wearily laugh depends chiefly on your chance state of mind.'—*James Agee*

Monsieur Hulot's Holiday***
France 1953 91m bw
Cady / Discina (Fred Orain)
original title: *Les Vacances de Monsieur Hulot*
An accident-prone bachelor arrives at a seaside resort and unwittingly causes havoc for himself and everyone else.
Despite lame endings to some of the jokes, this is a film to set the whole world laughing, Hulot himself being an unforgettable character and some of the timing magnificent. One feels that it could very nearly happen.
w Jacques Tati, Henri Marquet *d* Jacques Tati *ph* Jacques Mercanton, Jean Mouselle *m* Alain Romans
Jacques Tati, Nathalie Pascaud, Michèle Rolla, Valentine Camax
'The casual, amateurish air of his films clearly adds to their appeal: it also appears to explain their defects.'—*Penelope Houston, MFB*
'It had me laughing out loud with more enjoyment than any other comedy film this year.'—*Daily Express*
AAN: script

Monsieur Verdoux**
US 1947 125m bw
Charles Chaplin
A bank cashier marries and murders rich women to support his real wife.
Interesting but unsatisfactory redrafting of the Landru case; the star is more dapper than funny, the moral is unconvincing, and the slapstick sequences too often raise yawns.
wd / m Charles Chaplin *ph* Rollie Totheroh
Charles Chaplin, Martha Raye, Isobel Elsom
'The cleverest and most brilliant film I have yet made.'—*Charles Chaplin*
'Even today it will seem a failure to anyone who has taken half a dozen lessons in film technique.'—*Andrew Sarris, 1970*
AAN: Charles Chaplin (as writer)

Monsieur Vincent*
France 1947 113m bw
EDIC / UGC
The life of 17th-century St Vincent de Paul, who gave up all worldly goods to devote his life to the poor.
Earnest, realistic Catholic biopic.
w Jean-Bernard Luc, Jean Anouilh *d* Maurice Cloche *ph* Claude Renoir *m* J. J. Grunenwald
Pierre Fresnay, Aimé Clairiond, Jean Debucourt, Lise Delemare

Monsignor
US 1982 121m De Luxe
TCF / Frank Yablans (Kurt Neumann)
An Irish cardinal supports the Vatican by doubtful financial means.
A largely boring *roman à clef*, with a sluggish story and uninspired performances.
w Abraham Polonsky, Wendell Mayes, *novel* Jack Alain Leger *d* Frank Perry *ph* Billy Williams *m* John Williams *pd* John de Cuir
Christopher Reeve, Genevieve Bujold, Fernando Rey, Jason Miller, Joe Cortese, Adolfo Celi, Leonardo Cimino
'Irrevocably grounded in a hash of breastbeating and pious platitudes.'—*Sight and Sound*

The Monster
US 1925 70m approx at 24 fps bw silent
A scientist abducts passing motorists and uses them in his experiments at bringing the dead back to life. Typical star grotesquerie without much flair. Lon Chaney, Gertrude Olmstead, Hallam Cooley, Walter James. Written by Willard Mack and Albert Kenyon, from a play by Crane Wilbur; directed by Roland West; for MGM.

The Monster and the Ape
US 1946 bw serial: 15 eps
The Matelogen Man is coveted by enemy agents, who set a trained ape loose on it. Archetypal 'horror' serial. Robert Lowery, George Macready, Ralph Morgan, Carole Matthews, Willie Best. Directed by Howard Bretherton; for Columbia.

The Monster and the Girl
US 1940 64m bw
Paramount (Jack Moss)
A man is wrongfully executed and his brain is implanted in a gorilla, which goes on the rampage.
Curiously ineffectual considering its plot and cast, this little horror thriller seems to have been the first to use this particular situation, which became very well worn later.
w Stuart Anthony *d* Stuart Heisler *ph* Victor Milner *m* Sigmund Krumgold
Paul Lukas, Ellen Drew, Joseph Calleia, George Zucco, Robert Paige, Rod Cameron, Phillip Terry, Onslow Stevens, Gerald Mohr
'The ape steals the picture.'—*Variety*

The Monster Club
GB 1980 97m colour
ITC / Chips (Milton Subotsky)
A vampire introduces his victim to a club for ghouls and witches, who tell their stories.
A spoofy but not very entertaining variation on a too-familiar formula.
w Edward and Valerie Abraham, *stories* R. Chetwynd-Hayes *d* Roy Ward Baker *ph* Peter Jessop *md* Graham Walker
Vincent Price, John Carradine, Anthony Steel, Simon Ward, James Laurenson,

Geoffrey Bayldon, Donald Pleasence, Richard Johnson, Britt Ekland, Anthony Valentine, Stuart Whitman, Patrick Magee

The Monster Maker
US 1944 64m bw

A doctor frustrated in love turns his girl friend's father into a monster by injecting him with acromegaly, a distorting disease. Ludicrous tinpot shocker. Ralph Morgan, J. Carrol Naish, Tala Birell, Wanda McKay, Glenn Strange. Written by Pierre Gendron, Martin Mooney, Lawrence Williams; directed by Sam Newfield; for Sigmund Neufeld / PRC.

'Horror that waited 100 million years becomes a terrifying reality!'

Monster on the Campus
US 1958 76m bw

A college professor studies a prehistoric fossilized fish, which turns everything that touches it into monsters. Silly horror stuff with little to take the attention. Arthur Franz, Whit Bissell, Joanna Moore. Written by David Duncan; directed by Jack Arnold; for Joseph Gershenson / Universal.

The Monster Squad*
Canada 1987 81m Metrocolor Panavision

Dracula, Frankenstein's monster, the Wolf Man, the Gill Man and the Mummy take refuge in a small American town. Mildly amusing spoof for the teenage audience. Stephen Macht, Duncan Regehr, Andre Gower, Robby Kiger, Tom Noonan. Written by Shane Black and Fred Dekker; directed by Fred Dekker; for Keith Barish/Taft/Tri-Star.

The Monster that Challenged the World
US 1957 83m bw

A giant caterpillar lays eggs in California's Salton Sea: one hatches . . . Overlong shocker for kids. Tim Holt, Audrey Dalton, Hans Conried, Milton Parsons. Written by Pat Fielder; directed by Arnold Laven; for Levy-Gardner-Laven / United Artists.

The Monster Walks
US 1932 57m bw

A supposed paralytic plans the death of his rich niece. Spooky house murder mystery, too hammy by half. Sheldon Lewis, Mischa Auer, Martha Mattox, Vera Reynolds, Willie Best. Written by Robert Ellis; directed by Frank Strayer; for Like / Action. 'Not badly done, but lacking utterly in novelty.'—*Variety*

Montana
US 1950 76m Technicolor
Warner (William Jacobs)

An Australian sheepman fights the cattle barons of Montana.
Modest western from the star's declining years at Warner.

w James R. Webb, Borden Chase, Charles O'Neal, *story* Ernest Haycox *d* Ray Enright *ph* Karl Freund *m* David Buttolph

Errol Flynn, Alexis Smith, S. Z. Sakall, Douglas Kennedy, James Brown, Ian MacDonald

Montana Belle
US 1952 82m Trucolor
RKO (Howard Welsch)

The Daltons rescue Belle Starr and insist that she works with them on a dangerous raid. Warmed-over western melodramatics, quite unmemorable.

w Horace McCoy, Norman S. Hall *d* Allan Dwan *ph* Jack Marta *m* Nathan Scott

Jane Russell, George Brent, Scott Brady, Forrest Tucker, Andy Devine, Jack Lambert, John Litel, Ray Teal

† The film was completed in 1948, but held over.

Montana Moon
US 1930 88m bw

A wealthy rancher's spoiled daughter is about to leave for New York when she falls for a handsome cowboy. A long string of nothings with bursts of song; incompetent early talkie. Joan Crawford, Johnny Mack Brown, Ricardo Cortez, Lloyd Ingraham, Cliff Edwards. Written by Sylvia Thalberg and Frank Butler; directed by Malcolm St Clair; for MGM.

Monte Carlo*
US 1930 94m bw
Paramount (Ernst Lubitsch)

A count passes himself off as a hairdresser to win a gambling lady.
Faded but charming romantic comedy with music, the first to show its director's sound style in full throttle, notably in the final 'Beyond the Blue Horizon' sequence.

w Ernest Vajda, *play* The Blue Coast by Hans Muller, *novel* Monsieur Beaucaire by Booth Tarkington *d Ernst Lubitsch* *ph* Victor Milner *m* W. Franke Harling *songs* Leo Robin, Richard Whiting *ad* Hans Dreier

Jack Buchanan, Jeanette MacDonald, Zasu Pitts, Tyler Brooke, Claud Allister, Lionel Belmore

'Nothing extra beyond usual par programmer.'—*Variety*

'Very stylish and sly, not to be missed.'—*New Yorker, 1978*

The Monte Carlo Story
Italy / US 1956 101m Technirama
Tatanus (Marcello Girosi)

A gambler looks for a rich wife, and finds instead a glamorous woman as penniless as himself: they become confidence tricksters but suffer a change of heart.
Lubitsch might have made something of it, but this is a flavourless pudding of a film and the stars can do nothing with it.

wd Samuel Taylor, *story* Marcello Girosi, Dino Risi *ph* Giuseppe Rotunno *m* Renzo Rossellini

Marlene Dietrich, Vittorio de Sica, Arthur O'Connell, Mischa Auer, Natalie Trundy, Jane Rose, Renato Rascel

'He's a cowboy. She's a woman. He's the best at what he does. And so is she.'

Monte Walsh*
US 1970 108m Technicolor
Cinema Center (Hal Landis, Bobby Roberts)

Two ageing cowboys find life increasingly hard and hopeless; an old acquaintance kills one and is shot by the other.
'Realistic' western developed in leisurely style with the emphasis on character and on the real drudgery of frontier life.

w David Z. Goodman, Lukas Heller, *novel* Jack Schaefer *d* William A. Fraker *ph* David M. Walsh *m* John Barry

Lee Marvin, Jack Palance, Jeanne Moreau, Mitch Ryan, Jim Davis

'As boring a western as ever involved a bronco-busting scene that alone cost almost half a million dollars.'—*Judith Crist*

Montenegro*
Sweden / GB 1981 96m Eastmancolor
Viking / Europa / Smart Egg (Bo Jonsson)

A housewife driven mad by boredom takes a lover and murders him.
Another case history in which the creator finds more symbolic meaning than the audience is likely to see. On the surface, a mildly entertaining piece of near-pornography.

w,d Dusan Makavejev *ph* Tomislav Pinter *m* Kornell Kovach

Susan Anspach, Erland Josephson, Bora Todorovic, Per Oscarsson

A Month in the Country*
GB 1987 96m colour

In the English countryside, two men recover from the horrors of World War I. Traditional British teledrama with much going for it despite a final lack of direction. Colin Firth, Kenneth Branagh, Natasha Richardson, Patrick Malahide, Tony Haygarth, Richard Vernon. Written by Simon Gray from the novel by J. L. Carr; directed by Pat O'Connor; for Kenith Trodd/Euston Films.

'Makes *Ben-Hur* look like an epic!'

Monty Python and the Holy Grail**
GB 1975 90m Technicolor
EMI / Python (Monty) Pictures / Michael White (Mark Forstater)

King Arthur and his knights seek the Holy Grail.
Hellzapoppin-like series of linked sketches on a medieval theme; some slow bits, but often uproariously funny and with a remarkable visual sense of the middle ages.

w Graham Chapman, John Cleese, Terry Gilliam, Eric Idle, Michael Palin *d* Terry Gilliam, Terry Jones *ph* Terry Bedford *animation* Terry Gilliam *m* Neil Innes *pd Roy Smith*

Graham Chapman, John Cleese, Terry Gilliam, Eric Idle, Michael Palin

'The team's visual buffooneries and verbal rigmaroles are piled on top of each other with no attention to judicious timing or structure, and a form which began as a jaunty assault on the well-made revue sketch and an ingenious misuse of television's fragmented style of presentation, threatens to become as unyielding and unfruitful as the conventions it originally attacked.'—*Geoff Brown*

Monty Python's Life of Brian**
GB 1979 93m Eastmancolor
Hand Made Films (John Goldstone)

A contemporary of Jesus is mistaken for him and crucified.
Controversial middle-eastern romp which left its creators battered but extremely wealthy. In the face of such an onslaught of bad taste, criticism seems irrelevant.

written by and starring John Cleese, Graham Chapman, Eric Idle, Michael Palin, Terry Gilliam, Terry Jones *d* Terry Jones *ph* Peter Biziou *m* Geoffrey Burgon

Monty Python's the Meaning of Life
GB 1983 90m Technicolor
Universal / Celandine / The Monty Python Partnership (John Goldstone)

A series of sketches in questionable taste. Subjects include organ transplants, sex, death and the results of overeating.

d Terry Jones *w* and starring Graham Chapman, John Cleese, Terry Gilliam, Eric Idle, Michael Palin, Terry Jones *ph* Peter Hannan *pd* Harry Lange *m* various

The Moon and Sixpence***
US 1943 85m bw (colour sequence)
Albert Lewin / David L. Loew (Stanley Kramer)

A stockbroker leaves his wife and family, spends some selfish years painting in Paris and finally dies of leprosy on a South Sea island.
Pleasantly literary adaptation of an elegant novel based on the life of Gauguin; a little stodgy in presentation now, but much of it still pleases.

w Albert Lewin, *novel* W. Somerset Maugham *d* Albert Lewin *ph* John Seitz *m* Dmitri Tiomkin

George Sanders, Herbert Marshall (as Maugham), *Steve Geray*, Doris Dudley, Elena Verdugo, Florence Bates, Heather Thatcher, Eric Blore, Albert Basserman

'An admirable film until the end, when it lapses into Technicolor and techni-pathos.'—*James Agate*

AAN: Dmitri Tiomkin

The Moon Is Blue*
US 1953 99m bw
Otto Preminger

A spry young girl balances the attractions of a middle-aged lover against her young one.
Paper-thin comedy partly set on top of the Empire State Building (and thereafter in a dowdy set); mildly amusing in spots, it gained notoriety, and a Production Code ban, by its use of such naughty words as 'virgin' and 'mistress'.

w F. Hugh Herbert, from his play *d* Otto Preminger *ph* Ernest Laszlo *m* Herschel Burke Gilbert

Maggie McNamara, David Niven, William Holden, Tom Tully, Dawn Addams

PATTY (Maggie McNamara): Men are usually bored with virgins. I'm so glad you're not. . . . Have you a mistress?'

DONALD: 'Don't you think it's better for a girl to be preoccupied with sex than occupied with it?'

'It adds nothing to the art of cinema and certainly does not deserve the attention it will get for flouting the Production Code.'—*Philip T. Hartung*

† The film was made simultaneously in German, as *Die Jungfrau auf dem Dach*, with Hardy Kruger, Johanna Matz and Johannes Heesters.

AAN: Maggie McNamara; title song (*m* Herschel Burke Gilbert, *ly* Sylvia Fine)

The Moon Is Down**
US 1943 90m bw
TCF (Nunnally Johnson)

A Norwegian village resists the Nazis.
Sombre, talkative, intelligent little drama, the best of the resistance films, shot on the set of *How Green Was My Valley* (with snow covering).

w Nunnally Johnson, novel John Steinbeck *d Irving Pichel ph* Arthur Miller *m* Alfred Newman

Henry Travers, Cedric Hardwicke, Lee J. Cobb, Dorris Bowden, Margaret Wycherly, Peter Van Eyck, John Banner

'This may well be a true picture of Norway and its people. But it fails to strike fire, to generate passion. It leaves one feeling rather proud but also sad.'—*Bosley Crowther*

'Jungle love tease! It's hot!'

Moon over Burma
US 1940 76m bw
Paramount

Jungle lumbermen fight over a stranded American entertainer.
Routine adventure romance climaxing in a forest fire.

w Frank Wead, W. P. Lipscomb, Harry Clark *d* Louis King *ph* William Mellor *m* Victor Young

Dorothy Lamour, Robert Preston, Preston Foster, Doris Nolan, Albert Basserman, Frederick Worlock, Addison Richards

Moon over Miami*
US 1941 92m Technicolor
TCF (Harry Joe Brown)

Two sisters seek rich husbands in Florida.
Musical remake of *Three Blind Mice*, which was suspiciously similar to *Golddiggers of Broadway, The Greeks Had a Word for Them*, etc., and the later *How to Marry a Millionaire* and *Three Little Girls in Blue*. In short, a Hollywood standard, not too badly done.

w Vincent Lawrence, Brown Holmes *d* Walter Lang *ph* Peverell Marley, Leon Shamroy *md* Alfred Newman *songs* Leo Robin, Ralph Rainger

Don Ameche, Betty Grable, Carole Landis, Robert Cummings, Charlotte Greenwood, Jack Haley, Cobina Wright Jnr, Robert Greig

Moon Pilot**
US 1961 98m Technicolor
Walt Disney (Ron Miller)

A reluctant astronaut falls in love with a girl from outer space, who finally accompanies him on his mission.
Engaging science-fiction spoof with good performances.

w Maurice Tombragel, *serial* Robert Buckner *d* James Neilson *ph* William Snyder *m* Peter Smith *sp* Eustace Lycett

Edmond O'Brien, Tom Tryon, Brian Keith

The Moon Spinners*
GB 1964 119m Technicolor
Walt Disney (Bill Anderson)

A young girl holidaying in Crete becomes involved with jewel robbers.
Teenage adventure against attractive locations; quite agreeable but overlong.

w Michael Dyne, *novel* Mary Stewart *d* James Neilson *ph* Paul Beeson *m* Ron Grainer

Hayley Mills, Peter McEnery, Eli Wallach, Joan Greenwood, John Le Mesurier, *Pola Negri*

'The number one space western!'

Moon Zero Two
GB 1969 100m Technicolor
Hammer (Michael Carreras)

In 2021, the moon is being colonized and crooks are trying to get control of an asteroid.
A self-acknowledged 'space western' which has a few bright ideas but suffers from a childish script.

w Michael Carreras, *story* Gavin Lyall, Frank Hardman, Martin Davidson *d* Roy Ward Baker *ph* Paul Beeson *m* Don Ellis

James Olson, Catherina Von Schell, Warren Mitchell, Ori Levy, Adrienne Corri, Dudley Foster, Bernard Bresslaw, Neil McCallum

'It's all just about bad enough to fill older audiences with nostalgia for the inspired innocence of Flash Gordon, or even the good old days of Abbott and Costello in outer space.'—*MFB*

Moonfleet*
US 1955 87m Eastmancolor Cinemascope
MGM (John Houseman)

In Dorset in 1770 an orphan boy finds that his elegant guardian leads a gang of smugglers.
Period gothic melodrama which nearly, but not quite, comes off; the script simply doesn't build to the right climax, and too many characters come to nothing. But there are splendid moments.

w Margaret Fitts, Jan Lustig, *novel* J. Meade Faulkner *d* Fritz Lang *ph* Robert Planck *m* Miklos Rozsa

Stewart Granger, Jon Whiteley, George Sanders, Joan Greenwood, Viveca Lindfors, Liliane Montevecchi, Melville Cooper, Sean McClory, John Hoyt, Alan Napier

Moonlight in Havana
US 1942 63m bw

A baseball catcher goes to Havana for spring training. Another in the long line of light-weight musical supports from this studio. Allan Jones, Jane Frazee, Marjorie Lord, William Frawley, the Jiving Jacks and Jills. Written by Oscar Brodney; directed by Anthony Mann; for Bernard W. Burton / Universal.

Moonlight Sonata*
GB 1937 90m bw
Pall Mall (Lothar Mendes)

Stranded victims of a plane crash are affected by the art of a famous pianist.
Curious, slight, unexpected play-on-film designed to showcase the talent of Paderewski.

w Edward Knoblock, E. M. Delafield *d* Lothar Mendes *ph* Jan Stallich

Ignace Paderewski, Eric Portman, *Marie Tempest*, Charles Farrell, Barbara Greene, Binkie Stuart

'Should make good with class audiences.'—*Variety*

'Dame Marie is a sparking line-tosser who keeps the script alive when Paderewski (then 77) is not putting it to music.'—*New York Times*

The Moonlighter
US 1953 77m bw 3-D
Warner (Joseph Bernhard)

A cattle rustler moves towards reforming.
Ho-hum western which offers its stars little to work with and was not even very exciting in 3-D.

w Niven Busch *d* Roy Rowland *ph* Bert Glennon *m* Heinz Roemheld

Fred MacMurray, Barbara Stanwyck, Ward Bond, William Ching, John Dierkes, Morris Ankrum

Moonlighting**
GB 1982 97m colour
Michael White / Channel Four (Mark Shivas, Jerzy Skolimowski)

In 1981 four Polish building workers arrive in London to renovate a house for their boss and make a quick profit. The scheme is somewhat upset by the news of martial law at home . . .
Very interesting and well-acted anecdote, virtually constructed out of the headlines.

wd Jerzy Skolimowski ph Tony Pierce Roberts *m* Stanley Myers *pd* Tony Woollard *ed* Barrie Vince

Jeremy Irons, Eugene Lipinski, Jiri Stanislaw, Eugeniusz Haczkiewicz

The Moonraker*
GB 1958 82m Technicolor
ABPC (Hamilton Inglis)

During the English Civil War, a noble highwayman smuggles the king's son into France.
Likeable swashbuckler which confines its second half to suspense at an inn, a who-is-it rather than a whodunnit. Good fun.

w Robert Hall, Wilfred Eades, Alistair Bell, *play* Arthur Watkyn *d* David MacDonald *m* Laurie Johnson *ph* Max Greene

George Baker, Sylvia Syms, Marius Goring, Peter Arne, Richard Leech, Clive Morton, Paul Whitsun-Jones, Gary Raymond, John Le Mesurier (as Cromwell), Patrick Troughton, Michael Anderson Jnr

Moonraker
GB 1979 126m Technicolor Panavision
UA / Eon (Albert S. Broccoli)

James Bond investigates the disappearance of a space shuttle during a test flight.
Adventures in Venice, Rio and the upper Amazon; all very repetitive and no longer more than faintly amusing.

w Christopher Wood, *novel* Ian Fleming *d* Lewis Gilbert *ph* Jean Tournier *m* John Barry *pd* Ken Adam

Roger Moore, Lois Chiles, Michael Lonsdale, Richard Kiel, Geoffrey Keen, Lois Maxwell, Bernard Lee

'Conspicuously expensive production values but an unmistakably cut price plot.'—*Sight and Sound*

Moonrise*
US 1948 90m bw
Republic (Charles F. Haas)

A murderer's son is driven into violence by memories and fears of his childhood.
Broody melodrama set against a remote village and swamp background; not a very interesting story, but memorable detail.

w Charles Haas *d Frank Borzage ph* John L. Russell *m* William Lava

Gail Russell, Dane Clark, Ethel Barrymore, Allyn Joslyn, Rex Ingram

'If the world is sane—then they're completely mad!'

The Moon's Our Home*
US 1936 80m bw
Paramount (Walter Wanger)

A headstrong actress marries an adventurer on impulse, and they both try to work it out.
Light, bright romantic comedy with the zany tinge then in fashion.

w Isabel Dawn, Boyce DeGaw, *novel* Faith Baldwin *d* William A. Seiter *ph* Joseph Valentine *m* Gerard Carbonara

Margaret Sullavan, Henry Fonda, Beulah Bondi, Charles Butterworth, Margaret Hamilton, Dorothy Stickney, Lucien Littlefield

The Moonshine War
US 1970 100m Metrocolor Panavision
MGM / Filmways (James C. Pratt, Leonard Blair)

In Kentucky just before the repeal of prohibition, a corruptible revenue agent regrets bringing in a sadistic crook to help confiscate illegal whisky.
Downright peculiar hillbilly melodrama, neither straight nor satirical; interesting only in fits and starts.

w Elmore Leonard, from his novel *d* Richard Quine *ph* Richard H. Kline *m* Fred Karger

Patrick McGoohan, Richard Widmark, Alan Alda, Melodie Johnson, Will Geer

The Moonspinners see The Moon Spinners

Moonstruck*
US 1987 102m Technicolor
Patrick Palmer / Norman Jewison

Young widow falls for the estranged brother of her husband-to-be.
Noisy, sometimes heavy-handed romantic comedy of Italian-American manners.

w John Patrick Stanley *d* Norman Jewison *ph* David Watkin *m* Dick Hyman *pd* Philip Rosenberg

Cher, Nicolas Cage, Vincent Gardenia, Olympia Dukakis, Danny Aiello

Moontide*
US 1942 94m bw
TCF (Mark Hellinger)

A seaman cares for an unhappy waif.
A Hollywood attempt at romantic melodrama in the French manner. It looks good, and the cast is fine, but everything is just a bit too glum.

w John O'Hara, *novel* Willard Robertson *d* Archie Mayo *ph* Charles G. Clarke *m* Cyril Mockridge, David Buttolph

Jean Gabin, Ida Lupino, Claude Rains, Thomas Mitchell, Jerome Cowan, Sen Yung, Tully Marshall, Helen Reynolds

AAN: Charles G. Clarke

The Morals of Marcus
GB 1936 75m bw
Real Art (W. J. Locke)

A girl escapes from a Middle Eastern harem by stowing away with a British aristocrat.
Feeble 'naughty' comedy, killed by lack of wit and pace.

w Guy Bolton, Miles Mander, *play* W. J. Locke *d* Miles Mander *ph* John W. Boyle

Lupe Velez, Ian Hunter, Adrienne Allen, Noel Madison, J. H. Roberts, H. F. Maltby

'Acceptable feature for general consumption.'—*Variety*

More American Graffiti
US 1979 111m Technicolor
Universal / Lucasfilm (Howard Kazanjian)

In 1964, American small-town teenagers quarrel over drugs and dragracing.
Tedious sequel to a movie which was more than enough.

wd B. W. L. Norton *ph* Caleb Deschanel *m* various

Candy Clark, Bo Hopkins, Ron Howard, Paul Le Mat, Mackenzie Philips, Richard Bradford

'What once was a crate of dynamite has been cosmetically giftwrapped à la *Happy Days*.'—*Cynthia Rose, MFB*

More Dead Than Alive
US 1968 99m De Luxe
United Artists / Aubrey Schenck

Revenge erupts some years after a violent jail break.
Eccentric and pretentious western with a complex story which might have intrigued if handled better.

w George Schenck *d* Robert Sparr *ph* Jack Marquette *m* Philip Springer

Clint Walker, Vincent Price, Anne Francis, Paul Hampton, Mike Henry, Craig Littler

More Than a Secretary
US 1936 80m bw

A dowdy secretary loses her glasses and wins her boss. *That* old story, and the treatment isn't anything to get excited about either. Jean Arthur, George Brent, Lionel Stander, Ruth Donnelly, Reginald Denny, Dorothea Kent, Charles Halton. Written by Dale Van Every, Lynn Starling; directed by Alfred E. Green; for Columbia. 'Fair b.o. possibilities, but the story doesn't belong on the same block as the production afforded to it.'—*Variety*

The More the Merrier***
US 1943 104m bw
Columbia (George Stevens)

In crowded Washington during World War II, a girl allows two men to share her apartment and falls in love with the younger one.
Thoroughly amusing romantic comedy with bright lines and situations; remade less effectively as *Walk Don't Run* (qv).

w Robert Russell, Frank Ross, Richard Flournoy, Lewis R. Foster *d George Stevens* *ph* Ted Tetzlaff *m* Leigh Harline *md* Morris Stoloff

Jean Arthur, Joel McCrea, Charles Coburn, Richard Gaines, Bruce Bennett

'The gayest comedy that has come from Hollywood in a long time. It has no more substance than a watermelon, but is equally delectable.'—*Howard Barnes*

'Farce, like melodrama, offers very special chances for accurate observation, but here accuracy is avoided ten times to one in favour of the easy burlesque or the easier idealization which drops the bottom out of farce. Every good moment frazzles or drowns.'—*James Agee*

† Garson Kanin has claimed to have written virtually all the script.

AA: Charles Coburn
AAN: best picture; script; original story (Frank Ross, Robert Russell); George Stevens; Jean Arthur

Morgan—A Suitable Case for Treatment**
GB 1966 97m bw
British Lion / Quintra (Leon Clore)

A young woman determines to leave her talented but half-mad artist husband, who has a fixation on gorillas and behaves in a generally uncivilized manner.
Archetypal sixties marital fantasy, an extension of *Look Back in Anger* in the mood of swinging London. As tiresome as it is funny—but it *is* funny.

w David Mercer, from his play *d Karel Reisz* *ph Larry Pizer, Gerry Turpin* *m* Johnny Dankworth

Vanessa Redgrave, *David Warner*, Robert Stephens, Irene Handl, Newton Blick, Nan Munro

'Poor Morgan: victim of a satire that doesn't bite, lost in a technical confusion of means and ends, and emerging like an identikit photograph, all bits and pieces and no recognizable face.'—*Penelope Houston*

'The first underground movie made above ground.'—*John Simon*

'I think *Morgan* is so appealing to college students because it shares their self-view: they accept this mess of cute infantilism and obsessions and aberrations without expecting the writer and director to resolve it and without themselves feeling a necessity to sort it out.'—*Pauline Kael*

AAN: Vanessa Redgrave

The Morning After
US 1986 103m De Luxe
TCF / Lorimar / American Filmworks (Bruce Gilbert)

A drunken actress wakes up one morning next to a man with a dagger in his heart.
A mystery which starts as intriguing but is insufficiently developed and peters out into a series of casual encounters between unattractive people.

w James Hicks *d* Sidney Lumet *ph* Andrzej Bartkowiak *m* Paul Chihara *pd* Albert Brenner *ed* Joel Goodman

Jane Fonda, Jeff Bridges, Raul Julia, Diane Salinger

AAN: Jane Fonda

Morning Departure*
GB 1950 102m bw
Rank / Jay Lewis (Leslie Parkyn)
US title: *Operation Disaster*

Twelve men are caught in a trapped submarine, and only eight can escape.
Archetypal stiff-upper-lip service tragedy, which moves from briskness to a slow funereal ending.

w William Fairchild, *play* Kenneth Woolard *d* Roy Baker *ph* Desmond Dickinson

John Mills, Richard Attenborough, Nigel Patrick, Lana Morris, Peter Hammond, Helen Cherry, James Hayter, Andrew Crawford, George Cole, Michael Brennan, Wylie Watson, Bernard Lee, Kenneth More

Morning Glory**
US 1933 74m bw
RKO (Pandro S. Berman)

A young actress comes to New York determined to succeed.
Marvellously evocative theatrical drama which provided a strong star part for a fresh young actress and surrounded her with accomplished thespians. Remade to much less effect as *Stage Struck* (qv).

w Howard J. Green, *play* Zoe Akins *d* Lowell Sherman *ph* Bert Glennon *m* Max Steiner

Katharine Hepburn, Douglas Fairbanks Jnr, Adolphe Menjou, Mary Duncan, C. Aubrey Smith, Don Alvarado

'Star vastly superior to this sometimes misdirected arty story.'—*Variety*

AA: Katharine Hepburn

'Revealing the amazing things a woman will do for love!'

Morocco***
US 1930 97m bw
Paramount (Louis D. Lighton)

A cabaret singer arrives in Morocco and continues her wicked career by enslaving all the men in sight; but true love reaches her at last.
The star's first American film reveals her quintessence, and although wildly dated in subject matter remains a perversely enjoyable entertainment.

w Jules Furthman, *novel* Amy Jolly by Benno Vigny *d Josef Von Sternberg* *ph* Lee Garmes *m* Karl Hajos

Marlene Dietrich, Gary Cooper, Adolphe Menjou, Ullrich Haupt, Juliette Compton, Francis McDonald

'Lightweight story with good direction . . . needs plenty of exploitation to do over average.'—*Variety*

'A definite step forward in the art of motion pictures.'—*National Board of Review*

'A cinematic pattern brilliant, profuse, subtle, and at almost every turn inventive.'—*Wilton A. Barrett*

'Enchantingly silly, full of soulful grand passions, drifting cigarette smoke, and perhaps a few too many pictorial shots of the Foreign Legion marching this way and that.'—*New Yorker, 1979*

AAN: Josef Von Sternberg; Lee Garmes; Marlene Dietrich

Morons from Outer Space
GB 1985 91m colour
Thorn EMI (Barry Hanson)

Dopey space travellers arrive on earth.
Spoofy comedy which, apart from staging a spectacular motorway landing and mocking various popular film genres, never decides where to go.

w Griff Rhys Jones, Mel Smith *d* Michael Hodges *ph* Phil Meheux *m* Peter Brewis

Mel Smith, Griff Rhys Jones, Paul Bown, Joanne Pearce, Jimmy Nail, Dinsdale Landen, James B. Sikking

'It remains stuck on the launch pad.'—*Variety*

The Mortal Storm**
US 1940 100m bw
MGM (Sidney Franklin)

A German family in the thirties is split by Nazism.
Solid anti-Nazi melodrama typical of the period before America entered the war; good performances outweigh unconvincing studio sets.

w Claudine West, George Froeschel, Andersen Ellis, *novel* Phyllis Bottome *d Frank Borzage ph* William Daniels *m* Edward Kane

Margaret Sullavan, Robert Young, James Stewart, Frank Morgan, Robert Stack, Bonita Granville, Irene Rich, Maria Ouspenskaya

'The love story of today with the popular stars of *The Shop Around the Corner*!'—*publicity*

† The film caused Goebbels to ban the showing of MGM pictures in all German territories.

Moscow Distrusts Tears*
USSR 1979 148m Sovcolor
Mosfilm (V. Kuchinsky)
original title: *Moskva Slezam Ne Verit*

In Moscow in 1958, three working girls have love affairs. Twenty years later they compare notes.
Odd portmanteau drama, most interesting for its picture of life in Russia.

w Valentin Chernykh *d* Vladimir Menshov *ph* Igor Slabnevich *m* Sergei Nikitin

AAN: best foreign film

Moscow Nights
GB 1935 75m bw

A Russian girl sacrifices her virtue to save her lover from execution. Cardboard melodrama of pre-revolutionary Moscow; not by any means a classic. Laurence Olivier, Penelope Dudley Ward, Harry Baur, Robert Cochran, Morton Selten, Athene Seyler. Written by Erich Seipmann, from the novel by Pierre Benoit; directed by Anthony Asquith; for London Films / Capitol Films. (US title: *I Stand Condemned*.)

† This was based directly on a 1934 French film, *Nuits Moscovites*, with Annabella, Pierre-Richard Willm, and Harry Baur.

Moscow on the Hudson*
US 1984 117m Metrocolor
Columbia / Delphi (Paul Mazursky)

A Soviet circus artiste defects in New York but has second thoughts.
Not so much a political comedy as an immigrant one, with the Big Apple shown at its worst. As such, occasionally funny in a desperate way, but overlong.

w Paul Mazursky, Leon Capetanos *d* Paul Mazursky *ph* Donald McAlpine *m* David McHugh *pd* Pato Guzman

Robin Williams, Maria Conchita Alonso, Cleavant Derricks, Alejandro Rey, Savely Kramarov

The Mosquito Coast*
US 1986 117m Technicolor
Saul Zaentz / Jerome Hellman

A frustrated visionary packs up and moves his family to a remote Caribbean island, where he fails to notice the seeds of downfall.
An antidote to *Robinson Crusoe* which is often wryly amusing, but the leading character is too hysterical and his fall too complete to make good drama.

w Paul Schrader *novel* Paul Theroux *d* Peter Weir *ph* John Seale *m* Maurice Jarre *pd* John Stoddart *ed* Thom Noble

Harrison Ford, Helen Mirren, River Phoenix, Jadrien Steele, Andre Gregory

'In the end there is barely a thread of hope to take home, other than some strikingly beautiful and sad images of a man grasping for something just beyond his reach.'—*Variety*

Mosquito Squadron
GB 1968 90m De Luxe

In 1944, the RAF tries out bouncing bombs in a French offensive. Very minor and belated war heroics for double-billing. David McCallum, Suzanne Neve, David Buck, Dinsdale Landen, Charles Gray. Written by Donald Sanford and Joyce Perry; directed by Boris Sagal; for Lewis J. Rachmil / UA.

Moss Rose
US 1947 82m bw
TCF (Gene Markey)

A Victorian chorus girl suspects her aristocratic admirer of being a murderer.
Absurd, stilted mystery melodrama with a better-looking production than it deserves.

w Jules Furthman, Tom Reed *d* Gregory Ratoff *ph* Joe MacDonald *m* David Buttolph

Peggy Cummins, Victor Mature, Ethel Barrymore, Vincent Price

The Most Dangerous Game***
US 1932 63m bw
(RKO) Merian C. Cooper
GB title: *The Hounds of Zaroff*

A mad hunter lures guests on to his island so that he can hunt them down like animals.
Dated but splendidly shivery melodrama with moments of horror and mystery and a splendidly photographed chase sequence. Much imitated in curious ways, and not only by direct remakes such as *A Game of Death* and *Run for the Sun* (qv).

w James Creelman, story Richard Connell d Ernest B. Schoedsack, Irving Pichel ph Henry Gerrard m Max Steiner

Leslie Banks, Joel McCrea, Fay Wray, Robert Armstrong, Noble Johnson

'Futile stab at horror film classification, ineffective as entertainment and minus cast names to compensate.'—*Variety*

The Most Dangerous Man in the World
GB 1969 99m De Luxe Panavision
TCF / APJAC (Mort Abrahams)
US title: *The Chairman*

A top scientist is sent by western intelligence on a mission into Red China, with a transmitter and a detonator implanted in his skull.
Wild Boys' Own Paper adventure which regrettably slows down in the middle for political philosophizing.

w Ben Maddow, *novel* The Chairman by Jay Richard Kennedy *d* J. Lee-Thompson *ph* Ted Moore *m* Jerry Goldsmith

Gregory Peck, Anne Heywood, Arthur Hill, Conrad Yama, Francisca Tu, Keye Luke, Alan Dobie, Ori Levy

The Most Precious Thing
US 1934 67m bw

A college boy marries a waitress; his mother eases the girl out but keeps the baby. Unconvincing domestic drama, rather drab. Anita Louise, Mary Forbes, Jane Darwell, Ben Alexander, John Wray, Ward Bond. Written by Ethel Hill, Dore Schary, from a magazine story by Travis Ingham; directed by Lambert Hillyer; for Columbia. 'Not enough strength for the more important spots.'—*Variety*

'It takes all kinds of critters
To make Farmer Vincent's fritters!'

Motel Hell
US 1980 106m Technicolor
United Artists / Camp Hill (Herb Jaffe)

Benign motel owners are famous for their spiced meat, which is in fact made from their human guests.
Horror comic intended to amuse, but too repulsive to do so.

w Robert Jaffe, Steven-Charles Jaffe *d* Kevin Connor *ph* Thomas Del Ruth *m* Lance Rubin

Rory Calhoun, Paul Linke, Nancy Parsons, Nina Axelrod, Wolfman Jack

Mother***
USSR 1926 90m approx (24 fps) bw silent
Mezhrabpom–Russ
original title: *Mat*

A mother incriminates her strike-breaking son, but realizes her error.
Propagandist social melodrama which is also brilliantly conceived and edited, with sequences matching those of Eisenstein.

w N. Zarkhi, V. I. Pudovkin, *novel* Maxim Gorky *d V. I. Pudovkin ph* A. Golovnia

Vera Baranovskaya, Nikolai Batalov

† Other versions appeared in 1920 and (*d* Mark Donskoi) 1955.

Mother Carey's Chickens
US 1938 82m bw
RKO (Pandro S. Berman)

The tribulations of a small-town family in the nineties.
Modest domestic drama, not totally unpleasing.

w S. K. Lauren, Gertrude Purcell, *novel* Kate Douglas Wiggin *d* Rowland V. Lee *ph* Roy Hunt *m* Frank Tours

Anne Shirley, Ruby Keeler, Fay Bainter, James Ellison, Walter Brennan, Donnie Dunagan, Frank Albertson, Alma Kruger, Jackie Moran, Virginia Weidler, Margaret Hamilton

† Remade 1963 as *Summer Magic*.

Mother Didn't Tell Me
US 1950 88m bw
TCF (Fred Kohlmar)

A working girl marries a doctor and their off duty hours don't coincide.
Thin comedy.

wd Claude Binyon, *novel* The Doctor Wears Three Faces by Mary Baird *ph* Joseph La Shelle *m* Cyril Mockridge

Dorothy McGuire, William Lundigan, June Havoc, Gary Merrill, Jessie Royce Landis

Mother Is a Freshman
US 1948 80m Technicolor

A mother goes to college and falls for the teacher with whom her daughter is infatuated. Thin romantic comedy lacking the piquancy at which it aims. Loretta Young, Van Johnson, Rudy Vallee, Barbara Lawrence, Betty Lynn, Robert Arthur. Written by Mary Loos and Richard Sale; directed by Lloyd Bacon; for TCF. (GB title: *Mother Knows Best.*)

Mother, Jugs and Speed
US 1976 98m De Luxe Panavision
TCF (Joseph R. Barbera)

Comic and tragic events in the lives of Los Angeles drivers of private commercial ambulances.
Black comedy of incidents ranging from farcical to sentimental, sometimes funny but basically unacceptable in either vein.

w Tom Mankiewicz *d* Peter Yates *ph* Ralph Woolsey *m* various *md* Joel Sill

Bill Cosby, Raquel Welch, Harvey Keitel, *Allen Garfield*, Bruce Davison, Larry Hagman

'The writer has found a way to get into the underbelly of a city, to survey the twilight territory where tragedy and comedy trip over each other and make an unsightly mess.'—*Time*

'The lure of gold can make a man do anything!'

Mother Lode
US 1982 101m colour
Agamemnon / Martin Shafter, Andrew Scheinman (Fraser Clarke Heston, Andrew Snell)

A villainous miner stops at nothing to protect his goldfield.
More-or-less old fashioned western with a change of pace for the star. No world beater, but not bad.

w Fraser Clarke Heston, Peter Snell *d* Charlton Heston *ph* Richard Leiterman *m* Ken Wannberg *pd* Douglas Higgins

Charlton Heston, Nick Mancuso, Kim Basinger, John Marley

Mother Riley Meets the Vampire
GB 1952 74m bw
Renown (John Gilling)
US title: *My Son the Vampire*

An old washerwoman accidentally catches a robot-wielding crook called The Vampire.
Childish farce notable for Lucan's last appearance in his dame role, and Lugosi's last substantial appearance of any kind—two pros at the end of their tether.

w Val Valentine *d* John Gilling *ph* Stan Pavey *m* Linda Southworth

Arthur Lucan, Bela Lugosi, Dora Bryan, Richard Wattis

'Stupid, humourless and repulsive.'—*MFB*

Mother Wore Tights*
US 1947 109m Technicolor
TCF (Lamar Trotti)

Recollections of a vaudeville team and their growing family.
Well-mounted, reasonably charming family musical, one of the best of the many TCF examples of this genre.

w Lamar Trotti, *book* Miriam Young *d* Walter Lang *ph* Harry Jackson *md* Alfred Newman, Charles Henderson

Betty Grable, Dan Dailey, Mona Freeman, Connie Marshall, Vanessa Brown, Robert Arthur, Sara Allgood, William Frawley, Ruth Nelson

AA: Alfred Newman, Charles Henderson
AAN: Harry Jackson; song 'You Do' (*m* Josef Myrow, *ly* Mack Gordon)

Moulin Rouge
US 1934 69m bw
Twentieth Century (Darryl F. Zanuck)

The wife of a songwriter impersonates her own sister in order to revitalize her marriage and her stage career.
Predictable minor star vehicle, quite competently done.

w Nunnally Johnson, Henry Lehrman, *play* Lyon de Bri *d* Sidney Lanfield *ph* Charles Rosher *md* Alfred Newman *songs* Harry Warren, Al Dubin

Constance Bennett, Franchot Tone, Tullio Carminati, Helen Westley, Andrew Tombes, Hobart Cavanaugh

Moulin Rouge**
GB 1952 119m Technicolor
Romulus (Jack Clayton)

Fictional biopic of Toulouse Lautrec.
The dramatic emphasis is on the love affairs of the dwarfish artist, but the film's real interest is in its evocation of 19th-century Montmartre, and especially in the first twenty-minute can can sequence. Nothing later can stand up to the exhilaration of this, and the film slowly slides into boredom.

w John Huston, Anthony Veiller, *novel* Pierre La Mure *d* John Huston *ph Oswald Morris* *m* Georges Auric *ad Paul Sheriff*

Jose Ferrer, Zsa Zsa Gabor, Katherine Kath, Colette Marchand, Suzanne Flon

AAN: best picture; John Huston (as director); Jose Ferrer; Colette Marchand

The Mountain*
US 1956 105m Technicolor Vistavision
Paramount (Edward Dmytryk)

After an airplane crash the wreck is difficult to reach. A young man sets off alone to loot it, and his elder brother follows to stop him.
An indeterminate production in which one believes neither the setting, the plot nor the characters, especially not with Vistavision making everything sharply unreal and the brothers seeming two generations apart.

w Ranald MacDougall, *novel* Henri Troyat *d* Edward Dmytryk *ph* Franz Planer *m* Daniele Amfitheatrof

Spencer Tracy, Robert Wagner, Claire Trevor, William Demarest, E. G. Marshall

The Mountain Eagle
GB 1926 72m approx (24 fps) bw silent
Gainsborough / Emelka (Michael Balcon)
US title: *Fear o'God*

A young schoolmistress resists the attentions of a businessman, escapes to the mountains, and marries a recluse.
Unremarkable romantic drama; one of the lost Hitchcock films.

w Eliot Stannard *d* Alfred Hitchcock *ph* Baron Ventimiglia

Nita Naldi, Bernard Goetzke, Malcolm Keen

Mountain Justice
US 1937 82m bw

A frightened hillbilly girl kills her brutal father and is protected by a lawyer. Involved backwoods melodrama, not really worth the trouble. Josephine Hutchinson, George Brent, Robert Barrat, Guy Kibbee, Mona Barrie, Margaret Hamilton, Robert McWade. Written by Norman Reilly Raine, Luci Ward; directed by Michael Curtiz; for Warners. 'Too much plot, but okay for duals.'—*Variety*

The Mountain Men
US 1980 102m Metrocolor Panavision

Two nineteenth-century trappers have adventures with Indians. Rumbustious, foul-mouthed and lethargic western of the primitive kind; no possible interest. Charlton Heston, Brian Keith, Victoria Racino, Stephen Macht, John Glover. Written by Frazer Clarke Heston; directed by Richard Lang; for Martin Ransohoff / Columbia. 'It plays like a Sunn Classic four-waller uncomfortably spiced up with violence and profanity.'—*Variety.*

Mountain Music
US 1937 76m bw

A hillbilly runs from a marriage and loses his memory. Tiresome comedy with music. Martha Raye, Bob Burns, John Howard, George Hayes, Rufe Davis, Fuzzy Knight. Written by J. C. Moffitt, Duke Atteberry, Russel Crouse, Charles Lederer, from a story by Mackinlay Kantor; directed by Robert Florey; for Paramount. 'Burns and Raye have trouble topping a cast. Mild and minor.'—*Variety*

The Mountain Road
US 1960 102m bw
Columbia / William Goetz

In 1944 China, an American officer helps peasants against the Japanese.
Confused and rather dreary war adventure with pretensions.

w Alfred Hayes, *novel* Theodore White *d* Delbert Mann *ph* Burnett Guffey *m* Jerome Moross *md* Morris Stoloff

James Stewart, Lisa Lu, Glenn Corbett, Henry Morgan, Frank Silvera, James Best, Mike Kellin, Frank Maxwell, Alan Baxter

'Mother and daughter! Rivals in love!'

Mourning Becomes Electra*
US 1947 170m bw
RKO / Theatre Guild (Dudley Nichols)

Murder, doom and guilt affect a New England family at the end of the Civil War.
A mark for trying is all. This is a clearly fated attempt to film the unfilmable, a long and lugubrious updating of Sophocles with more than its share of risible moments.

wd Dudley Nichols, *play* Eugene O'Neill *m* Richard Hagemann *ph George Barnes* *ad* Albert D'Agostino

Michael Redgrave, Rosalind Russell, Katina Paxinou, Kirk Douglas, Raymond Massey, Nancy Coleman, Leo Genn

'A star cast fumbles with helpless and sometimes touching ineptitude.'—*Gavin Lambert*

'Within its own terms of mistaken reverence, a good, straight, deliberately unimaginative production.'—*James Agee*

'It is apparent from their accents that they have only recently become a family.'—*Pauline Kael, 70s*

AAN: Michael Redgrave; Rosalind Russell

The Mouse on the Moon
GB 1963 85m Eastmancolor
UA / Walter Shenson

The tiny duchy of Grand Fenwick discovers that its home-made wine makes excellent rocket fuel.
Piddling sequel to *The Mouse that Roared*, suffering from a hesitant script, too few jokes, and overacting.

w Michael Pertwee *d* Richard Lester *ph* Wilkie Cooper *m* Ron Grainer

Margaret Rutherford, Ron Moody, Bernard Cribbins, David Kossoff, Terry-Thomas, Michael Crawford

The Mouse that Roared**
GB 1959 85m Technicolor
Columbia / Open Road (Carl Foreman)

The tiny duchy of Grand Fenwick is bankrupt, and its minister decides to declare war on the United States, be defeated, and receive Marshall Aid.
Lively comedy which sounds rather better than it plays, but has bright moments.

w Roger Macdougall, Stanley Mann, *novel* Leonard Wibberley *d* Jack Arnold *ph* John Wilcox *m* Edwin Astley

Peter Sellers (playing three parts), Jean Seberg, David Kossoff, William Hartnell, Leo McKern, Macdonald Parke, Harold Kasket

'The kind of irrepressible topical satire whose artistic flaws become increasingly apparent but whose merits outlast them.'—*Peter John Dyer*

The Mouthpiece**
US 1932 90m bw
Warner (Lucien Hubbard)

A prosecuting counsel successfully turns to defence but becomes corrupt.
A hard-hitting and entertaining melodrama allegedly based on the career of William Fallon, a New York lawyer.

w Joseph Jackson, Earl Baldwin *d* James Flood, Elliott Nugent *ph* Barney McGill

Warren William, Sidney Fox, Aline MacMahon, John Wray, Ralph Ince, Guy Kibbee

'First-grade melodrama, a bet for all grades of houses.'—*Variety*

Move
US 1970 88m De Luxe Panavision

A frustrated playwright writes pornography to make money; he moves to a larger apartment but his mind is full of fantasies. None of which are of much interest to the paying customers, the movie being drenched with self-pity.
Elliott Gould, Paula Prentiss, Genevieve Waite, John Larch, Joe Silver. Written by Joel Lieber and Stanley Hart, from a novel by Joel Lieber; directed by Stuart Rosenberg; for TCF.

Move Over Darling**
US 1963 103m De Luxe Cinemascope
TCF / Arcola / Arwin (Aaron Rosenberg, Marty Melcher)

A wife who has spent five years shipwrecked on a desert island returns to find that her husband has just remarried.
Thin but fitfully amusing remake of *My Favorite Wife*; sheer professionalism gets it by.

w Hal Kanter, Jack Sher *d* Michael Gordon *ph* Daniel L. Fapp *m* Lionel Newman

Doris Day, James Garner, Polly Bergen, Thelma Ritter, Chuck Connors, Fred Clark

Movers and Shakers
US 1985 79m Metrocolor
MGM-UA / BHC (Charles Grodin, William Asher)

A Hollywood writer tries to cope with a difficult project while having personal problems with his wife.
Mishmash of unrealized anecdotes with pauses for studio in-jokes. Despite the talent, it could never have worked, not even under the previously announced title *Dreamers*.

w Charles Grodin *d* William Asher *ph* Robbie Greenberg *m* Ken and Mitzie Welch

Walter Matthau, Charles Grodin, Vincent Gardenia, Tyne Daly, Bill Macy, Gilda Radner, Steve Martin, Nita Talbot

'Only occasionally amusing: faces a bleak boxoffice future.'—*Variety*

Movie Crazy**
US 1932 82m bw
Harold Lloyd

A filmstruck young man is mistakenly invited to Hollywood for a film test.
The silent comedian is not quite at his best in this early sound comedy, but it contains his last really superb sequences and its picture of Hollywood is both amusing and nostalgic.

w Harold Lloyd and others *d* Clyde Bruckman *ph* Walter Lundin

Harold Lloyd, Constance Cummings

'A corking comedy, replete with wow belly laughs. Sure-fire.'—*Variety*

Movie Movie**
US 1978 106m part colour
ITC (Stanley Donen)

A pastiche of a thirties double bill, including a boxing yarn (*Dynamite Hands*) and a Busby-Berkeley style girlie show (*Baxter's Beauties of 1933*).
Unfortunately there weren't enough paying customers to appreciate the spoofs, which are pretty patchy anyway; but golden moments stay in the mind.

w Larry Gelbart, Sheldon Keller *d* Stanley Donen *ph* Chuck Rosher Jnr, Bruce Surtees *m* Ralph Burns *ch* Michael Kidd

George C. Scott, Trish Van Devere, Red Buttons, Eli Wallach, Michael Kidd, Barbara Harris, Barry Bostwick, Art Carney, Jocelyn Brando

'*Camp*, which has to do with a switch of vision from one era to another, cannot be created, and where it is, as this and previous attempts testify, it is immediately swallowed in its own idiocy.'—*Richard Combs, MFB*

Movietone Follies of 1930
US 1930 70m bw

A rich boy courts a chorus girl, and her friends give a show on his estate. Thin, fumbling drama which doesn't remember to become a musical till it's halfway through, and even then has little spark. El Brendel, Marjorie White, William Collier Jnr, Miriam Seegar, Frank Richardson. Written by William K. Wells; directed by Ben Stoloff; for Fox.

Moving Violation*
US 1976 91m De Luxe
TCF / Roger Corman

Small-town teenagers are pursued by the sheriff because they saw him commit a murder.
Old hat suspenser with a smart new line in thrills.

w David R. Osterhout, William Norton *d Charles S. Dubin* *ph* Charles Correll *m* Don Leake

Stephen McHattie, Kay Lenz, Eddie Albert, Lonnie Chapman, Will Geer

'Probably the most hair-raising pursuit sequences in the history of film.'—*Cleveland Amory*

Moving Violations
US 1985 90m De Luxe

Misadventures of trainee traffic school cops. Wasn't *Police Academy* bad enough? John Murray, Jennifer Tilly, James Keach, Brian

Backer. Written by Neal Israel, Pat Proft; directed by Neal Israel; for Ufland-Roth-IPI-James G. Robinson / TCF.

Much Too Shy
GB 1942 92m bw
Columbia (Ben Henry)

A gormless handyman gets into trouble when the portraits of his lady clients are sold to an advertising agency with nude bodies added to them.
A slightly vulgar and talkative farce which restricts the star.

w Ronald Frankau *d* Marcel Varnel
ph Arthur Crabtree

George Formby, Kathleen Harrison, Hylda Bayley, Eileen Bennett, Joss Ambler, Jimmy Clitheroe

The Mudlark**
GB 1950 98m bw
TCF (Nunnally Johnson)

A scruffy boy from the docks breaks into Windsor Castle to see Queen Victoria and ends her fifteen years of seclusion.
A pleasant whimsical legend which could have done without the romantic interest, but which despite an air of unreality provides warm-hearted, well upholstered entertainment for family audiences.

w Nunnally Johnson, novel Theodore Bonnet
d Jean Negulesco ph Georges Périnal
m William Alwyn *ad* C. P. Norman

Alec Guinness, Irene Dunne, *Andrew Ray*, Anthony Steel, Constance Smith, *Finlay Currie*, *Edward Rigby*

Mug Town
US 1943 60m bw

The Little Tough Guys get mixed up with hi-jackers. A failing entry in this series: the ageing teenagers shortly decided to play for laughs. Billy Halop, Huntz Hall, Bernard Punsley, Gabriel Dell, Grace McDonald, Edward Norris, Jed Prouty. Written by Brenda Weisberg, Harold Tarshis, Harry Sucher and Lewis Amster; directed by Ray Taylor; for Universal.

'It comes to life!'
'A love story that lived for three thousand years!'

The Mummy**
US 1932 72m bw
Universal (Stanley Bergerman)

An Egyptian mummy comes back to life and covets a young girl.
Strange dreamlike horror film with only fleeting frissons but plenty of narrative interest despite the silliest of stories and some fairly stilted acting.

w John L. Balderston d Karl Freund
ph Charles Stumar ad Willy Pogany
m Tchaikovsky

Boris Karloff, Zita Johann, David Manners, Arthur Byron, Edward Van Sloan

'Should show profit despite fairy tale theme.'—*Variety*

'It beggars description . . . one of the most unusual talkies ever produced.'—*New York Times*

'Editing very much in the Germanic style, magnificent lighting and a superb performance from Karloff make this a fantasy almost without equal.'—*John Baxter, 1968*

† The star was billed simply as 'Karloff the uncanny'.

The Mummy*
GB 1959 88m Technicolor
Hammer (Michael Carreras)

A mummy brought back to England by archaeologists wakes up and goes on the rampage.
Typical Hammer vulgarization of a Hollywood legend; starts slowly and unpleasantly, but picks up speed and resource in the last half hour.

w Jimmy Sangster *d* Terence Fisher *ph* Jack Asher *m* Frank Reizenstein

Peter Cushing, Christopher Lee, Yvonne Furneaux, Eddie Byrne, Felix Aylmer, Raymond Huntley, John Stuart
† Hammer sequels, of little interest, were *Curse of the Mummy's Tomb* (1964), *The Mummy's Shroud* (1966) and *Blood from the Mummy's Tomb* (1971).

Mummy's Boys
US 1936 68m bw

Two ditch diggers in Egypt encounter some dirty work by a mad archaeologist. Ho-hum comedy with tired old gags. Bert Wheeler, Robert Woolsey, Barbara Pepper, Moroni Olsen, Willie Best. Written by Jack Townley, Philip G. Epstein, Charles Roberts; directed by Fred Guiol; for Lee Marcus / RKO. 'Poorly acted, raggedly written . . . net result of the dialogue is about four snickers.'—*Variety*

'Tomb of a thousand terrors!'

The Mummy's Hand**
US 1940 67m bw
Universal (Ben Pivar)

The high priest of an evil sect revivifies an Egyptian mummy and uses it to kill off members of an archaeological expedition.
Semi-sequel to 1932's *The Mummy*, economically using the same flashback. It starts off in comedy vein, but the last half hour is among the most scary in horror film history.

w Griffin Jay, Maxwell Shane *d Christy Cabanne ph* Elwood Bredell

Dick Foran, Wallace Ford, *George Zucco*, Cecil Kellaway, Peggy Moran, *Tom Tyler, Eduardo Ciannelli*

† Sequels, of decreasing merit, were *The Mummy's Tomb* (1942) (in which the heroes of *The Mummy's Hand* are killed off), *The Mummy's Ghost* (1944) and *The Mummy's Curse* (1944). See also *Abbott and Costello Meet the Mummy*.

The Mummy's Tomb
US 1942 61m bw

The aged high priest sends a young disciple to America, where Kharis dutifully kills off those who violated his tomb. Shoddily made sequel to *The Mummy's Hand*, with much re-used footage; astonishingly, it broke box office records for its year, and provoked two more episodes. Turhan Bey, George Zucco, Dick Foran, Wallace Ford, Elyse Knox, Lon Chaney Jnr. Written by Griffin Jay and Henry Sucher; directed by Harold Young; for Ben Pivar / Universal.

'Nameless! Fleshless! Deathless!'

The Mummy's Ghost
US 1944 60m bw

The slow but unstoppable Kharis is now on the trail of his long-lost princess. A slight improvement on its predecessor. John Carradine, George Zucco, Ramsay Ames, Robert Lowery, Barton MacLane, Lon Chaney Jnr. Written by Griffin Jay, Henry Sucher, Brena Weisberg; directed by Reginald LeBorg; for Ben Pivar / Universal.

'Egypt's ancient loves live again in evil!'

The Mummy's Curse
US 1944 62m bw

Sequel to *The Mummy's Ghost*, notable for many loose ends of narrative. Last of the Universal mummy films (until Abbott and Costello met him). Peter Coe, Martin Kosleck, Kay Harding, Kurt Katch, Virginia Christine, Lon Chaney Jnr. Written by Bernardo Schubert (could he have existed?); directed by Leslie Goodwins; for Oliver Drake / Universal. 'This film contains the most nauseous horror imaginable and is not for the squeamish.'—*Monthly Film Bulletin*

'Buried alive for 3700 years! Brought back to live, love and kill!'

The Mummy's Shroud
GB 1966 84m Technicolor
Hammer (Anthony Nelson-Keys)

In the twenties, an exhumed mummy brought to the city museum is restored to life and slaughters those who disturbed his rest.
Uninventive rehash of every other mummy movie; too hackneyed to be saved even by a good cast and production values.

wd John Gilling *ph* Arthur Grant *m* Don Banks

John Phillips, André Morell, David Buck, Elizabeth Sellars, Catherine Lacey, Maggie Kimberley, Michael Ripper, Tim Barrett, Roger Delgado, Dickie Owen

'Beware the beat of the cloth-wrapped feet!'—*publicity*

Mumsy, Nanny, Sonny and Girly
GB 1959 102m Eastmancolor
CIRO / Brigitte (Ronald J. Kahn)
aka: *Girly*

Two adolescents bring home lonely people as playthings for a homicidal family.
Revolting black comedy for masochists, representing the British cinema at its lowest ebb.

w Brian Comport, *play* Maisie Mosco
d Freddie Francis *ph* David Muir *m* Bernard Ebbinghouse

Michael Bryant, Ursula Howells, Pat Heywood, Howard Trevor, Vanessa Howard

'More entertainment than humanly possible!'

The Muppet Movie**
GB 1979 97m Eastmancolor
ITC (Jim Henson)

Kermit the Frog and friends travel across America to Hollywood and are offered a film contract by Lew Lord, the famous impresario. Technically an adroit transfer of the celebrated puppets from their TV backstage milieu to a wider canvas; but the latter tends to dwarf them, the material is very variable, the guest stars look embarrassed and the show goes on too long.

w Jerry Juhl, Jack Burns *d* James Frawley *ph* Isidore Mankofsky *pd* Joel Schiller *m* Paul Williams, Kenny Ascher

Charles Durning, Edgar Bergen, Bob Hope, Milton Berle, Mel Brooks, James Coburn, Dom DeLuise, Elliott Gould, Cloris Leachman, Telly Savalas, Orson Welles

The Muppets Take Manhattan*
US 1984 94m Technicolor
Tri-Star (David Lazer)

The Muppets' varsity show is promised a New York opening.
Probably the best of the Muppet features, but by the time of its arrival the early brilliance had been forgotten and even Miss Piggy had worn out her welcome.

w Frank Oz, Tom Patchett, Jay Tarses *d* Frank Oz

AAN: Jeffrey Moss (music)

Murder**
GB 1930 92m bw
British International (John Maxwell)

A girl is convicted of murder, but one of the jurors sets out to prove her innocent.
Interesting early Hitchcock, a rare whodunnit for him.

w Alma Reville, *novel* Enter Sir John by Clemence Dane and Helen Simpson *d Alfred Hitchcock* *ph* Jack Cox

Herbert Marshall, Nora Baring, Phyllis Konstam, Edward Chapman, Miles Mander, Esmé Percy, Donald Calthrop

'If Hitchcock produced in Hollywood and was wise enough to keep his films to six or seven reels, he might be a rave anywhere.'—*Variety*

Murder Ahoy
GB 1964 74m bw
MGM (Lawrence P. Bachmann)

Miss Marple investigates murders on a naval cadet training ship.
Weakest of the Marple mysteries: all chat and no interest.

w David Pursall, Jack Seddon *d* George Pollock *ph* Desmond Dickinson *m* Ron Goodwin

Margaret Rutherford, Lionel Jeffries, Stringer Davis, Charles Tingwell, William Mervyn, Joan Benham, Nicholas Parsons, Miles Malleson, Henry Oscar, Derek Nimmo, Francis Matthews, Gerald Cross

Murder Among Friends
US 1941 61m bw

Subscribers to a 200,000-dollar insurance policy die one by one. Pleasingly efficient supporting mystery. John Hubbard, Marjorie Weaver, Cobina Wright Jnr, Mona Barrie, Douglass Dumbrille, Sidney Blackmer, Lucien Littlefield, Milton Parsons. Written by John Larkin; directed by Ray McCarey; for Ralph Dietrich-Walter Morosco / TCF.

Murder at Monte Carlo
GB 1934 70m bw
Warner (Irving Asher)

A professor is murdered for his roulette system.
Modest second feature notable only as a springboard for the career of its star.

w John Hastings Turner, Michael Barringer, *novel* Tom Van Dyke *d* Ralph Ince *ph* Basil Emmott

Errol Flynn, Eve Gray, Paul Graetz, Molly Lamont, Ellis Irving

'By the first lady of mystery—with the last word in detectives!'

Murder at the Gallop*
GB 1963 81m bw
MGM (Lawrence P. Bachmann)

Miss Marple investigates when an old man is apparently frightened to death by a cat.
Probably the best of the Marples, with a good sense of place and lively performances.

w James P. Cavanagh, *novel* After the Funeral by Agatha Christie *d* George Pollock *ph* Arthur Ibbetson *m* Ron Goodwin

Margaret Rutherford, Flora Robson, Robert Morley, Stringer Davis, Charles Tingwell, Duncan Lamont, James Villiers, Robert Urquhart, Katya Douglas

Murder at the Vanities*
US 1934 95m bw
Paramount (E. Lloyd Sheldon)

Murder backstage at the first night of Earl Carroll's Vanities.
Curious, stylish mixture of musical numbers, broad comedy and mystery. Dated, but fun.

w Carey Wilson, Joseph Gollomb, Sam Hellman *d Mitchell Leisen* *ph* Leo Tover *songs* Arthur Johnston, Sam Coslow *md* Rudolph Kopp

Jack Oakie, Victor McLaglen, Carl Brisson, Kitty Carlisle, Dorothy Stickney, Gertrude Michael, Jessie Ralph, Gail Patrick

'Above average and for the masses . . . long but does not drag.'—*Variety*

'It can boast lavish staging, tuneful melodies, and a host of attractive girls.'—*New York Times*

Murder at the Windmill
GB 1949 70m bw

At London's famous girlie show, a front row patron is murdered. Rather rushed-looking whodunnit with interesting detail. Garry Marsh, Jack Livesey, Jon Pertwee, Diana Decker, Jimmy Edwards, Eliot Makeham. Written and directed by Val Guest; for Daniel Angel and Nat Cohen. (US title: *Murder at the Burlesque*.)

Murder by Contract*
US 1958 81m bw
Columbia / Orbin (Leon Chooluck)

A professional killer makes a fatal mistake and is shot down by police.
Low-budgeter which seemed stark and original at the time, but television has familiarized its contents. Moody, contrasty photography and restrained style give it a minor distinction.

w Ben Simcoe *d Irving Lerner* *ph Lucien Ballard* *m* Perry Borkin

Vince Edwards, Philip Pine, Herschel Bernardi, Caprice Toriel

'Ice cold and completely unsentimental.'—*John Gillett*

'A bloody funny movie!'

Murder by Death*
US 1976 94m Metrocolor
Columbia / Ray Stark

Several (fictional) detectives are invited to stay at the home of a wealthy recluse, and mystery and murder follow.
Sometimes thin but generally likeable spoof of a longstanding genre; the stars seize their opportunities avidly, and the film does not outstay its welcome.

w Neil Simon *d* Robert Moore *ph* David M. Walsh *m* Dave Grusin *pd* Stephen Grimes

Peter Falk, Alec Guinness, Peter Sellers, Truman Capote, Estelle Winwood, Elsa Lanchester, Eileen Brennan, James Coco, David Niven, Maggie Smith, Nancy Walker

'Plenty of scene-stealing actors but not many scenes worth stealing.'—*Michael Billington, Illustrated London News*

'Polished performances fail to compensate for a vacuous and frustratingly tortuous plot.'—*Sight and Sound*

'It seems to me that if you haven't watched the real Thin Man and the real Bogie in the real *Maltese Falcon* you won't see the joke; and if you have watched them, the joke is not good enough.'—*Dilys Powell, Sunday Times*

Murder by Decree
GB / Canada 1978 112m Metrocolor
Avco / Decree Productions / Saucy Jack (Robert A. Goldstone)

Sherlock Holmes investigates the matter of Jack the Ripper and comes upon a Masonic conspiracy.
Interminably long and unpardonably muddled variation on this over-familiar theme, with halts for the performances of guest artists and no clear grip on narrative or character.

w John Hopkins *d* Bob Clark *ph* Reginald H. Morris *m* Carl Zittrer, Paul Zaza *pd* Harry Pottle

Christopher Plummer, James Mason, Anthony Quayle, David Hemmings, Susan Clark, John Gielgud, Donald Sutherland, Frank Finlay, Geneviève Bujold

Murder by the Clock
US 1931 76m bw
Paramount

Creepy goings on in an old house after the death of a dowager who has built herself a tomb from which she can escape if buried alive.
Tasteless chiller which had the distinction of being withdrawn from British circulation after public protests.

w Henry Myers, Rufus King, Charles Beahan, *play* Charles Beahan, *novel* Rufus King
d Edward Sloman *ph* Karl Struss

Lilyan Tashman, William 'Stage' Boyd, Regis Toomey, Irving Pichel, Blanche Frederici, Walter McGrail

'Lacking in punch as a strongie for first runs. Below that should do oke.'—*Variety*

Murder by Television
US 1935 60m bw

The inventor of a television process is murdered. Static whodunit with the star as twin brothers. Only a curio. Bela Lugosi, June Collyer, Huntley Gordon, George Meeker. Written by Joseph O'Donnell; directed by Clifford Sanforth; for Edward M. Spitz / Imperial.

Murder Goes to College
US 1937 77m bw

A reporter on vacation helps solve a campus killing. Reasonably lively comedy mystery which might have started a series, but didn't. Roscoe Karns, Lynne Overman, Marsha Hunt, Astrid Allwyn, Harvey Stephens, Larry Crabbe. Written by Brian Marlow, Eddie Welch, Robert Wyler, from a novel by Kurt Steele; directed by Charles Reisner; for Paramount. 'Dialogue crackles with humour . . . this whodunit will be welcome material on many programmes.'—*Variety*

'You'll die laughing!'
Murder He Says**
US 1945 91m bw
Paramount (E. D. Leshin)

An insurance salesman stays with a homicidal family of hillbillies.
A curious black farce which seems to be compounded of *Cold Comfort Farm* and *The Red Inn*. Very funny, and ahead of its time.

w Lou Breslow *d* George Marshall
ph Theodor Sparkuhl

Fred MacMurray, Marjorie Main, Helen Walker, Peter Whitney, Jean Heather, Porter Hall, Mabel Paige

MURDER AT THE GALLOP. Margaret Rutherford's Miss Marple was more Rutherford than Christie but enjoyable nonetheless. Robert Morley huffs and puffs but his co-star has his measure.

Murder in Reverse
GB 1945 88m bw

After long imprisonment for a supposed murder, a convict comes out and hunts down the victim, who isn't really dead. A reasonable crime entertainment of its day which seemed to introduce a new star; but it hasn't worn well. William Hartnell, Jimmy Hanley, Chili Bouchier, John Slater, Dinah Sheridan, Wylie Watson. Written and directed by Montgomery Tully, from a novel by 'Seamark'; for British National.

Murder in the Big House
US 1942 67m bw

Two reporters uncover a murder ring in a prison. Acceptable second feature which catapulted its star to fame—at another studio. Van Johnson, George Meeker, Faye Emerson, Frank Wilcox. Written by Raymond Schrock; directed by B. Reeves Eason; for Warner.

(NB: A previous 1936 version was called *Jailbreak* and starred Craig Reynolds. *Murder in the Big House* was reissued in 1945 as *Born for Trouble*.)

Murder in the Blue Room
US 1944 61m bw

Volunteering to sleep in a room where a murder was committed, a guest is found dead. Tepid remake of *The Secret of the Blue Room*.

Anne Gwynne, Donald Cook, John Litel, Grace MacDonald, June Preisser, Regis Toomey. Written by I. A. L. Diamond, Stanley Davis; directed by Leslie Goodwins; for Frank Gross / Universal.

Murder in the Cathedral
GB 1951 136m bw
Film Traders / George Hoellering

The 12th-century struggle between Henry II and his archbishop culminates in the assassination of Becket in Canterbury Cathedral.
Plainly filmed, slightly amateur version of the celebrated verse play; scarcely a rewarding cinematic experience.

wd George Hoellering, *play* T. S. Eliot *ph* David Kosky *m* Laszlo Lajtha *ad* Peter Pendrey

Father John Grosner, Alexander Gauge, David Ward, George Woodbridge, Basil Burton, Paul Rogers, Niall MacGinnis, Mark Dignam, Leo McKern

'A curious ordeal for the audience . . . a no-man's-land between cinema and drama has been discovered, rather than any extension of either.'—*Gavin Lambert*

Murder in the Family
GB 1938 75m bw

Who killed rich Aunt Octavia? Mild whodunnit with interesting cast. Barry Jones, Jessica Tandy, Evelyn Ankers, Donald Gray, David Markham, Glynis Johns, Roddy McDowall. Written by David Evans, from the novel by James Ronald; directed by Al Parker; for TCF.

Murder in the Fleet
US 1935 70m bw
MGM (Lucien Hubbard)

Sabotage on a navy cruiser turns out to be the work of a mad inventor.
Weak and confused mixture of melodrama and comedy.

wd Edward Sedgwick *ph* Milton Krasner

Robert Taylor, Jean Parker, Jean Hersholt, Ted Healy, Una Merkel, Nat Pendleton, Raymond Hatton, Donald Cook, Mischa Auer

Murder in the Music Hall
US 1946 84m bw
Republic (Herman Millakowsky)
reissue title: *Midnight Melody*

A former criminal, now Broadway producer, is murdered on opening night.
Humdrum extravaganza built round its star, whose last skating appearance this was.

w Frances Hyland, Laszlo Gorog *d* John English *ph* John Alton *md* Walter Scharf

Vera Hruba Ralston, William Marshall, Helen Walker, Nancy Kelly, William Gargan, Ann Rutherford, Julie Bishop, Jerome Cowan, Edward Norris, Paul Hurst, Jack La Rue

Murder in the Private Car*
US 1934 60m bw

Mysteries proliferate aboard a fast-moving train. Adequate second feature which builds up to a remarkably well-staged climax in a runaway carriage. Russell Hardie, Charles Ruggles, Mary Carlisle, Una Merkel, Porter Hall. Written by Ralph Spence, Edgar Allen Woolf, Al Boasberg, Harvey Threw; directed by Harry Beaumont; for Lucien Hubbard / MGM. (GB title: *Murder on the Runaway Train.*)

'About the swiftest 61 minutes of entertainment you are ever likely to see.'—*Picturegoer*

Murder in Times Square
US 1943 72m bw

An actor-playwright is suspected of four theatrical murders. Standard detection work with some slight claim to sophistication. Edmund Lowe, Sidney Blackmer, Marguerite Chapman, John Litel. Written by Stuart Palmer and Paul Gangelin; directed by Lew Landers; for Columbia.

Murder in Trinidad
US 1934 74m bw

A quiet detective solves a murder in the tropics. Modest whodunit with Nigel Bruce for once playing the sleuth instead of the Watson. Nigel Bruce, Heather Angel, Victor Jory, Murray Kinnell, Douglas Walton, J. Carrol Naish. Written by Seton I. Miller from the novel by John W. Vandercook; directed by Louis King; for Fox. 'Amusing, but not particularly intriguing.'—*Variety*

Murder, Incorporated
US 1960 103m bw Cinemascope
TCF (Burt Balaban)

In the thirties, Anastasia and Lepke build up their crime syndicate which spreads terror through New York.
Tedious and poorly made gangster thriller, unforgivable faults considering the many admirable models it has to follow.

w Irve Tunick, Mel Barr *d* Burt Balaban, Stuart Rosenberg *ph* Gayne Rescher *m* Frank de Vol

Stuart Whitman, Mai Britt, Henry Morgan, Peter Falk, David J. Stewart, Simon Oakland, Morey Amsterdam

AAN: Peter Falk

The Murder Man*
US 1935 84m bw
MGM (Harry Rapf)

A reporter commits murder and frames someone else.
Good low-key melodrama with an interesting cast.

w Tim Whelan, John C. Higgins *d* Tim Whelan *ph* Lester White *m* William Axt

Spencer Tracy, Virginia Bruce, Lionel Atwill, James Stewart, Harvey Stephens, William Collier Snr

'It will please in the lesser houses.'—*Variety*

Murder Most Foul
GB 1964 91m bw
MGM / Lawrence P. Bachmann (Ben Arbeid)

Refusing to return a guilty verdict, juror Miss Marple makes her own murder investigation backstage at a third-rate repertory company.
Moderate Marple mystery which hasn't quite found the light touch it seeks.

w David Pursall, Jack Seddon, *novel* Mrs McGinty's Dead by Agatha Christie *d* George Pollock *ph* Desmond Dickinson *m* Ron Goodwin

Margaret Rutherford, Ron Moody, Charles Tingwell, Andrew Cruickshank, Megs Jenkins, Ralph Michael, James Bolam, Stringer Davis, Francesca Annis, Dennis Price, Terry Scott

Murder My Sweet: see Farewell My Lovely

The Murder of Dr Harrigan
US 1935 67m bw

A hospital founder disappears while on his way to the operating room. Formula murder mystery without much special interest. Kay Linaker, Ricardo Cortez, Mary Astor, John Eldredge, Joseph Crehan, Frank Reicher. Written by Peter Milne and Sy Bartlett from a novel by Mignon G. Eberhart; directed by Frank McDonald; for Warners. 'Will probably do no better than mildly.'—*Variety*

Murder on the Blackboard
US 1934 71m bw

Hildegarde Withers solves a murder in school. Modest mystery with popular leads; it satisfied. Edna May Oliver, James Gleason, Bruce Cabot, Gertrude Michael, Regis Toomey, Edgar Kennedy. Written by Willis Goldbeck, Stuart Palmer; directed by George Archainbaud; for RKO. 'Moderate entertainment in its class.'—*Variety*

Murder on the Orient Express**
GB 1974 131m Technicolor
EMI / GW Films (John Brabourne, Richard Goodwin)

In the early thirties, Hercule Poirot solves a murder on a snowbound train.
Reasonably elegant but disappointingly slackly-handled version of a classic mystery novel. Finney overacts and his all-star support is distracting, while as soon as the train chugs into its snowdrift the film stops moving too, without even a dramatic 'curtain'.

w Paul Dehn, *novel* Agatha Christie *d* Sidney Lumet *ph* Geoffrey Unsworth *m* Richard Rodney Bennett *pd* Tony Walton

Albert Finney, *Ingrid Bergman*, Lauren Bacall, Wendy Hiller, Sean Connery, Vanessa Redgrave, Michael York, Martin Balsam, Richard Widmark, Jacqueline Bisset, Jean-Pierre Cassel, Rachel Roberts, George Coulouris, *John Gielgud*, Anthony Perkins, Colin Blakely, Jeremy Lloyd, Denis Quilley

'Audiences appear to be so hungry for this type of entertainment that maybe it hardly matters that it isn't very good.'—*Judith Crist*

AA: Ingrid Bergman
AAN: Paul Dehn; Geoffrey Unsworth; Richard Rodney Bennett; Albert Finney

Murder She Said*
GB 1961 87m bw
MGM (George H. Brown)

An elderly spinster investigates after seeing a woman strangled in a passing train.
Frightfully British and disappointingly tame adaptation of an Agatha Christie character, with only the star (who is somewhat miscast) holding one's attention.

w David Pursall, Jack Seddon, *novel* 4.50 from Paddington by Agatha Christie *d* George Pollock *ph* Geoffrey Faithfull *m* Ron Goodwin

Margaret Rutherford, Charles Tingwell, Muriel Pavlow, Arthur Kennedy, James Robertson Justice, Thorley Walters, Gerald Cross, Conrad Phillips
† Thanks to Miss Rutherford's popularity, three increasingly poor sequels were made: *Murder at the Gallop* (1963), *Murder Most Foul* (1964), *Murder Ahoy* (1964).

Murder without Crime
GB 1950 76m bw

A blackmailer extracts money for a crime not yet committed. Thin four-hander from a rather mysterious West End success. Dennis Price, Derek Farr, Joan Dowling, Patricia Plunkett. Written and directed by J. Lee-Thompson, from his play Double Error; for ABPC.

The Murderers Are Among Us*
Germany 1947 87m bw
Defa
original title: *Die Mörder Sind Unter Uns*

In the ruins of Berlin several post-war characters indulge in gloomy self-examination.
Almost a caricature of what one would expect from a defeated people, this now-curious item has a certain power of its own.

wd Wolfgang Staudte *ph* Friedl Behn-Grund, Eugen Klagemann *m* Ernst Roters

Hildegard Knef, Ernst Fischer, Arno Paulsen

Murderer's Row
US 1966 108m Technicolor
Columbia / Meadway–Claude / Euan Lloyd

Matt Helm tracks down an international villain who has kidnapped an inventor.
Witless and uninventive spy spoof which drags itself wearily along but never attempts an explanation of its own title.

w Herbert Baker, *novel* Donald Hamilton *d* Henry Levin *ph* Sam Leavitt *m* Lalo Schifrin

Dean Martin, Ann-Margret, Karl Malden, Camilla Sparv, James Gregory, Beverly Adams, Tom Reese

'The blood will run cold in your veins!'

Murders in the Rue Morgue*
US 1932 62m bw
Universal (Carl Laemmle Jnr)

A series of grisly murders prove to be the work of a trained ape.
A distant relation of the original story, mildly interesting for its obvious Caligari influences, but not very good in any way.

w Tom Reed, Dale Van Avery, John Huston, *story* Edgar Allan Poe *d Robert Florey* *ph* Karl Freund

Bela Lugosi, Sidney Fox, Leon Ames, Bert Roach, Brandon Hurst
Synthetic studio rewrite . . . Poe wouldn't recognize his story.'—*Variety*

'Where sights of passion end in screams of terror!'

Murders in the Rue Morgue*
US 1971 86m Foto Film Color
AIP (Louis M. Heyward)

Poe's story is being presented at a Grand Guignol theatre in Paris, and when murders happen within the company Inspector Vidocq comes to investigate.
Playfully plotted chiller which has more to do with *The Phantom of the Opera* than with Poe. A good time waster for addicts.

w Charles Wicking, Henry Slesar *d Gordon Hessler* *ph* Manuel Berengier *m* Waldo de Los Rios

Jason Robards Jnr, Herbert Lom, Lilli Palmer, Adolfo Celi, Michael Dunn, Christine Kaufman

Murders in the Zoo
US 1933 64m bw

A jealous zoologist finds interesting ways to murder any man who shows interest in his wife. Modest time-passer with a rampant star. Lionel Atwill, Charles Ruggles, Kathleen Burke, John Lodge, Randolph Scott, Gail Patrick. Written by Philip Wylie and Seton I. Miller; directed by Edward Sutherland; for Paramount. 'Has what it takes to chill and entertain.'—*Variety*

Muriel*
France / Italy 1963 116m Eastmancolor
Argos / Alpha / Eclair / Films de la Pléiade / Dear Films (Anatole Dauman)
aka: *Muriel, ou le Temps d'un Retour*

A widow and her stepson are both misled by memories of past loves.
Elusive character drama which, though over-generous in length, fails to satisfy.

w Jean Cayrol *d* Alain Resnais *ph* Sacha Vierny *m* Hans Werner Henze

Delphine Seyrig, Jean-Pierre Kérien, Nita Klein, Jean-Baptiste Thierrée
'One has to watch and listen with every nerve alert.'—*Tom Milne, MFB*

Murph the Surf
US 1975 101m colour

Two Miami playboys steal a famous sapphire from a museum. Criminal autobiography based on fact; but it never settles down to being comedy or drama. Robert Conrad, Don Stroud, Donna Mills, Luther Adler. Written by E. Arthur Kean, from a story by Allan Dale Kuhn; directed by Marvin Chomsky; for AIP. (Aka: *Live a Little, Steal a Lot.*)

Murphy's Law
US 1986 100m TVC colour
Cannon (Pancho Kohner)

A tough LA cop with a drink problem is arrested for his ex-wife's murder.
Unattractively violent and foul-mouthed urban thriller in the wake of *Dirty Harry*.

w Gail Morgan Hickman *d* J. Lee Thompson *ph* Alex Phillips *m* Marc Donahue, Valentine McCallum

Charles Bronson, Carrie Snodgrass, Kathleen Wilhoite, Robert F. Lyons, Richard Romanus

Murphy's Romance
US 1985 107m Metrocolor Panavision
Columbia / Martin Ritt-Fogwood (Laura Ziskin)

A divorcée determined to make a living as a horse trainer in rural Arizona falls for the ageing local chemist.
Well-meaning but somewhat yawnworthy romantic comedy-drama which might almost have strayed from the days of the Hardy family.

w Harriet Frank Jnr, Irving Ravetch *d* Martin Ritt *ph* William A. Fraker *m* Carole King *pd* Joel Schiller

Sally Field, James Garner, Brian Kerwin, Corey Haim
'Sweet and homey, but falls far short of compelling film-making.'—*Variety*

AAN: James Garner; photography

Murphy's War*
GB 1971 108m Eastmancolor Panavision
Hemdale / Yates–Deeley (Michael Deeley)

A torpedoed British merchantman in Venezuela devotes himself to bombing a U-boat from a home-made plane.
Modest adventure story with the star in better form than the script.

w Stirling Silliphant, *novel* Max Catto *d* Peter Yates *ph* Douglas Slocombe *m* John Barry

Peter O'Toole, Sian Phillips, Philippe Noiret, Horst Janson

The Music Box****
US 1932 30m bw

Two delivery men take a piano to a house at the top of a flight of steps. Quintessential Laurel and Hardy, involving almost all their aspects including a slight song and dance. With Billy Gilbert. Written by H. M. Walker; directed by James Parrott; for Hal Roach.
AA: best short.

Music for Madame
US 1937 81m bw
RKO (Jesse L. Lasky)

An opera singer goes to Hollywood and becomes the dupe of jewel thieves.
Tolerable star musical with rather stale comedy elements.

w Gertrude Purcell, Robert Harari *d* John G. Blystone

Nino Martini, Joan Fontaine, Alan Mowbray, Erik Rhodes, Alan Hale, Billy Gilbert, Grant Mitchell, Lee Patrick

'Seems that Nino just can't make the grade as a film star.'—*Variety*

Music for Millions*
US 1944 117m bw
MGM (Joe Pasternak)

A small girl helps her pregnant sister who is a member of Jose Iturbi's orchestra.
Dewy-eyed wartime musical, full of popular classics, sentimentality and child interest, all smoothly packaged. As an example of what the public wanted in 1944, quite an eye-opener.

w Myles Connelly *d* Henry Koster *ph* Robert Surtees *md* George Stoll

Margaret O'Brien, June Allyson, Jose Iturbi, Jimmy Durante, Marsha Hunt, Hugh Herbert, Henry Davenport, Connie Gilchrist

AAN: Myles Connelly

Music Hath Charms*
GB 1935 70m bw
BIP (Walter C. Mycroft)

A dance band's broadcast has various effects on listeners.
Pleasing, modest portmanteau of sketches with music.

w Jack Davies, Courtney Territt, L. Du Garde Peach *d* Thomas Bentley, Alexander Esway, Walter Summers, Arthur Woods

ph Jack Cox, Claude Friese-Greene, Ronald Neame

Henry Hall and his Orchestra, Carol Goodner, W. H. Berry, Arthur Margetson, Antoinette Cellier, Billy Milton

Music in My Heart
US 1940 70m bw

An alien singer wins the lead in a Broadway musical, which prevents him from being deported. Forgettable second feature which was its leading lady's last stepping stone before stardom. Rita Hayworth, Tony Martin, Edith Fellows, Alan Mowbray, George Tobias, Eric Blore, Andre Kostelanetz and his orchestra. Written by James Edward Grant; directed by Joseph Santley; for Columbia. AAN: song, 'It's a Blue World'.

Music in the Air
US 1934 85m bw
Fox (Erich Pommer)

An opera singer is torn between two men.
Heavy-going light entertainment.

w Howard Young, Billy Wilder, *play* Oscar Hammerstein II, Jerome Kern *ph* Ernest Palmer *d* Joe May

Gloria Swanson, John Boles, Douglass Montgomery, June Lang, Al Shean, Reginald Owen, Joseph Cawthorn, Hobart Bosworth

'Mild operetta of class appeal, which limits its b.o. sturdiness.'—*Variety*

Music Is Magic
US 1935 67m bw

By a series of unexpected events, a young girl becomes a Hollywood star. Unpretentious and fairly snappy musical which still provides moments to enjoy. Alice Faye, Bebe Daniels, Ray Walker, Frank Mitchell, Jack Durant, Hattie McDaniel. Written by Edward Eliscu and Lou Breslow; directed by George Marshall; for TCF. 'One of those flighty affairs that will have trouble getting past the dual barricade.'—*Variety*

'The story of a homosexual who married a nymphomaniac!'

The Music Lovers*
GB 1970 123m Eastmancolor Panavision
UA / Rossfilms (Roy Baird)

Homosexual composer Tchaikovsky is impelled to marry, loses his sponsor, drives his wife into an asylum and dies of cholera.
Absurd fantasia on the life of a great composer, produced in a manner reminiscent of MGM's sillier musicals; up to a point hysterically (and unintentionally) funny, then rather sickening.

w Melvyn Bragg, *book* Beloved Friend by C. D. Bowen, Barbara Von Meck *d Ken Russell* *ph* Douglas Slocombe *md* André Previn

Richard Chamberlain, *Glenda Jackson, Christopher Gable*, Max Adrian, Isabella Telezynska, Maureen Pryor, Andrew Faulds

'Tchaikovsky has been made the excuse for a crude melodrama about sex.'—*Konstantin Bazarov*

'Libellous not only to the composer but to his music.'—*Roger Ebert*

The Music Man***
US 1962 151m Technirama
Warner (Morton da Costa)

A confidence trickster persuades a small-town council to start a boys' band, with himself as the agent for all the expenses.
Reasonably cinematic, thoroughly invigorating transference to the screen of a hit Broadway musical. Splendid period 'feel', standout performances, slight sag in second half.

w Marion Hargrove, *book* Meredith Willson *d Morton da Costa* *ph* Robert Burks *md* Ray Heindorf *ch* Onna White *songs Meredith Willson*

Robert Preston, Shirley Jones, Buddy Hackett, *Hermione Gingold*, Pert Kelton, Paul Ford

'This is one of those triumphs that only a veteran performer can have; Preston's years of experience and his love of performing come together joyously.'—*Pauline Kael*

AA: Ray Heindorf
AAN: best picture

Muss 'em Up
US 1936 70m bw

A cop with a Philo Vance complex routs out gangsters. Competent crime programmer. Preston Foster, Margaret Callahan, Alan Mowbray, Ralph Morgan, Guinn Williams, Maxie Rosenbloom. Written by Erwin Gelsey, James Edward Grant; for Pandro S. Berman / RKO. 'Enough comedy and other values to make it fairly passable fare.'—*Variety*

Mustang Country
US 1976 79m Technicolor
Universal (John Champion)

In 1925 Montana, a rancher comes out of retirement to help to round up a wild stallion.
Mild outdoor yarn for family audiences.

wd John Champion *ph* J. Barry Herron *m* Lee Holdridge

Joel McCrea, Nika Mina, Robert Fuller, Patrick Wayne

The Mutations
GB 1974 92m Eastmancolor
Columbia / Getty (Robert D. Weinbach)

A bio-chemist uses circus freaks in his experiments to find the perfect synthesis of plant and animal.
Tasteless horror film with little style of any kind.

w Robert D. Weinbach, Edward Mann *d* Jack Cardiff *ph* Paul Beeson *m* Basil Kirchin

Donald Pleasence, Tom Baker, Brad Harris, Julie Ege, Michael Dunn, Scott Antony, Jill Haworth, Lisa Collings

Mutiny
US 1952 77m Technicolor

During the war of 1812, an American ship runs the English blockade to collect gold bullion from France. Fairly lively swashbuckler. Mark Stevens, Angela Lansbury, Patric Knowles, Gene Evans, Rhys Williams. Written by Philip Yordan and Sydney Harmon; directed by Edward Dmytryk; for King Brothers / United Artists.

Mutiny in the Big House
US 1939 83m bw

A chaplain is at the centre of a prison break, and tries to calm the mob. Archetypal cellblock movie, and not the worst of them. Charles Bickford, Barton Maclane. Written by Robert D. Andrews and Martin Mooney; directed by William Nigh; for Monogram. 'Will edge toward the profit side of the ledger for the pop-pricers.'—*Variety*

The Mutiny of the Elsinore
GB 1937 79m bw

A reporter on a sailing ship for a story finds himself in the middle of a mutiny. Very studio-bound seafaring adventure. Paul Lukas, Lyn Harding, Kathleen Kelly, Clifford Evans. Written by Walter Summers and Beaufoy Milton, from the novel by Jack London; directed by Roy Lockwood; for Argyle British.

'They'll take this town by storm . . . fighting, laughing, loving, breaking every law of the seven seas!'

Mutiny on the Bounty***
US 1935 135m bw
MGM (Irving Thalberg, Albert Lewin)

An 18th-century British naval vessel sets off for South America but during a mutiny the captain is cast adrift and the mutineers settle in the Pitcairn Islands.
A still-entertaining adventure film which seemed at the time like the pinnacle of Hollywood's achievement but can now be seen to be slackly told, with wholesale pre-release editing very evident. Individual scenes and performances are however refreshingly well-handled.

w Talbot Jennings, Jules Furthman, Carey Wilson, *book* Charles Nordhoff, James Hall *d Frank Lloyd ph* Arthur Edeson *m* Herbert Stothart

Charles Laughton, Clark Gable, Franchot Tone, Movita, Dudley Digges, Henry Stephenson, Donald Crisp, Eddie Quillan, Francis Lister, Spring Byington, Ian Wolfe

BLIGH (Charles Laughton): 'Casting me adrift 3,500 miles from a port of call! You're sending me to my doom, eh? Well, you're wrong, Christian. I'll take this boat, as she floats, to England if I must. I'll live to see you—all of you—hanging from the highest yardarm in the British fleet . . .'

'Nothing to stand in the way of a box office dynamite rating.'—*Variety*

'Incidents are made vivid in terms of the medium—the swish and pistol crack of the lash, the sweating lean bodies, the terrible labour, and the ominous judgment from the quarterdeck.'—*Otis Ferguson*

AA: best picture
AAN: script; Frank Lloyd; Herbert Stothart; Charles Laughton; Clark Gable; Franchot Tone (whose role was originally to have been played by Robert Montgomery)

Mutiny on the Bounty
US 1962 185m Technicolor Ultra Panavision 70
MGM / Arcola (Aaron Rosenberg)

Overlong and unattractive remake marred principally by Brando's English accent and various production follies, not to mention his overlong and bloody death scene. The shipboard sadism still works pretty well, but after the landing in Tahiti boredom takes over.

w Charles Lederer *d* Lewis Milestone *ph* Robert Surtees *m* Bronislau Kaper

Trevor Howard, Marlon Brando, Richard Harris, Hugh Griffith, Tarita, Richard Haydn, Percy Herbert, Duncan Lamont, Gordon Jackson, Chips Rafferty, Noel Purcell

AAN: best picture; Robert Surtees; Bronislau Kaper; song 'Follow Me' (*m* Bronislau Kaper, *ly* Paul Francis Webster)

My American Uncle*
France 1980 126m Eastmancolor
Andrea Films / TFI (Philippe Dussart)
Original title: *Mon Oncle Américain*

Professor Henri Laborit explains the lives of two men and a woman in terms of animal behaviour.
Fascinatingly assembled but basically pessimistic dissection of human life, in the director's most meticulous style. The American uncle is the piece of good luck which may be just around the corner (but probably isn't).

w Jean Gruault, from the works of Henri Laborit *d* Alain Resnais *ph* Sacha Vierny *m* Arié Dzierlatka

Gerard Depardieu, Nicole Garcia, Roger Pierre, Henri Laborit

AAN: screenplay

My Beautiful Laundrette*
GB 1985 97m colour
Working Title / SAF / Channel Four (Sarah Radclyffe, Tim Bevan)

A young south London Asian manages his uncle's launderette and falls for a white racist boy.
Made for TV, but fashionable enough to get critical acclaim and cinema distribution, this soft-centred anecdote was a bit of a puzzle to those neither Asian nor homosexual.

w Hanif Kureishi *d* Stephen Frears *ph* Oliver Stapleton *m* Ludus Tonalis

Saeed Jaffrey, Roshan Seth, Daniel Day-Lewis, Gordon Warnecke, Shirley Anne Field, Rita Wolf

AAN: best original screenplay

My Best Girl*
US 1927 84m (24 fps) bw silent
Mary Pickford Corporation

A shopgirl falls for a co-worker, unaware that he is the son of the owner.
The star's last silent film is a charming comedy which tends to fade in the memory.

w Allen McNeil, Tim Whelan *d* Sam Taylor *ph Charles Rosher m* Gaylord Carter

Mary Pickford, Charles 'Buddy' Rogers, Sunshine Hart, Lucien Littlefield, Hobart Bosworth

AAN: Charles Rosher

'Perhaps it is not for the living to know the truth about reincarnation!'
'If you give away the ending, may your blood run cold forever!'

My Blood Runs Cold
US 1965 108m bw Panavision
Warner (William Conrad)

A spoilt heiress meets a strange young man who claims she is the reincarnation of a long dead charmer; he turns out to be a madman who has come across an old diary.
Initially intriguing but eventually exhausting melodrama with a weak solution.

w John Mantley *d* William Conrad *ph* Sam Leavitt *m* George Duning

Troy Donahue, Joey Heatherton, Barry Sullivan, Jeanette Nolan

'Not all that bad, but not worth missing *I Love Lucy* for either.'—*Leonard Maltin*

My Blue Heaven
US 1950 96m Technicolor
TCF (Sol C. Siegel)

A pair of troupers want a family, by adoption if not otherwise.
Routine musical drenched in sentimentality.

w Lamar Trotti, Claude Binyon *d* Henry Koster *ph* Alfred E. Arling *m* Alfred Newman *songs* Harold Arlen (*m*), Ralph Blane (*ly*)

Betty Grable, Dan Dailey, Mitzi Gaynor, David Wayne, Jane Wyatt, Una Merkel

My Bodyguard
US 1980 96m CFI Color
Market Street / Melvin Simon

A 15-year-old Chicago boy has trouble at school.
Oddly titled, uncommercial but quite watchable drama of adolescence. Not surprisingly, it failed to find an audience.

w Alan Ormsby *d* Tony Bill *ph* Michael D. Margulies *m* Dave Grusin *pd* Jackson de Givia

Chris Makepeace, Adam Baldwin, Ruth Gordon, Matt Dillon, Martin Mull, John Houseman

My Brilliant Career*
Australia 1979 100m Eastmancolor
NSW Film Corporation / Margaret Fink

The daughter of an Australian bush farmer at the turn of the century dreams of the world beyond and writes a memoir.
Pleasing but very slow picture of a world gone by.

w Eleanor Witcombe, *novel* Miles Franklin *d* Gillian Armstrong *ph* Don McAlpine *m* Nathan Waks

Judy Davis, Sam Neill, Wendy Hughes, Robert Grubb, Max Cullen

BFA: Judy Davis

My Brother Jonathan
GB 1947 108m bw
ABP (Warwick Ward)

The life of a small-town doctor who wanted to be a great surgeon.
Unobjectionable, unexciting novel-on-film with the typically British artificial studio look of the time.

w Leslie Landau, Adrian Alington, *novel* Francis Brett Young *d* Harold French *ph* Derick Williams *m* Hans May

Michael Denison, Dulcie Gray, Ronald Howard, Stephen Murray

My Brother Talks to Horses
US 1946 93m bw
MGM (Samuel Marx)

A boy who can talk to horses finds himself in demand by racetrack gamblers.
Well-mounted but uninspired whimsy with a fatal lack of pace.

w Morton Thomson, from his novel Joe the Wounded Tennis Player *d* Fred Zinnemann *ph* Joseph Ruttenberg *m* Rudolph Kopp

Butch Jenkins, Peter Lawford, Charlie Ruggles, Edward Arnold, Beverly Tyler, Spring Byington

My Brother's Keeper
GB 1948 91m bw
GFD / Gainsborough (Anthony Darnborough)

Two convicts escape, handcuffed together; one is violent, the other innocent.
Pre-*Defiant Ones* social melodrama, quite well made but suffering from miscasting.

w Frank Harvey, *story* Maurice Wiltshire *d* Alfred Roome, Roy Rich *ph* Gordon Lang *m* Clifton Parker

Jack Warner, George Cole, Jane Hylton, David Tomlinson, Bill Owen, Raymond Lovell, Yvonne Owen, Beatrice Varley

My Buddy*
US 1944 67m bw

A World War I veteran is forced into crime. Not a new message, but a second feature with sincerity and conviction. A better title would have helped. Don Barry, Alexander Granach, Ruth Terry, Lynne Roberts, Emma Dunn, John Litel, George E. Stone. Written by Arnold Manoff, Prescott Chaplin; directed by Steve Sekely; for Eddy White / Republic.

My Cousin Rachel*
US 1952 98m bw
TCF (Nunnally Johnson)

A Cornish gentleman dies in Italy after marrying a mysterious lady; when she comes to England she arouses the hostility, and love, of her husband's foster son.
Well-wrought but dramatically unsatisfactory Victorian melodrama from a bestseller; plenty of suspicion but no solution makes Rachel a dull girl.

w Nunnally Johnson, *novel* Daphne du Maurier *d* Henry Koster *ph* Joseph La Shelle *m* Franz Waxman

Olivia de Havilland, Richard Burton, John Sutton, Audrey Dalton, Ronald Squire

AAN: Joseph La Shelle; Richard Burton

'She was everything the west was—young, fiery, exciting!'

My Darling Clementine***
US 1946 98m bw
TCF (Samuel G. Engel)

Wyatt Earp cleans up Tombstone and wipes out the Clanton gang at the OK corral.
Archetypal western mood piece, full of nostalgia for times gone by and crackling with memorable scenes and characterizations.

w Samuel G. Engel, Winston Miller, *book* Wyatt Earp, Frontier Marshal by Stuart N. Lake *d John Ford ph Joe MacDonald m Cyril Mockridge*

Henry Fonda, Victor Mature, Walter Brennan, Linda Darnell, Cathy Downs, Tim Holt, Ward Bond, *Alan Mowbray*, John Ireland, Jane Darwell

'Every scene, every shot is the product of a keen and sensitive eye.'—*Bosley Crowther*

'Considerable care has gone to its period reconstruction, but the view is a poetic one.'—*Lindsay Anderson*

My Daughter Joy
GB 1950 81m bw
London Films / Gregory Ratoff
US title: *Operation X*

In order to cement a new trade pact, an international financier plans to marry his daughter to the son of an African sultan.
Turgid melodrama swamping some good actors.

w Robert Thoeren, William Rose, *novel* David Golder by Irene Neirowsky *d* Gregory Ratoff *ph* Georges Périnal *m* Raymond Gallois-Montbrun

Edward G. Robinson, Peggy Cummins, Nora Swinburne, Richard Greene, Finlay Currie, Gregory Ratoff, Ronald Adam, Walter Rilla, James Robertson Justice, David Hutcheson

My Dear Miss Aldrich
US 1937 73m bw

The glamorous new owner of a newspaper never agrees with its editor. Skilful light comedy with good work all round. Maureen O'Sullivan, Walter Pidgeon, Edna May Oliver, Rita Johnson, Janet Beecher. Written by Herman Mankiewicz; directed by George B. Seitz; for MGM.

My Dear Secretary
US 1948 96m bw

A secretary marries her boss and becomes jealous of his new secretary. Slow-paced, frivolous romantic comedy. Kirk Douglas, Laraine Day, Keenan Wynn, Rudy Vallee, Helen Walker, Florence Bates, Alan Mowbray. Written and directed by Charles Martin; for Cardinal/UA.

My Dinner with Andre*
US 1981 111m Movielab
Andre Company / George W. George / Michael White

Two men start a dinner table conversation which becomes a philosophical argument.
Curious two-hander which can please the right audience when it's in the mood; for selling tickets, forget it.

w Wallace Shawn, Andre Gregory *d* Louis Malle *ph* Jeri Sopanen *m* Allen Shawn

Wallace Shawn, Andre Gregory, Jean Lenauer, Roy Butler

'A magical mystery tour of thoughts, dreams, fantasies and emotions.'—*Time Out*

'An adventure through a magically cracked looking glass.'—*San Francisco Chronicle*

'A dazzling cerebral comedy of ideas.'—*Los Angeles Times*

My Dream Is Yours
US 1949 101m Technicolor
Warner (Michael Curtiz)

A Hollywood talent scout discovers a new singer.
Competent, forgettable musical.

w Harry Kurnitz, Dane Lussier *d* Michael Curtiz *ph* Ernest Haller *m* Harry Warren *ly* Ralph Blane *ch* Le Roy Prinz.

Doris Day, Jack Carson, Lee Bowman, Adolphe Menjou, Eve Arden, S. Z. Sakall
† A remake of *Twenty Million Sweethearts*.

My Fair Lady***
US 1964 175m Technicolor Super Panavision 70
CBS / Warner (Jack L. Warner)

Musical version of *Pygmalion*, about a flower girl trained by an arrogant elocutionist to pass as a lady.
Careful, cold transcription of a stage success; cinematically quite uninventive when compared with *Pygmalion* itself, but a pretty good entertainment.

w Alan Jay Lerner, *play* Pygmalion by Bernard Shaw *d* George Cukor *ph Harry Stradling m* Frederick Loewe ch Hermes Pan ad Gene Allen *costumes Cecil Beaton*

Rex Harrison, Audrey Hepburn, *Stanley Holloway*, Wilfrid Hyde White, Gladys Cooper, Jeremy Brett, Theodore Bikel, Isobel Elsom, Mona Washbourne, Walter Burke

'The property has been not so much adapted as elegantly embalmed.'—*Andrew Sarris*

AA: best picture; George Cukor; Harry Stradling; Rex Harrison
AAN: Alan Jay Lerner; Stanley Holloway; Gladys Cooper

My Favorite Blonde***
US 1942 78m bw
Paramount (Paul Jones)

A burlesque comic travelling by train helps a lady in distress and lives to regret it.
Smartly paced spy comedy thriller, one of its star's best vehicles.

w Don Hartman, Frank Butler, Melvin Frank, Norman Panama d Sidney Lanfield ph William Mellor *m* David Buttolph

Bob Hope, Madeleine Carroll, Gale Sondergaard, George Zucco, Lionel Royce, Walter Kingsford, Victor Varconi

My Favorite Brunette*
US 1947 87m bw
Paramount / Hope Enterprises (Daniel Dare)

A photographer gets mixed up with mobsters. Pretty fair star vehicle which half-heartedly spoofs *Farewell My Lovely*.

w Edmund Beloin, Jack Rose *d* Elliott Nugent *ph* Lionel Lindon *m* Robert Emmett Dolan

Bob Hope, Dorothy Lamour, Peter Lorre, Lon Chaney Jnr, John Hoyt, Charles Dingle, Reginald Denny

My Favorite Spy
US 1942 86m bw

The bandleader Kay Kyser has to postpone his honeymoon when he is called up and set to spy-catching. Fairly slick nonsense featuring a band popular at the time. Kay Kyser, Ginny Simms, Ish Kabibble, Ellen Drew, Jane Wyman. Written by Sig Herzig, William Bowers; directed by Tay Garnett; for RKO.

My Favorite Spy*
US 1951 93m bw
Paramount (Paul Jones)

A burlesque comic is asked by the US government to pose as an international spy who happens to be his double.
Moderately funny star vehicle with more willing hands than good ideas. The chase finale however is worth waiting for.

w Edmund Hartmann, Jack Sher *d* Norman Z. McLeod *ph* Victor Milner *m* Victor Young

Bob Hope, Hedy Lamarr, Francis L. Sullivan, Arnold Moss, Mike Mazurki, Luis Van Rooten

'The funniest, fastest honeymoon ever screened!'

My Favorite Wife***
US 1940 88m bw
RKO (Leo McCarey)

A lady explorer returns after several shipwrecked years to find that her husband has married again.
A well-worn situation gets its brightest treatment in this light star vehicle.

w Sam and Bella Spewack, Leo McCarey d Garson Kanin ph Rudolph Maté *m* Roy Webb

Cary Grant, Irene Dunne, Randolph Scott, Gail Patrick, Ann Shoemaker, Donald MacBride

'One of those comedies with a glow on it.'—*Otis Ferguson*

† Other variations (qv): *Too Many Husbands, Our Wife, Three for the Show, Move Over Darling.*

AAN: script; Roy Webb

'I can't go on *live*! I'm a movie star, not an actor!'

My Favorite Year**
US 1982 92m Metrocolor
MGM–UA / Brooksfilms / Michael Gruskoff

In 1954, a legendary Hollywood star noted for wine and women is unwisely invited to star in a television series.
A good-humoured and well-researched romp with a central character not too far removed from Errol Flynn.

w Norman Steinberg, Dennis Palumbo *d* Richard Benjamin *ph* Gerald Hirschfeld *m* Ralph Burns *pd* Charles Rosen *ed* Richard Chew

Peter O'Toole, Mark Linn-Baker, Jessica Harper, Joseph Bologna, Bill Macy, Lainie Kazan, Lou Jacobi, Cameron Mitchell

'A field day for a wonderful bunch of actors.'—*Variety*

AAN: Peter O'Toole

'I was a good girl—wasn't I?'

My Foolish Heart*
US 1949 98m bw
Samuel Goldwyn

A woman deceives her husband into thinking her forthcoming child is his.
A 'woman's picture' par excellence, and among the first to benefit from commercial plugging of a schmaltzy theme tune.

w Julius J. and Philip G. Epstein, *story* J. D. Salinger *d* Mark Robson *ph* Lee Garmes *m Victor Young*

Susan Hayward, Dana Andrews, Kent Smith, Robert Keith, Gigi Perreau, Lois Wheeler, Jessie Royce Landis

'Obviously designed to pull the plugs out of the tear glands and cause the ducts to overflow.'—*Bosley Crowther, New York Times*

'In its dry-eyed moments, this damp fable is brightened by some well-written patches of wryly amusing dialogue.'—*Time*

AAN: Susan Hayward; title song (*m* Victor Young, *ly* Ned Washington)

My Forbidden Past
US 1951 81m bw
RKO (Polan Banks)

A New Orleans beauty seeks vengeance when her cousin prevents her marriage.
Stuffy period melodrama with vigorous performances.

w Marion Parsonnet, *novel* Polan Banks *d* Robert Stevenson *ph* Harry J. Wild *m* Frederick Hollander *ad* Albert S. D'Agostino

Ava Gardner, Melvyn Douglas, Robert Mitchum, Janis Carter, Lucile Watson

My Friend Flicka*
US 1943 89m Technicolor
TCF

Adventures of a young boy and his pet colt.
Winsome boy-and-horse story, one of the most popular family films of the forties. Sequel 1945 with virtually the same cast: *Thunderhead Son of Flicka.*

w Mary O'Hara from her novel *d* Harold Schuster *m* Alfred Newman

Roddy McDowall, Preston Foster, Rita Johnson, James Bell, Jeff Corey

My Friend Irma*
US 1949 103m bw
Paramount / Hal B. Wallis

Dumb blonde Irma's con-man boy friend lends her apartment to two soda jerks.
Comic strip humour responsible for the screen debut of Martin and Lewis. Sequel 1950: *My Friend Irma Goes West.*

w Cy Howard, Parke Levy, *radio show* Cy Howard *d* George Marshall *ph* Leo Tover *m* Roy Webb

Marie Wilson, John Lund, Diana Lynn, *Dean Martin, Jerry Lewis*, Don Defore, Hans Conried, Kathryn Givney

My Friend Irma Goes West
US 1950 90m bw
Paramount / Hal Wallis

Irma's friends Steve and Seymour are offered a Hollywood contract and have adventures on the train.
Witless farce of mild historical interest.

w Cy Howard, Parke Levy *d* Hal Walker *ph* Lee Garmes *m* Leigh Harline

John Lund, Marie Wilson, Dean Martin, Jerry Lewis, Diana Lynn, Corinne Calvet, Lloyd Corrigan

'The general mental level can be judged from the fact that the performance of the chimpanzee seems the most natural thing in the film.'—*MFB*

'It takes a girl like Rita to play a gal like Sal!'

My Gal Sal*
US 1942 103m Technicolor
TCF (Robert Bassler)

The career and romances of songwriter Paul Dreiser.
Conventional nineties musical biopic, more vigorous and likeable than most.

w Seton I. Miller, Darrell Ware, Karl Tunberg, *book* My Brother Paul by Theodore Dreiser *d* Irving Cummings *ph* Ernest Palmer *md* Alfred Newman

Rita Hayworth, Victor Mature, John Sutton, Carole Landis, James Gleason, Phil Silvers, Walter Catlett, Mona Maris, Frank Orth

† The title role was intended for Alice Faye, but she was pregnant. Irene Dunne was too busy, Mae West refused, and Betty Grable didn't test well.

AAN: Alfred Newman

My Geisha
US 1962 120m Technirama
Paramount / Steve Parker

A director makes a film in Japan; his wife disguises herself as a geisha and gets the leading role.
Silly, overstretched comedy with pretty locations.

w Norman Krasna *d* Jack Cardiff *ph* Shunichuro Nakao *m* Franz Waxman

Shirley Maclaine, Yves Montand, Robert Cummings, Edward G. Robinson, Yoko Tani

My Girl Tisa***
US 1948 95m bw
United States Pictures (Milton Sperling)

An immigrant girl in New York in the nineties falls for an aspiring politician, is threatened with deportation but saved by the intervention of Theodore Roosevelt.
Charming period fairy tale with excellent background detail and attractive performances.

w Allen Boretz, *play* Lucille S. Prumbs, Sara B. Smith *d Elliott Nugent ph* Ernest Haller *m* Max Steiner

Lilli Palmer, Sam Wanamaker, Alan Hale, Stella Adler, Akim Tamiroff

My Gun Is Quick
US 1957 90m bw
United Artists / Victor Saville

Mike Hammer investigates the murder of a bar girl and is led to rival gangs of jewel thieves.
Impenetrably plotted but quite violent brew of typical Spillane ingredients.

w Richard Collins, Richard Powell, *novel* Mickey Spillane *d* George A. White, Phil Victor *ph* Harry Neuman *m* Marlin Skiles

Robert Bray, Whitney Blake, Pat Donahue, Pamela Duncan, Booth Colman

My Heart Belongs to Daddy
US 1942 73m bw

A cabby helps a pregnant widow to find shelter in the home of a professor. Unsparkling B romance with a totally unrelated title. Richard Carlson, Martha O'Driscoll, Cecil Kellaway, Frances Gifford, Florence Bates. Written by F. Hugh Herbert; directed by Robert Siodmak; for Sol C. Siegel / Paramount.

My Heart Is Calling
GB 1935 91m bw

An opera singer falls for a stowaway to Monte Carlo. Musical trifle with little to be said for or against it. Jan Kiepura, Marta Eggerth, Sonnie Hale, Hugh Wakefield, Ernest Thesiger, Marie Lohr. Written by Sidney Gilliat from a story by Ernst Marischka; directed by Carmine Gallone; for Cine-Allianz

My Kingdom for a Cook
US 1943 81m bw

An English author on a US lecture tour steals his hostess's cook. Curious comedy with the star seeming to play an unsympathetic Alexander Woollcott type. Charles Coburn, Marguerite Chapman, Bill Carter, Isobel Elsom, Ed Gargan. Written by Harold Goldman, Andrew Solt, Joseph Hoffman, Jack Henley; directed by Richard Wallace; for P. J. Wolfson / Columbia.

My Learned Friend***
GB 1943 76m bw
Ealing (Robert Hamer)

A shady lawyer is last on a mad ex-convict's murder list of those who helped get him convicted.
Madcap black farce, plot-packed and generally hilarious; the star's last vehicle, but one of his best, with superbly timed sequences during a pantomime and on the face of Big Ben.

w John Dighton, Angus Macphail d Basil Dearden, Will Hay ph Wilkie Cooper *m* Ernest Irving

Will Hay, Claude Hulbert, Mervyn Johns, Ernest Thesiger, Charles Victor, Lloyd Pearson, Maudie Edwards, G. H. Mulcaster, Gibb McLaughlin

My Life with Caroline*
US 1941 81m bw
RKO (Lewis Milestone)

An understanding husband thinks his high-spirited wife may be having an affair.
Very minor romantic comedy with an agreeable air but no substance whatever.

w John Van Druten, Arnold Belgard *d* Lewis Milestone *ph* Victor Milner *m* Werner Heymann

Ronald Colman, Anna Lee, Reginald Gardiner, Charles Winninger, Gilbert Roland

My Little Chickadee*
US 1939 83m bw
Universal (Lester Cowan)

A shady lady and an incompetent cardsharp unmask a villain in the old west.
A clash of comedy personalities which is affectionately remembered but in truth does not play very well apart from the odd line.

w Mae West, W. C. Fields d Edward Cline *ph* Joseph Valentine *m* Frank Skinner *md* Charles Previn

Mae West, W. C. Fields, Joseph Calleia, Dick Foran, Margaret Hamilton

'It obstinately refuses to gather momentum.'—*The Times*

'A classic among bad movies . . . the satire never really gets off the ground. But the ground is such an honest mixture of dirt, manure and corn that at times it is fairly aromatic.'—*Pauline Kael, 1968*

My Little Pony
US 1986 100m Technicolor

The inhabitants of Ponyland fear the wicked witch Hydia. Immensely distended cartoon meant to plug a fashionable line of children's dolls. Written by George Arthur Bloom; directed by Michael Jones; for Sunbow / Hasbro. (Animated in Japan.)

My Life as a Dog**
Sweden 1985 101m Fujicolor
Svensk Filmindustri / Film-Teknik

Twelve-year-old Ingemar learns to cope with his mother's illness and death, and his own propensity for getting into trouble, while staying with his aunt and uncle in the country. By turns painful and funny, the film manages to achieve genuine charm while steering clear of sentimentality.

w Lasse Hallstrom, Reidar Jonsson and others, from Jonsson's novel *d* Lasse Hallstrom *ph* Jorgen Persson, Rolf Lindstrom *m* Bjorn Isfalt

Anton Glanzelius, Manfred Serner, Anki Liden, Tomas von Bromssen, Melinda Kinnaman, Ing-Marie Carlsson

My Love Came Back
US 1940 85m bw

A millionaire helps the career of a pretty young violinist. Palatable comedy of its day, promptly forgotten. Olivia de Havilland, Jeffrey Lynn, Charles Winninger, Eddie Albert, Spring Byington, S. Z. Sakall, Jane Wyman. Written by Robert Buckner, Ivan Goff and Earl Baldwin; directed by Curtis Bernhardt; for Warner.

My Lucky Star*
US 1938 84m bw
TCF (Harry Joe Brown)

A shopgirl is innocently caught in a compromising situation with the owner's son. Fluffy comedy, acceptable as a background for skating sequences.

w Harry Tugend, Jack Yellen *d* Roy del Ruth *ph* John Mescall *songs* Mack Gordon, Harry Revel *m* Louis Silvers

Sonja Henie, Richard Greene, Joan Davis, Buddy Ebsen, Cesar Romero, Arthur Treacher, George Barbier, Louise Hovick, Billy Gilbert

'The characters act and talk like living people!'

My Man
US 1928 85m approx part talkie bw

A poor girl becomes a Broadway star. Lachrymose and technically primitive debut for the ebullient Fanny Brice; with Guinn Williams, Edna Murphy. Written by Joe Jackson, story by Robert Lord and Darryl F. Zanuck; directed by Archie Mayo; for Warner.

My Man and I
US 1952 99m bw
MGM (Stephen Ames)

A Mexican farm labourer, proud of his American citizenship, is drawn into trouble. Eccentric melodrama in which all the native Americans are whores, cheats or murderers; well enough made but not very interesting.

w John Fante, Jack Leonard *d* William Wellman *ph* William Mellor *m* David Buttolph

Ricardo Montalban, Shelley Winters, Claire Trevor, Wendell Corey

My Man Godfrey***
US 1936 90m bw
Universal (Gregory La Cava)

A zany millionaire family invite a tramp to be their butler and find he is richer than they are. Archetypal Depression concept which is also one of the best of the thirties crazy sophisticated comedies, though its pacing today seems somewhat unsure.

w Morrie Ryskind, Eric Hatch, Gregory La Cava d Gregory La Cava ph Ted Tetzlaff *m* Charles Previn

Carole Lombard, William Powell, Alice Brady, Mischa Auer, Eugene Pallette, Gail Patrick, Alan Mowbray, Jean Dixon

AAN: best picture; script; Gregory La Cava (as director); Carole Lombard; William Powell; Alice Brady; Mischa Auer

'The butler did it! He made every lady in the house oh so very happy!'

My Man Godfrey
US 1957 92m Technicolor Cinemascope
U-I (Ross Hunter)

Tepid remake which without the period background, and in unsuitable wide screen, raises very few laughs.

w Everett Freeman, Peter Berneis, William Bowers *d* Henry Koster *ph* William Daniels *m* Frank Skinner

June Allyson, David Niven, Jessie Royce Landis, Jay Robinson, Robert Keith, Martha Hyer, Eva Gabor

My Marriage
US 1936 68m bw

A girl finds that her marriage is not accepted by her high society in-laws. Satisfactory woman's picture. Claire Trevor, Kent Taylor, Pauline Frederick, Paul Kelly, Thomas Beck, Beryl Mercer. Written by Frances Hyland; directed by George Archainbaud; for TCF. 'Will get by with family audiences.'—*Variety*

My Name Is Julia Ross**
US 1945 65m bw
Columbia

A girl is kidnapped and forced to impersonate an heiress.
A very good second feature which has been culted into a reputation beyond its worth, though it is undeniably slick and entertaining.

w Muriel Roy Bolton, *novel* The Woman in Red by Anthony Gilbert *d Joseph H. Lewis* *ph* Burnett Guffey *md* Mischa Bakaleinikoff

Nina Foch, Dame May Whitty, George Macready, Roland Varno, Doris Lloyd

'A superior, well-knit thriller.'—*Don Miller*
'A likeable, unpretentious, generally successful attempt to turn good trash into decently artful entertainment.'—*James Agee*

My Old Dutch
GB 1934 82m bw

Ageing cockney parents see their son die a hero. Historically interesting sentimental wallow, built around a popular song; very primitive by most standards. Gordon Harker, Betty Balfour, Michael Hogan, Florrie Forde. Written by Bryan Wallace, Marjorie Gaffney, Mary Murillo and Michael Hogan; directed by Sinclair Hill; for Gainsborough. (NB: A 1915 version had starred the original singer, Albert Chevalier, with Florence Turner and Henry Edwards.)

My Outlaw Brother
US 1951 78m bw

A young man is shocked to find that his elder brother is a notorious bandit. Glum little semi-western, unpersuasively cast. Mickey Rooney, Robert Preston, Robert Stack, Wanda Hendrix. Written by Gene Fowler Jnr; directed by Elliott Nugent; for Eagle Lion.

'Desperately loved by two men—father and son!'
My Own True Love
US 1948 84m bw
Paramount (Val Lewton)

A lonely man home from the war quarrels with his son over a girl twenty years younger than himself.
Minor romantic drama, competently but coldly presented.

w Arthur Kober, *novel* Yolanda Foldes *d* Compton Bennett *ph* Charles Lang *m* Robert Emmett Dolan

Phyllis Calvert, Melvyn Douglas, Philip Friend, Wanda Hendrix, Binnie Barnes

My Pal Gus
US 1952 84m bw
TCF (Stanley Rubin)

A business man has a five-year-old problem son and in sorting him out falls in love with his schoolteacher.
Unrewarding domestic drama with actors who look as though they would rather be somewhere else.

w Fay and Michael Kanin *d* Robert Parrish *ph* Leo Tover *m* Leigh Harline

Richard Widmark, Joanne Dru, Audrey Totter, George Winslow, Joan Banks, Regis Toomey, Ludwig Donath

My Pal Trigger
US 1946 79m bw

A cowboy tracks down the man who killed his horse's sire. Folksy western drama, a cut above the usual Rogers episode. Roy Rogers, Dale Evans, Jack Holt, George 'Gabby' Hayes, Roy Barcroft. Written by Jack Townley and John K. Butler; directed by Frank McDonald; for Armand Schaefer / Republic.

My Reputation
US 1946 96m bw
Warner (Henry Blanke)

A widow is talked about for dispensing too soon with her weeds.
Dim drama, hastily shot on familiar sets with a reach-me-down script.

w Catherine Turney, *novel* Instruct My Sorrows by Clare Jaynes *d* Curtis Bernhardt *ph* James Wong Howe *m* Max Steiner

Barbara Stanwyck, George Brent, Warner Anderson, Lucile Watson, John Ridgely, Eve Arden, Jerome Cowan, Esther Dale, Scotty Beckett

My Science Project
US 1985 91m Technicolor

A high school student investigates an old UFO and finds an energy-absorbing machine which can materialize objects from the past and future. Disney-style fare with teenage sex: the mixture may not be for many. John Stockwell, Danielle Von Zerneck, Fisher Stevens, Raphael Sbarge, Richard Masur, Dennis Hopper. Written and directed by Jonathan R. Betuel; for Touchstone / Silver Screen Partners.

My Sin
US 1931 79m bw

A drunken lawyer helps a woman who has shot her husband. Turgid melodrama which failed to make a screen idol of its star. Tallulah Bankhead, Fredric March. Harry Davenport, Scott Kolk, Ann Sutherland. Written by Owen David and Adelaide Heilbron, from the story by Frederick Jackson; directed by George Abbott; for Paramount. 'Fair returns will be top.'—*Variety*

My Sister Eileen*
US 1942 96m bw
Columbia (Max Gordon)

Two Ohio girls come to New York and live with some zany friends in a Greenwich Village basement apartment.
Rather strained high jinks which were, not surprisingly, later musicalized.

w Ruth McKinney, Joseph Fields, Jerome Chodorov, *book* Ruth McKinney *d* Alexander Hall *ph* Joseph Walker *md* Morris Stoloff

Rosalind Russell, Janet Blair, Brian Aherne, Allyn Joslyn, George Tobias, Elizabeth Patterson, June Havoc

AAN: Rosalind Russell

My Sister Eileen*
US 1955 108m Technicolor Cinemascope
Columbia (Fred Kohlmar)

Musical version of the above, via a Broadway show. Watchable but hardly stimulating.

w Blake Edwards, Richard Quine, *play* Joseph Fields, Jerome Chodorov *d* Richard Quine *ph* Charles Lawton Jnr *m* George Duning *md* Morris Stoloff *ch Bob Fosse* *songs* Jule Styne, Leo Robin

Betty Garrett, Janet Leigh, Jack Lemmon, Bob Fosse, Kurt Kasznar, Horace MacMahon, Dick York

My Six Convicts*
US 1952 104m bw
Columbia / Stanley Kramer

A psychologist joins the staff of an American prison and gains the trust of six inmates.
Moderately interesting semi-documentary melodrama marred by a conventional prison break climax.

w Michael Blankfort, *book* Donald Powell Wilson *d* Hugo Fregonese *ph* Guy Roe *m* Dmitri Tiomkin

John Beal, *Millard Mitchell, Gilbert Roland*, Marshall Thompson, Regis Toomey

My Six Loves
US 1963 101m Technicolor
Paramount / Gant Gaither

A musical comedy star goes to the country for a rest and with the help of the local minister adopts six scruffy children.
Icky sentimental comedy for the easily pleased.

w John Fante, Joseph Calvelli, William Wood *d* Gower Champion *ph* Arthur E. Arling *m* Walter Scharf *songs* Jimmy Van Heusen, Sammy Cahn

Debbie Reynolds, David Janssen, Cliff Robertson, Eileen Heckart

'Enough to make you settle for cyclamates—or cyanide.'—*Judith Crist, 1973*

My Son John
US 1952 122m bw
Paramount / Rainbow (Leo McCarey)

An American Catholic family is horrified when its eldest son is revealed as a communist.
The lower depths of Hollywood's witch hunt cycle are marked by this Goldwynesque family saga, all sweetness and light, in which the commie son is treated as though he had rabies. Purely as entertainment the plot is pretty choppy and defeats all attempts at acting.

w Myles Connelly, Leo McCarey *d* Leo McCarey *ph* Harry Stradling *m* Robert Emmett Dolan

Helen Hayes, Robert Walker, Dean Jagger, Van Heflin, Minor Watson, Frank McHugh, Richard Jaeckel

AAN: Leo McCarey (original story)

'Their tangled loves wove a web of hate!'

My Son My Son*
US 1940 117m bw
Edward Small

A man who becomes rich spoils his son and lives to regret it.
Solid narrative from a bestseller.

w Lenore Coffee, *novel* Howard Spring *d* Charles Vidor *ph* Harry Stradling *m* Edward Ward

Brian Aherne, Madeleine Carroll, Louis Hayward, Laraine Day, Henry Hull

My Song for You
GB 1934 90m bw

A grand opera tenor tries to help a young girl and falls for her. The story is an excuse for the songs, and looks it. Jan Kiepura, Aileen Marson, Sonnie Hale, Emlyn Williams, Gina Malo. Written by Austin Melford, Robert Edmunds, Richard Benson, from a German original, *Ein Lied für Dich*, by Ernst Marischka and Irmgard Von Cube; directed by Maurice Elvey; for Gaumont-British.

My Teenage Daughter
GB 1956 100m bw
British Lion / Everest (Herbert Wilcox)
US title: *Teenage Bad Girl*

A widow's seventeen-year-old daughter meets an aggressive young man and ends up in court. Predictable domestic drama, a tame British version of *Rebel without a Cause*.

w Felicity Douglas *d* Herbert Wilcox *ph* Max Greene

Anna Neagle, Sylvia Syms, Kenneth Haigh, Norman Wooland, Wilfrid Hyde White, Julia Lockwood, Helen Haye

My Tutor
US 1982 97m De Luxe

Two teenage boys try to lose their virginity. As woeful as it sounds. Matt Lattanzi, Caren Kaye, Kevin McCarthy, Arlene Golonka. Written by Joe Roberts; directed by George Bowers; for Crown.

My Uncle Antoine
Canada 1971 110m Eastmancolor

In a Quebec village a young boy reluctantly helps his undertaker uncle to deliver a coffin. French-speaking comedy drama with a sour edge, as thoughts of death mar a family Christmas. Jacques Gagnon, Lyne Champagne, Jean Duceppe, Olivette Thibault. Written by Clément Perron; directed by Claude Jutra; for the National Film Board of Canada.

My Weakness*
US 1933 74m bw

As part of a joke, a hotel slavey is disguised as a grand lady, and warms to the part. Tolerable comedy with songs, using some ingenuity of presentation to ingratiate its German star with American audiences. *Lilian Harvey*, Lew Ayres, Charles Butterworth, Harry Langdon, Sid Silvers, Henry Travers. Written by B. G. De Sylva; directed by David Butler; for Fox.
'A highly favourable début.'—*Variety*

My Wife's Best Friend
US 1952 87m bw

A wife learns of her husband's infidelity, and imagines how Cleopatra, Joan of Arc and other historical figures might handle the situation. A sharp little comedy rather similar to *Unfaithfully Yours*. Anne Baxter, Macdonald Carey, Cecil Kellaway, Casey Adams, Catherine McLeod. Written by Isobel Lennart; directed by Richard Sale; for TCF.

My Wife's Family
GB 1931 80m bw

A wife thinks her husband has an illegitimate child. Archetypal British farce. This may be the best version; it was also made with Charlie Clapham in 1941 and with Ronald Shiner in 1956. Gene Gerrard, Muriel Angelus, Jimmy Godden, Amy Veness. Written by Fred Duprez and Val Valentine, from the play by Fred Duprez, Hal Stephens and Harry B. Linton; directed by Monty Banks; for BIP.

My Wild Irish Rose
US 1947 101m Technicolor
Warner (William Jacobs)

The ups and downs of Irish tenor Chauncey Olcott and his encounters with Lillian Russell. Inoffensive but not very exciting period musical, rather lacking in humour.

w Peter Milne, *book* Rita Ilcott *d* David Butler *ph* Arthur Edeson *m* Ray Heindorf, Max Steiner *ch* Le Roy Prinz

Dennis Morgan, Arlene Dahl, Andrea King, Alan Hale, George Tobias

AAN: Ray Heindorf, Max Steiner

'At last, the book that couldn't be written is now the motion picture that couldn't be made!'

Myra Breckinridge
US 1970 94m De Luxe Panavision
TCF (Robert Fryer)

After a sex change operation a film critic goes to Hollywood to accomplish the deflation of the American male.
A sharply satirical novel has been turned into a sleazy and aimless picture which became a watershed of permissiveness; after international outcry it was shunned even by its own studio. A few good laughs do emerge from the morass, but even the old clips are misused.

w Mike Sarne, David Giler, *novel* Gore Vidal *d* Mike Sarne *ph* Richard Moore *m* John Philips *md* Lionel Newman

Mae West, Raquel Welch, John Huston, Rex Reed, Jim Backus, John Carradine, Andy Devine

'Whatever the novel may be like, it surely cannot be this sort of witless, lip-smacking, continuously inept cop-out.'—*John Simon*

'About as funny as a child molester.'—*Time*

'A disjointed patchwork of leers, vulgarity and general ineptness.'—*Cue*

'An incompetent attempt at exploitation by an industry that knew once, at the very least, how to make a dishonest buck.'—*Newsweek*

'I don't want subtlety. I want vulgarity.'—*Michael Sarne*

The Mysterious Doctor
US 1942 57m bw

Nazis strike at an English village by staging a headless ghost. Risible propaganda hokum which somehow earned an 'H' certificate. John Loder, Eleanor Parker, Bruce Lester, Lester Matthews, Forrester Harvey. Written by Richard Weil; directed by Ben Stoloff; for Warner.

The Mysterious Dr Fu Manchu
US 1929 80m bw

After the Boxer rebellion an evil Chinese seeks the death of British officers. First but not the worst of the yellow peril's sinister adventures; to be taken for what it is, however. Warner Oland, Jean Arthur, Neil Hamilton, O. P. Heggie, William Austin. Written by Florence Ryerson and Lloyd Corrigan; directed by Rowland V. Lee; for Paramount.

The Mysterious Dr Satan
US 1940 bw serial: 15 eps

A master criminal invents a mechanical man. Rousing serial stuff with most of the regular elements. Eduardo Ciannelli, Robert Wilcox, William Newell, C. Montague Shaw. Directed by William Witney and John English; for Republic.

Mysterious Intruder
US 1946 62m bw

A private detective seeks a missing heiress. Intriguing minor thriller, part of the *Whistler* series. Richard Dix, Barton Maclane, Nina Vale, Regis Toomey. Written by Eric Taylor; directed by William Castle; for Columbia.

Mysterious Island
US 1951 bw serial: 15 eps

A serialization of the Jules Verne book, with Captain Nemo and a final volcano. Richard Crane, Marshall Reed, Karen Randle, Gene Roth, Leonard Penn. Directed by Spencer Bennet; for Columbia.

Mysterious Island*
GB 1961 101m Technicolor
Columbia / Ameran (Charles Schneer)

Confederate officers escape by balloon and join shipwrecked English ladies on a strange island where they are menaced by prehistoric monsters and helped by Captain Nemo.

Rambling, lively juvenile adventure with good moments and excellent monsters.

w John Prebble, Dan Ullman, Crane Wilbur, *novel* Jules Verne *d* Cy Endfield *ph* Wilkie Cooper *m* Bernard Herrmann *sp* Ray Harryhausen

Joan Greenwood, Michael Craig, Herbert Lom, Michael Callan, Gary Merrill

† An early sound version was made by MGM in 1929, directed by Lucien Hubbard. Despite Technicolor and a cast which included Lionel Barrymore it was judged unsatisfactory, and concentrated less on stop-frame monsters than on the submarine elements ignored in the above but remade in *Captain Nemo and the Underwater City* (qv).

The Mysterious Lady
US 1928 84m (24 fps) bw silent
MGM

A glamorous Russian spy has to save her lover from execution as a traitor.
Threadbare star melodrama.

w Bess Meredyth *d* Fred Niblo *ph* William Daniels

Greta Garbo, Conrad Nagel, Gustav Von Seyffertitz

The Mysterious Mr M
US 1946 bw serial: 13 eps

A submarine inventor is kidnapped and murdered by a master criminal. Predictable serial adventures. Richard Martin, Pamela Blake, Dennis Moore, Jane Randolph, Byron Foulger, Edmund MacDonald. Directed by Lewis D. Collins and Vernon Keays; for Universal.

Mysterious Mr Wong
US 1935 60m bw

A mandarin in New York's Chinatown will stop at nothing to collect the twelve coins of Confucius. Tolerable programme filler with old-fashioned thrills. Bela Lugosi, Wallace Ford, Arline Judge, Fred Warren. Written by Nina Howatt from a story by Stephen Keeler; directed by William Nigh; for Monogram. 'Passably exciting.'—*Variety*

The Mysterious Pilot
US 1937 bw serial: 15 eps

A villainous executive tries to kill his fiancée when she learns that he has murdered a man; but the Mounties help. Open-air serial adventures: one long chase. Frank Hawks, Dorothy Sebastian, Rex Lease, Guy Bates Post, Kenneth Harlan. Directed by Spencer Gordon Bennet; for Columbia.

Mystery Broadcast
US 1943 63m bw

A radio crime writer tackles a real case. Acceptable lower-case mystery. Frank Albertson, Ruth Terry, Nils Asther, Wynne Gibson, Addison Richards. Written by Dane Lussier; directed and produced by George Sherman; for Republic.

Mystery in Mexico
US 1948 65m bw

An insurance detective disappears in Mexico; another is sent to find him and uncovers a complex plot. Fairly effective time-passer shot on location. William Lundigan, Ricardo Cortez, Jacqueline White, Tony Barrett. Written by Lawrence Kimble; directed by Robert Wise; for RKO.

Mystery Junction
GB 1951 67m bw

Passengers stranded in a snowbound railway station solve a mystery. One of the better second features of its type. Sidney Tafler, Barbara Murray, Pat Owens, Martin Benson. Written and directed by Michael McCarthy; for Merton Park.

Mystery Liner
US 1934 62m bw

Several murders take place at sea on a passenger liner. Reputedly above-average whodunit. Noah Beery, Astrid Allwyn, Cornelius Keefe, Gustav Von Seyffertitz, Edwin Maxwell. Written by Wellys Totman from the novel The Ghost of John Holling by Edgar Wallace; directed by William Nigh; for Monogram. 'Too good for the lesser grinds: exceptional indie entertainment.'—*Variety*

Mystery Mountain
US 1934 bw serial: 12 eps

A master criminal named The Rattler has a mountain lair from which he directs attacks on a new western railroad. Modest serial hair-raiser. Kan Maynard, Eddie Cobb, Verna Hillie, Edward Earle. Directed by Otto Brower, B. Reeves Eason; for Mascot.

'A thing to bewitch your senses for days and days! Charming in the thrills! Gripping in the suspense!'

The Mystery of Edwin Drood*
US 1935 85m bw
Universal

In a cathedral town, a drug- addicted choirmaster is his nephew's rival for the hand of Rosa Bud.
Fairly creditable attempt to deal with a famous unfinished novel. Slightly stilted, but good visuals and performances.

w John L. Balderston, Gladys Unger, Bradley King, Leopold Atlas, *novel* Charles Dickens *d Stuart Walker* *ph* George Robinson *m* Edward Ward

Claude Rains, Douglass Montgomery, Heather Angel, David Manners, E. E. Clive, Valerie Hobson

The Mystery of Marie Roget
US 1942 61m bw
Universal (Paul Malvern)

A Parisian music hall star plots to kill her sister but herself disappears.
Ham-fisted, stilted mystery drama relying hardly at all on its original.

w Michael Jacoby, *story* Edgar Allan Poe *d* Phil Rosen *ph* Elwood Bredell *m* Hans Salter

Maria Montez, Patric Knowles, *Maria Ouspenskaya*, Lloyd Corrigan, John Litel, Edward Norris, Frank Reicher

The Mystery of Mr X*
US 1934 84m bw
MGM (Lawrence Weingarten)

In foggy London, a jewel thief protects himself by finding the murderer of several policemen. Passable mystery, later remade as *The Hour of Thirteen*.

w Howard Emmett Rogers, Philip MacDonald, Monckton Hoffe, *novel* X vs Rex by Philip MacDonald *d* Edgar Selwyn *ph* Oliver T. Marsh

Robert Montgomery, Elizabeth Allan, Lewis Stone, Ralph Forbes, Henry Stephenson, Forrester Harvey

'One of the best-made mystery mellers yet.'—*Variety*

The Mystery of the Mary Celeste
GB 1935 80m bw

A mad sailor kills his fellow crew members and jumps overboard. Unpersuasive solution to an unsolved mystery in a production which sounds more interesting than it is. Bela Lugosi, Shirley Grey, Arthur Margetson, Edmund Willard, Dennis Hoey. Written and directed by Denison Clift; for Hammer. (US title: *Phantom Ship*.) 'Very strong stuff for those who like tragic entertainment.'—*Variety*

Mystery of the River Boat
US 1944 bw serial: 13 eps

Three old Louisiana families control swampland containing valuable oil deposits, which a villain is after. Rather complicated basis for a serial, but the usual thrills evolve. Robert Lowery, Eddie Quillan, Marion Martin, Lyle Talbot, Arthur Hohl, Mantan Moreland. Directed by Ray Taylor and Lewis D. Collins; for Universal.

The Mystery of the 13th Guest
US 1943 60m bw

A girl beneficiary under her uncle's will is menaced when she goes to visit. Ham-fisted remake of *The Thirteenth Guest*, which was a mite too complex in the first place. This version makes no sense at all and is cheaply produced. Helen Parrish, Dick Purcell, Tim Ryan, Frank Faylen. Written by Charles Marion, Tim Ryan, from play by Armitage Trail; directed by William Beaudine; for Lindsley Parsons / Monogram.

'Images of wax that throbbed with human passion. Almost woman! What did they lack?'

Mystery of the Wax Museum***
US 1933 77m Technicolor
Warner (Henry Blanke)

A sculptor disfigured in a fire builds a wax museum by covering live victims in wax.

MYRA BRECKINRIDGE. Hollywood rightly bid farewell to director Mike Sarne after this fiasco. Film critic Rex Reed, here with Raquel Welch, would have been better advised to review the film than to appear in it.

Archetypal horror material is augmented by a sub-plot about drug-running and an authoritative example of the wisecracking reporter school of the early thirties. The film is also notable for its highly satisfactory use of two-colour Technicolor and for its splendid art direction. Remade 1953 as *House of Wax* (qv).

w Don Mullally, Carl Erickson, play Charles S. Belden *d Michael Curtiz ph Ray Rennahan ad Anton Grot*

Lionel Atwill, Fay Wray, *Glenda Farrell, Frank McHugh*, Gavin Gordon, Allen Vincent, Edwin Maxwell

ATWILL: 'I offer you immortality, my child. Think of it: in a thousand years you shall be as lovely as you are now!'

'Would have been certain of better gate support a year ago. Recognizing this, the Technicolor and hyper-weirdness were apparently mandatory studio precautions to offset the element of belated arrival.'—*Variety*

'Marvellously grisly chiller.'—*Judith Crist, 1977*

'Its most telling details are its horrific ones. The fire at the beginning, with lifelike figures melting into grisly ooze; night time in the city morgue, with a dead body suddenly popping up as a side effect of embalming fluid; chases through shadows as the ghoulish sculptor collects bodies for his exhibit; and the shock when Atwill's homemade wax face crumbles to the floor and exposes the hidden demon.'—*Tom Shales, The American Film Heritage, 1972*

The Mystery of the Yellow Room*
France 1931 96m bw

An attempt is made on the life of a scientist's daughter. Complex mystery which has maintained some reputation. Hugette Ex-Duclos, Roland Toutain, Maxime Desjardins. Written and directed by Marcel L'Herbier, from novel by Gaston Leroux; for Osso.

Mystery Sea Raider
US 1940 76m bw

A ship is hijacked and converted into a German raider in the Caribbean. Standard propaganda potboiler with little imagination. Carole Landis, Henry Wilcoxon, Onslow Stevens, Kathleen Howard, Henry Victor. Written by Edward E. Paramore Jnr; directed by Edward Dmytryk; for Eugene J. Zukor / Paramount.

Mystery Squadron
US 1933 bw serial: 12 eps

Mysterious airplane raids threaten destruction to a power dam: they are the wo.k of The Black Ace. Pot-boiling serial. Bob Steele, Big Boy Williams, Lucile Browne, Jack Mulhall. Directed by Colbert Clark and David Howard; for Mascot.

Mystery Street*
US 1950 93m bw
MGM (Frank E. Taylor)

Harvard medical scientists help solve a murder by examining the victim's bones.
Standard semi-documentary police thriller; well paced and quite entertaining.

w Sidney Boehm, Richard Brooks d John Sturges *ph* John Alton *m* Rudolph Kopp

Ricardo Montalban, Sally Forrest, Elsa Lanchester, Bruce Bennett, Marshall Thompson, Jan Sterling

AAN: Leonard Speigelgass (original story)

Mystery Submarine
GB 1962 92m bw
British Lion / Britannia / Bertram Ostrer
US title: *Decoy*

A Nazi submarine is captured and sent out again with a British crew.
Routine war adventure.

w Hugh Woodhouse, Bertram Ostrer, Jon Manchip White *d* C. M. Pennington-Richards *ph* Stan Pavey *m* Clifton Parker

Edward Judd, James Robertson Justice, Laurence Payne, Albert Lieven

Mystery Woman

US 1934 69m bw

Recovery of a secret document will mean freedom for a soldier sent to Devil's Island. Tolerable time-passer, with action mostly on a liner. Mona Barrie, Gilbert Roland, John Halliday, Rod La Rocque, Mischa Auer, Billy Bevan. Written by Philip MacDonald, Dudley Nichols, E. E. Paramore Jnr; directed by Eugene Forde; for Fox. 'Entertainment of a just passable sort.'—*Variety*

Nadine
US 1987 88m Metrocolor
Husband and wife on the brink of divorce are drawn together by a suspicious killing.
Unresolvedly old-fashioned comedy which seems to need the Cary Grant touch. Jeff Bridges, Kim Basinger, Rip Torn, Gwen Verdon, Glenne Headly, Jerry Stiller. Written and directed by Robert Benton; for Arlene Donovan/Tri-Star.

Nagana
US 1933 73m bw
Doctors in Africa try to cure sleeping sickness.
Dreary drama with cut-in animal footage. Tala Birell, Melvyn Dougas, M. Morita, Onslow Stevens. Written by James Light, Dale Van Every, Don Ryan, Lester Cohen; directed by Ernst L. Frank; for Universal.

Naked Alibi
US 1954 85m bw
U-I (Ross Hunter)
The police track a homicidal baker to a Mexican border town.
Modest police thriller which sags after it crosses the border.
w Lawrence Roman *d* Jerry Hopper *ph* Russell Metty *m* Hans Salter
Sterling Hayden, Gene Barry, Gloria Grahame, Marcia Henderson, Casey Adams, Chuck Connors

The Naked and the Dead
US 1958 131m Technicolor RKOscope
RKO Teleradio / Gregjac (Paul Gregory)
Adventures of an army platoon in the Pacific war.
Shorn of the four letter words which made the novel notorious, this is a routine war film, neither very good nor very bad.
w Denis and Terry Sanders, *novel* Norman Mailer *d* Raoul Walsh *ph* Joseph La Shelle *m* Bernard Herrmann
Aldo Ray, Cliff Robertson, Raymond Massey, William Campbell, Richard Jaeckel, James Best, Joey Bishop, Robert Gist, Jerry Paris, L. Q. Jones

The Naked City****
US 1948 96m bw
Universal (Mark Hellinger)
New York police track down a killer.
Highly influential documentary thriller which, shot on location in New York's teeming streets, claimed to be giving an impression of city life; actually its real mission was to tell an ordinary murder tale with an impressive accumulation of detail and humour. The narrator's last words became a cliché: 'There are eight million stories in the naked city. This has been one of them.'
w Malvin Wald, Albert Maltz d Jules Dassin ph William Daniels m Frank Skinner, Miklos Rozsa *md* Milton Schwarzwald
Barry Fitzgerald, Don Taylor, Howard Duff, Dorothy Hart, Ted de Corsia, Adelaide Klein
AA: William Daniels
AAN: original story (Malvin Wald)

The Naked Dawn
US 1956 82m Technicolor
A hired robber finds that his boss is not to be trusted. Heavy-going Mexican western. Arthur Kennedy, Eugene Iglesias, Betta St John. Written by Nina and Herman Schneider; directed by Edgar G. Ulmer; for Universal-International.

Naked Earth
GB 1958 96m bw Cinemascope
TCF / Foray Films (Adrian Worker)
In 1895 a young Irish farmer goes to Africa to grow tobacco, but moves on to crocodile hunting.
Predictable and uninteresting epic of endurance; not very convincing either.
w Milton Holmes *d* Vincent Sherman *ph* Erwin Hillier
Richard Todd, Juliette Greco, John Kitzmiller, Finlay Currie, Laurence Naismith, Christopher Rhodes, Orlando Martins

The Naked Edge
GB 1961 100m bw
UA/Pennebaker/Baroda (Walter Seltzer, George Glass)
A successful executive is suspected by his wife of an old murder in which he testified against the man who was convicted.
Dreary thriller which piles up red herrings in shoals, then abandons them all for a razor-and-bathroom finale.
w Joseph Stefano, *novel* First Train to Babylon by Max Ehrlich *d* Michael Anderson *ph* Erwin Hillier *m* William Alwyn
Gary Cooper, Deborah Kerr, Peter Cushing, Eric Portman, Diane Cilento, Hermione Gingold, Michael Wilding, Ronald Howard

The Naked Face
US 1984 106m Metrocolor
Cannon (Rony Yacov)
A Chicago psychiatrist finds himself a potential victim of the Mafia.
Muddled and violent mystery with a rather boring solution.
w,d Bryan Forbes, *novel* Sidney Sheldon *ph* David Gurfinkel *m* Michael J. Lewis *pd* William Fosser
Roger Moore, Rod Steiger, Elliott Gould, Anne Archer, David Hedison, Art Carney, Ron Parady

The Naked Hills
US 1955 73m Pathecolor
Allied Artists / La Salle (Josef Shaftel)
Starting in 1849, a young prospector spends his life looking for gold.
Curious, mildly interesting saga with an obsession instead of a plot.
wd Josef Shaftel *ph* Frederick Gately *m* Herschel Burke Gilbert
David Wayne, Marcia Henderson, Keenan Wynn, James Barton, Jim Backus, Denver Pyle

The Naked Jungle*
US 1954 95m Technicolor
Paramount / George Pal (Frank Freeman Jnr)
In 1901 a young woman is married by proxy to a South American cocoa planter, and when she arrives at his jungle home she has to conquer not only him but an army of soldier ants.
Mixture of *Rebecca* elements with a more unusual kind of thrill; all quite watchable, and the ant scenes very effective.
w Philip Yordan, Ranald MacDougall, *story* Leiningen Versus the Ants by Carl Stephenson *d* Byron Haskin *ph* Ernest Laszlo *m* Daniele Amfitheatrof
Charlton Heston, Eleanor Parker, William Conrad, Abraham Sofaer, John Dierkes, Douglas Fowley

The Naked Kiss
US 1964 92m bw
A prostitute tries to enter mainstream society.
Tough early work by a director who never compromised but seldom hit the public fancy. Constance Towers, Anthony Eisley, Michael Dante, Virginia Grey, Patsy Kelly, Betty Bronson. Written, directed and produced by Samuel Fuller; for F and F/AA.

The Naked Maja
Italy / US 1959 112m Technirama
MGM / Titanus (Goffredo Lombardo)

Peasant Francisco Goya becomes a famous painter through the influence of the Duchess of Alba.
Boring and unconvincing biopic.

w Giorgio Prosperi, Norman Corwin, Albert Lewin, Oscar Saul *d* Henry Koster *ph* Giuseppe Rotunno *m* Francesco Lavagnino

Anthony Franciosa, Ava Gardner, Amedeo Nazzari, Gino Cervi, Lea Padovani, Massimo Serrato

'This travesty of Goya's life, country and period adds up to nothing more entertaining than a perfunctory, heavy-handed pageant.'—*MFB*

The Naked Prey*
US 1966 94m Technicolor Panavision
Paramount / Theodora / Sven Persson (Cornel Wilde)

In 1840, a white hunter becomes brutalized when a tribe hunts him down as though he were a lion.
Savage adventure story with bloodthirsty detail; unusual and certainly effective.

w Clint Johnston, Don Peters *d Cornel Wilde* *ph* I. A. R. Thompson *md* Andrew Tracy, from African folk music

Cornel Wilde, Gert Van Den Berg, Ken Gampu

'Overtones pretentious, but it tries.'—*Sight and Sound*

AAN: script

The Naked Runner
GB 1967 104m Techniscope
Warner / Artanis (Brad Dexter)

British intelligence conceive a plan to turn an innocent businessman into a spy killer.
Silly espionage thriller further marred by its director's penchant for making a zany composition of every frame.

w Stanley Mann, *novel* Francis Clifford *d* Sidney J. Furie *ph* Otto Heller *m* Harry Sukman

Frank Sinatra, Peter Vaughan, Derren Nesbitt, Nadia Gray, Toby Robins, Cyril Luckham, Edward Fox, Inger Stratton

'It might be a good movie to read by if there were light in the theatre.'—*Pauline Kael*

The Naked Spur*
US 1953 91m Technicolor
MGM (William H. Wright)

A bounty hunter has trouble getting his quarry back to base.
Standard big studio western shot in Colorado, with all characters motivated by greed.

w Sam Rolfe, Harold Jack Bloom *d* Anthony Mann *ph* William Mellor *m* Bronislau Kaper

James Stewart, Robert Ryan, Janet Leigh, Millard Mitchell

AAN: script

The Naked Street
US 1955 83m bw
Edward Small

A racketeer's daughter marries a worthless crook: her father saves him from the electric chair but he murders again.
Semi-documentary exposé melodrama about unpleasant people; reasonably proficient on its level.

w Maxwell Shane, Leo Katcher *d* Maxwell Shane *ph* Floyd Crosby *m* Ernest Gold *md* Emil Newman, Anthony Quinn, Anne Bancroft, Farley Granger, Peter Graves

The Naked Truth*
GB 1957 92m bw
Rank / Mario Zampi
US title: *Your Past is Showing*

Celebrities band together to kill a blackmailer who threatens to expose unsavoury aspects of their lives.
Frenzied black farce, quite a lot of which comes off.

w Michael Pertwee *d* Mario Zampi *ph* Stan Pavey *m* Stanley Black

Peter Sellers, Terry-Thomas, Peggy Mount, Dennis Price, Shirley Eaton, Georgina Cookson

'Even men of God can trade with the Devil'
The Name of the Rose*
US 1986 130m colour
TCF / Bernd Eichinger / Bernd-Schaefers / Cristaldi / Ariane / ZDF

In the 14th century, an English monk's visit to an Italian abbey is soured by a series of murders.
Curious, remote, randomly developed and edited, this can never have been an obvious candidate for box office success: yet it did pretty well.

w Andrew Birkin, Gerard Brach, Howard Franklin, Alain Godard *novel* Umberto Eco *d* Jean-Jacques Annaud *ph* Tonio Delli Colli *m* James Horner *pd* Dante Ferretti *ed* Jane Seitz

Sean Connery, F. Murray Abraham, Christian Slater, Michael Lonsdale, Elya Baskin

'A plodding misfire . . . sorrowfully mediocre.'—*Variety*

Nana*
US 1934 89m bw
Samuel Goldwyn
GB title: *Lady of the Boulevards*

The high life and subsequent degradation of a Parisian demi-mondaine in the nineties.
Stylish yet stolid slice of *le beau monde*, intended to create a new star.

w Willard Mack, Harry Wagstaff Gribble, *novel* Emile Zola *d Dorothy Arzner* *ph Gregg Toland* *m* Alfred Newman

Anna Sten, Lionel Atwill, Phillips Holmes, Richard Bennett, Mae Clarke, Muriel Kirkland, Reginald Owen, Jessie Ralph

'The star's resources should be sufficient to offset some of the lesser script deficiencies.'—*Variety*

Nancy Drew
This series of second features starring Bonita Granville as a teenage small-town detective was moderately well received but quickly forgotten. The character was created in novels by Edward Stratemeyer and his daughter Harriet Evans; the films were all directed by William Clemens for Warners.

1938: NANCY DREW, DETECTIVE
1939: NANCY DREW, REPORTER; NANCY DREW, TROUBLE SHOOTER; NANCY DREW AND THE HIDDEN STAIRCASE

Nancy Goes to Rio
US 1950 99m Technicolor
MGM (Joe Pasternak)

Two actresses, mother and daughter, are both after the same part.
Mild shipboard musical.

w Sidney Sheldon *d* Robert Z. Leonard *ph* Ray June *m* George Stoll

Jane Powell, Ann Sothern, Carmen Miranda, Barry Sullivan, Louis Calhern, Fortunio Bonanova, Hans Conried

Nancy Steele Is Missing*
US 1937 85m bw
TCF (Nunnally Johnson)

Crooks try to pass off a girl as the long lost heir to a fortune.
Slightly unusual, well cast melodrama.

w Gene Fowler, Hal Long, *novel* C. F. Coe *d* George Marshall *ph* Barney McGill *m* David Buttolph

Victor McLaglen, Peter Lorre, June Lang, Jane Darwell, John Carradine, Walter Connolly

The Nanny*
GB 1965 93m bw
ABP / Hammer (Jimmy Sangster)

A ten-year-old boy hates his nanny, and with good reason, for she is a neurotic murderess.
Muted Hammer experiment in psychopathology, with too much equivocation before the dénouement; the star's role allows few fireworks, and the plot is rather unpleasant.

w Jimmy Sangster, *novel* Evelyn Piper *d Seth Holt* *ph* Harry Waxman *m* Richard Rodney Bennett

Bette Davis, Jill Bennett, William Dix, James Villiers, Wendy Craig, Pamela Franklin, Maurice Denham

Nanook of the North*
US 1921 57m (1947 sound version) bw silent
Revillon Freres

The life of an Eskimo and his family.
Primitive but trail-blazing documentary, hard to sit through for modern audiences.

w, d, ph, ed Robert Flaherty

'In a day of emotional and artistic deliquescence on the screen, a picture with the fresh strength and pictorial promise of *Nanook of the North* is in the nature of a revolution.'—*Frances Taylor Patterson*

† Nanook himself died of hunger on the ice shortly after the film was released.

Napoleon****
France 1927 378m approx (24 fps) bw (some colour) silent
WESTI / Société Générale de Films

The early life of Napoleon.
A cinematic epic which, although brilliant in most particulars, owes its greatest interest to its narrative sweep, its flair for composition and its use of triptych screens which at the end combine to show one giant picture, the clear precursor of Cinerama. In 1934 Gance revised his film and added stereophonic sound.

w, d, ed Abel Gance *ph* various *m* Arthur Honegger

Albert Dieudonné, Antonin Artaud, Pierre Batcheff

† The 1934 version ran 140m and included three-dimensional sound.

Napoleon and Samantha
US 1972 91m Technicolor
Walt Disney (Winston Hibler)

When his old guardian dies, a small boy and his girl friend run away with their pet lion.
Patchy, episodic action drama for older children, with a very sleepy lion.

w Stewart Raffil *d* Bernard McEveety *ph* Monroe Askins *m* Buddy Baker

Michael Douglas, Will Geer

AAN: Buddy Baker

The Narrow Corner
US 1933 71m bw

On an eastern island, a man on the run for murder finds he can't escape his fate.
Mediocre adaptation of a Somerset Maugham novel in which very little happens; the added love interest doesn't help. Douglas Fairbanks Jnr, Ralph Bellamy, Dudley Digges, Arthur Hohl, Patricia Ellis. Written by Robert Presnell; directed by Alfred E. Green; for Warner. (Remade three years later as *Isle of Fury* [qv].) 'Considerably better than fair.'—*Variety*

The Narrow Margin***
US 1950 70m bw
RKO (Stanley Rubin)

Police try to guard a prosecution witness on a train from Chicago to Los Angeles.
Tight little thriller which takes every advantage of its train setting. What the trade used to call a sleeper, it gave more satisfaction than many a top feature.

w Earl Felton *d Richard Fleischer* *ph George E. Diskant*

Charles McGraw, Marie Windsor, Jacqueline White, Queenie Leonard

'A taut, breathlessly fast and highly suspenseful "sleeper" par excellence.'—*Time Out, 1986*

AAN: original story (Martin Goldsmith, Jack Leonard)

The Narrowing Circle
GB 1955 66m bw

Murder on the staff of a magazine. Very tolerable mystery which wastes no time and plays fair. Paul Carpenter, Hazel Court, Ferdy Mayne, Russell Napier, Trevor Reid. Written by Doreen Montgomery, from the novel by Julian Symons; directed by Charles Saunders; for Fortress Films / Eros.

'The damnedest thing you ever saw!'

Nashville**
US 1975 161m Metrocolor Panavision
Paramount / ABC (Robert Altman)

A political campaign in Nashville organizes a mammoth pop concert to gain support.
Kaleidoscopic, fragmented, multi-storied musical melodrama, a mammoth movie which can be a bore or an inspiration according to taste. Certainly many exciting moments pass by, but the length is self-defeating.

w Joan Tewkesbury *d* Robert Altman *ph* Paul Lohmann *md* Richard Baskin

Geraldine Chaplin, David Arkin, Barbara Baxley, Ned Beatty, Karen Black, Keith Carradine, Henry Gibson, Keenan Wynn, Lily Tomlin, Ronee Blakley

'A gigantic parody . . . crammed with samples taken from every level of Nashville society, revealed in affectionate detail bordering on caricature in a manner that would surely delight Norman Rockwell.'—*Philip Strick*

'Wildly over-praised Altman, with all the defects we once looked on as marks of healthy ambitiousness: terrible construction, messy editing, leering jokes at its own characters, unending pomposity.'—*Time Out, 1980*

AA: song 'I'm Easy' (*m / ly* Keith Carradine)
AAN: best picture; Robert Altman; Lily Tomlin; Ronee Blakley

Nasty Habits*
GB 1976 92m Technicolor
Brut / Bowden (Robert Enders)

An abbess dies and the nuns vie for succession.
Satirical comedy rather obviously based on the Watergate scandals; initially amusing , but very tiresome by the end.

w Robert Enders, *novel* The Abbess of Crewe by Muriel Spark *d* Michael Lindsay-Hogg *ph* Douglas Slocombe *m* John Cameron

Glenda Jackson, Melina Mercouri, Geraldine Page, Sandy Dennis, Anne Jackson, Anne Meara, Edith Evans, Susan Penhaligon, Rip Torn, Eli Wallach, Jerry Stiller

'The sort of material just about fit for a half-hour TV sketch.'—*Richard Combs, MFB*

The National Health*
GB 1973 97m Eastmancolor
Columbia (Ned Sherrin, Terry Glinwood)

Life in the general men's ward of a large antiquated hospital.
Acerbic comedy from a National Theatre play which mixes tragedy and farce into a kind of *Carry on Dying*.

w Peter Nichols, from his play *d Jack Gold* *ph* John Coquillon *m* Carl Davis *pd* Ray Simm

Jim Dale, Lynn Redgrave, Eleanor Bron, Sheila Scott-Wilkinson, Donald Sinden, Colin Blakely, Clive Swift

National Lampoon's Animal House*
US 1978 109m Technicolor
Universal (Matty Simmons, Ivan Reitman)

On an American campus around 1962, scruffy newcomers challenge the elegant elite.
A ragbag of college gags, of interest only to those who have had the experience; but its success caused much imitation, especially in American television.

w Harold Ramis, Douglas Kenney, Chris Miller *d* John Landis *ph* Charles Correll *m* Elmer Bernstein

John Belushi, Tim Matheson, John Vernon, Donald Sutherland, Verna Bloom, Cesare Danova, Mary Louise Weller

National Lampoon's Class Reunion
US 1982 85m Metrocolor

The class of '72 foregathers at Lizzie Borden High, where a murderer is lurking. An entertainment in which the presentation is better than the material, which is a vague spoof of high school and horror films. Gerrit Graham, Michael Lerner, Fred McCarren, Miriam Flynn, Stephen Furst. Written by John Hughes; directed by Michael Miller; for Matty Simmons / ABC Motion Pictures.

National Lampoon's Vacation
US 1983 98m Technicolor

An inventor drives his family on a holiday starting in Chicago and ending in California, but the journey is fraught with disaster. Episodic, more or less straight black comedy, with detail more often boring or repellent than funny. Chavy Chase, Imogene Coca, Beverly D'Angelo, Randy Quaid, Eddie Bracken. Written by John Hughes; directed by Harold Ramis; for Matty Simmons / Warners.

National Lampoon's European Vacation
US 1985 94m Technicolor

An American family determines to see Europe. Hopelessly unfunny and simple-minded comedy, lacking even the usual schoolboy smut. Chevy Chase, Beverly D'Angelo, Jason Lively, Dana Hill, Eric Idle. Written by John Hughes, Robert Klane; directed by Amy Heckerling; for Matty Simmons / Warner.

National Velvet*
US 1945 125m Technicolor
MGM (Pandro S. Berman)

Children train a horse to win the Grand National.
A big bestseller from another era; its flaws of conception and production quickly became evident.

w Theodore Reeves, Helen Deutsch, *novel* Enid Bagnold *d* Clarence Brown *ph* Leonard Smith *m* Herbert Stothart

Mickey Rooney, Elizabeth Taylor, *Anne Revere*, Donald Crisp, Angela Lansbury, Jackie Jenkins, Reginald Owen, Terry Kilburn, Norma Varden, Alec Craig, Arthur Shields, Dennis Hoey
† Sequel 1978: *International Velvet.*

AA: Anne Revere
AAN: Clarence Brown; Leonard Smith

Native Son
US 1986 112m colour
Cinecom / Diane Silver / American Playhouse / Cinetudes

A poor black teenager commits murder.
Heavy-going adaptation of a novel seen in some American quarters as a symbol of classic guilt.

w Richard Wesley *novel* Richard Wright *d* Jerrold Freedman *ph* Thomas Burstyn *m* James Mtume

Carroll Baker, Akousuwa Busia, Matt Dillon, Art Evans, Elizabeth McGovern, John McMartin, Geraldine Page

† A low-budget Argentine version had been filmed in 1950 by Pierre Chenal, with the author in the leading role.

The Natural*
US 1984 137m Technicolor
Tri-Star / Delphi II (Mark Johnson)

The life of a baseball star who reaches the heights and can only fall.
Curious attempt to modernize the King Arthur legend, with a baseball bat substituting for Excalibur and hints of magic everywhere. A generally mystifying if occasionally an attractive experience.

w Roger Towne, Phil Dusenberry *d* Barry Levinson *ph* Caleb Deschanel *m* Randy Newman

Robert Redford, Robert Duvall, Glenn Close, Kim Basinger, Wilford Brimley, Barbara Hershey, Robert Prosky, Joe Don Baker, Richard Farnsworth

AAN: Glenn Close (supporting actress); photography; music; art direction

Naughty But Nice
US 1939 90m bw
Warner (Sam Bischoff)

A professor of classical music accidentally writes a popular song.
Mildly amusing comedy musical with all the tunes adapted from the classics (cf *That Night with You*).

w Jerry Wald, Richard Macaulay *d* Ray Enright *ph* Arthur L. Todd *songs* Harry Warren, Johnny Mercer

Dick Powell, Ann Sheridan, Ronald Reagan, Gale Page, Zasu Pitts, Jerry Colonna

Naughty Marietta**
US 1935 106m bw
MGM (Hunt Stromberg)

A French princess goes to America and falls in love with an Indian scout.
Period operetta which set the seal of success on the MacDonald-Eddy team. In itself, dated but quite pleasing for those who like the genre.

w John Lee Mahin, Frances Goodrich, Albert Hackett, *operetta* Rida Johnson Young *d* W. S. Van Dyke *ph* William Daniels *m* Victor Herbert *ad* Cedric Gibbons

Jeanette MacDonald, Nelson Eddy, Frank Morgan, Elsa Lanchester, Douglass Dumbrille, Joseph Cawthorn, Cecelia Parker, Walter Kingsford

'Slow-moving operetta which singing must sustain.'—*Variety*

'When these two profiles come together to sing Ah Sweet Mystery of Life, it's beyond camp, it's in a realm of its own.'—*Judith Crist, 1977*

AAN: best picture

The Naughty Nineties
US 1945 72m bw
Universal (Edward L. Hartmann, John Grant)

Two incompetents help an old showboat owner.
Dim star comedy apart from the team's rendition of their most famous routine, 'Who's On First'.

w Edmund L. Hartmann, John Grant, Edmund Joseph, Hal Fimburg *d* Jean Yarborough *ph* George Robinson

Bud Abbott, Lou Costello, Henry Travers, Alan Curtis, Rita Johnson, Joe Sawyer

The Navigator***
US 1924 63m approx (24 fps) bw silent
Metro-Goldwyn / Buster Keaton (Joseph M. Schenck)

A millionaire and his girl are the only people on a transatlantic liner marooned in mid-ocean.
A succession of hilarious sight gags: the star in top form.

w Jean Havez, Clyde Bruckman, J. A. Mitchell *d* Buster Keaton, Donald Crisp *ph* Elgin Lessley, Byron Houck

Buster Keaton, Kathryn McGuire

'Studded with hilarious moments and a hundred and one adroit gags.'—*Photoplay*

'It is not the victory that is important, it is how the game is played!'

Navy Blue and Gold
US 1937 93m bw

An unpopular naval cadet makes good.
Ingenuous flagwaver, like a wrap-up of umpteen others but with better production. Robert Young, James Stewart, Florence Rice, Billie Burke, Lionel Barrymore, Tom Brown, Samuel S. Hinds, Paul Kelly. Written by George Bruce; directed by Sam Wood; for Sam Zimbalist / MGM. 'Expertly made and sure box office.'—*Variety*

Navy Blues
US 1941 109m bw
Warner (Jerry Wald)

Naval ratings get into trouble in Honolulu.
Undernourished musical comedy with not too much of either commodity.

w Jerry Wald, Richard Macaulay, Arthur T. Horman *d* Lloyd Bacon *ph* Tony Gaudio *ch* Seymour Felix *songs* Arthur Schwarz, Johnny Mercer

Ann Sheridan, Jack Oakie, Martha Raye, Jack Haley, Herbert Anderson, Jack Carson, Richard Lane, Jackie Gleason, Howard da Silva

The Navy Comes Through
US 1942 81m bw

The story of a merchant marine ship.
Propaganda potboiler with a reasonably efficient cast and production. Pat O'Brien, George Murphy, Jane Wyatt, Jackie Cooper, Carl Esmond, Max Baer, Desi Arnaz, Ray Collins. Written by Roy Chanslor and Aeneas Mackenzie from a story by Borden Chase; directed by A. Edward Sutherland; for RKO.

Navy Wife
US 1935 72m bw

A girl who marries a navy doctor is unhappy with the life. Routine domestic drama with a propaganda angle. Claire Trevor, Ralph Bellamy, Jane Darwell, Ben Lyon, Warren Hymer, Kathleen Burke. Written by Sonya Levien from the novel Beauty's Daughter by Kathleen Norris; directed by Allan Dwan; for Fox. 'Problem play for the duals.'—*Variety*

Navy Wife
US 1956 83m bw

A commander's wife visits her husband in Japan and learns about Japanese attitudes. Silly hands-across-the-sea comedy which takes a long time to get nowhere. Joan Bennett, Gary Merrill, Shirley Yagamuchi, Judy Nugent. Written by Kay Lenard; directed by Edward Bernds; for Allied Artists. (GB title: *Mother, Sir!*)

Nazarin*
Mexico 1958 94m bw
Barbachano Ponce

A Catholic priest tries to take the teachings of Christ literally, but is drastically misunderstood.
A black atheistic satire pretty typical of its director, but not among his most enjoyable works.

w Julio Alejandro, Luis Bunuel, *novel* Benito Perez Galdos *d Luis Bunuel* *ph* Gabriel Figueroa

Francisco Rabal, Marga Lopez, Rita Macedo, Ignacio Lopez Tarso

Nazi Agent*
US 1942 84m bw
MGM (Irving Asher)

A German-American is forced by his Nazi twin to help a group of German spies.
Modest suspenser with a plot twist similar to *The Great Impersonation* and *Dead Ringer*.

w Paul Gangelin, John Meehan Jnr *d Jules Dassin* *ph* Harry Stradling *m* Lennie Hayton

Conrad Veidt, Ann Ayars, Frank Reicher, Dorothy Tree, Martin Kosleck

The Neanderthal Man
US 1953 75m bw

A scientist transforms a cat into a sabre-toothed tiger and himself into a neanderthal man; he is then eaten by the tiger. By no means as amusing as it sounds. Robert

Shayne, Richard Crane, Doris Merrick, Joyce Terry. Written by Aubrey Wisberg and Jack Pollexfen; directed by E. A. Dupont; photographed by Stanley Cortez; for Global / United Artists.

Nearly a Nasty Accident
GB 1961 91m bw
British Lion / Britannia / Marlow (Bertram Ostrer)

A mild-mannered aircraftman causes disaster wherever he goes.
Familiar faces just about save from disaster this underscripted comedy for indulgent audiences.

w Jack Davies, Hugh Woodruff, *play* Touch Wood by David Stringer, David Carr *d* Don Chaffey *ph* Paul Beeson *m* Ken Jones

Kenneth Connor, Jimmy Edwards, Shirley Eaton, Richard Wattis, Ronnie Stevens, Jon Pertwee, Eric Barker, Peter Jones, Jack Watling, Joyce Carey, Terry Scott

'Three men and a woman face death beside a man they want to kill!'

The Nebraskan
US 1953 66m Technicolor 3D

An army scout proves the innocence of an Indian supposed to have murdered a Sioux chief. Two-bit western which looked even worse in three dimensions. Phil Carey, Roberta Haynes, Wallace Ford, Richard Webb, Lee Van Cleef. Written by David Lang and Martin Berkeley; directed by Fred F. Sears; for Columbia.

Necromancy
US 1973 83m colour
Cinerama (Bert I. Gordon)

Two young people become involved in small-town witchcraft.
Low-key, low-talent thriller overbalanced by its star.

wd Bert I. Gordon *ph* Winton C. Hoch *m* Fred Karger

Orson Welles, Pamela Franklin, Michael Onthean, Lee Purcell

Ned Kelly
GB 1970 103m Technicolor
UA / Woodfall (Neil Hartley)

The career of a 19th-century Australian outlaw.
Obstinately unlikeable action picture with some kind of message which never becomes clear amid all the cleverness.

w Tony Richardson, Ian Jones *d* Tony Richardson *ph* Gerry Fisher *m* Shel Silverstein *pd* Jocelyn Herbert

Mick Jagger, Allen Bickford, Geoff Gilmour, Mark McManus

Negatives*
GB 1968 98m Eastmancolor
Crispin / Kettledrum (Judd Bernard)

Three people indulge in sexual fantasies involving Dr Crippen and Baron Von Richthofen.
Smoothly done but impenetrable psychological poppycock: what is fact and what is fancy, only the author knows.

w Peter Everett, Roger Lowry, *novel* Peter Everett *d* Peter Medak *ph* Ken Hodges *m* Basil Kirchin

Glenda Jackson, Peter McEnery, Diane Cilento, Maurice Denham, Steven Lewis, Norman Rossington

Neighbors*
US 1981 94m Technicolor
Columbia / Zanuck–Brown

A staid suburbanite is first irritated, then taken over by his splashy neighbours.
Hit-or-miss but generally quite funny comedy in a style familiar to viewers of American late night television.

w Larry Gelbart, *novel* Thomas Berger *d* John G. Avildsen *ph* Gerald Hirschfeld *m* Bill Conti *pd* Peter Larkin *ed* Jan Kurson

John Belushi, Dan Aykroyd, Kathryn Walker, Cathy Moriarty, Igors Gavon, Dru-Ann Chukron

Nell Gwyn**
GB 1934 85m bw
B and D (Herbert Wilcox)

The affair of Charles II and an orange seller.
Naïve, vivid account of a famous couple; physically cheap and rather faded, but the best film on the subject and one of the best covering this period.

w Miles Malleson d Herbert Wilcox
ph F. A. Young

Anna Neagle, Cedric Hardwicke, Jeanne de Casalis, Muriel George, Miles Malleson, Esmé Percy, Moore Marriott

'Slow costumer, also lacking marquee value.'—*Variety*

'Wherever you've been—this is where you've never been before!'

The Neptune Factor
Canada 1972 98m De Luxe Panavision
TCF / Quadrant / Bellevue–Pathe (Sanford Howard)
Later retitled: *The Neptune Disaster*

American oceanologists conduct an experiment in underwater living.
Wet 'actioner' in which very little happens except a few porthole views of magnified fish.

w Jack de Witt *d* Daniel Petrie *ph* Harry Makin *m* Lalo Schifrin

Ben Gazzara, Walter Pidgeon, Yvette Mimieux, Ernest Borgnine, Chris Wiggins

Neptune's Daughter*
US 1949 93m Technicolor
MGM (Jack Cummings)

A lady bathing suit designer has a South American romance.
Generally thought one of the better aquatic musicals, and certainly very typical of them and its studio at this time.

w Dorothy Kingsley *d* Edward Buzzell *ph* Charles Rosher *m* George Stoll *songs* Frank Loesser

Esther Williams, Red Skelton, Ricardo Montalban, Betty Garrett, Keenan Wynn, Xavier Cugat and his Orchestra, Mike Mazurki, Ted de Corsia, Mel Blanc

AA: song, 'Baby, It's Cold Outside'

The Net
GB 1953 86m bw
Rank / Two Cities (Anthony Darnborough)
US title: *Project M7*

Tension among boffins in an aviation research station leads to murder and the discovery of a spy.
Low-key suspenser, quite adequately presented.

w William Fairchild, *novel* John Pudney *d* Anthony Asquith *ph* Desmond Dickinson *m* Benjamin Frankel

Phyllis Calvert, Noel Willman, Herbert Lom, James Donald, Robert Beatty, Muriel Pavlow, Walter Fitzgerald, Maurice Denham

'Television will never be the same!'
'Prepare yourself for a perfectly outrageous motion picture!'

Network**
US 1976 121m Metrocolor Panavision
MGM / UA (Howard Gottfried, Fred Caruso)

A network news commentator begins to say what he thinks about the world and becomes a new messiah to the people and an embarrassment to his sponsors.
Overheated satire which in between its undoubted high points becomes noisy and tiresome, not helped by fuzzy photography. Its very existence in a commercial system, however, is as remarkable as its box-office success.

w Paddy Chayevsky d Sidney Lumet *ph* Owen Roizman *m* Elliot Lawrence

Peter Finch, William Holden, Faye Dunaway, Robert Duvall, Wesley Addy, Ned Beatty, Beatrice Straight, John Carpenter

HOWARD BEALE (Peter Finch) on live television: 'I don't know what to do about the depression and the inflation and the Russians and the crime in the streets. All I know is that first you've got to get mad. You've got to say: "I'm a human being, god damn it, my life has some value!" So I want you to get up now. I want all of you to get up out of your chairs. I want you to get up right now and go to the window, open it and stick your head out and yell "I'm mad as hell, and I'm not going to take this any more!" '

Ditto: 'Ladies and gentlemen, I would like at this moment to announce that I will be retiring from this programme in two weeks' time because of poor ratings. Since this show was the only thing I had going for me in my life, I have decided to kill myself. I'm going to blow my brains out right on this programme a week from today.'

MAX SCHUMACHER (William Holden): 'You're television incarnate, Diana, indifferent to suffering, insensitive to joy. All of life is reduced to the common rubble of banality. War, murder, death—all the same to you as bottles of beer, and the daily business of life is a corrupt comedy. You even shatter the sensations of time and space into split seconds and instant replays. You're madness, Diana.'

'The cast of this messianic farce take turns yelling at us soulless masses.'—*New Yorker*

'Too much of this film has the hectoring stridency of tabloid headlines.'—*Michael Billington, Illustrated London News*

† The theme was taken up a year later in the shortlived TV series *W.E.B.*

AA: Paddy Chayevsky; Peter Finch; Faye Dunaway; Beatrice Straight
AAN: best picture; Sidney Lumet; Owen Roizman; William Holden; Ned Beatty

Neutral Port
GB 1940 92m bw

A merchant navy captain avenges the loss of his ship by sabotaging a German U-boat. Unconvincing propaganda, rather stagily presented. Will Fyffe, Phyllis Calvert, Leslie Banks, Yvonne Arnaud, Hugh McDermott, Frederick Valk. Written by J. B. Williams and T. J. Morrison; directed by Marcel Varnel; for Gainsborough.

Nevada Smith*
US 1966 131m Eastmancolor Panavision
Avco / Solar (Joe Levine, Henry Hathaway)

A cowboy takes a long revenge on the outlaws who murdered his parents.
Violent, sour, occasionally lively but frequently boring western melodrama on a well worn theme.

w John Michael Hayes, from the 'early life' of a character in The Carpetbaggers by Harold Robbins *d* Henry Hathaway *ph* Lucien Ballard *m* Alfred Newman

Steve McQueen, Karl Malden, Brian Keith, Suzanne Pleshette, Arthur Kennedy, Janet Margolin, Howard da Silva, Raf Vallone, Pat Hingle

The Nevadan
US 1950 81m Cinecolor

A marshal recovers stolen gold. Solid western programmer, compromised by poor colour. Randolph Scott, Dorothy Malone, Forrest Tucker, Frank Faylen, George Macready. Written by George W. George and George F. Slavin; directed by Gordon Douglas; for Harry Joe Brown / Columbia. (GB title: *The Man from Nevada.*)

Never a Dull Moment
US 1943 60m bw

Three comedians prevent a nightclub owner from carrying out a robbery. The last thin vehicle for a famous comedy trio; even here they have their moments. The Ritz Brothers, Frances Langford, Mary Beth Hughes, George Zucco, Franklin Pangborn. Written by Mel Ronson and Stanley Roberts; directed by Edward Lilley; for Universal.

Never a Dull Moment
US 1950 89m bw
RKO (Harriet Parsons)

A lady music critic marries a rodeo cowboy and finds life hard down on the ranch.
Very mild star programmer.

w Lou Breslow, Doris Anderson, *novel* Who Could Ask for Anything More? by Kay Swift *d* George Marshall *ph* Joseph Walker *m* Frederick Hollander *md* Constantin Bakaleinikoff

Irene Dunne, Fred MacMurray, William Demarest, Andy Devine, Gigi Perreau, Natalie Wood, Philip Ober, Jack Kirkwood

Never a Dull Moment
US 1967 100m Technicolor
Walt Disney (Ron Miller)

An unsuccessful actor is mistaken for a notorious gangster.
Slapstick romp with vigour but not much flair.

w A. J. Carothers, *novel* John Godey *d* Jerry Paris *ph* William Snyder *m* Robert F. Brunner

Dick Van Dyke, Edward G. Robinson, Dorothy Provine, Henry Silva, Joanna Moore, Tony Bill, Slim Pickens, Jack Elam

'They thought he couldn't do the job: that's why they chose him!'

Never Cry Wolf
US 1983 105m Technicolor

A scientist is dumped alone in the Arctic to collect evidence against wolves. Weird fable whose comic asides diminish its serious intent, and whose leading characterization is so eccentric as to bewilder any audience. Charles Martin Smith, Brian Dennehy, Samson Jorah. Written by Curtis Hanson, Sam Hamm, Richard Kletter, from the book by Farley Mowat; directed by Carroll Ballard; for Walt Disney.

Never Give a Sucker an Even Break*
US 1941 70m bw
Universal
GB title: *What a Man*

W. C. Fields dives off an aeroplane into the lap of a young woman who has never seen a man; she falls in love with him.
Stupefyingly inept in its scripting and pacing, this comedy is often irresistibly funny because of the anti-everything personality of its writer-star. No one else could have got away with it, or would have been likely to try.

w John T. Neville, Prescott Chaplin, *story* Otis Criblecoblis (W. C. Fields) *d* Edward Cline *ph* Charles Van Enger *m* Frank Skinner

W. C. Fields, Gloria Jean, Leon Errol, Butch and Buddy, Franklin Pangborn, Anne Nagel, Mona Barrie, Ann Miller, Margaret Dumont

'A beautifully timed exhibition of mock pomposity, puzzled ineffectualness, subtle understatement and true-blue nonchalance.'—*James Agee*

Never Give an Inch: see Sometimes a Great Notion

Never Let Go
GB 1960 91m bw
Rank / Julian Wintle–Leslie Parkin (Peter de Sarigny)

A travelling salesman has his car stolen and stands up to the sadistic gang boss responsible.
Brutishly unattractive thriller, apparently designed for the sole purpose of giving Peter Sellers a villainous part.

w Alun Falconer *d* John Guillermin *ph* Christopher Challis *m* John Barry

Richard Todd, Peter Sellers, Elizabeth Sellars, Adam Faith, Carol White, Mervyn Johns, Noel Willman

Never Let Me Go
GB 1953 94m bw
MGM (Clarence Brown)

After World War II an American correspondent marries a Russian ballerina but is later deported by the authorities.
Ho-hum romantic melodrama, quite interestingly cast.

w Roland Millar, George Froeschel, *novel* Came the Dawn by Roger Bax *d* Delmer Daves *ph* Robert Krasker *m* Hans May

Clark Gable, Gene Tierney, Richard Haydn, Belita, Bernard Miles, Kenneth More, Karel Stepanek, Theodore Bikel, Frederick Valk

Never Look Back
GB 1952 73m bw

A lady barrister finds she must defend an old boy friend on a murder charge. Plausible drama which never quite comes to the boil. Rosamund John, Hugh Sinclair, Guy Middleton, Henry Edwards, Terence Longdon. Written by John Hunter, Guy Morgan and Francis Searle; directed by Francis Searle; for Michael Carreras / Hammer.

Never Love a Stranger
US 1958 93m bw
Harold Robbins / Allied Artists (Peter Gettlinger)

A Catholic boy who has become a gangster helps his Jewish friend who has become assistant district attorney to trap a vicious hoodlum.
The old *Manhattan Melodrama* theme is dusted off once again, this time to very little effect.

w Harold Robbins, Richard Day, *novel* Harold Robbins *d* Robert Stevens *ph* Lee Garmes *m* Raymond Scott

John Drew Barrymore, Steve McQueen, Robert Bray, Lita Milan, R. G. Armstrong, Salem Ludwig

Never on Sunday*
Greece 1959 97m bw
Lopert / Melinafilm (Jules Dassin)
original title: *Pote tin Kyriaki*

An American scholar in Greece is infatuated by a prostitute and sets about improving her. Amiable if rather shoddy variation on

Pygmalion: the star performance and the music carried it, along with its own naughtiness, to success.

wd Jules Dassin *ph* Jacques Natteau *m Manos Hadjidakis*

Melina Mercouri, Jules Dassin, Georges Foundas, Tito Vandis, Despo Diamantidou

'It barely stands scrutiny, but it communicates cheerfulness, and this in itself is no mean achievement.'—*Penelope Houston, MFB*

AA: title song (Manos Hadjidakis)
AAN: direction; script; Melina Mercouri

Never Put it in Writing*
GB 1963 93m bw
MGM / Andrew Stone

A young executive tries to recover from the mails an indiscreet letter he has written to his boss.
Frantic hit-or-miss farcical comedy distinguished by Dublin locations and cast.

wd Andrew Stone *ph* Martin Curtis *m* Frank Cordell

Pat Boone, Fidelma Murphy, Reginald Beckwith, John Le Mesurier, Colin Blakely, Milo O'Shea

Never Say Die*
US 1939 80m bw
Paramount (Paul Jones)

A millionaire hypochondriac is convinced he is dying.
Thin farce with Hope on the very brink of stardom; some bright moments.

w Don Hartman, Frank Butler, Preston Sturges *d* Elliott Nugent *ph* Leo Tover *md* Boris Morros

Martha Raye, Bob Hope, Andy Devine, Alan Mowbray, Gale Sondergaard, Sig Rumann, Ernest Cossart, Monty Woolley, Christian Rub

'Needs strong support for top dual spots.'—*Variety*

'The most enjoyable film for weeks . . . consistently absurd . . . no dignity, no passion, and a magnificent cast.'—*Graham Greene*

Never Say Goodbye
US 1946 97m bw
Warner (William Jacobs)

A seven-year-old girl draws her divorced parents back together.
Highly derivative romantic comedy mishmash which did its star's career no good at all.

w James V. Kern, I. A. L. Diamond, Lewis R. Foster, Ben and Norma Barzman *d* James V. Kern *ph* Arthur Edeson *m* Frederick Hollander

Errol Flynn, Eleanor Parker, Lucile Watson, S. Z. Sakall, Donald Woods, Patti Brady, Forrest Tucker, Hattie McDaniel

Never Say Goodbye
US 1955 96m Technicolor
U-I (Albert J. Cohen)

In 1945 Berlin an American army doctor marries a pianist who is later trapped in the Russian zone; they meet years later in America.
Romantic drama aimed at a female audience, remade from *This Love of Ours* (qv).

w Charles Hoffman *d* Jerry Hopper *ph* Maury Gertsman *m* Frank Skinner

Rock Hudson, George Sanders, Cornell Borchers, Ray Collins, David Janssen

Never Say Never Again*
GB 1983 134m Technicolor Panavision
Warner / Woodcote / Taliafilm (Jack Schwartzman)

James Bond foils a world domination attempt by Blofeld.
Reasonably enjoyable mishmash of Bondery; the plot is technically a remake of *Thunderball*, not that it matters much until the end, when the underwater stuff becomes tiresome because one hardly knows who is under the masks.

w Lorenzo Semple Jnr *d* Irvin Kershner *ph* Douglas Slocombe *m* Michel Legrand *pd* Philip Harrison, Stephen Grimes

Sean Connery, Klaus Maria Brandauer, Max Von Sydow, Barbara Carrera, Kim Basinger, Bernie Casey, Alec McCowen, Edward Fox, Rowan Atkinson

'Q' (Alec McCowen): 'Good to see you again, Mr Bond. Let's get back to some gratuitous sex and violence, I say.'

Never So Few
US 1959 124m Metrocolor Cinemascope
MGM / Canterbury (Edmund Grainger)

Adventures of World War II Americans commanding Burmese guerrillas.
Jungle actioner with pauses for philosophizing; well enough made but not very interesting.

w Millard Kaufman, *novel* Tom Chamales *d* John Sturges *ph* William H. Daniels *m* Hugo Friedhofer

Frank Sinatra, Gina Lollobrigida, Peter Lawford, Steve McQueen, Paul Henreid, Richard Johnson, Brian Donlevy, Charles Bronson, Dean Jones

Never Steal Anything Small
US 1958 94m Eastmancolor Cinemascope
U-I (Aaron Rosenberg)

The reformation of a corrupt but sympathetic dockers' union boss.
Curious semi-musical which doesn't come off at all despite excellent credentials.

wd Charles Lederer, *play* The Devil's Hornpipe by Rouben Mamoulian, Maxwell Anderson *ph* Harold Lipstein *m* Allie Wrubel *ly* Maxwell Anderson *ch* Hermes Pan

James Cagney, Shirley Jones, Roger Smith, Cara Williams, Nehemiah Persoff, Royal Dano, Anthony Caruso

'The closest thing to it, I'd say, is *The Threepenny Opera*. It's witty, and it has some good radical lyrics. Films must have some comment to make.'—*James Cagney*

Never Take No for an Answer*
GB 1951 82m bw
Constellation (Anthony Havelock-Allan)

A small boy goes to Rome to get permission from the Pope to take his sick donkey to be blessed in the church.
Slight, easy-going whimsy with attractive sunlit locations.

w Paul and Pauline Gallico, *novel* The Small Miracle by Paul Gallico *d* Maurice Cloche, Ralph Smart *ph* Otto Heller *m* Nino Rota

Vittorio Manunta, Denis O'Dea, Guido Cellano, Nerio Bernardi

'The main pleasures of this slender film are visual ones.'—*MFB*

† Remade as a TV movie *Small Miracle*.

Never Take Sweets from a Stranger
GB 1960 81m bw Megascope

In a Canadian town, a respected elderly man is accused of improper sexual advances to a child. In the awful warning category, and rather predictable. Gwen Watford, Patrick Allen, Felix Aylmer, Niall MacGinnis, Bill Nagy, Janina Faye, Michael Gwynn. Written by John Hunter from play *The Pony Cart* by Roger Garis; directed by Cyril Frankel; for Hammer / Columbia.

Never the Twain Shall Meet
US 1931 89m bw

A young lawyer goes native when he falls for a South Sea island girl. Stilted misalliance melodrama, previously made in 1925 as a silent with Bert Lytell and Anita Stewart; its faded notions simply didn't survive sound. Leslie Howard, Conchita Montenegro, Karen Morley, C. Aubrey Smith. Written by Ruth Cummings and Edwin Justus Mayer, from the novel by Peter B. Kyne; directed by W. S. Van Dyke; for MGM.

Never Too Late
US 1965 104m Technicolor Panavision
Warner / Lear–Yorkin (Norman Lear)

A well-to-do middle-aged housewife discovers she is pregnant.
Predictable, rather hysterical domestic comedy, flatly developed from a successful play which offered two star parts for old stagers.

w Sumner Arthur Long, from his play *d* Bud Yorkin *ph* Philip Lathrop *m* David Rose

Paul Ford, Maureen O'Sullivan, Connie Stevens, Jim Hutton, Lloyd Nolan, Henry Jones, Jane Wyatt

Never Wave at a WAC
US 1952 87m bw
Independent Artists (Frederick Brisson)
GB title: *The Private Wore Skirts*

A Washington hostess joins the WACs and finds she can't get beyond the rank of private.
Pattern comedy, unconvincing in all respects but with a smattering of funny moments.
Flagwaving takes over towards the end.

w Ken Englund *d* Norman Z. McLeod *ph* William Daniels *m* Elmer Bernstein

Rosalind Russell, Paul Douglas, Marie Wilson, William Ching, Leif Erickson, Arleen Whelan, Charles Dingle

'A boy who needs a friend finds a world that needs a hero in a land beyond imagination!'

The Neverending Story*
West Germany 1984 94m Technicolor Technovision

A reluctant student reads a book instead: dealing with mystical monsters and make believe, it takes him back into their world. Slow-starting fantasy with agreeable enough creations but not a lot of humour despite its intended stimulus to the imagination. Barret Oliver, Gerald McRaney, Moses Gunn. Written and directed by Wolfgang Petersen, from book by Michael Ende; for Bavaria Studios / WDR / Neue Constantin Filmproduktion.

The New Adventures of Get-Rich-Quick Wallingford
US 1931 76m bw

Exploits of an attractive go-getter. Reliable comedy of its day. William Haines, Jimmy Durante, Leila Hyams, Guy Kibbee. Written by Charles MacArthur, from the novel by G. R. Chester; directed by Sam Wood; for MGM.

The New Adventures of Tarzan
US 1935 bw serial: 12 eps

Tarzan goes to Guatemala to find a friend captured by Mayans. Modestly intriguing serial which was also released as two features: the first under the above title and the second as *Tarzan and the Green Goddess*. Herman Brix, Ula Holt, Frank Baker, Dale Walsh. Directed by Edward Kull and W. F. McGaugh; for Dearholt-Stout and Cohen.

The New Babylon*
USSR 1929 80m approx (24 fps) bw silent
Sovkino
original title: *Novyi Vavilon*

The rise and fall of the 1871 French commune, seen through the eyes of a girl department store worker.
Propagandist socio-historical melodrama, most interesting now for its sub-Eisenstein technique.

wd Leonid Trauberg, Grigori Kozintsev *ph* Andrei Moskvin, Yevgeni Mikhailov *m* Dmitri Shostakovich *ad* Yevgeni Enei

Yelena Kuzmina, Pyotr Sobelevsky, Sophie Magarill

The New Centurions*
US 1972 103m Eastmancolor Panavision
Columbia / Chartoff–Winkler
GB title: *Precinct 45: Los Angeles Police*

An old cop teaches a new one.
'Realistic' crime prevention saga which spawned the TV series *Police Story* and *Police Woman*. Well done within its limits.

w Stirling Silliphant, *novel* Joseph Wambaugh *d* Richard Fleischer *ph* Ralph Woolsey *m* Quincy Jones

George C. Scott, Stacy Keach, Jane Alexander, Rosalind Cash, Scott Wilson

New Faces*
US 1954 99m Eastmancolor Cinemascope
Edward L. Alperson (Leonard Sillman)

A revue goes on despite money problems.
Five minutes of plot, ninety-five minutes of revue from the Broadway stage; mostly quite amusing, and chiefly notable for introducing Eartha Kitt with all her standards.

w various *d* Harry Horner *ph* Lucien Ballard *m* Raoul Kraushaar *revue deviser* John Murray Anderson

Eartha Kitt, Ronny Graham, Alice Ghostley, Robert Clary, Paul Lynde

New Faces of 1937
US 1937 105m bw

Talent auditions for a Broadway show. Shapeless agglomeration of variety acts with a wisp of story; the level of talent is not outstandingly high. Joe Penner, Milton Berle, Parkyakarkus, Harriet Hilliard, Jerome Cowan, Bert Gordon, Ann Miller, Richard Lane. Written by Nat Perrin, P. G. Epstein, Irving Brecher, Harold Russell, Harry Clork, Howard J. Green, from a story Shoestring by George Bradshaw; directed by Leigh Jason; for RKO. 'A hodgepodge of vaudeville, night club and radio talent, unskilfully blended and rather inanely promulgated.'—*Variety*

The New Gulliver*
USSR 1933 85m approx bw

Gulliver's Travels is retold in puppet form, but the plot has become a satire against capitalism. Interesting both as animation and as propaganda. Written by A. Ptoushko, B. Roshal; directed by A. Ptoushko, A. Vanitchkin.

The New Interns
US 1964 123m bw
Columbia (Robert Cohn)

Young doctors at a city hospital have trouble saving a rapist and his victim.
Unnecessary sequel to *The Interns*, its 'realism' requiring large pinches of salt.

w Wilton Schiller *d* John Rich *ph* Lucien Ballard *m* Earle Hagen

George Segal, Telly Savalas, Michael Callan, Dean Jones, Inger Stevens, Stefanie Powers, Lee Patrick

A New Kind of Love
US 1963 110m Technicolor
Paramount / Llenroc (Melville Shavelson)

An American dress designer in Paris is softened by a boorish newspaper columnist.
Very thin sex comedy, dressed to kill but with nowhere to go.

wd Melville Shavelson *ph* Daniel Fapp *m* Leith Stevens

Paul Newman, Joanne Woodward, Maurice Chevalier, Thelma Ritter, George Tobias

AAN: Leith Stevens

The New Land see The Emigrants

A New Leaf*
US 1970 102m Movielab
Paramount / Aries / Elkins (Joe Manduke)

A middle-aged playboy, close to bankruptcy, thinks of acquiring a wealthy wife.
Agreeably mordant comedy which sparkles in patches rather than as a whole.

wd Elaine May, story The Green Heart by Jack Ritchie *ph* Gayne Rescher *m* John Mandel, Neal Hefti *pd* Richard Fried

Walter Matthau, Elaine May, Jack Weston, George Rose, William Redfield, James Coco

'Unashamedly a thirties fairy tale in modern, but not fashionable, dress.'—*Jan Dawson*

New Mexico
US 1952 78m Anscocolor

A cavalry officer tries to make peace with the Indians, but when an Indian child is accidentally killed a savage war breaks out. Standard western, not badly made. Lew Ayres, Marilyn Maxwell, Robert Hutton, Andy Devine, Raymond Burr, Jeff Corey. Written by Max Trell; directed by Irving Reis; for Irving Allen / United Artists.

New Moon*
US 1940 105m bw
MGM (Robert Z. Leonard)

Romance in old French Louisiana.
Stalwart adaptation of an operetta previously filmed in 1930 with Lawrence Tibbett and Grace Moore.

w Jacques Deval, Robert Arthur *d* Robert Z. Leonard *ph* William Daniels *m / ly* Sigmund Romberg, Oscar Hammerstein

Jeanette MacDonald, Nelson Eddy, Mary Boland, George Zucco, H. B. Warner, Stanley Fields, Grant Mitchell

New Morals for Old
US 1932 77m bw

John Van Druten's play *After All*, about the generation gap in the London aristocracy, was here rather unwisely translated to the American middle class and emerged as a decided curiosity. Robert Young, Myrna Loy, Jean Hersholt, Lewis Stone, Laura Hope Crews, Elizabeth Patterson. Written by Zelda Sears and Wanda Tuchock; directed by Charles Brabin; for MGM. 'A weak sister, swathed in gloom, muddled, and without names that will draw.'—*Variety*

New Orleans*
US 1947 89m bw
Jules Levey

NEVER SAY NEVER AGAIN. Sean Connery, the original 007, returned in a virtual remake of *Thunderball* and, for good measure, provided the title as well.

How jazz was born, according to the movies. Routine low-budgeter enlivened by a splendid array of guest musicians.

w Elliot Paul, Dick Irving Hyland *d* Arthur Lubin *ph* Lucien Andriot *md* Nathaniel Finston

Louis Armstrong and his All Stars, Arturo de Cordova, Dorothy Patrick, *Billie Holiday, Meade Lux Lewis, Woody Herman* and his Orchestra

New Wine
US 1941 89m bw

Franz Schubert seeks the patronage of Beethoven and sacrifices his love life to music. Weirdly cast romantic drama, rather fumbling in all departments. Alan Curtis (as Schubert!), Ilona Massey, Albert Basserman, Binnie Barnes, Sterling Holloway. Written by Howard Estabrook and Nicholas Jory; directed by Reinhold Schunzel; for Gloria / UA. (GB title: *The Great Awakening*.)

New York Confidential
US 1955 87m bw
Warner / Russel Rouse, Clarence Greene

The head of a crime syndicate is assassinated by his own hired killer.

Unexciting 'realistic' thriller with the gangsters presented as family and businessmen; seventeen years later *The Godfather* did it rather better.

w Clarence Greene, Russel Rouse *d* Russel Rouse *ph* Edward Fitzgerald *m* Joseph Mullendore *pd* Fernando Carrere

Broderick Crawford, Richard Conte, Anne Bancroft, Marilyn Maxwell, Onslow Stevens, J. Carrol Naish, Barry Kelley, Mike Mazurki, Celia Lovsky

The New York Hat*
US 1912 10m approx (24 fps) bw silent
D. W. Griffith

A small-town minister is gossiped about when he buys a hat for a young girl.
Influential early short story film with good local backgrounds.

w Anita Loos *d D. W. Griffith* *ph* Billy Bitzer

Mary Pickford, Lionel Barrymore, Lillian Gish, Dorothy Gish, Robert Harron, Mack Sennett, Mae Marsh

New York, New York*
US 1977 153m Technicolor Panavision
UA / Chartoff–Winkler (Gene Kirkwood)

In the late forties in New York, a single-minded saxophonist fails to do right by his girl friend, who becomes a Hollywood star.
A clever recreation of the big band era, hampered by gross overlength, unattractive characters and a pessimistic plot.

w Earl Mac Rauch, Mardik Martin *d* Martin Scorsese *ph* Laszlo Kovacs *pd* Boris Leven *md* Ralph Burns

Liza Minnelli, Robert de Niro, Lionel Stander, Barry Primus

New York Nights
US 1929 81m bw

A musical comedy star has a husband who drinks, and she accepts help from a gangster. The star's sound début was a hit-and-miss affair composed of familiar elements. Norma Talmadge, Gilbert Roland, John Wray, Lilyan Tashman, Roscoe Karns. Written by Jules Furthman from the play Tin Pan Alley by Hugh Stanislaus Stange; directed by Lewis Milestone; for UA / Talmadge. 'Good performance, fair picture.'—*Variety*

New York Town
US 1941 94m bw
Paramount (Anthony Veiller)

A girl new to the Big Apple befriends a sidewalk photographer.
Flat romantic comedy, a soufflé which doesn't rise despite the talents involved.

w Lewis Seltzer (and, uncredited, Preston Sturges) *d* Charles Vidor (and Sturges) *ph* Charles Schoenbaum *m* Leo Shuken

Fred MacMurray, Mary Martin, Robert Preston, Akim Tamiroff, Lynne Overman, Eric Blore, Cecil Kellaway, Fuzzy Knight

Newman's Law
US 1974 99m Technicolor
Universal (Richard Irving)

A cop uses unconventional methods to trap drug smugglers.
Very routine police actioner, just above TV movie level.

w Anthony Wilson *d* Richard Heffron *ph* Vilis Lapenieks *m* Robert Prince

George Peppard, Roger Robinson, Eugene Roche, Gordon Pinsent, Abe Vegoda

News Is Made at Night
US 1939 72m bw

To boost circulation, a news editor pins a string of murders on a well-known gangster, and soon regrets it. Pacy crime comedy-drama, very acceptable as the lower half of a double bill. Preston Foster, Lynn Bari, Eddie Collins, Russell Gleason, George Barbier, Charles Halton. Written by John Larkin; directed by Alfred Werker; for TCF. 'Above average B; should do all right where properly placed.'—*Variety*

Newsboys' Home
US 1939 73m bw

A girl inherits a newspaper which sponsors a home for boys. Modest debut for the East Side Kids, a spin-off group from the Dead End Kids. Jackie Cooper, Edmund Lowe, Wendy Barrie, Edward Norris, Samuel S. Hinds; and Elisha Cook Jnr, Hally Chester, Harris Berger, David Gorcey, Billy Benedict, Charles Duncan. Written by Gordon Kahn; directed by Harold Young; for Universal. 'Another in the tough kid cycle. Will easily handle its end of dual depots.'—*Variety*

Newsfront*
Australia 1978 110m colour

In the fifties, rival news teams battle to get the best shots for cinema newsreels. Lively nostalgic feature with slick modern technique. Bill Hunter, Wendy Hughes, Gerald Kennedy, Chris Haywood. Written and directed by Phillip Noyce, from a concept by David Elfick; for Palm Beach Productions.

The Next Man
US 1976 107m Technicolor
Artists Entertainment Complex (Martin Bregman)

A female assassin is hired to kill the Saudi Arabian Minister of State at the United Nations.
Fractured and uninteresting thriller in which all manner of cinematic styles obscure the storyline but point up the lack of narrative skill.

w Mort Fine, Alan R. Trustman, David M. Wolf, Michael Chapman *d* Richard C. Sarafian *ph* Michael Chapman *m* Michael Kamen *pd* Gene Callahan

Sean Connery, Cornelia Sharpe, Albert Paulsen, Adolfo Celi, Charles Cioffi

'The director takes forever to set up the film's premise, and then he lingers over interminable street festivals and lush scenery.'—*Dave Pomeroy, Film Information*

The Next of Kin***
GB 1942 102m bw
Ealing (S. C. Balcon)

Careless talk causes loss of life in a commando raid.
A propaganda instructional film which was made so entertainingly that it achieved commercial success and remains an excellent example of how to make a bitter pill palatable.

w Thorold Dickinson, Basil Bartlett, Angus Macphail, John Dighton *d* Thorold Dickinson *ph* Ernest Palmer *m* William Walton

Mervyn Johns, Nova Pilbeam, Stephen Murray, Reginald Tate, Basil Radford, Naunton Wayne, Geoffrey Hibbert, Philip Friend, Mary Clare, Basil Sydney

'The detail everywhere is curious and surprising, with something of the fascination of a Simenon crime being unravelled.'—*William Whitebait*

Next of Kin
Australia 1982 86m Eastmancolor

A young girl teacher inherits an old people's home, and finds murder lurking. Slow-starting but finally over-the-top melodrama, with elements borrowed from *Psycho*, *Taste of Fear* and a score of other creepies. Kacjkie Kerin, John Jarratt, Alex Scott, Gerda Nicolson. Written by Michael Heath, Tony Williams; directed by Tony Williams; for SIS productions / Filmco. 'Genre awareness is one thing; a dreary sense of *déjà vu* is another matter entirely.'—*Paul Taylor, MFB*

Next Stop Greenwich Village*
US 1975 111m Movielab
TCF (Paul Mazursky, Tony Ray)

In 1953 in a poor quarter of New York, a young Jew tries to stretch his wings.
A bumper bundle of Jewish clichés dressed up as autobiography, and switching abruptly from comedy to tragedy and back. Vivid, but not exactly entertaining.

wd Paul Mazursky *ph* Arthur Ornitz *m* Bill Conti

Lenny Baker, Shelley Winters, Ellen Greene, Lois Smith, Dori Brenner

'Some tartly comic observation, but the fragmented structure keeps the mixture inert.'—*Sight and Sound*

The Next Time I Marry
US 1938 64m bw

In order to become the richest girl in America, an heiress must marry in haste. Tedious comedy which falls apart halfway. Lucille Ball, James Ellison, Lee Bowman, Granville Bates, Mantan Moreland. Written by John Twist and Helen Meinardi; directed by Garson Kanin; for RKO. 'A very poor entry. The story is banal, production values poor, direction sloppy and most of the performances bad.'—*Variety*

Next Time We Love
US 1936 87m bw
Universal (Paul Kohner)
GB title: *Next Time We Live*

The wife of a war-correspondent has plenty of time for romance.

Romantic drama which badly needs an injection of comedy.

w Melville Baker, *stories* Ursula Parrott *d* Edward H. Griffith *ph* Joseph Valentine *m* Franz Waxman

Margaret Sullavan, Ray Milland, James Stewart, Grant Mitchell, Robert McWade

'Draggy, complex tale . . . will have to be sold on the star's past performances.'—*Variety*

Next to No Time
GB 1958 93m Eastmancolor
British Lion / Montpelier (Albert Fennell)

A meek-and-mild engineer crossing the Atlantic gains confidence when told that anything is possible during the hour 'lost' every day.
Whimsical comedy which never gains momentum.

wd Henry Cornelius, *story* The Enchanted Hour by Paul Gallico *ph* Freddie Francis *m* Georges Auric

Kenneth More, Betsy Drake, Bessie Love, Harry Green, Roland Culver, Reginald Beckwith, John Welsh, John Laurie, Howard Marion-Crawford

The Next Voice You Hear*
US 1950 83m bw
MGM (Dore Schary)

God speaks to mankind on the radio, and the life of Joe Smith American is changed.
Soppy parable, the archetypal instance of Schary's reign of do-goodery at MGM. (He wrote a book about it, *Case History of a Movie*.) The idea is handled with deadly reverence, and falls quite flat, while the depiction of the inhabitants of American suburbia is depressing.

w Charles Schnee *d* William Wellman *ph* William Mellor *m* David Raksin

James Whitmore, Nancy Davis, Lillian Bronson, Jeff Corey

'The sins of the American working man are singularly uninteresting and their obliteration seems scarcely to require the very voice of God.'—*Henry Hart*

'A raging torrent of emotion that even nature can't control!'

Niagara***
US 1952 89m Technicolor
TCF (Charles Brackett)

While visiting Niagara Falls, a faithless wife is plotting to murder her husband, but he turns the tables.
Excellent suspenser with breathtaking locations; in the best Hitchcock class though slightly marred by the emphasis on Monroe's wiggly walk (it was her first big part).

w Charles Brackett, Walter Reisch, Richard Breen *d Henry Hathaway ph Joe MacDonald m* Sol Kaplan

Joseph Cotten, Jean Peters, *Marilyn Monroe*, Don Wilson, Casey Adams

'The story is most imaginatively treated, the production values are excellent.'—*CEA Film Report*

'Seen from any angle, the Falls and Miss Monroe leave little to be desired.'—*New York Times*

'A masterly example of fluid screen narrative.'—*Charles Higham*

'It would have turned out a much better picture if James Mason had played the husband as I wanted. He has that intensity, that neurotic edge. He was all set to do it, but his daughter Portland said she was sick of seeing him die in his pictures.'—*Henry Hathaway*

'This isn't a good movie but it's compellingly tawdry and nasty . . . the only movie that explored the mean, unsavoury potential of Marilyn Monroe's cuddly, infantile perversity.'—*Pauline Kael, 70s*

Niagara Falls
US 1941 43m bw

Confusion reigns in a hotel overlooking the falls. Potted farce in the producer's season of 'shorties'; not the worst, but far from brilliant. ZaSu Pitts, Slim Summerville, Tom Brown, Marjorie Woodworth, Chester Clute. Written by Paul Gerard Smith, Hal Yates, Eugene Conrad; directed by Gordon Douglas; for Hal Roach.

Nice Girl?*
US 1941 95m bw
Universal (Joe Pasternak)

A teenager finds herself in demand by two older men.
Amusing romantic trifle supposed to mark the growing up of Universal's great teenage star.
w Richard Connell, Gladys Lehman *d* William A. Seiter *ph* Joseph Valentine *md* Charles Previn

Deanna Durbin, Franchot Tone, Robert Stack, Walter Brennan, Robert Benchley, Helen Broderick, Ann Gillis

A Nice Girl Like Me
GB 1969 91m Eastmancolor
Anglo Embassy / Partisan (Roy Millichip)

A sheltered young lady sets out to see life but keeps getting pregnant.
Insufferable romantic whimsy, made to look like a marathon TV commercial but never so interesting.

w Anne Piper, Desmond Davis *d* Desmond Davis *ph* Gil Taylor, Manny Wynn *m* Pat Williams

Barbara Ferris, Harry Andrews, Gladys Cooper, Joyce Carey, Bill Hinnant, James Villiers, Christopher Guinee, Fabia Drake

'High-toned woman's magazine nostalgia.'—*MFB*

A Nice Little Bank That Should Be Robbed
US 1958 87m bw Cinemascope
TCF (Anthony Muto)
GB title: *How to Rob a Bank*

Two incompetent crooks rob a bank and buy a racehorse.
Feeble comedy, a sad waste of its stars.

w Sidney Boehm *d* Henry Levin *ph* Leo Tover *m* Lionel Newman

Mickey Rooney, Tom Ewell, Mickey Shaugnessy, Dina Merrill

Nicholas and Alexandra*
GB 1971 189m Eastmancolor Panavision
Columbia / Horizon (Sam Spiegel)

The life of Tsar Nicholas II from 1904 to the execution of the family in 1918.
Inflated epic of occasional interest, mainly for its sets; generally heavy going.

w James Goldman, *book* Robert K. Massie *d* Franklin Schaffner *ph Frederick A. Young m* Richard Rodney Bennett *pd John Box*

Michael Jayston, Janet Suzman, Laurence Olivier, Jack Hawkins, Tom Baker, Harry Andrews, Michael Redgrave, Alexander Knox

† Original preferred casting: Rex Harrison, Vanessa Redgrave.

AAN: best picture; Frederick A. Young; Richard Rodney Bennett; Janet Suzman

Nicholas Nickleby**
GB 1947 108m bw
Ealing (John Croydon)

The adventures of a Victorian schoolmaster, deprived of his rightful fortune, who joins a band of travelling entertainers.
Quite tasteful and expert but too light-handed potted version of Dickens, which suffered by comparison with the David Lean versions.

w John Dighton, *novel* Charles Dickens *d* Alberto Cavalcanti *ph* Gordon Dines *m* Lord Berners

Derek Bond, *Cedric Hardwicke, Alfred Drayton, Sybil Thorndike*, Stanley Holloway, James Hayter, Sally Ann Howes, Jill Balcon, Cyril Fletcher, Fay Compton

'Here's richness! Not all the novel, perhaps, but enough to make a film full of the Dickens spirit.'—*Star*

Nick Carter, Master Detective
US 1939 57m bw

Carter uncovers a spy ring in a plane factory. Dull, devitalized version of the old dime novel adventures; generally characterless and unmemorable. Walter Pidgeon, Rita Johnson, Henry Hull, Stanley Ridges, Donald Meek, Addison Richards, Milburn Stone, Martin Kosleck. Written by Bertram Millhauser, directed by Jacques Tourneur; for Lucien Hubbard / MGM. 'Just another screen sleuth.'—*Variety*

The Nickel Queen
Australia 1971 89m colour

A back country barmaid becomes a rich woman with a nickel share in the mineral boom; but she is swindled by con men. Mild comedy-drama. Googie Withers, John McCallum, John Laws, Ed Devereaux. Written by Henry C. James, John McCallum, Joy Cavill; directed and produced by John McCallum; for Woomera.

The Nickel Ride
US 1975 110m De Luxe

A wheeler dealer in downtown Los Angeles learns that he is marked for elimination. Unpleasant and entirely uninteresting low-life crime melodrama. Jason Miller, Linda Haynes, Victor French, John Hillerman, Bo Hopkins. Written by Eric Roth; directed by Robert Mulligan; for TCF.

Nickelodeon*
US / GB 1976 122m Metrocolor
Columbia / EMI / Chartoff–Winkler (Frank Marshall)

In 1910, various characters come together to make movies, finally attending the 1915 opening in Hollywood of *The Birth of a Nation.*
What should have been a hugely entertaining chunk of comic nostalgia is killed stone dead by embarrassed acting, poor timing, and a general lack of funny ideas, despite having so much to borrow from.

w W. D. Richter, Peter Bogdanovich *d* Peter Bogdanovich *ph* Laszlo Kovacs *md* Richard Hazard

Ryan O'Neal, Burt Reynolds, Tatum O'Neal, Brian Keith, Stella Stevens, John Ritter, Jane Hitchcock

'Ponderous slapstick and a pathetic parody of Harold Lloyd.'—*Sight and Sound*

'Another collection of scenes from other people's films.'—*Howard Kissel, Women's Wear Daily*

'The slightest familiarity with the early works of Hal Roach—not to mention D. W. Griffith, here pretentiously quoted—reveals how little Bogdanovich understands his vastly superior predecessors.'—*Robert Asahina, New Leader*

'The crudest, stupidest, unfunniest farce of this or any other year.'—*John Simon, New York*

The Niebelungen***
Germany 1924 bw silent
Decla-Bioscop (Erich Pommer)
Part One: 'Siegfried': 115m approx (24 fps)
Part Two: 'Kriemheld's Revenge': 125m approx (24 fps)

Siegfried kills a dragon and marries a princess of Burgundy but the fierce queen Brunhilde arranges his death. His widow marries Attila the Hun and they massacre the Burgundians. Stately, warlike legends are transformed into a slow, chilling, awe-inspiring sequence of films, the décor being of special interest. The films were conceived as a tribute to the German nation, and were among Hitler's favourites.

w Thea Von Harbou *d Fritz Lang* *ph* Carl Hoffman, Gunther Rittau *ad* Otto Hunte, Karl Vollbrecht, Erich Kettelhut

Paul Richter, Marguerite Schön, Theodor Loos, Hannah Ralph, Rudolph Klein-Rogge

'They all loved him—a schoolteacher, a night club hostess, and a luscious society bud!'

Night after Night*
US 1932 76m bw
Paramount

An ex-boxer seeking refinement buys a night club and falls for a socialite.
Dim little drama which is remembered for introducing Mae West to the screen with her famous line, 'Goodness had nothing to do with it'.

w Vincent Laurence, *novel* Single Night by Louis Bromfield *d* Archie Mayo *ph* Ernest Haller

George Raft, Constance Cummings, Wynne Gibson, *Mae West,* Alison Skipworth, Roscoe Karns, Louis Calhern

'Mae West stole everything but the cameras. I never made another picture with her. I knew she had me licked.'—*George Raft*

Night and Day*
US 1946 132m Technicolor
Warner (Arthur Schwarz)

The life of Cole Porter.
Or rather, a fictitious story about a composer who happens to be called Cole Porter. A careful but undistinguished musical with pleasant moments.

w Charles Hoffman, Leo Townsend, William Bowers *d* Michael Curtiz *ph* Peverell Marley, William V. Skall *m / ly Cole Porter* *md* Max Steiner, Ray Heindorf *ch* Le Roy Prinz

Cary Grant, Alexis Smith, Monty Woolley, Mary Martin, Ginny Simms, Jane Wyman, Eve Arden, Victor Francen, Alan Hale, Dorothy Malone

AAN: Max Steiner, Ray Heindorf

Night and Fog*
France 1955 31m Eastmancolor
Argos / Como
original title: *Nuit et Brouillard*

An account of the concentration camp at Auschwitz, contrasted with the peaceful surroundings ten years after its disbandment. An official film of great dignity.

d, ed Alain Resnais *ph* Ghislain Cloquet, Sacha Vierny

Night and the City
GB 1950 101m bw
TCF (Samuel G. Engel)

A crooked wrestling promoter is tracked down by an underworld gang.
A fated attempt to extend the success of *Naked City* in a London setting; the surface is accomplished enough, but the plot and characters are just plain dull, especially as little is seen of the police.

w Jo Eisinger, *novel* Gerald Kersh *d* Jules Dassin *ph Max Greene* *m* Benjamin Frankel

Richard Widmark, Gene Tierney, Googie Withers, Hugh Marlowe, Herbert Lom

'Brilliantly photographed, it is an example of neo-expressionist techniques at their most potent.'—*Richard Roud, 1964*

The Night Angel
US 1931 75m bw

A Prague lawyer falls for the daughter of the brothel keeper he has sent to prison, and after killing a jealous suitor is himself accused of murder. Would-be Dietrichean high-style melodrama which did its stars no good at all and virtually ended Miss Carroll's career. Fredric March, Nancy Carroll, Alan Hale, Alison Skipworth, Katherine Emmett. Written and directed by Edmund Goulding; for Paramount. 'Mild and frequently boring entertainment of the kind that can just about last a week in most of the de luxers.'—*Variety*

A Night at Earl Carroll's
US 1940 63m bw

When gangsters kidnap stars of Earl Carroll's nightclub, the restaurant staff put on their own show. Tinseltown time-passer which served a very small purpose. Ken Murray, J. Carrol Naish, Lilian Cornell, Blanche Stewart. Written by Lynn Starling; directed by Kurt Neumann; for Paramount.

A Night at the Opera****
US 1935 96m bw
MGM (Irving Thalberg)

Three zanies first wreck, then help an opera company.
Certainly among the best of the Marxian extravaganzas, and the first to give them a big production to play with as well as musical interludes by other than themselves for a change of pace. The mix plays beautifully.

w George S. Kaufman, Morrie Ryskind *d Sam Wood* *ph* Merritt Gerstad *md* Herbert Stothart

Groucho, Chico, Harpo (Zeppo absented himself from here on), *Margaret Dumont*, Kitty Carlisle, Allan Jones, Walter Woolf King, *Sig Rumann*

'Corking comedy with the brothers at par and biz chances excellent . . . songs in a Marx picture are generally at a disadvantage because they're more or less interruptions, the customers awaiting the next laugh.'—*Variety*

Night Beat
GB 1948 91m bw

Demobbed, a commando becomes a policeman and his friend becomes a crook. *Manhattan Melodrama*, British style; no more than an adequate offering of its type. Anne Crawford, Maxwell Reed, Ronald Howard, Christine Norden, Hector Ross, Sidney James. Written by T. J. Morrison, Roland Pertwee and Robert Westerby; directed by Harold Huth; for BLPA.

Night Boat to Dublin
GB 1945 99m bw
ABP (Hamilton Inglis)

An MI5 man saves an atom scientist from kidnapping.
Generally watchable low key thriller with familiar British ingredients.

w Lawrence Huntington, Robert Hall *d* Lawrence Huntington *ph* Otto Heller

Robert Newton, Raymond Lovell, Muriel Pavlow, Guy Middleton, Herbert Lom, Martin Miller, Marius Goring

The Night Caller*
GB 1965 84m bw

An alien being arrives on earth to abduct girls for genetic purposes. Reasonably well made science fiction thriller. John Saxon, Maurice Denham, Patricia Haines, Alfred Burke, John Carson, Jack Watson, Warren Mitchell. Written by Jim O'Connelly from novel by Frank Crisp; directed by John Gilling; for New Art / Armitage. (US title: *Blood Beast from Outer Space*.)

Night-Club Lady
US 1932 66m bw

A police commissioner solves the murder of a night-club hostess. Straightforward cops and killers melodrama with the star in his first non-romantic role. Adolphe Menjou, Mayo Methot, Skeets Gallagher, Blanche Friderici, Nat Pendleton. Written by Robert Riskin from a novel by Anthony Abbott; directed by Irving Cummings; for Columbia.

Night Club Scandal
US 1937 74m bw
Paramount

A society doctor murders his wife and incriminates her lover.
Smooth second feature remake of *Guilty as Hell*, chiefly notable for its star's last controlled performance.

w Lillie Hayward, *play* Riddle Me This by Daniel Rubin *d* Ralph Murphy *ph* Leo Tover

John Barrymore, Lynne Overman, Charles Bickford, Elizabeth Patterson, Evelyn Brent, Louise Campbell, J. Carrol Naish

Night Court
US 1932 90m bw

A corrupt judge frames a girl on a prostitution charge. Tough star melodrama. Walter Huston, Lewis Stone, Anita Page, Phillips Holmes, Jean Hersholt. Written by Mark Hellinger, Bayard Veiller, Charles Beehan and Lenore Coffee; directed by W. S. Van Dyke; for MGM. (GB title: *Justice for Sale*).
'Political frame-up of women is made the subject of a vigorous melodrama, though it comes after the New York scandal on the subject is largely forgotten.'—*Variety*

Night Crossing
US 1982 106m Technicolor
Walt Disney (Tom Leetch)

East Germans escape to the west via air balloon.
Well-meaning melodrama which sadly lacks plot development and suspense, and is also rather miserable to look at.

w John McGreevey *d* Delbert Mann *ph* Tony Imi *m* Jerry Goldsmith

John Hurt, Jane Alexander, Doug McKeon, Frank McKeon, Beau Bridges, Glynnis O'Connor, Ian Bannen

The Night Digger
GB 1971 100m colour

A frustrated spinster protects a handyman clearly guilty of murder, and runs away with him. How this came to be made at all when the Finney version of *Night Must Fall* had recently flopped is a mystery; it had so little box office appeal that it was barely released. Patricia Neal, Nicholas Clay, Pamela Browne, Jean Sanderson, Yootha Joyce, Peter Sallis, Graham Crowden. Written by Roald Dahl, from a story by Joy Cowley; directed by Alastair Reid; for MGM.

Night Flight*
US 1933 84m bw
MGM (David O. Selznick)

The president of a civil airline insists that dangerous night flights must continue as a mark of progress.
Spurious, unsatisfactory, multi-star air melodrama lacking both narrative flow and the common touch.

w Oliver H. P. Garrett, *stories* Antoine de St Exupéry *d* Clarence Brown *ph* Oliver T. Marsh, Elmer Dyer, Charles Marshall

John Barrymore, Helen Hayes, Lionel Barrymore, Clark Gable, Robert Montgomery, Myrna Loy, William Gargan, C. Henry Gordon

'Punch aviation film with a flock of potent marquee names.'—*Variety*

'It is in the sense it conveys of human beings caught in the swift machinery of modern living that *Night Flight* soars above other pictures of its kind.'—*James Shelley Hamilton*

Night Games*
Sweden 1966 105m bw
Sandrews (Lena Malmsjö)
original title: *Nattlek*

A 35-year-old man is sexually inhibited by memories of his dead mother's passions and perversions.
Curious Freudian parable apparently intended as a comment on the state of Europe. Audiences found it merely peculiar.

wd Mai Zetterling, from her novel *ph* Rune Ericson *m* Jan Johansson, George Riedel

Ingrid Thulin, Keve Hjelm, Lena Brundin, Naima Wifstrand

'The best one can say is that it never lets up for a moment.'—*David Wilson, MFB*

Night Games
US 1980 100m Technicolor

A neurotic Beverly Hills housewife is terrified of men. Crazy mix of case history, eroticism and suspense with insufficient of any to satisfy fans. Cindy Pickett, Joanna Cassidy, Barry Primus. Written by Anton Diether and Clarke Reynolds; directed by Roger Vadim; for Golden Harvest / Avco.

Night Hair Child
GB 1971 89m Movielab
Leander / Harry Alan Towers (Graham Harris)

A 12-year-old boy makes sexual advances to his stepmother.
Corrupt voyeuristic weirdie which has to be seen to be believed.

w Trevor Preston *d* James Killy *ph* Harry Waxman *m* Stelvio Cipriani

Mark Lester, Britt Ekland, Hardy Kruger, Harry Andrews, Lilli Palmer

'Was his strange power a blessing or a curse? He was a refugee from love—because he could foretell that their marriage and their kisses would dissolve in a tragedy of tears!'

Night Has a Thousand Eyes
US 1948 80m bw
Paramount (André Boehm)

A vaudeville mentalist finds that he really does have the power to predict the future.
Predictable supernatural melodrama closely modelled on *The Clairvoyant* (qv); quite nicely made but simply not exciting.

w Barre Lyndon, Jonathan Latimer, *novel* Cornell Woolrich *d* John Farrow *ph* John F. Seitz *m* Victor Young

Edward G. Robinson, Gail Russell, John Lund, Virginia Bruce, William Demarest, Richard Webb, Jerome Cowan

'For those who like sweet hocus-pocus and Edward G. Robinson.'—*Sunday Express*

The Night Has Eyes*
GB 1942 79m bw
ABP (John Argyle)
US title: *Terror House*

A young teacher disappears on the Yorkshire moors; her friend goes in search, and comes under the influence of a strange young man and his sinister housekeeper.
Stagey but effective little thriller, with oodles of fog and bog to help the suspense.

w Alan Kennington *d* Leslie Arliss *ph* Gunther Krampf *m* Charles Williams

James Mason, Joyce Howard, *Wilfrid Lawson, Mary Clare,* Tucker McGuire, John Fernald

'Some ingenuity and not a little style.'—*The Times*

The Night Holds Terror*
US 1955 86m bw
Columbia (Andrew Stone)

Three gunmen on the run kidnap a factory worker and hold him to ransom.
Effective, detailed, low-budget police melodrama; its plot may be over familiar now, but at the time it was refreshing and the whole film an intelligent exercise in suspense.

wd Andrew Stone *ph* Fred Jackman Jnr *m* Lucien Calliet

Jack Kelly, Hildy Parks, John Cassavetes, David Cross, Edward Marr, Jack Kruschen

A Night in Casablanca**
US 1946 85m bw
David L. Loew

Three zanies rout Nazi refugees in a North African hotel.
The last authentic Marxian extravaganza; it starts uncertainly, builds to a fine sustained frenzy, then peters out in some overstretched airplane acrobatics.

w Joseph Fields, Roland Kibbee, Frank Tashlin *d* Archie Mayo *ph* James Van Trees *m* Werner Janssen *pd* Duncan Cramer

Groucho, Chico, Harpo, Sig Rumann, Lisette Verea, Charles Drake, Lois Collier, Dan Seymour

KORNBLOW (Groucho Marx): 'I don't mind being killed, but I resent hearing it from a character whose head comes to a point.'

KORNBLOW: 'From now on the essence of this hotel will be speed. If a customer asks you for a three-minute egg, give it to him in two minutes. If he asks you for a two-minute egg, give it to him in one minute. If he asks you for a one-minute egg, give him the chicken and let him work it out for himself.'

BEATRICE (Lisette Verea): 'My name's Beatrice Ryner. I stop at the hotel.'

KORNBLOW: 'My name's Ronald Kornblow. I stop at nothing.'

'It is beside the main point to add that it isn't one of their best movies; for the worst they might ever make would be better worth seeing than most other things I can think of.'—*James Agee*

'It's a swell night for kissing or killing—or both!'

A Night in New Orleans
US 1942 75m bw

A policeman goes after gamblers and finds one of them murdered. Routine mystery, competently made. Preston Foster, Albert Dekker, Patricia Morison, Charles Butterworth, Dooley Wilson. Written by Jonathan Latimer; directed by William C. Clemens; for Paramount.

A Night in Paradise
US 1946 84m Technicolor
(Universal) Walter Wanger

Aesop falls in love at the court of King Croesus.
Deadly boring, unintentionally funny Arabian Nights farrago without the saving grace of action.

w Ernest Pascal, Emmet Lavery, *novel* Peacock's Feather by George S. Hellman *d* Arthur Lubin *ph* Hal Mohr *m* Frank Skinner

Merle Oberon, Turhan Bey, Thomas Gomez, Gale Sondergaard, Ray Collins, George Dolenz, John Litel, Ernest Truex, Jerome Cowan, Douglass Dumbrille

Night into Morning
US 1951 86m bw
MGM (Edwin H. Knopf)

A college professor loses his wife and son in an accident; despair drives him to drink and attempted suicide.
Well-made and well meaning melodrama whose virtual absence of plot makes it seem by the end merely maudlin.

w Karl Tunberg, Leonard Spiegelgass *d* Fletcher Markle *ph* George Folsey *m* Carmen Dragon

Ray Milland, Nancy Davis, John Hodiak, Lewis Stone, Jean Hagen, Rosemary de Camp

'Tediously uneventful, as sincere and futile as a note of condolence.'—*Time*

The Night Invader
GB 1942 81m bw

A Britisher in an occupied country is helped to capture a Nazi count. Propaganda potboiler for double billing. Anne Crawford, David Farrar, Carl Jaffe, Sybilla Binder, Marius Goring. Written by Brock Williams, Edward Dryhurst and Roland Pertwee, from the novel *Rendezvous with Death* by John Bentley; directed by Herbert Mason; for Warner.

Night Is My Future
Sweden 1947 87m bw
Terra Film (Lorens Marmstedt)
original title: *Musik I Mörker*

A war veteran learns to live with his blindness and finds romance.
Cliché romantic melodrama suffused by Scandinavian gloom. An unmemorable early work from this director.

w Dagmar Edqvist *d* Ingmar Bergman *ph* Göran Strindberg *m* Erland von Koch

Mai Zetterling, Birger Malmsten, Bengt Eklund, Gunnar Björnstrand, Naima Wifstrand

The Night Is Young
US 1934 82m bw

A European archduke loves a ballerina. High-class musical which failed despite an intriguing cast and a Romberg and Hammerstein score. Evelyn Laye, Ramon Novarro, Una Merkel, Edward Everett Horton, Rosalind Russell, Charles Butterworth, Herman Bing, Henry Stephenson, Donald Cook. Written by Vicki Baum; directed by Dudley Murphy; for MGM. 'Disappointing entertainment . . . feeble in plot, with a cast struggling to carry assignments and failing to ignite any real romantic fire, film also seems to lack a single strong musical number.'—*Variety*

Night Key
US 1937 67m bw
Universal (Robert Presswell)

An inventor's idea is stolen by his former partner, and he takes an appropriate revenge.
Low-key star melodrama: competent, but no great shakes.

w Tristam Tupper, John C. Moffit *d* Lloyd Corrigan *ph* George Robinson *m* Louis Forbes *make up* Jack Pierce

Boris Karloff, Jean Rogers, Warren Hull, Samuel S. Hinds, Alan Baxter, Ward Bond, Edwin Maxwell

'Mildly entertaining dualler . . . one of those impossible gadget yarns with liberal injections of cops and robbers stuff.'—*Variety*

The Night Life of the Gods
US 1935 75m bw

An inventor turns statues into people, and vice versa. Fantasy comedy from a well-known comic novel; interesting despite low level of invention. Alan Mowbray, Florine McKinney, Richard Carle, Peggy Shannon. Written by Barry Trivers, from Thorne Smith's novel; directed by Lowell Sherman; for Universal. 'Universal has managed to keep in the fun and restrain it from getting too rough.'—*Variety*

A Night Like This
GB 1932 74m bw

An Irish policeman breaks up a crooked gambling club. Minor Aldwych farce which hasn't worn well. Tom Walls, Ralph Lynn, Robertson Hare, Winifred Shotter, Mary Brough, Claude Hulbert. Written by Ben Travers, from his play; directed by Tom Walls; for British and Dominions.

Night Mail***
GB 1936 24m bw
GPO Film Unit (John Grierson)

A 'film poem' showing the journey of the mail train from London to Glasgow.
One of the best and most influential of British documentaries: despite a few absurdities, it remains a pleasure to watch.

wd Basil Wright, Harry Watt ph J. Jones, H. E. Fowle m Benjamin Britten poem W. H. Auden *sound arrangements* Alberto Cavalcanti

Night Mayor
US 1932 65m bw

The Mayor of New York pays too much attention to night life and not enough to his desk. Thinly veiled account of the Jimmy Walker affair, released after Walker had been discredited. As entertainment, punchy, but in the end only fair. Lee Tracy, Evalyn Knapp, Eugene Pallette, Warren Hymer, Donald Dillaway, Astrid Allwyn. Written by Gertrude Purcell, Sam Marx; directed by Ben Stoloff; for Columbia. 'It is a safe general statement that the screen ought never to exploit a public character who is the centre of debate.'—*Variety*

Night Monster
US 1942 73m bw
Universal (Ford Beebe)
GB title: *House of Mystery*

Murders are committed in a spooky house by a cripple who produces synthetic legs by self-hypnotism.
Stilted, creaky would-be thriller with a good cast and an impertinent plot.

w Clarence Upson Young *d* Ford Beebe *ph* Charles Van Enger

Ralph Morgan, Don Porter, Irene Hervey, Bela Lugosi, Lionel Atwill, Nils Asther, Leif Erickson, Frank Reicher

'Night, Mother
US 1986 96m De Luxe
Universal / Aaron Spelling, Alan Greisman

A mother gets to grips with the problems of her suicidal daughter.
Rueful drama which pares down the nerve ends but was clearly not designed for box office, and remains a play rather than a film.

w Marsha Norman, from her play *d* Tom Moore *ph* Stephen M. Katz *m* David Shire

Anne Bancroft, Sissy Spacek, Ed Berke, Carol Robbins

'Maybe he would find the girl—maybe he would find himself!'

Night Moves*
US 1975 99m Technicolor
Warner / Hillier / Layton (Robert M. Sherman)

A private eye is engaged to find a runaway teenager.
Apparently a Chandlerish mystery, this is really a Pinterish audience-teaser with obsessions about communication and the meaning of life. A smart-ass entertainment for eager trendies.

w Alan Sharp *d* Arthur Penn *ph* Bruce Surtees *m* Michael Small *pd* George Jenkins

Gene Hackman, Jennifer Warren, Edward Binns, Harris Yulin, Kenneth Mars

'Beneath the complicated unravelling of a mystery, an anti-mystery, with the hero's detection registering as an evasion of his own problems; beneath a densely charted intrigue of betrayals and cross purposes, a cryptic void . . .'—*Jonathan Rosenbaum*

'A suspenseless suspenser . . . there's very little rhyme or reason for the plot's progression.'—*Variety*

'Rich and dense enough to set up reverberations long after one has left the cinema.'—*Michael Billington, Illustrated London News*

Night Must Fall**
US 1937 117m bw
MGM (Hunt Stromberg)

A bland young bellboy who is really a psychopathic murderer attaches himself to the household of a rich old lady.
Unconvincing but memorable Hollywood expansion of an effective British chiller.

w John Van Druten, *play* Emlyn Williams *d* Richard Thorpe *ph* Ray June *m* Edward Ward

Robert Montgomery, Rosalind Russell, *May Whitty*, Alan Marshal, Merle Tottenham, Kathleen Harrison, Matthew Boulton, E. E. Clive

'Too long and not box office . . . tedious, slow, and even dull in spots.'—*Variety*

'A pretty little murder play has made a long dim film.'—*Graham Greene*

'The most exhilarating shrouds of horror hang over it. It represents a provocative imagination, a skilled adapter, a sensitive director, a splendid acting job.'—*Bland Johaneson, New York Daily Mirror*

† Louis B. Mayer so disliked this film that at the New York première he ordered the distribution of leaflets disowning it on behalf of MGM.

AAN: Robert Montgomery; May Whitty

Night Must Fall
GB 1964 105m bw
MGM (Albert Finney, Karel Reisz)

Dreary remake with a mannered star performance and the emphasis on axe murders. A mistake from beginning to end.

w Clive Exton *d* Karel Reisz *ph* Freddie Francis *m* Ron Grainer

Albert Finney, Susan Hampshire, Mona Washbourne, Sheila Hancock, Michael Medwin, Joe Gladwin, Martin Wyldeck

'Not so much a thriller as a typically humourless example of that overworked genre known as psychological drama . . . (Finney) constantly recalls a ventriloquist's dummy.'—*MFB*

The Night My Number Came Up*
GB 1954 94m bw
Ealing (Tom Morahan)

A man dreams that his plane will crash, and the dream begins to come true.
Intriguing little melodrama which badly lacks a twist ending and foxes itself by a flashback construction which leaves very little open to doubt. Production generally good.

w R. C. Sherriff *d* Leslie Norman *ph* Lionel Banes *m* Malcolm Arnold

Michael Redgrave, Alexander Knox, Sheila Sim, Denholm Elliott, Ursula Jeans, George Rose, Nigel Stock, Michael Hordern, Ralph Truman, Victor Maddern, Bill Kerr, Alfie Bass

'A story which, in its delicately measured suspenses and reliefs, has been beautifully built.'—*Times Educational Supplement*

'The idea of destiny as predestiny is an old psychological trump, but it still takes tricks.'—*Time*

† The story was taken from a personal account by Sir Victor Goddard.

Night Nurse*
US 1931 72m bw
Warner

A nurse uncovers a plot by other members of the household against her patient's children.
Fast-moving melodrama with solid star performances; just what the public wanted in 1931.

w Oliver H. P. Garrett, *novel* Dora Macy *d* William Wellman *ph* Chick McGill

Barbara Stanwyck, Ben Lyon, Joan Blondell, Clark Gable, Charles Winninger, Vera Lewis, Blanche Frederici, Charlotte Merriam

'A conglomeration of exaggerations, often bordering on serial dramatics.'—*Hollywood Reporter*

The Night of January 16th
US 1941 79m bw

A secretary is arrested for her boss's murder; but is he really dead? A stage thriller full of theatrical trickery becomes a very mundane film. Robert Preston, Ellen Drew, Nils Asther, Margaret Hayes. Written by Delmer Daves, Robert Pirosh and Eve Greene from a play by Ayn Rand; directed by William Clemens; for Paramount.

The Night of June 13th
US 1932 76m bw

A suburban street is transformed when one of its residents goes on trial for murder. Combination courtroom and slice-of-life drama which satisfied most audiences. Clive Brook, Lila Lee, Mary Boland, Adrienne Allen, Gene Raymond, Frances Dee, Charley Grapewin. Written by Agnes Brand Leahy, Brian Marlow, William Slavens McNutt, from a story by Vera Caspary; directed by Stephen Roberts; for Paramount. 'Absorbingly worked out with fascinating character study and a touch of satire.'—*Variety*

'What happens after they turn the lights out on Broadway?'

The Night of Nights
US 1939 86m bw

A once-famous Broadway writer, now a drunk, tries to ensure his daughter's fame. Curious downbeat melodrama without the courage of its convictions, or the actors to give the right bravura performances. Pat O'Brien, Olympe Bradna, Reginald Gardiner, Roland Young. Written by Donald Ogden Stewart; directed by Lewis Milestone; for Paramount.

'Backstage drama lightened by direction and cast performances. Nominal supporter for key duals.'—*Variety*

The Night of San Lorenzo*
Italy 1981 107m Agfacolor
RAI / Ager (Giuliani G. De Negri)

A Tuscan township suffers under the Nazis and is liberated by the Americans.
One would have to be Italian for full appreciation, but this affectionate memoir of the war years is clearly in the Rossellini tradition and it bursts with energy and memorable moments.

wd Paolo and Vittorio Taviani *ph* Franco Di Giacomo *m* Nicola Piovani *ed* Roberto Perpignani

Omero Antonutti, Margarita Lozano, Claudio Bigagli, Massimo Bonetti, Norma Martelli

Night of the Big Heat
GB 1967 94m Eastmancolor

Invaders from outer space take over a remote Scottish island and make it unbearably hot so that they can survive. Sloppily made and over-prolonged science fiction with far too much irrelevant talk. Christopher Lee, Peter Cushing, Patrick Allen, Sarah Lawson, Jane Merrow, William Lucas, Kenneth Cope. Written by Ronald Liles, from the novel by John Lymington; directed by Terence Fisher; for Tom Blakeley / Planet. (US title: *Island of the Burning Damned*.)

Night of the Demon***
GB 1957 87m bw
Columbia / Sabre (Frank Bevis)
US title: *Curse of the Demon*

An occultist despatches his enemies by raising a giant medieval devil.
Despite dim work from the leads, this supernatural thriller is intelligently scripted and achieves several frightening and memorable sequences in the best Hitchcock manner.

w Charles Bennett, Hal E. Chester, story Casting the Runes by *M. R. James* *d Jacques Tourneur* *ph* Ted Scaife *m* Clifton Parker *ad* Ken Adam

Dana Andrews, Peggy Cummins, *Niall MacGinnis, Athene Seyler*, Brian Wilde, Maurice Denham, Ewan Roberts, Liam Redmond, Reginald Beckwith

Night of the Eagle**
GB 1961 87m bw
Independent Artists (Albert Fennell)
US title: *Burn, Witch, Burn*

At a medical school, a jealous witch sets an evil force on her rival.
Pretty good supernatural thriller, let down by leading performances and sustained by character roles and solid production values in creepy sequences.

w Charles Beaumont, Richard Matheson, George Baxt, *novel* Conjure Wife by Fritz Leiber Jnr *d Sidney Hayers ph* Reg Wyer *m* William Alwyn

Margaret Johnston, Janet Blair, Peter Wyngarde, Anthony Nicholls, Reginald Beckwith, Kathleen Byron

The Night of the Following Day*
US 1969 100m Technicolor
Universal / Gina (Hubert Cornfield)

A young girl arriving in Paris to stay with her father is kidnapped and held to ransom by an eccentric gang.
Straightforward suspense thriller with delusions of grandeur; the second half bogs down in pretentious talk and the end suggests that the whole thing was a dream.

w Hubert Cornfield, Robert Phippeny, *novel* The Snatchers by Lionel White *d Hubert Cornfield ph* Willy Kurant *m* Stanley Myers

Marlon Brando, Richard Boone, Rita Moreno, Pamela Franklin, Jess Hahn

Night of the Garter
GB 1933 86m bw

A newly married man tries to retrieve an intimate gift from an old flame. One of the best-remembered comedies of Sydney Howard; with Winifred Shotter, Elsie Randolph, Austin Melford. Written by Austin Melford and Marjorie Gaffney, from the play *Getting Gertie's Garter* by Avery Hopwood and Wilson Collison; directed by Jack Raymond; for Herbert Wilcox/British and Dominions.

The Night of the Generals**
GB 1967 148m Technicolor Panavision
Columbia / Horizon / Filmsonor (Sam Spiegel)

A German intelligence agent tracks down a psychopathic Nazi general who started killing prostitutes in Warsaw during World War I.
A curiously bumpy narrative which is neither mystery nor character study but does provide a few effective sequences and impressive performances. The big budget seems well spent.

w Joseph Kessel, Paul Dehn, *novel* Hans Helmut Hirst *d* Anatole Litvak *ph* Henri Decaë *m* Maurice Jarre *pd* Alexander Trauner

Peter O'Toole, *Omar Sharif, Tom Courtenay,* Donald Pleasence, Joanna Pettet, *Philippe Noiret*, Charles Gray, Coral Brown, John Gregson, Harry Andrews, Nigel Stock, Christopher Plummer, Juliette Greco

'The "who" is obvious from the first and the "dunnit" interminable.'—*Judith Crist, 1973*

'Lurid and vivid, if nothing else.'—*Robert Windeler*

The Night of the Grizzly
US 1966 102m Techniscope
Paramount (Burt Dunne)

A Wyoming ex-sheriff kills a marauding bear and earns the respect of his son.
Stout-hearted family film, rather sluggishly made.

w Warren Douglas *d* Joseph Pevney *ph* Harold Lipstein, Loyal Griggs *m* Leith Stevens

Clint Walker, Martha Hyer, Keenan Wynn, Leo Gordon, Kevin Brodie, Nancy Kulp, Ellen Corby, Jack Elam, Ron Ely

'The scenes! The story! The stars! But above all—the suspense!'

The Night of the Hunter***
US 1955 93m bw
UA / Paul Gregory

A psychopathic preacher goes on the trail of hidden money, the secret of which is held by two children.
Weird, manic fantasy in which evil finally comes to grief against the forces of sweetness and light (the children, an old lady, water, animals). Although the narrative does not flow smoothly there are splendidly imaginative moments, and no other film has ever quite achieved its texture.

w James Agee, novel Davis Grubb *d Charles Laughton ph Stanley Cortez m* Walter Schumann

Robert Mitchum, Shelley Winters, Lillian Gish, Don Beddoe, Evelyn Varden, Peter Graves, James Gleason

PREACHER (Robert Mitchum): 'Lord, you sure knew what you was doing when you brung me to this very cell at this very time. A man with ten thousand dollars hid somewhere, and a widder in the makin'.'

'One of the most frightening movies ever made.'—*Pauline Kael, 1968*

'A genuinely sinister work, full of shocks and over-emphatic sound effects, camera angles and shadowy lighting.'—*NFT, 1973*

'One of the most daring, eloquent and personal films to have come from America in a long time.'—*Derek Prouse*

The Night of the Iguana***
US 1964 125m bw
MGM / Seven Arts (Ray Stark)

A disbarred clergyman becomes a travel courier in Mexico and is sexually desired by a teenage nymphomaniac, a middle-aged hotel owner and a frustrated itinerant artist.
The author is most tolerable when poking fun at his own types, and this is a sharp, funny picture with a touch of poetry.

w Anthony Veiller, *play Tennessee Williams d John Huston ph Gabriel Figueroa m* Benjamin Frankel *ad* Stephen Grimes

Richard Burton, Deborah Kerr, Ava Gardner, Sue Lyon, *Grayson Hall, Cyril Delevanti*

'One man . . . three women . . . one night!'—*publicity*

'Whatever poetry it had seems to have leaked out.'—*New Yorker, 1982*

AAN: Gabriel Figueroa; Grayson Hall

Night of the Juggler
US 1980 100m Technicolor

A New Yorker relentlessly pursues the kidnapper of his daughter. Average chase thriller with good location staging of car crashes. James Brolin, Cliff Gorman, Richard Castellano, Abby Bluestone. Written by Bill Norton Snr and Rick Natkin; directed by Robert Butler; for Columbia.

'There's a herd of killer rabbits heading this way!'

Night of the Lepus
US 1972 88m Metrocolor
MGM (A. C. Lyles)

A serum meant to control a surplus of rabbits instead produces monster varieties four feet tall.
Tolerable sci-fi tailored to a very tired formula.

w Don Holiday, Gene R. Kearney, *novel* The Year of the Angry Rabbit by Russell Braddon *d* William F. Claxton *ph* Ted Voigtlander *m* Jimmie Haskell

Stuart Whitman, Rory Calhoun, Janet Leigh, Paul Fix, De Forrest Kelley

'For insomniacs with lax standards.'—*Judith Crist*

The Night of the Living Dead
US 1968 98m bw

Flesh-eating zombies, activated by radiation from a space rocket, ravage the countryside. Gruesome horror comic with effective moments; the director was still doing the same schtick ten years later. Judith O'Dea, Duane Jones, Karl Hardman, Keith Wayne. Written by John A. Russo; directed by George A. Romero; for Image Ten. 'The best film ever made in Pittsburgh.'—*Anon.*

Night of the Party
GB 1934 60m bw

A game of murder at a dinner party leads to a real one. Solid supporting thriller with interesting credits. Leslie Banks, Jane Baxter, Viola Keats, Ian Hunter, Ernest Thesiger, Malcolm Keen. Written by Roland Pertwee and John Hastings Turner; directed by Michael Powell; for Gaumont-British.
'Nothing original, but good entertainment.' —*Variety*

Night Owls*
US 1930 20m bw

A policeman wanting to record an arrest bribes two tramps to burgle a house. The stars at their most hilariously incompetent, unable

THE NIGHT OF THE HUNTER. Film critic James Agee's script showed he knew of what he wrote, Robert Mitchum gave one of his finest performances and Charles Laughton proved as inventive behind the camera as in front of it.

even to get through a doorway efficiently. Laurel and Hardy, Edgar Kennedy, James Finlayson. Written by Leo McCarey and H. M. Walker; directed by James Parrott; for Hal Roach.

Night Passage*
US 1957 90m Technirama
U-I (Aaron Rosenberg)

A railroad worker entrusted with a payroll finds that the bandits trying to rob it are led by his own brother.
Obscurely titled and rather empty western providing standard excitements.

w Borden Chase *d* James Neilson *ph* William Daniels *m* Dmitri Tiomkin

James Stewart, Audie Murphy, Dan Duryea, Brandon de Wilde, Dianne Foster, Elaine Stewart

'You have never really seen Gregory Peck until you see him in CinemaScope!'
'We didn't say nice people, we said *night people*!'

Night People*
US 1954 93m Technicolor Cinemascope
TCF (Nunnally Johnson)

When a US corporal stationed in Berlin is kidnapped by the Russians, his influential father flies into action.
Curiously titled cold war suspenser which would have been more memorable if not in Cinemascope; the pace and talent are visible, but the wide screen and poor colour dissipate them.

wd Nunnally Johnson ph Charles G. Clarke *m* Cyril Mockridge

Gregory Peck, Broderick Crawford, Anita Bjork, Walter Abel, Rita Gam, Buddy Ebsen, Jill Esmond, Peter Van Eyck

AAN: original story (Jed Harris, Tom Reed)

'Seven in the skies over China—and one of them a dangerous Axis spy!'

Night Plane from Chungking
US 1942 69m bw
Paramount

Assorted international passengers are flown from Chungking to India, but one of their number is a German spy who will kill to get his hands on vital information.
A lower-case 'who is it' based on *Shanghai Express*. Not bad according to its lights.

w Earl Felton, Theodore Reeves, Lester Cole *d* Ralph Murphy *ph* Theodor Sparkuhl *m* Gerard Carbonara

Ellen Drew, Robert Preston, Otto Kruger, Steve Geray, Ernest Dorian, Tamara Geva, Sen Yung

'The most controversial film of our time!'

The Night Porter
Italy 1973 118m Technicolor
Lotar Films (Robert Gordon Edwards, Esa De Simone)

The wife of an opera conductor recognizes a hotel porter as the sadistic SS commandant of a concentration camp in which she spent the war years; they now resume a sado-masochistic love affair.
A downright deplorable film, with no cinematic skill or grace to excuse it; the visuals are as loathsome as the sound is indecipherable, and the sheer pointlessness of it is insulting.

w Liliana Cavani, Italo Moscati *d* Liliana Cavani *ph* Alfio Contini *m* Daniele Paris

Dirk Bogarde, Charlotte Rampling, Philippe Leroy, Gabriele Ferzetti, Isa Miranda

'Its claim to be saying something important is offensive, but the picture is too crudely trumped up to be a serious insult.'—*New Yorker*

Night Ride
GB 1937 70m bw

Unemployed lorry drivers start an independent co-operative. Brisk action programmer. Julian Vedey, Wally Patch, Jimmy Hanley, Joan Ponsford. Written by Ralph Bettinson; directed by John Paddy Carstairs; for Paramount.

Night Shift
US 1982 106m Technicolor
Warner / Ladd (Brian Grazer)

A weary financial analyst becomes a morgue attendant and finds himself involved with gangsters and pimps.
Unattractive comedy which outstays its welcome, which wasn't very enthusiastic in the first place.

w Lowell Ganz, Babaloo Mandel *d* Ron Howard *ph* James Crabe *m* Burt Bacharach *pd* Jack Collis

Henry Winkler, Michael Keaton, Shelley Long, Gina Hecht

Night Song
US 1947 101m bw
RKO (Harriet Parsons)

A wealthy socialite falls for a blind pianist and pretends to be blind also, and poor to boot.
Silly, pretentious soaper, moodily photographed.

w Frank Fenton, Irving Hyland, De Witt Bodeen *d* John Cromwell *ph Lucien Ballard* *m* Leith Stevens

Dana Andrews, Merle Oberon, Hoagy Carmichael, Ethel Barrymore, Artur Rubenstein, Eugene Ormandy

The Night They Raided Minsky's**
US 1968 99m De Luxe
UA / Tandem (Norman Lear)
GB title: *The Night They Invented Striptease*

Various human problems are posed and solved during a night at a burlesque theatre.
Marvellous kaleidoscopic ragbag of brilliant fragments which unfortunately don't cohere in the mind into a really memorable film, though it gives detailed pleasure on every viewing.

w Arnold Schulman, Sidney Michaels, Norman Lear, *book* Rowland Barber *d William Friedkin ph Andrew Laszlo m Charles Strouse pd William Eckart, Jean Eckar ch* Danny Daniels *narrator* Rudy Vallee

Jason Robards, Britt Ekland, *Norman Wisdom*, Forrest Tucker, Joseph Wiseman, Bert Lahr, Harry Andrews, Denholm Elliott, Elliot Gould, Jack Burns

'The Fanny Brice country stunningly brought to life—every face a snapshot of yesterday.'—*Alexander Walker*

'It's lightweight and disorganized; it's a shambles; yet a lot of it is charming, and it has a wonderful seedy chorus line—a row of pudgy girls with faces like slipped discs.'—*Pauline Kael, New Yorker*

'A brilliant pastiche of classic American burlesque on the lower east side in the twenties.'—*Time*

'An entire way of life is encapsulated'—*Morning Star*

Night Tide
US 1961 84m bw

A sailor falls in love with a fairground freak show girl who may be a real mermaid.
Cheaply made and very derivative romantic fantasy which seemed to hold a promise never fulfilled. Dennis Hopper, Linda Lawson, Gavin Muir, Luana Anders. Written and directed by Curtis Harrington; for Virgo Films.

A Night to Remember*
US 1943 91m bw
Columbia (Samuel Bischoff)

A Greenwich Village mystery-writing couple try to solve a murder.
Reasonably sparkling comedy whodunnit with a zany tinge.

w Richard Flournoy, Jack Henley *d* Richard Wallace *ph* Joseph Walker *m* Werner Heymann *md* Morris Stoloff

Loretta Young, Brian Aherne, Jeff Donnell, William Wright, Sidney Toler, Gale Sondergaard, Donald MacBride, Lee Patrick, Blanche Yurka

'A first-rate gloom chaser.'—*Picture Show*

A Night to Remember***
GB 1958 123m bw
Rank (William Macquitty)

The story of the 1912 sea disaster when the *Titanic* struck an iceberg.
A major film enterprise featuring hundreds of cameos, none discernibly more important than the other. On this account the film seems alternately stiff and flabby as narrative, but there is much to enjoy and admire along the way, though the sense of awe is dissipated by the final model shots.

w Eric Ambler, book Walter Lord *d Roy Baker ph Geoffrey Unsworth m* William Alwyn

Kenneth More, Honor Blackman, Michael Goodliffe, David McCallum, George Rose, Anthony Bushell, Ralph Michael, John Cairney, Kenneth Griffith, Frank Lawton, Michael Bryant

'A worthy, long-drawn-out documentary, with noticeably more honesty about human nature than most films, but little shape or style.'—*Kenneth Cavender*

Night Train to Munich***
GB 1940 93m bw
TCF (Edward Black)
aka: *Gestapo; Night Train*

A British agent poses as a Nazi in order to rescue a Czech inventor.
First-rate comedy suspenser obviously inspired by the success of *The Lady Vanishes* and providing much the same measure of thrills and laughs.

w Frank Launder, Sidney Gilliat, novel Report on a Fugitive by Gordon Wellesley *d Carol Reed ph* Otto Kanturek *m* Charles Williams *md* Louis Levy

Margaret Lockwood, *Rex Harrison, Basil Radford, Naunton Wayne,* Paul Henreid, Keneth Kent, Felix Aylmer, Roland Culver, *Eliot Makeham, Raymond Huntley*, Wyndham Goldie

'A very nice triumph of skill and maturity in films, and thus a pleasure to have.'—*Otis Ferguson*

AAN: Gordon Wellesley

Night unto Night*
US 1949 85m bw
Warner (Owen Crump)

An epileptic scientist falls for a girl hallucinated by the ghost of her dead husband.
Cheerless nuthouse melodrama, one of the well-meant aberrations which Hollywood studios used to produce as a sop to conscience.

w Kathryn Scola, *novel* Philip Wylie *d Don Siegel ph* Peverell Marley *m* Franz Waxman

Ronald Reagan, Viveca Lindfors, Rosemary de Camp, Broderick Crawford, Osa Massen, Craig Stevens, Erskine Sanford

'Locked in the cold asylum of the mind—a sane man stalks his prey!'
The Night Visitor
Sweden US 1970 102m Eastmancolor

Imprisoned for an axe murder he didn't commit, a man escapes and takes revenge.
Overdone Grand Guignol which simply doesn't come off. Max Von Sydow, Trevor Howard, Liv Ullmann, Rupert Davies, Per Oscarsson, Andrew Keir. Written by Guy Elmes from the story Salem Came to Supper by Samuel Roecca; directed by Laslo Benedek; for Hemisphere / UMC.

'Do you know that a dream can kill you?'
The Night Walker*
US 1964 86m bw
U-I / William Castle

The widow of a tough executive, killed and disfigured in an explosion, is haunted in her dreams not only by him but by a mysterious lover who turns up in reality.
Stiff and unconvincing but still fairly frightening low-budget shocker with a plot twist or two.

w Robert Bloch d William Castle *ph* Harold Stine *m* Vic Mizzy

Robert Taylor, *Barbara Stanwyck*, Lloyd Bochner, Rochelle Hudson, Judi Meredith, Hayden Rorke

Night Watch
GB 1973 98m Technicolor
Avco / Brut (David White)

A widow recovering from a nervous breakdown keeps seeing bodies in the night. Her friends try to help, but things are not quite what they seem.
Predictable coiled-spring shocker which goes curiously flat despite a star cast and lashings of blood. Perhaps we have all been here once too often.

w Tony Williamson, *play* Lucille Fletcher *d* Brian G. Hutton *ph* Billie Williams *m* John Cameron

Elizabeth Taylor, Laurence Harvey, Billie Whitelaw, Robert Lang, Tony Britton, Bill Dean

'It has all the trappings of a Joan Crawford vehicle of the forties, with numerous elegant dresses for Miss Taylor, an appropriately unbecoming wardrobe for Miss Whitelaw, and a set which is an art director's dream.'—*Brenda Davies*

'Elizabeth Taylor's gowns are by Valentino, her jewellery is by Van Cleef and Arpels, even her kitchen is by Westinghouse. And she is *still* going out of her mind.'—*Alexander Walker*

The Night We Dropped a Clanger
GB 1959 86m bw

During World War II, a wing commander's double is accidentally sent to the front line in his place. Feeble take-off on *I Was Monty's Double*; a few bright gags survive. Brian Rix, Cecil Parker, William Hartnell, Leslie Phillips, Leo Franklyn, John Welsh, Liz Fraser. Written by John Chapman; directed by Darcy Conyers; for Sidney Box / Four Star / Rank. (US title: *Make Mine a Double.*)

The Night We Got the Bird
GB 1960 82m bw

A husband is driven bonkers by a talking parrot which he believes to be the reincarnation of his predecessor. Pretty awful farce with the sole virtue of a frantic pace. Brian Rix, Dora Bryan, Ronald Shiner, Leo Franklyn, Irene Handl, John Slater, Liz Fraser, Reginald Beckwith, Robertson Hare, John Le Mesurier, Terry Scott. Written by Ray Cooney, Tony Hilton and Darcy Conyers; directed by Darcy Conyers; for Rix–Conyers / British Lion.

Night without Sleep
US 1952 77m bw
TCF (Robert Bassler)

A man reconstructs his drunken actions the night before, and fears he has committed a murder.
Dreary melodrama, all frayed tempers, drunkenness and cigarette smoke.

w Frank Partos, Elick Moll *d* Roy Baker *ph* Lucien Ballard *m* Cyril Mockridge

Gary Merrill, Linda Darnell, Hildegarde Neff, Hugh Beaumont, Mae Marsh

Night Without Stars
GB 1951 86m bw

A blind lawyer solves the death of a traitor.
Enervated romantic melodrama. David Farrar, Nadia Gray, Maurice Teynac, Gilles Queyant. Written by Winston Graham, from his novel; directed by Anthony Pelissier; for Hugh Stewart / GFD.

Night World
US 1932 58m bw

Characters with an assortment of problems congregate in a nightclub. Tolerable slice-of-life drama with interesting cast. Lew Ayres, Boris Karloff, Mae Clarke, Russell Hopton, George Raft, Dorothy Revier, Bert Roach, Hedda Hopper. Written by Richard Schayer from story by P. J. Wolfson and Allen Rivkin; directed by Hobart Henley; for Universal.
'Sum total is an impression that this was a two-reeler blown up into five.'—*Variety*

The Nightcomers*
GB 1971 96m Technicolor
Scimitar / Kastner–Kanter–Ladd (Michael Winner)

How the ghost-ridden children in *The Turn of the Screw* became evil; they became involved in aberrant sexual activities between the gardener and the housekeeper, and finally murdered the former.
Despite its unexpected literariness this is unpleasant and unconvincing nonsense with a boring script punctuated by shock cuts and very little period feel.

w Michael Hastings *d* Michael Winner *ph* Robert Paynter *m* Jerry Fielding

Stephanie Beacham, Marlon Brando, Thora Hird, Harry Andrews, Verna Harvey, Christopher Ellis

'It leaves the viewer cold—perhaps even repelled. How could anybody think this movie would be entertaining?'—*Pauline Kael, New Yorker*

Nightfall*
US 1956 78m bw
Columbia (Ted Richmond)

The police and two bank robbers chase an innocent artist who happens to know that the loot is hidden in a Wisconsin snowdrift.
Occasionally stylish but obscurely narrated suspenser.

w Stirling Silliphant, *novel* David Goodis *d Jacques Tourneur* *ph* Burnett Guffey *m* George Duning

Anne Bancroft, Aldo Ray, Brian Keith, James Gregory, Jocelyn Brando, Frank Albertson

Nighthawks
GB 1978 113m Eastmancolor

The life of an actively homosexual schoolteacher. Painful low-life drama with many signs of its amateur status. Ken Robertson and non-professionals. Written and directed by Ron Peck and Paul Hallam; for Nashburgh / Four Corner Films.

Nighthawks
US 1981 99m Technicolor
Universal / Herb Nanas (Martin Poll)

New York cops track an international terrorist.
Kojak-style thriller with a rather glum attitude to its subject.

w David Shaber *d* Bruce Malmuth *ph* James A. Contner *m* Keith Emerson

Sylvester Stallone, Billy Dee Williams, Rutger Hauer, Lindsay Wagner, Persis Khambatta, Nigel Davenport

Nightmare
US 1942 81m bw
Universal (Dwight Taylor)

A gambler in wartime London helps a beautiful girl escape from Nazi spies.
Thin espionage thriller with a good sequence or two and a smooth villain.

w Dwight Taylor, *novel* Escape by Philip MacDonald *d* Tim Whelan *ph* George Barnes *m* Frank Skinner

Brian Donlevy, Diana Barrymore, *Gavin Muir*, Henry Daniell, Hans Conried, Arthur Shields

Nightmare*
US 1956 89m bw
UA / Pine–Thomas / Shane (Maxwell Shane)

A young musician is hypnotized into committing a murder, and reconstructs his actions with the help of his policeman brother-in-law.
Lethargic remake of the ingenious *Fear in the Night* (qv). Watchable.

wd Maxwell Shane, *novel* Cornell Woolrich *ph* Joseph Biroc *m* Herschel Burke Gilbert

Edward G. Robinson, Kevin McCarthy, Virginia Christine, Connie Russell

'A chilling, highly suspenseful little item.'—*Motion Picture Herald*

Nightmare*
GB 1964 82m bw Hammerscope
U-I / Hammer (Jimmy Sangster)

18-year-old Janet still has nightmares after seeing her mad mother kill her father six years ago; brought home, even more frightening visions afflict her.
Genuinely scary *Diabolique*-type mystery with the usual Hammer borrowings put to good use.

w Jimmy Sangster *d* Freddie Francis *ph* John Wilcox *m* Don Banks

Moira Redmond, David Knight, Brenda Bruce, John Welsh, *Jennie Linden*

Nightmare Alley**
US 1947 112m bw
TCF (George Jessel)

A fairground barker becomes a successful confidence trickster dealing with the supernatural, but finally sinks to the depths.
Unusual road to ruin melodrama, a striking oddity from Hollywood at the time, and still quite interesting and well done.

w Jules Furthman, novel William Lindsay Gresham *d Edmund Goulding* *ph Lee Garmes* *m* Cyril Mockridge

Tyrone Power, Coleen Gray, Joan Blondell, *Taylor Holmes*, Helen Walker, Mike Mazurki, Ian Keith

'The picture goes just short of all that might have made it very interesting . . . even so, two or three sharply comic and cynical scenes make it worth seeing.'—*James Agee*

Nightmare in the Sun*
US 1963 81m De Luxe
Afilmco (Marc Lawrence, John Derek)

A rich man kills his wife and blames a hitch-hiker who has had a brief affair with her.
Modest independent melodrama, quite interestingly made though not entirely effective.

w Ted Thomas *d* Marc Lawrence *ph* Stanley Cortez *m* Paul Glass

John Derek, Ursula Andress, Arthur O'Connell, Aldo Ray

'See Freddy—before he sees you!'
A Nightmare on Elm Street
US 1984 91m De Luxe
New Line / Media / Smart Egg / Elm Street Venture / Robert Shaye

Suburban teenagers find their communal dreams becoming reality when they are menaced by a creepy figure with knives for fingernails.
Unpleasant semi-splatter movie which was well enough made to take a lot of money.

w,d Wes Craven *ph* Jacques Haitkin *m* Charles Bernstein *pd* Greg Fonseca

John Saxon, Ronee Blakely, Heather Langenkamp, Amanda Wyss, Nick Corri, Robert Englund (as Freddy)

† Freddy was back in 1988 with *Nightmare on Elm Street 4: The Dream Master*.

A Nightmare on Elm Street Part Two: Freddy's Revenge
US 1985 84m De Luxe

Freddy comes back and tries to take over the mind and body of a young boy. More horror nonsense in the same mould as the above. Mark Patton, Kim Myers, Hope Lange, Clu Gulager, Robert Englund. Written by David Chaskin; directed by Jack Sholder; for Robert Shaye / Heron / Smart Egg / New Line.

'Much as one loves watching unpleasant American teenagers ripped to death, the slasher formula has worn thin of late.'—*Time Out*

A Nightmare on Elm Street Part Three: Dream Warriors
US 1987 96m De Luxe

Freddy now invades the minds of teenagers under group hypnosis for nightmares.
Diminishing returns set in as this tedious bloodbath (all in the mind) gets under way. Heather Langenkamp, Patricia Arquette, Larry Fishburne, Robert Englund, Priscilla Pointer, Craig Wasson. Written by Wes Craven and others; directed by Chuck Russell; for Robert Shaye/Heron/Smart Egg/New Line.

Nightwing
Netherlands 1979 105m Metrocolor
Columbia / Polyc / Martin Ransohoff

In Arizona, mysterious deaths turn out to be caused by plague-bearing vampire bats.
Tedious shocker in the vein of *Them* but with 'modern' unpleasantness of detail.

w Steve Shagan, Bud Shrake, *novel* Martin Cruz Smith *d* Arthur Hiller *ph* Charles Rosher *m* Henry Mancini

David Warner, Kathryn Harrold, Steven Macht, Strother Martin, Nick Mancuso, Ben Piazza

Nijinsky*
US 1980 125m Metrocolor
Paramount / Hera (Harry Saltzman)

The rise and fall of a great dancer groomed for stardom in the Ballets Russes by the impresario Diaghilev.
Rather boringly scripted with the emphasis on homosexual love, this film finally survives through its electrifying personalities and its strong sense of period.

w Hugh Wheeler *d* Herbert Ross *ph* Douglas Slocombe *md* John Lanchbery *pd John Blezard*

Alan Bates, George de la Pena, Leslie Brown, *Alan Badel*, Colin Blakely, Ronald Pickup, Ronald Lacey, Jeremy Irons, Anton Dolin, Janet Suzman, Sian Phillips, members of the London Festival Ballet

'The impression is left of a fascinating subject which proved too challenging for its makers, who settle eventually for what is uncomfortably near *All About Eve* with Bette Davis in a dinner jacket and Anne Baxter in a jock strap.'—*Alan Brien, Sunday Times*

Nikki, Wild Dog of the North*
US 1961 74m Technicolor
Walt Disney (Winston Hibler)

The life of a Canadian trapper's wolf dog.
Pleasing 'true life fiction' which didn't quite reach top feature status.

w Ralph Wright, Winston Hibler, *novel* James Oliver Curwood *d* Jack Couffer *m* Oliver Wallace

Emile Genest, Jean Coutu

Nine and a Half Weeks
US 1986 113m colour
MGM / UA / PSO / Sidney Kimmel / Keith Barish / Jonesfilm / Galactic Films / Triple Ajaxx (Anthony Rufus Isaacs, Zalman King)

A Wall Street executive and an art gallery employee embark upon a passionate affair.
Crash course in hot sex for those who wish to major in such studies; of no other interest despite its aspirations to being some sort of art.

w Patricia Knop, Zalman King, Sarah Kernochan *novel* Elizabeth McNeill *d* Adrian Lyne *ph* Peter Biziou *m* Jack Nitzsche *pd* Ken Davis

Mickey Rourke, Kim Basinger, Margaret Whitton, David Margulies, Christine Baranski

'The virtual absence of anything happening between them—like plausible attraction, amazing sex or, God forbid, good dialogue—leaves one great hole on the screen for two hours.'—*Variety*

Nine Girls
US 1944 78m bw
Columbia (Burt Kelly)

College girls are murdered in a sorority house.
Cheapjack whodunnit with a cardboard look and feel.

w Karen de Wolff, Connie Lee, *play* Wilfred H. Pettit *d* Leigh Jason *ph* James Van Trees *m* John Leopold

Ann Harding, Evelyn Keyes, Jinx Falkenberg, Anita Louise, Leslie Brooks, Lynn Merrick, Jeff Donnell, Nina Foch, Marcia Mae Jones, William Demarest

Nine Hours to Rama
GB 1962 125m De Luxe Cinemascope
TCF / Red Lion (Mark Robson)

Events leading to the assassination of Mahatma Gandhi.
Fictionalized, sensationalized and very dull, this multi-character drama holds interest only for snatches of acting and location backgrounds.

w Nelson Gidding, *novel* Stanley Wolpert *d* Mark Robson *ph* Arthur Ibbetson *m* Malcolm Arnold

Jose Ferrer, Diane Baker, Robert Morley, J. S. Casshyap, Horst Buchholz, Harry Andrews

'The only interesting line in the movie is the thick brown one visible on the inside of every white collar.'—*John Simon*

Nine Lives Are Not Enough
US 1941 63m bw

A reporter solves a multi-murder in a boarding house. Lively second feature which moves at a commendable pace. Ronald Reagan, Howard da Silva, James Gleason, Ed Brophy, Faye Emerson, Peter Whitney, Charles Drake. Written by Fred Niblo Jnr; directed by A. Edward Sutherland; for Warner.

Nine Men*
GB 1943 68m bw

A sergeant and a handful of men in an old fort hold off the Italians in the Libyan desert.
Sharp semi-documentary of the war which paled against the mightier epics to follow. Jack Lambert, Gordon Jackson, Frederick Piper, Grant Sutherland, Bill Blewett. Written and directed by Harry Watt; for Ealing.

Nine to Five*
US 1980 110m De Luxe
TCF / IPC (Bruce Gilbert)

Three office women plot to get rid of their boss, and nearly make it.
Sporadically agreeable comedy somewhat reminiscent of Sturges' *Unfaithfully Yours*.

w Colin Higgins, Patricia Resnick *d* Colin Higgins *ph* Reynaldo Villalobos *m* Charles Fox *pd* Dean Mitzner

Jane Fonda, Dolly Parton, Lily Tomlin, Dabney Coleman, Sterling Hayden, Elizabeth Wilson, Henry Jones

'An effective escapist feast with lotsa funny physical schtick.'—*Variety*

AAN: best song (Dolly Parton)

1984*
GB 1955 91m bw
Holiday (N. Peter Rathvon)

Europe has become the fascist state of Oceania, ruled by Big Brother; Winston Smith yearns for the old days, and is brainwashed.
The famous prophecy of a dehumanized future is followed with reasonable fidelity apart from the defiant ending, but the novel is too literary for cinematic success and the result is too often both downbeat and boring.

w William P. Templeton, Ralph Bettinson, *novel George Orwell d Michael Anderson* *ph* C. Pennington Richards *m* Malcolm Arnold

Michael Redgrave, Edmond O'Brien, Jan Sterling, David Kossoff, Mervyn Johns, Donald Pleasence

'Will ecstasy be a crime—in the terrifying world of the future?'

1984*
GB 1984 110m Eastmancolor
Umbrella / Rosenblum / Virgin (Simon Perry)

Winston Smith comes to love Big Brother after being brainwashed and taught Doublethink.
Pointless, perhaps, to make a prophetic film in the year it was supposed to be prophesying, but this version adds a few twists to Orwell's nightmarish original and is well if sometimes confusingly made.

w Michael Radford, *novel* George Orwell *d Michael Radford* *ph* Roger Deakins *m* Dominic Muldowney *pd* Allan Cameron *ed* Tom Priestley

John Hurt, Richard Burton, Suzanna Hamilton, Cyril Cusack, Gregor Fisher, James Walker

1941*
US 1979 118m Metrocolor Panavision
Columbia / Universal / A-Team (John Milius)

Just after Pearl Harbor, a stray Japanese submarine terrorizes Hollywood.
Absurdly over-budgeted manic farce which substitutes noise for wit and slapstick for comedy; it fails on every level.

w Robert Zemeckis, Bob Gale *d* Steven Spielberg *ph* William A. Fraker *m* John Williams *pd* Dean Edward Mitzner

Dan Aykroyd, Ned Beatty, John Belushi, Lorraine Gary, Murray Hamilton, Christopher Lee, Tim Matheson, Toshiro Mifune, Warren Oates, Robert Stack, Elisha Cook Jnr

'So overloaded with visual humour of rather monstrous nature that the feeling emerges that once you've seen ten explosions, you've seen them all.'—*Variety*

'Aimed at young audiences, who deserve better fun.'—*New Yorker*

'Its sheer relentless physicality, its elaborately orchestrated pointlessness on every other level, make it probably the purest demonstration of what it means to have two of the all-time commercial blockbusters to one's record and one's hands firmly on the fantasy machine.'—*Richard Combs, MFB*

'Spielberg intended it as "a stupidly outrageous celebration of paranoia" . . . audiences found it curiously unfunny and elephantine.'—*Les Keyser, Hollywood in the Seventies*

AAN: William A. Fraker

1900*
Italy / France / West Germany 1976
320m Technicolor
TCF / PEA / Artistes Associés / Artemis (Alberto Grimaldi)
original title: *Novecento*

The political and personal vicissitudes of a noble Italian family between 1900 and 1945. Immensely long and heavy-going study of the rise of fascism in the form of a family saga. For specialists only.

w Bernardo Bertolucci, Franco Arcalli, Giuseppe Bertolucci *d* Bernardo Bertolucci *ph* Vittorio Stovaro *m* Ennio Morricone *ad* Enzo Frigiero

Burt Lancaster, Robert de Niro, Gerard Depardieu, Dominique Sanda, Donald Sutherland, Sterling Hayden

'Exasperatingly uneven, but its most powerful moments can't be matched by any movie since *Godfather Two*.'—*Time*

'Bertolucci tried to write a 19th-century novel on film: the result is appalling, yet it has the grandeur of a classic visionary folly.'—*New Yorker*

† The film was normally shown in two separate parts.

99 and 44 / 100 Per Cent Dead
US 1974 98m De Luxe Panavision
TCF / Joe Wizan / Vashon
aka: *Call Harry Crown*

A losing gang boss hires a trouble shooter. Violent gangster melodrama apparently intended as a black comedy; if so, as clumsy as its title.

w Robert Dillon *d* John Frankenheimer *ph* Ralph Woolsey *m* Henry Mancini

Richard Harris, Edmond O'Brien, Bradford Dillman, Ann Turkel, Chuck Connors, Constance Ford

'Esthetically, commercially and morally, a quintessential fiasco.'—*Variety*

† The title in fact spoofs an ad familiar to Americans for a soap which was said to be '99 and 44 / 100 per cent pure'.

99 River Street*
US 1953 83m bw
UA / Edward Small

A taxi driver becomes involved in a diamond robbery.
Adequate thick ear with quite good detection and action sequences.

w Robert Smith *d Phil Karlson* *ph* Franz Planer

John Payne, Evelyn Keyes, Frank Faylen, Brad Dexter, Peggie Castle

'The picture that kids the commissars!'
'Garbo laughs!'
'Don't pronounce it—see it!'

Ninotchka***
US 1939 110m bw
MGM (Ernst Lubitsch)

A Paris playboy falls for a communist emissary sent to sell some crown jewels.
Sparkling comedy on a theme which has been frequently explored; delicate pointing and hilarious character comedy sustain this version perfectly until the last half hour, when it certainly sags; but it remains a favourite Hollywood example of this genre.

w Charles Brackett, Billy Wilder, Walter Reisch, story Melchior Lengyel *d Ernst Lubitsch* *ph William Daniels* *m* Werner Heymann

Greta Garbo, Melvyn Douglas, Sig Rumann, Alexander Granach, Felix Bressart, Ina Claire, Bela Lugosi

PROLOGUE: This picture takes place in Paris in those wonderful days when a siren was a brunette and not an alarm—and if a Frenchman turned out the light it was not on account of an air raid!

NINOTCHKA (Greta Garbo): 'I must have a complete report of your negotiations and a detailed expense account.'

BULJANOFF (Felix Bressart): 'No, non, Ninotchka. Don't ask for it. There is an old Turkish proverb that says, if something smells bad, why put your nose in it?'

NINOTCHKA: 'And there is an old Russian saying, the cat who has cream on his whiskers had better find good excuses.'

NINOTCHKA: 'The last mass trials were a great success. There are going to be fewer but better Russians.'

'High calibre entertainment for adult audiences, and a top attraction for the key de-luxers.'—*Variety*

'The Lubitsch style, in which much was made of subtleties—glances, finger movements, raised eyebrows—has disappeared. Instead we have a hard, brightly lit, cynical comedy with the wisecrack completely in control.'—*John Baxter, 1968*

† William Powell and Robert Montgomery were formerly considered for the Melvyn Douglas role.

AAN: best picture; script; story; Greta Garbo

The Ninth Configuration
US 1980 105m Metrocolor

A new psychiatrist in a compound of military misfits becomes the victim of a terror campaign. Weirdly obscure would-be thriller which only mystifies and annoys. Stacy Keach, Scott Wilson, Jason Miller, Ed Flanders, Neville Brand, Moses Gunn. Written, directed and produced by William Peter Blatty; for Lorimar. 'Quite astonishingly garbled, trailing yards of portentous religious allegory.'—*Observer*. 'The pretensions are enough to raise the *Titanic*—and sink it again.'—*Guardian*

The Ninth Guest
US 1934 65m bw

Eight people are trapped by a murderer in a penthouse suite. Whodunit which must have been seen by Agatha Christie before she wrote And Then There Were None. This version however is flatly scripted and characterized, with no real interest in the (unlikely) outcome. Donald Cook, Genevieve Tobin, Hardie Albright, Edward Ellis, Edwin Maxwell, Vince Barnett, Samuel S. Hinds. Written by Garnett Weston from the stage play by Owen Davis and the novel by Gene Bristow; directed by Roy William Neill; for Columbia. 'It ought to get a neat return in most spots.'—*Variety*

The Nitwits
US 1935 81m bw

Two cigar-stand assistants solve the murder of a music publisher. Overlong crime comedy with a good finale. Bert Wheeler, Robert Woolsey, Fred Keating, Betty Grable, Evelyn Brent. Written by Fred Guiol, Al Boasberg, Stuart Palmer; directed by George Stevens; for RKO. 'Fair.'—*Variety*

No Blade of Grass
GB 1970 97m Metrocolor Panavision
MGM (Cornel Wilde)

Industrial pollution sets a destructive virus ruining the crops of the world; anarchy spreads through Britain and one family takes refuge in the Lake District.
Apocalyptic sci-fi, moderately well done though so humourless as to be almost funny.

w Sean Forestal, Jefferson Pascal, *novel* John Christopher *d* Cornel Wilde *ph* H. A. R. Thompson *m* Burnell Whibley

Nigel Davenport, Jean Wallace, Patrick Holt, John Hamill

No Deposit, No Return
US 1976 112m Technicolor
Walt Disney (Ron Miller)

Airport confusion causes crooks to abduct (unwittingly) a millionaire's grandchildren; the millionaire gives chase.
Overlong and tedious action comedy which makes little sense.

w Arthur Alsberg, Don Nelson *d* Norman Tokar *ph* Frank Phillips *m* Buddy Baker

David Niven, Darren McGavin, Don Knotts, Herschel Bernardi, Barbara Feldon, John Williams, Vic Tayback, Kim Richards

'Once again one is left wondering why there should be such an unbridgeable gulf between the brilliant professionalism and sometimes innovative genius of the Disney animated films, and the dull artlessness of the majority of their live-action pictures.'—*Philip French, The Times*

'You can't throw so many young couples together and not expect explosions!'
No Down Payment**
US 1957 105m bw Cinemascope
TCF (Jerry Wald)

Tension among smart suburban couples in a Los Angeles housing development.
Lively domestic melodrama, very useful to sociologists as a mirror of its times.

w Philip Yordan, novel John McPartland *d Martin Ritt ph* Joseph La Shelle *m* Leigh Harline

Joanne Woodward, Tony Randall, Sheree North, Jeffrey Hunter, Cameron Mitchell, Patricia Owens, Barbara Rush, Pat Hingle

No Escape
GB 1936 85m bw

A man pretends to be dead as a hoax, and when he is found so, his accomplice is suspected. Twisty thriller from a popular play. Valerie Hobson, Leslie Perrins, Robert Cochran, Billy Milton, Henry Oscar. Written by George Goodchild and Frank Witty from their play No Exit; directed by Norman Lee; for Pathé Welwyn. 'Good programme picture for almost anywhere.'—*Variety*

No Funny Business
GB 1933 75m bw
John Stafford

Two professional co-respondents are sent to the Riviera; each mistakes the other as his client.
Stagey farce, notable for its unlikely star teaming and its hilariously dated style.

w Victor Hanbury, Frank Vosper, Dorothy Hope *d* John Stafford, Victor Hanbury

Gertrude Lawrence, Laurence Olivier, Jill Esmond, Edmund Breon, Gibb McLaughlin, Muriel Aked

No Greater Glory
US 1934 78m bw

Boys learn through their play that there is no greater glory than to die for one's country. Glum parable which probably worked better in the original German. George Breakston, Jimmy Butler, Jackie Searl, Frankie Darro, Ralph Morgan, Christian Rub. Written by Jo Swerling from the film script The Paul Street Boys by Ferenc Molnar; directed by Frank Borzage; for Columbia. 'Not for the general trade, but a prospective hit in the arties.'—*Variety*

No Hands on the Clock
US 1941 76m bw

A private eye on honeymoon steps right into a kidnapping. Rather flat timepasser with too many loose ends. Chester Morris, Jean Parker, Rose Hobart, Dick Purcell, Astrid Allwyn, Rod Cameron. Written by Maxwell Shane from novel by Geoffrey Homes; directed by Frank McDonald; for Pine-Thomas / Paramount.

'Turn back, I tell you! Any minute may be too late!'
No Highway**
GB 1951 98m bw
TCF (Louis D. Lighton)
US title: *No Highway in the Sky*

During a transatlantic flight, a boffin works out that the plane's tail is about to fall off from metal fatigue.
The central premise of this adaptation from a popular novel is fascinating, but the romantic asides are a distraction and the characters cardboard; the film still entertains through sheer professionalism.

w R. C. Sherriff, Oscar Millard, Alec Coppel, *novel* Nevil Shute *d* Henry Koster *ph* Georges Périnal

James Stewart, Marlene Dietrich, Glynis Johns, Jack Hawkins, Janette Scott, Elizabeth Allan, Kenneth More, Niall MacGinnis, Ronald Squire

No Kidding
GB 1960 86m bw

An old house is turned into a holiday home for deprived rich children. Strained comedy with agreeable cast. Leslie Phillips, Geraldine McEwan, Julia Lockwood, Noel Purcell, Irene Handl, Joan Hickson, Cyril Raymond. Written by Norman Hudis, Robin Estridge, from novel by Verity Anderson; directed by Gerald Thomas; for Peter Rogers / GHW / Anglo Amalgamated. (US title: *Beware of Children.*)

No Leave, No Love
US 1946 118m bw
MGM (Joe Pasternak)

Sailors on leave meet an English girl.
Witless, overlong musical extravaganza.

w Charles Martin, Leslie Karkos *d* Charles Martin *ph* Harold Rosson, Robert Surtees *md* Georgie Stoll

Van Johnson, Pat Kirkwood, Keenan Wynn, Guy Lombardo and his Orchestra, Edward Arnold, Marie Wilson, Leon Ames

No Limit*
GB 1935 79m bw
ATP (Basil Dean)

A motor mechanic enters for the TT Races.
Lively star comedy with Isle of Man locations.

w Tom Geraghty, Fred Thompson, *story* Walter Greenwood *d* Monty Banks *ph* Bob Martin

George Formby, Florence Desmond, Edward Rigby, Jack Hobbs, Peter Gawthorne, Alf Goddard

No Love for Johnnie*
GB 1960 111m bw Cinemascope
Rank / Five Star (Betty E. Box)

The personal and political problems of a Labour MP.
Predictable but quite lively study of ambition and frustration, with good cameos; Cinemascope all but ruins its impact.

w Nicholas Phipps, Mordecai Richler, *novel* Wilfred Fienburgh *d* Ralph Thomas *ph* Ernest Steward *m* Malcolm Arnold

Peter Finch, Mary Peach, *Stanley Holloway*, Donald Pleasence, Billie Whitelaw, Hugh Burden, Rosalie Crutchley, Michael Goodliffe, Mervyn Johns, Geoffrey Keen, Paul Rogers, Dennis Price, Peter Barkworth, Fenella Fielding, Gladys Henson

No Man Is an Island
US 1962 114m Eastmancolor
U-I / Gold Coast (John Monks Jnr, Richard Goldstone)
GB title: *Island Escape*

After the Japanese attack on Guam, a radioman finds refuge in a leper colony and sets up his own resistance unit.
Unexceptionable war adventure in the jungle.

wd John Monks Jnr, Richard Goldstone *ph* Carl Kayser *m* Restie Umali

Jeffrey Hunter, Marshall Thompson, Barbara Perez, Ronald Remy

'Good clean fun for right-minded teenagers.'—*MFB*

'He was a hit and run lover . . . personally, he preferred a cigarette to any dame!'
No Man of Her Own*
US 1932 98m bw
Paramount

A big-time gambler marries a local girl on a bet and tries to keep her innocent of his activities.
Star romantic comedy drama, quite professionally assembled and played.

w Maurine Watkins, Milton H. Gropper *d* Wesley Ruggles *ph* Leo Tover

Clark Gable, Carole Lombard, Dorothy Mackail, Grant Mitchell, George Barbier, Elizabeth Patterson, J. Farrell MacDonald

'Entertaining film with national appeal.'—*Variety*

'Just about everything that the ordinary picture fan looks for: drama, romance, comedy, strong build-ups, exciting climaxes, a fine line of human interest.'—*Film Daily*

No Man of Her Own*
US 1949 98m bw
Paramount (Richard Maibaum)

A pregnant wanderer is involved in a train crash and assumes the identity of the wife of a dead passenger.
Glossy star melodrama, very watchable.

w Catherine Turney, Sally Benson, Mitchell Leisen *d Mitchell Leisen ph* Daniel L. Fapp *m* Hugo Friedhofer

Barbara Stanwyck, John Lund, Lyle Bettger, *Jane Cowl*, Phyllis Thaxter, Henry O'Neill, Richard Denning

No Mercy
US 1986 105m Metrocolor
Tri-Star / Delphi IV (D. Constantine Conte)

Policemen pretend to be hit men in an attempt to infiltrate a murder-by-contract organization. Fashionable violence, slick production, nothing new.

w Jim Carabatsos *d* Richard Pearce *ph* Michael Brault *m* Alan Silvestri

Richard Gere, Kim Basinger, Jeroen Krabbe, George Dzundza, Gary Basaraba, William Atherton

No Minor Vices
US 1948 96m bw
(MGM) Enterprise (Lewis Milestone)

A doctor brings home an artist friend who proceeds to wreck his household.
Interminable thin comedy which gives no clue as to what the talent involved thought it was doing.

w Arnold Manoff *d* Lewis Milestone *ph* George Barnes *m* Franz Waxman

Dana Andrews, Lilli Palmer, Louis Jourdan, Jane Wyatt, Norman Lloyd

No More Ladies
US 1935 79m bw
MGM

A society girl thinks that by marrying a rake she can reform him.
Breezy sophisticated comedy which doesn't quite maintain its impetus.

w Donald Ogden Stewart, Horace Jackson, *play* A. E. Thomas *d* Edward H. Griffith, George Cukor *ph* Oliver T. Marsh *m* Edward Ward

Joan Crawford, Robert Montgomery, Franchot Tone, Charles Ruggles, Edna May Oliver, Gail Patrick, Reginald Denny, Arthur Treacher

'Sophistication plus in society setting and probably too much on the ultra side for sock appreciation. But okay.'—*Variety*

No More Women
US 1934 73m bw

Deep sea divers compete for jobs and a woman. Flagg and Quirt in all but name, with action melodrama largely substituted for skirt-chasing. Edmund Lowe, Victor McLaglen, Sally Blane, Minna Gombell, Harold Huber. Written by Delmer Daves, Lou Beslow, from a story by John M. Strong; directed by Al Rogell; for Paramount. 'Quirt and Flagg under the Hays morality code, and they can't take it.'—*Variety*

No, My Darling Daughter
GB 1961 96m bw
Rank / Five Star / Betty E. Box–Ralph Thomas

Chaos ensues when a tycoon's daughter is thought to be eloping with an American boy friend.
Clumsy comedy with moments of brightness provided by the actors.

w Frank Harvey, *play* A Handful of Tansy by Harold Brooke, Kay Bannerman *d* Ralph Thomas *ph* Ernest Steward *m* Norrie Paramor

Michael Redgrave, Michael Craig, Roger Livesey, Rad Fulton, Juliet Mills, Renee Houston, Joan Sims, Peter Butterworth

No Name on the Bullet
US 1958 77m Eastmancolor Cinemascope
Universal (Howard Christie, Jack Arnold)

A hired gunman books into the hotel of a small western town, and everybody wonders who he is after.
Tolerable western programmer with more emphasis than usual on characterization.

w Gene L. Coon *d* Jack Arnold *ph* Harold Lipstein *m* Herman Stein

Audie Murphy, Charles Drake, Joan Evans, R. G. Armstrong, Willis Bouchey, Karl Swenson

No No Nanette
US 1930 90m approx bw with Technicolor sequences

A married bible publisher secretly helps three girls, who all visit him on the same day. Early talkie version of the rather naïve musical hit, with a priceless moment or two among the dross. Bernice Claire, Lucien Littlefield, Lilyan Tashman, Bert Roach, Zasu Pitts. Written by Howard Emmett Rogers, from the play by Otto Harbach and Frank Mandel; directed by Clarence Badger; for Warner.

No No Nanette
US 1940 90m bw
RKO / Suffolk (Herbert Wilcox)

Slightly altered remake with too little attention to the musical numbers.

w Ken Englund *d* Herbert Wilcox *md* Anthony Collins

Anna Neagle, Richard Carlson, Victor Mature, Helen Broderick, Roland Young, Zasu Pitts, Eve Arden, Billy Gilbert

'It's overboard on inaction, with most of the dead wood up front.'—*Variety*

No Orchids for Miss Blandish
GB 1948 102m bw
Alliance / Tudor (A. R. Shipman, Oswald Mitchell)

An heiress is kidnapped by gangsters and falls for their psychopathic leader.
Hilariously awful gangster movie from a bestselling shocker. Everyone concerned is all at sea, and the result is one of the worst films ever made.

wd St John L. Clowes, *novel* James Hadley Chase *ph* Gerald Gibbs

Jack La Rue, Linden Travers, Hugh McDermott, Walter Crisham, Lily Molnar, Zoe Gail

'This must be the most sickening exhibition of brutality, perversion, sex and sadism ever to be shown on a cinema screen . . . with pseudo-American accents the actors literally battle their way through a script laden with suggestive dialogue.'—*MFB*

'A most vicious display of sadism, brutality and suggestiveness.'—*Milton Shulman, Evening Standard*

'The morals are about level with those of a scavenger dog.'—*Daily Express*

'It has all the morals of an alley cat and all the sweetness of a sewer.'—*Observer*

'The worst film I have ever seen.'—*Sunday Express*

† Remade as *The Grissom Gang* (qv).

No Parking
GB 1938 72m bw
Herbert Wilcox

A car park attendant is mistaken for an American killer.
Modest, entertaining star comedy.

w Gerald Elliott, *story* Carol Reed *d* Jack Raymond *ph* Francis Carver

Gordon Harker, Leslie Perrins, Irene Ware, Cyril Smith

No Peace among the Olives
Italy 1950 99m bw
Lux (Domenico Davanzati)

A young shepherd goes home after the war and finds himself at war again—against a local racketeer.
A rather crude melodrama comparable with the American *Thieves' Highway* and other *films noirs* of the time.

w Giuseppe de Santis and others *d* Giuseppe de Santis *ph* Pietro Portalupi *m* Goffredo Petrassi

Lucia Bose, Raf Vallone, Folco Lulli, Dante Maggio

No Place for Jennifer
GB 1949 90m bw

Divorcing parents think again when their twelve-year-old daughter runs away. Very predictable tearjerker which kept box offices busy in its day. Leo Genn, Rosamund John, Janette Scott, Beatrice Campbell, Guy Middleton, Anthony Nicholls, Jean Cadell. Written by J. Lee-Thompson, from the novel *No Difference to Me* by Phyllis Hambledon; directed by Henry Cass; for ABPC.

No Questions Asked
US 1951 80m bw
MGM (Nicholas Nayfack)

A young lawyer undertakes shady business and finds himself framed for murder.
Well made second feature on conventional lines.

w Sidney Sheldon *d* Harold Kress *ph* Harold Lipstein *m* Leith Stevens

Barry Sullivan, George Murphy, Arlene Dahl, Jean Hagen, William Reynolds, Mari Blanchard

No Resting Place
GB 1951 77m bw
Colin Lesslie

A wandering Irish tinker accidentally kills a man and is hounded by a Civil Guard.
Interesting attempt at realistic location drama, suffering from a dejected plot and unsympathetic characters.

w Paul Rotha, Colin Lesslie, Michael Orrom, *novel* Ian Niall *d* Paul Rotha *ph* Wolfgang Suschitsky *m* William Alwyn

Michael Gough, Noel Purcell, Jack McGowran

No Room at the Inn
GB 1948 82m bw
British National (Ivan Foxwell)

A monstrous woman half-starves evacuees and turns her house into a brothel.
Absurd melodrama from a play which was popular because it offered a full-blooded star performance. The film is less convincing but works pretty well on its level.

w Ivan Foxwell, Dylan Thomas, *play* Joan Temple *d* Dan Birt *ph* James Wilson

Freda Jackson, Joy Shelton, Hermione Baddeley, Joan Dowling, Harcourt Williams, Sydney Tafler, Frank Pettingell, Niall MacGinnis

No Room for the Groom*
US 1952 82m bw
Universal-International (Ted Richmond)

An army veteran returns to his wife, who has moved in with her family without telling them of her marriage.
Amiable comedy which rises to a fair pitch of frenzy.

w Joseph Hoffman, *story* Darwin H. Teilhet *d* Douglas Sirk *ph* Clifford Stine *m* Frank Skinner

Tony Curtis, Piper Laurie, Don Defore, *Spring Byington*, Lee Aaker, Jack Kelly, Lillian Bronson

No Sad Songs for Me
US 1950 89m bw
Columbia (Buddy Adler)

A young wife discovers she has only eight months to live, and spends it planning her husband's future.
Well-meant but rather icky melodrama featuring one of those beautiful illnesses that appear to have no physical effect.

w Howard Koch, *novel* Ruth Southard *d* Rudolph Maté *ph* Joseph Walker *m* George Duning

Margaret Sullavan, Wendell Corey, Viveca Lindfors, Natalie Wood, John McIntire

AAN: George Duning

No Sex Please, We're British
GB 1973 91m Technicolor
Columbia / BHP (John R. Sloan)

Confusion ensues when a wrongly addressed parcel of dirty postcards arrives at a bank.
Fairly lively farce with everything from mistaken identity to falling trousers.

w Anthony Marriott, Johnnie Mortimer, Brian Cooke, from the play by Anthony Marriott and Alistair Foot *d* Cliff Owen *ph* Ken Hodges *m* Eric Rogers

Ronnie Corbett, Arthur Lowe, Beryl Reid, Ian Ogilvy, Susan Penhaligon, David Swift, Michael Bates

No Surrender*
GB 1985 104m colour
Dumbarton / NFFC / Lauron / Film Four International (Mamoun Hassan)

Irish factions collide in a Liverpool club.
Black comedy typical of the author of *Boys from the Black Stuff.*

w Alan Bleasdale *d* Peter Smith *ph* Mick Coulter *m* Daryl Runswick

Michael Angelis, Avis Bunnage, James Ellis, Ray McAnally, Tom Georgeson, Bernard Hill, J. G. Devlin

'Monstrous and marvellous, it combines the disturbing, the disorienting and the downright daft.'—*Paul Taylor, Monthly Film Bulletin*

No Time for Comedy*
US 1940 93m bw
Warner (Robert Lord)

A playwright is depressed by the times and has lost the knack of making people laugh.
Smooth film version of a thoughtful romantic comedy play.

w Julius J. and Philip G. Epstein, *play S. N. Behrman* *d* William Keighley *ph* Ernest Haller *m* Heinz Roemheld

James Stewart, Rosalind Russell, Charles Ruggles, Genevieve Tobin, Allyn Joslyn, Clarence Kolb, Louise Beavers

'Claudette loves the men with muscles!'
No Time for Love*
US 1943 83m bw
Paramount (Mitchell Leisen)

A lady photographer falls for the foreman of a crew digging a tunnel under the Hudson.
Agreeable romantic slapstick farce.

w Claude Binyon *d* Mitchell Leisen *ph* Charles Lang Jnr *m* Victor Young

Claudette Colbert, Fred MacMurray, Ilka Chase, Richard Haydn, June Havoc, Marjorie Gateson, Bill Goodwin

No Time for Sergeants
US 1958 111m bw
Warner (Mervyn Le Roy)

Adventures of a hillbilly army conscript.
Heavy-handed adaptation of the stage success, a real piece of filmed theatre with not much sparkle to it.

w John Lee Mahin, *play* Ira Levin, *novel* Mac Hyman *d* Mervyn Le Roy *ph* Harold Rosson *m* Ray Heindorf

Andy Griffith, William Fawcett, Murray Hamilton, Nick Adams, Myron McCormick, Bartlett Robinson

No Time for Tears
GB 1957 86m Eastmancolor Cinemascope
ABPC (W. A. Whittaker)

Problems of a children's hospital.
Totally predictable British tearjerker with a happy ending.

w Anne Burnaby *d* Cyril Frankel *ph* Gilbert Taylor *m* Francis Chagrin

Anna Neagle, Anthony Quayle, Sylvia Syms, Flora Robson, George Baker, Alan White, Daphne Anderson, Michael Hordern, Joan Hickson, Sophie Stewart, Rosalie Crutchley

No Trees in the Street
GB 1958 96m bw
ABP / Allegro (Frank Godwin)

Problems of a London slum family in the thirties.
Artificial and unconvincing attempt at a London *Love on the Dole*, dragged up and redigested in a later era when 'realism' was thought to be fashionable.

w Ted Willis, from his play *d* J. Lee-Thompson *ph* Gilbert Taylor *m* Laurie Johnson

Sylvia Syms, Herbert Lom, Joan Miller, Melvyn Hayes, Stanley Holloway, Liam Redmond, Ronald Howard, Carole Lesley, Lana Morris, Lily Kann

'Nothing remains but crude sensationalism and several moments of unconscious humour.'—*MFB*

No Way Out*
US 1950 106m bw
TCF (Darryl F. Zanuck)

A crook stirs up racial feeling against a black doctor in whose hands his brother has died.
Vivid, hard-hitting melodrama with a hospital background and a strong sociological flavour.

w Joseph L. Mankiewicz, Lesser Samuels *d* Joseph L. Mankiewicz *ph Milton Krasner* *m* Alfred Newman

Richard Widmark, Sidney Poitier, Linda Darnell, Stephen McNally, Harry Bellaver, Stanley Ridges, Ossie Davis, Ruby Dee

'A production designed solely for purposes of agitation and propaganda, unworthy of literary or cinematic consideration.'—*Henry Hart, Films in Review*

AAN: script

No Way Out*
US 1987 116m Metrocolor
Orion / Neufeld / Ziskin / Garland (Laura Ziskin, Robert Garland)

A Pentagon officer is convinced his boss is guilty of murder, but the evidence points to himself.
Fast-paced remake of *The Big Clock* (qv) which does not efface the memory of the original.

w Robert Garland, from Kenneth Fearing's novel *d* Roger Donaldson *ph* John Alcott *m* Maurice Jarre *pd* Dennis Washington

Kevin Costner, Gene Hackman, Sean Young, Will Patton, Howard Duff, George Dzundza

No Way to Treat a Lady*
US 1968 108m Technicolor
Paramount / Sol C. Siegel

A mass murderer of women who is also a master of disguise has a running battle with a police detective.
Curious mixture of star show-off piece, murder mystery, black farce, suspense melodrama and Jewish comedy. Bits of it come off very well, but it's a bumpy ride.

w John Gay, *novel* William Goldman *d* Jack Smight *ph* Jack Priestley *m* Stanley Myers

Rod Steiger, George Segal, Lee Remick, Eileen Heckart, Murray Hamilton, Michael Dunn

'The sweetest love story ever told! The epic drama of the age! Drama with a world sweep, colossal and sublime!'

Noah's Ark**
US 1929 135m bw
Warner

The biblical story of Noah is paralleled, rather loosely, with a tragedy of World War I.
Naïve but fascinating Hollywood epic which in patches triumphantly overcomes the problems of the part-talkie period and is always fascinating to look at.

w Anthony Coldeway, Darryl F. Zanuck *d Michael Curtiz ph Hal Mohr, Barney McGill ph Anton Grot*

Dolores Costello, Noah Beery, Louise Fazenda, Guinn Williams, Paul McAllister, Myrna Loy, George O'Brien

'The biggest and best edited picture of the industry . . . mobs, Niagaras, train wrecks, war aplenty, crashes, deluges and everything that goes to give the picture fan a thrill.'—*Variety*

'Staggering . . . the greatest thing the screen has done.'—*The Film Spectator*

† On première it was Warners' longest film, but the release version was cut by nearly half.

Nob Hill*
US 1945 95m Technicolor
TCF (André Daven)

In the gay nineties, a San Francisco saloon owner tries to step into society and win one of its most eligible young ladies.
Engaging period musical drama with all talents working well.

w Wanda Tuchock, Norman Reilly Raine *d* Henry Hathaway *ph* Edward Cronjager *md* Emil Newman, Charles Henderson *m* David Buttolph

George Raft, Joan Bennett, Peggy Ann Garner, Vivian Blaine, Alan Reed, B. S. Pully, Edgar Barrier

Nobody Lives Forever
US 1946 100m bw
Warner (Robert Buckner)

A con man fleeces a rich widow, then falls in love with her.
Forgettable romantic melodrama.

w W. R. Burnett *d* Jean Negulesco *ph* Arthur Edeson *m* Adolph Deutsch

John Garfield, Geraldine Fitzgerald, Walter Brennan, Faye Emerson, George Coulouris, George Tobias

Nobody Runs Forever*
GB 1968 101m Eastmancolor
Rank / Selmur (Betty E. Box)
US title: *The High Commissioner*

An Australian detective is sent to arrest the high commissioner in London on a charge of murdering his first wife.
Sub-Hitchcock thriller which comes to life in patches but has a plot and dialogue which obviously embarrass the actors.

w Wilfred Greatorex, *novel* The High Commissioner by Jon Cleary *ph* Ernest Steward *m* Georges Delerue

Rod Taylor, Christopher Plummer, Lilli Palmer, Camilla Sparv, Daliah Lavi, Clive Revill, Lee Montague, Calvin Lockhart, Derren Nesbitt, Leo McKern, Franchot Tone

Nobody's Baby
US 1937 67m bw

Girls at a training school for nurses find themselves looking after a baby. Lightweight comedy filler. Lyda Roberti, Patsy Kelly, Lynne Overman, Robert Armstrong, Rosina Lawrence, Don Alvarado, Tom Dugan. Written by Harold Law, Hal Yates, Pat C. Flick; directed by Gus Meins; for Hal Roach / MGM. 'Agreeable enough number two feature for duals.'—*Variety*

Nobody's Fool
US 1986 107m CFI colour

A small-town girl with a mild past falls for a lighting technician with a visiting theatrical troupe. Much ado about nothing; good observant touches don't stifle the yawns. Rosanna Arquette, Eric Roberts, Mare Winningham, Jim Youngs, Louise Fletcher, Gwen Welles. Written by Beth Henley; directed by Evelyn Purcell; for Katz / Denny / Island.

Nobody's Perfect
US 1968 103m Techniscope
Universal (Howard Christie)

An ex-naval officer returns to Japan to make amends for stealing a buddha.
Flatfooted comedy adventure.

w John D. F. Black, *novel* The Crows of Edwina Hill by Allan R. Bosworth *d* Alan Rafkin *ph* Robert H. Wyckoff *m* Irving Gertz

Doug McClure, Nancy Kwan, Steve Carlson, James Whitmore, David Hartman, Gary Vinson, James Shigeta

Nocturne*
US 1946 87m bw
RKO (Joan Harrison)

A police detective investigates the death of a composer.
Amusingly self-mocking crime thriller, quite smoothly done in all departments.

w Jonathan Latimer d Edwin L. Marin ph Harry J. Wild *m* Leigh Harline

George Raft, Lynn Bari, Virginia Huston, Joseph Pevney, Myrna Dell, Edward Ashley, Walter Sande, Mabel Paige

Nomads
US 1985 100m Eastmancolor
PSO / Elliott Kastner / Cinema 7 (George Pappas, Cassian Elwes)

An anthropologist settling in Los Angeles is haunted by vengeful spirits of remote tribes he had investigated.
Stylish nonsense, but nonsense none the less: it would have seemed more striking if it hadn't been five-hundredth in line.

w,d John McTiernan *ph* Stephen Ramsey *m* Bill Conti *pd* Marcia Hinds

Pierce Brosnan, Lesley-Anne Down, Anna Maria Monticelli, Adam Ant, Hector Mercado.

Non Stop New York
GB 1937 71m bw
GFD / Gaumont (Michael Balcon)

In 1940, gangsters on a transatlantic airliner try to kill a key witness.
Slightly futuristic thriller of its time, now hilariously dated but quite entertaining as well as giving a rare picture of air travel in the thirties.

w Curt Siodmak, Roland Pertwee, J. O. C. Orton, Derek Twist, *novel* Sky Steward by Ken Attiwill *d* Robert Stevenson

John Loder, Anna Lee, Francis L. Sullivan, Frank Cellier, Desmond Tester, Athene Seyler, Jerry Verno

None But the Brave
US 1965 105m Technicolor Panavision
Warner / Eiga / Toho / Artanis (Frank Sinatra)

During World War II a plane carrying US Marines to the Pacific front crashlands on an island held by Japanese.
Anti-war melodrama in which the action scenes are more memorable than the admirable sentiments.

w John Twist, Katsuya Susaki *d* Frank Sinatra *ph* Harold Lipstein *m* Johnny Williams

Frank Sinatra, Clint Walker, Tommy Sands, Tony Bill, Brad Dexter

'When is the world coming out of its midnight? When is the human race going to get off its knees?'

None But the Lonely Heart*
US 1944 113m bw
RKO (David Hempstead)

In the thirties, a cockney drifter finds himself when he learns that his mother is dying.
Wildly astonishing moodpiece to come from Hollywood during World War II; its picture of East End low life is as rocky as its star performance, but it started Miss Barrymore on the west coast career which sustained her old age.

wd Clifford Odets, *novel* Richard Llewellyn *ph* George Barnes *m* Hanns Eisler *md* Constantin Bakaleinikoff

Cary Grant, *Ethel Barrymore*, June Duprez, Barry Fitzgerald, Jane Wyatt, George Coulouris, Dan Duryea, Konstantin Shayne, Morton Lowry, Helene Thimig

'A perplexing mixture of good and bad, authentic and phony.'—*Hermione Rich Isaacs, Theatre Arts*

AA: Ethel Barrymore
AAN: Hanns Eisler; Cary Grant

None Shall Escape*
US 1944 85m bw
Columbia (Sam Bischoff)

The career of a Nazi officer shown as flashbacks from his trial as a war criminal.
Taut topical melodrama reflecting the mood of the time.

w Lester Cole *d* André de Toth *ph* Lee Garmes *m* Ernst Toch

Alexander Knox, Marsha Hunt, Henry Travers, Dorothy Morris, Richard Crane

AA: Lester Cole; original story (Alfred Neumann, Joseph Thau)

Noose
GB 1948 98m bw
ABPC / Edward Dryhurst

A Soho black market gang is exposed.
Vivid though rather tatty film version of a West End play success.

w Richard Llewellyn, from his play *d* Edmond T. Greville *ph* Hone Glendining *m* Charles Williams

Nigel Patrick, Carole Landis, Derek Farr, Joseph Calleia, Stanley Holloway, Hay Petrie, John Slater

The Noose Hangs High
US 1948 77m bw

Two window washers are hired by a crooked bookie who finds their incompetence hard to tolerate when they lose his winnings. Thin star comedy filled with the team's cornier routines, not too cleverly revived. Bud Abbott, Lou Costello, Leon Errol, Joseph Calleia, Murray Leonard, Cathy Downs, Mike Mazurki, Fritz Feld. Written by John Grant and Howard Harris; directed by Charles Barton; for Eagle-Lion. (A previous film of the same story was made in 1939 under the title *For Love or Money*, with June Lang, Robert Kent and Ed Brophy.)

Nor the Moon By Night
GB 1958 92m Eastmancolor
Rank (John Stafford)
US title: *Elephant Gun*

An African game warden marries a longtime penfriend who finds that Africa presents unexpected problems.
Paperback romance with pleasant backgrounds.

w Guy Elmes, *novel* Joy Packer *d* Ken Annakin *ph* Harry Waxman *m* James Bernard

Belinda Lee, Michael Craig, Patrick McGoohan, Anna Gaylor, Eric Pohlmann

'Neither character nor incident nor theme has any coherence or interest.'—*MFB*

'A mouth like hers is just for kissing . . . not for telling!'

Nora Prentiss*
US 1946 117m bw
Warner (William Jacobs)

A doctor falls for a café singer who ruins his life.
Standard star melodrama aimed at women, and appreciated by them.

w N. Richard Nash, *story* Paul Webster, Jack Sobell *d* Vincent Sherman *ph* James Wong Howe *m* Franz Waxman

Ann Sheridan, Kent Smith, Bruce Bennett, Robert Alda, Rosemary de Camp, John Ridgely, Wanda Hendrix

Norma Rae*
US 1979 114m De Luxe Panavision
TCF / Martin Ritt / Rose and Asseyev

A southern girl becomes an angry union organizer.
Well-intentioned and well-acted pamphlet of political enlightenment with an inevitably ambivalent attitude.

w Irving Ravetch, Harriet Frank Jnr *d* Martin Ritt *ph* John A. Alonzo *m* David Shire *pd* Walter Scott Herndon

Sally Field, Beau Bridges, Ron Leibman, Pat Hingle, Barbara Baxley
AA: Sally Field
AAN: best picture

Norman, Is That You?
US 1976 92m Metrocolor

Adulterous parents find that their son is a homosexual. Unattractive comedy roughly filmed and given a black ambience. Not worth buying a ticket. Redd Foxx, Pearl Bailey, Dennis Dugan, Michael Warren, Tamara Dobson. From the play by Ron Clark and Sam Bobrick; directed by George Schlatter; for George Schlatter / MGM.

The Norseman
US 1978 90m Movielab
AIP / Charles B. Pierce / Fawcett Majors

A Viking heads across the sea to America in search of his long lost father.
Low grade hokum for the easily pleased.

wd Charles B. Pierce *ph* Robert Bethard *m* Jaime Mendoza-Nava

Lee Majors, Cornel Wilde, Mel Ferrer, Jack Elam, Chris Connelly

The North Avenue Irregulars
US 1978 99m Technicolor

A Presbyterian minister becomes an undercover agent for the FBI, helping to expose a crooked gambling syndicate. Very heavy comedy which seems to find itself much funnier than the audience does. Edward Herrmann, Barbara Harris, Susan Clark, Karen Valentine, Michael Constantine, Cloris Leachman, Patsy Kelly, Douglas Fowley, Alan Hale Jnr. Written by Don Tait, from the novel by the Rev. Albert Fay Hill; directed by Bruce Bilson; for Disney. (GB title: *Hill's Angels.*)

North by Northwest****
US 1959 136m Technicolor Vistavision
MGM (Alfred Hitchcock)

A businessman is mistaken for a spy, and enemy agents then try to kill him because he knows too much.
Delightful chase comedy-thriller with a touch of sex, a kind of compendium of its director's best work, with memories of *The 39 Steps*, *Saboteur* and *Foreign Correspondent* among others.

w Ernest Lehman d Alfred Hitchcock ph Robert Burks m Bernard Herrmann

Cary Grant, Eva Marie Saint, James Mason, Leo G. Carroll, Martin Landau, Jessie Royce Landis, Adam Williams

'It is only when you adopt the basic premise that Cary Grant could not possibly come to harm that the tongue in Hitchcock's cheek becomes plainly visible.'—*Hollis Alpert, Saturday Review*

AAN: Ernest Lehman

North Dallas Forty
US 1979 118m Metrocolor
Paramount (Frank Yablans)

The gruelling life of a professional football player, laced with drugs, sex and alcohol.
Well made but generally unattractive, the kind of movie for which one wouldn't expect to find an audience.

w Frank Yablans, Ted Kotcheff, Peter Gent, *novel* Peter Gent *d* Ted Kotcheff *ph* Paul Lohmann *m* John Scott *pd* Alfred Sweeney

Nick Nolte, Mac Davis, Charles Durning, Dayle Haddon, Bo Swenson

North Sea Hijack
GB 1979 100m Technicolor
Universal / Cinema Seven (Mo Rothman)
US title: *ffoulkes*

A British oil rig in the North Sea is held for ransom.
Asinine *Boy's Own Paper* adventure story with the very minimum of thrills and a totally miscast hero.

w Jack Davies, from his novel Esther, Ruth and Jennifer *d* Andrew V. McLaglen *ph* Tony Imi *m* Michael J. Lewis *pd* Maurice Carter

Roger Moore, Anthony Perkins, James Mason, Michael Parks, David Hedison, Jack Watson, George Baker, Faith Brook

North Star*
US 1943 105m bw
Samuel Goldwyn (William Cameron Menzies)
aka: *Armored Attack*

A Russian village defends itself against the Nazi onslaught.
Highly artificial propaganda piece later disowned by its makers and retitled. Good acting can't make its mark when the Russian steppes become a never-never land.

w Lillian Hellman *d* Lewis Milestone *ph* James Wong Howe *m* Aaron Copland

Anne Baxter, Farley Granger, Jane Withers, Dana Andrews, Walter Brennan, Erich Von Stroheim, Dean Jagger, Ann Harding, Carl Benton Reid, Walter Huston

'Putting American villagers into Russian costumes and calling them by Russian names is never going to deceive this old bird.'—*James Agate*

'Its failure is the case history of every Hollywood film that steps out of its scope.'—*Richard Winnington*

'Something to be seen more in sorrow than in anger and more in the attitude of the diagnostician in any emotion at all.'—*James Agee*

AAN: Lillian Hellman; James Wong Howe; Aaron Copland

North to Alaska*
US 1960 122m De Luxe Cinemascope
TCF (Henry Hathaway)

In 1900, two successful gold prospectors have woman trouble.
Good-natured brawling adventure story which could do with cutting but is certainly the type of action movie they don't make 'em like any more.

w John Lee Mahin, Martin Rackin, Claude Binyon, *play* Birthday Gift by Ladislas Fodor *d* Henry Hathaway *ph* Leon Shamroy *m* Lionel Newman

John Wayne, Stewart Granger, Fabian, Capucine, Ernie Kovacs, Mickey Shaughnessy, Karl Swenson, Joe Sawyer, John Qualen

North to the Klondike
US 1942 60m bw

Gold hunters protect the rights of a girl who has made a strike. Typical economy size programme filler with a studio look and a stalwart cast. Broderick Crawford, Lon Chaney Jnr, Andy Devine, Evelyn Ankers, Keye Luke. Written by Clarence Upson Young, Lew Sarecky, George Bricker and William Castle; directed by Erle C. Kenton; for Universal.

Northern Pursuit*
US 1943 94m bw
Warner (Jack Chertok)

A Mountie tracks a stranded Nazi pilot through the Canadian wastes.
Rather unusual star actioner, not badly done.

w Frank Gruber, Alvah Bessie *d* Raoul Walsh *ph* Sid Hickox *m* Adolph Deutsch

Errol Flynn, Helmut Dantine, Julie Bishop, John Ridgely, Gene Lockhart, Tom Tully, Bernard Nedell

Northwest Frontier***
GB 1959 129m Eastmancolor Cinemascope
Rank / Marcel Hellman
US title: *Flame Over India*

In 1905 an English officer during a rebellion escorts a young Hindu prince on a dangerous train journey.
Thoroughly enjoyable Boys' Own Paper adventure story with excellent set pieces and a spot-the-villain mystery.

w Robin Estridge d J. Lee-Thompson ph Geoffrey Unsworth m Mischa Spoliansky

Kenneth More, Lauren Bacall, Herbert Lom, Ursula Jeans, Wilfrid Hyde White, I. S. Johar, Eugene Deckers, Ian Hunter

'*Northwest Frontier* seems to have borrowed its eccentric engine from *The General*, its hazardous expedition from *Stagecoach* and its background of tribal violence from *The Drum*.'—*Penelope Houston*

'Ten stars! Two love stories! One thousand thrills!'

Northwest Mounted Police*
US 1940 125m Technicolor
Paramount (Cecil B. de Mille)

A Texas Ranger seeks a fugitive in Canada. Typical big-scale action concoction by de Mille, but in this case none of it's very memorable and the detail is poor.

w Alan Le May, Jesse Lasky Jnr, C. Gardner Sullivan *d* Cecil B. de Mille *ph* Victor Milner, Howard Greene *m* Victor Young

Gary Cooper, Paulette Goddard, Madeleine Carroll, Preston Foster, Robert Preston, George Bancroft, Lynne Overman, Akim Tamiroff, Walter Hampden, Lon Chaney Jnr, Montagu Love, George E. Stone

'Two hours of colour, killing, kindness and magnificent country.'—*Otis Ferguson*

'A movie in the grand style. God's own biggest trees and mountains for prop and backdrop; staunch courage and lofty aims among the good people; cunning and treachery lurking within the sinister forces; the ominous note of doom finally stifled by the fortitude of noble men.'—*Time*

AAN: Victor Milner, Howard Greene; Victor Young

Northwest Outpost
US 1947 91m bw
Republic (Allan Dwan)
GB title: *End of the Rainbow*

Adventures of California cavalrymen.
Milk-and-water adventures in a forgettable operetta.

w Elizabeth Meehan, Richard Sale *d* Allan Dwan *ph* Reggie Lanning *m* Rudolf Friml

Nelson Eddy, Ilona Massey, Hugo Haas, Elsa Lanchester

Northwest Passage***
(Part One, Rogers' Rangers)
US 1940 126m Technicolor
MGM (Hunt Stromberg)

Colonial rangers fight it out with hostile Indians.
Part Two was never made, but no one seemed to mind that the characters in Part One never got round to seeking the titular sea route. The adventures depicted had the feel of historical actuality, and the star was well cast.

w Lawrence Stallings, Talbot Jennings, *novel* Kenneth Roberts *d King Vidor ph* Sidney Wagner, William V. Skall *m* Herbert Stothart

Spencer Tracy, Robert Young, Ruth Hussey, Walter Brennan, Nat Pendleton, Robert Barrat, Lumsden Hare, Donald MacBride

'Half men, half demons, warriors such as the world has never known . . . they lived with death and danger for the women who hungered for their love!'—*publicity*

AAN: Sidney Wagner, William V. Skall

Norwood
US 1969 95m Technicolor
Paramount / Hal B. Wallis

A Vietnam veteran returns to his Texas home but feels restless and decides to become a radio singer.
A rather ordinary film about an innocent abroad, neither very funny nor very moving.

w Marguerite Roberts *d* Jack Haley Jnr *ph* Robert B. Hauser *m* Al de Lory

Glen Campbell, Kim Darby, Joe Namath, Carol Lynley, Pat Hingle, Tisha Sterling, Dom De Luise, Jack Haley, Cass Daley, Gil Lamb

Nosferatu***
Germany 1921 72m approx (24 fps) bw
Prana

Count Dracula goes to Bremen and is destroyed by sunlight.
An unofficial treatment of the Bram Stoker novel, with a terrifying count and several splendid moments. It took its director to Hollywood.

w Henrik Galeen *d F. W. Murnau ph* Fritz Arno Wagner *ad Albin Grau*

Max Schreck, Gustav Von Wangenheim, Greta Schroeder, Alexander Granach

Nosferatu the Vampyre*
West Germany / France 1979 107m Eastmancolor

Excruciatingly slow retread of the German silent film. Despite the star's splendidly loathsome appearance, the overall is no improvement, and the colour in the English prints is quite dreadful. *Klaus Kinski*, Isabelle Adjani, Bruno Ganz, Walter Ladengast. Written and directed by Werner Herzog; for Gaumont / Werner Herzog Filmproduktion.
'Like a dream from which you keep waking with indigestion.'—*Guardian*. (Original title: *Nosferatu, Phantom der Nacht*.)

Nostalgia*
Italy 1983 126m Eastmancolor

A Russian writer in Italy meets a social outcast who is expecting the end of the world. Indescribably doomladen, occasionally beautiful, stylistically interesting and for the most part very boring parable of a kind unique to this director. Oleg Jankovsky, Erland Josephson, Domiziana Giordano. Written by Andrei Tarkovsky, Tonino Guerra; directed by Andrei Tarkovsky; for Opera Film / Sovin Film / RAI

Not as a Stranger**
US 1955 135m bw
UA / Stanley Kramer

A medical student has professional and personal struggles.
Earnest filming of a bestseller, with all the actors too old for their parts.

w Edna and Edward Anhalt, *novel* Morton Thompson *d* Stanley Kramer *ph* Franz Planer *m* George Antheil *pd* Rudolph Sternad

Robert Mitchum, Olivia de Havilland, Broderick Crawford, Frank Sinatra, Gloria Grahame, Charles Bickford, Myron McCormick, Lon Chaney Jnr, Jesse White, Henry Morgan, Lee Marvin, Virginia Christine

NORTHWEST FRONTIER. Herbert Lom has a temporarily supine Kenneth More in a tight spot but Lauren Bacall has her trusty rifle at the ready.

Not Now, Darling
GB 1972 97m Eastmancolor

A furrier gets into a complicated situation when he arranges for his mistress to have a cheap mink coat. Interminable film version (in Multivista, a shoot-and-edit equivalent to TV taping which gives a dingy look and can only work in a single set) of a West End farce which wasn't marvellous to begin with. Leslie Phillips, Ray Cooney, Moira Lister, Julie Ege, Joan Sims, Derren Nesbitt, Barbara Windsor, Jack Hulbert, Cicely Courtneidge, Bill Fraser. Written by John Chapman, from the play by Ray Cooney; directed by Ray Cooney and David Croft; for LMG / Sedgemoor / Not Now Films.

Not of This Earth**
US 1957 72m bw
AA (Roger Corman)

An alien comes to earth in human form in search of blood which may save his planet. Modestly budgeted minor sci-fi; ruthless, original and competent.

w Charles Griffith, Mark Hanna d Roger Corman ph John Mescall *m* Ronald Stein

Paul Birch, Beverly Garland, Morgan Jones

Not Quite Jerusalem
GB 1985 114m colour
Rank / Acorn / Lewis Gilbert

An Israeli girl and an American volunteer fall in love on the kibbutz.
A curious misfire. Interest in the subject is cancelled out by unattractive, slangy or caricatured people and by a muddled approach suggesting that a fairer title might have been *Carry on Terrorist.*

w Paul Kember, from his play *d* Lewis Gilbert *ph* Tony Imi *m* Rondo Veneziano

Joanna Pacula, Sam Robards, Kevin McNally, Todd Graff, Selina Cadell

Not So Dumb
US 1929 80m approx at 24 fps bw silent

A naïve girl throws a big party in the hope of advancing her boy friend's career. Popular comedy of its time. Marion Davies, Elliott Nugent, Raymond Hackett, Franklin Pangborn, Julia Faye. Written by Wanda Tuchock and Edwin Justus Mayer, from the play *Dulcy* by George S. Kaufman and Marc Connolly; directed by King Vidor; for MGM. (NB: Previously made as *Dulcy* by Warner in 1923, directed by Sidney Franklin, with Constance Talmadge.)

Not Wanted on Voyage
GB 1957 82m bw

A necklace is stolen on an ocean liner. Feeble fun from an old play. Ronald Shiner, Brian Rix, Griffith Jones, Katie Boyle, Fabia Drake, Michael Brennan. Written by Michael and Ronald Pertwee and others from the play by Evadne Price and Ken Attiwill; directed by Maclean Rogers; for Renown.

Not with My Wife You Don't
US 1966 119m Technicolor
Warner / Fernwood / Reynard (Norman Panama, Joel Freeman)

A Korean war veteran is furious when an old rival turns up in London and again makes eyes at his wife.
Extraordinarily flat star comedy of cross and double cross among friends.

w Norman Panama, Larry Gelbart, Peter Barnes *d* Norman Panama *ph* Charles Lang, Paul Beeson *m* Johnny Williams

Tony Curtis, George C. Scott, Virna Lisi, Carroll O'Connor, Richard Eastham

'About as frothy as a tin of dehydrated milk.'—*MFB*

'It has all the verve, subtlety and sophistication of its title.'—*Judith Crist*

Nothing Barred
GB 1961 83m bw

A burglar helps a noble lord steal one of his own paintings. Leaden-footed farce. Brian Rix, Leo Franklyn, Naunton Wayne, Charles

Heslop, John Slater, Vera Pearce. Written by John Chapman; directed by Darcy Conyers; for Rix-Conyers/British Lion.

Nothing But the Best**
GB 1964 99m Eastmancolor
Anglo Amalgamated / Domino (David Deutsch)

An ambitious clerk learns to fight his way to the top by cheek and one-upmanship.
Hard, skilful, rather unattractive comedy with interesting social comments on its time.

w Frederic Raphael d Clive Donner
ph Nicolas Roeg *m* Ron Grainer *ad* Reece Pemberton

Alan Bates, Denholm Elliott, Harry Andrews, Millicent Martin, Pauline Delany

'The nightmare has already killed five people. Now it's yours to live!'

Nothing But the Night*
GB 1972 90m Eastmancolor
Rank / Charlemagne (Anthony Nelson Keys)

The trustees of an orphanage die off mysteriously, and it seems that the orphans themselves are responsible.
Convoluted murder mystery with horror elements and a twist hardly worth waiting for; earnest performances help.

w Brian Hayles, *novel* John Blackburn
d Peter Sasdy *ph* Ken Talbot *m* Malcolm Williamson

Christopher Lee, Peter Cushing, Diana Dors, Georgia Brown, Keith Barron, John Robinson

Nothing But the Truth
US 1941 90m bw
Paramount (Arthur Hornblow Jnr)

A stockbroker takes a bet that he can tell the absolute truth for twenty-four hours.
Rather unsurprising version of a stage comedy previously filmed as a silent. It lacks the style one might expect from the team which made *The Cat and the Canary*.

w Don Hartman, Ken Englund, *play* James Montgomery, *novel* Frederic S. Isham
d Elliott Nugent *ph* Charles Lang

Bob Hope, Paulette Goddard, Edward Arnold, Leif Erickson, Glen Anders, Helen Vinson, Grant Mitchell, Willie Best

Nothing But Trouble
US 1945 70m bw
MGM (B. F. Ziedman)

A chef and butler accidentally prevent a poison plot against a young king.
Feebly-devised star comedy, their last for a big studio.

w Russel Rouse, Ray Golden *d* Sam Taylor
ph Charles Salerno Jnr *m* Nathaniel Shilkret

Stan Laurel, Oliver Hardy, Mary Boland, Henry O'Neill, David Leland

Nothing in Common
US 1986 118m Metrocolor
Tri-Star / Rastar (Alexandra Rose)

Problems of an eccentric family when mum decides to walk out after 36 years.
Edgy comedy which misfires in all directions.

w Rick Podell, Michael Preminger *d* Garry Marshall *ph* John A. Alonzo *m* Patrick Leonard

Jackie Gleason, Eva Marie Saint, Tom Hanks, Hector Elizondo, Barry Corbin, Bess Armstrong

Nothing Personal
US 1980 97m Movielab

A professor and a lady lawyer try to stop seal hunting. The subject is an unsuitable starting point for a thin and zany comedy which gets nowhere and stays there. Donald Sutherland, Suzanne Somers, Larence Dane, Roscoe Lee Browne. Written by Robert Kaufman; directed by George Bloomfield; for David M. Perlmutter / AIP.

Nothing Sacred***
US 1937 77m Technicolor
David O. Selznick

A girl thought to be dying of a rare disease is built up by the press into a national heroine; but the diagnosis was wrong.
Hollywood's most bitter and hilarious satire, with crazy comedy elements and superb wisecracks; a historical monument of screen comedy, though its freshness at the time can't now be recaptured.

w Ben Hecht, story Letter to the Editor by James H. Street *d* William Wellman
ph W. Howard Greene *m* Oscar Levant

Carole Lombard, Fredric March, Walter Connolly, Charles Winninger, Sig Rumann, Frank Fay, Maxie Rosenbloom, Margaret Hamilton, Hedda Hopper, Monty Woolley, Hattie McDaniel, Olin Howland, John Qualen

DOCTOR (Charles Winninger): 'I'll tell you briefly what I think of newspapermen. The hand of God, reaching down into the mire, couldn't elevate one of them to the depths of degradation.'

EDITOR (Walter Connolly): 'I am sitting here, Mr Cook, toying with the idea of cutting out your heart and stuffing it—like an olive!'

'Hit comedy . . . will be one of the big grossers of the year.'—*Variety*

'Because it does hold up a mirror, even though a distorting mirror, to a very real world of ballyhoo and cheap sensationalism, the pleasure to be obtained from it is something more than the usual mulish guffaw.'—*Spectator*

† Refashioned in 1953 as a stage musical, *Hazel Flagg*, with music by Jule Styne; this in turn became a Martin and Lewis comedy *Living It Up* (Jerry Lewis in the Carole Lombard part).

Notorious***
US 1946 101m bw
RKO (Alfred Hitchcock)

In Rio, a notorious lady marries a Nazi renegade to help the US government but finds herself falling in love with her contact.
Superb romantic suspenser containing some of Hitchcock's best work.

w Ben Hecht d Alfred Hitchcock ph Ted Tetzlaff *m* Roy Webb

Cary Grant, Ingrid Bergman, Claude Rains, Louis Calhern, Leopoldine Konstantin, Reinhold Schunzel

'Velvet smooth in dramatic action, sharp and sure in its characters, and heavily charged with the intensity of warm emotional appeal.'—*Bosley Crowther*

'The suspense is terrific.'—*New Yorker, 1976*

'A film in the supercharged American idiom which made *Casablanca* popular.'—*Hermione Rich Isaacs, Theatre Arts*

AAN: Ben Hecht; Claude Rains

A Notorious Gentleman
US 1935 73m bw

A man plans murder and incriminates the victim's fiancée. Basically intriguing crime yarn spoiled by over-enthusiastic direction. Charles Bickford, Helen Vinson, Sidney Blackmer, Onslow Stevens, Dudley Digges. Written by Leopold Atlas, Robert Trasker; directed by Edward Laemmle; for Universal. 'Too heavily handled for first consideration.'—*Variety*

The Notorious Landlady
GB 1962 127m bw
Columbia / Kohlmar / Quine (Fred Kohlmar)

An American diplomat in London takes rooms with a murder suspect; after many mysterious happenings he helps to clear her.
Flatly whimsical goings on in comical old London, complete with fog and eccentrics. The actors all try hard but are deflated by the script.

w Larry Gelbart, Richard Quine *d* Richard Quine *ph* Arthur E. Arling *m* George Duning

Kim Novak, Jack Lemmon, Fred Astaire, Lionel Jeffries, Estelle Winwood, Maxwell Reed

The Notorious Sophie Lang
US 1934 60m bw

A lady jewel thief matches wits with a rival from abroad. Frothy crime comedy which isn't quite smart enough to avoid boredom. Gertrude Michael, Paul Cavanagh, Arthur Byron, Alison Skipworth, Leon Errol. Written by Anthony Veiller; directed by Ralph Murphy; for Paramount. 'No marquee strength, but nice pace and some genuine amusement.'—*Variety*

† There was a sequel in 1937, *Sophie Goes West*, also starring Gertrude Michael, directed by Charles Reisner.

La Notte*
Italy / France 1960 121m bw
Nepi / Sofitedip / Silver

A moderately successful novelist and his wife begin to question their marriage and their life. Slow but engaging character drama set during one night in Milan.

w Michelangelo Antonioni, Ennio Flaiano, Antonio Guerra *d Michelangelo Antonioni*
ph Gianni di Venanzo *m* Giorgio Gaslini

Marcello Mastroianni, Jeanne Moreau, Monica Vitti, Bernhard Wicki

Nous Sommes Tous les Assassins*
France 1952 108m bw
UGC
aka: *Are We All Murderers?*

An illiterate youth is taught to kill during the war; afterwards he kills again for money and is sent for execution.
A solemn sermon on capital punishment, and a powerful though rather glib one.

w André Cayatte, Charles Spaak *d* André Cayatte *ph* Jean Bourgoin

Marcel Mouloudji, Raymond Péllégrin, Antoine Balpêtre, Claude Laydu

Les Nouveaux Messieurs*
France 1928 135m approx (24 fps) bw silent
Albatros / Séquance

A glamorous dancer forsakes a count for a rising trade union official.
Lengthy political satire which caused a few headlines when first released.

w Charles Spaak, Jacques Feyder, *play* Robert de Flers, Francis de Grosset *d* Jacques Feyder *ph* Georges Périnal, Maurice Defassiaux *ad* Lazare Meerson

Albert Préjean, Gaby Morlay, Henri Roussel

Now About These Women . . .*
Sweden 1964 80m Eastmancolor
Svensk Filmindustri
aka: *All These Women*

A critic comes to stay with a famous cellist whose biography he is writing, but his efforts are hampered by all the women in the house.
Virtually indescribable black farce comedy which doesn't really work, yet, as always with this director, is continually of interest.

w Erland Josephson, Ingmar Bergman *d* Ingmar Bergman *ph* Sven Nykvist *m* Erik Nordgren

Jarl Kulle, Georg Funkquist, Eva Dahlbeck, Karen Kavli, Harriet Andersson, Bibi Andersson, Gertrud Fridh

Now and Forever*
US 1934 82m bw
Paramount (Louis D. Lighton)

A jewel thief and his mistress are taught a thing or two by his small daughter.
Odd mixture of comedy and drama which was box office at the time but seems pretty dated after nearly fifty years, though technically very smooth.

w Vincent Lawrence, Sylvia Thalberg *d* Henry Hathaway *ph* Harry Fischbeck

Gary Cooper, Carole Lombard, Shirley Temple, Guy Standing, Charlotte Granville, Gilbert Emery, Henry Kolker

'Cinch b.o. entertainment.'—*Variety*

'Expertly contrived to furnish first-rate entertainment.'—*Thornton Delehanty, New York Post*

Now and Forever
GB 1955 91m Technicolor
ABPC / Mario Zampi

A lonely schoolgirl plans an elopement and is chased across England by two sets of parents.
Teenage romance with elements of both farce and melodrama. It seemed to please at the time.

w R. F. Delderfield, Michael Pertwee, *play* The Orchard Walls by R. F. Delderfield *d* Mario Zampi *ph* Erwin Hillier *m* Stanley Black

Janette Scott, Vernon Gray, Kay Walsh, Jack Warner, Pamela Brown, Charles Victor, Wilfrid Lawson, Marjorie Rhodes, Sonia Dresdel, Ronald Squire, David Kossoff

Now Barabbas . . .
GB 1949 87m bw
Warner / Anatole de Grunwald
aka: *Now Barabbas Was a Robber*

Stories of men in prison.
Thinly intercut dramas; from a stage success.

w Anatole de Grunwald, *play* William Douglas Home *d* Gordon Parry *ph* Otto Heller

Richard Greene, Cedric Hardwicke, William Hartnell, Kathleen Harrison, Leslie Dwyer, Richard Burton, Kenneth More, Ronald Howard, Stephen Murray, Beatrice Campbell, Betty Ann Davies, Alec Clunes

Now I'll Tell
US 1934 72m bw
Fox (Winfield Sheehan)
GB title: *When New York Sleeps*

The story of Arnold Rothstein, gambler-racketeer of the twenties, as told by his widow.
Competent crime / domestic programmer.

wd Edwin Burke *ph* Ernest Palmer *m* Hugo Friedhofer

Spencer Tracy, Helen Twelvetrees, Hobart Cavanaugh, Alice Faye, G. P. Huntley Jnr, Shirley Temple, Leon Ames

'In spite of the breezy sequences with which it starts, it quickly gets improbable and goes from bad to maudlin.'—*Otis Ferguson*

Now Voyager***
US 1942 117m bw
Warner (Hal B. Wallis)

A dowdy frustrated spinster takes the psychiatric cure and embarks on a doomed love affair.
A basically soggy script still gets by, and how, through the romantic magic of its stars, who were all at their best; and suffering in mink went over very big in wartime.

w Casey Robinson, *novel* Olive Higgins Prouty *d Irving Rapper* *ph* Sol Polito *m* Max Steiner

Bette Davis, Claude Rains, Paul Henreid, Gladys Cooper, John Loder, Bonita Granville, Ilka Chase, Lee Patrick, Charles Drake, Franklin Pangborn

CHARLOTTE (Bette Davis): 'Oh, Jerry, don't let's ask for the moon. We have the stars!'

'If it were better, it might not work at all. This way, it's a crummy classic.'—*New Yorker, 1977*

AA: Max Steiner
AAN: Bette Davis; Gladys Cooper

Now You See Him Now You Don't
US 1972 88m Technicolor
Walt Disney

Two students discover an elixir of invisibility and help prevent a gangster from taking over the college.
Flat Disney frolic with fair trick effects.

w Joseph L. McEveety *d* Robert Butler *ph* Frank Phillips *m* Robert F. Brunner *sp* Eustace Lycett, Danny Lee

Kurt Russell, Cesar Romero, Joe Flynn, Jim Backus, William Windom, Edward Andrews, Richard Bakalyan

Nowhere to Go
GB 1958 87m bw
Ealing (Eric Williams)

A thief escapes from prison but can get no help from the underworld and is accidentally shot after being sheltered by a socialite.
Glum character melodrama which fails to sustain interest despite the best intentions.

w Seth Holt, Ken Tynan, *book* Donald MacKenzie *d* Seth Holt *ph* Paul Beeson *m* Dizzy Reece

George Nader, Maggie Smith, Bernard Lee, Geoffrey Keen, Andree Melly, Bessie Love, Howard Marion Crawford

The Nude Bomb
US 1980 94m Technicolor

An incompetent secret agent chases a missile-launching villain. Curious and unsatisfactory attempt to revive a twenty-year-old TV situation comedy minus half its personnel. Don Adams, Sylvia Kristel, Dana Elcar, Rhonda Fleming, Andrea Howard, Norman Lloyd. Written by Arne Sultan, Bill Dana and Leonard B. Stern; directed by Clive Donner (aka: *The Return of Maxwell Smart*.) 'Fans of the vidshow will derive much more enjoyment by crowding round their television sets with a bowl of popcorn watching *Get Smart* re-runs.'—*Variety*.

Number One
GB 1984 106m Technicolor

Adventures of a snooker hall hustler. Unappetizingly foul-mouthed low-life saga. Bob Geldof, Mel Smith, Alison Steadman, P. H. Moriarty, Phil Daniels. Written by G. F. Newman; directed by Les Blair; for Videoform.

Number One With a Bullet
US 1987 101m colour

An LA detective is obsessed with busting a big drug dealer who is also a pillar of the community. Ho-hum *policier* with routine violence. Robert Carradine, Billy Dee Williams, Valerie Bertinelli, Peter Graves, Doris Roberts. Written by Gail Morgan Hickman and others; directed by Jack Smight; for Cannon.

Number Seventeen*
GB 1932 63m bw
BIP (John Maxwell)

A girl jewel thief reforms and helps the police track down her former gang.
Minor Hitchcock thriller largely confined to a single interior until the final train chase, which despite obvious models remains exhilarating.

w Alfred Hitchcock, Alma Reville, Rodney Ackland, *play* J. Jefferson Farjeon *d Alfred Hitchcock* *ph* Jack Cox

Leon M. Lion, Anne Grey, John Stuart, Donald Calthrop, Barry Jones, Garry Marsh

'Only spasmodically good photography and usual slow tempo British direction. Wonder why they can't speed up a picture? Maybe it's the tea.'—*Variety*

† The same play had been filmed as a silent in 1928 by Geza Bolvary, with Guy Newall; it was shot in Germany.

The Nun and the Sergeant
US 1962 74m bw
UA / Springfield

In Korea, a tough sergeant commanding a 'dirty dozen' mission is joined by a schoolgirl and a nun.
Minor war adventure, moderately well done but highly unconvincing.

w Don Cerveris *d* Franklin Adreon *ph* Paul Ivano *m* Jerry Fielding

Anna Sten, Robert Webber, Leo Gordon, Hari Rhodes

'Filmed in Belgium, Italy, Africa . . . and mostly in the conscience of a beautiful young girl!'

The Nun's Story***
US 1959 151m Technicolor
Warner (Henry Blanke)

A Belgian girl joins a strict order, endures hardship in the Congo, and finally returns to ordinary life.
The fascinating early sequences of convent routine are more interesting than the African adventures, but this is a careful, composed and impressive film with little Hollywood exaggeration.

w Robert Anderson, book Kathryn C. Hulme d Fred Zinnemann ph Franz Planer m Franz Waxman

Audrey Hepburn, Peter Finch, Edith Evans, Peggy Ashcroft, Dean Jagger, Mildred Dunnock, Patricia Collinge, Beatrice Straight

'A major directorial achievement . . . the best study of the religious life ever made in the American cinema.'—*Albert Johnson, Film Quarterly*

AAN: best picture; Robert Anderson; Fred Zinnemann; Franz Planer; Franz Waxman; Audrey Hepburn

Nurse Edith Cavell
US 1939 98m bw

The story of a British nurse executed as a spy during World War I; previously filmed in 1930 as *Dawn* with Sybil Thorndike. This is a moderately touching but uninspired treatment. Anna Neagle, George Sanders, May Robson, Edna May Oliver, Alan Marshal. Written by Michael Hogan from the novel *Dawn* by Reginald Berkeley; directed by Herbert Wilcox; for Imperator / RKO. AAN: music by Anthony Collins. 'Excellently produced documentary film, but not for general audience appeal . . . no light moments to relieve the tragic aspects.'—*Variety*

Nurse on Wheels
GB 1963 86m bw
Anglo Amalgamated / GHW (Peter Rogers)

Adventures of a young District Nurse.
Part sentimental, part Carry On; watchable of its curious kind.

w Norman Hudis, *novel* Nurse Is a Neighbour by Joanna Jones *d* Gerald Thomas *ph* Alan Hume *m* Eric Rogers

Juliet Mills, Ronald Lewis, Joan Sims, Raymond Huntley, Athene Seyler

The Nursemaid Who Disappeared
GB 1939 86m bw

A domestic agency hides a gang of kidnappers. Fairly pleasing mystery of the old school. Arthur Margetson, Peter Coke, Lesley Brook, Edward Chapman, Coral Browne, Martita Hunt. Written by Paul Gangelin and Connery Chappell, from the novel by Philip MacDonald; directed by Arthur Woods; for Warner.

The Nurse's Secret
US 1941 56m bw

A hired nurse solves her patient's murder. Potboiling remake of *Miss Pinkerton*, rather better written than the original. Lee Patrick, Regis Toomey, Julie Bishop, Charles D. Waldron, Charles Trowbridge, Leonard Mudie. Written by Anthony Coldeway; directed by Noel M. Smith; for First National / Warner.

Nutcracker
GB 1982 101m Eastmancolor
Rank / Ezshaw (Panos Nicolaou)

A Russian ballerina defects in London but finds that she is being used for business / political purposes.
Weird, dated and utterly mediocre melodrama with pauses for sexual revels. Not a goer.

w Raymond Christodoulou *d* Anwar Kawadri *ph* Peter Jessop *m* Simon Park

Joan Collins, Carol White, Paul Nicholas, Finola Hughes, William Franklyn, Murray Melvin

The Nutty Professor
US 1963 107m Technicolor
Paramount / Jerry Lewis (Ernest D. Glucksman)

An eccentric chemistry professor discovers an elixir which turns him into a pop idol.
Long dreary comedy which contains patches of its star at somewhere near his best; but even *Dr Jekyll and Mr Hyde* is funnier.

w Jerry Lewis, Bill Richmond *d* Jerry Lewis *ph* W. Wallace Kelley *m* Walter Scharf

Jerry Lewis, Stella Stevens, Howard Morris, Kathleen Freeman

Nuts
US 1987 116m Technicolor
Warner (Barbra Streisand)

Classy prostitute kills a client; at her trial she battles against attempts to find her mentally unstable.
Star vehicle, strictly for fans.

w Tom Topor and others, from his play *d* Martin Ritt *ph* Andrzej Bartkowiak *m* Barbra Streisand *pd* Joel Schiller

Barbra Streisand, Richard Dreyfuss, Maureen Stapleton, Karl Malden, Eli Wallach

O. Henry's Full House**
US 1952 117m bw
TCF (André Hakim)
GB title: *Full House*

John Steinbeck introduces five stories by O. Henry.
Modelled on the success of *Quartet* (qv), this compendium was less successful because these turn-of-the century tales of New York depend less on character than on the sting in the tail; but the cast and production were lavish.

m Alfred Newman

THE COP AND THE ANTHEM *w* Lamar Trotti *d* Henry Koster *ph* Lloyd Ahern
Charles Laughton, David Wayne, Marilyn Monroe
THE CLARION CALL *w* Richard Breen *d* Henry Hathaway *ph* Lucien Ballard
Dale Robertson, Richard Widmark
THE LAST LEAF *w* Ivan Coff, Ben Roberts *d* Jean Negulesco *ph* Joe MacDonald
Anne Baxter, Jean Peters, Gregory Ratoff
THE RANSOM OF RED CHIEF *w* Nunnally Johnson *d* Howard Hawks *ph* Milton Krasner
Fred Allen, Oscar Levant
THE GIFT OF THE MAGI *w* Walter Bullock *d* Henry King *ph* Joe MacDonald
Jeanne Crain, Farley Granger

O.H.M.S.
GB 1936 86m bw
Gaumont (Geoffrey Barkas)
US title: *You're in the Army Now*

British forces fighting in China are joined by an American gangster on the run, who dies a hero.
Stiff-upper-lip adventure of no particular interest.

w Bryan Edgar Wallace, Austin Melford, A. R. Rawlinson, Lesser Samuels, Ralph Bettinson *d* Raoul Walsh *ph* Roy Kellino

John Mills, Wallace Ford, Anna Lee, Frank Cellier, Grace Bradley, Frederick Leister
'As near 100% entertainment value as can reasonably be hoped for without the employment of a superstar, super-cast, super-director and super-production.'—*Variety*

'Smile while you're makin' it,
Laugh while you're takin' it,
Even though you're fakin' it,
Nobody's gonna know . . .'

O Lucky Man**
GB 1973 174m Eastmancolor
Warner / Memorial / Sam (Michael Medwin, Lindsay Anderson)

The odyssey of a trainee salesman who after a while as an international financier settles down to be a do-gooder.
Modern revue-style version of *Candide / Decline and Fall*; very hit or miss in style and effect, and hellishly overlong, but with good things along the way.

w David Sherwin *d* Lindsay Anderson *ph* Miroslav Ondricek *m Alan Price* *pd* Jocelyn Herbert

Malcolm McDowell, Arthur Lowe, Ralph Richardson, Rachel Roberts, Helen Mirren, Mona Washbourne, Dandy Nichols
'A sort of mod *Pilgrim's Progress*.'—*New Yorker*

'He's deep in danger, deeper in love!'

O.S.S.*
US 1946 107m bw
Paramount (Richard Maibaum)

American spies are parachuted into France in 1943.
Espionage heroics with an unhappy ending and a slight documentary flavour. Not bad of its kind.

w Richard Maibaum *d Irving Pichel* *ph* Lionel Lindon *m* Daniele Amfitheatrof, Heinz Roemheld

Alan Ladd, Geraldine Fitzgerald, Patric Knowles, John Hoyt, Don Beddoe

Oasis
France / Germany 1956 100m approx Eastmancolor Cinemascope
TCF / Roxy / Criterion (Gerd Oswald, Luggi Waldleitner)

An ex-pilot gets involved with two attractive women who are smuggling gold across the Sahara.
Glum romantic adventure.

w Joseph and Georges Kessel *d* Yves Allégret *ph* Roger Hubert *m* Paul Misraki

Pierre Brasseur, Michèle Morgan, Cornell Borchers, Grégoire Aslan

Objective Burma*
US 1944 142m bw
Warner (Jerry Wald)

Exploits of an American platoon in the Burma campaign.
Overlong but vivid war actioner which caused a diplomatic incident by failing to mention the British contribution.

w Ranald MacDougall, Lester Cole, Alvah Bessie *d Raoul Walsh* *ph* James Wong Howe *m* Franz Waxman

Errol Flynn, James Brown, William Prince, George Tobias, Henry Hull, Warner Anderson, John Alwin
'At the rate Errol Flynn and co. knock off the Japanese, it may make you wonder why the war need outlast next weekend.'—*Time*
'I am amazed that Warner Brothers ever made it, or having made it failed to think again and smother it.'—*Reynolds News*

† The film was not released in Britain until 1952, and then with an apologetic prologue.

AAN: original story (Alvah Bessie); Franz Waxman

The Obliging Young Lady
US 1941 80m bw

A secretary escorts a wealthy child out of town while her parents wrangle over custody.
Tedious comedy with interest occasionally provided by the supporting cast. Joan Carroll, Ruth Warrick, Edmond O'Brien, Eve Arden, Franklin Pangborn, Marjorie Gateson, John Miljan, George Cleveland. Luis Alberni, Charles Lane. Written by Frank Ryan and Bert Granet; directed by Richard Wallace; for RKO.

The Oblong Box
GB 1969 95m Eastmancolor
AIP (Gordon Hessler)

One of two 19th-century brothers is mysteriously disfigured and buried alive; he recovers and runs amok.
Nastily effective horror film with a frail story but good background detail.

w Lawrence Huntington *d Gordon Hessler* *ph* John Coquillon *m* Harry Robinson

Vincent Price, Christopher Lee, Alastair Williamson, Hilary Dwyer, Peter Arne, Maxwell Shaw, Rupert Davies
'A pervasive aura of evil.'—*MFB*

Obsession*
GB 1948 98m bw
GFD / Independent Sovereign (Nat Bronsten)
US title: *The Hidden Room*

A doctor decides to kill his wife's lover by imprisoning him in a lonely cellar while he accumulates enough acid to destroy all traces of his body.

Implausible, overstretched thriller, carefully enough done to be bearable.

w Alec Coppel, from his play A Man About a Dog *d* Edward Dmytryk *ph* C. Pennington Richards *m* Nino Rota

Robert Newton, Sally Gray, Phil Brown, Naunton Wayne

Obsession*
US 1976 98m Technicolor Panavision
Columbia (Robert S. Bremson)

A widower with guilt feelings meets the double of his dead wife and is drawn into a strange plot.
Hitchcockian adventure with a few unwise attempts at seriousness, à la *Don't Look Now*. Generally entertaining, skilled and quite rewarding.

w Paul Schrader *d* Brian de Palma *ph* Vilmos Zsigmond *m* Bernard Herrmann

Cliff Robertson, Geneviève Bujold, John Lithgow, Sylvia Williams, Wanda Blackman, Patrick McNamara

'An unholy mess. Intended as an *hommage* to Hitchcock . . . it attitudinizes [also] towards the old-fashioned tearjerker and towards the sophisticated European film, with cultural references strewn like breadcrumbs along the way of Hansel and Gretel . . .'—*John Simon, New York*

'Merely a mannered cerebral exercise without any emotional underpinning or unconscious feeling of its own.'—*Andrew Sarris, Village Voice*

AAN: Bernard Herrmann

Occupe-Toi d'Amélie***
France 1949 95m bw
Lux (Louis Wipf)
aka: *Keep an Eye on Amelia*

A Parisian cocotte agrees to go through a mock marriage ceremony with her lover's best friend to fool his uncle: but the ceremony turns out to be real.
Hilarious and superbly stylized adaptation of a period boulevard farce: the play starts in a theatre, showing the audience, but gradually cinema technique takes over. Acting, timing and editing are all impeccable, and the production stands as a model of how such things should be done.

w Jean Aurenche, Pierre Bost, play Georges Feydeau *d Claude Autant-Lara ph* André Bac *m* René Cloërc

Danielle Darrieux, Jean Desailly, Bourvil, Carette, Grégoire Aslan

'Even those who do not respond to the artificialities of French vaudeville will admire the ingenuity and elegance of treatment.'—*Gavin Lambert, MFB*

'Most people, I think, could see it with considerable enjoyment even twice on the same evening.'—*Richard Mallett, Punch*

Ocean's Eleven*
US 1960 128m Technicolor Panavision
Warner / Dorchester (Lewis Milestone)

A gang of friends plan to rob a Las Vegas casino.
Self-indulgent and overlong caper comedy which marked Hollywood's entry into a subsequently much overworked field. In this case the plot stops all too frequently for guest spots and in-jokes.

w Harry Brown, Charles Lederer *d* Lewis Milestone *ph* William H. Daniels *m* Nelson Riddle

Frank Sinatra, Peter Lawford, Sammy Davis Jnr, Richard Conte, Dean Martin, Angie Dickinson, Cesar Romero, Joey Bishop, Patrice Wymore, Akim Tamiroff, Henry Silva, Ilka Chase

October****
USSR 1927 95m approx bw silent
Sovkino

In 1917, the Kerensky regime is overthrown by the Bolsheviks.
A propaganda masterpiece whose images have all too often been mistaken and used for genuine newsreel. Cinematically, an undoubted masterpiece.

w Sergei M. Eisenstein, Grigory Alexandrov *d Sergei M. Eistenstein ph* Edouard Tissé, V. Popov

The October Man**
GB 1947 98m bw
GFD / Two Cities (Eric Ambler)

After an accident which causes a head injury and subsequent depression, a lonely man staying at a small hotel is suspected of a local murder.
Nice blend of character study, mystery and suspense, with excellent attention to suburban detail.

w Eric Ambler d Roy Baker ph Erwin Hillier

John Mills, Joan Greenwood, Edward Chapman, Kay Walsh, Catherine Lacey, Joyce Carey, Adrianne Allen, Felix Aylmer

'This film of psychological suspense tells its complicated story with complete clarity, but it is mainly to be noted for its settings.'—*Basil Wright, 1972*

'A new type of thriller in which tension is heightened by the vivid realism of its setting and the complete credibility of its characters.'—*Reynolds News*

October Moth
GB 1959 54m bw

A mentally retarded farmhand goes berserk after causing a fatal car crash. Unattractive and singularly pointless little melodrama which neither edifies nor entertains. Lana Morris, Lee Patterson, Peter Dynely, Robert Cawdron. Written and directed by John Kruse; for Independent Artists.

Octopussy
GB 1983 131m Technicolor Panavision
Eon / Danjaq (Albert R. Broccoli)

James Bond takes on an evil Afghan prince and a glamorous woman who plan between them to plunder Tsarist treasures.
Bond at the end of his tether: such far-stretched adventures have become merely a tedious way of passing the time.

w George MacDonald Fraser, Richard Maibaum, Michael G. Wilson *d* John Glen *ph* Alan Hume *m* John Barry *pd* Peter Lamont

Roger Moore, Maud Adams, Louis Jourdan, Kristina Wayborn, Kabir Bedi, Desmond Llewellyn, Lois Maxwell

'As the films drift further and further into self-parody, no one seems to notice and no one (at any rate in box office terms) seems to mind.'—*Nick Roddick, MFB*

The Odd Couple**
US 1968 105m Technicolor Panavision
Paramount (Howard W. Koch)

A fussy divorce-shocked newswriter moves in with his sloppy sportscaster friend, and they get on each other's nerves.
Straight filming of a funny play which sometimes seems lost on the wide screen, but the performances are fine.

w Neil Simon, from his play *d* Gene Saks *ph* Robert B. Hauser *m* Neal Hefti

Jack Lemmon, Walter Matthau, John Fiedler, Herb Edelman, David Sheiner, Larry Haines, Monica Evans, Carole Sheely, Iris Adrian

OSCAR (Walter Matthau): 'I can't take it anymore, Felix. I'm crackin' up. Everything you do irritates me. And when you're not here, the things I know you're gonna do when you come in irritate me. You leave me little notes on my pillow. I told you 158 times I cannot stand little notes on my pillow. "We are all out of cornflakes, F.U." It took me three hours to figure out that F.U. was Felix Ungar. It's not your fault, Felix. It's a rotten combination, that's all.'

AAN: Neil Simon

Odd Man Out***
GB 1946 115m bw
GFD / Two Cities (Carol Reed)
US title: *Gang War*

An IRA gunman, wounded and on the run in Belfast, is helped and hindered by a variety of people.
Superbly crafted but rather empty dramatic charade, visually and emotionally memorable but with nothing whatever to say.

w F. L. Green, R. C. Sherriff, *novel* F. L. Green *d Carol Reed ph Robert Krasker* *m* William Alwyn

James Mason, Robert Newton, Kathleen Ryan, F. J. McCormick, Cyril Cusack, Robert Beatty, Fay Compton, Dan O'Herlihy, Denis O'Dea, Maureen Delany, Joseph Tomelty, William Hartnell

'The story seems to ramify too much, to go on too long, and at its unluckiest to go arty. Yet detail by detail *Odd Man Out* is made with great skill and imaginativeness and with a depth of ardour that is very rare.'—*James Agee*

'Quite simply the most imaginative film yet produced in England, comparable with *Quai des Brumes* and *Le Jour se Lève*.'—*William Whitebait, New Statesman*

Odds against Tomorrow*
US 1959 96m bw
UA / Harbel (Robert Wise)

Three crooks plan to rob a bank, but two of them cause the enterprise to fail because of their own racist hatreds.
Sour, glossy crime thriller with elementary social significance.

w John O. Killens, Nelson Gidding, *novel* John P. McGivern *d Robert Wise ph Joseph Brun m* John Lewis

Robert Ryan, Harry Belafonte, *Ed Begley*, Shelley Winters, Gloria Grahame, Will Kuluva, Kim Hamilton

'An efficient but unnecessarily portentous thriller.'—*Penelope Houston*

† The writer was actually Abraham Polonsky, who was blacklisted at the time.

The Odessa File**
GB 1974 129m Eastmancolor Panavision
Columbia / Domino / Oceanic (John Woolf)

In 1963, a young German reporter tracks down a gang of neo-Nazis.
Elaborate but uninvolving suspenser with several excellent cliffhanging sequences and a let-down climax.

w Kenneth Ross, George Markstein, *novel* Frederick Forsyth *d* Ronald Neame *ph* Oswald Morris *m* Andrew Lloyd Webber *pd* Rolf Zeherbauer

Jon Voight, Maria Schell, Maximilian Schell, Mary Tamm, Derek Jacobi, Peter Jeffrey, *Noel Willman*

'As resistible a parcel of sedative entertainment as ever induced narcolepsy in a healthy man.'—*Benny Green, Punch*

Odette*
GB 1950 123m bw
Herbert Wilcox

A Frenchwoman with an English husband spies for the French resistance, is caught and tortured.
Deglamorized true life spy story with emotional moments let down by generally uninspired handling, also by the too well-known image of its star, who however gives a remarkable performance.

w Warren Chetham Strode, *book* Jerrard Tickell *d* Herbert Wilcox *ph* Max Greene *m* Anthony Collins

Anna Neagle, Trevor Howard, Peter Ustinov, Marius Goring

'As a work of art, pretty flat . . . though innumerable people will find it moving and impressive, they will have done the work themselves.'—*Richard Mallett, Punch*

Odongo
GB 1956 85m Technicolor Cinemascope

A collector of animals for zoos runs into various kinds of trouble during an African safari. Elementary jungle adventure centring on a small Sabu-like jungle boy. For the now extinct family audience. Macdonald Carey, Rhonda Fleming, Juma, Eleanor Summerfield, Francis de Wolff, Earl Cameron. Written and directed by John Gilling; for Warwick / Columbia.

Of Human Bondage**
US 1934 83m bw
(RKO) Pandro S. Berman

A well-to-do Englishman is brought down by his infatuation with a sluttish waitress.
This version of the famous novel brought Bette Davis to prominence but is not otherwise any better than the others.

w Lester Cohen, *novel* W. Somerset Maugham *d* John Cromwell *ph* Henry W. Gerrard *m* Max Steiner

Leslie Howard, Bette Davis, Frances Dee, Reginald Owen, Reginald Denny, Kay Johnson, Alan Hale

'Stars and the novel rep will have to carry a lethargic romance.'—*Variety*

'A totally obtuse concoction, serving only to demonstrate how untalented an actress Bette Davis was before she perfected those camp mannerisms.'—*John Simon, 1967*

Of Human Bondage*
US 1946 105m bw
Warner (Henry Blanke)

Good-looking but thoroughly dull remake.

w Catherine Turney *d* Edmund Goulding *ph* Peverell Marley *m* Erich Wolfgang Korngold

Paul Henreid, Eleanor Parker, Alexis Smith, Edmund Gwenn, Patric Knowles, Janis Paige, Henry Stephenson

Of Human Bondage
GB 1964 99m bw
MGM / Seven Arts (James Woolf)

Disastrous remake with both star roles miscast.

w Bryan Forbes *d* Henry Hathaway, Ken Hughes *ph* Oswald Morris *m* Ron Goodwin *pd* John Box

Laurence Harvey, Kim Novak, Nanette Newman, Roger Livesey, Jack Hedley, Robert Morley, Siobhan McKenna, Ronald Lacey

Of Human Hearts*
US 1938 100m bw
MGM (John Considine Jnr)

A 19th-century idyll of middle America and especially of a preacher and his wayward son. Curious all-American moral fable, splendidly made and acted.

w Bradbury Foote, *novel* Benefits Forgot by Honoré Morrow *d* Clarence Brown *ph* Clyde de Vinna *m* Herbert Stothart

Walter Huston, James Stewart, Beulah Bondi, Gene Reynolds, Charles Coburn, Guy Kibbee, John Carradine, Gene Lockhart, Ann Rutherford

'Long on narrative and short on romance . . . the box office reaction is likely to dampen the enthusiasm of those who believe the film possesses any wide public appeal.'—*Variety*

† The title was chosen via a radio contest, the winner being a high-school student.

AAN: Beulah Bondi

Of Love and Desire
US 1963 97m De Luxe
New World (Victor Stoloff)

An engineer in Mexico takes up with the boss's nymphomaniac sister.
Unwise sensationalist vehicle for an ageing leading lady who is past such carryings on.

w Laslo Gorag, Richard Rush *d* Richard Rush *ph* Alex Phillips *m* Ronald Stein

Merle Oberon, Steve Cochran, John Agar, Curt Jurgens

'I'm decent, I tell ya! Nobody's got the right to call me names!'

'The picture Hollywood said could never be made!'

Of Mice and Men***
US 1939 107m bw
Hal Roach (Lewis Milestone)

An itinerant worker looks after his mentally retarded cousin, a giant who doesn't know his own strength.
A strange and unexpected tragedy which has strength and is very persuasively made but seems somehow unnecessary.

w Eugene Solow, *novel* John Steinbeck *d Lewis Milestone ph Norbert Brodine m* Aaron Copland

Burgess Meredith, Lon Chaney Jnr, Betty Field, Charles Bickford, Roman Bohnen, Bob Steele, Noah Beery Jnr

AAN: best picture; Aaron Copland

Off Limits
US 1953 89m bw
Paramount (Harry Tugend)
GB title: *Military Policemen*

A boxing manager trains a young fighter in the military police.
Flat star comedy.

w Hal Kanter, Jack Sher *d* George Marshall *ph Peverell Marley m* Van Cleave

Bob Hope, Mickey Rooney, Marilyn Maxwell, Marvin Miller

Off the Dole
GB 1935 89m bw

An amateur detective catches burglars. Artless comedy shot on a minuscule budget; it helped to make George Formby a star. With Beryl Formby, Constance Shotter, Dan Young. Written and directed by Arthur Mertz; for Mancunian.

Off the Record
US 1939 71m bw

A star reporter exposes the mob's use of youngsters as spotters in the gambling racket. Predictable crime support. Pat O'Brien, Joan Blondell, Bobby Jordan, Alan Baxter, Morgan Conway. Written by Niven Busch, Lawrence Kimble, Earl Baldwin; directed by James Flood; for Warners. 'Stereotype dualler.'—*Variety*

Offbeat*
GB 1960 72m bw
British Lion / Northiam (M. Smedley Aston)

An MI5 undercover man finds himself sympathizing with a gang of robbers and falling in love with one of them.

Sharply observed thriller which gets a bit glum in dealing with its rather contrived 'switch'.

w Peter Barnes *d* Cliff Owen *ph* Geoffrey Faithfull *m* Ken Jones

William Sylvester, Mai Zetterling, Anthony Dawson, John Meillon, John Phillips, Victor Brooks, Joseph Furst, Neil McCarthy, Harry Baird

The Offence*
GB 1972 113m De Luxe
United Artists / Tantallon (Denis O'Dell)

A tough police inspector bullies a suspected child molester.
Tortuous psychological study on the fringe of hysteria; good performances.

w John Hopkins, from his play This Story of Yours *d* Sidney Lumet *ph* Gerry Fisher *m* Harrison Birtwistle

Sean Connery, Trevor Howard, Ian Bannen, Vivien Merchant

An Officer and a Gentleman*
US 1982 126m Metrocolor
Paramount / Lorimar (Martin Elfand)

A potential officer suffers thirteen weeks of agony at the Naval Aviation Officer Candidate School.
Old-hat stuff given a fresh look and some smart acting.

w Douglas Day Stewart *d* Taylor Hackford *ph* Donald Thorin *m* Jack Nitzsche *pd* Philip M. Jefferies

Richard Gere, Debra Winger, *Louis Gossett Jnr*, David Keith, Lisa Blount, Lisa Eilbacher

'Shamelessly manipulative, but whether the manipulations are funny, dramatic or tear-jerking, it knows exactly what and how to deliver.'—*Sunday Telegraph*

AA: Louis Gossett Jnr (as supporting actor); *song* 'Up Where We Belong' by Jack Nitzche, Buffy Sainte-Marie (*m*), Will Jennings (*ly*)
AAN: Debra Winger; original screenplay; editing (Peter Zinner); music

Oh Dad, Poor Dad, Mamma's Hung You in the Closet and I'm Feelin' So Sad
US 1966 86m Technicolor
Paramount / Seven Arts (Ray Stark, Stanley Rubin)

A dead father helps his son to get married despite his mother's influence to the contrary.
Zany black comedy which never really worked on the stage, let alone the screen.

w Ian Bernard, *play* Arthur Kopit *d* Richard Quine *ph* Geoffrey Unsworth *m* Neal Hefti

Rosalind Russell, Jonathan Winters, Robert Morse, Hugh Griffith, Barbara Harris, Lionel Jeffries, Cyril Delevanti, Hiram Sherman

Oh Doctor
US 1937 67m bw

A rich hypochondriac is the target of confidence tricksters. Moderate star comedy. Edward Everett Horton, Donrue Leighton, Eve Arden, Thurston Hall, William Demarest. 'Smooth dialogue keeps this hokey picture from going completely corkscrew.'—*Variety*

'It's an almighty laugh!'
Oh, God*
US 1977 104m Technicolor
Warner (Jerry Weintraub)

A bewildered supermarket manager is enlisted by God to prove to the world that it can only work if people try.
Overlong but generally amiable reversion to the supernatural farces of the forties: its success seems to show that people again need this kind of comfort.

w Larry Gelbart, *novel* Avery Corman *d* Carl Reiner *ph* Victor Kemper *m* Jack Elliott

George Burns, John Denver, Ralph Bellamy, Donald Pleasence, Teri Garr, William Daniels, Barnard Hughes, Paul Sorvino, Barry Sullivan, Dinah Shore, Jeff Corey, David Ogden Stiers

'Undeniably funny and almost impossible to dislike.'—*Tom Milne, MFB*

'Basically a single-joke movie: George Burns is God in a football cap.'—*Pauline Kael, New Yorker*

AAN: Larry Gelbart

Oh God Book Two
US 1980 94m Technicolor

God enlists a child to remind people that he is still around. Crass sequel with sentiment replacing jokes. George Burns, Suzanne Pleshette, David Birney, Louanne, Howard Duff, Hans Conried, Wilfrid Hyde White. Written by Josh Greenfield, Hal Goldman, Fred S. Fox, Seaman Jacobs and Melissa Miller; directed by Gilbert Cates; for Warner.

Oh God, You Devil
US 1984 96m Technicolor
Warner (Robert M. Sherman)

A struggling musician sells his soul to the devil in exchange for success.
A comic version of Faust, appended to the two films in which George Burns played God; he now puts on the other hat to fairly, but not very, comic effect.

w Andrew Bergman *d* Paul Bogart *ph* King Baggot *m* David Shire *pd* Peter Wooley *ed* Andy Zall

George Burns, Ted Wass, Ron Silver, Roxanne Hart, Eugene Roche

Oh Heavenly Dog
US 1980 103m De Luxe

A private eye is reincarnated as a dog and solves his own murder. Witless fantasy comedy, an uncredited remake of *You Never Can Tell* which also rates as a Benji movie with curious additions of sex and profanity. A total muddle. Chevy Chase, Jane Seymour, Omar Sharif, Robert Morley, Alan Sues. Written by Rod Browning and Joe Camp; directed by Joe Camp; for Mulberry Square / TCF.

Oh Men! Oh Women!
US 1957 90m Eastmancolor Cinemascope
TCF (Nunnally Johnson)

A psychoanalyst discovers that his wife is involved with two of his patients.
Scatty Broadway comedy which strains the patience.

wd Nunnally Johnson, *play* Edward Chodorov *ph* Charles G. Clarke *m* Cyril Mockridge

David Niven, Ginger Rogers, Dan Dailey, Barbara Rush, Tony Randall

'The ugliest sort of fun.'—*Observer*

'Cinemascope discovers a solution to the problem of filling its wide screen; the characters spend most of their time full length on the psychoanalyst's couch.'—*Sunday Times*

Oh Mr Porter****
GB 1937 84m bw
GFD / Gainsborough (Edward Black)

The stationmaster of an Irish halt catches gun-runners posing as ghosts.
Marvellous star comedy showing this trio of comedians at their best, and especially Hay as the seedy incompetent. The plot is borrowed from *The Ghost Train*, but each line and gag brings its own inventiveness. A delight of character comedy and cinematic narrative.

w Marriott Edgar, Val Guest, J. O. C. Orton, story Frank Launder *d Marcel Varnel* *ph* Arthur Crabtree *md* Louis Levy

Will Hay, Moore Marriott, Graham Moffatt, Dave O'Toole, Dennis Wyndham

'That rare phenomenon: a film comedy without a dud scene.'—*Peter Barnes, 1964*

'Behind it lie the gusty uplands of the British music hall tradition, whose rich soil the British film industry is at last beginning to exploit.'—*Basil Wright*

Oh Rosalinda!
GB 1955 105m Technicolor Cinemascope
ABP / Powell and Pressburger

A playboy in four-power Vienna plays a practical joke on four officers and the flirtatious wife of one of them.
Lumbering attempt to modernize *Die Fledermaus*, unsuitably wide-screened and totally lacking the desired Lubitsch touch. A monumental step in the decline of these producers, and a sad stranding of a brilliant cast.

wd Michael Powell, Emeric Pressburger *ph* Christopher Challis *m* Johann Strauss *ad* Hein Heckroth

Anton Walbrook, Michael Redgrave, Anthony Quayle, Mel Ferrer, Dennis Price, Ludmilla Tcherina

Oh What a Lovely War**
GB 1969 144m Technicolor Panavision
Paramount / Accord (Brian Duffy, Richard Attenborough)

A fantasia with music on World War I.

A brave all-star attempt which comes off only in patches; the pier apparatus from the stage show really doesn't translate, the piece only works well when it becomes cinematic, as in the recruiting song and the final track-back from the graves. But there are many pleasures, as well as yawns, along the way.

w Len Deighton, *stage show* Joan Littlewood, Charles Chilton *d* Richard Attenborough *ph Gerry Turpin* *m* various *md* Alfred Ralston *pd Don Ashton*

Ralph Richardson, Meriel Forbes, John Gielgud, Kenneth More, John Clements, Paul Daneman, Joe Melia, Jack Hawkins, John Mills, Maggie Smith, Michael Redgrave, Laurence Olivier, Susannah York, Dirk Bogarde, Phyllis Calvert, Vanessa Redgrave

'This musical lampoon is meant to stir your sentiments, evoke nostalgia, and make you react to the obscenity of battles and bloodshed, and apparently it does all that for some people.'—*New Yorker, 1977*

'A naïve, sentimental, populist affair, using many (too many) clever devices yet making the same old simplistic statements.'—*John Simon*

'An overlong and rarely cinematic musical satire that ladles its anti-war message on by the bucketload.'—*Time Out, 1984*

Oh You Beautiful Doll*
US 1949 93m Technicolor
TCF (George Jessel)

Fred Fisher wants to write opera but is more successful with pop songs.
Standard turn of the century biopic, very pleasantly handled and performed.

w Albert and George Lewis *d* John M. Stahl *ph* Harry Jackson *md* Alfred Newman

S. Z. Sakall, Mark Stevens, June Haver, *Charlotte Greenwood*, Jay C. Flippen, Gale Robbins

O'Hara's Wife
US 1983 87m De Luxe

A widower is helped by his wife's ghost. Rather icky sentimental comedy. Ed Asner, Mariette Hartley, Jodie Foster, Perry Lang, Tom Bosley, Ray Walston. Written by James Nasella and William S. Bartman; directed by William S. Bartman; for David-Panzer.

Oil for the Lamps of China*
US 1935 98m bw
Warner (Robert Lord)

The career in China of an American oil company representative.
Adequate general audience picture from a bestseller.

w Laird Doyle, *novel* Alice Tisdale Hobart *d* Mervyn Le Roy *ph* Tony Gaudio *m* Heinz Roemheld *md* Leo F. Forbstein

Pat O'Brien, Josephine Hutchinson, Jean Muir, Lyle Talbot, Arthur Byron, John Eldredge, Henry O'Neill, Donald Crisp

'Long and choppy version of a best-seller novel. Little marquee strength will probably mean light returns.'—*Variety*

'Far above average in performance, direction and content.'—*John Baxter, 1968*

† Remade 1941 as *Law of the Tropics*.

Okay America
US 1932 80m bw

A brash reporter saves a politician's daughter from kidnapping. Okay melodrama remade in 1939 as *Risky Business*. Lew Ayres, Maureen O'Sullivan, Louis Calhern, Walter Catlett, Edward Arnold. Written by William Anthony McGuire; directed by Tay Garnett; for Universal. (GB title: *Penalty of Fame.*)

Okay for Sound*
GB 1937 85m bw
GFD / Gainsborough (Edward Black)

The Crazy Gang runs amok in a film studio. Patchy farce with music hall talents of the time.

w Marriott Edgar, Val Guest, R. P. Weston, Bert Lee *d* Marcel Varnel *ph* Jack Cox *md* Louis Levy

Bud Flanagan, Chesney Allen, Jimmy Nervo, Teddy Knox, Charlie Naughton, Jimmy Gold, Fred Duprez, Enid Stamp-Taylor, Graham Moffatt, Meinhart Maur, H. F. Maltby, Peter Dawson, The Radio Three, The Sherman Fisher Girls

Okinawa
US 1952 67m bw

Adventures of the gun crew of a Pacific destroyer. Routine war actioner with much newsreel padding. Pat O'Brien, Richard Denning, Cameron Mitchell, Rhys Williams. Written by Jameson Bewer, Arthur Ross, Leonard Stern; directed by Leigh Jason; for Columbia.

'A picture straight from the heart of America!'

Oklahoma!**
US 1955 143m Technicolor Todd-AO
Magna / Rodgers and Hammerstein (Arthur Hornblow Jnr)

A cowboy wins his girl despite the intervention of a sinister hired hand.
Much of the appeal of the musical was in its simple timeworn story and stylized sets; the film makes the first merely boring and the latter are replaced by standard scenery, not even of Oklahoma. The result is efficient rather than startling or memorable.

w Sonya Levien, William Ludwig, *'book'* Oscar Hammerstein, *play* Green Grow the Rushes by Lynn Riggs *d* Fred Zinnemann *ph* Robert Surtees *songs* Richard Rodgers, Oscar Hammerstein II *m* Robert Russell Bennett, Jay Blackton, Adolph Deutsch *pd* Oliver Smith

Gordon Macrae, Shirley Jones, Rod Steiger, Gloria Grahame, Charlotte Greenwood, Gene Nelson, Eddie Albert

AA: music score
AAN: Robert Surtees; Robert Russell Bennett, Jay Blackton, Adolph Deutsch

'A story of wooden derricks, iron men, and a defiant woman!'

Oklahoma Crude*
US 1973 111m Technicolor
Columbia / Stanley Kramer

In 1913, a drifting oil man stops to help a girl develop her rig.
Dour, downbeat melodrama with restricted action and much bad language; within its lights quite entertaining, but odd.

w Marc Norman *d* Stanley Kramer *ph* Robert Surtees *m* Henry Mancini *pd* Alfred Sweeney

Faye Dunaway, George C. Scott, John Mills, Jack Palance, Woodrow Parfrey

The Oklahoma Kid**
US 1939 80m bw
Warner (Samuel Bischoff)

During the settlement of the Cherokee Strip a cowboy avenges the unjust lynching of his father.
Competent but slightly disappointing star western memorable for the clash in this guise of its protagonists, more usually seen as gangsters.

w Warren Duff, Robert Buckner, Edward E. Paramore *d* Lloyd Bacon *ph* James Wong Howe *m* Max Steiner

James Cagney, Humphrey Bogart, Rosemary Lane, Donald Crisp, Harvey Stephens, Charles Middleton, Edward Pawley, Ward Bond

'Its b.o. potency will depend on Cagney's name and draw, rather than story or production, neither of which is commendable.'—*Variety*

'There's something entirely disarming about the way he has tackled horse opera, not pretending for a minute to be anything but New York's Jimmy Cagney all dressed up as a Robin Hood of the old west.'—*Frank Nugent*

The Oklahoman
US 1956 78m De Luxe Cinemascope

A widowed doctor becomes the subject of gossip when he takes an Indian girl for his housekeeper. Rather curious domestic western which erupts into action sequences but devotes too much time to talk and romance. Joel McCrea, Barbara Hale, Brad Dexter, Gloria Talbott, Michael Pate. Written by Daniel B. Ullman; directed by Francis D. Lyon; for Walter Mirisch / Allied Artists.

Old Acquaintance**
US 1943 110m bw
Warner (Henry Blanke)

Two jealous lady novelists interfere in each other's love lives.
A dated but rather splendid battle of the wild cats, with two stars fighting their way through a plush production and a rather overlong script.

w John Van Druten, Lenore Coffee, *play* John Van Druten *d* Vincent Sherman *ph* Sol Polito *m* Franz Waxman

Bette Davis, Miriam Hopkins, Gig Young, John Loder, Dolores Moran, Philip Reed, Roscoe Karns, Anne Revere

'The odd thing is that the two ladies and the director can make the whole business look fairly intelligent, detailed and plausible; and that on the screen such trash can seem, even, mature and adventurous.'—*James Agee*

'Trashy fun, on an unusually literate level.'—*New Yorker, 1978*

Old Bill and Son
GB 1940 96m bw

Too old for active duty, a veteran follows his son to Flanders. Ineffective screen version of a popular newspaper strip. Morland Graham, John Mills, Mary Clare, Renée Houston, Rene Ray, Roland Culver. Written by Bruce Bairnsfather and Ian Dalrymple, from Bairnsfather's cartoons; directed by Ian Dalrymple; for Legeran Films.

Old Bones of the River*
GB 1938 90m bw
GFD / Gainsborough (Edward Black)

A teacher in Africa accidentally quells a native rising.
Tediously funny star comedy; enough said.

w Marriott Edgar, Val Guest, J. O. C. Orton *character* Edgar Wallace *d* Marcel Varnel *ph* Arthur Crabtree *m* Louis Levy *ad Vetchinsky*

Will Hay, Moore Marriott, Graham Moffatt, Robert Adams, Jack Livesey

Old Boyfriends*
US 1978 103m Technicolor
Edward R. Pressman Productions (Paul Schrader)

A divorcee survives a nervous breakdown and goes on a journey of her past life to find out where she went wrong.
Low-key and somehow rather flat romantic odyssey, with interesting sequences and characters muted by the director's jaundiced eye.

w Paul and Leonard Schrader *d* Joan Tewkesbury *ph* William A. Fraker *m* David Shire

Talia Shire, Richard Jordan, John Belushi, Keith Carradine, John Houseman, Buck Henry, Bethel Leslie

The Old Curiosity Shop*
GB 1934 95m bw
BIP (Walter C. Mycroft)

The lives of a gambler and his granddaughter are affected by a miserly dwarf.
Heavy-going Dickens novel given reasonably rich production and well enough acted; sentimentality prevented a remake until the unsuccessful *Mister Quilp* (qv) in 1975.

w Margaret Kennedy, Ralph Neale, *novel* Charles Dickens *d* Thomas Bentley *ph* Claude Friese-Greene

Hay Petrie, Ben Webster, Elaine Benson, Beatrice Thompson, Gibb McLaughlin, Reginald Purdell, Polly Ward

The Old Dark House****
US 1932 71m bw
Universal (Carl Laemmle Jnr)

Stranded travellers take refuge in the house of a family of eccentrics.
Marvellous horror comedy filled with superb grotesques and memorable lines, closely based on a Priestley novel but omitting the more thoughtful moments. A stylist's and connoisseur's treat.

w Benn W. Levy, R. C. Sherriff, novel Benighted by *J. B. Priestley d James Whale ph Arthur Edeson ad Charles D. Hall*

Melvyn Douglas, Charles Laughton, Raymond Massey, Boris Karloff, Ernest Thesiger, Eva Moore, Gloria Stuart, Lilian Bond, Brember Wills, John Dudgeon (Elspeth Dudgeon)

'Somewhat inane, it's a cinch for trick ballyhooing. Better for the nabes than the big keys.'—*Variety*

'An unbridled camp fantasy directed with great wit.'—*Charles Higham*

'Each threat as it appears is revealed to be burlap and poster paint . . . despite storm, attempted rape and a remarkable final chase, the film is basically a confidence trick worked with cynical humour by a brilliant technician.'—*John Baxter, 1968*

'Basically a *jeu d'esprit* in which comedy of manners is edged into tragedy of horrors, the film never puts a foot wrong.'—*Tom Milne, MFB, 1978*

'The ghost doesn't walk in this family—it runs riot!'

The Old Dark House
GB 1962 86m Eastmancolor
Columbia / Hammer / William Castle

An American accepts an invitation to visit Femm Manor and finds the inhabitants either mad or homicidal.
A travesty which has nothing to do with the 1932 film and possesses no merit of its own. The cast is left floundering.

w Robert Dillon *d* William Castle *ph* Arthur Grant *m* Benjamin Frankel

Tom Poston, Janette Scott, Robert Morley, Joyce Grenfell, Mervyn Johns, Fenella Fielding, Peter Bull

'Come and meet a grand old sinner!'

Old English
US 1930 87m bw

In order to provide for his grandchildren, a financier makes certain illegal arrangements which involve his prearranged death.
Satisfying pattern play arranged for its star. *George Arliss,* Leon Janney, Doris Lloyd, Betty Lawford, Ivan Simpson. Written by Walter Anthony and Maude Howell, from the play by John Galsworthy; directed by Alfred E. Green; for Warner. 'Will call for most careful placement by chains and indies to draw the class trade it will only appeal to.'—*Variety*

'You dastard! Get thee hence or I shall smite thee in the puss!'

The Old-Fashioned Way*
US 1934 74m bw
Paramount / (William Le Baron)

Adventures of The Great McGonigle and his troupe of travelling players.
Period comedy tailored for its star and incorporating fragments of *The Drunkard.* Not so funny as it might be, but essential for students.

w Garnett Weston, Jack Cunningham, Charles Bogle (W. C. Fields) *d* William Beaudine *ph* Benjamin Reynolds *m* Harry Revel

W. C. Fields, Joe Morrison, Judith Allen, Jan Duggan, Jack Mulhall, Baby Leroy

Old Hutch
US 1936 80m bw

An idler finds a fortune but can't spend it because everybody knows he hasn't worked for years. Satisfactory star comedy. Wallace Beery, Elizabeth Patterson, Eric Linden, Cecilia Parker, Donald Meek, Virginia Grey. Written by George Kelly; directed by J. Walter Ruben; for MGM. 'Hasn't the backbone usually associated with Wallace Beery's vehicles. A nice light comedy which will doubtless garner fair box office.'—*Variety*

Old Iron
GB 1938 80m bw

A shipping magnate disowns his son for marrying against his will, but a car accident reconciles them. Very boring drama, an odd choice for this star, who can't cope with it. Tom Walls, Eva Moore, Cecil Parker, Richard Ainley, David Tree, Enid Stamp-Taylor. Written by Ben Travers; directed by Tom Walls; for TW Productions / British Lion.

The Old Maid**
US, 1939 95m bw
Warner (Henry Blanke)

When her suitor is killed in the Civil War, an unmarried mother lets her childless cousin bring up her daughter as her own.
A 'woman's picture' par excellence, given no-holds-barred treatment by all concerned but a little lacking in surprise.

w Casey Robinson, *play* Zoe Akins, *novel* Edith Wharton *d Edmund Goulding ph Tony Gaudio m* Max Steiner *md* Leo F. Forbstein

Bette Davis, Miriam Hopkins, George Brent, Jane Bryan, Donald Crisp, Louise Fazenda, Henry Stephenson, Jerome Cowan, William Lundigan, Rand Brooks

'Stagey, sombre and generally confusing fare. Must aim for the femme trade chiefly.'—*Variety*

'It is better than average and sticks heroically to its problem, forsaking all delights and filling a whole laundry bag with wet and twisted handkerchiefs.'—*Otis Ferguson*

'The picture isn't bad, but it trudges along and never becomes exciting.'—*New Yorker, 1977*

The Old Man and the Sea*
US 1958 89m Technicolor
Warner / Leland Hayward

An old fisherman dreams of hooking a great fish.
Expensive but poor-looking and stultifyingly dull one-character drama with variable production effects, a low key *Moby Dick.* Interesting but not effective.

w Peter Viertel from the novella by Ernest Hemingway *d* John Sturges *ph* James Wong Howe, Floyd Crosby, Tom Tutweiler, Larna Boren *m* Dimitri Tiomkin

Spencer Tracy, Felipe Pazos, Harry Bellaver

'A literary property about as suited for the movie medium as *The Love Song of J. Alfred Prufrock.*'—*Time*

THE OLD MAID. Clash of the Titans. Miriam Hopkins and Bette Davis.

'A strange amalgam of practically unassisted acting, good camerawork and editing, and a lot of special effects.'—*Ernest Callenbach, Film Quarterly*

'Tracy struggles valiantly with the endless monologues . . . misguided in the extreme.'—*Time Out, 1984*

'This is not a picture audiences are going to tear down the doors to see.'—*Motion Picture Herald*

AA: Dmitri Tiomkin
AAN: James Wong Howe; Spencer Tracy

Old Mother Riley

This Irish washerwoman with flailing arms and a nice line in invective was a music hall creation of Arthur Lucan, a variation of a pantomime dame. His wife Kitty Macshane played Mother Riley's daughter, and despite personal difficulties they were top of the bill for nearly 30 years. The films were very cheaply made and the padding is difficult to sit through, but Lucan at his best is a superb comedian: they were made for small independent companies such as Butcher's and usually directed by Maclean Rogers.

1937: OLD MOTHER RILEY
1938: OLD MOTHER RILEY IN PARIS
1939: OLD MOTHER RILEY MP, OLD MOTHER RILEY JOINS UP
1940: OLD MOTHER RILEY IN BUSINESS, OLD MOTHER RILEY'S GHOSTS
1941: OLD MOTHER RILEY'S CIRCUS
1942: OLD MOTHER RILEY IN SOCIETY
1943: OLD MOTHER RILEY DETECTIVE
1943: OLD MOTHER RILEY OVERSEAS
1944: OLD MOTHER RILEY AT HOME
1945: OLD MOTHER RILEY HEADMISTRESS
1947: OLD MOTHER RILEY'S NEW VENTURE
1949: OLD MOTHER RILEY'S JUNGLE TREASURE
1952: MOTHER RILEY MEETS THE VAMPIRE

Old Yeller*

US 1957 83m Technicolor
Walt Disney

The love of a boy for his dog.
Archetypal family movie set in a remote rural area.

w Fred Gipson, William Tubberg, *novel* Fred Gipson *d* Robert Stevenson *ph* Charles P. Boyle *m* Oliver Wallace

Dorothy McGuire, Fess Parker, Tommy Kirk, Kevin Corcoran, Jeff York, Chuck Connors

The Oldest Profession

France / West Germany / Italy 1967
115m Eastmancolor

Six sketches about prostitution. Very variable portmanteau, with moments of interest towards the end. Michele Mercier, Elsa Martinelli, Jeanne Moreau, Jean-Claude Brialy, Raquel Welch, Nadia Gray, Anna Karina. Written by Ennio Flaiano, Daniel Boulanger, Georges and André Tabet, Jean Aurenche, Jean-Luc Godard; directed by Franco Indovina, Mauro Bolognini, Philippe de Broca, Michel Pfleghar, Claude Autant-Lara, Jean-Luc Godard; for Gibe / Francoriz / Rialto / Rizzoli.

'Much much more than a musical!'
Oliver!***

GB 1968 146m Technicolor
Panavision 70
Columbia / Warwick / Romulus (John Woolf)

A musical version of *Oliver Twist.*
The last, perhaps, of the splendid film musicals which have priced themselves out of existence; it drags a little in spots but on the whole it does credit both to the show and the original novel, though eclipsed in style by David Lean's straight version.

w Vernon Harris, *play* Lionel Bart, *novel Charles Dickens d Carol Reed ph Oswald Morris m* Lionel Bart *md* John Green *pd John Box ch Onna White*

Ron Moody, Oliver Reed, Harry Secombe, *Mark Lester,* Shani Wallis, *Jack Wild,* Hugh Griffith, Joseph O'Conor, Leonard Rossiter, Hylda Baker, Peggy Mount, Megs Jenkins

'Only time will tell if it is a great film but it is certainly a great experience.'—*Joseph Morgenstern*

'There is a heightened discrepancy between the romping jollity with which everyone goes about his business and the actual business being gone about . . . such narrative elements as the exploitation of child labour, pimping, abduction, prostitution and murder combine to make *Oliver!* the most non-U subject ever to receive a U certificate.'—*Jan Dawson*

AA: best picture; Carol Reed; John Green
AAN: Vernon Harris; Oswald Morris; Ron Moody; Jack Wild

Oliver the Eighth

US 1933 20m bw

Ollie goes on a blind date, and the lady turns out to be homicidal. Star farce which never quite rises to the occasion; pleasant fooling but no more. Laurel and Hardy, Mae Busch, Jack Barty. Written by anon; directed by Lloyd French; for Hal Roach.

Oliver Twist****

GB 1948 116m bw
GFD / Cineguild (Ronald Neame)

A foundling falls among thieves but is rescued by a benevolent old gentleman.
Simplified, brilliantly cinematic version of a voluminous Victorian novel, beautiful to look at and memorably played, with every scene achieving the perfect maximum impact.

w David Lean, Stanley Haynes, novel Charles Dickens d David Lean ph Guy Green m Arnold Bax pd John Bryan

Alec Guinness, Robert Newton, Francis L. Sullivan, John Howard Davies, Kay Walsh, Anthony Newley, Henry Stephenson, Mary Clare, Gibb McLaughlin, Diana Dors

'A thoroughly expert piece of movie entertainment.'—*Richard Winnington*

'A brilliant, fascinating movie, no less a classic than the Dickens novel which it brings to life.'—*Time*

Oliver's Story
US 1978 92m Technicolor
Paramount (David V. Picker)

A sequel to *Love Story*, showing how Oliver succumbed to depression but finally found another girl friend.
Love means never having to watch this trendy rubbish.

w Erich Segal, John Korty *d* John Korty *ph* Arthur Ornitz *m* Francis Lai, Lee Holdridge

Ryan O'Neal, Candice Bergen, Nicola Pagett, Edward Binns, Ray Milland

Olly Olly Oxen Free
US 1978 93m Metrocolor
Rico Lion (Richard A. Colla)

A junkyard proprietress helps two young children to launch a decrepit hot-air balloon.
Simpleminded children's adventure with a surprising star.

w Eugene Poinc *d* Richard A. Colla *ph* Gayne Rescher *m* Bob Alcivar *pd* Peter Wooley

Katharine Hepburn, Kevin McKenzie, Dennis Dimster

Los Olvidados*
Mexico 1951 88m bw
Utramar / Oscar Dancigers
aka: *The Young and the Damned*

A good boy is contaminated by the young thugs in Mexico City's slums, and both he and his tormentor die violently.
Sober but penetrating analysis of social conditions leading to violence. The film was widely acclaimed, yet its very proficiency and excellent photography tend to glamorize its subject. Compare, however, the Hollywood resolutions of *Dead End*, on a similar subject.

w Luis Bunuel, Luis Alcoriza, Oscar Dancigers *d* Luis Bunuel *ph* Gabriel Figueroa *m* Gustavo Pitaluga

Alfonso Mejia, Miguel Inclan, Estela Inda, Roberto Cobo

Olympische Spiele***
Germany 1936 Part 1, 118m; Part 2, 107m bw
Leni Riefenstahl

An account of the Berlin Olympic Games.
This magnificent film is in no sense a mere reporting of an event. Camera movement, photography and editing combine with music to make it an experience truly olympian, especially in the introductory symbolic sequence suggesting the birth of the games. It was also, dangerously, a hymn to Nazi strength.

d, ed Leni Riefenstahl assistant Walter Ruttman *ph* Hans Ertl, Walter Franz and 42 others *m* Herbert Windt

'Here is the camera doing superbly what only the camera can do: refashioning the rhythms of the visible; of the moment seen.'—*Dilys Powell*

The Omaha Trail
US 1942 62m bw

The laying of train track across the west causes Indian wars. Brisk second feature western with good production values. James Craig, Dean Jagger, Edward Ellis, Chill Wills, Donald Meek, Pamela Blake, Howard da Silva. Written by Jesse Lasky Jnr and Hugo Butler; directed by Edward Buzzell; for MGM.

'One thousand years ago, Omar Khayyam was a poet, a scientist and military leader so great that an army of Assassins dedicated to world domination fell before his genius!'

Omar Khayyam
US 1956 101m Technicolor Vistavision
Paramount (Frank Freeman Jnr)

The Persian poet and philosopher defends his Shah against the Assassins.
Clean but dull Arabian Nights fantasy with pantomime sets and no humour.

w Barre Lyndon *d* William Dieterle *ph* Ernest Laszlo *m* Victor Young

Cornel Wilde, Michael Rennie, Raymond Massey, John Derek, Yma Sumac, Sebastian Cabot, Debra Paget

The Omega Man*
US 1971 98m Technicolor Panavision
Warner / Walter Seltzer

In 1977 a plague resulting from germ warfare has decimated the world's population; in Los Angeles, one man wages war against loathsome carriers of the disease.
'Realistic' version of a novel which was about vampires taking over, and was previously filmed unsatisfactorily as *The Last Man on Earth*. This nasty version rises to a few good action sequences but is bogged down by talk in between.

w John William Corrington and Joyce M. Corrington, *novel* I am Legend by Richard Matheson *d* Boris Sagal *ph* Russell Metty *m* Ron Grainer

Charlton Heston, Rosalind Cash, Anthony Zerbe

'Good morning. You are one day closer to the end of the world!'

The Omen**
US 1976 111m De Luxe Panavision
TCF (Harvey Bernhard)

The adopted child of an ambassador to Great Britain snows unnerving signs of being diabolically inspired.
Commercially successful variation on *The Exorcist*, quite professionally assembled and more enjoyable as entertainment than its predecessor.

w David Seltzer *d Richard Donner ph* Gil Taylor *m* Jerry Goldsmith

Gregory Peck, Lee Remick, David Warner, Billie Whitelaw, Leo McKern, Harvey Stevens, Patrick Troughton, Anthony Nicholls, Martin Benson

'A cut above the rest in that it has an ingenious premise, a teasingly labyrinthine development, a neat sting in its tail, and enough confidence in its own absurdities to carry them off.'—*David Robinson, The Times*

'Dreadfully silly . . . its horrors are not horrible, its terrors are not terrifying, its violence is ludicrous.'—*New York Times*

'More laughs than an average comedy.'—*Judith Crist*

'I did it strictly for the money.'—*David Seltzer*

† See *Damien: Omen II* and *The Final Conflict*.

†† Gregory Peck inherited his role from Charlton Heston, who turned it down.

AA: Jerry Goldsmith
AAN: song *'Ave Satani'*

On a Clear Day You Can See For Ever*
US 1970 129m Technicolor Panavision
Paramount (Howard Koch)

A psychiatric hypnotist helps a girl to stop smoking, and finds that in trances she remembers previous incarnations.
Romantic musical which tries, and fails, to substitute wispy charm for its original Broadway vitality. There are compensations.

w Alan Jay Lerner, from his play *d* Vincente Minnelli *ph* Harry Stradling *m* Burton Lane

Barbra Streisand, Yves Montand, Bob Newhart, Larry Blyden, Jack Nicholson, Simon Oakland

On an Island with You
US 1948 104m Technicolor
MGM (Joe Pasternak)

A film actress on location in the South Seas is chased by a naval officer.
Below par musical which far outstays its welcome.

w Dorothy Kingsley, Dorothy Cooper, Charles Martin, Hans Wilhelm *d* Richard Thorpe *ph* Charles Rosher *md* George Stoll

Esther Williams, Peter Lawford, Jimmy Durante, Ricardo Montalban, Cyd Charisse, Xavier Cugat and his Orchestra

On Approval***
GB 1943 80m bw
(GFD) Clive Brook

An Edwardian duke and an American heiress plan a chaperoned trial marriage in a remote Scottish castle.
Sparkling comedy of manners made even more piquant by careful casting and mounting; a minor delight.

w Clive Brook, Terence Young, play Frederick Lonsdale d Clive Brook ph C. Friese-Greene *m* William Alwyn

Clive Brook, Beatrice Lillie, Googie Withers, Roland Culver, O. B. Clarence, Lawrence Hanray, Hay Petrie

'Totally diverting, highly cinematic.'—*NFT, 1974*

'There has probably never been a richer, funnier anthology of late-Victorian mannerisms.'—*Time*

'I enjoyed it so thoroughly that I have to fight off superlatives.'—*James Agee*

† Also filmed in 1930 by Tom Walls for Herbert Wilcox, with Walls, Yvonne Arnaud, Winifred Shotter and Edmund Breon.

On Borrowed Time*
US 1939 98m bw
MGM (Sidney Franklin)

An old man refuses to die and chases Death up the apple tree.
Amiable, very American fantasy with much sentiment and several effective moments.

w Alice Duer Miller, Frank O'Neill, Claudine West, *novel* Lawrence Edward Watkin *d* Harold S. Bucquet *ph* Joseph Ruttenberg *m* Franz Waxman

Lionel Barrymore, Bobs Watson, Beulah Bondi, *Cedric Hardwicke* (as Mr Brink), Una Merkel, Ian Wolfe, Philip Terry, Eily Malyon

'General audiences may cotton to the novelty . . . artistically fine prestige production.'—*Variety*

'A weird, wild, totally unpredictable fantasy with dream sequences more like Bunuel than anything in the cinema.'—*John Russell Taylor, 1965*

On Dangerous Ground
US 1951 82m bw
RKO (John Houseman)

A tough cop falls in love with the blind sister of a mentally defective murderer.
Pretentious Hollywood *film noir* in the Gabin manner, partly redeemed by its glossy surface.

w A. I. Bezzerides, *novel* George Butler *d* Nicholas Ray *ph George E. Diskant* *m* Bernard Herrmann

Robert Ryan, Ida Lupino, Ward Bond, Ed Begley, Cleo Moore, Charles Kemper

On Dress Parade
US 1939 62m bw

The Dead End Kids go to military school. Cleaned-up comedy-drama, the last for the Kids before they split up. Billy Halop, Leo Gorcey, Huntz Hall, Bobby Jordan, Gabriel Dell, Bernard Punsley, John Litel, Frankie Thomas. Written by Tom Reed, Charles Balden; directed by William Clemens; for Warners. 'It just doesn't ring true. Dualler.'—*Variety*

On Friday at Eleven
West Germany / France / Italy 1960 93m bw
Corona / Criterion / Erredi (Alexander Gruter)
aka: *The World in My Pocket*

A cold-hearted gang plans to rob a heavily armoured American army truck.
Unsurprising but vaguely unpleasant thriller with nary a character left alive at the end.

w Frank Harvey, *novel* James Hadley Chase *d* Alvin Rakoff *ph* Vaclav Vich *m* Claude Bolling

Rod Steiger, Nadja Tiller, Peter Van Eyck, Jean Servais, Ian Bannen

'Growing up isn't easy at any age.'
On Golden Pond***
US 1981 109m colour
ITC / IPC (Bruce Gilbert)

An 80-year-old, his wife and his daughter spend a holiday at their New England lakeside cottage.
A film remarkable not so much for what it is—a well-acted, decent screen presentation of a rather waffling and sentimental play—as for the fact that in the sophisticated eighties enough people paid to see it to make it a box office record breaker. This was mainly due to affection for its star, whose last film it was, but also to an American desire for a reversion to the old values of warmth and humanity after the sex and violence which the screen had lately been offering.

w Ernest Thompson, from his play *d* Mark Rydell *ph* Billy Williams *m* Dave Grusin

Henry Fonda, Katharine Hepburn, Jane Fonda, Doug McKeon, Dabney Coleman

'Moments of truth survive some cloying contrivance; Rydell directs on bended knees.'—*Sight and Sound*

'Two of Hollywood's best-loved veterans deserve a far better swansong than this sticky confection.'—*Time Out*

'The kind of uplifting twaddle that traffics heavily in rather basic symbols: the gold light on the pond stands for the sunset of life, and so on.'—*Pauline Kael, New Yorker*

AA: Ernest Thompson; Henry Fonda; Katharine Hepburn

AAN: best film; Mark Rydell; editing (Robert L. Wolfe); Dave Grusin; Jane Fonda; Billy Williams

BFA: best actress (Katharine Hepburn)

On Her Majesty's Secret Service**
GB 1969 140m Technicolor Panavision
UA / Eon / Danilaq (Harry Saltzman, Albert R. Broccoli)

James Bond tracks down master criminal Blofeld in Switzerland.
Perhaps to compensate for no Sean Connery and a tragic ending, the producers of this sixth Bond opus shower largesse upon us in the shape of no fewer than four protracted and spectacular climaxes. Splendid stuff, but too much of it, and the lack of a happy centre does show.

w Richard Maibaum, *novel* Ian Fleming *d* Peter Hunt *ph* Michael Reed, Egil Woxholt, Roy Ford, John Jordan *m* John Barry *pd* Syd Cain

George Lazenby, Diana Rigg, Telly Savalas, Ilse Steppat, Gabriele Ferzetti, Yuri Borienko, Bernard Lee, Lois Maxwell

On Moonlight Bay**
US 1951 95m Technicolor
Warner (William Jacobs)

Family crises, to do with growing up and young love, in a 1917 Indiana town.
Pleasant musical, competently made, from the Penrod stories, with the emphasis switched to big sister.

w Melville Shavelson, Jack Rose, *stories* Booth Tarkington *d* Roy del Ruth *ph* Ernest Haller *md* Ray Heindorf

Doris Day, Gordon Macrae, Leon Ames, Rosemary de Camp, Billy Gray

† See also *By the Light of the Silvery Moon*, a companion piece.

On Our Merry Way*
US 1948 107m bw
Miracle Productions (Benedict Bogeaus, Burgess Meredith)
aka: *A Miracle Can Happen*

A reporter is urged by his wife to dig up some human interest stories.
Frail compendium of anecdotes which barely work.

w Laurence Stallings, *story* Arch Oboler *d* King Vidor, Leslie Fenton (also John Huston, George Stevens, uncredited) *ph* Joseph August, Gordon Avil, John Seitz, Edward Cronjager *m* Heinz Roemheld *md* David Chudnow, Skitch Henderson

Burgess Meredith, Paulette Goddard, Fred MacMurray, Hugh Herbert, James Stewart, Dorothy Lamour, Victor Moore, Henry Fonda, William Demarest

On Our Selection
Australia 1932 99m bw

The life of the Rudd family in rural Queensland. Predictable plot complications and loveable characters. Bert Bailey, Fred McDonald, Afreda Bevan, Jack McGowan. Written by Bert Bailey and Ken G. Hall; directed by Ken G. Hall; for Australasian Films. † Subsequent Rudd adventures included *Dad and Dave Come to Town* (1938) and *Dad Rudd M.P.* (1940).

On Stage Everybody
US 1945 65m bw

A vaudevillian helps youngsters put on a radio show. Tired musical support. Jack Oakie, Peggy Ryan, Johnny Coy, Julie London, Otto Kruger. Written by Warren Wilson and Oscar Brodney; directed by Jean Yarbrough; for Universal.

On Such a Night
US 1937 71m bw

Gangsters get caught in a Mississippi flood. Confusing action yarn which fizzles out before it gets going. Grant Richards, Roscoe Karns, Karen Morley, Eduardo Ciannelli, Alan Mowbray, Robert McWade. Written by Doris Malloy, William Lipman, and various hands; directed by E. A. Dupont; for Emmanuel Cohen / Paramount. 'So many baffling twists that the thread of the narrative is soon lost.'—*Variety*

On Such a Night*
GB 1955 37m Eastmancolor

An American is initiated into the splendours of Glyndebourne Opera. Modestly pleasing

documentary with fictionalized bookends.
David Knight, Josephine Griffin, Marie Lohr. Written by Paul Dehn; directed by Anthony Asquith; for Screen Audiences / Rank.

On the Avenue**
US 1937 89m bw
TCF (Gene Markey)

An heiress rages because she is being satirized in a revue, but later falls in love with the star.
Bright musical which keeps moving and uses its talents wisely.

w Gene Markey, William Conselman d Roy del Ruth ph Lucien Andriot *m / ly Irving Berlin ch* Seymour Felix

Dick Powell, Madeleine Carroll, The Ritz Brothers, George Barbier, Alice Faye, Walter Catlett, Joan Davis, E. E. Clive
Songs include 'He Ain't Got Rhythm'; 'The Girl on the Police Gazette'; 'This Year's Kisses'; 'I've Got My Love to Keep Me Warm'. The title song was dropped before release

'An amusing revue, with a pleasant score and a disarming informality in its production to lure us into liking it.'—*New York Times*

† Revamped as *Let's Make Love* (qv).

On the Beach**
US 1959 134m bw
United Artists / Stanley Kramer

When most of the world has been devastated by atomic waste, an American atomic submarine sets out to investigate.
Gloomy prophecy which works well in spasms but is generally too content to chat rather than imagine. A solid prestige job nevertheless.

w John Paxton, James Lee Barrett, *novel* Nevil Shute *d Stanley Kramer ph Giuseppe Rotunno, Daniel Fapp m* Ernest Gold *pd Rudolph Sternad*

Gregory Peck, Ava Gardner, *Fred Astaire,* Anthony Perkins, Donna Anderson, John Tate, Lola Brooks

'Its humanism is clearly of the order that seeks the support of a clamorous music score. The characters remain little more than spokesmen for timid ideas and Salvation Army slogans, their emotions hired from a Hollywood prop room; which is all pretty disturbing in a film about nothing less than the end of the world.'—*Robert Vas*

AAN: Ernest Gold

On the Beat
GB 1962 105m bw
Rank (Hugh Stewart)

A Scotland Yard car park attendant manages to capture some crooks and become a policeman.
Busy but flat comedy vehicle, never very likeable.

w Jack Davies *d* Robert Asher *ph* Geoffrey Faithfull *m* Philip Green

Norman Wisdom, Jennifer Jayne, Raymond Huntley, David Lodge

On the Black Hill*
GB 1987 117m Eastmancolor
BFI / Channel Four (Colin MacCabe)

Eighty years of a farming family on the Welsh borders.
Lyrical and often poignant account of the impact of history on rural life.

w,d Andrew Grieve, from novel by Bruce Chatwin *ph* Thaddeus O'Sullivan *m* Robert Lockhart *ad* Jocelyn James

Mike Gwilym, Robert Gwilym, Bob Peck, Gemma Jones

On the Buses
GB 1971 88m Technicolor
EMI / Hammer (Ronald Woolfe, Ronald Chesney)

Women drivers cause trouble at a bus depot.
Grotesque, ham-handed farce from a TV series which was sometimes funny; this is merely vulgar.

w Ronald Woolfe, Ronald Chesney *d* Harry Booth *ph* Mark MacDonald *m* Max Harris

Reg Varney, Doris Hare, Anna Karen, Michael Robbins, Stephen Lewis
† *Mutiny on the Buses* followed in 1972 and *Holiday on the Buses* in 1973. Both were deplorably witless.

On the Double*
US 1961 92m Technicolor Panavision
Paramount / Dena–Capri (Jack Rose)

During World War II, an American private is asked to impersonate a British intelligence officer.
From the plot and the talents it seems one might start laughing at this while still in the queue, but in fact most of it goes sadly awry and it never quite comes to the boil.

w Jack Rose, Melville Shavelson *d* Melville Shavelson *ph* Harry Stradling, Geoffrey Unsworth *m* Leith Stevens

Danny Kaye, Dana Wynter, Wilfrid Hyde White, Diana Dors, Margaret Rutherford, Allan Cuthbertson, Jesse White

On the Fiddle*
GB 1961 97m bw
Anglo-Amalgamated / S. Benjamin Fisz
US title: *Operation Snafu*

A wide boy and a slow-witted gypsy have comic and other adventures in the RAF.
Curious mixture of farce and action, more on American lines than British, but quite entertainingly presented.

w Harold Buchman, *novel* Stop at a Winner by R. F. Delderfield *d* Cyril Frankel *ph* Ted Scaife *m* Malcolm Arnold

Alfred Lynch, Sean Connery, Cecil Parker, Wilfrid Hyde White, Kathleen Harrison, Alan King, Eleanor Summerfield, Eric Barker, Terence Longdon, John Le Mesurier, Harry Locke

On the Night of the Fire*
GB 1939 94m bw
GFD / G & S (Josef Somlo)
US title: *The Fugitive*

A barber kills the blackmailer of his wife.
Dour little drama, rather unusual for pre-war British studios.

w Brian Desmond Hurst, Terence Young, *novel* F. L. Green *d* Brian Desmond Hurst *ph* Gunther Krampf

Ralph Richardson, Diana Wynyard, Romney Brent, Mary Clare, Henry Oscar, Frederick Leister

'The kind of film either liked very much or very little . . . absorbingly entertaining, and b.o. should profit considerably by word of mouth.'—*Variety*

On the Riviera**
US 1951 90m Technicolor
TCF (Sol C. Siegel)

A cabaret artist is persuaded to pose as a philandering businessman.
Remake of *Folies Bergère* and *That Night in Rio* (see also *On the Double*); disliked at the time and accused of tastelessness, it now seems smarter and funnier than comparable films of its era.

w Valentine Davies, Phoebe and Henry Ephron *d Walter Lang ph* Leon Shamroy *m* Alfred Newman

Danny Kaye, Corinne Calvet, Gene Tierney, Marcel Dalio, Jean Murat

AAN: Alfred Newman

On the Threshold of Space
US 1956 96m Eastmancolor Cinemascope
TCF (William Bloom)

The USAF medical corps explores human reactions at high altitudes.
Semi-documentary flagwaver with dreary domestic asides; very dated now, and of no particular nostalgic interest.

w Simon Wincelberg, Francis Cockrill *d* Robert D. Webb *ph* Joe MacDonald *m* Lyn Murray

Guy Madison, Virginia Leith, John Hodiak, Dean Jagger, Warren Stevens

On the Town****
US 1949 98m Technicolor
MGM (*Arthur Freed*)

Three sailors enjoy twenty-four hours' leave in New York.
Most of this brash location musical counts as among the best things ever to come out of Hollywood; the serious ballet towards the end tends to kill it, but it contains much to be grateful for.

w Betty Comden, Adolph Green, ballet Fancy Free by Leonard Bernstein *d / ch Gene Kelly, Stanley Donen ph Harold Rosson md* Lennie Hayton, Roger Edens *songs* various

Gene Kelly, Frank Sinatra, Jules Munshin, Vera-Ellen, Betty Garrett, Ann Miller, Tom Dugan, Florence Bates, Alice Pearce

'A film that will be enjoyed more than twice.'—*Lindsay Anderson*

'So exuberant that it threatens at moments to bounce right off the screen.'—*Time*

'The speed, the vitality, the flashing colour and design, the tricks of timing by which motion is fitted to music, the wit and invention and superlative technical accomplishment make it a really exhilarating experience.'—*Richard Mallett, Punch*

AA: Lennie Hayton, Roger Edens

On the Twelfth Day*
GB 1956 23m Eastmancolor

A balletic presentation of the song about the twelve days of Christmas, with plenty of maids a'milking and lords a'leaping. A refreshing and extravagant novelty. Wendy Toye, Franklin Bennett, David O'Brien. Written by James Matthews and Val Valentine; directed by *Wendy Toye*; for George K. Arthur / Bahamian.

On the Waterfront***
US 1954 108m bw
Columbia / Sam Spiegel

After the death of his brother, a young stevedore breaks the hold of a waterfront gang boss.
Intense, broody dockside thriller with 'method' performances; very powerful of its kind, and much imitated.

w Budd Schulberg, from his novel *d Elia Kazan ph Boris Kaufman m* Leonard Bernstein *ad* Richard Day

Marlon Brando, Eva Marie Saint, *Lee J. Cobb*, Rod Steiger, Karl Malden, Pat Henning, Leif Erickson, James Westerfield, John Hamilton

'An uncommonly powerful, exciting and imaginative use of the screen by gifted professionals.'—*New York Times*

'A medley of items from the Warner gangland pictures of the thirties, brought up to date.'—*Steven Sondheim, Films in Review*
† Sample dialogue: 'Charlie, oh Charlie, you don't understand. I coulda had class. I coulda been a contender.'

AA: best picture; Budd Schulberg; Elia Kazan; Boris Kaufman; Richard Day; Marlon Brando; Eva Marie Saint
AAN: Leonard Bernstein; Lee J. Cobb; Rod Steiger; Karl Malden

On Trial
US 1939 60m bw

A man kills his wife's lover and is put on trial for murder. Dozy film version of a once sensational play. John Litel, Margaret Lindsay, Edward Norris, James Stephenson. Written by Don Ryan from the play by Elmer Rice; directed by Terry Morse; for Warners. 'Strictly dual fodder, talking along for an hour without going anywhere.'—*Variety*

On with the Show
US 1929 98m Technicolor (two-colour)
Warner

Crude early talkie musical revue with historical interest.

w Robert Lord, *play* Shoestring by Humphrey Pearson *d* Alan Crosland *ph* Tony Gaudio *ch* Larry Ceballos *songs* Grant Clarke, Harry Akst

Betty Compson, Louise Fazenda, Sally O'Neil, Joe E. Brown, Ethel Waters, Arthur Lake

On Your Toes*
US 1939 94m bw
Warner (Robert Lord)

Backstage jealousies at the ballet.
Smooth film version of a top Broadway show of its time.

w Jerry Wald, Richard Macaulay, *play* George Abbott *d* Ray Enright *ph* James Wong Howe, Sol Polito *m / ly Richard Rodgers, Lorenz Hart*

Vera Zorina, Eddie Albert, Alan Hale, Frank McHugh, James Gleason, Donald O'Connor, Gloria Dickson

'Box office prospects appear to be pretty good, but more than the average campaigning should be indulged.'—*Variety*

Once a Crook
GB 1941 81m bw

A publican with a shady past helps his son who is in trouble with the law. Low-key character comedy for two stars who would benefit from a greater tendency to farce. Gordon Harker, Sydney Howard, Frank Pettingell, Carla Lehmann, Bernard Lee, Kathleen Harrison, Cyril Cusack. Written by Roger Burford, from the play by Evadne Price and Ken Attiwill; directed by Herbert Mason; for TCF.

Once a Jolly Swagman*
GB 1948 100m bw
GFD / Wessex (Ian Dalrymple)
US title: *Maniacs on Wheels*

A factory worker becomes a speedway rider. Competent sporting drama of no particular interest.

w William Rose, Jack Lee *d* Jack Lee *ph* H. E. Fowle *m* Bernard Stevens

Dirk Bogarde, Renée Asherson, Bonar Colleano, Bill Owen

Once a Lady
US 1931 65m bw

An illegitimate baby grows up to meet her mother without recognizing her. A plot that was often tried out during the early thirties, seldom more boringly than on this occasion. Ruth Chatterton, Ivor Novello, Jill Esmond, Geoffrey Kerr, Doris Lloyd. Written by Zoe Akins and Samuel Hoffenstein from the play The Second Life by Rudolf Bernauer and Rudolf Oesterreicher; directed by Guthrie McClintic; for Paramount. 'Another crying towel special.'—*Variety*

Once a Sinner
US 1930 71m bw

A girl criminal reforms but almost loses the love of her new boy friend when he finds out about her past. Transparent melodrama, strictly for indulgent ladies. Dorothy Mackail, Joel McCrea, John Halliday, C. Henry Gordon, Ilka Chase, Clara Blandick, George Brent. 'Slow drama that needs plenty of support.'—*Variety*

Once a Sinner
GB 1950 80m bw

A girl with a shady past finds her husband is being threatened by her ex-partner. Uninteresting character melodrama which defeats its lightweight stars. Pat Kirkwood, Jack Watling, Joy Shelton, Sidney Tafler, Thora Hird. Written by David Evans, from the novel *Irene* by Ronald Marsh; directed by Lewis Gilbert; for John Argyle / Butcher.

Once a Thief
US 1965 107m bw Panavision
MGM / Cipra / RN / Fred Engel (Jacques Bar)

An ex-convict is hounded by a vengeful cop. Glum crime melodrama gleamingly photographed but otherwise quite routine.

w Zekial Marko *d* Ralph Nelson *ph Robert Burks m* Lalo Schifrin

Alain Delon, Ann-Margret, Van Heflin, Jack Palance, John David Chandler

Once Before I Die
US 1966 97m Eastmancolor
F.8 Productions (John Derek)

In the Philippines, after a Jap aerial attack, a cavalry major's girl friend causes complications in her bids to escape.
Mildly hilarious action melodrama in which the star's superstructure is made the focus of the action.

w Vance Skarstedt *d* John Derek *ph* Arthur Arling *m* Emmanuel Vardi

Ursula Andress, John Derek, Richard Jaeckel, Rod Lauren

Once Bitten
US 1985 93m Metrocolor

Teenage sex problems are complicated by a visiting vampiress who needs the blood of a virgin three times before Hallowe'en. Dispiriting attempt to mix genres without even a tinge of talent or sophistication. Lauren Hutton, Jim Carrey, Karen Kopins, Cleavon Little. Written by David Hines, Jeffrey Hause, Jonathan Roberts; directed by Howard Storm; for Villard-Wald-Hilderbrand.

'Mr Storm might have found his ideas for the tone of this movie written on high school locker walls.'—*People*

Once in a Blue Moon
US 1936 (produced 1934) 65m bw

Adventures of an innocent abroad in contemporary Russia. Would-be satire which was seen by very few people indeed. Jimmy Savo, Nikita Balieff, Whitney Bourne, Cecilia Loftus. Written and directed by Ben Hecht and Charles MacArthur; for Paramount. 'A dud. The exhibitors who are kidded into playing it won't be very happy afterwards.'—*Variety*

Once in a Lifetime*
US 1933 80m approx bw
Universal (Carl Laemmle Jnr)

How a script was sold in old-time Hollywood. Half good-humoured, half-scathing satire on Hollywood; technique dated, content still amusing.

w Seton I. Miller, *play* Moss Hart, George S. Kaufman *d* Russell Mack *ph* George Robinson

Jack Oakie, Sidney Fox, Aline MacMahon, Russell Hopton, Zasu Pitts, Louise Fazenda, Gregory Ratoff, Onslow Stevens
'Idol-smashing satire, strictly for the initiated.'—*Variety*

Once in Paris
US 1978 100m TVC color
A naïve American writer is introduced to the delights of Paris by a worldly chauffeur and an amorous British noblewoman. A movie that adds up to very little, but pleases along the way. Wayne Rogers, Gayle Hunnicutt, Jack Lenoir, Philippe Hart, Tanya Lopert. Written and directed by Frank D. Gilroy, for his own company.

'The darkest alleys of love among the international set!'
Once Is Not Enough
US 1975 122m Movielab Panavision
Paramount / Sujac / Aries (Howard W. Koch)
aka: *Jacqueline Susann's Once Is Not Enough*
The daughter of a movie producer is corrupted by his circle.
Old-fashioned jet-set melodrama with new-fashioned sexual novelties.
w Julius J. Epstein, *novel* Jacqueline Susann *d* Guy Green *ph* John A. Alonzo *m* Henry Mancini *pd* John de Cuir
Kirk Douglas, Alexis Smith, David Janssen, George Hamilton, Melina Mercouri, Gary Conway, Brenda Vaccaro, Deborah Raffin
AAN: Brenda Vaccaro

Once More My Darling
US 1949 92m bw
Universal (Joan Harrison)
A young girl is romantically pursued by an older man.
Tame comedy.
w Robert Carson *d* Robert Montgomery *ph* Franz Planer *m* Elizabeth Firestone
Robert Montgomery, Ann Blyth, Jane Cowl, Taylor Holmes, Charles McGraw

Once More with Feeling
GB 1960 92m Technicolor
Columbia / Stanley Donen
The volatile private life of an orchestral conductor.
Thin comedy from a West End play, something between a shouting match and a fashion show.
w Harry Kurnitz, from his play *d* Stanley Donen *ph* Georges Périnal *md* Muir Mathieson *pd* Alexander Trauner
Yul Brynner, Kay Kendall, Geoffrey Toone, Maxwell Shaw, Mervyn Johns, Martin Benson, Gregory Ratoff

Once to Every Woman
US 1934 70m bw
A young doctor saves a patient's life by pushing his ailing chief aside during an operation. Tedious, routine hospital stuff. Walter Connolly, Ralph Bellamy, Fay Wray, Mary Carlisle, Walter Byron. Written by Jo Swerling from a story by A. J. Cronin; directed by Lambert Hillyer; for Columbia. 'A programmer which won't make the grade in key houses.'—*Variety*

Once Upon a Dream
GB 1948 84m bw
An officer's wife has a romantic dream about her husband's batman, and comes to believe it true. Very wispy comedy which does none of its principals any good. Googie Withers, Griffith Jones, Guy Middleton, Raymond Lovell, Hubert Gregg. Written by Patrick Kirwan and Victor Katona; directed by Ralph Thomas; for Triton / Rank.

Once Upon a Honeymoon*
US 1942 116m bw
RKO (Leo McCarey)
An American radio correspondent and an ex-burlesque queen cheat the Nazis—and her husband—in Europe during World War II.
Smooth but curious mixture of comedy and drama, a satisfactory but unmemorable star vehicle.
w Sheridan Gibney, Leo McCarey *d* Leo McCarey *ph* George Barnes *m* Robert Emmett Dolan
Cary Grant, Ginger Rogers, Walter Slezak, Albert Dekker, Albert Bassermann, Ferike Boros, Harry Shannon
'The attempt to play for both laughs and significance against a terrifying background of Nazi aggression is on the whole a little disappointing.'—*Newsweek*

Once Upon a Horse
US 1958 85m bw Cinemascope
Two cowboys steal a herd of cattle but can't afford to feed them. Unprepossessing comedy vehicle for a team which found success only on television. Dan Rowan, Dick Martin, Martha Hyer, Leif Erickson, Nita Talbot, James Gleason. Written, directed and produced by Hal Kanter; for Universal.

Once Upon a Time*
US 1944 89m bw
Columbia (Louis Edelman)
A luckless producer makes a sensation out of a boy and his dancing caterpillar.
Thin whimsical comedy, too slight to come off given such standard treatment, but with nice touches along the way.
w Lewis Meltzer, Oscar Saul, *radio play* My Client Curley by Norman Corwin, Lucille F. Herrmann *d* Alexander Hall *ph* Franz Planer *m* Frederick Hollander
Cary Grant, Janet Blair, James Gleason, Ted Donaldson, Howard Freeman, William Demarest, Art Baker, John Abbott
'There just isn't enough material here for a full-length feature.'—*Philip T. Hartung*
'It would be nice to see some screen fantasy if it were done by anyone with half a heart, mind and hand for it. But when the studios try to make it, duck and stay hid till the mood has passed.'—*James Agee*

'As boys they said they would die for each other. As men, they did.'
Once Upon a Time in America*
US 1984 228m (also in 147m version) Technicolor
Warner / Embassy / Ladd / PSO (Arnon Milchan)
The lives of four gangsters between 1922 and 1968.
Vast, sprawling, violent crime saga with a pretentious approach and a confusing time scheme. Some scenes have great power but the total effect is overwhelming in the wrong way.
w Leonardo Benvenuti, Piero de Bernardi, Enrico Medioli, Franco Arcalli, Franco Ferrini, Sergio Leone, from The Hoods by David Aaronson ('Harry Grey') *d Sergio Leone* *ph* Tonino Delli Colli *m* Ennio Morricone *ed* Nino Baragli
Robert de Niro, James Woods, Elizabeth McGovern, Treat Williams, Tuesday Weld, Burt Young, Danny Aiello, William Forsythe
'It is, finally, a heart-breaking story of mutual need. By matching that need with his own need to come to terms with his own cultural memories, Leone has made his most oneiric and extraordinary film.'—*Tony Rayns, MFB*
BFA: music

Once Upon a Time in the West*
Italy / US 1969 165m Techniscope
Paramount / Rafran / San Marco (Fulvio Morsella)
A lonely woman in the old west is in danger from a band of gunmen.
Immensely long and convoluted epic western marking its director's collaboration with an American studio and his desire to make serious statements about something or other. Beautifully made, empty, and very violent.
w Sergio Leone, Sergio Donati *d* Sergio Leone *ph* Tonino Delli Colli *m* Ennio Morricone
Henry Fonda, Claudia Cardinale, Jason Robards, Charles Bronson, Gabriele Ferzetti, Keenan Wynn, Paolo Stoppa, Lionel Stander, Jack Elam, Woody Strode
† This film has the longest credits of all: they sprawl through the first twelve minutes.

The One and Only
US 1978 98m Movielab
Paramount / First Artists (Steve Gordon, David V. Picker)
A stage-struck egomaniac finds success at the expense of happiness with his wife.
Uneasy mixture of farce and sentiment intended as a star vehicle, but not a very successful one.
w Steve Gordon *d* Carl Reiner *ph* Victor J. Kemper *m* Patrick Williams
Henry Winkler, Kim Darby, Gene Saks, William Daniels, Polly Holiday, Herve Villechaize, Harold Gould, Richard Lane

The One and Only Genuine Original Family Band
US 1968 110m Technicolor

Adventures of a Republican family at the 1888 convention. Long and rather muddled family comedy with politics and music; not a winner anywhere. Walter Brennan, Buddy Ebsen, John Davidson, Lesley Ann Warren, Janet Blair, Kurt Russell, Richard Deacon. Written by Lowell S. Hawley from a book by Laura Bower Van Nuys; directed by Michael O'Herlihy; for Disney.

One Body Too Many
US 1944 74m bw

An insurance salesman arrives at a spooky house to find his prospect murdered. Comedy melodrama which could have been a lot funnier and more melodramatic; once more, the butler didn't do it. Jack Haley, Bela Lugosi, Jean Parker, Bernard Nedell, Blanche Yurka, Douglas Fowley, Lyle Talbot. Written by Winston Miller and Maxwell Shane; directed by Frank McDonald; for Pine-Thomas/Paramount.

One Brief Summer
GB 1969 86m Eastmancolor
TCF / Twickenham (Guido Coen)

A wealthy man loses interest in his mistress and begins courting his daughter's friend.
Odd, downbeat melodrama with hints of incest; a sophisticated time-passer.

w Wendy Marshall, *play* Valkyrie's Armour by Harry Tierney *d* John Mackenzie *ph* David MacDonald *m* Roger Webb

Clifford Evans, Felicity Gibson, Jennifer Hilary, Jan Holden, Peter Egan, Fanny Carby, Richard Vernon, Brian Wilde

One Day in the Life of Ivan Denisovich*
GB 1971 105m Eastmancolor
Group W / Leontes / Norsk (Caspar Wrede)

Life in a Siberian labour camp in 1950.
A fairly successful book adaptation, as far as mere pictures can cope with the harrowing detail.

w Ronald Harwood, *novel* Alexander Solzhenitsyn *d* Caspar Wrede *ph Sven Nykvist* *m* Arne Nordheim

Tom Courtenay, Espen Skjonberg, James Maxwell, Alfred Burke, Eric Thompson, Matthew Guinness

'The film's general air of earnestness deflects rather than stimulates involvement.'—*David Wilson*

One Deadly Summer*
France 1983 133m Eastmancolor

In a Provençal village, a girl's strange behaviour turns out to have a revenge motive. Complex and overlong thriller which loses most of its interest once one knows what it is about. Written by Sébastien Japrisot, from his novel; directed by Jean Becker; for SNC / CAPAC / TFI. 'That the film could have been worse does not make it any better.'—*Gilbert Adair, MFB*. (Original title: *L'Eté Meurtrier*.)

One Desire
US 1955 94m Technicolor
U-I (Ross Hunter)

The romantic career of the lady owner of a gambling saloon.
Tawdry nineties drama which never really gets going.

w Lawrence Roman, Robert Blees, *novel* Tacey Cromwell by Conrad Richter *d* Jerry Hopper *ph* Maury Gertsman *m* Frank Skinner *md* Joseph Gershenson

Anne Baxter, Rock Hudson, Julia Adams, Natalie Wood, Barry Curtis, William Hopper, Carl Benton Reid

'The standards of writing and characterization belong to a Victorian servant girl's paper-covered romance.'—*MFB*

One Exciting Night
GB 1944 89m bw

A singing welfare worker averts a plan to steal a Rembrandt. Very ho-hum stuff for a very popular but histrionically untried star. Vera Lynn, Donald Stewart, Mary Clare, Frederick Leister, Richard Murdoch. Written by Howard Irving Young, Peter Fraser, Margaret Kennedy and Emery Bonnet; directed by Walter Forde; for Columbia British.

One Eyed Jacks
US 1961 141m Technicolor Vistavision
Paramount / Pennebaker (Frank P. Rosenberg)

An outlaw has a running battle with an old friend.
Grossly self-indulgent western controlled (unwisely) by its star, full of solemn pauses and bouts of violence.

w Guy Trosper, Calder Willingham, *novel* The Authentic Death of Hendry Jones by Charles Neider *d* Marlon Brando *ph* Charles Lang Jnr *m* Hugo Friedhofer

Marlon Brando, Karl Malden, Pina Pellicier, Katy Jurado, Slim Pickens, Ben Johnson, Timothy Carey, Elisha Cook Jnr

AAN: Charles Lang Jnr

One Flew over the Cuckoo's Nest***
US 1975 134m De Luxe
UA / Fantasy Films (Paul Zaentz, Michael Douglas)

A cheerful immoralist imprisoned for rape is transferred for observation to a state mental hospital.
Wildly and unexpectedly commercial film of a project which had lain dormant for fourteen years, this amusing and horrifying film conveniently sums up anti-government attitudes as well as make love not war and all that. It's certainly impossible to ignore.

w Laurence Hauben, Bo Goldman, *novel Ken Kesey* *d Milos Forman* *ph* Haskell Wexler *m* Jack Nitzche *pd* Paul Sylbert

Jack Nicholson, Louise Fletcher, William Redfield, Will Sampson, Brad Dourif, Christopher Lloyd

'Lacks the excitement of movie art, but the story and the acting make the film emotionally powerful.'—*New Yorker*

AA: best picture; script; Milos Forman; Jack Nicholson; Louise Fletcher
AAN: Haskell Wexler; Jack Nitzche; Brad Dourif

One Foot in Heaven*
US 1941 108m bw
Warner (Robert Lord, Irving Rapper)

The small-town doings of a methodist minister.
Slow but pleasing chronicle, nicely assembled.

w Casey Robinson, *biography* (of his father) Hartzell Spence *d* Irving Rapper *ph* Charles Rosher *m* Max Steiner

Fredric March, Martha Scott, Beulah Bondi, Gene Lockhart, Elizabeth Fraser, Harry Davenport, Laura Hope Crews, Grant Mitchell, Moroni Olsen, Ernest Cossart, Jerome Cowan

'A clean, sweet, decent picture.'—*Cecilia Ager*

AAN: best picture

One Foot in Hell
US 1960 89m De Luxe Cinemascope
TCF (Sydney Boehm)

The sheriff of a small western town is secretly plotting revenge on the townsfolk for their long-ago treatment of his wife.
Unusual western suspenser with plenty of violent action and an extremely equivocal hero.

w Aaron Spelling, Sydney Boehm *d* James B. Clark *ph* William C. Mellor *m* Dominic Frontière

Alan Ladd, Dan O'Herlihy, Don Murray, Dolores Michaels, Barry Coe, Larry Gates, John Alexander

One Frightened Night
US 1935 67m bw

Relatives assemble in a spooky house in the hope of inheriting an old man's wealth. Low-budget thriller that sometimes seems like a spoof of *The Cat and the Canary*. Charles Grapewin, Mary Carlisle, Arthur Hohl, Evalyn Knapp, Wallace Ford, Hedda Hopper, Lucien Littlefield, Regis Toomey, Rafaela Ottiano. Written by Wellyn Totman; directed by Christy Cabanne; for Mascot.

One from the Heart*
US 1982 101m Metrocolor
Zoetrope Studios (Gray Frederickson, Fred Roos, Armyan Bernstein)

On Independence Day in Las Vegas, a pair of lovers quarrel and make up.
Extraordinarily slim (for its cost) romantic fantasy which makes one wonder why, of all stories in the world, its creator chose this one. It does however boast attractive visuals.

w Armyan Bernstein, Francis Coppola *d* Francis Coppola *ph* Vittorio Storaro *m* Tom Waits *pd* Dean Tavoularis

Frederic Forrest, Teri Garr, Raul Julia, Nastassja Kinski, Lainie Kazan, Harry Dean Stanton

'Giddy heights of visual imagination and technical brilliance are lavished on a wafer-thin story.'—*Variety*

'If this is the essence of cinema, then Salvador Dali is the essence of painting.'—*Sunday Times*

'A very beautiful film, the background of which totally drowns a wafer-thin plot. A musical non-musical, a spectacular non-spectacular, a fantasy with realist aspirations.'—*Guardian*

'Escapism running away with itself.'—*Standard*

AAN: original song score

One Good Turn
US 1931 20m bw

Two odd job men see their benefactress rehearsing a play, and think she is really being evicted. Moderate star comedy with nice moments. Laurel and Hardy, Mary Carr, Billy Gilbert. Written by H. M. Walker; directed by James W. Horne; for Hal Roach.

One Good Turn
GB 1954 90m bw
GFD / Two Cities (Maurice Cowan)

An orphan stays on to become an odd job man, and tries to raise money to buy an old car.
The star's second comedy is an almost unmitigated disaster, disjointed and depending too much on pathos.

w Maurice Cowan, John Paddy Carstairs, Ted Willis *d* John Paddy Carstairs *ph* Jack Cox *m* John Addison

Norman Wisdom, Joan Rice, Shirley Abicair, Thora Hird, William Russell, Richard Caldicot

One Heavenly Night
US 1930 82m bw

A flower girl in a Budapest music hall finds herself imitating the absent star. Would-be-Lubitsch-like musical comedy which doesn't quite succeed in its pleasant aims. Evelyn Laye, John Boles, Leon Errol, Lilyan Tashman, Hugh Cameron, Lionel Belmore. Written by Sidney Howard from a story by Louis Bromfield; directed by George Fitzmaurice; for Samuel Goldwyn. 'It will satisfy the customers, but lacks the intrinsic quality that makes 'em talk and recommends it as an entertainment for big grosses.'—*Variety*

'Gayest screen event of the year!'
One Hour with You***
US 1932 84m bw
Paramount (*Ernst Lubitsch*)

The affairs of a philandering Parisian doctor.
Superbly handled comedy of manners in Lubitsch's most inventive form, handled by a most capable cast. Unique entertainment of a kind which is, alas, no more.

w Samson Raphaelson, play Only a Dream by Lothar Schmidt *d George Cukor, Ernst Lubitsch ph* Victor Milner *m Oscar Straus, Richard Whiting ly Leo Robin ad Hans Dreier*

Maurice Chevalier, Jeanette MacDonald, Genevieve Tobin, Roland Young, Charles Ruggles, George Barbier

'Sure fire if frothy screen fare, cinch b.o. at all times.'—*Variety*

'A brand new form of musical entertainment . . . he has mixed verse, spoken and sung, a smart and satiric musical background, asides to the audience, and sophisticated dialogue, as well as lilting and delightful songs . . . The result is something so delightful that it places the circle of golden leaves jauntily upon the knowing head of Hollywood's most original director.'—*Philadelphia Inquirer*

† A remake of Lubitsch's silent success *The Marriage Circle.*

AAN: best picture

One Hundred and One Dalmatians***
US 1961 79m Technicolor
Walt Disney

The dogs of London help save puppies which are being stolen for their skins by a cruel villainess.
Disney's last really splendid feature cartoon, with the old flexible style cleverly modernized and plenty of invention and detail in the story line. The London backgrounds are especially nicely judged.

w Bill Peet, *novel* Dodie Smith *d* Wolfgang Reitherman, Hamilton S. Luske, Clyde Geronimi

120 Days of Sodom
Italy / France 1975 117m Technicolor

After the Italian campaign of 1944, four local dignitaries marry each other's daughters, withdraw with a bevy of nubile girls to a mountain retreat, and tell each other sado-masochistic sexual adventures. Thoroughly revolting and much banned piece with no perceptible point but a good deal of emetic detail. Paolo Bonacelli, Giorgio Cataldi, Uberto P. Quintavalle, Aldo Valetti. Written and directed by Pier Paolo Pasolini, from the novel by the Marquis de Sade; for PEA / PAA.

One Hundred Men and a Girl***
US 1937 84m bw
Universal (*Joe Pasternak*)

A young girl persuades a great conductor to form an orchestra of unemployed musicians.
Delightful and funny musical fable, an instance of the Pasternak formula of sweetness and light at its richest and best.

w Bruce Manning, Charles Kenyon, Hans Kraly d Henry Koster ph Joseph Valentine *m* Charles Previn *songs* various

Deanna Durbin, Adolphe Menjou, Leopold Stokowski, Alice Brady, Mischa Auer, Eugene Pallette, Billy Gilbert, Alma Kruger, Jed Prouty, Frank Jenks, Christian Rub

'Smash hit for all the family . . . something new in entertainment.'—*Variety*

'Apart from its value as entertainment, which is considerable, it reveals the cinema at its sunny-sided best.'—*New York Times.*

'An original story put over with considerable skill.'—*Monthly Film Bulletin*

AA: Charles Previn
AAN: best picture; original story (Hans Kraly)

100 Rifles*
US 1969 109m De Luxe
TCF / Marvin Schwartz

In war-torn Mexico, a black American sheriff and his prisoner become involved in a girl's fight for vengeance after her father's death.
Blood-soaked adventure with plenty of tough action and tight pace. A little too purposeful in its unpleasantness to be very entertaining.

w Clair Huffaker, Tom Gries, *novel* Robert MacLeod *d Tom Gries ph* Cecilio Paniagua *m* Jerry Goldsmith

Jim Brown, Raquel Welch, Burt Reynolds, Fernando Lamas, Dan O'Herlihy, Hans Gudegast

One in a Million**
US 1936 94m bw
TCF (Raymond Griffith)

The daughter of a Swiss innkeeper becomes an Olympic ice-skating champion.
Sonja Henie's film debut shows Hollywood at its most professional, making entertainment out of the purest moonshine with considerable injections of novelty talent.

w Lenore Praskins, Mark Kelly *d* Sidney Lanfield *ph* Edward Cronjager *md* Louis Silvers *songs* Sidney Mitchell, Lew Pollack

Sonja Henie, Don Ameche, *The Ritz Brothers*, Jean Hersholt, Ned Sparks, Arline Judge, Dixie Dunbar, Borrah Minnevitch and his Rascals, Montagu Love

'A very entertaining, adroitly mixed concoction of romance, music, comedy and skating. . . Miss Henie is a screen find.'—*Variety*

One Is a Lonely Number*
US 1972 97m Metrocolor
MGM (Stan Margulies)

When her husband leaves her, a woman tries to develop new interests.
Satirical sentimental view of American divorce, with interesting moments.

w David Seltzer, *novel* Rebecca Morris *d* Mel Stuart *ph* Michel Hugo *m* Michel Legrand

Trish Van Devere, Monte Markham, Melvyn Douglas, Janet Leigh

One Little Indian
US 1973 91m Technicolor
Walt Disney (Winston Hibler)

A cavalry corporal escapes from jail and falls in with a ten-year-old Indian.
Sentimental semi-western, a bit dull for Disney apart from a camel.

w Harry Spalding *d* Bernard McEveety *ph* Charles F. Wheeler *m* Jerry Goldsmith

James Garner, Vera Miles, Pat Hingle, Morgan Woodward, John Doucette

One Magic Christmas
Canada 1985 88m De Luxe

An angel interferes in the lives of a family with problems. Decidedly downbeat Christmas fantasy: daddy gets drowned, mother is a nut, and the angel looks like a tramp. Santa Claus puts in an appearance for a happy finale, but *It's a Wonderful Life* should sue for plagiarism. Mary Steenburgen, Gary Basaraba, Harry Dean Stanton, Arthur Hill. Written by Thomas Meehan; directed by Phillip Borsos; for Peter O'Brian / Fred Roos / Silver Screen / Telefilm Canada / Walt Disney.

One Man's Journey
US 1933 72m bw

The career of a rural doctor for whom fame arrives too late. Pleasant, predictable, rather downbeat small-town drama. Lionel Barrymore, May Robson, Dorothy Jordan, Joel McCrea, Frances Dee, David Landau, Samuel S. Hinds. Written by Lester Cohen and Sam Ornitz from a story Failure by Katherine Haviland Taylor; directed by John Robertson; for RKO. 'Carries sympathetic interest and appeal.'—*Variety*

One Man's Way
US 1964 105m bw

A crime reporter becomes a priest. Rather self-conscious biography of Norman Vincent Peale, adequately assembled but containing no surprises. Don Murray, Diana Hyland, William Windom, Virginia Christine, Carol Ohmart. Written by Eleanore Griffin and John W. Bloch, from the book *Minister to Millions* by Arthur Gordon; directed by Denis Sanders; for UA.

One Mile from Heaven
US 1937 68m bw

A girl reporter makes hay with the story of a black woman who is raising a white child. Curious mixture of melodrama and wisecracking farce, with tap dancing from Bill Robinson thrown in. Claire Trevor, Sally Blane, Douglas Fowley, Fredi Washington, Ralf Harolde. Written by Lou Breslow and John Patrick; directed by Allan Dwan; for TCF. 'Whether the theme fits into the popular groove is something to think about.'—*Variety*

'The most exciting adventure in a million years!'
One Million BC*
US 1940 80m bw
Hal Roach
GB title: *Man and His Mate*
aka: *The Cave Dwellers*

Life between warring tribes of primitive man in the stone age.
Impressive-looking but slow-moving grunt-and-groan epic originally based on D. W. Griffith's *Man's Genesis* and on which Griffith did some work. The totally unhistoric dinosaurs (which had disappeared long before man arrived) are impressively concocted by magnifying lizards.

w Mickell Novak, George Baker, Joseph Frickert *d* Hal Roach, Hal Roach Jnr, D. W. Griffith *ph Norbert Brodine* *m* Werner R. Heymann

Victor Mature, Carole Landis, Lon Chaney Jnr, John Hubbard, Nigel de Brulier, Conrad Nagel

AAN: Werner R. Heymann

'This is the way it was!'
One Million Years BC*
GB 1966 100m Technicolor
Hammer (Michael Carreras)

A vague remake of the above, with animated monsters. Not badly done, with some lively action.

w Michael Carreras *d* Don Chaffey *ph* Wilkie Cooper *m* Mario Nascimbene

John Richardson, Raquel Welch, Robert Brown, Percy Herbert, Martine Beswick

'Very easy to dismiss the film as a silly spectacle; but Hammer production finesse is much in evidence and Don Chaffey has done a competent job of direction. And it is all hugely enjoyable.'—*David Wilson*

One Minute to Zero
US 1952 105m bw
RKO (Edmund Grainger)

In Korea a US colonel is evacuating American civilians but is forced to bomb refugees.
Flat war film with Something To Say and the star at his most humourless.

w Milton Krims, William Haines *d* Tay Garnett *ph* William E. Snyder *m* Victor Young *md* Constantin Bakaleinikoff

Robert Mitchum, Ann Blyth, William Talman, Charles McGraw, Richard Egan

One More River*
US 1934 88m bw
Universal (James Whale)
GB title: *Over the River*

A wife runs away from her husband, and he sets detectives on her and her lover.
Old-fashioned, well made picturization of a novel.

w R. C. Sherriff, *novel* John Galsworthy *d* James Whale *ph* John Mescalle *m* W. Franke Harling

Colin Clive, Diana Wynyard, C. Aubrey Smith, Jane Wyatt, Lionel Atwill, Mrs Patrick Campbell, Frank Lawton, Reginald Denny, Henry Stephenson, Alan Mowbray, E. E. Clive

'Galsworthy beautifully transmuted to the screen . . . Very British and ultra, but should prove nice enough b.o.'—*Variety*

'Taste, elegance, narrative drive and a deliberate nostalgia for the Galsworthy period.'—*Peter John Dyer, 1966*

'One of the finest courtroom episodes ever projected on a screen.'—*Motion Picture Herald*

One More Spring*
US 1935 87m bw
Fox (Winfield Sheehan)

Three strangers, in reduced circumstances due to the Depression, meet in Central Park and pool their resources.
Topical serio-comedy which looks pretty dated but still serves as a summation of American mid-thirties attitudes.

w Edwin Burke, novel Robert Nathan *d* Henry King *ph* John Seitz *md* Arthur Lange

Janet Gaynor, Warner Baxter, Walter Woolf King, Grant Mitchell, Jane Darwell, Roger Imhof, John Qualen, Dick Foran, Stepin Fetchit

'Whimsical comedy with plenty of laughs. Should do well.'—*Variety*

One More Time
GB 1969 93m De Luxe
UA / Chrislaw–Tracemark (Milton Ebbins)

More crime-solving adventures of Salt and Pepper.
Even less funny than before; see *Salt and Pepper*.

w Michael Pertwee *d* Jerry Lewis *ph* Ernest Steward *m* Les Reed

Peter Lawford, Sammy Davis Jnr, Esther Anderson, Maggie Wright

One More Tomorrow*
US 1946 89m bw
Warner (Henry Blanke)

A wealthy playboy marries a left-wing photographer and buys up her magazine.
An interesting but dated play fails to come to life because neither cast nor director seem to understand what it's about.

w Charles Hoffman, Catherine Turney, Julius J. and Philip G. Epstein, *play* The Animal Kingdom by Philip Barry *d* Peter Godfrey *ph* Bert Glennon *m* Max Steiner

Ann Sheridan, Dennis Morgan, Jack Carson, Alexis Smith, Jane Wyman, Reginald Gardiner, John Loder, Marjorie Gateson

One More Train to Rob
US 1971 108m Technicolor
Universal (Robert Arthur)

A train robber comes out of prison and warily takes up with his old partners.
Undistinguished western which tries to be funny and serious at the same time.

w Don Tait, Dick Nelson *d* Andrew V. McLaglen *ph* Alric Edens *m* David Shire

George Peppard, Diana Muldaur, John Vernon, France Nuyen, Steve Sandor

One New York Night*
US 1935 80m bw
MGM (Bernard Hyman)
GB title: *The Trunk Mystery*

A young farmer in Manhattan on a visit finds a body in the hotel room next to his.
Slick comedy thriller very typical of its date and studio.

w Frank Davis *play* Edward Childs Carpenter *d* Jack Conway

Franchot Tone, Una Merkel, Steffi Duna, Conrad Nagel, Charles Starrett, Harold Huber

'Sprightly devised murder mystery accounting for plenty of laughs . . . studded with multiple touches of production value.'—*Variety*

'A comedy of astonishing intelligence and finish . . . it ought to take its place immediately with the classics.'—*Graham Greene*

One Night in Lisbon
US 1941 97m bw
Paramount (Edward H. Griffith)

During World War II an American flier falls for a British socialite who is being used by the government as a decoy for spies.
Flabby romantic comedy-drama which mostly wastes a good cast.

w Virginia Van Upp, *play* There's Always Juliet by John Van Druten *d* Edward H. Griffith *ph* Bert Glennon *m* Sigmund Krumgold

Madeleine Carroll, Fred MacMurray, Edmund Gwenn, Patricia Morison, Billie Burke, John Loder, Dame May Whitty, Reginald Denny, Billy Gilbert

One Night in the Tropics
US 1940 69m bw
Universal (Leonard Spiegelgass)

Holidays on a Caribbean island lead to a double wedding.
Very lightweight comedy-musical notable only for introducing Abbott and Costello.

w Gertrude Purcell, Charles Grayson, *play* Love Insurance by Earl Derr Biggers *d* A. Edward Sutherland *ph* Joseph Valentine *md* Charles Previn *songs* Oscar Hammerstein II, Jerome Kern, Otto Harbach, Dorothy Fields

Allan Jones, Nancy Kelly, Bud Abbott, Lou Costello, Robert Cummings, Leo Carillo, Peggy Moran, Mary Boland

One Night of Love**
US 1934 95m bw
Columbia (Harry Cohn)

An opera star rebels against her demanding teacher.
Light classical musical which was a surprising box office success and brought Hollywood careers for Lily Pons, Gladys Swarthout, Miliza Korjus, etc.

w Dorothy Speare, Charles Beahan, S. K. Lauren, James Gow, Edmund North *d Victor Schertzinger* *ph* Joseph Walker *songs* Victor Schertzinger, Gus Kahn *m* Louis Silvers *md* Pietro Cimini

Grace Moore, Tullio Carminati, Lyle Talbot, Mona Barrie, Nydia Westman, Jessie Ralph, Luis Alberni, Jane Darwell

AA: Victor Schertzinger, Gus Kahn (as songwriters)
AAN: best picture; direction; Louis Silvers; Grace Moore

One Night With You
GB 1948 92m bw

An English girl and an Italian tenor, stranded by a train failure, are taken for forgers. Rather frantic but occasionally amusing Italian-set comedy. Nino Martini, Patricia Roc, Hugh Wakefield, Bonar Colleano, Guy Middleton, Stanley Holloway, Irene Worth, Charles Goldner. Written by Caryl Brahms and S. J. Simon; directed by Terence Young; for Two Cities / Rank.

One of Our Aircraft Is Missing*
GB 1941 102m bw
British National (Michael Powell, Emeric Pressburger)

A bomber is grounded after a raid and its crew is helped by the Dutch resistance.
Efficient propaganda piece which starts vigorously but gets bogged down in talk.

wd Michael Powell, Emeric Pressburger *ph* Ronald Neame

Godfrey Tearle, Eric Portman, Hugh Williams, Bernard Miles, Hugh Burden, Emrys Jones, Googie Withers, Pamela Brown, Peter Ustinov, Joyce Redman, Hay Petrie, Robert Helpmann, Alec Clunes

AAN: script

One of Our Dinosaurs Is Missing*
US 1975 94m Technicolor
Walt Disney (Bill Walsh)

In the 1920s a strip of secret microfilm is smuggled out of China and hidden in a dinosaur's skeleton in the Natural History Museum.
Unexceptionable family comedy with everyone trying hard; somehow it just misses, perhaps because it is told through talk rather than cinematic narrative.

w Bill Walsh, *novel* The Great Dinosaur Robbery by David Forrest *d* Robert Stevenson *ph* Paul Beeson *m* Ron Goodwin

Helen Hayes, Peter Ustinov, Derek Nimmo, Clive Revill, Joan Sims, Bernard Bresslaw, Roy Kinnear, Deryck Guyler, Richard Pearson

One Rainy Afternoon*
US 1935 79m bw

In a cinema one afternoon, a gigolo kisses the wrong girl. Rather heavy-handed light comedy with interesting credentials. Francis Lederer, Ida Lupino. Written by Stephen Morehouse Avery and Maurice Hamline from a play by Emeric Pressburger and René Pujal ; directed by Rowland V. Lee; for Pickford-Lasky.

One Summer Love
US 1976 97m colour Panavision

A young man leaves mental hospital for his Connecticut home, only to find everyone there nuttier than he is. Over-the-top melodrama. Beau Bridges, Susan Sarandon, Mildred Dunnock, Michael B. Miller. Written by N. Richard Nash; directed by Gilbert Cates; for AIP. (Aka: *Dragonfly*.)

One Sunday Afternoon**
US 1933 93m bw
Paramount (Louis D. Lighton)

In 1910, a Brooklyn dentist feels he has married the wrong girl, but discovers that his choice was the right one.
Pleasant period comedy drama which was twice remade; as *The Strawberry Blonde* (qv) and see below.

w William Slavens McNutt, Grover Jones, *play* James Hagan *d* Stephen Roberts *ph* Victor Milner

Gary Cooper, Frances Fuller, Fay Wray, Neil Hamilton, Roscoe Karns

'Still pitched in stage tempo and unfolds haltingly.'—*Variety*

One Sunday Afternoon
US 1948 90m Technicolor
Warner (Jerry Wald)

Pleasant but undistinguished musical remake of the above.

w Robert L. Richards *d* Raoul Walsh *ph* Sid Hickox, Wilfrid M. Cline *md* Ray Heindorf *ad* Anton Grot

Dennis Morgan, Dorothy Malone, Janis Paige, Don Defore, Ben Blue

'A lackadaisical and uninspired jaunt down memory lane.'—*New Yorker, 1978*

The One That Got Away**
GB 1957 111m bw
Rank (Julian Wintle)

A German flier, Franz Von Werra, is captured and sent to various British prisoner-of-war camps, from all of which he escapes.
True-life biopic, developed in a number of suspense and action sequences, all very well done.

w Howard Clewes, book Kendal Burt, James Leasor *d Roy Baker* *ph* Eric Cross *m* Hubert Clifford

Hardy Kruger, Michael Goodliffe, Colin Gordon, *Alec McCowen*

One Third of a Nation*
US 1939 79m bw
Federal Theatre (Dudley Murphy)

A shopgirl persuades a landlord to tear down his dangerous slums and put up good buildings.
Naïve do-goodery, not too persuasively managed.

w Dudley Murphy, Oliver H. P. Garrett, *play* Arthur Arent *d* Dudley Murphy *ph* William Mellor *m* Nathaniel Shilkret

Sylvia Sidney, Leif Erickson, Myron McCormick, Hiram Sherman, Sidney Lumet, Percy Waram

'No worse and rather better than a commensurate modest-budgeter essayed on the coast . . . the cinematic transition however seems to have almost wholly ditched the Federal Housing "living newspaper" purpose of the stage version, emphasizing the boy-meets-girl premise against the shocking slum background.'—*Variety*

The One Thousand Plane Raid
US 1969 94m De Luxe

An American colonel persuades top brass of the need for daylight bombing of Germany.

Reasonable routine war action drama. Christopher George, Laraine Stephens, J. D. Cannon, Gary Marshall, Michael Evans, Ben Murphy. Written by Donald S. Sanford; directed by Boris Sagal; for Oakwood / UA.

One Touch of Venus*
US 1948 82m bw
Universal / Lester Cowan

In a fashionable department store, a statue of Venus comes to life and falls for a window dresser.
Pleasant satirical comedy, watered down from the Broadway original.

w Harry Kurnitz, Frank Tashlin, *play* S. J. Perelman, Ogden Nash *d* William A. Seiter *ph* Franz Planer *songs* Kurt Weill *ad* Bernard Herzbrun, Emrich Nicholson

Ava Gardner, Robert Walker, Eve Arden, Dick Haymes, Olga San Juan, Tom Conway

One, Two, Three**
US 1961 115m bw Panavision
United Artists / Mirisch / Pyramid (Billy Wilder)

An executive in West Berlin is trying to sell Coca Cola to the Russians while preventing his boss's daughter from marrying a communist.
Back to *Ninotchka* territory, but this time the tone is that of a wild farce which achieves fine momentum in stretches but also flags a lot in between, teetering the while on the edge of taste.

w Billy Wilder, I. A. L. Diamond, *play* Ferenc Molnar *d Billy Wilder ph* Daniel Fapp *m* André Previn

James Cagney, Horst Buchholz, Arlene Francis, Pamela Tiffin, Lilo Pulver, Howard St John, Leon Askin

'A sometimes bewildered, often wonderfully funny exercise in nonstop nuttiness.'—*Time*

'This first-class featherweight farce is a serious achievement.'—*Stanley Kauffmann*

AAN: Daniel Fapp

One Way Passage*
US 1932 69m bw
Warner (Robert Lord)

On an ocean voyage, a dying girl falls in love with a crook going home to face a life sentence.
Pattern melodrama which stood Hollywood in good stead.

w Wilson Mizner, Joseph Jackson, Robert Lord *d* Tay Garnett *ph* Robert Kurrie *m* W. Franke Harling

William Powell, Kay Francis, Frank McHugh, Aline MacMahon, Warren Hymer, Herbert Mundin, Roscoe Karns, Stanley Fields

'Will reach house averages for this time of year.'—*Variety*

† Remade as *'Til We Meet Again* (qv).

AA: original story (Robert Lord)

One Way Pendulum
GB 1964 85m bw
UA / Woodfall (Michael Deeley)

A suburban clerk leads a dream existence; his son teaches speak-your-weight machines to sing, while he sets an imaginary murder trial in motion.
A nonsense play (which has many adherents) resists the literalness of the camera eye.

w N. F. Simpson, from his play *d* Peter Yates *ph* Denys Coop *m* Richard Rodney Bennett

Eric Sykes, George Cole, Julia Foster, Jonathan Miller, Peggy Mount, Alison Leggatt, Mona Washbourne

One Way Street
US 1950 79m bw
U-I / Leonard Goldstein (Sam Goldwyn Jnr)

A disillusioned doctor steals a fortune and hides out in a Mexican village, where he regains his self-respect.
Thin and pointless melodrama.

w Lawrence Kimble *d* Hugo Fregonese *ph* Maury Gertsman *m* Frank Skinner

James Mason, Marta Toren, Dan Duryea, William Conrad, King Donovan, Jack Elam

'It is reported that James Mason chooses his own parts, and if this is true I have to report that he is a glutton for punishment.'—*Daily Herald*

'One of the dullest, most stupid films of the year.'—*Sunday Pictorial*

One-Way Ticket
US 1935 66m bw

A convicted bank robber falls in love with the warden's daughter. Prison break drama which seems to be trying to make a point but is not sure what. Lloyd Nolan, Walter Connolly, Peggy Conklin, Edith Fellows, Nana Bryant, Thurston Hall. Written by Vincent Lawrence, Joseph Anthony, Oliver H. P. Garrett, Grover Jones, from a novel by Ethel Turner; directed by Herbert Biberman; for Columbia. 'It is "different" at the cost of credulity.'—*Variety*

One Way to Love
US 1945 83m bw

A Chicago radio writer gets a chance in Hollywood. Hit-and-miss romantic comedy which takes place largely on a westbound train. Willard Parker, Marguerite Chapman, Hugh Herbert, Chester Morris, Jerome Cowan, Janis Carter. Written by Joseph Hoffman, Jack Henley, Lester Lee, Larry Marks; directed by Ray Enright; for Burt Kelly / Columbia.

One Wild Night
US 1938 63m bw

Four small-town citizens anxious for vacations away from their wives plot their own kidnapping. Tolerable second feature comedy, but the plot might have been better developed. June Lang, Dick Baldwin, Lyle Talbot, J. Edward Bromberg, Sidney Toler, William Demarest, Andrew Tombes, Spencer Charters. Written by Charles Belden and Jerry Cady; directed by Eugene Forde; for John Stone / TCF.

One Wild Oat
GB 1951 78m bw

An old flame tries to blackmail a highly respectable solicitor. Modest film version of a popular West End farce. Robertson Hare, Stanley Holloway, Sam Costa, Andrew Crawford, Vera Pearce, Robert Moreton, Irene Handl. Written by Vernon Sylvaine and Lawrence Huntingdon, from the play by Vernon Sylvaine; directed by Charles Saunders; for Coronet / Eros.

Onibaba*
Japan 1964 104m bw Tohoscope
Kindai Eiga Kyokai / Tokyo Eiga
aka: *The Hole*

In medieval times on a remote marshy plain, mother and daughter live by killing stray soldiers and selling their armour, until daughter takes one for a lover and mother becomes jealous.
A kind of original horror legend is told by this strange, compelling piece with its frequent moments of nastiness. It remains, perhaps mercifully, unique.

wd Kaneto Shindo *ph* Kiyomi Juroda *m* Hikaru Hayashi

Nobuko Otowa, Jitsuko Yoshimura, Kei Sato

'What happened is true . . . but the real crime is what happened after!'

The Onion Field
US 1979 126m Eastmancolor
Black Marble (Walter Coblenz)

Two policemen are shot at by a manic killer, and the one who survives finds that he is suspected of cowardice and has to resign from the force.
Well meaning but lumbering case history. The author must carry the blame, as for once the picture was made exactly on his terms.

w Joseph Wambaugh, from his novel *d* Harold Becker *ph* Charles Rosher *m* Eumir Depdato *pd* Brian Eatwell

John Savage, James Woods, Franklyn Seales, Ted Danson, Ronny Cox, David Huffman

Onionhead
US 1958 110m bw
Warner (Jules Schermer)

Adventures of a ship's cook in the US Coastguard.
Service comedy that must have seemed funnier in the US than in Britain.

w Nelson Gidding, *novel* Weldon Hill *d* Norman Taurog *ph* Harold Rosson *md* Ray Heindorf

Andy Griffith, Felicia Farr, Walter Matthau, Erin O'Brien, Joe Mantell, Ray Danton, Roscoe Karns, James Gregory, Tige Andrews

† An attempt to cash in on the success of *No Time for Sergeants*.

'Romance as glorious as the towering Andes!'

Only Angels Have Wings**
US 1939 121m bw
Columbia (Howard Hawks)

Tension creeps into the relationships of the men who fly cargo planes over the Andes when a stranded showgirl sets her cap at the boss.
For an action film this is really too restricted by talk and cramped studio sets, and its theme was more entertainingly explored in *Red Dust*. Still, it couldn't be more typical of the Howard Hawks film world, where men are men and women have to be as tough as they are.

w Jules Furthman, *story* Howard Hawks *d* Howard Hawks ph Joseph Walker, Elmer Dyer *m* Dmitri Tiomkin *md* Morris Stoloff

Cary Grant, Jean Arthur, Rita Hayworth, Richard Barthelmess, Thomas Mitchell, Sig Rumann, Victor Kilian, John Carroll, Allyn Joslyn

'All these people did the best they could with what they were given—but look at it.'—*Otis Ferguson*

The Only Game in Town
US 1969 113m De Luxe
TCF (Fred Kohlmar)

A Las Vegas chorus girl and a piano player have an unhappy life because of his gambling fever.
Uninteresting two-header from a play that didn't make it; no light relief, no action, and not even very good acting.

w Frank D. Gilroy, from his play *d* George Stevens *ph* Henri Decaë *m* Maurice Jarre

Elizabeth Taylor, Warren Beatty, Charles Braswell, Hank Henry

'It epitomizes the disaster the studio and star systems foist on films . . . the only two-character tale around to cost $11 million.'—*Judith Crist*

† Frank Sinatra was originally cast but walked out after production started; Warren Beatty astonishingly chose to do this rather than *Butch Cassidy and the Sundance Kid*.

'They were six and they fought like six hundred!'
Only the Valiant
US 1950 105m bw
(Warner) William Cagney

A tough cavalry officer in a lonely fort wins a battle against Indians.
Standard top-of-the-bill western; competent but not very gripping.

w Edmund H. North, Harry Brown *d* Gordon Douglas *ph* Lionel Lindon *m* Franz Waxman

Gregory Peck, Ward Bond, Gig Young, Lon Chaney Jnr, Barbara Payton, Neville Brand

Only Two Can Play***
GB 1962 106m bw
British Lion / Vale (Launder and Gilliat)

A much married assistant librarian in a Welsh town has an abortive affair with a councillor's wife.
Well characterized and generally diverting 'realistic' comedy which slows up a bit towards the end but contains many memorable sequences and provides its star's last good character performance.

w Bryan Forbes, novel That Uncertain Feeling by *Kingsley Amis d Sidney Gilliat ph* John Wilcox *m* Richard Rodney Bennett *ad* Albert Witherick

Peter Sellers, Mai Zetterling, Virginia Maskell, Richard Attenborough, Raymond Huntley, John Le Mesurier, *Kenneth Griffith*

Only When I Larf*
GB 1968 103m Eastmancolor
Paramount / Beecord (Len Deighton, Brian Duffy, Hugh Attwooll)

The adventures of three confidence tricksters. Quite likeable but unmemorable 'with it' comedy of the sixties; the tricks are more amusing than the characterization.

w John Salmon, *novel* Len Deighton *d* Basil Dearden *ph* Anthony Richmond *m* Ron Grainer

Richard Attenborough, David Hemmings, Alexandra Stewart, Nicholas Pennell, Melissa Stribling, Terence Alexander, Edric Connor, Calvin Lockhart, Clifton Jones

Only When I Laugh
US 1981 120m Metrocolor
Columbia (Roger M. Rothstein, Neil Simon)
GB title: *It Hurts Only When I Laugh*

An alcoholic actress tries to rebuild her life. Last desperate fling (one hopes) of the Neil Simon industry, dispensing in this case more bitter tears than laughs, and generally failing to stay the course.

w Neil Simon, from his play The Gingerbread Lady *d* Glenn Jordan *ph* David M. Walsh *m* David Shire

Marsha Mason, Kristy McNichol, James Coco, Joan Hackett, David Dukes, John Bennett Perry

'One can almost hear the click of typewriter keys.'—*Geoff Brown, MFB*

AAN: Marsha Mason; James Coco (supporting actor); Joan Hackett (supporting actress)

Only Yesterday*
US 1933 105m bw

An unmarried mother is seduced twice by the same man. One that Ross Hunter didn't get around to remaking . . . and a good job too. Margaret Sullavan, John Boles, Billie Burke, Reginald Denny, Edna May Oliver, Benita Hume. Written by William Hurlbut, George O'Neill and Arthur Richman; directed by John M. Stahl; for Universal. 'The film needs little more praise than that it warrants its unusual length.'—*Variety*

† The original intention seems to have been to mirror recent history as in Frederick Lewis Allen's book of the same title.

Ooh, You Are Awful*
GB 1972 97m Eastmancolor
British Lion / Quintain (E. M. Smedley Aston)
US title: *Get Charlie Tully*

A London con man seeks a fortune, the clue to which is tattooed on the behind of one of several girls.
Amusing star vehicle with plenty of room for impersonations and outrageous jokes.

w John Warren, John Singer *d Cliff Owen ph* Ernest Stewart *m* Christopher Gunning

Dick Emery, Derren Nesbitt, Ronald Fraser, Pat Coombs, William Franklyn, Brian Oulton, Norman Bird

Open City**
Italy 1945 101m bw
Minerva
original title: *Roma, Città Aperta*

Italian underground workers defy the Nazis in Rome towards the end of the war.
A vivid newsreel quality is achieved by this nerve-stretching melodrama in which all the background detail is as real as care could make it.

w Sergio Amidei, Federico Fellini *d Roberto Rossellini ph* Ubaldo Arata *m* Renzo Rossellini

Aldo Fabrizzi, *Anna Magnani*, Marcello Pagliero, Maria Michi

AAN: script

Open Season
US / Spain / Switzerland 1974 104m Eastmancolor Panavision
Impala / Arpa (George H. Brown, Jose S. Vicuna)

Three young criminals hunt human prey, but one of their victims takes his own revenge.
Rough, flashy, violent melodrama which pretends to have something to say but in fact is merely sensationalist.

w David Osborn, Liz Charles Williams *d* Peter Collinson *ph* Fernando Arribas *m* Ruggero Cini

Peter Fonda, Cornelia Sharp, John Phillip Law, Richard Lynch, Albert Mendoza, William Holden

'An offensive, gamy potboiler.'—*Variety*

'Both patience and the plot line are severely strained by the artiness Collinson frequently indulges, with frozen shots to mark the moments of truth and a meaningless punctuation throughout of long shots, angles and flashes.'—*Tom Milne*

Opening Night
US 1978 144m Metrocolor
Faces Distribution (Al Ruban)

A Broadway actress is on the point of a nervous breakdown.
Interminable addition to the director's list of unwatchable personal films.

wd John Cassavetes *ph* Al Ruban *m* Bo Horwood

Gena Rowlands, Ben Gazzara, John Cassavetes, Joan Blondell, Paul Stewart, Zohra Lampert, Laura Johnson

'Shrill, puzzling, depressing and overlong.'—*Variety*

L'Opéra de Quat' Sous see Die Dreigroschenoper

Operation Amsterdam*
GB 1958 104m bw
Rank / Maurice Cowan

In 1940 spies are sent into Holland to prevent the invading Germans from finding Amsterdam's stock of industrial diamonds.
Semi-documentary war adventure, well mounted and played.

w Michael McCarthy, John Eldridge, *book* Adventure in Diamonds by David Walker *d Michael McCarthy* *ph* Reg Wyer, *m* Philip Green

Peter Finch, Tony Britton, Eva Bartok, Alexander Knox, Malcolm Keen, Tim Turner, John Horsley, Melvyn Hayes, Christopher Rhodes

Operation Bullshine
GB 1959 84m Technicolor

In 1942, complications ensue when an ATS private suspects her husband of infidelity.
Flabby army comedy with a few laughs.
Donald Sinden, Barbara Murray, Carole Lesley, Ronald Shiner, Naunton Wayne, Daniel Massey, Dora Bryan. Written by Anne Burnaby, Rupert Lang and Gilbert Gunn; directed by Gilbert Gunn; for ABPC.

Operation CIA
US 1965 90m bw

An agent is rushed to Saigon to find a secret message which was never delivered. Crude thick-ear with a few suspenseful moments.
Burt Reynolds, John Hoyt, Daniele Aubry, Kieu Chinh, Cyril Collick. Written by Bill S. Ballinger and Peer J. Oppenheimer; directed by Christian Nyby; for Allied Artists.

Operation Crossbow*
GB 1965 116m Metrocolor Panavision
MGM / Carlo Ponti
aka: *The Great Spy Mission*

In World War II, trained scientists are parachuted into Europe to destroy the Nazi rocket-making plant at Peenemunde.
Unlikely, star-packed war yarn with more passing tragedy than most, all obliterated by a shoot-em-up James Bond finale.

w Robert Imrie (Emeric Pressburger), Derry Quinn, Ray Rigby *d* Michael Anderson *ph* Erwin Hillier *m* Ron Goodwin

George Peppard, Tom Courtenay, John Mills, Sophia Loren, Lilli Palmer, Anthony Quayle, Patrick Wymark, Jeremy Kemp, Paul Henreid, Trevor Howard, Sylvia Sims, Richard Todd

Operation Daybreak
US 1975 119m Technicolor
Warner / Howard R. Schuster / American Allied (Carter de Haven)

In 1941, Czech patriots kill the hated Nazi Heydrich and are hunted down.
Curiously-timed evocation of wartime resistance adventures, too realistic for the squeamish and certainly not very entertaining despite a fair level of professionalism.

OPERATION AMSTERDAM. Director Michael McCarthy's death robbed the British cinema of an accomplished craftsman. Peter Finch, Tony Britton, Alexander Knox.

w Ronald Harwood, *novel* Seven Men at Daybreak by Alan Burgess *d* Lewis Gilbert *ph* Henri Decaë *m* David Hentschel

Timothy Bottoms, Martin Shaw, Joss Ackland, Nicola Pagett, Anthony Andrews, Anton Diffring, Carl Duering, Diana Coupland

Operation Eichmann
US 1961 94m bw

After the war, the Nazi who exterminated six million Jews escapes from Europe but is eventually recaptured. Crude exploitation item designed to cash in on Eichmann's trial, a documentary on which would have been much more interesting. Werner Klemperer (as Eichmann), Ruta Lee, Donald Buka, John Banner. Written by Lewis Copley; directed by R. G. Springsteen; for Allied Artists.

Operation Kid Brother
Italy 1967 105m Techniscope

007's brother defeats an international mastermind with the help of a Scottish archery team. Very elementary James Bond spoof, with a confusing array of old and new elements but less than the required minimum of style. Neil Connery (Sean's kid brother), Daniela Bianchi, Adolfo Celi, Bernard Lee, Lois Maxwell, Agata Flori. Written by Paolo Levi, Vincenzo Mannino and Carlo Tritto; directed by Alberto de Martino; for Dario Sabatello. (Aka: *OK Connery*.) 'A grotesque parody of a parody . . . bad enough to be hysterically funny.'—*MFB.*

Operation Mad Ball*
US 1957 105m bw
Columbia (Jed Harris)

American troops in Normandy are forbidden to fraternize with nurses, but a clandestine dance is arranged.
Madcap army farce which keeps promising to be funnier than it is.

w Arthur Carter, Jed Harris, Blake Edwards, *play* Arthur Carter *d Richard Quine* *ph* Charles Lawton Jnr *m* George Duning

Jack Lemmon, Ernie Kovacs, Kathryn Grant, Mickey Rooney, James Darren, Arthur O'Connell

Operation Pacific
US 1950 109m bw
Warner (Louis F. Edelmann)

Adventures of a submarine commander in the Pacific war.
Routine war heroics, tolerably done but overstretched.

wd George Waggner *ph* Bert Glennon *m* Max Steiner

John Wayne, Patricia Neal, Ward Bond, Scott Forbes, Phil Carey, Paul Picerni, William Campbell, Martin Milner

Operation Petticoat*
US 1959 124m Eastmancolor
Universal / Granart (Robert Arthur)

During World War II, a crippled submarine is refloated by fair means and foul, and a party of nurses is taken aboard.
Flabby comedy with good moments, but not many.

w Stanley Shapiro, Maurice Richlin *d* Blake Edwards *ph* Russell Harlan *m* David Rose

Cary Grant, Tony Curtis, Joan O'Brien, Dina Merrill, Gene Evans, Arthur O'Connell, Richard Sargent

'Grant is a living lesson in getting laughs without lines.'—*Variety*

AAN: script

Operation St Peter's
Italy 1968 100m colour

Three thieves steal Michelangelo's *Pietà* and sell it for forty dollars to an American gangster. Rather surprisingly watchable comedy chase, with the star parodying his past roles. Edward G. Robinson, Lando Buzzanca, Heinz Ruhmann, Jean-Claude Brialy. Written by Ennio de Concini, Adriano Baracco, Roberto Gianviti and Lucio Fulci; directed by Lucio Fulci; for Turi Vasile / Paramount.

Operation Secret
US 1952 108m bw
Warner (Henry Blanke)

A traitor in the French resistance movement shoots a colleague, and the wrong man is accused.
Belated World War II adventure which gives the impression of having been discarded by Errol Flynn.

w James R. Webb, Harold Medford *d* Lewis Seiler *ph* Ted McCord m Roy Webb

Cornel Wilde, Steve Cochran, Paul Picerni, Karl Malden

Operation Thunderbolt*
Israel 1977 117m Eastmancolor Panavision
GS Films (Menahem Golan, Yoram Globus)
aka: *Entebbe: Operation Thunderbolt*

An account of the rescue of Israeli hostages from terrorists who have hijacked their plane to Entebbe.
Victory at Entebbe and *Raid on Entebbe* were made with all-star casts for American television. This home-grown account of a famous deed is more modest yet more authoritative.

w Clarke Reynolds *d* Menahem Golan *ph* Adam Greenberg *m* Dov Seltzer

Klaus Kinski, Assaf Dayan, Ori Levy, Yehoram Geon, Mark Heath
AA: best foreign film

Operator 13
US 1934 86m bw
MGM / Cosmopolitan (Lucien Hubbard)
GB title: *Spy 13*

During the Civil War an actress becomes a Union spy.
Elaborate period romance with action highlights.

w Harry Thew, Zelda Sears, Eve Greene *d* Richard Boleslawski *ph George Folsey* *m* William Axt

Marion Davies, Gary Cooper, Jean Parker, Katherine Alexander, Ted Healy, Russell Hardie, Henry Wadsworth, Douglass Dumbrille

'Will please generally . . . one of Davies' best.'—*Variety*

AAN: George Folsey

The Opposite Sex
US 1956 116m Metrocolor Cinemascope
MGM (Joe Pasternak)

A New York socialite divorces her unfaithful husband but finally takes him back.
Softened, musicalized version of *The Women* (qv); very patchy, shapeless, and not nearly sharp enough.

w Fay and Michael Kanin, *play* Clare Boothe *d* David Miller *ph* Robert Bronner *m* Nicholas Brodszky *songs* Nicholas Brodszky, Sammy Cahn

June Allyson, Dolores Gray, Joan Collins, Ann Sheridan, Agnes Moorehead, Joan Blondell, Barbara Jo Allen, Charlotte Greenwood

The Optimists of Nine Elms*
GB 1973 110m Eastmancolor
Cheetah / Sagittarius (Adrian Gaye, Victor Lyndon)

Children of a London slum make friends with an old busker.
Gentle, sentimental, quite well-observed piece of wistful melancholia, falsified by its star performance.

wd Anthony Simmons, from his novel *co-w* Tudor Gates *ph* Larry Pizer *m* George Martin

Peter Sellers, Donna Mullane, John Chaffey, David Daker, Marjorie Yates

The Oracle
GB 1952 83m bw
Group Three (Colin Lesslie)
US title: *The Horse's Mouth*

A reporter discovers that a village well in Ireland contains an oracle which can predict the future.
Weak sub-Ealing comedy which aims to please and gets a few laughs. All very British.

w Patrick Campbell *d* C. M. Pennington-Richards *ph* Wolfgang Suschitsky *m* Temple Abady

Robert Beatty, Virginia McKenna, Mervyn Johns, Gilbert Harding

Orca—Killer Whale
US 1977 92m Technicolor Panavision
Famous Films / Dino de Laurentiis (Luciano Vincenzoni)

Off Newfoundland, a killer whale takes revenge for its mate's death.
A rather unpleasant attempt to mix horror and thrills with ecology: not very entertaining, and not for the squeamish.

w Luciano Vincenzoni, Sergio Donati *d* Michael Anderson *ph* Ted Moore, J. Barry Herron *m* Ennio Morricone

Richard Harris, Charlotte Rampling, Will Sampson, Keenan Wynn

'The biggest load of cod imaginable.'—*Philip Bergson, Sunday Times*

'There are more thrills to be had in the average dolphinarium.'—*Sight and Sound*

Orchestra Wives**
US 1942 97m bw
TCF (William Le Baron)

A small town girl marries the trumpet player of a travelling swing band.
Fresh and lively musical of its period, full of first-class music and amusing backstage backbiting.

w Karl Tunberg, Darrell Ware *d* Archie Mayo *ph* Lucien Ballard *md* Alfred Newman

Ann Rutherford, George Montgomery, Lynn Bari, *Glenn Miller and his Orchestra,* Carole Landis. Jackie Gleason, Cesar Romero

'A natural for any theatre that hasn't got an ironclad rule against jive.'—*Hollywood Reporter*

AAN: song 'I've Got a Girl in Kalamazoo' (*m* Harry Warren, *ly* Mack Gordon)

Orchids to You*
US 1935 74m bw

A florist pulls several strokes to prevent an attorney from taking over her lease. Amusing comedy drama which failed through lack of strong names. John Boles, Jean Muir, Charles Butterworth, Ruthelma Stevens, Arthur Lake, Spring Byington. Written by William Hurlbut, Bartlett Cormack, Glenn Tryon, Howard Estabrook; directed by William A. Seiter; for Robert T. Kane / Fox. 'One of those productions that just misses the top rung.'—*Variety*

Ordeal By Innocence
US 1985 88m Eastmancolor
Cannon (Jenny Craven)

An explorer returning from an Antarctic trip discovers that an acquaintance has been two years in prison for murder, and he might have saved him.
Rather dim Agatha Christie adaptation (though set in her favourite Devon from her

favourite book), with workaday actors and a most unsuitable music score. By the time the end comes, nobody could possibly care who done it.

w Alexander Stuart *d* Desmond Davis *ph* Billy Williams *m* Dave Brubeck

Donald Sutherland, Christopher Plummer, Faye Dunaway, Sarah Miles, Ian MacShane, Diana Quick, Annette Crosbie, Michael Elphick, Phoebe Nichols

Orders Are Orders
GB 1954 78m bw
Group 3 (Donald Taylor)

Flabby update of *Orders Is Orders* with an interesting cast below par.

w Donald Taylor, Geoffrey Orme *d* David Paltenghi *ph* Arthur Grant *m* Stanley Black

Peter Sellers, Brian Reece, Sid James, Tony Hancock, Margot Grahame, Raymond Huntley, Maureen Johnson, June Thorburn, Bill Fraser

Orders is Orders*
GB 1933 88m bw
Gaumont British (Michael Balcon)

An army barracks is disrupted when an American film company gets permission to work there.
Breezy farce which pleased at the time.

w Leslie Arliss, Sidney Gilliat, *play* Ian Hay, Anthony Armstrong *d* Walter Forde *ph* Glen MacWilliams

Charlotte Greenwood, James Gleason, Cedric Hardwicke, Cyril Maude, Ian Hunter, Ray Milland, Jane Carr, Donald Calthrop, Eliot Makeham, Wally Patch, Finlay Currie

'A wow from start to finish.'—*Variety*

'They made this boy a cold-blooded killer!'
Orders to Kill*
GB 1958 111m bw
British Lion / Lynx (Anthony Asquith, Anthony Havelock-Allan)

During World War II a bomber pilot undertakes a mission to parachute into occupied France and kill a double agent, who turns out afterwards to have been innocent.
Strong, hard-to-take but well made war story about the effect of war on conscience.

w Paul Dehn d Anthony Asquith
ph Desmond Dickinson *m* Benjamin Frankel

Paul Massie, Irene Worth, James Robertson Justice, *Leslie French*, Eddie Albert, Lillian Gish, John Crawford, Jacques Brunius, Lionel Jeffries

Ordet*
Denmark 1957 126m bw

In a God-fearing village, a father and his three sons have various religious experiences. Hard-to-take intellectual drama of the faith, very slow and austere but strangely compelling. Henrik Malberg, Emil Hass Christensen, Preben Lerdorff-Rye, Cay Kristensen. Written, directed and produced by Carl Theodor Dreyer; for Palladium.

'Everything is in its proper place—except the past!'
Ordinary People**
US 1980 124m Technicolor
Paramount / Wildwood (Ronald L. Schwary)

The eldest son of a well-heeled American family is drowned, and the survivors take stock and indulge in recriminations.
An actor's piece which on that level succeeds very well, and accurately pins down a certain species of modern American family.

w Alvin Sargent, novel Judith Guest *d Robert Redford ph* John Bailey *m* Marvin Hamlisch

Donald Sutherland, *Mary Tyler Moore, Timothy Hutton*, Judd Hirsch, Elizabeth McGovern, M. Emmet Walsh

'This is an academic exercise in catharsis: it's earnest, it means to improve people, and it lasts a lifetime.'—*New Yorker*

AA: best film; Alvin Sargent; Robert Redford; Timothy Hutton
AAN: Mary Tyler Moore; Judd Hirsch (supporting actor)

The Oregon Trail
US 1939 bw serial: 15 eps

Outlaws and Indians harass pioneer wagon trains. Well-mounted serial. John Mack Brown, Louis Stanley, Bill Cody Jnr, Fuzzy Knight, Roy Barcroft. Directed by Ford Beebe; for Universal.

The Oregon Trail
US 1959 86m De Luxe Cinemascope

A New York reporter in 1846 is sent to cover a westward trek. Prototype settlers vs Indians western with all the expected incident. Fred MacMurray, William Bishop, Nina Shipman, Gloria Talbot, Henry Hull, John Carradine, Elizabeth Patterson. Written by Louis Vittes and Gene Fowler Jnr; directed by Gene Fowler Jnr; for TCF.

The Organization
US 1971 108m De Luxe
UA / Mirisch (Walter Mirisch)

San Francisco policemen combat an international drug smuggling organization. The third and weakest adventure of Virgil Tibbs, black policeman of *In the Heat of the Night*. Absolutely routine.

w James R. Webb *d* Don Medford
ph Joseph Biroc *m* Gile Melle

Sidney Poitier, Barbara McNair, Sheree North, Gerald S. O'Loughlin

Orient Express*
US 1934 71m bw

Various stories conflict on the Orient Express. Moderately successful multi-drama in the wake of *Grand Hotel*. Heather Angel, Ralph Morgan, Norman Foster, Herbert Mundin, Una O'Connor, Irene Ware, Dorothy Burgess. Written by Paul Martin, Carl Hovey, Oscar Levant, William Conselman, from the novel by Graham Greene; directed by Paul Martin; for Fox. 'Rather too much story all of a sudden; auditors may be lulled to quiet by the easy, non-exciting early action.'—*Variety*

Orion's Belt
Norway 1985 103m Eastmancolor

Spitzbergen seamen stumble upon a Russian spy base. Slow-moving cold-war saga with an ironic finale: the scenery is the best part. Helge Jordal, Sverre Anker Ousdal, Hans Ola Sorlie. Written by 'Richard Harris'; directed by Ola Solum; for Filmeffekt.

Orphans
US 1987 120m colour

Two outcast brothers have their lives transformed by a gangster. Photographed talk-piece which could hope for few takers among the general audience: one for actor-fanciers. Albert Finney, Matthew Modine. Kevin Anderson, John Kellogg. Written by Lyle Kessler from his play; directed by Alan J. Pakula; for Lorimar.

'Can a woman love more than one man?'
Orphans of the Storm*
US 1921 124m (24 fps) bw silent
D. W. Griffith

Two sisters are caught up in the French revolution of 1789.
Half melodrama, half epic, this celebrated film survives chiefly by its careful attention to historical detail and by the excitement of its crowd scenes.

w D. W. Griffith, *play* Adolph Ennery
d D. W. Griffith ph Henrick Sartov

Lillian Gish, Dorothy Gish, Joseph Schildkraut, Lucille La Verne, Morgan Wallace, Frank Puglia, Creighton Hale

'There is scarcely a scene or an effect in the entire production that is not beautiful to look upon, and there is scarcely a moment that is not charged with intense dramatic power.'—*Robert E. Sherwood, Life*

Orphée***
France 1949 112m bw
André Paulvé 1 / Films du Palais Royal

Death, represented by a princess, falls in love with Orpheus, a poet, and helps him when he goes into hell in pursuit of his dead love.
Fascinating poetic fantasy which may have been finally unintelligible but was filled to overflowing with memorable scenes and cinematic tricks, from the entry to the hereafter through a mirror to intercepted code messages such as 'L'oiseau compte avec ses doigts'. The closest the cinema has got to poetry.

wd Jean Cocteau, from his play *ph Nicolas Hayer m Georges Auric ad Jean d'Eaubonne*

Jean Marais, François Périer, Maria Casarès, Marie Déa, Edouard Dermithe, Juliette Greco

'It is a drama of the visible and the invisible . . . I interwove many myths. Death condemns herself in order to help the man she is duty bound to destroy. The man is saved but Death dies: it is the myth of immortality.'—*Jean Cocteau*

† See the sequel *Le Testament d'Orphée*.
†† The film was dedicated to its designer Christian Bérard (1902–49).

The Oscar*
US 1966 118m Pathecolor
Paramount / Greene-Rouse (Russel Rouse)

On the night of the Academy Awards his friend recalls a heel's rise to stardom. Squalid, sensationalist account of Hollywood mores; one hopes it isn't quite true.

w Harlan Ellison, Russel Rouse, Clarence Greene, *novel* Richard Sale *d* Russel Rouse *ph* Joseph Ruttenberg *m* Percy Faith

Stephen Boyd, Elke Sommer, Tony Bennett, Eleanor Parker, Milton Berle, Joseph Cotten, Jill St John, Edie Adams, Ernest Borgnine, Ed Begley, Walter Brennan, Broderick Crawford, James Dunn, Peter Lawford, Edith Head, Hedda Hopper, Merle Oberon, Bob Hope, Frank Sinatra

'This is the sort of film that only Hollywood could make, and on that level it is preposterously enjoyable.'—*David Wilson*

'That true movie rarity—a picture that attains a perfection of ineptitude quite beyond the power of words to describe.'—*Richard Schickel*

Oscar Wilde**
GB 1959 96m bw
Vantage (William Kirby)

Scandal strikes Oscar Wilde through his involvement with Lord Alfred Douglas. Competent, well acted version of well-known events of the nineties, with Morley in his original stage role; generally more satisfactory than *The Trials of Oscar Wilde* which was shot simultaneously.

w Jo Eisinger *d* Gregory Ratoff *ph* Georges Périnal *m* Kenneth V. Jones

Robert Morley, John Neville, Phyllis Calvert, *Ralph Richardson*, Dennis Price, Alexander Knox, Edward Chapman, Martin Benson, Robert Harris, Henry Oscar, William Devlin

O'Shaughnessy's Boy
US 1935 88m bw

A circus performer is reunited with the son his wife took away in childhood. Shameless sentiment which failed to repeat for its stars the success of *The Champ*. Wallace Beery, Jackie Cooper, Leona Maricle, Sara Haden, Henry Stephenson, Spanky MacFarland. Written by Leonard Praskins and Otis Garrett; directed by Richard Boleslawski; for MGM.

'Far too much crying. Good production will help.'—*Variety*

Ossessione*
Italy 1942 135m bw
ICI

A wanderer falls for the wife of an innkeeper and they murder him, but fate takes a hand. Unofficial remake of *The Postman Always Rings Twice*, barely released outside Italy. A powerful melodrama credited with starting the neo-realist school.

w Antonio Pietrangeli, Giuseppe de Santis, Gianni Puccini, Luchino Visconti, Mario Alicata *d Luchino Visconti ph* Aldo Tonti, Domenico Scala *m* Giuseppe Rosati

ORDINARY PEOPLE. Actually, the family under the microscope was far from ordinary but let it pass. Oscar-winning director Robert Redford gives hand signals to another Oscar-winner, Timothy Hutton.

Massimo Girotti, Clara Calamai, Elio Marcuzzo

† Other versions: *Le Dernier Tournant* (France 1939); *The Postman Always Rings Twice* (US 1945).

The Osterman Weekend
US 1983 102m De Luxe

A CIA chief tries to convince a powerful TV journalist that several of his trusted informants are Soviet agents. Convoluted bloodbath with absolutely nothing new in its locker. Rutger Hauer, John Hurt, Burt Lancaster, Craig T. Nelson, Dennis Hopper, Chris Sarandon, Meg Foster, Helen Shaver. Written by Alan Sharp, Ian Masters, from the novel by Robert Ludlum; directed by Sam Peckinpah; for Davis-Panzer / Fox. 'A competent, professional, but thoroughly impersonal meller.'—*Variety*

Otello*
US / Italy 1986 120m Eastmancolor
Cannon / RAI (John Thompson, Fulvio Lucisano)

Verdi's opera based on Shakespeare's play, adapted and directed by Franco Zeffirelli. A visually splendid transcription which however did not hit the mark with audiences.

ph Ennio Guarnieri

Placido Domingo, Katia Ricciarelli, Justino Diaz, Petra Malakova

AA: costumes (Anna Anni, Maurizio Millenotti)

Othello*
US / France 1951 91m bw
Mercury / Films Marceau (Orson Welles)

Shakespeare's play as rearranged by Orson Welles at the start of his European wanderings; modest budget, flashes of brilliance, poor technical quality, variable acting. Not really the best way to film Shakespeare.

w Orson Welles, *play* William Shakespeare *d* Orson Welles *ad* Alexander Trauner *ph* Anchise Brizzi, George Fanto, Obadan Troania, Roberto Fusi, G. Araldo *m* Francesco Lavagnino, Alberto Barberis

Orson Welles, Micheal MacLiammoir, Fay Compton, Robert Cook, Suzanne Cloutier, Michael Laurence, Hilton Edwards, Doris Dowling

Othello*
GB 1965 166m Technicolor Panavision
BHE (Richard Godwin)

A record of the National Theatre production, disappointing in terms of cinema but a valuable record of a famous performance.

d Stuart Burge *ph* Geoffrey Unsworth *md* Richard Hampton

Laurence Olivier, Frank Finlay, Joyce Redman, Maggie Smith, Derek Jacobi, Robert Lang, Anthony Nicholls

AAN: Laurence Olivier; Frank Finlay; Joyce Redman; Maggie Smith

'What the director does is keep the camera moving among the actors with the most intelligent precision.'—*Observer*

The Other*
US 1972 100m De Luxe
TCF / Rex-Benchmark (Tom Tryon)

A boy insists that his dead twin is responsible for several unexplained deaths.
Subtle family ghost story for intellectuals; a bit pretentious and restrained for popular success.

w Tom Tryon, from his novel *d* Robert Mulligan *ph* Robert Surtees *m* Jerry Goldsmith *pd* Albert Brenner

Uta Hagen, Diana Muldaur, Chris Connelly, Victor French

'Her every exciting moment was an unforgettable experience!'
The Other Love
US 1947 96m bw
Enterprise (David Lewis)

At a Swiss sanatorium, a lady concert pianist who is dying falls in love with her doctor.
Fairly icky 'woman's picture' with uncomfortable performances.

w Ladislas Fodor, Harry Brown, *story* Erich Maria Remarque *d* André de Toth *ph* Victor Milner *m* Miklos Rozsa

Barbara Stanwyck, David Niven, Richard Conte, Gilbert Roland, Joan Lorring, Lenore Aubert

Other Men's Women
US 1931 70m bw

A train driver falls for his partner's wife.
Stilted heavy-breathing melodrama. Grant Withers, James Cagney, Mary Astor, Joan Blondell, Regis Toomey. Written by William K. Wells; directed by William A. Wellman; for Warner. 'Good railroad melo for the lesser run theatres.'—*Variety*

'The romance of passion and power!'
The Other Side of Midnight
US 1977 166m De Luxe Panavision
TCF / Frank Yablans, Martin Ransohoff (Howard W. Koch Jnr)

Before and after World War II a young Parisienne courts an American flyer, but her tycoon husband eventually exacts a grim revenge on both of them.
Turgid and interminable adaptation of a best-seller, with no likeable characters and several unpleasant sequences.

w Herman Raucher, Daniel Taradash, *novel* Sidney Sheldon *d* Charles Jarrott *ph* Fred J. Koenekamp *m* Michel Legrand *pd* John De Cuir

Marie-France Pisier, John Beck, Susan Sarandon, Raf Vallone, Clu Gulager, Christian Marquand

'After 166 minutes the feeling that one has actually lived through it all is a little too real for comfort.'—*David Badder, MFB*

'A fatuous, money-spinning film from the fatuous, money-spinning book.'—*New Yorker*

'Right down to the nonsense title, this epic of schlock restores the era of *Now Voyager* . . . the movie equivalent of a good bad read.'—*Time Out*

'Once in your life—may someone love you like this!'
The Other Side of the Mountain
US 1975 102m Technicolor
Universal / Filmways / Larry Peerce (Edward S. Feldman)
GB title: *A Window to the Sky*

A girl skiing champion is paralysed by polio.
Maudlin tearjerker based on a real case; altogether too much of a good thing.

w David Seltzer, *book* A Long Way Up by E. G. Valens *d* Larry Peerce *ph* David M. Walsh *m* Charles Fox

Marilyn Hassett, Beau Bridges, Belinda Montgomery, Nan Martin, William Bryant, Dabney Coleman

AAN: song 'Richard's Window' (*m* Charles Fox, *ly* Norman Gimbel)

'For everyone who believes in happy endings!'
The Other Side of the Mountain Part Two
US 1977 99m Technicolor
Universal / Filmways (Edward S. Feldman)

Crippled skier Jill Kinmont becomes a teacher and falls in love again.
More true-life weepie material spun out from the first successful film; the sequel is quickly forgettable.

w Douglas Day Stewart *d* Larry Peerce *ph* Ric Waite *m* Lee Holdridge

Marilyn Hassett, Timothy Bottoms, Nan Martin, Belinda J. Montgomery

Otley**
GB 1968 91m Technicolor
Columbia / Open Road (Bruce Cohn Curtis)

An inoffensive Londoner falls in with spies and murderers.
Semi-spoof comedy thriller taking in James Bondery and the swinging London set. Generally pretty funny, but not entirely certain of its own motives.

w Ian La Frenais, Dick Clement, *novel* Martin Waddell *d* Dick Clement *ph* Austin Dempster *m* Stanley Myers

Tom Courtenay, Romy Schneider, Alan Badel, James Villiers, Leonard Rossiter, Freddie Jones, James Bolam, Fiona Lewis

Our Betters*
US 1933 83m bw
RKO (David O. Selznick)

An American woman in London finds her titled husband is unfaithful and sets about causing society scandals.
Dimly adapted West End success makes an interesting but unamusing film.

w Jane Murfin, Harry Wagstaff Gribble, *play* W. Somerset Maugham *d* George Cukor *ph* Charles Rosher *md* Max Steiner

Constance Bennett, Violet Kemble Cooper, Alan Mowbray, Gilbert Roland, Phoebe Foster, Charles Starrett, Grant Mitchell, Anita Louise, Minor Watson, Hugh Sinclair

'It's all very English and so sophisticated . . . they will really have to go for Constance Bennett to go for this picture.'—*Variety*

'One of those familiar dreams of high life in which we are asked to admire even while we condemn the superb immorality of our almost godlike betters.'—*The Times*

Our Blushing Brides see Our Dancing Daughters

Our Daily Bread*
US 1934 80m bw
(UA) Viking / King Vidor

A young couple in the Depression inherit a broken-down farm and make it work.
A rather drab sequel to *The Crowd*, with an irrigation ditch finale in clear imitation of Eisenstein.

w Elizabeth Hill, *story* King Vidor *d King Vidor* *ph* Robert Planck *m* Alfred Newman

Karen Morley, Tom Keene, John Qualen, Barbara Pepper, Addison Richards

'Regardless of the scepticism on the matter of box office, and its chances seem thin, it ranks as a fine effort.'—*Variety*

'With the arrival of the ditchdigging sequence, all that has gone before seems but buildup for this compelling climax.'—*Eileen Bowser, Film Notes, 1969*

† Vidor so desperately wanted to make the film that, discovering its theme to be unpopular with sponsors, he pawned everything he owned to finance it.

Our Dancing Daughters*
US 1928 86m approx (24 fps) bw silent
MGM / Cosmopolitan (Hunt Stromberg)

A wild young socialite knows when to stop, and makes a good marriage; her friend doesn't and falls to her death while drunk.
Mild exploitation piece of its time which swept Joan Crawford to stardom after her dance in her underwear.

w Josephine Lovett *d* Harry Beaumont *ph* George Barnes

Joan Crawford, Johnny Mack Brown, Dorothy Sebastian, Anita Page, Nils Asther
† Sequels: *Our Modern Maidens* (silent, 1929) with JC, Rod La Rocque, Douglas Fairbanks Jnr, Anita Page, *w* Josephine Lovett; *Our Blushing Brides* (sound, 1930) with JC, Robert Montgomery, Anita Page, Dorothy Sebastian, Raymond Hackett, *w* Bess Meredyth and John Howard Lawson. Neither was remarkable.

AAN: Josephine Lovett; George Barnes.

Our Fighting Navy
GB 1937 75m bw

In South America, a British naval captain saves the consul's daughter from a revolutionary. Tuppenny blood heroics, unconvincingly staged. Robert Douglas, H. B. Warner, Noah Beery, Richard Cromwell, Hazel Terry, Esme Percy. Written by 'Bartimeus', Guy Pollock, H. T. Bishop, Gerald Elliott and Harrison Owens; directed by Norman Walker; for Herbert Wilcox. (US title: *Torpedoed.*)

Our Girl Friday
GB 1953 87m Eastmancolor

Four shipwrecked survivors are washed up on a desert island. Coy sex comedy for the family; pretty unbearable. Kenneth More, Joan Collins, George Cole, Robertson Hare, Hermione Gingold, Walter Fitzgerald. Written and directed by Noel Langley; for Renown. (US title: *The Adventures of Sadie.*)

Our Hearts Were Young and Gay*
US 1944 81m bw
Paramount (Sheridan Gibney)

Two well-to-do flappers of the twenties find fun and romance in Paris.
A pleasant, undemanding piece of nostalgia based on a popular biography.

w Sheridan Gibney, *book* Cornelia Otis Skinner, Emily Kimbrough *d* Lewis Allen *ph* Theodor Sparkuhl *m* Werner Heymann

Gail Russell, Diana Lynn, Charles Ruggles, Dorothy Gish, Beulah Bondi, James Brown, Bill Edwards, Jean Heather

Our Hearts Were Growing Up
US 1946 83m bw

Our two heroines experience their college days during the roaring twenties. Rather stiffly made but fitfully amusing sequel to the above. Gail Russell, Diana Lynn, Brian Donlevy, James Brown, William Demarest, Bill Edwards, Billy DeWolfe, Sara Haden. Written by Norman Panama and Melvin Frank; directed by William D. Russell; for Daniel Dare / Paramount.

Our Hospitality***
US 1923 70m approx (24 fps) bw silent
Metro / Buster Keaton (Joseph M. Schenck)

Around 1850, a southerner returns home to claim his bride and finds himself in the middle of a blood feud.
Charming rather than hilarious star comedy with a splendid ancient train and at least one incredible stunt by the star.

w Jean Havez, Joseph Mitchell, Clyde Bruckman *d* Buster Keaton, Jack Blystone *ph* Elgin Lessley, Gordon Jennings

Buster Keaton, Natalie Talmadge, Joe Keaton, Buster Keaton Jnr

'A novelty mélange of dramatics, low comedy, laughs and thrills . . . one of the best comedies ever produced.'—*Variety*

Our Leading Citizen
US 1939 87m bw

A philosophical lawman tries to deal with labour unrest in his community. Another attempt to make a star out of a character who appealed only in rural districts. Bob Burns, Susan Hayward, Joseph Allen, Charles Bickford, Elizabeth Patterson, Clarence Kolb, Paul Guilfoyle. Written by John C. Moffitt from stories by Irvin S. Cobb; directed by Alfred Santell; for George Arthur / Paramount. 'Confusing and burdensome script . . . programme supporter.'—*Variety*

Our Little Girl
US 1935 63m bw
Fox (Edward Butcher)

A doctor's daughter brings her parents together.
One of the child star's thinner and more sentimental vehicles.

w Stephen Morehouse Avery, Allen Rivkin, Jack Yellen, *story* Heaven's Gate by Florence Leighton Pfalzgraf *d* John Robertson *ph* John Seitz *md* Oscar Bradley

Shirley Temple, Joel McCrea, Rosemary Ames, Lyle Talbot, Erin O'Brien-Moore

'She should easily satisfy her following and assure business.'—*Variety*

Our Man Flint*
US 1965 108m De Luxe Cinemascope
TCF (Saul David)

An American secret agent and super stud fights an organization bent on controlling the world through its weather.
Comic strip imitation of James Bond; in its wild way the first instalment scored a good many laughs, but the sequel, *In Like Flint* (qv), quickly ended the series.

w Hal Fimberg, Ben Starr *d* Daniel Mann *ph* Daniel L. Fapp *m* Jerry Goldsmith

James Coburn, Lee J. Cobb, Gila Golan, Edward Mulhare, Benson Fong, Sigrid Valdis

'Despite the fact that everyone from designers to actors seems to be having a ball, the film somehow goes over the edge of parody—ultimately it looks suspiciously like a case of wish-fulfilment.'—*John Gillett*

Our Man in Havana*
GB 1959 112m bw Cinemascope
Columbia / Kingsmead (Carol Reed)

A British vacuum cleaner salesman in Havana allows himself to be recruited as a spy, and wishes he hadn't.
The wry flavour of the novel does not really translate to the screen, and especially not to the wide screen, but a few lines and characters offer compensation.

w Graham Greene, from his novel *d* Carol Reed *ph* Oswald Morris *m* Hermanos Deniz Cuban Rhythm Band

Alec Guinness, *Noel Coward*, Burl Ives, Maureen O'Hara, Ernie Kovacs, *Ralph Richardson*, Jo Morrow, Paul Rogers, Grégoire Aslan, Duncan Macrae

'The main weakness is the absence of economic, expressive cutting and visual flow. As a result . . . stretches of dialogue become tedious to watch; and the essential awareness of the writer's shifting tensions yields disappointingly to the easier mannerisms of any conventional comedy-thriller.'—*Peter John Dyer*

Our Man in Marrakesh
GB 1966 92m Technicolor

A tourist becomes involved with gangsters. Thin comedy-thriller with exotic locations. Tony Randall, Senta Berger, Terry-Thomas, Herbert Lom, Wilfrid Hyde White, Gregoire Aslan, Klaus Kinski. Written by Peter Yeldham; directed by Don Sharp; for Harry Alan Towers. (US title: *Bang Bang, You're Dead.*)

Our Miss Brooks
US 1955 85m bw

A lady teacher finds that the professor to whom she is engaged is tied to mother's apron strings. Verbose comedy considerably less funny than the TV series from which it was spun off. Eve Arden, Gale Gordon, Robert Rockwell, Don Porter, Jane Morgan, Richard Crenna, Nick Adams. Written by Al Lewis and Joseph Quillan; directed by Al Lewis; for Warner.

Our Miss Fred*
GB 1972 96m Technicolor
EMI / Willis World Wide (Josephine Douglas)

In World War II France, an actor escapes in women's clothes when his troupe is captured by the Nazis.
A carefully nurtured vehicle for Britain's top female impersonator somehow doesn't come off; celluloid both constrains his range and reveals his inadequacies.

w Hugh Leonard *d* Bob Kellett *ph* Dick Bush *m* Peter Greenwell

Danny La Rue, Alfred Marks, Lance Percival, Lally Bowers, Frances de la Tour, Walter Gotell

Our Modern Maidens see Our Dancing Daughters

Our Mother's House
GB 1967 105m Metrocolor
MGM / Filmways (Jack Clayton)

When mother dies, seven children, who don't want to go to an orphanage, bury her in the garden. Then their ne'er-do-well father turns up.
Unpleasant and rather boring melodrama, too silly to have much dramatic impact.

w Jeremy Brooks, Haya Harareet, *novel* Julian Gloag *d* Jack Clayton *ph* Larry Pizer *m* Georges Delerue

Dirk Bogarde, Margaret Brooks, Pamela Franklin, Mark Lester, Yootha Joyce, Anthony Nicholls

'The children begin to display an alarming variety of accents . . . and when Dirk Bogarde enters, doing a rich Bill Sykes act as the long lost wicked father to a predominantly genteel family, the whole structure collapses.'—*Tom Milne*

Our Neighbours the Carters
US 1939 85m bw

A small-town pharmacist is so poor that he considers an offer from a wealthy friend to adopt one of his children. A small-town saga of smiles and tears, much appreciated at the time. Fay Bainter, Frank Craven, Genevieve Tobin, Edmund Lowe. Written by S. K. Lauren and Renaud Hoffman; directed by Ralph Murphy; for Paramount. 'Neatly set up as a programmer for the family trade.'—*Variety*

Our Relations***
US 1936 65m bw
Hal Roach / Stan Laurel Productions

Two sailors entrusted with a diamond ring get mixed up with their long lost and happily married twin brothers.
A fast-moving comedy which contains some of Laurel and Hardy's most polished work as well as being their most satisfying production.

w Richard Connell, Felix Adler, Charles Roger, Jack Jevne, *story* The Money Box by W. W. Jacobs *d Harry Lachman ph Rudolph Maté*

Stan Laurel, Oliver Hardy, James Finlayson, Alan Hale, Sidney Toler, Daphne Pollard, Iris Adrian, Noel Madison, Ralf Harolde, *Arthur Housman*

'The story of a love affair that lasted a lifetime!'

Our Town**
US 1940 90m bw
Principal Artists / Sol Lesser

Birth, life and death in a small New Hampshire community.
One of the main points of the play, the absence of scenery, is abandoned in this screen version, and the graveyard scene has to be presented as a dream, but the film retains the narrator and manages to make points of its own while absorbing the endearing qualities which made the play a classic.

w Thornton Wilder, Frank Craven, Harry Chantlee, *play* Thornton Wilder *d Sam Wood ph* Bert Glennon *m* Aaron Copland *pd William Cameron Menzies*

Frank Craven, William Holden, *Martha Scott, Thomas Mitchell, Fay Bainter, Guy Kibbee, Beulah Bondi*, Stuart Erwin

'You can nearly smell things cooking, and feel the night air.'—*Otis Ferguson*

AAN: best picture; Aaron Copland; Martha Scott

Our Very Own
US 1950 93m bw
Samuel Goldwyn

A girl is shocked to discover that she is adopted.
Another Goldwyn foray into chintzy, middle-class, small-town America, but not a winning example.

w F. Hugh Herbert *d* David Miller *ph* Lee Garmes *m* Victor Young *ad* Richard Day

Ann Blyth, Farley Granger, Joan Evans, Jane Wyatt, Ann Dvorak, Donald Cook, Natalie Wood, Gus Schilling, Phyllis Kirk

Our Vines Have Tender Grapes*
US 1945 105m bw
MGM (Robert Sisk)

Life in a Norwegian farm community in southern Wisconsin.
Unexceptionable family picture produced in MGM's best manner.

w Dalton Trumbo, *novel* George Victor Martin *d* Roy Rowland *ph* Robert Surtees *m* Bronislau Kaper

Edward G. Robinson, Margaret O'Brien, James Craig, Agnes Moorehead, Jackie 'Butch' Jenkins, Morris Carnovsky, Frances Gifford, Sara Haden

Our Wife*
US 1931 20m bw

Stan helps Ollie to elope. Good standard star comedy with a rather disappointing third sequence as three people try to get into a car designed for one. Laurel and Hardy, James Finlayson, Jean London. Written by H. M. Walker; directed by James W. Horne; for Hal Roach.

Our Wife
US 1941 95m bw
Columbia (John M. Stahl)

A composer is romantically torn between a lady scientist and his own ex-wife.
Middling romantic comedy of a kind very familiar at the time.

w P. J. Wolfson, *play* Lillian Day by Lyon Mearson *d* John M. Stahl *ph* Franz Planer *m* Leo Shuken

Melvyn Douglas, Ruth Hussey, Ellen Drew, Charles Coburn, John Hubbard, Harvey Stephens

Ourselves Alone
GB 1936 87m bw

An Irish colleen has a brother in the IRA and a lover in the British Army. Rather tired hawking of a theme already treated in *Beloved Enemy*. Antoinette Cellier, Niall MacGinnis, John Lodge, John Loder, Clifford Evans. Written by Dudley Leslie, Marjorie Jeans, Dennis Johnston from the play by Dudley Sturrock and Noel Scott; directed by Brian Desmond Hurst, Walter Summers; for British International. 'Will find tough sledding because of the subject matter.'—*Variety*

Out of Africa**
US/GB 1985 150m Rank colour Technovision
Mirage / Sydney Pollack

In 1914 Karen Blixen arrives in Africa for a marriage of convenience with a German baron who ignores her; a white hunter remedies the situation.
Heavy going but critically lauded transcription of a semi-classic which ambles along for an extremely long time without really getting anywhere.

w Kurt Luedtke, from writings of 'Isak Dinesen' (Karen Blixen) *d* Sydney Pollack *ph* David Watkin *m* John Barry *pd* Stephen Grimes

Meryl Streep, Robert Redford, Klaus Maria Brandauer, Michael Kitchen, Michael Gough

'It's a long way to go for a downbeat ending.'—*Variety*

'The film purrs pleasantly along like one of its own big cats.'—*Sight and Sound*

AA: best picture; direction; photography; music; art direction; adapted screenplay

AAN: Meryl Streep; Klaus Maria Brandauer (supporting actor)

Out of Season*
GB 1975 90m Technicolor
EMI / Lorimar (Robert Enders, Merv Adelson)

One winter in an English seaside resort, an old love is rekindled.
Restrained sexual fireworks in the old French manner, well enough done with excellent atmosphere but a shade overlong and marred by the need to indulge in modern tricks such as a deliberately ambiguous ending.

w Reuben Bercovitch, Eric Bercovici *d Alan Bridges ph* Arthur Ibbetson *m* John Cameron

Cliff Robertson, Vanessa Redgrave, Susan George, Edward Evans

Out of the Blue
GB 1931 88m bw

An aristocrat's daughter loves the radio singer who is engaged to her sister. Dated frou-frou with interesting talent. Jessie Matthews, Gene Gerrard, Kay Hammond, Kenneth Kove, Binnie Barnes. Written by R. P. Weston, Frank Miller and Bert Lee, from the play *Little Tommy Tucker* by Caswell Garth and Desmond Carter; directed by Gene Gerrard and John Orton; for BIP.

Out of the Blue
US 1947 86m bw

A Greenwich village artist thinks a girl who has passed out in his apartment is dead, and tries to hide the body. Tasteless and very unfunny farce. George Brent, Carole Landis, Ann Dvorak, Turhan Bey, Virginia Mayo, Elizabeth Patterson, Julia Dean, Richard Lane. Written by Vera Caspary, Walter Bullock and Edward Eliscu; directed by Leigh Jason; for Eagle Lion.

Out of the Clouds
GB 1954 88m Eastmancolor
Ealing (Michael Relph, Basil Dearden)

Several personal stories mesh against a background of London airport during a fog.
A dull compendium of stories with a background of documentary detail which is now fascinating because it's so dated.

w John Eldridge, Michael Relph *d* Michael Relph, Basil Dearden *ph* Paul Beeson *m* Richard Addinsell

Anthony Steel, Robert Beatty, David Knight, Margo Lorenz, James Robertson Justice, Eunice Gayson, Isabel Dean, Gordon Harker, Bernard Lee, Michael Howard, Marie Lohr, Esme Cannon, Abraham Sofaer

'The film relies considerably on small-time players and marginal incidents; the detail, however, never looks like adding up to a satisfactory whole.'—*Penelope Houston*

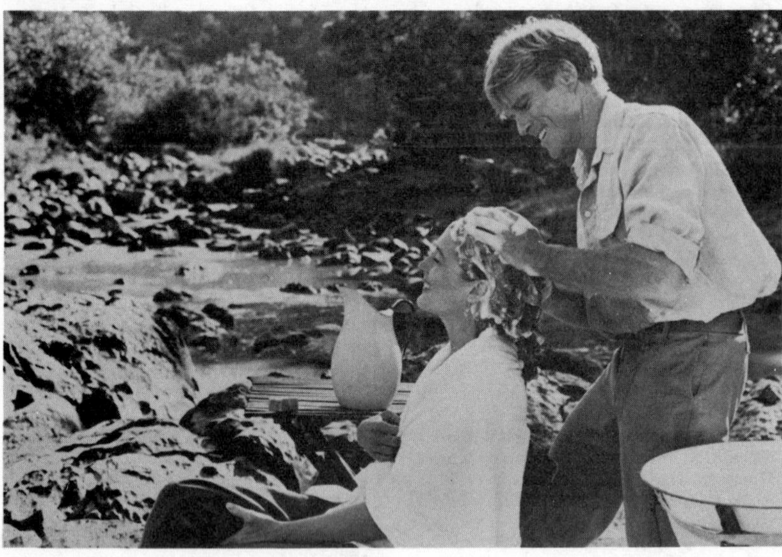

OUT OF AFRICA. Meryl Streep was an excellent Karen Blixen but few were convinced by Robert Redford's Hollywood-style White Hunter.

Out of the Fog*
US 1941 86m bw
Warner (Henry Blanke)

Gangsters move in to terrorize an innocent Brooklyn family.
Standard exploration of a situation which became routine.

w Robert Rossen, Jerry Wald, Richard Macaulay, *play* The Gentle People by Irwin Shaw *d* Anatole Litvak *ph* James Wong Howe

Ida Lupino, John Garfield, Thomas Mitchell, Eddie Albert, George Tobias, Aline MacMahon, Jerome Cowan, John Qualen, Leo Gorcey

'You're no good and neither am I. We deserve each other!'
Out of the Past**
US 1947 97m bw
RKO (Warren Duff)
GB title: *Build My Gallows High*

A private detective is hired by a hoodlum to find his homicidal girl friend; he does, and falls in love with her.
Moody *film noir* with Hollywood imitating French models; plenty of snarling and a death-strewn climax.

w Geoffrey Homes, from his novel Build My Gallows High *d Jacques Tourneur*
ph Nicholas Musuraca *m* Roy Webb

Robert Mitchum, Jane Greer, Kirk Douglas, Rhonda Fleming, Richard Webb, Steve Brodie, Virginia Huston, Dickie Moore

'Is this not an outcrop of the national masochism induced by a quite aimless, newly industrialized society proceeding rapidly on its way to nowhere?'—*Richard Winnington*

'Mitchum is so sleepily self-confident with the women that when he slopes into clinches you expect him to snore in their faces.'—*James Agee*

'The laugh-a-minute lowdown on the birth of swoon!'
Out of this World
US 1945 96m bw
Paramount (Sam Coslow)

A Western Union messenger becomes a hit crooner and a national phenomenon.
Very mild comedy with the gimmick that Bing Crosby dubbed the singing.

w Walter de Leon, Arthur Phillips *d* Hal Walker *ph* Stuart Thompson *m* Victor Young

Eddie Bracken, Veronica Lake, Diana Lynn, Cass Daley, Parkyakarkus, Donald MacBride, Florence Bates, Carmen Cavallero

The Out of Towners*
US 1970 98m Movielab
Paramount / Jalem (Paul Nathan)

An executive and his wife fly into New York for an interview, but their encounter with the city is a mounting series of traumatic disasters.
A love-hate relationship with a city demonstrated by a resident is something of an in-joke and becomes increasingly hysterical and unsympathetic, but there are bright moments in this company.

w Neil Simon *d* Arthur Hiller *ph* Andrew Laszlo *m* Quincy Jones

Jack Lemmon, Sandy Dennis

Outback*
Australia 1970 109m Technicolor
NIT / Group W (George Willoughby)

A young teacher becomes involved in the rougher side of life in a remote Australian village.
A convincingly brutal picture of a community whose interests range from homosexuality to a bloody kangaroo hunt.

w Evan Jones, *novel* Wake in Fright by Kenneth Cook *d Ted Kotcheff ph* Brian West *m* John Scott

Gary Bond, Donald Pleasence, Chips Rafferty

Outcast Lady
US 1934 79m bw

A spoilt rich girl goes from man to man but helps her drunken brother. Modest remake of the Garbo vehicle *A Woman of Affairs.*
Constance Bennett, Hugh Williams, Mrs Patrick Campbell, Elizabeth Allan, Henry Stephenson, Leo G. Carroll. Written by Zoe Akins, from the novel *The Green Hat* by Michael Arlen; directed by Robert Z. Leonard; for MGM. (GB title: *A Woman of the World.*)

'Even her love was primitive!'
An Outcast of the Islands**
GB 1951 102m bw
London Films (Carol Reed)

A shiftless trader finds a secret Far Eastern trading post where he can be happy – but even here he becomes an outcast.
An interesting but not wholly successful attempt to dramatize a complex character study. It looks great and is well acted.

w William Fairchild, *novel* Joseph Conrad *d* Carol Reed *ph John Wilcox m* Brian Easdale

Trevor Howard, Ralph Richardson, Kerima, Robert Morley, Wendy Hiller, George Coulouris, Frederick Valk, Wilfrid Hyde White, Betty Ann Davies

'The script is so overwhelmed by the narrative itself that the characters and relationships fail to crystallize . . . while the handling is often intelligent, ingenious, and has its effective moments, no real conception emerges.'—*Gavin Lambert*

'Its sordidness is not veneered by the usual lyricism of Hollywood.'—*London Evening News*

'The most powerful film ever made in this country.'—*Observer*

The Outcasts of Poker Flat
US 1937 68m bw
RKO (Robert Sisk)

Four undesirables are run out of town and stuck in a mountain cabin during a snowstorm. Overstretched anecdote with a predictably downbeat finale and not much action.

w John Twist, Harry Segall, *story* Bret Harte *d* Christy Cabanne *ph* Robert de Grasse

Preston Foster, Jean Muir, Van Heflin

The Outcasts of Poker Flat
US 1952 80m bw
TCF (Julian Blaustein)

Good-looking but equally undramatic remake of the above.

w Edmund H. North *d* Joseph M. Newman *ph* Joseph La Shelle *m* Hugo Friedhofer

Dale Robertson, Anne Baxter, Cameron Mitchell, Miriam Hopkins

'Fails badly either as dramatic or as western fare . . . best where two features prevail.'—*Variety*

The Outfit
US 1973 103m Metrocolor
MGM (Carter de Haven)

A criminal just out of prison finds himself in danger from the Syndicate.
Unattractive rehash of *Point Blank* with much gratuitous violence.

wd John Flynn, *novel* Richard Stark *ph* Bruce Surtees *m* Jerry Fielding

Robert Duvall, Karen Black, Robert Ryan, Joe Don Baker, Timothy Carey, Richard Jaeckel, Sheree North, Marie Windsor, Jane Greer, Elisha Cook Jnr

'A nice profusion of Hollywood character actors makes up for the overall lack of drive.'—*Sight and Sound*

'Even in space, the ultimate enemy is man!'
'On Jupiter's moon, something deadly is happening!'

Outland
GB 1981 109m Technicolor Panavision
Warner / Ladd (Richard A. Roth)

The marshal of a mining base on the third moon of Jupiter waits for hired killers to arrive from Earth and try to assassinate him.
Ludicrous, over-plotted outer-space version of *High Noon*, in such thick colour that the action is hard to follow.

w,d Peter Hyams *ph* Stephen Goldblatt *m* Jerry Goldsmith *pd* Philip Harrison

Sean Connery, Peter Boyle, Francis Sternhagen, James B. Sikking, Kika Markham, Clarke Peters

'Acres of footage are expended on the same old dreary electronic gadgetry and the same old hollowly echoing metalwork sets.'—*Tom Milne, MFB*

'Action! Thrills! Sensations! Primitive Love!'

The Outlaw*
US 1943 126m bw
Howard Hughes

Billy the Kid, Doc Holliday and Pat Garrett meet up at a way station and quarrel over a half-breed girl.
Half-baked western with much pretentious chat and the main interest squarely focused on the bosom of the producer's new discovery. This aspect kept censorship ballyhoo going for six years before the film was finally released in truncated form, and audiences found it not worth the wait, though it does look good.

w Jules Furthman *d* Howard Hughes *ph Gregg Toland* *md* Victor Young

Jack Beutel, Jane Russell, Thomas Mitchell, Walter Huston

Outlaw Blues
US 1977 101m Technicolor
Warner / Fred Weintraub–Paul Heller (Steve Tisch)

An ex-con finds that a singing star has stolen his song.
Fashionable comedy-melodrama with no great entertainment value despite action scenes towards the end.

w B. W. L. Norton *d* Richard T. Heffron *ph* Jules Brenner *m* Charles Bernstein

Peter Fonda, Susan Saint James, John Crawford, James Callahan, Michael Lerner

The Outlaw Josey Wales*
US 1976 135m De Luxe Panavision
Warner / Malpaso (Robert Daley)

A westerner gradually avenges the death of his wife at the hands of bandits.
Bloodthirsty actioner in the star's usual mould; likely to prove unintentionally funny for hardened addicts.

w Phil Kaufman, Sonia Chernus, *novel* Gone to Texas by Forrest Carter *d* Clint Eastwood *ph* Bruce Surtees *m* Jerry Fielding

Clint Eastwood, Chief Dan George, Sondra Locke, John Vernon, Bill McKinney

'If only the actors hadn't got in the way of the scenery, it would have been a very beautiful film indeed.'—*Benny Green, Punch*

AAN: Jerry Fielding

Outpost in Morocco
US 1949 92m bw
Joseph N. Ermolieff

A romantic Foreign Legion officer falls for the daughter of an enemy Arab.
Despite authentic locations and the co-operation of the Legion this is a stolid piece of work, too dull even for children's matinees.

w Charles Grayson, Paul de St Columbe *d* Robert Florey *ph* Lucien Andriot

George Raft, Akim Tamiroff, Marie Windsor, John Litel, Eduard Franz

Outrage
US 1950 75m bw
Filmmakers (Collier Young)

A girl who has been raped is almost unhinged by the experience.
Well-meaning low-budgeter, thin in entertainment value.

w Ida Lupino, Collier Young, Marvin Wald *d* Ida Lupino *ph* Archie Stout *m* Paul Sawtell *md* Constantin Bakaleinikoff *pd* Harry Horner

Mala Powers, Tod Andrews, Robert Clarke, Raymond Bond, Lilian Hamilton

'An unconvincing mixture of sensationalism, sentiment and half-baked sociology.'—*MFB*

The Outrage*
US 1964 97m bw Panavision
MGM / Harvest / February / Ritt / Kayos (A. Ronald Lubin)

Conflicting views of a western murder.
Wildly ineffective remake of *Rashomon*, with everyone strangely overacting and little sense of the west as it is normally depicted.

w Michael Kanin *d* Martin Ritt *ph* James Wong Howe *m* Alex North

Paul Newman, Edward G. Robinson, Laurence Harvey, Claire Bloom, William Shatner, Albert Salmi

Outrageous Fortune*
US 1986 100m De Luxe
Touchstone / Interscope (Ted Field, Robert Cort)

Two disparate women are in love with the same man, who is wanted by the CIA and the KGB.
Chase comedy with sex elements and plenty going on: old-fashioned jokes wrapped up in a modern package.

w Leslie Dixon *d* Arthur Hiller *ph* David M. Walsh *m* Alan Silvestri *pd* James D. Vance

Shelley Long, Bette Midler, Peter Coyote, Robert Prosky, John Schick

'Really a risqué film for a conservative audience.'—*Daily Variety*

The Outriders
US 1950 93m Technicolor
MGM (Richard Goldstone)

Three Confederate soldiers escape from a yankee prison camp.
Competent star western with solid production values.

w Irving Ravetch *d* Roy Rowland *ph* Charles Schoenbaum *m* André Previn

Joel McCrea, Arlene Dahl, Barry Sullivan, Claude Jarman Jnr, Ramon Novarro

The Outside Man
US / France 1973 104m colour

A French hit man comes to Los Angeles on a mission. Tough gangster movie which will satisfy fans. Jean-Louis Trintignant, Roy Scheider, Ann-Margret, Angie Dickinson, Georgia Engel. Written by Jacques Deray, Ian McLellan Hunter, Jean-Claude Carrière; directed by Jacques Deray; for Jacques Bar / UA.

Outside the Law
US 1930 76m bw

A girl becomes involved between two crooks planning a bank robbery. Incompetent early talkie with some familiar talents all at sea. Mary Nolan, Edward G. Robinson, Owen Moore, Edwin Sturgis. Written by Tod Browning, Garrett Fort; directed by Tod Browning; for Universal. 'One of the worst examples of claptrap since sound came in . . . no continuity and the director lets the cast run wild.'—*Variety*

The Outsider
GB 1931 93m bw

A 'quack' osteopath is finally able to make a surgeon's crippled daughter walk. Cast-iron theatre and a fairly successful quota quickie which was also released in America. Harold Huth, Joan Barry, Norman McKinnel, Frank Lawton, Mary Clare. Written by Harry Lachman and Alma Reville, from the play by Dorothy Brandon; directed by Harry Lachman; for Cinema House / MGM.

The Outsider
GB 1939 90m bw

Sturdy remake of the above. George Sanders, Mary Maguire, Frederick Leister, Peter Murray Hill, Kathleen Harrison. Written by Dudley Leslie; directed by Paul Stein; for ABPC. 'Up-to-date and should appeal to popular-priced audiences.'—*Variety*

The Outsider
US 1961 108m bw
U-I (Sy Bartlett)

Ira Hayes, a simple Red Indian, becomes a war hero but cannot reconcile himself to living in a white society.
Prolonged biopic which proves a shade too much for an eager star; it's all earnest and mildly interesting but not cinematically compulsive.

w Stewart Stern *d* Delbert Mann *ph* Joseph La Shelle *m* Leonard Rosenman

Tony Curtis, James Franciscus, Bruce Bennett, Gregory Walcott, Vivian Nathan, Edmund Hashim, Stanley Adams

The Outsiders
US 1983 91m Technicolor Panavision

A young punk leads a high school gang against another rather higher in the social scale. Oddball youth melodrama, a curious choice for a director with big successes behind him. Matt Dillon, Ralph Macchio, C. Thomas Howell, Patrick Swayze, Rob Lowe, Emilio Estevez, Tom Cruise. Written by Katherine Knutsen Rowell, from the novel by S. E. Hinton; directed by Francis Ford Coppola; for Zoetrope/Warner. 'No more than a well-acted teen film.'—*Motion Picture Guide*

Outward Bound*
US 1930 82m bw
Warner

Passengers on a strange liner discover that they are all dead and heading for purgatory. Early sound version of a popular twenties play which does not translate too well to cinematic forms and now seems very dated apart from a couple of performances; remade as *Between Two Worlds* (qv).

w J. Grubb Alexander, *play* Sutton Vane *d* Robert Milton *ph* Hal Mohr

Leslie Howard, Douglas Fairbanks Jnr, Alec B. Francis, Helen Chandler, Beryl Mercer, Alison Skipworth, Montagu Love, Dudley Digges

'Intelligentsia subject that must be spotted carefully . . . seems to lack the essentials of mass entertainment.'—*Variety*

Over My Dead Body
US 1942 67m bw

A writer plans commercial success by pleading guilty to an imaginary crime, but truth is stranger than fiction. Over-talkative crime comedy. Milton Berle, Mary Beth Hughes, Reginald Denny, Frank Orth, J. Pat O'Malley. Written by Edward James, from novel by James O'Hanlon; directed by Mal St Clair; for Walter Morosco / TCF.

Over She Goes*
GB 1937 74m bw

An old friend helps a nobleman to thwart a blackmailer. Lively comedy vehicle for a forgotten star. Stanley Lupino, Laddie Cliff, Gina Malo, Clare Luce, Max Baer, Sally Gray, Syd Walker. Written by Elizabeth Meehan and Hugh Brooke, from the play by Stanley Lupino; directed by Graham Cutts; for ABPC.

Over the Brooklyn Bridge
US 1983 106m Metrocolor

Misadventures of a family-ridden Jewish restaurant owner in New York. Frantic ethnic comedy with an unsympathetic hero. Elliott Gould, Margaux Hemingway, Sid Caesar, Shelley Winters, Burt Young, Carol Kane. Written by Arnold Somkin; directed by Menahem Golan; for Golan-Globus. 'The film's lip service to liberalism is offset by a blatantly sexist storyline.'—*Ruth Baumgarten, MFB*

Over the Hill
US 1931 87m bw

An ageing mother is sent to the poorhouse by her hard-hearted older son, but rescued by her ne'er-do-well younger one. Sound remake of a silent success which in 1920 made a star of Mary Carr, who thereafter specialized in playing dear old ladies. James Dunn, Sally Eilers, Mae Marsh, Edward Crandall, James Kirkwood. Written by Tom Barry and Jules Furthman from poems by Will Carleton; directed by Henry King; for Fox. 'There isn't a single overacted scene and there isn't a sequence that doesn't reach straight to the heart.'—*Variety*

Over the Moon
GB 1937 78m Technicolor
London Films (Alexander Korda)

A poor girl comes into a fortune but this does not help her romance with a proud young doctor.
Insubstantial comedy which turns itself into a European travelogue before petering out.

w Anthony Pelissier, Arthur Wimperis, Alec Coppel *d* Thornton Freeland *ph* Harry Stradling *m* Mischa Spoliansky

Merle Oberon, Rex Harrison, Ursula Jeans, Robert Douglas, Louis Borell, Zena Dare, Peter Haddon, David Tree

Over The Top
US 1987 93m Metrocolor Panavision

An arm wrestler tries to win the love of his son. Mundane melodrama which its star couldn't carry. Sylvester Stallone, Robert Loggia, Susan Blakely, Rick Zumwalt, David Mendenhall. Written by Stirling Silliphant, Sylvester Stallone; directed by Menaham Golan; for Cannon. 'Routinely made in every respect.'—*Daily Variety*.

Over the Wall
US 1938 72m bw

A man wrongly convicted of murder fights the prison system. Predictable semi-documentary thriller from the prolific pen of Warden Lewis E. Lawes; just an efficient second feature. Dick Foran, John Litel, June Travis, Dick Purcell, Veda Ann Borg, George E. Stone. Written by Crane Wilbur, George Bricker; directed by Frank MacDonald; for Warners. 'Authentic melodrama, headed for nice biz.'—*Variety*

Over Twenty-One
US 1945 102m bw
Columbia (Sidney Buchman)

A famous lady screenwriter copes with wartime domestic problems while her husband is off at the war.
Thin star comedy based on Ruth Gordon's play about her own predicament; not for the wider audience, and not very good anyway.

w Sidney Buchman, *play* Ruth Gordon *d* Alexander Hall *ph* Rudolph Maté *m* Marlin Skiles

Irene Dunne, Alexander Knox, Charles Coburn, Jeff Donnell, Lee Patrick, Phil Brown, Cora Witherspoon

Overland Mail
US 1942 bw serial: 15 eps

A western frontiersman investigates mail thefts. Strongly cast but otherwise ordinary serial. Lon Chaney Jnr, Noah Beery, Noah Beery Jnr, Helen Parrish, Don Terry. Directed by Ford Beebe and John Rawlins; for Universal.

Overland with Kit Carson
US 1939 bw serial: 15 eps

West of the Mississippi, a mysterious outlaw named Pegleg builds a corrupt empire. Rather yawnworthy adventures. Bill Elliott, Iris Meredith, Richard Fiske, Trevor Bardette. Directed by Sam Nelson and Norman Denning; for Columbia.

The Overlanders**
Australia 1946 91m bw
Ealing (Ralph Smart)

In 1943 a drover saves a thousand head of cattle from the Japanese by taking them two thousand miles across country.
Attractive, easy-going semi-western, the first and best of several films made by Ealing Studios in Australia.

wd Harry Watt ph Osmond Borradaile
m John Ireland

Chips Rafferty, John Heyward, Daphne Campbell

Overlord*
GB 1975 83m bw
EMI / Jowsend (James Quinn)

An eighteen-year-old is called up in early 1944 and killed in the D-Day landings.
Semi-documentary recreating a time in history (with much aid from newsreels) but making no discernible point. Interesting, though.

w Stuart Cooper, Christopher Hudson
d Stuart Cooper *ph* John Alcott *m* Paul Glass

Brian Stirner, Davyd Harries, Nicholas Ball, Julie Neesam

Owd Bob*
GB 1938 78m bw
GFD / Gainsborough (Edward Black)
US title: *To the Victor*

A Cumberland farmer's faithful dog is accused of killing sheep.
Sentimental yarn with good location backgrounds; the plot was later reused as *Thunder in the Valley*.

w Michael Hogan, J. B. Williams,
novel Alfred Olivant *d* Robert Stevenson
ph Jack Cox *md* Louis Levy

Will Fyffe, John Loder, Margaret Lockwood, Moore Marriott, Graham Moffatt, Wilfred Walter, Elliot Mason

The Owl and the Pussycat*
US 1970 96m Eastmancolor
Panavision
Columbia / Rastar (Ray Stark)

A bookstore assistant reports a fellow tenant for prostitution, and when she is evicted she moves in with him.
Wacky, bawdy double act which starts promisingly but outstays its welcome. A solid step forward in permissiveness, with kinky behaviour as well as four-letter words.

w Buck Henry, *play* Bill Manhoff *d* Herbert Ross *ph* Harry Stradling, Andrew Laszlo
m Richard Halligan

Barbra Streisand, George Segal, Robert Klein, Allen Garfield

'If computers ever turn out romantic comedies, the results will look like this.'—*Stanley Kauffmann*

The Ox-Bow Incident**
US 1943 75m bw
TCF (Lamar Trotti)
GB title: *Strange Incident*

A cowboy is unable to prevent three wandering travellers being unjustly lynched for murder.
Stark lynch law parable, beautifully made but very depressing.

w Lamar Trotti, *novel* Walter Van Tilburg Clark *d William Wellman ph Arthur Miller*
m Cyril Mockridge

Henry Fonda, Henry Morgan, Jane Darwell, Anthony Quinn, Dana Andrews, Mary Beth Hughes, William Eythe, Harry Davenport, *Frank Conroy*

'Realism that is as sharp and cold as a knife.'—*Frank S. Nugent, New York Times*

'Very firm, respectable, and sympathetic; but I still think it suffers from *rigor artis*.'—*James Agee*

AAN: best picture

Oxford Blues
US 1984 97m colour
Winkast / Baltic Industrial (Peter Kohn, David Wimbury)

A Los Angeles casino worker wins enough to finance an Oxford education.
Sexed-up version of *A Yank at Oxford*; only tolerable when the tone gets close to the original.

w,d Robert Boris *ph* John Stanier *m* John Du Prez

Rob Lowe, Ally Sheedy, Alan Howard, Amanda Pays, Julian Sands, Julian Firth, Michael Gough, Aubrey Morris

'Gun in one hand—woman in the other!'

P.J.
US 1967 109m Techniscope
Universal (Edward J. Montagne)
GB title: *New Face in Hell*

A down-at-heel private eye takes a job as bodyguard to a boorish businessman.
Routine thick-ear with a predictable turnabout plot.

w Philip Reisman Jnr *d* John Guillermin *ph* Loyal Griggs *m* Neal Hefti

George Peppard, Gayle Hunnicutt, Raymond Burr, Susan St James, Coleen Gray, Jason Evers, Wilfrid Hyde White, Severn Darden

'Enough action to keep you from noticing that the plot doesn't make any sense.'—*Judith Crist*

'A killer and a girl—trapped in America's first air raid!'

Pacific Blackout
US 1942 76m bw
Paramount (Sol C. Siegel)

An inventor escapes from jail and proves his innocence during a practice air raid blackout.
Minor melo which proved profitably topical, being released shortly after the Japanese attack on Pearl Harbor.

w Lester Cole, W. P. Lipscomb *d* Ralph Murphy *ph* Theodor Sparkuhl

Robert Preston, Martha O'Driscoll, Philip Merivale, Eva Gabor, Louis Jean Heydt, Thurston Hall

Pacific Destiny
GB 1956 97m Eastmancolor Cinemascope
James Lawrie

Experiences of a British colonial servant in the South Seas.
Pleasant episodic drama which needed a firmer hand all round.

w Richard Mason, *autobiography* A Pattern of Islands by Sir Arthur Grimble *d* Wolf Rilla *ph* Martin Curtis *m* James Bernard

Denholm Elliott, Susan Stephen, Michael Hordern

Pacific Liner
US 1938 73m bw

Cholera breaks out on a ship bound from Shanghai to San Francisco. Rather a depressing melodrama with all the action below decks, and very slow at that. Victor McLaglen, Chester Morris, Wendy Barrie, Alan Hale, Barry Fitzgerald, Halliwell Hobbes, Cy Kendall. Written by John Twist, Anthony Coldeway, Henry Roberts Symonds; directed by Lew Landers; for RKO. 'Drab melodrama with little of interest to hold attention.'—*Variety*

AAN: music (Robert Russell Bennett)

Pacific Rendezvous
US 1942 76m bw

A coding expert breaks up an enemy spy ring. Competent propaganda potboiler, rehashed from the rather smarter *Rendezvous*, which was set one war earlier. Lee Bowman, Jean Rogers, Mona Maris, Carl Esmond, Paul Cavanagh, Blanche Yurka. Written by Harry Kurnitz, P. J. Wolfson, George Oppenheimer; directed by George Sidney; for MGM.

The Pack
US 1977 99m colour

Abandoned dogs on a remote island turn on holidaymakers. *The Birds* becomes *The Dogs*; competently made but unsurprising thriller. Joe Don Baker, Hope Alexander Willis, Richard B. Shull, R. G. Armstrong. Written and directed by Robert Clouse, from the novel by Dave Fisher; for Warner.

Pack Up Your Troubles*
US 1931 68m bw
Hal Roach

Two World War I veterans try to look after their late pal's orphan daughter.
Patchy comedy vehicle in which too many gags are not fully thought out or timed.

w H. M. Walker *d* George Marshall, Ray McCarey *ph* Art Lloyd

Stan Laurel, Oliver Hardy, Donald Dillaway, Mary Carr, Charles Middleton, Dick Cramer, James Finlayson, Tom Kennedy, Billy Gilbert

Pack Up Your Troubles*
US 1939 75m bw
GB title: *We're In the Army Now*

Exploits in Flanders of three zany soldiers. Good slapstick antics in an unfamiliar venue. The Ritz Brothers, Jane Withers, Joseph Schildkraut, Lynn Bari, Stanley Fields. Written by Lou Breslow and Owen Francis; directed by H. Bruce Humberstone; for TCF. 'A pretty good programmer in the B division.'—*Variety*

The Pad, and How to Use It*
US 1966 86m Technicolor
Universal (Ross Hunter)

A shy young man has his first date.
Pleasant, odd little comedy apparently made in emulation of *The Knack*.

w Thomas C. Ryan, Benn Starr, *play* The Private Ear by Peter Shaffer *d* Brian C. Hutton *ph* Ellsworth Fredericks *m* Russ Garcia

Brian Bedford, James Farentino, Julie Sommars, Edy Williams, Nick Navarro

Paddy O'Day
US 1935 73m bw

An Irish child emigrates to America to find that her mother has died. One of the more satisfactory vehicles for a child star maintained by the studio as an antidote to the cuter antics of Shirley Temple. *Jane Withers*, Pinky Tomlin, Rita Hayworth, Jane Darwell, Francis Ford. Written by Lou Breslow and Edward Eliscu; directed by Lewis Seiler; for TCF.

Paddy the Next Best Thing
US 1933 75m bw
Fox

Adventures of an Irish tomboy in New York.
Modest star comedy from a popular play.

w Edwin Burke, *play* Gertrude Page *d* Harry Lachman *ph* John Seitz

Janet Gaynor, Warner Baxter, Walter Connolly, Harvey Stephens, Margaret Lindsay

'Easy entertainment: excellent, wholesome and amusing.'—*Variety*

Padre Padrone**
Italy 1977 113m Eastmancolor
Radiotelevisione Italia (Tonino Paoletti)
aka: *Father and Master*

The author recounts how he grew up with a violent and tyrannical father.
A vivid chunk of autobiography with food for thought on several levels, and a clever piece of film-making to boot.

wd Paolo Taviani, Vittorio Taviani, *book* Gavino Ledda *ph* Mario Masini *md* Egisto Macchi

Omero Antonutti, Saverio Marconi, Marcella Michelangeli

The Pagan
US 1929 85m approx bw

A South Sea islander falls for the daughter of a white trader. Highly commercial star vehicle apparently made as an afterthought to *White Shadows in the South Seas*. Ramon Novarro, Renee Adoree, Dorothy Janis, Donald Crisp. Written by Dorothy Farnum; directed by W. S. Van Dyke; for MGM.

Pagan Lady
US 1931 70m bw

A nice American boy in Havana falls for a girl who is no better than she should be. Sultry melodrama reminiscent of *Rain* but of no intrinsic merit. Evelyn Brent, Conrad Nagel, Charles Bickford, Roland Young, William Farnum. Written by Ben Glazer from the play by William Dubois; directed by John Francis Dillon; for Columbia. 'Something of a lightweight; the storm is quite the best thing in the picture.'—*Variety*

Pagan Love Song
US 1950 76m Technicolor
MGM (Arthur Freed)

An American schoolteacher marries a Tahitian girl.
Very mild musical potboiler using familiar talents.

w Robert Nathan, Jerry Davis *d* Robert Alton *ph* Charles Rosher *m* Harry Warren *ly* Arthur Freed

Esther Williams, Howard Keel, Rita Moreno, Minna Gombell

Page Miss Glory*
US 1935 90m bw
Warner / Cosmopolitan

A con man wins a beauty contest with a composite photograph of a non-existent girl.
Amusing comedy-musical, unjustly forgotten.

w Delmer Daves, Robert Lord, *play* Joseph Schrank, Philip Dunning *d* Mervyn Le Roy *ph* George Folsey *m / ly* Harry Warren, Al Dubin

Dick Powell, Marion Davies, Frank McHugh, Pat O'Brien, Mary Astor, Lyle Talbot, Patsy Kelly, Allen Jenkins, Barton MacLane

Pagliacci*
GB 1936 92m colour

A jealous clown kills his wife and her lover. A surprising British enterprise of the time which did fairly well at the box office, presumably because of the colour. Richard Tauber, Steffi Duna, Diana Napier, Arthur Margetson, Esmond Knight, Jerry Verno. Written by Monckton Hoffe, John Drinkwater, Roger Burford and Ernest Betts, from the opera by Ruggiero Leoncavallo; directed by Karl Grune; for Trafalgar. (US title: *A Clown Must Laugh*.)

Paid*
US 1930 80m bw
MGM
GB title: *Within the Law*

A woman sent to prison unjustly plots revenge on those responsible.
Reliable melodrama with the heroine eventually forgiving and forgetting.

w Charles MacArthur, Lucien Hubbard, *play* Within the Law by Bayard Veiller *d* Sam Wood *ph* Charles Rosher

Joan Crawford, Kent Douglass, Robert Armstrong, Marie Prévost, John Miljan, Polly Moran

Paid in Full
US 1949 105m bw
Paramount / Hal B. Wallis

A woman is responsible for the death of her sister's child, and becomes pregnant herself in the knowledge that giving birth will be fatal to her.
Stolid, contrived tearjerker.

w Robert Blees, Charles Schnee *d* William Dieterle *ph* Leo Tover *m* Victor Young

Lizabeth Scott, Diana Lynn, Robert Cummings, Eve Arden, Ray Collins, Frank McHugh, Stanley Ridges, Louis Jean Heydt

'Ben and pardner shared everything—even their wife!'

Paint Your Wagon*
US 1969 164m Technicolor
Panavision 70
Paramount / Alan Jay Lerner (Tom Shaw)

During the California Gold Rush, two prospectors set up a Mormon menage with the same wife.
Good-looking but uncinematic and monumentally long version of an old musical with a new plot and not much dancing. There are minor pleasures, but it really shouldn't have been allowed.

w Paddy Chayevsky, *musical play* Alan Jay Lerner, Frederick Loewe *d* Joshua Logan *ph* William A. Fraker *md* Nelson Riddle *pd* John Truscott

Lee Marvin, Clint Eastwood, Jean Seberg, Harve Presnell, Ray Walston

'One of those big movies in which the themes are undersized and the elements are juggled around until nothing fits together right and even the good bits of the original show you started with are shot to hell.'—*Pauline Kael*

AAN: Nelson Riddle

Painted Boats
GB 1945 63m bw

Romance among the bargees. Excessively thin location drama, which nevertheless has an early place in the Ealing tradition. Jenny Laird, Bill Blewett, Robert Griffith, May Hallatt. Written by Louis MacNeice and Michael McCarthy; directed by Charles Crichton; for Ealing. (US title: *The Girl on the Canal*.)

The Painted Stallion
US 1937 bw serial: 12 eps

Jim Bowie and Kit Carson lead the first wagon train to Santa Fe, and are helped by a mysterious girl rider. Adequate serial western. Ray Corrigan, Hoot Gibson, Sammy McKim, Leroy Mason, Duncan Renaldo. Directed by William Witney and Ray Taylor; for Republic.

The Painted Veil*
US 1934 84m bw
MGM (Hunt Stromberg)

In China, a doctor's wife gives up her lover to join her husband fighting an epidemic.
Soulful melodrama which seemed much more acceptable in this version than in the summer stock style remake *The Seventh Sin*.

w John Meehan, Salka Viertel, Edith Fitzgerald, *novel* W. Somerset Maugham *d* Richard Boleslawski *ph* William Daniels *m* Herbert Stothart

Greta Garbo, George Brent, Herbert Marshall, Warner Oland, Jean Hersholt

'Confused and slow, but extra heavy name cast should get it by.'—*Variety*

Painted Woman
US 1932 73m bw

A floozie stranded on a South Sea island resists offers of help from several men.
Another variation on *Rain*, and not the best. Spencer Tracy, Peggy Shannon, William Stage Boyd, Irving Pichel, Raul Roulien. Written by Guy Bolton, Leon Gordon, from A. C. Kennedy's After the Rain; directed by John Blystone; for Fox. 'It's hard to see how the studio figured a good picture would result from the material at hand.'—*Variety*

Painting the Clouds with Sunshine
US 1951 86m Technicolor
Warner (William Jacobs)

Three singing sisters go to Las Vegas in search of rich husbands.
Yet another revamp of the original *Gold Diggers* (qv), and not a very lively one.

w Henry Clark, Roland Kibbee, Peter Milne *d* David Butler *ph* Wilfred Cline

Virginia Mayo, Gene Nelson, Dennis Morgan, S. Z. Sakall, Lucille Norman, Tom Conway

A Pair of Briefs
GB 1961 90m bw
Rank / Betty E. Box–Ralph Thomas

Barristers Tony and Frances fall in love while opposing each other in court.
Adam's Rib need have no fears; this is the palest of imitations.

w Nicholas Phipps, *play* How Say You by Harold Brooke, Kay Bannerman *d* Ralph Thomas *ph* Ernest Steward *m* Norrie Paramor

Michael Craig, Mary Peach, Brenda de Banzie, James Robertson Justice, Roland Culver, Liz Fraser, Ron Moody, Jameson Clark, Charles Heslop

Paisà*
Italy 1946 115m bw
Foreign Film Productions / OFI

Six episodes in the Battle of Italy between 1943 and 1945.
More important historically than dramatically, *Paisà* was always a somewhat disappointing experience, especially as the earlier episodes are stronger than the later ones. Like *Open City*, it was partly improvised and had a gritty documentary quality.

w Federico Fellini, Roberto Rossellini *d* Roberto Rossellini *ph* Otello Martelli *m* Renzo Rossellini

William Tubbs, Gar Moore, Maria Michi and non-professionals

AAN: script

The Pajama Game***
US 1957 101m Warnercolor
Warner / George Abbott

Workers in a pajama factory demand a pay rise, but their lady negotiator falls for the new boss.
Brilliantly conceived musical on an unlikely subject, effectively concealing its Broadway origins and becoming an expert, fast-moving, hard-hitting piece of modern musical cinema.

w George Abbott, Richard Bissell, book Seven and a Half Cents by Richard Bissell *d Stanley Donen, ph* Harry Stradling *songs Richard Adler, Jerry Ross ch Bob Fosse*

Doris Day, John Raitt, *Eddie Foy Jnr,* Reta Shaw, Carol Haney

Pal Joey**
US 1957 109m Technicolor
Columbia / Essex–Sidney (Fred Kohlmar)

The rise of a nightclub entertainer who is also a heel.
Smart musical which begins very brightly indeed but slides off alarmingly into conventional sentiment.

w Dorothy Kingsley, *play* John O'Hara, *stories* John O'Hara *d* George Sidney *ph* Harold Lipstein *songs Richard Rodgers, Lorenz Hart*

Frank Sinatra, Rita Hayworth, Kim Novak, Bobby Sherwood, Hank Henry, Elizabeth Patterson, Barbara Nichols

Pale Rider
US 1985 115m Technicolor Panavision
Warner / Malpaso (Clint Eastwood)

Harassed gold prospecting families are helped by a mysterious avenger.
Unreeling like a supernatural *Shane*, this is a violent and pretentious western with nothing to be pretentious about.

w Michael Butler, Dennis Shryack *d* Clint Eastwood *ph* Bruce Surtees *m* Lennie Niehaus *pd* Edward Carfagno *ed* Joel Cox

Clint Eastwood, Michael Moriarty, Carrie Snodgrass, Christopher Penn, Richard Dysart, Richard Kiel

The Paleface***
US 1948 91m Technicolor
Paramount (Robert L. Welch)

Calamity Jane undertakes an undercover mission against desperadoes, and marries a timid dentist as a cover.
Splendid wagon train comedy western with the stars in excellent form. Sequel, *Son of Paleface* (qv); remake, *The Shakiest Gun in the West* (1968).

w Edmund Hartman, Frank Tashlin *d* Norman Z. McLeod *ph* Ray Rennahan *m* Victor Young

Bob Hope, Jane Russell, Robert Armstrong, Iris Adrian, Robert Watson, Jack Searle, Joe Vitale, Clem Bevans, Charles Trowbridge

AA: song 'Buttons and Bows' (*m* Jay Livingston, *ly* Ray Evans)

The Palm Beach Story***
US 1942 88m bw
Paramount (Paul Jones)

The wife of a penurious engineer takes off for Florida to set her sights on a millionaire.
Flighty comedy, inconsequential in itself, but decorated with scenes, characters and zany touches typical of its creator, here at his most brilliant if uncontrolled.

wd Preston Sturges ph Victor Milner *m* Victor Young

Claudette Colbert, Joel McCrea, Rudy Vallee, Mary Astor, Sig Arno, Robert Warwick, Torben Meyer, Jimmy Conlin, William Demarest, Jack Norton, Robert Greig, Roscoe Ates, Chester Conklin, Franklin Pangborn, Alan Bridge, *Robert Dudley*

HACKENSACKER (Rudy Vallee): 'That's one of the tragedies of this life, that the men most in need of a beating up are always enormous.'

WEENIE KING (Robert Dudley): 'Anyway, I'd be too old for you. Cold are the hands of time that creep along relentlessly, destroying slowly but without pity that which yesterday was young. Alone, our memories resist this disintegration and grow more lovely with the passing years. That's hard to say with false teeth.'

'Surprises and delights as though nothing of the kind had been known before . . . farce and tenderness are combined without a fault.'—*William Whitebait*

'Minus even a hint of the war . . . packed with delightful absurdities.'—*Variety*

Palm Springs
US 1936 74m bw

An elderly Englishman becomes a gambler in order to give his daughter the appropriate upbringing. Slight romantic comedy which gave a young Englishman a foothold in Hollywood. David Niven, Sir Guy Standing, Frances Langford, Ernest Cossart, Spring Byington. Written by Joseph Fields; directed by Aubrey Scotto; for Paramount. (GB title: *Palm Springs Affair.*)

Palm Springs Weekend
US 1963 100m Technicolor
Warner (Michael Hoey)

Various holidaymakers at Palm Springs get romantically involved.
Youth-oriented farce, better produced than most but basically a depressing experience.

w Earl Hanmer Jnr *d* Norman Taurog *ph* Harold Lipstein *m* Frank Perkins

Troy Donahue, Ty Hardin, Connie Stevens, Stefanie Powers, Robert Conrad, Jack Weston, Andrew Duggan

Palmy Days
US 1932 77m bw
Samuel Goldwyn

Shady fortune tellers find a willing stooge.
Dated star comedy.

w Eddie Cantor, Morrie Ryskind, David Freedman, Keene Thompson *d* A. Edward Sutherland *ph* Gregg Toland *ch* Busby Berkeley

Eddie Cantor, Charlotte Greenwood, Charles Middleton, George Raft, Walter Catlett

'Heavily hoked but funny throughout.'—*Variety*

Palooka
US 1934 80m bw

An eccentric manager makes a prizefighter of a country cousin. Fairly amusing first-feature version of the strip cartoon hero Joe Palooka. Jimmy Durante (as Knobby Walsh), Stuart Erwin, Lupe Velez, Marjorie Rambeau, Robert Armstrong, Mary Carlisle, William Cagney, Thelma Todd. Written by Jack Jevne, Arthur Kober, Gertrude Purcell, from Ham Fisher's strip; directed by Ben Stoloff; for Reliance (Edward Small). (GB title: *The Great Schnozzle.*) 'A laugh riot, the nearest approach to a Marx picture that's been around.'—*Variety*

Pan-Americana*
US 1945 85m bw
RKO (Sid Rogell)

A New York magazine sends editors around South America to choose the prettiest girl of each nation.
Slick, mindless musical with good numbers.

w Laurence Kimble *d* John H. Auer *ph* Frank Redman *md* Constantin Bakaleinikoff *ch* Charles O'Curran

Audrey Long, Philip Terry, Robert Benchley, Eve Arden, Ernest Truex, Marc Cramer

Panama Hattie
US 1942 79m bw
MGM (Arthur Freed)

A showgirl in Panama helps to capture Nazis.
Dim film version of a Broadway musical, stripped of most of its music and more like a *Maisie* comedy.

w Jack McGowan, Wilkie Mahoney, *musical play* Herbert Fields, B. G. De Sylva, Cole Porter *d* Norman Z. McLeod *ph* George Folsey *md* George Stoll

Ann Sothern, Dan Dailey, Red Skelton, Marsha Hunt, Rags Ragland, Virginia O'Brien, Alan Mowbray, Ben Blue, Carl Esmond

Pancho Villa
Spain 1972 93m Technicolor
Granada Films (Bernard Gordon)

In 1916 Villa is rescued from execution and starts a reign of terror.
Mexican banditry played half for laughs and half for real; not a successful compromise.

w Julian Halevy *d* Eugenio Martin *ph* Allejandro Ulloa *m* Anton Garcia-Abril

Telly Savalas, Clint Walker, Chuck Connors

Pandora and the Flying Dutchman*
GB 1950 122m Technicolor
Romulus (Albert Lewin)

A cold but beautiful American woman in Spain falls for a mystery man who turns out to be a ghostly sea captain; she dies so as to be with him.
Pretentious, humourless, totally unpersuasive fantasy of the kind much better done in *Portrait of Jennie*. The writer-director wears Omar Khayyam's moving finger to the bone, and the actors look thoroughly unhappy; even the colour is a bit thick.

wd Albert Lewin ph Jack Cardiff *m* Alan Rawsthorne *ad* John Bryan

James Mason, Ava Gardner, Harold Warrender, Nigel Patrick, Sheila Sim, Mario Cabre, John Laurie, Pamela Kellino, Marius Goring

'Conspicuous in its confident assumption of scholarship and its utter poverty of imagination and taste.'—*C. A. Lejeune*

'It might have been enjoyably silly but for Lewin's striving to be classy and an air of third-rate decadence that hangs about it. This is an Anglo-American co-production and one of the occasions, I think, when we might be generous and let Hollywood have all the credit.'—*Richard Winnington*

Pandora's Box*
Germany 1929 97m approx (24 fps) bw silent
Nero Film
original title: *Die Büchse der Pandora*
aka: *Lulu*

A woman murders her lover, becomes a prostitute, and is murdered in London by Jack the Ripper.
Oddball fantasy on a few favourite German themes: very watchable, and benefiting from its star performance.

w G. W. Pabst, Laszlo Wajda, *plays* Erdgeist and Pandora's Box by Franz Wedekind *d G. W. Pabst ph* Günther Krampf

Louise Brooks, Fritz Kortner, Franz Lederer, Gustav Diessi
† Remade in Austria in 1962 as *No Orchids for Lulu*, with Nadja Tiller.

Panhandle
US 1948 84m bw

A reformed gunman avenges the murder of his brother. Solid co-feature western. Rod Cameron, Cathy Downs, Reed Hadley, Anne Gwynne, Blake Edwards. Written by Blake Edwards and John C. Champion; directed by Lesley Selander; for Champion-Edwards / Allied Artists.

Panic Button
US 1963 98m bw

A hasbeen film star is hired by gangsters to star in a film which must lose money; but it wins the Venice Festival award. Artless and padded comedy with good moments provided by an intriguing cast. Maurice Chevalier, Akim Tamiroff, Jayne Mansfield, Eleanor Parker, Michael Connors. Written by Hal Biller; directed by George Sherman; for Gorton Associates.

The Panic in Needle Park
US 1971 110m De Luxe
Gadd Productions (Dominick Dunne)

Drug addiction problems in a New York ghetto.
Vivid, intimate but overlong and unsympathetic account of a junkie and his mistress.

w Joan Didion, John Gregory Dunne, *novel* James Mills *d* Jerry Schatzberg *ph* Adam Holender *m* none

Al Pacino, Kitty Winn, Adam Vint, Richard Bright, Kiel Martin

Panic in the Streets***
US 1950 96m bw
TCF (Sol C. Siegel)

On the New Orleans waterfront, public health officials seek a carrier of bubonic plague.
Semi-documentary suspenser in the *Naked City* manner; location Hollywood at its best.

w Richard Murphy, Edward and Edna Anhalt *d Elia Kazan ph Joe MacDonald m* Alfred Newman

Richard Widmark, Jack Palance, Paul Douglas, Barbara Bel Geddes, Zero Mostel

'A model of what an action story should be . . . every department is admirably handled.'—*Richard Mallett, Punch*

AA: original story (Edward and Edna Anhalt)

Panic in Year Zero*
US 1962 93m bw Cinemascope
AIP (Lou Rusoff, Arnold Houghland)

Adventures of a family on a fishing trip in the mountains when Los Angeles is blasted by a nuclear attack.
Mildly interesting catalogue of predictable events—thugs, looting, fear of fall-out—in a simple-minded script finishing with a hopeful meeting of the UN.

w Jay Simms, John Morton *d* Ray Milland *ph* Gil Warrenton *m* Les Baxter

Ray Milland, Jean Hagen, Frankie Avalon, Joan Freeman

Panique*
France 1946 98m bw
Filmsonor

A respectable man knows who committed a murder, and the murderer cunningly swings the blame onto him.
Careful suspenser with a twist ending.

w Charles Spaak, Julien Duvivier, *novel* Georges Simenon *d* Julien Duvivier *ph* Nicolas Hayer

Michel Simon, Viviane Romance, Paul Bernard

'Whether you like it or not, you may be forced to agree that it's a near-perfect movie.'—*Pauline Kael, 1972*

The Panther's Claw
US 1942 73m bw

Thatcher Colt solves a blackmail case which ends in murder. Unassuming but efficient second-feature mystery. Sidney Blackmer, Byron Foulger, Rick Vallin. Written by Martin Mooney and Athony Abbott; directed by William Beaudine; for PRC.

Panther Girl of the Congo
US 1955 bw serial: 12 eps

A villainous chemist grows monster crawfish which frighten natives away from an African diamond mine. One of the last half-dozen serials made, and a silly one. Phyllis Coates, Myron Healey, Arthur Space, Roy Glenn Snr. Directed by Franklin Adreon; for Republic.

Papa's Delicate Condition
US 1963 98m Technicolor
Paramount / Amro (Jack Rose)

At the turn of the century in a small Texas town an amiable family man gets into scrapes when he drinks too much.
Basically pleasing period comedy which suffers from slow, stiff treatment.

w Jack Rose, *book* Corinne Griffith *d* George Marshall *ph* Loyal Griggs *m* Joseph J. Lilley

Jackie Gleason, Glynis Johns, Charles Ruggles, Charles Lane, Laurel Goodwin, Juanita Moore, Elisha Cook Jnr, Murray Hamilton

AA: song 'Call Me Irresponsible' (*m* James Van Heusen, *ly* Sammy Cahn)

Paper Bullets
US 1941 69m bw

Three orphanage pals grow up to be involved in crime. Fast-moving second feature. Joan Woodbury, Jack La Rue, Alan Ladd, Linda Ware, Vince Barnett, Gavin Gordon, John Archer. Written by Martin Mooney; directed by phil Rosen; for King Brothers / PRC.

The Paper Chase**
US 1973 111m De Luxe Panavision
TCF (Robert C. Thompson, Rodrick Paul)

A Harvard law graduate falls in love with the divorced daughter of his tetchiest professor.
A thoughtful analysis of attitudes to learning turns into just another youth movie.

wd James Bridges, *novel* John Jay Osborn Jnr *ph* Gordon Willis *m* John Williams

Timothy Bottoms, Lindsay Wagner, *John Houseman*, Graham Bickel

'A slightly unfocused account of conformism and milk-mild rebellion on the campus.'—*Sight and Sound*

'A worthy film which engages the eye and the brain.'—*Benny Green, Punch*

AA: John Houseman
AAN: James Bridges (as writer)

PAPER MOON. Tatum O'Neal, here with father Ryan, had no reason to look glum: she was the youngest-ever winner of the supporting actress Oscar.

Paper Lion
US 1968 105m colour

The training of a professional football player. Rather single-minded sporting biography from a book by George Plimpton. Alan Alda, Lauren Hutton, David Doyle, Sugar Ray Robinson. Written by Lawrence Roman; directed by Alex March; for Stuart Millar / United Artists

Paper Moon**
US 1973 103m bw
Paramount / Saticoy (Peter Bogdanovich)

In the American midwest in the thirties, a bible salesman and a plain little girl make a great con team.
Unusual but overrated comedy, imperfectly adapted from a very funny book, with careful but disappointing period sense and photography. A lot more style and gloss was required.

w Alvin Sargent, *novel* Addie Pray by *Joe David Brown* *d* Peter Bogdanovich *ph* Laszlo Kovacs *m* popular songs and recordings

Ryan O'Neal, Tatum O'Neal, Madeleine Kahn, John Hillerman

'I've rarely seen a film that looked so unlike what it was about.'—*Stanley Kauffmann*

'At its best the film is only mildly amusing, and I'm not sure I could recall a few undeniable highlights if pressed on the point.'—*Gary Arnold*

'Bogdanovich once again deploys the armoury of nostalgia with relentless cunning to evoke the threadbare side of American life forty years ago . . . one of those rare movies which engages at least two of the senses.'—*Benny Green, Punch*

'It is so enjoyable, so funny, so touching that I couldn't care less about its morals.'—*Daily Telegraph*

AA: Tatum O'Neal
AAN: Alvin Sargent; Madeleine Kahn

Paper Orchid
GB 1949 86m bw

A girl reporter is suspected of murdering an actor. Mystery programmer which did not displease. Hugh Williams, Hy Hazell, Sidney James, Garry Marsh, Andrew Cruickshank, Ivor Barnard, Walter Hudd. Written by Val Guest, from the novel by Arthur La Bern; directed by Roy Baker; for Ganesh / Columbia.

Paper Tiger
GB 1975 99m Technicolor
Maclean and Co (Euan Lloyd)

An ageing Englishman becomes tutor to the son of the Japanese ambassador in a Pacific state, and finds he has to live his heroic fantasies in reality.
Uneasy adventure comedy drama which might, given more skilled handling, have been much better than it is.

w Jack Davies *d* Ken Annakin *ph* John Cabrera *m* Roy Budd

David Niven, Toshiro Mifune, Hardy Kruger, Ando, Ivan Desny, Irene Tsu, Miiko Taka, Ronald Fraser, Jeff Corey

'Makes no demands, except on 99 minutes of our time.'—*Michael Billington, Illustrated London News*

Papillon*
US 1973 150m Technicolor Panavision
Papillon Partnership / Corona / General Production Co (Robert Dorfmann)

Filmed autobiography of life on Devil's Island. Overlong and rather dreary film of a bestseller; it determinedly rubs the audience's nose in ordure from the start, and the final successful escape is one try too many.

w Dalton Trumbo, Lorenzo Semple Jnr, *book* Henri Charrière *d* Franklin Schaffner *ph* Fred Koenekamp *m* Jerry Goldsmith

Steve McQueen, Dustin Hoffman, Victor Jory, Don Gordon, Anthony Zerbe, George Coulouris, Woodrow Parfrey

'A 2½-hour epic trampling the corn growing round the theme of man's inhumanity to man.'—*Sight and Sound*

'Papillon offers torture as entertainment but winds up making entertainment a form of torture . . . a tournament of brutality unrelieved by imagination.'—*Paul D. Zimmermann*

'So overloaded with details that the stars are almost lost in exposition, repetition and unfocused drama.'—*Judith Crist, 1977*

'So solemn one would think it the story of a pope at the very least.'—*New Yorker, 1980*

AAN: Jerry Goldsmith

Parachute Battalion
US 1941 75m bw

Three boys go through parachute training school. Propaganda quickie. Robert Preston, Nancy Kelly, Edmond O'Brien, Harry Carey, Buddy Ebsen, Paul Kelly, Richard Cromwell, Robert Barrat. Written by John Twist and Major Hugh Fite; directed by Leslie Goodwins; for Howard Benedict / RKO. 'It would make a nice educational short, but as feature material it rates in the secondary dual category.'—*Variety*

Parachute Jumper
US 1932 70m bw

Ex-flying Marines out of a job fall in with gangsters. Easy-going adventure yarn with agreeable players. Douglas Fairbanks Jnr, Bette Davis, Leo Carrillo, Claire Dodd, Frank McHugh, Harold Huber. Written by Rian James, John Francis Larkin; directed by Alfred E. Green; for Warners. 'Breezy treatment of a not very brilliant yarn.'—*Variety*

Parade*
France / Sweden 1974 85m Technicolor

Jacques Tati introduces a series of acts in a small-scale circus. Pleasant, sometimes boring variety show, to be included in the Tati canon for completeness; it does include some of his unique pieces of mime. Written and directed by Jacques Tati; for Gray Film / Sveriges Radio. 'A curious, unresolved *envoi*.'—*John Pym, MFB*. 'Moments of great good humour and flashes of incomparable magic.'—*Sight and Sound*

The Paradine Case**
US 1947 115m bw
Selznick

A barrister falls in love with his client, a murder suspect who, it turns out, is actually guilty.
A stodgy and old-fashioned script is given gleaming treatment; this and the acting make it seem better thirty years later than it did on release.

w David O. Selznick, *novel* Robert Hichens *d Alfred Hitchcock ph Lee Garmes m* Franz Waxman

Gregory Peck, *Alida Valli*, Ann Todd, Louis Jourdan, *Charles Laughton*, Charles Coburn, Ethel Barrymore, Leo G. Carroll

'This is the wordiest script since the death of Edmund Burke.'—*James Agee*

'The characters and their problems don't make much imprint on a viewer; if you can't remember whether you've seen the picture or not, chances are you did and forgot it.'—*New Yorker, 1976*

† Original choices were Olivier instead of Peck, Garbo instead of Valli, and Robert Newton instead of Jourdan.

AAN: Ethel Barrymore

Paradise Alley
US 1978 107m Technicolor
Universal / Force Ten (John F. Roach, Ronald A. Suppa)

The adventures of three wrestling brothers in New York's Hell's Kitchen during the forties.
Fashionable update of the *City for Conquest* school, not in itself very interesting despite amusing bits.

wd Sylvester Stallone *ph* Laszlo Kovacs *m* Bill Conti *pd* John W. Corso

Sylvester Stallone, Kevin Conway, Anne Archer, Joe Spinell, Armand Assante, Lee Canalito

Paradise for Three
US 1937 78m bw

A businessman goes to Germany to find out how the workers live. An interesting premise leads inevitably into a flimsy romantic comedy. Robert Young, Frank Morgan, Mary Astor, Edna May Oliver, Florence Rice, Reginald Owen, Henry Hull, Sig Rumann, Herman Bing. Written by George Oppenheimer and Harry Ruskin; directed by Edward Buzzell; for MGM. (GB title: *Romance for Three*.)

Paradise for Two
GB 1937 77m bw
US title: *Gaiety Girls*

A millionaire posing as a reporter is asked to pose as a millionaire. Cheerful comedy-romance. Jack Hulbert, Patricia Ellis, Arthur Riscoe, Googie Withers, Sidney Fairbrother, Wylie Watson, David Tree. Written by Robert Stevenson and Arthur Macrae; directed by Thornton Freeland; for Gunther Stapenhorst / Denham

Paradise Hawaiian Style
US 1965 91m Technicolor
(Paramount) Hal Wallis / Joseph H. Hazen

An amorous airline pilot returns to Hawaii and sets up a helicopter service.
Mindless musical vehicle for an increasingly resistible star.

w Allan Weiss, Anthony Lawrence *d* Michael Moore *ph* W. Wallace Kelley *md* Joseph J. Lilley

Elvis Presley, Suzanna Leigh, James Shigeta, Irene Tsu

The Parallax View*
US 1974 102m Technicolor Panavision
Paramount / Gus / Harbour / Doubleday (Alan J. Pakula)

Witnesses to a political assassination are systematically killed, despite the efforts of a crusading journalist.
Stylish, persuasive political thriller with a downbeat ending; the villains win.

w David Giler, Lorenzo Semple Jnr, *novel* Loren Singer *d* Alan J. Pakula *ph* Gordon Willis *m* Michael Small

Warren Beatty, Paula Prentiss, William Daniels, Hume Cronyn, Walter McGinn

'Pakula at his best . . . the test sequence is one of the most celebrated, manipulating the audience as it bombards Beatty's psyche.'—*Les Keyser, Hollywood in the Seventies*

'It is terribly important to give an audience a lot of things they may not get as well as those they will, so that finally the film does take on a texture and is not just simplistic communication.'—*Alan J. Pakula*

Paramount on Parade*
US 1930 102m bw (Technicolor sequence)
Paramount (Elsie Janis)

A revue featuring Paramount contract stars.
A ragged affair by any standard, but worth a look for a couple of Chevalier's numbers.

w various *d* Dorothy Arzner, Otto Brower, Edmund Goulding, Victor Heerman, Edwin H. Knopf, Rowland V. Lee, Ernst Lubitsch, Lothar Mendes, Victor Schertzinger, Edward Sutherland, Frank Tuttle *ph* Harry Fischbeck, Victor Milner *m* various

Richard Arlen, Jean Arthur, George Bancroft, Clara Bow, Nancy Carroll, Ruth Chatterton, Maurice Chevalier, Gary Cooper, Leon Errol, Kay Francis, Harry Green, Mitzi Green, Dennis King, Fredric March, Nino Martini, Jack Oakie, Charles 'Buddy' Rogers, Lillian Roth, Fay Wray, Clive Brook, Warner Oland, Eugene Pallette, William Powell

'Pip revue packed with laughs and talent.'—*Variety*

'Suddenly, she knew the lips burning on hers did not belong to any normal man!'

Paranoiac*
GB 1963 80m bw Cinemascope
U-I / Hammer (Anthony Hinds)

An heiress is saved from a suicide attempt by a young man claiming to be her dead brother.
A complex maze of disguise, mistaken identity, family curses and revelations of something nasty in the woodshed, out of *Psycho* by *Taste of Fear*. Not very good in itself, but interesting in its borrowings.

w Jimmy Sangster *d* Freddie Francis *ph* Arthur Grant *m* Elisabeth Lutyens

Oliver Reed, Janette Scott, Alexander Davion, Sheila Burrell, Liliane Brousse, Maurice Denham, John Bonney

Les Parapluies de Cherbourg**
France / West Germany 1964 92m Eastmancolor
Parc / Madeleine / Beta
aka: *The Umbrellas of Cherbourg*

A shopgirl loves a gas station attendant. He goes on military service; she finds she is pregnant and marries for security. Years later they meet briefly by accident.
Unexpected, charming, pretty successful screen operetta with only sung dialogue. Careful acting and exquisite use of colour and camera movement paste over the thinner sections of the plot.

wd Jacques Demy ph Jean Rabier m Michel Legrand ad Bernard Evein

Catherine Deneuve, *Anne Vernon*, Nino Castelnuovo

'Poetic neo-realism.'—*Georges Sadoul*

'We are told that in Paris the opening night audience wept and the critics were ecstatic. It would have made a little more sense the other way round.'—*John Simon*

AA: best foreign film

AAN: script; Michel Legrand; song, 'I Will Wait for You'

Pardners
US 1956 88m Technicolor Vistavision
Paramount (Paul Jones)

An incompetent idiot goes west and accidentally cleans up the town.
Stiff western star burlesque, a remake of *Rhythm on the Range*.

w Sidney Sheldon *d* Norman Taurog *ph* Daniel Fapp *songs* Sammy Cahn, Jimmy Van Heusen

Dean Martin, Jerry Lewis, Agnes Moorehead, Lori Nelson, John Baragrey, Jeff Morrow, Lon Chaney Jnr

Pardon My Past*
US 1945 88m bw
Columbia

A man unwittingly takes on the problems of his double, a shady playboy.
Amusing mistaken identity comedy.

w Earl Felton, Karl Kamb *d* Leslie Fenton *ph* Russell Metty *m* Dmitri Tiomkin

Fred MacMurray, Marguerite Chapman, Akim Tamiroff, Rita Johnson, William Demarest, Harry Davenport

Pardon My Rhythm
US 1944 61m bw

A kid orchestra participates in a national radio contest. We have all been here before. Gloria Jean, Mel Tormé, Patric Knowles, Evelyn Ankers, Marjorie Weaver, Walter Catlett, Bob Crosby and his orchestra. Written by Val Burton, Eugene Conrad; directed by Felix Feist; for Bernard W. Burton / Universal.

Pardon Us*
US 1931 55m bw
Hal Roach
aka: *Jailbirds*

Two zany bootleggers find themselves in and out of prison.
Patchy star comedy which finds the boys on the whole not in quite their best form.

w H. M. Walker *d* James Parrott *ph* Jack Stevens

Stan Laurel, Oliver Hardy, Wilfred Lucas, Walter Long, James Finlayson

'Their first full-length, with not over two reels of value.'—*Variety*

The Parent Trap*
US 1961 129m Technicolor
Walt Disney (George Golitzen)

Twin daughters of separated parents determine to bring the family together again.
Quite bright but awesomely extended juvenile romp.

wd David Swift, *novel* Das Doppelte Lottchen by Erich Kastner *ph* Lucien Ballard *m* Paul Smith

Hayley Mills, Maureen O'Hara, Brian Keith, Charles Ruggles, Leo G. Carroll, Una Merkel, Joanna Barnes, Cathleen Nesbitt, Ruth McDevitt, Nancy Kulp

Les Parents Terribles**
France 1948 98m bw
Sirius

Life with a family in which the children are as neurotic as the parents.
Alternately hilarious and tragic, this is a fascinating two-set piece of filmed theatre, with every performance a pleasure.

wd Jean Cocteau, from his play *ph* Michel Kelber *m* Georges Auric *ad* Christian Bérard, Guy de Gastyne

Jean Marais, Yvonne de Bray, Gabrielle Dorziat, Marcel André, Josette Day

† In 1953 a curious and unsatisfactory British version was made by Charles Frank under the title *Intimate Relations,* with Marian Spencer, Russell Enoch, Ruth Dunning, Harold Warrender and Elsy Albiin.

Paris
US 1929 88m part colour

An American stage star, her fiancé, her partner and her mother-in-law-to-be converge on the Champs Elysées. Shaky musical with interesting talent, but bereft of its original Cole Porter score. Irene Bordoni, Jack Buchanan, Louise Closser Hale, Jason Robards. Written by Hope Loring; directed by Clarence Badger; for Warner.

Paris after Dark
US 1943 85m bw

In wartime Paris a doctor leads the resistance forces. Propaganda potboiler, quite neatly made and cast. George Sanders, Philip Dorn, Brenda Marshall, Marcel Dalio, Madeleine LeBeau. Written by Howard Buchman; directed by Leonide Moguy; for TCF. (GB title: *The Night Is Ending.*)

Paris Blues*
US 1961 98m Technicolor
UA / Pennebaker / Diane / Jason / Monica / Monmouth (Sam Shaw)

Two jazz musicians have romantic problems in Paris.
Semi-serious mini-drama with emphasis on the music; one is not quite sure what the actors thought they were up to.

w Jack Sher, Irene Kamp, Walter Bernstein, *novel* Harold Flender *d* Martin Ritt *ph* Christian Matras *m* Duke Ellington

Paul Newman, Joanne Woodward, Sidney Poitier, Louis Armstrong, Diahann Carroll, Serge Reggiani, Barbara Laage

AAN: Duke Ellington

Paris Calling
US 1941 95m bw
Universal / Charles K. Feldman

When the Nazis invade Paris, a woman discovers that her husband is a traitor.
Totally predictable flagwaver.

w Benjamin Glazer, Charles Kaufmann *d* Edwin L. Marin *ph* Milton Krasner *m* Richard Hageman

Elisabeth Bergner, Basil Rathbone, Randolph Scott, Gale Sondergaard, Lee J. Cobb, Eduardo Ciannelli, Charles Arnt

Paris Holiday*
US 1957 101m Technirama
UA / Tolda (Bob Hope)

An American comedian meets a French one in Paris, and both have narrow escapes because their script contains the clue to a gang of counterfeiters.
Amiable location romp with the stars in pretty good form.

w Edmund Beloin, Dean Riesner *d* Gerd Oswald *ph* Roger Hubert *m* Joseph J. Lilley

Bob Hope, Fernandel, Anita Ekberg, Martha Hyer, André Morell, Maurice Teynac, Jean Murat, Preston Sturges

Paris Honeymoon
US 1938 85m bw

An American in Paris persuades his fiancée to forget a French nobleman. Candy floss musical for star fans. Bing Crosby, Franciska Gaal, Akim Tamiroff. Written by Frank Butler and Don Hartman; directed by Frank Tuttle; for Paramount. 'Entertaining offering that will click substantially at the box office.'—*Variety*

Paris in Spring
US 1935 81m bw
GB title: *Paris Love Song*

Four visitors change partners in the romantic city. Predictable romance with good ingredients. Mary Ellis, Tullio Carminati, Lynne Overman, Ida Lupino. Written by Samuel Hoffenstein, Franz Schulz and Keene Thompson, from the play by Dwight Taylor; directed by Lewis Milestone; for Paramount.

'In everything except the unhappy choice of narrative it comes close to being an ideal production.'—*Variety*

Paris Interlude
US 1934 72m bw

American newspapermen hang out in a Paris bar. Aimless comedy-drama which fails to achieve the intended mood of world-weariness. Madge Evans, Otto Kruger, Robert Young, Una Merkel, Ted Healy, Louis Henry, Edward Brophy. Written by Wells Root from the play All Good Americans by S. J. and Laura Perelman; directed by Edwin L. Marin; for MGM. '60 minutes instead of 72 would still have left something to be desired—further cutting.'—*Variety*

Paris Model
US 1953 88m bw

Stories involving four copies of the same Paris gown. Depressing dramatic package with production values at a low ebb and some pleasant talents going awry. Paulette Goddard, Eva Gabor, Marilyn Maxwell, Barbara Lawrence, Tom Conway, Leif Erickson, Florence Bates, Cecil Kellaway, Robert Hutton. Written by Robert Smith; directed by Alfred E. Green; for Albert Zugsmith / Columbia.

Paris Qui Dort*
France 1923 40m approx (24 fps) bw silent
Films Diamant (Maurice Diamant-Berger)
aka: *The Crazy Ray*

A mad scientist invents a ray which brings everyone but six people in Paris to a halt.
Mildly entertaining semi-professional comedy showing several of its director's most engaging traits.

wd, ed René Clair ph Maurice Défassiaux, Paul Guichard

Henri Rollan, Albert Préjean, Marcel Vallée, Madeleine Rodrigue

Paris, Texas**
West Germany / France 1984 148m colour
Road Movies / Argos (Don Guest, Anatole Dauman)

After separating from his wife a man goes missing and is later found in the small town where he was born.
Long, enigmatic but generally fascinating puzzle-without-a-solution, about people who never find what they want.

w Sam Shepard *d Wim Wenders ph* Robby Müller *m* Ry Cooder

Harry Dean Stanton, Dean Stockwell, Aurore Clement, Hunter Carson, Nastassja Kinski, Bernhard Wicki
† NB: Filmed in English.

BFA: best director

Paris Underground
US 1945 97m bw
(UA) Constance Bennett
GB title: *Madame Pimpernel*

Two women caught in Paris when the Nazis invade continue their resistance activities.
Artificial and not very exciting flagwaver.

w Boris Ingster, Gertrude Purcell, *novel* Etta Shiber *d* Gregory Ratoff *ph* Lee Garmes *m* Alexander Tansman

Constance Bennett, Gracie Fields, George Rigaud, Kurt Kreuger, Leslie Vincent

'Mainly trash, involving enough handsome young men, in various poses of gallant gratitude, to satisfy Mae West in her prime.'—*James Agee*

AAN: Alexander Tansman

Paris When It Sizzles
US 1963 110m Technicolor
Paramount (Richard Quine, George Axelrod)

A film writer tries out several script ideas with his secretary as heroine and himself as hero or villain.
As a French film called *La Fête à Henriette* this was a charming whimsy, but Hollywood made it heavy-handed and boring, especially as no one in it seems to be having much fun.

w George Axelrod, *screenplay* Julien Duviver, Henri Jeanson *d* Richard Quine *ph* Charles Lang Jnr *m* Nelson Riddle

William Holden, Audrey Hepburn, Grégoire Aslan, Noel Coward, Raymond Bussières

'The new script embalms the original instead of reviving it.'—*Stanley Kauffmann, New Republic*

Park Row
US 1952 83m bw
UA / Samuel Fuller

Conflict breaks out between two newspapers in 1886 New York.
Earnest but flat low-budgeter of a rather unusual kind.

wd Samuel Fuller *ph* Jack Russell *ad* Ray Robinson

Gene Evans, Mary Welch, Herbert Hayes, Forrest Taylor

Parker
GB 1984 97m colour
Moving Picture Company (Nigel Stafford-Clark)

A British businessman turns up after claiming to have been kidnapped in Munich, but the police don't necessarily believe him.
Suspense thriller hampered by overblown bits of ambivalence which prevent sympathy from lodging in any quarter.

w Trevor Preston *d* Jim Goddard *ph* Peter Jessop *m* Richard Hartley

Bryan Brown, Cherie Lunghi, Kurt Raab, Bob Peck, Beate Finkh

Parlor, Bedroom and Bath
US 1931 72m bw

A mild-mannered husband has trouble when he becomes a landlord. Rather flatfooted farce, on a par with the star's other talkies. Buster Keaton, Charlotte Greenwood, Reginald Denny, Cliff Edwards. Written by Richard Schayer, Robert Hopkins, from the farce by Charles W. Bell and Mark Swan; directed by Edward Sedgwick; for MGM. NB: The film was largely shot on location in Keaton's own house. 'Funny, clean enough for kids, and generally well made.'—*Variety*. (GB title: *Romeo in Pyjamas*.)

'As though torn from life's pages!'
Parnell*
US 1937 115m bw
MGM (John M. Stahl)

A 19th-century Irish politician comes to grief through his love for a married woman.
Well made but miscast biopic, a resounding thud at the box office.

w John Van Druten, S. N. Behrman, *play* Elsie T. Schauffler *d* John M. Stahl *ph* Karl Freund *m* William Axt

Clark Gable, Myrna Loy, Edmund Gwenn, Edna May Oliver, Alan Marshal, Donald Crisp, Billie Burke, Berton Churchill, Donald Meek, Montagu Love, George Zucco

'Dull and overlong historical drama . . . word of mouth is likely to be poor.'—*Variety*

'A singularly pallid, tedious and unconvincing drama.'—*Frank Nugent*

'Poor though the picture may be, it is pleasing to think how clean a film magnate's wish-fulfilments are, how virginal and high-minded the tawdry pathetic human past becomes when the Mayers and Goldwyns turn the magic ring.'—*Graham Greene*

Parole, Inc
US 1948 71m bw

A racketeer arranges to spring hardened criminals from the state prison. Routine crime stuff, quite efficiently handled. Michael O'Shea, Turhan Bey, Evelyn Ankers, Virginia Lee, Lyle Talbot. Written by Sherman T. Lowe; directed by Alfred Zeisler; for Orbit / Eagle Lion.

Parrish
US 1961 137m Technicolor
Warner (Delmer Daves)

A young tobacco plantation worker has an ample sex life and the luck to become boss.
Predictable trudge through scenes from a bestselling novel, less offensive than most such adaptations.

wd Delmer Daves, *novel* Mildred Savage *ph* Harry Stradling *m* Max Steiner

Troy Donahue, Claudette Colbert, Karl Malden, Dean Jagger, Connie Stevens, Diane McBain, Sharon Hugueny

The Parson of Panamint
US 1941 84m bw
Paramount (Harry Sherman)

A gold rush mountain town is corrupted by success until a two-fisted parson puts things right.
Middling western morality play.

w Harold Shumate, Adrian Scott, *novel* Peter B. Kyne *d* William McGann *ph* Russell Harlan *m* Irwin Talbot

Charles Ruggles, Ellen Drew, Philip Terry, Joseph Schildkraut, Henry Kolker, Janet Beecher, Paul Hurst

Une Partie de Campagne***
France 1936 40m bw
Pantheon / Pierre Braunberger
aka: *A Day in the Country*

Around 1880, a Parisian tradesman and his family picnic one Sunday in the country, and one of the daughters falls in love.
An unfinished film which was much admired for its local colour, like an impressionist picture come to life.

wd Jean Renoir, story Guy de Maupassant *ph* Claude Renoir, Jean Bourgoin *m* Joseph Kosma

Sylvie Bataille, Georges Darnoul, Jane Marken, Paul Temps

Une Partie de Plaisir*
France 1975 100m colour
La Boétie / Sunchild / Gerico (André Genoves)

The analysis of a divorce.
Bitter comedy drama, with the director's usual scriptwriter playing out his own life story. A little too incestuous for its own good, but with striking moments.

w Paul Gegauff *d* Claude Chabrol *ph* Jean Rabier

Paul Gegauff, Danielle Gegauff, Paula Moore, Michel Valette

Partners
US 1982 98m Movielab
Titan (Aaron Russo)

Two Los Angeles police officers, one straight and one gay, investigate the murder of a homosexual.
Uneasy comedy-melodrama of somewhat mysterious purpose.

w Francis Veber *d* James Burrows *ph* Victor J. Kemper *m* Georges Delerue

John Hurt, Ryan O'Neal, Kenneth McMillan, Robyn Douglass, Jay Robinson

Partners in Crime
US 1937 66m bw

A private eye stumbles on a plot to victimize the reform candidate in a local election. Reliable second feature with few surprises. Lynne Overman, Roscoe Karns, Muriel Hutchinson, Anthony Quinn, Inez Courtney, Charles Halton, Lucien Littlefield. Written by Garnett Weston from the novel by Kurt Steel; directed by Ralph Murphy; for Paramount. 'A cockeyed affair, perforated with surprises.'—*Variety*

The Party*
US 1968 98m De Luxe Panavision
UA / Mirisch / Geoffrey (Blake Edwards)

An accident-prone Indian actor is accidentally invited to a swank Hollywood party and wrecks it.
Would-be Tatiesque comedy of disaster, occasionally well-timed but far too long for all its gloss.

w Blake Edwards, Tom and Frank Waldman *d* Blake Edwards *ph* Lucien Ballard *m* Henry Mancini *pd* Fernando Carrere

Peter Sellers, Claudine Longet, Marge Champion, Fay McKenzie, Steve Franken, Buddy Lester

'One thing the old movie makers did know is that two reels is more than enough of this stuff.'—*Wilfred Sheed*

'It is only rarely that one laughs or even smiles; mostly one just chalks up another point for ingenuity.'—*Tom Milne*

Party Girl
US 1958 98m Metrocolor Cinemascope
MGM / Euterpe (Joe Pasternak)

In twenties Chicago, a lawyer wins a girl from a gangster.
Heavy-handed Scarface-style saga which at one time won a curious reputation for being a satire.

w George Wells *d* Nicholas Ray *ph* Robert Bronner *m* Jeff Alexander

Robert Taylor, Cyd Charisse, Lee J. Cobb, John Ireland, Kent Smith, Claire Kelly, Corey Allen

Party, Party
GB 1983 98m colour

A teenager throws a drunken party while his parents are out. Ghastly British rubbish: no plot and nothing to laugh at at all, just young people making asses of themselves. Daniel Peacock, Karl Howman, Perry Fenwick, Sean Chapman, Phoebe Nicholls, Caroline Quentin. Written by Daniel Peacock, Terry Winsor; directed by Terry Winsor; for A & M Records.

Party Wire
US 1935 70m bw

Small-town gossipers listen in on party wires and draw the wrong conclusions. Multi-stranded comedy-drama; not important but quite pleasant. Jean Arthur, Victor Jory, Helen Lowell, Charley Grapewin, Clara Blandick, Maude Eburne. Written by Ethel Hill, John Howard Lawson, Bruce Manning; directed by Erle C. Kenton; for Columbia. 'Entertaining for the family trade.'—*Variety*

The Party's Over
GB 1963 94m bw
Tricastle (Anthony Perry)

An American girl joins a group of Chelsea beatniks and dies in a fall from a balcony; her father investigates.
Tasteless and boring swinging London trash which became notorious when its producers (Rank) disowned it because it features a party at which a man makes love to a dead girl. An unattractive display of moral squalor.

w Marc Behm *d* Guy Hamilton *ph* Larry Pizer *m* John Barry

Oliver Reed, Eddie Albert, Ann Lynn, Louise Sorel

Pascali's Island**
GB 1988 104m Agfacolor / Metrocolor
Avenue / Film Four International / Dearfilm

On an island in the Dodecanese in the last days of Ottoman rule, a spy for the Turkish authorities becomes entangled with a British confidence man. Atmospheric, ambiguous mood-piece with strong performances, let down by an overly melodramatic ending.

w,d James Dearden, from novel by Barry Unsworth *ph* Roger Deakins *m* Loek Dikker *pd* Andrew Mollo

Ben Kingsley, *Charles Dance*, *Helen Mirren*, Stefan Gryff, George Murcell

The Passage
GB 1978 98m Eastmancolor Technovision
Hemdale / Passage / Lester Goldsmith-Maurice Binder (John Quested)

A Basque shepherd guides a scientist and his family from occupied France over the mountains into Spain.
Routine war suspenser given an unnecessary taint of sadism. Only those addicted to unpleasant detail will enjoy it.

w Bruce Micolaysen from his novel The Perilous Passage *d* J. Lee Thompson *ph* Michael Reed *m* Michael J. Lewis

Anthony Quinn, James Mason, Malcolm McDowell, Patricia Neal, Kay Lenz, Paul Clemens, Christopher Lee

Passage Home
GB 1955 102m bw
GFD / Group Films (Julian Wintle)

In 1931, tensions run high on a merchant ship when the captain accepts an attractive girl as passenger from South America.
Obvious melodrama complete with drunken captain and storm at sea; not badly done if it must be done at all.

w William Fairchild, *novel* Richard Armstrong *d* Roy Baker *ph* Geoffrey Unsworth *m* Clifton Parker

Peter Finch, Anthony Steel, Diane Cilento, Cyril Cusack, Geoffrey Keen, Hugh Griffith, Duncan Lamont, Bryan Forbes, Gordon Jackson, Michael Craig

A Passage to India**
GB 1984 163m Technicolor
EMI / John Brabourne-Richard Goodwin / HBO / John Heyman / Edward Sands

An English girl in India accuses an Indian doctor of rape.
Another film about India under the Raj seems somewhat redundant after *The Jewel in the Crown*, *Gandhi* and *The Far Pavilions*, but at least under David Lean's direction this is intelligent and good to look at.

w,d,ed David Lean, *novel* E. M. Forster *ph* Ernest Day *m* Maurice Jarre *pd* John Box

Judy Davis, Alec Guinness, Victor Bannerjee, Peggy Ashcroft, James Fox, Nigel Havers, Richard Wilson, Antonia Pemberton, Michael Culver, Art Malik

AA: Peggy Ashcroft (supporting actress); music

AAN: best picture; direction; Judy Davis; adapted screenplay; photography; editing; art direction

BFA: Peggy Ashcroft

Passage to Marseilles*
US 1944 110m bw
Warner (Hal B. Wallis)

Convicts escape from Devil's Island and join the Free French.
A rare example of a film boasting flashbacks within flashbacks within flashbacks, this confusing if sometimes entertaining all-star saga is done to death by its unconvincing flagwaving endpapers which prevent it from being at all comparable with *Casablanca*, as was clearly intended.

w Casey Robinson, Jack Moffitt, *story* Charles Nordhoff, James Hall *ph* James Wong Howe *d* Michael Curtiz *m* Max Steiner

Humphrey Bogart, Michèle Morgan, Claude Rains, Philip Dorn, Sidney Greenstreet, Peter Lorre, Helmut Dantine, George Tobias, John Loder, Victor Francen, Eduardo Ciannelli

'Invincibly second rate.'—*Richard Mallet, Punch*

Passage West
US 1951 81m Technicolor

Religious pioneers headed west are menaced by escaped convicts. Entertaining minor western. John Payne, Dennis O'Keefe, Arleen Whelan, Peter Hanson. Written by Lewis R. Foster and Nedrick Young; directed by Lewis R. Foster; for Pine-Thomas / Paramount.

Passenger*
Poland 1963 63m bw Dyaliscope
Kadr
original title: *Pasazerka*

A German woman on a liner sees a woman she thinks she recognizes, and realizes that it is one of her charges when she was an official in a concentration camp.
Minor but effective character drama, in essence an investigation of guilt. The director died during its making, so some scenes are replaced by still photographs.

wd Andrzej Munk, play Zofia Posmysz-Piasecka *ph* Krzysztof Winiewicz

Aleksandra Slaska, Anna Ciepielewska

'I used to be somebody else; but I traded myself in . . .'

The Passenger*
Italy / France / Spain 1975 119m Metrocolor
MGM / CCC / Concordia / CIPI (Carlo Ponti)
aka: *Profession: Reporter*

A TV reporter in a desert hotel changes identities with a dead man and finds he is now an African gun runner being drawn irresistibly towards his own death.
Pretty much in the style of *Blow Up*, but this time with no frills of fashion or nudity to bring the public in. After this, Antonioni was given up by the commercial cinema.

w Mark Peploe, Peter Wollen, Michelangelo Antonioni *d* Michelangelo Antonioni *ph* Luciano Tovoli *md* Ivan Vandor

Jack Nicholson, Maria Schneider, Jenny Runacre, Ian Hendry

'A film of real romance, depth and power . . . the very quintessence of cinema.'—*Michael Billington, Illustrated London News*

The Passing of the Third Floor Back*
GB 1935 90m bw
Gaumont (Ivor Montagu)

A Christ-like visitor stays at a London boarding house and changes the lives of the inmates.
Competent film version of a famous, sentimental, dated play.

w Michael Hogan, Alma Reville, *play* Jerome K. Jerome *d* Berthold Viertel *ph* Curt Courant *m* Hubert Bath

Conrad Veidt, René Ray, Anna Lee, Frank Cellier, Mary Clare, Beatrix Lehmann, Cathleen Nesbitt, Sara Allgood

'Drawing power of the book, the play, the picturization and the star should, on form, be invincible.'—*Variety*

'The pious note has been toned down, the milk of human kindness has been agreeably watered, and the types in the small London private hotel are observed with malicious realism.'—*Graham Greene*

Passion
US 1954 84m Technicolor

Jealousy erupts between ranchers in Spanish California. Peculiarly titled western of no merit whatsoever. Yvonne de Carlo, Cornel Wilde, Raymond Burr, Lon Chaney Jnr, Rodolfo Acosta, John Qualen. Written by Beatrice A. Dresher and Joseph Leytes; directed by Allan Dwan; for Benedict Bogeaus / RKO.

Passion Flower
US 1930 78m bw

Two rich girls marry beneath them. Tedious romantic drama about class and true love. Kay Francis, Kay Johnson, Charles Bickford, Lewis Stone, Zasu Pitts, Dickie Moore, Winter Hall. Written by Martin Flavin, L. E. Johnson, Edith Fitzgerald, from the novel by Kathleen Norris; directed by William de Mille; for MGM. 'A flock of talent, but talent doesn't always count on a marquee.'—*Variety*

The Passionate Friends**
GB 1948 91m bw
GFD / Cineguild (Eric Ambler)
US title: *One Woman's Story*

A woman marries an older man, then meets again her young lover.
A simple and obvious dramatic situation is tricked out with flashbacks and the inimitable high style of its director to make a satisfying entertainment.

w Eric Ambler, *novel* H. G. Wells *d* David Lean *ph Guy Green m* Richard Addinsell

Ann Todd, Trevor Howard, Claude Rains, Betty Ann Davies, Isabel Dean, Arthur Howard, Wilfrid Hyde White

'Mr Lean plants his clues with the certainty of a master of the detective story, and heightens their effect with a sure handling of camera and sound track.'—*The Times*

The Passionate Plumber
US 1932 73m bw

A woman hires a professional lover to fend off the man she really loves but thinks she shouldn't have. Much revamped farce version of a comedy made straight in 1927 and 1942. All flopped, but this is the worst. Buster Keaton, Jimmy Durante, Irene Purcell, Polly Moran, Gilbert Roland, Mona Maris, Maude Eburne. Written by Laurence E. Johnson from the play Her Cardboard Lover by Frederick Lonsdale; directed by Edgar Sedgwick; for MGM. 'Another lay-me-down-to-sleeper for box offices.'—*Variety*

The Passionate Stranger
GB 1956 97m part bw, part Eastmancolor
British Lion / Beaconsfield (Peter Rogers, Gerald Thomas)
US title: *A Novel Affair*

A lady novelist bases a character on her virile chauffeur; he reads the book and thinks she fancies him.
Feeble comedy, half of it consisting of a dramatization of the heroine's very dull novel.

w Muriel and Sydney Box *d* Muriel Box *ph* Otto Heller *m* Humphrey Searle

Ralph Richardson, Margaret Leighton, Carlo Justini, Patricia Dainton, Marjorie Rhodes, Thorley Walters, Frederick Piper

Passionate Summer
GB 1958 104m Eastmancolor
Briar / Kenneth Harper

A divorced headmaster at a Jamaican school is loved by three women.
Silly melodrama with splendid backgrounds ruined by poor colour.

w Joan Henry, *novel* The Shadow and the Peak by Richard Mason *d* Rudolph Cartier *ph* Ernest Steward *m* Angelo Lavagnino

Virginia McKenna, Bill Travers, Yvonne Mitchell, Alexander Knox, Ellen Barrie, Carl Mohner.

'The climactic hurricane does little to dispel the overall feeling of emotional suffocation.'—*MFB*

Passport to Hell
US 1932 72m bw

A woman tainted by scandal moved from country to country and marries a German commandant in the Cameroons to avoid internment. Reasonably lively drama which ends less well than it began. Elissa Landi, Paul Lukas, Warner Oland, Alexander Kirkland, Donald Crisp. Written by Bradley King, Leon Gordon, Harry Hervey; directed by Frank Lloyd; for Fox. 'Not a de luxer; Broadway spotted because of the product shortage.'—*Variety*

Passport to Pimlico****
GB 1949 84m bw
Ealing (E. V. H. Emmett)

Part of a London district is discovered to belong to Burgundy, and the inhabitants find themselves free of rationing restrictions.
A cleverly detailed little comedy which inaugurated the best period of Ealing, its preoccupation with suburban man and his foibles. Not exactly satire, but great fun, and kindly with it.

w T. E. B. Clarke d Henry Cornelius ph Lionel Banes *m Georges Auric*

Stanley Holloway, *Margaret Rutherford,* Basil Radford, Naunton Wayne, Hermione Baddeley, John Slater, Paul Dupuis, Jane Hylton, Raymond Huntley, Betty Warren, Barbara Murray, Sidney Tafler

† The film was based on a genuine news item. The Canadian government presented to the Netherlands the room in which Princess Juliana was to bear a child.

AAN: T. E. B. Clarke

Passport to Shame
GB 1959 88m bw

A taxi driver rescues his girl from the white slave business. Would-be seamy melodrama which just about serves its purpose. Eddie Constantine, Diana Dors, Odile Versois, Herbert Lom, Brenda de Banzie, Robert

Brown. Written by Patrick Alexander; directed by Alvin Rakoff; for United/Cory/Eros. (US title: *Room 43*.)

Passport to Treason
GB 1956 80m bw

A detective traces the death of his colleague to fascists working within an alleged peace group. Stock melodramatic situations straightforwardly presented make this a watchable support. Rod Cameron, Lois Maxwell, Clifford Evans, John Colicos, Ballard Berkeley. Written by Kenneth Hales and Norman Hudis; directed by Robert S. Baker; for Mid Century / Eros.

The Password Is Courage*
GB 1962 116m bw
MGM / Andrew and Virginia Stone

In Europe during World War II, Sgt-Major Charles Coward has a career of escapes and audacious anti-Nazi exploits.
Lively, slightly over-humorous account of one man's war, well mounted and shot entirely on location.

wd Andrew L. Stone, *biography* John Castle *ph* David Boulton

Dirk Bogarde, Maria Perschy, Alfred Lynch, Nigel Stock, Reginald Beckwith

'The experiences are, it seems, mainly true but they do not seem so.'—*Guardian*

Pastor Hall*
GB 1940 97m bw
Charter (John Boulting)

The story of German village pastor Niemoller, who in 1934 was shot for denouncing the Nazis.
A courageous film of its time, not very interesting dramatically or cinematically.

w Leslie Arliss, Haworth Bromley, Anna Reiner, *play* Ernst Toller *d* Roy Boulting *ph* Max Greene

Wilfrid Lawson, Nova Pilbeam, Seymour Hicks, Marius Goring, Percy Walsh, Brian Worth, Peter Cotes, Hay Petrie

'Not much meat on her, but what there is is cherce!'

Pat and Mike**
US 1952 95m bw
MGM (Lawrence Weingarten)

A small-time sports promoter takes on a female intellectual multi-champion.
A comedy which amuses because of its star playing, but doesn't really develop. All very easy going, with guest appearances from sporting personalities.

w Ruth Gordon, Garson Kanin *d* George Cukor *ph* William Daniels *m* David Raksin

Spencer Tracy, Katharine Hepburn, Aldo Ray, William Ching, Sammy White, Jim Backus, Phyllis Povah

'They do not, like the Lunts, give the impression of a rigid calculated effect; rather, they complement and stimulate each other.'—*Monthly Film Bulletin*

AAN: script

Pat Garrett and Billy the Kid
US 1973 106m Metrocolor Panavision
MGM (Gordon Carroll)

Blood-spattered version of a western legend, with violence always to the fore, accentuated by the impossibility of listening to the dialogue because of poor direction and recording.

w Rudolph Wurlitzer *d* Sam Peckinpah *ph* John Coquillon *m* Bob Dylan

James Coburn, Kris Kristofferson, Bob Dylan, Richard Jaeckel, Katy Jurado, Slim Pickens, Chill Wills, Jason Robards Jnr

'A sombre, intense, downbeat essay on the truth behind the legend and the legend behind the truth.'—*Sight and Sound*

'Shows what Peckinpah can do when he doesn't put his mind to it.'—*Stanley Kauffmann*

'A rash adventure in inadvertent self-parody.'—*William S. Pechter*

'Ambitious, erotic, peculiarly unrealized . . .'—*Pauline Kael, New Yorker*

A Patch of Blue*
US 1965 105m bw Panavision
MGM / Pandro S. Berman

A blind girl who lives in a slum is helped by a negro with whom she falls in love without realizing his colour.
Polished tearjerker with racial overtones; nicely done for those who can take it.

d Guy Green, *novel* Be Ready with Bells and Drums by Elizabeth Kata *ph* Robert Burks *m* Jerry Goldsmith

Sidney Poitier, Elizabeth Hartman, Shelley Winters, Wallace Ford, Ivan Dixon, Elizabeth Fraser, John Qualen

AA: Shelley Winters
AAN: Robert Burks; Jerry Goldsmith; Elizabeth Hartman

'He wants YOU to have his baby!'

Paternity
US 1981 93m Movielab
Paramount (Jerry Tokofsky)

A middle-aged bachelor decides to father a son via a hired mother, who will then return the child to him.
Tastelessly up-dated Hollywood romance with predictable complications. Not worth sitting through.

w Charlie Peters *d* David Steinberg *ph* Bobby Byrne *m* David Shire

Burt Reynolds, Beverly D'Angelo, Norman Fell, Paul Dooley, Elizabeth Ashley, Lauren Hutton, Juanita Moore

Pather Panchali**
India 1955 115m bw
Government of West Bengal

In a small Bengal village, the son of a would-be writer grows up in poverty and tragedy before setting off with what remains of the family to seek a living in Benares.
A remarkable first film of a director now famous, showing that people are much the same though the details of their daily lives may be different. The pace may be slow but the content is mainly absorbing.

wd Satyajit Ray, novels Bhibuti Bashan Bannerjee *ph* Subrata Mitra *m* Ravi Shankar

Kanu Bannerjee, Karuna Bannerjee, Uma Das Gupta, Subir Bannerjee, Chunibala

Paths of Glory***
US 1957 86m bw
UA / Bryna (James B. Harris)

In 1916 in the French trenches, three soldiers are courtmartialled for cowardice.
Incisive melodrama chiefly depicting the corruption and incompetence of the high command; the plight of the soldiers is less interesting. The trench scenes are the most vivid ever made, and the rest is shot in genuine castles, with resultant difficulties of lighting and recording; the overall result is an overpowering piece of cinema.

w Stanley Kubrick, Calder Willingham, Jim Thompson, *novel* Humphrey Cobb *d Stanley Kubrick ph Georg Krause m* Gerald Fried

Kirk Douglas, Adolphe Menjou, George Macready, Wayne Morris, Richard Anderson, Ralph Meeker, Timothy Carey

'A bitter and biting tale, told with stunning point and nerve-racking intensity.'—*Judith Crist*

'Beautifully performed, staged, photographed, cut and scored.'—*Colin Young*

Patrick the Great*
US 1944 88m bw
Universal (Howard Benedict)

An actor whose career is waning is jealous of his young son.
Slick teenage family comedy, virtually a one-man show for O'Connor.

w Jane Hall, Bertram Millhauser, Dorothy Bennett, Frederick and Ralph Block *d* Frank Ryan *ph* Frank Redman *m* Hans Salter

Donald O'Connor, Donald Cook, Peggy Ryan, Frances Dee, Eve Arden, Thomas Gomez, Gavin Muir, Andrew Tombes

The Patriot**
US 1928 110m approx (24 fps) bw silent
Paramount (Ernst Lubitsch)

Mad Czar Paul I is assassinated by his chief adviser for the good of the state.
Historical melodrama with a good many comedy touches: the director makes the most of both aspects, but they don't in the end hang together despite bravura acting.

w Hans Kraly, novel Alfred Neumann *d Ernst Lubitsch ph* Bert Glennon *ad* Hans Dreier

Emil Jannings, Lewis Stone, Florence Vidor, Neil Hamilton

'I believe this picture the most suggestive we ever ran. Just another reason why we need censorship. Small-town exhibitors need clean pictures.'—*Ohio exhibitor's report in Motion Picture Herald*

AA: Hans Kraly
AAN: best picture; Ernst Lubitsch; Lewis Stone

The Patsy*
US 1927 80m approx (24 fps) bw silent
MGM (Irving Thalberg)
GB title: *The Politic Flapper*

Tired of being taken for granted, a girl puts on a surprising show for her family.
Amusing comedy which, in sound, might have made Miss Davies a bigger star than she ever became.

w Agnes Christine Johnson, *play* Barry Connors *d* King Vidor

Marion Davies, Marie Dressler, Lawrence Gray, Del Henderson, Jane Winton

'Marion Davies is in my opinion Filmland's Funniest Female, the only one I would mention in the same breath as Charlie Chaplin.'—*A. P. Herbert, Punch*

The Patsy
US 1964 101m Technicolor
Paramount / Jerry Lewis (E. J. Glicksman)

Hollywood executives try to mould a bellboy to replace a deceased comedian.
A few mildly funny scenes scarcely atone for a long raucous comedy in which the star upstages his betters.

wd Jerry Lewis *ph* Wallace Kelley *m* David Raksin

Jerry Lewis, Everett Sloane, Peter Lorre, John Carradine, Phil Harris, Hans Conried, Ina Balin

'Inside the skyscraper jungle! Ruthless men and ambitious women clawing for control of a billion-dollar empire!'

Patterns***
US 1956 88m bw
UA / Jed Harris, Michael Myerberg
GB title: *Patterns of Power*

The tough boss of a New York corporation forces a showdown between a young executive and the older ineffectual man who he hopes will resign.
Tense little boardroom melodrama with domestic asides, one of the best of the filmed TV plays of the mid-fifties.

w Rod Serling, from his play *d Fielder Cook ph* Boris Kaufman

Van Heflin, Everett Sloane, Ed Begley, Beatrice Straight, Elizabeth Wilson

'Nobody ever won a war by dying for his country. He won it by making the other poor dumb bastard die for his country!'

Patton***
US 1970 171m De Luxe Dimension 150
TCF (Frank McCarthy)
GB title: *Patton—Lust for Glory*

World War II adventures of an aggressive American general.
Brilliantly handled wartime character study which is also a spectacle and tries too hard to have it both ways, but as a piece of film-making is hard to beat.

w Francis Ford Coppola, Edmund H. North *d Franklin Schaffner ph Fred Koenekamp m Jerry Goldsmith*

George C. Scott, Karl Malden, Michael Bates, Stephen Young, Michael Strong, Frank Latimore

'Here is an actor so totally immersed in his part that he almost makes you believe he is the man himself.'—*John Gillett*

AA: best picture; script; Franklin Schaffner; George C. Scott
AAN: Fred Koenekamp; Jerry Goldsmith

Paula
US 1952 80m bw
Columbia (Buddy Adler)
GB title: *The Silent Voice*

A barren wife causes a boy's deafness in an accident; she cures and adopts him.
Adequate woman's picture, a vehicle for a star and a luxuriant wardrobe.

w James Poe, William Sackheim *d* Rudolph Maté *ph* Charles Lawton Jnr *m* George Duning

Loretta Young, Kent Smith, Alexander Knox, Tommy Rettig

The Pawnbroker**
US 1965 114m bw
Landau–Unger (Worthington Miner)

A Jew in slummy New York is haunted by his experiences in Nazi prison camps.
Engrossing, somewhat over-melodramatic character study, generally well done.

w David Friedkin, Morton Fine, *novel* Edward Lewis Wallant *d* Sidney Lumet *ph* Boris Kaufman *m* Quincy Jones

Rod Steiger, Brock Peters, Geraldine Fitzgerald, Jaime Sanchez, Thelma Oliver, Juano Hernandez

AAN: Rod Steiger

Pay or Die!*
US 1960 109m bw
Allied Artists (Richard Wilson)

In 1906, a New York Italian police detective forms a special squad to combat the Black Hand.
Tough, convincing period melodrama.

w Richard Wilson, Bertram Millhauser *d Richard Wilson ph* Lucien Ballard *m* David Raksin *ad* Fernando Carrere

Ernest Borgnine, Alan Austin, Zohra Lampert, Robert F. Simon, Renata Vanni

Payday
US 1972 103m colour
Cinerama / Pumice / Fantasy (Ralph J. Gleason)

An over-age pop singer has personal problems which erupt into violence.
Well made, dislikeable melodrama.

w Don Carpenter *d* Daryl Duke *ph* Richard C. Glouner *md* Ed Bogas

Rip Torn, Ahna Capri, Elayne Heilveil, Michael C. Gwynn

Payment Deferred*
US 1932 75m bw
MGM (Irving Thalberg)

A man desperate for money poisons his wealthy nephew.
Watchable photographed play.

w Ernest Vajda, Claudine West, *play* Jeffrey Dell *d* Lothar Mendes *ph* Merritt Gerstad

Charles Laughton, Maureen O'Sullivan, Ray Milland, Dorothy Peterson, Veree Teasdale, Billy Bevan, Halliwell Hobbes

'In spite of its excellence, it will probably prove indifferent box office.'—*Variety*

Payment on Demand*
US 1951 90m bw
RKO / Jack H. Skirball

A happy wife and mother is appalled when her husband asks for a divorce.
A star suffers her way through luxury to a happy ending; good enough stuff for its intended audience.

w Bruce Manning, Curtis Bernhardt *d* Curtis Bernhardt *ph* Leo Tover *m* Victor Young

Bette Davis, Barry Sullivan, Jane Cowl, Kent Taylor, Betty Lynn, John Sutton, Frances Dee, Otto Kruger

'An absolutely typical Joan Crawford picture except that Bette Davis happens to be in the Joan Crawford part.'—*Richard Mallett, Punch*

The Payoff
US 1943 74m bw

A star reporter nabs the killer of a prosecuting attorney. A fading star in a role he had played several times before. Lee Tracy, Tom Brown, Tina Thayer, Evelyn Brent, Jack La Rue. Written by Edward Dein; directed by Arthur Dreifuss; for Jack Schwarz / PRC.

Payroll*
GB 1961 105m bw
Anglo Amalgamated / Lynx (Norman Priggen)

Small-time crooks snatch £100,000, but after the getaway things begin to go wrong.
Tense, vivid, thoroughly predictable *Rififi*-style thriller, handled with solid professionalism.

w George Baxt, *novel* Derek Bickerton *d Sidney Hayers ph Ernest Steward m* Reg Owen

Michael Craig, Billie Whitelaw, Françoise Prévost, Kenneth Griffith, William Lucas, Tom Bell, Barry Keegan, Joan Rice, Glyn Houston

Peach O'Reno
US 1931 66m bw

Two incompetent lawyers work on a divorce case. Burlesque-style comedy with cabaret asides. Thin stuff. Bert Wheeler, Robert Woolsey, Dorothy Lee, Joseph Cawthorn, Cora Witherspoon, Zelma O'Neal. Written by Ralph Spence, Tim Whelan; directed by William Seiter; for RKO-Pathé. 'Less than average; low comedy laughs for the minor spots.'—*Variety*

The Pearl*
US / Mexico 1948 72m bw
RKO / Oscar Dancigers

In a remote Mexican village, a simple shell diver finds a pearl of great price, but finds his life complicated as a result.
A fable which at the time seemed to have considerable quality, being the first Mexican film to receive international distribution.

w John Steinbeck, Emilio Fernandez, Kack Wagner *d* Emilio Fernandez *ph* Gabriel Figueroa *m* Antonio Diaz Conde

Pedro Armendariz, Maria Elena Marques, Alfonso Bedoya

The Pearl of Death**
US 1944 67m bw
Universal (Howard S. Benedict)

When a valuable pearl is stolen, Sherlock Holmes has only his own cleverness to blame; but he redeems himself by trapping 'The Creeper'.
An amusing picturization of Doyle's *The Six Napoleons*, with the addition of a horror figure; it plays very well and is certainly among the best of this series.

w Bertram Millhauser d Roy William Neill ph Virgil Miller *m* Paul Sawtell

Basil Rathbone, *Nigel Bruce*, Dennis Hoey, Miles Mander, Rondo Hatton, Evelyn Ankers

Peck's Bad Boy
US 1934 70m bw

Adventures of a well-intentioned but accident-prone boy in a midwestern town. Old-fashioned American juvenile classic, modestly well done. Jackie Cooper, Jackie Searle, Dorothy Peterson, Thomas Meighan, Written by Bernard Schubert and Marguerite Roberts from the story by G. W. Peck; directed by Edward Cline; for Sol Lesser / Fox. (Previously made in 1921 with Jackie Coogan.)

† Cline also directed a sequel, *Peck's Bad Boy With the Circus* starring Tommy Kelly, in 1938.

Peeper
US 1975 87m De Luxe Panavision
TCF / Chartoff–Winkler (Ron Buck)

In 1947 Los Angeles, a poor British private eye gets into trouble when he seeks a man's lost daughter.
Semi-spoofing Chandleresque caper which is never quite funny or quite thrilling enough.

w W. D. Richter, *novel* Deadfall by Keith Laumer *d* Peter Hyams *ph* Earl Rath *m* Richard Clements

Michael Caine, Natalie Wood, Kitty Winn, Thayer David, Liam Dunn
'Flimsy whimsy.'—*Variety*

'More horrible than horror! More terrible than terror!'

Peeping Tom*
GB 1959 109m Eastmancolor
Anglo Amalgamated / Michael Powell

A film studio focus puller is obsessed by the lust to murder beautiful women and photograph the fear on their faces.
Thoroughly disagreeable suspenser, a kind of compendium of the bad taste the director showed in flashes during his career.

w Leo Marks *d* Michael Powell *ph* Otto Heller *m* Brian Easdale

Carl Boehm, Moira Shearer, Anna Massey, Maxine Audley, Esmond Knight, Michael Goodliffe, Shirley Ann Field, Jack Watson
'Of enormous and deserved reputation.'—*Time Out, 1982*

Peg of Old Drury*
GB 1935 76m bw
British and Dominions / Herbert Wilcox

The romance of 18th-century actress Peg Woffington with David Garrick.
Primitive but vivacious historical romp with adequate star performances.

w Miles Malleson, *play* Masks and Faces by Charles Reade, Tom Taylor *d* Herbert Wilcox *ph* F. A. Young

Anna Neagle, Cedric Hardwicke, Jack Hawkins, Margaretta Scott, Hay Petrie

Peg o' My Heart
US 1933 86m bw

To the concern of his family, an English nobleman falls for an Irish colleen. Half-hearted version of a famous lavender-tinted stage hit previously filmed in the twenties with its original star Laurette Taylor; but by 1933 its time was past. Marion Davies, Onslow Stevens, Alan Mowbray, Robert Greig, Irene Browne, J. Farrell MacDonald, Juliette Compton. Written by Frances Marion, from the play by J. Hartley Manners; directed by Robert Z. Leonard; for MGM. 'Just an 86-minute Irish monologue . . . undeservedly flattered by an almost perfect production.'—*Variety*

Peggy Sue Got Married**
US 1986 104m De Luxe
Tri-Star / Rastar (Paul R. Gurian)

A disillusioned woman goes to her 25th high school reunion and finds herself reliving her young life.
It plays like an extended *Twilight Zone*, but with plenty of interesting details to back up an excellent leading performance.

w Jerry Leichtling, Arlene Sarner *d Francis Coppola ph* Jordan Cronenweth *m* John Barry *pd* Dean Tavoularis *ed* Barry Malkin

Kathleen Turner, Nicholas Cage, Barry Miller, Catherine Hicks, Maureen O'Sullivan, Leon Ames, Helen Hunt, Don Murray, Barbara Harris, Kevin J. O'Connor
'Provocative, well acted, stylish and uneven.'—*Variety*

AAN: Jordan Cronenweth; Theodora Van Runkle (costumes); Kathleen Turner

Peking Express
US 1951 90m bw
Paramount / Hal B. Wallis

In communist China, an assortment of people are aboard a train which is diverted by outlaws.
Pot-boiling remake of *Shanghai Express* (qv); an adequate time-passer.

w John Meredyth Lucas *d* William Dieterle *ph* Charles Lang *m* Dmitri Tiomkin

Joseph Cotten, Corinne Calvet, Edmund Gwenn, Marvin Miller
'Lacks flavour or distinction.'—*Leonard Maltin*

The Penalty
US 1941 81m bw
MGM (Jack Chertok)

The son of a gangster is regenerated by farm life and turns against his father.
Antediluvian sweetness and light which wastes a good cast.

w Harry Ruskin, John C. Higgins *d* Harold S. Bucquet *ph* Harold Rosson *m* David Snell

Edward Arnold, Lionel Barrymore, Marsha Hunt, Robert Sterling, Gene Reynolds

Pendulum*
US 1969 102m Technicolor
Columbia / Pendulum (Stanley Niss)

A convicted murderer and rapist is freed on appeal and kills the wife of the detective who arrested him.
Heavy-going police melodrama, efficient but not very interesting.

w Stanley Niss *d* George Schaefer *ph* Lionel Lindon *m* Walter Scharf

George Peppard, Jean Seberg, Richard Kiley, Charles McGraw, Robert F. Lyons, Madeleine Sherwood

Penelope
US 1966 98m Metrocolor Panavision
MGM / Euterpe (Joe Pasternak, Arthur Loew Jnr)

The wife of a bank vice-president is a bank robber and kleptomaniac.
Would be cute comedy which only sickens one for wasting its talent.

w George Wells, *novel* E. V. Cunningham *d* Arthur Hiller *ph* Harry Stradling *m* Johnny Williams

Natalie Wood, Ian Bannen, Dick Shawn, Peter Falk, Jonathan Winters, Lila Kedrova, Lou Jacobi, Norma Crane, Arthur Malet, Jerome Cowan

The Penguin Pool Murder*
US 1932 69m bw

Inspector Piper on a murder case is outsmarted by schoolmarm Hildegarde Withers. Mystery comedy which started a short series: plot smothered by wisecracks. *Edna May Oliver*, *James Gleason*, Mae Clarke, Robert Armstrong, Donald Cook, Edgar Kennedy. Written by Willis Goldbeck from the novel by Stuart Palmer; directed by George Archainbaud; for RKO. 'An odd blend of illogical happenings, but basically broad comedy.'—*Variety*

Penitentiary
US 1938 78m bw

A district attorney becomes prison warden, and his daughter falls for a convict. Scene-for-scene remake of *The Criminal Code* (*qv*) but considerably less dynamic. Walter Connolly, John Howard, Jean Parker, Robert Barrat, Marc Lawrence, Arthur Hohl, Paul Fix. Written by Fred Niblo Jnr and Seton I. Miller from a play by Martin Flavin; directed by John Brahm; for Columbia.

Penn of Pennsylvania
GB 1941 79m bw
British National (Richard Vernon)
US title: *The Courageous Mr Penn*

Persecuted Quakers leave England for America.
Stodgily fictionalized history.

w Anatole de Grunwald, *book* William Penn by C. E. Vulliamy *d* Lance Comfort *ph* Ernest Palmer

Clifford Evans, Deborah Kerr, Denis Arundell, Aubrey Mallalieu, Henry Oscar, Max Adrian

Pennies from Heaven
US 1936 81m bw

A wanderer protects a homeless little girl from the truant officer. Mild star musical, lucky enough to have a hit title song. Bing Crosby, Edith Fellows, Madge Evans, Louis Armstrong and his band. Written by Katherine Leslie Moore, William Rankin and Jo Swerling; directed by Norman Z. McLeod; for Columbia.

Pennies from Heaven*
US 1982 108m Metrocolor
MGM / Hera (Nora Kaye, Herbert Ross)

In 1934 Chicago, a sheet music salesman consoles himself for his drab and tragic life by fantasies induced by his songs.
The essence of Dennis Potter's British TV serial was hard enough to get at; transposed to America it becomes unattractive nonsense, and the song sequences are not even well staged despite the enormous expense.

w Dennis Potter *d* Herbert Ross *ph* Gordon Willis *md* Marvin Hamlisch, Billy May *pd* Ken Adam

Steve Martin, Bernadette Peters, Christopher Walken, Jessica Harper, John McMartin

'All flash and style and no heart.'—*Roger Ebert*

AAN: Dennis Potter

Penny Paradise
GB 1938 72m bw

A tugboat captain thinks he has won the football pools; but the coupon wasn't posted. An old, old story, put over with modest effectiveness. Edmund Gwenn, Betty Driver, Jimmy O'Dea, Maire O'Neill, Jack Livesey. Written by Tommy Thompson, W. L. Meade and Thomas Browne; directed by Carol Reed; for ATP.

PEGGY SUE GOT MARRIED. Kathleen Turner's fine performance helped director Francis Coppola to return to form after a long dry spell.

Penny Points to Paradise
GB 1951 77m bw

A pools winner takes cash but nearly loses it to a forger. Abysmally made comedy, only interesting as an early teaming of the Goons. Harry Secombe, Peter Sellers, Spike Milligan, Alfred Marks, Bill Kerr, Freddie Frinton, Paddy O'Neil. Written by John Ormonde; directed by Tony Young; for Advance / Adelphi.

Penny Princess
GB 1952 94m Technicolor
Rank / Conquest (Frank Godwin)

A New York shopgirl inherits a tiny European state and boosts its economy by marketing a mixture of cheese and schnapps.
Thin, spoofy comedy with mild moments of fun.

wd Val Guest *ph* Geoffrey Unsworth
m Ronald Hamner

Dirk Bogarde, Yolande Donlan, A. E. Matthews, Anthony Oliver, Edwin Styles, Reginald Beckwith, Kynaston Reeves, Peter Butterworth, Laurence Naismith, Mary Clare, Desmond Walter-Ellis

Penny Serenade*
US 1941 120m bw
Columbia (Fred Guiol)

Courtship, marriage and the death of two children are recollected by a woman contemplating divorce.
Well-played but uneasy film which veers suddenly and disconcertingly from light comedy into tragedy.

w Morrie Ryskind *d* George Stevens
ph Joseph Walker *m* W. Franke Harling

Cary Grant, Irene Dunne, Beulah Bondi, Edgar Buchanan, Ann Doran

'To make something out of very little, and that so near at hand, is one of the tests of artistry.'—*Otis Ferguson*

'A tear compeller showing how Cary Grant and Irene Dunne lose first their own baby and then the one they adopt. Which, as Lady Bracknell would certainly have observed, looks like carelessness.'—*James Agate*

AAN: Cary Grant

Penrod and Sam
US 1937 68m bw

Exploits of a club for juvenile sleuths. Start of a second feature series which had little to do with the original period characters but was generally well received. Later the same year came *Penrod and his Twin Brother*, and in 1938 *Penrod's Double Trouble*. Billy Mauch, Frank Craven, Spring Byington, Craig Reynolds, Charles Halton. Written by Lillie Hayward and Hugh Cummings from the characters created by Booth Tarkington; directed by William McGann; for Warners. 'Should serve as a nucleus for swell exploitation tie-ups.'—*Variety*.
† There had been an earlier version in 1931, starring Leon Janney; and the family turned up again in the Doris Day musicals *On Moonlight Bay* and *By the Light of the Silvery Moon*.

Penthouse*
US 1933 90m bw
GB title: *Crooks in Clover*

When he outlives his usefulness to the underworld, a lawyer is framed for murder. Sprightly murder comedy-drama which plays like a try-out for *The Thin Man*. Warner Baxter, Myrna Loy, C. Henry Gordon, Nat Pendleton, Charles Butterworth, George E. Stone. Written by Frances Goodrich and Albert Hackett; directed by W. S. Van Dyke; for Hunt Stromberg / MGM. 'Well-sustained crime solution with smashing climax and arresting title.'—*Variety*

The Penthouse
GB 1967 96m Eastmancolor
Paramount / Tahiti (Harry Fine)

Illicit lovers in an unfinished block of flats are terrorized by intruders.
Thoroughly objectionable and unpleasant melodrama with no attractive characters and no attempt to explain itself.

wd Peter Collinson, *play* The Meter Man by J. Scott Forbes *ph* Arthur Lavis *m* John Hawkesworth

Suzy Kendall, Terence Morgan, Tony Beckley, Norman Rodway, Martine Beswick

'Pornography in Pinter's clothing.'—*MFB*

The People against O'Hara*
US 1951 102m bw
MGM (William H. Wright)

An ex-alcoholic defence lawyer sacrifices himself to prove his client's innocence.
Formula drama, well made and entertainingly performed, with snatches of bright dialogue.

w John Monks Jnr, *novel* Eleanor Lipsky
d John Sturges *ph* John Alton *m* Carmen Dragon

Spencer Tracy, Diana Lynn, Pat O'Brien, John Hodiak, James Arness, Arthur Shields, Eduardo Ciannelli, Louise Lorimer

The People Next Door
US 1970 93m De Luxe
Avco Embassy (Herb Brodkin)

Suburban parents have trouble with their drug-addicted teenage daughter.
Hysterical melodrama with good credentials.

w J. P. Miller, from his TV play *d* David Greene *ph* Gordon Willis *m* Don Sebesky

Eli Wallach, Julie Harris, Hal Holbrook, Cloris Leachman, Stephen McHattie, Nehemiah Persoff

'As unlovely a picture of suburban living as one is likely to see.'—*Judith Crist*

People on Sunday*
Germany 1929 72m approx (24 fps) bw silent
Filmstudio 1929
original title: *Menschen am Sonntag*

Two couples spend a day in Berlin's countryside.
Influential semi-documentary with fascinating credits.

w Billy Wilder, Curt Siodmak d Robert Siodmak, Fred Zinnemann, Edgar G. Ulmer ph Eugen Schüfftan

Brigitte Borchert, Christl Ehlers, Annie Schreyer

The People That Time Forgot
GB 1977 90m Technicolor
AIP / Amicus (John Dark)

Major McBride tries to rescue his old friend from a prehistoric island on which he disappeared in 1916.
Tepid sequel to *The Land That Time Forgot*: even the dinosaurs don't rise to the occasion.

w Patrick Tilley *d* Kevin Connor *ph* Alan Hume *m* John Scott *pd* Maurice Carter

Patrick Wayne, Sarah Douglas, Dana Gillespie, Doug McClure, Thorley Walters, Shane Rimmer, Tony Britton

People Will Talk
US 1935 60m bw

Mr and Mrs Wilton try to patch up their daughter's failing marriage. Slight domestic comedy with popular leads. Charles Ruggles, Mary Boland, Leila Hyams, Dean Jagger, Edward Brophy. Written by Herbert Fields, Sophie Kerr, F. Hugh Herbert; directed by Al Santell; for Paramount. 'Strictly light summer fare and not solid enough to stand alone.'—*Variety*

People Will Talk**
US 1951 110m bw
TCF (Darryl F. Zanuck)

A surgeon's unorthodox psychological methods cause jealousy among his colleagues, especially when he falls in love with a pregnant patient.
Oddly entertaining jumble of melodrama, comedy, romance, speeches and a little mystery, all quite typical of its director.

wd Joseph L. Mankiewicz, play Dr Praetorius by Curt Goetz *ph* Milton Krasner *md* Alfred Newman

Cary Grant, Jeanne Crain, Finlay Currie, Hume Cronyn, Walter Slezak, Sidney Blackmer, Basil Ruysdael

'A picture so mature and refreshingly frank as to hold that an erring young woman might be rewarded with a wise and loving mate is most certainly a significant milestone in the moral emancipation of American films.'—*New York Times*

Pepe
US 1960 195m Eastmancolor Cinemascope
Columbia / George Sidney (Jacques Gelman)

A Mexican peasant in Hollywood gets help from the stars.
Feeble and seemingly endless extravaganza in which the boring stretches far outnumber the rest, and few of the guests have anything worthwhile to do.

w Dorothy Kingsley, Claude Binyon
d George Sidney *ph* Joe MacDonald
md Johnny Green

Cantinflas, Dan Dailey, Shirley Jones, Ernie Kovacs, Jay North, William Demarest, Michael Callan, Maurice Chevalier, Bing Crosby, Richard Conte, Bobby Darin, Sammy

Davis Jnr, Jimmy Durante, Zsa Zsa Gabor, Judy Garland, Hedda Hopper, Joey Bishop, Peter Lawford, Janet Leigh, Jack Lemmon, Kim Novak, André Previn, Donna Reed, Debbie Reynolds, Greer Garson, Edward G. Robinson, Cesar Romero, Frank Sinatra, Billie Burke, Tony Curtis, Dean Martin, Charles Coburn

AAN: Joe MacDonald; Johnny Green; song, 'Faraway Part of Town' (*m* André Previn, *ly* Dory Langdon)

Pépé le Moko**
France 1936 90m bw
Paris Film

A Parisian gangster lives in the Algerian casbah where the police can't get at him; but love causes him to emerge and be shot.
Romantic melodrama modelled on the American gangster film but with a decided poetic quality of its own: the Americans promptly paid it the compliment of remaking it as the not-too-bad *Algiers*.

w Henri Jeanson, Roger d'Ashelbe, *novel* Roger d'Ashelbe (Henri La Barthe) *d Julien Duvivier ph* Jules Kruger *m* Vincent Scotto *ad* Jacques Krauss

Jean Gabin, Mireille Ballin, Gabriel Gabrio, Lucas Gridoux

'One of the most compelling of all French films.'—*New Yorker, 1977*

'Perhaps there have been pictures as exciting on the thriller level . . . but I cannot remember one which has succeeded so admirably in raising the thriller to a poetic level.'—*Graham Greene*

Percy
GB 1971 103m Eastmancolor
Anglo EMI / Welbeck (Betty E. Box)

After an unfortunate accident, a young man undergoes a successful penis transplant, and sets out to discover who the donor was.
Barrage of phallic jokes, some quite funny, but mostly as witless as the whole idea.

w Hugh Leonard, *novel* Raymond Hitchcock *d* Ralph Thomas *ph* Ernest Steward *m* Ray Davies

Hywel Bennett, Elke Sommer, *Denholm Elliott*, Britt Ekland, Cyd Hayman

Percy's Progress
GB 1974 101m Eastmancolor
EMI (Betty E. Box)

A chemical causes impotence in all males except the owner of the first transplanted penis.
Percy dug deep, but this is really the bottom of the barrel.

w Sid Colin *d* Ralph Thomas *ph* Tony Imi *m* Tony Macauley

Leigh Lawson, Elke Sommer, Denholm Elliott, Judy Geeson, Harry H. Corbett, Vincent Price, Adrienne Posta, Julie Ege, James Booth

'Health clubs—more sex than sweat?'
Perfect
US 1985 115m Technicolor

An aerobics instructor (female) meets a reporter (male) doing a story on health clubs, but it isn't love at first sight.
Nervy, unattractive drama which didn't find an audience.

w Aaron Latham, James Bridges *d* James Bridges *ph* Gordon Willis *m* Ralph Burns

John Travolta, Jamie Lee Curtis, Anne de Salvo, Marilu Henner, Laraine Newman

'Guilty of the sins it condemns—superficiality, manipulation and smugness.'—*Variety*

A Perfect Couple*
US 1979 112m De Luxe
TCF / Lions Gate (Robert Altman)

A middle-aged Greek much dependent on his family meets a jazz singer through a dating service.
A free-speaking update of *Marty*, featuring the Altman repertory company; intelligent sequences are muffled by the familiar Altman messiness of approach.

w Robert Altman, Allan Nicholls *d* Robert Altman *ph* Edmond L. Koons *md* Tom Pierson, Tony Berg

Paul Dooley, Marta Heflin, Titos Vandis, Belita Moreno, Henry Gibson, Dimitra Arliss

Perfect Day*
US 1929 20m bw

Various problems delay a family's departure for a picnic. Technically a most adept star comedy but its repetition can annoy. Laurel and Hardy, Edgar Kennedy. Written by Hal Roach, Leo McCarey and H. M. Walker; directed by James Parrott; for Hal Roach. (NB: The picnic was originally to have occupied the second reel, but the departure gags swelled to occupy the entire footage.)

Perfect Friday*
GB 1970 95m Eastmancolor
London Screenplays / Sunnymede (Dimitri de Grunwald)

A bank manager engages aristocratic help to rob his own bank.
Middling comedy caper.

w Anthony Greville-Bell, J. Scott Forbes *d* Peter Hall *ph* Alan Hume *m* Johnny Dankworth *pd* Terence Marsh

Stanley Baker, Ursula Andress, David Warner, Patience Collier, T. P. McKenna, David Waller, Joan Benham, Julian Orchard

The Perfect Furlough
US 1958 93m Eastmancolor Cinemascope
U-I (Robert Arthur)
GB title: *Strictly for Pleasure*

To help morale at a remote Arctic army unit, one of the men is selected to enjoy the perfect leave in Paris on behalf of the others.
Amiable farce which entertains while it's on but is quickly forgotten.

w Stanley Shapiro *d* Blake Edwards *ph* Philip Lathrop *m* Frank Skinner

Tony Curtis, Janet Leigh, Elaine Stritch, Keenan Wynn, Troy Donahue, King Donovan, Linda Cristal

The Perfect Gentleman
US 1935 73m bw

A retired officer helps an actress make a comeback. Genial comedy which didn't quite work well enough to make an English variety star popular on both sides of the Atlantic. Cicely Courtneidge, Frank Morgan, Heather Angel, Herbert Mundin, Henry Stephenson. Written by Edward Childs Carpenter; directed by Tim Whelan; for MGM. (GB title: *The Imperfect Lady*.)

The Perfect Marriage
US 1946 88m bw
Paramount / Hal B. Wallis

On their tenth wedding anniversary, a happy couple have a row and start divorce proceedings.
Wispy comedy, unmemorable and rather tiresome.

w Leonard Spiegelgass, *play* Samson Raphaelson *d* Lewis Allen *ph* Russell Metty *m* Frederick Hollander

David Niven, Loretta Young, Eddie Albert, Nona Griffith, Virginia Field, Jerome Cowan, Rita Johnson, Charles Ruggles, Nana Bryant, Zasu Pitts

'Another film about disillusionment and reconciliation in a mansion with constant evening dress.'—*Sunday Times*

The Perfect Snob
US 1941 63m bw

A woman tosses her daughter at millionaires. The girl settles on a poor boy . . . who turns out to be a millionaire after all. Predictable comedy with competent cast. Charles Ruggles, Charlotte Greenwood, Lynn Bari, Cornel Wilde, Anthony Quinn, Alan Mowbray. Written by Lee Loeb and Harold Buchman; directed by Ray McCarey; for Walter Morosco / TCF.

The Perfect Specimen
US 1937 82m bw
Warner (Harry Joe Brown)

The grandmother of a rich young man brings him up uncontaminated by the world, but when a girl crashes her car into his fence he proves fitted to deal with the situation.
Fantasticated comedy a long way after *Mr Deeds* and too slow by half.

w Norman Reilly Raine, Lawrence Riley, Brewster Morse, Fritz Falkenstein, Samuel Hopkins Adams *d* Michael Curtiz *ph* Charles Rosher

Errol Flynn, Joan Blondell, Hugh Herbert, Edward Everett Horton, May Robson, Dick Foran, Beverly Roberts, Allen Jenkins

'Upper bracket comedy for the family trade.'—*Variety*

Perfect Strangers**
GB 1945 102m bw
MGM / London Films (Alexander Korda)
US title: *Vacation from Marriage*

A downtrodden clerk and his dowdy wife go to war, and come back unrecognizably improved. Pleasant comedy with good actors; but the turnabout of two such caricatures really strains credibility.

w Clemence Dane, Anthony Pelissier *d* Alexander Korda *ph* Georges Périnal *m* Clifton Parker

Robert Donat, Deborah Kerr, Glynis Johns, Ann Todd, Roland Culver, Elliot Mason, Eliot Makeham, Brefni O'Rourke, Edward Rigby

'War is supposed to be the catalyst, the sportsman's bracer; and the film's chief weakness is its failure to show the briefly exalted couple sinking back, uncontrollably, under their peacetime stone.'—*James Agee*

'It glows with laughter and honest sentiment.'—*New York Times*

AA: original story (Clemence Dane)

'They met by chance, and once they kissed, they knew they never should have!'

Perfect Strangers
US 1950 87m bw
Warner (Jerry Wald)
GB title: *Too Dangerous to Love*

Two jurors on a murder case fall in love. Talkative, unlikely, and rather boring potboiler.

w Edith Sommer, *play* Ladies and Gentlemen by Charles MacArthur, Ben Hecht *d* Bretaigne Windust *ph* Peverell Marley *m* Leigh Harline

Ginger Rogers, Dennis Morgan, Thelma Ritter, Margalo Gillmore, Howard Freeman, Alan Reed, Paul Ford, George Chandler

Perfect Understanding*
GB 1933 80m bw
Gloria Swanson British Pictures Ltd

A couple agree to marry on condition that they will never disagree with each other. Silly comedy with a unique star combination looking acutely uncomfortable.

w Miles Malleson, Michael Powell *d* Cyril Gardner *ph* Curt Courant

Gloria Swanson, Laurence Olivier, John Halliday, Nigel Playfair, Michael Farmer, Genevieve Tobin, Nora Swinburne

'Dull and talky picture, done in the uninspiring British style.'—*Variety*

The Perfect Woman*
GB 1949 89m bw
GFD / Two Cities (George and Alfred Black)

A girl changes places with her inventor uncle's robot woman.
Described as a romp, this is in fact a pretty good farce, very fast moving and well played after the usual expository start.

w George Black, Bernard Knowles, J. B. Boothroyd, *play* Wallace Geoffrey, Basil Mitchell *d* Bernard Knowles *ph* Jack Hildyard *m* Arthur Wilkinson

Patricia Roc, Nigel Patrick, Stanley Holloway, David Hurst, Miles Malleson, Irene Handl

Performance*
GB 1970 105m Technicolor
Warner / Goodtimes (Donald Cammell)

A vicious gangster moves in with an ex-pop star.
Dense, Pinterish melodrama about alter egos; not really worth the trouble it takes, but superficially very flashily done.

w Donald Cammell *d Nicolas Roeg, Donald Cammell ph Nicolas Roeg m* Jack Nitzche *md* Randy Newman

James Fox, Mick Jagger, Anita Pallenberg, Michèle Breton, Stanley Meadows, Allan Cuthbertson

'A humourless, messy mixture of crime and decadence and drug-induced hallucination.'—*New Yorker, 1980*

'You don't have to be a drug addict, pederast, sado-masochist or nitwit to enjoy it, but being one or more of these things would help.'—*John Simon*

Perilous Holiday
US 1946 89m bw

A newly acquainted couple become involved with counterfeiters in Mexico City. Passable comedy-crime programme filler. Pat O'Brien, Ruth Warrick, Alan Hale, Minna Gombell. Written by Robert Carson and Roy Chanslor; directed by Edward H. Griffith; for Columbia.

A Perilous Journey
US 1953 87m bw
Republic (W. J. O'Sullivan)

A party of women sail to the California goldfields to sell themselves into marriage. Reasonably lively action drama.

w Richard Wormser, *novel* The Golden Tide by Virgie Roe *d* R. G. Springsteen *ph* Jack Marta *m* Victor Young

Vera Ralston, David Brian, Charles Winninger, Scott Brady, Virginia Grey, Ben Cooper

Perils of Nyoka
US 1942 bw serial: 15 eps

Archaeologists seek the long lost Tablets of Hippocrates, and are helped by a girl explorer seeking her lost father. Wildly plotted serial; incidents routine. Kay Aldridge, Clayton Moore, William Benedict, Charles Middleton. Directed by William Witney; for Republic.

The Perils of Pauline
US 1934 bw serial: 12 eps

The daughter of a noted scientist seeks a deadly gas formula in Indo-China. Semi-remake of the famous silent serial. Evalyn Knapp, Robert Allan, James Durkin, Sonny Ray, Frank Lackteen. Directed by Ray Taylor; for Universal.

The Perils of Pauline*
US 1947 96m Technicolor
Paramount (Sol C. Siegel)

The career of silent serial queen Pearl White. An agreeable recreation of old time Hollywood, with plenty of slapstick chases but a shade too much sentiment also.

w P. J. Wolfson *d* George Marshall *ph* Ray Rennahan *md* Robert Emmett Dolan

Betty Hutton, John Lund, Billy de Wolfe, William Demarest, Constance Collier, Frank Faylen, William Farnum, Paul Panzer, Snub Pollard, Creighton Hale, Chester Conklin, James Finlayson, Hank Mann, Bert Roach, Francis McDonald, Chester Clute

'People who can accept such stuff as solid gold have either forgotten a lot, or never knew first-rate slapstick when they saw it, twenty or thirty years ago, when it was one of the wonders of the world.'—*James Agee*

AAN: song 'I Wish I Didn't Love You So' (*m / ly* Frank Loesser)

Perils of the Royal Mounted
US 1942 bw serial: 15 eps

Indians accused of massacring settlers turn out to have been white outlaws in disguise. The Mounties get their man once more. Robert Stevens, Kenneth MacDonald, Herbert Rawlinson, Nell O'Day. Directed by James W. Horne; for Columbia.

Perils of the Wilderness
US 1956 bw serial: 15 eps

The Mounties pursue a ruthless crime lord in the Canadian Northwest. Unsurprising serial, one of the last to be made. Dennis Moore, Richard Emory, Eve Anderson, Kenneth MacDonald. Directed by Spencer Bennet: for Columbia.

Period of Adjustment
US 1962 122m bw Panavision
MGM / Marton (Lawrence Weingarten)

A Korean War veteran has the shakes and his sexual adequacy is effected, as his wife furiously discovers.
Comedy of maladjustment, tolerably witty but unsuitably widescreened.

w Isabel Lennart, *play* Tennessee Williams *d* George Roy Hill *ph* Paul bc. Vogel *m* Lyn Murray

Tony Franciosa, Jane Fonda, Jim Hutton, Lois Nettleton

Les Perles de la Couronne*
France 1937 118m bw

The history over four centuries of seven pearls given by Pope Clement VII to Catherine de Medici. Generally amusing series of historical sketches in Guitry's inimitable style. Sacha Guitry, Renée Saint-Cyr, Lyn Harding, Percy Marmont, Arletty, Claude Dauphin, Raimu, Jean-Louis Barrault, Jacqueline Delubac. Written by *Sacha Guitry*; directed by Sacha Guitry and Christian-Jaque; for Serge Sandburg / Tobis. 'Headed to bring in returns both at home and abroad.'—*Variety*.

† The picture tried, but failed, to be intelligible without sub-titles to all language-speakers.

Permission to Kill
US / Austria 1975 97m Technicolor Panavision
Warner / Sascha (Paul Mills)

British agents try to stop a communist returning home from the west.
Prolonged, confusing and boring spy melodrama in which everyone looks understandably glum.

w Robin Estridge, from his novel *d* Cyril Frankel *ph* Freddie Young *m* Richard Rodney Bennett

Bekim Fehmiu, Dirk Bogarde, Ava Gardner, Timothy Dalton, Frederic Forrest

'Pretentious political mishmash.'—*MFB*

Perri**
US 1957 75m Technicolor
Walt Disney (Winston Hibler)

The life of a squirrel.
Disney's first True Life Fantasy, in which live footage of animals is manipulated against artificial backgrounds to produce an effect as charming and unreal as a cartoon.

w Ralph Wright, Winston Hibler, *novel* Felix Salten *d* Ralph Wright *ph* various *m* Paul Smith

AAN: Paul Smith

Persecution
GB 1974 96m Eastmancolor
Fanfare / Tyburn (Kevin Francis)

A rich American woman in England is hated by her son and fearful that her murky past will be revealed.
Rich but not engrossing nonsense, somewhat à la *Baby Jane*, with hazy script and stolid production.

w Robert B. Hutton, Rosemary Wootten *d* Don Chaffey *ph* Ken Talbot *m* Paul Ferris

Lana Turner, Ralph Bates, Olga Georges-Picot, Trevor Howard, Suzan Farmer, Ronald Howard, Patrick Allen

'Gives off the unmistakable odour of damp mothballs.'—*Michael Billington, Illustrated London News*

Persona**
Sweden 1966 81m bw
Svensk Filmindustri (Lars-Owe Carlberg)

A nurse begins to identify with her mentally ill patient, and herself has a nervous breakdown.
Intense clinical study presented in a very complex cinematic manner which tends to obscure the main theme while providing endless fascination for cinéastes.

wd Ingmar Bergman ph Sven Nykvist *m* Lars Johan Werle, *Liv Ullmann, Bibi Andersson*, Gunnar Bjornstrand

'Reactions have ranged from incomprehension to irritation with what is dismissed as a characteristic piece of self-indulgence on Bergman's part—Bergman talking to himself again.'—*David Wilson, MFB*

'A puzzling, obsessive film that Bergman seems not so much to have worked out as to have torn from himself.'—*New Yorker, 1977*

Personal Affair
GB 1953 83m bw
Rank / Two Cities (Anthony Darnborough)

A schoolmaster and his neurotic wife run into trouble when a girl pupil develops a crush on him.
Preposterous domestic drama making much ado about nothing.

w Lesley Storm, from her play *d* Anthony Pelissier *ph* Reg Wyer *m* William Alwyn

Leo Genn, Gene Tierney, Glynis Johns, Pamela Brown

Personal Best
US 1982 122m Technicolor
Warner (Robert Towne)

A female Olympic track star has a lesbian relationship.
So what, is the response to two numbing hours of tedium.

wd Robert Towne *ph* Michael Chapman *m* Jack Nitzsche

Mariel Hemingway, Scott Glenn, Patrice Donnelly, Kenny Moore, Jim Moody

'There's an undercurrent of flabbergasted awe in this celebration of women's bodies, and everything in the movie is physically charged.'—*Pauline Kael, New Yorker*

Personal Maid's Secret
US 1935 60m bw

A maid's financial tips keep her master and mistress solvent. Modest comedy which was well liked at the time. Ruth Donnelly, Anita Louise, Warren Hull, Margaret Lindsay, Frank Albertson, Arthur Treacher. Written by F. Hugh Herbert, Lillie Hayward, from story by Lillian Day; directed by Arthur Greville Collins; for Bryan Foy / Warner.

Personal Property*
US 1937 84m bw
MGM (John W. Considine Jnr)
GB title: *The Man in Possession*

An American widow in England, in financial straits, falls for the bailiff sent to keep an eye on her.
Moderate star comedy which still amuses.

w Hugh Mills, Ernest Vajda, *play* The Man in Possession by H. M. Harwood *d* W. S. Van Dyke II *ph* William Daniels *m* Franz Waxman

Jean Harlow, Robert Taylor, Reginald Owen, Una O'Connor, Henrietta Crosman, E. E. Clive, Cora Witherspoon, Barnett Parker

'Harmless boudoir farce, for the undergraduates.'—*Variety*

Personal Services*
GB 1987 105m Eastmancolor
Zenith (Tim Bevan)

Adventures of a London madam.
Rather astonishing study of British attitudes to sex: not for Aunt Edna, but with a fair measure of interest for many.

w David Leland *d* Terry Jones *ph* Roger Deakins *ed* George Akers

Julie Walters, Alec McCowen, Shirley Stelfox, Danny Schiller, Victoria Hardcastle

The Personality Kid
US 1934 70m bw

A prizefighter becomes intoxicated by his own success and ignores his faithful wife. Mediocre filler wasting reliable stars. Pat O'Brien, Glenda Farrell, Claire Dodd, Henry O'Neill, Robert Gleckler, Thomas Jackson. Written by F. Hugh Herbert, Erwin Gelsey, Gene Towne, Graham Baker; directed by Alan Crosland; for Warners. 'Rates poorly: strictly cuffo yarn.'—*Variety*

'She's the woman behind the killer behind the gun!'

Persons in Hiding*
US 1939 71m bw
Paramount

A bored girl absconds with gangsters and becomes a public enemy.
Interesting programmer which led to several sequels using the same book as source; this one was vaguely inspired by the story of Bonnie and Clyde.

w William R. Lipman, Horace McCoy, *book* J. Edgar Hoover *d* Louis King *ph* Harry Fischbeck *m* Boris Morros

Patricia Morison, J. Carrol Naish, Lynne Overman, William Henry, Helen Twelvetrees, William Frawley

'Strong supporter for the duals . . . will depend entirely on rep of J. Edgar Hoover to attract.'—*Variety*

'A little on the tame side, but distinguished by the presence of a crooked and merciless heroine.'—*Graham Greene*

Persons Unknown*
Italy 1958 105m bw
Lux / Vides / Cinecittà (Franco Cristaldi)
original title: *I Soliti Ignoti;* US title: *Big Deal on Madonna Street*

Adventures of a gang of incompetent thieves, who get arrested more often than they get away, and finally, elaborately drill through a wall into the bank . . . only to find it's the wrong wall and they are in another room of the same flat.
Spoof black comedy working up to an elaborate take-off of *Rififi*; a great success in Italy and the USA, mildly received elsewhere.

w Age Scarpelli, Suso Cecchi d'Amico, Mario Monicelli *d* Mario Monicelli *ph* Gianni di Venanzo *m* Piero Umiliani

Vittorio Gassman, Renato Salvatori, Toto, Marcello Mastroianni, Memmo Carotenuto, Carla Gravina, Rosanna Rory

'Honeymoon's over—time to get married!'

Pete 'n Tillie*
US 1972 100m Technicolor Panavision
Universal (Julius J. Epstein)

The tragi-comic marriage of two eccentrics. Curious: plain drama treated as comedy, with surprisingly satisfactory results, but not an example to be followed.

w Julius J. Epstein, *novel* Witch's Milk by Peter de Vries *d* Martin Ritt *ph* John Alonzo *m* John T. Williams

Walter Matthau, Carol Burnett, Geraldine Page, René Auberjonois, Barry Nelson, Henry Jones

'For the most part an amusing, moving, sentimental comedy. The wisecracks stay on this side of human possibility – that is, we don't feel, as we do so often with Neil Simon, that the characters have private gag writers in their homes.'—*Stanley Kauffmann*

AAN: Julius J. Epstein; Geraldine Page

Pete Kelly's Blues*

US 1955 95m Warnercolor Cinemascope

(Warner) Mark VII Ltd (Jack Webb)

Jazz musicians in the twenties get involved with gangsters.

Minor cult film, mainly for the score; dramatically it is not exactly compelling.

w Richard L. Breen *d* Jack Webb *ph* Hal Rosson *ph* Harper Goff *m* Sammy Cahn, Ray Heindorf, Arthur Hamilton, Matty Matlock

Jack Webb, Edmond O'Brien, Janet Leigh, Peggy Lee, Andy Devine, *Ella Fitzgerald,* Lee Marvin, Martin Milner

'Concerned with striking attitudes and establishing an atmosphere rather than developing anything very coherent in the way of narrative . . . one remains aware of an over-deliberate straining after effect.'—*Penelope Houston*

AAN: Peggy Lee

'The most beautiful romance in all modern literature!'

Peter Ibbetson*

US 1935 85m bw

Paramount (Louis D. Lighton)

Childhood sweethearts meet again as adults, are separated when he is imprisoned for her husband's murder, but are reunited in heaven.

Downright peculiar romantic fantasy, even more oddly cast, but extremely well produced.

w Vincent Lawrence, Waldemar Young, Constance Collier, *novel* George du Maurier *d* Henry Hathaway *ph* Charles Lang *m* Ernst Toch

Gary Cooper, Ann Harding, Ida Lupino, John Halliday, Douglass Dumbrille, Virginia Weidler, Dickie Moore, Doris Lloyd

'In a day and a world hard-boiled and realistic Paramount hopes to sell a picture about dreams and beauty and love. It just isn't in the cards.'—*Variety*

'A triumph of surrealist thought.'—*André Breton*

'One of the world's ten best films.'—*Luis Bunuel*

AAN: Ernst Toch

Peter Pan***

US 1953 76m Technicolor

Walt Disney

Three London children are taken into fairyland by a magic flying boy who cannot grow up.

Solidly crafted cartoon version of a famous children's play; not Disney's best work, but still miles ahead of the competition.

supervisor Ben Sharpsteen *d* Wilfred Jackson, Clyde Geronomi, Hamilton Luske

Peter the Great*

USSR 1937 96m bw

The rise to power of the famous autocrat. Standard Russian first feature with plenty of action and striking composition, but not really memorable. Nikolai Simonov, Nikolai Cherkassov, Alla Tarasova, M. Zharov. Written by Alexei Tolstoy and Vladimir Petrov; directed by Vladimir Petrov; for Lenfilm. 'Surprisingly strong: a cinch in Russian-languagers.'—*Variety*

The Peterville Diamond

GB 1942 85m bw

Warner (A. H. Salomon)

A bored wife revives her husband's interest by cultivating the advances of a jewel thief.

Modest comedy-drama, smoothly presented: the same play formed the basis of Dieterle's *Jewel Robbery*.

w Brock Williams, Gordon Wellesley, *play* Jewel Robbery by Ladislas Fodor *d* Walter Forde *ph* Basil Emmott *md* Jack Beaver

Anne Crawford, Donald Stewart, Renee Houston, Oliver Wakefield, Charles Heslop, William Hartnell, Felix Aylmer, Charles Victor

Pete's Dragon

US 1977 127m Technicolor

Walt Disney (Ron Miller, Jerome Courtland)

In Maine in 1900, a nine-year-old boy escapes from grasping foster-parents with his pet dragon, which no one but himself can see.

A kind of juvenile rewrite of *Harvey*. The dragon is drawn (rather poorly) and the human characters are not exactly three-dimensional. A long way from *Mary Poppins*.

w Malcolm Marmorstein, *story* Seton I. Miller, S. S. Field *d* Don Chaffey *ph* Frank Phillips *anim* Ken Anderson *md* Irwin Kostal *songs* Al Kasha, Joel Hirschhorn *ch* Onna White

Sean Marshall, Mickey Rooney, Jim Dale, Helen Reddy, Red Buttons, Shelley Winters, Jim Backus, Joe E. Ross, Ben Wrigley

'For a Disney film it's terribly badly made, in parts so clumsy that it looks like the work of the Burbank Amateur Camera Club.'—*Barry Took, Punch*

AAN: music; song, 'Candle on the Water'

The Petrified Forest**

US 1936 83m bw

Warner (Henry Blanke)

Travellers at a way station in the Arizona desert are held up by gangsters.

Rather faded melodrama (it always was), which is important to Hollywood for introducing such well used figures as the poet idealist hero and the gangster anti-hero, and for giving Bogart his first meaty role. Otherwise, the settings are artificial, the acting theatrical, the development predictable and the dialogue pretentious.

w Charles Kenyon, Delmer Daves, *play* Robert E. Sherwood *d* Archie Mayo *ph* Sol Polito *md* Leo F. Forbstein

Leslie Howard, Bette Davis, *Humphrey Bogart,* Genevieve Tobin, Dick Foran, Joe Sawyer, Porter Hall, Charley Grapewin

ALAN SQUIER (Leslie Howard): 'Let there be killing. All this evening I've had a feeling of destiny closing in.'

JACKIE (Joe Sawyer): 'Now, just behave yourself and nobody'll get hurt. This is Duke Mantee, the world-famous killer, and he's hungry.'

'Marquee draft should offset the philosophic meanderings which minimize appeal.'—*Variety*

'Drama slackens under the weight of Mr Sherwood's rather half-baked philosophy.'—*Alistair Cooke*

'There is good dramatic material here, but Mr Sherwood doesn't see his play as certain things happening, but as ideas being expressed, "significant" cosmic ideas. . . . Life itself, which crept in during the opening scene, embarrassed perhaps at hearing itself so explicitly discussed, crept out again, leaving us only with the symbols, the too pasteboard desert, the stunted cardboard studio trees.'—*Graham Greene*

† Remade as *Escape in the Desert* (qv).

Petticoat Fever

US 1936 80m bw

MGM (Frank Davis)

A girl and her stuffy fiancé crash land their plane in sub-Arctic Labrador and are helped by a wireless operator who has not seen a woman for two years.

Pert, slightly unusual comedy which comes off pretty well.

w Harold Goldman, *play* Mark Reed *d* George Fitzmaurice *ph* Ernest Haller *m* William Axt

Robert Montgomery, Myrna Loy, Reginald Owen, Winifred Shotter

Petticoat Pirates

GB 1961 87m Technicolor CinemaScope

Women naval officers mutiny and take a nervous male stoker with them. Uncertain comedy fantasy. Charlie Drake, Cecil Parker, Anne Heywood, John Turner, Maxine Audley, Thorley Walters. Written by Lew Schwarz and Charlie Drake; directed by David MacDonald; for Gordon L. T. Scott / ABPC.

The Petty Girl
US 1950 88m Technicolor
Columbia (Nat Perrin)
GB title: *Girl of the Year*

A calendar artist takes a staid college professor as his model, and causes a scandal.
Witless comedy musical which barely lingers in the memory.

w Nat Perrin, *story* Mary McCarthy *d* Henry Levin *ph* William Snyder *m* George Duning *songs* Harold Arlen, Johnny Mercer

Robert Cummings, Joan Caulfield, Melville Cooper, Elsa Lanchester, Audrey Long, Mary Wickes, Frank Orth

Petulia*
US 1968 105m Technicolor
Warner / Petersham (Raymond Wagner)

A doctor's life is disrupted by his meeting and loving a kooky girl who has family problems.
Swinging London melodrama which happens to be set in San Francisco. All very flashy, and occasionally arresting or well acted, but adding up to nothing.

w Lawrence B. Marcus, *novel* Me and the Arch Kook Petulia by John Haase *d* Richard Lester *ph* Nicolas Roeg *m* John Barry

George C. Scott, Julie Christie, Richard Chamberlain, Joseph Cotten, Arthur Hill, Shirley Knight, Kathleen Widdoes, Pippa Scott

'A sad and savage comment on the ways we waste our time and ourselves in upper-middle-class America.'—*Richard Schickel*

'A soulless, arbitrary, attitudinizing piece of claptrap.'—*John Simon*

'Everybody in this town hides behind plain wrappers!'

Peyton Place**
US 1957 157m De Luxe Cinemascope
TCF (Jerry Wald)

Sex, frustration and violence ferment under the placid surface of a small New England town.
Well-made film of what was at the time a scandalous bestseller, one of the first to reveal those nasty secrets of 'ordinary people'.

w John Michael Hayes, *novel* Grace Metalious *d* Mark Robson *ph* William Mellor *m* Franz Waxman

Lana Turner, Arthur Kennedy, Hope Lange, Lee Philips, Lloyd Nolan, Diane Varsi, Russ Tamblyn, Terry Moore, Barry Coe, David Nelson, Betty Field, Mildred Dunnock, Leon Ames, Lorne Greene

AAN: best picture; John Michael Hayes; Mark Robson; William Mellor; Lana Turner; Arthur Kennedy; Hope Lange; Diane Varsi; Russ Tamblyn

Phaedra*
US / Greece 1961 116m bw
UA / Melinafilm (Jules Dassin)

A tycoon's wife falls in love with her stepson.
Ludicrous, awesomely folly-filled attempt to modernize and sex up Greek tragedy.

wd Jules Dassin *ph* Jacques Natteau *m* Mikis Theodorakis

Melina Mercouri, Anthony Perkins, Raf Vallone, Elizabeth Ercy

'Unfortunately unforgettable.'—*John Simon*

'If this one doesn't scare you . . . you're already dead!'

Phantasm
US 1979 90m Technicolor

A 16-year-old has nightmares which seem to come true. Cleverly assembled horror comic with many nasty moments. Not for the squeamish, and with no real merit except the power to frighten. Michael Baldwin, Bill Thornbury, Reggie Bannister, Angus Scrimm. Written, directed, edited and photographed by Don Coscarelli (who was 20 at the time); for Avco Embassy.

The Phantom
US 1943 bw serial: 15 eps

Various factions seek the lost city of Zoloz. Fantasy serial with Ace the Wonder Dog and everything but the kitchen sink. Tom Tyler, Kenneth MacDonald, Frank Shannon, Jeanne Bates. Directed by B. Reeves Eason; for Columbia.

The Phantom Creeps
US 1939 bw serial: 12 eps

Dr Alex Zorka has invented a giant robot and can also turn whole armies into zombies. Silly serial which was also cut into an indecipherable feature. Bela Lugosi, Robert Kent, Regis Toomey, Dorothy Arnold, Edward Van Sloan. Directed by Ford Beebe and Saul Goodkind; for Universal.

Phantom Empire
US 1935 bw serial: 12 eps

Western crooks covet radium-covered land. Elementary serial adventures. Gene Autry, Frankie Darro, Betsy King Ross, Dorothy Christy, Smiley Burnette. Directed by Otto Brewer and B. Reeves Eason; for Mascot.

Phantom Killer
US 1942 57m bw

A young district attorney uncovers an ingenious criminal ruse by twin brothers. Better-than-average crime filler. Dick Purcell, Joan Woodbury, John Hamilton, Warren Hymer, J. Farrell MacDonald, Mantan Moreland. Written by Karl Brown; directed by William Beaudine; for A. W. Hackel / Monogram.

Phantom Lady**
US 1944 87m bw
Universal (Joan Harrison)

A man is accused of murder and his only alibi is a mysterious lady he met in a bar.
Odd little thriller which doesn't really hold together but is made for the most part with great style.

w Bernard C. Schoenfeld, *novel* William Irish *d* Robert Siodmak *ph* Woody Bredell *m* Hans Salter

Franchot Tone, Alan Baxter, Ella Raines, Elisha Cook Jnr, Fay Helm, Andrew Tombes

The Phantom Light
GB 1934 75m bw

Wreckers try to scare off a new lighthouse keeper. Effective minor comedy-thriller with good credentials. Gordon Harker, Binnie Hale, Ian Hunter, Donald Calthrop, Milton Rosmer, Herbert Lomas. Written by Austin Melford and Ralph Smart, from the play *The Haunted Light* by Evadne Price and Joan Roy Byford; directed by Michael Powell; for Gainsborough. 'A very strong melodrama, atmospheric to a marked degree.'—*Variety*

Phantom of Crestwood*
US 1932 77m bw
RKO (David O. Selznick)

Murder strikes when a blackmailer assembles her victims.
Lively mystery with spoof elements.

w Bartlett Cormack, J. Walter Ruben *d* J. Walter Ruben *ph* Henry Gerrard *m* Max Steiner

Ricardo Cortez, H. B. Warner, Anita Louise, Karen Morley, Pauline Frederick, Robert McWade, Skeets Gallagher

'Below the deluxe classification it should give a good account of itself.'—*Variety*

Phantom of 42nd Street
US 1945 58m bw

A young Broadway star is suspected when her uncle is murdered backstage. Lightweight but amiable mystery. Dave O'Brien, Kay Aldredge, Alan Mowbray, Frank Jenks, Jack Mulhall. Written by Milton Ralson; directed by Albert Herman; for Mooney-Herman / PRC.

Phantom of Paris
US 1931 73m bw

A magician proves by a complex plan that he did not kill his fiancée's father. Unusual but tortuous thriller which fails to thrill. John Gilbert, Leila Hyams, Ian Keith, C. Aubrey Smith, Lewis Stone, Jean Hersholt. Written by Bess Meredyth, John Meehan and Edwin Justus Mayer; directed by John S. Robertson; for MGM. 'It isn't Gilbert that makes the picture, it makes itself. Merits above-average gross.'—*Variety*

The Phantom of the Air
US 1933 bw serial: 12 eps

Various criminals covet a new airplane which can defy gravity. Standard serial exploits. Tom Tyler, Gloria Shea, LeRoy Mason, William Desmond. Directed by Ray Taylor; for Universal.

Phantom of the Opera***
US 1925 94m (24 fps) bw (Technicolor sequence) silent
Universal

A disfigured man in a mask abducts the prima donna of the Paris Opera House to his lair in the sewers below.
Patchy but often splendid piece of Grand

THE PHANTOM OF THE OPERA (1943). In the first colour *Phantom* Claude Rains, behind the mask, intends to bring down the house.

Guignol which not only provided its star with a famous role but was notable for its magnificent visual style.

w Raymond Shrock, Elliot Clawson, *novel* Gaston Leroux *d Rupert Julian ph Charles Van Enger, Virgil Miller ad Dan Hall*

Lon Chaney, Mary Philbin, Norman Kerry, Gibson Gowland

'The greatest inducement to nightmare that has yet been screened.'—*Variety*

† The chase was directed by Edward Sedgwick

†† In 1930 an 89m talkie version was issued, with approximately 35% dialogue which had been recorded by the surviving actors, and some new footage.

The Phantom of the Opera*
US 1943 92m Technicolor
Universal (George Waggner)

This version is more decorous and gentlemanly, with much attention paid to the music, but it certainly has its moments.

w Erich Taylor, Samuel Hoffenstein, *d* Arthur Lubin *ph Hal Mohr, W. Howard Greene m* Edward Ward *ad John B. Goodman, Alexander Golitzen*

Claude Rains, Nelson Eddy, Susanna Foster, Edgar Barrier, Leo Carrillo, J. Edward Bromberg, Jane Farrar, Hume Cronyn

AA: Hal Mohr, W. Howard Greene; John B. Goodman, Alexander Golitzen

'A grand and gaudy entertainment.'—*Manchester Guardian*

Phantom of the Opera
GB 1962 90m Technicolor
U-I / Hammer (Anthony Hinds)

Stodgy remake with the accent on shock.

w John Elder *d* Terence Fisher *ph* Arthur Grant *m* Edwin Astley

Herbert Lom, Edward de Souza, Heather Sears, Thorley Walters, Michael Gough, Ian Wilson, Martin Miller, John Harvey, Miriam Karlin

'The only shock is that the British, who could have had a field day with this antique, have simply wafted it back with a lick and a promise.'—*New York Times*

Phantom of the Paradise*
US 1974 91m Movielab
TCF / Pressman Williams (Edward R. Pressman)

A modern satirical remake of *Phantom of the Opera* in rock opera terms, set in a pop music palace. Not bad in spots, but it doesn't really know where it's going.

wd Brian de Palma ph Larry Pizer *m* Paul Williams *pd* Jack Fisk

Paul Williams, William Finley, Jessica Harper, George Memmoli, Gerrit Graham

'Too broad in its effects and too bloated in style to cut very deeply as a parody . . . closer to the anything goes mode of a *Mad* magazine lampoon.'—*Richard Combs*

AAN: Paul Williams

Phantom of the Rue Morgue
US 1954 84m Warnercolor 3-D
Warner (Henry Blanke)

In old Paris, a killer of pretty girls turns out to be an ape.
Dull revamping of a rather dull story, with boring characters and little horror.

w Harold Medford, James R. Webb, *story* Murders in the Rue Morgue by Edgar Allan Poe *d* Roy del Ruth *ph* Peverell Marley *m* David Buttolph

Karl Malden, Claude Dauphin, Steve Forrest, Patricia Medina, Allyn McLerie, Dolores Dorn

The Phantom of the West
US 1931 bw serial: 10 episodes

A mysterious Phantom haunts a western town where one of the townsmen is a murderer. A serial somewhat more straightforward than usual in its plotting. Tom Tyler, Dorothy Gulliver, William Desmond, Tom Santschi, Tom Dugan. Directed by Ross Lederman; for Mascot.

The Phantom President*
US 1932 78m bw
Paramount

A fast-talking quack doubles for a lacklustre presidential candidate.
A likely but in fact unsuccessful film debut for a famous Broadway star: many points of interest.

w Walter de Leon, Harlan Thompson *d* Norman Taurog *ph* David Abel *songs* Richard Rodgers, Lorenz Hart

George M. Cohan, Claudette Colbert, Jimmy Durante, George Barbier, Sidney Toler, Jameson Thomas, Paul Hurst, Alan Mowbray

'A lot of smart stuff is packed into the footage . . . should do well without threatening to rate itself a smash.'—*Variety*

'For anyone who cares about American theatrical history, it's an indispensable record of Cohan's style.'—*New Yorker, 1978*

The Phantom Rider
US 1936 bw serial: 15 eps

The state governor sends Buck Grant on a secret mission to investigate outlaw activity in Maverick. Serial chapters with a stalwart hero. Buck Jones, Maria Shelton, Diana Gibson, Joey Ray. Directed by Ray Taylor; for Universal.

The Phantom Rider
US 1946 bw serial: 12 eps

Dr Jim Sterling poses as a phantom rider to deal with western outlaws. Or, Zorro Rides Again. Formula stuff. Robert Kent, Peggy Stewart, LeRoy Mason, George J. Lewis. Directed by Spencer Bennet and Fred Brannon; for Republic.

The Phantom Tollbooth**
US 1969 90m Metrocolor
MGM / Animation Visual Arts

A bored boy goes through a magic tollbooth to land beyond his wildest imagination, rescues Rhyme and Reason, and defeats the Demons of Ignorance.
Ambitious and well-devised, though rather slow-starting, cartoon feature which falls in style somewhere between *Alice in Wonderland* and *The Wizard of Oz* but is more intellectual than either and would be beyond the reach of most children. Discerning adults may have a ball.

w Chuck Jones, Sam Rosen, *novel* Norton Juster *d* Chuck Jones, Abe Levitow *ph* Maurice Noble

Butch Patrick

Phar Lap
Australia 1983 118m colour Panavision
TCF / Michael Edgley International (John Sexton)
GB title: *Phar Lap—Heart of a Nation*

The story of a crack racehorse which was the talk of the world in the early thirties but died of a mysterious disease.
The film, though adequately textured, won't win any races.

w David Williamson *d* Simon Wincer *ph* Russell Boyd *m* Bruce Rowland

Tom Burlinson, Martin Vaughan, Judy Morris, Celia de Burgh, Ron Liebman, Vincent Ball

'The day the earth was turned into a cemetery!'

Phase IV
GB 1973 84m Technicolor
Paramount / Alced (Paul B. Radin)

In the Arizona desert, ants attack a scientific installation.
Oddly effective if repulsive science fiction; the ants are all the more unpleasant because they stay the normal size.

w Mayo Simon *d Saul Bass* *ph* Dick Bush *m* Brian Gascoyne

Nigel Davenport, Lynne Frederick, Michael Murphy, Alan Gifford

'Sin City of Alabama!'

The Phenix City Story*
US 1955 100m bw
Allied Artists (Sam Bischoff, David Diamond)

A young lawyer fights the racketeers who control his town.
Goodish example of the semi-documentary melodramas of small-town corruption which swarmed out of Hollywood following the Kefauver investigations.

w Crane Wilbur, Dan Mainwaring *d Phil Karlson* *ph* Harry Neumann *m* Harry Sukman

Richard Kiley, *Edward Andrews*, John McIntire, Kathryn Grant

Phffft
US 1954 91m bw
Columbia (Fred Kohlmar)

The title refers to the sound of an expiring match; the story tells of a couple who get divorced and try to find out what they have been missing.
Champagne comedy with no bubbles.

w George Axelrod *d* Mark Robson *ph* Charles Lang *m* Frederick Hollander

Jack Lemmon, Judy Holliday, Kim Novak, Jack Carson, Luella Gear, Donald Randolph, Donald Curtis, Merry Anders

The Philadelphia Experiment*
US 1984 101m CFI colour
New World / Cinema Group (Joel B. Michaels, Douglas Curtis)

Seamen on a 1943 destroyer fall through a time warp into 1984, and have one hell of a job getting back.
Science fiction, *Outer Limits / Final Countdown* style; quite watchable, and technically proficient, but the claim that it was based on an actual incident seems a bit tall.

w William Gray, Michael Janover, *book* William I. Moore, Charles Berlitz *d* Stewart Raffill

Michael Paré, Nancy Allen, Eric Christmas, Bobby di Cicco, Louise Latham

'Uncle Leo's bedtime story for you older tots! The things they do among the playful rich—oh, boy!'

The Philadelphia Story****
US 1940 112m bw
MGM (Joseph L. Mankiewicz)

A stuffy heiress, about to be married for the second time, turns human and returns gratefully to number one.
Hollywood's most wise and sparkling comedy, with a script which is even an improvement on the original play. Cukor's direction is so discreet you can hardly sense it, and all the performances are just perfect.

w Donald Ogden Stewart, play Philip Barry *d George Cukor* *ph* Joseph Ruttenberg *m Franz Waxman* *ad* Cedric Gibbons

Katharine Hepburn, Cary Grant, James Stewart, Ruth Hussey, Roland Young, John Halliday, Mary Nash, Virginia Weidler, John Howard, Henry Daniell

'There are just not enough superlatives sufficiently to appreciate this show.'—*Hollywood Reporter*

'An exceptionally bright job of screenplay writing . . . though films like this do little to advance the art of motion pictures, they may help to convince some of the more discerning among cultural slugabeds that when movies want to turn their hand to anything, they can turn it.'—*Otis Ferguson*

† Cary Grant donated his salary to war relief.

AA: Donald Ogden Stewart; James Stewart
AAN: best picture; George Cukor; Katharine Hepburn; Ruth Hussey

Philo Vance

The smooth sleuth created by S. S. Van Dine was a popular film hero of the thirties, for several different companies and with several different actors. As a series it was very variable indeed.

1929: THE CANARY MURDER CASE (Paramount: William Powell); THE GREENE MURDER CASE (Paramount: William Powell)
1930: THE BISHOP MURDER CASE (MGM: Basil Rathbone); THE BENSON MURDER CASE (Paramount: William Powell)
1933: THE KENNEL MURDER CASE (qv) (Warner: William Powell)
1934: THE DRAGON MURDER CASE (Warner: Warren William)
1935: THE CASINO MURDER CASE (MGM: Paul Lukas)
1936: THE GARDEN MURDER CASE (MGM: Edmund Lowe)
1937: NIGHT OF MYSTERY (Paramount: Grant Richards)
1937: THE SCARAB MURDER CASE (British: Wilfrid Hyde White)
1939: THE GRACIE ALLEN MURDER CASE (Paramount: Warren William); CALLING PHILO VANCE (Warner: James Stephenson)
1947: PHILO VANCE RETURNS (PRC: William Wright); PHILO VANCE'S GAMBLE (PRC: Alan Curtis); PHILO VANCE'S SECRET MISSION (PRC: Alan Curtis)

Phobia
Canada 1980 90m colour
Borough Park (Zale Magder)

Five volunteer phobics, released from jail for experiments, are killed one by one.
Unprepossessing whodunit with horror touches but none of the style one might expect from its director.

w Lew Lehman, Jimmy Sangster, Peter Bellwood *d* John Huston *ph* Reginald H. Morris *m* Andre Gagnon

Paul Michael Glaser, John Colicos, Susan Hogan, Alexandra Stewart, David Bolt

Phone Call from a Stranger
US 1952 96m bw
TCF (Nunnally Johnson)

Of four airplane acquaintances, only one survives a crash; he visits the families of the others.
Four stories with an unlikely link. (The compendium craze, which had started in 1948 with *Quartet*, was now straining itself.) Nothing to remember except Miss Davis.

w Nunnally Johnson *d* Jean Negulesco *ph* Milton Krasner *m* Franz Waxman

Bette Davis, Gary Merrill, Michael Rennie, Shelley Winters, Keenan Wynn, Evelyn Varden, Warren Stevens, Craig Stevens

'A cinematic party line on which several conversations are going at once, none of them coming across very distinctly.'—*Time*

Piccadilly*
GB 1929 105m (24 fps) bw silent
BIP (E. A. Dupont)

A club owner's fiancée is accused of killing his Chinese mistress.
Sub-Edgar Wallace melodrama, no longer watchable with a straight face.

w Arnold Bennett *d* E. A. Dupont *ph* Werner Brandes

Gilda Gray, Anna May Wong, Jameson Thomas, Cyril Ritchard, Ellen Pollock, Charles Laughton, Debroy Somers and his Band

† Sound added in 1930.

Piccadilly Incident*
GB 1946 102m bw
ABP (Herbert Wilcox)

During World War II, a girl believed drowned returns from the front to find her husband remarried.
The Enoch Arden theme again, and the first of the Wilcox-Neagle 'London' films, though untypically a melodrama with a sad ending. Efficient enough for its chosen audience.

w Nicholas Phipps *d* Herbert Wilcox *ph* Max Greene *m* Anthony Collins

Anna Neagle, Michael Wilding, Michael Laurence, Frances Mercer, Coral Browne, A. E. Matthews, Edward Rigby, Brenda Bruce

† Michael Wilding was cast only after Rex Harrison and John Mills had proved unavailable.

Piccadilly Jim*
US 1936 100m bw
MGM (Harry Rapf)

A cartoonist helps his father to marry by making the bride's stuffy family objects of ridicule.
Amiable comedy with a diverting London setting.

w Charles Brackett, Edwin Knopf, *novel* P. G. Wodehouse *d* Robert Z. Leonard *ph* Joseph Ruttenberg *m* William Axt

Robert Montgomery, Madge Evans, Frank Morgan, Billie Burke, Eric Blore, Robert Benchley, Ralph Forbes, Cora Witherspoon, E. E. Clive

Piccadilly Third Stop
GB 1960 90m bw
Rank / Sydney Box / Ethiro (Norman Williams)

A smooth crook seduces the daughter of an eastern ambassador in London to gain entry to the embassy and rob it.
Boring and rather unpleasant thriller partly redeemed by a final chase through the Underground.

w Leigh Vance *d* Wolf Rilla *ph* Ernest Steward *m* Philip Green

Terence Morgan, Yoko Tani, John Crawford, William Hartnell, Mai Zetterling, Dennis Price, Ann Lynn

Pick a Star
US 1937 76m bw
MGM / Hal Roach

An innocent girl in Hollywood achieves stardom with the help of a publicity man.
Perfectly awful Cinderella story with interesting glimpses behind the studio scenes and (if you can wait that long) a couple of good Laurel and Hardy sequences.

w Richard Flournoy, Arthur Vernon Jones, Thomas J. Dugan *d* Edward Sedgwick *ph* Norbert Brodine *m* Marvin Hatley, Arthur Morton

Rosina Lawrence, Jack Haley, Patsy Kelly, Mischa Auer, *Stan Laurel, Oliver Hardy,* Charles Halton, Lyda Roberti

'Part farce, part comedy, part musical and three parts dull.'—*Variety*

Pick Up
US 1933 80m bw

A girl released from jail picks up with a truck driver, but her crooked husband reappears.
Sob story of the Peg's Paper type; a yawn.
Sylvia Sidney, George Raft, William Harrigan, Lillian Bond. Written by S. K. Lauren, Agnes Leahy, Vina Delmar; directed by Marion Gering; for B. P. Schulberg / Paramount.
'Good title and cast, weakish film.'—*Variety*

Pick Up
US 1951 78m bw
Columbia (Hugo Haas)

A lonely middle-aged man falls for a tart who is interested only in his money.
Modest variation on *The Blue Angel*, the first of several second features made by Haas to feature himself as a second Emil Jannings. They got progressively more maudlin.

wd Hugo Haas *ph* Paul Ivano

Hugo Haas, Beverly Michaels, Allan Nixon, Howard Chamberlin

'Anybody's back seat will do—as long as he's going her way!'

Pickup on 101
US 1972 93m Movielab

A lady hitchhiker picks up with an old hobo and an unemployed rock 'n' roller. Sentimental rather than sensational is this small drama which starts slowly and goes nowhere. Lesley Warren, Jack Albertson, Martin Sheen, Michael Ontkean. Written by Anthony Blake; directed by John Florea; for AIP.

Pickup on South Street*
US 1953 80m bw
TCF (Jules Schermer)

A pickpocket steals a girl's wallet and finds himself up to his neck in espionage.
Over-rich mixture of crime, violence and anti-communism, smartly made without being very interesting.

wd Samuel Fuller *ph* Joe MacDonald *m* Leigh Harline

Richard Widmark, Jean Peters, *Thelma Ritter*, Richard Kiley
† Remade 1968 as *Capetown Affair*.

AAN: Thelma Ritter

The Pickwick Papers*
GB 1952 115m bw
George Minter (Bob McNaught)

Various adventures of the Pickwick Club culminate in Mrs Bardell's suit for breach of promise.
Flatly conceived and loosely constructed Dickensian comedy; good humour and lots of well-known faces do not entirely atone for lack of artifice.

wd Noel Langley *ph* Wilkie Cooper
m Antony Hopkins *ad* Fred Pusey

James Hayter, James Donald, Donald Wolfit, Hermione Baddeley, Hermione Gingold, Kathleen Harrison, *Nigel Patrick*, Alexander Gauge, Lionel Murton

'As welcome as the sun in the morning and as British as a cup of tea.'—*Daily Mirror*

'A town—a stranger—and the things he does to its people! Especially its women!'

Picnic***
US 1956 113m Technicolor Cinemascope
Columbia (Fred Kohlmar)

A brawny wanderer causes sexual havoc one summer in a small American town.
Seminal melodrama setting new directions for Hollywood and illustrating the side of life the Hardy family never showed. Generally quite compulsive despite some overacting.

w Daniel Taradash, *play William Inge*
d Joshua Logan *ph James Wong Howe*
m George Duning *pd* Jo Mielziner
ad William Flannery

William Holden, Kim Novak, Rosalind Russell, *Susan Strasberg*, Arthur O'Connell, Cliff Robertson, Betty Field, Verna Felton, Reta Shaw

'Mr Logan's idea of an outing in the corn country includes a choir of at least a hundred voices, a camera so alert that it can pick up the significance of the reflection of a Japanese lantern in a pool (futility, wistfulness, the general transience of life, as I get it) and a sound track let loose in the most formidable music I've heard in my time at the movies.'—*New Yorker*

AAN: best picture; Joshua Logan; George Duning; Arthur O'Connell

'A recollection of evil . . .'

Picnic at Hanging Rock*
Australia 1975 115m Eastmancolor
Picnic Productions / Australia Film Corporation (Hal and Jim McElroy)

In 1900, schoolgirls set out for a picnic; some disappear and are never found.
An intriguing but finally irritating puzzle with no answer; the atmosphere is nicely calculated, but as in *L'Avventura* the whole thing outstays its welcome.

w Cliff Green, *novel* Joan Lindsay *d* Peter Weir *ph* Russell Boyd *m* Bruce Smeaton

Rachel Roberts, Dominic Guard, Helen Morse, Jacki Weaver, Vivean Gray, Kirsty Child

'Atmospherically vivid, beautifully shot, and palpably haunting.'—*Michael Billington, Illustrated London News*

'If this film *had* a rational and tidy conclusion, it would be a good deal less interesting. But as a tantalizing puzzle, a tease, a suggestion of forbidden answer just out of earshot, it works hypnotically and very nicely indeed.'—*Roger Ebert*

Picture Mommy Dead
US 1966 88m Pathecolor
Embassy / Berkeley (Bert I. Gordon)

A girl who has been hospitalized following the death of her mother in a fire returns home to find, apparently, that her father's new wife is trying to kill her.
Twist-ending shocker with tired stars, from the tag end of the *Baby Jane* cycle.

w Robert Sherman *d* Bert I. Gordon
ph Ellsworth Fredericks *m* Robert Drasnin

Don Ameche, Martha Hyer, Zsa Zsa Gabor, Susan Gordon, Maxwell Reed, Signe Hasso, Wendell Corey

The Picture of Dorian Gray***
US 1945 110m bw (Technicolor inserts)
MGM (Pandro S. Berman)

A Victorian gentleman keeps in the attic a picture of himself, which shows his age and depravity while he stays eternally young.
Elegant variation on *Dr Jekyll and Mr Hyde*, presented in portentous style which suits the subject admirably.

wd Albert Lewin, novel Oscar Wilde
ph Harry Stradling *m* Herbert Stothart

George Sanders, Hurd Hatfield, Donna Reed, Angela Lansbury, Peter Lawford

SIR HENRY (George Sanders): 'If I could get back my youth, I'd do anything in the world—except get up early, take exercise or be respectable.'

SIR HENRY: 'I apologize for the intelligence of my remarks, Sir Thomas, I had forgotten that you were a Member of Parliament.'

DORIAN (Hurd Hatfield): 'If only the picture could change and I could be always what I am now. For that, I would give anything. Yes, there's nothing in the whole world I wouldn't give. I'd give my soul for that.'

'Respectful, earnest, and, I'm afraid, dead.'—*James Agee*

'Loving and practised hands have really improved Wilde's original, cutting down the epigrammatic flow . . . and rooting out all the preciousness which gets in the way of the melodrama.'—*Richard Winnington*

AA: Harry Stradling
AAN: Angela Lansbury

The Picture Show Man*
Australia 1977 98m Eastmancolor
Limelight (Joan Long)

Adventures of a travelling picture show troupe in the 1920s.
Agreeably nostalgic incidents, not very dramatically connected.

w Joan Long *d* John Power *ph* Geoffrey Burton *m* Peter Best

Rod Taylor, John Meillon, John Ewart, Harold Hopkins, Judy Morris, Patrick Cargill

The Picture Snatcher**
US 1933 77m bw
Warner

An ex-racketeer just out of prison becomes a scandal photographer.
Lively star vehicle, interesting for period detail.

w Allen Rivkin, P. J. Wolfson *d* Lloyd Bacon *ph* Sol Polito *md* Leo F. Forbstein

James Cagney, Ralph Bellamy, Patricia Ellis, Alice White, Ralf Harolde, Robert Emmett O'Connor, Robert Barrat

'A vulgar but generally funny collection of blackouts.'—*Time*

'Fast, snappy, tough and packed with action.'—*New York Herald Tribune*

† Remade 1947 as *Escape from Crime*, with Richard Travis.

A Piece of the Action
US 1977 135m Metrocolor
Warner / First Artists / Verdon (Melville Tucker)

Crooks are blackmailed into helping rebellious adolescents.
A black version, at immense length, of the hoodlum comedies in which the Dead End Kids so often featured. Not badly made, but out of date without being nostalgic.

w Charles Blackwell, *story* Timothy March
d Sidney Poitier *ph* Don Morgan *m* Curtis Mayfield

Sidney Poitier, James Earl Jones, Bill Cosby, Denise Nicholas, Hope Clarke, Tracy Reed, Jason Evers, Marc Lawrence

The Pied Piper**
US 1942 86m bw
TCF (Nunnally Johnson)

An elderly man who hates children finds himself smuggling several of them out of occupied France.
Smart, sentimental, occasionally funny war adventure.

w Nunnally Johnson, *novel* Nevil Shute
d Irving Pichel *ph* Edward Cronjager
m Alfred Newman

Monty Woolley, Anne Baxter, Roddy McDowall, Otto Preminger, J. Carrol Naish, Lester Matthews, Jill Esmond, Peggy Ann Garner

AAN: best picture; Edward Cronjager; Monty Woolley

The Pied Piper
GB 1971 90m Eastmancolor Panavision
Sagittarius / Goodtimes (David Puttnam, Sanford Lieberson)

In 1349 a strolling minstrel rids Hamelin of a plague of rats.
Paceless, slightly too horrific, and generally disappointing fantasy, especially from this director; poor sets and restricted action.

w Jacques Demy, Mark Peploe, Andrew Birkin *d* Jacques Demy *ph* Peter Suschitsky
m Donovan *pd* Assheton Gorton

Donovan, Donald Pleasence, Michael Hordern, Jack Wild, Diana Dors, John Hurt

Pierre of the Plains
US 1942 66m bw

Adventures of a cheerful trapper in Canada's northwest territory. Unashamed second-feature version of a play which its producer, Edgar Selwyn, had written in 1907 and which had been filmed in 1918 (as *Hearts of the Wild*)

PICNIC. William Holden and Susan Strasberg have something to cheer about.

and in 1922 (as *Over the Border*). (Selwyn was the man who once merged with Goldfish to form Goldwyn, a name which Goldfish then kept.) John Carroll, Ruth Hussey, Bruce Cabot, Reginald Owen, Henry Travers, Evelyn Ankers. Written by Bertram Millhauser and Laurence Kimble; directed by George B. Seitz; for MGM.

The Pigeon That Took Rome
US 1962 101m bw Panavision
Paramount / Llenroc (Melville Shavelson)

American undercover agents are smuggled into Rome during the German occupation.
Heavy-going war comedy-drama with bright sequences countered by too little wit and too many voluble Italians.

wd Melville Shavelson, *novel* The Easter Dinner by Donald Downes *ph* Daniel Fapp *m* Alessandro Cicognini

Charlton Heston, Elsa Martinelli, Brian Donlevy, Harry Guardino, Baccaloni

Pigskin Parade
US 1936 93m bw
TCF (Bogart Rogers)
GB title: *Harmony Parade*

A country farmer becomes a college football hero.
Livelier-than-average college comedy.

w Harry Tugend, Jack Yellen, William Conselman *d* David Butler *ph* Arthur Miller *md* David Buttolph *songs* Sidney Mitchell, Lew Pollack

Stuart Erwin, Patsy Kelly, Jack Haley, Johnny Downs, Betty Grable, Arline Judge, Dixie Dunbar, Judy Garland, Tony Martin, Elisha Cook Jnr

AAN: Stuart Erwin

The Pilgrim*
US 1923 38m approx (24 fps) bw silent
First National / Charles Chaplin

An escaped convict disguises himself as a minister and does a few good deeds.
Star comedy with more sentiment than laughter.

wd Charles Chaplin *ph* Rollie Totheroh

Charles Chaplin, Edna Purviance, Kitty Bradbury, Mack Swain

Pilgrimage*
US 1933 95m bw

A selfish mother sees the error of her ways when she makes a post-war journey to her son's grave. Strong character study, put across with style. *Henrietta Crosman*, Heather Angel, Norman Foster, Marian Nixon, Maurice Murphy, Charley Grapewin, Hedda Hopper. Written by Dudley Nichols, Philip Klein, Barry Conners, from the story by I. A. R. Wylie; directed by John Ford; for Fox. 'A natural for residential clienteles: mother love from a new angle.'—*Variety*

Pillars of the Sky
US 1956 95m Technicolor Cinemascope
U-I (Robert Arthur)
GB title: *The Tomahawk and the Cross*

An indian scout and a missionary help bring peace between cavalry and indians.
Modest western, adequately done.

w Sam Rolfe *d* George Marshall *ph* Harold Lipstein *m* Joseph Gershenson

Jeff Chandler, Dorothy Malone, Ward Bond, Keith Andes, Lee Marvin, Sydney Chaplin, Michael Ansara, Willis Bouchey

Pillow of Death
US 1945 66m bw

A lawyer is suspected when his wife is murdered. First fumbling story in the Inner Sanctum series, of which the title sequence was always the most entertaining portion. Lon Chaney Jnr, Brenda Joyce, J. Edward Bromberg, Rosalind Ivan, Clara Blandick. Written by George Bricker; directed by Wallace Fox; for Universal.

Pillow Talk**
US 1959 110m Eastmancolor Cinemascope
Universal / Arwin (Ross Hunter, Martin Melcher)

Two people who can't stand each other fall in love via a party line.
Slightly elephantine romantic comedy which nevertheless contains a number of funny scenes and was notable for starting off the Hudson-Day partnership and a run of similar comedies which survived the sixties.

w Stanley Shapiro, Maurice Richlin
d Michael Gordon *ph* Arthur E. Arling
m Frank de Vol

Doris Day, Rock Hudson, Tony Randall, Thelma Ritter, Nick Adams, Julia Meade, Allen Jenkins, Marcel Dalio, Lee Patrick

AA: Stanley Shapiro, Maurice Richlin
AAN: Frank de Vol; Doris Day; Thelma Ritter

Pillow to Post
US 1945 96m bw
Warner (Alex Gottlieb)

A girl poses as a soldier's wife to get a hotel room.
World War II comedy on a familiar theme (*The More the Merrier, Standing Room Only, The Doughgirls,* etc). Uninspired.

w Charles Hoffman, *play* Pillar to Post by Rose Simon Kohn *d* Vincent Sherman *ph* Wesley Anderson *m* Frederick Hollander

Ida Lupino, Sidney Greenstreet, William Prince, Stuart Erwin, Ruth Donnelly, Barbara Brown, Frank Orth

The Pilot*
US 1979 92m colour

A once great pilot insists on working despite an alcohol problem. Not enough meat on the story bones is enough to ground this dismal drama, but the air scenes look terrific and the actors seem to believe in what they're doing. *Cliff Robertson*, Frank Converse, Diane Baker, Gordon MacRae, Dana Andrews, Milo O'Shea. Written and directed by Cliff Robertson from the novel by Robert P. Davis; photographed by *Walter Lassally*; music by John Addison; for Summit/New Line.

Pilot Number Five
US 1943 71m bw
MGM (B. P. Fineman)

A pilot in the South Pacific volunteers for a desperate mission because—we learn in flashback—he hates fascists.
Rather unpalatable propaganda encased in dim drama.

w David Hertz *d* George Sidney *ph* Paul C. Vogel *m* Lennie Hayton

Franchot Tone, Gene Kelly, Marsha Hunt, Van Johnson, Alan Baxter, Dick Simmons, Steve Geray

Pimpernel Smith**
GB 1941 121m bw
British National (Leslie Howard)
US titles: *Mister V; The Fighting Pimpernel*

A professor of archaeology goes into war-torn Europe to rescue refugees.
The Scarlet Pimpernel unassumingly and quite effectively brought up to date, with memorable scenes after a slow start.

w Anatole de Grunwald, Roland Pertwee, Ian Dalrymple *d* Leslie Howard *ph* Max Greene *m* John Greenwood

Leslie Howard, Mary Morris, Francis L. Sullivan, Hugh McDermott, Raymond Huntley, Manning Whiley, Peter Gawthorne, David Tomlinson

Pin Up Girl
US 1944 83m Technicolor
TCF (William Le Baron)

A Washington secretary becomes a national celebrity when she meets a navy hero.
Adequate star flagwaver, mildly interesting for its new streamlined set designs.

w Robert Ells, Helen Logan, Earl Baldwin
d Bruce Humberstone *ph* Ernest Palmer
md Emil Newman, Charles Henderson
songs James V. Monaco, Mack Gordon
ch Hermes Pan ad James Basevi, Joseph C. Wright

Betty Grable, John Harvey, Martha Raye, Joe E. Brown, Eugene Pallette, Dave Willcock, Charles Spivak and his Orchestra
'A spiritless blob of a musical, and a desecration of a most inviting theme.'—*Bosley Crowther*

Pink Floyd The Wall*
GB 1982 95m Metrocolor
MGM / Tin Blue / Goldcrest (Alan Marshall)

A washed-up pop star finds his life a mixture of fact and fiction, of reality and animation.
Dislikeable self-pitying dirge, accompanied by animation which will not be to everybody's taste but is sometimes brilliantly arranged.

w Roger Waters *d* Alan Parker *ph* Peter Biziou *m* Roger Waters *animation designer* Gerald Scarfe

Bob Geldof, Christine Hargreaves, James Laurenson, Eleanor David, Kevin McKeon, Bob Hoskins
'A vacuous, bombastic and humourless piece of self-indulgence.'—*Steve Jenkins, MFB*
'Roger Waters flounders in woman-hating self-pity; Gerald Scarfe turns up particularly weedy examples of his animated savagery; and Alan Parker revels in the chance to make a feature-length TV commercial.'—*Sight and Sound*

The Pink Jungle
US 1968 104m Techniscope
Universal / Cherokee (Stan Margulies)

A photographer and his model are stranded in a South American village and become involved in a diamond hunt.
Curious mixture of adventure and light comedy that works only in patches.

w Charles Williams, *novel* Snake Water by Alan Williams *d* Delbert Mann *ph* Russell Metty *m* Ernie Freeman

James Garner, Eva Renzi, George Kennedy, Nigel Green, Michael Ansara, George Rose
'Another backlot cheapie.'—*Robert Windeler*

The Pink Panther**
US 1963 113m Technirama
UA / Mirisch (Martin Jurow)

An incompetent *sûreté* inspector is in Switzerland on the trail of a jewel thief called The Phantom.
Sporadically engaging mixture of pratfalls, Raffles, and Monsieur Hulot, all dressed to kill and quite palatablc for the uncritical. Inspector Clouseau later became a cartoon

character and also provoked five sequels: *A Shot in the Dark, Inspector Clouseau, The Return of the Pink Panther, The Pink Panther Strikes Again* and *The Revenge of the Pink Panther.*

w Maurice Richlin, Blake Edwards *d* Blake Edwards *ph* Philip Lathrop *m* Henry Mancini *ad* Fernando Carrere *animation* De Patie-Freleng

David Niven, Peter Sellers, Capucine, Claudia Cardinale, Robert Wagner, Brenda de Banzie, Colin Gordon

AAN: Henry Mancini

The Pink Panther Strikes Again*
GB 1976 103m De Luxe Panavision
United Artists / Amjo (Blake Edwards)

After a nervous breakdown, Chief Inspector Dreyfus builds up a vast criminal organization devoted to the extermination of Inspector Clouseau.
Zany pratfall farce with signs of overconfidence since the success of *The Return of the Pink Panther.* But some gags are funny, despite a rather boring star.

w Frank Waldman, Blake Edwards *d* Blake Edwards *ph* Harry Waxman *m* Henry Mancini

Peter Sellers, Herbert Lom, Colin Blakely, Leonard Rossiter, Lesley-Anne Down, Burt Kwouk

AAN: song, 'Come To Me' (*ly* Don Black, *m* Henry Mancini)

Pink String and Sealing Wax*
GB 1945 89m bw
Ealing (S. C. Balcon)

In 1880 Brighton, a publican's wife plans to have her husband poisoned.
Unusual, carefully handled period crime melodrama which needed a slightly firmer grip.

w Diana Morgan, Robert Hamer, *play* Roland Pertwee *d* Robert Hamer *ph* Stanley Pavey *m* Norman Demuth

Googie Withers, Mervyn Johns, Gordon Jackson, Sally Ann Howes, Mary Merrall, John Carol, Catherine Lacey, Gary Marsh

'She passed for white!'
Pinky**
US 1949 102m bw
TCF (Darryl F. Zanuck)

In the American south, a negro girl who passes for white has romantic problems.
Rather blah problem picture which seemed brave at the time; a highly professional piece of work nevertheless.

w Philip Dunne, Dudley Nichols, *novel* Quality by Cid Ricketts Summer *d Elia Kazan ph Joe MacDonald m* Alfred Newman

Jeanne Crain, Ethel Barrymore, Ethel Waters, William Lundigan, Basil Ruysdael, Nina Mae McKinney, Frederick O'Neal, Evelyn Varden

AAN: Jeanne Crain; Ethel Barrymore; Ethel Waters

'Out of a dream world into yours!'
Pinocchio****
US 1940 77m Technicolor
Walt Disney

The blue fairy breathes life into a puppet, which has to prove itself before it can turn into a real boy.
Charming, fascinating, superbly organized and streamlined cartoon feature without a single second of boredom.

supervisors Ben Sharpsteen, Hamilton Luske *m / ly Leigh Harline, Ned Washington, Paul J. Smith*

'A film of amazing detail and brilliant conception.'—*Leonard Maltin*

'A work that gives you almost every possible kind of pleasure to be got from a motion picture.'—*Richard Mallett, Punch*

'The limits of the animated cartoon have been blown so wide open that some of the original wonder of pictures has been restored.'—*Otis Ferguson*

AA: Leigh Harline (*m*); song 'When You Wish Upon a Star' (*m* Leigh Harline, *ly* Ned Washington)

'Lost River Lake was a thriving resort—until they discovered . . .'
Piranha*
US 1978 92m Metrocolor
New World (Roger Corman, Jeff Schechtman, Jon Davison)

A mad doctor's stock of man-eating fish is accidentally released into the local rivers.
Slightly spoofy thriller with a high death rate and a better than usual script. On the whole, an improvement on *Jaws.*

w John Sayles *d* Joe Dante *ph* Jamie Anderson *m* Pino Danaggio *sp* Jon Berg

Bradford Dillman, Heather Menzies, Kevin McCarthy, Bruce Gordon, Barbara Steele, Keenan Wynn, Dick Miller

The Pirate**
US 1948 102m Technicolor
MGM (Arthur Freed)

In a West Indian port, a girl imagines that a wandering player is a famous pirate, who in fact is her despised and elderly suitor.
Minor MGM musical with vivid moments and some intimation of the greatness shortly to come; all very set-bound, but the star quality is infectious.

w Albert Hackett, Frances Goodrich, *play* S. N. Behrman *d* Vincente Minnelli *ph* Harry Stradling *m / ly* Cole Porter *md* Lennie Hayton

Gene Kelly, Judy Garland, Walter Slezak, Gladys Cooper, Reginald Owen, George Zucco, *the Nicholas Brothers*

AAN: Lennie Hayton

The Pirate Movie
Australia 1982 105m Colorfilm

A girl dreams herself back into *The Pirates of Penzance* but changes some of the details.
Galumphing fantasy which suggests that Australian film-makers had better stick to *Botany Bay, Gallipoli* and sheep shearing.
Kristy McNichol, Christopher Atkins, Ted Hamilton, Bill Kerr, Maggie Kirkpatrick, Garry Macdonald Written by Trevor Farrant; directed by Ken Annakin; for Joseph Hamilton International. 'The slapstick and the swordplay are as ineptly choreographed as the production numbers.'—*Kim Newman, MFB*

Pirate Treasure
US 1934 bw serial: 12 eps

An adventurer finds a treasure map and heads for a tropical island, but is followed by a criminal lawyer with ideas of his own. A serial which plays like a modernized *Treasure Island.*
Richard Talmadge, Lucile Lund, Walter Miller, Pat O'Malley. Directed by Ray Taylor; for Universal.

Pirates
France / Tunisia 1986 124m Eclaircolor Panavision
Cannon / Carthago / Accent Dominco (Tarak Ben Ammar)

A British buccaneer, cast adrift on a raft, is taken aboard a Spanish galleon and causes mayhem.
A disaster from a director who should never be allowed to attempt comedy. This one is revolting when it is not a crashing bore.

w Gerard Brach, Roman Polanski *d* Roman Polanski *ph* Witold Sobocinski *m* Philippe Garde

Walter Matthau, Damien Thomas, Richard Pearson, Roy Kinnear, Ferdy Mayne, Charlotte Lewis

† The galleon, which cost 8 million dollars, was not wasted. It was given to the municipality of Cannes and became a tourist attraction.

AAN: costumes (Anthony Powell)

Pirates of Blood River*
GB 1961 84m Technicolor Hammerscope
Hammer (Anthony Nelson Keys)

Pirates in search of gold terrorize a Huguenot settlement.
Land-locked blood and thunder for tough schoolboys.

w John Hunter, John Gilling *d* John Gilling *ph* Arthur Grant

Christopher Lee, Andrew Keir, Kerwin Mathews, Glenn Corbett, Peter Arne, Oliver Reed, Marla Landi, Michael Ripper

Pirates of Monterey
US 1947 72m Technicolor

A Spanish girl goes to California to marry a soldier but is romanced by an outlaw.
Predictable action hokum. Maria Montez, Rod Cameron, Mikhail Rasumny, Philip Reed, Gilbert Roland, Gale Sondergaard, Tamara

Shayne, Robert Warwick. Written by Sam Hellman and Margaret Buell Wilder; directed by Alfred Werker; for Paul Malvern / Universal-International.

The Pirates of Penzance
GB 1982 112m Technicolor Panavision

An adaptation of the Gilbert and Sullivan operetta in the form of the Joseph Papp Broadway revival. What was tolerably pretty and witty on the stage is a great bore on wide film. Kevin Kline, Angela Lansbury, Linda Ronstadt, George Rose, Tony Azito, Rex Smith. Written and directed by Wilford Leach; for Universal. 'Not the slightest trace of imagination.'—*MFB*. 'Anyone who thinks Gilbert and Sullivan indestructible should see this.'—*Observer*

Pirates of the High Seas
US 1950 bw serial: 15 eps

A one-ship Pacific freight line is under constant attack from a pirate cruiser; an adventurer buddy comes to help. A serial for its times: the villain turns out to be an escaped war criminal. Buster Crabbe, Lois Hall, Tommy Farrell, Gene Roth, Tristram Coffin. Directed by Spencer Bennet and Thomas Carr; for Columbia.

Pirates of Tortuga
US 1961 97m De Luxe Cinemascope

In the 17th-century Caribbean, a privateer is ordered by the king to go undercover and rout Sir Henry Morgan. Listless swashbuckler with inferior talent. Ken Scott, Dave King, Letitia Roman, John Richardson, Robert Stephens, Edgar Barrier. Written by Melvin Levy, Jesse L. Lasky Jnr and Pat Silver; directed by Robert D. Webb; for Sam Katzman / TCF.

Pirates of Tripoli
US 1955 72m Technicolor

A pirate captain comes to the aid of an oriental princess. More akin to the Arabian Knights than Blackbeard, but not bad for a double-biller. Paul Henreid, Patricia Medina, Paul Newland, John Miljan, Lillian Bond. Written by Allen March; directed by Felix Feist; for Sam Katzman / Columbia.

The Pit and the Pendulum*
US 1961 85m Pathecolor Panavision
AIP / Alta Vista (Roger Corman)

Lovers plan to drive her brother mad; he responds by locking them in his torture chamber.
The centrepiece only is borrowed from Poe; the rest is lurid but mostly ineffective. Still, its commercial success started the Poe cycle of the sixties.

w Richard Matheson *d* Roger Corman
ph Floyd Crosby *m* Les Baxter

Vincent Price, Barbara Steele, John Kerr

'As in *House of Usher*, the quality of the film is its full-blooded feeling for Gothic horror—storms and lightning, mouldering castles and cobwebbed torture chambers, bleeding brides trying to tear the lids from their untimely tombs.'—*David Robinson*

Pitfall
US 1948 85m bw
Samuel Bischoff

An insurance investigator proves easy prey for a grasping woman.
Modest suspenser, quite efficiently made.

w Jay Dratler, from his novel *d* André de Toth *ph* Harry Wild *md* Louis Forbes

Dick Powell, Lizabeth Scott, Jane Wyatt, Raymond Burr, John Litel, Byron Barr, Ann Doran

Pittsburgh
US 1942 91m bw
Universal (Charles K. Feldman)

A coal miner's daughter has two loves, all of them trying to improve their social status as Pittsburgh becomes a world centre of steel production.
Routine melodrama ending as a flagwaver, and allowing none of its stars any opportunity.

w Kenneth Gamet, Tom Reed *d* Lewis Seiler
ph Robert de Grasse *m* Hans Salter

Marlene Dietrich, Randolph Scott, John Wayne, Frank Craven, Louise Allbritton, Shemp Howard, Ludwig Stossel, Thomas Gomez

'They do it in the name of love!'
A Place for Lovers
US 1969 102m colour

A dying American fashion designer retires to her Italian villa and has a high old time with an Italian engineer. Incomparably crass tearjerker which seems eager to offer too many morals about life and love and art. Faye Dunaway, Marcello Mastroianni, Caroline Mortimer, Karin Engh. Written by Peter Baldwin, Ennio de Concini, Tonino Guerra, Julian Halevy, Cesare Zavattini; directed by Vittorio de Sica; for MGM. 'The most God-awful piece of pseudo-romantic slop I've ever seen.'—*Roger Ebert, Chicago Sun Times*. 'The worst movie I have seen all year and possibly since 1926.'—*Charles Champlin, L.A. Times*. 'The five scriptwriters who supposedly worked on the film must have spent time enough at the watercooler to flood a camel.'—*Time*

A Place in the Sun**
US 1951 122m bw
Paramount / George Stevens

A poor young man, offered the chance of a rich wife, allows himself to be convicted and executed for the accidental death of his former fiancée.
Overblown, overlong and over-praised melodrama from a monumental novel of social guilt; sometimes visually striking, this version alters the stresses of the plot and leaves no time for sociological detail. A film so clearly intended as a masterpiece could hardly fail to be boring.

w Michael Wilson, Harry Brown, *novel* An American Tragedy by Theodore Dreiser
d George Stevens ph William C. Mellor
m Franz Waxman *ad* Hans Dreier, Walter Tyler

Montgomery Clift, Elizabeth Taylor, Shelley Winters, Anne Revere, Keefe Brasselle, Fred Clark, Raymond Burr, Frieda Inescort, Shepperd Strudwick, Kathryn Givney, Walter Sande

'An almost incredibly painstaking work . . . mannered enough for a very fancy Gothic murder mystery. This version gives the story a modern setting, but the town is an arrangement of symbols of wealth, glamour and power versus symbols of poor, drab helplessness—an arrangement far more suitable to the thirties than to the fifties.'—*Pauline Kael*

AA: script; George Stevens; William C. Mellor; Franz Waxman
AAN: best picture; Montgomery Clift; Shelley Winters

A Place of One's Own**
GB 1944 92m bw
GFD / Gainsborough (R. J. Minney)

In Edwardian times, an old house is taken over by an elderly couple, and their young companion is possessed by the spirit of a murdered girl.
Charming little ghost story, not quite detailed enough to be totally effective.

w Brock Williams, *novel* Osbert Sitwell
d Bernard Knowles *ph Stephen Dade*
m Hubert Bath *md* Louis Levy

James Mason, Barbara Mullen, Margaret Lockwood, Dennis Price, Helen Haye, Michael Shepley, Dulcie Gray, Moore Marriott

'A fine piece of work . . . gripping, marvellous, outstanding, eerie, perky, beautiful, lovely and different.'—*C. A. Lejeune*

'One comes away with an impression of elegance which has not so far been frequent in the British cinema.'—*Dilys Powell*

A Place to Go
GB 1963 86m bw
British Lion / Excalibur (Michael Relph, Basil Dearden)

A young man depressed by his urban environment turns to crime.
Panorama of London low life, efficiently varied and well made but not in any way memorable. *It Always Rains on Sunday*, fifteen years earlier, wears better.

w Michael Relph, Clive Exton, *novel* Bethnal Green by Michael Fisher *d* Basil Dearden
ph Reg Wyer *m* Charles Blackwell

Rita Tushingham, Mike Sarne, Doris Hare, John Slater, Bernard Lee, Barbara Ferris, Roy Kinnear

Places in the Heart
US 1984 111m Technicolor
Tri-Star / Delphi (Arlene Donovan)

In 1935 Texas, the sheriff's widow struggles to maintain the family farm.
All-American saga with asides including the Ku Klux Klan; though based on the author's recollections of childhood, it all seems predictable.

A PLACE IN THE SUN. Oscar-nominee Montgomery Clift and Elizabeth Taylor.

w,d Robert Benton *ph* Nestor Almendros *m* John Kander *pd* Gene Callahan

Sally Field, Lindsay Crouse, Ed Harris, Amy Madigan, John Malkovitch, Danny Glover

'Basically just another calculated tug at the heartstrings.'—*Tom Milne, Monthly Film Bulletin*

AA: Sally Field; original screenplay

AAN: best picture; John Malkovitch (supporting actor); Lindsay Crouse (supporting actress); direction

The Plague Dogs
GB / US 1982 103m Technicolor

Two dogs escape from a research laboratory and are in danger of infecting the country with a deadly virus. Misguided and woefully overlong attempt to preach a message through a cartoon. Like *Watership Down*, it needs the printed word and is deflected by the inevitably cuddly look of the animated animals. Written and directed by Martin Rosen, from the book by Richard Adams; for Nepenthe Productions.

The Plague of the Zombies*
GB 1965 91m Technicolor
Hammer (Anthony Nelson Keys)

A voodoo-practising Cornish squire raises zombies from the dead and uses them to work his tin mine.

They don't explain why he didn't simply hire the living; apart from that this is Hammer on its better side, with a charming elderly hero and good suspense sequences.

w Peter Bryan *d* John Gilling *ph* Arthur Grant *m* James Bernard

André Morell, John Carson, Diane Clare, Brook Williams, Jacqueline Pearce, Alex Davion, Michael Ripper

'Visually the film is splendid . . . the script manages several offbeat strokes.'—*MFB*

'Grandest love story ever told!'

The Plainsman**
US 1936 113m bw
Paramount / Cecil B. de Mille

The life of Wild Bill Hickok and his friends Buffalo Bill and Calamity Jane.
Standard big-scale thirties western; narrative lumpy, characters idealized, spectacle impressive, technical credits high.

w Waldemar Young, Lynn Riggs, Harold Lamb *d Cecil B. de Mille* *ph* Victor Milner, George Robinson *m* George Antheil *md* Boris Morros

Gary Cooper, James Ellison, Jean Arthur, Charles Bickford, Helen Burgess, Porter Hall, Paul Harvey, Victor Varconi

'It should do all right for business, ranging from big to good, possibly irregular in spots.'—*Variety*

'Certainly the finest western since *The Virginian*; perhaps the finest western in the history of the film.'—*Graham Greene*

† The story was remade as a TV movie in 1966, with Don Murray.

The Plainsman and the Lady
US 1946 84m bw

In 1847, the Pony Express is threatened by stagecoach owners. Moderate western for family consumption. William Elliott, Gail Patrick, Vera Ralston, Joseph Schildkraut. Written by Richard Wormser; directed by Joseph Kane; for Republic.

Le Plaisir*
France 1952 97m bw
Stera / CCFC

Three stories by Guy de Maupassant, about the search for pleasure: 'Le Masque', 'La Maison Tellier', 'Le Modèle'.
Stylish but rather subdued compendium, with no highlights to stay in the memory.

w Jacques Natanson, Max Ophuls *d* Max Ophuls *ph* Christian Matras, Philippe Agostini *m* Joe Hajos

Claude Dauphin, Gaby Morlay; Madeleine Renaud, Danielle Darrieux, Ginette Leclerc, Jean Gabin, Pierre Brasseur; Simone Simon, Daniel Gélin

'An attractive theme tune, good performances, and the pleasure itself of virtuosity.'—*Gavin Lambert, MFB*

'There comes a time in every man's life when he just can't believe his eyes!'

Plan 9 from Outer Space
US 1956 79m bw

Space people try to resurrect the Earth's dead and turn them against the world. Inept mini-budgeter often hailed as the worst film ever made. It is certainly among the most boring. Bela Lugosi (who died after four days of shooting and is mostly represented by a double), Tor Johnson, Gregory Walcott, Mona McKinnon, Vampira, Lyle Talbot. Written and directed by Edward D. Wood Jnr; for William J. Reynolds. (aka: *Grave Robbers from Outer Space*.)

SAMPLE DIALOGUE: 'One thing's sure, Inspector Clay's dead. Murdered. And someone's responsible.'

'Somewhere in the universe, there must be something better than man!'

Planet of the Apes***
US 1968 119m De Luxe Panavision
TCF / Apjac (Mort Abrahams)

Astronauts caught in a time warp land on a planet which turns out to be Earth in the distant future, when men have become beasts and the apes have taken over.
Stylish, thoughtful science fiction which starts and finishes splendidly but suffers from a sag in the middle. The ape make-up is great.

w Michael Wilson, Rod Serling, novel Monkey Planet by Pierre Boulle *d Franklin Schaffner ph Leon Shamroy m* Jerry Goldsmith

Charlton Heston, Roddy McDowall, *Kim Hunter,* Maurice Evans, James Whitmore, James Daly, Linda Harrison

'One of the most telling science fiction films to date.'—*Tom Milne*

† Sequels, in roughly descending order of interest, were BENEATH THE PLANET OF THE APES (1969), ESCAPE FROM THE PLANET OF THE APES (1970), CONQUEST OF THE PLANET OF THE APES (1972) and BATTLE FOR THE PLANET OF THE APES (1973). A TV series followed in 1974, and a cartoon series in 1975.

AAN: Jerry Goldsmith

The Planter's Wife
GB 1952 91m bw
Rank / Pinnacle (John Stafford)
US title: *Outpost in Malaya;* original title: *White Blood*

Malaya under the terrorists. A wife is planning to leave but changes her mind after she and her husband defend their home in a siege.
Superficial studio-bound melodrama unworthy of its subject but a good star vehicle.

w Peter Proud, Guy Elmes *d* Ken Annakin *ph* Geoffrey Unsworth *m* Allan Gray

Claudette Colbert, Jack Hawkins, Ram Gopal, Jeremy Spenser, Tom Macauley, Helen Goss

Platinum Blonde*
US 1931 92m bw
Columbia

A newspaper reporter falls for an heiress.
Limp romantic comedy with interesting performances: the film which established Jean Harlow.

w Robert Riskin, Jo Swerling, *story* Harry E. Chandler, Doug Churchill *d* Frank Capra *ph* Joseph Walker

Robert Williams, Loretta Young, Jean Harlow, Halliwell Hobbes, Reginald Owen

'A programmer that fully entertains, is laughy and represents what cast, dialogue and direction can do with a lean story.'—*Variety*

Platinum High School
US 1960 96m bw

A father investigates his son's death at a military academy for rich juvenile delinquents.
Hilarious serial-like melodrama with the worm turning to some effect. Mickey Rooney, Dan Duryea, Terry Moore, Warren Berlinger, Yvette Mimieux, Conway Twitty, Elisha Cook Jnr, Richard Jaeckel. Written by Robert Smith; directed by Charles Haas; for Albert Zugsmith / MGM. (GB title: *Rich, Young and Deadly*.)

Platoon**
US 1986 120m CFI colour
Hemdale / Arnold Kopelson

Experiences of infantrymen during the Vietnam war. Not badly done in the style of *Bataan* (plus brutality and gore). One would have thought it too late to do it at all, but the American public made it a box-office hit. Tom Berenger, William DaFoe, Charlie Sheen, Forest Whitaker, Francesco Quinn.

w,d Oliver Stone *ph* Robert Richardson *m* Georges Delerue

AA: best picture; Oliver Stone as director; Claire Simpson (editor)
AAN: Tom Berenger, William DaFoe; Oliver Stone for original screenplay; Robert Richardson

Play Dirty*
GB 1969 118m Technicolor Panavision
UA / Lowndes (Harry Saltzman)

During World War II, a squad of ex-criminals is given the job of destroying an enemy oil depot in North Africa.
Small-scale *Dirty Dozen* with would-be ironic twists; well made entertainment for the stout-hearted.

w Lotte Colin, Melvyn Bragg *d* André de Toth *ph* Edward Scaife *m* Michel Legrand

Michael Caine, Nigel Davenport, Nigel Green, Harry Andrews, Bernard Archard, Daniel Pilon

Play It Again Sam*
US 1972 86m Technicolor Panavision
Paramount / APJAC / Rollins–Joffe (Arthur P. Jacobs)

A neurotic film critic is abandoned by his wife and seeks fresh companionship, with help from the shade of Humphrey Bogart.
Random comedy for star fans, mainly quite lively and painless.

w Woody Allen, from his play *d* Herbert Ross *ph* Owen Roizman *m* Billy Goldenberg

Woody Allen, Diane Keaton, Jerry Lacy, Susan Anspach

Play It as It Lays
US 1972 94m Technicolor Panavision

An unsuccessful actress takes stock of her wrecked life. With-it melodrama which audiences preferred to be without. Anthony Perkins, Tuesday Weld, Tammy Grimes, Adam Roarke, Ruth Ford. Written by Joan Didion and John Gregory Dunne, from the novel by Joan Didion; directed by Frank Perry; for Universal.

'The scream you hear may be your own!'
Play Misty for Me*
US 1971 102m Technicolor
Universal / Malpaso (Robert Daley)

A radio disc jockey is pestered by a girl who turns out to be homicidally jealous.
Smartly made if over-extended psycho melodrama with good suspense sequences and a fair quota of shocks.

w Jo Heims, Dean Reisner *d* Clint Eastwood *ph* Bruce Surtees *m* Dee Barton

Clint Eastwood, Jessica Walter, Donna Mills, John Larch

'Maurice brings a new kind of love to you!'
Playboy of Paris
US 1930 82m bw

A waiter inherits a million but finds he can't leave his job, so he becomes a playboy by night only. Rather rickety star vehicle which demands attention only when he is on screen. *Maurice Chevalier*, Frances Dee, O. P. Heggie, Stuart Erwin, Eugene Pallette. Written by Percy Heath from the play The Little Café by Tristan Bernard; directed by Ludwig Berger; for Paramount. 'Light, amusing farce story doesn't help and may hurt . . . Chevalier's the only draw.'—*Variety*

Players
US 1979 120m Metrocolor
Paramount (Robert Evans)

A pro tennis player is trained for top stardom by a sculptress with a mysterious past.
Entirely uninvolving romantic drama stretched around a Wimbledon match; slickness does not compensate for a gaping hole at the centre.

w Arnold Schulman *d* Anthony Harvey *ph* James Crabe *m* Jerry Goldsmith *pd* Richard Sylbert

Ali MacGraw, Dean-Paul Martin, Maximilian Schell, Pancho Gonzalez

Playgirl
US 1954 85m bw

A small-town girl becomes a good-time girl in the big city. Totally unsurprising melodrama. Shelley Winters, Barry Sullivan, Colleen Miller, Gregg Palmer, Richard Long, Kent Taylor. Written by Robert Blees; directed by Joseph Pevney; for Universal-International.

Playmates*
US 1941 96m bw
RKO (Cliff Reid)

For the sake of a lucrative radio contract, John Barrymore agrees to turn bandleader Kay Kyser into a Shakespearian actor.
Barrymore's last film is a weird comedy concoction, awesome in its waste of his talents but fairly funny in a high school kind of way.

w James V. Kern *d* David Butler *ph* Frank Redman *songs* James Van Heusen, Johnny Burke

Kay Kyser and his Band, *John Barrymore,* Ginny Simms, Lupe Velez, May Robson, Patsy Kelly, Peter Lind Hayes, George Cleveland

Playtime*
France 1968 152m Eastmancolor 70mm
Specta Films (René Silvera)

Hulot and a group of American tourists are bewildered by life in an airport, a business block and a restaurant.
Incredibly extended series of sketches, none of which is devastatingly funny, The irritation is that the talent is clearly there but needs control.

w Jacques Tati, Jacques Lagrange *d* Jacques Tati *ph* Jean Badal, Andreas Winding *m* Francis Lemarque *pd* Eugene Roman

Jacques Tati, Barbara Dennek, Jacqueline Lecomte, Henri Piccoli

'Tati still seems the wrong distance from his audience: not so far that we cannot see his gifts, not close enough so that they really touch.'—*Stanley Kauffmann*

'How sad that the result of all this, though it includes a great deal of intermittent pleasure, comes at times so dangerously close to boredom.'—*Brenda Davies, MFB*

'A series of brilliant doodles by an artist who has earned the right to indulge himself on such a scale.'—*Alexander Walker*

Plaza Suite*
US 1971 114m Technicolor
Paramount (Howard B. Koch)

Three sketches set in the same suite at New York's Plaza Hotel, with Walter Matthau appearing in all three but in different character.
A highly theatrical entertainment which was bound to seem flattened on the screen, but emerges with at least some of its laughs intact.

w Neil Simon, from his play *d* Arthur Hiller *ph* Jack Marta *m* Maurice Jarre

Walter Matthau, Maureen Stapleton, Barbara Harris, Lee Grant, Louise Sorel

† In the play, Maureen Stapleton played all three female roles.

Please Believe Me
US 1950 87m bw
MGM (Val Lewton)

An English girl inherits an American ranch and is chased by a millionaire, a con man and a lawyer.
Dullsville comedy which failed to establish its star in America.

w Nathaniel Curtis *d* Norman Taurog *ph* Robert Planck *m* Hans Salter

Deborah Kerr, Robert Walker, Mark Stevens, Peter Lawford, James Whitmore, Spring Byington

Please Don't Eat the Daisies
US 1960 111m Metrocolor Panavision
MGM (Joe Pasternak)

The family of a drama critic move to the country.
Thin, obvious comedy, all dressed up but with nowhere to go.

w Isobel Lennart, *book* Jean Kerr *d* Charles Walters *ph* Robert Bronner *m* David Rose

Doris Day, David Niven, Janis Paige, Spring Byington, Patsy Kelly, Richard Haydn, Jack Weston, John Harding, Margaret Lindsay

Please Murder Me
US 1956 78m bw
DCA (Donald Hyde)

An attorney defends an accused murderess, at great cost to himself.
Adequate Poverty Row suspenser with a foreseeable trick ending.

w Al C. Ward, Donald Hyde *d* Peter Godfrey *ph* Allen Stensvold

Angela Lansbury, Raymond Burr, Dick Foran, John Dehner, Lamont Johnson, Denver Pyle

Please Sir
GB 1971 101m Eastmancolor
Rank / LWL / Leslie Grade (Andrew Mitchell)

The masters and pupils of Fenn Street school go on an annual camp.
Grossly inflated, occasionally funny big-screen version of the TV series.

w John Esmonde, Bob Larbey *d* Mark Stuart *ph* Wilkie Cooper *m* Mike Vickers

John Alderton, Deryck Guyler, Joan Sanderson, Noel Howlett, Eric Chitty, Richard Davies

Please Teacher
GB 1937 75m bw

An heir tries to find his bequest in the country house he has sold as a girls' school. Cheerful star farce with songs. Bobby Howes, René Ray, Vera Pearce, Wylie Watson, Bertha Belmore, Lyn Harding. Written by Stafford Dickens from the musical by K. R. G. Browne and R. P. Weston; directed by Stafford Dickens; for Associated British. 'Plenty of laughs.'—*Variety*

Please Turn Over
GB 1959 87m bw

A teenager writes a sexy best-seller clearly featuring her family and friends. Acceptable but uninspired comedy from a West End success. Ted Ray, Jean Kent, Leslie Phillips, Joan Sims, Julia Lockwood, Charles Hawtrey, Lionel Jeffries. Written by Norman Hudis, from the play *Book of the Month* by Basil Thomas; directed by Gerald Thomas; for Beaconsfield / Anglo Amalgamated.

The Pleasure Garden
GB / Germany 1925 74m approx (24 fps) bw silent
Gainsborough / Emelka (Michael Balcon, Erich Pommer)

A chorus girl marries a rich colonial who goes native.
Boring melodrama with a few touches typical of its director, whose first film it is.

w Eliot Stannard, *novel* Oliver Sandys *d* Alfred Hitchcock *ph* Baron Ventigmilia

Virginia Valli, John Stuart, Miles Mander, Carmelita Gerghty

The Pleasure Girls
GB 1965 88m bw
Compton Tekli (Harry Fine)

Girl flatmates in London have trouble with their boy friends.
The road to ruin sixties style, hackneyed but quite well observed.

wd Gerry O'Hara ph Michael Reed *m* Malcolm Lockyer

Ian McShane, Francesca Annis, Tony Tanner, Klaus Kinski, Mark Eden, Suzanna Leigh

The Pleasure of His Company
US 1961 114m Technicolor
Paramount / Perlberg–Seaton

An ageing playboy arrives unexpectedly in San Francisco for his daughter's wedding.
Tame family comedy, very flatly adapted from the stage; dressed to kill, but with no narrative or cinematic drive.

w Samuel Taylor, *play* Samuel Taylor, Cornelia Otis Skinner *d* George Seaton *ph* Robert Burks *m* Alfred Newman

Fred Astaire, Lilli Palmer, Debbie Reynolds, Charles Ruggles, Tab Hunter, Gary Merrill, Harold Fong

'Smart comedy in its most diluted form.'—*MFB*

The Pleasure Seekers
US 1964 107m De Luxe Cinemascope
TCF (David Weisbart)

Three girls in Madrid find boy friends.
Dim remake of *Three Coins in the Fountain,* adequate but unstimulating on all levels.

w Edith Sommer *d* Jean Negulesco *ph* Daniel L. Fapp *m* Lionel Newman, Alexander Courage

Ann-Margret, Tony Franciosa, Carol Lynley, Gene Tierney, Brian Keith, Gardner McKay, Isobel Elsom

AAN: Lionel Newman, Alexander Courage

Plenty*
US 1985 124m Technicolor Panavision
TCF / RKO / Edward R. Pressman

After World War II, the career of a neurotic society woman has parallels with the problems of western Europe.
Heavy-going allegory which should have stayed on the stage.

w David Hare, from his play *d* Fred Schepisi *ph* Ian Baker *m* Bruce Smeaton *pd* Richard MacDonald *ed* Peter Honess

Meryl Streep, Charles Dance, Tracey Ullman, John Gielgud, Sting, Ian McKellen, Sam Neill

The Plot Thickens
US 1936 69m bw

A murder proves to be connected with an art swindle. Another minor case for Hildegarde Withers. James Gleason, ZaSu Pitts, Owen Davis Jnr, Louise Latimer. Written by Clarence Upson Young and Jack Townley from novel by Stuart Palmer; directed by Ben Holmes; for William Sistrom / RKO.

The Plough and the Stars*
US 1936 72m bw
RKO (Cliff Reid, Robert Sisk)

In 1916, a Dublin marriage is threatened by the husband's appointment as commander of the citizen army.
Rather elementary film version of the play about the Troubles; interesting for effort rather than performance, and for the talent involved.

w Dudley Nichols, *play* Sean O'Casey *d* John Ford *ph* Joseph August *m* Roy Webb

Barbara Stanwyck, Preston Foster, Barry Fitzgerald, Denis O'Dea, Eileen Crowe, F. J. McCormick, Arthur Shields, Una O'Connor, Moroni Olsen, J. M. Kerrigan, Bonita Granville

'Skilfully made but not impressive as a money entry.'—*Variety*

The Ploughman's Lunch*
GB 1983 107m colour
Goldcrest / Greenpoint / AC & D (Simon Relph, Ann Scott)

Media people find their cynicism deepened after the Falklands War.
An essentially trivial work, too deep in its own despair, but with nice observation and twists of detail.

w Ian McEwan *d* Richard Eyre *ph* Clive Tickner *m* Dominic Muldowney

Jonathan Pryce, Tim Curry, Rosemary Harris, Frank Finlay, Charlie Dore, David De Keyser, Nat Jackley

'You don't have to agree with it, but you can't ignore it.'—*Daily Mail*

'It quietly and persuasively suggests that we get precisely the media we deserve.'—*Guardian*

The Plow That Broke the Plains**
US 1936 28m bw

The story of how overcultivation of America's Great Plains resulted in the Dust Bowl. Classic documentary which inevitably means less now than it did at the time but is still an impressive counterpoint to *The Grapes of Wrath*. Written and directed by Pare Lorenz; for Resettlement Administration Film Unit.

Plunder*
GB 1930 98m bw

Two society friends turn jewel thieves to help an heiress. Primitive talkie version of a Ben Travers farce which veered towards melodrama but had a successful stage revival at the National Theatre in 1978; valuable as a record of the original performances. Tom Walls, Ralph Lynn, Robertson Hare, Winifred Shotter, Sydney Lynn, Ethel Coleridge. Written by W. P. Lipscomb; directed by Tom Walls; for Herbert Wilcox / British and Dominions. 'Just a photographic record of the stage success.'—*Variety*

Plunder of the Sun*
US 1953 81m bw
Warner (Robert Fellows)

Various criminal elements seek buried treasure among the Mexican Aztec ruins. Interestingly located, well made, unconvincingly scripted melodrama, yet another borrowing from *The Maltese Falcon*.

w Jonathan Latimer, *novel* David Dodge *d* John Farrow *ph* Jack Draper *m* Antonio D. Conde

Glenn Ford, Diana Lynn, Francis L. Sullivan, Patricia Medina, Sean McClory, Douglass Dumbrille, Eduardo Noriega

The Plunderers
US 1947 87m bw

An undercover cavalry officer becomes friends with an outlaw who saves his life. Routine western, just about watchable. Rod Cameron, Ilona Massey, Adrian Booth. Written by Gerald Geraghty and Gerald Drayson Adams; directed by Joseph Kane; for Republic.

The Plunderers
US 1960 94m bw
Allied Artists / August (Joseph Pevney)

In the old west, four juvenile delinquents take over a town.
The Wild One in period dress. Nothing in particular.

w Bob Barbash *d* Joseph Pevney *ph* Eugene Polito *m* Leonard Rosenman

Jeff Chandler, John Saxon, Ray Sticklyn, Roger Torrey, Dee Pollock, Marsha Hunt, Dolores Hart, Jay C. Flippen, James Westerfield

Plymouth Adventure*
US 1952 105m Technicolor
MGM (Dore Schary)

The Pilgrim Fathers sail from Plymouth on the Mayflower and spend their first months ashore on the coast of America.
Well-meaning schoolbook history, totally unconvincing and very dull despite obvious effort all round. One or two of the actors have their moments.

w Helen Deutsch, *novel* Ernest Gebler *d* Clarence Brown *ph* William Daniels *m* Miklos Rozsa

Spencer Tracy, Gene Tierney, Van Johnson, Leo Genn, Dawn Addams

'It demonstrates how Hollywood can dull down as well as jazz up history.'—*Judith Crist, 1973*

Pocket Money
US 1972 100m Technicolor
First Artists / Coleytown (John Foreman)

Two slow-thinking Arizona cowboys try to make money herding cattle.
Peculiar modern western comedy drama which doesn't work.

w Terry Malick, *novel* Jim Kane by J. K. S. Brown *d* Stuart Rosenberg *ph* Laszlo Kovacs *m* Alex North

Paul Newman, Lee Marvin, Strother Martin, Kelly Jean Peters, Wayne Rogers

Pocketful of Miracles
US 1961 136m Technicolor Panavision
UA / Franton (Frank Capra)

Kindly gangsters help an old apple seller to persuade her long lost daughter that she is a lady of means.
Boring, overlong remake of *Lady for a Day*, showing that Capra's touch simply doesn't work on the wide screen, that his themes are dated anyway, and that all the fine character actors in Hollywood are a liability unless you find them something to do.

w Hal Kanter, Harry Tugend, *scenario* Robert Riskin, *story* Damon Runyon *d* Frank Capra *ph* Robert Bronner *m* Walter Scharf

Bette Davis, Glenn Ford, Hope Lange, Arthur O'Connell, Peter Falk, Thomas Mitchell, Edward Everett Horton, Sheldon Leonard, Barton MacLane, Jerome Cowan, Fritz Feld, Snub Pollard, David Brian, Ann-Margret, John Litel, Jay Novello, Willis Bouchey, George E. Stone, Mike Mazurki, Jack Elam, Mickey Shaughnessy, Peter Mann, Frank Ferguson

'The effect is less one of whimsy than of being bludgeoned to death with a toffee apple.'—*Peter John Dyer*

'The story has enough cracks in it for the syrup to leak through.'—*Playboy*

AAN: title song (*m* James Van Heusen, *ly* Sammy Cahn); Peter Falk

Poet's Pub
GB 1949 79m bw
GFD / Aquila (Donald B. Wilson)

A rowing blue takes over a Tudor inn and discovers a priceless jewelled gauntlet, the wearer of which is kidnapped during the performance of a pageant.
Very thin, naive treatment of a whimsical novel. The last film to use the Independent Frame process.

w Diana Morgan, *novel* Eric Linklater *d* Frederick Wilson *ph* George Stretton *m* Clifton Parker

Derek Bond, Rona Anderson, Barbara Murray, Leslie Dwyer, Joyce Grenfell

Poil de Carotte*
France 1932 94m bw

A small boy is picked on by his ageing mother to the point where he attempts suicide.
Country melodrama which made its director's name but seems a little faded now despite bravura sequences.

w Jules Renard *d* Julien Duvivier *ph* Thirard Monniot

Harry Baur, Robert Lynen, Catherine Fontenoy

'Looks like the best chance ever for a French film to get American distribution on the grand scale.'—*Variety*

Point Blank*
US 1967 92m Metrocolor Panavision
MGM / Judd Bernard, Irwin Winkler

A gangster takes an elaborate revenge on his cheating partner.
Extremely violent gangster thriller, well shot on location and something of a cult, but with irritating pretentiousness and obscure plot points.

w Alexander Jacobs, David Newhouse, Rafe Newhouse, *novel* The Hunter by Richard Stark *d* John Boorman *ph* *Philip Lathrop* *m* Johnny Mandel

Lee Marvin, Angie Dickinson, Keenan Wynn, Carroll O'Connor, Lloyd Bochner, Michael Strong, John Vernon, Sharon Acker

'The fragmentation was necessary to give the characters and the situation ambiguity, to suggest another meaning beyond the immediate plot.'—*John Boorman*

†*The Outfit* (qv) is a kind of sequel / reprise.

Pointed Heels
US 1929 61m bw (colour sequence)

A theatrical producer loves a musical comedy star but loses her to a young composer. Predictable backstage drama. William Powell, Fay Wray, Helen Kane, Phillips Holmes, Richard 'Skeets' Gallagher, Eugene Pallette. Written by Florence Ryerson and John V. A. Weaver, from a story by Charles Brackett; directed by A. Edward Sutherland; for Paramount. 'Moderate business likely for a light comedy that choked on too big a mouthful.'—*Variety*

Poison Pen*
GB 1939 79m bw
ABP (Walter C. Mycroft)

A village community is set at odds by a writer of vindictive anonymous letters.
Effective minor drama, with good location atmosphere.

w Doreen Montgomery, William Freshman, N. C. Hunter, Esther McCracken, *play* Richard Llewellyn *d* Paul Stein

Flora Robson, Reginald Tate, Robert Newton, Ann Todd, Geoffrey Toone, Belle Chrystal, Edward Chapman, Edward Rigby

'Sordid theme makes it doubtful film fare.'—*Variety*

'A lamentably artificial piece.'—*Richard Mallett, Punch*

'Call them what you like. Just don't call them when you're in trouble!'
Police Academy
US 1984 96m Technicolor

The mayor of an American city lifts all restrictions on entry to the police force. Appallingly unfunny series of snippets about police training, like an American Carry On with few jokes leading to a punch line and occasional resorting to dirty bits. Steve Guttenberg, Kim Cattrall, G. W. Bailey, Bubba Smith, Donovan Scott, George Gaynes. Written by Neal Israel, Pat Proft, Hugh Wilson; directed by Hugh Wilson; for Paul Maslansky / Ladd Company / Warner Brothers. 'Hit or miss comic juvenilia . . . pure popcorn fantasy fodder.'—*Paul Taylor, MFB*

† Within two years *Police Academy 2* and *Police Academy 3* had followed; neither requires detailed examination. *Police Academy 4* (1988) was the limpest to date—until *Police Academy 5: Assignment Miami Beach* appeared in the same year.

Politics
US 1931 71m bw

Two small-town women get into politics to fight racketeers. Scrappy star comedy which probably seemed funnier at the time. Marie Dressler, Polly Moran, Roscoe Ates, Karen Morley, William Bakewell, John Miljan. Written by Robert E. Hopkins, Wells Root, Zelda Sears, Malcolm Stuart Boylan; directed by Charles F. Reisner; for MGM. 'Loaded with technical faults, but it has too many laugh moments to fail to sock the b.o.'—*Variety*

Polly of the Circus
US 1932 72m bw
MGM (Paul Bern)

A trapeze artiste falls for the local minister, but incurs disapproval from his bishop.
Elementary romance reminiscent of silent drama.

w Carey Wilson, *play* Margaret Mayo *d* Alfred Santell *ph* George Barnes *m* William Axt

Marion Davies, Clark Gable, C. Aubrey Smith, Raymond Hatton, David Landau, Maude Eburne, Guinn Williams, Ray Milland

'Frail entertainment with both leads miscast.'—*Variety*

Pollyanna*
US 1960 134m Technicolor
Walt Disney (George Golitzen)

A 12-year-old orphan girl cheers up the grumps of the small town where she comes to live.
Well cast but overlong and rather humourless remake of a children's classic from an earlier age.

wd David Swift, *novel* Eleanor Porter *ph* Russell Harlan *m* Paul Smith *ad* Carroll Clark, Robert Clatworthy

Hayley Mills, Jane Wyman, Karl Malden, Nancy Olson, Adolphe Menjou, Donald Crisp, Agnes Moorehead, Richard Egan, Kevin Corcoran, James Drury, Reta Shaw, Leora Dana

'Even Hayley Mills can neither prevent one from sympathizing with the crusty aunts, hermits, vicars and hypochondriacs who get so forcibly cheered up, nor from feverishly speculating whether films like this don't run the risk of inciting normally kind and gentle people into certain excesses of violent crime – child murder, for instance.'—*MFB*

'It knows what scares you!'
Poltergeist**
US 1982 114m Metrocolor Panavision
MGM / SLM (Steven Spielberg)

Suburban life is disrupted when through her TV set a young girl releases unpleasant forces from the cemetery over which the modern estate was built.
Skilful but dramatically thin and sometimes rather nasty horror movie in which the producer's hand seems often to have controlled the director's. Misjudgment must be the reason that it was not the huge success intended.

w Steven Spielberg, Michael Grais, Mark Victor *d* Tobe Hooper *ph* Matthew F. Leonetti *m* Jerry Goldsmith *ed* Michael Kahn

Jobeth Williams, Craig T. Nelson, Beatrice Straight, Dominique Dunne, Oliver Robbins

AAN: music, visual effects (Richard Edlund, Michael Wood, Bruce Nicholson)

Poltergeist II
US 1986 90m Metrocolor Panavision
MGM-UA / Freddie Fields / Victor-Grais

The family from *Poltergeist* is in for more trouble when Grandma dies and they begin receiving phone messages from the other side.
More pointless spine-shivering: good technical effects but no message of any kind, not even entertainment.

w Mark Victor, Michael Grais *d* Brian Gibson *ph* Andrew Laszlo *pd* Ted Haworth

JoBeth Williams, Craig T. Nelson, Heather O'Rourke, Oliver Robins, Julian Beck

† *Poltergeist III* came along in 1988.

Pony Express*
US 1953 101m Technicolor
Paramount (Nat Holt)

In 1860 Buffalo Bill Cody and Wild Bill Hickok are sent to establish pony express stations across California.
Standard western which tells a factual tale adequately if rather slowly.

w Charles Marquis Warren *d* Jerry Hopper *ph* Ray Rennahan *m* Paul Sawtell

Charlton Heston, Forrest Tucker, Rhonda Fleming, Jan Sterling

Pony Soldier
US 1952 82m Technicolor
TCF (Samuel G. Engel)
GB title: *MacDonald of the Canadian Mounties*

The mounties settle the hash of Canadian Indian renegades who have been causing trouble on the American border.
Mediocre outdoor adventure.

w John C. Higgins *d* Joseph M. Newman *ph* Harry Jackson *m* Alex North

Tyrone Power, Cameron Mitchell, Robert Horton, Thomas Gomez, Penny Edwards, *Adeline de Walt Reynolds*

Pool of London
GB 1950 85m bw
Ealing (Michael Relph)

A smuggling sailor gets involved in murder.
Routine semi-documentary police thriller with locations in London docks decorating a standard piece of thick ear.

w Jack Whittingham, John Eldridge *d* Basil Dearden *ph* Gordon Dines *m* John Addison

Bonar Colleano, Susan Shaw, Earl Cameron, Renée Asherson, Moira Lister, Max Adrian, James Robertson Justice, Joan Dowling

'Done with such imagination, humour and visual attractiveness as to hold the pleased attention of all who like to use their eyes and their ears.'—*Richard Mallett, Punch*

Poor Cow*
GB 1967 101m Eastmancolor
Anglo Amalgamated / Vic / Fenchurch (Joe Janni)

The dismal life of a young London mother who lives in squalor with her criminal husband.
Television-style fictional documentary determined to rub one's nose in the mire. Innovative and occasionally striking but not very likeable.

w Nell Dunn, Ken Loach, *novel* Nell Dunn *d Ken Loach* *ph* Brian Probyn *m* Donovan

Carol White, Terence Stamp, John Bindon, Kate Williams, Queenie Watts

'A superficial, slightly patronizing excursion into the nether realms of social realism.'—*Jan Dawson*

Poor Little Rich Girl*
US 1936 79m bw
TCF (Darryl F. Zanuck)

A child is separated from her father and joins a radio singing act.
Pleasing star vehicle with all the expected elements, adapted from a Mary Pickford vehicle of 1917.

w Sam Hellman, Gladys Lehman, Harry Tugend *d* Irving Cummings *ph* John Seitz *songs* Mack Gordon, Harry Revel

Shirley Temple, Jack Haley, Alice Faye, Gloria Stuart, Michael Whalen, Sara Haden, Jane Darwell, Claude Gillingwater, Henry Armetta

Pop Always Pays
US 1940 65m bw

Pop promises to match his future son-in-law's savings, but runs into a business slump. Minor comedy which accelerates into frantic farce, but the star was always funnier at two-reel length. Leon Errol, Dennis O'Keefe, Adele Pearce, Walter Catlett, Marjorie Gateson, Tom Kennedy. Written by Charles E. Roberts; directed by Leslie Goodwins; for Bert Gilroy / RKO.

Pope Joan
GB 1972 132m Eastmancolor Panavision
Big City Productions / Kurt Unger
aka: *The Devil's Imposter*

The legend of a 9th-century German semi-prostitute who discovered a vocation to preach and was made Pope.
Uninspiring pageant, brutish and rather silly, full of would-be medieval sensationalism.

w John Briley *d* Michael Anderson *ph* Billy Williams *m* Maurice Jarre *pd* Elliott Scott

Liv Ullmann, Trevor Howard, Olivia de Havilland, Maximilian Schell, Keir Dullea, Robert Beatty, Franco Nero, Patrick Magee

The Pope of Greenwich Village
US 1984 120m Metrocolor
MGM-UA / Koch-Kirkwood (Benjy Rosenberg)

In New York, Charlie and his cousin Paulie become thieves and fall foul of the Mafia.
Back again to the mean streets of the east side, but with nothing at all new to add to the scores of indistinguishable real-life melodramas of this kind.

w Vincent Patrick, from his novel *d* Stuart Rosenberg *ph* John Bailey *m* Dave Grusin *pd* Paul Sylbert

Eric Roberts, Mickey Rourke, Daryl Hannah, Geraldine Page, Kenneth McMillan, Tony Musante, M. Emmet Walsh, Burt Young
AAN: Geraldine Page (supporting actress)

Popeye
US 1980 114m colour
Paramount / Disney (Robert Evans)

Popeye returns to Sweethaven in search of the father who abandoned him.
Lamentable attempt by an ill-chosen director to humanize and sentimentalize a celebrated cartoon character who doesn't get into the expected physical action until the film is nearly over.

w Jules Feiffer, from characters created by E. C. Segar *d* Robert Altman *ph* Giuseppe Rotunno *m / ly* Harry Nilsson *pd* Wolf Kroeger

Robin Williams, Shelley Duvall, Ray Walston, Paul Dooley

'The picture doesn't come together, and much of it is cluttered, squawky, and eerily unfunny.'—*Pauline Kael, New Yorker*

Popi*
US 1969 113m De Luxe
UA / Leonard Films (Herbert B. Leonard)

Adventures of a cheerful inhabitant of New York's Puerto Rican ghetto.
Ethnic comedy-drama of the kind that has since found its way in abundance into American TV series. Very competently done for those who like it, e.g. Puerto Ricans.

w Tina and Lester Pine *d* Arthur Hiller *ph* Ross Lowell *m* Dominic Frontière

Alan Arkin, Rita Moreno, Miguel Alejandro, Ruben Figuero

'An appropriately disenchanted view of an immigrant's struggling ambitions in the Promised Land.'—*Richard Combs*

Poppy*
US 1936 74m bw
Paramount (Paul Jones)

An itinerant medicine-seller sets up his stall in a small town where his daughter falls in love with the mayor's son.
Clumsily but heavily plotted vehicle for W. C. Fields, who as usual has great moments but seems to rob the show of its proper pace.

w Waldemar Young, Virginia Van Upp, *play* Dorothy Donnelly *d* A. Edward Sutherland *ph* William Mellor *m* Frederick Hollander

W. C. Fields, Rochelle Hudson, Richard Cromwell, Granville Bates, Catherine Doucet, Lynne Overman, Maude Eburne

'Antique hokum trussed up for a Fields vehicle.'—*Literary Digest*

Porgy and Bess*
US 1959 138m Technicolor Todd-AO
Samuel Goldwyn

A slum girl falls in love with a crippled beggar.
Negro opera about the inhabitants of Catfish Row; full of interest for music lovers, but not lending itself very readily to screen treatment.

w N. Richard Nash, *libretto* Du Bose Heyward, *play* Porgy by Du Bose and Dorothy Heyward *d* Otto Preminger *ph* Leon Shamroy *m George Gershwin* *md* André Previn, Ken Darby *ch* Hermes Pan

Sidney Poitier, Dorothy Dandridge, Sammy Davis Jnr, Pearl Bailey, Brock Peters, Diahann Carroll, Clarence Muse
AA: André Previn, Ken Darby
AAN: Leon Shamroy

'Bold! blunt! blustering! the battle picture without equal!'

Pork Chop Hill*
US 1959 97m bw
United Artists / Melville / Lewis Milestone

The Americans in Korea take a vital hill but the colonel in command finds it difficult to hold.
Ironic war film with vivid spectacle separated by much talk.

w James R. Webb *d Lewis Milestone* *ph Sam Leavitt* *m* Leonard Rosenman *pd* Nicolai Remisoff

Gregory Peck, Harry Guardino, George Shibata, Woody Strode, James Edwards, Rip Torn, George Peppard, Barry Atwater, Robert Blake

Porky's
Canada 1982 98m colour
Melvin Simon / Astral Bellevue Pathe / Porky's Productions / (Don Carmody, Bob Clark)

In Florida in the early fifties, high school boys try to get into a local brothel.
Ghastly teenage goings-on taking cinema bad taste just about as far as it will get.

wd Bob Clark *ph* Reginald H. Morris *m* Carl Zittrer, Paul Zaza *pd* Reuben Freed

Dan Monahan, Mark Herrier, Wyatt Knight, Roger Wilson, Kim Cattrall, Art Hindle, Wayne Maunder, Alex Karras, Nancy Parsons

'It is difficult to say which is the more depressing: the technical expertise with which this mind-numbing tripe has been put together, or its great success at the US box office.'—*Jo Imeson, MFB*

'One of those movies that makes you weep for the state of the contemporary commercial cinema—and, even more, for the gullibility of the public that pays to see it.'—*Margaret Hinxman, Daily Mail*

† *Porky's 2* followed in 1983 and was even worse. 1985 brought *Porky's Revenge*, about which there is nothing to be said.

Porridge*
GB 1979 93m Eastmancolor
Black Lion / Witzend

Old lags at Slade Prison try to arrange an escape for a first offender.
Genial expansion of a successful TV series to the big screen; alas, as usual the material is stretched to snapping point, and the welcome irony of the original becomes sentimentality. Still, the film is a valuable record of memorable characters.

w Dick Clement, Ian La Frenais *d* Dick Clement *ph* Bob Huke *md* Terry Oates

Ronnie Barker, Richard Beckinsale, Fulton Mackay, Brian Wilde, Peter Vaughan, Geoffrey Bayldon, Julian Holloway

Port Afrique
GB 1956 92m Technicolor

In Morocco, an American pilot solves the shooting of his wife. Tropical variation on *The Maltese Falcon* and *The Blue Dahlia*; not much cop on its own account. Phil Carey, Pier Angeli, Dennis Price, Eugene Deckers, James Hayter, Rachel Gurney, Anthony Newley. Written by Frank Partos and John Cresswell, from a novel by Bernard Victor Dyer; directed by Rudolph Maté; for David E. Rose / Columbia.

Port of New York*
US 1949 82m bw
Eagle Lion (Aubrey Schenck)

A woman narcotics smuggler determines to betray her colleagues to the authorities. Good routine semi-documentary thick ear, notable for an early appearance by Yul Brynner as villain-in-chief.

w Eugene Ling *d* Laslo Benedek *ph* George E. Diskant *w* Sol Kaplan

Scott Brady, Richard Rober, K. T. Stevens, Yul Brynner

Port of Seven Seas*
US 1938 81m bw
MGM (Henry Henigson)

Love on the Marseilles waterfront.
Stagey Hollywoodization of Pagnol's *Marius* trilogy: some vigour shows through.

w Preston Sturges *d* James Whale *ph* Karl Freund *m* Franz Waxman

Wallace Beery, Frank Morgan, Maureen O'Sullivan, John Beal, Jessie Ralph, Cora Witherspoon

'Genuine and touching drama . . . strong solo biller.'—*Variety*

Porte des Lilas*
France / Italy 1957 95m bw
Filmsonor / Rizzoli (Jacques Plante)
aka: *Gate of Lilacs*

A gangster on the run shelters in a poor quarter of Paris, but his treachery is his undoing.
Atmospheric comedy-drama put across with the expected style but providing very little to smile at.

w René Clair, Jean Aurel, *novel* La Grande Ceinture by René Fallet *d* René Clair *ph* Robert Le Fèbvre *m* Georges Brassens

Pierre Brasseur, Georges Brassens, Henri Vidal, Dany Carrel, Raymond Bussières, Amedée, Alain Bouvette

Les Portes de la Nuit*
France 1946 106m bw
Pathé Cinema
aka: *Gates of Night*

Various people in post-war Paris are drawn into a pattern woven by Destiny—who appears as a melancholy tramp.
A polished piece of post-war gloom, and the archetype of all *films noirs* of the period. The beginning, also, of its director's decline.

w Jacques Prévert *d Marcel Carné*
ph Philippe Agostini *m* Joseph Kosma
ad Alexander Trauner

Pierre Brasseur, Yves Montand, Nathalie Nattier, Serge Reggiani, Jean Vilar, Saturnin Fabre, Mady Berry, Dany Robin

† One of the few films to have been based on a ballet—*Le Rendezvous* by Prévert. Oddly enough its realistic scenes of daily life are among its most successful elements.

Portia on Trial*
US 1937 83m bw

A lady lawyer uses her skills in the courtroom to right the personal wrongs done to her years before. Efficient tearjerker, *Madame X* style, and one of the comparatively big productions Republic occasionally tried. Frieda Inescort, Walter Abel, Neil Hamilton, Heather Angel, Ruth Donnelly, Barbara Pepper, Clarence Kolb. Written by Sam Ornitz, E. E. Paramore Jnr, from the novel by Faith Baldwin; directed by George Nicholls Jnr; for Republic. 'A distinguished production: exploitation required to overcome title and no-name handicap.'—*Variety*
(GB title: *The Trial of Portia Merriman.*)

Portnoy's Complaint
US 1972 101m Technicolor Panavision
Warner / Chehnault (Ernest Lehman)

A young New York Jewish boy has mother and masturbation problems.
Foolhardy attempt to film a fashionably sensational literary exercise; one of Hollywood's last attempts – thank goodness – to be 'with it'.

wd Ernest Lehman, *novel* Philip Roth
ph Philip Lathrop *m* Michel Legrand

Richard Benjamin, Karen Black, Lee Black, Jack Somack, Jill Clayburgh, Jeannie Berlin

'The spectator is forced into the doubly uncomfortable position of a voyeur who can't actually see anything.'—*Jan Dawson*

Portrait from Life
GB 1948 90m bw
GFD / Gainsborough (Antony Darnborough)
US title: *The Girl in the Painting*

In an art gallery, a German professor recognizes a portrait as that of his daughter, lost during the war in Germany, and after a search discovers her to have been an amnesiac under the protection of a leading Nazi.
Tolerable melodrama with similarities to *The Seventh Veil* (the girl has to choose between four men).

w Frank Harvey Jnr, Muriel and Sydney Box *d* Terence Fisher *ph* Jack Asher *m* Benjamin Frankel

Mai Zetterling, Robert Beatty, Guy Rolfe, Herbert Lom, Patrick Holt

Portrait in Black*
US 1960 113m Eastmancolor
U-I / Ross Hunter

An elderly shipping tycoon is murdered by his wife and doctor, but they are blackmailed.
Absurd old-fashioned melodrama of dark doings among the idle rich. Quite entertaining for addicts.

w Ivan Goff, Ben Roberts *d* Michael Gordon
ph Russell Metty *m* Frank Skinner

Lana Turner, Anthony Quinn, Richard Basehart, Anna May Wong, Lloyd Nolan, Sandra Dee, John Saxon, Ray Walston, Virginia Grey

'Connoisseurs of the higher tosh should find it irresistible.'—*Penelope Houston*

Portrait of a Mobster
US 1961 108m bw
Warner

The career of twenties gangster Dutch Schultz. Over-familiar, warmed over racketeering stuff with no particular edge or style.

w Howard Browne *d* Joseph Pevney
ph Eugene Polito *m* Max Steiner

Vic Morrow, Leslie Parrish, Peter Breck, Ray Danton (repeating as Legs Diamond), Norman Alden, Ken Lynch

Portrait of Alison*
GB 1955 84m bw
Anglo-Amalgamated / Insignia (Frank Godwin)
aka: *Postmark for Danger*

A journalist dies while investigating an international smuggling ring, and his brother takes up the case.
Solidly carpentered mystery with all the twists expected from this source.

w Guy Green, Ken Hughes, *radio serial* Francis Durbridge *d* Guy Green
ph Wilkie Cooper *m* John Veale

Robert Beatty, Terry Moore, William Sylvester, Josephine Griffin, Geoffrey Keen, Allan Cuthbertson, Henry Oscar

Portrait of Clare
GB 1950 98m bw
ABPC (Leslie Landau)

In 1900, a woman looks back on her three marriages.
High school novelette for easily pleased female audiences.

w Leslie Landau, Adrian Arlington, *novel* Francis Brett Young *d* Lance Comfort
ph Gunther Krampf *ad* Don Ashton

Margaret Johnston, Richard Todd, Robin Bailey, Ronald Howard, Mary Clare, Marjorie Fielding, Anthony Nicholls, Lloyd Pearson

Portrait of Jennie***
US 1948 86m bw (tinted sequence)
David O. Selznick
GB title: *Jennie*

A penniless artist meets a strange girl who seems to age each time he sees her; they fall in

love and he discovers that she has long been dead, though she finally comes to life once more during a sea storm like the one in which she perished.
A splendid example of the higher Hollywood lunacy: a silly story with pretensions about life and death and time and art, presented with superb persuasiveness by a first-class team of actors and technicians.

w Peter Berneis, Paul Osborn, Leonard Bernovici, *novel* Robert Nathan *d William Dieterle ph Joseph August m Dmitri Tiomkin*, after Debussy

Jennifer Jones, Joseph Cotten, Ethel Barrymore, David Wayne, Lillian Gish, Henry Hull, Florence Bates

PROLOGUE: Since time began man has looked into the awesome reaches of infinity and asked the eternal questions: What is time? What is life? What is space? What is death? Through a hundred civilizations, philosophers and scientists have come together with answers, but the bewilderment remains. . . . Science tells us that nothing ever dies but only changes, that time itself does not pass but curves around us, and that the past and the future are together at our side for ever. Out of the shadows of knowledge, and out of a painting that hung on a museum wall, comes our story, the truth of which lies not on our screen but in your hearts.

JENNIE'S SONG: 'Where I come from, nobody knows . . .
And where I'm going, everything goes . . .
The wind blows,
The sea flows . . .
And nobody knows . . .'

EBEN (Joseph Cotten): 'I want you, not dreams of you.'

JENNIE (Jennifer Jones): 'There is no life, my darling, until you love and have been loved. And then there is no death.'

'Easily the Selznick masterpiece, rich in superb performances, tasteful direction and superb photography.'—*Motion Picture Herald*

'One of the most exquisite fantasy films ever made . . . a milieu rich in visual and aural imagery . . . a sensuous evocation of time and timelessness.'—*Cinefantastique*

'Though the story may not make sense, the pyrotechnics, joined to the dumbfounded silliness, keep one watching.'—*New Yorker 1976*

AAN: Joseph August

The Poseidon Adventure**
US 1972 117m De Luxe Panavision
TCF / Kent (Irwin Allen)

A luxury liner is capsized, and trapped passengers have to find their way to freedom via an upside down world.
Tedious disaster movie which caught the public fancy and started a cycle. Spectacular moments, cardboard characters, flashes of imagination.

w Stirling Silliphant, Wendell Mayes, *novel* Paul Gallico *ph* Harold Stine *d* Ronald Neame *m* John Williams *pd* William Creber

Gene Hackman, Ernest Borgnine, Shelley Winters, Red Buttons, Carol Lynley, Leslie Nielson, Arthur O'Connell, Pamela Sue Martin, Roddy McDowall, Eric Shea, Jack Albertson, Stella Stevens

'The script is the only cataclysm in this waterlogged *Grand Hotel.*'—*New Yorker*

† See also: *Beyond the Poseidon Adventure.*

AA: song 'The Morning After' (*m / ly* Al Kasha, Joel Hirschhorn)

AAN: Harold Stine; John Williams; Shelley Winters

Posse**
US 1975 93m Technicolor Panavision
Paramount / Bryna (Kirk Douglas)

A US marshal seeking higher office vows to capture a railroad bandit, but the tables are smartly turned.
Unusual minor western, quite pleasing in all departments and neither mindless nor violent.

w William Roberts, Christopher Knopf d Kirk Douglas ph Fred Koenekamp *m* Maurice Jarre

Kirk Douglas, Bruce Dern, Bo Hopkins, James Stacy, Luke Askey, David Canary

Posse from Hell
US 1961 89m Technicolor

Four killers escape from jail and take over a town. Moderate western programmer with more violence than usual. Audie Murphy, John Saxon, Zohra Lampert, Vic Morrow, Robert Keith. Written by Clair Huffaker; directed by Herbert Coleman; for Universal / International.

Possessed*
US 1931 76m bw
MGM

A factory girl goes to New York in search of riches.
Reasonably gutsy Depression melodrama which moves at a fair pace.

w Lenore Coffee, *play* The Mirage by Edgar Selwyn *d* Clarence Brown *ph* Oliver T. Marsh

Joan Crawford, Clark Gable, Wallace Ford, Skeets Gallagher, Frank Conroy, Marjorie White, John Miljan

'Lots of luxury; lots of charm; lots of smooth talk about courage and marriage and what women want.'—*James R. Quirk*

'You'll be possessed by its love madness!'
Possessed*
US 1947 108m bw
Warner (Jerry Wald)

An emotionally unstable nurse marries her employer but retains a passionate love for an engineer whom she kills when he does not respond.
Extremely heavy, almost Germanic, flashback melodrama with everyone tearing hammer and tongs at the rather ailing script. Fun if you're in that mood, and an interesting example of the American *film noir* of the forties.

w Silvia Richards, Ranald MacDougall, *novel* One Man's Secret by Rita Weiman *d Curtis Bernhardt ph Joseph Valentine m* Franz Waxman

Joan Crawford, Raymond Massey, Van Heflin, Geraldine Brooks, Stanley Ridges, John Ridgely, Moroni Olsen

'Acting with bells on.'—*Richard Winnington*

'Miss Crawford performs with the passion and intelligence of an actress who is not content with just one Oscar.'—*James Agee*

AAN: Joan Crawford

The Possession of Joel Delaney
US 1971 108m Eastmancolor
ITC / Haworth (George Justin)

A wealthy New York divorcee tries to save her brother from death at the hands of a Puerto Rican occult group who believe in ritual murder and demonic possession.
Unpleasant, frightening and overlong horror film with some kind of message struggling to get out but precious little entertainment value.

w Matt Robinson, Grimes Grice, *novel* Ramona Stewart *d* Waris Hussein *ph* Arthur J. Ornitz *m* Joe Ragoso

Shirley Maclaine, Perry King, Lisa Kohane, David Ellacott

'Some see the film as a political allegory; I see it as a piece of political tosh.'—*Michael Billington, Illustrated London News*

The Postman Always Rings Twice*
US 1946 113m bw
MGM (Carey Wilson)

A guilty couple murder her husband but get their come-uppance.
Pale shadow of *Double Indemnity,* efficient but not interesting or very suspenseful.

w Harry Ruskin, Niven Busch, *novel* James M. Cain *d* Tay Garnett *ph Sidney Wagner m* George Bassman

Lana Turner, John Garfield, Cecil Kellaway, Hume Cronyn, Leon Ames, Audrey Totter, Alan Reed

'It was a real chore to do *Postman* under the Hays Office, but I think I managed to get the sex across.'—*Tay Garnett*

'You will feel the heat!'
'Their love was a war that destroyed!'
The Postman Always Rings Twice*
US 1981 121m Metrocolor

A remake of the above with more heavy breathing and some table-ending. Not otherwise any better, but an interesting measure of the times. Jack Nicholson, Jessica Lange, John Colicos, Michael Lerner, John P. Ryan, Anjelica Huston. Written by David Mamet; directed by Bob Rafelson; for Northstar International / Lorimar. 'Too cheerless to be erotic, too charmless to be titillating.'—*Margaret Hinxman, Daily Mail*

Postman's Knock*
GB 1961 88m bw
MGM (Ronald Kinnoch)

A village postman is transferred to London, finds life and work bewildering, but captures some crooks and ends up a hero.
Mildly amusing star vehicle rising to good comic climaxes.

w John Briley, Jack Trevor Story *d* Robert Lynn *ph* Gerald Moss *m* Ron Goodwin

Spike Milligan, Barbara Shelley, Wilfrid Lawson

The Pot Carriers
GB 1962 84m bw

A sensitive young man is debased by prison routine. Odd little comedy-drama with comedy moments seeming to set the mood. Paul Massie, Ronald Fraser, Carole Lesley, Dennis Price, Paul Rogers, Davy Kaye, Eddie Byrne. Written by T. J. Morrison and Mike Watts from the latter's play; directed by Peter Graham Scott; for Associated British.

Pot Luck*
GB 1936 71m bw

A Scotland Yard inspector enlists the aid of department store staff to recover a stolen Chinese vase. Surprisingly not from a stage original, this action farce gets better as it goes along and finds time for a quick spoof of *The Old Dark House.* Tom Walls, Ralph Lynn, Robertson Hare, Diana Churchill, Gordon James, Martita Hunt. Written by Ben Travers; directed by Tom Walls; for Gainsborough.

Pot o' Gold
US 1941 87m bw
Globe / James Roosevelt
GB title: *The Golden Hour*

A radio giveaway show finds work for idle musicians.
Thin Capraesque comedy which needed more determined handling.

w Walter de Leon *d* George Marshall *ph* Hal Mohr *md* Lou Forbes

James Stewart, Paulette Goddard, Horace Heidt, Charles Winninger, Mary Gordon, Frank Melton, Jed Prouty

Potemkin: see The Battleship Potemkin

Powder River
US 1953 77m Technicolor

A marshal finds that an embittered doctor is the killer he is seeking. Satisfactory programmer, more of a suspense drama than a western. Rory Calhoun, Cameron Mitchell, Corinne Calvet, Penny Edwards, Carl Betz, John Dehner. Written by Geoffrey Holmes, from a novel by Stuart Lake; directed by Louis King; for TCF.

Powder Town
US 1942 79m bw

A scientist in a munitions plant comes into conflict with a tough foreman. Propaganda action programmer. Victor McLaglen, Edmond O'Brien, June Havoc. Written by David Boehm and Vicki Baum from a novel by Max Brand; directed by Rowland V. Lee; for RKO.

The Power*
US 1967 109m Metrocolor Cinemascope
MGM / George Pal

Scientists researching into human endurance are menaced by one of their number who has developed the ability to kill by will power.
Interesting but finally unexciting and exasperating science fiction which badly lacks a gimmick one can actually see.

w John Gay, *novel* Frank M. Robinson *d* Byron Haskin *ph* Ellsworth Fredericks *m* Miklos Rozsa

Michael Rennie, George Hamilton, Suzanne Pleshette, Nehemiah Persoff, Earl Holliman, Arthur O'Connell, Aldo Ray, Barbara Nichols, Yvonne de Carlo, Richard Carlson, Gary Merrill, Ken Murray, Miiko Taka, Celia Lovsky

'The movie takes itself very seriously. We don't have to.'—*Robert Windeler*

Power
US 1985 111m Technicolor
TCF / Lorimar / Polar (Reene Schisgal, Mark Tarlov)

A political PR man takes on an industrialist of dubious background.
Slick and punchy but somewhat unnecessary investigation of corruption in the media, an American version of *The Ploughman's Lunch.*

w David Himmelstein *d* Sidney Lumet *ph* Andrzej Bartkowiak *m* Cy Coleman *pd* Peter Larkin *ed* Andrew Mondsheim

Richard Gere, Julie Christie, Gene Hackman, Kate Capshaw, Denzel Washington, E. G. Marshall, Beatrice Straight, Fritz Weaver, Michael Learned

The Power and the Glory*
US 1933 76m bw
Fox (Jesse L. Lasky)

The flashback story of a tycoon who rose from nothing and was corrupted by power.
Often noted as a forerunner of *Citizen Kane,* this is in fact a disappointing film with a very thin script and a general sense of aimlessness. 'Presented in narratage' meant that the characters voice their unspoken thoughts. Most interesting for its credits.

w Preston Sturges *d* William K. Howard *ph* James Wong Howe

Spencer Tracy, Colleen Moore, Ralph Morgan, Helen Vinson

'Débuting at two dollars on Broadway. Not two dollars but decidedly above-average film fare. Packs plenty of appeal, even with a not too punch marquee cast.'—*Variety*

The Power and the Prize*
US 1956 98m bw Cinemascope
MGM (Nicholas Nayfack)

An ambitious company executive is criticized by his president for wanting to marry a European refugee, but the other executives support him.
Unconvincing big business fairy tale which passes the time competently enough, though Taylor is a humourless hero.

w Robert Ardrey, *novel* Howard Swiggett *d* Henry Koster *ph* George Folsey *m* Bronislau Kaper

Robert Taylor, Elizabeth Mueller, Mary Astor, Burl Ives, Charles Coburn, Cedric Hardwicke

Power of the Press
US 1943 63m bw

The owner of a New York paper kills to maintain its isolationist line. Hard-hitting melodrama which overdoes the propaganda. Lee Tracy, Guy Kibbee, Otto Kruger, Gloria Dickson. Written by Samuel Fuller and Robert D. Andrews; directed by Lew Landers; for Columbia.

Power Play
GB / Canada 1978 109m colour
Robert Cooper / Canada United Kingdom (Christopher Dalton)

In a mythical country, a tank commander joins the leaders of a coup d' ètat only to doublecross them.
Uninteresting mixture of violent action and verbosity.

wd Martyn Burke *ph* Ousama Rawi *m* Ken Thorne

Peter O'Toole, David Hemmings, Donald Pleasence, Barry Morse

The Powers Girl
US 1942 92m bw
UA / Charles R. Rogers
GB title: *Hello Beautiful*

Girls come to New York to become models for John Robert Powers.
Extremely thin and forgettable musical.

w Edwin Moran, Harry Segall, *book* John Robert Powers *d* Norman Z. McLeod *ph* Stanley Cortez *md* Louis Silvers

George Murphy, Anne Shirley, Carole Landis, Alan Mowbray (as Powers), Dennis Day, Benny Goodman and his Orchestra, Mary Treen

Practically Yours
US 1944 89m bw
Paramount (Mitchell Leisen)

A war hero comes back after being supposed dead, and finds himself with a fiancée he never met.
Silly romantic comedy which never gets going.

w Norman Krasna *d* Mitchell Leisen *ph* Charles Lang Jnr *m* Victor Young

Claudette Colbert, Fred MacMurray, Gil Lamb, Cecil Kellaway, Robert Benchley, Rosemary de Camp, Tom Powers, Jane Frazee

A Prayer for the Dying
GB 1987 107m Metrocolor

An ex-IRA gunman feels unable to silence a priest witness of a killing, and confesses his sins instead. Convoluted melodrama which kills its chances as a thriller by striving to say something meaningful. Mickey Rourke, Bob

Hoskins, Alan Bates, Sammi Davis, Christopher Fulford. Written by Edmund Ward, Martin Lynch from Jack Higgins's novel; directed by Mike Hodges (who disowned the version released); for Peter Snell/ Samuel Goldwyn Co.

Predator
US 1987 107m De Luxe

An allied military rescue team gets into trouble in South America. Lethargic action thriller with unpleasant moments. Arnold Schwarzenegger, Carl Weathers, Bill Duke, Elpidia Carrillo, Jesse Ventura. Written by Jim and John Thomas; directed by John McTiernan; for Gordon-Silver-Davis/TCF.

Prelude to Fame
GB 1950 88m bw
Rank / Two Cities (Donald B. Wilson)

The health of a child musical prodigy is endangered by an ambitious woman who pushes him to the top.
Banal drama with classical music, generally overacted by the adults.

w Robert Westerby, *story* Young Archimedes by Aldous Huxley *d* Fergus McDonell *ph* George Stretton

Jeremy Spenser, Guy Rolfe, Kathleen Ryan, Kathleen Byron, James Robertson Justice, Henry Oscar, Rosalie Crutchley

Prelude to War***
US 1943 53m bw

First in the Why We Fight series, produced by Frank Capra for the US Signal Corps. A brilliant assemblage of newsreel, diagrams, and March of Time techniques which pointed a new way for documentary. 'There isn't a dull second.'—*Variety*

The Premature Burial
US 1961 81m Eastmancolor Panavision
AIP (Roger Corman)

A man afraid of being buried alive suffers just that fate, but later comes to and wreaks revenge on his tormentors.
Gloomy Gothic horror based vaguely on Edgar Allan Poe: the ultimate in graveyard ghoulishness.

w Charles Beaumont, Ray Russell *d* Roger Corman *ph* Floyd Crosby *m* Ronald Stein *ad* Daniel Haller

Ray Milland, Heather Angel, Hazel Court, Richard Ney, Alan Napier, John Dierkes

Premiere
GB 1938 71m bw

The principal backer of a stage show is shot during the first performance. Slightly unusual mystery drama. John Lodge, Judy Kelly, Joan Marion, Hugh Williams, Edmund Breon, Steven Geray, Edward Chapman. Written by F. McGrew Willis; directed by Walter Summers; for ABPC.

Presenting Lily Mars*
US 1943 104m bw
MGM (Joe Pasternak)

A girl from the sticks hits it big on Broadway. No, the plot wasn't new, but some of the numbers were nice.

w Richard Connell, Gladys Lehman, *novel* Booth Tarkington *d* Norman Taurog *ph* Joseph Ruttenberg *md* George Stoll

Judy Garland, Van Heflin, Fay Bainter, Richard Carlson, Martha Eggerth, Spring Byington, Bob Crosby and his band, Tommy Dorsey and his band

The President Vanishes
US 1934 80m bw

The president of the US agrees to drop out of sight for a few days, pretending to have been kidnapped, so that his country will not be drawn into a European war. Reasonably intriguing political fantasy with good production and performances. Arthur Byron, Janet Beecher, Paul Kelly, Peggy Conklin, Rosalind Russell, Sidney Blackmer, Walter Kingsford, Charley Grapewin, Edward Arnold. Written by Lynn Starling, Carey Wilson, Cedric Worth, from the anonymous novel; directed by William A. Wellman; for Walter Wanger (Paramount). 'Provocative topical meller, but likely to be spotty.'—*Variety* (GB title: *Strange Conspiracy*.)

The President's Analyst*
US 1967 104m Technicolor Panavision
Paramount / Panpiper (Stanley Rubin)

A psychiatrist who has been asked to treat the President is pursued by spies of every nationality.
Wild political satirical farce which finally unmasks as its chief villain the telephone company. Laughs along the way, but it's all rather too much.

wd Theodore J. Flicker *ph* William A. Fraker *m* Lalo Schifrin *pd* Pato Guzman

James Coburn, Godfrey Cambridge, Severn Darden, Joan Delaney, Pat Harrington, Eduard Franz, Will Geer

The President's Lady*
US 1953 96m bw
TCF (Sol C. Siegel)

An account of the early career of Andrew Jackson, a lawyer whose frail wife died shortly after he became president.
Well-produced political historical romance.

w John Patrick, *novel* Irving Stone *d* Henry Levin *ph Leo Tover* *m Alfred Newman*

Charlton Heston, Susan Hayward, John McIntire, Fay Bainter, Carl Betz

'History plays a curious second fiddle to love's old sweet song.'—*New York Times*

Press for Time
GB 1966 102m Eastmancolor
Rank / Ivy / Titan (Robert Hartford Davis, Peter Newbrook)

The prime minister's grandson is a newspaper seller, and is quietly promoted to be a journalist in a seaside town where it is thought he can do no harm.
The star's last comedy in his original style; competent but nothing special.

w Norman Wisdom, Eddie Leslie *novel* Yea Yea Yea by Angus McGill *d* Robert Asher *ph* Peter Newbrook *m* Mike Vickers

Norman Wisdom, Derek Bond, Angela Browne, Derek Francis, Noel Dyson, Peter Jones, David Lodge

Pressure Point*
US 1962 89m bw
UA / Larcas / Stanley Kramer

A black prison psychiatrist has longstanding trouble with a violent racist inmate.
Curious, quite compelling case history, told in pointless and confusing flashback; sharply made and photographed, melodramatically acted.

w Hubert Cornfield, S. Lee Pogositin *d Hubert Cornfield* *ph Ernest Haller* *m* Ernest Gold

Sidney Poitier, Bobby Darin, Peter Falk, Carl Benton Reid

Prestige
US 1932 71m bw

A woman follows her fiancé to a Malayan prison colony where he is on the staff, and finds he has become an alcoholic. Tediously stilted romantic melodrama which seems at least twice as long as its actual running time. Ann Harding, Melvyn Douglas, Adolphe Menjou, Guy Bates Post, Clarence Muse. Written by Francis Edwards Faragoh, from the novel *Lips of Steel* by Harry Hervey; directed by Tay Garnett; for RKO.

Pretty Baby*
US 1950 92m bw
Warner (Harry Kurnitz)

A girl finds it easier to get a seat on the subway if she is carrying a (dummy) baby, but gets into complications when she meets a baby food king.
Silly but quite pleasant comedy variation on *Bachelor Mother*.

w Everett Freeman, Harry Kurnitz *d* Bretaigne Windust *ph* Peverell Marley *m* David Buttolph

Betsy Drake, Edmund Gwenn, Dennis Morgan, Zachary Scott, William Frawley

Pretty Baby
US 1978 109m Metrocolor
Paramount (Louis Malle)

A 12-year-old girl grows up in a New Orleans brothel.
Tedious elaboration of a sensational subject; neither good art nor good commerce.

w Polly Platt, Louis Malle *d* Louis Malle *ph* Sven Nykvist *md* Jerry Wexler

Keith Carradine, Susan Sarandon, Brooke Shields, Francis Faye, Antonio Fargas

AAN: Jerry Wexler

Pretty in Pink
US 1986 96m Technicolor

A pretty girl from the wrong side of the tracks begins to find herself when she goes to a classy high school. Slick but not very interesting look at the insecurities of American adolescents. Molly Ringwald, Harry Dean Stanton, Jon Cryer, Andrew McCarthy, Annie Potts. Written by John Hughes; directed by Howard Deutch; for Lauren Shuler/Paramount.

Pretty Ladies
US 1925 70m at 24 fps bw silent

The husband of a Broadway actress leaves her for a chorus girl. Heavy-going melodrama with a star who later turned comedienne and a couple of stars-to-be playing bits. Zasu Pitts, Tom Moore, Norma Shearer, Lilyan Tashman, Conrad Nagel, George K. Arthur, Myrna Loy, Joan Crawford. Written by Adela Rogers St John; directed by Monta Bell; for MGM.

Pretty Maids All in a Row
US 1971 95m Metrocolor
MGM (Gene Roddenberry)

High school girl students are being murdered by their guidance counsellor.
Uneasy murder comedy with few laughs, casting its star as a most unlikely villain. An interesting if unsuccessful attempt to be different.

w Gene Roddenberry, *novel* Francis Pollini *d* Roger Vadim *ph* Charles Rosher *m* Lalo Schifrin

Rock Hudson, Angie Dickinson, Telly Savalas, Roddy McDowall, Keenan Wynn

Pretty Poison*
US 1968 89m De Luxe
TCF / Lawrence Turman / Mollino (Marshal Backlar, Noel Black)

A psychotic arsonist enlists the aid of a teenager but soon discovers she is kinkier than he and has murder in mind.
Bizarre black comedy-melodrama, quite successfully mixed and served.

w Lorenzo Semple Jnr, *novel* She Let Him Continue by Stephen Geller *d Noel Black* *ph* David Quaid *m* Johnny Mandel

Anthony Perkins, Tuesday Weld, Beverly Garland, John Randolph, Dick O'Neill, Clarice Blackburn

Pretty Polly
GB 1967 102m Techniscope
Universal / George W. George, Frank Granat
US title: *A Matter of Innocence*

On a world tour with her vulgar aunt, a timid maiden finds romance in Singapore.
Slight romantic fable decked out with travel guide backgrounds and at odds with the cynicism of the short story from which it originates.

w Keith Waterhouse, Willis Hall, *story* Noel Coward *d* Guy Green *ph* Arthur Ibbetson *m* Michel Legrand

Hayley Mills, Trevor Howard, Shashi Kapoor, Brenda de Banzie, Dick Patterson, Peter Bayliss, Patricia Routledge, Dorothy Alison

'It came and went this winter, leaving a slight trace of camphor and old knitting needles.'—*Wilfrid Sheed*

The Price of Fear
US 1956 79m bw
Universal-International (Howard Christie)

A lady hit-and-run driver falls for a man on the run from racketeers but plans to give him away in order to save herself.
Vaguely unpleasing programmer in which nobody is sympathetic.

w Robert Tallman *d* Abner Biberman *ph* Irving Glassberg *md* Joseph Gershenson

Merle Oberon, Lex Barker, Charles Drake, Gia Scala, Warren Stevens

Prick up your Ears**
GB 1987 108m Eastmancolor
Zenith / Civilhand (Andrew Brown)

The life and violent death of Joe Orton, playwright. Raunchy homosexual saga of a writer who became a cult figure with the sophisticated; treatment full of vigour for those who can take the pace.

w Alan Bennett from the biography by John Lahr *d* Stephen Frears *ph* Oliver Stapleton *m* Stanley Myers *pd* Hugo Luczyc-Wyhowski

Gary Oldman, Alfred Molina, Vanessa Redgrave, Wallace Shawn, Julie Walters, James Grant

'Five charming sisters on the gayest, merriest manhunt that ever snared a bewildered bachelor! Girls! take a lesson from these husband hunters!'

Pride and Prejudice***
US 1940 116m bw
MGM (Hunt Stromberg)

An opinionated young lady of the early 19th-century wins herself a rich husband she had at first despised for his pride.
A pretty respectable version of Jane Austen's splendid romantic comedy, with a generally excellent cast; full of pleasurable moments.

w Aldous Huxley, Jane Murfin, *play* Helen Jerome, *novel Jane Austen* *d Robert Z. Leonard* *ph* Karl Freund *m* Herbert Stothart

Laurence Olivier, Greer Garson, Edmund Gwenn, Mary Boland, Melville Cooper, Edna May Oliver, Karen Morley, Frieda Inescort, Bruce Lester, Edward Ashley, Ann Rutherford, Maureen O'Sullivan, E. E. Clive, Heather Angel, Marsha Hunt

'The most deliciously pert comedy of old manners, the most crisp and crackling satire in costume that we can remember ever having seen on the screen.'—*Bosley Crowther*

'Animated and bouncing, the movie is more Dickens than Austen; once one adjusts to this, it's a happy and carefree viewing experience.'—*New Yorker, 1980*

The Pride and the Passion*
US 1957 131m Technicolor Vistavision
UA / Stanley Kramer

In 1810 Spain a British naval officer helps Spanish guerrillas, by reactivating an old cannon, to win their fight against Napoleon.
Stolid, miscast adventure spectacle, its main interest being the deployment of the gun across country by surging throngs of peasants.

w Edna and Edward Anhalt, *novel* The Gun by C. S. Forester *d* Stanley Kramer *ph Franz Planer* *m* Georges Antheil

Cary Grant, Sophia Loren, Frank Sinatra, Theodore Bikel, John Wengraf, Jay Novello, Philip Van Zandt

'The whirr of the cameras often seems as loud as the thunderous cannonades. It evidently takes more than dedication, co-operative multitudes and four million dollars to shoot history in the face.'—*Time*

The Pride of St Louis
US 1952 93m bw
TCF (Jules Schermer)

The life of baseball star Dizzy Dean, who injured himself and became a commentator.
Sporting biopic of clearly restricted interest; modestly well done.

w Herman J. Mankiewicz *d* Harmon Jones *ph* Leo Tover *m* Arthur Lange

Dan Dailey, Joanne Dru, Richard Haydn, Richard Crenna, Hugh Sanders

AAN: original story (Guy Trosper)

Pride of the Marines*
US 1945 120m bw
Warner (Jerry Wald)
GB title: *Forever in Love*

The story of Marine Al Schmid, blinded while fighting the Japanese.
Over-dramatic, sudsy biopic which is well enough mounted to carry quite an impact in the flagwaving Hollywood style.

w Albert Maltz *d* Delmer Daves *ph* Peverell Marley *m* Franz Waxman

John Garfield, Eleanor Parker, Dane Clark, John Ridgely, Rosemary de Camp, Ann Doran, Warren Douglas, Tom D'Andrea

'Long drawn out and never inspired, but very respectably honest and dogged.'—*James Agee*

AAN: Albert Maltz

'The most wonderful story America ever took to its heart!'

The Pride of the Yankees*
US 1942 128m bw
Samuel Goldwyn

The story of baseball star Lou Gehrig, who died of amytropic lateral sclerosis at the height of his powers.
Standard sporting biopic ending on Gehrig's famous speech to the crowd; emotion covers the film's other deficiencies.

w Jo Swerling, Herman J. Mankiewicz, *story* Paul Gallico *d* Sam Wood *ph* Rudolph Maté *m* Leigh Harline *pd* William Cameron Menzies *ed* Daniel Mandell

Gary Cooper, Teresa Wright, Babe Ruth, Walter Brennan, Dan Duryea, Elsa Janssen, Ludwig Stossel, Virginia Gilmore

'A simple, tender, meticulous and explicitly narrative film . . . a real saga of American life, homey, humorous, sentimental, and composed in patient detail.'—*New York Times*

AA: Daniel Mandell

THE PRIME MINISTER. Queen Victoria (Fay Compton, with a patently false nose) and Disraeli (John Gielgud) try to outstare each other.

AAN: best picture; script; Paul Gallico; Rudolph Maté; Leigh Harline; Gary Cooper; Teresa Wright

'Their extravagant romance was more tempestuous than anything he wrote!'

Priest of Love
GB 1981 125m colour
Ronceval / Milesian (Stanley J. Seeger)

The last years of D. H. Lawrence, when his books were banned and he was seeking warmer climes to help his TB.
An extremely disappointing film, seeming to consist of aimless travelling by fractious people who never have anything interesting to say. Stilted in all departments.

w Alan Plater *d* Christopher Miles *ph* Ted Moore *m* Joseph James

Ian McKellen, Janet Suzman, Helen Mirren, Penelope Keith, Jorge Rivero, John Gielgud
'Miles has assigned himself a missionary role but he is just not up to the task.'—*Jill Forbes, MFB*

Prime Cut
US 1972 91m Technicolor Panavision
Cinema Center (Joe Wizan)

A Kansas gangster incurs the wrath of his Chicago bosses, and a hired killer is sent to eliminate him.
Gory cat-and-mouse chase melodrama with no interest save its excesses.

w Robert Dillon *d* Michael Ritchie *ph* Gene Polito *m* Lalo Schifrin

Gene Hackman, Lee Marvin, Angel Tompkins, Sissy Spacek

The Prime Minister*
GB 1940 109m bw
Warner (Max Milder)

Episodes in the life of Disraeli.
Modestly budgeted historical pageant notable only for performances.

w Brock Williams, Michael Hogan *d* Thorold Dickinson *ph* Basil Emmott

John Gielgud, Diana Wynyard, Will Fyffe, Stephen Murray, Owen Nares, Fay Compton (as Queen Victoria), Lyn Harding, Leslie Perrins

The Prime of Miss Jean Brodie*
GB 1969 116m De Luxe
TCF (Robert Fryer)

A sharp-minded Edinburgh schoolmistress of the thirties is a bad influence on her more easily-swayed pupils.
Interesting but slackly handled and maddeningly played character drama.

w Jay Presson Allen, *novel* Muriel Spark *d* Ronald Neame *ph* Ted Moore *m* Rod McKuen *pd* John Howell

Maggie Smith, Robert Stephens, Pamela Franklin, Celia Johnson, Gordon Jackson, Jane Carr

'The novel lost a good deal in its stage simplification, and loses still more in its movie reduction of that stage version.'—*John Simon*

AA: Maggie Smith
AAN: song 'Jean' (*m* / *ly* Rod McKuen)

The Primrose Path
US 1940 92m bw
RKO (Gregory La Cava)

The youngest of a family of shanty-town prostitutes falls in love with an honest hamburger stand proprietor.
Downright peculiar melodrama for its day and age, and not very entertaining either, spending most of its time being evasive.

w Allan Scott, Gregory La Cava, *play* Robert Buckner, Walter Hart, *novel* February Hill by Victoria Lincoln *d* Gregory La Cava *ph* Joseph H. August *m* Werner Heymann

Ginger Rogers, Joel McCrea, Marjorie Rambeau, Henry Travers, Miles Mander, Queenie Vassar, Joan Carroll

'The story isn't good enough, the direction isn't sincere enough, to give any pain to the lumps in the throat which its designers obviously had in mind.'—*Richard Mallett, Punch*

AAN: Marjorie Rambeau

The Prince and the Pauper*
US 1937 118m bw
Warner (Robert Lord)

In Tudor London, young Edward VI changes places with a street urchin who happens to be his double.
Well-produced version of a famous story; it never quite seems to hit the right style or pace, but is satisfying in patches.

w Laird Doyle, *novel* Mark Twain *d* William Keighley *ph* Sol Polito *m Erich Wolfgang Korngold*

Errol Flynn, Claude Rains, Billy and Bobby Mauch, Henry Stephenson, Barton MacLane, Alan Hale, Eric Portman, Montagu Love (as Henry VIII), Lionel Pape, Halliwell Hobbes, Fritz Leiber

'Lavish but not convincing. Doubtful box office: the commercial aspect seems wholly concerned in the timeliness of a Coronation sequence and the name of Errol Flynn. It is not enough.'—*Variety*

The Prince and the Pauper*
Panama 1977 121m Technicolor Panavision
International Film Production / Ilya and Alexander Salkind (Pierre Spengler)
US title: *Crossed Swords*

Young Edward VI changes place with a beggar, who helps to expose a traitor.
Moderately well-made swashbuckler with an old-fashioned air, not really helped by stars in cameo roles or by the poor playing of the title roles.

w George MacDonald Fraser, *novel* Mark Twain *d* Richard Fleischer *ph* Jack Cardiff *m* Maurice Jarre *pd* Anthony Pratt

Mark Lester, Oliver Reed, Raquel Welch, Ernest Borgnine, George C. Scott, Rex Harrison, David Hemmings, Charlton Heston (as Henry VIII), Harry Andrews, Murray Melvin, Julian Orchard

The Prince and the Showgirl*
GB 1957 117m Technicolor
Warner / Marilyn Monroe Productions (Laurence Olivier)

In London for the 1911 coronation, a Ruritanian prince picks up a chorus girl and they come to understand and respect each other.
Heavy-going comedy, rich in production values but weak in dramatic style and impact.

w Terence Rattigan, from his play The Sleeping Prince *d* Laurence Olivier *ph* Jack Cardiff *m* Richard Addinsell *pd* Roger Furse *ad* Carmen Dillon

Laurence Olivier, Marilyn Monroe, Sybil Thorndike, Richard Wattis, Jeremy Spenser, Esmond Knight, Rosamund Greenwood, Maxine Audley

'A saga of scoundrels in a century of infamy!'
Prince of Foxes*
US 1949 107m bw
TCF (Sol. C. Siegel)

A wandering adventurer in medieval Italy gets mixed up with the Borgias.
Good-looking historical fiction with a slight edge to it.

w Milton Krims, *novel* Samuel Shellabarger *d* Henry King *ph* Leon Shamroy *m* Alfred Newman

Tyrone Power, Orson Welles, Wanda Hendrix, Felix Aylmer, Everett Sloane, Katina Paxinou, Marina Berti

'Plot, counterplot, action and vengeance.'—*MFB*

'This pretentious chapter of pseudo-history never rises above the merely spectacular, hovers mostly around the conventionally banal, and descends once to the unpardonably crude.'—*Richard Mallett, Punch*

AAN: Leon Shamroy

Prince of Pirates
US 1953 80m Technicolor

A young prince of the Netherlands turns pirate when his brother allies with the Spanish invader. Fast-moving costume potboiler with lavish use of action scenes from *Joan of Arc*. John Derek, Barbara Rush, Carla Balenda, Whitfield Connor, Edgar Barrier. Written by John O'Dea and Samuel Newman; directed by Sidney Salkow; for Columbia.

Prince of Players*
US 1955 102m De Luxe Cinemascope
TCF (Philip Dunne)

Episodes in the life of actor Edwin Booth, brother of the man who killed Abraham Lincoln.
Earnest but ham-fisted biopic more notable, as a Hollywood entertainment, for its dollops of straight Shakespeare than for any dramatic interest.

w Moss Hart, *book* Eleanor Ruggles *d* Philip Dunne *ph* Charles G. Clarke *m* Bernard Herrmann

Richard Burton, Eva Le Gallienne, Maggie McNamara, John Derek, Raymond Massey, Charles Bickford, Elizabeth Sellars, Ian Keith

Prince of the City*
US 1981 167m Technicolor
Warner / Orion (Jay Presson Allen)

A New York policeman on the drug beat is induced to inform on his corrupt colleagues.
Punishingly long police semi-documentary based on real events and apparently filmed with a political motive. Excellent acting and production detail do not prevent the enterprise from seeming like a half-speed version of *Serpico*.

w Jay Presson Allen, Sidney Lumet, *book* Robert Daley *d* Sidney Lumet

Treat Williams, Jerry Orbach, Don Billett, Richard Foronjy, Carmine Caridi, Kenny Marino

AAN: screenplay

Prince of Thieves
US 1948 72m bw

Robin Hood saves a nobleman's intended from Baron Tristram. Tatty second-feature version of a legendary figure. Jon Hall, Patricia Morison, Alan Mowbray, Michael Duane, Adele Jergens. Written by Maurice Tombragel; directed by Howard Bretherton; for Sam Katzman / Columbia.

Prince Valiant*
US 1954 100m Technicolor Cinemascope
TCF (Robert L. Jacks)

The son of the exiled king of Scandia seeks King Arthur's help against the usurper, and becomes involved in a court plot.
Agreeable historical nonsense for teenagers, admittedly and sometimes hilariously from a comic strip.

w Dudley Nichols, *comic strip* Harold Foster *d* Henry Hathaway *ph* Lucien Ballard *m* Franz Waxman

Robert Wagner, James Mason, Debra Paget, Janet Leigh, Sterling Hayden, Victor McLaglen, Donald Crisp, Brian Aherne, Barry Jones, Primo Carnera

The Prince Who Was a Thief
US 1951 88m Technicolor
U-I (Leonard Goldstein)

An Arabian Nights prince is lost as a baby and brought up by thieves, but finally fights back to his rightful throne.
Given the synopsis, any viewer can write the script himself. Standard eastern western romp.

w Gerald Drayson Adams, Aeneas Mackenzie, *story* Theodore Dreiser *d* Rudolph Maté *ph* Irving Glassberg *m* Hans Salter

Tony Curtis, Piper Laurie, Everett Sloane, Jeff Corey

The Princess and the Pirate*
US 1944 94m Technicolor
Samuel Goldwyn (Don Hartman)

An impostor is on the run from a vicious pirate.
Typical star costume extravaganza with fewer laughs than you'd expect.

w Don Hartman, Melville Shavelson, Everett Freeman *d* David Butler *ph* William Snyder, Victor Milner *m* David Rose

Bob Hope, Virginia Mayo, Victor McLaglen, Walter Slezak, Walter Brennan, Marc Lawrence, Hugo Haas, Maude Eburne

'From start to finish, Hope dominates the action with well-timed colloquial nifties.'—*Variety*

AAN: David Rose

The Princess Bride*
US 1987 98m De Luxe
Act III (Andrew Scheinmann, Rob Reiner)

Grandfather tells a fairy tale of good and evil.
Rather strained fantasy with occasional bright moments.

w William Goldman from his novel *d* Rob Reiner *ph* Adrian Biddle *m* Mark Knopfler *pd* Norman Garwood

Cary Elwes, Mandy Patinkin, Chris Sarandon, Christopher Guest, Peter Falk, Wallace Shawn

AAN: song 'Storybook Love'

Princess Charming
GB 1934 78m bw

A Ruritanian revolution forces a princess to escape in disguise. Light operetta with an intriguing cast. Evelyn Laye, Yvonne Arnaud, George Grossmith, Max Miller, Henry Wilcoxon, Ivor Barnard, Francis L. Sullivan. Written by L. DuGarde Peach, Arthur Wimperis and Lauri Wylie, from the play *Alexandra* by F. Martos; directed by Maurice Elvey; for Gainsborough. 'Still just below the peak of excellence for which Hollywood is noted.'—*Variety*

The Princess Comes Across*
US 1936 76m bw
Paramount (Arthur Hornblow Jnr)

A starstruck Brooklyn girl makes a transatlantic liner voyage disguised as a princess, and finds herself involved in a murder mystery.
Zany comedy thriller with plenty of jokes.

w Walter de Leon, Frances Martin, Frank Butler, Don Hartman, Philip MacDonald, *novel* Louis Lucien Rogger *d* William K. Howard *ph* Ted Tetzlaff *m* Phil Boutelje

Carole Lombard, Fred MacMurray, Alison Skipworth, Douglass Dumbrille, William Frawley, Porter Hall, George Barbier, Lumsden Hare, Sig Rumann, Mischa Auer, Tetsu Komai

Princess of the Nile
US 1954 71m Technicolor

An Egyptian princess of the middle ages leads her country against the invasion of a bedouin prince. Lethargic costume piece with hopelessly miscast actors. Debra Paget, Michael Rennie, Jeffrey Hunter, Dona Drake, Edgar Barrier, Jack Elam, Lee Van Cleef. Written by Gerald Drayson Adams; directed by Harmon Jones; for TCF.

Princess O'Hara
US 1935 79m bw

In her father's memory a girl steals the racehorse he loved. Sentimental comedy from Damon Runyon, later remade for Abbott and Costello as *Money from Home*. Not up to much in either version. Jean Parker, Chester Morris, Leon Errol, Vince Barnett, Henry Armetta, Ralph Remley, Clara Blandick. Written by Doris Malloy, Harry Clork; directed by David Burton; for Universal. 'Poor construction limits this one's chances . . . not likely to go above average grosses.'—*Variety*

Princess O'Rourke
US 1943 94m bw
Warner (Hal B. Wallis)

An ace pilot falls for a princess and causes diplomatic complications.
Very thin wartime comedy with a propaganda ending involving Franklin Roosevelt.

wd Norman Krasna *ph* Ernest Haller *m* Frederick Hollander

Olivia de Havilland, Robert Cummings, Charles Coburn, Jack Carson, Jane Wyman, Harry Davenport, Gladys Cooper, Minor Watson, Curt Bois

AA: Norman Krasna (as writer)

Priorities on Parade
US 1942 79m bw

Members of a swing band get jobs in a munitions factory. Inept propaganda musical. Ann Miller, Johnnie Johnston, Jerry Colonna, Betty Jane Rhodes, Vera Vague, Eddie Quillan, The Debonaires. Written by Art Arthur and Frank Loesser; directed by Albert S. Rogell; for Sol C. Siegel / Paramount. 'Manifestly just another of the misfortunes of war.'—*Variety*

Prison Farm
US 1938 69m bw

A girl denounces her boy friend when he is wanted for robbery and murder. Good example of this studio's tour of criminals and penal institutions. Lloyd Nolan, Shirley Ross, John Howard, J. Carrol Naish, Porter Hall, Anna Q. Nilsson, Esther Dale, May Boley. Written by Eddie Welch, Robert Yost, Stuart Anthony; directed by Louis King; for Paramount. 'First-rate entertainment despite lightweight star names.'—*Variety*

Prison without Bars
GB 1938 80m bw

The newest inmate of a reform school for girls vies with the superintendent for the love of the doctor. Basically paperback trash, this film of a notorious original was shot in three languages, but the English version at least omitted the lesbianism, except by implication. Cinematically it was without style. Edna Best, Corinne Luchaire, Barry K. Barnes, Mary Morris, Lorraine Clewes, Martita Hunt, Glynis Johns. Written by Hans Wilhelm, Margaret Kennedy and Arthur Wimperis, from the play by Kaus, Eis and Koveloff; directed by Brian Desmond Hurst; for Alexander Korda / Irving Asher.

The Prisoner*
GB 1955 91m bw
(Columbia) Facet / London Independent Producers (Vivian A. Cox)

In a European totalitarian state, a Cardinal is tortured and brainwashed.
Virtually a two-character talkpiece from an offbeat play which should have stayed in the theatre.

w Bridget Boland, from her play *d* Peter Glenville *ph* Reg Wyer *m* Benjamin Frankel

Alec Guinness, Jack Hawkins, Wilfrid Lawson, Kenneth Griffith, Ronald Lewis, Raymond Huntley

'And you think you've got problems?'
The Prisoner of Second Avenue*
US 1975 98m Technicolor Panavision
Warner (Melvin Frank)

A New York clerk and his wife are driven to distraction by the problems of urban living.
Gloomier-than-usual (from this author) collection of one-liners which almost turns into a psychopathic melodrama and causes its amiable leading players to overact horrendously.

w Neil Simon, from his play *d* Melvin Frank *ph* Philip Lathrop *m* Marvin Hamlisch

Jack Lemmon, Anne Bancroft, Gene Saks, Elizabeth Wilson

The Prisoner of Shark Island**
US 1936 95m bw
TCF (Darryl F. Zanuck)

The story of the doctor who treated the assassin of President Lincoln.
Well-mounted historical semi-fiction with excellent detail.

w Nunnally Johnson d John Ford ph Bert Glennon md Louis Silvers

Warner Baxter, Gloria Stuart, Joyce Kay, Claude Gillingwater, Douglas Wood, Harry Carey, Paul Fix, John Carradine

'Strong film fare for men; will have to be sold for femme appeal.'—*Variety*

'A powerful film, rarely false or slow, maintaining the relentless cumulative pressure, the logical falling of one thing into another, until the audience is included in the movement and carried along with it in some definite emotional life that is peculiar to the art of motion pictures at its best.'—*Otis Ferguson*

Prisoner of War
US 1954 81m bw
MGM (Henry Berman)

Life in a communist prison camp in Korea. Sensational propaganda, reduced to comic strip level.

w Allen Rivkin *d* Andrew Marton *ph* Robert Planck *m* Jeff Alexander

Ronald Reagan, Steve Forrest, Dewey Martin, Oscar Homolka, Robert Horton, Paul Stewart, Henry Morgan, Stephen Bekassy

'It presents its catalogue of horrors in a manner unworthy of the cause it attempts to uphold.'—*John Gillett*

The Prisoner of Zenda****
US 1937 101m bw
David O. Selznick

An Englishman on holiday in Ruritania finds himself helping to defeat a rebel plot by impersonating the kidnapped king at his coronation.
A splendid schoolboy adventure story is perfectly transferred to the screen in this exhilarating swashbuckler, one of the most entertaining films to come out of Hollywood.

w John Balderston, Wills Root, Donald Ogden Stewart, novel Anthony Hope d John Cromwell ph James Wong Howe m Alfred Newman

Ronald Colman, Douglas Fairbanks Jnr, Madeleine Carroll, David Niven, Raymond Massey, Mary Astor, *C. Aubrey Smith*, Byron Foulger, Montagu Love

'The most pleasing film that has come along in ages.'—*New York Times*

'One of those rare movies that seem, by some magic trick, to become more fascinating and beguiling with each passing year.'—*John Cutts, 1971*

† Previously filmed in 1913 and 1922.

AAN: Alfred Newman

The Prisoner of Zenda*
US 1952 100m Technicolor
MGM (Pandro S. Berman)

A costly scene-for-scene remake which only goes to show that care and discretion are no match for the happy inspiration of the original.

w John Balderston, Noel Langley *d* Richard Thorpe *ph* Joseph Ruttenberg *m Alfred Newman*

Stewart Granger, James Mason, Deborah Kerr, Robert Coote, Robert Douglas, Jane Greer, Louis Calhern, Francis Pierlot, Lewis Stone

The Prisoner of Zenda
US 1979 108m Technicolor
Universal (Walter Mirisch)

Palpably uneasy version of the above which teeters between comedy and straight romance, with barely a moment of real zest creeping in. The star is way off form in both roles.

w Dick Clement, Ian La Frenais *d* Richard Quine *ph* Arthur Ibbetson *m* Henry Mancini *pd* John J. Lloyd

Peter Sellers, Lynne Frederick, Lionel Jeffries, Elke Sommer, Gregory Sierra, Stuart Wilson, Jeremy Kemp, Catherine Schell, Simon Williams, Norman Rossington, John Laurie

'Flatly directed, leadenly unfunny.'—*Paul Taylor, MFB*

Prisoners of the Casbah
US 1953 78m Technicolor

An Eastern princess and her lover take refuge from the evil Grand Vizier in the Casbah, a haven for outcasts. Inept sword and sandal actioner; you can almost smell the Turkish delight. Gloria Grahame, Cesar Romero, Turhan Bey, Nestor Paiva. Written by DeVallon Scott; directed by Richard Bare; for Sam Katzman / Columbia.

Private Affairs
US 1940 74m bw

A girl with problems seeks out the father she has never met. Thin comedy with a pleasant cast. Nancy Kelly, Robert Cummings, Roland Young, Hugh Herbert, Montagu Love, Jonathan Hale. Written by Charles Grayson, Leonard Spiegelgass and Peter Milne, from a story by Walter Green; directed by Albert S. Rogell; for Universal.

'All women take to men who have the appearance of wickedness!'

The Private Affairs of Bel Ami*
US 1947 119m bw
UA / David L. Loew (Ray Heinz)

In nineties Paris, a career journalist climbs to fame over the ruined lives of his friends. Tame and stuffy adaptation of an incisive novel, rather poorly produced.

wd Albert Lewin, *novel* Guy de Maupassant *ph* Russell Metty *m* Darius Milhaud

George Sanders, Angela Lansbury, Ann Dvorak, Frances Dee, John Carradine, Hugo Haas, Marie Wilson, Albert Basserman, Warren William

Private Angelo
GB 1949 106m bw
Pilgrim (Peter Ustinov)

An Italian soldier hates war and spends World War II on the run from both sides.
Listless satirical comedy that just isn't funny enough.

w Peter Ustinov, Michael Anderson, *novel* Eric Linklater *d* Peter Ustinov *ph* Erwin Hillier

Peter Ustinov, Godfrey Tearle, Robin Bailey, Maria Denis, Marjorie Rhodes, James Robertson Justice, Moyna McGill

Private Benjamin
US 1980 110m Technicolor
Warner / Hawn–Myers–Shyer–Miller

A well-heeled Jewish widow, at a crossroads in her life, joins the army.
Half-assed attempt at combining slapstick, character study, sentiment, sex and a recruiting poster. Some funny moments don't really make it worth sitting through.

w Nancy Meyers, Charles Shyer, Harvey Miller *d* Howard Zieff *ph* David M. Walsh *m* Bill Conti

Goldie Hawn, Eileen Brennan, Armand Assante, Robert Webber, Sam Wanamaker, Barbara Barrie, Harry Dean Stanton

AAN: screenplay; Goldie Hawn; Eileen Brennan (supporting actress)

Private Buckaroo
US 1942 68m bw

The difficulties of putting on shows for soldiers. Slaphappy second feature worth preserving for the talent. The Andrews Sisters, Harry James and his Orchestra, Joe E. Lewis, Donald O'Connor, Peggy Ryan, Huntz Hall, Ernest Truex, Shemp Howard. Written by Edmund Kelso and Edmund James; directed by Edward Cline; for Universal.

The Private Files of J. Edgar Hoover*
US 1978 112m Movielab
AIP / Larco (Larry Cohen)

The supposedly true facts of the career of the longtime head of the FBI.
Unreliable exposé with some interesting bits.

wd Larry Cohen *ph* Paul Glickman *m* Miklos Rosza

Broderick Crawford, Jose Ferrer, Michael Parks, Ronee Blakely, Rip Torn, Celeste Holm, Dan Dailey, Raymond St Jacques, Howard Da Silva, June Havoc, John Marley, Andrew Duggan, Lloyd Nolan

A Private Function**
GB 1984 94m colour
Handmade (Mark Shivas)

In 1947 Yorkshire, a doctor and his family secretly fatten an unlicensed pig.
Sharply-detailed comedy typical of its author, but less likeable than many.

w Alan Bennett *d* Malcolm Mowbray *ph* Tony Pierce-Roberts *m* John Du Prez *pd* Stuart Walker *ed* Barrie Vince

Michael Palin, Maggie Smith, Denholm Elliott, Richard Griffiths, Tony Haygarth, *Liz Smith*, John Normington

BFA: Maggie Smith; Liz Smith (supporting actress); Denholm Elliott (supporting actor)

Private Hell 36*
US 1954 81m bw

Two cops on a robbery trail find the loot and keep it for themselves. Predictable but stylish *film noir*, still moderately watchable. Ida Lupino, Steve Cochran, Howard Duff, Dean Jagger, Dorothy Malone. Written by Collier Young, Ida Lupino; directed by *Don Siegel*; for Filmakers.

Private Izzy Murphy
US 1926 80m approx at 24 fps bw silent

A Jewish boy loves a Catholic girl. Dreary variant on *Abie's Irish Rose,* popular enough for a 1927 sequel called *Sailor Izzy Murphy*. George Jessel, Patsy Ruth Miller, Vera Gordon. Written by Philip Lonergan; directed by Lloyd Bacon; for Warner.

The Private Life of Don Juan
GB 1934 90m bw
London Films (Alexander Korda)

In 17th-century Spain, the famous lover fakes death and makes a comeback in disguise. Lacklustre frolic by an overage star through dismal sets. The production was meant to extend the success of *The Private Life of Henry VIII*, but totally failed to do so.

w Lajos Biro, Frederick Lonsdale, *play* Henri Bataille *d* Alexander Korda *ph* Georges Périnal *m* Ernst Toch

Douglas Fairbanks, Merle Oberon, Binnie Barnes, Benita Hume, Joan Gardner, Melville Cooper, Athene Seyler, Owen Nares

'Technically it has so much in its favour that it's too bad it doesn't promise solid b.o. attraction.'—*Variety*

'One of those ideas that never really take off.'—*New Yorker, 1977*

'The things I do for England!'

The Private Life of Henry VIII***
GB 1933 97m bw
London Films (*Alexander Korda*)

How Henry beheaded his second wife and acquired four more.
This never was a perfect film, but certain scenes are very funny and its sheer sauciness established the possibility of British films making money abroad, as well as starting several star careers. It now looks very dated and even amateurish in parts.

w Lajos Biro, Arthur Wimperis d Alexander Korda *ph* Georges Périnal *m* Kurt Schroeder

Charles Laughton, Elsa Lanchester, Robert Donat, Merle Oberon, Binnie Barnes, Franklin Dyall, Miles Mander, Wendy Barrie, Claud Allister, Everly Gregg

'Among the best anywhere and by far the top British picture . . . figures a sock entry, especially for the best houses.'—*Variety*

AA: Charles Laughton
AAN: best picture

The Private Life of Sherlock Holmes***
GB 1970 125m De Luxe Panavision
UA / Phalanx / Mirisch / Sir Nigel (Billy Wilder)

A secret Watson manuscript reveals cases in which Sherlock Holmes became involved with women.
What started as four stories is reduced to two, one brightly satirical and the other no more than a careful and discreet recreation, with the occasional jocular aside, of the flavour of the stories themselves. A very civilized and pleasing entertainment except for the hurried rounding-off which is a let-down.

w Billy Wilder, I. A. L. Diamond d Billy Wilder *ph* Christopher Challis *m* Miklos Rozsa *ad Alexander Trauner*

Robert Stephens, Colin Blakely, Genevieve Page, Clive Revill, Christopher Lee, Catherine Lacey, Stanley Holloway

'Affectionately conceived and flawlessly executed.'—*NFT, 1974*

'Wilder's least embittered film, and by far his most moving. Great.'—*Time Out, 1984*

Private Lives*
US 1931 82m bw
MGM (Albert Lewin)

Ex-marrieds desert their intended new spouses to try each other again.
An essentially theatrical comedy, and a great one, seems somewhat slow-witted on film.

w Hans Kraly, Richard Schayer, *play* Noel Coward *d* Sidney Franklin *ph* Ray Binger

Norma Shearer, Robert Montgomery, Reginald Denny, Una Merkel, Jean Hersholt

'Stars are a big asset to this parlour comedy which will amuse the women more than the men.'—*Variety*

'For polish, few comedies of the thirties can equal this early alliance of cinema and stage.'—*John Baxter, 1968*

The Private Lives of Elizabeth and Essex**
US 1939 106m Technicolor
Warner (Robert Lord)
reissue title: *Elizabeth the Queen*

Elizabeth I falls in love with the Earl of Essex, but events turn him into a rebel and she has to order his execution.
Unhistorical history given the grand treatment; a Hollywood picture book, not quite satisfying dramatically despite all the effort.

w Norman Reilly Raine, Aeneas Mackenzie, *play* Elizabeth the Queen by Maxwell Anderson *d* Michael Curtiz *ph* Sol Polito *m* Erich Wolfgang Korngold

Bette Davis, Errol Flynn, Olivia de Havilland, Donald Crisp, Vincent Price, Alan Hale, Henry Stephenson, Henry Daniell, Leo G. Carroll, Nanette Fabray, Robert Warwick, John Sutton

'Solid box office material, with fine grosses and holdovers indicated . . . in all technical departments, picture has received topnotch investiture.'—*Variety*

'A rather stately, rigorously posed and artistically technicolored production.'—*Frank S. Nugent*

AAN: Sol Polito; Erich Wolfgang Korngold

The Private Navy of Sergeant O'Farrell
US 1968 92m Technicolor
Hope Enterprises (John Beck)

After World War II, military personnel congregate on an island which has been by-passed by hostilities.
Nothing much wrong with the plot, but at this time in his career Hope seemed unable to do anything right, and the film was barely released.

wd Frank Tashlin *ph* Alan Stensvold *m* Harry Stikman

Bob Hope, Gina Lollobrigida, Phyllis Diller, Jeffrey Hunter, Mylene Demongeot, Henry Wilcoxon

Private Number
US 1936 80m bw
TCF (Raymond Griffith)
GB title: *Secret Interlude*

A wealthy young man keeps a secret of his marriage to a housemaid.
Warmed-over class melodrama previously filmed in 1930 as *Common Clay*. Adequate within its lights.

w Gene Markey, William Conselman, *play* Common Clay by Cleves Kinkead *d* Roy del Ruth *ph* Peverell Marley *m* Louis Silvers

Loretta Young, Robert Taylor, Basil Rathbone, Patsy Kelly, Marjorie Gateson, Paul Harvey, Monroe Owsley, John Miljan

Private Potter
GB 1962 89m bw
MGM / Ben Arbeid

A young soldier is court-martialled for cowardice but claims he had a vision of god. Stilted morality play, unpersuasively made and acted.

w Ronald Harwood, from his TV play *d* Caspar Wrede *ph* Arthur Lavis *m* George Hall

Tom Courtenay, Mogens Wieth, Ronald Fraser, James Maxwell, Ralph Michael, Brewster Mason

The Private Secretary
GB 1935 70m bw

A clerical gentleman is duped into protecting a rich young idler from his creditors. Moderately effective filming of a popular stage farce from a German original. Edward Everett Horton, Barry Mackay, Judy Gunn, Oscar Asche, Sydney Fairbrother, Alastair Sim, Michael Shepley. Written by Arthur Macrae, George Broadhurst and H. Fowler Mear, from the play by Van Moser; directed by Henry Edwards; for Twickenham.

The Private War of Major Benson
US 1955 105m Technicolor Cinemascope
U-I (Howard Pine)

A soldier with outspoken views is sent to cool off as commander of a military academy run by an order of nuns.
Cute and sentimental nonsense with unlikely situations, a martinet becoming soft-centred and a happy-ever-after finale.

w William Roberts, Richard Alan Simmons *d* Jerry Hopper *ph* Harold Lipstein *m* Henry Mancini, Herman Stein

Charlton Heston, Julie Adams, Tim Hovey, William Demarest, Tim Considine, Sal Mineo, Nana Bryant, Milburn Stone, Mary Field

AAN: original story (Bob Mosher, Joe Connelly)

'She loved a man who did not exist—except in her own private world!'

Private Worlds*
US 1935 84m bw
Paramount (Walter Wanger)

Romance among the doctors at a mental hospital.
Melodrama treated with what was at the time unexpected seriousness.

w Lynn Starling, *novel* Phyllis Bottome *d* Gregory La Cava *ph* Leon Shamroy *m* Heinz Roemheld

Claudette Colbert, Charles Boyer, Joel McCrea, Joan Bennett, Helen Vinson, Esther Dale, Samuel S. Hinds

'Fine but not too artistic production . . . woman's picture of fair b.o. potentialities.'—*Variety*

AAN: Claudette Colbert

A Private's Affair
US 1959 92m De Luxe Cinemascope
TCF (David Weisbart)

Three army recruits form a close harmony trio and get into various scrapes.
Thin service comedy for the 'new' youth audience.

w Winston Miller *d* Raoul Walsh *ph* Charles G. Clarke *m* Cyril Mockridge

Sal Mineo, Christine Carere, Barry Coe, Barbara Eden, Gary Crosby, Terry Moore, Jim Backus, Jessie Royce Landis

Privates on Parade*
GB 1982 113m colour
Handmade (Simon Relph)

Farcical and serious incidents in the lives of an army concert party in 1948 Singapore.
Rather heavy-going comedy with much bad language and an overdose of effeminacy; on the whole no funnier than *It Ain't Half Hot, Mum*.

w Peter Nichols from his play *d* Michael Blakemore *ph* Ian Wilson *m* Denis King

John Cleese, *Denis Quilley*, Michael Elphick, Nicola Pagett, Bruce Payne, Joe Melia

Private's Progress***
GB 1956 97m bw
British Lion / Charter (Roy Boulting)

An extremely innocent young national serviceman is taught a few army dodges and becomes a dupe for jewel thieves.
Celebrated army farce with satirical pretensions; when released it had something to make everyone in Britain laugh.

w Frank Harvey, John Boulting, novel Alan Hackney *d John Boulting* *ph* Eric Cross *m* John Addison

Ian Carmichael, Terry-Thomas, Richard Attenborough, *Dennis Price,* Peter Jones, William Hartnell, Thorley Walters, Ian Bannen, Jill Adams, Victor Maddern, Kenneth Griffith, Miles Malleson, *John Le Mesurier*

Privilege*
GB 1967 103m Technicolor
Universal / Worldfilm / Memorial (John Heyman)

The publicity campaign for a pop star turns him into a religious messiah.
Rather hysterical fable for our time, undeniably forceful in spots and yawnful in others.

w Norman Bogner, *story* Johnny Speight *d Peter Watkins* *ph* Peter Suschitsky *m* Mike Leander

Paul Jones, Jean Shrimpton, Mark London, Max Bacon, Jeremy Child, James Cossins, Victor Henry

'Everything in it goes wrong, and one can do little but catalogue the failures.'—*MFB*

Privileged*
GB 1982 96m Technicolor

Oxford undergraduates rehearsing *The Duchess of Malfi* become involved in sexual intrigues which result in suicide. Highly unusual because made and funded by the students themselves, this melodrama has vivid patches but generally lacks a professional eye. Robert Woolley, Diana Katis, Hughie Grant, Victoria Studd, James Wilby. Written by Michael Hoffman, David Woollcombe and Rupert Walters; directed by Michael Hoffman; for The Oxford Film Company.

The Prize***
US 1963 135m Metrocolor Panavision
MGM / Roxbury (Pandro S. Berman)

In Stockholm during the Nobel Prize awards, a drunken American author stumbles on a spy plot.
Whatever the original novel is like, the film is a Hitchcock pastiche which works better than most Hitchcocks: suspenseful, well characterized, fast moving and funny from beginning to end.

w Ernest Lehman, novel Irving Wallace *d Mark Robson* *ph* William Daniels *m* Jerry Goldsmith

Paul Newman, Elke Sommer, *Edward G. Robinson,* Diane Baker, Kevin McCarthy, *Leo G. Carroll,* Micheline Presle

A Prize of Arms
GB 1961 105m bw
British Lion / Interstate (George Maynard)

An ex-army officer and an explosives expert plan to steal an army payroll.
Standard, pacy caper melodrama offering nothing at all new.

w Paul Ryder *d* Cliff Owen *ph* Gilbert Taylor *m* Robert Sharples

Stanley Baker, Tom Bell, Helmut Schmid, John Phillips

A Prize of Gold
GB 1955 100m Technicolor
Columbia / Warwick (Phil C. Samuel)

An American army sergeant in Berlin decides to steal a cargo of Nazi loot.
Routine caper thriller with sentimental leanings.

w Robert Buckner, John Paxton, *novel* Max Catto *d* Mark Robson *ph* Ted Moore *m* Malcolm Arnold

Richard Widmark, Mai Zetterling, Nigel Patrick, George Cole, Donald Wolfit, Andrew Ray, Joseph Tomelty, Karel Stepanek

The Prizefighter and the Lady
US 1933 102m bw
MGM (Hunt Stromberg)
GB title: *Every Woman's Man*

A boxer falls for a high class gangster's girl.
Plodding romantic melodrama, popular because it starred a real boxer.

w John Meehan, John Lee Mahin *d* W. S. Van Dyke *ph* Lester White *m* David Snell

Myrna Loy, Max Baer, Otto Kruger, Walter Huston, Jack Dempsey, Primo Carnera

'Freak Max Baer starrer, a picture that entertains in high-pressure manner.'—*Variety*

AAN: original story (Frances Marion)

Prizzi's Honor*
US 1985 129m De Luxe
ABC / John Foreman

Male and female hired killers for Mafia families fall in love but are assigned to 'hit' each other.
Critically lauded but puzzling and unsatisfactory black comedy which takes far too long to get going, is muddled in narrative, and leaves an unpleasant taste.

w Richard Condon, Janet Roach, from Condon's novel *d* John Huston *ph* Andrzej Bartkowiak *m* Alex North *pd* Dennis Washington *ed* Rudi and Kaja Fehr

Jack Nicholson, *Kathleen Turner*, Robert Loggia, William Hickey, John Randolph, *Anjelica Huston*

'Certainly one of the most curious films to kick off the summer season by an American major.'—*Variety*

AA: Anjelica Huston (supporting actress)

AAN: best picture; direction; Jack Nicholson; William Hickey; adapted screenplay; editing

BFA: adapted screenplay

The Prodigal
US 1931 76m bw

The scion of a southern plantation becomes a tramp. Pleasant minor musical with a star who never really caught on. Lawrence Tibbett, Esther Ralston, Roland Young, Cliff Edwards, Purnell Pratt, Hedda Hopper, Stepin Fetchit. Written by Bess Meredyth, Wells Root; directed by Harry Pollard; for MGM. 'Between average and good . . . should top the normal gross.'—*Variety*

'The story of woman's beauty and man's temptation!'

The Prodigal
US 1955 115m Eastmancolor Cinemascope
MGM (Charles Schnee)

The son of a Hebrew farmer falls for the high priestess of a pagan cult.
Wildly apocryphal 'biblical' story of obvious expensiveness but no merit.

w Maurice Zimm *d* Richard Thorpe *ph* Joseph Ruttenberg *m* Bronislau Kaper

Lana Turner, Edmund Purdom, Louis Calhern, James Mitchell, Walter Hampden, Francis L. Sullivan, Joseph Wiseman, Audrey Dalton, Taina Elg, Neville Brand, Cecil Kellaway

'A few lines of dialogue derive from the Bible; the rest is pure Hollywood, but

THE PRIVATE LIVES OF ELIZABETH AND ESSEX. Historically dubious but lavishly costumed: Bette Davis and Errol Flynn confront one another while Robert Warwick looks concerned.

Hollywood in its mood of sham solemnity when even the unintentional jokes are not funny.'—*MFB*

'A costume stinker . . . it should have played Disneyland!'—*Lana Turner*

The Producers*
US 1967 88m Pathecolor
Avco / Springtime / MGM / Crossbow (Sidney Glazier)

A Broadway producer seduces elderly widows to obtain finance for his new play, sells 25000 per cent in the expectation that it will flop, and is horrified when it succeeds.
Dismally unfunny satire except for the play itself, *Springtime for Hitler,* which is neatly put down. This has, however, become a cult film, so that criticism is pointless.

wd Mel Brooks *ph* Joseph Coffey *m* John Morris

Zero Mostel, Gene Wilder, Kenneth Mars, Estelle Winwood, Renee Taylor, Dick Shawn

'Over and over again promising ideas are killed off, either by over-exposure or bad timing.'—*Tom Milne*

'An almost flawless triumph of bad taste, unredeemed by wit or style.'—*Arthur Schlesinger Jnr*

AA: Mel Brooks (as writer)
AAN: Gene Wilder

Professional Soldier
US 1936 75m bw
TCF (Darryl F. Zanuck)

A kidnapper befriends the young prince who is his victim.
Predictable, polished family film.

w Gene Fowler, Howard Willis Smith, *story* Damon Runyon *d* Tay Garnett *ph* Rudolph Maté *m* Louis Silvers

Victor McLaglen, Freddie Bartholemew, Constance Collier, Gloria Stuart, Michael Whalen

'Some of the sequences are amusing; some of the action is very fast. But fundamentally the story is not believable.'—*Variety*

Professional Sweetheart
US 1933 70m bw
RKO (Merian C. Cooper)
GB title: *Imaginary Sweetheart*

A radio 'purity girl' seeks some real life romance.
Modestly smart comedy of no lasting merit.

w Maurine Watkins *d* William Seiter *ph* Edward Cronjager *m* Max Steiner

Ginger Rogers, Betty Furness, Gregory Ratoff, Sterling Holloway, Frank McHugh, Zasu Pitts, Allen Jenkins, Norman Foster, Edgar Kennedy, Franklin Pangborn

'After a fast start this radio satire loses a lot of ground . . . but comedy's there all the way.'—*Variety*

The Professionals**
US 1966 123m Technicolor Panavision
Columbia / Pax (Richard Brooks)

Skilled soldiers of fortune are hired by a millionaire rancher to get back his kidnapped wife.
Strong-flavoured star western with good suspense sequences.

wd Richard Brooks, novel A Mule for the Marquesa by Frank O'Rourke *ph* Conrad Hall *m* Maurice Jarre

Burt Lancaster, Lee Marvin, Robert Ryan, Jack Palance, Ralph Bellamy, Claudia Cardinale, Woody Strode

'After the *Lord Jim* excursion, it is good to see Brooks back on his own professional form, filming the tight, laconic sort of adventure which usually seems to bring out the best in Hollywood veterans.'—*Penelope Houston*

'It has the expertise of a cold old whore with practised hands and no thoughts of love.'—*Pauline Kael, 1968*

AAN: Richard Brooks (as writer and as director); Conrad Hall

Professor Beware*
US 1938 93m bw
Paramount

A staid professor finds himself on the run across America in pursuit of an Egyptian artefact.
Slow-starting comedy with only moments of the comedian at his best.

w Delmer Daves, Jack Cunningham, *story* Crampton Harris, Francis M. and Marian B. Cockrell *d* Elliott Nugent *ph* Archie Stout

Harold Lloyd, Phyllis Welch, Raymond Walburn, Lionel Stander, William Frawley, Thurston Hall, Cora Witherspoon, Sterling Holloway

'Both Lloyd and the audience are out of breath after 3000 miles cross country, but most of it is exhaustion from laughing.'—*Variety*

Professor Mamlock**
USSR 1938 100m bw

The leading surgeon of a Berlin hospital is driven to attempt suicide because he is a Jew.
Ironic in all kinds of ways, this quite devastating film was a unique attack by one government on a neighbouring one. S. Mezhinski, E. Nikitina, O. Zhakov. Written by Friedrich Wolf, Adolph Minkin, Herbert Rappaport; directed by Adolph Minkin and Herbert Rappaport; for Lenfilm. 'An arresting picture which is sure to arouse strenuous comment.'—*Variety*

Project X*
US 1968 97m Technicolor
Paramount / William Castle

In the year 2118, a man is scientifically induced to think he lives in the 1960s so that he can recover a lost secret.

Fearsomely complex science fiction, cheaply made but on the whole intriguingly imagined.

w Edmund Morris, *novels* Leslie P. Davies *d* William Castle *ph* Harold Stine *m* Van Cleave

Christopher George, Greta Baldwin, Henry Jones, Monte Markham, Harold Gould

The Promise
GB 1969 98m Eastmancolor
Commonwealth United / Howard and Wyndham

Two young men and a girl share a flat after the 1942 siege of Leningrad; thirteen years later, their dreams of life considerably modified, they meet again and change partners.
Talky and too carefully budgeted screen version of a somewhat pretentious play.

w Michael Hayes, *play* Aleksei Arbuzov *d* Michael Hayes *ph* Brendan Stafford *m* Iwan Williams *pd* William McCrow

Ian McKellen, John Castle, Susan Macready, Mary Jones, David Mettheim

The Promise
US 1978 97m Technicolor Panavision
Universal (Fred Weintraub, Paul Heller)
GB TV title: *Face of a Stranger*

A young man fails to recognize his lost love when her face has been rebuilt after an accident.
Rambling teenage variation on *Random Harvest*, not very well done and about forty years behind its proper times.

w Garry Michael White *d* Gilbert Cates *ph* Ralph Woolsey *m* David Shire

Kathleen Quinlan, Stephen Collins, Beatrice Straight, Larry Luckinbill, William Prince
'Appalling romantic tushery by any standards.'—*Tom Milne, MFB*

Promise at Dawn
US / France 1970 102m De Luxe
Avco / Nathalie (Jules Dassin)

The boyhood of novelist Romain Gary and the last years of his fearsome Russian Jewish actress mother with whom he traipses around Europe.
Scrappy star vehicle and unnecessary biopic in a variety of indulgent styles.

w Jules Dassin, *play* First Love by Samuel Taylor *d* Jules Dassin *ph* Jean Badal *m* Georges Delerue

Melina Mercouri, Assef Dayan

Promise Her Anything
GB 1966 97m Technicolor
Seven Arts (Stanley Rubin)

A mail order movie maker falls for a young French widow in the next flat.
Scatty comedy set in Greenwich Village and aiming in vain for a kind of frantic bohemian charm, with a baby as deus ex machina.

w William Peter Blatty *d* Arthur Hiller *ph* Douglas Slocombe *m* Lynn Murray

Warren Beatty, Leslie Caron, Hermione Gingold, Lionel Stander, Robert Cummings, Keenan Wynn, Cathleen Nesbitt

Promises in the Dark
US 1979 115m Metrocolor
Warner / Orion (Jerome Hellman)

A young girl dies of cancer.
Depressing and not particularly well done case history, a curious enterprise in view of the hundreds of television movies relentlessly exploring the same field.

w Loring Mandel *d* Jerome Hellman *ph* Adam Holender *m* Leonard Rosenman

Marsha Mason, Ned Beatty, Susan Clark, Michael Brandon, Kathleen Beller, Paul Clemens

Prophecy
US 1979 102m Movielab Panavision
Paramount (Robert L. Rosen)

In rural Maine, mercury poisoning produces huge animal mutants.
Unpleasant ecological shocker with no particular talent in evidence.

w David Seltzer *d* John Frankenheimer *ph* Harry Stradling Jnr *m* Leonard Rosenman *pd* William Craig Smith

Talia Shire, Robert Foxworth, Armand Assante, Richard Dysart

Prosperity
US 1932 90m bw

Mothers-in-law disagree about the marriage of their children. Reliable comedy of the depression, marking the last teaming of its popular stars. *Marie Dressler*, *Polly Moran,* Anita Page, Norman Foster, Henry Armetta. Written by Eve Greene and Zelda Sears; directed by Sam Wood; for MGM. 'Sure-fire money picture . . . could stand a little cutting but on the whole it's a workmanlike production.'—*Variety*

Prostitute
GB 1980 96m colour
Kestrel (Tony Garnett)

A provincial tart moves into the West End.
Downbeat, supposedly realistic documentary drama which ends up being depressing but not in the least titillating.

w Tony Garnett *ph* Charles Stewart *m* The Gangsters

Eleanor Forsythe, Kate Crutchley, Kim Lockett, Nancy Samuels

'There's something funny going on in the world of diplomacy!'

Protocol
US 1984 96m Technicolor
Warner (Anthea Sylbert)

A cocktail waitress thwarts an assassination and becomes a career diplomat.
Star comedy with Something to Say and not much to laugh at; a step down even from *Private Benjamin.*

w Buck Henry *d* Herbert Ross *ph* William A. Fraker *m* Basil Poledouris *pd* Bill Malley *ed* Paul Hirsch

Goldie Hawn, Chris Sarandon, Gail Strickland, Richard Romanus, André Gregory, Cliff de Young

The Proud and Profane
US 1956 112m bw Vistavision
Paramount (William Perlberg)

In the Pacific War a Roman Catholic widow falls for a tough Lieutenant Colonel. ('My pleasure is physical; my men call me The Beast.')
Unlikely romantic melodrama with a certain amount of plain speaking, otherwise routine.

wd George Seaton, *novel* The Magnificent Bastards by Lucy Herndon Crockett *ph* John F. Warren *m* Victor Young

William Holden, Deborah Kerr, Thelma Ritter, Dewey Martin, William Redfield

The Proud Ones
US 1956 94m Eastmancolor Cinemascope
TCF (Robert L. Jacks)

A marshal cleans up a crooked town despite the hazards of his own physical disability and a deputy who hates him.
Entertaining though rather foolishly scripted western.

w Edmund North, Joseph Patracca *d* Robert D. Webb *ph* Lucien Ballard *m* Lionel Newman

Robert Ryan, Jeffrey Hunter, Virginia Mayo, Robert Middleton

The Proud Rebel
US 1958 103m Technicolor
MGM / Sam Goldwyn Jnr

After the Civil War, a southerner wanders the Yankee states in search of a doctor to cure his mute son; he falls for a lady farmer and his son finds his voice at a crucial moment.
Pretty dim family western for pretty dim families; everything happens precisely according to plan.

w Joseph Patracca, Lillie Hayward *d* Michael Curtiz *ph* Ted McCord *m* Jerome Moross

Alan Ladd, Olivia de Havilland, David Ladd, Dean Jagger, Cecil Kellaway, Dean Stanton, Henry Hull, John Carradine, James Westerfield

The Proud Valley*
GB 1939 76m bw
Ealing (Sergei Nolbandov)

A black stoker helps unemployed Welsh miners reopen their pits.
Neat little propaganda drama.

w Roland Pertwee, Louis Golding, Jack Jones *d Pen Tennyson* *ph* Roy Kellino, Glen MacWilliams *m* Ernest Irving

Paul Robeson, Edward Chapman, Edward Rigby, *Rachel Thomas,* Simon Lack, Clifford Evans, Allan Jeayes

Providence*
France / Switzerland 1977 107m Eastmancolor
Action Film / Société Française de Production / FR3 / Citel (Philippe Dussart)

A famous writer, dying, spends a painful night in unpleasant and sometimes fantastic

recollections of his sons and their women; but the reality, when they come to lunch next day, is somewhat different.
Despite its cast and other credits, this is a repellent and not too well acted study in the lack of communication, told at undue length and in turgid colour.

w David Mercer *d* Alain Resnais *ph* Ricardo Aronovitch *m* Miklos Rozsa *ad* Jacques Saulnier

John Gielgud, Dirk Bogarde, Ellen Burstyn, David Warner, Elaine Stritch

'The movie is peculiarly fastidious and static: you feel as if it were going to dry up and blow away.'—*New Yorker*

The Prowler*
US 1951 92m bw
Horizon (Sam Spiegel)

A discontented wife thinks she sees a prowler and calls a cop; they have an affair and murder her husband.
Another variant on *Double Indemnity* and *The Postman Always Rings Twice*; the script is terse and the actors well-handled.

w Hugo Butler *d Joseph Losey* *ph* Arthur Miller *m* Lyn Murray

Van Heflin, Evelyn Keyes, John Maxwell, Katharine Warren

'A rivetingly cool, clean thriller.'—*NFT, 1973*

Prudence and the Pill*
GB 1968 92m De Luxe
TCF / Kenneth Harper, Ronald Kahn

A girl borrows her mother's contraceptive pills and replaces them with aspirin, causing no end of complications.
Self-consciously naughty sex comedy with a long dénouement and some stiff patches to affect one's enjoyment of the brighter moments.

w Hugh Mills, from his play *d* Fielder Cook *ph* Ted Moore *m* Bernard Ebbinghouse

David Niven, Deborah Kerr, Edith Evans, Keith Michell, Robert Coote, Irina Demick, Joyce Redman, Judy Geeson

'Everybody winds up pregnant to clutter the earth, apparently, with people as obnoxious as their progenitors.'—*Judith Crist*

Psyche 59
GB 1964 94m bw
Columbia / Troy / Schenck (Philip Hazelton)

A wife recovers from blindness after realizing that her husband is in love with her sister.
Pretentious melodrama with stuffy dialogue, pompous direction and irritating characters.

w Julian Halevy, *novel* Françoise de Ligneris *d* Alexander Singer *ph* Walter Lassally *m* Kenneth V. Jones

Patricia Neal, Curt Jurgens, Samantha Eggar, Ian Bannen, Beatrix Lehmann

'The screen's master of suspense moves his camera into the icy blackness of the unexplained!'
'Don't give away the ending—it's the only one we have!'

Psycho***
US 1960 109m bw
Shamley / Alfred Hitchcock

At a lonely motel vicious murders take place and are attributed to the manic mother of the young owner.
Curious shocker devised by Hitchcock as a tease and received by most critics as an unpleasant horror piece in which the main scene, the shower stabbing, was allegedly directed not by Hitchcock but by Saul Bass. After enormous commercial success it achieved classic status over the years; despite effective moments of fright, it has a childish plot and script, and its interest is that of a tremendously successful confidence trick, made for very little money by a TV crew.

w Joseph Stefano, *novel* Robert Bloch *d Alfred Hitchcock* (and *Saul Bass*) *ph* John L. Russell *m Bernard Herrmann*

Anthony Perkins, Vera Miles, John Gavin, Janet Leigh, John McIntire, Martin Balsam, Simon Oakland

'Probably the most visual, most cinematic picture he has ever made.'—*Peter Bogdanovich*

'I think the film is a reflection of a most unpleasant mind, a mean, sly, sadistic little mind.'—*Dwight MacDonald*

† When asked by the press what he used for the blood in the bath, Mr Hitchcock said: 'Chocolate sauce'.

†† This is the whole text of Hitchcock's trailer, in which he audaciously wandered round the sets and practically gave away the entire plot: Here we have a quiet little motel, tucked away off the main highway, and as you see perfectly harmless looking, whereas it has now become known as the scene of a crime. . . . This motel also has an adjunct, an old house which is, if I may say so, a little more sinister looking. And in this house the most dire, horrible events took place. I think we can go inside because the place is up for sale—though I don't know who would buy it now.

In that window in the second floor, the one in front, that's where the woman was first seen. Let's go inside. You see, even in daylight this place looks a bit sinister. It was at the top of these stairs that the second murder took place. She came out of that door there and met the victim at the top. Of course in a flash there was the knife, and in no time the victim tumbled and fell with a horrible crash. . . . I think the back broke immediately it hit the floor. It's difficult to describe the way . . . the twisting of the . . . I won't dwell on it.

Come upstairs. Of course the victim, or should I say victims, hadn't any idea of the kind of people they'd be confronted with in this house. Especially the woman. She was the weirdest and the most . . . well, let's go into her bedroom.

Here's the woman's room, still beautifully preserved. And the imprint of her body on the bed where she used to lie. I think some of her clothes are still in the wardrobe. (He looks, and shakes his head.) Bathroom.

This was the son's room but we won't go in there because his favourite spot was the little parlour behind the office in the motel. Let's go down there. This young man . . . you have to feel sorry for him. After all, being dominated by an almost maniacal woman was enough to . . . well, let's go in. I suppose you'd call this his hideaway. His hobby was taxidermy. A crow here, an owl there. An important scene took place in this room. There was a private supper here. By the way, this picture has great significance because . . . let's go along into cabin number one. I want to show you something there.

All tidied up. The bathroom. Oh, they've cleaned all this up now. Big difference. You should have seen the blood. The whole place was . . . well, it's too horrible to describe. Dreadful. And I tell you, a very important clue was found here. (Shows toilet.) Down there. Well, the murderer, you see, crept in here very slowly—of course, the shower was on, there was no sound, and . . .

MUSIC WELLS UP FIERCELY, SHOWER CURTAIN SWISHES ACROSS, BLACKOUT.

Voice: THE PICTURE YOU MUST SEE FROM THE BEGINNING—OR NOT AT ALL.

AAN: Alfred Hitchcock; John L. Russell; Janet Leigh

'It's 22 years later and Norman Bates is coming home!'

Psycho 2*
US 1983 113m Technicolor
Universal / Oak (Hilton A. Green)

Despite protests from the sister of one of his victims, Norman Bates is released after 22 years in a mental institution . . . and the murders begin again.
A reasonably inventive sequel, if on the gory side. It probably holds the record for the longest delayed follow-up.

w Tom Holland *d* Richard Franklin *ph* Dean Cundey *m* Jerry Goldsmith *pd* John W. Corso

Anthony Perkins, Vera Miles, Meg Tilly, Robert Loggia, Dennis Franz

'It's all very well having your tongue in your cheek, but it helps to have a brain in your head.'—*Sunday Times*

Psycho 3
US 1986 93m colour
Universal / Hilton A. Green

A suicidal novice flees after unwittingly causing the death of another nun, and takes refuge at the Bates Motel.
More variations on the original Psycho murders, with invention wearing a bit thin by now.

w Charles Edward Pogue d Anthony Perkins *ph* Bruce Surtees *m* Carter Burwell *pd* Henry Bumstead *ed* David Blewitt

Anthony Perkins, Diana Scarwid, Jeff Fahey, Roberta Maxwell

Psychomania
GB 1972 91m Technicolor
Benmar (Andrew Donally)

A Hells Angels motor cyclist commits suicide and returns from the dead an invulnerable monster.
Arrant nonsense of the macabre sort, sometimes irresistibly amusing.

w Armand d'Usseau *d* Don Sharp *ph* Ted Moore *m* David Whitaker

George Sanders, Nicky Henson, Beryl Reid, Robert Hardy

The Psychopath
GB 1966 83m Techniscope
Paramount / Amicus (Milton Subotsky)

Men are found dead in London, each with a doll beside him.
Complicated horror thriller in which the actors go further over the top the more the plot winds down.

w Robert Bloch *d* Freddie Francis *ph* John Wilcox *m* Philip Martell

Patrick Wymark, Margaret Johnston, John Standing, Alexander Knox, Judy Huxtable, Don Borisenko, Thorley Walters, Colin Gordon

PT 109
US 1963 140m Technicolor Panavision
Warner (Brian Foy)

Adventures of president-to-be John F. Kennedy when he was a naval lieutenant in the Pacific during World War II.
Extraordinarily protracted and very dull action story which seems to have been overawed by its subject.

w Richard L. Breen *d* Leslie H. Martinson *ph* Robert Surtees *m* William Lava, David Buttolph

Cliff Robertson, Ty Hardin, James Gregory, Robert Blake

Puberty Blues
Australia 1982 81m Eastmancolor Panavision

Teenage girls aim to become beach groupies. Both repellent and boring, this mindless sex movie has little more to offer than the beach extravaganzas of the sixties. Nell Schofield, Jad Capelja, Geoff Rhoe, Tony Hughes, Sandy Paul. Written by Margaret Kelly, from the novel by Kathy Lette and Gabrielle Carey; directed by Bruce Beresford; for Limelight.

Public Deb Number One
US 1940 80m bw

A waiter spanks a spoiled society girl at a communist rally, and accepts a job which makes him a capitalist. Lively comedy packed with familiar faces. Brenda Joyce, George Murphy, Ralph Bellamy, Elsa Maxwell, Mischa Auer, Charles Ruggles, Maxie Rosenbloom, Berton Churchill, Franklin Pangborn, Hobart Cavanaugh, Lloyd Corrigan, Elisha Cook Jnr. Written by Karl Tunberg and Darrell Ware; directed by Gregory Ratoff; for TCF.

'Drama that hurls a mighty challenge to all humanity!'

The Public Enemy***
US 1931 84m bw
Warner
GB title: *Enemies of the Public*

Two slum boys begin as bootleggers, get too big for their boots, and wind up dead.
Although it doesn't flow as a narrative, this early gangster film still has vivid and startling scenes and was most influential in the development of the urban American crime film.

w Harvey Thew, Kubec Glasmon, John Bright *d William Wellman ph Dev Jennings* *m* David Mendoza

James Cagney, Edward Woods, Jean Harlow, Joan Blondell, Beryl Mercer, Donald Cook, Mae Clarke, Leslie Fenton

'Roughest, most powerful and best gang picture to date. So strong as to be repulsive in some aspects, plus a revolting climax. No strong cast names but a lot of merit.'—*Variety*

'The real power of *The Public Enemy* lies in its vigorous and brutal assault on the nerves and in the stunning acting of James Cagney.'—*James Shelley Hamilton*

'A postscript said that the producers wanted to "depict honestly an environment that exists today in certain strata of American life, rather than glorify the hoodlum or the criminal". The film had a different effect: Cagney was playful and dynamic, and so much more appealing than the characters opposed to him that audiences rooted for him in spite of themselves.'—*Martin Quigley Jnr, 1970*

'What not many people know is that right up to two days before shooting started, I was going to play the good guy, the pal. Edward Woods played it in the end.'—*James Cagney*

AAN: Kubec Glasmon, John Bright

Public Enemy's Wife
US 1936 78m bw
Warner (Sam Bischoff)
GB title: *G-Man's Wife*

A girl agrees to marry an escaped convict so that the FBI can track him down.

Lower-berth gangster thrills culminating in a chase climax; neatly enough done.

w Abem Finkel, Harold Buckley, *story* David O. Selznick, P. J. Wolfson *ph* Ernest Haller *d* Nick Grinde

Pat O'Brien, Margaret Lindsay, Robert Armstrong, Cesar Romero, Dick Foran, Dick Purcell

† Remade as *Bullets for O'Hara* (1942).

Public Hero Number One
US 1935 89m bw
MGM (Lucien Hubbard)

A G-man goes undercover to track down the Purple Gang.
Moderate thick ear dating from the time when studios tried to smother public outcry against gangster films by presenting the cop as the hero.

w Wells Root *d* J. Walter Ruben *ph* Gregg Toland

Chester Morris, Jean Arthur, Joseph Calleia, Lionel Barrymore, Paul Kelly, Lewis Stone, Paul Hurst

'Rates with the best of the G-men pictures.'—*Variety*

'The best picture on criminal life I've seen.'—*Otis Ferguson*

Pufnstuf
US 1970 98m Technicolor
Universal / Krofft Enterprises

A dejected boy is led by his talking flute on a talking boat to Living Island, full of strange but friendly animals in fear of an incompetent witch.
Amalgam of a TV series using life-size puppets to project a mildly pleasing variation on *The Wizard of Oz*, without quite achieving the right blend of wit and charm.

w John Fenton Murray, Si Rose *d* Hollingsworth Morse *ph* Kenneth Peach *m* Charles Fox *ad Alexander Golitzen*

Jack Wild, Billie Hayes, Martha Raye, Mama Cass

Pulp*
GB 1972 95m colour
UA / Klinger–Caine–Hodges (Michael Klinger)

An ex-funeral director now living in the Mediterranean as a successful pulp fiction writer gets involved with gangsters and weirdos.
Occasionally funny pastiche which sorely lacks shape and is sustained by guest appearances and zany ideas.

wd Mike Hodges ph Ousama Rawi *m* George Martin

Michael Caine, *Mickey Rooney*, Lizabeth Scott, Lionel Stander, Nadia Cassini, Al Lettieri, Dennis Price

'Various eccentrics act out their "turns", but never quite lift a light comedy-thriller through the more playful and productive inversions of parody.'—*Richard Combs*

The Pumpkin Eater***
GB 1964 118m bw
Columbia / Romulus (James Woolf)

A compulsive mother (of eight children) finds her third marriage rocking when she gets evidence of her husband's affairs.
Brilliantly made if basically rather irritating kaleidoscope of vivid scenes about silly people, all quite recognizable as sixties Londoners; very well acted.

w Harold Pinter, *novel* Penelope Mortimer *d Jack Clayton ph Oswald Morris m* Georges Delerue

Anne Bancroft, Peter Finch, James Mason, Maggie Smith, Cedric Hardwicke, Richard Johnson, Eric Porter

'There never was a film so rawly memorable.'—*Evening Standard*

'It is solid, serious, intelligent, stylish. It is also, for the most part, quite dead.'—*The Times*

'It plays like a house afire.'—*Time*

AAN: Anne Bancroft

THE PUBLIC ENEMY. James Cagney as audiences wanted to see him—tough, mean and carrying a gun. Eddie Woods is carrying the liquor.

The Punch and Judy Man*
GB 1962 96m bw
(ABP) Macconkey (Gordon L. T. Scott)

A seashore children's entertainer tries and fails to establish himself as an important citizen.
Melancholy comedy of failure which did not please its star's adherents and indeed just missed the style it was seeking.

w Philip Oakes, Tony Hancock *d* Jeremy Summers *ph* Gilbert Taylor *m* Derek Scott, Don Banks

Tony Hancock, Sylvia Syms, Ronald Fraser, Barbara Murray, John Le Mesurier, Hugh Lloyd

Puppet on a Chain*
GB 1970 98m Technicolor
Big City (Kurt Unger)

An American Interpol agent hunts down drug smugglers in Amsterdam.
Sadistic adventure thriller, a toughened version of James Bond, climaxing in a splendid boat chase through Amsterdam.

w Alistair MacLean, Don Sharp, Paul Wheeler, *novel* Alistair MacLean *d* Geoffrey Reeve, *Don Sharp* *ph* Jack Hildyard, Skeets Kelly *m* Piero Piccioni

Sven Bertil Taube, Barbara Parkins, Patrick Allen, Alexander Knox, Vladek Sheybal
'One suspects that a marionette also sat in for Alistair MacLean.'—*Judith Crist*

The Purple Gang
US 1960 85m bw

In Detroit during prohibition a gang of juvenile delinquents become as powerful as the gangsters. Unpleasant detail mars this cops-and-robbers subject; twenty years later it would have been even more of a shocker, but it's bad enough as it is. Robert Blake, Barry Sullivan, Elaine Edwards, Marc Cavell, Jody Lawrance, Susie Marquette, Paul Dubov. Written by Jack DeWitt; directed by Frank McDonald; for Allied Artists.

The Purple Heart*
US 1944 99m bw
TCF (Darryl F. Zanuck)

American prisoners of war in Japan are tried and executed.
Relentlessly sombre flagwaver, extremely persuasively presented.

w Jerome Cady, Darryl F. Zanuck *d Lewis Milestone* *ph* Arthur Miller *m* Alfred Newman

Dana Andrews, Richard Conte, Farley Granger, Kevin O'Shea, Sam Levene, Don Barry, Richard Loo
'It is unusually edged, well organized and solidly acted. But I feel extremely queasy watching fiction—especially persuasive fiction—which pretends to clarify facts that are not clear, and may never become so.'—*James Agee*

Purple Heart Diary
US 1951 73m bw

Entertainers tour war zones and bring various comforts. Sentimental piece which the USO picked up as useful propaganda. Frances Langford, Ben Lessy, Tony Romano, Judd Holdren. Written by William Sackheim; directed by Richard Quine; for Sam Katzman/Columbia. (GB title: *No Time for Tears*.)

The Purple Mask
US 1955 82m Technicolor Cinemascope
U-I (Howard Christie)

In 1802 Paris the Royalist resistance to Napoleon is led by the mysterious Purple Mask, who also disguises himself as a foppish dandy.
Cheeky rewrite of *The Scarlet Pimpernel*, with plenty of gusto but not much style.

w Oscar Brodney *d* Bruce Humberstone *ph* Irving Glassberg *m* Joseph Gershenson

Tony Curtis, Dan O'Herlihy, Colleen Miller, Gene Barry, Angela Lansbury, George Dolenz, John Hoyt
'Sir Percy, one feels, would have personally conducted this lot to the guillotine.'—*MFB*

The Purple Monster Strikes
US 1945 bw serial: 15 eps

A Martian kills a great scientist and enters his body. Early example of unpleasant aliens, a precursor of *It Came from Outer Space* and *Invasion of the Body Snatchers*. Dennis Moore, Linda Stirling, Roy Barcroft. Directed by Spencer Bennet and Fred Brannon; for Republic.

The Purple Plain*
GB 1954 100m Technicolor
GFD / Two Cities (John Bryan)

During the Burma campaign, a Canadian squadronleader regains his shattered nerves during an arduous trek across country.
Psychological study and eastern adventure combined; not the best of either, but a potent crowd-puller.

w Eric Ambler, *novel* H. E. Bates *d* Robert Parrish *ph* Geoffrey Unsworth *m* John Veale

Gregory Peck, Maurice Denham, Win Min Than, Lyndon Brook, Brenda de Banzie, Bernard Lee, Anthony Bushell, Ram Gopal

The Purple Rose of Cairo*
US 1984 82m De Luxe
Orion / Jack Rollins-Charles H. Joffe (Robert Greenhut)

In the thirties, a film-struck woman is confronted in reality by the hero of her dreams.
Amusing but slight comedy: several good jokes, but in sum no more than an elongated sketch.
w,d Woody Allen *ph* Gordon Willis *m* Dick Hyman *pd* Stuart Wurtzel *ed* Susan E. Morse
Mia Farrow, Jeff Daniels, Danny Aiello, Dianne Wiest, Van Johnson, Zoe Caldwell, John Wood, Milo O'Shea
BFA: best picture, original screenplay

Pursued*
US 1947 101m bw
(Warner) United States (Milton Sperling)
A revenge-seeking cowboy accidentally causes a tragedy in his adopted family.
Glum, good-looking revenge western.
w Niven Busch *d* Raoul Walsh *ph James Wong Howe* *m* Max Steiner
Robert Mitchum, Teresa Wright, Judith Anderson, Dean Jagger, Alan Hale, Harry Carey Jnr

Pursuit
US 1935 73m bw
A child is kidnapped, and several people want the reward for restoring him. Rather frantic chase thriller with insufficient variety. Chester Morris, Sally Eilers, Scotty Beckett, Henry Travers, C. Henry Gordon, Dorothy Peterson, Harold Huber. Written by Wells Root, Lawrence G. Blochman; directed by Edwin L. Marin; for Lucien Hubbard-Ned Marin / MGM.

The Pursuit of D. B. Cooper
US 1981 100m Metrocolor
Polygram (Daniel Wigutow, Michael Taylor)
A skyjacker bails out with his loot and is chased by various people after the reward.
Fantasy variation on a real case which was never solved; of no interest whatever despite the talent involved.
w Jeffrey Alan Fiskin, *book* Free Fall by J. D. Reed *d* Roger Spottiswoode (also John Frankenheimer, Buzz Kulik) *ph* Harry Stradling *m* James Horner *pd* Preston Ames
Robert Duvall, Treat Williams, Kathryn Harrod, Ed Flanders, Paul Gleason, R. G. Armstrong
'Doubtless a law-enforcement ploy to lure the skyjacker out of hiding: surely after seeing this mess he will want to surface and sue somebody.'—*Variety*

The Pursuit of Happiness
US 1934 75m bw
Paramount (Arthur Hornblow Jnr)
In 1776 Connecticut a Puritan maid falls for a Hessian soldier.
Mildly pleasing romantic comedy centring on the ancient practice of 'bundling' in which betrothed couples might sleep together fully clothed.
w Stephen Morehouse Avery, Jack Cunningham, J. P. McEvoy, Virginia Van Upp, *play* Lawrence Langner, Armina Marshall *d* Alexander Hall *ph* Karl Struss
Francis Lederer, Joan Bennett, Charles Ruggles, Mary Boland, Walter Kingsford, Minor Watson
'A comedy that will entertain and merits business.'—*Variety*

The Pursuit of Happiness*
US 1970 98m Eastmancolor
Columbia / TA Films / Norton–Simon (David Susskind)
A New York college dropout is sent to prison after a hit and run accident.
Smooth, watchable but empty youth movie.
w Sidney Carroll, George L. Sherman *d* Robert Mulligan *ph* Dick Kratina *m* Dave Grusin
Michael Sarrazin, Barbara Hershey, Robert Klein, Ruth White, E. G. Marshall, Arthur Hill

Pursuit to Algiers
US 1945 65m bw
Universal (Roy William Neill)
Sherlock Holmes guards the young king of Ruritania on a sea voyage.
After an amiably lunatic first reel, this settles down as one of the dullest of the series, but it never entirely taxes the patience.
w Leonard Lee *d* Roy William Neill *ph* Paul Ivano *md* Edgar Fairchild *m* Hans Salter
Basil Rathbone, Nigel Bruce, Martin Kosleck, Marjorie Riordan, Rosalind Ivan, John Abbott, Frederic Worlock, Morton Lowry

Pushover*
US 1954 91m bw
Columbia (Jules Schermer)
An honest policeman involves himself in murder for loot.
Another variation on *Double Indemnity*, smoothly carpentered as the first appearance of newly-groomed star Kim Novak. The events of a night were familiar and watchable.

PYGMALION. Eliza Doolittle (Wendy Hiller) dislikes the idea of a bath but Jean Cadell will brook no refusal.

w Roy Huggins, *novels* The Night Watch by Thomas Walsh, Rafferty by William S. Ballinger *d Richard Quine ph* Lester B. White *m* Arthur Morton

Fred MacMurray, Kim Novak, Phil Carey, Dorothy Malone, E. G. Marshall

Puttin' on the Ritz
US 1930 88m bw (colour sequence)
(UA) Joseph M. Schenck

A has-been vaudevillian gets a second chance but succumbs to the demon rum.
Primitive early musical melodrama valuable only as an example of the work of its star.

w, p John W. Considine Jnr *d* Edward Sloman *ph* Ray June *ad* William Cameron Menzies

Harry Richman, Joan Bennett, James Gleason, Aileen Pringle, Lilyan Tashman, Purnell Pratt

'Entertaining backstage story with ultra production values.'—*Variety*

Putting Pants on Philip*
US 1927 20m bw silent

A respectable man meets his randy Scottish nephew who wears nothing under his kilt.
Early star comedy, allegedly their first as a team but before their more recognizable characteristics had developed. Not at all bad in its way, though developing into one long chase. Laurel and Hardy, Sam Lufkin, Harvey Clark. Written by H. M. Walker; directed by Clyde Bruckman; for Hal Roach.

Puzzle of a Downfall Child
US 1970 104m Technicolor
Universal / Newman–Foreman

Fantasy reminiscences of a top fashion model.
Pretentious, fashionable, seemingly interminable collage of sex and high living.

w Adrien Joyce (Carol Eastman) *d Jerry Schatzberg ph* Adam Holender *m* Michael Small

Faye Dunaway, Barry Primus, Viveca Lindfors, Barry Morse, Roy Scheider

Pygmalion****
GB 1938 96m bw
Gabriel Pascal

A professor of phonetics takes a bet that he can turn a cockney flower seller in six months into a lady who can pass as a duchess.
Perfectly splendid Shavian comedy of bad manners, extremely well filmed and containing memorable lines and performances; subsequently turned into the musical *My Fair Lady* (qv). One of the most heartening and adult British films of the thirties.

w Anatole de Grunwald, W. P. Lipscomb, Cecil Lewis, Ian Dalrymple, *play Bernard Shaw d Anthony Asquith, Leslie Howard ph* Harry Stradling *m Arthur Honegger*

Leslie Howard, Wendy Hiller, Wilfrid Lawson, Scott Sunderland, Marie Lohr, David Tree, Esmé Percy, Everley Gregg, Jean Cadell

HIGGINS (Leslie Howard): 'Yes, you squashed cabbage leaf, you disgrace to the noble architecture of these columns, you incarnate insult to the English language, I can pass you off as the Queen of Sheba.'

HIGGINS: 'Where the devil are my slippers, Eliza?'

'Ought to have big potentialities in the US, with some cutting. . . . An introductory title briefly gives the source of the play, which was Shakespeare's *Pygmalion*.' (!)—*Variety*

'An exhibition of real movie-making – of a sound score woven in and out of tense scenes, creating mood and tempo and characterization.'—*Pare Lorentz*

'Every possible care has been taken in the presentation of what may well prove to have a significant effect on future British film production, for it is live, human entertainment, flawlessly presented and making an obvious appeal to all kinds of audiences.'—*The Cinema*

AAN: best picture; script; Bernard Shaw; Leslie Howard; Wendy Hiller

Q Planes**
GB 1939 82m bw
Harefield / London Films (Irving Asher, Alexander Korda)
US title: *Clouds over Europe*

A secret ray helps spies to steal test aircraft during proving flights.
Lively comedy thriller distinguished by a droll leading performance.

w Ian Dalrymple, Brock Williams, Jack Whittingham, Arthur Wimperis *d Tim Whelan ph* Harry Stradling *md* Muir Mathieson

Ralph Richardson, Laurence Olivier, Valerie Hobson, George Merritt, George Curzon, Gus McNaughton, David Tree

Q—The Winged Serpent
US 1982 100m colour

An ex-con on the run finds a prehistoric bird in the spire of the Chrysler building. Slow horror film with flashes of brightness. Michael Moriarty, Candy Clark, David Carradine, Richard Roundtree, James Dixon. Written and directed by Larry Cohen; photographed by Fred Murphy; for United FD (aka: *The Winged Serpent*.)

Quackser Fortune Has a Cousin in the Bronx*
US 1970 90m Eastmancolor
UMC (John H. Cushingham)

An Irish layabout strikes up an acquaintance with an American student.
Likeable if plotless Dublin comedy, pleasantly photographed.

w Gabriel Walsh *d* Waris Hussein *ph* Gil Taylor *m* Michael Dress

Gene Wilder, Margot Kidder, Eileen Colgen, Seamus Ford

Quadrophenia
GB 1979 120m Eastmancolor

A drama of bitter rivalry between Mods and Rockers on the Brighton beaches in 1964.
What passes for a successful musical at the end of the seventies is typified by this violent, screaming and wholly unattractive amalgam of noise, violence, sex and profanity. The Who, Kate Williams, Michael Elphick. Written by Dave Humphries, Martin Stellman and Franc Roddam; directed by Franc Roddam; for Polytel.

Quai des Brumes***
France 1938 89m bw
Rabinovitch
US title: *Port of Shadows*

An army deserter rescues a girl from crooks but is killed before they can escape.
Artificial, set-bound, but at the time wholly persuasive melodrama which became one of the archetypal French films of the thirties, its doomed lovers syndrome not being picked up by Hollywood until after World War II.

w Jacques Prévert, novel Pierre MacOrlan *d Marcel Carné ph Eugen Schüfftan m Maurice Jaubert ad Alexander Trauner*

Jean Gabin, Michèle Morgan, Michel Simon, Pierre Brasseur

'Unity of space, time and action give the film a classical finish.'—*Georges Sadoul*

† The plot was in fact almost identical with that of *Pépé le Moko*. The romantic pessimism of these films, plus *Le Jour Se Lève*, so suited the mood of France that Vichy officials later said: 'If we have lost the war it is because of *Quai des Brumes*.'

Quai des Orfèvres*
France 1947 105m bw
Majestic

A music hall artiste is accused of murdering the man he took to be seducing his mistress.
The equivalent of many a British Scotland Yard thriller, but a good one, with excellent acting, atmosphere and suspense.

w Henri-Georges Clouzot, Jean Ferry, *novel* Legitime Défense by Stanislas-André Steeman *d Henri-Georges Clouzot ph* Armand Thirard *m* Francis Lopez

Louis Jouvet, Bernard Blier, Suzy Delair, Pierre Larquey, Simone Rennant

'The wonder of *Quai des Orfèvres* is the way Clouzot has pricked it with life.'—*Guardian*

'A stunningly well made entertainment.'—*New Yorker, 1982*

'Two love experts in a daring game of hearts!'

Quality Street*
US 1937 84m bw
RKO (Pandro S. Berman)

When an officer returns from the Napoleonic wars, he does not recognize his sweetheart, whose beauty has faded, so she masquerades as her own capricious niece.
Fairly successful attempt to capture on screen the essence of Barrie whimsy; everyone tries hard, anyway.

w Mortimer Offner, Allan Scott, *play* J. M. Barrie *d* George Stevens *ph* Robert de Grasse *m* Roy Webb

Katharine Hepburn, Franchot Tone, Fay Bainter, Eric Blore, Cora Witherspoon, Estelle Winwood, Florence Lake, Joan Fontaine

'Hepburn and Tone unable to instil any life, and little entertainment, into this old-timer from legit . . . one for the bonnet and shawl trade.'—*Variety*

'It is strictly a self-propelled picture, tearing breathlessly, even hysterically, through Barrie's quizzical account of a man-hunt. . . . But we were exhausted by the intensity of Miss Hepburn's concentration on it. Her Phoebe needs a neurologist far more than a husband. Such flutterings and jitterings and twitchings, such hand-wringings and mouth-quiverings, such runnings-about and eyebrow-raisings have not been on the screen in many a moon.'—*Frank Nugent, New York Times*

† Previously made by MGM in 1927 (silent), with Marion Davies and Conrad Nagel; directed by Sidney Franklin.

AAN: Roy Webb

Quantez
US 1957 80m Eastmancolor Cinemascope

Robbers hiding for the night in a frontier town become involved in an Indian attack. Curious, slow-paced attempt to redo *The Gunfight* with inferior materials; not a profitable experience. Fred MacMurray, Dorothy Malone, James Barton, Sydney Chaplin, John Gavin, John Larch, Michael Ansara. Written by R. Wright Campbell; directed by Harry Keller; for Universal-International.

The Quare Fellow
GB 1962 90m bw
BLC / Bryanston (Anthony Havelock-Allan)

Life in a Dublin prison when two men are to be hanged, as experienced by a new young warder.
Watered-down version of a rumbustious stage tragi-comedy, with not much but the gloom left.

wd Arthur Dreifuss, *play* Brendan Behan *ph* Peter Hennessey *m* Alexander Faris

Patrick McGoohan, Sylvia Syms, Walter Macken, Dermot Kelly, Hilton Edwards

Q PLANES. Laurence Olivier turns his matinee idol profile to the camera which clearly upsets the assembled onlookers.

Quartet***
GB 1948 120m bw
GFD / Gainsborough (Anthony Darnborough)

Four stories introduced by the author.
This entertaining production began the compendium fashion (*Full House, Phone Call from a Stranger,* etc) and is fondly remembered, though all the stories had softened endings and the middle two did not work very well as drama. Subsequent Maugham compilations were *Trio* and *Encore* (both qv).

w R. C. Sherriff, stories W. Somerset Maugham m John Greenwood

THE FACTS OF LIFE *d* Ralph Smart *ph* Ray Elton

Basil Radford, Naunton Wayne, Mai Zetterling, Jack Watling, James Robertson Justice

THE ALIEN CORN *d* Harold French *ph* Ray Elton

Dirk Bogarde, Françoise Rosay, Raymond Lovell, Honor Blackman, Irene Browne

THE KITE *d* Arthur Crabtree *ph* Ray Elton

George Cole, Hermione Baddeley, Susan Shaw, Mervyn Johns, Bernard Lee

THE COLONEL'S LADY *d* Ken Annakin *ph* Reg Wyer

Cecil Parker, Linden Travers, Nora Swinburne, Ernest Thesiger, Felix Aylmer, Henry Edwards, Wilfrid Hyde White

Quartet*
GB / France 1981 101m GTC colour
TCF / Merchant Ivory (Ismail Merchant, Jean Pierre Mahot de la Querantonnais)

In 1927 Paris, a convict's wife finds herself part of a *ménage à trois*.
Slow-moving, good-looking study of characters in a milieu; as usual with films from this stable, it has nothing to please the majority.

w Ruth Prawer Jhabvala, *novel* Jean Rhys *d* James Ivory *ph* Pierre Lhomme *m* Richard Robbins

Isabelle Adjani, Maggie Smith, Alan Bates, Anthony Higgins

Quatermass and the Pit**
GB 1967 97m Technicolor
Hammer / Anthony Nelson Keys
US title: *Five Million Years to Earth*

Prehistoric skulls are unearthed during London Underground excavations, and a weird and deadly force makes itself felt.
The third film of a Quatermass serial is the most ambitious, and in many ways inventive and enjoyable, yet spoiled by the very fertility of the author's imagination: the concepts are simply too intellectual to be easily followed in what should be a visual thriller. The climax, in which the devil rears over London and is 'earthed', is satisfactorily harrowing.

w Nigel Kneale, from his TV serial *d Roy Ward Baker ph* Arthur Grant *m* Tristam Cary

Andrew Keir, James Donald, Barbara Shelley, Julian Glover, Duncan Lamont, Edwin Richfield, Peter Copley

The Quatermass Experiment**
GB 1955 82m bw
Exclusive / Hammer (Anthony Hinds)
US title: *The Creeping Unknown*

When a rocketship returns from space, two of its three crew members have disappeared and the third is slowly taken over by a fungus which thrives on blood.
Intelligent science fiction based on a highly successful BBC TV serial; the film version is generally workmanlike despite its obvious low budget.

w Richard Landau, Val Guest, *serial Nigel Kneale d* Val Guest *ph* Jimmy Harvey

Brian Donlevy, Jack Warner, Margia Dean, *Richard Wordsworth,* David King Wood, Thora Hird, Gordon Jackson

Quatermass II**
GB 1957 85m bw
Hammer (Anthony Hinds)
US title: *Enemy from Space*

A research station operating under military secrecy is supposed to be making synthetic foods, but is in fact an acclimatization centre for invaders from outer space.
Simplified version of a TV serial, a bit stodgy in the talk scenes, but building into sequences of genuine alarm and based on an idea of lingering persuasiveness.

w Nigel Kneale, Val Guest, *serial Nigel Kneale d Val Guest ph* Gerald Gibbs *m* James Bernard

Brian Donlevy, John Longden, Sidney James, Bryan Forbes, William Franklyn, Charles Lloyd Pack, Percy Herbert, Tom Chatto

Quebec
US 1951 85m Technicolor

The wife of the loyalist governor of Quebec is in love with the leader of the rebels. Ho-hum period actioner with some pretty backgrounds and not much personality. Corinne Calvet, John Barrymore Jnr, Barbara Rush, Patric Knowles, John Hoyt, Arnold Moss. Written by Alan Le May; directed by George Templeton; for Paramount.

'She's so excitingly good when she's so wonderfully bad!'

Queen Bee*
US 1955 95m bw
Columbia (Jerry Wald)

A wealthy woman has a compulsion to dominate everyone around her.
Claustrophobic southern-set melodrama obviously created for its star.

wd Ranald MacDougall, *novel* Edna Lee
ph Charles Lang *m* George Duning
md Morris Stoloff

Joan Crawford, Barry Sullivan, Betsy Palmer, John Ireland, Lucy Marlow, William Leslie, Fay Wray

AAN: Charles Lang

Queen Christina***
US 1933 101m bw
MGM (Walter Wanger)

The queen of 17th-century Sweden, distressed at the thought of a political marriage, goes wandering through her country in men's clothes and falls in love with the new Spanish ambassador.
The star vehicle par excellence, superb to look at and one of its star's most fondly remembered films. Historically it's nonsense, but put across with great style.

w Salka Viertel, H. M. Harwood, S. N. Behrman d Rouben Mamoulian ph William Daniels m Herbert Stothart

Greta Garbo, John Gilbert, Ian Keith, Lewis Stone, C. Aubrey Smith, Reginald Owen, Elizabeth Young

ANTONIO (John Gilbert): 'It's all a question of climate. You cannot serenade a woman in a snowstorm. All the graces in the art of love—elaborate approaches that will make the game of love amusing—can only be practised in those countries that quiver in the heat of the sun.'

CHRISTINA (Greta Garbo): 'I have been memorizing this room. In the future, in my memory, I shall live a great deal in this room.'

'The shortcomings, such as they are, are so far overshadowed by the potency of the premier satellite, the sterling support, the Mamoulian montage and the Behrman crisp dialogue that they're relatively unimportant; for *Christina* is cinch b.o.'—*Variety*

'Garbo, as enchanting as ever, is still enveloped by her unfathomable mystery.'—*Photoplay*

'An unending series of exceptional scenes.'—*Modern Screen*

† The leading male role was announced in turn for Leslie Howard, Franchot Tone, Nils Asther, Bruce Cabot and Laurence Olivier: Garbo turned them all down.

Queen Elizabeth*
France 1912 35m approx (24 fps) bw silent
Histrionic Film
original title: *Les Amours de la Reine Elisabeth*

Scenes from the life of the queen.
Abysmally boring now, this film is important in several ways. It is our best record of Sarah Bernhardt. It was immensely successful throughout the world. It made cinema interesting to all classes, not just the hoi polloi. It made the fortunes of Adolph Zukor, who bought it cheaply and went on to found Paramount Pictures. (Bernhardt is said to have remarked to him: 'You have put me in pickle for all time!')

w Eugene Moreau *d* Henri Desfontaines, Louis Mercanton

Sarah Bernhardt, Lou Tellegen

Queen Kelly**
US 1928 100m approx (24 fps) (unfinished version) bw silent
United Artists / Gloria Productions / Joseph Kennedy

A convent girl goes to the bad, is ill-used by a prince, becomes a white slave in Africa but finally inherits a fortune.
Sexually-oriented extravaganza, the last great folly of its director but never finished by him. Various versions exist: in all of them individual scenes are more entertaining than the whole. Extracts were shown in *Sunset Boulevard.*

wd Erich Von Stroheim ph Gordon Pollock, Paul Ivano, Ben Reynolds *m* Adolf Tandler
ad Harry Miles

Gloria Swanson, Walter Byron, Seena Owen

Queen of Atlantis see L'Atlantide

Queen of Hearts*
GB 1936 80m bw
ATP (Basil Dean)

A working girl poses as a socialite and wins a matinee idol.
Stalwart romantic comedy with its star slightly more glamorized than usual.

w Clifford Grey, H. F. Maltby, Douglas Furber, Anthony Kimmins, Gordon Wellesley *d* Monty Banks

Gracie Fields, John Loder, Enid Stamp Taylor, Fred Duprez, Edward Rigby, Hal Gordon

The Queen of Spades**
GB 1948 96m bw
ABP / World Screen Plays (Anatole de Grunwald)

A Russian officer tries to wrest from an ancient countess the secret of winning at cards, in return for which he has sold his soul to the devil; but she dies of fright and haunts him.
Disappointingly slow-moving but splendidly atmospheric recreation of an old Russian story with all the decorative stops out; the chills when they come are quite frightening, the style is impressionist and the acting suitably extravagant.

w Rodney Ackland, Arthur Boys, *novel* Alexander Pushkin *d Thorold Dickinson ph Otto Heller m Georges Auric ad Oliver Messel*

Anton Walbrook, Edith Evans, Ronald Howard, Yvonne Mitchell, Mary Jerrold

'The photography is adventurous, the cutting imaginative and the sets startling.'—*Evening Standard*

'It is fine to come across such distinguished filmcraft.'—*Evening News*

Queen of the Mob*
US 1940 61m bw
Paramount

A murderess and her three sons are captured by the FBI.
Pacy crime melodrama from the *Persons in Hiding* series, based on the exploits of Ma Barker.

w Horace McCoy, William R. Lippmann
d James Hogan *ph* Theodor Sparkuhl

Blanche Yurka, Ralph Bellamy, Jack Carson, Richard Denning, Paul Kelly, J. Carrol Naish, Jeanne Cagney, William Henry, James Seay, Hedda Hopper

The Queen's Guards
GB 1960 112m Technicolor Cinemascope
TCF / Imperial (Michael Powell)

Reminiscences during trooping the colour of father and son guardsmen.
Incredibly old-fashioned family melodrama complete with skeleton in family closet; despite its date it has a decidedly pre-war air, except that it might have been more smartly done then.

w Roger Milner *d* Michael Powell *ph* Gerald Turpin *m* Brian Easdale

Raymond Massey, Daniel Massey, Robert Stephens, Ursula Jeans, Judith Stott, Elizabeth Shepherd, Duncan Lamont, Ian Hunter, Jack Watling

'This flagwaving museum piece would be distressing if it weren't so inept . . . [the actors] battle manfully with dialogue and characters as dated as a Crimean cavalry charge. The film could scarcely be taken as a tribute to the Guards except, just possibly, by elderly aunts in Cheltenham.'—*MFB*

Queimada!
France / Italy 1968 132m De Luxe
PEA / PPA (Alberto Grimaldi)
aka: *Burn!*

A diplomat is sent to a Caribbean island to break the Portuguese sugar monopoly and becomes involved with revolutionaries.
An indigestible attempt to combine adventure with the film of ideas; very tedious.

w Franco Solinas, Giorgio Arlorio *d* Gillo Pontecorvo *ph* Marcello Gatti *m* Ennio Morricone

Marlon Brando, Renato Salvatori, Norman Hill, Evaristo Marquez

'Theirs was a time of love and violence!'

Quentin Durward*
GB 1955 101m Eastmancolor Cinemascope
MGM (Pandro S. Berman)
aka: *The Adventures of Quentin Durward*

An elderly English lord sends his nephew to woo a French lady on his behalf; but the boy falls in love with her himself.
Haphazardly constructed and produced, but quite enjoyable, period romp, with a bold black villain and several rousing set pieces including a final set-to on bell ropes.

w Robert Ardrey, *novel* Sir Walter Scott *d* Richard Thorpe *ph* Christopher Challis *m* Bronislau Kaper

Robert Taylor, Kay Kendall, Robert Morley, Alec Clunes, Marius Goring, Wilfrid Hyde White, Ernest Thesiger, Duncan Lamont, Harcourt Williams, Laya Raki, George Cole

Querelle
West Germany / France 1982 108m Eastmancolor
Planet / Albatross / Gaumont

A homosexual sailor has a mystical quest which involves murder.
Overheated fantasy which may have something to say to gays, but not much to other audiences.

wd Rainer Werner Fassbinder, *book* Jean Genet *ph* Xaver Schwarzenberger *m* Peer Raben

Brad Davis, Franco Nero, Jeanne Moreau, Laurent Malet

Quest for Fire
Canada / France 1981 100m Bellevue-Pathecolor Panavision
ICC / Cine Trail / Belstar / Stephan (Michael Gruskoff)

Eighty thousand years ago, a primitive tribe uses the discovery of fire to defeat its enemies.
Scientifically cosseted but sometimes unintentionally funny attempt to make us care about the problems of primitive man. Lively sequences are separated by longueurs.

w Gérard Brach, *novel* La Guerre du Feu by J. H. Rosny *d* Jean-Jacques Annaud *ph* Claude Agostini *m* Philippe Sarde *pd* Guy Comtois, Brian Morris *special language* Anthony Burgess *body movement* Desmond Morris

Everett McGill, Ron Perlman, Rae Dawn, Nameer El-Kadi

'He had seen her, felt her touch, knew she existed . . .'

Quest for Love*
GB 1971 90m Eastmancolor
Rank / Peter Rogers Productions (Peter Eton)

After an explosion during an experiment, a young physicist finds himself living a different life, in love with a dying girl; returning to normal, he finds the girl and saves her.
Pleasing variation on *Berkeley Square*, quite well staged and played.

w Terence Feely, *story* Random Quest by John Wyndham *d* Ralph Thomas *ph* Ernest Steward *m* Eric Rogers

Tom Bell, Joan Collins, Denholm Elliott, Laurence Naismith, Lyn Ashley

A Question of Adultery
GB 1958 84m bw
Eros / Connaught Place / Raymond Stross

When a husband is discovered to be sterile, his wife suggests artificial insemination, but when she seems to have a lover he institutes divorce proceedings.
Opportunist melodrama from the headlines. Not even interesting *then*.

w Anne Edwards, *play* Breach of Marriage by Dan Sutherland *d* Don Chaffey *ph* Stephen Dale *m* Philip Green

Julie London, Anthony Steel, Basil Sidney, Donald Houston, Anton Diffring, Andrew Cruickshank, Conrad Philips, Kynaston Reeves

Quick before It Melts
US 1964 97m Metrocolor Panavision
MGM / Biography (Douglas Lawrence, Delbert Mann)

A journalist is sent to cover a naval enterprise in the Antarctic, and gets a scoop despite his shyness.
Noisy service comedy with precious little plot.

w Dale Wasserman, *novel* Philip Benjamin *d* Delbert Mann *ph* Russell Harlan *m* David Rose

George Maharis, Robert Morse, Anjanette Comer, James Gregory, Howard St John, Janine Gray, Michael Constantine

'The combination of romantic dalliance, service high jinks and hectic journalism remains uniformly flat all through.'—*MFB*

The Quick Gun
US 1964 88m Techniscope

A gunfighter gets an icy welcome when he returns home to claim his father's farm.
Standard western with the hero redeemed and elected sheriff at the end. Audie Murphy, Merry Anders, James Best, Ted de Corsia, Walter Sande, Frank Ferguson. Written by Robert E. Kent; directed by Sidney Salkow; for Admiral / Columbia.

Quick Let's Get Married
US 1965 100m colour
Golden Eagle (William Marshall)
aka: *The Confession, Seven Different Ways*

The voice of a sneak thief in a ruined church is taken by an unwed mother as a miracle.
Downright peculiar mishmash wasting intesting stars; an independent production by Rogers and husband in Jamaica.

w Allen Scott *d* William Dieterle *ph* Robert Bronner *m* Michael Colicchio

Ginger Rogers, Ray Milland, Barbara Eden, Walter Abel, Cecil Kellaway, Elliott Gould, Michael Ansara, David Hurst

Quick Millions**
US 1931 69m bw
Fox

An ambitious truck driver becomes a ruthless racketeer.
Fast-moving, otherwise naïve early gangster melodrama notable for Tracy's first star performance.

w Courtney Terrett, Rowland Brown, John Wray *d Rowland Brown* *ph* Joseph August

Spencer Tracy, Marguerite Churchill, Sally Eilers, Robert Burns, John Wray, George Raft

'This film is in the money. Ranks with the best of the gangster items.'—*Variety*

Quicksand
US 1950 79m bw

A garage mechanic gets involved in crime for the sake of an unworthy girl. Lower-case melodrama of no notable merit. Mickey Rooney, Jeanne Cagney, Barbara Bates, Peter Lorre. Written by Robert Smith; directed by Irving Pichel; for Mort Briskin / UA.

The Quiet American**
US 1957 122m bw
UA / Figaro (Joseph L. Mankiewicz)

An American in Saigon has naïve ideas for ending the war; he saves the life of a journalist who for various reasons becomes jealous and is duped into betraying the American to the communists.
Semi-successful excursion into the territory of Graham Greene, who as in *Brighton Rock* has allowed his ironic ending to be totally re-emphasized, here making the film anti-communist instead of anti-American.

wd Joseph L. Mankiewicz, novel Graham Greene *ph* Robert Krasker *m* Mario Nascimbene

Michael Redgrave, Audie Murphy, Claude Dauphin, Giorgia Moll, Bruce Cabot, Fred Sadoff, Richard Loo

The Quiet Man***
US 1952 129m Technicolor
Republic / Argosy (John Ford, Merian C. Cooper)

An Irish village version of *The Taming of the Shrew*, the tamer being an ex-boxer retired to the land of his fathers and in need of a wife.
Archetypal John Ford comedy, as Irish as can be, with everything but leprechauns and the Blarney Stone on hand. Despite some poor sets the film has a gay swing to it, much brawling vigour and broad comedy, while the actors all give their roistering best.

w Frank Nugent, story Maurice Walsh *d John Ford* *ph Winton C. Hoch, Archie Stout* *m Victor Young*

John Wayne, Maureen O'Hara, Barry Fitzgerald, Victor McLaglen, Ward Bond, Mildred Natwick, Francis Ford, Arthur Shields, Eileen Crowe, Sean McClory, Jack McGowran

'Ford's art and artifice . . . are employed to reveal a way of life—stable, rooted, honourable, purposeful in nature's way, and thereby rhythmic. Everyone is an individual, yet everyone and everything has a place.'—*Henry Hart, Films in Review*

AA: John Ford; Winton C. Hoch, Archie Stout
AAN: best picture; Frank Nugent; Victor McLaglen

Quiet Please, Murder*
US 1943 70m bw
TCF (Ralph Dietrich)

Nazis and art thieves cause a high death rate in a public library.
Unusual, stylish second feature.

wd John Larkin ph Joe MacDonald
m Arthur Lange *md* Emil Newman

George Sanders, Kurt Katch, Gail Patrick, Richard Denning, Lynne Roberts, Sidney Blackmer, Byron Foulger

Samples of quirky dialogue:
PATRICK TO SANDERS: 'How many butterflies did you torture since lunch, hoping one would turn on you?'
SANDERS: 'I am a punishment in your life. Your conscience demands it. The unconscious instinct to punish ourselves sometimes becomes self-destructive. The way we live is a constant threat to our own security. We love it. Giving and taking pain.'
PATRICK: 'You hate because you fear love—and the thought of desiring.'

Quiet Wedding***
GB 1940 80m bw
Paramount / Conqueror (Paul Soskin)

Middle-class wedding preparations are complicated by family guests.
A semi-classic British stage comedy is admirably filmed with a splendid cast.

w Terence Rattigan, Anatole de Grunwald, play Esther McCracken d Anthony Asquith

Margaret Lockwood, Derek Farr, *A. E. Matthews, Marjorie Fielding, Athene Seyler, Peggy Ashcroft*, Margaretta Scott, Frank Cellier, Roland Culver, Jean Cadell, David Tomlinson, Bernard Miles

'A completely unpretentious and charming film, the components of which are as delicately balanced as the mechanism of a watch.'—*New York Times*

'No subtlety of glance, movement or dialogue has been missed, no possible highlight omitted.'—*Monthly Film Bulletin*

† Production was halted five times when bombs fell on the studio.
†† Remade as *Happy is The Bride* (qv).

Quiet Weekend
GB 1946 92m bw
Associated British (Warwick Ward)

The Royds spend a weekend at their country cottage and get involved with poachers.
Trivial and poorly-made sequel, not up to the standard of *Quiet Wedding* as a comic study of British types.

w Victor Skuzetsky, *play* Esther McCracken
d Harold French *ph* Eric Cross

Derek Farr, Marjorie Fielding, George Thorpe, Frank Cellier

The Quiller Memorandum*
GB 1966 105m Eastmancolor
Panavision
Rank / Ivan Foxwell / Carthay

A Britisn secret service man is sent to Berlin to combat a neo-Nazi organization.
Disappointingly thin but smooth and watchable spy story.

w Harold Pinter, *novel* The Berlin Memorandum by Adam Hall (Elleston Trevor) *d* Michael Anderson *ph Erwin Hillier m* John Barry

George Segal, Max Von Sydow, Alec Guinness, Senta Berger, George Sanders, Robert Helpmann, Robert Flemyng

'In disposing of most of the storyline Pinter has virtually thrown out the baby with the bathwater; all that remains is a skeleton plot which barely makes sense and is totally lacking in excitement.'—*Brenda Davies*

'Harold Pinter wrote the screenplay and for each word of dialogue there has to be a separate scene involving several different camera angles, which is perhaps why they asked him to do it as the story is pretty thin.'—*J. A., Illustrated London News*

Quintet
US 1979 118m De Luxe
TCF / Lions Gate (Robert Altman)

In an icebound city of the future, citizens play a death game and a survivor hunts down a killer who plays for real.
Dismayingly pretentious claptrap which did its star's career no good at all.

w Frank Barhydt, Robert Altman, Patricia Resnick *d* Robert Altman *ph* Jean Boffety *m* Tom Pierson *pd* Leon Ericksen

Paul Newman, Vittorio Gassman, Fernando Rey, Bibi Andersson, Brigitte Fossey, Nina Van Pallandt

Quo Vadis**
US 1951 171m Technicolor
MGM (Sam Zimbalist)

A Roman commander under Nero falls in love with a Christian girl and jealous Poppea has them both thrown to the lions.
Spectacular but stagey and heavy-handed Hollywood version of a much-filmed colossus which shares much of its plot line with *The Sign of the Cross*. Three hours of solemn tedium with flashes of vigorous acting and a few set pieces to take the eye; but the sermonizing does not take away the bad taste of the emphasis on physical brutality.

w John Lee Mahin, S. N. Behrman, Sonya Levien *d* Mervyn Le Roy *ph* Robert Surtees, William V. Skall *m* Miklos Rozsa *ad* Cedric Gibbons, Edward Carfagno, William Horning

Robert Taylor, Deborah Kerr, *Peter Ustinov, Leo Genn, Patricia Laffan*, Finlay Currie, Abraham Sofaer, Marina Berti, Buddy Baer, Felix Aylmer, Nora Swinburne, Ralph Truman, Norman Wooland

'In making this film, MGM feel privileged to add something of permanent value to the cultural treasure house of mankind . . .'—*publicity*

'Ancient Rome is going to the dogs, Robert Taylor is going to the lions, and Peter Ustinov is going crazy!'—*publicity*

AAN: best picture; Robert Surtees, William V. Skall; Miklos Rozsa; Peter Ustinov; Leo Genn

RPM (Revolutions Per Minute)
US 1970 97m colour
Columbia / Stanley Kramer

At an American college, a middle-aged professor teaches liberal ideas.
Dim, thankfully forgotten addition to the *Strawberry Statement* cycle.

w Erich Segal *d* Stanley Kramer *ph* Michel Hugo, Perry Botkin Jnr *m* Barry de Vorzon

Anthony Quinn, Ann-Margret, Gary Lockwood, Paul Winfield, Alan Hewitt

'Three years ago Rabbit Angstrom ran out to buy his wife cigarettes. He hasn't come back yet . . .'

Rabbit, Run
US 1970 94m Technicolor Panavision
Warner (Howard Kreitsek)

A man leaves his pregnant wife for a prostitute.
Uninteresting sex melodrama without any of the wit which distinguishes the book; hard to sit through.

w Howard B. Kreitsek, *novel* John Updike *d* Jack Smight *ph* Philip Lathrop *m* Ray Burton, Brian King

James Caan, Anjanette Comer, Arthur Hill, Jack Albertson, Carrie Snodgress

The Rabbit Trap*
US 1959 76m bw
UA / Canon (Harry Kleiner)

A hardworking draughtsman finally defies his boss and completes his holiday with his family.
Watchable minor drama just about marking the end of Hollywood's infatuation with TV plays which had begun with *Marty*; the moral and family problems of ordinary people were beginning to prove a shade lacking in excitement.

w J. P. Miller, from his TV play *d Philip Leacock* *ph* Irving Glassberg *m* Jack Marshall

Ernest Borgnine, Bethel Leslie, David Brian, Kevin Corcoran

Race for the Yankee Zephyr
New Zealand / Australia 1981 108m Eastmancolor Panavision

Adventurers discover an American aircraft wrecked in 1944, and argue over the loot without knowing that it contains a 50-million-dollar payroll.
Very moderate adventure story distinguished only by good locations.

w Everett de Roche *d* David Hemmings *ph* Vincent Monton *m* Brian May

Kan Wahl, Lesley Ann Warren, Donald Pleasence, George Peppard, Bruno Lawrence, Robert Bruce

Race Street
US 1948 79m bw
RKO (Nat Holt)

A bookie vows revenge when his pal is killed by an extortionist gang, but discovers that his girl friend is married to the leader.
Routine thick-ear, quite adequately handled.

w Martin Rackin, *story* Maurice Davis *d* Edwin L. Marin *ph* J. Roy Hunt *m* Roy Webb

George Raft, Marilyn Maxwell, William Bendix, Frank Faylen, Henry Morgan, Gale Robbins

Race with the Devil
US 1975 88m De Luxe
TCF / Saber / Maslansky (Wes Bishop)

Holidaymakers witness a black mass and are pursued by the diabolists.
Silly melodrama which resolves into a wild car chase and much violence.

w Lee Frost, Wes Bishop *d* Jack Starrett *ph* Robert Jessup *m* Leonard Rosenman

Peter Fonda, Warren Oates, Loretta Swit, Lara Parker, R. G. Armstrong

'Why do you need a woman when death is your mistress every afternoon?'
'A love story that hurtles full speed across the barriers of convention!'

The Racers
US 1955 112m De Luxe Cinemascope
TCF (Julian Blaustein)
GB title: *Such Men Are Dangerous*

A Monte Carlo Rally contestant is financed by an attractive lady gambler.
Routine racing car melodrama, totally unmemorable but impersonally efficient.

w Charles Kaufman, *novel* Hans Ruesch *d* Henry Hathaway *ph* Joe MacDonald *m* Alex North

Kirk Douglas, Bella Darvi, Gilbert Roland, Cesar Romero, Lee J. Cobb, Katy Jurado, Charles Goldner, George Dolenz

Rachel and the Stranger*
US 1948 92m bw
RKO (Richard H. Berger)

A western farmer feels real love for his wife for the first time when an attractive stranger seems likely to take her away from him.
Modestly appealing romantic drama in a western setting.

w Martin Rackin, *novel* Howard Fast *d* Norman Foster *ph* Maury Gertsman *m* Roy Webb *md* Constantin Bakaleinikoff

Loretta Young, Robert Mitchum, William Holden, Gary Gray, Tom Tully, Sara Haden, Frank Ferguson

Rachel, Rachel**
US 1968 101m Eastmancolor
Warner / Kayos (Paul Newman)

Events in the life of a middle-aged schoolmistress in a small New England town.
Appealing and freshly observed study of a limited personality in a small community.

w Stewart Stern, novel A Jest of God by Margaret Laurence *d Paul Newman* *ph Gayne Rescher* *m* Jerome Moross

Joanne Woodward, Estelle Parsons, James Olson, Kate Harrington, Donald Moffat, Geraldine Fitzgerald, Bernard Barrow

'It could all very easily degenerate into a woman's weepy; and the fact that it doesn't is due largely to Newman's refusal to treat Manawaka as another Peyton Place.'—*Jan Dawson*

'It tends to verge on dullness, but something always saves it.'—*John Simon*

AAN: best picture; Stewart Stern; Joanne Woodward; Estelle Parsons

Racing with the Moon
US 1984 108m Movielab
Paramount / Jaffe-Lansing (Alain Bernheim, John Kohn)

In 1942 California, two young men await induction into the Marines and say goodbye to their girl friends.
Disappointing flashback by people who fail to capture the spirit of the time, and replace it by conventional boy-girl teenage antics.

w Steven Kloves *d* Richard Benjamin *ph* John Bailey *m* Dave Grusin *pd* David L. Snyder

Sean Penn, Elizabeth McGovern, Nicolas Cage, John Karlen, Max Showalter

The Rack
US 1956 100m bw
MGM (Arthur M. Loew Jnr)

A veteran of the Korean War is courtmartialled for collaborating with the enemy under torture.
Dullish courtroom melodrama overstretched from a TV play.

w Stewart Stern *TV play* Rod Serling *d* Arnold Laven *ph* Paul Vogel *m* Adolph Deutsch

Paul Newman, Walter Pidgeon, Edmond O'Brien, Lee Marvin, Cloris Leachman, Wendell Corey

The Racket*
US 1951 88m bw
RKO / Edmund Grainger

Police break up the empire of a powerful gangster.
Oddly timed and rather weak remake of the 1928 film; glossy but very old-fashioned in treatment.

w William Wister Haines, *play* Bartlett Cormack *d* John Cromwell *ph* George E. Diskant *m* Constantin Bakaleinikoff

Robert Ryan, Robert Mitchum, Ray Collins, Lizabeth Scott, William Talman

Racket Busters
US 1938 71m bw
Warner (Samuel Bischoff)

A gangster aiming to take over a trucking enterprise is opposed by the special prosecutor's office.
Routine cops and robbers, still very watchable but also forgettable.

w Robert Rossen, Leonardo Bercovici *d* Lloyd Bacon *ph* Arthur Edeson *m* Adolph Deutsch

George Brent, Humphrey Bogart, Gloria Dickson, Allen Jenkins, Walter Abel, Penny Singleton, Henry O'Neill

Rackety Rax
US 1932 65m bw

Gangster methods are applied to college football. Stiff burlesque which didn't transfer well from the printed page. Victor McLaglen, Greta Nissen, Nell O'Day, Alan Dinehart, Allen Jenkins. Written by Ben Markson and Lou Breslow, from novel by Joel Sayre; directed by Alfred Werker; for Fox.

Radar Men from the Moon
US 1952 bw serial: 12 eps

Commander Cody, Sky Marshal of the Universe, settles the hash of moonmen who plan to conquer the earth. Hilarious comic strip stuff played with straight faces. George Wallace, Aline Towne, Roy Barcroft, William Blakewell, Clayton Moore. Directed by Fred Brannon; for Republic.

Radar Patrol vs Spy King
US 1950 bw serial: 12 eps

International saboteurs threaten America's defence system. Lively thick ear on formula serial lines. Kirk Alyn, Jean Dean, Anthony Warde, George J. Lewis, Tristram Coffin. Directed by Fred C. Brannon; for Republic.

Radio City Revels
US 1938 90m bw

A songwriter can work only in his sleep. A wisp of plot is the peg for a very moderate revue. Bob Burns, Jack Oakie, Kenny Baker, Victor Moore, Ann Miller, Milton Berle, Helen Broderick, Jane Froman, Buster West, Richard Lane. Written by Matt Brooks, Eddie Davis, Anthony Veiller, Mortimer Offner; directed by Ben Stoloff; for RKO. 'Should do well at b.o., but no smash.'—*Variety*

Radio Days**
US 1986 85m Du Art
Orion (Robert Greenhut)

At the beginning of World War II, families near New York are affected by what they hear on the radio.
Shapeless montage of funny bits, best appreciated by those who lived through the time at somewhere near the place.

w,d Woody Allen ph Carlo Di Palma *m ed* Dick Hyman *ed* Susan E. Morse *pd* Santo Loquasto

Mia Farrow, Dianne Wiest, Seth Green, Julie Kavner, Josh Mostel, Michael Tucker, Wallace Shawn

'One of his most purely entertaining pictures.'—*Daily Variety*

AAN: best original screenplay, art direction (Speed Hopkins)

Radio Parade of 1935
GB 1934 96m bw with colour sequence

Amateur talent makes it big for a radio station. Historically interesting revue which unfortunately requires its comic lead to play straight. Will Hay, Helen Chandler, Clifford Mollison, Davy Burnaby, The Western Brothers, Alfred Drayton, Lily Morris, Nellie Wallace, Clapham and Dwyer, Claude Dampier, Ronald Frankau, Ted Ray, Beryl Orde, Stanelli. Written by Jack Davies, Paul Perez, Arthur Woods and James Bunting; directed by Arthur Woods; for BIP. (US title: *Radio Follies*.)

Radio Patrol
US 1937 bw serial: 12 eps

Radio cops foil international crooks who seek a formula for flexible bulletproof steel. Average serial chapters. Grant Withers, Catherine Hughes, Adrian Morris, Frank Lackteen. Directed by Ford Beebe and Cliff Smith; for Universal.

Radio Stars on Parade
US 1945 69m bw

Agents fix up a show despite threats from gangsters. Slim excuse for a revue including talent popular at the time. Wally Brown, Alan Carney, Frances Langford, Don Wilson, Tony Romano, Rufe Davis, Sheldon Leonard, Ralph Edwards, Skinnay Ennis and his band. Written by Robert E. Kent and Monty Brice; directed by Leslie Goodwins; for Ben Stoloff / RKO.

Rafferty and the Gold Dust Twins
US 1975 92m Technicolor Panavision
Warner / Gruskoff-Venture-Linson

A drifter encounters two female vagrants who force him at gunpoint to drive them to New Orleans and get him into various adventures.
Indulgent and unattractive 'road' movie which despite occasional amusing incident gets nowhere very slowly.

w John Kaye *d* Dick Richards *ph* Ralph Woolsey *m* Artie Butler

Alan Arkin, Sally Kellerman, MacKenzie Phillips, Alex Rocco, Charlie Martin Smith, Harry Dean Stanton, John McLiam

Raffles*
US 1939 72m bw
Samuel Goldwyn

Raffles the famous cricketer is also a compulsive and daring amateur thief.
Slight, modernized version of the turn-of-the century stories; very palatable, but it could have been better.

w John Van Druten, Sydney Howard, *novel* Raffles the Amateur Cracksman by E. W. Hornung *d* Sam Wood *ph* Gregg Toland *m* Victor Young

David Niven, Olivia de Havilland, *Dudley Digges*, May Whitty, Douglas Walton, Lionel Pape, E. E. Clive, Peter Godfrey

'Fair remake . . . moderate b.o. potential.'—*Variety*

† This was virtually a scene-for-scene remake of the 1930 Goldwyn version starring Ronald Colman, Kay Francis and Alison Skipworth. It was written by Sidney Howard and directed by George Fitzmaurice.

Rage
US 1966 103m Technicolor
Columbia / Joseph M. Schenck / Cinematografico Jalisco (Gilberto Gazcon)

A drunken doctor finds a new will to live during a difficult journey to avert a rabies epidemic.
Pattern melodrama with no surprises, but gripping most of the way.

w Teddi Sherman, Gilberto Gazcon, Fernando Mendez *d* Gilberto Gazcon *ph* Rosalio Solano *m* Gustavo Cesar Carreon

Glenn Ford, Stella Stevens, David Reynoso, Armando Silvestre

Rage
US 1972 99m De Luxe Panavision
Warner (Fred Weintraub)

A father takes revenge when his son dies after a chemical warfare accident.
Well-meaning but turgid and boring melodrama.

RAFFLES. Gentlemen crooks don't come any suaver than David Niven who seems to be looking at May Whitty's jewels with an appraiser's eye.

w Philip Friedman, Dan Kleinman *d* George C. Scott *ph* Fred Koenekamp *m* Lalo Schifrin

George C. Scott, Richard Basehart, Martin Sheen, Barnard Hughes, Stephen Young

'Sluggish, tired and tiring.'—*Variety*

Rage at Dawn
US 1955 86m Technicolor

Detectives stage a fake train robbery to attract the evil Reno brothers. Very moderate western programmer. Randolph Scott, Forrest Tucker, J. Carrol Naish, Mala Powers, Edgar Buchanan, Ray Teal. Written by Horace McCoy; directed by Tim Whelan; for Nat Holt / RKO.

Rage in Heaven
US 1941 82m bw
MGM (Gottfried Reinhardt)

An unstable millionaire becomes jealous of his wife and arranges his own death so that her supposed lover will be suspected.
Stilted melodrama with the stars more or less at sea.

w Christopher Isherwood, Robert Thoeren, *novel* James Hilton *d* W. S. Van Dyke II *ph* Oliver T. Marsh *m* Bronislau Kaper

Robert Montgomery, Ingrid Bergman, George Sanders, Lucile Watson, Oscar Homolka, Philip Merivale, Matthew Boulton, Aubrey Mather

'Nothing happens but the obvious, and that only after a long and confused struggle.'—*Otis Ferguson*

The Rage of Paris*
US 1938 78m bw
Universal (B. G. De Sylva)

Confidence tricksters invest their money in a French girl who is out to nail a millionaire.
If memory serves right, an amusingly amoral trifle in the best style of its year.

w Bruce Manning, Felix Jackson *d* Henry Koster

Danielle Darrieux, Douglas Fairbanks Jnr, Louis Hayward, Mischa Auer, Helen Broderick, Harry Davenport, Samuel S. Hinds, Mary Martin (in a bit part)

'Smart comedy of first-run calibre . . . a finished and polished job.'—*Variety*

'The names and the places didn't matter—only when!'

A Rage to Live
US 1965 101m bw Panavision
UA / Mirisch (Lewis J. Rachmil)

The unhappy college and married life of a nymphomaniac.
Well made but deliberately 'daring' case history which becomes too obvious and silly.

w John T. Kelley, *novel* John O'Hara *d* Walter Grauman *ph* Charles Lawton *m* Nelson Riddle

Suzanne Pleshette, Bradford Dillman, Ben Gazzara, Peter Graves, Bethel Leslie, James Gregory, Ruth White

'Stuff like this needs the exuberance of grand opera; sadly, all it gets here is a blue note.'—*MFB*

Raggedy Ann and Andy*
US 1977 85m Movielab Panavision
Lester Osterman (Richard Horner)

Toys come to life and have their own adventures while their owner is absent.
Attractive fully animated cartoon feature in which only the central story is lacking in pace and humour.

w Patricia Thackray, Max Wilk, *stories* Johnny Gruelle *d Richard Williams* *m* Joe Raposo

Raggedy Man
US 1981 94m Technicolor
Universal / William D. Wittliff, Burt Weissbourd

In 1944, a small-town switchboard operator and her two children are protected by a mysterious stranger.
Curious and quite unnecessary melodrama of some skill but very dubious appeal.

w William D. Wittliff *d* Jack Fisk *ph* Ralf Bode *m* Jerry Goldsmith *ed* Edward Warschilka

Sissy Spacek, Eric Roberts, Sam Shepard, William Sanderson, Tracey Walter, R. G. Armstrong

'Despite the casual, unhurried pace of the film, it doesn't seem to observe much.'—*Richard Combs, MFB*

Raging Bull*
US 1980 119m colour
UA / Chartoff-Winkler

The rise to fame of an unlikeable middle-weight boxer, based on the autobiography of Jake La Motta.
Powerfully made but very violent and alienating ringside melodrama.

w Paul Schrader, Mardik Martin *d Martin Scorsese* *ph* Michael Chapman *m* from library sources *pd* Gene Rudolf

Robert De Niro, Cathy Moriarty, Joe Pesci, Frank Vincent, Nicholas Colasanto

'Scorsese makes pictures about the kind of people you wouldn't want to know.'—*Variety*

AA: editing (Thelma Schoonmaker); Robert De Niro
AAN: best film; best direction; Cathy Moriarty; Joe Pesci; Michael Chapman
BFA: editing

'A bravura display of cinematic skill.'—*Daily Mail*

The Raging Moon*
GB 1970 111m Technicolor
EMI (Bruce Cohn Curtis)
aka: *Long Ago Tomorrow*

A love affair develops between two inmates of a home for the physically handicapped. Appealing romantic drama which nearly became a big commercial success.

wd Bryan Forbes, novel Peter Marshall
ph Tony Imi *m* Stanley Myers

Malcolm McDowell, Nanette Newman, Georgia Brown, Bernard Lee, Gerald Sim, Michael Flanders

The Raging Tide
US 1951 93m bw
U-I (Aaron Rosenberg)

A San Francisco gangster stows away on a fishing trawler and redeems himself when he perishes saving the life of a fisherman. Fearfully old-fashioned seafaring melodrama, rather well made.

w Ernest K. Gann, from his novel Fiddler's Green *d* George Sherman *ph Russell Metty*
m Frank Skinner

Richard Conte, Charles Bickford, Shelley Winters, Stephen McNally, Alex Nicol, Jesse White, John McIntire

The Ragman's Daughter
GB 1972 94m Technicolor
TCF / Penelope (Harold Becker)

A Nottingham layabout falls in love with an exciting middle-class girl; they fail to overcome parental opposition and she is killed in a road accident.
Wispy drama framed in pointless flashbacks; done on the cheap, it never seems to get anywhere and even fails to use its locations to advantage.

w Alan Sillitoe, from his short story *d* Harold Becker *ph* Michael Seresin *m* Kenny Clayton

Simon Rouse, Victoria Tennant, Patrick O'Connell, Leslie Sands

'What a time it was, an incredible time, a good time, a bad time . . .'

Ragtime*
US 1981 155m Technicolor Todd-AO
Ragtime / Sunley (Dino de Laurentiis)

Just before World War I, various Americans are affected by world events, and a chapter of accidents turns a placid negro into a revolutionary.
The fascinating patchwork of the novel has been virtually abandoned in favour of its least interesting episode, which is even further drawn out by the decision to bring on the aged James Cagney as a comic turn not in the novel. The early sequences show what might have been.

w Michael Weller, *novel* E. L. Doctorow
d Milos Forman *ph Miroslav Ondricek*
m Randy Newman

James Olson, Mary Steenburgen, James Cagney, Pat O'Brien, Elizabeth McGovern, *Howard E. Rollins Jnr*, Brad Dourif, Moses Gunn, Kenneth McMillan, Donald O'Connor

'It's limp . . . it always seems to be aiming about halfway toward the effects that Doctorow achieved in his literary extravaganza.'—*New Yorker*

'The book, despite its defects, was funny, radical and angry. The film, despite its virtues, is solemn, liberal and passive.'—*Sunday Times*

† The film cost 32 million dollars and took eleven.

AAN: screenplay; Miroslav Ondricek; Randy Newman; Elizabeth McGovern (supporting actress); Howard E. Rollins Jnr

The Raid*
US 1954 83m Technicolor
TCF (Robert L. Jacks)

In 1864 six confederate soldiers escape from a union prison, and from a Canadian refuge carry out a revenge raid on a small Vermont town.
Interesting little action drama, crisply characterized and plotted, and based on a historical incident.

w Sidney Boehm, story Affair at St Albans by Herbert Ravenal Sass *d Hugo Fregonese*
ph Lucien Ballard *m* Roy Webb

Van Heflin, Anne Bancroft, Richard Boone, Lee Marvin, Tommy Rettig, Peter Graves, Douglas Spencer, Will Wright, John Dierkes

Raid on Rommel
US 1971 99m Technicolor
Universal (Harry Tatelman)

In North Africa during World War II, a British officer releases prisoners of war and leads them in an assault on Tobruk.
Dispirited low-budget actioner apparently first intended for television.

w Richard Bluel *d* Henry Hathaway *ph* Earl Rath *m* Hal Mooney

Richard Burton, John Colicos, Clinton Greyn, Wolfgang Preiss

The Raiders
US 1964 75m Technicolor

Cattle drovers enlist the aid of famous western characters to persuade the railroad company to extend its line through dangerous country. Slightly oddball western with endearing moments amid the miscalculations. Robert Culp (as Wild Bill Hickok), Judi Meredith (as Calamity Jane), James McMullan (as Buffalo Bill Cody). Brian Keith, Alfred Ryder, Simon Oakland. Written by Gene L. Coon; directed by Herschel Daugherty; for Revue / Universal.

Raiders of Ghost City
US 1944 bw serial: 13 eps

During the Civil War, fake confederates steal bullion shipments, and a Union secret service agent is sent to investigate. Solid western adventures. Dennis Moore, Wanda McKay, Lionel Atwill, Joe Sawyer, Regis Toomey. Directed by Ray Taylor and Lewis D. Collins; for Universal.

Raiders of the Lost Ark**
US 1981 115m Metrocolor Panavision
Paramount / Lucasfilm (Frank Marshall)

In the thirties, an American archaeologist and explorer beats the Nazis to a priceless artifact, the magical box containing fragments of the stones on which God wrote his laws. Commercially very successful, this attempted wrap-up of the Saturday morning serials of two generations ago spends a great deal of money and expertise on frightening us rather than exciting us; in Dolby sound the experience is horrendous. Second time round, one can better enjoy the ingenious detail of the hero's exploits and ignore the insistence on unpleasantness; still, there are boring bits in between, and the story doesn't make a lot of sense.

w Lawrence Kasdan *d Steven Spielberg*
ph Douglas Slocombe *pd Norman Reynolds*
m John Williams

Harrison Ford, Karen Allen, Ronald Lacey, Paul Freeman, John Rhys-Davies, Denholm Elliott

'Both de trop and not enough.'—*Sight and Sound*

'Children may well enjoy its simple-mindedness, untroubled by the fact that it looks so shoddy and so uninventive.'—*Observer*

'Kinesthetically, the film gets to you, but there's no exhilaration, and no surge of feeling at the end.'—*Pauline Kael, New Yorker*

'An out of body experience, a movie of glorious imagination and breakneck speed that grabs you in the first shot, hurtles you through a series of incredible adventures, and deposits you back in reality two hours later—breathless, dizzy, wrung-out, and with a silly grin on your face.'—*Roger Ebert*

† Tom Selleck was the first choice for the lead, but was tied up with his TV series *Magnum*.

AA: editing (Michael Kahn); visual effects
AAN: best picture; Steven Spielberg; Douglas Slocombe; John Williams
BFA: Norman Reynolds

Railroaded*
US 1947 72m bw

A detective is on the trail of a ruthless mobster. A new post-war toughness was evident in this sharply made second feature. John Ireland, Sheila Ryan, Hugh Beaumont, Jane Randolph, Ed Kelly, Charles D. Brown. Written by John C. Higgins, Gertrude Walker; directed by Anthony Mann; for Charles F. Reisner / Eagle Lion.

Rails into Laramie
US 1954 81m Technicolor

Railway construction is hampered in Laramie by a saloon keeper who keeps the workers too happy. Solid co-feature western, quite enjoyable. John Payne, Dan Duryea, Mari Blanchard, Barton Maclane, Harry Shannon, Lee Van Cleef. Written by D. D. Beauchamp and Joseph Hoffman; directed by Jesse Hibbs; for Universal-International.

'A film for adults to take their children, too!'

The Railway Children***
GB 1970 108m Technicolor
EMI (Robert Lynn)

Three Edwardian children and their mother move into Yorkshire when their father is imprisoned as a spy, and have adventures on the railway line while helping to prove his innocence.
Fresh and agreeable family film with many pleasing touches to compensate for its meandering plot.

wd Lionel Jeffries, novel E. Nesbit *ph Arthur Ibbetson m* Johnny Douglas

Dinah Sheridan, William Mervyn, Jenny Agutter, Bernard Cribbins, Iain Cuthbertson, Gary Warren, Sally Thomsett

Rain*
US 1932 92m bw
(UA)
Art Cinema Corporation (Joseph Schenck)

Stranded passengers in Pago Pago during an epidemic include a prostitute and a missionary who lusts after her.
Early talkie version of a much filmed story; interesting but not very entertaining now that the sensational aspects have worn off.

w Maxwell Anderson, *play* John Colton, Clemence Randolph, *story* W. Somerset Maugham *d* Lewis Milestone *ph* Oliver T. Marsh *m* Alfred Newman

Joan Crawford, Walter Huston, William Gargan, Beulah Bondi, Matt Moore, Guy Kibbee, Walter Catlett

'A b.o. disappointer. Only the play's rep and Joan Crawford's personal pull will save it.'—*Variety*

† Other versions: *Sadie Thompson* (1928) with Gloria Swanson; *Miss Sadie Thompson* (1953) (qv).

The Rain People
US 1969 101m Technicolor
Warner / American Zoetrope (Bart Patton, Ronald Colby)

A depressed housewife leaves home, drives across country, and picks up a mentally retarded hitch-hiker who tries to protect her.
Slow, pretentious character drama which strains after art but only presents an unedifying study of failure.

wd Francis Ford Coppola *ph* Wilmer Butler *m* Ronald Stein

Shirley Knight, James Caan, Robert Duvall, Tom Aldredge, Marya Zimmet

'The rain people are people made of rain and when they cry they disappear because they cry themselves away.'—*sample dialogue*

'The siren of the sarongs is calling you!'

Rainbow Island
US 1944 95m Technicolor
Paramount (I. D. Leshin)

A white girl brought up by her doctor father on a Pacific island is pursued by three sailors escaping from the Japanese.
Cheerful spoof of the sarong cycle with the star seeing the joke; otherwise a silly service farce with South Sea trimmings.

w Walter de Leon, Seena Owen, Arthur Phillips *d* Ralph Murphy *ph* Karl Struss *m* Roy Webb *songs* Burton Lane, Ted Koehler

Dorothy Lamour, Eddie Bracken, Gil Lamb, Barry Sullivan, Forrest Orr, Anne Revere, Reed Hadley, Marc Lawrence

The Rainbow Jacket
GB 1954 99m Technicolor
Ealing (Michael Relph)

A boy jockey is blackmailed into losing a big race.
Disappointing racecourse drama which packs in all the expected ingredients.

w T. E. B. Clarke *d* Basil Dearden *ph* Otto Heller *m* William Alwyn

Kay Walsh, Bill Owen, Edward Underdown, Robert Morley, Wilfrid Hyde White, Charles Victor, Honor Blackman, Sidney James

Rainbow on the River
US 1936 83m bw

After the Civil War, an orphan is brought up by a Black mammy and later discovered to be rich. Sentimental drama with songs from its boy star; not much, but popular. Bobby Breen, May Robson, Charles Butterworth, Louise Beavers, Alan Mowbray, Benita Hume, Henry O'Neill. Written by Earle Snell, William Hurlbut, from a story by Mrs C. V. Jamison; directed by Kurt Neumann; for Sol Lesser (RKO). 'Phoney and over-sugared sentimentality.'—*Variety*

Rainbow Round My Shoulder
US 1952 78m Technicolor

A society girl breaks into show business.
Agreeable light musical for the easily pleased. Frankie Laine, Billy Daniels, Charlotte Austin, Arthur Franz, Ida Moore, Lloyd Corrigan. Written by Blake Edwards and Richard Quine; directed by Richard Quine; for Columbia.

The Rainmaker
US 1956 121m Technicolor
Vistavision
Paramount / Hal B. Wallis (Paul Nathan)

In 1913 Kansas, a fake rainmaker has more success melting the heart of a confirmed spinster.
Such a whimsical play is too talky to make a good movie, especially as the actors are over-age, their performances are mannered, the dialogue seems interminable and the production is too stagey.

w N. Richard Nash, from his play *d* Joseph Anthony *ph* Charles Lang Jnr *m* Alex North

Katharine Hepburn, Burt Lancaster, Wendell Corey, Lloyd Bridges, Earl Holliman, Cameron Prud'homme, Wallace Ford

AAN: Alex North; Katharine Hepburn

The Rainmakers
US 1935 79m bw

Fake rainmakers are chased by midwestern farmers to California, where they get involved in an irrigation scheme. Slow-paced comedy with a train chase finale which comes too late. Bert Wheeler, Robert Woolsey, Dorothy Lee, Berton Churchill, George Meeker. Written by Grant Garrett, Leslie Goodwins; directed by Fred Guiol; for RKO. 'May appeal mildly to their fans, but won't make new business.'—*Variety*

The Rains Came***
US 1939 103m bw
TCF (Harry Joe Brown)

High-class parasites in India during the Raj redeem themselves when a flood disaster strikes.
Wholly absorbing disaster spectacular in which the characterization and personal plot development are at least as interesting as the spectacle, and all are encased in a glowingly professional production.

w Philip Dunne, Julien Josephson, novel Louis Bromfield *d Clarence Brown ph Arthur Miller m Alfred Newman sp Fred Sersen*

Myrna Loy, *George Brent*, Tyrone Power, Brenda Joyce, *Maria Ouspenskaya, Joseph Schildkraut*, H. B. Warner, Nigel Bruce, Mary Nash, Jane Darwell, Marjorie Rambeau, Henry Travers

'A big box-office picture with the advantage of a new locale.'—*Variety*

'It would be difficult to improve on the direction, the outbreak of the monsoon, a curtain billowing in the breeze, a lamp casting the shadow of lattice work against white silk, servants scattering for cover . . .'—*Charles Higham, 1972*

'Slick Hollywood film-making at its professional best.'—*Channel 4, 1982*

† Myrna Loy was third choice after Dietrich and Lamarr; Brent second choice after Ronald Colman.

AAN: Alfred Newman

The Rains of Ranchipur
US 1955 104m Eastmancolor
Cinemascope
TCF (Frank Ross)

Dismal remake of *The Rains Came*, with bored actors and inferior production, all the character of the original being wiped out by badly processed wide-screen spectacle.

w Merle Miller *d* Jean Negulesco *ph* Milton Krasner *m* Hugo Friedhofer

Lana Turner, Fred MacMurray, Richard Burton, Joan Caulfield, Eugenie Leontovich, Michael Rennie

Raintree County
US 1958 166m Technicolor
Panavision (Camera 65)
MGM (David Lewis)

During the Civil War a southern belle gets the man she thinks she wants, but subsequently finds life as a schoolmaster's wife boring.
Dreary attempt by MGM to out-do *Gone with the Wind*, with neither characters nor plot one third as interesting and the production values merely expensive.

THE RAINS CAME. *Après moi, le deluge*. Myrna Loy with Maria Ouspenskaya and George Brent.

w Millard Kaufman, *novel* Ross Lockridge *d* Edward Dmytryk *ph* Robert Surtees *m* Johnny Green

Montgomery Clift, Elizabeth Taylor, Eva Marie Saint, Nigel Patrick, Lee Marvin, Rod Taylor, Agnes Moorehead, Walter Abel, Jarma Lewis, Tom Drake, Gardner McKay, Rhys Williams

AAN: Johnny Green; Elizabeth Taylor

Raise the Roof
GB 1930 77m bw

An actress is bribed to sabotage a touring show. Early talkie which retains surprising freshness. Betty Balfour, Maurice Evans, Jack Raine, Sam Livesey, Ellis Jeffreys. Written by Walter Summers, Philip MacDonald; directed by Walter Summers; for BIP.

† Credited as the first British musical.

Raise the Titanic!
US 1980 122m De Luxe
Lord Grade / Martin Starger (William Frye)

Assorted Americans try to recover rare minerals from the wreck of the ship which sank in the North Atlantic in 1912.

Heavy-going exploiter with little action and even less plot.

w Adam Kennedy, Eric Hughes, *novel* Clive Cussler *d* Jerry Jameson *ph* Matthew F. Leonetti *second unit ph* Rex Metz *underwater ph Bob Steadman* *m* John Barry *pd* John F. DeCuir

Jason Robards, Richard Jordan, Alec Guinness, David Selby, Anne Archer, J. D. Cannon

'Hits new depths hitherto unexplored by the worst of Lew Grade's overloaded ark melodramas. This one wastes a potentially intriguing premise with dull scripting, a lacklustre cast, laughably phony trick work and clunky direction that makes *Voyage of the Damned* seem inspired by comparison.'—*Variety*

'The longer it all goes on, the more one hopes that, if they ever do raise the *Titanic*, they'll heave the film overboard to replace it.'—*Guardian*

† The film cost 40 million dollars and took 7 million.

A Raisin in the Sun*
US 1961 128m bw
Columbia / Paman–Doris (David Susskind, Philip Rose)

The life of a struggling black family in a cramped Chicago flat.
Earnest but claustrophobic play-on-film which long outstays its welcome but contains good performances.

w Lorraine Hansberry, from her play *d* Daniel Petrie *ph* Charles Lawton Jnr *m* Laurence Rosenthal

Sidney Poitier, Ruby Dee, Claudia McNeil, Diana Sands, Ivan Dixon, John Fielder, Lou Gossett

Raising Arizona*
US 1987 94m Du Art

In the American heartlands, a petty crook falls for the lady cop who regularly checks him into jail. Zany collection of incidents which scarcely welds itself into a story but offers a few laughs along the way. Nicholas Cage, Holly Hunter, Trey Wilson, John Goodman, William Forsythe. Written by Ethan and Joel Coen; directed by Joel Coen; for Circle Films/TCF.

Raising the Wind
GB 1961 91m colour

Misadventures of students at a music academy. A Carry On in all but name, from the same stable; good moments among the dross. James Robertson Justice, Leslie Phillips, Kenneth Williams, Sidney James, Paul Massie, Liz Fraser, Eric Barker, Jennifer Jayne, Geoffrey Keen, Esma Cannon. Written by Bruce Montgomery; directed by Gerald Thomas; for GHW / Anglo Amalgamated.
(US title: *Roommates*.)

The Rake's Progress*
GB 1945 123m bw
GFD / Individual (Frank Launder, Sidney Gilliat)
US title: *Notorious Gentleman*

The career of a cheerful ne'er-do-well playboy of the thirties.
The road to ruin played for light comedy, with silly endpapers in which, quite out of character, the rake becomes a war hero. Generally good production, witty script.

w Frank Launder, Sidney Gilliat, *story* Val Valentine *d* Sidney Gilliat *ph* Wilkie Cooper *m* William Alwyn *pd* David Rawnsley

Rex Harrison, Lilli Palmer, Margaret Johnston, Godfrey Tearle, Griffith Jones, Guy Middleton, Jean Kent, Marie Lohr, Garry Marsh, David Horne, Alan Wheatley

† In the American version Harrison crowned the Martyrs' Memorial not with a chamber pot but with a top hat.

Rally Round the Flag Boys
US 1958 106m De Luxe Cinemascope
TCF (Leo McCarey)

A small community protests at the siting nearby of a missile base.
Raucous service and sex comedy which becomes frenetic without ever being very funny.

w Claude Binyon, Leo McCarey, *novel* Max Shulman *d* Leo McCarey *ph* Leon Shamroy *m* Cyril Mockridge

Paul Newman, Joanne Woodward, Joan Collins, Jack Carson, Dwayne Hickman, Tuesday Weld, Gale Gordon, Murvyn Vye

Rambo: First Blood Part Two
US 1985 92m Technicolor
Anabasis Investments NV / Buzz Feitshans

A special ops veteran is sent to spring POWs in Vietnam.
Absurdly overwrought comic strip action which shamefully caught the mood of America at the time of its release.

w Sylvester Stallone, James Cameron *d* George Pan Cosmatos *ph* Jack Cardiff *m* Jerry Goldsmith

Sylvester Stallone, Richard Crenna, Charles Napier, Julia Nickson, Steven Berkoff

'One mounting fireball . . . risible production, comic book heroics.'—*Variety*

Rambo III in 1988 took state-of-the-art pyrotechnics to Afghanistan.

Ramona
US 1936 90m Technicolor
TCF (Sol M. Wurtzel)

A half-breed girl and an Indian chief's son combat the greed of white pioneers.
Old-fashioned, stuffy adventure romance, much filmed in silent days.

w Lamar Trotti, *novel* Helen Hunt Jackson *d* Henry King *ph* William Skall, Chester Lyons *m* Alfred Newman

Loretta Young, Don Ameche, Kent Taylor, Pauline Frederick, Jane Darwell, Katherine de Mille, Victor Kilian, John Carradine

Rampage
US 1963 98m Technicolor
Warner Seven Arts / Talbot (William Fadiman)

Two white hunters love the same girl; one releases a tiger to harm the other, but it escapes.
Silly, unconvincing, old-style melodrama in which even the animals seem to overact.

w Robert Holt, Marguerite Roberts, *novel* Alan Caillou *d* Phil Karlson *ph* Harold Lipstein *m* Elmer Bernstein

Robert Mitchum, Jack Hawkins, Elsa Martinelli, Sabu, Emile Genest

The Ramparts We Watch*
US 1940 87m bw

A typical American family exemplifies the need for military preparedness. A feature acted by amateurs, produced by the March of Time unit; interesting rather than influential, as it still took Pearl Harbor to bring the Americans into the war. Written by Robert Richards and Cedric B. Worth; produced and directed by Louis de Rochemont; for RKO. 'It enters the fray with frankness in its favour.'—*Variety*

'A woman is soft and warm . . . and deadlier than steel!'
Ramrod
US 1947 94m bw
(MGM) Enterprise

A predatory lady ranch owner hires a tough foreman and her ruthlessness causes several deaths and a stampede.
Ho-hum minor western with fading stars.

w Jack Moffit, Graham Baker, Cecile Kramer, *story* Luke Short *d* André de Toth *ph* Russell Harlan *m* Adolph Deutsch

Veronica Lake, Joel McCrea, Preston Foster, Charles Ruggles, Donald Crisp, Arleen Whelan, Lloyd Bridges

Ran***
Japan 1985 161m colour
Herald-Ace / Nippon-Herald / Greenwich (Masato Hara, Serge Silberman)

A Japanese version of *King Lear*, with three sons instead of three daughters.
Predictable bloodshed and tremendous style are evident in this oriental epic from a master hand at the age of 75.

w Akiro Kurosawa, Hideo Oguni, Masato Ide *d Akiro Kurosawa ph Takao Saito m* Toru Takemitsu

Tatsuya Nakadai, Satoshi Terao, Jinpachi Nezu, Daisuke Ryu

'Prepare to be astonished . . . a towering achievement in any language.'—*People*

AAN: direction, photography, art direction

Rancho De Luxe
US 1974 95m De Luxe
UA / EK (Anthony Ray)

Cheerful cattle rustlers go on a binge and end up in prison.
Modern anti-everything western; it's anti-entertainment as well.

w Thomas McGuane *d* Frank Perry *ph* William A. Fraker *m* Jimmy Buffett

Sam Waterston, Jeff Bridges, Elizabeth Ashley, Charlene Dallas, Clifton James, Slim Pickens

'Where anything goes . . . for a price!'
Rancho Notorious
US 1952 89m Technicolor
RKO / Fidelity (Howard Welsch)

A cowboy seeking revenge for his girl friend's murder follows a clue to a lonely ranch run by a saloon singer.
Curious western which seems to have been intended as another *Destry Rides Again* but is made in a hard inflexible style which prevents it from appealing.

w Daniel Taradash *d* Fritz Lang *ph* Hal Mohr *m* Hugo Friedhofer *md* Emil Newman

Marlene Dietrich, Arthur Kennedy, Mel Ferrer, Gloria Henry, William Frawley, Jack Elam

'Every quality you might ask of a western is in lavish supply—except entertainment value.'—*Alton Cook*

Random Harvest***
US 1942 126m bw
MGM (Sidney Franklin)

A shell-shocked officer in the 1914–18 war escapes from an asylum, marries a music hall singer and is idyllically happy until a shock makes him remember that he is the head of a noble family. His wife, whom he does not now remember, dutifully becomes his secretary and years later another shock brings memory and happiness back.
A silly enough story works remarkably well in this rather splendid, no holds barred, roses round the door romance in Hollywood's best style with incomparable stars. A triumph of the Peg's Paper syndrome, and hugely enjoyable because it is done so enthusiastically.

w Claudine West, George Froeschel, Arthur Wimperis, *novel* James Hilton *d Mervyn Le Roy ph* Joseph Ruttenberg *m* Herbert Stothart

Ronald Colman, Greer Garson, Susan Peters, Philip Dorn, Reginald Owen, Henry Travers, Margaret Wycherly, Bramwell Fletcher, Arthur Margetson

'I would like to recommend this film to those who can stay interested in Ronald Colman's amnesia for two hours and who could with pleasure eat a bowl of Yardley's shaving soap for breakfast.'—*James Agee*

'A strangely empty film . . . its characters are creatures of fortune, not partisans in determining their own fates.'—*Bosley Crowther, New York Times*

'It is cast with pearly players in every part. Its pedigreed plot is savoured with just the right mixture of ups and downs, ecstasy and well-bred anguish, implausibility and psyche. And it moves towards its climax with the measured tread and nicely timed emotional bumps of a Hearst Cosmopolitan serial. It is perhaps the clearest example of the year of how a studio possessing lion's shares of movie-making capital and ingratiating talent can mate these two to synthesize a magnificent neuter, which will predictably bring in vast box office returns with which to produce more neuters.'—*John McManus, PM*

AAN: best picture; script; Mervyn Le Roy; Herbert Stothart; Ronald Colman; Susan Peters

Rangers of Fortune
US 1940 79m bw

Three amiable gun-runners clean up a southwest town. Good reliable western with star appeal. Fred MacMurray, Albert Dekker, Gilbert Roland, Patricia Morison, Joseph Schildkraut, Dick Foran, Betty Brewer. Written by Frank Butler; directed by Sam Wood; for Dale Van Every / Paramount.

Rango
US 1931 70m bw

An old man and a boy in Sumatra go about their business of killing tigers. Faded semi-documentary by the man who was about to direct *King Kong*. Claude King, Douglas Scott. Written and directed by Ernest B. Schoedsack; for Paramount.

Ransom*
US 1955 104m bw
MGM (Nicholas Nayfack)

A rich man takes desperate measures to rescue his son from a kidnapper.
Solid but overlong suspenser, virtually a vehicle for a star at his twitchiest and most dogged.

w Cyril Hume, Richard Maibaum *d* Alex Segal *ph* Arthur E. Arling *m* Jeff Alexander

Glenn Ford, Donna Reed, Leslie Nielsen, Juano Hernandez, Robert Keith

'He faced a decision that someday may be yours to make!'—*publicity*

Ransom*
GB 1975 98m Eastmancolor
Lion International (Peter Rawley)
aka: *The Terrorists*

A British ambassador to Scandinavia is kidnapped by terrorists and a Norwegian security chief gives chase.
Topical but unconvincing action thriller with unfamiliar detail; builds up to exciting sequences but is quickly forgotten.

w Paul Wheeler *d* Caspar Wrede *ph Sven Nykvist m* Jerry Goldsmith

Sean Connery, Ian McShane, Norman Bristow, John Cording, Isabel Dean, William Fox, Robert Harris

Rapture
US / France 1965 104m bw
International Classics / TCF (Christian Ferry)

A mentally unstable girl has a tragic romance with a fugitive murderer.
Gloomy all the way, and if it's art it needs explaining.

w Stanley Mann, *novel* Rapture in My Rags by Phyllis Hastings *d* John Guillermin *ph* Marcel Grignon

Patricia Gozzi, Dean Stockwell, Melvyn Douglas, Gunnel Lindblom

The Rare Breed
US 1966 97m Technicolor Panavision
Universal (William Alland)

An English bull is taken by its woman owner to St Louis to breed with American longhorns, and various frictions are caused among the ranchers.
Amusing western idea which misses fire by not coming down firmly as either drama or comedy; it does however pass the time amiably enough.

w Ric Hardman *d* Andrew V. McLaglen *ph* William H. Clothier *m* Johnny Williams

James Stewart, Maureen O'Hara, Brian Keith, Juliet Mills, Don Galloway, David Brian, Jack Elam, Ben Johnson

Rascals
US 1938 77m bw

A rich young man and a girl suffering from amnesia join a gypsy troupe. Absurdly cast and plotted semi-musical with a certain liveliness to keep it going. Jane Withers, Borrah Minevitch and his Rascals, Robert Wilcox, Rochelle Hudson, Steffi Duna. Written by Robert Ellis, Helen Logan; directed by H. Bruce Humberstone; for TCF.
'In the main amusing and entertaining.'—*Variety*

Rashomon***
Japan 1951 83m bw
Daiei (Jingo Minoura)
aka: *In the Woods*

In medieval Japan, four people have different versions of a violent incident when a bandit attacks a nobleman in the forest.
Indescribably vivid in itself, and genuinely strange (one of the versions is told by a ghost), *Rashomon* reintroduced Japanese films to the world market and was remade (badly) in Hollywood as *The Outrage*.

wd Akira Kurosawa, story Inside a Bush by Ryunosuke Akutagawa *ph* Kazuo Matsuyama *m* Takashi Matsuyama

Toshiro Mifune, Machiko Kyo, Masayuki Mori, Takashi Shimura

'A masterpiece, and a revelation.'—*Gavin Lambert, MFB*

AA: best foreign film

Raskolnikov*
Germany 1923 80m approx (at 24 fps) bw silent
Neumann (Robert Wiene)

A student kills a pawnbroker and is hounded by a police inspector until he confesses.
Interesting adaptation of *Crime and Punishment* with some of the expressionist aspects of the same director's *The Cabinet of Dr Caligari.*

wd Robert Wiene ph Willy Godberger *ad Andre Andreyev*

Gregory Khmara, Michael Tarkhanov, Pavel Pavlov, Vera Toma

Rasputin and the Empress*
US 1932 133m bw
MGM (Irving Thalberg)
GB title: *Rasputin the Mad Monk*

The story of the last years of the Russian court, when a sinister monk gained influence over the empress.
An unhappy film which was besieged by lawsuits and never generated much drama of its own despite starring the three Barrymores, who all seemed to be acting in separate rooms. Production values are the most impressive thing about it.

w Charles MacArthur *d* Richard Boleslawski *ph* William Daniels *m* Herbert Stothart

John Barrymore, Ethel Barrymore, Lionel Barrymore, Diana Wynyard, Ralph Morgan, C. Henry Gordon, Edward Arnold, Jean Parker, Gustav Von Seyffertitz, Anne Shirley (Dawn O'Day)

† The lawsuit was by Prince Youssoupoff (portrayed as Chegodieff), who claimed that although he did kill Rasputin his wife was never raped. He was awarded one million dollars.

AAN: Charles MacArthur

Rasputin the Mad Monk
GB 1966 92m De Luxe CinemaScope

A recapitulation of well-known events with fictional trimmings. Dreary excuse for Christopher Lee to go berserk. Also in cast: Barbara Shelley, Richard Pasco, Francis Matthews, Renee Asherson. Written by John Elder; directed by Don Sharp; for Hammer/7 Arts.

The Rat*
GB 1937 72m bw

A Parisian thief takes the blame for murder, but is saved by the socialite who loves him. Rather smart talkie version of a well-worn theatrical hit, previously filmed in 1925 as a silent, with Ivor Novello as star. Anton Walbrook, Ruth Chatterton, Rene Ray, Beatrix Lehmann, Felix Aylmer, Mary Clare. Written by Hans Rameau, Marjorie Gaffney, Miles Malleson and Romney Brent, from the play by Ivor Novello and Constance Collier; directed by Jack Raymond; for Herbert Wilcox/Imperator.

The Rat Race*
US 1960 105m Technicolor
Paramount / Perlberg–Seaton

A young jazz musician and a dance hall hostess share a flat and face the adversities of New York.
A kind of sour fairy tale of the big city which has neither enough jokes nor enough incident but purveys the kind of charm that grows on one despite oneself.

w Garson Kanin, from his play *d* Robert Mulligan *ph* Robert Burks *m* Elmer Bernstein

Tony Curtis, Debbie Reynolds, Jack Oakie, Kay Medford, Don Rickles

'The New Yorkers of *The Rat Race* – noisy soft-hearted landlady, philosophical bartender, backchatting taxi driver – are as familiar as the settings of shabby apartment house and quiet little bar across the street. Film makers no longer need to invent here – they simply move in for a few weeks.'—*Penelope Houston*

Ratboy
US 1986 104m Technicolor

A half-rodent alien gets the anticipated rough treatment when he visits Earth. Clint Eastwood's favourite co-star was given leave to make the film of her choice, but the choice is inexplicable in the wake of so many other *E.T.* imitations. Sondra Locke, Robert Townsend, Christopher Hewett, Larry Hankin. Written by Rob Thompson; directed by Sondra Locke; for Malpaso / Warner.

Rationing
US 1943 93m bw

A small-town shopkeeper is frustrated by wartime restrictions. Amiable comedy for established stars. Wallace Beery, Majorie Main, Donald Meek, Howard Freeman, Connie Gilchrist. Written by William Lipman, Grant Garrett and Harry Ruskin; directed by Willis Goldbeck; for MGM.

Raton Pass
US 1951 84m bw

A greedy wife swindles her husband out of his share in their ranch. Unusual western melodrama; quite entertaining. Dennis Morgan, Patricia Neal, Steve Cochran, Scott Forbes, Dorothy Hart. Written by Tom

Blackburn and James Webb; directed by Edwin L. Marin; for Warner. (GB title: *Canyon Pass.*)

Rattle of a Simple Man
GB 1964 95m bw
Sydney Box (William Gell)

A shy football supporter in London spends the night with a tart for a bet.
Archetypal farcical situation with sentiment added to string it out to twice its proper length. Production values modest but adequate.

w Charles Dyer, from his play *d* Muriel Box *ph* Reg Wyer *m* Stanley Black

Harry H. Corbett, *Diane Cilento,* Thora Hird, Charles Dyer

The Raven*
US 1935 61m bw
Universal

A doctor obsessed by Poe-inspired torture devices transforms a gangster on the run into a hideous mutant.
Silly but quite effective horror film with memorable sequences.

w David Boehm *d* Lew Landers *ph* Charles Stumar *md* Gilbert Kurland

Bela Lugosi, Boris Karloff, Samuel S. Hinds, Irene Ware, Lester Matthews

'Maintains Universal's high batting average with the shockers . . . should come through with nice grosses.'—*Variety*

The Raven*
US 1963 86m Pathecolor Panavision
AIP / Alta Vista (Roger Corman)

Two 15th-century conjurors fight a deadly duel of magic.
The rather splendid duel is a long time coming; the preliminaries are largely confined to chat in a single set, and the random jokes do not quite atone for the boredom.

w Richard Matheson *d* Roger Corman *ph Floyd Crosby m* Les Baxter

Vincent Price, Peter Lorre, Boris Karloff, Hazel Court, Jack Nicholson

Raw Deal
US 1948 78m bw

A convict is helped by his girl friend to escape, and the police chase them across country.
Fairly violent crime melodrama which holds the attention. Dennis O'Keefe, Claire Trevor, Marsha Hunt, John Ireland, Raymond Burr. Written by Leopold Atlas and John C. Higgins; directed by Anthony Mann; for Reliance / Eagle Lion.

Raw Deal
US 1986 106m Technicolor JDC Wide Screen
De Laurentiis / International (Martha Schumacher)

An ex-FBI man is recruited to infiltrate Chicago's biggest mob.
Violent crime hokum with momentary amusements.

w Gary M. DeVore, Norman Wexler *d* John Irvin *ph* Alex Thomson *m* Cinemascore

Arnold Schwarzenegger, Kathryn Harrold, Sam Wanamaker, Paul Shenar, Ed Lauter, Darren McGavin, Joe Regalbuto

'Comic book crime meller suffers from an irredeemable script'—*Variety*

Raw Edge
US 1956 76m Technicolor

A rancher's workers plan to kill him. Tense, fairly adult western. Rory Calhoun, Yvonne de Carlo, Mara Corday, Rex Reason, Neville Brand. Written by Harry Essex and Robert Hill; directed by John Sherwood; for Universal-International.

Raw Wind in Eden
US 1958 93m Eastmancolor Cinemascope
U-I (William Alland)

A model is stranded on a Sardinian island, and falls in love with a mysterious American who turns out to be a disillusioned millionaire.
Wish-fulfilment woman's picture with the occasional relief of a smart line.

w Elizabeth and Richard Wilson *d* Richard Wilson *ph* Enzo Serafin *m* Hans Salter

Esther Williams, Jeff Chandler, Carlos Thompson, Rossana Podesta, Eduardo de Filippo, Rik Battaglia

Rawhide**
US 1950 86m bw
TCF (Samuel G. Engel)
TV title: *Desperate Siege*

Four escaped convicts terrorize a stagecoach stop.
Good suspense western with excellent technical credits.

w Dudley Nichols d Henry Hathaway ph Milton Krasner m Sol Kaplan

Tyrone Power, Susan Hayward, Hugh Marlowe, Jack Elam, Dean Jagger, George Tobias, Edgar Buchanan, Jeff Corey

Razorback
Australia 1984 95m colour Panavision

In a small outback town a man is tried for the murder of his grandson, actually carried off by a wild boar. Grim images of Australian life pepper this cross between *Jaws* and the dingo baby case. Not, as they say, for the squeamish. Gregory Harrison, Arkie Whiteley, Bill Kerr, Chris Haywood. Written by Everett De Roche, from novel by Peter Brennan; directed by Russell Mulcahy; for UAA / Western.

'Between love and hatred there is a line as sharp as a razor's edge!'

The Razor's Edge*
US 1946 146m bw
TCF (Darryl F. Zanuck)

A well-to-do young man spends the years between the wars first idling, then looking for essential truth.
The novel was an empty parable with amusing trimmings. In the film the trimmings seem less amusing, but the presentation is glossy.

w Lamar Trotti, *novel* W. Somerset Maugham *d* Edmund Goulding *ph* Arthur Miller *m* Alfred Newman *ad* Richard Day, Nathan Juran

Tyrone Power, Gene Tierney, *Clifton Webb, Herbert Marshall,* John Payne, Anne Baxter, Lucile Watson, Frank Latimore, Elsa Lanchester, Fritz Kortner

'I like Somerset Maugham when he's looking through keyholes or down cracks, not at vistas.'—*Richard Winnington*

'Almost as irresistibly funny and terrible as *The Fountainhead*.'—*Pauline Kael, 70s*

† Maugham has a different source for his title, in the shape of an Oriental proverb, probably invented: 'The sharp edge of a razor is difficult to pass over; thus the wise say that the path to salvation is hard.'

AA: Anne Baxter
AAN: best picture; Clifton Webb

The Razor's Edge
US 1984 128m colour
Columbia (Robert P. Marucci, Harry Benn)

An unlikely remake which came into being because the star persuaded the studio to do it, then failed in his attempt to convey the necessary spirituality. As for the rest, the time is out of joint (except for Denholm Elliott).

w John Byrum, Bill Murray *d* John Byrum *ph* Peter Hannan *m* Jack Nietzche *pd* Philip Harrison *ed* Peter Boyle

Bill Murray, Denholm Elliott, Theresa Russel, Catherine Hicks, James Keach, Peter Vaughan, Faith Brook

Reach for Glory*
GB 1962 86m bw
Columbia / Blazer (John Kohn, Jud Kinberg)

During World War II, evacuee boys play war games and a German refugee is accidentally killed.
Grim and unpalatable parable, competently rather than excitingly made.

w John Rae, from his novel The Custard Boys *d* Philip Leacock *ph* Bob Huke *m* Bob Russell

Kay Walsh, Harry Andrews, Michael Anderson Jnr, Oliver Grimm, Alexis Kanner, Martin Stephenson, Richard Vernon

Reach for the Sky*
GB 1956 135m bw
Rank / Pinnacle (Daniel M. Angel)

Douglas Bader loses both legs in a 1931 air crash, learns to walk on artificial limbs and flies again in World War II.

Box office exploitation of one man's personal heroism, adequately but not inspiringly put together with many stiff upper lips and much jocular humour.

wd Lewis Gilbert, *book* Paul Brickhill *ph* Jack Asher *m* John Addison

Kenneth More, Muriel Pavlow, Lyndon Brook, Lee Patterson, Alexander Knox, Dorothy Alison, Sydney Tafler, Howard Marion Crawford

Reaching for the Moon
US 1931 90m bw
United Artists (Douglas Fairbanks)

On a transatlantic liner, a new cocktail has a sensational effect on a mild-mannered hero.
Very flimsy comedy with songs and some athletic stunts for its hero.

wd Edmund Goulding *ph* Ray June *song* Irving Berlin

Douglas Fairbanks, Bebe Daniels, Edward Everett Horton, Claud Allister, Jack Mulhall, Bing Crosby

'Not a smash entry, but should do moderately and perhaps a little better than that.'—*Variety*

'You'll love them as much as they love each other!'
Reaching for the Sun
US 1941 90m bw

A clam digger who needs an outboard motor goes to work in a Detroit car plant. Easygoing comedy, too muted to recommend itself widely. Joel McCrea, Ellen Drew, Eddie Bracken, Albert Dekker. Written by W. L. River from a novel by Wessel Smitter; directed by William Wellman; for Paramount.

Ready Willing and Able
US 1937 93m bw
Warner (Samuel Bischoff)

Two songwriters import an English leading lady for their new show.
Lightweight star musical with no outstanding qualities except a number in which girls dance on the keys of a huge typewriter.

w Sig Herzig, Jerry Wald, Warren Duff *d* Ray Enright *ph* Sol Polito *ch* Bobby Connelly *songs* Johnny Mercer, Richard Whiting

Ruby Keeler, Ross Alexander, Lee Dixon, Wini Shaw, Jane Wyman, Allen Jenkins

'Too many numbers and a slow script.'—*Variety*

'Always outnumbered! Never outfought!'
'One of the most stunning dramas of love and courage ever brought to the screen!'
The Real Glory*
US 1939 96m bw
Samuel Goldwyn

Soldiers of fortune help the American Army to quell a terrorist uprising in the Philippines just after the Spanish-American War.
Well made Gunga Dinnery.

w Jo Swerling, Robert R. Presnell *d* Henry Hathaway *ph* Rudolph Maté *m* Alfred Newman *ad* James Basevi

Gary Cooper, David Niven, Broderick Crawford, Andrea Leeds, Reginald Owen, Kay Johnson, Russell Hicks, Vladimir Sokoloff

'Moro uprisings, guerrilla warfare, cholera epidemics, and fancy exhibitions of inhuman cruelty are the frame against which an innocuous melodramatic yarn is told.'—*Variety*

'The same sort of picture as *Gunga Din.*'—*Richard Mallett, Punch*

'Recommended to adolescents of all ages.'—*New Statesman*

'In times like these, we question the wisdom of rattling the bones in Yankee imperialism's closet.'—*Daily Worker*

Real Life
GB 1983 93m colour

An estate agent's assistant with a vivid imagination becomes involved in thefts. Clumsy, witless comedy which quickly bores. Rupert Everett, Cristina Raines, Norman Beaton, Warren Clarke, Isla Blair, James Faulkner. Written by Francis Megahy, Bernie Cooper; directed by Francis Megahy; for The Real Life Partnership. 'Try as one may to look sympathetically on this brand of independent British venture, the resolute lack of wit or style wipes the indulgent smile from one's lips early on, and it never returns.'—*Guardian*

'Death is just the beginning!'
Re-animator
US 1985 86m De Luxe

When a crazy scientist brings people back to life, they come back violent. Gross and grisly horror comic which amused some critics. Jeffrey Combs, Bruce Abbott, Barbara Crampton. Written by Dennis Paoli, William J. Norris, Stuart Gordon, from story by H. P. Lovecraft; directed by Stuart Gordon; for Empire International. 'For those with a strong sense of humour, and a stomach stronger still.'—*Sunday Times.* 'A cheap smell of excess.'—*Observer*

'Man against terrifying monster—in the most spectacular underwater scenes ever filmed!'
Reap the Wild Wind**
US 1942 124m Technicolor
Paramount / Cecil B. de Mille

Seafaring salvage engineers fight over a southern belle.
Georgia-set period adventure; intended as another *Gone with the Wind,* it simply doesn't have the necessary, but on its level it entertains solidly, climaxing with the famous giant squid fight.

w Alan le May, Jesse Lasky Jnr *d Cecil B. de Mille* *ph* Victor Milner, Dewey Wrigley, William V. Skall *m* Victor Young *ad* Hans Dreier, Roland Anderson

Ray Milland, John Wayne, *Paulette Goddard,* Raymond Massey, Robert Preston, Lynne Overman, Susan Hayward, Charles Bickford, Walter Hampden, Louise Beavers, Martha O'Driscoll, Hedda Hopper

'The essence of all his experience, the apogee of all his art, and as jamfull a motion picture as has ever played two hours upon a screen.'—*Howard Barnes, New York Herald Tribune*

† The underwater scenes were filmed in the Santa Monica Pan Pacific Marine Museum, which had a pool 100 feet long and 50 feet wide. The 50-foot giant squid was operated by a 24-button electronic keyboard.

AAN: photography

Rear Window***
US 1954 112m Technicolor
Alfred Hitchcock

A news photographer, confined to his room by a broken leg, sees a murder committed in a room on the other side of the court.
Artificial but fairly gripping suspenser of an unusual kind; with such restricted settings, all depends on the script and the acting, and they generally come up trumps.

w John Michael Hayes, novel Cornell Woolrich *d Alfred Hitchcock* *ph* Robert Burks *m* Franz Waxman

James Stewart, Grace Kelly, Raymond Burr, Judith Evelyn, Wendell Corey, Thelma Ritter

AAN: John Michael Hayes; Alfred Hitchcock; Robert Burks

Rebecca****
US 1940 130m bw
David O. Selznick

The naïve young second wife of a Cornish landowner is haunted by the image of his glamorous first wife Rebecca.
The supreme Hollywood entertainment package, set in Monte Carlo and Cornwall, with generous helpings of romance, comedy, suspense, melodrama and mystery, all indulged in by strongly-drawn characters, and directed by the new English wizard for the glossiest producer in town, from a novel which sold millions of copies. It really couldn't miss, and it didn't.

w Robert E. Sherwood, Joan Harrison, novel Daphne du Maurier *d Alfred Hitchcock* *ph George Barnes* *m Franz Waxman*

Laurence Olivier, Joan Fontaine, George Sanders, Judith Anderson, Nigel Bruce, Gladys Cooper, Florence Bates, Reginald Denny, C. Aubrey Smith, Melville Cooper, Leo G. Carroll, Leonard Carey

NARRATOR: 'Last night I dreamed I went to Manderley again . . .'

FAVELL (George Sanders) to Mrs De Winter: 'I say, marriage with Max is not exactly a bed of roses, is it?'

MRS DANVERS (Judith Anderson): 'You're overwrought, madam. I've opened a window for you. A little air will do you good. Why don't you go? Why don't you leave Manderley? He doesn't need you. He's got his memories. He doesn't love you—he wants to be alone again with *her*. You've nothing to stay for. You've nothing to live for, have you, really? Look down there. It's easy, isn't it? Why don't you? Go on, go on. Don't be afraid . . .'

MAXIM (Laurence Olivier): 'You thought I loved Rebecca? You thought that? I hated her. Oh, I was carried away by her—enchanted by her, as everyone was—and when I was married, I was told I was the luckiest man in the world. She was so lovely, so accomplished, so amusing. "She's got the three things that really matter in a wife," everyone said, "breeding, brains and beauty." And I believed them completely. But I never had a moment's happiness with her. She was incapable of love, or tenderness, or decency.'

'A carefully considered trying out of the superior technical resources now at Hitchcock's disposal.'—*George Perry, 1965*

'Hitchcock fans will have to put up with a surprising lack of the characteristic Hitchcock improvisations in the way of salty minor personages and humorous interludes, and satisfy themselves with a masterly exhibition of the Hitchcock skill in creating suspense and shock with his action and his camera.'—*National Board of Review*

'Riveting and painful—a tale of fear and guilt, class and power.'—*Time Out, 1988*

'Hitch kept me off balance, much to his own delight . . . he would constantly tell me that no one thought I was very good except himself.'—*Joan Fontaine*

† Original casting thoughts, all rejected, were Ronald Colman, William Powell and Leslie Howard for Maxim; Anne Baxter, Margaret Sullavan, Loretta Young, Vivien Leigh and Olivia de Havilland (for the second Mrs De Winter).

AA: best picture; George Barnes
AAN: script; Alfred Hitchcock; Franz Waxman; Laurence Olivier; Joan Fontaine; Judith Anderson

Rebecca of Sunnybrook Farm
US 1932 75m bw

A rural glad girl wins over her dour aunt and reforms an atheist. Routine sound remake of the children's classic in a 1921 silent version of which Mary Pickford starred. Marian Nixon, Ralph Bellamy, Mae Marsh, Louise Closser Hale, Alan Hale, Charlotte Henry. Written by S. N. Behrman, Sonya Levien, from the novel by Kate Douglas Wiggin and Charlotte Thompson; directed by Alfred Santell; for Fox.

Rebecca of Sunnybrook Farm
US 1938 80m bw
TCF (Raymond Griffith)

A child performer becomes a pawn in the fight to exploit her talents on radio.
Unrecognizable revamping of a famous story makes a very thin star vehicle.

w Karl Tunberg, Don Ettlinger, *novel* Kate Douglas Wiggin *d* Allan Dwan *ph* Arthur Miller *m* Arthur Lange *songs* various

Shirley Temple, Randolph Scott, Jack Haley, Gloria Stuart, Phyllis Brooks, Helen Westley, Slim Summerville, Bill Robinson

'More fitting title would be *Rebecca of Radio City* . . . a weak story, indifferently directed and acted.'—*Variety*

The Rebel*
GB 1960 105m Technicolor
Associated British (W. A. Whitaker)
US title: *Call Me Genius*

A suburban businessman goes to Paris to become an artist.
A kind of farcical *The Moon and Sixpence*, insufficiently well tailored to the requirements of a very specialized comic, but occasionally diverting none the less.

w Alan Simpson, Ray Galton *d* Robert Day *ph* Gilbert Taylor *m* Frank Cordell

Tony Hancock, George Sanders, Paul Massie, Margit Saad, Grégoire Aslan, Dennis Price, Irene Handl, Mervyn Johns, Peter Bull, John Le Mesurier, Nanette Newman, Oliver Reed, John Wood

'The more prosaic the setting, the funnier Hancock seems; transplanted into a conventionally silly screen art world, he is submerged among the other grotesques.'—*Penelope Houston*

Rebel in Town
US 1956 78m bw

A bank robber accidentally kills a small boy and is hunted down by the father. Surprisingly stark western with no particular merit. John Payne, John Smith, Ruth Roman, J. Carrol Naish, Ben Cooper. Written by Danny Arnold; directed by Alfred Werker; for Bel Air / UA.

The Rebel Son
GB 1939 90m bw
London Films Omnia (E. C. Molinier, Charles David)

A Tartar leader's son falls in love with the daughter of the opposing leader.
Resistible grafting of the Romeo and Juliet story into the barbarians of the Steppes, with much carousing and threatened violence surrounding a good central performance. It includes much footage from a 1936 French film, *Taras Bulba*.

w Adrian Brunel, *story* Gogol *d* Alexis Granowsky and Adrian Brunel *ph* Franz Planer and Bernard Browne

Harry Baur, Patricia Roc, Roger Livesey, Anthony Bushell, Joan Gardner

'The bad boy from a good family!'
Rebel without a Cause**
US 1955 111m Warnercolor Cinemascope
Warner (David Weisbart)

The adolescent son of a well-to-do family gets into trouble with other kids and the police.
The first film to suggest that juvenile violence is not necessarily bred in the slums, this somewhat dreary melodrama also catapulted James Dean to stardom as the prototype fifties rebel.

w Stewart Stern *d* Nicholas Ray *ph* Ernest Haller *m* Leonard Rosenman

James Dean, Natalie Wood, Jim Backus, Sal Mineo, Ann Doran, Dennis Hopper

AAN: original story (Nicholas Ray); Natalie Wood; Sal Mineo

Rebound
US 1931 88m bw

A woman tries to forgive her husband when he is jilted by a girl friend. A sophisticated stage comedy presented with the minimum of alteration. Ina Claire, Robert Williams, Robert Ames, Myrna Loy, Hedda Hopper, Louise Closser Hale. Written by Horace Jackson from the play by Donald Ogden Stuart; directed by E. H. Griffith; for RKO-Pathé. 'A splendidly made picture which will delight smart audiences.'—*Variety*

'The biggest musical show of the century, with a throbbing love story as exciting as its title!'
Reckless
US 1935 96m bw
MGM (David O. Selznick)

A theatrical agent loves the glamorous star he represents, but she marries a drunken millionaire.
Remarkably flat backstage melodrama with music, based on the life of Libby Holman.

w P. J. Wolfson *d* Victor Fleming *ph* George Folsey *songs* various *md* Edward Ward

Jean Harlow, William Powell, Franchot Tone, May Robson, Ted Healy, Nat Pendleton, Rosalind Russell, Henry Stephenson

'Several sets of dramatic premises are established and then permitted to wander aimlessly, making the 93 minutes seem much longer than that.'—*Variety*

The Reckless Moment*
US 1949 82m bw
Columbia (Walter Wanger)

A woman accidentally kills her daughter's would-be seducer, and is then trailed by a blackmailer.
Uninteresting melodrama electrified by Ophuls' direction, which might have been applied to something more worthwhile.

w Henry Garson, R. W. Soderborg, *novel* The Blank Wall by Elizabeth Sanxay Holding *d Max Ophuls* *ph* Burnett Guffey *m* Hans Salter *md* Morris Stoloff

Joan Bennett, James Mason, Geraldine Brooks, Henry O'Neill, Shepperd Strudwick

'Swift, sure narrative and solidly pleasurable detail.'—*Richard Winnington*

The Reckoning**
GB 1969 108m Technicolor
Columbia / Ronald Shedlo (Hugh Perceval)

A tough London executive with a Liverpool-Irish background has a brutal streak and a self-destructive urge, but goes on narrowly averting misfortune.

Interesting melodrama of a man disgusted with both bourgeois and working-class values; slickly made and fast-moving.

w John McGrath, novel The Harp That Once by Patrick Hall *d Jack Gold ph Geoffrey Unsworth m* Malcolm Arnold

Nicol Williamson, Rachel Roberts, Paul Rogers, Zena Walker, Ann Bell, Gwen Nelson, J. G. Devlin

The Red Badge of Courage**
US 1951 69m bw
MGM (Gottfried Reinhardt)

A youth called up during the Civil War gets his first taste of battle.
Fresh, poetic, but dramatically unsatisfactory filming of a classic American novel. The story of its production is fascinatingly told in *Picture,* a book by Lillian Ross.

wd John Huston, novel Stephen Crane *ph Harold Rosson m Bronislau Kaper*

Audie Murphy, Bill Mauldin, Douglas Dick, Royal Dano, John Dierkes, Andy Devine, Arthur Hunnicutt

Red Ball Express
US 1952 83 bw
U-I (Aaron Rosenberg)

A supply column runs from the Normandy beachhead to Patton's army on the outskirts of Paris.
Standard war adventure, not too convincingly mounted but providing the usual excitements.

w John Michael Hayes *d* Budd Boetticher *ph* Maury Gertsman

Jeff Chandler, Sidney Poitier, Alex Nicol, Judith Braun, Hugh O'Brian, Jack Kelly, Jack Warden

The Red Balloon****
France 1955 34m Technicolor

A lonely boy finds a balloon which becomes his constant companion and finally lifts him to the skies. Absorbing and quite perfectly timed fantasy, one of the great film shorts. With Pascal Lamorisse; written and directed by *Albert Lamorisse*; photographed by *Edmond Sechan*; music by *Maurice Le Roux*; for Films Montsouris.

Red Barry
US 1938 bw serial: 13 eps

A famous detective chases villains named Natacha and Chong Lee. Acceptable serial thick ear. Buster Crabbe, Frances Robinson, Edna Sedgwick, Cyril Delevanti, Frank Lackteen. Directed by Ford Beebe and Alan James; for Universal.

The Red Beret
GB 1953 88m Technicolor
Warwick (Irving Allen, Albert R. Broccoli)
US title: *Paratrooper*

In 1940, an American with a guilt complex joins the British paratroopers.
Routine war action flagwaver; good battle scenes, rubbish in between.

w Richard Maibaum, Frank Nugent, *book* Hilary St George Saunders *d* Terence Young *ph* John Wilcox *m* John Addison

Alan Ladd, Susan Stephen, Leo Genn, Harry Andrews, Donald Houston, Anthony Bushell, Patric Doonan, Stanley Baker, Lana Morris

Red Canyon
US 1949 82m Technicolor

A cowboy drifter sets out to corral a famous wild stallion. Old-fashioned family western. Howard Duff, George Brent, Ann Blyth, Edgar Buchanan, John McIntire, Chill Wills, Jane Darwell, Lloyd Bridges. Written by Maurice Geraghty, from novel by Zane Grey; directed by George Sherman; for Leonard Goldstein / Universal.

The Red Danube
US 1950 119m bw
MGM (Carey Wilson)

In occupied Vienna, citizens are being returned to Russia against their will.
Tedious and silly Red-baiting cold war charade.

w Gina Kaus, Arthur Wimperis, *novel* Vespers in Vienna by Bryan Marshall *d* George Sidney *ph* Charles Rosher m Miklos Rozsa

Ethel Barrymore, Walter Pidgeon, Janet Leigh, Peter Lawford, Francis L. Sullivan, Angela Lansbury, Louis Calhern, Melville Cooper

Red Dawn
US 1984 114m Metrocolor
MGM-UA / Valkyrie (Buzz Feitshans, Barry Beckerman)

Russians lead a violent invasion into Colorado and are wiped out by the locals.
Ludicrous and somewhat dangerous Cold War throwback with little entertainment value to commend it. Violent teenage nonsense.

w Kevin Reynolds, John Milius *d* John Milius *ph* Ric Waite *m* Basil Poledouris *pd* Jackson de Govia *ed* Thom Noble

Patrick Swayze, C. Thomas Howell, Lea Thompson, Charlie Sheen, Darren Dalton, Jennifer Grey, Ben Johnson, Harry Dean Stanton, Ron O'Neal, Vladek Sheybal, Powers Boothe

The Red Desert*
Italy / France 1964 116m Eastmancolor
Duemila / Federiz (Angelo Rizzoli)
original title: *Il Deserto Rosso*

A wife suffers from depression, and a brief affair with her husband's friend doesn't help.
Elongated character study, very talkative but rather decoratively designed with the same subtle use of colour in an urban landscape as was seen later in *Blow Up.*

w Michelangelo Antonioni, Tonino Guerra *d Michelangelo Antonioni ph* Carlo di Palma *m* Giovanni Chionetti

Monica Vitti, Richard Harris, Carlos Chionetti

'The beauty is stationary, painterly; and the arresting image precisely arrests and retards the already moribund thrust of the film.'—*John Simon*

'Boredom in Ravenna, and it seeps into the viewer's bones.'—*Pauline Kael, New Yorker, 1984*

'He treated her rough—and she loved it!'

Red Dust***
US 1932 86m bw
MGM (Hunt Stromberg)

On a rubber plantation in Indo-China, the overseer is pursued by his engineer's bride but himself falls for a stranded prostitute.
Vigorous romantic melodrama with echoes of *Rain;* remade as *Congo Maisie* (1940) and *Mogambo* (1954).

w John Lee Mahin, *play* Wilson Collison *d Victor Fleming ph* Harold Rosson

Clark Gable, Jean Harlow, Mary Astor, Gene Raymond, Donald Crisp, Tully Marshall, Forrester Harvey

'Lots of pash, sex and undress . . . an exhib's delight and a cinch for fancy takings. Done so expertly it almost overcomes the basic script shortcomings.'—*Variety*

'Gable and Harlow have full play for their curiously similar sort of good-natured toughness.'—*Time*

† The Gable role was first announced for John Gilbert.

†† Scenes showing the shooting of *Red Dust* are included in *Bombshell.*

Red Garters**
US 1954 91m Technicolor
Paramount (Pat Duggan)

Various familiar types congregate in the western town of Paradise Lost, and settle matters by the Code of the West.
Amusing western musical spoof slightly deadened by its pretty but finally boring theatrically stylized scenery. Songs are catchy, performances good natured.

w Michael Fessier d George Marshall *ph Arthur E. Arling m* Joseph J. Lilley *songs Jay Livingston, Ray Evans*

Rosemary Clooney, Guy Mitchell, Gene Barry, Jack Carson, Pat Crowley, Cass Daley, Frank Faylen, Reginald Owen

'A musical of considerable freshness and gaiety.'—*MFB*

Red Headed Woman*
US 1932 74m bw
MGM (Albert Lewin)

A shopgirl marries the boss but is rejected in his social circles.
Unconvincing but occasionally entertaining melodrama.

w Anita Loos, *novel* Katharine Brush *d* Jack Conway *ph* Harold Rosson

Jean Harlow, Chester Morris, Lewis Stone, Leila Hyams, Una Merkel, Henry Stephenson, Charles Boyer, May Robson

'Gingery treatment of a controversial subject that is bound to engage femme interest.'—*Variety*

The Red House*
US 1947 100m bw
(UA) Thalia (Sol Lesser)

A moody farmer's guilty obsession with an old house in the woods is that he murdered his parents in it.
Psycho-like suspense melodrama, too extended for comfort and too restricting for the actors, but effective in spurts.

wd Delmer Daves, *novel* George Agnew Chamberlain *ph* Bert Glennon *m* Miklos Rozsa

Edward G. Robinson, Judith Anderson, Lon McCallister, Allene Roberts, Rory Calhoun, Julie London, Ona Munson

The Red Inn*
France 1951 95m bw
Memnon
original title: *L'Auberge Rouge*

In 1833, stagecoach travellers stay at a remote inn, where the owners intend to rob and murder them.
Extreme black farce which manages to be pretty funny for those who can take this kind of thing: even the survivors of the night's massacre fall down a ravine.

w Jean Aurenche, Pierre Bost d Claude Autant-Lara *ph* André Bac *m* René Cloërc *ad* Max Douy

Fernandel, Françoise Rosay, Carette, Grégoire Aslan

The Red Light
US 1949 83m bw
UA / Pioneer (Roy Del Ruth)

An industrialist tracks down his brother's murderer.
Competent routine detection piece with engaging clues.

w George Callahan *d* Roy Del Ruth *ph* Bert Glennon *m* Dmitri Tiomkin

George Raft, Virginia Mayo, Raymond Burr, Gene Lockhart, Henry Morgan, Arthur Franz

Red Line 7000
US 1965 110m Technicolor
Paramount / Laurel (Howard Hawks)

The career and loves of a stock car racer.
Very routine romantic actioner full of the director's favourite situations but failing to find any fresh slant.

w George Kirgo *d* Howard Hawks *ph* Milton Krasner *m* Nelson Riddle

James Caan, Laura Devon, Gail Hire, Charlene Holt, John Robert Crawford

The Red Menace
US 1949 87m bw

A discontented war veteran is preyed on by communists. An odd piece of anti-Red propaganda to come from an action studio, but it had some effect on thinking at the time. Robert Rockwell, Hanne Axman, Shepard Menken. (Cast deliberately chosen from unknowns.) Written by Albert DeMond, Gerald Geraghty; directed by R. G. Springsteen; for Republic. (GB title: *The Enemy Within*.) 'It waves the flag at the proper times and is an okay melodrama on other points.'—*Variety*

Red Mountain
US 1951 84m Technicolor
Paramount / Hal B. Wallis

A Confederate captain joins Quantrell's Raiders but is horrified by their brutality.
Fast-moving action western.

w John Meredyth Lucas, George W. George, George F. Slavin *d* William Dieterle *ph* Charles Lang Jnr *m* Franz Waxman

Alan Ladd, Lizabeth Scott, Arthur Kennedy, John Ireland, Jeff Corey, James Bell

Red Planet Mars
US 1952 87m bw
UA / Donald Hyde, Anthony Veiller

Americans and Russians both tune in to Mars and learn that it is a powerful Christian planet; the news causes first panic, then a religious revival and a determination to live more harmoniously on earth.
Lunatic farrago that has to be seen to be believed.

w Anthony Veiller, John L. Balderston *d* Harry Horner *ph* Joseph Biroc *m* Mahlon Merrick *md* David Chudnow *ad* Charles D. Hall

Herbert Berghof, Peter Graves, Andrea King, Marvin Miller

The Red Pony
US 1949 88m Technicolor
Republic (Lewis Milestone)

When his pet pony dies after an illness, a farmer's son loses faith in his father.
Sincere but rather obvious little fable which although capably made does not make inspiring film drama.

w John Steinbeck *d* Lewis Milestone *ph* Tony Gaudio *m* Aaron Copland pd Nicolai Remisoff

Myrna Loy, Robert Mitchum, Peter Miles, Louis Calhern, Shepperd Strudwick, Margaret Hamilton

The Red Rider
US 1934 bw serial: 15 eps

A western sheriff saves his best pal from the noose and proves him innocent. Adequate western serial. Buck Jones, Grant Withers, Marion Shilling, Walter Miller, Richard Cramer. Directed by Louis Friedlander; for Universal.

Red River**
US 1948 133m bw
UA / Monterey (Howard Hawks)

How the Chisholm Trail was developed as a cattle drive.
Brawling western, a bit serious and long drawn out but with splendid action sequences.

w Borden Chase, Charles Schnee *d Howard Hawks ph Russell Harlan m Dmitri Tiomkin*

John Wayne, Montgomery Clift, Joanne Dru, Walter Brennan, Colleen Gray, John Ireland, Noah Beery Jnr, Harry Carey Jnr

AAN: original story (Borden Chase)

Red Salute*
US 1935 78m bw
Edward Small
aka: *Runaway Daughter*; GB title: *Arms and the Girl*

A college girl with communist leanings takes a cross country trip with an American soldier.
Odd little romantic comedy modelled on *It Happened One Night*; it was picketed for its inconsequential attitude to politics.

w Humphrey Pearson, Manuel Seff *d* Sidney Lanfield *ph* Robert Planck

Barbara Stanwyck, Robert Young, Hardie Albright, Cliff Edwards, Ruth Donnelly, Gordon Jones, Henry Kolker

'Tepid comedy romance wrapped up in a preachment against campus agitators who oppose militarism.'—*Variety*

The Red Shoes****
GB 1948 136m Technicolor
GFD / The Archers *(Michael Powell, Emeric Pressburger)*

A girl student becomes a great ballet star but commits suicide when torn between love and her career.
Never was a better film made from such a penny plain story so unpersuasively written and performed; the splendour of the production is in the intimate view it gives of life backstage in the ballet world with its larger-than-life characters. The ballet excerpts are very fine, and the colour discreet; the whole film is charged with excitement.

wd Michael Powell, Emeric Pressburger ph Jack Cardiff m Brian Easdale pd Hein Heckroth

Anton Walbrook, Moira Shearer, Marius Goring, Robert Helpmann, Albert Basserman, Frederick Ashton, Leonide Massine, Ludmilla Tcherina, Esmond Knight

'In texture, like nothing the British cinema has ever seen.'—*Time Out, 1981*

AA: Brian Easdale
AAN: best picture; original story (Michael Powell, Emeric Pressburger)

Red Skies of Montana
US 1952 99m Technicolor
TCF (Samuel G. Engel)
aka: *Smoke Jumpers*

Tension among firefighting crews in the mountains of Montana.
Adequate, routine action melodrama with semi-documentary touches.

w Harry Kleiner *d* Joseph M. Newman *ph* Charles G. Clarke *m* Sol Kaplan

Richard Widmark, Jeffrey Hunter, Constance Smith, Richard Boone, Richard Crenna

'A man's desperation—a woman's passion—a boy's awakening—a girl's desire!'

Red Sky at Morning
US 1970 113m Technicolor
Universal / Hal Wallis

During World War II the family of an officer on active service find life in New Mexico not what they've been used to.
Peyton Place by any other name, well produced but of little real interest.

w Marguerite Roberts, *novel* Richard Bradford *d* James Goldstone *ph* Vilmos Zsigismond *m* Billy Goldenberg

Claire Bloom, Richard Thomas, Richard Crenna, Catherine Burns, Desi Arnaz Jnr, John Colicos, Harry Guardino

Red Sonja
US 1985 89m Metrocolor

In the times of sword and sorcery, Sonja avenges her sister's death and deposes an evil queen. Absolute comic strip nonsense: even the monsters look mechanical. Brigitte Nielsen, Arnold Schwarzenegger, Sandahl Bergman, Paul Smith, Ronald Lacey. Written by Clive Exton, George MacDonald Fraser, from stories by Robert E. Howard; directed by Richard Fleischer; for Christian Ferry / MGM-UA.

Red Sun
France / Italy / Spain 1971 108m Eastmancolor
Corona / Oceania / Balcazar (Robert Dorfman)

In 1870 Arizona, an outlaw is forced to accompany a Japanese samurai to recover a ceremonial sword which his partner has stolen.
Unusual but generally ineffective western with a fashionable international cast.

w Lair Koenig, D. B. Petitclerc, W. Roberts, L. Roman *d* Terence Young *ph* Henri Alekan *m* Maurice Jarre

Charles Bronson, Toshiro Mifune, Alain Delon, Ursula Andress, Capucine

'A nice exotic item ruined by suburban direction.'—*Sight and Sound*

Red Sundown
US 1956 81m Technicolor

A gunslinger becomes a deputy and tames a lawless town. Elementary western action piece, not unentertaining. Rory Calhoun, Martha Hyer, Dean Jagger, Robert Middleton, James Millican, Grant Williams. Written by Martin Berkeley; directed by Jack Arnold; for Universal-International.

The Red Tent*
Italy / USSR 1970 121m Technicolor
Paramount / Vides / Mosfilm (Franco Cristaldi)

The story of General Nobile's ill-fated 1928 expedition by dirigible to the Arctic.
Stiffly-conceived international spectacular with one striking sequence but not much good cheer.

w Ennio de Concini, Richard Adams *d* Mikhail Kalatozov *ph Leonid Kalashnikov* *m* Ennio Morricone

Peter Finch, Sean Connery, Hardy Kruger, Claudia Cardinale, Mario Adorf, Massimo Girotti

Red Tomahawk
US 1967 80m Technicolor

The small town of Deadwood is caught up in the aftermath of Little Big Horn. Talkative western filled with old faces, as is this producer's wont. Howard Keel, Joan Caulfield, Broderick Crawford, Scott Brady, Wendell Corey, Richard Arlen, Tom Drake. Written by Steve Fisher; directed by R. G. Springsteen; for A. C. Lyles / Paramount.

Red Wagon
GB 1933 107m bw

Passions mount in a travelling circus. Gypsies and jealousies are the ingredients of a melodrama aimed at the international market. It failed. Charles Bickford, Raquel Torres, Greta Nissen, Don Alvarado, Anthony Bushell, Paul Graetz, Jimmy Hanley, Frank Pettingell. Written by Roger Burford, Edward Knoblock and Arthur Woods, from the novel by Lady Eleanor Smith; directed by Paul Stein; for BIP.

Redbeard*
Japan 1965 165 bw Tohoscope
Toho-Kurosawa
original title: *Akahige*

Problems of a 19th-century doctor.
Almost a Japanese version of *The Citadel*: Kurosawa himself called it 'a monument to goodness in man'. Rather heavy-going, but sporadically compelling.

w Masato Ide, Hideo Oguni, Akira Kurosawa, *novel* Shugoro Yamamoto *d* Akira Kurosawa *ph* A. Nakai, T. Saito *m* M. Sato

Toshiro Mifune, Yuzo Kayama

'A three-hour excursion into nineteenth-century hospital soap opera; a mediocre enough script, but beautifully directed and flawlessly acted.'—*John Simon*

Redemption
US 1930 82m bw

A man thought dead commits suicide rather than interrupt his wife's new life. Elaborate but unsuccessful talkie debut of a waning star; very hard going. John Gilbert, Renee Adoree, Eleanor Boardman, Conrad Nagel. Written by Dorothy Farnum and Edwin Justus Mayer, from *The Living Corpse* by Leo Tolstoy; directed by Fred Niblo; for MGM.

'Not since *Gone with the Wind* has there been a great romantic epic like it!'

Reds**
US 1981 196m Technicolor
Paramount (Warren Beatty)

The last years of John Reed, an American writer who after stormy romantic vicissitudes goes with his wife to Russia and writes *Ten Days That Shook the World*.
Interminably long but full of quality, this immensely detailed work was a most unlikely project to succeed in the eighties, but its very strangeness enabled it to break even.

w Warren Beatty, Trevor Griffiths *d Warren Beatty* *ph Vittorio Storaro* *m* Stephen Sondheim *pd Richard Sylbert*

Warren Beatty, Diane Keaton, Edward Herrman, Jerzy Kosincki, Jack Nicholson, Maureen Stapleton, Paul Sorvino

AA: Warren Beatty (as director); Vittorio Storaro; Maureen Stapleton (supporting actress)
AAN: best picture; screenplay; editing (Dede Allen, Craig McKay); Warren Beatty (as actor); Diane Keaton; Jack Nicholson
BFA: best supporting actor (Jack Nicholson); best supporting actress (Maureen Stapleton)

Reducing
US 1931 73m bw

The proprietress of a beauty parlour sends for an old family servant to help her. Loosely plotted comedy consisting largely of slapstick in a Turkish bath. Marie Dressler, Polly Moran, Anita Page, Lucien Littlefield, Sally Eilers. Written by Willard Mack, Beatrice Banyard; directed by Charles F. Reisner; for MGM. 'Rough and tumble hoke comedy addressed to the banana peel sense of humour.'—*Variety*

Reflection of Fear
US 1971 90m Eastmancolor
Columbia (Howard B. Jaffe)

A retarded teenage girl kills her mother and her grandmother.
Psycho thriller of little interest or suspense.

w Edward Hume, Lewis John Carlino, *novel* Go to Thy Deathbed by Stanton Forbes *d* William A. Fraker *ph* Laszlo Kovacs *m* Fred Myrow

Robert Shaw, Mary Ure, Signe Hasso, Sondra Locke, Mitch Ryan

Reflections in a Golden Eye*
US 1967 108m Technicolor
Warner Seven Arts (Ray Stark)

Repressions at a peacetime army camp in Georgia. A private soldier rides nude on horseback, a major has the hots for him, the major's wife has an affair with their neighbour, whose wife has cut off her nipples with garden shears.
A film as idiotic as its story line, but smoothly marshalled so that at least it's more amusing than boring.

w Chapman Mortimer, Gladys Hill, *novel* Carson McCullers *d John Huston* *ph Aldo Tonti* *pd* Stephen Grimes *m* Toshiro Mayuzumi

Marlon Brando, Elizabeth Taylor, Brian Keith, Julie Harris, Robert Forster, Zorro David

'One feels trapped in a huge overheated hothouse containing nothing but common snapdragons. Pedestrian, crass, and uninvolving to the point of repellence.'—*John Simon*

'Nothing more than nutty people and pseudo porn.'—*Judith Crist*

The Reformer and the Redhead*
US 1950 90m bw
MGM (Norman Panama, Melvin Frank)

A small-town reform candidate abandons his crooked protector and wins under his own steam, helped by the daughter of the zoo superintendent.
Scatty sub-Capra comedy with a lightweight script but good production and playing.

wd Norman Panama, Melvin Frank *ph* Ray June *m* David Raksin

Dick Powell, June Allyson, Cecil Kellaway, David Wayne, Ray Collins, Robert Keith, Marvin Kaplan

La Règle du Jeu***
France 1939 113m bw
La Nouvelle Edition Française (Claude Renoir)
aka: *The Rules of the Game*

A count organizes a weekend shooting party which results in complex love intrigues among servants as well as masters.
Celebrated satirical comedy with a uniquely bleak outlook.

w Jean Renoir, Carl Koch d Jean Renoir *ph* Jean Bachelet, Alain Renoir *m* Joseph Kosma, Roger Desormières *ad* Eugène Lourié, Max Douy

Marcel Dalio, Nora Gregor, Jean Renoir, Mila Parély, Julien Carette, Gaston Modot, Roland Toutain

'It is a question of panache, of preserving a casual indifference to the workings of fate.'—*The Times*

'How brilliantly Renoir focuses the confusion! The rather fusty luxury of the chateau, the constant mindless slaughter of wild animals, the minuets of adultery and seduction, the gavottes of mutual hatred or mistrust. . .'—*Basil Wright, 1972*

† The film was originally banned as indicting the corruption of France, and during the war the negative was destroyed during an air raid; but eventually a full version was pieced together from various materials.

The Reincarnation of Peter Proud
US 1974 104m Technicolor
Avco Embassy / Bing Crosby (Frank P. Rosenberg)

A history professor is troubled by recurring dreams of his former existence.
Hysterical psychic melodrama which pretty well ruins its own chances by failing to explain its plot.

w Max Ehrlich, from his novel *d* J. Lee-Thompson *ph* Victor J. Kemper *m* Jerry Goldsmith

Michael Sarrazin, Jennifer O'Neill, Margot Kidder, Cornelia Sharpe, Paul Hecht

'It may well be the silliest approach to the subject in any medium . . . all flashbacks trampling the action with the finesse of a rogue elephant.'—*Tom Milne*

The Reivers*
US 1969 111m Technicolor Panavision
Cinema Center / Duo / Solar (Irving Ravetch)

In Mississippi at the turn of the century a hired hand borrows the new family auto for a trip into Memphis with the grandson of the family and a black stablehand.
Pleasant but insubstantial yarn of more gracious days; most attractive to look at, it entertains gently without ever reaching a point.

w Irving Ravetch, Harriet Frank Jnr, *novel* William Faulkner *d* Mark Rydell *ph Richard Moore m* John Williams

Steve McQueen, Sharon Farrell, Will Geer, Rupert Crosse, Mitch Vogel, Michael Constantine, Juano Hernandez, Clifton James

AAN: John Williams; Rupert Crosse

Relentless
US 1948 93m Technicolor

A cowboy framed for murder must clear himself before the posse catches up with him.
Brisk western copy of *The 39 Steps.* Robert Young, Marguerite Chapman, Willard Parker, Barton Maclane, Will Wright. Written by Winston Miller; directed by George Sherman; for Columbia.

The Reluctant Astronaut
US 1967 101m Technicolor

By a series of accidents a man with vertigo becomes an astronaut. Feeble vehicle for a comedian briefly popular. Don Knotts, Leslie Nielsen, Joan Freeman, Jesse White, Jeanette Nolan, Arthur O'Connell. Written by Jim Fritzell, Everett Greenbaum; directed by Edward J. Montagne; for Universal.

The Reluctant Debutante*
US 1958 96m Metrocolor Cinemascope
MGM / Avon (Pandro S. Berman)

A noble couple have difficulty in steering their American-educated daughter through the intricacies of the London season.
A slight but pleasing British comedy has become a rather strident example of lend-lease, but still affords minor pleasures.

w William Douglas Home, from his play *d* Vincente Minnelli *ph* Joseph Ruttenberg *md* Eddie Warner *ad* Jean d'Aubonne

Rex Harrison, Kay Kendall, Sandra Dee, Peter Myers, Angela Lansbury, John Saxon, Diane Clare

The Reluctant Dragon**
US 1941 72m Technicolor
Walt Disney

A tour of the Disney Studios affords some glimpses of how cartoons are made.
Amiable pot-pourri of cartoon shorts *(Baby Weems, How to Ride a Horse* and the title story) linked by a studio tour of absorbing interest.

w various *d* Alfred Werker (live action), various

Robert Benchley, Frances Gifford, Nana Bryant

Reluctant Heroes*
GB 1951 80m bw
Byron (Henry Halstead)

Comedy of national servicemen and their misdemeanours.
Simple-minded army farce which was popular for years as play and film.

w Colin Morris, from his play *d* Jack Raymond *ph* James Wilson

Brian Rix, Ronald Shiner, Derek Farr, Christine Norden, Larry Noble

The Reluctant Widow
GB 1950 91m bw
Rank / Two Cities (Gordon Wellesley)

During the Napoleonic wars a governess is co-opted as a spy.
Thin romantic drama which despite nice art direction never really sparks into life.

w Gordon Wellesley, J. B. Boothroyd, *novel* Georgette Heyer *d* Bernard Knowles *ph* Jack Hildyard *ad Carmen Dillon*

Jean Kent, Guy Rolfe, Kathleen Byron, Paul Dupuis, Lana Morris, Julian Dallas, Peter Hammond, Andrew Cruickshank

Remains to be Seen
US 1953 88m bw
MGM (Arthur Hornblow Jnr)

The manager of an apartment house finds a dead body, and before the police arrive someone sticks a knife into it.
Flabby comedy-thriller giving the cast little to work on.

w Sidney Sheldon, *play* Howard Lindsay, Russel Crouse *d* Don Weis *ph* Robert Planck *md* Jeff Alexander

June Allyson, Van Johnson, Angela Lansbury, Louis Calhern, John Beal, Dorothy Dandridge

'By thunderation, I'll show America how to get tough!'

The Remarkable Andrew*
US 1942 80m bw
Paramount (Richard Blumenthal)

A young municipal bookkeeper is framed by local politicians but helped by the ghost of Andrew Jackson and friends.
Pleasant, rather faded, whimsical comedy which also managed to be propaganda for the war effort.

w Dalton Trumbo *d* Stuart Heisler *ph* Theodor Sparkuhl *m* Victor Young

William Holden, Ellen Drew, Brian Donlevy, Rod Cameron, Richard Webb, Porter Hall, Frances Gifford, Nydia Westman, Montagu Love

'About all that comes through in the juxtaposition of these lithograph characters over modern Shale City is Franklin's delight over the electric light and Jackson's alarm over the radio.'—*John McManus, PM*

The Remarkable Mr Pennypacker
US 1958 87m Technicolor Cinemascope
TCF (Charles Brackett)

A Pennsylvania businessman leads two lives with two separate families.
Feeble and obvious period comedy of bigamy; very few laughs.

w Walter Reisch, *play* Liam O'Brien *d* Henry Levin *ph* Milton Krasner *m* Leigh Harline

Clifton Webb, Dorothy McGuire, Charles Coburn, Ray Stricklyn, Jill St John, Ron Ely, David Nelson

Rembrandt****
GB 1936 85m bw
London Films (Alexander Korda)

Episodes in the life of the 17th-century painter.
Austerely comic, gently tragic character piece, superbly staged and photographed, with a great performance at its centre.

w Lajos Biro, June Head, Carl Zuckmayer d Alexander Korda ph Georges Perinal, Richard Angst m Geoffrey Toye

Charles Laughton, Elsa Lanchester, Gertrude Lawrence, Edward Chapman, Walter Hudd, Roger Livesey, Herbert Lomas, Allan Jeayes, Sam Livesey, Raymond Huntley, John Clements

'Never exciting, and only partly believable . . . a feature film without a story plot.'—*Variety*

'Amazingly full of that light which the great master of painting subdued to his supreme purpose.'—*James Agate*

'The film is ruined by lack of story and continuity: it has no drive. Like *The Private Life of Henry the Eighth* it is a series of unrelated tableaux.'—*Graham Greene*

Remember?
US 1939 83m bw
MGM (Milton Bren)

A newly married couple do not get on, so a friend gives them a potion which makes them lose their memories and fall in love all over again.
Silly, witless comedy which did no good for anyone concerned.

w Corey Ford, Norman Z. McLeod *d* Norman Z. McLeod *ph* George Folsey *m* Edward Ward

Robert Taylor, Greer Garson, Lew Ayres, Billie Burke, Reginald Owen, George Barbier, Henry Travers, Richard Carle, Laura Hope Crews, Halliwell Hobbes, Sig Rumann

'Many bright episodes contrast with some bumpy and over-dialogued stretches.'—*Variety*

Remember Last Night?**
US 1936 80m bw
Universal

Socialites with hangovers find that murder was committed during their party.
Ingenious but overlong mixture of styles: farce, *Thin Man* comedy, murder mystery, satire, fantasy. Very well worth looking at.

w Harry Clark, Dan Totheroh, Doris Malloy, *novel* The Hangover Murders by Adam Hobhouse *d* James Whale *ph* Joseph Valentine *m* Franz Waxman

Robert Young, Edward Arnold, Arthur Treacher, Constance Cummings, Robert Armstrong, Sally Eilers, Reginald Denny, Ed Brophy, Jack La Rue, Gustav Von Seyffertitz, Gregory Ratoff

'It will be hard to sell because it is hard to understand . . . the basic story can scarcely be followed, while the superficial gloss of phoney sophistication neither fits a narrative in which four murders and two suicides are recorded, nor carries conviction of itself.'—*Variety*

'Parodying the detective thriller in a dazzling cascade of gags, this brilliant divertissement eventually takes off into pure surrealism.'—*Tom Milne, MFB, 1974*

Remember My Name*
US 1978 94m De Luxe
Lion's Gate (Robert Altman)

After twelve years in prison, a woman takes calm revenge on the man who allowed her to take the blame for his crime.
Basically reminiscent of a Barbara Stanwyck vehicle of the forties, this interesting film is finally too concerned to strike on all levels, including satire, social awareness and fashionable pessimism.

wd Alan Rudolph *ph* Tak Fujimoto

Geraldine Chaplin, Anthony Perkins, Moses Gunn, Berry Berenson, Jeff Goldblum

Remember the Day*
US 1941 86m bw
TCF (William Perlberg)

An elderly schoolteacher recollects her past life.
Pleasant sentimental drama, very well mounted.

w Tess Schlesinger, Frank Davis, Allan Scott, *play* Philo Higley *d* Henry King *ph* George Barnes *m* Alfred Newman

Claudette Colbert, John Payne, Shepperd Strudwick, Jane Seymour, Anne Revere, Frieda Inescort

Remember the Night*
US 1940 94m bw
Paramount (Mitchell Leisen)

An assistant district attorney takes a lady shoplifter home with him for Christmas.
Eccentric but winning blend of comedy, romance and drama, deftly mixed by master chefs.

w Preston Sturges d Mitchell Leisen ph Ted Tetzlaff *m* Frederick Hollander

Barbara Stanwyck, Fred MacMurray, Beulah Bondi, Elizabeth Patterson, Sterling Holloway, Paul Guilfoyle, Willard Robertson

'Rarely has such a theme been so smoothly advanced and so pleasantly played out to so sensible and credible a conclusion.'—*New York Times*

Remembrance
GB 1982 117m Eastmancolor
Colin Gregg / Channel Four

Young sailors in Plymouth enjoy a last night's leave before a six-month tour of duty with the NATO forces.
A few slices of what in the eyes of film-makers passes for realism these days; boozing, violence and bad language. The film seems to make no point and certainly doesn't entertain, though the components are slickly enough assembled.

w Hugh Stoddart *d* Colin Gregg *ph* John Metcalfe *m* various pop performances *ed* Peter Delfgou

John Altman, Al Ashton, Martin Barrass, Nick Dunning, Sally Jane Jackson, David John, Peter Lee-Wilson, Kenneth Griffith

'A clear and disheartening case of ambition exceeding grasp.'—*Geoff Brown, MFB*

Remo Williams: The Adventure Begins
US 1985 121m De Luxe
Orion / Dick Clark, Larry Spiegel, Mel Bergman
GB title: *Remo: Unarmed and Dangerous*

A New York cop is recruited by the CIA to learn martial arts which will help him to fight an evil arms manufacturer.
Po-faced and oddly unlikeable, this elaborate adventure movie never really finds a style, and is dislocated by a middle section in which our hero is taught by an elderly Korean.

w Christopher Wood, from the *Destroyer* books by Richard Sapir, Warren Murphy *d* Guy Hamilton *ph* Andrew Laszlo *m* Craig Safan *pd* Jackson de Govia

Fred Ward, Joel Grey, Wilford Brimley, J. A. Preston, Charles Cioffi, Kate Mulgrew, George Coe

Remorques*
France 1941 80m bw
MAIC
US title: *Stormy Waters*

A tugboat captain falls in love with a mysterious woman but remains faithful to his invalid wife.
Effective, minor, romantic melodrama.

w Jacques Prévert, André Cayatte, *novel* Roger Vercel *d* Jean Grémillon *ph* Armand Thirard, Louis Née *m* Roland Manuel

Jean Gabin, Michèle Morgan, Madeleine Renaud, Fernand Ledoux

Rendezvous
US 1935 106m bw
MGM (Lawrence Weingarten)

A decoding expert breaks an enemy spy ring.
Agreeable light romantic comedy drama with an espionage plot.

w Bella and Samuel Spewack, *novel* Black Chamber by Herbert Yardley *d* William K. Howard *ph* William Daniels *m* William Axt

William Powell, Rosalind Russell, Binnie Barnes, Lionel Atwill, Cesar Romero, Samuel S. Hinds, Henry Stephenson, Frank Reicher

'Another chill-and-chuckle play aiming at the *Thin Man* trade and scoring a bull's-eye.'—*Variety*

Rendezvous at Midnight
US 1935 60m bw

A police commissioner investigates the murder of his predecessor. Modest mystery co-feature which wastes time up front on a fashion show. Ralph Bellamy, Valerie Hobson, Catherine Doucet, Irene Ware, Helen Jerome Eddy. Written by Gladys Unger from the play The Silver Fox by Gaetano Sazlo; directed by Christy Cabanne; for Universal. 'The woeful lack of action drags it down.'—*Variety*

Rendezvous de Juillet**
France 1949 110m bw
UGC–SNEG (René G. Vuattoux)

A group of young people in post-war St Germain-des-Pres plan an expedition to the Congo.
Highly likeable series of impressions of interesting people, a little indeterminate and possibly dated now, but in its time extremely fresh and vital.

wd Jacques Becker *ph* Claude Renoir *m* Jean Wiener, Mezzmezzrow

Daniel Gelin, Maurice Ronet, Brigitte Auber, Pierre Trabaud, Nicole Courcel

Les Rendezvous du Diable**
France 1958 80m colour
Union Générale Cinématographique / Jacques Constant / Haroun Tazieff
aka: *Volcano*

Adventures of a Belgian volcanologist.
Daring exploits on the rims of the world's most active volcanoes, including Etna and Stromboli in eruption. Fascinating footage is urbanely presented.

w, d, ph Haroun Tazieff *m* Marius-François Gaillard

'Beauty blends with horror, romantic grandeur with fear.'—*MFB*

Rendezvous 24
US 1946 70m bw

American secret agents track down post-war Nazis who are working on atomic explosions from a remote base in the Harz mountains. Routine thick-ear despite claims of timeliness; as such, quite tolerable. William Gargan, Maria Palmer, Pat O'Moore, David Leonard, Kurt Katch, Herman Bing. Written by Aubrey Wisberg; directed by James Tinling; for Sol M. Wurtzel / TCF.

Rendezvous with Annie
US 1946 89m bw

An American soldier in England goes absent without leave to see his wife in New York, an exploit which later nearly loses him a fortune. An engaging comedy idea filmed with insufficient wit, this gets by on charm. Eddie Albert, Faye Marlowe, C. Aubrey Smith. Written by Mary Loos and Richard Sale; directed by Allan Dwan; for Republic.

Renegades
US 1930 84m bw

A disgraced French officer becomes a hero of the Foreign Legion. Satisfying romantic melodrama of its period. Warner Baxter, Myrna Loy, Bela Lugosi, Noah Beery, C. Henry Gordon, Gregory Gaye. Written by Jules Furthman from a novel by André Armandy; directed by Victor Fleming; for Fox. 'Everyone in the picture dies in the last few feet.'—*Variety*

Renegades
US 1946 88m Technicolor

An outlaw's son tries in vain to go straight. Unsurprising but efficient bill-topping western of its day. Evelyn Keyes, Larry Parks, Willard Parker, Edgar Buchanan. Written by Melvin Levey and Francis Faragoh; directed by George Sherman; for Columbia.

Reno
US 1939 72m bw

As Reno becomes a great city for gambling and divorce, a lawyer becomes a gambling hall proprietor. Mildly interesting romantic drama in a flashback format. Richard Dix, Gail Patrick, Anita Louise, Paul Cavanagh, Laura Hope Crews, Louis Jean Heydt, Hobart Cavanaugh, Charles Halton. Written by John Twist, Ellis St Joseph; directed by John Farrow; for RKO. 'Capable handling of an interesting story against a colourful background.'—*Variety*

Rentadick
GB 1972 94m Eastmancolor
Rank / Paradine / Virgin (Ned Sherrin)

Incompetent private eyes become involved in the battle for a deadly nerve gas.
Ineffective crazy comedy which never takes shape, preferring to aim barbs of satire in all directions.

w John Wells, John Fortune *d* Jim Clarke *ph* John Coquillon *m* Carl Davis

James Booth, Richard Briers, Julie Ege, Donald Sinden, Roy Kinnear

Repeat Performance*
US 1947 93m bw
Eagle Lion / Aubrey Schenck

People in trouble find they can repeat the previous year.
Adequate flashback fantasy, very dated now.

w Walter Bullock *d* Alfred L. Werker *ph* Lew O'Connell *m* George Antheil

Louis Hayward, Joan Leslie, Tom Conway, Richard Basehart, Virginia Field

Repo Man*
US 1984 92m De Luxe
Universal / Edge City (Peter McCarthy, Jonathan Wacks)

A repossessor of cars finds himself on the run from all manner of dangers.
Nightmarish *film noir* with nods to many predecessors and some elements of black fantasy.

w,d Alex Cox *ph* Robby Muller *m* Tito Larriva, Steven Hufsteter

Harry Dean Stanton, Emilio Estevez, Tracey Walter, Olivia Barash, Sy Richardson, Susan Barnes

Report from the Aleutians**
US 1943 45m colour

American forces live under tough conditions on a group of Arctic islands from which they raid Japanese bases. Simple and somewhat overlong, but still one of the better US documentaries to come out of World War II. Written, narrated and directed by John Huston; additional narration by Walter Huston; for US Signal Corps.

Report to the Commissioner
US 1974 112m Metrocolor
UA / M. J. Frankovich
GB title: *Operation Undercover*

A policeman's son follows in father's footsteps but finds life around Times Square dismaying.
Realistic, concerned crime melodrama with nothing very new to say.

w Abby Mann, Ernest Tidyman, *novel* James Mills *d* Milton Katselas *ph* Mario Tosi *m* Elmer Bernstein

Michael Moriarty, Yaphet Kotto, Susan Blakely, Hector Elizondo, Tony King, Michael McGuire

'A clear also-ran in the police thriller stakes.'—*Verina Glaessner*

'A bit too full of sweat and frenzy.'—*Michael Billington, Illustrated London News*

The Reptile*
GB 1966 90m Technicolor
Hammer (Anthony Nelson Keys)

A Cornish village is terrified by several mysterious and unpleasant deaths; it turns out

that the daughter of the local doctor, victim of a Malayan sect, periodically turns into a deadly snake.
Silly horror story most effectively filmed as a mixture of chills, detection and good characterization.

w John Elder d John Gilling ph Arthur Grant *m* Don Banks

Noel Willman, Jennifer Daniel, Ray Barrett, Jaqueline Pearce, Michael Ripper, John Laurie, Marne Maitland

Repulsion**
GB 1965 105m bw
Compton / Tekli (Gene Gutowski)

A Belgian manicurist in London is driven by pressures into neurotic withdrawal; terrified above all by sex, she locks herself up in her gloomy flat and murders her boy friend and landlord when they try to approach her.
Weird, unmotivated but undeniably effective Grand Guignol in the form of a case history; little dialogue, which is just as well as the director at that time clearly had no ear for the language.

w Roman Polanski, Gerard Brach *d Roman Polanski ph Gilbert Taylor m* Chico Hamilton

Catherine Deneuve, Ian Hendry, John Fraser, Patrick Wymark, Yvonne Furneaux

'An unashamedly ugly film, but as a lynx-eyed view of a crumbling mind it is a masterpiece of the macabre.'—*Daily Mail*

Requiem for a Heavyweight*
US 1962 87m bw
Columbia (David Susskind)
GB title: *Blood Money*

The last bouts of a prizefighter who will not realize his career is over.
Tough, effective melodrama, extremely well acted.

w Rod Serling, from his TV play *d Ralph Nelson ph Arthur J. Ornitz m* Laurence Rosenthal

Anthony Quinn, *Jackie Gleason, Mickey Rooney*, Julie Harris, Stan Adams, Madame Spivy, Jack Dempsey, Cassius Clay

The Rescuers*
US 1977 77m Technicolor
Walt Disney (Ron Miller)

The Mouse Rescue Aid Society volunteer to bring back a girl lost in a swamp.
Feature-length cartoon which, while by no means as bad as some of Disney's very routine seventies product, still seems light years away from his classics of the thirties.

w various, from stories by Margery Sharp *d* Wolfgang Reitherman, John Lounsbery, Art Stevens *m* Artie Butler

'The people who really need rescuing are the Disney animators and cameramen.'—*Time Out*

'It's no *Snow White* but there are long moments when its inventiveness and skill are entirely captivating. I have only this one lingering doubt: if you are going to put this amount of effort into a movie shouldn't you have more at the end than a snappy collection of 330,000 drawings and a bill for six million dollars?'—*Barry Took, Punch*

AAN: song, 'Someone's Waiting for You'

'Torn from the blazing pages of Texas history!'
The Restless Breed
US 1957 81m Eastmancolor by Pathé

The son of a secret service agent arrives in a frontier town to avenge his father's death. Standard star western full of expected elements. Scott Brady, Anne Bancroft, Jay C. Flippen, Jim Davis, Rhys Williams. Written by Steve Fisher; directed by Allan Dwan; for Edward L. Alperson.

Restless Natives
GB 1985 89m Technicolor

Two young idlers set up as modern highwaymen, robbing American visitors on coach tours; to their surprise, they become a tourist attraction. Irritatingly patchy and amoral comedy which wastes a potentially interesting idea. Vincent Friell, Joe Mullaney, Teri Lally, Ned Beatty, Robert Urquhart. Written by Ninian Dunet; directed by Michael Hoffman; for Oxford Film Company / Thorn EMI.

The Restless Years
US 1959 86m bw Cinemascope

A small-town dressmaker tries to prevent her daughter from discovering that she is illegitimate. Antediluvian sudser with second-string talent. John Saxon, Sandra Dee, Margaret Lindsay, Luana Patten, Virginia Grey. Written by Edward Anhalt, from the play *Teach Me How to Cry* by Patricia Joudry; directed by Helmut Kautner; for Universal-International.

Resurrection
US1931 81m bw
Universal

In 1870s Russia, a peasant girl is seduced by a prince and bears his child.
Unremarkable version of a much-filmed melodrama.

w Finis Fox, *novel* Leo Tolstoy *d* Edwin Carewe *ph* Robert B. Kurrle, Al Green *m* Dmitri Tiomkin

Lupe Velez, John Boles, Nance O'Neil, William Keighley, Rose Tapley
† See also: *We Live Again.*

Resurrection
US 1981 103m Technicolor
Universal (Renee Missel, Howard Rosenman)

A woman who has escaped death in a car crash finds herself miraculously able to heal others.
Curious modern parable with nowhere to go; even religious reactionaries may find it rather boring.

w Lewis John Carlino *d* Daniel Petrie *ph* Mario Tosi *m* Maurice Jarre

Ellen Burstyn, Sam Shepard, Richard Farnsworth, Eva LeGallienne, Roberts Blossom, Clifford David

AAN: Ellen Burstyn; Eva LeGallienne (supporting actress)

Retreat, Hell!
US 1952 95m bw
(Warner) United States (Milton Sperling)

Adventures of a Marine unit in the Korean War.
Standard war film.

w Milton Sperling, Ted Sherdeman *d* Joseph H. Lewis *ph* Warren Lynch *m* William Lava

Frank Lovejoy, Richard Carlson, Anita Louise, Russ Tamblyn

Return from the Ashes*
GB 1965 104m bw Panavision
UA / Mirisch (J. Lee-Thompson)

A woman returns from Dachau to find that her husband is living with her step-daughter and that they plan to murder her.
Broken-backed thriller melodrama, the first half of which is quite irrelevant to the second. The whole is modestly inventive for those who don't mind a mixture of *Enoch Arden, Psycho* and *Dial M for Murder* with a touch of the concentration camps and a background of post-war misery.

w Julius J. Epstein, *novel* Hubert Monteilhet *d* J. Lee-Thompson *ph Christopher Challis m* Johnny Dankworth

Ingrid Thulin, Maximilian Schell, Samantha Eggar, Herbert Lom

Return from Witch Mountain
US 1978 93m Technicolor
Walt Disney (Ron Miller, Jerome Courtland)

A brother and sister from outer space come back to earth for a vacation and are used by crooks for their own purposes.
Acceptable sequel to *Escape from Witch Mountain*, with improved special effects.

w Malcolm Marmorstein *d* John Hough *ph* Frank Phillips *m* Lalo Schifrin *sp* Eustace Lycett, Art Cruickshank, Danny Lee

Bette Davis, Christopher Lee, Ike Eisenmann, Kim Richards, Jack Soo

The Return of a Man Called Horse*
US 1976 125m De Luxe Panavision
UA / Sandy Howard / Richard Harris

The English nobleman of *A Man Called Horse* goes back to the west to save his adopted Indian tribe from extinction.
Another 'realistic' action adventure with torture highlights; nicely made, but not for the squeamish.

w Jack de Witt *d* Irvin Kershner *ph Owen Roizman m Laurence Rosenthal*

RETURN OF THE PINK PANTHER. Peter Sellers as accident-prone Inspector Clouseau about to show off his Martial Arts expertise.

Richard Harris, Gale Sondergaard, Geoffrey Lewis, Bill Lucking, Jorge Luke

'Maintains a tidy balance between nausea and boredom.'—*Judith Crist*

† At 17 minutes, this pre-title sequence must be the longest so far.

The Return of Bulldog Drummond
GB 1934 71m bw

Drummond forms a society to oust crooked foreigners from Britain. Thin Drummond exploit with traces of the original Fascism. Ralph Richardson, Ann Todd, Francis L. Sullivan, Claud Allister, Joyce Kennedy. Written and directed by Walter Summers, from the novel *The Black Gang* by 'Sapper'; for BIP.

The Return of Captain Invincible
Australia 1982 91m Eastmancolor Panavision

An American superhero is discovered in the back streets of Sydney, a down-and-out drunk; but his skills are needed for the fight against Mr Midnight. Occasionally agreeable spoof which for most of its length is too frantic. Alan Arkin, Christopher Lee, Kate Fitzpatrick, Bill Hunter, Michael Pate, John Bluthal. Written by Steven E. De Souza, Andrew Gaty; directed by Philippe Mora; for Seven Keys / Willarra.

The Return of Chandu
US 1934 bw serial: 12 eps

A supernatural magician rescues a princess from the Black Magic Cult of Ubasti. Lively nonsense emanating from the feature film *Chandu the Magician*. Bela Lugosi, Maria Alba, Clara Kimball Young, Luvien Prival, Phyllis Ludwig. Directed by Ray Taylor; for Principal.

The Return of Dr X*
US 1939 62m bw
Warner (Bryan Foy)

A modern vampire terrorizes the city.
Minor thriller which doesn't get going till the last reel; only notable for Bogart's appearance as the monster. Nothing to do with *Dr X*.

w Lee Katz, *novel* The Doctor's Secret by William J. Makin *d* Vincent Sherman *ph* Sid Hickox *m* Bernhard Kaun

Dennis Morgan, Rosemary Lane, Wayne Morris, Humphrey Bogart, Olin Howland, John Litel

The Return of Dracula*
US 1958 77m bw
UA / Gramercy (Jules V. Levy, Arthur Gardner)
GB title: *The Fantastic Disappearing Man*

A European vampire makes his way to an American small town in the guise of a refugee Iron Curtain painter.
Quite nicely made low-budget horror film with a good balance of the supernatural and the ordinary.

w Pat Fielder *d Paul Landres* *ph* Jack McKenzie *m* Gerald Fried

Francis Lederer, Norman Eberhardt, Ray Stricklyn, Jimmie Baird, John Wengraf

The Return of Frank James*
US 1940 92m Technicolor
TCF (Darry F. Zanuck)

A sequel to *Jesse James* (qv).
Moody, nicely photographed western in which Jesse's brother avenges his murder.

w Sam Hellman *d Fritz Lang* *ph* George Barnes, William V. Skall *m* David Buttolph

Henry Fonda, Gene Tierney, Jackie Cooper, Henry Hull, John Carradine, J. Edward Bromberg, Donald Meek, Eddie Collins, George Barbier

'I doubt if any character was ever as lily white as that of Frank James here, but that is a present from the Hays Office to you, and anyway the part is played by Henry Fonda. Durn if I don't like that boy.'—*Otis Ferguson*

The Return of Martin Guerre*
France 1982 123m Fujicolor

In the sixteenth century, a man comes to a French village claiming to be the one who left his wife and child eight years before. Complaints are laid that he is an impostor . . . Mildly intriguing story which falls apart because one is never sure where the film's sympathies lie. Gérard Depardieu, Nathalie Baye, Sylvie Meda, Maurice Barrier. Written by Jean-Claude Carrière, Daniel Vigne; directed by Daniel Vigne; for Marcel Dassault / SFP. 'By far the most enigmatic film seen in London this year.'—*Sunday Times*. 'A plodding, confusing narrative that neither does proper justice to the story nor really teases out the complex historical, moral and psychological issues which it raises.'—*Observer* (Original title: *Le Retour de Martin Guerre*.)

The Return of Monte Cristo*
US 1946 92m bw
Columbia / Edward Small-Grant Whytock
GB title: *Monte Cristo's Revenge*

The grandson of the original count is framed and sent to Devil's Island, but escapes.
Very tolerable action romp of its time, with a fair troupe of actors enjoying themselves.

w George Bruce, Alfred Neumann, Kurt Siodmak *d* Henry Levin *ph* Charles Lawton Jnr *m* Lucien Moraweck

Louis Hayward, Barbara Britton, George Macready, Una O'Connor, Henry Stephenson, Steve Geray, Ray Collins, Ludwig Donath, Ivan Triesault

The Return of October
US 1948 89m Technicolor

A girl's inheritance is contested on the grounds that she thinks a horse is the reincarnation of her Uncle Willie. Thin whimsy which leaves its stars with egg on their faces. Glenn Ford, Terry Moore, Dame May Whitty, James Gleason, Albert Sharpe. Written by Norman Panama and Melvin Frank; directed by Joseph H. Lewis; for Columbia. (GB title: *A Date with Destiny*.)

The Return of Peter Grimm
US 1935 82m bw

A strong-minded family man returns as a ghost to see how his family is getting on without him. Fairly satisfying fantasy with good performances. Lionel Barrymore, Helen Mack, Edward Ellis, Donald Meek. Written by Francis Edwards Faragoh from the play by David Belasco; directed by George Nicholls Jnr; for RKO. (Previously filmed in 1925 with Alec B. Francis and Janet Gaynor.) 'Sombre fantasy . . . pretty dull and boresome.'—*Variety*

Return of the Ape Man: see The Ape Man

The Return of the Bad Men
US 1948 90m bw
RKO (Nat Holt)

A farmer tries to reform the female leader of a terrorist outlaw gang, but she is killed in a bank raid.
Standard, well shot western which contrives to introduce a number of well-known historical bandits.

w Charles O'Neal, Jack Netteford, Luci Ward *d* Ray Enright *ph* J. Roy Hunt *m* Roy Webb *md* Constantin Bakaleinikoff

Randolph Scott, Robert Ryan, Anne Jeffreys, Jacqueline White, Steve Brodie

'Riding to greater glory as the gay O. Henry hero!'
The Return of the Cisco Kid
US 1939 70m bw

The Kid escapes a Mexican firing squad into Arizona and defeats swindlers. Modest western with plenty of zip. Warner Baxter, Lynn Bari, Cesar Romero, Henry Hull, Kane Richmond, C. Henry Gordon, Robert Barrat. Written by Milton Sperling; directed by Herbert I. Leeds; for Kenneth MacGowan / TCF. 'Substantial fare for adventure audiences.'—*Variety*

Return of the Fly
US 1959 80m bw

The son of the original fly man meets the same fate as his father. Cheerless follow-up. Vincent Price, Brett Halsey, John Sutton, David Frankham, Dan Seymour. Written and directed by Edward Bernds; for Bernard Glasser/TCF.

Return of the Frontiersman
US 1950 74m Technicolor

A man escapes from prison to prove himself innocent of the bank robbery for which he was convicted. Goodish double-bill western with no surprises. Gordon Macrae, Julie London, Rory Calhoun, Fred Clark, Edwin Rand. Written by Edna Anhalt; directed by Richard Bare; for Warner.

Return of the Jedi*
US 1983 132m De Luxe Panavision
TCF / Lucasfilm (Howard Kazanjian)

'Episode 6' of the *Star Wars* serial: our heroes combat Darth Vader and Jabba the Hutt. More expensive fantasy for the world's children of all ages, especially the undemanding ones.

w Lawrence Kasdan, George Lucas *d* Richard Marquand *ph* Alan Hume *pd* Norman Reynolds *m* John Williams

Mark Hamill, Harrison Ford, Carrie Fisher, Billy Dee Williams, Anthony Daniels, Peter Mayhew, Kenny Baker

'I admire the exquisite skill and talent which have been poured into these films, while finding the concepts behind these gigantic video games in the sky mindlessly tedious.'—*Margaret Hinxman, Daily Mail*

'An impersonal and rather junky piece of moviemaking.'—*Pauline Kael, New Yorker*

'Only the effects are special.'—*Sight and Sound*

AAN: John Williams; art direction

'They're back—and they're hungry!'
The Return of the Living Dead
US 1985 90m De Luxe

The army is called in to repel a zombie onslaught. Cult horror movie hailed by some as a black comedy, but likely to repel most audiences. Clu Gulager, James Karen, Don Calfa, Thom Matthews. Written and directed by Dan O'Bannon; for Tom Fox / Hemdale / Orion.

The Return of the Pink Panther*
GB 1974 113m De Luxe Panavision
UA / Jewel / Pimlico / Mirisch / Geoffrey (Blake Edwards)

When the Pink Panther diamond – national treasure of the Eastern state of Lugash – is once again stolen, bungling Inspector Clouseau is called in.
Rehash of jokes from *The Pink Panther* (qv), not bad in parts but a rather tedious whole.

w Frank Waldman, Blake Edwards *d* Blake Edwards *ph* Geoffrey Unsworth *m Henry Mancini*

Peter Sellers, Christopher Plummer, Herbert Lom, Catherine Schell, Peter Arne, Peter Jeffrey, Grégoire Aslan, David Lodge, Graham Stark

'The film never comes fully to the boil, but simmers in a series of self-contained, self-destructing little set pieces.'—*Richard Combs*

'The first film in history to be upstaged by its own credit titles.'—*Benny Green, Punch*

The Return of the Scarlet Pimpernel*
GB 1937 94m bw
London Films (Alexander Korda, Arnold Pressburger)

Sir Percy Blakeney saves his wife and other French aristos from the guillotine.
Predictable, stylish revolutionary romance, much thinner in plot and performance than its predecessor.

w Lajos Biro, Arthur Wimperis, Adrian Brunel *d* Hans Schwarz *ph* Mutz Greenbaum *m* Arthur Benjamin

Barry K. Barnes, Sophie Stewart, Margaretta Scott, James Mason, *Henry Oscar,* Francis Lister, Anthony Bushell

The Return of the Seven*
US 1966 95m Technicolor Panavision
UA / Mirisch / CB (Ted Richmond)

The seven gunmen, slightly reconstituted, fight again to rescue some kidnapped farmers.
The mixture as before (see *The Magnificent Seven*); adequate but scarcely inspired.

w Larry Cohen *d* Burt Kennedy *ph* Paul Vogel *m* Elmer Bernstein

Yul Brynner, Robert Fuller, Julian Mateos, Warren Oates, Claude Akins, Virgilio Texeira, Emilio Fernandez, Jordan Christopher

AAN: Elmer Bernstein

The Return of the Soldier*
GB 1982 102m Technicolor
Brent Walker / Barry R. Cooper (Ann Skinner, Simon Relph)

In 1916, a shellshocked soldier returns home, able to remember his old sweetheart but not his wife.
Overcast and heavy-handed treatment of a classy novella.

w Hugh Whitemore, *novel* Rebecca West *d* Alan Bridges *ph* Stephen Goldblatt *m* Richard Rodney Bennett *pd* Luciana Arrighi

Alan Bates, Ann-Margret, Julie Christie, Glenda Jackson, Jeremy Kemp, Edward de Souza, Frank Finlay, Jack May, Ian Holm

'The film has nowhere to go except into rhetorical bluster about class distinctions.'—*Tom Milne, MFB*

The Return of the Terror
US 1934 65m bw

A scientist feigns insanity to avoid prosecution for murder, and escapes to his old sanatorium, where murder strikes again. Barnstorming murder mystery borrowing its title and nothing else from Edgar Wallace. John Halliday, Mary Astor, Lyle Talbot, Frank McHugh, Irving Pichel, J. Carrol Naish. Written by Eugene Solow and Peter Milne; directed by Howard Bretherton; for Warner. 'Formula mystery, but speedy.'—*Variety*

'Terrifying! Paralysing! Horrifying!'
The Return of the Vampire*
US 1943 69m bw
Columbia (Sam White)

Dracula reappears amid the London blitz. Surprisingly well made and complexly plotted horror film; it looks good and only lacks humour. The wolf man, however, is a regrettable intrusion.

w Griffin Jay *d Lew Landers ph John Stumar, L. J. O'Connell m* Mario Castelnuovo-Tedesco *md* Morris Stoloff

Bela Lugosi, Nina Foch, Frieda Inescort, Miles Mander, Matt Willis, Roland Varno, Ottola Nesmith

Return to Glennascaul*
Eire 1951 23m bw
Dublin Gate Theatre

Orson Welles gives a man a lift and is told a gentle ghost story.
Neither very satisfying nor very well done, this little film deserves a niche in history because of the talents involved. It was apparently made during one of the many intervals in the filming of *Othello.*

wd Hilton Edwards *narrator* Orson Welles

Return to Macon County
US 1975 89m Movielab
AIP / Macon Service Company (Eliot Schick)

In the fifties, two wandering youths pick up a waitress and have serious trouble with a manic policeman in America's unfriendliest area.
Slam-bang sequel to *Macon County Line,* rather unintentionally comic.

wd Richard Compton *ph* Jacques Marquette *m* Robert O. Ragland

Nick Nolte, Don Johnson, Robin Mattson, Robert Viharo

Return to Oz
US 1985 110m Technicolor
Walt Disney / Silver Screen Partners (Paul Maslansky)

Dorothy has traumas because of her Oz experiences, and suffers further nightmares under shock treatment.
A weird way to treat a children's classic, the result being a movie which appealed strongly to nobody except, possibly, the producer. The Disney people should have known better.

w Walter Murch, Gill Dennis *d* Walter Murch *ph* David Watkin *m* David Shire

Fairuza Balk, Jean Marsh, Nicol Williamson, Piper Laurie, Matt Clark, Emma Ridley

'Astonishingly sombre, melancholy, and sadly unengaging.'—*Variety*

'Without musical numbers this narrative seems a perilously thin journey with no particular purpose.'—*Time Out*

Return to Paradise*
US 1953 109m Technicolor
UA / Aspen (Theron Warth)

A peace seeker settles on a tiny South Sea island and leaves when his wife dies; he returns after World War II with his daughter.
Curious idyll, slow but not displeasing.

w Charles Kaufman, *novel* James Michener *d* Mark Robson *ph* Winton Hoch *m* Dmitri Tiomkin

Gary Cooper, Barry Jones, Roberta Haynes, Moira MacDonald

Return to Peyton Place*
US 1961 122m De Luxe Cinemascope
TCF / API (Jerry Wald)

Constance Mackenzie's daughter writes a novel about Peyton Place and falls in love with the publisher.
More closets are unlocked, more skeletons fall out; for addicts, the sequel does not disappoint, and it's all very glossy.

w Ronald Alexander *d* Jose Ferrer *ph* Charles G. Clarke *m* Franz Waxman

Jeff Chandler, Carol Lynley, Eleanor Parker, *Mary Astor,* Robert Sterling, Luciana Paluzzi, Brett Halsey, Tuesday Weld

'Enough soap suds to pollute the Mississippi along with the mind.'—*Judith Crist, 1973*

Return to Yesterday
GB 1940 68m bw

A bored Hollywood star seeks anonymity in a seaside repertory company. Mild comedy, not without interest. Clive Brook, Anna Lee, Dame May Whitty, Hartley Power, Milton Rosmer, David Tree, Olga Lindo. Written by Robert Stevenson, Margaret Kennedy, Roland Pertwee and Angus MacPhail, from the play *Goodness How Sad* by Robert Morley; directed by Robert Stevenson; for Ealing.

Reuben, Reuben*
US 1982 101m CFI colour
Saltair / Taft (Walter Shenson)

A drunken British poet upsets a New England community.
Oddball comedy at which one laughs without much enthusiasm.

w Julius J. Epstein, *novel* Peter de Vries and *play* Spofford by Herman Shumlin *d* Robert Ellis Miller *ph* Peter Stein *m* Billy Goldenberg *pd* Peter Larkin

Tom Conti, Kelly McGillis, Roberts Blossom, Cynthia Harris, Joel Fabiani

AAN: Tom Conti; adaptation

Reunion
US 1936 83m bw

When a doctor retires, the townsfolk reunite him with many of the children he has brought into the world. Tiresome second attempt to cash in on the Dionne Quintuplets, who make several appearances. Jean Hersholt, Rochelle Hudson, Helen Vinson, Slim Summerville, J. Edward Bromberg, Sara Haden. Written by Sam Hellman, Gladys Lehman, Sonya Levien; directed by Norman Taurog; for Darryl Zanuck / TCF. (GB title: *Hearts in Reunion.*)
'Too episodic to command interest or supply suspense.'—*Variety*
† NB: a sequel to *The Country Doctor.*

Reunion in France
US 1943 104m bw
MGM (Joseph L. Mankiewicz)
GB title: *Mademoiselle France*

A selfish Parisian dress designer gradually realizes that her world has changed when the Nazis invade and she is asked to help an American flier.
Action flagwaver which tries also to be a woman's picture and goes pretty soppily about it.

w Jan Lustig, Marvin Borowsky, Marc Connelly, *story* Ladislas Bus-Fekete *d* Jules Dassin *ph* Robert Planck *m* Franz Waxman

Joan Crawford, John Wayne, Philip Dorn, Reginald Owen, Albert Basserman, John Carradine, Ann Ayars, J. Edward Bromberg, Henry Daniell, Moroni Olsen, Howard da Silva

'Miss Crawford isn't making all the sacrifices implied in the script . . . Dressing like a refugee is certainly not in her contract.'—*New York Herald Tribune*

Reunion in Vienna*
US 1933 100m bw
MGM

A long-exiled nobleman tries to take up an old romance even though the lady is married.
Lacklustre adaptation of a play which must have style; the performances remain interesting.

w Ernest Vajda, Claudine West, *play* Robert E. Sherwood *d* Sidney Franklin *ph* George Folsey *m* William Axt

John Barrymore, Diana Wynyard, Frank Morgan, May Robson, Eduardo Ciannelli, Una Merkel, Henry Travers

'Unlikely money film outside a few of the larger cities.'—*Variety*

AAN: George Folsey

Reveille With Beverly*
US 1943 78m bw

A girl disc jockey runs a programme for soldiers. Thin excuse for a musical, but the result was pretty popular. Ann Miller, William Wright, Dick Purcell, Franklin Pangborn, Tim Ryan, Larry Parks. Written by Howard J. Green, Jack Henley, Albert Duffy; directed by Charles Barton; for Sam White/Columbia.

Revenge
GB 1971 89m Eastmancolor
Rank / Peter Rogers Productions (George H. Brown)

When children are raped and murdered in a north country town, two men take the law into their own hands.
Crude melodrama set in Cold Comfort Farm country; efficient but unrewarding.

w John Kruse *d* Sidney Hayers *ph* Ken Hodges *m* Eric Rodgers

Joan Collins, Sinead Cusack, James Booth, Ray Barrett, Kenneth Griffith

'If you go alone—you'll find yourself running all the way home!'

The Revenge of Frankenstein
GB 1958 89m Technicolor
Columbia / Hammer (Anthony Hinds)

Baron Frankenstein evades the guillotine and makes a new creature with the brain of a homicidal dwarf.
Dullish horror farrago with a few indications of quirkish humour.

w Jimmy Sangster, Hurford Janes *d* Terence Fisher *ph* Jack Asher *m* Leonard Salzedo

Peter Cushing, Michael Gwynn, Oscar Quitak, Francis Matthews, Eunice Gayson, John Welsh, Lionel Jeffries, Richard Wordsworth, Charles Lloyd Pack, John Stuart, Arnold Diamond

† This second Hammer Frankenstein set the tone for the rest; see *The Curse of Frankenstein*.

The Revenge of the Pink Panther
US 1978 98m Technicolor Panavision
UA / Blake Edwards

Inspector Clouseau tracks down a drug-smuggling industrialist.
Feeble addition to a series which was always too pleased with itself.

w Frank Waldman, Ron Clarke, Blake Edwards *d* Blake Edwards *ph* Ernie Day *m* Henry Mancini

Peter Sellers, Herbert Lom, Robert Webber, Dyan Cannon, Burt Kwouk, Paul Stewart, Robert Loggia, Graham Stark

Revenge of the Zombies
US 1943 61m bw

A Nazi scientist in Mexico tries to convert an army of the dead for Hitler's use.
Unpersuasive horror cheapie. John Carradine, Robert Lowery, Gale Storm, Veda Ann Borg, Mantan Moreland. Written by Edmund Kelso and Van Norcross; directed by Steve Sekely; for Lindsley Parsons / Monogram.

The Revengers
US 1972 108m De Luxe Panavision
Cinema Center / Martin Rackin

A rancher gathers a posse to hunt down the Indians who have allegedly murdered his wife and family.
Standard major western with a dismal script which echoes *The Dirty Dozen* and *The Wild Bunch*: sometimes repulsive, seldom exciting.

w Wendell Mayes *d* Daniel Mann *ph* Gabriel Torres *m* Pino Calvi

William Holden, Ernest Borgnine, Susan Hayward, Woody Strode, Roger Hanin

The Revolt of Mamie Stover
US 1956 93m Eastmancolor Cinemascope
TCF (Buddy Adler)

A dance hall girl leaves San Francisco for Honolulu, makes money there but reforms for love of a rich novelist.
Absurdly bowdlerized and boring film version of a novel about a sleazy prostitute; hardly worth making at all in this form, especially as the cast seems well capable of a raunchier version.

w Sidney Boehm, *novel* William Bradford Huie *d* Raoul Walsh *ph* Leo Tover *m* Hugo Friedhofer

Jane Russell, Agnes Moorehead, Richard Egan, Joan Leslie

The Revolutionary
US 1970 101m Technicolor
(UA) Pressman–Williams (Edward R. Pressman)

Episodes in the life of a revolutionary, from distributing leaflets to attempted assassination.
A rather casual study of one man's radicalism, in no particular time or place; no doubt of great interest to other revolutionaries.

w Hans Konigsberger *d* Paul Williams *ph* Brian Probyn *m* Michael Small

Jon Voight, Jennifer Salt, Robert Duvall

The Reward
US 1965 92m De Luxe Cinemascope
TCF / Aaron Rosenberg

A mixed group of adventurers set out across the desert to capture a murderer; but thieves fall out.
Pretentious and talky melodrama which quickly scuttled its director's chances in Hollywood. Little action, obvious outcome, attractive Death Valley locations.

w Serge Bourgignon, Oscar Mullard, *novel* Michael Barrett *d* Serge Bourgignon *ph Joe MacDonald* *m* Elmer Bernstein

Max Von Sydow, Efrem Zimbalist Jnr, Yvette Mimieux, Gilbert Roland, Emilio Fernandez, Henry Silva

'Emotions clash in a crescendo of drama!'
Rhapsody
US 1954 116m Technicolor
MGM (Lawrence Weingarten)

A wealthy woman affects the lives of two quite different musicians, each of whom has his weakness.
Tedious romantic drama which vainly attempted a smart veneer but boasted a splendid musical sound track.

w Fay and Michael Kanin, *novel* Maurice Guest by Henry Handel Richardson *d* Charles Vidor *ph* Robert Planck *md* Johnny Green, Bronislau Kaper *pianist* Claudio Arrau *violinist* Michael Rabin

Elizabeth Taylor, Vittorio Gassman, John Ericson, Louis Calhern, Michael Chekhov, Barbara Bates, Celia Lovsky, Richard Hageman

Rhapsody in Blue**
US 1945 139m bw
Warner (Jesse L. Lasky)

The life story of composer George Gershwin.
No more trustworthy on factual matters than other Hollywood biopics of its era, this rather glum saga at least presented the music and the performers to excellent advantage.

w Howard Koch, Elliot Paul *d Irving Rapper ph Sol Polito* *md* Ray Heindorf, Max Steiner *ch* Le Roy Prinz *ad* Anton Grot, John Hughes

Robert Alda, Joan Leslie, Alexis Smith, Charles Coburn, Julie Bishop, *Albert Basserman, Oscar Levant, Herbert Rudley*, Rosemary de Camp, Morris Carnovsky, *Al Jolson, Paul Whiteman*, George White, Hazel Scott

'With no story at all, this two-hour concert of Gershwin music would be well worth the price of admission '—*Daily Mail*

AAN: Ray Heindorf, Max Steiner

Rhinestone
US 1984 111m De Luxe
TCF / Howard Smith, Marvin Worth

A night club singer bets her obnoxious employer that she can turn a cab driver into a star.
Crude and witless *Pygmalion* variation with unsympathetic leads.

w Phil Alden Robinson, Sylvester Stallone *d* Bob Clark *ph* Timothy Galfas *m* Dolly Parton

Dolly Parton, Sylvester Stallone, Richard Farnsworth, Ron Leibman, Tim Thomerson

Rhino
US 1964 91m Metrocolor
MGM / Ivan Tors (Ben Chapman)

A scientist working with white rhinos is joined by an unscrupulous big game hunter.
Inoffensive African adventure.

w Art Arthur, Arthur Weiss *d* Ivan Tors *ph* Sven Persson, Lamar Boren *m* Lalo Schifrin

Harry Guardino, Robert Culp, Shirley Eaton

Rhodes of Africa*
GB 1936 91m bw
Gaumont (Geoffrey Barkas)
US title: *Rhodes*

A rough-hewn diamond miner becomes Prime Minister of Cape Colony.
Heavy-going but generally interesting historical drama shot on location.

w Michael Barringer, Leslie Arliss, Miles Malleson, *book* Sarah Millin *d* Berthold Viertel *ph* Bernard Knowles *m* Hubert Bath

Walter Huston, Oscar Homolka, Basil Sydney, Peggy Ashcroft, Frank Cellier, Bernard Lee, Lewis Casson

'One of the better English-made pictures . . . should do all right even if it doesn't get the women.'—*Variety*

'Solid, worthy, humourless, it unrolls its eleven well-bred reels with all the technical advantages of 1936.'—*Graham Greene*

Rhubarb
US 1951 94m bw
Paramount (Perlberg–Seaton)

A millionaire leaves his fortune, including a baseball team, to a wild ginger cat, which means problems for his publicity agent.
Typical scatty farce of the early fifties, held together by the splendid performance of the disdainful feline in the title role rather than by any special merit in the handling.

w Dorothy Reid, Francis Cockrill, *novel* H. Allen Smith *d* Arthur Lubin *ph* Lionel Lindon *m* Van Cleave

Ray Milland, Jan Sterling, Gene Lockhart, William Frawley

Rhubarb
GB 1969 37m Technicolor

Various village notables congregate on the golf course. Virtually silent comedy (nobody says anything but 'rhubarb') which could have been very funny with better jokes. A TV remake in 1979 was however much worse. Harry Secombe, Eric Sykes, Jimmy Edwards, Hattie Jacques, Gordon Rollins, Graham Stark, Kenneth Connor. Written and directed by Eric Sykes; for Avalon / ABPC.

Rhythm of the Islands
US 1943 60m bw

A rather dull south sea island sets itself up to attract tourists. Moderate musical programmer, one of many from this studio during the war. Allan Jones, Jane Frazee, Andy Devine, Ernest Truex, Marjorie Gateson, Mary Wickes. Written by Oscar Brodney, M. M. Musselman; directed by Roy William Neill; for Bernard Burton / Universal. 'Acceptably fulfils its purpose of providing an hour's diverting footage for dual support in the general runs.'—*Variety*

Rhythm on the Range*
US 1936 87m bw
Paramount (Benjamin Glazer)

A hired hand saves the boss's daughter when she is kidnapped by local badmen.
Easy-going musical comedy with a western background, later remade as *Pardners* (qv).

w John C. Moffett, Sidney Salkow, Walter de Leon, Francis Martin *d* Norman Taurog *ph* Karl Struss *songs* various

Bing Crosby, Martha Raye, Frances Farmer, Bob Burns, Lucile Watson, Samuel S. Hinds, George E. Stone, Warren Hymer

'Bing Crosby as a cowboy; Bing Crosby crooning a prize bull to sleep on a freight car; Bing Crosby more than ever like Walt Disney's Cock Robin; it needs some stamina to be a film reviewer.'—*Graham Greene*

Rhythm on the River*
US 1940 92m bw
Paramount (William Le Baron)

A song writer employs 'ghosts' to produce his music and lyrics; they discover this fact and go into business for themselves.
Cheerful musical with strong billing.

w Dwight Taylor, Billy Wilder, Jacques Théry *d* Victor Schertzinger *ph* Ted Tetzlaff *m* Johnny Burke, James V. Monaco

Bing Crosby, Mary Martin, Basil Rathbone, Oscar Levant, Oscar Shaw, Charley Grapewin, William Frawley

AAN: song 'Only Forever'

'From the very beginning, they knew they'd be friends to the end. What they didn't count on was everything in between!'

Rich and Famous
US 1981 117m Metrocolor
MGM / Jaquet / William Allyn

Two girl friends meet again years after college; one has become a famous highbrow novelist, and with her help the other becomes a lowbrow one.
Unattractively sexed-up remake of *Old Acquaintance*, with even more talk than the original, and much less style.

w Gerald Ayres *d* George Cukor *ph* Don Peterman, Peter Eco *m* Georges Delerue *pd* Jan Scott *ed* John F. Burnett

Candice Bergen, Jacqueline Bisset, David Selby, Hart Bochner, Steven Hill, Meg Ryan

'A sadly dispiriting occasion . . . a jumbled conflation of *The Group* and a female version of *Carnal Knowledge*.'—*Tim Pulleine, MFB*

† The director was 82 when the film was shot, which must be some kind of record.

Rich and Strange*
GB 1931 83m bw
BIP (John Maxwell)
US title: *East of Shanghai*

A young couple come into money and take a trip around the world.
Slight, agreeable early talkie with a few Hitchcock touches.

w Alma Reville, Val Valentine, Alfred Hitchcock, *novel* Dale Collins *d Alfred Hitchcock* *ph* Jack Cox, Charles Martin *m* Hal Dolphe

Henry Kendall, Joan Barry, Percy Marmont, Betty Amann, Elsie Randolph

'Hitchcock, being Britain's D. W. Griffith, according to the press agents around here, usually gets a rave as his pictures take the screen. Here's one where the admirers will have difficulty knowing what to say.'—*Variety*

'Perhaps his bravest failure.'—*George Perry, 1965*

The Rich Are Always with Us
US 1932 73m bw
Warner (Sam Bischoff)

A socialite determines on a divorce but her new love is annoyed by her concern for her ex-husband.
Cocktail drama of a kind which totally disappeared from the screen.

w Austin Parker, *novel* E. Pettit *d* Alfred E. Green *ph* Ernest Haller *m* W. Franke Harling

Ruth Chatterton, George Brent, John Miljan, Bette Davis, Adrienne Dore, Mae Madison, Robert Warwick

'Chiefly a femme picture . . . the title's appropriateness is as obscure as the wisdom of so metaphoric a label for a flicker.'—*Variety*

Rich Kids
US 1979 96m Technicolor

An adolescent boy and girl are mildly corrupted by the behaviour of their parents. Spasmodically interesting comedy-drama which seems ill at ease among the rich and alternates between exploitation, satire and whimsy. Trini Alvarado, Jeremy Levy, Kathryn Walker, John Lithgow, Terry Kiser, David Selby. Written by Judith Ross; directed by Robert M. Young; for Robert Altman / Lion's Gate / UA.

Rich Man, Poor Girl
US 1938 72m bw

Consternation takes a white-collar family when a millionaire takes a fancy to one of its daughters. Unexciting comedy-drama vaguely modelled on *You Can't Take It With You.* Lew Ayres, Ruth Hussey, Robert Young, Don Castle, Guy Kibbee, Lana Turner, Rita Johnson. Written by Joseph Fields and Jerome Chodorov, from a play by Edith Ellis; directed by Reinhold Schunzel; for MGM. 'Lightweight in marquee strength but should build through word of mouth.'—*Variety*

Rich Man's Folly
US 1931 80m bw
Paramount

A rich man has no time for his children.
Curious updating of Dickens' *Dombey and Son*; not really a success.

w Grover Jones, Edward Paramore Jnr *d* John Cromwell *ph* David Abel

George Bancroft, Frances Dee, Robert Ames, Juliette Compton, Dorothy Peterson

'Splendid cast and serviceable product anywhere.'—*Variety*

Rich, Young and Pretty
US 1951 95m Technicolor
MGM (Joe Pasternak)

A Texas rancher takes his young daughter to Paris, where she meets her real mother.
Moderate musical.

w Dorothy Cooper, Sidney Sheldon *d* Norman Taurog *ph* Robert Planck *m* Nicholas Brodszky *ly* Sammy Cahn *ch* Nick Castle

Danielle Darrieux, Wendell Corey, Jane Powell, Fernando Lamas, Vic Damone

AAN: song 'Wonder Why' (*m* Nicholas Brodszky, *ly* Sammy Cahn)

Richard III***
GB 1955 161m Technicolor Vistavision
London Films (Laurence Olivier)

Shakespeare's play about Richard Crookback, his seizure of the throne and his defeat at Bosworth.
Theatrical but highly satisfying filming of a splendidly melodramatic view of history. Interesting but not fussy camera movement, delightful sets (followed by a disappointingly 'realistic' battle) and superb performances.

w William Shakespeare (adapted by Laurence Olivier, Alan Dent, with additions) *d Laurence Olivier* *ph Otto Heller* *pd Roger Furse* *m William Walton* *ad Carmen Dillon*

Laurence Olivier, Claire Bloom, *Ralph Richardson, Cedric Hardwicke*, Stanley Baker, Alec Clunes, John Gielgud, Mary Kerridge, Pamela Brown, Michael Gough, Norman Wooland, Helen Haye, Patrick Troughton, Clive Morton, Andrew Cruickshank

'Wherever the play was loose-jointed or ill-fitting. Sir Laurence has been its tinker and its tailor, but never once its butcher.'—*Paul Dehn, News Chronicle*

AAN: Laurence Olivier

The Richest Girl in the World
US 1934 80m bw

A millionairess changes places with her secretary to find a man who will love her for herself. Rose-coloured romance, remade in 1944 as *Bride by Mistake*. Miriam Hopkins, Joel McCrea, Fay Wray, Henry Stephenson, Reginald Denny, Beryl Mercer. Written by Norman Krasna; directed by William A. Seiter; for RKO. AAN: Norman Krasna.

'Eighty minutes of unerring entertainment . . . a pip picture for Miriam Hopkins.'—*Variety*

The Richest Man in Town
US 1941 70m bw

A small-town newspaper publisher feuds with an old friend over his prepared obituary of the latter. A fragment of Americana with an unfinished feel. Frank Craven, Edgar Buchanan, Eileen O'Hearn, Roger Pryor, Tom Dugan. Written by Farnya Foss, Jerry Sackheim; directed by Charles Barton; for Jack Fier / Columbia.

Ricochet Romance
US 1954 80m bw

The new cook transforms a dude ranch which had been allowed to run down. Modest programme filler on well-established lines. Marjorie Main, Chill Wills, Rudy Vallee, Pedro Gonzales-Gonzales, Alfonso Bedoya, Ruth Hampton. Written by Kay Lennard; directed by Charles Lamont; for Universal.

The Riddle of the Sands*
GB 1978 102m Eastmancolor Panavision
Rank / Worldmark (Drummond Challis)

In 1901 a British yachtsman in the North Sea hits upon a German trial invasion.
Rather too placid adaptation of a semi-classic adventure story in which too little happens to make a rousing action film; points of interest along the way, though.

w Tony Maylam, John Bailey, *novel* Erskine Childers *d* Tony Maylam *ph* Christopher Challis *m* Howard Blake *ph* Hazel Peiser

Michael York, Simon MacCorkindale, Jenny Agutter, Alan Badel, Jurgen Andersen

Ride a Crooked Mile*
US 1938 70m bw

An ex-Cossack cattle hijacker is disappointed when jailed to find that his son will not help him escape. Lively crime melodrama with an unusual twist. Akim Tamiroff, Leif Erickson, Frances Farmer, Lynne Overman, John Miljan, Vladimir Sokoloff. Written by Ferdinand Reyher, John C. Moffitt; directed by Alfred E. Green; for Jeff Lazarus / Paramount. 'Fine melodrama, handicapped by lack of cast strength and so-so title.'—*Variety*

Ride a Crooked Trail
US 1958 88m Eastmancolor Cinemascope

A crook takes refuge in a small town and becomes its honest marshal. One we've heard before, and seen better done. Audie Murphy, Walter Matthau, Gia Scala, Henry Silva. Written by Borden Chase; directed by Jesse Hibbs; for Universal-International.

The Ride Back*
US 1957 79m bw
UA / Associates and Aldrich (William Conrad)

A lawman arrests an outlaw wanted for murder, but has the problem of getting him back to base.
Slightly offbeat low-budget western, well enough done if it had to be done at all.

w Anthony Ellis *d* Allen H. Miner *ph* Joseph Biroc *m* Frank de Vol

Anthony Quinn, William Conrad, George Trevino, Lita Milan

Ride beyond Vengeance
US 1966 100m Technicolor
Columbia / Tiger / Goodson / Todman / Sentinel / Fenady

A young westerner, accused of cattle rustling and branded, vows revenge.
Dourly brutal but studio-bound and very padded western; if there is any entertainment value it doesn't emerge for more than a few moments.

w Andrew J. Fenady, *novel* The Night of the Tiger by Al Dewlen *d* Bernard McEveety *ph* Lester Shorr *m* Richard Markowitz

Chuck Connors, Michael Rennie, Kathryn Hays, Claude Akins, Bill Bixby, Paul Fix, Gary Merrill, Joan Blondell, Gloria Grahame, Ruth Warrick, Arthur O'Connell, Frank Gorshin, James MacArthur

† Probably intended as a TV movie and found too violent.

Ride Clear of Diablo
US 1954 80m Technicolor

A young man seeking vengeance on his father's murderer becomes deputy to a sheriff hired to kill him too. Lively enough star western. Audie Murphy, Dan Duryea, Susan Cabot, Abbe Lane, Russell Johnson, Paul Birch, Jack Elam. Written by George Zuckerman; directed by Jesse Hibbs; for Universal-International.

Ride 'Em Cowboy
US 1941 82m bw
Universal (Alex Gottlieb)

Two hot dog vendors find themselves working on an Arizona dude ranch.
Slick but routine comedy star vehicle with no outstanding sequences.

w True Boardman, John Grant *d* Arthur Lubin *ph* John W. Boyle *m* Frank Skinner *songs* Don Raye, Gene de Paul

Bud Abbott, Lou Costello, Dick Foran, Anne Gwynne, Samuel S. Hinds, Richard Lane, Johnny Mack Brown, Ella Fitzgerald

Ride Lonesome
US 1959 73m Eastmancolor Cinemascope

A bounty hunter catches a killer as bait to trap the criminal's brother against whom he plots vengeance. Mildly suspenseful western, rather lost on the wide screen. Randolph Scott, Karen Steele, Pernell Roberts, James Best, James Coburn, Lee Van Cleef. Written by Burt Kennedy; directed by Budd Boetticher; for Columbia.

Ride Out for Revenge
US 1957 79m bw

Gold is discovered on land to which the army is moving Indians, and this causes second thoughts. Low-key, rather brooding western which aims to be different. Rory Calhoun, Lloyd Bridges, Gloria Grahame, Joanne Gilbert, Vince Edwards. Written and produced by Norman Retchin; directed by Bernard Girard; for Bryna/UA.

Ride the High Country**
US 1962 94m Metrocolor Cinemascope
MGM (Richard E. Lyons)
GB title: *Guns in the Afternoon*

Two retired lawmen help transport gold from a mining camp to the bank, but one has ideas of his own.
Thoughtful western graced by ageing star presences; generally well done.

w N. B. Stone Jnr *d Sam Peckinpah* *ph* Lucien Ballard *m* George Bassman

Joel McCrea, Randolph Scott, Edgar Buchanan, Mariette Hartley, James Drury

'A nice little conventional unconventional western.'—*Stanley Kauffmann*

'The movie that rocked the debutantes—down to their last martini!'

Ride the High Iron
US 1957 74m bw

A war veteran gets into the seamier side of public relations. Curious little urban melodrama with a high moral tone, like a cut-price *Sweet Smell of Success*. Don Taylor, Raymond Burr, Sally Forrest. Written by Milton Gelman; directed by Don Weis; for Columbia.
(NB: originally made for TV.)

Ride the Man Down
US 1952 90m Trucolor

The death of a rancher sets off a bitter fight for his lands. Flat and uninteresting western melodrama. Brian Donlevy, Ella Raines, Rod Cameron, Forrest Tucker, Barbara Britton, James Bell, Chill Wills, J. Carrol Naish, Jim Davis. Written by Mary McCall Jnr; directed by Joe Kane; for Republic.

Ride the Pink Horse*
US 1947 101m bw
U-I (Joan Harrison)

An ex-serviceman visits a New Mexican town in search of the gangster who killed his buddy. Dour, complex melodrama with a certain amount of style but not enough substance.

w Charles Lederer, *novel* Dorothy B. Hughes *d* Robert Montgomery *ph* Russell Metty *m* Frank Skinner

Robert Montgomery, Wanda Hendrix, Andrea King, Thomas Gomez, Fred Clark, Art Smith

'One of a kind: no one in his right mind would imitate it.'—*Pauline Kael, 70s*

AAN: Thomas Gomez

Ride the Wild Surf
US 1964 101m Eastmancolor
Columbia / Jana (Jo and Art Napoleon)

Surf riders go to Hawaii and find romance. Pleasant, overlong, open air fun and games.

w Jo and Art Napoleon *d* Don Taylor *ph* Joseph Biroc *m* Stu Phillips

Fabian, Shelley Fabares, Tab Hunter, Barbara Eden

The Ride to Hangman's Tree
US 1967 90m Technicolor

Three bandits never quite manage to reform. Easy-going western, played on the light side in a vein later developed in *Butch Cassidy and the Sundance Kid*. Jack Lord, James Farentino, Don Galloway, Melody Johnson, Richard Anderson. Written by Luci Ward, Jack Natteford and William Bowers; directed by Alan Rafkin; for Universal.

Ride, Vaquero
US 1953 90m Anscocolor
MGM (Stephen Ames)

Ranchers settling in New Mexico after the Civil War cause some natives to turn bandit; one of them has a mysterious American associate called Rio.
Very mildly interesting western with the stars rather swamping a humourless script.

w Frank Fenton *d* John Farrow *ph* Robert Surtees *m* Bronislau Kaper

Robert Taylor, Ava Gardner, Howard Keel, Anthony Quinn, Charlita

Rider on a Dead Horse
US 1962 72m bw

A prospector murders one partner for his gold and tries to pin the blame on the other. Watchable minor western with good use of location. John Vyvyan, Bruce Gordon, Kevin Hagen, Lisa Lu. Written by Stephen Longstreet; directed by Herbert L. Strock; for Allied Artists.

Riders of Death Valley
US 1941 bw serial: 15 eps

During the California gold rush, vigilantes protect the mines against raiders. Fairly vigorous serial action with good locations. Dick Foran, Leo Carrillo, Buck Jones, Charles Bickford, Lon Chaney Jnr, Noah Beery Jnr, Guinn 'Big Boy' Williams, Monte Blue, Glenn Strange. Directed by Ford Beebe and Ray Taylor; for Universal.

Riders of the Purple Sage
US 1931 58m bw

A rootin', tootin' cowboy traps a villain and weathers a stampede and an avalanche. Good standard western previously filmed in 1918 with William Farnum and in 1925 with Tom Mix. This version was premièred on the wide screens of the period. George O'Brien, Marguerite Churchill, Noah Beery, Yvonne Pelletier, Stanley Fields. From the novel by Zane Grey; directed by Hamilton McFadden; for Fox. 'Still a good western and okay outside the de luxers.'—*Variety*

Riders of Vengeance
US 1952 80m Technicolor

During the California gold rush, a prospector takes revenge on a local dictator. Standard western themes against a colourful background. Richard Conte, Barbara Britton, Viveca Lindfors, Hugh O'Brian, Morris Ankrum, William Reynolds, Dennis Weaver. Written by Polly James and Lillie Hayward; directed by Lesley Selander; for Universal-International. (GB title: *The Raiders*.)

Riders to the Stars*
US 1954 81m Color Corporation
UA / Ivan Tors

Rocket scientists investigate the problems of cosmic bombardment.
Enjoyably straightforward science fiction with no monsters or political problems; it has decided historic interest as a record of what scientists in 1954 thought rocket travel would be like.

w Curt Siodmak *d* Richard Carlson *ph* Stanley Cortez *m* Harry Sukman

Richard Carlson, Herbert Marshall, William Lundigan, Dawn Addams, Martha Hyer, Robert Karnes, Lawrence Dobkin

'It's a rootin', tootin', six-gun shootin' musicalallapalooza!'

Riding High
US 1943 88m Technicolor
Paramount (Fred Kohlmar)
GB title: *Melody Inn*

A burlesque queen goes home to Arizona and helps ranchers by performing at a dude ranch. Dim formula musical with exuberance but neither wit nor style.

w Walter de Leon, Arthur Phillips, Art Arthur, *play* Ready Money by James Montgomery *d* George Marshall *ph* Karl Struss, Harry Hallenberger *md* Victor Young

Dorothy Lamour, Dick Powell, Victor Moore, Gil Lamb, Cass Daley, Bill Goodwin, Rod Cameron, Glenn Langan, Andrew Tombes, Tim Ryan, Douglas Fowley, Milt Britton and his Band

Riding High*
US 1950 112m bw
Paramount (Frank Capra)

An easygoing racing man forsakes the chance of wealth to train his beloved horse for the Imperial Derby.
The director's familiar ingredients—farce, sentimentality, fast cutting, nice people and a lot of noise—seem a shade too tried and tested in this remake of his 1934 success *Broadway Bill*. Despite the cast, the result is only moderately entertaining.

w Robert Riskin *d* Frank Capra *ph* George Barnes, Ernest Laszlo *m* James Van Heusen *ly* Johnny Burke

Bing Crosby, Coleen Gray, Charles Bickford, Raymond Walburn, James Gleason, Oliver Hardy, Frances Gifford, William Demarest, Ward Bond, Clarence Muse, Percy Kilbride, Harry Davenport, Margaret Hamilton, Douglass Dumbrille, Gene Lockhart

Riding Shotgun
US 1954 75m Warnercolor

A shotgun stagecoach guard carries on a long vendetta against an outlaw. Routine western excitements, played mainly indoors. Randolph Scott, Wayne Morris, Joan Weldon, Joe Sawyer, James Millican, Charles Bronson, James Bell. Written by Tom Blackburn; directed by André de Toth; for Warner.

Riding with Buffalo Bill
US 1954 bw serial: 15 eps

The famous Indian scout helps a miner against outlaws. Unremarkable western serial. Marshall Reed, Rick Vallin, Joanne Rio, Shirley Whitney. Directed by Spencer Bennet; for Columbia.

Riff Raff*
US 1935 90m bw
MGM (Irving Thalberg)

A con man and his wife end up on the wrong side of the law.
Modest comedy drama that never quite sparks.

w Frances Marion, H. W. Haneman, Anita Loos *d* J. Walter Ruben *m* Edward Ward

Jean Harlow, Spencer Tracy, Joseph Calleia, Una Merkel, Mickey Rooney, Victor Kilian, J. Farrell MacDonald

'It ain't art, but it's box office.'—*Variety*

Riff Raff*
US 1947 80m bw
RKO (Nat Holt)

A dying man hands a Panama City con man a map to valuable oil deposits, and various shady people are after it.
Rather heavy but well made comedy-drama with some striking scenes.

w Martin Rackin *d* Ted Tetzlaff *ph* George E. Diskant *m* Roy Webb

Pat O'Brien, Walter Slezak, Anne Jeffreys, Percy Kilbride, Jerome Cowan

Rififi**
France 1955 116m bw
Indus / Pathé / Prima
original title: *Du Rififi chez les Hommes*

After an elaborate raid on a jewellery store, thieves fall out and the caper ends in bloodshed.
A film with much to answer for, in the form of hundreds of imitations showing either detailed accounts of robberies (*Topkapi, Gambit*) or gloomy looks at the private lives of criminals. At the time it seemed crisp and exciting, and the 25-minute silent robbery sequence is quite something.

w René Wheeler, Jules Dassin, Auguste le Breton, *novel* Auguste le Breton *d Jules Dassin* *ph* Philippe Agostini *m* Georges Auric

Jean Servais, Carl Mohner, Robert Manuel, Marie Sabouret, Perlo Vita (Jules Dassin)

'I sometimes ask myself whether so much of the film is silent because of my own lack of French.'—*Jules Dassin*

† Several 'sequels' were made using the word *rififi* (criminal argot for 'trouble') in the title, but in plot terms they were entirely unrelated.

The Right Approach
US 1961 92m bw Cinemascope
TCF (Oscar Brodney)

A Hollywood opportunist tries to make it as a star.
A potentially witty Hollywood story is sabotaged by a style which is as naïve as it is dismal; and Mr Vaughan's hopes of stardom unfairly ended right here.

w Fay and Michael Kanin, *play* Garson Kanin *d* David Butler *ph* Sam Leavitt *m* Dominic Frontière

Frankie Vaughan, Martha Hyer, Juliet Prowse, Gary Crosby, David MacLean, Jesse White, Jane Withers

Right Cross
US 1950 90m bw
MGM (Armand Deutsch)

A boxing champion injures his hand and has to abandon his career.
Rather dull sporting melodrama with a Mexican background, saved by good production values.

w Charles Schnee *d* John Sturges *ph* Norbert Brodine *m* David Raksin

Dick Powell, June Allyson, Lionel Barrymore, Ricardo Montalban

The Right Stuff*
US 1983 193m Technicolor
Warner / Ladd (Irwin Winkler, Robert Chartoff)

Test pilots are recruited and trained as astronauts.
A reasonably factual account of the Mercury programme: extremely well made but somehow too brash and inhuman to provide much entertainment. An unexpected commercial flop.

w,d Philip Kaufman, *book* Tom Wolfe *ph* Caleb Deschanel *m* Bill Conti *pd* Geoffrey Kirkland

Sam Shepard, Scott Glenn, Ed Harris, Dennis Quaid, Fred Ward, Barbara Hershey, Kim Stanley, Veronica Cartwright

AA: Bill Conti; editing; art direction
AAN: best picture; Sam Shepard; Caleb Deschanel

The Right to Live
US 1935 75m bw

Someone in the family mercifully kills a crippled war hero. Uninspired rendering of Somerset Maugham's play *The Sacred Flame*, previously filmed under its own title in 1929 (with Pauline Frederick, Henrietta Crosman, George Brent). Colin Clive, Josephine Hutchinson, Peggy Wood, C. Aubrey Smith, Leo G. Carroll, Halliwell Hobbes. Written by Ralph Block; directed by William Keighley; for Warner. (GB title: *The Sacred Flame.*)

The Right to Love*
US 1930 79m bw

A mother has a strong affinity with her illegitimate daughter who is a missionary on the other side of the world. Curious mystic melodrama which adds a twist to the popular mother-love devices. Technically it introduced the Bell light valve which improved sound reproduction, and also the Dunning process which improved the presentation of dual roles. (The star played mother and daughter.) Charles Lang, the cinematographer, was nominated for an Academy Award. *Ruth Chatterton*, Paul Lukas, David Manners, Irving Pichel, George Baxter. Written by Zoe Akins from the novel Brook Adams by Susan Glaspell; directed by Richard Wallace; for Paramount. 'A profound and thoughtful romantic drama treated with utmost refinement of sophistication and still possessing elements which will appeal to the broadest kind of screen audience.'—*Variety*

The Ring
US 1952 79m bw
King Brothers

A young Mexican becomes a prizefighter in the hope of winning greater respect for Mexican-Americans.
Well-meant low-budget programmer.

w Irving Shulman *d* Kurt Neumann *ph* Russell Harlan *m* Herschel Burke Gilbert

Gerald Mohr, Lalo Rios, Rita Moreno, Robert Arthur

Ring of Bright Water*
GB 1969 107m Technicolor
Palomar / Brightwater (Joseph Strick)

A civil servant buys a pet otter and moves to a remote cottage in the western Highlands.
Disneyesque fable for animal lovers, from a bestselling book.

w Jack Couffer, Bill Travers, *book* Gavin Maxwell *d* Jack Couffer *ph* Wolfgang Suschitsky *m* Frank Cordell

Bill Travers, Virginia McKenna, Peter Jeffrey, Roddy McMillan, Jameson Clark

Ring of Fear
US 1954 88m Warnercolor Cinemascope
Warner / Wayne–Fellows (Robert M. Fellows)

A homicidal maniac returns to the circus where he used to work and causes various 'accidents'.
Tediously predictable circus melodrama with a curious but not very likeable cast.

w Paul Fix, Philip MacDonald, James Edward Grant *d* James Edward Grant *ph* Edwin DuPar *m* Emil Newman, Arthur Lange

Clyde Beatty, Pat O'Brien, Mickey Spillane, Sean McClory, Marion Carr, John Bromfield, Pedro Gonzalez Gonzalez, Emett Lynn

Ring of Fire
US 1961 90m Metrocolor
MGM / Andrew and Virginia Stone

An Oregon sheriff is kidnapped by teenage delinquents but manages to lead them into both a police trap and a forest fire.
Outdoor action thriller with a plot which is ludicrously unconvincing in detail, though the fire scenes impress.

wd Andrew L. Stone *ph* William H. Clothier *m* Duane Eddy

David Janssen, Joyce Taylor, Frank Gorshin, Joel Marston

Ring of Spies*
GB 1963 90m bw
British Lion (Leslie Gilliatt)
US title: *Ring of Treason*

How the Portland spy ring was tracked down.
Documentary drama, rather less intriguing, somehow, than the actual facts; but the sheer thought of spies in the suburbs keeps interest going.

w Frank Launder, Peter Barnes *d* Robert Tronson *ph* Arthur Lavis

Bernard Lee, Margaret Tyzack, David Kossoff, Nancy Nevinson, William Sylvester

The Ringer*
GB 1952 78m bw
BL / London (Hugh Perceval)

A dangerous criminal known only as The Ringer threatens to kill the crooked lawyer responsible for his sister's death.
Artful old-fashioned mystery, quite well restaged, and in fact the best extant example of filmed Wallace.

w Val Valentine, *novel* and *play* Edgar Wallace *d* Guy Hamilton *ph* Ted Scaife *m* Malcolm Arnold

Donald Wolfit, Mai Zetterling, Herbert Lom, Greta Gynt, William Hartnell, Norman Wooland

† The play was also filmed in 1931 with Patrick Curwen, Franklin Dyall and Gordon Harker; and in 1938 as *The Gaunt Stranger* (qv).

Rings on Her Fingers*
US 1942 85m bw
TCF (Milton Sperling)

The front girl for a couple of confidence tricksters falls in love with their first victim.
Lively comedy which drags into drama in its second half.

w Ken Englund *d* Rouben Mamoulian *ph* George Barnes *m* Cyril Mockridge

Gene Tierney, Henry Fonda, Laird Cregar, Spring Byington, Shepperd Strudwick, Frank Orth, Henry Stephenson, Marjorie Gateson

Rio
US 1939 78m bw
Universal

A crooked financier escapes from Devil's Island to join his wife in Rio, only to find she has been unfaithful.
Modest but well made melodrama.

w Stephen Morehouse Avery, Frank Partos, Edwin Justus Mayer, Abem Kandel, Jean Negulesco *d John Brahm* *ph* Hal Mohr *m* Frank Skinner *md* Charles Previn

Basil Rathbone, Victor McLaglen, Sigrid Gurie, Robert Cummings, Leo Carrillo, Billy Gilbert, Irving Bacon, Irving Pichel

'A fair programmer with a blend of romance and adventure . . . should stand up satisfactorily as a top dualler in most situations.'—*Variety*

Rio Bravo**
US 1959 141m Technicolor
Warner / Armada (Howard Hawks)

A wandering cowboy and a drunken sheriff hold a town against outlaws.
Cheerfully overlong and slow-moving western in which everybody, including the director, does his thing. All very watchable for those with time to spare, but more a series of revue sketches than an epic.

w Jules Furthman, Leigh Brackett *d Howard Hawks* *ph* Russell Harlan *m* Dmitri Tiomkin

John Wayne, Dean Martin, Ricky Nelson, Angie Dickinson, Walter Brennan, Ward Bond, John Russell, Pedro Gonzalez Gonzalez, Claude Akins, Harry Carey Jnr, Bob Steele

'After we finished we found we could have done it a lot better . . . and that's why we went ahead and made *El Dorado*.'—*Howard Hawks*

† More or less remade in 1966 as *El Dorado* and in 1970 as *Rio Lobo*.

Rio Conchos*
US 1964 107m De Luxe Cinemascope
TCF (David Weisbart)

Two thousand rifles are stolen from an army command port and traced to the hide-out of a former Confederate colonel who wants to continue the Civil War.
Good standard western which shares much of its story line with *The Comancheros*.

w Clair Huffaker, Joseph Landon *d* Gordon Douglas *ph* Joe MacDonald *m* Jerry Goldsmith

Richard Boone, Edmond O'Brien, Stuart Whitman, Tony Franciosa

Rio Grande*
US 1950 105m bw
Republic / Argosy (John Ford, Merian C. Cooper)

A Cavalry unit on the Mexican border in the 1880s conducts a vain campaign against marauding Indians.
Thin Ford western on his favourite theme, with too many pauses for song, too many studio sets, and too little plot. *Aficionados*, however, will find much to admire.

w James Kevin McGuinness, *story* James Warner Bellah *d* John Ford *ph* Bert Glennon, Archie Stout *m* Victor Young

John Wayne, Maureen O'Hara, Ben Johnson, Claude Jarman Jnr, Harry Carey Jnr, Chill Wills, J. Carrol Naish, Victor McLaglen

Rio Lobo*
US 1970 114m Technicolor
Cinema Center (Howard Hawks)

A union colonel near the end of the Civil War recovers a gold shipment and exposes a traitor.
Rambling western with traces of former glory, enjoyable at least for its sense of humour.

w Leigh Brackett, Burton Wohl *d* Howard Hawks *ph* William Clothier *m* Jerry Goldsmith

John Wayne, Jorge Rivero, Jennifer O'Neill, *Jack Elam,* Victor French, Chris Mitchum, Mike Henry

Rio Rita
US 1929 135m bw and Technicolor
RKO (William Le Baron)

Romance on a ranch near the Mexican border.
Very early talkie version of a popular Broadway operetta of the twenties; historical interest only.

w Luther Reed, Russell Mack, *book* Guy Bolton, Fred Thomson, as produced by Florenz Ziegfeld *d* Luther Reed *ph* Robert Kurle, Lloyd Knetchel *md* Victor Baravalle *songs* Harry Tierney, Joe McCarthy

Bebe Daniels, John Boles, Bert Wheeler, Robert Woolsey, Dorothy Lee, Don Alvarado, George Renavent

Rio Rita
US 1942 91m bw
MGM (Pandro S. Berman)

Flat-footed remake bringing in Nazi spies; poor comedy even by Abbott and Costello standards.

w Richard Connell, Gladys Lehman *d* S. Sylvan Simon *ph* George J. Folsey *m* Herbert Stothart

Bud Abbott, Lou Costello, John Carroll, Kathryn Grayson, Tom Conway, Barry Nelson

Riot
US 1968 98m Technicolor
Paramount / William Castle

While the warden is away, thirty-five convicts take over a state penitentiary and are violently subdued.
Strikingly bloody melodrama set in an actual prison in Arizona; well made, but less entertaining than Cagney and Raft used to be.

w James Poe, *novel* Frank Elli *d* Buzz Kulik *ph* Robert B. Hauser *m* Christopher Komeda

Gene Hackman, Jim Brown, Ben Carruthers, Mike Kellin, Gerald O'Loughlin, Clifford David

Riot in Cell Block Eleven*
US 1954 80m bw
Allied Artists / Walter Wanger

In a big American prison three convicts seize their guards, free the other prisoners and barricade themselves in their block.
Socially concerned low-budgeter, quite nicely made and persuasive of the need for prison reform.

w Richard Collins *d Don Siegel* *ph* Russell Harlan *m* Herschel Burke Gilbert

Neville Brand, *Emile Meyer*, Frank Faylen, Leo Gordon, Robert Osterloh, Paul Frees, Don Keefer

'As a compassionate, angry, unsensational account of an episode of violence it makes considerably more impact than many of the overblown melodramas currently in fashion.'—*Penelope Houston*

Riptide*
US 1934 90m bw
MGM (Irving Thalberg)

A British diplomat weds a Manhattan chorus girl, but she later falls for an old flame.
Elegantly set, star-packed drawing-room drama which somehow didn't click.

wd Edmund Goulding *ph* Ray June *m* Herbert Stothart

Norma Shearer, Robert Montgomery, Herbert Marshall, Mrs Patrick Campbell, Skeets Gallagher, Ralph Forbes, Lilyan Tashman, Helen Jerome Eddy, George K. Arthur, Halliwell Hobbes

'Has all the earmarks of box office . . . a commendable job all round.'—*Variety*

The Rise and Fall of Legs Diamond
US 1960 101m bw
Warner / United States (Milton Sperling)

The career of a New York hoodlum of the twenties.
Inspired, like *King of the Roaring Twenties*, by the TV success of *The Untouchables*, this was part of a brief attempt by Warners to recapture its pre-war gangster image. Alas, stars and style were equally lacking.

w Joseph Landon *d* Budd Boetticher *ph* Lucien Ballard *m* Leonard Rosenman

Ray Danton, Karen Steele, Elaine Stewart, Jesse White, Simon Oakland, Robert Lowery, Warren Oates, Judson Pratt

The Rise and Rise of Michael Rimmer
GB 1970 101m Technicolor
Warner / David Frost (Harry Fine)

An efficiency expert takes over an advertising agency and is soon an MP, a cabinet minister, and PM.
Satirical comedy which quickly goes overboard and is only occasionally funny; it does, however, mark the final death throes of the swinging sixties, and the changeover to *Monty Python*.

w Peter Cook, John Cleese, Kevin Billington, Graham Chapman *d* Kevin Billington *ph* Alex Thompson *m* John Cameron

Peter Cook, John Cleese, Arthur Lowe, Denholm Elliott, Ronald Fraser, Vanessa Howard, George A. Cooper, Harold Pinter, James Cossins, Roland Culver, Dudley Foster, Julian Glover, Dennis Price, Ronnie Corbett

Rise and Shine
US 1941 93m bw
TCF (Mark Hellinger)

A dumb but brilliant football player is kidnapped by the other side.
Drab collegiate comedy, disappointing considering the credits.

w Herman J. Mankiewicz, *novel* My Life and Hard Times by James Thurber *d* Allan Dwan *ph* Edward Cronjager *m* Emil Newman *songs* Leo Robin, Ralph Rainger

Linda Darnell, Jack Oakie, George Murphy, Walter Brennan, Milton Berle, Sheldon Leonard, Donald Meek, Ruth Donnelly, Donald MacBride, Raymond Walburn, Emma Dunn

Rising Damp
GB 1980 98m colour
ITC / Black Lion (Roy Skeggs)

The amorous and conniving landlord of a slum boarding house develops a passion for one of his tenants.
A useful reminder of a TV sitcom worth remembering, but handicapped by restriction of action, paucity of plot and the overlength usual in film versions of such things, not to mention the premature death of its original co-star Richard Beckinsale.

w Eric Chappell *d* Joe McGrath *ph* Frank Watts *m* David Lindup

Leonard Rossiter, Frances de la Tour, Don Warrington, Denholm Elliott, Christopher Strauli

'Unforgettably John Ford's finest film!'
The Rising of the Moon
Eire 1957 81m bw
Warner / Four Provinces (Lord Killanin)

Three Irish short stories.
Curiously dull John Ford portmanteau with the Abbey players.

w Frank Nugent, *stories* Frank O'Connor, Malcolm J. McHugh, Lady Gregory *d* John Ford *ph* Robert Krasker *m* Eamonn O'Gallagher *narrator* Tyrone Power

Maureen Connell, Eileen Crowe, Cyril Cusack, Maureen Delany, Donald Donelly, Frank Lawton, Edward Lexy, Jack MacGowran, Denis O'Dea, Jimmy O'Dea, Noel Purcell

Risky Business
US 1939 67m bw

A crusading radio columnist tracks down a kidnapper. Tolerable crime programmer. George Murphy, Dorothea Kent, Eduardo Ciannelli, Leon Ames, El Brendel, John Wray. Written by Charles Grayson from a previous script by William Anthony McGuire; directed by Arthur Lubin; for Universal. 'It will garner nice business in city spots, where they like their melodrama realistic.'—*Variety*

Risky Business
US 1983 99m Technicolor

A 17-year-old is left in charge of his parents' house and fills it with pimps and prostitutes . . . a lucrative business. Would-be outrageous teenage comedy which is pretty well made but soon wears out its welcome. Tom Cruise, Rebecca de Mornay, Joe Pantoliano, Richard Masur, Bronson Pinchot, Curtis Armstrong, Nicholas Pryor. Written and directed by Paul Brickman; for Tisch-Avnet / Geffen.

Rita, Sue and Bob Too*
GB 1987 95m Eastmancolor

Schoolgirl babysitters are introduced to sex by their employer on the way home. Raunchy yet appealing study of British attitudes to sex, in the tradition of *Letter to Brezhnev*. Michelle Holmes, Siobhan Finneran, George Costigan, Lesley Sharp. Written by Andrea Dunbar from her plays; directed by Alan Clarke; for Umbrella/British Screen/Film Four.

The Ritz*
US 1976 90m Technicolor
Warner / Courtyard (Denis O'Dell)

A comedy of mistaken identities in a gay New York turkish bath.
An adaptation of a stage success which doesn't seem nearly as funny as it thinks it is; but some of it does work.

w Terrance McNally, from his play *d* Richard Lester *ph* Paul Wilson *m* Ken Thorne *pd* Phillip Harrison

Jack Weston, Rita Moreno, Jerry Stiller, Kaye Ballard, Bessie Love, George Coulouris, F. Murray Abrahams, Treat Williams

The River*
India 1951 87m Technicolor
Oriental / International / Theatre Guild (Kenneth McEldowney)

Episodes in the life of a small English community living on the banks of the Ganges.
A slight and surprising work from this director, superbly observed and a pleasure to watch but dramatically very thin.

w Rumer Godden, Jean Renoir, *novel* Rumer Godden *d Jean Renoir ph Claude Renoir* *m* M. A. Partha Sarathy *pd Eugene Lourié*

Nora Swinburne, Esmond Knight, Arthur Shields, Adrienne Corri
† Renoir's assistant was Satyajit Ray.

The River
US 1984 122m Technicolor
Universal / Edward Lewis

The Garveys battle flood waters to save the family farm.
Old-fashioned rural drama, at times reminiscent of *Way Down East* plus a dash of symbolism. A surprise in 1984, and not a very pleasant one, despite or because of its political awareness.

w Robert Dillon, Julian Barry *d* Mark Rydell *ph* Vilmos Zsigmond *m* John Williams *pd* Charles Rosen *ed* Sidney Levin

Mel Gibson, Sissy Spacek, Shane Bailey, Becky Jo Lynch, Scott Glenn, Billy Green Bush

AAN: Sissy Spacek; photography; music

River Lady
US 1948 78m Technicolor

The beautiful owner of a Mississippi gambling boat tries to buy up all her rivals. Routine romantic drama. Yvonne de Carlo, Rod Cameron, Dan Duryea, Helena Carter, Lloyd Gough, Florence Bates, John McIntire. Written by D. D. Beauchamp and William Bowers; directed by George Sherman; for Universal-International.

River of No Return*
US 1954 91m Technicolor Cinemascope
TCF (Stanley Rubin)

During the California gold rush a widower and his 10-year-old son encounter a saloon singer with a gold claim.
Cheerful, clichéd star western designed to exploit the splendours of early Cinemascope, and very adequate for this purpose.

w Frank Fenton *d* Otto Preminger *ph* Joseph La Shelle *m* Cyril Mockridge *md* Lionel Newman

Robert Mitchum, Marilyn Monroe, Tommy Rettig, Rory Calhoun, Murvyn Vye

Riverboat Rhythm
US 1946 65m bw

A Mississippi riverboat captain is financially embarrassed. Very mild comedy with the star in dual roles. Leon Errol, Walter Catlett, Glenn Vernon, Marc Cramer, Jonathan Hale, Joan Newton. Written by Robert Faber, Charles Roberts; directed by Leslie Goodwins; for RKO.

The River's Edge
US 1956 87m Eastmancolor Cinemascope
TCF (Benedict Bogeaus)

A fugitive bank robber forces a farmer to guide him over the mountains into Mexico.
Sluggish open-air character melodrama.

w Harold J. Smith *d* Allan Dwan *ph* Harold Lipstein *m* Lou Forbes

Ray Milland, Anthony Quinn, Debra Paget, Byron Foulger

River's End
US 1930 74m bw

A Mountie dies chasing his man, who then impersonates him. Popular, contrived, outdoor thriller, previously filmed in 1922 with Lewis Stone, and subsequently in 1940 with Dennis Morgan (this version became known as *Double Identity*). Charles Bickford, Evalyn Knapp, J. Farrell MacDonald, Zasu Pitts, David Torrence. Written by Charles Kenyon, from the story by James Oliver Curwood; directed by Michael Curtiz; for Warner.

The Road Back**
US 1937 105m bw
Universal (James Whale)

After World War I, German soldiers go home to problems and disillusion.
A major work, intended as a sequel to *All Quiet on the Western Front*. Despite impressive sequences, it doesn't quite reach inspiring heights.

w R. C. Sherriff, Charles Kenyon, *novel* Erich Maria Remarque *d James Whale ph John Mescall, George Robinson* *m* Dmitri Tiomkin *ad* Charles D. Hall

Richard Cromwell, John King, Slim Summerville, Andy Devine, Barbara Read, Louise Fazenda, Noah Beery Jnr, Lionel

Atwill, John Emery, Etienne Girardot, Spring Byington, Laura Hope Crews

'Big and frequently effective, but a let-down in toto . . . does not compare with *All Quiet* in quality or power.'—*Variety*

'They call it an all-star cast and that means there isn't a single player of any distinction to be picked out of the herd. . . . It might be funny if it wasn't horrifying. This is America seeing the world in its own image.'—*Graham Greene*

† The film is said to have been extensively reshot after protests from the German consul in Los Angeles. No 35mm negative now exists, as it reverted to Remarque and was lost.

Road Games
Australia 1981 110m colour

A long-distance truck-driver unwittingly picks up a murderer on the run. Tolerable but overlong road thriller. Stacy Keach, Jamie Lee Curtis, Marion Edwards, Grant Page. Written by Everett De Roche; directed by Richard Franklin; for Quest.

Road Gang
US 1936 60m bw

Penal corruption and brutality in a southern state is exposed by the *Chicago Sun*. A rough ride over familiar ground. Donald Woods, Carlyle Moore Jnr, Kay Linaker, Harry Cording, Marc Lawrence. Written by Abem Finkel, Dalton Trumbo, Harold Buckley; directed by Louis King; for First National. (GB title: *Injustice*.)

Road House
GB 1934 76m bw

A barmaid helps to track down a murderer. Mild comedy melodrama with music. Violet Loraine, Gordon Harker, Emlyn Williams, Aileen Marson, Hartley Power, Stanley Holloway, Marie Lohr. Written by Austin Melford and Leslie Arliss, from play by Walter Hackett; directed by Maurice Elvey; for Michael Balcon / Gaumont.

Road House*
US 1948 95m bw
TCF (Edward Chodorov)

A road house owner is jealous of his manager and frames him for murder.
Dated but watchable *film noir* of its era, with all characters cynical or homicidal.

w Edward Chodorov *d* Jean Negulesco *ph* Joseph La Shelle *m* Cyril Mockridge

Richard Widmark, Ida Lupino, Cornel Wilde, Celeste Holm

Road Show*
US 1941 86m bw
Hal Roach

A young man wrongly committed to an insane asylum escapes with another inmate and joins a travelling circus.
Engaging scatty comedy on familiar Roach lines which suffers from lame pacing but manages some likeable moments.

w Arnold Beldard, Harry Langdon, Mickell Novak, *novel* Eric Hatch *d* Gordon Douglas *ph* Norbert Brodine *m* George Stoll

John Hubbard, Adolphe Menjou, Carole Landis, Patsy Kelly, George E. Stone

Road to Denver
US 1955 90m Trucolor

An honest ranch hand gets into trouble when he tries to help his lawless brother. Uninspired western which just about passes the time. John Payne, Lee J. Cobb, Skip Homeier, Mona Freeman, Ray Middleton, Andy Clyde, Lee Van Cleef. Written by Horace McCoy and Allen Rivkin; directed by Joe Kane; for Republic.

The Road to Glory*
US 1936 103m bw
TCF (Darryl F. Zanuck)

Adventures of a French regiment in World War I.
Meticulously produced war movie which bears comparison with *All Quiet on the Western Front*.

w Joel Sayre, William Faulkner *d Howard Hawks ph Gregg Toland m* Louis Silvers

Fredric March, Warner Baxter, Lionel Barrymore, June Lang, Gregory Ratoff, Victor Kilian, John Qualen, Julius Tannen, Leonid Kinskey

The Road to Life*
USSR 1930 100m bw

Moscow street children are rounded up and reformed. A kind of Russian prequel to the *Dead End Kids*, presented with much style. Mikhail Zharov, Maria Gonfa, Tsifan Kyrla. Written and directed by Nikolai Ekk; for Mejrabpom. 'Judged purely as entertainment the film recedes quickly, as do most Russian films.'—*Variety*

'Where the human wreckage of the seven seas foregather, this powerful tale of love and intrigue is told!'

Road to Mandalay
US 1926 77m at 24 fps bw silent

Two eastern planters quarrel over a girl. Potboiling star vehicle. Lon Chaney, Lois Moran, Owen Moore, Henry B. Walthall. Written by Elliott Clawson and Herman Mankiewicz; directed by Tod Browning; for MGM.

The Road to Reno
US 1938 69m bw

A rancher won't give his wife the divorce she thinks she wants. Combination comedy, drama, romance and horse opera which doesn't gel. Randolph Scott, Hope Hampton, Glenda Farrell, Helen Broderick, Alan Marshal, Samuel S. Hinds. Written by Roy Chanslor, Adele Comandini, Brian Marlowe, from the novel by I. A. R. Wylie; directed by S. Sylvan Simon; for Universal.

The Road to Salina
France / Italy 1971 96m colour Panavision

The proprietress of a roadside café recognizes a drifter as her long-lost son. Boring emotional drama stymied by the multi-language problem. Rita Hayworth, Mimsy Farmer, Robert Walker Jnr, Ed Begley, Sophie Hardy. Written by Georges Lautner, Pascal Jardin and Jack Miller; directed by Georges Lautner; for Robert Dorfmann. (Original title: *Quando il Sola Scotta*.)

Road to Singapore
US 1931 70m bw

A doctor's wife is caught with her lover, and her life falls to pieces. Tensions among the oriental upper crust: very dated and not very convincing. William Powell, Louis Calhern, Doris Kenyon, Marian Marsh, Alison Skipworth. Written by J. Grubb Alexander, from a play by Roland Pertwee; directed by Alfred E. Green; for Warner.

THE 'ROAD' SERIES:

Road to Singapore*
US 1940 84m bw
Paramount (Harlan Thompson)

Two rich playboys swear off women until they quarrel over a Singapore maiden.
The first Hope–Crosby–Lamour 'road' picture is basically a light romantic comedy and quite forgettable; the series got zanier as it progressed.

w Don Hartman, Frank Butler, *story* Harry Hervey *d* Victor Schertzinger *ph* William C. Mellor *m* Victor Young

Bing Crosby, Bob Hope, Dorothy Lamour, Charles Coburn, Judith Barrett, Anthony Quinn, Jerry Colonna

'A deft blend of romance and comedy, songs and fisticuffs.'—*Picture Show*

'Two of the most congenially harmonized performances caught by the camera in recent years.'—*Motion Picture Herald*

† The script was originally designed for Fred MacMurray and Jack Oakie, who weren't available; then for Burns and Allen, who turned it down.

Road to Zanzibar**
US 1941 92m bw
Paramount (Paul Jones)

The trio on safari in Africa, with *Hellzapoppin* gags breaking in and an anything-goes atmosphere.

w Frank Butler, Don Hartman *d* Victor Schertzinger *ph* Ted Tetzlaff *m* Victor Young *songs* Johnny Burke, Jimmy Van Heusen

Hope, Crosby, Lamour, Una Merkel, Eric Blore, Luis Alberni, Douglass Dumbrille

'The funniest thing I've seen on the screen in years. Years.'—*Otis Ferguson*

Road to Morocco**
US 1942 83m bw
Paramount (Paul Jones)

Hollywood Arab palaces, a captive princess, topical gags and talking camels.

w Frank Butler, Don Hartman *d* David Butler *ph* William C. Mellor *md* Victor Young *songs* Johnny Burke, Jimmy Van Heusen

Hope, Crosby, Lamour, Anthony Quinn, Dona Drake

'A bubbly spontaneous entertainment without a semblance of sanity.'—*Variety*

'It would be difficult to find a screen pantomime with better wartime credentials.'—*Kine Weekly*

'This is the screwiest picture I've ever been in.'—*Camel*

AAN: script

Road to Utopia**
US 1945 89m bw
Paramount (Paul Jones)

The California gold rush, with all the previous gag styles in good order, capped by a cheeky epilogue and constant explanatory narration by Robert Benchley.

w Norman Panama, Melvin Frank *d* Hal Walker *ph* Lionel Lindon *m* Leigh Harline *songs* Johnny Burke, Jimmy Van Heusen

Hope, Crosby, Lamour, Douglass Dumbrille, Hillary Brooke, Jack La Rue

AAN: script

Road to Rio**
US 1947 100m bw
Paramount (Daniel Dare)

Guest stars are given their head, plot intrudes again in the shape of a hypnotized heiress, and the style is more constrained (but still funny).

w Edmund Beloin, Jack Rose *d* Norman Z. McLeod *ph* Ernest Laszlo *md* Robert Emmett Dolan *songs* Johnny Burke, Jimmy Van Heusen

Hope, Crosby, Lamour, Gale Sondergaard, Frank Faylen, the Wiere Brothers, the Andrews Sisters

'Enough laughs to pass the time easily and to remind you how completely, since sound came in, the American genius for movie comedy has disintegrated.'—*James Agee*

AAN: Robert Emmett Dolan

Road to Bali*
US 1952 91m Technicolor
Paramount (Harry Tugend)

In and around the South Seas, with colour making the sets obvious and the gags only tediously funny. The team's zest was also flagging.

w Frank Butler, Hal Kanter, William Morrow *d* Hal Walker *ph* George Barnes *md* Joseph J. Lilley *songs* Johnny Burke, Jimmy Van Heusen

Hope, Crosby, Lamour, Murvyn Vye, Peter Coe

Road to Hong Kong
GB 1962 91m bw
UA / Melnor (Norman Panama)

Curious, slightly dismal-looking attempt to continue the series in a British studio and on a low budget. A few good gags, but it's all very tired by now, and the space fiction plot makes it seem more so.

w Norman Panama, Melvin Frank *d* Melvin Frank *ph* Jack Hildyard *m* Robert Farnon *pd* Roger Furse

Hope, Crosby, Lamour, Joan Collins, Robert Morley, Walter Gotell, Felix Aylmer and guests Peter Sellers, David Niven, Frank Sinatra, Dean Martin, Jerry Colonna

Roadhouse Nights*
US 1930 71m bw
Paramount

A reporter exposes a gangster operating from a country nightclub.
Experimental mingling of elements which later become very familiar.

w Garrett Fort, *story* Ben Hecht *d* Hobart Henley *ph* William Steiner

Helen Morgan, Charles Ruggles, Fred Kohler, Jimmy Durante, Fuller Mellish Jnr

Roar*
US 1981 102m colour Panavision
Noel Marshall / Banjiro Uemura

A research biologist lives in the African bush with assorted wild animals. He is expecting his family, but they arrive a day early when he is out . . .
A rather silly story takes in some of the most remarkable animal photography on record, and there is a sub-plot involving villainous game hunters.

wd Noel Marshall *ph* Jan de Bont *m* Dominic Frontière

Noel Marshall, Tippi Hedren, and family

† The Marshalls live with their 150 lions and other wild animals in a ranch near Los Angeles. During production the film, which eventually cost 17 million dollars, was halted by flood, fire, epidemic and injury.

Roar of the Dragon
US 1932 70m bw

Passengers in a Chinese river boat are menaced by bandits. Curious water-set version of *Shanghai Express*, with a good cast its best recommendation. Richard Dix, Edward Everett Horton, Gwili Andre, ZaSu Pitts, Arline Judge, Dudley Digges, C. Henry Gordon. Written by Howard Estabrook from a story by George Kibbee Turner, Merian C. Cooper and Jane Bigelow; directed by Wesley Ruggles; for Radio.

Roar of the Iron Horse
US 1951 bw serial: 15 eps

A railroad engineer goes out west to find why the new line is subject to so many accidents. Tolerable iron horse serial saga. Jock O'Mahoney, Virginia Herrick, William Fawcett, Hal Landon. Directed by Spencer G. Bennet and Thomas Carr; for Columbia.

'The land of the free gone wild! The heyday of the hotcha! The shock-crammed days G-men took ten whole years to lick!'

The Roaring Twenties***
US 1939 106m bw
Warner (Hal B. Wallis)

A World War I veteran returns to New York, innocently becomes involved in bootlegging, builds up an empire and dies in a gang war. Among the last of the Warner gangster cycle, this was perhaps the best production of them all, despite the familiar plot line: stars and studio were in cracking form.

w Jerry Wald, Richard Macaulay, Robert Rossen, *story* Mark Hellinger *d Raoul Walsh, Anatole Litvak ph Ernest Haller m* Heinz Roemheld

James Cagney, Humphrey Bogart, Priscilla Lane, Jeffrey Lynn, Gladys George, Frank McHugh, Paul Kelly, Elizabeth Risdon

† The James Cagney character was based on Larry Fay, who was Texas Guinan's partner, and Gladys George is clearly Guinan herself.

The Roaring West
US 1935 bw serial: 15 eps

Cowboys participating in a land rush hope that a map will lead them to the most valuable sites. Routine star western serial. Buck Jones, Muriel Evans, Walter Miller, Frank McGlynn Snr, William Desmond. Directed by Ray Taylor; for Universal.

Rob Roy the Highland Rogue
GB 1953 81m Technicolor
Walt Disney (Perce Pearce)

After the defeat of the clans in the 1715 rebellion, their leader escapes and after several adventures is granted a royal pardon. A kind of Scottish Robin Hood, so stiffly acted and made that it might as well—or better—be a cartoon.

w Lawrence E. Watkin *d* Harold French *ph* Guy Green *m* Cedric Thorpe Davie

Richard Todd, Glynis Johns, James Robertson Justice, Michael Gough, Finlay Currie, Geoffrey Keen, Archie Duncan

Robbers' Roost
US 1955 82m De Luxe

An honest cowboy is employed by cattle rustlers and strives to clear his name. Fair western programmer. George Montgomery, Richard Boone, Sylvia Findley, Bruce Bennett, Peter Graves, Warren Stevens, William Hopper. Written by John O'Dea, Sidney Salkow and Maurice Geraghty, from a novel by Zane Grey; directed by Sidney Salkow; for Leonard Goldstein / UA.

Robbery*
GB 1967 113m Eastmancolor
Joseph E. Levine / Oakhurst (Michael Deeley, Stanley Baker)

Criminals conspire to rob the night mail train from Glasgow.

Heavy-going fictionalized account of the famous train robbery of 1963; best seen as standard cops and robbers, with some good chase sequences.

w Edward Boyd, Peter Yates, George Markstein *d Peter Yates ph* Douglas Slocombe *m* Johnny Keating

Stanley Baker, James Booth, Frank Finlay, Joanna Pettet, Barry Foster, William Marlowe, Clinton Greyn, George Sewell

Robbery under Arms
GB 1957 99m Eastmancolor
Rank (Joe Janni)

In 19th-century Australia, two farming brothers join the notorious outlaw Captain Starlight.
Howlingly dull film version of a semi-classic adventure novel; a rambling story with no unity of viewpoint is saved only by excellent photography.

w Alexander Baron, W. P. Lipscomb, *novel* Rolf Boldrewood *d* Jack Lee *ph Harry Waxman m* Matyas Seiber

Peter Finch, David McCallum, Ronald Lewis, Maureen Swanson, Jill Ireland, Laurence Naismith, Jean Anderson

Robbery under Arms
Australia 1985 141m colour

Adventures of two young followers of the highwayman Captain Starlight. Uninteresting cut-down of a TV mini-series; earlier versions were made in 1907, 1911, 1920 and 1957 (above). Sam Neill, Steven Vidler, Christopher Cummins, Liz Newman, Ed Devereux. Written by Graeme Koestveld, Tony Morphett, from novel by Rolf Boldrewood; directed by Ken Hannam, Donald Crombie; for Jock Blair / South Australia Film Corporation.

'The miracle story of all time!'
The Robe**
US 1953 135m Technicolor Cinemascope
TCF (Frank Ross)

Followers and opponents of Jesus are affected by the robe handed down by him at his crucifixion.
The first film in Cinemascope was, surprisingly, a biblical bestseller, but the crowded Roman sets hid most of the flaws in the process. The film itself was competent and unsurprising in the well-tried *Sign of the Cross* manner.

w Philip Dunne, *novel* Lloyd C. Douglas *d* Henry Koster *ph Leon Shamroy m* Alfred Newman

Richard Burton, Jean Simmons, Michael Rennie, *Victor Mature*, Jay Robinson, Torin Thatcher, Dean Jagger, Richard Boone, Betta St John, Jeff Morrow, Ernest Thesiger, Dawn Addams

† Power was originally cast in the Burton role, and Burt Lancaster in Mature's.

AAN: best picture; Leon Shamroy; Richard Burton

Roberta*
US 1935 105m bw (Technicolor sequence)
RKO (Pandro S. Berman)

An American inherits a Parisian fashion house.
Thin and remarkably flatly-handled musical romance of the old school, charged only by the occasional appearances in supporting roles of Astaire and Rogers, then on the brink of stardom.

w Jane Murfin, Sam Mintz, Allan Scott, *play* Otto Harbach, *book* Gowns by Roberta by Alice Duer Miller *d* William A. Seiter *ph* Edward Cronjager *m Jerome Kern md* Max Steiner *ch* Fred Astaire *ad* Van Nest Polglase

Irene Dunne, *Fred Astaire, Ginger Rogers,* Randolph Scott, Helen Westley, Claire Dodd, Victor Varconi, Torben Meyer

'Musical picture-making at its best—fast, smart, good-looking and tuneful.'—*Variety*

† Remade as *Lovely to Look At* (qv).

AAN: song 'Lovely to Look At' (*m* Jerome Kern, *ly* Dorothy Fields, Jimmy McHugh)

Robin and Marian*
US 1976 107m Technicolor
Columbia / Rastar (Dennis O'Dell)

Robin Hood returns from the Crusades and finds conditions in Britain depressing; he finally conquers the evil Sheriff but dies in the attempt.
A kind of serious parody of medieval life, after the fashion of *The Lion in Winter* but much glummer; in fact, nothing to laugh at at all.

w James Goldman *d* Richard Lester *ph* David Watkin *m* John Barry *pd* Michael Stringer

Sean Connery, Audrey Hepburn, Robert Shaw, Ronnie Barker, Nicol Williamson, Richard Harris, Denholm Elliott, Kenneth Haigh, Ian Holm, Bill Maynard, Esmond Knight, Peter Butterworth

'Surface realism only hides a core of mush, suddenly revealed when the hero and heroine settle down for love-making in a field of corn.'—*Geoff Brown*

'Whimsical jokiness is a bit hard to reconcile with the final plunge into sacrificial romance.'—*Michael Billington, Illustrated London News*

Robin and the Seven Hoods*
US 1964 123m Technicolor Panavision
Warner / PC (Howard W. Koch, William H. Daniels)

A spoof of the Robin Hood legend set in gangland Chicago of the twenties.
Too flabby by far to be as funny as it thinks it is, this farrago of cheerful jokes has effective moments and lively routines, but most of them are nearly swamped by flat treatment and the wide screen.

w David Schwartz *d* Gordon Douglas *ph* William H. Daniels *m* Nelson Riddle *songs* Sammy Cahn, James Van Heusen

Frank Sinatra, Dean Martin, Bing Crosby, Sammy Davis Jnr, Peter Falk, Barbara Rush, Edward G. Robinson, Victor Buono, Barry Kelley, Jack La Rue, Allen Jenkins, Sig Rumann, Hans Conried

AAN: Nelson Riddle; song 'My Kind of Town' (*m* James Van Heusen, *ly* Sammy Cahn)

Robin Hood**
US 1922 127m approx (24 fps) bw silent
Douglas Fairbanks

Robin Hood combats Prince John and the Sheriff of Nottingham.
An elaborate version of the legend which featured some of Hollywood's most celebrated sets and allowed the star to perform a selection of exhilarating stunts.

w Douglas Fairbanks *d* Allan Dwan *ph* Arthur Edeson *ad* Wilfrid Buckland, Irvin J. Martin

Douglas Fairbanks, Wallace Beery, Alan Hale, Enid Bennett

'The high water mark of film production. It did not grow from the bankroll, it grew from the mind.'—*R. E. Sherwood*

'A story book picture, as gorgeous and glamorous a thing in innumerable scenes as the screen has yet shown . . . thrilling entertainment for the whole family group.'—*National Board of Review*

† See also *The Adventures of Robin Hood* and *The Story of Robin Hood and his Merrie Men.*

Robin Hood
US 1973 83m Technicolor
Walt Disney (Wolfgang Reitherman)

Alarmingly poor cartoon feature with all the characters 'played' by animals; songs especially dim and treatment quite lifeless

w Larry Clemmons, Ken Anderson, others *d* Wolfgang Reitherman *voices* Brian Bedford, Peter Ustinov, Terry-Thomas, Phil Harris, Andy Devine, Pat Buttram

AAN: song 'Love' (*m* George Bruns, *ly* Floyd Huddleston)

Robin Hood of El Dorado*
US 1936 86m bw

Joaquin Murieta turns bandit to avenge himself on the men who killed his wife.
Whitewashed biopic of a notorious western desperado, played mainly for action and light relief. Warner Baxter, Bruce Cabot, Margo, Eric Linden, J. Carrol Naish, Ann Loring. Written by William Wellman, Melvin Levy and Joseph Calleia; directed by William Wellman; for MGM.

Robinson Crusoe: see The Adventures of Robinson Crusoe

Robinson Crusoe and the Tiger
Mexico 1969 110m Eastmancolor

Simple but extremely handsome version of the famous story, with the addition of a tiger

ROAD TO UTOPIA. Judging by Bing Crosby's disbelieving expression, his *Road* partner Bob Hope is revealing what Paramount is paying him.

which Crusoe takes as a pet. Hugo Stieglitz, Ahui. Written by Mario Marzac and Rene Cardona Jnr, from the novel by Daniel Defoe; directed by Rene Cardona Jnr; for Avant / Avco Embassy.

Robinson Crusoe of Clipper Island
US 1936 bw serial: 14 eps

A search for an international spy group which has wrecked a giant dirigible. Lively serial with animal interest. Mala (a Polynesian), Rex (a horse), Buck (a dog), Mamo Clark, Herbert Rawlinson, William Newell. Directed by Mack V. Wright and Ray Taylor; for Republic.

Robinson Crusoe on Mars**
US 1964 110m Techniscope
Paramount / Devonshire (Aubrey Schenck)

An astronaut lands on Mars and learns to survive until rescue comes.
Remarkably close to Defoe (Man Friday being a refugee in an interplanetary war) this is an absorbing, entertaining and well-staged piece of science fiction, strikingly shot in Death Valley.

w Ib Melchior John C. Higgins *d Byron Haskin ph Winton C. Hoch m* Van Cleave *sp Lawrence Butler ad* Hal Pereira, Arthur Lonergan

Paul Mantee, Adam West, Vic Lundin

Robocop*
US 1987 103m Du Art

Detroit in the future: a badly injured cop is reconstructed by science, and goes on the rampage. Violent fantasy, slick and good-looking but full of jolts. Peter Weller, Nancy Allen, Ronny Cox, Kurtwood Smith, Dan O'Herlihy. Written by Edward Neumeier, Michael Miner; directed by Paul Verhoeven; for Arne Schmidt/Orion. 'A comic book film that's definitely not for kids.'—*Daily Variety*. 'Very violent and very funny.'—*Time Out*.
AAN: editing (Frank J. Urioste).

Robinson Crusoeland
France / Italy 1950 98m bw
Sirius / Franco-London / Fortezza
aka: *Atoll K; Escapade; Utopia*

Stan and Ollie inherit an island in the Pacific, but uranium is discovered on it.
Laurel and Hardy's last film is a dispiriting mess, and the less said about it the better.

w unknown, *d* Leo Joannon, John Berry *ph* Armand Thirard, Louis Née *m* Paul Misraki

Stan Laurel, Oliver Hardy, Suzy Delair

'Here comes a pleasant surprise, a piece of science fiction based on valid speculation . . . modest yet provocative.'—*Time*

Rocco and his Brothers**
Italy / France 1960 180m bw
Titanus / Les Films Marceau (Goffredo Lombardo)

A peasant family moves into Milan, and each of its five brothers has his problems.
Massive portmanteau of realistic stories, a bit hard to take despite its undoubted brilliance.

w Luchino Visconti, Suso Cecchi d'Amico, Vasco Pratolini *d Luchino Visconti*
ph Giuseppe Rotunno *m* Nino Rota

Alain Delon, Renato Salvatori, Annie Girardot, Katina Paxinou, Roger Hanin, Paolo Stoppa, Suzy Delair, Claudia Cardinale

Rock a Bye Baby
US 1958 107m Technicolor Vistavision
Paramount (Jerry Lewis)

A film star asks her devoted schoolday admirer to look after her triplets by a secret marriage.
Tasteless jazzing-up of *The Miracle of Morgan's Creek* by talents distinctly unsympathetic.

wd Frank Tashlin *ph* Haskell Boggs
m Walter Scharf

Jerry Lewis, Marilyn Maxwell, Reginald Gardiner, Salvatore Baccaloni, Hans Conried, Isobel Elsom, James Gleason, Isa Moore, Connie Stevens

Rock around the Clock*
US 1956 74m bw
Columbia (Sam Katzman)

A band playing a new form of jive—rock 'n roll—becomes a nationwide sensation.
A cheap second feature with guest artists, this cheerful little movie deserved at least a footnote in the histories because it spotlights the origins and the leading purveyors of rock 'n roll. It also caused serious riots in several countries. A sequel in 1957, *Don't Knock the Rock*, was merely cheap.

w Robert E. Kent, James B. Gordon *d* Fred F. Sears *ph* Benjamin H. Kline

Bill Haley and the Comets, the Platters, Little Richard, Tony Martinez and his Band, Freddie Bell and the Bellboys, Johnny Johnson, Alan Freed, Lisa Gaye, Alix Talton

Rockabye
US 1932 70m bw

A great actress who has scratched her way up is unhappy because of frustrated mother love. One of many tearjerkers of its type produced in the first three years of the thirties: it doesn't travel well across the decades. Constance Bennett, Joel McCrea, Paul Lukas, Walter Pidgeon, Jobyna Howland, Walter Catlett. Written by Jane Murfin and Kubec Glasmon from the play by Lucia Bronder; directed by George Cukor; for Radio. 'Moderate grosser, best for the neighbourhood mats.'—*Variety*

The Rocket Man
US 1954 79m bw

A visitor from outer space gives a magic ray gun to an orphan boy and tells him to use it only for good. Elementary fantasy with amusing moments. Charles Coburn, George 'Foghorn' Winslow, Spring Byington, Anne Francis, John Agar. Written by Lenny Bruce and Jack Henley; directed by Oscar Rudolph; for TCF.

Rockets Galore
GB 1958 94m Technicolor
Rank / Relph and Dearden
US title: *Mad Little Island*

The Scottish island of Todday resists the installation of a rocket-launching site.
Amiable but disappointingly listless sequel to *Whisky Galore*.

w Monja Danischewsky *d* Michael Relph *ph* Reg Wyer *m* Cedric Thorpe Davie

Jeannie Carson, Donald Sinden, Roland Culver, Noel Purcell, Ian Hunter, Duncan Macrae, Jean Cadell, Carl Jaffe, Gordon Jackson, Catherine Lacey

Rocketship XM*
US 1950 79m bw
Lippert (Kurt Neumann)

An expedition to the moon lands by accident on Mars.
The first post-war space adventure is sheer hokum, quite likeable for its cheek though not for its cheap sets.

wd Kurt Neumann *ph* Karl Struss *m* Ferde Grofe

Lloyd Bridges, Osa Massen, John Emery, Hugh O'Brian

The Rocking Horse Winner*
GB 1949 90m bw
Rank / Two Cities (John Mills)

A boy discovers he can predict winners while riding an old rocking horse; his mother's greed has fatal results.
A very short story is fatally over-extended and becomes bathetic; but the production is solid and the film deserves a mark for trying.

wd Anthony Pelissier, *story* D. H. Lawrence *ph* Desmond Dickinson *m* William Alwyn *ad* Carmen Dillon

John Mills, Valerie Hobson, John Howard Davies, Ronald Squire, Hugh Sinclair, Cyril Smith

'His whole life was a million-to-one shot!'
Rocky**
US 1976 119m Technicolor
UA / Chartoff-Winkler (Gene Kirkwood)

A slightly dimwitted Philadelphia boxer makes good.
Pleasantly old-fashioned comedy-drama with rather unattractive characters in the modern manner. Despite the freshness, on the whole *Marty* is still preferable.

w Sylvester Stallone *d John G. Avildsen* *ph* James Crabe *m* Bill Conti

Sylvester Stallone, Burgess Meredith, Talia Shire, Burt Young, Carl Weathers, Thayer David

AA: best picture; John G. Avildsen
AAN: Sylvester Stallone (as writer); song 'Gonna Fly Now' (*m* Bill Conti, *ly* Carol Connors, Ayn Robbins); Sylvester Stallone (as actor); Burgess Meredith; Talia Shire; Burt Young

Rocky II
US 1979 119m Technicolor
UA / Irwin Winkler, Robert Chartoff

After success comes failure; then Rocky marries his sweetheart and works for another big fight.
Over-inflated but under-nourished sequel with absolutely nothing new to offer.

wd Sylvester Stallone *ph* Bill Butler *m* Bill Conti

Sylvester Stallone, Talia Shire, Burt Young, Carl Weathers, Burgess Meredith

Rocky III
US 1982 99m Technicolor
United Artists / Chartoff–Winkler (James D. Brubaker)

Rocky is challenged by a brutal slugger who beats him at the first match . . .
Unnecessary regurgitation of bits and pieces from the first two Rocky movies.

wd Sylvester Stallone *ph* Bill Butler *m* Bill Conti *pd* William J. Cassidy *ed* Don Zimmerman, Mark Warner

Sylvester Stallone, Talia Shire, Burt Young, Burgess Meredith, Carl Weathers, Tony Burton, Mr T, Hulk Hogan

'The time has surely come for Rocky Balboa to take the final count.'—*Tom Milne, MFB*

'The first *Rocky* was primitive in a relatively innocent way. This picture is primitive too, but it's also shrewd and empty and inept.'—*New Yorker*

AAN: original song, 'Eye of the Tiger' by Jim Peterik and Frankie Sullivan III

Rocky IV
US 1985 91m Metrocolor

Rocky takes on a Russian champion.
Hilarious, hysterical, would-be allegorical, this is the pits; but it took a lot of money. Sylvester Stallone, Dolph Lundren, Carl Weathers, Talia Shire, Burt Young, Brigitte Nielsen. Written and directed by Sylvester Stallone; for Winkler-Chartoff / MGM-UA. 'Ludicrous rubbish, but efficient with it.'—*Shaun Usher, Daily Mail*

Rocky Mountain
US 1950 83m bw
Warner (William Jacobs)

A Confederate horseman gets involved in an Indian war.
Routine star western with unusual tragic ending.

w Winston Miller, Alan le May *d* William Keighley *ph* Ted McCord *m* Max Steiner

Errol Flynn, Patrice Wymore, Scott Forbes, Guinn Williams, Slim Pickens

Rocky Mountain Mystery
US 1935 64m bw

An engineer solves a number of murders at a radium mine. Routine whodunit in an unfamiliar setting. Randolph Scott, Charles Chic Sale, Mrs Leslie Carter (a rare screen appearance, and just as well to judge from her performance), Kathleen Burke, Ann Sheridan. Written by Edward E. Paramore Jnr, from the novel Golden Dreams by Zane Grey; directed by Charles Barton; for Paramount. 'Good entertainment in spite of minor shortcomings.'—*Variety*

Roger Touhy, Gangster
US 1944 73m bw

An associate of Al Capone is finally cornered by the FBI. Unsurprising, competent cops-and-robbers melodrama, based more or less on fact. Preston Foster, Victor McLaglen, Lois Andrews, Kent Taylor, Anthony Quinn, Henry Morgan. Written by Crane Wilbur and Jerry Cady; directed by Robert Florey; for TCF. (GB title: *The Last Gangster.*)

Rogue Cop
US 1954 92m bw
MGM (Nicholas Nayfack)

A police detective is on the payroll of a crime syndicate.
Uncompelling star melodrama.

w Sidney Boehm, *novel* William P. McGivern *d* Roy Rowland *ph* John Seitz *m* Jeff Alexander

Robert Taylor, George Raft, Janet Leigh, Steve Forrest, Anne Francis

'Another of the sour, disillusioned crime stories which have recently been coming into fashion.'—*Penelope Houston*

AAN: John Seitz

The Rogue Song*
US 1930 115m Technicolor
MGM (Lionel Barrymore)

A bandit wins the hand of a Russian princess.
Primitive early sound operetta, not salvaged by a few Laurel and Hardy scenes added as an afterthought.

w Frances Marion, John Colton, *operetta* Gypsy Love by Franz Lehar, Robert Bodansky *d* Lionel Barrymore, Hal Roach *ph* Percy Hilburn, C. Edgar Schoenbaum *m* Dmitri Tiomkin

Lawrence Tibbett, Catherine Dale Owen, Florence Lake, Judith Voselli, Nance O'Neill, Stan Laurel, Oliver Hardy

'Slow unto dullness outside of Tibbett's singing; Laurel and Hardy names draw but their comedy is very weak.'—*Variety*

† No print is known to exist, but in 1980 the sound track was issued on record.

AAN: Lawrence Tibbett

Rogue's March
US 1953 84m bw
MGM (Leon Gordon)

A British army officer is unjustly accused of espionage but becomes a hero in India.
Victorian comedy adventure set on a never-never frontier. Not much.

w Leon Gordon *d* Allan Davis *ph* Paul C. Vogel *m* Alberto Columbo

Peter Lawford, Richard Greene, Janice Rule, Leo G. Carroll, John Abbott, Patrick Aherne

Rogues of Sherwood Forest*
US 1950 80m Technicolor
Columbia (Fred M. Packard)

Robin Hood's son helps the barons to force the signing of Magna Carta.
Satisfactory action adventure.

w George Bruce *d* Gordon Douglas *ph* Charles Lawton Jnr *m* Heinz Roemheld, Arthur Morton

John Derek, Diana Lynn, George Macready, Alan Hale, Paul Cavanagh, Lowell Gilmore, Billy House

Rogues' Regiment
US 1948 86m bw
Universal–International (Robert Buckner)

An intelligence man joins the French Foreign Legion in Saigon to track down an ex-Nazi.
Keen but rather muddled actioner.

w Robert Buckner *d* Robert Florey *ph* Maury Gertsman *m* Daniele Amfitheatrof

Dick Powell, Marta Toren, Vincent Price, Stephen McNally

Rollerball*
US 1975 129m Technicolor Scope
UA / Norman Jewison

In the 21st century an ultra-violent game is used to release the anti-social feelings of the masses.
A one-point parable, and an obvious point at that, is stretched out over more than two hours of violence in which the rules of the game are not even explained. A distinctly unlikeable film.

w William Harrison *d* Norman Jewison *ph* Douglas Slocombe *md* André Previn *pd* John Box

James Caan, John Houseman, Ralph Richardson, Maud Adams, John Beck, Moses Gunn

'A classic demonstration of how several millions of dollars can be unenjoyably wasted.'—*Jonathan Rosenbaum*

Rollercoaster
US 1977 118m Technicolor Panavision Sensurround
Universal (Jennings Lang)

A saboteur blows up rollercoasters if his blackmail demands are not met.
Limp, unsuspenseful, would-be spectacular in which a stalwart cast struggles with inane dialogue and situations.

w Richard Levinson, William Link *d* James Goldstone *ph* David M. Walsh *m* Lalo Schifrin

George Segal, Timothy Bottoms, Richard Widmark, Susan Strasberg, Harry Guardino, Henry Fonda

Rollover
US 1981 115m Technicolor Panavision
Orion / IPC (Bruce Gilbert)

The widow of a murdered bank president exposes various kinds of financial chicanery on an international scale.
So complexly plotted as to be virtually unintelligible, this slick romantic melodrama was caviare to the general despite its stars.

w David Shaber *d* Alan J. Pakula *ph* Giuseppe Rotunno, William Garroni *m* Michael Small

Jane Fonda, Kris Kristofferson, Hume Cronyn, Josef Sommer, Bob Gunton

Le Roman d'un Tricheur*
France 1936 83m bw
Cinéas
aka: *The Story of a Cheat*

A reformed elderly cardsharp writes his memoirs.
First person singular comedy, a *tour de force* in which only the narrator speaks, the rest use pantomime only.

wd Sacha Guitry ph Marcel Lucien

Sacha Guitry, Marguerite Moreno, Serge Grave

Roman Holiday**
US 1953 118m bw
Paramount (William Wyler)

A princess on an official visit to Rome slips away incognito and falls in love with a newspaperman.
Wispy, charming, old-fashioned romantic comedy shot in Rome and a little obsessed by the locations; one feels that a studio base would have resulted in firmer control of the elements. The stars, however, made it memorable.

w Ian McLellan Hunter, John Dighton *d William Wyler ph* Franz Planer, Henri Alekan *m* Georges Auric

Gregory Peck, Audrey Hepburn, Eddie Albert, Hartley Power, Harcourt Williams

'While Capra, or in a different way Lubitsch, could have made something wholly enjoyable from it, it would seem that Wyler's technique is now too ponderously inflexible for such lightweight material.'—*MFB*

AA: original story (Ian McLellan Hunter); Audrey Hepburn
AAN: best picture; script; William Wyler; photography; Eddie Albert

Roman Scandals**
US 1933 93m bw
Samuel Goldwyn

A troubled young man dreams himself back in ancient Rome.
Musical farce which is not only pretty entertaining on its own account but remains interesting for a number of reasons; as its star's best vehicle, for its Depression bookends, as a spoof on *The Sign of the Cross* and the inspiration of scores of other comedies in which the heroes dreamed themselves back into other times. Note also the musical numbers, the chariot race finale, and the rare appearance of Ruth Etting.

w William Anthony McGuire, George Oppenheimer, Arthur Sheekman, Nat Perrin, *story* George S. Kaufman, Robert E. Sherwood *d* Frank Tuttle *chariot sequence Ralph Cedar ph Gregg Toland m* Alfred Newman *ch Busby Berkeley songs* Harry Warren (*m*), Al Dubin, L. Wolfe Gilbert (*ly*)

Eddie Cantor, Gloria Stuart, Ruth Etting, Edward Arnold, Alan Mowbray, Verree Teasdale

'An extraordinary rigmarole containing everything from chariot races to a torch song.'—*Time*

The Roman Spring of Mrs Stone*
GB 1961 104m Technicolor
Warner Seven Arts / AA (Louis de Rochemont)

A widowed American actress in Rome begins to drift into lassitude and moral decline.
Vivien Leigh gets degraded again in this rambling novella complete with mysterious dark stranger waiting at the end. Nice to look at, and occasionally compelling, but unsuccessful as a whole.

w Gavin Lambert, *novel* Tennessee Williams *d* José Quintero *ph* Harry Waxman *m* Richard Addinsell *pd* Roger Furse *ad* Herbert Smith

Vivien Leigh, Warren Beatty, Lotte Lenya, Jeremy Spenser, Coral Browne, Ernest Thesiger

AAN: Lotte Lenya

Romance*
US 1930 76m bw
MGM

A clergyman falls in love with the opera singer mistress of an industrialist.
Simple-minded romantic drama with the star not at her best; but an interesting example of 'high class' romance of the time.

w Bess Meredyth, Edwin Justus Mayer, *play* Edward Sheldon *d* Clarence Brown *ph* William Daniels

Greta Garbo, Lewis Stone, Gavin Gordon, Elliott Nugent, Clara Blandick, Florence Lake, Henry Armetta

'A first-run hit of the sort that won't miss.'—*Variety*

AAN: Clarence Brown; Greta Garbo

Romance in Flanders
GB 1937 73m bw

Two sergeants fall for a Belgian farmer's daughter; she marries the one she doesn't love, thinking the other is dead. Rose-coloured romantic hokum, of no sustaining interest. Paul Cavanagh, Marcelle Chantal, Garry Marsh, Olga Lindo, Alastair Sim.

Written by Harold Simpson, from book by Mario Fort and Ralph E. Vanloc; directed by Maurice Elvey; for Franco-London / British Lion.
(US title: *Romance on the Western Front*.)

Romance in Manhattan
US 1934 78m bw

A New York girl helps a Czech immigrant to find work in the metropolis. Slim, sentimental movie novelette without a touch of sophistication. Ginger Rogers, Francis Lederer, Arthur Hohl, J. Farrell MacDonald, Eily Malyon, Donald Meek. Written by Jane Murfin and Edward Kaufmann; directed by Stephen Roberts; for RKO.

Romance in the Dark
US 1938 78m bw

A famous baritone helps a singing servant to get famous. Musical romance for the carriage trade, with apparently more comedy asides than were originally intended. Gladys Swarthout, John Boles, John Barrymore, Claire Dodd, Fritz Field, Curt Bois. Written by Frank Partos and Anne Morrison Chapin; directed by H. C. Potter; for Paramount.
'Biz will be good, if no wow. Boles and Barrymore will give some tug to the tide against the turnstiles.'—*Variety*

Romance in the Rain
US 1934 74m bw

A girl from the slums wins a Cinderella contest and falls for the press agent. Lightweight romantic concoction which pleased at the time. Roger Pryor, Heather Angel, Victor Moore, Esther Ralston, Ruth Donnelly, Christian Rub. Written by Barry Trivers, Gladys Unger, John V. A. Weaver, Sig Herzig. Jay Gorney; directed by Stuart Walker; for Universal.

Romance of a Horse Thief
US / Yugoslavia 1971 100m Technicolor
Allied Artists / Jadran / Emmanuel L. Wolf (Gene Gutowski)

In a Polish village in 1904 there is dismay when horses are commandeered by Cossacks for service in the Russo-Japanese war. Nostalgic Jewish drama which ends up rather like *Fiddler on the Roof* without the music.

w David Opatoshu, based on his father's novel *d* Abraham Polonsky *ph* Piero Portalupsisic *m* Mort Shuman

Yul Brynner, Eli Wallach, Jane Birkin, Oliver Tobias, Lainie Kazan, David Opatoshu

The Romance of Rosy Ridge
US 1947 103m bw
MGM (Jack Cummings)

After the Civil War, farmers make their own peace.
Mild period romance with everything settled by a betrothal.

w Lester Cole, *novel* Mackinlay Kantor *d* Roy Rowland *ph* Sidney Wagner *m* George Bassman

Van Johnson, Thomas Mitchell, Janet Leigh, Selena Royle, Marshall Thompson, Dean Stockwell

'Rustic charm spread through it like molasses.'—*Douglas Eames*

Romance on the High Seas*
US 1948 99m Technicolor
Warner (Alex Gottleib, George Amy)
GB title: *It's Magic*

Various romances mesh on an ocean voyage. Lightweight musical which introduces Doris Day and generally manages to keep afloat.

w Julius J. and Philip G. Epstein, I. A. L. Diamond *d* Michael Curtiz *ph* Elwood Bredell *m* Ray Heindorf *songs* Jule Styne, Sammy Cahn

Jack Carson, Janis Paige, Don Defore, Doris Day, Oscar Levant, S. Z. Sakall, Eric Blore, Franklin Pangborn, Fortunio Bonanova

AAN: Ray Heindorf; song 'It's Magic' (*m* Jule Styne, *ly* Sammy Cahn)

Romancing the Stone*
US 1984 106m De Luxe Panavision
TCF / El Corazon (Michael Douglas)

A best-selling lady romance novelist gets more than she bargained for when she tries to find her kidnapped sister in Colombia.
Spoof adventure thriller which takes too long to get going and then finds it has nowhere to go. But commercial . . .

w Diane Thomas *d* Robert Zemeckis *ph* Dean Cundey *m* Alan Silvestri *pd* Lawrence G. Paull

Michael Douglas, Kathleen Turner, Danny DeVito, Zack Norman, Alfonso Arau

'The picture has a bravura opening and a jolly kind of movement, but it becomes too slambang.'—*Pauline Kael, New Yorker*

Romanoff and Juliet*
US 1961 103m Technicolor
U-I / Pavla (Peter Ustinov)

Both Americans and Russians woo the tiny country of Concordia, and war threatens while the ambassadors' children fall in love.
Despite the author's wit this pattern comedy became something of a bore as a stylized stage piece, and the film is not smartly enough handled to be anything but a yawn; the humour never becomes cinematic.

wd Peter Ustinov, from his play *ph* Robert Krasker *m* Mario Nascimbene *ad* Alexander Trauner

Peter Ustinov, Sandra Dee, John Gavin, Akim Tamiroff, Tamara Shayne, John Phillips, Alix Talton, Peter Jones

The Romantic Age
GB 1949 86m bw

A precocious French student sets her cap at the art teacher. Fluffy farce in which all the adults behave like children; not well regarded. Mai Zetterling, Hugh Williams, Margot Grahame, Petula Clark, Carol Marsh, Raymond Lovell, Paul Dupuis. Written by Edward Dryhurst and Peggy Barwell, from a novel by Serge Weber; directed by Edmond T. Greville; for Pinnacle - Rank. (US title: *Naughty Arlette*.)

Romantic Comedy
US 1983 102m Metrocolor
MGM-UA / Taft Entertainment / The Mirisch Corporation (Walter Mirisch, Morton Gottlieb)

A Broadway playwright and a New England schoolteacher have a creative partnership that is more personal than professional.
Tedious film version of a play which wallows in autobiography.

w Bernard Slade, from his play *d* Arthur Hiller *ph* David M. Walsh *m* Marvin Hamlisch *pd* Alfred Sweeney

Dudley Moore, Mary Steenburgen, Frances Sternhagen, Janet Eilber, Robyn Douglass, Ron Leibman

'When a movie's production notes wax lyrical about the pile of the living room carpet, one senses that they're in trouble.'—*Nick Roddick, MFB*

The Romantic Englishwoman*
GB 1975 116m Eastmancolor
Dial / Meric–Matalon (Daniel M. Angel)

A discontented woman, holidaying at Baden Baden, falls in love with a stranger while her husband completes a novel on the same theme.
Almost as ambiguous as *Last Year in Marienbad*, this annoying film wastes good actors in a script which hovers uncertainly between fantasy, melodrama and reality, intending one supposes to make humourless and obvious comparisons between romance and life.

w Tom Stoppard, Thomas Wiseman, *novel* Thomas Wiseman *d* Joseph Losey *ph* Gerry Fisher *m* Richard Hartley

Glenda Jackson, Michael Caine, Helmut Berger, Marcus Richardson, Kate Nelligan, René Kolldehoff, Michel Lonsdale

'The central trio bite off their lines, play deviously with hypocrisies and humiliations, and seem slightly aware that they're creations by artifice out of artificiality.'—*Penelope Houston*

'An itsy-bitsy, fragmented film that seems less than the sum of its parts.'—*Michael Billington, Illustrated London News*

Rome Adventure
US 1962 119m Warnercolor

A pretty American librarian goes to Rome to learn about love, and does. Sluggish and overstretched travelogue with dollops of arch romance; hard to take. Suzanne Pleshette, Troy Donahue, Angie Dickinson, Rossano Brazzi, Constance Ford, Chad Everett. Written and directed by Delmer Daves; for Warner. (GB title: *Lovers Must Learn*.)

Rome Express***
GB 1932 94m bw
Gaumont (Michael Balcon)

Thieves and blackmail victims are among the passengers on an express train.
Just a little faded now as sheer entertainment, this remains the prototype train thriller from which *The Lady Vanishes, Murder on the Orient Express* and a hundred others are all borrowed; it also spawned a myriad movies in which strangers are thrown together in dangerous situations. Technically it still works very well, though the script needs modernizing.

w Clifford Grey, Sidney Gilliat, Frank Vosper, Ralph Stock *d* Walter Forde *ph* Gunther Krampf

Conrad Veidt, Gordon Harker, Esther Ralston, Joan Barry, Harold Huth, Cedric Hardwicke, Donald Calthrop, Hugh Williams, Finlay Currie, Frank Vosper, Muriel Aked, Eliot Makeham

'A first class craftsman's job.'—*Basil Wright*

'Technically, and in a sense intellectually speaking, this film puts Forde into Class A1.'—*Cinema Quarterly*

HARKER: 'Discretion is the better part of Wagons Lits.'

† Remade 1948 as *Sleeping Car to Trieste* (qv).

Romeo and Juliet*
US 1936 127m bw
MGM (Irving Thalberg)

Hollywood Shakespeare with a super production and a rather elderly cast. Not entertaining in the strict sense, but full of interest.

w Talbot Jennings *d* George Cukor
ph William Daniels *m* Herbert Stothart
ad Cedric Gibbons

Leslie Howard, Norma Shearer, John Barrymore, Basil Rathbone, Edna May Oliver, Henry Kolker, C. Aubrey Smith, Violet Kemble-Cooper, Robert Warwick, Virginia Hammond, Reginald Denny, Ralph Forbes, Andy Devine, Conway Tearle

'Unimaginative, coarse-grained, a little banal, it is frequently saved—by Shakespeare—from being a bad film.'—*Graham Greene*

'It is impossible to realize how bad this film was unless you reflect on how good it might have been.'—*Alberto Cavalcanti*

† Fredric March, Robert Donat and Robert Montgomery all refused the lead before Leslie Howard accepted.

AAN: best picture; Norma Shearer; Basil Rathbone

Romeo and Juliet
GB 1954 138m Technicolor
Rank / Verona (Joe Janni, Sandro Ghenzi)

Good-looking but extremely boring version shot on Italian locations with quite unacceptable leads.

wd Renato Castellani *ph* Robert Krasker
m Roman Vlad

Laurence Harvey, Susan Shentall, Aldo Zollo, Enzo Fiermonte, Flora Robson, Mervyn Johns, Sebastian Cabot, Lydia Sherwood, Giulio Garbinetti, Nietta Zocchi, Bill Travers, Norman Wooland, John Gielgud as prologue speaker

Romeo and Juliet*
GB 1968 152m Technicolor
Paramount / BHE / Verona / Dino de Laurentiis (Anthony Havelock-Allan, John Brabourne, Richard Goodwin)

The with-it version for modern youngsters; unfortunately the admirably rapid style does not suit the verse, and long before the much-deferred end the thing becomes just as tiresome as the other versions.

w Franco Brusati, Masolino D'Amico
d Franco Zeffirelli *ph* Pasquale de Santis
m Nino Rota

Leonard Whiting, Olivia Hussey, John McEnery, Michael York, Pat Heywood, Milo O'Shea, Paul Hardwick, Natasha Parry, Antonio Pierfederici, Esmeralda Ruspoli, Bruce Robinson, Roberto Bisacco, Laurence Olivier as prologue speaker

'A large gold watch should be tossed to Zeffirelli for his part in reversing the movies' reputation for emasculating the classics.'—*Newsweek*

AA: Pasquale de Santis
AAN: best picture; Franco Zeffirelli

La Ronde***
France 1950 100m bw
Sacha Gordine

In 1900 Vienna, an elegant compère shows that love is a merry-go-round: prostitute meets soldier meets housemaid meets master meets married woman meets husband meets midinette meets poet meets actress meets officer meets prostitute meets soldier . . .
Superb stylized comedy with a fine cast, subtle jokes, rich decor and fluent direction; not to mention a haunting theme tune.

w Jacques Natanson, Max Ophuls,
novel Arthur Schnitzler *d Max Ophuls*
ph Christian Matras *m* Oscar Straus

Anton Walbrook, Simone Signoret, Serge Reggiani, Simone Simon, Daniel Gélin, Danielle Darrieux, Fernand Gravey, Odette Joyeux, Jean-Louis Barrault, Isa Miranda, Gérard Philipe

'One of the most civilized films to have come from Europe in a long time.'—*Gavin Lambert, MFB*

'A film that drags on and on by what seems like geometric progression.'—*John Simon, 1968*

AAN: script

La Ronde
France 1964 110m Eastmancolor Franscope
Robert and Raymond Hakim

Vulgarization of the above, reset in Paris in 1913. The lack of a compère vastly reduces the number of jokes.

w Jean Anouilh *d* Roger Vadim *ph* Henri Decaë *m* Michel Magne

Marie Dubois, Claude Giraud, Anna Karina, Jean-Claude Brialy, Jane Fonda, Maurice Ronet, Catherine Spaak, Bernard Noel, Francine Bergé, Jean Sorel

Rookery Nook**
GB 1930 107m bw
British and Dominions (Herbert Wilcox)

A nervous husband on holiday tries to hide a runaway girl who has asked for protection against her stepfather.
Primitive talkie technique cannot entirely conceal the brilliance of the original Aldwych farce team in their most enduring vehicle.

w Ben Travers, from his play *d* Tom Walls
ph Dave Kessan

Ralph Lynn, Tom Walls, Robertson Hare, Winifred Shotter, Mary Brough, Ethel Coleridge, Griffith Humphreys, Margot Grahame

'As a talker it is the best specimen so far made on this side.'—*Variety*

Rookies
US 1927 75m at 24 fps bw silent

Army adventures of a tough sergeant and a bumbling recruit. Popular comedy of its day which established the new team of Karl Dane and George K. Arthur; also with Marceline Day, Louise Lorraine, Tom O'Brien. Written by Byron Morgan; directed by Sam Wood; for MGM.

Room at the Top***
GB 1958 117m bw
Remus (John and James Woolf)

An ambitious young clerk causes the death of his real love but manages to marry into a rich family.
Claimed as the first British film to take sex seriously, and the first to show the industrial north as it really was, this melodrama actually cheats on both counts but scene for scene is vivid and entertaining despite a weak central performance.

w Neil Paterson, novel John Braine *d Jack Clayton ph Freddie Francis m* Mario Nascimbene

Laurence Harvey, *Simone Signoret,* Heather Sears, Donald Wolfit, Ambrosine Philpotts, Donald Houston, Raymond Huntley, John Westbrook, Allan Cuthbertson, Hermione Baddeley, Mary Peach

'A drama of human drives and torments told with maturity and precision.'—*Stanley Kauffmann*

AA: Neil Paterson; Simone Signoret
AAN: best picture; Jack Clayton; Laurence Harvey; Hermione Baddeley

Room for One More
US 1952 95m bw
Warner (Henry Blanke)

A married couple adopt several underprivileged children.
Slightly mawkish family movie redeemed by star performances.

w Jack Rose, Melville Shavelson *d* Norman Taurog *ph* Robert Burks *m* Max Steiner

Cary Grant, Betsy Drake, Lurene Tuttle, Randy Stuart, George Winslow

Room Service*
US 1938 78m bw
RKO (Pandro S. Berman)

Penniless theatricals find ways of staying in a hotel until they can find a backer.
Claustrophobic Broadway farce unsuitably adapted for the Marx Brothers, who are constrained by having to play characters with a passing resemblance to human beings.

w Morrie Ryskind, *play* John Murray, Allen Boretz *d* William A. Seiter *ph* Russell Metty *m* Roy Webb

Groucho, Chico, Harpo, Lucille Ball, *Donald MacBride,* Frank Albertson, Ann Miller, Philip Loeb

'A natural for the box office . . . the change of pace is a good idea.'—*Variety*

'It should also be noted . . . that there is a scene in which a turkey is chased around a room. Not everybody will care for this.'—*MFB*

† Remade as *Step Lively* (qv).

A Room with a View***
GB 1985 115m colour
Merchant Ivory / Goldcrest (Ismail Merchant)

An innocent Edwardian girl travelling in Italy has her eyes opened to real life and romance.
Competent, unexciting equivalent of a television classic mini-series which so perfectly filled a need as to become a runaway commercial success.

w Ruth Prawer Jhabvala *novel* E. M. Forster *d James Ivory* *ph* Tony Pierce-Roberts *m* Richard Robbins *pd* Gianna Quaranta, Brian Ackland-Snow *ed* Humphrey Dixon

Maggie Smith, Denholm Elliott, Helena Bonham Carter, Julian Sands, Daniel Day Lewis, Simon Callow, Judi Dench, Rosemary Leach, Rupert Graves

'Quality-starved filmgoers will welcome it.'—*Variety*

AA: art direction; adapted screenplay; costumes (Jenny Beavan, John Bright)
AAN: James Ivory as director; Tony Pierce-Roberts; best picture; Maggie Smith; Denholm Elliott

Rooney*
GB 1958 88m bw
Rank (George H. Brown)

Adventures of a bachelor Irish dustman.
Moderately charming, though unconvincing, Dublin comedy.

w Patrick Kirwan, *novel* Catherine Cookson *d* George Pollock *ph* Christopher Challis *m* Philip Green

John Gregson, Barry Fitzgerald, Muriel Pavlow, June Thorburn, Noel Purcell, Marie Kean, Liam Redmond, Jack MacGowan, Eddie Byrne

Rooster Cogburn*
US 1975 108m Technicolor Panavision
Universal (Paul Nathan)

An elderly marshal after a gang of outlaws is helped by the Bible-thumping daughter of a priest.
Disappointing western too obviously patterned after *True Grit* and *The African Queen*. Having had the idea for outrageous star casting, the producers obviously decided erroneously that the film would make itself.

w Martin Julien *d* Stuart Millar *ph* Harry Stradling Jnr *m* Laurence Rosenthal

John Wayne, Katharine Hepburn, Anthony Zerbe, Richard Jordan, John McIntyre, Strother Martin

'Like one of those infuriating exhibition bouts in which two resilient old pros bob, weave and spar without ever landing any punches.'—*Michael Billington, Illustrated London News*

† 'Martin Julien' allegedly covers the writing talents of Hal Wallis, his wife Martha Hyer, and some friends.

The Root of All Evil
GB 1946 110m bw

A jilted woman becomes unscrupulous in business in order to get even with her ex-boyfriend. Incredible farrago with a star ill at ease. Phyllis Calvert, Michael Rennie, John McCallum, Moore Marriott, Brefni O'Rourke, Hazel Court, Edward Rigby. Written and directed by Brock Williams, from the novel by J. S. Fletcher; for Gainsborough.

The Roots of Heaven*
US 1958 125m Eastmancolor Cinemascope
TCF / Darryl F. Zanuck

A white man in central Africa dedicates himself to prevent the slaughtering of elephants.
Curiously patchy version of a novel which was a strange choice for filming; so many side issues are introduced that at times it takes on the look of another jolly safari adventure.

w Romain Gary, Patrick Leigh-Fermor, *novel* Romain Gary *d* John Huston *ph* Oswald Morris *m* Malcolm Arnold

Trevor Howard, Juliette Greco, Errol Flynn, Eddie Albert, Orson Welles, Paul Lukas, Herbert Lom, Grégoire Aslan, Friedrich Ledebur, Edric Connor

'The Huston who did *Sierra Madre* would have lighted his cigar with this script.'—*Stanley Kauffmann*

Rope**
US 1948 80m Technicolor
Transatlantic (Sidney Bernstein, Alfred Hitchcock)

Two homosexuals murder a friend for the thrill of it and conceal his body in a trunk from which they serve cocktails to a party including his father and girl friend.
An effective piece of Grand Guignol on the stage, this seemed rather tasteless when set in a New York skyscraper, especially when the leading role of the investigator was miscast and Hitch had saddled himself with the ten-minute take, a short-lived technique which made the entire action (set in one room) cinematically continuous (and dizzy-making). Of considerable historic interest, nevertheless.

w Arthur Laurents, *play* Patrick Hamilton *d Alfred Hitchcock* *ph* Joseph Valentine, William V. Skall *md* Leo F. Forbstein *theme* François Poulenc

James Stewart, John Dall, Farley Granger, Joan Chandler, Cedric Hardwicke, Constance Collier, Edith Evanson, Douglas Dick

'It was a limiting use of the medium, and parts of the film are unbearably tedious.'—*George Perry, 1965*

'A mighty story of savage greed and sultry love!'

Rope of Sand*
US 1949 105m bw
Paramount (Hal B. Wallis)

Various factions seek hidden diamonds in a prohibited South African area.
Ham-fisted adventure story which suggests at times that a violent parody of *Casablanca* was intended. The stars carry it through.

w Walter Doniger *d* William Dieterle *ph* Charles Lang *m* Franz Waxman

Burt Lancaster, Paul Henreid, Claude Rains, Peter Lorre, Corinne Calvet, Sam Jaffe

'The entertainment world is ablaze!'

Rosalie*
US 1937 118m bw
MGM (William Anthony McGuire)

A college football hero falls for an incognito Balkan princess.
Ambitious light musical with a wispy plot but satisfying numbers.

w William Anthony McGuire, *play* William Anthony McGuire, Guy Bolton *d* W. S. Van Dyke *ph* Oliver T. Marsh *m* Herbert Stothart *songs* Cole Porter

Nelson Eddy, Eleanor Powell, Frank Morgan, Ray Bolger, Ilona Massey, Reginald Owen, Edna May Oliver, Jerry Colonna

'The most lavish, ornate, tinselled and glittering production which has come from Hollywood.'—*Variety*

The Rosary Murders
US 1987 105m colour

In Detroit, murders are committed by someone with a grudge against the Catholic Church. Lax thriller with a priest detective. Donald Sutherland, Charles Durning, Josef Sommer, Belinda Bauer. Written by Elmore Leonard, Fred Walton; directed by Fred Walton; for Laurel-Mihalich / Samuel Goldwyn.

'She gave . . . and gave . . . and gave . . . until there was nothing left to give!'

The Rose
US 1979 134m De Luxe
TCF (Tony Ray)

Drink and drugs cause the decline and death of a famous rock singer.
An unattractive, hysterical, foul-mouthed show business biopic roughly based on Janis Joplin, this does afford an undisciplined nightclub talent a role to get her teeth into.

w Bill Kerby, Bo Goodman *d* Mark Rydell *ph* Vilmos Zsigmond *md* Paul A. Rothchild *pd* Richard MacDonald

Bette Midler, Alan Bates, Frederic Forrest, Harry Dean Stanton, Barry Primus

AAN: Frederic Forrest

Rose Marie*
US 1936 113m bw
MGM (Hunt Stromberg)

A Canadian Mountie gets his man—and a lady.
Backwoods romance from a stage success, filmed mostly on location and quite successfully.

w Frances Goodrich, Albert Hackett, Alice Duer Miller, *play* Otto Harbach, Oscar Hammerstein II *d* W. S. Van Dyke *ph* William Daniels *m* Rudolf Friml *md* Herbert Stothart *songs* various

Nelson Eddy, Jeanette MacDonald, James Stewart, Reginald Owen, Allan Jones, Gilda Gray, George Regas, Alan Mowbray, Robert Greig, Una O'Connor, David Niven, Herman Bing

'An operatic honey with MacDonald and Eddy for the tungstens.'—*Variety*

† Previously filmed in 1928—and see below.

Rose Marie
US 1954 115m Technicolor Cinemascope
MGM (Mervyn Le Roy)

Dull remake with stodgy handling and poor sets.

w Ronald Millar *d* Mervyn Le Roy *ph* Paul C. Vogel *md* Georgie Stoll *ch* Busby Berkeley

Howard Keel, Ann Blyth, Fernando Lamas, Bert Lahr, Marjorie Main, Ray Collins

'The wildcat of the west has the outlaws in her gunsights!'

Rose of Cimarron
US 1952 72m Natural Color

A girl tracks down the killers of her Indian foster-parents. Routine lower-berth western. Mala Powers, Jack Buetel, Bill Williams, Jim Davis. Written by Maurice Geraghty; directed by Harry Keller; for Edward L. Alperson / TCF.

Rose of the Rancho
US 1935 83m bw

Spanish settlers in California fight landgrabbers. Romantic musical with interesting if seldom-used talent. John Boles, Gladys Swarthout, Willie Howard, Charles Bickford, Herb Williams, H. B. Warner. Written by Frank Partos, Charles Brackett, Arthur Sheekman, Nat Perrin, Harlan Thompson, Brian Hooker, from play by Richard Walton Tully and David Belasco; directed by Marion Gering; for William LeBaron / Paramount. 'A fandango mustang meller . . . a tango version of a bronc opera.'—*Variety*

'Song by song . . . scene by scene . . . the thrill grows greater!'

Rose of Washington Square**
US 1939 86m bw
TCF (Nunnally Johnson)

Tribulations of a Broadway singer in love with a worthless husband.
Revamping of the Fanny Brice story; smartly done, but the material interpolated for Jolson is what makes the film notable.

w Nunnally Johnson *d* Gregory Ratoff *ph* Karl Freund *m* Louis Silvers *songs* various

Alice Faye, Tyrone Power, *Al Jolson, Hobart Cavanaugh,* William Frawley, Joyce Compton, Louis Prima and his band

'This is Jolson's picture . . . the rest is also-ran.'—*Variety* .

'Jolson's singing is something for the memory book.'—*New York Times*

† Fanny Brice sued TCF for 75,000 dollars for invasion of privacy; the defendants settled.

'The boldest story of love you have ever been permitted to see!'

The Rose Tattoo
US 1955 117m bw Vistavision
Paramount / Hal B. Wallis

A Sicilian woman on the gulf coast is tormented by the infidelity of her dead husband, but a brawny truckdriver makes her forget him.
Heavily theatrical material, unsuited to the big screen for all the powerful acting (or perhaps because of it).

w John Michael Hayes, *play* Tennessee Williams *d* Daniel Mann *ph* James Wong Howe *m* Alex North

Anna Magnani, Burt Lancaster, Marisa Pavan, Ben Cooper, Virginia Grey, Jo Van Fleet

AA: James Wong Howe; Anna Magnani
AAN: best picture; Alex North; Marisa Pavan

Roseanna McCoy
US 1949 89m bw
Samuel Goldwyn

In old Virginia the Hatfields and the McCoys continue their feud with tragic results.
Hillbilly Romeo and Juliet saga, a shade too cornfed despite the credits.

w John Collier *d* Irving Reis *ph* Lee Garmes *m* David Buttolph

Joan Evans, Farley Granger, Charles Bickford, Raymond Massey, Richard Basehart, Aline MacMahon

Rosebud
US 1975 126m Eastmancolor Panavision
UA / Otto Preminger

Five girls of wealthy families are kidnapped by the Palestine Liberation Army.
Overlong topical suspenser which goes awry by not being very suspenseful, and by packing in too many irrelevant satirical jibes.

w Erik Lee Preminger, *novel* Joan Hemingway, Paul Bonnecarrere *d* Otto Preminger *ph* Denys Coop *m* Laurent Petitgerard *titles* Saul Bass

Peter O'Toole, Richard Attenborough, Cliff Gorman, Claude Dauphin, John V. Lindsay, Peter Lawford, Raf Vallone, Adrienne Corri

Roseland*
US 1977 103m color
Cinema Shares / Merchant Ivory (Ismail Merchant)

Generation after generation, the lonely and the loving come to a New York ballroom.
Pleasantly intentioned slice-of-life drama which is rather slackly written and handled, with unprofessionalism showing through at several points.

w Ruth Prawer Jhabvala *d* James Ivory *ph* Ernest Vincze *m* Michael Gibson

Geraldine Chaplin, Teresa Wright, Lou Jacobi, Don de Natale, Louise Kirkland, Helen Gallagher, Joan Copeland, Conrad Janis, Lilia Skala, Christopher Walken

'Typically discreet and dull film from Merchant-Ivory . . . what one might call over-decorous.'—*Time Out, 1984*

Rosemary's Baby**
US 1968 137m Technicolor
Paramount / William Castle

After unwittingly becoming friendly with diabolists, an actor's wife is impregnated by the Devil.
Seminal gothic melodrama which led in due course to the excesses of *The Exorcist*; in itself well done in a heavy-handed way, the book being much more subtle.

wd Roman Polanski, *novel Ira Levin* *ph* William Fraker *m* Krzysztof Komeda *pd* Richard Sylbert

Mia Farrow, John Cassavetes, Ruth Gordon, Sidney Blackmer, Patsy Kelly, Ralph Bellamy, Maurice Evans, Angela Dorian, Elisha Cook, Charles Grodin

'It may not be for the very young, and perhaps pregnant women should see it at their own risk.'—*Motion Picture Herald*

'Tension is sustained to a degree surpassing Alfred Hitchcock at his best.'—*Daily Telegraph*

† William Castle, the producer, is glimpsed outside a phone booth.
†† A TV sequel followed: *Look What Happened to Rosemary's Baby.*

AA: Ruth Gordon
AAN: Roman Polanski (as writer)

Rosie
US 1967 98m Techniscope
Universal / Ross Hunter (Jacque Mapes)

A rich woman spends wildly and her daughters try to have her committed to safeguard their inheritance.
Hopelessly muddled comedy drama which flits from one mood to the other without making a success of either.

w Samuel Taylor, *play* Ruth Gordon, *French original* Les Joies de la Famille by Philippe Heriat *d* David Lowell Rich *ph* Clifford Stine *m* Lyn Murray

Rosalind Russell, Brian Aherne, Sandra Dee, Vanessa Brown, Audrey Meadows, James Farentino, Leslie Nielsen, Margaret Hamilton, Reginald Owen, Juanita Moore, Virginia Grey
'A mawkish mixture of *Auntie Mame* and *King Lear.*'—*MFB*

Rosie the Riveter
US 1944 75m bw

Warplant workers have to share rooms in a boarding house. Easy-going wartime comedy. Jane Frazee, Frank Albertson, Vera Vague, Frank Jenks, Lloyd Corrigan, Frank Fenton, Maude Eburne, Carl 'Alfalfa' Switzer. Written by Jack Townley and Aileen Leslie, from story by Dorothy Curnow Handley; directed by Joseph Santley; for Armand Schaefer/ Republic. (GB title: *In Rosie's Room.*)

Rotten to the Core
GB 1965 88m bw
Panavision
BL / Tudor (The Boulting Brothers)

Ex-convicts plan an army payroll robbery. Routine caper comedy, unsuitably widescreened, with a few good jokes along the way.

w Jeffrey Dell, Roy Boulting, John Warren, Len Heath *d* John Boulting *ph* Freddie Young *m* Michael Dress

Anton Rodgers, *Thorley Walters,* Eric Sykes, Kenneth Griffith, Charlotte Rampling, Ian Bannen, Avis Bunnage, Raymond Huntley
† The original title, *Rotten to the Corps,* was more apt but plainly seemed too subtle.

Le Rouge et le Noir*
France / Italy 1954 170m approx
Eastmancolor
Franco London / Documento
aka: *Scarlet and Black*

A carpenter's son becomes a private tutor, seduces his master's wife and is sent to study for the priesthood . . .
Massive attempt to conquer an unfilmable novel. Some enjoyable scenes and decor are the best it can offer.

w Jean Aurenche, Pierre Bost, Claude Autant-Lara, *novel* Stendhal *d* Claude Autant-Lara *ph* Michel Kelber *m* René Cloërc *ad* Max Douy

Gérard Philipe, Danielle Darrieux, Antonella Lualdi, Jean Martinelli

The Rough and the Smooth
GB 1959 99m bw
Renown (George Minter)
US title: *Portrait of a Sinner*

An archaeologist about to marry the niece of a press lord falls for a mysterious nymphomaniac.
Preposterous melodrama about unreal people; its very excesses become enjoyable for those who can stay the course.

w Audrey Erskine-Lindop, Dudley Leslie, *novel* Robin Maugham *d* Robert Siodmak *ph* Otto Heller *md* Muir Mathieson *m* Douglas Gamley

Tony Britton, Nadja Tiller, William Bendix, Natasha Parry, Norman Wooland, Donald Wolfit, Tony Wright, Adrienne Corri, Joyce Carey
'The script is never even on nodding terms with life, and tries to make up for this deficiency by a candidly explosive vocabulary which gives the production a weirdly old-fashioned air.'—*MFB*

Rough Cut
US 1980 112m Movielab
Paramount / David Merrick

A retiring Scotland Yard inspector spars with a jewel thief and finally changes sides.
Dated comedy which required a much lighter touch in all departments.

w Francis Burns, *novel* Touch the Lion's Paw by Derek Lambert *d* Don Siegel *ph* Frederick Young *m* Nelson Riddle, from Duke Ellington themes *pd* Ted Haworth

Burt Reynolds, Lesley Anne Down, David Niven, Timothy West, Patrick Magee, Joss Ackland
'All surface smartness without a single structural idea.'—*Richard Combs, MFB*

Rough Night in Jericho
US 1967 97m Techniscope
Universal (Martin Rackin)

A stagecoach man rids a cattle town of a villain.
Totally uninteresting star western with glum performances.

w Sidney Boehm, Marvin H. Albert, *novel* The Man in Black by Marvin H. Albert *d* Arnold Laven *ph* Russell Metty *m* Don Costa

George Peppard, Dean Martin, Jean Simmons, John McIntire, Slim Pickens, Don Galloway, Brad Weston

Rough Shoot*
GB 1952 86m bw
Raymond Stross
US title: *Shoot First*

A retired US officer in Dorset thinks he has shot a poacher—but the dead man is a spy, and someone else shot him.
Minor Hitchcock-style thriller with a climax in Madame Tussaud's. Generally efficient and entertaining.

w Eric Ambler, novel Geoffrey Household *d Robert Parrish ph* Stan Pavey *m* Hans May

Joel McCrea, Evelyn Keyes, Marius Goring, Roland Culver, Frank Lawton, Herbert Lom

Rough, Tough and Ready
US 1945 64m bw

Two members of the Army engineers' port repair service fall out over a girl. A faint echo of the old Flagg and Quirt comedies. Victor McLaglen, Chester Morris, Veda Ann Borg, Jean Rogers. Written by Edward T. Lowe; directed by Del Lord; for Alexis Thurn-Taxis / Columbia.

Roughly Speaking*
US 1945 117m bw
Warner (Henry Blanke)

Oddball, overlong domestic comedy drama about father's wild and impractical schemes.

w Louise Randall Pierson, from her book *d* Michael Curtiz *ph* Joseph Walker *m* Max Steiner

Rosalind Russell, Jack Carson, Robert Hutton, Jean Sullivan, Alan Hale, Donald Woods, Andrea King, Ray Collins, Kathleen Lockhart

Roughshod
US 1949 88m bw
RKO (Richard H. Berger)

Two cowboys journeying to California with a herd of horses come up against villains intent on revenge.
Likeable old-fashioned western.

w Geoffrey Homes, Hugo Butler *d* Mark Robson *ph* Joseph F. Biroc *m* Roy Webb

Robert Sterling, Gloria Grahame, Claude Jarman Jnr, John Ireland, Jeff Donnell, Martha Hyer

Round Midnight**
France 1986 133m Eastmancolor
Warner / Little Bear / PECF (Irwin Winkler)

A black American jazz musician spends his last days in Paris.
A jazz buff's tribute to Bud Powell and Lester Young; acclaimed by the critics but essentially a film for minorities.

w Bertrand Tavernier, David Rayfiel *d Bertrand Tavernier ph* Bruno de Keyzer *m,md Herbie Hancock pd* Alexandre Trauner

Dexter Gordon, François Cluzet, Gabrielle Haker, John Berry, Martin Scorsese

AA: Herbie Hancock
AAN: Dexter Gordon

The Rounders
US 1965 85m Metrocolor Panavision
MGM (Richard E. Lyons)

Two modern cowboys mean to settle down but never get around to it.
Pale comedy western which never gets going.

wd Burt Kennedy, *novel* Max Evans *ph* Paul C. Vogel *m* Jeff Alexander

Henry Fonda, Glenn Ford, Chill Wills, Sue Anne Langdon, Edgar Buchanan

Roustabout
US 1964 101m Techniscope
Hal B. Wallis

A wandering tough guy joins a travelling carnival.
Dreary star vehicle momentarily salvaged by its co-star.

w Allan Weiss, Anthony Lawrence *d* John Rich *ph* Lucien Ballard *m* Joseph L. Lilley

Elvis Presley, Barbara Stanwyck, Sue Ann Langdon, Joan Freeman, Leif Erickson

Roxanne*
US 1987 107m De Luxe
Columbia / Michael Rachmil, Daniel Melnick

An ugly man writes love letters for his friend . . . but true love will find a way.
Zany modernization of Rostand's Cyrano de Bergerac, funny in spots but way overlong.

w Steve Martin *d* Fred Schepisi *ph* Ian Baker *m* Bruce Smeaton *pd* Jack DeGovia

Steve Martin, Daryl Hannah, Rick Rossovich, Shelley Duvall, John Kapelos, Fred Willard, Michael J. Pollard

'The low down story of a high class gal!'
Roxie Hart**
US 1942 72m bw
TCF (Nunnally Johnson)

A twenties showgirl confesses for the sake of publicity to a murder of which she is innocent.
Crowded Chicago burlesque which now seems less funny than it did but is full of smart moments.

w Nunnally Johnson, play Chicago by Maurine Watkins *d William Wellman ph Leon Shamroy m* Alfred Newman

Ginger Rogers, George Montgomery, *Adolphe Menjou*, Lynne Overman, Nigel Bruce, Spring Byington, Sara Allgood, William Frawley

DEDICATION: To all the beautiful women in the world who have shot their husbands full of holes out of pique.

'A masterpiece of form, of ensemble acting, of powerhouse comedy and scripting.'—*NFT, 1974*

† The play was also filmed in 1927 under its original title, with Phyllis Haver.

Royal African Rifles
US 1954 75m Cinecolor

In British East Africa in 1914, a lieutenant tracks down a consignment of stolen guns.
Mini-budget *Boys Own Paper* heroics; quite enjoyable on its level. Louis Hayward, Veronica Hurst, Michael Pate, Angela Greene, Steve Geray, Bruce Lester. Written by Dan Ullman; directed by Lesley Selander; for Allied Artists. (GB title: *Storm over Africa*.)

The Royal Bed
US 1931 74m bw

The king and queen of a European country lead their own private lives. Insufficient wit graces this would-be daring romantic drama from a Broadway hit. Mary Astor, Lowell Sherman, Nance O'Neill, Anthony Bushell, Robert Warwick. Written by J. Walter Ruben, from the play *The Queen's Husband* by Robert E. Sherwood; directed by Lowell Sherman; for RKO. (GB title: *The Queen's Husband*.)

Royal Cavalcade
GB 1935 104m bw

A chronicle of the events of the reign of King George V. Thoroughly embarrassing jubilee tribute, of historical interest only. Marie Lohr, Hermione Baddeley, Esme Percy, John Mills, Reginald Gardiner, Syd Walker, Seymour Hicks, Owen Nares, Matheson Lang, George Robey, Florrie Forde, many others. Written by Marjorie Deans; directed by Marcel Varnel, Thomas Bentley, Herbert Brenon, Norman Lee, Walter Summers and Will Kellino; for BIP.

A Royal Divorce
GB 1938 85m bw

Napoleon Bonaparte in 1809 marries a widow whose reputation isn't exactly spotless. Heavy comedy or light drama, take your pick; not exactly riveting as either. Pierre Blanchar, Ruth Chatterton, Frank Cellier, Carol Goodner, George Curzon, John Laurie, Jack Hawkins. Written by Miles Malleson, from the novel *Josephine* by Jacques Thery; directed by Jack Raymond; for Herbert Wilcox/Imperator.

The Royal Family of Broadway*
US 1930 82m bw
Paramount
GB title: *Theatre Royal*

The off-stage escapades of a famous family of actors.
Fairly funny lampoon of the Barrymores, primitively staged and very talky but still entertaining for those in the joke.

w Herman J. Mankiewicz, Gertrude Purcell, *play* George S. Kaufman, Edna Ferber *d* George Cukor, Cyril Gardner *ph* George Folsey

Fredric March, Henrietta Crosman, Ina Claire, Mary Brian, Charles Starrett, Frank Conroy

'Lionel does not come into the burlesque at all, and I can quite believe that he is the most damaged of the entire family.'—*James Agate*

'Stagebound and awkward, but great fun anyway.'—*New Yorker, 1977*

AAN: Fredric March

Royal Flash
GB 1975 118m Technicolor
TCF / Two Roads (David V. Picker, Denis O'Dell)

A Victorian bully and braggart has various adventures in Europe and Ruritania.
A rather unsatisfactory romp which takes pot shots at every 19th-century person and object in the encyclopaedia, but is never as funny as it intends to be.

w George Macdonald Fraser, from his novel *d* Richard Lester *ph* Geoffrey Unsworth *m* Ken Thorpe *ph* Terence Marsh

Malcolm McDowall, Oliver Reed, Alan Bates, Florinda Bolkan, Britt Ekland, Lionel Jeffries, Tom Bell, Joss Ackland, Leon Greene, Richard Hurndall, Alastair Sim, Michael Hordern

The Royal Hunt of the Sun
GB 1969 121m Technicolor
Security Pictures (Eugene Frenke, Philip Yordan)

How the Spanish soldier Pizarro on his South American trek overcame the Inca god-king Atahualpa.
Deadly literal rendering with nothing to replace the play's theatrical splendour, resembling nothing so much as an opera without the music.

w Philip Yordan, *play* Peter Shaffer *d* Irving Lerner *ph* Roger Barlow *m* Marc Wilkinson

Robert Shaw, Christopher Plummer, Nigel Davenport, Michael Craig, Leonard Whiting, Andrew Keir, James Donald, Percy Herbert, Alexander Davion

The Royal Mounted Rides Again
US 1945 bw serial: 13 eps

Captain Decker of the Mounties seeks the true culprit of a murder for which his father is prime suspect. Adequate chapter play with location settings. George Dolenz, Bill Kennedy, Addison Richards, Daun Kennedy. Directed by Ray Taylor and Lewis D. Collins; for Universal.

A Royal Scandal
US 1945 94m bw
TCF (Ernst Lubitsch)
GB title: *Czarina*

The illicit loves of Catherine the Great.
Censored romps around some chilly court sets; very few moments of interest, and none of the style of the silent version *Forbidden Paradise*.

w Edwin Justus Mayer, *play* Lajos Biro, Melchior Lengyel *d* Otto Preminger *ph* Arthur Miller *m* Alfred Newman

Tallulah Bankhead, Charles Coburn, Anne Baxter, William Eythe, Vincent Price, Mischa Auer, Sig Rumann, Vladimir Sokoloff

'Nothing is one-tenth well enough done, and all the laughs are played for at their cheapest, far down the ramp.'—*James Agee*

Royal Wedding
US 1951 93m Technicolor
MGM (Arthur Freed)
GB title: *Wedding Bells*

Journalists congregate in London for the royal wedding.
Thin musical with acceptable numbers.

w Alan Jay Lerner *d* Stanley Donen *ph* Robert Planck *md* Johnny Green *songs* Alan Jay Lerner, Burton Lane

Fred Astaire, Jane Powell, Sarah Churchill, Peter Lawford, Keenan Wynn

AAN: song 'Too Late Now' (*m* Burton Lane, *ly* Alan Jay Lerner)

'Dangerous . . . destructive . . . deadly to love!'
Ruby Gentry
US 1952 82m bw
Joseph Bernhard / King Vidor

A tempestuous girl, brought up as a boy in the Carolina swamps, has a love-hate relationship with a local aristocrat, revenges herself on the

people who scorn her, loses her lover in a swamp shooting, and becomes a sea captain.
Richly absurd sex melodrama typical of its director and star yet not very entertaining.

w Sylvia Richards *d* King Vidor *ph* Russell Harlan *m* Heinz Roemheld *ad* Dan Hall

Jennifer Jones, Charlton Heston, Karl Malden, Josephine Hutchinson

Rue de l'Estrapade*
France 1953 95m bw
Cinephonic / SGGC / Filmsonor
aka: *Françoise Steps Out*

A young Parisienne suspects her husband of having an affair.
Lightly likeable domestic comedy in the vein of *Edouard et Caroline*, but not quite up to its standard.

w Annette Wademant *d* Jacques Becker *ph* Marcel Grignon *m* Georges Van Parys, Marguerite Monnot

Louis Jourdan, Anne Vernon, Daniel Gelin, Jean Servais, Micheline Dax

'Five comedy stars in a five-star comedy!'
Ruggles of Red Gap**
US 1935 90m bw
Paramount (Arthur Hornblow Jnr)

A British butler has a startling effect on the family of an American rancher who takes him out west.
A famous comedy which seemed hilarious at the time but can now be seen as mostly composed of flat spots; the performances however are worth remembering.

w Walter de Leon, Harlan Thompson, Humphrey Pearson, *novel* Harry Leon Wilson *d* Leo McCarey *ph* Alfred Gilks

Charles Laughton, Mary Boland, Charles Ruggles, Zasu Pitts, Roland Young, Leila Hyams, James Burke, Maude Eburne, Lucien Littlefield

'Plenty of marquee strength, and dynamite on the inside. An A1 comedy.'—*Variety*

'A sane, witty, moving and quite unusual picture of Anglo-American relations.'—*C. A. Lejeune*

'The most heart-warming comedy of the season . . . there is about it a sympathetic and even a patriotic quality which is touching.'—*Literary Digest*

'The archetypal film they don't make any more, partly because comedy has now grown too raucous to favour the quiet drollery of players like Charlie Ruggles and Mary Boland, partly because even McCarey himself had trouble after the thirties separating sentiment from sentimentality.'—*Time Out, 1980*

† Remade as *Fancy Pants* (qv).

AAN: best picture

Rulers of the Sea*
US 1939 96m bw
Paramount (Frank Lloyd)

Problems surround the first steamship voyage across the Atlantic.
Well-made period action drama.

w Talbot Jennings, Frank Cavett, Richard Collins *d* Frank Lloyd *ph* Theodor Sparkuhl, Archie Stout *m* Richard Hageman

Douglas Fairbanks Jnr, Margaret Lockwood, Will Fyffe, Montagu Love, George Bancroft, Mary Gordon, Alan Ladd

'Timely in content and grand for exploitation. In the British Empire it will be greeted as inspirational entertainment.'—*Variety*

The Ruling Class*
GB 1972 155m De Luxe
Keep Films (Jules Buck, Jack Hawkins)

The fetishistic Earl of Gurney is succeeded by his mad son Jack who believes he is God.
An overlong satirical play with brilliant patches is hamfistedly filmed but boasts some bright performances. The hits are as random as the misses, however.

w Peter Barnes, from his play *d* Peter Medak *ph* Ken Hodges *m* John Cameron

Peter O'Toole, Harry Andrews, *Arthur Lowe, Alastair Sim,* Coral Browne, Michael Bryant

'This irritating and unsatisfying film is worth being irritated and unsatisfied by.'—*Stanley Kauffmann*

AAN: Peter O'Toole

'This is the dance of love!'
Rumba*
US 1935 71m bw
Paramount (William Le Baron)

A society girl has a yen for a Broadway hoofer.
Streamlined star vehicle which attempts to recapture the success of *Bolero* (qv).

w Howard J. Green *d* Marion Gering *ph* Ted Tetzlaff

Carole Lombard, George Raft, Margo, Lynne Overman, Monroe Owsley, Iris Adrian, Gail Patrick, Samuel S. Hinds, Jameson Thomas

Rumble Fish
US 1983 94m bw (with colour inserts)

A Tulsa teenager survives local gang violence and while working in a petshop sees himself in the rumble fish, which fights even its own image in a glass. Glum piece of self-absorption by a director going rapidly downhill. Matt Dillon, Mickey Rourke, Diane Lane, Dennis Hopper, Diana Scarwid. Written and directed by Francis Ford Coppola from the novel by S. E. Hinton; for Zoetrope.

Run for Cover*
US 1955 92m Technicolor Vistavision
Paramount (William H. Pine)

An ex-convict becomes innocently involved in a train robbery.
Adequate star western.

w William C. Thomas, *story* Harriet Frank Jnr, Irving Ravetch *d* Nicholas Ray *ph* Daniel Fapp *md* Howard Jackson

James Cagney, Viveca Lindfors, John Derek, Jean Hersholt, Grant Withers, Ernest Borgnine, Jack Lambert

Run for the Sun
US 1956 99m Technicolor Superscope
UA / Russ–Field (Harry Tatelman)

Crashlanding in the Mexican jungle, a disillusioned author and a lady journalist find themselves at the mercy of renegade Nazis.
Tame remake of *The Most Dangerous Game* with Count Zaroff replaced by Lord Haw-Haw. Sluggish plot development mars the action.

w Dudley Nichols, Roy Boulting *d* Roy Boulting *ph* Joseph La Shelle *m* Fred Steiner

Richard Widmark, Jane Greer, Trevor Howard, Peter Van Eyck

A Run for Your Money*
GB 1949 83m bw
Ealing (Leslie Norman)

Welsh Rugby supporters have various adventures on their one day in London.
Slight, bright, British chase comedy with characterizations as excellent as they are expected.

w Richard Hughes, Charles Frend, Leslie Norman *d* Charles Frend *ph* Douglas Slocombe *m* Ernest Irving

Alec Guinness, Meredith Edwards, Moira Lister, Donald Houston, Hugh Griffith, Clive Morton, Joyce Grenfell

Run of the Arrow
US 1956 85m Technicolor RKOscope
Global (Samuel Fuller)

An ex-Civil War soldier is captured by Indians and accepted by them, but sickened by their violence.
Bloody little western in the accustomed Fuller vein of unpleasantness.

wd Samuel Fuller *ph* Joseph Biroc *m* Victor Young

Rod Steiger, Sarita Montiel, Charles Bronson, Tim McCoy, Ralph Meeker

Run Silent Run Deep*
US 1958 93m bw
UA / Hecht–Hill–Lancaster (William Schorr)

Antagonisms flare up between the officers of a US submarine in Tokyo Bay during World War II.
Competent, unsurprising war actioner trading on its stars.

w John Gay *d* Robert Wise *ph* Russell Harlan *m* Franz Waxman

Clark Gable, Burt Lancaster, Jack Warden, Brad Dexter, Nick Cravat, Joe Maross, H. M. Wynant

'Mostly good sea fights. Otherwise it's damn the torpedoes, half speed ahead.'—*Time*

Run Wild, Run Free*
GB 1969 98m Technicolor
Columbia / Irving Allen (John Danischewsky)

A mute boy living on Dartmoor gains self-confidence through the love of animals.
Rather vaguely developed family film with agreeable sequences.

w David Rook, from his novel The White Colt, *d* Richard C. Sarafian *ph* Wilkie Cooper *m* David Whitaker

John Mills, Sylvia Syms, Mark Lester, Bernard Miles, Gordon Jackson, Fiona Fullerton

The Runaround*
US 1946 100m bw
Universal (Joseph Gershenson)

Two rival detectives are hired to find a missing heiress.
Peripatetic comedy on the lines of *It Happened One Night*; unexpectedly enjoyable.

w Arthur T. Horman, Sam Hellman *d* Charles Lamont *ph* George Robinson *m* Frank Skinner

Rod Cameron, Broderick Crawford, Ella Raines, Samuel S. Hinds, Frank McHugh, George Cleveland

Runaway
US 1984 100m Metrocolor
Tri-Star / Michael Crichton (Michael Rachmil)

An electronics wizard sets a half-perfected robot on the rampage.
Simple-minded comedy-melodrama which feels as though it ought to have been played entirely for laughs.

w,d Michael Crichton *ph* John A. Alonzo *m* Jerry Goldsmith *pd* Douglas Higgins *ed* Glenn Farr

Tom Selleck, Cynthia Rhodes, Gene L. Simmons, Kirstie Alley, Stan Shaw

The Runaway Bus*
GB 1954 78m bw
Eros / Conquest–Guest (Val Guest)

Passengers at London Airport are fogbound, and a relief bus driver takes some of them to Blackbushe. Incognito among them are robbers and detectives . . .
Vaguely plotted variation on *The Ghost Train*, with fair production, a good smattering of jokes, and a hilarious view of a great airport in its earlier days.

wd Val Guest *ph* Stan Pavey *m* Ronald Binge

Frankie Howerd, Margaret Rutherford, George Coulouris, Petula Clark, Terence Alexander, Toke Townley, Belinda Lee

'Once it starts, nothing can stop it!'
Runaway Train*
US 1985 111m Rank colour
Cannon / Northbrook (Menahem Golan, Yoram Globus)

Prison breakers escape into the Alaskan wilderness and commandeer a train which can't stop.
Violent, foul-mouthed melodrama with no interest beyond breathtaking photography of the speeding train. Its general pretentiousness, perhaps, is also something to experience.

w Djordje Milicevic, Paul Zindel, Edward Bunker, from screenplay by Akira Kurosawa *d Andrei Konchalovsky ph Alan Hume* *m* Trevor Jones *pd* Stephen Marsh

Jon Voight, Eric Roberts, Rebecca DeMornay, Kyle T. Heffner

'The most exciting epic since *The Road Warrior*.'—*Variety*

'Nervy, exciting violence; immaculate, metallic camerawork; unstoppable pace.'—*Sight and Sound*

AAN: Jon Voight; Eric Roberts (supporting actor); editing

The Runner Stumbles
US 1979 110m CFI color
Melvin Simon Productions (Stanley Kramer)

In the mid-twenties, a Catholic priest is accused of the murder of a nun for whom he had felt a strong romantic attraction.
Musty exhumation of a genuine case which has little dramatic interest and even less wider significance. Good acting does not atone.

w Milan Stiff, from his play *d* Stanley Kramer *ph* Laszlo Kovacs *m* Ernest Gold *pd* Alfred Sweeney Jnr

Dick Van Dyke, Kathleen Quinlan, Maureen Stapleton, Ray Bolger, Tammy Grimes, Beau Bridges

'The reanimated corpse of middlebrow Hollywood pretension . . . funereal pacing, portentous low angles and symbolic overkill.'—*Paul Taylor, MFB*

Runners
GB 1983 106m colour
Goldcrest (Barry Hanson)

Distraught parents try to trace their missing children in London.
Heavy-going realistic drama with apparent inner meanings which are not brought to the surface.

w Stephen Poliakoff *d* Charles Sturridge *ph* Howard Atherton *m* George Fenton *pd* Arnold Chapkis

James Fox, Kate Hardie, Jane Asher, Eileen O'Brien, Ruti Simon

Running Brave
US 1983 106m colour

A young Sioux from the reservation faces the pressures of the white world and becomes an Olympic runner. The terrible punning title is the best thing in this very predictable piece of do-goodery, which would just about have passed muster as a TV movie. Robby Benson, Pat Hingle, Claudia Cron, Jeff McCracken. Written by Henry Bean, Shirl Hendrix; directed by D. S. Everett; for Englander Productions. 'This is in essence a propaganda film for the American way, masked as a piece of liberal sentiment, and I distrust it thoroughly.'—*Observer*

'Time is running out for him!'
The Running Man*
GB 1963 103m Technicolor Panavision
Columbia / Peet (Carol Reed, John R. Sloan)

A private airline pilot fakes an accident and disappears, leaving his wife to collect the insurance and meet him in Spain.
Flabby, expensive suspenser; both plot and character take a back seat to scenic views.

w John Mortimer, *novel* The Ballad of the Running Man by Shelley Smith *d* Carol Reed *ph* Robert Krasker *m* William Alwyn

Laurence Harvey, Alan Bates, Lee Remick, Felix Aylmer, Eleanor Summerfield, Allan Cuthbertson

'There seems to be something about the panoramic screen that seduces film-makers into filling it with irrelevant local colour and drawing the whole proceedings out to a length that matches its width.'—*Brenda Davies*

Running Scared
GB 1972 98m Technicolor Panavision
Paramount / Wigan / Hemmings / O'Toole (Gareth Wigan)

A university student is generally condemned for allowing his friend to commit suicide; eventually he takes his own life.
Depressing and rather pointless exercise in death wish complicated by a doomed love affair.

w Clive Exton, David Hemmings, *novel* Gregory MacDonald *d* David Hemmings *ph* Ernest Day *m* Michael J. Lewis

Robert Powell, Gayle Hunnicutt, Barry Morse, Stephanie Bidmead, Edward Underdown, Maxine Audley, Georgia Brown

Running Scared
US 1986 106m Metrocolor Panavision
MGM-UA / Turman-Foster (Peter Hyams)

Accident-prone Chicago cops nevertheless succeed in getting their man.
Crime comedy-melodrama of a type seen far too often before.

w Guy Devore, Jimmy Huston *d* Peter Hyams *ph* Peter Hyams *m* Rod Temperton *pd* Albert Brenner

Gregory Hines, Billy Crystal, Steven Bauer, Joe Pantoliano, Tracy Reed, Darlanne Fluegel

Russian Roulette
US 1975 90m Eastmancolor
ITC / Elliott Kastner / Bulldog

Real and fake secret agents shoot it out when the Russian premier is about to visit Vancouver.
Fast-moving but impossible to follow location thriller which resolves itself into a series of chases.

w Tom Ardies, Stanley Mann, Arnold Margolin, *novel* Kosygin is Coming by Tom Ardies *d* Lou Lombardo *ph* Brian West *m* Michael J. Lewis

George Segal, Gordon Jackson, Denholm Elliott, Cristina Raines, Richard Romanus, Louise Fletcher, Nigel Stock

'A stale, mechanical espionage caper that wastes its star.'—*Kevin Thomas*

The Russians Are Coming, The Russians Are Coming*
US 1966 126m De Luxe Panavision
UA / Mirisch (Norman Jewison)

Russian submariners make a forced landing on a Connecticut holiday island and cause panic. 'Daring' cold war comedy which turns out to be of the most elementary and protracted nature, saved from boredom only by a few cameos.

w William Rose, *novel* The Off-Islanders by Nathaniel Benchley *d* Norman Jewison *ph* Joseph Biroc *m* Johnny Mandel

Carl Reiner, Eva Marie Saint, Alan Arkin, John Philip Law, Paul Ford, Tessie O'Shea, Brian Keith, Jonathan Winters, Theodore Bikel, Ben Blue

'Rather amiable, though the film, like its title, seems to repeat most things twice.'—*Sight and Sound*

'Why the crazy title? If we told you, you'd only laugh!'—*publicity*

AAN: best picture; William Rose; Alan Arkin

Rustlers of Red Dog
US 1935 bw serial: 12 eps

Three musketeers of the old west find plenty of action with rustlers and renegade Indians. Western serial with all the expected elements. John Mack Brown, Joyce Compton, Walter Miller, Raymond Hatton, H. L. Woods. Directed by Louis Friedlander; for Universal.

'Love betrayed them—power destroyed them!'
Ruthless*
US 1948 104m bw
Eagle Lion / Arthur S. Lyons

A conniver breaks several lives on his way to the top.
Rich melodrama with some entertaining moments.

w S. K. Lauren, Gordon Kahn, *novel* Prelude to Night by Dayton Stoddert *d* Edgar G. Ulmer *ph* Bert Glennon *m* Werner Janssen

Zachary Scott, Sidney Greenstreet, Diana Lynn, Louis Hayward, Martha Vickers, Lucille Bremer, Edith Barrett, Raymond Burr, Dennis Hoey

'Beginning pictures at the end
Is, I'm afraid, the modern trend.
But I'd find *Ruthless* much more winning
If it could end at the beginning.'
—*C. A. Lejeune*

Ruthless People*
US 1986 93m De Luxe
Touchstone / Silver Screen Partners / Wagner-Lancaster

Comic kidnappers find they have on their hands a troublesome woman whose husband won't pay for her return.
Raucous comedy which packs a few good laughs before wearing out its welcome.

w Dane Launer *d* Jim Abrahams, David and Jerry Zucker *ph* Jan DeBont *m* Michel Colombier

Danny DeVito, Bette Midler, Judge Reinhold, Helen Slater, Anita Morris, Bill Pulman

RX Murder
GB 1958 85m bw Cinemascope

The doctor of a small seaside resort has had four wives die on him. Could it be murder? Modest mystery with an obvious outcome. Marius Goring, Rick Jason, Lisa Gastoni, Mary Merrall, Vida Hope, Phyllis Neilson-Terry, Frederick Leister, Nicholas Hannen. Written and directed by Derek Twist, from the novel *The Deeds of Dr Deadcert* by Joan Fleming; for TCF. (GB release title: *Family Doctor.*)

Ryan's Daughter**
GB 1970 206m Metrocolor Panavision 70
MGM / Faraway (Anthony Havelock-Allan)

1916 Ireland: a village schoolmaster's wife falls for a British officer.
A modestly effective pastoral romantic melodrama, stretched on the rack of its director's meticulous film-making technique and unnecessarily big budget. A beautiful, impressive, well-staged and well-acted film, but not really four hours' worth of drama.

w Robert Bolt *d David Lean ph Frederick A. Young* *m* Maurice Jarre *pd* Stephen Grimes (who created an entire village)

Sarah Miles, Robert Mitchum, Chris Jones, John Mills, Trevor Howard, Leo McKern

'Instead of looking like the money it cost to make, the film feels like the time it took to shoot.'—*Alexander Walker*

'Gush made respectable by millions of dollars tastefully wasted.'—*Pauline Kael*

AA: Frederick A. Young; John Mills
AAN: Sarah Miles

S.O.B.
US 1981 121m Metrocolor Panavision
Lorimar / Geoffrey (Blake Edwards, Tony Adams)

A Hollywood director goes bananas when his much-touted epic is a fiasco, and decides to remake it as a sex picture.
Tasteless, vulgar and unfunny comedy, with everybody shouting at once and most of the jokes about vomiting, farting and funerals. Julie Andrews, who is made to bare her breasts, could surely use it as grounds for divorce.

wd Blake Edwards *ph* Harry Stradling *m* Henry Mancini

Julie Andrews, Richard Mulligan, *Robert Preston*, William Holden, Robert Vaughn, Robert Webber, Larry Hagman, Shelley Winters, Marisa Berenson, Loretta Swit, Craig Stevens, Robert Loggia

'One feels that this in-house comedy was in some way intended as a purge and not an entertainment.'—*John Pym, MFB*

'At best the humour is cheap and at worst unnecessarily vulgar.'—*Margaret Hinxman, Daily Mail*

† S.O.B., it seems, stands no longer for Son Of a Bitch but for Standard Operational Bullshit.

SOS Coast Guard
US 1937 bw serial: 12 eps

The coast guards combat a half-mad inventor who is prepared to sell to all comers his deadly disintegrating gas. Hilarious thick ear, one of the more revivable serials. Ralph Byrd, Bela Lugosi, Maxine Doyle, Herbert Rawlinson, Lawrence Grant. Directed by William Witney and Alan James; for Republic.

SOS Iceberg*
US 1933 117m (at first showings) bw

A young scientist seeks to recover the records of the lost Wegener expedition to the Arctic.
At the time this was a spectacular semi-documentary, but it did no business. Rod la Rocque, Leni Riefenstahl, Sepp Rist, Gibson Gowland. Written by Tom Reed, Edwin H. Knopf; directed by Tay Garnett, for Universal.
† The production was begun in Berlin and taken over by Universal when the producers ran out of money.

SOS Pacific*
GB 1959 91m bw
Rank / Sydney Box (John Nasht, Patrick Filmer-Sankey)

Survivors of a Pacific plane crash await rescue on a small island which is the site of an imminent H-bomb test.
Satisfactory open-air thick ear with strongly deployed types and a suspense climax.

w Robert Westerby *d* Guy Green *ph* Wilkie Cooper *m* Georges Auric

Eddie Constantine, Pier Angeli, John Gregson, Richard Attenborough, Eva Bartok, Clifford Evans, Jean Anderson, Cec Linder

Saadia
US 1953 87m Technicolor
MGM (Albert Lewin)

A young French doctor in the Sahara has trouble with the local witch doctor.
Pretentious and ill-considered multi-national romance from the champion of Omar's Rubaiyat.

wd Albert Lewin, *novel* Echec au Destin by Francis D'Autheville *ph* Christopher Challis *m* Bronislau Kaper

Cornel Wilde, Mel Ferrer, Rita Gam, Michel Simon, Wanda Rotha, Cyril Cusack, Marcel Poncin, Peter Bull

Sabotage***
GB 1936 76m bw
Gaumont British (Michael Balcon, Ivor Montagu)
US title: *A Woman Alone*

The proprietor of a small London cinema is a dangerous foreign agent.
Unattractively plotted but fascinatingly detailed Hitchcock suspenser with famous sequences and a splendidly brooding melodramatic atmosphere.

w Charles Bennett, Ian Hay, Helen Simpson, E. V. H. Emmett, *novel* The Secret Agent by Joseph Conrad *d Alfred Hitchcock* *ph* Bernard Knowles *md* Louis Levy

Oscar Homolka, Sylvia Sidney, John Loder, Desmond Tester, Joyce Barbour, Matthew Boulton

'Tightly packed, economical, full of invention and detail.'—*NFT, 1961*

Saboteur***
US 1942 108m bw
Universal (Frank Lloyd, Jack H. Skirball)

A war worker unjustly suspected of sabotage flees across the country and unmasks a spy ring.
Flawed Hitchcock action thriller, generally unsatisfactory in plot and pace but with splendid sequences at a ball, in Radio City Music Hall, and atop the Statue of Liberty.

w Peter Viertel, Joan Harrison, Dorothy Parker, *story* Alfred Hitchcock *d Alfred Hitchcock* *ph* Joseph Valentine *m* Frank Skinner *md* Charles Previn

Robert Cummings, Priscilla Lane, Otto Kruger, Alan Baxter, Alma Kruger, *Norman Lloyd*

'It throws itself forward so rapidly that it allows slight opportunity for looking back.'—*New York Times*

'The drama of a nation stirred to action, of a people's growing realization of themselves and their responsibilities.'—*Motion Picture Herald*
† Hitchcock wanted for the three leading roles Gary Cooper, Barbara Stanwyck and Harry Carey, but all refused or were unavailable.

'World War II espionage adventure and human lives have never before been combined so explosively!'

The Saboteur, Code Name Morituri*
US 1965 122m bw
TCF / Arcola / Colony (Aaron Rosenberg)
aka: *Morituri; The Saboteur*

In 1942 a German pacifist working for the allies is actually a German spy.
Dreary as a whole, suspenseful in snatches, this shipboard melodrama is full of irrelevancies and is in any case played much more seriously than the matter demands.

w Daniel Taradash, *novel* Werner Jeorg Kosa *d* Bernhard Wicki *ph* Conrad Hall *m* Jerry Goldsmith

Yul Brynner, Marlon Brando, Trevor Howard, Janet Margolin

AAN: Conrad Hall

Sabre Jet
US 1953 96m Cinecolor

A US Air Force colonel in Korea has trouble with his career-hunting wife as well as with the enemy. Propaganda cheapie with a few stirring aerial moments. Robert Stack, Coleen Gray,

Richard Arlen, Julie Bishop, and Leon Ames, Amanda Blake. Written by Dale Eunson and Katherine Albert; directed by Louis King; for Krueger Productions / UA.

Sabrina*
US 1954 113m bw
Paramount (Billy Wilder)
GB title: *Sabrina Fair*

The chauffeur's daughter is wooed by both her brother employers.
Superior comedy, rather uneasily cast.

w Billy Wilder, *play* Samuel Taylor *d* Billy Wilder *ph* Charles Lang Jnr *m* Frederick Hollander

Humphrey Bogart, William Holden, Audrey Hepburn, Walter Hampden, John Williams, Martha Hyer, Joan Vohs, Marcel Dalio

'This is never less than a glittering entertainment, but somehow a certain measure of lead has found its way into the formula.'—*Time*

† Cary Grant was sought for the role played by Bogart.

AAN: Billy Wilder (as writer and director); Charles Lang Jnr; Audrey Hepburn

The Sad Sack
US 1957 98m bw Vistavision
Paramount (Paul Nathan)

Adventures of an army misfit.
Resistible star comedy.

w Edmund Beloin, Nate Monaster, *cartoon* George Baker *d* George Marshall *ph* Loyal Griggs *m* Walter Scharf

Jerry Lewis, David Wayne, Phyllis Kirk, Peter Lorre, Joe Mantell, Gene Evans, George Dolenz, Liliane Montvecchi, Shepperd Strudwick

Saddle the Wind*
US 1958 84m Metrocolor Cinemascope
MGM (Armand Deutsch)

A reformed gunman's young brother gets into bad company.
Modestly effective, humourless western drama.

w Rod Serling *d* Robert Parrish *ph* George J. Folsey *m* Jeff Alexander

Robert Taylor, John Cassavetes, Julie London, Donald Crisp, Charles McGraw, Royal Dano, Richard Erdman

Saddle Tramp
US 1950 76m Technicolor

A wandering cowboy adopts four orphan children and after various adventures marries the eldest of them. Mild family western for star fanciers. Joel McCrea, Wanda Hendrix, John Russell, John McIntire, Jeanette Nolan, Russell Simpson. Written by Harold Shumate; directed by Hugo Fregonese; for Universal-International.

Sadie McKee*
US 1934 88m bw
MGM (Lawrence Weingarten)

A maid at various times loves her master, a young ne'er-do-well, and a middle-aged millionaire.
Solidly carpentered millgirl's romance of the period.

w John Meehan, *story* Vina Delmar
d Clarence Brown *ph* Oliver T. Marsh
m William Axt

Joan Crawford, Franchot Tone, Gene Raymond, Edward Arnold, Esther Ralston, Jean Dixon, Leo Carrillo, Akim Tamiroff

'The stuff the fans cry for.'—*Hollywood Reporter*

Sadie Thompson*
US 1928 95m (24 fps) bw silent
Gloria Swanson

In the South Seas, a fire-and-brimstone missionary is attracted to a prostitute.
Steamy, much-filmed melodrama (see *Rain, Miss Sadie Thompson*). This version has long been unavailable for revaluation.

w G. Gardner Sullivan, *story* Rain by W. Somerset Maugham *d* Raoul Walsh
ph George Barnes, Robert Kurrle *ad* William Cameron Menzies

Gloria Swanson, Lionel Barrymore, Blanche Frederici, Charles Lane, Florence Midgley, Raoul Walsh

'It's stirring and ironic and funny. You couldn't ask more.'—*Photoplay*

AAN: George Barnes; Gloria Swanson

'Her hungry heart beat to tom-tom rhythm!'
Safari
US 1940 82m bw

A disillusioned girl goes to Africa with her sportsman fiancé, but falls for the hired white hunter. We had heard that before, even in 1940. Moderate time-passer. Douglas Fairbanks Jnr, Madeleine Carroll, Tullio Carminati, Billy Gilbert, Muriel Angelus, Lynne Overman. Written by Delmer Daves, from story by Paul Hervey Fox; directed by Edward H. Griffith; for Anthony Veiller / Paramount.

Safari
GB 1956 91m Technicolor Cinemascope
Warwick (Adrian Worker)

A white hunter falls in love with the wife of his employer and luckily the latter is killed by the Mau Mau.
Feeble adventure story exploiting political tensions.

w Anthony Veiller *d* Terence Young
ph John Wilcox, Fred Ford, Ted Moore
m William Alwyn

Victor Mature, Janet Leigh, Roland Culver, John Justin, Earl Cameron, Liam Redmond, Orlando Martins

The Safecracker
GB 1958 96m bw
MGM / Coronado (David E. Rose)

A safecracker is released to help in a commando raid during World War II.
One-twelfth of a dirty dozen, with a long indecisive lead-up and not much pull as drama or comedy.

w Paul Monash, *story* Rhys Davies *d* Ray Milland *ph* Gerald Gibbs *m* Richard Rodney Bennett

Ray Milland, Barry Jones, Jeanette Sterke, Victor Maddern, Ernest Clark, Cyril Raymond, Melissa Stribling

Safety Last***
US 1923 70m (24 fps) bw silent
Harold Lloyd

A small-town boy goes to the big city and to impress his girl friend enters a contest to climb a skyscraper.
Marvellous star comedy which set a new standard not only in sight gags but in the comedy-thrill stunts which became Lloyd's stock-in-trade.

w Harold Lloyd, Sam Taylor, Tim Whelan, Hal Roach *d* Sam Taylor, Fred Newmeyer
ph Walter Lundin

Harold Lloyd, Mildred Davis, Noah Young

The Saga of Anatahan
Japan 1953 90m bw

During the Pacific war, castaways on a remote island kill each other for the sake of one woman. A curious footnote to its director's career, this mannered film is entirely in Japanese with English commentary, and does not recommend itself to western audiences. Written and directed by Josef Von Sternberg; for Daiwa productions.

Sahara**
US 1943 97m bw
Columbia (Harry Joe Brown)

During the retreat from Tobruk a group of men of mixed nationality find water for themselves and harass the Nazis.
Good, simple war actioner with a realistic feel and strong characters deployed in melodramatic situations.

w John Howard Lawson, Zoltan Korda
d Zoltan Korda *ph* Rudolph Maté *m* Miklos Rozsa

Humphrey Bogart, Bruce Bennett, Lloyd Bridges, Rex Ingram, J. Carrol Naish, Dan Duryea, Kurt Kreuger

'It borrows, chiefly from the English, a sort of light-alloy modification of realism which makes the traditional Hollywood idiom seem as obsolete as a minuet.'—*James Agee*

'The tank keeps rolling, picking up strays along the way until it has a full Hollywood ethnic complement.'—*Pauline Kael, 70s*

AAN: Rudolph Maté; J. Carrol Naish

Said O'Reilly to MacNab
GB 1937 83m bw

A rich Scot is afflicted by an Irish conman. Lively ethnic comedy, a good vehicle for two stars. Will Mahoney, Will Fyffe, Ellis Drake,

Sandy McDougal. Written by Leslie Arliss, Howard Irving Young; directed by William Beaudine; for Gainsborough. (US title: *Sez O'Reilly to McNab*.) 'Most hinterland exhibs have the quakes and headaches when it comes time on their sked to play a British film, but here's one, if sold along American lines, which may be found acceptable to the patrons in most places.'—*Variety*

'It's dynamite—when these two come together in the powderkeg city of the Far East!'

Saigon
US 1947 93m bw
Paramount (P. J. Wolfson)

Veteran airmen in Saigon are offered half a million to help in a robbery.
Tired studio-set star actioner.

w P. J. Wolfson, Arthur Sheekman *d* Leslie Fenton *ph* John Seitz *m* Robert Emmett Dolan

Alan Ladd, Veronica Lake, Douglas Dick, Wally Cassell, Luther Adler, Morris Carnovsky, Mikhail Rasumny

Sail a Crooked Ship
US 1961 88m bw
Columbia / Philip Barry Jnr

A shipowner unwittingly takes on a crew of crooks intending to use the boat as a getaway after a bank robbery.
Flimsy comedy sustained by a star comedian.

w Ruth Brooks Flippen, Bruce Geller, *novel* Nathaniel Benchley *d* Irving Brecher *ph* Joseph Biroc *m* George Duning

Robert Wagner, *Ernie Kovacs,* Dolores Hart, Carolyn Jones, Frank Gorshin

Sailing Along
GB 1938 90m bw
Gaumont-British (Michael Balcon)

A girl barge hand meets an impresario and becomes a dancing star.
Rather deadly British musical romance with the star not at her best, the supporting talents wasted, and a generally heavy hand in evidence.

wd Sonnie Hale *ph* Glen MacWilliams *m / ly* Arthur Johnston, Maurice Sigler *ad* Alfred Junge

Jessie Matthews, Roland Young, Barry Mackay, Jack Whiting, Noel Madison, Alastair Sim, Athene Seyler, Frank Pettingell

Sailor Beware
US 1952 103m bw
Paramount / Hal B. Wallis

Martin and Lewis in the navy.
Unlovable star antics.

w James Allardice, Martin Rackin, *play* Kenyon Nicholson, Charles Robinson *d* Hal Walker *ph* Daniel L. Fapp *m* Joseph J. Lilley

Dean Martin, Jerry Lewis, Corinne Calvet, Marion Marshall, Robert Strauss, Leif Erickson

Sailor Beware*
GB 1956 80m bw
Romulus (Jack Clayton)
US title: *Panic in the Parlor*

A young sailor has trouble with his mother-in-law-to-be.
Plain but adequate film version of a successful lowbrow stage farce about an archetypal female dragon.

w Philip King and Falkland L. Cary, from their play *d* Gordon Parry *ph* Douglas Slocombe *m* Peter Akister

Peggy Mount, Esma Cannon, Cyril Smith, Shirley Eaton, Ronald Lewis

'It's the music-hall mother-in-law joke inflated to gigantic proportions.'—*The Times*

The Sailor Takes a Wife
US 1945 91m bw

A sailor on leave gets married and finds he has acquired a few problems. Rather self-consciously cute sentimental comedy, proficiently staged. June Allyson, Robert Walker, Reginald Owen, Hume Cronyn, Eddie Anderson, Audrey Totter, Gerald Oliver Smith. Written by Anne Chapin and Whitfield Cook, from a play by Chester Erskine; directed by Richard Whorf; for MGM.

'He gave his soul to the sea and his heart to a woman! Their love will arouse you—their story will disturb you—the ending will startle you!'

The Sailor Who Fell from Grace with the Sea
GB 1976 105m Technicolor
AVCO / Sailor Company (Martin Poll)

A precocious boy interferes with his widowed mother's affair with a sailor by castrating the latter.
Weird and unattractive sex fantasy set in Dartmouth of all places and not helped by tiresome sex scenes.

wd Lewis John Carlino, *novel* Gogo No Eiko by Mishima Yukio *ph* Douglas Slocombe *m* John Mandel

Sarah Miles, Kris Kristofferson, Jonathan Kahn, Margo Cunningham, Earl Rhodes

'Like the act of love, this film must be experienced from beginning to end!'—*publicity*

'This everyday tale of torture, scopophilia, copulation, masturbation, dismemberment and antique dealing deserves to be traded back to the Japs and made required viewing for timorous kamikaze pilots.'—*Benny Green, Punch*

The Sailor's Return
GB 1978 100m colour

A Victorian seaman returns to his native village with a black bride, and opens a pub. Lame-paced and highly predictable yarn of prejudice and doomed love, assembled with almost no cinematic flair. Tom Bell, Shope Sodeinde, Elton Charles, Mick Ford, Clive Swift. Written by James Saunders from the novel by David Garnett; directed by Jack Gold; for Euston Films. (As a theatrical film it found no takers, and in GB was first shown on television in 1980.)

Sailors Three**
GB 1940 86m bw
Ealing (Culley Forde)
US title: *Three Cockeyed Sailors*

Drunken sailors capture a German battleship by mistake.
Low service comedy which keeps moving, is brightly played and reaches a good standard. Sequel: *Fiddlers Three* (qv).

w Angus Macphail, John Dighton, Austin Melford *d* Walter Forde *ph* Gunther Krampf *md* Ernest Irving

Tommy Trinder, Claude Hulbert, Michael Wilding, Carla Lehmann, Jeanne de Casalis, James Hayter, John Laurie

The Saint

Leslie Charteris' famous character, the reformed British gentleman crook who becomes a Robin Hood of crime, has been most popular in the long-running sixties TV series starring Roger Moore. The films which featured him never seemed to hit quite the right note, and now seem slow. All were made for RKO, who later switched allegiance to THE FALCON (qv).

1938: THE SAINT IN NEW YORK
1939: THE SAINT STRIKES BACK, THE SAINT IN LONDON
1940: THE SAINT'S DOUBLE TROUBLE, THE SAINT TAKES OVER
1941: THE SAINT IN PALM SPRINGS, THE SAINT'S VACATION
THE SAINT MEETS THE TIGER
1953: THE SAINT'S RETURN (US: THE SAINT'S GIRL FRIDAY)

Louis Hayward played the role in the first and last; Hugh Sinclair in VACATION and TIGER; George Sanders in the rest.

St Benny the Dip
US 1951 79m bw
Danzigers
GB title: *Escape If You Can*

Gamblers learn to escape the law by dressing as priests, but circumstance converts them to good works.
Unfunny comedy notable only for its cast.

w John Roeburt *d* Edgar G. Ulmer *ph* Don Malkames *m* Robert Stringer

Freddie Bartholemew, Roland Young, Dick Haymes, Lionel Stander, Nina Foch

'The passion burns deep!'

St Elmo's Fire
US 1985 108m Metrocolor
Columbia / Lauren Shuler

A group of college graduates drift apart as realities impinge on their lives.

Nobody explained why audiences should want to interest themselves in such a group of objectionable people; and they didn't.

w Joel Schumacher, Carl Kurlander *d* Joel Schumacher *ph* Stephen H. Burum *m* David Foster

Rob Lowe, Demi Moore, Andrew McCarthy, Judd Nelson, Ally Sheedy, Emilio Estevez, Mare Winningham, Martin Balsam

'He's clean! He's mean! He's the go-between!'

St Ives

US 1976 93m Technicolor

Warner (Pancho Kohner, Stanley Kanter)

An ex-police reporter gets involved in a complex murder puzzle.

Soporific suspenser with every tired situation in the book.

w Barry Beckerman, *novel* The Procane Chronicle by Oliver Bleeck *d* J. Lee-Thompson *ph* Lucien Ballard *m* Lalo Schifrin

Charles Bronson, Harry Guardino, John Houseman, Jacqueline Bisset, Maximilian Schell, Harris Yulin, Dana Elcar, Elisha Cook Jnr

'Much cross-cutting of the sort where the only events you care less about than the ones you cut from are the ones you cut to.'—*John Simon*

'People make love for so many crazy reasons—why shouldn't money be one of them?'

Saint Jack

US 1979 115m colour

New World / Shoals Creek / Playboy / Copa de Oro (Roger Corman)

An American wanderer in Singapore finds his metier as a pimp.

Whimsical, loquacious black comedy which failed to set its wavering director back on the firm ground he needed.

w Peter Bogdanovich, Howard Sackler, Paul Theroux, *novel* Paul Theroux *d* Peter Bogdanovich *ph* Robby Muller *m* various

Ben Gazzara, Denholm Elliott, James Villiers, Joss Ackland, Rodney Bewes, Mark Kingston, Lisa Lu, George Lazenby, Peter Bogdanovich

Saint Joan

GB 1957 110m bw

Wheel (Otto Preminger)

Glumly assembled screen version of the brilliantly argumentative play about the Maid of Orleans. Plenty of talent, but neither wit nor style.

w Graham Greene, *play* Bernard Shaw *d* Otto Preminger *ph* Georges Périnal *m* Mischa Spoliansky *pd* Roger Furse

Jean Seberg, Anton Walbrook, Richard Widmark, John Gielgud, Felix Aylmer, Harry Andrews, Richard Todd

St Louis Blues*

US 1939 92m bw

Paramount (Jeff Lazarus)

A Broadway musical star finds new fame down south.

Moderate star entertainment with good guest artists.

w John C. Moffitt, Malcolm Stuart Boylan, Frederick Hazlitt Brennan *d* Raoul Walsh *ph* Theodor Sparkuhl *songs* Frank Loesser, Burton Lane

Dorothy Lamour, Lloyd Nolan, Tito Guizar, Jerome Cowan, Jessie Ralph, William Frawley, the King's Men, Matty Melneck and his Orchestra

'It doesn't quite jell but will suffice as passable divertissement.'—*Variety*

St Louis Blues

US 1958 93m bw VistaVision

Paramount (Robert Smith)

W. C. Handy, son of a black Memphis preacher, becomes a blues composer.

Unsurprising biopic with some good music and the usual strained plot about father's disapproval of the new music.

w Robert Smith, Ted Sherdeman *d* Allen Reisner *ph* Haskell Boggs *md* Nelson Riddle

Nat King Cole, Eartha Kitt, Pearl Bailey, Cab Calloway, Mahalia Jackson, Ruby Dee, Juano Hernandez, Ella Fitzgerald

The St Louis Kid

US 1934 67m bw

Warner (Sam Bischoff)

GB title: *A Perfect Weekend*

A hot-headed truck driver takes the side of milk farmers in a trade dispute.

Modest star action comedy with a fair amount to amuse.

w Seton I. Miller, Warren Duff *d* Ray Enright *ph* Sid Hickox

James Cagney, Patricia Ellis, Hobart Cavanaugh, Spencer Charters, Addison Richards

'Jimmy in another slugger role, with results this time not so satisfactory.'—*Variety*

St Martin's Lane*

GB 1938 85m bw

Mayflower (Erich Pommer)

US title: *Sidewalks of London*

A middle-aged busker falls in love with a brilliant girl dancer who becomes a star.

Well-made romantic drama with star performances and interesting theatrical background.

w Clemence Dane *d* Tim Whelan *ph* Jules Kruger *m* Arthur Johnson

Charles Laughton, Vivien Leigh, Rex Harrison, Tyrone Guthrie, Larry Adler, Gus MacNaughton

'In its choice of subject, its overwhelming interest in character and its introspective, uncompromising treatment, it is experimental in a courageous fashion.'—*Film Weekly*

The St Valentine's Day Massacre

US 1967 99m De Luxe Panavision

TCF / Los Altos (Roger Corman)

The twenties gang war between Al Capone and Bugs Moran.

The director's first big studio film is disappointing; stagey, poorly developed, unconvincing-looking and overacted.

w Howard Browne *d* Roger Corman *ph* Milton Krasner *m* Fred Steiner *md* Lionel Newman

Jason Robards Jnr, George Segal, Ralph Meeker, Jean Hale, Clint Ritchie, Joseph Campanella, Richard Bakalyan, David Canary, Bruce Dern, Harold J. Stone, Kurt Kreuger, John Agar, Alex D'Arcy

'You'll love every illegal inch of 'em!'

The Sainted Sisters

US 1948 89m bw

Paramount (Richard Maibaum)

Two New York con girls find themselves taken in by the inhabitants of the small town in which they are hiding out.

Unfunny period comedy which misses on all cylinders.

w Harry Clark *d* William D. Russell *ph* Lionel Lindon *m* Van Cleave

Veronica Lake, Joan Caulfield, Barry Fitzgerald, William Demarest, George Reeves, Beulah Bondi, Chill Wills, Darryl Hickman

'Lake, Caulfield, and a swarm of clichés, pleasantly kidded in a manner derived from Preston Sturges.'—*James Agee*

Saints and Sinners

GB 1948 85m bw

An ex-convict comes back to his home town to prove that those who condemned him were fools or knaves. Curious slice of Irish whimsy mixed with Ealing comedy; not very satisfactory. Kieron Moore, Christine Norden, Sheila Manahan, Michael Dolan, Maire O'Neill, Noel Purcell. Written by Paul Vincent Carroll and Leslie Arliss; directed by Leslie Arliss; for London Films / BLPA.

Sally

US 1930 *c.* 90m Technicolor

Warner

A waitress makes it to the lights of Broadway.

Lightweight musical play, previously filmed in 1925 with Colleen Moore and Leon Errol, here the basis of an elaborate colour production with its original star, who however did not take too kindly to the camera.

w Waldemar Young, *play* Guy Bolton and Jerome Kern *d* John Francis Dillon *ph* Dev Jennings, E. E. Schoenbaum *ch* Larry Ceballos

Marilyn Miller, Joe E. Brown, Alexander Grey, T. Roy Barnes, Pert Kelton, Ford Sterling.

Sally and St Anne

US 1952 90m bw

U-I (Leonard Goldstein)

When an Irish-American family is threatened

with eviction, the daughter appeals to St Anne for help.
Whimsical comedy, quite nimbly performed.

w James O'Hanlon, Herb Meadow
d Rudolph Maté *ph* Irving Glassberg
m Frank Skinner

Ann Blyth, Edmund Gwenn, Hugh O'Brian, John McIntire, Jack Kelly

Sally in Our Alley*
GB 1931 77m bw
ATP / Basil Dean

Poor girl loves wounded soldier.
Early talkie drama with music which made Gracie Fields a star and gave her a theme song.

w Miles Malleson, Archie Pitt, Alma Reville, *play* The Likes of 'Er by Charles McEvoy
d Maurice Elvey *ph* Robert G. Martin, Alex Bryce

Gracie Fields, Ian Hunter, Florence Desmond, Ivor Barnard

'The songs are just numbers, the general standard nothing to shout about.'—*Variety*

Sally, Irene and Mary
US 1938 86m bw
TCF (Gene Markey)

Three girls try to break into show business.
Simple-minded romantic comedy-musical, well enough done.

w Harry Tugend, Jack Yellen *d* William A. Seiter *ph* Peverell Marley *md* Arthur Lange

Alice Faye, Tony Martin, Fred Allen, Jimmy Durante, Gregory Ratoff, Joan Davis, Marjorie Weaver, Gypsy Rose Lee

'Palatable light entertainment that is no Pulitzer prizer but prize b.o.'—*Variety*

Sally of the Sawdust
US 1925 78m at 24 fps bw silent

A circus juggler and faker tries to prevent his daughter from discovering that she is adopted. Silent version of the stage hit *Poppy*, remade under its own title in 1936 (qv). In both versions W. C. Fields takes over the whole show (not to one's entire satisfaction) and the director's name in this case should not lead one to expect a film of significance, as he seems to have been glad of the work. With Carol Dempster, Alfred Lunt, Effie Shannon, Erville Anderson. Written by Forrest Halsey, from the play by Dorothy Donnelly; directed by D. W. Griffith; for Paramount / United Artists.

Salome
US 1923 80m at 24 fps bw silent

Almost unendurable as an entertainment, this stylized silent provided a famous role for its star against backgrounds in Aubrey Beardsley style, and is much illustrated in film histories. The *New Yorker* commented on a 1980 revival: 'The movie looks better in stills than when one actually sees it, but a folly like this should probably be experienced.' Nazimova, Mitchell Lewis, Nigel de Brulier, Based on Aubrey Beardsley's drawings and Oscar Wilde's play; sets and costumes by Natacha Rambova; directed by Charles Bryant; for Nazimova.

'The supreme screen achievement of our time!'
Salome
US 1953 103m Technicolor
Columbia / Beckworth (Buddy Adler)

Princess Salome of Galilee eludes her licentious stepfather, falls in love with a secret Christian, and leaves home when her dancing fails to save the life of John the Baptist.
Distorted biblical hokum with an interesting cast frozen into unconvincing attitudes.

w Harry Kleiner, Jesse Lasky Jnr *d* William Dieterle *ph* Charles Lang *m* George Duning *md* Daniele Amfitheatrof *ad* John Meehan

Rita Hayworth, Charles Laughton, Stewart Granger, Judith Anderson, Cedric Hardwicke, Alan Badel, Basil Sydney, Maurice Schwartz, Rex Reason, Arnold Moss

'Pomp and splendour are paraded across the screen as a background to the story's combination of sex and religion.'—*Variety*

Salome Where She Danced*
US 1945 90m Technicolor
Universal (Walter Wanger, Alexander Golitzen)

During the Austro-Prussian war a dancer is suspected of being a spy and flees to Arizona, where she affects the lives of the citizenry.
Absurdly plotted and stiffly played romantic actioner whose sheer creakiness made it a minor cult film.

w Laurence Stallings, *story* Michael J. Phillips *d* Charles Lamont *ph* Hal Mohr, W. Howard Green *m* Edward Ward

Yvonne de Carlo, Rod Cameron, Albert Dekker, David Bruce, Walter Slezak, Marjorie Rambeau, J. Edward Bromberg, Abner Biberman, John Litel, Kurt Katch

'I gratefully salute it as the funniest dead-pan parody I have ever seen.'—*James Agee*

Saloon Bar*
GB 1940 76m bw
Ealing (Michael Balcon)

A murder is solved during an evening in a pub.
Amusing, well-made little suspenser from a West End success.

w Angus MacPhail, John Dighton, *play* Frank Harvey *d* Walter Forde *ph* Ronald Neame *md* Ernest Irving

Gordon Harker, Elizabeth Allen, Mervyn Johns, Joyce Barbour, Anna Konstam, Judy Campbell, Norman Pierce, Alec Clunes, Felix Aylmer, Mavis Villiers, Torin Thatcher, O. B. Clarence

'The detail has been sought lovingly and with exactitude . . . this is a modest and endearing film.'—*New Statesman*

Salt and Pepper
GB 1968 101m De Luxe
UA / Chrislaw / Tracemark (Milton Ebbins)

Soho nightclub proprietors solve a murder.
Infuriating throwaway star vehicle set in the dregs of swinging London. The sequel, *One More Time* (1970), was quite unnecessary.

w Michael Pertwee *d* Richard Donner
ph Ken Higgins *m* Johnny Dankworth

Sammy Davis Jnr, Peter Lawford, Michael Bates, Ilona Rodgers, John Le Mesurier, Graham Stark, Ernest Clark

Salty O'Rourke
US 1945 100m bw
Paramount / E. D. Leshin

A racetrack con man is reformed by a schoolteacher.
Very moderate and overlong star vehicle.

w Milton Holmes *d* Raoul Walsh
ph Theodor Sparkuhl *m* Robert Emmett Dolan

Alan Ladd, Gail Russell, William Demarest, Bruce Cabot, Spring Byington, Stanley Clements

AAN: Milton Holmes

Saludos Amigos*
US 1943 43m Technicolor
Walt Disney

Donald Duck has various South American adventures with a parrot named Joe Carioca.
Basically a naïve implementation of the good neighbour policy, but with flashes of brilliant animation and some mingling of live-action with cartoon.

Production supervisor Norman Ferguson

'Self-interested, belated ingratiation embarrasses me, and Disney's famous cuteness, however richly it may mirror national infantilism, is hard on my stomach.'—*James Agee*

AAN: music (Edward J. Plumb, Paul J. Smith, Charles Wolcott); title song (*m* Charles Wolcott, *ly* Ned Washington)

Salute for Three
US 1943 75m bw

An all-girl orchestra opens a canteen for servicemen. Modest, middling propaganda musical with minimum talents. Betty Jane Rhodes, Macdonald Carey, Dona Drake and her orchestra, Marty May, Lorraine and Rognan. Written by Davis Anderson, Curtis Kenyon, Hugh Wedlock Jnr and Howard Snyder; directed by Ralph Murphy; for Paramount.

Salute John Citizen
GB 1942 98m bw
British National (Wallace Orton)

A clerk and his family suffer cheerfully through the blitz.
Modest, competent propaganda piece.

w Clemence Dane, Elizabeth Baron, *novel* Mr Bunting at War by Robert Greenwood
d Maurice Elvey *ph* James Wilson

Edward Rigby, Stanley Holloway, George Robey, Mabel Constanduros, Jimmy Hanley, Dinah Sheridan, Peggy Cummins, Stewart Rome

Salute to the Marines
US 1943 101m Technicolor
MGM (John Considine Jnr)

A sergeant-major struggles to get his family out of the Philippines when the Japs attack.
Recruiting poster heroics with comedy interludes.

w Wells Root, George Bruce, *story* Robert Andrews *d* S. Sylvan Simon *ph* Charles Schoenbaum, W. Howard Green *m* Lennie Hayton

Wallace Beery, Fay Bainter, Marilyn Maxwell, William Lundigan, Keye Luke, Reginald Owen, Ray Collins, Noah Beery, Russell Gleason

Salvador*
US 1986 123m colour
Hemdale / Gerald Green, Oliver Stone

Adventures of an American photo-journalist in Central America.
Drama torn from the headlines; it should perhaps have stayed there, as few people proved to be interested in paying to see it. One cannot, however, deny its brilliant if superficial technical command.

w Oliver Stone, Richard Boyle *d* Oliver Stone *ph* Robert Richardson *m* Georges Delerue

James Woods, James Belushi, Michael Murphy, John Savage

'As raw, difficult, compelling, unreasonable, reckless and vivid as its protagonist.'—*Variety*

AAN: best original screenplay; James Woods

The Salvation Hunters**
US 1925 65m (24 fps) bw silent
Academy Photoplays (Josef Von Sternberg, George K. Arthur)

Among the mud flats of San Pedro, a boy wins his girl from a brute.
Mini-budgeted minor classic whose very artiness and pretentiousness were keys to its director's later development.

wd Josef Von Sternberg ph Josef Von Sternberg, Edward Gheller

George K. Arthur, Georgia Hale, Bruce Guerin

'Audience reaction was: even *our* lives are not so drab as this, and if they are we don't want to know about it. Asked to comment on the failure of a film he had praised so highly, Chaplin said, "Well, you know I was only kidding. They all take everything I say so seriously. I thought I'd praise a bad picture and see what happened." '—*Richard Griffith and Arthur Mayer, The Movies*

Salvation Nell
US 1931 83m bw

A wronged girl sinks lower and lower until she joins the Salvation Army. One thinks it must have been meant as a spoof, but apparently not. Helen Chandler, Ralph Graves, Sally O'Neill, Jason Robards, Dewitt Jennings. Written by Selma Stein, Walter Woods, from the play by Edward Sheldon; directed by James Cruze; for Tiffany. 'It probably will be livelier in the states, where the Mme Cloquette scene is not cut out.'—*Variety*

Salvatore Giuliano*
Italy 1961 125m bw
Lux / Vides / Galatea (Franco Cristaldi)

The bullet-ridden body of key Sicilian Mafia leader Giuliano triggers flashbacks to his complex and brutal career.
Vivid, sometimes obscure, politically oriented melodrama based on fact. Undoubtedly a local classic, but not an easy film to appreciate.

w Francesco Rosi, Suso Cecchi d'Amico, Enzo Provenzale, Franco Solinas *d Francesco Rosi ph* Gianni di Venanzo *m* Piero Piccioni

Frank Wolff, Salvo Randone, Federico Zardi

'Epic reportage in the twentieth-century manner of a society reminiscent of some backward corner of the nineteenth century.'—*Peter John Dyer, MFB*

The Salzburg Connection
US 1972 93m De Luxe Panavision
TCF (Ingo Preminger)

An American lawyer on holiday in Salzburg finds himself suspected by spies of both sides.
Turgid, routine action thriller with attractive locations.

w Oscar Millard, *novel* Helen MacInnes *d* Lee H. Katzin *ph* Wolfgang Treu *md* Lionel Newman

Barry Newman, Anna Karina, Maria Brandauer, Karen Jensen, Wolfgang Preiss

'So dull you can't tell the CIA agents from the neo-Nazis or double agents—or the inept actors from the blocks and stones in the handsome Austrian locales.'—*Judith Crist*

Sam Whiskey
US 1969 96m De Luxe
UA / Brighton (Jules Levy, Arthur Gardner, Arnold Laven)

An itinerant gambler is paid to recover a fortune in gold bars from the bottom of a Colorado river.
Easy-going but rather slackly-handled western.

w William W. Norton *d* Arnold Laven *ph* Robert Moreno *m* Herschel Burke Gilbert

Burt Reynolds, Clint Walker, Ossie Davis, Angie Dickinson, Rick Davis, William Schallert

'The story of the longest-run date in the history of non-marriage!'

Same Time, Next Year*
US 1978 119m colour
Universal / Walter Mirisch, Robert Mulligan

An illicit affair is carried on for twenty-five years, the couple confining themselves to one annual meeting in a hotel.
Careful film version of a smash Broadway comedy; the flimsiness of the premise is well concealed, but it remains a one-set play.

w Bernard Slade, from his play *d* Robert Mulligan *ph* Robert Surtees *m* Marvin Hamlisch *pd* Henry Bumstead

Ellen Burstyn, Alan Alda

AAN: Bernard Slade; Robert Surtees; Ellen Burstyn; song, 'The Last Time I Felt Like This'

Sammy and Rosie Get Laid*
GB 1987 100m colour

A young Pakistani accountant in London is confused by the return of his long-lost father, and vice versa. Those who liked the harsh conflicts of *My Beautiful Laundrette* will get similar frissons from this; others will be as confused as the characters. Shashi Kapoor, Claire Bloom, Ayub Khan Din, Frances Barber, Roland Gift. Written by Hanif Kureishi; directed by Stephen Frears; for Cinecom / Film Four.

Sammy Going South*
GB 1963 128m Eastmancolor Cinemascope
Bryanston (Hal Mason)
US title: *A Boy Ten Feet Tall*

A 10-year-old boy is orphaned in Port Said and hitch-hikes to his aunt in Durban.
Disappointing family-fodder epic in which the mini-adventures follow each other too predictably.

w Denis Cannan, *novel* W. H. Canaway *d* Alexander Mackendrick *ph* Erwin Hillier *m* Tristam Cary

Fergus McClelland, Edward G. Robinson, Constance Cummings, Harry H. Corbett

'A story as timeless and tumultuous as the violent age it spreads before you!'

Samson and Delilah
US 1949 128m Technicolor
Paramount / Cecil B. de Mille

Delilah, rejected by religious strong man Samson, cuts his hair and delivers him to his enemies.
Absurd biblical hokum, stodgily narrated and directed, monotonously photographed and edited, and notable only for the 30-second destruction of the temple at the end.

w Jesse L. Lasky Jnr, Fredric M. Frank *d* Cecil B. de Mille *ph* George Barnes *m* Victor Young *ad* Hans Dreier, Walter Tyler

Hedy Lamarr, Victor Mature, Angela Lansbury, George Sanders, Henry Wilcoxon, Olive Deering, Fay Holden, Russ Tamblyn

'To ignore so enormous, over-coloured, over-stuffed, flamboyant an "epic" would be almost as absurd as taking it seriously.'—*Richard Mallett, Punch*

'Perhaps de Mille's survival is due to the fact that he decided in his movie nonage to ally himself with God as his co-maker and get his major scripts from the Bible, which he has always handled with the proprietary air of a gentleman fondling old love letters.'—*New Yorker*

AAN: George Barnes; Victor Young

San Antone
US 1952 90m bw

During the Civil War a Texas rancher antagonizes an army lieutenant. Very routine, competent western without any moment of inspiration. Rod Cameron, Forrest Tucker,

Arleen Whelan, Katy Jurado, Rodolfo Acosta. Written by Steve Fisher, from the novel *Golden Herd* by Curt Carroll; directed by Joe Kane; for Republic.

San Antonio*
US 1945 109m Technicolor
Warner (Robert Buckner)

A cowboy incurs the jealousy of a saloon owner
Typically thinly-plotted Warner star western which works well enough sequence by sequence, climaxing with a fight in the deserted Alamo.

w Alan le May, W. R. Burnett *d* David Butler *ph* Bert Glennon *m* Max Steiner

Errol Flynn, Alexis Smith, Paul Kelly, Victor Francen, S. Z. Sakall, John Litel, Florence Bates, Robert Shayne, Monte Blue, Robert Barrat

AAN: song 'Some Sunday Morning' (*m* Ray Heindorf, M. K. Jerome, *ly* Ted Koehler)

San Demetrio London*
GB 1943 105m bw
Ealing (Robert Hamer)

In 1940, the survivors of a crippled tanker bring it back home.
Rather flat and dated propaganda piece which seemed much more vivid at the time.

w Robert Hamer, Charles Frend, *story* F. Tennyson Jesse *d* Charles Frend *ph* Ernest Palmer, Roy Kellino *m* John Greenwood

Walter Fitzgerald, Mervyn Johns, Ralph Michael, Robert Beatty, Charles Victor, Frederick Piper, Gordon Jackson.

San Diego I Love You*
US 1944 83m bw
Universal (Michael Fessier, Ernest Pagano)

A family travels to San Diego to promote father's inventions.
Pleasing, easy-come-easy-go comedy full of memorable incident and characterization.

w Michael Fessier, Ernest Pagano *d* Reginald Le Borg *ph* Hal Mohr *m* Hans Salter

Louise Allbritton, Edward Everett Horton, Jon Hall, Eric Blore, *Buster Keaton*, Irene Ryan

'She fell in love with the toughest guy on the toughest street in the world!'

San Francisco****
US 1936 117m bw
MGM (John Emerson, Bernard Hyman)

The loves and career problems of a Barbary Coast saloon proprietor climax in the 1906 earthquake.
Incisive, star-packed, superbly-handled melodrama which weaves in every kind of appeal and for a finale has some of the best special effects ever conceived.

w Anita Loos, story Robert Hopkins *d W. S. Van Dyke ph Oliver T. Marsh m* Edward Ward *md Herbert Stothart montage John Hoffman title song* Bronislau Kaper

Clark Gable, Spencer Tracy, Jeanette MacDonald, Jack Holt, Jessie Ralph, Ted Healy, Shirley Ross, Al Shean, Harold Huber

'Prodigally generous and completely satisfying.'—*Frank S. Nugent*

AAN: best picture; Robert Hopkins; W. S. Van Dyke; Spencer Tracy

San Francisco Docks
US 1940 64m bw

A man accused of killing a crooked politician proves he didn't do it. Curiously pretentious melodrama with suggestions of Group Theater style; not for the action buffs, or anybody else. Burgess Meredith, Irene Hervey, Raymond Walburn, Barry Fitzgerald, Robert Armstrong, Lewis Howard. Written by Stanley Crea Rubin and Edmund L. Hartmann; directed by Arthur Lubin; for Marshall Grant / Universal.

'Between the sea and the Sierras stood the brawling gateway to gold!'

The San Francisco Story*
US 1952 90m bw
Warner / Fidelity–Vogue (Howard Welsch)

In 1856, a wanderer bound for China stops in San Francisco to get involved in politics.
Lively melodrama with good period feel.

w D. D. Beauchamp, *novel* Richard Summers *d* Robert Parrish *ph* John Seitz *m* Paul Dunlap *md* Emil Newman

Joel McCrea, Yvonne de Carlo, Sidney Blackmer, Florence Bates

San Quentin*
US 1937 70m bw
Warner (Sam Bischoff)

A convict's sister loves the warden.
Standard tough prison melodrama, competently done.

w Peter Milne, Humphrey Cobb, *story* John Bright, Robert Tasker *d* Lloyd Bacon *ph* Sid Hickox *m* Heinz Roemheld, David Raksin

Pat O'Brien, Ann Sheridan, Humphrey Bogart, Barton MacLane, Joseph Sawyer, Veda Ann Borg

'Fairly good appeal but will need pushing.'—*Variety*

San Quentin
US 1946 66m bw

A convict starts a movement for the rehabilitation of prisoners after release, but despite himself is caught up in a prison break. Tolerable support of a familiar kind. Lawrence Tierney, Barton Maclane, Marian Carr, Raymond Burr, Joe Devlin. Written by Lawrence Kimble, Arthur A. Ross and Howard J. Green; directed by Gordon Douglas; for RKO.

Sanctuary
US 1960 90m bw Cinemascope
TCF (Richard D. Zanuck)

The governor's daughter is seduced by a bootlegger, and her life goes from one tragedy to another.
Confused adaptation of unadaptable material, full of pussyfoot daring but little sense.

w James Poe, *novel* William Faulkner *d* Tony Richardson *ph* Ellsworth Fredericks *m* Alex North

Lee Remick, Bradford Dillman, Yves Montand, Odetta, Harry Townes, Howard St John, Reta Shaw, Strother Martin

The Sand Pebbles*
US 1966 193m De Luxe Panavision
TCF / Argyle / Solar (Robert Wise)

In 1926 an American gunboat patrolling the Yangtze river gets involved with Chinese warlords.
Confused action blockbuster with Vietnam parallels for those who care to pick them up; pretty thinly stretched entertainment despite the tons of explosive.

w Robert Anderson, *novel* Richard McKenna *d* Robert Wise *ph* Joseph MacDonald *m* Jerry Goldsmith

Steve McQueen, Candice Bergen, Richard Attenborough, Richard Crenna, Marayat Andriane, Mako, Larry Gates. Simon Oakland

'If it had been done twenty years ago, it would have been fast and unpretentious, with some ingeniously faked background shots . . . and we would never have asked for larger historical meanings.'—*Pauline Kael*

AAN: best picture; Joseph MacDonald; Jerry Goldsmith; Steve McQueen; Mako

Sanders of the River*
GB 1935 98m bw
London (Alexander Korda)
US title: *Bosambo*

Problems of a British colonial servant in keeping peace among the tribes.
Much-caricatured African adventure of the very old school, helped by Robeson's personality.

w Lajos Biro, Jeffrey Dell, Arthur Wimperis *stories* Edgar Wallace *d* Zoltan Korda *ph* Georges Perinal *m* Mischa Spoliansky

Leslie Banks, Paul Robeson, Nina Mae McKinney, Robert Cochran

'It will interest those who are sincerely interested in the cinema as an art form, but it will suffer the hazards of all pioneers.'—*Variety*

Sandokan the Great
Italy / France / Spain 1963 114m Techniscope

The son of the Sultan of Borneo wages jungle war against the oppressive British. A curious mixture of Tarzan and Robin Hood, this character appeared in several adventures before expiring; the first chapter is the best, or least worst. Steve Reeves, Genevieve Grad, Rik Battaglia, Andrea Bosic. Written by Fulvio Gicca and Umberto Lenzi, from the novel by Emilio Salgari; directed by Umberto Lenzi; for Filmes / CCF / Ocean.

The Sandpiper
US 1965 116m Metrocolor Panavision
MGM / Filmways (John Calley)

An artist lives with her illegitimate son in a Monterey beach shack; when she is forced to send the boy to school he attracts the attention of the minister in charge.
Absurd novelettish love story basically copied from *The Garden of Allah;* pretty seascapes are the most rewarding aspect.

w Dalton Trumbo, Michael Wilson
d Vincente Minnelli *ph* Milton Krasner
m Johnny Mandel

Elizabeth Taylor, Richard Burton, Eva Marie Saint, Charles Bronson, Robert Webber

'Straight Louisa May Alcott interlarded with discreet pornographic allusions.'—*John Simon*

'Sex-on-the-sand soap opera.'—*Robert Windeler*

AA: song 'The Shadow of Your Smile' (*m* Johnny Mandel, *ly* Paul Francis Webster)

'My name is Stryker. Sgt John M. Stryker. You're gonna be my squad!'

Sands of Iwo Jima*
US 1949 109m bw
Republic (Edmund Grainger)

During World War II in the Pacific, a tough sergeant of marines moulds raw recruits into fighting men but is himself shot by a sniper.
Celebrated star war comic, still quite hypnotic in its flagwaving way.

w Harry Brown, James Edward Grant
d Allan Dwan *ph* Reggie Lanning *m* Victor Young

John Wayne, John Agar, Adele Mara, Forrest Tucker, Arthur Franz, Julie Bishop, Richard Jaeckel

'The battle sequences are terrifyingly real . . . but the personal dramatics make up a compendium of war-picture clichés.'—*Variety*

'Say what you like about the sentimental flavour of war pictures such as this, there's no denying they keep you in your seat.'—*Richard Mallett, Punch*

AAN: Harry Brown (original story); John Wayne

Sands of the Desert
GB 1960 92m Technicolor

A diminutive travel agent goes out to investigate a desert holiday camp which has suffered from sabotage. Limp star comedy with poor studio work and meandering script. Charlie Drake, Peter Arne, Sarah Branch, Raymond Huntley, Peter Illing, Harold Kasket. Written and directed by John Paddy Carstairs; for Associated British.

Sands of the Kalahari
GB 1965 119m Technicolor
Panavision
Pendennis (Cy Endfield, Stanley Baker)

Survivors of a plane crash trek across the desert and are menaced by baboons and each other.
Hysterical melodrama with predictable heebie-jeebies by all concerned and the baddie finally left to the mercy of the monkeys. For hardened sensationalists.

wd Cy Endfield, *novel* William Mulvihill
ph Erwin Hillier *m* Johnny Dankworth

Stanley Baker, Stuart Whitman, Harry Andrews, Susannah York, Theodore Bikel, Nigel Davenport, Barry Lowe

The Sandwich Man*
GB 1966 95m Eastmancolor
Rank / Titan (Peter Newbrook)

In the course of a walking day around London a sandwich man encounters many of his eccentric acquaintances.
Spurned when it was first released, this comedy variety show, mostly in mime, can now be seen to be of a kind popularized by TV, and may have been simply ahead of its time. It certainly seems funnier than it did.

w Michael Bentine, Robert Hartford-Davis
d Robert Hartford-Davis *ph* Peter Newbrook *m* Mike Vickers

Michael Bentine, Dora Bryan, Suzy Kendall, Norman Wisdom, Harry H. Corbett, Bernard Cribbins, Ian Hendry, Stanley Holloway, Alfie Bass, Diana Dors, Ron Moody, Wilfrid Hyde White, Donald Wolfit, Max Bacon, Fred Emney, Frank Finlay, Peter Jones, Michael Medwin, Ronnie Stevens, John Le Mesurier, Sidney Tafler, John Junkin, Warren Mitchell

Sandy Gets Her Man
US 1940 65m bw

A councilman's baby gets involved in the rival claims of police and fire departments for the best funding. Rather complex excuse for a slight family comedy. Baby Sandy, Stuart Erwin, Edgar Kennedy, Una Merkel, William Frawley, Edward Brophy. Written by Sy Bartlett and Jane Storm; directed by Otis Garrett and Paul Gerard Smith; for Burt Kelly / Universal.

Sandy is a Lady
US 1940 62m bw

A baby is responsible for her father's promotion. Third of a series featuring the gurgling infant introduced in *East Side of Heaven.* (The others: *Little Accident, Unexpected Father, Sandy Gets Her Man.*) This one is an excuse for slapstick comedy situations. Baby Sandy, Butch and Buddy, Eugene Pallette, Nan Grey, Tom Brown, Mischa Auer, Billy Gilbert, Edgar Kennedy. Written by Charles Grayson; directed by Charles Lamont; for Burt Kelly / Universal.

Sangaree
US 1953 95m Technicolor 3-D
Paramount / Pine–Thomas

Trouble ensues when a plantation owner wills his wealth to the son of a slave.
Period skullduggery rather hammily presented.

w David Duncan, *novel* Frank G. Slaughter
d Edward Ludwig *ph* Lionel Lindon, W. Wallace Kelley *m* Lucien Caillet

Fernando Lamas, Arlene Dahl, Patricia Medina, Francis L. Sullivan, Charles Korvin, Tom Drake, John Sutton, Willard Parker, Lester Matthews

Sans Lendemain*
France 1940 83m bw

A night club hostess with a mysterious past is troubled when an old lover turns up. Moody melodrama in the *Quai des Brumes* tradition. Edwige Feuillère, Georges Rigaud, Georges Lannes, Paul Azais. Written by Jean Wilhelm and Max Colpet; directed by *Max Ophuls*; for Gregor Rabinovitch / Cine Alliance.

Santa Claus
GB 1985 112m Rank colour
Panavision
Alexander Salkind (Ilya Salkind, Pierre Spengler)

An old woodcutter is given immortality by the elves and turned into Santa Claus; in modern times, he goes to New York to rescue a discontented elf from the clutches of a demon toymaker.
Utterly charmless treatment of an extremely vague legend, with the two halves entirely failing to coalesce and the level of invention low throughout.

w David Newman *d* Jeannot Szwarc
ph Arthur Ibbetson *m* Henry Mancini
pd Anthony Pratt *ed* Peter Hollywood

David Huddleston, Dudley Moore, John Lithgow, Judy Cornwell, Christian Fitzpatrick, Burgess Meredith

'For children of all ages, but it skews best towards infancy or senility.'—*Variety*

Santa Fe
US 1951 89m Technicolor

After the Civil War, the eldest of four westbound brothers tries to prevent the others from becoming outlaws.
Regulation star western, with action sequences a little under par. Randolph Scott, Jerome Courtland, Janis Carter, Peter Thompson, John Archer, Warner Anderson, Roy Roberts. Written by Kenneth Gamet; directed by Irving Pichel; for Harry Joe Brown / Columbia.

Santa Fe Passage
US 1954 89m Trucolor

An Indian-hating scout with a bad record is hired to transport arms to Santa Fe. Rough-and-ready brawling western with very little going for it. John Payne, Rod Cameron, Faith Domergue, Slim Pickens, Leo Gordon. Written by Lillie Hayward; directed by William Witney; for Republic.

'The thundering story that challenges all filmdom to match its excitement!'

Santa Fe Trail**
US 1940 110m bw
Warner (Robert Fellows)

A cavalry officer is responsible for the final capture of John Brown.
The most solemn western from star or studio has impressive patches amid routine excitements.

w Robert Buckner *d Michael Curtiz* *ph* Sol Polito *m* Max Steiner

Errol Flynn, Olivia de Havilland, Raymond Massey, Ronald Reagan, Alan Hale, Van Heflin, Gene Reynolds, Henry O'Neill

Santee
US 1972 93m colour
Vagabond (Deno Paoli, Edward Platt)

A boy goes west to find his father and befriends the bounty hunter who has killed him.
Personable, violent western with adequate style and performances.

w Brand Bell *d* Gary Nelson *ph* Donald Morgan *m* Don Randi

Glenn Ford, Michael Burns, Dana Wynter, Jay Silverheels, Harry Townes, John Larch

Santiago
US 1956 92m Warnercolor Cinemascope
Warner (Martin Rackin)
GB title: *The Gun Runner*

A Mississippi paddle-boat sets out for Cuba with a consignment of guns for the rebels.
Stiff period actioner of no particular merit.

w Martin Rackin, John Twist *d* Gordon Douglas *ph* John Seitz *m* David Buttolph

Alan Ladd, Rossana Podesta, Lloyd Nolan, Chill Wills, Paul Fix, L. Q. Jones, Frank de Kova

The Saphead*
US 1920 70m (24 fps) bw silent
Metro / Buster Keaton

A shy young man reads a manual on how to win the modern girl.
Interesting early star comedy: quite winning in its way, but without the spectacular moments which were a feature of his later films.

w June Mathis, *play* The New Henrietta by Winchell Smith, Victor Mapes *d* Herbert Blache *ph* Harold Wenstrom

Buster Keaton, Beula Booker, William H. Crane, Irving Cummings

Sapphire**
GB 1959 92m Eastmancolor
Rank / Artna (Michael Relph)

Scotland Yard solves the murder of a coloured music student.
Efficient police thriller with a strong race angle.

w Janet Green *d* Basil Dearden *ph* Harry Waxman *m* Philip Green

Nigel Patrick, Michael Craig, Yvonne Mitchell, Paul Massie, Bernard Miles, Olga Lindo, Earl Cameron, Gordon Heath, Robert Adams

'A dandy murder mystery—taut, tantalizing and beautifully done.'—*Judith Crist, 1980*

Saps at Sea
US 1940 60m bw
Hal Roach

Olly needs a rest after working in a horn factory, so he and Stan take a boating holiday but are kidnapped by a gangster.
Disappointing star comedy with gags too few and too long drawn out.

w Charles Rogers, Harry Langdon, Gil Pratt, Felix Adler *d* Gordon Douglas *ph* Art Lloyd *m* Marvin Hatley

Stan Laurel, Oliver Hardy, James Finlayson, Dick Cramer, Ben Turpin

Saraband for Dead Lovers*
GB 1948 96m Technicolor
Ealing (Michael Relph)
US title: *Saraband*

The tragic love affair of Konigsmark and Sophie Dorothea, wife of the Elector of Hanover who later became George I of England.
Gloomy but superb-looking historical love story; it just misses being a memorable film.

w John Dighton, Alexander Mackendrick, *novel* Helen Simpson *d* Basil Dearden, Michael Relph *ph Douglas Slocombe* *m* Alan Rawsthorne

Stewart Granger, Joan Greenwood, Françoise Rosay, Flora Robson, Peter Bull

'Suspense, romance, interest and excitement in full measure.'—*MFB*

The Saracen Blade
US 1954 76m Technicolor

In the thirteenth century a young Italian crusader devotes himself to avenging the murder of his father. Cut-price swashbuckler full of unintentional laughs and therefore quite watchable. Ricardo Montalban, Betta St John, Rick Jason, Carolyn Jones, Michael Ansara. Written by DeVallon Scott and Worthing Yates, from the novel by Frank Yerby; directed by William Castle; for Sam Katzman / Columbia.

Sarah and Son
US 1930 85m bw
Paramount (David O. Selznick)

A widow seeks the baby her husband took away from her.
Mother love saga; soppy but with good credits.

w Zoe Akins, *novel* Timothy Shea *d* Dorothy Arzner *ph* Charles Lang

Ruth Chatterton, Fredric March, Fuller Mellish Jnr, Gilbert Emery, Doris Lloyd

'*Madame X* with a slightly varied theme. Photography and recording par.'—*Variety*

AAN: Ruth Chatterton

Saratoga*
US 1937 102m bw
MGM (Bernard H. Hyman)

A bookmaker helps the daughter of a horse breeder.
Forgettable racetrack drama notable chiefly as the last film of Jean Harlow who died before it was completed.

w Anita Loos, Robert Hopkins *d* Jack Conway *ph* Ray June *m* Edward Ward

Clark Gable, Jean Harlow, Lionel Barrymore, Frank Morgan, Walter Pidgeon, Una Merkel, Cliff Edwards, George Zucco, Jonathan Hale

'Glib, forthright, knowing and adroit.'—*Time*

'Surefire box office, and tastefully produced.'—*Variety*

'Their times were violent—and so was their love!'

Saratoga Trunk*
US 1943 135m bw
Warner (Hal B. Wallis)

A notorious woman comes back to New Orleans and falls for a cowboy helping a railroad combine against their rivals.
Curious, unsatisfactory, miscast and overlong film version of a bestseller; there are enjoyable sequences, but it simply fails to come alive.

w Casey Robinson, *novel* Edna Ferber *d* Sam Wood *ph Ernest Haller* *m* Max Steiner *ph Joseph St Amaad*

Ingrid Bergman, Gary Cooper, Flora Robson, Jerry Austin, Florence Bates, John Warburton, John Abbott, Curt Bois, Ethel Griffies

'It lacks a logical pattern of drama and character . . . a piece of baggage labelled solely for the stars.'—*Bosley Crowther*

AAN: Flora Robson

Saskatchewan
US 1954 87m Technicolor
U-I (Aaron Rosenberg)
GB title: *O'Rourke of the Royal Mounted*

A mountie helps the lady survivor of an Indian attack.
Standard star actioner.

w Gil Doud *d* Raoul Walsh *ph* John Seitz *m* Hans Salter

Alan Ladd, Shelley Winters, J. Carrol Naish, Hugh O'Brian, Robert Douglas, Richard Long, Jay Silverheels

The Satan Bug*
US 1965 114m De Luxe Panavision
UA / Mirisch / Kappa (John Sturges)

At a top-secret desert research station, one scientist is a traitor, and a deadly virus has been stolen for use by a mad millionaire.
Slow-moving, portentous, gadget-filled actioner which looks good but seldom stimulates.

w James Clavell, Edward Anhalt, *novel* Alistair MacLean *d* John Sturges *ph Robert Surtees* *m* Jerry Goldsmith

George Maharis, Richard Basehart, Anne Francis, Dana Andrews, Ed Asner

Satan Met a Lady*
US 1936 74m bw
Warner (Henry Blanke)

Various crooks and a private detective pursue a rare artifact.
Perversely rewritten version of *The Maltese Falcon* (qv). Fascinating but not really successful

w Brown Holmes *w* William Dieterle *ph* Arthur Edeson *m* Leo F. Forbstein

Bette Davis, Warren William, Alison Skipworth, Arthur Treacher, Wini Shaw, Marie Wilson, Porter Hall

'One lives through it in constant expectation of seeing a group of uniformed individuals appear suddenly from behind the furniture and take the entire cast into protective custody.'—*Bosley Crowther*

Satan Never Sleeps
US / GB 1962 126m De Luxe Cinemascope
TCF / Leo McCarey
GB title: *The Devil Never Sleeps*

In the late forties in China, Catholic missionaries defy the communists.
Failed anti-Red imitation of *Inn of the Sixth Happiness* with the priests from *Going My Way*. Has to be seen to be believed.

w Claude Binyon, Leo McCarey *d* Leo McCarey *ph* Oswald Morris *m* Richard Rodney Bennett

Clifton Webb, William Holden, France Nuyen, Weaver Lee, Athene Seyler, Martin Benson

'For all its superficial smirk of piety, this is just a prurient, soft-soapy and holy water version of the spicy story about the lonely missionary and the beautiful native girl.'—*Time*

The Satanic Rites of Dracula
GB 1973 88m Technicolor
Hammer (Roy Skeggs)
US title: *Dracula is Alive and Well and Living in London*

When vampires infest London, a property speculator proves to be Dracula himself.
Intriguingly plotted screamer with more mystery than horror.

w Don Houghton *d* Alan Gibson *ph* Brian Probyn *m* John Cacavas

Peter Cushing, Christopher Lee, Michael Coles, William Franklyn, Freddie Jones, Richard Vernon, Patrick Barr

'Never told till now! The world's most guarded secret!'

Satellite in the Sky
GB 1956 85m Warnercolor Cinemascope
Warner / Tridelta / Danziger

A rocketship is ordered to lose a tritonium bomb in space, but the device attaches itself to the side of the ship.
Boringly talkative low-budget science fiction with ideas beyond its station but not enough talent to put them over.

w John Mather, J. T. McIntosh, Edith Dell *d* Paul Dickson *ph* Georges Périnal *m* Albert Elms

Kieron Moore, Lois Maxwell, Donald Wolfit, Bryan Forbes, Jimmy Hanley, Alan Gifford

Saturday Island
GB 1951 102m Technicolor
Coronado (David E. Rose)
US title: *Island of Desire*

In 1943 a supply boat is torpedoed and a Canadian nurse finds romance on a desert island with a US marine and a one-armed RAF pilot.
Unlikely, conversational, old-fashioned love story.

wd Stuart Heisler, *novel* Hugh Brooke *ph* Oswald Morris *m* William Alwyn

Linda Darnell, Tab Hunter, Donald Gray

Saturday Night and Sunday Morning****
GB 1960 89m bw
Bryanston / Woodfall (Harry Salzman, Tony Richardson)

A Nottingham factory worker is dissatisfied with his lot, gets into trouble through an affair with a married woman, but finally settles for convention.
Startling when it emerged, this raw working-class melodrama, with its sharp detail and strong comedy asides, delighted the mass audience chiefly because of its strong central character thumbing his nose at authority. Matching the mood of the times, and displaying a new attitude to sex, it transformed British cinema and was much imitated.

w Alan Sillitoe, from his novel *d Karel Reisz ph Freddie Francis m* Johnny Dankworth

Albert Finney, Shirley Anne Field, *Rachel Roberts,* Bryan Pringle, Norman Rossington, Hylda Baker

'Here is a chance for our own new wave.'—*Evening Standard*

† Warwickshire never showed the film because the producers refused to delete two love scenes. David Kingsley of British Lion said: 'We are not prepared to agree that a film of outstanding importance and merit should be re-edited by the Mrs Grundys of the Warwickshire County Council. It is fortunate for the world that Warwickshire's greatest and often bawdy son, William Shakespeare, was not subject in his day to the restrictions of prim and petty officialdom.'

Saturday Night Fever*
US 1978 119m Movielab
Paramount / Robert Stigwood (Milt Felsen)

Italian roughnecks in Brooklyn live for their Saturday night disco dancing, and one of them falls in love with a girl who makes him realize there are better things in life.
Foul-mouthed, fast-paced slice of life which plays like an updated version of *Marty* except that all the characters seem to have crawled from under stones. The slick direction, fast editing and exciting dance numbers do something to take away the sour taste.

w Norman Wexler, *story* Nik Cohn *d John Badham ph* Ralf D. Bode *m* David Shire *songs* Barry, Robin and Maurice Gibb (and others), performed by the Bee Gees *ed* David Rawlins *pd* Charles Bailey

John Travolta, Karen Lynn Gorney, Barry Miller, Joseph Cali, Paul Pape, Bruce Ornstein

'A stylish piece of contemporary anthropology, an urban safari into darkest America, a field study of the mystery cults among the young braves and squaws growing up in North Brooklyn.'—*Alan Brien, Sunday Times*

AAN: John Travolta

Saturday Night Out
GB 1963 96m bw

Five sailors spend an overnight leave in London. Portmanteau drama in which all elements are equally uninteresting. Bernard Lee, Heather Sears, John Bonney, Francesca Annis, Erika Remberg, Colin Campbell, David Lodge. Written by Donald and Derek Ford; directed by Robert Hartford-Davis; for Compton-Tekli.

Saturday's Children
US 1940 101m bw
Warner (Henry Blanke)

An impractical young inventor marries an ambitious young woman, but depressed finances lead to discord.
Glum, dated rehash of a 1929 silent; watchable but not compelling.

w Julius J. and Philip G. Epstein, *play* Maxwell Anderson *d* Vincent Sherman *ph* James Wong Howe

John Garfield, Claude Rains, Anne Shirley, Lee Patrick, George Tobias, Roscoe Karns, Elizabeth Risdon, Berton Churchill

† The story was also made in 1935 as *Maybe It's Love,* with Ross Alexander, Henry Travers and Gloria Stuart; William McGann directed without flair.

Saturday's Hero
US 1951 110m bw
Columbia (Sidney Buchman)
GB title: *Idols in the Dust*

A poor boy wins a football scholarship but finds his value to the college is purely commercial and he isn't given time to learn anything.
A spirited attack on the American sporting system, but a dull and overlong film.

w Millard Lampell, Sidney Buchman, *novel* The Hero by Millard Lampell *d* David Miller *ph* Lee Garmes *m* Elmer Bernstein

John Derek, Donna Reed, Sidney Blackmer, Alexander Knox, Elliott Lewis, Howard St John

Saturn Three
GB 1980 87m colour
ITC / Transcontinental (Stanley Donen)

A maniac builds a robot on a remote space station, and they both go berserk.
Rather unpleasant blend of space fiction, horror and suspense, with some nasty detail and a general feeling that the actors wish they were elsewhere.

w Martin Amis, *story* John Barry *d* Stanley Donen *ph* Billy Williams *m* Elmer Bernstein *pd* Stuart Craig

Kirk Douglas, Farrah Fawcett, Harvey Keitel, Ed Bishop

Satyricon*
Italy / France 1969 129m De Luxe Panavision
UA / PAA / PEA (Alberto Grimaldi)
aka: *Fellini Satyricon*

Sexual adventures of a Roman student.
Garish, sporadically enjoyable sketches on a very thin thread of plot: a more benevolent version of the usual Fellini nightmare.

w Federico Fellini, Bernandino Zapponi *d* Federico Fellini *ph* Giuseppe Rotunno *m* Nino Rota, Ilhan Mimaroglu, Tod Dockstader, Andrew Rudin *pd* Danilo Donati

Martin Potter, Hiram Keller, Salvo Randone, Max Born

'A picaresque satire in fragments . . . a series of tableaux which carry the poetry visually at the price of coherence.'—*Mike Wallington, MFB*

'Part of the gradual decomposition of what once was one of the greatest talents in film history . . . a gimcrack, shopworn nightmare.'—*John Simon*

AAN: Federico Fellini (as director)

Le Sauvage
France / Italy 1978 107m Eastmancolor
Lira / PAI (Raymond Danon)

A business executive has opted out of life to be alone on a desert island, but on his last night in the city accidentally helps a runaway heiress who follows him.
A promising and amusing start is squandered in the tedious island sequences of this patchy romantic comedy, which does however leave one with a sense of freshness and optimism rare in the cinema of the seventies.

w Jean-Paul Rappeneau, Elizabeth Rappeneau, Jean-Loup Dabadie *d* Jean-Paul Rappeneau *ph* Pierre Lhomme *m* Michel Legrand

Yves Montand, Catherine Deneuve, Luigi Vannucchi, Dana Wynter

The Savage
US 1952 95m Technicolor
Paramount (Mel Epstein)

A white boy grows up with Indians and later suffers from divided loyalties.
Solemn, rather tedious but well produced western.

w Sidney Boehm, *novel* L. L. Foreman *d* George Marshall *ph* John F. Seitz *m* Paul Sawtell

Charlton Heston, Susan Morrow, Peter Hanson, Joan Taylor, Richard Rober, Don Porter

The Savage Eye*
US 1959 68m bw
City Film Corporation (Ben Maddow, Joseph Strick, Sidney Meyers)

An unhappily married young woman takes a jaundiced view of life around her in Los Angeles.
The wisp of plot is merely an excuse to present a documentary exposé of the seamier side of life in America's most eccentric city, with its faith healers and revellers. Much of it is fascinating, though the film is not a cohesive whole and the would-be poetic commentary falls on its face.

wd, ed Ben Maddow, Joseph Strick, Sidney Meyers *m* Leonard Rosenman *ph* Jack Couffer, Haskell Wexler, Helen Levitt

Barbara Baxley, Gary Merrill, Herschel Bernardi

The Savage Guns
US / Spain 1961 83m Metrocolor Cinemascope

After the Civil War, an American rancher settles in Mexico but finds his pacifist principles tested by bandits. Unappealing, stodgy western with the Hammer horror team rather curiously cast as co-producers. Richard Basehart, Don Taylor, Alex Nicol, Jose Nieto, Fernando Rey. Written by Edmund Morris (?Jimmy Sangster); directed by Michael Carreras; for Capricorn / Tecisa / MGM.

The Savage Innocents
GB / France / Italy 1960 107m Super Technirama 70
Joseph Janni / Magic Film / Playart / Gray Films (Maleno Malenotti)
aka: *Ombre Bianchi*

Trials of an Eskimo and his wife in Canada's frozen north.
Conscientious, determined and very boring account of Eskimo life played by actors talking pidgin English. Not a success despite the magnificent photography.

w Nicholas Ray, *novel* Top of the World by Hans Ruesch *d* Nicholas Ray, Baccio Bandini *ph Aldo Tonti, Peter Hennessy* *m* Angelo Lavagnino

Anthony Quinn, Yoko Tani, Marie Yang, Peter O'Toole, Carlo Justini, Anna May Wong, Lee Montague, Ed Devereaux

† The Anna May Wong in the cast is not the famous silent star.

Savage Messiah*
GB 1972 103m Metrocolor
MGM / Russ–Arts (Ken Russell)

The life together (1910–14) of the 18-year-old painter Gaudier and 38-year-old Sophie Brzeska.
Intense, fragmentary art film about two eccentrics; would have better suited TV.

w Christopher Logue, *book* H. S. Ede *d* Ken Russell *ph* Dick Bush *m* Michael Garrett *pd* Derek Jarman

Dorothy Tutin, Scott Anthony, Helen Mirren, Lindsay Kemp, Michael Gough, John Justin

Savage Pampas
Spain / Argentina / US 1967 108m Eastmancolor Superpanorama
Jaime Prados–Dasa–Sam Bronston

In 19th-century Argentina the commander of an isolated fort finds that a bandit is bribing his men to desert.
Densely plotted semi-western, sometimes good to look at but slow and lugubrious.

w Hugo Fregonese, John Melson *d* Hugo Fregonese *ph* Marcel Berenguer *m* Waldo de los Rios

Robert Taylor, Ron Randell, Ty Hardin, Rosenda Monteros, Marc Lawrence

Savage Sam*
US 1962 104m Technicolor
Walt Disney (Bill Anderson)

The youngest son of a homesteading family has a troublesome dog which redeems itself by tracking down Apaches.
Folksy boy-and-dog western, good of its kind, with adequate suspense and scenery.

w Fred Gipson, William Tunberg *d* Norman Tokar *ph* Edward Colman *m* Oliver Wallace

Brian Keith, Tommy Kirk, Kevin Corcoran, Dewey Martin, Jeff York

'A cadet edition of the best of Ford.'—*MFB*

Savage Wilderness
US 1956 98m Technicolor Cinemascope
Columbia (William Fadiman)
GB title: *The Last Frontier*

An Indian-hating fort commander puts himself and his charges in jeopardy.
Standard western with good performances and excellent action scenes.

w Philip Yordan, Russell S. Hughes, *novel* The Gilded Rooster by Richard Emery Roberts *d* Anthony Mann *ph* William Mellor *m* Leigh Harline

Victor Mature, *Robert Preston*, Guy Madison, Anne Bancroft, James Whitmore, Peter Whitney

Savages
US 1972 106m colour
Angelika / Merchant–Ivory (Joseph Saleh)

Forest wanderers take over a deserted mansion and begin to feel its civilizing influence.
Mild fable which needed a Bunuel to do it justice; a few lively moments.

w George Swift Trow, Michael O'Donoghue *d* James Ivory *ph* Walter Lassally *m* Joe Raposo

Louis Stadlen, Anne Francine, Thayer David, Salome Jens, Neil Fitzgerald

Save the Tiger*
US 1973 100m Movielab
Paramount / Jalem / Filmways / Cirandinha (Steve Shagan)

A middle-aged businessman regrets the slack morality of modern America.
Self-adulatory drama which really has little point but gets a few marks for meaning well and for vivid scenes.

w Steve Shagan *d* John G. Avildsen *ph* Jim Crabe *m* Marvin Hamlisch

Jack Lemmon, Jack Gilford, Laurie Heineman, Norman Burton, Thayer David

'A scathing indictment of the US, of materialism, war, marriage—the works. Wordy, literate and deeply felt.'—*NFT, 1974*

AA: Jack Lemmon
AAN: Steve Shagan; Jack Gilford

Saving Grace
US 1986 112m Technicolor Technovision
Columbia / Embassy (Herbert F. Solow)

A Pope escapes from office to meet the real people.
The trouble with this movie is, he learns nothing by doing so.

w Joaquin Montana *novel* Celia Gittelson *d* Robert M. Young *ph* Reynaldo Villalobos

Tom Conti, Fernando Rey, Erland Josephson, Giancarlo Giannini, Donald Hewlett

'More sleeping draught than balm for the spirits.'—*Sight and Sound*

Sawdust and Tinsel*
Sweden 1953 95m bw
Svensk Filmindustri
aka: *The Naked Night;* original title: *Gycklarnas Afton*

The owner of a travelling circus leaves his mistress for his separated wife, and is challenged to fight by the mistress's new lover.
Powerfully-made yet rather pointless melodrama about unpleasant people.

wd Ingmar Bergman ph Sven Nykvist *m* Karl-Birger Blomdahl

Harriet Andersson, Ake Grönberg, Hasse Ekman, Annika Tretow

'One of the extremely rare instances of a film's elements all blending perfectly.'—*John Simon*

The Saxon Charm
US 1948 88m bw
Universal (Joseph Sistrom)

A Broadway impresario dominates the lives of those around him.
Rather heavy-going comedy drama which could have done with more malicious wit; allegedly based on Jed Harris.

wd Claude Binyon, *novel* Frederick Wakeman *ph* Milton Krasner *m* Walter Scharf

Robert Montgomery, Susan Hayward, John Payne, Audrey Totter, Henry Morgan, Harry Von Zell, Cara Williams, Chill Wills, Heather Angel

Say Hello to Yesterday
GB 1970 92m Eastmancolor
Josef Shaftel (William Hill)

A middle-aged married woman goes to London for shopping and is pursued by a strange young man whom she allows to seduce her.
Unattractive 'with it' romantic drama with a swinging London setting, a long way after *Brief Encounter.*

w Alvin Rakoff, Peter King *d* Alvin Rakoff *ph* Geoffrey Unsworth *m* Riz Ortolani

Jean Simmons, Leonard Whiting, *Evelyn Laye*, John Lee, Jack Woolgar

Say It in French
US 1938 67m bw

A golf champion marries a French girl, but on his return, in order to help his father's finances, has to pretend to be marrying a rich girl, so his wife pretends to be a maid. Thin comedy which has a job to sustain its short running time. Ray Milland, Olympe Bradna, Irene Hervey, Janet Beecher, Mary Carlisle, Holmes Herbert, Erik Rhodes. Written by Frederick Jackson, from a play by Jacques Deval; directed by Andrew L. Stone; for Paramount. 'The harder it strives for hare-brained badinage, the more laboured it becomes.'—*Variety*

Say It with Songs
US 1929 89m bw
Warner

A radio singer accidentally kills a man and is jailed for manslaughter.
Miscalculated star vehicle with a few good moments among the sentiment and melodrama.

w Darryl F. Zanuck, Joseph Jackson, Harvey Gates *d* Lloyd Bacon *ph* Lee Garmes

Al Jolson, Davey Lee, Marian Nixon, Fred Kohler, Holmes Herbert

† Though Jolson was paid half a million dollars to do it, the film was a tremendous flop. The songs were again by De Sylva, Brown and Henderson, but 'Little Pal' was not another 'Sonny Boy'.

Say One for Me
US 1959 117m De Luxe Cinemascope
TCF / Bing Crosby (Frank Tashlin)

Adventures of a parish priest in New York's theatrical quarter.
Unconvincing, unattractive imitation of *Going My Way* which counters bad taste with religiosity.

w Robert O'Brien *d* Frank Tashlin *ph* Leo Tover *songs* Sammy Cahn, James Van Heusen *md* Lionel Newman

Bing Crosby, Robert Wagner, Debbie Reynolds, Ray Walston, Les Tremayne, Connie Gilchrist, Frank McHugh, Joe Besser, Sebastian Cabot

'Tasteless and disturbing.'—*Variety*

AAN: Lionel Newman

'I am not allowed to love. But I will love you if that is your desire!'

Sayonara**
US 1957 147m Technirama
Goetz Pictures–Pennebaker (William Goetz)

An American air force major in Tokyo after the war falls in love with a Japanese actress.
A lush travelogue interrupted by two romances, one tragic and one happy. A great success at the time, though mainly of interest to Americans; now vaguely dated.

w Paul Osborn, *novel* James A. Michener *d* Joshua Logan *ph Ellsworth Fredericks* *m* Franz Waxman *ad* Ted Haworth

Marlon Brando, Miyoshi Umeki, Miiko Taka, Red Buttons, Ricardo Montalban, Patricia Owens, Kent Smith, Martha Scott, James Garner

AA: Miyoshi Umeki; Red Buttons
AAN: best picture; Paul Osborn; Joshua Logan; Ellsworth Fredericks; Marlon Brando

Scalawag
US / Italy 1973 93m Technicolor
Bryna / Inex–Oceania (Anne Douglas)

Mexico 1840: a one-legged pirate and a boy try to trace a hidden treasure.
Flagrant reworking of *Treasure Island*, heavily overdone by stars and rhubarbing extras alike.

w Albert Maltz, Sid Fleischman *d* Kirk Douglas *ph* Jack Cardiff *m* John Cameron

Kirk Douglas, Mark Lester, Neville Brand, David Stroud, Lesley-Anne Down, Phil Brown

The Scalphunters*
US 1968 102m De Luxe Panavision
UA / Bristol / Norlan (Levy–Gardner–Laven)

An old cowboy and a black ex-slave track down a gang who kill Indians for their scalps.
Vigorous, aimless, likeable comedy western with the emphasis on brawling.

w William Norton *d* Sydney Pollack *ph* Duke Callaghan, Richard Moore *m* Elmer Bernstein

Burt Lancaster, Ossie Davis, Telly Savalas, Shelley Winters, Nick Cravat, Paul Picerni

'It is the sort of frolic where bodies litter the ground, but you know they'll get up and draw their pay. And where even a villain can crack a joke without losing face.'—*Robert Ottaway*

Scandal at Scourie
US 1953 90m Metrocolor
MGM (Edwin H. Knopf)

The wife of the Protestant reeve of a Scottish-Canadian Protestant community adopts a Catholic child.
Sentimental whimsy with no holds barred, but with rather jaded acting and production.

w Norman Corwin, Leonard Spiegelgass, Karl Tunberg *d* Jean Negulesco *ph* Robert Planck *m* Daniele Amfitheatrof

Greer Garson, Walter Pidgeon, Agnes Moorehead, Arthur Shields, Philip Ober, Donna Corcoran

A Scandal in Paris*
US 1946 100m bw
UA / Arnold Pressburger
aka: *Thieves' Holiday*

Adventures of Vidocq, a 19th-century rogue who became Paris chief of police.
The actors look uneasy in their costumes, and

the sets are cardboard, but there is fun to be had from this light comedy-drama.

w Ellis St Joseph *d* Douglas Sirk *ph* Guy Roe *m* Hans Eisler

George Sanders, Signe Hasso, Carole Landis, Akim Tamiroff, Gene Lockhart

Scandal Sheet
US 1931 77m bw

A newspaper editor with principles prints scandal involving his wife. Dated star drama. George Bancroft, Kay Francis, Regis Toomey, Clive Brook. Written by Vincent Lawrence and Max Marcin; directed by John Cromwell; for Paramount.

Scandal Sheet
US 1939 67m bw

A ruthless publisher sacrifices himself to save his son. Uninteresting star quickie. Otto Kruger, Ona Munson, Edward Norris. Written by Joseph Carole; directed by Nick Grinde; for Columbia.

Scandal Sheet
US 1952 81m bw
Columbia (Edward Small)
GB title: *The Dark Page*

An editor has to allow his star reporter to expose a murderer—himself.
Obvious, reasonably holding melodrama with familiar characters.

w Ted Sherdeman, Eugene Ling, James Poe, *novel* Samuel Fuller *d* Phil Karlson *ph* Burnett Guffey *m* George Duning

Broderick Crawford, John Derek, Donna Reed, Rosemary de Camp, Henry O'Neill, Henry Morgan

Scandal Street
US 1937 63m bw

The arrival in a small town of an innocent young girl causes gossip which leads to murder. Satisfactory mini-drama for the easily pleased. Lew Ayres, Louise Campbell, Roscoe Karns, Porter Hall, Virginia Weidler, Edgar Kennedy, Elizabeth Patterson. Written by Bertram Millhauser and Eddie Welch, from a story by Vera Caspary; directed by James Hogan; for Paramount. 'A curiously beguiling little hodge-podge.'—*Variety*

Scandalous!
GB 1984 92m Technicolor
Hemdale / Raleigh / Angeles Cinema Investors (Arlene Sellers, Alex Winitsky)

A TV reporter becomes involved with two con artists, who seem to have some connection with the murder of his wife.
Frantic black comedy which never even begins to be funny.

w Rob Cohen, John Byrum *d* Rob Cohen *ph* Jack Cardiff *m* Dave Grusin *pd* Peter Mullins

Robert Hays, John Gielgud, Pamela Stephenson, M. Emmet Walsh, Nancy Wood, Jim Dale

Scandalous John
US 1971 117m Technicolor
Walt Disney (Bill Walsh)

The elderly owner of a derelict ranch resists all efforts to close him up.
Unsatisfactory Disney attempt to capture a more adult audience than usual; overlong, repetitious and dreary.

w Bill Walsh, Don da Gradi, *novel* Richard Gardner *d* Robert Butler *ph* Frank Phillips *m* Rod McKuen

Brian Keith, Alfonso Arau, Michele Carey, Rick Lenz, Henry Morgan, Simon Oakland

Scanners
Canada 1980 103m Eastmancolor
Filmplan International (Claude Heroux)

Certain people are found to be telepathic 'scanners' able to lock at will into other people's nervous systems. This has the occasional result of blowing apart the other people's heads.
Overlong science fiction which concentrates on the nastier elements.

wd David Cronenberg *ph* Mark Irwin *m* Howard Shore

Jennifer O'Neill, Patrick McGoohan, Stephen Lack, Lawrence Dane, Michael Ironside

The Scapegoat*
GB 1959 92m bw
MGM / Du Maurier–Guinness (Dennis Van Thal)

A quiet bachelor on a French holiday is tricked into assuming the identity of a lookalike aristocrat who wants to commit a murder.
Disappointing adaptation of a good story, with much evidence of re-cutting and an especially slack middle section.

w Gore Vidal, Robert Hamer, *novel* Daphne du Maurier *d* Robert Hamer *ph* Paul Beeson *m* Bronislau Kaper

Alec Guinness, Bette Davis, Irene Worth, Nicole Maurey, Pamela Brown, Geoffrey Keen

The Scar
US 1948 83m bw
Eagle–Lion (Bryan Foy, Paul Henreid)
aka: *Hollow Triumph*

A fugitive kills his psychoanalyst double and takes his place, but is caught for the double's crimes.
Cheap suspense thriller with no suspense and no surprises.

w Daniel Fuchs, *novel* Murray Forbes *d* Steve Sekely *ph* John Alton *m* Sol Kaplan

Joan Bennett, Paul Henreid, Eduard Franz, Leslie Brooks, John Qualen, Mabel Paige, Herbert Rudley

Scaramouche**
US 1952 115m Technicolor
MGM (Carey Wilson)

A young man disguises himself as an actor to avenge the death of his friend at the hands of a wicked marquis.
Cheerful swashbuckler set in French revolutionary times, first filmed in the twenties with Ramon Novarro. MGM costume production at somewhere near its best.

w Ronald Millar, George Froeschel, *novel* Rafael Sabatini *d* George Sidney *ph* Charles Rosher *m* Victor Young *ad Cedric Gibbons, Hans Peters*

Stewart Granger, Mel Ferrer, Eleanor Parker, Janet Leigh, Henry Wilcoxon, Nina Foch, Lewis Stone, Robert Coote, Richard Anderson

† The sword fight, at 6½ minutes, is credited with being the longest in cinema history.

Scarecrow*
US 1973 112m Technicolor Panavision
Warner (Robert M. Sherman)

Two of the world's losers hitch-hike across America.
Well-shot but eventually dreary parable of friendship, a pedestrian *Easy Rider*.

w Garry Michael White *d* Jerry Schatzberg *ph* Vilmos Zsigmond *m* Fred Myrow

Gene Hackman, Al Pacino

'Here's a picture that manages to abuse two American myths at once—the Road and the Male Pair.'—*Stanley Kauffmann*

The Scarecrow*
New Zealand 1981 88m colour
Oasis / New Zealand National Film Unit (Rob Whitehouse)

In a small town in the early fifties, a strange chain of events is set in motion by the disappearance of six chickens.
A curious mix of sinister atmosphere which seems mystical and sinister events which are all too real. Interesting but unsatisfying, both as a murder mystery and as a study in evil.

w Michael Heath, Sam Pilsbury, *novel* Ronald Hugh Morrieson *d* Sam Pilsbury *ph* James Bartle *m* Schtung

John Carradine, Tracy Mann, Jonathan Smith, Daniel McLaren, Denise O'Connell, Anne Flannery

Scared Stiff
US 1945 65m bw

A timid reporter stumbles over a murder on a bus and finds the culprit before the sheriff arrives. Tedious comedy mystery. Jack Haley, Ann Savage, Barton Maclane, Veda Ann Borg, George E. Stone, Lucien Littlefield. Written by Geoffrey Homes and Maxwell Shane; directed by Frank McDonald; for Pine-Thomas / Paramount.

'They're making a spook-tacle of themselves!'

Scared Stiff
US 1953 108m bw
Paramount (Hal B. Wallis)

Nightclub entertainers get involved with a girl who has inherited a spooky castle off the Cuban coast.

Stretched-out remake of *The Ghost Breakers*; the last half hour, being closest to the original, is the most nearly funny.

w Herbert Baker, Walter de Leon *d* George Marshall, Ed Simmons, Norman Lear *ph* Ernest Laszlo *md* Joseph J. Lilley

Dean Martin, Jerry Lewis, Lizabeth Scott, Carmen Miranda, George Dolenz, Dorothy Malone, William Ching, Jack Lambert

The Scarf
US 1951 86m bw
UA / Gloria (I. G. Goldsmith)

A man escapes from a lunatic asylum and proves himself innocent of the crime for which he was committed.
Glum and pretentious murder mystery with a pictorial style to match its flowery dialogue.

wd E. A. Dupont *ph* Franz Planer *m* Herschel Burke Gilbert

John Ireland, Mercedes McCambridge, Emlyn Williams, James Barton, Lloyd Gough, Basil Ruysdael

'I'm going to run the whole works. There's only one law: do it first, do it yourself, and keep doing it!'

Scarface****
US 1932 99m bw
Howard Hughes
aka: *The Shame of a Nation*

The life and death of a Chicago gangster of the twenties.
Obviously modelled on Al Capone, with an incestuous sister thrown in, this was perhaps the most vivid film of the gangster cycle, and its revelling in its own sins was not obscured by the subtitle, *The Shame of a Nation*.

w Ben Hecht, Seton I. Miller, John Lee Mahin, W. R. Burnett, Fred Pasley, *novel* Armitage Traill *d Howard Hawks ph Lee Garmes, L. W. O'Connell m* Adolph Tandler, Gus Arnheim

Paul Muni, Ann Dvorak, George Raft, Boris Karloff, Osgood Perkins, Karen Morley, C. Henry Gordon, Vince Barnett, Henry Armetta, Edwin Maxwell

'Presumably the last of the gangster films, on a promise, it is going to make people sorry that there won't be any more. Should draw wherever it can play.'—*Variety*

'More brutal, more cruel, more wholesale than any of its predecessors.'—*James Shelley Hamilton*

'Because it was so close to the actual events, it possesses a kind of newsreel quality which cannot be recaptured or imitated. It vibrates with the impact of things that were real and deeply felt.'—*National Film Theatre programme, 1961*

† On original release added scenes showed Tony tried, convicted and hanged, though since Muni is never seen, it appears that they were an afterthought made when he was not available.

Scarface
US 1983 170m Technicolor Panavision
Universal (Martin Bregman)

Absurdly brutalized version of the above, with detailed violence and a superabundance of foul language. Scarface has now become an emigré Cuban, and the film seems to want to make a political statement.

w Oliver Stone *d* Brian de Palma *ph* John A. Alonzo *m* Giorgio Moroder

Al Pacino, Steven Bauer, Michelle Pfeiffer, Mary Elizabeth Mastrantonio, Robert Loggia, Paul Shenar, Harris Yulin

The Scarface Mob*
US 1958 96m bw
Desilu (Quinn Martin)

Al Capone's empire thrives while he is in Alcatraz, and prohibition agent Eliot Ness recruits a tough squad to fight the gangsters. Though released theatrically, this was in effect a pilot film for the successful TV series *The Untouchables*, well enough done within its limits.

w Paul Monash, *novel* The Untouchables by Eliot Ness *d* Phil Karlson *ph* Charles Straumer *m* Wilbur Hatch

Robert Stack, Neville Brand, Keenan Wynn, Barbara Nichols, Joe Mantell, Pat Crowley, Bruce Gordon, Paul Picerni, Abel Fernandez

Scarlet Angel
US 1952 81m Technicolor
U-I (Leonard Goldstein)

A saloon hostess presents herself to a wealthy family as their dead son's wife.
Modest, satisfactorily plotted woman's picture with action interludes.

w Oscar Brodney *d* Sidney Salkow *ph* Russell Metty *m* Joseph Gershenson

Yvonne de Carlo, Rock Hudson, Richard Denning, Henry O'Neill, Amanda Blake

The Scarlet Blade*
GB 1963 82m Technicolor Hammerscope
Hammer (Anthony Nelson Keys)
US title: *The Crimson Blade*

In 1648, a Cromwellian colonel plans to hang every royalist rebel.
Adequate swashbuckler.

wd John Gilling ph Jack Asher *m* Gary Hughes

Lionel Jeffries, Oliver Reed, Jack Hedley, June Thorburn, Duncan Lamont

The Scarlet Claw**
US 1944 74m bw
Universal (Roy William Neill)

Grisly revenge murders take place in the fog-bound Canadian village of Le Mort Rouge.
Possibly the best of the modernized Sherlock Holmes series, with a plot hastily borrowed from *The Hound of the Baskervilles*.

w Edmund L. Hartmann, Roy William Neill *d Roy William Neill ph George Robinson md* Paul Sawtell *m* Hans Salter

Basil Rathbone, Nigel Bruce, Miles Mander, Gerald Hamer, Paul Cavanagh, Kay Harding, Arthur Hohl

The Scarlet Coat
US 1955 99m Eastmancolor Cinemascope
MGM (Nicholas Nayfack)

During the American War of Independence, an American officer deserts to the British in order to unmask a traitor.
Rather talky historical actioner with too much time spent on friendship and romance.

w Karl Tunberg *d* John Sturges *ph* Paul C. Vogel *m* Conrad Salinger

Cornel Wilde, Michael Wilding, George Sanders, Anne Francis, Robert Douglas, Bobby Driscoll, John McIntire

Scarlet Dawn*
US 1932 76m bw
Warner (Hal Wallis)

During the Russian revolution, an exiled aristocrat loves a serving maid.
Heavy-going romantic drama distinguished by stylish direction and sets.

w Niven Busch, Erwin Gelsey, Douglas Fairbanks Jnr, *novel* Revolt by Mary McCall Jnr *d William Dieterle ph* Ernest Haller *ad Anton Grot*

Douglas Fairbanks Jnr, Nancy Carroll, Lilyan Tashman, Guy Kibbee, Sheila Terry, Frank Reicher

'The story starts off to get somewhere but fails to arrive.'—*Variety*

'Based on a private diary of Catherine the Great!'
'The screen's reigning beauty in a wild pageant of barbaric splendour!'
'A cavalcade of fury led by a woman of fire!'

The Scarlet Empress***
US 1934 109m bw
Paramount

A fantasia on the love life of Catherine the Great.
A marvellous, overwhelming, dramatically insubstantial but pictorially brilliant homage to a star; not to everyone's taste, but a film to remember.

w Manuel Komroff *d Josef Von Sternberg ph Bert Glennon md* W. Franke Harling, John M. Leipold, Milan Roder *ad Hans Dreier, Peter Ballbusch, Richard Kollorsz costumes Travis Banton*

Marlene Dietrich, John Lodge, Sam Jaffe, Louise Dresser, C. Aubrey Smith, Gavin Gordon, Jameson Thomas

'She's photographed behind veils and fishnets, while dwarfs slither about and bells ring and everybody tries to look degenerate.'—*New Yorker, 1975*

'A ponderous, strangely beautiful, lengthy and frequently wearying production.'—*Mordaunt Hall, New York Times*

The Scarlet Horseman
US 1946 bw serial: 13 eps

An undercover agent assumes the identity of The Scarlet Horseman in order to identify gun smugglers. Adequate western serial. Peter Cookson, Paul Guilfoyle, Virginia Christine, Victoria Horne. Directed by Ray Taylor and Lewis Collins; for Universal.

The Scarlet Hour
US 1955 93m bw Vistavision
Paramount (Michael Curtiz)

A bored wife persuades her lover to turn thief; her husband misconstrues the situation and is accidentally killed.
Complex suspenser designed to introduce new talent; rather too smooth, and pretty boring.

w Rip van Ronkel, Frank Tashlin, Meredyth Lucas *d* Michael Curtiz *ph* Lionel Lindon *m* Leith Stevens

Carol Ohmart, Tom Tryon, James Gregory, Jody Lawrance, E. G. Marshall, *Elaine Stritch*

The Scarlet Letter*
US 1926 90m (24 fps) bw silent
MGM / Jury

In Puritan New England, the mother of an illegitimate child wears the scarlet A (for adulteress) for years rather than reveal that her lover was the village priest.
Celebrated 17th-century melodrama, quite powerfully made in the best silent tradition, but of little intrinsic interest for modern audiences.

w Frances Marion, *novel* Nathaniel Hawthorne *d* Victor Sjostrom *ph* Henrik Sartov *ad* Cedric Gibbons

Lillian Gish, Lars Hanson, Karl Dane, Henry B. Walthall
† Other versions include the following: US 1910, US 1911, US 1913, US 1917, US 1920, GB 1922, US 1934, Germany 1971, US (TV) 1979

The Scarlet Letter
US 1934 70m bw

A lightened version with an attempt at comedy relief. Not in any way remarkable. Colleen Moore, Hardie Albright, Henry B. Walthall, William Farnum, Alan Hale. Written by Leonard Fields, David Silverstein; directed by Robert G. Vignola; for Darmour / Majestic.

The Scarlet Pimpernel***
GB 1934 98m bw
London Films (Alexander Korda)

In the early days of the French revolution, an apparently foppish Englishman leads a daring band in rescuing aristocrats from the guillotine.
First-class period adventure with a splendid and much imitated plot, strong characters, humour and a richly detailed historical background.

w Robert E. Sherwood, Sam Berman, Arthur Wimperis, Lajos Biro, *novel* Baroness Orczy *d Harold Young* *ph* Harold Rosson *m* Arthur Benjamin

Leslie Howard, Merle Oberon, Raymond Massey, Nigel Bruce, Bramwell Fletcher, Anthony Bushell, Joan Gardner, Walter Rilla

'Excellent British import that will do business.'—*Variety*

'One of the most romantic and durable of all swashbucklers.'—*New Yorker, 1976*

'A triumph for the British film world.'—*Sunday Times*

† Some scenes were directed by Alexander Korda, others by Rowland Brown.
†† The story was remade as *The Elusive Pimpernel* (*qv*) and in 1982 in a TV version starring Anthony Andrews. See also *The Return of the Scarlet Pimpernel.*

'I've been wanting to laugh in your face ever since I met you. You're old and ugly and I'm sick of you—sick, sick, sick!'

Scarlet Street**
US 1945 103m bw
(Universal) Walter Wanger (Fritz Lang)

A prostitute is murdered by her client and her pimp is executed for the crime.
Daring but rather gloomy Hollywood melodrama, the first in which a crime went unpunished (though the culprit was shown suffering remorse). Interesting and heavily Teutonic, but as entertainment not a patch on the similar but lighter *The Woman in the Window*, which the same team had made a year previously.

w Dudley Nichols, *play* La Chienne by George de la Fouchardière (filmed by Jean Renoir in 1932) *d Fritz Lang* *ph* Milton Krasner *m* Hans Salter *ad* Alexander Golitzen

Edward G. Robinson, Joan Bennett, Dan Duryea, Jess Barker, Margaret Lindsay, Rosalind Ivan, Samuel S. Hinds, Arthur Loft

'The director unerringly chooses the right sound and image to assault the spectator's sensibilities.'—*C. A. Lejeune*

The Scarlet Thread
GB 1950 84m bw

Jewel thieves take refuge in a Cambridge college. Flabby melodrama featuring emergent young talent. Kathleen Byron, Laurence Harvey, Sidney Tafler, Arthur Hill, Dora Bryan. Written by A. R. Rawlinson, from a play by A. R. Rawlinson and Moie Charles; directed by Lewis Gilbert; for Nettlefold / Butcher.

Scars of Dracula
GB 1970 96m Technicolor
Hammer / EMI (Aida Young)

A young man on the run finds himself an unwitting guest of Count Dracula.
Overpadded vampire saga, its few effective moments stemming directly from the original novel.

w John Elder *d* Roy Ward Baker *ph* Moray Grant *m* James Bernard

Christopher Lee, Dennis Waterman, Christopher Matthews, Jenny Hanley, Patrick Troughton, Michael Gwynn, Bob Todd

Scattergood Baines
US 1941 69m bw

The new owner of a small-town hardware store takes an interest in his fellow men. First of several second features featuring the exploits of a likeable busybody. *Guy Kibbee*, Carol Hughes, John Archer, Emma Dunn. Written by Michael L. Simmons and Edward T. Lowe, from the stories by Clarence Budington Kelland; directed by Christy Cabanne; for RKO. (The succeeding episodes were as follows: *Scattergood Pulls the Strings*, 1941; *Scattergood Meets Broadway*, 1941; *Scattergood Rides High*, 1942; *Scattergood Survives a Murder*, 1942; *Cinderella Swings It*, 1943.)

Scavenger Hunt
US 1979 116m De Luxe
TCF / Melvin Simon

A rich man leaves a fortune to the member of his family who can collect most of the useless objects in a list provided.
Depressing cheapjack imitation of Kramer's *It's a Mad Mad Mad Mad World*, which itself was not free from fault.

w Steven A. Vail, Henry Harper *d* Michael Schultz *ph* Ken Lamkin *m* Billy Goldenberg

Richard Benjamin, James Coco, Scatman Crothers, Cloris Leachman, Cleavon Little, Roddy McDowall, Robert Morley, Richard Mulligan, Tony Randall, Dirk Benedict, Vincent Price

'Loud, obnoxious, and above all unfunny.'—*Variety*

'First they moved (1895)! Then they talked (1927)! Now they smell!'

Scent of Mystery*
US 1959 125m Technicolor Cinerama (70mm)
Cinerama / Mike Todd Jnr
aka: *Holiday in Spain*

An Englishman on holiday in Spain protects a mysterious girl.
More of a travelogue than a thriller, but worth a note as the cinema's first 'smellie'. A process called Smell-o-Vision released appropriate odours throughout the auditorium . . .

w William Rose *d* Jack Cardiff *ph* John Von Kotze *m* Mario Nascimbene

Denholm Elliott, Peter Lorre, Beverly Bentley, Paul Lukas, Liam Redmond, Leo McKern, Peter Arne, Mary Laura Wood, Elizabeth Taylor
† The first film to credit its providers of shoe polish.

School for Husbands
GB 1937 71m bw
Wainwright (Richard Wainwright)

A romantic novelist annoys the husbands of his adoring fans.
Would-be champagne comedy which bubbles pretty well for most of its length.

w Frederick Jackson, Gordon Aherry, Austin Melford, *play* Frederick Jackson *d* Andrew Marton *ph* Phil Tannura

Rex Harrison, Henry Kendall, Romney Brent, Diana Churchill, June Clyde

The School for Scandal
GB 1930 73m Raycol Colour

Two brothers have characters opposite to their appearances. Doomed attempt to film the famous 18th-century comedy of manners. Madeleine Carroll, Basil Gill, Henry Hewitt, Ian Fleming. Written by Jean Jay from play by Richard Brinsley Sheridan; directed by Maurice Elvey; for Albion Film Syndicate. 'Its value in the States looks like exactly nothing.'—*Variety*

School for Scoundrels*
GB 1960 94m bw
ABP / Guardsman (Hal E. Chester)

A failure reports to the College of One-Upmanship and his life is transformed. Amusing trifle, basically a series of sketches by familiar comic actors.

w Patricia Mayes, Hal E. Chester, *books* Stephen Potter *d* Robert Hamer *ph* Erwin Hillier *m* John Addison

Ian Carmichael, Alastair Sim, Terry-Thomas, Janette Scott, Dennis Price, Peter Jones, Edward Chapman, John Le Mesurier

School for Secrets
GB 1946 108m bw
Rank / Two Cities (George H. Brown, Peter Ustinov)
US title: *Secret Flight*

The boffins who invented radar find themselves in a little war action of their own. An unsatisfactory entertainment which, with the best intentions, shuffles between arch comedy, character drama, war action and documentary, doing less than justice to any of these aspects.

wd Peter Ustinov *ph* Jack Hildyard

Ralph Richardson, Raymond Huntley, Richard Attenborough, Marjorie Rhodes, John Laurie, Ernest Jay, David Tomlinson, Finlay Currie

Schweik's New Adventures
GB 1943 84m bw

An unassuming Czechoslovakian writer gently kids the Nazi occupiers and manages to save some of his friends from the concentration camp. Curious English attempt to film a popular Czechoslovakian character; it made mildly effective wartime propaganda, though few went to see it. Lloyd Pearson, George Carney, Julien Mitchell, Richard Attenborough, Margaret McGrath. Written by Karel Lamac and Con West, from the novel by Jaroslav Hasek; directed by Karel Lamac; for Eden Films.

'When Scorpio wants you, there is nowhere to hide!'
Scorpio
US 1972 114m Technicolor
UA / Scimitar (Walter Mirisch)

CIA agents doublecross each other. Incredibly complex spy thriller in which it's difficult to know, or care, who's following whom. The brutalities, however, are capably staged.

w David W. Rintels, Gerald Wilson *d* Michael Winner *ph* Robert Paynter *m* Jerry Fielding

Burt Lancaster, Alain Delon, Paul Scofield, John Colicos, Gayle Hunnicutt, J. D. Cannon
'Strictly zoom and thump.'—*Sight and Sound*

'Relying on moments of violence for effect, Winner directs with typically crass abandon.'—*Time Out, 1984*

Scotland Yard
US 1941 68m bw
TCF (Sol M. Wurtzel)

The Nazis capture a London banker and use his double to turn funds over to them. Outlandish spy melodrama which certainly keeps the interest.

w Samuel G. Engel, John Balderston, *play* Deniston Clift *d* Norman Foster *ph* Virgil Miller *m* Emil Newman

Nancy Kelly, Edmund Gwenn, Henry Wilcoxon, John Loder, Melville Cooper, Gilbert Emery, Norma Varden

Scotland Yard Investigator
US 1945 68m bw

Frenchmen attempt to steal the Mona Lisa from its wartime home in the National Gallery. Very passable programme filler with stalwart actors enjoying themselves. Sir Aubrey Smith, Erich Von Stroheim, Stephanie Bachelor, Forrester Harvey, Richard Fraser, Frederick Worlock. Written by Randall Faye; directed and produced by George Blair; for Republic.

Scott of the Antarctic**
GB 1948 111m Technicolor
Ealing (Sidney Cole)

After long preparation, Captain Scott sets off on his ill-fated 1912 expedition to the South Pole.
The stiff-upper-lip saga par excellence; inevitable knowledge of the end makes it pretty downbeat, and the actors can only be sincere; but the snowscapes, most of them artificial, are fine.

w Ivor Montagu, Walter Meade, Mary Hayley Bell *d* Charles Frend *ph* Geoffrey Unsworth, Jack Cardiff, Osmond Borradaile *m* Ralph Vaughan Williams

John Mills, James Robertson Justice, Derek Bond, Harold Warrender, Reginald Beckwith, Kenneth More, James McKechnie, John Gregson

The Scoundrel**
US 1935 74m bw
Paramount (Ben Hecht, Charles MacArthur)

A famous writer dies; his ghost comes back to find the meaning of love.
Unique thirties supernatural melodrama with barbs of dated wit despatched by a splendid cast. Nonsense, but great nonsense.

wd Ben Hecht, Charles MacArthur *ph* Lee Garmes *m* George Antheil

Noel Coward, Alexander Woolcott, Julie Haydon, Stanley Ridges, Eduardo Ciannelli
'Good Hotel Algonquin literati stuff, but not for the Automat trade.'—*Variety*

'An unmistakeable whiff from a gossip column world which tries hard to split the difference between an epigram and a wisecrack.'—*William Whitebait*

'Practically flawless drama. It's arty, but if this is art, let us have more of it.'—*Photoplay*
'An impudent work . . . but there are brains in it, and observation, and even a kind of stunted poetry.'—*Observer*

† Helen Hayes and Edna Ferber made cameo appearances.

AA: original story
AAN: script

Scouts to the Rescue
US 1939 bw serial: 12 eps

Eagle Scouts find buried treasure in a ghost town. Juvenile serial. Jackie Cooper, Frank Coghlan Jnr, Bill Cody Jnr, Vondell Darr, Edwin Stanley. Directed by Ray Taylor and Alan James; for Universal.

Scram!*
US 1932 20m bw

Two vagrants are ordered out of town but by a series of misadventures are found drunk with the judge's wife. Generally sprightly star comedy culminating in a marathon laughing session. Laurel and Hardy, Arthur Housman, Rychard Cramer, Vivien Oakland. Written by H. M. Walker; directed by Ray McCarey; for Hal Roach.

Scream and Scream Again*
GB 1969 94m Eastmancolor
AIP / Amicus (Milton Subotsky)

Murders are traced to superhuman composite beings created by a mad scientist.
Energetic and well-staged though rather humourless shocker.

w Christopher Wicking, *novel* The Disorientated Man by Peter Saxon *d* Gordon Hessler *ph* John Coquillon *m* David Whittaker *ad* Don Mingaye

Vincent Price, Christopher Lee, Peter Cushing, Alfred Marks, Anthony Newlands, David Lodge

Scream for Help
US 1984 90m colour

A teenager becomes convinced that her stepfather is trying to murder her mother. Crude splatter movie which the director presumably undertook as a joke. Rachael Kelly, David Brooks, Marie Masters, Rocco Sisto, Lolita Lorre. Written by Tom Holland; directed by Michael Winner; for Lorimar.
'Over the moronic characterization, daft dialogue, inept performances and opportunistic camerawork, music has been poured like a constant stream of cold gravy, making a sound that on occasion resembles, not inappropriately, a growling stomach.'—*Philip Strick, Monthly Film Bulletin*

A Scream in the Dark
US 1943 53m bw

A private eye tracks down a constant widow with a trail of dead husbands. Lightweight mystery which might have been better. Robert Lowery, Marie McDonald, Edward S. Brophy, Wally Vernon, Hobart Cavanaugh, Jack La Rue, Elizabeth Russell. Written by Gerald Schnitzer, Anthony Coldeway, from Jerome Odlum's novel *The Morgue is Always Open*; directed and produced by George Sherman; for Republic.

Screaming Mimi
US 1958 79m bw

After being sexually assaulted a dancer comes to believe she has committed murder . . . and later we learn that she has. Sub-Freudian melodrama on the comic strip level. Anita Ekberg, Phil Carey, Harry Townes, Gypsy Rose Lee, Romney Brent, Alan Gifford. Written by Robert Blees, from the book by Frederic Brown; directed by Gerd Oswald; for Sage / Columbia.

Scrooge*
GB 1935 78m bw
Twickenham (Julius Hagen, John Brahm)

A miser reforms after ghosts haunt him on Christmas Eve.
Acceptable unambitious version with interesting performances.

w Seymour Hicks, H. Fowler Mear, *novel* Charles Dickens *d* Henry Edwards *ph* Sidney Blythe, William Luff

Seymour Hicks, Donald Calthrop (Cratchit), Athene Seyler, Oscar Asche, Barbara Everest, Maurice Evans, C. V. France, Marie Ney

Scrooge***
GB 1951 86m bw
Renown (Brian Desmond Hurst)
US title: *A Christmas Carol*

By far the best available version of the classic parable; casting, art direction, pace and general handling are as good as can be.

w Noel Langley *d Brian Desmond Hurst* *ph C. Pennington-Richards* *m* Richard Addinsell

Alastair Sim, Mervyn Johns, Kathleen Harrison, Jack Warner, Michael Hordern, Hermione Baddeley, George Cole, Miles Malleson

Scrooge*
GB 1970 113m Technicolor
Panavision
Cinema Center / Waterbury (Richard H. Solo)

Dim musical version, darkly coloured and quite lost on the wide screen; but it has its macabre moments of trick photography.

w / m / ly Leslie Bricusse *d* Ronald Neame *ph* Oswald Morris *pd* Terry Marsh

Albert Finney, Michael Medwin, Alec Guinness, Edith Evans, Kenneth More, David Collings, Laurence Naismith, Kay Walsh

† Richard Harris and Rex Harrison were both sought before Finney was signed.
AAN: song 'Thank You Very Much' (*m / ly* Leslie Bricusse); music

Scrooged*
US 1988 101m Technicolor
Paramount / Mirage

Updated version of Dickens's *A Christmas Carol*, centring on the president of a New York television company.
Energetic and sometimes genuinely scary seasonal entertainment for modern kids.

w Mitch Glazer, Michael O'Donoghue *d* Richard Donner *ph* Michael Chapman *m* Danny Elfman *pd* J. Michael Riva

Bill Murray, Karen Allen, John Forsythe, Robert Mitchum, John Housman, Lee Majors

Scrubbers
GB 1982 93m Eastmancolor
Handmade (Don Boyd)

Sensational events in a girls' borstal.
Wild-eyed melodrama which seems to serve no sort of purpose and is certainly not entertaining.

w Roy Minton, Jeremy Watt, Mai Zetterling *d* Mai Zetterling *ph* Ernest Vincze *m* Michael Hurd

Amanda York, Chrissie Cotterill, Elizabeth Edmonds, Kate Ingram, Honey Bane, Eva Motley

Scudda Hoo, Scudda Hay
US 1948 98m Technicolor
TCF (Walter Morosco)
GB title: *Summer Lightning*

A farmer's son is less interested in girls than in the welfare of his two mules.
Antediluvian rural romance for the simple-minded.

wd F. Hugh Herbert, *novel* George Agnew Chamberlain *ph* Ernest Palmer *m* Cyril Mockridge

June Haver, Lon McCallister, Walter Brennan, Anne Revere, Natalie Wood, Robert Karnes, Henry Hull, Tom Tully, Marilyn Monroe

Scum
GB 1979 97m Eastmancolor

Injustices in a Borstal institution lead to a riot. Gorily overstated view of boys' prison life from the inside, with the camera gloating over each violent close-up. (The original TV play had been made, then banned, by the BBC.) Ray Winstone, Mick Ford, Julian Firth, John Blundell. Written by Roy Minton; directed by Alan Clarke; for Berwick Street Films.

The Sea Bat
US 1930 69m bw

Mexican fishermen compete to kill a deadly sting-ray. The *Jaws* of its time; box office hokum. Charles Bickford, Raquel Torres, Nils Asther, John Miljan, Gibson Gowland, Boris Karloff. Written by Bess Meredyth and John Howard Lawson; directed by Wesley Ruggles; for MGM.

The Sea Beast*
US 1926 125m approx bw silent
In this version of Moby Dick, Ahab gets to settle down at the end with his lady love. Memorable sea scenes and a star performance. *John Barrymore*, Dolores Costello, George O'Hara, Mike Donlin, Sam Baker. Written by Bess Meredyth; directed by Millard Webb; for Warners.

The Sea Chase*
US 1955 117m Warnercolor
Cinemascope
Warner (John Farrow)

In 1939 a German freighter tries to make it from Sydney harbour back to Germany.
Unusual but not very compelling naval melodrama, chiefly because the leads are miscast.

w James Warner Bellah, John Twist, *novel* Andrew Geer *d* John Farrow *ph* William Clothier *m* Roy Webb

John Wayne, Lana Turner, David Farrar, Lyle Bettger, Tab Hunter, James Arness, Dick Davalos, John Qualen

'A film compounded of monotonously familiar ingredients.'—*Penelope Houston*

Sea Devils
US 1937 88m bw

Exploits of the ice patrols of the US Coast Guard. Flagwaving action hokum for popular stars. Victor McLaglen, Preston Foster, Ida Lupino, Donald Woods. Written by Frank Wead, John Twist and P. J. Wolfson; directed by Ben Stoloff; for RKO.

Sea Devils
GB 1953 90m Technicolor
Coronado (David E. Rose)

Spies prevent Napoleon's invasion of England. Cheerful, forgettable swashbuckler.

w Borden Chase *d* Raoul Walsh *ph* Wilkie Cooper *m* Richard Addinsell

Yvonne de Carlo, Rock Hudson, Maxwell Reed, Denis O'Dea, Michael Goodliffe, Bryan Forbes, Ivor Barnard, Arthur Wontner

Sea Fury
GB 1958 97m bw
Rank (Benjamin Fisz)

Rivalry strikes up between an old and a young sailor on tugboats plying between Spain and England.
Shapeless, leery melodrama with strong performances and an exciting storm-at-sea climax.

w John Kruse, Cy Endfield *d* Cy Endfield *ph* Reg Wyer *m* Philip Green

Stanley Baker, Victor McLaglen, Luciana Paluzzi, Grégoire Aslan, Francis de Wolff, David Oxley, Rupert Davies, Robert Shaw

'They stand side by side. Young and old. Rich and poor. They gather together for a single purpose. Survival.'

The Sea Gull*
GB 1968 141m Technicolor
Warner / Sidney Lumet

Loves and hates on a 19th-century Russian estate.
Rather heavily star-studded, but certainly proficient film version of a Chekhov favourite.

w Moura Budberg, *play* Anton Chekhov *d* Sidney Lumet *ph* Gerry Fisher *m* none *pd* Tony Walton

James Mason, Simone Signoret, Vanessa Redgrave, David Warner, Harry Andrews, Ronald Radd, Eileen Herlie, Kathleen Widdoes, Denholm Elliott, Alfred Lynch

'The camera cannot capture the hollowness of space, the oppressive immoveableness of a seemingly harmless enclosure, stasis settling on everything like a fine, corrosive dust.'—*John Simon*

'If you miss it, you will owe yourself an apology!'

The Sea Hawk***
US 1940 122m bw
Warner (Hal B. Wallis, Henry Blanke)

Elizabeth I encourages one of her most able captains to acts of piracy against the Spanish.
Wobbly-plotted but stirring and exciting seafaring actioner, with splendid battle and duel scenes.

w Seton I. Miller, Howard Koch *d Michael Curtiz ph Sol Polito m Erich Wolfgang Korngold ad Anton Grot*

Errol Flynn, Flora Robson, Brenda Marshall, *Henry Daniell,* Claude Rains, Donald Crisp, Alan Hale, Una O'Connor, James Stephenson, Gilbert Roland, William Lundigan

'Endless episodes of court intrigue tend to diminish the effect of the epic sweep of the high seas dramatics.'—*Variety*

AAN: Erich Wolfgang Korngold

The Sea Hound
US 1947 bw serial: 15 eps

The owner of a private schooner tracks down modern pirates in search of Spanish gold.
Tolerable adventure serial. Buster Crabbe, Jimmy Lloyd, Pamela Blake, Rick Vallin. Directed by Walter B. Eason, Mack Wright; for Columbia.

'A man who loved as ruthlessly as he ruled. A woman whose indiscretions cost a lifetime of happiness!'

The Sea of Grass
US 1947 131m bw
MGM (Pandro S. Berman)

A cattle tycoon is so obsessed by his work that he alienates his family.
Brooding, overlong semi-western with an unexpected cast.

w Marguerite Roberts, Vincent Lawrence, *novel* Conrad Richter *d* Elia Kazan *ph Harry Stradling m* Herbert Stothart

Spencer Tracy, Katharine Hepburn, Melvyn Douglas, Phyllis Thaxter, Robert Walker, Edgar Buchanan, Harry Carey, Ruth Nelson, James Bell

'In spite of all the sincerity and talent involved, an epically dreary film.'—*Time*

Sea of Lost Ships
US 1953 85m bw

The US Coast Guard saves a passenger ship from an iceberg. Scrappy, semi-documentary account punctuated by rough action highlights. Walter Brennan, John Derek, Wanda Hendrix, Richard Jaeckel, Barton Maclane, Darryl Hickman. Written by Steve Fisher; directed by Joe Kane; for Republic.

Sea of Sand*
GB 1958 98m bw
Rank / Tempean (Robert Baker, Monty Berman)
US title: *Desert Patrol*

Just before Alamein an Eighth Army desert group plans to destroy one of Rommel's last petrol dumps.
Good standard war suspenser.

w Robert Westerby *d* Guy Green *ph* Wilkie Cooper *m* Clifton Parker

Richard Attenborough, John Gregson, Vincent Ball, Percy Herbert, Michael Craig, Barry Foster, Andrew Faulds, Dermot Walsh

The Sea Shall Not Have Them
GB 1954 93m bw
Eros / Daniel M. Angel

Survivors of a seaplane crash await rescue in a dinghy.
Rather dim computerized compendium of flashback mini-dramas.

w Lewis Gilbert, Vernon Harris *d* Lewis Gilbert *ph* Stephen Dade *m* Malcolm Arnold

Dirk Bogarde, Michael Redgrave, Bonar Colleano, Jack Watling, Anthony Steel, Nigel Patrick, James Kenney, Sidney Tafler, George Rose

'One of the most challenging stories of faith ever told! What happened out there . . . in the surging vastness of the Indian Ocean?'

Sea Wife
GB 1957 82m De Luxe Cinemascope
TCF / Sumar (André Hakim)

Survivors of a shipwreck near Singapore in 1942 are rescued, not before the bosun has fallen in love with the only lady, not knowing she is a nun.
Flashbacked, uncertain, intermittently effective film of a popular minor novel.

w George K. Burke, *novel* Sea Wyf by J. M. Scott *d* Bob McNaught *ph* Ted Scaife *m* Kenneth V. Jones, Leonard Salzedo

Richard Burton, Joan Collins, Basil Sydney, Cy Grant

The Sea Wolf**
US 1941 90m bw
Warner (Henry Blanke)

Survivors of a ferry crash in San Francisco Bay are picked up by a psychopathic freighter captain who keeps them captive.
Much filmed action suspenser which in this version looks great but overdoes the talk.

w Robert Rossen, *novel* Jack London *d Michael Curtiz ph Sol Polito m Erich Wolfgang Korngold*

Edward G. Robinson, Alexander Knox, Ida Lupino, John Garfield, Gene Lockhart, Barry Fitzgerald, Stanley Ridges, David Bruce, Howard da Silva

'A Germanic, powerful work almost devoid of compromise.'—*Charles Higham, 1972*

† Other versions appeared in 1913, with Hobart Bosworth; in 1920, with Noah Beery; in 1925, with Ralph Ince; in 1930, with Milton Sills; in 1950 (as *Barricade*, turned into a western), with Raymond Massey; in 1958 (as *Wolf Larsen*), with Barry Sullivan; and in 1975 (Italian), as *Wolf of the Seven Seas*, with Chuck Connors.

The Sea Wolves*
GB-US-Switzerland 1980 122m Eastmancolor
Richmond-Lorimar-Varius (Euan Lloyd)

In 1943, elderly British territorials living in India dispose of a Nazi transmitter in neutral Goa.
Mildly larkish *Boy's Own Paper* adventure with a somewhat geriatric air; an interesting 1980 throwback to the films of 1950.

w Reginald Rose *novel* Boarding Party by James Leasor *d* Andrew McLaglen *ph* Tony Imi *m* Roy Budd

Gregory Peck, Roger Moore, Trevor Howard, David Niven, Barbara Kellerman, Patrick MacNee, Patrick Allen, Bernard Archard, Faith Brook, Martin Benson, Allan Cuthbertson, Kenneth Griffith, Donald Houston, Glyn Houston, Percy Herbert, Patrick Holt, Terence Longdon, John Standing, Michael Medwin

'As a genre—the arterio-sclerotic war movie—it'll never catch on.'—*Time Out*

† The film was dedicated to Earl Mountbatten after his assassination.

Seagulls over Sorrento
GB 1954 92m bw
MGM (John and Roy Boulting)
US title: *Crest of the Wave*

Life on a naval research station on a small Scottish island.
A long-running British service comedy has been Americanized to little effect, but it remains just about watchable.

w Frank Harvey, Roy Boulting, *play* Hugh Hastings *d* John and Roy Boulting *ph* Gilbert Taylor *m* Miklos Rozsa

Gene Kelly, John Justin, Bernard Lee, Sidney James, Jeff Richards, Patric Doonan, Patrick Barr

Seal Island see The Living Desert

'What is the truth about fraternization?'

Sealed Verdict
US 1948 83m bw
Paramount (Robert Fellows)

An American officer in Germany falls in love with the ex-girl friend of a Nazi war criminal.
Routine melodrama, as boring as it sounds.

w Jonathan Latimer, *novel* Lionel Shapiro *d* Lewis Allen *ph* Leo Tover *m* Hugo Friedhofer

Ray Milland, Florence Marly, Broderick Crawford, John Hoyt, John Ridgely, Ludwig Donath

Seance on a Wet Afternoon*
GB 1964 121m bw
Rank / Allied Film Makers (Richard Attenborough, Bryan Forbes, Jack Rix)

A fake medium persuades her husband to kidnap a child so that she can become famous by revealing its whereabouts in a trance.
Overlong character melodrama in which the suspense is better than the psychopathology. A mannered performance from the lady, a false nose from the gentleman, and a general air of gloom.

wd Bryan Forbes *ph* Gerry Turpin *m* John Barry

Kim Stanley, Richard Attenborough, Nanette Newman, Patrick Magee

AAN: Kim Stanley

The Search*
US / Switzerland 1948 105m bw
MGM / Praesens Film (Lazar Wechsler)

An American soldier in Germany cares for a war orphan.
Vivid semi-documentary post-war drama which falls down in its elementary dramatics but sent audiences home wiping away tears.

w Richard Schweizer, David Wechsler, Paul Jarrico *d Fred Zinnemann ph Emil Berna* *m* Robert Blum

Montgomery Clift, Aline MacMahon, Ivan Jandl, Wendell Corey

AA: original story (Richard Schweizer, David Wechsler)
AAN: script; Fred Zinnemann; Montgomery Clift

'You never saw so many skins you'd like to touch!'

Search for Beauty
US 1934 77m bw

A physical culture magazine sponsors an international contest for beauties of both sexes. Mildly amusing extravaganza staking its popularity on girls in bathing dress. Larry Buster Crabbe, Ida Lupino, Toby Wing, James Gleason, Robert Armstrong, Gertrude Michael, Roscoe Karns. Written by Claude Binyon, Sam Hellman, Frank Butler and others from a play by Schuyler E. Gray and Paul R. Milton; directed by Erle C. Kenton; for Paramount. 'A couple of years ago so many girls in abbreviated dress would have been enough for one picture . . . but they've seen massed pulchritude quite often lately, so the girls here are just trimmings.'—*Variety*

The Search for Bridey Murphy*
US 1956 84m bw Vistavision
Paramount (Pat Duggan)

A Colorado businessman and amateur hypnotist finds a lady neighbour so good a subject that he is able to delve into her previous incarnation as a long-dead Irish peasant.
Adequately presented with alienation effects, but mainly consisting of two-shots and fuzzy flashbacks, this treatment of an actual case (subsequently discredited) works up to a fine pitch of frenzy when the subject seems unable to come back from her previous life.

wd Noel Langley, book Morey Bernstein *ph* John F. Warren *m* Irving Talbot

Teresa Wright, Louis Hayward, Kenneth Tobey, Nancy Gates, Richard Anderson

The Searchers**
US 1956 119m Technicolor Vistavision
Warner / C. V. Whitney (Merian C. Cooper)

A Confederate war veteran tracks down the Indians who have slaughtered his brother and sister-in-law and carried off their daughter.
Desultory, easy-going, good-looking western in typical Ford style; a bit more solemn than usual.

w Frank S. Nugent, *novel* Alan le May *d John Ford ph Winton C. Hoch m* Max Steiner

John Wayne, Jeffrey Hunter, Natalie Wood, Vera Miles, Ward Bond, John Qualen, Henry Brandon, Antonio Moreno

'You can read a lot into it, but it isn't very enjoyable.'—*Pauline Kael, 70s*

'What strange power could drive this man from the lips of the woman he married to the arms of the woman he loved?'

The Searching Wind*
US 1946 107m bw
Paramount (Hal B. Wallis)

Affairs of an American diplomat in Europe during the thirties.
Earnest melodrama which would have been better timed six years earlier. Excellent production, though.

w Lillian Hellman, from her play *d* William Dieterle *ph* Lee Garmes *m* Victor Young *ad* Hans Drier, Franz Bachelin

Robert Young, Sylvia Sidney, Ann Richards, Douglas Dick, Dudley Digges, Albert Basserman, Dan Seymour

The Seashell and the Clergyman*
France 1928 30m approx (24 fps) bw silent
(Producer unknown)

A clergyman is afflicted by sexual torments.
Celebrated surrealist short with memorable images and a great deal of confusion.

w Antonin Artaud *d Germaine Dulac* *ph* Paul Guichard

Alix Allin

† In GB the film was banned by the censor with the famous comment: 'It is so cryptic as to have no apparent meaning. If there is a meaning, it is doubtless objectionable.'

Sebastian
GB 1968 100m Eastmancolor
Paramount / Maccius (Herb Brodkin, Michael Powell)

An Oxford professor and code expert is appointed to the secret service.
Mildly spoofy spy yarn: style but not much substance.

w Gerald Vaughan-Hughes *d David Greene* *ph* Gerry Fisher *m* Jerry Goldsmith *pd* Wilfred Shingleton

Dirk Bogarde, *John Gielgud,* Lilli Palmer, Susannah York, Janet Munro, Margaret Johnston, Nigel Davenport, Ronald Fraser

'One of the problems with this kind of movie is the enormous pressure put on the audience to have a good time over practically nothing.'—*Renata Adler*

Second Best Bed
GB 1938 74m bw

A magistrate is suspected of adultery. Cheerful star comedy with a touch of sophistication. Tom Walls, Jane Baxter, Veronica Rose, Carl Jaffe, Greta Gynt. Written by Ben Travers; directed by Tom Walls; for Capitol.

Second Chance
US 1953 82m Technicolor 3-D
RKO (Edmund Grainger)

In South America, a professional killer stalks a gangster's moll.
Comic strip antics with a climax on a stalled cable car.

w Oscar Millard, Sidney Boehm, *story* D. M. Marshman Jnr *d* Rudolph Maté *ph* William Snyder *m* Roy Webb

Robert Mitchum, Linda Darnell, Jack Palance, Reginald Sheffield, Roy Roberts

Second Chorus
US 1940 84m bw
Paramount (Boris Morros)

Two trumpeters and their lady manager hit Broadway.
Mild musical.

w Elaine Ryan, Ian McClellan Hunter, Frank Cavett *d* H. C. Potter *ph* Theodor Sparkuhl *songs* various *m* Artie Shaw

Fred Astaire, Burgess Meredith, Paulette Goddard, Charles Butterworth, Artie Shaw and his Band, Frank Melton, Jimmy Conlon

AAN: Artie Shaw; song 'Love of my Life' (*m* Artie Shaw, *ly* Johnny Mercer)

Second Fiddle
US 1939 86m bw
TCF (Gene Markey)

A Minnesota skating schoolteacher goes to Hollywood and becomes a star.
Routine star vehicle.

w Harry Tugend *d* Sidney Lanfield *ph* Leon Shamroy *md* Louis Silvers *songs* Irving Berlin

Sonja Henie, Tyrone Power, Edna May Oliver, Rudy Vallee, Mary Healy, Lyle Talbot, Alan Dinehart

AAN: song 'I Poured My Heart into a Song' (*m / ly* Irving Berlin)

The Second-Floor Mystery
US 1930 56m bw

Correspondents through an agony column find themselves enmeshed in mystery and murder. Burlesque whodunit which seemed a smart trick at the time. Loretta Young, Grant Withers, H. B. Warner, Clare McDowell, John Loder. Written by Joseph Jackson from the novel The Agony Column by Earl Derr Biggers; directed by Roy del Ruth; for Warners.

The Second Greatest Sex
US 1955 87m Technicolor Cinemascope
U-I (Albert J. Cohen)

Western women emulate Lysistrata to stop their men from feuding.
Flat attempt to cash in on *Seven Brides for Seven Brothers*; some good acrobatic dancing but no style.

w Charles Hoffman *d* George Marshall *ph* Wilfrid M. Cline *md* Joseph Gershenson *ch* Lee Scott

Jeanne Crain, George Nader, Bert Lahr, Kitty Kallen, Paul Gilbert, Keith Andes, Mamie Van Doren, Tommy Rall

Second Honeymoon
US 1937 79m bw
TCF (Raymond Griffith)

A man tries to win back his ex-wife.
Moderate star romantic comedy.

w Kathryn Scola, Darrell Ware, *story* Philip Wylie *d* Walter Lang *ph* Ernest Palmer *m* David Buttolph

Tyrone Power, Loretta Young, Stuart Erwin, Claire Trevor, Marjorie Weaver, Lyle Talbot, J. Edward Bromberg

The Second Mrs Tanqueray
GB 1952 75m bw
Vandyke (Roger Proudlock)

A Victorian society widower marries a notorious lady.
Stiff-backed penny-pinching version of an interestingly antiquated play.

play Arthur Wing Pinero *d* Dallas Bower

Pamela Brown, Hugh Sinclair, Ronald Ward, Virginia McKenna, Andrew Osborn

Second Thoughts
US 1982 98m Movielab

A lady lawyer gets into complex trouble when she bails out her inconsiderate lover from a Santa Fe jail. An absurd series of situations is played for drama rather than comedy, and the feminist flag is frequently waved. The result is an unlikeable muddle. Lucie Arnaz, Craig Wasson, Ken Howard, Anne Schedeen. Written by Steve Brown; directed by Lawrence Turman; for Turman-Foster / EMI.
'Alternately dull and risible.'—*Chris Auty, MFB*

The Second Time Around
US 1961 99m De Luxe Cinemascope
TCF / Cummings / Harman (Jack Cummings)

In 1912 Arizona, a widow stands for sheriff and has plenty of choice for a husband.
Light-hearted western fun mixed with family sentimentality.

w Oscar Saul, Cecil Van Heusen, *novel* Richard Emery Roberts *d* Vincent Sherman *ph* Ellis W. Carter *m* Gerald Fried

Debbie Reynolds, Steve Forrest, Andy Griffith, Juliet Prowse, Thelma Ritter, Ken Scott, Isobel Elsom

'Keep a lemon handy for sucking to ward off an attack of the terminal cutesies.'—*Judith Crist, 1973*

The Second Victory
GB 1986 112m Rank colour

In Austria after World War II, British occupation forces try to keep order in face of unrest following the murder of a sergeant. Curiously timed return to the Third Man era, with a plotline unlikely to appeal to modern filmgoers; technical resources adequate rather than inspired. Anthony Andrews, Helmut Griem, Max von Sydow, Mario Adorf, Birgit Doll. Written by Morris West from his novel; directed and produced by Gerald Thomas for Lelaleuka / J and M.

The Second Woman
US 1950 91m bw
United Artists / Cardinal (Mort Briskin)
GB title: *Ellen*

An architect, apparently paranoic, is proved to be the victim of a revenge plot.
Tolerable semi-star melodrama with a deliberate 'film noir' look.

w Robert Smith *d* James V. Kern *ph* Hal Mohr *md* Nat Finston

Robert Young, Betsy Drake, John Sutton, Florence Bates, Morris Carnovsky, Henry O'Neill

Seconds**
US 1966 106m bw
Paramount / Joel / Gibraltar (Edward Lewis)

A secret organization sells a special service to the jaded rich; apparent death followed by physical rejuvenation.
An intriguing half-hour is followed by a glum new life for our hero, capped by a horrifying finale in which, dissatisfied, he learns he is to become one of the corpses necessary to the organization's continuance.

w Lewis John Carlino, *novel* David Ely *d John Frankenheimer ph James Wong Howe* *m* Jerry Goldsmith *titles* Saul Bass

Rock Hudson, *John Randolph, Will Geer*, Salome Jens, Jeff Corey, Richard Anderson, Murray Hamilton, Wesley Addy

'A really horrifying piece of science fiction that burns its way into your mind like a gnawing headache.'—*Sunday Express*

'An ending that is one of the most terrifying episodes I have ever seen on the screen.'—*Daily Express*

AAN: James Wong Howe

The Secret Agent**
GB 1936 83m bw
Gaumont British (Michael Balcon, Ivor Montagu)

A reluctantly recruited spy is ordered to kill a man.
Unsatisfactory in casting and writing, this Hitchcock suspenser nevertheless has many typically amusing moments.

w Charles Bennett, *play* Campbell Dixon, *story* Ashenden by Somerset Maugham *d Alfred Hitchcock ph* Bernard Knowles *md* Louis Levy

John Gielgud, Robert Young, *Peter Lorre*, Madeleine Carroll, Percy Marmont, Lilli Palmer, Florence Kahn

'As uncommon as it is unsentimentally cruel.'—*Peter John Dyer, 1964*

'Many sequences which show Hitchcock at his very best: the fake funeral, the murder on the mountainside, the riverside café, and the climax in a chocolate factory.'—*NFT, 1961*

'How unfortunate it is that Mr Hitchcock, a clever director, is allowed to produce and even to write his own films, though as a producer he has no sense of continuity and as a writer he has no sense of life. His films consist of a series of small "amusing" melodramatic situations: the murderer's button dropped on the baccarat board; the strangled organist's hands prolonging the notes in the empty church; the fugitives hiding in the bell tower when the bell begins to swing. Very perfunctorily he builds up to these tricky situations . . . and then drops them.'—*Graham Greene*

'Hitch said he was offering me *Hamlet* in modern dress. But when we came to make it, all the psychological interest was dissipated.'—*John Gielgud*

Secret Agent of Japan
US 1942 72m bw

A female British agent tangles with Japanese in the Shanghai international settlement. Standard propaganda filler with caricature Japs. Preston Foster, Lynn Bari, Noel Madison, Sen Yung, Janis Carter, Steve Geray, Kurt Katch. Written by John Larkin; directed by Irving Pichel; for TCF.

Secret Agent X9
US 1937 bw serial: 12 eps

A G-man goes undercover to track down the Belgravian crown jewels. Mildly amusing adventures. Scott Kolk, Jean Rogers, Henry Hunter, Henry Brandon, Monte Blue. Directed by Ford Beebe and Cliff Smith; for Universal.

Secret Agent X9
US 1945 bw serial: 13 eps

More adventures of the G-man, this time sent to the China coast to destroy the Black Dragon Intelligence service. Predictable propaganda serial. Lloyd Bridges, Keye Luke, Jan Wiley, Victoria Horne, Samuel S. Hinds, Cy Kendall. Directed by Ray Taylor and Lewis Collins; for Universal.

'Behind a locked door—the relentless evil of his past!'

The Secret beyond the Door
US 1948 98m bw
Universal / Walter Wanger (Fritz Lang)

An heiress marries a moody millionaire with a death fixation, and comes to think of herself as his next potential victim.
Silly melodrama with much chat and little suspense.

w Sylvia Richards, *story* Rufus King *d* Fritz Lang *ph* Stanley Cortez *m* Miklos Rozsa

Joan Bennett, Michael Redgrave, Anne Revere, Barbara O'Neil, Natalie Schaefer, Paul Cavanagh

'A dog-wagon *Rebecca* with a seasoning of psychiatrics.'—*Otis L. Guernsey Jnr*

'Lang gets a few wood-silky highlights out of this sow's ear, but it is a hopeless job and a worthless movie.'—*James Agee*

The Secret Bride
US 1935 63m bw
Warner
GB title: *Concealment*

A District Attorney is secretly married to the daughter of the politician he is trying to convict.
Dismal melodrama, tritely scripted.

w Tom Buckingham, F. Hugh Herbert, Mary McCall Jnr, *play* Concealment by Leonard Ide *d* William Dieterle *ph* Ernest Haller

Barbara Stanwyck, Warren William, Glenda Farrell, Grant Mitchell, Arthur Byron, Henry O'Neill, Douglass Dumbrille

'Fast moving melodrama, well above average.'—*Variety*

Secret Ceremony
GB 1969 109m Eastmancolor
Universal / World Films / Paul M. Heller (John Heyman, Norman Priggen)

A prostitute mothers a young girl with a strange past.
Nuthouse melodrama for devotees of the director.

w George Tabori, *short story* Marco Denevi *d* Joseph Losey *ph* Gerry Fisher *m* Richard Rodney Bennett

Elizabeth Taylor, Robert Mitchum, Mia Farrow, Pamela Brown, Peggy Ashcroft

'This piece of garbage is so totally ridiculous that I can't imagine why anyone would want to be in it, let alone see it.'—*Rex Reed*

The Secret Code
US 1942 bw serial: 15 eps

A police lieutenant arranges to be thrown off the force in disgrace so that he can infiltrate an enemy sabotage ring. Standard wartime thick-ear. Paul Kelly, Anne Nagel, Clancy Cooper, Trevor Bardette. Directed by Spencer G. Bennet; for Columbia.

Secret Command
US 1944 92m bw
Columbia (Phil L. Ryan)

An ex-foreign correspondent goes undercover at a shipyard to track down saboteurs.
Routine wartime thick ear.

w Roy Chanslor, *story* The Saboteurs by John and Ward Hawkins *d* Eddie Sutherland *ph* Franz Planer *m* Paul Sawtell

Pat O'Brien, Carole Landis, Chester Morris, Ruth Warrick, Barton MacLane, Tom Tully, Wallace Ford, Howard Freeman

The Secret Fury
US 1950 86m bw
RKO (Jack H. Skirball, Bruce Manning)

A successful pianist is deliberately driven insane by her fiancé.
Derivative melodrama of no great interest.

w Lionel House *d* Mel Ferrer *ph* Leo Tover *m* Roy Webb *md* Constantin Bakaleinikoff

Claudette Colbert, Robert Ryan, Jane Cowl, Paul Kelly, Philip Ober, Elizabeth Risdon, Doris Dudley

The Secret Garden*
US 1949 92m bw (Technicolor sequence)
MGM (Clarence Brown)

An orphan girl goes to stay with her moody uncle and brightens up the lives of those around her.
Subdued, richly produced, rather likeable Victorian fable with the same moral as *The Bluebird* and *The Wizard of Oz*: happiness is in your own back yard.

w Robert Ardrey, *novel* Frances Hodgson Burnett *d* Fred M. Wilcox *ph* Ray June *m* Bronislau Kaper

Margaret O'Brien, Herbert Marshall, Gladys Cooper, Elsa Lanchester, Dean Stockwell, Brian Roper

'Uneven, but oddly and unexpectedly interesting.'—*Richard Mallett, Punch*

'Let's have more pictures in this kindly vein.'—*Picturegoer*

The Secret Heart
US 1946 97m bw
MGM (Edwin H. Knopf)

A widow has problems with her emotionally disturbed daughter.
Old-fashioned woman's picture.

w Rose Franken, William Brown Meloney *d* Robert Z. Leonard *ph* George Folsey *m* Bronislau Kaper

Claudette Colbert, Walter Pidgeon, June Allyson, Robert Sterling, Marshall Thompson, Elizabeth Patterson, Richard Derr, Patricia Medina

' "There are three things you can't hide," says Walter Pidgeon in one of his bantering moments; "love, smoke, and a man riding a camel." I would add a fourth—that old MGM touch.'—*Richard Winnington*

'The daring plan—the staggering odds—the incredible five!'

The Secret Invasion
US 1964 98m De Luxe Panavision
UA / San Carlos (Gene Corman)

During World War II five convicted criminals become commandos.
Cut price *Dirty Dozen*, quite well made and exciting.

w R. Wright Campbell *d* Roger Corman *ph* Arthur E. Arling *m* Hugo Friedhofer

Stewart Granger, Raf Vallone, Henry Silva, Mickey Rooney, Edd Byrnes, William Campbell, Peter Coe

The Secret Life of an American Wife**
US 1968 92m De Luxe
TCF / Charlton (George Axelrod)

A bored suburban housewife sets out to seduce a movie star.
Sympathetic comedy of sixties suburban manners.

wd George Axelrod *ph* Leon Shamroy *m* Billy May

Walter Matthau, Anne Jackson, Patrick O'Neal, Edy Williams

'Both a first-class satire on American mores and a compassionate study of wish-fulfilment.'—*NFT, 1970*

The Secret Life of Walter Mitty**
US 1947 110m Technicolor
Samuel Goldwyn

A mother's boy dreams of derring-do, and eventually life catches up with fiction.
This pleasantly remembered star comedy, though it never had much to do with Thurber, can now be seen to have missed most of its opportunities, though the nice moments do tend to compensate.

w Ken Englund, Everett Freeman, *story* James Thurber *d* Norman Z. McLeod *ph* Lee Garmes *m* David Raksin

Danny Kaye, Virginia Mayo, Boris Karloff, Florence Bates, Fay Bainter, *Thurston Hall*, Ann Rutherford, Gordon Jones, Reginald Denny

Secret Mission
GB 1942 94m bw
GFD / Marcel Hellman / Excelsior

During World War II four British Intelligence officers are landed in occupied France to discover the truth about German defences.
Stilted war suspenser.

w Anatole de Grunwald, Basil Bartlett, Terence Young *d* Harold French *ph* Bernard Knowles *m* Mischa Spoliansky

Hugh Williams, Carla Lehmann, James Mason, Roland Culver, Nancy Price, Michael Wilding, Percy Walsh

The Secret of Blood Island
GB 1964 84m Technicolor
U-I / Hammer (Anthony Nelson Keys)

A girl parachutist secret agent is smuggled into a Japanese POW camp and out again.
Absurd blood and thunder, almost perversely enjoyable—but not quite.

w John Gilling *d* Quentin Lawrence *ph* Jack Asher *m* James Bernard

Barbara Shelley, Jack Hedley, Charles Tingwell, Bill Owen, Lee Montague

The Secret of Convict Lake*
US 1951 83m bw
TCF (Frank P. Rosenberg)

In the 1870s, escaped convicts take over a California town.
Brooding, snowy, set-bound western melodrama; predictable but watchable.

w Oscar Saul *d* Michael Gordon *ph* Leo Tover *m* Sol Kaplan *md* Lionel Newman

Glenn Ford, Gene Tierney, Ann Dvorak, Ethel Barrymore, Zachary Scott, Barbara Bates, Cyril Cusack, Jeanette Nolan, Ruth Donnelly

The Secret of Madame Blanche
US 1933 85m bw

The woman who takes the blame for murder committed by a young man is the mother he never knew. Or, *Madame X* unofficially revisited: all-stops-out melodrama very typical of its time. Irene Dunne, Phillips Holmes, Lionel Atwill, Douglas Walton, Jean Parker, Una Merkel. Written by Frances Goodrich and Albert Hackett; directed by Charles Brabin; for MGM.

The Secret of My Success
GB 1965 105m Metrocolor Panavision
MGM / Andrew and Virginia Stone

A village policeman follows his mother's dictum that he should not think ill of others, and accidentally goes from success to success. Flabby portmanteau comedy full of in-jokes and flat-footed farce; satire is not evident.

wd Andrew L. Stone *ph* David Boulton *m* Lucien Caillet and others *md* Roland Shaw

James Booth, Lionel Jeffries, *Amy Dalby*, Stella Stevens, Honor Blackman, Shirley Jones, Joan Hickson

The Secret of My Success*
US 1987 110m De Luxe
Universal / Rastar (Herbert Ross)

A country cousin in New York is determined to hit the big time.
An amiable melange of familiar situations with just a touch of *Midnight Cowboy* and a sharp edge to some of the writing; but not enough to keep its star at the top.

w Jim Cash, Jack Epps, A. J. Carothers *d* Herbert Ross *ph* Carlo Di Palma *m* David Foster

Michael J. Fox, Helen Slater, Richard Jordan, Margaret Whitton, John Pankow, Christopher Murney

'A bedroom farce with a leaden touch, a corporate comedy without teeth.'—*Daily Variety*

The Secret of Nimh*
US 1982 82m Technicolor
Aurora / Don Bluth

Forced out of her cosy field, a widowed mouse seeks the help of Nicodemus, king of the rat pack.
Animated cartoon by Disney artists who rejected that company's declining standards and set up their own factory. Alas, though they have the skills, the narrative they have chosen needed refining.

w Don Bluth, John Pomeroy, Gary Foldman, Will Finn, *novel* Mrs Frisby and the Rats of Nimh by Robert C. O'Brien *d* Don Bluth *m* Jerry Goldsmith

'Vintage techniques are proudly invoked, but the story desperately needs loving care.'—*Sight and Sound*

The Secret of St Ives
US 1949 76m bw

During the Napoleonic War, a French prisoner-of-war escapes from Edinburgh Castle, only to be accused of murder. Modest swashbuckler with a somewhat lacklustre atmosphere. Richard Ney, Vanessa Brown, Henry Daniell, Aubrey Mather. Written by Eric Taylor, from the story by Robert Louis Stevenson; directed by Phil Rosen; for Columbia.

The Secret of Santa Vittoria*
US 1969 140m Technicolor Panavision
UA / Stanley Kramer

In 1945 an Italian village hides its wine from the occupying Germans.
Expected, exhausting epic comedy with everyone talking at once.

w William Rose, Ben Maddow, *novel* Robert Crichton *d* Stanley Kramer *ph* Giuseppe Rotunno *m* Ernest Gold

Anthony Quinn, Anna Magnani, Virna Lisi, Hardy Kruger, Sergio Franchi, Renato Rascel

'A brainless farrago of flying rolling pins and rotten vegetables, filled with the kind of screaming, belching, eye-rolling fictional Italians only Stanley Kramer could invent.'—*Rex Reed*

AAN: Ernest Gold

The Secret of Stamboul
GB 1936 93m bw

An English adventurer foils a Turkish revolution. Pale rendering of a full-blooded best-seller. Valerie Hobson, Frank Vosper, James Mason, Kay Walsh, Peter Haddon. Written by Richard Wainwright, Howard Irving Young and Noel Langley, from the novel *The Eunuch of Stamboul* by Dennis Wheatley; directed by Andrew Marton; for Wainwright. (NB: Reissue title: *The Spy in White.*)

The Secret of the Blue Room
US 1933 66m bw

An heiress's three suitors all volunteer to spend the night in the haunted room of her mansion. Murderous malarkey without the courage of its convictions. Lionel Atwill, Gloria Stuart, Paul Lukas, Edward Arnold, Onslow Stevens, Robert Barrat, Elizabeth Patterson. Written by William Hurlbut; directed by Kurt Neumann; for Universal. (NB: Remade in 1938 as *The Missing Guest* and in 1944 as *Murder in the Blue Room.*)
'Americanization of a German mystery yarn which ought to do well in the smaller spots.'—*Variety*

The Secret of the Incas
US 1954 101m Technicolor
Paramount (Mel Epstein)

Various adventurers seek a priceless Inca jewel.
Boys' Own Paper yarn which sounds a good deal more exciting than it is: too much talk and a few choice studio backcloths drop the tension alarmingly, and the script lacks humour and conciseness.

w Ranald MacDougall, Sidney Boehm *d* Jerry Hopper *ph* Lionel Lindon *m* David Buttolph

Charlton Heston, Robert Young, Thomas Mitchell, Nicole Maurey, Yma Sumac, Glenda Farrell, Michael Pate

The Secret of the Loch
GB 1934 80m bw
ABFD / Bray Wyndham

A diver thinks he finds a prehistoric monster in Loch Ness.
Mildly amusing exploitation item following the 1934 rebirth of interest in the old legend.

w Charles Bennett, Billie Bristow *d* Milton Rosmer

Seymour Hicks, Nancy O'Neil, Gibson Gowland, Frederick Peisley, Rosamund John, Ben Field

The Secret of Treasure Island
US 1938 bw serial: 15 eps

A reporter investigates a friend's disappearance in the Caribbean. Juvenile serial with plenty of action involving a sinister Doctor X and some skull-faced pirates. Don Terry, Gwen Gaze, Grant Withers, Hobart Bosworth, William Farnum, Dave O'Brien. Directed by Elmer Clifton; for Columbia.

'Run for your life! You must find the secret before it finds you!'

The Secret Partner*
GB 1961 91m bw
MGM (Michael Relph)

A blackmailing dentist is visited by a mysterious hooded stranger who forces him to rob one of his businessman victims.
Complex puzzle thriller, neatly made in sub-Hitchcock style.

w David Pursall, Jack Seddon *d* Basil Dearden *ph* Harry Waxman *m* Philip Green

Stewart Granger, Haya Harareet, Bernard Lee, Hugh Burden, Melissa Stribling, Norman Bird, Conrad Philips

The Secret People*
GB 1951 96m bw
Ealing (Sidney Cole)

European refugees in London during the thirties become members of a ring of anarchists.
Downbeat political melodrama which pleased neither the masses nor the highbrows, despite plaudits for sensitive direction and performances.

w Thorold Dickinson, Wolfgang Wilhelm *d Thorold Dickinson* *ph* Gordon Dines *m* Roberto Gerhard

Valentina Cortese, Serge Reggiani, Audrey Hepburn, Charles Goldner, Megs Jenkins, Irene Worth, Athene Seyler, Reginald Tate

'The tension and power of the film make it one of the most remarkable British productions for some time.'—*Penelope Houston*

'That *Secret People*, despite the creative agonies recorded by Mr Lindsay Anderson [in a book on the making of the film] should turn out to be a confused, unco-ordinated spy thriller concealing a tentative message deep down below some strained effects of style is another tragedy of British film hopes.'—*Richard Winnington*

Secret Service
US 1931 67m bw
During the Civil War a Yankee officer goes behind enemy lines and falls in love with a southern girl. Sluggish romantic adventure. Richard Dix, Shirley Grey, William Post Jnr, Gavin Gordon. Written by Bernard Schubert from a play by William Gillette; directed by J. Walter Ruben; for RKO. 'Dix does a good character. It's all the picture has.'—*Variety*

Secret Service in Darkest Africa
US 1943 bw serial: 15 eps
An American undercover agent posing as a member of the Gestapo in Berlin learns of a plan to convert the Arabs to the Nazi cause by means of a forged scroll and the dagger of Solomon. Lively cliffhanging adventures. Rod Cameron, Joan Marsh, Duncan Renaldo, Lionel Royce, Kurt Kreuger, Kurt Katch. Directed by Spencer G. Bennet; for Republic.

Secret Service of the Air
US 1939 61m bw
A government agent tracks down smugglers. Serial-like thrills and comedy, adequately presented. Ronald Reagan, Eddie Foy Jnr, John Litel, Ila Rhodes, James Stephenson. Written by Raymond Shrock; directed by Noel Smith; for Warners. 'No marquee names, but a better than average story of its kind.'—*Variety*

The Secret Six*
US 1931 83m bw
MGM
A syndicate of businessmen finance two reporters to get evidence against a gang of bootleggers.
Solidly carpentered gangster thriller.
w Frances Marion *d* George Hill *ph* Harold Wenstrom
Wallace Beery, Lewis Stone, Clark Gable, John Mack Brown, Jean Harlow, Marjorie Rambeau, Paul Hurst, Ralph Bellamy, John Miljan
'A gangster talker too rough, crude and familiar. In big cities it may pull the roughneck trade . . . but the vocalized expression for it will be adverse.'—*Variety*

'It's not who you con—it's how you do it!'
The Secret War of Harry Frigg
US 1967 109m Techniscope
Universal / Albion (Hal E. Chester)
In 1943 a private engineers the escape of five captured generals.
Unattractive war comedy; slow, uninventive and overlong.
w Peter Stone, Frank Tarloff *d* Jack Smight *ph* Russell Metty *m* Carlo Rustichelli
Paul Newman, *John Williams*, Sylva Koscina, Andrew Duggan, Tom Bosley, Charles D. Gray, Vito Scotti, James Gregory

The Secret Ways*
US 1961 112m bw
U-I / Heath (Richard Widmark)
An American reporter is recruited to rescue a scholar from communist Hungary.
Pretentious Iron Curtain melodrama, quite good to look at but overlong and no *Third Man*.
w Jean Hazelwood, *novel* Alistair MacLean *d* Phil Karlson *ph* Max Greene *m* Johnny Williams
Richard Widmark, Sonja Ziemann, Charles Regnier, Walter Rilla, Howard Vernon, Senta Berger

Secrets*
US 1933 85m bw
A pioneering couple stick together despite the husband's infidelities. Curiously mixed-up star vehicle, part romantic comedy, part western, part sob-stuff. Interesting rather than entertaining. Mary Pickford, Leslie Howard, C. Aubrey Smith, Blanche Friderici, Doris Lloyd, Ned Sparks. Written by Frances Marion from the play by Rudolf Besier and May Edgington; directed by Frank Borzage; for Mary Pickford/UA. 'Singularly uneven . . . but at least the story is given fine production and interesting playing.'—*Variety*. 'You can be sure you won't make any mistake by taking the family to see it.'—*Photoplay*. NB: Norma Talmadge starred in a 1923 silent version.

Secrets of a Secretary
US 1931 76m bw
A social secretary discovers that her ex-husband is blackmailing her employer's daughter. *Peg's Paper* romance of a heroine who rises above her many problems. Claudette Colbert, Herbert Marshall, George Metaxas, Mary Boland, Berton Churchill. Written by Dwight Taylor and Charles Brackett; directed by George Abbott; for Paramount.

Secrets of a Soul**
Germany 1926 95m (24 fps) bw silent
UFA / Hans Neumann
A chemist develops a knife phobia, has hallucinations, and tries to cut his wife's throat.
A lesson in elementary psychology which was innovatory at the time and survives as cinema for its stylish and impressionist use of visual techniques.
w Colin Ross, Hans Neumann, G. W. Pabst *d G. W. Pabst* *ph* Guido Seeber, Curt Oertel, Robert Lach
Werner Krauss, Jack Trevor, Ruth Weyher, Pawel Pawlow

Secrets of an Actress
US 1938 70m bw
A star actress falls for one of her backers, a married architect. High-life suffering of a familiar kind: it satisfied the Peg's Paper audience. Kay Francis, George Brent, Ian Hunter, Gloria Dickson, Isabel Jeans, Peggy Singleton. Written by Milton Krims, Rowland Leigh, Julius J. Epstein; directed by William Keighley; for Warners. 'Miss Francis may be able to live up to all requirements except an acrobatic dance on the toes, but it's no use hitching race horses to milk wagons.'—*Variety*

Secrets of Scotland Yard
US 1944 68m bw
A British secret service man is impersonated by his Nazi twin brother. Likeable absurdities with a strong cast. C. Aubrey Smith, Edgar Barrier, Stephanie Bachelor, Lionel Atwill, Henry Stephenson, John Abbott, Walter Kingsford, Martin Kosleck. Written by Denison Clift, from his novel *Room 40, O.B.*; directed and produced by George Blair; for Republic.

Secrets of the French Police
US 1932 55m bw
The Sûreté tracks down a hypnotist and murderer. Rather wildly-imagined suspenser with points of interest. Gwili André, Frank Morgan, Gregory Ratoff, Murray Kinnell, John Warburton. Written by Samuel Ornitz, Robert Tasker; directed by Edward Sutherland; for RKO. 'Hodge-podge of melodramatics . . . hardly enough for the de luxers.'—*Variety*

Secrets of the Underground
US 1943 70m bw
The proprietor of a fashionable gown shop is a Nazi agent. Nifty second feature on predictable wartime lines. John Hubbard, Virginia Grey, Lloyd Corrigan, Miles Mander, Ben Welden. Written by Robert Tasker and Geoffrey Homes; directed by William Morgan; for Republic.

'There are many ways to be seduced. Fame . . . power . . . love!'
The Seduction of Joe Tynan*
US 1979 107m Technicolor
Universal (Martin Bregman)
A young senator alienates his wife when he sacrifices his principles for advancement.
Fairly arresting political character drama with strong narrative and acting
w Alan Alda *d* Jerry Schatzberg *ph* Adam Holender *m* Bill Conti
Alan Alda, Barbara Harris, Meryl Streep, *Melvyn Douglas,* Rip Torn, Carrie Nye, Charles Kimbrough

See America Thirst
US 1930 71m bw
Two hoboes become involved with rum runners. Poorly constructed talkie début for a silent comedian who never made it. Harry Langdon, Slim Summerville, Bessie Love, Mitchell Lewis, Stanley Fields. Written by Edward Luddy, Vin Moore, C. J. Horwin; directed by W. J. Craft; for Universal. 'Direction shows silent technique throughout, and is unmindful of the talkie advent. Rub is that this system got reversed in the important sequences.'—*Variety*

See Here Private Hargrove*
US 1944 102m bw
MGM (George Haight)

Adventures of a raw recruit in the US army. Standard transcription of a humorous bestseller which did its best to make the war painless for Americans.

w Harry Kurnitz, *book* Marion Hargrove *d* Wesley Ruggles *ph* Charles Lawton *m* David Snell

Robert Walker, Donna Reed, Robert Benchley, Keenan Wynn, Bob Crosby, Ray Collins, Chill Wills, Grant Mitchell

† Sequel 1945: *What Next, Corporal Hargrove?*

See How They Run
GB 1955 84m bw

A country vicarage gets lively when several miscreants pretend to be the vicar. Reliable stage farce which doesn't get the laughs on screen. Ronald Shiner, Greta Gynt, James Hayter, Wilfrid Hyde White, Dora Bryan, Richard Wattis, Viola Lyel. Written by Leslie Arliss, Philip King, Val Valentine from a play by Philip King; for Winwell (BL).

See My Lawyer
US 1945 67m bw

Comedians try to get out of a nightclub commitment by insulting the customers. Thin vehicle for a team that wasn't going anywhere: too many variety acts got in their way. Ole Olsen, Chic Johnson, Grace McDonald, Franklin Pangborn, Alan Curtis, Noah Beery Jnr, Ed Brophy. Written by Edmund L. Hartmann and Stanley Davis; directed by Edward Cline; for Universal.

Seed
US 1931 96m bw

A husband leaves his family to become a novelist, but returns ten years later. Long-drawn-out domestic drama whose few virtues have not weathered the years. John Boles, Genevieve Tobin, Lois Wilson, Raymond Hackett, Bette Davis, Zasu Pitts. Written by Gladys Lehman from the novel by Charles G. Norris; directed by John Stahl; for Universal. 'Good woman's picture that will strike generous b.o. anywhere.'—*Variety*

The Seekers
GB 1954 90m Eastmancolor
GFD / Fanfare (George H. Brown)
US title: *Land of Fury*

In 1820 a British sailor and his family emigrate to New Zealand.
Stilted epic which never gains the viewer's sympathy or interest.

w William Fairchild *d* Ken Annakin *ph* Geoffrey Unsworth *m* William Alwyn

Jack Hawkins, Glynis Johns, Inia Te Wiata, Noel Purcell, Kenneth Williams, Laya Raki

Seems Like Old Times*
US 1980 102m Metrocolor
Columbia / Ray Stark

An innocently involved bank robber takes refuge with his ex-wife, a lady lawyer married to the district attorney.
Nostalgic farce which doesn't quite live up to the old skills and often bogs down in talk. Funny moments, though.

w Neil Simon *d* Jay Sandrich *ph* David M. Walsh *m* Marvin Hamlisch *pd* Gene Callahan

Goldie Hawn, Chevy Chase, Charles Grodin, Robert Guillaume, Harold Gould, George Grizzard

The Sellout
US 1951 82m bw
MGM (Nicholas Nayfack)

A newspaper editor exposes a corrupt administration.
Competent melodrama with no surprises.

w Charles Palmer *d* Gerald Mayer *ph* Paul Vogel *m* David Buttolph

Walter Pidgeon, John Hodiak, Audrey Totter, Thomas Gomez, Everett Sloane, Cameron Mitchell, Karl Malden, Paula Raymond

The Sellout
GB / Italy 1975 102m colour
Warner / Oceanglade / Amerifilm (Josef Shaftel)

Russians and Americans lure a double agent to Jerusalem in order to eliminate him.
Unsmiling spy melodrama with a complex plot, a bagful of clichés and some unnecessarily unpleasant violence.

w Judson Kinberg, Murray Smith *d* Peter Collinson *ph* Arthur Ibbetson *m* Mike Green, Colin Frechter

Richard Widmark, Oliver Reed, Gayle Hunnicutt, Sam Wanamaker, Vladek Sheybal, Ori Levy, Assef Dayan

Seminole
US 1953 86m Technicolor

A West Point graduate goes to Florida to make peace with the Indians. Slightly unusual but not very interesting semi-western with the usual clichés. Rock Hudson, Anthony Quinn, Barbara Hale, Richard Carlson, Hugh O'Brian, Russell Johnson, Lee Marvin, James Best. Written by Charles K. Peck Jnr; directed by Budd Boetticher; for Universal-International.

Semi-Tough*
US 1977 107m De Luxe
UA / David Merrick

The manager's daughter decides between two star members of a football team.
Rambling satiric comedy which takes jabs at various states of mind in America today, notably the fashionable forms of self-help therapy. Much of it comes off quite well.

w Walter Bernstein, *novel* Dan Jenkins *d* Michael Ritchie *ph* Charles Rosher Jnr *m* Jerry Fielding

Burt Reynolds, Kris Kristofferson, Jill Clayburgh, Bert Convy, Robert Preston, Lotte Lenya, Roger E. Mosley

The Senator Was Indiscreet*
US 1947 95m bw
U-I (Nunnally Johnson)
GB title: *Mr Ashton Was Indiscreet*

A foolish politician determines to become president and hires a press agent.
Satirical political farce which hurls its shafts wide and doesn't seem to mind how few of them hit.

w Charles MacArthur, *story* Edwin Lanham *d* George S. Kaufman *ph* William Mellor *m* Daniele Amfitheatrof

William Powell, Ella Raines, Peter Lind Hayes, Ray Collins, Arleen Whelan, Allen Jenkins, Hans Conried, Charles D. Brown

Send Me No Flowers*
US 1964 100m Technicolor
U-I / Martin Melcher (Harry Keller)

A hypochondriac mistakenly thinks he is dying and tries to provide another spouse for his wife.
A timeworn farcical situation is handled in the glossy Doris Day manner; it all starts quite brightly but gradually fizzles out.

w Julius Epstein, *play* Norman Barrasch, Carroll Moore *d* Norman Jewison *ph* Daniel Fapp *m* Frank de Vol *ad* Alexander Golitzen, Robert Clatworthy

Doris Day, Rock Hudson, Tony Randall, Paul Lynde, Clint Walker, Hal March, Edward Andrews

Sensation
GB 1936 67m bw

A village barmaid is murdered and only our reporter hero sees the wider implications. Presentable murder mystery. John Lodge, Diana Churchill, Francis Lister, Joan Marion, Margaret Vyner, Athene Seyler, Richard Bird. Written by Dudley Leslie, Marjorie Deans and William Freshman, from the play *Murder Gang* by Basil Dean and George Munro; directed by Brian Desmond Hurst; for BIP. 'The genuine situation is lost in false trials, in an absurd love story, in humour based on American films, and in the complete unreality of the "murder gang".'—*Graham Greene*.

Sensations of 1945
US 1944 87m bw
Andrew L. Stone

Father and son disagree over the handling of their publicity agency.
Slim plot holds together a ragbag of variety acts, some quite choice.

w Dorothy Bennett *d* Andrew L. Stone *ph* Peverell Marley, John Mescall *md* Mahlon Merrick

Eleanor Powell, W. C. Fields, Sophie Tucker, Dennis O'Keefe, Eugene Pallette, C. Aubrey Smith, Lyle Talbot, Dorothy Donegan, Cab Calloway and his band, Woody Herman and his band

AAN: Mahlon Merrick

Senso*
Italy 1953 115m Technicolor
Lux
aka: *The Wanton Countess* (cut version)

In 1866 Venice a noblewoman falls in love with an officer of the invading Austrian army, but finally denounces him.
The melodramatic plot is less important than the portrait of a period, for this is an expensive film in the grand style, often breathtaking to look at.

w Luchino Visconti, Suso Cecchi d'Amico and others *story* Camilla Botto *d Luchino Visconti ph G. R. Aldo, Robert Krasker m* Anton Bruckner *ad* Ottavio Scotti

Alida Valli, Farley Granger, Massimo Girotti, Christian Marquand

Sentimental Journey
US 1946 94m bw
TCF (Walter Morosco)

An actress who knows she is dying arranges for a little orphan girl to take her place in her husband's affections.
Hollywood's most incredible three-handkerchief picture; nicely made, but who dared to write it?

w Samuel Hoffenstein, Elizabeth Reinhardt, *story* Nelia Gardner White *d* Walter Lang *ph* Norbert Brodine *m* Cyril Mockridge

Maureen O'Hara, John Payne, William Bendix, Cedric Hardwicke, Glenn Langan, Mischa Auer, Connie Marshall, Kurt Kreuger

'In twenty years of filmgoing I can't remember being so slobbered at: the apotheosis of the weepie.'—*Richard Winnington*

'It may not be for the critics, but who are critics? Just a lot of Joes, with passes.'—*Variety*

† Remade as *The Gift of Love* (qv).

'Doomed to guard the gates of Hell forever!'
The Sentinel
US 1976 92m Technicolor
Universal / Jeffrey Konvitz

A disturbed girl in an old apartment house is haunted by walking corpses: the house turns out to be the gateway to hell and she its appointed sentinel.
Vulgarly modish rip-off of several fashionable themes, notably *Rosemary's Baby* and *The Exorcist.*

w Michael Winner, Jeffrey Konvitz, *novel* Jeffrey Konvitz *d* Michael Winner *ph* Dick Kratina *m* Gil Melle

Chris Sarandon, Cristina Raines, Martin Balsam, John Carradine, Jose Ferrer, Ava Gardner, Arthur Kennedy, Burgess Meredith, Sylvia Miles, Deborah Raffin, Eli Wallach, Jerry Orbach

'Moral or ironic points are hard to discern in the eye-wrenching flux of a Michael Winner movie, which drifts and zooms across its polished people and places in a continual caressing motion, as crudely excitatory as any sex movie when the climaxes are approaching.'—*Richard Combs, MFB*

'A man with a face that looks like chicken giblets, a naked whore with a mouse on her thigh, a cat devouring a canary and Sylvia Miles in a tight leotard—these are some of the highlights of *The Sentinel,* a perfect film for those who like to slow down and look at traffic accidents.'—*Janet Maslin, Newsweek*

Separate Tables**
US 1958 98m bw
UA / Hecht–Hill–Lancaster (Harold Hecht)

Emotional tensions among the boarders at a British seaside guest house.
The genteel melodramas seem less convincing on the Hollywood screen than they did on the London stage, but the handling is thoroughly professional.

w Terence Rattigan, John Gay, *play* Terence Rattigan *d* Delbert Mann *m* David Raksin *ph* Charles Lang

Burt Lancaster, Rita Hayworth, *David Niven*, Deborah Kerr, *Wendy Hiller, Gladys Cooper, Cathleen Nesbitt, Felix Aylmer*, Rod Taylor, Audrey Dalton, *May Hallatt*

AA: David Niven; Wendy Hiller
AAN: best picture; script; Charles Lang; David Raksin; Deborah Kerr

September
US 1987 83m Du Art / De Luxe
Orion (Jack Rollins, Charles H. Joffe)

Enclosed family drama: Allen in his melancholy Bergman mode.

w,d Woody Allen *ph* Carlo Di Palma *m* various *ad* Speed Hopkins *ed* Susan E. Morse

Denholm Elliott, Dianne Wiest, Mia Farrow, Elaine Stritch, Sam Waterston

'The debts to Chekhov are everywhere.'—*Variety*

September Affair
US 1950 104m bw
Paramount (Hal B. Wallis)

Two married people fall in love and a plane crash in which they are reported dead gives them their chance.
Turgid romantic melodrama, not very well made despite the background tour of Capri; what made it a hit was the playing of the old Walter Huston record of the title song.

w Robert Thoeren *d* William Dieterle *ph* Charles B. Lang *m* Victor Young

Joseph Cotten, Joan Fontaine, Françoise Rosay, Jessica Tandy, Robert Arthur, Jimmy Lydon

'A smooth surface mirrors the film's essential superficiality.'—*Penelope Houston*

September Storm
US 1960 110m De Luxe Cinemascope 3-D
TCF / Alco (Edward L. Alperson)

A New York model and two adventurers search for sunken treasure off an uncharted Mediterranean island.
Thin actioner originally intended to marry 3-D and Cinemascope, but failed to do so.

w W. R. Burnett, *novel* The Girl in the Red Bikini by Steve Fisher *d* Byron Haskin *ph* Jorge Stahl Jnr, Lamar Boren *m* Edward L. Alperson Jnr

Joanne Dru, Mark Stevens, Robert Strauss

Sequoia
US 1934 73m bw

A girl living in the High Sierras defends wild animals from hunters. Refreshingly unusual outdoor drama with good location photography. Jean Parker, Russell Hardie, Samuel S. Hinds, Paul Hurst. Written by Ann Cunningham, Sam Arnstrong and Carey Wilson; directed by Chester Franklin; photographed by Chester Lyons; for MGM. 'It was unlikely that either Miss Parker or the deer would eat the puma, but I hung on hoping that the puma would eat the deer or Miss Parker.'—*James Agate.*

Serenade
US 1956 121m Warnercolor
Warner (Henry Blanke)

A vineyard worker becomes a successful opera singer and is desired by two women.
Cliché success story with plot taking second place to singing.

w Ivan Goff, Ben Roberts, John Twist, *novel* James M. Cain *d* Anthony Mann *ph* Peverell Marley *md* Ray Heindorf *songs* Nicholas Brodszky (*m*), Sammy Cahn (*ly*)

Mario Lanza, Joan Fontaine, Sarita Montiel, Vincent Price, Joseph Calleia, Harry Bellaver, Vince Edwards, Silvio Minciotti

The Sergeant
US 1968 108m Technicolor
Warner / Robert Wise (Richard Goldstone)

France, 1952. In a dreary army camp, a tough army sergeant with a guilt complex is brought face to face with his own homosexuality.
Well-made but very ponderous and limited melodrama which could have been told in half the time.

w Dennis Murphy, from his novel *d* John Flynn *ph* Henri Persin *m* Michel Mayne

Rod Steiger, John Philip Law, Frank Latimore, Ludmila Mikael

'The funniest foul-up of the space age!'
Sergeant Deadhead
US 1965 89m CFI colour

An army sergeant is accidentally sent into orbit and undergoes a personality change. Clumsy comedy partially redeemed by its supporting players. Frankie Avalon, Deborah Walley, Fred Clark, Cesar Romero, Eve Arden, Gale Gordon, Buster Keaton, Harvey Lembeck, John Ashley. Written by Louis M. Heyward; directed by Norman Taurog; for AIP.

Sergeant Madden
US 1939 78m bw
MGM (J. Walter Ruben)

A policeman's son becomes a gangster. Routine crime melodrama with sentimental trimmings, quite untypical of its director.

w Wells Root, *story* A Gun in His Hand by William A. Ulman *d* Josef Von Sternberg *ph* John Seitz *m* William Axt

Wallace Beery, Tom Brown, Alan Curtis, Laraine Day, Fay Holden, Marc Lawrence, Marion Martin

'Good programme drama, geared to supply strong support in the key duals.'—*Variety*

Sgt Pepper's Lonely Hearts Club Band
US 1978 111m Technicolor Panavision
Universal / Robert Stigwood (Dee Anthony)

A family band finds a new sound despite the activities of villains.
Oddball hotch-potch of middle-aged comedy and youth nostalgia with an American small-town setting. Some moments please, but most of it simply doesn't gell.

w Henry Edwards *d* Michael Schultz *ph* Owen Roizman *m* various (mostly the Beatles) *pd* Brian Eatwell

Peter Frampton, Barry Gibb, Robin Gibb, Maurice Gibb, George Burns, Frankie Howerd, Donald Pleasence, Paul Nicholas, Sandy Farina, Alice Cooper, Steve Martin, Earth Wind and Fire

'Another of those films which serve as feature-length screen advertising for an album.'—*Variety*

Sergeant Rutledge*
US 1960 111m Technicolor
Warner / John Ford (Willis Goldbeck, Patrick Ford)

In 1881 a black army sergeant is on trial for rape and murder, but his defence counsel reveals the real culprit.
Flashback western; not the director's best, but generally of some interest.

w James Warner Bellah, Willis Goldbeck *d* John Ford *ph* Bert Glennon *m* Howard Jackson

Woody Strode, Jeffrey Hunter, Constance Towers, Willis Bouchey, Billie Burke, Carleton Young, Juano Hernandez, Mae Marsh

Sergeant Steiner
West Germany 1979 115m Eastmancolor Panavision
Palladium / Rapidfilm (Arlene Sellers, Alex Winitsky)

The German sergeant hero of *Cross of Iron* survives the Western Front and involvement in an anti-Hitler conspiracy.
Somewhat bloodless though interesting sequel to an exceptionally nasty war film, with an international cast aiming at better box office.

w Tony Williamson *d* Andrew McLaglen *ph* Tony Imi *m* Peter Thomas

Richard Burton, Robert Mitchum, Curt Jurgens, Rod Steiger, Helmut Griem, Michael Parks

Sergeant York**
US 1941 134m bw
Warner (Jesse L. Lasky)

The story of a gentle hillbilly farmer who became a hero of World War I.
Standard real-life fiction given the big treatment; a key Hollywood film of its time in several ways.

w Abem Finkel, Harry Chandler, Howard Koch, John Huston *d Howard Hawks ph Arthur Edeson m Max Steiner*

Gary Cooper, Joan Leslie, Walter Brennan, George Tobias, David Bruce, Stanley Ridges, Margaret Wycherly, Dickie Moore, Ward Bond

'I hardly think the effect is any different from that of a parade, with colours and a band; it is stirring and it is too long; there are too many holdups and too many people out of step, and your residue of opinion on the matter is that it will be nice to get home and get your shoes off.'—*Otis Ferguson*

'It has all the flavour of true Americana, the blunt and homely humour of backwoodsmen and the raw integrity peculiar to simple folk.'—*Bosley Crowther, New York Times*

AA: Gary Cooper
AAN: best picture; script; Howard Hawks; Sol Polito; Max Steiner; Walter Brennan; Margaret Wycherly

Sergeants Three
US 1961 112m Technicolor Panavision
(UA) Essex–Claude (Frank Sinatra)

Just after the Civil War three cavalry sergeants, with the help of an ex-slave bugler, dispose of some hostile Indians.
High-spirited but exhausting parody of *Gunga Din*, with bouts of unfunny bloodthirstiness separated by tedious slabs of dialogue.

w W. R. Burnett *d* John Sturges *ph* Winton Hock, Carl Guthrie *m* Billy May

Frank Sinatra, Dean Martin, Peter Lawford, Sammy Davis Jnr, Joey Bishop, Henry Silva, Ruta Lee

'The participants have a better time than the onlookers.'—*Judith Crist, 1973*

Serial*
US 1980 91m Movielab
Paramount / Sidney Beckerman

Well-heeled Californians in a high suburban community go in for various cults and fashions.
Amusing satire on everything from *Peyton Place* to *Bob and Carol and Ted and Alice*. Just a little late in coming, that's all.

w Rich Eustis, Michael Elias, *novel* Cyra McFadden *d* Bill Persky *ph* Rexford Metz *m* Lalo Schifrin

Martin Mull, Tuesday Weld, Jennifer McAllister, Sam Chew Jnr, Sally Kellerman, Nita Talbot, Bill Macy, Christopher Lee, Pamela Bellwood, Peter Bonerz, Tom Smothers

Serious Charge
GB 1959 99m bw
Alva (Mickey Delamar)

A small-town troublemaker, accused by his priest of being responsible for the death of a young girl, amuses himself by accusing the priest of making homosexual advances.
A sensational play of its time makes a dull film despite earnest performances.

w Guy Elmes, Mickey Delamar, *play* Philip King *d* Terence Young *ph* Georges Périnal *m* Leighton Lucas

Anthony Quayle, Andrew Ray, Sarah Churchill, Irene Browne, Percy Herbert, Cliff Richard

The Serpent
France / Italy / Germany 1974 124m colour
Films La Boetie (Henri Verneuil)

A top KGB official defects to the west.
Complicated, humourless, multi-lingual spy capers.

w Henri Verneuil, Gilles Perrault, *novel* Pierre Nord *d* Henri Verneuil *ph* Claude Renoir *m* Ennio Morricone

Yul Brynner, Henry Fonda, Dirk Bogarde, Philippe Noiret, Farley Granger, Virna Lisi

The Serpent's Egg*
West Germany / US 1977 120m Eastmancolor
Rialto-Dino de Laurentiis

An American trapeze artist has a hard time in Berlin at the time of Hitler's rise to power.
More of a curate's egg, really, with a poor leading performance and too many lapses into nastiness, but much incidental interest of the kind one associates with the director.

wd Ingmar Bergman *ph* Sven Nykvist *m* Rolf Wilhelm *pd* Rolf Zehetbauer

David Carradine, Liv Ullmann, Gert Frobe, James Whitmore, Heinz Bennent

'A crackpot tragedy: everything is strained, insufficient, underfelt.'—*New Yorker*

Serpico*
US 1973 130m Technicolor
Paramount / Artists Entertainment Complex / Dino de Laurentiis (Martin Bregman)

A New York cop reveals police corruption and is eventually forced to leave the country.
A harrowing true story played with authentic gloom and violence.

w Waldo Salt, Norman Wexler, *book* Peter Maas *d Sidney Lumet ph* Arthur J. Ornitz *m* Mikis Theodorakis

Al Pacino, John Randolph, Jack Kehoe, Biff McGuire

'There's nothing seriously wrong with *Serpico* except that it's unmemorable, and not even terribly interesting while it's going on.'—*Stanley Kauffmann*

AAN: script; Al Pacino

The Servant**
GB 1963 116m bw
Elstree / Springbok (Joseph Losey, Norman Priggen)

A rich, ineffectual young man is gradually debased and overruled by his sinister manservant and his sexy 'sister'.

Acclaimed in many quarters on its first release, this downbeat melodrama now seems rather naïve and long drawn out; its surface gloss is undeniable, but the final orgy is more risible than satanic.

w Harold Pinter, *novel* Robin Maugham *d* Joseph Losey *ph Douglas Slocombe* *m* Johnny Dankworth

Dirk Bogarde, James Fox, Sarah Miles, Wendy Craig, Catherine Lacey, Richard Vernon

'Moodily suggestive, well acted, but petering out into a trickle of repetitious unmeaningful nastiness.'—*John Simon*

Servants' Entrance
US 1934 88m bw
Fox

A maid falls in love with a chauffeur. Upstairs downstairs style comedy drama; passable.

w Samson Raphaelson, *novel* Sigrid Boo *d* Frank Lloyd *ph* Hal Mohr *m* Arthur Lange

Janet Gaynor, Lew Ayres, Walter Connolly, G. P. Huntley Jnr, Sig Rumann, Louise Dresser, Astrid Allwyn, Ned Sparks

'Capable production, directing and casting manages to make it fair entertainment.'—*Variety*

Service De Luxe*
US 1938 85m bw

Adventures of the members of a super-secretarial agency. Very tolerable but uninspired comedy which doesn't really allow its acting talent full rein. Constance Bennett, Vincent Price, Charles Ruggles, Helen Broderick, Mischa Auer, Halliwell Hobbes. Written by Gertrude Purcell and Leonard Spiegelgass; directed by Rowland V Lee; for Universal. 'A speedy comedy-drama . . . will hold its own as a leadoff attraction in the keys.'—*Variety*

Service for Ladies
GB 1932 93m bw
Paramount (Alexander Korda)
US title: *Reserved for Ladies*

A waiter has a way with his rich lady clients. Tenuous satirical comedy, a variation on the American silent *The Grand Duchess and the Waiter*.

w Eliot Crawshay-Williams, Lajos Biro, *novel* The Head Waiter by Ernst Vajda *d* Alexander Korda

Leslie Howard, George Grossmith, Benita Hume, Elizabeth Allan, Morton Selten, Cyril Ritchard, Martita Hunt, Merle Oberon

'Too talky and English for general American consumption.'—*Variety*

The Set Up***
US 1949 72m bw
RKO (Richard Goldstone)

An ageing boxer refuses to pull his last fight, and is beaten up by gangsters.
One of the most brilliant little *films noirs* of the late forties; thoroughly studio-bound, yet evoking a brilliant feeling for time and place. Photography, direction, editing, acting are all of a piece.

w Art Cohn, *poem* Joseph Moncure March *d Robert Wise ph Milton Krasner* *md* Constantin Bakaleinikoff

Robert Ryan, Audrey Totter, George Tobias, Alan Baxter, Wallace Ford

Seven Angry Men*
US 1954 90m bw
Allied Artists (Vincent M. Fennelly)

In Kansas, John Brown determines to abolish slavery by violence.
Low-budget, intensely felt little biopic of the celebrated 19th-century fanatic and his sons.

w Daniel B. Ullman *d* Charles Marquis Warren *ph* Ellsworth Fredericks *m* Carl Brandt

Raymond Massey, Jeffrey Hunter, Larry Pennell, Debra Paget, Leo Gordon, John Smith, James Best, Dennis Weaver

Seven Beauties*
Italy 1975 115m Technicolor
Medusa (Lina Wertmuller, Giancarlo Giannini, Arrigo Colombo)
original title: *Pasqualino Settebellezze*

An incorrigible survivor manages to get through the rigours of World War II and scarcely notices the damage to his honour. *Candide*-like mixture of farce and satire with the addition of a good deal of unpleasantness. Less meaningful abroad than on its home ground.

wd Lina Wertmuller *ph* Tonino delli Colli *m* Enzo Jannacci

Giancarlo Giannini, Fernando Rey, Shirley Stoler, Piero di Iorio

AA: best foreign film

AAN: Lina Wertmuller (as writer and as director); Giancarlo Giannini

'I now pronounce you—men and wives!'
Seven Brides for Seven Brothers**
US 1954 104m Anscocolor Cinemascope
MGM (Jack Cummings)

In the old west, seven hard-working brothers decide they need wives, and carry off young women from the villages around.
Disappointingly studio-bound western musical, distinguished by an excellent score and some brilliant dancing, notably the barn-raising sequence.

w Frances Goodrich, Albert Hackett, *story* Sobbin' Women by Stephen Vincent Benet *d Stanley Donen ph* George Folsey *ch Michael Kidd songs Johnny Mercer, Gene de Paul m* Adolph Deutsch, Saul Chaplin

Howard Keel, Jane Powell, Jeff Richards, Russ Tamblyn, Tommy Rall, Howard Petrie, Marc Platt, Jacques d'Amboise, Matt Mattox

AA: Adolph Deutsch, Saul Chaplin
AAN: best picture; script; George Folsey

Seven Chances**
US 1925 69m (24 fps) bw silent
Buster Keaton / Joseph M. Schenck

A meek young man finds that he is to inherit seven million dollars if he is married within a few hours.
Slim and rather slow comedy which builds to a fine climax as the hero is pursued first by hordes of women and then by rolling boulders.

w Clyde Bruckman, Jean Havez, Joseph A. Mitchell, *play* Roi Cooper Megrue *d* Buster Keaton *ph* Elgin Lessley, Byron Houck

Buster Keaton, Ruth Dwyer, Ray Barnes, Snitz Edwards

† The rocks sequence, which makes the film, was added only after a disappointing sneak preview.

'The sword and the cross battle for California's soul!'
Seven Cities of Gold*
US 1955 103m De Luxe Cinemascope
TCF (Robert D. Webb, Barbara McLean)

In 1796, a Spanish expedition sets out from Mexico to annex California, but with it goes Father Junipero Serra . . .
A semi-historical, semi-religious western which ends up not being much of anything but has interesting sequences.

w Richard L. Breen, John C. Higgins, *novel* Isabelle Gibson Ziegler *d* Robert D. Webb *ph* Lucien Ballard *m* Hugo Friedhofer

Michael Rennie, Richard Egan, Anthony Quinn, Rita Moreno, Jeffrey Hunter, Eduardo Noriega, John Doucette

Seven Days in May***
US 1964 120m bw
Seven Arts / Joel / John Frankenheimer (Edward Lewis)

An American general's aide discovers that his boss intends a military takeover because he considers the President's pacifism traitorous. Absorbing political mystery drama marred only by the unnecessary introduction of a female character. Stimulating entertainment.

w Rod Serling, novel Fletcher Knebel, Charles W. Bailey II *d John Frankenheimer ph Ellsworth Fredericks m* Jerry Goldsmith

Kirk Douglas, Burt Lancaster, *Fredric March*, Ava Gardner, Martin Balsam, *Edmond O'Brien*, George Macready, John Houseman

'A political thriller which grips from start to finish.'—*Penelope Houston*

'It is to be enjoyed without feelings of guilt, there should be more movies like it, and there is nothing first class about it.'—*John Simon*

'In the best tradition of the suspense thriller, with the ultimate thrill our awareness of its actual potential.'—*Judith Crist*

'An entertainment, in Graham Greene's sense of the word, and an intelligent one.'—*Monthly Film Bulletin*

AAN: Edmond O'Brien

Seven Days Leave
US 1929 83m bw
Paramount (Louis D. Lighton)
GB title: *Medals*

A London charlady 'adopts' a soldier, and both their lives are changed.
Sentimental melodrama which suited the times and confirmed Cooper's stardom.

w John Farrow, Dan Totheroh, *play* The Old Lady Shows Her Medals by J. M. Barrie *d* Richard Wallace *ph* Charles Lang

Gary Cooper, Beryl Mercer, Daisy Belmore, Nora Cecil, Tempe Piggott, Arthur Hoyt, Basil Radford

Seven Days Leave
US 1942 87m bw
RKO (Tim Whelan)

In order to inherit a hundred thousand dollars, a soldier must marry within a week.
Cheerful frivolity featuring radio stars of the time.

w William Bowers, Ralph Spence, Curtis Kenyon, Kenneth Earl *d* Tim Whelan *ph* Robert de Grasse *md* Roy Webb *songs* Frank Loesser, Jimmy McHugh

Lucille Ball, Victor Mature, Harold Peary, Mary Cortes, Ginny Simms, Ralph Edwards, Peter Lind Hayes, Marcy McGuire, Wallace Ford

Seven Days to Noon**
GB 1950 94m bw
London Films (Roy Boulting)

A professor engaged on atomic research threatens to blow up London unless his work is brought to an end.
Persuasively understated suspense piece which was subsequently much copied, so that it now seems rather obvious.

w Frank Harvey, Roy Boulting, Paul Dehn, James Bernard d John Boulting ph Gilbert Taylor *m* John Addison

Barry Jones, Olive Sloane, André Morell, Joan Hickson, Sheila Manahan, Hugh Cross, Ronald Adam, Marie Ney

'A first rate thriller that does not pretend to a serious message, but yet will leave a query in the mind.'—*Richard Winnington*

'A film of great tension and excitement with a climax that is reached after breathless suspense.'—*Star*

AA: script

The Seven Deadly Sins*
France / Italy 1952 150m bw
Franco London / Costellazione

The master of ceremonies introduces seven stories and an epilogue.
Among the most successful compendiums of its kind, partly because of cast and credits and partly because it came when French naughtiness was appealing to a wide international audience.

w Jean Aurenche, Pierre Bost, Roberto Rossellini, Leo Joannon, Carlo Rim, Diego Fabbri, Liana Ferri, Eduardo de Filippo, Charles Spaak, Turi Vaselle, René Wheeler *d* Eduardo de Filippo, Jean Dréville, Yves Allégret, Roberto Rossellini, Carlo Rim, Claude Autant-Lara, Georges Lacombe

Gérard Philipe, Isa Miranda, Eduardo de Filippo, Noel-Noel, Louis de Funès, Viviane Romance, Frank Villard, Henri Vidal, Michèle Morgan, Françoise Rosay

Seven Doors to Death
US 1944 60m bw

The owners of six exclusive shops and an apartment house are all murder suspects.
Flabby little bottom-biller which never gets going. Chick Chandler, June Clyde, George Meeker, Gregory Gay, Edgar Dearing. Written and directed by Elmer Clifton; for Alfred Stern / PRC.

711 Ocean Drive*
US 1950 102m bw
Columbia (Frank N. Seltzer)

A wireless expert is drawn into the bookie racket.
Overlong but vigorous crime exposé melodrama with excellent location sequences, notably a climax on Hoover Dam.

w Richard English, Francis Swann *d Joseph H. Newman ph* Franz Planer *m* Sol Kaplan

Edmond O'Brien, Joanne Dru, Otto Kruger, Don Porter, Sammy White, Dorothy Patrick, Barry Kelley, Howard St John

Seven Faces of Dr Lao*
US 1964 100m Metrocolor
MGM / George Pal

An elderly Chinaman with a penchant for spectacular disguise solves the problems of a western desert town.
A pleasant idea and excellent production are submerged in a sloppily sentimental and verbose script.

w Charles G. Finney, from his novel *d* George Pal *ph* Robert Bronner *m* Leigh Harline *make up* William Tuttle

Tony Randall, Arthur O'Connell, John Ericson, Barbara Eden, Noah Beery Jnr, Lee Patrick, Minerva Urecal, John Qualen

Seven Footsteps to Satan
US 1929 70m bw

A rich recluse plays an elaborate and macabre joke on his niece and nephew. Richly-designed but dramatically disappointing haunted house spoof. Thelma Todd, Creighton Hale, Sheldon Lewis, Ivan Christie, Sojin. Written by Richard Bee; directed by Benjamin Christensen; for Warner.

Seven Golden Men*
Italy / France / Spain 1965 91m Eastmancolor

Seven master criminals plot to rob a bank of its gold. Simple-minded but slickly handled caper story with many visual pleasures. Rossana Podesta, Philippe Leroy, Gastone Moschin, Gabriele Tinti. Written and directed by Marco Vicario; for Atlantica / PUF / Asfilm / Warner. (A sequel, *Seven Golden Men Strike Again,* was less successful.)

Seven Hills of Rome
US / Italy 1957 104m Technirama
MGM / Titanus (Lester Welch)

An American singer in Italy is pursued by the fiancée with whom he has quarrelled.
Thin travelogue with several halts for the star to sing; production very patchy.

w Art Cohn, Giorgio Prosperi *d* Roy Rowland *ph* Tonino Delli Colli *md* George Stoll

Mario Lanza, Renato Rascel, Marisa Allasio, Peggie Castle

Seven Keys to Baldpate*
US 1935 69m bw
RKO

A novelist retiring to a lonely inn for inspiration finds it full of criminals and damsels in distress.
An old theatrical warhorse with a trick ending, also filmed in 1929 (with Richard Dix; *Variety* said 'it all happens like a synopsis of what might have occurred') and in 1947 with Philip Terry. There was also a horror variation in 1982, *House of the Long Shadows* (*qv*). None was as satisfying as a good stage production.

play George M. Cohan, *story* Earl Derr Biggers *d* William Hamilton, Edward Killy *ph* Robert de Grasse

Gene Raymond, Margaret Callahan, Eric Blore, Grant Mitchell, Moroni Olsen, Henry Travers

'Too much conversation and too little action.'—*Variety*

† The 1935 version at least will be found to have lost its trick ending, without which it ends lamely. A curious executive decision.

The Seven Little Foys*
US 1955 95m Technicolor Vistavision
Paramount (Jack Rose)

The story of a family vaudeville act.
Routine showbiz biopic, a little heavy on the syrup.

w Melville Shavelson, Jack Rose *d* Melville Shavelson *ph* John F. Warren *md* Joseph J. Lilley

Bob Hope, Milly Vitale, George Tobias, Angela Clarke, Herbert Heyes, *James Cagney* as George M. Cohan

AAN: script

Seven Men from Now
US 1956 78m Warnercolor
Batjac (Andrew V. McLaglen, Robert E. Morrison)

A sheriff seeks revenge when his wife is killed by bandits.
Good western programmer.

w Burt Kennedy *d* Budd Boetticher *ph* William H. Clothier *m* Henry Vars

Randolph Scott, Gail Russell, Lee Marvin, Walter Reed, Don Barry, John Larch

Seven Miles from Alcatraz
US 1942 62m bw

Prison escapees take over an offshore lighthouse. Compact melodrama with the lifers heroically catching spies. James Craig, Bonita Granville, Frank Jenks, Cliff Edwards, George Cleveland, Tala Birell, John Banner. Written by Joseph Krumgold, John D. Klorer; directed by Edward Dmytryk; for Herman Schlom / RKO.

SEVEN FACES OF DR LAO. William Tuttle's impressive character make-up for Tony Randall, seen in the centre as the mysterious Dr Lao himself.

The Seven Minutes
US 1971 102m De Luxe
TCF (Russ Meyer)

A bookseller is arrested for distributing an obscene novel, and many people are unexpectedly involved in the court case.
A fascinating piece of old-fashioned hokum, full of 'daring' words and cameo performances.

w Richard Warren Lewis, *novel* Irving Wallace *d* Russ Meyer *ph* Fred Mandl *m* Stu Philips

Wayne Maunder, Marianne MacAndrew, Yvonne de Carlo, Phil Carey, Jay C. Flippen, Edy Williams, Lyle Bettger, Ron Randell, David Brian, Charles Drake, John Carradine, Harold J. Stone

Seven Nights in Japan
GB / France 1976 104m Eastmancolor
EMI–Marianne (Lewis Gilbert)

The heir to the British throne has shore leave in Tokyo and falls in love with a geisha.
Tediously daring romance with a banal script which seems over impressed by its own barely-existent controversial qualities.

w Christopher Wood *d* Lewis Gilbert *ph Henri Decaë* *m* David Hentschel

Michael York, Hidemi Aoki, James Villiers, Peter Jones, Charles Gray

The Seven Per Cent Solution
US 1976 114m Technicolor
Universal (Herbert Ross)

Dr Watson lures Sherlock Holmes to Vienna so that Professor Freud can cure him of persecution complex and cocaine addiction.
Drearily serious spoof with only a glimmer of the required style and a totally miscast Holmes.

w Nicholas Meyer, from his novel *d* Herbert Ross *ph* Oswald Morris *m* John Addison *pd* Ken Adam

Nicol Williamson, Robert Duvall, Alan Arkin, Vanessa Redgrave, Laurence Olivier, Jeremy Kemp, Samantha Eggar, Joel Grey, Charles Gray, Georgia Brown, Regine

'Sorrily botched all-star extravaganza.'—*Sight and Sound*

'Comes into the category of hit and myth . . . A heavyweight spoof in which Sherlock Holmes is placed under hypnosis by Sigmund Freud. The audience is then placed under hypnosis by director Herbert Ross.'—*Michael Billington, Illustrated London News*

AAN: script

Seven Samurai***
Japan 1954 155m bw
Toho (Shojiro Motoki)
original title: *Shichi-nin no Samurai*

16th-century villagers hire samurai to defend their property against an annual raid by bandits.
Superbly strange, vivid and violent medieval adventure which later served as the basis for the western *The Magnificent Seven*.

w Akira Kurosawa, Shinobu Hashimoto, Hideo Oguni *d Akira Kurosawa* *ph* Asaichi Nakai *m* Fumio Hayasaka

Toshiro Mifune, Takashi Shimura, Kuninori Kodo

'It is as sheer narrative, rich in imagery, incisiveness and sharp observation, that it makes its strongest impact . . . It provides a fascinating display of talent, and places its director in the forefront of creative film-makers of his generation.'—*Gavin Lambert, Sight and Sound*

'This, on the surface, is a work of relentless, unmitigated action, as epic as any film ever made, and, again on the surface, sheer entertainment. Yet it is also an unquestionable triumph of art.'—*John Simon*

Seven Seas to Calais
US / Italy 1962 103m Eastmancolor Cinemascope
MGM / Adelphia (Paolo Moffa)

In 1577, Sir Francis Drake follows the Spanish treasure route.
Ho-hum swashbuckler with a background of schoolboy history.

w Filippo Sanjust *d* Rudolph Maté *ph* Giulio Gianini *m* Franco Mannino

Rod Taylor, Keith Michell, Irene Worth, Anthony Dawson, Basil Dignam

Seven Sinners*
GB 1936 70m bw
Gaumont (Michael Balcon)
US title: *Doomed Cargo*

Gunrunners wreck trains to cover traces of murder.
Fascinatingly dated comedy suspenser with excellent sub-Hitchcock sequences, the whole thing having a strong flavour of *The 39 Steps*.

w Frank Launder, Sidney Gilliat, L. DuGarde Peach, Austin Melford, *play* The Wrecker by Arnold Ridley, Bernard Merivale *d Albert de Courville* *ph* Mutz Greenbaum (Max Greene)

Edmund Lowe, Constance Cummings, Thomy Bourdelle, Henry Oscar, Felix Aylmer, Allan Jeayes, O. B. Clarence

Seven Sinners*
US 1940 86m bw
Universal (Joe Pasternak)
GB title: *Café of Seven Sinners*

A cabaret singer is deported from several South Sea islands for causing too many fights among the naval officers.
Ho-hum hokum with an amiable cast and a good-natured final free-for-all.

w John Meehan, Harry Tugend *d* Tay Garnett *ph* Rudolph Maté *m* Frank Skinner

Marlene Dietrich, John Wayne, Albert Dekker, Broderick Crawford, Mischa Auer, Billy Gilbert, Oscar Homolka, Anne Lee, Samuel S. Hinds

'Nothing to worry about, unless you happen to be in the theatre, watching it go from fairly good to worse than worse.'—*Otis Ferguson*

Seven Sweethearts
US 1942 98m bw
MGM (Joe Pasternak)

Seven daughters must marry in sequence, eldest first.
Period musical frou-frou inspired by *Pride and Prejudice*. So light it almost floats.

w Walter Reisch, Leo Townsend *d* Frank Borzage *ph* George Folsey *m* Franz Waxman

Kathryn Grayson, Marsha Hunt, Van Heflin, Cecelia Parker, S. Z. Sakall, Peggy Moran, Isobel Elsom, Diana Lewis, Donald Meek, Louise Beavers

Seven Thieves*
US 1960 102m bw Cinemascope
TCF (Sidney Boehm)

An elderly crook conceives a last plan to rob the Monte Carlo casino.
Routine caper story, efficiently presented with some humour.

w Sidney Boehm, *novel* Lions at the Kill by Max Catto *d* Henry Hathaway *ph* Sam Leavitt *m* Dominic Frontière

Edward G. Robinson, Rod Steiger, Joan Collins, Eli Wallach, Michael Dante, Alexander Scourby, Berry Kroeger, Sebastian Cabot

'Christ, it was supposed to be a fun film, and Steiger is far, far from having a sense of humour.'—*Henry Hathaway*

Seven Thunders
GB 1957 100m bw

In wartime Marseilles, escaped POWs are helped by a doctor who turns out to have sinister intent. Slow chiller which telegraphs its surprises but gets by on good production values. James Robertson Justice, Stephen Boyd, Kathleen Harrison, Anna Gaylor, Tony Wright, Eugene Deckers, Rosalie Crutchley. Written by John Baines from a novel by Rupert Croft-Cooke; directed by Hugo Fregonese; for Daniel M. Angel/Rank. (US title: *The Beasts of Marseilles*.)

'They take the third degree one step further!'

The Seven-Ups
US 1973 103m De Luxe
TCF / Philip D'Antoni

Gangsters are hunted down by a secret force of the New York police.
Formulary realistic rough stuff in the wake of *The French Connection*.

w Albert Ruben, Alexander Jacobs *d* Philip D'Antoni *ph* Urs Furrer *m* *Don Ellis*

Roy Scheider, Victor Arnold, Jerry Leon, Tony Lo Bianco, *Richard Lynch*

Seven Waves Away
GB 1956 95m bw
Columbia / Copa (John R. Sloan)
US title: *Abandon Ship*

After the sinking of a luxury liner, the officer in charge of a lifeboat has to make life or death decisions.
Initially gripping but finally depressing open sea melodrama derived from *Souls at Sea* and later remade for TV as *The Last Survivors*.

wd Richard Sale *ph* Wilkie Cooper *m* Arthur Bliss

Tyrone Power, Mai Zetterling, Lloyd Nolan, Stephen Boyd, Moira Lister, James Hayter, Marie Lohr, Moultrie Kelsall, Noel Willman, Gordon Jackson, Clive Morton, John Stratton

'Eventually one is bludgeoned into a grudging admiration for the film's staying power.'—*Peter John Dyer*

'It jabs at your entrails with a cold unrelenting spear.'—*New York Times*

Seven Ways from Sundown
US 1960 87m Eastmancolor

A Texas Ranger befriends an outlaw, but has twinges of conscience. Straightforward character western with the inevitable shootout finale. Audie Murphy, Barry Sullivan, Venetia Stevenson, John McIntire, Kenneth Tobey. Written by Clair Huffaker; directed by Harry Keller; for Universal-International.

'Love, lust, courage and cowardice! Faith, fury and sacrifice!'

Seven Women*
US 1966 100m Metrocolor Panavision
MGM / John Ford / Bernard Smith

In 1935, an isolated Chinese mission staffed by American women is overrun by bandits.
Dusty melodrama which might have appealed in the thirties but was quite out of tune with the sixties. Well enough made and acted, but a strange choice for Ford's last film.

w Janet Green, John McCormick, *story* Chinese Finale by Norah Lofts *d* *John Ford* *ph* Joseph La Shelle *m* Elmer Bernstein

Anne Bancroft, Flora Robson, Margaret Leighton, Sue Lyon, Mildred Dunnock, Betty Field, Anna Lee, Eddie Albert, Mike Mazurki, Woody Strode, Irene Tsu

The Seven Year Itch*
US 1955 105m De Luxe Cinemascope
TCF (Charles K. Feldman, Billy Wilder)

A married man has a fling with the girl upstairs.
An amusing theatrical joke, with dream sequences like revue sketches, is really all at sea on the big screen, especially as the affair remains unconsummated, but direction and performances keep the party going more or less.

w Billy Wilder, George Axelrod, *play* George Axelrod *d* *Billy Wilder* *ph* Milton Krasner *m* Alfred Newman

Tom Ewell, *Marilyn Monroe*, Sonny Tufts, Evelyn Keyes, Robert Strauss, Oscar Homolka, Marguerite Chapman, Victor Moore

Seventeen
US 1940 76m bw

Adolescent problems of a midwestern small town boy. Old-fashioned family entertainment, smartly cast and filmed. Jackie Cooper, Betty Field, Otto Kruger, Ann Shoemaker, Norma Nelson. Written by Agnes Christine Johnson and Stuart Palmer from the novel by Booth Tarkington; directed by Louis King; for Stuart Walker / Paramount.

1776*
US 1972 141m Eastmancolor Panavision
Columbia / Jack L. Warner

The thirteen American colonies prepare to declare their independence of Great Britain.
Plain, low-key filming of the successful Broadway musical showing the domestic lives of the historical figures concerned. Splendid moments alternate with stretches of tedium.

w Peter Stone, from his play *d* Peter Hunt *ph* Harry Stradling Jnr *m / ly* Sherman Edwards *ad* George Jenkins *md* Ray Heindorf

William Daniels, Howard da Silva, Ken Howard, Donald Madden, Blythe Danner

AAN: Harry Stradling Jnr

Seventh Cavalry
US 1956 75m Technicolor
Columbia / Scott–Brown

An officer accused of cowardice volunteers to bring back General Custer's body after Little Big Horn.
Lively co-feature with a good traditional action climax.

w Peter Packer *d* Joseph H. Lewis *ph* Ray Rennahan *m* Mischa Bakaleinikoff

Randolph Scott, Barbara Hale, Jay C. Flippen, Jeanette Nolan, Frank Faylen

The Seventh Cross**
US 1944 112m bw
MGM (Pandro S. Berman)

Seven Germans escape from a concentration camp, and the Nazis threaten to execute them all. Just one escapes.
Impressive melodrama, brilliantly limiting its escape / suspense story to studio sets. Old-style Hollywood production at its best; but a rather obviously contrived story.

w Helen Deutsch, *novel* Anna Seghers *d* *Fred Zinnemann* *ph* *Karl Freund* *m* Roy Webb *ad* *Cedric Gibbons, Leonid Vasian*

Spencer Tracy, Signe Hasso, Hume Cronyn, Jessica Tandy, Agnes Moorehead, Felix Bressart, George Macready, George Zucco

AAN: Hume Cronyn

The Seventh Dawn
GB 1964 123m Technicolor
UA / Holden / Charles K. Feldman (Karl Tunberg)

In the early fifties a Malayan rubber planter finds that his best friend is a leading terrorist. Doom-laden romantic adventure drama with a lot of suffering and too little entertainment value.

w Karl Tunberg, *novel* The Durian Tree by Michael Keon *d* Lewis Gilbert *ph* Freddie Young *m* Riz Ortolani

William Holden, Tetsuro Tamba, Capucine, Susannah York, Michael Goodliffe, Allan Cuthbertson, Maurice Denham

'Echoes of *The Ugly American, Love Is a Many-Splendored Thing*, and many another adventure East of Sumatra, with every character running absolutely true to form.'—*MFB*

'An interminable melange of political, racial and romantic clichés, with performances and dialogue as overripe as the jungle setting.'—*Judith Crist, 1973*

Seventh Heaven**
US 1927 93m approx (24 fps) bw silent
Fox (William Fox)

A Paris sewer worker shelters a street waif, marries her and after idyllic happiness goes off to war, returning blinded.
All softness, sweetness and light, a very typical—and attractive—film of its director and a big influence on Hollywood's European period.

w Benjamin Glazer, *play* Austin Strong *d Frank Borzage ph* Ernest Palmer, J A. Valentine

Janet Gaynor, Charles Farrell, Gladys Brockwell, David Butler

AA: Benjamin Glazer; Frank Borzage; Janet Gaynor
AAN: best picture

Seventh Heaven*
US 1937 102m bw
TCF (Raymond Griffith)

Dewy-eyed remake; the mood is antediluvian but the production impresses.

w Melville Baker *d Henry King ph Merritt Gerstad md* Louis Silvers *ad William Darling*

James Stewart, Simone Simon, Jean Hersholt, Gale Sondergaard, J. Edward Bromberg, Gregory Ratoff, John Qualen, Victor Kilian, Sig Rumann, Mady Christians

'A romance that can stand another telling . . . the older element will join in making it a bracer for the box office.'—*Variety*

The Seventh Seal***
Sweden 1957 95m bw
Svensk Filmindustri (Allan Ekelund)
original title: *Det Sjunde Inseglet*

Death comes for a knight, who challenges him to a game of chess while he tries to show illustrations of goodness in mankind: but Death takes them all away in the end.
A modestly budgeted minor classic which, because of its international success and its famous shots, is seldom analysed in detail. In fact its storyline is meandering and apparently pointless, and it is kept going by its splendid cinematic feel and its atmosphere is that of a dark world irrationally sustained by religion.

wd Ingmar Bergman ph Gunnar Fischer m Erik Nordgren

Max Von Sydow, Bengt Ekerot, Gunnar Bjornstrand, Nils Poppe, Bibi Andersson, Gunnel Lindblom

'The most extraordinary mixture of beauty and lust and cruelty, Odin-worship and Christian faith, darkness and light.'—*Alan Dent, Illustrated London News*

'You know where they dance along the horizon? We'd packed up for the evening and were about to go home. Suddenly I saw a cloud, and Fischer swung his camera up. Some actors had gone, so grips had to stand in. The whole scene was improvised in ten minutes flat.'—*Ingmar Bergman*

The Seventh Sin
US 1957 94m bw Cinemascope
MGM (David Lewis)

A faithless wife accompanies her bacteriologist husband to fight a Chinese cholera epidemic, and regains her self-respect.
Tatty remake of a Garbo vehicle which was dated even in 1934. (See *The Painted Veil.*)

w Karl Tunberg, *novel* The Painted Veil by Somerset Maugham *d* Ronald Neame *ph* Ray June *m* Miklos Rozsa

Eleanor Parker, Bill Travers, George Sanders, Jean-Pierre Aumont, Françoise Rosay

The Seventh Survivor
GB 1941 75m bw

Survivors of a shipwreck gather in a lighthouse and discover that one of them is a Nazi agent. Adequate mystery potboiler, comparable with Hitchcock's talkier *Lifeboat.* Linden Travers, Austin Trevor, John Stuart, Martita Hunt, Frank Pettingell, Jane Carr, Felix Aylmer, Wally Patch, Henry Oscar. Written by Michael Barringer; directed by Leslie Hiscott; for British National.

The Seventh Veil**
GB 1945 94m bw
Theatrecraft / Sydney Box / Ortus

A concert pianist is romantically torn between her psychiatrist, her guardian, and two other fellows.
A splendid modern melodrama in the tradition of *Jane Eyre* and *Rebecca*; it set the seal of moviegoing approval on psychiatry, classical music, and James Mason, and it is the most utter tosh.

w Muriel and Sydney Box d Compton Bennett ph Reg Wyer *m Benjamin Frankel*

James Mason, Ann Todd, Herbert Lom, Albert Lieven, Hugh McDermott, Yvonne Owen, David Horne, Manning Whiley

'An example of the intelligent, medium-priced picture made with great technical polish which has represented for Hollywood the middle path between the vulgar and the highbrow.'—*Spectator*

'A popular film that does not discard taste and atmosphere.'—*Daily Mail*

'A rich, portentous mixture of Beethoven, Chopin, Kitsch and Freud.'—*Pauline Kael, 1968*

'An odd, artificial, best sellerish kind of story, with reminiscences of *Trilby* and *Jane Eyre* and all their imitations down to *Rebecca*.'—*Richard Mallett, Punch*

'Maybe, with a few veils stripped away, all of us have a fantasist inside who gobbles up this sadomasochistic sundae.'—*Pauline Kael, 70s*

AA: script

The Seventh Victim*
US 1943 71m bw
RKO (*Val Lewton*)

A girl goes to New York in search of her sister, who is under the influence of Satanists. Much praised but in effect rather boring little thriller, with rather stately acting and ponderous direction and dialogue. Censorship made the plot so obscure that it's difficult to follow.

w Charles O'Neal, De Witt Bodeen *d* Mark Robson *ph* Nicholas Musuraca *m* Constantin Bakaleinikoff

Kim Hunter, Tom Conway, Jean Brooks, Hugh Beaumont, Erford Gage, Isabel Jewell, Evelyn Brent

'It is the almost oppressive mood, the romantic obsession with death-in-life, which dominates the film.'—*NFT, 1973*
† Note the use in the first scene of the staircase from *The Magnificent Ambersons.*

The Seventh Voyage of Sinbad*
US 1958 89m Technicolor
Columbia / Morningside (Charles Schneer)

Sinbad seeks a roc's egg which will restore his fiancée from the midget size to which an evil magician has reduced her.
Lively fantasy with narrative drive and excellent effects.

w Kenneth Kolb *d* Nathan Juran ph Wilkie Cooper *m* Bernard Herrmann *sp Ray Harryhausen*

Kerwin Mathews, Kathryn Grant, Torin Thatcher, Richard Eyer, Alec Mango

70,000 Witnesses
US 1932 69m bw

A football star is murdered in the middle of a game. Okay for sports fans, but not much of a murder mystery. Phillips Holmes, Johnny Mack Brown, Charles Ruggles, Dorothy Jordan, J. Farrell MacDonald, Lew Cody. Written by Garrett Fort, P. J. Wolfson, Allen Rivkin, from the novel by Cortland Fitzsimmons; directed by Ralph Murphy; for Harry Joe Brown / Paramount. 'Will make money and please . . . enough comedy interwoven to satisfy on laughs alone.'—*Variety*

A Severed Head*
GB 1970 98m Technicolor
Columbia / Winkast (Alan Ladd Jnr)

A wine merchant has a long-standing affair which he thinks is secret, but is annoyed when his wife tries the same game.
Unwisely boisterous screen version of a slyly academic novel; tolerably sophisticated for those who don't know the original.

w Frederic Raphael, *novel* Iris Murdoch *d* Dick Clement *ph* Austin Dempster *m* Stanley Myers *pd* Richard Macdonald

Lee Remick, Richard Attenborough, Ian Holm, Claire Bloom, Jennie Linden, Clive Revill

Sex and the Single Girl
US 1964 114m Technicolor
Warner / Richard Quine / Reynard (William T. Orr)

A journalist worms his way into the life of a lady sexologist in order to unmask her—but guess what.
Coy sex comedy with noise substituting for wit and style, all pretence being abandoned in a wild chase climax.

w Joseph Heller, David R. Schwarz, *book* Helen Gurley Brown *d* Richard Quine *ph* Charles Lang Jnr *m* Neal Hefti

Natalie Wood, Tony Curtis, Henry Fonda, Lauren Bacall, Mel Ferrer, Fran Jeffries, Edward Everett Horton, Otto Kruger

'For those willing to devote two hours of their lives to a consideration of Natalie Wood's virginity.'—*Judith Crist, 1973*

Sextette*
US 1978 91m Metrocolor
Briggs and Sullivan (Warren G. Toub)

The honeymoon of a Hollywood film star is interrupted by her previous husbands.
An amazing last stab at her old métier by an 86-year-old ex-star. It doesn't work, of course, and most of it is embarrassing, but the attempt is in itself remarkable.

w Herbert Baker, *play* Mae West *d* Ken Hughes *ph* James Crabe *m* Artie Butler

Mae West, Tony Curtis, Ringo Starr, Dom de Luise, Timothy Dalton, George Hamilton, Alice Cooper, Rona Barrett, Walter Pidgeon, George Raft

Sexton Blake and the Hooded Terror
GB 1938 70m bw

A millionaire is unmasked as the head of a criminal gang. Rather unyielding series melodrama, chiefly interesting for the casting of Tod Slaughter as Blake's Moriarty. George Curzon, Tod Slaughter, Greta Gynt, Charles Oliver, David Farrar. Written by A. R. Rawlinson; directed by George King; for George King.

TERROR: 'You little fool! Don't you realise that the game is up? The Black Quorum has seen through your treacheries. I alone can save you from their revenge!'
GIRL: 'I'd rather die.'
(NB: Other Sexton Blake movies, all cheaply made by British independents, include six 1928 two-reelers starring Langhorne Burton; *Sexton Blake and the Bearded Doctor* and *Sexton Blake and the Mademoiselle*, both 1935, both with Curzon; *Meet Sexton Blake* and *The Echo Murders*, both 1943, both with David Farrar; and *Murder on Site Three*, 1963 with Geoffrey Toone.)

Sh! The Octopus
US 1937 54m bw

Lamebrain detectives fight a giant octopus in a lighthouse. Footling remake of *The Gorilla*, (*qv*). Hugh Herbert, Allen Jenkins, Marcia Ralston, John Eldredge, George Rosener. Written by George Bricker; directed by William McGann; for First National. 'This bit of grist for the double-feature mills is so feeble even the actors seem embarrassed.'—*Variety*

Shack Out on 101*
US 1955 80m bw
AA / William F. Broidy

A waitress at a café near a research establishment unmasks two spies.
Modest suspenser which seemed at the time to have some fresh and realistic attitudes.

w Ed and Mildred Dein *d Ed Dein ph Floyd Crosby* *m* Paul Dunlap

Frank Lovejoy, Lee Marvin, Keenan Wynn, Terry Moore, Whit Bissell

Shadey
GB 1985 106m colour
Larkspur / Otto Plashkes

A bankrupt car mechanic will do almost anything to finance his sex change operation.
Weird, utterly unprovoked and unmotivated black comedy which confounded all comers.

w Snoo Wilson *d* Philip Saville *ph* Roger Deakins *m* Colin Towns

Anthony Sher, Billie Whitelaw, Patrick MacNee, Leslie Ash, Bernard Hepton, Larry Lamb, Katherine Helmond

The Shadow
US 1940 bw serial: 15 eps

A scientist and criminologist assumes the guise of The Shadow in order to combat The Black Tiger. Archetypal silly season serial. Victor Jory, Weda Ann Borg, Robert Moore, Robert Fiske, J. Paul Jones. Directed by James W. Horne; for Columbia.

Shadow in the Sky
US 1951 78m bw
MGM (William H. Wright)

A shell-shocked marine moves from a psychiatric hospital to live with his sister.
Low-key drama, plainly but quite well done, though of little continuing interest.

w Ben Maddow *d* Fred M. Wilcox *ph* George Folsey *m* Bronislau Kaper

Ralph Meeker, Nancy Davis, James Whitmore, Jean Hagen

Shadow of a Doubt***
US 1943 108m bw
Universal (Jack H. Skirball)

A favourite uncle comes to visit his family in a small Californian town. He is actually on the run from police, who know him as the Merry Widow murderer.
Hitchcock's quietest film is memorable chiefly for its depiction of small-town life; but the script is well written and keeps the suspense moving slowly but surely.

w Thornton Wilder, Sally Benson, Alma Reville, story Gordon McDonell *d Alfred Hitchcock ph* Joe Valentine *m* Dmitri Tiomkin

Joseph Cotten, Teresa Wright, Hume Cronyn, Macdonald Carey, Patricia Collinge, Henry Travers, Wallace Ford

'Some clever observation of rabbity white-collar life which, in spite of a specious sweetness, is the best since *It's a Gift*.'—*James Agee*
† Remade in 1959 as *Step Down to Terror*, with Charles Drake.

AAN: original story

Shadow of a Woman
US 1946 78m bw

A woman suspects her husband of trying to murder his son by a former marriage. Poor melodrama on *Love from a Stranger* lines. Andrea King, Helmut Dantine, Don McGuire, Richard Erdman, William Prince. Written by Whitman Chambers and C. Graham Baker; directed by Joseph Santley; for Warner.

Shadow of Chinatown
US 1936 bw serial: 15 eps

A master villain is employed by international businessmen to close down the trade of Chinatown. Inept but action-packed serial with unintentional laughs. Bela Lugosi, Joan Barclay, Herman Brix, Luana Walters. Directed by Bob Hill; for Victory.

Shadow of Doubt
US 1935 71m bw

An actress suspected of murder is cleared by the efforts of her fiancé's aunt. Routine mystery with a strong part for a new character actress from England. Ricardo Cortez, Virginia Bruce, *Constance Collier*, Arthur Byron, Isabel Jewell, Regis Toomey, Edward Brophy. Written by Wells Root, Arthur Somers Roche; directed by George B. Seitz; for MGM. 'Passable murder mystery.'—*Variety*

Shadow of the Cat
GB 1961 79m bw
U-I / BHP (Jon Penington)

A cat appears to wreak vengeance on those who murdered its mistress.
Tolerable old dark house shocker with an amusing theme not too well sustained.

w George Baxt *d* John Gilling *ph* Alec Grant *m* Mikis Theodorakis

André Morell, William Lucas, Barbara Shelley, Conrad Phillips, Alan Wheatley, Vanda Godsell, Richard Warner, Freda Jackson

The Shadow of the Eagle
US 1932 bw serial: 12 eps

An airborne criminal sends his threats by skywriting. Silly adventure serial. John Wayne, Dorothy Gulliver, Walter Miller, Kenneth Harlan, Yakima Canutt. Directed by Ford Beebe; for Mascot.

Shadow of the Eagle
GB 1950 92m bw

In 1770, a Russian envoy to Venice falls for the princess he is supposed to kidnap. Limp swashbuckler based on a deservedly shadowy corner of European history. Richard Greene, Valentina Cortese, Greta Gynt, Binnie Barnes, Charles Goldner, Walter Rilla. Written by Doreen Montgomery and Hagar Wilde; directed by Sidney Salkow; for Anthony Havelock-Allan / Valiant.

Shadow on the Wall
US 1949 84m bw
MGM (Robert Sisk)

A child is traumatized by the accidental witnessing of the murder of her unpleasant stepmother.
Forgettable melodramatic suspenser.

w William Ludwig *d* Pat Jackson *ph* Ray June *m* André Previn

Ann Sothern, Zachary Scott, Gigi Perreau, Nancy Davis, Kristine Miller, John McIntire

The Shadow on the Window
US 1957 73m bw
Columbia (Jonie Taps)

Three teenage thugs break into a lonely house, murder its owner and hold a girl hostage.
Routine crime programmer, rather boringly unravelled.

w Leo Townsend, David Harmon *d* William Asher *ph* Kit Carson *m* George Duning

Betty Garrett, Phil Carey, John Barrymore Jnr, Corey Allen, Gerald Saracini

Shadows*
US 1959 81m bw
Cassavetes / Cassel / Maurice McEndree

Two blacks and their sister find their identities in Manhattan.
16mm realistic drama which began a new and essentially dreary trend of grainily true-life pictures with improvised dialogue and little dramatic compression.

w the cast *d* John Cassavetes *ph* Erich Kollmar *m* Charles Mingus

Ben Carruthers, Leila Goldoni, Hugh Hurd, Rupert Crosse, Anthony Ray

'I don't so much object to its mindlessness as to its formlessness, regardless of the practical excuses that may be advanced for its rambling incoherence.'—*William S. Pechter*

'A picture of startling immediacy and shocking power.'—*Robert Hatch, Nation*

'We were improvising . . . every scene was very simple. They were predicated on people having problems that were overcome with other problems. At the end of the scene another problem would come in and overlap.'—*John Cassavetes*

Shady Lady
US 1945 90m bw

An elderly cardsharp is persuaded to help the district attorney nab others of his kind.
Poorish comedy which offers its star little support. Charles Coburn, Ginny Simms, Robert Paige, Martha O'Driscoll, Alan Curtis. Written by Curt Siodmak, Gerald Geraghty and M. M. Musselman; directed by George Waggner; for Universal.

Shaft*
US 1971 100m Metrocolor
MGM / Shaft Productions (Joel Freeman)

A black private eye finds himself at odds with a powerful racketeer.
Violent, commercial action thriller which spawned two sequels and a tele-series as well as stimulating innumerable even more violent imitations.

w Ernest Tidyman, John D. F. Black *d* Gordon Parks *ph* Urs Furrer *m* Isaac Hayes

Richard Roundtree, Moses Gunn, Charles Cioffi, Christopher St John

'Relentlessly supercool dialogue, all throwaway colloquialisms and tough Chandlerian wisecracks.'—*MFB*

AA: title song (*m / ly* Isaac Hayes)
AAN: Isaac Hayes (musical score)

Shaft in Africa
US 1973 112m Metrocolor Panavision
(MGM) Shaft Productions (Roger Lewis)

Shaft is kidnapped by an Ethiopian emir who wants him to track down a gang of slavers.
More miscellaneous violence, rather shoddily assembled, with a few good jokes.

w Stirling Silliphant *d* John Guillermin *ph* Marcel Grignon *m* Johnny Pate

Richard Roundtree, Frank Finlay, Vonetta McGee

Shaft's Big Score
US 1972 105m Metrocolor Panavision
MGM / Shaft Productions (Richard Lewis, Ernest Tidyman)

Shaft avenges the death of a friend and comes up against the numbers racket.
Violent footage and an incomprehensible plot.

w Ernest Tidyman *d* Gordon Parks *ph* Urs Furrer *m* Gordon Parks

Richard Roundtree, Moses Gunn, Drew Bundini Brown, Joseph Mascolo

The Shaggy DA
US 1976 92m Technicolor
Walt Disney (Ron Miller)

A magic ring enables a young lawyer to become a talking dog and thus expose corruption.
Rather feeble sequel to *The Shaggy Dog*, with overtones of Watergate.

w Don Tait *d* Robert Stevenson *ph* Frank Phillips *m* Buddy Baker *sp* Eustace Lycett, Art Cruickshank, Danne Lee

Dean Jones, Tim Conway, Suzanne Pleshette, Jo Anne Worley, Vic Tayback, Keenan Wynn, Dick Van Patten

The Shaggy Dog*
US 1959 101m bw
Walt Disney (Bill Walsh)

A small boy turns into a big shaggy dog and catches some crooks.
Simple-minded, overlong Disney comedy for kids and their indulgent parents; good laughs in the chase scenes.

w Bill Walsh, Lillie Hayward, *novel* The Hound of Florence by Felix Salten *d* Charles Barton *ph* Edward Colman *m* Paul Sawtell

Fred MacMurray, Jean Hagen, Tommy Kirk, Cecil Kellaway, Annette Funicello, Tim Considine, Kevin Corcoran, Alexander Scourby

Shake Hands with Murder
US 1944 61m bw

Bailbondsmen get involved in murder.
Tolerable little mystery for the bottom of the bill. Frank Jenks, Iris Adrian, Douglas Fowley, Jack Raymond. Written by John T. Neville, Martin Mooney; directed by Albert Herman; for American Productions / PRC.

Shake Hands with the Devil*
Eire 1959 110m bw
UA / Troy / Pennebaker (Michael Anderson)

In 1921 Dublin a surgeon is the secret leader of the IRA, and comes to cherish violence as an end rather than a means.
Downbeat action melodrama, politically very questionable but well made.

w Ivan Goff, Ben Roberts, *novel* Rearden Connor *d* Michael Anderson *ph* Erwin Hillier *m* William Alwyn

James Cagney, Glynis Johns, Don Murray, Dana Wynter, Michael Redgrave, Sybil Thorndike, Cyril Cusack, Niall MacGinnis, Richard Harris, Ray McAnally, Noel Purcell

Shakedown
US 1950 80m bw
U-I (Ted Richmond)

A ruthless press photographer becomes a blackmailer.
Routine crime melodrama, adequately done.

w Alfred Lewis, Martin Goldsmith *d* Joseph Pevney *ph* Irving Glassberg *m* Joseph Gershenson

Howard Duff, Brian Donlevy, Anne Vernon, Peggy Dow, Lawrence Tierney, Bruce Bennett

The Shakedown
GB 1959 92m bw
Rank / Alliance / Ethiro (Norman Williams)

A Soho vice boss photographs prominent people in compromising situations and blackmails them.
A semi-remake set in the squalid London so beloved of film makers at the time, before it became 'swinging'. Of no interest or entertainment value.

w Leigh Vance *d* John Lemont *ph* Brendan J. Stafford *m* Philip Green

Terence Morgan, Hazel Court, Donald Pleasence, Bill Owen, Robert Beatty, Harry H. Corbett, Gene Anderson, Eddie Byrne

Shaker Run
New Zealand 1985 90m colour

Two American stunt car drivers help a girl who for the best political reasons has stolen a deadly virus. Harebrained excuse for car chases against beautiful scenery; quite exhausting. Cliff Robertson, Leif Garrett, Lisa Harrow, Shane Briant. Written by James Kouf Jnr, Henry Fownes, Bruce Morrison; directed by Bruce Morrison; for Laurelwood / Aviscom / Mirage.

Shakespeare Wallah*
India 1965 125m bw
Merchant Ivory (Ismail Merchant)

A troupe of English actors find their Indian tour interrupted by romance.
Interesting but sluggish drama on an unusual subject. Not by any means a classic, but it set off this partnership on an enduring wave of critical acclaim and public indifference.

w Ruth Prawer Jhabvala, James Ivory *d* James Ivory *ph* Subrata Mitra *m* Satyajit Ray

Felicity Kendal, Shashi Kapoor, Laura Liddell, Geoffrey Kendal, Madhur Jaffrey, Utpal Dutt

The Shakiest Gun in the West
US 1967 101m Techniscope
Universal (Edward J. Montagne)

A cowardly dentist becomes a western hero.
Dreary farce, an unsubtle remake of *The Paleface*.

w Jim Fritzell, Everett Greenbaum *d* Alan Rafkin *ph* Andrew Jackson *m* Vic Mizzy

Don Knotts, Barbara Rhoades, Jackie Coogan, Don Barry

Shalako
GB 1968 118m Technicolor Franscope
Kingston / Dimitri de Grunwald (Euan Lloyd)

New Mexico, 1880: a cowboy acts as guide to European aristocratic big game hunters, but the Indians become annoyed and attack.
A cute idea is given routine treatment; though packed with stars, the action never becomes very exciting despite incidental brutalities.

w J. J. Griffith, Hal Hopper, Scot Finch, *novel* Louis L'Amour *d* Edward Dmytryk *ph* Ted Moore *m* Robert Farnon

Sean Connery, Brigitte Bardot, Jack Hawkins, Stephen Boyd, Peter Van Eyck, Honor Blackman, Eric Sykes, Alexander Knox, Woody Strode, Valerie French

Shall We Dance?**
US 1937 116m bw
RKO (Pandro S. Berman)

Dancing partners pretend to be married but are not; until they both get the same idea.
A light musical which was full of good things but nevertheless began the decline of Astaire-Rogers films; repetition was obvious, as was ostentation for its own sake, and the audience was expecting too much.

w Allan Scott, Ernest Pagano *d* Mark Sandrich *ph* David Abel *m / ly George and Ira Gershwin* *md* Nathaniel Shilkret *ad* Van Nest Polglase

Fred Astaire, Ginger Rogers, Edward Everett Horton, Eric Blore, Harriet Hoctor, Jerome Cowan, Ketti Gallian, Ann Shoemaker

'Another holdover musical in the Astaire-Rogers string . . . it has everything it needs on production.'—*Variety*

AAN: song 'They Can't Take That Away From Me'

Shampoo*
US 1975 110m Technicolor
Columbia / Persky–Bright / Vista (Warren Beatty)

A Beverly Hills hairdresser seduces his most glamorous clients.
Ugly little sex farce with few laughs but much dashing about and bad language. Its setting on election eve 1968 has made some people think it a political satire.

w Robert Towne, Warren Beatty *d* Hal Ashby *ph* Laszlo Kovacs *m* Paul Simon

Warren Beatty, Julie Christie, Lee Grant, Goldie Hawn, Jack Warden, Tony Bill, Jay Robinson

'It has the bursting-with-talent but fuzziness-of-effect aspect of a movie made by a group of friends for their own amusement.'—*Richard Combs*

AA: Lee Grant
AAN: script; Jack Warden

Shamus
US 1972 98m Eastmancolor
Columbia / Robert M. Weitman

A private eye is hired by a wealthy man to recover stolen jewels and find a murderer.
A forties retread with seventies violence; junky stuff, with a few laughs for buffs who can spot the in-jokes.

w Barry Beckerman *d* Buzz Kulik *ph* Victor J. Kemper *m* Jerry Goldsmith

Burt Reynolds, Dyan Cannon, John Ryan, Joe Santos, Giorgio Tozzi, Ron Weyland

'Very hectic, very vividly New York and as idiotic as Reynolds' physical resiliency.'—*Judith Crist*

Shane***
US 1953 118m Technicolor
Paramount (George Stevens, Ivan Moffat)

A mysterious stranger helps a family of homesteaders.
Archetypal family western, but much slower and statelier than most, as though to emphasize its own quality, which is evident anyway.

w A. B. Guthrie Jnr, *novel* Jack Schaefer *d George Stevens* *ph* Loyal Griggs *m* Victor Young

Alan Ladd, Jean Arthur, Van Heflin, *Jack Palance*, Brandon de Wilde, Ben Johnson, Edgar Buchanan, Emile Meyer, Elisha Cook Jnr, John Dierkes

'A kind of dramatic documentary of the pioneer days of the west.'—*MFB*

'Westerns are better when they're not too self-importantly self-conscious.'—*New Yorker, 1975*

'Stevens managed to infuse a new vitality, a new sense of realism into the time-worn story through the strength and freshness of his visuals.'—Arthur Knight

AA: Loyal Griggs
AAN: best picture; A. B. Guthrie Jnr; George Stevens; Jack Palance; Brandon de Wilde

Shanghai
US 1935 77m bw
(Paramount) Walter Wanger

A visiting American lady falls in love with a half caste.
Romantic drama programmer.

w Gene Towne, Graham Baker, Lynn Starling *d* James Flood *ph* James Van Trees

Loretta Young, Charles Boyer, Warner Oland, Alison Skipworth, Fred Keating, Charles Grapewin, Walter Kingsford

Shanghai Express***
US 1932 84m bw
Paramount

A British officer and his old flame meet on a train which is waylaid by Chinese bandits.
Superbly pictorial melodrama which set the pattern for innumerable train movies to come, though none matched its deft visual quality and few sketched in their characters so neatly. Plot and dialogue are silent style, but refreshingly so.

w Jules Furthman *d Josef Von Sternberg* *ph Lee Garmes* *m* W. Franke Harling *ad Hans Dreier*

Marlene Dietrich, Clive Brook, Warner Oland, Anna May Wong, Eugene Pallette, Lawrence Grant, Louise Closser Hale, Gustav Von Seyffertitz

LILY (Marlene Dietrich): 'It took more than one man to change my name to Shanghai Lily.'

'Good programme picture bolstered by the Dietrich name . . . Excellent camerawork overcomes really hoke melodramatic story.'—*Variety*

'A limited number of characters, all meticulously etched, highly atmospheric sets and innumerable striking photographic compositions.'—*Curtis Harrington, 1964*

AA: Lee Garmes
AAN: best picture; Josef Von Sternberg

The Shanghai Gesture*
US 1941 90m bw
Arnold Pressburger (Albert de Courville)

The proprietress of a Shanghai gambling casino taunts her ex-husband by showing him his daughter in a state of degradation; but he proves that the girl is her daughter also.
An ancient theatrical shocker was completely bowdlerized and chopped into nonsense for the screen; but the director's hand showed in the handling of the vast casino set.

w Josef Von Sternberg, Geza Herczeg, Karl Vollmoeller, Jules Furthman, *play* John Colton *d Josef Von Sternberg* *ph* Paul Ivano *m* Richard Hageman *ad Boris Leven*

Ona Munson, Victor Mature, Walter Huston, Gene Tierney, Albert Basserman, Phyllis Brooks, Maria Ouspenskaya, Eric Blore, Ivan Lebedeff, Mike Mazurki

'The effect of a descent into a maelstrom of iniquity.'—*Curtis Harrington, 1962*

'In spite of all the changes necessitated by the Hays Office, seldom have decadence and sexual depravity been better suggested on the screen.'—*Richard Roud, 1966*

'Hilariously, awesomely terrible.'—*New Yorker, 1977*

AAN: Richard Hageman

Shanghai Madness
US 1933 63m bw

A naval officer is cashiered in Shanghai and gets mixed up with Communists. Weakish melodrama which goes the long way round to a happy ending. Spencer Tracy, Fay Wray, Ralph Morgan, Eugene Pallette, Herbert Mundin. Written by Frederick Hazlitt Brennan, Austin Parker, Gordon Wellesley; directed by John G. Blystone; for Fox. 'Okay generally but in big spots will need stage support.'—*Variety*

Shanghai Surprise
GB 1986 97m Technicolor
HandMade / Vista / John Kohn

A lady missionary hires an adventurer to track down a stack of opium before it falls into the wrong hands.
Astonishingly abysmal adventure romance set rather uncertainly in the 1937 Orient. Nothing matches the so-called talents involved.

w John Kohn, Robert Bentley
novel Faraday's Flowers by Tony Kenrick
d Jim Goddard *ph* Ernest Vincze *m* George Harrison, Michael Kamen

Madonna, Sean Penn, Paul Freeman, Richard Griffiths

'A silly little trifle which wouldn't even have passed muster as a 1930s programmer.'—*Variety*

Shark
US / Mexico 1969 88m Eastmancolor
Heritage / Cinematografica Calderon

A gunrunner in the Sudan becomes involved with unscrupulous divers after wrecks.
Tepid adventure yarn allegedly damaged by recutting but showing very little sign of original talent.

w Samuel Fuller, John Kingsbridge, *novel* His Bones Are Coral by Victor Canning *d* Samuel Fuller *ph* Raul Martinez Solares *m* Rafael Moroyoqui

Burt Reynolds, Arthur Kennedy, Barry Sullivan, Silvia Pinal, Enrique Lucero

The Sharkfighters
US 1956 72m Technicolor
Cinemascope
(UA) Formosa (Samuel Goldwyn Jnr)

To save the lives of fliers forced down into the sea, navy scientists experiment with a shark repellent.
Straightforward semi-documentary with suspenseful action sequences.

w Lawrence Roman, John Robinson *d* Jerry Hopper *ph* Lee Garmes *m* Jerome Moross

Victor Mature, Karen Steele, James Olson, Claude Akins

Shark's Treasure*
US 1974 95m De Luxe
UA / Symbol (Cornel Wilde)

Treasure hunters seek buried gold in the Caribbean where sharks abound.
Fairly thrilling action hokum.

wd Cornel Wilde *ph* Jack Atcheler, Al Giddings
m Robert O. Ragland

Cornel Wilde, Yaphet Kotto, John Neilson, David Canary, Cliff Osmond

'Wilde maintains his reputation for making the most likeable bad movies around.'—*Tom Milne*

Sharky's Machine
US 1981 120m Technicolor
Warner / Orion / Deliverance (Hank Moonjean)

A vice squad policeman builds up a new team. Exceptionally violent cop thriller on the lines of *Dirty Harry*

w Gerald Di Pego, *novel* William Diehl
d Burt Reynolds *ph* William A. Fraker
md Al Capps

Burt Reynolds, Vittorio Gassman, Brian Keith, Charles Durning, Earl Holliman, Bernie Casey, Henry Silva

Sharpshooters
US 1938 63m bw

Adventures of a newsreel cameraman who saves a young prince from kidnapping. Serial-like action and comedy very palatably blended: the first of a short series. Brian Donlevy, Lynn Bari, Wally Vernon, John King, Douglass Dumbrille, C. Henry Gordon, Sidney Blackmer. Written by Robert Ellis, Helen Logan; directed by James Tinling; for TCF . 'A standard programmer to entertain, and a natural for the juve trade.'—*Variety*

'Young and beautiful for 500 years—and wicked every one of them!'

She*
US 1935 89m bw
RKO (Merian C. Cooper)

Ancient papers lead a Cambridge professor and his friends to the lost city where dwells a queen who cannot die—until she falls in love. The producers have the right spirit for this Victorian fantasy, but tried too hard to emulate the mood of their own *King Kong*, and it was a mistake to transfer the setting from Africa to the Arctic. One for connoisseurs, though.

w Ruth Rose, Dudley Nichols, *novel* H. Rider Haggard *d* Irving Pichel, Lansing G. Holden *ph* J. Roy Hunt *m* Max Steiner

Randolph Scott, Nigel Bruce, Helen Gahagan

'Beautiful production, but story dubious for discriminating adults.'—*Variety*

'To an unrepentant Haggard fan it does sometimes seem to catch the thrill as well as the childishness of his invention.'—*Graham Greene*

'A spectacle of magnificent proportions with the decadent effluvium of the tomb period.'—*Photoplay*

'The stagey décor of Kor is in the art deco style of Radio City Music Hall, and you keep expecting the Rockettes to turn up.'—*Pauline Kael, 70s*

She
GB 1965 105m Technicolor
Hammerscope
ABP / Hammer (Aida Young)

Flat, uninventive and tedious remake which reverts to Africa but does nothing else right; it ignores the essential Cambridge prologue and ignores all suggestions of fantasy.

w David T. Chantler *d* Robert Day *ph* Harry Waxman *m* James Bernard

Peter Cushing, Ursula Andress, Christopher Lee, John Richardson, Bernard Cribbins, André Morell, Rosenda Monteros

She Couldn't Say No
US 1952 89m bw
RKO (Robert Sparks)
GB title: *Beautiful But Dangerous*

An heiress returns to the town of her childhood to distribute anonymous gifts to those who had helped her.
Moderate Capraesque comedy which doesn't quite come off.

w D. D. Beauchamp, William Bowers, Richard Flournoy *d* Lloyd Bacon *ph* Harold J. Wild *m* Roy Webb

Jean Simmons, Robert Mitchum, Arthur Hunnicutt, Edgar Buchanan, Wallace Ford, Raymond Walburn

She Couldn't Take It*
US 1935 89m bw
Columbia (B. P. Schulberg)

A rich old reprobate meets a gangster in prison and puts him in charge of his rebellious family.
Little-known crazy comedy with touches of melodrama; not a success, but with interesting elements.

w Gene Towne, Oliver H. P. Garrett, *story* Graham Baker *d* Tay Garnett *ph* Leon Shamroy

George Raft, Joan Bennett, Walter Connelly, Billie Burke, Lloyd Nolan, Wallace Ford, Alan Mowbray, Donald Meek

She Didn't Say No!
GB 1958 97m Technicolor
GW Films (Sergei Nolbandov)

A young Irish widow has five illegitimate children, each by a different father.
Coyly daring comedy full of stage Oirishisms and obvious jokes, a few of which work.

w T. J. Morison, Una Troy, from her novel We Are Seven *d* Cyril Frankel *ph* Gilbert Taylor *m* Tristam Cary

Eileen Herlie, Jack MacGowran, Perlita Neilson, Niall MacGinnis, Ian Bannen

She Done Him Wrong***
US 1933 68m bw
Paramount (William Le Baron)

A lady saloon keeper of the Gay Nineties falls for the undercover cop who is after her.
As near undiluted Mae West as Hollywood ever came: fast, funny, melodramatic and pretty sexy; also a very atmospheric and well-made movie.

w Mae West, from her play Diamond Lil (with help on the scenario from Harry Thew, John Bright) *d Lowell Sherman ph* Charles Lang *songs* Ralph Rainger (*m*), Leo Robin (*ly*)

Mae West, Cary Grant, Owen Moore, Gilbert Roland, Noah Beery, David Landau, Rafaela Ottiano, Rochelle Hudson, Dewey Robinson

'Only alternative to a strong drawing cast, nowadays if a picture wants business, is strong entertainment. This one has neither.'—*Variety*

AAN: best picture

She Gets Her Man*
US 1945 73m bw
Universal (Warren Wilson)

A country girl in New York tracks down a blowgun murderer.
Disarming mystery farce which tries every slapstick situation known to gag writers, and gets away with it.

w Warren Wilson, Clyde Bruckman *d* Erle C. Kenton *ph* Jerry Ash

Joan Davis, William Gargan, Leon Errol, Milburn Stone, Russell Hicks

She Has What It Takes
US 1943 66m bw

A small-time singer masquerades as the long-lost daughter of a famous stage star. An excuse for musical padding, for indulgent audiences. Jinx Falkenberg, Tom Neal, Constance Worth, Joe King, The Radio Rogues, The Vagabonds. Written by Paul Yawitz; directed by Charles Barton; for Colbert Clark / Columbia.

She Knew All the Answers
US 1941 84m bw

Prevented by his uncle from marrying a playboy, a chorine falls for the uncle. Mildly merry comedy which came and went without being noticed. Joan Bennett, Franchot Tone, John Hubbard, Eve Arden, William Tracy. Written by Harry Segall, Kenneth Earl, Curtis Kenyon, from story by Jane Allen; directed by Richard Wallace; for Charles R. Rogers / Columbia.

She Learned about Sailors
US 1934 82m bw

In Shanghai, a couple get married so that they will be permitted to leave; back home, they're not sure they want an annulment. Mild comedy with music. Alice Faye, Lew Ayres, Harry Green, Mitchell and Durant. Written by William Conselman and Henry Johnson from a story by Randall H. Faye; directed by George Marshall; for Fox.

'The hi-de-hi of higher education!'
She Loves Me Not*
US 1934 85m bw
Paramount (Benjamin Glazer)

A showgirl murder witness takes refuge in a men's college.
Larky musical farce later remade as *True to the Army* and *How to be Very Very Popular*; this first version is perhaps the most nearly amusing.

w Ben Glazer, *novel* Edward Hope, *play* Howard Lindsay *d* Elliott Nugent *ph* Charles Lang *songs* various

Bing Crosby, Miriam Hopkins, Kitty Carlisle, Edward Nugent, Lynne Overman, Henry Stephenson, Warren Hymer, George Barbier

AAN: song 'Love in Bloom'

She Married an Artist
US 1938 78m bw

A wife becomes jealous of her husband's models. Very mild romantic comedy. John Boles, Francis Drake, Albert Dekker. Written by Avery Strakosch, Delmer Daves and Gladys Lehman; directed by Marion Gering; for Columbia.

She Married Her Boss
US 1935 90m bw

A secretary marries her boss and finds herself taken for granted. Pleasant but rather thin romantic comedy with amiable stars. Claudette Colbert, Melvyn Douglas, Raymond Walburn, Edith Fellows, Jean Dixon, Katherine Alexander. Written by Sidney Buchman; directed by Gregory La Cava; for Columbia.

She Shall Have Murder
GB 1950 90m bw

A law clerk helps to solve the murder of an elderly client. Old-fashioned light comedy whodunnit, the equivalent of reading a Crime Club thriller. Rosamund John, Derrick de Marney, Mary Jerrold, Felix Aylmer, Joyce Heron, Beatrice Varley. Written by Allan Mackinnon, from a novel by Delano Ames; directed by Daniel Birt; for Concanen / IFD.

She Wanted a Millionaire
US 1932 74m bw

A girl spurns her childhood sweetheart for a rich man who turns out to be dangerous. Curious comedy–melodrama which confuses its watchers. Joan Bennett, Spencer Tracy, James Kirkwood, Una Merkel, Dorothy Peterson. Written by Sonja Levien, from story by William Anthony McGuire; directed by John G. Blystone; for Fox.

The She-Wolf
US 1931 90m bw

A woman gets rich but neglects her children. Talkative filmed play, almost redeemed by its star performance. May Robson, James Hall, Lawrence Gray, Frances Dade. Written by Winfred Dunn, from stage play *Mother's Millions*; directed by James Flood; for Universal.

'Beauty or beast? Woman or monster?'
She Wolf of London
US 1946 61m bw

A girl thinks she must be the family werewolf. Risibly inept semi-horror melodrama with a highly implausible solution and poor production. June Lockhart, Don Porter, Sara Haden, Lloyd Corrigan, Dennis Hoey, Martin Kosleck. Written by George Bricker; directed by Jean Yarbrough; for Universal. (GB title: *The Curse of the Allenbys*.)

She Wore a Yellow Ribbon**
US 1949 103m Technicolor
RKO / Argosy (John Ford, Merian C. Cooper)

Problems of a cavalry officer about to retire. Fragmentary but very enjoyable western with all Ford ingredients served piping hot.

w Frank Nugent, Laurence Stallings, *story* James Warner Bellah *d John Ford ph Winton C. Hoch m* Richard Hageman

John Wayne, Joanne Dru, John Agar, Ben Johnson, Harry Carey Jnr, Victor McLaglen, Mildred Natwick, George O'Brien, Arthur Shields

AA: Winton C. Hoch

She Wouldn't Say Yes
US 1945 87m bw

A lady psychiatrist falls for the subject of an experiment. Star comedy vehicle which falls rather flat. Rosalind Russell, Lee Bowman, Charles Winninger, Adele Jergens. Written by Laslo Gorog, William Thiele, Virginia Van Upp, John Jacoby and Sarett Tobias; directed by Alexander Hall; for Columbia.

She Wrote the Book
US 1946 72m bw

A lady professor imagines herself to be the glamorous femme fatale heroine of a lurid novel. Adventures of a female Walter Mitty; one of the star's better comedies. Joan Davis, Mischa Auer, Jack Oakie, Kirby Grant, John Litel, Gloria Stuart, Thurston Hall. Written by Warren Wilson and Oscar Brodney; directed by Charles Lamont; for Universal.

'When paradise became a battleground, she led the fight for survival!'
Sheena, Queen of the Jungle
US 1984 115m Metrocolor Panavision
Columbia / Delphi II (Paul Aratow)

Orphaned when her explorer parents are killed, a white girl is raised by an African tribe.
Female Tarzan stuff from a comic strip, smoothly made but too rough and slightly too sexy for the family audience which must have been intended.

w David Newman, Lorenzo Semple Jnr *d* John Guillermin *ph* Pasqualino de Santis *m* Richard Hartley

Tanya Roberts, Ted Wass, Donovan Scott

THE SHINING. Bartender Joe Turkel remains commendably inscrutable in the face of an over-the-top Jack Nicholson.

The Sheep Has Five Legs*
France 1954 96m bw
Raoul Ploquin
original title: *Le Mouton a Cinq Pattes*

A town seeking publicity tries to bring together the five quintuplet grandsons of its oldest inhabitant.
Mildly saucy star vehicle which was in fact most notable for introducing Fernandel to an international audience.

w Albert Valentin *d* Henri Verneuil
ph Armand Thirard *m* Georges Van Parys

Fernandel, Françoise Arnoul, Delmont, Paulette Dubost, Louis de Funès

AAN: original story

The Sheepman*
US 1958 91m Metrocolor
Cinemascope
MGM (Edmund Grainger)

A tough sheep farmer determines to settle in a cattle town.
Easy-going western with humorous moments.

w William Bowers, James Edward Grant
d George Marshall *ph* Robert Bronner
m Jeff Alexander

Glenn Ford, Shirley Maclaine, Leslie Nielsen, Mickey Shaughnessy, Edgar Buchanan

AAN: script

'When an Arab sees a woman he wants, he takes her!'—ancient Arabian proverb

The Sheik*
US 1921 73m (24 fps) bw silent
Famous Players-Lasky / George Melford

An English heiress falls for a desert chieftain.
Archetypal romantic tosh which set the seal on Valentino's superstardom.

w Monte M. Katterjohn, *novel* E. M. Hull
d George Melford *ph* William Marshall

Rudolph Valentino, Agnes Ayres, Adolphe Menjou, Walter Long, Lucien Littlefield

'A photoplay of tempestuous love between a madcap English beauty and a bronzed Arab chief!'—*publicity*

† *Son of the Sheik*, released in 1926, was even more popular.

The Sheik Steps Out
US 1937 68m bw
Republic (Herman Schlom)

A modern sheik has a riotous time in the big city.
Uninventive spoof of the Valentino myth.

w Adele Buffington, Gordon Kahn *d* Irving Pichel *ph* Jack Marta *md* Alberto Columbo

Ramon Novarro, Lola Lane, Gene Lockhart, Kathleen Burke, Stanley Fields

'Novarro in a comeback start. An action picture of the desert for the lower half of the duals.'—*Variety*

She'll Be Wearing Pink Pajamas
GB 1985 90m Eastmancolor

Women go on an outdoor survival course.
Basically an excuse for a lot of female nattering; it might have seemed more appealing under a more sensible title. Julie Walters, Anthony Higgins, Jane Evers, Janet Henfrey, Paula Jacobs. Written by Eva Hardy; directed by John Goldschmidt; for Pink Pajamas / Film Four International.

Shenandoah**
US 1965 105m Technicolor
Universal (Robert Arthur)

How the American Civil War affected the lives of a Virginia family.
Surprisingly hard-centred and moving semi-western for the family; excellent performances and well-controlled mood.

w James Lee Barrett d Andrew V. McLaglen
ph William Clothier *m* Frank Skinner
md Joseph Gershenson

James Stewart, Rosemary Forsyth, Doug McClure, Glenn Corbett, Katharine Ross, Philip Alford

Shepherd of the Hills*
US 1941 98m Technicolor
Paramount / Jack Moss

Ozarkian backwoodsmen enjoy their lifestyle except for the intrusions of the revenue men and a mysterious stranger. Early colour adaptation of a long-favourite American story, deliberately styled for rural audiences.

w Grover Jones, Stuart Anthony
novel Harold Bell Wright Jnr *d* Henry Hathaway *ph* Charles Lang Jnr, W. Howard Greene *m* Gerard Carbonara

John Wayne, Betty Field, Harry Carey, Beulah Bondi, James Barton, Samuel S. Hinds, Marjorie Main, Ward Bond, Marc Lawrence, John Qualen, Fuzzy Knight.

The Sheriff of Fractured Jaw
GB 1958 103m Eastmancolor
Cinemascope
TCF / Daniel M. Angel

A London gunsmith in the old west accidentally becomes a hero.
Tame, predictable comedy with a clear lack of invention.

w Arthur Dales *d* Raoul Walsh *ph* Otto Heller
m Robert Farnon

Kenneth More, Jayne Mansfield, Robert Morley, Ronald Squire, David Horne, Henry Hull, Eynon Evans, Bruce Cabot, William Campbell

Sherlock Holmes
The innumerable Sherlock Holmes films are noted in *Filmgoer's Companion*, and in this volume the appropriate films are listed under their own titles including the modernized dozen made in the forties by Universal, starring Basil Rathbone as Holmes and Nigel Bruce as Watson. These followed on from Fox's two period pieces, THE HOUND OF THE BASKERVILLES and THE ADVENTURES OF SHERLOCK HOLMES (qv). The series started and ended somewhat lamely but several of the episodes remain highly enjoyable, for performances and dialogue rather than plot or pacing. All but the first were directed by Roy William Neill.

1942: SHERLOCK HOLMES AND THE VOICE OF TERROR (*d* John Rawlins *with* Reginald Denny, Thomas Gomez); SHERLOCK HOLMES AND THE SECRET WEAPON* (with Lionel Atwill as Moriarty)
1943: SHERLOCK HOLMES IN WASHINGTON* (*with* Henry Daniell, George Zucco); SHERLOCK HOLMES FACES DEATH** (*with* Halliwell Hobbes, Dennis Hoey)
1944: SHERLOCK HOLMES AND THE SPIDER WOMAN** (*with* Gale Sondergaard, Dennis Hoey); THE SCARLET CLAW** (*with* Gerald Hamer); THE PEARL OF DEATH** (*with* Miles Mander, Dennis Hoey, Rondo Hatton)
1945: THE HOUSE OF FEAR* (*with* Aubrey Mather, Dennis Hoey); THE WOMAN IN GREEN* (*with* Henry Daniell as Moriarty); PURSUIT TO ALGIERS (*with* Martin Kosleck)
1946: TERROR BY NIGHT* (*with* Alan Mowbray), DRESSED TO KILL (GB title: SHERLOCK HOLMES AND THE SECRET CODE; *with* Patricia Morison)

Sherlock Holmes*
US 1932 68m bw
Fox

Moriarty brings Chicago gangsters into London.
Interesting but rather unsatisfactory Holmes adventure.

w Bertram Milhauser *d* William K. Howard
ph George Barnes

Clive Brook, Reginald Owen, Ernest Torrence, Miriam Jordan, Alan Mowbray, Herbert Mundin

'Old-fashioned artificial stage play with modern trimmings that only muddle it. The interpolated modern gangster angle will mystify the mugs who go for underworld and it's a late day to offer the Conan Doyle thing straight to educated clienteles.'—*Variety*

Sherlock Holmes and the Secret Weapon*
US 1942 68m bw
Universal (Howard Benedict)

Sherlock Holmes saves a stolen bombsight from Nazi agents.
Slightly stiff modernized Holmes story with amusing ingredients.

w Edward T. Lowe, W. Scott Darling, Edmund L. Hartmann, vaguely based on The Dancing Men by Sir Arthur Conan Doyle
d Roy William Neill *ph* Les White *m* Frank Skinner

Basil Rathbone, Nigel Bruce, Lionel Atwill (as Moriarty), Dennis Hoey, Karen Verne, William Post Jnr, Mary Gordon

Sherlock Holmes and the Voice of Terror
US 1942 65m bw
Universal (Howard Benedict)

Sherlock Holmes unmasks a Lord Haw Haw in the war cabinet.
Fairly risible first entry in the modernized series, with a Hollywood view of London and a singular haircut for the star.

w Lynn Riggs, from His Last Bow by Sir Arthur Conan Doyle *d* John Rawlins
ph Woody Bredell *m* Frank Skinner

Basil Rathbone, Nigel Bruce, Hillary Brooke, Reginald Denny, Evelyn Ankers, Montagu Love, Thomas Gomez, Mary Gordon

Sherlock Holmes Faces Death**
US 1943 68m bw
Universal (Roy William Neill)

Weird murders occur in a convalescent home for retired officers.
One of the better entries in this rather likeable modernized series; fairly close to the original story except that the events don't make a lot of sense.

w Bertram Millhauser, from The Musgrave Ritual by Sir Arthur Conan Doyle *d* Roy William Neill *ph* Charles Van Enger *m* Hans Salter

Basil Rathbone, Nigel Bruce, Hillary Brooke, Milburn Stone, Halliwell Hobbes, Arthur Margetson, Dennis Hoey, Gavin Muir, Frederic Worlock, Olaf Hytten, Gerald Hamer, Mary Gordon, Vernon Downing

Sherlock Holmes in Washington*
US 1943 70m bw
Universal (Howard Benedict)

Sherlock Holmes flies west and prevents Nazi spies from grabbing a microfilmed document concealed in a match folder.
Moderate adventure in the modernized series, with a good beginning and end but a sag in the middle.

w Bertram Millhauser, Lynn Riggs *d* Roy William Neill *ph* Lester White *m* Frank Skinner

Basil Rathbone, Nigel Bruce, Henry Daniell, George Zucco, Marjorie Lord, John Archer, Gavin Muir

Sherlock Junior**
US 1924 45m (24 fps) bw silent
Metro / Buster Keaton (Joseph M. Schenck)

A film projectionist, unjustly accused of stealing a watch, has dreams of being a great detective.
Fast-moving, gag-filled comedy which ranks among its star's best.

w Clyde Bruckman, Jean Haves, Joseph Mitchell *d, ed* Buster Keaton *ph* Elgin Lessley, Bryon Houck

Buster Keaton, Kathryn McGuire, Ward Crane, Joseph Keaton

She's Got Everything
US 1937 70m bw

A young woman in debt meets a stuffed shirt coffee planter. Mild comedy which never seems to jell despite the talent assembled. Ann Sothern, Gene Raymond, Victor Moore, Helen Broderick, Parkyakarkus, Billy Gilbert. Written by Harry Segal, Maxwell Shane; directed by Joseph Santley; for RKO.

'She shakes the student body like it's never been shook before!'

She's Working Her Way through College
US 1952 101m Technicolor
Warner (William Jacobs)

A burlesque queen goes to college and brings out the beast in an English professor.
Limp and vulgar musical remake of a well-liked play and film; just about gets by as a lowbrow timekiller.

w Peter Milne, *play* The Male Animal by James Thurber, Elliott Nugent *d* Bruce Humberstone *ph* Wilfrid Cline *md* Ray Heindorf *ch* Le Roy Prinz *songs* Sammy Cahn, Vernon Duke

Virginia Mayo, Ronald Reagan, Don Defore, Gene Nelson, Phyllis Thaxter, Patrice Wymore

† Sequel 1953: *She's Back on Broadway.*

Shine on Harvest Moon*
US 1944 112m bw (Technicolor sequence)
Warner (William Jacobs)

The life and times of vaudeville singer Nora Bayes.
Standard ragtime biopic, very adequately made.

w Sam Hellman, Richard Weil, Francis Swan, James Kern *d* David Butler *ph* Arthur Edeson *md* Heinz Roemheld

Ann Sheridan, Dennis Morgan, Jack Carson, Irene Manning, S. Z. Sakall, Marie Wilson, Robert Shayne

The Shining*
GB 1980 119m (general release; cut from première length of 146m) colour
Warner / Stanley Kubrick

Under the influence of a desolate hotel where murders had occurred, a caretaker goes berserk and threatens his family.
Uninteresting ghost story sparked by meticulous detail and sets but finally vitiated by overlength and an absurdly over-the-top star performance.

w Stanley Kubrick, Diane Johnson *novel* Stephen King *d* Stanley Kubrick *ph John Alcott* *m* Bela Bartok (on record) *pd Roy Walker*

Jack Nicholson, Shelley Duvall, Danny Lloyd, Barry Nelson, Scatman Crothers, Philip Stone

'The truly amazing question is why a director of Kubrick's stature would spend his time and effort on a novel that he changes so much it's barely recognizable, taking away whatever originality it possessed while emphasizing its banality. The answer presumably is that Kubrick was looking for a "commercial" property he could impose his own vision on, and Warners, not having learned its lesson with *Barry Lyndon*, was silly enough to let him do it.'—*Variety*

'A grandiose horror tale which consumes itself, snake-like, swallowing its own tail in a series of narrowing spirals.'—*Sunday Times*

The Shining Hour
US 1938 76m bw

A nightclub dancer marries a gentleman farmer, but has trouble with his family. Overcast melodrama with insufficient basic interest in the characters. Joan Crawford, Melvyn Douglas, Margaret Sullavan, Robert Young, Fay Bainter, Allyn Joslyn, Hattie McDaniel. Written by Ogden Nash and Jane Murfin, from the play by Keith Winter; directed by Frank Borzage; for MGM.

'A confused jumble of cross-purpose motivations and situations that fail entirely to arouse interest.'—*Variety*

Shining Victory
US 1941 80m bw
Warner (Robert Lord)

A psychiatrist is torn between love and duty. Adequate romantic programmer.

w Howard Koch, Ann Froelick, *play* Jupiter Laughs by A. J. Cronin *d* Irving Rapper *ph* James Wong Howe *m* Max Steiner

James Stephenson, Geraldine Fitzgerald, Donald Crisp, Barbara O'Neil, Montagu Love, Sig Rumann

Ship Ahoy
US 1942 95m bw
MGM (Jack Cummings)

On a trip to Puerto Rico, a tap dancer is enlisted as a spy.
Tepid musi-comedy.

w Harry Clark *d* Eddie Buzzell *ph* Leonard Smith *md* George Stoll *ad* Merrill Pye

Eleanor Powell, Red Skelton, Bert Lahr, Virginia O'Brien, William Post Jnr, James Cross

Ship Cafe
US 1935 65m bw

A singing stoker wins a rich girl. Musical star vehicle of the lower class. Carl Brisson, Arline Judge, Mady Christians, William Frawley, Eddie Davis. Written by Harlan Thompson, Herbert Fields; directed by Robert Florey; for Harold Hurley / Paramount.

Ship of Fools***
US 1965 150m bw
Columbia / Stanley Kramer

In 1933 a German liner leaves Vera Cruz for Bremerhaven with a mixed bag of passengers. Ambitious, serious, quite fascinating slice-of-life shipboard multi-melodrama. Capable mounting, memorable performances and a bravura finale erase memories of padding and symbolic pretensions.

w Abby Mann, novel Katherine Anne Porter *d Stanley Kramer* *ph Ernest Laszlo* *m Ernest Gold*

Vivien Leigh, Simone Signoret, Oskar Werner, Heinz Ruhmann, Jose Ferrer, Lee Marvin, Elizabeth Ashley, *Michael Dunn*, George Segal, Jose Greco, Charles Korvin, Alf Kjellin, Werner Klemperer, John Wengraf, Lilia Skala, Karen Verne

GLOCKEN (Michael Dunn): 'My name is Karl Glocken, and this is a ship of fools. I'm a fool. You'll meet more fools as we go along. This tub is packed with them. Emancipated ladies and ballplayers. Lovers. Dog lovers. Ladies of joy. Tolerant Jews, Dwarfs. All kinds. And who knows—if you look closely enough, you may even find yourself on board!'

'When you're not being hit over the head with the symbolism, you're being punched in the stomach by would-be inventive camera work while the music score unremittingly fills your nostrils with acrid exhalations.'—*John Simon*

'There is such wealth of reflection upon the human condition, so subtle an orchestration of the elements of love and hate, that it is not fair to tag this with the label of any other film.'—*New York Times*

AA: Ernest Laszlo
AAN: best picture; Abby Mann; Simone Signoret; Oskar Werner; Michael Dunn

The Ship That Died of Shame
GB 1955 91m bw
Ealing (Michael Relph, Basil Dearden)

The wartime crew of a motor gunboat buy the vessel and go into postwar business as smugglers.
Thin and rather obvious melodramatic fable.

w John Whiting, Michael Relph, Basil Dearden, *novel* Nicholas Monsarrat *d* Michael Relph, Basil Dearden *ph* Gordon Dines *m* William Alwyn

Richard Attenborough, George Baker, Bill Owen, Virginia McKenna, Roland Culver, Bernard Lee, Ralph Truman, John Chandos

'A sentimental fantasy tacked on to a basically conventional thriller.'—*Penelope Houston*

Shipbuilders
GB 1943 89m bw

A cavalcade of the problems of a Clydeside tycoon in the thirties. Plodding propaganda piece ending with masters and unions working for Britain. Clive Brook, Morland Graham, Finlay Currie, Maudie Edwards. Written by Gordon Wellesley, Stephen Potter and Reginald Pound; directed by John Baxter; for British National.

Shipmates Forever
US 1935 124m bw

An admiral's son disappoints his dad by preferring song and dance to the navy. Very stretched light musical without any overpowering talents. Dick Powell, Ruby Keeler, Lewis Stone, Ross Alexander, Eddie Acuff, Dick Foran. Written by Delmer Daves; directed by Frank Borzage; for Warner.

Ships with Wings*
GB 1941 103m bw
Ealing (S. C. Balcon)

Aircraft carriers prepare for World War II. Historically interesting, dramatically insubstantial flagwaver.

w Sergei Nolbandov, Patrick Kirwan, Austin Melford, Diana Morgan *d* Sergei Nolbandov *ph* Max Greene, Eric Cross, Roy Kellino, Wilkie Cooper *m* Geoffrey Wright

John Clements, Leslie Banks, Jane Baxter, Ann Todd, Basil Sydney, Edward Chapman, Hugh Williams, Frank Pettingell, Michael Wilding

Shipyard Sally
GB 1939 79m bw

A barmaid persuades a shipyard owner to reopen. Sub-Ealing style comedy with music which manages to bring in management and man as well as waving a flag or two. Gracie Fields, Sydney Howard, Morton Selten, Norma Varden, Oliver Wakefield. Written by Karl Tunberg and Don Ettlinger; directed by Monty Banks; for TCF.

The Shiralee*
GB 1957 99m bw
Ealing (Jack Rix)

An Australian swagman leaves his wife and takes to the road with his small daughter. Episodic character comedy-drama throwing a fairly sharp light on the Australian scene.

w Neil Paterson, Leslie Norman, *novel* D'Arcy Niland *d Leslie Norman ph* Paul Beeson *m* John Addison

Peter Finch, Dana Wilson, Elizabeth Sellars, George Rose, Russell Napier, Nial MacGinnis, Tessie O'Shea

Shoah
France 1985 Part 1 274m / Part 2 292m colour

Massive documentary history of the Holocaust, using survivors' testimony and some re-enactment but no historical footage. Directed by Claude Lanzmann; for Aleph/Historia.

Shock
US 1946 70m bw
TCF

A girl in a hotel sees a murder committed, and an elaborate plan is concocted to silence her. Flat treatment ruins a good suspense situation.

w Eugene Ling *d* Alfred Werker *ph* Glen MacWilliams, Joe MacDonald *m* David Buttolph

Vincent Price, Lynn Bari, Frank Latimore, Annabel Shaw

'Extreme improbabilities and a general lack of finish.'—*MFB*

Shock Corridor
US 1963 101m bw (colour sequence)
Leon Fromkess / Sam Firks (Samuel Fuller)

A journalist gets himself admitted to a mental asylum to solve the murder of an inmate. Sensational melodrama, a cinematic equivalent of the yellow press, and on that level quite lively.

wd Samuel Fuller *ph* Stanley Cortez *m* Paul Dunlap

Peter Breck, Constance Towers, Gene Evans, James Best, Hari Rhodes, Philip Ahn

Shock Treatment
US 1964 94m bw
Warner (Aaron Rosenberg)

Murders are committed in a mental institution. Tasteless thriller, not even very arresting as a yarn.

w Sidney Boehm *d* Denis Sanders *ph* Sam Leavitt *m* Jerry Goldsmith

Lauren Bacall, Roddy MacDowall, Carol Lynley, Ossie Davis, Stuart Whitman, Douglass Dumbrille

The Shocking Miss Pilgrim
US 1946 85m Technicolor
TCF (William Perlberg)

In 1894 Boston, a lady typist (stenographer) fights for women's rights.
Period comedy with music; not nearly as sharp as it thinks it is.

wd George Seaton *ph* Leon Shamroy *ad* James Basevi, Boris Leven *songs* George and Ira Gershwin *md* David Raksin

Betty Grable, Dick Haymes, Anne Revere, Allyn Joslyn, Gene Lockhart, Elizabeth Patterson, Arthur Shields, Elizabeth Risdon

Shockproof
US 1949 79m bw
Columbia (S. Sylvan Simon)

A parole officer falls in love with his protégée and becomes corrupted.
Predictable programmer with a few pleasant touches.

w Helen Deutsch, Samuel Fuller *d* Douglas Sirk *ph* Charles Lawton Jnr *m* George Duning

Cornel Wilde, Patricia Knight, John Baragrey, Esther Minciotti, Howard St John, Russell Collins

The Shoes of the Fisherman**
US 1968 157m Metrocolor Panavision
MGM (George Englund)

After twenty years as a political prisoner, a Russian bishop becomes Pope.
Predigested but heavy-going picturization of a bestseller; big budget, big stars, big hopes. In fact a commercial dud, with plenty of superficial interest but more dramatic contrivance than religious feeling.

w John Patrick, James Kennaway, *novel* Morris West *d Michael Anderson ph Erwin Hiller m* Alex North *ad Edward Carfagno, George W. Davis*

Anthony Quinn, David Janssen, Laurence Olivier, Oskar Werner, John Gielgud, Barbara Jefford, Leo McKern, Vittorio de Sica, Clive Revill, Paul Rogers

'A splendidly decorated curate's egg.'—*MFB*

AAN: Alex North

Shoeshine**
Italy 1946 90m bw
Paolo W. Tamburella
original title: *Sciuscià*

In Nazi-occupied Rome two shoeshine boys become involved in black marketeering, with tragic consequences.
Not especially rewarding to watch now, this was a key film in the development of Italian neo-realism.

w Cesare Zavattini, Sergio Amidei, Adolfe Franci, C. G. Viola *d Vittorio de Sica ph* Anchise Brizzi, Elio Paccara

Franco Interlenghi, Rinaldo Smordoni

'It is filled in every scene with an awareness of the painful complexity of even simple evil.'—*James Agee*

AAN: script

Shoot the Moon*
US 1981 123m Metrocolor
MGM (Alan Marshall)

The family is affected when well-heeled parents decide to split up.
A halfway decent actors' piece which doesn't really justify its time or leave affectionate memories behind. In essence it adds nothing except noise to what was being done in this field forty years ago.

w Bo Goldman *d* Alan Parker *ph* Michael Seresin *m* no credit *pd* Geoffrey Kirkland

Albert Finney, Diane Keaton, Karen Allen, Peter Weller, Dana Hill, Leora Dana

'Despite their superficial sophistication, these are immature creatures playing grown-up games which would be thought childish in *Bugsy Malone*.'—*Sunday Times*

Shoot the Pianist*
France 1960 80m bw Dyaliscope
Films de la Pléiade (Pierre Braunberger)
original title: *Tirez sur le Pianiste*

A bar-room piano player becomes involved with gangsters and his girl friend is killed. Fair copy of an American *film noir*, not especially interesting except for its sharp observation.

w Marcel Moussy, François Truffaut, *novel* Down There by David Goodis *d François Truffaut ph* Raoul Coutard *m* Jean Constantin, Georges Deleru

Charles Aznavour, Nicole Berger, Marie Dubois, Michèle Mercier, Albert Rémy

'Pictorially it is magnificent, revealing Truffaut's brilliant control over his images; emotionally, it is all a little jejeune.'—*John Gillett, MFB*

Shoot the Works
US 1934 82m bw

A band leader and a gossip columnist stage a fake feud. Anaemic Hollywood version of a rather sharp Broadway play which in this form means less than nothing. Jack Oakie, Ben Bernie, Dorothy Dell, Arline Judge, Alison Skipworth, Roscoe Karns, William Frawley, Paul Cavanaugh, Lew Cody. Written by Howard J. Green and Claude Binyon, from play *The Great Magoo* by Ben Hecht and Gene Fowler; directed by Wesley Ruggles; for Albert Lewis / Paramount.

The Shooting
US 1966 82m De Luxe
Santa Clara (Jack Nicholson, Monte Hellman)

An ex-bounty hunter is trailed by a hired killer.
Simplistic semi-professional western which achieves some power despite poor technical quality and a deliberately obscure ending.

w Adrien Joyce *d* Monte Hellman *ph* Gregory Sandor *m* Richard Markowitz

Warren Oates, Will Hutchins, Jack Nicholson, Millie Perkins

The Shooting Party*
GB 1984 96m Technicolor
Edenflow / Geoff Reeve (Peter Dolman)

In 1913 Sir Randolph Nettleby invites guests for a weekend at his country estate, but the coming war is foretold in their behaviour.
Mild little symbolic play which provides the expected minor pleasures.

w Julian Bond *novel* Isabel Colegate *d* Alan Bridges *ph* Fred Tammes *m* John Scott

James Mason, Edward Fox, Dorothy Tutin, John Gielgud, Gordon Jackson, Cheryl Campbell, Robert Hardy

Shooting Stars*
GB 1928 80m (24 fps) bw silent
British Instructional (H. Bruce Woolf)

The wife of a film star puts real bullets in a prop gun but her lover is killed by mistake.
Late silent drama with comedy touches: its main interest lies in its behind-the-scenes background and in the emergence of a new director.

w John Orton, Anthony Asquith *d* Anthony Asquith, A. V. Bramble

Annette Benson, Brian Aherne, Donald Calthrop, Wally Patch, Chili Bouchier

The Shootist**
US 1976 100m Technicolor Panavision
Paramount / Frankovich-Self

In 1901, a dying ex-gunfighter arrives in a small town to set his affairs in order.
Impressive semi-western melodrama, very well written and acted all round; the kind of solidly entertaining and thoughtful movie one imagined they didn't make any more.

w Miles Hood Swarthout, Scott Hale, novel Glendon Swarthout *d Don Siegel ph* Bruce Surtees *m* Elmer Bernstein

John Wayne, Lauren Bacall, James Stewart, Ron Howard, Bill McKinney, Richard Boone, John Carradine, Scatman Crothers, Harry Morgan, Hugh O'Brian, Sheree North

'Just when it seemed that the western was an endangered species, due for extinction because it had repeated itself too many times, Wayne and Siegel have managed to validate it once more.'—*Arthur Knight*

'Watching this film is like taking a tour of Hollywood legends.'—*Frank Rich*

'Three fast guns against one determined man!'

Shootout
US 1971 94m Technicolor
Universal (Hal B. Wallis)

After seven years in prison, a bank robber seeks out his betrayer.
Routine, flatly-handled revenge western.

w Marguerite Roberts, *novel* The Lone Cowboy by Will James *d* Henry Hathaway *ph* Earl Rath *m* Dave Grusin

Gregory Peck, Pat Quinn, Robert F. Lyons, Susan Tyrell, Jeff Corey, James Gregory, Rita Gam

Shootout at Medicine Bend
US 1957 87m bw

Three ex-soldiers clean up a corrupt community. Entertaining western programmer. Randolph Scott, James Craig, Angie Dickinson, James Garner, Gordon Jones. Written by John Tucker Battle and D. D. Beauchamp; directed by Richard Bare; for Warner.

The Shop around the Corner**
US 1940 97m bw
MGM (Ernst Lubitsch)

In a Budapest shop, the new floorwalker and a girl who dislikes him find they are pen pals.
Pleasant period romantic comedy which holds no surprises but is presented with great style.

w Samson Raphaelson, play Nikolaus Laszlo *d Ernst Lubitsch ph* William Daniels *m* Werner Heymann

James Stewart, Margaret Sullavan, *Frank Morgan*, Joseph Schildkraut, Sara Haden, *Felix Bressart*, William Tracy

'It's not pretentious but it's a beautiful job of picture-making, and the people who did it seem to have enjoyed doing it just as much as their audiences will enjoy seeing it.'—*James Shelley Hamilton*

'An agreeably bittersweet example of light entertainment.'—*Charles Higham, 1972*

'One of the most beautifully acted and paced romantic comedies ever made in this country.'—*New Yorker, 1978*

† Remade as *In The Good Old Summertime* (qv).

The Shop at Sly Corner
GB 1946 92m bw
Pennant (George King)
US title: *Code of Scotland Yard*

An antique dealer who is also a fence kills a blackmailer in order to shield his daughter.
Competent but stagey version of a West End success, giving full rein to a bravura star performance.

w Katherine Strueby, *play* Edward Percy *d* George King *ph* Hone Glendinning *m* George Melachrino

Oscar Homolka, Muriel Pavlow, Derek Farr, Manning Whiley, Kenneth Griffith, Kathleen Harrison, Garry Marsh, Irene Handl

The Shop on Main Street*
Czechoslovakia 1965 128m bw
Ceskoslovensky Film
original title: *Obchod na Korze*; aka: *The Shop on the High Street*

During the German invasion of Czechoslovakia, a well-meaning carpenter tries to shield an old Jewish lady, but his own rough treatment kills her.
A rather obvious sentimental fable, developed at too great length, but with bravura acting.

w Ladislav Grosman, Jan Kadar, Einar Klos *d* Jan Kadar, Einar Klos *ph* Vladimir Novotny *m* Zdenek Liska

Ida Kaminska, Jozef Kroner, Hana Slivkova, Martin Holly

'Overlong, derivative, ploddingly directed.'—*John Simon*

AA: best foreign film
AAN: Ida Kaminska

Shopworn Angel*
US 1928 90m approx bw part-talkie
Paramount (Louis D. Lighton)

A showgirl meets a naïve young soldier off to war and forsakes her man about town.
Hard-boiled, soft-centred romantic drama remade as below and later as *That Kind of Woman* (qv).

w Howard Estabrook, Albert Shelby Le Vino, *play* Private Pettigrew's Girl by Dana Burnet *d* Richard Wallace *ph* Charles Lang

Nancy Carroll, Gary Cooper, Paul Lukas, Emmett King

Shopworn Angel*
US 1938 85m bw
MGM (Joseph L. Mankiewicz)

Smooth, close remake of the above.

w Waldo Salt *d* H. C. Potter *ph* Joseph Ruttenberg *m* Edward Ward *montage* Slavko Vorkapitch

Margaret Sullavan, James Stewart, Walter Pidgeon, Hattie McDaniel, Sam Levene

Short Cut to Hell
US 1957 89m bw Vistavision
Paramount (A. C. Lyles)

A racketeer hires a gunman to commit a double murder, then doublecrosses him.
Rough and ready remake of *This Gun for Hire*

(qv), less arresting than the original.

w Ted Berkeman, Raphael Blau, W. R. Burnett, *novel* A Gun for Sale by Graham Greene *d James Cagney* *ph* Haskell Boggs *md* Irvin Talbot

Robert Ivers, Georgeann Johnson, William Bishop, Murvyn Vye

A Shot in the Dark*
US 1964 101m De Luxe Panavision
UA / Mirisch / Geoffrey (Blake Edwards)

A woman is accused of shooting her lover; accident-prone Inspector Clouseau investigates.
Further adventures of the oafish, Tatiesque clodhopper from *The Pink Panther*; mildly funny for those in the mood for pratfalls.

w Blake Edwards, William Peter Blatty *d* Blake Edwards *ph* Christopher Challis *m* Henry Mancini *pd* Michael Stringer

Peter Sellers, Elke Sommer, George Sanders, Herbert Lom, Tracy Reed, Graham Stark

Shotgun
US 1954 81m Technicolor print

A deputy marshal avenges the death of his boss. Rather violent western with a few unusual angles. Sterling Hayden, Zachary Scott, Yvonne de Carlo, Guy Prescott, Robert Wilke. Written by Clark E. Reynolds and Rory Calhoun; directed by Lesley Selander; for Allied Artists.

Should Ladies Behave?
US 1933 90m bw

A young girl falls for her aunt's lover. Brittle comedy of manners which transferred poorly from Broadway with a star well over the top. Alice Brady, Lionel Barrymore, Conway Tearle, Katherine Alexander, Halliwell Hobbes, Mary Carlisle. Written by Sam and Bella Spewack, from the play *The Vinegar Tree* by Paul Osborn; directed by Harry Beaumont; for MGM.

Should Married Men Go Home?
US 1928 20m bw silent

Tribulations on the golf course end in a mud-slinging contest. Goodish star slapstick, but the preliminary domestic scene is the funniest. Laurel and Hardy, Edgar Kennedy. Written by Leo McCarey, James Parrott and H. M. Walker, directed by *d* James Parrott; for Hal Roach.

Shoulder Arms*
US 1918 24m (24 fps) bw silent
Charles Chaplin / First National

A soldier in the trenches dreams of winning the war single-handedly.
A comedy which meant a great deal at the time of its release but now provides precious little to laugh at.

wd Charles Chaplin *ph* Rollie Totheroh

Charles Chaplin, Edna Purviance, Sydney Chaplin, Henry Bergman, Albert Austin

The Shout*
GB 1978 87m colour
Rank / Recorded Picture (Jeremy Thomas)

A man who may be mad claims that, like the old aborigine magicians, he can kill by shouting.
Curiously gripping but ultimately pointless fable, very well done to little purpose.

w Michael Austin, Jerzy Skolimovsky, *story* Robert Graves *d* Jerzy Skolimovsky *ph* Mike Molloy *m* Rupert Hine, Anthony Banks, Michael Rutherford

Alan Bates, Susannah York, John Hurt, Robert Stephens, Tim Curry

'Poorly acted, incoherent and unendurably loud.'—*Pauline Kael, New Yorker*

Shout at the Devil*
GB 1976 147m Technicolor Panavision
Tonav (Michael Klinger)

In 1913 Zanzibar, a hard-drinking American and an old Etonian Englishman join forces to rout a brutal German commissioner who resents their poaching ivory in his territory.
The main characters are respectively repellent, effete, and just plain nasty, but the action scenes are vivid and the production is mainly notable as an expensive old-fashioned British film made at a time when there were few British films of any kind.

w Wilbur Smith, Stanley Price, Alastair Reid, *novel* Wilbur Smith *d* Peter Hunt *ph* Mike Reed *m* Maurice Jarre

Lee Marvin, Roger Moore, Barbara Parkins, René Kolldehoff, Ian Holm, Karl Michael Vogler, Maurice Denham, Jean Kent, Robert Lang, Murray Melvin, George Coulouris

'Elephantine plod through the action highlights of a best seller.'—*Sight and Sound*

Show Business***
US 1944 92m bw
RKO (Eddie Cantor)

The careers of four friends in vaudeville.
Lively low-budget period musical which probably presents the best picture of what old-time vaudeville was really like; a lot of fun when the plot doesn't get in the way.

w Joseph Quillan, Dorothy Bennett *d Edwin L. Marin* *ph* Robert de Grasse, Vernon L. Walker *m* George Duning *md* Constantin Bakaleinikoff *ch Nick Castle*

Eddie Cantor, Joan Davis, George Murphy, Constance Moore, Don Douglas, Nancy Kelly

'Bits of archaic vaudeville which give off a moderately pleasant smell of peanuts and cigar smoke.'—*James Agee*

Show Girl in Hollywood
US 1930 77m bw (colour sequence)

Adventures of a New York girl on the west coast. Comedy with music; it seems content to wallow in supposed Hollywood glamour without contributing much by way of wit or storyline. Alice White, Jack Mulhall, Blanche Sweet, Ford Sterling, John Miljan, Herman Bing. Written by Harvey Thew, James A. Starr, J. P. McEvoy; directed by Mervyn Le Roy; for First National.

The Show Goes On
GB 1937 93m bw
ATP (Basil Dean)

A mill girl becomes a star singer with the help of a dying composer.
An attempt to turn Gracie Fields into a serious performer, this was not much enjoyed by her fans.

w Austin Melford, Anthony Kimmins, E. G. Valentine *d* Basil Dean *ph* Jan Stallich

Gracie Fields, Owen Nares, Edward Rigby, John Stuart, Horace Hodges, Amy Veness, Cyril Rutchard

The Show-Off
US 1934 80m bw

A girl's blundering new husband alienates his in-laws and nearly wrecks his brother-in-law's career. Surefire satirical comedy-drama from a Broadway staple, this low-budget item gave MGM a new star. *Spencer Tracy*, Madge Evans, Clara Blandick, Henry Wadsworth, Grant Mitchell, Lois Wilson. Written by Herman Mankiewicz from the play by George Kelly; directed by Charles Riesner; for MGM. (NB: The play had been filmed twice in silent days by Paramount, and turned up again in 1946 as a Red Skelton vehicle.)

'In Vitaphone, it eclipses the sun in splendour!'

Show of Shows**
US 1929 128m Technicolor
Warner (Darryl F. Zanuck)

A big musical show put on by Warner contract artists.
Primitive early talkie, of vital historical interest but mostly photographed from a seat in the stalls.

w / *m* various *d* John G. Adolfi *ph* Barney McGill

Frank Fay, H. B. Warner, Monte Blue, Lupino Lane, Ben Turpin, Chester Morris, Ted Lewis and his band, Georges Carpentier, Patsy Ruth Miller, Beatrice Lillie, Winnie Lightner, Irene Bordoni, Myrna Loy, Douglas Fairbanks Jnr, John Barrymore, Betty Compson

'Colour photography of the crudest, most garish kind, the resulting impression being that a child of seven has been let loose with a shilling box of paints.'—*James Agate*

Show People
US 1928 80m at 24 fps bw silent

A naïve young actress makes it in Hollywood. Historically important comedy with cameo appearances by many stars of the time. Marion Davies, William Haines. Written by Wanda Tuchock, Agnes Christine Johnson and Lawrence Stallings; directed by *King Vidor*; for MGM.

Show Them No Mercy*
US 1935 76m bw
TCF (Raymond Griffith)
GB title: *Tainted Money*

Kidnappers are rounded up by G-men.
Lively crime thriller typical of its time.

w Kubec Glasmon, Henry Lehrman *d* George Marshall *ph* Bert Glennon *m* David Buttolph

Rochelle Hudson, Cesar Romero, Bruce Cabot, Edward Norris, Edward Brophy, Warren Hymer

'Direct, surely dramatic, inevitable and full of terror.'—*Otis Ferguson*

Showboat***
US 1936 110m bw
Universal (Carl Laemmle Jnr)

Lives and loves of the personnel on an old-time Mississippi showboat.
Great style and excellent performances mark this version, which still suffers from longueurs in the middle followed by the rapid passage of many years to provide a happy ending.

w Oscar Hammerstein II, from his book for the Broadway musical from Edna Ferber's novel *d James Whale ph John Mescall m Jerome Kern ly Oscar Hammerstein II*

Irene Dunne, Allan Jones, Helen Morgan, Paul Robeson, Charles Winninger, Hattie McDaniel, Donald Cook, Sammy White

'For three quarters of its length good entertainment: sentimental, literary, but oddly appealing.'—*Graham Greene*

† A primitive talkie version of *Showboat*, now lost, was made in 1929.

†† Before Allan Jones was cast, Walter Pidgeon, Robert Taylor, John Boles, Fredric March and Nelson Eddy were all considered.

Showboat**
US 1951 108m Technicolor
MGM (Arthur Freed)

Vigorous remake with good ensemble dancing; otherwise inferior to the 1936 version.

w John Lee Mahin *d* George Sidney *ph* Charles Rosher *md* Conrad Salinger, Adolph Deutsch *ch Robert Alton*

Kathryn Grayson, *Howard Keel*, Ava Gardner, William Warfield, *Joe E. Brown*, Robert Sterling, Marge and Gower Champion, Agnes Moorehead

AAN: Charles Rosher; Conrad Salinger, Adolph Deutsch

The Showdown
US 1950 86m bw

A trail boss seeks revenge on his brother's killer. Routine western with a touch of mystery. Wild Bill Elliott, Marie Windsor, Walter Brennan, Henry Morgan, William Ching, Rhys Williams. Written by Richard Wormser and Dan Gordon; directed by Darrell and Stuart McGowan; for Republic.

Showdown
US 1963 79m Technicolor

Two wandering cowboys become involved with a criminal. Below-par western with little action and rather boring characters. Audie Murphy, Charles Drake, Harold J. Stone, Kathleen Crowley, Skip Homeier, L. Q. Jones, Strother Martin. Written by Bronson Howitzer; directed by R. G. Springsteen; for Universal.

Showdown
US 1972 99m Technicolor Todd-AO 35
Universal (George Seaton)

A sheriff finds that his old friend is leader of an outlaw gang.
Routine star western adequately done.

w Theodore Taylor *d* George Seaton *ph* Ernest Laszlo *m* David Shire

Rock Hudson, Dean Martin, Susan Clark, Donald Moffat, Don McLiam

Showdown at Abilene
US 1956 80m Technicolor

A shellshocked Civil War veteran, returning home to find his girl married, reluctantly takes a job as sheriff. Fairly lively western remade eleven years later as *Gunfight in Abilene*. Jock Mahoney, David Janssen, Martha Hyer, Lyle Bettger, Grant Williams. Written by Bernie Giler, from the novel *Gun Shy* by Clarence Upson Young; directed by Charles Haas; for Universal-International.

Showgirl in Hollywood
US 1930 80m bw and Technicolor

A girl singer is spotted and trained for movie stardom. Naïve look behind the studio scenes, historically fascinating but dramatically dull. Alice White, Jack Mulhall, Blanche Sweet, Ford Sterling, John Miljan, Herman Bing. Written by Harvey Thew and James A. Starr, from the novel *Hollywood Girl* by J. P. McEvoy; directed by Mervyn LeRoy; for Warner.

The Shrike
US 1955 88m bw
U-I (Aaron Rosenberg)

A brilliant theatre man has a nervous breakdown because his wife is a vindictive harpy.
Theatrical two-hander, aridly filmed, of little interest except to show that both stars are capable of sustained emotional acting.

w Ketti Frings, *play* Joseph Kramm *d* Jose Ferrer *ph* William Daniels *m* Frank Skinner *titles Saul Bass*

Jose Ferrer, June Allyson, Joy Page, Jacqueline de Wit, Kendall Clark

'The film is unvaryingly paced, the result, one feels, of a respectable but far from invigorating honesty of purpose.'—*MFB*

The Shuttered Room
GB 1967 110m Technicolor
Warner / Troy–Schenck (Philip Hazelton)

Returning to her childhood home on an island off the New England coast, a girl and her husband are subjected to terror and violence.
Stretched out suspenser which looks good and is carefully made but fails in its effort to combine the menace of teenage yobboes with that of the monster lurking upstairs.

w D. B. Ledrov, Nathaniel Tanchuck, *story* H. P. Lovecraft, August Derleth *d David Greene ph Ken Hodges m* Basil Kirchin

Gig Young, Carol Lynley, Flora Robson, Oliver Reed, William Devlin

Une Si Jolie Petite Plage*
France 1948 91m bw
CICC (Emile Darbon)
aka: *Such a Pretty Little Beach*

A murderer returns to the small seaside town where he spent his childhood, befriends the maid at the hotel, and after a few days kills himself.
A melancholy anecdote which works both as a character study and pictorially.

w Jacques Sigurd *d* Yves Allégret *ph* Henri Alekan *m* Maurice Thiriet

Gérard Philipe, Jean Servais, *Madeleine Robinson*, Jane Marken, Carette

'Shows fine craftsmanship and is beautifully sensitive to place and atmosphere.'—*Gavin Lambert, MFB*

Si Tous les Gars du Monde . . .*
France 1956 108m bw
Ariane / Filmsonor / Francinex (Alexandre Mnouchkine)
aka: *Race for Life*

When members of a French trawler crew fall ill in mid-Atlantic, amateur radio operators around the world arrange rescue.
Well-meaning realistic melodrama with a hands-across-the-sea message.

w Jacques Remy *d* Christian-Jaque *ph* Armand Thiraud *m* Georges Van Parys

Andre Valmy, Jean Gaven, Doudou-Babet, Jean-Louis Trintignant

Sid and Nancy
GB 1986 111m colour
Zenith / Initial (Eric Feliner)

An account of the self-destruction of the leader of a punk rock group and his American girl friend.
Some have said stimulating, most have preferred revolting. Consensus, an example of the dregs to which cinema has been reduced.

w Alex Cox, Abbe Wool *d* Alex Cox *ph* Roger Deakins *m* The Pogues

Gary Oldman, Chloe Webb, David Hayman

'The dialogue is extremely rough, the settings sordid, the theme of wasted lives depressing.'—*Variety*

'Relentlessly whingeing performances and a lengthy slide into drugs, degradation and death make this a solemnly off-putting moral tract.'—*Sight and Sound*

Side Street
US 1950 83m bw
MGM (Sam Zimbalist)

A petty thief finds himself involved with big-time crooks.
Well-made but rather boring crime melodrama with an excellent car chase finale.

w Sidney Boehm *d* Anthony Mann *ph* Joseph Ruttenberg *m* Lennie Hayton

Farley Granger, Cathy O'Donnell, James Craig, Paul Kelly, Jean Hagen, Edmon Ryan, Paul Harvey

Side Streets
US 1934 63m bw

A lady furrier takes pity on a sailor, and finally marries him, only to find that he has a past.
Strange, rather tedious, and quite unconvincing character drama. Aline MacMahon, Paul Kelly, Ann Dvorak, Helen Lowell, Henry O'Neill, Marjorie Gateson. Written by Manuel Seff from a story by Ann Garrick and Ethel Hill; directed by Alfred E. Green; for First National. (GB title: *A Woman in her Thirties*.)

Sidewalks of New York*
US 1931 73m bw
MGM (Lawrence Weingarten)

The playboy owner of some tenement apartments falls in love with the daughter of one of the tenants.
Interesting rather than wholly successful early sound comedy which marked the beginning of Keaton's decline; he was not allowed full control and the comedy scenes are thinly spaced.

w George Landy, Paul Gerard Smith, Eric Hatch, Robert E. Hopkins *d* Jules White, Zion Myers *ph* Leonard Smith

Buster Keaton, Anita Page, Cliff Edwards, Frank Rowan

The Siege at Red River
US 1954 86m Technicolor
TCF / Panoramic (Leonard Goldstein)

During the American Civil War a Confederate agent behind northern lines defeats a treacherous helper and escapes to the south.
Modest, generally watchable, and quite forgettable western.
w Sidney Boehm *d* Rudolph Maté
ph Edward Cronjager *m* Lionel Newman

Van Johnson, Joanne Dru, Richard Boone, Milburn Stone, Jeff Morrow, Craig Hill

The Siege of Pinchgut
GB 1959 104m bw
Ealing (Eric Williams)
US title: *Four Desperate Men*

Escaped convicts take over a small island in Sydney harbour.
Disappointingly obvious location melodrama with routine excitements.

w Harry Watt, Jon Cleary *d* Harry Watt
ph Gordon Dines *m* Kenneth V. Jones

Aldo Ray, Heather Sears, Neil McCallum, Victor Maddern, Carlo Justini

The Siege of Sidney Street*
GB 1960 92m bw Dyaliscope
Midcentury (Robert S. Baker, Monty Berman)

An account of the anarchists who infiltrated London in 1912.
Detailed but not dramatically absorbing historical reconstruction with unsatisfactory fictional trimmings.

w Jimmy Sangster, Alexander Baron *d / ph* Robert S. Baker, Monty Berman
m Stanley Black

Peter Wyngarde, Donald Sinden, Nicole Berger, Kieron Moore, Leonard Sachs, Tutte Lemkow

The Siege of the Saxons
GB 1963 85m Technicolor
Columbia / Ameran (Jud Kinberg)

When King Arthur is ill, the Saxons plot his overthrow but are foiled by a handsome outlaw.
Comic strip adventure with action highlights borrowed from older and better films.

w John Kohn, Jud Kinberg *d* Nathan Juran
ph Wilkie Cooper, Jack Willis *m* Laurie Johnson

Ronald Lewis, Janette Scott, Ronald Howard, Mark Dignam, John Laurie, Richard Clarke, Jerome Willis

The Sign of Four
GB 1932 75m bw

Sherlock Holmes clears up a mystery including a hidden fortune, a secret pact, revenge from the east, and a pygmy who blows poison darts through a pipe. Very acceptable version of the famous story, previously filmed as a silent. Arthur Wontner, Ian Hunter, Isla Bevan, Miles Malleson, Herbert Lomas, Roy Emerton. Written by W. P. Lipscomb, from the novel by Sir Arthur Conan Doyle; directed by Rowland V. Lee and Graham Cutts; for ATP.

'A picture which will proudly lead all the entertainments the world has ever seen!'
'Like a shining light—the simple faith that was mightier than a pagan empire!'

The Sign of the Cross***
US 1932 123m bw
Paramount (Cecil B. de Mille)

In the days of Nero, a Roman officer is converted to Christianity.
A heavily theatrical play becomes one of de Mille's most impressive films, the genuine horror of the arena mingling with the debauched humour of the court. A wartime prologue added in 1943 prolongs the film without improving it.

w Waldemar Young, Sidney Buchman, *play* Wilson Barrett *d Cecil B. de Mille ph Karl Struss m* Rudolph Kopp

Fredric March, Elissa Landi, *Charles Laughton, Claudette Colbert*, Ian Keith, Harry Beresford, Arthur Hohl, Nat Pendleton

'A beautiful film to watch . . . a triumph of popular art.'—*Charles Higham, 1972*

'However contemptible one may find de Mille's moralizing, it is impossible not to be impressed by *The Sign of the Cross*.'—*John Baxter, 1968*

'De Mille's bang-them-on-the-head-with-wild-orgies-and-imperilled-virginity style is at its ripest.'—*New Yorker, 1976*

'Preposterous, but the laughter dies on the lips.'—*NFT, 1974*

'This slice of "history" has it all: Laughton's implicitly gay Nero fiddling away while an impressive miniature set burns, Colbert bathing up to her nipples in asses' milk, Christians and other unfortunates thrown to a fearsome menagerie, much suggestive slinking about in Mitchell Leisen's costumes, much general debauchery teetering between the sadistic and the erotic. Not for people with scruples.'—*Geoff Brown, Time Out, 1980*

AAN: Karl Struss

'Against his ruthless pagan lusts—the power of a woman's love!'

The Sign of the Pagan
US 1954 92m Technicolor Cinemascope
U-I (Albert J. Cohen)

Attila the Hun is defeated by the Romans.
Historic horse opera, rather cheaply done.

w Oscar Brodney, Barre Lyndon *d* Douglas Sirk *ph* Russell Metty *m* Frank Skinner, Hans Salter

Jeff Chandler, Jack Palance, Rita Gam, Ludmilla Tcherina, Jeff Morrow, George Dolenz, Eduard Franz, Alexander Scourby

The Sign of the Ram
US 1948 84m bw
Columbia (Irving Cummings Jnr)

A selfish invalid interferes in her family's affairs.
Stultifying melodrama in the wake of *Guest in the House*, devised for the unfortunate Miss Peters who was crippled after an accident. Poor production values don't help.

w Charles Bennett *d* John Sturges
ph Burnett Guffey *m* Hans Salter

Susan Peters, Alexander Knox, Peggy Ann Garner, May Whitty

Signpost to Murder
US 1964 74m bw Panavision
MGM / Martin (Lawrence Weingarten)

A convicted murderer escapes after ten years and a lonely wife promises to help him.
Tricksy mystery set in a never-never English village.

w Sally Benson, *play* Monte Doyle *d* George Englund *ph* Paul C. Vogel *m* Lyn Murray

Joanne Woodward, Stuart Whitman, Edward Mulhare, Alan Napier, Murray Matheson

The Silence*
Sweden 1963 96m bw
Svensk Filmindustri
original title: *Tystnaden*

Of two women in a large hotel in a foreign city where the military are dominant, one masturbates while the other sleeps with a barman.
Bergman may know what this was all about, but it's a certainty that no one else did: so everyone thought it must be very clever and went to see it. Superficially, as usual, it is careful and fascinating.

wd Ingmar Bergman ph Sven Nykvist
m from Bach

Ingrid Thulin, Gunnel Lindblom

SILK STOCKINGS. Fred Astaire and Janis Paige dance up a storm in the movie-mocking number 'Stereophonic Sound'.

'There is not enough forward thrust, not enough momentum to unite the specific points, the complementary but discrete images. The pearls are there, but the string is too weak to hold them.'—*John Simon*

Le Silence est d'Or*
France 1947 99m bw
Pathé / RKO Radio (René Clair)

In 1906 a comedian becomes a film producer and as a result falls into an affair with a young girl.
Somehow not an important film, but quite a delightful one, especially for its local colour and for the combination of Clair and Chevalier up to their old tricks.

wd René Clair *ph* Armand Thirard
m Georges Van Parys

Maurice Chevalier, François Périer, Marcelle Derrien

The Silence of Dean Maitland
Australia 1934 97m bw

A clergyman sires an illegitimate baby, kills the girl's father and allows another man to be convicted. Once sensational stuff which almost caused an Australian scandal. John Longden, Charlotte Francis, Jocelyn Howarth, Patricia Minchin. Written by Gayne Dexter, Edmund Barclay; directed and produced by Ken G. Hall; for Cinesound.

Silence of the North
Canada 1981 94m colour
Universal (Canada) (Murray Shostak)

In 1919 a city girl is courted by a trapper and joins him in the north country.
Nicely filmed but utterly predictable romantic melodrama, based on a biography but not carrying much conviction. D. W. Griffith would have liked it.

w Patricia Louisiana Knop, *book* Olive Fredrickson, Ben East *d* Allan Winton King *ph* Richard Leiterman *m* Allan MacMillan

Ellen Burstyn, Tom Skerritt, Gordon Pinsent, Jennifer McKinney

'Follow his secret from bedroom to bedlam, with guns, girls and dynamite!'

The Silencers*
US 1966 103m Technicolor
Columbia / Irving Allen (Jim Schmerer)

Adventures of a sexy secret agent.
Or, James Bond sent up rotten. Plenty of fun along the way, with in-jokes and characters like Lovey Kravezit, but the plot could have done with more attention, and the sequels (*Murderers Row, The Ambushers, Wrecking Crew*) were uncontrolled disaster areas.

w Oscar Saul, *novel* Donald Hamilton *d* Phil Karlson *ph* Burnett Guffey *m* Elmer Bernstein

Dean Martin, Stella Stevens, Victor Buono, Daliah Lavi, Cyd Charisse, Robert Webber, James Gregory, Nancy Kovack

The Silent Battle
GB 1939 84m bw

A French agent battles revolutionaries in the Balkans. Unconvincing spy stuff with an uncertain tone. Rex Harrison, Valerie Hobson, John Loder, Muriel Aked, John Salew, George Devine. Written by Wolfgang Wilhelm and Rodney Ackland, from the novel by Jean Bommart; directed by Herbert Mason; for Anthony Havelock-Allan / Pinebrook.

Silent Dust*
GB 1947 82m bw
ABP / Independent Sovereign (Nat Bronsten)

A baronet builds a memorial to his son who has apparently been killed in action, but the son turns up and proves to be an absolute bounder.
Effective stage melodrama, quite neatly filmed.

w Michael Pertwee, *play* The Paragon by Roland and Michael Pertwee *d* Lance Comfort *ph* Wilkie Cooper *m* Georges Auric

Sally Gray, Derek Farr, Stephen Murray, Nigel Patrick, Seymour Hicks

The Silent Enemy
GB 1958 112m bw
Romulus (Bertram Ostrer)

The World War II exploits of a naval frogman in the Mediterranean.
Stereotyped naval underwater adventures, adequately presented.

wd William Fairchild *ph* Egil Woxholt, Otto Heller *m* William Alwyn

Laurence Harvey, John Clements, Michael Craig, Dawn Addams, Sidney James, Alec McCowen, Nigel Stock

The Silent Flute
US 1978 95m colour
Volare (Richard St Johns)

In a martial arts tournament, a hero is chosen to challenge the wizard Zetan.
Curiously mystical adventure allegory with an unhelpful title. Not too bad for those in the mood.

w Stirling Silliphant, Stanley Mann *d* Richard Moore *ph* Ronnie Taylor *m* Bruce Smeaton

Jeff Cooper, David Carradine, Roddy McDowall, Christopher Lee, Eli Wallach

Silent Movie*
US 1976 87m De Luxe
TCF / Crossbow (Michael Hertzberg)

An alcoholic producer gets the idea that a silent movie would be a great novelty, and tries to get stars to take part.
Fairly lively spoof with the talents concerned in variable form. The shortage of laughter made it a hit in the seventies, but at no time does it approach the Keaton or Laurel and Hardy level.

w Mel Brooks, Ron Clark, Rudy de Luca, Barry Levinson *d* Mel Brooks *ph* Paul Lohmann *m* John Morris

Mel Brooks, Marty Feldman, Dom De Luise, Bernardette Peters, Sid Caesar, Harold Gould, Fritz Feld, Harry Ritz, Henny Youngman *guest stars* Anne Bancroft, Paul Newman, Burt Reynolds, James Caan, Liza Minnelli, Marcel Marceau

† Marcel Marceau utters the only word in the movie, which is '*Non*'.

The Silent Partner
Canada 1978 105m colour
Carolco (Garth H. Drabinsky)

A bank teller foils an attempted raid and steals the money himself.
A suspense thriller of a familiar kind; it might have been entertaining but elects instead to be unpleasant.

w Curtis Hanson, *novel* Think of a Number by Anders Bodelson *d* Daryl Duke *ph* Stephen Katz *m* Oscar Peterson

Christopher Plummer, Elliott Gould, Susannah York, Celine Lomez, Michael Kirby

The Silent Passenger
GB 1935 75m bw

Lord Peter Wimsey clears a man of a murder charge. Not an unappealing presentation of Dorothy Sayers' famous detective, though he is presented as too much the silly ass and the story is weak. Peter Haddon, John Loder, Mary Newland, Austin Trevor, Donald Wolfit, Leslie Perrins, Robb Wilton. Written by Basil Mason; directed by Reginald Denham; for Phoenix.

Silent Running*
US 1971 90m Technicolor
Universal / Michel Gruskoff / Douglas Trumbull

Members of a space station crew in 2001 are space gardening to replenish nuclear-devasted earth.
Sombre futuristic fantasy, well made but slow and muddled in development.

w Deric Washburn, Mike Cimino, Steve Bocho *d* Douglas Trumbull *ph* Charles F. Wheeler *m* Peter Schickele

Bruce Dern, Cliff Potts, Ron Rifkin, Jesse Vint

The Silent Village**
GB 1943 35m bw

Harrowing depiction, by the members of a Welsh village, of what happened to the Czech population of Lidice after the assassination of Heydrich. A chilling documentary at the time, this little classic has kept its kick. Written, directed and produced by Humphrey Jennings; edited by Stewart McAllister; for the Ministry of Information.

The Silent Witness
US 1932 73m bw

A man confesses to murder in order to protect his son. Solid courtroom stuff of its day, built for a new star who never quite made it. Lionel Atwill, Helen Mack, Greta Nissen, Bramwell Fletcher, Alan Mowbray. From the play by Jack de Leon and Jack Celestin; directed by Marcel Varnel; for Fox. 'A gripping talker that rates well above most of the creep releases.'—*Variety*

The Silk Hat Kid
US 1935 70m bw

A settlement housekeeper accepts help from a racketeer. Thin little drama, perfunctorily played. Lew Ayres, Mae Clarke, Paul Kelly, Ralf Harolde, William Harrigan. Written by Edward Eliscu, Lou Breslow, Dore Schary, from a story by Gerald Beaumont; directed by H. Bruce Humberstone; for Joseph Engel / Fox. 'It hasn't the story nor the entertainment weight to lift it out of the double feature classification.'—*Variety*

Silk Stockings*
US 1957 116m Metrocolor Cinemascope
MGM (Arthur Freed)

A Russian composer in Paris agrees to write music for a Hollywood film; a lady commissar is sent to get him back.
Musical rewrite of *Ninotchka* via a Broadway show; good moments but generally very stretched.

w Leonard Gershe, Leonard Spiegelgass, *play* George S. Kaufman, Leueen McGrath, Abe Burrows, *original play* Melchior Lengyel *d* Rouben Mamoulian *ph* Robert Bronner *m / ly* Cole Porter *md* André Previn

Fred Astaire, Cyd Charisse, Peter Lorre, Janis Paige, George Tobias, Jules Munshin, Joseph Buloff

The Silken Affair
GB 1956 96m bw
Dragon (Fred Feldkamp)

An accountant decides to live it up, and finds himself on trial for manipulating the firm's books.
Unsatisfactory mix of comedy and fantasy, with a dim plot and virtually no comic ideas.

w Robert Lewis Taylor *d* Roy Kellino *ph* Gilbert Taylor *m* Peggy Stuart

David Niven, Genevieve Page, Wilfrid Hyde White, Ronald Squire, Beatrice Straight, Howard Marion Crawford, Dorothy Alison

Silken Skin*
France 1964 118m bw
Films du Carrosse / SEDIF
original title: *La Peau Douce*

A middle-aged married man leaves his wife for an attractive young girl, but the latter leaves him and his wife shoots him.
Carefully balanced mixture of comedy and melodrama which rings almost every possible change on the theme of adultery and does so with wit.

w François Truffaut, Jean-Louis Richard *d* François Truffaut *ph* Raoul Coutard *m* Georges Delerue

Jean Desailly, Françoise Dorléac, Nelly Benedetti

'Very funny, very touching, very wise about human beings.'—*New York Herald Tribune*

Silkwood*
US 1983 131m Technicolor
ABC (Mike Nichols, Michael Hausman)

The true story, more or less, of a girl worker in a nuclear processing plant who mysteriously dies in an accident just before she is going to talk to a reporter about a safety problem.
Despite the historical interest of the case, it is too simple to merit a film of this length, which is filled with pregnant pauses and romantic asides. Nor are the actors quite so charismatic as they think they are.

w Nora Ephron, Alice Arlen *d* Mike Nichols *ph* Miroslav Ondricek *m* Georges Delerue *pd* Patrizia Von Brandenstein

Meryl Streep, Cher, Kurt Russell, Craig T. Nelson, Diana Scarwid, Fred Ward

'A movie with a preordained conclusion but nowhere to go . . . it submerges what could have been its most telling points in a kind of concentrated soap opera.'—*Richard Combs, MFB*

AAN: Meryl Streep; Cher; direction; screenplay; editing (Sam O'Steen)

Silver Bears
GB 1977 113m Technicolor
EMI / Raleigh (Martin Schute)

A Las Vegas money man invests money in various European outlets and makes a killing.
Extraordinarily complex financial jape which tries the patience of all but financiers.

w Peter Stone, *novel* Paul Erdman *d* Ivan Passer *ph* Anthony Richmond *m* Claude Bolling

Michael Caine, Louis Jourdan, Cybill Shepherd, Stephane Audran, David Warner, Tom Smothers, Martin Balsam, Charles Gray

Silver Blaze
GB 1937 70m bw

Sherlock Holmes clears a racehorse of having killed its trainer. Not the best of the Holmes series, but this is a very satisfying Holmes. Arthur Wontner, Ian Fleming, Lyn Harding, Judy Gunn, Lawrence Grossmith, Arthur Macrae. Written by Arthur Macrae and H. Fowler Mear, from the story by Sir Arthur Conan Doyle; directed by Thomas Bentley; for Twickenham. (US title: *Murder at the Baskervilles.*)

Silver Bullet
US 1985 95m Technicolor
Paramount / Dino de Laurentiis (Martha Schumacher)

Murders at Tarker's Mill turn out to be the work of a werewolf.
Dreary, unimaginative rendition of a theme that was more entertaining in 1941.

w Stephen King, from his novelette *Cycle of the Werewolf* *d* Daniel Attias *ph* Armando Nannuzzi *m* Jay Chataway

Corey Haim, Gary Busey, Megan Follows, Everett McGill

'It's a Stephen King filmette from his novelette which may sell some tickettes but not without regrettes.'—*Variety*

'I bid you seek the lost silver cup . . . for sin is rising like the swollen rivers!'
'Against the broad canvas of history's mad era of splendour and seduction—here is the story of the sacred cup of silver that challenged the iron sword of tyranny—the mighty struggle to possess it—and the loves and the faith that triumphed in humanity's darkest hour!'

The Silver Chalice
US 1954 142m Warnercolor Cinemascope
Warner (Victor Saville)

Adventures of a slave freed by Luke the apostle to fashion a chalice to hold the cup used at the Last Supper.
Po-faced biblical hokum, slower and deadlier than most, with howlingly bad casting and direction. On reflection, interesting things are being attempted with limbo set design, but in this sea of boredom the attempt only raises an eyebrow.

w Lesser Samuels, *novel* Thomas B. Costain *d* Victor Saville *ph* William V. Skall *m* Franz Waxman *pd Rolf Gerard*

Paul Newman, Pier Angeli, Jack Palance, Virginia Mayo, Walter Hampden, Joseph Wiseman, Alexander Scourby, Lorne Greene, Michael Pate, E. G. Marshall

AAN: William V. Skall; Franz Waxman

Silver City
US 1951 90m Technicolor

A mining assayer helps a farmer and his daughter protect the ore found on their land. Standard western programmer with plenty of action. Yvonne de Carlo, Edmond O'Brien, Barry Fitzgerald, Richard Arlen, Gladys George, Laura Elliot, Edgar Buchanan, John Dierkes. Written by Frank Gruber, from a story by Luke Short; directed by Byron Haskin; for Nat Holt / Paramount. (GB title: *High Vermilion.*)

The Silver Cord
US 1933 74m bw
RKO (Pandro S. Berman)

A young wife threatens to leave her husband because of his excessive devotion to his mother.
Stilted version of an old theatrical warhorse.

w Jane Murfin, *play* Sidney Howard *d* John Cromwell *ph* Charles Rosher

Irene Dunne, Joel McCrea, Laura Hope Crews, Frances Dee, Eric Linden, Helen Cromwell

The Silver Darlings
GB 1947 84m bw

Hebridean islanders take to herring fishing as a last chance to avoid emigration. Uneventful island mood piece which lacks the poetic quality which might have made it memorable. Clifford Evans, Helen Shingler, Carl Bernard, Norman Shelley, Simon Lack, Hugh Griffith. Written by Clarence Elder, from the novel by Neil Gunn; directed by Clarence Elder and Clifford Evans; for Holyrood.

Silver Dollar*
US 1932 84m bw
Warner

A poor farmer goes to Colorado for the gold rush, strikes it rich, and learns that money doesn't bring happiness.
Packed biopic of one H. A. W. Tabor, an excellent star vehicle.

w Carl Erickson, Harvey Thew *d* Alfred E. Green *ph* James Van Trees *m* Milan Roder

Edward G. Robinson, Bebe Daniels, Aline MacMahon, Jobyna Howland, Robert Warwick, Russell Simpson

'Historical subject admirably done as to its variety but not so strong on its commercial side.'—*Variety*

Silver Dream Racer
GB 1980 111m Eastmancolor Panavision
Rank / David Wickes (Rene Dupont)

A garage mechanic becomes a racing motorcyclist and is killed at the peak of success.
One wonders who can have thought there was any box office appeal in this cliché-ridden, derivative, flashily made update of the Road to Ruin.

wd David Wickes *ph* Paul Beeson *m* David Essex

David Essex, Beau Bridges, Cristina Raines, Harry H. Corbett, Lee Montague, Clark Peters.

'Watching this grotesque hotch-potch of implausible characters being shunted through improbable situations is uncannily akin to being assaulted by a non-stop stream of TV commercials.'—*Tom Milne, MFB*

The Silver Fleet*
GB 1943 87m bw
GFD / Archers (Michael Powell, Emeric Pressburger, Ralph Richardson)

In occupied Holland, a shipping magnate destroys his new U-boat and himself and his Nazi mentors with it.
Slow-starting, rather stilted melodrama which when it gets into its stride provides good acting and gripping propaganda.

wd Vernon Sewell, Gordon Wellesley *ph* Erwin Hillier

Ralph Richardson, Esmond Knight, Googie Withers, Beresford Egan, Frederick Burtwell, Kathleen Byron

Silver Lode
US 1954 80m Technicolor print

A respected citizen of Silver Lode proves that the marshal who rides into town on his wedding day to accuse him of murder is a civilian bent on revenge. Broody little western melodrama, not half bad. John Payne, Dan Duryea, Lizabeth Scott, Dolores Moran, Emile Meyer, Robert Warwick. Written by Karen de Wolf; directed by Allan Dwan; for Benedict Bogeaus / RKO.

Silver Queen
US 1942 80m bw
UA / Harry Sherman

A chivalrous western gambler rescues a girl from the wiles of a villain.
Standard romantic melodrama mainly set in saloons.

w Bernard Schubert, Cecile Kramer *d* Lloyd Bacon *ph* Russell Harlan *m* Victor Young

George Brent, Priscilla Lane, Bruce Cabot, Lynne Overman, Eugene Pallette, Janet Beecher, Guinn Williams, Roy Barcroft

AAN: Victor Young

Silver River
US 1948 110m bw
Warner (Owen Crump)

A ruthless gambler becomes powerful but loses everything because of his character defects.
Meandering western drama with a few good highlights dissipated by long chunks of

character building and a rehash of the David and Bathsheba story.

w Stephen Longstreet, Harriet Frank Jnr *d* Raoul Walsh *ph* Sid Hickox *m* Max Steiner

Errol Flynn, Ann Sheridan, Thomas Mitchell, Bruce Bennett, Tom D'Andrea, Barton Maclane, Monte Blue, Alan Bridge

Silver Skates
US 1942 73m bw

A touring ice revue is lapsing into debt. Novelties on ice occupy more screen time than the story, which is just as well. Competent small-scale musical filler. Kenny Baker, Patricia Morison, Belita, Frick and Frack. Written by Jerry Cady; directed by Leslie Goodwins; for Lindsley Parsons / Monogram.

The Silver Streak*
US 1934 85m bw

A streamlined train makes its first run from Chicago to Boulder Dam, where a victim of infantile paralysis must be got into an iron lung. Historically interesting melodrama which seldom pauses for breath. Sally Blane, Charles Starrett, Hardie Albright, William Farnum, Irving Pichel, Arthur Lake, Edgar Kennedy. Written by H. W. Hanemann, Jack O'Donnell, Roger Whately; directed by Tommy Atkins; for RKO. 'Pretty absurd, yet exciting and fast . . . there's scarcely a stunt known to the railroad picture formula that hasn't been employed.'—*Variety*

Silver Streak*
US 1976 113m De Luxe
TCF / Martin Ransohoff, Frank Yablans

On a trans-continental train, a young publisher discovers a murder and is at the mercy of the culprits.
Rather like an update of a Bob Hope comedy-thriller with a whiff of sex, this amiable spoof goes on too long, brings in a second comic too late, and ends with fashionable but irrelevant violence.

w Colin Higgins *d* Arthur Hiller *ph* David M. Walsh *m* Henry Mancini *pd* Alfred Sweeney

Gene Wilder, Jill Clayburgh, Richard Pryor, Patrick McGoohan, Ned Beatty, Clifton James, Ray Walston, Richard Kiel

'Nineteen-seventies performers are trapped in this fake thirties mystery comedy, which is so inept you can't even get angry.'—*New Yorker*

Silverado*
US 1985 132m Technicolor Super Techniscope
Writer and Director / Lawrence Kasdan

In the 1880s, various pioneers try to establish a future in the west.
Interesting but not wholly successful attempt to revive in one movie various western myths and legends; a little more conscious humour might have helped.

w Lawrence and Mark Kasdan *d* Lawrence Kasdan *ph* John Bailey *m* Bruce Broughton *pd* Ida Random *ed* Carol Littleton

Kevin Kline, Scott Glenn, Kevin Costner, Danny Glover, John Cleese, Rosanna Arquette, Brian Dennehy, Linda Hunt, Jeff Goldblum

'Less like the film westerns of imagination and more like something more common. Maybe it was that way in real life.'—*Variety*

AAN: music

Simba
GB 1955 99m Eastmancolor
GFD / Group Film (Peter de Sarigny)

An English farmer in Kenya fights the Mau Mau.
Savagely topical melodrama which tends to cheapen a tragic situation.

w John Baines *d* Brian Desmond Hurst *ph* Geoffrey Unsworth *m* Francis Chagrin

Dirk Bogarde, Donald Sinden, Virginia McKenna, Basil Sydney, Marie Ney, Joseph Tomelty, Earl Cameron, Orlando Martins

Simon*
US 1980 97m Technicolor
Warner / Orion (Louis A. Stroller, Martin Bregman)

Corrupt scientists brainwash a psychology professor into thinking he's from another planet.
Solemn comic fantasy which doesn't seem to make much of a point and only superficially entertains, but is well made and well acted.

wd Marshall Brickman *ph* Adam Holender *m* Stanley Silverman *pd* Stuart Wurtzel

Alan Arkin, Madeleine Kahn, Austin Pendleton, Judy Graubert, William Finley, Fred Gwynne

Simon and Laura*
GB 1955 91m Technicolor Vistavision
GFD / Group Films (Teddy Baird)

The actors who play husband and wife in a TV series are married in reality and hate each other, a fact that shows in the live Christmas episode.
Adequate film of a reasonably sophisticated West End comedy; good lines and performances.

w Peter Blackmore, *play* Alan Melville *d* Muriel Box *ph* Ernest Steward *m* Benjamin Frankel

Peter Finch, Kay Kendall, Ian Carmichael, Alan Wheatley, Richard Wattis, Muriel Pavlow, Maurice Denham, Hubert Gregg

The Sin of Madelon Claudet
US 1931 74m bw
MGM (Harry Rapf)
GB title: *The Lullaby*

A mother is separated from her illegitimate baby.
Sob stuff for a rising star: hilarious now.

w Charles MacArthur, *play* Eward Knoblock *d* Edgar Selwyn

Helen Hayes, Robert Young, Neil Hamilton, Lewis Stone, Marie Prevost, Cliff Edwards, Jean Hersholt, Karen Morley

'Natural sobber for women and grosses . . . but you don't have to go back as far as *Madame X* to find a parallel for the plot.'—*Variety*

AA: Helen Hayes

Sin Town
US 1942 74m bw
Universal (George Waggner)

Two confidence tricksters arrive in a western town and solve a murder.
Members of the studio repertory company in a passable western discarded by Marlene Dietrich.

w Gerald Geraghty, W. Scott Darling, Richard Brooks *d* Ray Enright *m* Hans Salter

Constance Bennett, Broderick Crawford, Leo Carrillo, Anne Gwynne, Patric Knowles, Andy Devine, Ward Bond, Ralf Harolde

Sinbad and the Eye of the Tiger
GB 1977 113m Metrocolor
Columbia / Andor (Charles H. Schneer, Ray Harryhausen)

Sinbad frees a city from a wicked woman's spell.
Lumpish sequel to a sequel: even the animated monsters raise a yawn this time.

w Beverly Cross *d* Sam Wanamaker *ph* Ted Moore *m* Roy Budd *sp* Ray Harryhausen

Patrick Wayne, Taryn Power, Jane Seymour, Margaret Whiting, Patrick Troughton

Sinbad the Sailor
US 1947 117m Technicolor
RKO (Stephen Ames)

Sinbad sets off on his eighth voyage to find the lost treasure of Alexander.
Well-staged but humourless Arabian Nights swashbuckler.

w John Twist *d* Richard Wallace *ph* George Barnes *m* Roy Webb

Douglas Fairbanks Jnr, Walter Slezak, Maureen O'Hara, Anthony Quinn, George Tobias, Jane Greer, Mike Mazurki, Sheldon Leonard

Since You Went Away***
US 1944 172m bw
David O. Selznick

When hubby is away at the war, his wife and family adopt stiff upper lips.
Elaborate flagwaving investigation of the well-heeled American home front in World War II, with everyone brimming with goodwill and not a dry eye in the place. Absolutely superbly done, if it must be done at all, and a symposium of Hollywood values and techniques of the time.

w David O. Selznick, *book* Margaret Buell Wilder *d John Cromwell ph Stanley Cortez, Lee Garmes* *m* Max Steiner *pd William L. Pereira*

Claudette Colbert, Joseph Cotten, Jennifer Jones, Shirley Temple, Agnes Moorehead, Monty Woolley, Lionel Barrymore, Guy

Madison, Robert Walker, Hattie McDaniel, Craig Stevens, Keenan Wynn, Albert Basserman, Nazimova, Lloyd Corrigan

PREFACE: 'This is the story of the unconquerable fortress—the American home, 1943.'

'A deft, valid blend of showmanship, humour, and yard-wide Americanism.'—*James Agee*

'The whole litany of that middle-class synthetic emotionalism, meticulously annotated over a decade by tough and sentimental experts, has been procured for us.'—*Richard Winnington*

'A rather large dose of choking sentiment.'—*Bosley Crowther*

'It is not an average US reality. It is an average US dream.'—*Time*

'Selznick wrote the script himself, intending his story to be moving and simple, along epic lines; the result is pedestrian in a peculiarly grandiose manner.'—*Pauline Kael, 70s*

AA: Max Steiner
AAN: best picture; Stanley Cortez; Claudette Colbert; Jennifer Jones; Monty Woolley

Sincerely Yours
US 1955 115m Warnercolor
Warner (Henry Blanke)

A concert pianist goes deaf and retires to his penthouse, but with the help of binoculars lipreads the humble folk below. Helping them anonymously gives him courage to have an operation.
Absurd updating for a modern non-star of a creaky old George Arliss vehicle *The Man Who Played God*.

w Irving Wallace *d* Gordon Douglas *ph* William H. Clothier *m adviser* George Liberace

Liberace, Joanne Dru, Dorothy Malone, Alex Nicol, William Demarest

'Drenched in coy bathos to the point of embarrassment.'—*Films and Filming*

'Given sufficient intoxication, you could find this movie amusing.'—*Saturday Review*

Sinful Davey
GB 1968 95m Eastmancolor Panavision
UA / Mirisch / Webb (William N. Graf)

In 1821 a young Scotsman determines to become a criminal like his father, but falls in love.
Thin imitation of *Tom Jones*, highly implausible but played with some zest.

w James R. Webb, based on the autobiography of David Haggart *d* John Huston *ph* Ted Scaife, Freddie Young *m* Ken Thorne *pd* Stephen Grimes

John Hurt, Pamela Franklin, Nigel Davenport, Ronald Fraser, Robert Morley, Maxine Audley, Noel Purcell

Sing and Be Happy
US 1937 67m bw

A young man is too irresponsible to work in his father's advertising agency. A wisp of a plot with some wisps of music attached; nothing to remember next day. Tony Martin, Leah Ray, Joan Davis, Chick Chandler, Helen Westley, Allan Lane, Berton Churchill. Written by Ben Markson, Lou Breslow, John Patrick; directed by James Tinling; for Milton H. Feld / Fox. 'This musical will require plenty of exploitative pressure by exhibs.'—*Variety*

Sing As We Go***
GB 1934 80m bw
ATP (Basil Dean)

An unemployed millgirl gets various holiday jobs in Blackpool.
A splendid, pawky star vehicle which is also the best picture we have of industrial Lancashire in the thirties. Great fun.

w J. B. Priestley, Gordon Wellesley d Basil Dean ph Robert G. Martin

Gracie Fields, John Loder, *Frank Pettingell*, Dorothy Hyson, Stanley Holloway

'We have an industrial north that is bigger than Gracie Fields running around a Blackpool fun fair.'—*C. A. Lejeune*

Sing Baby Sing*
US 1936 87m bw
TCF (Darryl F. Zanuck)

A drunken Shakespearian actor sets his sights on a night club singer.
Reasonably hilarious take-off on the John Barrymore-Elaine Barrie affair, with several Fox contractees fooling to the top of their bent with the help of good musical numbers.

w Milton Sperling, Jack Yellen, Harry Tugend *d* Sidney Lanfield *ph* Peverell Marley *songs* various *md* Louis Silvers

Alice Faye, Adolphe Menjou, Gregory Ratoff, Patsy Kelly, Ted Healy, The Ritz Brothers, Montagu Love, Dixie Dunbar

AAN: song 'When Did You Leave Heaven?' (*ly* Walter Bullock, *m* Richard Whiting)

Sing, Boy, Sing
US 1958 91m bw Cinemascope
TCF (Henry Ephron)

A rock and roll star comes close to a nervous breakdown because of an unscrupulous manager and a revivalist grandfather.
Fairly painless vehicle for a singing star.

w Claude Binyon *d* Henry Ephron *ph* William C. Mellor *m* Lionel Newman

Tommy Sands, Edmond O'Brien, John McIntire, Lili Gentle, Nick Adams, Josephine Hutchinson

Sing Me a Love Song
US 1936 78m bw

A reformed playboy starts at the bottom as a clerk in his father's department store. Thin but mildly pleasing musical with good comedy support. James Melton, Patricia Ellis, *Hugh Herbert*, Zasu Pitts, Allen Jenkins, Nat Pendleton, Ann Sheridan, Walter Catlett, Hobart Cavanaugh, Charles Halton. Written by Sig Herzig, Jerry Wald, Harry Sauber; directed by Ray Enright; for Cosmopolitan / First National. 'Story isn't much and the dialogue fails to sparkle, yet there's a constant stream of laughs.'—*Variety*

'The gol-darnedest family in the whole USA!'

Sing You Sinners**
US 1938 88m bw
Paramount (Wesley Ruggles)

The adventures of a happy-go-lucky family and their racehorse.
Cheerful family musical with amiable cast and good tunes.

w Claude Binyon *d* Wesley Ruggles *ph* Karl Struss *md* Boris Morros *songs* James V. Monaco, Johnny Burke

Bing Crosby, Donald O'Connor, Fred MacMurray, Elizabeth Patterson, Ellen Drew, John Gallaudet

'Homespun, down to earth, and as natural as eggs for breakfast.'—*Variety*

Sing Your Worries Away
US 1941 71m bw

A debt-ridden songwriter has a girlfriend unaware of a huge pending inheritance.
Rather ribby comedy material which adds up to very little. Bert Lahr, Buddy Ebsen, June Havoc, Patsy Kelly, Sam Levene, Margaret Dumont. Written by Monte Brice; directed by Edward Sutherland; for Cliff Reid / RKO.

Singapore Woman
US 1941 65m bw

A slightly fallen woman is redeemed by a plantation owner. Hasty and uninteresting remake of the Bette Davis vehicle *Dangerous*. Brenda Marshall, David Bruce, Virginia Field, Jerome Cowan, Rose Hobart, Heather Angel. Written by Laird Doyle; directed by Jean Negulesco; for Harlan Thompson / Warner.

The Singer Not the Song
GB 1960 132m colour Cinemascope
Rank (Roy Baker)

In an isolated Mexican town a priest defies an outlaw who oddly respects him.
Lengthy character drama with little action or humour but a great deal of moody introspection and a suggestion of homosexuality.

w Nigel Balchin, *novel* Audrey Erskine Lindop *d* Roy Baker *ph* Otto Heller *m* Philip Green

John Mills, Dirk Bogarde, Mylene Demongeot, John Bentley, Laurence Naismith, Eric Pohlmann

'A rewarding film, as startling as a muffled scream from the subconscious.'—*Peter John Dyer*

The Singing Fool**
US 1928 110m bw
Warner

A successful singer goes on the skids when his small son dies.

Early talkie musical, a sensation because of its star's personality, but a pretty maudlin piece of drama.

w C. Graham Baker, *play* Leslie S. Barrows *d* Lloyd Bacon *ph* Byron Haskin *songs* Lew Brown, Ray Henderson, B. G. De Sylva

Al Jolson, Davey Lee, Betty Bronson, Josephine Dunn, Arthur Housman

'Obvious and tedious as the climax is, when the black-faced comedian stands before the camera and sings "Sonny Boy" you know the man is greater, somehow, than the situation, the story or the movie.'—*Pare Lorentz*

Singin' in the Rain****
US 1952 102m Technicolor
MGM (Arthur Freed)

When talkies are invented, the reputation of one female star shrivels while another grows. Brilliant comic musical, the best picture by far of Hollywood in transition, with the catchiest tunes, the liveliest choreography, the most engaging performances and the most hilarious jokes of any musical.

w Adolph Green, Betty Comden d / ch Gene Kelly, Stanley Donen ph Harold Rosson m Nacio Herb Brown md Lennie Hayton ly Arthur Freed

Gene Kelly, Donald O'Connor, Debbie Reynolds, Millard Mitchell, Jean Hagen, Rita Moreno, Cyd Charisse, *Douglas Fowley*

'Perhaps the most enjoyable of all movie musicals.'—*New Yorker, 1975*

AAN: Lennie Hayton; Jean Hagen

The Singing Kid
US 1936 83m bw
Warner (Robert Lord)

A cocky night club singer takes a talented juvenile under his wing.
Routine star vehicle most notable for a string of standards sung by him right after the credits.

w Warren Duff, Pat C. Flick *d* William Keighley *ph* George Barnes *md* Leo F. Forbstein *songs* E. Y. Harburg, Harold Arlen

Al Jolson, Sybil Jason, Allen Jenkins, Lyle Talbot, Edward Everett Horton, Beverly Roberts, Claire Dodd

The Singing Marine
US 1937 107m bw

A marine singer wins a talent contest and success goes to his head. Light musical of very little interest save two dance sequences by Busby Berkeley. Dick Powell, Doris Weston, Jane Darwell, Hugh Herbert, Lee Dixon, Dick Wesson, Allen Jenkins, Jane Wyman, Larry Adler. Written by Delmer Daves; directed by Ray Enright; for Warner.

The Singing Nun
US 1966 98m Metrocolor Panavision
MGM (Jon Beck)

Adventures of a nun who takes her music to the outside world.
Icky musical drama based on a true character.

w Sally Benson, John Furia *d* Henry Koster *ph* Milton Krasner *md* Harry Sukman *songs* Soeur Sourire

Debbie Reynolds, Greer Garson, Ricardo Montalban, Agnes Moorehead, Chad Everett, Katharine Ross, Ed Sullivan, Juanita Moore

AAN: Harry Sukman

The Sinister Man*
GB 1961 60m bw
Anglo Amalgamated / Merton Park (Jim O'Connelly)

The murder of an Oxford scholar is linked to the archaeological relics which are coveted for political purposes.
Very tolerable minor thriller in the Edgar Wallace series: short, sharp and snappy.

w Robert Banks Stewart *d* Clive Donner *ph* Bert Mason *m* Charles Blackwell

Patrick Allen, John Bentley, Jacqueline Ellis, Eric Young, Arnold Lee, John Glyn-Jones, William Gaunt, Wilfrid Brambell

'Personal! Powerful! Human! Heroic!'
Sink the Bismarck**
GB 1960 97m bw Cinemascope
TCF / John Brabourne

In 1941, Britain's director of naval operations arranges the trapping and sinking of Germany's greatest battleship.
Tight little personal drama which would have been better on a standard screen, as its ships are plainly models and much of the footage stretched-out newsreel. Nevertheless, a good example of the stiff-upper-lip school.

w Edmund H. North *d* Lewis Gilbert *ph* Christopher Challis *m* Clifton Parker *md* Muir Mathieson

Kenneth More, Dana Wynter, Karel Stepanek, Carl Mohner, Laurence Naismith, Geoffrey Keen, Michael Hordern, Maurice Denham, Esmond Knight

Sinner Take All
US 1937 74m bw

Members of a family are murdered one by one. Moderate puzzler with a reporter sharing solving honours with the police. Bruce Cabot, Margaret Lindsay, Joseph Calleia, Stanley Ridges, Vivienne Osborne, Charley Grapewin, Edward Pawley, George Zucco. Written by Leonard Lee, Walter Wise, from the novel Murder of a Wanton by Whitman Chambers; directed by Errol Taggart; for Lucien Hubbard / Sam Marx / MGM. 'Above the usual whodunit average . . . able to make its way alone in the less exacting spots.'—*Variety*

Sinner's Holiday
US 1930 55m bw
Warner

A fairground barker loves the daughter of a penny arcade owner, but is framed by her brother.
Early talkie quickie using Bradway talent, and introducing James Cagney to the screen. It still has vigour if little else.

w Harvey Thew, George Rosener, *play* Penny Arcade by Marie Baumer *d* John G. Adolfi *ph* Ira Morgan

Grant Withers, Evalyn Knapp, James Cagney, Joan Blondell, Lucille La Verne, Warren Hymer, Noel Madison

Sinners in Paradise
US 1938 65m bw

Air travellers are wrecked on a South Sea island. Much ado about very little, and a grave disappointment from its director. Madge Evans, John Boles, Bruce Cabot, Marion Martin, Gene Lockhart, Charlotte Wynters, Nana Bryant. Written by Lester Cole, Harold Buckley, Louis Stevens; directed by James Whale; for Ken Goldsmith / Universal. 'Melodrama sufficiently lurid to be cut into several parts and released as a serial.'—*Variety*

Sinners in the Sun
US 1932 69m bw

A young couple break up; each has romantic adventures, but eventually they come together again. Blah comedy-drama with the defects of its period. Carole Lombard, Chester Morris, Adrienne Allen, Alison Skipworth, Walter Byron, Cary Grant. Written by Vincent Lawrence, Waldemar Young, Samuel Hoffenstein, Mildred Cram; directed by Alexander Hall; for Paramount. 'Only high-powered selling will aid a dull and poorly-handled story.'—*Variety*

The Sins of Rachel Cade
US 1960 123m Technicolor
Warner (Henry Blanke)

An American missionary nurse in the Belgian Congo falls in love with a crashed flier and has a baby.
Romantic melodrama which starts like *The Nun's Story* and ends like Peg's Paper; competent on its level.

w Edward Anhalt, *novel* Charles Mercer *d* Gordon Douglas *ph* Peverell Marley *m* Max Steiner

Angie Dickinson, Roger Moore, Peter Finch, Errol John, Woody Strode, Juano Hernandez, Frederick O'Neal, Mary Wickes

Sir Henry at Rawlinson's End
GB 1980 71m bw

A grossly eccentric English aristocrat lays a family ghost. Weirdly isolated, semi-professional comedy with elements of everything from Ealing to Monty Python. Trevor Howard, Patrick Magee, Denise Coffey, J. G. Devlin. Written by Vivien Stanshall and Steve Roberts from Stanshall's radio play; directed by Steve Roberts; for Charisma.

Siren of Atlantis see L'Atlantide

Siren of Bagdad
US 1953 72m Technicolor

A travelling magician helps reinstate a deposed sultan. Flippant oriental extravaganza aiming at the Hope–Crosby style but falling sadly short of it. Paul Henreid, Patricia Medina, Hans Conried, Charlie Lung. Written by Robert E. Kent; directed by Richard Quine; for Same Katzman / Columbia.

Sirocco
US 1951 98m bw
Columbia / Santana (Robert Lord)

In 1925 Damascus, an American runs guns for the rebels.
Tedious romantic drama in the *Casablanca* vein but with none of the magic.

w A. I. Bezzerides, Hans Jacoby, *novel* Coup de Grâce by Joseph Kessel *d* Curtis Bernhardt *ph* Burnett Guffey *m* George Antheil

Humphrey Bogart, Marta Toren, Lee J. Cobb, Everett Sloane, Gerald Mohr, Zero Mostel, Onslow Stevens

Sister Kenny*
US 1946 116m bw
RKO (Dudley Nichols)

The career of a nurse who instigated treatment for polio.
Standard, well-done biopic.

w Dudley Nichols, Alexander Knox, Mary McCarthy *d* Dudley Nichols *ph* George Barnes *m* Alexander Tansman

Rosalind Russell, Alexander Knox, Dean Jagger, Philip Merivale, Beulah Bondi, Dorothy Peterson

† From the autobiography of Australian nurse Mary Kenny: *And They Shall Walk.*

AAN: Rosalind Russell

The Sisters*
US 1938 98m bw
Warner (Hal B. Wallis)

The marriages of three sisters from a small Montana town.
Well-made potboiler for women; it even brings in the San Francisco earthquake, and the star teaming is piquant to say the least.

w Milton Krims, *novel* Myron Brinig *d* Anatole Litvak *ph* Tony Gaudio *m* Max Steiner

Bette Davis, Errol Flynn, Anita Louise, Ian Hunter, Donald Crisp, Beulah Bondi, Jane Bryan, Alan Hale, Dick Foran, Henry Travers, Patric Knowles, Lee Patrick, Harry Davenport

Sisters under the Skin
US 1934 65m bw

An older man loses his mistress to a bohemian composer. Surprise, surprise: and the screenplay does not enliven the situation. Frank Morgan, Elissa Landi, Joseph Schildkraut, Doris Lloyd, Clara Blandick, Samuel S. Hinds. Written by Jo Swerling, S. K. Lauren; directed by David Burton; for Columbia. 'Mild flicker of obvious triangle story texture.'—*Variety*

Sitting Bull
US 1954 106m Eastmancolor Cinemascope
United Artists / W. R. Frank / Televoz of Mexico

Despite the massacre of Custer's men, a cavalry officer strives to establish a relationship with Sitting Bull.
Sloppy and undernourished western epic in abysmal colour, not helped by Mexicans pretending to be Indians.

w Jack De Witt, Sidney Salkow *d* Sidney Salkow *ph* Charles Van Enger, Victor Herrara *m* Raoul Kraushaar

Dale Robertson, Mary Murphy, J. Carrol Naish, Iron Eyes Cody, John Litel, William Hopper, Douglas Kennedy (as Custer)

Sitting Ducks
US 1978 88m De Luxe
Sunny Side Up (Meira Atta Dor)

Two men steal a fortune and abscond to Miami with two women who turn out to have a contract on them.
Endlessly talkative sex comedy from a practitioner who scorns built-up gags. The kind of movie that puts people off movies.

wd Henry Jaglom *ph* Paul Glickman *m* Richard Romanus

Michael E. Jaglom, Zack Norman, Patrice Townsend, Irene Forrest, Richard Romanus, Henry Jaglom

Sitting Pretty
US 1933 85m bw
Paramount (Charles R. Rogers)

Two songwriters strike it rich in Hollywood.
Cheerful comedy musical, interesting for its backgrounds.

w Jack McGowan, S. J. Perelman, Lou Breslow *d* Harry Joe Brown *ph* Milton Krasner *songs* Mack Gordon, Harry Revel

Jack Oakie, Jack Haley, Ginger Rogers, Thelma Todd, Gregory Ratoff, Lew Cody, Harry Revel, Mack Gordon

'Should please all over.'—*Variety*

Sitting Pretty***
US 1948 84m bw
TCF (Samuel G. Engel)

A young couple acquire a most unusual male baby sitter, a self-styled genius who sets the neighbourhood on its ears by writing a novel about it.
Out of the blue, a very funny comedy which entrenched Clifton Webb as one of Hollywood's great characters and led to two sequels, *Mr Belvedere Goes to College* and *Mr Belvedere Rings the Bell* (qv).

w F. Hugh Herbert, *novel* Belvedere by Gwen Davenport *d* Walter Lang *ph* Norbert Brodine *m* Alfred Newman

Clifton Webb, Robert Young, Maureen O'Hara, *Richard Haydn*, Louise Allbritton, Ed Begley, Randy Stuart, Larry Olsen

AAN: Clifton Webb

Sitting Target
GB 1972 92m Metrocolor
MGM (Barry Kulick)

A violent killer escapes from jail and seeks revenge on those who 'shopped' him.
Rough, tough action thriller; passes the time for hardened addicts.

w Alexander Jacobs, *novel* Lawrence Henderson *d* Douglas Hickox *ph* Ted Scaife *m* Stanley Myers *pd* Jonathan Barry

Oliver Reed, Jill St John, Edward Woodward, Frank Finlay, Ian McShane, Freddie Jones, Robert Beatty

Situation Hopeless But Not Serious
US 1965 97m bw
Paramount / Castle (Gottfried Reinhardt)

In 1944, two American fliers are captured by a friendly, lonely mild-mannered German, who keeps them in his cellar and hasn't the heart to tell them when the war is over . . .
Flat little comedy which leaves a talented cast no room for manoeuvre.

w Silvia Reinhardt, *novel* The Hiding Place by Robert Shaw *d* Gottfried Reinhardt *ph* Kurt Hasse *m* Harold Byrne

Alec Guinness, Robert Redford, Mike Connors, Anita Hoefer

Six Black Horses
US 1962 80m Eastmancolor

A girl hires a gunslinger and a horse thief to escort her across Indian territory. Rather glum western programmer. Audie Murphy, Dan Duryea, Joan O'Brien, George Wallace, Roy Barcroft. Written by Burt Kennedy; directed by Harry Keller; for Universal-International.

Six Bridges to Cross
US 1955 96m bw
U-I (Aaron Rosenberg)

The criminal career of a young hoodlum in Boston in the thirties.
Public Enemy reprise with a sentimental veneer, smooth but uninteresting.

w Sidney Boehm, *novel* They Stole Two and a Half Million Dollars and Got Away with It by Joseph F. Dineen *d* Joseph Pevney *ph* William Daniels *m* Joseph Gershenson

Tony Curtis, George Nader, Julie Adams, Jay C. Flippen, Sal Mineo, Jan Merlin

Six Day Bike Rider
US 1934 69m bw
Warner (Sam Bischoff)

One of life's failures impresses his girl by entering a cycling contest.
One of the star's stronger comedy vehicles.

w Earl Baldwin *d* Lloyd Bacon *ph* Warren Lynch

Joe E. Brown, Maxine Doyle, Frank McHugh, Gordon Westcott

Six Hours to Live*
US 1932 78m bw

A scientist revives a diplomat for six hours so that his murderer can be traced. Fanciful

hokum set at a Geneva peace conference. Warner Baxter, John Boles, Miriam Jordan, Irene Ware, George Marion. From the story by Gordon Morris and Morton Barteaux; directed by William Dieterle; for Fox.
'A strong box office title which together with an aggressive sales campaign should bring picture into the money.'—*Variety*

Six Lessons from Madame La Zonga
US 1941 62m bw
A Cuban nightclub proprietress causes mix-ups on a pleasure boat. Witless vehicle for two stars popular at another studio in the *Mexican Spitfire* series. Lupe Velez, Leon Errol, William Frawley, Helen Parrish, Charles Lang, Eddie Quillan, Quinn Williams. Written by Stanley Rubin, Marion Orth, Larry Rhine and Ben Chapman; directed by John Rawlins; for Universal.

'Their first honeymoon was so much fun They're off to have another one!'
Six of a Kind*
US 1934 69m bw
Paramount
Comic adventures of six people driving across America.
Minor comedy which doesn't come off as a whole but adequately displays the talents of its stars.
w Walter de Leon, Harry Ruskin *d* Leo McCarey *ph* Henry Sharp *m* Ralph Rainger
Charles Ruggles, Mary Boland, W. C. Fields, Alison Skipworth, George Burns, Gracie Allen
'Another pleasing film . . . it reminds the Englishman of *Three Men in a Boat*.'—*E. V. Lucas, Punch*
'Old-fashioned farce that gets a lot of laughs. Better for duals than de luxers.'—*Variety*

Six Pack
US 1982 110m De Luxe
TCF / Lion Share (Michael Trikilis)
A loner stock car driver finds himself fathering six orphan kids.
Old-fashioned family picture built around a country singer.
w Mike Marvin, Alex Matter *d* Daniel Petrie *ph* Mario Tosi *m* Charles Fox
Kenny Rogers, Diane Lane, Erin Gray, Barry Corbin

6,000 Enemies
US 1939 61m bw
A district attorney is framed for a prison stretch and finds himself hated by every convict inside. Formula support climaxing in a prison break: well enough done. Walter Pidgeon, Rita Johnson, Paul Kelly, Nat Pendleton, Harold Huber, Grant Mitchell. Written by Bertram Millhauser; directed by George B. Seitz; for Lucien Hubbard / MGM.
'Prison meller with action aplenty.'—*Variety*

633 Squadron*
GB 1964 94m Technicolor Panavision
UA / Mirisch (Cecil F. Ford)
In 1944 Mosquito aircraft try to collapse a cliff overhanging a munitions factory in a Norwegian fjord.
Standard war heroics with enough noise and disorder to keep most audiences hypnotized.
w James Clavell, Howard Koch, *novel* Frederick E. Smith *d* Walter Grauman *ph* Ted Scaife, John Wilcox *m Ron Goodwin*
Cliff Robertson, George Chakiris, Maria Perschy, Harry Andrews, Donald Houston, Michael Goodliffe

Six Weeks
US 1982 107m Metrocolor
Polygram (Peter Guber, Jon Peters)
A lady cosmetics tycoon whose ten-year-old daughter is dying of leukaemia enlists the aid of a politician to make what's left of her life a triumph.
Icky tearjerker on the lines of *The Christmas Tree*. Everything is done to make it palatable, but it won't be many people's cup of bromide.
w David Seltzer, *novel* Fred Mustard Stewart *d* Tony Bill *ph* Michael D. Margulies *m* Dudley Moore *ad* Hilyard Brown *ed* Stu Linder
Dudley Moore, Mary Tyler Moore, Katherine Healy, Shannon Wilcox, Bill Calvert
'Very sleek and very sickmaking.'—*Observer*

Sixty Glorious Years**
GB 1938 95m Technicolor
Imperator (Herbert Wilcox)
US title: *Queen of Destiny*
Scenes from the life of Queen Victoria.
A stately pageant apparently composed of material which couldn't be fitted into the previous year's black-and-white success *Victoria the Great*. Fascinating, though the camerawork is not very nimble.
w Robert Vansittart, Miles Malleson, Charles de Grandcourt *d* Herbert Wilcox *ph* Frederick A. Young
Anna Neagle, Anton Walbrook, C. Aubrey Smith, Walter Rilla, Charles Carson, Felix Aylmer, Lewis Casson
'One of the most artistic and expensive films made in England.'—*Variety*
† The two films were edited together in 1943 to make a new selection called *Queen Victoria*, and in the process the original negatives were accidentally destroyed, so that both films now have to be printed from unattractive dupes.

Skateboard
US 1977 95m Technicolor
A small-time theatrical agent in trouble builds up a professional skateboard team. Unsatisfactory exploitation item which devotes more time to its plot than to its sport. Allen Garfield, Kathleen Lloyd, Leif Garrett, Richard Van Der Wyk. Written by Richard A. Wolf, George Gage; directed by George Gage; for Universal.

The Ski Raiders
US 1972 90m Technicolor Panavision
Warner (Edward L. Rissien)
aka: *Snow Job*
An alpine ski instructor devises a scheme to rob a bank.
Very medium caper thriller with a breathtaking opening sequence.
w Ken Kolb, Jeffrey Bloom *d* George Englund *ph* Gabor Pogany, Willy Bogner *m* Jacques Loussier
Jean Claude Killy, Cliff Potts, Vittorio de Sica, Daniele Gaubert

Skidoo
US 1968 98m Technicolor Panavision
Paramount / Sigma (Otto Preminger)
Active and reformed gangsters get involved with hippies and preach universal love.
Abysmal mishmash with top talent abused; clearly intended as satirical farce, but in fact one of the most woebegone movies ever made.
w Doran William Cannon *d* Otto Preminger *ph* Leon Shamroy *m* Harry Nilsson
Jackie Gleason, Carol Channing, Groucho Marx, Frankie Avalon, Fred Clark, Michael Constantine, Frank Gorshin, John Philip Law, Peter Lawford, Burgess Meredith, George Raft, Cesar Romero, Mickey Rooney
'Unspeakable.'—*Michael Billington, Illustrated London News*

The Skin Game
GB 1932 85m bw
BIP (John Maxwell)
A landowner hates his self-made neighbour.
Stiff picturization of a well-known stage play.
w Alfred Hitchcock, Alma Reville, *play* John Galsworthy *d* Alfred Hitchcock *ph* Jack Cox
Edmund Gwenn, John Longden, Jill Esmond, C. V. France, Helen Haye, Phyllis Konstam, Frank Lawton

The Skin Game*
US 1971 102m Technicolor Panavision
Warner / Cherokee (Harry Keller)
A white and a black con man have near escapes in many a western town.
Amusing comedy western with good pace and a few shafts of wit.
w Peter Stone, Richard Alan Simmons *d* Paul Bogart *ph* Fred Koenekamp *m* David Shire
James Garner, Lou Gossett, Susan Clark, Brenda Sykes, Ed Asner, Andrew Duggan, Henry Jones, Neva Patterson

Skippy*
US 1931 88m bw
Paramount
The young son of a local health inspector makes friends in the slums.
Standard, blameless family entertainment.
w Joseph L. Mankiewicz, Norman McLeod, *comic strip* Percy Crosby *d* Norman Taurog *ph* Karl Struss

SKY RIDERS. After the aerial adventures rescue is at hand for the kidnapped children.

Jackie Cooper, Robert Coogan, Mitzi Green, Jackie Searl, Willard Robertson

'A great kid talker, but not for kids only . . . if there is such a thing as being 100% inhuman, only then is it possible for anyone to dislike *Skippy* as entertainment.'—*Variety*

AA: Norman Taurog
AAN: best picture; script; Jackie Cooper

Skirts Ahoy
US 1952 105m Technicolor
MGM (Joe Pasternak)

Three girls join the navy and get their men.
Musical recruiting poster, quite devoid of interest.

w Isobel Lennart *d* Sidney Lanfield *ph* William Mellor *m* Harry Warren *ly* Ralph Blane *ch* Nick Castle

Esther Williams, Vivian Blaine, Joan Evans, Barry Sullivan, Keefe Brasselle, Dean Miller, Debbie Reynolds, Bobby Van, Billy Eckstine

The Skull
GB 1965 83m Techniscope
Paramount / Amicus (Milton Subotsky)

The skull of the Marquis de Sade haunts two antiquarians.
Clodhopping horror with very visible wires.

w Milton Subotsky, *story* Robert Bloch *d* Freddie Francis *ph* John Wilcox *m* Elisabeth Lutyens

Peter Cushing, Christopher Lee, Patrick Wymark, Jill Bennett, Nigel Green, Michael Gough, George Coulouris

Skullduggery
US 1969 105m Technicolor Panavision
Universal (Saul David)

Archaeologists and adventurers clash on a trek in New Guinea.
Fashionable oddball adventure about the discovery of an unspoiled primitive tribe; the elements don't jell.

w Nelson Gidding *d* Gordon Douglas *ph* Robert Moreno *m* Oliver Nelson

Burt Reynolds, Susan Clark, Roger C. Carmel, Paul Hubschmid, Chips Rafferty, Alexander Knox, Edward Fox, Wilfrid Hyde White, Rhys Williams

Sky Bandits
GB 1986 93m Rank colour
London Front Ltd (Richard Herland)

Adventures of World War I flyers.
An attempt at a light-hearted *Hell's Angels*. It misfires on all cylinders.

w Thom Keyes *d* Zoran Perisic *ph* David Watkin *m* Alfie Kabilje *pd* Tony Woollard *ed* Peter Tanner

Scott McGinnis, Jeff Osterhage, Ronald Lacey, Miles Anderson, Valerie Steffen, Ingrid Held

Sky Bride
US 1932 75m bw

An aerial barnstormer loses his nerve after an accident. Formula melodrama with aerobatics. Richard Arlen, Jack Oakie, Virginia Bruce, Robert Coogan, Charles Starrett. Written by Joseph L. Mankiewicz, Agnes Brand Leahy and Grover Jones; directed by Stephen Roberts; for Paramount. 'Lack of romantic interest is somewhat of a handicap to a conventional air plot with a suspensive finish.'—*Variety*

Sky Devils
US 1931 89m bw
Caddo / Howard Hughes

Two draft dodgers find themselves heroes of the Army Air Corps in World War I France.
Little-seen but unremarkable adventure comedy in the Flagg and Quirt tradition.

w Joseph Moncure March, Edward Sutherland *d* Edward Sutherland *ph* Tony Guadio *md* Alfred Newman *ch* Busby Berkeley

Spencer Tracy, William Boyd, Ann Dvorak, George Cooper, Billy Bevan, Forrester Harvey

'A hodge-podge of all the laugh war stuff . . . and how they want something to laugh about right now. Psychologically and in a material way, it should do nicely.'—*Variety*

Sky Full of Moon
US 1952 73m bw
MGM (Sidney Franklin Jnr)

A rodeo cowboy wins money and a showgirl in Las Vegas.
Ambling comedy with an agreeable air of innocence.

wd Norman Foster *ph* Ray June *m* Paul Sawtell

Carleton Carpenter, Jan Sterling, Keenan Wynn

Sky Giant
US 1938 80m bw

Romance and adventure at a flying school. Unremarkable melodrama with expected heroics. Richard Dix, Joan Fontaine, Chester Morris, Harry Carey, Paul Guilfoyle. Written by Lionel Houser; directed by Ken Landers; for Robert Sisk / RKO. 'Good for the lighter weight first run houses and the upper berth of double deckers.'—*Variety*

Sky Raiders
US 1941 bw serial: 12 eps

Airplane manufacturers combat enemy agents. Routine thick-ear with a better than average cast. Donald Woods, Billy Halop, Robert Armstrong, Eduardo Ciannelli, Kathryn Adams, Reed Hadley. Directed by Ford Beebe and Ray Taylor; for Universal.

'He'll try anything once . . . even if it's impossible!'

Sky Riders*
US 1976 91m De Luxe Todd-AO 35
TCF (Terry Morse Jnr)

In Athens, the family of an American businessman is kidnapped by terrorists and rescued by hang gliders led by a soldier of fortune.
Old-fashioned actioner with new-fashioned political concern.

w Jack de Witt, Stanley Mann, Gary Michael White, Hall T. Sprague, Bill McGaw
d Douglas Hickox *ph* Ousama Rawi *m* Lalo Schifrin

James Coburn, Susannah York, Robert Culp, Charles Aznavour, Werner Pochath, Kenneth Griffith, Harry Andrews

Sky West and Crooked
GB 1965 102m Eastmancolor
Rank / John Mills (Jack Hanbury)
US title: *Gypsy Girl*

A mentally retarded girl falls in love with a gypsy.
Eccentric rural melodrama with echoes of *Cold Comfort Farm* and *Les Jeux Interdits*. Interesting, but scarcely a runaway success.

w Mary Hayley Bell, John Prebble *d* John Mills *ph* Arthur Ibbetson *m* Malcolm Arnold

Hayley Mills, Ian McShane, Laurence Naismith, *Geoffrey Bayldon*, Annette Crosbie, Norman Bird

'Behind the overwhelming feyness of it all lurk assumptions which in cold blood look almost sinister.'—*MFB*

Skyjacked*
US 1972 101m Metrocolor Panavision
MGM / Walter Seltzer

A Boeing 707 on a flight from Los Angeles to Minneapolis is forced by a mad bomber to fly to Moscow.
Shamelessly hackneyed aeroplane adventure with quite enjoyable elements.

w Stanley R. Greenberg, *novel* Hijacked by David Harper *d* John Guillermin *ph* Harry Stradling Jnr *m* Perry Botkin Jnr

Charlton Heston, Yvette Mimieux, James Brolin, Claude Akins, Jeanne Crain, Rosey Grier, Walter Pidgeon, Leslie Uggams

Skylark
US 1941 94m bw
Paramount (Mark Sandrich)

A wife decides on her fifth anniversary that she is tired of being secondary to her husband's career, and needs a fling.
Formula matrimonial comedy; plenty of talent but no sparkle.

w Z. Myers, *play* Samson Raphaelson *d* Mark Sandrich *ph* Charles Lang *m* Victor Young

Claudette Colbert, Ray Milland, Brian Aherne, Binnie Barnes, Walter Abel, Grant Mitchell, Mona Barrie, Ernest Cossart

Skyliner
US 1949 61m bw

The FBI nabs a spy on a transcontinental plane. Second feature chiefly interesting for its setting. Richard Travis, Pamela Blake, Rochelle Hudson, Steve Geray, Greg McClure. Written by Maurice Tombragel; directed by William Berke; for William Stephens / Lippert.

The Sky's the Limit
GB 1937 79m bw

A sacked aircraft designer suddenly finds himself in demand. Amiable star musical. Jack Buchanan, Mara Loseff, William Kendall, David Hutcheson, H. F. Maltby, Athene Seyler, Sara Allgood. Written by Jack Buchanan and Douglas Furber; directed by Lee Garmes and Jack Buchanan; for Jack Buchanan.

The Sky's the Limit*
US 1943 89m bw
RKO (David Hempstead)

A flier on leave meets and falls for a news photographer.
Thin musical with incidental compensations.

w Frank Fenton, Lynn Root *d* Edward H. Griffith *ph* Russell Metty *m* Leigh Harline *md* Leo F. Forbstein

Fred Astaire, Joan Leslie, *Robert Benchley*, Robert Ryan, Elizabeth Patterson

AAN: Leigh Harline; song 'My Shining Hour' (*m* Harold Arlen, *ly* Johnny Mercer)

Skyscraper Souls
US 1932 100m bw

In an office building, several personal dilemmas interlock. Portmanteau drama in the *Grand Hotel* mould, and quite comparable. Warren William, Maureen O'Sullivan, Verree Teasdale, Gregory, Ratoff, Jean Hersholt, Norman Foster, Anita Page, George Barbier, Wallace Ford, Hedda Hopper. Written by C. G. Sullivan and Elmer Harris, from the book by Faith Baldwin; directed by Edgar Selwyn; for MGM.

Slander
US 1956 81m bw
MGM (Armand Deutsch)

Revelations about a film star in a scandal

magazine lead to blackmail and murder.
Unlikely melodrama, routinely assembled, based on the Confidential Magazine lawsuits.

w Jerome Weidman *d* Roy Rowland *ph* Harold J. Marzerati *m* Jeff Alexander

Van Johnson, Ann Blyth, Steve Cochran, *Marjorie Rambeau*, Harold J. Stone

Slap Shot*
US 1977 124m Technicolor
Universal / Robert J. Wunsch, Stephen Friedman

The wily player-coach of a fading ice hockey team finds ways, including dirty play, of keeping it going.
Violent, foul-mouthed comedy which works as it goes but leaves a bad taste in the mouth.

w Nancy Dowd *d* George Roy Hill *ph* Victor Kemper, Wallace Worsley *md* Elmer Bernstein

Paul Newman, Michael Ontkean, Lindsay Crouse, Jennifer Warren, Strother Martin

'Fast, noisy, profane . . . gets you laughing, all right, but you don't necessarily enjoy yourself.'—*New Yorker*

'Both indulgent and moralizing, the self-consciously racy script ends up looking merely opportunistic.'—*Time Out*

Slattery's Hurricane
US 1949 87m bw
TCF (William Perlberg)

Loves of a storm-spotting pilot with the US Weather Bureau in Florida.
Forgettable programmer with good storm sequences.

w Herman Wouk, Richard Murphy, *novel* Herman Wouk *d* André de Toth *ph* Charles G. Clarke *m* Cyril Mockridge

Richard Widmark, Linda Darnell, Veronica Lake, John Russell, Gary Merrill, Walter Kingsford

Slaughter
US 1972 90m De Luxe Todd-AO 35
AIP / Slaughter United (Monroe Sachson)

A black Vietnam veteran hunts down the underworld syndicate which killed his mother and father.
Hectic crime yarn with a pitilessly violent hero and not enough style to relieve the unappetizing monotony.

w Mark Hanna, Don Williams *d* Jack Starrett *ph* Rosanio Solano *m* Luchi de Jesus

Jim Brown, Rip Torn, Don Gordon, Cameron Mitchell

'The cast perform their trigger-happy tasks with all the passionate conviction of a team of well-oiled robots.'—*Jan Dawson*

Slaughter on Tenth Avenue
US 1957 103m bw
U-I (Albert Zugsmith)

The New York DA's office investigates union murders on the docks.
Uninteresting imitation of *On the Waterfront.*

w Lawrence Roman, *novel* The Man Who Rocked the Boat by William J. Keating, Richard Carter *d* Arnold Laven *ph* Fred Jackman *m* Richard Rodgers

Richard Egan, Jan Sterling, Dan Duryea, Julie Adams, Walter Matthau, Charles McGraw, Sam Levene, Mickey Shaughnessy, Harry Bellaver

Slaughter Trail
US 1952 78m Cinecolor

Three outlaws cause trouble between white man and Indian. Rough-hewn western strung together by verses of a ballad. Brian Donlevy, Gig Young, Virginia Grey, Andy Devine, Robert Hutton. Written by Sid Kuller; directed by Irving Allen; for RKO.

Slaughterhouse Five*
US 1972 104m Technicolor
Universal / Vanadas (Paul Monash)

A suburban optometrist has nightmare space / time fantasies involving Nazi POW camps and a strange futuristic planet.
Interesting but infuriating anti-war fantasy for intellectuals.

w Stephen Geller, *novel* Kurt Vonnegut Jnr *d* George Roy Hill *ph* Miroslav Ondricek *m* J. S. Bach, performed by Glen Gould *pd Henry Bumstead*

Michael Sacks, Ron Leibman, Eugène Roche, Sharon Gans, Valerie Perrine, Sorrell Booke, John Dehner

'A lot of good makings in this picture; but very little is made.'—*Stanley Kauffmann*

Slaughter's Big Rip-Off
US 1973 93m Movielab Todd-AO 35
AIP (Monroe Sachson)

Still on the run from gangsters who have killed his best friend, Slaughter violently disposes of a number of adversaries.
More routine black violence, a rampage of senseless brutality against sunny Los Angeles backgrounds.

w Charles Johnson *d* Gordon Douglas *ph* Charles Wheeler *m* Jim Brown, Fred Wesley

Jim Brown, Ed MacMahon, Brock Peters, Don Stroud

Slave Girl
US 1947 79m Technicolor
U-I (Michael Fessier, Ernest Pagano)

In the early 1800s, a diplomat is sent to Tripoli to ransom sailors held by the power-mad potentate.
Criticism would be superfluous: when the film was finished it was obviously so bad that executives ordered the addition of a talking camel and other *Hellzapoppin*-type jokes in order to turn it into a comedy.

w Michael Fessier, Ernest Pagano *d* Charles Lamont *ph* George Robinson, W. Howard Greene *m* Milton Rosen

George Brent, Yvonne de Carlo, Albert Dekker, Broderick Crawford, Lois Collier, Andy Devine, Carl Esmond, Arthur Treacher

Slave Girls
GB 1966 95m Technicolor Cinemascope
Hammer (Aida Young)
US title: *Prehistoric Women*

A hunter seeking white rhinoceros finds himself in a lost valley ruled by a tribe of women.
Feebly preposterous comic strip farrago without the saving grace of humour.

wd Michael Carreras *ph* Michael Reed *m* Carlo Mantelli

Michael Latimer, Martine Beswick, Edina Ronay

Slave Ship**
US 1937 100m bw
TCF (Darryl F. Zanuck)

An American slave captain decides to become respectable but finds a mutiny on his hands.
Well-made adventure movie in the old tradition, a model of studio production.

w Sam Hellman, Lamar Trotti, Gladys Lehman, *story* William Faulkner, based on a novel by George S. King *d* Tay Garnett *ph* Ernest Palmer *m* Alfred Newman

Wallace Beery, Warner Baxter, Elizabeth Allen, Mickey Rooney, George Sanders, Jane Darwell, Joseph Schildkraut, Arthur Hohl, Minna Gombell, Billy Bevan, Francis Ford, Edwin Maxwell, J. Farrell MacDonald, Paul Hurst, Holmes Herbert

'Plenty of action and de luxe scenic trimmings . . . good box office blood and thunder.'—*Variety*

Slaves
US 1969 110m Eastmancolor
Slaves Company / Theatre Guild / Walter Reade (Philip Langner)

In 1850 Kentucky a slave stands up for his rights and plans escape.
Well-meaning but muddled and old-fashioned melodrama, hardly well enough done to raise comparison with *Gone with the Wind.*

wd Herbert J. Biberman *ph* Joseph Brun *m* Bobby Scott

Stephen Boyd, Ossie Davis, Dionne Warwick, Shepperd Strudwick, Nancy Coleman, David Huddleston, Gale Sondergaard

Slayground
GB 1983 89m Technicolor
EMI / Jennie and Co. (John Dark, Gower Frost)

A rich man hires an assassin to track down a criminal who accidentally killed his daughter.
One of those tedious and violent films in which the criminal wins out; slickness seems to make it worse.

w Trevor Preston, *novel* Richard Stark *d* Terry Bedford *ph* Stephen Smith, Herb Wagreich *m* Colin Towns *pd* Keith Wilson

Peter Coyote, Mel Smith, Billie Whitelaw, Philip Sayer, Bill Luhrs

'A disappointingly lame front runner for the new EMI stable.'—*Philip Strick, MFB*

Sleep My Love*
US 1948 96m bw
(UA) Mary Pickford (Charles 'Buddy' Rogers)

A man plots to murder his wife, but is foiled. Thin suspenser, rather splendidly photographed in the expressionist manner.

w St Clair McKelway, *novel* Leo Rosten *d Douglas Sirk ph Joseph Valentine m* Rudy Schrager

Claudette Colbert, Don Ameche, Robert Cummings, Rita Johnson, George Coulouris, Hazel Brooks, Keye Luke

'A love story about two people who hate each other!'

Sleeper*
US 1973 88m De Luxe
UA / Jack Rollins, Charles Joffe (Jack Grossberg)

A health food store owner is deep frozen after an operation and wakes two hundred years in the future.
Predictable star vehicle with an agreeable string of bright gags.

w Woody Allen, Marshall Brickman d Woody Allen *ph* David M. Walsh *m* Woody Allen *pd* Dale Hennesy

Woody Allen, Diane Keaton, John Beck, Mary Gregory

'Verbal and visual gags rain down like hailstones.'—*Michael Billington, Illustrated London News*

The Sleeping Beauty*
US 1959 75m Technirama 70
Walt Disney (Ken Peterson)

Rather stodgy, unwisely Cinemascoped feature cartoon of the old legend; very fashionable and detailed, but somehow lifeless.

d Clyde Geronomi *md* George Bruns *pd* Don da Gradi, Ken Anderson

AAN: George Bruns

Sleeping Car
GB 1933 82m bw

A woman on the run pretends to marry a sleeping car attendant, then finds they really are married. Artificial comedy with interesting cast from London stage. Madeleine Carroll, Ivor Novello, Laddie Cliff, Kay Hammond, Claud Allister, Stanley Holloway. Written by Franz Schultz; directed by Anatole Litvak; for Gaumont.

The Sleeping Car Murders*
France 1965 95m bw Cinemascope
PECF (Julien Derode)
original title: *Compartiment Tueurs*

When the overnight express from Marseilles reaches Paris, a girl is found dead in the sleeping car.
Rather long-winded whodunnit with an unlikely solution: a good pace helps, however, as do skilful borrowings from American police films of the forties.

wd Costa-Gavras, *novel* Sebastien Japrisot *ph* Jean Tournier *m* Michel Magne

Yves Montand, Simone Signoret, Pierre Mondy, Catherine Allégret, Jacques Pérrin, Jean-Louis Trintignant, Michel Piccoli

Sleeping Car to Trieste*
GB 1948 95m bw
GFD / Two Cities (George H. Brown)

Spy melodrama, a slow-starting but generally entertaining remake of *Rome Express* (qv).

w Allan Mackinnon *d* John Paddy Carstairs *ph* Jack Hildyard *m* Benjamin Frankel

Albert Lieven, Jean Kent, David Tomlinson, David Hutcheson, Rona Anderson, Paul Dupuis, Finlay Currie, *Alan Wheatley*, Derrick de Marney, Grégoire Aslan, Hugh Burden

The Sleeping Cardinal
GB 1931 84m bw

Sherlock Holmes exposes a smuggling ring. Slow-paced but interesting adaptation, vaguely based on *The Empty House*. Arthur Wontner, Ian Fleming, Norman McKinnel, Jane Welsh, Louis Goodrich. Written by Cyril Twyford and H. Fowler Mear, from stories by Sir Arthur Conan Doyle; directed by Leslie Hiscott; for Twickenham.

The Sleeping City**
US 1950 85m bw
U-I (Leonard Goldstein)

A policeman disguises himself as a medical student to learn more about a murder in a general hospital.
A location melodrama of modest excellence.

w Jo Eisinger d George Sherman ph William Miller m Frank Skinner

Richard Conte, Richard Taber, Coleen Gray, John Alexander, Peggy Dow, Alex Nicol

The Sleeping Tiger
GB 1954 89m bw
Anglo-Amalgamated / Insignia (Victor Hanbury)

A psychiatrist overpowers a criminal and takes him home as a guinea pig; the criminal then falls in love with the psychiatrist's wife.
Turgid and unconvincing melodrama, a thoroughgoing bore.

w Harold Buchman, Carl Foreman, *novel* Maurice Moiseiwitch *d* Joseph Losey *ph* Harry Waxman *m* Malcolm Arnold

Dirk Bogarde, Alexander Knox, Alexis Smith, Hugh Griffith, Maxine Audley, Glyn Houston, Billie Whitelaw

'There is a splendour about this film, which has one of the most absurdly extravagant plots on record, and never flinches from it.'—*Gavin Lambert*

The Slender Thread*
US 1966 98m bw
Paramount / Athene (Stephen Alexander)

A volunteer social worker tries to prevent a woman from committing suicide while police track her down from their phone conversations.
Acceptable star melodrama, curiously artificially styled.

w Stirling Silliphant *d Sydney Pollack ph* Loyal Griggs *m* Quincy Jones

Anne Bancroft, Sidney Poitier, Steven Hill, Telly Savalas

'Think of the crime . . . then go one step further . . . If it was murder, where's the body? If it was for a woman, which woman? If it's only a game, why the blood?'

Sleuth**
GB 1972 139m colour
Palomar (Morton Gottlieb)

A successful thriller writer invents a murder plot which rebounds on himself.
Well-acted version of a highly successful piece of stage trickery; despite hard work all round it seems much less clever and arresting on the screen, and the tricks do show.

w Anthony Shaffer, from his play *d* Joseph L. Mankiewicz *ph* Oswald Morris *m* John Addison

Laurence Olivier, Michael Caine

AAN: Joseph L. Mankiewicz; John Addison; Laurence Olivier; Michael Caine

A Slight Case of Larceny
US 1952 71m bw

Garage proprietors find a way of tapping their rivals' supply of petrol. Laboured comedy for two rather tiresome stars. Mickey Rooney, Eddie Bracken, Elaine Stewart, Marilyn Erskine, Douglas Fowley. Written by Jerry Davis; directed by Don Weis; for MGM.

A Slight Case of Murder***
US 1938 85m bw
Warner (Sam Bischoff)

When a beer baron tries to go legitimate his colleagues attempt to kill him, but end up shooting each other.
Amusing black farce, remade to less effect as *Stop, You're Killing Me* (qv).

w Earl Baldwin, Joseph Schrank, *play* Damon Runyon, Howard Lindsay *d Lloyd Bacon* *ph* Sid Hickox
m M. K. Jerome, Jack Scholl

Edward G. Robinson, Jane Bryan, Willard Parker, *Ruth Donnelly*, Allen Jenkins, John Litel, Harold Huber, Edward Brophy, Bobby Jordan

'Nothing funnier has been produced by Hollywood for a long time . . . a mirthful and hilarious whimsy.'—*Variety*

'The complications crazily mount, sentiment never raises its ugly head, a long nose is made at violence and death.'—*Graham Greene*

Slightly Dangerous
US 1943 94m bw

A small-town girl goes to New York and establishes herself by fraudulent impersonation; meanwhile a boy back home is suspected of being involved in her disappearance. Unsatisfactory comedy-drama. Lana Turner, Robert Young, Dame May Whitty, Walter Brennan, Eugene Pallette, Alan Mowbray, Florence Bates. Written by Charles Lederer, George Oppenheimer, Ian McLellan Hunter, Aileen Hamilton; directed by Wesley Ruggles; for Pandro S. Berman / MGM.

Slightly French
US 1948 81m bw

A film director in trouble passes off a Bowery-born carnival dancer as an exotic French star. Rather tedious comedy which lively performances can't sustain. Dorothy Lamour, Don Ameche, Janis Carter, Jeanne Manet, Willard Parker. Written by Karen de Wolf; directed by Douglas Sirk; for Columbia.

'Her heart belongs to daddy, and she calls everybody daddy!'

Slightly Honorable
US 1940 85m bw
(UA) Walter Wanger (Tay Garnett)

Lawyer partners set out to break a crime syndicate.
Fair crime thriller which can't decide whether it's comedy or drama.

w John Hunter Lay, Robert Tallman, Ken Englund, *novel* Send Another Coffin by F. G. Presnell *d* Tay Garnett *ph* Merritt Gerstad *m* Werner Janssen

Pat O'Brien, Broderick Crawford, Edward Arnold, Eve Arden, Claire Dodd, Ruth Terry, Bernard Nedell, Alan Dinehart, Douglass Dumbrille, Ernest Truex

'The story skips along without deftness between serious drama and comedy, and winds up in the aggregate as a whatisit.'—*Variety*

Slightly Scarlet
US 1930 72m bw

Two jewel thieves outwit a malicious mastermind. Somewhat effete comedy-drama in a long bygone style. Clive Brook, Evelyn Brent, Paul Lukas, Eugene Pallette, Helen Ware, Virginia Bruce, Henry Wadsworth, Claud Allister. Written by Howard Estabrook, Joseph L. Mankiewicz, Percy Heath; directed by Louis Gasnier, Edwin H. Knopf; for Paramount. 'Fair general programme feature.'—*Variety*

Slightly Scarlet
US 1956 92m Technicolor Superscope
(RKO) Benedict Bogeaus

The mayor's secretary loves the leader of a criminal gang.
Competent but uninteresting crime romance.

w Robert Blees, *novel* James A. Cain *d* Allan Dwan *ph* John Alton *m* Louis Forbes

Arlene Dahl, John Payne, Rhonda Fleming, Kent Taylor, Ted de Corsia

'So complicated that it is difficult to sort out which characters are supposed to be sympathetic.'—*MFB*

Slim
US 1937 85m bw

Electric linesmen argue about their work and their women. A reworking of *Tiger Shark* which itself later became *Manpower*; competent action stuff. Pat O'Brien, Margaret Lindsay, Henry Fonda, Stuart Erwin, J. Farrell MacDonald, Jane Wyman. Written by William Wister Haines; directed by Ray Enright; for Warner. 'A comedy drama which will do all right without setting off fireworks.'—*Variety*

Slim Carter
US 1957 82m Eastmancolor

A playboy is signed up by a Hollywood studio and required to change his image. Curious sentimental comedy which might have worked with stronger casting. Jock Mahoney, Julie Adams, Tim Hovey, William Hopper, Ben Johnson, Barbara Hale. Written by Montgomery Pitman; directed by Richard H. Bartlett; for Universal-International.

'You'll forget every love story you ever saw—or sang to!'

The Slipper and the Rose*
GB 1976 146m Technicolor Panavision
Paradine Co-Productions (David Frost, Stuart Lyons)

The story of Cinderella.
The elements are charming, but the treatment is fussy yet uninventive and the film is immensely overlong and lacking in magic and wit. Alas, not the renaissance of the family film that was hoped for.

w Bryan Forbes, Robert and Richard Sherman *d* Bryan Forbes *ph* Tony Imi *songs* Robert and Richard Sherman *pd Ray Simm*

Richard Chamberlain, Gemma Craven, Kenneth More, Michael Hordern, Edith Evans, Annette Crosbie, Margaret Lockwood, *Christopher Gable*, Julian Orchard, Lally Bowers, John Turner

'The tunes, I'm afraid, go in one ear and out the other; and, as Dr Johnson said of *Paradise Lost*, no man wished it a minute longer.'—*Michael Billington, Illustrated London News*

AAN: music; song, 'He Danced with Me'

Slither*
US 1972 96m Metrocolor
MGM / Talent Associates / Jack Sher

An ex-con, some gangsters, and a few mobile homes are involved in a chase across California for some hidden loot.
Wackily with-it comedy-thriller ranging from violence to slapstick, the former always undercut into the latter. Pretty funny, once you get the idea.

w W. D. Richter *d* Howard Zieff *ph* Laszlo Kovacs *m* Tom McIntosh

James Caan, Peter Boyle, Sally Kellerman, Louise Lasser

Slow Dancing in the Big City
US 1978 110m Technicolor
UA / CIP (Michael Levee, John G. Avildsen)

A New York newspaper columnist is affected by a dying eight-year-old drug addict and an ailing girl ballet dancer.
Warners in the thirties might have got away with this corn, but in 1978, played against a realistic backdrop, it seems merely silly and indigestible, its title as pretentious as its use of four-letter words.

w Barra Grant *d* John G. Avildsen *ph* Ralf D. Bode *m* Bill Conti

Paul Sorvino, Anne Ditchburn, Nicholas Coster, Anita Dangler

'The earnestness and shamelessness of the director are so awesome that if the picture fails as romance, it succeeds as camp.'—*New Yorker*

The Small Back Room**
GB 1949 106m bw
London Films / The Archers
US title: *Hour of Glory*

A bomb expert with a lame foot and a drink problem risks his life dismantling a booby bomb and returns to his long-suffering girl friend.
Rather gloomy suspense thriller with ineffective personal aspects but well-made location sequences and a fascinating background of boffins at work in post-war London.

wd Michael Powell, Emeric Pressburger, *novel* Nigel Balchin *ph Christopher Challis* *m* Brian Easdale

David Farrar, Kathleen Byron, Jack Hawkins, Leslie Banks, Robert Morley, Cyril Cusack

Small Change*
France 1976 105m Eastmancolor
Films du Carosse / Artistes Associés (Marcel Berbert, Roland Thenot)
original title: *L'Argent de Poche*

Linked incidents affecting a class of small boys in provincial France.
Competent if rather ordinary little portmanteau which one can't imagine adults actually paying to see.

w François Truffaut, Susan Schiffman *d* François Truffaut *ph* Pierre-William Glenn *m* Maurice Jaubert

Geory Desmouceaux, Philippe Goldman, Claudio Deluca

A Small Circle of Friends
US 1980 112m Technicolor

Adventures of Harvard men at the end of the sixties. Comedy, sex, politics and melodrama are all ploughed into this tiresome and predictable mixture. Brad Davis, Karen Allen, Jameson Parker, Shelley Long, John Friedrich. Written by Ezra Sacks; directed by Rob Cohen; for United Artists. 'Sacks' recreation of his college days relies on a mistaken belief that an audience will love his characters as much as they love each other.'—*John Pym, MFB.*

Small Town Girl*
US 1936 90m bw
MGM (Hunt Stromberg)

A girl traps a handsome stranger into offering marriage when he's drunk, then sets out to win him when he's sober.
Thin but adequate romantic comedy, a good example of MGM's production line of the mid-thirties, with established star and character players helping upcoming talents.

w John Lee Mahin, Edith Fitzgerald, *novel* Ben Ames Williams *d* William A. Wellman *ph* Oliver Marsh, Charles Rosher *m* Edward Ward

Janet Gaynor, Robert Taylor, James Stewart, Binnie Barnes, Frank Craven, Elizabeth Patterson, Lewis Stone, Andy Devine, Isabel Jewell, Charley Grapewin, Robert Greig, Agnes Ayres

Small Town Girl*
US 1953 93m Technicolor
MGM (Joe Pasternak)

Musical remake of the above.
Willing hands make the most of it, but the songs are not the best.

w Dorothy Cooper, Dorothy Kingsley *d* Leslie Kardos *ph* Joseph Ruttenberg *songs* Leo Robin, Nicholas Brodszky *md* André Previn *ch* Busby Berkeley

Jane Powell, Farley Granger, *Bobby Van,* Ann Miller, Robert Keith, Billie Burke, S. Z. Sakall, Fay Wray, Nat King Cole

AAN: song, 'My Flaming Heart'

A Small Town in Texas
US 1976 96m colour

An ex-convict returns to his hometown seeking revenge on those who framed him. Unpleasant shock thriller with much violence. Susan George, Timothy Bottoms, Bo Hopkins, Art Hindle. Written by William Norton; directed by Jack Starrett; for AIP.

The Small Voice*
GB 1948 83m bw
British Lion / Constellation (Anthony Havelock-Allan)
US title: *Hideout*

Escaped convicts hold up a playwright and his wife in their country cottage.
Gripping, well-characterized version of a very well worn plot.

w Derek Neame, Julian Orde, *novel* Robert Westerby *d* Fergus McDonell *ph* Stan Pavey

James Donald, Valerie Hobson, Howard Keel, David Greene, Michael Balfour, Joan Young

The Small World of Sammy Lee
GB 1962 107m bw
Bryanston / Seven Arts / Ken Hughes (Frank Godwin)

A small-time Soho crook tries desperately to raise money to pay off threatening bookies.
Overlong 'realist' comedy-melodrama based on a TV play and filled with low-life 'characters'; vivid but cursed with a tedious hero.

wd Ken Hughes, from his TV play *ph* Wolfgang Suschitsky *m* Kenny Graham *ad* Seamus Flannery

Anthony Newley, Julia Foster, Robert Stephens, Wilfrid Brambell, Warren Mitchell, Miriam Karlin, Kenneth J. Warren

The Smallest Show on Earth*
GB 1957 81m bw
British Lion / Launder and Gilliat (Michael Relph)
US title: *Big Time Operators*

Two young marrieds inherit a decayed cinema and make it pay.
Amiable caricature comedy with plenty of obvious jokes and a sentimental attachment to old cinemas but absolutely no conviction, little plot, and a very muddled sense of the line between farce and reality.

w William Rose, John Eldridge *d* Basil Dearden *ph* Douglas Slocombe *m* William Alwyn

Bill Travers, Virginia McKenna, Margaret Rutherford, Bernard Miles, Peter Sellers, Leslie Phillips, Francis de Wolff

Smart Blonde*
US 1936 57m bw

A female reporter beats the cops to the solution of a murder. Slick second feature, first in the Torchy Blane series. Glenda Farrell, Barton MacLane, Wini Shaw, Craig Reynolds, Addison Richards, Jane Wyman. Written by Don Ryan, Kenneth Gamet, Frederick Nebel; directed by Frank McDonald; for Warners. 'Fairly well paced with gunplay, an amount of smart talk, but no mountings to mention.'—*Variety*

Smart Girl
US 1935 78m bw

Girls left orphaned and penniless get their men—each other's. Very mild comedy. Ida Lupino, Kent Taylor, Gail Patrick, Joseph Cawthorn, Sidney Blackmer, Pinky Tomlin. Written by Frances Hyland, Wilson Collison; directed by Aubrey Scotto; for Walter Wanger / Paramount.

Smart Girls Don't Talk
US 1948 81m bw

A society girl rats on her gangster boy friend after her brother has been killed. Flatly handled underworld melodrama, as uninteresting as its cast. Virginia Mayo, Bruce Bennett, Robert Hutton, Richard Rober, Tom D'Andrea. Written by William Sackheim; directed by Richard Bare; for Warner.

'A fool in love! A sap for women!'
Smart Money
US 1931 67m bw
Warner

A gambler hits the big time but finally goes to jail.
Rather ordinary crime drama, a distinct letdown for its star after *Little Caesar.*

w Kubec Glasmon, John Bright, Lucien Hubbard, Joseph Jackson *d* Alfred E. Green *ph* Robert Kurrie

Edward G. Robinson, James Cagney, Evalyn Knapp, Ralf Harolde, Noel Francis, Margaret Livingstone, Boris Karloff, Billy House
'It will have no trouble upholding its title at the box office.'—*Variety*

† This film marks the only teaming of Robinson and Cagney.

AAN: script

Smart Woman
US 1948 93m bw
Monogram (Hal E. Chester)

A crafty lady lawyer becomes romantically involved with a crusading district attorney.
What to Monogram was a high-class production would have been a very routine programmer from anyone else.

w Alvah Bessie, Louise Morheim, Herbert Margolis *d* Edward A. Blatt *ph* Stanley Cortez *m* Louis Gruenberg *md* Constantin Bakaleinikoff

Constance Bennett, Brian Aherne, Barry Sullivan, Michael O'Shea, James Gleason, Otto Kruger, Isobel Elsom, Taylor Holmes, John Litel

Smash and Grab
GB 1937 76m bw

A detective's wife helps him track down a criminal mastermind. Agreeable star comedy. Jack Buchanan, Elsie Randolph, Arthur Margetson, Antony Holles, Zoe Wynn, Edmund Willard, David Burns. Written by Ralph Spence; directed by Tim Whelan; for Jack Buchanan / GFD. (US title: *Larceny Street.*)

Smash Palace*
New Zealand 1981 108m colour

The owner of a car-wrecking business goes to pieces when his wife leaves him. Downbeat character study of the kind of psychopath who doesn't arouse much sympathy; but the film is well mounted. Bruno Lawrence, Anna Jemison, Keith Aberdein, Greer Robson. Written and directed by Roger Donaldson; for Aardvark Films.

Smash-up, The Story of a Woman
US 1947 113m bw
Universal-International (Walter Wanger)
GB title: *A Woman Destroyed*

The story of a lady alcoholic.
Tedious distaff side of *The Lost Weekend.*

w John Howard Lawson *d* Stuart Heisler *ph* Stanley Cortez *m* Daniele Amfitheatrof

Susan Hayward, Lee Bowman, Eddie Albert, Marsha Hunt, Carl Esmond, Carleton Young, Charles D. Brown

AAN: original story (Dorothy Parker, Frank Cavett); Susan Hayward

Smashing the Money Ring
US 1939 57m bw

The Secret Service investigates gambling ships. Fast-moving serial-like action. Ronald Reagan, Eddie Foy Jnr, Margot Stevenson, Charles D. Brown. Written by Anthony Coldeway and Raymond Shrock; directed by Terry Morse; for Bryan Foy / First National / Warner.

Smashing Time
GB 1967 96m Eastmancolor
Paramount / Partisan / Carlo Ponti (Ray Millichip)

Two north country girls have farcical adventures in swinging London, including paint squirting and pie throwing.
Horrendous attempt to turn two unsuitable actresses into a female Laurel and Hardy; plenty of coarse vigour but no style or sympathy.

w George Melly *d* Desmond Davis *ph Manny Wynn* *m* John Addison

Rita Tushingham, Lynn Redgrave, Ian Carmichael, Anna Quayle, Michael York, Irene Handl, Jeremy Lloyd

Smile*
US 1975 113m De Luxe
UA (Michael Ritchie)

A bird's eye view of the Young Miss America pageant in a small California town.
A witty series of sketches in the form of a drama-documentary or satirical mosaic. Highly polished fun for those who can stay the course.

w Jerry Belson *d Michael Ritchie* *ph* Conrad Hall *m* various

Bruce Dern, Barbara Feldon, Michael Kidd, Geoffrey Lewis, Nicholas Pryor

'A beady, precise, technically skilful movie.'—*Michael Billington, Illustrated London News*

Smiles of a Summer Night**
Sweden 1955 105m bw
Svensk Filmindustri
original title: *Sommarnattens Leende*

A country lawyer meets again a touring actress who was once his mistress, and accepts an invitation for him and his young wife to stay at her mother's country home for a weekend.
Comedy of high period manners with an admirable detached viewpoint and elegant trappings. It later formed the basis of Stephen Sondheim's *A Little Night Music*, a stage musical which was later filmed.

wd Ingmar Bergman *ph* Gunnar Fischer *m* Erik Nordgren

Gunnar Bjornstrand, Eva Dahlbeck, Ulla Jacobsson, Harriet Andersson, Margit Carlquist, Naima Wifstrand, Jarl Kulle

Smiley*
GB 1956 97m Technicolor Cinemascope
TCF / London Films (Anthony Kimmins)

An adventurous Australian boy has various adventures and finally gets the bicycle he wants.
An open-air 'William'-type story for children, quite nicely made and generally refreshing. *Smiley Gets a Gun* was a less effective sequel.

w Moore Raymond, Anthony Kimmins from Raymond's novel *d* Anthony Kimmins *ph* Ted Scaife, Russ Wood *m* William Alwyn

Colin Petersen, Ralph Richardson, Chips Rafferty, John McCallum

Smiley Gets a Gun
Australia 1958 90m Technicolor CinemaScope

Smiley is promised a rifle if he can keep out of trouble. Unexceptional sequel. Keith Calvert, Bruce Archer, Sybil Thorndike, Chips Rafferty. Written by Anthony Kimmins, Rex Rienits; directed by Anthony Kimmins; for Canberra Films.

Smilin' Through*
US 1932 97m bw
MGM (Irving Thalberg)

Three generations of complications follow when a Victorian lady is accidentally killed by a jealous lover on her wedding day.
Archetypal sentimental romantic drama, wholly absorbing to the mass audience and extremely well done; originally a 1922 Norma Talmadge vehicle.

w Ernest Vajda, Claudine West, Donald Ogden Stewart, J. B. Fagan, *play* Jane Cowl, Jane Murfin *d* Sidney Franklin *ph Lee Garmes* *m* William Axt

Norma Shearer, Leslie Howard, Fredric March, O. P. Heggie, Ralph Forbes, Beryl Mercer

'A big women's picture of tear-drawing power, done with satisfying sincerity by a cast which spells money.'—*Variety*

'A sensitive and beautiful production distinguished by excellent settings and rich photography.'—*New York Mirror*

AAN: best picture

Smilin' Through*
US 1941 100m Technicolor
MGM (Victor Saville)

Flat but adequate remake of the above.

w Donald Ogden Stewart, John Balderston *d* Frank Borzage *ph* Leonard Smith *m* Herbert Stothart

Jeanette MacDonald, Gene Raymond, Brian Aherne, Ian Hunter, Frances Robinson, Patrick O'Moore

The Smiling Ghost
US 1941 71m bw

A girl reporter solves a haunted house mystery. Moderate comedy chiller with plenty going on. Alexis Smith, Wayne Morris, Brenda Marshall, Alan Hale, Willie Best, David Bruce, Helen Westley, Richard Ainley. Written by Kenneth Gamet; directed by Lewis Seiler; for Warner.

'His intimate and roguish romance will break your heart—with love and laughter!'

The Smiling Lieutenant**
US 1931 88m bw
Paramount (Ernst Lubitsch)

A Viennese guards officer leaves his mistress to become consort to a visiting princess.
A sophisticated soufflé in Lubitsch's best style, naughty but quite nice, with visual effects largely replacing dialogue.

w Ernest Vajda, Samson Raphaelson, *operetta* A Waltz Dream *d Ernst Lubitsch* *ph* George Folsey *m* Oscar Straus *md* Adolph Deutsch

Maurice Chevalier, Miriam Hopkins, Claudette Colbert, Charles Ruggles, George Barbier, Elizabeth Patterson

'Will delight smart audiences and figures to be liked well enough by the average fan. A good but not a smash picture.'—*Variety*

'All the shrewd delights that were promised in *The Love Parade* all realized with an economy and sureness that give it a luster which no other American-made comedy satire has achieved. One must look to *Le Million* to find its peer.'—*Richard Watts, New York Post*

AAN: best picture

Smokey and the Bandit*
US 1977 97m Technicolor
Universal / Rastar (Robert L. Levy)

A Georgia bootlegger on a mission picks up a girl in distress and is chased by her irate sheriff fiancé.
Frantic chase comedy full of car crashes and low lines: a surprise box office smash.

w James Lee Barrett, Charles Shyer, Alan Mandel *d* Hal Needham *ph* Bobby Byrne *m* Bill Justis, Jerry Reed, Art Feller

Burt Reynolds, Jackie Gleason, Sally Field, Jerry Reed, Mike Henry, Pat McCormick, Paul Williams

Smokey and the Bandit II
US 1980 101m Technicolor
Universal / Rastar / Mort Engelberg
GB title: *Smokey and the Bandit Ride Again*

A trucker is hired to take a pregnant elephant to the Republican convention.
More mindless chasing and crashing, with even less wit than before and rather more wholesale destruction.

w Jerry Belson, Brock Yates *d* Hal Needham *ph* Michael Butler *md* Snuff Garrett

Burt Reynolds, Jackie Gleason, Sally Field, Jerry Reed, Dom DeLuise, Paul Williams

Smokey and the Bandit III
US 1983 88m Technicolor

Sheriff Justice mistakes an innocent driver for his old enemy. A rather random car chase movie, obviously the last of a short line. Jackie Gleason, Jerry Reed, Mike Henry, Pat McCormick, Burt Reynolds (for a cameo). Written by Stuart Birnbaum, David Dashev;

directed by Dick Lowry; for Mort Engelberg / Universal. 'A patchwork of arbitrary mayhem.'—*Variety*

Smoky
US 1946 87m Technicolor
TCF (Robert Bassler)

An especially independent horse virtually runs the ranch on which he lives.
Family saga of the great outdoors, well enough assembled.

w Dwight Cummings, Lillie Hayward, Dorothy Yost, *novel* Will James *d* Louis King *ph* Charles Clarke *m* David Raksin *md* Emil Newman

Fred MacMurray, Anne Baxter, Burl Ives, Bruce Cabot, Esther Dale
† The story was also made by Fox in 1933 with Victor Jory, and in 1966 with Fess Parker.

Smooth as Silk
US 1946 64m bw

When his girl friend jilts him, a criminal lawyer plans to murder her new sweetheart.
Watchable supporting feature. Kent Taylor, Virginia Grey, Jane Adams, Milburn Stone, John Litel. Written by Dane Lussier and Kerry Shaw; directed by Charles Barton; for Jack Bernhard / Universal.

Smooth Talk
US 1985 92m colour

A mixed-up 15-year-old girl has a dangerous encounter with a mildly psychopathic male.
Unattractive scenario about thoroughly dislikeable people. Treat Williams, Laura Dern, Mary Kay Place, Levon Helm. Written by Tom Cole, from story by Joyce Carol Oates; directed by Joyce Chopra; for Nepenthe / American Playhouse / Goldcrest.

SNAFU
US 1945 85m bw
Columbia
GB title: *Welcome Home*

Middle-class parents rescue their difficult 15-year-old son from the army, then wish they hadn't.
Predictable, well-greased comedy of a rebellious teenager.

w Louis Solomon, Harold Buchman, from their play *d* Jack Moss *ph* Franz Planer *m* Paul Sawtell

Robert Benchley, Vera Vague, Conrad Janis, Nanetta Parks
† The title can be bowdlerized as 'Situation Normal, All Fouled Up'.

The Snake Pit**
US 1948 108m bw
TCF (Anatole Litvak, Robert Bassler)

A girl becomes mentally deranged and has horrifying experiences in an institution.
A headline-hitting film which made a stirring plea for more sympathetic treatment of mental illness. Very well made, and arrestingly acted, but somehow nobody's favourite movie.

w Frank Partos, Millen Brand, *novel* Mary Jane Ward *d Anatole Litvak* *ph* Leo Tover *m* Alfred Newman

Olivia de Havilland, Leo Genn, Mark Stevens, Celeste Holm, Glenn Langan, Leif Erickson, Beulah Bondi, Lee Patrick, Natalie Schaefer
'A film of superficial veracity that requires a bigger man than Litvak; a good film with bad things.'—*Herman G. Weinberg*

† The British censor insisted on a foreword explaining that everyone in the film was an actor and that conditions in British mental hospitals were unlike those depicted.

AAN: best picture; script; Anatole Litvak; Alfred Newman; Olivia de Havilland

The Sniper**
US 1952 87m bw
Columbia / Stanley Kramer (Edna and Edward Anhalt)

A psychopath kills a succession of blondes with a high-powered rifle.
Semi-documentary police drama which was quite startling and influential when released but seems quite routine now.

w Harry Brown *d Edward Dmytryk* *ph* Burnett Guffey *m* George Antheil

Adolphe Menjou, Arthur Franz, Gerald Mohr, Richard Kiley, Frank Faylen, Marie Windsor

AAN: original story (Edna and Edward Anhalt)

The Snorkel
GB 1958 80m bw
Columbia / Hammer (Michael Carreras)

A man murders his wife and is given away by his observant young stepdaughter.
Tenuous suspenser which outstays its welcome.

w Peter Myers, Jimmy Sangster, Anthony Dawson *d* Guy Green *ph* Jack Asher

Peter Van Eyck, Mandy Miller, William Franklyn, Grégoire Aslan

Snow Treasure
US 1968 95m Eastmancolor
Sagittarius (Irving Jacoby)

In Nazi-occupied Norway a teenage boy finds gold hidden in the snow; an underground agent helps him get it to safety.
Curiously undernourished but attractively made adventure film.

w Irving Jacoby, Peter Hansen, *novel* Marie McSwigan *d* Irving Jacoby *ph Sverre Bergli* *m* Egil Monn-Iversen

James Franciscus, Paul Anstad, Paoul Oyen, Randi Borch

Snow White and the Seven Dwarfs****
US 1937 82m Technicolor
Walt Disney

Disney's first feature cartoon, a mammoth enterprise which no one in the business thought would work. The romantic leads were wishy-washy but the splendid songs and the marvellous comic and villainous characters turned the film into a world-wide box office bombshell which is almost as fresh today as when it was made.

w Ted Sears, Otto Englander, Earl Hurd, Dorothy Ann Blank, Richard Creedon, Dick Richard, Merrill de Maris, Webb Smith, from the fairy tale by the brothers Grimm *supervising director David Hand* *m* Frank Churchill, Leigh Harline, Paul Smith *songs Larry Morey, Frank Churchill*
'The first full-length animated feature, the turning point in Disney's career, a milestone in film history, and a great film.'—*Leonard Maltin*
'Sustained fantasy, the animated cartoon grown up.'—*Otis Ferguson*

AAN: Frank Churchill, Leigh Harline, Paul Smith

Snow White and the Three Stooges*
US 1961 107m De Luxe Cinemascope
(TCF) Chanford (Charles Wick)
GB title: *Snow White and the Three Clowns*

The old story retold as a vehicle for a champion skater and three veteran clowns.
Surprisingly tolerable as a holiday attraction, once you get over the shock.

w Noel Langley, Elwood Ullman *d* Walter Lang *ph* Leon Shamroy *m* Lyn Murray *ad* Jack Martin Smith, Maurice Ransford

Carol Heiss, Moe Howard, Larry Fine, Joe de Rita, Edson Stroll, Patricia Medina, Guy Rolfe, Buddy Baer, Edgar Barrier

Snowball Express
US 1972 99m Technicolor
Walt Disney (Ron Miller)

An insurance accountant inherits a dilapidated skiing hotel in the Colorado Rockies.
Uninspired family comedy with slapstick on the snow slopes.

w Don Tait, Jim Parker, Arnold Margolin, *novel* Château Bon Vivant by Frankie and John O'Rear *d* Norman Tokar *ph* Frank Phillips *m* Robert F. Brunner

Dean Jones, Nancy Olson, Henry Morgan, Keenan Wynn, Mary Wickes, Johnny Whittaker
'As wholesome and bland as that old American favourite the peanut butter and jelly sandwich.'—*MFB*

Snowbound
GB 1948 87m bw
GFD / Gainsborough

Various people congregate at a ski hut in the Swiss Alps; all are after buried Nazi loot.
A rather foolish story which provides little in the way of action but at least assembles a fine crop of character actors.

w David Evans, Keith Campbell, *novel* The Lonely Skier by Hammond Innes *d* David MacDonald *ph* Stephen Dade

Robert Newton, Dennis Price, Herbert Lom, Stanley Holloway, Marcel Dalio, Mila Parely, Guy Middleton

'Out of one masterpiece, another has been created!'

The Snows of Kilimanjaro**
US 1952 117m Technicolor
TCF (Darryl F. Zanuck)

A hunter lies wounded in Africa and while waiting for help looks back over his life and loves.
Hollywood version of a portable Hemingway, with reminiscences of several novels stirred into a lush and sprawling mix of action and romance, open spaces and smart salons. A big popular star film of its time, despite constricted and unconvincing characters.

w Casey Robinson, *story* Ernest Hemingway *d Henry King* *ph* Leon Shamroy *m* Bernard Herrmann

Gregory Peck, Susan Hayward, Ava Gardner, Hildegard Neff, Leo G. Carroll, Torin Thatcher, Marcel Dalio

'A naïve kind of success story with a conventional boy-meets-lots-of-girls plot.'—*Karel Reisz*

'The succinct and vivid qualities associated with Hemingway are rarely evoked, and what has been substituted is for the most part meandering, pretentious and more or less maudlin romance.'—*Newsweek*

AAN: Leon Shamroy

So Big*
US 1932 80m bw
Warner (Lucien Hubbard)

A schoolteacher marries a farmer, has trouble with her son, falls in love with a sculptor.
Watchable, superficial, top-talented adaptation of a best-seller, first filmed in 1925 with Colleen Moore.

w J. Grubb Alexander, Robert Lord, *novel* Edna Ferber *d* William Wellman *ph* Sid Hickox *m* W. Franke Harling

Barbara Stanwyck, George Brent, Dickie Moore, Guy Kibbee, Bette Davis, Hardie Albright

'Too long getting started, and only has moments towards the end . . . somewhat of a bore for the major part of its footage.'—*Variety*

So Big
US 1953 101m bw
Warner (Henry Blanke)

By the time this inflated remake came along, the story was just too corny despite careful production.

w John Twist *d* Robert Wise *ph* Ellsworth Fredericks *m* Max Steiner

Jane Wyman, Sterling Hayden, Richard Beymer, Nancy Olson, Steve Forrest, Elizabeth Fraser, Martha Hyer

So Dark the Night*
US 1946 71m bw
Columbia

A detective tracks down a murderer whom he finds to be himself.
Smart second feature with a likeable leading performance.

w Aubrey Wisberg, Martin Berkeley, Dwight Babcock *d* Joseph H. Lewis *m* Hugo Friedhofer

Steven Geray, Ann Codee, Micheleine Cheirel

So Dear to My Heart*
US 1948 84m Technicolor
Walt Disney

Life on a country farm in 1903.
Live action nostalgia with a few cartoon segments; well enough done, but mainly appealing to well brought up children.

w John Tucker Battle, *novel* Midnight and Jeremiah by Sterling North *d* Harold Schuster *ph* Winton C. Hoch *m* Paul Smith

Burl Ives, Beulah Bondi, Harry Carey, Luana Patten, Bobby Driscoll

AAN: song 'Lavender Blue' (*m* Eliot Daniel, *ly* Larry Morey)

So Ends Our Night*
US 1941 120m bw
(UA) David L. Loew, Albert Lewin

Refugees from Nazi Germany are driven from country to country and meet persecution everywhere.
Worthy but rather drab and unfocused melodrama from the headlines.

w Talbot Jennings, *novel* Flotsam by Erich Maria Remarque *d* John Cromwell *ph* William Daniels *m* Louis Gruenberg

Fredric March, Margaret Sullavan, Glenn Ford, Frances Dee, Anna Sten, Erich Von Stroheim, Joseph Cawthorn, Leonid Kinskey, Alexander Granach, Sig Rumann

'It ought to be a great picture but it isn't.'—*Archer Winsten, New York Post*

AAN: Louis Gruenberg

So Evil My Love*
GB 1948 100m bw
Paramount (Hal B. Wallis)

A missionary's widow is enticed into a life of crime and immorality by a scoundrelly artist.
Curious Victorian melodrama with a Wildean flavour; doesn't quite come off.

w Leonard Spiegelgass, Ronald Miller, *novel* Joseph Shearing *d* Lewis Allen *ph* Max Greene *m* Victor Young, William Alwyn

Ray Milland, Ann Todd, Geraldine Fitzgerald, Leo G. Carroll, Raymond Huntley, Martita Hunt, Moira Lister, Raymond Lovell, Muriel Aked, Finlay Currie, Hugh Griffith

'There's only one thing that can keep them apart—the seven-foot thing she's married to!'

So Fine
US 1981 91m Technicolor
Warner / Lobell–Bergman (Mike Lobell)

A professor of literature trying to save his father from gangsters becomes involved in strange adventures.
Weirdly titled action comedy which tries to be far too clever for its own good.

wd Andrew Bergman *ph* James A. Contner *m* Ennio Morricone

Ryan O'Neal, Jack Warden, Mariangela Melato, Richard Kiel, Fred Gwynne, Mike Kellin

'A visual insult, crudely lighted and framed, and jumping out at you.'—*Pauline Kael, New Yorker*

So Goes My Love
US 1946 88m bw
(U-I) Jack H. Skirball / Bruce Manning
GB title: *A Genius in the Family*

The domestic life of inventor Hiram Maxim.
Formula period family film with pleasant moments.

w Bruce Manning, James Clifden *d* Frank Ryan *ph* Joseph Valentine *m* Hans Salter

Myrna Loy, Don Ameche, Rhys Williams, Bobby Driscoll, Richard Gaines

So Little Time
GB 1952 88m bw
ABP / Mayflower (Aubrey Baring, Maxwell Setton)

In occupied Belgium an aristocratic lady falls in love with a Nazi colonel.
Doomed love story with musical accompaniment; tolerable but slow.

w John Cresswell *d* Compton Bennett *ph* Oswald Morris *m* Robert Gill

Marius Goring, Maria Schell, Gabrielle Dorziat, Barbara Mullen

So Long at the Fair*
GB 1950 86m bw
Rank / Gainsborough / Sydney Box (Betty E. Box)

During the 1889 Paris Exposition a girl books into a hotel with her brother, and next day finds that he has totally disappeared and his existence is denied by all concerned.
Straightforward version of an old yarn which has turned up in such varied forms as *The Lady Vanishes* and *Bunny Lake is Missing*. This modest production is pleasant enough but badly lacks drive.

w Hugh Mills, Anthony Thorne *d* Terence Fisher, Anthony Darnborough *ph* Reginald Wyer *m* Benjamin Frankel *ad* Cedric Dawe

Jean Simmons, Dirk Bogarde, David Tomlinson, Marcel Poncin, Cathleen Nesbitt, Honor Blackman, Betty Warren, Felix Aylmer, André Morell

'A foxhole was her honeymoon hotel!'
'The first great story of our women at the fighting front!'

So Proudly We Hail*
US 1943 125m bw
Paramount (Mark Sandrich)

The self-sacrifice of war nurses in the Pacific.
Fairly harrowing and well-meant but studio-bound and unconvincing flagwaver.

w Allan Scott *d* Mark Sandrich *ph* Charles Lang *m* Miklos Rozsa

Claudette Colbert, Paulette Goddard, Veronica Lake, George Reeves, Barbara Britton, Walter Abel, Sonny Tufts, John Litel

'Probably the most deadly accurate picture ever made of what war looks like through the lenses of a housewives' magazine romance.'—*James Agee*

'The stars are devotedly, almost gallantly, deglamorized and dishevelled but they cannot escape the smell of studio varnish.'—*Richard Winnington*

AAN: Allan Scott; Charles Lang; Paulette Goddard

'The flower of southern chivalry dewed with the shining glory of a woman's tears!'

So Red the Rose*
US 1935 82m bw
Paramount (Douglas MacLean)

The life of a southern family during the Civil War.
Quiet, pleasing historical romance.

w Laurence Stallings, Maxwell Anderson, Edwin Justus Mayer, *novel* Stark Young *d* King Vidor *ph* Victor Milner *m* W. Franke Harling

Margaret Sullavan, Randolph Scott, Walter Connolly, Elizabeth Patterson, Janet Beecher, Robert Cummings

'Certain to go better in the Dixie belt than north, but okay on average.'—*Variety*

So This Is London
GB 1939 89m bw

An American magnate visits his English rival, and romance springs up between their children. Brightish comedy with a fair scattering of funny lines. Robertson Hare, Alfred Drayton, George Sanders, Berton Churchill, Fay Compton, Carla Lehmann, Stewart Granger, Ethel Revnell, Gracie West. Written by William Conselman, Ben Travers, Tom Phipps and Douglas Furber; directed by Thornton Freeland; for TCF.

So This Is Love
US 1953 101m Technicolor
Warner (Henry Blanke)
GB title: *The Grace Moore Story*

Events leading up to Grace Moore's debut at the Metropolitan Opera in 1928.
Acceptable musical biopic full of the usual Hollywood contrivances.

w John Monks Jnr, from Grace Moore's autobiography *d* Gordon Douglas *ph* Robert Burks *md* Ray Heindorf, Max Steiner *ch* Le Roy Prinz *ad* Edward Carrere

Kathryn Grayson, Merv Griffin, Joan Weldon, Walter Abel, Rosemary de Camp, Jeff Donnell, Douglas Dick, Mabel Albertson, Fortunio Bonanova

So This Is New York*
US 1948 78m bw
Stanley Kramer / Enterprise

In 1919 some country cousins who have come into money have a big time in the gay city.
Curious, sporadically effective, silent-style comedy which doesn't quite come off.

w Carl Foreman, Herbert Baker, *novel* The Big Town by Ring Lardner *d* Richard Fleischer *ph* Jack Russell *m* Dmitri Tiomkin

Henry Morgan, Rudy Vallee, Hugh Herbert, Bill Goodwin, Virginia Grey, Dona Drake, Leo Gorcey

So This Is Paris
US 1955 96m Technicolor
U-I (Albert J. Cohen)

Three American sailors on leave in Paris meet girls and help war orphans.
Very thin imitation of *On the Town*, bogged down by sentimentality and lack of sparkle. The musical numbers, however, are not bad.

w Charles Hoffman *d* Richard Quine *ph* Maury Gertsman *md* Joseph Gershenson *ch* Gene Nelson, Lee Scott

Tony Curtis, Gloria de Haven, Gene Nelson, *Corinne Calvet*, Paul Gilbert, Mara Corday, Allison Hayes

So Well Remembered*
GB 1947 114m bw
(RKO) Alliance (Adrian Scott)

The ambitious daughter of a mill-owner marries a rising politician but almost ruins his life.
Rather routine treatment of a three-decker north country novel; humdrum incident and unsympathetic characters, but full of minor British virtues.

w John Paxton, *novel* James Hilton *d* Edward Dmytryk *ph* Frederick A. Young

John Mills, Martha Scott, Trevor Howard, Patricia Roc, Richard Carlson

Soak the Rich*
US 1935 74m bw
Paramount (Ben Hecht, Charles MacArthur)

A rebellious rich girl is cured when she is rescued from kidnapping.
Smartly written social comedy-melodrama.

wd Ben Hecht, Charles MacArthur *ph* Leon Shamroy

Walter Connolly, John Howard, Mary Taylor, Lionel Stander, Ilka Chase

'Hecht and MacArthur have not been very successful in their attempts to gauge public opinion . . . inadequate entertainment.'—*Variety*

Social Register
US 1934 71m bw

A chorus girl fights the prejudices of her in-laws to be. Dull and obvious romantic drama mainly notable for its cast, and for the star who failed to make a comeback. Colleen Moore, Charles Winninger, Pauline Frederick, Alexander Kirkland, Robert Benchley, Ross Alexander. Written by Clara Beranger, Anita Loos, John Emerson; directed by Marshall Neilan; for William de Mille / Columbia. 'Good players lost in a trite story.'—*Variety*

Society Doctor
US 1935 63m bw
MGM (Lucien Hubbard)
GB title: *After Eight Hours*

A doctor's modern ideas incur hostility: he goes into private practice, but returning to the hospital is wounded by a gangster and supervises his own operation under spinal anaesthetic.
Melodramatic hokum with most attention going to the second male lead, the young and rising Robert Taylor.

w Sam Marx, Michael Fessier, *novel* The Harbor by Theodore Reeves *d* George B. Seitz *ph* Lester White *m* Oscar Radin

Chester Morris, Virginia Bruce, Robert Taylor, Billie Burke, Raymond Walburn, Henry Kolker, William Henry

Society Girl
US 1932 72m bw

A prizefighter falls for a society girl. Weak melodrama whose best scenes are in the ring. James Dunn, Spencer Tracy, Peggy Shannon, Walter Byron, Marjorie Gateson. Written by Charles Benhan, Elmer Harris, from the play by John Larkin Jnr; directed by Sidney Lanfield; for Fox. 'Falls short of first-rate classification.'—*Variety*

Society Lawyer
US 1939 77m bw

A lawyer is embarrassed by the gratitude of a racketeer. Tolerable co-feature with class production. Walter Pidgeon, Virginia Bruce, Leo Carrillo, Eduardo Ciannelli, Lee Bowman, Herbert Mundin. Written by Frances Goodrich, Albert Hackett, Leon Gordon, Hugo Butler; directed by Edwin L. Marin; for John W. Considine Jnr / MGM. 'Fairish murder mystery with sophisticated background. For duals.'—*Variety*

Sodom and Gomorrah
Italy / France 1962 154m colour
Titanus / S. N. Pathe (Gottfredo Lombardo)

Lot and the Hebrews become involved in a Helamite plan to take over the rich sinful cities of Sodom and Gomorrah.
Dreary biblical blood-and-thunder; an international muddle, tedious in the extreme outside a few hilariously misjudged moments.

w Hugo Butler, Giorgio Prosperi *d* Robert Aldrich *ph* Silvano Ippoliti, Cyril Knowles *m* Miklos Rozsa *ad* Ken Adam

Stewart Granger, Stanley Baker, Pier Angeli, Anouk Aimée, Rossana Podesta

Soft Beds, Hard Battles
GB 1973 107m colour
Rank / Charter (John Boulting)
US title: *Undercovers Hero*

Inhabitants of a Paris brothel help to win World War II.
Ragbag of poor sketches and dirty jokes, with the star in several ineffective roles including Hitler.

w Leo Marks, Roy Boulting *d* Roy Boulting *ph* Gil Taylor *m* Neil Rhoden

Peter Sellers, Lila Kedrova, Curt Jurgens, Gabriella Licudi, Jenny Hanley

Sol Madrid
US 1968 90m Metrocolor Panavision
MGM / Gershwin–Kastner (Hall Bartlett)
GB title: *The Heroin Gang*

An undercover narcotics agent is assigned to track down an elusive Mafia executive.
Humdrum, predictable, brutishly violent international crime caper.

w David Karp, *novel* Fruit of the Poppy by Robert Wilder *d* Brian G. Hutton *ph* Fred Koenekamp *m* Lalo Schifrin

David McCallum, Telly Savalas, Stella Stevens, Ricardo Montalban, Rip Torn, Pat Hingle, Paul Lukas, Perry Lopez, Michael Ansara.

Solaris**
USSR 1972 165m Sovcolor 'Scope
Mosfilm

A psychologist is sent to investigate the many deaths in a space station orbiting a remote planet.
Heavy-going but highly imaginative space fiction in which the menaces are ghosts materialized from the subjects' guilty pasts. The technology is superbly managed, but the whole thing is rather humourless.

w Andrei Tarkovsky, Friedrich Gorenstein, *novel* Stanislaw Lem *d* Andrei Tarkovsky *ph* Vadim Yusov *m* Eduard Artemyev

Natalya Bondarchuk, Donatas Banionis, Yuri Yarvet

The Soldier and the Lady*
US 1937 85m bw
RKO (Pandro S. Berman)
GB title: *Michael Strogoff*

In Napoleonic times, a messenger from the Czar sees more trouble than he expected.
Mildly ambitious swashbuckler from a story much remade in Europe; the elements jelled quite well in the Hollywood fashion.

w Mortimer Offner, Anthony Veiller and Anne Morrison Chapin from the novel by Jules Verne *d* George Nicholls Jnr *ph* Joseph H. August

Anton Walbrook, Elizabeth Allan, Akim Tamiroff

'Spectacle film lacking strength and names. Will have its troubles.'—*Variety*

† Exteriors were taken from a German / French film of 1936, *Courier to the Star*

'Stained with the blood of the innocent!'
Soldier Blue*
US 1970 114m Technicolor Panavision
Avco (Gabriel Katzka, Harold Loeb)

A paymaster's detachment of the US cavalry is attacked by Indians seeking gold, and two white survivors trek through the desert.
Extremely violent 'anti-violence' western with a particularly nauseating climax following clichés all the way. From a director with pretensions.

w John Gay, *novel* Arrow in the Sun by Theodore V. Olsen *d* Ralph Nelson *ph* Robert Hauser *m* Roy Budd

Candice Bergen, Peter Strauss, Donald Pleasence

'One is more likely to be sickened by the film itself than by the wrongs it tries to right.'—*Tom Milne*

Soldier in the Rain
US 1963 87m bw
AA / Cedar / Solar (Martin Jurow)

Two army sergeants have wild plans for their demob, but one dies.
Curious sentimental tragi-comedy which misfires on all cylinders.

w Blake Edwards, Maurice Richlin, *novel* William Goldman *d* Ralph Nelson *ph* Philip Lathrop *m* Henry Mancini

Steve McQueen, Jackie Gleason, Tuesday Weld, Tony Bill, Tom Poston, Ed Nelson, John Hubbard

Soldier of Fortune*
US 1955 96m De Luxe Cinemascope
TCF (Buddy Adler)

When a photographer disappears in Red China, his wife comes to Hong Kong to institute a search, enlists the aid of an amiable smuggler.
Cheerful Boys' Own Paper adventure romance with attractive locations and some silly anti-Red dialogue.

w Ernest K. Gann, from his novel *d* Edward Dmytryk *ph* Leo Tover *m* Hugo Friedhofer

Clark Gable, Susan Hayward, Gene Barry, Alex D'Arcy, Michael Rennie, Tom Tully, Anna Sten, Russell Collins, Leo Gordon

'A very good adventure film but not one of the Gable smashes.'—*Hollywood Reporter*

Soldiers of the King
GB 1933 80m bw

A guards lieutenant causes trouble when he wants to marry a music hall star. Sprightly star vehicle with all talents in good form. Cicely Courtneidge, Edward Everett Horton, Anthony Bushell, Frank Cellier, Dorothy Hyson, Leslie Sarony. Written by J. O. C. Orton, Jack Hulbert and W. P. Lipscomb; directed by Maurice Elvey; for Gainsborough.

A Soldier's Story*
US 1984 101m Metrocolor
Columbia / Delphi (Norman Jewison, Patrick Palmer)

In 1944 Louisiana, a hated sergeant at a small army post is shot dead.
Investigative melodrama on the old lines of *Boomerang*; quite watchable and well acted.

w Charles Fuller, from his play *d* Norman Jewison *ph* Russell Boyd *m* Herbie Hancock

Howard E. Rollins Jnr, Adolph Caesar, Art Evans, David Alan Grier, David Harris, Denzel Washington

AAN: best picture; Adolph Caesar (supporting actor); adapted screenplay

Soldiers Three
US 1951 87m bw
MGM (Pandro S. Berman)

Adventures of three roistering British officers on the North-West Frontier.
A kind of unofficial remake of *Gunga Din* without the title character; one suspects it was meant seriously and found to be so bad that the only way out was strenuously to play it for laughs.

w Marguerite Roberts, Tom Reed, Malcolm Stuart Boylan *d* Tay Garnett *ph* William Mellor *m* Adolph Deutsch

Stewart Granger, David Niven, Robert Newton, Walter Pidgeon, Cyril Cusack, Greta Gynt, Frank Allenby, Robert Coote, Dan O'Herlihy

'Kipling fans will probably have a fit but my guess is that it will have most people in fits of laughter.'—*Daily Mail*

The Solid Gold Cadillac**
US 1956 99m bw
Columbia (Fred Kohlmar)

A very minor stockholder upsets the crooked board of a large corporation.
Vaguely Capraesque comedy which begins brightly but peters out; performances sustain passing interest.

w Abe Burrows, *play* George S. Kaufman, Howard Teichmann *d* Richard Quine *ph* Charles Lang *m* Cyril Mockridge

Judy Holliday, Paul Douglas, *John Williams*, *Fred Clark*, Hiram Sherman, Neva Patterson, Ralph Dumke, Ray Collins, Arthur O'Connell

The Solitaire Man*
US 1933 68m bw

Crooks doublecross each other on a Paris–London aeroplane. Smart little comedy with top talent. Herbert Marshall, Elizabeth Allan, Mary Boland, Lionel Atwill, May Robson, Ralph Forbes. Written by James Kevin McGuinness, from the play by Bella and Samuel Spewack; directed by Jack Conway; for MGM. 'Diverting crook melodrama in the drawing room manner . . . a lot better than the grosses it will probably get.'—*Variety*

'Only once in 3000 years—anything like it!'
Solomon and Sheba
US 1959 142m Super Technirama 70
UA / Edward Small (Ted Richmond)

When David names his younger son as heir, his older son plots revenge.
Dullish biblical spectacle, alternating between pretentiousness and cowboys and Indians.

w Anthony Veiller, Paul Dudley, George Bruce *d* King Vidor *ph* Frederick A. Young *m* Mario Nascimbene *ad* Richard Day, Alfred Sweeney

Yul Brynner, Gina Lollobrigida, George Sanders, Marisa Pavan, David Farrar, John Crawford, Laurence Naismith, Alejandro Rey, Harry Andrews

'Penance is due.'—*Hollis Alpert*

'Watch out it doesn't put you to sleep.'—*New York Times*

SOLARIS. Intellectual science fiction: Natalya Bondarchuk models the Soviet idea of what the well-dressed spacewoman should be wearing.

Sombrero
US 1953 103m Technicolor
MGM (Jack Cummings)

Two Mexican villages feud over the burial place of a famous poet.
Rather self-consciously unusual musical which never catches fire but certainly keeps one watching its incredible mixture of music and melodrama.

w Norman Foster, Josefina Niggli, from her novel A Mexican Village *d* Norman Foster *ph* Ray June *m* Leo Arnaud

Ricardo Montalban, Pier Angeli, Yvonne de Carlo, Nina Foch, Cyd Charisse, Rick Jason, Jose Greco, Thomas Gomez, Kurt Kasznar, Walter Hampden, John Abbott

'Staggering is the only word for the hokum of this extraordinary film.'—*Gavin Lambert*

Some Call It Loving
US 1973 103m Technicolor
Pleasant Pastures / James B. Harris

A young man buys a 'sleeping beauty' at a fair but is sorry when he wakes her up.
Fashionable fantasy, amplified from a slender, winning short story.

wd James B. Harris, *story* Sleeping Beauty by John Collier *ph* Mario Tosi *m* Richard Hazard

Zalman King, Carol White, Tisa Farrow, Richard Pryor, Veronica Anderson

Some Came Running
US 1959 136m Metrocolor Cinemascope
MGM / Sol C. Siegel

A disillusioned writer returns after service to his home town and takes up with a gambler and a prostitute.
Strident and rather pointless melodrama with solid acting and production values.

w John Patrick, Arthur Sheekman, *novel* James Jones *d* Vincente Minnelli *ph* William H. Daniels *m* Elmer Bernstein

Frank Sinatra, Dean Martin, Shirley Maclaine, Martha Hyer, Arthur Kennedy, Nancy Gates, Leora Dana

AAN: song 'To Love and Be Loved' (*m* James Van Heusen, *ly* Sammy Cahn); Shirley Maclaine; Martha Hyer; Arthur Kennedy

Some Girls Do
GB 1969 93m Eastmancolor
Rank / Ashdown (Betty E. Box)

Bulldog Drummond traces the sabotage of a supersonic airliner to a gang of murderous women.
Abysmal spoof melodrama in the swinging sixties mould; a travesty of a famous character.

w David Osborn, Liz Charles-Williams *d* Ralph Thomas *ph* Ernest Steward *m* Charles Blackwell

Richard Johnson, Daliah Lavi, Bebi Loncar, James Villiers, Sydne Rome, Robert Morley, Maurice Denham, Florence Desmond, Ronnie Stevens

Some Kind of a Nut
US 1969 89m De Luxe
UA / Mirisch / TFT / DFI (Walter Mirisch)

When a bank teller grows a beard because of an unsightly bee sting, he is thought to be flouting authority and his whole life changes.
Laboured, cliché-ridden anti-establishment comedy, a waste of the talent involved.

wd Garson Kanin *ph* Burnett Guffey, Gerald Hirschfeld *m* Johnny Mandel

Dick Van Dyke, Angie Dickinson, Rosemary Forsyth, Zohra Lampert, Elliot Reid, Dennis King

Some Kind of Hero
US 1981 97m Movielab
Paramount (Howard W. Koch)

After six years as a prisoner of the Vietcong, an army veteran returns home to find his life no bed of roses.
Weird mixture of comedy and melodrama which simply doesn't jell, especially when it tries to get earnest.

d James Kirkwood, Robert Boris, *novel* James Kirkwood *d* Michael Pressman *ph* King Battot *m* Patrick Williams

Richard Pryor, Margot Kidder, Ray Sharkey, Ronny Cox, Lynne Moody, Olivia Cole

'The killer-diller of all swing shows!'

Some Like It Hot
US 1939 65m bw
Paramount (William C. Thomas)
TV reissue title: *Rhythm Romance*

A sideshow owner runs out of money.
Very mild comedy, one of several which helped to establish Hope's star potential.

w Lewis R. Foster, *play* Wilkie C. Mahoney, Ben Hecht, Gene Fowler *d* George Archainbaud *ph* Karl Struss

Bob Hope, Shirley Ross, Una Merkel, Gene Krupa, Richard Denning

'Turned out deliberately to catch the jitterbug devotees . . . will satisfy moderately.'—*Variety*

† The play, *The Great Magoo*, was previously filmed in 1934 as *Shoot the Works*.

Some Like It Hot***
US 1959 122m bw
UA / Mirisch (Billy Wilder)

Two unemployed musicians accidentally witness the St Valentine's Day Massacre and flee to Miami disguised as girl musicians.
Overstretched but sporadically very funny comedy which constantly flogs its central idea to death and then recovers with a smart line or situation. It has in any case become a milestone of film comedy.

w Billy Wilder, I. A. L. Diamond d Billy Wilder ph Charles Lang Jnr *m* Adolph Deutsch

Jack Lemmon, Tony Curtis, Marilyn Monroe, Joe E. Brown, George Raft, Pat O'Brien, Nehemiah Persoff, George E. Stone, Joan Shawlee

'Hectic slapstick, smartass movie pardies, sexist stereotyping, crass one-liners, and bad taste galore.'—*Time Out, 1984*

AAN: script; Billy Wilder (as director); Charles Lang Jnr; Jack Lemmon

Some People
GB 1962 93m Eastmancolor
Vic Films (James Archibald)

Troublesome teenage factory workers are helped by a church organist and become model citizens.
Bland propaganda for the Duke of Edinburgh's Award scheme for young people, quite acceptably presented, with pop music ad lib.

w John Eldridge *d* Clive Donner *ph* John Wilcox *m* Ron Grainer

Kenneth More, Ray Brooks, Annika Wells, David Andrews, Angela Douglas, David Hemmings, Harry H. Corbett

Some Will, Some Won't
GB 1969 90m Technicolor
ABP / Transocean (Giulio Zampi)

In order to inherit under an eccentric will, four people have to perform tasks out of character.
Thin remake of *Laughter in Paradise* (qv); funny moments extremely few.

w Lew Schwarz *d* Duncan Wood *ph* Harry Waxman *m* Howard Blake

Ronnie Corbett, Thora Hird, Michael Hordern, Leslie Phillips, Barbara Murray, James Robertson Justice, Dennis Price, Wilfrid Brambell, Eleanor Summerfield, Arthur Lowe

Somebody Killed Her Husband
US 1978 96m Movielab
Columbia / Melvin Simon (Martin Poll)

The title tells what happened when an unhappily married young mother falls in love.
Very thin suspense comedy which starts as it ends, uncertainly.

w Reginald Rose *d* Lamont Johnson *ph* Andrew Laszlo, Ralf D. Bode *m* Alex North *ph* Ted Haworth

Farrah Fawcett-Majors, Jeff Bridges, John Wood, Tammy Grimes, John Glover, Patricia Elliott

Somebody Loves Me
US 1952 97m Technicolor
Paramount / Perlberg–Seaton

First successful in San Francisco at earthquake time, Blossom Seeley climbs to Broadway success with her partner Benny Fields, then retires to become his wife.
Adequate, unsurprising star musical of the second or third rank.

wd Irving Brecher *ph* George Barnes *songs* Jay Livingston, Ray Evans

Betty Hutton, Ralph Meeker, Robert Keith, Adele Jergens, Billie Bird, Sid Tomack, Ludwig Stossel

Somebody Up There Likes Me*
US 1956 112m bw
MGM (Charles Schnee)

An East Side kid with reform school experience becomes middleweight boxing champion of the world.
A sentimental fantasia on the life of Rocky Graziano, expertly blending violence, depression, prizefight sequences and fake uplift.

w Ernest Lehman *d* Robert Wise *ph* Joseph Ruttenberg *m* Bronislau Kaper

Paul Newman, Pier Angeli, Everett Sloane, Eileen Heckart, Sal Mineo, Joseph Buloff, Harold J. Stone, Robert Loggia

AA: Joseph Ruttenberg

Someone at the Door
GB 1936 74m bw

The new owner of a spooky house invents a murder which seems to come true. Derivative but quite amusing comedy thriller. Billy Milton, Aileen Marson, Noah Beery, Edward Chapman, Hermione Gingold, John Irwin. Written by Jack Davies and Marjorie Deans, from the play by Dorothy and Campbell Christie; directed by Herbert Brenon; for BIP. (NB: Remade in 1950 with Michael Medwin, Yvonne Owen and Garry Marsh; directed by Francis Searle; for Hammer.)

Someone behind the Door
France 1971 97m colour

A brain surgeon takes a psychopathic patient home and tries to make him commit murder. Adequate but somehow unexciting suspenser. Charles Bronson, Anthony Perkins, Jill Ireland. Written by Mark Boehm and Jacques Robert; directed by Nicolas Gessner; for Lira Film. (Aka: *Two Minds for Murder*.)

Someone to Watch Over Me*
US 1987 106m De Luxe
Columbia / Thierry de Ganay

A New York cop falls for the witness he must protect from a vicious killer.
Lively thriller with slick technicalities.

w Howard Franklin *d Ridley Scott ph* Steven Poster *m* Michael Kamen *pd* Jim Bissell

Tom Berenger, Mimi Rogers, Lorraine Bracco, Jerry Orbach, John Rubinstein, Andreas Katsulas

'Stylish and romantic . . . manages to triumph over several hard-to-swallow plot developments.'—*Daily Variety*

Something Big
US 1971 108m Technicolor
Cinema Center / Stanmore and Penbar (Andrew V. McLaglen)

A retiring cavalry colonel has a last battle with his old enemy.
Wry serio-comic western in the Ford tradition.

w James Lee Barrett *d* Andrew V. McLaglen *ph* Harry Stradling Jnr *m* Marvin Hamlisch

Dean Martin, Brian Keith, Honor Blackman, Carol White, Ben Johnson, Albert Salmi, Denver Pyle

Something for Everyone*
US 1970 110m colour
National General (John Flaxman)
GB title: *Black Flowers for the Bride*

A young con man insinuates himself into the household of a widowed Austrian countess.
Unusual black comedy which doesn't quite come off.

w Hugh Wheeler, *novel* The Cook by Harry Kressing *d* Harold Prince *ph* Walter Lassally *m* John Kander

Angela Lansbury, Michael York, Anthony Corlan, Heidelinde Weis

'Nothing much for anyone, actually.'—*New Yorker*

Something for the Birds
US 1952 81m bw
TCF (Samuel G. Engel)

An elderly fraud is of help to a Washington girl trying to save a bird sanctuary.
Derivative, competent but slightly boring political whimsy on Capra lines.

w I. A. L. Diamond, Boris Ingster *d* Robert Wise *ph* Joseph La Shelle *m* Sol Kaplan

Edmund Gwenn, Victor Mature, Patricia Neal, Larry Keating, Christian Rub

Something for the Boys
US 1944 87m Technicolor
TCF (Irving Starr)

A southern plantation is turned into a retreat for army wives.
Modest musical, vaguely based on a Broadway success.

w Robert Ellis, Helen Logan, Frank Gabrielson, *musical comedy* Cole Porter, Herbert and Dorothy Fields *d* Lewis Seiler *ph* Ernest Palmer *title song* Cole Porter *other songs* Harold Adamson, Jimmy McHugh *m* Cyril Mockridge

Carmen Miranda, Michael O'Shea, Vivian Blaine, Phil Silvers, Sheila Ryan, Perry Como, Glenn Langan, Cara Williams

Something in the Wind
US 1947 89m bw
U-I (Joseph Sistrom)

A lady disc jockey is mistaken for her aunt, who has been seeing too much for the heirs' liking of a wealthy old man.
Poorish star musical comedy.

w Harry Kurnitz, William Bowers *d* Irving Pichel

Deanna Durbin, Donald O'Connor, John Dall, Charles Winninger, Helena Carter

Something Money Can't Buy
GB 1952 82m bw
Rank / Vic (Joe Janni)

After World War II a young couple find civilian life difficult and dreary, but finally start a catering and secretarial business.
Weakly contrived comedy which makes nothing of its possibilities and is limply handled all round.

w Pat Jackson, James Lansdale Hodson *d* Pat Jackson *ph* C. Pennington-Richards *m* Nino Rota

Patricia Roc, Anthony Steel, A. E. Matthews, Moira Lister, David Hutcheson, Michael Trubshawe, Diane Hart, Charles Victor, Henry Edwards

Something of Value
US 1957 113m bw
MGM (Pandro S. Berman)

A young African with many English friends is initiated into the Kikuyu.
An attempt to see all sides in the case of the African ritual murders of the fifties; bloodthirsty and unconvincing as well as dull.

wd Richard Brooks, *novel* Robert Ruark *ph* Russell Harlan *m* Miklos Rozsa

Rock Hudson, Sidney Poitier, Dana Wynter, Wendy Hiller, Robert Beatty, Juano Hernandez, William Marshall, Walter Fitzgerald, Michael Pate

Something to Hide
GB 1971 99m Eastmancolor
Avton (Michael Klinger)

A civil servant has a row with his wife, kills her and buries her body on the Isle of Wight.
Unpleasant and uninteresting melodrama demanding a hysterical performance from its star. Pleasant photography is its only asset.

w,d Alastair Reid, *novel* Nicholas Monsarrat *ph Wolfgang Suschitzky* *m* Roy Budd, Jack Fishman

Peter Finch, Colin Blakely, John Stride, Shelley Winters, Linda Hayden, Harold Goldblatt

Something to Live For
US 1952 (completed 1950) 89m bw
Paramount (George Stevens)

A commercial artist member of Alcoholics Anonymous falls for a dipsomaniac actress but refuses to break up his marriage.
Glossy romantic melodrama with some style but no depth; the casting makes it seem like a sequel to *The Lost Weekend*.

w Dwight Taylor *d* George Stevens *ph* George Barnes *m* Victor Young

Ray Milland, Joan Fontaine, Teresa Wright, Richard Derr, Douglas Dick

'The victory over alcohol becomes a somewhat woebegone business.'—*Penelope Houston*

Something to Shout About
US 1943 93m bw
Columbia (Gregory Ratoff)

A press agent tries to get rid of an untalented star.
Tolerable musical comedy.

w Fred Shiller, Lou Breslow, Edward Eliscu, George Owen *d* Gregory Ratoff *m* Victor Schertzinger *songs* Cole Porter *md* Morris Stoloff

Don Ameche, Janet Blair, William Gaxton, Perry Como

AAN: Victor Schertzinger; Morris Stoloff; song, 'You'd Be So Nice to Come Home To'

Something to Sing About*
US 1937 90m bw
Grand National (Zion Myers)

A New York bandleader decides to take a fling at Hollywood.
Lightweight but reasonably pleasing musical, made by the star as an independent during a rift with his studio, Warners.

w Austin Parker *d, songs* Victor Schertzinger *ph* John Stumar *md* Constantin Bakaleinikoff

James Cagney, Evelyn Daw, Mona Barrie, William Frawley, Gene Lockhart

'A first-class comedy with music; will please everywhere.'—*Variety*

Something Wicked This Way Comes*
US 1983 95m Technicolor
Walt Disney / Bryna (Peter Vincent Douglas)

A sinister carnival with a power over time and age visits a small town in Illinois.
A curious departure for the Disney studio is this grim fairy tale from a novel which was probably intractable. In the cinema, this is the sort of film very lucky to find an audience despite its good qualities.

w Ray Bradbury, from his novel *d* Jack Clayton *ph* Stephen H. Burum *m* James Horner *pd* Richard MacDonald

Jason Robards, Jonathan Pryce, Diane Ladd, Pam Grier, Royal Dano, Vidal Peterson, Shawn Carson

Something Wild
US 1961 112m bw
(UA) Prometheus (George Justin)

A girl's life and attitudes change after she is raped, and she moves in with a garage mechanic.
A bit of a wallow, with much method acting but no clear analysis of the central relationship.

w Jack Garfein, Alex Karmel, *novel* Mary Ann by Alex Karmel *d* Jack Garfein *ph* Eugene Schufftan *m* Aaron Copland *ad* Richard Day

Carroll Baker, Ralph Meeker, Mildred Dunnock, Charles Watts, Martin Kosleck, Jean Stapleton

Something Wild
US 1986 113m colour
Orion / Religioso Primitiva Du Art (Jonathan Demme, Kenneth Utt)

Two irresponsible young people find themselves on the run from police and criminals.
Unremarkable melodrama with trendy musical trappings.

w E. Max Frye *d* Jonathan Demme *ph* Tak Fujimoto *m* John Cale, Laurie Anderson

Jeff Daniels, Melanie Griffith, Ray Liotta, Margaret Colin

Sometimes a Great Notion*
US 1971 114m Technicolor Panavision
Universal / Newman–Foreman
GB title: *Never Give an Inch*

In a small Oregon township, trouble is caused by an independent family of lumberjacks.
Freewheeling but unsatisfactorily eccentric comedy-melodrama which never quite jells but has flashes of individuality.

w John Gay, *novel* Ken Kesey *d Paul Newman* *ph* Richard Moore *m* Henry Mancini

Paul Newman, Henry Fonda, Lee Remick, Michael Sarrazin, Richard Jaeckel, Linda Lawson, Cliff Potts

AAN: song 'All His Children' (*m* Henry Mancini, *ly* Alan and Marilyn Bergman); Richard Jaeckel

Somewhere I'll Find You*
US 1942 108m bw
MGM (Pandro S. Berman)

Brother war correspondents quarrel over a girl and later find her in Indo-China smuggling Chinese babies to safety.
Absurd but satisfactory star vehicle of the second rank, with the theme designed to prepare America for war.

w Marguerite Roberts, *story* Charles Hoffman *d* Wesley Ruggles *ph* Harold Rosson *m* Bronislau Kaper

Clark Gable, Lana Turner, Robert Sterling, Patricia Dane, Reginald Owen, Lee Patrick, Charles Dingle, Rags Ragland, William Henry

Somewhere in England
GB 1940 79m bw
Mancunian (John E. Blakeley)

High jinks among army recruits staging a show.
One of a series of misshapen and badly made regional comedies which afflicted British cinemas in the forties and should be mentioned for their immense popularity, their new-style vulgarity (later to be refined by the Carry On series) and their highly popular stars.

w Arthur Mertz, Rodney Parsons *d* John E. Blakeley *ph* Geoffrey Faithfull

Frank Randle, Harry Korris, Robbie Vincent, Winki Turner, Dan Young

† Subsequently released, or allowed to escape, between 1941 and 1949 were *Somewhere in Camp, Somewhere on Leave, Somewhere in Civvies* and *Somewhere in Politics*.

Somewhere in the Night*
US 1946 111m bw
TCF (Anderson Lawler)

An amnesiac war veteran tries to discover his true identity and discovers he is a crook with much-wanted information.
Overlong suspenser with a tentative *film noir* atmosphere. A few nice touches partly atone for a tediously conversational plot.

w Howard Dimsdale, Joseph L. Mankiewicz, *story* The Lonely Journey by Marvin Borowsky *d* Joseph L. Mankiewicz *ph* Norbert Brodine *m* David Buttolph

John Hodiak, Nancy Guild, Lloyd Nolan, Richard Conte, Josephine Hutchinson, *Fritz Kortner*

Somewhere in Time*
US 1980 104m Technicolor
Universal / Rastar (Stephen Deutsch)

A playwright finds a way back in time for another encounter with the girl he loved and lost in a previous incarnation.
Rather a charming variation on *Berkeley Square*, but hardly a theme to do well in the hardnosed eighties.

w Richard Matheson, from his novel Bid Time Return *d* Jeannot Szwarc *ph* Isidore Mankofsky *m* John Barry

Christopher Reeve, Christopher Plummer, Jane Seymour, Teresa Wright, Bill Erwin, George Voskovec

The Son-Daughter
US 1932 79m bw

True love among the San Francisco Chinese is affected by warring Tongs. Ill-advised oriental romance which failed to please. Ramon Novarro, Helen Hayes, Lewis Stone, Warner Oland, Ralph Morgan, H. B. Warner, Louise Closser Hale. Written by Claudine West, Leon Gordon and John Goodrich, from a play by David Belasco and George Scarborough; directed by Clarence Brown; for MGM.
'Old-time stuff, moving slowly and laboriously towards a sad climax.'—*Variety*

Son of a Gunfighter
US / Spain 1964 90m Metrocolor Cinemascope

A young westerner stalks the outlaw responsible for his mother's death. Tolerable international western. Russ Tamblyn, Kieron Moore, James Philbrook, Fernando Rey. Written by Clarke Reynolds; directed by Paul Landres; for Lester Welch / Zurbano / MGM.

Son of Ali Baba
US 1952 75m Technicolor
U-I (Leonard Goldstein)

A cadet of the military academy outwits a wicked caliph.
Routine Arabian Nights hokum.

w Gerald Drayson Adams *d* Kurt Neumann *ph* Maury Gertsman *m* Joseph Gershenson

Tony Curtis, Piper Laurie, Susan Cabot, Victor Jory

Son of Captain Blood
Italy / Spain 1962 95m Eastmancolor Dyaliscope

Captain Blood's son routs his father's enemies. Lively swashbuckler with the original star's son rather unhappily cast. Sean Flynn, Ann Todd, Jose Nieto, John Kitzmiller. Written by Mario Caiano; directed by Tullio Demichelli; for Harry Joe Brown / CCM / BP.

Son of Dr Jekyll
US 1951 77m bw

Dr Jekyll's son worries about developing a split personality, but discovers that his father's supposed friend Dr Lanyon is the nigger in the woodpile. Irresistibly silly elaboration of a famous story; no thrills but several good unintentional laughs. Louis Hayward, Alexander Knox, Jody Lawrance, Lester Matthews, Paul Cavanagh, Gavin Muir, Rhys Williams. Written by Mortimer Braus and Jack Pollexfen; directed by Seymour Friedman; for Columbia.

'Searing the screen with new terror!'
Son of Dracula*
US 1943 80m bw
Universal (Ford Beebe)

A mysterious stranger named Alucard, with a penchant for disappearing in puffs of smoke, turns up on a southern plantation.
Stolid series entry with a miscast lead; nicely handled moments.

w Eric Taylor *d Robert Siodmak ph George Robinson m* Hans Salter

Lon Chaney Jnr, Louise Allbritton, Robert Paige, Samuel S. Hinds, Evelyn Ankers, Frank Craven, J. Edward Bromberg
† The title cheats: he isn't the son of, but the old man himself . . .

'The black shadows of the past bred this half-man, half-demon!'
Son of Frankenstein***
US 1939 99m bw
Universal (Rowland V. Lee)

The old baron's son comes home and starts to dabble, with the help of a broken-necked and vindictive shepherd.
Handsomely mounted sequel to *Bride of Frankenstein* and the last of the classic trio. The monster is less interesting, but there are plenty of other diversions, including the splendid if impractical sets.

w Willis Cooper d Rowland V. Lee ph George Robinson m Frank Skinner ad Jack Otterson

Basil Rathbone, Boris Karloff, Bela Lugosi, Lionel Atwill, Josephine Hutchinson, Donnie Dunagan, Emma Dunn, *Edgar Norton*, Lawrence Grant
'Rather strong material for the top keys, picture will still garner plenty of bookings in the secondary first runs along the main stem.'—*Variety*
'The slickness of production gives a kind of refinement to the horrific moments and a subtlety to the suspense.'—*Film Weekly*

Son of Fury*
US 1942 102m bw
TCF (William Perlberg)

An 18th-century Englishman is deprived of his inheritance, flees to a South Sea island but comes back seeking restitution.
Elaborate costumer which suffers from loss of suspense during the central idyll. Much to enjoy along the way.

w Philip Dunne, *novel* Benjamin Blake by Edison Marshall *d John Cromwell ph* Arthur Miller *m* Alfred Newman

Tyrone Power, Gene Tierney, George Sanders, Frances Farmer, Roddy McDowall, John Carradine, Elsa Lanchester, *Dudley Digges*, Harry Davenport, Halliwell Hobbes
† Remade as *Treasure of the Golden Condor* (qv).

Son of Geronimo
US 1952 bw serial: 15 eps

Jim Scott seeks to end the bloodshed between whites and Indians. Rather solemn western serial. Clayton Moore, Bud Osborne, Tommy Farrell, Rodd Redwing. Directed by Spencer Bennet; for Columbia.

Son of Kong*
US 1933 69m bw
RKO (Merian C. Cooper)

After Kong has wrecked New York, producer Carl Denham flees from his creditors and finds more monsters on the old island.
Hasty sequel to the splendid *King Kong*; the results were so tame and unconvincing that the film was sold as a comedy, but it does have a few lively moments after four reels of padding.

w Ruth Rose *d* Ernest B. Schoedsack *ph* Eddie Linden, Vernon Walker, J. O. Taylor *m* Max Steiner *sp Willis O'Brien*

Robert Armstrong, Helen Mack, Frank Reicher, John Marston, Victor Wong
'The sequel to and wash-up of the *King Kong* theme, consisting of salvaged remnants from the original production . . . the punch is no longer there.'—*Variety*

Son of Lassie
US 1945 100m Technicolor
MGM (Samuel Marx)

A dog follows its young master to the war and helps settle the hash of a few Nazis.
Silly dog story, the first sequel to *Lassie Come Home*; far too slow to start with, then packed with serial-like action.

w Jeanne Bartlett *d* S. Sylvan Simon *ph* Charles Schoenbaum *m* Herbert Stothart

Peter Lawford, Donald Crisp, June Lockhart, Nigel Bruce, Leon Ames, Nils Asther
'Good old sentimental hokum.'—*Variety*

Son of Monte Cristo*
US 1940 102m bw
(UA) Edward Small

The masked avenger who quashes a dictatorship in 1865 Lichtenstein is none other than the son of Edmond Dantes.
Cheerful swashbuckler of the second class.

w George Bruce *d* Rowland V. Lee *ph* George Robinson *m* Edward Ward

Louis Hayward, Joan Bennett, George Sanders, Florence Bates, Lionel Royce, Montagu Love, Clayton Moore, Ralph Byrd

Son of Paleface*
US 1952 95m Technicolor
(Paramount) Bob Hope (Robert L. Welch)

A tenderfoot and a government agent compete for the attentions of a lady bandit.
Gagged-up sequel to *The Paleface*; much of the humour now seems self-conscious and dated in the *Road* tradition which it apes, but there are still moments of delight.

w Frank Tashlin, Joseph Quillan, Robert L. Welch *d* Frank Tashlin *ph* Harry J. Wild *m* Lyn Murray

Bob Hope, Roy Rogers, Jane Russell, Trigger, Douglass Dumbrille, Harry Von Zell, Bill Williams, Lloyd Corrigan

AAN: song 'Am I in Love' (*m / ly* Jack Brooks)

Son of Robin Hood
GB 1958 77m Eastmancolor Cinemascope
TCF / Argo (George Sherman)

Robin's daughter joins with the Regent's brother to overthrow the Black Duke.
Empty-headed romp, more or less in the accepted tradition.

w George George, George Slavin *d* George Sherman *ph* Arthur Grant *m* Leighton Lucas

David Hedison, June Laverick, David Farrar, Marius Goring, Philip Friend, Delphi Lawrence, George Coulouris, George Woodbridge

Son of Sinbad*
US 1955 88m Technicolor Superscope
RKO (Robert Sparks)

Sinbad and Omar Khayyam are imprisoned by the Caliph but escape with the secret of green fire.
Arabian Nights burlesque, mainly quite bright, with the forty thieves played by harem girls.

w Aubrey Wisberg, Jack Pollexfen *d* Ted Tetzlaff *ph* William Snyder *m* Victor Young

Dale Robertson, Vincent Price, Sally Forrest, Lili St Cyr, Mari Blanchard, Leon Askin, Jay Novello

Son of the Gods
US 1930 90m bw

A Chinaman falls in love with a white girl . . . but turns out not to be a Chinaman after all.
Antediluvian miscegenation melodrama with an unconvincing twist. Richard Barthelmess, Constance Bennett, Geneva Mitchell, E. Alyn Warren. Written by Bradley King from a novel by Rex Beach; directed by Frank Lloyd; for First National. 'High-class general programme release.'—*Variety*

Son of the Guardsman
US 1946 bw serial: 15 eps

In medieval England, David Trent turns against his thieving uncle and joins a band of outlaws. Muddled serial antics in the style of Robin Hood. Robert Shaw, Daun Kennedy, Robert 'Buzz' Henry, Jim Diehl. Directed by Derwin Abrahams; for Columbia.

'An eye feast of virile action, colourful settings and glowing climaxes!'

The Son of the Sheik*
US 1926 74m at 24 fps bw silent
(UA) J. M. Schenck

Ahmed protects a dancing girl from a band of renegades.
Tongue-in-cheek desert romp which was probably its star's best film. He plays a dual role of father and son.

w Frances Marion, George Marion Jnr, Frederick Gresac *d* George Fitzmaurice *m* (1934 sound version) Jack Ward

Rudolph Valentino, Vilma Banky, Agnes Ayres

'The very picture for which the world's wife, mother and daughter have been waiting!'—*Louella Parsons*

'We expect every fan in the country to be saying: It is Rudy's best. We can never forget him.'—*Photoplay*

Son of Zorro
US 1947 bw serial: 13 eps

After the Civil War, a Southern officer takes on a ring of crooked politicians who are bleeding his home town dry. Reasonably lively treading on familiar waters. George Turner, Peggy Stewart, Roy Barcroft. Directed by Spencer Bennet and Fred Brannon; for Republic.

The Song and Dance Man
US 1936 72m bw

A vaudeville dancer goes on the skids but turns up when his former partner needs him.
Hokey backstage drama with interesting detail.
Paul Kelly, Claire Trevor, Michael Whalen, Ruth Donelly, James Burke. Written by Maude Fulton, from a play by George M. Cohan; directed by Allan Dwan; for TCF

A Song Is Born*
US 1948 113m Technicolor
Samuel Goldwyn

Flat remake of *Ball of Fire* (qv), graced by an array of top-flight musical talent.

w Harry Tugend *d* Howard Hawks *ph* Gregg Toland *m* Hugo Friedhofer *md* Emil Newman *songs* Don Raye, Gene de Paul

Danny Kaye, Virginia Mayo, Hugh Herbert, Steve Cochran, Felix Bressart, J. Edward Bromberg, Mary Field, Ludwig Stossel, Louis Armstrong, Charlie Barnet, Benny Goodman, Lionel Hampton, Tommy Dorsey, Mel Powell

Song o' My Heart
US 1930 85m bw

A professional singer looks after the orphaned children of his former love. A thin story is the excuse for a great tenor to sing eleven songs. *John McCormack*, Maureen O'Sullivan, John Garrick, J. M. Kerrigan, Alice Joyce. Written by Tom Barry, J. J. McCarthy; directed by Frank Borzage; for Fox. 'A simple tale charmingly told . . . sitting through it is no hardship.'—*Variety*

'We're going to see Jennifer Jones again in . . .'

The Song of Bernadette**
US 1943 156m bw
TCF (William Perlberg)

A peasant girl has a vision of the Virgin Mary at what becomes the shrine of Lourdes.
Hollywood religiosity at its most commercial; but behind the lapses of taste and truth is an excellent production which was phenomenally popular and created a new star.

w George Seaton, *novel* Franz Werfel *d Henry King ph Arthur Miller m* Alfred Newman *ad James Basevi, William Darling*

Jennifer Jones, William Eythe, Charles Bickford, Vincent Price, Lee J. Cobb, Gladys Cooper, Anne Revere, Roman Bohnen, Patricia Morison, Aubrey Mather, Charles Dingle, Mary Anderson, Edith Barrett, Sig Rumann

PROLOGUE: 'For those who believe in God, no explanation is necessary. For those who do not believe in God, no explanation is possible.'

'A tamed and pretty image, highly varnished, sensitively lighted, and exhibited behind immaculate glass, the window at once of a shrine and of a box office.'—*James Agee*

'It contains much to conciliate even the crustiest and most prejudiced objector.'—*Richard Mallett, Punch*

AA: Arthur Miller; Alfred Newman; Jennifer Jones
AAN: best picture; George Seaton; Henry King; Charles Bickford; Gladys Cooper; Anne Revere

Song of Ceylon**
GB 1934 40m bw
Ceylon Tea Board (John Grierson)

A pictorial, almost sensuous, but not very informative documentary in four sections: 'The Buddha', 'The Virgin Island', 'The Voices of Commerce', 'The Apparel of a God'. Its influence was immense.

wd, ph Basil Wright m Walter Leigh

Song of Freedom*
GB 1936 80m bw
Hammer (J. Fraser Passmore)

A black London docker becomes an opera singer, then goes to Africa to free the tribe of which he has discovered himself to be the head.
A weird fable but a good star vehicle and a surprisingly smart production for the time.

w Fenn Sherie, Ingram d'Abbes, Michael

Barringer, Philip Lindsay *d* J. Elder Wills *ph* Eric Cross

Paul Robeson, Elizabeth Welch, George Mosart, Esmé Percy

Song of India
US 1949 77m bw

An Indian prince protects his land against a big game hunter. Not much singing, but lots of animals and a fight with knives: tolerable programme filler. Sabu, Gail Russell, Turhan Bey, Anthony Caruso, Aminta Dyne, Fritz Leiber. Written by Art Arthur, Kenneth Perkins; directed and produced by Albert S. Rogell; for Columbia.

Song of Love*
US 1947 118m bw
MGM (Clarence Brown)

The story of Clara and Robert Schumann and their friend Johannes Brahms.
Dignified musical biopic which unfortunately falls into most of the pitfall clichés of the genre. Dull it may be, but it looks good and the music is fine.

w Ivan Tors, Irmgard Von Cube, Allen Vincent, Robert Ardrey *d* Clarence Brown *ph* Harry Stradling *md* Bronislau Kaper *ad* Cedric Gibbons *piano* Artur Rubenstein

Katharine Hepburn, Paul Henreid, Robert Walker, Henry Daniell, Leo G. Carroll, Else Janssen, Gigi Perreau

'This is how Brahms and the Schumanns might very possibly have acted if they had realized that later on they would break into the movies.'—*Time*

Song of Norway*
US 1970 141m De Luxe Super Panavision 70
ABC / Andrew and Virginia Stone

A fantasia on the life of Grieg.
Multinational hodgepodge, mostly in the *Sound of Music* style but with everything from cartoons to Christmas cracker backgrounds. Quite watchable, and the landscapes are certainly splendid.

wd Andrew Stone *ph* Davis Boulton *stage musical* Milton Lazarus *(book)* Robert Wright, George Forrest *(m / ly)*

Toralv Maurstad, Florence Henderson, Christina Schollin, Frank Poretta, Harry Secombe, Edward G. Robinson, Robert Morley, Elizabeth Larner, Bernard Archard, Oscar Homolka, Richard Wordsworth

Song of Russia
US 1944 107m bw
MGM (Joe Pasternak)

An American symphony conductor is in Russia when hostilities begin, and watches the citizens' war effort with admiration.
A terrible big-budget film which followed the wartime propaganda line but five years later was heavily criticized by the Unamerican Activities Committee (for the wrong reasons).

w Paul Jarrico, Richard Collins *d* Gregory Ratoff *ph* Harry Stradling *m* Herbert Stothart

Robert Taylor, Susan Peters, John Hodiak, Robert Benchley, Felix Bressart, Michael Chekhov, Darryl Hickman

'Film makers have evolved a new tongue—the broken accent deriving from no known language to be used by foreigners on all occasions.'—*Richard Winnington*

'MGM performs the neatest trick of the week by leaning over backward in Russia's favour without once swaying from right to left.'—*Newsweek*

Song of Scheherezade
US 1947 107m Technicolor
Universal (Edward Kaufman)

In 1865 naval cadet Rimsky-Korsakov falls in love with a dancer.
Yet another composer takes a drubbing in this dull and unconvincing hodgepodge.

wd Walter Reisch *ph* Hal Mohr, William V. Skall *md* Miklos Rozsa *ch* Tilly Losch *ad* Jack Otterson

Yvonne de Carlo, Jean-Pierre Aumont, Brian Donlevy, Eve Arden, Charles Kullman, John Qualen, Richard Lane, Terry Kilburn

'One of the world's great love stories comes to the star who can make it live!'

Song of Songs*
US 1933 89m bw
Paramount (Rouben Mamoulian)

A German peasant girl falls for a sculptor but marries a lecherous baron.
Pretentious romantic nonsense, made fairly palatable by the director's steady hand.

w Leo Birinsky, Samuel Hoffenstein, *play* Edward Sheldon, *novel* Das hohe Lied by Herman Sudermann w Rouben Mamoulian *ph* Victor Milner *m* Karl Hajos, Milien Rodern *ad* Hans Dreier

Marlene Dietrich, Brian Aherne, Lionel Atwill, Alison Skipworth, Hardie Albright

'An ornate and irresistible slice of outright hokum.'—*Peter John Dyer, 1966*

'From the moment she heard this strange, compelling music of love—she was lost!'

Song of Surrender
US 1949 93m bw
Paramount (Richard Maibaum)

In turn-of-the-century New England, a sophisticated visitor from New York falls for the wife of the museum curator.
Ho-hum romantic drama, well enough presented.

w Richard Maibaum *d* Mitchell Leisen *ph* Daniel L. Fapp *m* Victor Young

Wanda Hendrix, Claude Rains, Macdonald Carey, Andrea King, Henry Hull, Elizabeth Patterson, Art Smith

Song of the City
US 1937 73m bw

Italian fisherfolk in San Francisco pull a socialite out of the bay and make a man of him. Unlikely and unlovable moral tale, full of warm-hearted simple people. Margaret Lindsay, Jeffrey Dean, J. Carrol Naish, Nat Pendleton, Stanley Morner, Edward Norris. Written by Michael Fessier; directed by Errol Taggart; for Lucien Hubbard / MGM. 'Elemental stuff with some nice photography but needs bolstering for b.o. allure.'—*Variety*

Song of the Eagle
US 1933 65m bw

Racketeers try to control the supply of beer both after and during prohibition. Tolerable crime / family saga which becomes sentimental. Charles Bickford, Richard Arlen, Jean Hersholt, Mary Brian, Louise Dresser, George E. Stone, Andy Devine. Written by Casey Robinson, Willard Mack, Gene Towne, Graham Baker; directed by Ralph Murphy; for Charles R. Rogers / Paramount. 'Fairly good programmer and timely. What hurts is the title. Remember *Animal Kingdom*.'—*Variety*

Song of the Islands*
US 1942 75m Technicolor
TCF (William Le Baron)

On a South Sea island, the daughter of an Irish beachcomber falls for the son of an American cattle king.
Wispy musical with agreeable settings and lively songs.

w Joseph Schrank, Robert Pirosh, Robert Ellis, Helen Logan *d* Walter Lang *ph* Ernest Palmer *md* Alfred Newman *songs* various

Betty Grable, Victor Mature, Jack Oakie, Thomas Mitchell, *Hilo Hattie*, Billy Gilbert, George Barbier

Song of the Open Road
US 1944 93m bw

A dissatisfied child movie star goes off to help volunteers to save a tomato crop. Thin youth drama enlivened by a putting-on-a-show finale. Jane Powell, Bonita Granville, Jackie Moran, W. C. Fields, Edgar Bergen and Charlie McCarthy, Sammy Kaye and his orchestra. Written by Albert Mannheimer; directed by S. Sylvan Simon; for Charles R. Rogers (UA). AAN: Charles Previn (music direction); song 'Too Much in Love' (*m* Walter Kent, *ly* Kim Gannon)

Song of the South*
US 1946 94m Technicolor
Walt Disney (Perce Pearce)

On a long-ago southern plantation, small boys listen to the Brer Rabbit stories from an elderly black servant.
Too much Uncle Remus and not enough Brer Rabbit, we fear, but children liked it. The cartoons were actually very good.

w Dalton Raymond *d* Harve Foster *ph* Gregg Toland *m* Daniele Amfitheatrof, Paul J. Scott, Charles Wolcott *cartoon credits* various

Ruth Warrick, Bobby Driscoll, James Baskett, Luana Patten, Lucile Watson, Hattie McDaniel

'The ratio of live to cartoon action is approximately two to one, and that is the ratio of the film's mediocrity to its charm.'—*Bosley Crowther*

SONS AND LOVERS. Hollywood's Dean Stockwell fitted in well with an otherwise British cast. Here he is with Mary Ure.

AA: song 'Zip a Dee Do Dah' (*m* Allie Wrubel, *ly* Ray Gilbert)
AAN: Daniele Amfitheatrof, Paul J. Scott, Charles Wolcott

A Song to Remember**
US 1944 113m Technicolor
Columbia (Louis F. Edelman)

The life and death of Chopin and his liaison with George Sand.
Hilarious classical musical biopic which was unexpectedly popular and provoked a flood of similar pieces. As a production, not at all bad, but the script . . .

w Sidney Buchman *d* Charles Vidor *ph* Tony Gaudio *md* Miklos Rozsa, Morris Stoloff *piano José Iturbi ad* Lionel Banks, Van Nest Polglase

Cornel Wilde, Merle Oberon, Paul Muni, Stephen Bekassy, Nina Foch, George Coulouris, Sig Arno, Howard Freeman, George Macready

'It is the business of Hollywood to shape the truth into box-office contours.'—*Richard Winnington*

'This glorious picture is a major event in film history.'—*Hollywood Reporter*

'As infuriating and funny a misrepresentation of an artist's life and work as I have seen.'—*James Agee*

AAN: original story (Ernest Marischka); Tony Gaudio; Miklos Rozsa, Morris Stoloff; Cornel Wilde

Song without End
US 1960 142m Eastmancolor Cinemascope
Columbia (William Goetz)

The life and loves of Franz Liszt.
What worked at the box office for Chopin failed disastrously for Liszt; famous people are turned into papier mâché dullards. Again, the production is elegance itself.

w Oscar Millard *d* Charles Vidor, George Cukor *ph* James Wong Howe *md* Morris Stoloff, Henry Sukman *piano* Jorge Bolet *ad Walter Holscher*

Dirk Bogarde, Capucine, Genevieve Page, Patricia Morison, Ivan Desny, Martita Hunt, Lyndon Brook, Alex Davion (as Chopin)

AA: Morris Stoloff, Henry Sukman

Songwriter
US 1984 94m Metrocolor
Tri-Star (Sydney Pollack)

Adventures of a country-music duo.
Very moderate entertainment which gives the impression of stars doing their own thing.

w Bud Shrake *d* Alan Rudolph *ph* Matthew Leonetti *m* Kris Kristofferson *pd* Joel Schiller *ed* Stuart Pappe

Willie Nelson, Kris Kristofferson, Melinda Dillon, Rip Torn, Lesley Ann Warren, Richard C. Sarafian

AAN: Kris Kristofferson (for music)

'The first experiences of a young man in the mysteries of woman!'

Sons and Lovers***
GB 1960 103m bw Cinemascope
TCF / Company of Artists / Jerry Wald

A Nottingham miner's son learns about life and love.
Well-produced and generally absorbing, if unsurprising, treatment of a famous novel.

w Gavin Lambert, T. E. B. Clarke, novel D. H. Lawrence *d Jack Cardiff ph Freddie Francis m* Mario Nascimbene

Dean Stockwell, Trevor Howard, Wendy Hiller, Mary Ure, Heather Sears, William Lucas, Donald Pleasence, Ernest Thesiger

'An album of decent Edwardian snapshots.'—*Peter John Dyer*

'A rare, remarkable and courageous film.'—*Daily Herald*

AA: Freddie Francis
AAN: best picture; script; Jack Cardiff; Trevor Howard; Mary Ure

Sons o' Guns
US 1936 79m bw

A Broadway dancer in uniform finds himself accidentally enlisted and sent to France.
Among the better comedies of this star. Joe E. Brown, Joan Blondell, Eric Blore, Wini Shaw, Robert Barrat. Written by Julius J. Epstein and Jerry Wald; directed by Lloyd Bacon; for Warner.

The Sons of Katie Elder*
US 1965 122m Technicolor Panavision
Paramount / Hal B. Wallis (Paul Nathan)

At Katie Elder's funeral, her four troublesome wandering sons find themselves on the verge of further trouble.
Sluggish all-star western with predictable highlights.

w Allan Weiss, William H. Wright, Harry Essex *d* Henry Hathaway *ph* Lucien Ballard *m* Elmer Bernstein

John Wayne, Dean Martin, Michael Anderson Jnr, Earl Holliman, Martha Hyer, Jeremy Slate, James Gregory, George Kennedy, Paul Fix

Sons of the Desert****
US 1934 68m bw
Hal Roach
GB title: *Fraternally Yours*

Stan and Ollie want to go to a Chicago convention, but kid their wives that they are going on a cruise for health reasons.
Archetypal Laurel and Hardy comedy, unsurpassed for gags, pacing and sympathetic characterization.

w Frank Craven, Byron Morgan d William A. Seiter ph Kenneth Peach

Stan Laurel, Oliver Hardy, Charlie Chase, Mae Busch, Dorothy Christie

Sons of the Sea
GB 1939 82m Dufaycolor

Life at the Royal Naval College in Dartmouth. Simple-minded recruiter with a top dressing of spy stuff: naive but well liked at the time. Leslie Banks, Mackenzie Ward, Kay Walsh, Simon Lack, Cecil Parker, Ellen Pollock, Nigel Stock. Written by Gerald Elliott, Maurice Elvey, D. William Woolf, George Barraud; directed by Maurice Elvey; for British Consolidated.

Sophie's Choice*
US 1982 157m Technicolor
Universal / AFD / ITC / Keith Barish

In 1947, a Polish girl who has been in a concentration camp finds that her past still haunts her in New York.
Glum romantic drama about guilt and retribution, long and uncinematic as well as rather poorly done; but its intentions are doubtless honourable.

wd Alan J. Pakula, *novel* William Styron *ph* Nestor Almendros *m* Marvin Hamlisch *pd* George Jenkins *ed* Evan Lottman

Meryl Streep, Kevin Kline, Peter MacNicol, Rita Karin, Stephen D. Newman, Josh Mostel

'Handsome, doggedly faithful and astoundingly tedious.'—*Variety*

'Not boring, simply unilluminating. By the end, only one question remains: why did Pakula have to make this movie?'—*Sight and Sound*

AA: Meryl Streep
AAN: screenplay (adaptation); cinematography; costume design; music

Sorcerer
US 1977 121m Technicolor
Universal / Film Properties International (William Friedkin)
GB title: *Wages of Fear*

Volunteers are needed to drive nitro-glycerine to an outpost in the South American jungle. Why anyone should have wanted to spend twenty million dollars on a remake of *The Wages of Fear*, do it badly, and give it a misleading title is anybody's guess. The result is dire.

w Walon Green, *novel* Georges Arnaud (and the film by Henri-Georges Clouzot) *d* William Friedkin *ph* John M. Stephens, Dick Bush *m* Tangerine Dream, Keith Jarrett, Charlie Parker *pd* John Box

Roy Scheider, Bruno Cremer, Francisco Rabal, Amidou, Ramon Bieri

The Sorcerers
GB 1967 85m Eastmancolor
Tigon / Curtwel / Global (Patrick Curtis, Tony Tenser)

An old couple find a way of regaining their youth through hypnotizing a young man to do their bidding.
Rather slight but oddly memorable horror film, with an elegant old lady becoming the real monster.

w Michael Reeves, Tom Baker, John Burke *d* Michael Reeves *ph* Stanley Long *m* Paul Ferris

Boris Karloff, *Catherine Lacey,* Ian Ogilvy, Elizabeth Ercy, Victor Henry, Susan George, Meier Tzelniker

Sorrell and Son
GB 1933 97m bw

When his wife leaves them, a man devotes his life to his worthless son. Fair picturization of a popular novel. H. B. Warner, Hugh Williams, Winifred Shotter, Margot Grahame, Donald Calthrop, Louis Hayward. Written by Lydia Hayward, from the novel by Warwick Deeping; directed by Jack Raymond; for Herbert Wilcox / B and D. 'Insufficient in action for the average American screen devotee.'—*Variety*

† H. B. Warner played the same role in the silent version of 1927.

Sorrowful Jones
US 1949 88m bw
Paramount (Robert L. Welch)

A racetrack tout unofficially adopts an orphan girl.
Heavy-going sentimental comedy peopled by comic gangsters, a remake of *Little Miss Marker* with the emphasis changed.

w Melville Shavelson, Edmund Hartmann, Jack Rose, *story* Damon Runyon *d* Sidney Lanfield *ph* Daniel L. Fapp *m* Robert Emmett Dolan

Bob Hope, Lucille Ball, William Demarest, Bruce Cabot, Thomas Gomez, Tom Pedi, Houseley Stevenson, Mary Jane Saunders

The Sorrows of Satan*
US 1926 115m approx bw silent

A struggling writer accepts success in the form of a fortune offered to him by a prince who is in fact Satan. Smooth Faust derivative with a few choice scenes of special effects. Adolphe Menjou, Ricardo Cortez, Lya de Putti, Carol Dempster, Ivan Lebedeff. Written by Forrest Halsey, John Russell, George Hull, from the novel by Marie Corelli; directed by D. W. Griffith (who didn't want to do it); for Famous Players/Paramount.

Sorry Wrong Number**
US 1948 89m bw
Paramount (Hal B. Wallis, Anatole Litvak)

A bedridden neurotic woman discovers she is marked for murder and tries to summon help.
Artificial but effective suspenser, extended from a radio play.

w Lucille Fletcher, from her play *d* Anatole Litvak *ph* Sol Polito *m* Franz Waxman

Barbara Stanwyck, Burt Lancaster, Ann Richards, Wendell Corey, Ed Begley, Harold Vermilyea, Leif Erickson, William Conrad

AAN: Barbara Stanwyck

The Soul of a Monster
US 1944 61m bw

A rich man is saved from death by a female hypnotist, who keeps him under her spell. Unusual but not very interesting thriller. Rose Hobart, George Macready, Jim Bannon, Jeanne Bates. Written by Edward Dein; directed by Will Jason; for Ted Richmond / Columbia.

'Out of the secret annals of the sea comes the strangest story ever told!'

Souls at Sea*
US 1937 93m bw
Paramount (Henry Hathaway)

In a 19th-century shipwreck an intelligence officer must save himself, and his mission, at the cost of other lives, and is courtmartialled. A lively seafaring melodrama produced on a fairly impressive scale.

w Grover Jones, Dale Van Every *d* Henry Hathaway *ph* Charles Lang Jnr *m* Milan Roder, W. Franke Harling *md* Boris Morros

Gary Cooper, George Raft, Frances Dee, Henry Wilcoxon, Harry Carey, Olympe Bradna, Robert Cummings, Porter Hall, George Zucco, Virginia Weidler, Joseph Schildkraut, Gilbert Emery

'First rate slave ship adventure.'—*Variety*

AAN: Milan Roder, W. Franke Harling

The Sound and the Fury
US 1959 117m Eastmancolor Cinemascope
TCF / Jerry Wald

A once proud southern family has sunk low in finance and moral stature, and a stern elder son tries to do something about it.
Heavy melodrama with performances to match.

w Irving Ravetch, Harriet Frank Jnr, *novel* William Faulkner *d* Martin Ritt *ph* Charles G. Clarke *m* Alex North

Yul Brynner, Joanne Woodward, Margaret Leighton, Stuart Whitman, Ethel Waters, Jack Warden, Françoise Rosay, John Beal, Albert Dekker

'A fourth carbon copy of Chekhov in Dixie.'—*Stanley Kauffmann*

The Sound Barrier**
GB 1952 118m bw
London Films (David Lean)
US title: *Breaking the Sound Barrier*

An aircraft manufacturer takes risks with the lives of his family and friends to prove that the sound barrier can be broken.
Riveting, then topical, melodrama with splendid air sequences; a bit upper crust, but with well-drawn characters.

w Terence Rattigan d David Lean ph Jack Hildyard m Malcolm Arnold

Ralph Richardson, Nigel Patrick, Ann Todd, John Justin, Dinah Sheridan, Joseph Tomelty, Denholm Elliott

'The most exciting film about the air that has ever been produced anywhere.'—*Daily Express*

'A peacetime film as exciting as any wartime one.'—*Sunday Dispatch*

AAN: Terence Rattigan

The Sound of Music***
US 1965 172m De Luxe Todd-AO
TCF / Argyle (Robert Wise)

In 1938 Austria, a trainee nun becomes governess to the Trapp family, falls in love with the widower father, and helps them all escape from the Nazis.
Slightly muted, very handsome version of an enjoyably old-fashioned stage musical with splendid tunes.

w Ernest Lehman, *book* Howard Lindsay, Russel Crouse *d Robert Wise ph Ted McCord m / ly Richard Rodgers, Oscar Hammerstein II md Irwin Kostal pd Boris Leven*

Julie Andrews, Christopher Plummer, Richard Haydn, Eleanor Parker, *Peggy Wood*, Anna Lee, Marni Nixon

'. . . sufficient warning to those allergic to singing nuns and sweetly innocent children.'—*John Gillett*

AA: best picture; Robert Wise; Irwin Kostal
AAN: Ted McCord; Julie Andrews; Peggy Wood

Sound Off
US 1952 83m Supercinecolor
Columbia (Jonie Taps)

An entertainer is recruited into the army and has predictable difficulties.
Dishevelled service farce with funny moments.

w Blake Edwards, Richard Quine *d* Richard Quine *ph* Ellis Carter *m* George Duning *md* Morris Stoloff

Mickey Rooney, Anne James, Sammy White, John Asher, Gordon Jones

Sounder*
US 1972 105m De Luxe Panavision
TCF / Radnitz–Mattel (Robert B. Radnitz)

During the thirties Depression, black sharecroppers in the deep south endure various tribulations.
Well made liberated family movie . . . but not very exciting.

w Lonnie Elder III, *novel* William H. Armstrong *d* Martin Ritt *ph* John Alonzo *m* Taj Mahal

Paul Winfield, Cicely Tyson, Kevin Hooks, Carmen Mathews, James Best, Taj Mahal

AAN: best picture; Lonnie Elder III; Paul Winfield; Cicely Tyson

Sous le Ciel de Paris Coule la Seine
France 1951 111m bw
Regina Filmsonor (Pierre O'Connell and Arys Nisotti)

The adventures of a variety of characters during a day in Paris.
The director is back on his multi-story band wagon, but in this case the stories are undeveloped and the handling less than interesting.

w René Lefèvre, Julien Duvivier *d* Julien Duvivier *ph* Nicholas Hayer *m* Jean Winer

Brigitte Auber, Jean Brochard, René Blancard, Paul Frankeur, Sylvie

'A hotchpotch of familiar story devices, camera tricks and picturesque characterizations and settings, bundled together with an old hand's facility.'—*MFB*

Sous les Toits de Paris*
France 1930 92m bw
Tobis (Frank Clifford)

A Parisian street singer falls in love with a girl, fights her lover, and proves himself innocent of theft.
Surprisingly serious and darkly lit little comedy-drama which, while well enough directed, hardly seems to merit its classic status.

wd René Clair ph Georges Périnal *m* Armand Bernard *pd* Lazare Meerson

Albert Préjean, Pola Illery, Gaston Modot, Edmond Gréville

'Real film fare of quality . . . a talker which is intelligible to any country.'—*Variety*

'It is far more movie than talkie, which exercises the imagination and rests the ear.'—*National Board of Review*

South American George
GB 1941 93m bw

An unsuccessful singer poses as a South American opera star. Not among the star's best. George Formby, Linden Travers, Enid Stamp-Taylor, Jacques Brown, Felix Aylmer. Written by Leslie Arliss, Norman Lee and Austin Melford; directed by Marcel Varnel; for Ben Henry / Columbia.

South of Algiers
GB 1952 95m Technicolor
ABP / Mayflower (Aubrey Baring, Maxwell Setton)
US title: *The Golden Mask*

Archaeologists and thieves search the Sahara for a priceless mask.
Schoolboy adventure story with a straightforward plot and plenty of local colour.

w Robert Westerby *d* Jack Lee *ph* Oswald Morris *m* Robert Gill

Van Heflin, Wanda Hendrix, Eric Portman, Charles Goldner, Jacques François, Jacques Brunius, Alec Mango, Marne Maitland

'A thousand thundering terrific thrills in a fight-swept tropic paradise!'

South of Pago Pago
US 1940 96m bw
(UA) Edward Small (Erle C. Kenton)

Greedy white men seek riches in pearls by cheating and overworking the natives.
Slightly unfamiliar backgrounds and a fair supply of two-fisted action gave this romantic adventure drama plenty of box office pull.

w George Bruce *d* Alfred E. Green *ph* John Mescall *m* Edward Ward

Victor McLaglen, Jon Hall, Frances Farmer, Olympe Bradna, Gene Lockhart, Douglass Dumbrille, Francis Ford

South of St Louis
US 1948 88m Technicolor

Before the Civil War starts, southern farmers are plagued by Union guerrillas. Pretty good western with plenty of action. Joel McCrea, Zachary Scott, Victor Jory, Douglas Kennedy, Dorothy Malone, Alexis Smith, Alan Hale. Written by Zachary Gold and James R. Webb; directed by Ray Enright; for Milton Sperling / Warner.

South of Suez
US 1940 85m bw

A diamond miner falls for the daughter of a man he is accused of murdering. Watchable melodrama with pleasing actors, George Brent, Brenda Marshall, George Tobias, James Stephenson, Lee Patrick, Eric Blore, Cecil Kellaway. Written by Barry Triver; directed by Lewis Seiler; for Warner.

South of Tahiti
US 1941 75m bw

Four adventurers drift ashore on a tropical island. Penny-pinching hokum without even the colour to make it watchable. Brian Donlevy, Maria Montez, Broderick Crawford, Andy Devine, Henry Wilcoxon, H. B. Warner. Written by Gerald Geraghty; directed by George Waggner; for Universal. (GB title: *White Savage*.)

South Pacific**
US 1958 170m Technicolor Todd-AO
Magna / S. P. Enterprises (Buddy Adler)

In 1943 an American navy nurse on a South Pacific island falls in love with a middle-aged French planter who becomes a war hero.
Overlong, solidly produced film of the musical stage hit, with great locations, action climaxes and lush photography (also a regrettable tendency to use alarming colour filters for dramatic emphasis).

w Paul Osborn, Richard Rodgers, Oscar Hammerstein II, Joshua Logan, *stories* Tales of the South Pacific by James A. Michener *d* Joshua Logan *ph Leon Shamroy* *m / ly Richard Rodgers, Oscar Hammerstein II* *md* Alfred Newman, Ken Darby *ch* Le Roy Prinz

Mitzi Gaynor, Rossano Brazzi, Ray Walston, John Kerr, France Nuyen, Juanita Hall

AAN: Leon Shamroy; Alfred Newman, Ken Darby

South Riding**
GB 1937 91m bw
London Films (Alexander Korda, Victor Saville)

A schoolmistress in a quiet Yorkshire dale exposes crooked councillors and falls for the depressed local squire.
Dated but engrossing multi-drama from a famous novel; a good compact piece of film-making.

w Ian Dalrymple, Donald Bull, novel Winifred Holtby d Victor Saville ph Harry Stradling *m* Richard Addinsell

Ralph Richardson, Edna Best, Edmund Gwenn, Ann Todd, Glynis Johns, John Clements, Marie Lohr, Milton Rosmer, Edward Lexy

'Another artistic Korda film . . . lacking in a story of popular appeal.'—*Variety*

'A convincing and dramatic picture of English provincial life.'—*Film Weekly*

South Sea Sinner
US 1949 88m bw

On a South Sea island, a fugitive from justice is blackmailed by a café owner. Hackneyed elements are strung together without much flair in this routine melodrama. Macdonald Carey, Shelley Winters, Luther Adler, Helena Carter, Frank Lovejoy, Art Smith, Liberace. Written by Joel Malone and Oscar Brodney; directed by Bruce Humberstone; for Universal-International. (GB title: *East of Java*.)

South Sea Woman
US 1953 99m bw
Warner (Sam Bischoff)
aka: *Pearl of the South Pacific*

Adventures of a fight-loving marine in the Pacific war.
Unlovable mixture of brawling, romancing and war-winning.

w Edwin Blum, *play* William M. Rankin *d* Arthur Lubin *ph* Ted McCord *m* David Buttolph

Burt Lancaster, Virginia Mayo, Chuck Connors, Arthur Shields, Barry Kelley, Leon Askin

Southern Comfort
US 1981 106m De Luxe
EMI / Phoenix / Cinema Group Venture (David Giler)

National Guardsmen go on a routine exercise into swampland, and after a brush with Louisiana Indians succumb to violence.
Brutish retread of *Deliverance* with a few nods to Vietnam.

w Michael Kane, Walter Hill, David Giler *d* Walter Hill *ph* Andrew Laszlo *m* Ry Cooder

Keith Carradine, Powers Boothe, Fred Ward, Franklyn Seales, T. K. Carter, Lewis Smith

'Africa explodes with a thousand surprises!'

The Southern Star*
GB / France 1968 105m Techniscope
Columbia / Eurofrance / Capitole (Roger Duchet)

In French West Africa in 1912, a penniless American finds a huge diamond which several crooks are after.
Quite a likeable adventure romp, with good suspense sequences and convincing jungle settings.

w David Pursall, Jack Seddon, *novel* Jules Verne *d* Sidney Hayers *ph* Raoul Coutard *m* Georges Garvarentz

George Segal, Ursula Andress, Orson Welles, Ian Hendry, Michael Constantine, Johnny Sekka, Harry Andrews

A Southern Yankee*
US 1948 90m bw
MGM (Paul Jones)
GB title: *My Hero*

During the Civil War a southern bellboy masquerades as a spy and finds himself behind enemy lines.
A rather feeble reworking of Buster Keaton's *The General*, with some excellent gags supervised by the master himself.

w Harry Tugend *d* Edward Sedgwick *ph* Ray June *m* David Snell

Red Skelton, Brian-Donlevy, Arlene Dahl, George Coulouris, Lloyd Gough, John Ireland, Minor Watson, Charles Dingle

'She was his woman! And he was her man! That's all they had to fight with—against the world, the flesh, and the devil!'

The Southerner***
US 1945 91m bw
(UA) David Loew, Robert Hakim

Problems of penniless farmers in the deep south.
Impressive, highly pictorial outdoor drama, more poetic than *The Grapes of Wrath* and lacking the acting strength.

wd Jean Renoir, novel Hold Autumn in Your Hand by George Sessions Perry *ph Lucien Andriot m* Werner Janssen

Zachary Scott, Betty Field, *Beulah Bondi*, J. Carrol Naish, Percy Kilbride, Blanche Yurka, Norman Lloyd

'I cannot imagine anybody failing to be spellbound by this first successful essay in Franco-American screen collaboration.'—*Richard Winnington*

'You can smell the earth as the plough turns it up; you can sense the winter and the rain and the sunshine.'—*C. A. Lejeune*

† Some sources state that the script was by William Faulkner.

AAN: Jean Renoir (as director); Werner Janssen

Soylent Green*
US 1973 97m Metrocolor Panavision
MGM (Walter Seltzer, Russell Thatcher)

In 2022, the population of New York exists in perpetual heat on synthetic foods; a policeman hears from his elderly friend about an earlier time when things were better.
Lively futuristic yarn with a splendid climax revealing the nature of the artificial food; marred by narrative incoherence and by direction which fails to put plot points clearly across.

w Stanley R. Greenberg, *novel* Make Room, Make Room by Harry Harrison *d* Richard Fleischer *ph* Richard H. Kline *m* Fred Myrow

Charlton Heston, *Edward G. Robinson*, Leigh Taylor-Young, Chuck Connors, Brock Peters, Joseph Cotten

The Space Children
US 1958 71m bw VistaVision

Children at a rocket testing site sabotage equipment on the instructions of a strange pulsating object. Naïve moral fable, not badly done on its level. Adam Williams, Peggy Webber, Michel Ray, Jackie Coogan. Written by Bernard Schoenfeld; directed by Jack Arnold; for William Alland / Paramount.

Spaceballs
US 1987 96m Metrocolor

A ruthless race is out to steal the air supply from the planet Druidia. Flabby spoof of *Star Wars*, without any funny ideas. Mel Brooks, John Candy, Rick Moranis, Bill Pullman, Daphne Zuniga. Written, directed and produced by Mel Brooks; for MGM/UA. 'At its worst, it displays a colossal ego at work and humour better left to home movies.'—*Daily Variety*

Spacehunter: Adventures in the Forbidden Zone
US 1983 90m Metrocolor 3-D
Columbia / Delphi (Don Carmody, Andre Link, John Dunning)

In the 22nd century, a spaceship salvage expert lands on a long-forgotten planet to rescue three earthwomen from the tyrants of Graveyard City.
Mindless and rather unattractive space fantasy, far less likeable than *Flash Gordon*.

w David Preston, Edith Rey, Dan Goldbert, Len Blum *d* Lamont Johnson *ph* Frank Tidy *m* Elmer Bernstein *pd* Jackson de Govia

Peter Strauss, Molly Ringwald, Ernie Hudson, Andrea Marcovicci, Michael Ironside

The Spaceman and King Arthur
GB 1979 93m Technicolor

An astronaut and his robot accidentally land themselves back at the court of King Arthur.
Mindless but occasionally funny rewrite of

Mark Twain's *A Connecticut Yankee*. Dennis Dugan, Jim Dale, Ron Moody, Kenneth More, John Le Mesurier, Rodney Bewes, Robert Beatty. Written by Don Tait; directed by Russ Mayberry; for Walt Disney. (US title: *Unidentified Flying Oddball*.)

Spanish Affair
US 1958 92m Technicolor Vistavision
Paramount / Nomad (Bruce Odlum)

An American architect in Madrid falls in love with his interpreter and is pursued by her lover.
Curiously plotless excuse for a travelogue, lushly photographed but not exactly gripping.

w Richard Collins *d* Don Siegel *ph* Sam Leavitt *m* Daniele Amfitheatrof

Richard Kiley, Carmen Sevilla, Jose Guardiola

Spanish Fly
GB 1975 86m Technicolor

An Englishman in Majorca tries to improve a purchase of local wine by putting an aphrodisiac in it, with predictable results.
Crude, tatty comedy by people who should know better. Terry-Thomas, Leslie Phillips, Graham Armitage, Frank Thornton, Sue Lloyd. Written by Robert Ryerson; directed by Bob Kellett; for Winkle / EMI.

The Spanish Gardener
GB 1956 97m Technicolor Vistavision
Rank (John Bryan)

The British consul in Spain is annoyed when his young son develops a strong friendship with the gardener.
Slow, understated study in human relationships which doesn't come off; any sexual relevance is well concealed.

w Lesley Storm, John Bryan, *novel* A. J. Cronin *d* Philip Leacock *ph* Christopher Challis *m* John Veale

Dirk Bogarde, Michael Hordern, Jon Whiteley, Cyril Cusack, Geoffrey Keen, Maureen Swanson, Lyndon Brook, Josephine Griffin, Bernard Lee, Rosalie Crutchley

The Spanish Main*
US 1945 101m Technicolor
RKO (Robert Fellows)

In the Caribbean, the fiancée of the Spanish viceroy is kidnapped by a pirate who determines to tame her before marrying her.
Slightly tongue-in-cheek pirate hokum; generally good value for the easily amused.

w George Worthing Yates, Herman J. Mankiewicz *d* Frank Borzage *ph* George Barnes *m* Hanns Eisler *md* Constantin Bakaleinikoff

Paul Henreid, Maureen O'Hara, Binnie Barnes, Walter Slezak, John Emery, Barton MacLane, J. M. Kerrigan, Nancy Gates, Fritz Leiber, Jack La Rue, Mike Mazurki, Victor Kilian

AAN: George Barnes

Spare a Copper*
GB 1940 77m bw

A police war reservist catches saboteurs. One of the last good Formby comedies, with everything percolating as it should. George Formby, Dorothy Hyson, Bernard Lee, John Warwick, John Turnbull, George Merritt. Written by Roger MacDougall, Austin Melford and Basil Dearden; directed by John Paddy Carstairs; for Ealing.

Spare the Rod
GB 1961 93m bw
British Lion / Bryanston / Weyland (Victor Lyndon)

At an East End school, a novice master wins the confidence of tough pupils.
A British *Blackboard Jungle*, paving the way for *To Sir with Love*; not exciting on its own account.

w John Cresswell, *novel* Michael Croft *d* Leslie Norman *ph* Paul Beeson *m* Laurie Johnson

Max Bygraves, Geoffrey Keen, Donald Pleasence, Richard O'Sullivan, Betty McDowall, Eleanor Summerfield, Mary Merrall

Sparrows Can't Sing
GB 1962 94m bw
Elstree / Carthage (Donald Taylor)

Returning after two years at sea, a sailor searches for his wife and threatens vengeance on her lover.
Relentlessly caricatured cockney comedy melodrama, too self-conscious to be effective, and not at all likeable anyway.

w Stephen Lewis, Joan Littlewood *d* Joan Littlewood *ph* Mac Greene *m* James Stevens

James Booth, Barbara Windsor, Roy Kinnear, Avis Bunnage, George Sewell, Barbara Ferris, Murray Melvin, Arthur Mullard

Spartacus**
US 1960 196m Super Technirama 70
U-I / Bryna (Edward Lewis)

The slaves of ancient Rome revolt and are quashed.
Long, well-made, downbeat epic with deeper than usual characterization and several bravura sequences.

w Dalton Trumbo, *novel* Howard Fast *d Stanley Kubrick ph Russell Metty m* Alex North *pd* Alexander Golitzen

Kirk Douglas, Laurence Olivier, Charles Laughton, Tony Curtis, Jean Simmons, Peter Ustinov, John Gavin, Nina Foch, Herbert Lom, John Ireland, John Dall, Charles McGraw, Woody Strode

'Everything is depicted with a lack of imagination that is truly Marxian.'—*Anne Grayson*

'A lot of first-rate professionals have pooled their abilities to make a first-rate circus.'—*Stanley Kauffmann*

'One comes away feeling rather revolted and not at all ennobled.'—*Alan Dent, Illustrated London News*

AA: Russell Metty; Peter Ustinov
AAN: Alex North

Spartacus the Gladiator
Italy 1953 103m bw
Consorzio Spartacus

Action-oriented remake of a familiar story.

w Jean Ferry, Mario Bori *d* Riccardo Freda *ph* Gabor Pigany *m* Renzo Rossellini

Massimo Girotti, Ludmilla Tcherina, Maria Canala

'A love story stormy as raging Arctic seas!'

Spawn of the North**
US 1938 110m bw
Paramount (Albert Lewin)

In 1890s Alaska, American fishermen combat Russian poachers.
Solidly carpentered all-star action melodrama, a sizzler of its day. Remade 1953 as *Alaska Seas*.

w Talbot Jennings, Jules Furthman *d Henry Hathaway ph Charles Lang m* Dmitri Tiomkin

George Raft, Henry Fonda, Dorothy Lamour, *John Barrymore*, Akim Tamiroff, Louise Platt, Lynne Overman, Fuzzy Knight, Vladimir Sokoloff, Duncan Renaldo, John Wray

'The visual features are so realistic and terrifying that audiences will find complete satisfaction in the production.'—*Variety*

'This film has something which the cinema of bygone days used to supply as a matter of course—action and thrills, the quickened pulse and the lump in the throat.'—*Basil Wright*

'Rousing old-fashioned spectacle.'—*New York Times*

Speak Easily*
US 1932 83m bw
MGM (Lawrence Weingarten)

A professor inherits a Broadway musical and falls for the lure of the bright lights.
Interesting Keaton talkie at the point of his decline.

w Ralph Spence, Lawrence E. Johnson, *novel* Footlights by Clarence Budington Kelland *d* Edward Sedgwick *ph* Harold Wentstrom

Buster Keaton, Jimmy Durante, Hedda Hopper

Special Agent
US 1935 74m bw

A special investigator pretends to be a newspaperman. Routine rough stuff, quite watchable. Bette Davis, George Brent, Ricardo Cortez, Jack La Rue, Henry O'Neill, J. Carrol Naish. Written by Laird Doyle, Abem Finkel; directed by William Keighley; for Cosmopolitan / Warners. 'Indifferent entertainment but Bette Davis may help.'—*Variety*

Special Delivery
US 1976 99m De Luxe
TCF / Bing Crosby Productions (Richard Berg)

Three disabled Vietnam veterans rob a bank, and the consequences are complicated.
Unremarkable suspenser which takes itself too seriously.

w Don Gazzaniga *d* Paul Wendkos *ph* Harry Stradling Jnr *m* Lalo Schifrin

Bo Svenson, Cybill Shepherd, Michael C. Gwynne, Vic Tayback, Sorrell Booke

The Speckled Band
GB 1931 80m bw
Sherlock Holmes saves an heiress from a horrible death. Limp and overstretched version of Conan Doyle's story, interesting only for the actors. Raymond Massey, Athole Stewart (as Watson), Lyn Harding (as Rylott), Angela Baddeley, Nancy Price. Written by W. P. Lipscomb; directed by Jack Raymond; for Herbert Wilcox / B and D.

The Specter of the Rose*
US 1946 90m bw
Republic (Ben Hecht)
A schizophrenic ballet dancer lives his role and nearly murders his wife.
A rather hilarious bid for culture: hard to sit through without laughing, but unique.
wd Ben Hecht *ph* Lee Garmes *m* Georges Antheil
Viola Essen, Ivan Kirov, Michael Chekhov

Speedy**
US 1928 90m approx bw silent
A young man saves his girl's grandfather's trolley car business. One of its star's most stylish comedies, and his last silent film, with a trolley car ride for climax. *Harold Lloyd*, Ann Christy, Bert Woodruff, Brooks Benedict, Babe Ruth. Written by John Grey, Lex Neal, Howard Emmett Rogers, Jay Howe; directed by *Ted Wilde*; for Harold Lloyd (Paramount).

Spell of the Circus
US 1931 bw serial: 10 eps
A scheming circus manager wants to marry the owner's daughter, but she loves the cowboy star. Slight basis for a serial. Francis X. Bushman Jnr, Alberta Vaughn, Tom London, Walter Shumway. Directed by Robert F. Hill; for Universal.

The Spellbinder
US 1939 68m bw
A criminal lawyer full of tricks finds himself on trial for murder. Contrived courtroom drama tailored to its star. Lee Tracy, Barbara Read, Patric Knowles, Allan Lane, Morgan Conway. Written by Thomas Lennon and Joseph A. Fields; directed by Jack Hively; for RKO.
'Average supporter for duals.'—*Variety*

Spellbound
GB 1940 82m bw
Pyramid Amalgamated (R. Murray Leslie)
aka: *Passing Clouds*; US title: *The Spell of Amy Nugent*
A young man is in despair when his fiancée dies, and nearly goes mad when a medium materializes her from the dead.
Very odd, very naïve, but somehow rather winning.
w Miles Malleson, *novel* The Necromancers by Robert Benson *d* John Harlow *ph* Walter Harvey
Derek Farr, Vera Lindsay, Frederick Leister, Hay Petrie, Diana King, Felix Aylmer

Spellbound**
US 1945 111m bw
David O. Selznick
The new head of a mental institution is an impostor and an amnesiac; a staff member falls in love with him and helps him recall the fate of the real Dr Edwardes.
Enthralling and rather infuriating psychological mystery; the Hitchcock touches are splendid, and the stars shine magically, but the plot could have stood a little more attention.
w Ben Hecht, Angus MacPhail, *novel* The House of Dr Edwardes by Francis Beeding *d Alfred Hitchcock ph George Barnes dream sequence Salvador Dali m* Miklos Rozsa *ad* James Basevi
Ingrid Bergman, Gregory Peck, Leo G. Carroll, Michael Chekhov, Rhonda Fleming, John Emery, Norman Lloyd, Steve Geray
'Just about as much of the id as could be safely displayed in a Bergdorf Goodman window.'—*James Agee*
'Glossily produced and wildly improbable.'—*George Perry, 1965*
'Bergman's apple-cheeked sincerity has rarely been so out of place as in this confection whipped up by jaded chefs.'—*New Yorker, 1976*
AA: Miklos Rozsa
AAN: best picture; Alfred Hitchcock; George Barnes; Michael Chekhov

Spencer's Mountain*
US 1963 121m Technicolor Panavision
Warner (Delmer Daves)
Life in rural America in the thirties with a poor quarry worker and his family of nine.
Sentimental rose-tinted hokum which later became TV's *The Waltons*. Expertly concocted, Hollywood style.
wd Delmer Daves, *novel* Earl Hanmer Jnr *ph* Charles Lawton, H. F. Koenekamp *m* Max Steiner
Henry Fonda, Maureen O'Hara, James MacArthur, Donald Crisp, Wally Cox, Mimsy Farmer, Lilian Bronson

Spendthrift
US 1936 80m bw
A millionaire playboy runs out of cash. Mild romantic comedy. Henry Fonda, Pat Paterson, Mary Brian, George Barbier, Ed Brophy. Written by Raoul Walsh and Bert Hanlon; directed by Raoul Walsh; for Paramount.

The Sphinx
US 1933 63m bw
A murderer uses his deaf mute brother as an alibi. Mildly ingenious low-budget thriller. Lionel Atwill, Sheila Terry, Theodore Newton, Paul Hurst, Luis Alberni. Written by Albert DeMond; directed by Phil Rosen; for Monogram. 'Fair returns are probable if dated properly.'—*Variety*

Sphinx
US 1980 118m Technicolor Panavision
Warner / Orion (Stanley O'Toole)
Archaeologists in modern Cairo find clues to an ancient treasure.
Expensive penny dreadful which lurches about from comedy to horror but is often well worth looking at.
w John Byrum, *novel* Robin Cook *d* Franklin J. Schaffner *ph* Ernest Day *m* Michael J. Lewis *pd* Terence Marsh
Lesley-Anne Down, Frank Langella, Maurice Ronet, John Gielgud, Vic Tablian, Martin Benson, John Rhys-Davies
'A glossily-packaged exercise in random-selection box-office formulae.'—*Jo Imeson, MFB*

The Spider
US 1931 65m bw
A theatre magician traps a killer. Rather flat transcription of a play which in its original form took every advantage of the audience and other elements. Edmund Lowe, Howard Philips, Lois Moran, George E. Stone, El Brendel. From play by Fulton Oursler and Lowell Brentano; directed by William Cameron Menzies and Kenneth MacKenna; for Fox.

The Spider
GB 1940 81m bw
A theatrical agent kills his partner on a train. Barely competent murder thriller. Derrick de Marney, Diana Churchill, Cecil Parker, Jean Gillie, Frank Cellier, Allan Jeayes. Written by Kenneth Horne, Reginald Holt from novel by Henry Holt; directed by Maurice Elvey; for Victor M. Greene / Admiral Films.

The Spider and the Fly
GB 1949 95m bw
GFD / Maxwell Setton, Aubrey Baring
In 1913 a Parisian safecracker constantly outwits an inspector of the Sûreté, but war brings changes.
Coldly ironic comedy drama which really, regrettably, doesn't work.
w Robert Westerby *d* Robert Hamer *ph* Geoffrey Unsworth *m* Georges Auric
Eric Portman, Guy Rolfe, Nadia Gray, George Cole, Edward Chapman, John Carol, Maurice Denham
'Not sufficiently exciting for a thriller, not quite sharp enough for a real drama of character.'—*Gavin Lambert, MFB*

The Spider Returns
US 1941 bw serial: 15 eps
A wealthy socialite dons disguises to fight the underworld. Enjoyable comic strip hokum; a feature version was also released. Warren Hull, Mary Ainslee, Dave O'Brien, Joe Girard. Directed by James W. Horne; for Columbia. (Sequel to *The Spider's Web*.)

Spider Woman**
US 1944 62m bw
Universal (Roy William Neill)

A female Moriarty kills her victims with spiders so that she can collect on their insurance policies.
Lively episode in the modernized series, which packs in several suspenseful episodes borrowed from a variety of Conan Doyle originals.

w Bertram Millhauser d Roy William Neill ph Charles Van Enger *m* Hans Salter

Basil Rathbone, Nigel Bruce, Gale Sondergaard, Dennis Hoey, Vernon Downing, Alec Craig, Mary Gordon

The Spider Woman Strikes Back
US 1946 59m bw

An innocent girl is used as decoy by a conniving female criminal. Boring crime filler, scarcely a worthy sequel to *Spider Woman.* Gale Sondergaard, Brenda Joyce, Rondo Hatton, Milburn Stone, Kirby Grant, Hobart Cavanaugh. Written by Eric Taylor; directed by Arthur Lubin; for Howard Welsch / Universal.

The Spider's Stratagem*
Italy 1970 97m Eastmancolor
Radiotelevisione Italiana / Red Film (Giovanni Bertolucci)

Revisiting the village in the Po valley where his father was murdered by fascists in 1936, our gradually disillusioned hero learns that his father was really a traitor executed by his own men.
Elaborately mysterious puzzle play for intellectuals, with infinite shades of meaning which few will bother to explore. The atmosphere, however, is superbly caught.

w Bernardo Bertolucci, Eduardo de Gregorio, Marilu Parolini, *story* The Theme of the Traitor and the Hero by Jorge Luis Borges *d* Bernardo Bertolucci *ph* Vittorio Storaro, Franco di Giacomo

Giulio Brogi, Alida Valli, Tino Scotti, Pino Campanini

The Spider's Web
US 1938 bw serial: 15 eps

The Spider (see *The Spider Returns*) fights The Octopus, an outlaw demoralizing the nation's transport system. Predictable adventures, less lively than the sequel. Warren Hull, Iris Meredith, Richard Fiske, Marc Lawrence. Directed by Ray Taylor and James W. Horne; for Columbia.

The Spider's Web
GB 1960 89m colour

A diplomat's wife has an unwanted corpse on her hands. Fairly standard who-done-it played unwisely for comedy. Glynis Johns, John Justin, Cicely Courtneidge, Jack Hulbert, Ronald Howard, David Nixon. Written by Albert G. Miller, Eldon Howard from the play by Agatha Christie; directed by Godfrey Grayson; for Danzigers.

Spies Like Us
US 1985 109m Technicolor

Bumbling bureaucrats are mistakenly chosen for a spy mission. Inept attempts at humour fall flat throughout this dreary venture, which is as though Hope and Crosby had set out on the Road to Morocco without a script. Chevy Chase, Dan Aykroyd, Steve Forrest, Donna Dixon, Bruce Davison, William Prince, Bernie Casey. Written by Dan Aykroyd, Lowell Ganz, Babaloo Mandel; directed by John Landis; for Brian Grazer-George Folsey Jnr / Warner.

Spies of the Air
GB 1939 77m bw

A test pilot turns out to be an enemy agent. Moderate programmer with an engaging cast. Barry K. Barnes, Roger Livesey, Joan Marion, Basil Radford, Felix Aylmer, John Turnbull, Henry Oscar. Written by A. R. Rawlinson and Bridget Boland from Jeffrey Dell's play *Official Secrets*; directed by David MacDonald; for John Corfield / British National.

The Spikes Gang
US 1974 96m De Luxe
UA / Mirisch / Duo / Sanford (Walter Mirisch)

Three boys shelter a bank robber and join his gang.
Doom-laden, violent western with a few comic lines.

w Irving Ravetch, Harriet Frank Jnr, *novel* The Bank Robber by Giles Tippette *d* Richard Fleischer *ph* Brian West *m* Fred Karlin

Lee Marvin, Gary Grimes, Ron Howard, Charles Martin Smith, Arthur Hunnicutt, Noah Beery Jnr

Spinout
US 1966 93m Metrocolor Panavision
MGM / Euterpe (Joe Pasternak)
GB title: *California Holiday*

A carefree touring singer agrees to drive an experimental car in a road race.
Mild star musical which at least stays in the open air.

w Theodore J. Flicker, George Kirgo *d* Norman Taurog *ph* Daniel L. Fapp *md* Georgie Stoll

Elvis Presley, Shelley Fabares, Carl Betz, Cecil Kellaway, Diane McBain, Deborah Walley, Jack Mullaney, Will Hutchins, Una Merkel

The Spiral Road
US 1962 145m Eastmancolor
U-I (Robert Arthur)

In 1936 Java, an atheist medical man fights a leprosy epidemic and eventually becomes a missionary.
A long slog through jungle / religious clichés, with a hilariously miscast star and an almost Victorian script.

w John Lee Mahin, Neil Paterson, *novel* Jan de Hartog *d* Robert Mulligan *ph* Russell Harlan *m* Jerry Goldsmith

Rock Hudson, Burl Ives, Geoffrey Keen, Gena Rowlands, Will Kuluva, Neva Patterson, Philip Abbott

The Spiral Staircase***
US 1945 83m bw
RKO (Dore Schary)

A small town in 1906 New England is terrorized by a psychopathic killer of deformed girls.
Archetypal old dark house thriller, superbly detailed and set during a most convincing thunderstorm. Even though the identity of the villain is pretty obvious, this is a superior Hollywood product.

w Mel Dinelli, novel Some Must Watch by Ethel Lina White *d Robert Siodmak ph Nicholas Musuraca m Roy Webb ad Albert S. D'Agostino, Jack Okey*

Dorothy McGuire, George Brent, Kent Smith, Ethel Barrymore, Rhys Williams, Rhonda Fleming, Gordon Oliver, Sara Allgood, James Bell

'A nice, cosy and well-sustained atmosphere of horror.'—*C. A. Lejeune*

AAN: Ethel Barrymore

The Spiral Staircase
GB 1975 89m Technicolor
Warner / Raven (Peter Shaw)

Modernized remake of the above using virtually the same script, and apparently determined to prove how badly it can be presented.

w Allan Scott, Chris Bryant *d* Peter Collinson *ph* Ken Hodges *m* David Lindup

Jacqueline Bisset, Christopher Plummer, Sam Wanamaker, Mildred Dunnock, Gayle Hunnicutt, Sheila Brennan, Elaine Stritch, John Ronane, Ronald Radd, John Phillip Law

'I don't think this needless remake is going to set anyone's flesh creeping, except at the vulgar flashiness of the whole enterprise.'—*Michael Billington, Illustrated London News*

The Spirit Is Willing
US 1966 100m Technicolor
Paramount / William Castle

A family finds that its holiday home is haunted by the ghosts of a *crime passionel*.
Overlong, overlayed and witless farce with virtually no opportunity well taken.

w Ben Starr, *novel* The Visitors by Nathaniel Benchley *d* William Castle *ph* Hal Stine *m* Vic Mizzy

Sid Caesar, Vera Miles, John McGiver, Cass Daley, John Astin, Mary Wickes, Jesse White

Spirit of Culver
US 1939 89m bw

A boy grows up at Culver Military Academy. Very humdrum flagwaver combined with a last attempt to maintain stardom for two child performers. Jackie Cooper, Freddie Bartholomew, Tim Holt, Henry Hull, Andy Devine, Gene Reynolds. Written by Nathaniel West, Whitney Bolton; directed by Joseph Santley; for Universal. 'Mild entertainment for duals and kids.'—*Variety*

The Spirit of St Louis*
US 1957 135m Warnercolor Cinemascope
Warner (Leyland Hayward)

In 1927 Charles Lindbergh flies a specially constructed plane 3,600 miles nonstop New York to Paris in 33½ hours.
Impeccably in its period, this needlessly Cinemascoped reconstruction can scarcely avoid dull patches since for long stretches its hero is on screen solo apart from a fly, and his monologues become soporific.

w Billy Wilder, Wendell Mayes, *book* Charles Lindbergh *d* Billy Wilder *ph* Robert Burks, Peverell Marley *m* Franz Waxman

James Stewart, Murray Hamilton, Marc Connelly

The Spirit of the Beehive*
Spain 1973 98m Eastmancolor
Elias Querejeta

In 1940 in a remote village, two children see a travelling film show of Frankenstein, and their imaginations run riot; or do they?
Sensitive story of childish imagination, reminiscent of *Jeux Interdits* and yet very much its own vision.

w Francisco J. Querejeta *d* Victor Erice *ph* Luis Cuadrado *m* Luis de Pablo

Fernando Fernan Gomez, Teresa Gimpera, Ana Torrent, Isabel Telleria

The Spiritualist*
US 1948 79m bw

A medium finds that his client's 'dead' husband is very much alive and planning to grab her estate. Once it gets past its pretentious beginning, this is quite a lively mystery thriller. Written by Muriel Roy Bolton and Ian Hunter, from story by Crane Wilbur; directed by Bernard Vorhaus; for Ben Stoloff / Eagle Lion.

Spite Marriage*
US 1929 77m (24 fps) bw silent
MGM / Buster Keaton (Lawrence Weingarten)

A tailor's assistant loves an actress, who marries him to spite someone else.
For a Keaton comedy from his great period, this is remarkably thin on invention, and its pleasures, though undeniable, are minor.

w Richard Schayer, Lew Lipton *d* Edward Sedgwick *ph* Reggie Lanning

Buster Keaton, Dorothy Sebastian, Edward Earle, Leila Hyams

Spitfire*
US 1934 88m bw
RKO (Pandro S. Berman)

An Ozark mountain girl believes herself to be a faith healer and is driven from the community.
Curious star melodrama with effective moments.

w Jane Murfin, *play* Trigger by Lula Vollmer *d* John Cromwell *ph* Edward Cronjager *m* Max Steiner

Katharine Hepburn, Robert Young, Ralph Bellamy, Martha Sleeper, Louis Mason

'The veins of the story carry thin milk rather than heavy corpuscles.'—*Variety*

'The picture would suggest that Katharine Hepburn is condemned to elegance, doomed to be a lady for the rest of her natural life, and that her artistry does not extend to the interpretation of the primitive or the uncouth. That her producers have not bothered to give her a scenario of any interest or quality is another aspect of the situation.'—*The New Yorker*

'She was the woman of his dreams. She had large dark eyes, a beautiful smile, and a great pair of fins.'

Splash!*
US 1984 110m Technicolor
Touchstone / Buena Vista (Brian Grazer)

A New York wholesaler on holiday off Cape Cod falls in love with a mermaid.
A kind of updated and mildly sexed-up *Miranda*: occasionally funny but far too long.

w Lowell Ganz, Babaloo Mandel, Bruce Jay Friedman, Brian Grazer *d* Ron Howard *ph* Don Peterman *m* Lee Holdridge

Tom Hanks, Daryl Hannah, Eugene Levy, John Candy, Dody Goodman, Shecky Greene, Richard B. Shull, Howard Morris

'A typically Disney subject trying to be grown up.'—*Kim Newman, MFB*

'The picture is frequently on the verge of being more wonderful than it is . . . more lyrical, a little wilder.'—*Pauline Kael, New Yorker*

AAN: screenplay

Splendor
US 1935 77m bw
Samuel Goldwyn

The son of a once-wealthy Park Avenue family marries a poor girl.
Dated romantic drama.

w Rachel Crothers, from her play *d* Elliott Nugent *ph* Gregg Toland *md* Alfred Newman

Joel McCrea, Miriam Hopkins, Helen Westley, Katherine Alexander, David Niven, Paul Cavanagh, Billie Burke, Arthur Treacher

'An unusually good production, but probably too quiet for the lesser spots.'—*Variety*

'A model of dramatic exposition, but it suffers from inaction and its theme is too commonplace.'—*New York Times*

Splendor in the Grass*
US 1961 124m Technicolor
Warner / NBI (Elia Kazan)

Adolescent love in a small Kansas town in the twenties.
Impressive though curiously unmemorable addition to a nostalgic young sex cycle which was already played out; production and performances well up to scratch.

w William Inge *d Elia Kazan* *ph* Boris Kaufman *m* David Amram

Natalie Wood, Warren Beatty, Pat Hingle, Audrey Christie, Barbara Loden, Zohra Lampert, Sandy Dennis

'Less like a high-school version of *Summer and Smoke* than [like] an Andy Hardy story with glands.'—*Stanley Kauffmann*

AA: William Inge
AAN: Natalie Wood

Splinters
GB 1929 82m bw

Soldiers at the front in 1915 form a concert party. Easy-going crowd-pleaser of its time. Nelson Keys, Sidney Howard, Lew Lake, Hal Jones. Written by W. P. Lipscomb; directed by Jack Raymond; for Herbert Wilcox / B and D. (NB: Sequels, of roughly the same standard, included *Splinters in the Navy,* 1931, and *Splinters in the Air*, 1937; both with Sidney Howard.)

The Split
US 1968 90m Metrocolor Panavision
MGM / Spectrum (Robert Chartoff, Irwin Winkler)

A black criminal plans to rob the Los Angeles Coliseum during a football match.
Busy, brutal crime thriller, well enough done but totally unsympathetic.

w Robert Sabaroff, *novel* The Seventh by Richard Stark *d* Gordon Flemyng *ph* Burnett Guffey *m* Quincy Jones

Jim Brown, Diahann Carroll, Ernest Borgnine, Julie Harris, Gene Hackman, Jack Klugman, Warren Oates, James Whitmore, Donald Sutherland

Split Second
US 1953 85m bw
RKO (Edmund Grainger)

An escaped convict hides out with four hostages in an Arizona ghost town which has been cleared in preparation for an atom bomb test.
Routine suspenser.

w William Bowers, Irving Wallace *d* Dick Powell *ph* Nicholas Musuraca *m* Roy Webb

Stephen McNally, Alexis Smith, Jan Sterling, Keith Andes, Arthur Hunnicutt, Paul Kelly, Richard Egan, Robert Paige

The Spoilers*
US 1930 86m bw
Paramount (Lloyd Sheldon)

In Alaska during the gold rush, crooked government officials begin despoiling the richest claims.
Early talkie version of a famous brawling saga.

w Bartlett Cormack, Agnes Brand Leahy, *novel* Rex Beach *d* Edward Carewe *ph* Harry Fischbeck

Gary Cooper, William 'Stage' Boyd, Betty Compson, Kay Johnson, Harry Green, Slim Summerville

'Fair for a week in the de luxers, but made to order for the neighbourhoods and grinds everywhere.'—*Variety*

The Spoilers**
US 1942 87m bw
Universal (Frank Lloyd)

Two adventurers in the Yukon quarrel over land rights and a saloon entertainer.

Well-packaged mixture of saloon brawls, romance and adventure, much filmed as a silent.

w Lawrence Hazard, Tom Reed *d* Ray Enright *ph* Milton Krasner *m* Hans Salter *ad* Jack Otterson

Marlene Dietrich, Randolph Scott, John Wayne, Margaret Lindsay, Harry Carey, Richard Barthelmess, George Cleveland, Samuel S. Hinds

'All concerned have kept their tongues firmly in their cheeks.'—*New York Times*

The Spoilers*
US 1955 82m Technicolor
U-I (Ross Hunter)

Adequate, unmemorable remake of the above.

w Oscar Brodney, Charles Hoffman *d* Jesse Hibbs *ph* Maury Gertsman *m* Joseph Gershenson

Anne Baxter, Jeff Chandler, Rory Calhoun, Barbara Britton, Carl Benton Reid, Ray Danton, John McIntire, Raymond Walburn, Wallace Ford

The Sport of Kings
GB 1931 98m bw

A strict JP inherits a bookie business. Heavy-going adaptation of a stage comedy warhorse, which nevertheless paved the way for many screen farces of the thirties. Leslie Henson, Gordon Harker, Hugh Wakefield, Dorothy Boyd. Written by Angus MacPhail, from the play by Ian Hay; directed by Victor Saville; for Gainsborough.

Sporting Blood
US 1931 80m bw

A horse passes through various hands and finally wins the Kentucky Derby. Unremarkable programme fodder. Clark Gable, Ernest Torrence, Madge Evans, Lew Cody, Marie Prevost. Written by Charles Brabin, Wanda Tuchock, Willard Mack, from the story Horseflesh by Frederick Hazlitt Brennan; directed by Charles Brabin; for MGM. 'Racetrack romance with a different twist and only name Clark Gable.'—*Variety*

Sporting Love
GB 1936 70m bw

Two owners of a bankrupt racing stable try to kidnap their prize horse which has been mortgaged. Thin musical farce from a stage success. Stanley Lupino, Laddie Cliff, Henry Carlisle, Edna Peel. Written by Fenn Sherie, Ingram D'Abbes from play by Stanley Lupino; directed by J. Elder Wills; for Hammer.

Spring and Port Wine
GB 1970 101m Technicolor
EMI / Memorial (Michael Medwin)

A Lancashire family runs into trouble when stern father insists that teenage daughter should eat a meal she refuses.
A popular old-fashioned stage comedy which simply doesn't work on film, partly from being set in a too-real town (Bolton) and partly because of a miscast lead.

w Bill Naughton, from his play *d* Peter Hammond *ph* Norman Warwick *m* Douglas Gamley *pd* Reece Pemberton

James Mason, Diana Coupland, Susan George, Rodney Bewes, Hannah Gordon, Adrienne Posta, Arthur Lowe

Spring in Park Lane**
GB 1948 92m bw
Imperadio / Herbert Wilcox

A diamond merchant's niece falls for a footman who just happens to be an impoverished lord in disguise.
Flimsy but highly successful romantic comedy which managed to get its balance right and is still pretty entertaining, much more so than its sequel *Maytime in Mayfair*.

w Nicholas Phipps, play Come Out of the Kitchen by Alice Duer Miller *d Herbert Wilcox ph* Max Greene *m* Robert Farnon

Anna Neagle, Michael Wilding, Tom Walls, Nicholas Phipps, Peter Graves, Marjorie Fielding, *Nigel Patrick*, Lana Morris

'A never-failing dream of Olde Mayfaire and its eternally funny butlers and maids, its disguised lords and ladies.'—*Richard Winnington*

'A gag comedy which absolutely sparkles.'—*Picture Show*

'The best comedy any British studio has produced for more years than I care to remember.'—*News of the World*

Spring Madness
US 1938 66m bw

The romance of a Harvard man and a student in the nearby women's college. Very thin comedy material, stretched to its tearing point. Maureen O'Sullivan, Lew Ayres, Ruth Hussey, Burgess Meredith, Joyce Compton. Written by Edward Chodorov, from play *Spring Dance* by Philip Barry; directed by S. Sylvan Simon; for MGM.

Spring Meeting
GB 1940 93m bw

In Ireland, an impecunious widow wants her son to marry the daughter of an old flame. Staid film version of a comedy whose characters turned up again in *Treasure Hunt*. Nova Pilbeam, Basil Sydney, Henry Edwards, Sarah Churchill, Michael Wilding, *Margaret Rutherford,* Enid Stamp Taylor, Hugh McDermott. Written by Walter C. Mycroft and Norman Lee, from the play by M. J. Farrell and John Perry; directed by Walter C. Mycroft; for ABPC.

Spring Parade*
US 1940 89m bw
Universal (Joe Pasternak)

A single baker's assistant falls for a prince. Pleasing, artificial Austrian frou-frou with star and support in good escapist form.

w Bruce Manning, Felix Jackson, *story* Ernst Marischka *d* Henry Koster *ph* Joseph Valentine *m* Robert Stolz *md* Charles Previn

Deanna Durbin, Robert Cummings, S. Z. Sakall, Mischa Auer, Henry Stephenson, Anne Gwynne, Butch and Buddy

AAN: Joseph Valentine; Charles Previn; song 'Waltzing in the Clouds' (*m* Robert Stolz, *ly* Gus Kahn)

Spring Reunion
US 1956 79m bw
UA / Bryna (Jerry Bresler)

College classmates fall in love all over again at a reunion fifteen years later.
Romantic fiction for the middle-aged, performed with bare competence.

wd Robert Pirosh *ph* Harold Lipstein *m* Herbert Spencer, Earle Hagen

Betty Hutton, Dana Andrews, Jean Hagen, Robert Simon, James Gleason, Laura La Plante, Irene Ryan

Spring Tonic
US 1935 55m bw

An escaped tigress causes various farcical episodes. Comedy extravaganza on modest lines, like a stretched-out two-reeler. Lew Ayres, Claire Trevor, Walter Woolf King, Zasu Pitts, Jack Haley, Tala Birell, Sig Rumann. Written by Patterson McNutt and H. W. Hanemann from the play Man Eating Tiger by Ben Hecht and Rose Caylor; directed by S. Sylvan Simon; for Fox. 'Hodge-podge of hokum that offers no hope to distraught exhibitors.'—*Variety*

'The gun . . . the girl . . . they made one man the equal of five!'

Springfield Rifle
US 1952 93m Warnercolor
Warner (Louis E. Edelman)

A Union officer gets himself cashiered, joins the Confederates as a spy, and unmasks a traitor.
Stolid Civil War western with Grade A production but not much individuality.

w Charles Marquis Warren, Frank Davis *d* André de Toth *ph* Edwin DuPar *m* Max Steiner

Gary Cooper, Phyllis Thaxter, David Brian, Lon Chaney Jnr, Paul Kelly, Phil Carey, James Millican, Guinn Williams

Springtime for Henry
US 1935 73m bw

A rich man makes a vocation of woman chasing. Modest version of a play which was toured for many years with Edward Everett Horton in the lead. Otto Kruger, Nancy Carroll, Nigel Bruce, Heather Angel, Herbert Mundin. Written by Keene Thompson, Frank Tuttle, from the play by Benn W. Levy; directed by Frank Tuttle; for Jesse L. Lasky / Fox. 'Farcical intent, but only a few snickers.'—*Variety*

Springtime in the Rockies
US 1942 91m Technicolor
TCF (Darryl F. Zanuck)

Romances blossom on a mountain holiday. Flimsily-plotted, studio-bound, absolutely routine musical.

THE SPY IN BLACK. Love among the spies—Conrad Veidt and Valerie Hobson.

w Walter Bullock, Ken Englund *d* Irving Cummings *ph* Ernest Palmer *m* Alfred Newman *songs* Mack Gordon, Harry Warren

Betty Grable, John Payne, Carmen Miranda, Edward Everett Horton, Cesar Romero, Charlotte Greenwood, Frank Orth, Harry James and his Music Makers

Spy for a Day
GB 1939 71m bw

A farm hand is discovered to be the exact double of a spy. The only screen vehicle for this 'gormless' comedian, and not a bad one. Duggie Wakefield, Paddy Browne, Jack Allen, Albert Lieven, Nicholas Hannen, Gibb McLaughlin. Written by Anatole de Grunwald, Hans Wilhelm, Emeric Pressburger, Ralph Block and Tommy Thompson, from a story by Stacy Aumonier; directed by Mario Zampi; for Two Cities.

Spy Hunt*
US 1950 74m bw
Universal (Ralph Dietrich)
GB title: *Panther's Moon*

Secret microfilm is stowed in the collar of one of two panthers being transported out of Europe by train for circus use.
Slick minor espionage thriller.

w George Zuckerman, Leonard Lee, *novel* Panther's Moon by Victor Canning *d* George Sherman, *ph* Irving Glassberg *m* Walter Scharf *md* Joseph Gershenson

Howard Duff, Marta Toren, Philip Friend, Robert Douglas, Philip Dorn, Walter Slezak, Kurt Kreuger

The Spy in Black**
GB 1939 82m bw
Harefield / Alexander Korda (Irving Asher)
US title: *U-Boat 29*

In the Orkneys in 1917, German spies don't trust each other.
Unusual romantic melodrama which provided an unexpectedly interesting romantic team.

w Emeric Pressburger, Roland Pertwee, novel J. Storer Clouston *d Michael Powell* *ph* Bernard Browne *m* Miklos Rosza

Conrad Veidt, Valerie Hobson, Hay Petrie, Helen Haye, Sebastian Shaw, Marius Goring, June Duprez, Athole Stewart, Cyril Raymond

Spy of Napoleon
GB 1936 101m bw

A dancer saves Louis Napoleon from assassination. Solidly mounted period piece without much sense of humour. Richard Barthelmess, Dolly Haas, Frank Vosper, Francis L. Sullivan, Lyn Harding, Henry Oscar. Written by L. DuGarde Peach, Frederick Merrick and Harold Simpson; directed by Maurice Elvey; for JH Productions.

Spy Smasher
US 1942 bw serial: 12 eps

An American agent in occupied France is captured by Nazis while trying to unmask The Mask. Busy, peripatetic serial adventures. Kane Richmond, Sam Flint, Marguerite Chapman, Tristram Coffin. Directed by William Witney; for Republic.

'Brace yourself for greatness!'

The Spy Who Came in from the Cold**
GB 1966 112m bw
Paramount / Salem (Martin Ritt)

A British master spy is offered a chance to get even with his East German opponent by being apparently sacked, disillusioned, and open for recruitment.
The old undercover yarn with trimmings of such sixties malaises as death wish, anti-establishmentism and racial problems. As a yarn, quite gripping till it gets too downbeat, but very harshly photographed.

w Paul Dehn, Guy Trosper, *novel* John Le Carré *d* Martin Ritt *ph* Oswald Morris *m* Sol Kaplan *pd* Tambi Larsen

Richard Burton, Claire Bloom, *Oskar Werner*, Peter Van Eyck, Sam Wanamaker, Rupert Davies, George Voskovec, Cyril Cusack, Michael Hordern, Robert Hardy, Bernard Lee, Beatrix Lehmann
AAN: Richard Burton

The Spy Who Loved Me
GB 1977 125m Eastmancolor Panavision
UA / Eon (Albert R. Broccoli)

James Bond and a glamorous Russian spy combine forces to track down and eliminate a megalomaniac shipping magnate with an undersea missile base.
Witless spy extravaganza in muddy colour, with the usual tired chases and pussyfoot violence but no new gimmicks except a seven-foot villain with steel teeth.

w Christopher Wood, Richard Maibaum, *novel* Ian Fleming *d* Lewis Gilbert *ph* Claude Renoir *m* Marvin Hamlisch *pd* Ken Adam

Roger Moore, Barbara Bach, Curt Jurgens, Richard Kiel, Caroline Munro, Walter Gotell, Bernard Lee, Lois Maxwell, George Baker, Desmond Llewellyn, Edward De Souza, Sydney Tafler

'The film, bearing no relation to its nominal source, seems to do nothing more than anthologize its forerunners.'—*Tim Pulleine, MFB*

AAN: Marvin Hamlisch; song, 'Nobody Does It Better'

The Spy with a Cold Nose
GB 1966 93m Eastmancolor
Paramount / Associated London / Embassy (Robert Porter)

A fashionable vet is blackmailed by MI5 into inserting a radio transmitter into a bulldog.
Rather painful, overacted and overwritten farce full of obvious jokes masquerading as satire.

w Ray Galton, Alan Simpson *d* Daniel Petrie *ph* Kenneth Higgins *m* Riz Ortolani

Lionel Jeffries, Laurence Harvey, Daliah Lavi, Eric Sykes, Eric Portman, Colin Blakely, Denholm Elliott, Robert Flemyng, Paul Ford, Bernard Lee, June Whitfield, Bernard Archard

S*P*Y*S
GB 1974 100m Technicolor
Dymphana / C-W / American Film Properties (Irwin Winkler, Robert Chartoff)

Clumsy CIA agents in Paris come across a list of KGB agents in China.
Surprisingly dull and unfashionable parade of comic spy clichés; the talents involved obviously intended something closer to M*A*S*H.

w Malcolm Marmorstein, Lawrence J. Cohen, Fred Freeman *d* Irwin Kershner *ph* Gerry Fisher *m* John Scott

Elliott Gould, Donald Sutherland, Zouzou, Joss Ackland, Kenneth Griffith, Vladek Sheybal

'Seems to have arrived several years too late to find its true niche.'—*Sight and Sound*

Squadron Leader X
GB 1942 100m bw
RKO (Victor Hanbury)

A Nazi hero poses as a British pilot but has difficulty getting back home.
Tall war story with dreary romantic trimmings.

w Wolfgang Wilhelm, Miles Malleson
d Lance Comfort *ph* Mutz Greenbaum (Max Greene)

Eric Portman, Ann Dvorak, Walter Fitzgerald, Barry Jones, Henry Oscar, Beatrice Varley

The Squall
US 1929 105m bw

A Hungarian gypsy girl attracts all the male members of a farming family, and causes trouble. Perfectly awful melodrama made worse by early sound techniques. Myrna Loy, Alice Joyce, Loretta Young, Richard Ticker, Carroll Nye, Zasu Pitts, Harry Cording. Written by Bradley King, from the play by Jean Bart; directed by Alexander Korda; for First National.

Square Dance*
GB 1986 112m Metrocolor

An awkward 13-year-old girl in rural Texas leaves her gruff grandfather for a visit to the mother she dislikes. Unremarkable but cohesive family drama which most will feel they have seen before. Jason Robards, Jane Alexander, Winona Ryder, Rob Lowe, Deborah Richter. Written by Alan Hines, from his novel; directed by Daniel Petrie; for NBC/ Michael Nesmith/Island.

The Square Jungle
US 1955 85m bw
U-I (Albert Zugsmith)

A conceited boxer gets his come-uppance.
Tailor-made studio co-feature.

w George Zuckerman *d* Jerry Hopper
ph George Robinson *m* Heinz Roemheld

Tony Curtis, Ernest Borgnine, Pat Crowley, Jim Backus, Paul Kelly

The Square Peg*
GB 1958 89m bw
Rank (Hugh Stewart)

An army recruit finds he is the double of a German general.
Slam-bang star slapstick, shorter than usual and with a few jokes that can't fail.

w Jack Davies *d* John Paddy Carstairs
ph Jack Cox *m* Philip Green

Norman Wisdom, Edward Chapman, Campbell Singer, Hattie Jacques, Brian Worth, Terence Alexander

The Square Ring*
GB 1953 83m bw

One night at a boxing stadium. An assortment of anecdotes does not constitute one of Ealing's best films, but the competence level is high. Jack Warner, Robert Beatty, Maxwell Reed, Bill Owen, Joan Collins, Kay Kendall, Bernadette O'Farrell, Eddie Byrne, Sid James, Alfie Bass. Written by Robert Westerby, Peter Myers, Alec Grahame from a play by Ralph Peterson; directed by Basil Dearden; for Relph-Dearden/Ealing.

The Squaw Man
US 1931 .106m bw
MGM (Cecil B. de Mille)
GB title: *The White Man*

An Indian maiden saves the life of a British aristocrat, bears his child and commits suicide.
Third outing for a hoary miscegenation drama filmed in 1914 with Dustin Farnum and Red Wing, and in 1918 with Elliott Dexter and Ann Little. This talkie version sank without trace.

w Lucien Hubbard, Lenore Coffee, *play* Edwin Milton Royle *d* Cecil B. de Mille
ph Harold Rosson *m* Herbert Stothart

Warner Baxter, Lupe Velez, Charles Bickford, Eleanor Boardman, Roland Young, Paul Cavanagh, Raymond Hatton

'Should be generally fair b.o. in the smaller localities and perhaps not so hot for the diffident big-town show shoppers.'—*Variety*

The Squeaker*
GB 1937 77m bw
London Films (Alexander Korda)
US title: *Murder on Diamond Row*

A dangerous diamond fence is unmasked by a discredited policeman.
Typical Edgar Wallace who-is-it, performed with old-fashioned bravura.

w Edward O. Berkman, Bryan Wallace, *novel* Edgar Wallace *d* William K. Howard

Edmund Lowe, Sebastian Shaw, Ann Todd, Tamara Desni, Alastair Sim, Robert Newton, Allan Jeayes, Stewart Rome
† Previously filmed in 1930, directed by Edgar Wallace for British Lion; with Percy Marmont, Eric Maturin, Anne Grey and Nigel Bruce.

The Squeeze
GB 1977 107m Technicolor
Warner / Martinat (Stanley O'Toole)

An alcoholic ex-cop rescues his ex-wife from kidnappers.
Sleazy action thriller which despite efficient production goes over the top in its search for unpleasant detail.

w Leon Griffiths, *novel* David Craig
d Michael Apted *ph* Dennis Lewiston
m David Hentschel

Stacy Keach, David Hemmings, Stephen Boyd, Edward Fox, Carol White, Freddie Starr

Squibs*
GB 1935 77m bw

A cockney flowergirl wins a sweepstake.
Acceptable sound version of a series of rather naïve silents which pleased the crowds in the early twenties with the same star: they were *Squibs, Squibs MP, Squibs' Honeymoon* and *Squibs Wins the Calcutta Sweep. Betty Balfour*, Gordon Harker, Stanley Holloway, Margaret Yarde, Michael Shepley. Written by Michael Hogan and H. Fowler Mear, from the play by Clifford Seyler and George Pearson; directed by Henry Edwards; for Twickenham.

Squirm
US 1976 92m Movielab
AIP / The Squirm Company (Edgar Lansbury, Joseph Beruh)

A power cable cut in a storm turns worms into maneaters.
Revolting shocker with a few funny moments for those who can take it.

wd Jeff Lieberman *ph* Joseph Mangine
m Robert Prince

John Scardino, Patricia Pearcy, R. A. Dow, Jean Sullivan

Stablemates
US 1938 89m bw

A broken-down vet saves a stableboy's racehorse. Sentimental comedy vehicle for two masters of the surreptitious tear. Wallace Beery, Mickey Rooney, Margaret Hamilton, Minor Watson, Marjorie Gateson. Written by Reginald Owen and William Thiele; directed by Sam Wood; for MGM.

Stage Door***
US 1937 93m bw
RKO (Pandro S. Berman)

Life in a New York theatrical boarding house for girls.
Melodramatic, sharply comedic, always fascinating slice of stagey life from a Broadway hit; the performances alone make it worth preserving.

w Morrie Ryskind, Anthony Veiller, play Edna Ferber, George S. Kaufman d Gregory La Cava ph Robert de Grasse *m* Roy Webb
ad Van Nest Polglase

Katharine Hepburn, Ginger Rogers, Adolphe Menjou, Gail Patrick, Constance Collier, Andrea Leeds, Lucille Ball, Samuel S. Hinds, Jack Carson, Franklin Pangborn, Eve Arden

'It is a long time since we have seen so much feminine talent so deftly handled.'—*Otis Ferguson*

'Zest and pace and photographic eloquence.'—*Frank S. Nugent, New York Times*

'A rare example of a film substantially improving on a stage original and a remarkably satisfying film on all levels.'—*NFT, 1973*

'One of the flashiest, most entertaining comedies of the 30s, even with its tremolos and touches of heartbreak.'—*Pauline Kael, 70s*

AAN: best picture; script; Gregory La Cava; Andrea Leeds

'48 stars plus a great love story!'

Stage Door Canteen*
US 1943 132m bw
Sol Lesser (Barnett Briskin)

How the stars in New York entertained the armed forces during World War II.
Nothing as a film, mildly interesting as sociology and for some rarish appearances.

w Delmer Daves *d* Frank Borzage *ph* Harry Wild *m* Freddie Rich *pd* Harry Horner

Cheryl Walker, Lon McCallister, Judith Anderson, Tallulah Bankhead, Ray Bolger, Katherine Cornell, Helen Hayes, George Jessel, Alfred Lunt, Harpo Marx, Yehudi Menuhin, Elliott Nugent, Cornelia Otis Skinner, Ethel Waters, May Whitty, William Demarest, Gracie Fields, Katharine Hepburn, Gertrude Lawrence, Ethel Merman, Merle Oberon, Johnny Weissmuller, Edgar Bergen, Jane Cowl, Lynn Fontanne, Paul Muni, Gypsy Rose Lee, George Raft, etc; Count Basie, Benny Goodman, Xavier Cugat, Guy Lombardo, Kay Kyser and their bands

'A nice harmless picture for the whole family, and a goldmine for those who are willing to go to it in the wrong spirit.'—*James Agee*

AAN: Freddie Rich; song 'We Mustn't Say Goodbye' (*m* James V. Monaco, *ly* Al Dubin)

Stage Fright*
GB 1950 110m bw
Warner / ABPC (Alfred Hitchcock)

A man is on the run for a backstage murder, and his girl friend takes a job as maid to the great star he says is responsible.
Creaky Hitchcock thriller in which you can see all the joins and the stars seem stuck in treacle; but a few of the set pieces work well enough.

w Whitfield Cook, *novel* Man Running by Selwyn Jepson *d* Alfred Hitchcock *ph* Wilkie Cooper *m* Leighton Lucas

Marlene Dietrich, Jane Wyman, Richard Todd, Alastair Sim, Michael Wilding, Sybil Thorndike, Kay Walsh, Miles Malleson

Stage Mother
US 1933 85m bw

The mother of a young actress is not above sacrificing her daughter for financial gain.
Wisecracking comedy-romance, rather similar to the later *Gypsy*. Alice Brady, Maureen O'Sullivan, Franchot Tone, Phillips Holmes, Ted Healy, C. Henry Gordon. Written by John Meehan, Bradford Ropes, from the latter's novel; directed by Charles Brabin; for MGM. 'Packed with colour, not a little s.a., and certain of adequate b.o. attention.'—*Variety*

Stage Struck
US 1936 95m bw
Warner (Robert Lord)

Young people put on a show and become instant hits.
Dim musical oddly shorn of production numbers.

w Tom Buckinham, Pat C. Flick, Robert Lord *d / ch* Busby Berkeley *ph* Byron Haskin *m* Leo F. Forbstein *songs* Harold Arlen, E. Y. Harburg

Dick Powell, Joan Blondell, Jeanne Madden, the Yacht Club Boys, Warren William, Frank McHugh

Stage Struck**
US 1957 95m Technicolor
RKO (Stuart Millar)

A young actress comes to New York intent on stardom . . .
Careful, slightly arid remake of *Morning Glory* marred by a tiresome central performance; good theatrical detail.

w Ruth and Augustus Goetz, *play* Zoe Akins *d Sidney Lumet ph Franz Planer m* Alex North *ad* Kim Edgar Swados

Susan Strasberg, Henry Fonda, Herbert Marshall, *Joan Greenwood*, Christopher Plummer

Stage to Thunder Rock
US 1964 89m Techniscope
Paramount / A. C. Lyles

An ageing sheriff takes a bank robber back to jail by stagecoach.
Acceptable lower-berth western with the producer's usual roster of half-forgotten character actors.

w Charles Wallace *d* William F. Claxton *ph* W. Wallace Kelley *m* Paul Dunlap

Barry Sullivan, Marilyn Maxwell, Scott Brady, Keenan Wynn, Allan Jones, Lon Chaney Jnr, John Agar, Wanda Hendrix, Anne Seymour, Robert Lowery

Stagecoach****
US 1939 99m bw
(UA) Walter Wanger

Various western characters board a stagecoach in danger from an Indian war party.
What looked like a minor western with a plot borrowed from Maupassant's *Boule de suif*, became a classic by virtue of the firm characterization, restrained writing, exciting climax and the scenery of Monument Valley. Whatever the reasons, it damn well works.

w Dudley Nichols, story Stage to Lordsburg by Ernest Haycox *d John Ford ph* Bert Glennon, Ray Binger *m* Richard Hageman, W. Frank Harling, John Leopold, Leo Shuken, Louis Gruenberg *md* Boris Morros

Claire Trevor, John Wayne, Thomas Mitchell, George Bancroft, Andy Devine, *Berton Churchill*, Louise Platt, *John Carradine, Donald Meek*, Tim Holt, Chris-Pin Martin

'It displays potentialities that can easily drive it through as one of the surprise big grossers of the year.'—*Variety*

'The basic western, a template for everything that followed.'—*John Baxter, 1968*

'Grand Hotel on wheels.'—*New Yorker, 1975*

'A motion picture that sings a song of camera.'—*Frank S. Nugent, New York Times*

AA: music; Thomas Mitchell
AAN: best picture; John Ford; Bert Glennon; Ray Binger

Stagecoach
US 1966 114m De Luxe Cinemascope
TCF / Martin Rackin

Absolutely awful remake of the above; costly but totally spiritless, miscast and uninteresting.

w Joseph Landon *d* Gordon Douglas *ph* William H. Clothier *m* Jerry Goldsmith

Ann-Margret, Alex Cord, Bing Crosby, Van Heflin, Slim Pickens, Robert Cummings, Stefanie Powers, Michael Connors, Red Buttons, Keenan Wynn

Staircase*
US / France 1969 101m De Luxe Panavision
TCF / Stanely Donen

The problems of two ageing homosexual hairdressers.
Unsatisfactorily opened-out and over-acted version of an effective two-handler play. Oddly made in France, so that the London detail seems all wrong.

w Charles Dyer, from his play *d* Stanley Donen *ph* Christopher Challis *m* Dudley Moore

Richard Burton, Rex Harrison, Cathleen Nesbitt, Beatrix Lehmann

'The shape is smashed . . . no longer a graceful duet, it becomes a waddling tale, spattered with ugliness, that falls into the biggest sentimental trap for homosexual material: it pleads for pity.'—*Stanley Kauffmann*

Stakeout
US 1987 115m De Luxe

One of two Seattle cops engaged in a long stakeout falls in love with a suspect. Ho-hum *policier* with insufficient plot for its length. Richard Dreyfuss, Emilio Estevez, Madeleine Stowe, Aidan Quinn, Dan Lauria. Written by Jim Kouf; directed by John Badham; for Touchstone.

Stakeout on Dope Street*
US 1958 83m bw
Warner (Andrew J. Fenady)

Three young men find a briefcase containing heroin and are attacked by the gangsters who lost it.
Lively little crime morality, uneven but worth a look.

w Irwin Schwartz, Irvin Kershner, Andrew J. Fenady *d Irvin Kershner ph Mark Jeffrey m* Richard Markowitz

Yale Wexler, Jonathon Haze, Morris Miller, Abby Dalton

Stalag 17**
US 1953 120m bw
Paramount (Billy Wilder)

Comedy and tragedy for American servicemen in a Nazi prisoner-of-war camp.
High jinks, violence and mystery in a sharply calculated mixture; an atmosphere quite different from the understated British films on the subject.

w Billy Wilder, Edwin Blum, play Donald Bevan, Edmund Trzinski *d* Billy Wilder *ph* Ernest Laszlo *m* Franz Waxman

William Holden, Don Taylor, Otto Preminger, *Robert Strauss*, Harvey Lembeck, Richard Erdman, Peter Graves, Neville Grand, Sig Rumann

'A facility for continuous rapid-fire action which alternately brings forth the laughs and tingles the spine.'—*Otis L. Guernsey Jnr*

'Raucous and tense, heartless and sentimental, always fast-paced, it has already been assigned by critics to places on their lists of the year's ten best movies.'—*Life*

AA: William Holden
AAN: Billy Wilder (as director), Robert Strauss

Stalker*
USSR 1979 161m colour
Mosfilm Unit 2

In the centre of an industrial wasteland there appears a mysterious zone where all normal laws of life are suspended.
Part political allegory, part personal fantasy, all very fascinating but rather hard tack for anybody in search of entertainment.

w Arkady Strugatsky, Boris Strugatsky, from their story *d/ph Andrei Tarkovsky* *m* Eduard Artemyev

Aleksandr Kaidanovsky, Anatoly Solonitsin, Nikolai Grinko, Alisa Freindlikh

The Stalking Moon*
US 1968 109m Technicolor Panavision
National General / Stalking Moon Company (Alan J. Pakula)

An ageing scout escorts home a white woman who has escaped from the Indians, and kills a murderous Apache.
Slow, thoughtful western with effective moments.

w Alvin Sargent, *novel* Theodore V. Olsen *d* Robert Mulligan *ph* Charles Lang *m* Fred Karlin

Gregory Peck, Eva Marie Saint, Robert Forster, Frank Silvera

Stallion Road
US 1947 97m bw
Warner (Alex Gottlieb)

An outbreak of anthrax threatens a racing stable.
Routine romantic drama with sporting background.

w Stephen Longstreed *d* James V. Kern *ph* Arthur Edeson *m* Frederick Hollander

Ronald Reagan, Alexis Smith, Zachary Scott, Peggy Knudsen, Patti Brady, Harry Davenport, Frank Puglia

Stamboul Quest
US 1934 88m bw
MGM (Walter Wanger)

During World War I, Germany's most notorious lady spy falls for an American medical student.
Modest variation on the true story twice filmed as *Fraülein Doktor*; standard Hollywood values.

w Herman J. Mankiewicz *d* Sam Wood *ph* James Wong Howe *m* Herbert Stothart

Myrna Loy, George Brent, Lionel Atwill, C. Henry Gordon, Douglass Dumbrille, Mischa Auer.

The Stand at Apache River
US 1953 77m Technicolor

Apaches attack a reservation when the army won't listen to reason. Conventional western with sympathy for the Indians. Stephen McNally, Julie Adams, Hugh Marlowe, Hugh O'Brian, Jack Kelly. Written by Arthur Ross; directed by Lee Sholem; for Universal-International.

Stand by for Action
US 1943 109m bw
MGM (Robert Z. Leonard, Orville O. Dull)
GB title: *Cargo of Innocents*

A Harvard graduate learns the realities of war on an old destroyer.
Studio-bound war heroics slurping into sentiment.

w George Bruce, Herman J. Mankiewicz, John L. Balderston *d* Robert Z. Leonard *ph* Charles Rosher *m* Lennie Hayton

Robert Taylor, Charles Laughton, Brian Donlevy, Walter Brennan, Marilyn Maxwell, Henry O'Neill

Stand by Me*
US 1986 89m Technicolor / De Luxe
Columbia / Act III

A boys' gang finds the body of a missing teenager.
Less macabre than its source would suggest, the film is mostly concerned with the friendships and tensions within the group; nostalgia for 50s childhood is nicely conveyed.

w Raynold Gideon and others, from story The Body by Stephen King *d* Rob Reiner *ph* Thomas Del Ruth *m* Jack Nitsche *pd* Dennis Washington

Wil Wheaton, River Phoenix, Corey Feldman, Jerry O'Connell, Kiefer Sutherland, Richard Dreyfuss

Stand In*
US 1937 90m bw
Walter Wanger

An efficiency expert is sent to save a Hollywood studio from bankruptcy.
Amusing satire which could have done with sharper scripting and firmer control but is pleasantly remembered.

w Gene Towne, Graham Baker, *serial* Clarence Budington Kelland *d* Tay Garnett *ph* Charles G. Clarke *m* Heinz Roemheld

Leslie Howard, Joan Blondell, Humphrey Bogart, Alan Mowbray, Marla Shelton, C. Henry Gordon, Jack Carson, Tully Marshall

'A joyous and nonsensical Hollywood fantasia.'—*Spectator*

Stand Up and Be Counted*
US 1971 99m Eastmancolor
Columbia / Mike Frankovich

An international woman journalist returns to Denver and becomes involved in women's lib.
A glamoured-up flirtation with a fashionable theme, quite nicely done but instantly dated—and sociologically interesting.

w Bernard Slade *d* Jackie Cooper *ph* Fred Koenekamp *m* Ernie Wilkins

Jacqueline Bisset, Stella Stevens, Steve Lawrence, Gary Lockwood, *Loretta Swit*, Lee Purcell, Madlyn Rhue

Stand Up and Cheer*
US 1934 80m bw
Fox (Winfield Sheehan)

The new US Secretary of Amusement attempts to shake the country's Depression blues by staging a mammoth revue.
Naïve propaganda, but the whole world was swept away to cloud nine—by Shirley Temple.

w Ralph Spence, Will Rogers, Philip Klein *d* Hamilton McFadden *ph* Ernest Palmer *md* Arthur Lange

Warner Baxter, Madge Evans, Nigel Bruce, Stepin Fetchit, Frank Melton, Lila Lee, Ralph Morgan, James Dunn, *Shirley Temple*, John Boles, George K. Arthur

'Its intrinsic merits do not quite match its pretentiousness.'—*Variety*

'Impossible to file it away in an ordinary drawer marked 'Stinkers'. This one is extra, it is super, and it butters itself very thickly with the most obvious sort of topical significance.'—*Otis Ferguson*

† The original title was Fox Follies.

Stand Up and Fight*
US 1938 99m bw
MGM (Mervyn Le Roy)

A southern aristocrat comes into conflict with a stagecoach operator used as transportation for stolen slaves.
Superior star action piece with plenty of vigorous brawls.

w James M. Cain, Jane Murfin, Harvey Ferguson *d W. S. Van Dyke II* *ph* Leonard Smith *m* William Axt

Wallace Beery, Robert Taylor, Florence Rice, Helen Broderick, Charles Bickford, Barton MacLane, Charley Grapewin, John Qualen

'An action thriller that will please the muggs more than the dames . . . should prove strong at the b.o.'—*Variety*

Stand Up Virgin Soldiers
GB 1977 90m Technicolor
Warner / Greg Smith / Maidenhead

More sexual adventures of National Servicemen in Singapore in 1950.
The Virgin Soldiers had a certain authenticity behind the fooling; this is a bawdy romp, and not a very efficient one.

w Leslie Thomas, from his novel *d* Norman Cohen *ph* Ken Hodges *m* Ed Welch

Nigel Davenport, Robin Askwith, George Layton, Robin Nedwell, Warren Mitchell, John Le Mesurier, Edward Woodward, Irene Handl

'The hilarious story of what a girl will do to get her boss a bed in Washington!'

Standing Room Only*
US 1944 83m bw
Paramount (Paul Jones)

Hotel rooms being hard to find in wartime Washington, a resourceful secretary hires out herself and her boss as a servant couple.
Moderate romantic farce with a few good laughs.

w Darrell Ware, Karl Tunberg *d* Sidney Lanfield *ph* Charles Lang *m* Robert Emmett Dolan

Paulette Goddard, Fred MacMurray, Edward Arnold, Roland Young, Hillary Brooke, Porter Hall, Clarence Kolb, Anne Revere

Stanley and Livingstone***
US 1939 101m bw
TCF (Kenneth MacGowan)

An American journalist goes to Africa to find a lost Victorian explorer.
A prestige picture which played reasonably fair with history and still managed to please the masses.

w Philip Dunne, Julien Josephson *d Henry King ph George Barnes m* David Raksin, David Buttolph, Cyril Mockridge, Alfred Newman *ad* Thomas Little

Spencer Tracy, Cedric Hardwicke, Richard Greene, Nancy Kelly, Walter Brennan, Charles Coburn, Henry Hull, Henry Travers, Miles Mander, Holmes Herbert

'Sound, worthy, interesting.'—*Richard Mallett, Punch*

'Most of the film consists of long shots of stand-ins moving across undistinguished scenery. . . . Mr Tracy is always a human being, but Sir Cedric is an elocution lesson, a handclasp.'—*Graham Greene*

'Holds box office promise for socko biz . . . it's absorbing and adventurous drama.'—*Variety*

'When the star fades, the woman is born!'
'The story of every woman who ever climbed the stairway to the stars—and found herself at the bottom looking up!'

The Star*
US 1952 91m bw
TCF / Bert E. Friedlob

A once famous Hollywood star is financially and psychologically on her uppers.
A movie apparently tailor-made for its star turns out to be a disappointingly plotless wallow.

w Katherine Albert, Dale Eunson *d* Stuart Heisler *ph* Ernest Laszlo *m* Victor Young

Bette Davis, Sterling Hayden, Natalie Wood, Warner Anderson, Minor Watson

† The role was originally designed for Joan Crawford.

AAN: Bette Davis

Star!**
US 1968 194m De Luxe Todd-AO
TCF / Robert Wise (Saul Chaplin)

Revue artist Gertrude Lawrence rises from poverty to international stardom and a measure of happiness.
Elephantiasis finally ruins this patient, detached, generally likeable recreation of a past theatrical era. In the old Hollywood style, it would probably have been even better on a smaller budget; but alas the star would still have been ill at ease with the drunken termagant scenes.

w William Fairchild *d Robert Wise ph* Ernest Laszlo *md* Lennie Hayton *ch* Michael Kidd *pd* Boris Leven

Julie Andrews, Richard Crenna, Michael Craig, *Daniel Massey* (as Noel Coward), John Collin, Robert Reed, Bruce Forsyth, Beryl Reid, Jenny Agutter

† Short version: *Those Were the Happy Days.*

†† The film cost 14 million and took four.

AAN: Ernest Laszlo; Lennie Hayton; title song (*m* James Van Heusen, *ly* Sammy Cahn); Daniel Massey

The Star Chamber
US 1983 109m De Luxe Panavision
TCF / Frank Yablans

Judges get together to retry defendants who have been unjustly freed, and then have them executed by hired assassins.
A bit hard to swallow; also overlong and rather unpleasant.

w Roderick Taylor, Peter Hyams *d* Peter Hyams *ph* Richard Hannah *m* Michael Small *pd* Bill Malley

Michael Douglas, Hal Holbrook, Yaphet Kotto, Sharon Gless, James B. Sikking, Joe Regalbuto

'Michael Winner territory with a veneer of conscience.'—*Sight and Sound*

'Small-screen material suffering from crippling inflation.'—*Steve Jenkins, MFB*

Star Dust*
US 1940 85m bw
TCF (Kenneth MacGowan)

A talent scout discovers a new Hollywood star.
Light, amusing studio comedy, a pleasing addition to Hollywood mythology.

w Robert Ellis, Helen Logan *d* Walter Lang *ph* Peverell Marley *m* David Buttolph

Linda Darnell, John Payne, Roland Young, Charlotte Greenwood, William Gargan, Mary Beth Hughes, Donald Meek, Jessie Ralph

Star 80
US 1983 103m Technicolor
Warner / Ladd (Wolfgang Glattes, Kenneth Utt)

The murder by her husband of Dorothy Stratten, the playboy centrefold model.
Unappetizing recounting, made less palatable by flashy direction, of a story with no possible moral.

w,d Bob Fosse *ph* Sven Nykvist *m* Ralph Burns *pd* Tony Walton

Mariel Hemingway, Eric Roberts, Cliff Robertson (as Hugh Hefner), Carroll Baker, Roger Rees

'A mishmash of embarrassments.'—*Tom Milne, MFB*

'Obviously intended as a cautionary tale for our times, with the beautiful dreamers and ruthless schemers peopling a colour supplement world of success.'—*Sight and Sound*

A Star Is Born***
US 1937 111m Technicolor
David O. Selznick

A young actress meets Hollywood success and marries a famous leading man, whose star wanes as hers shines brighter.
Abrasive romantic melodrama which is also the most accurate study of Hollywood ever put on film.

w Dorothy Parker, Alan Campbell, Robert Carson, story William A. Wellman, based partly on *What Price Hollywood* (1932) (qv) *d William A. Wellman ph W. Howard Greene m* Max Steiner

Janet Gaynor, Fredric March, Adolphe Menjou, Lionel Stander, Andy Devine, May Robson, Owen Moore, Franklin Pangborn

'One of those rare ones which everyone will want to see and talk about . . . disproves the tradition that good pictures can't be made with a Hollywood background.'—*Variety*

'Good entertainment by any standards.'—*Frank S. Nugent, New York Times*

'A peculiar sort of masochistic self-congratulatory Hollywood orgy.'—*New Yorker, 1975*

'The first colour job that gets close to what colour must eventually come to: it keeps the thing in its place, underlining the mood and situation of the story rather than dimming everything else out in an iridescent razzle-dazzle.'—*Otis Ferguson*

AA: original story; W. Howard Greene
AAN: best picture; script; William A. Wellman; Janet Gaynor; Fredric March

'Fate raised her to fame—and killed the man she loved!'

A Star Is Born**
US 1954 181m Technicolor Cinemascope
Warner / Transcona (Sidney Luft)

Musical version of the above which begins very strongly and has two splendid performances, but suffers in the second half from a lack of writing strength and heavy post-production cutting. The numbers add very little except length.

w Moss Hart *d George Cukor ph* Sam Leavitt *md Ray Heindorf*

Judy Garland, James Mason, Charles Bickford, Jack Carson, Tommy Noonan, Amanda Blake, Lucy Marlow

'Maintains a skilful balance between the musical and the tear jerker.'—*Penelope Houston*

† Cary Grant and Humphrey Bogart were both sought before James Mason was signed.

AAN: Ray Heindorf; song 'The Man that Got Away' (*m* Harold Arlen, *ly* Ira Gershwin); Judy Garland; James Mason

A Star Is Born*

US 1976 140m Metrocolor

Warner / Barwood / First Artists (Barbra Streisand, Jon Peters)

Interminable remake set in the pop world amid screaming crowds and songs at high decibel level; also an insufferable piece of showing off by the star. But some of the handling has style.

w John Gregory Dunne, Joan Didion, Frank Pierson *d* Frank Pierson *ph* Robert Surtees *md* Paul Williams *pd* Polly Platt

Barbra Streisand, Kris Kristofferson, Paul Mazursky, Gary Busey

'A clear case for the monopolies commission.'—*Michael Billington, Illustrated London News*

'A bore is starred.'—*Village Voice*

AA: song 'Evergreen' (*m* Barbra Streisand, *ly* Paul Williams)

AAN: Robert Surtees; Roger Kellaway (music underscoring)

The Star Maker*

US 1939 94m bw

Paramount (Charles R. Rodgers)

A songwriter makes the big time by organizing kid acts.

Pleasant minor musical based on the career of Gus Edwards.

w Frank Butler, Don Hartman, Arthur Caesar *d* Roy del Ruth *ph* Karl Struss

Bing Crosby, Louise Campbell, Linda Ware, Ned Sparks, Laura Hope Crews, Janet Waldo, Walter Damrosch

'A rollicking filmusical, first-class entertainment.'—*Variety*

Star of Midnight*

US 1935 90m bw

RKO (Pandro S. Berman)

A New York attorney solves the disappearance of a leading lady.

Wisecracking, debonair murder mystery modelled on *The Thin Man*.

w Howard J. Green, Anthony Veiller, Edward Kaufman *d* Stephen Roberts *ph* J. Roy Hunt *m* Max Steiner

William Powell, Ginger Rogers, Paul Kelly, Gene Lockhart, Ralph Morgan, Leslie Fenton, J. Farrell MacDonald

'Too bad the title isn't more attractive, but the picture is excellent otherwise and should be a snappy grosser.'—*Variety*

'It is all suavity and amusement, pistol shots and cocktails.'—*Graham Greene*

'One of the best sophisticated comedy-mysteries in a period full of such films.'—*NFT, 1973*

The Star Spangled Girl

US 1971 92m colour

Paramount (Howard W. Koch)

A sweet old-fashioned girl is fought for by two young radicals.

Unamusingly 'with it' comedy from an unsuccessful play.

w Arnold Margolin, Jim Parker, *play* Neil Simon *d* Jerry Paris *ph* Sam Leavitt *m* Charles Fox

Sandy Duncan, Tony Roberts, Todd Susman, Elizabeth Allen

Star Spangled Rhythm***

US 1942 99m bw

Paramount (Joseph Sistrom)

The doorman of Paramount Studios pretends to his sailor son that he is a big producer.

Frenetic farce involving most of the talent on Paramount's payroll and culminating in an 'impromptu' show staged for the navy. A good lighthearted glimpse of wartime Hollywood.

w Harry Tugend *d* George Marshall *ph* Leo Tover, Theodor Sparkuhl *md* Robert Emmett Dolan *songs* Johnny Mercer, Harold Arlen

Betty Hutton, Eddie Bracken, *Victor Moore, Walter Abel,* Anne Revere, Cass Daley, Gil Lamb, Macdonald Carey, Bob Hope, Bing Crosby, Paulette Goddard, Veronica Lake, Dorothy Lamour, Vera Zorina, Fred MacMurray, Ray Milland, Lynne Overman, Franchot Tone, Dick Powell, *Walter Dare Wahl and Co, Cecil B. de Mille, Preston Sturges,* Alan Ladd, Rochester, Katherine Dunham, Susan Hayward

AAN: Robert Emmett Dolan; song 'Black Magic' (*m* Harold Arlen, *ly* Johnny Mercer)

'The human adventure is just beginning!'

Star Trek: The Motion Picture

US 1979 132m Metrocolor Panavision

Paramount (Gene Roddenberry)

In the twenty-third century, Admiral Kirk resumes command of the *Enterprise* to combat an alien force.

And a surprisingly boring one. Vast sets and big-screen solemnity hardly make this more enjoyable than some of the TV episodes which got more tricks and philosophical fun into one-third of the length.

w Harold Livingstone, Alan Dean Foster *d* Robert Wise *ph* Richard H. Kline, Richard Yuricich *m* Jerry Goldsmith *pd* Harold Michelson

William Shatner, Leonard Nimoy, DeForest Kelley, Stephen Collins, Persis Khambatta

'At the end of the universe lies the beginning of vengeance!'

Star Trek: The Wrath of Khan

US 1982 114m Movielab Panavision

Paramount (Harve Bennett)

The crew of the starship *Enterprise* counter the wiles of an evil genius on a distant planet.

Comic strip capers a long way from the controlled intelligence of some episodes of the TV series; but more entertaining than the first movie.

w Jack B. Sowards *d* Nicholas Meyer *ph* Gayne Rescher *m* James Horner *pd* Joseph R. Jennings

William Shatner, Leonard Nimoy, Ricardo Montalban, DeForest Kelley, Ike Eisenmann

'A pitiful snack for the eyes with some unappetizing crumbs left over for the mind to chew on.'—*Philip Strick, MFB*

Star Trek 3: The Search for Spock

US 1984 105m Metrocolor Panavision

Paramount / Cinema Group Venture (Harve Bennett)

Admiral Kirk discovers that Spock is not dead but has been reborn as a Vulcan child . . .

Very silly, empty and unamusing follow-up. Let us hope fervently that the adventure does not continue.

w Harve Bennett *d* Leonard Nimoy *ph* Charles Correll *m* James Horner

William Shatner, De Forrest Kelley, James Doohan, Walter Koenig, Michelle Nichols, Robert Hooks, Leonard Nimoy

Star Trek IV: The Voyage Home*

US 1986 119m Technicolor Panavision

Paramount / Harve Bennett

GB title: *The Voyage Home: Star Trek IV*

The Enterprise crew is called home to face trial for mutiny: they find a very alien world.

The best of the series: it isn't saying much, but at least there are shreds of wit in the script.

w Harve Bennett, Steve Meerson, Peter Krikes, Nicholas Meyer *d* Leonard Nimoy *ph* Don Peterman *m* Leonard Rosenman *pd* Jack T. Collis *ed* Peter E. Berger

William Shatner, Leonard Nimoy, DeForest Kelley, James Doohan, George Takei, Walter Koenig, Jane Wyatt, Catherine Hicks

AAN: Don Peterman; Leonard Rosenman

Star Wars***

US 1977 121m Technicolor Panavision

TCF / Lucasfilm (Gary Kurtz)

A rebel princess in a distant galaxy escapes, and with the help of her robots and a young farmer overcomes the threatening forces of evil.

Flash Gordon rides again, but with timing so impeccably right that the movie became a phenomenon and one of the top grossers of all time. In view of the hullaballoo, some disappointment may be felt with the actual experience of watching it . . . but it's certainly good harmless fun, put together with style and imagination.

wd George Lucas ph Gilbert Taylor *m* John Williams *pd* John Barry *sp* many and various

Mark Hamill, Harrison Ford, Carrie Fisher, Peter Cushing, Alec Guinness, Anthony Daniels (See Threepio), Kenny Baker (Artoo Detoo), Dave Prowse (Darth Vader)

'A great work of popular art, fully deserving the riches it has reaped.'—*Time*

'Acting in this movie I felt like a raisin in a giant fruit salad. And I didn't even know who the coconuts or the canteloups were.'—*Mark Hamill*

'He intended his film, Lucas confesses, for a generation growing up without fairy tales. His target audience was fourteen years and younger. . . It was a celebration, a social affair, a collective dream, and people came again and again, dragging their friends and families with them.'—*Les Keyser, Hollywood in the Seventies*

'The loudness, the smash and grab editing and the relentless pacing drive every idea from your head, and even if you've been entertained you may feel cheated of some dimension—a sense of wonder, perhaps.'—*New Yorker, 1982*

'Heartless fireworks ignited by a permanently retarded director with too much clout and cash.'—*Time Out, 1984*

AA: John Williams
AAN: best picture; script; direction; Alec Guinness

The Star Witness*
US 1931 68m bw
Warner

An old man witnesses a crime and threatened by gangsters.
Pacy melodrama with good performances.

w Lucien Hubbard *d* William Wellman *ph* James Van Trees

Walter Huston, Chic Sale, Grant Mitchell, Frances Starr, Sally Blane

'Plenty of action, laughs, and a tear.'—*Variety*

AAN: Lucien Hubbard

Stardust
GB 1974 111m Technicolor
EMI / Goodtimes (David Puttnam, Sandy Lieberson)

The rise and fall of a pop singer.
Unappetizing rehash of the road to ruin, pop music style.

w Ray Connolly *d* Michael Apted *ph* Tony Richmond *md* Dave Edmunds, David Puttnam

David Essex, Adam Faith, Larry Hagman, Marty Wilde, Rosalind Ayres

Stardust Memories*
US 1980 88m bw
UA / Jack Rollins, Charles H. Joffe

An increasingly melancholy comedian attends a retrospective of his work and is plagued by real and imaginary fears.
A plainly autobiographical work which, while amusing and moving in spots, makes it doubtful that the writer / director / star can even now shake off his obsessions.

wd Woody Allen ph Gordon Willis *m* Dick Hyman

Woody Allen, Charlotte Rampling, Jessica Harper, Marie-Christine Barrault, Tony Roberts, Helen Hanft

'Its posturing pyrotechnics seem more the symptom of a crisis than its controlled expression.'—*Gilbert Adair, MFB*

Starlift
US 1951 102m bw
Warner (Robert Arthur)

Movie stars entertain at Travis Air Base, where the boys are constantly leaving for Korea.
Insipid musical with even more insipid romantic interludes.

w John Klorer, Karl Kamb *d* Roy del Ruth *ph* Ted McCord *md* Ray Heindorf

Janice Rule, Dick Wesson, Richard Webb, Howard St John; and guest stars Doris Day, Gordon MacRae, Virginia Mayo, Gene Nelson, Ruth Roman, James Cagney, Gary Cooper, Phil Harris, Louella Parsons, Randolph Scott, Jane Wyman

Starman
US 1984 115m MGM color
Columbia / Delphi (Larry J. Franco)

An alien arrives in Wisconsin and takes human form, falling in love with the widow of the man he impersonates.
Derivative but eccentric science-fiction fantasy with lapses of narrative and a general attempt to make the love story predominant over the hardware.

w Bruce A. Evans, Raynold Gideon *d* John Carpenter *ph* Donald M. Morgan *m* Jack Nitzche *pd* Daniel Lomino *ed* Marion Rothman

Jeff Bridges, Karen Allen, Charles Martin Smith, Richard Jaeckel, Robert Phalen, Tony Edwards
AAN: Jeff Bridges

Stars and Bars
US 1988 94m Du Art / De Luxe

Cliché Englishman's encounters with stereotyped Americans in search for long-lost Renoir painting. Daniel Day-Lewis, Harry Dean Stanton, Martha Plimpton, Joan Cusack. Written by William Boyd, from his novel; directed by Pat O'Connor; for Columbia.
'Unhappy mixture of farce and misdirected satire.'—*Variety*

Stars and Stripes Forever*
US 1952 89m Technicolor
TCF (Lamar Trotti)
GB title: *Marching Along*

In the 1890s John Philip Sousa, a bandmaster who wants to write ballads, finds success as a writer of marches.
Low-key musical biopic with predictably noisy numbers.

w Lamar Trotti, from Sousa's autobiography *d* Henry Koster *ph* Charles G. Clarke *md* Alfred Newman

Clifton Webb, Debra Paget, Robert Wagner, Ruth Hussey, Finlay Currie, Roy Roberts, Lester Matthews

The Stars Are Singing
US 1952 99m Technicolor
Paramount (Irving Asher)

A Polish refugee girl illegally enters the US and becomes an opera star.
Painless Cinderella fantasy in which everybody sings.

w Liam O'Brien *d* Norman Taurog *ph* Lionel Lindon *md* Victor Young

Anna Maria Alberghetti, Lauritz Melchior, Rosemary Clooney, Fred Clark, Mikhail Rasumny

Stars in My Crown*
US 1950 89m bw
MGM (William H. Wright)

A two-gun parson brings peace to a Tennessee town after the Civil War.
Sentimental family western, quite pleasantly made and performed.

w Margaret Fitts, *novel* Joe David Brown *d Jacques Tourneur ph* Charles Schoenbaum *m* Adolph Deutsch

Joel McCrea, Ellen Drew, Dean Stockwell, Juano Hernandez, James Mitchell, Lewis Stone, Alan Hale, Amanda Blake

The Stars Look Down**
GB 1939 110m bw
Grafton (Isadore Goldschmidt)

The son of a coal miner struggles to become an MP.
Economically but well made social drama from a popular novel, with good pace and backgrounds.

w J. B. Williams, A. J. Cronin, novel A. J. Cronin *d Carol Reed ph* Max Greene *m* Hans May

Michael Redgrave, Margaret Lockwood, Edward Rigby, Emlyn Williams, Nancy Price, Allan Jeayes, Cecil Parker, Linden Travers

'Dr Cronin's mining novel has produced a very good film—I doubt whether in England we have ever produced a better.'—*Graham Greene*

'A splendidly directed portrait of those who burrow for the black diamond in England's northland . . . the picture is mounted with exactness of detail and technique.'—*Variety*

Stars over Broadway
US 1935 89m bw
Warner (Sam Bischoff)

Agent turns hotel porter into radio star.
Unremarkable musical, with unusual talent.

w Jerry Wald, Julius J. Epstein, Pat C. Flick *d* William Keighley *ph* George Barnes *md* Leo F. Forbstein *ch* Busby Berkeley, Bobby Connolly *songs* Harry Warren, Al Dubin

James Melton, Jane Froman, Pat O'Brien, Jean Muir, Frank McHugh, Marie Wilson, Frank Fay

'A far from inspired backstage yarn with pleasant dialogue and fancy trimmings.'—*Variety*

Start Cheering
US 1938 78m bw

An actor's agent has problems when his potential star decides to go to college. Fairly amusing low-budget musical with some surprises. Jimmy Durante, Walter Connolly, Joan Perry, Charles Starrett, the Three Stooges, Hal Leroy, Ernest Truex, Gertrude Niesen, Raymond Walburn, Broderick Crawford. Written by Eugene Solow, Richard E. Wormser, Philip Rapp, Corey Ford; directed by Albert S. Rogell; for Columbia. 'Longer on entertainment satisfaction than many of the more formidable pricers.'—*Variety*

Start the Revolution without Me*
US 1969 90m Technicolor
Warner / Norbud (Norman Lear)

Two sets of twins get mixed up at the court of Louis XVI.
Historical spoof of the kind subsequently made familiar by Mel Brooks; the script might have suited Abbott and Costello better than these two actors.

w Fred Freeman, Lawrence J. Cohen *d* Bud Yorkin *ph* Jean Tournier *m* John Addison

Donald Sutherland, Gene Wilder, Hugh Griffith, Jack McGowran, Billie Whitelaw, Victor Spinetti, Ewa Aulin

Starting Over*
US 1979 106m Movielab
Paramount / Century Associates (Alan J. Pakula, James L. Brooks)

A divorced man nearly goes back to his wife but finally plumps for a nursery school teacher.
Plain-speaking sex comedy-drama with accomplished stars giving rather more than the script is worth.

w James L. Brooks, *novel* Dan Wakefield *d* Alan J. Pakula *ph* Sven Nykvist *m* Marvin Hamlisch *pd* George Jenkins

Burt Reynolds, Jill Clayburgh, Candice Bergen, Charles Durning, Austin Pendleton

State Fair**
US 1933 98m bw
Fox (Winfield Sheehan)

Dad wants his prize pig to win at the fair, but the younger members of his family have romance in mind.
Archetypal family film, much remade but never quite so pleasantly performed.

w Paul Green, Sonya Levien, *novel* Phil Stong *d* Henry King *ph* Hal Mohr *md* Louis de Francesco

Will Rogers, Janet Gaynor, Lew Ayres, Sally Eilers, Norman Foster, Louise Dresser, Frank Craven, Victor Jory, Hobart Cavanaugh

'A pungent, good-humoured motion picture.'—*Pare Lorentz*

'Vigour, freshness and sympathy abound in its admittedly idealized fantasy treatment of small-town life.'—*Charles Higham, 1972*

AAN: best picture; script

State Fair**
US 1945 100m Technicolor
TCF (William Perlberg)
TV title: *It Happened One Summer*

Musical remake with an amiable cast and a rousing score.

w / ly Oscar Hammerstein II *d* Walter Lang *ph* Leon Shamroy *m Richard Rodgers* *md* Alfred Newman

Charles Winninger, Jeanne Crain, Dana Andrews, Vivian Blaine, Dick Haymes, Fay Bainter, Frank McHugh, Percy Kilbride, Donald Meek

'Surely the sort of theme that clamours for movie treatment. But no, say Twentieth Century Fox: let's make the fair look like a night club. Let's look around for stars of pristine nonentity. Let's screw the camera down to the studio floor. The result, "an epic that sings to the skies . . . with glorious, glamorous new songs".'—*Richard Winnington*

'Comes pretty close to being another *Oklahoma*.'—*Motion Picture Herald*

AA: song 'It Might As Well Be Spring'
AAN: Alfred Newman

State Fair
US 1962 118m De Luxe Cinemascope
TCF (Charles Brackett)

Dullsville modernized version, condescending towards the rurals and peopled by unattractive youngsters.

w Richard Breen *d* Jose Ferrer *ph* William C. Mellor *md* Alfred Newman

Pat Boone, Alice Faye, Tom Ewell, Pamela Tiffin, Ann-Margret, Bobby Darin, Wally Cox

State of the Union***
US 1948 110m bw
(MGM) Liberty Films (Frank Capra)
GB title: *The World and His Wife*

An estranged wife rejoins her husband when he is running for president.
Brilliantly scripted political comedy which unfortunately goes soft at the end but offers stimulating entertainment most of the way.

w Anthony Veiller, Myles Connelly, *play Howard Lindsay, Russel Crouse* *d Frank Capra* *ph* George J. Folsey *m* Victor Young

Spencer Tracy, Katharine Hepburn, Adolphe Menjou, Van Johnson, Angela Lansbury, Lewis Stone, Howard Smith, Raymond Walburn, Charles Dingle

'A triumphant film, marked all over by Frank Capra's artistry.'—*Howard Barnes*

State Secret**
GB 1950 104m bw
British Lion / London (Frank Launder, Sidney Gilliat)
US title: *The Great Manhunt*

In a Ruritanian country, spies pursue a surgeon, the only man who knows that the dictator is dead.
Hitchcockian chase comedy-thriller which is well detailed and rises to the heights on occasion.

wd Sidney Gilliat, *novel* Appointment with Fear by Roy Huggins *ph* Robert Krasker *m* William Alwyn

Douglas Fairbanks Jnr, Glynis Johns, Herbert Lom, Jack Hawkins, Walter Rilla, Karel Stepanek, Carl Jaffe

'An admirably fast-moving diversion in the Hitchcock tradition.'—*Richard Mallett, Punch*

State's Attorney*
US 1932 79m bw
GB title: *Cardigan's Last Case*

A prosecuting counsel nearly pays the penalty for arrogance. Good star melodrama. John Barrymore, Jill Esmond, William Boyd, Helen Twelvetrees. Written by Rowland Brown and Gene Fowler; directed by George Archainbaud; for RKO. 'Good programme box office stuff if not particularly smashing.'—*Variety*

Station Six Sahara
GB 1962 101m bw
British Lion / CCC / Artur Brauner (Victor Lyndon)

Five men working on a remote Saharan pipeline quarrel over the favours of an American girl whose car crashes nearby.
Raging old-fashioned melodrama with the courage of its lack of convictions.

w Bryan Forbes, Brian Clemens *d* Seth Holt *ph* Gerald Gibbs *m* Ron Grainer

Carroll Baker, Ian Bannen, Peter Van Eyck, Denholm Elliott, Mario Adorf, Jorg Felmy, Biff McGuire

Station West
US 1948 91m bw
RKO (Robert Sparks)

A saloon queen is the secret head of a gang of gold robbers.
Predictable but well made western patterned after *Destry Rides Again*.

w Frank Fenton, Winston Miller, *novel* Luke Short *d* Sidney Lanfield *ph* Harry J. Wild *m* Heinz Roemheld

Dick Powell, Jane Greer, Agnes Moorehead, Burl Ives, Tom Powers, Gordon Oliver, Steve Brodie, Guinn Williams, Raymond Burr, Regis Toomey

'The face was his . . . the body was his . . . but suddenly, Hello, Charlie!'

The Statue
US 1970 89m Eastmancolor
Cinerama / Josef Shaftel (Anis Nohra)

A languages professor is embarrassed when his sculptress wife makes an immense nude statue of him—with someone else's private parts.
Strained phallic comedy which doesn't even make the most of its one joke.

w Alec Coppel, Denis Norden *d* Rod Amateau *ph* Piero Portalupi *m* Riz Ortolani

David Niven, Virna Lisi, Robert Vaughn, Ann Bell, John Cleese, Hugh Burden

Stay Away Joe
US 1968 102m Metrocolor Panavision
MGM (Douglas Lawrence)

An Indian rodeo rider returns to his reservation, makes several romantic conquests, and helps a government rehabilitation scheme.
Thin if surprising vehicle for a singing star; all rather tedious.

w Michael A. Hoey, *novel* Dan Cushman *d* Peter Tewkesbury *ph* Fred Koenekamp *m* Jack Marshall

Elvis Presley, Burgess Meredith, Joan Blondell, Katy Jurado, Thomas Gomez, Henry Jones, L. Q. Jones

Stay Hungry
US 1976 102m De Luxe
UA / Outov (Harold Schneider, Bob Rafaelson)

The heir to an Alabama estate annoys the locality by assembling a curious bunch of friends and making unexpected use of his money.
Rather obvious and pointless fable; well made but not very stimulating.

w Charles Gaines, Bob Rafaelson, *novel* Charles Gaines *d* Bob Rafaelson *ph* Victor Kemper *m* Bruce Langhorne, Byron Berline

Jeff Bridges, Sally Field, Arnold Schwarzenegger, R. G. Armstrong, Robert Englund, Roger E. Mosley

'It's five years later for Tony Manero. The fever still burns!'

Staying Alive
US 1983 96m Metrocolor
Paramount / Robert Stigwood / Cinema Group Venture (Sylvester Stallone)

Tony Manero becomes a Broadway dancer.
Fragile sequel to *Saturday Night Fever*, with some of its frenetic quality but none of its impact.

w Sylvester Stallone, Norman Wexler *d* Sylvester Stallone *ph* Nick McLean *m* Johnny Mandel, Robin Garb, others *pd* Robert Boyle

John Travolta, Cynthia Rhodes, Finola Hughes, Steve Inwood, Julie Bovasso

'By turns exhilarating and absurd.'—*Nick Roddick, MFB*

'Stallone doesn't bother much with character, scenes or dialogue. He just puts the newly muscle-plated Travolta in front of the camera, covers him with what looks like oil slick, and goes for the whambams.'—*Pauline Kael, New Yorker*

Steamboat Bill Jnr*
US 1928 71m (24 fps) bw silent
UA / Buster Keaton / Joseph Schenck

A student takes over his father's old Mississippi steamboat, and wins the daughter of his rival.
Rather flat comedy redeemed by a magnificent cyclone climax.

w Carl Harbaugh, Buster Keaton *d* Charles Riesner *ph* J. Devereaux Jennings, Bert Haines

Buster Keaton, Ernest Torrence, Marion Byron

Steamboat Round the Bend*
US 1935 80m bw
TCF (Sol M. Wurtzel)

A Mississippi steamboat captain defeats his rival and finds evidence to clear his nephew of a murder charge.
Rather heavily-scripted star vehicle which sacrifices fun for atmosphere but is often good to look at.

w Dudley Nichols, Lamar Trotti, *novel* Ben Lucien Berman *d John Ford* *ph* George Schneiderman *m* Samuel Kaylin

Will Rogers, Anne Shirley, Eugene Pallette, John McGuire, Irvin S. Cobb, Berton Churchill, Stepin Fetchit, Roger Imhof, Raymond Hatton

'Will Rogers' final picture . . . in the money despite a drab theme.'—*Variety*

Steaming
GB 1985 95m colour

Women in a rundown steam bath confide in each other. Excessively dreary talk piece which apparently seemed crisper on the stage. Vanessa Redgrave, Sarah Miles, Diana Dors, Patti Love, Brenda Bruce. Written by Patricia Losey, from play by Nell Dunn; directed by Joseph Losey (his last film); photographed by Chris Challis; for Paul Mills / World Film Services / Columbia.

Steel
US 1979 101m Movielab
Columbia / Panzer / Davis / Fawcett-Majors (Lee Majors)

When a construction boss is killed, his daughter vows to complete his last project. Flashy, foul-mouthed, but basically old-fashioned hokum climaxing in a race to complete before foreclosure.

w Leigh Chapman *d* Steve Carver *ph* Roger Shearman *m* Michael Colombier *pd* Ward Preston

Lee Majors, Jennifer O'Neill, Art Carney, George Kennedy, Harris Yulin, Terry Kiser, Richard Lynch, Albert Salmi

The Steel Bayonet
GB 1957 85m bw Hammerscope
(UA) Hammer (Michael Carreras)

During the assault on Tunis a battle-weary platoon holds a farm against enemy attack.
Dreary cliché-ridden war melodrama peopled by all the usual types.

w Howard Clewes *d* Michael Carreras *ph* Jack Asher *m* Leonard Salzedo

Leo Genn, Kieron Moore, Michael Medwin, Robert Brown, Michael Ripper, John Paul, Bernard Horsfall

Steel Town
US 1952 84m Technicolor
U-I (Leonard Goldstein)

A steel president's nephew joins the company as a furnace hand.
Routine drama with an unusual background.

w Gerald Drayson Adams, Lou Breslow *d* George Sherman *ph* Charles P. Boyle *m* Joseph Gershenson

Ann Sheridan, John Lund, Howard Duff, James Best, Nancy Kulp

The Steel Trap*
US 1952 85m bw
TCF / Thor (Bert E. Friedlob)

An assistant bank manager steals half a million dollars from the vault but is troubled by conscience and manages to put it back before the loss is discovered.
Solidly competent little suspenser with plenty of movement.

wd Andrew Stone *ph* Ernest Laszlo *m* Dmitri Tiomkin

Joseph Cotten, Teresa Wright, Jonathan Hale, Walter Sande

Steelyard Blues
US 1972 92m Technicolor
Warner / S. B. Productions (Tony Bill, Michael and Julia Phillips)

An ex-con and his call-girl friend are an embarrassment to his DA brother.
Bits and pieces of anti-establishment comedy are tacked on to a thin plot; a few of them work.

w David S. Ward *d* Alan Myerson *ph* Laszlo Kovacs, Steven Larner *m* Nick Gravenites

Donald Sutherland, Jane Fonda, Peter Boyle, Howard Hesseman

Stella Dallas*
US 1925 110m approx (24 fps) bw silent
Samuel Goldwyn

An uncouth woman loses both husband and daughter.
Standard weepie complete with 'out into the cold cold snow' ending, but handled here with tact and discretion. A seminal film of its time.

w Frances Marion, *novel* Olive Higgins Prouty *d* Henry King *ph* Arthur Edeson

Belle Bennett, Ronald Colman, Lois Moran, Jean Hersholt, Douglas Fairbanks Jnr, Alice Joyce

Stella Dallas*
US 1937 106m bw
Samuel Goldwyn

Fashionable remake with excellent talent; 1937 audiences came to sneer and stayed to weep.

w Victor Heerman, Sara Y. Mason *d King Vidor* *ph* Rudolph Maté *m* Alfred Newman

Barbara Stanwyck, John Boles, Anne Shirley, Barbara O'Neil, Alan Hale, Marjorie Main, Tim Holt

'A tear-jerker of A ranking. There are things about the story that will not appeal to some men, but no one will be annoyed or offended by it. And the wallop is inescapably there for femmes.'—*Variety*

† Goldwyn's premier choices for the lead were Ruth Chatterton and Gladys George.

AAN: Barbara Stanwyck; Anne Shirley

Step by Step*
US 1946 62m bw

The FBI gives chase to a young couple who may or may not have stolen government plans.
Trim second feature melodrama with nice touches. Lawrence Tierney, Anne Jeffreys, Lowell Gilmore, George Cleveland, Jason Robards. Written by Stuart Palmer; directed by Phil Rosen; for Sid Rogell / RKO.

Step Down to Terror
US 1959 76m bw
U-I (Joseph Gershenson)
GB title: *The Silent Stranger*

A man returns to his home town and is discovered to be a psychopathic killer on the run.
Dismal reworking of *Shadow of a Doubt*; strictly second feature stuff.

w Mel Dinelli, Czenzi Ormonde, Chris Cooper *d* Harry Keller *ph* Russell Metty *m* Joseph Gershenson

Charles Drake, Coleen Miller, Rod Taylor, Josephine Hutchinson, Jocelyn Brando

Step Lively*
US 1944 88m bw
RKO (Robert Fellows)

Gleaming musical remake of *Room Service* (qv); all very efficient if witless.

w Warren Duff, Peter Milne *d* Tim Whelan *ph* Robert de Grasse *md* Constantin Bakaleinikoff *songs* Jule Styne, Sammy Cahn

Frank Sinatra, George Murphy, Adolphe Menjou, Gloria de Haven, Anne Jeffreys, Walter Slezak, Eugene Pallette

The Stepfather
US 1986 88m CFI colour

A teenage girl discovers that her new stepfather is a psychopath who may make her his victim.
Well enough done but rather obvious suspenser on the lines of *Love from a Stranger*. Terry O'Quinn, Jill Schoelen, Shelley Hack, Charles Lanyer. Written by Donald E. Westlake; directed by Joseph Ruben; for Jay Benson / Vista / New World.

The Stepford Wives*
US 1974 115m TVC
Fadsin / Palomar (Edgar J. Sherick)

A new wife in a commuter village outside New York finds all her female friends too good to be true . . . because their husbands have had them replaced by computerized models.
An attractive idea which needs a much lighter and pacier touch but entertains in patches and shows agreeable sophistication.

w William Goldman, *novel* Ira Levin *d* Bryan Forbes *ph* Owen Roizman *m* Michael Small *pd* Gene Callahan

Katharine Ross, Paula Prentiss, Nanette Newman, Peter Masterson, Patrick O'Neal, Tina Louise, William Prince

'It was hard to tell Katharine Ross playing a robot from Katharine Ross playing a normal housewife.'—*Les Keyser, Hollywood in the Seventies*

'The first women's lib gothic—hardly the landmark the world had been waiting for.'—*Pauline Kael, New Yorker*

Steppin' in Society
US 1945 72m bw

A judge is caught in a storm and takes refuge in a low club frequented by criminals.
Uncertain comedy which never really works. Edward Everett Horton, Gladys George, Ruth Terry, Robert Livingston, Jack La Rue, Lola Lane. Written by Bradford Ropes, from novel by Marcel Arnac; directed by Alexandre Esway; for Joseph Bercholtz / Republic.

Steptoe and Son
GB 1972 98m Technicolor
EMI / Associated London Films (Aida Young)

Harold gets married, mislays his wife but thinks he is a father.
Strained attempt to transfer the TV rag-and-bone comedy (which in the US became *Sanford and Son*) to the big screen. Not the same thing at all.

w Ray Galton, Alan Simpson *d* Cliff Owen *ph* John Wilcox *m* Roy Budd, Jack Fishman

Wilfrid Brambell, Harry H. Corbett, Carolyn Seymour, Arthur Howard, Victor Maddern

† *Steptoe and Son Ride Again*, which followed in 1973, was even more crude and out of character.

The Sterile Cuckoo
US 1969 107m Technicolor
Paramount / Boardwalk (Alan J. Pakula)
GB title: *Pookie*

A talkative but insecure college girl has her first sexual adventures.
Rather tiresome comedy drama with good scenes; general handling far too restrained.

w Alvin Sargent, *novel* John Nicholson *d* Alan J. Pakula *ph* Milton Krasner *m* Fred Karlin

Liza Minnelli, Tim McIntire, Wendell Burton, Austin Green, Sandra Faison

AAN: song 'Come Saturday Morning' (*m* Fred Karlin, *ly* Dory Previn); Liza Minnelli

Stevie*
US / GB 1978 102m Technicolor
First Artists / Grand Metropolitan (Robert Enders)

An account of the uneventful life of poetess Stevie Smith, lived out mainly in a London suburb under the fear of death.
Claustrophobic showcase for a whimsical lady; interesting for some specialized audiences.

w Hugh Whitemore, from his play *d* Robert Enders *ph* Freddie Young *m* Marcus Gowers

Glenda Jackson, Mona Washbourne, Trevor Howard, Alec McCowen

Stick
US 1985 109m Technicolor
Universal / Jennings Lang (Robert Daley)

A hardboiled ex-con goes to Miami's low-life district in search of the man who killed his friend.
Wearisome crime melodrama with too many pauses for the hero's self-examination.

w Elmore Leonard, Joseph C. Stinson *novel* Elmore Leonard *d* Burt Reynolds *ph* Nick McLean *m* Barry de Vorzon, Joseph Conlan

Burt Reynolds, Candice Bergen, George Segal, Charles Durning.

'Plot is of the convoluted kind beloved by exhibitors since patrons can wander out for popcorn and come back without missing anything.'—*Variety*

The Stick Up
GB 1977 101m colour
Backstage (Elliott Kastner, Danny O'Donovan)

In Devon in 1935, an American gives a lift to a café waitress and finds she is a thief on the run.
Numbingly peculiar comedy melodrama which tries too hard to have any chance of succeeding.

wd Jeffrey Bloom *ph* Michael Reed *m* Michael J. Lewis

David Soul, Pamela McMyler, Johnny Wade, Michael Balfour

'The worst film of this or possibly any year.'—*Barry Took, Punch*

Stiletto
US 1969 99m Berkey–Pathe
Avco / Harold Robbins (Norman Rosemont)

A wealthy playboy racing driver is in fact a Mafia executioner.
Dreary, violent, fashionable Mafioso melodrama with international jet set trimmings.

w A. J. Russsell, *novel* Harold Robbins *d* Bernard Kowalski *ph* Jack Priestly *m* Sid Ramin

Alex Cord, Britt Ekland, Barbara McNair, Patrick O'Neal, Joseph Wiseman, John Dehner, Eduardo Ciannelli, Roy Scheider

Still of the Night*
US 1982 91m Technicolor
MGM / UA (Arlene Donovan)

A psychiatrist finds himself in danger when one of his patients is murdered.
Hitchcock-style mystery melodrama with the villain fairly well concealed . . . but somehow not very entertaining. The actors all take their characters too seriously.

w Robert Benton, David Newman *d* Robert Benton *ph* Nestor Almendros *m* John Gibson *pd* Mel Bourne

Roy Scheider, Meryl Streep, Jessica Tandy, Sara Botsford, Josef Somner, Joe Grifasi

'A lifeless and frustrating muddle.'—*Steve Jenkins, MFB*

'All it takes is a little confidence!'

The Sting**
US 1973 129m Technicolor
Universal / Richard Zanuck, David Brown (Tony Bill, Michael S. Phillips)

In twenties Chicago, two con men stage an elaborate revenge on a big time gangster who caused the death of a friend.
Bright, likeable, but overlong, unconvincingly studio-set and casually developed comedy suspenser cashing in on star charisma but riding to enormous success chiefly on its tinkly music and the general lack of simple entertainment.

w David S. Ward *d George Roy Hill* *ph* Robert Surtees *m Scott Joplin* (arranged by Marvin Hamlisch) *ad* Henry Bumstead

Paul Newman, *Robert Redford*, Robert Shaw, Charles Durning, Ray Walston, Eileen Brennan

'A visually claustrophobic, mechanically plotted movie that's meant to be a roguishly charming entertainment.'—*New Yorker*

'It demonstrates what can happen when a gifted young screenwriter has the good fortune to fall among professionals his second time out.'—*Judith Crist*

'A testament to the value of blue eyes and bright smiles.'—*Les Keyser, Hollywood in the Seventies*

AA: best picture; David S. Ward; George Roy Hill; Marvin Hamlisch
AAN: Robert Surtees; Robert Redford

'The con is on—place your bets!'

The Sting 2
US 1983 102m Technicolor
Universal (Jennings Lang)

Lonnegan plots his revenge on the two who stung him in twenties Chicago.
Boring reprise of an overrated movie: though efficiently made, it never catches fire, and the cast is indisputably a second team.

w David S. Ward *d* Jeremy Paul Kagan *ph* Bill Butler *m* Lalo Schifrin *pd* Edward C. Carfagno

Jackie Gleason, Mac Davis, Karl Malden, Oliver Reed, Bert Remsen, Teri Garr

'The vivid minor characters have been squeezed into lifelessness by the python-like plot.'—*Tom Milne, MFB*

AAN: Lalo Schifrin

Stingaree
US 1934 76m bw (colour sequence)
RKO (Pandro S. Berman)

An Australian outlaw of the eighties falls for a rancher's daughter.
Unexciting but unobjectionable piece of Robin Hoodery.

w Becky Gardiner, *stories* E. W. Hornung *d* William A. Wellman *ph* James Van Trees *m* Max Steiner

Irene Dunne, Richard Dix, Mary Boland, Conway Tearle, Andy Devine, Henry Stephenson, Una O'Connor, Reginald Owen, Snub Pollard, George Barraud

'Should bring medium results. It does not promise to rise to greater heights.'—*Variety*

Stir Crazy
US 1980 111m Metrocolor
Columbia / Hannah Weinstein

Two New Yorkers heading for California to try their luck are wrongly convicted of a bank robbery but plan escape from prison.
Extended farce giving rather too free rein to its stars' potential for mugging, and polishing up every prison gag in the book.

w Bruce Jay Friedman *d* Sidney Poitier *ph* Fred Schuler *m* Tom Scott *pd* Alfred Sweeney

Gene Wilder, Richard Pryor, George Stanford Brown, Jobeth Williams

A Stitch in Time
GB 1963 94m bw
Rank (Hugh Stewart)

A butcher's boy goes into hospital and falls for a nurse.
Thin star slapstick; all one can say is that it's marginally preferable to Jerry Lewis.

w Jack Davies *d* Robert Asher *ph* Jack Asher *m* Philip Green

Norman Wisdom, Edward Chapman, Jerry Desmonde, Jeanette Sterke, Jill Melford

Stolen Face
GB 1952 72m bw

Via plastic surgery a girl criminal is given another face, which produces a different kind of trouble. Quickie melodrama which proved fairly popular because of its Hollywood stars. Paul Henreid, Lizabeth Scott, André Morell, Susan Stephen, Mary Mackenzie, Arnold Ridley. Written by Martin Berkeley and Richard Landau; directed by Terence Fisher; for Hammer-Lippert.

Stolen Harmony
US 1935 79m bw

An ex-con becomes a saxophonist with a band and is suspected of a robbery. Tedious mix-up of mayhem and music. George Raft, Ben Bernie, Grace Bradley, Iris Adrian, Lloyd Nolan, Ralf Harolde. Written by Leon Gordon, Harry Ruskin, Claude Binyon, Lewis Foster; directed by Alfred Werker; for Paramount. 'Once under way it provides some exciting entertainment; but the poor beginning isn't easily tossed off.'—*Variety*

'Its surprise finish will lift you to amazing emotional peaks!'

Stolen Heaven
US 1931 72m

A boy and girl decide to commit suicide after spending the twenty thousand dollars they've stolen, but neither can go through with it. A very silly idea, ineptly presented. Nancy Carroll, Phillips Holmes, Louis Calhern, Edward Keane. Written by Dana Burnet; directed by George Abbott; for Paramount. 'It will range down from moderate figures.'—*Variety*

Stolen Heaven
US 1938 88m bw

Two jewel thieves in love are harboured on the run by an old concert pianist. Sentimental melodrama which almost works, with its backing of classical piano pieces. Gene Raymond, Olympe Bradna, Lewis Stone, Glenda Farrell, Porter Hall, Douglass Dumbrille. Written by Eve Greene, Frederick Jackson, Andrew L. Stone; directed by Andrew L. Stone; for Paramount. 'Pleasing entertainment all the way.'—*Variety*

Stolen Holiday
US 1937 82m bw

A model marries a fortune hunter to protect him from the law. Slightly unusual romantic drama based on the career of Alexander Stavisky. *Claude Rains*, Kay Francis, Ian Hunter, Alison Skipworth, Charles Halton, Alex D'Arcy. Written by Casey Robinson; directed by Michael Curtiz; for Warner.

Stolen Hours
GB 1963 97m De Luxe
UA / Mirisch / Barbican (Denis Holt)

An American divorcee with only a year to live falls in love with her surgeon.
Tired remake of *Dark Victory*; pleasant Cornish backgrounds.

w Jessamyn West *d* Daniel Petrie *ph* Harry Waxman *m* Mort Lindsey

Susan Hayward, Michael Craig, Diane Baker, Edward Judd, Paul Rogers

Stolen Kisses*
France 1968 91m Eastmancolor
Films du Carrosse / Artistes Associés (Marcel Berbert)
original title: *Baisers Volés*

An ineffective young man can find neither work nor love.
A pleasing, rather sad little comedy which has almost the feel of a Keaton; but one is not quite sure at the end what its creator intended.

w François Truffaut, Claude de Givray, Bernard Revon *d* François Truffaut *ph* Denys Clerval *m* Antoine Duhamel

Jean-Pierre Léaud, Delphine Seyrig, Michel Lonsdale, Claude Jade

AAN: best foreign film

A Stolen Life*
GB 1939 91m bw
(Paramount) Orion (Anthony Havelock-Allan)

In Brittany, a woman deceives her husband by exchanging identities with her dead twin.
An actress's showcase, quite satisfactorily mounted.

w Margaret Kennedy, George Barraud, *novel* Karel J. Benes *d* Paul Czinner *ph* Philip Tannura *m* William Walton

Elisabeth Bergner, Michael Redgrave, Wilfrid Lawson, Richard Ainley, Mabel Terry-Lewis, Clement McCallin

A Stolen Life*
US 1946 107m bw
Warner (Bette Davis)

Enjoyable if slightly disappointing remake with New England backgrounds.

w Catherine Turney *d* Curtis Bernhardt *ph* Sol Polito, Sid Hickox *m* Max Steiner

Bette Davis, Glenn Ford, Dane Clark, Walter Brennan, Charles Ruggles, Bruce Bennett, Peggy Knudsen, Esther Dale

'A distressingly empty piece of show-off.'—*Bosley Crowther*

'What I'm waiting for is a film about beautiful identical quintuplets who all love the same man.'—*Richard Winnington*

'Take away his badge and he'd top the ten most wanted list!'

The Stone Killer*
US 1973 96m Technicolor
Columbia / Dino de Laurentiis (Michael Winner)

A brutal Los Angeles police detective takes on the Mafia.
Fast-moving amalgam of chases and violence with a downbeat hero.

w Gerald Wilson, *novel* A Complete State of Death by John Gardner *d* Michael Winner *ph* Richard Moore *m* Roy Budd

Charles Bronson, Martin Balsam, Ralph Waite, David Sheiner, Norman Fell

'Film-making as painting by numbers.'—*Sight and Sound*

The Stooge
US 1951 100m bw
Paramount / Hal B. Wallis

In 1930 a conceited song and dance man fails to realize that his moronic stooge is the act's real attraction.
Typical, and particularly resistible, Martin and Lewis concoction: whenever one thinks of laughing, a dollop of sentimentality comes along and promptly quashes the idea.

w Fred Finkelhoffe, Martin Rackin *d* Norman Taurog *ph* Daniel L. Fapp *m* Joseph J. Lilley

Dean Martin, Jerry Lewis, Polly Bergen, Marie McDonald, Eddie Mayehoff, Marion Marshall, Richard Erdman

Stop Press Girl
GB 1949 78m bw

A girl finds she has the unconscious power to bring all machinery to a halt. Weary comedy which has nowhere to go after its first silly idea. Sally Ann Howes, Gordon Jackson, Basil Radford, Naunton Wayne, James Robertson Justice, Sonia Holm, Nigel Buchanan, Kenneth More. Written by Basil Thomas and T. J. Morrison; directed by Michael Barry; for Aquila / Rank.

Stop You're Killing Me
US 1953 86m Warnercolor
Warner (Louis F. Edelman)

At the end of prohibition a beer baron decides to go straight, but finds his house filled with the corpses of rival gangsters.
Frantic remake of *A Slight Case of Murder* with a few musical numbers added; all rather messy.

w James O'Hanlon *d* Roy del Ruth *ph* Ted McCord *md* Ray Heindorf

Broderick Crawford, Claire Trevor, Virginia Gibson, Bill Hayes, Sheldon Leonard, Joe Vitale, Howard St John, Henry Morgan, Margaret Dumont

Stopover Tokyo
US 1957 100m Eastmancolor Cinemascope
TCF (Walter Reisch)

An American spy in Tokyo seeks to capture a communist undercover man.
Sprawling espionage stuff with frequent halts for scenic tours.

w Richard L. Breen, Walter Reisch, *novel* John P. Marquand *d* Richard L. Breen *ph* Charles G. Clarke *m* Paul Sawtell

Robert Wagner, Joan Collins, Edmond O'Brien, Ken Scott, Larry Keating

Stories from a Flying Trunk
GB 1979 88m Technicolor
EMI / Sands (John Brabourne, Richard Goodwin)

Three Hans Andersen stories are performed by stop frame animation and by ballet dancers dressed as vegetables.
Lugubrious attempt to repeat the success of *Tales of Beatrix Potter;* moments to make one smile, but on the whole a depressing experience.

wd Christine Edzard *m* Gioacchino Rossini *ph* Robin Browne, Brian West

Murray Melvin, Ann Firbank, Johanna Sonnex, Tasneem Maqsood

Stork Bites Man
US 1948 67m bw

An apartment house manager has a pregnant wife and a baby-hating boss. Threadbare farce, not enlivened by wit or pacing. Jackie Cooper, Gene Roberts, Gus Schilling, Emory Parnell. Written and directed by Cyril Endfield; for Ralph Cohn / Buddy Rogers.

The Stork Club
US 1945 98m bw
Paramount (B. G. De Sylva)

A nightclub hat-check girl saves an elderly millionaire from drowning.
Very light comedy with music, a great ad for a once famous night haunt.

w B. G. De Sylva, John McGowan *d* Hal Walker *ph* Charles Lang Jnr *md* Robert Emmett Dolan

Betty Hutton, Barry Fitzgerald, Don Defore, Robert Benchley, Bill Goodwin, Iris Adrian, Mary Young, Mikhail Rasumny

The Storm
US 1930 76m bw

An orphan girl left with a trapper becomes an object of jealousy between him and his partner. Old-fashioned outdoor melodrama, previously filmed in 1916 and 1922. Not really talkie material. Lupe Velez, Paul Cavanagh, William Boyd, Alphonse Ethier. Written by Wells Root from the play by Langdon McCormick; directed by William Wyler; for Universal. 'A fairly good programmer . . . the fight is a pip.'—*Variety*

The Storm
US 1938 79m bw

Tensions lead to violence among shipboard radio operators. Lively action melodrama culminating in a storm at sea. Charles Bickford, Barton MacLane, Preston Foster, Tom Brown, Nan Grey, Andy Devine, Frank Jenks. Written by Daniel Moore, Hugh King, Theodore Reeves; directed by Harold Young; for Ken Goldsmith / Universal. 'Good enough for the duals, but too weak for solo billing.'—*Variety*

Storm at Daybreak
US 1932 80m bw

A fanciful reconstruction of events leading up to the Sarajevo assassination which precipitated World War I. Unlikely melodrama with stars forced to overact; still, a rich and historically interesting slice of ham. Walter Huston, Kay Francis, Nils Asther, Phillips Holmes, Eugene Pallette, C. Henry Gordon, Jean Parker. Written by Bertram Millhauser, from a play by Sandor Hunyady; directed by Richard Boleslawski; for MGM.

'A good cast unwisely spent on weak material: doubtful as a grosser.'—*Variety*

'Who really set the town aflame?'

Storm Center
US 1956 87m bw
Columbia / Phoenix (Julian Blaustein)

A small-town librarian is dismissed when she refuses to remove a communist book from the shelves.
Formula anti-McCarthy melodrama originally designed for Mary Pickford's comeback; not very absorbing and rather dingily produced.

w Daniel Taradash Elick Moll *d* Daniel Taradash *ph* Burnett Guffey *m* George Duning

Bette Davis, Brian Keith, Kim Hunter, Paul Kelly, Joe Mantell

Storm Fear
US 1955 88m bw
(UA) Theodora (Cornel Wilde)

Three fugitives from justice hide in a mountain cabin, but all meet violent deaths.
Gloomy, strenuous melodrama, partly shot outdoors.

w Horton Foote, *novel* Clinton Seeley *d* Cornel Wilde *ph* Joseph La Shelle *m* Elmer Bernstein

Cornel Wilde, Jean Wallace, Dan Duryea, Lee Grant, Steven Hill, Dennis Weaver

Storm in a Teacup*
GB 1937 87m bw
Alexander Korda / Victor Saville

A national sensation ensues when a Scottish provost fines an old lady for not licensing her dog, and she refuses to pay.

Early Ealing-type comedy, a bit emaciated by later standards.

w Ian Dalrymple, Donald Bull, *play* Sturm in Wasserglass by Bruno Frank *d* Ian Dalrymple, Victor Saville *ph* Max Greene *m* Frederic Lewis

Vivien Leigh, Rex Harrison, Cecil Parker, Sara Allgood, Ursula Jeans, Gus McNaughton, Arthur Wontner

Storm over Asia*
USSR 1928 93m approx (24 fps) bw silent
Mezhrabpomfilm
original title: *Potomok Chingis-Khana*; aka: *The Heir to Genghis Khan*

A Mongolian trapper is discovered to be descended from Genghis Khan and made puppet emperor of a Soviet province.
Curious yarn without much discernible point though with the usual patches of propagandizing. It certainly looks good.

w Osip Brik *d* V. I. Pudovkin *ph* A. L. Golovnya

I. Inkizhinov, Valeri Inkizhinov, A. Dedintsev

'Fetid with propaganda and thematically ridiculous to any semi-intelligent audience. The more illiterate a man is in these Russian blurbs, the better his chances to make a name for himself in the Red World.'—*Variety*

Storm over Lisbon
US 1944 86m bw
Republic (George Sherman)

An international spy mastermind runs a Lisbon night club and sells documents to the highest bidder.
Feeble copy of *Casablanca.*

w Doris Gilbert, Dane Lussier *d* George Sherman *ph* John Alton *m* Walter Scharf

Vera Hruba Ralston, Erich Von Stroheim, Richard Arlen, Eduardo Ciannelli, Otto Kruger, Robert Livingston, Mona Barrie, Frank Orth

Storm over the Andes
US 1935 82m bw

An American flyer helps Bolivia against Paraguay. Thick-ear melodrama about a forgotten local war; soundly made of its kind. Jack Holt, Antonio Moreno, Mona Barrie, Gene Lockhart, Grant Withers. Written by Eliot Gibbons, Laclede Christy, Frank Wead, Al De Mond, Eva Greene; directed by Christy Cabanne; for Maurice Pivar / Universal.

Storm over the Nile
GB 1955 107m Technicolor Cinemascope
Independent / London (Zoltan Korda)

Feeble remake of *The Four Feathers* (qv), using most of that film's action highlights stretched out to fit the wide screen.

w R. C. Sherriff *d* Terence Young *ph* Ted Scaife, Osmond Borradaile *m* Benjamin Frankel

Anthony Steel, Laurence Harvey, Ronald Lewis, Ian Carmichael, James Robertson Justice, Mary Ure, Geoffrey Keen, Jack Lambert, Ferdy Mayne, Michael Hordern

'The material appears not so much dated as fossilized within its period.'—*Penelope Houston*

Storm over Tibet
US 1951 87m bw
Columbia / Summit (Ivan Tors, Laslo Benedek)

An explorer steals a holy mask which brings bad luck.
Slight adventure yarn ingeniously built around an old German documentary.

w Ivan Tors, Sam Mayer *d* Andrew Marton *ph* George E. Diskant, Richard Angst *m* Arthur Honegger

Rex Reason, Diana Douglas, Myron Healey

Storm Warning*
US 1950 93m bw
Warner (Jerry Wald)

A New York model goes south to visit her sister, and finds that her brother-in-law is an oversexed brute and a Ku Klux Klan killer.
Heavy melodrama disguised as a social document; sufficiently arresting for its purposes.

w Daniel Fuchs, Richard Brooks *d* Stuart Heisler *ph* Carl Guthrie *m* Daniele Amfitheatrof

Ginger Rogers, Doris Day, *Steve Cochran*, Ronald Reagan, Hugh Sanders, Raymond Greenleaf, Ned Glass

Stormy Weather
GB 1935 74m bw

A top executive foils a blackmail racket in Chinatown. Very presentable vehicle for the Aldwych team of farceurs. Tom Walls, Ralph Lynn, Robertson Hare, Yvonne Arnaud, Gordon James, Graham Moffatt. Written by Ben Travers, from his play; directed by Tom Walls; for Gainsborough.

Stormy Weather***
US 1943 77m bw
TCF (Irving Mills)

A backstage success story lightly based on the career of Bill Robinson.
Virtually a high-speed revue with all-black talent, and what talent! The production is pretty slick too.

w Frederick Jackson, Ted Koehler *d Andrew Stone ph Leon Shamroy, Fred Sersen md Benny Carter ch* Clarence Robinson

Bill Robinson, Lena Horne, Fats Waller, Ada Brown, Cab Calloway, Katherine Dunham and her Dancers, Eddie Anderson, Flournoy Miller, *The Nicholas Brothers*, Dooley Wilson

'A first-rate show, a spirited divertissement . . . a joy to the ear.'—*New York Times*

The Story of a Woman
US / Italy 1969 101m Technicolor
Universal / Westward (Leonardo Bercovici)

A Swedish girl pianist in Rome falls in love with a fashionable doctor, then back in Sweden meets an American diplomat.
Intermezzo-type romantic drama with colour supplement trappings. Tolerable of its kind.

wd Leonardo Bercovici *ph* Piero Portalupi *m* John Williams

Robert Stack, Bibi Andersson, James Farentino, Annie Girardot, Frank Sundstrom

The Story of Adèle H*
France 1975 98m Eastmancolor
Films du Carrosse / Artistes Associés (Marcel Berbert, Claude Miller)

In 1863, the daughter of Victor Hugo follows her lover to Nova Scotia.
Surprisingly slow and stilted version of a true story, though with a few of the expected subtleties.

w François Truffaut, Jean Gruault, Suzanne Schiffman *d* François Truffaut *ph* Nestor Almendros *m* Maurice Jaubert

Isabelle Adjani, Bruce Robinson, Sylvia Marriott

AAN: Isabelle Adjani

'America's most thrilling story! Of love so great and faith so strong that it inspired this man to endure ridicule, privation and hunger—to achieve the miracle of wings for the human voice!'

The Story of Alexander Graham Bell**
US 1939 97m bw
TCF (Kenneth MacGowan)
GB title: *The Modern Miracle*

The inventor of the telephone marries a deaf girl.
Acceptable history lesson with dullish principals but excellent production.

w Lamar Trotti *d* Irving Cummings *ph* Leon Shamroy *m* Louis Silvers

Don Ameche, Henry Fonda, Loretta Young, Charles Coburn, Gene Lockhart, Spring Byington, Bobs Watson

'Production will need teasing to get the women.'—*Variety*

The Story of Dr Wassell*
US 1944 140m Technicolor
Paramount / Cecil B. de Mille

The adventures of a naval doctor who heroically saved men during the Pacific war.
Long, slogging, glamorized account of real events which is typical de Mille and very unconvincing physically, but keeps one watching simply as a story.

w Alan le May, Charles Bennett, *book* James Hilton *d* Cecil B. de Mille *ph* Victor Milner, William Snyder *m* Victor Young

Gary Cooper, Laraine Day, Signe Hasso, Dennis O'Keefe, Carol Thurston, Carl Esmond, Paul Kelly, Stanley Ridges

'The director has taken a true story of heroism . . . and jangled it into a cacophony of dancing girls, phoney self-sacrifice and melodramatic romance.'—*Howard Barnes*

'To be regretted beyond qualification. It whips the story into a nacreous foam of lies whose speciousness is only the more painful because Mr de Mille is so obviously free from any desire to alter the truth except for what he considers to be its own advantage.'—*James Agee*

'Close to the last word in honest understanding and convincing production.'—*Motion Picture Herald*

The Story of Esther Costello*
GB 1957 103m bw
Columbia / Romulus (James Woolf)
US title: *The Golden Virgin*

A blind Irish deaf mute girl is adopted by an American socialite and her plight becomes an international cause.
Rich melodrama develops from this unlikely premise and the star enjoys it hugely.

w Charles Kaufman, *novel* Nicholas Monsarrat *d* David Miller *ph* Robert Krasker *m* Georges Auric

Joan Crawford, Heather Sears, Rossano Brazzi, Ron Randell, Lee Patterson, Fay Compton, John Loder, Denis O'Dea, Sidney James, Maureen Delany

The Story of GI Joe**
US 1945 108m bw
(UA) Lester Cowan (David Hall)
aka: *War Correspondent*

Journalist Ernie Pyle follows fighting men into the Italian campaign.
Slow, convincing, sympathetic war film with good script and performances; not by any means the usual action saga.

w Leopold Atlas, Guy Endore, Philip Stevenson, *book Ernie Pyle d William A. Wellman ph Russell Metty m* Ann Ronell, Louis Applebaum

Burgess Meredith, Robert Mitchum, Freddie Steele, Wally Cassell, Jimmy Lloyd, Jack Reilly

'It is humorous, poignant and tragic, an earnestly human reflection of a stern life and the dignity of man.'—*Thomas M. Pryor*

'A tragic and eternal work of art.'—*James Agee*

'One of the best films of the war.'—*Richard Mallett, Punch*

AAN: script; music score; song 'Linda' (*m / ly* Ann Ronell); Robert Mitchum

The Story of Gilbert and Sullivan*
GB 1953 109m Technicolor
British Lion / London Films (Frank Launder, Sidney Gilliat)

In 1875 a young composer named Arthur Sullivan and a librettist named William Gilbert come together under the auspices of Rupert D'Oyly Carte and write the Savoy Operas.
Light, accurate, well-cast and well-produced Victorian musical which somehow fails to ignite despite the immense talent at hand.

w Sidney Gilliat, Leslie Baily *d* Sidney Gilliat *ph* Christopher Challis *md* Sir Malcolm Sargent *pd* Hein Heckroth

Robert Morley, Maurice Evans, Peter Finch, Eileen Herlie, Dinah Sheridan, Isabel Dean, Wilfrid Hyde White, Muriel Aked

The Story of Louis Pasteur***
US 1936 85m bw
Warner / Cosmopolitan (Henry Blanke)

How the eminent 19th-century French scientist overcomes obstacles in finding cures for various diseases.
Adequate biopic which caused a sensation and started a trend; some of the others were better but this was the first example of Hollywood bringing schoolbook history to box office life.

w Sheridan Gibney, Pierre Collins *d William Dieterle ph* Tony Gaudio *m* Bernhard Kaun, Heinz Roemheld

Paul Muni, Josephine Hutchinson, Anita Louise, Donald Woods, Fritz Leiber, Henry O'Neill, Porter Hall, Akim Tamiroff, Walter Kingsford

'Probably limited b.o. but a creditable prestige picture.'—*Variety*

'What should be vital and arresting has been made hollow and dull . . . we are tendered something that is bright and stagey for something out of life.'—*Otis Ferguson*

'More exciting than any gangster melodrama.'—*C. A. Lejeune*

AA: script; Paul Muni
AAN: best picture

'Men and their women from the beginning of creation! Never so vast an undertaking!'

The Story of Mankind
US 1957 100m Technicolor
Warner / Cambridge (Irwin Allen)

A heavenly tribunal debates whether to allow man to destroy himself, and both the Devil and the Spirit of Man cite instances from history.
Hilarious charade, one of the worst films ever made, but full of surprises, bad performances, and a wide range of stock shots.

w Irwin Allen, Charles Bennett, *book* Henrik Van Loon *d* Irwin Allen *ph* Nicholas Musuraca *m* Paul Sawtell

Ronald Colman, Vincent Price, Cedric Hardwicke, the Marx Brothers, Hedy Lamarr, Agnes Moorehead, Reginald Gardiner, Peter Lorre, Virginia Mayo, Charles Coburn, Francis X. Bushman

'A poor excuse to use a batch of available actors in some of the weirdest casting ever committed.'—*Newsweek*

The Story of Molly X
US 1949 82m bw

When a criminal is killed, his wife masterminds the gang to find out who killed him. Silly melodrama, generally ineptly presented. June Havoc, John Russell, Dorothy Hart, Elliott Lewis, Connie Gilchrist. Written and directed by Crane Wilbur; for Universal / International.

The Story of Robin Hood and his Merrie Men
GB 1952 84m Technicolor
Walt Disney (Perce Pearce)

When Prince John starts a ruthless taxation campaign, Robert Fitzooth turns outlaw.
Fairly competent but quite forgettable version of the legend, softened for children.

w Laurence E. Watkin *d* Ken Annakin *ph* Guy Green *m* Clifton Parker

Richard Todd, Joan Rice, James Hayter, Hubert Gregg, James Robertson Justice, Martita Hunt, Peter Finch

The Story of Ruth
US 1960 132m De Luxe Cinemascope
TCF (Samuel G. Engel)

Ruth becomes the favourite of a pagan king but eventually flees to Israel.
Tedious, portentous bible-in-pictures, of virtually no interest or entertainment value.

w Norman Corwin *d* Henry Koster *ph* Arthur E. Arling *m* Franz Waxman

Elana Eden, Peggy Wood, Viveca Lindfors, Stuart Whitman, Tom Tryon, Jeff Morrow, Thayer David, Eduard Franz

The Story of Seabiscuit
US 1949 98m Technicolor
Warner (William Jacobs)
GB title: *Pride of Kentucky*

The success story of a racehorse.
Blue grass vapidities, the kind of family entertainment that drove the families away.

w John Taintor Foote *d* David Butler *ph* Wilfrid Cline *md* David Buttolph

Shirley Temple, Barry Fitzgerald, Lon McCallister, Rosemary de Camp, Donald McBride, Pierre Watkin

The Story of Shirley Yorke
GB 1948 92m bw

A nobleman tries to blame his wife's nurse for her death by poison. Lethargic version of a play previously filmed as *Lord Camber's Ladies* (qv). Derek Farr, Dinah Sheridan, Margaretta Scott, John Robinson, Barbara Couper, Valentine Dyall. Written by A. R. Rawlinson, Maclean Rogers and Kathleen Butler, from the play *The Case of Lady Camber* by H. A. Vachell; directed by Maclean Rogers; for Nettlefold

The Story of Temple Drake*
US 1933 71m bw
Paramount (Ben Glazer)

A neurotic southern flapper is abducted by gangsters, and likes it.
Deliberately shocking melodrama of its time, restructured from a notorious book later filmed under its own title. Very dated, but interesting.

w Oliver H. P. Garrett, *novel* Sanctuary by William Faulkner *d* Stephen Roberts *ph* Karl Struss

Miriam Hopkins, Jack La Rue, William Gargan, William Collier Jnr, Irving Pichel, Guy Standing, Elizabeth Patterson, Florence Eldridge

'Under Haysian ban the title of the novel can't be ballyhooed, but any whispering campaign about this is the picture's best b.o. asset. It has little else to commend it.'—*Variety*

The Story of Three Loves
US 1953 122m Technicolor
MGM (Sidney Franklin)

Three love stories concerning the passengers on a transatlantic liner.
Three bits of old-fashioned kitsch, one tragic, one whimsical, one melodramatic, all rather slow and dull though well produced.

w John Collier, Jan Lustig, George Froeschel *d* Gottfried Reinhardt, Vincente Minnelli *ph* Charles Rosher, Harold Rosson *m* Miklos Rozsa

Ethel Barrymore, James Mason, Moira Shearer, Pier Angeli, Leslie Caron, Kirk Douglas, Farley Granger, Agnes Moorehead, Zsa Zsa Gabor

The Story of Vernon and Irene Castle**
US 1939 93m bw
RKO (George Haight, Pandro S. Berman)

The story of a husband and wife dance team who had their first success in Paris and became influential international celebrities before he was killed as a flier in World War I.
Pleasant understated musical with very agreeable dance sequences and a firm overall style. The last of the main stream of Astaire-Rogers musicals.

w Richard Sherman, Oscar Hammerstein II, Dorothy Yost, *books* Irene Castle *d H. C. Potter ph Robert de Grasse md* Victor Baravalle *ch Hermes Pan ad Van Nest Polglase*

Fred Astaire, Ginger Rogers, Edna May Oliver, Walter Brennan, Lew Fields, Etienne Girardot, Donald MacBride

'One of the best Astaire-Rogers musicals . . . a wealth of nostalgic appeal.'—*Variety*

† The title was devised and insisted on by Mrs Castle.

The Story of Will Rogers
US 1950 109m Technicolor
Warner (Robert Arthur)

A wild west performer becomes a Ziegfeld star and pop philosopher.
Bland, unshaped biopic of one of American show business's best loved figures, who died in an air crash in 1935.

w Frank Davis, Stanley Roberts *d* Michael Curtiz *ph* Wilfrid M. Cline *md* Victor Young

Will Rogers Jnr, Jane Wyman, James Gleason, Eddie Cantor (as himself), Carl Benton Reid

The Story on Page One
US 1960 123m bw Cinemascope
TCF / Company of Artists (Jerry Wald)

A lawyer undertakes the defence of a woman who with her lover is charged with the murder of her husband.
Long drawn out and not very interesting courtroom drama, performed and presented with some style.

wd Clifford Odets *ph* James Wong Howe *m* Elmer Bernstein

Rita Hayworth, Tony Franciosa, Gig Young, Mildred Dunnock, Hugh Griffith, Sanford Meisner, Alfred Ryder

Stowaway*
US 1936 86m bw
TCF (Earl Carroll, Harold Wilson)

The orphan daughter of a Shanghai missionary stows away on an American pleasure ship.
Very good star vehicle in which Shirley performs some of her best musical numbers.

w William Conselman, Arthur Sheekman, Nat Perrin *d* William A. Seiter *ph* Arthur Miller *md* Louis Silvers *songs* Mack Gordon, Harry Revel

Shirley Temple, Robert Young, Alice Faye, Eugene Pallette, Helen Westley, Arthur Treacher, J. Edward Bromberg, Astrid Allwyn

'No exhib worrying necessary for this one.'—*Variety*

La Strada*
Italy 1954 94m bw
Ponti / de Laurentiis
aka: *The Road*

A half-witted peasant girl is sold to an itinerant strong man and ill-used by him.
Curious attempt at a kind of poetic neo-realism, saved by style and performances.

w Federico Fellini, Ennio Flaiano, Tullio Pinelli *d Federico Fellini ph* Otello Martelli *m* Nino Rota

Giulietta Masina, Anthony Quinn, Richard Basehart

AA: best foreign film
AAN: script

Straight on Till Morning
GB 1972 96m Technicolor
EMI / Hammer (Roy Skeggs)

A Liverpool girl in London meets a dangerous psychotic.
Unattractive suspenser, wildly directed.

w Michael Peacock *d* Peter Collinson *ph* Brian Probyn *m* Roland Shaw

Rita Tushingham, Shane Briant, Tom Bell, Annie Ross, James Bolam

Straight, Place and Show*
US 1938 66m bw

Three pony-ride proprietors impersonate Russian jockeys to save a race. Lively, unpretentious vehicle for three zanies, with a further bonus in its lead singer. The Ritz Brothers, Ethel Merman, Richard Arlen, Phyllis Brooks, George Barbier, Sidney Blackmer. Written by M. M. Musselman and Allen Rivkin, from a play by Damon Runyon and Irving Caesar; directed by David Butler; for TCF. (GB title: *They're Off*.)

Straight Time
US 1978 114m Technicolor
Warner / First Artist / Sweetwall (Stanley Beck, Tim Zinnemann)

A psychotic parolee fails to go straight.
Unappetizing social melodrama with an irresolute leading performance.

w Alvin Sargent, Edward Bunker, Jeffrey Boam, *novel* No Beast So Fierce by Edward Bunker *d* Ulu Grosbard *ph* Owen Roizman *m* David Shire

Dustin Hoffman, Theresa Russell, Gary Busey, Harry Dean Stanton

'One leaves the theatre hoping the character will die painfully and slowly in a hail of bullets.'—*Variety*

'Just keep saying to yourself—it's only a film, it's only a film!'

Strait Jacket
US 1963 92m bw
Columbia / William Castle

A woman who murdered her faithless husband with an axe is released twenty years later, and more axe murders occur.
Dull and unattractive shocker in which all concerned lean over backwards to conceal the trick ending.

w Robert Bloch *d* William Castle *ph* Arthur E. Arling *m* Van Alexander

Joan Crawford, Diane Baker, Leif Erickson, Howard St John, Rochelle Hudson, George Kennedy

Stranded
US 1936 73m bw

A woman working for Traveller's Aid meets an old school beau. Much ado about nothing, the kind of movie that loses stars their reputations. Kay Francis, George Brent, Patricia Ellis, Donald Woods, Robert Barrat, Barton MacLane. Written by Delmer Daves, Carl Erickson, Frank Wead, Ferdinand Reyher; directed by Frank Borzage; for Warners. 'Limited chances.'—*Variety*

The Strange Affair
GB 1968 106m Techniscope
Paramount (Howard Harrison, Stanley Mann)

A young London policeman finds that his superiors are almost as corrupt as the villains.
Stylishly made melodrama of despair, with a sexy nymphet heroine straight from swinging London. It all leaves a sour taste in the mouth.

w Stanley Mann, *novel* Bernard Toms *d David Greene ph* Alex Thompson *m* Basil Kirchin

Michael York, Jeremy Kemp, Susan George, Jack Watson, George A. Cooper

The Strange Affair of Uncle Harry
US 1945 82m bw
Universal (Joan Harrison)
aka: *Uncle Harry*

A man henpecked by his two sisters plans to murder one of them.
Stilted melodrama from an uninspired stage original, with a cop-out dream ending tacked on.

w Stephen Longstreet, Keith Winter, *play* Thomas Job *d* Robert Siodmak *ph* Woody Bredell *m* Hans Salter

George Sanders, Geraldine Fitzgerald, Ella Raines, Sara Allgood, Moyna MacGill, Samuel S. Hinds, Harry Von Zell, Ethel Griffies

Strange Bargain
US 1949 68m bw

A lowly bookkeeper finds himself accomplice in an insurance swindle. Watchable second feature suspenser. Jeffrey Lynn, Henry Morgan, Martha Scott, Katherine Emery, Richard Gaines, Henry O'Neill. Written by Lillie Hayward; directed by Will Price; for Sid Rogell / RKO.

Strange Bedfellows
US 1965 99m Technicolor
U-I / Panama–Frank (Melvin Frank)

An American executive in London nearly divorces his fiery Italian wife.
Frantic sex comedy with picture postcard background; fatiguing rather than funny, but with minor compensations.

w Melvin Frank, Michael Pertwee *d* Melvin Frank *ph* Leo Tover *m* Leigh Harline

Rock Hudson, Gina Lollobrigida, Gig Young, Edward Judd, Howard St John, Arthur Haynes, Dave King, Terry-Thomas

'The grind of predictable situations is further afflicted by considerable lapses in taste.'—*MFB*

Strange Boarders*
GB 1938 79m bw
GFD / Gainsborough (Edward Black)

A police detective postpones his honeymoon to book into a boarding house and discover which of the guests is a spy.
Quite engaging comedy-thriller in the Hitchcock mould, with entertaining performances and incidents.

w A. R. Rawlinson, Sidney Gilliatt, *novel* The Strange Boarders of Paradise Crescent by E. Phillips Oppenheim *d* Herbert Mason *ph* Jack Cox

Tom Walls, Renee Saint-Cyr, Leon M. Lion, Googie Withers, C. V. France, Ronald Adam, Irene Handl, George Curzon, Martita Hunt

Strange Cargo*
US 1940 105m bw
MGM (Joseph L. Mankiewicz)

Eight convicts escape from Devil's Island and are influenced by a Christ-like fugitive.
One of Hollywood's occasional lunacies; one doubts whether even the author knew the point of this cockamamy parable, but it was well produced and acted.

w Lawrence Hazard, *novel* Not Too Narrow, Not Too Deep by Richard Sale *d* Frank Borzage *ph* Robert Planck *m* Franz Waxman

Clark Gable, Joan Crawford, Ian Hunter, Peter Lorre, Paul Lukas, Albert Dekker, J. Edward Bromberg, Eduardo Ciannelli, Frederick Worlock

'Even the most hardened mystics may blush.'—*New Yorker, 1978*

The Strange Case of Clara Deane
US 1932 60m bw

A young mother is unjustly convicted of a crime which she didn't commit and bids a tearful farewell to her child . . . Hilariously inept and theatrical rendering of a very outmoded play. Wynne Gibson, Pat O'Brien, Frances Dee, Dudley Digges. Written by Max Marcin from the play by Arthur M. Brillant; directed by Louis Gasnier and Max Marcin; for Paramount. 'Strictly for the minors where the clientele is elderly and naive.'—*Variety*

The Strange Case of Doctor RX
US 1942 66m bw

A mysterious murderer eliminates criminals whom the law can't touch. Inept semi-horror which wastes a good cast, as did the same author's *Night Monster*. Lionel Atwill, Patric Knowles, Anne Gwynne, Samuel S. Hinds, Shemp Howard, Mona Barrie, Paul Cavanagh, Mantan Moreland. Written by Clarence Upson Young; directed by William Nigh; for Universal.

Strange Conquest: see The Crime of Dr Hallet

The Strange Death of Adolf Hitler*
US 1943 74m bw
Universal (Ben Pivar)

A stage impressionist murders the Führer and takes his place, steering Germany deliberately into losing the war.
One of the more eccentric curios of World War II, especially from a mundane studio like Universal. Once one recovers from the shock of its existence, the thing is moderately well done. See also *The Magic Face*.

w Fritz Kortner *d* James Hogan *m* Hans Salter

Ludwig Donath, Gale Sondergaard, Fritz Kortner, George Dolenz

The Strange Door*
US 1951 81m bw
U-I (Ted Richmond)

A young nobleman, passing through the one-way door of a castle, finds himself the prisoner of a madman.
Torture-chamber suspenser, adequately if rather tediously developed, with most of its interest reposing in the cast.

w Jerry Sackheim, *story* The Sire de Maletroit's Door by Robert Louis Stevenson *d* Joseph Pevney *ph* Irving Glassberg *m* Hans Salter

Charles Laughton, Boris Karloff, Michael Pate, Sally Forrest, Richard Stapley, Alan Napier

Strange Evidence
GB 1932 71m bw

When an invalid dies, his adulterous wife is suspected. Mildly interesting quickie whodunnit. Leslie Banks, Carol Goodner, George Curzon, Frank Vosper, Norah Baring, Diana Napier. Written by Miles Malleson, from a story by Lajos Biro; directed by Robert Milton; for Alexander Korda/London Films.

Strange Holiday
US 1945 61m bw

A man back from holiday discovers that American Nazis have taken over the country. Over-talkative fantasy which barely scraped a release, especially since it was made in 1940 but not offered until five years later. Claude Rains, Gloria Holden, Milton Kibbee. Written, directed and produced by Arch Oboler; for General Motors.

'A woman suspected! A woman desired! A woman possessed!'
'The film in which you hear the characters think!'

Strange Interlude**
US 1932 110m bw
MGM (Irving Thalberg)
GB title: *Strange Interval*

Problems of an unfulfilled wife and her lover.
Surprising film version of a very heavy modern classic, complete with asides to the audience; very dated now, but a small milestone in Hollywood's development.

w Bess Meredyth, C. Gardner Sullivan, *play* Eugene O'Neill *d* Robert Z. Leonard *ph* Lee Garmes

Norma Shearer, Clark Gable, May Robson, Alexander Kirkland, Ralph Morgan, Robert Young, Maureen O'Sullivan, Henry B. Walthall

'Chiefly a reserved seat attraction, dubious for general release appeal.'—*Variety*

'A cinematic novelty to be seen by discerning audiences.'—*Film Weekly*

'More exciting than a thousand "action" movies.'—*Pare Lorentz*

Strange Intruder
US 1957 78m bw
AA (Lindsley Parsons)

A psychopathic ex-POW menaces the children of his dead friend's wife.
Gloomy second feature melodrama, rather well presented.

w David Evans, Warren Douglas, *novel* Helen Fowler *d* Irving Rapper *ph* Ernest Haller *m* Paul Dunlap

Edmund Purdom, Ida Lupino, Ann Harding, Jacques Bergerac, Carl Benton Reid

Strange Invaders*
US 1983 93m De Luxe
EMI / Orion / Michael Laughlin (Walter Coblenz)

An Illinois town is taken over by beings from outer space.
Patchy but often amusing take-off of the *Invasion of the Body Snatchers* genre.

w William Condon, Michael Laughlin *d* Michael Laughlin *ph* Louis Horvath, Zoltan Vidor *m* John Addison *pd* Susanna Moore

Paul Le Mat, Nancy Allen, Diana Scarwid, Michael Lerner, Louise Fletcher, Fiona Lewis, Kenneth Tobey

Strange Lady in Town
US 1955 118m Warnercolor Cinemascope
Warner (Mervyn Le Roy)

Adventures of a woman doctor in 1880 Santa Fe.
Quaint western drama which is never any more convincing than its star.

w Frank Butler *d* Mervyn Le Roy *ph* Harold Rosson *m* Dmitri Tiomkin

Greer Garson, Dana Andrews, Cameron Mitchell, Lois Smith, Walter Hampden

'Fate drew them together and only murder can part them!'
'Whisper her name!'

The Strange Love of Martha Ivers**
US 1946 116m bw
Paramount / Hal B. Wallis

A murderous child becomes a wealthy woman with a spineless lawyer husband; the melodrama starts when an ex-boy friend returns to town.
Irresistible star melodrama which leaves no stone unturned; compulsive entertainment of the old school.

w Robert Rossen *d* Lewis Milestone *ph* Victor Milner *m* Miklos Rozsa

Barbara Stanwyck, Van Heflin, Kirk Douglas, Lizabeth Scott, Judith Anderson, Roman Bohnen

AAN: original story (Jack Patrick)

The Strange Love of Molly Louvain
US 1932 72m bw

A young mother has gone to the bad through men. Hoary melodrama which the cast seem forever on the point of sending up. Lee Tracy, Ann Dvorak, Richard Cromwell, Guy Kibbee, Leslie Fenton, Frank McHugh. Written by Maurine Watkins and Erwin Gelsey from the play The Tinsel Girl by Maurine Watkins; directed by Michael Curtiz; for Warners. 'A lightweight yarn which never takes a toehold to deliver a sock.'—*Variety*

The Strange Mr Gregory
US 1945 63m bw

In pursuit of a murder fraud, a magician feigns his own death and poses as his brother. Complex but watchable little crime thriller. Edmund Lowe, Jean Rogers, Don Douglas, Frank Reicher, Robert Emmett Keane. Written by Myles Connelly, Charles S. Belden; directed by Phil Rosen; for Louis Berkoff / Monogram.

The Strange One*
US 1957 99m bw
Columbia / Sam Spiegel
GB title: *End as a Man*

A sadistic cadet causes trouble at a southern military college.
A weird and unsavoury but rather compelling melodrama which unreels like a senior version of *Tom Brown's Schooldays*.

w Calder Willingham, from his novel End as a Man *d* Jack Garfein *ph* Burnett Guffey *m* Kenyon Hopkins

Ben Gazzara, George Peppard, Mark Richman, Pat Hingle, Arthur Storch, Paul Richards, Geoffrey Horne, James Olson

'The film's brilliance is in its persuasive depiction of a highly controversial, artificially organized world; its failure is to make any dramatic statement about it.'—*MFB*

The Strange Woman
US 1946 100m bw
(UA) Hunt Stromberg (Jack Chertok)

A scheming woman plays with the lives of three men.
Star wish-fulfilment; otherwise a hammy costume piece.

w Herb Meadows, *novel* Ben Ames Williams *d* Edgar G. Ulmer *ph* Lucien Andriot *m* Carmen Dragon

Hedy Lamarr, George Sanders, Louis Hayward, Gene Lockhart, Hillary Brooke

The Stranger*
US 1946 95m bw
International (Sam Spiegel)

An escaped Nazi criminal marries an American woman and settles in a Connecticut village.
Highly unconvincing and artificial melodrama enhanced by directorial touches, splendid photography and no-holds-barred climax involving a church clock.

w Anthony Veiller, *story* Victor Trivas, Decia Dunning *d Orson Welles ph Russell Metty* *m* Bronislau Kaper

Edward G. Robinson, Orson Welles, Loretta Young, Philip Merivale, Richard Long, Konstantin Shayne

'Some striking effects, with lighting and interesting angles much relied on.'—*Bosley Crowther*

'A film of confused motivations and clumsy effects.'—*Basil Wright, 1972*

AAN: original story

Stranger at My Door
US 1956 85m bw
Republic (Sidney Picker)

A gunman takes refuge in the house of a preacher who tries to convert him.
Odd, sentimental little western morality play, not badly presented.

w Barry Shipman *d* William Witney *ph* Bud Thackery *m* Dale Butts

Macdonald Carey, Skip Homeier, Patricia Medina, Louis Jean Heydt

The Stranger Came Home
GB 1954 80m bw

After being assaulted in the Far East, a financier loses his memory and does not return home until three years later, when murder ensues. Muddled mystery quickie, only notable as the film which persuaded its star to retire. Paulette Goddard, William Sylvester, Patrick Holt, Paul Carpenter, Russell Napier, Alvys Maben. Written by Michael Carreras, from the novel *Stranger at Home* by George Sanders; directed by Terence Fisher; for Hammer. (US title: *The Unholy Four*.)

A Stranger in My Arms
US 1958 88m bw Cinemascope
U-I (Ross Hunter)

A test pilot falls in love with his dead friend's widow and helps her face up to her in-laws.
Dreary romantic drama.

w Peter Berneis, *novel* And Ride a Tiger by Robert Wilder *d* Helmut Kautner *ph* William Daniels *m* Joseph Gershenson

June Allyson, Jeff Chandler, *Mary Astor*, Sandra Dee, Charles Coburn, Conrad Nagel, Peter Graves

A Stranger in Town
US 1943 67m bw

A supreme court judge on vacation finds himself sorting out crooked local politicians. Interesting second feature with good cast and production values. Frank Morgan, Richard Carlson, Jean Rogers, Porter Hall, Robert Barrat, Donald MacBride, Andrew Tombes, John Hodiak. Written by Isobel Lennart, William Koslenko; directed by Roy Rowland; for Robert Sisk / MGM.

A Stranger Is Watching
US 1981 92m Metrocolor

A small girl is terrified by the psychopath who raped and murdered her mother. Unpleasant thriller in the modern manner. Kate Mulgrew, Rip Torn, James Naughton, Shawn Van Schreiber. Written by Earl MacRaugh and Victor Miller, from the novel by Mary Higgins Clark; directed by Sean S. Cunningham; for Sidney Beckerman / MGM–UA.

The Stranger Left no Card**
GB 1952 23m bw

A weirdly dressed eccentric comes to a small town and is accepted by the townspeople; but his real purpose is murder. Smart little trick film which as a novelty has not been surpassed. *Alan Badel*, Cameron Hall, Eileen Way. Written by *Sidney Carroll*; directed by *Wendy Toye*; for George K. Arthur / Meteor / British Lion.

Stranger on the Prowl
Italy / US 1952 83m bw
UA / CPCT (Noel Calef)

In an Italian port, a stranger helps a boy but is shot by the police.
Ineffective melodrama, a sad comedown for its star.

wd Andrea Forzano *ph* Henri Alekan *m* C. G. Sonzogno

Paul Muni, Joan Lorring, Vittorio Manunta, Aldo Silvani

† Most of the picture was directed by Joseph Losey while he was technically unemployable owing to Hollywood's red-baiting.

Stranger on the Third Floor*
US 1940 64m bw
RKO (Lee Marcus)

A reporter finds that he was wrong in the well-intentioned testimony which helps convict an innocent man for murder.

Stylish B feature with a striking dream scene and a curious fleeting performance by Lorre as the real murderer.

w Frank Partos *d* Boris Ingster *ph* Nicholas Musuraca *m* Roy Webb

Margaret Tallichet, Peter Lorre, John McGuire, Charles Waldron, Elisha Cook Jnr, Charles Halton, Ethel Griffies

'For him death has two faces—and he faces them both, alone!'

The Stranger Wore a Gun
US 1953 83m Technicolor 3-D

An honest adventurer finds that the man who once saved his life has become a stagecoach robber. Routine western with many objects hurled at the audience to show off the 3-D process. Randolph Scott, George Macready, Claire Trevor, Joan Weldon, Lee Marvin, Ernest Borgnine, Alfonso Bedoya. Written by Kenneth Gamet; directed by André de Toth; for Columbia.

The Stranger's Hand
GB 1953 85m bw
Independent Film Producers / John Stafford, Peter Moore
aka: *Mano della Straniero*

A schoolboy is due to meet his father in Venice, but the father is kidnapped by enemy agents.
Rather tentative suspense thriller with a vague plot which seems to defeat an excellent cast.

w Guy Elmes, Giorgio Bassani, *story* Graham Greene *d* Mario Soldati *ph* Enzo Serafin *m* Nino Rota

Trevor Howard, Richard O'Sullivan, Francis L. Sullivan, Alida Valli, Eduardo Ciannelli, Richard Basehart, Stephen Murray

Strangers in Love
US 1932 68m bw

A ne'er-do-well has some difficulties when he tries to step into his dead twin's shoes. Predictable comedy-melodrama, quite well acted. Fredric March, Kay Francis, Stuart Erwin, Juliette Compton, George Barbier, Sidney Toler. Written by Grover Jones and William Slavens McNutt from the play The Shorn Lamb by William J. Locke; directed by Lothar Mendes; for Paramount. 'All the qualities that bespeak wide appeal.'—*Variety*

Strangers May Kiss
US 1931 82m bw
MGM

A sophisticated wife takes love and fidelity lightly.
Dated romantic drama.

w John Meehan, *novel* Ursula Parrott *d* George Fitzmaurice *ph* William Daniels

Norma Shearer, Robert Montgomery, Neil Hamilton, Marjorie Rambeau, Irene Rich

'Outstanding money picture. It'll sell itself.'—*Variety*

'It begins with the scream of a train whistle—and ends with screaming excitement!'

Strangers on a Train***
US 1951 101m bw
Warner (Alfred Hitchcock)

A tennis star is pestered on a train by a psychotic who wants to swap murders, and proceeds to carry out his part of the bargain. This quirky melodrama has the director at his best, sequence by sequence, but the story is basically unsatisfactory. It makes superior suspense entertainment, however.

w Raymond Chandler, Czenzi Ormonde, *novel* Patricia Highsmith *d Alfred Hitchcock ph Robert Burks m Dmitri Tionkin md* Ray Heindorf

Farley Granger, *Robert Walker*, Ruth Roman, Leo G. Carroll, Patricia Hitchcock, *Marion Lorne*, Howard St John, Jonathan Hale, Laura Elliott

BRUNO (Robert Walker): 'Some people are better off dead—like your wife and my father, for instance.'

'You may not take it seriously, but you certainly don't have time to think about anything else.'—*Richard Mallett, Punch*

'The construction seems a little lame, but Hitch takes delight in the set pieces.'—*Time Out, 1985*

† Remade 1970 as *Once You Kiss A Stranger*.
AAN: Robert Burks

The Stranger's Return
US 1933 89m bw

An old farmer disapproves of his granddaughter's affair with a married man. An American view of Cold Comfort Farm country, too heavy to click at the box office. Lionel Barrymore, Miriam Hopkins, Franchot Tone, Beulah Bondi, Stuart Erwin, Irene Hervey. Written by Brown Holmes and Phil Stong; directed by King Vidor; for MGM.

Strangers When We Meet*
US 1960 117m Technicolor Cinemascope
Columbia / Bryna (Richard Quine)

A successful architect starts an affair with a beautiful married neighbour.
Beverly Hills soap opera with lots of romantic suffering in luxury. Lumpy but generally palatable.

w Evan Hunter, from his novel *d* Richard Quine *ph* Charles Lang Jnr *m* George Duning

Kirk Douglas, Kim Novak, *Ernie Kovacs, Walter Matthau,* Barbara Rush, Virginia Bruce, Helen Gallagher, Kent Smith

The Strangler
US 1963 80m bw
AA

An obese lab technician murders nurses who help his hated mother.
Modest, lively shocker.

w Bill S. Ballinger *d* Burt Topper *ph* Jacques Marquette *m* Marlin Skiles

Victor Buono, David McLean, Ellen Corby, Diane Sayer

The Stranglers of Bombay
GB 1959 81m bw Megascope
Columbia / Hammer (Anthony Hinds)

In 1826 travellers are waylaid and sacrificially killed by a cult of stranglers.
Semi-historical parade of atrocities, repellent but scarcely exciting.

w David Z. Goodman *d* Terence Fisher *ph* Arthur Grant *m* James Bernard

Guy Rolfe, Allan Cuthbertson, Andrew Cruickshank, Marne Maitland, Jan Holden, George Pastell, Paul Stassino

Strategic Air Command
US 1955 114m Technicolor Vistavision
Paramount (Samuel J. Briskin)

A baseball player is recalled to air force duty.
Sentimental flagwaver featuring the newest jets of the fifties.

w Valentine Davies, Beirne Lay Jnr *d* Anthony Mann *ph* William Daniels *m* Victor Young

James Stewart, June Allyson, Frank Lovejoy, Barry Sullivan, Alex Nicol, Bruce Bennett, Jay C. Flippen, James Millican, James Bell

AAN: original story (Beirne Lay Jnr)

The Stratton Story
US 1949 106m bw
MGM (Jack Cummings)

An amateur baseball enthusiast becomes a famous professional, but suffers an accident which involves the amputation of a leg.
Mild sentimental biopic, well made but not very interesting.

w Douglas Morrow, Guy Trosper *d* Sam Wood *ph* Harold Rosson *m* Adolph Deutsch

James Stewart, June Allyson, Frank Morgan, Agnes Moorehead, Bill Williams

AA: original story (Douglas Morrow)

'The knock at the door meant the birth of one man and the death of seven others!'

Straw Dogs
GB 1971 118m Eastmancolor
Talent Associates / Amerbroco (Daniel Melnick)

In a Cornish village, a mild American university researcher erupts into violence when taunted by drunken villagers who commit sustained assaults on himself and his wife.
Totally absurd, poorly contrived, hilariously overwritten Cold Comfort Farm melodrama with farcical violence.

w David Zelag Goodman, Sam Peckinpah, *novel* The Siege of Trencher's Farm by Gordon M. Williams *d* Sam Peckinpah *ph* John Coquillon, *m* Jerry Fielding

Dustin Hoffman, Susan George, Peter Vaughan, David Warner, T. P. McKenna, Colin Welland

AAN: Jerry Fielding

The Strawberry Blonde**
US 1941 97m bw
Warner (William Cagney)

A dentist in turn-of-the-century Brooklyn wonders whether he married the right woman. Pleasant period comedy drama, a remake of *One Sunday Afternoon* (qv).

w Julius J. and Philip G. Epstein *d* Raoul Walsh *ph James Wong Howe* *m* Heinz Roemheld

James Cagney, Olivia de Havilland, *Rita Hayworth, Alan Hale,* George Tobias, Jack Carson, Una O'Connor, George Reeves

'It not only tells a very human story, it also creates an atmosphere, recreates a period.'—*New York Sun*

'A blithe, sentimental, turn-of-the-century buggy ride.'—*Time*

AAN: Heinz Roemheld

Strawberry Roan
GB 1944 84m bw

A farmer weds a showgirl who ruins his life. Rather glum rural drama with some style but little entertainment value. William Hartnell, Carol Raye, Walter Fitzgerald, Sophie Stewart, John Ruddock, Wylie Watson, Petula Clark. Written by Elizabeth Baron, from the novel by A. G. Street; directed by Maurice Elvey; for British National.

The Strawberry Statement
US 1970 109m Metrocolor
MGM / Robert Chartoff, Irwin Winkler

Student rebels occupy a university administration building.
One of a short-lived group of student anti-discipline films of the early seventies, and about the most boring.

w Israel Horowitz, *novel* James Simon Kunen *d* Stuart Hagmann *ph* Ralph Woolsey *m* Ian Freebairn Smith

Bruce Davison, Kim Darby, Bud Cort, Murray MacLeod

Streamers
US 1983 118m Movielab

Tensions mount at a training camp for the 83rd Airborne Division. Claustrophobic photographed play about generally worthless people. Matthew Modine, Michael Wright, Mitchell Lichtenstein, David Alan Grier, Guy Boyd, George Dzundza. Written by David Rabe from his play; directed by Robert Altman; for Streamers International Distributors.

'A thing of beauty is a joy for ever . . .'
Street Angel*
US 1928 101m bw part-talkie
Fox

An unwilling prostitute becomes a circus artiste.
A sentimental and tawdry tale becomes a vehicle for good typical work by director and stars.

w Marion Orth *play* Lady Cristallinda by Monckton Hoffe *d Frank Borzage* *ph* Ernest Palmer, Paul Ivano *ad* Harry Oliver

Janet Gaynor, Charles Farrell, Henry Armetta, Guido Trento

AA: Ernest Palmer; Janet Gaynor

Street Corner
GB 1953 94m bw
Rank / LIP / Sydney Box (William MacQuitty)
US title: *Both Sides of the Law*

Days in the lives of the women police of Chelsea.
Patter-plotted female *Blue Lamp*; just about watchable.

w Muriel and Sydney Box *d* Muriel Box *ph* Reg Wyer *m* Temple Abady

Rosamund John, Anne Crawford, Peggy Cummins, Terence Morgan, Barbara Murray, Sarah Lawson, Ronald Howard, Eleanor Summerfield, Michael Medwin

Street of Chance
US 1930 78m bw
Paramount (David O. Selznick)

A New York gambler gets his come-uppance. Dullish family melodrama with gangsters as *dei ex machina.*

w Howard Estabrook, Lenore Coffee *d* John Cromwell *ph* Charles Lang

William Powell, Kay Francis, Regis Toomey, Jean Arthur

'Strong exploitation can cinch this one. Strongly hints at recent murder of well-known gambler.'—*Variety*

AAN: script

'Where women came to forget—one man came to remember!'
Street of Chance*
US 1942 74m bw

An amnesia case discovers that he is wanted for murder. The plot was fairly original at the time, and the treatment maintains interest. Burgess Meredith, Claire Trevor, Sheldon Leonard, Jerome Cowan, Frieda Inescort, Louise Platt. Written by Garrett Fort, from story by Cornell Woolrich; directed by Jack Hively; for Burt Skelly / Sol C. Siegel / Paramount.

Street of Shame*
Japan 1956 85m bw
Daiei (Masaichi Nagata)
original title: *Akasen Chitai*

Stories of women in a Tokyo brothel. Unremarkable material executed with the style expected of the director.

w Masashige Narusawa *d* Kenji Mizoguchi *ph* Kazuo Miyagawa *m* Toshiro Mayazumi

Machiko Kyo, Ayako Wakao, Aiko Mimasu

Street of Women
US 1932 59m bw

A property developer is torn between his wife and his mistress. Choppily developed drama which starts haltingly and gets nowhere. Kay Francis, Alan Dinehart, Roland Young, Marjorie Gateson, Gloria Stuart. Written by Mary McCall Jnr from the novel by Polan Banks; directed by Archie Mayo; for Warners.
'Just a programme picture.'—*Variety*

Street Scene*
US 1931 80m bw
Samuel Goldwyn

In a New York slum street on a hot summer night, an adulterous woman is shot by her husband.
Slice-of-life drama from an influential play; never much of a film, and very dated.

w Elmer Rice, from his play *d* King Vidor *ph* George Barnes *m* Alfred Newman

Sylvia Sidney, William Collier Jnr, Max Mantor, David Landau, Estelle Taylor, Russell Hopton

'Whenever the camera starts to focus on two or three characters, the plot thickens and *Street Scene* flies out the window; petty domestic tragedy supplants the original slice-of-life conception.'—*National Board of Review*

'As a commercial proposition it will cause talk and reap honours, but whether it will prove an exceptional box office attraction remains to be seen.'—*Variety*

The Street Singer
GB 1937 85m bw

A musical comedy star is mistaken for a beggar by a girl with whom he falls in love. Rather tiresome star vehicle. Arthur Tracy, Margaret Lockwood, Arthur Riscoe, Hugh Wakefield. Written by Reginald Arkell; directed by Jean de Marguenat; for British National.

Street Smart
US 1987 95m TVC

A top journalist turns in a story that gets him involved with pimps and prostitutes. Unpersuasive crime melodrama in which the star seems surprised to find himself. Christopher Reeve, Kathy Baker, Mimi Rogers, Jay Patterson, Andre Gregory, Morgan Freeman. Written by David Freeman; directed by Jerry Schatzberg; for Cannon.
AAN: Morgan Freeman.

The Street with No Name*
US 1948 93m bw
TCF (Samuel G. Engel)

An FBI man goes undercover to unmask a criminal gang.
The oldest crime plot in the world, applied with vigour to the documentary realism of *The House on 92nd Street* and built around the *Kiss of Death* psychopathic character created by Richard Widmark.

w Harry Kleiner *d* William Keighley *ph Joe MacDonald* *m* Lionel Newman

Richard Widmark, Mark Stevens, Lloyd Nolan, Barbara Lawrence, Ed Begley
† Remade 1955 as *House of Bamboo.*

A Streetcar Named Desire**
US 1951 122m bw
Charles K. Feldman / Elia Kazan

A repressed southern widow is raped and driven mad by her brutal brother-in-law.
Reasonably successful, decorative picture from a highly theatrical but influential play; unreal sets and atmospheric photography vaguely Sternbergian.

w Tennessee Williams, from his play *d Elia Kazan ph Harry Stradling m* Alex North *ad* Richard Day

Vivien Leigh, Marlon Brando, Kim Hunter, Karl Malden

AA: Vivien Leigh; Kim Hunter; Karl Malden
AAN: best picture; Tennessee Williams; Elia Kazan; Harry Stradling; Alex North; Marlon Brando

Streets of Fire
US 1984 94m Technicolor
Universal / RKO / Hill-Gordon-Silver (Lawrence Gordon, Joel Silver)

A rock singer is kidnapped and a professional trouble shooter takes on the job of recovery.
Violent melodrama with an unsuccessful comic strip approach which fails to raise the material into the realm of myth.

w Walter Hill, Larry Gross *d* Walter Hill *ph* Andrew Laszlo *pd* John Vallone *m* Ry Cooder *ed* Freeman Davies, Michael Ripps

Michael Paré, Diane Lane, Rick Moranis, Andy Madigan, Willem Dafoe

Streets of Gold*
US 1986 95m De Luxe
TCF / James G. Robinson / Ufland-Roth

A disenchanted immigrant finds an unexpected road to success as a boxing coach for two streetwise kids.
Unappealing variation on the Rocky movies, good to look at but devoid of content.

w Heywood Gould, Richard Price, Tom Cole *d* Joe Roth *ph* Arthur Albert *m* Jack Nitzche *pd* Marcos Flaksman *ed* Richard Chew

Klaus Maria Brandauer, Adrian Pasdar, Wesley Snipes, Angela Molina

Streets of Laredo
US 1949 92m Technicolor
Paramount (Robert Fellows)

Two of three bandit friends become Texas Rangers.
Adequate star western, a remake of *The Texas Rangers*.

w Charles Marquis Warren *d* Leslie Fenton *ph* Ray Rennahan *m* Victor Young

William Holden, William Bendix, Macdonald Carey, Mona Freeman

Streets of New York
US 1939 72m bw

The teenage owner of a newsstand studies law at night school. Unconvincing street-life drama, an obvious vehicle for a boy star. Jackie Cooper, Martin Spellman, George Cleveland, Dick Purcell. Written by Robert Andrews; directed by William Nigh; for Monogram. 'Should do all right if not pointed too high.'—*Variety*

Strictly Dishonourable
US 1951 94m bw
MGM (Melvin Frank, Norman Panama)

A young girl falls in love with a rakish Italian opera star; he is such a sentimentalist that he marries her.
Emasculated sentimental version of the sharp Preston Sturges comedy.

wd Norman Panama, Melvin Frank *ph* Ray June *m* Lennie Hayton

Ezio Pinza, Janet Leigh, Millard Mitchell, Maria Palmer

† Previously filmed in 1931 by Universal, with Paul Lukas, Sidney Fox and Lewis Stone.

Strictly Unconventional: see The Circle

Strike***
USSR 1924 70m approx (24 fps) bw silent
Goskino / Proletkult

A 1912 strike of factory workers is brutally put down by the authorities.
Brilliant propaganda piece with superbly cinematic sequences.

wd Sergei M. Eisenstein ph Edouard Tissé, Vassili Khvatov

Grigori Alexandrov, Maxim Strauch, Mikhail Gomarov

Strike Me Pink*
US 1935 104m bw
Samuel Goldwyn

A timid amusement park owner is threatened by crooks.
Acceptable star comedy with music.

w Frank Butler, Walter de Leon, Francis Martin *d* Norman Taurog *ph* Gregg Toland, Merritt Gerstad *m* Alfred Newman *songs* Harold Arlen, Lew Brown

Eddie Cantor, Sally Eilers, Ethel Merman, William Frawley, Parkyakarkus

'At the box office both here and abroad the take will be big.'—*Variety*

Strike Up the Band*
US 1940 120m bw
MGM (Arthur Freed)

A high-school band takes part in a nationwide radio contest.
Rather tiresomely high-spirited musical with the stars at the top of their young form.

w Fred Finklehoffe, John Monks Jnr *d / ch* Busby Berkeley *ph* Ray June *m* Roger Edens, *ly* Arthur Freed

Judy Garland, Mickey Rooney, Paul Whiteman and his Orchestra, June Preisser, William Tracy, Larry Nunn

AAN: Georgie Stoll, Roger Edens; song 'Our Love Affair' (*m / ly* Roger Edens, Georgie Stoll)

The Strip*
US 1951 85m bw
MGM (Joe Pasternak)

A band drummer is accused of the murder of a racketeer.
Minor mystery melodrama intriguingly set on Sunset Strip, with jazz accompaniment.

w Allen Rivkin *d* Leslie Kardos *ph* Robert Surtees *m* George Stoll

Mickey Rooney, Sally Forrest, William Demarest, James Craig, Kay Brown; and Louis Armstrong, Earl Hines, Jack Teagarden

AAN: song 'A Kiss To Build a Dream On (*m / ly* Bert Kalmar, Harry Ruby, Oscar Hammerstein II)

'Today's army needs men of courage—honesty—integrity—ambition. Instead, they got John Winger . . .'

Stripes
US 1981 106m Metrocolor
Columbia (Ivan Reitman, Dan Goldberg)

Sergeant Hulka tries to train a platoon of misfit volunteers.
Ancient army wheezes dressed up with fashionable black comedy and sex, but no funnier than *Carry On Sergeant*.

w Len Blum, Dan Goldberg, Harold Ramis *d* Ivan Reitman *ph* Bill Butler *m* Elmer Bernstein

Bill Murray, Harold Ramis, Warren Oates, P. J. Soles, John Larroquette, Sean Young

The Stripper*
US 1963 95m bw Cinemascope
TCF (Jerry Wald)
GB title: *Woman of Summer*

An ageing beauty queen returns to her Kansas hometown and has an affair with a 19-year-old garage hand.
Downbeat character melodrama typical of its time and its author; competent but sterile and rather tedious.

w Meade Roberts, *play* A Loss of Roses by William Inge *d Franklin Schaffner* *ph* Ellsworth Fredericks *m* Jerry Goldsmith

Joanne Woodward, Richard Beymer, *Claire Trevor*, Carol Lynley, Robert Webber, Louis Nye, Gypsy Rose Lee, Michael J. Pollard

Stromboli
Italy 1949 107m bw
RKO / Be-Ro (Roberto Rossellini)

A Lithuanian refugee accepts the protection of marriage to an Italian fisherman, but resents the barrenness and hostility of her life, especially when the local volcano erupts.
Sloppy melodrama with pretensions, interesting but not even attractive to the eye.

w Roberto Rossellini and others *d* Roberto Rossellini *ph* Otello Martelli *m* Renzo Rossellini

Ingrid Bergman, Mario Vitale, Renzo Cesana

† The international version was cut to 81m.

The Strong Man*
US 1926 75m approx (24 fps) bw (colour sequence) silent
First National / Harry Langdon

A war veteran returns and searches the city for his female penfriend.
Quite charming star comedy, probably Langdon's best.

w Frank Capra, Arthur Ripley, Hal Conklin, Robert Eddy *d* Frank Capra *ph* Elgin Lessley, Glenn Kershner

Harry Langdon, Gertrude Astor, Tay Garnett

Stronger than Desire
US 1939 82m bw

A lawyer's wife gets into trouble and lets him try an innocent man for her crime. Fast remake of *Evelyn Prentice*; a good half-bill. Walter Pidgeon, Virginia Bruce, Ann Dvorak, Lee Bowman, Rita Johnson, Ilka Chase. Written by David Hertz and William Ludwig; directed by Leslie Fenton; for MGM.

The Strongest Man in the World
US 1976 92m Technicolor
Walt Disney (Bill Anderson)

An accident in a science lab gives a student superhuman strength.
Formula comedy for older children.

w Joseph L. McEveety, Herman Groves *d* Vincent McEveety *ph* Andrew Jackson *m* Robert F. Brunner

Kurt Russell, Joe Flynn, Eve Arden, Cesar Romero, Phil Silvers, Dick Van Patten, Harold Gould, William Schallert, James Gregory, Roy Roberts, Fritz Feld, Raymond Bailey, Eddie Quillan, Burt Mustin

Strongroom*
GB 1961 80m bw
Bryanston / Theatrecraft (Guido Coen)

Two car breakers plan a once-for-all bank robbery but get involved with potential murder when their hostages get locked in. Suspenseful second feature with gloss and pace.

w Max Marquis, René Harris *d Vernon Sewell* *ph* Basil Emmott *m* Johnny Gregory

Colin Gordon, Ann Lynn, Derren Nesbitt, Keith Faulkner

The Struggle*
US 1931 88m bw
UA / D. W. Griffith

A New Yorker goes to the bad on bootleg liquor.
The director's last film reveals many of his old skills allied to a Victorian tract.

w Anita Loos, John Emerson *d* D. W. Griffith *ph* Joseph Ruttenberg

Hal Skelly, Zita Johann, Charlotte Wynters, Jackson Halliday

'A dull and sodden rendering with old-time ranting and little drama . . . just dull when it isn't in the highest degree maudlin.'—*Dwight MacDonald*

It was based on The Drunkard by Emile Zola.
† The picture failed and was re-released as *Ten Nights in a Bar-room.*

The Stud
GB 1978 90m colour
Brent Walker / Artoc (Edward D. Simons)

A millionaire's wife installs her lover as manager of a discotheque, but he becomes bored and wants a place of his own.
Life among the unpleasant rich. A surprise box office success, richly undeserved.

w Jackie Collins, from her novel *d* Quentin Masters *ph* Peter Hannan *m* Biddu

Joan Collins, Oliver Tobias, Sue Lloyd, Mark Burns, Doug Fisher, Walter Gotell

'Watching it is rather like being buried alive in a coffin stuffed with back numbers of *Men Only*.'—*Alan Brien*

The Student Prince
US 1954 107m Anscocolor
Cinemascope
MGM (Joe Pasternak)

A prince studies in Heidelberg and falls for a barmaid.
Ruritanian operetta, lumpishly filmed, with Mario Lanza providing only the voice of the hero as he got too fat to play the part.

w William Ludwig, Sonya Levien, *play* Old Heidelberg by Wilhelm Meyer-Foerster *operetta* Dorothy Donnelly *d* Richard Thorpe *ph* Paul C. Vogel *m Sigmund Romberg* *md* George Stoll

Edmund Purdom, Ann Blyth, John Williams, Edmund Gwenn, S. Z. Sakall, John Ericson, Louis Calhern, Betta St John, Evelyn Varden
† Without the music, the play had been filmed at MGM in 1926, with Ramon Novarro and Norma Shearer under Ernst Lubitsch's direction.

Student Tour
US 1934 80m bw

A professor of philosophy chaperones a world tour by collegiates. Very thin comedy yarn with songs. Jimmy Durante, Charles Butterworth, Maxine Doyle, Phil Regan, Douglas Fowley, Betty Grable, Nelson Eddy. Written by Ralph Spence, Philip Dunne; directed by Charles F. Reisner; for MGM. 'Long, slow, and of mild entertainment appeal.'—*Variety*

The Studio Murder Mystery
US 1929 62m bw

An actor is murdered on a film set. Primitive talkie comedy mystery now interesting only for its studio backgrounds. Neil Hamilton, Florence Eldridge, Warner Oland, Eugene Pallette, Fredric March, Doris Hill, Chester Conklin. Written by Frank Tuttle, from a magazine serial by the Edingtons; directed by Frank Tuttle; for Paramount.

Studs Lonigan
US 1960 95m bw

The growing up of an unlettered Chicago Irishman in the twenties. Rough-and-ready version of a celebrated novel, not a bad try but insufficiently detailed to be any kind of classic. Christopher Knight, Jack Nicholson, Frank Gorshin. Written by Philip Yordan, from the novel by James T. Farrell; directed by Irving Lerner; for Philip Yordan.

A Study in Scarlet
US 1933 71m bw

Sherlock Holmes solves a mysterious murder. Rather emaciated version of a spirited yarn. Reginald Owen, Warburton Gamble, Anna May Wong, June Clyde, Alan Dinehart, Alan Mowbray. Written by Robert Florey from the story by Sir Arthur Conan Doyle; directed by Edwin L. Marin; for KBS. 'Okay for secondary houses.'—*Variety*

A Study in Terror*
GB 1965 95m Eastmancolor
Compton-Tekli / Sir Nigel (Henry E. Lester)

Sherlock Holmes discovers the identity of Jack the Ripper.
A reasonably good Holmes pastiche marred by a surfeit of horror and over-riotous local colour; quite literate, but schizophrenic.

w Donald and Derek Ford, *novel* Ellery Queen *d* James Hill *ph* Desmond Dickinson *m* John Scott *ad* Alex Vetchinsky

John Neville, Donald Houston, John Fraser, Robert Morley, Cecil Parker, Anthony Quayle, Barbara Windsor, Adrienne Corri, Judi Dench, Frank Finlay, Barry Jones, Kay Walsh, Georgia Brown

The Stuff
US 1985 93m Technicolor

A monstrous yogurt-like goo eats people from the inside out. Messy comedy-horror without benefit of much plotline. Michael Moriarty, Andrea Marcovicci, Paul Sorvino, Scott Bloom, Danny Aiello, Alexander Scourby. Written and directed by Larry Cohen; for New World.

The Stunt Man*
US 1978 129m Metrocolor
Melvin Simon (Richard Rush)

A Vietnam veteran on the run from the police finds refuge as a star stunt man for a sinister film director.
Overlong, curious, but sometimes compelling melodrama which entertains on the surface while its actual aims are harder to fathom.

w Lawrence B. Marcus *novel* Paul Brodeur *d Richard Rush* *ph* Mario Tosi *m* Dominic Frontière

Peter O'Toole, Steve Railsback, Barbara Hershey, Allen Goorwitz, Alex Rocco, Sharon Farrell

'It's like one of those sets of Chinese boxes, each one with another box inside, growing smaller and smaller until finally there is nothing left at all.'—*Roger Ebert*

AAN: screenplay; Richard Rush; Peter O'Toole

The Subject Was Roses*
US 1968 107m Metrocolor
MGM (Edgar Lansbury)

A young war veteran finds he can't communicate with his parents, and vice versa. Photographed play notable for its performances.

w Frank D. Gilroy, from his play *d* Ulu Grosbard *ph* Jack Priestley

Patricia Neal, Jack Albertson, Martin Sheen, Don Saxon, Elaine Williams

AA: Jack Albertson
AAN: Patricia Neal

Submarine Command
US 1951 87m bw
Paramount (John Farrow, Joseph Sistrom)

A submarine officer who considers himself a coward becomes a hero in Korea.
Very routine soul-searching actioner.

w Jonathan Latimer *d* John Farrow
ph Lionel Lindon *m* David Buttolph

William Holden, Don Taylor, Nancy Olsen, William Bendix, Moroni Olsen, Peggy Webber

Submarine D1
US 1937 93m bw

Adventures of recruits to the naval submarine service. Standard flagwaver of no intrinsic interest. Pat O'Brien, George Brent, Wayne Morris, Frank McHugh, Doris Weston, Ronald Reagan, Henry O'Neill, Regis Toomey, Broderick Crawford. Written by Frank Wead, Warren Duff, Lawrence Kimble; directed by Lloyd Bacon; for Cosmopolitan / Warners. 'An instructive and illuminating document . . . film waves its own flag, the best on earth, and with some exhibitor push it should do business.'—*Variety*

Submarine Patrol
US 1938 93m bw

Recruits learn to handle sub-chasing boats at Annapolis. Cheerful propaganda comedy-drama with familiar faces on hand and some good thrill sequences. Richard Greene, Nancy Kelly, Preston Foster, George Bancroft, Slim Summerville, John Carradine, Henry Armetta, Warren Hymer, Elisha Cook Jnr, E. E. Clive, Ward Bond, George E. Stone. Written by Rian James, Darrell Ware, Jack Yellen, from a book by Ray Milholland; directed by John Ford; for Gene Markey / TCF. 'Surefire film entertainment directed by a veteran who knows all the tricks.'—*Variety*

Submarine Raider
US 1942 65m bw

An American sub learns too late about the attack on Pearl Harbor. Stodgy wartime filler with unconvincing action sequences. John Howard, Marguerite Chapman, Bruce Bennett, Warren Ashe. Written by Aubrey Wisberg; directed by Lew Landers; for Wallace MacDonald / Columbia.

Submarine X-I
GB 1967 90m Eastmancolor
UA / Mirisch (John C. Champion)

A submarine commander in World War II trains men to attack the *Lindendorf* in midget submarines.
Belated quota quickie, routine in every department.

w Donald S. Sanford, Guy Elmes *d* William Graham *ph* Paul Beeson

James Caan, Norman Bowler, David Sumner

'We are the new Bohemians!'
The Subterraneans
US 1960 89m Metrocolor
Cinemascope
MGM (Arthur Freed)

The love affairs of San Francisco bohemians.
A boring oddity with lashings of eccentric behaviour and sexual hang-ups; MGM venturing very timidly outside its field.

w Robert Thom, *novel* Jack Kerouac
d Ranald MacDougall *ph* Joseph Ruttenberg
m André Previn

George Peppard, Leslie Caron, Janice Rule, Roddy McDowall, Anne Seymour, Jim Hutton

Subway
France 1985 104m colour
CinemaScope

An eccentric hero on the run from thugs takes refuge overnight in the Paris Metro. Oddball melodrama with more style than substance. Christophe Lambert, Isabelle Adjani, Richard Bohringer. Written by Luc Besson and others; directed by Luc Besson; for Gaumount / Films du Loup / TSF / TFI.

Subway in the Sky
GB 1958 87m bw
Orbit (John Temple-Smith, Patrick Filmer-Sankey)

A Berlin cabaret star finds her landlady's ex-husband, a deserter, hiding in her apartment and sets out to prove his innocence of drug smuggling.
Tedious photographed play with precious few points of dramatic interest.

w Jack Andrews, *play* Ian Main *d* Muriel Box *ph* Wilkie Cooper *m* Mario Nascimbene

Hildegarde Neff, Van Johnson, Katherine Kath, Cec Linder, Albert Lieven, Edward Judd

Success at Any Price
US 1934 74m bw

A young man climbs to great business heights by crushing those around him, then attempts suicide when the crash comes. Slackly handled drama with an unsympathetic hero. Douglas Fairbanks Jnr, Genevieve Tobin, Frank Morgan, Colleen Moore, Edward Everett Horton, Nydia Westman, Henry Kolker. Written by John Howard Lawson, Howard J. Green; directed by J. Walter Ruben; for RKO. 'Episodic, unreasonable and anything but audience proof.'—*Variety*

Success Is the Best Revenge
GB / France 1984 91m Technicolor
De Vere / Gaumont (Jerzy Skolimowski)

A Polish theatre director in London stages a symbolic show but alienates his son.
Another study of Polish exiles to follow *Moonlighting*, but this time with surrealist elements.

w Jerzy Skolimowski, Michael Lyndon
d Jerzy Skolimowski *ph* Mike Fash
m Stanley Myers, Hans Zimmer

Michael York, Joanna Szczerbic, Michael Lyndon, Jerry Skol, Michel Piccoli, John Hurt, Anouk Aimée, Jane Asher

A Successful Calamity
US 1931 75m bw

A millionaire discovers the true worth of his family when he pretends to be poor. Good star vehicle which pleases despite its predictability. George Arliss, Mary Astor, Evalyn Knapp, Grant Mitchell, William Janney. Written by Maude Howell, Julien Josephson and Austin Parker, from the play by Clare Kummer; directed by John G. Adolfi; for Warner.

Such Good Friends*
US 1971 102m Movielab
Paramount / Sigma (Otto Preminger)

A successful man has a mysterious illness and his wife enlists help from his friends.
Satirical parable which alternates between sex comedy and medical exposé; generally heavy-going but with good moments.

w Elaine May, *novel* Lois Gould *d* Otto Preminger *ph* Gayne Rescher *m* Thomas Z. Shepherd

Dyan Cannon, James Coco, Jennifer O'Neil, Nina Foch, Laurence Luckinbill, Ken Howard, Burgess Meredith, Louise Lasser, Sam Levene, Rita Gam, Nancy Guild

Such Men Are Dangerous
US 1930 83m bw

A crooked financier undergoes plastic surgery and leads a new life. Phoney melodrama with slow pace and unconvincing details. Warner Baxter, Catherine Dale Owen, Albert Conti, Hedda Hopper, Claud Allister, Bela Lugosi. Written by Ernest Vajda, Elinor Glyn; directed by Kenneth Hawks; for Fox. 'Will bore intelligent fans and impress even the gullible with its implausibilities.'—*Variety*

Such Women Are Dangerous
US 1934 81m bw

Through circumstances an innocent man about town is accused of murder. Mild drama which fails through slack handling. Warner Baxter, Rosemary Ames, Rochelle Hudson, Mona Barrie, Herbert Mundin, Henrietta Crosman. Written by Jane Storm, Oscar M. Sheridan, from the story Odd Thursday by Vera Caspary; directed by James Flood; for Fox. 'Just fair screen amusement.'—*Variety*

Sudden Fear**
US 1952 111m bw
RKO / Joseph Kaufman

A playwright heiress finds that her husband is plotting to kill her.
Archetypal star suspenser, glossy and effectively climaxed.

w Lenore Coffee, Robert Smith *d David Miller ph Charles Lang Jnr m* Elmer Bernstein

Joan Crawford, Jack Palance, Gloria Grahame, Bruce Bennett, Mike Connors

AAN: Charles Lang Jnr; Joan Crawford; Jack Palance

'Go on—make his day!'

Sudden Impact
US 1983 117m Technicolor
Warner / Malpaso (Clint Eastwood)

San Francisco detective Harry Callahan goes after a lady killer of men who raped her.
Unattractive and overlong cop show featuring an increasingly tired Dirty Harry.

w Joseph C. Stinson *d* Clint Eastwood *ph* Bruce Surtees *m* Lalo Schifrin *pd* Edward Carfagno

Clint Eastwood, Sondra Locke, Pat Hingle, Bradford Dillman, Paul Drake

'Eastwood presumably takes credit for such gems of authorial self-awareness as replacing the orang-outang of the *Which Way* films, with a farting dog.'—*Paul Taylor, MFB*

'To all those cowboy movies we saw in our youth, all those TV westerns and cop dramas and war movies, Dirty Harry has brought a great simplification: A big man, a big gun, a bad guy, and instant justice.'—*Roger Ebert.*

Suddenly*
US 1954 75m bw
UA / Robert Bassler

Gunmen take over a suburban house and plan to assassinate the President who is due to pass by.
Moderately effective minor suspenser with rather too much psychological chat.

w Richard Sale *d* Lewis Allen *ph* Charles G. Clarke *m* David Raksin

Frank Sinatra, Sterling Hayden, James Gleason, Nancy Gates, Kim Charney

'What she doesn't know about spring—neither does Cupid!'

Suddenly It's Spring
US 1947 87m bw
Paramount (Claude Binyon)

A WAC captain comes home to find that her husband wants a divorce.
Tired romantic comedy with no fizz at all.

w Claude Binyon *d* Mitchell Leisen *ph* Daniel L. Fapp *m* Victor Young

Paulette Goddard, Macdonald Carey, Fred MacMurray, Arleen Whelan, Lillian Fontaine, Frank Faylen, Victoria Horne

Suddenly Last Summer*
GB 1959 114m bw
Columbia / Horizon (Sam Spiegel)

A homosexual poet's young cousin goes mad when she sees him raped and murdered by beach boys.
Arty flashback talk-piece from a one-act play, padded out with much sub-poetic mumbo jumbo; it takes too long to get to the revelation, which is ambiguously presented anyway.

w Gore Vidal, *play* Tennessee Williams *d* Joseph L. Mankiewicz *ph Jack Hildyard* *m* Buxton Orr, Malcolm Arnold *pd Oliver Messel*

Katharine Hepburn, Elizabeth Taylor, Montgomery Clift, Albert Dekker, Mercedes McCambridge, Gary Raymond

'A short play turns into a ludicrous, lumbering horror movie.'—*New Yorker, 1978*

'I loathe this film, I say so candidly. To my mind it is a decadent piece of work, sensational, barbarous and ridiculous.'—*C. A. Lejeune, Observer*

'A wholly admirable rendering into film of a work at once fascinating and nauseating, brilliant and immoral.'—*Arthur Knight*

AAN: Katharine Hepburn; Elizabeth Taylor

Suez*
US 1938 104m bw
TCF (Gene Markey)

The career of French engineer Ferdinand de Lesseps, who built the Suez Canal.
Superbly mounted but rather undramatic fictionalized biopic.

w Philip Dunne, Julien Josephson *d* Allan Dwan *ph* Peverell Marley *md* Louis Silvers *m* David Raksin, David Buttolph, Cyril Mockridge

Tyrone Power, Annabella, Loretta Young, J. Edward Bromberg, Joseph Schildkraut, Henry Stephenson, Sidney Blackmer, Maurice Moscovitch, Sig Rumann, Nigel Bruce, Miles Mander, George Zucco, Leon Ames, Rafaela Ottiano

'It's a big film in its attempt, but it misses out on its epic aims.'—*Variety*

AAN: Peverell Marley; Louis Silvers

Sugarfoot
US 1951 80m Technicolor

Two men meet on a train for Prescott, Arizona, and each determines to make the town his own. Unusual but fatally sluggish western. Randolph Scott, Raymond Massey, Adele Jergens, S. Z. Sakall, Robert Warwick, Arthur Hunnicutt. Written by Russell Hughes, from a novel by Clarence Budington Kelland; directed by Edwin L. Marin; for Warner. (TV title: *Swirl of Glory*.)

'The true story of a girl who took on all of Texas . . . and almost won.'

Sugarland Express*
US 1974 110m Technicolor Panavision
Universal (Richard Zanuck, David Brown)

A convict's wife persuades him to escape because their baby is being adopted, and they inadvertently leave behind them a trail of destruction, ending in tragedy.
Mainly comic adventures with a bitter aftertaste, very stylishly handled.

w Hal Barwood, Matthew Robbins *d Steven Spielberg* *ph* Vilmos Zsigmond *m* John Williams

Goldie Hawn, Ben Johnson, Michael Sacks, William Atherton

'*Ace in the Hole* meets *Vanishing Point*.'—*Sight and Sound*

The Suitor*
France 1962 85m bw
CAPAC
original title: *Le Soupirant*

A nervous young man makes several attempts to get married.
The most successful feature of Pierre Etaix, a student of Tati: his jokes are more polished but in the end his own personality seems rather lacking.

w Pierre Etaix, Jean-Claude Carrière *d* Pierre Etaix *ph* Pierre Levant *m* Jean Paillaud

Pierre Etaix, Laurence Lignères, France Arnell

The Sullivans*
US 1944 111m bw
TCF (Sam Jaffe)
Reissue title: *The Fighting Sullivans*

Five sons of the same family are killed in World War II.
Inspirational true story which had a wide appeal.

w Mary C. McCall Jnr *d* Lloyd Bacon *ph* Lucien Andriot *m* Alfred Newman

Anne Baxter, Thomas Mitchell, Selena Royle, Edward Ryan, Trudy Marshall, John Campbell, James Cardwell, John Alvin, George Offerman Jnr, Roy Roberts

AAN: original story (Jules Schermer, Edward Doherty)

'There's no speed limit and no brake When Sullivan travels with Veronica Lake!'

Sullivan's Travels****
US 1941 90m bw
Paramount (Paul Jones)

A Hollywood director tires of comedy and goes out to find real life.
Marvellously sustained tragi-comedy which ranges from pratfalls to the chain gang and never loses its grip or balance.

wd Preston Sturges ph John Seitz m Leo Shuken

Joel McCrea, Veronica Lake, Robert Warwick, William Demarest, Franklin Pangborn, Porter Hall, Byron Foulger, Eric Blore, Robert Greig, Torben Meyer, *Jimmy Conlin*, Margaret Hayes

DEDICATION: 'To all the funny men and clowns who have made people laugh.'

'A brilliant fantasy in two keys—slapstick farce and the tragedy of human misery.'—*James Agee*

'The most witty and knowing spoof of Hollywood movie-making of all time.'—*Film Society Review*

'A deftly sardonic apologia for Hollywood make-believe.'—*New York Times*

'Reflecting to perfection the mood of wartime Hollywood, it danced on the grave of thirties social cinema.'—*Eileen Bowser, 1969*

'Bold ideas . . . bolder people!'

Summer and Smoke
US 1961 118m Technicolor Panavision
Paramount / Hal B. Wallis

In a small Mississippi town in 1916, the minister's spinster daughter nurses an unrequited love for the local rebel.
Wearisome screen version, in hothouse settings, of a pattern play about earthly and spiritual love.

w James Poe, Meade Roberts, *play* Tennessee Williams *d* Peter Glenville *ph* Charles Lang Jnr *m* Elmer Bernstein *ad* Walter Tyler

Geraldine Page, Laurence Harvey, Una Merkel, John McIntire, Pamela Tiffin, Rita Moreno, Thomas Gomez, Casey Adams, Earl Holliman, Lee Patrick, Malcolm Atterbury

AAN: Elmer Bernstein; Geraldine Page; Una Merkel

Summer Holiday**
US 1948 92m Technicolor
MGM (Arthur Freed)

Life for a small-town family at the turn of the century.
Musical version of a famous play: excellent individual numbers, warm playing and sympathetic scenes, but a surprising lack of overall style.

w Frances Goodrich, Albert Hackett, Ralph Blane, *play* Ah Wilderness by Eugene O'Neill *d Rouben Mamoulian ph Charles Schoenbaum md* Lennie Hayton *songs* Harry Warren, Ralph Blane *ch Charles Walters*

Walter Huston, Mickey Rooney, Frank Morgan, Agnes Moorehead, Butch Jenkins, Selena Royle, Marilyn Maxwell, Gloria de Haven, Anne Francis
† The film was finished in 1946 and held back because it seemed unlikely to succeed.

Summer Holiday*
GB 1962 109m Technicolor Cinemascope
ABP / Ivy (Kenneth Harper)

Four young London Transport mechanics borrow a double decker bus for a continental holiday.
Pacy, location-filmed youth musical with plenty of general appeal.

w Peter Myers, Ronnie Cass *d Peter Yates ph* John Wilcox *md* Stanley Black

Cliff Richard, Lauri Peters, Melvyn Hayes, Una Stubbs, Teddy Green, Ron Moody, Lionel Murton, David Kossoff

Summer Interlude*
Sweden 1950 97m bw
Svensk Filmindustri (Alan Ekelund)
original title: *Sommarlek*

A prima ballerina remembers a happy summer she spent with a boy who was tragically killed.
Melancholy romance quite typical of its creator but with less density of meaning than usual.

w Ingmar Bergman, Herbert Grevenius *d* Ingmar Bergman *ph* Gunnar Fischer, Bengt Jarnmark *m* Erik Nordgren

Maj-Britt Nilsson, Birger Malmsten, Alf Kjellin

Summer Madness: see Summertime

Summer Magic*
US 1963 104m Technicolor
Walt Disney (Ron Miller)

Children help their widowed mother in 1912 Boston.
Amiable remake of *Mother Carey's Chickens*, irreproachably presented.

w Sally Benson *d* James Neilson *ph* William Snyder *m* Buddy Baker *songs* the Sherman Brothers

Hayley Mills, Burl Ives, Dorothy McGuire, Darren McGavin, Deborah Walley, Una Merkel, Eddie Hodges, Michael J. Pollard

AAN: William Snyder

Summer of '42*
US 1971 103m Technicolor
Warner / Mulligan-Roth (Richard Alan Roth)

Adolescents make sexual explorations on a New England island in 1942.
Well-observed indulgence in the new permissiveness.

w Herman Raucher *d* Robert Mulligan *ph* Robert Surtees *m* Michel Legrand

Jennifer O'Neill, Gary Grimes, Jerry Houser, Oliver Conant, Lou Frizell

AA: Michel Legrand
AAN: Herman Raucher; Robert Surtees

Summer of the Seventeenth Doll
US / Australia 1959 94m bw
UA / Hecht–Hill–Lancaster (Leslie Norman)
US title: *Season of Passion*

Two cane-cutters on their annual city lay-off have woman trouble.
Miscast and unsatisfactory rendering of a good play; the humour has evaporated.

w John Dighton, *play* Ray Lawler *d* Leslie Norman *ph* Paul Beeson *m* Benjamin Frankel

Ernest Borgnine, John Mills, Angela Lansbury, Anne Baxter, Vincent Ball

A Summer Place
US 1959 130m Technicolor
Warner (Delmer Daves)

Romantic summer adventures of teenagers and their elders on an island off the coast of Maine.
Sex among the idle rich: a routine piece of Hollywood gloss, bowdlerized from a bestseller.

wd Delmer Daves, *novel* Sloan Wilson *ph* Harry Stradling *m* Max Steiner

Richard Egan, Dorothy McGuire, Sandra Dee, Arthur Kennedy, Troy Donahue, Constance Ford, Beulah Bondi

Summer Stock*
US 1950 109m Technicolor
MGM (Joe Pasternak)
GB title: *If You Feel Like Singing*

A theatre troupe takes over a farm for rehearsals, and the lady owner gets the bug.
Likeable but halting musical with the star's weight problems very obvious.

w George Wells, Sy Gomberg *d* Charles Walters *ph* Robert Planck *md* Johnny Green *ch* Nick Castle

Judy Garland, Gene Kelly, Gloria de Haven, Carleton Carpenter, Eddie Bracken, Phil Silvers, Hans Conried
† June Allyson was to have starred, but became pregnant.

Summer Storm*
US 1944 106m bw
(UA) Angelus

In 1912 Russia, a provincial judge falls for a local mancatcher.
One of Hollywood's occasional aberrations, an attempt to do something very European in typical west coast style. An interesting failure.

w Rowland Leigh, *story* The Shooting Party by Anton Chekhov *d* Douglas Sirk *ph* Archie Stout *md* Karl Hajos

George Sanders, Linda Darnell, *Edward Everett Horton,* Anna Lee, Hugo Haas, John Philiber, Sig Rumann, André Charlot
'There are bits of acting and photography which put it as far outside the run of American movies as it laudably tries to be. But most of it had for me the sporty speciousness of an illustrated drugstore classic.'—*James Agee*

AAN: Karl Hajos

Summer Wishes, Winter Dreams*
US 1973 88m Technicolor
Columbia / Rastar (Jack Brodsky)

A neurotic New York housewife goes to pieces when her mother dies but finds a new understanding of her husband when she accompanies him on a trip to the World War II battlefields.
Menopausal melodrama, well observed but disappointingly wispy and underdeveloped.

w Stewart Stern *d* Gilbert Cates *ph* Gerald Hirschfeld *m* Johnny Mandel

Joanne Woodward, Martin Balsam, Sylvia Sidney, Dori Brenner, Win Forman

AAN: Joanne Woodward; Sylvia Sidney

Summer with Monika*
Sweden 1952 97m bw
Svensk Filmindustri (Allan Ekelund)

A wild, restless girl defies her parents and goes off with her boy friend for an island holiday. Her subsequent pregnancy and motherhood don't in the least suit her, and the father is left alone with the baby.
Probably truthful but rather glum and unsophisticated drama of young love; not among Bergman's most interesting films.

w Ingmar Bergman, *novel* Per Anders Fogelstrom *ph* Gunnar Fischer *m* Erik Nordgren

Harriet Andersson, Lars Ekborg

Summertime***
US 1955 99m Eastmancolor
London Films / Lopert Productions (Ilya Lopert)
GB title: *Summer Madness*

An American spinster has a holiday in Venice and becomes romantically involved.
Delightful, sympathetic travelogue with dramatic asides, great to look at and hinging on a single superb performance.

w David Lean, H. E. Bates, *play* The Time of the Cuckoo by Arthur Laurents *d David Lean ph Jack Hildyard m* Sandro Cicognini

SULLIVAN'S TRAVELS. Joel McCrea and Veronica Lake, looking boyish in hat and man's jacket, discover the seriousness of real life.

Katharine Hepburn, Rossano Brazzi, Isa Miranda, Darren McGavin, Mari Aldon, André Morell

'The eye is endlessly ravished.'—*Dilys Powell*

AAN: David Lean; Katharine Hepburn

Summertree
US 1971 88m Eastmancolor
Warner / Bryna (Kirk Douglas)

A bored student learns about life and becomes a Vietnam casualty.
Well-made, rather tedious character study; good social observation.

w Edward Hume, Stephen Yafa, *play* Ron Cowen *d* Anthony Newley *ph* Richard C. Glouner *m* David Shire

Michael Douglas, Brenda Vaccaro, Jack Warden, Barbara Bel Geddes

The Sun Also Rises**
US 1957 129m Eastmancolor Cinemascope
TCF (Darryl F. Zanuck)

In Paris after World War I an impotent journalist meets a nymphomaniac lady of title, and they and their odd group of friends have various saddening adventures around Europe.
Not a bad attempt to film a difficult novel, though Cinemascope doesn't help and the last half hour becomes turgid. *The Last Flight* (qv) conveyed the same atmosphere rather more sharply.

w Peter Viertel, *novel* Ernest Hemingway *d Henry King* *ph* Leo Tover *m* Hugo Friedhofer

Tyrone Power, Ava Gardner, *Errol Flynn*, Eddie Albert, Mel Ferrer, Robert Evans, Juliette Greco, Gregory Ratoff, Marcel Dalio, Henry Daniell

The Sun Never Sets
US 1939 98m bw
Universal (Rowland V. Lee)

Two brothers in the African colonial service prevent a munitions baron from plunging the world into war.
Stiff upper lip melodrama, very dated.

w W. P. Lipscomb *d* Rowland V. Lee *ph* George Robinson *m* Frank Skinner *md* Charles Previn

Basil Rathbone, Douglas Fairbanks Jnr, Virginia Field, Lionel Atwill, Barbara O'Neil, C. Aubrey Smith, Melville Cooper

'Confusing script and poor direction relegate this to lower duals . . . brightest thing is the title.'—*Variety*

The Sun Shines Bright**
US 1953 92m bw
Republic / Argosy (John Ford, Merian C. Cooper)

Forty years after the Civil War, the judge of a Kentucky town still has trouble quelling the Confederate spirit.
Mellow anecdotes of time gone by, scrappily linked but lovingly polished; a remake of a Will Rogers vehicle *Judge Priest.*

w Lawrence Stallings, *stories* Irwin S. Cobb *d John Ford ph Archie Stout m Victor Young*

Charles Winninger, Arleen Whelan, John Russell, Stepin Fetchit, Milburn Stone, Grant Withers, Russell Simpson

'Passages of quite remarkable poetic feeling . . . alive with affection and truthful observation.'—*Lindsay Anderson*

Sun Valley Serenade*
US 1941 86m bw
TCF (Milton Sperling)

The band manager at an Idaho ice resort takes care of a Norwegian refugee.
Simple-minded musical which still pleases because of the talent involved.

w Robert Ellis, Helen Logan *d* H. Bruce Humberstone *ph* Edward Cronjager *songs* Mack Gordon, Harry Warren *m* Emil Newman

Sonja Henie, *Glenn Miller and his Orchestra*, John Payne, *Milton Berle*, Lynn Bari, Joan Davis, *The Nicholas Brothers*, Dorothy Dandridge

AAN: Edward Cronjager; Emil Newman; song 'Chattanooga Choo-Choo' (*m* Harry Warren, *ly* Mack Gordon)

Sunbonnet Sue
US 1945 89m bw

In the 1890s, a Park Avenue matron objects to her niece singing in a Bowery saloon. Old-fashioned family movie for the innocent-minded. Gale Storm, Phil Regan, Minna Gombell, George Cleveland, Raymond Hatton, Alan Mowbray. Written by Paul Gerard Smith, Bradford Ropes; directed by Ralph Murphy; for Scott R. Dunlap / Monogram. AAN: Edward J. Kay (music)

Sunburn
GB / US 1979 98m Technicolor
Hemdale / Bind Films (David Korda)

An insurance investigator hires a model to act as his wife while he trails a suspected murderer in Acapulco.
All sun and skin and swirling cameras, this entire movie is a seventies cliché, but it provides some fitful amusement.

w John Daly, Stephen Oliver, James Booth, *novel* The Bind by Stanley Ellin *d* Richard C. Sarafian *ph* Alex Phillips Jnr *m* John Cameron

Farrah Fawcett, Charles Grodin, Art Carney, Joan Collins, William Daniels, John Hillerman, Eleanor Parker, Keenan Wynn

'It's about three decent people. They will break your heart!'

Sunday, Bloody Sunday***
GB 1971 110m De Luxe
UA / Vectia (Joseph Janni)

A young designer shares his sexual favours equally between two loves of different sexes, a Jewish doctor and a lady executive.
Stylishly made character study with melodramatic leanings, rather self-conscious about its risky subject but, scene by scene, both adult and absorbing, with an overpowering mass of sociological detail about the way we live.

w Penelope Gilliatt d John Schlesinger ph Billy Williams m Ron Geesin *pd* Luciana Arrighi

Glenda Jackson, Peter Finch, Murray Head, Peggy Ashcroft, Maurice Denham, Vivian Pickles, Frank Windsor, Tony Britton, Harold Goldblatt

'This is not a story about the loss of love, but about its absence.'—*Roger Ebert*

AAN: Penelope Gilliatt; John Schlesinger; Glenda Jackson; Peter Finch

Sunday Dinner for a Soldier*
US 1944 86m bw
TCF (Walter Morosco)

A poor family living on a derelict Florida houseboat scrape together enough money to invite a soldier for a meal.
Sentimental little flagwaving romance, quite sympathetically presented and agreeably underacted.

w Wanda Tuchock, Melvin Levy *d* Lloyd Bacon *ph* Joe MacDonald *m* Alfred Newman

Anne Baxter, John Hodiak, Charles Winninger, Anne Revere, Connie Marshall, Chill Wills, Bobby Driscoll, Jane Darwell

'Simple, true and tender, the best propaganda America has put out in the current year.'—*Richard Winnington*

'Their eyes met! Their lips questioned! Their arms answered!'—*publicity*

Sunday in New York*
US 1963 105m Metrocolor
MGM / Seven Arts (Everett Freeman)

Complications in the love life of a brother and sister, each of whom thinks the other is very moral.
Fresh, fairly adult sex comedy with New York backgrounds.

w Norman Krasna, from his play *d* Peter Tewkesbury *ph* Leo Tover *m* Peter Nero

Cliff Robertson, Rod Taylor, Jane Fonda, Robert Culp, Jo Morrow, Jim Backus

Sunday in the Country**
France 1984 94m Eastmancolor
Sara Films / Films A2 / Little Bear (Alain Sarde)
Original title: *Un Dimanche à la Campagne*

An elderly artist enjoys a Sunday visit from his family.
Delightful, slight and moving sketch for a drama, which gives nothing but pleasure yet is hard to recapture.

w Bertrand and Colo Tavernier from a novella by Pierre Bost *d Bertrand Tavernier ph Bruno de Keyzer m* Gabriel Fauré

Louis Ducreux, Sabine Azema, Michel Aumont, Geneviève Mnich, Monique Chaumette, Claude Winter

Sunday Too Far Away
Australia 1977 94m colour

Itinerant sheep shearers become involved in an industrial dispute. Almost the archetypal Australian outback movie, good to look at but hard to care about. Jack Thompson, Max Cullen, Reg Lye, John Ewart. Written by John Dingwall; directed by Ken Hannam; for South Australian Film Corporation.

Sundays and Cybèle*
France 1962 110m bw Franscope
Terra / Fides / Orsa / Trocadéro (Romain Pinès)
original title: *Cybèle ou les Dimanches de Ville d'Avray*

An amnesiac ex-pilot strikes up a friendship with an abandoned 12-year-old girl, but the relationship is misunderstood and ends in tragedy.
A fashionable film of its time which now has little to offer: its director's reputation sagged alarmingly when he went to Hollywood.

w Serge Bourgignon, Antoine Tudal, *novel* Bernard Echasseriaux *d* Serge Bourgignon *ph* Henri Decaë *m* Maurice Jarre

Hardy Kruger, Nicole Courcel, Patricia Gozzi, Daniel Ivernel

'Studied charm and a creakingly melodramatic dénouement take the place of any serious attempt to probe the characters or situation . . . the film is so busily preoccupied with being as attractive, visually and sentimentally, as it possibly can, that it never has time to consider what it is being attractive about.''—*Tom Milne, MFB*

'Uneven but highly meritorious . . . a near-triumph of the intelligently mobile camera.'—*John Simon*

AA: best foreign film
AAN: script; Maurice Jarre

Sundown
US 1941 91m bw
Walter Wanger

The adopted daughter of an Arab trader assists British troops in Africa during World War II.
Artificial-looking romantic actioner with good cast.

w Barre Lyndon *d* Henry Hathaway *ph* Charles Lang *m* Miklos Rozsa

Gene Tierney, Bruce Cabot, George Sanders, Harry Carey, Joseph Calleia, Cedric Hardwicke, Carl Esmond, Reginald Gardiner

AAN: Charles Lang; Miklos Rozsa

The Sundowners**
GB / Australia 1960 133m Technicolor
Warner (Gerry Blatner)

In the twenties an Irish sheepdrover and his family travel from job to job in the Australian bush.
Easygoing, often amusing but lethargically developed family film with major stars somewhat ill at ease. Memorable sequences.

w Isabel Lennart, *novel* Jon Cleary *d Fred Zinnemann ph* Jack Hildyard *m* Dmitri Tiomkin

Robert Mitchum, Deborah Kerr, *Glynis Johns, Peter Ustinov*, Michael Anderson Jnr, Dina Merrill, *Wylie Watson*, Chips Rafferty

'For all Zinnemann's generous attention to character, the hints of longing, despair and indomitable spirit, the overall impression remains one of sheer length and repetition and synthetic naturalism.'—*Richard Winnington*

AAN: best picture; Isabel Lennart; Fred Zinnemann; Deborah Kerr; Glynis Johns

'In a world gone mad—a love story!'
Sunflower
France / Italy 1970 101m Technicolor

A man and wife are separated during World War II. Sudsy romantic drama, partly shot in Moscow but with no other redeeming feature. Sophia Loren, Marcello Mastroianni, Lyudmyla Savelyeva. Written by Tonino Guerra, Cesare Zavattini, Georgiy Mdivani; directed by Vittorio de Sica; for Champion/ Concordia.

Sunny*
US 1930 81m bw
Warner

A showgirl falls for a rich young man.
Tinny early musical notable for its star.

w Humphrey Pearson, Henry McCarthy, *musical play* Otto Harbach, Oscar Hammerstein II, Jerome Kern *ph* Ernest Haller *d* William A. Seiter

Marilyn Miller, Lawrence Grey, Jack Donahue, Mackenzie Ward, O. P. Heggie

Sunny*
US 1941 97m bw
RKO / Imperator (Herbert Wilcox)

Adequate remake of the above.

w Sig Herzig *d* Herbert Wilcox *ph* Russell Metty *m* Anthony Collins

Anna Neagle, Ray Bolger, John Carroll, Edward Everett Horton, Frieda Inescort, Grace and Paul Hartman

AAN: Anthony Collins

Sunny Side Up*
US 1929 80m bw ('Multicolor' sequence)
Fox

A slum girl falls for the son of a rich Southampton family.
Typical early musical of the softer kind; rewarding for those who can project themselves back.

w / m / ly B. G. De Sylva, Lew Brown, Ray Henderson d David Butler *ph* Ernest Palmer

Janet Gaynor, Charles Farrell, El Brendel, Marjorie White, Sharon Lynn

Sunnyside*
US 1919 27m approx (24 fps) bw silent
First National / Charles Chaplin

The overworked odd job man at a country hotel has a pastoral dream.
Very mildly funny star comedy which was intended as a satire on the D. W. Griffith / Charles Ray type of rural drama then popular. It doesn't work in this vein either.

wd Charles Chaplin *ph* Rollie Totheroh

Charles Chaplin, Edna Purviance, Tom Wilson, Albert Austin, Henry Bergman

Sunrise**
US 1927 97m (24 fps) bw silent
Fox

A villager in love with a city woman tries to kill his wife but then repents and spends a happy day with her.
Lyrical melodrama, superbly handled: generally considered among the finest Hollywood productions of the twenties.

w Carl Meyer, *novel* A Trip to Tilsit by Hermann Sudermann *d F. W. Murnau ph* Karl Struss, Charles Rosher *m* (sound version) Hugo Riesenfeld

Janet Gaynor, George O'Brien, Margaret Livingston

OPENING TITLE: 'This story of a man and his wife is of nowhere and everywhere, you might hear it anywhere and at any time.'

'It is filled with intense feeling and in it is embodied an underlying subtlety . . . exotic in many ways for it is a mixture of Russian gloom and Berlin brightness.'—*Mordaunt Hall, New York Times*

'Not since the earliest, simplest moving pictures, when locomotives, fire engines and crowds in streets were transposed to the screen artlessly and endearingly, when the entranced eye was rushed through tunnels and over precipices on runaway trains, has there been such joy in motion as under Murnau's direction.'—*Louise Bogan, The New Republic*

'The story is told in a flowing, lyrical German manner that is extraordinarily sensual, yet perhaps too self-conscious, too fable-like, for American audiences.'—*Pauline Kael, 70s*

AA: Karl Struss, Charles Rosher; Janet Gaynor

Sunrise at Campobello*
US 1960 143m Technicolor
Warner / Dore Schary

The early life of Franklin Roosevelt, including his battle against polio and return to politics. Static filming of a rather interesting Broadway success and of a memorable performance.

w Dore Schary, from his play *d* Vincent J. Donehue *ph* Russell Harlan *m* Franz Waxman

Ralph Bellamy, Greer Garson, Ann Shoemaker, Hume Cronyn, Jean Hagen

AAN: Greer Garson

'It happened in Hollywood . . . a love story . . . a drama real and ruthless, tender and terrifying!'
Sunset Boulevard***
US 1950 110m bw
Paramount (Charles Brackett)

A luckless Hollywood scriptwriter goes to live with a wealthy older woman, a slightly dotty and extremely possessive relic of the silent screen.
Incisive melodrama with marvellous moments but a tendency to overstay its welcome; the first reels are certainly the best, though the last scene is worth waiting for and the malicious observation throughout is a treat.

w Charles Brackett, Billy Wilder, D. M. Marshman Jnr d Billy Wilder ph John F. Seitz m Franz Waxman

Gloria Swanson, William Holden, Erich Von Stroheim, Fred Clark, Nancy Olson, Jack Webb, Lloyd Gough, *Cecil B. de Mille*, H. B. Warner, Anna Q. Nilsson, Buster Keaton, Hedda Hopper

'That rare blend of pungent writing, expert acting, masterly direction and unobtrusively artistic photography which quickly casts a spell over an audience and holds it enthralled to a shattering climax.'—*New York Times (T.M.P.)*

'Miss Swanson's performance takes her at one bound into the class of Boris Karloff and Tod Slaughter.'—*Richard Mallett, Punch*

'A weird, fascinating motion picture about an art form which, new as it is, is already haunted by ghosts.'—*Otis L. Guernsey Jnr, New York Herald Tribune*

AA: script; Franz Waxman
AAN: best picture; Billy Wilder (as director); John F. Seitz; Gloria Swanson; William Holden; Erich Von Stroheim; Nancy Olson

Sunset in Vienna
GB 1937 73m bw

An Italian cavalry officer finds that his wife's brother is a spy, and shoots him. Dated romantic melodrama with music. Lilli Palmer, Tullio Carminati, John Garrick, Geraldine Hislop. Written by Florence Tranter; directed by Norman Walker; for Herbert Wilcox.
(US title: *Suicide Legion*.)

'For the price of a movie, you'll feel like a million!'
The Sunshine Boys*
US 1975 111m Metrocolor
MGM / Rastar (Ray Stark)

Two feuding old vaudeville comedians come together for a television spot, and ruin it. Over-extended sketch in which one main role is beautifully underplayed, the other hammed up, and the production lacks any kind of style. The one-liners are good, though.

w Neil Simon, from his play *d* Herbert Ross *ph* David M. Walsh *md* Harry V. Lojewski

Walter Matthau, *George Burns*, Richard Benjamin, Carol Arthur

'It's just shouting, when it needs to be beautifully timed routines.'—*New Yorker*

'They feud with ill-matched resources, and the movie's visual delights vanish with the title sequence.'—*Sight and Sound*

† George Burns stepped in when Jack Benny became ill and died.

AA: George Burns
AAN: Neil Simon; Walter Matthau

Sunshine Susie
GB 1931 87m bw
A banker pretends to be a clerk in order to court a typist. Viennese-set comedy which worked at the time but quickly dated. Renate Muller, Jack Hulbert, Owen Nares, Morris Harvey, Sybil Grove. Written by Angus MacPhail, Robert Stevenson, Victor Saville and Noel Wood-Smith, from the play *The Private Secretary* by Franz Schultz; directed by Victor Saville; for Gainsborough.

Sunstruck
Australia 1972 92m Eastmancolor
Immigrant (Jack Neary, James Grafton)
A shy Welsh schoolmaster emigrates to the Australian outback.
Simple-minded, uninspired, predictable family comedy for star fans.

w Stan Mars *d* James Gilbert *ph* Brian West *m* Peter Knight

Harry Secombe, Maggie Fitzgibbon, John Meillon, Dawn Lake

The Super Cops
US 1974 94m Metrocolor
Two New York cops are suspended for breaking too many rules, but wage their private war on crime. Low-life crime melodrama which plays effectively enough as a lighter-hearted *Serpico*. Ron Leibman, David Selby, Sheila Frazier, Pat Hingle, Dan Frazer. Written by Lorenzo Semple Jnr, from the book by L. H. Whittemore; directed by Gordon Parks Jnr; for St Regis Films / UA.

Superdad
US 1974 95m Technicolor
A lawyer is determined to rule the life of his teenage daughter. Bumbling farce with frenzied and unattractive characters. Bob Crane, Barbara Rush, Kurt Russell, Joe Flynn, Kathleen Cody. Written by Joseph L. McEveety; directed by Vincent McEveety; for Walt Disney.

Superfly
US 1972 98m Technicolor
Warner (Sig Shore)
The New York adventures of black cocaine peddlers.
'Sensational' comedy with violence in which the pushers exit laughing. Tedious and deplorable.

w Philip Fenty *d* Gordon Parks *ph* James Signorelli *m* Curtis Mayfield

Ron O'Neal, Carl Lee, Sheila Frazier

'It suggests that New York is now nothing more than a concrete junkieyard.'—*Philip Strick*

Supergirl*
GB 1984 124m colour Panavision
Cantharus / Ilya Salkind (Pierre Spengler, Timothy Burrill)
A Krypton power source falls into the hands of a power-hungry witch, and Supergirl is sent to retrieve it.
Playful comic strip spectacular which entertains in *Wizard of Oz* style for most of its way but was savaged by the critics.

w David Odell *d* Jeannot Szwarc *ph* Alan Hume *m* Jerry Goldsmith *pd* Richard MacDonald

Helen Slater, Faye Dunaway, Peter O'Toole, Mia Farrow, Brenda Vaccaro, Peter Cook, Simon Ward, Marc McClure, Hart Bochner, David Healy

The Supergrass
GB 1985 105m colour
The police unwisely believe that a boaster can lead them to a drug ring. For those who enjoy the somewhat remote satirical humour of Channel Four's *The Comic Strip*. Adrian Edmondson, Jennifer Saunders, Peter Richardson, Dawn French. Written by Pete Richens, Peter Richardson; directed by Peter Richardson; for Recorded Releasing.

Superman
US 1948 bw serial: 15 eps
The man from Krypton who poses as mild-mannered Clark Kent combats The Spider Lady. The subject makes this serial fairly lively—livelier in fact than the multi-million-dollar 1978 film. Kirk Alyn, Noel Neill, Tommy Bond, Carol Forman, George Meeker. Directed by Spencer Bennet and Thomas Carr; for Columbia.

'You'll believe a man can fly!'
Superman
US / GB 1978 142m colour Panavision
Warner / Alexander Salkind (Pierre Spengler)
A baby saved from the planet Krypton when it explodes grows up as a newspaperman and uses his tremendous powers to fight evil and support the American way.
Long, lugubrious and only patchily entertaining version of the famous comic strip, with far too many irrelevant preliminaries and a misguided sense of its own importance.

w Mario Puzo, David Newman, Robert Benton, Leslie Newman *d* Richard Donner *ph* Geoffrey Unsworth *m* John Williams *pd* John Barry *sp* various

Christopher Reeve, Marlon Brando, Margot Kidder, Jackie Cooper, Glenn Ford, Phyllis Thaxter, Trevor Howard, Gene Hackman, Ned Beatty, Susannah York, Valerie Perrine

'Though one of the two or three most expensive movies made to date, it's cheesy-looking, and the plotting is so hit or miss that the story never seems to get started; the special effects are far from wizardly and the editing often seems hurried and jerky just at the crucial points.'—*New Yorker*

'It gives the impression of having been made in panic—in fear that style or too much imagination might endanger its approach to the literal-minded.'—*Pauline Kael, New Yorker*

'The epitome of supersell.'—*Les Keyser, Hollywood in the Seventies*

† Reprehensible records were set by Brando getting three million dollars for a ten-minute performance (and then suing for a share of the gross); and by the incredible 7½-minute credit roll at the end.

†† Tiny roles were played by Noel Neill, who was Lois Lane in the TV series, and by Kirk Alyn, who was Superman in two serials.

AAN: John Williams

Superman 2
US 1980 127m Technicolor Panavision
Warner / Alexander Salkind (Pierre Spengler)
Three renegade Kryptonians threaten Earth with a space bomb.
Half the first episode was devoted to a creaky and unnecessary setting up of plot and characters. This sequel is all the better for diving straight into action, but a classic it isn't, even of the comic strip kind.

w Mario Puzo, David Newman, Leslie Newman *d* Richard Lester *ph* Geoffrey Unsworth, Robert Paynter *m* Ken Thorne

Christopher Reeve, Gene Hackman, Ned Beatty, Jackie Cooper, Sarah Douglas, Margot Kidder, Valerie Perrine, Susannah York, Terence Stamp, Jack O'Halloran, E. G. Marshall

Superman 3
GB 1983 125m colour Panavision
Dovemead / Cantharus (Pierre Spengler)
Synthetic Kryptonite warps Superman's character, but his conscience is reawakened by a plea from a small boy.
Sometimes humorous but overwritten and overacted variation on a tired theme. The special effects are the thing, but there's too much padding in between.

w David Newman, Leslie Newman *d* Richard Lester *ph* Robert Paynter *m* Ken Thorne *pd* Peter Murton

Christopher Reeve, Richard Pryor, Jackie Cooper, Marc McClure, Annette O'Toole, Annie Ross, Pamela Stephenson, Robert Vaughn, Margot Kidder

Superman 4: The Quest for Peace
GB 1987 89m colour JDC widescreen
Superman determines that the world shall lay down its nuclear arms. Stolid dialogue and poor technicalities are evident throughout what will surely be the last of the series. Christopher Reeve, Gene Hackman, Jackie Cooper, Marc McClure, Sam Wanamaker, Mariel Hemingway, Margot Kidder. Written by Lawrence Konner, Mark Rosenthal, Christopher Reeve; directed by Sidney J. Furie; for Cannon.

'Her heart cried out for love—yet her hands reached out to destroy!'

Supernatural*
US 1933 67m bw
Paramount (Victor and Edward Halperin)

A girl is possessed by the soul of a dead murderess.
Mad doctor nonsense, interestingly but not very successfully styled.

w Harvey Thew, Brian Marlow *d Victor Halperin ph* Arthur Martinelli

Carole Lombard, H. B. Warner, Randolph Scott, Vivienne Osborne, Alan Dinehart

'A 65-minute ghost story that dies after the first half-hour.'—*Variety*

Support Your Local Gunfighter
US 1971 92m De Luxe
UA / Cherokee / Brigade (Burt Kennedy)

A con man jumps a train at a small mining town and is mistaken for a dreaded gunfighter.
Disappointing sequel to the following; just a couple of good jokes.

w James Edward Grant *d* Burt Kennedy *ph* Harry Stradling Jnr *m* Jack Elliott, Allyn Ferguson

James Garner, Suzanne Pleshette, Joan Blondell, Jack Elam, Chuck Connors, Harry Morgan, Marie Windsor, Henry Jones, John Dehner

Support Your Local Sheriff**
US 1968 92m Technicolor
UA / Cherokee (William Bowers)

Gold is found near a western village, and the resulting influx of desperate characters causes problems for the sheriff.
Amusing comedy, drawing on many western clichés.

w William Bowers d Burt Kennedy ph Harry Stradling Jnr *m* Jeff Alexander

James Garner, Joan Hackett, Walter Brennan, Jack Elam, Henry Morgan, Bruce Dern, Henry Jones

'It rejuvenates a stagnating genre by combining just the right doses of parody and affectionate nostalgia.'—*Jan Dawson*

Suppose They Gave a War and Nobody Came
US 1969 114m De Luxe
Engel–Auerbach / ABC (Fred Engel)

Three accident-prone PROs try to give the army a good name in a town which wishes it would go away; they eventually cause panic by arriving at a dance in a tank.
Muddled farce which may have hoped to be satire.

w Don McGuire, Hal Captain *d* Hy Averback *ph* Burnett Guffey *m* Jerry Fielding

Tony Curtis, Brian Keith, Ernest Borgnine, Ivan Dixon, Suzanne Pleshette, *Tom Ewell*, Bradford Dillman, Arthur O'Connell, Robert Emhardt, John Fiedler, Don Ameche

The Sure Thing
US 1985 94m De Luxe

Two uneasy couples travel west to California for Christmas. Slightly unsettling youth comedy which, in the form of *It Happened One Night*, seems to be saying that friendship is more important than sex. John Cusack, Daphne Zuniga, Anthony Edwards, Boyd Gaines, Tim Robbins, Lisa Jane Persky, Viveca Lindfors. Written by Steven L. Bloom, Jonathan Roberts; directed by Rob Reiner; for Roger Birnbaum / Monument / Embassy.
'Two sounds clash: old wine being poured into new bottles, and familiar barrels being scraped.'—*Philip French, Observer*

Surprise Package
GB 1960 100m bw
Columbia / Stanley Donen

An American gangster is deported to the same Mediterranean island as an exiled European king, whose crown gets stolen.
Flat and feeble comedy which defeats its stars.

w Harry Kurnitz, *novel* Art Buchwald *d* Stanley Donen *ph* Christopher Challis *m* Benjamin Frankel

Yul Brynner, Noel Coward, Mitzi Gaynor, Bill Nagy, Eric Pohlmann, George Coulouris, Warren Mitchell

Surrender
US 1931 69m bw

A French soldier in a German prison camp falls in love with a German girl at the nearby castle. Flabby drama which seems constantly about to make symbolic points. Warner Baxter, Leila Hyams, Ralph Bellamy, C. Aubrey Smith, William Pawley, Alexander Kirkland. Written by S. N. Behrman, Sonya Levien, from the play Axelle by Pierre Benoit; directed by William K. Howard; for Fox.
'Anaemic picture product, not for A houses in big towns.'—*Variety*

The Survivors
US 1983 102m Metrocolor
Columbia-Delphi-Rastar-William Sackheim

An executive and a gas station attendant, both potential victims of a hit man, take refuge in the snowy mountains of Vermont.
Bewilderingly unfocused black comedy with some pleasant barbs along the way.

w Michael Leeson *d* Michael Ritchie *ph* Billy Williams *m* Paul Chihara *pd* Gene Callahan *ed* Richard A. Harris

Walter Matthau, Robin Williams, Jerry Reed, James Wainwright, Kristen Vigard, Annie McEnroe

Susan and God*
US 1940 117m bw
MGM (Hunt Stromberg)
GB title: *The Gay Mrs Trexel*

A flighty society woman gets religion but fails to practise what she preaches.
Unusual comedy-drama for MGM to tackle, but a fairly successful one for high class audiences.

w Anita Loos, play Rachel Crothers *d George Cukor ph* Robert Planck *m* Herbert Stothart

Joan Crawford, Fredric March, Ruth Hussey, John Carroll, Rita Hayworth, Nigel Bruce, Bruce Cabot, Rita Quigley, Rose Hobart, Constance Collier, Gloria de Haven, Marjorie Main

'It's not a good comedy, but it has a certain fascination, because the theme is such an odd one for Hollywood to have attempted at all.'—*Pauline Kael, 70s*

'Thrill to them together!'

Susan Lenox, Her Fall and Rise*
US 1931 76m bw
MGM (Paul Bern)
GB title: *The Rise of Helga*

A farm girl flees to the city when her father tries to marry her off to a brute.
Moderate star melodrama with the star somewhat miscast.

w Wanda Tuchock, novel David Graham Phillips *d* Robert Z. Leonard *ph* William Daniels

Greta Garbo, Clark Gable, Jean Hersholt, John Miljan, Alan Hale

'A torrid romance that will fascinate the femmes.'—*Variety*

'If you like your romance spread thick, your passions strong and your Garbo hot, don't miss this.'—*Photoplay*

† The author of the book had been shot by a crank who disapproved of his treatment of women.

Susan Slade
US 1961 116m Technicolor
Warner (Delmer Daves)

An engineer brings his family back to San Francisco from Chile, and his teenage daughter runs into problems of the heart.
Stilted, busy sudser.

w Delmer Daves, *novel* Doris Hume *d* Delmer Daves *ph* Lucien Ballard *m* Max Steiner

Connie Stevens, Troy Donahue, Dorothy McGuire, Lloyd Nolan, Brian Aherne, Natalie Schaefer, Grant Williams, Bert Convy, Kent Smith

Susan Slept Here
US 1954 98m Technicolor
RKO (Harriet Parsons)

The Hollywood scriptwriter of a film about youth problems agrees to look after a delinquent teenage girl.
Skittish, would-be piquant comedy; quite unattractive.

w Alex Gottlieb *d* Frank Tashlin *ph* Nicholas Musuraca *md* Leigh Harline *songs* Jack Lawrence, Richard Myers

Dick Powell, Debbie Reynolds, Anne Francis, Glenda Farrell, Alvy Moore, Horace MacMahon

AAN: song 'Hold My Hand'

Susannah of the Mounties*
US 1939 78m bw
TCF (Kenneth MacGowan)

A little girl who is the only survivor of a wagon train massacre is looked after by the Canadian Mounties.
Adequate star action romance, Shirley's last real success.

w John Taintor Foote, Philip Dunne *d* William A. Seiter *ph* Bert Glennon *m* Louis Silvers

Shirley Temple, Randolph Scott, Margaret Lockwood, J. Farrell MacDonald, Maurice Moscovitch, Moroni Olsen, Victor Jory

'Strictly for the juvenile trade . . . illogical situations make it no more than a moderate fairy tale.'—*Variety*

'His was a strange secret! Hers was a strange love!'

The Suspect*
US 1944 84m bw
Universal (Islin Auster)

A henpecked husband kills his wife and is blackmailed.
Efficient studio-bound suspenser with theatrically effective acting.

w Bertram Millhauser, *novel* James Ronald *d* Robert Siodmak *ph* Paul Ivano *m* Frank Skinner

Charles Laughton, Henry Daniell, Rosalind Ivan, Ella Raines, Molly Lamont, Dean Harens

'High marks for tension, local colour, story.'—*William Whitebait*

Suspect*
GB 1960 81m bw
The Boulting Brothers / British Lion

Government research chemists find a traitor in their midst.
Entertaining but fairly routine spy melodrama, shot on an experimental low budget but confined to lower berth bookings.

w Nigel Balchin, from his novel Sort of Traitors *d* Roy and John Boulting *ph* Max Greene *m* John Wilkes

Tony Britton, Virginia Maskell, Peter Cushing, Ian Bannen, Raymond Huntley, Donald Pleasence, Thorley Walters, Spike Milligan, Kenneth Griffith

'A better standard of second feature film is badly needed, but the way to do it is not by making pictures which look as though they have strayed from TV.'—*Penelope Houston*

Suspected Person
GB 1943 78m bw

Thieves fall out and are tracked by police.
Slightly bitter crime drama which adequately filled half a bill. Clifford Evans, Patricia Roc, David Farrar, Robert Beatty. Written and directed by Lawrence Huntington; for Associated British.

'Unmasking a beautiful woman's secret and unholy desires!'

Suspense
US 1946 103m bw

A tough guy crashes an ice palace and makes a play for the boss's skating star wife. Heavy melodrama with skating interludes; remarkably similar in plot to the more famous *Gilda*. Chiefly remarkable as Monogram's most expensive film. Belita, Barry Sullivan, Albert Dekker, Bonita Granville, Eugene Pallette, George E. Stone, Leon Belasco. Written by Philip Yordan; directed by Frank Tuttle; photographed by Karl Struss; for Maurice and Frank King / Monogram.

Suspicion**
US 1941 99m bw
RKO (Alfred Hitchcock)

A sedate young girl marries a playboy, and comes to suspect that he is trying to murder her.
Rather artificial and stiff Hitchcock suspenser, further marred by an ending suddenly switched to please the front office. Full of the interesting touches one would expect.

w Samson Raphaelson, Alma Reville, Joan Harrison, *novel* Before the Fact by Francis Iles *d Alfred Hitchcock* *ph* Harry Stradling *m* Franz Waxman

Joan Fontaine, Cary Grant, Nigel Bruce, Cedric Hardwicke, May Whitty, Isabel Jeans, Heather Angel, Leo G. Carroll

'The fact that Hitchcock throws in a happy end during the last five minutes, like a conjuror explaining his tricks, seems to me a pity; but it spoils the film only in retrospect, and we have already had our thrills.'—*William Whitebait, New Statesman*

AA: Joan Fontaine
AAN: best picture; Franz Waxman

'The only thing more terrifying than the last twelve minutes of this film is the first eighty!'
'Once you've seen it you will never again feel safe in the dark!'

Suspiria*
Italy 1976 97m Eastmancolor Technovision
Seda Spettacoli (Claudio Argento)

A young American dance student arrives at dead of night at a continental academy where murder is the order of the day.
Psycho meets *The Exorcist*, with no holds barred: a genuinely scary thriller with gaudy visuals and a screaming sound track. A pyrotechnic display for those who can take it.

w Dario Argento, Dario Nicolodi *d* Dario Argento *ph* Luciano Tovoli *m* Dario Argento

Jessica Harper, Alida Valli, Joan Bennett, Stefania Casini, Udo Kier

'Thunderstorms and explicitly grotesque murders pile up as Argento happily abandons plot mechanics to provide a bravura display of his technical skill.'—*Time Out*

Sutter's Gold
US 1936 75m bw

During the California gold rush an immigrant has to fight for his rights when a strike starts on his land. Patchily arresting western which by costing much more than it should started the exit of Carl Laemmle from the chairman's office. Edward Arnold, Lee Tracy, Binnie Barnes, Katherine Alexander, Addison Richards, Montagu Love, John Miljan. Written by Jack Kirkland, Walter Woods and George O'Neil; directed by James Cruze; for Universal. (Most of the action footage was reused in a 1939 quickie, *Mutiny on the Blackhawk*.)

Suzy*
US 1936 95m bw
MGM (Maurice Revnes)

A French air ace of World War I marries an American showgirl; they then find that her former husband, thought dead, is still alive.
Proficient star comedy-drama with romance, action, comedy and a complex plot. A showcase for its stars.

w Dorothy Parker, Alan Campbell, Horace Jackson, Lenore Coffee, *novel* Herbert Gorman *d* George Fitzmaurice *ph* Ray June *m* William Axt

Jean Harlow, Cary Grant, Franchot Tone, Benita Hume, Lewis Stone

AAN: song 'Did I Remember' (*m* Walter Donaldson, *ly* Harold Adamson)

Svengali**
US 1931 81m bw
Warner

In nineties Paris, a hypnotist turns a girl into a great opera singer but she does not reciprocate his love.
Victorian fantasy melodrama with a great grotesque part for the star and interesting artwork.

w J. Grubb Alexander, *novel* Trilby by George du Maurier *d Archie Mayo* *ph* Barney McGill

John Barrymore, Marian Marsh, Luis Alberni, Lumsden Hare, Donald Crisp, Paul Porcasi

'A slow and old-fashioned melodrama.'—*Variety*

'Barrymore never needed occult powers to be magnetic, but interest flags when he's offscreen.'—*New Yorker, 1978*

AAN: Barney McGill

Svengali
GB 1954 82m Eastmancolor
Renown / Alderdale (Douglas Pierce)

Flatulent remake which does have the virtue of following the original book illustrations but is otherwise unpersuasive.

wd Noel Langley *ph* Wilkie Cooper *m* William Alwyn *ad Fred Pusey*

Donald Wolfit, Hildegarde Neff, Terence Morgan, Derek Bond, Paul Rogers, David Kossoff, Hubert Gregg, Noel Purcell, Alfie Bass, Harry Secombe

Swallows and Amazons
GB 1974 92m Eastmancolor
EMI / Theatre Projects (Richard Pilbrow)

In the twenties four children have adventures in the Lake District.

Mild family film, great to look at but lacking in real excitement or style.

w David Wood, *novel* Arthur Ransome *d* Claude Whatham *ph* Denis Lewiston *m* Wilfred Josephs

Virginia McKenna, Ronald Fraser, Simon West, Sophie Neville, Zanna Hamilton, Stephen Grenville

Swamp Fire
US 1946 68m bw

The rehabilitation of a war veteran bar pilot in the treacherous waters at the mouth of the Mississippi. Routine romantic melo, notable only as its star's only screen appearance in long trousers. Johnny Weissmuller, Buster Crabbe, Virginia Grey, Carol Thurston, Edwain Maxwell, Pedro de Cordoba. Written by Geoffrey Homes; directed by William Pine; for Pine-Thomas / Paramount.

Swamp Water**
US 1941 90m bw
TCF (Irving Pichel)
GB title: *The Man Who Came Back*

A fugitive holds out for years in the Okefenokee swamp, and affects the lives of the local township.
A strange little story, not very compelling as drama but with striking photography and atmosphere. Remade more straightforwardly as *Lure of the Wilderness* (qv).

w Dudley Nichols, *story* Vereen Bell *d Jean Renoir ph Peverell Marley m* David Buttolph

Walter Huston, Walter Brennan, Anne Baxter, Dana Andrews, Virginia Gilmore, John Carradine, Eugene Pallette, Ward Bond, Guinn Williams

'So bad it's terrific.'—*Otis Ferguson*

The Swan*
US 1956 108m Eastmancolor Cinemascope
MGM (Dore Schary)

In 1910 Hungary, a girl of noble stock is groomed to marry the crown prince.
Interesting chiefly for a typical Hollywood reaction to a news event; about to lose their top star to a real life prince, MGM dusted off this old and creaky property for her last film. The star cast can't make much of it and the treatment is very heavy.

w John Dighton, *play* Ferenc Molnar *d* Charles Vidor *ph* Robert Surtees *m* Bronislau Kaper *ad* Cedric Gibbons, Randall Duell

Grace Kelly, Alec Guinness, Louis Jourdan, Agnes Moorehead, Jessie Royce Landis, Brian Aherne, Leo G. Carroll, *Estelle Winwood*, Robert Coote

'Balancing between artificial comedy and a no less artificial romantic theme, the film ultimately requires considerably greater finesse and subtlety in the handling.'—*Penelope Houston*

Swanee River**
US 1939 84m Technicolor
TCF (Darryl F. Zanuck)

The life and loves of Stephen Foster.
Attractive, unsurprising family film in rich early colour, sparked by Jolson as E. P. Christy.

w John Taintor Foote, Philip Dunne *d* Sidney Lanfield *ph* Bert Glennon *md* Louis Silvers

Don Ameche, *Al Jolson*, Andrea Leeds, Felix Bressart, Russell Hicks

'An unimpressive story: will hit profitable but not big b.o.'—*Variety*

AAN: Louis Silvers

Swann in Love**
France 1983 111m colour
Gaumont / FR3 / SFPC / Bioskop / Films du Losange (Margaret Menegoz)
Original title: *Un Amour de Swann*

An elegant Jew in 19th-century Paris society becomes obsessed by a beautiful demi-mondaine.
Reasonably successful attempt to film part of an unfilmable book. Comparisons with *Letter from an Unknown Woman* are inevitable.

w Peter Brook, Jean-Claude Carrière, Marie-Hélène Estienne, from the works of Marcel Proust *d Volker Schlöndorff ph* Sven Nykvist *m* Hans Werner Henze

Jeremy Irons, Ornella Muti, Alain Delon, Fanny Ardant, Marie-Christine Barrault, Anne Bennent

'A film of more taste than vision.'—*Gilbert Adair, MFB*

'If you've read the original, forget it.'—*Volker Schlöndorff*

'A failure, maybe, but one that deserves to be seen.'—*Observer*

The Swarm
US 1978 116m Technicolor Panavision
Warner (Irwin Allen)

African killer bees menace the US.
Very obvious all-star disaster movie with risible dialogue. A box office flop, probably because several TV movies had already tackled the same subject.

w Stirling Silliphant, *novel* Arthur Herzog *d* Irwin Allen *ph* Fred J. Koenekamp *m* Jerry Goldsmith *sp* L. B. Abbott, Van Der Veer, Howard Jensen

Michael Caine, Katharine Ross, Richard Widmark, Richard Chamberlain, Olivia de Havilland, Fred MacMurray, Ben Johnson, Lee Grant, Jose Ferrer, Patty Duke Astin, Slim Pickens, Bradford Dillman, Henry Fonda, Cameron Mitchell

'You could pass it all off as a sick joke, except that it cost twelve million dollars, twenty-two million bees, and several years of someone's life.'—*Guardian*

'The story is of a banality matched only by the woodenness of the acting.'—*Barry Took, Punch*

Swashbuckler*
US 1976 101m Technicolor Panavision
Universal / Elliott Kastner (Jennings Lang)
GB title: *The Scarlet Buccaneer*

Rival pirates help a wronged lady.
Uninspired reworking of some old Errol Flynn ideas; the idea was pleasant, but the old styie is sadly lacking.

w Jeffrey Bloom *d* James Goldstone *ph* Philip Lathrop *m* John Addison *pd* John Lloyd

Robert Shaw, James Earl Jones, Peter Boyle, Geneviève Bujold, Beau Bridges, Geoffrey Holder

'This tacky pastepot job can't make up its mind whether it's serious, tongue-in-cheek, satirical, slapstick, burlesque, parody or travesty; but be assured it is all of the above.'—*Variety*

'The talented cast is left to play living statues, immobilized by dumb dialogue and awkward action.'—*Judith Crist*

Sweeney!*
GB 1976 89m Technicolor
EMI / Euston (Ted Childs)

Scotland Yard's Flying Squad investigates a suicide and uncovers an elaborate political blackmail scheme.
Enjoyable big screen version of a pacy, violent TV cop show.

w Ranald Graham *d* David Wickes *ph* Dusty Miller *m* Denis King

John Thaw, Dennis Waterman, Barry Foster, Ian Bannen, Colin Welland, Michael Coles, Joe Melia

Sweeney 2
GB 1978 108m Technicolor
Euston Films (Ted Childs)

The flying squad discovers that a series of armed bank robberies is being committed by a gang of expatriates who return from a luxurious Malta development for each caper.
Silly, sluggish and violent extension of thin material which would scarcely have made a good one-hour TV episode. There isn't even an exciting climax.

w Troy Kennedy Martin *d* Tom Clegg *ph* Dusty Miller *m* Tony Hatch

John Thaw, Dennis Waterman, Barry Stanton, Denholm Elliott, Nigel Hawthorne, John Flanagan, David Casey

Sweeney Todd, the Demon Barber of Fleet Street*
GB 1936 68m bw
George King

A barber kills his customers and makes them into 'mutton pies' for sale at the shop next door.
Decent version of a famous old melodrama; stilted as film-making, but preserving a swaggering star performance.

w Frederick Hayward, H. F. Maltby, *play* George Dibdin-Pitt *ph* Ronald Neame

Tod Slaughter, Bruce Seton, Eve Lister, Stella Rho, Ben Soutten

Sweepings*
US 1933 77m bw

An ambitious Chicago merchant finds that his sons do not wish to emulate him. Curious family melodrama based on fact; interesting but not exactly inspiring. Lionel Barrymore, Alan Dinehart, Eric Linden, William Gargan, Gloria Stuart, Gregory Ratoff. Written by Lester Cohen from his novel; directed by John Cromwell; for RKO. 'Nothing to interest the women and a subject too sombre to interest the men.'—*Variety*

Sweet Adeline
US 1934 85m bw
Warner (Edward Chodorov)

In the nineties, the daughter of a beer garden owner attracts the attention of a composer and becomes a Broadway star.
Unexceptionable, and quite forgotten, adaptation of a pleasant, old-fashioned Broadway musical.

w Erwin S. Gelsey, *play* Jerome Kern, Oscar Hammerstein II, Harry Armstrong, Dick Gerard *d* Mervyn Le Roy *m / ly* Jerome Kern, Oscar Hammerstein II *ph* Sol Polito *ch* Bobby Connolly *ad* Robert Haas

Irene Dunne, Donald Woods, Ned Sparks, Hugh Herbert, Wini Shaw, Louis Calhern, Nydia Westman, Joseph Cawthorn

'As a production in the bigtime musical class, but strictly on merit it rates no better than fair.'—*Variety*

'He used love like most men use money!'
Sweet Bird of Youth*
US 1962 120m Metrocolor Cinemascope
MGM / Roxbury (Pandro S. Berman)

A Hollywood drifter brings an ageing glamour star back to his home town, but runs into revenge from the father of a girl he had seduced.
Emasculated version of an overwrought play with the author's usual poetic squalor; comatose patches alternate with flashes of good acting and diverting dialogue, but the wide screen and heavy colour don't direct the attention.

wd Richard Brooks, *play* Tennessee Williams *ph* Milton Krasner *m* Harold Gellman *md* Robert Armbruster

Paul Newman, Geraldine Page, *Ed Begley*, Mildred Dunnock, Rip Torn, Shirley Knight, Madeleine Sherwood

AA: Ed Begley
AAN: Geraldine Page; Shirley Knight

'Love is what it's all about!'
Sweet Charity*
US 1969 149m Technicolor Panavision 70
Universal (Robert Arthur)

A New York taxi dancer dreams of love.
A revue-type musical bowdlerized from Fellini's *Le notti di Cabiria* accords ill with real New York locations, especially as its threads of plot come to nothing; but behind the camera are sufficient stylists to ensure striking success with individual numbers.

w Peter Stone, *play* Neil Simon *d Robert Fosse ph Robert Surtees m* Cy Coleman *ly* Dorothy Fields *md* Joseph Gershenson

Shirley Maclaine, Ricardo Montalban, John McMartin, *Chita Rivera*, Paula Kelly, Stubby Kaye, Sammy Davis Jnr

'The kind of platinum clinker designed to send audiences flying towards the safety of their television sets.'—*Rex Reed*

AAN: Cy Coleman (as music director)

Sweet Dreams
US 1985 115m / Technicolor
Tri-Star / HBO / Silver Screen (Bernard Schwartz)

The effect on her marriage of the rise to success of folk singer Patsy Cline.
Pleasant, muted, unremarkable modern biopic.

w Robert Getchell *d* Karel Reisz *ph* Robbie Greenberg *m* Charles Gross

Jessica Lange, Ed Harris, Ann Wedgeworth, David Clennon, James Staley

AAN: Jessica Lange

Sweet Kitty Bellairs
US 1930 60m Technicolor

A romance of stagecoach days set in an English seaside resort. A decided curiosity to come from this studio in *Little Caesar* days, and not a successful one. Claudia Dell, Ernest Torrence, Walter Pidgeon, June Collyer, Perry Askam, Lionel Belmore, Flora Finch. Written by Hermann Harrison, from the stage production of David Belasco; directed by Alfred E. Green; for Warners. 'Artistic achievement, but weak on fan pull.'—*Variety*

Sweet Liberty
US 1986 107m colour
Universal / Martin Bregman

A college professor is disgusted as he watches the Hollywood filming of his historical novel.
A good idea surprisingly wasted: the plot turns to tedium before the half-way mark.

w,d Alan Alda *ph* Frank Tidy *m* Bruce Broughton *pd* Ben Edwards *ed* Michael Economou

Alan Alda, Michael Caine, Michelle Pfeiffer, Lillian Gish, Bob Hoskins, Saul Rubinek, Lois Chiles, Lise Hilboldt

Sweet Music
US 1934 100m bw

An orchestra leader and a girl singer spar a lot but finally make it up. The slimmest of stories stretches over a few good numbers and some snappy dialogue; but it's all too long. Rudy Vallee, Ann Dvorak, Ned Sparks, Helen Morgan, Allen Jenkins, Alice White, Robert Armstrong. Written by Jerry Wald, Carl Erickson and Warren Duff; directed by Alfred E. Green; for Warner.

Sweet November
US 1968 113m Technicolor
Warner Seven Arts / Jerry Gershwin, Elliott Kastner

An English tycoon in New York meets a girl who takes a new lover every month because she hasn't long to live.
Irritating exercise in eccentric sentimentality, not helped by twitchy stars.

w Herman Raucher *d* Robert Ellis Miller *ph* Daniel L. Fapp *m* Michel Legrand

Anthony Newley, Sandy Dennis, Theodore Bikel, Burr de Benning

The Sweet Ride
US 1967 110m De Luxe Panavision
TCF (Joe Pasternak)

Surfers and drop-outs on a California beach have woman trouble.
Teenage melodrama, well produced but abysmal of content.

w Tom Mankiewicz, *novel* William Murray *d* Harvey Hart *ph* Robert B. Hauser *m* Pete Rugolo

Jacqueline Bisset, Tony Franciosa, Michael Sarrazin, Bob Denver, Michael Wilding

Sweet Rosie O'Grady*
US 1943 79m Technicolor
TCF (William Perlberg)

A Police Gazette reporter tries to uncover the past of a musical comedy star.
Pleasant nineties musical with plenty of zest but a lack of good numbers. A typical success of the war years.

w Ken Englund *d* Irving Cummings *ph Ernest Palmer ch* Hermes Pan *songs* Mack Gordon, Harry Warren *ad James Basevi, Joseph C. Wright*

Betty Grable, Robert Young, Adolphe Menjou, Reginald Gardiner, Virginia Grey, Phil Regan, Sig Rumann, Hobart Cavanaugh, Alan Dinehart
† Remake of *Love Is News*; remade as *That Wonderful Urge*.

'This is the story of J.J.—but not the way he wants it told!'
Sweet Smell of Success***
US 1957 96m bw
UA / Norma / Curtleigh (James Hill)

A crooked press agent helps a megalomaniac New York columnist break up his sister's marriage.
Moody, brilliant, Wellesian melodrama put together with great artificial style; the plot matters less than the photographic detail and the skilful manipulation of decadent characters, bigger than life-size.

w Clifford Odets, Ernest Lehman *d Alexander Mackendrick ph James Wong Howe m Elmer Bernstein ad* Edward Carrere

Burt Lancaster, *Tony Curtis*, Martin Milner, Sam Levene, Susan Harrison, Barbara Nichols, *Emile Meyer*

'A sweet slice of perversity, a study of dollar and power worship.'—*Pauline Kael*

Sweet William
GB 1980 90m Eastmancolor

A London girl discovers that her American lover is constantly unfaithful. A situation in search of a story makes this slight piece with its wry observations rather less memorable than the average TV play. Sam Waterston, Jenny Agutter, Anna Massey, Daphne Oxenford, Arthur Lowe, Geraldine James. Written by Beryl Bainbridge, from her novel; directed by Claude Whatham; for Kendon.

Sweetheart of the Campus
US 1941 64m bw

A college principal objects to Ozzie Nelson's band playing at a nearby night spot.
Evanescent musical filler. Ruby Keeler, Ozzie Nelson, Harriet Hilliard, Gordon Oliver, Don Beddoe, Kathleen Howard. Written by Robert D. Andrews, Edmund Hartmann; directed by Edward Dmytryk; for Jack Fier / Columbia.

(GB title: *Broadway Ahead*.)

Sweethearts**
US 1938 120m Technicolor
MGM (Hunt Stromberg)

Two stars of the musical stage never stop fighting each other.

The lightest and most successful of the MacDonald / Eddy musicals, with an excellent script, production and cast.

w Dorothy Parker, Alan Campbell d W. S. Van Dyke ph Oliver Marsh *m* Victor Herbert *md* Herbert Stothart

Jeanette MacDonald, Nelson Eddy, Frank Morgan, Ray Bolger, Florence Rice, Mischa Auer, Fay Holden, Reginald Gardiner, Herman Bing, Allyn Joslyn, Raymond Walburn, Lucile Watson, Gene Lockhart

'It will disappoint because of length, and general lethargy and sameness of production values.'—*Variety*

AA: Oliver Marsh
AAN: Herbert Stothart

Swell Guy
US 1946 86m bw

A war correspondent comes home to visit his family but turns out to be something of a heel.
Ironical drama which deserved better casting and handling. Sonny Tufts, Ann Blyth, Ruth Warrick, William Gargan, John Litel, Thomas Gomez, Millard Mitchell, Mary Nash. Written by Richard Brooks, from Gilbert Emery's play *The Hero*; directed by Frank Tuttle; for Mark Hellinger / Universal-International.

'They had the pools—but he had their wives!'

The Swimmer*
US 1968 94m Technicolor
Columbia / Horizon / Dover (Frank Perry, Roger Lewis)

A man clad only in trunks swims his way home via the pools of his rich friends, and arrives home to find that his success is a fantasy.
Strange but compelling fable, too mystifying for popular success, about the failure of the American dream. Annoyingly inexplicit, but well made and sumptuously photographed in a variety of Connecticut estates.

w Eleanor Perry, short story John Cheever *d* Frank Perry, Sydney Pollack *ph David L. Quaid m* Marvin Hamlisch

Burt Lancaster, Janice Rule, Kim Hunter, Diana Muldaur, Cornelia Otis Skinner, Marge Champion

Swing Fever
US 1943 80m bw

A bandleader uses hypnotism to train a boxer.
Witless farrago with sprightly musical numbers. Kay Kyser and his band, Marilyn Maxwell, Nat Pendleton, William Gargan, Lena Horne. Written by Nat Perrin and Warren Wilson; directed by Tim Whelan; for MGM.

Swing High Swing Low**
US 1937 97m bw
Paramount (Arthur Hornblow Jnr)

A talented trumpeter goes on a bender but is rescued by his wife.
Backstage comedy-drama, a beautifully cinematic version of a very tedious story also filmed as *Dance of Life* (1929) and *When My Baby Smiles at Me* (1948).

w Virginia Van Upp, Oscar Hammerstein II, *play* Burlesque by George Manker Walters, Arthur Hopkins *d Mitchell Leisen ph* Ted Tetzlaff *m* Victor Young *md* Boris Morros

Carole Lombard, Fred MacMurray, Charles Butterworth, Jean Dixon, Dorothy Lamour, Harvey Stephens, Franklin Pangborn, Anthony Quinn

'No reason to believe it won't jam 'em at the gate . . . it's a cinch for the younger trade, and will satisfy general audience standards.'—*Variety*

'Enough concentrated filmcraft to fit out half a dozen of those gentlemen who are always dashing around in an independent capacity making just the greatest piece of cinema ever.'—*Otis Ferguson*

Swing Shift
US 1984 100m Technicolor
Warner / Lantana / Hawn-Sylbert / Jerry Bick

During World War II, in her husband's absence at war, a woman factory hand has an affair with a co-worker.
Surprisingly dreary romantic drama on a subject which could at least have had a livelier surface despite the lack of surprise in what passes for plot.

w 'Rob Morton' (Ron Nyswaner, Bo Goldman, Nancy Dowd) *d* Jonathan Demme *ph* Tak Fujimoto *m* Patrick Williams *pd* Peter Jamison *ed* Craig McKay

Goldie Hawn, Kurt Russell, Christine Lahti, Fred Ward, Ed Harris

'Bland, muddled and inconclusive.'—*Steve Jenkins, Monthly Film Bulletin*

AAN: Christine Lahti (supporting actress)

Swing Time**
US 1936 103m bw
RKO (Pandro S. Berman)

A dance team can't get together romantically because he has a commitment to a girl back home.
Satisfactory but unexciting musical vehicle for two stars at the top of their professional and box-office form.

w Howard Lindsay, Allan Scott *d* George Stevens *ph* David Abel *md* Nathaniel Shilkret *songs* Jerome Kern, Dorothy Fields

Fred Astaire, Ginger Rogers, Victor Moore, Helen Broderick, Eric Blore, Betty Furness, Georges Metaxa

AA: song 'The Way You Look Tonight'

Swing Your Lady*
US 1937 77m bw
Warner (Sam Bischoff)

A promoter gets involved in the problems of a hillbilly wrestler.
Minor comedy with some laughs.

w Joseph Scrank, Maurice Leo, *story* Toehold on Artemus by H. R. Marsh *d* Ray Enright *ph* Arthur Edeson *m* Adolph Deutsch

Humphrey Bogart, Louise Fazenda, Nat Pendleton, Frank McHugh, Penny Singleton, Allen Jenkins, Ronald Reagan, The Weaver Brothers and Elviry

'A comedy of not immense proportions, it is nevertheless a rollicking, considerably different laugh-piece which should do from average to good business everywhere.'—*Variety*

The Swinger
US 1966 81m Technicolor
Paramount / George Sidney

When a girl writer's wholesome stories are rejected, she pretends to have a naughty past.
With-it comedy which audiences preferred to be without.

w Lawrence Roman *d* George Sidney *ph* Joseph Biroc *m* Marty Paich

Ann-Margret, Tony Franciosa, Robert Coote, Yvonne Romain, Horace MacMahon, Nydia Westman

'A hectically saucy mixture of lechery, depravity, perversion, voyeurism and girlie magazines . . . a heavy, witless pudding.'—*MFB*

The Swiss Family Robinson
US 1940 93m bw
(RKO) Gene Towne, Graham Baker

A shipwrecked family builds a new home on a desert island.
Pleasing low-budgeter.

w Gene Towne, Graham Baker, Walter Ferris, *novel* Johann Wyss *d* Edward Ludwig *ph* Nicholas Musuraca

Thomas Mitchell, Edna Best, Freddie Bartholemew, Tim Holt, Terry Kilburn

'In outlook, dialogue and manner it is frankly old-fashioned.'—*MFB*

The Swiss Family Robinson*
GB 1960 126m Technicolor Panavision
Walt Disney (Bill Anderson, Basil Keys)

Quite pleasing comedy adventure from the children's classic.

w Lowell S. Hawley *d* Ken Annakin *ph* Harry Waxman *m* William Alwyn

John Mills, Dorothy McGuire, James MacArthur, Tommy Kirk, Kevin Corcoran, Janet Munro, Sessue Hayakawa, Cecil Parker

Swiss Miss*
US 1938 73m bw
(MGM) Hal Roach

Two mousetrap salesmen in Switzerland run into trouble with a cook, a gorilla and two opera singers.
Operetta style vehicle which constrains its stars, since their material is somewhat below vintage anyway. Not painful to watch, but disappointing.

w James Parrott, Felix Adler, Charles Nelson *d* John G. Blystone *ph* Norbert Brodine

Stan Laurel, Oliver Hardy, Walter Woolf King, Della Lind, Eric Blore

'Story, production, acting and direction suggest a revival of early sound filmusicals presented with stage technique.'—*Variety*

The Swissmakers
Switzerland 1978 108m Eastmancolor

Cases of a department investigating applicants for naturalization. Amusing satirical comedy which presumably has more bite in its home territory. Walo Luond, Emil Steinberger, Beatrice Kessler. Written by Rolf Lyssy and Christa Maerker; directed by Rolf Lyssy; for Lyssy / Rex / Willora / Schoch / Ecco.

The Sword and the Rose
GB 1952 91m Technicolor
Walt Disney (Perce Pearce)

The romantic problems of young Mary Tudor. Unhistorical charade not quite in the usual Disney vein, and not very good.

w Laurence E. Watkin, *novel* When Knighthood Was in Flower by Charles Major *d* Ken Annakin *ph* Geoffrey Unsworth *m* Clifton Parker

Richard Todd, Glynis Johns, James Robertson Justice, Michael Gough, Jane Barrett, Peter Copley, Rosalie Crutchley, Jean Mercure, D. A. Clarke-Smith

The Sword and the Sorcerer
US 1982 99m De Luxe
Sorcerer Productions / Group One / Brandon Chase

A tyrant wins an idyllic kingdom with the help of an evil sorcerer; young Prince Talon gets it back.
Medieval magic and violence, laid on with a shovel; hopefully the last attempt to start an ill-fated cycle.

w Tom Karnowski, Albert Pyun, John Stuckmeyer *d* Albert Pyun *ph* Joseph Mangine *m* David Whitaker

Lee Horsley, Kathleen Beller, Simon MacCorkindale, George Maharis, Richard Lynch

Sword in the Desert
US 1949 100m bw

During World War II, Jewish refugees are smuggled to the Palestine coast. Dim topical melodrama with an anti-British slant which caused international embarrassment. Dana Andrews, Marta Toren, Jeff Chandler, Stephen McNally, Philip Friend. Written by Robert Buckner; directed by George Sherman; for Robert Arthur / Universal.

The Sword in the Stone**
US 1963 80m Technicolor
Walt Disney (Ken Peterson)

In the Dark Ages, a young forest boy named Wart becomes King Arthur.
Feature cartoon with goodish sequences but disappointingly showing a flatness and economy of draughtsmanship.

w Bill Peet, *novel* The Once and Future King by T. H. White *d* Wolfgang Reitherman *m* George Bruns *songs* The Sherman Brothers

AAN: George Bruns

Sword of Ali Baba
US 1965 81m Technicolor

Ali Baba is forced from the royal court to become a king of thieves. Cut-rate programme filler utilizing great chunks of *Ali Baba and the Forty Thieves* (twenty-one years older), with one actor, Frank Puglia, playing the same role in both films. Peter Mann, Jocelyn Lane, Peter Whitney, Gavin McLeod. Written by Edmund Hartmann and Oscar Brodney; directed by Virgil Vogel; for Universal.

Sword of Monte Cristo
US 1951 80m Supercinecolor

Virtuous rebels and a villainous minister all seek the fabulous treasure of Monte Cristo. Rubbishy sequel apparently shot in somebody's back garden by people only recently acquainted with film techniques. George Montgomery, Paula Corday, Berry Kroeger, Robert Warwick, William Conrad. Written and directed by Maurice Geraghty; for Edward L. Alperson.

Sword of Sherwood Forest
GB 1960 80m Technicolor Megascope
Columbia / Hammer / Yeoman (Richard Greene, Sidney Cole)

Robin Hood reveals the villainy of the Sheriff of Nottingham and the Earl of Newark.
This big-screen version of a popular TV series makes a rather feeble addition to the legend, but the actors try hard.

w Alan Hackney *d* Terence Fisher *ph* Ken Hodges *m* Alan Hoddinott

Richard Greene, Peter Cushing, Richard Pasco, Niall MacGinnis, Jack Gwyllim, Sarah Branch, Nigel Green

Sword of the Valiant
GB 1984 101m Fujicolor JDC Wide Screen
Cannon (Michael Kagan, Philip M. Breen)

In the mythical middle ages, squire Gawain takes on a challenge from the magical Green Knight.
An unsatisfactory mixture of realism, fantasy and deadly seriousness. Spoofing might have worked better.

w Stephen Weeks, Philip M. Breen, Howard C. Pen *d* Stephen Weeks *ph* Freddie Young, Peter Hurst *m* Ron Geesin *pd* Maurice Fowler, Derek Nice *ed* Richard Marden, Barry Peters

Miles O'Keeffe, Sean Connery, Trevor Howard, Leigh Lawson, Cyrielle Claire, Peter Cushing, Ronald Lacey, Lila Kedrova, John Rhys Davies, Douglas Wilmer, Wilfred Brambell

The Swordsman
US 1947 80m Technicolor
Columbia

A young 18th-century Scot tries to end a family feud so that he can marry the girl of his choice.
Amiable costume programmer, quite forgettable but mostly enjoyable while it's on.

w Wilfred Petitt *d* Joseph H. Lewis *ph* William Snyder *m* Hugo Friedhofer

Larry Parks, Ellen Drew, George Macready

Sylvia
US 1964 115m bw
Paramount / Joseph E. Levine (Martin H. Poll)

A millionaire with a mysterious fiancée hires a detective to discover the truth about her past.
Improbable story of a high-minded prostitute, sluggishly narrated and variably acted.

w Sidney Boehm, *novel* E. V. Cunningham *d* Gordon Douglas *ph* Joseph Ruttenberg *m* David Raksin

Carroll Baker, George Maharis, Peter Lawford, Joanne Dru, Ann Sothern, Viveca Lindfors, Edmond O'Brien, Aldo Ray

Sylvia and the Ghost*
France 1944 93m bw
Ecran Français / André Paulvé
Original title: *Sylvie et la Fantôme*

A sixteen-year-old girl lives in her father's castle and is friendly with the ghost of a man killed in a duel fought for love of her grandmother.
Melancholy comedy which despite some charming moments somehow misses the expected style which would have made it a minor classic.

w Jean Aurenche, *play* Alfred Adam *d* Claude Autant-Lara *ph* Philippe Agostini *m* René Cloerc

Odette Joyeux, François Périer, Jacques Tati, Louis Salou, Jean Desailly

'A charming film, written, handled and acted with wit, feeling and a beautiful lightness of touch.'—*Gavin Lambert*

'She's a boy! It's Mr Hepburn to you!'

Sylvia Scarlett*
US 1935 94m bw
RKO (Pandro S. Berman)

A girl masquerades as a boy in order to escape to France with her crooked father.
Strange, peripatetic English comedy-adventure which failed to ring any bells but preserves aspects of interest.

w Gladys Unger, John Collier, Mortimer Offner, *novel* Compton Mackenzie *d* George Cukor *ph* Joseph August *m* Roy Webb

Katharine Hepburn, Cary Grant, Edmund Gwenn, Brian Aherne, Lennox Pawle

'A story that's hard to believe. Dubious entertainment for the public.'—*Variety*

'It seems to go wrong in a million directions, but it has unusually affecting qualities.'—*New Yorker, 1978*

'A sprawling and ineffective essay in dramatic chaos.'—*Richard Watts Jnr, New York Herald Tribune*

'A tragic waste of time and screen talent.'—*Eileen Creelman, New York Sun*

'A much more polished comedy than most, and consistently engaging.'—*Winston Burdett, Brooklyn Daily Eagle*

La Symphonie Fantastique*
France 1947 90m bw

The life of Hector Berlioz. Stately but uninspired biopic chiefly notable for its leading performance. *Jean-Louis Barrault*, Renée Saint-Cyr, Jules Berry, Bernard Blier. Written by J. P. Feydeau and H. A. Legrand; directed by Christian-Jaque; for L'Atelier Français.

La Symphonie Pastorale*
France 1946 105m bw
Les Films Gibe

A Swiss pastor takes in an orphan child who grows up to be a beautiful girl and causes jealousy between himself and his son.
Curious mountain tragedy, a great visual pleasure with its symbolic use of snow and water.

w Jean Delannoy, Jean Aurenche, *novel* André Gide *d* Jean Delannoy *ph* Armand Thirard *m* Georges Auric

Pierre Blanchar, Michèle Morgan

Symphony of Six Million
US 1932 94m bw
RKO (Pandro S. Berman)
GB title: *Melody of Life*

A doctor drags himself from New York's slums to Park Avenue, but feels guilty and demoralized when he can't save the life of his own father.
Monumental tearjerker, not badly done.

w Bernard Schubert, J. Walter Ruben, *novel* Fannie Hurst *d* Gregory La Cava *ph* Leo Tover *m* Max Steiner

Irene Dunne, Ricardo Cortez, Gregory Ratoff, Anna Appel, Noel Madison, Julie Haydon

'Picture of Jewish home life in the familiar Hurst style . . . a good-looking picture without strongly marked cast names.'—*Variety*

Synanon
US 1965 106m bw
Columbia / Richard Quine
GB title: *Get Off My Back*

Stories of the inmates of a voluntary Californian institution for the rehabilitation of drug addicts.
Well-intentioned but rather dreary case histories, unconvincingly dramatized. The house and its leader subsequently came in for much press criticism.

w Ian Bernard, S. Lee Pogostin *d* Richard Quine *ph* Harry Stradling *m* Neal Hefti

Edmond O'Brien (as Chuck Dederich), Chuck Connors, Stella Stevens, Alex Cord, Eartha Kitt, Richard Conte, Barbara Luna

'The real drug addicts who appear in the background are plumpish, greyish and utterly ordinary; but the fictional ones are glamorously handsome, and lead lives which are full of throbbing emotion and upset.'—*Tom Milne, MFB*

Syncopation*
US 1942 88m bw

The career of a young trumpeter parallels the development of jazz. Somewhat disappointing musical considering the talents involved. Jackie Cooper, Adolphe Menjou, Bonita Granville, Connee Boswell, the Hall Johnson Choir, Benny Goodman, Harry James, Gene Krupa, Charlie Barnet. Written by Philip Yordan, Frank Cavett, Valentine Davies; directed by William Dieterle; Charles F. Glett for William Dieterle / RKO.

The System
US 1953 90m bw
Warner (Sam Bischoff)

A crime leader is softened by love, and allows himself to be convicted.
Strange nonsense inspired by the Kefauver investigations into American society; neither edifying nor entertaining.

w Jo Eisinger *d* Lewis Seiler *ph* Edwin DuPar *m* David Buttolph

Frank Lovejoy, Joan Weldon, Bob Arthur, Paul Picerni, Don Beddoe

The System
GB 1964 90m bw
British Lion / Bryanston / Kenneth Shipman
US title: *The Girl-Getters*

Seaside layabouts have a system for collecting and sharing rich girl visitors, but one of the latter traps the leader at his own game.
Adequate sexy showcase for some looming talents; all very unattractive, but smoothly directed in a number of imitated styles.

w Peter Draper *d Michael Winner ph Nicolas Roeg m* Stanley Black

Oliver Reed, Jane Merrow, Barbara Ferris, Julia Foster, Ann Lynn, Guy Doleman, Andrew Ray, David Hemmings, John Alderton, Derek Nimmo, Harry Andrews

'A modest, skilful, charming, inconsequential, and fairly dishonest little picture, to be enjoyed and deprecated in roughly equal measure.'—*John Simon*

T. R. Baskin
US 1971 89m Technicolor
Paramount (Peter Hyams)
GB title: *A Date with a Lonely Girl*

A businessman in Chicago meets an unhappy girl who tells him her story of loneliness and lack of communication.
Intolerable self-pitying mishmash with no place to go.

w Peter Hyams *d* Herbert Ross *ph* Gerald Hirschfeld *m* Jack Elliott

Candice Bergen, Peter Boyle, James Caan, Marcia Rodd, Erin O'Reilly

Table for Five
US 1983 124m De Luxe
CBS / Voight-Schaffel (Robert Schaffel)

A divorced husband takes his children on a European holiday and has to tell them that their mother has been killed.
Slow, sentimental domestic drama with attractive travel backgrounds, like a TV movie writ large.

w David Seltzer *d* Robert Lieberman *ph* Vilmos Zsigmond *m* John Morris *pd* Robert F. Boyle

Jon Voight, Richard Crenna, Marie-Christine Barrault, Millie Perkins, Roxana Zal, Robby Kiger, Son Hoang Bui, Maria O'Brien

'A family problem picture resolutely updated for the eighties.'—*Robert Brown, MFB*

Tabu*
US 1931 80m bw
Colorart Synchrotone

The life of a young Tahitian pearl fisherman. The plot is used only to bring together the elements of a superb travelogue, but the conflicts between the aims of the two directors are clearly seen.

wd F. W. Murnau, Robert Flaherty *ph* Floyd Crosby, Robert Flaherty *m* Hugo Riesenfeld

'Never more than interesting . . . it is not going to set anything on fire.'—*Variety*

AA: Floyd Crosby

Taggart
US 1965 85m Technicolor print

A young western squatter avenges his parents' murder but finds himself pursued by three professional gunslingers. Tough adult western, quite well made. Tony Young, Dan Duryea, Dick Foran, Emile Meyer, Elsa Cardenas, Jean Hale, David Carradine. Written by Robert Creighton Williams, from the novel by Louis L'Amour; directed by R. G. Springsteen; for Universal.

Tai-Pan
US 1986 127m Technicolor JDC Widescreen
Dino de Laurentiis (Rafaella de Laurentiis)

Various problems afflict the leader of the European community in Canton and Hong Kong.
Nineteenth-century soap opera with eighteenth-century plotting and dialogue.

w John Briley, Stanley Mann *novel* James Clavell *d* Daryl Duke *ph* Jack Cardiff *m* Maurice Jarre *pd* Tony Masters

Bryan Brown, Joan Chen, John Stanton, Tom Guinee, Bill Leadbitter, Russell Wong

'Underneath all the gloss the film isn't really about anything.'—*Variety*

'With some movies, you're forever checking your watch. With *Tai-Pan*, you'll be checking your calendar.'—*People*

'Miniseries kitsch which shortchanges on dramatic spectacle.'—*Sight and Sound*

Tail Spin
US 1938 83m bw
TCF (Harry Joe Brown)

The interwoven private lives of lady civilian air pilots.
Predictable romantic goings on; a tear, a smile, a song, etc.

w Frank Wead *d* Roy del Ruth *ph* Karl Freund *m* Louis Silvers

Alice Faye, Constance Bennett, Joan Davis, Nancy Kelly, Charles Farrell, Jane Wyman, Kane Richmond, Wally Vernon, Harry Davenport

'Story zooms and flutters to create many slow spots in between the spectacular flying sequences.'—*Variety*

Tailspin Tommy
US 1934 bw serial: 12 eps

A young auto mechanic learns to fly and battles aerial pirates. Juvenile serial comic strip. Maurice Murphy, Patricia Farr, Noah Beery Jnr, Grant Withers. Directed by Louis Friedlander; for Universal.

Tailspin Tommy in the Great Air Mystery
US 1935 bw serial: 12 eps

Our heroes prevent a villainous plan to steal oil reserves. More of the above. Clark Williams, Noah Beery Jnr, Jean Rogers, Bryant Washburn. Directed by Ray Taylor; for Universal.

Take a Giant Step
US 1958 100m bw
UA / Sheila / Hecht–Hill–Lancaster (Julius J. Epstein)

A young black person brought up in a white town feels ill at ease and runs into adolescent troubles.
Well-meaning racial drama with good detail but no real feeling.

w Louis S. Peterson, Julius J. Epstein *d* Philip Leacock *ph* Arthur Arling *m* Jack Marshall

Johnny Nash, Estelle Hemsley, Ruby Dee, Frederick O'Neal

Take a Girl Like You
GB 1970 101m Eastmancolor
Columbia / Albion (Hal E. Chester)

A north country girl comes to teach in London and has man trouble.
Old-fashioned novelette with sex trimmings and neither zest nor humour.

w George Melly, *novel* Kingsley Amis *d* Jonathan Miller *ph* Dick Bush *m* Stanley Myers

Hayley Mills, Oliver Reed, Noel Harrison, Sheila Hancock, John Bird, Aimi MacDonald

Take a Letter, Darling**
US 1942 94m bw
Paramount (Fred Kohlmar)
GB title: *Green-Eyed Woman*

A woman executive hires a male secretary.
Smartish romantic comedy.

w Claude Binyon d Mitchell Leisen ph John Mescall *m* Victor Young

Rosalind Russell, Fred MacMurray, Macdonald Carey, Constance Moore, Cecil Kellaway, Charles Arnt, Kathleen Howard, Dooley Wilson

AAN: John Mescall; Victor Young

Take Care of My Little Girl
US 1951 93m Technicolor
TCF (Julian Blaustein)

A university freshwoman gets into trouble with her sorority.

Ho-hum exposé of college conventions, of routine interest at best.

w Julius J. and Philip G. Epstein, *novel* Peggy Goodwin *d* Jean Negulesco *ph* Harry Jackson *m* Alfred Newman

Jeanne Crain, Mitzi Gaynor, Dale Robertson, Jean Peters, Jeffrey Hunter

'As is customary in college pictures, it appears that Tri U recruits most of its strength from the chorus.'—*Penelope Houston*

Take Her, She's Mine*
US 1963 98m De Luxe Cinemascope
TCF (Henry Koster)

A lawyer protects his teenage daughter from boys and causes.
Routine Hollywood family comedy with some laughs and an agreeable cast.

w Nunnally Johnson, *play* Phoebe and Henry Ephron *d* Henry Koster *ph* Lucien Ballard *m* Jerry Goldsmith

James Stewart, Sandra Dee, Robert Morley, Audrey Meadows, Philippe Forquet, John McGiver

Take It or Leave It
US 1944 68m bw

A sailor enters a quiz show to raise money for his expectant wife. Thin link for a string of old movie clips which form the questions; all from Fox films of course. Phil Baker, Phil Silvers, Edward Ryan, Marjorie Massow; with clips of Shirley Temple, the Ritz Brothers, Betty Grable, Alice Faye, Sonja Henie, Al Jolson, etc. Written by Harold Buchman, Snag Werris and Mac Benoff; directed by Ben Stoloff; for TCF.

Take Me High
GB 1973 90m Technicolor
EMI (Kenneth Harper)

A bank manager helps an unsuccessful restaurant to launch a new hamburger.
Jaded youth musical with no dancing but some zip and bounce to commend it to mums and dads if not to its intended young audience.

w Christopher Penfold *d* David Askey *ph* Norman Warwick *m / songs* Tony Cole

Cliff Richard, Debbie Watling, Hugh Griffith, George Cole, Anthony Andrews, Richard Wattis

Take Me Out to the Ball Game**
US 1949 93m Technicolor
MGM (Arthur Freed)
GB title: *Everybody's Cheering*

A woman takes over a baseball team and the players are antagonistic.
Lively, likeable nineties comedy musical which served as a trial run for *On the Town* and in its own right is a fast-moving, funny, tuneful delight with no pretensions.

w Harry Tugend, George Wells d Busby Berkeley ph George Folsey *md* Adolph Deutsch *songs Betty Comden, Adolph Green, Roger Edens*

Gene Kelly, Frank Sinatra, Esther Williams, *Betty Garrett,* Jules Munshin, Edward Arnold, Richard Lane, Tom Dugan

Take Me to Town
US 1953 81m Technicolor
U-I (Ross Hunter)

The three sons of a backwoods widower import a vaudeville artiste as their new mother.
Old-fashioned family schmaltz containing every known cliché professionally stitched into the plot.

w Richard Morris *d* Douglas Sirk *ph* Russell Metty *m* Joseph Gershenson

Ann Sheridan, Sterling Hayden, Philip Reed, Lee Patrick, Lee Aaker, Harvey Grant, Dusty Henley

Take My Life**
GB 1947 79m bw
GFD / Cineguild (Anthony Havelock-Allan)

A man is suspected of murdering an ex-girl friend, and his wife journeys to Scotland to prove him innocent.
Hitchcock-style thriller with excellent detail and performances.

w Winston Graham, Valerie Taylor *d Ronald Neame ph Guy Green m* William Alwyn

Hugh Williams, Greta Gynt, Marius Goring, Francis L. Sullivan, Rosalie Crutchley, Henry Edwards, Ronald Adam

Take My Tip
GB 1937 74m bw
Gaumont-British (Michael Balcon)

Lord Pilkington gets his revenge on a confidence trickster when they meet at a Dalmatian hotel.
Reasonably lively comedy musical adapted for the stars.

w Sidney Gilliat, Michael Hogan, Jack Hulbert *d* Herbert Mason *ph* Bernard Knowles *songs* Sam Lerner, Al Goodheart, Al Hoffman

Jack Hulbert, Cicely Courtneidge, Frank Cellier, Harold Huth, Frank Pettingell, Robb Wilton, H. F. Maltby

Take One False Step*
US 1949 94m bw
U-I (Chester Erskine)

An innocent middle-aged man who has befriended a girl is hunted by the police when she is murdered.
Fairly absorbing and well-cast chase thriller in a minor key.

w Irwin Shaw, Chester Erskine, *story* Night Call by Irwin and David Shaw *d* Chester Erskine *ph* Franz Planer *m* Walter Scharf

William Powell, Shelley Winters, Marsha Hunt, Dorothy Hart, James Gleason, Felix Bressart, Art Baker, Sheldon Leonard

Take the High Ground
US 1953 101m Anscocolor
MGM (Dore Schary)

A tough sergeant trains army conscripts for action in Korea.
Very routine flagwaver.

w Millard Kaufman *d* Richard Brooks *ph* John Alton *m* Dmitri Tiomkin

Richard Widmark, Karl Malden, Carleton Carpenter, Elaine Stewart, Russ Tamblyn, Jerome Courtland, Steve Forrest, Robert Arthur

AAN: Millard Kaufman

Take the Money and Run
US 1968 85m Technicolor
Palomar (Charles H. Joffe)

A social misfit becomes a bungling crook.
A torrent of middling visual gags, not the star's best vehicle.

wd Woody Allen *ph* Lester Shorr *m* Marvin Hamlisch

Woody Allen, Janet Margolin, Marcel Hillaire

The Taking of Pelham 123*
US 1974 104m Technicolor Panavision
UA / Palomar / Palladium (Gabriel Katzka)

Four ruthless gunmen hold a New York subway train to ransom and have an ingenious plan for escape.
Entertaining crime caper made less enjoyable by all the fashionable faults the script is deliberately hard to follow and full of four letter words, the sound track hard to hear, and the visuals ugly.

w Peter Stone, *novel* John Godey *d* Joseph Sargent *ph* Owen Roizman *m* David Shire

Walter Matthau, Robert Shaw, Martin Balsam, Hector Elizondo, Earl Hindman, James Broderick

'Full of noise and squalling and dirty words used for giggly shock effects.'—*New Yorker*

Taking Off**
US 1971 92m Movielab
Universal (Alfred W. Crown, Michael Hausman)

Suburban parents seek their errant daughter among the hippies, and gradually lose their own inhibitions.
Slight, formless, but amusing revue-style comment by a Czech director on the American scene.

w Milos Forman, John Guare, Jean-Claude Carrière, John Klein *d Milos Forman* *ph* Miroslav Ondricek

Lynn Carlin, Buck Henry, Linnea Heacock

A Tale of Five Cities
GB 1951 99m bw
Grand National (Alexander Paal)
US title: *A Tale of Five Women*

An amnesiac American seeks clues to his past in Rome, Vienna, Paris, Berlin and London.
Tedious pattern drama remarkable only for its then untried cast.

w Patrick Kirwan, Maurice J. Wilson *d* Montgomery Tully *ph* Gordon Lang *m* Hans May

Bonar Colleano, Gina Lollobrigida, Barbara Kelly, Lana Morris, Anne Vernon, Eva Bartok

'His love challenged the flames of revolution!'

A Tale of Two Cities**
US 1935 121m bw
MGM (David O. Selznick)

A British lawyer sacrifices himself to save another man from the guillotine.
Richly detailed version of the classic melodrama, with production values counting more than the acting.

w W. P. Lipscomb, S. N. Behrman, *novel* Charles Dickens *d Jack Conway* *ph* Oliver T. Marsh *m* Herbert Stothart

Ronald Colman, Elizabeth Allan, Basil Rathbone, Edna May Oliver, Blanche Yurka, Reginald Owen, Henry B. Walthall, Donald Woods, Walter Catlett, H. B. Warner, Claude Gillingwater, Fritz Leiber

'A screen classic . . . technically it is about as flawless as possible . . . it has been made with respectful and loving care.'—*Variety*

'A prodigiously stirring production . . . for more than two hours it crowds the screen with beauty and excitement.'—*New York Times*

† Originally prepared at Warners for Leslie Howard.

AAN: best picture

A Tale of Two Cities*
GB 1958 117m bw
Rank (Betty E. Box)

Modest but still costly remake with good moments but a rather slow pace.

w T. E. B. Clarke *d* Ralph Thomas *ph* Ernest Steward *m* Richard Addinsell

Dirk Bogarde, Dorothy Tutin, Christopher Lee, Athene Seyler, Rosalie Crutchley, Ernest Clark, Stephen Murray, Paul Guers, Donald Pleasence, Ian Bannen, Cecil Parker, Alfie Bass

'Serviceable rather than imaginative.'—*MFB*

A Talent for Loving
US 1969 101m colour

Two generations of an international jet-setting family have woman trouble. Little-seen melodrama apparently disowned by those who made it. Richard Widmark, Cesar Romero, Topol, Genevieve Page. From the novel by Richard Condon; directed by Richard Quine; for Walter Shenson / Paramount.

Tales from the Crypt*
GB 1972 92m Eastmancolor
Metromedia / Amicus (Milton Subotsky)

Five people get lost in catacombs and are shown the future by a sinister monk who turns out to be Satan.
Fair ghoulish fun; a quintet of stories with a recognizable Amicus link.

w Milton Subotsky, from comic strips by William Gaines *d* Freddie Francis *ph* Norman Warwick *m* Douglas Gamley

Ralph Richardson, Geoffrey Bayldon, Peter Cushing, Joan Collins, Ian Hendry, Robin Phillips, Richard Greene, Barbara Murray, Roy Dotrice, Nigel Patrick, Patrick Magee

Tales of Beatrix Potter**
GB 1971 90m Technicolor
EMI (Richard Goodwin)
US title: *Peter Rabbit and the Tales of Beatrix Potter*

Children's stories danced by the Royal Ballet in animal masks.
A charming entertainment for those who can appreciate it, though hardly the most direct way to tell these stories.

w Richard Goodwin, Christine Edward *d* Reginald Mills *ph* Austin Dempster *m* John Lanchbery *ch Frederick Ashton* *masks Rotislav Doboujinsky* *pd* Christine Edward

The Tales of Hoffman**
GB 1951 127m Technicolor
British Lion / London / Michael Powell, Emeric Pressburger

The poet Hoffman, in three adventures, seeks the eternal woman and is beset by eternal evil.
Overwhelming combination of opera, ballet, and rich production design, an indigestible hodgepodge with flashes of superior talent.

wd Michael Powell, Emeric Pressburger *ph* Christopher Challis *m Jacques Offenbach* *pd Hein Heckroth*

Robert Rounseville, Robert Helpmann, Pamela Brown, Moira Shearer, Frederick Ashton, Leonide Massine, Ludmilla Tcherina, Ann Ayars, Mogens Wieth; music conducted by Sir Thomas Beecham with the Royal Philharmonic Orchestra

'The most spectacular failure yet achieved by Powell and Pressburger, who seem increasingly to dissipate their gifts in a welter of aimless ingenuity.'—*Gavin Lambert*

'An art director's picnic: I marvelled without being enthralled.'—*Richard Mallett, Punch*

'Enchanting, a labour of love.'—*Sunday Telegraph*

'It echoes the peak of the Victorian spirit.'—*Time*

Tales of Manhattan**
US 1942 118m bw
TCF (Boris Morros, Sam Spiegel)

Separate stories of a tail coat, which passes from owner to owner.
The stories are all rather disappointing in their different veins, but production standards are high and a few of the stars shine. A sequence starring W. C. Fields was deleted before release.

w Ben Hecht, Ferenc Molnar, Donald Ogden Stewart, Samuel Hoffenstein, Alan Campbell, Ladislas Fodor, Laslo Vadnay, Laszlo Gorog, Lamar Trotti, Henry Blankfort *d Julien Duvivier* *ph* Joseph Walker *m* Sol Kaplan

Charles Boyer, Rita Hayworth, Thomas Mitchell, Eugene Pallette; Ginger Rogers, Henry Fonda, Cesar Romero, Gail Patrick, Roland Young; *Charles Laughton*, Elsa Lanchester, Victor Francen, Christian Rub; *Edward G. Robinson*, George Sanders, James Gleason, Harry Davenport; Paul Robeson, Ethel Waters, Eddie Anderson

† Duvivier was clearly chosen to make this film because of his success with the similar *Carnet de Bal*; he and Boyer went on to make the less successful *Flesh and Fantasy* on similar lines.

Tales of Ordinary Madness
Italy / France 1981 108m Eastmancolor English version
23 Giugno / Ginis (Jacqueline Ferreri)

A drunken poet is obsessed by sex but can't find a happy relationship with his women.
Outlandish, episodic wallow, mostly on Venice beach in California. Not for maiden aunts, and probably not for anyone else either.

w Marco Ferreri and others, from the book Erections, Ejaculations, Exhibitions and Tales of Ordinary Madness by Charles Bukowski *d* Marco Ferreri *ph* Tonino Delli Colli *m* Philippe Sarde

Ben Gazzara, Ornella Muti, Susan Tyrrell, Tanya Lopert, Katia Berger

'By turns repellent, naive and risible.'—*Sight and Sound*

Tales of Terror*
US 1962 90m Pathecolor Panavision
AIP (Roger Corman)

'Morella': a dying girl discovers the mummified body of her mother. 'The Black Cat': a henpecked husband kills his wife and walls up the body. 'The Facts in the Case of M Valdemar': an old man is hypnotized at the moment of death.
Tolerable short story compendium, rather short on subtlety and style.

w Richard Matheson, *stories* Edgar Allan Poe *d* Roger Corman *ph* Floyd Crosby *m* Les Baxter

Vincent Price, *Peter Lorre*, Basil Rathbone, Debra Paget

'An orgy of the damned!'

Tales That Witness Madness
GB 1973 90m colour
Paramount / Amicus (Milton Subotsky, Norman Priggen)

Five ghostly tales linked by an old bookshop.
Extreme example of the Amicus compendiums.

w Jay Fairbank *d* Freddie Francis *ph* Norman Warwick *m* Bernard Ebbinghouse

Jack Hawkins, Donald Pleasence, Georgia Brown, Donald Houston, Suzy Kendall, Peter McEnery, Joan Collins, Michael Jayston, Kim Novak, Michael Petrovitch, Mary Tamm

Talk About a Lady
US 1946 71m bw

A country cousin comes to town and makes

good. Easy-going musical filler, better than some. Jinx Falkenberg, Forrest Tucker, Joe Besser, Trudy Marshall, Richard Lane, Stan Kenton and his orchestra. Written by Richard Weil, Ted Thomas; directed by George Sherman; for Columbia.

Talk About a Stranger*
US 1952 65m bw
MGM (Richard Goldstone)

In a small town, gossip is unjustly aroused over a mysterious stranger who is suspected of various crimes.
Unusual though rather naïve second feature, directed for more than its worth.

w Margaret Fitts, *novel* Charlotte Armstrong *d* David Bradley *ph* John Alton *m* David Buttolph

George Murphy, Nancy Davis, Lewis Stone, Billy Gray, Kurt Kasznar

Talk About Jacqueline
GB 1942 84m bw

A girl is mistaken for her naughtier sister. Thin, very British comedy with nowhere to go. Hugh Williams, Carla Lehmann, Joyce Howard, Roland Culver, John Warwick, Mary Jerrold, Guy Middleton, Max Adrian. Written by Roland Pertwee and Marjorie Deans, from a novel by Katherine Holland; directed by Harold French; for Excelsior / Marcel Hellman.

Talk of the Devil
GB 1936 78m bw

An impersonator pins a crooked deal on a magnate, who kills himself. Glum drama chiefly notable as the first film to be shot at Pinewood Studios. Ricardo Cortez, Sally Eilers, Basil Sydney, Randle Ayrton, Charles Carson. Written by Carol Reed, George Barraud and Anthony Kimmins; directed by Carol Reed; for B and D.

The Talk of the Town***
US 1942 118m bw
Columbia (George Stevens, Fred Guiol)

A girl loves both a suspected murderer and the lawyer who defends him.
Unusual mixture of comedy and drama, delightfully handled by three sympathetic stars.

w Irwin Shaw, Sidney Buchman d George Stevens ph Ted Tetzlaff *m* Frederick Hollander

Roland Colman, Cary Grant, Jean Arthur, Edgar Buchanan, Glenda Farrell, Charles Dingle, Emma Dunn, Rex Ingram

'A rip-roaring, knock-down-and-drag-out comedy about civil liberties.'—*John T. McManus*

'Well tuned and witty, at its best when it sticks to the middle ground between farce and melodrama. The chief fault of the script is its excessive length and the fact that a standard lynching mob climax is followed by a prolonged anti-climax.'—*Newsweek*

'I can't take my lynching so lightly, even in a screwball. Still, I am all for this kind of comedy and for players like Arthur and Grant, who can mug more amusingly than most scriptwriters can write.'—*Manny Farber*

'Did the authors think they were writing a Shavian comedy of ideas? The ideas are garbled and silly, but the people are so pleasant that the picture manages to be quite amiable and high-spirited.'—*Pauline Kael, 70s*

'I knew it was going to come off all along: it didn't have that element of hazard in it. It was more of an understood flight with a take-off time and an arrival time and not too much headwind.'—*George Stevens*

† Two endings were filmed: the eventual choice of mate for Miss Arthur was determined by audience reaction at previews.

AAN: best picture; original story (Sidney Harmon); script; Ted Tetzlaff; Frederick Hollander

Tall, Dark and Handsome
US 1941 78m bw

In 1929 Chicago, a gangster aspires to be a gentleman. Moderate crime comedy. Cesar Romero, Virginia Gilmore, Charlotte Greenwood, Milton Berle, Sheldon Leonard. Written by Karl Tunberg and Darrell Ware; directed by H. Bruce Humberstone; for TCF.

The Tall Headlines
GB 1952 100m bw
Grand National / Raymond Stross
aka: *The Frightened Bride*

A family is affected when the eldest son is executed for murder.
Glum, boring, badly cast, badly written and generally inept melodrama.

w Audrey Erskine Lindop (from her novel), Dudley Leslie *d* Terence Young *ph* C. M. Pennington-Richards *m* Hans May

Flora Robson, Michael Denison, Mai Zetterling, Jane Hylton, André Morell, Dennis Price, Mervyn Johns, Naunton Wayne

'A falsity which will surely surprise even those familiar with the conventions of British middle-class cinema.'—*Lindsay Anderson*

Tall in the Saddle
US 1944 87m bw
RKO (Robert Fellows)

The newly-arrived ranch foreman finds that his boss has been murdered.
Quite a watchable, and forgettable, mystery western.

w Michael Hogan, Paul J. Fix *d* Edwin L. Marin *ph* Robert de Grasse *m* Roy Webb *md* Constantin Bakaleinikoff

John Wayne, Ella Raines, Ward Bond, George 'Gabby' Hayes, Audrey Long, Elizabeth Risdon, Don Douglas, Paul Fix, Russell Wade

Tall Man Riding
US 1955 83m Warnercolor

An adventurer feuds with a rancher but in the end marries his daughter. Unremarkable star western. Randolph Scott, Robert Barrat, Dorothy Malone, Peggie Castle, John Dehner. Written by Joseph Hoffman; directed by Lesley Selander; for Warner.

The Tall Men*
US 1955 122m De Luxe Cinemascope
TCF (William A. Bacher, William B. Hawks)

After the Civil War, two Texans head north for the Montana goldfields.
Solid star western.

w Sidney Boehm, Frank Nugent, *novel* Clay Fisher *d* Raoul Walsh *ph* Leo Tover *m* Victor Young

Clark Gable, Jane Russell, Robert Ryan, Cameron Mitchell, Juan Garcia, Harry Shannon, Emile Meyer

'A big action feast and value for anyone's money.'—*Newsweek*

Tall Story
US 1960 91m bw
Warner / Mansfield (Joshua Logan)

A college basketball player faces various kinds of trouble when he marries.
Dislikeable campus comedy with leading players miscast.

w Julius J. Epstein, *novel* The Homecoming Game by Howard Nemoor *d* Joshua Logan *ph* Ellsworth Fredericks *m* Cyril Mockridge

Anthony Perkins, Jane Fonda, Ray Walston, Anne Jackson, Marc Connelly, Murray Hamilton, Elizabeth Patterson

The Tall Stranger
US 1957 83m De Luxe Cinemascope

Cared for by wagon train pioneers after being mysteriously shot, a rancher tries to help them settle. Fair star western with some tough action. Joel McCrea, Virginia Mayo, Barry Kelley, Michael Ansara, Whit Bissell. Written by Christopher Knopf, from a story by Louis L'Amour; directed by Thomas Carr; for Allied Artists.

The Tall T*
US 1957 78m Technicolor
Columbia / Scott–Brown (Harry Joe Brown)

Three bandits hold up a stagecoach and take a hostage, but are outwitted by a rancher.
Good small-scale suspense western with plenty of action and a blood-spattered finale.

w Burt Kennedy d Budd Boetticher ph Charles Lawton Jnr *m* Heinz Roemheld

Randolph Scott, Richard Boone, Maureen O'Sullivan, Arthur Hunnicutt, Skip Homeier, John Hubbard, Henry Silva

The Tall Target**
US 1951 78m bw
MGM (Richard Goldstone)

A discredited police officer tries to stop the assassination of Abraham Lincoln on a train to Washington.
Lively period suspenser with excellent attention to detail and much of the attraction of *The Lady Vanishes*. The plot slightly relaxes its hold before the end.

w George Worthing Yates, Art Cohn d Anthony Mann ph Paul C. Vogel ad Cedric Gibbons, Eddie Imazu

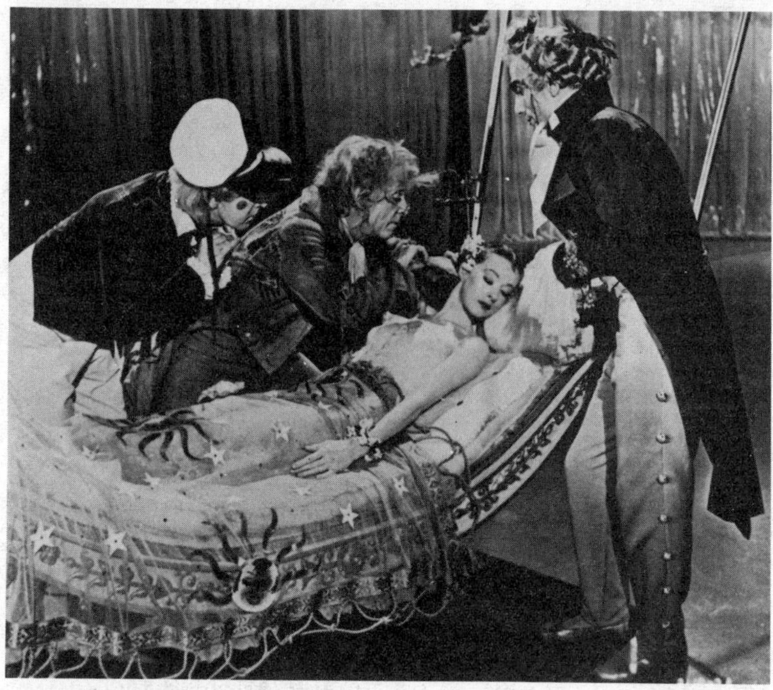

THE TALES OF HOFFMAN. Moira Shearer takes Powell and Pressburger's fascinating misfire lying down: audiences were similarly unmoved.

Dick Powell, Adolphe Menjou, Paula Raymond, Marshall Thompson, *Ruby Dee*, Richard Rober, Will Geer, Florence Bates

'An intelligent minor picture which makes good use of its material.'—*MFB*

Tamahine
GB 1962 95m Technicolor Cinemascope
ABP (John Bryan)

The headmaster of a boys' school is visited by his glamorous half-caste Polynesian cousin.
Simple-minded school comedy with predictable situations.

w Denis Cannan, *novel* Thelma Niklaus *d* Philip Leacock *ph* Geoffrey Unsworth *m* Malcolm Arnold

John Fraser, Nancy Kwan, Dennis Price, Derek Nimmo, Justine Lord, James Fox, Coral Browne, Michael Gough, Allan Cuthbertson

The Tamarind Seed*
GB 1974 125m Eastmancolor Panavision
Jewel / Lorimar / Pimlico (Ken Wales)

While holidaying in Barbados, a British widow falls for a Russian military attaché.
Old-fashioned romance which turns into a mild spy caper. A well-heeled time-passer.

w Blake Edwards, *novel* Evelyn Anthony *d* Blake Edwards *ph* Frederick A. Young *m* John Barry

Julie Andrews, Omar Sharif, Sylvia Syms, Dan O'Herlihy, Anthony Quayle, Oscar Homolka

'A painless timekiller, but one wishes Miss Andrews didn't always give the impression that she had just left her horse in the hallway.'—*Michael Billington, Illustrated London News*

The Taming of the Shrew*
US 1929 68m bw
United Artists / Pickford / Elton

A condensed version of the play which did not do much in its day for its stars' then declining reputations, but can now be watched with a fair measure of enjoyment.

w William Shakespeare, 'with additional dialogue by Sam Taylor' *d* Sam Taylor *ph* Karl Struss *pd* William Cameron Menzies, Laurence Irving

Douglas Fairbanks, Mary Pickford, Edwin Maxwell, Joseph Cawthorn, Clyde Cook, Dorothy Jordan

† A 'widescreen' version was issued in 1976.

'In the war between the sexes, there always comes a time to surrender unconditionally!'

The Taming of the Shrew*
US 1967 122m Technicolor Panavision
Columbia / Royal / FAI (Richard McWhorter)

Petruchio violently tames his shrewish wife.
Busy version of one of Shakespeare's more proletarian comedies; the words in this case take second place to violent action and rioting colour.

w Suso Cecchi d'Amico, Paul Dehn, Franco Zeffirelli *d Franco Zeffirelli ph* Oswald Morris, Luciano Trasatti *m* Nino Rota

Richard Burton, Elizabeth Taylor, Michael York, Michael Hordern, Cyril Cusack, Alfred Lynch, Natasha Pyne, Alan Webb, Victor Spinetti

'As entertainment *Kiss Me Kate* is infinitely better but then Cole Porter was a real artist and Burton is a culture vulture.'—*Wilfrid Sheed*

'The old warhorse of a comedy has been spanked into uproarious life.'—*Hollis Alpert*

Tam-Lin
GB 1971 106m Technicolor Panavision
Winkast (Jerry Gershwin, Elliott Kastner) / Commonwealth United
aka: *The Devil's Widow; The Ballad of Tam-Lin*

A sinister, beautiful, middle-aged widow has a diabolic influence on the bright young people she gathers around her.
Self-indulgent melodrama which might have worked with a shorter running time and a tighter script; as it was, it sank almost without trace.

w William Spier, *poem* Robert Burns *d* Roddy McDowall *ph* Willy Williams *m* Stanley Myers

Ava Gardner, Ian MacShane, Richard Wattis, Cyril Cusack, Stephanie Beacham, David Whitman, Fabia Drake, Sinead Cusack, Joanna Lumley, Jenny Hanley

Tammy and the Bachelor*
US 1957 89m Technicolor Cinemascope
U-I (Ross Hunter)
GB title: *Tammy*

A backwoods tomboy falls for a stranded flier.
Whimsical romance for middle America, which started Hollywood's last series of proletarian family appeal before the family was entirely forsaken for four letter words.

w Oscar Brodney, from stories by Cid Ricketts Summer *d* Joseph Pevney *ph* Arthur E. Arling *m* Frank Skinner *md* Joseph Gershenson

Debbie Reynolds, Walter Brennan, Leslie Nielsen, Mala Powers, Fay Wray, Sidney Blackmer, Mildred Natwick

Tammy and the Doctor
US 1963 88m Eastmancolor
U-I / Ross Hunter

Tammy leaves her riverboat to accompany an old lady who needs an operation in the big city.
More artless family fodder.

w Oscar Brodney *d* Harry Keller *ph* Russell Metty *m* Frank Skinner

Sandra Dee, Peter Fonda, Macdonald Carey, Beulah Bondi, Margaret Lindsay, Reginald Owen, Adam West

'The aura of simple religion and naïve philosophy remains singularly charmless.'—*MFB*

Tammy and the Millionaire
US 1967 88m Technicolor

Tammy becomes a private secretary in the big city. A re-edit from four half-hour TV shows; not at all watchable. Debbie Watson, Donald Woods, Dorothy Green, Denver Pyle, Frank McGrath. Written by George Tibbles; directed by Sidney Miller, Leslie Goodwins and Ezra Stone; for Universal.

Tammy Tell Me True
US 1961 97m Eastmancolor
U-I (Ross Hunter)

Tammy gets a college education and charms all comers.
Sugar-coated sequel to the original.

w Oscar Brodney *d* Harry Keller *ph* Clifford Stine *m* Percy Faith

Sandra Dee, John Gavin, Charles Drake, Virginia Grey, *Beulah Bondi*, Julia Meade, Cecil Kellaway, Edgar Buchanan

'The heroine appears to be not so much old-fashioned as positively retarded.'—*MFB*

Tampico
US 1944 75m bw
TCF (Robert Bassler)

A tanker captain picks up survivors from a torpedoed ship and finds himself involved with spies.
Very minor action melodrama, efficiently made.

w Kenneth Gamet, Fred Niblo Jnr, Richard Macaulay *d* Lothar Mendes *ph* Charles G. Clarke *m* David Raksin

Edward G. Robinson, Lynn Bari, Victor McLaglen, Marc Lawrence, E. J. Ballentine, Mona Maris

Tanganyika
US 1954 81m Technicolor

A 1900 settler finds that the African colony of his choice is terrorized by a murderer. Curious blend of outdoor action and who-is-it; not at all bad. Van Heflin, Howard Duff, Ruth Roman, Jeff Morrow, Joe Comadaore. Written by Richard Alan Simmons and William Sackheim; directed by André de Toth; for Universal-International.

Tangier
US 1946 74m bw

A dancer hunts for the Nazi war criminal responsible for her father's death. You can tell returns had been bad from the fact that the queen of Technicolor was sentenced to monochrome, and in a two-bit *Casablanca*. Maria Montez, Kent Taylor, Robert Paige, Sabu, Preston Foster, Louise Allbritton, Reginald Denny, J. Edward Bromberg. Written by M. M. Musselman and Monty Collins; directed by George Waggner; for Universal-International.

Tank
US 1984 113m Metrocolor
Lorimar / Universal (Irwin Yablans)

A retired army sergeant lovingly restores an old tank and uses it to secure justice for his wrongly imprisoned son.
Fairly lively if predictable American fantasy in which one just man stands up against the uncaring and / or corrupt mob.

w Dan Gordon *d* Marvin Chomsky *ph* Don Birnkrant *m* Lalo Schifrin *pd* Bill Kenney

James Garner, Shirley Jones, C. Thomas Howell, Mark Herrier, Dorian Harewood, G. D. Spradlin

'Further dispiriting evidence of the new reactionary spirit of Reagan's America.'—*Tom Milne, MFB*

Tanks a Million
US 1941 50m bw

An army recruit has a freak memory which keeps him out of trouble. Acceptable programme filler. William Tracy, James Gleason, Noah Beery Jnr, Joe Sawyer, Elyse Knox, Douglas Fowley. Written by Paul Gerard Smith, Warren Wilson, Edward E. Seabrook; directed by Fred Guiol; for Hal Roach.
AAN: Edward Ward (music)

The Tanks Are Coming
US 1951 90m bw

A tough sergeant learns humility during the race to Berlin. Tedious war drama which tries in vain to interest us in non-characters. Steve Cochran, Paul Picerni, Mari Aldon, Harry Bellaver, Philip Carey. Written by Robert Hardy Andrews; directed by D. Ross Lederman and Lewis Seiler; for Warner.

Tap Roots
US 1948 109m Technicolor
Universal-International (Walter Wanger)

A southern family tries to remain neutral in the Civil War.
Minor *Gone with the Wind* saga, quite expensively produced but not very exciting.

w Alan le May, *novel* James Street *d* George Marshall *ph* Winton C. Hoch, Lionel Lindon *m* Frank Skinner

Susan Hayward, Van Heflin, Boris Karloff, Julie London, Whitfield Connor

Taps
US 1981 126m De Luxe
TCF / Stanley Jaffe

Cadets at a military academy go on strike when the site is sold for development, and violence ensues.
Rather uninteresting moral fable, comparable with the British *If*. The moral attitudes are worked out on entirely predictable lines.

w Darryl Ponicsan, Robert Mark Kamen, *novel* Father Sky by Devery Freeman *d* Harold Becker *ph* Owen Roizman *m* Maurice Jarre

Timothy Hutton, George C. Scott, Ronny Cox, Sean Penn, Tom Cruise, Brendan Ward

'Even science was stunned!'
Tarantula
US 1955 80m bw
U-I (William Alland)

Scientists working on an artificial food become grossly misshapen, and an infected spider escapes and grows to giant size.
Moderate monster hokum with the desert setting which became a cliché; the grotesque faces are more horrific than the spider, which seldom seems to touch the ground.

w Robert M. Fresco, Martin Berkeley *d* Jack Arnold *ph* George Robinson *md* Joseph Gershenson

Leo G. Carroll, John Agar, Mara Corday, Nestor Paiva

'It's a great children's picture . . . particularly for bad children. It'll scare hell out of the little monsters.'—*Hollywood Reporter*

Taras Bulba*
US 1962 124m Eastmancolor Panavision
UA / H-H / Avala (Harold Hecht)

A cossack leader has bitter disagreements with his rebellious son.
Violent action epic based on a well-worn story; plenty of spectacular highlights.

w Waldo Salt, Karl Tunberg, *novel* Nicolai Gogol *d* J. Lee-Thompson *ph* Joe MacDonald *m* Franz Waxman *pd* Edward Carrere

Yul Brynner, Tony Curtis, Christine Kaufmann, Sam Wanamaker, Guy Rolfe, George Macready, Vladimir Sokoloff, Abraham Sofaer

'Now! Add a motion picture to the wonders of the world!'—*publicity*

AAN: Franz Waxman

Target
US 1985 117m Technicolor
CBS / Richard Zanuck, David Brown

When his wife is kidnapped, an ex-spy goes back into action.
Lethargic, simple-minded, and often ludicrous melodrama: the intent seems to be to pile up as many clichés of the genre as the writers can remember.

w Howard Berk, Don Petersen *d* Arthur Penn *ph* Jean Tournier *m* Michael Small

Gene Hackman, Matt Dillon, Gayle Hunnicutt, Josef Sommer, Guy Boyd, Herbert Berghof

Target for Tonight****
GB 1941 48m bw

The story of a bombing raid over Germany. Classic RAF semi-documentary, not quite so genuine as it seems since many scenes were re-created in the studio. Written by Harry Watt and B. Cooper; directed by Harry Watt; for the Crown Film Unit. Special AA. 'It looks like a sure grosser . . . one of the must-see films of 1941.'—*Variety*

Target Zero
US 1955 93m bw
Warner (David Weisbart)

An infantry patrol in Korea is cut off behind enemy lines.
Routine battle exploits with a highly unlikely superimposed romance.

w Sam Rolfe *d* Harmon Jones *ph* Edwin DuPar *m* David Buttolph

Richard Conte, Charles Bronson, Richard Stapley, Chuck Connors, L. Q. Jones, Peggie Castle

Targets*
US 1967 90m Pathecolor
(Paramount) Peter Bogdanovich

An elderly horror film star confronts and disarms a mad sniper at a drive-in movie.
Oddball melodrama apparently meant to contrast real and fantasy violence; it doesn't quite work despite effective moments, and the low budget shows.

wd Peter Bogdanovich *ph* Laszlo Kovacs

Boris Karloff, Tim O'Kelly, James Brown, Sandy Baron

The Tarnished Angels
US 1957 91m bw Cinemascope
U-I (Albert Zugsmith)

A reporter falls in with a self-torturing family of circus air aces.
Unsatisfactory attempt to reunite the talents of *Written on the Wind*; a dull story, very boringly presented.

w George Zuckerman, *novel* Pylon by William Faulkner *d* Douglas Sirk *ph* Irving Glassberg *m* Frank Skinner *md* Joseph Gershenson

Rock Hudson, Robert Stack, Dorothy Malone, Jack Carson, Robert Middleton

'Married to a man she doesn't love! Loving a man she can't have! What does life hold for this pampered beauty of the drawing rooms?'

Tarnished Lady
US 1931 80m bw
Paramount

Two society women and their lovers cross each other's paths. Exaggerated melodrama which failed to justify the London stage reputation of its American star. Tallulah Bankhead, Clive Brook, Phoebe Foster, Alexander Kirkland, Osgood Perkins, Elizabeth Patterson. Written by Donald Ogden Stewart; directed by George Cukor; for Paramount. 'A poor picture that fits the straight grinds best. Heavy production but too ponderous to mean anything.'—*Variety*

Tars and Spars
US 1945 86m bw

Adventures of members of the Coast Guard's touring wartime revue. Limp musical with interesting talent. Alfred Drake, Sid Caesar, Janet Blair, Marc Platt, Jeff Donnell. Written by John Jacoby, Sarett Tobias, Decla Dunning, Barry Trivers; directed by Alfred E. Green; for Milton H. Bren / Columbia.

The Tartars
Italy 1960 105m Technicolor Totalscope
Lux (Riccardo Gualino)

Viking settlers on the Russian steppes fight Tartar invaders.
Action-packed comic strip.

d Richard Thorpe *ph* Amerigo Genarelli *m* Renzo Rossellini

Orson Welles, Victor Mature, Folco Lulli, Arnoldo Foa

Tarzan
The talkie *Tarzans* began with Johnny Weissmuller and tailed off from there. (See *Filmgoer's Companion* for the silents.) The 1932 version more or less followed the original Edgar Rice Burroughs novel, and all the MGM entries had a special vivid quality about them, but subsequently the productions, usually produced under the aegis of Sol Lesser, tailed off towards the standard of the TV series of the sixties starring Ron Ely.

1929: TARZAN THE TIGER (*qv*)

1932: TARZAN THE APE MAN** (MGM: Weissmuller with Maureen O'Sullivan: *d* W. S. Van Dyke: 99m)

Publicity line: 'Mothered by an ape—he knew the law of the jungle—to seize what he wanted!'

1933: TARZAN THE FEARLESS (*qv*)
1934: TARZAN AND HIS MATE*** (MGM: Weissmuller with Maureen O'Sullivan: *d* Cedric Gibbons: 105m)

'Certainly one of the funniest things you'll ever see.'—*Otis Ferguson*

1935: THE NEW ADVENTURES OF TARZAN (*qv*)

1936: TARZAN ESCAPES** (MGM: Weissmuller with Maureen O'Sullivan: *d* Richard Thorpe: 95m)
1938: TARZAN'S REVENGE (Sol Lesser: Glenn Morris: *d* D. Ross Lederman: 70m); TARZAN AND THE GREEN GODDESS (Principal: Herman Brix: *d* Edward Kull: 72m: largely a re-edit of NEW ADVENTURES)
1939: TARZAN FINDS A SON (MGM: Weissmuller with O'Sullivan: Richard Thorpe: 90m)
1941: TARZAN'S SECRET TREASURE (MGM: Weissmuller with O'Sullivan: *d* Richard Thorpe: 81m)
1942: TARZAN'S NEW YORK ADVENTURE (MGM: Weissmuller with O'Sullivan: *d* Richard Thorpe: 71m)
1943: TARZAN TRIUMPHS (RKO: Weissmuller: *d* William Thiele: 78m); TARZAN'S DESERT MYSTERY (RKO: Weissmuller: *d* William Thiele: 70m)
1945: TARZAN AND THE AMAZONS (RKO: Weissmuller: *d* Kurt Neumann: 76m)
1946: TARZAN AND THE LEOPARD WOMAN (RKO: Weissmuller: *d* Kurt Neumann: 72m)
1947: TARZAN AND THE HUNTRESS (RKO: Weissmuller: *d* Kurt Neumann: 72m)
1948: TARZAN AND THE MERMAIDS (RKO: *d* Robert Florey: Weissmuller: 68m)
1949: TARZAN'S MAGIC FOUNTAIN (RKO: Lex Barker: *d* Lee Sholem: 73m)
1950: TARZAN AND THE SLAVE GIRL (RKO: Lex Barker: *d* Lee Sholem: 74m)
1951: TARZAN'S PERIL (RKO: Lex Barker: *d* Byron Haskin: 79m)
1952: TARZAN'S SAVAGE FURY (RKO: Lex Barker: *d* Cy Endfield: 80m)
1953: TARZAN AND THE SHE-DEVIL (aka: *Tarzan Meets the Vampire*)
(RKO: Lex Barker: *d* Kurt Neumann: 76m)
1955: TARZAN'S HIDDEN JUNGLE (RKO: Gordon Scott: *d* Harold Schuster: 73m)
1957: TARZAN AND THE LOST SAFARI (colour) Solar: Gordon Scott: *d* Bruce Humberstone: 84m)
1958: TARZAN'S FIGHT FOR LIFE (colour) (MGM: Gordon Scott: *d* Bruce Humberstone: 86m)
1959: TARZAN'S GREATEST ADVENTURE (colour) (Solar: Gordon Scott: *d* John Guillermin: 90m)
1959: TARZAN THE APE MAN (colour: remake of the original story) (MGM: Denny Miller: *d* Joseph Newman: 82m)
1960: TARZAN THE MAGNIFICENT (colour) (Paramount: Gordon Scott: *d* Robert Day: 88m)
1962: TARZAN GOES TO INDIA (colour) (MGM: Jock Mahoney: *d* John Guillermin: 86m)
1963: TARZAN'S THREE CHALLENGES (colour) (MGM: Jock Mahoney: *d* Robert Day: 92m)
1966: TARZAN AND THE VALLEY OF GOLD (colour) (NatGen: Mike Henry: Robert Day: 90m)
1967: TARZAN AND THE GREAT RIVER (colour) (Paramount: Mike Henry: *d* Robert Day: 88m)
1968: TARZAN AND THE JUNGLE BOY (colour) (Paramount: Mike Henry: *d* Robert Day: 90m)
1981: TARZAN THE APE MAN (colour)
1983: GREYSTOKE
(MGM: Miles O'Keefe; *d* John Derek; 112m).
A debased version with the emphasis on the undressed Jane played by Bo Derek.

Publicity line: 'The most exciting pair in the jungle!'

1984: GREYSTOKE: THE LEGEND OF TARZAN, LORD OF THE APES (*qv*). A pretentious retelling of the original story.

Tarzan the Fearless
US 1933 bw serial: 15 eps

Tarzan rescues explorers from the lost city of Zar, God of the Jewelled Fingers. Lively serial version of a production also released as a feature. Buster Crabbe, Jacqueline Wells, E.

Alyn Warren, Edward Woods, Mischa Auer (as high priest). Directed by Robert Hill; for Principal.

Tarzan the Tiger
US 1929 bw serial: 10 eps

Tarzan rescues Jane from slave traders. Primitive talkie serial. Frank Merrill, Natalie Kingston, Lillian Worth, Al Ferguson. Directed by Henry McRae; for Universal.

'It's that rare kind of movie that lights the spark that lights the heart!'

Task Force
US 1949 116m bw (Technicolor sequences)
Warner (Jerry Wald)

An admiral about to retire recalls his struggle to promote the cause of aircraft carriers.
Stilted and long-drawn-out flagwaver with too much chat and action highlights borrowed from wartime newsreel.

wd Delmer Daves *ph* Robert Burks, Wilfrid M. Cline *m* Franz Waxman

Gary Cooper, Walter Brennan, Jane Wyatt, Wayne Morris, Julie London, Bruce Bennett, Stanley Ridges, Jack Holt

A Taste of Excitement
GB 1968 99m Eastmancolor
Trio Films (George Willoughby)

An English girl holidaying on the Riviera suspects that someone is trying to kill her.
Standard frightened lady / 'they won't believe me' mystery with enough twists to satisfy addicts.

w Brian Carton, Don Sharp, *novel* Waiting for a Tiger by Ben Healey *d* Don Sharp *ph* Paul Beeson *m* Keith Mansfield

Eva Renzi, David Buck, Peter Vaughan, Sophie Hardy, Paul Hubschmid, Kay Walsh

Taste of Fear**
GB 1961 82m bw
Columbia / Hammer (Jimmy Sangster)
US title: *Scream of Fear*

A crippled heiress visits her long-lost father and is haunted by his corpse.
Smartly tricked-out sub-Hitchcock screamer with sudden shocks among the Riviera settings and a plot which Hammer borrowed from *Les Diaboliques* and used again and again.

w Jimmy Sangster d Seth Holt ph Douglas Slocombe m Clifton Parker

Susan Strasberg, Ann Todd, Ronald Lewis, Christopher Lee, Leonard Sachs

'All those creaking shutters, flickering candles, wavering shadows and pianos playing in empty rooms still yield a tiny frisson.'—*Penelope Houston*

'It plays its particular brand of the three-card trick with ingenuity and without scruple.'—*The Times*

A Taste of Honey***
GB 1961 100m bw
British Lion / Bryanston / Woodfall (Tony Richardson)

Adventures of a pregnant Salford teenager, her sluttish mother, black lover and homosexual friend.
Fascinating offbeat comedy drama with memorable characters and sharply etched backgrounds.

w Shelagh Delaney, Tony Richardson, *play* Shelagh Delaney *d Tony Richardson ph Walter Lassally m* John Addison

Rita Tushingham, Dora Bryan, Murray Melvin, Robert Stephens, Paul Danquah

'Tart and lively around the edges and bitter at the core.'—*Peter John Dyer*

'Rich, full work, directed with an unerring sense of rightness.'—*New Yorker*

Taste the Blood of Dracula
GB 1969 95m Technicolor
Hammer (Aida Young)

A depraved peer involves three Victorian businessmen in the reactivation of Dracula.
Latterday vampire saga, initially lively but mainly dreary.

w John Elder *d* Peter Sasdy *ph* Arthur Grant *m* James Bernard

Christopher Lee, Geoffrey Keen, Gwen Watford, Linda Hayden, Peter Sallis, Anthony Corlan, John Carson, Ralph Bates

The Tattered Dress
US 1957 93m bw Cinemascope
U-I (Albert Zugsmith)

While conducting a murder defence, a criminal lawyer annoys a vindictive small-town sheriff, who plots revenge.
Silly melodrama which rapidly loses interest after a promising start.

w George Zuckerman *d* Jack Arnold *ph* Carl Guthrie *m* Frank Skinner

Jeff Chandler, Jack Carson, Jeanne Crain, Gail Russell, George Tobias, Edward Andrews, Philip Reed

'Every great love leaves its mark!'

Tattoo
US 1980 103m Technicolor
Joseph E. Levine (Robert F. Colesberry)

A mad tattooist kidnaps a cover girl and tattoos her all over before forcing her to have sex. She kills him.
And not before time.

w Joyce Bunuel *d* Bob Brooks *ph* Arthur Ornitz *m* Barry de Vorzon *pd* Stuart Wurtzel

Bruce Dern, Maud Adams, Leonard Frey, Rikke Borge

'*The Collector* crossed with *Ai No Corrida* . . . a sensational package for the eighties confected from ideas half remembered from other films.'—*Mark Lefanu, MFB*

Tawny Pipit*
GB 1944 85m bw
GFD / Two Cities (Bernard Miles)

The life of a village in wartime is disrupted when two rare birds nest in a local meadow.
Pleasant, thin little comedy, a precursor of the Ealing school.

w Bernard Miles, Charles Saunders *d* Bernard Miles, Charles Saunders *ph* Eric Cross *m* Noel Mewton-Wood

Bernard Miles, Rosamund John, Niall MacGinnis, Jean Gillie, Christopher Steele, Lucie Mannheim, Brefni O'Rourke, Marjorie Rhodes

'Almost unimaginably genteel.'—*James Agee*

'Not quite dry enough for the epicures nor sweet enough for the addicts.'—*C. A. Lejeune*

'Seldom does such a piece of unsophisticated charm and humour reach the screen.'—*New York Times*

Taxi!
US 1931 68m bw
Warner (Robert Lord)

Independent cab drivers defy a powerful trust.
Sassy comedy drama with plenty going on.

w Kubec Glasmon, John Bright, *play* The Blind Spot by Kenyon Nicholson *d* Roy del Ruth *ph* James Van Trees *md* Leo Forbstein

James Cagney, Loretta Young, George E. Stone, Guy Kibbee, David Landau, Leila Bennett, Matt McHugh

'As a deese, dem and dose, chip-on-the-shoulder, on-the-make example of young America the audience knows no better interpretation on the screen than that which Cagney gives it. The populace are now expectant of this player socking all and sundry including all the women in the cast.'—*Variety*

'A sordid but amusing observation on minor metropolitan endeavours.'—*Time*

Taxi
US 1952 77m bw
TCF (Samuel G. Engel)

A taxi driver helps a young mother find her husband, and falls for her himself.
Practised sentimental guff, Hollywoodized from the French film *Sans Laisser d'Adresse*.

w D. M. Marshman Jnr, Daniel Fuchs *d* Gregory Ratoff *ph* Milton Krasner *m* Leigh Harline

Dan Dailey, Constance Smith, Neva Patterson, Blanche Yurka, Walter Woolf King

The Taxi Dancer
US 1926 64m at 24 fps bw silent

A Virginia girl in the big city rises from dime-a-dance joints to the big time. Mildly suggestive star melodrama which promises more than it gives. Joan Crawford, Owen Moore, Douglas Gilmore, Marc McDermott, Gertrude Astor. Written by A. P. Younger and Robert Terry Shannon; directed by Harry Millarde; for MGM.

Taxi Driver**
US 1976 114m Metrocolor
Columbia / Italo–Judeo (Michael and Julia Philips)

A lonely Vietnam veteran becomes a New York taxi driver and allows the violence and squalor around him to explode in his mind.

The epitome of the sordid realism of the seventies, this unlovely but brilliantly made film haunts the mind and paints a most vivid picture of a hell on earth. Unfortunately the plot in the latter stages makes no sense.

w Paul Schraeder d Martin Scorsese ph Michael Chapman m Bernard Herrmann

Robert de Niro, Jodie Foster, Cybill Shepherd, Peter Boyle, Leonard Harris, Harvey Keitel

'I don't question the truth of this material. I question Scorsese's ability to lift it out of the movie gutters into which less truthful directors have trampled it.'—*Stanley Kauffmann*

† Schraeder says the story was modelled after the diaries of would-be assassin Arthur Bremer.

AAN: best picture; Bernard Herrmann; Robert de Niro; Jodie Foster

Taza, Son of Cochise
US 1954 79m Technicolor

Peace-loving Taza succeeds his dad and tries not to be influenced by Geronimo. Routine pro-Indian western. Rock Hudson (as Taza), Barbara Rush, Gregg Palmer, Bart Roberts, Morris Ankrum. Written by George Zuckerman and Gerald Drayson Adams; directed by Douglas Sirk; for Universal-International.

'Years from now, when you talk about this—and you will—be kind!'

Tea and Sympathy
US 1956 122m Metrocolor Cinemascope
MGM (Pandro S. Berman)

A sensitive teenage schoolboy is scorned by his tougher classmates, but his housemaster's wife takes him in hand . . .
Overblown and bowdlerized version of a quiet little Broadway play; impeccable production values, but no spark.

w Robert Anderson (and the Hays office), from his play *d* Vincente Minnelli *ph* John Alton *m* Adolph Deutsch

Deborah Kerr, *John Kerr*, Leif Erickson, Edward Andrews, Darryl Hickman

'Even the most daring story can be brought onto the screen when done with courage, honesty and good taste.'—*publicity*

'. . . mounted for the screen as if it were a precious *objet d'art* in danger from rioting but miraculously saved. Besides being archaic, the film is a prodigiously silly fable, pulling the realities with which it deals dishonestly, systematically out of whack.'—*Parker Tyler*

Tea for Two*
US 1950 97m Technicolor
Warner (William Jacobs)

A nearly bankrupt financier promises his niece 25,000 dollars for her new musical show if she can say no to every question for twenty-four hours.
Tinkly, quite amusing light musical which has little to do with *No No Nanette* on which it is allegedly based.

w Henry Clark *d* David Butler *ph* Wilfrid Cline *md* Ray Heindorf *ch* Le Roy Prinz

Doris Day, Gordon Macrae, Gene Nelson, Eve Arden, Billy de Wolfe, S. Z. Sakall, Bill Goodwin, Patrice Wymore

Teachers
US 1984 106m Metrocolor
MGM-UA (Aaron Russo)

A burnt-out teacher is drawn back to his ideas despite, or because of, apparent lunacy in the administration.
Wildly unconsidered black comedy which takes stabs at everything and hits nothing.

w W. R. McKinney *d* Arthur Hiller *ph* David M. Walsh *m* Sandy Gibson *pd* Richard MacDonald *ed* Don Zimmermann

Nick Nolte, JoBeth Williams, Judd Hirsch, Ralph Macchio, Richard Mulligan, Allen Garfield, Royal Dano

Teacher's Pet*
US 1958 120m bw Vistavision
Paramount / Perlberg–Seaton (William Perlberg)

A tough city editor falls for a lady professor of journalism and enrols as a student.
Overlong one-joke comedy which quickly reneges on its early promise; but the principals play up divertingly.

w Fay and Michael Kanin *d* George Seaton *ph* Haskell Boggs *m* Roy Webb

Clark Gable, Doris Day, Gig Young, Mamie Van Doren, Nick Adams

AAN: Fay and Michael Kanin; Gig Young

The Teahouse of the August Moon*
US 1956 123m Metrocolor Cinemascope
MGM (Jack Cummings)

Okinawa 1944: a wily interpreter helps American troops succumb to the oriental way of life.
Adequate, well-acted screen version of a Broadway comedy which succeeded largely because of its theatricality. A few good jokes remain.

w John Patrick, from his play *d* Daniel Mann *ph* John Alton *m* Saul Chaplin

Marlon Brando, Glenn Ford, Eddie Albert, *Paul Ford*, Michiko Kyo, Henry Morgan

The Teckman Mystery
GB 1954 90m bw
British Lion / London Films / Corona (Josef Somlo)

An author commissioned to write the biography of a dead airman finds him very much alive and his own life in danger.
Peripatetic spy story with the twists expected of this author; all quite enjoyable.

w Francis Durbridge, James Matthews, *BBC serial* Francis Durbridge *d* Wendy Toye *ph* Jack Hilyard *m* Clifton Parker

Margaret Leighton, John Justin, Michael Medwin, Meier Tzelniker, Roland Culver, George Coulouris, Raymond Huntley, Duncan Lamont

Teen Wolf
US 1985 91m United Color Lab Color

An ineffective college basketball player finds he is a hereditary werewolf, and in his altered form becomes a star. Bewilderingly silly teenage variation on a famous legend, good-natured but totally empty. Michael J. Fox, James Hampton, Scott Paulin, Susan Ursitti. Written by Joseph Loeb III, Matthew Weisman; directed by Rod Daniel; for Coleman-Rosenblatt / Atlantic Releasing.

Teenage Rebel
US 1956 94m bw Cinemascope
TCF (Charles Brackett)

A wealthy California woman is visited by her teenage daughter from a former marriage; the girl proceeds to make difficulties for everyone. The first film in black-and-white Cinemascope is a tedious drama of unreal people.

w Walter Reisch, Charles Brackett, *play* Edith Sommer *d* Edmund Goulding *ph* Joe MacDonald *m* Leigh Harline

Ginger Rogers, Michael Rennie, Mildred Natwick, Betty Lou Keim, Warren Berlinger, Louise Beavers, Irene Hervey

Teheran
GB 1947 86m bw

A correspondent in Iran foils an assassination plot. Low-key blood and thunder; passable time-filler. Derek Farr, Marta Labarr, Manning Whiley, John Slater, John Warwick. Written by Akos Tolnay and William Freshman; directed by William Freshman and Giacomo Gentilomo; for Pendennis. (US title: *The Plot to Kill Roosevelt*.)

'Your next phone call may be your last!'

Telefon*
US 1977 103m Metrocolor Panavision
MGM (James B. Harris)

A Russian agent is instructed to seek out and destroy a ring of hard liners who are opposing detente with the west.
Moderately watchable espionage capers with a slightly new twist.

w Peter Hyams, Stirling Silliphant, *novel* Walter Wager *d* Don Siegel *ph* Michael Butler *m* Lalo Schifrin

Charles Bronson, Lee Remick, Donald Pleasence, Tyne Daly, Alan Badel, Patrick Magee, Sheree North

Television Spy
US 1939 58m bw

Enemy agents compete for the secret of long-range television transmission. Watchable pocket thriller, with the hero and heroine getting acquainted only by television from a 3000-mile distance. William Henry, Judith Barrett, William Collier Snr, Anthony Quinn,

Richard Denning, John Eldredge. Written by Horace McCoy, William R. Lipman, Lillie Hayward; directed by Edward Dmytryk; for Paramount. 'It may move slowly, but it does avoid the absurdity that goes with the average film crack at television.'—*Variety*

Tell England
GB 1931 88m bw
US title: *The Battle of Gallipoli*
In 1914, school chums join up and mostly die at Gallipoli. Even the most patriotic audiences ended up roaring with laughter at this stiff-upper-lip charade. Carl Harbord, Fay Compton, Tony Bruce, Dennis Hoey, Gerald Rawlinson, Wally Patch. Written by Anthony Asquith, from the novel by Ernest Raymond; directed by Anthony Asquith and Gerald Barkas; for British Instructional. 'Not likely to bring in any money.'—*Variety*

Tell It to a Star
US 1945 67m bw
A cigarette girl in a Florida hotel aspires to be a vocalist. The plot sets the level: minor musical. Ruth Terry, Robert Livingston, Alan Mowbray, Franklin Pangborn, Isabel Randolph. Written by John K. Butler; directed by Frank McDonald; for Walter H. Goetz / Republic.

Tell It to the Judge
US 1949 87m bw
Columbia (Buddy Adler)
A female candidate for judicial honours is suddenly re-attracted to her divorced husband. Leaden farce, relying entirely on its stars.
w Nat Perrin, Devery Freeman, Roland Kibbee *d* Norman Foster *ph* Joseph Walker *m* Werner Heyman
Rosalind Russell, Robert Cummings, Gig Young, Marie McDonald, Harry Davenport

Tell It to the Marines
US 1926 75m at 24 fps bw silent
A marine sergeant has an eventful time during training and in the Philippines. Lively war action piece with a more or less straight role for its star. Lon Chaney, William Haines, Eleanor Boardman, Carmel Myers, Warner Oland. Written by Richard Schayer; directed by George Hill; for MGM.

Tell Me a Riddle
US 1980 90m CFI color
A dying old woman, long a recluse, is reconciled with her family. Adequate if not exciting treatment of a very downbeat subject. Lila Kedrova, Melvyn Douglas, Brooke Adams, Dolores Dorn, Lili Valenty, Zalman King. Written by Joyce Eliason and Alev Lytle, from the novel by Tillie Olsen; directed by Lee Grant; for Godmother / Filmways.

Tell Me That You Love Me, Junie Moon
US 1969 113m Technicolor
Paramount / Sigma (Otto Preminger)
A disfigured girl, a homosexual paraplegic and an introvert epileptic set up house together. Absurd tragicomedy which remains disturbingly icky in conception and execution.
w Marjorie Kellogg, from her novel *d* Otto Preminger *ph* Boris Kaufman *m* Philip Springer
Liza Minnelli, Ken Howard, Robert Moore, Kay Thompson, Leonard Frey, James Coco, Fred Williamson
'Like seeing a venerated senior citizen desperately trying to show he's in love with today by donning see-through clothes.'—*Michael Billington, Illustrated London News*
'It slushes us with sentimentality to the point past compassion.'—*Judith Crist*

Tell Me Tonight
GB / Germany 1932 91m bw
An Italian tenor falls in love with a Swiss mayor's daughter, but complicates matters by pretending to be someone else. Bi-lingual operetta, fondly remembered for its singing star. *Jan Kiepura*, Sonnie Hale, Magda Schneider, Edmund Gwenn, Athene Seyler. Written by John Orton; directed by Anatole Litvak; for Herman Fellner-Josef Somlo / Cine Alliance.
(US title: *Be Mine Tonight*.)

Tell No Tales**
US 1939 68m bw
MGM (Edward Chodorov)
A managing editor seeks a big scoop to save his newspaper, and solves a kidnap-murder case.
Intriguingly written and handled second feature, with excellent pace, performance and entertainment value.
w Lionel Houser d Leslie Fenton ph Joseph Ruttenberg *m* William Axt
Melvyn Douglas, Louise Platt, Gene Lockhart, Douglass Dumbrille, Zeffie Tilbury, Halliwell Hobbes
'Full of excellent detail, and the smallest part is a genuine character. Add these qualities to its pace and excitement and you have something well worth seeing.'—*Richard Mallett, Punch*

Tell Them Willie Boy is Here*
US 1969 97m Technicolor
Universal / Jennings Lang (Philip A. Waxman)
In 1909 an Indian turned cowboy comes up against old prejudices and is pursued into the desert after an accidental death.
Boringly predictable story of white man's guilt, very professionally made.
wd Abraham Polonsky, novel Willie Boy by Harry Lawton *ph Conrad Hall m* Dave Grusin
Robert Redford, Robert Blake, Katharine Ross, Susan Clark, Barry Sullivan, Charles McGraw, Charles Aidman, John Vernon

The Tempest
GB 1980 95m Eastmancolor
A punk version of Shakespeare's play; less horrendous than might have been supposed, but far from interesting in its own right. Heathcote Williams, Karl Johnson, Toyah Willcox, Peter Bull, Richard Warwick, Elisabeth Welch. Written and directed by Derek Jarman; photographed by Peter Middleton; music by Wavemaker; for Boyd's Company.

Tempest
Italy / France / Yugoslavia 1958 123m Technirama
(Paramount) Dino de Laurentiis / Gray / S. N Pathe / Bosnia
Adventures of a Russian ensign banished by Catherine the Great.
Expensive but sloppy epic which fails to generate much interest.
w Louis Peterson, Alberto Lattuada, Ivo Perelli, *novel* The Captain's Daughter by Alexander Pushkin *d* Alberto Lattuada *ph Aldo Tonti m* Piero Piccioni
Van Heflin, Geoffrey Horne, Silvana Mangano, Oscar Homolka, Viveca Lindfors, Robert Keith, Vittorio Gassman, Finlay Currie, Agnes Moorehead, Helmut Dantine, Laurence Naismith

'Most men dream their fantasies. Philip decided to live his!'
Tempest
US 1982 142m De Luxe
Columbia (Paul Mazursky)
An architect leaves his unfaithful wife and takes his daughter to live on a Greek island attended only by a half-witted shepherd.
Absurd attempt to update Shakespeare; any initial amusement quickly gives way to abject boredom.
w Paul Mazursky, Leon Capetanos *d* Paul Mazursky *ph* Don McAlpine *m* Stomu Yamashta *pd* Pato Guzman
John Cassavetes, Gena Rowlands, Susan Sarandon, Vittorio Gassman, Raul Julia, Jerry Hardin, Molly Ringwald, Paul Stewart
'An aura of dottiness hangs over it . . . the fact remains that it is handsomely visualized and, within the limits of the material, excellently played.'—*Tim Pulleine, MFB*

Temptation
US 1946 92m bw
Universal (Edward Small)
An archaeologist's wife takes to poisoning both her husband and her blackmailing lover.
Hoary Edwardian melodrama, unpersuasively restaged.
w Robert Thoeren, *novel* Bella Donna by Robert Hichens *d* Irving Pichel *ph* Lucien Ballard *m* Daniele Amfitheatrof
Merle Oberon, George Brent, Charles Korvin, Paul Lukas, Lenore Ulric, Arnold Moss, Ludwig Stossel, Gavin Muir, Ilka Gruning, André Charlot

Temptation Harbour
GB 1946 104m bw
ABP (Victor Skutesky)

A railway signalman finds and keeps stolen money.
Well-presented but boringly predictable melodrama with an overwrought leading performance set against yards of studio fog.

w Victor Skutesky, Frederic Gotfurt, Rodney Ackland, *novel* Newhaven/Dieppe by Georges Simenon *d* Lance Comfort

Robert Newton, Simone Simon, William Hartnell, Marcel Dalio, Margaret Barton, Edward Rigby, Joan Hopkins, Charles Victor, Kathleen Harrison

The Temptress*
US 1927 80m (24 fps) bw silent
MGM

An immoral woman drives men to disgrace, murder and suicide.
No-holds-barred melodrama which, being Garbo's second American film, fully confirmed her stardom.

w Dorothy Farnum *d* Mauritz Stiller, Fred Niblo

Greta Garbo, Antonio Moreno, Lionel Barrymore, Roy D'Arcy, Marc McDermott

'10'
US 1979 122m Metrocolor Panavision
Warner / Orion / Geoffrey (Blake Edwards, Tony Adams)

A sex-mad middle-aged composer marks his girls from one to ten according to their performance.
Randy farce which struck some, but not all, audiences as the funniest thing since sliced bread.

wd Blake Edwards *ph* Frank Stanley *m* Henry Mancini *pd* Rodger Maus

Dudley Moore, Julie Andrews, Bo Derek, Robert Webber, Dee Wallace, Sam Jones

Ten Cents a Dance
US 1931 75m bw

A dance hostess is desired by a rich man but marries a ne'er-do-well. Rubbishy story inspired by a then-popular song. Barbara Stanwyck, Monroe Owsley, Ricardo Cortez, Sally Blane, Blanche Friderici. Written by Jo Swerling; directed by Lionel Barrymore; for Columbia. 'It lacks the magic of fancy that makes for universal entertainment.'—*Variety*

'The mightiest dramatic spectacle of all the ages!'

The Ten Commandments**
US 1923 150m approx (24 fps) part Technicolor silent
Paramount / Famous Players–Lasky (Cecil B. de Mille)

Moses leads the Israelites into the promised land in modern San Francisco; a story of two brothers shows the power of prayer and truth. The two halves in fact are totally disconnected; but this is a de Mille spectacular and therefore beyond reproach, while as a Hollywood milestone it cannot be denied a place in the Hall of Fame.

w Jeanie MacPherson *d* Cecil B. de Mille *ph* Bert Glennon and others (*colour,* Ray Renahan)

Theodore Roberts, Richard Dix, Rod la Rocque, Edythe Chapman, Leatrice Joy, Nita Naldi

'It will last as long as the film on which it is recorded.'—*James R. Quirk, Photoplay*

The Ten Commandments*
US 1956 219m Technicolor Vistavision
Paramount / Cecil B. de Mille (Henry Wilcoxon)

The life of Moses and his leading of the Israelites to the Promised Land.
Popular but incredibly stilted and verbose bible-in-pictures spectacle. A very long haul along a monotonous route, with the director at his pedestrian worst.

w Aeneas Mackenzie, Jesse L. Lasky Jnr, Jack Gariss, Frederic M. Frank *d* Cecil B. de Mille *ph* Loyal Griggs *m* Elmer Bernstein

Charlton Heston, Yul Brynner, Edward G. Robinson, Anne Baxter, Nina Foch, Yvonne de Carlo, John Derek, H. B. Warner, Henry Wilcoxon, Judith Anderson, John Carradine, Douglass Dumbrille, Cedric Hardwicke, Martha Scott, Vincent Price, Debra Paget

'De Mille not only moulds religion into a set pattern of Hollywood conventions; he has also become an expert at making entertainment out of it.'—*Gordon Gow, Films and Filming*

'The result of all these stupendous efforts? Something roughly comparable to an eight-foot chorus girl—pretty well put together, but much too big and much too flashy. . . . What de Mille has really done is to throw sex and sand into the moviegoers' eyes for almost twice as long as anyone else has ever dared to.'—*Time*

'What a story it tells! What majesty it encompasses! What loves it unveils! What drama it unfolds!'—*publicity*

AAN: best picture; Loyal Griggs

Ten Days in Paris
GB 1939 82m bw
Columbia / Irving Asher (Jerome J. Jackson)
US titles: *Missing Ten Days / Spy in the Pantry*

An amnesiac wakes up in Paris and finds he has been involved in espionage activities.
Modest, quite likeable little comedy suspenser.

w John Meehan Jnr, James Curtis, *novel* The Disappearance of Roger Tremayne by Bruce Graeme *d* Tim Whelan *ph* Otto Kanturek *m* Miklos Rozsa

Rex Harrison, Karen Verne, Leo Genn, Joan Marion, Anthony Holles, John Abbott, Hay Petrie

Ten Days That Shook the World: see October

Ten Gentlemen from West Point**
US 1942 104m bw
TCF (William Perlberg)

Adventures in Indian territory, and back at West Point, of the first recruits to that military academy in the early 1800s.
Likeable mixture of comedy and flagwaving adventure, with excellent production values and a dominating performance.

w Richard Maibaum, George Seaton *d* Henry Hathaway *ph* Leon Shamroy *m* Alfred Newman

Laird Cregar, George Montgomery, Maureen O'Hara, John Sutton, Shepperd Strudwick, Victor Francen, Harry Davenport, Ward Bond, Douglass Dumbrille, Ralph Byrd, Louis Jean Heydt

AAN: Leon Shamroy

Ten Little Indians*
GB 1966 91m bw
Tenlit (Harry Alan Towers)

Ten people, including two servants invited to a remote house in the Austrian Alps are murdered one by one.
Fair copy of a classic whodunnit.

w Peter Yeldham, Harry Alan Towers, *novel* Agatha Christie *d* George Pollock *ph* Ernest Steward *m* Malcolm Lockyer

Wilfrid Hyde White, Dennis Price, Stanley Holloway, Leo Genn, Shirley Eaton, Hugh O'Brian, Daliah Lavi, Fabian, Mario Adorf, Marianne Hoppe

† Made also in 1945 and 1975, as *And Then There Were None* (qv).

Ten North Frederick*
US 1958 102m bw Cinemascope
TCF (Charles Brackett)

At the funeral of a local politico, his family and friends think back to the events of his life.
Small beer, but a generally adult and entertaining family drama despite a miscast lead.

wd Philip Dunne, novel John O'Hara *ph* Joe MacDonald *m* Leigh Harline

Gary Cooper, Geraldine Fitzgerald, Diane Varsi, Stuart Whitman, Suzy Parker, Tom Tully, Ray Stricklyn, John Emery

Ten Rillington Place*
GB 1970 111m Eastmancolor
Columbia / Filmways (Basil Appleby)

An account of London's sordid Christie murders of the forties.
Agreeably seedy reconstruction of a *cause célèbre*, carefully built around the star part of a murderous aberrant landlord. Too long, however, and finally too lacking in detail.

w Clive Exton, *book* Ludovic Kennedy *d* Richard Fleischer *ph* Denys Coop *m* Johnny Dankworth

Richard Attenborough, *John Hurt*, Judy Geeson, Pat Heywood, Isobel Black, Geoffrey Chater, André Morell, Robert Hardy

Ten Seconds to Hell
US 1959 93m bw
Hammer / Seven Arts (Michael Carreras)

Bomb disposal experts in post-war Berlin quarrel over a girl.
Boring, harsh, hollow melodrama, so artificially constructed that no one can possibly care who gets exploded.

w Robert Aldrich, Teddi Sherman, *novel* The Phoenix by Lawrence Bachmann *d* Robert Aldrich *ph* Ernest Laszlo *m* Kenneth V. Jones

Jack Palance, Jeff Chandler, Martine Carol, Robert Cornthwaite, Dave Willock, Wesley Addy

Ten Tall Men
US 1951 97m Technicolor
Columbia / Norma (Harold Hecht)

A Foreign Legion patrol prevents a Riff attack.
Comic strip adventures, efficiently handled.

w Roland Kibbee, Frank Davis *d* Willis Goldbeck *ph* William Snyder *m* David Buttolph

Burt Lancaster, Gilbert Roland, Kieron Moore, John Dehner, Jody Lawrance, George Tobias, Mike Mazurki

10.30 pm Summer
US / Spain 1966 85m Technicolor
UA / Jorill / Argos (Jules Dassin, Anatole Litvak)

The neurotic Greek wife of an Englishman travelling in Spain becomes obsessed with a murderer on the run.
Preposterously overwrought romantic melodrama.

w Jules Dassin, Marguerite Duras, *novel* Marguerite Duras *d* Jules Dassin *ph* Gabor Pogany *m* Christobel Hallfter

Peter Finch, Melina Mercouri, Romy Schneider, Julian Mateos

Ten Thousand Bedrooms
US 1956 114m Metrocolor Cinemascope
MGM (Joe Pasternak)

An American millionaire finds romance when he buys a Rome hotel.
Old-fashioned, unfunny comedy sadly lacking pace and style.

w Laslo Vadnay, Art Cohn, William Ludwig, Leonard Spiegelgass *d* Richard Thorpe *ph* Robert Bronner *m* George Stoll *songs* Nicholas Brodszky, Sammy Cahn

Dean Martin, Eva Bartok, Anna Maria Alberghetti, Walter Slezak, Paul Henreid, Jules Munchin, Marcel Dalio

Ten to Midnight
US 1983 102m Metrocolor

A sexual deficient kills girls who reject him, but is tracked down and shot by a cop who is the father of one of the threatened girls.
Crude and rather nasty vigilante melodrama. Charles Bronson, Lisa Eilbacher, Andrew Stevens, Gene Davis, Geoffrey Lewis. Written by William Roberts; directed by J. Lee Thompson; for Golan-Globus. 'Too slow, slick and semi-respectable to live down to its inspirations.'—*Kim Newman, MFB*

Ten Wanted Men
US 1955 80m Technicolor

A rancher and his family are besieged by bandits in a lady's house. Rather elementary but efficient and good-looking western programmer. Randolph Scott, Jocelyn Brando, Richard Boone, Alfonso Bedoya, Donna Martell, Skip Homeier. Written by Kenneth Gamet, from a story by Irving Ravetch and Harriet Frank Jnr; directed by Bruce Humberstone; for Harry Joe Brown / Columbia.

Ten Who Dared
US 1960 92m Technicolor
Walt Disney (James Algar)

In 1869 a scientific expedition sets out to chart the Colorado River.
Tedious and unconvincing adventures.

w Lawrence E. Watkin, from the journal of Major John Wesley Powell *d* William Beaudine *ph* Gordon Avil *m* Oliver Wallace

Brian Keith, John Beal, James Drury, R. G. Armstrong, Ben Johnson, L. Q. Jones

The Tenant
France 1976 126m Eastmancolor
Paramount / Marianne (Andrew Braunsberg)
Original title: *Le Locataire*

A displaced person becomes convinced that his fellow lodgers are out to murder him.
Rather like a male version of the same director's *Repulsion*, this wearisome case history shows the total dissipation of whatever talent he once had.

w Gerard Brach, Roman Polanski, *novel* Roland Topor *d* Roman Polanski *ph* Sven Nykvist *m* Philippe Sarde

Roman Polanski, Melvyn Douglas, Isabelle Adjani, Shelley Winters, Jo Van Fleet, Lila Kedrova, Claude Dauphin

'It does not seem to have been designed as self-parody, but it certainly comes across that way.'—*Janet Maslin, Newsweek*

'A long-winded exercise in tedium and morbidity.'—*Kevin Thomas, LA Times*

Tender Comrade
US 1943 101m bw
RKO (David Hempstead)

Lady welders whose husbands are fighting men keep their chins up during World War II.
Dim tearjerker.

w Dalton Trumbo *d* Edward Dmytryk *ph* Russell Metty *m* Leigh Harline

Ginger Rogers, Robert Ryan, Ruth Hussey, Patricia Collinge, Mady Christians, Kim Hunter, Jane Darwell

Tender Is the Night*
US 1961 146m De Luxe Cinemascope
TCF (Henry T. Weinstein)

Adventures around Europe between the wars of a rich American psychiatrist who has married his patient.
Patchy, fairly literal transcription of a patently unfilmable novel about defiantly unreal people in what would now be the jet set. About half the result is superficially entertaining.

w Ivan Moffat, *novel* F. Scott Fitzgerald *d* Henry King *ph* Leon Shamroy *m* Bernard Herrmann

Jennifer Jones, Jason Robards Jnr, *Joan Fontaine, Tom Ewell*, Cesare Danova, Jill St John, Paul Lukas

AAN: title song (*m* Sammy Fain, *ly* Paul Francis Webster)

Tender Mercies*
US 1982 92m Movielab
EMI / Antron Media (Horton Foote, Robert Duvall)

An ex-alcoholic resumes his former career as a country and western singer.
Quiet, downbeat character study with scenic Texas backgrounds. Mildly impressive, but no real reason to go to the cinema.

w Horton Foote *d* Bruce Beresford *ph* Russell Boyd *m* George Dreyfus

Robert Duvall (who sang his own songs), Tess Harper, Betty Buckley, Wilford Brimley, Ellen Barkin

'It conceals its deficiencies behind heartfelt performances . . . the construction is so rickety that it seems at times entirely to lack a plot.'—*Kim Newman, MFB*

AA: Robert Duvall; Horton Foote
AAN: best picture; Bruce Beresford; song 'Over You' (Austin Roberts, Bobby Hart)

The Tender Trap*
US 1955 111m Eastmancolor Cinemascope
MGM (Lawrence Weingarten)

A smart New York agent has a way with women which annoys his friend; but Casanova gets his come-uppance when he sets his sights on an apparently naïve young actress.
Thin comedy with agreeable moments, not helped by the wide screen.

w Julius J. Epstein, *play* Max Shulman, Robert Paul Smith *d* Charles Walters *ph* Paul Vogel *m* Jeff Alexander

Frank Sinatra, Debbie Reynolds, David Wayne, Celeste Holm, Lola Albright, Carolyn Jones

AAN: title song (*m* James Van Heusen, *ly* Sammy Cahn)

The Tenderfoot
US 1931 73m bw

Adventures of a cowboy in New York.
Slapstick version of George Kaufman's often-remade comedy *The Butter and Egg Man*; not remarkable in any way. Joe E. Brown, Ginger Rogers, Lew Cody, Vivian Oakland, Robert Greig. Written by Arthur Caesar, Monty Banks, Earl Baldwin; directed by Ray Enright; for Warners. 'It ought to do well where they like lowdown comedy.'—*Variety*

Tenderloin
US 1928 88m bw

A dancer is accused of stealing a fortune and finds gangsters suddenly interested in her.

Primitive part-talkie (15 minutes of dialogue), unspeakably hammy to listen to though visually it had some inventiveness. Dolores Costello, Conrad Nagel, Mitchell Lewis, George E. Stone, Dan Wolheim. Written by Edward T. Lowe, from a story by Darryl Zanuck; directed by Michael Curtiz; for Warner.

Tendre Ennemie*
France 1938 66m bw

A woman's three dead lovers return to prevent her daughter from making a romantic mistake. Decorative whimsy which is not among its director's best, but mildly amusing none the less. Simone Berriau, Jacqueline Daix, Georges Vitray, Marc Valbel, Lucien Nat. Written by Max Ophuls, Kurt Alexander, from the play L'Ennemie by A. P. Antoine; directed by *Max Ophuls*; for World Pictures.
'Story is sacrificed for camera angles . . . weak even for the arties.'—*Variety*

Tennessee Champ
US 1954 75m Anscocolor

The Lord helps a religious boxer to win a few fights. Tedious sentimental square ring melodrama. Earl Holliman, Dewey Martin, Keenan Wynn, Shelley Winters, Yvette Dugay. Written by Art Cohn; directed by Fred M. Wilcox; for MGM.

Tennessee Johnson*
US 1943 102m bw
MGM (J. Walter Ruben)
GB title: *The Man on America's Conscience*

The rise and the problems of President Andrew Johnson.
Sincere, straightforward, well-produced historical drama which failed to set the Thames—or the Hudson—on fire.

w John Balderston, Wells Root *d* William Dieterle *ph* Harold Rosson *m* Herbert Stothart

Van Heflin, Ruth Hussey, Lionel Barrymore, Marjorie Main, Regis Toomey, Montagu Love, Porter Hall, Charles Dingle, J. Edward Bromberg

'Dieterle's customary high-minded, high-polished mélange of heavy touches and intelligent performances.'—*James Agee*

Tennessee's Partner
US 1955 87m Technicolor Superscope

A gambling queen and a tenderfoot are involved in a double cross which leads to murder. Predictable western from a story by Bret Harte. Ronald Reagan, John Payne, Rhonda Fleming, Colleen Gray. Written by Milton Krims, D. D. Beauchamp, Graham Baker and Teddi Sherman; directed by Allan Dwan; for RKO.

Tension
US 1950 91m bw
MGM (Robert Sisk)

A chemist plans the perfect murder of his wife's lover, loses his nerve, then finds himself suspected when the man is murdered after all.
Disappointing suspenser which starts well but outstays its welcome.

w Allen Rivkin *d* John Berry *ph* Harry Stradling *m* André Previn

Richard Basehart, Audrey Totter, Barry Sullivan, Cyd Charisse, Lloyd Gough, Tom d'Andrea

Tension at Table Rock
US 1956 93m Technicolor

When a stagecoach station owner is killed, a gunman takes care of his small son and at the same time rids a town of outlaws. All the clichés are in this one, fairly neatly amassed in corners labelled *High Noon, Hondo* and *Shane*. Written by Winston Miller, from a novel by Frank Gruber; directed by Charles Marquis Warren; for RKO.

Tentacles
Italy 1976 102m Technicolor Technovision
Esse Cinematografica (E. F. Doria)

A deadly menace which leaves its victims as skeletons washed up on the California beach turns out to be a giant octopus . . .
Dreary *Jaws* rehash. Sadly there is no element of spoofing, it's all deadly serious.

w Jerome Max, Tito Carpi, Steve Carabatsos, Sonia Molteni *d* Oliver Hellman (Sonia Assonitis) *ph* Roberto d'Ettore Piazzoli *m* S. W. Cipriani

Shelley Winters, John Huston, Bo Hopkins, Henry Fonda, Claude Akins, Cesare Danova, Delia Boccardo

Tenth Avenue Angel
US 1948 74m bw
MGM (Ralph Wheelwright)

The little daughter of poor parents loses her faith in life.
Icky sentimental piece for a waning child star.

w Angna Enters, Craig Rice, Harry Ruskin, Eleanore Griffin *d* Roy Rowland *ph* Robert Surtees *m* Rudolph G. Kopp

Margaret O'Brien, Angela Lansbury, George Murphy, Phyllis Thaxter, Rhys Williams, Warner Anderson, Audrey Totter, Connie Gilchrist

The Tenth Man
GB 1936 68m bw

A wife shows faith in her husband even though she knows him to be a crook. Stock film version of one of Somerset Maugham's less pungent plays. John Lodge, Antoinette Cellier, Aileen Marson, Clifford Evans, George Graves. Written by Geoffrey Kerr, Dudley Leslie, Marjorie Deans and Jack Davies; directed by Brian Desmond Hurst; for BIP.

The Tenth Victim
Italy / France 1965 92m Technicolor
Avco / CC Champion / Concordia (Carlo Ponti)

In the 21st century murder is legalized to avoid birth control and war, and ten killings bring a fabulous prize.
Science fiction satire which just about gets by.

w Tonina Guerra, Giorgio Salvioni, Ennio Flaiano, Elio Petri, *story* The Seventh Victim by Robert Sheckley *d* Elio Petri *ph* Gianni di Venanzo *m* Piero Piccioni

Ursula Andress, Marcello Mastroianni, Elsa Martinelli, Massimo Serato

Teresa**
US 1951 101m bw
MGM (Arthur M. Loew)

A soldier with mother problems brings home an Italian bride.
Careful, sensitive, intelligent variation on a problem frequently considered by films of this period (*Frieda, Fräulein, Japanese War Bride*).

w Stewart Stern d Fred Zinnemann
ph William J. Miller *m* Louis Applebaum

Pier Angeli, John Ericson, Patricia Collinge, Richard Bishop, Peggy Ann Garner, Ralph Meeker, Bill Mauldin

AAN: original story (Arthur Hayes, Stewart Stern)

Term of Trial*
GB 1962 130m bw
Romulus (James Woolf)

An unsuccessful schoolmaster is accused of rape by a nymphomaniac schoolgirl he has scorned.
Rather flabby 'adult' drama, too schematic to be really interesting despite the best that acting can do.

wd Peter Glenville, *novel* The Burden of Proof by James Barlow *ph* Oswald Morris *m* Jean-Michel Demase *ad* Antony Woolard

Laurence Olivier, Sarah Miles, Simone Signoret, Hugh Griffith, Terence Stamp, Roland Culver, Frank Pettingell, Thora Hird, Dudley Foster, Norman Bird

The Terminator*
US 1984 108m CFI colour
Orion / Hemdale / Pacific Western (Gale Anne Hurd)

A man from the future is sent back on a mission of extermination.
Slick rather nasty but undeniably compelling comic book adventures.

w James Cameron, Gale Anne Hurd *d* James Cameron *ph* Adam Greenberg *m* Brad Fiedel *ed* Mark Goldblatt

Arnold Schwarzenegger, Michael Biehn, Linda Hamilton, Paul Winfield, Rick Rossovich, Lance Henriksen

Terminus***
GB 1961 30m bw
British Transport Films

Twenty-four hours in the life of Waterloo Station.
An excellent 'fly-on-the-wall' documentary which launched the feature film career of its director and is still both funny and moving.

wd John Schlesinger *ph* Ken Phipps, Robert Paynter *m* Ron Grainer

Terms of Endearment**
US 1983 132m Metrocolor
Paramount (James L. Brooks)

An eccentric widow fends off suitors while interfering with her daughter's marriage; but all is forgiven when the daughter dies.
This shapeless film is little more than an excuse for actors and writer to show off, which they do to great excess; but parts of it are entertaining enough and it certainly impressed the Academy Award committee.

w,d James L. Brooks, *novel* Larry McMurtry *ph* Andrzej Bartkowiak *m* Michael Gore *pd* Polly Platt

Shirley Maclaine, *Jack Nicholson*, *Debra Winger*, Danny DeVito, Jeff Daniels, John Lithgow

'An outsize sitcom and a crassly constructed slice of anti-feminism that contrives to rub liberal amounts of soap in the viewer's eyes.'—*Sight and Sound*

AA: best picture; Shirley Maclaine; Jack Nicholson; direction; adaptation
AAN: John Lithgow; editing (Richard Marks); Michael Gore; art direction; Debra Winger

'There isn't a thing I would change.'—*Roger Ebert*

La Terra Trema*
Italy 1948 160m bw
Universalia

The life of a Sicilian fisherman and his family.
Seriously intended, carefully composed semi-documentary stressing the economic problems of the simple life. A commercial disaster: even the Italians couldn't understand the accents of the local actors.

wd Luchino Visconti *ph* G. R. Aldo *m* Luchino Visconti, Willy Ferrero

† The cast was drawn from the inhabitants of Aci Trezza, Sicily.

A Terrible Beauty
GB 1960 90m bw
UA / Raymond Stross
US title: *Night Fighters*

In a north Irish village, the IRA revive their activities on the outbreak of World War II.
Heavily Oirish melodrama with a muddled message.

w Robert Wright Campbell, *novel* Arthur Roth *d* Tay Garnett *ph* Stephen Dade *m* Cedric Thorpe Davie

Robert Mitchum, Anne Heywood, Dan O'Herlihy, Cyril Cusack, Richard Harris, Marianne Benet

The Terror
US 1928 82m approx bw
Warner

A mysterious killer lurks in the cellars of a country house.
Primitive talkie which attempted a few new styles but showed that more were needed, also that some silent actors could not make the transfer.

w Harvey Gates, *novel* and *play* Edgar Wallace *d* Roy del Ruth *ph* Barney McGill

May McAvoy, Edward Everett Horton, Louise Fazenda, Alec B. Francis, John Miljan, Frank Austin

'The only terrible thing about this talkie Terror is its unnatural slowness . . . the characters speak as if they were dictating important letters.'—*A. P. Herbert, Punch*

† The first film without a single subtitle: all the credits were spoken.
†† *Return of the Terror* (US 1934) has little to do with it.

The Terror
GB 1938 73m bw

Stilted remake of the above. Wilfrid Lawson, Arthur Wontner, Alastair Sim, Linden Travers, Bernard Lee, Henry Oscar. Written by William Freshman; directed by Richard Bird, for Associated British.

The Terror
US 1963 81m Pathecolor
AIP / Filmgroup (Roger Corman, Francis Ford Coppola)

A baron lives for twenty years in a creepy castle, mourning the death of his wife . . .
Shoddy horror improvised over a weekend on the set of *The Raven*. It looks it.

w Leo Gordon, Jack Hill *d* Roger Corman *ph* John Nickolaus *m* Ronald Stein

Boris Karloff, Jack Nicholson, Sandra Knight, Dorothy Neumann

Terror Aboard
US 1933 70m bw

Gruesome murders occur during a pleasure cruise. Fair murder mystery. Charles Ruggles, John Halliday, Shirley Grey, Neil Hamilton, Verree Teasdale, Jack La Rue. Written by Harvey Thew and Manuel Seff; directed by Paul Sloane; for Paramount.

Terror by Night*
US 1946 60m bw
Universal (Howard Benedict)

Sherlock Holmes recovers a stolen jewel and solves a murder or two aboard a speeding train.
An amusing entry in the modernized series despite some bad support acting and hilarious interposed shots of the supposed scenery between London and Edinburgh.

w Frank Gruber *d* Roy William Neill *ph* Maury Gertsman *m* Hans Salter

Basil Rathbone, Nigel Bruce, Dennis Hoey, Alan Mowbray, Renee Godfrey, Bill Bevan, Mary Forbes, Frederic Worlock

Terror in a Texas Town*
US 1958 81m bw
UA / Frank N. Seltzer

A Swedish seaman arrives in a small western town and avenges the death of his brother.
Stylish second feature western, a genuine sleeper which holds the interest throughout.

w Ben L. Perry *d Joseph H. Lewis* *ph Ray Rennahan* *m* Gerald Fried

Sterling Hayden, Sebastian Cabot, Carol Kelly, Eugene Martin, Ned Young

Terror in the Aisles
US 1984 82m CFI color

A compilation of fragments from mainly shock films, of no great interest even to film buffs because in most cases the scenes are wrenched out of context to fit a fatuous commentary. Written by Margery Doppelt; directed by Andrew Kuehn; for TEM / Kaleidoscope / Universal.

Terror in the Haunted House
US 1958 81m bw

A bride finds that her honeymoon mansion is one about which she has been having recurring nightmares. The plot has everything, even an axe murderer, but the treatment is soporific. Gerald Mohr, Cathy O'Donnell, William Ching, John Qualen, Barry Bernard. Written by Robert C. Dennis; directed by Harold Daniels; for Howco. (Alternative title: *My World Dies Screaming*.)

Terror in the Wax Museum
US 1973 94m De Luxe
Bing Crosby Productions / Fenady Associates (Andrew J. Fenady)

In Victorian London a waxworks owner is murdered . . .
Cheaply produced murder mystery (even the waxworks can't stand still) with horror asides and a cast of elderly hams.

w Jameson Brewer *d* George Fenady *ph* William Jurgensen *m* George Duning

Ray Milland, Broderick Crawford, Elsa Lanchester, Louis Hayward, John Carradine, Shani Wallis, Maurice Evans, Patric Knowles

'Drug-crazed assassins carrying out their hate-filled ritual murders!'

The Terror of the Tongs
GB 1960 79m Technicolor
Hammer / Merlin (Kenneth Hyman)

In 1910 Hong Kong a merchant avenges the death of his daughter at the hands of a villainous secret society.
Gory melodrama with dollops of screams, torture and vaguely orgiastic goings-on.

w Jimmy Sangster *d* Anthony Bushell *ph* Arthur Grant *m* James Bernard

Geoffrey Toone, Christopher Lee, Yvonne Monlaur, Brian Worth, Richard Leech

Terror Train
Canada 1980 97m De Luxe

Participants in a wild party aboard a train are decimated by a mysterious psychotic. Shocks and blood in the Carpenter tradition, adequately mounted. Ben Johnson, Jamie Lee Curtis, David Copperfield, Hart Bochner. Written by T. Y. Drake; directed by Roger Spottiswoode; for Astral.

TERMS OF ENDEARMENT. Superior soap opera, Hollywood-style. Debra Winger embraces Oscar-winner Shirley Maclaine.

Terry and the Pirates
US 1940 bw serial: 15 eps

The son of an American archaeologist in Asia fights Fang and the Tiger Men. Colourful nonsense for the kiddies. William Tracy, Granville Owen, Joyce Bryan, Allen Jung. Directed by James W. Horne; for Columbia.

The Terry Fox Story
Canada 1983 97m colour

A young man dying of cancer has a leg amputated, but still runs across Canada in aid of research. True it may be, but dramatically this is a one-note film with endless pretty pictures of countryside and in the foreground signs of failing health. Eric Fryer, Robert Duvall, Christopher Makepeace, Rosalind Chao. Written by Edward Hume; directed by Ralph L. Thomas; for Robert Cooper / CTV.

Terry of the Times
US 1930 bw serial: 10 eps

The son of a newspaper publisher overthrows a criminal league called The Mystic Mendicants. Early talkie serial which fulfilled its purpose. Reed Howes, Lotus Thompson, Sheldon Lewis, John Oscar, Will Hays. Directed by Henry McRae; for Universal.

Tess*
France-GB 1979 180m colour
Renn-Burrill (Claude Berri)

A peasant girl tries to prove her noble heritage but finds herself with an illegitimate child.
Solid, unexciting version of a classic Wessex novel; a hard sell for 1980 audiences.

w Roman Polanski, Gerard Brach, John Brownjohn *novel* Tess of the D'Urbervilles by Thomas Hardy *d* Roman Polanski
ph Geoffrey Unsworth, Ghislain Cloquet
m Philippe Sarde *pd* Pierre Guffroy

Nastassja Kinski, Leigh Lawson, Peter Firth, John Collin, David Markham, Richard Pearson

'It emerges without a hint of what might have drawn Polanski to the material.'—*Sight and Sound*

AA: Geoffrey Unsworth, Ghislain Cloquet; art direction (Pierre Guffroy, Jack Stevens); costume design (Anthony Powell)
AAN: best film; Roman Polanski; Philippe Sarde
BFA: best photography

Tess of the Storm Country
US 1932 80m bw
Fox

A retired sea captain's daughter loves the lord of the manor.
Antiquated tushery first filmed as a Mary Pickford silent.

w S. N. Behrman, Sonya Levien, Rupert Hughes, *novel* Grace Miller White *d* Alfred Santell *ph* Hal Mohr

Janet Gaynor, Charles Farrell, Dudley Digges, June Clyde, George Meeker

Test Pilot**
US 1938 118m bw
MGM (Louis D. Lighton)

A brilliant but unpredictable test pilot is helped by his wife and his self-sacrificing friend.
A big box-office star vehicle of its time, still interesting as a highly efficient product.

w Waldemar Young, Vincent Lawrence, *story* Frank Wead *d Victor Fleming* *ph* Ray June
m Franz Waxman

Clark Gable, Myrna Loy, Spencer Tracy, Lionel Barrymore, Samuel S. Hinds, Marjorie Main, Gloria Holden

'B.o. potential of above-average calibre . . . could have been cut 10–15 minutes without spoiling.'—*Variety*

'The picture is so noisy with sure-fire elements—box office cast, violent excitement, glycerine tears and such—that it may be hard to keep the ear attuned to the quieter, more authentically human things in it.'—*James Shelley Hamilton*

AAN: best picture; Frank Wead

Testament*
US 1983 90m CFI

A small California town is hit by a nuclear attack. Probably better than the TV movie *The Day After*, this was less well publicized and therefore lost out. *Jane Alexander*, William Devane, Ross Harris, Roxana Zal, Lukas Haas, Lilia Skala, Leon Ames. Written by John Sacret Young from a story by Carol Amen; directed by Lynne Littman; for Entertainment Events / American Playhouse. 'After thirty years of learning to live with the Bomb, we still lack ways of conceiving the Unthinkable.'—*Sheila Johnston, MFB*

AAN: Jane Alexander

Le Testament d'Orphée*
France 1959 83m bw
Editions Cinégraphiques (Jean Thullier)
aka: *The Testament of Orpheus*

The poet, as an 18th-century man, dies, enters space time, is revived, and seeks his identity. Rather like a melancholy madman's *Alice in Wonderland*, this bizarre jumble has its fascinations but misses by a mile the arresting qualities of *Orphée*.

wd Jean Cocteau *ph* Roland Pointoizeau
m Georges Auric and others

Jean Cocteau, Edouard Dermithe, Maria Casarès, François Périer, Henri Crémieux, Yul Brynner, Jean-Pierre Léaud, Daniel Gélin, Jean Marais, Pablo Picasso, Charles Aznavour

The Testament of Dr Mabuse**
Germany 1933 122m bw
Nero (Fritz Lang)

A sequel to *Dr Mabuse the Gambler*: the criminal mastermind dies in an asylum, and his assistant takes over his identity.
Fast-moving penny dreadful, alleged by its director to be a denouncing of the doctrines of Hitler, but showing little evidence of being more than a very slick entertainment.

w Thea Von Harbou, Fritz Lang *d Fritz Lang* *ph* Fritz Arno Wagner *m* Hans Erdmann *ad Karl Vollbrecht, Emil Hassler*

Rudolf Klein-Rogge, Otto Wernicke, Gustav Diesl

† On arrival in America Lang claimed that 'slogans of the Third Reich have been put into the mouths of criminals in the film'. Yet his wife, who co-scripted it, stayed behind as a confirmed Nazi.

Tevya the Milkman*
US 1939 93m bw

A Russian village milkman watches with awe as the pogroms begin to affect his people. One of the best Yiddish films with the best Yiddish actor, this pleasing comedy-drama was the basis for the musical *Fiddler on the Roof*. *Maurice Schwarz*, Miriam Riselle, Rebecca Weintraub, Paula Lubelska. Written and directed by Maurice Schwarz, from a story by Sholem Aleichem; for Henry Ziskin.

Tex Granger
US 1948 bw serial: 15 eps

A wandering western hero buys a newspaper and vanquishes various villains. Unremarkable sagebrush serial. Robert Kellard, Peggy Stewart, Buzz Henry, Smith Ballew, I. Stanford Jolley. Directed by Derwin Abrahams; for Columbia.

The Texan
US 1930 79m bw
Paramount (Hector Turnbull)

The Llano Kid absolves his bandit past.
Early sound western, an interesting curiosity.

w Daniel Nathan Rufin, *story* The Double-Dyed Deceiver by O. Henry *d* John Cromwell *ph* Victor Milner

Gary Cooper, Fay Wray, Emma Dunn, Oscar Apfel

'Few westerns are as well made and rate as high in every particular.'—*Variety*

'Love and glory on America's last frontier!'
The Texans
US 1938 92m bw
Paramount (Lucien Hubbard)

Problems of the post-Civil War years include new railroads, the Ku Klux Klan, and the new cattle drive routes.
Formula western with fairly well staged excitements backing a routine romantic triangle.

w Bertram Millhauser, Paul Sloane, William Wister Haines *d* James Hogan *ph* Theodor Sparkuhl *m* Gerard Carbonara

Joan Bennett, Randolph Scott, May Robson, Walter Brennan, Robert Cummings, Raymond Halton, Robert Barrat, Francis Ford

'Enough sweep and thrills to justify generally good business.'—*Variety*

Texas
US 1941 94m bw (released in sepia)
Columbia (Sam Bischoff)

Two veteran Civil War southerners head for Texas to set up a cattle business.
Western vehicle for two young stars, now very ordinary-looking.

w Horace McCoy, Lewis Meltzer, Michael Blankfort *d* George Marshall *ph* George Meehan

William Holden, Glenn Ford, Claire Trevor, George Bancroft, Edgar Buchanan, Don Beddoe, Andrew Tombes, Addison Richards

'While spoofing a little along the way, it observes the etiquette and tradition of an accepted cinema form. It has rough riding, cattle rustling, shooting and a story that leaves out only the Indian raid and the rescue by the US Cavalry.'—*Christian Science Monitor*

Texas across the River
US 1966 101m Techniscope
Universal (Harry Keller)

A Texan, an Indian and a Spanish nobleman on the run from jealous rivals have various adventures.
Sloppy western which seems to have had jokes added when someone realized it wasn't good enough to be taken seriously.

w Wells Root, Harold Greene, Ben Starr
d Michael Gordon *ph* Russell Metty
m Frank de Vol *md* Joseph Gershenson

Dean Martin, Alain Delon, Joey Bishop, Rosemary Forsyth, Tina Marquand, Peter Graves, Andrew Prine, Michael Ansara

Texas, Brooklyn and Heaven
US 1948 76m bw

A Texas boy meets a Texas girl in New York; after various eccentric encounters, they end up riding the range again. Would-be Saroyanesque dalliance with odd characters which never begins to come off and has been abruptly edited into the bargain. Guy Madison, Diana Lynn, James Dunn, Lionel Stander, Florence Bates, Michael Chekov, Margaret Hamilton, Moyna McGill, Irene Ryan, Roscoe Karns, William Frawley. Written by Lewis Meltzer, from story by Barry Benefield; directed by William Castle; for Robert S. Golden / United Artists.

(GB title: *The Girl from Texas*.)

Texas Carnival
US 1951 77m Technicolor
MGM (Jack Cummins)

A fairground showman is mistaken for a millionaire and runs up debts.
Very thin comedy musical relying entirely on its stars.

w Dorothy Kingsley *d* Charles Walters
ph Robert Planck *m* Harry Warren
ly Dorothy Fields *ch* Hermes Pan

Esther Williams, Red Skelton, Howard Keel, Ann Miller, Paula Raymond, Keenan Wynn, Tom Tully

The Texas Chainsaw Massacre
US 1974 81m CFI Color
Vortex (Tobe Hooper)

Visitors to a cemetery in rural Texas find their house occupied by a homicidal maniac.
Cheapjack horror thriller adapted from real events which also inspired *Psycho*. Nothing but shocks and gore, but the beginning of the wave of such deplorable movies which flooded the world's screens towards the end of the decade.

w Kim Henkel, Tobe Hooper *d* Tobe Hooper *ph* Daniel Pearl *m* Tobe Hooper, Wayne Bell

Marilyn Burns, Allen Danziger, Paul A. Partain, William Vail

'An absolute must for all maniacs and blood drinkers in need of a few tips.'—*Benny Green, Punch*

'It's without any apparent purpose, unless the creation of disgust and fright is a purpose.'—*Roger Ebert*

The Texas Chainsaw Massacre Part 2
US 1986 95m TVC colour

A family of Sweeney Todds lives in an abandoned Alamo theme park, and woe betide the stray visitor. Splatter shocker on predictable lines. Dennis Hopper, Caroline Williams, Bill Johnson, Jim Siedow. Written by L. M. Kit Carson; directed by Tobe Hooper; for Cannon.

Texas Lady
US 1955 85m Technicolor Superscope
RKO (Nat Holt)

A lady newspaper owner runs an anti-corruption campaign.
Mild family western.

w Horace McCoy *d* Tim Whelan *ph* Ray Rennahan *m* Paul Sawtell

Claudette Colbert, Barry Sullivan, Grey Walcott, James Bell, Horace MacMahon, Ray Collins, Walter Sande, Douglas Fowley

'They wrote their story in words of fire!'
The Texas Rangers*
US 1936 95m bw
Paramount (King Vidor)

Three wandering ne'er-do-wells break up; two join the Texas Rangers and hunt down the third, who is an outlaw.
Pleasantly remembered star western, later remade as *The Streets of Laredo* (qv).

w Louis Stevens *d* King Vidor *ph* Edward Cronjager

Fred MacMurray, Jack Oakie, Lloyd Nolan, Jean Parker, Edward Ellis

† Another film called *The Texas Rangers* came from Columbia in 1952 and had a similar plot to the original; otherwise it was a shoddy piece of work in Supercinecolor, with George Montgomery and Jerome Courtland.

Texas Rangers Ride Again
US 1940 67m bw

Modern Rangers capture cattle rustlers. Second-feature 'sequel' with no relation to the original. John Howard, Ellen Drew, Akim Tamiroff, May Robson, Broderick Crawford, Charley Grapewin, John Miljan, Anthony Quinn. Written by William R. Lipman and Horace McCoy; directed by James Hogan; for Paramount.

Thank God It's Friday
US 1978 89m Metrocolor
Columbia / Motown / Casablanca (Rob Cohen)

Problems of a disc jockey in a Hollywood disco.
Routine youth programmer, rather like *Rock Around the Clock* twenty years after.

w Barry Armyan Bernstein *d* Robert Klane *ph* James Crabe *pd* Tom H. John *m* various

Valerie Landsburg, Terri Nunn, Chick Vennera, Donna Summer, The Commodores

AA: song, 'Last Dance'

Thank You, Jeeves*
US 1936 57m bw
TCF (Sol M. Wurtzel)

A valet helps prevent his master from becoming involved in gun-running.
Competent second feature notable as Niven's first leading role; also one of the very few attempts to film Wodehouse.

w Joseph Hoffman, Stephen Gross, *story* P. G. Wodehouse *d* Arthur Greville Collins *ph* Barney McGill *m* Samuel Kaylin

David Niven, Arthur Treacher, Virginia Field, Lester Matthews, Colin Tapley

Thank Your Lucky Stars***
US 1943 127m bw
Warner (Mark Hellinger)

Eddie Cantor and his double get involved in planning a patriotic show.
All-star wartime musical with some unexpected turns and a generally funny script.

w Norman Panama, Melvin Frank, James V. Kern *d* David Butler *ph Arthur Edeson* *md* Leo F. Forbstein *ch* Le Roy Prinz *songs Frank Loesser, Arthur Schwartz*

Eddie Cantor, Dennis Morgan, Joan Leslie, Edward Everett Horton, S. Z. Sakall, Humphrey Bogart, Jack Carson, *Bette Davis*, Olivia de Havilland, *Errol Flynn*, John Garfield, Alan Hale, Ida Lupino, *Ann Sheridan*, Dinah Shore, George Tobias, Spike Jones and his City Slickers, Willie Best, Hattie McDaniel

'The loudest and most vulgar of the current musicals, it is also the most fun, if you are amused when show people kid their own idiom.'—*James Agee*

'An all-star show with the conspicuous flavour of amateur night at the studio.'—*New York Times*

'Everyone had a good time making it.'—*Motion Picture Herald*

AAN: song 'They're Either Too Young or Too Old'

Thanks a Million**
US 1935 87m bw
TCF (Darryl F. Zanuck)

A crooner runs for governor.
Smart, amusing political musical.

w Nunnally Johnson *d Roy del Ruth* *ph* Peverell Marley *songs* Arthur Johnston, Gus Kahn *m* Arthur Lange

Dick Powell, Fred Allen, Ann Dvorak, Patsy Kelly, Phil Baker, Paul Whiteman and his band, the Yacht Club Boys, Benny Baker, Raymond Walburn, Alan Dinehart

'Socko filmusical for big grosses . . . an example of canny showmanship and presentation.'—*Variety*

Thanks for Everything*
US 1938 70m bw
TCF (Darryl F. Zanuck)

Mr Average American is discovered, promoted and merchandized.
Very acceptable satirical comedy of the advertising world.

w Harry Tugend *d* William A. Seiter *ph* George Meehan *m* Abe Meyer

Adolphe Menjou, Jack Haley, Jack Oakie, Arleen Whelan, Tony Martin, Binnie Barnes, George Barbier

'Light and breezy, a cinch for popular audience appeal.'—*Variety*

'The funniest film I can remember seeing for many months, with something of the old Kaufman touch.'—*Graham Greene*

Thanks for the Memory*
US 1938 75m bw
Paramount (Mel Shaver)

A smart novelist has trouble with his marriage.
Light, agreeable domestic comedy on familiar lines.

w Lynn Starling, *play* Up Pops the Devil by Frances Goodrich, Albert Hackett *d* George Archainbaud *ph* Karl Struss *m* Boris Morros

Bob Hope, Shirley Ross

'Although lightweight, it will please if not exactly boff them.'—*Variety*

Thark*
GB 1932 79m bw
British and Dominion (Herbert Wilcox)

The heir to an old mansion spends a night in it to prove it is not haunted.
Very funny Aldwych farce, plainly transferred to the screen with the original stage team intact. One's only regret is that it peters out at the end.

w Ben Travers, from his play *d* Tom Walls *ph* F. A. Young

Ralph Lynn, Tom Walls, Robertson Hare, Mary Brough, Claude Hulbert, Gordon James

'Scream after scream of laughter of the wobbling midriff variety.'—*Variety*

That Brennan Girl
US 1946 97m bw

A young mother neglects her baby for the sake of a good time. Absurdly padded-out moral tract. Mona Freeman, James Dunn, William Marshall, June Duprez. Written by Doris Anderson; directed by Alfred Santell; for Republic.

That Certain Age*
US 1938 100m bw
Universal (Joe Pasternak)

A girl gets a crush on an older man.
Pleasant, well-cast star musical for the family.

w Bruce Manning *d* Edward Ludwig *ph* Joseph Valentine *songs* Jimmy McHugh, Harold Adamson

Deanna Durbin, Melvyn Douglas, Jackie Cooper, Irene Rich, Nancy Carroll, John Halliday, Juanita Quigley, Jackie Searl, Charles Coleman

'Certain for top grosses and extended runs.'—*Variety*

AAN: song 'My Own'

That Certain Feeling
US 1956 102m Technicolor Vistavision
Paramount (Melvin Frank, Norman Panama)

An arrogant comic strip artist loses his touch and hires a 'ghost'—the ex-husband of his secretary / fiancée.

Arid comedy from a mild Broadway play, totally miscast and lacking any kind of interest.

w Norman Panama, Melvin Frank, I. A. L. Diamond, William Altman, *play* King of Hearts by Jean Kerr, Eleanor Brooke *d* Norman Panama, Melvin Frank *ph* Loyal Griggs *m* Joseph J. Lilley

Bob Hope, George Sanders, Eva Marie Saint, Pearl Bailey, Al Capp

'She got all the breaks—in her heart!'

That Certain Woman*
US 1937 91m bw
Warner (Hal B. Wallis)

A gangster's widow goes straight but runs into complex marriage trouble.
Self-sacrifice and mother love are rewarded by two convenient deaths and a happy ending in this routine romantic melodrama remade from a silent success.

wd Edmund Goulding, from his original screen play The Trespasser *ph* Ernest Haller *m* Max Steiner

Bette Davis, Henry Fonda, Ian Hunter, Anita Louise, Donald Crisp, Katherine Alexander, Mary Philips, Minor Watson

'Big-time cast in a well-made first run film.'—*Variety*

That Championship Season*
US 1982 108m Metrocolor
Cannon–Golan–Globus (Menahem Golan)

Five rather unlikeable middle-aged men live by recreating the glory of a team basketball victory 25 years ago.
Unimaginative film version of a play which had dramatic strength but very limited general appeal. Rather less can be said of the film, as the acting shows a lack of team spirit.

wd Jason Miller, from his play *ph* John Bailey *m* Bill Conti *pd* Ward Preston *ed* Richard Halsey

Bruce Dern, Stacy Keach, Robert Mitchum, Martin Sheen, Paul Sorvino, Arthur Franz

That Cold Day in the Park
Canada 1969 115m Eastmancolor
(Commonwealth United) Donald Factor / Robert Altman / Leon Mirrell

A spinster invites a lonely wandering boy into her home, makes him a prisoner and becomes possessively jealous.
A companion piece to *The Collector*, rather better done for those who like morbid psychology.

w Gillian Freeman, *novel* Richard Miles *d* Robert Altman *ph* Laszlo Kovacs *m* Johnny Mandel

Sandy Dennis, Michael Burns, Suzanne Benton, Luana Anders, John Garfield Jnr

'About as pretentious, loathsome and stupid as a film can get.'—*John Simon*

That Dangerous Age
GB 1949 98m bw
London Films (Gregory Ratoff)
US title: *If This Be Sin*

Recovering from a breakdown, a KC discovers that his daughter wants to marry a man with whom his wife once had an affair.
Purple patch melodrama which sympathetic actors can't quite freshen up.

w Gene Markey, *play* Autumn by Margaret Kennedy and Ilya Surgutchoff *d* Gregory Ratoff *ph* Georges Périnal *m* Mischa Spoliansky

Roger Livesey, Myrna Loy, Peggy Cummins, Richard Greene, Elizabeth Allan, Gerard Heinz, Jean Cadell, G. H. Mulcaster

That Darn Cat!*
US 1965 116m Technicolor
Walt Disney (Bill Walsh, Ron Miller)

A troublesome cat inadvertently helps to trail bank robbers.
Overlong but generally pleasing small-town comedy with well-paced sequences and a fascinating feline hero.

w The Gordons, Bill Walsh, *novel* Undercover Cat by the Gordons *d Robert Stevenson* *ph* Edward Colman *m* Bob Brunner

Hayley Mills, Dean Jones, Dorothy Provine, Roddy McDowall, Neville Brand, Elsa Lanchester, William Demarest, Frank Gorshin, Grayson Hall, Ed Wynn

That Forsyte Woman*
US 1949 114m Technicolor
MGM (Leon Gordon)
GB title: *The Forsyte Saga*

The wife of an Edwardian man of property falls in love with her niece's fiancé.
Moderately successful American attempt to film the first part of a very British novel sequence; so genteel, however, that it becomes dull.

w Jan Lustig, Ivan Tors, James B. Williams, *novel* A Man of Property by John Galsworthy *d* Compton Bennett *ph* Joseph Ruttenberg *m* Bronislau Kaper

Greer Garson, *Errol Flynn*, Robert Young, Janet Leigh, Walter Pidgeon, Harry Davenport, Aubrey Mather

That Funny Feeling
US 1965 92m Technicolor
U-I (Harry Keller)

A maid pretends she lives in her boss's apartment.
Makeshift romantic comedy which barely takes the attention even while it's on.

w David R. Schwarz *d* Richard Thorpe *ph* Clifford Stine *m* Joseph Gershenson

Sandra Dee, Bobby Darin, Donald O'Connor, Nita Talbot, Larry Storch, Leo G. Carroll, James Westerfield

That Girl from Paris
US 1936 105m bw
RKO (Pandro S. Berman)

A Paris opera singer falls for a swing band leader and stows away on a transatlantic liner to be near him.
Comedy-accented musical romance: not bad but not memorable.

w P. J. Wolfson, Dorothy Yost, Jane Murfin *d* Leigh Jason *ph* J. Roy Hunt *m* Edward Heyman *md* Nathaniel Shilkret

Lily Pons, Gene Raymond, Jack Oakie, Herman Bing, Lucille Ball, Mischa Auer, Frank Jenks

'When it's good it's very very good, and when it's bad it's pretty awful.'—*Variety*

'Around her young heart she wore the scarlet letter of another woman's shame!'

That Hagen Girl
US 1947 83m bw
Warner (Alex Gottlieb)

A girl is convinced she is the illegitimate daughter of her teacher.
Stale teenage drama with odd anti-establishment overtones.

w Charles Hoffman, *novel* Edith Kneipple Roberts *d* Peter Godfrey *ph* Karl Freund *m* Franz Waxman

Shirley Temple, Ronald Reagan, Rory Calhoun, Lois Maxwell, Dorothy Peterson, Charles Kemper, Conrad Janis, Harry Davenport

'Less a film than a series of false situations.'—*MFB*

'They shouldn't do such things to Shirley.'—*Bosley Crowther, New York Times*

That Hamilton Woman**
US 1941 128m bw
Alexander Korda Films
GB title: *Lady Hamilton*

The affair of Lord Nelson and Emma Hamilton.
Bowdlerized version of a famous misalliance; coldly made but quite effective scene by scene, with notable performances.

w Walter Reisch, R. C. Sherriff *d* Alexander Korda *ph* Rudolph Maté *m* Miklos Rozsa

Laurence Olivier, Vivien Leigh, Gladys Cooper, Alan Mowbray, Sara Allgood, Henry Wilcoxon, Halliwell Hobbes

AAN: Rudolph Maté

That Kind of Woman
US 1959 92m bw
Paramount / Ponti–Girosi

World War II remake of *Shopworn Angel* (qv); rather well made but basically dated and dull.

w Walter Bernstein *d* Sidney Lumet *ph* Boris Kaufman *m* Daniele Amfitheatrof

Sophia Loren, Tab Hunter, George Sanders, Jack Warden, Barbara Nicholas, Keenan Wynn

'The romantic reunion of Tab Hunter and Sophia Loren resembles nothing so much as a sea scout given a luxury liner for Christmas.'—*Peter John Dyer*

That Lady
GB 1955 100m Eastmancolor Cinemascope
TCF / Atlanta (Sy Bartlett)

A noble widow at the court of Philip II of Spain loves a minister but incurs the king's jealous hatred.
Tepid historical romance which never flows as a film should.

w Anthony Veiller, Sy Bartlett, *novel* Kate O'Brien *d* Terence Young *ph* Robert Krasker *m* John Addison

Olivia de Havilland, Gilbert Roland, *Paul Scofield*, Françoise Rosay, Dennis Price, Anthony Dawson, Robert Harris, Peter Illing, Christopher Lee

'Somehow, somewhere, one feels, something went very wrong.'—*MFB*

That Lady in Ermine
US 1948 89m Technicolor
TCF (Ernst Lubitsch)

Two generations of European noblewomen learn to repel invaders.
Cheerless musical comedy which never gets started, what with the director dying during production and unsuitable stars lost in tinselly sets; the result can have appealed to no one.

w Samson Raphaelson *d* Ernst Lubitsch, Otto Preminger *ph* Leon Shamroy *songs* Leo Robin, Frederick Hollander *m* Alfred Newman

Betty Grable, Douglas Fairbanks Jnr, Cesar Romero, Walter Abel, Reginald Gardiner, Harry Davenport

AAN: song 'This Seems to be the Moment' (*m* Frederick Hollander, *ly* Leo Robin)

That Lucky Touch
GB 1975 93m Technicolor
Rank / Gloria (Dimitri de Grunwald)

During NATO war games in Brussels, a lady correspondent falls for an arms dealer.
Dim romantic farce which gives the impression of emanating from a dog-eared script written for the kind of stars who no longer shine.

w John Briley, *story* Moss Hart *d* Christopher Miles *ph* Douglas Slocombe *m* John Scott

Roger Moore, Susannah York, Lee J. Cobb, Shelley Winters, Jean-Pierre Cassel, Raf Vallone, Sydne Rome, Donald Sinden

That Man Bolt
US 1973 103m Technicolor
Universal (Bernard Schwarz)

Adventures of a professional black courier skilled in the martial arts.
Black Kung Fu hokum from a major company; tolerable of its debased kind.

w Quentin Werty, Charles Johnson *d* Henry Levin, David Lowell Rich *ph* Gerald Perry Finnerman *m* Charles Bernstein

Fred Williamson, Bryon Webster, Miko Mayama, Teresa Graves

'Gives every indication of having been devised by a computer fed with a variety of ingredients currently thought to guarantee box office success.'—*John Raisbeck, MFB*

That Man from Rio
France / Italy 1964 120m Eastmancolor
Ariane / Artistes Associés / Dear Film / Vides (Alexander Mnouchkine, Georges Danciger)
original title: *L'Homme de Rio*

An airforce pilot finds himself helping his girl friend in a worldwide search for stolen statuettes.
Elaborate mock thriller which is never quite as much fun as those involved seem to think. It provoked several inferior sequels.

w J. P. Rappeneau, Ariane Mnouchkine, Daniel Boulanger, Philippe de Broca *d* Philippe de Broca *ph* Edmond Séchan *m* Georges Delerue

Jean-Paul Belmondo, Jean Servais, Françoise Dorléac, Adolfo Celi, Simone Renant

'Fantasy takes over, with Belmondo outdoing Fairbanks in agility, Lloyd in cliffhanging, and Bond in indestructibility.'—*Brenda Davies, MFB*

AAN: script

That Midnight Kiss
US 1949 98m Technicolor
MGM (Joe Pasternak)

An unknown becomes a great singing star.
Simple-minded vehicle for the first appearance of Mario Lanza.

w Bruce Manning, Tamara Hovey *d* Norman Taurog *ph* Robert Surtees *m* Bronislau Kaper

Kathryn Grayson, Ethel Barrymore, Jose Iturbi, Mario Lanza, Keenan Wynn, J. Carrol Naish, Jules Munshin, Thomas Gomez, Marjorie Reynolds

That Night*
US 1957 88m bw
Galahad (Himan Brown)

An overwhelmed TV writer has a heart attack, and recovers after a series of medical setbacks.
Impressive minor case history, hardly entertainment but quite arresting.

w Robert Wallace, Burton J. Rowles *d* John Newland *ph* Maurice Hartzband *m* Mario Nascimbene

John Beal, Augusta Dabney, Shepperd Strudwick, Ralph Murphy

That Night in Rio*
US 1941 90m Technicolor
TCF (Fred Kohlmar)

A nightclub entertainer is paid to impersonate a lookalike count, but this causes complications with the countess.
Zippy musical based on a story first used in *Folies Bergère* (qv) and later in *On the Riviera* (qv).

w George Seaton, Bess Meredyth, Hal Long, *play* Rudolph Lothar, Hans Adler *d* Irving Cummings *ph* Leon Shamroy *songs* Mack Gordon, Harry Warren *md* Alfred Newman

Don Ameche, Alice Faye, Carmen Miranda, S. Z. Sakall, J. Carrol Naish, Curt Bois, Leonid Kinskey, Maria Montez

'An eye-filling and ear-filling musical comedy extravaganza.'—*Motion Picture Herald*

That Night with You
US 1945 84m bw
Universal (Michael Fessier, Ernest Pagano)

A girl singer anxious to get on tells a producer that she is his illegitimate daughter.
Mindless farce with music, its gimmick being that all the songs are set to Tchaikovsky's music. Otherwise very dull.

w Michael Fessier, Ernest Pagano *d* William A. Seiter *ph* Woody Bredell

Franchot Tone, Susanna Foster, David Bruce, Louise Allbritton, Buster Keaton, Irene Ryan, Jacqueline de Wit

That Obscure Object of Desire*
France / Spain 1978 103m Eastmancolor
Greenwich / Galaxie / In Cine (Serge Silberman)

A middle-aged gentleman suffers continual humiliations from the girl he loves.
Unrecognizable remake of a novel previously filmed as a vehicle for Dietrich and Bardot. Despite the tricking out with surrealist touches (the girl is played by two different actresses) it is not one of Bunuel's best, and amuses only on the surface.

w Luis Bunuel, Jean-Claude Carrière, *novel* La Femme et le Pantin by Pierre Louys *d* Luis Bunuel *ph* Edmond Richard *m* from Richard Wagner

Fernando Rey, Carole Bouquet, Angela Molina, Julien Bertheau

AA: best foreign film

AAN: script

That Riviera Touch
GB 1966 98m Eastmancolor
Rank (Hugh Stewart)

Two tourists in the south of France get mixed up with jewel thieves.
Disappointing star comedy ending in a surfboard chase.

w S. C. Green, R. M. Hills, Peter Blackmore *d* Cliff Owen *ph* Otto Heller *m* Ron Goodwin

Eric Morecambe, Ernie Wise, Suzanne Lloyd, Paul Stassino, Armand Mestral

That Touch of Mink**
US 1962 99m Eastmancolor Panavision
U-I / Granley / Arwin / Nob Hill (Stanley Shapiro, Martin Melcher)

Bachelor tycoon pursues virginal secretary.
Jaded sex comedy (or what passed for it in nudge-nudge 1962) enlivened by practised star performances and smart timing.

w Stanley Shapiro, Nate Monaster *d* Delbert Mann *ph* Russell Metty *m* George Duning

Cary Grant, Doris Day, Gig Young, Audrey Meadows, Dick Sargent, *John Astin*

'Too often there's a hampering second-hand air about situation and joke. Throughout, the determination is to keep faith with the American sex mythology at all costs.'—*Jack Pitman, Variety*

AAN: script

That Uncertain Feeling*
US 1941 84m bw
(UA) Sol Lesser (Ernst Lubitsch)

A wife with insomnia and hiccups befriends a wacky concert pianist who proceeds to move into her home.
Although Lubitsch had made this story before, as the silent *Kiss Me Again*, the elements didn't really jell in this version, which seemed silly rather than funny.

w Donald Ogden Stewart, Walter Reisch, *play* Divorçons by Victorien Sardou, Emile de Najac *d Ernst Lubitsch ph* George Barnes *m* Werner Heymann *pd* Alexander Golitzen

Merle Oberon, Melvyn Douglas, Burgess Meredith, Alan Mowbray, Olive Blakeney, Harry Davenport, Eve Arden, Sig Rumann

'Gay entertainment.'—*Picture Show*

AAN: Werner Heymann

That Was Then . . . This Is Now
GB 1985 102m TVC colour
Urban youths growing into manhood find the world a gloomy place. Highly resistible chunk of pessimistic philosophizing with a few fights thrown in. Emilio Estevez, Craig Sheffer, Kim Delaney, Jill Schoelen, Barbara Babcock, Morgan Freeman. Written by Emilio Estevez, from novel by S. E. Hinton; directed by Christopher Cain; for Media Ventures / Alan Belkin / Paramount. 'God save the kids who live in an S. E. Hinton novel. They're firecrackers waiting to go off.'—*Variety*

That Way With Women
US 1947 84m bw
Warner (Charles Hoffman)

A millionaire amuses himself by playing Cupid to a young couple.
Routine remake of *The Millionaire*: just about watchable.

w Leo Townsend *d* Frederick de Cordova *ph* Ted McCord *m* Frederick Hollander

Sidney Greenstreet, Dane Clark, Martha Vickers, Alan Hale, Craig Stevens, Barbara Brown

That Woman Opposite
GB 1957 83m bw
Monarch (William Gell)
US title: *City after Midnight*

In a small French town, a killer returns to silence a witness.
Slow-paced semi-mystery, reasonably well done.

wd Compton Bennett, *story* The Emperor's Snuff Box by John Dickson Carr *ph* Lionel Banes *m* Stanley Black

Phyllis Kirk, Dan O'Herlihy, Wilfrid Hyde White, Petula Clark, Jack Watling, William Franklyn, Margaret Withers

That Wonderful Urge
US 1948 82m bw
TCF (Fred Kohlmar)

A newspaperman is forced into marriage with a publicity-shy heiress.
Tepid romantic comedy, a remake of *Love Is News* (qv).

w Jay Dratler *d* Robert B. Sinclair *ph* Charles Clarke *m* Cyril Mockridge

Gene Tierney, Tyrone Power, Reginald Gardiner, Arleen Whelan, Lucile Watson, Gene Lockhart, Porter Hall, Taylor Holmes

That'll Be the Day*
GB 1973 91m Technicolor
EMI / Goodtimes (David Puttnam, Sanford Lieberson)

In 1958, a young drifter becomes a fairground worker, and eventually walks out on his wife and family to become a pop star.
Spirited return to British realism, with well-sketched cameos, a likeable dour viewpoint, and a cheerful pop music background.

w Ray Connolly *d* Claude Whatham *ph* Peter Suschitsky *md* Neil Aspinall, Keith Moon

David Essex, Ringo Starr, Rosemary Leach, James Booth, Billy Fury, Keith Moon, Rosalind Ayres

'As insubstantial as one of its own attempts at a statement.'—*Tony Rayns*

That's a Good Girl*
GB 1933 83m bw

A man about town seeks ways of making money. Archetypal vehicle for a debonair song and dance man. *Jack Buchanan,* Elsie Randolph, Dorothy Hyson, Garry Marsh, Vera Pearce, William Kendall. Written by Douglas Furber, Donovan Pedelty and Jack Buchanan; directed by Jack Buchanan; for Herbert Wilcox/ British and Dominions.

That's Dancin'!**
US 1985 105m Metrocolor
MGM–UA / David Niven Jnr, Jack Haley Jnr

Selections from the golden age of the movie musical, featuring the likes of Fred Astaire, Gene Kelly, Eleanor Powell, Busby Berkeley.
Fascinating compilation which made little impact at the box office.

narrators: Gene Kelly, Sammy Davis Jnr, Mikhail Baryshnikov, Liza Minnelli, Ray Bolger

'Boy! do we need it now!'
That's Entertainment**
US 1974 137m Metrocolor 70mm (blown up) / scope
MGM (Daniel Melnick, Jack Haley Jnr)

Fred Astaire, Gene Kelly, Elizabeth Taylor, James Stewart, Bing Crosby, Liza Minnelli, Donald O'Connor, Debbie Reynolds, Mickey Rooney and Frank Sinatra introduce highlights from MGM's musical past.
A slapdash compilation which was generally very big at the box office and obviously has fascinating sequences, though the narration is sloppily sentimental and the later wide-screen sequences let down the rest.

wd Jack Haley Jnr *ph* various *m* various

principal stars as above plus Judy Garland, Esther Williams, Eleanor Powell, Clark Gable, Ray Bolger

'While many ponder the future of MGM, none can deny that it has one hell of a past.'—*Variety*

'It is particularly gratifying to get the key sequences from certain movies without having to sit through a fatuous storyline.'—*Michael Billington, Illustrated London News*

'No other film in town offers such a harvest of undiluted joy.'—*Sunday Express*

That's Entertainment Part Two**
US 1976 133m Metrocolor 70mm (blown up) / scope
MGM (Saul Chaplin, Daniel Melnick)

More of the above, introduced by Fred Astaire and Gene Kelly, with comedy and drama sequences as well as musical.

d Gene Kelly *titles Saul Bass ph* various

principal stars as above plus Jeanette MacDonald, Nelson Eddy, the Marx Brothers, Laurel and Hardy, Jack Buchanan, Judy Garland, Ann Miller, Mickey Rooney, Oscar Levant, Louis Armstrong, etc.

That's Life!
US 1986 102m De Luxe Panavision
Columbia / Paradise Cove / Ubilam (Tony Adams)

An architect touching sixty, with a sick wife, pours out all his fears of old age and mortality.
Blake Edwards exposing himself again; the movie was even shot in his own house.
Somewhat embarrassing to watch, and overwrought, it does have a few good moments.

w Milton Wexler, Blake Edwards *d* Blake Edwards *ph* Anthony Richmond *m* Henry Mancini

Jack Lemmon, Julie Andrews, Sally Kellerman, Robert Loggia, Jennifer Edwards.
AAN: song 'Life in a Looking Glass' (Mancini, Leslie Bricusse)

That's My Boy
US 1951 98m bw
Paramount / Hal B. Wallis (Cy Howard)

An athletic father tries to press his hypochondriac teenage son into the same mould.
American college comedy of no international interest.

w Cy Howard *d* Hal Walker *ph* Lee Garmes *m* Leigh Harline

Dean Martin, Jerry Lewis, Eddie Mayehoff, Ruth Hussey, Polly Bergen, John McIntire

That's My Man
US 1946 98m bw
Republic (Frank Borzage)
GB title: *Will Tomorrow Ever Come?*

A racing man is reunited with his wife when their son has pneumonia.
A compendium of clichés, with everything but a title card reading *Came the Dawn*. Of no real interest.

w Steve Fisher, Bradley King *d* Frank Borzage *ph* Tony Gaudio *m* Cy Feuer

Don Ameche, Catherine McLeod, Roscoe Karns, John Ridgely

That's My Wife*
US 1929 20m bw silent

Stan dresses up as Ollie's wife to impress his rich uncle. Lesser-known star comedy which well sustains its basic joke and includes some splendidly timed farce in a restaurant. Laurel and Hardy, Vivien Oakland, William Courtright. Written by Leo McCarey and H. M. Walker; directed by Lloyd French; for Hal Roach.

That's Right, You're Wrong*
US 1939 91m bw
RKO (David Butler)

A band leader gets a Hollywood contract but is hated by the studio head.
Typical of the nonsense musicals featuring Kay Kyser and his radio Kollege of Musical Knowledge. The movie background and self-spoofing made this first attempt one of the best.

w William Conselman, James V. Kern
d David Butler *ph* Russell Metty *m* George Duning *songs* various

Kay Kyser, Adolphe Menjou, Lucille Ball, Dennis O'Keefe, May Robson, Edward Everett Horton, Ish Kabibble, Ginny Simms, Roscoe Karns, Moroni Olsen, Hobart Cavanaugh, Sheilah Graham, Hedda Hopper

'Moderate entertainment which will satisfy as a bill-topper.'—*Variety*

That's the Spirit
US 1943 87m bw

A ghost comes back to tell his actress wife he didn't desert her as she thought. Rather heavy comedy of the *Here Comes Mr Jordan* school. Jack Oakie, Peggy Ryan, June Vincent, Gene Lockhart, Andy Devine, Arthur Treacher, Irene Ryan, Buster Keaton. Written by Michael Fessier and Ernest Pagano; directed by Charles Lamont; for Universal.

Theatre of Blood*
GB 1973 102m De Luxe
UA / Cineman (John Kohn, Stanley Mann)

A Shakespearean actor uses appropriate murder methods on the various critics who have ridiculed his performances.
Spoof horror picture which goes too far with some sick visuals; the idea and some of the performances are fine.

w Anthony Greville-Bell *d* Douglas Hickox
ph Wolfgang Suschitsky *m* Michael J. Lewis
pd Michael Seymour

Vincent Price, Diana Rigg, Ian Hendry, Harry Andrews, Coral Browne, Robert Coote, Jack Hawkins, Michael Hordern, Arthur Lowe, Robert Morley, Dennis Price, Diana Dors, Joan Hickson, Renée Asherson, Milo O'Shea, Eric Sykes

Theatre of Death
GB 1966 91m Techniscope

Vampire-like murders in Paris are eventually connected with a Grand Guignol theatre. Dreary backstage shocker with inadequate production values. Christopher Lee, Jenny Till, Lelia Goldoni, Julian Glover, Ivor Dean, Evelyn Laye. Written by Roger Marshall and Ellis Kadison; directed by Sam Gallu; for Michael Smedley—Aston/Pennea. (US title: *Blood Fiend*.)

Theatre Royal
GB 1943 92m bw

A revue and a theatre are saved by a sentimental prop man. Shapeless star comedy with music; not their best. Bud Flanagan and Chesney Allen, Peggy Dexter, Lydia Sherwood, Horace Kenney, Marjorie Rhodes, Finlay Currie. Written by Bud Flanagan, Austin Melford and Geoffrey Orme; directed by John Baxter; for British National.

Their Big Moment
US 1934 68m bw

Phoney mindreaders solve a murder mystery in a spooky house. Quite good, well-organized fun of its type. Zasu Pitts, Slim Summerville, William Gaxton, Ralph Morgan, Bruce Cabot, Julie Haydon, Kay Johnson. Written by Arthur Caesar, Marian Dix, Walter Hackett; directed by James Cruze; for RKO. 'Should have fairly good audience strength.'—*Variety*

Their First Mistake**
US 1932 20m bw

Ollie decides to improve his marriage by adopting a baby, only to find that his wife has left him. Sublimely silly but endearing star comedy with brilliant passages of imbecilic conversation followed by well-timed farce. Laurel and Hardy, Mae Busch. Written by H. M. Walker; directed by George Marshall (who also plays a bit); for Hal Roach.

Their Purple Moment
US 1928 20m bw silent

Stan and Ollie go out on the town, only to discover that Stan's wife has replaced his money with grocery coupons. Minor star comedy with efficient but predictable restaurant scenes ending in a pie fight. Laurel and Hardy, Anita Garvin, Kay Deslys. Written by H. M. Walker; directed by James Parrott; for Hal Roach.

'Kill one and two others take its place!
Don't turn your back or you're doomed!
And don't tell anyone what Them are!'

Them!**
US 1954 94m bw
Warner (David Weisbart)

Atomic bomb radiation causes giant ants to breed in the New Mexico desert.
Among the first, and certainly the best, of the post-atomic monster animal cycle, this durable thriller starts with several eerie desert sequences and builds up to a shattering climax in the Los Angeles sewers. A general air of understatement helps a lot.

w Ted Sherdeman, *story* George Worthing Yates *d Gordon Douglas ph Sid Hickox*
m Bronislau Kaper

Edmund Gwenn, James Whitmore, Joan Weldon, James Arness, Onslow Stevens

'I asked the editor: How does it look? And he said: Fine. I said: Does it look honest? He said: As honest as twelve foot ants can look.'—*Gordon Douglas*

Them Thar Hills**
US 1934 20m bw

Stan and Ollie go camping, drink from a well full of moonshine whisky, and get drunk with another camper's wife. Consistently funny star comedy culminating in a tit-for-tat routine which was reprised in *Tit for Tat* the following year. Laurel and Hardy, Charlie Hall, Mae Busch, Billy Gilbert. Written by Stan Laurel and H. M. Walker; directed by Charles Rogers; for Hal Roach.

Theodora Goes Wild*
US 1936 94m bw
Columbia (Everett Riskin)

A small-town girl writes a titillating bestseller.
Mildly crazy comedy which helped develop the trend for stars performing undignified antics but today seems rather slow and dated.

w Sidney Buchman, story Mary McCarthy
d Richard Boleslawski *ph* Joseph Walker
m Morris Stoloff

Irene Dunne, Melvyn Douglas, Thomas Mitchell, Thurston Hall, Rosalind Keith, Spring Byington, Elizabeth Risdon, Nana Bryant

AAN: Irene Dunne

Theorem*
Italy 1968 98m Eastmancolor
Aetos Film

A handsome young man arrives unexpectedly to stay with a Milan industrialist and his family, gratifying their desires but leaving them tragically unhappy.
Moderately amusing fable with the presumed intent of decrying all universal panaceas, including Christianity.

wd Pier Paolo Pasolini, from his novel
ph Giuseppe Ruzzolini *m* Ennio Morricone

Terence Stamp, Silvana Mangano, Massimo Girotti, Anne Wiazemsky, Laura Betti

There Ain't No Justice
GB 1939 83m bw

A young boxer refuses to throw a fight. Minor sporting drama, well praised at the time but later forgotten. Jimmy Hanley, Edward Rigby, Mary Clare, Edward Chapman, Phyllis Stanley, Michael Wilding. Written by Pen Tennyson, James Curtis and Sergei Nolbandov; directed by Pen Tennyson; for Ealing.

There Goes My Heart
US 1938 81m bw
Hal Roach

A reporter is assigned to track down a runaway heiress.
Very pale imitation of *It Happened One Night*.

w Jack Jevne, Eddie Moran *d* Norman Z. McLeod *ph* Norbert Brodine *m* Marvin Hatley

Fredric March, Virginia Bruce, Patsy Kelly, Nancy Carroll, Eugene Pallette, Claude Gillingwater, Arthur Lake, Harry Langdon, Etienne Girardot

'A comedy clicko . . . plenty of zip and zing.'—*Variety*

AAN: Marvin Hatley

There Goes the Bride
GB 1980 91m Eastmancolor
Lonsdale (Martin Schute, Ray Cooney)

A harassed advertising executive suffers hallucinations about a lifesize cardboard cut-out of a twenties flapper.
Embarrassingly witless and plotless revamp of innumerable better comedies in the *Topper* tradition; it has to be seen to be believed.

w Terence Marcel, Ray Cooney *play* Ray Cooney and John Chapman *d* Terence Marcel *ph* James Devis *m* Harry Robinson *pd* Peter Mullins

Tom Smothers, Twiggy, Sylvia Syms, Martin Balsam, Michael Whitney, Geoffrey Sumner, Hermione Baddeley, Phil Silvers, Broderick Crawford, Jim Backus

'The whole thing would be laughable if it weren't so unfunny.'—*Gilbert Adair, MFB*

There Goes the Groom
US 1937 64m bw

A young man comes back rich from the Alaskan gold fields and reminds an old girl friend of her promise to marry him. A well-played comedy which can't conceal its threadbare situations. Ann Sothern, Burgess Meredith, Mary Boland, Onslow Stevens, Louise Henry. Written by S. K. Lauren, Dorothy Yost, Harold Kusell, David Garth; directed by Joseph Santley; for Albert Lewis / RKO.

There Is Another Sun
GB 1951 95m bw

A fairground wall of death rider turns to crime. Glum quickie which was oddly popular. Maxwell Reed, Susan Shaw, Laurence Harvey, Hermione Baddeley, Leslie Dwyer. Written by Guy Morgan; directed by Lewis Gilbert; for Nettlefold. (US title: *Wall of Death*.)

There Was a Crooked Man*
GB 1960 107m bw
UA / Knightsbridge (John Bryan)

An ex-safecracker outwits the crooked mayor of an industrial town.
Semi-happy attempt to humanize a knockabout clown; good supporting performances and production.

w Reuben Ship *d* Stuart Burge *ph* Arthur Ibbetson *m* Kenneth V. Jones

Norman Wisdom, Andrew Cruickshank, Alfred Marks, Susannah York, Reginald Beckwith

There Was a Crooked Man*
US 1970 126m Technicolor Panavision
Warner Seven Arts (Joseph L. Mankiewicz)

In 1883 Arizona a murderer tries to escape from jail and recover hidden loot but is constantly thwarted by the sheriff who arrested him, now a warden.
Curious black comedy melodrama with lots of talent going nowhere in particular; hard to endure as a whole but with entertaining scenes.

w David Newman, Robert Benton *d* Joseph L. Mankiewicz *ph* Harry Stradling Jnr *m* Charles Strouse *ad* Edward Carrere

Kirk Douglas, Henry Fonda, Hume Cronyn, Warren Oates, Burgess Meredith, John Randolph, Arthur O'Connell, Martin Gabel, Alan Hale

'This example of commercialized black comedy nihilism seems to have been written by an evil two-year-old, and it has been directed in the Grand Rapids style of moviemaking.'—*Pauline Kael, New Yorker*

There's a Girl in my Heart
US 1949 82m bw

The attractive widow who owns a music hall finds the site in demand. Slight, artificial but mildly pleasing musical extravaganza of the gay nineties. Lee Bowman, Elyse Knox, Lon Chaney Jnr, Gloria Jean, Peggy Ryan, Ludwig Donath, Ray McDonald, Irene Ryan. Written by Arthur Hoerl, John Eugene Hasty; directed and produced by Arthur Dreifuss; for Allied Artists.

There's a Girl in My Soup*
GB 1970 96m Eastmancolor
Columbia / Ascot (John Boulting)

A randy TV personality finds himself outplotted by a waif he picks up.
Flimsy screen version of a long-running sex comedy; some laughs, but the star is uncomfortably miscast.

w Terence Frisby, from his play *d* Roy Boulting *ph* Harry Waxman *m* Mike D'Abo

Peter Sellers, Goldie Hawn, Tony Britton, Nicky Henson, John Comer, Diana Dors, Judy Campbell

There's Always a Woman*
US 1938 81m bw

A private detective's wife beats him to the solution of a murder. Amiably scatty crime comedy in the *Thin Man* tradition. Joan Blondell, Melvyn Douglas, Mary Astor, Frances Drake, Jerome Cowan, Robert Paige, Thurston Hall, Pierre Watkin. Written by Gladys Lehman, Wilson Collison; directed by Alexander Hall; for Columbia. 'Will provide general satisfaction as entertainment and as a grosser.'—*Variety*

There's Always Tomorrow
US 1934 86m bw

A depressed family man is cheered up by a former sweetheart. Basically rather a dull drama, but with sincere performances which lift it. Frank Morgan, Binnie Barnes, Lois Wilson, Louise Latimer, Alan Hale, Robert Taylor. Written by William Hurlbut from the novel by Ursula Parrott; directed by Edward Sloman; for Universal. 'Attractive screen material, it weighs in for what looks like a favourable sprint for coin.'—*Variety*. (NB: Remade 1956 as *These Wilder Years*, with James Cagney and Barbara Stanwyck.)

There's Always Tomorrow
US 1956 84m bw
Universal (Ross Hunter)

A married man falls for another woman.
Very flat variation on *Brief Encounter*, with stars going through mechanical paces.

w Bernard Schoenfeld, *story* Ursula Parrott *d* Douglas Sirk *ph* Russell Metty *m* Herman Stein, Heinz Roemheld

Barbara Stanwyck, Fred MacMurray, Joan Bennett, Pat Crowley, William Reynolds, Gigi Perreau, Jane Darwell

† Previously made by Universal in 1934 with Frank Morgan and Binnie Barnes.

There's No Business like Show Business**
US 1954 117m De Luxe Cinemascope
TCF (Sol C. Siegel)

The life and times of a family of vaudevillians.
Mainly entertaining events and marvellous tunes make up this very Cinemascoped musical, in which the screen is usually filled with six people side by side.

w Phoebe and Henry Ephron *d Walter Lang* *ph* Leon Shamroy *m / ly Irving Berlin* *ad* John de Cuir, Lyle Wheeler *m* Lionel Newman, Alfred Newman

Ethel Merman, Dan Dailey, Marilyn Monroe, Donald O'Connor, Johnny Ray, Mitzi Gaynor, Hugh O'Brian, Frank McHugh

AAN: original story (Lamar Trotti); Lionel Newman, Alfred Newman

There's Something about a Soldier
US 1943 81m bw

The destinies of five officer candidates at the Anti-Aircraft Training School. Transparent recruiting poster dramatics. Tom Neal, Evelyn Keyes, Bruce Bennett, John Hubbard, Jeff Donnell, Frank Sully. Written by Horace McCoy, Barry Trivers; directed by Alfred E. Green; for Samuel Bischoff / Columbia.

There's That Woman Again
US 1938 75m bw

A district attorney is hampered by his meddlesome spouse. Half-hearted follow-up to *There's Always a Woman*; the *McMillan and Wife* of its day. Melvyn Douglas, Virginia Bruce, Margaret Lindsay, Stanley Ridges, Gordon Oliver, Tom Dugan, Don Beddoe. Written by Philip G. Epstein, James Edward Grant and Ken Englund; directed by Alexander Hall; for Columbia.

Therese*
France 1986 91m colour
AFC / Films AZ / CNC

A 19th-century Normandy girl becomes a nun, dies at 24, and is canonized.
Straightforward, austere biographical account which weaves a curious spell.

w,d Alain Cavalier *ph* Philippe Rousselot *m* Offenbach, Fauré

Catherine Mouchet, Aurore Prieto, Sylvie Habault

These Dangerous Years
GB 1957 92m bw
Everest/Anna Neagle
US title: *Dangerous Youth*

A Liverpool teenage gang leader is called up and becomes a better guy.
Dim drama with music marking the debut of a singing star.

w John Trevor Story *d* Herbert Wilcox *ph* Gordon Dines *m* Stanley Black

Frankie Vaughan, George Baker, Carole Lesley, Jackie Lane, Katherine Kath, Eddie Byrne, Kenneth Cope

These Glamour Girls
US 1939 78m bw

A drunken college student invites a dime-a-dance girl for a festive weekend with his snobbish friends. Wincingly predictable romantic comedy-drama with no outstanding talent displayed from any quarter. Lew Ayres, Lana Turner, Tom Brown, Richard Carlson, Jane Bryan, Anita Louise, Ann Rutherford, Marsha Hunt. Written by Marion Parsonnet and Jane Hall; directed by S. Sylvan Simon; for MGM. 'Silly situations and mawkish lines. A dualler.'—*Variety*

These Thousand Hills
US 1958 96m Eastmancolor Cinemascope
TCF (David Weisbart)

A successful cattle rancher finds that his best friend is a rustler.
Large-scale but somehow unimpressive western variant on *The Virginian*, cluttered with sub-plots.

w Alfred Hayes, *novel* A. B. Guthrie Jnr *d* Richard Fleischer *ph* Charles G. Clarke *m* Leigh Harline

Richard Egan, Stuart Whitman, Don Murray, Lee Remick, Albert Dekker, Harold J. Stone, Patricia Owens

These Three**
US 1936 93m bw
Samuel Goldwyn

A lying schoolgirl accuses two schoolmistresses of scandalous behaviour.
Bowdlerized version of a famous play (instead of lesbianism we have extra-marital affairs). It worked well enough at the time but now seems dated; oddly enough when the play was filmed full strength in 1962 it didn't work at all.

w Lillian Hellman, from her play *The Children's Hour* *d* William Wyler *ph* Gregg Toland *m* Alfred Newman

Merle Oberon, Miriam Hopkins, Joel McCrea, *Bonita Granville*, Catherine Doucet, Alma Kruger, Marcia Mae Jones, Margaret Hamilton, Walter Brennan

AAN: Bonita Granville

These Wilder Years
US 1956 91m bw
MGM (Jules Schermer)

A wealthy industrialist returns to his home town to trace his illegitimate son.
Modest sentimental drama with practised stars.

w Frank Fenton *d* Roy Rowland *ph* George Folsey *m* Jeff Alexander

James Cagney, Barbara Stanwyck, Walter Pidgeon, Betty Lou Keim, Don Dubbins, Edward Andrews

They All Kissed the Bride
US 1942 86m bw
Columbia (Edward Kaufman)

A woman executive falls in love with the crusading writer who is out to expose working conditions in her company.
No surprises are expected or provided in this very ho-hum romantic comedy.

w P. J. Wolfson *d* Alexander Hall *ph* Joseph Walker *m* Werner Heyman *md* Morris Stoloff

Joan Crawford, Melvyn Douglas, Roland Young, Billie Burke, Allen Jenkins, Andrew Tombes, Helen Parrish, Mary Treen

AAN: Joan Crawford

They All Laughed*
US 1982 115m Movielab
Time-Life / Moon (George Morfogen, Blaine Novak)

Three agency detectives fall in and out of love in the course of their duties.
It has the air of a somewhat misshapen and Americanized *La Ronde*, with added suggestions of *On the Town*, but it adds up to very little and provides only a few laughs on the way.

w,d Peter Bogdanovich *ph* Robby Muller *m* various

Audrey Hepburn, Ben Gazzara, John Ritter, Dorothy Stratten, Colleen Camp, Patti Hansen, George Morfogen, Blaine Novak

'One tires of long looks that speak volumes, of endless successions of meeting cute.'—*John Pym, MFB*

They Call It Sin
US 1932 68m bw

A Kansas girl joins a New York chorus and needs to be rescued from a villainous producer. Ho-hum romantic drama without much substance. Loretta Young, George Brent, Louis Calhern, David Manners, Una Merkel. Written by Lillie Hayward and Howard Green from the novel by Alberta Steadman Eagan; directed by Thornton Freeland; for First National. (GB title: *The Way of Life*.) 'It needs the sexy title to bolster a just so-so flicker.'—*Variety*

They Call Me Mister Tibbs!
US 1970 108m De Luxe
UA / Mirisch (Herbert Hirshman)

A San Francisco police lieutenant suspects a crusading local minister of murder.
Flat, dispirited police melodrama with irrelevant domestic asides, a long way after *In the Heat of the Night* which introduced the main character. (*The Organization* was the third and last in the so-called series.)

w Alan R. Trustman, James R. Webb *d* Gordon Douglas *ph* Gerald Finnerman *m* Quincy Jones

Sidney Poitier, Martin Landau, Barbara McNair, Anthony Zerbe, Jeff Corey, Juano Hernandez, Ed Asner

They Came by Night
GB 1939 72m bw

A jeweller pretends to be a crook in order to lure the men who killed his brother. Smart little suspense yarn. Will Fyffe, Phyllis Calvert, Anthony Hulme, George Merritt, Athole Stewart, John Glyn Jones. Written by Frank Launder, Sidney Gilliatt, Michael Hogan and Roland Pertwee; directed by Harry Lachman; for TCF.

They Came to a City*
GB 1944 77m bw
Ealing (Sidney Cole)

Assorted people find themselves outside the gates of a mysterious city.
The *Outward Bound* format applied to post-war reconstruction, with characters deciding what kind of a world they want. Good talk and good acting, but not quite cinema.

w Basil Dearden, Sidney Cole, *play J. B. Priestley* *d* Basil Dearden *ph* Stan Pavey

Googie Withers, John Clements, Raymond Huntley, Renée Gadd, A. E. Matthews, Mabel Terry-Lewis, *Ada Reeve*, Norman Shelley, Frances Rowe

They Came to Blow Up America
US 1943 73m bw

An FBI man of German parentage goes to Nazi Germany and trains with a group of saboteurs, who are arrested when they set foot in the US. Tolerable propaganda potboiler. George Sanders, Anna Sten, Ward Bond, Dennis Hoey, Sig Rumann, Ludwig Stossel. Written by Aubrey Wisberg; directed by Edward Ludwig; for TCF.

They Came to Cordura*
US 1959 123m Technicolor Cinemascope
Columbia / Goetz–Baroda (William Goetz)

In 1916 Mexico, six American military heroes are recalled to base, but the hardships of the journey reveal their true colours.
Watchable adventure epic, not so arresting as was intended but quite professional.

w Ivan Moffat, Robert Rossen, *novel* Glendon Swarthout *d* Robert Rossen *ph* Burnett Guffey *m* Elie Siegmeister

Gary Cooper, Rita Hayworth, Van Heflin, Richard Conte, Tab Hunter, Michael Callan, Dick York, Robert Keith

They Came to Rob Las Vegas*
Spain / France / Germany / Italy 1969 128m Techniscope
Warner / Isasi / Capitoli / Eichberg / Franca

THEY DIED WITH THEIR BOOTS ON. Errol Flynn prepares to ride into history as General Custer accompanied by President-to-be Ronald Reagan.

Criminals ambush a security truck in the Nevada desert.
Long-winded, flashily directed, gleamingly photographed, occasionally lively, frequently violent, finally tedious caper melodrama with a multi-lingual cast.

w Antonio Isasi, Jo Eisinger *d* Antonio Isasi *ph Juan Gelpi m* Georges Gavarentz

Jack Palance, Lee J. Cobb, Elke Sommer, Gary Lockwood, Georges Geret, Jean Servais

They Dare Not Love
US 1941 76m bw
Columbia (Sam Bischoff)

An Austrian prince flees the Nazis, but they force him to return and he has to leave his fiancée in America.
Curiously naïve romantic propaganda from this director; not at all memorable.

w Charles Bennett, Ernest Vajda *d* James Whale *ph* Franz Planer *m* Morris Stoloff

George Brent, Martha Scott, Paul Lukas, Egon Brecher, Roman Bohnen, Edgar Barrier, Frank Reicher

They Died with Their Boots On**
US 1941 140m bw
Warner (Robert Fellows)

The life of General Custer and his death at Little Big Horn.
It seems it all happened because of an evil cadet who finished up selling guns to the Indians. Oh, well! The first half is romantic comedy, the second steels itself for the inevitable tragic outcome, but it's all expertly mounted and played in the best old Hollywood style.

w Wally Kline, Aeneas Mackenzie *d Raoul Walsh ph Bert Glennon m* Max Steiner

Errol Flynn, Olivia de Havilland, Arthur Kennedy, Charles Grapewin, Anthony Quinn, Sidney Greenstreet, Gene Lockhart, Stanley Ridges, John Litel, Walter Hampden, Regis Toomey, Hattie McDaniel

They Drive by Night**
GB 1938 84m bw
Warner (Jerome Jackson)

An ex-convict is helped by lorry drivers to solve the silk stocking murders of which he is suspected.
Excellent, little-seen British suspenser of the Hitchcock school.

w Derek Twist, novel James Curtis *d* Arthur Woods *ph* Basil Emmott

Emlyn Williams, Ernest Thesiger, Anna Konstam, Allan Jeayes, Antony Holles, Ronald Shiner

'Dialogue, acting and direction put this picture on a level with the French cinema.'—*Graham Greene*

They Drive by Night**
US 1940 97m bw
Warner (Mark Hellinger)
GB title: *The Road to Frisco*

A truck driver loses his brother in an accident, and in an attempt to improve his lot becomes involved with a scheming murderess.
Solid melodramatic entertainment which borrows the second half of its plot from *Bordertown*.

w Jerry Wald, Richard Macaulay, *novel* Long Haul by A. I. Bezzerides *d Raoul Walsh ph* Arthur Edeson *md* Adolph Deutsch

George Raft, Humphrey Bogart, *Ann Sheridan, Ida Lupino*, Gale Page, Alan Hale, Roscoe Karns, John Litel, Henry O'Neill, George Tobias

They Flew Alone*
GB 1941 103m bw
RKO / Imperator (Herbert Wilcox)
US title: *Wings and the Woman*

The story of Amy Johnson and Jim Mollison, married flying pioneers of the thirties.
Adequate fictionalized history with interesting historical detail.

w Miles Malleson *d* Herbert Wilcox *ph* Frederick A. Young

Anna Neagle, Robert Newton, Edward Chapman, Nora Swinburne, Joan Kemp-Welch, Charles Carson, Brefni O'Rourke

They Gave Him a Gun
US 1937 94m bw
MGM (Harry Rapf)

Despite the efforts of his friend, a war-hardened veteran turns to crime and comes to a sticky end.
Dullish moral melodrama with its stars looking as though stuck in glue.

w Cyril Hume, Richard Maibaum, Maurice Rapf, *novel* William Joyce Cowan *d* W. S. Van Dyke II *ph* Harold Rosson

Spencer Tracy, Franchot Tone, Gladys George, Edgar Dearing, Mary Treen, Cliff Edwards

'Meller overboard on grief. Does not sum up as having b.o. punch.'—*Variety*

They Go Boom
US 1929 20m bw

Stan's nocturnal efforts to cure Ollie's cold nearly bring down the house about their ears.
Average, rather protracted star comedy.
Laurel and Hardy, Charlie Hall. Written by Leo McCarey and H. M. Walker; directed by James Parrott; for Hal Roach.

They Got Me Covered*
US 1943 93m bw
Samuel Goldwyn

An incompetent foreign correspondent inadvertently breaks up a spy ring in Washington.
One of Hope's better and most typical comedy-thriller vehicles.

w Harry Kurnitz *d* David Butler *ph* Rudolph Maté *m* Leigh Harline

Bob Hope, Dorothy Lamour, Otto Preminger, Lenore Aubert, Eduardo Ciannelli, Marion Martin, Donald Meek, Donald MacBride, Walter Catlett, John Abbott, Florence Bates, Philip Ahn

They Just Had to Get Married
US 1933 69m bw

A butler and maid come into money and rise in the social scale. Rather muddled comedy for star fans. Zasu Pitts, Slim Summerville, C. Aubrey Smith, Roland Young, Verree Teasdale, Fifi D'Orsay, Robert Greig, David Landau, Elizabeth Patterson. Written by Gladys Lehman and H. M. Walker from the play by Syril Harcourt; directed by Edward Ludwig; for Universal. 'Not for big town first runs, but a booker's selection for B houses or less.'—*Variety*

They Knew Mr Knight
GB 1945 93m bw

A clerk and his family become rich, then poor, through listening to a speculator. Slightly oddball domestic drama reminiscent of Priestley's *Angel Pavement*. Mervyn Johns, Alfred Drayton, Nora Swinburne, Joyce Howard, Joan Greenwood, Olive Sloane, Peter Hammond. Written by Norman Walker and Victor MacClure, from the novel by Dorothy Whipple; directed by Norman Walker; for IP / GHW.

They Knew What They Wanted**
US 1940 96m bw
RKO (Erich Pommer)

A waitress agrees by mail to marry a California-Italian vineyard owner, but is aghast when she arrives to discover that he sent his handsome foreman's photograph.
First-rate minor drama, expertly handled by stars and production team alike.

w Robert Ardrey, *play* Sidney Howard *d Garson Kanin* *ph* Harry Stradling *m* Alfred Newman

Charles Laughton, Carole Lombard, William Gargan, Harry Carey, Frank Fay

'For dialogue, acting, background and film creation it's a honey.'—*Otis Ferguson*

† Previous versions include *The Secret Love* (1928) with Pola Negri and *A Lady to Love* (1930) with Vilma Banky (and Edward G. Robinson).

AAN: William Gargan

They Live by Night*
US 1948 96m bw
RKO

A young man imprisoned for an accidental killing escapes with two hardened criminals and is forced to take part in their crimes.
Well-made if basically uninteresting melodrama with a draggy romantic interest; its 'realistic' yet impressionist style drew attention on its first release, and it was remade in the seventies as *Thieves like Us* (qv).

w Charles Schnee *d Nicholas Ray* *ph George E. Diskant* *m* Leigh Harline

Farley Granger, Cathy O'Donnell, Howard da Silva

They Made Me a Criminal*
US 1939 92m bw
Warner (Benjamin Glazer)

When he thinks he has killed a boxing opponent, a young man flees to the west and settles on a farm.
Competent remake of *The Life of Jimmy Dolan*, a tribute to the American way.

w Sig Herzig *d* Busby Berkeley *ph* James Wong Howe *m* Max Steiner

John Garfield, Claude Rains, Gloria Dickson, May Robson, Billy Halop, Bobby Jordan, Leo Gorcey, Huntz Hall, Gabriel Dell, Ann Sheridan

'Handsomely mounted and printed on sepia stock—all of which helps.'—*Variety*

They Made Me a Fugitive*
GB 1947 104m bw
Warner / Alliance (Nat Bronsten, James Carter)
US title: *I Became a Criminal*

An ex-RAF pilot is drawn into black marketeering. Framed for a killing, he escapes from Dartmoor and takes revenge on the gang leader.
Deliberately squalid thriller which began a fashion for British realism, but now seems only momentarily entertaining.

w Noel Langley, *novel* A Convict Has Escaped by Jackson Budd *d* Alberto Cavalcanti *ph* Otto Heller

Trevor Howard, Sally Gray, *Griffith Jones*, René Ray, Mary Merrall, Vida Hope, Ballard Berkeley, Phyllis Robins

They Made Me a Killer
US 1946 65m bw

A young man framed by bank robbers proves his innocence. Elementary cops-and-robbers, not too badly presented for a second feature. Robert Lowery, Barbara Britton, Frank Albertson, Lola Lane, James Bush. Written by Geoffrey Homes, Winston Miller, Kae Salkow, Owen Francis; directed by William C. Thomas; for Pine–Thomas / Paramount.

They Met in Argentina
US 1941 76m bw

A Texas oil millionaire sends his representative to buy a horse which has been winning races in Buenos Aires. Thin romantic comedy in pursuance of the good neighbour policy. Maureen O'Hara, James Ellison, Alberto Vila, Buddy Ebsen, Robert Barrat, Joseph Buloff. Written by Jerry Cady, Lou Brock, Harold Daniels; directed by Leslie Goodwins, Jack Hively; for Lou Brock / RKO.

They Met in Bombay*
US 1941 86m bw
MGM (Hunt Stromberg)

Jewel thieves on the run in the East fall in love.
A rather unusual romantic comedy chase which provides pretty satisfactory star entertainment.

w Edwin Justus Mayer, Anita Loos, Leon Gordon *d Clarence Brown* *ph* William Daniels *m* Herbert Stothart

Clark Gable, Rosalind Russell, Peter Lorre, Reginald Owen, Jessie Ralph, Matthew Boulton, Eduardo Ciannelli, Luis Alberni

They Met in the Dark
GB 1943 104m bw

A Blackpool theatrical agent is really a master spy. Elementary spy romance with a richly villainous performance from *Tom Walls*. Joyce Howard, James Mason, Phyllis Stanley, Edward Rigby, Ronald Ward, David Farrar. Written by Anatole de Grunwald, Miles Malleson, Basil Bartlett, Victor MacClure and

James Seymour, from the novel *The Vanishing Corpse* by Anthony Gilbert; directed by Karel Lamac; for Marcel Hellman / Rank.

They Might be Giants*
US 1972 88m Technicolor
Universal / Paul Newman, John Foreman

A lawyer imagines he is Sherlock Holmes, and is taken in hand by Dr Mildred Watson.
Curious fantasy comedy which rather tentatively satirizes modern life and the need to retreat into unreality. Mildly pleasing entertainment for intellectuals.

w James Goldman, from his play *d* Anthony Harvey *ph* Victor Kemper *m* John Barry

George C. Scott, Joanne Woodward, Jack Gilford, Lester Rawlins

They Only Kill Their Masters*
US 1972 98m Metrocolor
MGM (William Belasco)

A village police chief doggedly solves a series of murders.
Atmospheric, serio-comic murder mystery with a cast of old hands.

w Lane Slate *d* James Goldstone *ph* Michel Hugo *m* Perry Botkin Jnr

James Garner, Katharine Ross, Hal Holbrook, June Allyson, Harry Guardino, Tom Ewell, Peter Lawford, Ann Rutherford, Chris Connelly, Edmond O'Brien, Art Metrano, Arthur O'Connell

'The lovers of *The Caine Mutiny* have a picture all their own!'

They Rode West
US 1954 84m Technicolor

A cavalry doctor at a frontier fort gets into trouble by trying to help the Indians. Western programmer whose sights are higher than its achievement. Robert Francis, Donna Reed, May Wynn, Phil Carey, Onslow Stevens, Jack Kelly. Written by De Vallon Scott and Frank Nugent; directed by Phil Karlson; for Columbia.

They Shall Have Music
US 1939 105m bw
Samuel Goldwyn
GB title: *Melody of Youth*

Jascha Heifetz conducts a charity concert to help a music school for slum children.
Formula family film given the best possible production.

w John Howard Lawson, Irmgard Von Cube *d* Archie Mayo *ph* Gregg Toland *md* Alfred Newman

Joel McCrea, Jascha Heifetz, Andrea Leeds, Gene Reynolds, Walter Brennan, Porter Hall, Terry Kilburn, Diana Lynn (Dolly Loehr)

'A natural for the musically minded . . . elemental and surefire audience appeal.'—*Variety*

AAN: Alfred Newman

They Shoot Horses, Don't They?*
US 1969 129m De Luxe Panavision
Palomar / Chartoff–Winkler–Pollack

Tragedy during a six-day marathon dance contest in the early thirties.
An unrelievedly harrowing melodrama about dreary people, confused by 'flashforwards' but full of skilled technique, entertaining detail, and one brilliant performance.

w James Poe, Robert E. Thompson, *novel* Horace McCoy *d Sydney Pollack* *ph Philip Lathrop* *m* John Green *md* John Green, Albert Woodbury *pd* Harry Horner

Gig Young, Jane Fonda, Susannah York, Michael Sarrazin, Red Buttons, Bonnie Bedelia, Bruce Dern

COMPÈRE (Gig Young): 'There can only be one winner, folks, but isn't that the American way?'

AA: Gig Young
AAN: script; John Green, Albert Woodbury; Sydney Pollack; Jane Fonda; Susannah York

They Were Expendable*
US 1945 135m bw
MGM (John Ford, Cliff Reid)

Life in and around motor torpedo boats in the Pacific War.
Long drawn out flagwaver with some nice moments.

w Frank Wead, *book* William L. White *d* John Ford *ph* Joseph H. August *m* Herbert Stothart

John Wayne, Robert Montgomery, Donna Reed, Jack Holt, Ward Bond, Marshall Thompson, Leon Ames, Cameron Mitchell, Jeff York

'For what seems at least half its dogged, devoted length all you have to watch is men getting on or off PT boats and other men watching them do so. But this is made so beautiful and so real that I could not feel one foot of the film was wasted.'—*James Agee*

They Were Not Divided*
GB 1950 102m bw
Rank / Two Cities (Herbert Smith)

The life of a Guards officer is paralleled with that of his American friend; they both die on a reconnaissance during the advance on Berlin.
Odd mixture of barrack room comedy, semi-documentary action, propaganda and the most appalling sentimentality. No one questioned it at the box office, though.

wd Terence Young *ph* Harry Waxman *m* Lambert Williamson

Edward Underdown, Ralph Clanton, Helen Cherry, Stella Andrews, Michael Brennan, Michael Trubshaw, R.S.M. Brittain

'It is a rather curious experience to see a film made with all the best trappings of realism containing so many of the clichés of the studio.'—*Gavin Lambert*

They Were Sisters
GB 1945 115m bw
GFD / Gainsborough (Harold Huth)

The problems of three married sisters.
Flatly handled multi-melodrama, the chief attraction being 'wicked' James Mason as a sadist.

w Roland Pertwee, *novel* Dorothy Whipple *d* Arthur Crabtree *ph* Jack Cox *m* Louis Levy

James Mason, Phyllis Calvert, Dulcie Gray, Hugh Sinclair, Anne Crawford, Peter Murray Hill, Pamela Kellino

They Who Dare
GB 1953 107m Technicolor
British Lion / Mayflower (Aubrey Baring, Maxwell Setton)

During World War II a group of British soldiers are sent on a raiding expedition to Rhodes.
Grimmish war actioner with plenty of noise but not much holding power.

w Robert Westerby *d* Lewis Milestone *ph* Wilkie Cooper *m* Robert Gill

Dirk Bogarde, Denholm Elliott, Akim Tamiroff, Gérard Oury, Eric Pohlmann, Alec Mango

They Won't Believe Me*
US 1947 95m bw
RKO (Joan Harrison)

A playboy finds himself on trial for murder because of his philandering with three women.
Unusual suspenser with Hitchcock touches; quite neatly packaged, complete with twist ending.

w Jonathan Latimer *d* Irving Pichel *ph* Harry J. Wild *m* Roy Webb

Robert Young, Susan Hayward, Rita Johnson, Jane Greer, Tom Powers, Don Beddoe, Frank Ferguson

'Talk and die! Until now their lips were frozen with fear!'

They Won't Forget***
US 1937 94m bw
Warner (Mervyn Le Roy)

The murder of a girl in a southern town leads to a lynching.
Finely detailed social drama, a classic of American realism; harrowing to watch.

w Robert Rossen, Aben Kandel, novel Death in the Deep South by Ward Greene *d Mervyn Le Roy* *ph* Arthur Edeson, Warren Lynch *m* Adolph Deutsch *md* Leo F. Forbstein

Claude Rains, Gloria Dickson, Edward Norris, Otto Kruger, Allyn Joslyn, Linda Perry, Elisha Cook Jnr, Lana Turner, Cy Kendall, Elizabeth Risdon

'Not only an honest picture, but an example of real movie-making.'—*Pare Lorenz*

They're a Weird Mob
Australia 1966 112m colour

An Italian journalist goes to Australia and doesn't get on at first. Patchy comedy from a local best-seller. Walter Chiari, Clare Dunne, Chips Rafferty, Alida Chelli, Ed Devereaux, John Meillon. Written by Nino Culotta (John O'Grady); directed by Michael Powell; for Williamson–Powell.

Thicker than Water
US 1924 20m bw silent

Ollie spends his savings on a grandfather clock which is promptly destroyed by a passing truck. Well made but slightly tiresome star comedy, the last short ever made featuring Stan and Ollie. Laurel and Hardy, Daphne Pollard, James Finlayson. Written by Stan Laurel; directed by James W. Horne; for Hal Roach.

The Thief*
US 1952 86m bw
Harry M. Popkin (Clarence Greene)

A nuclear physicist is on the run from the FBI, who suspect him of being a spy.
Curious attempt to produce a thriller with no dialogue whatever; parts are well done, but the strain eventually shows, as the makers are not quite clever enough to flesh out the trickery with human interest.

w Clarence Greene, Russel Rouse *d* Russel Rouse *ph Sam Leavitt m* Herschel Gilbert

Ray Milland, Martin Gabel, Rita Gam, Harry Bronson, John McKutcheon

AAN: Herschel Gilbert

Thief
US 1981 123m Astrocolor
United Artists / Michael Mann / Caan Productions
GB title: *Violent Streets*

A high class thief's professional life is contrasted with his personal problems.
And at far too great a length, with the additional problem that few people are really interested. A slick but empty melodrama.

wd Michael Mann, *novel* The Home Invaders by Frank Hohimer *ph* Donald Thorin *m* Tangerine Dream *pd* Mel Bourne

James Caan, Tuesday Weld, Willie Nelson, James Belushi

'It promises too much and delivers too little.'—*Richard Combs, MFB*

The Thief of Bagdad***
US 1924 approx 135m (24fps) bw silent
Douglas Fairbanks

In old Bagdad, a thief uses magic to outwit the evil Caliph.
Celebrated silent version of the old fable, its camera tricks a little timeworn now but nevertheless maintaining the air of a true classic by virtue of its leading performance and driving narrative energy.

w Lotta Woods, Douglas Fairbanks *d Raoul Walsh ph Arthur Edeson m* Mortimer Wilson *ad William Cameron Menzies*

Douglas Fairbanks, Snitz Edwards, Charles Belcher, Anna May Wong, Julanne Johnston, Etta Lee, Brandon Hurst, Sojin

'An entrancing picture, wholesome and compelling, deliberate and beautiful, a feat of motion picture art which has never been equalled.'—*New York Times*

'Here is magic. Here is beauty. Here is the answer to cynics who give the motion picture no place in the family of the arts . . . a work of rare genius.'—*James Quirk, Photoplay*

The Thief of Baghdad****
GB 1940 109m Technicolor
London Films (Alexander Korda)

A boy thief helps a deposed king thwart an evil usurper.
Marvellous blend of magic, action and music, the only film to catch on celluloid the overpowering atmosphere of the Arabian Nights.

w Miles Malleson, Lajos Biro d Michael Powell, Ludwig Berger, Tim Whelan ph Georges Périnal, Osmond Borradaile m Miklos Rozsa sp Lawrence Butler

Conrad Veidt, Sabu, John Justin, June Duprez, Morton Selten, Miles Malleson, *Rex Ingram*, Mary Morris

ABU (Sabu): 'I'm Abu the thief, son of Abu the thief, grandson of Abu the thief, most unfortunate of ten sons with a hunger that yearns day and night . . .'

AGED KING (Morton Selten): 'This is the Land of Legend, where everything is possible when seen through the eyes of youth.'

'The true stuff of fairy tale.'—*Basil Wright*

'Both spectacular and highly inventive.'—*NFT, 1969*

'Magical, highly entertaining, and now revalued by Hollywood moguls Lucas and Coppola.'—*Time Out, 1980*

AA: Georges Périnal, Osmond Borradaile
AAN: Miklos Rozsa

The Thief of Baghdad
Italy / France 1960 100m Eastmancolor / Cinemascope

A very moderate remake in the form of an action star vehicle. Steve Reeves, Georgia Moll, Arturo Dominici. Written by Augusto Frassinetti, Filippo Sanjust and Bruno Vailati; directed by Arthur Lubin; for Titanus / Lux.

Thief of Damascus
US 1952 78m Technicolor
Columbia / Sam Katzman

The wicked ruler of Damascus is deposed by his own general, in league with Sinbad, Aladdin, and Scheherezade.
Mindless bosh, interesting only for its liberal use of scenes from *Joan of Arc*; the mind boggles at the costume compromise.

w Robert E. Kent *d* Will Jason *ph* Ellis W. Carter *m* Mischa Bakaleinikoff

Paul Henreid, Lon Chaney Jnr, Jeff Donnell, John Sutton, Elena Verdugo

The Thief Who Came to Dinner
US 1973 105m De Luxe
Warner / Tandem (Bud Yorkin)

A computer analyst determines to become a jewel thief.
Tedious comedy aping the *Raffles* school but saddled with a complex plot and listless script.

w Walter Hill, *novel* Terence L. Smith *d* Bud Yorkin *ph* Philip Lathrop *m* Henry Mancini

Ryan O'Neal, Jacqueline Bisset, Warren Oates, Jill Clayburgh, Charles Cioffi

Thieves Fall Out
US 1941 72m bw

An old lady lends her grandson money to start his business, but he has to rescue her when she's kidnapped. Fairly amusing goings-on to fill the lower half of a bill. Jane Darwell, Eddie Albert, Joan Leslie, Alan Hale, William T. Orr, John Litel, Anthony Quinn, Edward Brophy. Written by Charles Grayson and Ben Markson, from play by Irving Gaumont and Jack Sobel; directed by Ray Enright; for First National / Warner.

Thieves' Highway**
US 1949 94m bw
TCF (Robert Bassler)

A truck driver tracks down the racketeers who cheated and maimed his father.
Glossy, highly professional thick ear shedding a convincing light into one of America's less salubrious corners.

w A. I. Bezzerides, from his novel Thieves' Market *d Jules Dassin ph Norbert Brodine m* Alfred Newman

Richard Conte, Valentina Cortesa, Lee J. Cobb, Jack Oakie, Millard Mitchell, Joseph Pevney, Barbara Lawrence, Hope Emerson

'You will never be able to eat an apple again without calling up visions of trickery, mayhem, vandalism and violent death.'—*New York Times*

'The action sequences are brilliantly done.'—*Daily Mail*

Thieves Like Us*
US 1974 123m De Luxe
United Artists / Jerry Bick–George Litto (Robert Eggenwiler)

Three convicts break jail, and the youngest is attracted to the daughter of the farmer who helps them escape.
Gloomy romantic melodrama, agreeably set in the thirties and feelingly acted, but otherwise inferior to the much shorter version released in the forties as *They Live by Night*.

w Calder Willingham, Joan Tewkesbury, Robert Altman, *novel* Edward Anderson *d* Robert Altman *ph* Jean Boffety *m* various songs *ed* Lou Lombardo

Keith Carradine, Shelley Duvall, John Schuck, Bert Remsen, Louise Fletcher, Tom Skerritt

Thin Ice*
US 1937 78m bw
TCF (Raymond Griffith)
GB title: *Lovely to Look At*

A skating instructress at an Alpine resort falls in love with a visiting prince.
Light-hearted musical vehicle for Hollywood's newest novelty—a skating star.

w Boris Ingster, Milton Sperling, *novel* Der Komet by Attilla Orbok *d* Sidney Lanfield *ph* Robert Planck, Edward Cronjager *md* Louis Silvers *songs* Lew Pollack, Sidney Mitchell

Sonja Henie, Tyrone Power, Arthur Treacher, Raymond Walburn, Joan Davis, Sig Rumann, Alan Hale, Melville Cooper

'She's a flash of winter lightning, a great combination of muscle and music, a Pavlova on ice . . . production wallop is the staging of three elaborate ice ballets.'—*Variety*

'A laugh tops every thrilling moment!'
The Thin Man***
US 1934 93m bw
MGM / Cosmopolitan (Hunt Stromberg)

In New York over Christmas, a tipsy detective with his wife and dog solves the murder of an eccentric inventor.
Fast-moving, alternately comic and suspenseful mystery drama developed in brief scenes and fast wipes. It set a sparkling comedy career for two stars previously known for heavy drama, it was frequently imitated, and it showed a wisecracking, affectionate married relationship almost for the first time.

w Frances Goodrich, Albert Hackett, novel Dashiell Hammett d W. S. Van Dyke ph James Wong Howe *m* William Axt

William Powell, Myrna Loy, Maureen O'Sullivan, Nat Pendleton, Minna Gombell, Edward Ellis, Porter Hall, Henry Wadsworth, William Henry, Harold Huber, Cesar Romero, Edward Brophy

'A strange mixture of excitement, quips and hard-boiled sentiment . . . full of the special touches that can come from nowhere but the studio, that really make the feet a movie walks on.'—*Otis Ferguson*

† Sequels, on the whole of descending merit, included the following, all made at MGM with the same star duo: 1936: *After the Thin Man* (110m). 1939: *Another Thin Man* (102m). 1941: *Shadow of the Thin Man* (97m). 1944: *The Thin Man Goes Home* (100m). 1947: *Song of the Thin Man* (86m).

AAN: best picture; script; W. S. Van Dyke; William Powell

The Thin Red Line
US 1964 99m bw Cinemascope
Security / ACE (Sidney Harmon)

Raw recruits land on Guadalcanal and most of them are killed.
Weary, routine, realistic war drama.

w Bernard Gordon, *novel* James Jones *d* Andrew Marton *ph* Manuel Berenguer *m* Malcolm Arnold

Keir Dullea, Jack Warden, James Philbrook, Kieron Moore

The Thing**
US 1951 87m bw
RKO / Winchester (Howard Hawks)
GB title: *The Thing from Another World*

A US scientific expedition in the Arctic is menaced by a ferocious being they inadvertently thaw out from a spaceship.
Curiously drab suspense shocker mainly set in corridors, with insufficient surprises to sustain its length. It does, however, contain the first space monster on film, and is quite nimbly made, though it fails to use the central gimmick from its original story.

w Charles Lederer, *story* Who Goes There by J. W. Campbell Jnr *d* Christian Nyby (with mysterious help, either Hawks or Orson Welles) *ph* Russell Harlan *m* Dmitri Tiomkin

Robert Cornthwaite, Kenneth Tobey, Margaret Sheridan, Bill Self, Dewey Martin, James Arness (as the thing)

LAST SPEECH OF FILM: 'I bring you warning—to every one of you listening to the sound of my voice. Tell the world, tell this to everyone wherever they are: watch the skies, watch everywhere, keep looking—watch the skies!'

'There seems little point in creating a monster of such original characteristics if he is to be allowed only to prowl about the North Pole, waiting to be destroyed by the superior ingenuity of the US Air Force.'—*Penelope Houston*

'A monster movie with pace, humour and a collection of beautifully timed jabs of pure horror.'—*NFT, 1967*

'Man is the warmest place to hide!'
The Thing
US 1982 109m Technicolor Panavision
Universal / Lawrence Turman, David Foster

A remake using the basis of the original story (the thing conceals itself within each of the characters in turn) but filled with revolting detail which alienated many audiences.

w Bill Lancaster *d* John Carpenter *ph* Dean Cundey *m* Ennio Morricone *sp* Albert Whitlock

Kurt Russell, A. Wilford Brimley, T. K. Carter, David Clennon, Richard Dysart, Richard Masur

'The doctor blew it—he transplanted a white bigot's head onto a soul brother's body!'
The Thing with Two Heads
US 1972 89m colour

A racist brain surgeon with terminal cancer arranges to have his head transplanted on to the body of a convict; but the convict turns out to be black. Bad taste comedy-horror with a great many frantic action sequences. Beyond criticism. Ray Milland, Rosey Grier, Roger Perry, William Smith. Written by Lee Frost, Wes Bishop, James Gordon White; directed by Lee Frost; for AIP.

'Every bit as preposterous as it sounds.'—*LA Times*

Things Are Looking Up
GB 1935 78m bw

A circus horsewoman has to pose as her schoolmistress sister. Lively star vehicle for an oddly matched team. Cicely Courtneidge, William Gargan, Max Miller, Mary Lawson, Dick Henderson, Dick Henderson Jnr, Judy Kelly, Suzanne Lenglen, Vivien Leigh. Written by Stafford Davies and Con West; directed by Albert de Courville; for Gaumont.

Things to Come****
GB 1936 113m bw
London Films (Alexander Korda)

War in 1940 is followed by plague, rebellion, a new glass-based society, and the first rocketship to the moon.
Fascinating, chilling and dynamically well-staged vignettes tracing mankind's future. Bits of the script and acting may be wobbly, but the sets and music are magnificent, the first part of the prophecy chillingly accurate, and the whole mammoth undertaking almost unique in film history.

w H. G. Wells, from his book The Shape of Things to Come *d / pd William Cameron Menzies ph Georges Périnal m Arthur Bliss sp Harry Zech, Ned Mann ad Vincent Korda*

Raymond Massey, Edward Chapman, Ralph Richardson, Margaretta Scott, Cedric Hardwicke, Sophie Stewart, Derrick de Marney, John Clements

CABAL (Raymond Massey): 'It is this or that—all the universe or nothing. Which shall it be, Passworthy? Which shall it be?'

THEOTOCOPULOS (Cedric Hardwicke): 'What is this progress? What is the good of all this progress onward and onward? We demand a halt. We demand a rest . . . an end to progress! Make an end to this progress now! Let this be the last day of the scientific age!'

'Successful in every department except emotionally. For heart interest Mr Wells hands you an electric switch . . . It's too bad present-day film distribution isn't on a Wells 2040 basis, when the negative cost could be retrieved by button pushing. It's going to be harder than that. It's going to be almost impossible.'—*Variety*

'An amazingly ingenious technical accomplishment, even if it does hold out small hope for our race . . . the existence pictured is as joyless as a squeezed grapefruit.'—*Don Herold*

'A leviathan among films . . . a stupendous spectacle, an overwhelming, Dorean, Jules Vernesque, elaborated *Metropolis*, staggering to eye, mind and spirit, the like of which has never been seen and never will be seen again.'—*The Sunday Times*

The Third Day
US 1965 119m Technicolor Panavision
Warner (Jack Smight)

An amnesiac learns that he is a rich unpopular tycoon facing a major crisis.
Glum melodrama which suggests domestic mystery but provides only interminable chat.

w Burton Wohl, Robert Presnell Jnr, *novel* Joseph Hayes *d* Jack Smight *ph* Robert Surtees *m* Percy Faith

George Peppard, Elizabeth Ashley, Roddy McDowall, Herbert Marshall, Mona Washbourne, Robert Webber, Charles Drake, Sally Kellerman, Arte Johnson, Vincent Gardenia

Third Finger Left Hand
US 1940 96m bw
MGM (John W. Considine Jnr)

A lady fashion editor fends off unwanted suitors by saying she is already married, but a commercial artist trumps this card by claiming to be the long lost husband of her invention. Cheerful but overstretched romantic comedy.

w Lionel Houser *d* Robert Z. Leonard *ph* George Folsey *m* David Snell

Myrna Loy, Melvyn Douglas, Lee Bowman, Bonita Granville, Raymond Walburn, Felix Bressart, Sidney Blackmer

The Third Generation
West Germany 1979 111m colour

A Berlin executive becomes the victim of a gang of terrorists. Realistic melodrama, curiously muted in its satire and its anger, watchable more as an entertainment than as a polemic. Volker Spengler, Bulle Ogier, Harry Baer, Eddie Constantine. Written, directed, photographed and produced by Rainer Werner Fassbinder; for Tango / Project / FDA.

The Third Man****
GB 1949 100m bw
British Lion / London Films / David O. Selznick / Alexander Korda (Carol Reed)

An unintelligent but tenacious writer of westerns arrives in post-war Vienna to join his old friend Harry Lime, who seems to have met with an accident . . . or has he?
Totally memorable and irresistible romantic thriller. Stylish from the first to the last, with inimitable backgrounds of zither music and war-torn buildings pointing up a then-topical black market story full of cynical characters but not without humour. Hitchcock with feeling, if you like.

w Graham Greene d Carol Reed ph Robert Krasker m Anton Karas

Joseph Cotten, Trevor Howard, Alida Valli, Orson Welles, Bernard Lee, Wilfrid Hyde White, Ernst Deutsch, Siegfried Breuer, Erich Ponto, Paul Hoerbiger

HARRY LIME (Orson Welles): 'Look down there. Would you really feel any pity if one of those dots stopped moving for ever? If I offered you twenty thousand pounds for every dot that stopped, would you really, old man, tell me to keep my money, or would you calculate how many dots you could afford to spare? Free of income tax, old man, free of income tax. It's the only way to save money nowadays.'

LIME: 'In Italy for thirty years under the Borgias they had warfare, terror, murder and bloodshed, but they produced Michelangelo, Leonardo da Vinci and the Renaissance. In Switzerland, they had brotherly love; they had five hundred years of democracy and peace—and what did that produce? The cuckoo clock.'

'Sensitive and humane and dedicated, [Reed] would seem to be enclosed from life with no specially strong feelings about the stories that come his way other than that they should be something he can perfect and polish with a craftsman's love.'—*Richard Winnington*

'Crammed with cinematic plums which could do the early Hitchcock proud.'—*Time*

AA: Robert Krasker
AAN: Carol Reed

Third Man on the Mountain
GB 1959 103m Technicolor
Walt Disney (Bill Anderson)

In 1865 a Swiss dishwasher dreams of conquering the local mountain, and befriends a distinguished mountaineer.
Handsomely photographed boys' adventure story.

w Eleanore Griffin, *novel* Banner in the Sky by James Ramsay Ullman *d* Ken Annakin *ph* Harry Waxman, *George Tairraz* *m* William Alwyn

James MacArthur, Michael Rennie, Janet Munro, James Donald, Herbert Lom, Laurence Naismith, Walter Fitzgerald, Nora Swinburne

'The story of a man searching for a killer—who might even be himself!'

The Third Secret
GB 1964 103m bw Cinemascope
TCF / Hubris (Robert L. Joseph)

A psychiatrist apparently commits suicide; a patient who has relied on his strength finds the truth by interviewing other patients.
Pretentious package of short stories, only one of which is relevant to the frame (yet another one featuring Patricia Neal was shot but discarded); full of philosophical conversations on a Thames mudbank and other absurdities, but well enough put together.

w Robert L. Joseph d Charles Crichton *ph* Douglas Slocombe *m* Richard Arnell

Stephen Boyd, *Pamela Franklin*, Jack Hawkins, Richard Attenborough, Rachel Kempson, Diane Cilento, Paul Rogers, Freda Jackson

'An unappealing and irritatingly muddled scribble of a film, thoroughly lacking in suspense, veracity and justification.'—*MFB*

The Third Voice**
US 1959 80m bw Cinemascope
TCF (Maury Dexter, Hubert Cornfield)

A woman kills her wealthy lover and an accomplice impersonates him through a series of complex negotiations.
Superstylish minor thriller, with a plot fascinating as it unfolds and a climax which is only a slight letdown.

wd Hubert Cornfield, novel All the Way by Charles Williams *ph* Ernest Haller *m* Johnny Mandel

Edmond O'Brien, Laraine Day, Julie London

Thirteen*
USSR 1937 90m approx bw

Red Army soldiers are trekking from well to well through the desert. When help arrives only one is left. Russian adventure film which was supposedly copied from *The Lost Patrol* but itself inspired *Sahara*. Good stuff, anyway. Written by L. Prout, Mikhail Romm; directed by Mikhail Romm; for Mosfilm.

Thirteen Ghosts
US 1960 88m bw (colour sequence)
Columbia / William Castle

A penniless scholar inherits a haunted house. Childish thriller for which the audience was issued with a 'ghost viewer' (anaglyph spectacles) so that they could see the 'spirits'. The gimmick was called Illusion-O.

w Robb White *d* William Castle *ph* Joseph Biroc *m* Von Dexter

Charles Herbert, Jo Morrow, Martin Milner, Rosemary de Camp, Donald Woods, Margaret Hamilton

'Hurtling through space, eight people live fifteen dangerous, unforgettable hours!'

Thirteen Hours by Air*
US 1936 80m bw
Paramount (E. Lloyd Sheldon)

A transcontinental plane is hijacked by an ex-convict.
Solidly carpentered minor thriller which is also an interesting record of the early days of commercial aviation.

w Bogart Rogers, Kenyon Nicholson *d Mitchell Leisen* *ph* Theodor Sparkhul

Fred MacMurray, Joan Bennett, Zasu Pitts, Alan Baxter, Fred Keating, Brian Donlevy, John Howard, Ruth Donnelly, Dean Jagger

13 Rue Madeleine*
US 1946 95m bw
TCF (Louis de Rochemont)

Four trained American espionage agents locate a Nazi rocket site in France.
Semi-documentary spy stuff in the tradition of *The House on 92nd Street* but rather less satisfactory despite excellent technique.

w John Monks Jnr, Sy Bartlett *d* Henry Hathaway *ph* Norbert Brodine *m* David Buttolph *md* Alfred Newman

James Cagney, Annabella, Richard Conte, Frank Latimore, Walter Abel, Melville Cooper, Sam Jaffe, Blanche Yurka

'Far and away the roughest, toughest spy chase yet gleaned from the bulging files of the OSS.'—*Time*

'I stole the plot of *The Virginian* and used it. I'd always wanted to make that story anyway.'—*Henry Hathaway*

'It carries the kick of a mule.'—*Kine Weekly*

† Rex Harrison rejected the role taken by Cagney.

'This is where evil lurks!'

13 West Street*
US 1962 80m bw
Columbia / Ladd Enterprises (William Bloom)

An engineer is attacked on the street by teenage hoodlums and becomes obsessed by revenge.
Competent, darkly photographed, rather dislikeable little thriller, a kind of trial run for *Death Wish*.

w Bernard Schoenfeld, Robert Presnell Jnr *d* Philip Leacock *ph* Charles Lawton Jnr *m* George Duning

Alan Ladd, Rod Steiger, Dolores Dorn, Michael Callan, Kenneth MacKenna, Margaret Hayes

Thirteen Women
US 1932 73m bw

One of thirteen boarding school graduates is trying to murder the others. Thin mystery which wastes its cast. Ricardo Cortez, Irene Dunne, Myrna Loy, Jill Esmond, Florence Eldridge, Julie Haydon, Marjorie Gateson, C. Henry Gordon. Written by Bartlett Cormack, from a novel by Tiffany Thayer; directed by George Archainbaud; for RKO.

The Thirteenth Chair
US 1929 85m bw

A medium holds a seance to unmask a murderer. Effective though now very dated chiller from a Broadway hit. Margaret Wycherly, Bela Lugosi, Holmes Herbert, Conrad Nagel, Leila Hyams. Written by Elliott Clawson, from the play by Bayard Veiller; directed by Tod Browning; for MGM. (NB: The same studio remade the vehicle in 1936 with Dame May Whitty, Henry Daniell, Holmes Herbert—again—Elissa Landi and Lewis Stone; the director was George B. Seitz.) 'Playgoer type will get more enjoyment from it than the moviegoer.'—*Variety*

The Thirteenth Guest
US 1932 70m bw
Monogram (M. H. Hoffman)

A haunted house, a will at midnight, and a frightened lady.
Archetypal comedy thriller, shot on Poverty Row but still watchable.

w Francis Hyland, Arthur Hoerl, *novel* Armitage Traill *d* Albert Ray *ph* Harry Neumann, Tom Galligan

Ginger Rogers, Lyle Talbot, J. Farrell MacDonald, James Eagles, Eddie Phillips, Erville Alderson

'For all classes of houses a positive money maker.'—*Variety*

The Thirteenth Letter*
US 1951 85m bw
TCF (Otto Preminger)

A small French-Canadian town suffers from an outbreak of poison pen letters.
Moderate transcription of a memorable French film, *Le Corbeau*; in this version the events seem all too predictable and the performances dull.

w Howard Koch *d* Otto Preminger *ph* Joseph La Shelle *m* Alex North

Charles Boyer, Linda Darnell, Constance Smith, Michael Rennie, Françoise Rosay, Judith Evelyn

–30–
US 1959 96m bw
Warner / Mark VII (Jack Webb)
GB title: *Deadline Midnight*

A night in the newsroom of a paper preoccupied with scoops.
Not very dramatic, oddly titled and rather pretentious newspaper melodrama confined largely to one set.

w William Bowers *d* Jack Webb *ph* Edward Colman *m* Ray Heindorf

Jack Webb, William Conrad, David Nelson, Whitney Blake, James Bell, Nancy Valentine

Thirty Day Princess*
US 1934 74m bw
Paramount (B. P. Schulberg)

An actress is hired to impersonate a princess who gets mumps while visiting New York in hope of a loan.
Modest comedy which needed a wittier script but is stylishly played.

w Preston Sturges, Frank Partos, *novel* Clarence Budington Kelland *d* Marion Gering *ph* Leon Shamroy

Sylvia Sidney, Cary Grant, Edward Arnold, Henry Stephenson, Vince Barnett, Edgar Norton, Lucien Littlewood

'A compact little picture which will entertain generally.'—*Variety*

Thirty Is a Dangerous Age, Cynthia
GB 1967 84m Technicolor
Columbia / Walter Shenson

A timid nightclub pianist has trouble with women but sells his first musical.
Mild star vehicle for a very mild star, basically a few thin sketches, frantically overdirected.

w Dudley Moore, Joe McGrath, John Wells *d* Joe McGrath *ph* Billy Williams *m* Dudley Moore *titles* Richard Williams

Dudley Moore, Eddie Foy Jnr, Suzy Kendall, John Bird, Duncan Macrae, Patricia Routledge, John Wells

The Thirty-Nine Steps****
GB 1935 81m bw
Gaumont British (Ivor Montagu)

A spy is murdered; the man who has befriended her is suspected, but eludes the police until a chase across Scotland produces the real villains.
Marvellous comedy thriller with most of the gimmicks found not only in Hitchcock's later work but in anyone else's who has tried the same vein. It has little to do with the original novel, and barely sets foot outside the studio, but it makes every second count, and is unparalleled in its use of timing, atmosphere and comedy relief.

w Charles Bennett, Alma Reville, novel John Buchan *d Alfred Hitchcock ph Bernard Knowles m* Hubert Bath, Jack Beaver *md* Louis Levy

Robert Donat, Madeleine Carroll, Godfrey Tearle, Lucie Mannheim, Peggy Ashcroft, John Laurie, *Wylie Watson, Helen Haye*, Frank Cellier

'A narrative of the unexpected—a humorous, exciting, dramatic, entertaining, pictorial, vivid and novel tale told with a fine sense of character and a keen grasp of the cinematic idea.'—*Sydney W. Carroll*

'A miracle of speed and light.'—*Otis Ferguson*

'Such is the zest of the Hitchcock plot that the original point of the title was totally forgotten, and half a line had to be added at the end by way of explanation.'—*George Perry, 1965*

The Thirty-Nine Steps
GB 1959 93m Eastmancolor
Rank (Betty E. Box)

Just to show that stars and story aren't everything, this scene-for-scene remake muffs every opportunity for suspense or general effectiveness, and is practically a manual on how not to make a thriller.

w Frank Harvey *d* Ralph Thomas *ph* Ernest Steward *m* Clifton Parker

Kenneth More, Taina Elg, Barry Jones, Faith Brook, Brenda de Banzie, Duncan Lamont, James Hayter, Michael Goodliffe, Reginald Beckwith

The Thirty-Nine Steps*
GB 1978 102m Eastmancolor
Rank / Norfolk International (James Kenelm Clarke)

Eager-to-please remake which goes back to the original period and more or less the original story, but rather spoils itself by a cliffhanger climax on the face of Big Ben, absurdly borrowed from Will Hay's *My Learned Friend*.

w Michael Robson, *d* Don Sharp *ph* John Coquillon *m* Ed Welch *pd* Harry Pottle

Robert Powell, Karen Dotrice, John Mills, Eric Porter, David Warner, George Baker, Ronald Pickup, Timothy West, Donald Pickering, Andrew Keir, Robert Flemyng, Miles Anderson

Thirty Seconds over Tokyo**
US 1944 138m bw
MGM (Sam Zimbalist)

How the first American attack on Japan was planned.
Sturdy World War II action flagwaver, with Tracy guesting as Colonel Dolittle.

w Dalton Trumbo *d* Mervyn Le Roy *ph* Harold Rosson, Robert Surtees *m* Herbert Stothart

Spencer Tracy, Van Johnson, Robert Walker, Phyllis Thaxter, Tim Murdock, Don Defore, Robert Mitchum

'All of the production involving planes and technical action is so fine that the film has the tough and literal quality of an air force documentary.'—*Bosley Crowther, New York Times*

'A big studio, big scale film, free of artistic pretensions, it is transformed by its not very imaginative but very dogged sincerity into something forceful, simple and thoroughly sympathetic.'—*James Agee*

AAN: Harold Rosson, Robert Surtees

Thirty-Six Hours*
US 1964 115m bw Panavision
MGM / Perlberg–Seaton / Cherokee (William Perlberg)

In 1944 an American major is kidnapped by the Nazis and after drugging is made to think that the war is over.
Well-detailed spy suspenser.

wd George Seaton, *stories* Roald Dahl, Carl K. Hittleman *ph* Philip Lathrop *m* Dmitri Tiomkin

James Garner, Rod Taylor, Eva Marie Saint, Werner Peters, John Banner

Thirty Years of Fun**
US 1962 85m bw
Robert Youngson Productions

A compilation of silent comedy, including Chaplin's *The Floorwalker*, *Easy Street*, *The Pawnshop* and *The Rink*; Keaton's *The Balloonatic* and *Daydreams*; Langdon's *Smile Please*; and Laurel and Hardy's first meeting in *Lucky Dog*.

Not the most hilarious of the compilations, but historically important, with the usual high quality prints which Youngson alone seemed able to provide.

wd Robert Youngson film quality control Paul Guffanti

'What we're fighting for is bigger than you or me!'
This above All*
US 1942 110m bw
TCF (Darryl F. Zanuck)

A surgeon's daughter on active service during World War II falls in love with a conscientious objector who is also an army deserter: he proves his bravery during an air raid.
Superior studio-set war romance.

w R. C. Sheriff, *novel* Eric Knight *d* Anatole Litvak *ph* Arthur Miller *m* Alfred Newman

Tyrone Power, Joan Fontaine, Thomas Mitchell, Henry Stephenson, Nigel Bruce, Gladys Cooper, Philip Merivale, Alexander Knox, Melville Cooper

'Beautiful, stimulating and occasionally powerful.'—*New York Herald Tribune*

'One of the truly great pictures to come out of this war.'—*Motion Picture Herald*

AAN: Arthur Miller

This Angry Age
Italy 1957 104m Technirama

A French widow in Indo-China struggles to keep her rice fields going despite her family's waning interest. Curious international production which suffers from the audience's lack of interest in the central situation. Moments of interest and even beauty, though. Silvana Mangano, Jo Van Fleet, Anthony Perkins, Alida Valli, Richard Conte, Nehemiah Persoff. Written by Irwin Shaw, René Clément, Ivo Perelli and Diego Fabbri, from the novel *Barrage Contre Le Pacifique* by Marguerite Duras; directed by René Clément; for Dino de Laurentiis. (Alternative title: *The Sea Wall*. Original title: *La Diga sul Pacifico*.)

This Could Be the Night
US 1957 104m bw Cinemascope
MGM (Joe Pasternak)

A schoolteacher becomes secretary to a gangster in his Broadway night club.
Unlikely romantic melodrama with music, like a more solemn *Guys and Dolls*.

w Isabel Lennart, *story* Cornelia Baird Gross *d* Robert Wise *ph* Russell Harlan *m* George Stoll

Jean Simmons, Paul Douglas, Tony Franciosa, Julie Wilson, Joan Blondell, J. Carrol Naish, Zasu Pitts

'The master of inspiring spectacle makes his first great spectacle of modern times!'
This Day and Age*
US 1933 98m bw
Paramount / Cecil B. de Mille

During a youth week, boys put a gangster on trial and by his own methods force him to confess to murder.
A curious aberration for de Mille, this fairly powerful movie was condemned in some quarters as an incitement to fascism.

w Bartlett Cormack *d* Cecil B. de Mille *ph* Peverell Marley *m* Howard Jackson, L. W. Gilbert, Abel Baer

Charles Bickford, Richard Cromwell, Judith Allen, Harry Green, Ben Alexander

'A highly improbable and fantastic story but, as done by de Mille, carries more than average audience appeal.'—*Variety*

'Loaded with that power which excites emotional hysteria . . . should stimulate audiences to the same pitch of enthusiasm as it did the preview crowd.'—*Motion Picture Herald*

'A strange tale from the Hollywood hills . . . the technical work is beyond reproach, but the story is excessively melodramatic.'—*Mordaunt Hall, New York Times*

This Earth Is Mine
US 1959 124m Technicolor Cinemascope
U-I / Vintage (Casey Robinson, Claude Heilman)

A French-American vineyard owner in California brings out his granddaughter from England in the hope that she will consolidate his dynasty.
Solidly efficient film of a solidly efficient novel.

w Casey Robinson, *novel* The Cup and the Sword by Alice Tisdale Hobart *d* Henry King *ph* Winton Hoch, Russell Metty *m* Hugo Friedhofer

Jean Simmons, *Claude Rains*, Rock Hudson, Dorothy McGuire, Kent Smith, Anna Lee, Ken Scott

This England
GB 1941 84m bw

Landowner and labourer express contrary views through five periods of English history. Unintentionally hilarious charade with all concerned left with egg on their faces. With propaganda like this, it's a wonder we still won the war. John Clements, Emlyn Williams, Constance Cummings, Frank Pettingell, Roland Culver, Esmond Knight, Morland Graham, Leslie French. Written by Emlyn Williams, A. R. Rawlinson and Bridget Boland; directed by David MacDonald; for British National.

† In Scotland the film was known as *Our Heritage*.

This Gun for Hire***
US 1942 81m bw
Paramount (Richard M. Blumenthal)

A professional killer becomes involved in a fifth columnist plot.
Efficient Americanization of one of its author's more sombre entertainments. The melodrama has an authentic edge and strangeness to it, and it established the star images of both Ladd and Lake, as well as being oddly downbeat for a Hollywood product of this jingoistic time.

w Albert Maltz, W. R. Burnett, novel A Gun for Sale by *Graham Greene d Frank Tuttle ph John Seitz m* David Buttolph

Alan Ladd, Veronica Lake, Robert Preston, *Laird Cregar*, Tully Marshall, Mikhail Rasumny, Marc Lawrence

This Happy Breed**
GB 1944 114m Technicolor
GFD / Two Cities / Cineguild (Noel Coward, Anthony Havelock-Allan)

Life between the wars for a London suburban family.
Coward's domestic epic is unconvincingly written and largely miscast, but sheer professionalism gets it through, and the decor is historically interesting.

w David Lean, Ronald Neame, Anthony Havelock-Allan, *play* Noel Coward *d David Lean ph Ronald Neame*

Robert Newton, Celia Johnson, Stanley Holloway, John Mills, Kay Walsh, Amy Veness, Alison Leggatt

'Nearly two hours of the pleasure of recognition, which does not come very far up the scale of aesthetic values.'—*Richard Mallett, Punch*

This Happy Feeling
US 1958 92m Eastmancolor Cinemascope
U-I (Ross Hunter)

An ageing actor is invigorated by a mild affair with his secretary.
Flat romantic comedy: the bubbles obstinately refuse to rise.

wd Blake Edwards, *play* For Love or Money by F. Hugh Herbert *ph* Arthur E. Arling *m* Frank Skinner

Curt Jurgens, Debbie Reynolds, John Saxon, Alexis Smith, *Mary Astor, Estelle Winwood*

This Is My Affair**
US 1937 102m bw
TCF (Kenneth MacGowan)
GB title: *His Affair*

When President McKinley is assassinated, one

of his top undercover agents is suspected of being a criminal, and threatened with execution.
Jolly good romantic melodrama with excellent period trappings; Hollywood of the thirties at its routine best.

w Allen Rivkin, Lamar Trotti d William A. Seiter ph Robert Planck md Arthur Lange

Robert Taylor, Barbara Stanwyck, Victor McLaglen, Brian Donlevy, Sidney Blackmer, John Carradine, Sig Rumann, Alan Dinehart, Douglas Fowley

'Something of a G-man story in a costume setting.'—*Variety*

'The best American melodrama of the year . . . admirable acting, quick and cunning direction . . . a sense of doom, of almost classic suspense.'—*Graham Greene*

This Is My Love
US 1954 91m Technicolor

A sensitive young writer gives up everything to help her sister and crippled husband run a restaurant. Weird, miscast melodrama which ends with Cinderella murdering the ugly sister. Linda Darnell, Faith Domergue, Dan Duryea, Rick Jason. Written by Hagar Wilde and Hugh Brooke; directed by Stuart Heisler; for RKO.

This Is My Street
GB 1963 94m bw
Anglo-Amalgamated / Adder (Jack Hanbury)

A Battersea wife has a fling with her mother's lodger.
Unremarkable low-life drama.

w Bill MacIlwraith, *novel* Nan Maynard *d* Sidney Hayers *ph* Alan Hume *m* Eric Rogers

June Ritchie, Ian Hendry, Avice Landon, Meredith Edwards, Madge Ryan, John Hurt, Mike Pratt, Tom Adams

This Is the Army**
US 1943 121m Technicolor
Warner (Jack L. Warner, Hal B. Wallis)

Army recruits put on a musical revue.
Mammoth musical flagwaver.

w Casey Robinson, Claude Binyon *d* Michael Curtiz *ph* Bert Glennon, Sol Polito *songs Irving Berlin m* Ray Heindorf

George Murphy, Joan Leslie, Irving Berlin, George Tobias, Alan Hale, Charles Butterworth, Rosemary de Camp, Dolores Costello, Una Merkel, Stanley Ridges, Ruth Donnelly, Kate Smith, Frances Langford, Gertrude Niesen, Ronald Reagan, Joe Louis

AA: Ray Heindorf

This Is the Life
US 1943 87m bw

A young girl singer gets a crush on an older man. Lively youth musical from better-mannered days. Donald O'Connor, Susanna Foster, Peggy Ryan, Patric Knowles, Louise Allbritton, Dorothy Peterson, Jonathan Hale. Written by Wanda Tuchock, from the play *Angela Is 22* by Fay Wray and Sinclair Lewis; directed by Felix Feist; for Universal.

This is the Night*
US 1932 73m bw

A married lady with an eye for other men has an unfortunate habit of getting her dress caught in doors. Forgotten high comedy in the Lubitsch style, but without his command. Lili Damita, Charles Ruggles, Roland Young, Thelma Todd, Cary Grant. Written by George Marion Jnr, from play *Naughty Cinderella* by Avery Hopwood; directed by Frank Tuttle; for Paramount.

'The supreme entertainment of our time! Two and a half years in the making!'

This Island Earth**
US 1955 86m Technicolor
U-I (William Alland)

Scientists at a mysterious research station are really visitors from a planet in outer space, to which they kidnap brilliant minds who they hope can help them.
Absorbing science fiction mystery with splendid special effects and only one mutant monster to liven the last reels.

w Franklin Coen, Edward G. O'Callaghan, novel Raymond F. Jones *d Joseph Newman ph / sp* Clifford Stine, David S. Horsley *m* Joseph Gershenson *ad* Alexander Golitzen, Richard H. Riedel *m* Henry Mancini, Herman Stein, Hans Salter

Jeff Morrow, Faith Domergue, Rex Reason, Lance Fuller, Russell Johnson, Robert Nicholas, Karl Lindt

'We women who have known love—have learned how to hate!'

This Land Is Mine*
US 1943 103m bw
RKO (Jean Renoir, Dudley Nichols)

A European village fights for freedom under occupying Nazis, and a schoolmaster becomes a hero.
Rather superfluous flagwaver with good performances wasted in a totally predictable and rather uninspiring script which gives the director little scope.

w Dudley Nichols *d* Jean Renoir *ph* Frank Redman *m* Lothar Perl

Charles Laughton, Maureen O'Hara, George Sanders, Walter Slezak, Una O'Connor, Kent Smith, Philip Merivale, Thurston Hall, George Coulouris

'Directed with the same Zolaesque intensity, the same excited obsession with locomotives, the same exquisite pictorial sense, that informed *La Bête Humaine*.'—*Guardian*

'Dull, prolix and unamusing.'—*James Agate*

'You cannot afford to dislocate or internationalize your occupied country; or to try to sell it to Americans by making your citizens as well fed, well dressed and comfortably idiomatic as Americans; or to treat the show to the corrupted virtuosities of studio lighting and heavy ballet composition.'—*James Agee*

This Love of Ours
US 1945 90m bw
U-I (Edward Dodds)

A jealous doctor leaves his wife but years later saves her from an unhappy second marriage.
Stupid romantic melodrama with characters in whose idiotic behaviour one can take no interest. Remade as *Never Say Goodbye* (qv).

w Bruce Manning, John Klorer, Leonard Lee, *play* Comè Prima Meglio di Prima by Luigi Pirandello *d* William Dieterle *ph* Lucien Ballard *m* Hans Salter

Merle Oberon, Charles Korvin, Claude Rains, Carl Esmond, Jess Barker, Harry Davenport, Ralph Morgan, Fritz Leiber

'About as captivating as a funeral dirge.'—*Thomas M. Pryor, New York Times*

'A juicy example of masochistic team work . . . my favourite bad film in two years.'—*Richard Winnington*

AAN: Hans Salter

This Man in Paris
GB 1939 86m bw

A London reporter in Paris exposes a counterfeiting gang. Slightly disappointing sequel to the spruce *This Man Is News*; no more were made. Barry K. Barnes, Valerie Hobson, Alastair Sim, Edward Lexy, Garry Marsh. Written by Allan McKinnon and Roger MacDougall; directed by David MacDonald; for Pinebrook. 'Five years have passed since *The Thin Man*, and this particular uxurious relationship of loving insults, hygienic sex, and raillery from twin beds is period enough for *Punch*.'—*Graham Greene*.

This Man Is Dangerous
GB 1941 82m bw

A police inspector's son solves the case of a fake doctor and a mysterious nursing home. Nostalgically innocent crime caper; still quite entertaining. James Mason, Mary Clare, Margaret Vyner, Gordon McLeod, Frederick Valk. Written by John Argyle and Edward Dryhurst, from the novel *They Called Him Death* by David Hume; directed by Lawrence Huntington; for Rialto. (Aka: *The Patient Vanishes*.)

This Man Is Mine
US 1934 76m bw

A woman wins back her wandering playboy husband. Tedious marital drama which might have fared better as farce. Irene Dunne, Ralph Bellamy, Constance Cummings, Kay Johnson, Sidney Blackmer, Charles Starrett. Written by Jane Murfin, from the play *Love Flies in the Window* by Anne Morrison Chapin; directed by John Cromwell; for RKO.

This Man Is Mine
GB 1946 103m bw

A family invites a Canadian soldier for Christmas. Moderate heartwarmer which still exudes a patriotic sentimental glow. Tom Walls, Glynis Johns, Jeanne de Casalis, Hugh McDermott, Nova Pilbeam, Barry Morse.

THOROUGHLY MODERN MILLIE. Mary Tyler Moore never quite made it as a big-screen star but she gave her all to this mock-Twenties musical. John Gavin simply looks stolid.

Written by Doreen Montgomery, Nicholas Phipps, Reginald Beckwith, Mabel Constanduros, Val Valentine and David Evans, from the play *A Soldier for Christmas* by Reginald Beckwith; directed by Marcel Varnel; for Columbia.

This Man Is News**
GB 1938 77m bw
(Paramount) Pinebrook (Anthony Havelock-Allan)

A reporter tracks down jewel thieves.
Thoroughly brisk and lively comedy-thriller on *Thin Man* lines. (See *This Man in Paris.*)

w Allan MacKinnon, Roger Macdougall, Basil Dearden d David MacDonald ph Henry Harris *md* Percival Mackey

Barry K. Barnes, Valerie Hobson, Alastair Sim, John Warwick, Garry Marsh

This Man's Navy
US 1945 100m bw

Two old navy men compare their sons' exploits, especially in the matter of how many submarines destroyed. Easy-going star flagwaver. Wallace Beery, James Gleason, Tom Drake, Noah Beery, Selena Royle. Written by Borden Chase; directed by William Wellman; for MGM.

This Modern Age
US 1931 68m bw
MGM

The socialite child of divorced parents goes to Paris to stay with her sophisticated mother.
Mildly daring melodrama typical of its star and year.

w Sylvia Thalberg, Frank Butler, *story* Mildred Cram *d* Nick Grinde *ph* Charles Rosher

Joan Crawford, Pauline Frederick, Monroe Owsley, Neil Hamilton, Hobart Bosworth, Emma Dunn

'Alva was growing up the only way she knew how!'

This Property Is Condemned*
US 1966 110m Technicolor
Paramount / Seven Arts / Ray Stark (John Houseman)

Sexual adventures of a tubercular but beautiful girl in her mother's boarding house in a Mississippi town.
The Tennessee Williams mixture as before, quite well done but almost entirely resistible.

w Francis Ford Coppola, Fred Coe, Edith Sommer, *play* Tennessee Williams *d* Sydney Pollack *ph* James Wong Howe *m* Kenyon Hopkins

Natalie Wood, Robert Redford, Mary Badham, Kate Reid, Charles Bronson, Jon Provost, John Harding, Alan Baxter, Robert Blake

This Side of Heaven
US 1934 78m bw

A slightly whacky family gets together when father is accused of embezzlement.
Unmemorable but enjoyable domestic comedy drama. Lionel Barrymore, Fay Bainter, Mae Clarke, Tom Brown, Una Merkel, Mary Carlisle, Onslow Stevens. Written by Zelda Sears and Eve Greene from a novel by Marjorie Paradis; directed by William K. Howard; for MGM. 'The type of clean picture Will Hays has been telling Hollywood about.'—*Variety*

This Sporting Life**
GB 1963 134m bw
Rank / Independent Artists (Karel Reisz)

A tough miner becomes a successful rugby player, but his inner crudeness and violence keep contentment at bay.
Skilful movie-making around an unattractive hero in dismal settings; for all the excellent detail, we do not care sufficiently for the film to become any kind of classic.

w David Storey *d Lindsay Anderson ph Denys Coop m* Roberto Gerhard

Richard Harris, Rachel Roberts, Alan Badel, William Hartnell, Colin Blakely, Vanda Godsell, Arthur Lowe

AAN: Richard Harris; Rachel Roberts

This Thing Called Love*
US 1941 98m bw
Columbia (William Perlberg)
GB title: *Married But Single*

A lady executive insists on proving that marriage is best if the partners start out just good friends.
Amusing comedy which at the time seemed a little saucy, and got itself banned by the Legion of Decency.

w George Seaton, Ken Englund, P. J. Wolfson *d* Alexander Hall *ph* Joseph Walker *m* Werner Heyman *md* Morris Stoloff

Rosalind Russell, Melvyn Douglas, Binnie Barnes, Allyn Joslyn, Gloria Dickson, Lee J. Cobb, Gloria Holden, Don Beddoe

'One of those laborious forties comedies in which the independent-minded woman has no common sense.'—*New Yorker, 1979*

This Time for Keeps
US 1947 105m Technicolor
MGM (Joe Pasternak)

The son of a famous singer falls in love with a swimming star.
Dim star musical with no outstanding sequences.

w Gladys Lehman *d* Richard Thorpe *ph* Karl Freund *songs* various

Esther Williams, Jimmy Durante, Lauritz Melchior, Johnnie Johnston, Xavier Cugat and his Orchestra

'The money spent on this production might easily have kept Mozart and Schubert alive and busy to the age of sixty, with enough left over to finance five of the best movies ever made. It might even have been invested in a good movie musical.'—*James Agee*

This Was a Woman
GB 1948 104m bw

A paranoid wife, prevented from running the lives of her offspring, tries to poison her husband. Intolerable, interminable melodrama; a stage event makes a very stagey film. Sonia Dresdel, Barbara White, Walter Fitzgerald, Cyril Raymond, Marjorie Rhodes, Emrys Jones. Written by Val Valentine, from the play by Joan Morgan; directed by Tim Whelan; for Excelsior.

This Was Paris
GB 1941 88m bw

Spies suspect each other in Paris just before the Nazi occupation. Unpersuasive studio-bound potboiler. Ben Lyon, Ann Dvorak, Griffith Jones, Robert Morley, Harold Huth, Mary Maguire. Written by Brock Williams and Edward Dryhurst; directed by John Harlow; for Warner.

This Way Please
US 1937 72m bw

Romance backstage at a cine–variety theatre. Uninspired musical now interesting for its sociological detail. Charles Buddy Rogers, Betty Grable, Ned Sparks, Jim and Marion Jordan, Porter Hall, Lee Bowman, Wally Vernon. Written by Maxwell Shane, Bill Thomas, Grant Garret, Seena Owen, Howard J. Green; directed by Robert Florey; for Mel Shauer / Paramount.

This Week of Grace
GB 1933 92m bw

An unemployed factory girl goes into service. Very typical but underproduced star vehicle. Gracie Fields, Frank Pettingell, Henry Kendall, John Stuart, Douglas Wakefield, Minnie Rayner. Written by H. Fowler Mear and Jack Marks; directed by Maurice Elvey; for Real Art.

'Every inch a lady—till you look at the record!'

This Woman Is Dangerous
US 1952 97m bw
Warner (Robert Sisk)

A woman gangster goes blind and falls in love with her doctor.
Glossy hokum without much dramatic movement; strictly for star fans.

w Geoffrey Homes, George Worthing Yates *d* Felix Feist *ph* Ted McCord *m* David Buttolph

Joan Crawford, David Brian, Dennis Morgan, Mari Aldon, Phil Carey

This Woman Is Mine
US 1941 92m bw

Fur traders fall out over a beautiful stowaway. Fairly well-produced but unexciting period drama. Franchot Tone, John Carroll, Walter Brennan, Carol Bruce, Nigel Bruce, Leo G. Carroll, Sig Rumann. Written by Seton I. Miller, from the novel *I, James Lewis* by Gilbert Wolff Gabriel; directed by Frank Lloyd; for Universal.

This'll Make You Whistle*
GB 1936 78m bw

A playboy pretends to be a crook so as to shock his unwanted fiancée's guardian. Rather flat comedy from a stage musical; all depends on the star. *Jack Buchanan*, Elsie Randolph, Jean Gillie, William Kendall, David Hutcheson, Anthony Holles. Written by Guy Bolton, Fred Thompson; directed by Herbert Wilcox; for Herbert Wilcox Productions.

The Thomas Crown Affair**
US 1968 102m De Luxe Panavision
UA / Mirisch / Simkoe / Solar (Norman Jewison)

A bored property tycoon masterminds a bank robbery and is chased by a glamorous insurance investigator.
Not so much a movie as an animated colour supplement, this glossy entertainment makes style its prime virtue, plays cute tricks with multiple images and has a famous sexy chess game, but is not above being boring for the rest of the way.

w Alan R. Trustman *d Norman Jewison ph Haskell Wexler m* Michel Legrand *ad Robert Boyle*

Steve McQueen, Faye Dunaway, Paul Burke, Jack Weston, Yaphet Kotto

'Jewison and Wexler seem to have gone slightly berserk, piling up tricks and mannerisms until the film itself sinks out of sight, forlorn and forgotten.'—*Tom Milne*

'A glimmering, empty film reminiscent of an *haute couture* model—stunning on the surface, concave and undernourished beneath.'—*Stefan Kanter*

AA: song 'The Windmills of Your Mind' (*m* Michel Legrand, *ly* Alan and Marilyn Bergman)
AAN: Michel Legrand

Thoroughbreds Don't Cry
US 1937 80m bw

Jockeys fight for the chance to ride a valuable English horse. Ho-hum racetrack yarn significant as the first teaming of two young stars. Mickey Rooney, Judy Garland, Ronald Sinclair, Sophie Tucker, C. Aubrey Smith. Written by Lawrence Hazard, J. Walter Ruben and Eleanor Griffin; directed by Alfred E. Green; for MGM.

Thoroughly Modern Millie*
US 1967 138m Technicolor
Universal (Ross Hunter)

In the twenties, a young girl comes to New York, becomes thoroughly modern, falls for her boss, and has various adventures unmasking a white slave racket centring on a Chinese laundry.
Initially most agreeable but subsequently very patchy spoof of twenties fads and films, including a Harold Lloyd thrill sequence which just doesn't work and a comedy performance from Beatrice Lillie which does. Tunes and performances are alike variable.

w Richard Morris *d* George Roy Hill *ph Russell Metty ad* Alexander Golitzen, George Webb *m* Elmer Bernstein *md* André Previn, Joseph Gershenson *ch* Joe Layton *songs* various

Julie Andrews, Mary Tyler Moore, *John Gavin*, James Fox, Carol Channing, *Beatrice Lillie*, Jack Soo, Pat Morita, Anthony Dexter

'What a nice 65-minute movie is buried therein!'—*Judith Crist*

AA: Elmer Bernstein
AAN: André Previn, Joseph Gershenson; title song (*m* James Van Heusen, *ly* Sammy Cahn); Carol Channing

Those Calloways
US 1964 131m Technicolor
Walt Disney (Winston Hibler)

Adventures of a marsh trapper and his family who live near a Maine village and try to protect wild geese from hunters.
Predictable family saga with pleasant backgrounds.

w Louis Pelletier, *novel* Swift Water by Paul Annixter *d* Norman Tokar *ph* Edward Colman *m* Max Steiner

Brian Keith, Vera Miles, Brandon de Wilde, Walter Brennan, Ed Wynn, Linda Evans, Philip Abbott, John Larkin, John Qualen

Those Daring Young Men in Their Jaunty Jalopies
US / Italy / France 1969 125m Technicolor Panavision
Paramount / Dino de Laurentiis / Marianne (Ken Annakin, Basil Keys)
GB title: *Monte Carlo or Bust*

Accidents befall various competitors in the Monte Carlo Rally.
Rough-edged imitation of *The Great Race* and *Those Magnificent Men in Their Flying Machines*, much feebler than either but with the waste of a big budget well in evidence.

w Jack Davies, Ken Annakin *d* Ken Annakin *ph* Gabor Pogany *m* Ron Goodwin

Peter Cook, Dudley Moore, Tony Curtis, Bourvil, Walter Chiari, Terry-Thomas, Gert Frobe, Susan Hampshire, Jack Hawkins, Eric Sykes

Those Endearing Young Charms
US 1945 81m bw

An air corps mechanic loves a shopgirl. Nothing to remember about this light star time-passer. Robert Young, Laraine Day, Bill Williams, Ann Harding, Marc Cramer, Anne Jeffries. Written by Jerome Chodorov, from the play by Edward Chodorov; directed by Lewis Allen; for RKO. 'Well played, well directed, and not quite interesting enough to be worth the time it takes.'—*James Agee.*

Those High Grey Walls
US 1939 80m bw

A doctor is convicted for aiding a criminal. Modest variation on a plot used for *Prisoner of Shark Island*, *Devil's Island*, and so on. Walter Connolly, Onslow Stevens, Iris Meredith, Paul Fix, Bernard Nedell, Don Beddoe. Written by William A. Ullman, Lewis Meltzer; directed by Charles Vidor; for Columbia. 'Effective prison melodrama . . . will do all right where properly booked.'—*Variety*

Those Kids from Town
GB 1941 82m bw

An earl takes in a group of noisy cockney kids evacuated from the city. Sentimental wartime crowdpleaser, not especially good but a fairly rare record of one aspect of the war. Shirley Lenner, Jeanne de Casalis, Percy Marmont, Maire O'Neill, George Cole, Charles Victor. Written by Adrian Arlington, from his novel *These Our Strangers*; directed by Lance Comfort; for British National.

Those Magnificent Men in Their Flying Machines, or How I Flew from London to Paris in 25 hours and 11 Minutes**
GB 1965 133m Technicolor Todd-AO
TCF (Stan Marguilies, Jack Davies)

In 1910, a newspaper owner sponsors a London to Paris air race.
Long-winded, generally agreeable knockabout comedy with plenty to look at but far too few jokes to sustain it.

w Jack Davies, Ken Annakin *d Ken Annakin ph Christopher Challis m Ron Goodwin pd Tom Morahan*

Sarah Miles, Stuart Whitman, Robert Morley, Eric Sykes, Terry-Thomas, James Fox, Alberto Sordi, Gert Frobe, Jean-Pierre Cassel, Karl Michael Vogler, Irina Demich, Benny Hill, Flora Robson, Sam Wanamaker, Red Skelton, Fred Emney, Cicely Courtneidge, Gordon Jackson, John Le Mesurier, Tony Hancock, William Rushton

'There is many a likely gag, but none that survives the second or third reprise. It could have been a good bit funnier by being shorter: the winning time is 25 hours 11 minutes, and by observing some kind of neo-Aristotelian unity the film seems to last exactly as long.'—*John Simon*

AAN: script

Those Marvellous Benchley Shorts: see Benchley

Those Were the Days*
GB 1934 80m bw
BIP (Walter C. Mycroft)

In the nineties, a magistrate seeks out his teenage stepson in a music hall.
Lively comedy which is valuable as giving the screen's best recreation of an old-time music hall.

w Fred Thompson, Frank Miller, Frank Launder, Jack Jordan, *play* The Magistrate by Arthur Wing Pinero *d Thomas Bentley ph* Otto Kanturek *md* Idris Lewis

Will Hay, John Mills, Iris Hoey, Angela Baddeley, Claud Allister, George Graves, Jane Carr, H. F. Maltby

† Music hall acts include Gaston and Andrée, Lily Morris, G. H. Elliott, Sam Curtis, Frank Boston and Betty.

Those Were the Days
US 1940 74m bw
Paramount (J. Theodore Reed)
GB title: *Good Old Schooldays*

During their 40th anniversary celebrations, a married couple look back to their courtship days at college.
Pleasant, light, nostalgic escapades.

w Don Hartman, *stories* George Fitch *d* J. Theodore Reed *ph* Victor Milner

William Holden, Bonita Granville, Ezra Stone, Judith Barrett, Vaughan Glazer, Lucien Littlefield, Richard Denning

Those Wonderful Movie Cranks*
Czechoslovakia 1978 88m colour
Barrandov (Jan Suster)

A travelling conjuror at the turn of the century introduces short cinema films into his act, and solves his woman trouble meanwhile.
Charming melancholy comedy which adds a little to art as well as to history.

w Oldrich Vlcek, Jiri Menzel *d Jiri Menzel ph* Jaromir Sofr *m* Jiri Sust

Rudolf Hrusinsky, Vlasta Fabianova, Blazena Holisova

A Thousand and One Nights*
US 1945 92m Technicolor

Aladdin seeks his princess. Amusing take-off on the Arabian Nights, with good jokes and music. Cornel Wilde, Phil Silvers, Evelyn Keyes, Adele Jergens, Dusty Anderson, Dennis Hoey. Written by Wilfrid H. Pettitt, Richard English, Jack Henley; directed by Alfred E. Green; for Samuel Bischoff / Columbia.

A Thousand Clowns*
US 1965 115m bw
UA / Harell (Fred Coe)

A New Yorker who has abdicated from work leads a cheerful, useless life with his young nephew, but the school board have their doubts.
Imitative nonconformist comedy with frequent reminiscences of older, better plays such as *You Can't Take It with You*. Good lines occasionally make themselves felt, but the overall effect is patchy, the lead is miscast, and the location montages only emphasize the basic one-room set.

w Herb Gardner, from his play *d* Fred Coe *ph* Arthur J. Ornitz *m* Don Walker

Jason Robards, Martin Balsam, Barry Gordon, Barbara Harris, *William Daniels*, Gene Saks

AA: Martin Balsam
AAN: best picture; Herb Gardner; Don Walker

The Thousand Eyes of Dr Mabuse*
France / Italy / Germany 1960 103m bw

Murders in a Berlin hotel are attributed to a reincarnation of the evil Dr Mabuse. Lively if belated sequel to the director's silent films. Dawn Addams, Peter Van Eyck, Gert Frobe, Wolfgang Preiss, Werner Peters. Written by Fritz Lang, Jeinz Oskar Wuttig; directed by Fritz Lang; for CCC / Filmkunst / Incom Criterion / Ajay.

Thousands Cheer*
US 1943 126m Technicolor
MGM (Joe Pasternak)

An army base stages an all-star variety show. Ho-hum studio extravaganza with some good numbers.

w Paul Jarrico, Richard Collins *d* George Sidney *ph* George Folsey *md* Herbert Stothart *songs* various

Kathryn Grayson, Gene Kelly, John Boles, Mary Astor, Jose Iturbi, Kay Kyser and his Orchestra, Lionel Barrymore, Margaret O'Brien, June Allyson, Mickey Rooney, Judy Garland, Red Skelton, Eleanor Powell, Bob Crosby and his Orchestra, Lena Horne, Frank Morgan

'A thoroughly routine musical distinguished only by Gene Kelly with nothing to use his talents on, a terrible piece of trash by Shostakovich, and the unpleasant sight of Jose Iturbi proving he is a real guy by playing the sort of boogie woogie anyone ought to be able to learn through a correspondence course.'—*James Agee*

AAN: George Folsey; Herbert Stothart

The Three Ages*
US 1923 80m approx bw silent

Three stories parodying Griffith's *Intolerance*. The star's first feature film, not his strongest, is saved by the final chases, *Buster Keaton*, Wallace Beery, Margaret Leahy, Joe Roberts. Written by Clyde Bruckman, Jean Havez, Joseph Mitchell; directed by Buster Keaton, Eddie Cline; for Joseph Schenck / Metro.

Three Amigos
US 1986 105m Technicolor

Three wimpish cowboy stars find themselves hired to defend a desert town from a bandit. Weak take-off of *The Magnificent Seven*, with performances that grate. Chevy Chase, Steve Martin, Martin Short, Patrice Martinez, Alfonso Arau. Written by Martin, Lorne Michaels, Randy Newman; directed by John Landis; for Michaels/Folsey and Orion.

Three Bites of the Apple
US 1966 98m Metrocolor Panavision
MGM (Alvin Ganzer)

An English travel courier wins a lot of money in a Rome casino, and nearly loses it all.
Very dull comedy perked up by attractive locations.

w George Wells *d* Alvin Ganzer *ph* Gabor Pogany *m* Eddy Manson

David McCallum, Sylva Koscina, Tammy Grimes, Harvey Korman, Aldo Fabrizi

Three Blind Mice*
US 1938 75m bw
TCF (Raymond Griffith)

Three Kansas girls in the big city seek rich husbands.
Mild comedy remade as *Three Little Girls in Blue* and *How to Marry a Millionaire*, and not all that different from any of the *Gold Diggers* comedy musicals.

w Brown Holmes, Lynn Starling *d* William A. Seiter *ph* Ernest Palmer *m* Charles Maxwell

Loretta Young, Joel McCrea, David Niven, Stuart Erwin, Marjorie Weaver, Pauline Moore, Binnie Barnes, Jane Darwell, Leonid Kinskey

'More names than can be handled on the marquee . . . good summer entertainment.'—*Variety*

Three Brave Men*
US 1956 88m bw Cinemascope
TCF (Herbert B. Swope Jnr)

A civilian employee in the US Navy is suspended as a security risk and it takes a lawsuit to set things straight.
Semi-factual anti-McCarthy drama proving that America is a great place to live—when you're winning. Good courtroom scenes.

wd Philip Dunne, *articles* Anthony Lewis *ph* Charles G. Clarke *m* Hans Salter

Ray Milland, Ernest Borgnine, Nina Foch, Dean Jagger, Frank Lovejoy, Edward Andrews, Frank Faylen, James Westerfield, Joseph Wiseman

The Three Caballeros***
US 1945 70m Technicolor
Walt Disney (Norman Ferguson)

A programme of shorts about South America, linked by Donald Duck as a tourist.
Rapid-fire mélange of fragments supporting the good neighbour policy, following the shorter *Saludos Amigos* of 1943. The kaleidoscopic sequences and the combination of live action with cartoon remain of absorbing interest.

w various *d* various *m* Edward Plumb, Paul J. Smith, Charles Wolcott

† Stories include Pablo the Penguin, Little Gauchito, a Mexican sequence and some adventures with Joe Carioca.

AAN: Edward Plumb, Paul J. Smith, Charles Wolcott

Three Came Home**
US 1950 106m bw
TCF (Nunnally Johnson)

In 1941 writer Agnes Newton Keith tries to escape from Borneo but is interned and ill-used by the Japanese.
Well-made, harrowing war adventure.

w Nunnally Johnson, *book* Agnes Newton Keith *d Jean Negulesco ph Milton Krasner* *m* Hugo Friedhofer *md* Lionel Newman

Claudette Colbert, Patric Knowles, Sessue Hayakawa, Florence Desmond, Sylvia Andrew, Phyllis Morris

'It will shock you, disturb you, tear your heart out. But it will fill you with great respect for a heroic soul.'—*New York Times*

Three Cases of Murder*
GB 1954 99m bw
British Lion / Wessex / London Films (Ian Dalrymple, Hugh Perceval)

'In the Picture': a painting comes to life. 'You Killed Elizabeth': a man suspects himself of his faithless fiancée's murder. 'Lord Mountdrago': the foreign secretary dreams of killing an MP he hates.
Unlinked compendium, in which the first and third stories are quite interesting and well done, the second very commonplace.

w Donald Wilson, Sidney Caroll, Ian Dalrymple (original stories Roderick Wilkinson, Brett Halliday, W. Somerset Maugham) *d* Wendy Toye, David Eady, George More O'Ferrall *ph* Georges Périnal *m* Doreen Carwithen

Alan Badel, Hugh Pryse, Leueen MacGrath, Elizabeth Sellars, John Gregson, Emrys Jones, Orson Welles, André Morell

Three Cheers for the Irish
US 1940 100m bw
Warner (Sam Bischoff)

An Irishman's daughter causes family trouble when she falls for a Scot.
Pleasant, unpretentious but overlong romantic comedy.

w Richard Macaulay, Jerry Wald *d* Lloyd Bacon *ph* Charles Rosher *m* Adolph Deutsch

Thomas Mitchell, Priscilla Lane, Dennis Morgan, Alan Hale, Virginia Grey, Irene Hervey, William Lundigan

Three Coins in the Fountain**
US 1954 102m De Luxe Cinemascope
TCF (Sol C. Siegel)

Three American girls find romance in Rome.
An enormous box office hit, the pattern of which was frequently repeated against various backgrounds; it was actually remade in Madrid as *The Pleasure Seekers*. In itself a thin entertainment, but the title song carried it.

w John Patrick, *novel* John H. Secondari *d* Jean Negulesco *ph Milton Krasner* *m* Victor Young *song Jule Styne, Sammy Cahn*

Clifton Webb, Dorothy McGuire, Louis Jourdan, Jean Peters, Rossano Brazzi, Maggie McNamara, Howard St John, Kathryn Givney, Cathleen Nesbitt

AA: Milton Krasner; title song
AAN: best picture

'Out of the inferno of war came three men and a woman—to live their lives, to strive for happiness, to seek love!'

Three Comrades**
US 1938 98m bw
MGM (Joseph L. Mankiewicz)

In twenties Germany, three friends find life hard but derive some joy from their love for a high-spirited girl who is dying of tuberculosis.
Despairing romance becomes a sentimental tearjerker with all the stops out; immaculately produced and very appealing to the masses, but prevented by censorship from being the intended indictment of Nazi Germany. The final scene in which the two surviving comrades are joined in the churchyard by their ghostly friends still packs a wallop.

w F. Scott Fitzgerald, Edward A. Paramore, novel Erich Maria Remarque *d Frank Borzage ph* Joseph Ruttenberg *m* Franx Waxman

Margaret Sullavan, Robert Taylor, Robert Young, Franchot Tone, Guy Kibbee, Lionel Atwill, Henry Hull, Charley Grapewin

'Just what Frank Borzage is trying to prove is very difficult to fathom . . . there must have been some reason for making this picture, but it certainly isn't in the name of entertainment.'—*Variety*

'A remarkably high combination of talents has made it all very impressive and moving—good writing, a good man at the camera, good actors, and presiding over them a good director . . . such unforgettable bits as the pursuit of the boy who shot Gottfried, a glimpse from under the muffling blanket of the girl's stricken face, the startling downswoop of the camera's eye upon the girl getting up from bed to remove the burden of her illness from those who love her. These are high moments in a film full of beauty.'—*National Board of Review*

'A love story, beautifully told and consummately acted, but so drenched in hopelessness and heavy with the aroma of death, of wasted youth in a world of foggy shapes and nameless menaces, that its beauty and strength are often clouded and betrayed.'—*Time*

AAN: Margaret Sullavan

'They might be the family next door—but if they were, you'd move!'

Three Cornered Moon*
US 1933 72m bw
Paramount

A newly-poor Depression family has trouble finding work.

Slightly screwball romantic comedy, a predecessor of *You Can't Take It with You*; the humour now seems very faded, but it was a signpost of its day.

w S. K. Lauren, Ray Harris, *play* Gertrude Tonkonogy *d* Elliott Nugent *ph* Leon Shamroy

Claudette Colbert, Mary Boland, Richard Arlen, Wallace Ford, Lyda Roberti, Tom Brown, Hardie Albright

Three Daring Daughters
US 1948 115m Technicolor
MGM (Joe Pasternak)
GB title: *The Birds and the Bees*

Three girls are dismayed to hear that their mother is remarrying.
Cheerful comedy with music, but nothing to write home about.

w Albert Mannheimer, Frederick Kohner, Sonya Levien, John Meehan *d* Fred M. Wilcox *ph* Ray June *md* Georgie Stoll

Jeanette MacDonald, Jose Iturbi, Jane Powell, Anne Todd, Mary Elinor Donahue, Larry Adler, Edward Arnold, Harry Davenport, Moyna MacGill

'His code name is Condor. In the next twenty-four hours everyone he trusts will try to kill him.'

Three Days of the Condor**
US 1975 118m Technicolor Panavision
Paramount/ Dino de Laurentiis / Wildwood (Stanley Schneider)

An innocent researcher for a branch of the CIA finds himself marked for death by assassins employed by another branch.
Entertaining New York-based thriller which shamelessly follows most of the twists of *The 39 Steps*. It is just possible to follow its complexities, and the dialogue is smart.

w Lorenzo Semple Jnr, David Rayfiel, novel Six Days of the Condor by James Grady *d Sydney Pollack ph* Owen Roizman *m* Dave Grusin

Robert Redford, Faye Dunaway, Cliff Robertson, Max Von Sydow, John Houseman, Walter McGinn

Three Faces East*
US 1930 71m bw
Warner (Darryl F. Zanuck)

The butler to the British war minister is a German spy, and the German nurse sent to help him is really a British agent . . .
Slow , melodramatic remake of 1926 silent, later turned into a Karloff vehicle, *British Intelligence* (qv).

w Oliver H. P. Garrett, Arthur Caesar, *play* Anthony Paul Kelly *d* Roy del Ruth *ph* Chick McGill

Constance Bennett, Erich Von Stroheim, Anthony Bushell, William Holden

'Bennett and Von Stroheim guarantee a better than average week.'—*Variety*

The Three Faces of Eve**
US 1957 95m bw Cinemascope
TCF (Nunnally Johnson)

A psychiatrist discovers that a female patient has three distinct personalities: a drab housewife, a good time girl and a mature sophisticated woman.
Alistair Cooke introduces this tall tale as if he believed it; as presented, it is entertaining but not very convincing. Its box office success was sufficient to start a schizophrenia cycle.

w Nunnally Johnson, *book* Corbett H. Thigpen MD, Hervey M. Cleckley MD *d Nunnally Johnson ph Stanley Cortez* *m* Robert Emmett Dolan

Joanne Woodward, Lee J. Cobb, David Wayne, Nancy Kulp, Edwin Jerome

AA: Joanne Woodward

Three Faces West
US 1940 79m bw
Republic (Sol C. Siegel)

A dust bowl community is helped by an Austrian doctor fleeing from the Nazis, but his daughter is followed by a Nazi suitor.
Unusual modern western, blandly told.

w F. Hugh Herbert, Joseph Moncure March, Samuel Ornitz *d* Bernard Vorhaus *ph* John Alton *m* Victor Young

John Wayne, Charles Coburn, Sigrid Gurie, Roland Varno, Spencer Charters, Sonny Bupp

Three for Bedroom C
US 1952 74m Natural Color
Brenco (Edward L. Alperson Jnr)

Confusion reigns on a train when a film star takes a compartment booked for a Harvard scientist.
Inept farce which never rises above mediocrity and coasts along well below it.

wd Milton H. Bren *ph* Ernest Laszlo *m* Heinz Roemheld

Gloria Swanson, Fred Clark, James Warren, Hans Conried, Steve Brodie, Margaret Dumont

Three for Jamie Dawn
US 1956 81m bw
AA (Hayes Goetz)

A crooked lawyer bribes three members of a murder jury.
Minor courtroom melodrama, limply developed.

w John Klempner *d* Thomas Carr *ph* Duke Green *m* Walter Scharf

Laraine Day, Ricardo Montalban, Richard Carlson, June Havoc

Three for the Show*
US 1955 93m Technicolor Cinemascope
Columbia (Jonie Taps)

A married Broadway star finds that her first husband is still alive.
Adequate musical remake of *Too Many Husbands* (qv); not bad, not good.

w Edward Hope, Leonard Stern, *play* Too Many Husbands by W. Somerset Maugham *d* H. C. Potter *ph* Arthur E. Arling *ch* Jack Cole *songs* Various *md* George Duning

Betty Grable, Jack Lemmon, Marge Champion, Gower Champion, Myron McCormick, Paul Harvey

Three Girls about Town*
US 1942 71m bw
Columbia

Three sisters in New York find a corpse in their hotel bedroom.
A funny 'B' picture: fast paced and lively from start to finish.

w Richard Carroll *d* Leigh Jason *ph* Franz Planer

Joan Blondell, Binnie Barnes, Janet Blair, John Howard, Robert Benchley, Eric Blore, Una O'Connor

Three Godfathers*
US 1948 106m Technicolor
MGM / Argosy (John Ford)

Three outlaws escaping across the desert take charge of an orphan baby.
'Orrible sentimental parable partly redeemed by splendid scenery.

w Laurence Stallings, Frank S. Nugent, *story* Frank B. Kyne *d John Ford ph Winton Hoch* *m* Richard Hageman

John Wayne, Pedro Armendariz, Harry Carey Jnr, Ward Bond

† The story also appeared in 1909 as *Bronco Billy and the Baby*; in 1916 as *Three Godfathers*, with Harry Carey; in 1920 as *Marked Men*, with Harry Carey; in 1929 as *Hell's Heroes*, with Charles Bickford; in 1936 as *Three Godfathers*, with Chester Morris; and in 1975 as a TV movie, *The Godchild*, with Jack Palance.

†† The film is dedicated 'to the memory of Harry Carey, bright star of the early western sky'.

Three Guys Named Mike
US 1951 90m bw
MGM (Armand Deutsch)

An accident-prone air hostess has three suitors.
Inconsequential romantic comedy which shows the effort of stretching its thin material to feature length.

w Sidney Sheldon, *story* Ruth Brooks Flippen *d* Charles Walters *ph* Paul Vogel *m* Bronislau Kaper

Jane Wyman, Barry Sullivan, Van Johnson, Howard Keel, Phyllis Kirk, Jeff Donnell

Three Hats for Lisa*
GB 1965 99m Eastmancolor

A docker and a taxi driver help a foreign film star to steal three typically English hats. Minor musical, silly but good to look at. Joe Brown, Sid James, Sophie Hardy, Una Stubbs, Dave Nelson, Peter Bowles. Written by Leslie Bricusse, Talbot Rothwell; directed by Sidney Hayers; for Seven Hills / Jack Hanbury.

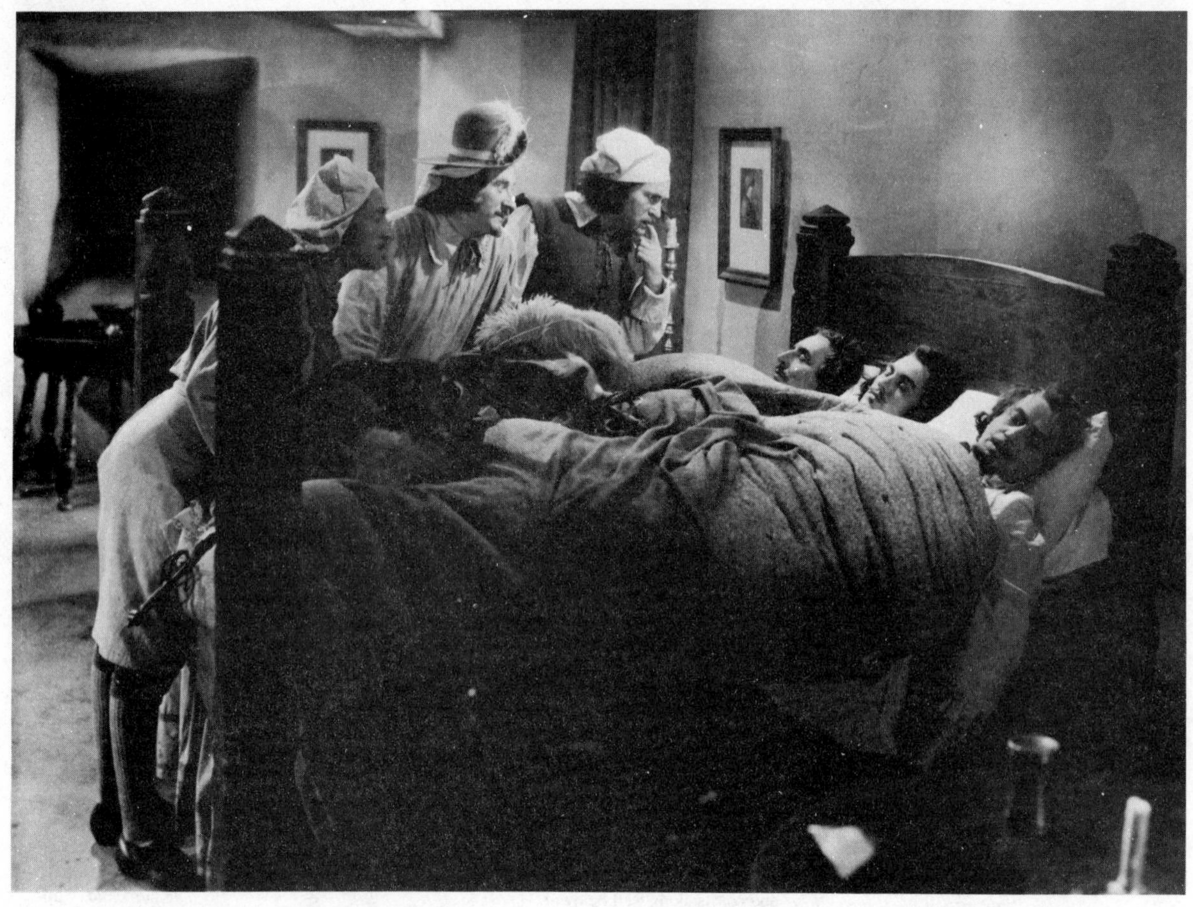

THE THREE MUSKETEERS. Dumas's celebrated swashbuckler proved sturdy enough even to survive the slapstick attentions of the Ritz Brothers and Don Ameche as a singing D'Artagnan.

Three Hearts for Julia
US 1943 90m bw

A reporter courts his wife all over again when she threatens to divorce him. One of those thin romantic comedies which sent its male lead back to the theatre. Melvyn Douglas, Ann Sothern, Lee Bowman, Felix Bressart, Reginald Owen, Richard Ainley. Written by Lionel Houser; directed by Richard Thorpe; for MGM.

365 Nights in Hollywood
US 1934 77m bw

A down-and-out becomes a director of a fake school of acting. Slight and casually developed comedy-romance, with comedy interludes by Mitchell and Durant. James Dunn, Alice Faye, John Bradford, Grant Mitchell. Written by William Conselman, Henry Johnson; directed by George Marshall; for Sol M. Wurtzel / Fox. 'A picture with no punch and little appeal.'—*Variety*

The 300 Spartans*
US 1962 114m De Luxe Cinemascope
TCF (Rudolph Maté, George St George)

Sparta leads the ancient Greek states against Persia's attack at Thermopylae.
Quite a lively epic with some dignity.

w George St George *d* Rudolph Maté
ph Geoffrey Unsworth *m* Manos Hadjikakis

Richard Egan, Ralph Richardson, David Farrar, Diane Baker, Barry Coe, Donald Houston, Kieron Moore, John Crawford, Robert Brown

Three Husbands
US 1950 76m bw
UA / Gloria (I. G. Goldsmith)

Three husbands receive letters from a dead friend claiming that he had affairs with each of their wives.
Silly copy of *A Letter to Three Wives*, with neither style nor sophistication.

w Vera Caspary, Edward Eliscu *d* Irving Reis *ph* Franz Planer *m* Herschel Burke Gilbert

Emlyn Williams, Eve Arden, Howard da Silva, Ruth Warrick, Shepperd Strudwick, Vanessa Brown, Billie Burke, Jonathan Hale

Three in the Attic
US 1968 90m Pathecolor
AIP - Hermes (Richard Wilson)

A college Casanova is locked in an attic by three girls who seduce him by rota until he cries for mercy.
One of the first outspoken comedies of the sexual revolution, but not a particularly funny one.

w Stephen Yafa, from his novel Paxton Quigley's Had the Course *d* Richard Wilson *ph* J. Burgi Contner *m* Chad Stuart

Chris Jones, Yvette Mimieux, Judy Pace, Maggie Turett, Nan Martin

'Hello, Mrs Howard, I'm a friend of Mr Howard!'
Three into Two Won't Go*
GB 1969 100m Technicolor
Universal (Julian Blaustein)

An executive has an affair with a girl hitch-hiker who later moves into his house to his wife's astonishment.
Palatable sex drama with good performances, rather flabbily written and directed.

w Edna O'Brien, *novel* Andrea Newman *d* Peter Hall *ph* Walter Lassally *m* Francis Lai

Rod Steiger, Claire Bloom, Judy Geeson, Peggy Ashcroft, Paul Rogers

Three is a Family*
US 1944 81m bw

A henpecked husband having made some unwise investments is relegated by his wife to the spouse position. Quite amusing comedy on a familiar theme. Charles Ruggles, Fay Bainter, Marjorie Reynolds, Helen Broderick, Arthur Lake, Hattie McDaniel, John Philliber, Jeff Donnell, Walter Catlett, Clarence Kolb, Warren Hymer. Written by Harry Chandlee, Marjorie L. Pfaelzer, from play by Phoebe and Henry Ephron; directed by Edward Ludaig; for Sol Lesser / United Artists.

Three Kids and a Queen
US 1935 85m bw

Three boys decide to kidnap a rich old lady, but are dismayed to find that she enjoys the experience. Sentimental comedy which seemed to hit the right note. May Robson, Frankie Darro, Billy Burrud, Billy Benedict, Charlotte Henry, Herman Bing, Henry Armetta, John Miljan, Hedda Hopper. Written by Barry Trivers, Samuel Ornitz, Harry Poppe, Chester Beecroft; directed by Edward Ludwig; for Universal. 'A cinch for box office satisfaction.'—*Variety*

Three Little Girls in Blue
US 1946 90m Technicolor
TCF (Mack Gordon)

Musical remake of *Three Blind Mice* (qv); adequate and quite forgettable.

w Valentine Davies *d* Bruce Humberstone *ph* Ernest Palmer *songs* Mack Gordon, Joseph Myrow

June Haver, George Montgomery, Vivian Blaine, Celeste Holm, Vera-Ellen, Frank Latimore, Charles Smith, Charles Halton

Three Little Words*
US 1950 102m Technicolor
MGM (Jack Cummings)

The careers of songwriters Bert Kalmar and Harry Ruby.
Disappointingly ordinary musical in which two witty people are made to seem dull, and the plot allows Fred Astaire only one dance.

w George Wells *d* Richard Thorpe *ph* Harry Jackson *md* André Previn *ch* Hermes Pan *songs Bert Kalmar, Harry Ruby* and various collaborators

Fred Astaire, Red Skelton, Vera-Ellen, Arlene Dahl, Keenan Wynn, Gale Robbins, Gloria de Haven, Phil Regan, *Debbie Reynolds*

AAN: André Previn

The Three Lives of Thomasina
GB 1963 97m Technicolor
Walt Disney

In a Scottish village in 1912, a vet finds that his methods are no match for a local girl who treats animals by giving them love.
Syrupy film for children: the animals are the main interest and one of them narrates . . .

w Robert Westerby, *novel* Thomasina by Paul Gallico *d* Don Chaffey *ph* Paul Beeson *m* Paul Smith

Susan Hampshire, Patrick McGoohan, Karen Dotrice, Vincent Winter, Laurence Naismith, Finlay Currie, Wilfrid Brambell

Three Loves Has Nancy
US 1938 69m bw
MGM (Norman Krasna)

A jilted bride takes her time about her next selection.
Adequate star comedy.

w Bella and Sam Spewack, George Oppenheimer, David Hertz *d* Richard Thorpe *ph* William Daniels

Janet Gaynor, Robert Montgomery, Franchot Tone, Guy Kibbee, Claire Dodd, Reginald Owen, Charley Grapewin, Emma Dunn, Cora Witherspoon

'This may not be the funniest picture of the season, but it's certainly one of the wackiest.'—*Variety*

The Three Maxims
GB 1937 87m bw
GFD / Pathé Consortium (Herbert Wilcox)

Two trapezists love the girl member of the team, and the situation leads to attempted murder.
Effective Paris-set treatment of a well worn theme (see *Trapeze*).

w Herman Mankiewicz *d* Herbert Wilcox *ph* Frederick A. Young, Jack Cox

Anna Neagle, Tullio Carminati, Leslie Banks, Horace Hodges

'They changed her diapers—she changed their lives!'
Three Men and a Baby
US 1987 102m De Luxe
Touchstone / Silver Screen III (Ted Field, Robert W. Cort)

Three swinging bachelors find a baby on their doorstep.
Slight comedy, given some momentum by a heroin-dealing subplot, which proved surprisingly successful with audiences thanks to energetic playing.

w James Orr, Jim Cruickshank *d* Leonard Nimoy *ph* Adam Greenberg *m* Marvin Hamlisch *pd* Peter Larkin

Tom Selleck, Steve Guttenberg, Ted Danson, Nancy Travis

† Remake of the more thoughtful and elegant *Trois Hommes et un Couffin* of 1985, whose director Coline Serreau was to have directed the US version but backed out.

Three Men in a Boat
GB 1956 94m Eastmancolor Cinemascope
Romulus (Jack Clayton)

In the 1890s, misadventures befall three men holidaying on the Thames.
Flabby burlesque of a celebrated comic novel whose style is never even approached.

w Hubert Gregg, Vernon Harris, *novel* Jerome K. Jerome *d* Ken Annakin *ph* Eric Cross *m* John Addison *ad* John Howell

David Tomlinson, Jimmy Edwards, Laurence Harvey, Shirley Eaton, Robertson Hare, Jill Ireland, Lisa Gastoni, Martita Hunt, A. E. Matthews, Ernest Thesiger, Adrienne Corri
† A previous version in 1933 starred William Austin, Edmond Breon and Billy Milton; directed by Graham Cutts for ATP.

Three Men on a Horse*
US 1936 85m bw
Warner (Sam Bischoff)

A timid Brooklynite finds he can always pick winners, and gangsters get interested.
Smooth New Yorkish comedy which pleased at the time.

w Laird Doyle, *play* John Cecil Holm, George Abbott *d* Mervyn Le Roy *ph* Sol Polito

Frank McHugh, Sam Levene, Joan Blondell, Guy Kibbee, Carol Hughes, Allen Jenkins, Edgar Kennedy, Eddie Anderson, Harry Davenport

The Three Mesquiteers
A three-man cowboy team who operated in popular B features at the Hopalong Cassidy level. The make-up of the team varied: the actors most often found in it were John Wayne, Max Terhune, Bob Livingston, Ray Corrigan, Bob Steele, Rufe Davis, Tom Tyler, Raymond Hatton, Duncan Renaldo and Jimmy Dodd. The first film was made for RKO, all the rest for Republic: most frequent directors were George Sherman, Mack V. Wright, Joseph Kane, John English and Lester Orlebeck.

1935: POWDERSMOKE RANGE, THE THREE MESQUITEERS
1936: GHOST TOWN, GOLD, ROARIN' LEAD
1937: RIDERS OF THE WHISTLING SKULL, HIT THE SADDLE, GUNSMOKE RANCH, COME ON COWBOYS, RANGE DEFENDERS, HEART OF THE ROCKIES, THE TRIGGER TRIO, WILD HORSE RODEO
1938: THE PURPLE VIGILANTES, CALL THE MESQUITEERS, CALL OF THE MESQUITEERS, OUTLAWS OF SONORA, RIDERS OF THE BLACK HILLS, HEROES OF THE HILLS, PALS OF THE SADDLE, OVERLAND STAGE RAIDERS, SANTA FE STAMPEDE, RED RIVER RANGE
1939: THE NIGHT RIDERS, THREE TEXAS STEERS, WYOMING OUTLAW, NEW FRONTIER, THE KANSAS TERRORS, COWBOYS FROM TEXAS
1940: HEROES OF THE SADDLE, PIONEERS OF THE WEST, COVERED WAGON DAYS, ROCKY MOUNTAIN RANGERS, OKLAHOMA RENEGADES, UNDER TEXAS SKIES, THE TRAIL BLAZERS, LONE STAR RAIDERS
1941: PRAIRIE PIONEERS, PALS OF THE PECOS, SADDLEMATES, GANGS OF SONORA, OUTLAWS OF THE CHEROKEE TRAIL, GAUCHOS OF EL DORADO, WEST OF CIMARRON
1942: CODE OF THE OUTLAW, RIDERS OF THE RANGE, WESTWARD HO, THE PHANTOM PLAINSMAN, SHADOWS ON THE SAGE, VALLEY OF HUNTED MEN
1943: THUNDERING TRAILS, THE BLOCKED TRAIL, SANTA FE SCOUTS, RIDERS OF THE RIO GRANDE

The Three Musketeers
US 1933 bw serial: 12 eps

Three Foreign Legionnaires defy the Devil of the Desert. Adequate serial with interesting cast. John Wayne, Ruth Hall, Jack Mulhall, Raymond Hatton, Francis X. Bushman Jnr, Lon Chaney Jnr, Noah Beery Jnr. Directed by Armand Schaefer and Colbert Clark; for Mascot.

The Three Musketeers
US 1935 97m bw

See below for synopsis. A thin and poorly handled version. Walter Abel (D'Artagnan), Paul Lukas (Athos), Moroni Olson (Porthos), Onslow Stevens (Aramis), Margot Grahame (Milady), Heather Angel (Constance), Ian Keith (de Rochefort), Miles Mander (King), Nigel de Brulier (Richelieu). Written by Dudley Nichols, Rowland V. Lee; directed by Rowland V. Lee; for RKO. 'Ineffective and disappointing adaptation . . . dull entertainment.'—*Variety*

The Three Musketeers**
US 1939 73m bw
TCF (Raymond Griffith)
GB title: *The Singing Musketeer*

A burlesque of the familiar story with pauses for song.
A very satisfactory entertainment with all concerned in top form.

w M. M. Musselman, William A. Drake, Sam Hellman *d Allan Dwan* *ph* Peverell Marley *songs* Samuel Pokrass, Walter Bullock

Don Ameche, the Ritz Brothers, Binnie Barnes, *Joseph Schildkraut*, Lionel Atwill, Miles Mander, Gloria Stuart, Pauline Moore, John Carradine

'Whenever the action lags, the trio take the rostrum for a slapstick specialty . . . moderate b.o., a topper for the key duals.'—*Variety*

The Three Musketeers***
US 1948 125m Technicolor
MGM (Pandro S. Berman)

High-spirited version of the famous story, with duels and fights presented like musical numbers. Its vigour and inventiveness is a pleasure to behold.

w Robert Ardrey *d George Sidney* *ph Robert Planck* *m Herbert Stothart*

Gene Kelly, Lana Turner, June Allyson, Frank Morgan, Van Heflin, Angela Lansbury, Vincent Price, Keenan Wynn, John Sutton, Gig Young, Robert Coote, Reginald Owen, Ian Keith, Patricia Medina

'A heavy, rough-housing mess. As Lady de Winter, Lana Turner sounds like a drive-in waitress exchanging quips with hotrodders, and as Richelieu, Vincent Price might be an especially crooked used car dealer. Angela Lansbury wears the crown of France as though she had won it at a county fair.'—*New Yorker, 1980*

AAN: Robert Planck

The Three Musketeers (The Queen's Diamonds)**
Panama 1973 107m Technicolor
Film Trust (Alex Salkind)

Jokey version with realistic blood; despite very lively highlights it wastes most of its high production cost by not giving its plot a chance; but money was saved by issuing the second half separately as *The Four Musketeers* (*The Revenge of Milady*). The latter section was less attractive.

w George MacDonald Fraser *d Richard Lester* *ph David Watkin* *m* Michel Legrand *pd Brian Eatwell*

Michael York, Oliver Reed, Richard Chamberlain, Frank Finlay, Raquel Welch, Geraldine Chaplin, Spike Milligan, Faye Dunaway, Charlton Heston, Christopher Lee, Jean-Pierre Cassel

'It's one dragged-out forced laugh. No sweep, no romance, no convincing chivalric tradition to mock.'—*Stanley Kauffmann*

'Move over, Casanova!'
Three on a Couch
US 1966 109m Technicolor

An artist tries to cure the sexual hang-ups of his psychiatrist fiancée's three female patients. Intolerably lengthy and witless comedy. Jerry Lewis, Janet Leigh, James Best, Mary Ann Mobley, Gila Golan, Leslie Parrish, Kathleen Freeman, Fritz Feld. Written by Bob Ross, Samuel A. Taylor, Arne Sultan, Marvin Worth; directed and produced by Jerry Lewis; for Jerry Lewis Productions / Columbia. 'A long drag through stock situations.'—*MFB*. 'Unintentionally unfunny.'—*Leonard Maltin*. 'Stay on your own couch and don't bother with Jerry's.'—*Steven Scheuer*

Three on a Match*
US 1932 63m bw
Warner (Sam Bischoff)

Three schoolgirl friends meet again in the big city, after which their paths cross melodramatically.
Predictable, watchable multi-story dramatics with an ironic twist: remade in 1938 as *Broadway Musketeers*.

w Lucien Hubbard *d* Mervyn Le Roy *ph* Sol Polito

Joan Blondell, Bette Davis, Ann Dvorak, Warren William, Grant Mitchell, Lyle Talbot, Humphrey Bogart, Glenda Farrell, Clara Blandick

'A nice picture descending to mediocrity in its final two reels.'—*Variety*

Three Ring Circus
US 1954 103m Technicolor
Vistavision
Paramount / Hal B. Wallis

Ex-army veterans join a circus.
The mixture as before from Martin and Lewis: variety acts interspersed with sentiment and heavy mugging.

w Don McGuire, Joseph Pevney *ph* Loyal Griggs *d* Joseph Pevney *m* Walter Scharf

Dean Martin, Jerry Lewis, Joanne Dru, Zsa Zsa Gabor, Wallace Ford, Sig Rumann, Gene Sheldon, Nick Cravat, Elsa Lanchester

Three Russian Girls
US 1943 80m bw

A remake of the Russian film *Girl from Stalingrad*, about a nurse called for duty at the front. Sheer propaganda, almost unwatchable now. Anna Sten, Kent Smith, Mimi Forsythe, Alexander Granach, Kathy Frye, Paul Guilfoyle, Feodor Chaliapin. Written by Maurice Clark, Victor Trivas, Aben Kandel, Dan James; directed by Fedor Ozep and Henry Kesler; for Gregor Rabinovitch / United Artists. (GB title: *She Who Dares*.)
AAN: W. Franke Harling (music)

Three Sailors and a Girl
US 1953 95m Technicolor
Warner (Sammy Cahn)

A ship's funds are unofficially invested in a musical show.
Undernourished comedy musical.

w Roland Kibbee, Devery Freeman, *play* The Butter and Egg Man by George S. Kaufman *d* Roy del Ruth *ph* Carl Guthrie *songs* Sammy Fain, Sammy Cahn

Jane Powell, Gordon Macrae, Gene Nelson, Sam Levene, George Givot, Veda Ann Borg

Three Secrets*
US 1949 98m bw
(Warner) US Pictures (Milton Sperling)

Three women wait anxiously to find out whose child survived a plane crash.
Well-made, formula woman's picture.

w Martin Rackin, Gina Kaus *d Robert Wise ph Sid Hickox m* Davis Buttolph

Eleanor Parker, Patricia Neal, Ruth Roman, Frank Lovejoy, Leif Erickson, Ted de Corsia, Edmon Ryan, Larry Keating

The Three Sisters*
GB 1970 165m Eastmancolor
Alan Clore Films

At the turn of the century, three fatherless sisters dream of abandoning Russian provincial life for the big city.
Filmed Chekhov, better than most but still lacking cinematic vigour.

translator Moura Budberg *d* Laurence Olivier *ph* Geoffrey Unsworth *m* William Walton

Laurence Olivier, Joan Plowright, Jeanne Watts, Louise Purnell, Derek Jacobi, Alan Bates, Ronald Pickup

Three Smart Girls**
US 1936 86m bw
Universal (Joe Pasternak)

Three sisters bring their parents back together.
Pleasant, efficient family film which made a world star of Deanna Durbin.

w Adele Comandini, Austin Parker *d* Henry Koster *ph* Joseph Valentine *md* Charles Previn

Deanna Durbin, Barbara Read, Nan Grey, Charles Winninger, Binnie Barnes, Ray Milland, Alice Brady, Mischa Auer, Ernest Cossart, Hobart Cavanaugh

'Surefire entertainment for any and all types of audiences. It also has that rare quality of making an audience feel better for having seen it.'—*Variety*

'Idiotically tuned in to happiness, but it isn't boring.'—*New Yorker, 1978*

'Clever, intelligent and witty, this delightful bit of entertainment has a genuineness which is rare.'—*Photoplay*

† Remade as *Three Daring Daughters.*

AAN: best picture; script

Three Smart Girls Grow Up*
US 1939 87m bw
Universal (Joe Pasternak)

A girl helps her sisters to find beaus.
More of the above, quite palatable but inevitably warmed over.

w Bruce Manning, Felix Jackson *d* Henry Koster *ph* Joe Valentine

Deanna Durbin, Helen Parrish, Nan Grey, Charles Winninger, Robert Cummings, William Lundigan, Ernest Cossart, Nella Walker

'The white feminine room which the three sisters share, the quilted beds, the little furry jackets over the pajamas—the whole upholstery is so virginal that it evokes little twitters of nostalgia from the stalls. Pillow fights and first love and being sent to bed without any dinner—the awkward age has never been so laundered and lavendered and laid away.'—*Graham Greene*

Three Strangers*
US 1946 92m bw
Warner (Wolfgang Reinhardt)

A sweepstake ticket brings fortune and tragedy to three ill-assorted people.
Humdrum pattern play: the stars work hard to bring a little magic to it.

w John Huston, Howard Koch *d* Jean Negulesco *ph* Arthur Edeson *m* Adolph Deutsch

Sidney Greenstreet, Peter Lorre, Geraldine Fitzgerald, Joan Lorring, Robert Shayne, Marjorie Riordan, Arthur Shields

Three Stripes in the Sun
US 1955 93m bw
Columbia (Fred Kohlmar)
GB title: *The Gentle Sergeant*

After World War II, a Japanese-hating sergeant in the US occupation forces helps a poverty-stricken orphanage.
Predictable sentimentality based on fact, with good background detail.

wd Richard Murphy, *articles* E. J. Kelly *ph* Burnett Guffey *m* George Duning

Aldo Ray, Phil Carey, Dick York, Chuck Connors, Mitsuko Kimura

3.10 to Yuma**
US 1957 92m bw
Columbia (David Heilwell)

A sheriff has to get his prisoner on to a train despite the threatening presence of the prisoner's outlaw friends.
Tense, well-directed but rather talky low-budget western: excellent performances and atmosphere flesh out an unconvincing physical situation.

w Halsted Welles *d Delmer Daves ph Charles Lawton Jnr m* George Duning

Glenn Ford, Van Heflin, Felicia Farr, Leora Dana, Henry Jones, Richard Jaeckel, Robert Emhardt

'A vivid, tense and intelligent story about probable people, enhanced by economical writing and supremely efficient direction and playing.'—*Guardian*

'We experimented by not filling the shadows with reflected light.'—*Delmer Daves*

Three Violent People
US 1956 100m Eastmancolor Vistavision
Paramount (Hugh Brown)

Brother ranchers quarrel over the wife of one of them, an ex-saloon hostess.
Characterless 'character' western, a long way after *Duel in the Sun.*

w James Edward Grant *d* Rudolph Maté *ph Loyal Griggs m* Walter Scharf

Charlton Heston, Anne Baxter, *Gilbert Roland*, Tom Tryon, Bruce Bennett, Forrest Tucker, Elaine Stritch, Barton MacLane

The Three Weird Sisters
GB 1948 82m bw
British National (Louis H. Jackson)

Three old maids in a Welsh village plot to kill their rich half-brother but are swept away by a flood.
All-stops-out melodrama which doesn't quite work and is generally remembered, if at all, for the last third of its writing team.

w Louise Birt, David Evans, Dylan Thomas, *novel* Charlotte Armstrong *d* Dan Birt *ph* Ernest Palmer

Nancy Price, Mary Clare, Mary Merrall, Nova Pilbeam, Raymond Lovell, Anthony Hulme

Three Wise Fools
US 1946 90m bw
MGM (William Wright)

Three crusty old gents adopt an orphan, who softens them.
Antediluvian whimsy without the expected fun, remade from a silent.

w John McDermott, James O'Hanlon, *play* Austin Strong *d* Edward Buzzell *m* Bronislau Kaper

Margaret O'Brien, Lionel Barrymore, Thomas Mitchell, Edward Arnold, Lewis Stone, Jane Darwell, Harry Davenport, Cyd Charisse

Three Wise Girls
US 1932 80m approx bw
Columbia

Three small-town girls gain wisdom in New York.
Three millgirls' romances for the price of one. Adequate, predictable romantic fodder of its time.

w Robert Riskin, Agnes C. Johnson *d* William Beaudine *ph* Ted Tetzlaff

Jean Harlow, Mae Clarke, Walter Byron, Marie Prevost, Andy Devine, Natalie Moorhead, Jameson Thomas

'Should turn in a respectable score . . . Miss Harlow fails to be convincing.'—*Variety*

Three Women*
US 1924 60m approx (24 fps) bw silent
Warner

A rake charms three women, each for a different purpose.
Subtle satirical comedy; not one of the

director's masterpieces, but with enough barbs to keep one watching.

w Ernst Lubitsch, Hans Kraly, from The Lilie by Yolanthe Marees *d Ernst Lubitsch* *ph* Charles Van Enger

Lew Cody, Pauline Frederick, May McAvoy, Marie Prevost

Three Women
US 1977 123m De Luxe Panavision
TCF / Lion's Gate (Robert Altman)

Three women come to California for different reasons; when their problems become insurmountable they rely on each other.
Tiresomely somnambulistic multi-character drama, half a satire, half a wallow, and never an entertainment.

wd Robert Altman *ph* Charles Rosher *m* Gerald Busby

Sissy Spacek, Janice Rule, Shelley Duvall, Robert Fortier, Ruth Nelson, John Cromwell, Sierra Pecheur

The Three Worlds of Gulliver
US / Spain 1959 100m Technicolor
Columbia / Morningside (Charles Schneer)

Gulliver's adventures in Lilliput and Brobdingnag.
Flat treatment of marvellous material, with all the excitement squeezed out of it and not even much pizazz in the trick photography.

w Arthur Ross, Jack Sher *d* Jack Sher *ph* Wilkie Cooper *m* Bernard Herrmann *sp* Ray Harryhausen

Kerwin Mathews, Basil Sydney, Mary Ellis, Jo Morrow, June Thorburn, Grégoire Aslan, Charles Lloyd Pack, Martin Benson

Thrill of a Lifetime
US 1937 72m bw

Summer campers put on a show which goes to Broadway. Stereotyped lower-case musical with agreeable acts. Judy Canova, Ben Blue, the Yacht Club Boys, Eleanore Whitney, Betty Grable, Johnny Downs, Dorothy Lamour (guest), Larry Crabbe. Written by Seena Owen, Grant Garrett, Paul Gerard Smith; directed by George Archainbaud; for Paramount. 'Lightweight but pleasant.'—*Variety*

Thrill of a Romance
US 1945 105m Technicolor
MGM (Joe Pasternak)

A lady swimmer falls for a returning serviceman.
Empty musical vehicle with nothing memorable about it except the waste of time and money.

w Richard Connell, Gladys Lehmann *d* Richard Thorpe *ph* Harry Stradling *md* George Stoll

Esther Williams, Van Johnson, Lauritz Melchior, Frances Gifford, Henry Travers, Spring Byington, Tommy Dorsey

The Thrill of Brazil
US 1946 90m bw

An American impresario in Brazil tries to win back his estranged wife. Efficient but unpersuasive musical, another result of the good neighbour policy. Evelyn Keyes, Keenan Wynn, Ann Miller, Allyn Joslyn, Tito Guizar, Veloz and Yolanda, Felix Bressart. Written by Allen Rivkin, Harry Clork, Devery Freeman; directed by S. Sylvan Simon; for Sidney Biddell / Columbia.

The Thrill of it All*
US 1963 104m Eastmancolor
U-I / Ross Hunter / Arwin (Ross Hunter, Marty Melcher)

The wife of a gynaecologist becomes an advertising model, and work pressures disrupt her marriage.
Glossy matrimonial farce which starts brightly but eventually flags and becomes exhausting. Its better jokes linger in the memory.

w Carl Reiner *d* Norman Jewison *ph* Russell Metty *m* Frank de Vol

Doris Day, James Garner, Arlene Francis, Edward Andrews, Reginald Owen, Zasu Pitts, Elliot Reid

'Pleasantly reminiscent of some of the screwball comedies of the thirties.'—*MFB*

Throne of Blood*
Japan 1957 105m bw
Toho (Akira Kurosawa, Sojiro Motoki)
original title: *Kumonosu-Jo*

A samurai, spurred on by his wife and an old witch, murders his lord at Cobweb Castle.
A Japanese version of *Macbeth* with a savage and horrifying final sequence. The whole film is a treat to look at.

w Hideo Oguni, Shinobu Hashimoto, Ryuzo Kikushima, Akira Kurosawa, from Shakespeare's play *d* Akira Kurosawa *ph* Asaichi Nakai *m* Masaru Sato

Toshiro Mifune, Isuzu Yamada

'Its final impression is of a man who storms into a room with an impassioned speech to deliver and then discovers that he has forgotten what he came to say.'—*Kenneth Cavander, MFB*

Through a Glass Darkly*
Sweden 1961 91m bw
Svensk Filmindustri

Four unfulfilled people on a remote island fail to communicate with each other or to understand what God is.
It sounds like a parody Bergman film, and it almost is. The same themes were carried through in *Winter Light* and *The Silence*.

wd Ingmar Bergman *ph* Sven Nykvist *m* Bach

Harriet Andersson, Gunnar Bjornstrand, Max Von Sydow, Lars Passgard

AA: best foreign film
AAN: Ingmar Bergman (as writer)

Through Different Eyes
US 1943 65m bw

A veteran DA cites an old murder case to illustrate the dangers of circumstantial evidence. Neat and peppy crime programme filler. Frank Craven, Donald Woods, Vivian Blaine, Mary Howard, Jerome Cowan. Written by Samuel G. Engel; directed by Thomas Z. Loring; for TCF.

Throw Momma from the Train*
US 1987 88m De Luxe
Orion (Larry Brezner)

After seeing *Strangers on a Train*, a student tries to persuade his professor to 'swap' murders.
Cheerful black comedy-cum-homage to Hitchcock.

w Stu Silver *d* Danny DeVito *ph* Barry Sonnenfeld *m* David Newman *pd* Ida Random

Danny DeVito, Billy Crystal, Anne Ramsey, Kim Greist, Kate Mulgrew

'Very clever and engaging from beginning to end.'—*Variety*

Thumb Tripping*
US 1972 94m De Luxe
Avco (Robert Chartoff, Irwin Winkler)

A boy and a girl hitch-hiker in California have a variety of violent adventures.
Tail end of the *Easy Rider* fashion, with odd moments of interesting detail.

w Don Mitchell, from his novel *d* Quentin Masters *ph* Harry Stradling Jnr *m* Bob Thompson

Michael Burns, Meg Foster, Marianna Hill, Bruce Dern

Thumbs Up
US 1943 67m bw

An American singing star in London is passed over in favour of talent from the war factories. Curious hands-across-the-sea filler which gives the wierdest impression of Britain at war. Brenda Joyce, Richard Fraser, Elsa Lanchester, Arthur Margetson, J. Pat O'Malley, Gertrude Niesen, Andre Charlot. Written by Frank Gill Jnr; directed by Joseph Santley; for Albert J. Cohen / Republic.

Thunder
US 1929 90m at 24 fps bw silent

A train driver has trouble with his sons. Almost forgotten star melodrama, his last silent one, made when his health was already failing. Lon Chaney, James Murray, George Duryea, Phyllis Haver. Written by Byron Morgan and Ann Price; directed by William Nigh; for MGM.

Thunder Afloat
US 1939 95m bw

Rival boat owners vie for a 1918 navy contract, and the winner finds he has been trapped into enlisting. Rumbustious Flagg-and-Quirt style comedy, good enough value for the undemanding. Wallace Beery, Chester Morris, Virginia Grey, Douglass Dumbrille, Regis Toomey, Henry Victor, Jonathan Hale. Written by Ralph Wheelwright, Wells Root and Harvey Haislip; directed by George B. Seitz; for MGM. 'Timely actioner, cinch for exploitation.'—*Variety*

Thunder Bay*
US 1953 102m Technicolor
U-I (Aaron Rosenberg)

An engineer is convinced that oil can be raised from the Louisiana sea-bed.
Well-produced outdoor actioner.

w Gil Doud, John Michael Hayes *d* Anthony Mann *ph* William Daniels *m* Frank Skinner

James Stewart, Joanne Dru, Dan Duryea, Jay C. Flippen, Anthony Moreno, Gilbert Roland, Marcia Henderson

Thunder Below
US 1932 71m bw

A wife loves her husband's best friend. Dreary melodrama with a star already seen to be box office poison. Tallulah Bankhead, Charles Bickford, Paul Lukas. From a novel by Thomas Rourke; directed by Richard Wallace; for Paramount. 'Star as weak as story . . . dull and uneventful.'—*Variety*

Thunder Birds: see Thunderbirds

Thunder in the City
GB 1937 88m bw
Atlantic (Akos Tolnay, Alexander Esway)

An American salesman in London helps a penniless duke promote a non-existent metal.
Mild satire on British and American idiosyncrasies, now very faded.

w Robert Sherwood, Abem Kandel, Akos Tolnay *d* Marion Gering *ph* Al Gilks *m* Miklos Rozsa

Edward G. Robinson, Lulu Deste, Ralph Richardson, Nigel Bruce, Constance Collier, Arthur Wontner

'Cinch to be an important feature and satisfactory booking.'—*Variety*

Thunder in the East
US 1951 98m bw
Paramount (Everett Riskin)

When India becomes independent in 1947, an American wanting to sell arms clashes with the peace-loving chief of a principality, but the arms are needed when rebels attack.
Artificial and boring action melodrama with platitudinous conversations.

w Jo Swerling, *novel* Rage of the Vulture by Alan Moorehead *d* Charles Vidor *ph* Lee Garmes *m* Hugo Friedhofer

Alan Ladd, Charles Boyer, Deborah Kerr, Corinne Calvet, Cecil Kellaway

Thunder in the Night
US 1935 69m bw

A police captain solves the murder of a blackmailer. Reasonably snappy mystery set in Budapest. Edmund Lowe, Karen Morley, Paul Cavanagh, Una O'Connor, Gene Lockhart, John Qualen, Russell Hicks. Written by Frances Hyland, Eugene Solow, from the play A Woman Lies by Ladislas Fodor; directed by George Archainbaud; for Fox. 'Tops average: deserves to do fairly well.'—*Variety*

Thunder in the Sun
US 1958 81m Technicolor
Seven Arts / Carollton (Clarence Greene)

In 1847 an Indian scout guides a group of Basques to California with their vines.
Overwritten and melodramatic wagon train story.

wd Russel Rouse *ph* Stanley Cortez *m* Cyril Mockridge

Susan Hayward, Jeff Chandler, Jacques Bergerac, Blanche Yurka, Carl Esmond

'I'll make a soldier of you, Mr McQuade—if you don't break first!'

A Thunder of Drums*
US 1961 97m Metrocolor Cinemascope
MGM (Robert J. Enders)

Trouble with Apaches at a frontier post in 1870.
Solid, unexciting first feature western, some way after Ford.

w James Warner Bellah *d* Joseph Newman *ph* William Spencer *m* Harry Sukman

Richard Boone, George Hamilton, Arthur O'Connell, Luana Patten, Richard Chamberlain, Charles Bronson

Thunder on the Hill
US 1951 84m bw
U-I (Michael Kraike)
GB title: *Bonaventure*

In Norfolk, a nun solves a murder mystery during a flood.
Modest whodunnit with an unusual background but not much suspense.

w Oscar Saul, André Solt, *play* Bonaventure by Charlotte Hastings *d* Douglas Sirk *ph* William Daniels *m* Hans Salter

Claudette Colbert, Ann Blyth, Robert Douglas, Anne Crawford, Philip Friend, Gladys Cooper, John Abbott, Connie Gilchrist, Gavin Muir

Thunder over Mexico**
US 1933 60m bw silent (with music score)

The Upton Sinclair version of the troubled Eisenstein travelogue. Packed with moments of genius, but not really a finished film in any sense. Music by Hugo Reisenfeld; for Principal Pictures. See also *Time in the Sun*. 'It will not get to first base either as a critic's picture, or in straight box office parlance . . . beautiful, slow and dull.'—*Variety*

Thunder over the Plains
US 1953 82m Warnercolor

After the Civil War, a Union officer is posted with his family to the southwest territory, and finds tension. Busy but uninvolving western programmer with a reliable star. Randolph Scott, Phyllis Kirk, Lex Barker, Charles McGraw, Elisha Cook Jnr, Fess Parker. Written by Russell Hughes; directed by André de Toth; for Warner.

Thunder Road*
US 1958 92m bw
UA / DRM (Robert Mitchum)

Hillbilly bootleggers defy a Chicago gangster. Downbeat but actionful crime melodrama with an unusual background and plenty of car chases.

w James Arlee Philips, Walter Wise *d Arthur Ripley* *ph* Alan Stensvold *m* Jack Marshall

Robert Mitchum, Gene Barry, Jacques Aubuchon, Keely Smith

Thunder Rock***
GB 1942 112m bw
Charter Films (John Boulting)

A journalist disgusted with the world of the thirties retires to a lighthouse on Lake Michigan and is haunted by the ghosts of immigrants drowned a century before.
Subtle adaptation of an impressive and topical anti-isolationist play, very well acted and presented.

w Jeffrey Dell, Bernard Miles, *play Robert Ardrey* *d Roy Boulting* *ph* Mutz Greenbaum (Max Greene) *m* Hans May

Michael Redgrave, Lilli Palmer, Barbara Mullen, James Mason, Frederick Valk, Frederick Cooper, Finlay Currie, Sybilla Binder

'Boldly imaginative in theme and treatment.'—*Sunday Express*

'More interesting technically than anything since *Citizen Kane*.'—*Manchester Guardian*

'If I thought it wouldn't keep too many people away, I'd call it a work of art.'—*Daily Express*

'What a stimulus to thought it is, this good, brave, outspoken, unfettered picture.'—*Observer*

Thunderball**
GB 1965 132m Technicolor Panavision
UA / Eon / Kevin McClory

James Bond goes underwater.
Commercially the most successful Bond, but certainly not the best despite a plethora of action sequences.

w Richard Maibaum, John Hopkins, *novel* Ian Fleming *d* Terence Young *ph Ted Moore* *m* John Barry

Sean Connery, Adolfo Celi, Claudine Auger, Luciana Paluzzi, Rik Van Nutter, Bernard Lee, Lois Maxwell, Martine Beswick

'The screenplay stands on tiptoe at the outermost edge of the suggestive and gazes yearningly down into the obscene.'—*John Simon*

Thunderbird Six
GB 1968 90m Techniscope
UA / AP / Century 21 (Gerry and Sylvia Anderson)

International Rescue combats the Black Phantom.
Bright, suspenseful puppetoon based on the TV series.

w Gerry and Sylvia Anderson *d* David Lane *ph* Harry Oakes *m* Barry Gray *ad* Bob Bell
'Holds some charm for adults, or at least for those who enjoy playing with miniature trains.'—*MFB*

Thunderbirds
US 1942 79m Technicolor
TCF (Lamar Trotti)

Problems of Arizona flight instructors during World War II.
Very minor flagwaver.

w Lamar Trotti *d* William A. Wellman *ph* Ernest Palmer *m* David Buttolph

Gene Tierney, Preston Foster, John Sutton, Jack Holt, May Whitty, George Barbier, Richard Haydn, Reginald Denny, Ted North

Thunderbirds
US 1952 99m bw
Republic (John H. Auer)

An Oklahoma unit covers itself in glory during World War II.
Scrappy, noisy war actioner with much newsreel footage.

w Mary McCall Jnr *d* John H. Auer *ph* Reggie Lanning *m* Victor Young

John Derek, John Barrymore Jnr, Mona Freeman, Ward Bond, Gene Evans

Thunderbolt**
US 1929 94m bw
Paramount

A gangster is caught, tried, and repents.
Gloomy melodrama with interesting style and credits.

w Jules Furthman, Herman J. Mankiewicz *d Josef Von Sternberg* *ph* Henry Gerrard

George Bancroft, Fay Wray, Richard Arlen, Tully Marshall, Eugénie Besserer

AAN: George Bancroft

Thunderbolt and Lightfoot*
US 1974 115m De Luxe Panavision
UA / Malpaso (Robert Daley)

A bank robber escapes prison, disguises himself as a preacher, befriends a young drifter, and discovers that a new building stands on the spot where the loot is hidden.
Violent melodrama reworking an ancient comedy situation; well made on its level.

wd Michael Cimino *ph* Frank Stanley *m* Dee Barton

Clint Eastwood, Jeff Bridges, George Kennedy, Geoffrey Lewis, Catherine Bach

AAN: Jeff Bridges

Thunderhead, Son of Flicka*
US 1945 78m Technicolor
TCF (Robert Bassler)

More where *My Friend Flicka* came from.
Unexceptionable family film with excellent outdoor photography.

w Dwight Cummins, Dorothy Yost, *novel* Mary O'Hara *d* Louis King *ph Charles Clarke* *m* Cyril Mockridge

Roddy McDowall, Preston Foster, Rita Johnson, James Bell, Carleton Young

Thunderstorm
GB 1955 88m bw
Hemisphere / Binnie Barnes

A Spanish fisherman rescues a mysterious girl from a derelict yacht and falls in love with her although the villagers regard her as a witch.
Heady stuff on a low budget, quite smoothly done for lovers of peasant drama.

w George St George, Geoffrey Holmes *d John Guillermin* *ph* Manuel Berenguer *m* Paul Misraki

Linda Christian, Carlos Thompson, Charles Korvin

Thursday's Child
GB 1942 81m bw

A child from an ordinary family has success in films and it goes to her head. Predictable domestic drama with some good moments, but rather overpraised at the time. Sally Ann Howes, Wilfrid Lawson, Kathleen O'Regan, Eileen Bennett, Stewart Granger, Felix Aylmer. Written by Donald Macardle and Rodney Ackland, from the novel by Donald Macardle; directed by Rodney Ackland; for ABPC.

'Visit the future where love is the ultimate crime!'

THX 1138*
US 1970 95m Technicolor / scope
Warner / American Zoetrope (Francis Ford Coppola, Lawrence Sturhahn)

In a future society, computer programmed and emotionless, an automated human begins to break the rules.
Orwellian science fiction; a thoughtful, rather cold affair which is always good to look at.

w George Lucas, Walter Murch *d George Lucas* *ph* Dave Meyers, Albert Kihn *m* Lalo Schifrin

Robert Duvall, Donald Pleasence, Pedro Colley, Maggie McOmie, Ian Wolfe

Thy Soul Shall Bear Witness*
Sweden 1920 70m approx (24 fps) bw silent Svensk Filmindustri
original title: *Korkarlen;* aka: *The Phantom Carriage*

A drunkard is knocked senseless, retraces his misspent life, hears the carriage of death approaching and returns to his family.
Old-fashioned moralistic saga which hit the right note at the time and has scenes which still impress.

wd Victor Sjostrom, *novel* Selma Lagerlöf *ph* J. Julius Jaenzon

Victor Sjostrom, Hilda Borgstrom, Astrid Holm

† Remade in France in 1939 by Julien Duvivier, as *La Charette Fantôme*, with Pierre Fresnay and Louis Jouvet; and again in Sweden in 1958 as *Korkarlen*, by Arne Mattson.

Tiara Tahiti*
GB 1962 100m Eastmancolor
Rank / Ivan Foxwell

An up-from-the-ranks colonel and an aristocratic smoothie captain continue their antipathy in peacetime Tahiti, where one is nearly murdered and the other gets his come-uppance.
Uneasy mixture of light comedy and character drama; enjoyable in parts, but flabbily assembled and muddily photographed.

w Geoffrey Cotterell, Ivan Foxwell, *novel* Geoffrey Cotterell *d* William T. Kotcheff *ph* Otto Heller *m* Philip Green

John Mills, James Mason, Herbert Lom, Claude Dauphin, Rosenda Monteros

Tick, Tick, Tick . . .*
US 1969 100m Metrocolor Panavision
MGM / Nelson-Barrett (Ralph Nelson, James Lee Barrett)

The first black sheriff in a southern community has trouble with murder and rape cases.
Socially conscious suspenser, well enough made from predictable elements and leading surprisingly to an upbeat ending.

w James Lee Barrett *d* Ralph Nelson *ph* Loyal Griggs *m* Jerry Stynes

Jim Brown, George Kennedy, Fredric March, Lynn Carlin, Don Stroud, Clifton James

Ticket to Heaven*
Canada 1981 108m colour

A rootless young man is taken over by a religious co-operative. Thinly veiled attack on the Moonies, quite well handled but perhaps better as a straight documentary. Nick Mancuso, Saul Rubinek, Meg Foster, Kim Cattrall. Written by Ralph L. Thomas and Anne Cameron from the book *Moonwebs* by Josh Freed; directed by Ralph L. Thomas; for Ronald Cohen Productions.

A Ticket to Tomahawk*
US 1950 90m Technicolor
TCF (Robert Bassler)

A stagecoach line defies the new western railroad.
Would-be satirical western which doesn't quite have the stamina and after some pleasing touches settles for dullness.

w Mary Loos *d* Richard Sale *ph* Harry Jackson *m* Cyril Mockridge

Anne Baxter, Dan Dailey, Rory Calhoun, Walter Brennan, Charles Kemper, Connie Gilchrist, Arthur Hunnicutt, Sen Yung

Tickle Me
US 1965 90m De Luxe Panavision
AA (Ben Schwalb)

An unemployed rodeo star accepts a job at a health ranch and helps a girl escape from villains after hidden treasure.
Wispy star vehicle with an unexpected haunted ghost town climax.

w Elwood Ullman, Edward Bernds *d* Norman Taurog *ph* Loyal Griggs *m* Walter Scharf

Elvis Presley, Julia Adams, Jocelyn Lane, Jack Mullaney, Merry Anders, Connie Gilchrist

A Ticklish Affair
US 1963 95m Metrocolor Panavision
MGM / Euterpe (Joe Pasternak)

A naval commander in San Diego falls for a widow with several children.
Thin romantic comedy with too many juvenile antics.

w Ruth Brooks Flippen *d* George Sidney *ph* Milton Krasner *m* George Stoll, Robert Van Eyps

Shirley Jones, Gig Young, Red Buttons, Carolyn Jones, Edgar Buchanan

Tiger Bay**
GB 1959 105m bw
Rank / Wintle–Parkyn (John Hawkesworth)

A Polish seaman in Cardiff kills his faithless girl friend and kidnaps a child who proves more than a match for him.
Generally very proficient police chase melodrama with strong characterizations: a considerable box office success of its time.

w John Hawkesworth, Shelley Smith *d J. Lee-Thompson ph Eric Cross m* Laurie Johnson

Hayley Mills, John Mills, Horst Buchholz, Megs Jenkins, Anthony Dawson, Yvonne Mitchell

Tiger in the Smoke*
GB 1956 94m bw
Rank (Leslie Parkyn)

Ex-commando criminals comb London for hidden loot and threaten a young girl.
Odd little melodrama with a complex plot and a different, Graham Greene-like atmosphere.

w Anthony Pelissier, *novel* Marjorie Allingham *d* Roy Baker *ph* Geoffrey Unsworth *m* Malcolm Arnold

Tony Wright, Muriel Pavlow, Donald Sinden, Bernard Miles, Alec Clunes, Laurence Naismith, Christopher Rhodes, Kenneth Griffith, Beatrice Varley

The Tiger Makes Out*
US 1967 94m Technicolor
Columbia / Elan (George Justin)

A middle-aged New York postman takes revenge on society by kidnapping a young girl—who rather enjoys the experience.
Semi-surrealist comedy misguidedly extended from a two-character play; frantic pace prevents more than a few effective moments.

w Murray Shisgal, from his play *d* Arthur Hiller *ph* Arthur J. Ornitz *m* Milton Rogers

Eli Wallach, Anne Jackson, Bob Dishy, David Burns, Charles Nelson Reilly

Tiger Shark*
US 1932 80m bw
Warner

A tuna fisherman who has lost a hand to a shark marries the daughter of an old friend, finds she loves someone else, and is conveniently killed by another shark.
Vivid melodrama with a plot partly borrowed from *Moby Dick* and itself partly borrowed by innumerable other Warner films including *Kid Galahad, The Wagons Roll at Night, Slim* and *Manpower.*

w Wells Root, *story* Tuna by Houston Branch *d Howard Hawks ph* Tony Gaudio

Edward G. Robinson, J. Carrol Naish, Zita Johann

'Strong and exceedingly well played and directed sea drama.'—*Variety*

A Tiger Walks*
US 1963 91m Technicolor
Walt Disney (Ron Miller)

In a small western town, a tiger escapes from the circus.
A splendid animal and a happy ending help to make this a pretty good film for children.

w Lowell S. Hawley, *novel* Ian Niall *d* Norman Tokar *ph* William Snyder *m* Buddy Baker

Sabu, Brian Keith, Vera Miles, Pamela Franklin, Kevin Corcoran, Edward Andrews, Una Merkel, Frank McHugh

'The Disney message runs true to form—grown-ups should practise what they preach and children are right about animals.'—*MFB*

The Tiger Woman
US 1944 bw serial: 12 eps

Oil drillers are delayed by jungle people led by a strange white woman who proves to be an heiress lost as a child in a plane crash. Ho-hum hokum. Allan Lane, Linda Stirling, Duncan Renaldo, George J. Lewis, LeRoy Mason. Directed by Spencer Bennet and Wallace Grissell; for Republic.

Tight Shoes
US 1941 67m bw

A political grafter buys tight shoes which have a series of dramatic consequences. Moderately witty little comedy which conveyed the Runyon flavour as well as any. Broderick Crawford, Binnie Barnes, John Howard, Anne Gwynne, Leo Carrillo, Samuel S. Hinds, Shemp Howard. Written by Leonard Spiegelgass and Art Arthur from the story by Damon Runyon; directed by Albert S. Rogell; for Jules Levey / Mayfair / Universal.

Tight Spot
US 1955 97m bw
Columbia (Lewis J. Rachmil)

A material witness in the trial of a gangster is released from prison in the custody of an attorney.
Fairly routine crime melodrama with unexciting star performances.

w William Bowers, *play* Dead Pigeon by Leonard Kantor *d* Phil Karlson *ph* Burnett Guffey *m* Morris Stoloff

Edward G. Robinson, Ginger Rogers, Brian Keith, Lorne Greene, Lucy Marlow, Katherine Anderson

Tightrope
US 1984 114m Technicolor
Warner / Malpaso (Clint Eastwood, Fritz Manes)

A New Orleans detective investigating a series of sex murders finds that his own impulses are none too healthy.
Boring, dimly lit and generally unappealing low life thriller.

w,d Richard Tuggle *ph* Billy Bragg *m* Lennie Niehaus

Clint Eastwood, Genevieve Bujold, Dan Hedaya, Alison Eastwood, Jennifer Beck

'Til We Meet Again
US 1940 99m bw
Warner (David Lewis)

On a ship bound from Hong Kong to San Francisco, a dying woman falls for a crook about to be executed.
Stolid remake of *One Way Passage* (qv).

w Warren Duff, *story* Robert Lord *d* Edmund Goulding *ph* Tony Gaudio *m* Ray Heindorf

Merle Oberon, George Brent, Frank McHugh, Pat O'Brien, Geraldine Fitzgerald, Eric Blore, Binnie Barnes, Henry O'Neill, George Reeves

† Marlene Dietrich was originally scheduled for the lead.

Till Death Us Do Part*
GB 1968 100m Eastmancolor
British Lion / Associated London Films (Jon Pennington)

From the thirties to the sixties with loud-mouthed, bigoted Londoner Alf Garnett.
Unremarkable and frequently misguided opening-up of a phenomenally successful TV series, adapted for the US as *All in the Family*
The original cast wades cheerfully enough through a bitty script; the sequel, *The Alf Garnett Saga*, defeated them.

w Johnny Speight *d* Norman Cohen *ph* Harry Waxman *m* Wilfrid Burns

Warren Mitchell, Dandy Nichols, Anthony Booth, Una Stubbs, Liam Redmond, Bill Maynard, Sam Kydd, Brian Blessed

Till the Clouds Roll By**
US 1946 137m Technicolor
MGM (Arthur Freed)

The life and times of composer Jerome Kern.
Better-than-average biopic with better-than-average tunes and stars.

w Myles Connolly, Jean Holloway *d* Richard Whorf *ph* Harry Stradling, George J. Folsey *md* Lennie Hayton

Robert Walker, Judy Garland, Lucille Bremer, Van Heflin, Mary Nash, Dinah Shore, Van Johnson, *June Allyson*, Tony Martin, Kathryn Grayson, *Lena Horne, Frank Sinatra, Virginia O'Brien*

'A little like sitting down to a soda fountain de luxe atomic special of maple walnut on vanilla on burnt almond on strawberry on butter pecan on coffee on raspberry sherbert on tutti frutti with hot fudge, butterscotch, marshmallow, filberts, pistachios, shredded pineapple, and rainbow sprills on top, go double on the whipped cream.'—*James Agee*

Till the End of Time*
US 1946 105m bw
RKO (Dore Schary)

Three returning GIs find romance and problems in their small town.
Downbeat variation on *The Best Years of Our Lives* with a theme tune which puts words to a Chopin Polonaise.

w Allen Rivkin *d* Edward Dmytryk *ph* Harry J. Wild *m* Leigh Harline

Dorothy McGuire, Guy Madison, Robert Mitchum

Till We Meet Again
US 1936 87m bw

Former sweethearts find themselves both spies, but on opposing sides. Unconvincing but climactically suspenseful romantic drama. Herbert Marshall, Gertrude Michael, Lionel Atwill. Written by Edwin Justus Mayer, Franklin Coen and Brian Marlow from a play by Alfred Davis; directed by Robert Florey; for Paramount.

'She came from a woman's world—into his world of men—and danger!'

Till We Meet Again
US 1944 88m bw
Paramount (David Lewis)

A French nun helps an American aviator escape from the Nazis.
Very moderate, nicely photographed, romantic war actioner.

w Lenore Coffee, *play* Alfred Maury *d* Frank Borzage *ph Theodor Sparkuhl* *m* David Buttolph

Ray Milland, Barbara Britton, Walter Slezak, Lucile Watson, Konstantin Shayne, Vladimir Sokoloff, Mona Freeman

Tillie and Gus*
US 1933 61m bw
Paramount (Douglas MacLean)

Two middle-aged cardsharps return home, help their niece and nephew win an inheritance, and come first in a paddleboat race.
Jumbled comedy with good moments and a rousing climax.

w Walter de Leon, Francis Martin *d* Francis Martin *ph* Benjamin Reynolds

W. C. Fields, Alison Skipworth, Baby Le Roy, Jacqueline Wells, Clifford Jones, Clarence Wilson, Edgar Kennedy, Barton MacLane

'Very funny in spots, but not enough spots.'—*Variety*

Tillie's Punctured Romance*
US 1914 60m approx (24 fps) bw silent
Keystone / Mack Sennett

A country maid falls for a con man who steals her money; but she finally gets her revenge.
Museum piece comedy which no longer irritates the funny bone but has clear historical interest.

w Hampton Del Ruth, *play* Tillie's Nightmare by Edgar Smith *d* Mack Sennett *ph* Frank D. Williams

Marie Dressler, Charles Chaplin, Mabel Normand, Mack Swain

Tilly of Bloomsbury
GB 1940 83m bw

The daughter of a boarding house keeper falls for a rich young man. Basically a millgirl's romance, remembered for one final drunk scene for the star comedian. Sydney Howard, Jean Gillie, Henry Oscar, Athene Seyler, Michael Wilding, Kathleen Harrison, Michael Denison, Martita Hunt, Athole Stewart. Written by Nils Hostius and Jack Marks, from the play by Ian Hay; directed by Leslie Hiscott; for Hammersmith. (Previous versions: 1921, with Tom Reynolds and Edna Best, for Samuelson; 1931, with Sydney Howard and Phyllis Konstam, for Sterling.)

Tim Tyler's Luck
US 1937 bw serial: 12 eps

Tim goes to gorilla country in search of his father, and finds a criminal who steals ivory and diamonds. Standard thick-ear from the Hollywood jungle. Frankie Thomas, Al Shean, Frances Robinson, Norman Willis. Directed by Ford Beebe; for Universal.

Timberjack
US 1954 94m Trucolor

A young man seeks his father's killer among forest lumberjacks. Resiliently cast action story of no great interest. Sterling Hayden, Vera Ralston, Adolphe Menjou, David Brian, Hoagy Carmichael, Chill Wills, Jim Davis, Elisha Cook Jnr. Written by Allen Rivkin, from the novel by Dan Cushman; directed by Joe Kane, for Republic.

Timbuktu
US 1958 92m bw

A gun runner quells a desert revolt in the French Sudan during World War II. Leaden-footed melodrama full of stock characters despite its complex plot. Yvonne de Carlo, Victor Mature, George Dolenz, John Dehner, Marcia Henderson. Written by Anthony Veiller; directed by Jacques Tourneur; for Edward Small.

Time after Time*
US 1980 112m Metrocolor Panavision
Warner / Orion (Charles Jaffe)

Jack the Ripper escapes via H. G. Wells' time machine from Victorian London to modern San Francisco; Wells gives chase and eventually projects him into limbo.
Amusing fantasy for those with light literary inclinations, marred by too much gore and a wandering middle section.

wd Nicholas Meyer, *story* Karl Alexander and Steve Hayes *ph* Paul Lohmann *m* Miklos Rozsa *pd* Edward Carfagno

Malcolm McDowell, David Warner, Mary Steenburgen, Charles Cioffi, Kent Williams

Time Bandits*
GB 1981 113m Technicolor
HandMade Films (Terry Gilliam)

A schoolboy is taken through time by a group of demonic dwarfs.
Curious tall tale in which schoolboy fantasy alternates with violence and black comedy. In general, much less funny than it intended to be, but with some hilarious moments.

w Michael Palin, Terry Gilliam *d* Terry Gilliam *ph* Peter Biziou *m* Mike Moran *pd* Millie Burns

John Cleese (as Robin Hood), Sean Connery (as Agamemnon), Ian Holm (as Napoleon), Ralph Richardson (as God), David Warner (as Satan), Shelley Duvall, Katherine Helmond, Michael Palin, Peter Vaughan, David Rappaport

Time Bomb*
GB 1952 72m bw
MGM (Richard Goldstone)
US title: *Terror on a Train*

A saboteur places a bomb on a goods train travelling from the north of England to Portsmouth.
Tolerable suspenser padded out with domestic asides.

w Ken Bennett from his novel Death at Attention *d* Ted Tetzlaff *ph* Frederick A. Young *m* John Addison

Glenn Ford, Anne Vernon, Maurice Denham, Harcourt Williams, Harold Warrender, Bill Fraser, John Horsley, Victor Maddern

Time Flies*
GB 1944 88m bw
GFD / Gainsborough (Edward Black)

A professor invents a time machine and takes his friends back to the court of Good Queen Bess.
Very passable star farce.

w J. O. C. Orton, Ted Kavanaugh, Howard Irving Young *d* Walter Forde *ph* Basil Emmott *md* Louis Levy

Tommy Handley, Felix Aylmer, Evelyn Dall, George Moon, Moore Marriott, Graham Moffatt, John Salew, Olga Lindo. Stephane Grappelly

A Time for Killing
US 1967 83m Pathecolor Panavision
Columbia / Sage Western (Harry Joe Brown)
GB title: *The Long Ride Home*

Confederate prisoners escape from a Union fort and the commander sets off in pursuit.
Fairly savage western with Something to Say about the corruption of war.

w Halsted Welles, *novel* Southern Blade by Nelson and Shirley Wolford *d* Phil Karlson *ph* Kenneth Peach *m* Mundell Lowe

Glenn Ford, George Hamilton, Inger Stevens, Max Baer, Paul Petersen, Timothy Carey, Todd Armstrong

A Time for Loving
GB 1971 104m colour
London Screen Plays / Mel Ferrer

Short romantic comedies set at different times in the same Paris flat.
Portmanteau ooh-la-la, quite neat but pitifully undernourished; certainly no *Plaza Suite.*

w Jean Anouilh *d* Christopher Miles *ph* Andreas Winding *m* Michel Legrand *pd* Theo Meurisse

Joanna Shimkus, Mel Ferrer, Britt Ekland, Philippe Noiret, Lila Kedrova, Robert Dhery, Mark Burns, Susan Hampshire

Time Gentlemen Please
GB 1952 83m bw
Group Three (Herbert Mason)

A lazy tramp is the one blot on a prize-winning English village.
Artificial, thinly scripted and overlit sub-Ealing comedy with familiar characters and situations.

w Peter Blackmore, *novel* Nothing to Lose by R. J. Minney *d* Lewis Gilbert *ph* Wilkie Cooper *m* Antony Hopkins

Eddie Byrne, Hermione Baddeley, Jane Barrett, Robert Brown, Raymond Lovell, Marjorie Rhodes, Dora Bryan, Thora Hird, Sidney James, Edie Martin, Ivor Barnard, Sidney Tafler

'Quite a nice little picture.'—*Karel Reisz*

Time in the Sun***
Mexico 1933 60m bw
Marie Seton

Unfinished fragments of Eisenstein's incomplete *Que Viva Mexico*, snippets from which were later released in various forms. This is the longest and presumably best version, with splendidly pictorial sequences of peasant and Indian life culminating with *Death Day*, all skulls and fireworks. Clearly the work of a master, though if completed the film might well have been a bore.

w Marie Seton, Paul Burnford *d Sergei Eisenstein* *ph* Edouard Tissé

Time Limit*
US 1957 95m bw
UA / Richard Widmark, William Reynolds

During the Korean war an officer is courtmartialled for suspected collaboration.
Suspenseful talk piece from a somewhat intellectualized play.

w Henry Denker, *play* Henry Denker, Ralph Berkey *d Karl Malden* *ph* Sam Leavitt *m* Fred Steiner

Richard Widmark, Richard Basehart, Dolores Michaels, June Lockhart, Carl Benton Reid, Martin Balsam, Rip Torn

'The tightly constructed story leads logically and unfalteringly to a tense climax.'—*Lindsay Anderson*

Time Lock*
GB 1957 73m bw
Romulus (Peter Rogers)

A small boy is trapped in a bank vault just as it is being locked for the weekend.
Acceptable expansion of a Canadian TV suspenser.

w Peter Rogers, *play* Arthur Hailey *d* Gerald Thomas *ph* Peter Hennessy *m* Stanley Black

Robert Beatty, Betty McDowall, Vincent Winter, Lee Patterson, Alan Gifford, Robert Ayres

The Time Machine*
US 1960 103m Metrocolor
MGM / Galaxy (George Pal)

A Victorian scientist builds a machine which after some trial and error transports him into the year 802701.
Surprisingly careful recreation of a period, and an undeniably charming machine, go for little when the future, including the villainous Morlocks, is so dull.

w David Duncan, *novel* H. G. Wells *d* George Pal *ph* Paul C. Vogel *m* Russell Garcia *ad George W. Davis, William Ferrari*

Rod Taylor, Yvette Mimieux, Alan Young, Sebastian Cabot, Tom Helmore, Whit Bissell, Doris Lloyd

The Time of Their Lives*
US 1946 82m bw
Universal (Val Burton)

Revolutionary ghosts haunt a country estate.
Unusual, quite effective Abbott and Costello vehicle with the comedians not playing as a team.

w Val Burton, Walter de Leon, Bradford Ropes, John Grant *d* Charles Barton *ph* Charles Van Enger *m* Milton Rosen

Bud Abbott, Lou Costello, Marjorie Reynolds, Binnie Barnes, Gale Sondergaard, John Shelton

The Time of Your Life*
US 1948 109m bw
William Cagney

A group of lovable eccentrics spend much of their time philosophizing in a San Francisco bar.
Not really a film at all, this essence of Saroyan contains much to enjoy or to annoy. The performances are pretty good.

w Nathaniel Curtis, *play William Saroyan* *d* H. C. Potter *ph* James Wong Howe *m* Carmen Dragon

James Cagney, William Bendix, Wayne Morris, Jeanne Cagney, Gale Page, Broderick Crawford, *James Barton*, Ward Bond, Paul Draper, James Lydon, Richard Erdman, Natalie Schaefer

'They have done so handsomely by Saroyan that in the long run everything depends on how much of Saroyan you can take.'—*Time*

Time out of Mind
US 1947 88m bw
Universal-International (Robert Siodmak)

The housekeeper's daughter finances music studies for the master's ungrateful son.
Silly romantic melodrama with few visible compensations.

w Abem Finkel, Arnold Phillips, *novel* Rachel Field *d* Robert Siodmak *ph* Maury Gertsman *m* Miklos Rozsa

Phyllis Calvert, Robert Hutton, Ella Raines, Eddie Albert, Leo G. Carroll

Time Out for Romance
US 1937 75m bw

A millionairess runs from the altar and teams up with a car factory driver. Weakish rehash of *It Happened One Night*, but the script isn't up to the intention. Claire Trevor, Michael Whalen, Joan Davis, Chick Chandler, Douglas Fowley, William Demarest, Andrew Tombes. Written by Lou Breslow, John Patrick, Eleanore Griffin, William Rankin; directed by Malcolm St Clair; for TCF. 'Just misses being able to stand on its own legs as a solo performer.'—*Variety*

A Time Out of War*
US 1954 20m bw

Two men on opposite sides of a river during the American Civil War strike up a brief friendship. Interesting but overpraised student piece. Barry Atwater, Robert Sherry, Alan Cohen. Written and directed by Denis Sanders, from the story *Pickets* by Robert W. Chambers; for Terry and Denis Sanders.

The Time, the Place and the Girl
US 1946 105m Technicolor
Warner (Alex Gottlieb)

Two nightclub owners have problems.
Lightweight musical, indistinguishable from a dozen others.

w Francis Swann, Agnes Christine Johnson, Lynn Starling *d* David Butler *ph* William V. Skall *m* Arthur Schwartz

Dennis Morgan, Jack Carson, Janis Paige, Martha Vickers, S. Z. Sakall, Alan Hale, Donald Woods, Angela Greene, Florence Bates

AAN: song 'A Gal in Calico' (*m* Arthur Schwartz, *ly* Leo Robin)

A Time to Love and a Time to Die*
US 1958 132m Eastmancolor Cinemascope
U-I (Robert Arthur)

During World War II, a German officer on his last leave solves problems at home but is killed on his return to the front.
Interesting but preachy and generally misguided attempt, by the studio which made *All Quiet on the Western Front* and *The Road Back*, to repeat the dose in colour and wide screen.

w Orin Jannings, *novel* Erich Maria Remarque *d* Douglas Sirk *ph* Russell Metty *m* Miklos Rozsa

John Gavin, Lilo Pulver, Keenan Wynn, Jock Mahoney, Thayer David, Agnes Windeck, Erich Maria Remarque

The Time Travelers*
US 1964 84m Pathecolor
AIP / Dobie (William Redlin)

Scientists venture 107 years into the future, and on escaping find themselves in a time trap.
Ingenious and lively low-budget science fiction with a sobering ending.

wd Ib Melchior *ph* William Zsigismond *m* Richard La Salle

Preston Foster, Phil Carey, Merry Anders, John Hoyt, Joan Woodbury

Time without Pity*
GB 1957 88m bw
Harlequin (John Arnold, Anthony Simmons)

An alcoholic arrives in London to seek new evidence which will prevent his son from being executed for murder.
Heavy-going, introspective, hysterical, downbeat melodrama which takes itself with a seriousness which is almost deadly.

w Ben Barzman *play* Someone Waiting by Emlyn Williams *d* Joseph Losey *ph* Freddie Francis *m* Tristam Cary

Michael Redgrave, Alec McCowen, Leo McKern, Renée Houston, Ann Todd, Peter Cushing, Paul Daneman, Lois Maxwell, George Devine, Richard Wordsworth, Joan Plowright

'It hammers home its effects with the concentration of a heavyweight out for the kill.'—*Philip Oakes*

Times Square
US 1980 113m Technicolor
EMI / Robert Stigwood

Two ill-matched teenage girls form a shabby nightclub act and soon have New York by its ears.
Sometimes sharply made but generally unpleasant urban fairy story with suicide as the end, like a cross between *Saturday Night Fever* and *Midnight Cowboy*. Among a number of forgettable songs is one called 'Pissing in the River'.

w Jacob Brackman *story* Alan Moyle and Leanne Unger
d Alan Moyle *ph* James A. Contner *m* Blue Weaver

Tim Curry, Trini Alvarado, Robin Johnson, Peter Coffield, Herbert Berghof, David Margulies

Times Square Lady
US 1935 69m bw

The daughter of a Broadway hustler, being chiselled by her father's attorney, is helped by one of his employees. Flat romantic drama designed as a test for young stars. Robert Taylor, Virginia Bruce, Pinky Tomlin, Helen Twelvetrees, Isabel Jewell, Nat Pendleton, Henry Kolker, Jack La Rue. Written by Albert Cohen, Robert Shannon; directed by George B. Seitz; for MGM. 'Not sufficient heft to be important.'—*Variety*

Times Square Playboy: see The Home Towners

Timetable*
US 1955 79m bw
(UA) Mark Stevens

An insurance investigator is assigned to a train robbery which he actually committed himself.
Concise suspenser with good script and treatment.

w Aben Kandel *d* Mark Stevens *ph* Charles Van Enger *m* Walter Scharf

Mark Stevens, Felicia Farr, King Calder, Wesley Addy

The Tin Drum*
West Germany / France 1979 142m Eastmancolor
UA / Franz Seitz / Bioskop / GGB 14 KG / Hallelujah / Artemis / Argos / Jadran / Film PolskiOriginal title: *Die Blechtrommel*

Not caring for the world he is growing up in, a small boy determines to remain a child.
Fairly brilliantly made version of a labyrinthine satire; the emphasis on sex and scatological detail, however, eventually defeats its own objects.

w Jean-Claude Carrière, Franz Seitz, Volker Schlöndorff, *novel* Gunter Grass *d Volker Schlöndorff ph* Igor Luther *m* Maurice Jarre *pd* Nicos Perakis

David Bennent, Mario Adorf, Angela Winkler, Daniel Olbrychski

Tin Men**
US 1987 112m De Luxe
Touchstone / Silver Screen Partners II (Mark Johnson)

In 1960s Baltimore, two aluminium salesmen have a series of feuds.
A comedy enjoyable not for its plot but for its authentic period backgrounds and characters.

w,d Barry Levinson ph Peter Sova *m* David Steele *pd* Peter Jamison *ed* Stu Linder

Richard Dreyfuss, Danny DeVito, Barbara Hershey, John Mahoney, Jackie Gayle, Stanley Brock

Tin Pan Alley***
US 1940 95m bw
TCF (Kenneth MacGowan)

During World War I and after, two dancing girls love the same composer.
Archetypal musical, full of Broadway clichés, razzmatazz and zip. Remade 1950 as *I'll Get By*, not to such peppy effect.

w Robert Ellis, Helen Logan *d Walter Lang ph Leon Shamroy ch* Seymour Felix *songs* Mack Gordon, Harry Warren *m* Alfred Newman

Alice Faye, Betty Grable, John Payne, Jack Oakie, Allen Jenkins, Esther Ralston, The Nicholas Brothers, John Loder, Elisha Cook Jnr

AA: Alfred Newman

The Tin Star*
US 1957 93m bw Vistavision
Paramount / Perlberg–Seaton

An ex-sheriff turned bounty hunter helps a new young sheriff to catch bandits.
Dignified and well-characterized western with customary pleasures.

w Dudley Nichols d Anthony Mann ph Loyal Griggs *m* Elmer Bernstein

Henry Fonda, Anthony Perkins, Betsy Palmer, Michel Ray, Neville Brand, John McIntire

AAN: original story (Barney Slater, Joel Kane); script

'Do you have the guts to sit in this chair?'

The Tingler
US 1959 82m bw
Columbia / William Castle

Fear (it says here) can create on the spinal column a parasite removable only by screaming. A scientist isolates it and it runs amok in a silent cinema.
Ridiculous shocker with generally dull handling but effective moments.

w Robb White *d* William Castle *ph* Wilfrid Cline *m* Von Dexter

Vincent Price, Judith Evelyn, Darryl Hickman, Patricia Cutts

'The sheer effrontery of this piece of hokum is enjoyable in itself.'—*MFB*

Tip-off Girls*
US 1938 61m bw

Gangsters use girl employees to get tips on merchandise shipments. Routine but watchable G-man second. Lloyd Nolan, Mary Carlisle, J. Carrol Naish, Harvey Stephens, Roscoe Karns, Larry Crabbe, Anthony Quinn. Written by Maxwell Shane, Robert Yost, Stuart Anthony; directed by Louis King; for Paramount. 'Excellent meller . . . bristles with action, tensity and suspense.'—*Variety*

Tip on a Dead Jockey
US 1957 99m bw
MGM (Edwin H. Knopf)
GB title: *Time for Action*

A flier loses his nerve and turns international smuggler, but reforms.
Gloomy, pedestrian star melodrama, dully cast.

w Charles Lederer, *novel* Irwin Shaw
d Richard Thorpe *ph* George J. Folsey
m Miklos Rozsa

Robert Taylor, Dorothy Malone, Gia Scala, Martin Gabel, Marcel Dalio, Jack Lord

Tish
US 1942 84m bw

A maiden aunt tries to guide her family's life. Boring domestic taradiddles which waste a good cast. Marjorie Main, Zasu Pitts, Aline MacMahon, Susan Peters, Lee Bowman, Guy Kibbee, Virginia Grey, Richard Quine, Al Shean. Written by Harry Ruskin, from stories by Mary Roberts Rinehart; directed by S. Sylvan Simon; for Orville O. Dull / MGM.

Tit for Tat*
US 1934 20m bw

Adjoining shopkeepers violently settle an old difference. Archetypal late star comedy: brilliant timing, but the warmth and sympathy have begun to ebb. Laurel and Hardy, Charlie Hall, Mae Busch. Written by Stan Laurel; directed by Charles Rogers; for Hal Roach.
AAN: best short.

Titanic*
US 1953 98m bw
TCF (Charles Brackett)

Personal dramas aboard the *Titanic* in 1912 come to a head as the ship hits an iceberg.

An excellent example of studio production is squandered on a dim script which arouses no excitement.

w Charles Brackett, Walter Reisch, Richard Breen *d* Jean Negulesco *ph Joe MacDonald m* Sol Kaplan *ad* Lyle Wheeler, Maurice Ransford

Clifton Webb, Barbara Stanwyck, Robert Wagner, Audrey Dalton, Thelma Ritter, Brian Aherne, Richard Basehart, Allyn Joslyn

AA: script

The Titfield Thunderbolt***
GB 1952 84m Technicolor
Ealing (Michael Truman)

When a branch railway line is threatened with closure, the villagers take it over as a private concern.
Undervalued on its release in the wake of other Ealing comedies, this now seems among the best of them as well as an immaculate colour production showing the England that is no more; the script has pace, the whole thing is brightly polished and the action works up to a fine climactic frenzy.

w T. E. B. Clarke d Charles Crichton ph Douglas Slocombe m Georges Auric

Stanley Holloway, George Relph, John Gregson, Godfrey Tearle, *Edie Martin*, Naunton Wayne, Gabrielle Brune, Hugh Griffith, Sidney James, Jack McGowran, Ewan Roberts, Reginald Beckwith

T-Men*
US 1947 96m bw
Eagle Lion (Aubrey Schenck)

Treasury Department detectives trail a gang of counterfeiters.
Tough, well-made crime melodrama which still packs a punch in the traditional vein.

w John C. Higgins *d* Anthony Mann *ph* John Alton *m* Paul Sawtell

Dennis O'Keefe, Alfred Ryder, Mary Meade, Wallace Ford, June Lockhart, Charles McGraw, Jane Randolph, Art Smith

To Be or Not to Be****
US 1942 99m bw
(Alexander Korda) Ernst Lubitsch

Warsaw actors get involved in an underground plot and an impersonation of invading Nazis, including Hitler.
Marvellous free-wheeling entertainment which starts as drama and descends through romantic comedy and suspense into farce; accused of bad taste at the time, but now seen as an outstanding example of Hollywood moonshine, kept alight through sheer talent and expertise.

w Edwin Justus Mayer, story Ernst Lubitsch, Melchior Lengyel *d Ernst Lubitsch ph Rudolph Maté m Werner Heymann ad Vincent Korda*

Jack Benny, Carole Lombard, Robert Stack, *Stanley Ridges, Felix Bressart, Lionel Atwill, Sig Rumann, Tom Dugan*, Charles Halton

TURA in disguise (Jack Benny): 'That great, great Polish actor Joseph Tura—you must have heard of him.'

ERHARDT (Sig Rumann): 'Ah, yes . . . what he did to Shakespeare, we are now doing to Poland!'

ERHARDT (and others): 'So they call me Concentration Camp Erhardt!'

'The comedy is hilarious, even when it is hysterically thrilling.'—*Commonweal*

'As effective an example of comic propaganda as *The Great Dictator* and far better directed.'—*Charles Higham, 1972*

'Based on an indiscretion, but undoubtedly a work of art.'—*James Agee*

'In any other medium it would be acknowledged as a classic to rank with *The Alchemist* or *A Modest Proposal*.'—*Peter Barnes*

'Lubitsch's comic genius and corrosive wit are displayed at every turn.'—*John Baxter*

'The actual business at hand . . . is nothing less than providing a good time at the expense of Nazi myth . . . Lubitsch distinguishes the film's zanier moments with his customary mastery of sly humour and innuendo, and when the story calls for outright melodrama he is more than equal to the occasion.'—*Newsweek*

AAN: Werner Heymann

To Be or Not to Be
US 1983 107m De Luxe
TCF / Brooksfilms (Mel Brooks)

Flat-footed remake of the above, with stagey sets, unconvincing acting (including the unnecessary addition of a gay dresser) and a leading comedian who won't stay still in case his lack of style should be noticed.

w Thomas Meehan, Ronnie Graham *d* Alan Johnson *ph* Gerald Hirschfeld *m* John Morris *pd* Terence Marsh

Mel Brooks, Anne Bancroft, Tim Matheson, Charles Durning, Jose Ferrer, George Gaynes, Christopher Lloyd, James Haake

AAN: Charles Durning

To Catch a Thief*
US 1955 97m Technicolor Vistavision
Paramount / Alfred Hitchcock

A famous cat burglar who has retired to the Riviera catches a thief who is imitating his old style.
Very slow, floppy and rather boring entertainment enlivened by the scenery and the odd Hitchcock touch.

w John Michael Hayes, *novel* David Dodge *d* Alfred Hitchcock *ph* Robert Burks *m* Lyn Murray

Cary Grant, Grace Kelly, *Jessie Royce Landis, John Williams*, Charles Vanel, Brigitte Auber

'Why should I steal? I'm rich.'
—'How did you get rich?'
'By stealing.'

'Billed as a comedy-mystery, it stacks up as a drawn-out pretentious piece that seldom hits the comedy level.'—*Variety*

AA: Robert Burks

'As long as there are lovers—this picture will live!'

To Each His Own**
US 1946 100m bw
Paramount (Charles Brackett)

During World War II, a middle-aged woman in London meets the soldier who is her own illegitimate and long-since-adopted-son.
The woman's picture par excellence, put together with tremendous Hollywood flair and extremely enjoyable to watch.

w Charles Brackett, Jacques Théry d Mitchell Leisen ph Daniel L. Fapp *m Victor Young ad* Hans Dreier, Roland Anderson

Olivia de Havilland, John Lund, Roland Culver, Mary Anderson, Philip Terry, Bill Goodwin, Virginia Welles, Virginia Horne

'Paramount proudly brings to the screens of America one of the three great love stories of all time!'—*publicity*

AA: Olivia de Havilland
AAN: original story (Charles Brackett)

To Find a Man*
US 1971 93m Eastmancolor
Columbia / Rastar (Irving Pincus)

The spoiled daughter of a rich family becomes pregnant and is helped by a young chemist.
Quiet, well-made minor drama about maturity, with good small-town atmosphere.

w Arnold Schulman, novel S. J. Wilson *d* Buzz Kulik *ph* Andy Laszlo *m* David Shire

Pamela Martin, Darrell O'Connor, *Lloyd Bridges*, Phyllis Newman, Tom Ewell, Tom Bosley

To Have and Have Not**
US 1945 100m bw
Warner (Howard Hawks)

An American charter boat captain in Martinique gets involved with Nazis.
Fairly routinely made studio adventure notable for first pairing of Bogart and Bacall, as an imitation of *Casablanca*, and for its consistent though not outstanding entertainment value. Remade later as *The Breaking Point* (qv) and *The Gun Runners* (qv), and not dissimilar from *Key Largo* (qv).

w Jules Furthman, William Faulkner, novel Ernest Hemingway *d Howard Hawks ph* Sid Hickox *m* Franz Waxman (uncredited) *md* Leo F. Forbstein

Humphrey Bogart, Lauren Bacall, Walter Brennan, Hoagy Carmichael, Dolores Moran, Sheldon Leonard, Dan Seymour, Marcel Dalio

'Remarkable for the ingenuity and industry with which the original story and the individualities of Ernest Hemingway have been rendered down into Hollywood basic.'—*Richard Winnington*

'Sunlight on the lattice, sex in the corridors, a new pianist at the café, pistol shots, the fat sureté man coming round after dark.'—*William Whitebait*

To Hell and Back
US 1955 106m Technicolor Cinemascope
U-I (Aaron Rosenberg)

The war career of America's most decorated infantryman.
Routine war story which happens to be about a fellow who later became a film star.

w Gil Doud, *book* Audie Murphy *d* Jesse Hibbs *ph* Maury Gertsman *m* Joseph Gershenson

Audie Murphy, Marshall Thompson, Charles Drake, Gregg Palmer, Jack Kelly, Paul Picerni, Susan Kohner

'The emotion is congealed and there is no real personal response to the anguish of war.'—*John Gillett*

To Kill a Clown
GB 1971 104m De Luxe
Palomar (Theodore Sills)

A painter and his wife move to a New England isle and are menaced by a crippled Vietnam veteran and his vicious dogs.
Pretentious, politically oriented rehash of *The Most Dangerous Game* (qv), carefully made but too slow for suspense.

w George Bloomfield, I. C. Rapoport, *novel* Master of the Hounds by Algis Budrys *d* George Bloomfield *ph* Walter Lassally *m* Richard Hill, John Hawkins

Alan Alda, Blythe Danner, Heath Lamberts, Eric Clavering

To Kill a Mockingbird**
US 1962 129m bw
U-I (Alan Pakula)

A lawyer in a small southern town defends a black man accused of rape.
Familiar dollops of social conscience, very well presented with a child interest and excellent atmosphere, but a mite overlong.

w Horton Foote, *novel* Harper Lee *d Robert Mulligan* *ph* Russell Harlan *m* Elmer Bernstein

Gregory Peck, Mary Badham, Philip Alford, John Megna, Frank Overton, Rosemary Murphy, Ruth White, Brock Peters

† The narrator is Kim Stanley.

AA: script; Gregory Peck
AAN: best picture; Robert Mulligan; Russell Harlan; Elmer Bernstein; Mary Badham

To Live and Die in L.A.
US 1985 116m Technicolor
MGM–UA / New Century / SLM / Irving H. Levin

A secret service agent nails the counterfeiter who killed his partner.
High-gloss, foul-mouthed, hysterical crime melo, a kind of west coast *French Connection*.

w William Friedkin, Gerald Petievich, from the latter's novel *d* William Friedkin *ph* Robby Muller *m* Wang Chung *pd* Lilly Kilvert *ed* Scott Smith

William L. Petersen, William Dafoe, John Pankow, Debra Feuer, Dean Stockwell, John Turturro, Darlanne Fluegel.

'The intense vulgarity of the characters and virtuoso stylistic overkill will turn off mainstream audiences.'—*Variety*

To Mary with Love
US 1936 87m bw

A businessman thinks back affectionately over ten years of married life. Harmless romantic comedy-drama. Warner Baxter, Myrna Loy, Ian Hunter, Claire Trevor, Jean Dixon. Written by Richard Sherman and Howard Ellis Smith; directed by John Cromwell; for TCF.

To Paris with Love
GB 1954 78m Technicolor
GFD / Two Cities (Anthony Darnborough)

A middle-aged widower and his son go to Paris on holiday and devise matrimonial plans for each other.
Thin, disappointing taradiddle which is short but seems long.

w Robert Buckner *d* Robert Hamer *ph* Reg Wyer *m* Edwin Astley

Alec Guinness, Vernon Gray, Odile Versois, Jacques François, Elina Labourdette, Austin Trevor

'The general impression is somehow too aimless, too muted.'—*Gavin Lambert*

'John Davis came on the set one day and said: Give us some pratfalls, Alec, give us some laughs. I realized there and then that I was not going to fit in.'—*Alec Guinness*

To Please a Lady*
US 1950 91m bw
MGM (Clarence Brown)

A ruthless midget-car racer falls for the lady journalist who is hounding him.
Good action programmer with no frills.

w Barre Lyndon, Marge Decker *d* Clarence Brown *ph* Harold Rosson *m* Bronislau Kaper

Clark Gable, Barbara Stanwyck, Adolphe Menjou, Will Geer, Roland Winters, Emory Parnell, Frank Jenks

'A story as fresh as the girls in their minis!'

To Sir with Love
GB 1967 105m Technicolor
Columbia (James Clavell)

A West Indian teacher comes to a tough East End school.
Sentimental non-realism patterned after *The Blackboard Jungle* but much softer; its influence led to a TV situation comedy, *Please Sir*.

w James Clavell, *novel* E. R. Braithwaite *d* James Clavell *ph* Paul Beeson *m* Ron Grainer

Sidney Poitier, Christian Roberts, Judy Geeson, Suzy Kendall, Lulu, Faith Brook, Geoffrey Bayldon, Patricia Routledge

'The sententious script sounds as if it has been written by a zealous Sunday school teacher after a particularly exhilarating boycott of South African oranges.'—*MFB*

To the Devil a Daughter
GB / Germany 1975 93m Technicolor
EMI / Hammer–Terra Filmkunst (Roy Skeggs)

An occult novelist is asked to take care of a girl who has been 'promised' to a group of Satanists.
Confusingly told, high camp diabolic thriller.

w Chris Wicking, *novel* Dennis Wheatley *d* Peter Sykes *ph* David Watkin *m* Paul Glass

Richard Widmark, Christopher Lee, Denholm Elliott, Honor Blackman, Michael Goodliffe, Anthony Valentine, Derek Francis, Nastassja Kinski

To the Ends of the Earth**
US 1948 107m bw
Columbia (Sidney Buchman)

A government agent follows a world-wide trail after a narcotics gang.
Thoroughly riveting conventional thriller, nicely made and photographed.

w Jay Richard Kennedy *d Robert Stevenson* *ph Burnett Guffey* *m* George Duning

Dick Powell, Signe Hasso, Ludwig Donath, Vladimir Sokoloff, Edgar Barrier

To the Shores of Tripoli
US 1942 82m Technicolor
TCF (Milton Sperling)

A cocky playboy becomes a tough marine.
Despite the title, this modest flagwaver with romantic trimmings never moves out of the San Diego training grounds.

w Lamar Trotti *d* Bruce Humberstone *ph* Edward Cronjager *m* Alfred Newman

Maureen O'Hara, John Payne, Randolph Scott, Nancy Kelly, William Tracy, Maxie Rosenbloom, Henry Morgan, Russell Hicks, Minor Watson

AAN: cinematography

To the Victor
US 1948 100m bw
Warner (Jerry Wald)

French collaborators stand trial for war crimes.
Glum melodrama with inadequate cast.

w Richard Brooks *d* Delmer Daves *ph* Robert Burks *m* David Buttolph

Dennis Morgan, Viveca Lindfors, Bruce Bennett, Victor Francen, Dorothy Malone, Tom d'Andrea, Eduardo Ciannelli, Joseph Buloff, Luis Van Rooten, William Conrad

To What Red Hell
GB 1929 100m bw

A young epileptic kills a prostitute and is protected by his mother. Unpalatable melodrama which failed to be as significant as it wished. Sybil Thorndike, John Hamilton, Bramwell Fletcher, Janice Adair. Written by Leslie Hiscott, from the play by Percy Robinson; directed by Edwin Greenwood; for Strand / Twickenham.

The Toast of New Orleans
US 1950 97m Technicolor
MGM (Joe Pasternak)

A Bayou villager becomes a star of the New Orleans opera.
Very ordinary setting for a new singing star.

w Sy Gomberg, George Wells *d* Norman Taurog *ph* William Snyder *md* George Stoll *ch* Eugene Loring

Kathryn Grayson, David Niven, Mario Lanza, J. Carrol Naish, James Mitchell, Richard Hageman, Clinton Sundberg, Sig Arno

'Sheer excruciation.'—*Pauline Kael, New Yorker*

AAN: song 'Be My Love' (*m* Nicholas Brodszky, *ly* Sammy Cahn)

'The screen sensation of a decade, played by a galaxy of stars in a hell-bent world of wine and women!'

The Toast of New York**
US 1937 109m bw
RKO (Edward Small)

A 19th-century medicine showman becomes a notorious Wall Street financier.
Smart biopic of Jim Fisk; good entertainment with accomplished production.

w Dudley Nichols, John Twist, Joel Sayre *d* Rowland V. Lee *ph* Peverell Marley *m* Nathaniel Shilkret

Edward Arnold, Cary Grant, Frances Farmer, Jack Oakie, Donald Meek, Clarence Kolb, Thelma Leeds

'Making no pretence for serious consideration as a faithful and accurate reflection of life and manners in the period it depicts, it rates as a piece of hokum aimed at the box office. It will do business.'—*Variety*

Tobacco Road***
US 1941 84m bw
TCF (Jack Kirkland, Harry H. Oshrin)

Poor whites in Georgia are turned off their land.
This bowdlerized version of a sensational book and play has superbly orchestrated farcical scenes separated by delightfully pictorial quieter moments: it isn't what was intended, but in its own way it's quite marvellous.

w Nunnally Johnson, novel Erskine Caldwell, *play* Jack Kirkland *d John Ford ph Arthur Miller m David Buttolph*

Charley Grapewin, Elizabeth Patterson, Dana Andrews, Gene Tierney, *Marjorie Rambeau*, Ward Bond, William Tracy, Zeffie Tilbury, Slim Summerville, Grant Mitchell, Russell Simpson, Spencer Charters

Tobruk
US 1967 110m Techniscope
Universal / Corman / Gibraltar (Gene Corman)

During the North African war, a British major and some German Jews try to blow up the Nazi fuel bunkers.
Routine war adventure, quite tough and spectacular but undistinguished.

w Leo V. Gordon *d* Arthur Hiller *ph* Russell Harlan *m* Bronislau Kaper

Rock Hudson, George Peppard, Nigel Green, Guy Stockwell, Jack Watson, Liam Redmond, Leo Gordon, Norman Rossington, Percy Herbert

Toby Tyler*
US 1959 96m Technicolor
Walt Disney (Bill Walsh)

In 1910, a young orphan runs away to join a travelling circus in the midwest, and with the help of a chimp becomes a famous star.
Acceptable, predictable family fare.

w Bill Walsh, Lillie Hayward, *novel* James Otis Kaler *d* Charles Barton *ph* William Snyder *m* Buddy Baker

Kevin Corcoran, Henry Calvin, Gene Sheldon, Bob Sweeney, James Drury

Today We Live*
US 1933 113m bw
MGM (Howard Hawks)

During World War I, an aristocratic English girl and her three lovers all find themselves at the front, and two fail to return.
Stilted romantic melodrama with imposing credentials.

w Edith Fitzgerald, Dwight Taylor, William Faulkner, *story* Turnabout by William Faulkner *d* Howard Hawks *ph* Oliver T. Marsh

Joan Crawford, Gary Cooper, Robert Young, Franchot Tone, Roscoe Karns, Louise Closser Hale, Rollo Lloyd

'One of those overly long features which would serve the purpose better in 2000 or more less feet . . . but the action, the men and the Crawford name should translate into satisfying figures.'—*Variety*

† Much of the flying footage was taken from the *Hell's Angels* stock.

The Todd Killings*
US 1970 93m Technicolor Panavision
National General (Barry Shear)

In a small American town, a 23-year-old boy starts out on a rampage of rape and murder.
Violent psychclogical melodrama, based on fact, with inventive direction.

w Dennis Murphy, Joe L. Oliansky *d Barry Shear ph* Harold E. Stine *m* Leonard Rosenman

Robert F. Lyons, Richard Thomas, Belinda Montgomery, Barbara Bel Geddes, Gloria Grahame

'The most striking of the many recent film versions of the souring of the American dream.'—*Tony Rayns*

Together Again
US 1944 93m bw
Columbia (Virginia Van Upp)

The widow of a New England mayor commissions a statue in his honour.
The title refers to the reteaming of the stars who were so popular in *Love Affair* and *When Tomorrow Comes*, which is a sign of the lack of invention elsewhere. A comedy without laughs.

w Virgina Van Upp, F. Hugh Herbert *d* Charles Vidor *ph* Joseph Walker *m* Werner Heymann

Charles Boyer, Irene Dunne, Charles Coburn, Mona Freeman, Jerome Courtland, Elizabeth Patterson, Charles Dingle, Walter Baldwin

Tokyo Joe
US 1949 88m bw
Columbia / Santana (Robert Lord)

A former nightclub owner returns to postwar Japan to reclaim his fortune and his ex-wife.
Dispirited star melodrama.

w Cyril Hume, Bertram Millhauser *d* Stuart Heisler *ph* Charles Lawton Jnr *m* George Antheil

Humphrey Bogart, Florence Marly, Alexander Knox, Sessue Hayakawa, Lora Lee Michel, Jerome Courtland

Tol'able David*
US 1921 80m approx (24 fps) bw silent
First National / Inspiration

A quiet farming community is disrupted by three marauding convicts, who are finally despatched by the peace-loving youngest son.
Fresh, sympathetic David-and-Goliath story which was a huge popular success on its release.

w Edmund Goulding, Henry King, *novel* Joseph Hergesheimer *d Henry King ph* Henry Cronjager

Richard Barthelmess, Gladys Hulette, Ernest Torrence, Warner Richmond

'It is sentimental in places, but not sloppy. It is bucolic, but its rusticity is not rubbed in . . . it is restrained, imaginatively suggestive when not briefly literal. For all these reasons it is stimulating.'—*New York Times*

† Columbia remade the story in 1930 with Richard Cromwell, but its time had passed.

Tom Brown of Culver
US 1932 79m bw

Life at a military cadet school. Idealized propaganda, with the hero a boy subsidized by the local legion because his dead father was a war hero. Tom Brown, H. B. Warner, Slim Summerville, Richard Cromwell, Ben Alexander, Sidney Toler, Betty Blythe. Written by Tom Beckingham; directed by William Wyler; for Universal. 'It will probably make acceptable film fare to other than irritated cadets.'—*Variety*

Tom Brown's Schooldays*
US 1940 86m bw
(RKO) The Play's the Thing (Gene Towne, Graham Baker)

Tom Brown finds life at Rugby brutal, but helps to become a civilizing influence.
Pretty lively Hollywood version of a rather unattractive semi-classic.

w Walter Ferris, Frank Cavell, *novel* Thomas Hughes *d* Robert Stevenson *ph* Nicholas Musuraca *m* Anthony Collins

Jimmy Lydon, Cedric Hardwicke, Billy Halop, Freddie Bartholemew, Gale Storm, Josephine Hutchinson

Tom Brown's Schooldays
GB 1951 96m bw
Talisman (George Minter)

Unexciting remake featuring one surprisingly strong performance.

w Noel Langley *d* Gordon Parry *ph* C. Pennington-Richards *m* Richard Addinsell

Robert Newton, John Howard Davies, Diana Wynyard, Francis de Wolff, Kathleen Byron, Hermione Baddeley, James Hayter, Rachel Gurney, Amy Veness, Max Bygraves, Michael Hordern, John Charlesworth, John Forrest

'An odd mixture of the brutal and the solemnly improving.'—*Richard Mallett, Punch*

Tom, Dick and Harry**
US 1940 86m bw
RKO (Robert Sisk)

A girl daydreams about her three boy friends, but can't make up her mind.
Brightly-handled comedy which became a minor classic but does seem to have faded a little. Remade as *The Girl Most Likely* (qv).

w Paul Jarrico d Garson Kanin ph Merrit Gerstad *m* Roy Webb

Ginger Rogers, Burgess Meredith, Alan Marshal, George Murphy, *Phil Silvers*, Joe Cunningham, Jane Seymour, Lenore Lonergan

'Foot by foot the best made picture of this year.'—*Otis Ferguson*

AAN: Paul Jarrico

Tom Horn
US 1979 97m Technicolor Panavision
Warner / Solar / First Artists (Fred Weintraub)

An ex-cavalry scout gets a job as a stock detective, is framed for murder, and allows himself to be hanged.
Curious pessimistic and unsatisfactory semi-western in which the star was found to have lost his old charisma after being too long away.

w Thomas McGuane, Bid Shrake, from the alleged autobiography of Tom Horn
d William Wiard *ph* John Alonzo *m* Ernest Gold

Steve McQueen, Linda Evans, Richard Farnsworth, Billy Green Bush, Slim Pickens, Elisha Cook Jnr.

'Imagine a film that opens up with dialogue that can't be heard at all, then proceeds to build up to a fist fight that's never seen, that cuts away to sunsets to fill in other scenes that have no dramatic point, that presents a meal where the sound of knives and forks drowns out what's being said, and you have just the beginning of what's wrong with *Tom Horn*.'—*Variety*

'The whole world loves him!'
Tom Jones***
GB 1963 129m Eastmancolor
UA / Woodfall (Tony Richardson)

In 18th-century England a foundling is brought up by the squire and marries his daughter after many adventures.
Fantasia on Old England, at some distance from the original novel, with the director trying every possible jokey approach against a meticulously realistic physical background. Despite trade fears, the *Hellzapoppin* style made it an astonishing box office success (the sex helped), though it quickly lost its freshness and was much imitated.

w John Osborne, *novel* Henry Fielding
d Tony Richardson ph Walter Lassally, Manny Wynn m John Addison pd Ralph Brinton

Albert Finney, Susannah York, Hugh Griffith, Edith Evans, Joan Greenwood, Diane Cilento, George Devine, Joyce Redman, David Warner, Wilfrid Lawson, Freda Jackson, Rachel Kempson

'Uncertainty, nervousness, muddled method . . . desperation is writ large over it.'—*Stanley Kauffmann*

'Much of the time it looks like a home movie, made with sporadic talent by a group with more enthusiasm than discipline.'—*Tom Milne*

'It is as though the camera had become a method actor: there are times when you wish you could buy, as on certain juke boxes, five minutes' silence . . . Obviously a film which elicits such lyric ejaculations from the reviewers cannot be all good.'—*John Simon*

'I just felt I was being used. I wasn't involved . . . I was bored most of the time.'—*Albert Finney*

† The narrator was Micheal MacLiammoir.

AA: best picture; John Osborne; Tony Richardson; John Addison
AAN: Albert Finney; Hugh Griffith; Edith Evans; Diane Cilento; Joyce Redman

Tom Sawyer
US 1973 103m De Luxe Panavision
UA / Readers Digest (Arthur P. Jacobs)

Reverential, rather tediously over-produced version for family audiences of the seventies, with brief songs and real Mississippi locations.

w / m / ly Richard and Robert Sherman
d Don Taylor *ph* Frank Stanley *md* John Williams *pd* Philip Jefferies

Johnnie Whitaker, Celeste Holm, Warren Oates, Jeff East, Jodie Foster

† There had been a version with Jackie Coogan in 1930. Selznick's *The Adventures of Tom Sawyer* followed in 1937. In 1939 Billy Cook was Tom Sawyer, Detective, with Donald O'Connor as Huckleberry Finn.

AAN: Richard and Robert Sherman; John Williams

Tom Thumb*
GB 1958 98m Eastmancolor
MGM / Galaxy (George Pal)

A tiny forest boy outwits a couple of thieves. Slight musical built round the legend of a two-inch boy; good trickwork and songs make it a delightful film for children.

w Ladislas Fodor *d* George Pal *ph* Georges Périnal *m* Douglas Gamley, Kenneth V. Jones *sp Tom Howard*

Russ Tamblyn, Jessie Matthews, Peter Sellers, Terry-Thomas, Alan Young, June Thorburn, Bernard Miles, Ian Wallace

† Donald O'Connor badly wanted the role, but it went to the MGM contractee.

Tomahawk
US 1951 82m Technicolor

An Indian scout helps the Sioux to get their territory rights. Competent small-scale western. Van Heflin, Yvonne De Carlo, Alex Nicol, Preston Foster, Jack Oakie, Tom Tully, Rock Hudson. Written by Silvia Richards and Maurice Geraghty; directed by George Sherman; for Universal-International. (GB title: *Battle of Powder River*.)

The Tomb of Ligeia**
GB 1964 81m Eastmancolor Cinemascope
American International (Roger Corman)

A brooding Victorian metamorphoses his dead wife into a cat, then into the beautiful Lady Rowena.
Complex but rather fascinating horror suspenser which rejogs familiar elements into something new; the best of the Corman Poes.

w Robert Towne, story Edgar Allan Poe
d Roger Corman ph Arthur Grant
m Kenneth V. Jones

Vincent Price, Elizabeth Shepherd, John Westbrook, Oliver Johnston, Richard Johnson, Derek Francis

'Good men (and women) live in Tombstone—but not for long!'
Tombstone (The Town Too Tough to Die)
US 1942 80m bw

How Wyatt Earp cleaned up the town. Lacklustre low-budget version of a famous story. Richard Dix, Frances Gifford, Kent Taylor, Edgar Buchanan, Don Castle, Victor Jory. Written by Albert Shelby Le Vino and Edward E. Paramore; directed by William McGann; for Paramount.

Tommy*
GB 1975 108m colour
Hemdale / Robert Stigwood

A deaf, dumb and blind child is eventually cured and becomes a rock celebrity.
Mystical rock opera screened with the director's usual barrage of effects and an ear-splitting score. Of occasional interest.

w Ken Russell, from the opera by Pete Townshend and the Who *d Ken Russell*
ph Dick Bush, Ronnie Taylor *m* Pete Townshend and the Who

Roger Daltrey, Ann-Margret, Oliver Reed, Elton John, Eric Clapton, Keith Moon

AAN: Ann-Margret

Tommy the Toreador
GB 1959 86m Technicolor

A seaman takes the place of a bullfighter framed for smuggling. Acceptable star comedy of its time. Tommy Steele, Sid James, Janet Munro, Pepe Nieto, Noel Purcell, Kenneth Williams, Eric Sykes. Written by Nicholas Phipps, Sid Colin, Talbot Rothwell; directed by John Paddy Carstairs; for Fanfare / AB.

Tomorrow and Tomorrow
US 1932 73m bw

A happily married woman suddenly falls for a foreign scientist. Sturdy woman's picture of its day. Ruth Chatterton, Paul Lukas, Robert Ames, Harold Minjir, Tad Alexander. Written by Josephine Lovett from the play by Philip Barry; directed by Richard Wallace; for Paramount. 'A screen play of the first grade . . . reflects credit on everybody concerned in its making.'—*Variety*

Tomorrow at Ten*
GB 1962 80m bw
Mancunian (Tom Blakeley)

A crook kidnaps a small boy and locks him up with a time bomb while he makes his demands in person. When the kidnapper is killed, the police have to hunt against time.
Tense second feature, well acted and efficiently done.

w Peter Millar, James Kelly *d Lance Comfort* *ph* Basil Emmott *m* Bernie Fenton

Robert Shaw, John Gregson, Alec Clunes, Alan Wheatley, Ernest Clark, Kenneth Cope

Tomorrow Is Another Day
US 1951 90m bw

An ex-convict is soon on the run for a crime he didn't commit. Miserable melodrama apparently left over from John Garfield days. Steve Cochran, Ruth Roman, Lurene Tuttle, Bobby Hyatt, Ray Teal. Written by Guy Endore and Art Cohn; directed by Felix Feist; for Warner.

Tomorrow Is Forever*
US 1945 105m bw
RKO–International (David Lewis)

A man supposed dead in the war returns with an altered face to find his wife has remarried.
Enoch Arden rides again in a rampant woman's picture which is well enough made to be generally entertaining.

w Lenore Coffee *d* Irving Pichel *ph* Joe Valentine *m* Max Steiner

Orson Welles, Claudette Colbert, George Brent, Lucile Watson, Richard Long, Natalie Wood

Tomorrow Never Comes
Canada / GB 1977 109m colour
Rank / Classic / Montreal Trust / Neffbourne (Michael Klinger, Julian Melzack)

A jealous lover shoots a caller at his girl's beach cabana and a police siege begins.
Far from the class of *Le Jour Se Lève*, this is an exploitative and violent melodrama which need never have been made.

w David Pursall, Jack Seddon, Sydney Banks *d* Peter Collinson *ph* François Protat *m* Roy Budd

Oliver Reed, Susan George, Raymond Burr, Stephen McHattie, John Ireland, Donald Pleasence, John Osborne, Cec Linder

Tomorrow the World*
US 1944 86m bw
UA / Lester Cowan

A college professor adopts his orphaned German nephew, who turns out to be an ardent 12-year-old Nazi.
Adequate, predictable screen version of a once-topical play.

w Ring Lardner Jnr, Leopold Atlas, *play* James Gow, Armand D'Usseau *d* Leslie Fenton *ph* Henry Sharp *m* Louis Applebaum

Fredric March, Betty Field, *Skip Homeier*, Agnes Moorehead, Joan Carroll

Tomorrow We Live
GB 1942 85m bw
British Aviation (George King)
US title: *At Dawn We Die*

French villagers help a spy escape to Britain. Minor flagwaver marred by cheap sets.

w Anatole de Grunwald, Katherine Strueby *d* George King

John Clements, Greta Gynt, Hugh Sinclair, Judy Kelly, Godfrey Tearle, Yvonne Arnaud, Bransby Williams

Tonight and Every Night
US 1945 92m Technicolor
Columbia (Victor Saville)

The lives and loves of London showgirls during the blitz.
Ludicrous concoction looking nothing like London and certainly nothing like the Windmill, the theatre to which it allegedly pays tribute. There are some tolerable numbers along the way.

w Lesser Samuels, Abem Finkel, *play* Heart of a City by Lesley Storm *d* Victor Saville *ph* Rudolph Maté *md* Morris Stoloff, Marlin Skiles

Rita Hayworth, Lee Bowman, Janet Blair, Marc Platt, Leslie Brooks, Dusty Anderson, Florence Bates, Ernest Cossart

AAN: Morris Stoloff, Marlin Skiles; song 'Anywhere' (*m* Jule Styne, *ly* Sammy Cahn)

Tonight Is Ours
US 1932 76m bw

A Balkan princess falls for a commoner in Paris. One of the master's less sparkling plays gets the heavy Hollywood treatment. Fredric March, Claudette Colbert, Alison Skipworth, Paul Cavanagh, Arthur Byron, Ethel Griffies. Written by Edwin Justus Mayer, from the play by Noel Coward; directed by Stuart Walker; for Paramount. 'Slow and talky flicker, better for the class houses.'—*Variety*

Tonight or Never
US 1931 80m bw
Samuel Goldwyn

A prima donna falls for a man she thinks is a Venetian gigolo, but he turns out to be an impresario from New York.
Flimsy comedy which turned out to be its star's last vehicle of any consequence for twenty years.

w Ernest Vajda, *play* Lily Hatvany *d* Mervyn Le Roy *ph* Gregg Toland *md* Alfred Newman

Gloria Swanson, Melvyn Douglas (debut), Ferdinand Gottschalk, Robert Greig, Alison Skipworth, Boris Karloff

Tonight We Raid Calais
US 1943 70m bw

A British agent lands in occupied France to pave the way for a bombing raid. Adequate low-budget morale booster. John Sutton, Annabella, Lee J. Cobb, Beulah Bondi, Blanche Yurka, Howard Da Silva, Marcel Dalio. Written by Waldo Salt; directed by John Brahm; for TCF.

Tonight We Sing*
US 1953 109m Technicolor
TCF (George Jessel)

Sol Hurok stifles his own talent to become a great musical impresario.
Blameless uppercrust biopic, with plenty of well-staged guest talent.

w Harry Kurnitz, George Oppenheimer *d* Mitchell Leisen *ph* Leon Shamroy *md* Alfred Newman *ch* David Lichine

David Wayne, Anne Bancroft, Ezio Pinza (Chaliapin), Roberta Peters, Tamara Toumanova (Pavlova), Isaac Stern (Eugene Ysaye), Jan Peerce

Tonka
US 1958 97m Technicolor
Walt Disney

A Sioux Indian tames a magnificent white horse, and after many adventures is reunited with him at Little Big Horn.
Unremarkable and overlong adventure story.

w Lewis R. Foster, Lillie Hayward, *novel* Comanche by David Appel *d* Lewis R. Foster *ph* Loyal Griggs

Sal Mineo, Phil Carey, Jerome Courtland, Rafael Campos, H. M. Wynant

Tons of Money
GB 1930 97m bw

An inventor poses as his own cousin, and in this guise achieves instant success. A long-running stage farce makes a grimly overlong movie. Ralph Lynn, Yvonne Arnaud, Mary Brough, Robertson Hare, Gordon James, Madge Saunders. Written by Herbert Wilcox and Ralph Lynn, from the play by Will Evans and Arthur Valentine; directed by Tom Walls; for Herbert Wilcox / B and D.

Tony Draws a Horse
GB 1950 91m bw

How to deal with a naughty boy causes mounting disagreement in the family. Very theatrical farce which on screen seems merely silly. Cecil Parker, Anne Crawford, Derek Bond, Barbara Murray, Mervyn Johns, Edward Rigby. Written by Brock Williams, from the play by Lesley Storm; directed by John Paddy Carstairs; for Pinnacle / GFD.

Tony Rome*
US 1967 111m De Luxe Panavision
TCF / Arcola / Millfield (Aaron Rosenberg)

A seedy Miami private eye runs into murder when he guards a millionaire's daughter.
Complex old-fashioned murder mystery decorated with the new amorality and fashionable violence. Tolerable for its backgrounds and professional expertise.
Sequel: *Lady in Cement* (qv).

w Richard L. Breen, *novel* Miami Mayhem by Marvin H. Albert *d* Gordon Douglas *ph* Joe Biroc *m* Billy May

Frank Sinatra, Jill St John, Richard Conte, Gena Rowlands, Simon Oakland, Jeffrey Lynn, Lloyd Bochner, Sue Lyon

Too Busy to Work
US 1932 76m bw

A tramp goes looking for his long lost wife.
Amiable remake of one of the star's most successful silents. *Will Rogers*, Marian Nixon, Dick Powell, Frederick Burton, Louise Beavers. Written by Barry Conners, Philip Klein, from the story Jubilo by Ben Ames Williams; directed by John Blystone; for Fox.
'A homey story of programmer weight . . . better than average business should be figured on.'—*Variety*

Too Hot to Handle*
US 1938 105m bw
MGM (Lawrence Weingarten)

Adventures of a scoop-seeking newsreel cameraman.
Boisterous comedy-melodrama with as many sags as highlights but generally making a cheerful star entertainment.

w Laurence Stallings, John Lee Mahin *d* Jack Conway *ph* Harold Rosson *m* Franz Waxman

Clark Gable, Myrna Loy, Walter Connolly, Walter Pidgeon, Leo Carrillo, Johnny Hines, Virginia Weidler

'Even more than *Test Pilot* it's hoked beyond the level of credibility. But it has a driving excitement, crackling dialogue, glittering performances and inescapable romantic pull. So it's a socko audience picture and should make a parachuteful of money.'—*Variety*

'It's like an old-fashioned serial . . . no one can call it dull.'—*Howard Barnes*

'Breathlessly paced, witty, and violent, this is one of the more acid comedies to have been produced by the Thirties.'—*John Baxter*

Too Hot to Handle
GB 1960 100m Eastmancolor
ABP / Wigmore (Selim Cattan)
aka: *Playgirl After Dark*

Two Soho strip club owners join forces to hunt down a blackmailer.
Rotten, hilarious British gangster film set in a totally unreal underworld and very uncomfortably cast.

w Herbert Kretzmer *d* Terence Young *ph* Otto Heller *m* Eric Spear

Leo Genn, Jayne Mansfield, Karl Boehm, Danik Patisson, Christopher Lee, Patrick Holt

Too Late Blues
US 1961 100m bw
Paramount (John Cassavetes)

A jazz musician falls for a neurotic girl and has fears of going commercial.
Uninteresting professional feature from a director whose reputation was made with the amateur *Shadows*.

w John Cassavetes, Richard Carr *d* John Cassavetes *ph* Lionel Lindon *m* David Raksin

John Cassavetes, Stella Stevens, Bobby Darin, Everett Chambers, Nick Dennis, Rupert Crosse, Vince Edwards

Too Late for Tears
US 1949 99m bw
(UA) Hunt Stromberg

A lady bluebeard disposes of both husbands and boyfriends.
Silly melodrama, poorly cast.

w Roy Huggins *d* Byron Haskin *ph* William Mellor *m* Dale Butts

Lizabeth Scott, Don Defore, Arthur Kennedy, Dan Duryea, Kristine Miller, Barry Kelley

Too Late the Hero*
US 1969 144m Technicolor 70mm
Associates and Aldrich / Palomar

In World War II the Japanese hold one end of a small Pacific island, British and Americans the other.
Semi-cynical, long and bloody war adventure of competence but no great merit.

w Robert Aldrich, Lukas Heller *d* Robert Aldrich *ph* Joseph Biroc *m* Gerald Fried

Michael Caine, Cliff Robertson, Ian Bannen, Henry Fonda, Harry Andrews, Denholm Elliott, Ronald Fraser, Percy Herbert

Too Many Crooks*
GB 1958 87m bw
Rank / Mario Zampi

Incompetent crooks plot a kidnapping.
Agreeable farce with black edges and an excellent chase sequence.

w Michael Pertwee *d* Mario Zampi *ph* Stan Pavey *m* Stanley Black

Terry-Thomas, George Cole, Brenda de Banzie, Bernard Bresslaw, Sidney James, Joe Melia, Vera Day, John Le Mesurier

Too Many Girls
US 1940 85m bw
RKO (Harry Edgington, George Abbott)

The father of a wealthy co-ed hires four football heroes to protect her.
Witless nonsense, flabbily derived from a Broadway show.

w John Twist, *play* George Marion Jnr, Richard Rodgers, Lorenz Hart *d* George Abbott *ph* Frank Redman *songs* Rodgers and Hart

Lucille Ball, Desi Arnaz, Richard Carlson, Ann Miller, Eddie Bracken, Frances Langford, Harry Shannon
† The film on which Ball and Arnaz first met.

Too Many Husbands*
US 1940 84m bw
Columbia (Wesley Ruggles)
GB title: *My Two Husbands*

Allegedly drowned on a boat cruise, a man turns up again after his wife has remarried.
Modest variation on a familiar theme, professional but unexciting; later remade as *Three for the Show* (qv).

w Claude Binyon, *play* Home and Beauty by W. Somerset Maugham *d* Wesley Ruggles *ph* Joseph Walker *m* Frederick Hollander

Jean Arthur, Melvyn Douglas, Fred MacMurray, Harry Davenport, Dorothy Peterson, Melville Cooper, Edgar Buchanan

Too Much Harmony
US 1933 76m bw

A star singer helps a promising girl to the top.
Routine light musical which filled a need. Bing Crosby, Jack Oakie, Judith Allen, Skeets Gallagher, Lilyan Tashman, Harry Green, Ned Sparks. Written by Harry Ruskin, Joseph L. Mankiewicz; directed by Eddie Sutherland; for Paramount. 'Should be an easy pleaser.'—*Variety*

'Always a man! Almost any man!'
Too Much Too Soon*
US 1958 121m bw
Warner (Henry Blanke)

Young actress Diana Barrymore goes to Hollywood to look after her alcoholic father John, but mild success goes to her head and she too turns to drink.
Rather dismal and murkily photographed account of an absorbing real-life situation; one performance holds the first half together.

wd Art Napoleon, *memoirs* Diana Barrymore *ph* Nicholas Musuraca, Carl Guthrie *m* Ernest Gold *ad* George James Hopkins

Dorothy Malone, *Errol Flynn*, Efrem Zimbalist Jnr, Neva Patterson, Martin Milner, Ray Danton, Murray Hamilton

Too Young to Kiss
US 1951 89m bw
MGM (Sam Zimbalist)

A girl pianist poses as an infant prodigy, and falls for the impresario who wants to adopt her.
Dull conveyor belt comedy.

w Frances Goodrich, Albert Hackett *d* Robert Z. Leonard *ph* Joseph Ruttenberg *m* Johnny Green

June Allyson, Van Johnson, Gig Young, Paula Corday, Larry Keating, Hans Conried

'If this happened to your daughter, would you be to blame?'

Too Young to Love
GB 1959 89m bw
Rank / Welbeck (Herbert Smith)

A 15-year-old prostitute is brought before a Brooklyn juvenile court.
Tepid filming of a popular exploitation play of the fifties, mysteriously made in England.

w Sydney and Muriel Box, *play* Pick Up Girl by Elsa Shelley *d* Muriel Box *ph* Gerald Gibbs *m* Bruce Montgomery

Thomas Mitchell, Pauline Hahn, Joan Miller, Austin Willis, Jess Conrad, Bessie Love, Alan Gifford

Tootsie**
US 1982 116m colour
Columbia / Mirage / Punch (Sydney Pollack)

An out-of-work actor pretends to be a woman in order to get a job in a soap opera.
As with *Genevieve* and *Whisky Galore*, an unlikely comedy subject makes an instant classic. It's all in the handling.

w Larry Gelbart, Murray Shisgal, story Don McGuire *d Sydney Pollack* *ph* Owen Roizman *m* Dave Grusin *pd* Peter Larkin *ed* Frederick and William Steinkamp

Dustin Hoffman, Jessica Lange, Teri Garr, Dabney Coleman, Charles Durning, Sydney Pollack, George Gaynes

AA: Jessica Lange
AAN: best picture; Dustin Hoffman; Teri Garr; Sydney Pollack as director; original screenplay; cinematography; editing; song, 'It Might Be You' (*m* Dave Grusin, *ly* Alan Bergman, Marilyn Bergman); sound
BFA: Dustin Hoffman

Top Banana*
US 1953 100m Color Corporation
Roadshow / Harry M. Popkin

A TV comedian invites an attractive salesgirl to join his show.
A wisp of plot is the excuse for a revue, and the interest is in the old-time burlesque acts, some of which survive the generally shoddy treatment.

w Gene Towne *d* Alfred E. Green *ph* William Bradford *m / ly* Johnny Mercer

Phil Silvers, Rose Marie, Danny Scholl, Jack Albertson

Top Gun
US 1986 110m Metrocolor
Paramount / Don Simpson, Jerry Bruckheimer

Adventures of naval fighter pilots.
A feast of hardware and noisy music; not much story.

TOP GUN. The story would have been told in half the time thirty years previously. Nevertheless the film flew high at the box office and Tom Cruise and Kelly McGillis helped it soar into popularity.

w Jim Cash, Jack Epps Jnr *d* Tony Scott *ph* Jeffrey Kimball *m* Harold Faltermeyer *pd* John F. De Cuir Jnr *ed* Billy Weber, Chris Lebenzon

Tom Cruise, Kelly McGillis, Val Kilmer, Anthony Edwards, Tom Skerritt

'Audiences prepared to go with it will be taken for a thrilling ride in the wild blue yonder.'—*Variety*

AA: song Take My Breath Away (Giorgio Moroder, Tom Whitlock)
AAN: editors

Top Hat****
US 1935 100m bw
RKO (Pandro S. Berman)

The path of true love is roughened by mistaken identities.
Marvellous Astaire-Rogers musical, with a more or less realistic London supplanted by a totally artificial Venice, and show stopping numbers in a style which is no more separated by amusing plot complications lightly handled by a team of deft *farceurs*.

w Dwight Taylor, Allan Scott d Mark Sandrich ph David Abel, Vernon Walker m / ly Irving Berlin ch Hermes Pan ad Van Nest Polglase, Carroll Clark

Fred Astaire, Ginger Rogers, Edward Everett Horton, Helen Broderick, Eric Blore, Erik Rhodes

'The theatres will hold their own world series with this one. It can't miss.'—*Variety*

'In 25 years *Top Hat* has lost nothing of its gaiety and charm.'—*Dilys Powell, 1960*

AAN: best picture; song 'Cheek to Cheek'

Top Man
US 1943 74m bw

When an officer is recalled to active duty his teenage son becomes head of the family.
Lively little putting-on-a-show comedy musical which established a new young star. *Donald O'Connor,* Richard Dix, Peggy Ryan, Lillian Gish, Susanna Foster, Anne Gwynne. Written by Zachary Gold; directed by Charles Lamont; for Universal.

Top o' the Morning
US 1949 100m bw
Paramount (Robert L. Welch)

Investigations follow the theft of the Blarney Stone.
More Irish whimsy from the *Going My Way* stars.

w Edmund Beloin, Richard Breen *d* David Miller *ph* Lionel Lindon *m* James Van Heusen

Bing Crosby, Barry Fitzgerald, Ann Blyth, Hume Cronyn, Eileen Crowe, John McIntire

Top of the Town
US 1937 86m bw

The daughter of the owner of the Moonbeam Room wants to oust the swing band and stage a symbolic ballet. A wisp of plot supports some expensive but not especially attractive numbers in a musical variety show that was supposed to be Universal's answer to other studios' biggies. George Murphy, Doris Nolan, Hugh Herbert, Gregory Ratoff, Ella Logan, Gertrude Niesen, Henry Armetta, Mischa Auer, Samuel S. Hinds, Peggy Ryan. Written by Brown Holmes, Charles Grayson, Lou Brock; directed by Ralph Murphy; for Universal. 'A bundle of mediocrity . . . it neither goes nor gets anywhere.'—*Variety*

Top Secret*
GB 1952 94m bw
ABP (Mario Zampi)
US title: *Mr Potts Goes to Moscow*

A sanitary engineer, mistaken for a spy, is kidnapped to Moscow when his blueprints are taken for atomic secrets.
Farcical satire full of chases and lavatory humour; much of it comes off nicely.

w Jack Davies, Michael Pertwee d Mario Zampi ph Stan Pavey *m* Stanley Black

George Cole, Oscar Homolka, Nadia Gray, Frederick Valk, Wilfrid Hyde White, Geoffrey Sumner, Ronald Adam

Top Secret!
US 1984 90m Metrocolor
Paramount / Kingsmere (Jon Davison, Hunt Lowry)

An American rock star in Germany gets involved with spies of both sides.
Dull spoof from the folks who gave us *Airplane!* A very few sight gags stand out among the dross.

w Jim Abrahams, David Zucker, Jerry Zucker, Martyn Burke *d* Jim Abrahams, David Zucker, Jerry Zucker *ph* Christopher Challis *m* Maurice Jarre *pd* Peter Lamont

Val Kilmer, Lucy Gutteridge, Peter Cushing, Jeremy Kemp, Warren Clarke, Michael Gough, Omar Sharif, Christopher Villiers

'Too far over the top to retain any comic sense of the targets it sets out to lampoon. The overwhelming impression is of a *Mad* magazine strip in a particularly poor week.'—*Martyn Auty, MFB*

Top Secret Affair*
US 1956 100m bw
Warner / United States (Martin Rackin)
GB title: *Their Secret Affair*

A female news publisher tries to discredit a military diplomat but falls in love with him.
Curious comedy adaptation of a rather heavy novel, moderately skilled in all departments.

w Roland Kibbee, Allan Scott, *novel* Melville Goodwin USA by John P. Marquand *d* H. C. Potter *ph* Stanley Cortez *m* Roy Webb

Kirk Douglas, Susan Hayward, Jim Backus, Paul Stewart, John Cromwell, Roland Winters

Topaz*
US 1969 124m Technicolor
Universal / Alfred Hitchcock

In 1962 the CIA enlists a French agent to break up a Russian spy ring.
Oddly halting, desultory and unconvincing spy thriller shot mainly in flat TV style, with just a few short sequences in its director's better manner. A measure of its unsatisfactoriness is that three different endings were shot and actually used at various points of release.

w Samuel Taylor, *novel* Leon Uris *d* Alfred Hitchcock *ph* Jack Hildyard *m* Maurice Jarre

Frederick Stafford, John Forsythe, John Vernon, *Roscoe Lee Browne*, Dany Robin, Karin Dor, Michel Piccoli, Philippe Noiret

'A larger, slower, duller version of the spy thrillers he used to make in the thirties.'—*New Yorker, 1975*

Topaze*
US 1933 78m bw
(RKO) David O. Selznick

A simple schoolmaster allows himself to be exploited.
Interesting little comedy with the star playing against type: remade as *Mr Topaze* (qv).

w Ben Hecht *play* Marcel Pagnol
d Harry d'Abbabie d'Arrast *ph* Lucien Andriot *m* Max Steiner

John Barrymore, Myrna Loy, Jobyna Howland, Jackie Searl

'Okay, for metropolitan spots, but scarcely for the subsequents . . . there haven't been half a dozen foreign dramas that have clicked on the screen.'—*Variety*

† In 1952 Howard Hughes announced a remake with Vincent Price, but it never happened.

Topkapi*
US 1964 119m Technicolor
UA / Filmways (Jules Dassin)

International thieves try to rob the Istanbul museum.
Light-hearted caper story which gets out of control because of the variety of styles and accents, the director's impression that his wife can do no wrong, and the general slowness and lack of wit; but there are bright moments, colourful backgrounds, and a final suspense sequence in the *Rififi* manner.

w Monja Danischewsky, *novel* The Light of Day by Eric Ambler *d* Jules Dassin *ph Henri Alekan m* Manos Hadjidakis

Melina Mercouri, Maximilian Schell, Peter Ustinov, Robert Morley, Akim Tamiroff, Gilles Segal, Jess Hahn

AA: Peter Ustinov

Topper**
US 1937 96m bw
(MGM) Hal Roach (Milton H. Bren)

A stuffy banker is haunted by the ghosts of his sophisticated friends the Kirbys, who are visible only to him.
Influential supernatural farce, still pretty funny and deftly acted though a shade slow to get going.

w Jack Jevne, Eric Hatch, Eddie Moran, *novel* The Jovial Ghosts by Thorne Smith
d Norman Z. McLeod *ph* Norbert Brodine
md Arthur Morton

Cary Grant, Constance Bennett, Roland Young, Billie Burke, Alan Mowbray, Eugene Pallette, Arthur Lake, Hedda Hopper

'How substantial the fan support will be is difficult to anticipate . . . None of the other films of similar theme aroused more than mild enthusiasm among a small group who patronize the arty theatres and talk about pictures in terms of art expression . . . Effort to excuse the story's absurdities on the theory that the intent is farce comedy does not entirely excuse the production from severe rebuke. Fact also that the living dead are always facetious may be shocking to sensibilities. Some of the situations and dialogue offend conventional good taste.'—*Variety*

AAN: Roland Young

Topper Returns**
US 1941 87m bw
Hal Roach

A girl ghost helps Topper solve her own murder.
Spirited supernatural farce which spoofs murder mysteries, spooky houses, frightened servants, dumb cops, etc, in a pacy, accomplished and generally delightful manner.

w Jonathan Latimer, Gordon Douglas, with additional dialogue by Paul Gerard Smith
d Roy del Ruth *ph* Norbert Brodine
m Werner Heyman

Roland Young, Joan Blondell, Eddie Anderson, Carole Landis, Dennis O'Keefe, *H. B. Warner*, Billie Burke, *Donald McBride*, Rafaela Ottiano

'Ectoplasm runs riot and blazes a trial of hilarity from 5th Avenue to the French Riviera!'

Topper Takes a Trip*
US 1938 85m bw
Hal Roach

Ghostly Mrs Kirby helps Topper to save his wife from a Riviera philanderer.
Mildly pleasant follow-up, with a dog replacing Cary Grant who had become too expensive.

w Eddie Moran, Jack Jevne, Corey Ford *d* Norman Z. McLeod *ph* Norbert Brodine *m* Hugo Friedhofer

Constance Bennett, Roland Young, Billie Burke, Alan Mowbray, Verree Teasdale, Franklin Pangborn, Alexander D'Arcy

'Dandy comedy sequel . . . can't miss at the b.o. . . . the original ended up a fine money-maker . . . no doubt one a year about Topper would be welcomed by exhibitors.'—*Variety*

Tora! Tora! Tora!*
US 1970 144m De Luxe Panavision
TCF (Elmo Williams)

A reconstruction from both sides of the events leading up to Pearl Harbor.
Immense, largely studio-bound, calcified war spectacle with much fidelity to the record but no villains and no hero, therefore no drama and no suspense.

w Larry Forrester, Hideo Oguni, Ryuzo Kikushima *d* Richard Fleischer, Ray Kellogg, Toshio Masuda, Kinji Fukasaku *ph* Charles F. Wheeler and Japanese crews *m* Jerry Goldsmith *sp L. B. Abbott, Art Cruickshank*

Martin Balsam, Joseph Cotten, James Whitmore, Jason Robards, Edward Andrews, Leon Ames, George Macready, Soh Yamamura, Takahiro Tamura

'One of the least stirring and least photogenic historical epics ever perpetrated on the screen.'—*Gary Arnold*

AAN: Charles F. Wheeler

'She sings torch songs to daddies and lullabies to babies!'

Torch Singer
US 1933 72m bw
Paramount (Albert Lewis)
aka: *Broadway Singer*

An unwed mother supports her child by singing in night clubs.
Banal melodrama.

w Lenore Coffee, Lynn Starling, *play* Mike by Grace Perkins *d* Alexander Hall *ph* Karl Struss

Claudette Colbert, Ricardo Cortez, David Manners, Lyda Roberti, Baby LeRoy, Florence Roberts, Ethel Griffies, Helen Jerome Eddy

'Unwed mother film not so forte.'—*Variety*

Torch Song
US 1953 90m Technicolor
MGM (Henry Berman, Sidney Franklin Jnr)

A temperamental musical comedy star falls for a blind pianist.
Ossified star vehicle which looks great but is too often unintentionally funny.

w John Michael Hayes, Jan Lustig, *story* Why Should I Cry? by I. A. R. Wylie *d* Charles Walters *ph* Robert Planck *m* Adolph Deutsch

Joan Crawford, Michael Wilding, Gig Young, Marjorie Rambeau, Henry Morgan, Dorothy Patrick

'Here is Joan Crawford all over the screen, in command, in love and in color.'—*Otis L. Guernsey Jnr*

AAN: Marjorie Rambeau

Torchy Blane

Glenda Farrell played the hard-boiled girl reporter and Barton MacLane the tough police inspector who puts up with her in seven out of the nine second features made by Warners in the late thirties. The characters were created in short stories by Frederick Nebel, and the films were mostly directed by William Beaudine or Frank McDonald.

1936: SMART BLONDE
1937: FLY AWAY BABY, THE ADVENTUROUS BLONDE
1938: BLONDES AT WORK, TORCHY BLANE IN PANAMA (with Lola Lane, Paul Kelly), TORCHY GETS HER MAN
1939: TORCHY BLANE IN CHINATOWN, TORCHY RUNS FOR MAYOR, TORCHY PLAYS WITH DYNAMITE (with Jane Wyman, Allen Jenkins)

Torn Curtain**
US 1966 119m Technicolor
Universal / Alfred Hitchcock

A defector who is really a double agent is embarrassed when his girl friend follows him into East Germany.
Patchy Hitchcock with some mechanically effective suspense sequences, a couple of efforts at something new, a few miscalculations, some evidence of carelessness, and a little enjoyable repetition of old situations.

w Brian Moore *d Alfred Hitchcock* *ph* John F. Warren *m* John Addison

Paul Newman, Julie Andrews, *Wolfgang Kieling*, Ludwig Donath, Lila Kedrova, Hans-Joerg Felmy, Tamara Toumanova

'The pace is plodding, the political background trite, and the actors stranded by their director's customary lack of concern with performance.'—*Time Out, 1984*

Torpedo Run*
US 1958 98m Metrocolor Cinemascope
MGM (Edmund S. Grainger)

A US submarine in World War II destroys a Japanese aircraft carrier in Tokyo Bay.
Well-staged potboiler with excellent action sequences marred slightly by excessive platitudinizing.

w Richard Sale, William Wister Haines *d* Joseph Pevney *ph* George J. Folsey

Glenn Ford, Ernest Borgnine, Diane Brewster, Dean Jones

The Torrent*
US 1925 75m (24 fps) bw silent
MGM (Hunt Stromberg)

Spanish sweethearts are parted by a domineering mother, and the girl consoles herself by becoming a Paris prima donna.
Adequate emotional vehicle of its day which happened to be Garbo's first American film.

w Dorothy Farnum, *novel* Vicente Blasco Ibanez *d* Monta Bell *ph* William Daniels

Ricardo Cortez, Greta Garbo, Gertrude Olmsted, Edward Connelly, Lucien Littlefield

Torrid Zone**
US 1940 88m bw
Warner (Mark Hellinger)

In Central America, a banana plantation manager is tricked by his boss into staying on, and helps a wandering showgirl as well as foiling bandits.
Enjoyable, fast-paced hokum with a plot borrowed from both *The Front Page* and *Red Dust*.

w Richard Macaulay, Jerry Wald *d* William Keighley *ph* James Wong Howe *m* Adolph Deutsch

James Cagney, Pat O'Brien, Ann Sheridan, Helen Vinson, Andy Devine, Jerome Cowan, George Tobias, George Reeves

Tortilla Flat*
US 1942 106m bw
MGM (Sam Zimbalist)

The problems of poor Mexican half-breeds in California.
Expensive but unappealing variation on *The Grapes of Wrath*, with none of the cast quite getting under the skin of their parts, and no sense of reality, rather that of a musical without music.

w John Lee Mahin, Benjamin Glazier, *novel* John Steinbeck *d* Victor Fleming *ph* Sidney Wagner *m* Franz Waxman

Spencer Tracy, Hedy Lamarr, John Garfield, Frank Morgan, Akim Tamiroff, Connie Gilchrist, John Qualen, Sheldon Leonard, Donald Meek, Allen Jenkins, Henry O'Neill

AAN: Frank Morgan

Torture Garden*
GB 1967 93m Technicolor
Columbia / Amicus (Milton Subotsky)

Five fairground visitors are told their future by the mysterious Dr Diablo.
Crude but effective horror portmanteau including one story about the resurrection of Edgar Allan Poe.

w Robert Bloch *d* Freddie Francis *ph* Norman Warwick *m* Don Banks, James Bernard

Burgess Meredith, Jack Palance, Peter Cushing, Beverly Adams, Michael Bryant, John Standing

The Touch*
Sweden / US 1970 112m Eastmancolor
ABC / Cinematograph AB (Lars/Owe Carlburg)

The wife of a provincial surgeon falls in love with an archaeologist.
Freedom versus security: the Bergman treatment is given to a familiar love story, but the expected finesse is lacking.

wd Ingmar Bergman *ph* Sven Nykvist *m* Jan Johansson

Bibi Andersson, Elliott Gould, Max Von Sydow

Touch and Go
GB 1955 85m Technicolor
Ealing (Seth Holt)
US title: *The Light Touch*

A family has doubts about its decision to emigrate to Australia.
Very mild comedy which fails to engage sympathy because the characters don't seem real.

w William Rose *d* Michael Truman
ph Douglas Slocombe *m* John Addison

Jack Hawkins, Margaret Johnston, June Thorburn, John Fraser, Roland Culver, Alison Leggatt, James Hayter

'They had the perfect love affair. Until they fell in love!'
A Touch of Class**
GB 1973 106m Technicolor Panavision
Avco / Brut / Gordon Films (Melvin Frank)

A married American businessman in London has a hectic affair with a dress designer.
Amiable and very physical sex farce with hilarious highlights and a few longueurs between; the playing keeps it above water.

w Melvin Frank, Jack Rose *d* Melvin Frank
ph Austin Dempster *m* John Cameron

Glenda Jackson, George Segal, Paul Sorvino, Hildegarde Neil

'Machine-tooled junk.'—*William S. Pechter*
'Brightly performed and quite engaging until it fades into vapid variations on a one-joke theme.'—*Sight and Sound*

AA: Glenda Jackson
AAN: best picture; script; John Cameron; song, 'All That Love Went to Waste' (*m* George Barrie, *ly* Sammy Cahn)

Touch of Evil**
US 1958 95m or 114m bw
U-I (Albert Zugsmith)

A Mexican narcotics investigator honeymooning in a border town clashes with the local police chief over a murder.
Overpoweringly atmospheric melodrama crammed with Wellesian touches, but very cold and unsympathetic, with rather restrained performances (especially his) and a plot which takes some following. Hardly the most auspicious return to Hollywood for a wanderer, but now becoming a cult classic.

wd Orson Welles, novel Badge of Evil by Whit Masterson *ph Russell Metty m* Henry Mancini

Charlton Heston, Orson Welles, Janet Leigh, Marlene Dietrich, Akim Tamiroff, Joseph Calleia, Ray Collins, Dennis Weaver

'Pure Orson Welles and impure balderdash, which may be the same thing.'—*Gerald Weales, Reporter*

A Touch of Larceny*
GB 1959 92m bw
Paramount / Ivan Foxwell

A naval commander mysteriously disappears in the hope that he will be branded a traitor and can sue for libel.
Fairly amusing light comedy with lively performances.

w Roger MacDougall, Guy Hamilton, Ivan Foxwell, *novel* The Megstone Plot by Andrew Garve *d* Guy Hamilton *ph* John Wilcox
m Philip Green

James Mason, Vera Miles, George Sanders, Robert Flemyng, Ernest Clark, Duncan Lamont, Peter Barkworth

'A beguilingly polished comedy, reminiscent in its style, urbanity and sheen of the sort of thing Lubitsch was doing in the 30s.'—*Daily Mail*

A Touch of Love
GB 1969 107m Eastmancolor
Amicus / Palomar (Milton Subotsky)
US title: *Thank You All Very Much*

A pregnant London student tries to get an abortion but later decides against it.
Curious bid for serious drama by horror producers; all very conscientious but rather dreary.

w Margaret Drabble, from her novel The Millstone *d* Waris Hussein *ph* Peter Suschitsky *m* Michael Dress

Sandy Dennis, Ian McKellen, Michael Coles, John Standing, Eleanor Bron

A Touch of the Sun
GB 1956 80m bw
Eros / Raystro (Raymond Stross)

A hall porter is left a fortune but after living it up for a while returns to his old hotel which is on the rocks.
Limp comedy vehicle.

w Alfred Shaughnessy *d* Gordon Parry
ph Arthur Grant *m* Eric Spear

Frankie Howerd, Ruby Murray, Dorothy Bromiley, Gordon Harker, Reginald Beckwith, Richard Wattis, Dennis Price, Alfie Bass, Willoughby Goddard

Touchez pas au Grisbi*
France / Italy 1953 90m approx bw
Del Duca / Antares
aka: *Honour among Thieves; Hands Off the Loot*

Two crooks succeed in stealing a consignment of gold, but that's only the start of their worries.
Smooth underworld hokum, with a slightly comic attitude implied if not stated.

w Jacques Becker, Maurice Griffe, *novel* Albert Simonin *d* Jacques Becker
ph Pierre Montazel *m* Jean Wiener

Jean Gabin, Jeanne Moreau, Gaby Basset, Daniel Cauchy, Marilyn Buferd, Lino Ventura, René Dary

Tough Guys
US 1986 104m De Luxe Panavision
Touchstone / Silver Screen / Brynal (Joe Wizan)

The last train robbers are released from prison after 30 years, and, finding that an old people's home is not for them, return to their old ways.
Slackly written caper comedy with two former stars in their seventh teaming.

w James Orr, Jim Cruickshank *d* Jeff Kanew
ph King Baggot *m* James Newton Howard

Burt Lancaster, Kirk Douglas, Charles Durning, Alexis Smith, Eli Wallach

Tough Guys Don't Dance
US 1987 108m TVC colour

A small businessman in Massachusetts gets involved in a drugs deal. Would-be parody of the Chandler style which works only fitfully and long outstays its welcome. Ryan O'Neal, Isabella Rossellini, Debra Sandlund, Wings Hauser, Lawrence Tierney. Written and directed by Norman Mailer from his novel; for Zoetrope/Cannon.

Toughest Man in Arizona
US 1952 90m Trucolor
Republic (Sidney Picker)

In 1861 a US marshal falls in love with the wife of an outlaw.
Easy-going, pleasant western aimed at the top half of a double bill.

w John K. Butler *d* R. G. Springsteen
ph Reggie Lanning *m* Dale Butts

Vaughn Monroe, Joan Leslie, Edgar Buchanan, Victor Jory, Jean Parker, Henry Morgan

'The most exciting screen event of all time!'
Tovarich**
US 1937 98m bw
Warner (Robert Lord)

A royal Russian husband and wife flee the revolution to Paris and take jobs as servants in an eccentric household.
A lively comedy of its time; though many of the jokes now seem obvious, the playing preserves its essential quality.

w Casey Robinson, *play adaptation Robert E. Sherwood, original* Jacques Deval *d* Anatole Litvak *ph* Charles Lang *m* Max Steiner

Claudette Colbert, Charles Boyer, Basil Rathbone, Anita Louise, Melville Cooper, Isabel Jeans, Maurice Murphy, Morris Carnovsky, Gregory Gaye, Montagu Love, Fritz Feld

'A yarn of charming and finely shaded characterizations. Both humour and heart appeal spring from intimate acquaintance with the background and motives of each player. Class production, magnet for first runs.'—*Variety*

Toward the Unknown
US 1956 115m Warnercolor Warnerscope
Warner / Toluca (Mervyn Le Roy)
GB title: *Brink of Hell*

An over-age officer takes part in the X2 experiments with rocket-firing aircraft. Humourless flagwaver, very forgettable.

w Beirne Lay Jnr *d* Mervyn Le Roy *ph* Harold Rosson *m* Paul Baron

William Holden, Lloyd Nolan, Virginia Leith, Charles McGraw, Murray Hamilton, L. Q. Jones, James Garner, Paul Fix, Karen Steele

Towed in a Hole***
US 1932 20m bw

Two would-be fishermen wreck the boat they have just bought. Brilliant star farce, filled with wonderfully lunatic dialogues and freshly conceived slapstick. Laurel and Hardy. Written by Stan Laurel; directed by George Marshall; for Hal Roach.

Tower of London**
US 1939 92m bw
Universal (Rowland V. Lee)

With the help of Mord the executioner, Richard Crookback kills his way to the throne but is destroyed at Bosworth.
The Shakespearean view of history played as a horror comic: despite an overall lack of pace, spirited scenes and good performances win the day.

w Robert N. Lee *d* Rowland V. Lee *ph George Robinson* *m* Charles Previn

Basil Rathbone, Boris Karloff, Barbara O'Neil, Ian Hunter, Vincent Price, Nan Grey, John Sutton, Leo G. Carroll, Miles Mander

'Spine-tingling horror picture . . . so strong that it may provide disturbing nightmares as aftermath.'—*Variety*

Tower of London*
US 1962 79m bw
AIP / Admiral (Gene Corman)

A variation on the same events, with Price graduating from Clarence to Crookback, and the addition of ghostly visions. All very cheap, but occasionally vivid melodrama, despite intrusive American accents.

w Leo V. Gordon, Amos Powell, James B. Gordon *d* Roger Corman *ph* Arch Dalzell *m* Michael Anderson

Vincent Price, Michael Pate, Joan Freeman, Robert Brown, Justice Eatson, Sara Salby, Richard McCauly, Bruce Gordon

The Tower of Terror
GB 1941 78m bw

British and German agents clash in a lighthouse tended by a mad keeper. Lurid penny-dreadful, quite amusing in its way. Wilfrid Lawson, Movita, Michael Rennie, Morland Graham, George Woodbridge. Written by John Argyle and John Reinhart; directed by Lawrence Huntington; for ABPC.

'One tiny spark becomes a night of towering suspense!'

The Towering Inferno***
US 1974 165m De Luxe Panavision
TCF / Warner (Irwin Allen)

The world's tallest building is destroyed by fire on the night of its inauguration.
Showmanlike but relentlessly padded disaster spectacular, worth seeing for its cast of stars, its sheer old-fashioned expertise, and its special effects.

w Stirling Silliphant, *novels* The Tower by Richard Martin Stern, The Glass Inferno by Thomas M. Scortia, Frank M. Robinson *d John Guillermin, Irwin Allen* *ph Fred Koenekamp, Joseph Biroc* *m* John Williams *sp Bill Abbott* *pd William Creber*

Paul Newman, Steve McQueen, William Holden, Faye Dunaway, Fred Astaire, Susan Blakely, Richard Chamberlain, Robert Vaughn, Jennifer Jones, O. J. Simpson, Robert Wagner

'Several generations of blue-eyed charmers act their roles as if each were under a separate bell jar.'—*Verina Glaessner*

'Each scene of someone horribly in flames is presented as a feat for the audience's delectation.'—*New Yorker*

'The combination of Grade A spectacle and B-picture characters induces a feeling of sideline detachment.'—*Michael Billington, Illustrated London News*

AA: photography; song 'We May Never Love Like This Again' (*m / ly* Al Kasha, Joel Hirschhorn)
AAN: best picture; John Williams; Fred Astaire

A Town Called Bastard
GB 1971 97m Technicolor Franscope
Benmar / Zurbano (Ben Fisz)
aka: *A Town Like Hell*

Mexican revolutionaries massacre a priest and his congregation and take over the town. Ten years later a widow arrives seeking vengeance. Sadistic western with an opening massacre followed by twenty-two killings (count 'em). Pretty dull otherwise.

w Richard Aubrey *d* Robert Parrish *ph* Manuel Berenguer *m* Waldo de Los Rios

Robert Shaw, Stella Stevens, Telly Savalas, Martin Landau, Michael Craig, Fernando Rey, Dudley Sutton

A Town like Alice**
GB 1956 117m bw
Rank / Vic Films (Joseph Janni)
US title: *The Rape of Malaya*

Life among women prisoners of the Japanese in Malaya, especially one who is finally reunited with her Australian lover.
Genteelly harrowing war film, formlessly adapted from the first part of a popular novel; a big commercial success of its day.

w W. P. Lipscomb, Richard Mason, *novel* Nevil Shute *d* Jack Lee *ph* Geoffrey Unsworth *m* Matyas Seiber

Virginia McKenna, Peter Finch, Takagi, Marie Lohr, Maureen Swanson, Jean Anderson, Renée Houston, Nora Nicholson

'There she lay, wearing her nylons—right around her neck!'

Town on Trial*
GB 1956 96m bw
Columbia / Marksman (Maxwell Setton)

A police inspector solves the murder of a girl after a tennis club dance in a British country town.
Straightforward murder mystery shot in Weybridge, with a wide variety of suspects having something to hide; settings and characters are quite realistic and also a little dreary.

w Ken Hughes, Robert Westerby *d John Guillermin* *ph* Basil Emmott *m* Tristam Cary

John Mills, Charles Coburn, Derek Farr, Barbara Bates, Alec McCowen, Geoffrey Keen, Elizabeth Seal, Margaretta Scott, Fay Compton

The Town Went Wild
US 1945 78m bw

Feuding next door neighbours have children in love. Romeo and Juliet in small-town America, and none of it sharp enough. Freddie Bartholomew, Edward Everett Horton, James Lydon, Tom Tully, Jill Browning, Minna Gombell, Maude Eburne, Charles Halton. Written by Bernard R. Roth, Clarence Greene, Russel Rouse; directed by Ralph Murphy; for PRC.

Town without Pity*
US / Switzerland / Germany 1961 103m bw
UA / Mirisch / Osweg / Gloria (Gottfried Reinhardt)

A German girl is raped and four American soldiers are accused; the defence counsel's wiles lead to the girl's suicide.
Dour drama with overpowering expressionist technique but not much real sympathy, interest or surprise.

w Silvia Reinhardt, George Hurdalek, *novel* The Verdict by Manfred Gregor *d* Gottfried Reinhardt *ph* Kurt Hasse *m* Dmitri Tiomkin

Kirk Douglas, E. G. Marshall, Christine Kaufmann, Barbara Rutting, Robert Blake, Richard Jaeckel

AAN: title song (*m* Dmitri Tiomkin, *ly* Ned Washington)

The Toy
US 1983 102m colour
Columbia / Rastar (Phil Feldman)

A black janitor is hired as a toy for a millionaire's nine-year-old son.
Feeble attempt to translate a 1976 French film by Francis Veber. The few laughs are laughs of embarrassment.

w Carol Sobieski *d* Richard Donner *ph* Laszlo Kovacs *m* Patrick Williams *pd* Charles Rosen

Richard Pryor, Jackie Gleason, Ned Beatty, Scott Schwarz, Teresa Ganzel, Wilfrid Hyde-White, Tony King

'Tasteless in implication, flavourless in execution.'—*Sight and Sound*

Toy Tiger
US 1956 88m Technicolor Cinemascope
U-I (Howard Christie)

The imaginative small son of a widow 'adopts' her business friend as his father.
Flat sentimental comedy off the studio's conveyor belt, a remake of *Mad about Music*.

w Ted Sherdeman *d* Jerry Hopper *ph* George Robinson *m* Joseph Gershenson

Jeff Chandler, Laraine Day, Tim Hovey, Cecil Kellaway, Richard Haydn, David Janssen

The Toy Wife*
US 1938 95m bw
MGM (Merian C. Cooper)
GB title: *Frou Frou*

In the early 19th century in Louisiana, a flirtatious girl causes jealousy and tragedy.
Another bid in the *Jezebel* / *Gone with the Wind* stakes, this handsome production proved a commercial misfire and hastened the end of its star's career.

w Zoe Akins *d* Richard Thorpe *ph* Oliver T. Marsh *m* Edward Ward

Luise Rainer, Melvyn Douglas, Robert Young, Barbara O'Neil, H. B. Warner, Alma Kruger, Walter Kingsford

'Old-fashioned melodrama, beautifully produced but creaky.'—*Variety*

Toys in the Attic*
US 1963 90m bw Panavision
UA / Claude / Mirisch

In a shabby New Orleans home, two ageing spinsters struggle to look after their ne'er-do-well brother.
Play into film doesn't go in this case, but the script and acting are interesting.

w James Poe, play Lillian Hellman d George Roy Hill *ph* Joseph Biroc *m* George Duning *ad* Cary Odell

Geraldine Page, Wendy Hiller, Dean Martin, Yvette Mimieux, Gene Tierney, Larry Gates

'A story of how men and women act when they think nobody is looking!'
Track of the Cat*
US 1954 102m Warnercolor Cinemascope
Warner / Wayne–Fellows / Batjac (Robert Fellows)

In the northern California backwoods one winter in the 1880s a farming family is menaced by a marauding mountain lion.
With the lion a symbol of evil, this is real Cold Comfort Farm country and despite good intentions all round becomes irresistibly funny before the end, largely because everyone moves and speaks so s-l-o-w-l-y. The bleached colour is interesting but would suit only snowy settings.

w A. I. Bezzerides, *novel* Walter Van Tilburg Clark *d William A. Wellman ph William H. Clothier m* Roy Webb

Robert Mitchum, Diana Lynn, Beulah Bondi, Teresa Wright, Tab Hunter, Philip Tonge, William Hopper, Carl Switzer

'Cinemascope's first genuine weirdie . . . the script is redolent of Eugene O'Neill, and to its presentation the director brings a touch of Poe . . . Despair hangs in the air like a curse . . . unfortunately ambition overreaches itself, and the film topples over into barnstorming melodrama.'—*MFB*

'Bill Wellman had the idea: he wanted to make a colour picture with very little colour.'—*William Clothier*

Trackdown
US 1976 98m De Luxe
UA / Essaness (Bernard Schwarz)

A Montana rancher follows his sister to Los Angeles and avenges her ill-treatment there by gangsters.
Routine action thriller with fashionable realism and violence.

w Paul Edwards *d* Richard T. Heffron *ph* Gene Polito *m* Charles Bernstein

Jim Mitchum, Karen Lamm, Anne Archer, Erik Estrada, Cathy Lee Crosby, Vince Cannon

Trade Winds
US 1939 93m bw
Walter Wanger

A girl who thinks she has committed murder flees to the Far East, and a cynical detective is sent to bring her back. Guess what happens. Smartly written mixture of comedy, drama, mystery and travelogue which comes off only in spots; it needed a firmer hand.

w Dorothy Parker, Alan Campbell, Frank R. Adams *d* Tay Garnett *ph* Rudolph Maté *m* Alfred Newman

Fredric March, Joan Bennett, Ralph Bellamy, Ann Sothern, Sidney Blackmer, Thomas Mitchell, Robert Elliott

'All the elements that provide broad entertainment are present in this picture, and it should reap healthy grosses.'—*Variety*

Trader Horn*
US 1930 120m bw
MGM (Irving Thalberg)

An experienced African trader overcomes tribal hostility.
Primitive talkie for which second units were sent to Africa amid much publicity hoo-ha. After fifty years, nothing of interest remains to be seen.

w Richard Schayer, Dale Van Every, Thomas Neville, *novel* Alfred Aloysius Horn, Etheldreda Lewis *d* W. S. Van Dyke *ph* Clyde de Vinna

Harry Carey, Edwina Booth, Duncan Renaldo, Mutia Omoolu, C. Aubrey Smith

'Sure money-getter. Outstanding animal stuff, great sound effects, and thin story, which has good-looking white girl romping around scantily clad.'—*Variety*

'A movie that contains all the best features of a zoo, a cannibal dance, and a big yarn by Rider Haggard.'—*National Board of Review*

AAN: best picture

Trader Horn
US 1973 105m Metrocolor
MGM (Lewis J. Rachmil)

Pitiful remake patched together largely from stock footage.

w William Norton, Edward Harper *d* Reza Badiyi *ph* Ronald W. Browne *m* Shelly Manne

Rod Taylor, Anne Heywood, Jean Sorel

'Laughably inept . . . it cannot face word of mouth for long.'—*Variety*

Trader Tom of the China Seas
US 1954 bw serial: 12 eps

A young trader scotches a plot to spread revolution in Sumatra. Among the last half dozen serials made, but far from the best. Harry Lauter, Aline Towne, Lyle Talbot, Robert Shayne, Victor Sen Yung. Directed by Franklin Adreon; for Republic.

Trading Places**
US 1983 116m Technicolor
Paramount / Landis-Folsey (Aaron Russo)

Two rich men arrange a wager on the effects of environment over heredity, and arrange for a con man and a stockbroker to change places. Surprisingly witty comedy, which while not aspiring to great heights, and marred by a few excesses, brought a refreshing breath of air to a declining genre.

w Timothy Harris, Herschel Weingrod *d John Landis ph* Robert Paynter *m* Elmer Bernstein *pd* Gene Rudolf

Dan Aykroyd, Eddie Murphy, *Ralph Bellamy, Don Ameche, Denholm Elliott*, Jamie Lee Curtis, Kristin Holby

'Proof positive that the genuine American populist comedy can still attract attention.'—*John Pym, MFB*

BFA: Jamie Lee Cúrtis, Denholm Elliott

Traffic*
France / Italy 1970 96m Eastmancolor
Corona / Gibe / Selenia (Robert Dorfman)

The designer of a camping car has various little accidents on the way from the works to a show.
Rambling comedy with understated jokes and an almost invisible star.

w Jacques Tati, Jacques Legrange *d* Jacques Tati (with Bert Haanstra) *ph* Edouard Van Den Enden, Marcel Weiss *m* Charles Dumont

Jacques Tati

The Trail of '98*
US 1928 90m at 24 fps bw silent

San Franciscans leave their homes for the Klondike gold rush. Impressive spectacular while it stays outdoors; not so good when the plot takes over. Dolores Del Rio, Ralph Forbes, Harry Carey, Karl Dane, Tully Marshall. Written by Waldmar Young and Ben Glazer, from the novel by Robert W. Service; directed by Clarence Brown; for MGM.

'The surging drama of love in the Kentucky hills springs to thrilling life as the first outdoor action romance filmed in colour!'

The Trail of the Lonesome Pine*
US 1936 102m Technicolor
Paramount (Walter Wanger)

A hillbilly girl goes back home when her brother is killed in a family feud.
Antediluvian Ozarkian melodrama, notable as the first outdoor film to be shot in three-colour Technicolor.

w Grover Jones, Horace McCoy, Harvey Thew, *novel* John Fox Jnr *d* Henry Hathaway *ph Howard Green* *m* Hugo Friedhofer, Gerrard Carbonara

Sylvia Sidney, Fred MacMurray, Henry Fonda, Fred Stone, Nigel Bruce, Beulah Bondi, Robert Barrat, Spanky McFarland, Fuzzy Knight

'A good show saleable for big grosses, a flicker the ballyhoo boys can and will do tricks with.'—*Variety*

'Unnatural as it is, the colour does no serious damage to the picture. This moldy bit of hokum . . . takes movies back to the days of their childhood.'—*Newsweek*

† The story was first filmed in 1915 by Cecil B. de Mille.

AAN: song 'A Melody from the Sky' (*m* Louis Alter, *ly* Sidney Mitchell)

Trail of the Pink Panther
GB 1982 97m Technicolor Panavision
MGM–UA / Titan (Blake Edwards, Tony Adams)

Inspector Clouseau is reported missing at sea and a television reporter interviews those who had known him.
Flimsy, necrophiliac excuse for a movie, with a star cast clearly failing to make bricks without straw two years after the nominal star's death.

w Frank and Tom Waldman, Blake Edwards, Geoffrey Edwards *d* Blake Edwards *ph* Dick Bush *m* Henry Mancini *pd* Peter Mullins *ed* Alan Jones

Peter Sellers, Joanna Lumley, Herbert Lom, David Niven, Richard Mulligan, Capucine, Robert Loggia, Harvey Korman, Burt Kwouk, Graham Stark, Leonard Rossiter, Peter Arne, Ronald Fraser

Trail of the Vigilantes*
US 1940 78m bw

In the old west, a reporter sets out to break up a band of outlaws. A mild western which at the time had some reputation as a wild comedy; the fact was that it turned out badly and the editors did the best they could.
Franchot Tone, Warren William, Broderick Crawford, Andy Devine, Mischa Auer, Porter Hall, Peggy Moran. Written by Harold Shumate; directed by Allan Dwan; for Universal. 'As light amusement it does all right, but it is amusement in confusion.'—*Otis Ferguson.*

Trail Street
US 1947 84m bw

Wheat is planted in Kansas by the early settlers. Pretty good, unpretentious western.
Randolph Scott, Robert Ryan, Anne Jeffreys, Billy House, George 'Gabby' Hayes. Written by Norman Houston and Gene Lewis; directed by Ray Enright; for Nat Holt / RKO.

'It carried their hopes, their nation's honour!'

The Train**
US 1964 140m bw
UA / Ariane / Dear (Jules Bricken)

In 1944, the French resistance tries to prevent the Nazis from taking art treasures back to Germany on a special train.
Proficient but longwinded suspense actioner with spectacular sequences; a safe bet for train enthusiasts.

w Franklin Coen, Frank Davis, Walter Bernstein *d John Frankenheimer* *ph* Jean Tournier, Walter Wottitz *m* Maurice Jarre

Burt Lancaster, *Paul Scofield*, Jeanne Moreau, Michael Simon, Wolfgang Preiss, Suzanne Flon

'Extraordinarily good in many of its parts but rather disappointing as a whole . . . its greatest virtue is an almost overpowering physical realism.'—*Moira Walsh, America*

AAN: script

Train of Events
GB 1949 89m bw
Ealing (Michael Relph)

Portmanteau of stories à la Friday the 13th or Dead of Night, linked by a train disaster.
A rather mechanical entertainment, proficiently made.

w Basil Dearden, T. E. B. Clarke, Ronald Millar, Angus MacPhail *d* Basil Dearden, Charles Crichton, Sidney Cole *ph* Lionel Banes, Gordon Dines *m* Leslie Bridgewater

Valerie Hobson, John Clements, Jack Warner, Gladys Henson, Peter Finch, Irina Baronova, Susan Shaw, Patric Doonan, Joan Dowling, Laurence Payne, Mary Morris

The Train Robbers
US 1973 92m Technicolor Panavision
Warner / Batjac (Michael Wayne)

A widow asks three gunmen to help her clear her husband's name by retrieving gold he had stolen.
Shaggy dog western, sadly lacking in comic situation and detail.

wd Burt Kennedy *ph* William Clothier *m* Dominic Frontière

John Wayne, Ann-Margret, Rod Taylor, Ben Johnson, Bobby Vinton, Christopher George

The Traitor*
GB 1957 88m bw
Fantur (E. J. Fancey)
US title: *The Accused*

At the annual reunion of a resistance group, the host announces that one of their number was a traitor.
Heavy-handed theatrical melodrama, helped by a stout plot and some directional flair.

wd Michael McCarthy *ph* Bert Mason *m* Jackie Brown

Donald Wolfit, Robert Bray, Jane Griffiths, Carl Jaffe, Anton Diffring, Oscar Quitak, Rupert Davies, John Van Eyssen

The Traitors*
GB 1962 69m bw
Ello (Jim O'Connelly)

A top scientist is killed and MI5 springs into action.
Commendable second feature with narrative virtues absent in most big films.

w Jim O'Connelly *d Robert Tronson* *ph* Michael Reed *m* Johnny Douglas

Patrick Allen, James Maxwell, Ewan Roberts, Zena Walker

Traitor's Gate
GB 1965 80m bw
Columbia / Summit (Ted Lloyd)

A London businessman organizes a gang to steal the Crown Jewels.
Modest caper melodrama, routine but watchable.

w John Sansom, *novel* Edgar Wallace *d* Freddie Francis *ph* Denys Coop

Albert Lieven, Gary Raymond, Margot Trooger, Klaus Kinski, Catherina Von Schell, Edward Underdown

The Tramp*
US 1915 20m approx (24 fps) bw silent
Mutual

A tramp saves a girl from crooks, is wounded and cared for by her, deliriously happy—until her lover arrives.
Fairly funny star comedy, the first with sentimental touches and the origin of the into-the-sunset fade-out.

wd Charles Chaplin *ph* Rollie Totheroh

Charles Chaplin, Edna Purviance, Bud Jamison, Leo White, Lloyd Bacon

Tramp Tramp Tramp*
US 1926 65m approx (24 fps) bw silent
Harry Langdon

Harry enters a cross-country walking contest in order to impress his girl.
Well-staged peripatetic comedy, the star's first feature.

w Frank Capra, Tim Whelan, Hal Conklin, Gerald Duffy, Murray Roth, J. Frank Holliday *d* Harry Edwards

Harry Langdon, Joan Crawford, Alec B. Francis

Transatlantic*
US 1931 74m bw

Various personal stories come to a climax aboard a transatlantic liner. Early attempt at what has now become a very worn format; quite lively it must have seemed then. Edmund Lowe, Lois Moran, John Halliday, Greta Nissen, Jean Hersholt, Myrna Loy, Earle Foxe, Billy Bevan. Written by Guy Bolton, Lynn Starling; directed by William K. Howard; for Fox. 'An aquatic *Grand Hotel*; should prosper.'—*Variety*

Transatlantic Merry Go Round
US 1934 92m bw

Romantic misunderstandings on an ocean liner. Patchy comedy with some good scenes. Jack Benny, Nancy Carroll, Gene Raymond, Sydney Howard. Written by Joseph Moncure March, Harry W. Conn and Leon Gordon; directed by Ben Stoloff; for Reliance. 'Good, popular screen entertainment; certain box office fodder.'—*Variety*

Trans-Europe Express*
France 1966 90m bw
Como Film (Samy Halfon)

Film-makers on a train invent a violent plot and then find life aping it.
A theme beloved of Hollywood is treated intellectually, and almost succeeds in attracting all classes.

wd Alain Robbe-Grillet *ph* Willy Kurant *m* Verdi

Jean-Louis Trintignant, Marie-France Pisier, Nadine Verdier, Christian Barbier, Charles Millot, Alain Robbe-Grillet

Transgression
US 1931 70m bw

During a Paris vacation, a man forgives his wife for her affair with a Spanish gigolo. Very routine, matinée drama. Kay Francis, Ricardo Cortez, Paul Cavanagh, Nance O'Neil. Written by Elizabeth Meehan from the novel by Kate Jordan; directed by Herbert Brenon; for RKO. 'Doubtful de luxe subject, principally because its story lacks conviction.'—*Variety*

The Trap*
US 1958 84m Technicolor
Paramount / Parkwood–Heath (Melvin Frank, Norman Panama)
GB title: *The Baited Trap*

A lawyer helps a vicious killer to escape into Mexico, but the plan backfires.
Reasonably tense action thriller with desert backgrounds.

w Richard Alan Simmons, Norman Panama *d* Norman Panama *ph* Daniel L. Fapp *m* Irvin Talbot

Richard Widmark, Lee J. Cobb, Earl Holliman, Tina Louise, Carl Benton Reid, Lorne Green

The Trap
GB / Canada 1966 106m Eastmancolor Panavision
Parallel (George H. Brown)

In nineteenth-century British Columbia a rough trapper takes a wife, who at first is terrified of him but nurses him when he is hurt . . .
Primitive open air melodrama with good action sequences; well made but hardly endearing.

w David Osborn *d* Sidney Hayers *ph* Robert Krasker *m* Ron Goodwin

Oliver Reed, Rita Tushingham, Rex Sevenoaks, Barbara Chilcott

Trapeze**
US 1956 105m De Luxe Cinemascope
UA / Hecht–Lancaster (James Hill)

A circus partnership almost breaks up when a voluptuous third member is engaged.
Concentrated, intense melodrama filmed almost entirely within a French winter circus and giving a very effective feel, almost a smell, of the life therein. Despite great skill in the making, however, the length is too great for a wisp of plot that goes back to *The Three Maxims* and doubtless beyond.

w James R. Webb *d Carol Reed ph Robert Krasker* *m* Malcolm Arnold

Burt Lancaster, Tony Curtis, Gina Lollobrigida, Thomas Gomez, Johnny Puleo, Katy Jurado, Sidney James

† This version was supposedly adapted from a Max Catto novel, *The Killing Frost*, but in 1932 Harmonie of Germany issued a film with the title *Trapeze* and a remarkably similar story. It had a scenario by Alfred Machard and was directed by E. A. Dupont. The Anna Neagle film *The Three Maxims* (*qv*) was also very similar, but that was supposedly an original by Herman Mankiewicz.

Traveller's Joy
GB 1949 78m bw

A divorced couple, stranded in Sweden by lack of funds, have to take joint action. Mild topical comedy from a popular play. Googie Withers, John McCallum, Yolande Donlan, Maurice Denham, Geoffrey Sumner, Colin Gordon, Dora Bryan. Written by Allan MacKinnon and Bernard Quayle, from the play by Arthur Macrae; directed by Ralph Thomas; for Gainsborough / Rank.

The Travelling Executioner*
US 1970 95m Metrocolor Panavision
MGM (Jack Smight)

In 1918 an ex-carnival showman travels the American south with his portable electric chair and charges a hundred dollars per execution, but falls for one of his proposed victims.
Oddball fable without apparent moral; neither fantastic nor funny enough.

w Garrie Bateson *d* Jack Smight *ph* Philip Lathrop *m* Jerry Goldsmith

Stacy Keach, Mariana Hill, Bud Cort, Graham Jarvis

Travelling North*
Australia 1986 96m Eastmancolor

A vigorous 70-year-old leaves Melbourne for sub-tropical Queensland, but his health gives out. Moving Australian mirror image of *On Golden Pond*, with good acting and direction. *Leo McKern*, Julia Blake, Graham Kennedy, Henri Szeps. Written by David Williamson from his play; directed by *Carl Schultz*; for View Pictures/CEL.

Travelling Saleslady
US 1935 75m bw

A toothpaste manufacturer's daughter shows her father the value of advertising. Warner stock company comedy which hits no heights but provided reliable entertainment. Joan Blondell, Hugh Herbert, Glenda Farrell, William Gargan, Al Shean, Grant Mitchell, Ruth Donnelly, Bert Roach. Written by Hugh Herbert, Manuel Seff, Benny Rubin, Frank Howard Clark; directed by Ray Enright; for Warners. 'It will please and should do all right at the wicket.'—*Variety*

Travels with My Aunt*
US 1972 109m Metrocolor Panavision
MGM (Robert Fryer, James Cresson)

A staid bank accountant is landed in a series of continental adventures by his eccentric life-loving aunt.
Busy but fairly disastrous adaptation of a delightful novel, ruined by ceaseless chatter, lack of characterization, shapeless incident and an absurdly caricatured central performance.

w Jay Presson Allen, Hugh Wheeler, *novel* Graham Greene *d* George Cukor *ph* Douglas Slocombe *m* Tony Hatch *pd* John Box

Maggie Smith, *Alec McCowen*, Lou Gossett, Robert Stephens, Cindy Williams

'It seems to run down before it gets started.'—*New Yorker, 1977*

AAN: Douglas Slocombe; Maggie Smith

La Traviata**
Italy 1982 109m colour

A much-acclaimed version of an opera which has previously defied transcription to the screen. Placido Domingo, Teresa Stratas, Cornell MacNeil, Allan Monk, Axell Gall. Written by Francesco Maria Piave from the opera by Verdi; designed and directed by *Franco Zeffirelli*; for Accent Films / RAI. 'Décors so opulent as on occasion to resemble a three-ring circus.'—*Sight and Sound*

AAN: costume design; art direction

Tread Softly Stranger*
GB 1958 91m bw
Alderdale (George Minter)

In a north country town, two brothers in love with the same girl rob a safe.
Hilarious murky melodrama full of glum faces, with a well-worn trick ending; rather well photographed.

w George Minter, Denis O'Dell, *play* Jack Popplewell *d* Gordon Parry *ph Douglas Slocombe* *m* Tristam Cary

George Baker, Terence Morgan, Diana Dors, Wilfrid Lawson, Patrick Allen, Jane Griffith, Joseph Tomelty, Norman Macowan

Treasure Hunt
GB 1952 79m bw
Romulus (Anatole de Grunwald)

The eccentric middle-aged members of an

Irish family find their father's fortune is missing.
Theatrical comedy with some charm and humour, but very much a photographed play.

w Anatole de Grunwald, *play* M. J. Perry *d* John Paddy Carstairs *ph* C. Pennington-Richards *m* Mischa Spoliansky

Jimmy Edwards, *Martita Hunt, Athene Seyler*, Naunton Wayne, June Clyde, Susan Stephen, Brian Worth

Treasure Island**
US 1934 105m bw
MGM (Hunt Stromberg)

An old pirate map leads to a long sea voyage, a mutiny, and buried treasure.
Nicely mounted Hollywood version of a classic adventure story, a little slow in development but meticulously produced.

w John Lee Mahin, novel Robert Louis Stevenson *d* Victor Fleming *ph* Ray June, Clyde de Vinna, Harold Rosson *m* Herbert Stothart

Wallace Beery, Jackie Cooper, Lewis Stone, *Lionel Barrymore*, Otto Kruger, Douglass Dumbrille, Nigel Bruce, Chic Sale

'While much of it entrances, the whole is somewhat tiring.'—*Variety*

'The first three-quarters is so lively and well established in its mood as to make the whole quite worth going to.'—*Otis Ferguson*

Treasure Island*
GB 1950 96m Technicolor
Walt Disney (Perce Pearce)

Cheerful Disney remake, poor on detail but transfixed by a swaggeringly overplayed and unforgettable leading performance.

w Lawrence Edward Watkin *d* Byron Haskin *ph* F. A. Young *m* Clifton Parker *pd* Thomas Morahan

Robert Newton, Bobby Driscoll, Walter Fitzgerald, Basil Sydney, Denis O'Dea, Geoffrey Wilkinson, Ralph Truman

'Serviceable rather than imaginative.'—*Lindsay Anderson*

Treasure Island
GB / France / Germany / Spain 1971 95m colour
Massfilms / FDL / CCC / Eguiluz (Harry Alan Towers)

Spiritless and characterless international remake with poor acting, production and dubbing.

w Wolf Mankowitz, O. W. Jeeves (Welles) *d* John Hough *ph* Cicilio Paniagua *m* Natal Massara

Orson Welles, Kim Burfield, Lionel Stander, Walter Slezak, Rik Battaglia

The Treasure of Lost Canyon
US 1952 82m Technicolor
U-I (Leonard Goldstein)

A small boy robbed of his inheritance finds it with the help of a country doctor who turns out to be his uncle.
Modest juvenile adventure, rather boringly narrated.

w Brainerd Duffield, Emerson Crocker, *story* by Robert Louis Stevenson *d* Ted Tetzlaff *ph* Russell Metty *m* Joseph Gershenson

William Powell, Julia Adams, Charles Drake, Rosemary de Camp, Henry Hull, Tommy Ivo

Treasure of Matecumbe
US 1976 116m Technicolor
Walt Disney (Bill Anderson)

Two boys seek buried gold in the Florida keys.
Cheerful adventure tale with a few nods to *Treasure Island*; all very competent in the Disney fashion.

w Don Tait *d* Vincent McEveety *ph* Frank Phillips *m* Buddy Baker

Robert Foxworth, Joan Hackett, Peter Ustinov, Vic Morrow, Jane Wyatt, Johnny Duran, Billy Attmore

Treasure of Monte Cristo
US 1949 76m bw

In modern San Francisco, a descendant of Monte Cristo is framed for murder. Mildly amusing but slackly made variant on a familiar theme. Glenn Langan, Adele Jergens, Steve Brodie, Robert Jordan, Michael Whalen. Written by Aubrey Wisberg, Jack Pollexfen; directed by William Berke; for Lippert / Screen Guild.

The Treasure of Pancho Villa
US 1955 96m Technicolor Superscope
RKO / Edmund Grainger

Mexico 1915: an American adventurer becomes involved with the revolutionary Pancho Villa; both seek a gold consignment but it is buried in an avalanche.
Modestly well made, routine action drama.

w Niven Busch *d* George Sherman *ph* William Snyder *m* Leith Stevens

Rory Calhoun, Shelley Winters, *Gilbert Roland*, Joseph Calleia

Treasure of San Teresa
GB 1959 81m bw
Orbit (John Nasht, Patrick Filmer-Sankey)

An American secret service agent finds Nazi loot in a Czech convent.
Roughly-made, watchable actioner.

w Jack Andrews, Jeffrey Dell *d* Alvin Rakoff *ph* Wilkie Cooper *m* Philip Martell

Eddie Constantine, Dawn Addams, Marius Goring, Christopher Lee, Walter Gotell

Treasure of the Golden Condor
US 1952 93m Technicolor
TCF (Jules Buck)

A young Frenchman flees to the South Seas but returns to discredit his wicked uncle.
Ineffectual remake of *Son of Fury* (qv) with Guatemalan backgrounds and no punch at all.

wd Delmer Daves *ph* Edward Cronjager *m* Sol Kaplan

Cornel Wilde, Finlay Currie, Constance Smith, George Macready, Walter Hampden, Anne Bancroft, Fay Wray, Leo G. Carroll

'Greed, gold and gunplay on a Mexican mountain of malice!'
'The nearer they got to their treasure the further they got from the law!'

The Treasure of the Sierra Madre**
US 1948 126m bw
Warner (Henry Blanke)

Three gold prospectors come to grief through greed.
Well-acted but partly miscast action fable on the oldest theme in the world; rather tedious and studio-bound for a film with such a high reputation.

wd John Huston, *novel* B. Traven *ph* Ted McCord *m* Max Steiner *md* Leo F. Forbstein

Humphrey Bogart, *Walter Huston*, Tim Holt, Alfonso Bedoya, John Huston, Bruce Bennett, Barton MacLane

'This bitter fable is told with cinematic integrity and considerable skill.'—*Henry Hart*

'The faces of the men, in close-up or in a group, achieve a kind of formal pattern and always dominate the screen.'—*Peter Ericsson*

'One of the very few movies made since 1927 which I am sure will stand up in the memory and esteem of qualified people alongside the best of the silent movies.'—*James Agee*

AA: John Huston (as writer and director); Walter Huston
AAN: best picture

A Tree Grows in Brooklyn***
US 1945 128m bw
TCF (Louis D. Lighton)

Life for an Irish family with a drunken father in New York's teeming slums at the turn of the century.
A superbly-detailed studio production of the type they don't make any more: a family drama with interest for everybody.

w Tess Slesinger, Frank Davis, novel Betty Smith d Elia Kazan ph Leon Shamroy m Alfred Newman

Peggy Ann Garner, James Dunn, Dorothy McGuire, Joan Blondell, Lloyd Nolan, Ted Donaldson, James Gleason, Ruth Nelson, John Alexander, Adeline de Walt Reynolds, Charles Halton

'He tells a maximum amount of story with a minimum of film. Little touches of humour and human understanding crop up throughout.'—*Frank Ward, NBR*

'An artistically satisfying and emotionally quickening tearjerker.'—*Kine Weekly*

'Its drabness is softened by a glow of love and hope.'—*Picture Show*

AA: James Dunn
AAN: script

The Tree of Wooden Clogs*
Italy 1978 186m Gevacolor
RAI / GPC

In nineteenth-century Lombardy the lives of four peasant families are interwined.
Sensitive, novel-like investigation of times gone by; never very exciting but certainly never dull, despite the limits of 16mm and a non-professional cast.

w, d, ph Ermanno Olmi *m* from Bach

Trent's Last Case
GB 1952 90m bw
Wilcox–Neagle (Herbert Wilcox)

A journalist suspects that the death of a tycoon was murder.
Desultory version of a famous novel, with none of the original style and a few naïveties of its own.

w Pamela Bower, *novel* E. C. Bentley *d* Herbert Wilcox *ph* Max Greene *m* Anthony Collins

Michael Wilding, Margaret Lockwood, Orson Welles, John McCallum, Miles Malleson

Trial*
US 1955 109m bw
MGM (Charles Schnee)

A young lawyer defends a Mexican boy accused of rape and murder.
Stereotyped but pacy and watchable racial drama with political overtones, Our Hero having to resist bigots, Commies *and* McCarthyites.

w Don M. Mankiewicz, from his novel *d* Mark Robson *ph* Robert Surtees *m* Daniele Amfitheatrof

Glenn Ford, Dorothy McGuire, Arthur Kennedy, John Hodiak, Katy Jurado, Rafael Campos, Juano Hernandez, Robert Middleton, John Hoyt

AAN: Arthur Kennedy

The Trial*
France / Italy / West Germany 1962 120m bw
Paris Europe / Ficit / Hisa (Alexander Salkind)
original title: *Le Procès*

Joseph K is tried and condemned for an unspecified crime.
Kafka's nightmares tend to go on too long, and this film of one of them is no exception, despite its pin-screen prologue by Alexeieff and its inventive setting in the old Gare d'Orsay. Once again Welles the magician badly needs a Hollywood studio behind him.

wd, ed Orson Welles *ph* Edmond Richard *m* Jean Ledrut *pd* Jean Mandarut

Orson Welles, Jeanne Moreau, Anthony Perkins, Madeleine Robinson, Elsa Martinelli, Suzanne Flon, Akim Tamiroff, Romy Schneider

'The elaboration of scale and decor is as boring as in any biblical spectacular and for the same reason: because it is used without mind or feeling, not to bring out meaning but to distract us from asking for it.'—*Dwight MacDonald*

Trial by Combat
GB 1976 90m Technicolor
Warner / Combat (Fred Weintraub, Paul Heller)
aka: *Choice of Weapons*

An apparently harmless secret society of 'medieval knights' rededicates itself to the ritual execution of criminals who have escaped the law.
A rare specimen of comic macabre apparently inspired by the TV series *The Avengers*. Sadly, not much of it really works.

w Julian Bond, Steven Rossen, Mitchell Smith *d* Kevin Conner *ph* Alan Hume *m* Frank Cordell *pd* Edward Marshall

John Mills, Donald Pleasence, Peter Cushing, Barbara Hershey, David Birney, Margaret Leighton, Brian Glover

The Trial of Mary Dugan
US 1929 120m bw

Prosecution and defence counsel both change their feelings towards the girl on trial for murder. A cast-iron audience pleaser, this adapted stage play was the studio's first all-talking picture. It wouldn't stand the test of time. Norma Shearer, H. B. Warner, Raymond Hackett, Lewis Stone, Lilyan Tashman. Written by Bayard Veiller (and Becky Gardner) from his play; directed by Bayard Veiller; for MGM. (A 1940 remake directed by Norman Z. McLeod starred Laraine Day, Tom Conway, Robert Young, John Litel and Frieda Inescort, but was not a particular success.)

The Trial of Vivienne Ware
US 1932 56m bw

An attempt is made to kill a woman witness during a murder trial. Fast, complex courtroom murder mystery which even finds time for frequent bouts of comic relief. Joan Bennett, Donald Cook, Skeets Gallagher, Zasu Pitts, Lillian Bond, Alan Dinehart, Herbert Mundin, Noel Madison. Written by Philip Klein, Barry Connors, from the novel by Kenneth M. Ellis; directed by William K. Howard; for Fox. 'A skilful bit of claptrap melodrama.'—*Variety*

Trial Run
New Zealand 1984 89m colour

An amateur photographer finds her metier photographing penguins, but in her remote retreat finds herself terrorized by a mysterious prowler. Suspenseful but overlong thriller with a weak ending and too much psychological probing. Annie Whittle, Judith Gibson, Christopher Broun, Philippa Mayne, Stephen Tozer. Written and directed by Melanie Read; for Don Reynolds / Cinema and Television / Double Feature.

The Trials of Oscar Wilde**
GB 1960 123m Super Technirama 70
Warwick / Viceroy (Harold Huth)
US title: *The Man with the Green Carnation*

Oscar Wilde fatally sues the Marquis of Queensberry for libel, and loses; he is then prosecuted for sodomy.
Plush account of a fascinating event; narrative drive is unfortunately lacking, but one is left with interesting performances.

wd Ken Hughes ph Ted Moore *m* Ron Goodwin *ad* Ken Adam, Bill Constable

Peter Finch, Yvonne Mitchell, *John Fraser*, Lionel Jeffries, *Nigel Patrick*, James Mason, Emrys Jones, Maxine Audley, Paul Rogers, James Booth

Tribute*
Canada 1980 122m colour
TCF / Joel B. Michaels, Garth B. Drabinsky

A Broadway press agent comes to know his son by his divorced wife just as he comes to know of his own fatal illness.
Satisfactory screen treatment of a play which is really a vehicle for a charismatic star.

w Bernard Slade, from his play *d* Bob Clark *ph* Reginald H. Morris *m* various

Jack Lemmon, Lee Remick, Robby Benson, Colleen Dewhurst, Kim Cattrall, John Marley

AAN: Jack Lemmon

Tribute to a Bad Man
US 1956 95m Eastmancolor Cinemascope
MGM (Sam Zimbalist)

A Wyoming horse breeder is callous in his treatment of rustlers, and wins the woman he wants when he becomes more understanding.
Somewhere behind an unsympathetic story and hesitant development lies a convincing picture of life in the old west.

w Michael Blankfort, *story* Jack Schaefer *d* Robert Wise *ph* Robert Surtees *m* Miklos Rozsa

James Cagney, Irene Papas, Don Dubbins, Stephen McNally, Vic Morrow, Royal Dano, Lee Van Cleef

Trio*
GB 1950 91m bw
Rank / Gainsborough (Antony Darnborough)

Following *Quartet* (qv), three more stories from Somerset Maugham: 'The Verger', 'Mr Knowall', and 'Sanatorium'.
An enjoyable package, unpretentiously handled but with full weight to the content.

w W. Somerset Maugham, R. C. Sherriff, Noel Langley, *stories* W. Somerset Maugham *d* Ken Annakin, Harold French *ph* Reg Wyer, Geoffrey Unsworth *m* John Greenwood *ad* Maurice Carter

James Hayter, Kathleen Harrison, Michael Hordern, Felix Aylmer; *Nigel Patrick*, Anne Crawford, Naunton Wayne, Wilfrid Hyde White; Michael Rennie, Jean Simmons, *John Laurie, Finlay Currie*, Roland Culver, Betty Ann Davies, Raymond Huntley, André Morell

'Listen to the sound of love! Feel people! Taste green!'

The Trip*
US 1967 85m Pathecolor
AIP (Roger Corman)

A director of TV commercials tries LSD and has hallucinations.
Much-banned plotless wallow, the ultimate opt-out movie; well done for those who can take it.

w Jack Nicholson *d* Roger Corman *ph Arch Dalzell psychedelic effects Peter Gardiner montage Dennis Jakob*

Peter Fonda, Susan Strasberg, Bruce Dern, Salli Sachse, Dennis Hopper

The Trip to Bountiful*
US 1985 106m Allied and WBS colour
Island / Film Dallas / Bountiful Film Partners (Sterling Vanwagenen, Horton Foote)

An old woman leaves her tiresome family to return by bus to the town where she was raised.
A relic of the fifties, when writers were mystical about mid-America, this oddity survives as an acting tour de force.

w Horton Foote, from his play *d* Peter Masterson *ph* Fred Murphy *m* J. A. C. Redford

Geraldine Page, John Heard, Carlin Glynn, Richard Bradford, Rebecca de Mornay

AA: Geraldine Page

AAN: adapted screenplay

Triple Cross
GB 1967 140m colour
Warner / Cineurop (Fred Feldkamp)

A small-time crook imprisoned on Jersey at the start of World War II offers to spy for the Nazis but reports to the English.
Ho-hum biopic of double agent Eddie Chapman; effective scenes merely interrupt the general incoherence.

w René Hardy, *book* The Eddie Chapman Story by Frank Owen *d* Terence Young *ph* Henri Alekan *m* Georges Garvarentz

Christopher Plummer, Yul Brynner, Trevor Howard, Romy Schneider, Gert Frobe, Claudine Auger

Triple Echo*
GB 1972 94m colour
Hemdale / Senta (Graham Cottle)

In 1942, a soldier's wife welcomes another soldier to her farm for tea; he deserts and poses as her sister.
Foolish story which would possibly have worked as a TV play but hardly justifies a film despite the talent on hand.

w Robin Chapman, *novel* H. E. Bates *d* Michael Apted *ph* John Coquillon *m* Marc Wilkinson

Glenda Jackson, Brian Deacon, Oliver Reed

The Triumph of Sherlock Holmes*
GB 1935 84m bw

Sherlock Holmes solves a murder stemming from enmity between Pennsylvania coal miners. Solidly satisfying adaptation of Conan Doyle's *The Valley of Fear*, with more of Moriarty added. Arthur Wontner, Ian Fleming, Lyn Harding, Jane Carr, Leslie Perrins, Michael Shepley. Written by H. Fowler Mear; directed by Leslie Hiscott; for Real Art.

Triumph of the Will****
Germany 1936 120m bw
Leni Riefenstahl / Nazi Party

The official record of the Nazi party congress held at Nuremberg in 1934.
A devastatingly brilliant piece of film-making—right from the opening sequence of Hitler descending from the skies, his plane shadowed against the clouds. The rally scenes are a terrifying example of the camera's power of propaganda. After World War II it was banned for many years because of general fears that it might inspire a new Nazi party.

d, ed Leni Riefenstahl ph Sepp Allgeier and 36 assistants *m* Herbert Windt

Triumphs of a Man Called Horse
Spain 1982 89m CFI

Third in a dispensable series (*A Man Called Horse*, *Return of a Man Called Horse*) of dour westerns. In this scrappy item the man dies early on, but his son upholds the tradition. Richard Harris, Michael Beck, Ana De Sade, Vaughn Armstrong, Buck Taylor. Written by Ken Blackwell, Carlos Aured, Jack De Witt; directed by John Hough; for Sandy Howard / Redwing / Transpacific / Hesperia.

Tripoli
US 1950 95m Technicolor

In 1805 the United States sends marines to rout the Barbary pirates. Not a superior actioner, but it passed the time. John Payne, Maureen O'Hara, Howard Da Silva, Philip Reed, Grant Withers, Lowell Gilmore. Written by Winston Miller; directed by Will Price; for Pine-Thomas / Paramount.

'From a million years back—horror explodes into today!'

Trog
GB 1970 91m Technicolor
Warner / Herman Cohen

A man-ape is discovered in a pothole and trained by a lady scientist.
Ridiculous semi-horror film which degrades its star.

w Aben Kandel *d* Freddie Francis *ph* Desmond Dickinson *m* John Scott

Joan Crawford, Michael Gough, Bernard Kay, David Griffin

The Trojan Women*
US 1971 111m Eastmancolor
Josef Shaftel (Michael Cacoyannis, Anis Nohra)

Troy has fallen to the Greeks and its women bemoan their fate.
And oh, how they bemoan! Even with this cast, Greek tragedy does not fill the big screen.

w Michael Cacoyannis, *play* Euripides *d* Michael Cacoyannis *ph* Alfio Contini *m* Mikis Theodorakis

Katharine Hepburn, Vanessa Redgrave, Geneviève Bujold, Irene Papas, Patrick Magee, Brian Blessed, Pauline Letts

The Trollenberg Terror
GB 1958 84m bw

Extraterrestrials invade Switzerland. Tolerable low-budget sci-fi from a BBC serial. Forrest Tucker, Laurence Payne, Janet Munro, Jennifer Jayne, Warren Mitchell. Written by Jimmy Sangster, from original by Peter Key; directed by Quentin Lawrence; for Tempean. (US title: *The Crawling Eye*.)

Tron*
US 1982 96m Technicolor Super Panavision 70mm
Walt Disney / Lisberger–Kushner

A computer games designer gets his revenge on an enemy by fighting things out in the computer world he has created.
Complicated science fantasy chiefly interesting for its computerized blend of live action and animation, which isn't always successful.

wd Steven Lisberger *ph* Bruce Logan *m* Michael Femer *associate producer (animation)* Harrison Ellenshaw *pd* Dean Edward Mitzner

Bruce Boxleitner, Jeff Bridges, David Warner, Barnard Hughes

'Loaded with the expected visual delights, but falls way short of the mark in story and viewer involvement.'—*Variety*

AAN: costume design; sound

Trooper Hook
US 1957 92m bw
UA / Sol Baer Fielding

A woman prisoner of the Indians has a half-breed son and becomes an outcast when returned to her people.
Peculiar western with good moments, but generally very slow and downbeat.

w Charles Marquis Warren, David Victor, Herbert Little Jnr, *story* Jack Schaefer *d* Charles Marquis Warren *ph* Ellsworth Fredericks *m* Gerald Fried

Barbara Stanwyck, Joel McCrea, Earl Holliman, Edward Andrews, John Dehner, Susan Kohner, Royal Dano

'Estupendo! Magnifico! Esplendido!'

Tropic Holiday
US 1938 78m bw

A Hollywood scriptwriter finds romance in Mexico. Musical time-filler with a bit of everything and not much of anything. Ray Milland, Dorothy Lamour, Bob Burns, Martha Raye, Binnie Barnes, Tito Guizar. Written by Don Hartman, Frank Butler, John C. Moffett and Duke Atteberry; directed by

Theodore Reed; for Paramount. 'Will need strong selling to top average business.'—*Variety*

AAN: Boris Morros (music direction)

Tropic Zone
US 1953 94m Technicolor

In a banana port a man wanted by the police saves a plantation from being taken over by crooks. Tropical thick-ear, not entirely unendurable. Ronald Reagan, Rhonda Fleming, Noah Beery Jnr, Estelita, Grant Withers, John Wengraf. Written and directed by Lewis R. Foster, from a novel by Tom Gill; for Pine-Thomas/Paramount.

Trottie True*
GB 1949 98m Technicolor
GFD / Two Cities (Hugh Stewart)
US title: *The Gay Lady*

Adventures of a Gaiety girl who married a lord.
Self-conscious period comedy which could have been highly diverting but manages only to be sporadically charming in a whimsically amateurish way.

w C. Denis Freeman, *novel* Caryl Brahms, S. J. Simon *d* Brian Desmond Hurst *ph* Harry Waxman *m* Benjamin Frankel *ad* Ralph Brinton

Jean Kent, James Donald, Hugh Sinclair, Bill Owen, Andrew Crawford, Lana Morris

Trouble along the Way
US 1953 110m bw
Warner (Melville Shavelson)

A famous football coach is co-opted to help a bankrupt college but some of his methods are not quite above board.
American college comedy with dollops of religiosity—a double threat.

w Melville Shavelson, Jack Rose *d* Michael Curtiz *ph* Archie Stout *m* Max Steiner

John Wayne, Donna Reed, Charles Coburn, Tom Tully, Sherry Jackson, Marie Windsor

'No opportunites for a laugh or a tear are missed by the entire cast.'—*MFB*

Trouble Brewing*
GB 1939 87m bw

A newspaper printer catches counterfeiters. Lively star comedy. George Formby, Googie Withers, Gus MacNaughton, Joss Ambler, Martita Hunt, Garry Marsh, Ronald Shiner, C. Denier Warren, Basil Radford. Written by Anthony Kimmins, Angus MacPhail and Michael Hogan; directed by Anthony Kimmins; for ATP.

Trouble for Two*
US 1936 75m bw
MGM (Louis D. Lighton)
GB title: *The Suicide Club*

A European prince in London for an arranged wedding gets involved with an ingenious organization for murder.
Light-hearted, black-edged Victorian literary spoof which starts nicely but can't quite keep up the pace.

w Manuel Seff, Edward Paramore Jnr, *stories* New Arabian Nights by Robert Louis Stevenson *d* J. Walter Rubin *ph* Charles G. Clarke *m* Franz Waxman

Robert Montgomery, Rosalind Russell, *Reginald Owen*, Frank Morgan, *Louis Hayward*, E. E. Clive, Walter Kingsford

Trouble in Paradise****
US 1932 86m bw
Paramount (Ernst Lubitsch)

Jewel thieves insinuate themselves into the household of a rich Parisienne, and one falls in love with her.
A masterpiece of light comedy, with sparkling dialogue, innuendo, great performances and masterly cinematic narrative. For connoisseurs, it can't be faulted, and is the masterpiece of American sophisticated cinema.

w Samson Raphaelson, Grover Jones, play The Honest Finder by Laszlo Aladar *d Ernst Lubitsch* *ph* Victor Milner *m* W. Franke Harling

Herbert Marshall, Miriam Hopkins, Kay Francis, Edward Everett Horton, Charles Ruggles, C. Aubrey Smith, Robert Greig, Leonid Kinskey

'Swell title, poor picture. Better for the class houses than the subsequents.'—*Variety*

'One of the gossamer creations of Lubitsch's narrative art . . . it would be impossible in this brief notice to describe the innumerable touches of wit and of narrative skill with which it is unfolded.'—*Alexander Bakshy*

'A shimmering, engaging piece of work . . . in virtually every scene a lively imagination shines forth.'—*New York Times*

'An almost continuous musical background pointed up and commented on the action. The settings were the last word in modernistic design.'—*Theodor Huff, 1948*

Trouble in Store*
GB 1953 85m bw
GFD / Two Cities (Maurice Cowan)

A stock assistant causes chaos in a department store.
First, simplest and best of the Wisdom farces.

w John Paddy Carstairs, Maurice Cowan, Ted Willis *d* John Paddy Carstairs *ph* Ernest Steward *m* Mischa Spoliansky

Norman Wisdom, Jerry Desmonde, Margaret Rutherford, Moira Lister, Derek Bond, Lana Morris, Megs Jenkins, Joan Sims

Trouble in the Glen
GB 1954 91m Trucolor
Republic / Wilcox–Neagle (Stuart Robertson)

An Argentinian laird in a Scottish glen causes ill-feeling.
Heavy-handed Celtic comedy whose predictability and sentimentality could have been forgiven were it not for the most garish colour ever seen.

w Frank S. Nugent, *novel* Maurice Walsh *d* Herbert Wilcox *ph* Max Greene *m* Victor Young

Margaret Lockwood, Orson Welles, Forrest Tucker, Victor McLaglen, John McCallum, Eddie Byrne, Archie Duncan, Moultrie Kelsall

The Trouble with Angels
US 1966 112m Pathecolor
Columbia / William Frye

Two mischievous new pupils cause trouble at a convent school.
Fun with the nuns, for addicts only.

w Blanche Hanalis, *novel* Life with Mother Superior by Jane Trahey *d* Ida Lupino *ph* Lionel Lindon *m* Jerry Goldsmith

Rosalind Russell, Hayley Mills, June Harding, Marge Redmond, Binnie Barnes, Gypsy Rose Lee, Camilla Sparv, Mary Wickes, Margalo Gillmore

'A relentless series of prankish escapades.'—*MFB*

The Trouble with Girls
US 1969 105m Metrocolor Panavision
MGM (Lester Welch)

In the twenties the manager of a travelling chautauqua (educational medicine show) gets involved in a small-town murder.
Curious vehicle for a very bored singing star, with some interesting background detail.

w Arnold and Lois Peyser, *novel* The Chautauqua by Day Keene, Dwight Babcock *d* Peter Tewksbury *ph* Jacques Marquette *m* Billy Strange

Elvis Presley, Marlyn Mason, Nicole Jaffe, Sheree North, Edward Andrews, John Carradine, Vincent Price, Joyce Van Patten

The Trouble with Harry**
US 1955 99m Technicolor Vistavision
(Paramount) Alfred Hitchcock

In the New England woods, various reasons cause various people to find and bury the same body.
Black comedy which never quite, despite bright moments, catches the style of the book; however, it is finely performed and the autumnal backgrounds are splendid.

w John Michael Hayes, *novel* Jack Trevor Story *d Alfred Hitchcock* *ph Robert Burks* *m Bernard Herrmann*

Edmund Gwenn, Mildred Natwick, John Forsythe, Shirley Maclaine, Mildred Dunnock

The Trouble with Women
US 1947 80m bw

A psychology professor thinks women enjoy being treated rough; a lady reporter tests his theories. Silly romantic comedy. Ray Milland,

Brian Donlevy, Teresa Wright, Rose Hobart, Charles Smith, Iris Adrian, Lloyd Bridges. Written by Arthur Sheekman, from a story by Ruth McKenney; directed by Sidney Lanfield; for Paramount.

† The film was completed in 1945, but held from release for two years because of overstock.

True as a Turtle
GB 1956 96m Eastmancolor
Rank (Peter de Sarigny)

Honeymooners join a variety of friends on a yacht crossing the Channel, and get involved in smuggling.
Artless, undemanding comedy for those who like messing about in boats.

w Jack Davies, John Coates, Nicholas Phipps *d* Wendy Toye *ph* Reg Wyer *m* Robert Farnon

John Gregson, June Thorburn, Cecil Parker, *Elvi Hale*, Keith Michell, Avice Landone

True Confession**
US 1937 85m bw
Paramount (Albert Lewin)

A fantasy-prone girl confesses to a murder she didn't commit, and her upright lawyer husband defends her.
Archetypal crazy comedy with fine moments despite longueurs and a lack of cinematic inventiveness. Remade as *Cross My Heart* (qv).

w Claude Binyon, *play* Mon Crime by Louis Verneuil, George Berr *d* Wesley Ruggles *ph* Ted Tetzlaff *m* Frederick Hollander

Carole Lombard, Fred MacMurray, *John Barrymore*, Una Merkel, Porter Hall, Edgar Kennedy, Lynne Overman, Fritz Feld, *Irving Bacon*

'Not a big bet but a favourable enough one . . . it just falls short of being a smash.'—*Variety*

'The best comedy of the year.'—*Graham Greene*

True Confessions*
US 1981 108m colour
United Artists / Chartoff–Winkler (James D. Brubaker)

A policeman working on a murder case finds that his brother, a priest, is involved.
Unnecessary fictional elaboration on a real Los Angeles murder case of the forties (the 'Black Dahlia'); chiefly notable for performances.

w John Gregory Dunne, Joan Didion, *novel* John Gregory Dunne *d* Ulu Grosbard *ph* Owen Roizman *m* Georges Delerue *pd* Stephen S. Grimes

Robert Duvall, *Robert De Niro*, Charles Durning, Kenneth McMillan, Ed Flanders, Cyril Cusack, Burgess Meredith

The True Glory****
GB / US 1945 90m bw
Ministry of Information / Office of War Information

The last year of the war, retold by edited newsreels: D-Day to the Fall of Berlin.
A magnificent piece of reportage, worth a dozen fiction films in its exhilarating Shakespearean fervour, though the poetic commentary does occasionally go over the top. One of the finest of all compilations.

w Eric Maschwitz, Arthur Macrae, Jenny Nicholson, Gerald Kersh, Guy Trosper d Carol Reed, Garson Kanin research Peter Cusick m William Alwyn

'Dwarfs all the fiction pictures of the year.'—*Richard Mallett, Punch*

'Bold, welcome but inadequate use of blank verse; much more successful use of many bits of individualized vernacular narration, unusually free of falseness. Very jab-paced, energetic cutting; intelligent selection of shots, of which several hundred are magnificent.'—*James Agee*

'An inspiring recital of human endeavour which all the world will want to see.'—*The Cinema*

True Grit*
US 1969 128m Technicolor
Paramount / Hal B. Wallis (Paul Nathan)

In the old west, a young girl wanting to avenge her murdered father seeks the aid of a hard-drinking old marshal.
Disappointingly slow-moving and uninventive semi-spoof western with a roistering performance from a veteran star, who won a sentimental Oscar for daring to look fat and old.

w Marguerite Roberts, *novel* Charles Portis *d* Henry Hathaway *ph* Lucien Ballard *m* Elmer Bernstein

John Wayne, Kim Darby, Glen Campbell, Dennis Hopper, Jeremy Slate, Robert Duvall, Strother Martin, Jeff Corey

'Readers may remember it as a book about a girl, but it's a film about John Wayne.'—*Stanley Kauffmann*

'There is a slight consistent heightening or lowering into absurdity, but there is also a strong feeling for the unvarnished preposterousness of everyday existence.'—*John Simon*

† *Rooster Cogburn* featured more adventures of the Wayne character, who also showed up on TV in 1978 in the guise of Warren Oates

AA: John Wayne
AAN: title song (*m* Elmer Bernstein, *ly* Don Black)

True Heart Susie*
US 1919 62m approx (24 fps) bw silent
D. W. Griffith / Artcraft

A country girl sells her cow to send her boy friend to college, but he is ungrateful.
Lavender-flavoured rustic romance, with the director at his most sentimental. But of its kind it is carefully done.

wd D. W. Griffith, *story* Marion Fremont *ph* Billy Bitzer

Lillian Gish, Robert Harron, Clarine Seymour

True Stories*
US 1986 89m Du Art
Warner / Edward R. Pressman / Gary Kurfirst

A narrator introduces people from the town of Virgil, Texas.
A curious entertainment which plays like a whimsical update of Thornton Wilder's *Our Town*, though without the subtlety.

w Stephen Tobolowsky, Beth Henley, David Byrne *d* David Byrne *ph* Ed Lachman *m* David Byrne

David Byrne, John Goodman, Annie McEnroe, Jo Harvey Allen, Spalding Gray, Alix Elias, Swoosie Kurtz

'The story is just a trick to get your attention. It opens the door and lets the real movie in.'—*David Byrne*

The True Story of Jesse James
US 1956 92m Eastmancolor Cinemascope
TCF (Herbert Swope Jnr)
GB title: *The James Brothers*

After the Civil War, Jesse and Frank James become outlaws and train robbers.
Fairly slavish remake of *Jesse James*, without the style.

w Walter Newman *d* Nicholas Ray *ph* Joe MacDonald *m* Leigh Harline

Robert Wagner, Jeffrey Hunter, Hope Lange, Agnes Moorehead, John Carradine, Alan Hale Jnr, Alan Baxter

True to Life*
US 1943 93m Technicolor
Paramount (Paul Jones)

The writer of a radio soap opera moves in with an average family to get the right atmosphere.
Quite a percipient comedy of its day, though it does not forgo the customary romantic entanglements.

w Don Hartman, Harry Tugend *d* George Marshall *ph* Charles Lang *m* Victor Young

Mary Martin, Dick Powell, Franchot Tone, Victor Moore, Mabel Paige, William Demarest, Clarence Kolb, Ernest Truex

True to the Navy
US 1930 70m bw

A drug store girl has too many sailor sweethearts for comfort. Very ordinary star vehicle, with little about it worth remembering next day. Clara Bow, Fredric March, Harry Green, Rex Bell, Eddie Fetherston. Written by Keene Thompson, Doris Anderson, Herman Mankiewicz; directed by Frank Tuttle; for Paramount. 'Hardly better than fair. Slow in tempo, sappy in story, and bearing the stamp of perfunctory production.'—*Variety*

The Trumpet Blows
US 1934 68m bw

A matador comes home to Mexico and quarrels with his bandit brother. Tedious melodrama with bullring scenes. George Raft, Adolphe Menjou, Frances Drake, Sidney Toler, Edward Ellis, Nydia Westman. Written by Bartlett Cormack, Wallace Smith, Porter Emerson Browne, J. Parker Read Jnr; directed by Stephen Roberts; for Paramount. 'Story weak, dialogue bad, casting hopeless.'—*Variety*

Trunk Crime
GB 1939 51m bw

A student goes mad and tries to bury his enemy alive. Now dated, but at the time a smart little programme-filler by an enterprising young producer-director team. Manning Whiley, Barbara Everest, Hay Petrie, Thorley Walters. Written by Francis Miller, from the play by Edward Percy and Reginald Denham; directed by Roy Boulting; produced by John Boulting; for Charter.

The Truth about Spring*
GB 1964 102m Technicolor
U-I / Quota Rentals (Alan Brown)

The bored nephew of a millionaire cruising in the Caribbean jumps at the chance to join friends on a scruffy yacht, but they all get involved with pirates.
Pleasing family film with good scenery and a friendly cast.

w James Lee Barrett, *novel* H. de Vere Stacpoole *d* Richard Thorpe *ph Ted Scaife* *m* Robert Farnon

Hayley Mills, James MacArthur, David Tomlinson, Lionel Jeffries, John Mills, Harry Andrews, Niall MacGinnis

The Truth about Women
GB 1957 107m Eastmancolor
British Lion / Beaconsfield (Sydney Box)

An old roué recounts to his son-in-law his early amorous adventures.
Tedious charade with neither wit nor grace.

w Muriel and Sydney Box *d* Muriel Box *ph* Otto Heller *m* Bruce Montgomery

Laurence Harvey, Julie Harris, Diane Cilento, Mai Zetterling, Eva Gabor, Michael Denison, Derek Farr, Roland Culver, Wilfrid Hyde White, Christopher Lee, Marius Goring, Thorley Walters, Ernest Thesiger, Griffith Jones

'It's amazing that with all those talented people nothing happens on the screen.'—*Pauline Kael, 70s.*

Try and Get Me*
US 1951 92m bw
(UA) Robert Stillman
GB title: *The Sound of Fury*

Two men are arrested for kidnapping and murder, and a journalist stirs the small town to lynch fury.
Harrowing, relentless melodrama, possibly the best on this subject.

w Jo Pagano, from his novel The Condemned *d Cyril Endfield* *ph* Guy Roe *m* Hugo Friedhofer

Frank Lovejoy, Lloyd Bridges, Kathleen Ryan, Richard Carlson, Katherine Locke, Adele Jergens, Art Smith

'The characterization and the handling of the drama are remarkable, at times reaching a complexity rare in films of this type.'—*Gavin Lambert*

'A strange, uncomfortable, sometimes brutal and depressing picture.'—*Richard Mallett, Punch*

The Trygon Factor*
GB 1966 88m Technicolor
Rank / Rialto Film / Preben Phillipsen (Ian Warren)

Bogus nuns plan a million pound bank raid. When you get used to its mixture of styles, this Anglo-German production is pretty good imitation Edgar Wallace, with bags of mystery and melodramatic goings-on involving larger than life characters most of whom come to sticky ends.

w Derry Quinn, Stanley Munro, Kingsley Amis *d* Cyril Frankel *ph* Harry Waxman *m* Peter Thomas

Stewart Granger, Susan Hampshire, Cathleen Nesbitt, Robert Morley, James Culliford, Brigitte Horney, Sophie Hardy, James Robertson Justice

Tudor Rose*
GB 1936 78m bw
GFD / Gainsborough (Michael Balcon)
US title: *Nine Days a Queen*

The brief life and reign of Lady Jane Grey. Modestly well made historical textbook.

w Robert Stevenson, Miles Malleson *d* Robert Stevenson *ph* Max Greene *m* Louis Levy

Cedric Hardwicke, Nova Pilbeam, John Mills, Felix Aylmer, Leslie Perrins, Frank Cellier, Desmond Tester, Gwen Frangcon Davïes, Sybil Thorndike, Martita Hunt, Miles Malleson, John Laurie

'There is not a character, not an incident in which history has not been altered for the cheapest of reasons.'—*Graham Greene*

Tuff Turf
US 1985 112m CFI colour

A street rebel and his moll have trouble understanding themselves and their world. Audiences had trouble getting interested. James Spader, Kim Richards, Paul Mones, Robert Downey, Matt Clark. Written by Jette Rick; directed by Fritz Kiersch; for Donald P. Borchers / New World.

Tugboat Annie**
US 1933 88m bw
MGM (Harry Rapf)

An elderly waterfront lady and her boozy friend smooth out the path of young love. Hilarious and well-loved comedy vehicle for two great stars of the period.

w Zelda Sears, Eve Greene, *stories* Norman Reilly Raine *d* Mervyn Le Roy *ph* Gregg Toland

Marie Dressler, Wallace Beery, Robert Young, Maureen O'Sullivan, Willard Robertson, Paul Hurst

'One of those rare naturals in the picture business—a flicker that sells itself immediately the stars' names go into the lights.'—*Variety*

'A bare outline of the story cannot convey the note of mother love that runs through it, the laughs, the pathos.'—*Picturegoer*

Tugboat Annie Sails Again
US 1940 75m bw

The river lady defeats all comers in her efforts to whip up trade. Badly developed sequel which isn't badly acted but gets nowhere. Marjorie Rambeau, Alan Hale, Jane Wyman, Ronald Reagan, Clarence Kolb, Charles Halton, Victor Kilian. Written by Walter DeLeon; directed by Lewis Seiler; for Edmund Grainger / Warner.

Tulsa*
US 1949 88m Technicolor
Eagle–Lion (Walter Wanger)

The daughter of a cattle owner builds an oil empire.
Splendid Hollywood hokum of the second grade, very predictable but well-oiled.

w Frank Nugent, Curtis Kenyon *d* Stuart Heisler *ph* Winton Hoch *m* Frank Skinner

Susan Hayward, Robert Preston, Pedro Armendariz, Lloyd Gough, Chill Wills, Ed Begley

'Like a damp fuse, it produces a loud bang at the end of a long splutter.'—*Time*

'Meet Cherokee Lansing . . . half wildcat . . . half angel . . . all woman!'—*publicity*

Tumbleweeds**
US 1925 80m (24 fps) bw silent
United Artists / William S. Hart

A wandering cowboy helps a family of settlers. The same plot as *Shane* works wonders in the last film of William S. Hart, which has the apparently authentic flavour of the old west.

w C. Gardner Sullivan, *story* Hal G. Evarts *d* King Baggott *ph* Joseph August

William S. Hart, Barbara Bedford, Lucien Littlefield, Monte Collins

† Reissued in 1939 with an added eight-minute introduction by Hart, showing how the west has changed.

Tunes of Glory**
GB 1960 107m Technicolor
UA / Knightsbridge (Albert Fennell)

The new disciplinarian CO of a highland regiment crosses swords with his lax, hard-drinking predecessor.
Wintry barracks melodrama, finely acted and well made with memorable confrontation scenes compensating for a somewhat underdeveloped script.

TRUE GRIT. John Wayne galloped to an Oscar as the drunken one-eyed marshal, Rooster Cogburn: neither the Bad Guys nor his co-stars stood a chance.

w James Kennaway, from his novel *d Ronald Neame ph Arthur Ibbetson*

Alec Guinness, John Mills, Susannah York, Dennis Price, Kay Walsh, *Duncan Macrae,* Gordon Jackson, John Fraser, Allan Cuthbertson

AAN: James Kennaway

The Tunnel*
GB 1935 94m bw
Gaumont (Michael Balcon)
US title: *Transatlantic Tunnel*

Crooked finances mar the completion of an undersea tunnel to America.

A rare example of British science fiction from this period, though the film was in fact first made in German and French versions, the latter with Jean Gabin.

w Curt Siodmak, L. DuGarde Peach, Clemence Dane, *novel* Bernard Kellerman *d* Maurice Elvey *ph* Gunther Krampf *m* Louis Levy

Richard Dix, Leslie Banks, Madge Evans, Helen Vinson, C. Aubrey Smith, George Arliss, Walter Huston, Basil Sydney, Jimmy Hanley

The Tunnel of Love
US 1958 98m bw Cinemascope
MGM / Joseph Fields

A husband applying to adopt an orphan thinks he may, while drunk, have seduced the glamorous orphan agency official.
Tasteless and not very funny comedy, somewhat miscast.

w Joseph Fields, *play* Joseph Fields, Peter de Vries, *novel* Peter de Vries *d* Gene Kelly *ph* Robert Bronner

Richard Widmark, Doris Day, Gig Young, Gia Scala, Elizabeth Fraser, Elizabeth Wilson

Turk 182*
US 1985 98m TVC colour

A mystery do-gooder embarrasses the city bureaucracy into doing right by citizens with a grievance. Interesting urban drama with a non-violent vigilante. Timothy Hutton, Robert Urich, Kim Cattrall, Robert Culp, Darren McGavin, Steven Keats, Peter Boyle, Paul Sorvino. Written by James Gregory Kingston and Denis and John Hamill; directed by Bob Clark; for Ted Field-Rene DuPont / TCF.

Turkey Time
GB 1933 73m bw

Family indiscretions come out at Christmas time. Vehicle for fruity characterizations by the popular Aldwych team, but not very strong as a farce. Tom Walls, Ralph Lynn, Robertson Hare, Dorothy Hyson, Mary Brough, Norma Varden. Written by Ben Travers, from his play; directed by Tom Walls; for Gaumont.

Turksib*
USSR 1929 60m approx (24 fps) bw silent
Vostok Kino

The making of the Turkestan–Siberia railway. A highly fluent and pictorial documentary with an especially famous climax as the men struggle to lay the last rails and meet a deadline.

w Victor Turin and others *d* Victor Turin *ph* Yevgeni Slavinsky, Boris Frantzisson

Turn Back the Clock*
US 1933 80m bw

A man dreams of changing places with his rich friend. Unusual, quite pleasing comedy-drama. Lee Tracy, Otto Kruger, Mae Clarke, C. Henry Gordon, George Barbier. Written by Edgar Selwyn and Ben Hecht; directed by Edgar Selwyn; for MGM. 'Neatly turned domestic comedy with a dramatic touch that will please all round.'—*Variety*

Turn of the Tide*
GB 1935 80m bw
British National (John Corfield)

A feud between two fishing families ends in marriage.
Low-key, location-set action drama with a moral. The film which brought J. Arthur Rank into the business, which he saw had religious possibilities.

w L. DuGarde Peach, J. O. C. Orton, *novel* Three Fevers by Leo Walmsley *d* Norman Walker

Geraldine Fitzgerald, John Garrick, Niall MacGinnis, J. Fisher White, Joan Maude, Sam Livesey, Wilfrid Lawson, Moore Marriott

'Cut to an hour, it should make an acceptable second feature.'—*Variety*

Turn Off the Moon
US 1937 79m bw

The proprietor of a department store is persuaded by an astrologer to stage a big show in celebration of his 25th anniversary. Thinly structured musical with some acceptable gags and turns. Charles Ruggles, Eleanore Whitney, Johnny Downs, Kenny Baker, Phil Harris and his Orchestra, Ben Blue, Andrew Tombes, Marjorie Gateson, Grady Sutton, Franklin Pangborn. Written by Marguerite Roberts, Harlan Ware, Paul Gerard Smith, Mildred Harrington; directed by Lewis Seiler; for Fanchon / Paramount. 'B from title to climax.'—*Variety*

Turn the Key Softly
GB 1953 81m bw
GFD / Chiltern (Maurice Cowan)

The problems of three women released from prison.
Soppy formula multi-drama with contrived and uninteresting plots and characters.

w Jack Lee, Maurice Cowan, *novel* John Brophy *d* Jack Lee *ph* Geoffrey Unsworth *m* Mischa Spoliansky

Yvonne Mitchell, Terence Morgan, Joan Collins, Kathleen Harrison, Thora Hird, Dorothy Alison, Glyn Houston, Geoffrey Keen, Clive Morton

'Pardon my error, the stork meekly smiled, I've overlooked wifey, gave hubby the child!'
Turnabout*
US 1940 83m bw
Hal Roach

A benevolent god enables a quarrelsome couple to change bodies and see how they like it.
'The man's had a baby instead of the lady', said the ads. Well, not quite, but it did seem pretty daring at the time, and it still provides a hilarious moment or two.

w Mickell Novak, Berne Giler, John McLain, *novel* Thorne Smith *d* Hal Roach *ph* Norbert Brodine *m* Arthur Morton

Adolphe Menjou, John Hubbard, Carole Landis, Mary Astor, Verree Teasdale, Donald Meek, William Gargan, Joyce Compton

Turned Out Nice Again
GB 1941 81m bw

An employee teaches an underwear firm to move with the times. Tolerable star comedy from his late period. George Formby, Peggy Bryan, Edward Chapman, Elliot Mason, Mackenzie Ward, O. B. Clarence. Written by Austin Melford, John Dighton and Basil Dearden, from the play *As You Are* by Hugh Mills and Wells Root; directed by Marcel Varnel; for ATP.

The Turners of Prospect Road
GB 1947 88m bw

A taxi driver's family greyhound wins a big race. Uneasily cast domestic comedy drama. Wilfrid Lawson, Jeanne de Casalis, Maureen Glynne, Helena Pickard, Leslie Perrins, Peter Bull. Written by Victor Katona and Patrick Kirwan; directed by Maurice J. Wilson; for Grand National.

The Turning Point*
US 1952 85m bw
Paramount (Irving Asher)
Original title: *This is Dynamite!*

A young lawyer is appointed by the state governor to smash a crime syndicate.
Familiar exposé drama of its time, quite crisply done.

w Warren Duff *w* William Dieterle *ph* Lionel Lindon *md* Irwin Talbot

William Holden, Alexis Smith, Edmond O'Brien, Tom Tully, Ray Teal

'A story of envy, hatred, friendship, triumph and love!'
The Turning Point*
US 1977 119m De Luxe
TCF / Hera (Nora Kaye)

The American Ballet Theatre visits Oklahoma City, and its ageing star revisits an ex-colleague, now a housewife.
Posh person's soap opera, rather boringly made and interesting only for its performances, which are certainly vivid.

w Arthur Laurents *d* Herbert Ross *ph* Robert Surtees *m* John Lanchbery *pd* Albert Brenner

Anne Bancroft, Shirley Maclaine, Mikhail Baryshnikov, Leslie Browne, Tom Skerritt, Martha Scott, Marshall Thompson

'A backstage musical dressed up with smart cultural trimmings.'—*Alan Brien*

'We get a glimpse of something great in the movie—Mikhail Baryshnikov dancing—and these two harpies out of the soaps block the view.'—*New Yorker, 1978*

AAN: best picture; Herbert Ross; Robert Surtees; Anne Bancroft; Shirley Maclaine; Mikhail Baryshnikov; Leslie Browne

Turtle Diary*
GB 1985 97m Technicolor
CBS / United British Artists / Britannic (Richard Johnson)

Two self-admitted eccentrics take it upon themselves to release turtles from captivity in the London Zoo.
Mainly ineffective character comedy, memorable only for fragments of dialogue and acting.

w Harold Pinter *novel* Russell Hoban *d* John Irvin *ph* Peter Hannan *m* Geoffrey Burgon *pd* Leo Austin *ed* Peter Tanner

Glenda Jackson, Ben Kingsley, Richard Johnson, Michael Gambon, Rosemary Leach, Eleanor Bron, Harriet Walter, Nigel Hawthorne, Michael Aldridge.

The Tuttles of Tahiti
US 1942 91m bw

The Tuttles have one ambition: to do no work. A negative prospect even for a light comedy, and this one rapidly sinks under a welter of flat dialogue. Charles Laughton, Jon Hall, Victor Francen, Peggy Drake, Florence Bates. Written by S. Lewis Meltzer, Robert Carson, James Hilton *novel* No More Gas by Charles Noordhof and James Norman Hall; directed by Charles Vidor; for Sol Lesser / RKO.

Twelve Angry Men****
US 1957 95m bw
(UA) Orion–Nova (Henry Fonda, Reginald Rose)

A murder case jury about to vote guilty is convinced otherwise by one doubting member. Though unconvincing in detail, this is a brilliantly tight character melodrama which is never less than absorbing to experience. Acting and direction are superlatively right, and the film was important in helping to establish television talents in Hollywood.

w Reginald Rose, from his play *d Sidney Lumet ph Boris Kaufman m* Kenyon Hopkins

Henry Fonda, Lee J. Cobb, E. G. Marshall, Jack Warden, Ed Begley, Martin Balsam, John Fiedler, Jack Klugman, George Voskovec, Robert Webber, Edward Binns, Joseph Sweeney

AAN: best picture; Reginald Rose; Sidney Lumet

The Twelve Chairs
US 1970 93m Movielab
UMC / Crossbow (Michael Hertzberg)

A Russian bureaucrat chases twelve dining chairs, in one of which is hidden the family jewels.
Tedious Mel Brooks romp with not too many laughs, from a yarn better handled in *Keep Your Seats Please* and *It's in the Bag,* from both of which he might have learned something about comedy timing.

w Mel Brooks, *novel* Ilf and Petrov *d* Mel Brooks *ph* Dorde Nikolic *m* John Morris

Ron Moody, Frank Langella, Dom De Luise, Bridget Brice, Diana Coupland, Mel Brooks

'In the end it runs out of both steam and jokes.'—*Michael Billington, Illustrated London News*

Twelve Good Men
GB 1936 64m bw

A convict escapes to murder the jury who convicted him. Solidly carpentered suspenser. Henry Kendall, Nancy O'Neill, Percy Parsons, Morland Graham, Bernard Miles. Written by *Sidney Gilliat* and *Frank Launder* from the novel *Murders in Praed Street* by John Rhode; directed by Ralph Ince; for Warner.

'A story of twelve men as their women never knew them!'

Twelve O'Clock High**
US 1949 132m bw
TCF (Darryl F. Zanuck)

During World War II, the commander of a US bomber unit in Britain begins to crack under the strain.
Absorbing character drama, justifiably a big box office success of its day, later revived as a TV series. All production values are excellent.

w Sy Bartlett, Beirne Lay Jnr d Henry King ph Leon Shamroy m Alfred Newman

Gregory Peck, Hugh Marlowe, Gary Merrill, Millard Mitchell, Dean Jagger, Robert Arthur, Paul Stewart, John Kellogg

'The best war film since the fighting stopped.'—*Daily Mirror*
'Integrity all the way down the line.'—*New York Times*

AA: Dean Jagger
AAN: best picture; Gregory Peck

Twentieth Century**
US 1934 91m bw
Columbia (Howard Hawks)

A temperamental Broadway producer trains an untutored actress, but when a star she proves a match for him.
Though slightly lacking in pace, this is a marvellously sharp and memorable theatrical burlesque, and the second half, set on the train of the title, reaches highly agreeable peaks of insanity.

w Ben Hecht, Charles MacArthur, play Napoleon of Broadway by Charles Bruce Millholland *d Howard Hawks ph* Joseph August

John Barrymore, Carole Lombard, Roscoe Karns, Walter Connolly, Ralph Forbes, *Etienne Girardot,* Charles Lane, Edgar Kennedy

'Probably too smart for general consumption . . . a long shot for grosses outside the large cities that boast a cosmopolitan clientele.'—*Variety*
'Notable as the first comedy in which sexually attractive, sophisticated stars indulged in their own slapstick instead of delegating it to their inferiors.'—*Andrew Sarris, 1963*
'In the role of Jaffe John Barrymore fits as wholly and smoothly as a banana in a skin.'—*Otis Ferguson*

The Twenty-Fifth Hour
France / Italy / Yugoslavia 1967 133m Eastmancolor Franscope
Concordia / CCC / Avala / Carlo Ponti

When the Nazis deport Rumanian Jews, a simple-minded farmer is sent with them because the officer desires his wife.
Peripatetic adventure with the storm-tossed hero flitting from one symbolic situation to another. All a bit much.

w Henri Verneuil, Wolf Mankowitz, François Boyer, *novel* C. Virgil Gheorghiu *d* Henri Verneuil *ph* Andreas Winding *m* Georges Delerue

Anthony Quinn, Virna Lisi, Grégoire Aslan, Michael Redgrave, Serge Reggiani, Marcel Dalio, Marius Goring, Alexander Knox, Liam Redmond, Meier Tzelniker, John Le Mesurier, Françoise Rosay

24 Hours
US 1931 65m bw

A day in the life of an ultra-rich couple whose marriage has gone sour. Fairly slick matrimonial drama with an attempt at filmic treatment. Written by Louis Witzenkorn, from the novel by Louis Bromfield; directed by Marion Gering; for Paramount. Clive Brook, Kay Francis, Miriam Hopkins, Regis Toomey, George Barbier, Adrienne Ames. 'An absorbing bit of fiction that should engage the attention of the fan regulars and register abundantly at the box office.'—*Variety*

Twenty-Four Hours of a Woman's Life
GB 1952 90m Technicolor
ABPC (Ivan Foxwell)
US title: *Affair in Monte Carlo*

A young widow tries to reform an inveterate gambler, but he kills himself.
Stilted, over-literary romantic melodrama with philosophical dialogue, flashback framing and Riviera settings.

w Warren Chetham Strode, *novel* Stefan Zweig *d* Victor Saville *ph* Christopher Challis *m* Robert Gill, Philip Green

Merle Oberon, Leo Genn, Richard Todd, Stephen Murray, Peter Illing, Isabel Dean

Twenty Million Miles to Earth
US 1957 82m bw
Columbia / Morningside (Charles Schneer)

An American rocket ship returning from Venus breaks open and a scaly monster escapes into the Mediterranean and is cornered in the Roman coliseum.
Cheeseparing monster fiction which doesn't wake up till the last five minutes, and looks pretty silly even then.

w Bob Williams, Chris Knopf *d* Nathan Juran *ph* Irving Lippmann *m* Mischa Bakaleinikoff *sp* Ray Harryhausen

William Hopper, Joan Taylor, Frank Puglia, John Zaremba

Twenty Million Sweethearts
US1934 89m bw
Warner

Singing radio sweethearts are kept apart because of their images.
Thin musical with moderate numbers, remade as *My Dream Is Yours.*

w Warren Duff, Harry Sauber *d* Ray Enright *ph* Sid Hickox *songs* Harry Warren, Al Dubin

Dick Powell, Ginger Rogers, Pat O'Brien, the Mills Brothers, Ted Fio Rito and his band, the Radio Rogues, Allen Jenkins, Grant Mitchell

'An entry the theatre boys won't have to worry about.'—*Variety*

Twenty Mule Team*
US 1940 84m bw
MGM (J. Walter Ruben)

Rivalry among the borax miners in Death Valley.
Adequate semi-western with an unusual theme and setting.

w Robert C. DuSoe, Owen Atkinson *d* Richard Thorpe *ph* Clyde De Vinna *m* David Snell

Wallace Beery, Leo Carrillo, Marjorie Rambeau, Anne Baxter, Douglas Fowley, Berton Churchill, Noah Beery Jnr, Arthur Hohl, Clem Bevans, Charles Halton, Minor Watson

29 Acacia Avenue
GB 1945 83m bw

Young people are having a good time when their parents return unexpectedly from holiday. Popular domestic comedy of its day. Gordon Harker, Betty Balfour, Carla Lehmann, Jimmy Hanley, Jill Evans, Hubert Gregg, Dinah Sheridan, Henry Kendall, Guy Middleton. Written by Muriel and Sydney Box, from the play by Mabel and Denis Constanduros; directed by Henry Cass; for Boca / Columbia.

Twenty-One Days*
GB 1937 75m bw
London Films (Alexander Korda)
aka: *The First and the Last*

A barrister's brother accidentally kills a man and lets an old eccentric take the blame.
Watchable but very stilted melodrama with interesting early performances by Olivier and Leigh and a few good moments.

w Graham Greene, *play* The First and the Last by John Galsworthy *d* Basil Dean *ph* Jan Stallich *m* John Greenwood

Laurence Olivier, Vivien Leigh, Leslie Banks, Hay Petrie, Francis L. Sullivan, Esmé Percy, Robert Newton, Victor Rietti

'I wish I could tell the extraordinary story that lies behind this shelved and resurrected picture, a story involving a theme song, and a bottle of whisky, and camels in Wales. Meanwhile let one guilty man, at any rate, stand in the dock, swearing never to do it again. . .'—*Graham Greene*

† The film was not shown until 1940.

The Twenty Questions Murder Mystery
GB 1949 95m bw

A killer taunts the police with clues sent to a radio quiz show. Somewhat heavy comedy mystery with interest arising from the broadcasting background. Robert Beatty, Rona Anderson, Clifford Evans, Edward Lexy, Olga Lindo, Richard Dimbleby, Jack Train, Stewart MacPherson, Daphne Padel, Norman Hackforth, Jeanne de Casalis. Written by Patrick Kirwan and Victor Katona; directed by Paul Stein; for Pax-Pendennis.

Twenty Thousand Leagues under the Sea**
US 1954 122m Technicolor
Cinemascope
Walt Disney

Victorian scientists at sea are wrecked and captured by the mysterious captain of a futuristic submarine.
Pretty full-blooded adaptation of a famous yarn, with strong performances and convincing art and trick work.

w Earl Felton, *novel Jules Verne d Richard Fleischer ph* Franz Planer, Franz Lehy, Ralph Hammeras, Till Gabbani *m* Paul Smith *ad John Meehan*

Kirk Douglas, James Mason, Paul Lukas, Peter Lorre, Robert J. Wilke, Carlton Young, Ted de Corsia

Twenty Thousand Men a Year
US 1939 83m bw

Experiences of recruits to college student aviation training. Very threadbare flagwaver. Randolph Scott, Preston Foster, Margaret Lindsay, Robert Shaw, Mary Healy, Kane Richmond, Maxie Rosenbloom, Sen Yung. Written by Lou Breslow, Owen Francis, Frank Wead; directed by Alfred E. Green; for Sol M. Wurtzel / Cosmopolitan / TCF. 'Needs exploitation as upper-bracket attraction.'—*Variety*

Twenty Thousand Years in Sing Sing**
US 1932 77m bw
Warner (Robert Lord)

A tough criminal escapes from prison but his girl kills a man during the attempt, and he takes the blame.
Dated but fast-moving and still-powerful crime melodrama, remade to less effect as *Castle on the Hudson* (qv).

w Wilson Mizner, Brown Holmes, *book* Lewis E. Lawes *d Michael Curtiz ph* Barney McGill *m* Bernhard Kaun

Spencer Tracy, Bette Davis, Arthur Byron, Lyle Talbot, Louis Calhern, Warren Hymer, Sheila Terry, Edward McNamara

'Good entertainment and good box office with that inside prison routine touch . . . Finally, it begins to appear Sing Sing wouldn't be a bad place at all to spend a vacation during the depression.'—*Variety*

'Somewhere in the fog there is a voice, a perfume, a glove, a knife—and a victim!'

Twenty-Three Paces to Baker Street*
US 1956 103m Eastmancolor
Cinemascope
TCF (Henry Ephron)

A blind playwright in a pub overhears a murder plot and follows the trail to the bitter end despite attacks on his life.
Sufficiently engrossing murder mystery with a weird idea of London's geography: the hero's Portman Square apartment has a balcony overlooking the Thames two miles away. Perhaps this is part of the script's light touch.

w Nigel Balchin, *novel* Philip MacDonald *d* Henry Hathaway *ph* Milton Krasner *m* Leigh Harline

Van Johnson, Vera Miles, *Cecil Parker,* Patricia Laffan, Maurice Denham, *Estelle Winwood,* Liam Redmond

Twice Blessed
US 1945 76m bw

Twin daughters of a divorced couple deliberately confuse their parents into a reconciliation. Paper-thin comedy without much wit. Preston Foster, Gail Patrick, Lee and Lyn Wilde, Richard Gaines, Jean Porter, Ethel Smith at the organ. Written by Ethel Hill; directed by Harry Beaumont; for Arthur L. Field / MGM.

Twice in a Lifetime
US 1985 117m colour

A man turns fifty and decides to make a clean break with his family. Comedy drama of the mid-life crisis: nothing new. Gene Hackman, Ellen Burstyn, Ann-Margret, Amy Madigan, Ally Sheedy. Written by Colin Welland; directed and produced by Bud Yorkin.

AAN: Amy Madigan (supporting actress)

Twice round the Daffodils
GB 1962 89m bw
Anglo Amalgamated / GHW (Peter Rogers)

Comic and serious episodes in the lives of male patients at a TB sanatorium.
Acceptable broadening, almost in *Carry On* style, of a modestly successful play.

w Norman Hudis, *play* Ring for Catty by Patrick Cargill, Jack Beale *d* Gerald Thomas *ph* Alan Hume *m* Bruce Montgomery

Juliet Mills, Donald Sinden, Donald Houston, Kenneth Williams, Ronald Lewis, Joan Sims, Andrew Ray, Lance Percival, Jill Ireland, Sheila Hancock, Nanette Newman

Twice Two
US 1933 20m bw

Stan and Ollie have each married the other's twin sister. . . . Strained and laboured trick comedy in which neither the double exposures nor the gags quite come off. Laurel and Hardy. Written by Stan Laurel; directed by James Parrott; for Hal Roach.

Twilight for the Gods
US 1958 120m Eastmancolor
U-I (Gordon Kay)

The captain of an old sailing ship takes her for a last voyage from Mexico to Tahiti.
Dull and miscast adventure story lacking the spark of the original novel; watchable only for the travelogue elements.

w Ernest K. Gann, from his novel *d* Joseph Pevney *ph* Irving Glassberg *m* David Raskin *md* Joseph Gershenson

Rock Hudson, Cyd Charisse, Arthur Kennedy, Leif Erickson, Charles McGraw, Ernest Truex, Richard Haydn, Wallace Ford, Celia Lovsky, Vladimir Sokoloff

'Rock Hudson has difficulty in suggesting a dedicated seaman who has served under sail for thirty years.'—*MFB*

The Twilight Hour
GB 1944 85m bw

A nobleman's gardener turns out to be the amnesiac father of the girl about to marry into the family. Plodding and very predictable drama with popular cast. Mervyn Johns, Basil Radford, Marie Lohr, A. E. Matthews, Lesley Brook, Grey Blake. Written by Jack Whittingham, from a novel by Arthur Valentine; directed by Paul Stein; for British National.

Twilight of Honor
US 1963 115m bw Panavision
MGM / Perlsea
GB title: *The Charge Is Murder*

A young small-town lawyer defends a neurotic no-good on a murder charge.
Modest courtroom melodrama in which the detail is better than the main plot.

w Henry Denker, *novel* Al Dewlen *d* Boris Sagal *ph* Philip Lathrop *m* John Green

Richard Chamberlain, *Claude Rains,* Joey Heatherton, Nick Adams, Joan Blackman, James Gregory, Pat Buttram, Jeanette Nolan

AAN: Nick Adams

Twilight's Last Gleaming
US / West Germany 1977 146m
Technicolor
Lorimar / Bavaria Studios (Helmut Jedele)

An ex-general commandeers an atomic missile plant and blackmails the president into telling some political truths.
Suspense thriller, fairly incompetent on its level and with ideas above its station. A distinctly overlong and unlikeable entertainment.

w Ronald M. Cohen, Edward Huebsch, *novel* Viper Three by Walter Wager *d* Robert Aldrich *ph* Robert Hauser *m* Jerry Goldsmith

Burt Lancaster, Richard Widmark, Charles Durning, Melvyn Douglas, Paul Winfield, Burt Young, Joseph Cotten, Roscoe Lee Brown, Gerald S. O'Loughlin, Charles Aidman

Twilight Zone: The Movie*
US 1983 101m Technicolor
Warner (Steven Spielberg, John Landis)

Four supernatural stories in the tradition of Rod Serling's long-running TV series of the fifties.
A disappointing collection on the whole, though with these talents what's on the screen is never quite boring.

w John Landis, George Clayton Johnson, Richard Matheson, Josh Rogan, Rod Serling *d* John Landis, Steven Spielberg, Joe Dante, George Miller *ph* Stevan Larner, Allen Daviau, John Hora *m* Jerry Goldsmith

Dan Aykroyd, Vic Morrow, Scatman Crothers, Bill Quinn, Kathleen Quinlan, Kevin McCarthy, John Lithgow

'If there is an overriding irony to this catalogue of misfortunes, it is that the desire of four up-and-coming directors to honour TV as an imaginative source should have rebounded so disastrously on their cinematic reputations.'—*Richard Combs, MFB*

Twin Beds*
US 1942 84m bw
Edward Small

A married couple are embarrassed by the antics of a drunken neighbour.
Slight pretext for a pretty funny old-fashioned farce.

w Curtis Kenyon, Kenneth Earl, E. Edwin Moran, *play* Margaret Mayo, Edward Salisbury Field *d Tim Whelan ph* Hal Mohr *m* Dmitri Tiomkin

George Brent, Joan Bennett, *Mischa Auer,* Una Merkel, Glenda Farrell, Ernest Truex, Margaret Hamilton, Charles Coleman

The Twinkle in God's Eye
US 1955 73m bw
Republic (Mickey Rooney)

A parson rebuilds a church in a western town where his father was killed by Indians.
Amiable if unlikely western drama with the star more convincing than one might expect.

w P. J. Wolfson *d* George Blair *ph* Bud Thackery *m* Van Alexander

Mickey Rooney, Hugh O'Brian, Colleen Gray, Michael Connors, Don Barry

Twinky
GB 1969 98m Technicolor
Rank / World Film Services (Clive Sharp)
US title: *Lola*

A 16-year-old London schoolgirl marries a dissolute 40-year-old American author.
Dreary sex comedy drama, the fag end of London's swinging sixties.

w Norman Thaddeus Vane *d* Richard Donner *ph* Walter Lassally *m* John Scott

Charles Bronson, Susan George, Trevor Howard, Michael Craig, Honor Blackman, Robert Morley, Jack Hawkins

'They use the satanic power of their bodies to turn men and women into their blood slaves!'

Twins of Evil
GB 1971 87m Eastmancolor
Rank / Hammer (Harry Fine, Michael Style)

Identical Austrian twins become devotees of a vampire cult.
Vampire-chasing Puritans add a little flavour to a routine Hammer horror.

w Tudor Gates *d* John Hough *ph* Dick Bush *m* Harry Robinson

Madeleine and Mary Collinson, Peter Cushing, Kathleen Byron, Dennis Price, Isobel Black

Twist around the Clock
US 1961 83m bw
Columbia / Sam Katzman

An astute manager discovers a small-town dance called the twist and promotes it nationally.
Rock around the Clock revisited, with an even lower budget and fewer shreds of talent.

w James B. Gordon *d* Oscar Rudolph *ph* Gordon Avil *md* Fred Karger

Chubby Checker, the Marcels, Dion, John Cronin, Mary Mitchell

A Twist of Sand
GB 1968 91m De Luxe
UA / Christina (Fred Engel)

An ill-matched set of criminals seek hidden diamonds on Africa's skeleton coast.
Pattern melodrama of thieves falling out, quite nicely put together but with performances too high pitched.

m Marvin H. Albert, *novel* Geoffrey Jenkins *d Don Chaffey ph* John Wilcox *m* Tristam Cary

Richard Johnson, Honor Blackman, Roy Dotrice, Peter Vaughan, Jeremy Kemp

'Enough to make even Hitchcock jump!'

Twisted Nerve
GB 1968 118m Eastmancolor
British Lion / Charter (John Boulting)

A rich, disturbed young man disguises himself as a retarded teenager in order to kill his hated stepfather.
Absurd, unpleasant, longwinded and naïvely scripted shocker, rightly attacked because it asserted that brothers of mongoloids are apt to become murderers. A long way behind the worst Hitchcock.

w Leo Marks, Roy Boulting *d* Roy Boulting *ph* Harry Waxman *m* Bernard Herrmann

Hayley Mills, Hywel Bennett, Phyllis Calvert, Billie Whitelaw, Frank Finlay, *Barry Foster*, Salmaan Peer

'Curious and in some respects disagreeable . . . never thrilling enough to reach the Hitchcock level and without sufficient medical credibility to be taken seriously as a case history.'—*Michael Billington, Illustrated London News*

Two a Penny
GB 1967 98m Eastmancolor
World Wide (Frank R. Jacobson)

An idle art student becomes involved in the drug racket but finally sees the light.
Naïve religious propaganda sponsored by the Billy Graham movement and featuring the evangelist in a cameo. A curiosity.

w Stella Linden *d* James F. Collier *ph* Michael Reed *m* Mike Leander

Cliff Richard, Dora Bryan, Ann Holloway, Avril Angers, Geoffrey Bayldon, Peter Barkworth

Two against the World
US 1936 64m bw
Warner (Bryan Foy)
GB title: *The Case of Mrs Pembroke*

A gutter newspaper unnecessarily digs up a sordid murder case and causes the suicide of two people involved.
Remake of *Five Star Final* with the interest boringly shifted to the do-gooders who *don't* want to publish the story.

w Michel Jacoby, *play* Louis Weitzenkorn *d* William McGann *ph* Sid Hickox *m* Heinz Roemheld

Humphrey Bogart, Beverly Roberts, Helen MacKellar, Henry O'Neill, Linda Perry, Virginia Brissac

Two Alone
US 1934 72m bw

The orphanage drudge on a remote farm gets herself pregnant. Heavy-going *Cold Comfort Farm* melodrama, with virtually no light relief in sight. Jean Parker, Tom Brown, Arthur Byron, Zasu Pitts, Beulah Bondi, Nydia Westman. Written by Josephine Lovett, Joseph Moncure March, from the play Wild Birds by Dan Totheroh; directed by Elliott Nugent; for RKO.

Two and Two Make Six
GB 1961 89m bw
Bryanston / Prometheus (Monja Danischewsky)

Two motor cycling couples almost accidentally swap partners.
Reasonably fresh little romantic comedy.

w Monja Danischewsky *d* Freddie Francis *ph* Desmond Dickinson, Ronnie Taylor *m* Norrie Paramor

George Chakiris, Janette Scott, Alfred Lynch, Jackie Lynch, Malcolm Keen, Ambrosine Philpotts, Bernard Braden

Two Bright Boys
US 1939 69m bw

A British boy and his father help an American boy save his oil ranch from a foreclosing villain. Traditional action stuff, quite pleasantly done for undemanding audiences. Jackie Cooper, Freddie Bartholomew, Melville Cooper, Dorothy Peterson, Alan Dinehart, Willard Robertson. Written by Val Burton, Edmund L. Hartman; directed by Joseph Santley; for Burt Kelly / Universal.
'Adequate support for the duals.'—*Variety*

The Two Faces of Dr Jekyll
GB 1960 88m Technicolor Megascope
Hammer (Anthony Nelson-Keys)
US title: *House of Fright*

A variation on the much-filmed story: the schizo's evil half is the more handsome.
Surprisingly flat and tedious remake.

w Wolf Mankowitz, *novel* Robert Louis Stevenson *d* Terence Fisher *ph* Jack Asher *m* David Heneker, Monty Norman

Paul Massie, Dawn Addams, Christopher Lee, David Kossoff, Francis de Wolff

Two-Faced Woman*
US 1941 90m bw
MGM (Gottfried Reinhardt)

A ski instructress who fears she may be losing her publisher husband to another woman poses as her own more vivacious twin sister.

The failure of this scatterbrained comedy is alleged to be the reason for Garbo's premature retirement. Looked at half a century later, it is no great shakes but harmless and eager to please; what sabotages it is a shoddy production and flagging pace.

w S. N. Behrman, Salka Viertel, George Oppenheimer, *play* Ludwig Fulda *d* George Cukor *ph* Joseph Ruttenberg *m* Bronislau Kaper

Greta Garbo, Melvyn Douglas, *Constance Bennett,* Roland Young, Robert Sterling, Ruth Gordon, George Cleveland

'It is almost as shocking as seeing your mother drunk.'—*Time*

Two Fisted
US 1935 60m bw

A prizefighter and his manager join a socialite's household as bodyguards. Flat comedy which doesn't get very far in any direction; a remake of the silent *Is Zat So?* Lee Tracy, Roscoe Karns, Grace Bradley, Kent Taylor, Gail Patrick. Written by Sam Hellman, Francis Martin, Eddie Moran, from the play by James Gleason and Richard Taber; directed by James Cruze; for Harold Hurley / Paramount. 'Some periods of hilarity.'—*Variety*

Two Flags West*
US 1950 92m bw
TCF (Casey Robinson)

Sixty Confederate prisoners of war are granted an amnesty and go west to fight the Indians. Laboured but good-looking Civil War western.

w Casey Robinson *d Robert Wise ph Leon Shamroy m* Hugo Friedhofer

Joseph Cotten, Jeff Chandler, Linda Darnell, Cornel Wilde, Dale Robertson, Jay C. Flippen, Noah Beery Jnr, Harry Von Zell

'Its period reconstruction is remarkable.'—*Gavin Lambert*

Two for the Road*
GB 1966 113m De Luxe Panavision
TCF / Stanley Donen

An architect and his wife motoring through France recall the first twelve years of their relationship.
Fractured, fashionable light romantic comedy dressed up to seem of more significance than the gossamer thing it really is; and some of the gossamer has a Woolworth look.

w Frederic Raphael *d* Stanley Donen *ph Christopher Challis m* Henry Mancini

Albert Finney, Audrey Hepburn, Eleanor Bron, William Daniels, Claude Dauphin

AAN: Frederic Raphael

Two for the Seesaw
US 1962 120m bw Panavision
UA / Seesaw / Mirisch / Argyle / Talbot (Robert Wise)

A New York dance instructress has a tempestuous affair with an Omaha attorney on the verge of divorce.
Serious comedy or light drama, meticulously detailed but immensely long for its content and too revealing of its stage origins.

w Isabel Lennart, *play* William Gibson *d* Robert Wise *ph* Ted McCord *m* André Previn *ad* Boris Leven

Robert Mitchum, Shirley Maclaine

AAN: Ted McCord; song 'Second Chance' (*m* André Previn, *ly* Dory Langdon)

Two for Tonight
US 1935 60m bw

Three half-brothers write a play for a temperamental star. Much ado about nothing, but not an unpleasant way of passing an hour. Bing Crosby, Joan Bennett, Mary Boland, Lynne Overman, Thelma Todd, Ernest Cossart. Written by George Marion Jnr, Jane Storm, from a play by Max and J. O. Lief; directed by Frank Tuttle; for Douglas MacLean / Paramount. 'No wow . . . the songs, the fetching title, the competent cast and mostly Crosby will have to offset the other deficiencies.'—*Variety*

Two Girls and a Sailor**
US 1944 124m bw
MGM (Joe Pasternak)

The title says it all.
Loosely-linked wartime musical jamboree with first-class talent; a lively entertainment of its type.

w Richard Connell, Gladys Lehman *d* Richard Thorpe *ph* Robert Surtees *m* George Stoll *songs* various

June Allyson, Gloria de Haven, Van Johnson, Xavier Cugat and his Orchestra, *Jimmy Durante*, Tom Drake, Lena Horne, Carlos Ramirez, Harry James and his Orchestra, Jose Iturbi, *Gracie Allen*, Virginia O'Brien, Albert Coates

AAN: script

Two Girls on Broadway
US 1940 73m bw

A song and dance man breaks up a sister act. Acceptable lower-case vaudeville musical which rewrites the already wispy plot of *Broadway Melody*. George Murphy, Joan Blondell, Lana Turner, Kent Taylor, Wallace Ford, Lloyd Corrigan. Written by Joseph Fields and Jerome Chodorov; directed by S. Sylvan Simon; for MGM. (GB title: *Choose Your Partner*.)

Two Guys from Milwaukee
US 1946 90m bw

A young Balkan prince goes incognito in Brooklyn and befriends a cab driver. Rumbustious comedy with an amiable cast and gag guest appearances. Dennis Morgan, Jack Carson, Joan Leslie, Janis Paige, S. Z. Sakall, Franklin Pangborn. Written by I. A. L. Diamond and Charles Hoffman; directed by David Butler; for Warner. (GB title: *Royal Flush*.)

Two Guys from Texas
US 1948 86m Technicolor

Two vaudevillians find themselves on the run from crooks. Little more than a peg on which to hang some clowning and a few musical numbers. Dennis Morgan, Jack Carson, Dorothy Malone, Penny Edwards, Fred Clark, Gerald Mohr, Forrest Tucker. Written by I. A. L. Diamond and Allen Boretz; directed by David Butler; for Warner. (GB title: *Two Texas Knights*.)

The Two-Headed Spy*
GB 1958 93m bw
Columbia (Hal E. Chester)

A bogus Nazi worms his way into the Gestapo hierarchy.
Adequate, not too exciting biopic of Colonel Alex Schottland; standard production values.

w James O'Donnell *d* André de Toth *ph* Ted Scaife *m* Bernard Schurmann

Jack Hawkins, Gia Scala, Alexander Knox, Erik Schumann, Felix Aylmer, Laurence Naismith, Donald Pleasence, Kenneth Griffith

Two in the Dark
US 1936 72m bw

An amnesiac tries to find out whether he was involved in the murder of a theatrical producer. Mildly intriguing mystery. Walter Abel, Margot Grahame, Wallace Ford, Gail Patrick, Alan Hale, Leslie Fenton, Eric Blore. Written by Seton I. Miller from the novel by Gelett Burgess; directed by Ben Stoloff; for RKO. 'A programmer that'll suit both audiences and b.o. outside of larger first runs.'—*Variety*

Two Lane Blacktop
US 1971 103m Technicolor scope
Universal / Michael S. Laughlin

In the American southwest, the aimless owners of two souped-up cars have an interminable race.
Occasionally arresting, generally boring eccentricity by a big studio looking for another *Easy Rider*.

w Rudolph Wurlitzer, Will Corry *d* Monte Hellman *ph* Jack Deerson *m* Billy James

James Taylor, Warren Oates, Laurie Bird, Dennis Wilson

Two Left Feet
GB 1963 93m bw
British Lion / Roy Baker (Leslie Gilliat)

A callow 19-year-old has girl trouble.
Ponderous sex comedy with no apparent purpose but some well observed scenes.

w Roy Baker, John Hopkins, *novel* In My Solitude by David Stuart Leslie *d* Roy Baker *ph* Wilkie Cooper *m* Philip Green

Michael Crawford, Nyree Dawn Porter, Julia Foster, David Hemmings, Dilys Watling, David Lodge, Bernard Lee

Two Loves
US 1961 100m Metrocolor Cinemascope
MGM / Julian Blaustein
GB title: *Spinster*

An American teacher in New Zealand teaches Maoris and whites and falls for two men.
Pretentious romantic drama with unspeakable dialogue and eccentric characters.

w Ben Maddow, *novel* Sylvia Ashton Warner *d* Charles Walters *ph* Joseph Ruttenberg *m* Bronislau Kaper

Shirley Maclaine, Jack Hawkins, Laurence Harvey, Nobu McCarthy

'91,000 people . . . 33 exit gates . . . one sniper!'

Two Minute Warning
US 1976 115m Technicolor Panavision
Universal / Filmways (Edward S. Feldman)

A sniper terrifies the crowd at a championship football game.
Smartly directed but weakly plotted and scripted disaster movie: the mystery gunman remains a mystery at the end.

w Edward Hume, *novel* George LaFountaine *d* Larry Peerce *ph* Gerald Hirschfeld *m* Charles Fox

Charlton Heston, John Cassavetes, Martin Balsam, Beau Bridges, David Janssen, Marilyn Hassett, Jack Klugman, Gena Rowlands, Walter Pidgeon, Brock Peters, Mitch Ryan

'Even by the standards of exploitation movies, this film is an unusually dehumanizing experience. Not only does it exist solely for its gore, but it reduces the victims to the dimensions of plastic ducks at a shooting gallery.'—*Frank Rich, New York Post*

The Two Mrs Carrolls
US 1945 (released 1947) 99m bw
Warner (Mark Hellinger)

A psychopathic artist paints his wives as the Angel of Death, then murders them with poisoned milk.
Stilted film of an old warhorse of a play, unhappily cast but working up some last-minute tension.

w Thomas Job, *play* Martin Vale *d* Peter Godfrey *ph* Peverell Marley *m* Franz Waxman

Barbara Stanwyck, Humphrey Bogart, Alexis Smith, Nigel Bruce, Isobel Elsom, Pat O'Moore, Peter Godfrey

Two Mules for Sister Sara
US 1969 116m Technicolor Panavision
Universal / Malpaso (Martin Rackin)

A wandering cowboy kills three men trying to rape a nun, but she is not what she seems.
Vaguely unsatisfactory western with patches of nasty brutality leading to an action-packed climax.

w Albert Maltz, Budd Boetticher *d* Don Siegel *ph* Gabriel Figueroa, Gabriel Torres *m* Ennio Morricone

Clint Eastwood, Shirley Maclaine, Manolo Fabregas, Alberto Morin

Two O'Clock Courage
US 1945 66m bw

An amnesia victim is suspected of killing a Broadway producer. Tepid murder mystery. Tom Conway, Ann Rutherford, Richard Lane, Roland Drew, Emory Parnell, Jane Greer. Written by Robert E. Kent, from a story by Gelett Burgess; directed by Anthony Mann; for Ben Stoloff / RKO.

Two of a Kind
US 1951 75m bw
Columbia (William Dozier)

A man is picked up by a glamorous girl who involves him in an elaborate scheme to defraud an elderly couple.
Modest suspenser.

w Lawrence Kimble, James Grunn *d* Henry Levin *ph* Burnett Guffey *m* George Duning

Edmond O'Brien, Lizabeth Scott, Terry Moore, Alexander Knox, Griff Barnett, Virginia Brissac

Two of a Kind
US 1983 87m De Luxe
TCF (Roger M. Rothstein, Joe Wizan)

Four angels propose that Earth be spared from a second flood if two arbitrarily chosen human beings can be seen to perform a great sacrifice for each other.
Curious reversion to angelic comedies of the thirties and forties. Lacking the right measures of wit and whimsy, it is totally unsuccessful.

w John Herzfeld *d* John Herzfeld *ph* Fred Koenekamp, Warren Rothenberger *md* Patrick Williams *pd* Albert Brenner

John Travolta, Olivia Newton-John, Charles Durning, Oliver Reed, Beatrice Straight, Scatman Crothers

'It feels as if it must be a remake of *something . . .'—Sheila Johnston, MFB*

Two on a Guillotine*
US 1965 107m bw Panavision
Warner (William Conrad)

An illusionist arranges to be chained into his coffin at his funeral but promises to return from the dead.
Longwinded and unconvincing shocker with some effectively scary sequences.

w Henry Slesar, John Kneubuhl *d* William Conrad *ph Sam Leavitt* *m* Max Steiner

Connie Stevens, Dean Jones, Cesar Romero, Parley Baer, Virginia Gregg, Connie Gilchrist, John Hoyt

'They had just 36 hours to share the love of a lifetime!'

Two People
US 1973 100m Technicolor
Universal (Robert Wise)

An army deserter returns home and falls for a fashion photographer.
Solemn, inconsequential topical drama which made no impact whatever.

w Richard de Roy *d* Robert Wise *ph* Gerald Hirschfeld *m* David Shire

Peter Fonda, Lindsay Wagner, Estelle Parsons, Alan Fudge

'Sluggish pacing, lifeless looping and terminally ludicrous dialogue eventually turn the film into a travesty of its own form.'—*Variety*

Two Rode Together
US 1961 109m Technicolor
Columbia / John Ford / Shpetner

An army commander and a tough marshal negotiate with Comanches for the return of prisoners.
Substandard Ford, moderately good-looking but uninteresting of plot and dreary of development.

w Frank Nugent, *novel* Will Cook *d* John Ford *ph* Charles Lawton Jnr *m* George Duning

James Stewart, Richard Widmark, Shirley Jones, Linda Cristal, Andy Devine, John McIntire

Two Seconds*
US 1932 68m bw
Warner

In the last two seconds of his life a criminal reviews the events leading up to his execution.
Competent, pacy crime melodrama.

w Harvey Thew, *play* Elliott Lester *d Mervyn Le Roy* *ph* Sol Polito *m* W. Franke Harling

Edward G. Robinson, Preston Foster, Vivienne Osborne, J. Carrol Naish, Guy Kibbee, Adrienne Dare

'General slowness and stodgy overdramatics won't draw the flaps, nor will a tragic finale help.'—*Variety*

'A film that compels attention.'—*Mordaunt Hall, New York Times*

Two Sinners
US 1935 71m bw

A man jailed for shooting his wife's lover makes a fresh start. Curious but tedious romantic drama. Otto Kruger, Martha Sleeper, Minna Gombell, Cora Sue Collins. Written by Jefferson Parker, from story *Two Black Sheep* by Warwick Deeping; directed by Arthur Lubin; for Republic.

Two Sisters from Boston*
US 1946 112m bw
MGM (Joe Pasternak)

Two girls visiting New York find work in a Bowery saloon.
Nicely-detailed turn-of-the-century musical with pleasant talent.

w Myles Connolly *d* Henry Koster *ph* Robert Surtees *md* Charles Previn *songs* Sammy Fain, Ralph Freed

June Allyson, Kathryn Grayson, Lauritz Melchior, Jimmy Durante, Peter Lawford, Ben Blue

Two Smart People
US 1946 93m bw
MGM (Ralph Wheelwright)

TWO FOR THE ROAD. More style than substance with the light playing of Albert Finney and Audrey Hepburn decorating the fashionable frolics.

A con man on parole in New Orleans is chased by a lady crook in search of his hidden loot.
Dog-eared comedy drama.

w Ethel Hill, Leslie Charteris *d* Jules Dassin *ph* Karl Freund *m* George Bassman

Lucille Ball, John Hodiak, Lloyd Nolan, Hugo Haas, Lenore Ulric, Elisha Cook Jnr, Lloyd Corrigan, Vladimir Sokoloff

Two Tars****
US 1928 20m bw silent

Two sailors in an old banger cause a traffic jam and a consequent escalation of violence.
Marvellous elaboration of a tit-for-tat situation, with the stars already at their technical best. Laurel and Hardy, Edgar Kennedy, Charley Rogers. Written by Leo McCarey and H. M. Walker; directed by James Parrott; for Hal Roach.

2001: A Space Odyssey***
GB 1968 141m Metrocolor Panavision
MGM / Stanley Kubrick (Victor Lyndon)

From ape to modern space scientist, mankind has striven to reach the unattainable.
A lengthy montage of brilliant model work and obscure symbolism, this curiosity slowly gathered commercial momentum and came to be cherished by longhairs who used it as a trip without LSD.

w Stanley Kubrick, Arthur C. Clarke, *story* The Sentinel by Arthur C. Clarke *d* Stanley Kubrick *ph Geoffrey Unsworth, John Alcott* *m* various classics *pd Tony Masters, Harry Lange, Ernie Archer* *ad* John Hoesli
Gary Lockwood, Keir Dullea, William Sylvester, Leonard Rossiter, Robert Beaty, Daniel Richter

'Somewhere between hypnotic and immensely boring.'—*Renata Adler*

'Morally pretentious, intellectually obscure and inordinately long . . . intensely exciting visually, with that peculiar artistic power which comes from obsession . . . a film out of control, an infuriating combination of exactitude on small points and incoherence on large ones.'—*Arthur Schlesinger Jnr*

'The satire throughout is tepid and half-hearted, and tends to look like unintended stupidity.'—*John Simon*

AAN: script; Stanley Kubrick

2010
US 1984 114m Metrocolor Panavision
MGM-UA (Peter Hyams)

With Earth on the brink of war, scientists return to Jupiter to decide on the fate of *Discovery* and the meaning of the black monolith.
Tame, almost flatfooted sequel to *2001: A Space Odyssey*, with none of the supposed significance and not much else to offer.

w,d Peter Hyams, *novel* Arthur C. Clarke *m* David Shire *pd* Albert Brenner *ed* James Mitchell

Roy Scheider, John Lithgow, Helen Mirren, Bob Balaban, Keir Dullea, Dana Elcar, Madolyn Smith

AAN: art direction

Two Thousand Women
GB 1944 97m bw
GFD / Gainsborough (Edward Black)

Two pilots try to rescue British women from a French concentration camp.
Routine mix of laughter and tears; hardly an outstanding film of its time, but mildly entertaining.

wd Frank Launder *ph* Jack Cox md Louis Levy

Phyllis Calvert, Flora Robson, Patricia Roc, Renée Houston, Anne Crawford, Jean Kent, James McKechnie, Reginald Purdell, Robert Arden, Thora Hird, Dulcie Gray, Carl Jaffe, Muriel Aked

Two Tickets to Broadway
US 1951 106m Technicolor
RKO (Jerry Wald)

Small-town college girl finds romance and success in the big city.
Very mild musical with TV studio backdrop.

w Sid Silvers, Hal Kanter *d* James V. Kern *ph* Edward Cronjager, Harry J. Wild *m* Walter Scharf

Janet Leigh, Eddie Bracken, Gloria de Haven, Tony Martin, Barbara Lawrence, *Joe Smith and Charlie Dale*

Two Tickets to London
US 1943 78m bw

A sailor accused of aiding an enemy submarine escapes and finds the true villain.
Routine wartime thick-ear. Alan Curtis, Michele Morgan, C. Aubrey Smith, Barry Fitzgerald, Dooley Wilson, Mary Gordon. Written by Tom Reed; directed by Edwin L. Marin; for Universal.

Two Way Stretch**
GB 1960 87m bw
British Lion / Shepperton (M. Smedley Aston)

Three convicts break jail to rob a maharajah.
Amusing comedy with good performances and situations, unofficially borrowed in part from *Convict 99*.

w John Warren, Len Heath d Robert Day *ph* Geoffrey Faithfull *m* Ken Jones

Peter Sellers, *Lionel Jeffries*, Wilfrid Hyde White, Bernard Cribbins, David Lodge, Maurice Denham, Beryl Reid, Liz Fraser, Irene Handl, George Woodbridge

Two Weeks in Another Town*
US 1962 107m Metrocolor Cinemascope
MGM (John Houseman)

An ex-alcoholic film director gets his

comeback chance in Rome but is plagued by old memories.
Self-indulgent melodrama with entertaining patches for *cinéastes*, especially those who saw *The Bad and the Beautiful*.

w Charles Schnee, novel Irwin Shaw
d Vincente Minnelli *ph* Milton Krasner
m David Raksin

Kirk Douglas, Edward G. Robinson, Cyd Charisse, Daliah Lavi, George Hamilton, Claire Trevor, Rosanna Schiaffino, James Gregory, George Macready

Two Weeks with Love*
US 1950 92m Technicolor
MGM (Jack Cummings)

Adventures on a family summer holiday at the turn of the century.
Pleasant family musical.

w John Larkin, Dorothy Kingsley *d* Roy Rowland *ph* Al Gilks *m* Georgie Stoll

Jane Powell, Ricardo Montalban, Louis Calhern, Ann Harding, Phyllis Kirk, Debbie Reynolds, Carleton Carpenter, Clinton Sundberg

Two Women*
Italy / France 1960 110m bw
Champion / Marceau / Cocinor / SGC (Carlo Ponti)
original title: *La Ciociara*

During the Allied bombing of Rome a woman and her daughter travel arduously south and have a hard time at the hands of invading soldiers.
Rather hysterical character drama allowing for a splendid top-note performance from its star.

w Cesare Zavattini, Vittorio de Sica, *novel* Alberto Moravia *d* Vittorio de Sica *ph* Gabor Pogany *m* Armando Trovaioli

Sophia Loren, Eleonora Brown, Jean-Paul Belmondo, Raf Vallone

AA: Sophia Loren

Two Yanks in Trinidad
US 1942 82m bw

Minor racketeers join the army and capture a German agent. One of the many variations on the Flagg and Quirt formula, and not a bad one. Pat O'Brien, Brian Donlevy, Janet Blair, Roger Clark, Donald MacBride, John Emery. Written by Sy Bartlett, Richard Carroll, Harry Segal; directed by Gregory Ratoff; for Samuel Bischoff / Columbia.

Two Years before the Mast*
US 1946 98m bw
Paramount (Seton I. Miller)

In the mid-19th century, a writer becomes a sailor to expose bad conditions.
Well-made but unconvincing-looking picturization of a famous book.

w Seton I. Miller, George Bruce, *book* Richard Henry Dana *d* John Farrow *ph* Ernest Laszlo *m* Victor Young

Alan Ladd, Brian Donlevy, William Bendix, Barry Fitzgerald, Howard da Silva, Albert Dekker, Luis Van Rooten, Darryl Hickman

Two's Company
GB 1936 74m bw

An earl's son loves the daughter of an American millionaire. Not particularly successful hands-across-the-sea comedy. Gordon Harker, Ned Sparks, Mary Brian, Patric Knowles, Robb Wilton, Morton Selten. Written by Tom Geraghty. Roland Pertwee, J. B. Morton, John Paddy Carstairs and Tim Whelan, from the novel *Romeo and Julia* by Sidney Horler; directed by Tim Whelan; for Paul Soskin / B and D.

Tycoon
US 1947 129m Technicolor
RKO

An engineer is hired to drive a tunnel through the Andes, and starts a feud with his boss when he falls in love with his daughter.
Boring, studio-set action saga with too many stops for romance.

w Borden Chase, John Twist *d* Richard Wallace *ph* Harry J. Wild *m* Leigh Harline

John Wayne, Cedric Hardwicke, Laraine Day, James Gleason, Judith Anderson, Anthony Quinn, Grant Withers

Typhoon
US 1940 70m Technicolor
Paramount (Anthony Veiller)

On a Dutch Guianan island, two sailors find a girl who has been a castaway since childhood.
One of Lamour's several sarongers, quite entertaining in its way and commendably brisk.

w Allen Rivkin *d* Louis King *ph* William Mellor *m* Frederick Hollander

Dorothy Lamour, Robert Preston, Lynne Overman, J. Carrol Naish, Frank Reicher

'One of the most emphatically silly pictures I ever saw in my life.'—*Richard Mallet, Punch*

'The gem of pure, pellucid silliness.'—*James Agate*

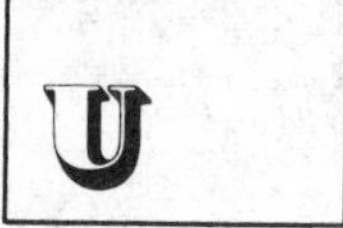

Ugetsu Monogatari*
Japan 1953 94m bw
Daiei (Masaichi Nagata)

During a 16th century civil war two potters find a way of profiteering, but their ambitions bring disaster on their families.
Unique mixture of action, comedy and the supernatural, with strong, believable characters participating and a delightfully delicate touch in script and direction. On its first release it began to figure in many best ten lists, but quickly seemed to fade from public approbation.

w Matsutaro Kawaguchi, from 17th-century collection by Akinara Ueda, Tales of a Pale and Mysterious Moon after the Rain *d Kenji Mizoguchi ph* Kazuo Miyagawa *m* Fumio Hayasaka

Masayuki Mori, Machiko Kyo, Sakae Ozawa, Mitsuko Mito

The Ugly American
US 1962 120m Eastmancolor
U-I / George Englund

A publisher is made ambassador to a south-east Asian state.
Self-dating anti-communist drama which was muddled and boring when new.

w Stewart Stern, *novel* William J. Lederer, Eugene Burdick *d* George Englund *ph* Clifford Stine *m* Frank Skinner

Marlon Brando, Eiji Okada, Sandra Church, Pat Hingle, Arthur Hill, Jocelyn Brando, *Kukrit Pramoj*

The Ugly Dachshund*
US 1965 93m Technicolor
Walt Disney (Winston Hibler)

A dachshund bitch fosters among its puppies an orphan Great Dane.
Cheerful, fast-moving animal farce.

w Albert Aley, *novel* G. B. Stern *d* Norman Tokar *ph* Edward Colman *m* George Bruns

Dean Jones, Suzanne Pleshette, Charles Ruggles, Kelly Thordsen, Parley Baer, Mako, Charles Lane

The Ultimate Warrior
US 1975 94m Technicolor
Warner (Fred Weintraub, Paul Heller)

In AD 2012 New York is ruled by a gangster, the atmosphere is poisoned, and the only hope is a new community on an island off North Carolina.
Curious pretentious fantasy without the courage of its convictions or much entertainment value.

wd Robert Clouse *ph* Gerald Hirschfeld *m* Gil Melle

Yul Brynner, Max Von Sydow, Joanna Miles, William Smith, Richard Kelton, Stephen McHattie

'Less a prophetic vision than a kind of thick-ear *West Side Story*.'—*Richard Combs*

'Actually filmed along the route he travelled 3000 years ago!'
Ulysses*
Italy 1954 103m Technicolor
Lux Film / Ponti–de Laurentiis (Fernando Cinquini)

Ulysses and his crew sail under the curse of Cassandra, and encounter Circe, the sirens and the cyclops.
Peripatetic adventure yarn not too far after Homer; narrative style uncertain but highlights good.

w Franco Brusati, Mario Camerini, Ennio de Concini, Hugh Gray, Ben Hecht, Ivo Perelli, Irwin Shaw, *poem* The Odyssey by Homer *d* Mario Camerini *ph Harold Rosson* *m* Alessandro Cicognini

Kirk Douglas, Silvana Mangano, Anthony Quinn, Rosanna Podesta

Ulysses*
GB 1967 132m bw Panavision
Walter Reade (Joseph Strick)

Twenty-four hours in Dublin with a young poet and a Jewish newspaper man.
A pleasant enough literary exercise, a decent précis of an unmanageably prolix classic novel, this specialized offering would have passed unnoticed were it not for its language, which got it banned in many places but now seems mild indeed.

w Joseph Strick, Fred Haines, *novel* James Joyce *d Joseph Strick ph Wolfgang Suschitsky m* Stanley Myers

Maurice Roeves, Milo O'Shea, Barbara Jefford, T. P. McKenna, Anna Manahan, Maureen Potter

'No amount of pious invoking of Joyce's name can disguise the fact that a cheaply produced film is being sold at exorbitant prices so that someone can make his boodle off "culture".'—*John Simon*

'An act of homage in the form of readings from the book plus illustrated slides.'—*Pauline Kael*

'A facile and ludicrous reduction.'—*Stanley Kauffmann*

AAN: script

'Only one man understood the savagery of the early American west!'
Ulzana's Raid
US 1972 103m Technicolor
Universal / Carter de Haven / Robert Aldrich

An ageing Indian fighter and a tenderfoot officer lead a platoon sent out to counter a murderous Apache attack.
Bloodthirsty, reactionary western with unpleasant shock moments.

w Alan Sharp *d* Robert Aldrich *ph* Joseph Biroc *m* Frank de Vol

Burt Lancaster, Bruce Davison, Jorge Luke, Richard Jaeckel, Lloyd Bochner

The Ultimate Solution of Grace Quigley: see Grace Quigley

Umberto D**
Italy 1952 89m bw
Dear Films

A retired civil servant can barely afford his rent but won't part with his dog.
Downbeat, immensely moving study of old age in a society which fails to provide for it.

w Cesare Zavattini, Vittorio de Sica *d Vittorio de Sica ph* G. R. Aldo *m* Alessandro Cicognini

Carlo Battista

AAN: Cesare Zavattini (original story)

Unaccustomed As We Are
US 1929 20m bw silent

Ollie takes a friend home to dinner, but his wife walks out, leaving him to get into all kinds of trouble. The team's first sound comedy, rather hesitant in its use of the new medium. The story was later reworked as the last half hour of *Blockheads*. Laurel and Hardy, Edgar Kennedy, Mae Busch, Thelma Todd. Written by Leo McCarey and H. M. Walker; directed by Lewis R. Foster; for Hal Roach.

The Unbearable Lightness of Being**
US 1987 172m Technicolor / De Luxe
Saul Zaentz

A womanizing brain surgeon and his two lovers painfully achieve maturity after the putting down of the Prague Spring by Soviet troops.
Brave and largely successful attempt to transfer a complex, ironic Czech novel to the screen.

w Jean-Claude Carrière, Philip Kaufman, from novel by Milan Kundera *d Philip Kaufman* *ph* Sven Nykvist *m* Leos Janacek *pd* Pierre Guffroy

Daniel Day-Lewis, Juliette Binoche, Lena Olin, Erland Josephson, Daniel Olbrychski

The Uncanny
Canada / GB 1977 85m colour
Rank / Cinevideo / Tor (Claude Héroux, Milton Subotsky)

An author tells his publisher three stories about evil cats.
Below-par horror compendium with crude effects failing to bolster a sagging script.

w Michael Parry *d* Denis Héroux *ph* Harry Waxman, James Bawden *m* Wilfred Josephs

Peter Cushing, Ray Milland, Susan Penhaligon, Joan Greenwood, Simon Williams, Roland Culver, Alexandra Stewart, Donald Pleasence, Samantha Eggar, John Vernon

Uncensored
GB 1942 108m bw
GFD / Gainsborough (Edward Black)

In Brussels during the Nazi occupation, the leader of a toe-the-line paper secretly leads the patriots.
Unconvincing underground melodrama with stilted presentation and performances.

w Wolfgang Wilhelm, Terence Rattigan, Rodney Ackland, *novel* Oscar Millard *d* Anthony Asquith *ph* Arthur Crabtree *m* Hans May

Eric Portman, Phyllis Calvert, Griffith Jones, Raymond Lovell, Peter Glenville, Irene Handl, Carl Jaffe, Felix Aylmer

Uncertain Glory
US 1944 102m bw
Warner (Robert Buckner)

During World War II, a French playboy sacrifices himself for his country.
Tame star vehicle needing more action and less philosophy.

w Laszlo Vadnay, Max Brand *d* Raoul Walsh *ph* Sid Hickox *m* Adolph Deutsch

Errol Flynn, Paul Lukas, Jean Sullivan, Lucile Watson, Faye Emerson, James Flavin, Douglass Dumbrille, Dennis Hoey

Uncertain Lady
US 1934 63m bw

An executive wife recovers her husband from the clutches of another woman. Transparent comedy with the principals ill cast. Edward Everett Horton, Genevieve Tobin, Renee Gadd, Paul Cavanagh, Mary Nash. Written by Daniel Evena and Martin Brown, from play by Harry Segal; directed by Karl Freund; for Universal.

Unchained
US 1955 75m bw
Warner / Hall Bartlett

A new governor experiments with a prison without bars.
Decent documentary drama which reaches no great heights.

wd Hall Bartlett, *book* Prisoners Are People by Kenyon J. Scudder *ph* Virgil Miller *m* Alex North

Chester Morris, Elroy Hirsch, Barbara Hale, Todd Duncan, Johnny Johnston, Peggy Knudsen, Jerry Paris, John Qualen

AAN: title song (*m* Alex North, *ly* Hy Zarek)

The Uncle
GB 1964 87m bw

A 7-year-old boy finds he is uncle to a boy the same age. Comedy-drama about the first stirrings of maturity; its failure to find a release got it championed by some critics, but it's essentially a thin piece of work. Rupert Davies, Brenda Bruce, Maurice Denham, Christopher Ariss. Written by Margaret Abrams and Desmond Davis, from her novel; directed by Desmond Davis; for Play-Pix.

Uncle Silas*
GB 1947 103m bw
GFD / Two Cities (Josef Somlo, Laurence Irving)
US title: *The Inheritance*

A young Victorian heiress finds herself menaced by her uncle and his housekeeper.
Slow-starting but superbly made period suspenser; unfortunately the characters are all sticks.

w Ben Travers, *novel* Sheridan Le Fanu *d* Charles Frank

Jean Simmons, Derrick de Marney, Katina Paxinou, Derek Bond, Esmond Knight, Sophie Stewart, Manning Whiley, Reginald Tate, Marjorie Rhodes

Uncommon Valor
US 1983 105m Movielab
Paramount / Ted Kotcheff (John Milius, Buzz Feitshans)

A retired colonel goes looking for his son, declared missing in action in Vietnam, and is helped by a similarly placed industrialist who backs a rescue raid.
Slam-bang action piece with the customary patriotic and personal sentiment.

w Joe Gayton *d* Ted Kotcheff *ph* Stephen H. Burum *m* James Horner *pd* James L. Schoppe

Gene Hackman, Robert Stack, Fred Ward, Reb Brown, Randall Cobb, Patrick Swayze

'Plunging over the falls—lashed at the stake—trapped by savages in the mightiest love-spectacle de Mille ever filmed!'

Unconquered
US 1947 146m Technicolor
Paramount / Cecil B. de Mille

An 18th-century English convict girl is deported to the American colonies and suffers various adventures before marrying a Virginia militiaman.
Cardboard epic, expensive and noisy but totally unpersuasive despite cannon, arrows, fire and dynamite.

w Charles Bennett, Frederic M. Frank, Jesse Lasky Jnr, *novel* Neil H. Swanson *d* Cecil B. de Mille *ph* Ray Rennahan *m* Victor Young

Paulette Goddard, Gary Cooper, Boris Karloff, Howard da Silva, Cecil Kellaway, Ward Bond, Katherine de Mille, Henry Wilcoxon, C. Aubrey Smith, Victor Varconi, Virginia Grey, Porter Hall, Mike Mazurki

'De Mille bangs the drum as loudly as ever but his sideshow has gone cold on us.'—*Richard Winnington*

'A five-million dollar celebration of Gary Cooper's virility, Paulette Goddard's femininity, and the American frontier spirit.'—*Time*

'I bought this woman for my own . . . and I'll kill the man who touches her!'—*publicity*

The Undefeated
US 1969 119m De Luxe Panavision
TCF (Robert L. Jacks)

After the Civil War, two colonels from opposite sides meet on the Rio Grande.
Sprawling, lethargic star western with moments of glory.

w James Lee Barrett *d* Andrew V. McLaglen *ph* William H. Clothier *m* Hugo Montenegro

John Wayne, Rock Hudson, Lee Meriwether, Tony Aguilar, Roman Gabriel

Under a Texas Moon
US 1930 70m Technicolor
Warner

A rancher of the Don Juan type makes hay with the ladies but also rounds up cattle rustlers.
Lightweight early talkie outdoor spectacle with music, not at all memorable.

w Gordon Rigby, Stewart Edward White *d* Michael Curtiz *ph* Bill Rees *songs* Ray Perkins

Frank Fay, Myrna Loy, Raquel Torres, Armida, Noah Beery, George E. Stone, Fred Kohler

'Unusually pleasing western . . . de luxe programmer of its kind.'—*Variety*

Under Capricorn
GB 1949 117m Technicolor
Transatlantic (Sidney Bernstein, Alfred Hitchcock)

In Australia in 1830 an English immigrant stays with his cousin Henrietta, who has become a dipsomaniac because of her husband's cruelty.

Cardboard 'woman's picture' with elements of *Rebecca,* shot with vestiges of Hitch's ten-minute take. A pretty fair disaster.

w James Bridie, *novel* Helen Simpson *d* Alfred Hitchcock *ph* Jack Cardiff, Paul Beeson, Ian Craig *m* Richard Addinsell

Ingrid Bergman, Joseph Cotten, Michael Wilding, Margaret Leighton, Jack Watling, Cecil Parker, Denis O'Dea

Under Cover of Night
US 1937 70m bw

A city detective and his wife nab a murderer. One of many to which this plot might be applied in the wake of The Thin Man, and not a good example. Edmund Lowe, Florence Rice, Henry Daniell, Nat Pendleton, Sara Haden, Dean Jagger, Frank Reicher. Written by Bertram Millhauser; directed by George B. Seitz; for Lucien Hubbard / MGM.

Under Fire*
US 1983 127m Technicolor
Orion / Lion's Gate / Greenberg Brothers (Jonathan Taplin)

War correspondents in Nicaragua become involved in the dirty politics on both sides.
A thinking man's action piece, but no help to anybody in finding the true facts.

w Ron Shelton, Clayton Frohman *d* Roger Spottiswoode *ph* John Alcott *m* Jerry Goldsmith

Gene Hackman, Nick Nolte, Joanna Cassidy, Jean-Louis Trintignant, Ed Harris, Richard Masur, Rene Enriquez

'A complex, genuinely thrilling drama of commitment, the mercenary mentality and the tortuous ironies of history.'—*Sight and Sound*

AAN: Jerry Goldsmith

Under Milk Wood*
GB 1971 88m Technicolor
Timon (Hugo French, Jules Buck)

Life in the Welsh village of Llareggub, as seen by the poet's eye.
Attractive but vaguely unsatisfactory screen rendering of an essentially theatrical event (originally a radio play); everything is much too literal, a real place instead of a fantasy.

wd Andrew Sinclair, *play Dylan Thomas* *ph* Bob Huke *m* Brian Gascoigne

Richard Burton, Elizabeth Taylor, Peter O'Toole, Glynis Johns, Vivien Merchant, Sian Phillips, Victor Spinetti, Rachel Thomas, Angharad Rees, Ann Beach

Under My Skin*
US 1949 86m bw
TCF (Casey Robinson)

A crooked jockey is idolized by his son and finally reforms rather than disillusion the boy.
Hokey sentimental melodrama with racetrack backgrounds.

w Casey Robinson, *short story* My Old Man by Ernest Hemingway *d* Jean Negulesco *ph* Joseph La Shelle *m* Daniele Amfitheatrof

John Garfield, Micheline Presle, Luther Adler, Orley Lindgren, Ann Codee

Under Ten Flags
US 1960 92m bw
Paramount / Dino de Laurentiis

In World War II, a German surface raider in disguise menaces British shipping.
Muddled naval epic with too many allegiances.

w Vittorio Petrilli, Duilio Coletti, Ulrich Mohr, William Douglas Home *d* Duilio Coletti, Silvio Narizzano *ph* Aldo Tonti *m* Nino Rota

Van Heflin, Charles Laughton, John Ericson, Mylène Demongeot, Cecil Parker, Folco Lulli, Alex Nicol, Liam Redmond

Under the Gun
US 1950 83m bw

A racketeer is jailed and tries to escape. Lower-case prison adventure without much conviction. Richard Conte, Audrey Totter, John McIntire, Sam Jaffe, Shepperd Strudwick, Written by George Zuckerman; directed by Ted Tatzlaff; for Universal-International.

Under the Pampas Moon
US 1935 78m bw

A gaucho leader recovers his stolen horse. Amiable modern adventure set in Argentina. Warner Baxter, Ketti Gallian, Rita Hayworth, Jack La Rue, J. Carrol Naish. Written by Ernest Pascal and Bradley King; directed by James Tinling; for Fox.

Under the Rainbow
US 1981 95m colour

Nazis and midgets mingle backstage while *The Wizard of Oz* is being filmed. Zany fantasy which someone must have thought was a good idea. Wrong. Chevy Chase, Carrie Fisher, Billy Barty, Eve Arden, Joseph Maher. Written by Pat McCormick, Harry Hurwitz, Martin Smith, Pat Bradley, Fred Bauer; directed by Steve Rash; for Orion/Warner.
† The film allegedly cost 20 million dollars and took eight.

Under the Red Robe*
GB 1937 82m bw
New World (Robert T. Kane)

A hell-raising nobleman is persuaded by Cardinal Richelieu to unmask the ringleader of an anti-monarchist conspiracy.
Smart, unusual swashbuckler on the lines of *The Prisoner of Zenda,* modestly but quite effectively made.

w Lajos Biro, Philip Lindsay, J. L. Hodson, *novel* Stanley J. Weyman *d Victor Sjostrom* *ph* Georges Périnal

Conrad Veidt, Raymond Massey, Annabella, Romney Brent, Sophie Stewart, Wyndham Goldie, Lawrence Grant

'Gripping meller of swashbuckling era . . . surprisingly fine entertainment.'—*Variety*

Under the Volcano*
US 1984 111m Technicolor
TCF / Ithaca / Michael and Kathy Fitzgerald (Moritz Borman, Wieland Schulz-Keil)

Mexico 1938: the ex-British consul, drinking himself to death, is surprised by a visit from his ex-wife.
A subtle novel has on film become a drunken monologue, fascinating as a *tour de force* but scarcely tolerable after the first half-hour.

w Guy Gallo, *novel* Malcolm Lowry *d* John Huston *ph* Gabriel Figueroa *m* Alex North *pd* Gunther Gerzso

Albert Finney, Jacqueline Bisset, Anthony Andrews, Katy Jurado, James Villiers

'Ultimately one is left not, as in the novel, with a man destroyed by the apocalypse of his own imagination, but with little more than another world-weary cuckold following in the wake of Greene's whisky priest and all those other drunkards who have mooned in Mexico.'—*Tom Milne, MFB*

AAN: Albert Finney; music

Under the Yum Yum Tree
US 1963 110m Eastmancolor
Columbia / Sonnis / Swift (Frederick Brisson)

Two college students have a trial marriage in an apartment block with a lecherous landlord. Coy, non-erotic and extremely tedious comedy which runs out of jokes after reel one.

w Lawrence Roman, David Swift *d* David Swift *ph* Joseph Biroc *m* Frank de Vol

Jack Lemmon, Carol Lynley, Dean Jones, Imogene Coca, Edie Adams, Paul Lynde, Robert Lansing

'Love as burning as Sahara's sands!'

Under Two Flags*
US 1936 111m bw
TCF (Raymond Griffith)

A dashing French Foreign Legionnaire is helped by a café girl.
Despite a highly predictable plot (of *Destry Rides Again)* this was a solidly-produced epic with a nice deployment of star talent.

w W. P. Lipscomb, Walter Ferris, *novel* 'Ouida' *d Frank Lloyd* *ph* Ernest Palmer *m* Louis Silvers

Ronald Colman, Claudette Colbert, Rosalind Russell, Victor McLaglen, J. Edward Bromberg, Nigel Bruce, Herbert Mundin, Gregory Ratoff, C. Henry Gordon, John Carradine, Onslow Stevens

'How Ouida would have loved the abandon of this picture, the thirty-two thousand rounds of ammunition shot off into the Arizona desert, the cast of more than ten thousand, the five thousand pounds which insured the stars against camel bites . . . and, in the words of the programme, a fort two hundred feet square, an Arabian oasis with eight full-sized buildings, a forest of transplanted date palms, two Arabian cities, a horse market and a smaller fort.'—*Graham Greene*

Under Your Hat*
GB 1940 79m bw
Grand National (Jack Hulbert)

Film stars chase spies and recover a stolen carburettor.

UNDER THE VOLCANO. Sombre stuff with a *tour de force* from Albert Finney, here with Jacqueline Bisset and Anthony Andrews.

Light-hearted adaptation of a stage musical, showing the stars in their best film form.

w Rodney Ackland, Anthony Kimmins, *play* Jack Hulbert, Archie Menzies, Geoffrey Kerr, Arthur Macrae *d* Maurice Elvey *ph* Mutz Greenbaum (Max Greene)

Jack Hulbert, Cicely Courtneidge, Austin Trevor, Leonora Corbett, Cecil Parker, H. F. Maltby, Glynis Johns, Charles Oliver

Undercover
GB 1943 80m bw

Yugoslavian partisans fight the Nazis. A rather obviously English cast doesn't help to make this flagwaver convincing. Tom Walls, Michael Wilding, Mary Morris, John Clements, Godfrey Tearle, Robert Harris, Rachel Thomas. Written by John Dighton, Monja Danischewsky, Sergei Nolbandov and Sergei Sokulich; directed by Sergei Nolbandov; for Ealing.

Undercover Girl
US 1950 80m bw

A New York policewoman goes undercover to avenge her father's murder. Rather tedious crime programmer. Alexis Smith, Scott Brady, Richard Egan, Gladys George, Edmon Ryan, Gerald Mohr. Written by Harry Essex; directed by Joseph Pevney; for Universal-International.

Undercover Man
US 1932 74m bw

A man avenges his father's death by going undercover for the FBI and nabbing a bond-stealing gang. Routine gangster thriller with situations well worn even in 1932. George Raft, Nancy Carroll, Roscoe Karns, Gregory Ratoff, Lew Cody. Written by Garrett Fort, Francis Faragoh; directed by James Flood; for Paramount.

Undercover Man*
US 1949 89m bw
Columbia (Robert Rossen)

US treasury agents indict a gang leader for tax evasion.
Good semi-documentary crime melodrama based on the Al Capone case.

w Sidney Boehm, Malvin Wald *d Joseph H. Lewis ph* Burnett Guffey *m* George Duning

Glenn Ford, Nina Foch, Barry Kelley, James Whitmore, David Wolf, Esther Minciotti

Undercurrent*
US 1946 116m bw
MGM (Pandro S. Berman)

A professor's daughter marries an industrialist and is frightened and finally endangered by the mystery surrounding his brother.
Overlong suspenser with solid performances and production values; a variation on *Gaslight.*

w Edward Chodorov, *story* Thelma Strabel *d* Vincente Minnelli *ph* Karl Freund *m* Herbert Stothart

Katharine Hepburn, Robert Taylor, Robert Mitchum, Edmund Gwenn, Marjorie Main, Jayne Meadows, Clinton Sundberg, Dan Tobin

'The indigestible plot, full of false leads and unkept promises, is like a woman's magazine serial consumed at one gulp.'—*Time*

Underground
US 1941 95m bw
Warner (William Jacobs)

Underground leaders in Germany during World War II send out radio messages under the noses of the Nazis.
Forgotten actioner, quite solidly made.

w Charles Grayson *d* Vincent Sherman *ph* Sid Hickox *m* Adolph Deutsch

Jeffrey Lynn, Philip Dorn, Karen Verne, Mona Maris, Frank Reicher, Martin Kosleck, Ilka Gruning

Underground
US 1970 100m De Luxe
UA / Levy–Gardner–Laven

An American paratrooper joins a French resistance group to kidnap a Nazi general.
Routine war actioner.

w Ron Bishop, Andy Lewis *d* Arthur H. Nader *ph* Ken Talbot *m* Stanley Myers

Robert Goulet, Danièle Gaubert, Laurence Dobkin, Carl Duering

Underneath the Arches
US 1937 71m bw

Ship stowaways help to prevent a peace gas from getting into the wrong hands. Moderate star comedy with music. Flanagan and Allen, Stella Moya, Enid Stamp Taylor, Lyn Harding, Edmund Willard, Edward Ashley. Written by H. Fowler Mear; directed by Redd David; for Julius Hagen / Twickenham.

The Underpup
US 1939 81m bw

A slum girl wins a country holiday among rich folk who ignore her. Light comedy-drama with music which seemed about to launch a rival to Deanna Durbin. Gloria Jean, Robert Cummings, Nan Grey, C. Aubrey Smith, Beulah Bondi, Virginia Weidler, Raymond Walburn, Margaret Lindsay. Written by Grover Jones; directed by Richard Wallace; for Joe Pasternak / Universal.

Undersea Kingdom
US 1936 bw serial: 12 eps

At the bottom of the ocean lies Atlantis, where the White Robes are in constant battle with the Black Robes. Slightly hilarious chapter play. Ray 'Crash' Corrigan, Lois Wilde, Monte Blue, William Farnum, Smiley Burnette, Lon Chaney Jnr, Raymond Hatton. Directed by B. Reeves Eason and Joseph Kane; for Republic.

Undertow
US 1949 70m bw

An ex-racketeer proves his innocence when a big-time gambler is murdered. Stock suspense crime story, not at all memorable. Scott Brady, John Russell, Dorothy Hart, Peggy Dow, Bruce Bennett. Written by Arthur T. Horman and Lee Loeb; directed by William Castle; for Universal-International.

Underwater
US 1955 99m Technicolor SuperScope
RKO / Howard Hughes

Treasure hunters dive in the Caribbean for sunken pirate treasure.
Flabby adventure yarn, badly designed for the purpose of showing off its star in a variety of dress and undress.

w Walter Newman, Hugh King, Robert B. Bailey *d* John Sturges *ph* Harry J. Wild, Lamar Boren *m* Roy Webb

Jane Russell, Gilbert Roland, Richard Egan, Lori Nelson, Robert Keith, Joseph Calleia

'This presentation of Miss Russell is like one of those fountain pens guaranteed to write under water—novel, but impractical.'—*Bosley Crowther, New York Times*

Underwater Warrior
US 1958 91m bw Cinemascope

A naval reserve commander trains frogmen. Dry semi-documentary drama, unlikely to win any recruits. Dan Dailey, Ross Martin, James Gregory, Claire Kelly. Written by Gene Levitt; directed by Andrew Marton; for Ivan Tors / MGM.

'Revolvers bark! Figures steal slowly among the shadows of the night! Then all is still . . . That's just a bit of the underworld!'

'It takes you to the haunts of the human birds of prey, to the refuge of the hunted!'

Underworld*
US 1927 82m (24 fps) bw silent
Paramount (Hector Turnbull)
GB title: *Paying the Penalty*

A gangster is rescued from prison by his moll and his lieutenant, and when he realizes they are in love he allows them to escape when the law closes in.
An innovative film in its time, this melodrama was the first to look at crime from the gangsters' point of view. Its main appeal now lies in its lush direction.

w Ben Hecht, Robert N. Lee, Josef Von Sternberg *d* Josef Von Sternberg *ph* Bert Glennon *ad* Hans Dreier

George Bancroft, Evelyn Brent, Clive Brook, Larry Semon

† The film was a great international success and had an influence on the pessimistic French school of the thirties.

AA: Ben Hecht

Underworld
GB 1985 100m colour

A mad doctor keeps his mutants underground. H. G. Wells up to date, but none the better for it. Denholm Elliott, Steven Berkoff, Larry Lamb, Miranda Richardson, Art Malik, Ingrid Pitt. Written by Clive Barker, James Caplin; directed by George Pavlou; for Limehouse / Green Man.

Underworld USA*
US 1960 99m bw
Columbia / Globe (Samuel Fuller)

A young gangster takes elaborate revenge for the killing of his father.
Violent syndicate melodrama with a semi-documentary veneer and some brutal scenes. Well done but heavy going.

wd Samuel Fuller ph Hal Mohr m Harry Sukman

Cliff Robertson, Beatrice Kay, Larry Gates, Dolores Dorn, *Robert Emhardt,* Paul Dubov, Richard Rust

'Savage! Sinister! Supernatural! The black fury of a werewolf—sacrificing life and love to the maddening evil that drove him to the most monstrous murders man ever committed!'

The Undying Monster*
US 1943 63m bw
TCF
GB title: *The Hammond Mystery*

A curse hangs over the English ancestral home of the Hammonds.
Silly but well-photographed and directed minor horror on wolf man lines.

w Lillie Hayward, Michel Jacoby, *novel* Jessie D. Kerruish *d John Brahm ph Lucien Ballard m* Emil Newman, David Raksin

James Ellison, John Howard, Heather Angel, Bramwell Fletcher, Heather Thatcher, Eily Malyon, Halliwell Hobbes, Aubrey Mather

THE FAMILY CURSE:
When stars are bright
On a frosty night,
Beware thy bane
On the rocky lane.

Unearthly Stranger*
GB 1963 75m bw
Independent Artists (Julian Wintle, Leslie Parkyn, Albert Fennell)

Scientists working on a time-space formula find that the bride of one of them is an alien in search of their secret.
Surprisingly effective minor science fiction, in some ways all the better for its modest, TV-style production values.

w Rex Carlton d John Krish ph Reg Wyer *m* Edward Williams

John Neville, Gabriella Licudi, Philip Stone, Jean Marsh, Patrick Newell, Warren Mitchell

Uneasy Terms
GB 1948 91m bw

Detective Slim Callaghan proves that a blackmail victim is not a murderer. The film which proved that the British simply can't make crime movies on the American model. Michael Rennie, Moira Lister, Faith Brook, Joy Shelton, Nigel Patrick, Paul Carpenter, Barry Jones. Written by Peter Cheyney, from his novel; directed by Vernon Sewell; for British National.

Unexpected Father
US 1939 78m bw

A dancer looks after his late partner's baby. Genial comedy introducing a baby star who was popular until she got out of diapers. Baby Sandy, Mischa Auer, Dennis O'Keefe, Shirley Ross, Mayo Methot. Written by Leonard Spiegelgass and Charles Grayson; directed by Charles Lamont; for Universal. (GB title: *Sandy Takes a Bow.*)

Unexpected Uncle
US 1941 67m bw

An elderly steel tycoon gives everything up to become a tramp and play Cupid. Money-is-not-everything fable, entirely dependent on amiable performances. Charles Coburn, Anne Shirley, James Craig, Ernest Truex, Russell Gleason, Jed Prouty. Written by Delmer Daves and Noel Langley, from the novel by Eric Hatch; directed by Peter Godfrey; for RKO.

The Unfaithful*
US 1947 109m bw
Warner (Jerry Wald)

A wife gets involved in a murder while her husband is out of town.
Glossy romantic melodrama, an unofficial remake of *The Letter*.

w David Goodis, James Gunn *d* Vincent Sherman *ph* Ernest Haller *m* Max Steiner

Ann Sheridan, Zachary Scott, Lew Ayres, Eve Arden, Steve Geray, Jerome Cowan, John Hoyt

'If she were yours, would you forgive?'—*publicity*

Unfaithfully Yours**
US 1948 105m bw
TCF (Preston Sturges)

An orchestral conductor believes his wife is unfaithful, and while conducting a concert thinks of three different ways of dealing with the situation.
A not entirely happy mixture of romance, farce, melodrama and wit, but in general a pretty entertaining concoction and the last major film of its talented writer-director.

wd Preston Sturges ph Victor Milner *m* Alfred Newman

Rex Harrison, Linda Darnell, Barbara Lawrence, Rudy Vallee, Kurt Kreuger, Lionel Stander, *Edgar Kennedy, Al Bridge*, Julius Tannen, Torben Meyer, Robert Greig

'Harrison discovers more ways of tripping over a telephone cable than one can count, and his efforts to falsify evidence through a recalcitrant tape recorder are as funny as anything thought up by Clair in *A Nous La Liberté* or by Chaplin in *Modern Times*.'—*Basil Wright, 1972*

† The Rex Harrison character is named Sir Alfred de Carter and is meant to be Sir Thomas Beecham. (In America the equivalent of Beecham's Pills is Carter's Little Liver Pills.)

†† The pieces of music played are as follows:
For murder: the Semiramide Overture by Rossini
For surrender: the Venusberg music from *Tannhäuser*, by Wagner
For Russian roulette: Francesca da Rimini by Tchaikovsky

Unfaithfully Yours
US 1983 96m De Luxe
TCF (Marvin Worth, Joe Wizan)

Modernized and simplified version of the above, with only one plot instead of three. This proves to be an advantage, and the film does deliver some laughs.

w Valerie Curtin, Barry Levinson, Robert Klane *d* Howard Zieff *ph* David M. Walsh *m* Bill Conti *pd* Albert Brenner

Dudley Moore, Nastassia Kinski, Armand Assante, Albert Brooks, Cassie Yates, Richard Libertini, Richard B. Shull

Unfinished Business
US 1941 95m bw
Universal (Gregory La Cava)

A wife has thoughts that she should have married her husband's brother.
Smooth but disappointing romantic comedy; the detail is good enough, but it sadly lacks drive.

w Eugene Thackery *d* Gregory La Cava *ph* Joseph Valentine *m* Franz Waxman

Irene Dunne, Robert Montgomery, Eugene Pallette, Preston Foster, Walter Catlett, June Clyde, Phyllis Barry, Esther Dale, Samuel S. Hinds

'Once sentiment gets the upper hand, reach for the exit.'—*Otis Ferguson*

The Unfinished Dance
US 1947 101m Technicolor
MGM (Joe Pasternak)

The young star of a ballet school becomes jealous of a talented newcomer, and causes her injury in an accident.
The delicacies of the French original, *La Mort du Cygne*, give way to standard Hollywood hokum and produce an accomplished but totally uninteresting film.

w Myles Connolly, *story* Paul Morand *d* Henry Koster *ph* Robert Surtees *md* Herbert Stothart

Margaret O'Brien, Cyd Charisse, Karin Booth, Danny Thomas, Esther Dale

'The same old story, with pathos, humour and ballet substituted for pathos, humour and chorus girls.'—*MFB*

The Unforgiven*
US 1960 125m Technicolor Panavision
UA / James Productions / Hecht–Hill–Lancaster (James Hill)

A rancher's daughter is suspected of being an Indian orphan, and violence results.
Good-looking, expensive but muddled racist western, hard to enjoy.

w Ben Maddow, *novel* Alan le May *d* John Huston *ph Franz Planer m* Dmitri Tiomkin

Burt Lancaster, Audrey Hepburn, Audie Murphy, Lillian Gish, Charles Bickford, Doug McClure, John Saxon, Joseph Wiseman, Albert Salmi

'How much strain can a director's reputation take? Of late, John Huston seems to have been trying to find out. I think he has carried the experiment too far with *The Unforgiven* . . . a work of profound phoniness, part adult western, part that *Oklahoma!* kind of folksy Americana.'—*Dwight MacDonald*

'Ludicrous . . . a hodgepodge of crudely stitched sententiousness and lame story-conference inspirations.'—*Stanley Kauffmann*

The Unguarded Hour*
US 1936 87m bw

A blackmailed woman has evidence to free a man accused of murder, but dare not reveal it.
Twisty suspense thriller with a rather splendid cast. Franchot Tone, Loretta Young, Roland Young, Henry Daniell, Jessie Ralph, Lewis Stone, Dudley Digges, E. E. Clive, Robert Greig, Aileen Pringle. Written by Howard Emmett Rogers and Leon Gordon, from the play by Ladislas Fodor / Bernard Merivale; directed by Sam Wood; for MGM.

The Unguarded Moment
US 1956 85m Technicolor
U-I (Gordon Kay)

A schoolmistress who receives anonymous love notes from a psychotic pupil is discredited by his even more unbalanced father.
Well-meaning but boring melodrama with the star attractively out of her usual element.

w Herb Meadow, Larry Marcus, *story* Rosalind Russell *d* Harry Keller *ph* William Daniels *m* Herman Stein

Esther Williams, George Nader, John Saxon, *Edward Andrews*, Jack Albertson

The Unholy Garden
US 1931 75m bw
Samuel Goldwyn

A gentleman thief hides out in a North African den of misfits.
Would-be romantic nonsense, much less interesting than its credits.

w Ben Hecht, Charles MacArthur *d* George Fitzmaurice *ph* Gregg Toland, George Barnes *m* Alfred Newman

Ronald Colman, Fay Wray, Estelle Taylor, Tully Marshall, Warren Hymer, Mischa Auer, Henry Armetta, Lawrence Grant

'Splendid presentation of an ordinary story.'—*Variety*

The Unholy Night
US 1929 94m bw

A strangler is caught in the London fog.
Clumsy and talkative early talkie, chiefly interesting for its cast. Lionel Barrymore, Roland Young, Boris Karloff, John Loder, Natalie Moorhead, Ernest Torrence, Polly Moran, John Miljan. Written by Ben Hecht; directed by Lionel Barrymore; for MGM.

Unholy Partners*
US 1941 95m bw
MGM (Samuel Marx)

The editor of a sensational newspaper has to accept finance from a gangster, but friction results when the newspaper exposes some of the gangster's activities.
Agreeable twenties melodrama with two solid stars battling it out.

w Earl Baldwin, Lesser Samuels, Bartlett Cormack *d* Mervyn Le Roy *ph* George Barnes *m* David Snell

Edward G. Robinson, Edward Arnold, Laraine Day, Marsha Hunt, William T. Orr, Don Beddoe, Charles Dingle, Walter Kingsford, Marcel Dalio

The Unholy Three*
US 1925 76m approx (24 fps) bw silent
MGM

A ventriloquist, a dwarf and a strong man carry out a series of crimes which end in murder.
Curious melodrama which set its star and director off on a series of seven more and even weirder eccentricities.

w Waldemar Young, *story* Clarence Robbins *d* Tod Browning *ph* David Kesson

Lon Chaney, Harry Earles, Victor McLaglen, Mae Busch, Matt Moore

The Unholy Three*
US 1930 74m bw

Remake of the above. The star's only talkie—he died before it was released—is less effective than the silent version. *Lon Chaney*, Lila Lee, Harry Earles, Ivan Linow, Elliott Nugent, John Miljan. Written by J. C. and Elliott Nugent from the novel by Clarence Robbins; directed by Jack Conway; for MGM.

The Unholy Wife
US 1957 94m Technicolor RKOscope
RKO / Treasure

A bored wife shoots a friend in mistake for her husband but is sentenced for the accidental death of her mother-in-law.
Totally uninteresting melodrama in the *Double Indemnity* style, professionally made but turgid.

w Jonathan Latimer *d* John Farrow *ph* Lucien Ballard *m* Daniele Amfitheatrof

Diana Dors, Rod Steiger, Tom Tryon, Beulah Bondi, Marie Windsor, Arthur Franz, Luis Van Rooten

'A love haunted by nameless evil which fought to live in their hearts!'
The Uninvited**
US 1944 98m bw
Paramount (Charles Brackett)

A girl returns to her family house and is haunted by her mother's spirit, which seems to be evil.
One of the cinema's few genuine ghost stories, and a good one, though encased in a rather stiff production; it works up to a fine pitch of frenzy.

w Dodie Smith, novel Uneasy Freehold by Dorothy Macardle *d Lewis Allen ph* Charles Lang *m* Victor Young

Ray Milland, Ruth Hussey, *Gail Russell*, Donald Crisp, Cornelia Otis Skinner, Dorothy Stickney, Barbara Everest, Alan Napier

'It will hold audiences glued to their seats.'—*Variety*

'It sets out to give you the shivers—and will do so, if you're readily disposed.'—*New York Times*

'I experienced thirty-five first class jolts, not to mention a well calculated texture of minor frissons.'—*Nation*

'Still manages to ice the blood with its implied horrors . . . you can almost smell the ghostly mimosa.'—*Peter John Dyer, 1966*

'A superior and satisfying shocker.'—*Newsweek*

† British critics of the time congratulated the director on not showing the ghosts: in fact the visible manifestations had been cut by the British censor.

AAN: Charles Lang

Union Depot
US 1932 68m bw

The fortunes of several people clash in a railway station. Pale but moderately interesting imitation of *Grand Hotel*. Douglas Fairbanks Jnr, Joan Blondell, Alan Hale, Frank McHugh, George Rosener, Guy Kibbee, David Landau. Written by Kenyon Nicholson and Walter De Leon, from the play by Gene Fowler, Douglas Durkin and Joe Laurie; directed by Alfred E. Green; for Warner. (GB title: *Gentleman for a Day*.)

Union Pacific**
US 1939 133m bw
Paramount / Cecil B. de Mille

Indians and others cause problems for the railroad builders.
Standard big-scale western climaxing in a spectacular wreck; not exactly exciting, but very watchable.

w Walter de Leon, C. Gardner Sullivan, Jesse Lasky Jnr *d Cecil B. de Mille ph* Victor Milner, Dewey Wrigley *m* John Leipold, Sigmund Krumgold *ad* Hans Dreier, Roland Anderson

Barbara Stanwyck, Joel McCrea, Akim Tamiroff, Robert Preston, Lynne Overman, Brian Donlevy, Robert Barrat, Anthony Quinn, Stanley Ridges, Henry Kolker, Evelyn Keyes, Regis Toomey

'A socko spectacular, surefire for big grosses right down the line.'—*Variety*

'This latest de Mille epic contains all the excelsior qualities we expect of his work—that sense of a Salvationist drum beating round the next corner—but it is never as funny as *The Crusades* and he has lost his touch with crowds.'—*Graham Greene*

'Excitement is the dominant emotion, with swift succession of contrasting materials and episodes, grim and gay, often furious, sometimes funny. The narrative and action take hold at the start and never let go.'—*Motion Picture Herald*

'The largest conglomeration of thrills and cold-blooded murder since Pauline was in peril.'—*Brooklyn Daily Eagle*

'A movie in the old tradition, melodramatic and breathtaking and altogether wonderful.'—*Photoplay*

† De Mille's last picture in black and white.

Union Station**
US 1950 80m bw
Paramount (Jules Schermer)

Kidnappers nominate a crowded railroad station as their ransom collection point.
Compelling little thriller modelled after *Naked City*, with real locations and plenty of excitement.

w Sidney Boehm, *novel* Thomas Walsh *d Rudolph Maté ph* Daniel L. Fapp *m* David Buttolph, Heinz Roemheld *md* Irvin Talbot

William Holden, *Barry Fitzgerald*, Nancy Olson, *Lyle Bettger*, Jan Sterling, Allene Roberts

Universal Soldier
GB 1971 96m colour
Appaloosa / Ionian (Frank J. Schwarz, Donald L. Factor)

A mercenary returns to London but can't escape his past.
Solemnly meaningful melodrama on a tight budget.

wd Cy Endfield *ph* Tony Imi *m* Philip Goodhand-Tait

George Lazenby, Edward Judd, Benito Carruthers, Germaine Greer, Rudolph Walker

The Unknown
US 1927 65m bw silent

A fake armless wonder has his arms amputated to please a girl who can't stand the touch of a man's hand. (She then changes her mind.) Weird melodrama which even this contortionist star can't save. Lon Chaney, Joan Crawford, Norman Kerry. Written by Waldemar Young; directed by Tod Browning; for MGM.

The Unknown
US 1946 70m bw

An amnesiac heiress returns to her family mansion. Twisty creeper in the *I Love a Mystery* series; not bad for a second feature. Karen Morley, Jeff Donnell, Jim Bannon. Written by Malcolm Stuart Boylan and Julian Harmon; directed by Henry Levin; for Columbia.

The Unknown Guest
US 1943 61m bw

A supposedly no-good young man is suspected of murdering his aunt and uncle. Rather tedious and silly mystery with little happening. Victor Jory, Pamela Blake, Harry Hayden, Veda Ann Borg, Nora Cecil. Written by Philip Yordan; directed by Kurt Neumann; for Maurice King / Monogram.

The Unknown Man
US 1951 86m bw
MGM (Robert Thomsen)

A civil court lawyer of high principles successfully undertakes a criminal case, finds his client was really guilty, and sets matters straight.
Contrived but entertaining morality with standard production and performances.

w Ronald Millar, George Froeschel *d* Richard Thorpe *ph* William Mellor *m* Conrad Salinger

Walter Pidgeon, Ann Harding, Lewis Stone, Barry Sullivan, Keefe Brasselle, Eduard Franz, Richard Anderson, Dawn Addams

Unman, Wittering and Zigo
GB 1971 102m colour
Paramount / Mediarts (Gareth Wigan)

A nervous schoolmaster discovers that his predecessor was murdered by the boys.
Macabre school story which overreaches itself and peters out.

w Simon Raven, *TV play* Giles Cooper *d* John Mackenzie *ph* Geoffrey Unsworth *m* Michael J. Lewis

David Hemmings, Douglas Wilmer, Hamilton Dyce, Carolyn Seymour

Unmarried
US 1939 66m bw

An ex-boxer, shy of marriage, raises an orphan boy. Modest domestic drama notable as one of the rare non-western appearances of its star. Buck Jones, Donald O'Connor, Helen Twelvetrees. Written by Lillie Hayward, Brian Marlow and Grover Jones; directed by Kurt Nuemann; for Paramount. (GB title: *Night Club Hostess*.)

An Unmarried Woman*
US 1978 124m Movielab
TCF (Paul Mazursky, Tony Ray)

A sophisticated New York woman is deserted by her husband, fights with her daughter, and takes up with two men.
Frank, well observed depiction of one woman in New York's new society; as modern as all get out but not very attractive.

wd Paul Mazursky ph Arthur J. Ornitz *m* Bill Conti *ph* Pato Guzman

Jill Clayburgh, Alan Bates, Michael Murphy, Cliff Gorman, Pat Quinn, Kelly Bishop

AAN: best picture; script; Jill Clayburgh

Unpublished Story
GB 1942 91m bw
Columbia / Two Cities (Anthony Havelock-Allan)

A reporter exposes the Nazis behind a pacifist organization.
Ho-hum formula flagwaver with generally stilted production.

w Anatole de Grunwald, Patrick Kirwan *d* Harold French *ph* Bernard Knowles *m* Nicholas Brodzky

Valerie Hobson, Richard Greene, Basil Radford, Roland Culver, Brefni O'Rourke, Miles Malleson, George Carney, André Morell

The Unseen
US 1945 82m bw
Paramount

A London governess comes to suspect that dark deeds have taken place in the empty house next door.
Period suspenser with good atmosphere but an insubstantial plot.

w Hagar Wilde, Raymond Chandler *d* Lewis Allen *ph* John Seitz *m* Ernst Toch

Joel McCrea, Gail Russell, Herbert Marshall, Richard Lyon, Nona Griffith
† The film seems to have been a hurried attempt to repeat and combine the previous year's success, *Gaslight* and *The Uninvited*.

The Unsinkable Molly Brown*
US 1964 128m Metrocolor Panavision
MGM / Marten (Lawrence Weingarten)

Western orphan Molly Brown grows up determined to become a member of Denver society.
Semi-western comedy-musical about a real lady who wound up surviving the *Titanic*. Bouncy and likeable but not at all memorable.

w Helen Deutsch, *musical play* Richard Morris *d* Charles Walters *ph* Daniel L. Fapp *md* Robert Armbruster *ad* George W. Davis, Preston Ames

Debbie Reynolds, Harve Presnell, *Ed Begley*, Jack Krischen, Hermione Baddeley, Martita Hunt

AAN: Daniel L. Fapp; Robert Armbruster; Debbie Reynolds

The Unsuspected*
US 1947 103m bw
Warner (Charles Hoffman)

A writer-producer of radio crime shows commits a murder and is forced to follow the clues on air.
Sleek, new look mystery thriller with a disappointing plot which gives its interesting cast little to do, and allows itself to peter out in chases.

w Ranald MacDougall, *novel* Charlotte Armstrong *d Michael Curtiz ph Woody Bredell m* Franz Waxman *ad* Anton Grot

Claude Rains, Joan Caulfield, Audrey Totter, Constance Bennett, Michael North, Hurd Hatfield, Fred Clark

Untamed
US 1940 83m Technicolor
Paramount (Paul Jones)

A doctor in the frozen north is beset by an epidemic as well as natural hazards.
Old-fashioned melodrama which found an eager audience.

w Frederick Hazlitt Brennan, Frank Butler, *novel* Mantrap by Sinclair Lewis *d* George Archainbaud *ph* Leo Tover, W. Howard Greene *m* Victor Young

Ray Milland, Patricia Morison, Akim Tamiroff, William Frawley, Jane Darwell, Esther Dale, J. M. Kerrigan, Eily Malyon
† A remake of Clara Bow's 1926 film *Mantrap*.

Untamed
US 1955 109m Technicolor Cinemascope
TCF (Bert E. Friedlob, William A. Bacher)

A Dutchman and an Irish girl meet again on a Boer trek to South Africa, and survive Zulu attacks.
A long and involved epic-style plot provides standard excitements and predictable romantic complications.

w Talbot Jennings, Michael Blankfort, Frank Fenton, *novel* Helga Moray *d* Henry King *ph* Leo Tover *m* Franz Waxman

Tyrone Power, Susan Hayward, Richard Egan, John Justin, Agnes Moorehead, Rita Moreno, Hope Emerson, Brad Dexter, Henry O'Neill
'A not unenjoyable essay in hokum.'—*MFB*

Untamed Frontier
US 1952 78m Technicolor
U-I (Leonard Goldstein)

The son of an unpopular Texan landowner commits murder.
Stolid minor western.

w Gerald Drayson Adams, Gwen and John Bagni *d* Hugo Fregonese *ph* Charles P. Boyle *m* Hans Salter

Joseph Cotten, Shelley Winters, Scott Brady, Suzan Ball, Minor Watson

Until They Sail
US 1957 95m bw Cinemascope
MGM (Charles Schnee)

Four New Zealand sisters have wartime romances.
Solid 'woman's picture', well enough presented.

w Robert Anderson, *novel* James A. Michener *d* Robert Wise *ph* Joseph Ruttenberg *m* David Raksin

Jean Simmons, Joan Fontaine, Paul Newman, Piper Laurie, Charles Drake, Wally Cassell, Sandra Dee

The Untouchables**
US 1987 119m Technicolor
Paramount / Art Linson

Law enforcers in 20s Chicago go after Al Capone and other mobsters.
The long-running tv show is given a new polish in this showy, violent gangster picture, which seemed to please all classes.

w David Marnet *d Brian De Palma ph* Stephen H. Burum *m* Ennio Morricone *pd* Patrizia Von Brandenstein *ed* Jerry Greenberg, Bill Pankow

Kevin Costner, *Sean Connery*, *Robert De Niro*, Charles Martin Smith, Andy Garcia, Richard Bradford
'Time honoured mayhem in the windy city.'—*Time Out*

AA: Sean Connery
AAN: Ennio Morricone; art direction (William A. Elliott); costume design (Marilyn Vance-Straker)

Up for the Cup
GB 1931 76m bw

A Yorkshireman gets into trouble when he comes to London for the Cup Final. Slap-happy star farce which pleased the public. Sydney Howard, Joan Wyndham, Stanley Kirk, Sam Livesey, Moore Marriott. Written by Con West, R. P. Weston and Bert Lee; directed by Jack Raymond; for Herbert Wilcox / B and D. (The same star appeared in *Up for the Derby* in the following year; and in 1950 the original, with much the same script, was refashioned for Albert Modley; it was also directed by Jack Raymond.)

'A lone American sergeant on the most impossible mission of the war!'

Up from the Beach*
US 1965 98m bw Cinemascope
TCF / Panoramic (Christian Ferry)

Just after D-Day, GIs have trouble in a Normandy village.
A kind of subdued sequel to *The Longest Day*, well made for war action addicts, but barely memorable.

w Stanley Mann, Claude Brule, *novel* Epitaph for an Enemy by George Barr *d Robert Parrish ph Walter Wottitz m* Edgar Cosma

Cliff Robertson, Red Buttons, Françoise Rosay, Marius Goring, Irina Demick, Broderick Crawford, James Robertson Justice, Slim Pickens

Up in Arms**
US 1944 106m Technicolor
Samuel Goldwyn

A hypochondriac joins the army.
Loose, generally pleasant introductory vehicle for Danny Kaye.

w Don Hartman, Robert Pirosh, Allen Boretz *d* Elliott Nugent *ph* Ray Rennahan *md* Ray Heindorf, Louis Forbes

Danny Kaye, Dinah Shore, Constance Dowling, Dana Andrews, Louis Calhern, Lyle Talbot
'Not since Greta Garbo made her bow has there been anything so terrific as the inimitable Danny, one of the most exhilarating and spontaneous personalities in film history.'—*New York Daily Mirror*

AAN: song 'Now I Know' (*m* Harold Arlen, *ly* Ted Koehler); Ray Heindorf, Louis Forbes

Up in Central Park
US 1948 88m bw
U-I (Karl Tunberg)

In turn-of-the-century New York, an Irish girl becomes involved in a crooked political set up. Stiff and unyielding star musical.

w Karl Tunberg *d* William A. Seiter *ph* Milton Krasner *songs* Sigmund Romberg *md* John Green

Deanna Durbin, Vincent Price, Dick Haymes, Albert Sharpe, Tom Powers

Up in Mabel's Room
US 1944 77m bw

A flustered professor has to retrieve incriminating evidence from an old flame's room. Antediluvian bedroom farce which keeps several ardent practitioners working happily. Dennis O'Keefe, Mischa Auer, Marjorie Reynolds, Gail Patrick. Written by Tom Reed from the play by Wilson Collinson and Otto Harbach; directed by Allan Dwan; for Edward Small. 'As horrible, and wonderful, as watching a Gopher Prairie dramatic club play a mail order farce (6m, 6f).'—*James Agee.*

AAN: editing (Edward Paul)

Up in the Cellar
US 1970 94m Movielab
AIP (William J. Immerman)

A dejected freshman tries various schemes to revenge himself on the college president. Youth satire aimed at a number of targets which quickly became obsolete; mildly interesting sociologically.

wd Theodore J. Flicker, *novel* The Late Boy Wonder by Angus Hall *ph* Earl Roth *m* Don Randi

Wes Stern, Joan Collins, Larry Hagman, Judy Pace

Up in the World
GB 1956 91m bw
Rank (Hugh Stewart)

A window cleaner becomes friendly with a boy millionaire.
Slow and unattractive comedy star vehicle.

w Jack Davies, Henry Blyth, Peter Blackmore *d* John Paddy Carstairs *ph* Jack Cox *m* Philip Green

Norman Wisdom, Martin Caridia, Jerry Desmonde, Maureen Swanson, Ambrosine Philpotts, Colin Gordon

Up Periscope
US 1959 111m Technicolor Warnerscope
Warner / Lakeside (Aubrey Schenck)

During World War II a submarine frogman is landed on a Pacific island to steal a Japanese code book.
Stock adventure story given stock presentation.

w Richard Landau, *novel* Robb White *d* Gordon Douglas *ph* Carl Guthrie *m* Ray Heindorf

James Garner, Edmond O'Brien, Alan Hale Jnr, Carleton Carpenter

Up Pompeii
GB 1971 90m Technicolor

A wily slave outwits Nero and escapes the eruption of Vesuvius.
Yawnmaking spinoff of a lively TV comedy series: the jokes just lie there, and die there.

w Sid Colin *d* Bob Kellett *ph* Ian Wilson *m* Carl Davis

Frankie Howerd, Patrick Cargill, Michael Hordern, Barbara Murray, Lance Percival, Bill Fraser, Adrienne Posta
† Sequels: *Up the Front, Up the Chastity Belt* (qv).

Up Pops the Devil
US 1931 74m bw

A wife supports her husband so that he can write novels. Odd little comedy-drama which struck most people as rather half-hearted. Carole Lombard, Norman Foster, Skeets Gallagher, Stuart Erwin, Lilyan Tashman. Written by Arthur Kober, Eve Unsell, from the play by Frances Goodrich and Albert Hackett; directed by A. Edward Sutherland; for Paramount. 'Here's a plenty satisfying strip of celluloid but it won't do any drawing unless it's by word-of-mouth advertising.'—*Variety*

Up the Chastity Belt*
GB 1971 94m Technicolor
EMI / Associated London Films (Ned Sherrin)

Medieval adventures of the serf Lurkalot and his master Sir Coward de Custard.
Patchy pantomime which doesn't always have the courage of its own slapdash vulgarity.

w Sid Colin, Ray Galton, Alan Simpson *d* Bob Kellett *ph* Ian Wilson *m* Carl Davis

Frankie Howerd, Graham Crowden, Bill Fraser, Roy Hudd, Hugh Paddick, Anna Quayle, Eartha Kitt, Dave King, Fred Emney

Up the Creek*
GB 1958 83m bw Hammerscope
Byron (Henry Halsted)

A none-too-bright naval lieutenant is assigned command of a broken-down shore establishment.
Cheeky remake of *Oh Mr Porter*. Jokes fair, atmosphere cheerful and easy-going.

wd Val Guest *ph* Arthur Grant

David Tomlinson, Peter Sellers, Wilfrid Hyde White, Vera Day, Tom Gill, Michael Goodliffe, Reginald Beckwith, Lionel Jeffries
† Sequel: *Further Up the Creek.*

Up the Down Staircase*
US 1967 124m Technicolor
Warner / Pakula–Mulligan

Problems of a schoolteacher in one of New York's tough sections.
Earnest, well-acted, not very likeable melodrama.

w Tad Mosel, *novel* Bel Kaufman *d* Robert Mulligan *ph* Joseph Coffey *m* Fred Karlin

Sandy Dennis, Patrick Bedford, Eileen Heckart, Ruth White, Jean Stapleton, Sorrel Booke, Roy Poole

'Sandy Dennis, blinking as if she'd taken pills and been awakened in the middle of the night. She reacts confusedly before the situations even develop, but the audience is ahead of her anyway.'—*Pauline Kael, New Yorker*

Up the Front
GB 1972 89m Technicolor
EMI / Associated London Films (Ned Sherrin)

A footman is hypnotized into enlisting in World War I and has an enemy 'plan' tattooed on his buttocks.
Threadbare end-of-the-pier romp.

w Sid Colin, Eddie Braben *d* Bob Kellett *ph* Tony Spratling *m* Patrick Greenwell *ad* Seamus Flannery

Frankie Howerd, Bill Fraser, Zsa Zsa Gabor, Stanley Holloway, Hermione Baddeley, Robert Coote, Lance Percival, Dora Bryan

'Don't get caught is what she wasn't taught!'

Up the Junction
GB 1967 119m Techniscope
Paramount / BHE (Anthony Havelock–Allan, John Brabourne)

A well-off girl crosses London's river to live among the workers of Clapham.
Socially obsolete sensationalism based on a television semi-documentary. An irritating heroine moves hygienically among motorbikes

w Roger Smith, *book* Nell Dunn *d* Peter Collinson *ph* Arthur Lavis *m* Mike Hugg, Manfred Mann

Suzy Kendall, Dennis Waterman, Adrienne Posta, Maureen Lipman, Michael Gothard, Liz Fraser, Hylda Baker, Alfie Bass

Up the River
US 1930 80m bw
Fox

An ex-convict is threatened with exposure, but his two pals escape to help him.
Very minor comedy with interesting credits.

w Maurine Watkins *d* John Ford *ph* Joseph August

Spencer Tracy, Warren Hymer, Claire Luce, Humphrey Bogart, William Collier Snr

'No cast names to draw, but if the exploitation can make 'em attend, the film will meet its entertainment obligations.'—*Variety*

† In 1938 TCF released a remake directed by Alfred Werker, with Preston Foster, Tony Martin, Slim Summerville and Arthur Treacher.

Up the Sandbox
US 1972 98m Technicolor
Barwood / First Artists (Robert Chartoff, Irwin Winkler)

A professor's wife finds she is pregnant again and fantasizes about her future life.
Muddled comedy-drama with little point and less entertainment value.

w Paul Zindel, *novel* Anne Richardson Roiphe *d* Irwin Kershner *ph* Gordon Willis, Andy Marton *m* Billy Goldenberg *ad* Harry Horner

Barbra Streisand, David Selby, Ariane Heller, Jane Hoffman

'A magical mystery tour through the picture book mind of one Manhattan housewife.'—*Richard Combs*

Up Tight
US 1968 104m Technicolor
Paramount / Marlukin (Jules Dassin)

A black street cleaner betrays his criminal pals for money and is hunted down by them.
Ponderous black remake of *The Informer*, too schematic to make any dramatic or human impression.

w Jules Dassin, Ruby Dee, Julian Mayfield *d* Jules Dassin *ph Boris Kaufman* *m* Booker T. Jones *pd* Alexander Trauner

Raymond St Jacques, Ruby Dee, Julian Mayfield, Frank Silvera, Roscoe Lee Browne, Juanita Moore

Upperworld
US 1934 75m bw

A society-conscious wife drives her husband into the arms of a girl from the Bronx. Smooth romantic melodrama with a murder angle; dated but enjoyable. Warren William, Mary Astor, Ginger Rogers, Andy Devine, J. Carrol Naish, Henry O'Neill. Written by Ben Markson, from a story by Ben Hecht; directed by Roy del Ruth; for Warner.

Upstairs and Downstairs
GB 1959 101m Eastmancolor
Rank (Betty E. Box)

Newlyweds have trouble with maids and au pair girls.
Glossy, cheerful, empty-headed domestic comedy.

w Frank Harvey, *novel* Ronald Scott Thorn *d* Ralph Thomas *ph* Ernest Steward

Michael Craig, Anne Heywood, Mylène Demongeot, James Robertson Justice, Sidney James, Daniel Massey, Claudia Cardinale, Joan Hickson, Joan Sims

Uptown Saturday Night*
US 1974 104m Technicolor
Warner / Verdon / First Artists (Melville Tucker)

Three friends pursue crooks who have inadvertently stolen a winning lottery ticket.
Witless but high-spirited star comedy for blacks, with a variety of sordid backgrounds.

w Richard Wesley *d* Sidney Poitier *ph* Fred J. Koenekamp *m* Tom Scott

Sidney Poitier, Bill Cosby, Harry Belafonte, Flip Wilson, Roscoe Lee Browne, Richard Pryor, Rosalind Cash, Paula Kelly

'If it had been filmed with a white cast this collection of atrophied comedy routines would have been indistinguishable from a Monogram farce of the forties.'—*David McGillivray*

The Upturned Glass*
GB 1947 86m bw
GFD / Triton (Sydney Box, James Mason)

A Harley Street surgeon murders the woman responsible for the death of the girl he loved.
Rather pointless psychopathology with an ill-explained title; an interesting example of a top star not knowing what's best for him.

w Jon P. Monaghan, Pamela Kellino *d* Lawrence Huntington *ph* Reg Wyer *m* Bernard Stevens

James Mason, Pamela Kellino, Rosamund John, Ann Stephens, Henry Oscar, Morland Graham, Brefni O'Rourke

'The psychology is genuine; so too is the tension; the camera plays some good quiet tricks.'—*William Whitebait*

Urban Cowboy
US 1980 135m Movielab Panavision
Paramount (Robert Evans, Irving Azoff)

A rural Texan finds it difficult to succeed in the big city.
Unpleasant and uninteresting star melodrama with a plot vaguely reminiscent of the first part of *An American Tragedy*.

w James Bridges, *novel* Aaron Latham *d* James Bridges *ph* Ray Villalobos *m* various songs *pd* Stephen Grimes

John Travolta, Debra Winger, Scott Glenn, Madolyn Smith

'A fatuous vehicle for John Travolta, requiring him to stride (stiffly and expressionlessly) through various macho torments . . . the two-hour-plus running time, incorporating a wealth of cliché characters, is excruciatingly protracted.'—*Tom Milne, MFB*

The Vagabond King
US 1956 88m Technicolor Vistavision
Paramount (Pat Duggan)

The life and loves of French medieval poet and rebel François Villon.
Shiny, antiseptic studio-set remake of an old musical warhorse.

w Ken Englund, Noel Langley, *operetta* Rudolf Friml *d* Michael Curtiz *ph* Robert Burks *md* Victor Young, *songs* Rudolf Friml (*m*), Brian Hooker, Johnny Burke (*ly*)

Oreste, Kathryn Grayson, Rita Moreno, *Walter Hampden*, Leslie Nielsen, Cedric Hardwicke, William Prince

† A 1930 version with Dennis King is lost. Non-musical versions of the story include 1928's *The Beloved Rogue* with John Barrymore, and *If I Were King*, in 1930 with William Farnum and in 1938 with Ronald Colman.

Vagabond Lady
US 1935 72m bw

The two sons of a department store owner fall for their father's secretary. Medium romantic comedy which didn't seem to stick in anyone's memory. Robert Young, Reginald Denny, Evelyn Venable, Frank Craven, Berton Churchill. Written by Frank Butler; directed by Sam Taylor; for MGM. 'This just misses being a charm picture, the kind they hold over or bring back for repeat dates.'—*Variety*

The Valachi Papers
France / Italy 1972 127m Technicolor
Euro France / de Laurentiis Intermarco (Dino de Laurentiis)

A convicted gangster talks to an FBI agent about his life in the Mafia.
Rough, violent gangster melodrama, none the better for being based on actual events.

w Stephen Geller, *book* Peter Maas *d* Terence Young *ph* Aldo Tonti *m* Riz Ortolani

Charles Bronson, Fred Valleca, Gerald S. O'Loughlin, Lino Ventura, Walter Chiari, Amedeo Nazzari, Joseph Wiseman

Valdez Is Coming
US 1970 90m De Luxe
UA / Norlan / Ira Steiner

A Mexican confronts a rancher who has double-crossed him.
Simply-conceived western which doesn't quite manage to be the classic intended.

w Roland Kibbee, David Rayfiel *d* Edwin Sherin *ph* Gabor Pogany *m* Charles Gross

Burt Lancaster, Susan Clark, Jon Cypher, Barton Heyman, Frank Silvera

Valentino
US 1951 105m Technicolor
Columbia (Edward Small)

An Italian immigrant to the US becomes a world-famous romantic film star but dies young.
Disastrously flat attempt to recapture the feel of Hollywood in the twenties as a background to a flatulent romance.

w George Bruce *d* Lewis Allen *ph* Harry Stradling *m* Heinz Roemheld

Anthony Dexter, Eleanor Parker, Richard Carlson, Patricia Medina, Joseph Calleia, Dona Drake, Lloyd Gough, Otto Kruger

'One can almost see the decorated border round the words . . . it mixes fact, speculation, needless inaccuracy and bathos.'—*Gavin Lambert*

'The dialogue is unbelievably ham, the "entirely imaginary" story commonplace; the players deserve sympathy.'—*Richard Mallett, Punch*

Valentino*
GB 1977 127m De Luxe
UA / Aperture / Chartoff–Winkler (Harry Benn)

Reporters quiz celebrities at a star's funeral, and his eccentric life unfolds.
Sensationalist 'exposé' of Valentino's rise to fame, with excellent period detail but no sympathy for its subject.

w Ken Russell, Mardik Martin, *book* Brad Steiger, Chaw Mank *d* Ken Russell *ph* Peter Suschitzky *m* Ferde Grofe, Stanley Black *ad* Philip Harrison

Rudolf Nureyev, Leslie Caron, Michelle Phillips, Carol Kane, Felicity Kendal, Huntz Hall, David de Keyser, Alfred Marks, Anton Diffring, Jennie Linden, John Justin

Valerie
US 1957 80m bw
UA / Hal R. Makelim

A western rancher is accused of wounding his wife and murdering her parents.
Curious little *Rashomon*-like courtroom melodrama, quite well made and acted.

w Leonard Heidemann, Emmett Murphy *d* Gerd Oswald *ph* Ernest Laszlo *m* Albert Glasser

Anita Ekberg, Sterling Hayden, Anthony Steel, John Wengraf

The Valiant
GB / Italy 1961 89m bw
(UA) BHP / Euro International (Jon Penington)

During World War II, a battleship in Alexandria harbour is mined, and the captain tries desperately to avert disaster.
Ill-made war fodder, of no interest at any level.

w Keith Waterhouse, Willis Hall *d* Roy Baker *ph* Wilkie Cooper, Egil Woxholt *m* Christopher Whelen

John Mills, Ettore Manni, Robert Shaw, Liam Redmond, Ralph Michael, Colin Douglas, Dinsdale Landen

'I, who have laughed at love, have fallen in love at last!'

Valiant Is the Word for Carrie
US 1936 110m bw
RKO (Wesley Ruggles)

A childless woman devotes her life to orphan children.
Tedious soap opera.

w Claude Binyon, *novel* Barry Benefield *d* Wesley Ruggles *ph* Leo Tover *m* Frederick Hollander

Gladys George, John Howard, Dudley Digges, Arline Judge, Harry Carey, Isabel Jewell

AAN: Gladys George

The Valley of Decision*
US 1945 119m bw
MGM (Edwin H. Knopf)

In old Pittsburgh, an Irish housemaid marries the master's son.
Trouble at t' mill epic romance, American style; starrily cast but not excitingly made.

w John Meehan, Sonya Levien, *novel* Marcia Davenport *d* Tay Garnett *ph* Joseph Ruttenberg *m* Herbert Stothart

Greer Garson, Gregory Peck, Lionel Barrymore, Donald Crisp, Preston Foster,

Gladys Cooper, Marsha Hunt, Reginald Owen, Dan Duryea, Jessica Tandy, Barbara Everest, Marshall Thompson

AAN: Herbert Stothart; Greer Garson

Valley of Eagles
GB 1951 86m bw

A Swedish scientist chases into Lapland after his wife and her lover who have stolen an important formula. Unconvincing scenery mars what might have been an unusual adventure drama. Jack Warner, John McCallum, Nadia Gray, Anthony Dawson, Mary Laura Wood, Christopher Lee. Written by Paul Tabori, Nat Bronsten and Terence Young; directed by Terence Young; for Independent Sovereign / GFD.

The Valley of Gwangi
US 1968 95m Technicolor
Warner / Morningside (Charles H. Schneer)

Cowboys and scientists discover prehistoric monsters in a 'forbidden' Mexican valley. Tedious adventure yarn enhanced by good special effects.

w William E. Bast *d* James O'Connelly *ph* Erwin Hillier *m* Jerome Moross *sp Ray Harryhausen*

Richard Carlson, Laurence Naismith, James Franciscus, Gila Golan, Freda Jackson

Valley of Song
GB 1953 74m bw

Members of a Welsh valley choir nearly come to blows over the interpretation of *The Messiah*. Neat, Ealing-style comedy from a well-known radio play. Mervyn Johns, Clifford Evans, Maureen Swanson, John Fraser, Rachel Thomas, Rachel Roberts, Kenneth Williams. Written by Cliff Gordon and Phil Park, from the play *Choir Practice* by Gordon; directed by Gilbert Gunn; for ABPC. (US title: *Men Are Children Twice*.)

Valley of the Dolls*
US 1967 123m De Luxe Panavision
TCF / Red Lion (David Weisbart)

An innocent young actress is corrupted by Broadway and Hollywood, and takes to drugs. Cliché-ridden but good-looking road-to-ruin melodrama from a bitchy bestseller; production values high, but the whole thing goes over the top at the end.

w Helen Deutsch, Dorothy Kingsley, *novel* Jacqueline Susann *d* Mark Robson *ph William H. Daniels* *m* André Previn *md* John Williams *ad* Jack Martin Smith, Richard Day

Barbara Parkins, Patty Duke, Susan Hayward, Paul Burke, Sharon Tate, Martin Milner, Tony Scotti, Charles Drake, Alex Davion, Lee Grant, Robert H. Harris

'What kind of pills do you take to sit through a film like this?'—*The Golden Turkey Awards*

'A skilfully deceptive imitation of a real drama . . . on a closer look the characters turn out to be images that have almost nothing to do with people.'—*Christian Science Monitor*

'One of the most stupefyingly clumsy films ever made by alleged professionals.'—*Joseph Morgenstern, Newsweek*

† Judy Garland was originally slated to play the Susan Hayward part.

AAN: John Williams

Valley of the Giants
US 1938 79m Technicolor

A lumberman fights pirates to preserve his beloved redwoods. Routine outdoor thick-ear to which colour lent the semblance of freshness. Wayne Morris, Claire Trevor, Frank McHugh, Alan Hale, Donald Crisp, Charles Bickford. Written by Seton I. Miller and Michael Fessier, from the novel by Peter B. Kyne; directed by William Keighley; for Warner. 'A yarn which contains nearly all the proven surefire elements of the successful outdoor picture.'—*Variety*

† This was the third version of the story; the first, in 1919, starred Wallace Reid; the second, in 1927, starred Milton Sills. The 1952 movie *The Big Trees*, with Kirk Douglas, had a suspiciously similar storyline.

Valley of the Kings
US 1954 86m Eastmancolor
MGM

Archaeologists fight looters in the tomb of a Pharaoh.
Thin as drama, with little action or suspense and dispirited acting, this hokum piece nevertheless benefits from splendid locations.

w Robert Pirosh, Karl Tunberg *d* Robert Pirosh *ph* Robert Surtees *m* Miklos Rozsa

Robert Taylor, Eleanor Parker, Carlos Thompson, Kurt Kasznar, Victor Jory

Valley of the Sun
US 1942 79m bw
RKO (Graham Baker)

A government spy in old Arizona outwits a crooked Indian agent.
Cheapjack western with nothing to commend it.

w Horace McCoy, *story* Clarence Budington Kelland *d* George Marshall *ph* Harry J. Wild *m* Paul Sawtell

James Craig, Lucille Ball, Dean Jagger, Billy Gilbert, Cedric Hardwicke, Peter Whitney, Tom Tyler, Antonio Moreno, George Cleveland

Valley of the Zombies
US 1946 56m bw

A big city zombie goes on a murder spree. Entirely unpersuasive hokum which wouldn't chill a baby. No valley is apparent. Ian Keith, Robert Livingston, Adrian Booth, Thomas Jackson, Charles Trowbridge. Written by the McGowans; directed by Philip Ford; for the McGowans / Republic.

The Valley of Vanishing Men
US 1942 bw serial: 15 eps

Adventurers in New Mexico trap a renegade European general who uses captive patriots as slaves. Less than eventful serial. Bill Elliott, Slim Summerville, Carmen Morales, Kenneth MacDonald. Directed by Spencer G. Bennet; for Columbia.

Value for Money
GB 1955 93m Technicolor Vistavision
Rank / Group Films (Sergei Nolbandov)

A Yorkshire businessman determines to broaden his outlook, and falls in love with a London showgirl.
Highly undistinguished north country romantic farce which wastes a good production and cast.

w R. F. Delderfield, William Fairchild, *novel* Derick Boothroyd *d* Ken Annakin *ph* Geoffrey Unsworth *m* Malcolm Arnold

John Gregson, Diana Dors, Susan Stephen, Derek Farr, Frank Pettingell, Jill Adams, *Ernest Thesiger*, Charles Victor, Joan Hickson

Vampira
GB 1974 88m colour
Columbia / World Film Services (Jack H. Wiener)
US title: *Old Dracula*

A vampire count lures beauty-contest winners to his castle and uses their blood to revive his dead wife.
Would-be spoof which falls flat on its fangs.

w Jeremy Lloyd *d* Clive Donner *ph* Tony Richmond *m* David Whitaker

David Niven, Teresa Graves, Peter Bayliss, Jennie Linden, Linda Hayden, Nicky Henson, Bernard Bresslaw, Veronica Carlson

The Vampire
US 1957 74m bw
UA / Gardner–Levy

A research scientist takes bat essence and becomes a vampire.
Silly attempt to turn a legend into science fiction: more risible than sinister.

w Pat Fielder *d* Paul Landres *ph* Jack Mackenzie *m* Gerald Fried

John Beal, Coleen Gray, Kenneth Tobey, Lydia Reed

'Mad? I, who have solved the secret of life, you call me mad?'

The Vampire Bat
US 1932 71m bw
Majestic (Phil Goldstone)

A mad doctor kills townsfolk in search of 'blood substitute'.
Primitive but vigorous low budget chiller.

w Edward Lowe *d* Frank Strayer *ph* Ira Morgan

Lionel Atwill, Fay Wray, Melvyn Douglas, Maude Eburne, George E. Stone, Dwight Frye, Lionel Belmore

'Shiver picture, well enough done but coming too late in the cycle to take any money.'—*Variety*

Vampire Circus
GB 1971 87m colour
Hammer (Wilbur Stark)

In 1825 a plague-ridden village is visited by a circus of animal vampires.
Silly but quite inventive horror thriller.

w Judson Kinberg *d* Robert Young *ph* Moray Grant *m* Philip Martell *ad* Scott MacGregor

Adrienne Corri, Laurence Payne, Thorley Walters, John Moulder Brown, Elizabeth Seal, Lynne Frederick, Robert Tayman, Robin Hunter

The Vampire Lovers
GB 1970 91m Technicolor
Hammer / AIP (Harry Fine, Michael Style)

A lady vampire worms her way into several noble households.
Reasonably close retelling of Sheridan Le Fanu's *Carmilla*, complete with lesbian love scenes. Adequate production but not much spirit.

w Tudor Gates, Harry Fine, Michael Styles *story* 'Carmilla' by Sheridan Le Fanu *d* Roy Ward Baker *ph* Moray Grant *m* Harry Robinson

Ingrid Pitt, Peter Cushing, Pippa Steele, Madeleine Smith, George Cole, Dawn Addams, Douglas Wilmer, Kate O'Mara

The Vampire's Ghost
US 1945 59m bw

A vampire takes control of a West African plantation. Unconvincing horror comic with no horror. John Abbott, Charles Gordon, Peggy Stewart, Grant Withers. Written by John K. Butler, Leigh Brackett; directed by Lesley Selander; for Rudolph E. Abel / Republic.

Vampyr**
Germany / France 1931 83m bw
Tobis Klangfilm / Carl Dreyer
US title: *Castle of Doom*
aka: *The Strange Adventure of David Gray*

A young man staying in a remote inn suspects that he is surrounded by vampires and has a dream of his own death.
Vague, misty, virtually plotless but occasionally frightening and always interesting to look at, this semi-professional film long since joined the list of minor classics for two scenes: the hero dreaming of his own death and the villain finally buried by flour in a mill.

w Christen Jul, Carl Dreyer, *story* 'Carmilla' by Sheridan Le Fanu *d Carl Dreyer* *ph Rudolph Maté, Louis Née* *m* Wolfgang Zeller

Julian West, Sybille Schmitz, Maurice Schutz, Jan Hieronimko

'It makes our contemporary, explicit Draculas look like advertisements for false teeth.'—*Sunday Times, 1976*

'It is intensely a film of hints, of eerie non sequiturs, of barely perceivable yet striking images . . . evil wafts off the screen like a smell of bad breath.'—*New Statesman, 1976*

'Imagine we are sitting in an ordinary room. Suddenly we are told there is a corpse behind the door. In an instant, the room is completely altered; everything in it has taken another look; the light, the atmosphere have changed, though they are physically the same. This is because *we* have changed, and the objects are as *we* perceive them. That is the effect I meant to get in my film.'—*Carl Dreyer*

† 'Julian West' was really Baron Nicholas de Gunsberg, who financed the project.

Vanessa, Her Love Story
US 1935 76m bw
MGM (David O. Selznick)

When her husband becomes insane, a Victorian lady falls for a gypsy.
Very dated romance which finished Helen Hayes's star career, for thirty years at least.

w Lenore Coffee, *novel* Hugh Walpole *d* William K. Howard *ph* Ray June *m* Herbert Stothart

Helen Hayes, Robert Montgomery, May Robson, Otto Kruger, Lewis Stone, Henry Stephenson, Violet Kemble-Cooper, Jessie Ralph

'It drips with agony and dullness.'—*Variety*

The Vanishing American
US 1925 110m at 24 fps bw silent

A history of the American Indian. Solid western epic, now of historical interest only. Richard Dix, Lois Wilson, Noah Beery, Malcolm McGregor, Charles Stevens. From a story by Zane Grey; directed by George B. Seitz; for Paramount.

The Vanishing Corporal*
France 1962 106m bw
Films du Cyclope (J. W. Beyer)
original title: *Le Caporal Epinglé*

After several attempts, three Frenchmen succeed in escaping from a detention camp.
Symbolic World War II drama told in mainly comic terms. Not one of its director's great films, but a warm and assured one.

w Jean Renoir, Guy Lefranc *d* Jean Renoir *ph* Georges Leclerc *m* Joseph Kosma

Jean-Pierre Cassel, Claude Brasseur, Claude Rich, O. E. Hasse

The Vanishing Legion
US 1931 bw serial: 12 eps

A western adventurer finds the reason for Indian raids on Milesburg. Modest western serial. Harry Carey, Edwina Booth, Rex the wild horse, Frankie Darro, William Desmond. Directed by B. Reeves Eason; for Mascot.

Vanishing Point*
US 1971 107m De Luxe
TCF / Cupid (Norman Spencer)

An ex-racing driver who delivers cars for a living becomes hepped up on benzedrine and leads police a rare chase through the Nevada desert.
Strange, fashionable action suspenser which is better to look at than to understand.

w Guillermo Cain *d Richard Sarafin* *ph John A. Alonzo* *md* Jimmy Brown

Barry Newman, Cleavon Little, Dean Jagger, Victoria Medlin, Paul Koslo, Bob Donner

'Uncomfortably reminiscent of *Easy Rider* as an odyssey through an unknown America in its discovery of strange alliances and unpredictable hostilities.'—*Tom Milne*

The Vanishing Shadow
US 1934 bw serial: 12 eps

A man sworn to revenge uses an array of scientific weapons against his father's enemies. Absurd chapter play with many unintentional laughs, especially at the gadgets. Onslow Stevens, Ada Ince, Walter Miller, James Durkin. Directed by Louis Friedlander; for Universal.

The Vanishing Virginian
US 1941 97m bw
MGM (Edwin H. Knopf)

A conservative Virginian finds that he harbours suffragettes in his household.
Life with Father in another setting; rather yawn-provoking.

w Jan Fortune, *novel* Rebecca Yancey Williams *d* Frank Borzage *ph* Charles Lawton Jnr *m* David Snell

Frank Morgan, Spring Byington, Kathryn Grayson, Elizabeth Patterson, Louise Beavers

Vanity Fair
US 1932 78m bw

The story of Becky Sharp is told in modern dress. A poorly made independent venture which rapidly dropped from sight. Myrna Loy, Conway Tearle, Barbara Kent, Walter Byron, Anthony Bushell. Written by F. Hugh Herbert from the novel by W. M. Thackeray; directed by Chester M. Franklin; for Hoffman / Allied.
'Poor photography, tepid direction, poor dialogue.'—*Variety*

The Vanquished
US 1953 84m Technicolor

After the Civil War, a returning Confederate officer finds corruption in his home town. Uninspiring semi-western. John Payne, Jan Sterling, Colleen Gray, Lyle Bettger, Willard Parker, Roy Gordon. Written by Winston Miller, Frank Moss and Lewis R. Foster, from a novel by Karl Brown; directed by Edward Ludwig; for Pine-Thomas / Paramount.

Variety**
Germany 1925 104m (24 fps) bw silent
UFA
aka: *Vaudeville*

An ageing acrobat seduces a young girl and later kills another man who is interested in her.
Crude, vivid backstage story, inventively presented to overcome the dullness and tawdriness of the plot.

w E. A. Dupont, Leo Birinsky, *novel* Frederick Hollander *d E. A. Dupont* *ph* Karl Freund

Emil Jannings, Lya de Putti, Maly Delschaft, Warwick Ward

'A continually roving lens seizes the best angle for every detail, expression and scene.'—*Leon Moussinac*

'The enduring power of the movie is not in its far from original story but in the restless, subjective camera and the fast editing which make it an almost voluptuous experience.'—*Pauline Kael, 70s*

'It was my aim to show a single childish grown-up, devoted, lovable, and his reaction to betrayal and duplicity.'—*E. A. Dupont*

Variety Girl
US 1947 83m bw
Paramount (Daniel Dare)

Of all the young hopefuls arriving in Hollywood, one girl becomes a star.
The slightest of excuses for a tour of the Paramount studios, with all the contract stars doing bits. It doesn't add up to much.

w Edmund Hartmann, Frank Tashlin, Monte Brice, Robert Welch *d* George Marshall *ph* Lionel Lindon, Stuart Thompson *md* Joseph J. Lilley, Troy Saunders

Mary Hatcher, Olga San Juan, De Forrest Kelley, Glenn Tryon; and Bob Hope, Bing Crosby, Gary Cooper, Ray Milland, Alan Ladd, Barbara Stanwyck, Paulette Goddard, Dorothy Lamour, Veronica Lake, Sonny Tufts, Joan Caulfield, William Holden, Lizabeth Scott, Burt Lancaster, Gail Russell, Diana Lynn, Sterling Hayden, Robert Preston, William Bendix, Barry Fitzgerald, Billy de Wolfe, George Pal Puppetoons, Cecil B. de Mille, Mitchell Leisen, George Marshall, Spike Jones and his City Slickers, etc.

Variety Jubilee
GB 1942 92m bw

Two generations in the life of a music hall.
Naïve romance with fascinating appearances by some famous names of variety. Lesley Brook, Ellis Irving, Reginald Purdell, George Robey, Charles Coborn, Ella Retford, Wilson Keppel and Betty, The Ganjou Brothers and Juanita, Slim Rhyder, Betty Warren as Florrie Forde; Marie Lloyd Jnr as Marie Lloyd; Tom Finglass as Eugene Stratton; John Rorke as Gus Elen. Written by Kathleen Butler; directed by Maclean Rogers; for Butcher's.

Varsity Show
US 1937 120m bw
Warner (Louis F. Edelman)

Collegians stage a revue.
Mild musical.

w Warren Duff, Richard Macaulay, Jerry Wald, Sig Herzig *d* William Keighley *ph* Sol Polito, George Barnes *ch* Busby Berkeley *songs* Richard Whiting, Johnny Mercer

Dick Powell, Priscilla Lane, Rosemary Lane, Fred Waring and his Pennsylvanians, Buck and Bubbles, Johnny 'Scat' Davis, Ted Healy, Walter Catlett

'A rah-rah musical entertainment made to order for early autumn business when college boys start pegging out the pigskin.'—*Variety*

'Everything that makes life worth leaving!'

Vault of Horror*
GB 1973 86m Eastmancolor
Metromedia / Amicus (Milton Subotsky)

Five men trapped in the basement of a skyscraper tell of their recurring dreams.
All-star horror omnibus, plainly but well staged.

w Milton Subotsky, *stories* William Gaines *d* Roy Ward Baker *ph* Denys Coop *m* Douglas Gamley

Daniel Massey, Anna Massey, Terry-Thomas, Glynis Johns, Curt Jurgens, Dawn Addams, Michael Craig, Edward Judd, Tom Baker, Denholm Elliott

The Velvet Touch*
US 1948 97m bw
RKO / Independent Artists (Frederick Brisson)

A famous actress murders her producer and is struck by conscience but allows a detective to find his own way to the truth.
Solid murder melodrama with an excellent theatrical atmosphere.

w Leo Rosten d John Gage *ph* Joseph Walker *m* Leigh Harline

Rosalind Russell, Leo Genn, Sidney Greenstreet, Claire Trevor, Leon Ames, Frank McHugh

'Child of the devil, she lives by a secret code!'

Vendetta
US 1950 84m bw
RKO / Howard Hughes

The daughter of an esteemed Corsican family takes vengeance on her father's enemies.
Outmoded ethnic melodrama with nothing to recommend it.

w W. R. Burnett, *novel* Columba by Prosper Mérimée *d* Mel Ferrer *ph* Franz Planer, Al Gilks *m* Roy Webb *md* Constantin Bakaleinikoff

Faith Domergue, George Dolenz, Donald Buka, Hilary Brooke, Nigel Bruce, Joseph Calleia, Hugo Haas

The Venetian Affair
US 1966 92m Metrocolor Panavision
MGM / Jerry Thorpe

A reporter investigates the death in Venice of an American diplomat.
Uninteresting and complicated spy thriller with pleasant locations.

w E. Jack Neuman, *novel* Helen MacInnes *d* Jerry Thorpe *ph* Milton Krasner, Enzo Serafin *m* Lalo Schifrin

Robert Vaughn, Karl Boehm, Elke Sommer, Ed Asner, Boris Karloff, Felicia Farr, Roger C. Carmel,Luciana Paluzzi, Joe de Santis

Venetian Bird*
GB 1952 95m bw
Rank / British Film Makers (Betty E. Box)
US title: *The Assassin*

A private detective goes to Venice to reward a wartime partisan, who turns out to have become a notorious criminal.
Standard action fare with a nod to *The Third Man* but not much excitement or sense of place.

w Victor Canning, from his novel *d* Ralph Thomas *ph* Ernest Steward *m* Nino Rota

Richard Todd, Eva Bartok, John Gregson, George Coulouris, Margot Grahame, Walter Rilla, Sidney James

Vengeance
GB / Germany 1962 83m bw
CCC / Raymond Stross
aka: *The Brain*

After a fatal accident, the brain of a tycoon is kept alive and persuades a doctor to find his murderer.
Twisty remake of *Donovan's Brain* (qv), not too badly done.

w Robert Stewart, Philip Mackie *d* Freddie Francis *ph* Bob Hulke *m* Ken Jones

Anne Heywood, Peter Van Eyck, Cecil Parker, Bernard Lee, Maxine Audley, Jeremy Spenser, Miles Malleson

The Vengeance of Fu Manchu
GB 1967 92m Eastmancolor
Anglo Amalgamated / Harry Alan Towers

The Yellow Peril plans a crime syndicate to counter Interpol, and creates a double for Nayland Smith . . .
Limp addition to a series which started well, but was subsequently robbed of period flavour.

w Harry Alan Towers, *novels* Sax Rohmer *d* Jeremy Summers *ph* John Von Kotze *m* Malcolm Lockyer

Christopher Lee, Douglas Wilmer, Tony Ferrer, Tsai Chin, Howard Marion Crawford, Wolfgang Kieling

The Vengeance of She
GB 1967 101m Technicolor
Hammer (Aida Young)

A girl is possessed by the spirit of long-dead Queen Ayesha.
Grotesquely unpersuasive reincarnation melodrama, a long long way from its inspiration.

w Peter O'Donnell *d* Cliff Owen *ph* Wolfgang Suschitsky *m* Mario Nascimbene

John Richardson, Olinka Berova, Edward Judd, Colin Blakely, Derek Godfrey, Noel Willman, André Morell, Jill Melford

Vengeance Valley
US 1951 82m Technicolor
MGM (Nicholas Nayfack)

A western rancher keeps his foster-brother's misdeeds from their father.
Well-made character western, a little short on action.

w Irving Ravetch, *novel* Luke Short *d* Richard Thorpe *ph* George Folsey *m* Rudolph G. Kopp

Burt Lancaster, Robert Walker, Ray Collins, Joanne Dru, Sally Forrest, John Ireland, Carleton Carpenter, Ted de Corsia

Venom
GB 1981 92m Technicolor
Aribage / Morison (Martin Bregman)

A kidnap plan goes awry when a deadly snake is let loose in a besieged house.
Hoary melodrama which veers between dullness, artificial suspense and unpleasant detail.

w Robert Carrington, *novel* Alan Scholefield *d* Piers Haggard *ph* Gilbert Taylor *m* Michael Kamen

Sterling Hayden, Klaus Kinski, Oliver Reed, Sarah Miles, Cornelia Sharpe, Nicol Williamson, Susan George

'Woefully archaic in its British B-picture reliance on very cheap thrills, and without any self-parodic saving grace.'—*Time Out*

Vera Cruz**
US 1953 94m Technicolor Superscope
UA / Hecht-Lancaster (James Hill)

Adventurers in 1860 Mexico become involved in a plot against Emperor Maximilian.
Terse, lively western melodrama with unusual locations and comedy and suspense touches. Great outdoor entertainment.

w Roland Kibbee, James R. Webb, Borden Chase d Robert Aldrich ph Ernest Laszlo m Hugo Friedhofer

Gary Cooper, Burt Lancaster, Denise Darcel, Cesar Romero, George Macready, Sarita Montiel, Ernest Borgnine, Morris Ankrum, Charles Bronson

The Verdict*
US 1946 86m bw
Warner (William Jacobs)

A retired Scotland Yard inspector continues to work on a case which vexes him.
Victorian murder mystery with very unconvincing Hollywood sets and curious casting, but rather nicely detailed.

w Peter Milne, *novel* The Big Bow Mystery by Israel Zangwill *d Don Siegel ph* Ernest Haller *m* Frederick Hollander

Sidney Greenstreet, Peter Lorre, Joan Lorring, George Coulouris, Rosalind Ivan, Paul Cavanagh, Arthur Shields

Verdict*
France / Italy 1974 97m Eastmancolor
Concordia / CCC (Carlo Ponti)

A gangster's widow kidnaps the judge who is trying her son for rape and murder.
Tortuous but watchable melodrama with star performances and the director's usual eagerness to exploit legal morality.

w Andre Cayatte, Henri Coupon, *novel* Henri Coupon *d Andre Cayatte ph* Jean Badal *m* Louiguy

Sophia Loren, Jean Gabin, Henri Garcin, Julien Bertheau

'Not exciting enough to qualify as a thriller nor penetrating enough to make you support Gallic penal reform.'—*Michael Billington, Illustrated London News*

The Verdict*
US 1982 128m Technicolor
TCF / Zanuck-Brown (Richard D. Zanuck, David Brown)

An ageing and failed attorney is unexpectedly handed a case of medical malpractice and successfully sues a hospital.
Complex and interesting but rather sombrely handled exposé of legal and medical ethics.

w David Mamet, *novel* Barry Reed *d* Sidney Lumet *ph* Andrzej Bartkowiak *m* Johnny Mandel *pd* Edward Pisoni

Paul Newman, James Mason, Charlotte Rampling, Jack Warden, Milo O'Shea, Lindsay Crouse, Edward Binns, Wesley Addy

AAN: best picture; Paul Newman; James Mason; Sidney Lumet; screenplay (adaptation)

Veronika Voss**
West Germany 1982 104m bw
Maura / Tango / Rialto / Trio / Maran (Thomas Schühly)

In the fifties, a distraught star of the previous decade flees from her own image, but finds that her psychiatrist is her own worst enemy.
Fascinatingly convoluted puzzle play with enough to say for a year of late-night discussions; but the bleached-out black and white photography is an unnecessary strain.

w Peter Märthesheimer, Pea Fröhlich, Rainer Werner Fassbinder *d* Rainer Werner Fassbinder *ph* Xaver Schwarzenberger *m* Peer Raben

Rosel Zech, Hilmar Thate, Annemarie Düringer, Doris Schade, Cornelia Froboess

'A dazzling parable of all cinema, of the penalties of living out one another's fantasies.'—*Sight and Sound*

Vertigo**
US 1958 128m Technicolor Vistavision
(Paramount) Alfred Hitchcock

A detective with a fear of heights is drawn into a complex plot in which a girl he loves apparently falls to her death. Then he meets her double . . .
Double identity thriller which doesn't really hang together but has many sequences in Hitchcock's best style despite central miscasting.

w Alec Coppel, Samuel Taylor, *novel* D'entre les Morts by Pierre Boileau, Thomas Narcejac *d Alfred Hitchcock ph Robert Burks m Bernard Herrmann*

James Stewart, Kim Novak, Barbara Bel Geddes, Tom Helmore, Henry Jones

'No woman should see this film without a man!'

The Very Edge
GB 1962 89m bw Cinevision
British Lion / Garrick / Raymond Stross

An obsessive young man menaces a mother-to-be.
Rather unpleasant suspenser, adequately presented.

w E. J. Howard *d* Cyril Frankel *ph* Bob Huke *m* David Lee

Anne Heywood, Richard Todd, Jack Hedley, Jeremy Brett, Nicole Maurey, Barbara Mullen, Maurice Denham, William Lucas

Very Important Person**
GB 1961 98m bw
Rank / Independent Artists (Julian Wintle, Leslie Parkyn)
US title: *A Coming-Out Party*

A senior British scientist is caught by the Nazis and has to be rescued.
Very satisfactory British comedy with a few suspense scenes; POW fare with a difference.

w Jack Davies d Ken Annakin *ph* Ernest Steward *m* Reg Owen

James Robertson Justice, Stanley Baxter, Leslie Phillips, Eric Sykes, Richard Wattis, Colin Gordon

A Very Special Favor*
US 1965 105m Technicolor
Universal / Lankershim (Robert Arthur)

A Frenchman with a spinster daughter asks an American lawyer to 'initiate' her.
Tasteless, smirking comedy with several funny scenes, glossily photographed in the lap of luxury and interesting in its early use of homosexuality as a comedy subject.

w Nate Monaster, Stanley Shapiro *d* Michael Gordon *ph Leo Tover m* Vic Mizzy

Rock Hudson, Charles Boyer, Leslie Caron, *Nita Talbot*, Dick Shawn, *Walter Slezak*, Larry Storch

The Very Thought of You
US 1944 99m bw
Warner (Jerry Wald)

Problems of a wartime marriage.
Tepid romantic potboiler.

w Alvah Bessie, Delmer Daves *d* Delmer Daves *ph* Bert Glennon *m* Franz Waxman

Dennis Morgan, Eleanor Parker, Dane Clark, Faye Emerson, Beulah Bondi, Henry Travers, William Prince, Andrea King

A Very Young Lady
US 1941 80m bw

A tomboy develops a crush on her headmaster. Remake of *Girls' Dormitory*, used as a vehicle for an ageing child star.
Predictable comedy, neatly made. Jane Withers, John Sutton, Nancy Kelly, Janet Beecher, Cecil Kellaway. Written by Ladislas Fodor, Elaine Ryan, from Fodor's play; directed by Harold Schuster; for Robert T. Kane / TCF.

Vessel of Wrath**
GB 1938 93m bw
Mayflower (Erich Pommer)
US title: *The Beachcomber*

In the Dutch East Indies, the missionary's spinster sister falls for a drunken beachcomber.
First-rate character comedy, remade as *The Beachcomber* (qv).

VERDICT. Sophia Loren is determined to do anything to protect her son (Michel Albertini), hence the original title *La Tigresse et l'éléphant*. Loren is, of course, the tigress.

w Bartlett Cormack, B. Van Thal, *story W. Somerset Maugham* *d* Erich Pommer *ph* Jules Kruger *m* Richard Addinsell

Charles Laughton, Elsa Lanchester, Robert Newton, Tyrone Guthrie, Dolly Mollinger, Eliot Makeham

'The moment this film starts you recognize the master touch.'—*Variety*

The Vicar of Bray
GB 1937 68m bw

The ex-tutor of Charles I persuades him to pardon a traitor. Mild historical fable with song; in its way quite refreshing. Stanley Holloway, Hugh Miller, Margaret Vyner, Felix Aylmer, Esmond Knight, Garry Marsh. Written by H. Fowler Mear; directed by Henry Edwards; for JH Productions.

The Vice Squad*
US 1931 78m bw

Stool pigeons account for many arrests of supposed prostitutes. Rather draggy exposé of police methods, allegedly torn from the headlines. Kay Francis, Paul Lukas, Judith Wood, William B. Davidson, Rockcliffe Fellowes, Esther Howard. Written by Oliver H. P. Garrett; directed by John Cromwell; for Paramount. 'Should draw adult attention in the large cities.'—*Variety*

Vice Squad
US 1953 88m bw
UA / Jules Levy, Arthur Gardner
GB title: *The Girl in Room 17*

A police captain tracks down two bank robbers who have killed a cop.
A day in the life of a police captain, quite watchable but scarcely engrossing.

w Lawrence Roman, *novel* Harness Bull by Leslie T. White *d* Arnold Laven *ph* Joseph C. Biroc *m* Herschel Burke Gilbert

Edward G. Robinson, Paulette Goddard, K. T. Stevens, Porter Hall, Adam Williams, Edward Binns, Lee Van Cleef

Vice Versa*
GB 1947 111m bw
Rank / Two Cities (Peter Ustinov, George H. Brown)

A magic stone enables an unhappy Victorian boy to change places with his pompous father.
Funny moments can't disguise the fact that this overlong comedy is a bit of a fizzle, its talented creator not being a film-maker. A pity, as British films have so rarely entered the realms of fancy.

w Peter Ustinov, *novel* F. Anstey *d* Peter Ustinov

Roger Livesey, Kay Walsh, Anthony Newley, *James Robertson Justice*, David Hutcheson, Petula Clark, Joan Young

'A repository of English oddities.'—*John Russell Taylor*

The Vicious Circle
US 1948 77m bw

Five Jewish farmers in Hungary are framed for murder. Well-meaning but tedious and very static melodrama. Conrad Nagel, Fritz Kortner, Reinhold Schunzel, Philip Van Zandt, Edwin Maxwell, Lyle Talbot. Written by Heinz Herald and Guy Endore, from play *The Burning Bush* by Herald and Geza Herczeg; directed and produced by W. Lee Wilder; for United Artists. (GB title: *The Woman in Brown*.)

The Vicious Circle*
GB 1957 84m bw
Romulus (Peter Rogers)
US title: *The Circle*

An actress is found dead in Dr Latimer's flat and the weapon turns up in the boot of his car . . .
Entertaining whodunnit from a TV serial.

w Francis Durbridge, from his serial The Brass Candlestick *d* Gerald Thomas *ph* Otto Heller *m* Stanley Black

John Mills, Derek Farr, Noelle Middleton, Roland Culver, Wilfrid Hyde White, Mervyn Johns, René Ray, Lionel Jeffries, Lisa Daniely

Vicki*
US 1953 85m bw
TCF (Leonard Goldstein)

A girl model is murdered, and her sister proves that her boy friend is innocent, despite the efforts of a brutal detective.
Very competent if uninspired remake of *I Wake Up Screaming* (qv).

w Dwight Taylor *d* Harry Horner *ph* Milton Krasner *m* Leigh Harline

Jeanne Crain, Jean Peters, Richard Boone, Elliott Reid, Casey Adams, Alex D'Arcy, Carl Betz, Aaron Spelling

'Fear is the oxygen of blackmail. If Barrett was paying, others are. Find me one!'

Victim***
GB 1961 100m bw
Rank / Allied Film Makers / Parkway (Michael Relph)

A barrister with homosexual inclinations tracks down a blackmailer despite the risk to his own reputation.
A plea for a change in the law is very smartly wrapped up as a murder mystery which allows all aspects to be aired, and the London locations are vivid.

w Janet Green, John McCormick d Basil Dearden ph Otto Heller m Philip Green

Dirk Bogarde, Sylvia Syms, John Barrie, Norman Bird, Peter McEnery, Anthony Nicholls, Dennis Price, *Charles Lloyd Pack*, Derren Nesbitt, John Cairney, Hilton Edwards, Peter Copley, Donald Churchill, Nigel Stock

'Ingenious, moralistic, and moderately amusing.'—*Pauline Kael, 70s*

Victor / Victoria*
GB 1982 134m Technicolor Panavision
MGM / Peerford / Ladbroke Entertainments / Blake Edwards

In 1934 Paris, a girl singer becomes successful when she poses as a female impersonator, but it causes complications in her love life.
The story was previously filmed more innocuously as a Jessie Matthews vehicle, *First a Girl*; Edwards makes it a sexually harping, grotesque low comedy, but there are pleasurable moments.

wd Blake Edwards, from the German film of 1933 Viktor und Viktoria *wd* Rheinhold Schunzel *ph* Dick Bush *m* Henry Mancini *pd* Rodger Maus

Julie Andrews, James Garner, *Robert Preston*, Lesley Anne Warren, Alex Karras, John Rhys-Davies, Graham Stark

'An audience pleaser in the worst sense.'—*New Yorker*

'Edwards' idea of European sophistication and Gallic naughtiness is seen throughout to be depressingly crude, parochial and second-hand, based on old American farces and reprises of his own Clouseau routines.'—*Sunday Times*

AA: original song score (Henry Mancini, Leslie Bricusse)
AAN: Julie Andrews; Robert Preston; Lesley Ann Warren; screenplay (adaptation); costume design; art direction

Victoria the Great***
GB 1937 112m bw (Technicolor sequence)
British Lion / Imperator / Herbert Wilcox

Episodes in the life of Queen Victoria.
A decent film with all the British virtues, and a milestone in the cinema of its time. Script and performances are excellent; production sometimes falters a little.

w Robert Vansittart, Miles Malleson, plays Victoria Regina by Laurence Housman *d* Herbert Wilcox *ph* F. A. Young, William V. Skall *m* Anthony Collins

Anna Neagle, Anton Walbrook, H. B. Warner, Walter Rilla, Mary Morris, C. V. France, Charles Carson, Felix Aylmer, Derrick de Marney

'The effect of the final colour reel is to make the picture look like something enamelled on pottery and labelled "A Present from Blackpool".'—*James Agate*

'The six most exciting women in the world—in the most expensive entertainment you have ever seen!'

The Victors*
GB 1963 175m bw Panavision
Columbia / Open Road (Carl Foreman)

World War II adventures of an American infantry platoon.
Patchy compendium with moral too heavily stressed but plenty of impressive scenes and performances along the way. The mixture of realism and irony, though, doesn't really mix.

w Carl Foreman, *novel* The Human Kind by Alexander Baron *d* Carl Foreman *ph* Christopher Challis *m* Sol Kaplan

George Peppard, George Hamilton, Albert Finney, Melina Mercouri, Eli Wallach, Vince Edwards, Rosanna Schiaffino, James Mitchum, *Jeanne Moreau*, Elke Sommer, Senta Berger, Peter Fonda, Michael Callan

'Doggerel epic.'—*John Coleman*

'War has revealed Mr Foreman as a pompous bore.'—*John Simon*

'Having made a point through an image it continually feels the need to state it all over again by way of dialogue.'—*Penelope Houston*

Victory*
US 1940 77m bw
Paramount (Anthony Veiller)

A Dutch East Indies recluse rescues a girl and is menaced by three villains who think he is wealthy.
Curious, ineffective but occasionally compelling attempt to translate the untranslatable to the screen.

w John L. Balderston, *novel* Joseph Conrad *d* John Cromwell *ph* Leo Tover *m* Frederick Hollander

Fredric March, Betty Field, *Cedric Hardwicke*, Sig Rumann, Margaret Wycherly, Jerome Cowan, Fritz Feld, Rafaela Ottiano

'There is achieved a combination of amateur theatricals and earnest emptiness of motive and motion that will throw a blanket of reminiscent affection around this solemn, unusual and exotic buffoonery.'—*Otis Ferguson*

'A mood of impending doom and horror more than makes up for its slow and deliberate action . . . a fine and penetrating motion picture melodrama.'—*New York World Telegram*

'This is an unusual film at almost every level, yet it's unusual and disturbing, too.'—*Pauline Kael, 70s*

'Not a film of flamboyant hues . . . but it has quality, weight, and above all, compelling drama.'—*Philadelphia Record*

† The story was previously filmed in 1919 by Maurice Tourneur (with Jack Holt) and in 1930 by William Wellman (with Richard Arlen)

Victory
US 1981 117m Metrocolor Panavision
Lorimar / Victory Company / Tom Stern (Freddie Fields)
alternative and GB release title: *Escape to Victory*

A German POW camp in 1943 houses many international football stars. A Nazi officer sees propaganda in a game against a German side, but the allies make it an opportunity for escape.

Flabby and unconvincing POW story with agreeably old-fashioned values sacrificed to trendy casting and a silly ending.

w Evan Jones, Yabo Yablonsky *d* John Huston *ph* Gerry Fisher *m* Bill Conti *pd* J. Dennis Washington

Sylvester Stallone, Michael Caine, Pele, Bobby Moore, Max Von Sydow, George Mikell, Daniel Massey

'Even readers of the *Boy's Own Paper* might have blenched . . . ludicrous beyond belief.'—*Tom Milne, MFB*

Victory through Air Power**

US 1943 65m Technicolor
Walt Disney

The history of aviation and the theories of Major Alexander de Seversky.
What was thought by many to be propaganda was in fact a demonstration of Disney's own fascination with the theories of a controversial figure. The cartoon segments are put together with the studio's accustomed brilliance.

w various *d* H. C. Potter (live action), various *m* Edward J. Plumb, Paul J. Smith, Oliver J. Wallace

AAN: Edward J. Plumb, Paul J. Smith, Oliver J. Wallace

Videodrome

Canada 1982 89m colour

A videodrome TV channel induced pornographic hallucinations in the viewer. Dangerous when it is not risible, this thoroughly tawdry concept is made worse by being slickly done. James Woods, Sonja Smits, Deborah Harry, Peter Dvorsky. Written and directed by David Cronenberg; for Filmplan International. 'Almost as incoherent as it is speculative.'—*Sight and Sound*

The View from Pompey's Head*

US 1955 97m Eastmancolor
Cinemascope
TCF (Philip Dunne)
GB title: *Secret Interlude*

A New York lawyer returns on a case to the small town of his youth, and falls in love again with his old sweetheart.
Routine Marquand-type novelette, long on atmosphere and short on plot.

wd Philip Dunne, *novel* Hamilton Basso *ph* Joe MacDonald *m* Elmer Bernstein

Richard Egan, Dana Wynter, Cameron Mitchell, *Sidney Blackmer, Marjorie Rambeau*

A View from the Bridge

France 1961 117m bw
Transcontinental (Paul Graetz)
original title: *Vu du Pont*

A longshoreman on the New York waterfront has passionate feelings for his wife's niece, and these erupt when she announces her engagement.
Solemn, self-examining melodrama, poorly adapted from the stage.

w Norman Rosten, *play* Arthur Miller *d* Sidney Lumet *ph* Michel Kelber *m* Maurice Leroux

Raf Vallone, Maureen Stapleton, Carol Lawrence, Jean Sorel, Raymond Péllégrin, Morris Carnovsky, Harvey Lembeck, Vincent Gardenia

† The film was shot in several languages.

A View to a Kill

GB 1985 121m Metrocolor Panavision
MGM–UA / Albert R. Broccoli

James Bond tangles with a ruthless international industrialist.
A tedious Bond adventure in which even the expensive highlights are unmemorable.

w Richard Maibaum, Michael G. Wilson *d* John Glen *ph* Alan Hume *m* John Barry *pd* Peter Lamont *ed* Peter Davies

Roger Moore, Christopher Walken, Grace Jones, Tanya Roberts, Patrick MacNee, David Yip, Fiona Fullerton

Vigil*

New Zealand 1984 90m Eastmancolor

On a remote farm, a teenage girl learns about life after her father is killed. Austere but vaguely impressive drama; one is pleased however when it ends. Bill Kerr, Fiona Kay, Gordon Shields, Penelope Stewart, Frank Whitten. Written by Vincent Ward, Graeme Tetley; directed by Vincent Ward; for First Blood / Last Rites / John Maynard.

Vigil in the Night

US 1940 96m bw
RKO (George Stevens)

Two nurses are attracted to the same doctor; one dies during an epidemic.
Dull, downbeat romantic melodrama with a miscast lead.

w Fred Guiol, P. J. Wolfson, Rowland Leigh, *novel* A. J. Cronin *d* George Stevens *ph* Robert de Grasse *m* Alfred Newman

Carole Lombard, Anne Shirley, Brian Aherne, Julien Mitchell, Robert Coote, Peter Cushing, Ethel Griffies

The Vigilante

US 1947 bw serial: 15 eps

A government undercover agent calls himself The Vigilante in his bid to protect a priceless string of pearls. The usual cliffhangers are spliced into an artless plot. Ralph Byrd, Ransay Ames, Lyle Talbot, Hugh Prosser. Directed by Wallace Fox; for Columbia.

The Vigilantes are Coming

US 1936 bw serial: 12 eps

In 1940 a wealthy California settler makes himself dictator, but is dislodged by a masked man called The Eagle. No credit given to *The Mark of Zorro*, but that's what it is. Bob Livingston, Kay Hughes, William Farnum, Guinn 'Big Boy' Williams, Raymond Hatton. Directed by Mack V. Wright and Ray Taylor; for Republic.

The Viking Queen

GB 1967 91m Technicolor
Warner / Hammer (John Temple-Smith)

During the first century AD, the queen of the Iceni tries to keep peace with the occupying Romans but has trouble with hot-headed Druids.
Stuff and nonsense from the Dark Ages; light should not have been shed upon it.

w Clarke Reynolds *d* Don Chaffey *ph* Stephen Dade *m* Gary Hughes

Don Murray, Carita, Donald Houston, Andrew Keir, Patrick Troughton, Adrienne Corri, Niall MacGinnis, Wilfrid Lawson, Nicola Pagett

The Vikings***

US 1958 116m Technirama
UA / KD Productions (Jerry Bresler)

Two Viking half-brothers quarrel over the throne of Northumbria.
Slightly unpleasant and brutal but extremely well-staged and good-looking epic in which you can almost feel the harsh climate. Fine colour, strong performances, natural settings, vivid action, and all production values as they should be.

w Calder Willingham, *novel* The Viking by Edison Marshall *d Richard Fleischer ph Jack Cardiff m Mario Nascimbene credit titles United Productions of America narrator* Orson Welles

Kirk Douglas, Tony Curtis, Ernest Borgnine, Janet Leigh, Alexander Knox, Frank Thring, James Donald, Maxine Audley, Eileen Way

Villa Rides!

US 1968 125m Technicolor
Panavision
Paramount (Ted Richmond)

1912 Mexico: an American pilot who has been gun-running for the rebels is pressed into more active service.
Bang-bang actioner which pauses too often for reflection and local colour.

w Robert Towne, Sam Peckinpah *d* Buzz Kulik *ph* Jack Hildyard *m* Maurice Jarre *ad* Ted Howarth

Yul Brynner, Robert Mitchum, Charles Bronson, Grazia Bucetta, Herbert Lom, Alexander Knox, Fernando Rey, Jill Ireland

Village of Daughters

GB 1961 86m bw
MGM (George H. Brown)

An unemployed commercial traveller in an Italian village finds himself choosing a bride for a successful emigré.
Voluble, gesticulating minor comedy.

w David Pursall, Jack Seddon *d* George Pollock *ph* Geoffrey Faithfull *m* Ron Goodwin

Eric Sykes, Warren Mitchell, Scilla Gabel, Carol White, Grégoire Aslan, John Le Mesurier

Village of the Damned**

GB 1960 78m bw
MGM (Ronald Kinnoch)

Children born simultaneously in an English village prove to be super-intelligent and deadly beings from another planet.

Modestly made but absorbing and logical science fiction, cleanly presented.

w Stirling Silliphant, Wolf Rilla, Geoffrey Barclay, novel The Midwich Cuckoos by *John Wyndham d Wolf Rilla ph* Geoffrey Faithfull *m* Ron Goodwin

George Sanders, Barbara Shelley, Michael Gwynn, Martin Stephens, Laurence Naismith
† Sequel: *Children of the Damned* (qv).

A Village Tale*
US 1935 79m bw
RKO (David Hempstead)

Envy leads to a clash between two rural landowners.
Unusual but very interesting attempt by Hollywood to film with integrity an old-fashioned country novel. Very dated, but pleasant to watch.

w Allan Scott, *novel* Phil Strong *d John Cromwell ph* Nicholas Musuraca *m* Alberto Columbo

Randoph Scott, Robert Barrat, Kay Johnson, Arthur Hohl, Janet Beecher, Edward Ellis, Donald Meek, Dorothy Burgess, Andy Clyde, Guinn Williams

'Depressing story without marquee strength. Restricted in appeal.'—*Variety*

Villain
GB 1971 98m Technicolor Panavision
EMI / Kastner / Ladd / Kanter

The come-uppance of a cowardly, sadistic, homosexual East End gang boss with a mother fixation.
Very unpleasant and unentertaining British low life shocker, plainly inspired by *White Heat.*

w Dick Clement, Ian La Frenais, *novel* The Burden of Proof by James Barlow *d* Michael Tuchner *ph* Christopher Challis *m* Jonathan Hodge

Richard Burton, Ian MacShane, Nigel Davenport, Joss Ackland, Cathleen Nesbitt, Donald Sinden, T. P. McKenna, Fiona Lewis

The Villain
US 1979 89m Metrocolor
Columbia / Rastar (Paul Maslansky, Mort Engelberg)
GB title: *Cactus Jack*

An incompetent outlaw rides from one disaster to another.
No doubt amusing in conception, this attempt to put the cartoon character Wile E. Coyote into human form lamentably misfires, six minutes being an ideal length for that kind of comedy.

w Robert G. Kane *d* Hal Needham
ph Bobby Byrne *m* Bill Justis

Kirk Douglas, Arnold Schwarzenegger, Ann-Margret, Paul Lynde, Ruth Buzzi, Jack Elam, Strother Martin

'Timing is entirely absent from this limp, laughless fiasco, as is any evidence of imagination . . . desperation is the keynote.'—*Paul Taylor, MFB*

The Villain Still Pursued Her*
US 1940 66m bw
(RKO) Harold B. Franklin

An innocent family suffers at the hands of a villainous landlord.
Clumsy burlesque of old time melodrama, interesting that it was done at all and with this cast.

w Elbert Franklin *d* Edward Cline *ph* Lucien Ballard *m* Frank Tours

Buster Keaton, Alan Mowbray, Anita Louise, Hugh Herbert, Joyce Compton, Margaret Hamilton, Billy Gilbert

The Vintage
US 1957 92m Metrocolor Cinemascope
MGM (Edwin H. Knopf)

Two fugitives from justice cause trouble when they become grape pickers.
Steamy drama with an unconvincing French setting; a Hollywood aberration.

w Michael Blankfort, *novel* Ursula Keir *d* Jeffrey Hayden *ph* Joseph Ruttenberg *m* David Raksin

Mel Ferrer, John Kerr, Michèle Morgan, Pier Angeli, Theodore Bikel, Leif Erickson

Violence
US 1947 72m bw

War veterans fall victim to a group spreading civil discord. Propaganda thick-ear. Nancy Coleman, Michael O'Shea, Sheldon Leonard, Peter Whitney, Emory Parnell. Written by Stanley Rubin, Louis Lantz; directed by Jack Bernhard; for Monogram.

The Violent Enemy
GB 1968 98m Eastmancolor
Trio / Group W. (Wilfrid Eades)

An IRA explosives expert escapes from a British jail but quarrels with his leaders.
Dullish political melodrama needlessly rubbing salt in old wounds.

w Edmund Ward, *novel* A Candle for the Dead by Hugh Marlowe *d* Don Sharp
ph Alan Hume *m* John Scott

Tom Bell, Ed Begley, Susan Hampshire, Noel Purcell, Michael Standing

The Violent Men*
US 1955 96m Technicolor Cinemascope
Columbia (Lewis J. Rachmil)
GB title: *Rough Company*

A crippled cattle baron drives small landowners from his valley, while his wife has an affair with his younger brother.
So much snarling goes on that this seems like a gangster film in fancy dress, but it does hold the attention.

w Harry Kleiner, *novel* Donald Hamilton *d* Rudolph Maté *ph* Burnett Guffey, W. Howard Greene *m* Max Steiner

Edward G. Robinson, Barbara Stanwyck, Glenn Ford, Brian Keith, Dianne Foster, May Wynn, Warner Anderson, Basil Ruysdael

The Violent Ones*
US 1967 90m Eastmancolor
Madison / Harold Goldman

In a small Mexican town, three American hobos are interrogated after the rape and murder of a local girl.
Rather well shot murder mystery with emphasis on character, leading to a desert chase climax.

w Doug Wilson, Charles Davis *d Fernando Lamas ph Fleet Southcott m* Martin Skiles

Fernando Lamas, Aldo Ray, David Carradine, Tommy Sands

Violent Playground
GB 1958 108m bw
Rank (Michael Relph)

A junior liaison officer in the Liverpool slums falls in love with the sister of a fire-raiser.
'Realistic' melodrama sabotaged by an entirely schematic and predictable plot; enervatingly dull until the siege climax.

w James Kennaway *d* Basil Dearden *ph Reg Wyer m* Philip Green

Stanley Baker, Anne Heywood, David McCallum, Peter Cushing, John Slater, Clifford Evans

'The bank robbers that caught a town with its morals down!'

Violent Saturday*
US 1955 90m De Luxe Cinemascope
TCF (Buddy Adler)

Crooks move quietly into a small town with the intention of robbing the bank.
Interesting little melodrama which the wide screen robs of its proper tension. Adequate presentation and performance.

w Sidney Boehm *d* Richard Fleischer
ph Charles G. Clarke *m* Hugo Friedhofer

Richard Egan, Victor Mature, Stephen McNally, Sylvia Sidney, Virginia Leith, Tommy Noonan, Lee Marvin, Margaret Hayes, J. Carrol Naish, Ernest Borgnine

Violette Nozière*
France / Canada 1977 122m Eastmancolor
Filmel / Cinevideo (Roger Morand)

In 1933 Paris, an eighteen-year-old girl leads a double life, gets syphilis, poisons her parents and is convicted of murder.
Oddly erratic but interesting recapitulation of a famous French murder case, not quite typical of its director.

w Odile Barski, Herve Bromberger, Frederic Grendel *d* Claude Chabrol *ph* Jean Rabier *m* Pierre Jansen *pd* Jacques Brizzio

Isabelle Huppert, Jean Carmier, Stephane Audran, Bernadette Lafont

The VIPs**
GB 1963 119m Metrocolor Panavision
MGM (Anatole de Grunwald)

Passengers at London Airport are delayed by fog and spend the night at a hotel.
Multi-story compendium cunningly designed to exploit the real-life Burton–Taylor romance. In itself, competent rather than stimulating.

w Terence Rattigan *d* Anthony Asquith *ph* Jack Hildyard *m* Miklos Rozsa

Richard Burton, Elizabeth Taylor, Maggie Smith, Rod Taylor, *Margaret Rutherford*, Louis Jourdan, Elsa Martinelli, Orson Welles, Linda Christian, Dennis Price, Richard Wattis, David Frost, Robert Coote, Joan Benham, Michael Hordern, Lance Percival, Martin Miller

'If Mr Rattigan's Aunt Edna still goes to the pictures she should like his latest offering, especially if she has a good lunch first.'—*Brenda Davies*

AA: Margaret Rutherford

The Virgin and the Gypsy*
GB 1970 95m colour
Kenwood / Dimitri de Grunwald (Kenneth Harper)

A Midlands clergyman's daughter falls in love with a gypsy fortune teller.
Slow, sensitive, stylish picturization of a Lawrence novella, with generally good performances.

w Alan Plater, story D. H. Lawrence d Christopher Miles ph Robert Huke *m* Patrick Gowers *pd* Terence Knight

Joanna Shimkus, Franco Nero, Honor Blackman, Mark Burns, Maurice Denham, Fay Compton, Kay Walsh, Norman Bird

Virgin Island
GB 1958 94m Eastmancolor
British Lion / Countryman (Leon Clore, Graham Tharp)
US title: *Our Virgin Island*

A young couple set up house on a tiny Caribbean island.
Pleasant comedy slowed down by lack of plot and too much conversation.

w Philip Rush, Pat Jackson, *book* Our Virgin Island by Robb White *d* Pat Jackson *ph* Freddie Francis *m* Clifton Parker

Virginia Maskell, John Cassavetes, Sidney Poitier, Isabel Dean, Colin Gordon

'Twentieth Century Fox spectacularly spreads before you the violent age and velvet cape of Sir Walter Raleigh!'

The Virgin Queen*
US 1955 92m De Luxe Cinemascope
TCF (Charles Brackett)

The relationship of Queen Elizabeth I and Sir Walter Raleigh.
Unhistorical charade, quite pleasantly made and worth noting for its star performance.

w Harry Brown, Mindret Lord *d* Henry Koster *ph* Charles G. Clarke *m* Franz Waxman

Bette Davis, Richard Todd, Joan Collins, Herbert Marshall, Jay Robinson, Dan O'Herlihy, Robert Douglas, Romney Brent

'Sooner or later they're going to get it!'

The Virgin Soldiers**
GB 1969 96m Technicolor
Columbia / Carl Foreman (Leslie Gilliat, Ned Sherrin)

Serio-comic adventures of recruits in the British army in 1960 Singapore.
Autobiographical fragments, mostly from below the belt, sharply observed and often very funny.

w John Hopkins, novel Leslie Thomas d John Dexter ph Ken Higgins m Peter Greenwell

Hywel Bennett, Nigel Patrick, *Lynn Redgrave*, Nigel Davenport, *Rachel Kempson*, Michael Gwynn, Tsai Chin

'A kind of monstrous mating of *Private's Progress* and *The Family Way*, with bits of *The Long and the Short and the Tall* thrown in for good measure.'—*David Pirie*

† Sequel 1977: *Stand Up Virgin Soldiers.*

The Virgin Spring*
Sweden 1959 87m bw
Svensk Filmindustri (Allan Ekelund)
original title: *Jungfraukällan*

When her murderers are killed, a spring bubbles up from the spot where a young maiden met her death.
Stark and rather lovely filming of a medieval legend, with heavy symbolism and a strong pictorial sense.

w Ulla Isaakson *d Ingmar Bergman ph* Sven Nykvist *m* Erik Nordgren

Max Von Sydow, Brigitta Valberg, Gunnel Lindblom, Brigitta Pettersson

AA: best foreign film

Virginia
US 1940 107m Technicolor
Paramount (Edward H. Griffith)

A showgirl goes home to claim her inheritance, but thinks of marrying a rich Yankee.
Languid post-Civil War romantic melodrama, only memorable for its colour.

w Virginia Van Upp *d* Edward H. Griffith *ph* Bert Glennon, William V. Skall

Madeleine Carroll, Fred MacMurray, Sterling Hayden, Helen Broderick, Paul Hurst, Marie Wilson, Carolyn Lee, Louise Beavers

Virginia City*
US 1940 121m bw
Warner (Robert Fellows)

A dance hall girl is really a southern spy helping a rebel colonel to steal a gold shipment from her Yankee boy friend.
Lumpy western in Warner's best budget but worst manner: the stars look unhappy and the plot progresses in fits and starts.

w Robert Buckner *d* Michael Curtiz *ph* Sol Polito *m* Max Steiner

Errol Flynn, Randolph Scott, Miriam Hopkins, Humphrey Bogart, Frank McHugh, Alan Hale, Guinn Williams, John Litel, Moroni Olsen, Russell Hicks, Douglass Dumbrille

The Virginia Judge
US 1935 70m bw

A southern judge's ne'er-do-well son gets deeper into trouble. Homely vehicle for a star whose 'judge' was for many years the centre of a vaudeville monologue. Walter C. Kelly, Marsha Hunt, Stepin Fetchit, Johnny Downs, Robert Cummings. Written by Henry Johnson, Frank Adams, Inez Lopez; directed by Edward Sedgwick; for Charles R. Rogers / Paramount.

The Virginian*
US 1929 95m bw
Paramount (Louis D. Lighton)

A stalwart ranch foreman has to see his best friend hanged for rustling, and defeats the local bad man.
Standard western with famous clichés, e.g. 'Smile when you say that . . .'

w Edward E. Paramore Jnr, Howard Estabrook, *novel* Owen Wister *d* Victor Fleming *ph* J. Roy Hunt

Gary Cooper, Walter Huston, Richard Arlen, Mary Brian, Chester Conklin, Eugene Pallette

The Virginian
US 1946 90m Technicolor
Paramount (Paul Jones)

Forgettable remake of the above.

w Frances Goodrich, Albert Hackett *d* Stuart Gilmore *ph* Harry Hallenberger *m* Daniele Amfitheatrof

Joel McCrea, Brian Donlevy, Sonny Tufts, Barbara Britton, William Frawley, Henry O'Neill, Fay Bainter

Viridiana**
Spain / Mexico 1961 91m bw
Uninci / Films 59 / Gustavo Alatriste (Munoz Suay)

A novice about to take her vows is corrupted by her wicked uncle and installs a load of beggars in his house.
Often hilarious surrealist melodrama packed with shades of meaning, most of them sacrilegious. A fascinating film to watch.

w Luis Bunuel, Julio Alajandro *d Luis Bunuel ph* José F. Agayo

Silvia Pinal, Francisco Rabal, Fernando Rey

'One of the cinema's few major philosophical works.'—*Robert Vas*

Virtue
US 1932 68m bw

A woman of the streets is regenerated through marriage. Routine matinée programmer. Carole Lombard, Pat O'Brien, Mayo Methot, Jack La Rue, Ward Bond. Written by Robert Riskin from a story by Ethel Hill; directed by Eddie Buzzell; for Columbia. 'A lot of plot is squeezed into the running time . . . the picture will be liked.'—*Variety*

The Virtuous Bigamist see Four Steps in the Clouds

The Virtuous Sin
US 1930 81m bw
Paramount
GB title: *Cast Iron*

A girl tries to help her student husband when war takes him away from bacteriology.
Stilted romantic drama.

w Martin Brown, Louise Long, *novel* Lajos Zilahy *d* George Cukor, Louis Gasnier *ph* David Abel

Walter Huston, Kay Francis, Kenneth MacKenna, Paul Cavanagh

'Average programme flicker . . . cast names all from legit . . . nor is there much excuse for the picture running 80 minutes when 70 would have been better.'—*Variety*

The Visit
US 1964 100m bw Cinemascope
TCF / Deutschefox / Cinecittà / Dear Film / Films du Siècle / PECF (Julien Derode, Anthony Quinn)

A millionairess offers a fortune to her home town, providing someone will kill her ex-lover.
A realistic production ill befits an essentially theatrical play, and all the effort goes for nothing.

w Ben Barzman, *play* Friedrich Durrenmatt *d* Bernhard Wicki *ph* Armando Nannuzzi *m* Hans-Martin Majewski

Ingrid Bergman, Anthony Quinn, Paolo Stoppa, Hans-Christian Blech, Valentina Cortesa, Irina Demick, Claude Dauphin, Eduardo Ciannelli

Visit to a Chief's Son
US 1974 92m De Luxe Panavision
UA / Robert Halmi

An American anthropologist and his son hope to film the rituals of an African tribe.
Minor adventure film with a happy resolution, based on a photomontage by the producer, a *Life* photographer.

w Albert Ruben *d Lamont Johnson* *ph* Ernest Day *m* Francis Lai

Robert Mulligan, Johnny Sekka, John Philip Hodgdon

Visit to a Small Planet
US 1960 101m bw
Paramount / Wallis–Hazen

A young man from outer space takes a look at Earth and falls in love.
A satirical play disastrously adapted for the moronic comedy of an unsuitable star.

w Edmund Beloin, Henry Garson, *play* Gore Vidal *d* Norman Taurog *ph* Loyal Griggs *m* Leigh Harline

Jerry Lewis, Joan Blackman, Earl Holliman, Fred Clark, John Williams, Jerome Cowan, Gavin Gordon, Lee Patrick

Les Visiteurs du Soir*
France 1942 110m bw
André Paulvé
aka: *The Devil's Envoys*

The devil sends messengers to earth to corrupt two lovers, but he fails: even though he turns them to stone, their hearts still beat.
Made during the Occupation, this stately medieval fable was intended to be significant: the devil was Hitler, and the heartbeat that of France. Perhaps because it is so conscious of hidden meanings, it moves rather stiffly but is often beautiful to behold.

w Jacques Prévert, Pierre Laroche *d Marcel Carné* *ph* Roger Hubert *m* Joseph Kosma, Maurice Thiriet *ad* Alexandre Trauner, Georges Wakhevitch

Arletty, *Jules Berry*, Marie Déa, Alain Cuny, Fernand Ledoux, Marcel Herrand

'There are wonderful images, but the movie is heavy on the allegorical and becomes rather slow and stylized.'—*Pauline Kael, 70s*

Visiting Hours
Canada 1981 105m colour Panavision
Filmplan International (Claude Héroux)

A homicidal maniac is at large in a hospital.
Tedious shocker wasting a reliable idea.

w Brian Taggert *d* Jean Claude Lord *ph* René Verzier *m* Jonathan Goldsmith

Michael Ironside, Lee Grant, Linda Purl, William Shatner, Lenore Zann, Harvey Atkin

I Vitelloni
Italy / France 1953 109m bw
Peg / Cité (Lorenzo Pegoraro)
aka: *Spivs*

In a small Italian resort, aimless young people get into various kinds of trouble.
Interesting in its realistic detail, this sharply observed slice of life is long enough for its basic purposelessness to become apparent.

w Federico Fellini, Ennio Flaiano, Tullio Pinelli *d* Federico Fellini *ph* Otello Martelli, Tasatti, Carlini *m* Nino Rota

Franco Fabrizi, Franco Interlenghi, Eleonora Ruffo, Alberto Sordi

AAN: script

Viva Knievel
US 1977 104m Technicolor Panavision

Evel Knievel becomes involved with drug smugglers. Abysmal attempt to turn a stuntman into an actor; a most ramshackle vehicle. Evel Knievel, Gene Kelly, Lauren Hutton, Leslie Nielsen, Red Buttons, Cameron Mitchell, Marjoe Gortner. Written by Antonio Santillan and Norman Katkov; directed by Gordon Douglas; for Warner. 'A paste-and-scissors B picture of quite breathtaking inanity.'—*Financial Times.*

Viva Las Vegas
US 1964 85m Metrocolor Panavision
MGM (Jack Cummins, George Sidney)
GB title: *Love in Las Vegas*

A sports car racer has fun in the gambling city.
Tolerable star musical.

w Sally Benson *d* George Sidney *ph* Joseph Biroc *md* George Stoll

Elvis Presley, Ann-Margret, Cesare Danova, William Demarest, Nicky Blair, Jack Carter

Viva Maria!
France / Italy 1965 120m Eastmancolor Panavision
Novelles Editions / Artistes Associés / Vides (Oscar Dancigers, Louis Malle)

An Irish anarchist girl arrives in Central America and joins a group of strolling players.
All show and no substance, this is a colour supplement of a film, neither fish, flesh nor good red herring.

w Louis Malle, Jean-Claude Carrière *d* Louis Malle *ph* Henri Decaë *m* Georges Delerue *ad* Bernard Evein

Jeanne Moreau, Brigitte Bardot, George Hamilton, Paulette Dubost, Claudio Brook

Viva Max
US 1969 93m Eastmancolor
Commonwealth United / Mark Carliner

A Mexican general marches his troops into Texas and seizes the Alamo.
Flat comedy with mildly amusing passages but too much noise, bluster and sentiment.

w Elliott Baker, *novel* James Lehrer *d* Jerry Paris *ph* Jack Richards *m* Hugo Montenegro

Peter Ustinov, *John Astin*, Pamela Tiffin, Jonathan Winters, Keenan Wynn, Henry Morgan, Alice Ghostley

'1001 nights of glorious romantic adventure!'

Viva Villa**
US 1934 110m bw
MGM (David O. Selznick)

The career of a Mexican rebel.
Gutsy action drama with some smoothing over of fact in the name of entertainment. A big, highly competent production of its year.

w Ben Hecht d Jack Conway ph James Wong Howe, Charles G. Clarke m Herbert Stothart

Wallace Beery, Fay Wray, Leo Carrillo, Donald Cook, Stuart Erwin, George E. Stone, Joseph Schildkraut, Henry B. Walthall, Katherine de Mille

'Glorified western . . . strong b.o. fodder, handicapped a bit perhaps by its abnormal masculine appeal.'—*Variety*

'A strange poem of violence.'—*John Baxter, 1968*

'A glorified horse opera . . . the spectator's excitement is incited by the purely physical impact of the furious riding and war sequences, by the frequent sadism, and by the lively musical score.'—*Irving Lerner*

AAN: best picture; script

Viva Zapata**
US 1952 113m bw
TCF (Darryl F. Zanuck)

A Mexican revolutionary is finally betrayed by a friend.
Moody, good-looking star vehicle taking a romanticized but glum view of history.

w John Steinbeck *d Elia Kazan ph Joe MacDonald* *m* Alex North *md* Alfred Newman

Marlon Brando, Jean Peters, Joseph Wiseman, Anthony Quinn, Arnold Moss, Margo, *Frank Silvera*

AA: Anthony Quinn
AAN: John Steinbeck; Alex North; Marlon Brando

Vivacious Lady*
US 1938 90m bw
RKO (George Stevens)

A nightclub singer marries a botany professor and has trouble with his parents.
Pleasant romantic comedy for two popular stars.

w P. J. Wolfson, Ernest Pagano *d* George Stevens *ph* Robert de Grasse *m* Roy Webb

Ginger Rogers, James Stewart, Charles Coburn, Beulah Bondi, James Ellison, Frances Mercer, Franklin Pangborn, Grady Sutton, Jack Carson

AAN: Robert de Grasse

Vogues of 1938*
US 1937 108m Technicolor
Walter Wanger
reissue title: *All This and Glamour Too*

Rival fashion houses compete at the Seven Arts Ball.
A fashion show with threads of plot, interesting for clothes and cast, all working hard.

w Bella and Samuel Spewack *d* Irving Cummings *ph* Ray Rennahan *m* Victor Young *md* Boris Morros *ch* Seymour Felix

Joan Bennett, Walter Baxter, Helen Vinson, Mischa Auer, Alan Mowbray, Jerome Cowan, Alma Kruger, Marjorie Gateson, Penny Singleton, Hedda Hopper

AAN: song 'That Old Feeling' (*m* Sammy Fain, *ly* Lew Brown)

The Voice in the Mirror
US 1958 102m bw Cinemascope

A reformed alcoholic thinks back on his past life. Glum case history of no particular point or persuasiveness. Richard Egan, Julie London, Walter Matthau, Arthur O'Connell, Troy Donahue, Mae Clarke, Ann Doran. Written by Larry Marcus; directed by Harry Keller; for Universal-International.

A Voice in the Wind
US 1944 85m bw

Two refugees from the Nazis meet again and die on a remote island. Pretentious romantic claptrap, fascinating only for a few of the impressionist effects it contrives on the lowest of budgets. Francis Lederer, Sigrid Gurie, J. Carrol Naish. Written by Frederick Torberg; directed by *Arthur Ripley*; for Arthur Ripley.
'Like a mid-thirties French melodrama drenched in the Rembrandt-and-molasses manner of German films of the early to middle twenties. Even within those terms it is much less good than it might be, solemn, unimaginative, thinly detailed; but it is also richly nostalgic if you have any feeling for bad period art.'—*James Agee.*

The Voice of Bugle Ann*
US 1936 70m bw
MGM (John Considine Jnr)

When a dog is killed its embittered owner seeks revenge.
Old-fashioned country tale, rather heavy-going but emotionally strong.

w Harvey Gates, Samuel Hoffenstein, *novel* Mackinlay Kantor *d* Richard Thorpe *ph* Ernest Haller

Lionel Barrymore, Maureen O'Sullivan, Eric Linden, Dudley Digges, Spring Byington, Charley Grapewin

'A very fine movie indeed.'—*Pare Lorentz*

The Voice of Merrill
GB 1952 84m bw
Tempean (Robert Baker, Monty Berman)
US title: *Murder Will Out*

Three men are suspected of murder but one becomes a potential victim.
Complicated murder thriller which intrigues but hardly satisfies.

wd John Gilling *ph* Monty Berman *m* Frank Cordell

Valerie Hobson, James Robertson Justice, Edward Underdown, Henry Kendall, Garry Marsh, Sam Kydd

The Voice of the Turtle**
US 1948 103m bw
Warner (Charles Hoffman)
aka: *One for the Book*

A girl shares her apartment with a soldier on leave.
A three-character play is smoothly filmed, slightly broadened, and burnished till its pale wit glows nicely.

w John Van Druten, from his play *d Irving Rapper* *ph* Sol Polito *m* Max Steiner

Eleanor Parker, Ronald Reagan, *Eve Arden,* Wayne Morris, Kent Smith

'A light and lovely comedy.'—*People*

Voices
GB 1973 91m Technicolor
(Hemdale) Warden (Robert Enders)

A young couple in an old country house are haunted by the voice of their dead son.
Twisty little ghost story which would have been more effective at one third of its length.

w George Kirgo, Robert Enders, *play* Richard Lortz *d* Kevin Billington *ph* Geoffrey Unsworth *m* Richard Rodney Bennett

Gayle Hunnicutt, David Hemmings

Voltaire*
US 1933 72m bw
Warner (Ray Griffith)

The life and times of the 18th-century French wit.
One of the better Arliss charades, because the film is as stagey as his performance.

w Paul Green, Maude T. Howell, *novel* George Gibbs, E. Laurence Dudley *d* John Adolfi *ph* Tony Gaudio

George Arliss, Doris Kenyon, Margaret Lindsay, Reginald Owen, Alan Mowbray, David Torrence, Douglass Dumbrille, Theodore Newton

'Sumptuously staged and photographed . . . sufficiently modern story to get interest.'—*Variety*

Volunteers
US 1985 106m Metrocolor

High jinks in the 1962 Peace Corps. Tawdry comedy about the exploits of a young Home Guard. Tom Hanks, John Candy, Rita Wilson, Tim Thomerson. Written by Ken Levine, David Isaacs; directed by Nicholas Meyer; for HBO / Tri-Star / Silver Screen.

Von Richthofen and Brown
US 1971 97m De Luxe
UA / Roger Corman (Gene Corman)
GB title: *The Red Baron*

During World War I, a Canadian pilot takes on Germany's air ace.
The airplanes are nice, but the film is grounded by plot and dialogue.

w John and Joyce Corrington *d* Roger Corman *ph* Michael Reed *m* Hugo Friedhofer

John Phillip Law, Don Stroud, Barry Primus, Karen Huston, Corin Redgrave, Hurd Hatfield

Von Ryan's Express**
US 1965 117m De Luxe Cinemascope
TCF (Saul David)

In an Italian POW camp during World War II, an unpopular American captain leads English prisoners in a train escape.
Exhilarating action thriller with slow spots atoned for by nail-biting finale, though the downbeat curtain mars the general effect.

w Wendell Mayes, Joseph Landon, *novel* Davis Westheimer *d Mark Robson* *ph* William H. Daniels, Harold Lipstein *m* Jerry Goldsmith

Frank Sinatra, Trevor Howard, Sergio Fantoni, Edward Mulhare, Brad Dexter, John Leyton, Wolfgang Preiss, James Brolin, Adolfo Celi, Rafaela Cara

Voodoo Man
US 1944 62m bw

A mad scientist kidnaps young girls and reduces them to zombies. Hopeless chiller wasting three stars. Bela Lugosi, John Carradine, George Zucco, Michael Ames, Wanda McKay. Written by Robert Charles; directed by William Beaudine; for Sam Katzman / Monogram.

Voyage of the Damned*
GB 1976 155m Eastmancolor
ITC / Associated General (Robert Fryer)

In 1939, a ship leaves Hamburg for Cuba with Jewish refugees; but Cuba won't take them.
High-minded, expensive, but poorly devised rehash of *Ship of Fools*, with too many stars in cameos and not enough central plot.

w Steve Shagan, David Butler, *book* Gordon Thomas, Max Morgan-Witts *d* Stuart Rosenberg *ph* Billy Williams *m* Lalo Schifrin

Faye Dunaway, Max Von Sydow, Oskar Werner, Malcolm McDowell, James Mason, Orson Welles, Katharine Ross, Ben Gazzara,

Lee Grant, Sam Wanamaker, Julie Harris, Helmut Griem, Luther Adler, Wendy Hiller, Nehemiah Persoff, Maria Schell, Fernando Rey, Donald Houston, Jose Ferrer, Denholm Elliott, Janet Suzman

'Not a single moment carries any conviction.'—*New Yorker*

'The movie stays surprisingly distanced and impersonal, like a panning shot that moves too quickly for all the details to register.'—*Charles Champlin, Los Angeles Times*

'With a story that is true (or thereabouts), tragic in its detail and implications, and about which it is impossible to take a neutral attitude, you feel an absolute bounder unless you give it the thumbs up.'—*Barry Took, Punch*

AAN: script; Lalo Schifrin; Lee Grant

Voyage to the Bottom of the Sea*
US 1961 105m De Luxe Cinemascope
TCF / Windsor (Irwin Allen)

USN Admiral Nelson takes scientists in his futuristic atomic submarine to explode a belt of radiation.
Childish but sometimes entertaining science fiction which spawned a long-running TV series.

w Irwin Allen, Charles Bennett *d* Irwin Allen *ph* Winton Hoch, John Lamb *m* Paul Sawtell, Bert Shefter *ad J. M. Smith, Herman A. Blumenthal*

Walter Pidgeon, Robert Sterling, Joan Fontaine, Peter Lorre, Barbara Eden, Michael Ansara, Henry Daniell, Regis Toomey, Frankie Avalon

The Vulture
GB 1967 92m bw

A family curse transforms a scientist into a giant vulture. Incredible nonsense—incredible that anyone should try to get away with it. Fun for those who like to watch actors in trouble.
Robert Hutton, Akim Tamiroff, Broderick Crawford, Diane Clare. Written and directed by Lawrence Huntington; for Lawrence Huntington Productions.

1086

W
US 1973 95m De Luxe
Bing Crosby Productions (Mel Ferrer)

A young wife is threatened by her psychotic first husband.
Tedious rehash of several frightened lady themes, all rather sick.

w Gerald di Pego, James Kelly *d* Richard Quine *ph* Gerry Hirschfeld *m* Johnny Mandell

Twiggy, Michael Witney, Eugene Roche, Dirk Benedict, John Vernon

The W Plan*
GB 1930 105m bw
BIP / Burlington (Victor Saville)

A British spy helps destroy Germany's secret tunnels.
Slightly fantasticated spy / war action which was a big popular success at the time.

w Victor Saville, Miles Malleson, Frank Launder, *novel* Graham Seton *d* Victor Saville *ph* F. A. Young, Werner Brandes

Brian Aherne, Madeleine Carroll, Gordon Harker, Gibb McLaughlin, George Merritt, Mary Jerrold

'One of the best pictures yet from England, but unconvincing b.o. for the US. Lacks punch.'—*Variety*

'Fast, spectacular action, fine acting and notably realistic war scenes.'—*NFT, 1971*

'On screen he played the child-hating, dog-hating, acid-tongued old swindler. It was no act!'

W. C. Fields and Me
US 1976 112m Technicolor Panavision
Universal (Jay Weston)

The rise to Hollywood fame of alcoholic comedian W. C. Fields.
Untruthful and rather boring biopic, with minor compensations.

w Bob Merrill, *book* Carlotta Monti *d* Arthur Hiller *ph* David M. Walsh *m* Henry Mancini *pd* Robert Boyle

Rod Steiger, Valerie Perrine, John Marley, Jack Cassidy (as John Barrymore), Paul Stewart (as Ziegfeld), Billy Barty, Bernadette Peters

'Steiger's impersonation largely keeps pace with the overriding vulgarity of the enterprise.'—*Sight and Sound*

'A stupid and pointless slander.'—*Judith Crist*

'Just the sort of memorial Fields might have wished for Baby Leroy.'—*Les Keyser, Hollywood in the Seventies*

WW and the Dixie Dancekings
US 1975 94m TVC
TCF (Stanley S. Canter)

In a southern state in the 1950s, a crook uses a travelling band as an alibi and stays to promote them.
Combination of *American Graffiti* and *Easy Rider,* either tiresome or tolerable according to one's mood. Very flashy, anyway.

w Thomas Rickman *d* John G. Avildsen *ph* Jim Crabe *m* Dave Grusin

Burt Reynolds, Art Carney, Conny Van Dyke, Jerry Reed, Ned Beatty

Wabash Avenue*
US 1950 92m Technicolor
TCF (William Perlberg)

During the Chicago World's Fair of 1892, a shimmy dancer is pursued by two men.
Bright rehash of *Coney Island* (qv), with solid tunes and performances.

w Harry Tugend, Charles Lederer *d* Henry Koster *ph* Arthur E. Arling *md* Lionel Newman

Betty Grable, Victor Mature, Phil Harris, Reginald Gardiner, Margaret Hamilton, James Barton, Barry Kelley

AAN: song 'Wilhelmina' (*m* Josef Myrow, *ly* Mack Gordon)

The Wackiest Ship in the Army
US 1960 99m Technicolor Cinemascope
Columbia / Fred Kohlmar

In the South Pacific during World War II a decrepit sailing ship with an inexperienced crew manages to confuse Japanese patrols and land a scout behind enemy lines.
Slapstick war comedy with fragments of action; effect rather muddled.

wd Richard Murphy, *story* Herbert Carlson *ph* Charles Lawton *m* George Duning

Jack Lemmon, Ricky Nelson, John Lund, Chips Rafferty, Tom Tully, Joby Baker, Warren Berlinger, Richard Anderson

Waco
US 1966 85m Technicolor

A gunfighter is hired to straighten out a corrupt town. Routine western programmer with familiar faces in cameo parts. Howard Keel, Jane Russell, Wendell Corey, Brian Donlevy, John Smith, Gene Evans, DeForest Kelley, Terry Moore, John Agar, Richard Arlen, Robert Lowery, Willard Parker, Fuzzy Knight. Written by Steve Fisher, from the novel *Emporia* by Harry Sanford and Max Lamb; directed by R. G. Springsteen; for A. C. Lyles / Paramount.

The Wages of Fear***
France / Italy 1953 140m bw
Filmsonor / CICC / Vera
original title: *Le Salaire de la Peur*

The manager of a Central American oilfield offers big money to drivers who will take nitro-glycerine into the jungle to put out an oil well fire.
After too extended an introduction to the less than admirable characters, this fascinating film resolves itself into a suspense shocker with one craftily managed bad moment after another.

wd Henri-Georges Clouzot, novel Georges Arnaud *ph Armand Thirard m* Georges Auric

Yves Montand, Folco Lulli, Peter Van Eyck, *Charles Vanel*, Vera Clouzot, William Tubbs

'As skilful as, in its preoccupation with violence and its unrelieved pessimism, it is unlikeable.'—*Penelope Houston, Sight and Sound*

'It has some claim to be the greatest suspense thriller of all time; it is the suspense not of mystery but of Damocles' sword.'—*Basil Wright, 1972*

† See *Sorcerer*, a lamentable remake.

Wagonmaster**
US 1950 86m bw
RKO / Argosy (John Ford, Merian C. Cooper)

Adventures of a Mormon wagon train journeying towards Utah in 1879.
Low-key Ford western, essentially a collection of incidents, fondly and enjoyably presented.

w Frank Nugent, Patrick Ford *d John Ford* *ph* Bert Glennon *m* Richard Hageman

Ben Johnson, Joanne Dru, Harry Carey Jnr, Ward Bond, Charles Kemper, Alan Mowbray, Jane Darwell, Russell Simpson

'The feel of the period, the poetry of space and of endeavour, is splendidly communicated.'—*Lindsay Anderson*

'What emerges at the end is nothing less than a view of life itself, the view of a poet.'—*Patrick Gibbs, 1965*

The Wagons Roll at Night
US 1941 83m bw
Warner (Harlan Thompson)

W. C. FIELDS AND ME. Even covering his face with a full deck fails to disguise Rod Steiger as the immortal W. C. Fields.

The sweetheart of a circus owner makes a pass at the new young lion-tamer.
Dull remake of *Kid Galahad* (qv), whose plot was borrowed from *Tiger Shark* (qv). Warners were good at this kind of retreading, but gradually poor quality began to show.

w Fred Niblo Jnr, Barry Trivers *d* Ray Enright *ph* Sid Hickox *m* Heinz Roemheld

Humphrey Bogart, Sylvia Sidney, Eddie Albert, Joan Leslie, Sig Rumann, Cliff Clark, Frank Wilcox

Waikiki Wedding*
US 1937 89m bw
Paramount (Arthur Hornblow Jnr)

A press agent in Hawaii promotes a Pineapple Queen contest.
Light-hearted, empty-headed musical very typical of this studio . . . except that this one is quite good.

w Frank Butler, Walter de Leon, Don Hartman, Francis Martin *d* Frank Tuttle *ph* Karl Struss *m* Leo Shukin *md* Boris Morros

Bing Crosby, Shirley Ross, Bob Burns, Martha Raye, George Barbier, Leif Erickson, Grady Sutton, Granville Bates, Anthony Quinn

'Shouldn't have any trouble getting by . . . it's saccharine celluloid, sugar-coated.'—*Variety*

AA: song 'Sweet Leilani' (*m / ly* Harry Owens)

Wait til the Sun Shines, Nellie*
US 1952 108m Technicolor
TCF (George Jessel)

The life of a small-town barber, from marriage through tragedy to retirement.
Amiable, leisurely family drama with pleasant settings; small beer, but oddly compulsive.

w Allan Scott, *novel* Ferdinand Reyher *d* Henry King *ph* Leon Shamroy *m* Alfred Newman

David Wayne, Jean Peters, Hugh Marlowe, Albert Dekker, Alan Hale Jnr, Helene Stanley

Wait until Dark**
US 1967 108m Technicolor
Warner Seven Arts (Mel Ferrer)

A photographer unwittingly smuggles a drug-filled doll into New York, and his blind wife, alone in their flat, is terrorized by murderous crooks in search of it.
Sharp suspenser with shock moments, from a successful play; in this case the claustrophobic atmosphere helps, though a lack of light relief makes itself felt.

w Robert and Jane Howard-Carrington, *play* Frederick Knott *d* Terence Young *ph* Charles Lang *m* Henry Mancini *ad* George Jenkins

Audrey Hepburn, Alan Arkin, Richard Crenna, Efrem Zimbalist Jnr, Jack Weston

AAN: Audrey Hepburn

Wake in Fright: see Outback

'It thrills the women!'
'To the last gun—to the last plane—to the last man!'

Wake Island*
US 1942 78m bw
Paramount (Joseph Sistrom)

During World War II, marines fight to hold an American base on a small Pacific island.
Terse, violent flagwaver, well done within its limits.

w W. R. Burnett, Frank Butler *d* John Farrow *ph* Theodor Sparkuhl, William C. Mellor *m* David Buttolph

Brian Donlevy, Macdonald Carey, Robert Preston, William Bendix, Albert Dekker, Walter Abel, Mikhail Rasumny, Rod Cameron, Barbara Britton

'Hollywood's first intelligent, honest and completely successful attempt to dramatize the deeds of an American force on a fighting front.'—*Newsweek*

AAN: best picture; script; John Farrow; William Bendix

Wake Me When It's Over
US 1960 126m De Luxe Cinemascope
TCF / Mervyn Le Roy

Soldiers holding a Pacific island build a de luxe hotel from surplus war material.
Aptly-titled army farce on the lines of *The Teahouse of the August Moon* but constructed from inferior material. Yawningly tedious.

w Richard Breen, *novel* Howard Singer *d* Mervyn Le Roy *ph* Leon Shamroy *m* Cyril Mockridge

Ernie Kovacs, Dick Shawn, Jack Warden, Margo Moore, Nobu McCarthy, Don Knotts, Robert Emhardt

Wake of the Red Witch**
US 1948 106m bw
Republic (Edmund Grainger)

The owner and captain of a ship settle their differences to seek treasure on an East Indian island.
Rattling good action yarn told in flashback, with adequate production and performances.

w Harry Brown, Kenneth Gamet, novel Garland Roark *d* Edward Ludwig *ph* Reggie Lanning *m* Nathan Scott

John Wayne, *Luther Adler*, Gail Russell, Gig Young, Adele Mara, Eduard Franz, Grant Withers, Henry Daniell, Paul Fix, Dennis Hoey

Wake Up and Dream
US 1946 92m Technicolor
TCF (Walter Morosco)

A little girl is determined to find her brother who is missing in action in World War II.
Ambitious but unappealing whimsy which descends into sentimentality; either way it bewildered audiences and critics.

w Elick Moll, *novel* The Enchanted Voyage by Robert Nathan *d* Lloyd Bacon *ph* Harry Jackson *m* Cyril Mockridge *md* Emil Newman

June Haver, John Payne, Connie Marshall, Charlotte Greenwood, John Ireland, Clem Bevans, Lee Patrick

Wake Up and Live*
US 1937 91m bw
TCF (Kenneth MacGowan)

Success and failure in the radio world as a commentator and a bandleader fight a verbal duel in public.
Fast-moving spoof in which something is always happening, and usually something funny.

w Harry Tugend, Jack Yellen, *book* Dorothea Brande *d* Sidney Lanfield *ph* Edward Cronjager *m* Louis Silvers *songs* Mack Gordon, Harry Revel

Walter Winchell, Ben Bernie and his band, Alice Faye, Jack Haley, Patsy Kelly, Ned Sparks, Grace Bradley, Walter Catlett, Joan Davis, Douglas Fowley, Miles Mander, Etienne Girardot

'Thoroughly satisfying film entertainment.'—*Variety*

Walk a Crooked Mile
US 1948 91m bw
Columbia (Edward Small)

British and American agents investigate the leakage of atomic secrets.
Moderate semi-documentary spy thriller.

w George Bruce *d* Gordon Douglas *ph* George Robinson *m* Paul Sawtell

Louis Hayward, Dennis O'Keefe, Louise Allbritton, Carl Esmond, Raymond Burr, Onslow Stevens

Walk a Crooked Path
GB 1969 88m Eastmancolor
Hanover (John Brason)

A housemaster at a boys' school is accused of homosexuality.
Po-faced melodrama in a minor key; reasonably effective but not exciting.

w Barry Perowne *d* John Brason *ph* John Taylor *m* Leslie Bridgewater

Tenniel Evans, Faith Brook, Christopher Coll, Patricia Haines, Pat Endersby, Margery Mason, Peter Copley

Walk, Don't Run*
US 1966 114m Technicolor Panavision
Columbia / Granley (Sol C. Siegel)

In Tokyo during the Olympics accommodation is hard to find, and two men move in with a girl.
Witless reprise of *The More the Merrier*, notable only for the Tokyo backgrounds and for Cary Grant's farewell appearance.

w Sol Saks *d* Charles Walters *ph* Harry Stradling *m* Quincy Jones

Cary Grant, Samantha Eggar, Jim Hutton, *John Standing*, Miiko Taka

'Too long as are most comedies today, it seems to take its title far too literally; but there are several very funny sequences, a jaunty score, and the unflawed elegance of Mr Grant.'—*Arthur Knight*

Walk East on Beacon*
US 1952 98m bw
Columbia (Louis de Rochemont)
GB title: *The Crime of the Century*

The FBI exposes communist spies in the US.
Fast-moving semi-documentary spy thriller modelled on the same producer's *The House on 92nd Street*.

w Leo Rosten *d* Alfred Werker *ph* Joseph Brun *m* Louis Applebaum

George Murphy, Finlay Currie, Virginia Gilmore, Karel Stepanek, Louisa Horton

'There weren't supposed to be any more surprises in their lives. And then they met each other!'

A Walk in the Spring Rain
US 1969 98m Technicolor Panavision
Columbia / Pingee (Stirling Silliphant)

A college lecturer's wife, on holiday in the mountains, falls in love with a local man.
Romance for the middle-aged, nicely done if lacking in surprise.

w Stirling Silliphant, *novel* Rachel Maddox *d* Guy Green *ph* Charles B. Lang *m* Elmer Bernstein

Ingrid Bergman, Anthony Quinn, Fritz Weaver, Katherine Crawford

'Not one line or scene is believably written or acted and the direction is so lazy it appears to have been mailed in during the postal strike.'—*Richard Roud*

A Walk in the Sun***
US 1946 117m bw
Lewis Milestone Productions

The exploits of a single army patrol during the Salerno landings of 1943, on one vital morning.
Vivid war film in a minor key, superbly disciplined and keenly acted.

w Robert Rossen, novel Harry Brown *d Lewis Milestone ph Russell Harlan m* Fredric Efrem Rich

Dana Andrews, Richard Conte, Sterling Holloway, John Ireland, George Tyne, Herbert Rudley, Richard Benedict, Norman Lloyd, Lloyd Bridges, Huntz Hall

'Concerned with the individual rather than the battlefield, the film is finely perceptive, exciting, and very moving.'—*Penelope Houston*

'A swiftly overpowering piece of work.'—*Bosley Crowther*

'A notable war film, if not the most notable war film to come from America.'—*Richard Winnington*

'After nearly two hours one is sorry when it ends.'—*Richard Mallett, Punch*

Walk like a Dragon
US 1960 95m bw
Paramount / James Clavell

In 1870 San Francisco, a cowboy sets free a Chinese slave girl but incurs racial intolerance when he takes her home.
Curious 'liberated' western which gets itself in a muddle and doesn't come off at all.

w James Clavell, Dan Mainwaring *d* James Clavell *ph* Loyal Griggs *m* Paul Dunlap

Jack Lord, James Shigeta, Nobu McCarthy, Mel Tormé, Josephine Hutchinson, Rodolfo Acosta

Walk on the Wild Side
US 1962 114m bw
Columbia / Famous Artists (Charles K. Feldman)

In the thirties, a penniless farmer finds the girl he once loved working in a New Orleans brothel.
A brilliant title sequence heralds the dreariest and most verbose of self-conscious melodramas, quite missing the sensational effect promised by the advertising.

w John Fante, Edmund Morris, *novel* Nelson Algren *d* Edward Dmytryk *ph* Joe MacDonald *m* Elmer Bernstein *credits Saul Bass*

Jane Fonda, Capucine, Barbara Stanwyck, Laurence Harvey, Anne Baxter, Richard Rust

'Since the film prides itself in calling a spade a spade, it is surprising to find all concerned reacting to their material as though they were up to their waists in a quagmire.'—*MFB*

'A side of life you never expected to see on the screen!'—*publicity*

AAN: title song (*m* Elmer Bernstein, *ly* Mack David)

Walk Softly Stranger
US 1950 81m bw
RKO (Robert Sparks)

A crook on the run falls for a crippled girl, who promises to wait for him.
Dismal love-conquers-all melodrama.

w Frank Fenton *d* Robert Stevenson *ph* Harry J. Wild *m* Frederick Hollander

Alida Valli, Joseph Cotten, Spring Byington, Paul Stewart, Jack Paar, Jeff Donnell, John McIntire

Walk the Proud Land
US 1956 88m Technicolor Cinemascope
U-I (Aaron Rosenberg)

An Indian agent persuades the army to use less violent methods.
Fair standard western with a thoughtful and sympathetic attitude.

w Gil Doud, Jack Sher *d* Jesse Hibbs *ph* Harold Lipstein *m* Hans Salter

Audie Murphy, Anne Bancroft, Pat Crowley, Robert Warwick, Charles Drake, Tommy Rall, Jay Silverheels

Walkabout*
Australia 1970 100m Eastmancolor
Max L. Raab / Si Litvinoff

A man kills himself in the desert and his small children trek among the aborigines to safety.
Eerily effective contrast of city with native life, a director's and photographer's experimental success.

w Edward Bond, *novel* James Vance Marshall *d / ph Nicolas Roeg* *m* John Barry

Jenny Agutter, Lucien John, David Gumpilil

The Walking Dead*
US 1936 66m bw
Warner (Louis F. Edelman)

A man is revived after electrocution and takes revenge on his enemies.
Dour but well mounted horror thriller in a shadowy style very typical of its director.

w Ewart Adamson, Peter Milne, Robert Adams, Lillie Hayward *d Michael Curtiz* *ph Hal Mohr*

Boris Karloff, Edmund Gwenn, Marguerite Churchill, Ricardo Cortez, Barton MacLane, Warren Hull, Henry O'Neill

'Weak story and haphazardly interpolated assortment of scientific abadaba prevent Karloff from making much of a shocker out of this one.'—*Variety*

The Walking Hills*
US 1949 78m bw

Various interests combine to locate gold bullion hidden in Death Valley . . . then thieves fall out. Elementary but fairly satisfying western. Randolph Scott, Ella Raines, William Bishop, Edgar Buchanan, Arthur Kennedy, John Ireland, Jerome Courtland, Josh White. Written by Alan LeMay; directed by John Sturges; for Harry Joe Brown / Columbia.

Walking My Baby Back Home*
US 1953 95m Technicolor
U-I (Ted Richmond)

Ex-army musicians hit on a combination of symphonic and dixieland jazz.
The lightest of light musicals, this highly polished offering remains mildly pleasing though thinly written throughout.

w Don McGuire, Oscar Brodney *d* Lloyd Bacon *ph* Irving Glassberg *md* Joseph Gershenson

Donald O'Connor, Janet Leigh, Buddy Hackett, Lori Nelson, Scat Man Crothers, Kathleen Lockhart, George Cleveland, John Hubbard

The Walking Stick*
GB 1970 101m Metrocolor Panavision
MGM / Winkast (Alan Ladd Jnr)

A repressed girl polio victim falls reluctantly in love with a painter who involves her in his criminal schemes.
Slow moving character romance which has its heart in the right place but too often promises suspense which never comes, and is made in a chintzy cigarette commercial style.

w George Bluestone, *novel* Winston Graham *d* Eric Till *ph* Arthur Ibbetson *m* Stanley Myers

David Hemmings, Samantha Eggar, Phyllis Calvert, Ferdy Mayne, Emlyn Williams, Francesca Annis, Dudley Sutton

Walking Tall*
US 1973 125m De Luxe
Bing Crosby Productions (Mort Briskin)

A Tennessee farmer-sheriff meets violence with violence and becomes a local hero.
True story of an American vigilante, made with modest competence; its great commercial success may have been due to the support of the righteous, or of those who revel in violence.

w Mort Briskin *d* Phil Karlson *ph* Jack Marta *m* Walter Scharf

Joe Don Baker, Elizabeth Hartman, Gene Evans, Noah Beery Jnr

'A terrifying image of Nixon's silent majority at work.'—*Gareth Jones*

'It generates a primitive, atavistic sort of power: it awakens more apprehension and dredges up more complicated and contradictory emotions than one anticipates.'—*Gary Arnold*

† Sequel 1976: *Part Two Walking Tall*. (GB title: *Legend of the Lawman*.) 1977: *Walking Tall: Final Chapter*

Wall of Noise
US 1963 112m bw
Warner (Joseph Landon)

A racehorse trainer falls for the boss's wife.
Complex but predictable melodrama of the old school, adequately presented and performed.

w Joseph Landon, *novel* Daniel Michael Stein *d* Richard Wilson *ph* Lucien Ballard *m* William Lava

Suzanne Pleshette, Ty Hardin, Dorothy Provine, Ralph Meeker, Simon Oakland, Murray Matheson, Robert F. Simon

Wallflower
US 1948 77m bw

Two sisters chase the same man; the less aggressive gets him. So-so comedy on familiar lines. Joyce Reynolds, Janis Paige, Robert Hutton, Edward Arnold, Jerome Cowan, Barbara Brown. Written by Phoebe and Henry Ephron, from the play by Reginald Denham and Mary Orr; directed by Frederick de Cordova; for Warner.

Wall Street**
US 1987 124m De Luxe
Edward R. Pressman / American Entertainment

An ambitious young financial broker is forced to choose between the values of his Wall Street hero and his own father, an aircraft mechanic.
Almost documentary in its detailed account of financial skulduggery but slipping ultimately into sentimentality, the film is marked by a brilliant performance from Michael Douglas as the scheming megalomaniac Gordon Gekko.

w Stanley Weiser, Oliver Stone *d* Oliver Stone *ph* Robert Richardson *m* Stewart Copeland *pd* Stephen Hendrickson

Charlie Sheen, *Michael Douglas*, Martin Sheen, Daryl Hannah, Terence Stamp

The Walls Came Tumbling Down*
US 1946 81m bw

A Broadway columnist tracks down the murderer of a priest. Very acceptable whodunit with familiar cast. Lee Bowman, Marguerite Chapman, George Macready, Edgar Buchanan, Lee Patrick, Jonathan Hale, J. Edward Bromberg, Elizabeth Risdon, Miles Mander, Moroni Olsen, Robert Ryan. Written by Wilfrid H. Pettitt, from novel by Jo Eisinger; directed by Lothar Mendes; for Albert J. Cohen / Columbia.

The Walls of Jericho
US 1948 106m bw
TCF (Lamar Trotti)

An influential small-town newspaperman is undermined by his vindictive wife.
Filmed novel of standard competence but minimum interest, ending in a courtroom scene.

w Lamar Trotti, *novel* Paul Wellman *d* John M. Stahl *ph* Arthur Miller *m* Cyril Mockridge

Cornel Wilde, Linda Darnell, Anne Baxter, Kirk Douglas, Ann Dvorak, Marjorie Rambeau, Henry Hull, Colleen Townsend

The Waltz King
US 1963 95m Technicolor
Walt Disney (Peter V. Herald)

The life of young Johann Strauss in 1850s Vienna.
Medium-budget international family musical, tolerably well done.

w Maurice Tombragel *d* Steve Previn *ph* Gunther Anders *md* Helmuth Froschauer

Kerwin Mathews, Brian Aherne, Senta Berger, Peter Kraus, Fritz Eckhardt

The Waltz of the Toreadors*
GB 1962 105m Technicolor
Rank / Wintle–Parkyn (Peter de Sarigny)

A lecherous retired general finds his past creeping up on him and loses his young mistress to his son.
Lukewarm adaptation of a semi-classic comedy, disastrously translated to English settings and characters.

w Wolf Mankowitz, *play* Jean Anouilh *d John Guillermin* *ph* John Wilcox *m* Richard Addinsell *pd* Wilfrid Shingleton

Peter Sellers, Margaret Leighton, Dany Robin, John Fraser, Cyril Cusack, Prunella Scales

Waltz Time
GB 1933 82m bw

Things are not what they seem to be at a Viennese masked ball. Pleasant but slight musical comedy vaguely derived from *Die Fledermaus*. Evelyn Laye, Fritz Schultz, Gina Malo, Jay Laurier, Frank Titterton. Written by A. P. Herbert; directed by William Thiele; for Gaumont.

Waltz Time
GB 1945 100m bw

At a Viennese ball, an Empress poses as her masked friend to win a philandering count. Rather plodding operetta which also has an unattributed allegiance to *Die Fledermaus*. Carol Raye, Peter Graves, Patricia Medina, Thorley Walters, Richard Tauber, Harry Welchman, George Robey, Anne Ziegler, Webster Booth. Written by Montgomery Tully, Jack Whittingham, Henry C. James and Karl Rossier; directed by Paul Stein; for British National.

Waltzes from Vienna
GB 1933 80m bw
Gaumont (Tom Arnold)
US title: *Strauss's Great Waltz*

A romance of the Strausses.
There is very little music and very little Hitchcock in this extremely mild romantic comedy.

w Alma Reville, Guy Bolton, *play* Guy Bolton *d* Alfred Hitchcock *ph* Glen MacWilliams

Jessie Matthews, Esmond Knight, Frank Vosper, Fay Compton, Edmund Gwenn, Robert Hale, Hindle Edgar

'I hate this sort of thing. Melodrama is the only thing I can do.'—*Alfred Hitchcock*

The Wanderers
US 1979 117m Technicolor

In 1963, teenage street gangs fight in the Bronx. A bad boys' *American Graffiti*, all violence and unpleasantness. Ken Wahl, John Friedrich, Karen Allen, Tonie Kalem, Linda Manz. Written by Rose and Philip Kaufman, from the novel by Richard Price; directed by Philip Kaufman; for PSO / Polyc.

The Wandering Jew*
GB 1933 111m bw
Gaumont / Twickenham (Julius Hagen)

A Jew is condemned to live forever, but dies in the Spanish Inquisition.
Ambitious fantasy which comes off pretty well for those in the mood, but was a curious choice for a British studio at the time.

w H. Fowler Mear, *play* E. Temple Thurston *d* Maurice Elvey *ph* Sydney Blythe

Conrad Veidt, Marie Ney, Basil Gill, Anne Grey, Dennis Hoey, John Stuart, Peggy Ashcroft, Francis L. Sullivan, Felix Aylmer, Abraham Sofaer

'A beautiful production, a historic triumph—and most likely a commercial error.'—*Variety*

Wanted for Murder*
GB 1946 103m bw
Marcel Hellman

A man, obsessed with the fact that his father was the public hangman, becomes a murderer himself.
Curiously stagey melodrama with intermittent use of London backgrounds; an interesting curiosity.

w Emeric Pressburger, Rodney Ackland, Maurice Cowan *d* Lawrence Huntington *ph* Max Greene *m* Mischa Spoliansky

Eric Portman, Dulcie Gray, Derek Farr, Roland Culver, Stanley Holloway, Barbara Everest, Bonar Colleano, Kathleen Harrison

'A pleasant and unpretentious thriller of the second or third grade.'—*James Agee*

Wanted: Jane Turner
US 1936 64m bw

The postal service tracks down mail van crooks. Familiar but lively action support. Lee Tracy, Gloria Stuart, Judith Blake, John McGuire, Frank M. Thomas. Written by John Twist; directed by Edward Killy; for Cliff Reid / RKO.

The War against Mrs Hadley*
US 1942 86m bw
MGM (Irving Asher)

A Washington matron tries to ignore the war and preserve her social life.
Efficient little propaganda piece with a middle-aged heroine.

w George Oppenheimer *d* Harold S. Bucquet *ph* Karl Freund *m* David Snell

Fay Bainter, Edward Arnold, Richard Ney, Jean Rogers, Sara Allgood, Spring Byington, Van Johnson, Isobel Elsom, Halliwell Hobbes, Miles Mander, Frances Rafferty, Connie Gilchrist

'If this film is, as some have labelled it, the American *Mrs Miniver*, then some of us must have grave illusions about our own (or the English) way of life.'—*Bosley Crowther*

AAN: George Oppenheimer

War and Peace**
US / Italy 1956 208m Technicolor Vistavision
Carlo Ponti / Dino de Laurentiis

A Russian family's adventures at the time of Napoleon's invasion.
Despite miscasting and heavy dubbing, the pictorial parts of this précis of a gargantuan novel are powerful and exciting enough; the human side drags a little.

w Bridget Boland, Robert Westerby, King Vidor, Mario Camerini, Ennio de Concini, Ivo Perelli, *novel* Leo Tolstoy *d King Vidor*, (battle scenes) *Mario Soldati* *ph Jack Cardiff*, (battle scenes) *Aldo Tonti* *m* Nino Rota *ad Mario Chiari*

Audrey Hepburn, Henry Fonda, Mel Ferrer, *Herbert Lom*, John Mills, Oscar Homolka, Wilfrid Lawson, Vittorio Gassman, Anita Ekberg, Helmut Dantine, Milly Vitale, Barry Jones

'The film has no more warmth than pictures in an art gallery.'—*Philip T. Hartung*

'When I first agreed to do it the screenplay by Irwin Shaw was fine, but what happened? King Vidor used to go home nights with his wife and rewrite it. All the genius of Tolstoy went out the window.'—*Henry Fonda*

AAN: King Vidor; Jack Cardiff

War and Peace***
USSR 1967 507m Sovcolor 'Scope 70mm
Mosfilm

An immensely long Russian version with some of the most magnificently spectacular battle scenes ever filmed. A treat for the eyes throughout, and perhaps less taxing than reading the novel, which it follows punctiliously.

w Sergei Bondarchuk, Vasili Solovyov *d Sergei Bondarchuk* *ph Anatoli Petritsky* *m* Vyacheslav Ovchinnikov

Lyudmila Savelyeva, Sergei Bondarchuk, Vyacheslav Tikhonov
† The film was five years in production and cost between 50 and 70 million dollars.

AA: best foreign film

The War between Men and Women
US 1972 105m Technicolor Panavision
National General / Jalem / Llenroc / 4D (Danny Arnold)

A half-blind cartoonist marries a divorcee and is troubled by her ex-husband.
Semi-serious comedy vaguely based on Thurber, but not so that you'd notice, apart from the blind hero; generally neither funny nor affecting.

w Mel Shavelson, Danny Arnold, based on the writings of James Thurber *d* Melville Shavelson *ph* Charles F. Wheeler *m* Marvin Hamlisch *pd* Stan Jolley

Jack Lemmon, Barbara Harris, Jason Robards Jnr, Herb Edelman, Lisa Gerritsen

War Games*
US 1983 113m Metrocolor
MGM-UA / Sherwood (Leonard Goldberg, Harold Schneider)

A teenager unwittingly taps his home computer into the Pentagon and pretends to be Russia on the point of launching missiles.
Mildly intriguing science fantasy which becomes uncomfortable and finally boring because of the excess of jargon and flashing lights.

w Lawrence Lasker, Walter F. Parkes *d* John Badham *ph* William A. Fraker *m* Arthur B. Rubenstein *pd* Angelo P. Graham

Matthew Broderick, Dabney Coleman, John Wood, Ally Sheedy, Barry Corbin, Kent Williams

'All the film's adventure and suspense is inevitably at odds with its ostensible sentiments . . . [but] the result has a kind of seamless efficiency.'—*Steve Jenkins, MFB*

AAN: screenplay, cinematography

War Hunt
US 1961 83m bw
TD Enterprises (Terry Sanders)

Korea 1953: a kill-crazy private is befriended by a war orphan but finally has to be shot.
Vaguely commendable but not very expert indictment of the realities of war.

w Stanford Whitmore *d* Denis Sanders *ph* Ted McCord *m* Bud Shank

John Saxon, Robert Redford, Sidney Pollack, Charles Aidman, Tommy Matsuda

The War Lord**
US 1965 121m Technicolor Panavision
Universal / Court (Walter Seltzer)

An officer of the Duke of Normandy has trouble with Druids and the law of *droit de seigneur.*
Complex medieval melodrama with an air of fantasy about it; generally likeably strange, but the production should have been more stylized and fanciful.

w John Collier, Millard Kaufman, *play* The Lovers by Leslie Stevens *d Franklin Schaffner ph Russell Metty m* Jerome Moross *ad* Alexander Golitzen, Henry Bumstead

Charlton Heston, Richard Boone, Rosemary Forsyth, Maurice Evans, Guy Stockwell, Niall MacGinnis, Henry Wilcoxon, James Farentino

The War Lover
GB 1962 105m bw
Columbia / Arthur Hornblow Jnr

In 1943, a Flying Fortress commander based in East Anglia has the wrong ideas about women and war.
Solemn character drama punctuated by aerial battles.

w Howard Koch, *novel* John Hersey *d* Philip Leacock *ph* Bob Huke *m* Richard Addinsell

Steve McQueen, Shirley Anne Field, Robert Wagner, Gary Cockrell, Michael Crawford

War Nurse
US 1930 79m bw

Problems of a nurse behind the lines in World War I. Ambitious but unsuccessful attempt to do another *Big Parade*; a lack of style and story kills it. Robert Montgomery, Anita Page, June Walker, Robert Ames, Zasu Pitts, Marie Prevost, Helen Jerome Eddy, Hedda Hopper. Written by Becky Gardner, Joe Farnham, from an anonymous autobiography, directed by Edgar Selwyn; for MGM. 'Won't get anywhere in the major houses; too filled with audible suffering to class as entertainment.'—*Variety*

War of the Wildcats
US 1943 102m bw
Republic (Robert North)
aka: *In Old Oklahoma*

A lady writer causes friction between an oil operator and a cowboy.
Action potboiler which once passed an hour and three-quarters quite painlessly.

w Ethel Hill, Eleanore Griffith, Thomson Burtis *d* Albert S. Rogell *ph* Jack Marta *m* Walter Scharf

John Wayne, Martha Scott, Albert Dekker, George 'Gabby' Hayes, Marjorie Rambeau, Dale Evans, Grant Withers, Sidney Blackmer

The War of the Worlds*
US 1953 85m Technicolor
Paramount / George Pal

Terrifying aliens invade Earth via the American midwest.
Spectacular battle scenes are the mainstay of this violent fantasy, which goes to pieces once the cardboard characters open their mouths.

w Barre Lyndon, *novel* H. G. Wells *d* Byron Haskin *ph* George Barnes *ad* Hal Pereira, Albert Nozaki *m* Leith Stevens

Gene Barry, Ann Robinson, Les Tremayne, Bob Cornthwaite, Sandra Giglio

The War Wagon**
US 1967 99m Technicolor Panavision
Universal / Batjac (Marvin Schwartz)

Two cowboys and an Indian plan to ambush the gold wagon of a crooked mining contractor.
Exhilarating but simply-plotted action western with strong comedy elements and a cast of old reliables.

w Clair Huffaker, from his novel Badman *d Burt Kennedy ph* William H. Clothier *m* Dmitri Tiomkin

John Wayne, Kirk Douglas, Howard Keel, Robert Walker, Keenan Wynn, Bruce Cabot, Gene Evans, Bruce Dern

'It all works splendidly.'—*MFB*

The Ware Case*
GB 1938 79m bw
Ealing / Capad (S. C. Balcon)

A nobleman is suspected of murdering his wife's rich brother.
Courtroom melodrama twice filmed as a silent; stagey but reasonably compelling in its way.

w Robert Stevenson, Roland Pertwee, E. V. H. Emmett, *play* G. P. Bancroft *d* Robert Stevenson *ph* Ronald Neame *m* Ernest Irving

Clive Brook, Jane Baxter, Barry K. Barnes, C. V. France, Francis L. Sullivan, Frank Cellier, Edward Rigby, Peter Bull, Athene Seyler, Ernest Thesiger
† Previous versions had been made in 1917 (with Matheson Lang) and 1930 (with Stewart Rome).

Warlock*
US 1959 123m De Luxe Cinemascope
TCF (Edward Dmytryk)

The cowardly citizens of a small western town hire a gunman as their unofficial marshal.
Overlong, talkative and somewhat pretentious star western with good sequences.

w Robert Alan Aurthur, *novel* Oakley Hall *d* Edward Dmytryk *ph* Joe MacDonald *m* Leigh Harline

Henry Fonda, Richard Widmark, Anthony Quinn, Dorothy Malone, Dolores Michaels, Wallace Ford, Tom Drake, Richard Arlen, Regis Toomey, Don Beddoe, De Forrest Kelley

Warlords of Atlantis
GB 1978 96m Technicolor
EMI / John Dark, Kevin Connor

Victorian sea scientists discover a lost land under the Mediterranean.
Predictable compote of monsters and unwearable costumes, without a trace of wit in the script. For infants only.

w Brian Hayles *d* Kevin Connor *ph* Alan Hume *m* Mike Vickers *pd* Elliot Scott

Doug McClure, Peter Gilmore, Shane Rimmer, Lea Brodie, Michael Gothard

A Warm December
GB / US 1972 101m Technicolor
First Artists / Verdon (Melville Tucker)

A widowed American doctor in London falls for a mysterious African girl who turns out to be the dying niece of a diplomat.
Weird mishmash of *Love Story, Brief Encounter* and *Dark Victory*, getting the worst of all worlds.

w Lawrence Roman *d* Sidney Poitier *ph Paul Beeson* *m* Coleridge-Taylor Parkinson

Sidney Poitier, Esther Anderson, George Baker, Johnny Sekka, Earl Cameron

Warn London
GB 1934 74m bw

A London policeman who is the double of a well-known burglar replaces him and infiltrates an international gang. Exuberant minor thriller which made a good novelty booking at the time. Edmund Gwenn, John Loder, Leonora Corbett, D. A. Clarke-Smith. Written by Charles Bennett, Billie Bristow, from the novel by Denison Clift; directed by T. Hayes Hunter; for British Lion.

Warn That Man
GB 1943 82m bw

German spies pose as an English nobleman and his staff but are routed by an unexpected guest. On the stage this must have been an effective comedy-thriller, but the film is stymied by stiff handling. Gordon Harker, Raymond Lovell, Jean Kent, Finlay Currie, Philip Friend, Frederick Cooper. Written by Vernon Sylvaine, Lawrence Huntington, from the play by Vernon Sylvaine; directed by Lawrence Huntington; for ABPC. 'Slick drama, mounting success, and spectacular military enterprise.'—*The Cinema*

WATCH ON THE RHINE. British character actor George Coulouris had one of his best Hollywood roles, here with Oscar nominee Paul Lukas and Bette Davis.

'What's a little bullet between friends?'
Warning Shot*
US 1966 100m Technicolor
Paramount / Bob Banner (Buzz Kulik)

While looking for a psychopathic killer, a cop shoots dead a man who draws a gun on him. But the dead man's gun cannot be found, and the officer is suspended . . .
Watchable mystery decked out with guest stars; possibly intended as a TV movie.

w Mann Rubin, *novel* 711—Officer Needs Help by Whit Masterson *d* Buzz Kulik *ph* Joseph Biroc *m* Jerry Goldsmith

David Janssen, Lillian Gish, Ed Begley, Keenan Wynn, Sam Wanamaker, Eleanor Parker, Stefanie Powers, Walter Pidgeon, George Sanders, George Grizzard, Steve Allen, Carroll O'Connor, Joan Collins

Warning Sign
US 1985 100m De Luxe

A solitary cop combats scientists who may unwittingly unleash a deadly plague. Unimpressive as propaganda and tedious as suspense. Sam Waterston, Kathleen Quinlan, Yaphet Kotto, Richard Dysart, Jeffrey De Munn. Written by Hal Barwood, Matthew Robbins; directed by Hal Barwood; for Barwood-Robbins / TCF.

Warning to Wantons
GB 1948 104m bw

A nobleman takes in a flirtatious girl and finds she causes trouble for him and his family. Interminable comedy-drama made even duller by the Independent Frame production method, which cut costs but restricted movement. Harold Warrender, Anne Vernon, David Tomlinson, Sonia Holm, Marie Burke, Judy Kelly. Written by Donald B. Wilson and James Laver, from the novel by Mary Mitchell; directed by Donald B. Wilson; for Aquila / GFD.

Warpath
US 1951 93m Technicolor
Paramount (Nat Holt)

An ex-army captain tracks down the outlaws who murdered his girl.
Goodish standard western.

w Frank Gruber *d* Byron Haskin *ph* Ray Rennahan *m* Paul Sawtell

Edmond O'Brien, Dean Jagger, Forrest Tucker, Harry Carey Jnr, Wallace Ford, Polly Bergen

'These are the armies of the night . . .'
The Warriors
US 1979 94m Movielab
Paramount (Laurence Gordon)

A New York street gang runs into trouble when making a cross-city journey.
A sick exploitation movie about urban violence, poorly made into the bargain.

w David Shaber, Walter Hill, *novel* Sol Yurick *d* Walter Hill *ph* Andrew Laszlo *m* Barry de Vorzon

Michael Beck, James Remar, Thomas Waites, Dorsey Wright, Brian Tyler, David Harris

The Warrior's Husband
US 1933 75m bw

The Greeks break into Amazonia and conquer the women, provoking a worm to turn. A weird attempt by Hollywood to film a whimsical comedy which belonged only on Broadway, where the Greeks no doubt have a word for it. Elissa Landi, Marjorie Rambeau, Ernest Truex, David Manners, Helen Ware, Maude Eburne. Written by Sonya Levien from the play by Julian Thompson; directed by Walter Lang; for Jesse L. Lasky / Fox. 'Novel farce will need astute exploitation aid.'—*Variety*

Washington Masquerade
US 1932 92m bw

A high-minded senator is corrupted by a worthless girl. Solid star melodrama. Lionel Barrymore, Karen Morley, Nils Asther, C. Henry Gordon, William Collier Snr. Written by John Meehan and Samuel Blythe, from the play *The Claw* by Henri Bernstein; directed by Charles Brabin; for MGM. (GB title: *Mad Masquerade.*)

Washington Merry-go-round*
US 1932 75m bw

A crusading young congressman attacks the crooks in the government. Naive comedy-drama with a miscast star. Lee Tracy, Constance Cummings, Alan Dinehart, Walter Connolly, Clarence Muse, Arthur Vinton. Written by Jo Swerling from an original by Maxwell Anderson; directed by James Cruze; for Columbia. 'Lots of flagwaving and political timeliness the chief appeal.'—*Variety*

Washington Story
US 1952 82m bw
MGM (Dore Schary)
GB title: *Target for Scandal*

A lady reporter goes to Washington to expose corruption, but falls for an honest congressman.
Standard flagwaver which takes itself a shade too seriously.

wd Robert Pirosh *ph* John Alton *m* Conrad Salinger

Van Johnson, Patricia Neal, Louis Calhern, Sidney Blackmer, Philip Ober, Patricia Collinge, Elizabeth Patterson, Moroni Olsen

Watch It, Sailor
GB 1961 81m bw

A sailor about to be married receives a paternity accusation. Glum farce with wasted talent. Dennis Price, Marjorie Rhodes, Irene Handl, Liz Fraser, Vera Day, John Meillon, Cyril Smith. Written by Falkland Cary and Phillip King from their play; directed by Wolf Rilla; for Cormorant/Hammer/Columbia.

Watch on the Rhine**
US 1943 114m bw
Warner (Hal B. Wallis)

A German refugee and his family are pursued by Nazi agents in Washington.
Talky play doesn't make much of a film, though the talk is good talk and the performances outstanding; but it made a prestige point or two for Hollywood.

w Dashiell Hammett, *play Lillian Hellman* *d* Herman Shumlin *ph* Merritt Gerstad, Hal Mohr *m* Max Steiner

Paul Lukas, Bette Davis, Lucile Watson, *George Coulouris*, Donald Woods, Geraldine Fitzgerald, Beulah Bondi, Henry Daniell

AA: Paul Lukas
AAN: best picture; script; Lucile Watson

Watch the Birdie
US 1950 71m bw
MGM (Harry Ruskin)

A photographer meets a rich girl and saves her from a crook.
Unhappy remake of Buster Keaton's *The Cameraman*, enlivened by a chase finale, but not helped by the star playing three members of the same family.

w Ivan Tors, Devery Freeman, Harry Ruskin *d* Jack Donohue *ph* Paul C. Vogel *m* George Stoll

Red Skelton, Arlene Dahl, Ann Miller, Leon Ames, Pamela Britton, Richard Rober

The Watcher in the Woods
US 1980 / 82 100m or 83m Technicolor
Walt Disney (Tom Leetch)

The teenage daughter of an American composer has strange and apparently supernatural experiences in the British countryside.
Unsatisfactory attempt by the Disney people to aim at a wider audience than is expected of them. The mixture of cuteness, menace and the supernatural simply doesn't gell, and the film was much re-edited between its two appearances.

w Brian Clemens, Harry Spaulding, Rosemary Anne Sisson, *novel* Florence Engel Randall *d* John Hough (and Vincent McEveety) *ph* Alan Hume *m* Stanley Myers

Bette Davis, Carroll Baker, David McCallum, Lynn-Holly Johnson, Kyle Richards, Ian Bannen, Richard Pasco

The Watchmaker of St Paul*
France 1973 105m Eastmancolor
Lira (Raymond Danon)
original title: *L'Horloger de St Paul*

A watchmaker's tranquil life is shattered when he learns that his son is wanted for murder.
Solid character drama with careful writing and acting.

w Jean Aurenche, Pierre Bost, Bertrand Tavernier, *novel* L'Horloger D'Everton by Georges Simenon *d* Bertrand Tavernier *ph* Pierre William Glenn *m* Philippe Sarde

Philippe Noiret, Jean Rochefort, Sylvain Rougerie, Christine Pascal

Water*
GB 1985 95m colour
HandMade (Ian La Frenais)

Chaos comes to a Caribbean island when industrialists check it for mineral springs.
Hysterical comedy which never develops a single line for long, and quickly wears out its welcome.

w Dick Clement, Ian La Frenais, Bill Bersky *d* Dick Clement *ph* Douglas Slocombe *m* Mike Moran

Michael Caine, Valerie Perrine, Brenda Vaccaro, Leonard Rossiter, Billy Connolly, Fred Gwynne, Maureen Lipman

The Water Babies
GB / Poland 1978 92m colour
Ariadne / Studio Miniatur Filmowych (Peter Shaw)

An 1850 chimney sweep evades his pursuers by jumping into a pool, where he becomes involved in an underwater adventure.
The live action bookends are strangely subdued, the animated middle totally characterless and seeming to bear little relation to the rest. A considerable disappointment.

w Michael Robson, *novel* Charles Kingsley *d* Lionel Jeffries *ph* Ted Scaife *m* Phil Coulter

James Mason, Billie Whitelaw, Bernard Cribbins, Joan Greenwood, David Tomlinson, Tommy Pender

Water Birds see The Living Desert

The Water Gypsies
GB 1932 80m bw

Adventures of two girls who live on a Thames barge. Rather naive and ordinary version of a successful book which many years later emerged as a stage musical; the film production has a stagey look throughout. Ann Todd, Sari Maritza, Richard Bird, Frances Doble, Ian Hunter, Anthony Ireland. Written by Basil Dean, Miles Malleson, Alma Reville, John Paddy Carstairs from the novel by A. P. Herbert; directed by Maurice Elvey; for ATP. 'Should do business in the best type of places.'—*Variety*

'The desires and loneliness of seafaring men and their women!'

Waterfront
GB 1950 80m bw
GFD / Conqueror / Paul Soskin
US title: *Waterfront Women*

A drunken ship's fireman comes back to Liverpool after many years and causes trouble.
Unintentionally funny melodrama which gives the actors a lot of trouble.

w John Brophy, Paul Soskin, *novel* John Brophy *d* Michael Anderson *ph* Harry Waxman *md* Muir Mathieson

Robert Newton, Richard Burton, Kathleen Harrison, Susan Shaw, Avis Scott, Kenneth Griffith

Waterhole Three
US 1967 100m Techniscope
Paramount

Sheriff, crooks and a gambler seek buried loot.
Rather irritatingly immoral western with a hero who defines rape as assault with a friendly weapon; in between it tries hard for the ballad style.

w Joseph Steck, Robert R. Young *d* William Graham *ph* Robert Burks *m* Dave Grusin

James Coburn, Carroll O'Connor, Margaret Blye, Claude Akins, Joan Blondell, Timothy Carey

'The men, the battle, the glory the world will remember forever!'

Waterloo*
Italy / USSR 1970 132m Technicolor Panavision
Columbia / DDL / Mosfilm (Dino de Laurentiis)

Historical events leading up to the 1815 battle. The battle forms the last hour of this historical charade, and looks both exciting and splendid, though confusion is not avoided. The rest is a mixed blessing.

w H. A. L. Craig, Sergei Bondarchuk *d Sergei Bondarchuk ph Armando Nannuzzi m* Nino Rota *pd* Mario Garbuglia

Rod Steiger, Christopher Plummer, Orson Welles, Jack Hawkins, Virginia McKenna, Dan O'Herlihy, Rupert Davies, Ian Ogilvy, Michael Wilding

Waterloo Bridge*
US 1931 72m bw
Universal (Carl Laemmle Jnr)

An army officer marries a ballerina; when he is reported missing his family ignore her and she sinks into prostitution.
One for the ladies, who lapped it up.

w Tom Reed, Benn W. Levy, *play* Robert E. Sherwood *d* James Whale *ph* Arthur Edeson

Mae Clarke, Kent Douglass, Doris Lloyd, Ethel Griffies, Enid Bennett, Frederick Kerr, Bette Davis

'Just fair programme fodder, and it ought to be better. Not helped by an uninspiring sad ending.'—*Variety*

Waterloo Bridge**
US 1940 103m bw
MGM (Sidney Franklin)

Lush, all-stops-out remake of the above; for yet another version see *Gaby*.

w S. N. Behrman, Hans Rameau, George Froeschel *d* Mervyn Le Roy *ph Joseph Ruttenberg m* Herbert Stothart

Vivien Leigh, Robert Taylor, Lucile Watson, Virginia Field, Maria Ouspenskaya, C. Aubrey Smith, Steffi Duna

'The director uses candlelight and rain more effectively than he does the actors.'—*New Yorker, 1977*

AAN: Joseph Ruttenberg; Herbert Stothart

The Waterloo Bridge Handicap*
GB 1978 21m colour

Commuters enjoy a daily race across Westminster Bridge. Amusing trifle, well shot and edited. Leonard Rossiter, Lynda Bellingham, John Quentin, Gordon Laye. Written and directed by *Ross Cramer*; edited by *Sean Barton*; for Fetter / Paramount.

Waterloo Road
GB 1944 76m bw
GFD / Gainsborough (Edward Black)

A soldier whose wife is enamoured of a petty crook absents himself to settle matters.
What at the time seemed cheerful realism now seems chronically forced, but amusing moments can still be found.

w Sidney Gilliat, *story* Val Valentine *d* Sidney Gilliat *ph* Arthur Crabtree *md* Louis Levy

John Mills, Stewart Granger, Joy Shelton, Alastair Sim, Beatrice Varley, Alison Leggatt, *Jean Kent*

'The harsh rattle of trains over a viaduct, the clamour of the street market, the wailing of sirens and the crash of bombs are the accompaniment of this wartime love story.'—*Richard Winnington*

'Unpretentious, credible, continuously entertaining and just the right length.'—*Richard Mallett, Punch*

Watermelon Man
US 1970 100m Technicolor
Columbia / Johanna (John B. Bennett)

A bigoted insurance salesman wakes up one morning to find he has turned into a black man.
Spasmodically funny racial comedy, compromised by the impossibility of a black man playing white even with heavy make-up.

w Herman Raucher *d* Melvin Van Peebles *ph* W. Wallace Kelley *m* Melvin Van Peebles

Godfrey Cambridge, Estelle Parsons, Howard Caine, Mantan Moreland

Waters of Time*
GB 1951 37m bw

A poetic impression of the Port of London, from the mouth of the Thames to Kingston. Notably stylish documentary, made to coincide with the Festival of Britain. Written, directed and edited by *Basil Wright* and *Bill Launder*; for the Port of London Authority.

Watership Down
GB 1978 92m Technicolor
Nepenthe (Martin Rosen)

A colony of rabbits seek a new home following a vision of the destruction of their warren.
A brilliantly written if somewhat pretentious parable becomes a rather flatly made cartoon in which it is difficult to distinguish one rabbit from another; the whole thing becomes a bit doomladen for family audiences, while adults will presumably prefer to re-read the novel.

wd Martin Rosen, *novel* Richard Adams *animation d* Tony Guy *m* Angela Morley

voices: John Hurt, Richard Briers, Ralph Richardson, Zero Mostel, Roy Kinnear, Denholm Elliott, John Bennett, Simon Cadell

Watusi
US 1959 85m Technicolor
MGM (Al Zimbalist)

Harry Quartermain retraces his father's footsteps to King Solomon's Mines.
Skilful re-use of *King Solomon's Mines* footage; acceptable Boys' Own Paper stuff.

w James Clavell *d* Kurt Neumann *ph* Harold E. Wellman

George Montgomery, Taina Elg, David Farrar, Rex Ingram, Dan Seymour

Waxworks*
Germany 1924 62m approx (24 fps) bw silent
Neptun-Film
original title: *Das Wachsfigurenkabinett*

A young poet in a fairground waxwork museum concocts stories about Haroun al Raschid, Ivan the Terrible and Jack the Ripper.
The form later became familiar in such horror films as *Torture Garden* and *Tales from the Crypt*, but here the emphasis is not on horror but on grotesquerie, and indeed the idea is somewhat more entertaining than the rather plodding execution.

w Henrik Galeen *d Paul Leni ph* Helmar Lerski *ad* Paul Leni, Ernst Stern, Alfred Junge

William Dieterle, Emil Jannings, Conrad Veidt, Werner Krauss

The Way Ahead***
GB 1944 115m bw
GFD / Two Cities (John Sutro, Norman Walker)
US title: *Immortal Battalion*

Adventures of a platoon of raw recruits during World War II.
Memorable semi-documentary originally intended as a training film; the warm humour of the early scenes, however, never leads quite naturally into the final action and tragedy.

w Eric Ambler, Peter Ustinov *d Carol Reed ph* Guy Green *m* William Alwyn

David Niven, Stanley Holloway, Raymond Huntley, *William Hartnell*, James Donald, John Laurie, Leslie Dwyer, Hugh Burden, Jimmy Hanley, Renée Asherson, Penelope Dudley Ward, Reginald Tate, Leo Genn, Mary Jerrold, Peter Ustinov

Way Back Home
US 1932 81m bw

Problems of a Maine preacher.
Unintentionally hilarious farrago of dark deeds in a small town, from a radio serial. Phillips Lord, Bette Davis, Effie Palmer, Bennett Kilpack, Frank Albertson, Mrs Phillips Lord. Written by Jane Murfin; directed by William A. Seiter; for RKO.

Way Down East**
US 1920 110m approx (24 fps) bw with colour sequence silent
D. W. Griffith

A country girl is seduced; her baby dies; her shame is revealed; but a kindly farmer rescues her from drowning and marries her.
Old-fashioned tearjerker impeccably mounted and very typical of its director in its sentimental mood. The ice floe sequence is famous for its excitement and realism.

w Anthony Paul Kelly, Joseph R. Grismer, D. W. Griffith, *play* Lottie Blair Parker *d D. W. Griffith* *ph* Billy Bitzer, Henrik Sortov

Lillian Gish, Richard Barthelmess, Lowell Sherman, Creighton Hale

'Griffith took a creaking, dated stage melodrama and turned it into a melodramatic epic.'—*Pauline Kael, 70s*

Way Down East
US 1935 85m bw
TCF (Winfield Sheehan)

Tedious and unwise remake.

w Howard Estabrook, William Hurlbut *d* Henry King

Rochelle Hudson, Henry Fonda, Slim Summerville, Edward Trevor, Margaret Hamilton, Andy Devine, Spring Byington, Russell Simpson, Sara Haden

Way for a Sailor
US 1930 83m bw
MGM

Adventures of a tough seafarer and a pet seal.
Thin vehicle for a declining star whose talkie voice was at odds with his image.

w Laurence Stallings, W. L. River, *novel* Albert Richard Wetjen *d* Sam Wood *ph* Percy Hilburn

John Gilbert, Wallace Beery, Leila Hyams, Jim Tully, Polly Moran, Doris Lloyd

'It throws John Gilbert for a loss, and it's not his fault. His voice is okay.'—*Variety*

Way of a Gaucho
US 1952 91m Technicolor
TCF (Philip Dunne)

An Argentine gaucho joins the militia and fights Indians.
Mildly interesting western-in-disguise.

w Philip Dunne, *novel* Herbert Childs *d* Jacques Tourneur *ph* Harry Jackson *m* Sol Kaplan

Rory Calhoun, Gene Tierney, Richard Boone, Hugh Marlowe, Everett Sloane, Enrique Chaico

The Way of All Flesh*
US 1928 94m (24 fps) bw silent
Paramount
(Adolph Zukor, Jesse L. Lasky)

A respectable man leaves his wife, goes to the dogs, and is too ashamed to come back.
Star character drama, most watchable now when it goes over the top.

d Victor Fleming

Emil Jannings, Belle Bennett, Phyllis Hayer

AA: Emil Jannings
AAN: best picture

'He left his heart behind when he took it!'

The Way of All Flesh
US 1940 82m bw
Paramount (Eugene Zukor)

Remake of the above, well enough done but clearly outmoded.

w Lenore Coffee, from treatment by Jules Furthman and Lajos Biro of novel by Perley Poore Sheehan *d* Louis King *ph* Theodor Sparkuhl

Akim Tamiroff, Gladys George, Muriel Angelus, Berton Churchill, Fritz Leiber

Way Out West****
US 1937 66m bw
Hal Roach (Stan Laurel)

Laurel and Hardy come to Brushwood Gulch to deliver the deed to a gold mine.
Seven reels of perfect joy, with the comedians at their very best in brilliantly-timed routines, plus two song numbers as a bonus.

w Jack Jevne, Charles Rogers, James Parrott, Felix Adler *d James Horne* *ph* Art Lloyd, Walter Lundin *m* Marvin Hatley

Stan Laurel, Oliver Hardy, James Finlayson, Sharon Lynne, Rosina Lawrence

'Thin returns indicated . . . for added feature on duallers.'—*Variety*

'Not only one of their most perfect films, it ranks with the best screen comedy anywhere.'—*David Robinson, 1962*

'The film is leisurely in the best sense; you adjust to a different rhythm and come out feeling relaxed as if you'd had a vacation.'—*New Yorker, 1980*

AAN: Marvin Hatley

'Of course he's naughty! But that's the way you love him best!'

The Way to Love
US 1933 80m bw
Paramount (Benjamin Glazer)

A would-be Paris tourist guide works as a pavement hawker and helps a showgirl evade her knife-thrower partner.
Thin star vehicle with a few pleasant moments.

w Gene Fowler, Benjamin Glazer *d* Norman Taurog *ph* Charles Lang *m / ly* Ralph Rainger, Leo Robin

Maurice Chevalier, Edward Everett Horton, Ann Dvorak, Arthur Pierson, Minna Gombell, Blanche Frederici, Douglass Dumbrille, John Miljan

'The poorest of the Chevaliers but poor entertainment which will get by on the strength of the star.'—*Variety*

The Way to the Gold
US 1957 94m bw
TCF (David Weisbart)

An ex-convict seeks hidden loot but is pursued by competitors.
Gloomy, self-pitying melodrama.

w Wendell Mayes, *novel* Wilber Steele *d* Robert D. Webb *ph* Leo Tover *m* Lionel Newman

Jeffrey Hunter, Sheree North, Barry Sullivan, Walter Brennan, Ruth Donnelly, Neville Brand

The Way to the Stars****
GB 1945 109m bw
Two Cities (Anatole de Grunwald)
US title: *Johnny in the Clouds*

World War II as seen by the guests at a small hotel near an airfield.
Generally delightful comedy drama suffused with tragic atmosphere but with very few flying shots, one of the few films which instantly bring back the atmosphere of the war in Britain for anyone who was involved.

w Terence Rattigan, Anatole de Grunwald poem John Pudney *d Anthony Asquith* *ph* Derrick Williams *m Nicholas Brodszky*

John Mills, Rosamund John, Michael Redgrave, Douglass Montgomery, Basil Radford, Stanley Holloway, Joyce Carey, Renée Asherson, Felix Aylmer, Bonar Colleano, Trevor Howard, Jean Simmons

'Not for a long time have I seen a film so satisfying, so memorable, or so successful in evoking the precise mood and atmosphere of the recent past.'—*Richard Mallett, Punch*

'Humour, humanity, and not a sign of mawkishness . . . a classic opening sequence, with the camera wandering through an abandoned air base, peering in at each detail in the nissen huts, the sleeping quarters, the canteens, noting all the time a procession of objects each of which will have its own special significance in the action of the film.'—*Basil Wright, 1972*

Way Way Out
US 1966 105m De Luxe Cinemascope
TCF / Coldwater / Jerry Lewis (Malcolm Stuart)

In 1994 a weather expert on the moon has woman trouble.
Dismal sex farce with an unusual backdrop; painful to sit through.

w William Bowers, Laslo Vadnay *d* Gordon Douglas *ph* William H. Clothier *m* Lalo Schifrin

Jerry Lewis, Connie Stevens, Robert Morley, Dick Shawn, Anita Ekberg, Dennis Weaver, Howard Morris, Brian Keith

'Everything seemed so important then—even love!'

The Way We Were**
US 1973 118m Eastmancolor Panavision
Columbia / Rastar (Ray Stark)

The romance and marriage of an upper-crust young novelist and a Jewish bluestocking girl, from college to Hollywood in the thirties, forties and fifties.
Instant nostalgia for Americans, some fun and a lot of boredom for everybody is provided by this very patchy star vehicle which makes a particular mess of the McCarthy witch hunt sequence but has undeniable moments of vitality.

w Arthur Laurents, from his novel *d* Sydney Pollack *ph* Harry Stradling Jnr *m* Marvin Hamlisch

Barbra Streisand, Robert Redford, Patrick O'Neal, Viveca Lindfors, Bradford Dillman, Lois Chiles, Allyn Ann McLerie, Herb Edelman, Murray Hamilton

'Not one moment of the picture is anything but garbage under the gravy of false honesty.'—*Stanley Kauffmann*

'A real curate's egg of a movie, composed of so many disparate parts as to put you in mind of Leacock's knight, who got on his horse and rode off furiously in all directions.'—*Benny Green, Punch*

AA: Marvin Hamlisch; title song (*m* Marvin Hamlisch, *ly* Alan and Marilyn Bergman)
AAN: Harry Stradling Jnr; Barbra Streisand

The Way West*
US 1967 122m De Luxe Panavision
UA / Harold Hecht

Hazards of a wagon train between Missouri and Oregon in 1843.
Semi-spectacular western which looks good but falls apart dramatically, especially in its insistence on a sub-plot about a most unlikely nymphet.

w Ben Maddow, Mitch Lindemann, *novel* A. B. Guthrie Jnr *d* Andrew V. McLaglen *ph William H. Clothier* *m* Bronislau Kaper

Kirk Douglas, Robert Mitchum, Richard Widmark, Lola Albright, Michael Witney, Sally Field, Stubby Kaye, Jack Elam

'A jerk's idea of an epic; big stars, big landscapes, bad jokes, folksy-heroic music to plug up the holes, and messy hang-ups.'—*Pauline Kael*

The Wayward Bus
US 1957 89m bw Cinemascope
TCF (Charles Brackett)

A landslide strands an assortment of bus passengers in a lonely farmhouse . . .
. . . but not the old dark house, unfortunately: this lot does nothing but talk, and the plot never really forms.

w Ivan Moffat, *novel* John Steinbeck *d* Victor Vicas *ph* Charles G. Clarke *m* Leigh Harline

Dan Dailey, Jayne Mansfield, Joan Collins, Rick Jason, Dolores Michaels, Larry Keating, Betty Lou Keim

We Are Not Alone*
US 1939 112m bw
Warner (Henry Blanke)

A man having an innocent affair is accused of murdering his wife.
Gloomy, well-acted drama with a rather uneasy English setting.

w James Hilton, Milton Krims, *novel* James Hilton *d* Edmund Goulding *ph* Tony Gaudio *m* Max Steiner

Paul Muni, Jane Bryan, Flora Robson, Raymond Severn, Una O'Connor, Henry Daniell, Montagu Love, James Stephenson, Cecil Kellaway

'It has dignity and warmth and is genuinely moving . . . handsomely produced, skilfully directed, and eloquently played.'—*Variety*

'An extraordinarily moving story, beautifully told and perfectly acted.'—*Monthly Film Bulletin*

We Dive at Dawn
GB 1943 98m bw
GFD / Gainsborough (Edward Black)

World War II adventures of a British submarine disabled in the Baltic.
Fairly routine war suspenser.

w J. P. Williams, Val Valentine, Frank Launder *d* Anthony Asquith *ph* Jack Cox *md* Louis Levy

John Mills, Eric Portman, Reginald Purdell, Niall MacGinnis, Joan Hopkins, Josephine Wilson, Jack Watling

We Faw Down
US 1928 20m bw silent

Stan and Ollie have an evening out, but their lies to their wives become apparent. Moderate star comedy, later elaborated in *Sons of the Desert*. Laurel and Hardy, Bess Flowers, Vivien Oakland. Written by H. M. Walker; directed by Leo McCarey; for Hal Roach.

We Have Our Moments
US 1937 63m bw

Gangsters hide their loot in the trunk of a schoolteacher going to Europe on a vacation. Rather slackly handled comedy with amusing bits. James Dunn, Sally Eilers, Mischa Auer, David Niven, Warren Hymer, Marjorie Gateson, Thurston Hall. Written by Bruce Manning, Charles Grayson, David Belden, Frederick Stephani; directed by Alfred Werker; for Edmund Grainger / Universal.
'As the number two feature on doubles it will manage to get by.'—*Variety*

We Joined the Navy
GB 1962 105m Eastmancolor Cinemascope
Dial / Daniel M. Angel

A carefree naval commander and three cadets get involved in the affairs of a small Mediterranean country.
Desperate naval farce which sinks from script malnutrition in reel two.

w Arthur Dales, *novel* John Winton *d* Wendy Toye *ph* Otto Heller *m* Ron Grainer

Kenneth More, Lloyd Nolan, Mischa Auer, Joan O'Brien, Jeremy Lloyd, Dinsdale Landen, Derek Fowlds

We Live Again*
US 1934 85m bw
Samuel Goldwyn

A Russian prince is brought up in the country and falls in love with a servant girl whose life later takes a downward path.
Beautifully made but dramatically uninteresting version of a Russian classic.

w Preston Sturges, Maxwell Anderson, Leonard Praskins, *novel* Resurrection by Leo Tolstoy *d Rouben Mamoulian* *ph Gregg Toland* *m* Alfred Newman

Fredric March, Anna Sten, Jane Baxter, C. Aubrey Smith, Ethel Griffies, Jessie Ralph, Sam Jaffe

'It's a class picture basically. That limits its mass b.o. appeal.'—*Variety*

We of the Never Never*
Australia 1982 134m Eastmancolor Technovision
Adams Packer / Film Corporation of Western Australia / GTC (Greg Tepper)

Around 1900, a city girl marries the owner of an isolated cattle station.
Longwinded but attractively photographed recollections of another time and another place. Not really very memorable despite a plethora of incident.

w Peter Schreck, *book* Mrs Aeneas Gunn *d* Igor Auzins *ph Gary Hansen* *m* Peter Best

Angela Punch McGregor, Arthur Dignam, Tony Barry, Tommy Lewis

'Tasteful period re-creation, choked-back emotionalism, a *Men of Two Worlds* attempt at assuaging colonial guilt, and the kind of tidily suffering heroine Deborah Kerr used to play.'—*Kim Newman, MFB*

We Were Dancing
US 1942 93m bw
MGM (Robert Z. Leonard, Orville Dull)

A Polish princess elopes from her engagement party with a gigolo.
Leaden romantic comedy produced in high style.

w Claudine West, Hans Rameau, George Froeschel, partly based on the play Tonight at 8.30 by Noel Coward *d* Robert Z. Leonard *ph* Robert Planck *m* Bronislau Kaper

Norma Shearer, Melvyn Douglas, Gail Patrick, Lee Bowman, *Marjorie Main*, Reginald Owen, Alan Mowbray, Florence Bates, Sig Rumann, Dennis Hoey, Heather Thatcher, Connie Gilchrist

We Were Strangers*
US 1949 105m bw
Columbia / Horizon (Sam Spiegel)

Cuban rebels in the thirties plan to assassinate a politician and have to build a tunnel through a cemetery.
Well-made but very downbeat adventure story, too cheerless to be exciting.

w Peter Viertel, John Huston, *novel* Rough Sketch by Robert Sylvester *d John Huston* *ph* Russell Metty *m* Georges Antheil

John Garfield, Jennifer Jones, Pedro Armendariz, Gilbert Roland, Wally Cassell, Ramon Novarro, David Bond, Jose Perez

'There is so much about this film I cannot swallow—the implausibilities of detail, the convention of broken accents, the literary conversaziones, the naïve doctrines of revolution . . . [but] it continues to haunt the mind and has therefore had its say.'—*Richard Winnington*

We Who Are about to Die
US 1937 82m bw

Life on Death Row. Modest prison melodrama with a lot of opportunity for character actors to display hysteria. Preston Foster, Ann Dvorak, John Beal, Ray Mayer, Gordon Jones, Russel Hopton, J. Carrol

Naish, Willie Fung, Paul Hurst, Frank Jenks, Barnett Parker, John Wray, John Carroll. Written by John Twist, David Lamson; directed by Christy Cabanne; for RKO. 'An action drama of considerable tension that should please the general run of fans with plenty of special charm for the kids and the menfolk.'—*Variety*

The Weak and the Wicked
GB 1953 88m bw
ABPC / Marble Arch (Victor Skutezky)

Flashbacks show how various women came to find themselves in prison.
Predictable portmanteau drama with stalwart performances.

w J. Lee Thompson, Anne Burnaby, *book* Who Lie in Gaol by Joan Henry *d* J. Lee Thompson *ph* Gilbert Taylor *m* Leighton Lucas

Glynis Johns, John Gregson, Diana Dors, Jane Hylton, Sidney James, Olive Sloane, Eliot Makeham, A. E. Matthews, Athene Seyler, Sybil Thorndike, Anthony Nicholls, Joan Haythorne

The Weaker Sex
GB 1948 84m bw

Day-to-day problems of a well-to-do war widow. Mild suburban comedy which sparkled more on stage, with such curtain lines as: 'Quick, the fishmonger's got fish!' Ursula Jeans, Cecil Parker, Joan Hopkins, Derek Bond, Lana Morris, Thora Hird, John Stone. Written by Esther McCracken and Paul Soskin, from the play *No Medals* by Esther McCracken; directed by Roy Baker; for Paul Soskin / Two Cities.

The Weapon
GB 1956 81m bw Superscope 235
Periclean (Frank Bevis)

A boy finds a loaded revolver on a bomb site and mistakenly thinks he has killed someone with it.
Standard suspenser with a cast worthy of something more interesting.

w Fred Freiburger *d* Val Guest *ph* Reg Wyer *m* James Stevens

Lizabeth Scott, Steve Cochran, George Cole, Herbert Marshall, Nicole Maurey, Jon Whiteley, Laurence Naismith

The Web*
US 1947 87m bw
Universal (Jerry Bresler)

A financier hires a young lawyer as his bodyguard and lures him into committing murder.
Modestly well staged and glossy thriller.

w William Bowers, Bertram Millhauser *d* Michael Gordon *ph* Irving Glassberg *m* Hans Salter

Edmond O'Brien, Vincent Price, Ella Raines, William Bendix

The Webster Boy
GB 1961 83m bw
Emmet Dalton
US title: *Middle of Nowhere*

A teenager suffers at the hands of a sadistic schoolmaster.
Curious, totally unbelievable melodrama.

w Ted Allen *d* Don Chaffey *ph* Gerald Gibbs *m* Wilfrid Joseph

Richard O'Sullivan, John Cassavetes, David Farrar, Elizabeth Sellars, Niall MacGinnis

A Wedding*
US 1978 125m De Luxe
TCF / Lion's Gate (Thommy Thompson, Robert Altman)

Two families converge for a fashionable wedding, but the day is beset by calamities.
Wide-ranging satirical comedy which despite excellent moments goes on far too long, is rather too black, and is sabotaged by the director's *penchant* for having fourteen people talking at the same time. An exhausting experience.

w John Considine, Patricia Resnick, Allan Nicholls, Robert Altman *d* Robert Altman *ph* Charles Rosher *md* Tom Walls

Carol Burnett, Paul Dooley, Amy Stryker, Mia Farrow, Peggy Ann Garner, Lillian Gish, Nina Van Pallandt, Vittorio Gassman, Howard Duff, Desi Arnaz Jnr, Dina Merrill, Geraldine Chaplin, Viveca Lindfors, Lauren Hutton, John Cromwell

The Wedding March**
US 1928 196m approx (24 fps) bw silent
Paramount / Celebrity

A Habsburg prince loves a poor girl but is forced to marry a crippled princess, who dies; he is then murdered by the poor girl's enraged defender.
A marathon dose of Stroheim's favourite subject, sex, with some violence and a few fetishes thrown in. Full of fascinating touches, but desperately overlong, it was originally released in two parts, but failed to draw.

w Harry Carr, Erich Von Stroheim *d Erich Von Stroheim* *ph* Hal Mohr, Ben Reynolds *ad* Erich Von Stroheim, Richard Day

Erich Von Stroheim, Fay Wray, Zasu Pitts, Matthew Betz, Maude George, Cesare Gravina, George Fawcett

'A pitilessly authentic portrait of decadent Imperialist Austria.'—*Georges Sadoul*

'The slowness, heaviness, mindlessness of this temple of unnaturalness through which man passes as through a forest of clichés defied description.'—*John Simon, 1967*

† In 1975 there was published a pictorial record, *The Complete Wedding March,* by Herman G. Weinberg.

The Wedding Night*
US 1935 83m bw
Samuel Goldwyn

A Connecticut author causes tragedy when he takes an interest in the local Polish immigrant farmers and especially in the daughter of one of them.
Interesting and unusual but slightly tediously told drama.

w Edith Fitzgerald *d* King Vidor *ph* Gregg Toland *m* Alfred Newman

Gary Cooper, Anna Sten, Sig Rumann, Helen Vinson, Ralph Bellamy, Esther Dale

'Fine artistic film, possibly too artistic.'—*Variety*

'Convincing and curiously powerful.'—*New York Herald Tribune*

The Wedding of Lilli Marlene
GB 1953 87m bw

The heroine of World War II becomes a success in show business. Poorly confected programme filler, an unnecessary sequel if ever there was one. Lisa Daniely, Hugh McDermott, Sid James, Gabrielle Brune, Robert Ayres. Written by John Baines; directed by Arthur Crabtree; for Monarch.

'He gave her something to remember him by!'

Wedding Present*
US 1936 81m bw
Paramount (B. P. Schulberg)

A pair of crack newspaper reporters take their jobs and themselves lightly.
Whimsical star comedy with some funny scenes.

w Joseph Anthony, *story* Paul Gallico *d* Richard Wallace *ph* Leon Shamroy

Cary Grant, Joan Bennett, George Bancroft, Conrad Nagel, Gene Lockhart, William Demarest, Edward Brophy

'Grant and Bennett try hard, but the combination of story, direction and whatnot is pretty much against them.'—*Variety*

Wedding Rehearsal
GB 1932 84m bw
London Films / Alexander Korda

A Guards officer foils his grandmother's plans to get him married by finding suitors for all the young ladies offered.
Frail comedy with unsure technique.

w Helen Gardom from story by Lajos Biro, George Grossmith *d* Alexander Korda *ph* Leslie Rowson *m* Kurt Schroeder

Roland Young, George Grossmith, John Loder, Lady Tree, Wendy Barrie, Maurice Evans, Joan Gardner, Merle Oberon, Kate Cutler, Edmund Breon

Wee Willie Winkie**
US 1937 99m bw
TCF (Gene Markey)

A small girl becomes the mascot of a British regiment in India.
Vaguely based on a Kipling tale, this was the most expensive Temple vehicle and a first-rate family action picture with sentimental asides.

w Ernest Pascal, Julien Josephson, *story* Rudyard Kipling *d John Ford* *ph Arthur Miller* *m* Alfred Newman

Shirley Temple, Victor McLaglen, C. Aubrey Smith, June Lang, Michael Whalen, Cesar Romero, Constance Collier, Gavin Muir

'Will add another clean-up to her cycle, but those knees are losing their contour . . . a pretentiously produced melodrama which launches the leading feminine box office star into a distinctly new phase of her career and story material.'—*Variety*

Weekend at the Waldorf*
US 1945 130m bw
MGM (Arthur Hornblow Jnr)

Four stories about guests at New York's largest hotel.
Disguised version of *Grand Hotel*, with the same stories twisted; the talent at hand, however, is serviceable rather than inspiring.

w Sam and Bella Spewack *d* Robert Z. Leonard *ph* Robert Planck *md* Johnny Green

Ginger Rogers, Walter Pidgeon, Van Johnson, Lana Turner, Robert Benchley, Edward Arnold, Constance Collier, Leon Ames, Warner Anderson, Phyllis Thaxter, Keenan Wynn, Porter Hall, Samuel S. Hinds, George Zucco, Xavier Cugat

Weekend for Three
US 1941 66m bw

A wife uses a male guest's attentions to excite her husband's jealousy. Fairly ordinary comedy with moments of wit in the script. Dennis O'Keefe, Jane Wyatt, Philip Reed, Edward Everett Horton, ZaSu Pitts, Franklin Pangborn. Written by Dorothy Parker and Alan Campbell; directed by Irving Reis; for Tay Garnett / RKO.

Weekend in Havana
US 1941 80m Technicolor
TCF (William Le Baron)

A shopgirl in Havana falls for a shipping executive.
Routine Fox musical showcasing familiar talents: adequate wartime escapist fare.

w Karl Tunberg, Darrell Ware *d* Walter Lang *ph* Ernest Palmer *md* Alfred Newman

Alice Faye, John Payne, Carmen Miranda, Cesar Romero, Cobina Wright Jnr, George Barbier, Sheldon Leonard, Leonid Kinskey

Weekend Marriage
US 1932 64m bw

A wife wants to remain independent. Comedy drama with nothing new to say about a familiar subject. Loretta Young, Norman Foster, George Brent, Aline MacMahon, Vivienne Osborne. Written by Sheridan Gibney from the novel Part-Time Wives by Faith Baldwin; directed by Thornton Freeland; for First National. (GB title: *Weekend Lives*.) 'Unimportant rewrite on familiar theme minus necessary key strength.'—*Variety*

Weekend with Father
US 1951 83m bw
U-I (Ted Richmond)

A widow and a widower fall in love when taking their respective children to a summer camp.
Mechanical comedy of upsets and embarrassments.

w Joseph Hoffman *d* Douglas Sirk *ph* Clifford Stine *m* Frank Skinner

Van Heflin, Patricia Neal, Gigi Perreau, Virginia Field, Richard Denning

Weird Science
US 1985 94m Technicolor

Teenage science students create a woman from a computer. Sex-obsessed frolics which go nowhere. Anthony Michael Hall, Kelly Le Brock, Ilan Mitchell-Smith, Bill Paxton. Written and directed by John Hughes; for Joel Silver / Universal.

'She strikes with the curse of voodoo!'
Weird Woman
US 1944 64m bw

A professor brings home from the South Seas a wife who seems to bring murder in her wake. Stiff and stilted thriller from an interesting original; one of the disappointing *Inner Sanctum* series. Lon Chaney, Evelyn Ankers, Anne Gwynne, Ralph Morgan, Elizabeth Risdon. Written by Brenda Weisberg, from the novel *Conjure Wife* by Fritz Leiber; directed by Reginald Le Borg; for Universal.

Welcome Danger*
US 1929 110m bw
Harold Lloyd

The meek son of a police chief gets involved in a tong war.
Moderate early talkie comedy showing the star in some trouble with pace and dialogue.

w Clyde Bruckman, Lex Neal, Felix Adler, Paul Gerard Smith *d* Clyde Bruckman *ph* Walter Lundin, Henry Kohler

Harold Lloyd, Barbara Kent, Noah Young, Charles Middleton

Welcome Home Soldier Boys
US 1972 92m De Luxe

Four war veterans go home and start a wave of violence. Clumsily brutal anti-war tract which merely repels. Joe Don Baker, Paul Koslo, Alan Vint, Billy Green Bush. Written by Guerdon Trueblood; directed by Richard Crompton; for TCF.

Welcome Mr Washington
GB 1944 90m bw

A US sergeant in an English village falls for a local lady. Mild plea for harmony between allies; rather embarrassing to watch even at the time. Barbara Mullen, Donald Stewart, Peggy Cummins, Graham Moffatt, Martita Hunt. Written by Jack Whittingham, from a novel by Noel Streatfeild; directed by Leslie Hiscott; for British National / Shaftesbury.

Welcome Stranger
US 1947 107m bw
Paramount (Sol C. Siegel)

A genial young doctor fills in for a crusty old one on vacation in a small town.
Formula sentimental comedy, one of several reuniting the stars of *Going My Way*.

w Arthur Sheekman *d* Elliott Nugent *ph* Lionel Lindon *m* Robert Emmett Dolan

Bing Crosby, Barry Fitzgerald, Joan Caulfield, Wanda Hendrix, Frank Faylen, Elizabeth Patterson, Robert Shayne, Percy Kilbride

Welcome to Arrow Beach
US 1973 99m colour
Brut (Jack Cushingham)

A photographer living in a California beach community has become a cannibal after his experiences in the Korean War.
Abysmal horror movie with insufficient plot.

w Wallace C. Bennett, Jack Gross Jnr *d* Laurence Harvey *ph* Gerald Perry Finnerman *m* Tony Camillo

Laurence Harvey, Joanna Pettet, Stuart Whitman, John Ireland, Meg Foster

Welcome to Hard Times*
US 1967 103m Metrocolor
MGM / Max E. Youngstein, David Carr
GB title: *Killer on a Horse*

A small western town arms itself against a mysterious bandit.
Curiously likeable, almost symbolic suspense western which has a good start and middle but not much idea how to end.

wd Burt Kennedy, novel E. L. Doctorow *ph* Harry Stradling Jnr *m* Harry Sukman

Henry Fonda, Janice Rule, Keenan Wynn, Janis Paige, John Anderson, Warren Oates, Fay Spain, Edgar Buchanan, Aldo Ray, Lon Chaney Jnr, Elisha Cook Jnr

Welcome to LA*
US 1976 106m De Luxe
Lion's Gate / Robert Altman

A young composer in Los Angeles has a varied sex life.
Fragmentary, vaguely mystical, momentarily interesting, frequently confusing slice of life as seen through misty glasses.

wd Alan Rudolph *ph* Dave Myers *m* Richard Baskin

Keith Carradine, Sally Kellerman, Geraldine Chaplin, Harvey Keitel, Lauren Hutton, Viveca Lindfors, Sissy Spacek, Denver Pyle

'The supposedly free-form, improvisational dynamics of an Altman movie have here become a strictly choreographed ballet.'—*Richard Combs, MFB*

Welcome to the Club
GB 1970 88m bw
Welcome (Sam Lomberg)

Hiroshima 1945; an American Quaker sergeant upsets military protocol.
Pale satirical comedy shot in Copenhagen.

w Clement Biddle Wood, from his novel *d* Walter Shenson *ph* Mikael Salomon *m* Ken Thomas

Brian Foley, Jack Warden, Lee Meredith, Andy Jarrett

The Well*
US 1951 85m bw
Cardinal / Harry M. Popkin (Clarence Greene, Leo Popkin)

A black child falls down a well, and the town unites to save her.
Forceful high-pitched melodrama, cut to a do-gooder pattern which became very familiar.

w Russel Rouse, Clarence Greene *d* Leo Popkin, Russel Rouse *ph* Ernest Laszlo *m* Dmitri Tiomkin

Richard Rober, Henry Morgan, Barry Kelley, Christine Larson

AAN: script

The Well Groomed Bride*
US 1946 75m bw
Paramount (Fred Kohlmar)

A naval officer searches San Francisco for a magnum of champagne with which to launch a ship.
Thin but cheerful star comedy.

w Claude Binyon, Robert Russell *d* Sidney Lanfield *ph* John F. Seitz *m* Roy Webb

Ray Milland, Olivia de Havilland, Sonny Tufts, James Gleason, Constance Dowling, Percy Kilbride, Jean Heather

We'll Meet Again
GB 1942 84m bw

A girl singer suffers while her boy friend loves another. Unassuming star vehicle for the Forces' Sweetheart. Vera Lynn, Geraldo, Patricia Roc, Ronald Ward, Donald Gray, Frederick Leister. Written by James Seymour and Howard Thomas; directed by Phil Brandon; for Columbia.

'Paramount's thundering romance of the winning of the west!'

Wells Fargo*
US 1937 115m bw
Paramount (Frank Lloyd)

How the express delivery service was built up.
Large-scale, entertaining western with overmuch emphasis on domestic issues.

w Paul Schofield, Gerald Geraghty, John Boland, *story* Stuart N. Lake *d* Frank Lloyd *ph* Theodor Sparkuhl *m* Victor Young

Joel McCrea, Bob Burns, Frances Dee, Lloyd Nolan, Henry O'Neill, Mary Nash, Ralph Morgan, John Mack Brown, Porter Hall, Clarence Kolb

'Big b.o. right across the playdate board.'—*Variety*

Went the Day Well?***
GB 1942 92m bw
Ealing (S. C. Balcon)
US title: *Forty-eight Hours*

Villagers resist when German paratroopers invade an English village and the squire proves to be a quisling.
Could-it-happen melodrama which made excellent wartime propaganda; generally well staged.

w Angus MacPhail, John Dighton, Diana Morgan, *story* Graham Greene *d Alberto Cavalcanti ph* Wilkie Cooper *m* William Walton

Leslie Banks, Elizabeth Allen, Frank Lawton, Basil Sydney, Valerie Taylor, Mervyn Johns, Edward Rigby, Marie Lohr, C. V. France, David Farrar

'At last, it seems, we are learning to make films with our own native material.'—*Sunday Times*

'It has the sinister, freezing beauty of an Auden prophecy come true.'—*James Agee*

'A refreshing, an exciting and an excellent film.'—*Documentary News Letter*

We're Going to Be Rich
GB 1938 80m bw

In the South African goldfields in 1880, a singer leaves her worthless husband for a publican. First American attempt to take over Our Gracie; it didn't work, but the damage was done. Gracie Fields, Victor McLaglen, Brian Donlevy, Coral Browne, Gus McNaughton. Written by Monty Banks, James Edward Grant, Rohama Siegel and Sam Hellman; directed by Monty Banks; for TCF. 'Will do well in England. In the States, will slide into the duals.'—*Variety*

We're in the Money
US 1935 65m bw

Adventures of female process servers working for a dizzy lawyer. Minor comedy using up contract artistes. Joan Blondell, Glenda Farrell, Hugh Herbert, Ross Alexander, Hobart Cavanaugh. Written by F. Hugh Herbert, Brown Holmes, Erwin Gelsey, George Bilson; directed by Ray Enright; for Warners. 'Only those exhibitors whose clients get hysterial on short notice will profit from it.'—*Variety*

We're No Angels*
US 1954 106m Technicolor Vistavision
Paramount (Pat Duggan)

Three escaped Devil's Island convicts help a downtrodden storekeeper and his family to outwit a scheming relative.
Whimsical, overstretched period comedy suffering from miscasting but with some pleasantries along the way.

w Ronald MacDougall, *play* La Cuisine des Anges by Albert Husson *d* Michael Curtiz *ph* Loyal Griggs *m* Frederick Hollander

Humphrey Bogart, *Peter Ustinov,* Aldo Ray, Joan Bennett, Basil Rathbone, Leo G. Carroll, John Smith

'It's a circus! Something doing every minute!'

We're Not Dressing*
US 1934 77m bw
Paramount (Benjamin Glazer)

A spoiled heiress shipwrecked on a Pacific island is tamed by an easy-going sailor.
Pleasant, madly dated, light-hearted variation on a much-filmed play, resolving itself into a series of comic turns.

w Horace Jackson, Francis Martin, George Marion Jnr, *play* The Admirable Crichton by J. M. Barrie *d* Norman Taurog *ph* Charles Lang *songs* Harry Revel, Mack Gordon

Bing Crosby, Carole Lombard, George Burns, Gracie Allen, Leon Errol, Ethel Merman, Jay Henry, Ray Milland

'Tiptop audience appeal musical.'—*Variety*

We're Not Married*
US 1952 85m bw
TCF (Nunnally Johnson)

Six couples find that they were never legally married.
Amiable, smartly-played compendium of sketches on a familiar theme.

w Nunnally Johnson *d* Edmund Goulding *ph* Leo Tover *m* Cyril Mockridge

Ginger Rogers, Fred Allen, Victor Moore, Paul Douglas, Eve Arden, Marilyn Monroe, David Wayne, Louis Calhern, Zsa Zsa Gabor, Mitzi Gaynor, Eddie Bracken, James Gleason, Jane Darwell

We're on the Jury
US 1937 71m bw

Disagreements break out in the jury room after a murder trial. More comedy than drama, a modest remake of *Ladies of the Jury* (*qv*). Helen Broderick, Victor Moore, Philip Huston, Louise Latimer, Robert McWade. Written by Franklin Coen from the play by John Frederick Ballard; directed by Ben Holmes; for RKO. 'Good secondary b.o. value.'—*Variety*

We're Only Human
US 1936 67m bw

A police sergeant loses a convicted prisoner and catches him again. Routine bang-bang melodrama with unconvincing dialogue. Preston Foster, Jane Wyatt, James Gleason, Arthur Hohl, Jane Darwell, Christian Rub, Moroni Olson, Mischa Auer. Written by Rian James from a story by Thomas Walsh; directed by James Flood; for Edward Kaufman / RKO. 'Nothing which will raise it above double-feature standards.'—*Variety*

The Werewolf
US 1956 80m bw
Columbia / Clover (Sam Katzman)

In a small mountain town, a victim of radiation exposure periodically becomes a werewolf and is hounded down.
Absurd and tedious thriller which wastes an interesting background.

w Robert E. Kent, James B. Gordon *d* Fred F. Sears *ph* Edwin Linden *m* Mischa Bakaleinikoff

Steven Ritch, Don McGowan, Joyce Holden

Werewolf of London*
US 1935 75m bw
Universal (Stanley Bergerman)

Werewolves fight for a rare Tibetan flower with curative properties.
Patchy horror film which lurches from excellent suspense scenes to tedious chunks of superfluous dialogue. In many ways a milestone in the history of its kind.

w Robert Harris *d Stuart Walker ph Charles Stumar m* Karl Hajos

Henry Hull, Warner Oland, Valerie Hobson, Spring Byington, Lester Matthews, Zeffie Tilbury, Ethel Griffies

'Horror attempt that doesn't horrify sufficiently. Requires a build-up and may disappoint.'—*Variety*

West Eleven
GB 1963 93m bw
(ABP) Daniel M. Angel (Vivian Cox)

A young London drifter is offered £10,000 to commit murder.
Dingy but not very convincing 'realist' melodrama with a jazzy style which induces weariness.

w Keith Waterhouse, Willis Hall, *novel* The Furnished Room by Laura del Rivo *d* Michael Winner *ph* Otto Heller *m* Stanley Black, Acker Bilk

Alfred Lynch, Eric Portman, Kathleen Harrison, Diana Dors, Kathleen Breck, Freda Jackson, Finlay Currie, Harold Lang

West of Broadway
US 1932 68m bw

A millionaire gets married while drunk and regrets it the next day. Unappetizing light drama which did no good to anyone concerned with it. John Gilbert, El Brendel, Lois Moran, Madge Evans, Ralph Bellamy, Frank Conroy, Hedda Hopper. Written by Gene Markey, J. K. McGuinness, Ralph Graves, Bess Meredyth; directed by Harry Beaumont; for MGM. 'Rates neighbourhood and grind spotting only.'—*Variety*

West of Shanghai
US 1937 64m bw

Fugitives in the Far East are saved by the self-sacrifice of a Chinese war lord.
Unpersuasive melodrama remade from *The Bad Man* (1930), heavily depending on a star performance. Boris Karloff, Beverly Roberts, Ricardo Cortez, Gordon Oliver, Vladimir Sokoloff. Written by Crane Wilbur; directed by John Farrow; for Warner.
† First released as *Warlord*.

West of the Pecos
US 1934 70m bw

In Texas after the Civil War a girl masquerades as a boy in order to get things done. Moderate western. Richard Dix, Martha Sleeper, Samuel S. Hinds, Fred Kohler, Louise Beavers, Willie Best ('Sleep 'n Eat'). Written by Milton Krims, John Twist, from the novel by Zane Grey; directed by Phil Rosen; for RKO. 'Superior entertainment of the horse opera type.'—*Variety*

West of Zanzibar
US 1928 70m at 24 fps bw silent

A paralysed magician turned ivory trader settles an old score. Corny star vehicle remade in 1932 as *Kongo*, with Walter Huston. Lon Chaney, Lionel Barrymore, Jacqueline Gadsden, Mary Nolan. Written by Waldemar Young and Elliott Clawson; directed by Tod Browning; for MGM.

West of Zanzibar
GB 1954 94m Technicolor
Ealing (Leslie Norman)

Native tribesmen move towards Mombasa and are drawn into ivory smuggling.
Fairly feeble follow-up to *Where No Vultures Fly*; quite good to look at but clearly not an original.

w Max Catto, Jack Whittingham *d* Harry Watt *ph* Paul Beeson *m* Alan Rawsthorne

Anthony Steel, Sheila Sim, William Simons, Orlando Martins, Martin Benson, Edric Connor, Howard Marion Crawford

West Point of the Air
US 1935 90m bw
MGM (Monta Bell)

The army sergeant father of an air cadet has great hopes for him.
Routine sentimental flagwaver.

w James J. McGuinness, John Monk Saunders, Frank Wead, Arthur J. Beckhard *d* Richard Rosson *ph* Clyde de Vinna, Charles A. Marshall, Elmer Dyer *m* Charles Maxwell

Wallace Beery, Robert Young, Maureen O'Sullivan, Lewis Stone, James Gleason, Rosalind Russell, Russell Hardie, Henry Wadsworth, Robert Taylor

'Trite story holds it down to just moderate entertainment rating.'—*Variety*

West Point Story*
US 1950 107m bw
Warner (Louis F. Edelman)
GB title: *Fine and Dandy*

A Broadway producer stages a show at the military academy.
Thin and rather tedious musical saved by its irrepressible star.

w John Monks Jnr, Charles Hoffman, Irving Wallace *d* Roy del Ruth *ph* Sid Hickox *md* Ray Heindorf *songs* Sammy Cahn, Jule Styne

James Cagney, Virginia Mayo, Doris Day, Gordon Macrae, Gene Nelson, Alan Hale Jnr, Roland Winters, Jerome Cowan

AAN: Ray Heindorf

West Side Story***
US 1961 155m Technicolor
Panavision 70
(UA) Mirisch / Seven Arts (Robert Wise)

The Romeo and Juliet story in a New York dockland setting.
The essentially theatrical conception of this entertainment is nullified by determinedly realistic settings which make much of it seem rather silly, but production values are fine and the song numbers electrifying.

w Ernest Lehman, *play* Arthur Laurents, after Shakespeare *d Robert Wise, Jerome Robbins ph* Daniel L. Fapp *m Leonard Bernstein ly Stephen Sondheim pd* Boris Leven

Natalie Wood (sung by Marni Nixon), Richard Beymer (sung by Jimmy Bryant), Russ Tamblyn, *Rita Moreno*, George Chakiris

AA: best picture; Robert Wise, Jerome Robbins; Daniel L. Fapp; Rita Moreno; George Chakiris; Saul Chaplin
AAN: Ernest Lehman; musical direction (Saul Chaplin, Johnny Green, Sid Ramin, Irwin Kostal)

Westbound
US 1959 69m Warnercolor

A stagecoach manager is entrusted with Californian gold, which attracts assorted villains. Stalwart star western which served its purpose. Randolph Scott, Virginia Mayo, Karen Steele, Andrew Duggan, Michael Pate. Written by Berne Giler; directed by Budd Boetticher; for Warner.

Western Approaches***
GB 1944 83m Technicolor
Crown Film Unit
US title: The Raider

Torpedoed merchantmen in the Atlantic are used by a U-boat as a decoy.
A fictional story is played to great documentary effect by men of the allied navies. One of the outstanding 'factual' films of the war years.

wd Pat Jackson ph Jack Cardiff m Clifton Parker

'Without a doubt the best sea film in existence.'—*Daily Mail*

Western Union**
US 1941 94m Technicolor
TCF (Harry Joe Brown)

Politicians and crooks hamper the laying of cross country cables.
First rate western with familiar excitements.

w Robert Carson, *novel* Zane Grey *d* Fritz Lang *ph* Edward Cronjager *m* David Buttolph

Randolph Scott, Robert Young, Dean Jagger, Virginia Gilmore, Slim Summerville, John Carradine, Chill Wills, Barton MacLane

'It is impossible to know what clichés the director may have prevented, but it is enough and too much to see those he left in.'—*Otis Ferguson*

'Two women helped him overthrow the most ruthless power in the west!'

The Westerner**
US 1940 99m bw
Samuel Goldwyn

Judge Roy Bean comes to grief through his love for Lily Langtry.
Moody melodramatic western with comedy touches; generally entertaining, the villain more so than the hero.

w Jo Swerling, Niven Busch, *story* Stuart N. Lake *d William Wyler ph Gregg Toland m* Dmitri Tiomkin

THE WESTERNER. Gary Cooper as the archetypal strong and silent Western hero takes time out with Walter Brennan's Judge Roy Bean.

Gary Cooper, *Walter Brennan*, Doris Davenport, Fred Stone, Paul Hurst, Chill Wills, Charles Halton, Forrest Tucker, Dana Andrews, Lilian Bond, Tom Tyler

AA: Walter Brennan
AAN: Stuart N. Lake

Westward Ho the Wagons
US 1956 85m Technicolor Cinemascope
Walt Disney (Bill Walsh)

A wagon train defends itself against Indians.
Slow and simple-minded family western.

w Tom Blackburn *d* William Beaudine *ph* Charles Boyle *m* Paul Smith

Fess Parker, Kathleen Crowley, Jeff York, David Stollery, Sebastian Cabot, George Reeves

Westward Passage
US 1932 73m bw
RKO (David O. Selznick)

A wealthy girl weds a poor novelist but wants the rich full life for their children.
Dogged romantic drama with only the casting of interest.

w Bradley and Humphrey King, *novel* Margaret Ayer Barnes *d* Robert Milton *ph* Lucien Andriot *m* Max Steiner

Ann Harding, Laurence Olivier, Zasu Pitts, Irving Pichel, Juliette Compton, Florence Roberts

'Slow, prone to be dull, and hardly warm weather theatre inducement.'—*Variety*

Westward the Women*
US 1951 118m bw
MGM (Dore Schary)

In the 1850s an Indian scout leads 150 Chicago women to meet husbands in California.
Good-looking episodic western, apparently intended mainly to amuse but seldom rising to the occasion.

w Charles Schnee *d* William Wellman *ph William Mellor* *m* Jeff Alexander

Robert Taylor, Denise Darcel, John McIntire, Marilyn Erskine, Hope Emerson, Lenore Lonergan, Julie Bishop

'Where nothing can possibly go wrongg . . .'

Westworld**
US 1973 89m Metrocolor Panavision
MGM (Paul N. Lazarus III)

In a millionaire holiday resort which recreates the past, a western badman robot goes berserk and relentlessly attacks two visitors.
Unusual and amusing but under-produced melodrama with slipshod story development and continuity, atoned for by memorable moments and underlying excitement.

wd Michael Crichton *ph* Gene Polito *m* Fred Karlin *ad* Herman Blumenthal

Yul Brynner, Richard Benjamin, James Brolin, Norman Bartold, Alan Oppenheimer

The Wet Parade*
US 1932 122m bw
MGM (Hunt Stromberg)

A politician points to the corruption caused by prohibition.
Sociologically interesting melodrama.

w John Lee Mahin, *novel* Upton Sinclair
d Victor Fleming *ph* George Barnes
m William Axt

Walter Huston, Myrna Loy, Neil Hamilton, Lewis Stone, Jimmy Durante, Wallace Ford, Dorothy Jordan, John Miljan, Robert Young

'Final impression strongly anti-liquor, but outside of reaction that may bring, picture hasn't much chance. What it lacks as entertainment isn't covered by propaganda possibilities.'—*Variety*

AAN: best picture

Wetherby*
GB 1985 97m Technicolor
Greenpoint / Film Four / Zenith (Simon Relph)

After a party at the home of a lonely and frustrated woman, a young man shoots himself.
Interesting if rather irritating drama which leaves as many puzzles as it solves.

w,d David Hare *ph* Stuart Harris *m* Nick Bicat *pd* Hayden Griffin

Vanessa Redgrave, Ian Holm, Judi Dench, Tim McInnery, Stuart Wilson

We've Never Been Licked
US 1943 103m bw

A young American raised in Japan finds himself on the wrong side after Pearl Harbor.
Shoddy flagwaver, low on talent and inspiration. Richard Quine, Anne Gwynne, Noah Beery Jnr, Harry Davenport, Martha O'Driscoll, William Frawley, Robert Mitchum. Written by Norman Reilly Raine and Nick Grinde; directed by John Rawlins; for Walter Wanger / Universal. (GB title: *Texas to Tokyo*.)

The Whales of August*
US 1987 90m TVC colour
Circle / Nelson (Carolyn Pfeiffer, Mike Kaplan)

Two elderly sisters live on the Maine coast and think of the past.
Edgy, sympathetic talk-piece in which old ladies prove that they are still stars.

w David Berry from his play *d* Lindsay Anderson *ph* Mike Fash *m* Alan Price *pd* Joselyn Herbert

Bette Davis, Lillian Gish, Vincent Price, Ann Sothern, Harry Carey Jnr, Mary Steenburgen, Tisha Stirling.

'Lovely on all counts.'—*Daily Variety*

AAN: Ann Sothern

'He had a price on his head . . . she had a price on her heart!'

Wharf Angel
US 1934 65m bw

To quote *Variety*, prostie goes softie for sailor with murder rap hanging over his head. Dim little fogbound melodrama. Victor McLaglen, Dorothy Dell, Preston Foster, Alison Skipworth. Written by Sam Hoffenstein, Frank Partos, Steve Avery, Frederick Schlick; directed by William Cameron Menzies and George Somnes; for Paramount. 'Poor stuff for de luxe audiences: old-fashioned, drab, lacking in box office draw.'—*Variety*

What a Carve Up
GB 1961 88m bw

A madman fakes his own death in order to murder his relatives. Spooky house farce, allegedly a remake of *The Ghoul* but bearing little resemblance to it. Sid James, Kenneth Connor, Shirley Eaton, Dennis Price, Donald Pleasence, Michael Gough, Valerie Taylor. Written by Ray Cooney, Tony Hilton, from the novel The Ghoul by Frank King; directed by Pat Jackson; for Baker-Berman (New World).

What a Crazy World
GB 1963 88m bw

A working-class London boy sets out to be a rock-and-roller. Unsurprising star musical, quite lively of its kind. Joe Brown, Susan Maughan, Marty Wilde, Harry H. Corbett, Avis Bunnage. Written by Alan Klein from his play; directed and produced by Michael Carreras; for Capricorn/AB Pathe.

What a Life
US 1939 75m bw

Henry Aldrich has difficulties in high school. First of the domestic comedy series (see under *Henry*) which became more farcical and had a different cast; this episode closely followed the Broadway success. Jackie Cooper, Betty Field, John Howard, Janice Logan, Lionel Stander, Hedda Hopper, Dorothy Stickney. Written by Charles Brackett and Billy Wilder from the play by Clifford Goldsmith; directed by Theodore Reed; for Paramount. 'A fine comedy drama, excellent for family trade.'—*Variety*

What a Way to Go*
US 1963 111m De Luxe Cinemascope
TCF / APJAC / Orchard (Arthur P. Jacobs)

An immensely rich girl tells her psychiatrist how all her husbands proved not only successful but accident-prone.
Wild, mainly agreeable, star-and-gag-laden black comedy which starts on too high a note and fails to sustain.

w Betty Comden, Adolph Green *d* J. Lee-Thompson *ph* Leon Shamroy *md* Nelson Riddle *ly* Comden and Green *songs* Jule Styne

Shirley Maclaine, Bob Cummings, Dick Van Dyke, Robert Mitchum, Gene Kelly, Dean Martin, Paul Newman, Reginald Gardiner, Margaret Dumont

What a Woman
US 1943 90m bw

An author's agent gets into romantic escapades with her writers. Ho-hum romantic comedy, quickly forgotten. Rosalind Russell, Brian Aherne, Willard Parker, Ann Savage, Alan Dinehart. Written by Therese Lewis and Barry Trivers; directed by Irving Cummings; for Columbia. (Aka: *The Beautiful Cheat.*)

'Off to grandmother's house they go,
For love in the attic and death down below!'

What Became of Jack and Jill?
GB 1971 90m De Luxe
Palomar / Amicus (Milton Subotsky)

A young man tries to hasten his grandmother's death but she has the last laugh.
Feeble suspenser with a dim ending.

w Roger Marshall, *novel* The Ruthless Ones by Laurence Moody *d* Bill Bain *ph* Gerry Turpin *m* Carl Davis

Vanessa Howard, Paul Nicholas, Mona Washbourne, Peter Copley, Peter Jeffrey

What Changed Charley Farthing
GB 1975 101m Eastmancolor
Patina–Hidalgo (Tristam Cones)

A philandering sailor has adventures in Cuba.
Weirdly ineffective comedy actioner which never gets started and should never have been thought of.

w David Pursall, Jack Seddon, *novel* Mark Hebdon *d* Sidney Hayers *ph* Graham Edgar *m* Angela Arteaga

Doug McClure, Lionel Jeffries, Warren Mitchell, Hayley Mills, Dilys Hamlett, Fernando Sancho

What Did You Do in the War, Daddy?
US 1966 115m De Luxe Panavision
UA / Mirisch / Geoffrey (Owen Crump, Blake Edwards)

In 1943, an Italian town surrenders readily to the Americans providing its wine festival and football match can take place.
Silly war comedy with insufficient jokes for its wearisome length. The performances are bright enough.

w William Peter Blatty *d* Blake Edwards *ph* Philip Lathrop *m* Henry Mancini

James Coburn, Dick Shawn, Sergio Fantoni, Giovanni Ralli, Aldo Ray, Harry Morgan, Carroll O'Connor, Leon Askin

What Every Woman Knows*
US 1934 90m bw

A quiet little wife encourages her husband into parliament. Adequate version of the sentimental play, very pleasantly acted. *Helen Hayes*, *Brian Aherne*, Madge Evans, Lucile Watson, Dudley Digges, Henry Stephenson, Donald Crisp, David Torrence. Written by Monckton Hoffe, John Meehan, James Kevin McGuinness, from the play by J. M. Barrie; directed by Gregory La Cava; for MGM. 'Cinch b.o., a swell woman's picture.'—*Variety*

What, No Beer?
US 1933 65m bw

A barber rushes to be first on the market with beer after its legalization, but finds himself premature and at odds with gangsters. Topical farce ending in a slapstick mêlée. Buster Keaton, Jimmy Durante, Rosco Ates, Phyllis Barry, John Miljan, Henry Armetta. Written by Carey Wilson, Jack Cluett, Robert E. Hopkins; directed by Edward Sedgwick; for MGM. 'A commercial little laugh picture.'—*Variety*

What Price Glory?*
US 1952 111m Technicolor
TCF (Sol. C. Siegel)

In 1917 France Captain Flagg and Sergeant Quirt spar for the same girl.
Stagey remake of the celebrated silent film and play; watchable if not exactly inspired.

w Phoebe and Henry Ephron, *play* Maxwell Anderson, Lawrence Stallings *d* John Ford *ph* Joe MacDonald *m* Alfred Newman

James Cagney, Dan Dailey, Corinne Calvet, William Demarest, Robert Wagner, Marisa Pavan, James Gleason

'A heart-touching drama of the world, the flesh and the movies!'

What Price Hollywood?*
US 1932 87m bw
RKO (Pandro S. Berman)

A waitress becomes a film star with the help of a drunken director who later commits suicide.
Fairly trenchant early study of the mores of the film city, later revamped as *A Star Is Born*.

w Jane Murfin, Ben Markson, Gene Fowler, Rowland Brown, *story* Adela Rogers St John *d George Cukor* *ph* Charles Rosher *m* Max Steiner *montage* Slavko Vorkapitch

Constance Bennett, Lowell Sherman, Neil Hamilton, Gregory Ratoff, Brooks Bendict, Louise Beavers, Eddie Anderson

'Many of the scenes are like sketches for the later versions, but this film has its own interest, especially because of its glimpses into the studio life of the time.'—*New Yorker, 1977*

AAN: Adela Rogers St John

Whatever Happened to Aunt Alice?*
US 1969 101m Metrocolor
Associates and Aldrich / Palomar

A genteel widow murders her housekeepers for their private incomes.
Ladylike shocker with some black humour and good performances.

w Theodore Apstein, *novel* The Forbidden Garden by Ursula Curtiss *d* Lee H. Katzin *ph* Joseph Biroc *m* Gerald Fried

Geraldine Page, Ruth Gordon, Rosemary Forsyth, Robert Fuller, Mildred Dunnock

'Sister, sister, oh so fair, why is there blood all over your hair?'
Whatever Happened to Baby Jane?*
US 1962 132m bw
Warner Seven Arts / Associates and Aldrich (Robert Aldrich)

In middle age, a demented ex-child star lives in an old Hollywood mansion with her invalid sister, and tension leads to murder.
Famous for marking the first time Hollywood's ageing first ladies stooped to horror, and followed by *Hush Hush Sweet Charlotte* and the other *Whatevers*, this dreary looking melodrama only occasionally grabs the attention and has enough plot for about half its length. The performances, however, are striking.

w Lukas Heller, *novel* Henry Farrell *d* Robert Aldrich *ph* Ernest Haller *m* Frank de Vol

Bette Davis, Joan Crawford, Victor Buono, Anna Lee

'It goes on and on, in a light much dimmer than necessary, and the climax, when it belatedly arrives, is a bungled, languid mingling of pursuers and pursued . . .'—*New Yorker*

AAN: Ernest Haller; Bette Davis; Victor Buono

What's Buzzin', Cousin?
US 1943 75m bw

An attorney turns band singer and helps revive a droopy hotel. Listless musical with a few good numbers. Ann Miller, John Hubbard, Eddie Anderson, Leslie Brooks, Jeff Donnell. Written by Harry Sauber; directed by Charles Barton; for Jack Fier / Columbia.

What's Good for the Goose
GB 1969 104m Eastmancolor
Tigon (Tony Tenser, Norman Wisdom)

An assistant bank manager falls for a girl hitch-hiker and tries to recover his youth.
Embarrassing attempt to build a sexy vehicle for a star whose sentimental mugging always appealed mainly to children.

w Norman Wisdom *d* Menahem Golan *ph* William Brayne *m* Reg Tilsley

Norman Wisdom, Sally Geeson, Sally Bazeley, Derek Francis, Terence Alexander

What's New Pussycat?
US / France 1965 108m Technicolor
UA / Famous Artists (Charles K. Feldman)

A fashion editor is distracted by beautiful girls.
Zany sex comedy with many more misses than hits, a product of the wildly swinging sixties when it was thought that a big budget and stars making fools of themselves would automatically ensure a success.

w Woody Allen *d* Clive Donner *ph* Jean Badal *m Burt Bacharach*

Peter O'Toole, Peter Sellers, Woody Allen, Ursula Andress, Romy Schneider, Capucine, Paula Prentiss

'Unfortunately for all concerned, to make something enjoyably dirty a lot of taste is required.'—*John Simon*

AAN: title song (*m* Burt Bacharach, *ly* Hal David)

What's So Bad About Feeling Good?
US 1965 94m Technicolor
Universal (George Seaton)

A 'happy virus' is carried into New York by a toucan, and affects the lives of various people.
Flimsy pretext for a comedy, further hampered by a less than sparkling script. The actors have their moments.

w George Seaton, Robert Pirosh *d* George Seaton *ph* Ernesto Caparros *m* Frank de Vol

George Peppard, Mary Tyler Moore, Dom De Luise, John McMartin, Susan St James, Don Stroud, Charles Lane

What's the Matter with Helen?*
US 1971 101m De Luxe
Filmways / Raymax (George Edwards, James C. Pratt)

In 1934 Hollywood, two women run a dancing school for child stars; one of them is a killer.
More *Baby Jane* melodramatics, quite lively and with interesting period detail.

w Henry Farrell *d* Curtis Harrington *ph* Lucien Ballard *m* David Raksin *pd Eugene Lourié*

Debbie Reynolds, Shelley Winters, Micheal MacLiammoir, Dennis Weaver, Agnes Moorehead

'A cast of seasoned troupers cannot quite alter the impression that they are all working to revive a stiff.'—*Bruce Williamson*

What's Up, Doc?**
US 1972 94m Technicolor
Warner / Saticoy (Peter Bogdanovich)

In San Francisco, an absent-minded young musicologist is troubled by the attentions of a dotty girl who gets him involved with crooks and a series of accidents.
Madcap comedy, a pastiche of several thirties originals. Spectacular slapstick and willing players are somewhat let down by exhausted patches and a tame final reel.

w Buck Henry, David Newman, Robert Benton *d Peter Bogdanovich* *ph* Laszlo Kovacs *m* Artie Butler *pd* Polly Pratt

Barbra Streisand, Ryan O'Neal, Kenneth Mars, Austin Pendleton, Madeleine Kahn, Mabel Albertson, Sorrell Booke

'A comedy made by a man who has seen a lot of movies, knows all the mechanics, and has absolutely no sense of humour. Seeing it is like shaking hands with a joker holding a joy buzzer: the effect is both presumptuous and unpleasant.'—*Jay Cocks*

'It's all rather like a 19th-century imitation of Elizabethan blank verse drama.'—*Stanley Kauffmann*

'It freely borrows from the best screen comedy down the ages but has no discernible style of its own.'—*Michael Billington, Illustrated London News*

The Wheeler Dealers
US 1963 106m Metrocolor Panavision
MGM / Filmways (Martin Ransohoff)
GB title: *Separate Beds*

A Texas tycoon with a flair for the stock market sets Wall Street agog by manipulating a mysterious and non-existent new product.
Fun for financiers, but barely worth following for the rest. A slick, loud, hollow show.

w G. J. W. Goodman, Ira Wallach *d* Arthur Hiller *ph* Charles Lang Jnr *m* Frank de Vol

James Garner, Lee Remick, Phil Harris, Chill Wills, Jim Backus, Louis Nye, John Astin

When a Man Loves
US 1927 83m at 24 fps bw silent with synchronized music

A hero escapes from a prison ship and gives his all for love of a worthless woman. Freely adapted version of *Manon Lescaut*, successful because of the real-life romance of the stars. John Barrymore, Dolores Costello, Warner Oland, Stuart Holmes, Holmes Herbert. Written by Bess Meredyth; directed by Alan Crosland; for Warner.

'Every baby sitter's nightmare becomes real!'
When a Stranger Calls
US 1979 97m colour

A policeman determinedly chases a baby-murdering maniac. Middling screamer extended from a short, *The Sitter*; a passive midsection separates a suspenseful start and finish. Charles Durning, Tony Beckley, Carol Kane, Colleen Dewhurst, Rachel Roberts. Written by Steve Feke and Fred Walton; directed by Fred Walton; for Melvin Simon / UA.

When Comedy Was King***
US 1959 84m bw
Robert Youngson Productions

Valuable compilation of silent comedy sequences, with the high print quality and poor commentary to be expected from this source. Extracts include Buster Keaton in *Cops*, Laurel and Hardy in *Big Business*, and a Fatty Arbuckle comedy.

ed Robert Youngson

When Dinosaurs Ruled the Earth
GB 1969 100m Technicolor
Hammer (Aida Young)

In prehistoric times, a girl is swept out to sea by a cyclone and adopted by a dinosaur. Sequel to *One Million Years BC*, all very silly but tolerably well done.

wd Val Guest *ph* Dick Bush *m* Mario Nascimbene *sp* Jim Danforth

Victoria Vetri, Patrick Allen, Robin Hawdon, Patrick Holt, Imogen Hassall

When Eight Bells Toll*
GB 1971 94m Eastmancolor Panavision
Winkast (Elliott Kastner)

A naval secret service agent investigates the pirating of gold bullion ships off the Scottish coast.
Acceptable kill-happy thriller: humourless James Bondery graced by splendid Scottish landscapes.

w Alistair MacLean, from his novel *d* Etienne Perier *ph* Arthur Ibbetson *m* Wally Stott

Anthony Hopkins, Robert Morley, Corin Redgrave, Jack Hawkins, Ferdy Mayne, Derek Bond, Nathalie Delon

When I Grow Up*
US 1951 90m bw
Horizon (S. P. Eagle)

A boy about to run away changes his mind after reading his grandfather's diaries.
Pleasant, sentimental family film with an unusual approach.

wd Michael Kanin *ph* Ernest Laszlo *m* Jerome Moross

Bobby Driscoll, Robert Preston, Charley Grapewin, Martha Scott, Ralph Dumke

When in Rome
US 1952 78m bw
MGM (Clarence Brown)

A gangster in Rome steals a priest's clothes and is accepted in his place.
Typically American religious comedy, nicely made but straying somewhat over the top when the gangster reforms and becomes a monk.

w Charles Schnee, Dorothy Kingsley, Robert Buckner *d* Clarence Brown *ph* William Daniels *m* Carmen Dragon

Van Johnson, Paul Douglas, Joseph Calleia, Carlo Rizzo, Tudor Owen, Aldo Silvani, Dono Nardi

When Johnny Comes Marching Home
US 1942 73m bw

A war hero on leave escapes formalities and returns to the theatrical boarding house he remembers. And so to the puttin'-on-a-show finale: not bad of its kind. Allan Jones, Jane Frazee, Gloria Jean, Donald O'Connor, Peggy Ryan, Phil Spitalny and his all-girl orchestra. Written by Oscar Brodney, Dorothy Bennett; directed by Charles Lamont; for Bernard W. Burton / Universal.

When Knights Were Bold
GB 1929 80m at 24 fps bw silent

An incompetent heir dreams that he lives in medieval times. Naïve romp which pleased at the time. Nelson Keys, Miriam Seeger, Eric Bransby Williams. Written by Tim Whelan and Herbert Wilcox, from a play by Charles Marlow; directed by Tim Whelan; for Herbert Wilcox. (Remade in 1936 with Jack Buchanan, Fay Wray and Garry Marsh; directed by Jack Raymond; for Max Schach.)

When Ladies Meet*
US 1933 73m bw
MGM

A successful lady novelist falls in love with her married publisher.
Smartish comedy of manners which still has a sting.

w John Meehan, Leon Gordon, *play* Rachel Crothers *d* Harry Beaumont *ph* Ray June

Ann Harding, Robert Montgomery, *Myrna Loy, Alice Brady*, Frank Morgan, Margaret Burton, Luis Alberni

'Nice production. Well-spaced comedy helps, and picture should be an outstander.'—*Variety*

When Ladies Meet
US 1941 108m bw
MGM (Robert Z. Leonard, Orville O. Dull)

Over-produced and very talkative remake of the above.

w S. K. Lauren, Anita Loos *d* Robert Z. Leonard *ph* Robert Planck *m* Bronislau Kaper

Joan Crawford, Robert Taylor, Greer Garson, Spring Byington, Herbert Marshall, Rafael Strom, Olaf Hytten

When Love Is Young
US 1937 75m bw

A Broadway stage star returns to her home town in hopes of marrying her old beau, but he is found wanting. Very moderate comedy to fill a programme. Virginia Bruce, Kent Taylor, Walter Brennan, Greta Meyer, Christian Rub, Sterling Holloway, Nydia Westman. Written by Eve Greene, Joseph Fields, from the story Class Prophecy by Eleanore Griffin; directed by Hal Mohr; for Robert Presnell / Universal. 'Will provide average filmgoers with averagely good amusement.'—*Variety*

When My Baby Smiles at Me
US 1948 98m Technicolor
TCF (George Jessel)

A vaudevillian goes on the skids but is saved by his wife.
Routine musical handling of a dreary drama previously filmed as *Dance of Life* (1929) and *Swing High Swing Low* (qv).

w Lamar Trotti, *play* Burlesque by George Manker Walters, Arthur Hopkins *d* Walter Lang *ph* Harry Jackson *md* Alfred Newman

Betty Grable, Dan Dailey, Jack Oakie, June Havoc, Richard Arlen, James Gleason, Jean Wallace

AAN: Alfred Newman; Dan Dailey

When Strangers Marry*
US 1944 67m bw
Monogram (Maurice King)
aka: *Betrayed*

A young bride in New York discovers that she may have married a murderer.
Much-praised second feature: a bit stodgy now, but still entertaining.

w Philip Yordan, Dennis Cooper *d William Castle* *ph* Ira Morgan *m* Dmitri Tiomkin

Dean Jagger, Kim Hunter, Robert Mitchum, Neil Hamilton, Lou Lubin, Milt Kibbee, Dewey Robinson

'The obviousness of the low budget is completely overcome by the solid craftsmanship of the direction, script, music, editing and performances.'—*Don Miller*

'Taking it as a whole I have seldom for years now seen one hour so energetically and sensibly used in a film.'—*James Agee*

When the Bough Breaks
GB 1947 81m bw
GFD / Gainsborough (Betty Box)

The bewildered wife of a bigamist allows her child to be adopted and then regrets it.
Peg's Paper stuff in the then-accepted Gainsborough tradition.

w Peter Rogers *d* Lawrence Huntington *ph* Bryan Langley *m* Clifton Parker

Patricia Roc, Rosamund John, Bill Owen, Patrick Holt, Brenda Bruce, Leslie Dwyer, Jane Hylton

When the Daltons Rode*
US 1940 80m bw
Universal

Adventures of the Dalton Gang.
Good standard western with whitewashed bad men for heroes.

w Harold Shumate, Stuart Anthony, Lester Cole *d* George Marshall *ph* Hal Mohr *m* Frank Skinner

Randolph Scott, Kay Francis, Brian Donlevy, Andy Devine, George Bancroft, Stuart Erwin

When the Legends Die*
US 1972 105m De Luxe
Sagoponack (Stuart Millar)

A young Indian boy, frustrated by life on the reservations, is helped by an old rodeo rider who becomes his guardian.
Dour modern western, rather stylishly done and an eloquent plea for freedom, but dramatically uncompelling.

w Robert Dozier, *novel* Hal Borland *d* Stuart Millar *ph* Richard Kline *m* Glenn Paxton

Richard Widmark, Frederic Forrest, Luana Anders, Vito Scotti

When the Lights go on Again
US 1944 70m bw

An ex-marine comes home with shell shock. One of the first films to deal with the problems of war veterans: a modest effort, but sincere. James Lydon, Barbara Belden, Grant Mitchell, Dorothy Peterson, Regis Toomey. Written by Milton Lazarus, from story by Frank Craven; directed by William K. Howard; for Leon Fromkess / PRC.

When the Wind Blows*
GB 1987 85m TVC colour

An elderly man and wife fail to cope with nuclear destruction. Cartoon picturization of a popular book; the film was less likely, despite its merits, to find an audience. Voices: John Mills, Peggy Ashcroft. Written by Raymond Briggs from his book; directed by Jimmy Murakami; for Film Four/Penguin/TVC/NFFC.

When Time Ran Out
US 1980 109m Technicolor Panavision
Warner / Irwin Allen

Inhabitants of a South Sea island are threatened by a volcano.
Incredibly inept disaster movie, with all clichés on hand in the characters of some downcast actors.

w Carl Foreman, Stirling Silliphant, *novel* The Day the World Ended by Max Morgan Witts and Gordon Thomas *d* James Goldstone *ph* Fred J. Koenekamp *m* Lalo Schifrin

Paul Newman, Jacqueline Bisset, William Holden, Edward Albert, Burgess Meredith, Valentina Cortesa, Red Buttons, Alex Carras, Ernest Borgnine, James Franciscus

'Disaster movies don't come any more disastrous than this.'—*Tom Milne, MFB*

† Said to have cost 22 million dollars and taken less than two.

When Tomorrow Comes**
US 1939 82m bw
Universal (John M. Stahl)

A waitress falls for a concert pianist with a mad wife.
Fascinating star romantic drama, a successful follow-up to *Love Affair*; full of clichés, but impeccably set and acted. The stuff that Hollywood dreams were made of.

w Dwight Taylor, *story* James M. Cain *d John M. Stahl ph* John Mescall *m* Charles Previn

Charles Boyer, Irene Dunne, Barbara O'Neil, Nydia Westman, Onslow Stevens

'A persuasive love story . . . a director's achievement.'—*Variety*

† The same story was remade twice in 1956, as *Serenade* and *Interlude*, and in 1968 as *Interlude* (all qv).

When We Are Married*
GB 1942 98m bw
British National (John Baxter)

In 1890s Yorkshire, three couples celebrating their silver wedding are told they were never legally married.
A very funny play smartly filmed with a superb cast of character actors.

w Austin Melford, Barbara K. Emery, *play J. B. Priestley d* Lance Comfort *ph* James Wilson

Raymond Huntley, Marian Spencer, Lloyd Pearson, Olga Lindo, Ernest Butcher, Ethel Coleridge, Sydney Howard, Barry Morse, Lesley Brook, Marjorie Rhodes, Charles Victor, Cyril Smith, George Carney

When Willie Comes Marching Home*
US 1950 82m bw
TCF (Fred Kohlmar)

During World War II, events suddenly transform a small-town air training instructor into a war hero.
Awkwardly paced comedy which could have been much funnier but does amuse in fits and starts.

w Mary Loos, Richard Sale *d* John Ford *ph* Leo Tover *m* Alfred Newman

Dan Dailey, Colleen Townshend, Corinne Calvet, William Demarest, Evelyn Varden, James Lydon, Mae Marsh, Lloyd Corrigan

AAN: original story (Sy Gomberg)

When Worlds Collide
US 1951 82m Technicolor
Paramount (George Pal)

Another planet is found to be rushing inevitably towards earth, but before the collision a few people escape in a space ship.
Stolid science fiction with a spectacular but not marvellous climax following seventy minutes of inept talk.

w Sidney Boehm, *novel* Philip Wylie, Edwin Balmer *d* Rudolph Maté *ph* John Seitz, W. Howard Greene *m* Leith Stevens

Richard Derr, Barbara Rush, Larry Keating, Peter Hanson, John Hoyt

AAN: John Seitz, W. Howard Greene

When You're in Love*
US 1937 110m bw
Columbia (Everett Riskin)
GB title: *For You Alone*

A European opera singer takes on a husband in order to get into the United States.
Pleasing musical star vehicle with comedy touches.

wd Robert Riskin *ph* Joseph Walker *md* Alfred Newman

Grace Moore, Cary Grant, Aline MacMahon, Henry Stephenson, Thomas Mitchell, Catherine Doucet, Luis Alberni, Emma Dunn

'Nice musical with fair quota of giggles . . . should do nice biz.'—*Variety*

Where Angels Go, Trouble Follows
US 1968 95m Eastmancolor
Columbia / William Frye

Nuns from a convent school take pupils to a California youth rally, and learn a thing or two.
Peripatetic comedy, rather frantically assembled; a sequel to *The Trouble with Angels*.

w Blanche Hanalis *d* James Neilson *ph* Sam Leavitt *m* Lalo Schifrin

Rosalind Russell, Stella Stevens, Binnie Barnes, Mary Wickes, Milton Berle, Arthur Godfrey, Robert Taylor, Van Johnson, Susan St James

Where are your Children?
US 1943 78m bw

A wandering rich boy takes up with a hash slinger, and they wind up suspected of murder . . . An 'awful warning' melodrama, risible now. Jackie Cooper, Gale Storm, Patricia Morison, John Litei, Gertrude Michael, Addison Richards, Betty Blythe. Written by Hilary Lynn, George W. Syre; directed by William Nigh; for Jeffrey Bernerd / Monogram.

Where Danger Lives
US 1950 84m bw
RKO (Irving Cummings Jnr)

A doctor falls in love with a murderous patient and is drawn into her schemes.
Standard *film noir* of its time, competent enough in its depressing way.

w Charles Bennett *d* John Farrow *ph* Nicholas Musuraca *m* Roy Webb

Faith Domergue, Robert Mitchum, Claude Rains, Maureen O'Sullivan, Charles Kemper

Where Do We Go from Here?*
US 1945 77m Technicolor
TCF (William Perlberg)

A writer stumbles on a genie who takes him through periods of American history, including a voyage with Christopher Columbus.
Well-staged and rather funny charade with at least one memorable song.

w Morrie Ryskind *d* Gregory Ratoff *ph* Leon Shamroy *songs* Kurt Weill, Ira Gershwin *m* David Raksin

Fred MacMurray, June Haver, Joan Leslie, Gene Sheldon, Anthony Quinn, Carlos Ramirez, Fortunio Bonanova, Alan Mowbray, Herman Bing, Otto Preminger

'Nine parts heavy facetiousness to one part very good fun.'—*James Agee*

'Don't tell your doctor about this film—it could give him ideas!'

Where Does it Hurt?
US 1971 88m colour
Josef Shaftel (Rod Amateau, William Schwarz)

Adventures of a profiteering hospital adminstrator.
Dislikeable, plodding smut in the form of black comedy.

wd Rod Amateau, *novel* The Operator by Budd Robinson, Rod Amateau *ph* Brick Marquard *m* Keith Allison

Peter Sellers, Jo Ann Pflug, Rick Lenz, Eve Druce

Where Eagles Dare**
GB 1969 155m Metrocolor Panavision 70
MGM / Winkast (Elliott Kastner)

During World War II, seven British paratroopers land in the Bavarian Alps to rescue a high-ranking officer from an impregnable castle.
Archetypal schoolboy adventure, rather unattractively photographed but containing a sufficient variety of excitements.

w Alistair MacLean, from his novel *d* Brian G. Hutton *ph* Arthur Ibbetson, H. A. R. Thompson *m* Ron Goodwin

Richard Burton, Clint Eastwood, Mary Ure, Patrick Wymark, Michael Hordern, Donald Houston, Peter Barkworth, Robert Beatty

Where It's At
US 1969 106m De Luxe
UA / Frank Ross

The owner of a Las Vegas gambling hotel tries to make his son take an interest in the business.
Flaccid comedy drama which belies its credits.

wd Garson Kanin *ph* Burnett Guffey *m* Benny Olsen

David Janssen, Rosemary Forsyth, Robert Drivas, Brenda Vaccaro

Where Love Has Gone*
US 1964 114m Techniscope
Paramount / Embassy (Joseph E. Levine)

A middle-aged man is appalled to hear that his teenage daughter has killed her mother's lover.
Squalid, glossy pulp fiction lightly based on the Lana Turner case, distinguished only by the game performances of its leading ladies.

w John Michael Hayes, *novel* Harold Robbins *d* Edward Dmytryk *ph* Joe MacDonald *m* Walter Scharf

Susan Hayward, Bette Davis, Mike Connors, Joey Heatherton, Jane Greer, George Macready

'A typical Robbins pastiche of newspaper clippings liberally shellacked with sentiment and glued with sex.'—*Newsweek*

AAN: title song (*m* James Van Heusen, *ly* Sammy Cahn)

Where No Vultures Fly*
GB 1951 107m Technicolor
Ealing (Leslie Norman)
US title: *Ivory Hunter*

Adventures of an East African game warden.
Pleasantly improving family film, nicely shot on location; a sequel, *West of Zanzibar,* was less impressive.

w W. P. Lipscomb, Ralph Smart, Leslie Norman *d* Harry Watt *ph* Geoffrey Unsworth *m* Alan Rawsthorne

Anthony Steele, Dinah Sheridan, Harold Warrender, Meredith Edwards

'These expeditionary films are really journalistic jobs. You get sent out to a country by the studio, stay as long as you can without getting fired, and a story generally crops up.'—*Harry Watt*

'No one will wonder why it was chosen for this year's royal film show. It is not sordid, as so many new films are; it has a theme that almost everyone will find appealing; and the corner of the Empire where it is set is fresh, beautiful and exciting to look at.'—*Daily Telegraph*

Where Sinners Meet
US 1934 68m bw

A millionaire eccentric kidnaps eloping couples to find out whether they are making a mistake. Stagebound whimsy saddled with an absurd American title. Diana Wynyard, Clive Brook, Billie Burke, Reginald Owen, Alan Mowbray, Gilbert Emery, Phyllis Barry. Written by H. W. Hanemann from the play The Dover Road by A. A. Milne; directed by J. Walter Ruben; for RKO. 'Despite fine performances and good production, very dubious.'—*Variety*. (GB title: *The Dover Road.*)

Where the Boys Are
US 1960 99m Metrocolor Cinemascope
MGM / Euterpe (Joe Pasternak)

Four college girls spend the Easter vacation near a Florida military post in search of conquests.
Mindless, frothy youth musical, quite smoothly done.

w George Wells, *novel* Glendon Swarthout *d* Henry Levin *ph* Robert Bronner *m* George Stoll

George Hamilton, Dolores Hart, Paula Prentiss, Jim Hutton, Yvette Mimieux, Connie Francis, Frank Gorshin, Chill Wills, Barbara Nichols

Where the Boys Are
US 1984 94m colour

The 1960 musical becomes a teenage sex movie; neither version has much to do with the original novel. Lisa Hartman, Lorna Luft, Wendy Schaal, Lynn-Holly Johnson, Russel Todd, Howard McGillin. Written by Stu Krieger, Jeff Burkhart; directed by Hy Averback; for ITC. 'A travesty . . . insufferably coy.'—*Tom Milne, MFB*

Where the Buffalo Roam
US 1980 99m Technicolor

Adventures of a mad attorney and an eccentric journalist. Way out black comedy, for connoisseurs only. Peter Boyle, Bill Murray, Bruno Kirby, René Auberjonois, R. G. Armstrong. Written by John Kaye; directed by Art Linson; for Blue Dolphin / Universal.

Where the Hot Wind Blows
France / Italy 1958 125m bw
MGM / Cité Films / Groupe des Quatre / Titanus (Jacques Bar)
original French title: *La Loi (The Law)*

In an Adriatic port, a voluptuous young girl is pursued by the aged local squire, a racketeer, her brother-in-law and a young agriculturist. Guess who wins her.
Hoary melodrama with the emphasis on virility and illicit passion. Long and tiresome, it failed to justify the pretensions with which it announced itself at the time.

w Jules Dassin, Diego Fabbri, *novel* Roger Vailland *d* Jules Dassin *ph* Otello Martelli *m* Roman Vlad

Gina Lollobrigida, Yves Montand, Marcello Mastroianni, Pierre Brasseur, Melina Mercouri, Paolo Stoppa

† An English version was generally available.

Where the Sidewalk Ends
US 1950 95m bw
TCF (Otto Preminger)

A tough policeman accidentally kills a suspect and tries to implicate a gang leader.
Gloomy *policier* with curious moral values.

w Rex Connor (Ben Hecht), *novel* William L. Stuart *d* Otto Preminger *ph* Joseph La Shelle *m* Cyril Mockridge

Dana Andrews, Gene Tierney, Gary Merrill, Bert Freed, Tom Tully, Karl Malden, Ruth Donnelly, Craig Stevens, Robert Simon

Where the Spies Are
GB 1965 113m Metrocolor Panavision
MGM / Val Guest

A country doctor is bribed to become a spy by the promise of a car he greatly covets.
Patchy spy adventure which never settles into a comfortable style but provides occasional entertainment along its bumpy way.

w Wolf Mankowitz, Val Guest, *novel* Passport to Oblivion by James Leasor *d* Val Guest *ph* Arthur Grant *m* Mario Nascimbene

David Niven, Françoise Dorleac, Nigel Davenport, John Le Mesurier, Ronald Radd, Cyril Cusack, Eric Pohlmann

Where There's a Will*
GB 1936 81m bw
Gainsborough (Edward Black, Sidney Gilliat)

A seedy education expert sponges on his rich relations but redeems himself by rounding up gangsters at a Christmas party.
Rather slapdash star comedy with very good scenes along the way.

w Will Hay, Robert Edmunds, Ralph Spence *d* William Beaudine *ph* Charles Van Enger *md* Louis Levy

Will Hay, Hartley Power, Gibb McLaughlin, Graham Moffatt, Norma Varden, Gina Malo

Where There's a Will
GB 1955 79m bw

A London family inherits a dilapidated Devon farm and makes a go of it. Slight comedy with pleasant players. Kathleen Harrison, George Cole, Leslie Dwyer, Dandy Nichols, Ann Hanslip, Michael Shepley. Written by R. F. Delderfield from his play; directed by Vernon Sewell; for Film Locations/ Eros.

'If you laugh yourself sick at this picture—sue Bob Hope!'

Where There's Life
US 1947 75m bw
Paramount (Paul Jones)

A timid New Yorker turns out to be heir to the throne of a Ruritanian country, and is harassed by spies of both sides.
Mild star comedy with slow patches.

w Allen Boretz, Melville Shavelson *d* Sidney Lanfield *ph* Charles Lang Jnr *m* Irwin Talbot

Bob Hope, Signe Hasso, William Bendix, George Coulouris

Where Were You When the Lights Went Out?*
US 1968 94m Metrocolor Panavision
MGM (Everett Freeman, Martin Melcher)

New York's famous electrical blackout in 1965 has its effect on the life of a musical comedy star.
Cheerful sex farce with intriguing beginnings; the later confinement to one set is just a bit harmful.

w Everett Freeman, Karl Tunberg, *play* Claude Magnier *d* Hy Averback *ph* Ellsworth Fredericks *m* Dave Grusin

Doris Day, Terry-Thomas, Patrick O'Neal, Robert Morse, Lola Albright, Jim Backus, Ben Blue

Where's Charley?*
GB 1952 97m Technicolor
Warner

An Oxford undergraduate impersonates the rich aunt of his best friend.
Slow and rather stately musical version of the famous farce *Charley's Aunt*, unsatisfactorily shot on a mixture of poor sets and sunlit Oxford locations; worth cherishing for the ebullient performance of its over-age star.

w John Monks Jnr, *play* Brandon Thomas (via stage musical, *book* George Abbott *m* Frank Loesser) *d* David Butler *ph* Erwin Hillier *ch* Michael Kidd

Ray Bolger, Robert Shackleton, Mary Germaine, Allyn McLerie, Margaretta Scott, Horace Cooper

Where's Jack?*
GB 1968 119m Eastmancolor
Paramount / Oakhurst (Stanley Baker)

In 18th-century London Jack Sheppard becomes a romantic highwayman at the behest of underworld leader Jonathan Wild.
Deliberately unromantic, squalid and 'realistic' period piece which takes no hold on the fancy despite the considerable care which was obviously taken in all departments.

w Rafe and David Newhouse *d* James Clavell *ph John Wilcox* *m* Elmer Bernstein *pd Cedric Dawe*

Tommy Steele, Stanley Baker, Fiona Lewis, Alan Badel, Dudley Foster, Sue Lloyd, Noel Purcell

Where's Poppa?*
US 1970 82m De Luxe
Jerry Tokovsky / Martin Worth

A Jewish lawyer's aged mother constantly harms his love life, and he considers various means of getting rid of her.
Much-censored black comedy which might have been funnier in a complete form. Even so, it has its moments.

w Robert Klane, from his novel *d* Carl Reiner *ph* Jack Priestly *m* Jack Elliott

George Segal, Ruth Gordon, Trish Van Devere, Ron Leibman

Where's That Fire?*
GB 1939 73m bw
TCF (Edward Black)

An incompetent village fire brigade accidentally saves the crown jewels from thieves.
Routine but not despicable star comedy, long thought lost; flat patches are well separated by hilarious sequences.

w Marriott Edgar, Val Guest, J. O. C. Orton *d* Marcel Varnel *ph* Arthur Crabtree

Will Hay, Moore Marriott, Graham Moffatt, Peter Gawthorne, Eric Clavering, Charles Hawtrey

W.H.I.F.F.S.
US 1975 92m Technicolor Panavision
Brut (C. O. Erickson)
GB title: *C.A.S.H.*

An impotent army veteran finds that a criminal career, helped by stolen army gas, helps his sex life.
Over-the-top comedy with vaguely anti-war and anti-pollution leanings.

w Malcolm Marmorstein *d* Ted Post *ph* David M. Walsh *m* John Cameron

Elliott Gould, Eddie Albert, Harry Guardino, Godfrey Cambridge, Jennifer O'Neill

† Rather typical of the film was its ambiguous catch line: 'The biggest bang in history!'

AAN: song, 'Now That We're in Love'

While I Live
GB 1947 85m bw
Edward Dryhurst
Reissue title: *The Dream of Olwen.*

A Cornishwoman believes an amnesiac girl to be the reincarnation of her dead sister.
Silly melodrama which achieved phenomenal popularity, despite poor production, because of its haunting theme tune *The Dream of Olwen* by Charles Williams.

w John Harlow, Doreen Montgomery, *play* This Same Garden by Robert Bell *d* John Harlow *ph* F. A. Young *m Charles Williams*

Tom Walls, Sonia Dresdel, Carol Raye, Clifford Evans, Patricia Burke, John Warwick, Edward Lexy

While the City Sleeps
US 1956 100m bw Superscope
RKO (Bert Friedlob)

Three chief executives of a newspaper empire are pitted against each other in a search for a murder scoop.
Star-packed but leaden-paced news bureau melodrama; a major disappointment considering the talent.

w Casey Robinson, *novel* The Bloody Spur by Charles Einstein *d* Fritz Lang *ph* Ernest Laszlo *m* Herschel Burke Gilbert

Dana Andrews, George Sanders, Ida Lupino, Sally Forrest, Thomas Mitchell, Rhonda Fleming, Vincent Price, Howard Duff, James Craig, Robert Warwick, John Barrymore Jnr

While the Patient Slept
US 1935 65m bw

A nurse hired to look after a stricken millionaire finds herself in the middle of a murder case. Announced as the first of a series of Clue Club Mysteries, this was derived from a source similar to, or possibly the same as, *Miss Pinkerton* (*qv*). It sufficed. Aline MacMahon, Guy Kibbee, Lyle Talbot, Patricia Ellis, Allen Jenkins, Gene Solow, Brown Holmes, Robert Barrat, Hobart Cavanaugh. Written by Robert N. Lee from a novel by Mignon G. Eberhart; directed by Ray Enright; for First National. 'Seems probable that it will please wherever mysteries are liked.'—*Variety*

While the Sun Shines
GB 1946 81m bw
ABPC / Anatole de Grunwald

An American soldier and a young Frenchman seek to woo Lady Elizabeth away from her intended.
Mild wartime comedy, rather stagey and considerably undercast.

w Terence Rattigan, from his play *d* Anthony Asquith *ph* Jack Hildyard

Brenda Bruce, Ronald Howard, Bonar Colleano, Ronald Squire, Barbara White, Margaret Rutherford, Miles Malleson, Joyce Grenfell

The Whip Hand
US 1951 82m bw
RKO (Lewis J. Rachmil)

A fisherman finds himself unwelcome in a lonely town run by ex-Nazi, now communist, bacteriologists.
Preposterous, pretentious anti-communist low-budgeter, mildly enjoyable for its sheer gall.

w George Bricker, Frank L. Moss *d / pd* William Cameron Menzies *ph* Nicholas Musuraca *m* Paul Sawtell

Elliott Reid, Carla Balenda, Edgar Barrier, Raymond Burr

Whiplash
US 1948 90m bw
Warner (William Jacobs)

A painter becomes a prizefighter.
Hokey, unpersuasive romantic melodrama.

w Maurice Geraghty, Harriet Frank Jnr *d* Lewis Seiler *ph* Peverell Marley *m* Franz Waxman

Dane Clark, Alexis Smith, Zachary Scott, Eve Arden, Jeffrey Lynn, S. Z. Sakall, Alan Hale, Douglas Kennedy

Whipsaw*
US 1935 88m bw
MGM (Harry Rapf)

A G-man infiltrates a gang by wooing its girl member.
Fairly snappy romantic drama which further established both its stars.

w Howard Emmett Rogers *d* Sam Wood *ph* James Wong Howe *m* William Axt

Spencer Tracy, Myrna Loy, Harvey Stephens, Clay Clements, William Harrigan

'Should do okay biz . . . romance and sex angles mingling with the light touch of sophistication so popular nowadays carries events along at a speedy pace that is unabated until the fadeout.'—*Variety*

Whirlpool
US 1934 69m bw

A convict is released and makes contact with the daughter who never knew him. Heavily plotted melodrama with an unhappy ending; technically quite proficient. Jack Holt, Jean Arthur, Allen Jenkins, Donald Cook, Lila Lee, John Miljan, Ward Bond. Written by Dorothy Howell, Ethel Hill, Howard Emmett Rogers; directed by Roy William Neill; for Columbia. 'One of the most surefire father and daughter stories ever screened, with heart interest running high throughout . . . well above fair in entertainment appeal.'—*Variety*

Whirlpool*
US 1950 98m bw
TCF (Otto Preminger)

A girl is accused of a murder committed by her hypnotist, who has willed himself out of a hospital bed.
Silly murder melodrama; glossy production makes it entertaining.

w Lester Barstow, Andrew Solt, *novel* Guy Endore *d* Otto Preminger *ph* Arthur Miller *m* David Raksin

Gene Tierney, *Jose Ferrer,* Richard Conte, Charles Bickford, Barbara O'Neil, Eduard Franz, Fortunio Bonanova

'It is sometimes difficult to discover from Miss Tierney's playing whether she is or is not under hypnosis.'—*MFB*
† Lester Barstow=Ben Hecht.

Whirlpool
GB 1959 95m Eastmancolor
Rank (George Pitcher)

A killer escapes in Cologne; his girl friend separates from him and gets a lift down the Rhine in a barge; the trip reforms her and she betrays her lover.
Modestly attractive travelogue with the burden of a very boring melodrama.

w Lawrence P. Bachmann from novel The Lorelei by Lawrence P. Bachmann *d* Lewis Allen *ph* Geoffrey Unsworth *m* Ron Goodwin

Juliette Greco, O. W. Fischer, William Sylvester, Marius Goring, Muriel Pavlow

Whisky Galore****
GB 1948 82m bw
Ealing (Monja Danischewsky)
US title: *Tight Little Island*

During World War II, a ship full of whisky is wrecked on a small Hebridean island, and the local customs and excise man has his hands full.
Marvellously detailed, fast-moving, well-played and attractively photographed comedy which firmly established the richest Ealing vein.

w Compton Mackenzie, Angus Macphail, novel Compton Mackenzie *d Alexander Mackendrick ph Gerald Gibbs m Ernest Irving*

Basil Radford, Joan Greenwood, Jean Cadell, Gordon Jackson, James Robertson Justice, Wylie Watson, John Gregson, Morland Graham, Duncan Macrae, Catherine Lacey, Bruce Seton, Henry Mollinson, Compton Mackenzie, A. E. Matthews

'Brilliantly witty and fantastic, but wholly plausible.'—*Sunday Chronicle*

The Whisperers
GB 1966 106m bw
UA / Seven Pines (Michael S. Laughlin, Ronald Shedlo)

An old lady hears voices and is put upon by her son, her wandering husband, and various others.
Interesting but cold and finally unsatisfactory character melodrama; even the acting, though in a sense admirable, is too genteel.

w Bryan Forbes, *novel* Robert Nicolson *d* Bryan Forbes *ph* Gerry Turpin *m* John Barry

Edith Evans, Eric Portman, Avis Bunnage, Nanette Newman, Gerald Sim, Ronald Fraser

AAN: Edith Evans

Whispering City
Canada 1947 95m bw

A girl reporter has dangerous information. Fairly watchable mystery, all Canadian apart from the three leads. Paul Lukas, Mary Anderson, Helmut Dantine, John Pratt, George Alexander. Written by Rian James. Leonard Lee; directed by Fedor Ozep; for Quebec / Eagle Lion.

Whispering Ghosts
US 1942 75m bw

A radio detective tackles the unsolved murder of an old sea captain. No ghosts are evident, and not much plot, in this slow mystery comedy which failed to do for Berle what *The Cat and the Canary* did for Hope. Milton Berle, Brenda Joyce, John Carradine, John Shelton, Willie Best. Written by Lou Breslow; directed by Alfred Werker; for Sol M. Wurtzel / TCF.

Whispering Shadows
US 1933 bw serial: 12 eps

A waxworks owner makes figures which speak and move; but he and they are prey to The Whispering Shadow. Quaint melodramatic serial, still good for a few laughs. Bela Lugosi, Henry B. Walthall, Karl Dane, Viva Tattersall, Robert Warwick. Directed by Albert Herman and Colbert Clark; for Mascot.

'The epic spectacle of America's most flaming era!'

Whispering Smith
US 1948 88m Technicolor
Paramount (Mel Epstein)

A government agent investigating robberies finds his friend is implicated.
Fairly entertaining detective western.

w Frank Butler, Karl Lamb, *novel* Frank H. Spearman *d* Leslie Fenton *ph* Ray Rennahan *m* Adolph Deutsch

Alan Ladd, Robert Preston, Brenda Marshall, Donald Crisp, William Demarest, Fay Holden, Murvyn Vye, Frank Faylen

Whispering Smith Hits London
GB 1951 82m bw
Exclusive / Hammer (Anthony Hinds)

An American detective in London investigates the case of a suicide which may be murder.
Tolerable programmer of its time: competence without inspiration.

w John Gilling *d* Francis Searle *ph* Walter Harvey *m* Frank Spencer

Richard Carlson, Greta Gynt, Herbert Lom, Rona Anderson, Alan Wheatley, Dora Bryan, Reginald Beckwith

The Whistle at Eaton Falls*
US 1951 96m bw
Columbia (Louis de Rochemont)
GB title: *Richer than the Earth*

The story of a strike at a small-town plastics factory.
Reasonably absorbing semi-documentary with a final 'solution' which rather evades the issues.

w Lemist Esler, Virginia Shaler *d* Robert Siodmak *ph* Joseph Brun *m* Louis Applebaum

Lloyd Bridges, Dorothy Gish, Carleton Carpenter, Murray Hamilton, James Westerfield, Lenore Lonergan

Whistle Down the Wind*
GB 1961 99m bw
Rank / Allied Film Makers / Beaver (Richard Attenborough)

Three north country children think a murderer on the run is Jesus Christ.
Charming allegorical study of childhood innocence, extremely well made, amusing, and avoiding sentimentality.

w Keith Waterhouse, Willis Hall, novel Mary Hayley Bell *d Bryan Forbes ph* Arthur Ibbetson *m* Malcolm Arnold

Hayley Mills, Bernard Lee, Alan Bates, Norman Bird, Elsie Wagstaff, Alan Barnes

Whistle Stop
US 1946 84m bw
United Artists / Nero / Seymour Nebenza

A city girl returns to her small-town home and finds herself torn between a night club proprietor and an indolent charmer.
Would-be *film noir*, miscast and rather glum when it isn't unintentionally funny.

w Philip Yordan, *novel* Maritta M. Wolff *d* Leonide Moguy *ph* Russell Metty *m* Dmitri Tiomkin

George Raft, Ava Gardner, Tom Conway, Victor McLaglen

The Whistler

Originally a radio series of suspense stories introduced by someone whistling the theme tune, this was turned by Columbia into a fairly workmanlike series of second features quite unrelated to each other except for the leading actor, Richard Dix, who alternated as hero and villain, and William Castle, who directed or produced most of them.

1944: THE WHISTLER, THE MARK OF THE WHISTLER
1945: THE POWER OF THE WHISTLER
1946: THE VOICE OF THE WHISTLER
1947: MYSTERIOUS INTRUDER, THE SECRET OF THE WHISTLER, THE 12th HOUR
1948: THE RETURN OF THE WHISTLER

Whistling in the Dark*
US 1941 77m bw
MGM (George Haight)

A radio detective is kidnapped by a criminal who wants him to devise a perfect murder which will then be pinned on him.
Scatty comedy-thriller which, though it now seems slow to start, was popular enough to warrant two sequels (*Whistling in Brooklyn, Whistling in Dixie*).

w Robert McGonigle, Harry Clark, Albert Mannheimer, *play* Laurence Gross, Edward Childs Carpenter *d* S. Sylvan Simon *ph* Sidney Wagner *m* Bronislau Kaper

Red Skelton, Conrad Veidt, Ann Rutherford, Virginia Grey, Eve Arden, Rags Ragland, Don Douglas, Lloyd Corrigan
† The play was previously filmed in 1933 with Ernest Truex, and this version is now shown on TV as *Scared*.

The White Angel*
US 1936 91m bw
Warner (Henry Blanke)

The life of Florence Nightingale.
Starchy biopic; the Victorian atmosphere is never quite caught.

w Mordaunt Shairp, Michael Jacoby *d* William Dieterle *ph* Tony Gaudio

Kay Francis, Ian Hunter, Donald Woods, Nigel Bruce, Donald Crisp, Henry O'Neill, Billy Mauch, Halliwell Hobbes

White Banners*
US 1938 88m bw
Warner (Henry Blanke)

A social worker tries to solve the problems of a troubled family among whom is her own son, a fact unknown to him.
Moderate middle-class drama.

w Lenore Coffee, Cameron Rogers, Abem Finkel, *novel* Lloyd C. Douglas *d* Edmund Goulding *ph* Charles Rosher *m* Max Steiner

Fay Bainter, Claude Rains, Jackie Cooper, Bonita Granville, Henry O'Neill, James Stephenson, Kay Johnson

'Emotional drama, okay for the family trade . . . there is something fine and tender about it.'—*Variety*

AAN: Fay Bainter

The White Buffalo
US 1977 97m Technicolor
Dino de Laurentiis (Pancho Kohner)

Wild Bill Hickok and Chief Crazy Horse join forces to kill a marauding white buffalo.
Ridiculous symbolic western, not helped by the very artificial looking beast of the title.

w Richard Sale, from his novel *d* J. Lee Thompson *ph* Paul Lohmann *m* John Barry

Charles Bronson, Jack Warden, Will Sampson, Kim Novak, Clint Walker, Stuart Whitman, John Carradine, Slim Pickens, Cara Williams, Douglas Fowley

'The dried husk of a *Moby Dick* allegory seems to be rattling around here amidst all the other dead wood.'—*Jonathan Rosenbaum, MFB*

White Cargo*
US 1942 90m bw
MGM (Victor Saville)

White rubber planters are driven mad with desire for a scheming native girl.
Antediluvian melodrama previously filmed in 1930. Good for laughing at, and the star looked great as Tondelayo.

w Leon Gordon, from his play and *novel* Hell's Playground by Vera Simonton *d* Richard Thorpe *m* Bronislau Kaper

Hedy Lamarr, Walter Pidgeon, Richard Carlson, Frank Morgan, Bramwell Fletcher, Richard Ainley, Reginald Owen
† There was also a British version in 1929 (silent) with Leslie Faber and Gypsy Rhouma; and a few months later it emerged with added dialogue.

White Christmas*
US 1954 120m Technicolor Vistavision
Paramount (Robert Emmett Dolan)

Two entertainers boost the popularity of a winter resort run by an old army buddy.
Humdrum musical lifted only by its stars; a revamp of *Holiday Inn*, which was much better.

w Norman Krasna, Norman Panama, Melvin Frank *d* Michael Curtiz *ph* Loyal Griggs *songs* Irving Berlin

Bing Crosby, Danny Kaye, Rosemary Clooney, Vera-Ellen, Dean Jagger, Mary Wickes, Sig Rumann, Grady Sutton

AAN: 'Count Your Blessings Instead of Sheep'

The White Cliffs of Dover*
US 1944 126m bw
MGM (Sidney Franklin)

An American girl who marries into the British aristocracy loses a husband in World War I and a son in World War II.
Tearful flagwaver with some entertaining scenes in the first half and the general sense of an all-stops-out production.

w Claudine West, Jan Lustig, George Froeschel, *poem* Alice Duer Miller *d* Clarence Brown *ph* George Folsey *m* Herbert Stothart

Irene Dunne, Alan Marshal, Frank Morgan, May Whitty, Roddy McDowall, C. Aubrey Smith, Gladys Cooper, Peter Lawford, Van Johnson

'A long, earnest, well-intentioned, over-emotionalized cliché.'—*Richard Mallett, Punch*

'This sterling silver picture . . . is such a tribute to English gentility as only an American studio would dare to make.'—*New York Times*

'Sentimental patriotism . . . a truly monstrous cultural artifact.'—*Pauline Kael, 70s*

AAN: George Folsey

The White Cockatoo
US 1935 72m bw

Male and female heirs to a will suffer death threats. Bland transcription of a popular mystery book. Ricardo Cortez, Jean Muir, Ruth Donnelly, Minna Gombell, Walter Kingsford, John Eldredge. Written by Ben Markson and Lillie Hayward, from novel by Mignon G. Eberhart; directed by Alan Crosland; for Warner.

White Corridors*
GB 1951 102m bw
GFD / Vic (Joseph Janni, John Croydon)

Life in a small Midlands hospital.
Competent multi-drama which found a big audience.

w Jan Read, Pat Jackson, *novel* Yeoman's Hospital by Helen Ashton *d* Pat Jackson *ph* C. Pennington-Richards

James Donald, Googie Withers, Godfrey Tearle, Petula Clark, Jack Watling, Moira Lister, Barry Jones, Megs Jenkins, Basil Radford

'This quality of professionalism is comparatively rare in British films.'—*Gavin Lambert*

White Cradle Inn
GB 1947 83m bw
British Lion / Peak (Ivor McLaren, A. G. Hardman)
US title: *High Fury*

A Swiss hotel owner adopts a refugee boy and is menaced by her ne'er-do-well husband, who finally sacrifices himself for the boy.
Unimpressive little drama which wastes its cast, but provides beautiful scenery.

w Harold French, Lesley Storm *d* Harold French *ph* Deric Williams

Madeleine Carroll, Michael Rennie, Ian Hunter, Anne Marie Blanc, Michael McKeag

The White Dawn
US 1976 110m Movielab
Paramount / American Film Properties (Martin Ransohoff)

In 1900, survivors from a whaling ship are cared for by Eskimos, who turn on them when nature proves unkind.
Unpleasant fable with lots of bitter weather and subtitled Eskimos. Scarcely an entertainment, and its message is mumbled.

w James Houston, Tom Rickman *d* Philip Kaufman *ph* Michael Chapman *m* Henry Mancini

Warren Oates, Timothy Bottoms, Lou Gossett, Eskimo cast

White Dog
US 1982 90m Metrocolor
Paramount / Edgar J. Scherick

A dog is trained to attack blacks only.
Oddball thriller with racist overtones; not a happy thought.

w Samuel Fuller, Curtis Hanson, *book* Romain Gary *d* Samuel Fuller *ph* Bruce Surtees *m* Ennio Morricone

Kristy McNichol, Paul Winfield, Burl Ives, Jameson Parker, Lynne Moody, Marshall Thompson

White Eagle
US 1941 bw serial: 15 eps

A pony express rider is threatened by revengeful crooks. Solid western serial with an Indian hero. Buck Jones, Raymond Hatton, Dorothy Fay, James Craven. Directed by James W. Horne; for Columbia.

White Feather*
US 1955 100m Technicolor Cinemascope
TCF / Panoramic (Robert L. Jacks)

A cavalry colonel tries to hold back gold prospectors until the Cheyenne have moved on to their new reservations.
Old-fashioned cowboys and (sympathetic) Indians, very efficiently done.

w Delmer Daves, Leo Townsend *d* Robert Webb *ph* Lucien Ballard *m* Hugo Friedhofer

Robert Wagner, John Lund, Jeffrey Hunter, Debra Paget, Eduard Franz, Noah Beery Jnr, Hugh O'Brian, Virginia Leith, Emile Meyer

'Pick up the pieces, folks, Jimmy's in action again!'

White Heat***
US 1949 114m bw
Warner (Louis F. Edelman)

A violent, mother-fixated gangster gets his comeuppance when a government agent is infiltrated into his gang.
This searing melodrama reintroduced the old Cagney and then some: spellbinding suspense sequences complemented his vivid and hypnotic portrayal.

w Ivan Goff, Ben Roberts, *story* Virginia Kellogg *d Raoul Walsh* *ph* Sid Hickox *m* Max Steiner

James Cagney, Edmond O'Brien, *Margaret Wycherly,* Virginia Mayo, Steve Cochran, John Archer

'The most gruesome aggregation of brutalities ever presented under the guise of entertainment.'—*Cue*

'In the hurtling tabloid traditions of the gangster movies of the thirties, but its matter-of-fact violence is a new post-war style.'—*Time*

'A wild and exciting picture of mayhem and madness.'—*Life*

AAN: Virginia Kellogg

The White Hell of Pitz Palu*
Germany 1929 approx 90m bw

Mountaineers have a difficult ascent of Pitz Palu. Classic semi-documentary, noted for its pictorial compositions more than its dramatic qualities. Written and directed by G. W. Pabst and Dr Arnold Fank; for UFA. 'An astonishing and, to me, wildly terrifying film.'—*James Agate.*

White Hunter
US 1936 65m bw

An African hunter is hired by an old enemy. Extremely predictable melodrama with poor technical work. Warner Baxter, Wilfrid Lawson, June Lang, Gail Patrick, Alison Skipworth. Written by Sam Duncan, Kenneth Earl, Gene Markey; directed by Irving Cummings; for Darryl F. Zanuck / TCF.

White Lightning
US 1973 101m De Luxe
United Artists / Levy–Gardner–Laven

A convict escapes to wreak vengeance on the corrupt sheriff who had killed his brother.
Heavy-going southern melodrama which comes to life only during its occasional fits of violence. *Gator* was a kind of sequel.

w William Norton *d* Joseph Sargent *ph* Edward Rosson *m* Charles Bernstein

Burt Reynolds, Jennifer Billingsley, Ned Beatty, Matt Clark, Bo Hopkins, Louise Latham, Diane Ladd

White Mischief
GB 1987 107m Agfa-Gevaert
Umbrella (Michael White)

Real-life unsolved murder of Lord Erroll in Kenya's Happy Valley.
Starry cast and slick direction fail to engage interest in the sybaritic lifestyle of white settlers in colonial Africa.

w Michael Radford, Jonathan Gems, from book by James Fox *d* Michael Radford *ph* Roger Deakins *m* George Fenton *pd* Roger Hall

Charles Dance, Greta Scacchi, Joss Ackland, Sarah Miles, John Hurt, Trevor Howard

White Nights
US 1985 135m Metrocolor
Columbia / New Visions / Delphi V (Taylor Hackford, William S. Gilmore)

A Russian emigré ballet star finds himself after a plane crash a prisoner in Leningrad.
Basically an escape story with silly details, this tries also to be a dance film about relationships. Despite the star's powerful presence, it fails on most counts.

w James Goldman, Eric Hughes *d* Taylor Hackford *ph* David Watkin *m* Michel Colombier *pd* Philip Harrison *ed* Fredric and William Steinkamp

Mikhail Baryshnikov, Gregory Hines, Jerzy Skolimowski, Helen Mirren, Geraldine Page, Isabella Rossellini

'Good looks but no style . . . neither fish nor fowl, good nor bad, box office gold nor poison.'—*Variety*

AA: song 'Say You, Say Me' (Lionel Richie)

The White Parade
US 1934 80m bw

Incidents at the nurses' training school of a midwestern hospital. Smooth but very predictable semi-documentary. Loretta Young, John Boles, Dorothy Wilson, Muriel Kirkland, Sara Haden, Astrid Allwyn, Jane Darwell, Frank Conroy. Written by Sonya Levien, Ernest Pascal, from the novel by Rian James; directed by Irving Cummings; for Jesse L. Lasky / Fox. 'Sympathetic comedy drama with strong *femme* draw value.'—*Variety*

AAN: best picture

White Savage
US 1943 75m Technicolor
Universal (George Waggner)
GB title: *White Captive*

The queen of a beautiful South Sea island has trouble with shark hunters and crooks after her mineral deposits.
Self-admitted hokum strung loosely and colourfully around its star: big box office in the middle of the war.

w Richard Brooks *d* Arthur Lubin *ph* Lester White, William Snyder *m* Frank Skinner

Maria Montez, Jon Hall, Sabu, Thomas Gomez, Sidney Toler, Paul Guilfoyle, Turhan Bey, Don Terry

'It may be that these semi-burlesques were more fun to make than to watch.'—*Pauline Kael, 70s*

White Shadows in the South Seas*
US 1927 88m (sound version) bw
MGM

An alcoholic doctor in Tahiti finds happiness with a native girl until he is killed by white colonials.

Rather boring melodrama illuminated by superb photography.

w Ray Doyle, Jack Cunningham, *book* Frederick J. O'Brien *d* W. S. Van Dyke (and Robert Flaherty) *ph* Clyde de Vinna and others (including Flaherty)

Monte Blue, Raquel Torres

AA: Clyde de Vinna

The White Sister
US 1933 110m bw
MGM (Hunt Stromberg)

When her lover is reported killed in the war, an Italian noblewoman takes the veil . . . but he comes back.
Tiresome romantic drama from another age, a big prestige production of its time.

w Donald Ogden Stewart, *novel* F. Marion Crawford, Walter Hackett *d* Victor Fleming *ph* William Daniels *m* Herbert Stothart

Helen Hayes, Clark Gable, Lewis Stone, Louise Closser Hale, May Robson, Edward Arnold

'An eloquent yoking of marquee names . . . certain money maker for general release.'—*Variety*

† The silent version of 1923 starred Lillian Gish and Ronald Colman, and bore the tagline: 'A love that outlived passion!'

White Tie and Tails
US 1946 81m bw

A butler left in charge of the house gets ideas above his station. Modest comedy which lacks the required high style. Dan Duryea, Ella Raines, William Bendix, Richard Gaines, Clarence Kolb, Frank Jenks. Written by Bertram Millhauser, from the novel *The Victoria Docks at Eight* by Rufus King and Charles Leakon; directed by Charles Barton; for Universal.

The White Tower
US 1950 98m Technicolor
RKO (Sid Rogell)

Various people have personal reasons for climbing an Alpine mountain.
Pretentiously symbolic melodrama with some good action sequences and curiously stilted performances.

w Paul Jarrico, *novel* James Ramsay Ullman *d* Ted Tetzlaff *ph* Ray Rennahan *m* Roy Webb

Glenn Ford, Claude Rains, Alida Valli, Oscar Homolka, Cedric Hardwicke, Lloyd Bridges, June Clayworth

'The main interest is a curiosity as to who will fall over which precipice when.'—*Penelope Houston*

The White Unicorn
GB 1947 97m bw
GFD / John Corfield (Harold Huth)
US title: *Bad Sister*

In a home for delinquent girls, the worst offender exchanges reminiscences with the warden.
Peg's Paper melodrama in complex flashback form.

w Robert Westerby, A. R. Rawlinson, Moie Charles, *novel* Flora Sandstrom *d* Bernard Knowles *ph* Reg Wyer *m* Bretton Byrd

Margaret Lockwood, Joan Greenwood, Ian Hunter, Dennis Price, Guy Middleton, Catherine Lacey, Mabel Constanduros, Paul Dupuis

White Witch Doctor
US 1953 96m Technicolor
TCF (Otto Lang)

A nurse in the Congo converts a gold-seeking adventurer.
Stale hokum in which the animals are the most interesting feature.

w Ivan Goff, Ben Roberts, *novel* Louise A. Stinetorf *d* Henry Hathaway *ph* Leon Shamroy *m* Bernard Herrmann

Susan Hayward, Robert Mitchum, Walter Slezak, Timothy Carey

'Alone among outcasts who hadn't seen a white woman in ten years!'

White Woman
US 1933 68m bw
Paramount

A cockney overseer in the Malaysian jungle takes back a cabaret singer as his bride.
Risible melodrama with an obvious outcome.

w Samuel Hoffenstein, Gladys Lehman from story by Norman Reilly Raine, Frank Butler *d* Stuart Walker *ph* Harry Fischbeck

Charles Laughton, Carole Lombard, Kent Taylor, Charles Bickford, Percy Kilbride, Charles Middleton, James Bell

'Bromidic South Sea stuff . . . seems best for dual bills.'—*Variety*

† Remade as *Island of Lost Men.*

White Zombie**
US 1932 74m bw
American Securities Corporation (Edward Halperin)

Haitian zombies work a sugar mill for a white schemer.
Genuinely eerie horror film with a slow, stagey, out-of-this world quality coupled with an interesting sense of composition.

w Garnett Weston *d* Victor Halperin *ph* Arthur Martinelli *md* Abe Meyer

Bela Lugosi, Madge Bellamy, John Harron, Joseph Cawthorn

'Fine work of Lugosi is backed by good cast and bizarre staging . . . not quite up to Broadway.'—*Variety*

'A Gothic fairy tale filled with dreamlike imagery, traditional symbols, echoes of Romanticism, and (probably unintentional) psychosexual overtones.'—*Carlos Clarens*

'For those absolutely dedicated to gothic silliness.'—*New Yorker, 1977*

Who?
GB 1974 93m Eastmancolor
British Lion / Hemisphere / Maclean

An American scientist is captured by the Russians after a car crash and returned six months later as a somewhat suspect android.
So-what mixture of character drama and James Bondery; aiming clearly at no particular audience, it failed to get a release.

w John Gould, *novel* Algis Budrys *d* Jack Gold *ph* Petrus Schloemp *m* John Cameron

Elliott Gould, Trevor Howard, Joseph Bova, Ed Grover, James Noble, Lyndon Brook

Who Dares Wins
GB 1982 125m colour
Rank / Richmond Light Horse / Euan Lloyd (Raymond Menmuir)
US title: *The Final Option*

An SAS captain infiltrates a ruthless anti-nuclear group which finally holds the American Secretary of State to ransom.
Crude exploitation of the SAS's successful relief of the Iranian Embassy. The entertainment is thick ear at best, and some of the dialogue and performances have to be seen to be believed.

w Reginald Rose *d* Ian Sharp *ph* Phil Meheux *m* Roy Budd, Jerry and Marc Donahue *pd* Syd Cain

Lewis Collins, Judy Davis, Ingrid Pitt, Richard Widmark, Edward Woodward, Robert Webber, Kenneth Griffith, Norman Rodway

'It should manage to offend anybody—punk, pacifist or policeman—inclined to take seriously the subject of global security.'—*Philip Strick, MFB*

'Cinematically antiquated and with hawkish politics poking unappealingly through the thin cloak of fiction.'—*Sight and Sound*

Who Done It?
US 1942 77m bw
Universal (Alex Gottlieb)

Soda jerks in a New York radio station catch a murderer.
So-so comedy thriller, fatally lacking atmosphere (and good jokes).

w Stanley Roberts, Edmund Joseph, John Grant *d* Erle C. Kenton *ph* Charles Van Enger *m* Frank Skinner

Bud Abbott, Lou Costello, William Gargan, Louise Allbritton, Patric Knowles, Don Porter, Jerome Cowan, William Bendix, Mary Wickes, Thomas Gomez

Who Done It?
GB 1956 85m bw
Ealing (Michael Relph, Basil Dearden)

An ice-rink sweeper sets up as a private eye and captures a ring of spies.
Lively but disappointing film debut for a star comic whose screen personality proved too bland.

w T. E. B. Clarke *d* Basil Dearden *ph* Otto Heller *m* Philip Green

Benny Hill, Belinda Lee, David Kossoff, Garry Marsh, Ernest Thesiger, Thorley Walters

Who Framed Roger Rabbit***
US 1988 103m Rank Color / Metrocolor / De Luxe
Touchstone / Amblin

Cartoon characters become involved in Dashiel Hammett-style whodunnit.
Criticisms of thin plotting are irrelevant: the seamless integration of animation and live-action enchanted audiences.

w Jeffrey Price, Peter S. Seaman from book Who Censored Roger Rabbit? by Gary K. Wold *d* Robert Zemeckis *ph* Dean Condey *m* Alan Silvestri *pd* Elliot Scott, Roger Cain *anim Richard Williams*

Bob Hoskins, Christopher Lloyd, Joanna Cassidy, Stubby Kaye *voices* Charles Fleischer, Kathleen Turner, Amy Irving, Lou Hirsch, Mel Blanc

Who Goes There?
GB 1952 85m bw
British Lion / London Films (Anthony Kimmins)
US title: *The Passionate Sentry*

In a Grace and Favour house near St James' Palace, a guardsman is involved in a trail of romantic intrigue.
Very British romantic farce, dully and quickly filmed from a West End success.

w John Dighton, from his play *d* Anthony Kimmins *ph* John Wilcox, Ted Scaife *m* Muir Mathieson

Peggy Cummins, Valerie Hobson, George Cole, Nigel Patrick, A. E. Matthews, Anthony Bushell

Who Is Harry Kellerman and Why Is He Saying These Terrible Things About Me?
US 1971 108m De Luxe
Cinema Center (Ulu Grosbard, Herb Gardner)

A New York composer is persecuted by a mysterious figure which turns out to be himself.
Wild, shapeless, satirical psycho-comedy-melodrama. Not very good.

w Herb Gardner *d* Ulu Grosbard *ph* Victor Kemper *pd* Harry Horner

Dustin Hoffman, Barbara Harris, Jack Warden, David Burns, Gabriel Dell, Dom De Luise

AAN: Barbara Harris

Who Is Killing the Great Chefs of Europe?*
US 1978 112m Metrocolor
Warner / Aldrich / Lorimar (Merv Adelson, Lee Rich, William Aldrich)
GB title: *Too Many Chefs*

A fast food entrepreneur in London finds himself at the centre of a series of grisly murders.
Unusual and lighthearted black comedy against the background of international gastronomy.

w Peter Stone, novel Nan and Ivan Lyons *d* Ted Kotcheff *ph* John Alcott *m* Henry Mancini

George Segal, Jacqueline Bisset, *Robert Morley*, Jean-Pierre Cassel, Philippe Noiret, Jean Rochefort, Madge Ryan

Who Killed Doc Robbin?
US 1948 55m Cinecolor

Local kids prowl a supposedly haunted mansion. Hesitant revival of the Our Gang comedy style in a semi-feature format; it had only mild success. George Zucco, Virginia Grey, Don Castle. Written by Maurice Geraghty, Dorothy Reid; directed by Bernard Carr; for Hal Roach.

Who Killed Mary What's Her Name?
US 1971 90m De Luxe
Cannon (George Manasse)

An ex-boxer determines to solve the murder of a prostitute.
Old-fashioned whodunnit with something to say grafted on every five minutes: an unsatisfactory mix.

w John O'Toole *d* Ernest Pintoff *ph* Greg Sandor *m* Gary McFarland

Red Buttons, Alice Playten, Sylvia Miles, Sam Waterston

Whoops Apocalypse
GB 1986 91m Eastmancolor

First woman president of the US tries to avert nuclear attack. Frenetic but pathetic attempt at Dr Strangelove for the 80s. Loretta Swit, Peter Cook, Rik Mayall, Alexei Sayle, Herbert Lom. Written by Andrew Marshall, David Renwick; directed by Tom Bussmann; for ITC.

Who Was That Lady?*
US 1960 115m bw
Columbia / Ansark / George Sidney (Norman Krasna)

A professor seen kissing a student persuades a friend to tell his wife that they are both FBI agents on duty. Foreign spies believe them . . .
Agreeably wacky comedy with a strained and prolonged middle section leading to a totally zany climax.

w Norman Krasna, from his play *d* George Sidney *ph* Harry Stradling *m* André Previn

Tony Curtis, Dean Martin, Janet Leigh, James Whitmore, John McIntire, Barbara Nichols, Larry Keating

'The hand that rocks the cradle has no flesh on it!'

Whoever Slew Auntie Roo?
GB 1972 91m Movielab
AIP / Hemdale (John Pellatt)
US title: *Who Slew Auntie Roo?*

A madwoman menaces two orphan children. Pointless and slenderly plotted adaptation of *Hansel and Gretel*, crude in all departments.

w Robert Blees, Jimmy Sangster *d* Curtis Harrington *ph* Desmond Dickinson *m* Ken Jones

Shelley Winters, Ralph Richardson, Mark Lester, Lionel Jeffries, Chloe Franks, Hugh Griffith, Rosalie Crutchley, Pat Heywood

'Not content with being a delicate fantasy of childish nightmare, it tries to add a totally inappropriate seasoning of Grand Guignol.'—*Tom Milne*

The Whole Town's Talking*
US 1935 86m bw
Columbia (Lester Cowan)
GB title: *Passport to Fame*

A gangster finds it convenient occasionally to pose as his double, a meek little clerk.
Pleasingly neat comedy, well staged and acted.

w Jo Swerling, Robert Riskin, *novel* W. R. Burnett *d* John Ford *ph* Joseph August

Edward G. Robinson, Jean Arthur, Arthur Hohl, Wallace Ford, Arthur Byron, Donald Meek, Edward Brophy, Etienne Girardot

'Wow comedy-melodrama . . . swell entertainment.'—*Variety*

'A lively and satisfactory combination of farce and melodrama.'—*Richard Watts Jnr*

The Whole Truth*
GB 1958 84m bw
Columbia / Romulus (Jack Clayton)

A jealous husband poses as a detective in order to murder his wife and incriminate a film producer.
A filmed play, but quite a solidly carpentered murder thriller with a couple of neat twists.

w Jonathan Latimer, *play* Philip Mackie *d* John Guillermin *ph* Wilkie Cooper *m* Mischa Spoliansky

Stewart Granger, George Sanders, Donna Reed, Gianna Maria Canale

Who'll Stop the Rain?
US 1978 125m colour
UA / Gabriel Katzka, Herb Jaffe
GB title: *Dog Soldiers*

A Vietnam veteran takes to smuggling heroin into the US, but gets his wife and friend involved with gangsters.
Heavy-going, downbeat character drama with action sequences; well enough done, but the kind of movie that does nothing for anybody.

w Judith Roscoe, *book* Dog Soldiers by Robert Stone *d* Karel Reisz *ph* Richard H. Kline *m* Laurence Rosenthal

Nick Nolte, Tuesday Weld, Michael Moriarty, Anthony Zerbe, Richard Masur, David Opatoshu, Roy Sharkey, Gail Strickland

'Just another ambition-downer, a wasted effort to make something meaningful out of wasted lives.'—*Richard Schickel, Time*

Wholly Moses
US 1980 109m Metrocolor Panavision

A shepherd hears God talking to Moses, and thinks he himself has been ordained to set his

people free. Inept and tasteless biblical spoof which must set back by about ten years the reputations of all connected with it. Dudley Moore, James Coco, Paul Sand, Jack Gilford, Dom DeLuise, John Houseman, Madeleine Kahn. Written by Guy Thomas; directed by Gary Weis; for David Begelman / Columbia.
'Deadly dullness of both writing and execution render pointless any attempt to single out blame for misfire, which leaves many talented performers flailing about in desperate attempts to generate laughs.'—*Variety*.

Whoopee*
US 1930 94m Technicolor
Samuel Goldwyn, Florenz Ziegfeld

A timid young man is catapulted into various adventures.
Early sound musical from a popular Broadway show, later remade as *Up in Arms* (qv).

w William Conselman, *musical play* William Anthony McGuire, *play* The Nervous Wreck by Owen Davis *d* Thornton Freeland *ph* Lee Garmes, Ray Rennahan, Gregg Toland *ch* Busby Berkeley *songs* Walter Donaldson, Gus Kahn

Eddie Cantor, Eleanor Hunt, Paul Gregory, Jack Rutherford, Ethel Shutta

'Dandiest of screen musicals and okay dough-getter.'—*Variety*

'You are cordially invited to George and Martha's for an evening of fun and games!'

Who's Afraid of Virginia Woolf?***
US 1966 129m bw
Warner (Ernest Lehman)

A college professor and his wife have an all-night shouting match and embarrass their guests.
As a film of a play, fair to middling; as a milestone in cinematic permissiveness, very important; as an entertainment, sensational for those in the mood.

w Ernest Lehman, *play Edward Albee* *d* Mike Nichols ph Haskell Wexler *m* Alex North

Richard Burton, Elizabeth Taylor, George Segal, Sandy Dennis

'A magnificent triumph of determined audacity.'—*Bosley Crowther*

'One of the most scathingly honest American films ever made.'—*Stanley Kauffmann*

AA: Haskell Wexler; Elizabeth Taylor; Sandy Dennis
AAN: best picture; Ernest Lehman; Mike Nichols; Alex North; Richard Burton; George Segal

Who's Been Sleeping in My Bed?
US 1963 103m Technicolor Panavision
Paramount / Amro (Jack Rose)

A TV matinee idol finds he is a sex symbol also in his private life.
Coy bedroom farce with no real action but a smattering of jokes.

w Jack Rose *d* Daniel Mann *ph* Joseph Ruttenberg *m* George Duning

Dean Martin, Elizabeth Montgomery, Martin Balsam, Jill St John, Richard Conte, Carol Burnett, Louis Nye, Yoko Tani, Elizabeth Fraser

'The most riotous bedtime story ever!'

Who's Got the Action?
US 1962 93m Technicolor Panavision
Paramount / Amro (Jack Rose)

A bored wife and her law partner husband have remarkable success betting on horses.
Badly cast and rather slow comedy with flashes of wit.

w Jack Rose, *novel* Four Horse Players Are Missing by Alexander Rose *d* Daniel Mann *ph* Joseph Ruttenberg *m* George Duning

Dean Martin, Lana Turner, Eddie Albert, Walter Matthau, Nita Talbot, Margo, Paul Ford, John McGiver

Who's Guilty?
US 1945 bw serial: 15 eps

Eerie happenings in a spooky house. Lively clutching hand serial. Robert Kent, Amelita Ward, Tim Ryan, Jayne Hazard, Minerva Urecal, Charles Middleton. Directed by Howard Bretherton and Wallace Grissell; for Columbia.

Who's Minding the Mint?*
US 1967 97m Technicolor
Columbia / Norman Maurer

An employee of the US mint and his friends find a means of printing bills at night.
Smartly-made action comedy with good performances.

w R. S. Allen, Harvey Bullock *d* Howard Morris *ph* Joseph Biroc *m* Lalo Schifrin

Jim Hutton, Dorothy Provine, Milton Berle, Joey Bishop, Bob Denver, Walter Brennan, Victor Buono, Jack Gilford

Who's Minding the Store?*
US 1963 90m Technicolor
Paramount / York / Jerry Lewis (Paul Jones)

An accident-prone young man gets a job in a department store.
Better-than-average star comedy, slapstick being allowed precedence over sentimentality.

w Frank Tashlin, Harry Tugend *d* Frank Tashlin *ph* W. Wallace Kelley *m* Joseph J. Lilley

Jerry Lewis, Jill St John, Agnes Moorehead, John McGiver, Ray Walston, Nancy Kulp

Who's That Girl?
US 1987 94m Technicolor
Warner / Peter Guber, Jon Peters, Roger Birnbaum

A mild lawyer finds an ex-jailbird starlet his hardest client to handle.
Muddled 'realistic' comedy which starts at screaming pitch and stays there.

w Andrew Smith, Ken Finkleman *d* James Foley *ph* Jan DeBont *ed* Pembroke J. Herring

Madonna, Griffin Dunne, Haviland Morris, John McMartin, Robert Swan, Drew Pilsbury

'What's lacking is pure and simple good humour.'—*Variety*

Whose Life Is It Anyway?
US 1981 118m Metrocolor
MGM / Martin C. Schute, Ray Cooney (Lawrence P. Bachmann)

Totally paralysed after a car crash, a young sculptor lies in hospital wanting to die.
Ill-advised film of a very static play which was a freak success on account of various very good leading performances. It makes a very uneasy movie.

w Brian Clark, Reginald Rose, *play* Brian Clark *d* John Badham *ph* Mario Tosi *m* Arthur B. Rubenstein

Richard Dreyfuss, John Cassavetes, Christine Lahti, Bob Balaban, Kenneth McMillan

Why Shoot the Teacher?
Canada 1976 99m colour
WSTT / Fraser Films (Lawrence Hertzog)

In 1935 a school teacher finds a chilly reception when he settles in a Saskatchewan village.
Unsatisfactory but occasionally quite entertaining comedy-drama which hovers around the *Cold Comfort Farm* mark.

w James Defilice, *novel* Max Braithwaite *d* Silvio Narizzano *ph* Marc Champion *m* Ricky Hyslop

Bud Cort, Samantha Eggar, Chris Wiggins, Gary Reineke

Why We Fight****
US War Office 1942–5 (*Frank Capra*) bw

A series of feature-length compilations for primary showing to the armed forces, these were superbly vigorous documentaries which later fascinated the public at large. Editing, music and diagrams were all used to punch home the message. Individual titles were:

'Prelude to War' (53m) *w Eric Knight, Anthony Veiller d Frank Capra*
'The Nazis Strike' (42m) *w* as above *d* as above
'Divide and Conquer' (58m) *w Anthony Veiller, Robert Heller d Frank Capra, Anatole Litvak*
'The Battle of Britain' (54m) *wd Anthony Veiller*
'The Battle of Russia' (80m) *w Anthony Veiller, Robert Heller, Anatole Litvak, d Anatole Litvak*
'The Battle of China (60m) *w Eric Knight, Anthony Veiller d Frank Capra, Anatole Litvak*
'War Comes to America' (70m) *w Anthony Veiller d Anatole Litvak*

All had editing by *William Hornbeck*, music by *Dmitri Tiomkin* and commentary by *Walter Huston*.

Why Worry?*
US 1923 60m approx (24 fps) bw silent Hal Roach - Harold Lloyd

A hypochondriac is cured when he gets mixed up in a South American revolution.
Moderate star comedy with highlights well spaced out.

d Sam Taylor, Fred Newmeyer

Harold Lloyd, Jobyna Ralston, Leo White

Wichita
US 1955 81m Technicolor CinemaScope

Wyatt Earp is hired to bring law and order to a wide-open cow town. Standard, i.e. romanticized, version of Earp's exploits: quite entertaining to watch. Joel McCrea, Vera Miles, Lloyd Bridges, Wallace Ford, Edgar Buchanan, Peter Graves, Keith Larsen, Carl Benton Reid. Written by Daniel Ullman; directed by Jacques Tourneur; for Walter Mirisch/AA.

Wicked
US 1931 57m bw

A woman is innocently sent to prison and when she comes out sets about finding the child she had to sign away. Woman's picture, packed with predictable incident. Elissa Landi, Victor McLaglen, Theodore Von Eltz, Alan Dinehart, Una Merkel, Oscar Apfel, Irene Rich. Written by anonymous hands; directed by Allan Dwan; for Fox. 'Old-fashioned tearjerker now too old to jerk tears or grosses.'—*Variety*

'If every woman has her price . . . there's a reason!'

Wicked as They Come
GB 1956 94m bw
Columbia / Film Locations (Maxwell Setton)
US title: *Portrait in Smoke*

A beauty contest winner from the slums makes money and luxury her goal.
Busy melodrama which interests without edifying.

wd Ken Hughes *co-w* Robert Westerby, Sigmund Miller *ph* Basil Emmott *m* Malcolm Arnold

Arlene Dahl, Herbert Marshall, Phil Carey, Michael Goodliffe, David Kossoff, Sidney James, Ralph Truman, Faith Brook

The Wicked Lady*
GB 1945 104m bw
GFD / Gainsborough (R. J. Minney)

In the days of Charles II, Lady Skelton befriends a highwayman and takes to crime.
The most commercially successful of the Gainsborough costume charades because of its atmosphere of gloomy sin. Dramatically turgid and surprisingly poorly acted and directed, but with good period detail. It had to be reshot for America because of the ladies' décolletage.

wd Leslie Arliss, *novel* The Life and Death of the Wicked Lady Skelton by Magdalen King-Hall *ph* Jack Cox *m* Hans May *md* Louis Levy

Margaret Lockwood, James Mason, Griffith Jones, Patricia Roc, Michael Rennie, Enid Stamp-Taylor, Felix Aylmer, Martita Hunt, David Horne

'A mixture of hot passion and cold suet pudding.'—*Manchester Guardian*

'Rather dull and juvenile in its determination to be daring.'—*Richard Mallett, Punch*

The Wicked Lady
GB 1983 99m colour

A remake with colour, sex and violence. Pictorially quite attractive, but that's about all. Faye Dunaway, Alan Bates, John Gielgud, Denholm Elliott, Prunella Scales, Oliver Tobias, Glynis Barber, Joan Hickson. Written by Leslie Arliss, Michael Winner; directed by Michael Winner; photographed by Jack Cardiff; for Cannon. 'The images look as cheap as expensive greetings cards.'—*Sunday Times*

A Wicked Woman
US 1934 71m bw
MGM (Harry Rapf)

A woman kills her drunken husband to protect her children, later confesses and is exonerated. The tail end of the mother love saga, better made than most.

w Florence Ryerson, Zelda Sears, *novel* Anne Austin *d* Charles Brabin *ph* Lester White *m* William Axt

Mady Christians, Charles Bickford, Betty Furness, William Henry, Jackie Searle, Robert Taylor, Paul Harvey

The Wicker Man*
GB 1973 86m Eastmancolor
British Lion (Peter Snell)

A policeman flies to a remote Scottish isle to investigate the death of a child, and finds himself in the hands of diabolists.
Old-fashioned but remarkably well made scare story, with effective shock moments.

w Anthony Shaffer d Robin Hardy ph Harry Waxman *m* Paul Giovanni *ad* Seamus Flannery

Edward Woodward, Britt Ekland, Christopher Lee, Ingrid Pitt, Diane Cilento

'An encouraging achievement for those who had begun to despair of the British cinema.'—*David McGillivray*

Wide Open Faces
US 1938 67m bw

Public enemies congregate in a wayside inn where missing loot is supposedly buried. Moderately amusing slapstick farce. Joe E. Brown, Jane Wyman, Alison Skipworth, Lyda Roberti, Alan Baxter, Lucien Littlefield, Sidney Toler, Berton Churchill. Written by Earle Snell, Clarence Marks, Joe Bigelow, Richard Flournoy; directed by Kurt Neumann; for David L. Loew (Columbia). 'On the corny side, strictly for dual bills.'—*Variety*

The Widow from Chicago
US 1930 63m bw

A woman mixes with a gang to avenge her brother's murder. Bottom-of-the-barrel gangster drama, presented with little flair. Alice White, Edward G. Robinson, Neil Hamilton, Frank McHugh, E. H. Calvert. Written by Earl Baldwin; directed by Edward Cline; for First National. 'Barely makes programme grade . . . will have to struggle to break even.'—*Variety*

Widow from Monte Carlo
US 1935 60m bw

The theft of an indiscreet letter causes much embarrassment in an English country house. Society comedy-drama with curious farcical asides: not an obvious success. Warren William, Dolores del Rio, Louise Fazenda, Colin Clive, Herbert Mundin, Warren Hymer. Written by F. Hugh Herbert, Charles Belden, from the play by Ian Hunter and A. E. W. Mason; directed by Arthur G. Collins; for Warners. 'Behind the eight ball where big-time dates are concerned.'—*Variety*

Wife, Doctor and Nurse*
US 1937 84m bw
TCF (Raymond Griffith)

A romantic triangle as the title suggests. Agreeable fluff with a mildly surprising end (for 1937) suggesting a *ménage à trois*.

w Kathryn Scola, Darrell Ware, Lamar Trotti *d* Walter Lang *ph* Edward Cronjager *m* Arthur Lange

Loretta Young, Warner Baxter, Virginia Bruce, Jane Darwell, Sidney Blackmer, Maurice Cass, Minna Gombell, Elisha Cook Jnr, Lon Chaney Jnr

'A smart comedy that will please all.'—*Variety*

Wife, Husband and Friend*
US 1939 80m bw
TCF (Nunnally Johnson)

A man sabotages his wife's efforts to become a professional singer.
Modestly agreeable romantic comedy later remade as *Everybody Does It* (qv).

w Nunnally Johnson, *story* James M. Cain *d* Gregory Ratoff *ph* Ernest Palmer *m* David Buttolph

Loretta Young, Warner Baxter, Binnie Barnes, Cesar Romero, George Barbier, J. Edward Bromberg, Eugene Pallette, Helen Westley

'Diverting farce comedy with appeal pointed to class audiences.'—*Variety*

The Wife of General Ling
GB 1937 72m bw

In China, a merchant's white wife unmasks him as a criminal. Stilted melodrama. Griffith Jones, Inkijinoff, Adrianne Renn, Alan Napier, Anthony Eustrel, Hugh McDermott, Gibson Gowland. Written by Akos Tolnay, Reginald Long, Peter Cheyney, Dorothy Hope; directed by Ladislas Vajda; for John Stafford / Premier. 'Hardly up to West End level.'—*Variety*

Wife of Monte Cristo
US 1946 83m bw

In 1832 Paris, the Count leads an underground movement against racketeers. And the film plays like a Brooklyn melodrama in fancy dress; as such, not too bad. John Loder, Lenore Aubert, Charles Dingle, Fritz Kortner, Martin Kosleck (as the Count!), Eduardo Ciannelli, Fritz Feld, Eva Gabor. Written by Dorcas Cochran; directed by Edgar G. Ulmer; for Leon Fromkess / PRC.

The Wife Takes a Flyer
US 1942 86m bw
Columbia (B. P. Schulberg)
GB title: *A Yank in Dutch*

A Dutchwoman whose husband is in the asylum takes in a fugitive USAF pilot in his place although a Nazi officer is billeted on the household.
Downright peculiar World War II comedy which at the time seemed the height of bad taste—and no laughs.

w Gina Kaus, Jay Dratler *d* Richard Wallace *ph* Franz Planer *m* Werner Heyman

Joan Bennett, Franchot Tone, Allyn Joslyn, Cecil Cunningham, Lloyd Corrigan, Georgia Caine

'Kicks in the pants, belching, and exaggerated face-making are lifted from burlesque to decorate this feeble attempt.'—*New York Post*

Wife versus Secretary*
US 1936 88m bw
MGM (Hunt Stromberg)

A publisher's wife starts to believe rumours about his attention to his secretary.
Practised star comedy drama which provided thoroughly satisfactory entertainment of a kind the cinema seems to have forgotten.

w Norman Krasna, Alice Duer Miller, John Lee Mahin, *novel* Faith Baldwin *d* Clarence Brown *ph* Ray June *m* Herbert Stothart, Edward Ward

Clark Gable, Myrna Loy, Jean Harlow, May Robson, George Barbier, James Stewart, Hobart Cavanaugh

'A real box office picture for the sticks and the stems.'—*Variety*

'See this picture if you enjoy the spectacle of three clever stars shining for all they are worth.'—*Film Weekly*

The Wilby Conspiracy*
GB 1975 105m De Luxe
UA / Optimus / Baum–Dantine (Stanley Sopel)

A British mining engineer is persuaded to help a black revolutionary in his flight from Cape Town to Johannesburg.
Reasonably exciting political chase thriller with a sufficiency of twists and action sequences; philosophy is present but secondary.

w Rod Amateau, Harold Nebenzal, *novel* Peter Driscoll *d* Ralph Nelson *ph* John Coquillon *m* Stanley Myers

Sidney Poitier, Michael Caine, Nicol Williamson, Prunella Gee, Saeed Jaffrey, Persis Khambatta

The Wild Affair*
GB 1965 87m bw
Seven Arts (Richard Patterson)

An office Christmas party nearly turns into an orgy.
Curious little comedy drama which plays almost like the Road to Ruin and has an attractive but miscast leading lady. Interesting elements.

wd John Krish, *novel* The Last Hours of Sandra Lee by William Sansom *ph* Arthur Ibbetson *m* Martin Slavin

Nancy Kwan, Terry-Thomas, Jimmy Logan, Bud Flanagan, Betty Marsden, Gladys Morgan, Paul Whitsun-Jones, Donald Churchill, Victor Spinetti

The Wild and the Innocent
US 1959 85m Eastmancolor Cinemascope

A trapper is torn between a mountain girl and a city tart. Oddly old-fashioned western, like *The Gold Rush* without laughs. Audie Murphy, Joanne Dru, Gilbert Roland, Sandra Dee, Jim Backus, Peter Breck. Written by Sy Gomberg and Jack Sher; directed by Jack Sher; for Universal-International.

The Wild and the Willing
GB 1962 112m bw
Rank / Box–Thomas (Betty E. Box)
US title: *Young and Willing*

A troublesome student at a provincial university seduces the wife of his professor.
Watchable sex melodrama with an interesting background on which no one seems to have quite enough grip; 'realism' is simply there to be exploited.

w Nicholas Phipps, Mordecai Richler, *play* The Tinker by Laurence Dobie, Robert Sloman *d* Ralph Thomas *ph* Ernest Steward *m* Norrie Paramor

Virginia Maskell, Paul Rogers, Ian McShane, Samantha Eggar, John Hurt, Catherine Woodville, John Standing, Jeremy Brett

Wild and Wonderful
US 1963 88m Eastmancolor
U-I / Harold Hecht

A French film star poodle makes friends with an American gambler.
Amiable zany comedy in a set-bound Gay Paree.

w Larry Markes, Michael Morris, Waldo Salt *d* Michael Anderson *ph* Joseph La Shelle *m* Morton Stevens

Tony Curtis, Christine Kaufmann, Larry Storch, Marty Ingels, Jacques Aubuchon, Jules Munshin

Wild and Woolly
US 1937 90m bw

During a small-town frontier celebration an attempt to rob the bank is thwarted. Pleasant family western with music. Jane Withers, Walter Brennan, Pauline Moore, Alfalfa Switzer, Jack Searl, Berton Churchill, Lon Chaney Jnr. Written by Lynn Root, Frank Fenton; directed by Alfred Werker; for John Stone / Fox. 'Whatever its companion feature happens to be, this is the one the audience talks about on the way home.'—*Variety*

The Wild Angels*
US 1966 85m Pathecolor Panavision
AIP (Roger Corman)

A Californian motorcycle gang is run on semi-religious, ritualistic, Nazi lines.
Much-banned melodrama, cheaply made but vigorously handled and of some interest on social and historical levels.

w Charles B. Griffith *d* Roger Corman *ph* Richard Moore *m* Mike Curb

Peter Fonda, Nancy Sinatra, Bruce Dern, Michael J. Pollard

Wild Bill Hickok Rides
US 1941 81m bw

Wild Bill helps a homesteader keep his land. Oddly cast, rather naïve little western. Constance Bennett, Bruce Cabot, Warren William, Ward Bond, Howard da Silva. Written by Charles Grayson, Paul Gerard Smith and Raymond Schrock; directed by Ray Enright; for Warner.

The Wild Blue Yonder
US 1952 98m bw
Republic (Herbert J. Yates)
GB title: *Thunder Across the Pacific*

Incidents in the lives of bomber pilots in the Pacific during World War II.
Routine action flagwaver.

w Richard Tregaskis *d* Allan Dwan *ph* Reggie Lanning *m* Victor Young

Wendell Corey, Vera Hruba Ralston, Forrest Tucker, Phil Harris, Walter Brennan, Ruth Donnelly

Wild Boys of the Road*
US 1933 88m bw
Warner (Robert Presnell)
GB title: *Dangerous Days*

Boys of poor families take to the road in gangs.
Vivid social melodrama of its day, now rather overstated.

w Earl Baldwin *d* William Wellman *ph* Arthur Todd

Frankie Darro, Rochelle Hudson, Edwin Philips, Arthur Hohl

'A depressing evening in the theatre, one which the general fan public will gladly avoid.'—*Variety*

Wild Brian Kent
US 1936 57m bw

An amiable western con man helps a town to rid itself of a villain. Mild comedy drama. Ralph Bellamy, Mae Clarke, Helen Lowell, Stanley Andrews, Lew Kelly. Written by Earle Snell, Don Swift, from the novel The Re-creation of Brian Kent by Harold Bell Wright; directed by Howard Bretherton; for Sol Lesser / TCF. 'Little to commend it.'—*Variety*

THE WILBY CONSPIRACY. East African location shooting gave an edge to a fairly facile political thriller. Michael Caine lets the heat get to him.

'Nine men who came too late and stayed too long!'
'The land had changed. They hadn't. The earth had changed. They couldn't!'

The Wild Bunch***

US 1969 145m Technicolor Panavision 70
Warner Seven Arts / Phil Feldman

In 1914, Texas bandits are ambushed by an old enemy and die bloodily in defence of one of their number against a ruthless Mexican revolutionary.
Arguably the director's best film, and one which set a fashion for blood-spurting violence in westerns. Undeniably stylish, thoughtful, and in places very exciting.

w Walon Green, Sam Peckinpah *d Sam Peckinpah ph Lucien Ballard m* Jerry Fielding *ad* Edward Carrere

William Holden, Ernest Borgnine, Robert Ryan, Edmond O'Brien, Warren Oates, Jaime Sanchez, Ben Johnson, Strother Martin, L. Q. Jones, Albert Dekker

'A western that enlarged the form aesthetically, thematically, demonically.'—*Stanley Kauffmann, 1972*

'We watch endless violence to assure us that violence is not good.'—*Judith Crist, 1976*

'The bloody deaths are voluptuous, frightening, beautiful. Pouring new wine into the bottle of the western, Peckinpah explodes the bottle; his story is too simple for this imagist epic.'—*Pauline Kael, New Yorker*

'One of the most moving elegies for a vanished age ever created within the genre.'—*Time Out, 1984*

AAN: script; Jerry Fielding

The Wild Country

US 1970 100m Technicolor
Walt Disney (Ron Miller)

In the late 1880s a farmer buys a dilapidated Wyoming ranch and falls foul of a local rancher who controls the water supply.
Predictable family western in the familiar Disney style.

w Calvin Clements Jnr, Paul Savage, *novel* Little Britches by Ralph Moody *d* Robert Totten *ph* Frank Phillips *m* Robert Bronner

Steve Forrest, Vera Miles, Jack Elam, Ronny Howard, Morgan Woodward

'The best ******* mercenaries in the business!'

The Wild Geese

GB 1978 134m Eastmancolor Panavision
Rank / Richmond (Euan Lloyd)

Adventures of four British mercenaries in a central African state.
All-star blood and guts with a few breezy touches in the script.

w Reginald Rose, *novel* Daniel Carney *d* Andrew V. McLaglen *ph* Jack Hildyard *m* Roy Budd

Roger Moore, Richard Burton, Richard Harris, Hardy Kruger, Stewart Granger, Jack Watson, Frank Finlay, Kenneth Griffith, Barry Foster, Jeff Corey, Ronald Fraser, Percy Herbert, Patrick Allen, Jane Hylton

Wild Geese II
GB 1985 125m Technicolor
Thorn EMI / Frontier / Euan Lloyd

A mercenary is commissioned by an American TV station to kidnap Rudolf Hess from Spandau jail.
Ingenious if unlikely premise for another tough adventure; it largely fails because of silly plotting.

w Reginald Rose *novel* The Square Circle by Daniel Carney *d* Peter Hunt *ph* Michael Reed *m* Roy Budd *pd* Syd Cain *ed* Keith Palmer

Scott Glenn, Barbara Carrera, Edward Fox, Laurence Olivier, Robert Webber, Kenneth Haigh, Stratford Johns

Wild Geese Calling
US 1941 77m bw
TCF (Harry Joe Brown)

A young adventurer in Oregon weds the girl friend of a conniving gambler.
Minor semi-western which never really finds a style.

w Horace McCoy, *novel* Stewart Edward White *d* John Brahm *ph* Lucien Ballard *m* Alfred Newman

Joan Bennett, Henry Fonda, Warren William, Ona Munson, Barton MacLane, Russell Simpson, Iris Adrian

Wild Harvest
US 1947 92m bw
Paramount (Robert Fellows)

A romantic triangle develops among wheat harvesters on the western plains.
Standard star hokum.

w John Monks Jnr *d* Tay Garnett *ph* John F. Seitz *m* Hugo Friedhofer

Alan Ladd, Dorothy Lamour, Robert Preston, Lloyd Nolan, Dick Erdman, Allen Jenkins, Will Wright

Wild in the Country
US 1961 114m De Luxe Cinemascope
TCF / Company of Artists (Jerry Wald)

A rebellious hillbilly is involved with three women.
Weird confection designed to show the star in all his facets.

w Clifford Odets, *novel* The Lost Country by J. R. Salamanca *d* Philip Dunne *ph* William C. Mellor *m* Kenyon Hopkins

Elvis Presley, Hope Lange, Tuesday Weld, Millie Perkins, John Ireland, Gary Lockwood

'One can't help feeling he was better off prior to this misguided bid for class.'—*MFB*

Wild in the Sky
US 1971 83m colour
AIP / Bald Eagle (William T. Naud, Dick Gautier)

Three young offenders skyjack a B52 jet bomber.
Black comedy melodrama, uncontrolled but with some engaging absurdities.

w William T. Naud, Dick Gautier *d* William T. Naud *ph* Thomas E. Spalding *m* Jerry Styner

Brandon de Wilde, Keenan Wynn, Dick Gautier, Tim O'Connor, James Daly, Robert Lansing

Wild in the Streets*
US 1968 97m Perfectcolor
AIP (Jack Cash)

In the imminent future, a pop singer becomes president and launches a campaign for teenage emancipation.
Satirical melodrama with a profusion of wild gags, some of which hit the target.

w Robert Thom *d* Barry Shear *ph* Richard Moore *m* Les Baxter

Shelley Winters, Chris Jones, Diane Varsi, Hal Holbrook, Millie Perkins

'Blatant, insensitive, crummy-looking . . . enjoyable at a pop, comic-strip level.'—*New Yorker, 1977*

Wild Is the Wind
US 1957 114m bw Vistavision
Paramount / Hal B. Wallis

A widowed Italian sheep rancher in Nevada marries his wife's sister from Italy, but she falls for his adopted son.
Intense Cold Comfort Farm melodrama with a strong similarity to *They Knew What They Wanted*; the strain shows, and the performances are tiresomely noisy.

w Arnold Schulman *d* George Cukor *ph* Charles Lang Jnr *m* Dmitri Tiomkin

Anna Magnani, Anthony Quinn, Tony Franciosa, Dolores Hart, Joseph Calleia

AAN: title song (*m* Dmitri Tiomkin, *ly* Ned Washington); Anna Magnani; Anthony Quinn

The Wild Man of Borneo
US 1941 78m bw
MGM (Joseph L. Mankiewicz)

An unsuccessful braggart comes to live with his daughter in a Manhattan boarding house.
Mildly likeable though very predictable sentimental comedy from an old Broadway warhorse.

w Waldo Scott, John McClain, *play* Herman J. Mankiewicz, Marc Connelly *d* Robert B. Sinclair *ph* Oliver T. Marsh *m* David Snell

Frank Morgan, Mary Howard, Dan Dailey, Billie Burke, Donald Meek, Bonita Granville, Marjorie Main, Connie Gilchrist, Walter Catlett, Andrew Tombes, Phil Silvers, Joe Yule

The Wild North
US 1951 97m Anscocolor
MGM (Stephen Ames)

A mountie gets his man but needs his help getting back to base.
Standard adventure story with avalanche and wolf attacks.

w Frank Fenton *d* Andrew Marton *ph* Robert Surtees *m* Bronislau Kaper

Stewart Granger, Wendell Corey, Cyd Charisse

'That streetcar man has a new desire!'
The Wild One**
US 1954 79m bw
Columbia / Stanley Kramer

Hoodlum motorcyclists terrorize a small town.
Brooding, compulsive, well-made little melodrama which was much banned because there was no retribution. As a narrative it does somewhat lack dramatic point.

w John Paxton, *story* The Cyclists' Raid by Frank Rooney *d* *Laslo Benedek* *ph* Hal Mohr *m* Leith Stevens

Marlon Brando, Lee Marvin, Mary Murphy, Robert Keith, Jay C. Flippen

'A picture that tries to grasp an idea, even though the reach falls short.'—*New York Times*

† 'What are you rebelling against?' 'What've you got?'—sample dialogue.
†† Sharpness of photography was achieved by the Garutso lens.

The Wild Party
US 1956 81m bw
UA / Security (Sidney Harmon)

An ex-football player and some Los Angeles layabouts plot a kidnap.
Unpleasant melodrama laced with sex, violence and loud music.

w John McPartland *d* Harry Horner *ph* Sam Leavitt *m* Buddy Bregman

Anthony Quinn, Carol Ohmart, Jay Robinson, Arthur Franz, Nehemiah Persoff, Kathryn Grant, Paul Stewart

The Wild Party
US 1974 91m Movielab
AIP / Edgar Lansbury, Joseph Beruh (Ismail Merchant)

In 1929, a silent film comedian on the skids throws a party to show his latest movie.
Evocative of its period but virtually confined to a single set which becomes boring, this collection of unlikely events and tedious people has only obvious points to make and its final descent into tragedy is not compelling.

w Walter Marks, *poem* Joseph Moncure March *d* James Ivory *ph* Walter Lassally *m* Larry Rosenthal

James Coco, Raquel Welch, Perry King, Tiffany Bolling, Royal Dano, David Dukes, Dena Dietrich

'Seems to promise a pointillist precision about its characters and milieu which it never quite delivers.'—*Jonathan Rosenbaum*

Wild River*
US 1960 115m De Luxe Cinemascope
TCF (Elia Kazan)

In 1933 a Tennessee Valley Authority inspector incurs the wrath of a local matriarch who will not leave her valley even though it is to be flooded.
Interesting liberal-minded sociological drama marred by an added love story, as the similar *Last Days of Dolwyn* was marred by melodrama. Well made but somehow unmemorable.

w Paul Osborn, *novels* Borden Deal, William Bradford Huie *d* Elia Kazan *ph* Ellsworth Fredericks *m* Kenyon Hopkins

Montgomery Clift, *Jo Van Fleet*, Lee Remick, Albert Salmi, Jay C. Flippen, James Westerfield, Bruce Dern

Wild Rovers
US 1971 132m Metrocolor
Panavision 70
MGM / Geoffrey (Blake Edwards, Ken Wales)

A middle-aged cowboy, depressed with the state of his life, joins with a younger man to become a bank robber.
Fashionable, derivative, quite unsuccessful western tragi-comedy mixing in shades of every director from Ford to Peckinpah.

wd Blake Edwards *ph* Philip Lathrop
m Jerry Goldsmith

William Holden, Ryan O'Neal, Karl Malden, Lynn Carlin, Tom Skerritt, Joe Don Baker, Rachel Roberts, Leora Dana, Moses Gunn

'An existentialist western which will not do much for existentialism, the western, or the box office.'—*Charles Champlin, Los Angeles Times*

Wild Strawberries***
Sweden 1957 93m bw
Svensk Filmindustri (Allan Ekelund)
original title: *Smultronstället*

An elderly professor has a nightmare and thinks back over his long life.
A beautifully paced and acted, but somewhat obscure piece of probing symbolism.

wd Ingmar Bergman *ph* Gunnar Fischer
m Erik Nordgren

Victor Sjostrom, Ingrid Thulin, Gunnar Bjornstrand, Bibi Andersson, Naima Wifstrand, Jullan Kindahl

'The work of a man obsessed by cruelty, especially spiritual cruelty, trying to find some resolution.'—*Kenneth Cavander, MFB*

AAN: script

Wild West Days
US 1937 bw serial: 13 eps

Three western friends outwit the scheming owner of *The Brimstone News*. Elementary but harmless western serial. Johnny Mack Brown, George Shelley, Robert Kortman, Russell Simpson, Frank Yaconelli. Directed by Ford Beebe and Cliff Smith; for Universal.

Wildcats
US 1986 107m Technicolor

A girl is appointed football coach at a ghetto school, and of course works wonders. Silly comedy with few laughs and not much plot development. Goldie Hawn, Swoosie Kurtz, Robyn Lively, Brandy Gold, James Keach, Bruce McGill. Written by Ezra Sacks; directed by Michael Ritchie; for Anthea Sylbert / Warner.

The Wildcats of St Trinian's
GB 1980 91m Technicolor
Wildcat (E. M. Smedley-Aston)

The awful schoolgirls get unionized, and kidnap an Arab's daughter to gain attention.
Crude and belated tailpiece to a series which was never very satisfactory. (See *The Belles of . . . , Blue Murder at . . . , The Pure Hell of . . . , The Great St Trinian's Train Robbery*.)

wd Frank Launder *ph* Ernest Steward
m James Kenelm Clarke

Sheila Hancock, Michael Hordern, Joe Melia, Thorley Walters, Rodney Bewes, Maureen Lipman, Ambrosine Philpotts

Will Any Gentleman?
GB 1953 84m Technicolor

A meek bank clerk is hypnotized and becomes a ladies' man. Efficient comedy from a stage success. George Cole, Veronica Hurst, Jon Pertwee, Heather Thatcher, James Hayter, William Hartnell, Diana Decker, Joan Sims, Alan Badel. Written by Vernon Sylvaine, from his play; directed by Michael Anderson; for ABPC.

'Will heats up slow, but when he gets there, he's hell with the hide off!'

Will Penny*
US 1967 109m Technicolor
Paramount / Fred Engel / Walter Seltzer / Tom Gries

A middle-aged cowpuncher falls foul of a family of maniacal cut-throats.
Realistically spare, laconic, uncomforting western with a curiously melodramatic set of villains.

wd Tom Gries *ph* Lucien Ballard *m* David Raksin

Charlton Heston, Joan Hackett, Donald Pleasence, Lee Majors, Bruce Dern, Anthony Zerbe, Clifton James, Ben Johnson

Will Success Spoil Rock Hunter?
US 1957 95m Eastmancolor
Cinemascope
TCF (Frank Tashlin)
GB title: *Oh! For a Man!*

A timid advertising executive is touted for a publicity stunt as the world's greatest lover.
A too-wild satire on TV commercials: less frenzied direction and gag-writing would have prised more humour from the situations.

w Frank Tashlin, *play* George Axelrod
d Frank Tashlin *ph* Joe MacDonald *m* Cyril Mockridge

Jayne Mansfield, Tony Randall, Betsy Drake, Joan Blondell, John Williams, Henry Jones, Mickey Hargitay

'The one film you should not see alone! Where your nightmare ends, *Willard* begins!'

Willard*
US 1971 95m De Luxe
Cinerama / Bing Crosby (Mort Briskin)

A shy, withdrawn young man breeds and trains rats to kill his enemies.
Modest, rather unusual suspenser which builds well after a slow start; only horrifying to people who can't stand rats. A sequel, *Ben* (qv), later appeared.

w Gilbert Ralston, *novel* Ratman's Notebooks by Stephen Gilbert *d* Daniel Mann
ph Robert B. Hauser *m* Alex North *rat trainer* Moe de Sesso

Bruce Davison, Elsa Lanchester, Ernest Borgnine, Sondra Locke, Michael Dante, J. Pat O'Malley

Willie and Phil
US 1980 116m De Luxe
TCF (Paul Mazursky, Tony Ray)

Two men and a woman enjoy a variable *ménage à trois* throughout the seventies.
Curious attempt at an American *Jules et Jim*; not badly done if you have to do it, but why do it?

wd Paul Mazursky *ph* Sven Nykvist
m Claude Bolling

Michael Ontkean, Margot Kidder, Ray Sharkey

'Truffaut's film existed both in the real world and in a world of the imagination. Mazursky's has no imagination and doesn't even touch a passable form of reality.'—*Sunday Times*

Willy Wonka and the Chocolate Factory*
US 1971 100m Technicolor
David Wolper

A boy wins a tour of the local chocolate factory and finds himself in the power of a magician.
Semi-satiric Grimms Fairy Tale pastiche which looks good but never seems quite happy with itself.

w Roald Dahl, from his novel *d* Mel Stuart
ph Arthur Ibbetson *songs* Leslie Bricusse, Anthony Newley *md* Walter Scharf
ad Harper Goff

Gene Wilder, Jack Albertson, Peter Ostrum, Roy Kinnear, Aubrey Woods

AAN: Walter Scharf

Wilson**
US 1944 154m Technicolor
TCF (Darryl F. Zanuck)

The rise and fall of an American president.
Admirably careful biopic which raises no particular excitement but entertains and instructs on various levels.

w Lamar Trotti d Henry King ph Leon Shamroy m Alfred Newman ad James Basevi, Wiard Ihnen

Alexander Knox, Charles Coburn, Cedric Hardwicke, Geraldine Fitzgerald, Thomas Mitchell, Ruth Nelson, William Eythe, Vincent Price, Mary Anderson, Ruth Ford, Sidney Blackmer, Stanley Ridges, Eddie Foy Jnr, Charles Halton, Thurston Hall, J. M. Kerrigan, Francis X. Bushman

'Not without tedium, but worth seeing as an enormous expensive curiosity.'—*Richard Mallett, Punch*

'Rich with the sense of movement and multitude.'—*Daily Sketch*

'Absorbing, significant and entertaining.'—*Time*

† Alexander Knox had 1194 lines in 294 scenes.

AA: Lamar Trotti; Leon Shamroy
AAN: best picture; Henry King; Alfred Newman; Alexander Knox

Winchester 73**
US 1950 92m bw
U-I (Aaron Rosenberg)

Long-time enemies settle an old grudge.
Entertaining, popular, hard-riding, hard-shooting western of the old school.

w Robert L. Richards, Borden Chase, *story* Stuart N. Lake *d Anthony Mann ph William Daniels m* Frank Skinner *md* Joseph Gershenson

James Stewart, Shelley Winters, Dan Duryea, Stephen McNally, Millard Mitchell, Charles Drake, John McIntire, Will Geer, Jay C. Flippen, Rock Hudson, Tony Curtis, John Alexander, Steve Brodie

The Wind***
US 1927 75m (sound version 1928) bw
MGM

A sheltered Virginia girl goes to live on the rough and windy Texas prairie, marries a man she doesn't love and kills a would-be rapist.
Heavy melodrama with a strong visual sense.

w Frances Marion, *novel* Dorothy Scarborough *d Victor Sjostrom ph* John Arnold

Lillian Gish, Lars Hanson, Montagu Love, Dorothy Cummings

'So penetrating is the atmosphere that one can almost feel the wind itself and taste the endless dust.'—*Georges Sadoul*

'Unrelieved by the ghost of a smile . . . but its relentlessness is gripping . . . a fine and dignified achievement.'—*Pictureplay*

† New version by Thames Silents 1984

Wind across the Everglades
US 1958 93m Technicolor
(Warner) Schulberg Productions (Stuart Schulberg)

Florida 1900: a young schoolteacher tracks down those responsible for hunting rare birds for their feathers, and becomes a game warden.
Dull, meandering adventure story with a purpose, relying heavily on violence and eccentric characters.

w Budd Schulberg *d* Nicholas Ray *ph* Joseph Brun

Christopher Plummer, Burl Ives, Gypsy Rose Lee, Emmett Kelly, George Voskovec, Tony Galento, Mackinlay Kantor

The Wind and the Lion
US 1975 119m Metrocolor Panavision
Columbia / MGM (Herb Jaffe, Phil Rawlins)

In 1904 Tangier, an American widow and her children are kidnapped by a Riffian chief, and the eyes of the world are focused on the incident.
Basing itself very lightly on an actual event, this adventure story is both confused as a narrative and unexciting as an action piece: the camera stops too often to look at sunsets, the plot stops too often for philosophizing, and there are too many underexplained characters and incidents fitting into the international jigsaw.

wd John Milius *ph* Billy Williams *m* Jerry Goldsmith

Sean Connery, Candice Bergen, Brian Keith, John Huston, Geoffrey Lewis, Steve Kanaly, Vladek Sheybal

'When the actors begin to talk (which they do incessantly) the flat-footed dialogue and the amateurish acting take one back to the low-budget buffoonery of Maria Montez and Turhan Bey.'—*Pauline Kael, New Yorker*

AAN: Jerry Goldsmith

The Wind Cannot Read
GB 1958 115m Eastmancolor
Rank (Betty E. Box)

In India and Burma during World War II, a flying officer falls in love with a Japanese language instructor suffering from a brain disease.
Or, love is a many-splendoured dark victory. Old-fashioned romance for addicts, well enough produced.

w Richard Mason, from his novel *d* Ralph Thomas *ph* Ernest Steward *m* Angelo Lavagnino

Dirk Bogarde, Yoko Tani, Ronald Lewis, John Fraser, Anthony Bushell, Michael Medwin

Windbag the Sailor
GB 1936 85m bw
Gainsborough (Edward Black)

An incompetent seaman is washed away on an old ketch and lands on a South Sea isle.
Rather uninventive star comedy with inevitable pleasing moments.

w Marriott Edgar, Stafford Dickens, Will Hay *d* William Beaudine *ph* Jack Cox *md* Louis Levy

Will Hay, Moore Marriott, Graham Moffatt, Norma Varden

Windom's Way*
GB 1957 108m Technicolor
Rank (John Bryan)

A doctor on a Far Eastern island tries to quell a native uprising.
Tolerably well intentioned action melodrama, topical because of Malaya; dramatically rather sober and predictable.

w Jill Craigie, *novel* James Ramsay Ullman *d* Ronald Neame *ph* Christopher Challis *m* James Bernard

Peter Finch, Mary Ure, Natasha Parry, Robert Flemyng, Michael Hordern

The Window***
US 1949 73m bw
RKO (Frederick Ullman)

A New York slum boy is always telling tall tales, so no one believes him when he actually witnesses a murder . . . except the murderer.
Classic little second feature, entertaining and suspenseful; unfortunately it had few successful imitators.

w Mel Dinelli d Ted Tetzlaff ph William Steiner *m* Roy Webb

Bobby Driscoll, Barbara Hale, Arthur Kennedy, Paul Stewart, Ruth Roman

'Logical, well-shaped, cohesive, admirably acted, beautifully photographed and cut to a nicety.'—*Richard Winnington*

A Window in London*
GB 1939 77m bw

A *crime passionel* is witnessed from a passing train. Modest Anglo-Saxon remake of the French film *Metropolitan*. Michael Redgrave, Sally Gray, Paul Lukas, Hartley Power, Patricia Roc. Written by Ian Dalrymple and Brigid Cooper; directed by Herbert Mason; for G and S / GFD. (US title: *Lady in Distress*.)

Wing and a Prayer*
US 1944 97m bw
TCF (William Becker, William Morosco)

Life aboard an aircraft carrier.
Standard action flagwaver.

w Jerome Cady *d* Henry Hathaway *ph* Glen MacWilliams *m* Hugo Friedhofer

Don Ameche, Cedric Hardwicke, Dana Andrews, Charles Bickford, Richard Jaeckel, Henry Morgan

AAN: Jerome Cady

The Winged Serpent*
US 1982 92m colour
Samuel Z. Arkoff / Larry Cohen
aka: *Q, The Winged Serpent*

A monstrous bird of prey terrorizes New York.
Old-fashioned monster movie with a few twists including religious allegory and a touch of political satire.

wd Larry Cohen *ph* Fred Murphy *m* Robert Ragland *sp* Randy Cook, David Allen, Peter Kuran

Michael Moriarty, David Carradine, Candy Clark, Richard Roundtree

Winged Victory**
US 1944 130m bw
TCF (Darryl F. Zanuck)

During World War II, pilots are inducted, trained and sent on dangerous missions.
Solid, competent, best-foot-forward flagwaver of the highest inspirational intention.

w Moss Hart, from his play *d* George Cukor *ph* Glen MacWilliams *m* David Rose

Lon McCallister, Jeanne Crain, Edmond O'Brien, Jane Ball, Mark Daniels, Don Taylor, Lee J. Cobb, Judy Holliday, Peter Lind Hayes, Alan Baxter, Red Buttons, Barry Nelson, Gary Merrill, Karl Malden, Martin Ritt, Jo-Carroll Dennison

'I suppose it is all right, but I don't enjoy having anyone tell me, so cheerfully and energetically, that the Air Force personnel is without exception composed of boy scouts old enough to shave.'—*James Agee*

'There is no question that Mr Hart captured much of the gallantry and pathos of youth rushing towards dangerous adventures with surface enthusiasm and inner dread.'—*Bosley Crowther, New York Times*

Wings*
US 1927 136m (24 fps) bw silent
Paramount (B. P. Schulberg)

Two young men join the Air Service during World War I, and one eventually shoots down the other by accident.
An epic of early aviation, still stirring in its action sequences.

w Hope Loring, Harry D. Lighton *d William Wellman ph Harry Perry*

Clara Bow, Charles Buddy Rogers, Richard Arlen, Gary Cooper, Jobyna Ralston, El Brendel

'Air battles are photographed from every conceivable angle, producing many bold cinematic effects . . . so much in fact happens in the air that it is impossible to take it all in.'—*National Board of Review*

AA: best picture; best engineering effects (Roy Pomeroy)

Wings for the Eagle
US 1942 85m bw
Warner (Robert Lord)

Aircraft workers do their bit during World War II.
Home Front propaganda, well enough produced.

w Byron Morgan, Harrison Orkow *d* Lloyd Bacon *ph* Tony Gaudio *m* Frederick Hollander

Ann Sheridan, Dennis Morgan, Jack Carson, George Tobias, Don Defore

Wings in the Dark*
US 1935 75m bw
Paramount (Arthur Hornblow Jnr)

Embittered after being blinded in an accident, a research flier finally leaps into action when his stranded girl friend needs help.
Satisfactory romantic melodrama.

w Jack Kirkland, Frank Partos *d* James Flood *ph* William C. Mellor

Cary Grant, Myrna Loy, Roscoe Karns, Hobart Cavanaugh, Dean Jagger, Bert Hanlon, Samuel S. Hinds

'Unconvincing and improbable story, but handled so deftly that it may nose through to moderate grosses.'—*Variety*

The Wings of Eagles*
US 1957 110m Metrocolor
MGM (Charles Schnee)

A navy flier breaks his neck in an accident and on recovery becomes a Hollywood writer.
Sentimental biopic of Frank 'Spig' Wead, a routine, easy-going assignment for its director (who is caricatured by Ward Bond as John Dodge).

w Frank Fenton, William Wister Haines *d* John Ford *ph* Paul C. Vogel *m* Jeff Alexander

John Wayne, Maureen O'Hara, Ward Bond, Dan Dailey, Ken Curtis, Edmund Lowe, Kenneth Tobey, Sig Rumann, Henry O'Neill

Wings of the Hawk
US 1953 81m Technicolor 3-D
U-I (Aaron Rosenberg)

Mexico 1911: a gold miner falls into the hands of revolutionaries.
Routine bang-bang, rather sloppily produced.

w James E. Moser *d* Budd Boetticher *ph* Clifford Stine *m* Frank Skinner

Van Heflin, Julie Adams, George Dolenz, Pedro Gonzales-Gonzales, Rodolfo Acosta, Antonio Moreno, Abbe Lane

Wings of the Morning*
GB 1937 89m Technicolor
New World (Robert T. Kane)

In 1899, a gypsy princess marries an Irish nobleman; in 1937, romance again blooms between their descendants.
Britain's first Technicolor film was great to look at and quite charming, though slight; its major attractions being horse races, songs from John McCormack, and a heroine dressed for plot purposes as a boy.

w Tom Geraghty, *story* Donn Byrne *d* Harold Schuster *ph* Ray Rennahan, Jack Cardiff *m* Arthur Benjamin

Henry Fonda, *Annabella*, Stewart Rome, John McCormack, Leslie Banks, Irene Vanbrugh, Harry Tate, Edward Underdown, Helen Haye

'A wholesome, refreshing and altogether likeable little romance.'—*Frank S. Nugent*

Wings of the Navy
US 1938 89m bw
Warner (Lou Edelman)

The loves and careers of navy pilots.
Competent animated recruiting poster.

w Michael Fessier *d* Lloyd Bacon *ph* Arthur Edeson, Elmer Dyer

George Brent, Olivia de Havilland, John Payne, Frank McHugh, John Litel, Victor Jory, Henry O'Neill, John Ridgely

'A convincer to mould public opinion and support in favour of current government plans for wide expansion of American air defence forces.'—*Variety*

Wings over Honolulu
US 1937 78m bw

A young naval airman is posted to Hawaii and followed by his bride. Lightweight flagwaver, all smiles at the end. Ray Milland, Wendy Barrie, William Gargan, Kent Taylor, Polly Knowles, Samuel S. Hinds. Written by Isabel Dawn, Boyce DeGaw, Mildred Cram; directed by H. C. Potter; for Universal.

Winner Take All*
US 1932 76m bw

A prizefighter rises to fame and helps a sick girl and her child. Slightly-plotted comedy-drama allowing its star full rein. *James Cagney*, Marian Nixon, Guy Kibbee, Clarence Muse, Virginia Bruce, Dickie Moore. Written by Wilson Mizner, Robert Lord, Gerald Beaumont; directed by Roy del Ruth; for Warners. 'Enjoyable prizefight talker: sprightly gags and bits bolster conventional story.'—*Variety*

Winners of the West
US 1940 bw serial: 13 eps

A self-styled ruler of the prairies tries to block the advance of the railroads. Predictable serial exploits. Dick Foran, Anne Nagel, James Craig, Tom Fadden, Trevor Bardette. Directed by Ford Beebe and Ray Taylor; for Universal.

Winning*
US 1969 123m Technicolor
Panavision 70
Universal / Newman–Foreman (John Foreman)

A racing driver's professional problems strain his relationship with his wife.
Cliché track melodrama with pretensions, well but needlessly made.

w Howard Rodman *d* James Goldstone *ph Richard Moore m* Dave Grusin

Paul Newman, Joanne Woodward, Richard Thomas, Robert Wagner, David Sheiner, Clu Gulager

The Winning of Barbara Worth*
US 1926 97m (24 fps) bw silent
Samuel Goldwyn

Desert engineers vie for the daughter of a landowner.
Forgettable action romance, a big hit in its day because of the climactic flood sequence, which still thrills.

w Frances Marion, *novel* Harold Bell Wright *d* Henry King *ph George Barnes m* Ted Henkel

Ronald Colman, Vilma Banky, Charles Lane, Gary Cooper, Paul McAllister

The Winning Team
US 1952 98m bw
Warner (Bryan Foy)

A telephone linesman becomes a great baseball player despite trouble with his vision after an accident.
Standard biopic of Grover Cleveland Alexander; all very pleasant but no surprises.

w Ted Sherdeman, Seeleg Lester, Merwin Gerard *d* Lewis Seiler *ph* Sid Hickox *m* David Buttolph

Doris Day, Ronald Reagan, Frank Lovejoy, Eve Miller, James Millican, Russ Tamblyn

The Winning Ticket
US 1935 69m bw

An Italian barber wins a sweepstake but can't find his ticket. Modest, lively comedy which pleased at the time. Leo Carrillo, Louise Fazenda, Ted Healy, Irene Hervey, James Ellison, Luis Alberni, Akim Tamiroff. Written by Ralph Spence, Richard Shayer, Robert Pirosh, George Seaton; directed by Charles F. Reisner; for MGM.

The Winslow Boy***
GB 1948 117m bw
British Lion / London Films (Anatole de Grunwald)

A naval cadet is expelled for stealing a postal order; his father spends all he had on proving his innocence.
Highly enjoyable middle-class British entertainment based on an actual case; performances and period settings are alike excellent, though the film is a trifle overlong.

w Terence Rattigan, Anatole de Grunwald, play Terence Rattigan *d Anthony Asquith ph* Frederick Young *m* William Alwyn

Robert Donat, Cedric Hardwicke, Margaret Leighton, Frank Lawton, Jack Watling, Basil Radford, Kathleen Harrison, Francis L. Sullivan, Marie Lohr, Neil North, Wilfrid Hyde White, Ernest Thesiger

'Only a clod could see this film without excitement, laughter and some slight moisture about the eyes.'—*Daily Telegraph*

Winter Carnival
US 1939 89m bw
(UA) Walter Wanger

College romances over a holiday weekend. Nondescript romantic comedy.

w Lester Cole, Budd Schulberg *d* Charles Riesner *ph* Merrit Gerstad *m* Werner Janssen

Ann Sheridan, Richard Carlson, Helen Parrish, Virginia Gilmore, Robert Walker

'Slick production of an undistinguished yarn about the annual Dartmouth winter sports.'—*Variety*

Winter Kills
US 1979 96m colour CinemaScope

The brother of an assassinated president tracks down the killers, but finds that his tycoon father is involved. Heavy-going and confusing melodrama with much flashy editing. Despite its cast, it was never satisfactorily released. Jeff Bridges, John Huston, Anthony Perkins, Elizabeth Taylor, Sterling Hayden, Eli Wallach, Dorothy Malone, Tomas Milian, Richard Boone. Written and directed by William Richert, from novel by Richard Condon; for Leonard Goldberg–Robert Sterling / Winter Gold.

Winter Light*
Sweden 1962 80m bw
Svensk Filmindustri (Allan Ekelund)
original title: *Nattvardsgasterna*

A widowed village pastor loses his vocation.
In a sense almost parody Bergman; in another, one of his clearest statements of despair. The middle section of a pessimistic trilogy which also included *Through a Glass Darkly* and *The Silence.*

wd Ingmar Bergman *ph* Sven Nykvist *m* none

Max Von Sydow, Ingrid Thulin, Gunnar Bjornstrand, Gunnel Lindblom

'The film-maker's mastery alone does not guarantee a great film. *Winter Light* is scarcely even a good one.'—*John Simon, 1967*

Winter Meeting
US 1948 104m bw
Warner (Henry Blanke)

A repressed spinster falls for a naval hero intent on becoming a priest.
Dreary talk marathon which did its star's career no good at all.

w Catherine Turney, *novel* Ethel Vance *d* Bretaigne Windust *ph* Ernest Haller *m* Max Steiner

Bette Davis, James Davis, Janis Paige, John Hoyt, Florence Bates, Walter Baldwin

Winter of Our Dreams*
Australia 1981 90m Eastmancolor
Vega Films (Richard Mason)

A bookseller investigates the suicide of an old girl friend, and becomes involved with an unhappy prostitute.
Intriguing character drama with a tendency to haunt the mind, though its effectiveness depends largely on its acting.

wd John Duigan ph Tom Cowan *m* Sharyn Calcraft

Judy Davis, Bryan Brown, Cathy Downes, Baz Luhrmann

'Like a thunderbolt of naked light it struck Broadway—now it tears at your heart on the screen!'

Winterset**
US 1936 78m bw
RKO

On the New York waterfront, a drifter determines to avenge his father's death.
Very dated poetic melodrama, here given a talky, artificial production which at the time impressed many critics but is now fairly difficult to endure.

w Anthony Veiller, *play* Maxwell Anderson *d* Alfred Santell *ph* Peverell Marley *md* Nathaniel Shilkret

Burgess Meredith, Eduardo Ciannelli, Margo, Paul Guilfoyle, John Carradine, Edward Ellis, Stanley Ridges, Maurice Moscovitch, Myron McCormick, Mischa Auer

'Not big box office . . . in certain locales they may even wonder what it's all about.'—*Variety*

'Still in a grand manner that just won't do on the screen . . . but there are fine moments in the performances, and there's something childishly touching in the florid dramatic effects.'—*New Yorker, 1978*

AAN: Nathaniel Shilkret

Wintertime
US 1943 82m bw
TCF (William Le Baron)

A Norwegian skating star comes to Canada where her uncle's winter resort is on its uppers.
The last of the star's Fox musicals is pure routine.

w Edward Moran, Jack Jevne, Lynn Starling *d* John Brahm *ph* Glen MacWilliams *m* Alfred Newman *md* Charles Henderson

Sonja Henie, Jack Oakie, Cesar Romero, S. Z. Sakall, Carole Landis, Cornel Wilde, Woody Herman and his Band

Wise Blood*
US/Germany 1979 108m colour

In the deep south, a war veteran with no beliefs becomes a travelling preacher. Odd story, not easy to like but with many impressive moments. Brad Dourif, Ned Beatty, Harry Dean Stanton, Daniel Shor, Amy Wright, John Huston. Written by Benedict Fitzgerald from the novel by Flannery O'Connor; directed by *John Huston*; for Anthea / Ithaca / New Line.

Wise Girl
US 1937 70m bw

A rich girl goes bohemian in Greenwich village. Pretty absurd romantic comedy which strains the patience. Miriam Hopkins, Ray Milland, Walter Abel, Henry Stephenson, Alec Craig, Guinn Williams, Margaret Dumont. Written by Allan Scott, Charles Norman; directed by Leigh Jason; for Edward Kaufman / RKO. 'Slow-moving narrative, considerable silliness, lack of convincing plot.'—*Variety*

Wise Guys
US 1986 91m Technicolor

Two small-time hoods unwittingly heist Mafia funds. Haven't we seen this somewhere before? And done better? Danny DeVito, Joe Piscopo, Harvey Keitel, Ray Sharkey. Written by George Gallo; directed by Brian de Palma; for Aaron Russo / MGM–UA.

The Wiser Sex
US 1932 72m bw

A society girl goes undercover to save her public prosecutor boy friend from smears. Unattractive comedy-melodrama which never seems to get going. Claudette Colbert, Melvyn Douglas, Lilyan Tashman, William Boyd, Ross Alexander, Douglass Dumbrille. Written by Harry Hervey, Caroline Franke from the play Her Confessions by Clyde Fitch; directed by Berthold Viertel; for Paramount. 'Story a handicap: picture suffers accordingly.'—*Variety*

Wish You Were Here**
GB 1987 81m colour

The growing pains of a teenage girl in a seaside town. Noted chiefly for its central performance, this is a film full of telling detail and compassion, despite its apparently defiant mood. *Emily Lloyd*, Tom Bell, Clare Clifford, Barbara Durkin, Geoffrey Hutchings. Written and directed by *David Leland*; for Zenith/Film Four.

The Wistful Widow of Wagon Gap*
US 1947 78m bw
U-I (Robert Arthur)

In old Montana, an accident-prone wayfarer accidentally kills a man and has to look after his family.
Tame and disappointing comedy vehicle.

w D. D. Beauchamp, William Bowers *d* Charles T. Barton, Robert Lees, Frederic I. Rinaldo, John Grant *ph* Charles Van Enger *m* Walter Shumann

Bud Abbott, Lou Costello, Marjorie Main, Audrey Young, George Cleveland

Witchcraft*
GB 1964 79m bw
TCF / Lippert (Robert Lippert, Jack Parsons)

A family of witches take revenge on their longtime enemies.
Spasmodically arresting horror film spoiled by too complex a plot line and some variable acting.

w Harry Spaulding *d Don Sharp* *ph* Arthur Lavis *m* Carlo Martelli

Jack Hedley, Lon Chaney Jnr, Marie Ney, Jill Dixon, David Weston

'Unpretentious and uncommonly gripping.'—*MFB*

Witchcraft through the Ages**
Sweden 1922 83m approx (24 fps) bw silent
Svensk Filmindustri
original title: *Haxan*

A 'documentary' investigation of the history of witchcraft, with acted examples.
Fascinating reconstruction of ancient rituals, still maintaining its power to frighten.

wd Benjamin Christensen *ph* Johan Ankarstjerne

Oscar Stribolt, Clara Pontoppidan, Karen Winther

The Witches
GB 1966 90m Technicolor
Hammer (Anthony Nelson Keys)
US title: *The Devil's Own*

A schoolmistress finds witchcraft in an English village.
Chintzy horror with predictable development and risible climax.

w Nigel Kneale, *novel* The Devil's Own by Peter Curtis *d* Cyril Frankel *ph* Arthur Grant *m* Richard Rodney Bennett

Joan Fontaine, Kay Walsh, Alec McCowen, Gwen Ffrangcon Davies, Ingrid Brett, John Collin, Michèle Dotrice, Leonard Rossiter, Martin Stephens, Carmel McSharry

The Witches of Eastwick**
US 1987 118m Technicolor
Warner / Guber-Peters / Kennedy Miller

Three divorcees on the make are seduced by the devil.
Horny fantasy, impeccably played, though it could have been shorter.

w Michael Cristofer from the novel by John Updike *d* George Miller *ph* Vilmos Zsigmond *m* John Williams *pd* Polly Platt

Jack Nicholson, Cher, Susan Sarandon, Michelle Pfeiffer, Veronica Cartwright, Richard Jenkins

AAN: John Williams

The Witches of Salem*
France / East Germany 1957 143m bw
Borderie / CICC / DEFA / Pathé (Raymond Borderie)
original title: *Les Sorcieres de Salem*

In 1692 Massachusetts, jealousies lead to accusations of witchcraft and multiple trials and executions.
An account of a horrifying historical fact which was also intended to reflect on the McCarthy witch hunts of the fifties; but the film, despite splendid acting, is too literal and slow-moving.

w Jean-Paul Sartre, *play* The Crucible by Arthur Miller *d* Raymond Rouleau *ph* Claude Renoir *m* Georges Auric

Simone Signoret, Yves Montand, Mylène Demongeot, Jean Debucourt

'Keep the children home! And if you're squeamish, stay home with them!'

Witchfinder General*
GB 1968 87m Eastmancolor
Tigon / American International (Arnold Miller, Philip Waddilove, Louis M. Heyward)
US title: *The Conqueror Worm*

In 1645 a villainous lawyer finds it profitable to travel the country instigating witch hunts.
Savage, stylish minor horror melodrama with a growing reputation as the best work of its young director. Not for the squeamish despite its pleasing countryside photography.

w Michael Reeves, Tom Baker, *novel* Ronald Bassett *d Michael Reeves* *ph John Coquillon* *m* Paul Ferris, Jim Morahan

Vincent Price, Rupert Davies, Ian Ogilvy, Patrick Wymark, Hilary Dwyer, Wilfred Brambell

'He made a murderer of the boy who was to marry his own daughter!'

The Witching Hour
US 1934 65m bw

A gambler hypnotizes a young man into taking the blame for a murder. Stalwart melodrama, reasonably well done. John Halliday, Guy Standing, Judith Allen, Tom Brown, William Frawley. Written by Anthony Veiller, Salisbury Field, from the play by Augustus Thomas; directed by Henry Hathaway; for Bayard Veiller / Paramount. NB: There was a previous (silent) version in 1921.

With a Song in My Heart*
US 1952 117m Technicolor
TCF (Lamar Trotti)

Singer Jane Froman is crippled in a plane crash but finally makes a comeback.
Romanticized showbiz biopic with the singer providing voice only. Adequate production and plenty of familiar tunes made this a successful mass appeal sob story.

w Lamar Trotti *d* Walter Lang *ph* Leon Shamroy *md* Alfred Newman

Susan Hayward, David Wayne, Rory Calhoun, Thelma Ritter, Una Merkel, Robert Wagner, Helen Westcott

AA: Alfred Newman
AAN: Susan Hayward; Thelma Ritter

With Six You Get Egg Roll
US 1968 99m De Luxe Panavision
Cinema Center / Arwin (Martin Melcher)

A widow with three sons marries a widower with one daughter.
Quite a bright and inventive family comedy.

w Gwen Bagni, Paul Dubov *d* Howard Morris *ph* Ellsworth Fredericks, Harry Stradling Jnr *m* Robert Mersey

Doris Day, Brian Keith, Pat Carroll, Barbara Hershey

Within the Law
US 1939 66m bw

A girl wrongly convicted studies law in prison and later takes her revenge on the real culprit. Reasonably interesting melodrama, filmed several times previously: in 1912, 1917, 1923 and in 1932 as *Paid*. Ruth Hussey, Tom Neal, Paul Kelly, William Gargan, Paul Cavanagh, Samuel S. Hinds, Rita Johnson, Sidney Blackmer. Written by Charles Lederer, Edith Fitzgerald, from the play by Bayard Veiller; directed by Gustav Machaty; for MGM.
'Certain of appeal where cops and robbers click.'—*Variety*

Within These Walls
US 1945 71m bw

A stern prison governor makes no exceptions when his son becomes a convict. Formula penitentiary drama with no surprises. Thomas Mitchell, Mary Anderson, Edward Ryan, Mark Stevens, Roy Roberts. Written by Charles Trapnell, James R. Fisher, Eugene Ling, Wanda Tuchock; directed by Bruce Humberstone; for Ben Silvey / TCF.

Withnail and I*
GB 1987 108m colour

In the 60s in Britain two out-of-work actors settle in a dilapidated country cottage. Deliberately seedy comedy which settles down as a study of character and contrives to be hard to forget. Richard E. Grant, Paul McGann, Richard Griffiths, Ralph Brown, Michael Elphick. Written and directed by Bruce Robinson; for HandMade Films.

Without a Trace
US 1983 120m De Luxe
TCF (Stanley R. Jaffe)

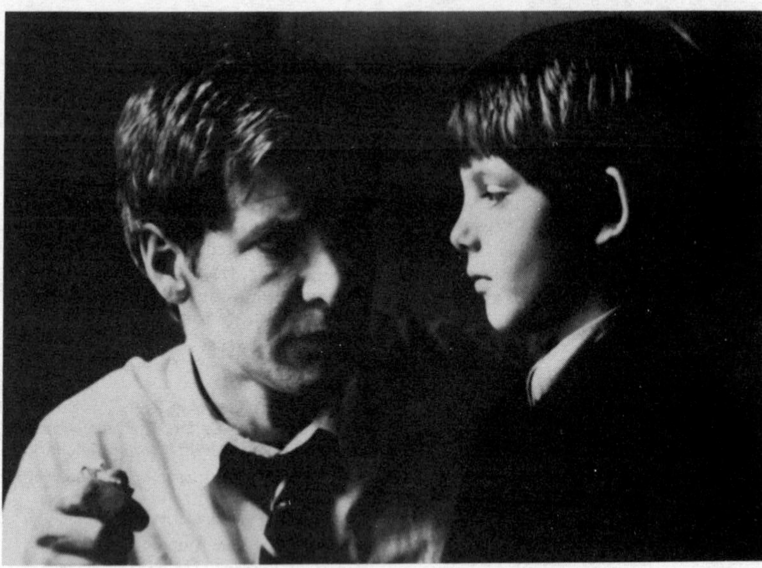

WITNESS. Harrison Ford, here with Lukas Haas, showed he could act (and was nominated for an Oscar) as well as swashbuckle his way through the *Indiana Jones* epics.

A mother solves the mystery of her missing child.
Fairly interesting modern melodrama with emphasis on character rather than the somewhat arbitrarily resolved plot.

w Beth Gutcheon, from her novel Still Missing *d* Stanley R. Jaffe *ph* John Bailey *m* Jack Nitsche *pd* Paul Sylbert

Kate Nelligan, Judd Hirsch, David Dukes, Stockard Channing, Jacqueline Brookes, Keith McDermott, Kathleen Widdoes

'Dignified understatement is the keynote.'—*Tom Milne, MFB*

Without Love*
US 1945 111m bw
MGM (Lawrence Weingarten)

The housing shortage in wartime Washington causes a widow to allow a scientist to move in with her, quite platonically.
Altered version of a popular play; rather long-drawn-out and disappointing considering the talent on hand.

w Donald Ogden Stewart, *play* Philip Barry *d* Harold S. Bucquet *ph* Karl Freund *m* Bronislau Kaper

Spencer Tracy, Katharine Hepburn, Lucille Ball, Keenan Wynn, Carl Esmond, Patricia Morison, Felix Bressart, Gloria Grahame

'One of those glossy conversation pieces that MGM does up so handsomely.'—*Rose Pelswick*

Without Reservations
US 1946 101m bw
RKO / Jesse L. Lasky

A famous woman writer heads for Hollywood by train and meets a marine who seems ideal for her male lead.
Would-be zany romantic comedy à la *It Happened One Night*; doesn't quite come off.

w Andrew Solt *d* Mervyn Le Roy *ph* Milton Krasner *m* Roy Webb

Claudette Colbert, John Wayne, Don Defore, Phil Brown, Frank Puglia

Without Warning
US 1952 70m bw
UA / Allart

A sex maniac murders a succession of blondes.
Semi-documentary, low-budget police thriller with all elements adequate for their purpose.

w Bill Raynor *d* Arnold Laven *ph* Joseph Biroc *m* Herschel Burke Gilbert

Adam Williams, Edward Binns, Meg Randall

'A big city cop who knows too much. His only witness—a small boy who's seen too much!'

Witness***
US 1985 112m Technicolor
Paramount / Edward S. Feldman

A young Amish boy witnesses a murder, and a big city detective hides out in the community to protect him.
As much about the meeting of cultures as about cops and robbers, this is one of those lucky movies which works out well on all counts and shows that there are still craftsmen lurking in Hollywood.

w Earl W. Wallace, William Kelley d Peter Weir ph John Seale *m* Maurice Jarre *pd* Stan Jolley *ed* Thom Noble

Harrison Ford, Kelly McGillis, Josef Sommer, Lukas Haas, Jan Rubes, Alexander Godunov

AA: editing

AAN: best picture; direction; Harrison Ford; original screenplay; photography; music; art direction

BFA: music

The Witness Chair
US 1936 64m bw

A secretary accidentally kills her nasty employer and almost allows an associate to take the blame. Stiff, old-fashioned melodrama which served its purpose. Ann Harding, Walter Abel, Douglass Dumbrille, Frances Sage, Moroni Olsen, Margaret Hamilton. Written by Rian James and Gertrude Purcell, from the story by Rita Weiman; directed by George Nicholls Jnr; for RKO.

Witness for the Prosecution***
US 1957 114m bw
UA / Theme / Edward Small (Arthur Hornblow Jnr)

A convalescent QC takes on a murder defence and finds himself in a web of trickery.
Thoroughly likeable though relentlessly over-expanded movie version of a clever stage thriller. Some miscasting and artificiality is condoned by smart dialogue and handling, one celebrated performance, and a handful of surprises.

w Billy Wilder, Harry Kurnitz, play Agatha Christie d Billy Wilder ph Russell Harlan *m* Matty Melneck

Charles Laughton, Tyrone Power, Marlene Dietrich, John Williams, Henry Daniell, Elsa Lanchester, Norma Varden, Una O'Connor, Ian Wolfe

AAN: best picture; Billy Wilder; Charles Laughton; Elsa Lanchester

Witness to Murder*
US 1954 81m bw
UA / Chester Erskine

A lonely woman sees a strangling in the flat across the street; the police don't believe her but the murderer does.
Predictable but quite effective screamer with a nick-of-time dénouement.

w Chester Erskine *d* Roy Rowland *ph* John Alton *m* Herschel Burke Gilbert

Barbara Stanwyck, George Sanders, Gary Merrill, Jesse White, Harry Shannon, Claire Carleton

'You can't tell them apart without a scorecard!'

Wives and Lovers
US 1963 103m bw
(Paramount) Hal B. Wallis

A successful author moves his family into Connecticut, where sex rears its ugly head.
Would-be sophisticated comedy with insufficient bubbles.

w Edward Anhalt, *play* The First Wife by Jay Presson Allen *d* John Rich *ph* Lucien Ballard *m* Lyn Murray

Van Johnson, Janet Leigh, Ray Walston, Shelley Winters, Martha Hyer, Jeremy Slate

Wives under Suspicion
US 1938 68m bw

A district attorney involved in a love-triangle murder discovers a similar situation developing in his own life. Flat remake of the same director's *The Kiss Before the Mirror*; of little interest. Warren William, Gail Patrick, Ralph Morgan, William Lundigan, Constance Moore. Written by Myles Connelly; directed by James Whale; for Universal.

The Wiz*
US 1978 134m Technicolor
Universal / Motown (Robert Cohen)

A black version of *The Wizard of Oz*, set in New York.
Glossy version of the Broadway musical hit; it offers some rewards, but on the whole the first is the best.

w Joel Schumacher, from play with ly / m by Charlie Smalls, book by William Brown *d* Sidney Lumet *ph* Oswald Morris *pd* Tony Walton *m* Quincy Jones *md* Quincy Jones *songs* Charlie Smalls

Diana Ross, Michael Jackson, Nipsey Russell, Ted Ross, Lena Horne, Richard Pryor, Mabel King, Theresa Merritt

AAN: Oswald Morris; Quincy Jones

The Wizard of Oz***
US 1939 102m Technicolor
MGM (Mervyn Le Roy)

Unhappy Dorothy runs away from home, has adventures in a fantasy land, but finally decides that happiness was in her own back yard all the time.
Classic fairy tale given vigorous straightforward treatment, made memorable by performances, art direction and hummable tunes.

w Noel Langley, Florence Ryerson, Edgar Allan Wolfe, *book* Frank L. Baum *d Victor Fleming* *ph* Harold Rosson *songs E. Y. Harburg, Harold Arlen* *md* Herbert Stothart *ad Cedric Gibbons, William A. Horning*

Judy Garland, Frank Morgan, Ray Bolger, Jack Haley, Bert Lahr, Margaret Hamilton, Billie Burke, Charley Grapewin, Clara Blandick

SCARECROW (Ray Bolger):
'I could while away the hours
Conversin' with the flowers,
Consultin' with the rain.
And perhaps I'd deserve you
And be even worthy erv you
If I only had a brain . . .'

COWARDLY LION (Bert Lahr):
'Oh, it's sad to be admittin'
I'm as vicious as a kitten
Widout de vim and voive;
I could show off my prowess,
Be a lion, not a mowess,
If I only had de noive.'

GLINDA, the good witch (Billie Burke): 'Close your eyes and tap your heels together three times. And think to yourself, there's no place like home.'

DOROTHY (Judy Garland): 'If I ever go looking for my heart's desire again, I won't look any further than my own back yard, because if it isn't there, I never really lost it to begin with.'

DOROTHY, LION, SCARECROW, TIN MAN:
'We're off to see the Wizard,
The wonderful Wizard of Oz.
We hear he is a whiz of a wiz,
If ever a wiz there was.
If ever a wever a wiz there was,
The Wizard of Oz is one because,
Because of the wonderful things he does . . .'

'There's an audience for it wherever there's a projection machine and a screen.'—*Variety*

'I don't see why children shouldn't like it, but for adults there isn't very much except Bert Lahr.'—*Richard Mallett, Punch*

'As for the light touch of fantasy, it weighs like a pound of fruitcake soaking wet.'—*Otis Ferguson*

† Ray Bolger was originally cast as the tin man but swapped roles with Buddy Ebsen who was to have been the scarecrow. Ebsen then got sick from the metal paint and was replaced by Jack Haley. Edna May Oliver was originally cast as the wicked witch. For Dorothy MGM wanted Shirley Temple, but Twentieth Century Fox wouldn't loan her.

†† The sepia scenes at beginning and end were directed by King Vidor.

AA: song 'Over the Rainbow'; Herbert Stothart
AAN: best picture

The Wolf Dog
US 1933 bw serial: 12 eps

An intelligent dog protects the inventor of an electric ray. Simple-minded action adventures. Rin Tin Tin Jnr, Frankie Darro, George Lewis, Boots Mallory, Henry B. Walthall, Fred Kohler. Directed by Harry Frazer and Colbert Clark; for Mascot.

Wolf Larsen
US 1958 83m bw
AA (Lindsley Parsons)

Serviceable remake of *The Sea Wolf* (qv) without the Nietzschean overtones.

w Jack de Witt, Turnley Walker *d* Harmon Jones *ph* Floyd Crosby *m* Paul Dunlap

Barry Sullivan, Peter Graves, Thayer David, Gita Hall

'His hideous howl a dirge of death!'
'Night monster with the blood lust of a savage beast!'

The Wolf Man*
US 1940 70m bw
Universal (George Waggner)

The son of an English squire comes home, is bitten by a gypsy werewolf, and becomes one himself.
Dazzlingly cast, moderately well staged, but dramatically very disappointing horror piece which established a new Universal monster who later met Frankenstein, Abbott and Costello, and several other eccentrics.

w Curt Siodmak *d* George Waggner *ph Joseph Valentine* *m* Hans Salter, Frank Skinner *md* Charles Previn

Lon Chaney Jnr, Claude Rains, Warren William, Ralph Bellamy, Bela Lugosi, *Maria Ouspenskaya*, Patric Knowles, Evelyn Ankers, Fay Helm

MALEVA (Maria Ouspenskaya):
'Even the man who is pure in heart
And says his prayers by night
May become a wolf when the wolf bane blooms
And the moon is pure and bright . . .'

'It will tear the scream from your throat!'

Wolfen
US 1981 115m Technicolor Panavision
Warner / Orion (Rupert Hitzig)

Mutilation murders in New York turn out to be the work of savage beasts descended from Indian hunters who went underground in despair at the future of mankind.
Nuthatch horror movie with a message, though providing little of either commodity. Clearly a waste of money.

w David Eyre, Michael Wadleigh, *novel* Whitley Strieber *d* Michael Wadleigh *ph* Gerry Fisher, Fred Abeles *m* James Horner *pd* Paul Sylbert

Albert Finney, Diane Venora, Edward James Olmos, Gregory Hines, Tom Noonan

'A thriller so slow, complicated and frankly rather dull that one's sympathy is all on the side of the predators.'—*Daily Mail*

Woman Accused*
US 1933 73m bw
Paramount

A woman kills her ex-lover in a struggle and goes on the run.
Intriguing rigmarole written as a magazine serial by ten well-known authors contributing a chapter each. The result confirms the method.

w Bayard Veiller, *serial* Rupert Hughes, Vicki Baum, Zane Grey, Vina Delmar, Irvin S. Cobb, Gertrude Atherton, J. P. McEvoy, Ursula Parrott, Polan Banks, Sophie Kerr *d* Paul Sloane *ph* Karl Struss

Nancy Carroll, Cary Grant, John Halliday, Irving Pichel, Louis Calhern, Jack La Rue, John Lodge

'It may convince producers and exhibitors that new writing talent should be encouraged . . . business possibilities anything but bright on so-so cast names.'—*Variety*

A Woman Alone
GB 1936 78m bw

In nineteenth-century Russia, a captain falls for a peasant girl. Uninteresting melodrama with stilted actors. Anna Sten, Henry Wilcoxon, Viola Keats, John Garrick, Rimilly Lunge. Written by Leo Lania and Warren Chetham Strode, from a novel by Fedor Ozep; directed by Eugene Frenke; for Garrett-Klement. (US title: *Two Who Dared*.)

Woman Chases Man
US 1937 71m bw
Samuel Goldwyn

A lady architect persuades a millionaire to help his land developer father.
Thin, lame comedy which constantly amazes by its lack of success.

w Joseph Anthony, Mannie Seff, David Hertz, *story* Lynn Root, Frank Fenton *d* John G. Blystone *ph* Gregg Toland *m* Alfred Newman

Miriam Hopkins, Joel McCrea, Charles Winninger, Erik Rhodes, Broderick Crawford, Leona Maricle, Ella Logan, Charles Halton

'Laughs stopped at the Music Hall when the action on the screen became so insanely illogical, and dull, that the amazed disappointment of the house expressed itself in chilly silence.'—*Variety*

'A pleasant warm weather fabrication—lightweight, attractively tailored and not meant to withstand the rigours of wear or the chill blasts of the critics.'—*Frank S. Nugent*

† The unhappy production began as a vehicle for Miss Hopkins. Writers who worked on it include Ben Hecht, Sam and Bella Spewack, and Dorothy Parker. Directors involved were Edward Ludwig, William Wyler and Gregory La Cava.

A Woman Commands
US 1932 85m bw

A cabaret entertainer rejects her lover for a king, but regains him when the king is murdered. Romantic melodrama of the silent school, quite unrevivable. Pola Negri, Basil Rathbone, Roland Young, H. B. Warner, Anthony Bushell, Reginald Owen. Written by Thilde Forster; directed by Paul Stein; for RKO Pathe.

Woman Doctor
US 1939 65m bw

Her career prospers, her marriage suffers. Old hat domestic drama, tolerably put over. Frieda Inescort, Henry Wilcoxon, Claire Dodd, Sybil Jason, Cora Witherspoon. Written by Joseph Moncure March; directed by Sidney Salkow; for Sol C. Siegel / Republic.

The Woman from Monte Carlo
US 1931 68m bw

The wife of a naval officer is suspected of adultery. Stiff marital melodrama based on a silent film *The Night Watch*; it worked no wonders for its German star. Lil Dagover, Walter Huston, Warren William, Robert Warwick, John Wray. Written by Harvey Thew; directed by Michael Curtiz; for Warner. 'Looks a light draw at best.'—*Variety*

Woman Hater
GB 1948 105m bw
GFD / Two Cities (William Sistrom)

An English nobleman tries to disprove a film star's statement that she hates men and loves solitude.
Incredibly slight material is interminably stretched out, well beyond an excellent cast's ability to help.

w Robert Westerby, Nicholas Phipps *d* Terence Young *ph* André Thomas *m* Lambert Williamson

Stewart Granger, Edwige Feuillère, Ronald Squire, Mary Jerrold, Jeanne de Casalis

The Woman I Love*
US 1937 85m bw
RKO (Albert Lewis)
GB title: *The Woman Between*

In World War I France, a pilot loves his superior officer's wife.
Well-made romantic action melodrama from a well-praised original.

w Mary Borden, French film L'Equipage and novel of same name by Joseph Kessel *d Anatole Litvak* *ph* Charles Rosher *m* Arthur Honegger, Maurice Thiriet

Paul Muni, Miriam Hopkins, Louis Hayward, Colin Clive, Minor Watson, Elizabeth Risdon, Paul Guilfoyle, Mady Christians

'Needs all the marquee help it can get . . . spotty business indicated.'—*Variety*

Woman in a Dressing Gown*
GB 1957 94m bw
Godwin / Willis / J. Lee-Thompson

After twenty years of marriage, a wife's slatternly ways alienate her once devoted husband, and he asks for a divorce.
Classic British TV play adequately filmed but now rather dated and irritating.

w Ted Willis, from his play *d* J. Lee-Thompson *ph* Gilbert Taylor *m* Louis Levy

Yvonne Mitchell, Anthony Quayle, Sylvia Syms, Andrew Ray, Carole Lesley

Woman in Hiding
US 1949 92m bw
U-I (Michael Kraike)

After escaping her husband's attempts to murder her, a woman goes into hiding while evidence is being accumulated against him.
Modest suspenser with too many near escapes and not much else.

w Oscar Saul *d* Michael Gordon *ph* William Daniels *m* Frank Skinner

Ida Lupino, Howard Duff, Stephen McNally, John Litel, Taylor Holmes, Irving Bacon, Peggy Dow, Joe Besser, Don Beddoe

'The detail is full of things interesting and amusing at the time and pleasant to remember afterwards.'—*Richard Mallett, Punch*

The Woman in Question*
GB 1949 88m bw
GFD / Javelin (Teddy Baird)
US title: *Five Angles on Murder*

Police investigating a woman's death build up several different impressions of her.
Multi-flashback melodrama which somehow doesn't quite come off despite effort all round.

w John Cresswell *d* Anthony Asquith *ph* Desmond Dickinson *m* John Wooldridge

Jean Kent, Dirk Bogarde, Susan Shaw, John McCallum, Hermione Baddeley, Charles Victor, Duncan Macrae, Lana Morris, Vida Hope

The Woman in Red
US 1935 68m bw

A professional horsewoman marries into society and is ill received. Stiff class melodrama partly redeemed by its star. Barbara Stanwyck, Genevieve Tobin, John Eldredge, Gene Raymond, Philip Reed. Written by Mary McCall Jnr and Peter Milne, from the novel *North Shore* by Wallace Irwin; directed by Robert Florey; for Warner.

The Woman in Red*
US 1984 86m De Luxe
Orion (Victor Drai)

A middle-aged married man has fantasies of infidelity.
Moderately successful transfer to America of a French comedy success.

w,d Gene Wilder, from the film *Un Eléphant Ça Trompe Enormement* by Jean-Loup Dabadie, Yves Robert *ph* Fred Schuler *m* John Morris *pd* David L. Snyder *ed* Christopher Greenbury

Gene Wilder, Charles Grodin, Joseph Bologna, Judith Ivey, Gilda Radner

AA: song 'I Just Called to Say I Love You' (Stevie Wonder)

The Woman in Room 13
US 1932 58m bw

The wife of an innocent convict tricks the real culprit into a confession. Stagey melodrama which just about fills an hour. Elissa Landi, Ralph Bellamy, Neil Hamilton, Myrna Loy, Gilbert Roland. Written by Guy Bolton from the play by Sam Shipman, Max Marcin and Percival Wilde; directed by Henry King; for Fox. 'Just another factory-made release.'—*Variety*

Woman in the Dark
US 1935 68m bw

A man convicted of manslaughter gets himself on his release into another awkward situation. Moderate semi-crime melodrama. Fay Wray, Melvyn Douglas, Ralph Bellamy, Roscoe Ates. Written by Sada Cowan from a story by Dashiell Hammett; directed by Phil Rosen; for Select / RKO. 'Marquee weakness only thing that may keep it out of single-feature houses . . . murder mystery fare of sufficient relish to keep 'em from leaving the table.'—*Variety*

The Woman in the Hall
GB 1947 93m bw
GFD / IP / Wessex (Ian Dalrymple)

THE WIZARD OF OZ. Wicked witch Margaret Hamilton lies in wait for hopeful travellers Judy Garland and Ray Bolger.

A well-intentioned woman takes to begging and becomes a bad influence on her daughter. Finger-wagging novelette makes an unrewarding film.

w G. B. Stern, Ian Dalrymple, Jack Lee *novel* G. B. Stern *d* Jack Lee *ph* C. Pennington-Richards and H. E. Fowle *m* Temple Abady

Ursula Jeans, Cecil Parker, Jean Simmons, Jill Raymond, Edward Underdown, Joan Miller

The Woman in the Moon*
Germany 1929 125m (24 fps) bw silent

Two scientists are forced to journey to the moon by criminals anxious to mine its gold deposits. Heavy-handed fantasy which is not among its director's best work. Willy Fritsch, Gerda Maurus, Gusti Stark-Gatettenbaur. Written by Thea Von Harbou; directed by Fritz Lang; for UFA. 'Half of it could be removed; as it is, it winds ponderously on.'—*Variety*. (Original title: *Frau im Mond*.)

'It was the look in her eyes that did it. How could he resist? How could he know it meant murder?'

The Woman in the Window***
US 1944 95m bw
International (Nunnally Johnson)

A grass widow professor befriends a girl who gets him involved with murder.
A refreshingly intelligent little thriller which was criticized at the time for a cop-out ending; this can now be seen as a decorative extra to a story which had already ended satisfactorily. Good middlebrow entertainment.

w Nunnally Johnson, novel Once Off Guard by J. H. Wallis *d Fritz Lang ph Milton Krasner m* Arthur Lang, Hugo Friedhofer

Edward G. Robinson, Joan Bennett, *Raymond Massey, Dan Duryea,* Edmund Breon, Thomas Jackson, Dorothy Peterson, Arthur Loft

'A perfect example of its kind, and a very good kind too.'—*James Shelley Hamilton*

'The accumulation of tiny details enlarged as though under a district attorney's magnifying glass gives reality a fantastic and anguishing appearance.'—*Jacques Bourgeois*

'In its rather artificial, club library style an effective and well made piece, absorbing, diverting and full of often painful suspense.'—*Richard Mallett, Punch*

'Art and Mammon, it seems to me, have been very prettily served.'—*Spectator*

AAN: Arthur Lang, Hugo Friedhofer

'Born in shame—living in mystery—what is her sinister secret?'

The Woman in White*
US 1948 109m bw
Warner (Henry Blanke)

The new tutor of a strange household finds himself among eccentrics, villains and ill-used ladies.
A Victorian thriller which is long on atmosphere but not so hot on suspense or plot development. The cast helps a lot.

w Stephen Morehouse Avery, *novel* Wilkie Collins *d* Peter Godfrey *ph Carl Guthrie* *m* Max Steiner

Gig Young, Eleanor Parker, *Sidney Greenstreet*, Alexis Smith, Agnes Moorehead, John Emery, *John Abbott*, Curt Bois

'The Wilkie Collins novel is given the studious, stolid treatment ordinarily reserved for the ritual assassination of a great classic. This is not intended as a recommendation.'—*James Agee*

'Greenstreet and others move through the murky passages of the story like visitors in some massive Gothic museum, and they move, on the whole, with stately discretion, and do not scribble on the objects or show anything but the greatest veneration for them.'—*C. A. Lejeune*

The Woman Next Door
France 1981 106m Fujicolor
Les Films du Carrosse / TF1

An engineer is embarrassed when an old flame, now married, comes to live next door; their love rekindles but ends in tragedy.
Rather uninteresting melodrama with a failure to communicate its apparent personal importance for the director.

w François Truffaut, Suzanne Schiffman, Jean Aurel *d* François Truffaut *ph* William Lubtchansky *m* Georges Delerue

Gérard Depardieu, Fanny Ardant, Henri Garcin, Michele Baumgarner

Woman Obsessed
US 1959 102m De Luxe Cinemascope
TCF (Sidney Boehm)

In the Canadian Rockies, a pioneer woman's small son does not take to his new stepfather.
Antediluvian pulp fiction with quicksand and a forest fire for highlights. Shades of D. W. Griffith, and badly done into the bargain.

w Sidney Boehm, *novel* John Mantley *d* Henry Hathaway *ph* William C. Mellor *m* Hugo Friedhofer

Susan Hayward, Stephen Boyd, Dennis Holmes, Theodore Bikel, Barbara Nichols, Ken Scott, Arthur Franz

A Woman of Affairs
US 1928 90m (24 fps) bw silent
MGM

A wild rich girl goes from man to man and finally kills herself in a car crash.
Romantic star tosh from a fashionable novel of the time.

w Bess Meredyth, *novel* The Green Hat by Michael Arlen *d* Clarence Brown *ph* William Daniels

Greta Garbo, Lewis Stone, John Gilbert, John Mack Brown, Douglas Fairbanks Jnr, Hobart Bosworth

A Woman of Distinction
US 1950 85m bw
Columbia (Buddy Adler)

The lady dean of a New England school falls for a British astronomer.
Pratfall farce for ageing stars. No go.

w Charles Hoffman *d* Edward Buzzell *ph* Joseph Walker *m* Werner Heymann *md* Morris Stoloff

Rosalind Russell, Ray Milland, Edmund Gwenn, Janis Carter, Mary Jane Saunders, Francis Lederer, Jerome Courtland

A Woman of Paris**
US 1923 85m (24 fps) bw silent (music track added 1976)
Charles Chaplin

A country girl goes to the city, becomes a demi-mondaine, and inadvertently causes the death of the one man she loves.
Remarkably simply-handled 'road to ruin' melodrama; its subtleties of treatment make it still very watchable for those so inclined.

wd Charles Chaplin *m* Rollie Totheroh, Jack Wilson

Edna Purviance, Adolphe Menjou, Carl Miller, Lydia Knott

'A thoroughly workmanlike entertainment and a candidate for honours and dollars entirely independent of the drawing power built up by Chaplin in other fields.'—*Variety*

'After five minutes of watching the sparkling new print, the spell begins to work. Chaplin is neatly turning the clichés inside out, like a glove.'—*Alan Brien, Sunday Times, 1980*

'Mr Chaplin as writer and director has not done anything radical or anything esoteric; he has merely used his intelligence to the highest degree, an act which for many years has ceased to be expected of motion picture people.'—*Robert E. Sherwood*

'The plot is desperately simple, but played with a control, a complete absence of histrionic vehemence, rare in the early twenties.'—*Dilys Powell, Punch, 1980*

† Chaplin appeared unbilled as a railway porter. The film was not a commercial success and he withdrew it for fifty years.

Woman of Straw*
GB 1964 114m Eastmancolor
UA / Novus (Michael Relph)

A rich old man's nurse conspires with his nephew in a murder plot.
Rather half-hearted but good-looking star melodrama which ventures into Hitchcock territory.

w Robert Muller, Stanley Mann, Michael Relph, *novel* Catherine Arley *d* Basil Dearden *ph* Otto Heller *m* Muir Mathieson *pd* Ken Adam

Gina Lollobrigida, Sean Connery, *Ralph Richardson,* Johnny Sekka, Laurence Hardy, Alexander Knox

Woman of the Dunes*
Japan 1964 127m bw
Teshigahara (Kiichi Ichikawa)
original title: *Suna no Onna*

An entomologist on a deserted beach finds an attractive young widow living in a shack at the bottom of a huge sand pit, spends the night with her, can't escape, and finally doesn't want to.
Unique sex melodrama, all shifting sand and picturesque angles, with a clear meaning; but far too long.

w Kobo Abe *d Hiroshi Teshigahara* *ph* Hiroshi Segawa

Eiji Okada, Kyoko Kishoda

'Teasingly opaque, broodingly erotic.'—*MFB*

AA: best foreign film
AAN: Hiroshi Teshigahara

Woman of the North Country
US 1952 90m Trucolor
Republic (Joseph Kane)

Minnesota 1890: rivalry over an iron ore mine erupts between a young engineer and an ambitious woman.
Standard western.

w Norman Reilly Raine *d* Joseph Kane *ph* Jack Marta *m* R. Dale Butts

Ruth Hussey, Rod Cameron, John Agar, Gale Storm, Jim Davis, J. Carrol Naish

Woman of the River*
Italy / France 1955 95m Technicolor
Ponti de Laurentiis / Films du Centaure

A peasant girl has nothing but trouble after falling for a handsome smuggler.
Lively melodrama whose primary purpose was to demonstrate the physical charms of its new star. It succeeded well enough in the *Bitter Rice* tradition.

w Basilio Franchina, Giorgio Bassani, Pier Paolo Pasolini, Florestano Vancini, Antonio Antoviti, Mario Soldati, *story* Alberto Moravia, Ennio Flainio *d* Mario Soldati *ph* Otello Martelli *m* Angelo Lavangini, Armando Trovaioli

Sophia Loren, Gerard Oury, Rik Battaglia, Lise Bourdin

The Woman of the Town*
US 1943 87m bw

Bat Masterson becomes marshal of Dodge and falls for a saloon singer. Busy, old-fashioned urban western with good entertainment values. Albert Dekker, Claire Trevor, Barry Sullivan, Henry Hull, Marion Martin, Porter Hall, Percy Kilbride. Written by Aeneas Mackenzie; directed by George Archainbaud; for Harry Sherman / United Artists.

Woman of the Year***
US 1942 114m bw
MGM (Joseph L. Mankiewicz)

A sports columnist marries a lady politician; they have nothing in common but love.
Simple, effective, mildly sophisticated comedy which allows two splendid stars, in harness for the first time, to do their thing to the general benefit.

w Ring Lardner Jnr, Michael Kanin d George Stevens ph Joseph Ruttenberg *m* Franz Waxman

Spencer Tracy, Katharine Hepburn, Fay Bainter, Reginald Owen, William Bendix, Dan Tobin, Minor Watson, Roscoe Karns

'Between them they have enough charm to keep any ball rolling.'—*William Whitebait*

AA: script
AAN: Katharine Hepburn

The Woman on Pier 13
US 1949 73m bw
RKO (Jack J. Gross)
aka: *I Married a Communist*

A shipping executive is blackmailed by communists, who know of a youthful crime, into helping them spy.
Laboured witch-hunt melodrama.

w Charles Grayson, Robert Hardy Andrews *d* Robert Stevenson *ph* Nicholas Musuraca *m* Leigh Harline

Laraine Day, Robert Ryan, John Agar, Thomas Gomez, Janis Carter, Richard Rober, William Talman

The Woman on the Beach
US 1947 71m bw
RKO (Jack J. Gross)

A mentally ailing coastguard meets a *femme fatale* and comes between her and her sadistic husband.
Nuthouse melodrama which neither convinces nor compels for a moment.

w Frank Davis, Jean Renoir, *novel* None So Blind by Mitchell Wilson *d* Jean Renoir *ph* Leo Tover, Harry Wild *m* Hanns Eisler

Joan Bennett, Robert Ryan, Charles Bickford, Nan Leslie, Walter Sande

'One may have to strain to see it as more than an over-aestheticized, interesting failure.'—*Pauline Kael, 70s*

Woman on the Run
US 1950 77m bw
Universal-International / Fidelity (Howard Welsch)

A man runs away after witnessing a murder; his wife is menaced by the killer.
Slightly unusual thriller which alas fails to thrill.

w Norman Foster, Alan Campbell *d* Norman Foster *ph* Hal Mohr *m* Emil Newman

Ann Sheridan, Dennis O'Keefe, Robert Keith, Ross Elliott

A Woman Rebels*
US 1936 88m bw
RKO (Pandro S. Berman)

A Victorian miss fights for women's rights and has an illegitimate baby.
Interesting, half-forgotten star drama.

w Anthony Veiller, Ernest Vajda, *novel* Portrait of a Rebel by Netta Syrett *d* Mark Sandrich *ph* Robert de Grasse *m* Roy Webb *ad* Van Nest Polglase

Katharine Hepburn, Herbert Marshall, Elizabeth Allan, Donald Crisp, Doris Dudley, David Manners, Van Heflin, Lucile Watson, Eily Malyon

'Delving into the fascinating ugliness of Victorian England, RKO Radio have found material that is picturesque, humorous and tragic.'—*Frank Nugent, New York Times*

The Woman They Almost Lynched
US 1952 90m bw

An innocent girl out west is blamed for a crime wave and almost executed as a spy. Incredible, random-plotted western with a few entertaining moments. Joan Leslie, Audrey Totter, John Lund, Brian Donlevy, Ben Cooper. Written by Steve Fisher, from a story by Michael Fessier; directed by Allan Dwan; for Republic.

'As naughty as a black lace nightgown!'
Woman Times Seven
US / France 1967 99m De Luxe
TCF / Embassy (Arthur Cohn)

Seven sketches, in each of which a woman behaves typically of her sex.
Humourless after-dinner entertainment.

w Cesare Zavattini *d* Vittorio de Sica *ph* Christian Matras *m* Riz Ortolani

Shirley Maclaine, Peter Sellers, Rossano Brazzi, Vittorio Gassman, Lex Barker, Elsa Martinelli, Robert Morley, Adrienne Corri, Patrick Wymark, Alan Arkin, Michael Caine, Anita Ekberg, Philippe Noiret

Woman to Woman
GB 1923 83m at 24 fps bw silent

A shell-shocked officer marries into Society and later adopts his son by a French ballerina. Far-fetched melodrama in what later became the *Random Harvest* style; a great box-office hit of its time. Betty Compson, Clive Brook, Josephine Earle, Marie Ault. Written by Alfred Hitchcock, from the play by Michael Morton; directed by Graham Cutts; for Balcon, Freedman and Saville. (Victor Saville directed a sound remake in 1929, with Betty Compson and George Barraud; and in 1946 Maclean Rogers had another shot with Adele Dixon and Douglass Montgomery.)

A Woman under the Influence*
US 1974 146m colour
Faces International (Sam Shaw)

A white collar worker's marriage goes sour. Insanely long case history in close up, with all parties constantly on the brink of hysteria. Often sharply observed, but hard to sit through.

wd John Cassavetes *ph* Mitch Breit *m* Bo Harwood

Peter Falk, Gena Rowlands

AAN: John Cassavetes (as director); Gena Rowlands

Woman Wanted
US 1935 65m bw

A girl accused of murder is helped by an attorney. Initially appealing comedy-thriller which moves fast enough but has a very muddled plotline. Maureen O'Sullivan, Joel McCrea, Lewis Stone, Louis Calhern, Edgar Kennedy, Adrienne Ames, Robert Greig, Noel Madison. Written by Leonard Fields, Dave Silverstein, Wilson Collison; directed by George B. Seitz; for MGM.

The Woman Who Came Back*
US 1945 68m bw

A girl returning to her home village in New England is made to think she is a witch. Quite an agreeably spooky second feature. Nancy Kelly, John Loder, Otto Kruger, Ruth Ford, Harry Tyler. Written by Dennis Cooper and Lee Willis; directed and produced by Walter Colmes; for Republic.

The Woman with No Name
GB 1950 83m bw

An amnesiac wife finds herself threatened from all sides. Hoary melodrama with some unintentional laughs. Phyllis Calvert, Edward Underdown, Helen Cherry, Richard Burton, Anthony Nicholls, James Hayter, Betty Ann Davies. Written by Ladislas Vajda and Guy Morgan, from the novel *Happy Now I Go* by Theresa Charles; directed by Ladislas Vajda and George More O'Ferrall; for IFP / ABP. (US title: *Her Panelled Door.*)

The Woman's Angle
GB 1952 86m bw
ABP / Leslie Arliss / Bow Belles (Walter Mycroft)

In a divorce court three flashbacks tell of the life of a composer.
Damp little formula drama for matinee audiences, refashioned from a successful silent film.

wd Leslie Arliss, *novel* Three Cups of Coffee by Ruth Feiner *ph* Erwin Hillier *m* Robert Gill; the Mansell Concerto by Kenneth Leslie Smith

Edward Underdown, Cathy O'Donnell, Lois Maxwell, Claude Farrell, Peter Reynolds, Marjorie Fielding

'Whatever I am, men made me!'
A Woman's Face**
US 1941 105m bw
MGM (Victor Saville)

A scarred and embittered woman turns to crime but jibs at murder.
Curious, unexpected but very entertaining melodrama with a courtroom frame, Swedish settings, an excellent cast and some bravura sequences.

w Donald Ogden Stewart, *play* Il Était une Fois by Francis de Croisset *d George Cukor ph Robert Planck m* Bronislau Kaper

Joan Crawford, Melvyn Douglas, *Conrad Veidt,* Osa Massen, Reginald Owen, Albert Basserman, Marjorie Main, Donald Meek, Connie Gilchrist

† Also involved in the script were Elliott Paul and Christopher Isherwood.

A Woman's Secret
US 1949 85m bw
RKO (Herman J. Mankiewicz)

An ex-singer grooms a girl as her successor but lives to regret it.
Downright peculiar little *film noir* by the co-author of *Citizen Kane* (though not so that you'd notice).

w Herman J. Mankiewicz, *novel* Mortgage on Life by Vicki Baum *d* Nicholas Ray *ph* George Diskant *m* Frederick Hollander *md* Constantin Bakaleinikoff

Maureen O'Hara, Gloria Grahame, Melvyn Douglas, Bill Williams, Victor Jory, Mary Phillips

A Woman's Vengeance*
US 1948 96m bw
Universal–International (Zoltan Korda)

A man is convicted for the murder of his invalid wife, actually committed by a jealous woman in love with him but later spurned.
Interesting but very stagey melodrama from one of its author's more commercial ventures.

w Aldous Huxley, from his story and play The Gioconda Smile *d* Zoltan Korda *ph* Russell Metty *m* Miklas Rozsa

Charles Boyer, Jessica Tandy, Ann Blyth, Cedric Hardwicke, Mildred Natwick
'A rather literary movie, but most movies aren't even that; much less are they real movies.'—*James Agee*

'It's a great big wonderful woman's world because men are in it!'
Woman's World**
US 1954 94m Technicolor Cinemascope
TCF (Charles Brackett)

Three top salesmen and their wives are summoned to New York by the boss, who seeks to choose a new general manager.
Amusing, superficial pattern comedy-drama for an all-star cast, backed by all-round technical competence.

w Claude Binyon, Mary Loos, Richard Sale *d Jean Negulesco* *ph* Joe MacDonald *m* Cyril Mockridge

Clifton Webb, Lauren Bacall, Van Heflin, June Allyson, Fred MacMurray, Arlene Dahl, Cornel Wilde, Elliott Reid, Margalo Gillmore

Wombling Free
GB 1977 96m Eastmancolor
Rank / Ian Shand

The furry creatures who live under Wimbledon Common at last make contact with humans.
Disastrous attempt to film a popular TV series for children. The series came in five-minute chunks; this elephantine transcription leaves several talents high and dry.

wd Lionel Jeffries, from characters created by Elizabeth Beresford *ph* Alan Hume *m* Mike Batt

David Tomlinson, Frances de la Tour, Bonnie Langford, Bernard Spear
'A fiasco. If you really must take your kids, it would be less of a pain to go shopping at the same time.'—*Derek Malcolm, Guardian*

'135 women with men on their minds!'
The Women***
US 1939 132m bw (Technicolor sequence)
MGM (Hunt Stromberg)

A New York socialite gets a divorce but later thinks better of it.
Bitchy comedy drama distinguished by an all-girl cast ('135 women with men on their minds'). An over-generous slice of real theatre, skilfully adapted, with rich sets, plenty of laughs, and some memorable scenes between the fighting ladies.

w Anita Loos, Jane Murfin, play Clare Boothe d George Cukor ph Oliver T. Marsh, Joseph Ruttenberg *m* Edward Ward, David Snell

Norma Shearer, Joan Crawford, *Rosalind Russell,* Mary Boland, Paulette Goddard, Joan Fontaine, Lucile Watson, Phyllis Povah, Virginia Weidler, Ruth Hussey, Margaret Dumont, Marjorie Main, Hedda Hopper
'Smash hit of solid proportions for extended runs and heavy profits . . . a strong woman entry but still has plenty of spicy lines and situations for the men.'—*Variety*
'A mordant, mature description of the social decay of one corner of the American middle class.'—*Time*
'So marvellous that we believe every Hollywood studio should make at least one thoroughly nasty picture a year.'—*New York Times*
'Whether you go or not depends on whether you can stand Miss Shearer with tears flowing steadily in all directions at once, and such an endless damn back fence of cats.'—*Otis Ferguson*

Women Are Like That
US 1938 78m bw

A separated couple meet again years later and find each other changed. Witless elaboration of a good idea: far too slow and talky. Kay Francis, Pat O'Brien, Ralph Forbes, Melville Cooper, Thurston Hall, Grant Mitchell. Written by Horace Jackson, Albert Z. Carr; directed by Stanley Logan; for Warners. 'Terribly tiresome, slow and talky.'—*Variety*

Women in Bondage
US 1943 72m bw

How the Nazis treat their women. Cheap but vigorous exploitation piece, not quite so sensational as it now sounds. Gail Patrick, Nancy Kelly, Gertrude Michael, Anne Nagel, Tala Birell, Maris Wrixon, William Henry, H. B. Warner, Alan Baxter. Written by Houston Branch, Frank Wisbar; directed by Steve Sekely; for Herman Millakowsky / Monogram.

Women in Love***
GB 1969 130m De Luxe
UA / Brandywine (Larry Kramer)

Two girls have their first sexual encounters in the Midlands during the twenties.
Satisfactory rendering of a celebrated novel, with excellent period detail atoning for rather irritating characters. The nude wrestling scene was a famous first.

w Larry Kramer, *novel D. H. Lawrence d Ken Russell ph Billy Williams m* Georges Delerue

Glenda Jackson, Jennie Linden, Alan Bates, Oliver Reed, Michael Gough, Alan Webb
'They should take all the pretentious dialogue off the soundtrack and call it Women in Heat.'—*Rex Reed*
'Two-thirds success, one-third ambitious failure.'—*Michael Billington, Illustrated London News*

AA: Glenda Jackson
AAN: Larry Kramer; Ken Russell; Billy Williams

Women in the Wind
US 1939 63m bw

Conflict arises between contestants in the Women's Air Derby. Formula multi-character picture, only moderately watchable. Kay Francis, William Gargan, Victor Jory, Maxie Rosenbloom, Eddie Foy Jnr, Eve Arden. Written by Lee Katz, Albert DeMond, from the novel by Francis Walton; directed by John Farrow; for Mark Hellinger / Warners. 'Good programmer for duals and cinch for action spots.'—*Variety*

Women in War
US 1942 71m bw

A socialite playgirl is recruited into war nursing in order to escape a prison sentence. Early World War II exploitation piece; lowish marks in its own right. Elsie Janis, Wendy Barrie, Patric Knowles, Mae Clarke, Dorothy Peterson, Billy Gilbert. Written by F. Hugh Herbert and Doris Anderson; directed by John H. Auer; for Sol C. Siegel / Republic.

Women of All Nations
US 1931 72m bw
Fox

Flagg and Quirt, back in the Marines, have amorous adventures in Sweden, Nicaragua and Egypt.
Routine fun and games with the heroes of *What Price Glory.*

w Barry Connors *d* Raoul Walsh *ph* Lucien Andriot *m* Reginald H. Bassett

Edmund Lowe, Victor McLaglen, Greta Nissen, El Brendel, Fifi D'Orsay, Bela Lugosi, Humphrey Bogart

Women of Glamour
US 1937 65m bw

A man is loved by a society flower and a gold-digger, and chooses the latter. Minor woman's picture. Melvyn Douglas, Virginia Bruce, Reginald Denny, Leona Maricle, Pert Kelton. Written by Lynn Starling, Mary McCall Jnr, from a story by Milton Herbert Gropper; directed by Gordon Wiles; for Columbia. 'Featherweight triangle headed for the dual round-up.'—*Variety*

Women of Twilight
GB 1952 89m bw
Romulus (Daniel M. Angel)

Unmarried mothers are victimized by a professional baby farmer.
Sordid, claustrophobic and ham-handed version of an exploitation play designed to provide another monstrous part for its star.

w Anatole de Grunwald, *novel* Sylvia Rayman *d* Gordon Parry *ph* Jack Asher *m* Alan Gray

Freda Jackson, René Ray, Lois Maxwell, Joan Dowling, Dora Bryan, Vida Hope, Mary Germaine, Laurence Harvey

'Caged emotions, yearning for love!'

Women Without Names

US 1940 62m bw

An innocent girl is accused of murder, is sent to prison, but saves her boy friend from the gallows. Eventful second feature; no one would complain. Ellen Drew, Robert Paige, Judith Barrett, John Miljan, Fay Helm, Louise Beavers, Marjorie Main, Esther Dale. Written by William H. Lipman and Horace McCoy; directed by Robert Florey; for Eugene Zukor / Paramount.

Won Ton Ton, the Dog Who Saved Hollywood

US 1976 92m colour
Paramount / David V. Picker, Arnold Schulman, Michael Winner

In twenties Hollywood, a lost Alsatian dog becomes a movie star but later suffers some ups and downs before being reunited with his mistress.
Scatty, unlikeable comedy with too frantic a pace, apparently in desperation at the dearth of funny lines and situations. The sixty 'guest stars' barely get a look in; the director seems to think (erroneously) that their appearance makes some kind of point even though they have nothing to do. Altogether, an embarrassment.

w Arnold Schulman, Cy Howard *d* Michael Winner *ph* Richard H. Kline *m* Neal Hefti

Madeleine Kahn, Art Carney, Bruce Dern, Ron Leibman; and Dennis Morgan, William Demarest, Virginia Mayo, Rory Calhoun, Henry Wilcoxon, Ricardo Montalban, Jackie Coogan, Johnny Weissmuller, Aldo Ray, Ethel Merman, Joan Blondell, Yvonne de Carlo, Andy Devine, Broderick Crawford, Richard Arlen, Jack La Rue, Dorothy Lamour, Phil Silvers, Gloria de Haven, Stepin Fetchit, Rudy Vallee, George Jessel, Ann Miller, Janet Blair, the Ritz Brothers, Victor Mature, Fernando Lamas, Cyd Charisse, Huntz Hall, Edgar Bergen, Peter Lawford, Regis Toomey, Alice Faye, Milton Berle, John Carradine, Walter Pidgeon, etc.

'The film tries to conceal its deficiencies in comic ideas and comic skill by doing everything at the pace of a clockwork toy with a too-tight spring.'—*Dave Robinson, Times*

Wonder Bar**

US 1934 84m bw
Warner (Robert Lord)

Love and hate backstage at a Paris night club.
Curious musical drama with an interesting cast and fairly stunning numbers.

w Earl Baldwin, *play* Geza Herczeg, Karl Farkas, Robert Katscher *d* Lloyd Bacon *ph* Sol Polito *ch Busby Berkeley* *songs* Harry Warren, Al Dubin *ad* Jack Okey

Al Jolson, Kay Francis, Dolores del Rio, Ricardo Cortez, Dick Powell, Guy Kibbee, Ruth Donnelly, Hugh Herbert, Louise Fazenda, Fifi D'Orsay

'Romance, flash, dash, colour, songs, star-studded talent, and almost every known requisite to ensure sturdy attention and attendance.'—*Variety*

'A tip-top musical.'—*Variety*

Wonder Man**

US 1945 97m Technicolor
Samuel Goldwyn

A mild-mannered student is persuaded by the ghost of his dead twin to avenge his murder.
Smooth, successful mixture of *Topper,* a nightclub musical, a gangster drama and the star's own brand of fooling; this is possibly his best vehicle after *The Court Jester*.

w Don Hartman, Melville Shavelson, Philip Rapp, story Arthur Sheekman *d Bruce Humberstone* *ph* Victor Milner, William Snyder *md* Louis Forbes, Ray Heindorf *sp* John Fulton

Danny Kaye, Vera-Ellen, Virginia Mayo, Steve Cochran, S. Z. Sakall, Allen Jenkins, Ed Brophy, Donald Woods, Otto Kruger, Richard Lane, Natalie Schaefer

AAN: Louis Forbes, Ray Heindorf; song 'So in Love' (*m* David Rose, *ly* Leo Robin)

The Wonderful Country

US 1959 96m Technicolor
UA / DRM (Chester Erskine)

A wandering gunman is offered a job by the Texas Rangers.
Complexly plotted western offering a range of familiar exploits.

w Robert Ardrey, *novel* Tom Lea *d* Robert Parrish *ph* Floyd Crosby, Alex Phillips *m* Alex North

Robert Mitchum, Julie London, Pedro Armendariz, Gary Merrill, Jack Oakie, Albert Dekker, Charles McGraw, John Banner, Jay Novello

Wonderful Life*

GB 1964 113m Techniscope
EMI / Elstree Distributors / Ivy (Kenneth Harper)

Four entertainers on a luxury liner are hired by a film crew in Africa.
Slight but zestful youth musical with highly illogical detail; the highlight is a ten-minute spoof history of the movies.

w Peter Myers, Ronald Cass *d* Sidney J. Furie *ph* Ken Higgins *pd* Stanley Dorfman

Cliff Richard, Walter Slezak, Susan Hampshire, Melvyn Hayes, Richard O'Sullivan, Una Stubbs, Derek Bond, Gerald Harper, the Shadows

The Wonderful World of the Brothers Grimm*

US 1962 134m Technicolor Cinerama
MGM / Cinerama / George Pal

An account of the lives of the German fairy tale writers is supplemented by three of their stories, *The Dancing Princess, The Cobbler and the Elves* and *The Singing Bone.*
Saccharine, heavy-handed pantomime with insufficient comedy, menace or spectacle.

w David P. Harmon, Charles Beaumont, William Roberts *d* Henry Levin, George Pal *ph* Paul C. Vogel *m* Leigh Harline *songs* Bob Merrill *ad* George W. Davis, Edward Carfagno

Laurence Harvey, Karl Boehm, Claire Bloom, Barbara Eden, Walter Slezak, Oscar Homolka, *Martita Hunt,* Russ Tamblyn, Yvette Mimieux, *Jim Backus,* Beulah Bondi, Terry-Thomas, Buddy Hackett, Otto Kruger

AAN: Paul C. Vogel; Leigh Harline

The Wonders of Aladdin

Italy 1961 92m Technicolor Cinemascope
Embassy / Lux

With the help of a genie, Aladdin defeats a usurper and wins the princess's hand.
Flat and disappointing pantomime with virtually no charm.

w Luther Davis *d* Henry Levin, Mario Bava *ph* Tonino Delli Colli *m* Angelo Lavagnino

Donald O'Connor, Vittorio de Sica, Aldo Fabrizi, Michèle Mercier

The Wooden Horse**

GB 1950 101m bw
British Lion / Wessex / London Films (Ian Dalrymple)

During World War II, British prisoners escape from Stalag Luft III by tunnelling under a vaulting horse.
Standard, solid POW drama with predictable but exciting and occasionally moving developments.

w Eric Williams, from his novel *d* Jack Lee *ph* C. Pennington-Richards *m* Clifton Parker

Leo Genn, David Tomlinson, Anthony Steele, David Greene, Michael Goodliffe, Bryan Forbes, Jacques Brunius

'All the suspense I care to take.'—*Sunday Chronicle*

Words and Music**

US 1948 121m Technicolor
MGM *(Arthur Freed)*

The songwriting collaboration of Richard Rodgers and Lorenz Hart.
Musical biopic which packs in a lot of good numbers and manages a script which is neither too offensive nor too prominent.

w Fred Finklehoffe *d* Norman Taurog *ph* Charles Rosher, Harry Stradling *md* Lennie Hayton *ch* Robert Alton, Gene Kelly

Tom Drake, Mickey Rooney, Perry Como, *Mel Tormé,* Betty Garrett, *June Allyson,* Lena

Horne, Ann Sothern, Allyn McLerie, *Gene Kelly,* Vera-Ellen, Cyd Charisse, Janet Leigh, Marshall Thompson

Work Is a Four-Letter Word
GB 1968 93m Technicolor
Universal / Cavalcade (Thomas Clyde)

A power station attendant is interested only in growing mushrooms, which have a chaotic effect on his private life.
Weakly futuristic industrial fantasy which the author would probably claim to be about lack of communication. Bored audiences might have a similar view.

w Jeremy Brooks, *play* Eh? by Henry Livings *d* Peter Hall *ph* Gilbert Taylor *m* Guy Woolfenden

David Warner, Cilla Black, Elizabeth Spriggs, Zia Mohyeddin, Joe Gladwin

The Working Man
US 1933 78m bw

A wealthy shoe manufacturer hands over his business, goes on holiday, and finds himself helping his bitterest rival. Palatable star parable. George Arliss, Bette Davis, Theodore Newton, J. Farrell MacDonald. Written by Maude T. Howell and Charles Kenyon, from the novel by Edgar Franklin; directed by John Adolfi; for Warner.

The World According to Garp*
US 1982 136m Technicolor
Warner / Pan Arts (George Roy Hill, Robert L. Crawford)

A young man grows up with a determination to become a writer.
Unlikely and uneasy film version of a somewhat cerebral novel; any drama there might have been in the original got lost in the transition, but at least the intention is to be applauded.

w Steve Tesich, *novel* John Irving *d* George Roy Hill *ph* Miroslav Ondricek *md* David Shire *pd* Henry Bumstead *ed* Stephen A. Rotter

Robin Williams, Mary Beth Hurt, Glenn Close, John Lithgow, Hume Cronyn, Jessica Tandy, Swoosie Kurtz

'Rather like watching a puppy chasing its own tail: engaging, touching, but pointless.'—*Margaret Hinxman, Daily Mail*

'When the movie was over, all I could find to ask myself was: What the hell was all that about?'—*Roger Ebert*

AAN: John Lithgow; Glenn Close (supporting actor)

A World Apart*
GB 1987 113m Eastmancolor
Working Title / Film Four International

A white South African journalist devoting her energies to supporting the ANC neglects her family.
Sincerity and fine acting are slightly contradicted by a ravishing visual style.

w Shawn Slovo *d* Chris Menges *ph* Peter Biziou *m* Hans Zimmer *pd* Brian Morris

Jodhi May, Jeroen Krabbé, Barbara Hershey, Nadine Chalmers

† Shawn Slovo is the daughter of Ruth First, on whose life the story is based.

The World Changes*
US 1933 91m bw
Warner (Robert Lord)

A simple farmer becomes a powerful executive, and success goes to his head.
Adequate moral drama of its time, well staged and acted.

w Edward Chodorov *d* Mervyn Le Roy *ph* Tony Gaudio

Paul Muni, Aline MacMahon, Mary Astor, Donald Cook, Patricia Ellis, Jean Muir, Margaret Lindsay, Guy Kibbee, Alan Dinehart

'It won't appeal to the hotsy-totsy type of fan, but the parents will bring the youngsters, which should sort of balance things.'—*Variety*

World in Flames*
US 1940 62m bw

A newsreel account of the rise to power of dictators during the thirties. Effective propaganda at the time, and a neat editing job. Produced by Albert J. Richard for Paramount.

The World in His Arms*
US 1952 104m Technicolor
Universal (Aaron Rosenberg)

In old San Francisco, a seal-poaching sea captain meets a Russian countess.
Romantic melodrama with plushy period backgrounds and a fair measure of action, climaxing in a boat race.

w Borden Chase *d* Raoul Walsh *ph* Russell Metty *m* Frank Skinner

Gregory Peck, Ann Blyth, Anthony Quinn, John McIntire, Andrea King, Carl Esmond, Eugenie Leontovitch

World in My Corner*
US 1955 85m bw
U-I (Aaron Rosenberg)

A penniless would-be prizefighter becomes the protégé of a millionaire and wins his daughter but not the crucial fight.
Well-done minor melodrama.

w Jack Sher *d* Jesse Hibbs *ph* Maury Gertsman *m* Joseph Gershenson

Audie Murphy, Barbara Rush, Jeff Morrow, John McIntire, Tommy Rall, Howard St John

The World Is Full of Married Men
GB 1979 106m Eastmancolor
New Realm / Married Men Productions (Adrienne Fancey)

The wife of an advertising executive tries to pay him out in kind for his infidelity.
Tedious jet-setting morality play which shows in great detail all the vices it wags a finger at.

w Jackie Collins, from her novel *d* Robert Young *ph* Ray Parslow *m* Frank Musker, Dominic Bugatti

Carroll Baker, Anthony Franciosa, Sherrie Cronn, Paul Nicholas, Gareth Hunt, Georgina Hale, Anthony Steel

The World Moves On*
US 1934 104m bw
Fox (Winfield Sheehan)

The saga of a Louisiana family up to World War I.
Careful, good-looking general entertainment.

w Reginald C. Berkeley *d* John Ford *ph* George Schneiderman *m* Louis de Francesco

Madeleine Carroll, Franchot Tone, Reginald Denny, Stepin Fetchit, Lumsden Hare, Louise Dresser, Sig Rumann

'Pacifistic picture inviting endorsement from all bodies. Big on production and cast with six minutes of superb war stuff.'—*Variety*

The World of Henry Orient**
US 1964 106m De Luxe Panavision
UA / Pan Arts (Jerome Hellman)

Two rich 14-year-old New York girls build fantasies around a concert pianist.
Charming, immaculately mounted, refreshingly unusual but overlong comedy.

w Nora and Nunnally Johnson, novel Nora Johnson *d George Roy Hill ph* Boris Kaufman, Arthur J. Ornitz *m* Elmer Bernstein *pd James Sullivan*

Tippy Walker, Merri Spaeth, Peter Sellers, Angela Lansbury, Paula Prentiss, Phyllis Thaxter, Tom Bosley, Bibi Osterwald

World of Plenty***
GB 1943 45m bw

How the distribution of food should be handled after the war. Classic documentary with many new film-making insights, including the use of statistical diagrams. Written by Paul Rotha, Eric Knight, Miles Malleson; directed by *Paul Rotha*; for the Ministry of Information. 'Any theatre audience will be grateful for seeing it. It is the epitome of educational picture-making.'—*Variety*

The World of Suzie Wong
GB 1960 129m Technicolor
Paramount / Ray Stark (Hugh Perceval)

A Hong Kong prostitute falls in love with the artist for whom she poses.
Dull, set-bound romantic melodrama without much gusto.

w John Patrick, *play* Paul Osborn *d* Richard Quine *ph* Geoffrey Unsworth *m* George Duning

William Holden, *Nancy Kwan*, Sylvia Syms, Michael Wilding, Laurence Naismith, Jackie Chan

'Maybe one day it will all make the grade as a musical.'—*MFB*

The World Owes Me a Living
GB 1944 91m bw

A man gets his memory back and recalls his air force career. Pointless flagwaving farrago. David Farrar, Judy Campbell, Sonia Dresdel, Jack Livesey, John Laurie, Wylie Watson. Written by Vernon Sewell and Erwin Reiner, from the novel by John Llewellyn Rhys; directed by Vernon Sewell; for British National.

World Premiere*
US 1940 70m bw
Paramount (Sol C. Siegel)

A zany film producer thinks up some wild publicity schemes for his new film and accidentally traps some Nazi spies.
Occasionally amusing farce mainly notable for its star.

w Earl Felton *d* Ted Tetzlaff *ph* Daniel Fapp

John Barrymore, Ricardo Cortez, Frances Farmer, Sig Rumann, Fritz Feld, Eugene Pallette, Luis Alberni, Virginia Dale, Don Castle

The World Ten Times Over
GB 1963 93m bw
Cyclops (Michael Luke)
US title: *Pussycat Alley*

Two semi-prostitutes try to improve their lot.
Dreary, derivative low-life drama with flashy technique.

wd Wolf Rilla *ph* Larry Pizer *m* Edwin Astley

Sylvia Syms, June Ritchie, Edward Judd, William Hartnell, Francis de Wolff

The World, the Flesh and the Devil*
US 1959 95m bw Cinemascope
MGM / Sol C. Siegel / Harbel

Trapped for five days in a mine cave-in, a man struggles to the surface to find a dead world devastated by atomic war; but still alive are the elements of an eternal triangle . . .
Enterprising but rather disappointing fantasy which tends to become merely glum and rather self-consciously carries a panic button message.

wd Ranald MacDougall *ph* Harold J. Marzorati *m* Miklos Rozsa *ad* William A. Horning, Paul Groesse

Harry Belafonte, Inger Stevens, Mel Ferrer

World without End
US 1956 80m Technicolor Cinemascope
AA (Richard Heermance)

A space ship breaks the time barrier and returns to earth in 2508, to find that intelligent humans have been driven underground by mutants.
Reasonably lively sci-fi with horror elements, and a plot borrowed from H. G. Wells.

wd Edward Bernds *ph* Ellsworth Fredericks *m* Leith Stevens

Hugh Marlowe, Nancy Gates, Rod Taylor

The World's Greatest Athlete
US 1973 92m Technicolor
Walt Disney (Bill Walsh)

An American sports coach on an African holiday finds a young Tarzan with amazing powers.
Simple-minded comedy with lame tomfoolery and trickwork.

w Gerald Gardiner, Dee Caruso *d* Robert Scheerer *ph* Frank Phillips *m* Marvin Hamlisch

Tim Conway, Jan-Michael Vincent, John Amos, Roscoe Lee Browne

The World's Greatest Lover
US 1977 89m De Luxe
TCF (Gene Wilder)

In the twenties, a rival studio starts a search for a man to surpass Valentino.
Imitative slapstick extravaganza in which anything goes but hardly anything pleases.

wd Gene Wilder *ph* Gerald Hirschfeld *m* John Morris

Gene Wilder, Carol Kane, Dom DeLuise, Fritz Feld

'Infantile humour for young, slow kids who want everything pounded at them.'—*Pauline Kael, New Yorker*

† The film carries a credit to Federico Fellini, 'for encouragement at the right time'.

Worm's Eye View
GB 1951 77m bw
ABFD / Byron (Henry Halsted)

Incidents in the lives of a group of RAF billetees.
Plotless comedy from a highly successful stage romp; plainly made and empty-headed but not disagreeable.

w R. F. Delderfield, from his play *d* Jack Raymond *ph* James Wilson *m* Tony Lowry, Tony Fones

Ronald Shiner, Garry Marsh, Diana Dors, Eric Davis, John Blythe

The Worst Woman in Paris
US 1933 75m bw

An American girl unfairly gets a bad reputation in Paris and on her way home becomes a heroine in Kansas. Silly, pointless story on which good production values are wasted. Benita Hume, Adolphe Menjou, Harvey Stephens, Helen Chandler, Margaret Seddon. Written by Marion Dix, Monta Bell, Martin Brown; directed by Monta Bell; for Jesse L. Lasky / Fox. 'Does not give promise of scoring in any placement.'—*Variety*

The Wrath of God
US 1972 111m Metrocolor Panavision
MGM / Rainbow / Cineman (William S. Gilmore Jnr)

During a twenties Central American revolution, a bootlegger joins forces with a defrocked priest.
Noisy, violent adventure yarn which works up to a gory climax but does not take itself too seriously.

wd Ralph Nelson, *novel* James Graham *ph* Alex Phillips Jnr *m* Lalo Schifrin

Robert Mitchum, Frank Langella, Rita Hayworth, Victor Buono, John Colicos

The Wreck of the Mary Deare*
US 1959 108m Metrocolor Cinemascope
MGM / Blaustein–Baroda (Julian Blaustein)

An insurance fraud comes to light when a salvage boat is rescued from high seas.
Curious, star-studded amalgam of seafaring action and courtroom melodrama, originally intended for Hitchcock.

w Eric Ambler, *novel* Hammond Innes *d* Michael Anderson *ph* Joseph Ruttenberg, F. A. Young *m* George Duning

Charlton Heston, Gary Cooper, Michael Redgrave, Emlyn Williams, Cecil Parker, Alexander Knox, Virginia McKenna, Richard Harris

The Wrecking Crew
US 1968 104m Technicolor
Columbia / Meadway / Claude (Irving Allen)

Special agent Matt Helm recovers bullion stolen from a Danish train.
Camped-up spy buffoonery with the usual nubile ladies and a production which seeks to be flashy but succeeds only in being tatty.

w William McGivern, *novel* Donald Hamilton *d* Phil Karlson *ph* Sam Leavitt *m* Hugo Montenegro

Dean Martin, Elke Sommer, Sharon Tate, Nancy Kwan, Nigel Green, Tina Louise

'The story of a family's ugly secret and the stark moment that thrust their private lives into public view!'

Written on the Wind**
US 1956 99m Technicolor
U-I (Albert Zugsmith)

A secretary marries her oil tycoon boss and finds herself the steadying force in a very rocky family.
The sheerest Hollywood moonshine: high-flying melodramatic hokum which moves fast enough to be very entertaining.

w George Zuckerman, *novel* Robert Wilder *d Douglas Sirk ph Russell Metty m* Frank Skinner

Lauren Bacall, *Robert Stack, Dorothy Malone*, Rock Hudson, Robert Keith, Grant Williams

AA: Dorothy Malone
AAN: title song (*m* Victor Young, *ly* Sammy Cahn); Robert Stack

Wrong Again
US 1929 20m bw silent

A horse instead of a painting is delivered to a rich man's house. Pleasing but not very inventive star comedy. Laurel and Hardy, Del Henderson. Written by Lewis R. Foster, Leo McCarey and H. M. Walker; directed by Leo McCarey; for Hal Roach.

The Wrong Arm of the Law*
GB 1962 94m bw
Romulus / Robert Verlaise (Aubrey Baring, E. M. Smedley Aston)

London gangsters plan retaliation against Australian interlopers, and offer Scotland Yard a temporary truce.
Forgettable but pretty funny crook comedy in the British vein, with pacy script and excellent comedy timing.

w John Warren, Len Heath *d Cliff Owen ph* Ernest Steward *m* Richard Rodney Bennett

Peter Sellers, Lionel Jeffries, Bernard Cribbins, Davy Kaye, Nanette Newman, Bill Kerr, John Le Mesurier

The Wrong Box*
GB 1966 110m Technicolor
Columbia / Salamander (Bryan Forbes)

Two elderly Victorian brothers are the last survivors of a tontine (an involved form of lottery) and try to murder each other.
Well-intentioned and star-studded black farce in which the excellent period trappings and stray jokes completely overwhelm the plot.

w Larry Gelbart, Burt Shevelove, *novel* Robert Louis Stevenson, Lloyd Osbourne *d* Bryan Forbes *ph Gerry Turpin m* John Barry *ad Ray Simm*

Ralph Richardson, John Mills, Michael Caine, *Wilfrid Lawson*, Nanette Newman, Peter Cook, Dudley Moore, Peter Sellers, Tony Hancock, Thorley Walters, Cicely Courtneidge, Irene Handl, John Le Mesurier, Gerald Sim, Norman Bird, Tutte Lemkow

'A slapdash affair in which anything goes, irrespective of whether or not it fits.'—*Tom Milne*

Wrong Is Right
US 1982 117m Metrocolor
Columbia / Richard Brooks
GB title: *The Man with the Deadly Lens*

An international TV commentator discovers that the world is being manipulated by the CIA.
Wild satiric melodrama which takes potshots at everything and usually misses.

wd Richard Brooks, *novel* The Deadly Angels by Charles McCarry *ph* Fred J. Koenekamp *m* Artie Kane *pd* Edward Carfagno *ed* George Grenville

Sean Connery, George Grizzard, Katharine Ross, Robert Conrad, G. D. Spradlin, John Saxon, Henry Silva, Leslie Nielsen, Robert Webber, Rosalind Cash, Hardy Kruger, Dean Stockwell, Ron Moody

'Intended as a sharply cynical overview of the current political scene, it emerges as a drearily murky thriller.'—*Sight and Sound*

The Wrong Man*
US 1957 105m bw
Warner (Herbert Coleman)

A New York musician is mistaken by police for an armed bandit, and both witnesses and circumstances prevent the truth from emerging.

WUTHERING HEIGHTS was voted best film of the year by the New York Film Critics in preference to the Oscar-garlanded *Gone With the Wind*. The still shows Laurence Olivier and Merle Oberon.

True but downbeat story from the headlines, filmed with remarkably little persuasion; not its director's *métier* despite evidence of his usual thoroughness.

w Maxwell Anderson, Angus MacPhail *d* Alfred Hitchcock *ph Robert Burks m* Bernard Herrmann

Henry Fonda, Vera Miles, Anthony Quayle, Harold J. Stone, Esther Minciotti

WUSA*
US 1970 117m Technicolor Panavision
Paramount / Mirror / Coleytown / Stuart Rosenberg (Paul Newman, John Foreman)

A penniless wanderer causes chaos when he becomes the announcer for a right-wing radio station.
A farcical melodrama for the intelligentsia, and for the most part a thoroughgoing bore. The last part offers a compensation or two.

w Robert Stone, from his novel Hall of Mirrors *d* Stuart Rosenberg *ph* Richard Moore *m* Lalo Schifrin

Paul Newman, Joanne Woodward, Laurence Harvey, Anthony Perkins, Pat Hingle, Cloris Leachman, Don Gordon, Robert Quarry, Bruce Cabot, Moses Gunn, Wayne Rogers

'The most significant film I've ever made and the best.'—*Paul Newman*

'Torn with desire . . . twisted with hate!'

Wuthering Heights***

US 1939 104m bw

Samuel Goldwyn

The daughter of an unhappy middle-class Yorkshire family falls passionately in love with a gypsy who has been brought up with her. Despite American script and settings, this wildly romantic film makes a pretty fair stab at capturing the power of at least the first half of a classic Victorian novel, and in all respects it's a superb Hollywood production of its day and a typical one, complete with ghostly finale and a first-rate cast.

w Ben Hecht, Charles MacArthur, novel Emily Brontë d William Wyler ph Gregg Toland m Alfred Newman

Laurence Olivier, Merle Oberon, David Niven, Hugh Williams, Flora Robson, Geraldine Fitzgerald, Donald Crisp, Leo G. Carroll, Cecil Kellaway, *Miles Mander*

CATHY (Merle Oberon): 'I don't think I belong in heaven, Ellen. I dreamt once I was there. I dreamt I went to heaven and that heaven didn't seem to be my home and I broke my heart with weeping to come back to earth and the angels were so angry they flung me out in the middle of the heath on top of Wuthering Heights and I woke up sobbing with joy.'

HEATHCLIFF (Laurence Olivier): 'What do they know of heaven or hell, Cathy, who know nothing of life? Oh, they're praying for you, Cathy. I'll pray one prayer with them. I'll repeat till my tongue stiffens: Catherine Earnshaw, may you not rest while I live on. I killed you. Haunt me, then! Haunt your murderer! I know that ghosts have wandered on the earth. Be with me always—take any form—drive me mad! Only do not leave me in this dark alone where I cannot find you. I cannot live without my life! I cannot die without my soul . . .'

'Sombre dramatic tragedy, productionally fine, but with limited appeal.'—*Variety*

'Unquestionably one of the most distinguished pictures of the year.'—*Frank S. Nugent, New York Times*

'A pattern of constant forward motion, with overtones maintained throughout the rise of interest and suspense.'—*Otis Ferguson*

'A strong and sombre film, poetically written as the novel not always was, sinister and wild as it was meant to be, far more compact dramatically than Miss Brontë had made it.'—*Richard Mallett, Punch*

AA: Gregg Toland
AAN: best picture; script; William Wyler; Alfred Newman; Laurence Olivier; Geraldine Fitzgerald

'The power, the passion, the terror!'

Wuthering Heights*

GB 1970 105m Movielab

AIP (John Pellatt)

Somewhat rewritten and overkeen to find a 1970 mood and interpretation for what can only be a period piece, this disappointing version marks a Z-film company's first determined effort to enter the big-time.

w Patrick Tilley *d* Robert Fuest *ph John Coquillon m* Michel Legrand

Anna Calder-Marshall, Timothy Dalton, Harry Andrews, Pamela Brown, Judy Cornwell, James Cossins, Rosalie Crutchley, Julian Glover, Hugh Griffith, Ian Ogilvy, Aubrey Woods

Wyoming

US 1940 88m bw

A Missouri badman is persuaded to try an honest life. Well-liked minor western responsible for the first teaming of its inelegant stars. Wallace Beery, Marjorie Main, Leo Carrillo, Ann Rutherford, Joseph Calleia, Lee Bowman, Henry Travers. Written by Jack Jevne and Hugo Butler; directed by Richard Thorpe; for MGM. (GB title: *Bad Man of Wyoming.*)

Wyoming

US 1947 84m bw

Early settlers in the west meet trouble from government squatters. Minor western for undemanding audiences. Bill Elliott, Vera Ralston, John Carroll, George 'Gabby' Hayes, Albert Dekker. Written by Lawrence Hazard and Gerald Geraghty; directed by Joe Kane; for Republic.

'If thine eye offends thee, pluck it out!'

X—The Man with X-Ray Eyes
US 1963 80m Pathecolor
'Spectarama'
AIP (Roger Corman)
GB title: *The Man with the X-Ray Eyes*

A scientist gives himself X-ray vision and goes mad.
Interesting but rather unpleasant horror story with moments of cleverness but a general air of disappointment.

w Robert Dillon, Ray Russell *d Roger Corman* *ph* Floyd Crosby *m* Les Baxter

Ray Milland, Diana Van Der Vlis, Harold J. Stone, John Hoyt, Don Rickles, John Dierkes

'When the dialogue suggests that Xavier is being driven insane by strange and satanic visions, what one actually sees is rather a comedown.'—*MFB*

'Concise, confident, and not an ounce overweight.'—*NFT, 1967*

X the Unknown*
GB 1956 81m bw
Hammer (Anthony Hinds)

A mysterious force feeds on radiation from a research station on a Scottish moor, and becomes a seeping mass.
Minor sci-fi horror with a monster like liquid lino, rushed into release to cash in on *The Quatermass Experiment*.

w Jimmy Sangster *d* Leslie Norman *ph* Gerald Gibbs *m* James Bernard

Dean Jagger, Edward Chapman, Leo McKern, William Lucas, John Harvey, Peter Hammond, Michael Ripper, Anthony Newley

Xanadu
US 1980 93m Technicolor
Universal / Lawrence Gordon

The muse Terpsichore comes to earth and becomes involved in the opening of a roller-derby disco.
Misguided attempt at a clean nostalgic musical, apparently conceived in a nightmare after somebody saw *Down to Earth* on the late show.

w Richard Christian Danus, Marc Reid Rubel *d* Robert Greenwald *ph* Victor J. Kemper *m* Barry de Vorzon *songs* Jeff Lynne, John Farrar *pd* John W. Corso

Olivia Newton-John, Gene Kelly, Michael Beck

'Truly a stupendously bad film whose only salvage is the music.'—*Variety*

'A forties musical submerged by contemporary tat.'—*Guardian*

'Mushy and limp, so insubstantial it evaporates before our eyes.'—*Roger Ebert*

† Gene Kelly uses the same character name, Danny McGuire, as he did in *Cover Girl*.

The Yakuza
US 1975 112m Technicolor Panavision
Warner (Sydney Pollack, Michael Hamilburg)

Japanese gangsters kidnap the daughter of a Los Angeles shipping magnate.
Violent thriller roughly exploiting an ancient Japanese genre.

w Paul Schrader, Robert Towne *d* Sydney Pollack *ph* Okazaki Kozo, Duke Callaghan *m* Dave Grusin

Robert Mitchum, Takakura Ken, Brian Keith, Kishi Keilo, Okada Eiji

'No more than a curious footnote to the western exploitation of oriental action movies.'—*Tony Rayns*

Yangtse Incident*
GB 1957 113m bw
British Lion / Wilcox/Neagle (Herbert Wilcox)
US title: *Battle Hell*; aka: *Escape of the Amethyst*

In 1949 a British frigate is shelled and held captive by communist shore batteries in the Yangtse.
Stalwart but not very exciting British war heroics.

w Eric Ambler, *book* Franklin Gollings *d* Michael Anderson *ph* Gordon Dines *m* Leighton Lucas

Richard Todd, William Hartnell, Akim Tamiroff, Donald Houston, Keye Luke, Sophie Stewart, Robert Urquhart, James Kenney, Barry Foster

A Yank at Eton
US 1942 88m bw
MGM (John Considine Jnr)

A rich, wild American boy is sent to Eton to cool down.
Tame, tasteless imitation of *A Yank at Oxford* with younger participants.

w George Oppenheimer, Lionel Houser, Thomas Phipps *d* Norman Taurog *ph* Karl Freund, Charles Lawton *m* Bronislau Kaper

Mickey Rooney, Freddie Bartholemew, Ian Hunter, Edmund Gwenn, Alan Mowbray, Tina Thayer, Marta Linden, Alan Napier, Terry Kilburn

A Yank at Oxford**
GB 1938 105m bw
MGM (Michael Balcon)

A cocky young American student comes to Oxford and meets all kinds of trouble.
A huge pre-war success which now seems naïve, this was the first big Anglo-American production from a team which went on to make *The Citadel* and *Goodbye Mr Chips* before war stymied them.

w Malcolm Stuart Boylan, Walter Ferris, George Oppenheimer, Leon Gordon, Roland Pertwee, John Monk Saunders, Sidney Gilliat, Michael Hogan *d* Jack Conway *ph* Harold Rosson Edward Ward

Robert Taylor, Vivien Leigh, Maureen O'Sullivan, Lionel Barrymore, Robert Coote, Edmund Gwenn, C. V. France, Griffith Jones, Morton Selten

'A draw picture for Taylor at a critical moment in his meteoric bid for fame.'—*Variety*

† A total of 31 writers are alleged to have worked without credit.

A Yank in Ermine
GB 1955 85m colour

An American finds that he is really an English earl. Thin comedy, thinly developed. Peter Thompson, Noelle Middleton. Harold Lloyd Jnr, Diana Decker, Jon Pertwee, Reginald Beckwith, Edward Chapman, Richard Wattis. Written by John Paddy Carstairs from his novel Solid Said the Earl; directed by Gordon Parry; for Monarch.

A Yank in the RAF*
US 1941 98m bw
TCF (Lou Edelman)

An American chorine stranded in London falls for the titular gentleman.
Silly but entertaining wartime flagwaver.

w Karl Tunberg, Darrell Ware, *story* Melville Crossman (Zanuck) *d* Henry King *ph* Leon Shamroy *m* Alfred Newman

Tyrone Power, Betty Grable, John Sutton, Reginald Gardiner, Donald Stuart, Morton Lowry, Richard Fraser, Bruce Lester

A Yank on the Burma Road
US 1942 66m bw
MGM (Samuel Marx)
GB title: *China Caravan*

A tough truck driver in the Far East abandons profit for heroism when he hears of Pearl Harbor.
Crass action flagwaver.

w George Kahn, Hugo Butler, David Lang *d* George B. Seitz *ph* Lester White

Barry Nelson, Laraine Day, Stuart Crawford, Keye Luke, Sen Yung

'Glib humbug, playing tiddleywinks with high stakes.'—*Theodore Strauss*

Yankee Doodle Dandy***
US 1942 126m bw
Warner (Hal B. Wallis, William Cagney)

The life story of dancing vaudevillian George M. Cohan.
Outstanding showbiz biopic, with unassuming but effective production, deft patriotic backdrops and a marvellous, strutting, magnetic star performance.

w Robert Buckner, Edmund Joseph *d Michael Curtiz ph James Wong Howe* *m* Heinz Roemheld *md* Heinz Roemheld, Ray Heindorf *songs George M. Cohan*

James Cagney, Joan Leslie, *Walter Huston*, Rosemary de Camp, Richard Whorf, George Tobias, Jeanne Cagney, Irene Manning, S. Z. Sakall, George Barbier, Frances Langford, Walter Catlett, Eddie Foy Jnr

COHAN (James Cagney) at end of vaudeville act: 'My mother thanks you. My father thanks you. My sister thanks you. And I thank you.'

COHAN: 'Where else in the world could a plain guy like me sit down and talk things over with the head man?'

ROOSEVELT (Captain Jack Young): 'Well now, you know, Mr Cohan, that's as good a description of America as I've ever heard.'

AA: music direction; James Cagney
AAN: best picture; original story (Robert Buckner); Michael Curtiz; Walter Huston

'Possibly the most genial screen biography ever made.'—*Time*

Yankee Pasha
US 1954 84m Technicolor

An American adventurer in nineteenth-century Marseilles saves his girl friend from pirates. Studio-bound hokum for double-featuring. Jeff Chandler, Rhonda Fleming, Mamie Van Doren, Lee J. Cobb, Bart Roberts, Hal March. Written by Joseph Hoffman, from the novel by Edison Marshall; directed by Joseph Pevney; for Universal-International.

Yanks**
GB 1979 141m Technicolor
United Artists / Joe Janni-Lester Persky / CIP

Romances of American GIs billeted on a

Lancashire town during World War II.
Not an entirely promising subject, this overlong piece maintains its interest by sheer skill of dramaturgy and cinematic narrative.

w Colin Welland, Walter Bernstein *d John Schlesinger ph* Dick Bush *m* Richard Rodney Bennett *pd* Brian Morris

Vanessa Redgrave, Richard Gere, William Devane, Lisa Eichhorn, Rachel Roberts, Chick Vennera

'Risking it was all part of the job!'
The Year of Living Dangerously*
Australia 1982 114m Eastmancolor
MGM / McElroy and McElroy / Peter Weir

A young Australian journalist takes his first international assignment in Indonesia.
Freshly observed but ultimately pointless political parable which undoubtedly means more to its maker than it will to audiences.

w David Williamson, Peter Weir, C. J. Koch, *novel* C. J. Koch *d Peter Weir ph* Russell Boyd *m* Maurice Jarre *ed* Bill Anderson

Mel Gibson, Sigourney Weaver, Linda Hunt, Michael Murphy, Bill Kerr, Noel Ferrier

AA: Linda Hunt

'It's Chinatown—and it's about to explode!'
The Year of the Dragon
US 1985 136m Technicolor Panavision
MGM–UA / Dino de Laurentiis

A tough cop clears Chinatown of a group of murderous youth gangs.
Extremely violent and convoluted thriller with an unpleasant hero.

w Oliver Stone, Michael Cimino *novel* Robert Daley *d* Michael Cimino *ph* Alex Thomson *m* David Mansfield *pd* Wolf Kroeger *ed* Noelle Boisson

Mickey Rourke, John Lone, Ariane, Leonard Termo, Ray Barry

'Never as important as the director thinks it is . . . nothing is clearly resolved beyond the last dead body.'—*Variety*

'They tamed a tropic wilderness!'
The Yearling**
US 1946 134m Technicolor
MGM (Sidney Franklin)

The son of an old-time country farmer is attached to a stray deer.
Excellent family film for four-handkerchief patrons.

w Paul Osborn, *novel* Marjorie Kinnan Rawlings *d Clarence Brown ph* Charles Rosher, Leonard Smith *m* Herbert Stothart

Gregory Peck, Jane Wyman, Claude Jarman Jnr, Chill Wills, Clem Bevans, Margaret Wycherly, Henry Travers, Forrest Tucker

AA: Charles Rosher, Leonard Smith (and Arthur Arling)
AAN: best picture; Clarence Brown; Gregory Peck; Jane Wyman

The Years Between
GB 1946 100m bw
GFD / Sydney Box

An MP returns after being presumed dead in the war and finds his wife has been elected in his place.
Stilted variation on the Enoch Arden theme; plot and performances alike unpersuasive.

w Muriel and Sydney Box, *play* Daphne du Maurier *d* Compton Bennett *ph* Reg Wyer

Michael Redgrave, Valerie Hobson, Flora Robson, Felix Aylmer, James McKechnie, Dulcie Gray, Edward Rigby

The Yellow Balloon
GB 1952 80m bw
ABP (Victor Skuzetsky)

A small boy who thinks he has killed his friend is terrorized by a murderer.
Tense but not especially rewarding suspenser, clearly borrowed from *The Window*.

w Anne Burnaby, J. Lee-Thompson *d* J. Lee-Thompson *ph* Gilbert Taylor *m* Philip Green

Kenneth More, William Sylvester, Kathleen Ryan, Andrew Ray, Bernard Lee, Veronica Hurst

The Yellow Cab Man
US 1950 84m bw
MGM (Richard Goldstone)

A taxi-driving inventor is pursued by crooks after his secret formula.
Moderate star comedy.

w Devery Freeman, Albert Beich *d* Jack Donohue *ph* Harry Stradling *m* Scott Bradley

Red Skelton, Gloria de Haven, Walter Slezak, Edward Arnold, James Gleason, Paul Harvey, Jay C. Flippen

Yellow Canary*
GB 1943 98m bw
RKO / Imperator (Herbert Wilcox)

A socialite suspected of being a Nazi sympathizer is really a British spy.
Mild wartime melodrama chiefly notable for allotting an apparently unsympathetic part to the beloved Miss Neagle.

w De Witt Bodeen, Miles Malleson, *story* Pamela Bower *d* Herbert Wilcox *ph* Max Greene

Anna Neagle, Richard Greene, Nova Pilbeam, Lucie Mannheim, Cyril Fletcher, Albert Lieven, Margaret Rutherford, Marjorie Fielding

Yellow Canary
US 1963 93m bw Cinemascope
TCF / Cooga Mooga (Maury Dexter)

The baby son of a singing idol is kidnapped.
Rather dreary suspenser with too much dialogue.

w Rod Serling, *novel* Easy Come Easy Go by Whit Masterson *d* Buzz Kulik *ph* Floyd Crosby *m* Kenyon Hopkins

Pat Boone, Barbara Eden, Steve Forrest, Jack Klugman, Jesse White, John Banner, Jeff Corey

Yellow Dog
GB 1973 101m Eastmancolor
Scotia–Barber / Akari (Terence Donovan)

A Japanese agent in London keeps watch on a mysterious scientist.
Incoherent spy thriller with a few hybrid oddities.

w Shinobu Hashimoto *d* Terence Donovan *ph* David Watkin *m* Ron Grainer

Jiro Tamiya, Robert Hardy, Carolyn Seymour, Joseph O'Conor

Yellow Jack*
US 1938 83m bw
MGM (Jack Cummings)

In 1899 Cuba a marine offers himself as a guinea pig to combat yellow fever.
Solid, unsurprising, period medical melodrama with conventional romantic sidelights.

w Edward Chodorov, *play* Sidney Howard, Paul de Kruif *d* George B. Seitz *ph* Lester White *m* William Axt

Robert Montgomery, Virginia Bruce, Lewis Stone, Andy Devine, Henry Hull, Charles Coburn, Buddy Ebsen, Henry O'Neill, Janet Beecher

'Okay for single billing, but no wow.'—*Variety*

The Yellow Rolls Royce*
GB 1964 122m Metrocolor Panavision
MGM (Anatole de Grunwald)

Three stories about the owners of an expensive car; an aristocrat, a gangster, and a wandering millionairess.
Lukewarm all-star concoction lacking either good stories or a connecting thread.

w Terence Rattigan *d* Anthony Asquith *ph* Jack Hildyard *m* Riz Ortolani *pd* Vincent Korda

Rex Harrison, Jeanne Moreau, Edmund Purdom, Moira Lister, Roland Culver, Shirley Maclaine, George C. Scott, Alain Delon, Art Carney, Ingrid Bergman, Omar Sharif, Joyce Grenfell

'Tame, bloodless, smothered in elegance and the worst kind of discreetly daring good taste.'—*Peter John Dyer*

Yellow Sands
GB 1938 68m bw

A Cornish family sets to bickering over a will.
Reliable comedy from a popular stage original. Marie Tempest, Wilfrid Lawson, Belle Chrystall, Robert Newton, Patrick Barr, Edward Rigby. Written by Michael Barringer and Rodney Ackland, from the play by Eden and Adelaide Phillpotts; directed by Herbert Brenon; for ABPC.

'It was a moment for being a woman . . . for only a woman's revenge could keep her alive—now!'
Yellow Sky**
US 1948 98m bw
TCF (Lamar Trotti)

Outlaws on the run take over a desert ghost town.

Gleaming, stylish western melodrama which benefits from its unusual and confined setting.

w Lamar Trotti, *story* W. R. Burnett *d William Wellman ph Joe MacDonald m* Alfred Newman

Gregory Peck, Anne Baxter, Richard Widmark, Robert Arthur, John Russell, Henry Morgan, James Barton

Yellow Submarine*
GB 1968 87m De Luxe
King Features / Apple (Al Brodax)

The happy kingdom of Pepperland is attacked by the Blue Meanies.
Way-out cartoon fantasia influenced by Beatlemania and the swinging sixties; hard to watch for non-addicts.

w Lee Minoff, Al Brodax, Jack Mendelsohn, Erich Segal *d* George Duning *m* John Lennon, Paul McCartney

The Yellow Ticket*
US 1931 76m bw
Fox
GB title: *The Yellow Passport*

In Russia during the pogroms, a Jewish girl pretends to be a prostitute in order to get a travel permit to see her dying father.
Curious anti-Russian melodrama deriving its plot from *La Tosca*.

w Jules Furthman, Guy Bolton, play Michael Morton *d* Raoul Walsh *ph* James Wong Howe

Elissa Landi, Laurence Olivier, Lionel Barrymore, Walter Byron, Sarah Padden, Mischa Auer, Boris Karloff

'A picture filled with swashbucklers, privateers, public floggings, saucy tarts, looney lords, beggars, queens, and even a very jolly Roger!'

Yellowbeard
US 1983 96m De Luxe
Orion / Seagoat (Carter de Haven Jnr)

Farcical adventures of a 17th-century pirate captain.
A spoofy saga in deliberately bad taste, this ragbag of old gags and new unpleasantness sank rapidly to the bottom of the box office barrel.

w Graham Chapman, Peter Cook, Bernard McKenna *d* Mel Damski *ph* Gerry Fisher *m* John Morris *pd* Joseph R. Jennings

Graham Chapman, Peter Boyle, Cheech and Chong, Peter Cook, Marty Feldman, Michael Hordern, Eric Idle, Madeline Kahn, James Mason, John Cleese, Kenneth Mars, Spike Milligan, Susannah York, Beryl Reid, Ferdy Mayne, Peter Bull.

'The atrocious script and haphazard direction elicit generally embarrassing performances from all concerned.'—*Kim Newman, MFB*

Yellowstone Kelly
US 1959 91m Technicolor
Warner

A fur trapper prevents war between Indians and whites.
Standard western with routine excitements and a cast of TV faces.

w Burt Kennedy *d* Gordon Douglas *ph* Carl Guthrie *m* Howard Jackson

Clint Walker, Edd Byrnes, John Russell, Ray Danton, Claude Akins

Yentl*
GB 1983 133m Technicolor
MGM-UA / Barwood / Ladbroke (Barbra Streisand, Rusty Lemorande)

Many years ago in Poland, a Jewish girl tries to get on in the world by dressing as a boy.
A personal and some would say megalomaniac extravagance by its producer-director-writer-star, who before embarking should have learned the value of brevity. Nevertheless there is about the enterprise a certain heavy style which may appeal strongly to Jews while precluding the interest and understanding of others.

w Jack Rosenthal, Barbra Streisand, *story* Isaac Bashevis Singer *d* Barbra Streisand *ph* David Watkin *m* Michel Legrand *pd* Roy Walker *ed* Terry Rawlings

Barbra Streisand, Mandy Patinkin, Amy Irving, Nehemiah Persoff, Steven Hill, David de Keyser, Bernard Spear

AA: music
AAN: Amy Irving; songs 'Papa, Can You Hear Me?' 'The Way He Makes Me Feel' (*m* Legrand, *ly* Alan Bergman, Marilyn Bergman); art director

'A glorious uproarious love story!'

Yes, Giorgio*
US 1982 110m Metrocolor
MGM–UA / Peter Fetterman

A top international tenor falls for the lady throat specialist who cures his ailment.
Nostalgic musical romance, fine in its way but out of key with the modern film business. A treat for television viewers.

w Norman Steinberg, *novel* Anne Piper *d* Franklin J. Schaffner *ph* Fred J. Koenekamp *m* John Williams *pd* William D. Creber

Luciano Pavarotti, Kathryn Harrold, Eddie Albert, Paola Borboni

AAN: original song, 'If We Were In Love' by John Williams, Alan and Marilyn Bergman
† The film allegedly cost 19 million and took only one.

Yes, Madam
GB 1938 77m bw

Heirs to a fortune are obliged to act as servants for three months. Agreeable minor comedy. Bobby Howes, Diana Churchill, Billy Milton, Fred Emney, Bertha Belmore, Wylie Watson, Vera Pearce. Written by Clifford Grey, Bert Lee and William Freshman, from the novel by K. R. G. Browne; directed by Norman Lee; for ABPC. (Previously filmed in 1933 with Frank Pettingell and Kay Hammond.)

Yes Mr Brown*
GB 1933 90m bw

A businessman's secretary pretends to be his wife after the latter has walked out on him.
One of its star's most fondly remembered musical farces, a thin thing but his own.
Jack Buchanan, Elsie Randolph, Hartley Power, Clifford Heatherley, Vera Pearce. Written by Douglas Furber from the play Business with America by Paul Frank, Ludwig Hershfield; directed by Herbert Wilcox, Jack Buchanan; for Herbert Wilcox / British and Dominions.

Yes My Darling Daughter
US 1939 86m bw
Warner (Ben Glazer)

Lovers elope and are pursued by her family.
Mildly amusing domestic comedy.

w Casey Robinson, *play* Mark Reed *d* William Keighley *ph* Charles Rosher

Priscilla Lane, Jeffrey Lynn, Roland Young, Fay Bainter, May Robson, Genevieve Tobin, Ian Hunter

Yes Sir, That's My Baby
US 1949 82m Technicolor
U-I (Leonard Goldstein)

Ex-service undergraduates and their wives have trouble settling down to studies.
Witless and exhausting college comedy.

w Oscar Brodney *d* George Sherman *ph* Irving Glassberg *m* Walter Scharf

Donald O'Connor, Gloria de Haven, Charles Coburn, Barbara Brown, Joshua Shelley

Yesterday, Today and Tomorrow
Italy / France 1963 119m Techniscope
CCC / Concordia / Joseph E. Levine (Carlo Ponti)

Three stories of naughty ladies.
A relentlessly boring compendium with everybody shouting at once.

w Eduardo de Fillipp, Cesare Zavattini, others *d* Vittorio de Sica *ph* Giuseppe Rotunno *m* Armando Trovajoli

Marcello Mastroianni, Sophia Loren

'A sad intimation of the sort of rainy day the Italian cinema is currently having.'—*MFB*

AA: best foreign film

Yesterday's Enemy
GB 1959 95m bw Megascope
Columbia / Hammer (T. S. Lyndon-Haynes)

In 1942 Burma, a British unit violently takes over a village and finds an unsolved puzzle.
Would-be ironic war suspenser, economically made but quite effective in putting its message across.

w Peter R. Newman, from his TV play *d* Val Guest *ph* Arthur Grant *m* none

Stanley Baker, Guy Rolfe, Leo McKern, Philip Ahn, Gordon Jackson, David Oxley, Richard Pasco, Russell Waters, Bryan Forbes, David Lodge, Percy Herbert

Yesterday's Hero
GB 1979 95m colour
Columbia / CinemaSeven (Elliott Kastner)

A successful footballer goes to the bad but redeems himself.
Totally uninteresting sporting version of the Road to Ruin.

w Jackie Collins *d* Neil Leifer *ph* Brian West *md* Stanley Myers *pd* Keith Wilson

Ian McShane, Suzanne Somers, Adam Faith, Paul Nicholas, Sam Kydd

Yield to the Night*
GB 1956 99m bw
ABP (Kenneth Harper)
US title: *Blonde Sinner*

A condemned murderess relives the events which led to her arrest.
Gloomy prison melodrama vaguely based on the Ruth Ellis case and making an emotional plea against capital punishment.

w John Cresswell, Joan Henry, *novel* Joan Henry *d* J. Lee-Thompson *ph* Gilbert Taylor *m* Ray Martin

Diana Dors, Yvonne Mitchell, Michael Craig, Marie Ney, Athene Seyler, Geoffrey Keen

Yokel Boy
US 1942 69m bw

A film buff from the sticks comes to Hollywood and gets involved with production. Spoofy comedy which doesn't come off despite the talent around. Eddie Foy Jnr, Joan Davis, Albert Dekker, Alan Mowbray, Roscoe Karns, Mikhail Rasumny, Marc Lawrence, Tom Dugan. Written by Isabel Dawn, from story by Russel Rouse (the legit musical by Lew Brown was thrown away, together with the songs); directed by Joseph Santley; for Robert North/Republic. (GB title: *Hitting the Headlines*.)

Yol**
Switzerland 1982 114m Fujicolor
Güney / Cactus / Maran / Antenne 2 / Swiss Television

Five convicts are released on a week's leave, and their various circumstances lead them to tragedy.
Rewarding if heavy-going Turkish saga which exhausts the spectator almost as much as its long-suffering characters. It feels and looks like an epic.

w Yilmaz Güney *d* Serif Gören *ph* Erdogan Engin *m* Sebastian Argol

Tarik Akan, Halil Ergün, Necmettin Cobanoglu, Serif Sezer

Yolanda and the Thief*
US 1945 108m Technicolor
MGM (Arthur Freed)

A con man poses as the guardian angel of a naïve heiress.
Laboured musical fantasy with arty Mexican settings; not a success in any way, but with a few effective moments.

w Irving Brecher, *story* Ludwig Bemelmans, Jacques Théry *d* Vincente Minnelli *ph* Charles Rosher *m* Lennie Hayton *songs* Harry Warren, Arthur Freed

Fred Astaire, Lucille Bremer, Frank Morgan, Leon Ames, Mildred Natwick

'The most extreme of the big musical mistakes.'—*New Yorker, 1979*

'Every time she says I love you, she breaks the law!'

You and Me
US 1938 90m bw
Paramount (Fritz Lang)

A department store owner employs ex-convicts, one of whom has not quite reformed. Curious comedy drama which never has a hope of coming off.

w Virginia Van Upp, *story* Norman Krasna *d* Fritz Lang *ph* Charles Lang Jnr *m* Kurt Weill

Sylvia Sidney, George Raft, Harry Carey, Barton MacLane, Warren Hymer, Roscoe Karns, George E. Stone, Adrian Morris

'Lang's individual touch is visible everywhere . . . but for the ordinary George Raft fan it will not only be unappreciated, it will be actually confusing.'—*National Board of Review*

You Belong to Me
US 1934 67m bw

An alcoholic vaudeville comic plays father to an orphan. Muddled backstage melodrama which would be enjoyed by fans of the star. Lee Tracy, Helen Mack, Helen Morgan, Lynne Overman, David Holt. Written by Walter DeLeon, Elizabeth Alexander; directed by Alfred Werker; for Louis D. Lighton / Paramount. 'Should gain attention in the nabe spots.'—*Variety*

You Belong to Me*
US 1941 94m bw
Columbia (Wesley Ruggles)
GB title: *Good Morning, Doctor*

A playboy becomes jealous of the male patients of his doctor wife.
Mild comedy for two stars who are well capable of keeping it afloat.

w Claude Binyon, Dalton Trumbo *d* Wesley Ruggles *ph* Joseph Walker *m* Frederick Hollander

Barbara Stanwyck, Henry Fonda, Edgar Buchanan, Roger Clark, Ruth Donnelly, Melville Cooper, Maude Eburne

You Came Along
US 1945 103m bw
Paramount (Hal B. Wallis)

A girl from the treasury department falls in love with one of three GIs she takes on a war bond tour, but he dies of leukemia.
Weird mishmash of farce and sentimentality; quite watchable in its way, but an odd showcase for a new female star.

w Robert Smith, Ayn Rand *d* John Farrow *ph* Daniel L. Fapp *m* Victor Young

Lizabeth Scott, Robert Cummings, Don Defore, Charles Drake, Julie Bishop, Kim Hunter, Rhys Williams, Franklin Pangborn, Minor Watson

You Can't Buy Everything*
US 1934 72m bw

A woman obsessed by her mounting bank balance almost ruins the lives of her family. Unusual and rather well-acted period melodrama with a pleasing cast. *May Robson*, Jean Parker, Lewis Stone, Mary Forbes, Reginald Mason. Written by Dudley Nichols, Lamar Trotti; directed by Charles F. Reisner; for MGM.

You Can't Cheat an Honest Man*
US 1939 79m bw
Universal (Lester Cowan)

Trials and tribulations of a circus owner.
Flat, desultory and generally disappointing comedy vehicle for an irresistible star combination.

w George Marion Jnr, Richard Mack, Everett Freeman, *story* Charles Bogle (W. C. Fields) *d* George Marshall *ph* Milton Krasner *m* Charles Previn

W. C. Fields, Edgar Bergen (with Charlie McCarthy and Mortimer Snerd), Constance Moore, Mary Forbes, Thurston Hall, Charles Coleman, Edward Brophy

'Fairly amusing but lacks sustained overall interest.'—*Variety*

You Can't Escape Forever
US 1942 77m bw

A girl reporter demoted to the lovelorn column exposes a racket boss. Untidy remake of *Hi Nellie*; tolerable on a double bill, but not for close criticism. George Brent, Brenda Marshall, Gene Lockhart, Roscoe Karns, Eduardo Ciannelli, Paul Harvey. Written by Fred Niblo Jnr and Hector Chevigny; directed by Jo Graham; for Warner.

You Can't Get Away with Murder
US 1939 78m bw
Warner (Sam Bischoff)

A juvenile delinquent teams up with a gangster and takes a prison rap for him. Standard post-Dead End crime melodrama with no surprises.

w Robert Buckner, Don Ryan, Kenneth Gamet, *play* Chalked Out by Lewis Lawes, Jonathan Finn *d* Lewis Seiler *ph* Sol Polito *m* Heinz Roemheld

Humphrey Bogart, Billy Halop, Gale Page, John Litel, Henry Travers, Harvey Stephens, Harold Huber

'Strictly a filler for the duals . . . ponderous and slow moving.'—*Variety*

You Can't Have Everything*
US 1937 99m bw
TCF (Lawrence Schwab)

A failed play is turned into a musical.
Lively backstage comedy with good moments.

w Harry Tugend, Jack Yellen, Karl Tunberg *d* Norman Taurog *ph* Lucien Andriot

YOU CAN'T TAKE IT WITH YOU. Monkey business from Frank Capra's entertaining film of the Moss Hart–George S. Kaufman stage hit. Donald Meek, Edward Arnold, Ann Miller and Spring Byington.

md David Buttolph *songs* Mack Gordon, Harry Revel

Alice Faye, *the Ritz Brothers,* Don Ameche, Charles Winninger, Gypsy Rose Lee, Tony Martin, Arthur Treacher, Louis Prima, Tip Tap and Toe, Wally Vernon

'An expert piecing together of story, melody, blackouts, night club specialties and production numbers.'—*Variety*

You Can't Have Everything
US 1970 90m Eastmancolor
Koala (Lou Brandt)
aka: *Cactus in the Snow*

An 18-year-old virgin GI is about to leave for Vietnam when he picks up a girl and spends a happy but platonic twenty-four hours.
An agreeably understated little love story for those absorbed by teenage sex problems.

wd Martin Zweibach *ph* David M. Walsh *m* Joe Parnello

Richard Thomas, Mary Layne, Lucille Benson, Oscar Beregi

You Can't Ration Love
US 1944 78m bw

It's wartime at college, and dates are rationed. Silly idea for a forgettable musical. Betty Jane Rhodes, Johnnie Johnston, Bill Edwards, Marjorie Weaver, Marie Wilson, Mabel Paige. Written by Val Burton, Hal Fimberg, Muriel Roy Bolton; directed by Lester Fuller; for Michel Kraike / Paramount.

You Can't Run Away from It
US 1956 96m Technicolor Cinemascope
Columbia (Dick Powell)

An heiress runs away from a marriage arranged by her father, and falls for an amiable reporter.
Flat remake of *It Happened One Night,* with practically no comic sense or talent.

w Claude Binyon, Robert Riskin *d* Dick Powell *ph* Charles Lawton Jnr *m* George Duning *md* Morris Stoloff

June Allyson, Jack Lemmon, Charles Bickford, Jim Backus, Stubby Kaye, Paul Gilbert, Allyn Joslyn

You Can't Take It with You**
US 1938 127m bw
Columbia (Frank Capra)

The daughter of a highly eccentric New York family falls for a rich man's son.
A hilarious, warm and witty play is largely changed into a tirade against big business, but the Capra expertise is here in good measure and the stars all pull their weight.

w Robert Riskin, *play* George S. Kaufman, Moss Hart *d Frank Capra* *ph* Joseph Walker *m* Dmitri Tiomkin

Jean Arthur, Lionel Barrymore, James Stewart, Edward Arnold, Spring Byington, Mischa Auer, Ann Miller, Samuel S. Hinds, Donald Meek, H. B. Warner, Halliwell Hobbes, Mary Forbes, Dub Taylor, Lillian Yarbo, Eddie Anderson, *Harry Davenport*

GRANDPA VANDERHOF (Lionel Barrymore) offering a prayer: 'Well, sir, here we are again. We had a little trouble, but that's not your fault. You spread the milk of human kindness, and if some of it gets curdled, that's our look-out. Anyway, things have turned out fine. Alice is going to marry Tony. The Kirbys are going to live with us for a while. And everybody on the block is happy. We've all got our health—and as far as anything else is concerned, we'll leave it up to you. Thank you.'

'The comedy is wholly American, wholesome, homespun, human, appealing, and touching in turn.'—*Variety*

'Shangri-La in a frame house.'—*Otis Ferguson*

AA: best picture; Frank Capra
AAN: Robert Riskin; Joseph Walker; Spring Byington

'It's bedlam in Islam!'

You Can't Win 'em All
GB 1970 99m Technicolor Panavision
Columbia / SRO (Gene Corman)

In 1922, two rival American mercenaries have adventures in the Mediterranean.
Hectic, overplotted comedy actioner.

w Leo V. Gordon *d* Peter Collinson *ph* Ken Higgins *m* Bert Kaempfert

Tony Curtis, Charles Bronson, Michèle Mercier, Grégoire Aslan, Patrick Magee

You for Me
US 1952 71m bw
MGM (Henry Berman)

A millionaire patient is courted by a needy hospital and falls for a popular nurse.
Cheerful but thin little programme-filler.

w William Roberts *d* Don Weis *ph* Paul Vogel *m* Alberto Columbo

Peter Lawford, Jane Greer, Gig Young, Paula Corday, Elaine Stewart

You Gotta Stay Happy
US 1948 100m bw
Universal (Karl Tunberg)

A runaway heiress joins cargo pilots on a transcontinental hop with some very queer passengers.
Ho-hum imitation of a Capra comedy; the effort shows.

w Karl Tunberg, *story* Robert Carson *d* H. C. Potter *ph* Russell Metty *m* Daniele Amfitheatrof

Joan Fontaine, James Stewart, Eddie Albert, Roland Young, Willard Parker, Percy Kilbride, Porter Hall, Paul Cavanagh, Halliwell Hobbes

You Live and Learn
GB 1937 80m bw

American night-club dancers are stranded in Paris and helped by a nitwit Englishman who turns out to be not what he seems. Rather flat comedy which gets flatter as it goes along. Glenda Farrell, Claude Hulbert, Glen Alyn, John Carol, James Stephenson, George Galleon. Written by Brock Williams and Tom Phipps from a story by Norma Petterson; directed by Arthur Woods; for Warners.

You Made Me Love You
GB 1934 69m bw

A temperamental heiress is tamed by an amorous songwriter. Flimsy comedy with amusing moments. Thelma Todd, Stanley Lupino, John Loder, James Carew, Gerald Rawlinson. Written by Frank Launder from a story by Stanley Lupino; directed by Monty Banks; for British International.

You Must Be Joking*
GB 1965 100m bw
Columbia / Ameran (Charles H. Schneer)

Assorted army personnel vie in an extended initiative test.
Slam-bang location comedy with more hits than misses: cheerful entertainment.

w Alan Hackney *d* Michael Winner *ph* Geoffrey Unsworth *m* Laurie Johnson

Terry-Thomas, Lionel Jeffries, Michael Callan, Gabriella Licudi, *Denholm Elliott,* Lee Montague, Bernard Cribbins, Wilfrid Hyde White, James Robertson Justice, Richard Wattis, James Villiers

You Never Can Tell*
US 1951 78m bw
U-I (Leonard Goldstein)
GB title: *You Never Know*

An Alsatian dog is murdered and is sent back from heaven in the guise of a private detective to expose his killer.
Self-confidently outrageous comedy fantasy in the wake of *Here Comes Mr Jordan;* not badly done if you accept the premise.

w Lou Breslow, David Chandler *d* Lou Breslow *ph* Maury Gertsman *m* Hans Salter

Dick Powell, Peggy Dow, Charles Drake, Joyce Holden, Albert Sharpe, Sara Taft

'Living, loving—as though any moment a vengeful world might tear her from his arms!'

You Only Live Once**
US 1937 85m bw
Walter Wanger

A petty crook framed for murder breaks out of prison and tries to escape to Canada with his wife.
Gloomy melodrama partly based on Bonnie and Clyde and incorporating a plea for justice; very well made and acted.

w Graham Baker, *story* Gene Towne *d Fritz Lang* *ph* Leon Shamroy *m* Alfred Newman

Sylvia Sidney, Henry Fonda, Barton MacLane, Jean Dixon, William Gargan, Jerome Cowan, Chic Sale, Margaret Hamilton, Warren Hymer

'Crack blend of spectacular drama and romance . . . good direction, strong scripting and an arresting production.'—*Variety*

'Again and again in this film we find what can only be described as camera style, the use of the pictorial image to narrate with the maximum of emotional impact.'—*Dilys Powell*

You Only Live Twice**
GB 1967 117m Technicolor Panavision
UA / Eon (Harry Saltzman, Albert R. Broccoli)

James Bond goes to Japan.
The Bond saga at its most expensive and expansive, full of local colour and in-jokes, with an enormously impressive set for the climactic action.

w Roald Dahl, *novel* Ian Fleming *d Lewis Gilbert* *ph* Freddie Young, Bob Huke *m* John Barry *pd Ken Adam*

Sean Connery, Tetsuro Tamba, Akiko Wakabayashi, Mie Hama, Karin Dor, Bernard Lee, Lois Maxwell, Desmond Llewellyn, *Charles Gray, Donald Pleasence*

You Said a Mouthful
US 1932 75m bw

The inventor of an unsinkable bathing suit is mistaken for a champion swimmer. Tepid star comedy. Joe E. Brown, Ginger Rogers, Sheila Terry, Guinn Williams, Oscar Apfel. Written by Robert Lord and Bolton Mallory; directed by Lloyd Bacon; for Warner.

You Were Meant for Me
US 1948 92m bw
TCF (Fred Kohlmar)

A small-town girl marries a bandleader.
Mildly pleasing, muted, musical romance, with good twenties atmosphere.

w Elick Moll, Valentine Davies *d* Lloyd Bacon *ph* Victor Milner *md* Lionel Newman *songs* various

Jeanne Crain, Dan Dailey, Oscar Levant, Barbara Lawrence, Selena Royle, Percy Kilbride, Herbert Anderson

You Were Never Lovelier*
US 1942 97m bw
Columbia (Louis F. Edelman)

An Argentinian hotel tycoon tries to interest his daughter in marriage by creating a mysterious admirer.
Pleasing musical, a follow up for the stars of *You'll Never Get Rich.*

w Michael Fessier, Ernest Pagano, Delmer Daves *d* William A. Seiter *ph* Ted Tetzlaff *songs* Jerome Kern, Johnny Mercer *m* Leigh Harline

Fred Astaire, Rita Hayworth, Adolphe Menjou, Leslie Brooks, Adele Mara, Isobel Elsom, Gus Schilling, Xavier Cugat and his Orchestra, Larry Parks

AAN: Leigh Harline; song 'Dearly Beloved'

You Will Remember
GB 1940 86m bw

The life of the late Victorian songwriter Leslie Stuart. Pleasant, rather surprising, minor British biopic. Robert Morley, Emlyn Williams, Dorothy Hyson, Tom E. Finglass, Nicholas Phipps, Allan Jeayes. Written by

Lydia Hayward; directed by Jack Raymond; for Jack Raymond Productions.

You'll Find Out*
US 1940 97m bw
RKO (David Butler)

Kay Kyser's band is hired to play for a 21st birthday party at a gloomy mansion; they help save the life of the girl concerned.
Cheerful if slow-starting spooky house send-up with a splendid trio of villains.

w James V. Kern, David Butler *d* David Butler *ph* Frank Redman *m* Roy Webb *songs* James McHugh, Johnny Mercer

Kay Kyser, Boris Karloff, Peter Lorre, Bela Lugosi, Dennis O'Keefe, Ginny Simms, Helen Parrish, Alma Kruger, Ish Kabibble

AAN: song, 'I'd Know You Anywhere'

You'll Like My Mother
US 1972 92m Technicolor
Universal / Bing Crosby Productions (Mort Briskin)

Pregnant widow visits neurotic mother-in-law in a snowbound mansion.
Predictable frightened lady shocker aiming somewhere between *Psycho* and *Fanatic*; of strictly routine interest.

w Jo Heims, *novel* Naomi Hintze *d* Lamont Johnson *ph* Jack Marta *m* Gil Melle

Rosemary Murphy, Patty Duke, Richard Thomas, Sian Barbara Allen

You'll Never Get Rich*
US 1941 88m bw
Columbia (Sam Bischoff)

A Broadway dance director helps his philandering producer by taking a romantically-inclined showgirl off his hands.
Smart comedy-musical which set its female lead as a top star.

w Michael Fessier, Ernest Pagano *d* Sidney Lanfield *ph* Philip Tannura *ch* Robert Alton *songs* Cole Porter *m* Morris Stoloff

Fred Astaire, Rita Hayworth, Robert Benchley, John Hubbard, Osa Massen, Frieda Inescort, Guinn Williams, Donald MacBride

AAN: Morris Stoloff; song 'Since I Kissed My Baby Goodbye'

Young America
US 1932 74m bw
Fox
GB title: *We Humans*

Two young boys get into trouble with the law.
Dog-eared domestic flagwaver.

w William Conselman, *play* John Frederick Ballard *d* Frank Borzage *ph* George Schneiderman *md* George Lipschultz

Spencer Tracy, Doris Kenyon, Tommy Conlon, Ralph Bellamy, Beryl Mercer, Sarah Padden

'Hokey propaganda for juvenile courts. Not for smart houses and doubtful elsewhere unless there is a preponderance of mothers.'—*Variety*

Young and Innocent***
GB 1937 80m bw
GFD / Gainsborough (Edward Black)
US title: *A Girl Was Young*

A girl goes on the run with her boy friend when he is suspected of murder.
Pleasant, unassuming chase melodrama with a rather weak cast but plenty of its director's touches.

w Charles Bennett, Alma Reville, *novel* A Shilling for Candles by Josephine Tey *d Alfred Hitchcock* *ph* Bernard Knowles *m* Louis Levy

Nova Pilbeam, Derrick de Marney, Mary Clare, Edward Rigby, Basil Radford, George Curzon, Percy Marmont, John Longden

Young and Willing
US 1942 83m bw
UA (made by Paramount) (Edward H. Griffith)

Impecunious actors in a New York boarding house hit on a great play.
Very mild, innocuous comedy which passed quickly from the public memory.

w Virginia Van Upp, *play* Francis Swann *d* Edward H. Griffith *ph* Leo Tover *m* Victor Young

William Holden, Susan Hayward, Eddie Bracken, Robert Benchley, Martha O'Driscoll, Barbara Britton, James Brown, Mabel Paige

Young as you Feel*
US 1931 78m bw

In order to reform his family a father pretends to be as irresponsible as they are. Medium star vehicle. Will Rogers, Fifi D'Orsay, Lucien Littlefield, Donald Dillaway. Written by Edwin Burke from the play Father and the Boys by George Ade; directed by Frank Borzage; for Fox. 'Looks fair b.o. due to star.'—*Variety*

Young at Heart**
US 1954 117m Warnercolor
(Warner) Arwin (Henry Blanke)

The daughters of a small-town music teacher have romantic problems.
Softened, musicalized remake of *Four Daughters* (qv), an old-fashioned treat with roses round the door and a high standard of proficiency in all departments.

w Julius J. Epstein, Lenore Coffee, *novel* Fannie Hurst *d* Gordon Douglas *ph* Ted McCord *md* Ray Heindorff

Doris Day, Frank Sinatra, Ethel Barrymore, Gig Young, Dorothy Malone, Robert Keith, Elizabeth Fraser, Alan Hale Jnr

Young Bess*
US 1953 112m Technicolor
MGM (Sidney Franklin)

The early years of Elizabeth I and her romance with Tom Seymour.
Historical fiction, wildly unreliable as to fact and dramatically not very rewarding. The character actors have the best of it.

w Arthur Wimperis, Jan Lustig, *novel* Margaret Irwin *d* George Sidney *ph* Charles Rosher *m* Miklos Rozsa

Jean Simmons, Stewart Granger, Charles Laughton (as Henry VIII), Kay Walsh, Deborah Kerr, Guy Rolfe, Kathleen Byron, Cecil Kellaway, Robert Arthur, Leo G. Carroll, Elaine Stewart, Dawn Addams, Rex Thompson

Young Billy Young
US 1969 89m De Luxe
UA / Talbot–Youngstein (Max Youngstein)

A young western gunman is helped out of scrapes by a mysterious stranger bent on revenge.
Good-looking but rather ineffective western which throws away good production values.

wd Burt Kennedy, *novel* Who Rides with Wyatt by Will Henry *ph* Harry Stradling Jnr *m* Shelly Manne

Robert Mitchum, Angie Dickinson, Robert Walker Jnr, David Carradine, John Anderson, Paul Fix

Young Cassidy*
GB 1964 110m Technicolor
MGM / Sextant (Robert D. Graff, Robert Emmett Ginna)

A romantic view of the early Dublin life of writer Sean O'Casey.
Ambling, unconvincing but generally interesting picture of a past time.

w John Whiting, from the writings of Sean O'Casey *d* Jack Cardiff, John Ford *ph* Ted Scaife *m* Sean O'Riada

Rod Taylor, Maggie Smith, Edith Evans, Flora Robson, Michael Redgrave, Julie Christie, Jack MacGowran, Sian Phillips, T. P. McKenna

Young Dillinger
US 1964 102m bw
Alfred Zimbalist

An embittered young convict becomes Public Enemy Number One.
Fantasized, forgettable biopic with violent moments.

w Arthur Hoerl, Don Zimbalist *d* Terry Morse *ph* Stanley Cortez *m* Shorty Rogers

Nick Adams, John Ashley, Robert Conrad, Mary Ann Mobley, Victor Buono, John Hoyt, Reed Hadley

The Young Doctors*
US 1961 102m bw
UA / Drexel / Stuart Millar / Laurence Turman

Old Dr Pearson resents his modern young assistant and almost causes a tragedy.
Routine medical melo of the Kildare / Gillespie kind, given a Grade A production and cast.

w Joseph Hayes, *novel* The Final Diagnosis by Arthur Hailey *d* Phil Karlson *ph* Arthur J. Ornitz *m* Elmer Bernstein

Fredric March, Ben Gazzara, Dick Clark, Eddie Albert, Ina Balin, Aline MacMahon, Edward Andrews, Arthur Hill, George Segal, Rosemary Murphy

Young Doctors in Love
US 1982 95m Metrocolor
TCF / ABC (Jerry Bruckheimer)

Goings-on in a modern hospital.
Spoof soap opera in the wake of *Airplane* but seeming more like a flat edition of *Carry On.*

w Michael Elias, Rich Eustis *d* Garry Marshall *ph* Don Peterman *m* Maurice Jarre

Michael McKean, Sean Young, Harry Dean Stanton, Patrick MacNee, Hector Elizondo, Dabney Coleman

Young Eagles*
US 1930 71m bw
Paramount

The adventures of American aviators in World War I.
Spirited early sound actioner.

w William McNutt, Grover Jones *d* William Wellman *ph* Archie Stout

Charles Rogers, Jean Arthur, Paul Lukas, Stuart Erwin, Virginia Bruce, James Finlayson
'Pint-sized version of *Wings.* Comedy and production almost square silly plot.'—*Variety*

Young Eagles
US 1934 bw serial: 12 eps

Two Eagle Scouts are awarded trips to South America and stumble across treasure.
Unremarkable juvenile serial dedicated by the scout movement to President Roosevelt.
Bobbie Cox, Jim Vance. For First Division.

Young Frankenstein**
US 1974 108m bw
TCF / Gruskoff / Venture / Jouer / Crossbow (Michael Gruskoff)

Young Frederick Frankenstein, a brain surgeon, goes back to Transylvania and pores over his grandfather's notebooks.
The most successful of Mel Brooks' parodies, Mad Magazine style; the gleamingly reminiscent photography is the best of it, the script being far from consistently funny, but there are splendid moments.

w Gene Wilder, Mel Brooks *d* Mel Brooks *ph Gerald Hirschfeld* *m* John Morris *ad Dale Hennesy*

Gene Wilder, Marty Feldman, Madeleine Kahn, *Peter Boyle,* Cloris Leachman, Kenneth Mars, Gene Hackman, Richard Haydn

AAN: script

Young Giants
US 1983 97m De Luxe Panavision

A San Diego priest helps a boys' home by re-organizing a football team so that an old priest can die happy. Shades of *Going My Way*, but somewhat ineptly done, with a guest appearance from Pele as *deus ex machina*. Peter Fox, John Huston, Lisa Wills, F. William Parker, Severn Darden. Written by Tom Moyer, Terrill Tannen, Mike Lammers; directed by Terrill Tannen; for Entertainment Enterprises. 'At least it has the courage of its throwback convictions.'—*Kim Newman, MFB*

The Young Girls of Rochefort
France 1967 126m Eastmancolor Franscope
Parc Film / Madeleine / Seven Arts (Mag Bodard, Gilbert de Goldschmidt)
original title: *Les Demoiselles de Rochefort*

Two country girls join a travelling dancing troupe, and find love on the day of the fair.
Flat, empty tribute to the Hollywood musical, which never inspires despite the presence of one of its greatest stars.

wd Jacques Demy *ph* Ghislain Cloquet *m* Michel Legrand

Catherine Deneuve, François Dorléac, George Chakiris, Gene Kelly, Danielle Darrieux, Grover Dale, Michel Piccoli

AAN: Michel Legrand

Young Ideas
US 1943 75m bw

The proposed marriage of two academics is interrupted by the protests of their children.
Predictable light concoction with practised players. Mary Astor, Herbert Marshall, Susan Peters, Elliott Reid, Richard Carlson, Allyn Joslyn. Written by Ian McLellan Hunter and Bill Noble; directed by Jules Dassin; for Robert Sisk / MGM.

The Young in Heart***
US 1938 91m bw
David O. Selznick

A family of charming confidence tricksters move in on a rich old lady but she brings out the best in them.
Delightful, roguish romantic comedy, perfectly cast and pacily handled.

w Paul Osborn, Charles Bennett, novel The Gay Banditti by I. A. R. Wylie *d Richard Wallace* *ph* Leon Shamroy *m* Franz Waxman

Douglas Fairbanks Jnr, Janet Gaynor, Roland Young, Billie Burke, Minnie Dupree, Paulette Goddard, Richard Carlson, Henry Stephenson
'Sentimental drama, vastly touching and entertaining . . . has everything to ensure box office success.'—*Variety*
'It comes as a gentle breeze in the hurricane of hurly burly comedies that have hurtled across the screen of late.'—*Motion Picture Herald*

AAN: Leon Shamroy; Franz Waxman

The Young Land
US 1957 89m Technicolor
(Columbia) C. V. Whitney (Patrick Ford)

A young sheriff arrests a gunman and after the trial has to save him from lynching.
Rather stiff attempt at a youth western.

w Norman Shannon Hall *d* Ted Tetzlaff *ph* Winton C. Hoch, Henry Sharp

Dan O'Herlihy, Patrick Wayne, Yvonne Craig, Dennis Hopper

AAN: song 'Strange Are the Ways of Love' (*m* Dmitri Tiomkin, *ly* Ned Washington)

The Young Lions**
US 1958 167m bw Cinemascope
TCF (Al Lichtman)

World War II adventures of two Americans and a German skiing instructor.
Three strands are loosely interwoven into a would-be modern epic; the result is well mounted and generally absorbing but uneven and decidedly overlong.

w Edward Anhalt, *novel* Irwin Shaw *d* Edward Dmytryk *ph* Joe MacDonald *m* Hugo Friedhofer

Marlon Brando, Montgomery Clift, Dean Martin, Hope Lange, Barbara Rush, May Britt, Maximilian Schell, Lee Van Cleef
'Episodic and overproduced, like a wartime *Grand Hotel.*'—*Pauline Kael, 70s*

AAN: Joe MacDonald; Hugo Friedhofer

The Young Lovers*
GB 1954 96m bw
GFD / Group Films (Anthony Havelock-Allan)
US title: *Chance Meeting*

A US Embassy man in London falls in love with the daughter of an Iron Curtain minister.
Romeo and Juliet, cold war style, quite nicely put together with a thriller climax.

w Robin Estridge, *story* George Tabori *d* Anthony Asquith *ph* Jack Asher *m* Tchaikovsky

Odile Versois, David Knight, David Kossoff, Joseph Tomelty, Paul Carpenter, Theodore Bikel, Jill Adams

'Put down your trumpet, jazz man—I'm in the mood for love!'
Young Man with a Horn*
US 1950 112m bw
Warner (Jerry Wald)
GB title: *Young Man of Music*

The professional and romantic tribulations of a trumpet player.
Overwrought character melodrama based on the life of Bix Beiderbecke; quite absorbing though occasionally risible.

w Carl Foreman, Edmund H. North, *novel* Dorothy Baker *d* Michael Curtiz *ph* Ted McCord *m* Ray Heindorf

Kirk Douglas, Lauren Bacall, Doris Day, Hoagy Carmichael, Juano Hernandez, Jerome Cowan, Mary Beth Hughes, Nestor Paiva

Young Man with Ideas*
US 1952 84m bw
MGM (Gottfried Reinhardt, William H. Wright)

A small-town lawyer tries to better himself in Los Angeles.
Modestly likeable comedy which doesn't add up to much.

w Arthur Sheekman *d* Mitchell Leisen *ph* Joseph Ruttenberg *m* David Rose

Glenn Ford, Ruth Roman, Nina Foch, Denise Darcel, Donna Corcoran, Mary Wickes, Sheldon Leonard

Young Man's Fancy
GB 1939 77m bw

A young Victorian lord avoids an unsuitable match by eloping to Paris. Rather pallid romantic comedy with likeable period detail. Griffith Jones, Anna Lee, Seymour Hicks, Billy Bennett, Edward Rigby, Francis L. Sullivan. Written by Roland Pertwee, Rodney Ackland and E. V. H. Emmett; directed by Robert Stevenson; for Ealing.

Young Mr Lincoln***
US 1939 100m bw
TCF (Kenneth MacGowan)

Abraham Lincoln as a young country lawyer stops a lynching and proves a young man innocent of murder.
Splendid performances and period atmosphere are rather nipped in the bud by second-feature courtroom twists, but this is a marvellous old-fashioned entertainment with its heart in the right place.

w Lamar Trotti *d John Ford* *ph Bert Glennon* *w* Alfred Newman

Henry Fonda, Alice Brady, Marjorie Weaver, Arleen Whelan, Eddie Collins, Richard Cromwell, Donald Meek, Eddie Quillan, Spencer Charters

'A dignified saga of early Lincolniana, paced rather slowly . . . lack of romance interest is one of the prime factors which deter the film from interpreting itself into big box office.'—*Variety*

'Its simple good faith and understanding are an expression of the country's best life that says as much as forty epics.'—*Otis Ferguson*

'Period details are lovingly sketched in—a log splitting contest, a tug of war, a tar barrel rolling match . . .'—*Charles Higham*

'Its source is a womb of popular and national spirit. This could account for its unity, its artistry, its genuine beauty.'—*Sergei Eisenstein*

'A film which indisputably has the right to be called Americana.'—*New York Times*

'In spite of the excitements of a murder, a near-lynching and a crackerjack trial, it remains a character study.'—*New York Sun*

'One of John Ford's most memorable films.'—*Pauline Kael, 70s*

AAN: Lamar Trotti

The Young Mr Pitt*
GB 1942 118m bw
TCF (Edward Black)

Britain's youngest prime minister quells the threat of invasion by Napoleon.
Shapeless and overlong but generally diverting historical pastiche timed as wartime propaganda against Hitler.

w Frank Launder, Sidney Gilliat *d* Carol Reed *ph* Frederick A. Young *m* Charles Williams *ad* Vetchinsky

Robert Donat, Robert Morley, Phyllis Calvert, John Mills, Raymond Lovell, Max Adrian, Felix Aylmer, Albert Lieven

The Young Ones*
GB 1961 108m Technicolor Cinemascope
ABP (Kenneth Harper)
US title: *Wonderful to be Young*

The son of a tycoon starts a youth club and puts on a musical to raise funds.
A shopworn idea is the springboard for a brave try in a field where Britain was presumed to have failed; despite the enthusiasm with which it was greeted at the time, it has dated badly.

w Peter Myers, Ronald Cass *d* Sidney J. Furie *ph* Douglas Slocombe *m* Stanley Black

Cliff Richard, Robert Morley, Carole Grey, Richard O'Sullivan, Melvyn Hayes, Gerald Harper, Robertson Hare

Young People
US 1940 78m bw
TCF (Harry Joe Brown)

Vaudevillians retire to give their daughter a proper upbringing, but find that showbiz is in her blood.
Pleasant but unremarkable comedy-drama with music, marking the end of its star's association with the studio.

w Edwin Blum, Don Ettlinger *d* Allan Dwan *ph* Edward Cronjager *md* Alfred Newman

Shirley Temple, Jack Oakie, Charlotte Greenwood, Arleen Whelan, George Montgomery, Kathleen Howard, Mae Marsh

The Young Philadelphians*
US 1959 136m bw
Warner (producer not credited)
GB title: *The City Jungle*

A forceful young lawyer pushes his way to the top of the snobbish Philadelphia heap despite threats to expose his illegitimacy.
Novel on film, gleamingly done and acted with assurance.

w James Gunn, *novel* The Philadelphian by Richard Powell *d* Vincent Sherman *ph* Harry Stradling *m* Ernest Gold

Paul Newman, Barbara Rush, Alexis Smith, Brian Keith, Billie Burke, John Williams, Otto Kruger, Diane Brewster, Robert Vaughn, Paul Picerni, Robert Douglas

AAN: Harry Stradling; Robert Vaughn

The Young Savages*
US 1961 103m bw
UA / Contemporary (Pat Duggan)

An assistant DA prosecutes three hoodlums for murder but begins to feel that one is not guilty.
Tough, realistic melodrama of the New York slums, with roughhouse climaxes and a political conscience.

w Edward Anhalt, J. P. Miller, *novel* A Matter of Conviction by Evan Hunter *d John Frankenheimer* *ph* Lionel Lindon *m* David Amram

Burt Lancaster, Shelley Winters, John David Chandler, Dina Merrill, Edward Andrews, Telly Savalas

Young Sherlock Holmes
US 1985 109m Technicolor
Paramount / Amblin (Mark Johnson)
GB title: *Young Sherlock Holmes and the Pyramid of Fear*

Holmes and Watson meet as teenage students, and trace some mysterious murders to an eastern cult.
More expensive gimmickry with acres of tedium in between the technical highlights. Nothing for Holmes buffs.

w Chris Columbus *d* Barry Levinson *ph* Stephen Goldblatt *m* Bruce Broughton *pd* Norman Reynolds *ed* Stu Linder

Nicholas Rowe, Alan Cox, Sophie Ward, Anthony Higgins, Freddie Jones, Nigel Stock

'Another Steven Spielberg version of those lamps made from driftwood and coffee tables from redwood burl. It's not art but they all serve their purpose and sell by millions.'—*Variety* (This one was a box-office disappointment.)

The Young Stranger*
US 1957 84m bw
RKO (Stuart Millar)

The 16-year-old son of a film executive gets into trouble with the police.
Reasonably stimulating film of a TV play about the kind of causeless rebel who quickly became a cliché.

w Robert Dozier *d* John Frankenheimer *ph* Robert Planck *m* Leonard Rosenman

James MacArthur, Kim Hunter, James Daly, James Gregory, Whit Bissell

Young Tom Edison*
US 1940 82m bw
MGM (John Considine Jnr)

First of a two-parter (see *Edison the Man*) tracing Edison's first experiments.
Reasonably factual and absorbing junior biopic.

w Bradbury Foote, Dore Schary, Hugo Butler *d* Norman Taurog *ph* Sidney Wagner *m* Edward Ward

Mickey Rooney, Eugene Pallette, George Bancroft, Fay Bainter, Virginia Weidler, Victor Kilian, Lloyd Corrigan

'A picture for all of the people in all of the places.'—*Motion Picture Herald*

Young Warriors
US 1983 103m colour

After the sister of one of them dies after being raped, high-school graduates set themselves up as vigilantes. Dangerous rubbish. Ernest Borgnine, Richard Roundtree, Lynda Day George, James Van Patten, Anne Lockhart, Tom Reilly, Dick Shawn. Written by Lawrence D. Foldes, Russell W. Colgin; directed by Lawrence D. Foldes; for Cannon.
'A lurid mishmash.'—*Jo Imeson, MFB*

The Young Widow
US 1946 100m bw
UA / Hunt Stromberg

The widow of a World War II flier returns to the Virginia farm where they had spent happy hours.
Glum sudser with talent all at sea.

w Richard Macaulay, Margaret Buell Wilder, *novel* Clarissa Fairchild Cushman *d* Edwin L. Marin *ph* Lee Garmes *m* Carmen Dragon *pd* Nicolai Remisoff

Jane Russell, Louis Hayward, Faith Domergue, Marie Wilson, Kent Taylor, Penny Singleton, Connie Gilchrist, Cora Witherspoon

Young Winston**
GB 1972 157m Eastmancolor Panavision
Columbia / Open Road / Hugh French (Carl Foreman)

The adventurous life of Winston Churchill up to his becoming an MP.
Generally engaging if lumpy film which switches too frequently from action to family drama to politics to character study and is not helped by irritating directorial tricks.

w Carl Foreman, *book* My Early Life by Winston Churchill *d* Richard Attenborough *ph* Gerry Turpin *m* Alfred Ralston *pd* Don Ashton, Geoffrey Drake

Simon Ward, Robert Shaw, Anne Bancroft, Jack Hawkins, Ian Holm, *Anthony Hopkins*, John Mills, Patrick Magee, Edward Woodward

AAN: Carl Foreman

Young Wives' Tale
GB 1951 79m bw

A playwright and his slaphappy wife share a house with a super-efficient couple. Very mild but palatable comedy set 'at the wrong end of St John's Wood'. Joan Greenwood, Nigel Patrick, Derek Farr, Guy Middleton, Athene Seyler, Helen Cherry, Audrey Hepburn, Irene Handl. Written by Anne Burnaby, from the play by Ronald Jeans; directed by Henry Cass; for ABPC.

Young Woodley
GB 1929 79m bw

A schoolboy falls in love with his teacher's wife. Modest early talkie version of a play thought mildly shocking at the time. Madeleine Carroll, Frank Lawton, Sam Livesey, Gerald Rawlinson, Billy Milton. Written by John Van Druten and Victor Kendall, from the play by John Van Druten; directed by Thomas Bentley; for BIP. (A silent version made earlier in the same year, with Marjorie Hume and Robin Irvine, was never released.)

Youngblood
US 1985 109m Metrocolor

Romances of a young hockey star, for those interested; it turned out that there weren't many. Rob Lowe, Cynthia Gibb, Patrick Swayze, Ed Lauter, Jim Youngs. Written and directed by Peter Markle; for Guber–Peters / United Artists.

Youngblood Hawke
US 1964 137m bw
Warner (Delmer Daves)

A Kentucky truck driver becomes a successful novelist and is spoiled by New York success. Absurdly archetypal soap opera from a bestseller, spilling over with every imaginable cliché; some of its excesses are glossily entertaining.

w Delmer Daves, *novel* Herman Wouk *d* Delmer Daves *ph* Charles Lawton *m* Max Steiner

James Franciscus, Genevieve Page, Suzanne Pleshette, Eva Gabor, *Mary Astor*, Lee Bowman, Edward Andrews, John Emery, Don Porter

The Younger Brothers
US 1949 76m Technicolor

A whitewashed version of the career of the legendary outlaws, who wind up expecting pardons; otherwise routine sagebrush stuff. Wayne Morris, Janis Paige, Bruce Bennett, Geraldine Brooks, Robert Hutton, Alan Hale, Fred Clark. Written by Edna Anhalt; directed by Edwin L. Marin; for Saul Elkins / Warner.

The Youngest Profession
US 1943 82m bw
MGM (B. F. Ziedman)

Teenage autograph hounds cause trouble at the MGM studio.
Innocuous comedy with guest stars.

w George Oppenheimer, Charles Lederer, Leonard Spiegelgass, *book* Lillian Day *d* Edward Buzzell *ph* Charles Lawton *m* David Snell

Virginia Weidler, Jean Porter, Edward Arnold, John Carroll, Agnes Moorehead, Greer Garson, William Powell, Lana Turner, Walter Pidgeon, Robert Taylor

Your Witness*
GB 1950 100m bw
Warner / Coronado (Joan Harrison)
US title: *Eye Witness*

An American lawyer comes to an English village to defend a war buddy on a murder charge.
Interesting but ineffective blend of comedy and courtroom procedure intended to contrast English and American ways.

w Hugo Butler, Ian Hunter, William Douglas Home *d* Robert Montgomery *ph* Gerald Gibbs *m* Malcolm Arnold

Robert Montgomery, Leslie Banks, Patricia Cutts, Felix Aylmer, Andrew Cruickshank, Harcourt Williams, Jenny Laird, Michael Ripper

You're a Big Boy Now*
US 1967 96m Eastmancolor
Warner Seven Arts (William Fadiman)

A young assistant librarian discovers girls.
Freewheeling semi-surrealist comedy with exhilarating moments and the inevitable letdowns associated with this kind of campy high style.

wd Francis Ford Coppola, *novel* David Benedictus *ph Andy Laszlo* *m* Bob Prince

Peter Kastner, Elizabeth Hartman, Geraldine Page, Julie Harris, Rip Torn, Tony Bill, Karen Black, Michael Dunn

AAN: Geraldine Page

You're a Lucky Fellow, Mr Smith
US 1943 63m bw

A girl must marry quickly in order to secure her inheritance. Very light musical support. Allan Jones, Evelyn Ankers, Billie Burke, David Bruce, Patsy O'Connor, Stanley Clements. Written by Lawrence Riley, Ben Narzman, Louis Lantz; directed by Felix Feist; for Edward Lilley / Universal.

You're a Sweetheart
US 1937 96m bw
Universal (B. G. De Sylva)

A Broadway star suffers from her press agent's bright ideas.
Muffed musical with all concerned ill at ease with below par material.

w Monte Brice, Charles Grayson *d* David Butler *ph* George Robinson *md* Charles Previn *songs* various

Alice Faye, George Murphy, Ken Murray, William Gargan, Frances Hunt, Frank Jenks, Andy Devine, Charles Winninger, Donald Meek

'Just what the doctor ordered for the holiday first runs . . . enough entertainers for two shows.'—*Variety*

You're Darn Tootin'***
US 1929 20m bw silent

Two musicians get into trouble at work, in their digs and in the street. Star comedy which though early in their teaming shows Stan and Ollie at their best in a salt shaker routine and in a surreal pants-ripping contest. Laurel and Hardy, Agnes Steele. Written by H. M. Walker; directed by Edgar Kennedy; for Hal Roach.

You're in the Army Now**
US 1941 79m bw
Warner (Ben Stoloff)

Two incompetent vacuum cleaner salesmen accidentally join the army.
An excellent vehicle for two star comedians who have often suffered from poor material, with a silent-comedy-style climax involving a house on wheels.

w Paul Gerard Smith, George Beatty *d* Lewis Seiler *ph* James Van Trees *m* Howard Jackson

Jimmy Durante, Phil Silvers, Donald MacBride, Jane Wyman, Regis Toomey

You're in the Navy Now*
US 1951 93m bw
TCF (Fred Kohlmar)
aka: *USS Teakettle*

Trouble results when the navy instals steam turbines in an experimental patrol craft.
Amusing service comedy with good script touches and capable performances.

w Richard Murphy *d* Henry Hathaway *ph* Joe MacDonald *m* Cyril Mockridge

Gary Cooper, Millard Mitchell, Jane Greer, Eddie Albert, John McIntire, Ray Collins, Harry Von Zell, Jack Webb, Richard Erdman

You're My Everything*
US 1949 94m Technicolor
TCF (Lamar Trotti)

A Boston socialite marries a hoofer and becomes a movie star.

Pleasant twenties comedy with good period detail and lively performances.

w Lamar Trotti, Will Hays Jnr *d* Walter Lang *ph* Arthur E. Arling *m* Alfred Newman

Anne Baxter, Dan Dailey, Anne Revere, Stanley Ridges, Shari Robinson, Henry O'Neill, Selena Royle, Alan Mowbray, Buster Keaton

You're Never Too Young
US 1955 103m Technicolor Vistavision
Paramount / Hal B. Wallis (Paul Jones)

An apprentice barber on the run from a murderer poses as a 12-year-old child to travel half fare.
Unattractive revamping of *The Major and the Minor* (qv), with the star team trying too obviously to make bricks with inferior straw.

w Sidney Sheldon *d* Norman Taurog *ph* Daniel L. Fapp *m* Arthur Schwarz

Dean Martin, Jerry Lewis, Diana Lynn, Nina Foch, Raymond Burr, Veda Ann Borg

You're Only Young Once see The Hardy Family

You're Only Young Twice
GB 1952 81m bw
Group Three (Terry Bishop)

The puritanical head of a Scottish university is laid low by circumstance and his own folly.
Misfire eccentric comedy which deserves marks for trying but fails to amuse.

w Reginald Beckwith, Lindsay Galloway, Terry Bishop, *play* What Say They by James Bridie *d* Terry Bishop *ph* Jo Jago

Duncan Macrae, Charles Hawtrey, Joseph Tomelty, Patrick Barr, Diane Hart, Robert Urquhart

You're Telling Me*
US 1934 66m bw
Paramount

A small-town inventor meets a princess and makes the social grade.
Meaninglessly-titled star vehicle which is often defiantly unamusing but does include the famous golf routine.

w Walter de Leon, Paul M. Jones *d* Erle C. Kenton *ph* Alfred Gilks *m* Arthur Johnston

W. C. Fields, Larry 'Buster' Crabbe, Joan Marsh, Adrienne Ames, Louise Carter

'The kind of comedy that Chaplin used to do in two reels, but stretched out like Carnera's suspenders to run an even six.'—*Variety*

Yours Mine and Ours*
US 1968 111m Technicolor
UA / Desilu / Walden (Robert F. Blumofe)

A widower with nine children marries a widow with eight, and they settle in an old San Francisco house.
Generally appealing comedy, based on fact and well suited to its stars.

w Mel Shavelson, Mort Lachman *d* Mel Shavelson *ph* Charles Wheeler *m* Fred Karlin

Lucille Ball, Henry Fonda, Van Johnson

Youth Runs Wild
US 1944 67m bw

Indifferent parents are responsible for the problems of teenagers. Dreary little sermon from the unit which produced semi-classic horrors. Bonita Granville, Kent Smith, Jean Brooks, Glenn Vernon, Arthur Shields. Written by John Fante, Herbert Kline; directed by Mark Robson; for Val Lewton / RKO.

Youth Takes a Fling
US 1938 77m bw

A reluctant truck driver is chased by a department store salesgirl. Mildy scatty comedy which failed to ring the bell. Joel McCrea, Andrea Leeds, Frank Jenks, Dorothea Kent, Isabel Jeans, Virginia Grey, Grant Mitchell, Willie Best. Written by Myles Connelly; directed by Archie Mayo; for Joe Pasternak / Universal. 'Good standard entertainment with many light and diverting passages.'—*Variety*

Z***
France / Algeria 1968 125m Eastmancolor
Reggane / ONCIC / Jacques Pérrin

A leading opposition MP is murdered at a rally. The police are anxious to establish the event as an accident, but the examining magistrate proves otherwise.
An exciting police suspense drama which also recalls events under the Greek colonels and was therefore highly fashionable for a while both as entertainment and as a political *roman à clef*.

w Costa-Gavras, Jorge Semprun, novel Vassili Vassilikos *d Costa-Gavras ph* Raoul Coutard *m* Mikis Theodorakis

Jean-Louis Trintignant, Jacques Pérrin, Yves Montand, François Périer, Irene Papas, Charles Denner

AAN: best picture; direction

'It will blow your mind!'
Zabriskie Point
US 1969 112m Metrocolor Panavision
MGM / Carlo Ponti

A rebellious Los Angeles student steals a private airplane, meets an aimless girl, and finds a revelation in Death Valley . . .
Highly self-indulgent and unattractive fantasy about escape from the crudities of our over-civilized world. An expensive failure and an awful warning of what happens if you give an arty director carte blanche.

w Michelangelo Antonioni, Fred Gardner, Sam Shepard, Tonino Guerra, Clare Peploe *d* Michelangelo Antonioni *ph* Alfio Contini *m* pop songs

Mark Frechette, Daria Halprin, Rod Taylor, Paul Fix

'Not even a good tourist's notebook . . . from the choice of Death Valley as a symbol of American civilization to the inclusion of gag signs on bar-room walls to the shots of garish billboards, this film sticks to the surface, stranded.'—*Stanley Kauffman*

'A huge, jerry-built, crumbling ruin of a movie.'—*Pauline Kael, New Yorker*

'A small, sad shambles of a film that has obviously been salvaged from a larger shambles. Bad enough to give anti-Americanism a bad name.'—*Joseph Morgenstern, Newsweek*

'He has tried to make a serious movie and hasn't even achieved a beach party level of insight.'—*Roger Ebert*

Zandy's Bride
US 1974 116m Technicolor Panavision
Warner (Harry Matofsky)

Life for a frontier family.
Dour semi-western.

w Marc Norman, *novel* The Stranger by Lillian Bos Ross *d* Joan Troell *ph* Jordan Cronenweth *m* Fred Karlin

Gene Hackman, Liv Ullmann, Eileen Heckart, Harry Dean Stanton, Joe Santos, Frank Cady

Zanzibar
US 1940 69m bw

European powers both want the sacred skull of an African chieftain, but so does a local tribe. Adventure nonsense patched together with stock shots, including a volcanic finale. Lola Lane, James Craig, Eduardo Ciannelli, Tom Fadden, Henry Victor, Samuel S. Hinds. Written by Maurice Tombragel and Maurice Wright; directed by Harold Schuster; for Warren Douglas / Universal.

Zapped!
US 1982 98m CFI

A high-school boffin discovers his own telekinetic powers, by which he is able to tear everyone's clothes off at the senior prom. Mild adolescent smut, half-way between *Porky's* and the unbearable Disney comedies of the sixties. Scott Baio, Willie Aames, Robert Mandan, Scatman Crothers. Written by Bruce Rubin, Robert J. Rosenthal; directed by Robert J. Rosenthal; for Thunder Associates.

Zarak*
GB 1956 99m Technicolor Cinemascope
Columbia / Warwick (Phil C. Samuel)

An Afghan outlaw finally saves a British officer at the cost of his own life.
Box-office actioner, shot in Morocco with a weird cast and the help of old movie clips.

w Richard Maibaum *d* Terence Young *2nd unit* Yakima Canutt *ph* John Wilcox, Ted Moore, Cyril Knowles *m* William Alwyn *ad* John Box

Victor Mature, Michael Wilding, Anita Ekberg, Bonar Colleano, Finlay Currie, Bernard Miles, Eunice Gayson, Peter Illing, Frederick Valk, André Morell

Zardoz
GB 1973 105m De Luxe Panavision
TCF / John Boorman

Life in 2293, when the earth has become wasteland and a mass of Brutals are ruled by a few Exterminators who have both memory and intelligence.
Pompous, boring fantasy for the so-called intelligentsia.

wd John Boorman *ph* Geoffrey Unsworth *m* David Munrow *pd* Anthony Pratt

Sean Connery, Charlotte Rampling, John Alderton

'A glittering cultural trash pile . . the most gloriously fatuous movie since *The Oscar*.'—*New Yorker*

Zaza
US 1938 83m bw
Paramount (Albert Lewin)

A 1904 French chanteuse is in love with a married aristocrat.
Rather flat period romantic drama with interesting credits.

w Zoe Atkins, *play* Pierre Berton, Charles Simon *d* George Cukor *ph* Charles Lang *songs* Frank Loesser, Frederick Hollander

Claudette Colbert, Herbert Marshall, Bert Lahr, Constance Collier, Helen Westley, Genevieve Tobin, Walter Catlett, Rex O'Malley

'Fine production with hefty woman-appeal.'—*Variety*

† The original David Belasco stage production made Mrs Leslie Carter famous. Silent film versions starred Pauline Frederick in 1915 and Gloria Swanson in 1923.

Zazie dans le Métro**
France 1960 88m Eastmancolor
Nouvelles Editions (Irène Leriche)

A naughty little girl has a day in Paris and causes chaos.
Inventive little comedy which almost turns into a French *Hellzapoppin*, with everybody chasing or fighting everybody else.

wd Louis Malle, novel Raymond Queneau *ph* Henri Raichi *m* Fiorenzo Capri

Catherine Demongeot, Philippe Noiret, Vittorio Caprioli

Zebra in the Kitchen
US 1965 93m Metrocolor
MGM / Ivan Tors

A young boy tries to improve the lot of zoo animals.
Pleasing family film.

w Art Arthur *d* Ivan Tors *ph* Lamar Boren

Jay North, Martin Milner, Andy Devine, Joyce Meadows, Jim Davis

A Zed and Two Noughts
GB 1985 115m colour

Quite indescribable surrealist farrago which seems principally to concern zoo images, with mankind sometimes behind the bars. At least Dali and Bunuel got through their private fantasies in half the time. Andrea Ferreol, Brian Deacon, Eric Deacon, Frances Barber, Joss Ackland. Written and directed by Peter Greenaway; for Allarts/VPRO/BFI/Channel Four. 'Cinema is far too rich and capable a medium to be merely left to the storytellers.'—*Peter Greenaway*

Zee and Co.*
GB 1971 109m colour
Columbia / Zee Films (Kastner–Ladd–Kanter)
US title: *X, Y and Zee*

A successful architect battles with his termagant wife and seeks an affair.
Overwritten but entertaining sexual melodrama about an absolute bitch. The flow of bad language was new at the time.

w Edna O'Brien *d* Brian G. Hutton *ph* Billy Williams *m* Stanley Myers *ad* Peter Mullins

Elizabeth Taylor, Michael Caine, Susannah York, Margaret Leighton, John Standing

'Miss Taylor is rapidly turning into a latterday Marie Dressler.'—*Tom Milne*

'A slice-of-jet-set-life nightmare far beyond the dreams of the piggiest male chauvinist . . . the distinction of this film is that its characters are repulsive, its style vulgar, its situations beyond belief and its dialogue moronic.'—*Judith Crist*

Zelig**
US 1983 79m (including about 5m of credits) bw/colour
Orion / Rollins-Joffe (Robert Greenhut)

A parody documentary tracing a chameleon-like nonentity who contrives to have been associated with all the major events of the twentieth century.
The central idea is more elusive than appealing, and the mid-section of psychiatric consultation is downright dull, but considerable amusement derives from the technical trickery which puts Woody Allen in pictorial association with Hitler, Roosevelt and Eugene O'Neill. In all, an after-dinner treat for the intellectuals.

w,d Woody Allen ph Gordon Willis m Dick Hyman *pd* Mel Bourne

Woody Allen, Mia Farrow

'We can all admire the brilliance and economy with which it is made. But is it funny enough? I take leave to doubt it.'—*Derek Malcolm, Guardian*

'*Citizen Kane* miraculously transformed into side-splitting comedy.'—*New York Times*

'The movie is a technical masterpiece, but in artistic and comic terms, only pretty good.'—*Roger Ebert*

AAN: cinematography; costume design

Zenobia
US 1939 83m bw
Hal Roach
GB title: *Elephants Never Forget*

A small-town doctor finds himself looking after a performing elephant.
Very mild small-town comedy made during a break-up in the Laurel and Hardy contract.

w Corey Ford, Arnold Belgard, Walter De Leon *d* Gordon Douglas *ph* Karl Struss *m* Marvin Hatley

Oliver Hardy, Harry Langdon, Jean Parker, Billie Burke, Alice Brady, James Ellison, Stepin Fetchit, Hattie McDaniel

Zeppelin*
GB 1971 97m Technicolor Panavision
Warner / Getty and Fromkess (Owen Crump)

In 1915, the British need to steal secrets from the zeppelin works at Friedrichshafen.
Undistinguished but entertaining period actioner with adequate spectacle but wooden performances.

w Arthur Rowe, Donald Churchill *d* Etienne Périer *ph* Alan Hume *m* Roy Budd *sp* Wally Veevers

Michael York, Elke Sommer, Peter Carsten, Marius Goring, Anton Diffring, Andrew Keir, Rupert Davies

Zéro de Conduite**
France 1933 45m approx bw
Gaumont / Franco Film / Aubert

Boys return from the holiday to a nasty little boarding school, where the headmaster is an unpleasant dwarf and all the staff are hateful. A revolution breaks out . . .
A clear forerunner of *If* . . . and one of the most famous of surrealist films, though it pales beside Bunuel and is chiefly valuable for being funny.

w,d Jean Vigo ph Boris Kaufman *m* Maurice Jaubert

Jean Dasté, Louis Lefébvre, Gilbert Pruchon, le nain Delphin

'One of the most influential films ever made.'—*New Yorker, 1978*

Zero Hour!
US 1957 83m bw
(Paramount) Bartlett / Champion (John Champion)

Half the passengers and all the crew of a jet plane are stricken with food poisoning and a shell-shocked ex-fighter pilot has to land the plane.
Adequate air melodrama with a premise which later served for *Terror in the Sky* (TV) and *Airport 75*.

w Arthur Hailey, John Champion, Hall Bartlett, *teleplay* Flight into Danger by Arthur Hailey *d* Hall Bartlett *ph* John F. Warren *m* Ted Dale

Dana Andrews, Linda Darnell, Sterling Hayden, Elroy Hirsch, Jerry Paris

Zero Population Growth
US 1971 96m Eastmancolor
Sagittarius (Thomas F. Madigan)

In the 21st century there is a death penalty for having children, but a young couple defy the authorities.
Good sci-fi quickly develops into sticky sentimentality.

w Max Ehrlich, Frank de Felita *d* Michael Campus *ph* Michael Reed *m* Jonathan Hodge *pd* Tony Masters

Oliver Reed, Geraldine Chaplin, Diane Cilento, Don Gordon, Bill Nagy, Aubrey Woods

Ziegfeld Follies**
US 1944 (released 1946) 110m Technicolor
MGM (Arthur Freed)

In heaven, Florenz Ziegfeld dreams up one last spectacular revue.
A rather airless all-star entertainment in which the comedy suffers from the lack of an audience but some of the production numbers are magnificently stylish.

w various *d Vincente Minnelli ph George Folsey, Charles Rosher m* various *md* Lennie Hayton *ad* Cedric Gibbons, Merrill Pye, Jack Martin Smith

Fred Astaire, Lucille Ball, Bunin's Puppets, William Powell, Jimmy Durante, Edward Arnold, *Fannie Brice*, Lena Horne, Lucille Bremer, Esther Williams, Judy Garland, *Red Skelton, Gene Kelly*, James Melton, Hume Cronyn, Victor Moore, Marion Bell

'Between opening and closing is packed a prodigious amount of material, some of which is frankly not deserving of the lavish treatment accorded it.'—*Film Daily*

'The fastidious are advised to head for the lobby while Kathryn Grayson sings 'There's Beauty Everywhere' against magenta foam skies.'—*Pauline Kael, 70s*

Ziegfeld Girl*
US 1941 131m bw
MGM (Pandro S. Berman)

The professional and romantic problems of Ziegfeld chorus girls.
Adequate big-budget drama with music.

w Marguerite Roberts, Sonya Levien *d* Robert Z. Leonard *ph* Ray June *m* Herbert Stothart *ch* Busby Berkeley *songs* various

James Stewart, Judy Garland, Hedy Lamarr, Lana Turner, Tony Martin, Jackie Cooper, Ian Hunter, *Charles Winninger*, *Al Shean*, Edward Everett Horton, Philip Dorn, Paul Kelly, Eve Arden, Dan Dailey, Fay Holden, Felix Bressart

'Heaping portions of show life in the opulent days of Flo Ziegfeld, the man who wanted bigger and better staircases.'—*C. A. Lejeune*

Zigzag*
US 1970 104m Metrocolor Panavision
MGM / Freeman–Enders
GB title: *False Witness*

A dying man frames himself for an unsolved murder so that the reward money, claimed under another name, will go to his wife.
Complex thriller which sustains itself pretty well most of the way, but lacks humour and character.

w John T. Kelley *d* Richard A. Colla *ph* James A. Crabe *m* Oliver Nelson

George Kennedy, Anne Jackson, Eli Wallach, Steve Ihnat, William Marshall, Joe Maross

The Zombies of Mora Tau
US 1957 71m bw

A diver plans to salvage a subterranean West African treasure; but it is guarded by zombies. Modest addition to the walking dead cycle. Gregg Palmer, Allison Hayes, Autumn Russell, Morris Ankrum. Written by Raymond T. Marcus; directed by Edward Cahn; for Sam Katzman / Columbia. (GB title: *The Dead That Walk.*)

Zombies of the Stratosphere
US 1952 bw serial: 12 eps

Invading rockets are intercepted by the Interplanetary Patrol and turn out to contain supernatural beings. Lively serial antics. Judd Holdren, Aline Towne; Wilson Wood, Lane Bradford, Leonard Nimoy. Directed by Fred Brannon; for Republic.

Zombies on Broadway
US 1945 70m bw

Press agents seek a real zombie for the opening of a new night club . . . and a mad professor provides one. Knockabout comedy-thriller, just tolerable for addicts of the genre. Wally Brown, Alan Carney, Bela Lugosi, Anne Jeffreys, Sheldon Leonard. Written by Lawrence Kimble; directed by Gordon Douglas; for Ben Stoloff / RKO.

Zoo in Budapest*
US 1933 83m bw
Fox (Jesse Lasky)

An orphan waif runs away to live with a zookeeper.
Curious little romance remembered for its luminescent photography.

w Dan Totheroh, Louise Long, Rowland V. Lee *d* Rowland V. Lee *ph Lee Garmes*

Loretta Young, Gene Raymond, O. P. Heggie, Wally Albright, Paul Fix

'Appeal for all classes . . . a subject of great photographic and pictorial beauty.—*Variety*

'Richly composed impressionistic images, assisted by highly imaginative use of sound and background music, create a poem that Murnau himself would have envied.'—*NFT, 1971*

Zorba the Greek**
GB 1964 142m bw
TCF / Rockley / Cacoyannis

A young English writer in Crete is befriended by a huge gregarious Greek who comes to dominate his life.
A mainly enjoyable character study of a larger-than-life character, this film made famous by its music does not really hang together dramatically and has several melodramatic excrescences.

wd Michael Cacoyannis, novel Nikos Kazantzakis *ph Walter Lassally m Mikis Theodorakis*

Anthony Quinn, Alan Bates, Lila Kedrova, Irene Papas

'For all its immense length, the film never gets down to a clear statement of its theme, or comes within measuring distance of its vast pretensions.'—*Brenda Davies*

AA: Walter Lassally; Lila Kedrova
AAN: best picture; Michael Cacoyannis (as writer and director); Anthony Quinn

Zorro Rides Again
US 1937 bw serial: 12 eps

A masked stranger helps the California–Tucatan railroad against the predations of a ruthless industrialist. Solidly carpentered serial. John Carroll, Helen Christian, Noah Beery, Duncan Renaldo, Nigel de Brulier. Directed by William Witney and John English; for Republic.

'Zany! Zexy! Zensational!'
Zorro the Gay Blade
US 1981 93m De Luxe
Melvin Simon (George Hamilton, C. O. Erickson)

Zorro, the masked avenger, not only pretends to be a fop but is one. Luckily he has a twin brother.
Abysmal attempt to do for Zorro what *Love at First Bite* did for Dracula.

w Hal Dresner *d* Peter Medak *ph* John A. Alonzo *m* Max Steiner themes

George Hamilton, Lauren Hutton, Brenda Vaccaro, Ron Leibman, James Booth

Zorro's Fighting Legion
US 1939 bw serial: 12 eps

While Don Diego masquerades as Zorro, his adversary in the San Mendolita Mines masquerades as a god named Don-deoro. Serial with most of the expected elements. Reed Hadley, Sheila Darcy, William Corson, Leander de Cordova. Directed by William Witney and John English; for Republic.

Zorro's Black Whip
US 1944 bw serial: 12 eps

In 1889 Idaho, sinister forces are opposed to the coming of law and order. Saturday morning serial adventures, quite adequate to their purpose. George J. Lewis, Linda Stirling, Lucien Littlefield, Francis McDonald. Directed by Spencer Bennet and Wallace Grissell; for Republic.

Zotz!
US 1962 87m bw
Columbia / William Castle

A professor finds a rare coin with occult powers.
Footling farce patterned after *The Absent-Minded Professor*. Poor, to say the least.

w Ray Russell, *novel* Walter Karig *d* William Castle *ph* Gordon Avil *m* Bernard Green

Tom Poston, Fred Clark, Jim Backus, Cecil Kellaway, Margaret Dumont

Zulu*
GB 1964 135m Technirama
Paramount / Diamond (Stanley Baker, Cyril Endfield)

In 1879 British soldiers stand fast against the Zulus at Rorke's Drift.
Standard period heroics, well presented and acted.

w John Prebble, Cy Endfield *d* Cy Endfield *ph* Stephen Dade *m* John Barry

Stanley Baker, Jack Hawkins, *Michael Caine*, Ulla Jacobsson, James Booth, Nigel Green, Ivor Emmanuel, Paul Daneman

Zulu Dawn
US / Netherlands 1979 117m Technicolor Panavision
Samarkand / Zulu Dawn NV (Barrie Saint Clair)

In 1878, 1,300 British troops are massacred at Isandlwhana.
Confusing historical action adventure, very similar to *Zulu* but failing in its cross-cut attempt to show both sides.

w Cy Enfield, Anthony Storey *d* Douglas Hickox *ph* Ousama Rawi *m* Elmer Bernstein *pd* John Rosewarne

Burt Lancaster, Denholm Elliott, Peter O'Toole, John Mills, Simon Ward, Nigel Davenport, Michael Jayston, Ronald Lacey, Freddie Jones, Christopher Cazenove, Ronald Pickup, Anna Calder-Marshall

Title Changes

The reason for changing any title is to make it more attractive at the box office. Even a famous play or novel may not be the right bait for film fans; so *The Private Ear and the Public Eye* became *The Pad and How to Use It*, *Orpheus Descending* turned into *The Fugitive Kind*, and *The Clansman* emerged as *The Birth of a Nation*. Even when a film has been well publicized during production, the title can be changed at the whim of the producer whenever he feels that what he has on his hands is by no means a one-hundred-per-cent copper-bottomed winner. Some very well-known films were rechristened at the very last moment. *Seven Brides for Seven Brothers* was made as *Sobbin' Women*, and *Three Coins in the Fountain* as *We Believe in Love. The Bad and the Beautiful* was almost released as *Tribute to a Bad Man*, a title which was later used for a different movie. And *I Love Louisa*, which has never in fact been used, was the working title for no fewer than three well-known movies: *Dancing in the Dark, The Band Wagon* and *What a Way to Go*.

Sometimes the new title seems weaker than the original, but decisions of this kind are far from easy, being usually taken at fraught moments. *Dr Goldfoot and the Sex Machine*, for instance, had to be changed because a real Dr Goldfoot protested; so it became *Dr G and the Bikini Machine*. For years British producers had been toying with a rustic love story called *Bats with Baby Faces*, but during production it was finally decided that people would take the film for a horror story, so it became, ill-advisedly, *Sky West and Crooked*; and after a fairly calamitous British release it was changed again for world markets into *Gypsy Girl*. A popular black comedy started production as *My Last Duchess*; this was felt to be too subtle to convey the theme of light-hearted wife murder, so the title became successively, in descending order of wit, *Arrivederci Baby*, *You Just Kill Me*, and *You're Dead Right*; but before release it reverted to *Arrivederci Baby* in most of the world and *See You Later Baby* for the apparently ignorant British. Then at the last minute it was shown to Londoners as *Drop Dead Darling*. Perhaps the most desperate last-minute change happened to *Morituri*, a title which had had world-wide publicity up to and including press shows. Suddenly the chill word came from New York: patrons were staying away from the movie like flies, ninety-nine per cent of them being unable to understand the title, and the few who could considering it less than entertaining to be reminded of their own mortality. So Fox changed the title, in one of the most drastic and expensive publicity actions of recent years; but so as to retain any goodwill they had accumulated for the old title, they incorporated it, with one of the clumsiest results ever perpetrated on the public: *The Saboteur, Code Name Morituri*.

Some other examples of re-thinking during production:

A modernization of *Volpone* began, unpromisingly, as *The Tale of a Fox*, brightened somewhat into *Anyone for Venice?*, and was released as *The Honey*

Pot; but after poor business it was shown in the States as *It Comes Up Murder*. The film of Tennessee Williams' *The Milk Train Doesn't Stop Here Any More* was announced at first as *Boom*, then *Goforth*, then *Sunburst*, before *Boom* was finally revived and given the accolade. *A Suitable Case for Treatment*, a title utterly unappealing except to the handful of TV cognoscenti, was personalized into *Morgan*, the name of the leading character – with the old title in small print underneath, presumably for luck.

When AIP began to film H. P. Lovecraft's *The House at the End of the World*, and publicized it under this title, it seemed that we might for once get a fairly subtle horror film. Alas, the treatment was more fitted to the titles under which the film was released: in Britain *Monster of Terror*, in America *Die, Monster, Die*. Then there was a film announced in Britain as *Jules Verne's Rocket to the Moon*, and in the US as *P. T. Barnum's Rocket to the Moon*. Owing to poor business the American title was abandoned and became *Those Fantastic Flying Fools*; this too was unsuccessful and the distributor finally settled on *Blast-Off*.

Incidentally, the notion of attaching author or director to a film title becomes popular occasionally, as in *Billy Rose's Jumbo*, *Sidney Sheldon's Bloodline*, and *Jacqueline Susann's Once is Not Enough*. They say it lost favour after Joshua Logan tried to have his new film released as *Joshua Logan's Fanny*.

When the Rank Organisation decided some years ago to film Rumer Godden's novel *An Episode of Sparrows*, about children who steal from church to feed starving animals, they made a most pleasing job of it. But John Davis as distributor had not much faith in John Davis as producer, and the film was released under the title *Innocent Sinners*, with a highly dubious publicity campaign which left no doubt that the sin involved was sexual. It is almost pleasing to record that the film failed at the box-office, whereas under its original title, with a tasteful campaign, it would certainly have had reasonable if limited success.

A 1969 ad in *Variety* spoofed this kind of indecision about titling a film; it purported to be a dialogue between Rowan and Martin of *Laugh-In*:

R: Guess what, Dick! MGM have taken a super survey to find a title for our new flick.

M: Well, ring my chimes! I thought it was called *The Strange Case of the @%!£&?*

R: No, dum-dum. That was last week's title. Only 9,673 people favoured it.

M: My aunt loves *Who Killed Cock Robin?*

R: 11,089 people voted for that, but we think your aunt stuffed the ballot box again.

M: My favourite is *The Farquahar Case*. Look that up in your Funk and Wagnalls.

R: It pulled very strong in the mid-west, with 18,909 votes.

M: I'll drink to that. So it's our new title?

R: No. And it's not *One of Our Bippies is Missing* either, even though it got 27,000½ votes.

M: ½? Sounds like one of our producers voted for it. Anyway, what *is* the new title? *The Monster Who Ate Beautiful Downtown Burbank*?

R: The new title is *The Maltese Bippy*. Leo the Lion roared his approval of it . . . and when he roars, you listen!

M: You bet your sweet bippy!

(And what, you may ask, happened to *The Maltese Bippy*? It was so poor that both theatrical and television buyers turned it down.)

Sometimes a film is hauled back and retitled after its first release, as a last trump card when nothing else will save the situation. John Huston's enterprising but ill-fated *Freud* was touted as *The Secret Passion*, or in some cases, even more meaninglessly, as *Freud – The Secret Passion*. (In no guise did it take money.) Billy Wilder's mordant *Ace in the Hole* reached the sticks as *The Big Carnival*. Danny Kaye's stolid-sounding *The Inspector General* was later corrected to *Happy Times* (the title of one of its songs). In America *Mr Topaze* became *I Like Money*, and *The Sea Wall* was shown as *This Angry Age* (a title justified by nothing in the movie). When William Dieterle's superb *All That Money Can Buy* failed to please the multitude, it was variously tried out as *The Devil and Daniel Webster* and *Daniel and the Devil*. A British drama called *The Tall Headlines* was about the effect on a family when its eldest son is hanged for murder. The title was commercially a non-starter, so the film was withdrawn and later revived under the utterly cheating tag *The Frightened Bride*. And a more recent ragbag of sensations which failed as *Our Incredible World* quickly re-emerged as *The Mystery and the Pleasure*.

Novels keep their original titles fairly seldom, being designed to attract a much more specialized public than the film version must command. But there may be other reasons. One presumes that Launder and Gilliat might have kept *That Uncertain Feeling* as the title of their adaptation from Kingsley Amis' book, had it not been for the constant reissues of an old Lubitsch film of the same name and for the more recent releases of similar-sounding films such as *That Certain Feeling* and *This Happy Feeling*. So they thought up a new joke and called it *Only Two Can Play*. A unique reason for not filming one novel under its original title was that the censor forbade it: so notorious in 1932 was William Faulkner's *Sanctuary* that it had to be filmed as *The Story of Temple Drake*. (Thirty years later it was remade under the original title.)

Very often a wily distributor with reissues to sell will alter the titles in the hope of persuading exhibitors that he is offering something new. A classic reissue bill of a few years back, presented as an all-action war show, consisted of two seriously-intentioned films with hardly a battle scene between them: *The Men*, which dealt with the hospital problems of paralysed veterans, became *Battle Stripe*, and *North Star*, Goldwyn's propaganda tribute to the Russian peasants in World War II, was carefully re-edited to avoid any suspicion of communist leanings and emerged as *Armoured Attack*. Another shining example of a publicist having an eye to the main chance dates from 1942, when President Roosevelt was asked to name the base from which US planes had bombed Tokyo. The President, who knew his movies, smiled and said: 'Shangri-La'. Columbia Pictures promptly put out a film called *The Lost Horizon at Shangri-La*, an edited version of their five-year-old classic *Lost Horizon*.

One British purveyor of Continental 'X' attractions hit upon the bright idea of reviving them under their original foreign titles if an English title was previously used – and sometimes vice versa. The advantage of this is that any patron complaining of having paid to see *Le Repos du Guerrier* and getting a second helping of *Warrior's Rest* has only his own ignorance to blame. (The distributors, incidentally, had hoped to issue this particular film under the title *Love on a Pillow*, but the censor wasn't having any.)

Retitling reissues is acknowledged in the trade to be a bit naughty, but Hollywood thinks remakes are fair game. Of course, the title of a really big film is still a strong drawing card when it is remade ten or twenty years later, so presumably *Cimarron* and *Stagecoach* and *The Four Horsemen of the Apocalypse* and *The Prisoner of Zenda* can go on being remade indefinitely under the same titles, but with a change of cast for each generation. It is different with medium-budget pictures which are likely to be forgotten within a year or two: if the plot has a clever twist, why waste it? Brush up the characters, vary the location, think of a fresh title and you have an original movie . . . more or less. Well-known though it is, the basic plot of *The Asphalt Jungle* has been re-used three times by Metro since the original came out in 1950: in *The Badlanders* it had a Western setting, and in *Cairo* an Eastern, while in *Cool Breeze* the orientation was black. *The More the Merrier*, a 1943 comedy, reappeared in 1966 as *Walk, Don't Run*, with Cary Grant replacing Charles Coburn. The first picture to exploit the situation in which a group of assorted people are marooned among savages after a plane crash was (probably) *Five Came Back* in 1939; it was remade as *Back from Eternity* in 1955, and ten years later *Sands of the Kalahari* trod very similar ground except that the savages had become baboons; while *The Flight of the Phoenix* was pretty similar, too, despite its emphasis on rebuilding the plane, and several TV movies including *Lost Flight* and *Valley of Mystery* have got in on the same act. The version of *The Maltese Falcon* which everyone remembers was made in 1941 by John Huston, but Warners had also made talkies of the story in 1932 and 1936, the latter disguised as *Satan Met a Lady*; and Huston himself spoofed the plot in *Beat the Devil* (1954). Warners, in fact, are way ahead in this particular field. The plot of *Kid Galahad*, a successful boxing picture, was remade four years later as *The Wagons Roll at Night*, with the sport changed to lion-taming; *Tiger Shark* was recast and became *Manpower*; while a 1932 gangster movie called *The Mouthpiece* turned up in 1940 as *The Man Who Talked Too Much* and in 1955 as *Illegal*. Raymond Chandler's detective stories *Farewell My Lovely* and *The High Window* (American titles: *Murder My Sweet* and *The Brasher Doubloon*) were filmed straight in the mid-40s, but each had in fact appeared twice before on celluloid, disguised as adventures of The Falcon and Michael Shayne. Four famous films remade as Westerns were *The Sea Wolf, The Petrified Forest, Kiss of Death* and *House of Strangers*; they became *Barricade, Escape in the Desert, The Fiend Who Walked the West* and *Broken Lance*.

It seems fair enough for a famous film to get a new title when music is added: *Pygmalion* can change to *My Fair Lady*, *The Women* to *The Opposite Sex, Anna and the King of Siam* to *The King and I*. But was it quite proper to remake *Love Affair* and call it *An Affair To Remember*, *Vessel of Wrath* and call it *The Beachcomber, My Favourite Wife* and call it *Move Over Darling*?

If the borrowing is admitted in the credits of the remake, it doesn't seem so much like cheating; but two fairly recent examples are inexcusable. One of Hitchcock's most celebrated thrillers, *Shadow of a Doubt*, was quietly remade by Universal as a second feature known in the US as *Step Down to Terror* and in Britain as *The Silent Stranger*; while anyone watching a Warner second called *Law versus Gangster* might recognize not only the storyline of *White Heat* (49) but most of the action sequences from the original, including long shots of Jimmy Cagney.

The most remade, and disguised, film, is probably the 1932 Cooper-Schoedsack thriller *The Most Dangerous Game*, released in Britain as *The Hounds of Zaroff*. It was remade in 1944 as *Johnny Allegro* (*Hounded* in Britain), and in 1946 as *A Game of Death*. In 1956 it was modernized as *Run for the Sun*; while in the seventies Alan Alda appeared in *To Kill a Clown* and Richard Basehart (for TV) in *Maneater*, both of which were disguised remakes.

There are, of course, cases where a change of title is logical, to avoid having two films of the same name in release. *Gaslight*, Thorold Dickinson's highly-acclaimed Victorian thriller, was released in Britain in 1940. Metro subsequently bought up the negative and released their remake in 1943, as *Gaslight* in the US, but in Britain, to avoid confusion, as *The Murder in Thornton Square*. Later some copies of the original were released in the US under the inexplicable title *Angel Street*. Similarly, the British farce *Sailor Beware* was released in the US as *Panic in the Parlor* to avoid confusion with a Martin and Lewis comedy. Universal's 1964 version of *The Killers* was first intended to be known as *Johnny North*, but the original title was adopted at the last minute; so when the 1947 version was released to TV, it had to be called *A Man Afraid*. And the Marilyn Monroe *Bus Stop* was shown on TV as *The Wrong Kind of Girl* because a TV series was thought to have worn out the welcome of the original title.

The case of *The Children's Hour* is complicated but instructive. When William Wyler first, in 1936, came to film this play about lesbians, the code compelled him to emasculate it, so rather than promise what he couldn't give he changed the title to *These Three*. In 1962 he remade it with full force and kept the original title; but in Britain, where the play was not widely known, *The Children's Hour* was felt not to accord with the film's 'X' certificate, and the picture was released as *The Loudest Whisper*.

The industry has long had its favourite title words, though most of them have no more justification in fact than superstitions. A producer is still encouraged by front office to call his film *The Big* this or *The Great* that, despite the fact that hundreds of others have done so before him and that even these trusted crowd-pulling epithets are subject to the law of diminishing returns. During the 30s, *Murder* and *Death* were surprisingly well thought of, and later we had epidemics of *Naked, Man, Woman, Girl, Lady, Violent, High, Long, Night, Song, Teenage, Party, Thunder, Beach* and *Spy*. (The most evocative Christian name, it seems, is *Johnny*, which during the last twenty years or so has been the word preceding such diverse title epithets as *Allegro, Angel, Belinda, O'Clock, Cool, Concho, Dark, Frenchman, Guitar, Holiday, In the Clouds, One-Eye, Rocco, Stool Pigeon, Tremain,* and *Trouble*.)

During the fifties and sixties the industry apparently found *Operation* to be a most useful ingredient of a title, almost a cure-all. You could tack it on to almost anything and come up with something appealing to the masses, as in *Operation Murder*, *Operation Bikini, Operation Eichmann, Operation Snatch, Operation Mad Ball, Operation Pacific, Operation Amsterdam, Operation Petticoat*. At the height of Sean Connery's sudden world-wide popularity, an old British service comedy called *On the Fiddle*, in which he appeared as a gormless private, was dusted off for the American market as *Operation SNAFU* and did big business. (SNAFU is an American army term which can be bowdlerized as 'situation normal, all fouled up'.) And when Cary Grant's comedy *Father Goose* did less than was expected at the box-office, the posters were redesigned to make the title look like *Operation Father Goose*. So imagine the shock MGM had when its all-star spy thriller *Operation Crossbow* failed to reach the box-office heights, and market research insisted that the title was to blame. 'It sounds like Robin Hood' was the cry from the Mid-West. A change was obviously in order, and what did the picture end up as? *The Great Spy Mission*. You can't beat subtlety.

There are unfavourite words too. Wherever films are bought and sold it has long been whispered that there can be no hope of box-office success when the title contains the word *Miracle*. Instances cited include *The Miracle of Morgan's Creek, The Modern Miracle, The Miracle Worker, Miracle in Milan, The Miracle of Fatima, The Miracle of the Bells, Miracle in the Rain,* and *The Miracle* itself. It isn't surprising that such films are sometimes retitled, but the odd thing is that the alternatives are so unappealing. The delightful *Miracle on 34th Street*, for instance, went out dolefully to Britishers as *The Big Heart, A Miracle Can Happen* became *On Our Merry Way, Miracle of the White Stallions* changed to *Flight of the White Stallions* (but still did no business).

Another highly suspect word in Britain is *Experiment*, despite the success of Quatermass; indeed there seems little reason for this phobia, but *Experiment in Terror* was changed to *The Grip of Fear* on account of it, and it is true that little trade was drummed up by *Experiment Perilous*, *Experiment Alcatraz* or *Experiment in Evil*.

Titles are often used again to cover plots quite different from the original. Since 1942, for instance, there have been three films and two TV movies called *Nightmare*, none of them in any way connected; indeed, one was a remake of another film called *Fear in the Night*, while a second owed more than a little of its plot to *The Thirty-nine Steps*. When *Monkey Business* appeared in 1951, it was a Cary Grant comedy about rejuvenation, not a remake of the Marx Brothers extravaganza released in 1931; but the latter movie, then being revived, was withdrawn by arrangement between the two renters concerned so that it should not harm the business of the new arrival.

By far the majority of title switches are in fact sea changes. When the title has to be translated into another language, it can be affected by anything from local idioms to national characteristics, and the often weird results are beyond the comfortable scope of these notes. But simple transatlantic changes, in the same language, between Great Britain and the US, are a study in themselves, and can offer a surprising amount of insight into national psychology (the list following this essay is pretty comprehensive).

Taking the eastward direction first, it is accepted that Hollywood gained its early stranglehold on British audiences because the audiences liked what they saw and clamoured for more. Yet to this day there are many facets of the American way of life which British renters think their customers won't stomach. Obviously, the names of American politicians, sportsmen and less familiar entertainers will be the first to go, with such transitions as *Tennessee Johnson* to *The Man on America's Conscience*, *Jim Thorpe, All-American* to *Man of Bronze*, *Abe Lincoln in Illinois* to *Spirit of the People*, and *The Bob Mathias Story* to *The Flaming Torch*.

Even the devil has a different nickname in the US, so *Alias Nick Beal* had to become *The Contact Man* (and the film lost some of its point).

Of course there are hundreds of American phrases and allusions incomprehensible to British ears. Some of the changes occasioned by that particular difficulty were *Buck Privates* to *Rookies*, *The Petty Girl* (in northern Britain a 'petty' is a lavatory) to *Girl of the Year*, *Hallelujah I'm a Bum* ('bum' in Britain is a vulgarism for backside) to *Hallelujah I'm a Tramp*, *A Girl, a Guy and a Gob* to *The Navy Steps Out*, and *Eight on the Lam* to *Eight on the Run*.

In 1951 a film called *The Enforcer* (which has no British equivalent) was translated as *Murder Inc*. This caused some confusion when a second film called *Murder Inc* came along a few years later, and even more when Clint Eastwood appeared in *The Enforcer* with a different plot.

Even American place-names are thought by British renters to be off-putting – despite the success of films like *Arizona, Texas, Union Pacific, In Old Oklahoma*, and hundreds of others. Anyway, a few examples: *The Doolins of Oklahoma* changed to *The Great Manhunt*, *Chicago Masquerade* to *Little Egypt*, *Kansas City Confidential* to *The Secret Four*, and *The Hawaiians* to *Master of the Islands*.

Even folksy humour as evidenced by *Aaron Slick from Punkin Creek*, or by *Curtain Call at Cactus Crick*, is thought to be impermissible. These two films came through, respectively, as *Marshmallow Moon* and *Take the Stage*.

The British are also very dubious of propaganda, or anything that smacks of old-fashioned Yankee jingoism. It just has to be put down, as follows: *America, America* to *The Anatolian Smile* (the thought processes involved here are beyond guesswork), *First Yank into Tokyo* to *Hidden Secret/Mask of Fury*, *The Magnificent Yankee* to *The Man with Thirty Sons* (the joke couldn't be intentional, one supposes), and *An American Dream* to *See You in Hell, Darling*.

How Britishers ever let *Yankee Doodle Dandy* through, I just don't know. But quotations from American patriotic songs are obviously OK as the British won't know the context: the fact that such titles as *Halls of Montezuma*, *To the Shores of Tripoli* and *So Proudly We Hail* are meaningless to them is apparently of no importance.

Sometimes there are censorship reasons, obvious or not, why an American title just won't do in Britain. Take *BF's Daughter*, for instance; although the title of a John Marquand novel, it had to become *Polly Fulton* in Britain, where a BF is a bloody fool. The monarchy must be protected, so *The Royal Bed* became *The Queen's Husband* and *Royal Wedding* turned into *Wedding Bells*. *A Royal Scandal* was obviously unthinkable: it turned up as *Czarina*. Religion sets similar problems: *The Man Who Played God*, in case anyone got the same idea, became *The Silent Voice*. *Damn Yankees*, being both offensive *and* over-American, was changed to *What Lola Wants*, and quickly sank without trace.

Suggestions of sex must obviously be toned down for strait-laced Britishers, in the golden age, at least, which saw such changes as *Vice Squad* to *The Girl in Room 17*, *I Was a Male War Bride* to *You Can't Sleep Here*, and *Professional Sweetheart* to *Imaginary Sweetheart*. Yet by the sixties *Any Wednesday* could show as *Bachelor Girl Apartment*.

Excess of any kind seems to scare British renters. When the gangster films of the early 30s were causing a press storm, the obvious solution was to tone down not the films but the titles. Who could object to *Public Enemy* when it became *Enemies of the Public*? This devious change technically made the public, not the gangster, into the hero. *The Hatchet Man* became *The Honourable Mr Wong, I am a Fugitive from a Chain Gang* lost its last four words, *Scarface* was subtitled *The Shame of a Nation*. Weirdest of all (it must have had a very adaptable plot-line), *Public Enemy's Wife* became *G-Man's Wife*.

Much later, *Confessions of an Opium Eater* became *Evils of Chinatown, Son of Slade* (a very violent Western) became *Texas Rose, The Bottom of the Bottle* became *Beyond the River, The Violent Men* became *Rough Company*, and

Scandal Sheet became *The Dark Page*. Even *The Killer That Stalked New York*, in which the killer was smallpox, became *Frightened City*; and a moving little drama called *The Judge Steps Out* was shown as *Indian Summer* (a British judge 'stepping out' was apparently unthinkable).

At least on one occasion the British were less sensitive than their American cousins. Agatha Christie's murder puzzle *Ten Little Niggers* was filmed by René Clair in 1945 – in America, where the title could not be used. The nursery rhyme was rewritten, and the picture became *Ten Little Indians*. This brought more protests from the minority groups, so it was released as *And Then There Were None*. But Britons staunchly saw it under the original title, despite the fact that the china figures were plainly Indians, and only Indians were mentioned in the dialogue. The sixties remake settled firmly on Indians all round, which made it less puzzling.

When two versions of a film exist, and both are sold to TV, the earlier one is sometimes given a different title. Thus you may come across something called *Forbidden Alliance* which turns out to be the Laughton version of *The Barretts of Wimpole Street*; similarly *Flight Commander* is the 1930 *Dawn Patrol*, *Tops is the Limit* is the Bing Crosby *Anything Goes*, and *Oriental Dream* is the Ronald Colman *Kismet*.

British renters seem convinced that no audience can see a joke in a title. This often deprives we Britishers of a choice morsel of wit. Not, I grant you, in *Who Killed Doc Robbin?* (shown as *Sinister House*) or *Callaway Went Thataway* (shown as *The Star Said No*). But surely we might have kept *State of the Union* rather than *The World and His Wife, The Desk Set* instead of *His Other Woman, Advance to the Rear* instead of *Company of Cowards, Take a Letter Darling* and not *Green-Eyed Woman*? I might have gone to see something called *The Bar Sinister*, but not *It's a Dog's Life*. And how dull for *I Can Get It For You Wholesale* (now on TV as *Only the Best*!) to be shown as *This Is My Affair* – especially as the latter is the rejected American title of a Robert Taylor movie shown in Britain as *His Affair*. (Got that?)

Indeed, when all allowances have been made, some title changes must remain inexplicable. It isn't surprising that Universal, having filmed J. M. Barrie's *Alice Sit by the Fire*, should feel like changing the title. But why, for America, did they settle on *Darling How Could You*, and for Britain, *Rendezvous*? One agrees with the British distributor that *Requiem for a Heavyweight* won't break any box-office records. But then, nor will *Blood Money*. Why did the concise *Edge of the City* revert in Britain to the title of its original story, *A Man Is Ten Feet Tall*? And at a time when Alan Ladd and others were doing very nicely with one-word titles like *Saigon*, *Calcutta*, *China* and *Santiago*, why was *Malaya* shown in Britain as *East of the Rising Sun* (which is geographically inaccurate of Malaya anyway)?

In particular, since horror films always keep their market, which is based on an appetite for excess, why the following attempts to tone down the bogeymen? *Frankenstein Versus the Space Monster* became *Duel of the Space Monsters*; *Blood of Dracula* became *Blood is My Heritage*, *The Astounding She-Monster* became *Mysterious Invader*, and *The Corpse Vanishes* became *The Case of the Missing Brides*.

It is rare for British renters deliberately to toughen up American titles. But it happened to *A Woman's Devotion* which became *War Shock*, to *Dino* (*Killer Dino*), and to *No Place To Land* (*Man Mad*). There were also two occasions when Hollywood chose British adventure themes but did them so badly that they had to be disguised: *Royal African Rifles* became *Storm Over Africa*, and *El Alamein* was released as *Desert Patrol*. The prize for falsification should probably go to the witch-hunting *I Married a Communist*, which RKO played in Britain as *The Woman on Pier 13* – a title 'justified' by an incident at the very end of the picture.

The westward traffic to America seems to keep relatively few British titles intact, the reasons for change being usually to stress the concrete rather than the allusive and action rather than subtlety, in other words to suggest excitements of the kind not provided by the picture. Consider the following examples in which sex has been made to rear its head: *Summer of the Seventeenth Doll* became *Season of Passion*, *The Romantic Age* became *Naughty Arlette*, *Who Goes There?* became *The Passionate Sentry*, *Love Story* became *A Lady Surrenders*, and *The Weak and the Wicked* became *Young and Willing*.

A general toughening process is evident in such changes as: *The Informers* (formerly *The Snout*) to *Underworld Informers*, *HMS Defiant* to *Damn the Defiant*, *Time Bomb* to *Terror on a Train*, *Serious Charge* to *A Touch of Hell*, and *The Late Edwina Black* to *Obsessed*.

More particularly, observe from the following changes how unacceptable are quotations and allusions, which are invariably replaced by something unmistakably personal, full of the promise of action: *Dangerous Moonlight* to *Suicide Squadron*, *Ill Met By Moonlight* to *Night Ambush*, *A Terrible Beauty* to *Night Fighters*, *Cry the Beloved Country* to *African Fury*, and *The First of the Few* to *Spitfire*.

It appears that America does not take to any title formed by a character's name: not, at least, if it's a British character, so *Father Brown* changed to *The Detective* and *Albert RN* to *Break for Freedom*. It seems too that when the British go in for horror they are a shade too reticent about it, which accounts for *The Quatermass Experiment* being changed to *The Creeping Unknown*, *City of the Dead* to *Horror Hotel* and *Fanatic* to *Die, Die, My Darling*.

Fashion has a lot to do with title changes. The spy vogue, for instance, produced such amendments as *The Intelligence Men* to *Spylarks* and *Licensed to Kill* to *The Second Best Secret Agent in the Whole Wide World*. But then it seems spies were just as popular way back in 1939, when a Rex Harrison comedy called *Ten Days in Paris* turned up in the US as *Spy in the Pantry*.

Sometimes American distributors of British films have the excuse of unintelligibility for their title changes. It was reasonable enough that *The Chiltern Hundreds* (pretty unintelligible to most Britons, too) should become *The Amazing Mr Beecham*, and that *The Card* should be translated as *The Promoter*. Similarly *The Guinea Pig* means less to an American audience than *The Outsider*. *The Battle of the River Plate* is how we remember the famous naval action of 1939; but to an American audience *Pursuit of the Graf Spee* pinpoints it better as well as being more actionful. And *I Live in Grosvenor Square* just might perplex mid-westerners, who can immediately grasp *A Yank in London*.

There are some words which the American code will not, or would not, allow. *Fanny by Gaslight*, having possibilities of *double entendre*, must change to *Man of Evil*; *The Rake's Progress*, Hogarth or not, emerges as *Notorious Gentleman*, and *The Passionate Friends* as *One Woman's Story*. The celebrated stand of the Hays Office to the effect that the word 'behind' is impermissible unless immediately followed by a noun, does not alas appear to have affected any

British titles. (Under this ruling, a certain well-known poem would have to begin: 'If winter comes, can spring be far in back of?')

Ealing's group of Scottish comedies survived the Atlantic crossing quite pleasingly: *Whisky Galore* changed to *Tight Little Island*, *Rockets Galore* to *Mad Little Island*, and *The Maggie* to *High and Dry*. But it would be interesting to hear, in view of the honourable box-office history of Stevenson's schizophrenic doctor, why *The Two Faces of Dr Jekyll* was changed to *House of Fright*. Even less understandable is the change of the British *Give Us This Day*, taken from a story called *Christ in Concrete*. One can sympathize with the distributor's reluctance to use either of these alternatives, but what he finally hit on, *Salt to the Devil*, is equally unlikely to have sold any tickets. And why did *I Was Happy Here* become *Time Lost and Time Remembered*?

A curious thing happened when the sombre historical romance *Saraband for Dead Lovers* crossed the water. One might reasonably have expected something more punchy, less downbeat; instead it was simply shortened to *Saraband*. Oddlier and oddlier, *Tomorrow We Live* was released in the States as *At Dawn We Die*.

Let me conclude with three personal favourites. Whoever rechristened the story of deaf little *Mandy* as *The Crash of Silence* surely deserves some kind of prize. The runner-up, perhaps, is the gentleman who discarded *The Woman with No Name* in favour of *Her Panelled Door*. And a special award for topicality. That mild theatrical comedy *The Amorous Prawn* would not normally have expected much American exposure. But its plot line made it possible to play it very profitably in the States, just after a certain well-reported British scandal of the sixties, as *The Playgirl and the War Minister*.

[Reprinted from *Halliwell's Filmgoer's Companion*]

The Decline and Fall of the Movie

It is only fair that the author of a book which categorizes fifty years of films should give some account of his own prejudices. I have spent more than forty years seeing, talking about and writing about films, so my affection for the medium in its 'golden age' can hardly be doubted. Even then, however, the worthwhile movies were the tip of the iceberg: probably eighty per cent of what was produced was ghastly rubbish, which is why this book deals with ten thousand movies, not all of them good, out of a total output of four times that number. The best kind of film buff loves the movie business for what it can be at its best, not for its journeyman 'B' features, its crackpot experiments, its cheapjack exploitation screamies or those relentlessly boring bottom-of-the-bill fillers.

Jonathan Swift said in 1725: 'I hate and detest that animal called man, although I heartily love John, Peter, Thomas and so forth.' This book encapsulates my Johns, my Peters and my Thomases; this essay complains bitterly that they have lately been so few in number, and attempts, admittedly by some slight use of exaggeration, to throw light on a confused and unhappy segment of cinema history.

When Sam Peckinpah made *Straw Dogs* from a novel called *The Siege of Trencher's Farm* he thought it unnecessary to explain to his audience the significance of his new title which, his publicists informed us on request, was taken from an old Chinese proverb. And when Stanley Kubrick made *A Clockwork Orange* he did not bother to retain the section of the Anthony Burgess novel which explained why it was so called. These almost identical incidents exemplify the kind of arrogance which besets film-makers in the seventies. Steeped in the history of Hollywood's golden age, they have no idea what made it work so well, and as soon as they become successful they begin to despise their audiences and are concerned only to over-spend enormous budgets while putting across some garbled self-satisfying message which is usually anti-establishment, anti-law-and-order and anti-entertainment.

In this they are assisted by such long-haired publications as *Sight and Sound* and a variety of earnest critics who bend over backwards to see 'significance' where none exists and to ascribe all the film's virtues and faults to the director, or in the current jargon the *auteur*. (Would any theatrical critic dream of judging a play solely on the director's contribution, or a literary critic of reviewing a book solely on the basis of its layout on the printed page?) If cinema, which is the creation of so many people, can be an art at all, it must be a folk art which appeals to innocent and sophisticate alike, and can be easily appreciated by both. This happy state of affairs was reached thirty-five years ago by unpretentious and slick productions of the studio system such as *The Maltese Falcon* and *Stagecoach*, which used every camera trick in the book without blinding the audience to the characters and the plot. Nowadays one has to fight one's way through the thick showy surface in order to get to a story which all too often is not worth following.

One problem is that modern films are largely made by people with no sense of humour, people who do not realize that they must please the mass audience if the industry in which they work is to survive. Old-time screenwriters such as Ben Hecht, Dudley Nichols and Lamar Trotti would no doubt be viewed by these young men as cynical hacks, but at least they took pains to please their audience with all the expertise at their command, and they still expressed their own views in a vein of sardonic humour which ran through most of the scripts of the thirties and forties and was there to please and satisfy the minority of film-goers who sought it out.

The absurd pretensions of some modern film-makers certainly cause amusement wherever sensible people congregate, but the advocates of sanity are in no position to have the last word. The present set-up of the film industry encourages wilder and wickeder sensations, from homicidal sharks to diabolical babies, as these are the only subjects which lure large audiences. The successes, however, are all one-offs: no one is much interested in sequels, preferring to wait for horrors of some other variety. The result is that only one film in twenty or thirty makes a profit, but the custodians of the cash have no option but to go on investing in the hope that the occasional fluke will make a fortune, which will then be quickly dissipated by a string of failures. Universal's phenomenally successful *Jaws*, for instance, was immediately followed by such commercial duds as *Gable and Lombard*, *W. C. Fields and Me*, *The Great Waldo Pepper* and *The Hindenberg*, and the studio is still looking for another hit. The sad fact is that no policy can be devised because the people in charge of the money have no idea what is likely to appeal, and they are forced to put their faith in reputedly brilliant directors who have no idea either but are quite prepared to spend large sums of other people's money in flying their own flimsy kites. The flimsiness is sometimes astonishing. The director of an abysmal 1976 comedy called *Harry and Walter go to New York* announced to the press, as a selling point, that it was 'Laurel and Hardy with real people.' Had he inquired of his mass audience, he would surely have been told that Stan and Ollie had more reality in their little fingers than was to be found in the entire crew of *Harry and Walter go to New York*, whether before or behind the camera.

One should of course add that many films these days are not supposed to make money. The adage which used to run 'you're only as good as your last picture' has been changed to 'you're only as big as your last budget', and it is no trick to get a big budget when many films are conceived by industrialists as tax losses: all you have to do is get in the news by holding outlandish views or even making pornography, and Hollywood these days opens its doors to you because at least you must have learnt how to point a camera or arrest public attention. The ones to suffer are the audiences, who have foisted upon them material which they have every right to expect to be professional, and which all too often is not, just the result of untalented exhibitionists spending someone else's money in whatever way happens to divert them most. Even if there is a profit, their habit is to take the money and run, not to invest it in better production facilities as used to happen in the good old days.

Work is thus produced for a small group of jet-setters; meanwhile that patient paying audience discovers that not only the films but the standards of physical cinema comfort are far worse than they were thirty years ago; since then the cost of admission has risen at a phenomenal rate, the average cost in Britain now being twenty times more than in 1956. What other commodity has risen in price to this extent? Television is infinitely cheaper and can be viewed in the comfort of one's own home: no wonder so many people prefer it.

So the movie industry hastens on its way to perdition and catastrophe, a fate which surely cannot be delayed more than another few years, and for which simple-minded greed, lack of foresight and a large measure of incompetence are chiefly responsible. Those of us who are old enough and who still care about the movies sigh frequently for the halcyon days when Harry Cohn and Louis B. Mayer sat in their front offices, for their intellectual limitations were far less harmful and sometimes far more stimulating to the medium than the excesses of the present incumbents, who seldom stay long enough to make their presences felt and certainly not long enough for any sense of continuity to develop. There is for instance no continuity of employment, which makes the unions tougher and tougher to deal with in an industry which was always volatile in its labour relations: every film is a fresh project for which cast and crew have to be accumulated, and the way things are there is no bank of trained talent to fall back on. As Billy Wilder said, you spend eighty per cent of your time making deals and twenty per cent making pictures. The old moguls had enough common sense and business acumen to keep the system working so that costs were comparatively low and one could afford the occasional interesting failure to please the intellectuals.

How did the movie world go so wrong? You can trace it to the restlessness after World War II, when the regular audience declined and television was a coming threat and the bosses knew that new trends had to be found but no one knew what they might be in a glum and depressed world. When actors began to want a say in production and seemed willing to risk their own money, the bosses were delighted to share the possible losses; instead they found themselves being eased out and their profits halved, their studios no longer vast employment centres with a constant production line but simply enclosed space and facilities which could be rented out to the highest bidder.

The old moguls were getting older and couldn't fight the developing situation, the new young ones were businessmen who often backed the wrong horse because they didn't understand the industry. Meanwhile the old showmen had one last irrelevant fling. If television was the enemy, they reasoned, then give the paying public what television cannot provide. Technology now allowed films to be shot on real locations, which was splendid but had two handicaps. First, the units were away from central control for a long time, and the costs were phenomenal; second, the magic was lost, for the real Paris was by no means so romantic or mysterious as Paramount's backlot which had served as Paris for so many years, nor could the lighting of it be so carefully controlled. The new realistic films were slower, because the travel costs had to be justified and travelogue largely took the place of drama. (Did anyone complain about the lack of shots of San Francisco in *The Maltese Falcon*?)

The other way to combat television was to change the shape and effect of the entertainment screen. 3-D was tried, but audiences hated wearing polaroid glasses in order to get a three-dimensional image which producers largely utilized by hurling knives, tennis balls, spiders and even grubby redskins into the audience's lap: this was fairground stuff. Cinemascope was then seized upon by Hollywood: twice as wide as the ordinary image and capable of the most spectacular effects. There is no record that the paying audience ever especially liked Cinemascope, or could even remember whether or not a film was in the process, but once the expensive equipment was installed in theatres there was no turning back. Unfortunately the technique involved a reversion in many cinematic effects to the days of D. W. Griffith. The compression of the wide image on to the film and its subsequent expansion in the projector made the photography grainy, especially in black and white, which was henceforth virtually abandoned. (At about the same time a transference to safety stock lost us the glamorous luminescent 'Feel' which had been possible with nitrate and which can still be seen in old prints.) The new shape was impossible to compose for; as Fritz Lang said, it was fine for funerals, but what painter through the ages had ever selected it unless to cut up into a triptych? Editing was cut to a minimum because on an image so large each cut made the audience jump. Instead, and cheaper, the camera stayed still while the cast roved around the empty spaces in front of it, and there was an absurd number of shots in which the leading actors reclined so as better to fit the frame. Close-ups and subtle nuances were forgotten: no longer did the camera direct you to the drama, you had to look around and find it yourself. It is rather astonishing that directors with an eye to their reputations still persist in using the scope format, for after initial release the future of any film these days is on television, and no scope film, will satisfactorily adapt to the TV screen.

In many cinemas Cinemascope was even a fraud, for it had to be on a screen smaller in area than the old image, which was now being referred to sneeringly as 'postage stamp'. This happened when the old screen had already occupied all the width allowed by the cinema's structure: to get the CinemaScope shape, if you could not go any wider, height had to be sacrificed, and audiences wondered why suddenly they were looking at a ribbon of picture across the middle of the space which the fine old screen had occupied.

Cinemascope was patented by Fox, so the other companies all hastened to produce their own variations: Warnerscope, Metroscope, Techniscope, Superscope, Megascope, Camerascope, Panavision, each with its own cheap colour process. Projectionists all over the world were confused by these new names, and seldom knew whether they were projecting a film as they were supposed to. The results were often truly appalling, with lack of focus, too much brightness and wrong screen masking among the most common faults. Paramount's Vistavision, a non-anamorphic process, used the full frame ratio but was intended for projection at anything between 1.33:1 and 2:1, so that the essential action had to take place in a strip along the centre of the picture; consequently, to see a Vistavision print on a 1.33:1 screen was painful indeed, as all the action seemed to take place in the middle distance with great areas of unused space at the top and bottom of the image, and composition, which any painter knows to be all-important, was no longer possible. By the mid-fifties, however, 1.33:1 was no longer generally available, as 'wide screen' had become *de rigueur* even for non-anamorphic films: these cut off the top and bottom of the frame and magnified the rest. This meant that revivals were impossible unless one was prepared to suffer dancers without feet and actors without heads!

The result of all this technical uncertainty was that by the mid-fifties movies were in danger of becoming mere expensive sideshows, uninteresting to anyone of sensitivity. At the same time, an element of sophistication crept away from the popular arts: whereas in the thirties and forties smooth and educated idols had been set up for general approbation, the fifties and sixties showed an alarming tendency not merely to make heroes of 'people like us' but to rub our noses firmly in the gutter by devising stories whose leading characters had few redeeming features. Censorship had been absurdly tight and must obviously relax, but it was unwise and unexpected that the floodgates should open as they did, to admit movies which would previously have been considered anti-social rubbish. It was right, for instance, for Otto Preminger to fight the idiocies of the Production Code with his *The Moon Is Blue* and *The Man with the Golden Arm*, but it was a pity he won his battle with a leaden piece of schoolboy smut and an absurdly melodramatic updating of The Road to Ruin. Such films simply made one yearn to go back to the days of *Trouble in Paradise* and *The Palm Beach Story*, or for the true social concern expressed in the considered, powerful and moving masterpieces of Frank Capra, John Ford, or the early Chaplin.

The talents which had made Hollywood great were certainly nearing retirement by now, but it was perhaps unwise as well as churlish for the new wave to pension them off quite as hurriedly as they did, because there was no comparable talent to take their place. Great art directors like Anton Grot and Hans Dreier, great cameramen like Arthur Miller and James Wong Howe, great directors like Michael Curtiz and William Dieterle were either tossed aside or forced to work on material totally unsuited to their talents and not at all comparable to the films which had made their names. The results were big-budget disasters such as *The Egyptian* and *Omar Khayyam*; meanwhile the young directors were copying low-budget television techniques which for every *Marty* produced a dozen flatly realistic bores.

By the early sixties Hollywood had decided on a new image, but it had lost its old loyalties – the golden age audiences as well as the talents were getting older – and had to appeal deliberately to the 'emancipated' young generation. This meant a virtual abolition of censorship, and from the release of *Who's Afraid of Virginia Woolf?* in 1966 to that of *The Texas Chainsaw Massacre* and *The Devil in Miss Jones* ten years later is but a short step. The film is no longer an art, or even a craft: after a brief 'swinging' period it became an exploitation industry designed to take quick money from suckers, led by maverick Ken Russells rather than conscientious Irving Thalbergs, to plaudits from irresponsible critics whenever some totally untalented new director 'does his thing'. There is no justification except box office for films like *The Exorcist* or *Mandingo*, none except self-indulgence for a $12 million coffee-table film like *Barry Lyndon*, while the popularity even in sophisticated circles of shoddy pornography like *Deep Throat* and *Death Weekend* should stand as an awful warning to the leaders of our society that a vivid young art form has overreached itself and is well and truly on the verge of disaster. It is all very well to say in defence of such films that large numbers of people flock to see them: so they did once to bear-baiting and public executions and witch hunts, but the human race long ago prided itself on having passed that stage.

The movies will be lucky if, in their search for sensationalism, they do not check themselves out altogether. Audiences have dwindled rapidly and are still dwindling; so is the number of cinemas. The lush old two-thousand seaters have turned into supermarkets, and instead each city has its ineptly-run boxes of mini-cinemas, the effect of which is rather like sitting in cheaply decorated funeral parlours and paying through the nose for the privilege. The family outing to the cinema is a thing of the past: few families can afford it or can find a suitable film, except once or twice a year when the Disney organization stirs itself; and *their* standards are by no means as high as they were, as a comparison of *Robin Hood* with *Bambi* or *Pinocchio* will immediately show. (The fact that such an uninventive computerized cartoon as *Robin Hood* can do well at the box office is an instance of how starved the public is for the older, gentler forms of entertainment.)

Another problem besetting the cinema in the sixties was its adoption by verbose and pompous critics who were determined to turn it into serious art. True art is the work of one man, or at least his personal vision: each film is the work of several hundred people. Of these, admittedly the director has the most control, but to assign to him the role of *auteur* and to ignore the contribution of producer, writer, photographer, composer and editor is arrant nonsense, except possibly in the cases of such as Hitchcock and Kubrick who do control almost every aspect of their output. The new cinema journalism simply encouraged the worst motives of the new breed of film-maker, who came to know that whatever idiocy he perpetrated would be staunchly defended, researched and psychoanalysed by one of these mercenaries in search of a cause. If a character spat on the pavement this would be taken as his final shedding of his working-class upbringing; if he went to bed with a girl it would symbolize his treachery to his own beliefs and his giving in to the snares of Mammon. Listen to a modern critic in the British Film Institute's *Monthly Film Bulletin*, once a terse and reliable guide to film trends, on *Alice Doesn't Live Here Any More*: 'What Scorsese has done, however, is to rescue an American cliché from the bland, flat but much more portentous naturalism of such as *Harry and Tonto* and restore it to an emotional and intellectual complexity through his particular brand of baroque realism.' Or on Rafelson's *Stay Hungry*: 'What distinguishes him from other film-makers of the "head" generation is both the poetic sureness of his fragmentary, allusive style, and the elliptical observation which prevents his social themes from being spiked too easily on the cultural antitheses of that bygone era.' Spare us.

Some of the elements missing from modern cinema are to be found in television, certainly in the UK with its brilliant documentaries, sharp comedies, serious art programmes and single plays; Americans are less lucky except on their public broadcasting system. But television is a private enjoyment, and one inevitably misses the sense of comradeship, of sharing a pleasure, that the cinema used to fulfil. Who having experienced them can forget the feeling of a full house being pleasurably chilled by *The Cat and the Canary*, or rolling in the aisles at Laurel and Hardy, or hoping against hope that Colman will find his *Lost Horizon*? What modern films can produce the sheer entertainment value and unforgettable, vivid scenes of such as *The Philadelphia Story*, *Stagecoach*, *Rebecca*, *Camille*, *Casablanca*, *Citizen Kane*, *Singin' in the Rain*, *A Night at the Opera*, *The Lady Vanishes*, and *The Third Man*? These were all intelligent films, all made for the despised mass audience, and they all made money because they were produced with impeccable professionalism and star talent, and because to these qualities they added heart and good humour. Where is the good humour in *Jaws*? Where is the heart in *The Exorcist*? These are rides on fairground ghost trains: one pays for the thrill, but one comes out more depressed than uplifted.

Of course there are some genuine talents at work in films today. One respects the likes of Jack Nicholson and Ellen Burstyn and Al Pacino and Glenda Jackson, but they are all depressingly committed to their own self-expression and to the depiction of mankind with warts and all, not to pleasing, stimulating or improving the public. They need control; but where are the likes of Lubitsch to control them? Of Sturges? Of Ben Hecht? Of James Whale? Of Donald Ogden Stewart? Of S. J. Perelman? Of Robert Benchley and Dorothy Parker? The films produced by Altman and Scorsese and Ashby are doubtless stimulating in their violent, abrasive way but they are not the whole of life. David Lean and John Schlesinger and Arthur Penn are meticulous craftsmen, but they are driven by commerce into the excesses of *Ryan's Daughter* and *Marathon Man* and *The Missouri Breaks*. In the acting league, where are our up-and-coming replacements for David Niven, Cary Grant, Melvyn Douglas, Katharine Hepburn, Ronald Colman? When again will it be the turn of grace and elegance? When indeed will actors want to work? Marlon Brando, Elizabeth Taylor and their like prefer to demand an impossibly high fee, and if they do not get it to sit comfortably at home on the proceeds of their previous hits.

Hollywood at its best – and for Hollywood also read Ealing and Tobis Klangfilm and Svenske Filmindustri – was the purveyor of an expensive and elegant craft which at times touched art, though seldom throughout a whole film. Reality was seldom sought, but why should it be? Real life is not dramatic anyway: even *Taxi Driver* is a heightening, a selection, an emphasis. So are all the great realist films from *The Battleship Potemkin* to *The Grapes of Wrath*. And so are the great works of Beethoven, of Rembrandt, of Michelangelo. Film stands to life as poetry to prose, and its comments were at their most apt and stylish when movies were confined to the sound stage and the backlot. Freedom from that confinement has not made them any better: it has only made them diffuse and patchy and overlong, and colour has made things worse because it apes reality whereas black and white conjured up its own mood and its own comment. Today's screens are too large for the eye to take in. Sound tracks are so 'realistic' as to be incoherent. Big budgets are wasted on movies which would have been ten times as effective if a little imagination had been used or required. Kaleidoscopic effects dazzle the eye and befuddle the brain; immensely long precredits sequences make one think the film is nearly over before it actually starts; characterization flies out the window because sex and violence must be fitted in somehow. Plot doesn't matter; since swinging London was invented every film has become a 'happening': which is another way of saying that anything goes and lack of professionalism cannot be criticized.

All right, this essay is a deliberate hatchet job by a disappointed fan who has turned devil's advocate. Some of the new films clearly have virtues which the old ones didn't possess: one is grateful for *The Graduate* and *Charlie Bubbles* and *Cabaret* and *One Flew over the Cuckoo's Nest*, which for various reasons could never have been made in the old Hollywood. But if my thesis were not largely true, how would one explain the enormous popularity of old movies on television, or the recent deluge of books about them? Why, out of more than sixty films on British television over the Christmas of 1976, were *White Heat* (1948), *A Night at the Opera* (1935) and *Yankee Doodle Dandy* (1942) the most discussed and appreciated? Nostalgia is only a trendy word to describe something which people have at last learned to appreciate because it has been taken away from them. No one in his right mind would be nostalgic for PRC second features or for much of the pure assembly line product which inevitably poured out of the studios when they were working at full pitch. And one must progress. But surely not to the wasteful ineptitude which confronts us at the cinema these days. Not to *Lucky Lady*, *Mother Jugs and Speed*, *At Long Last Love* or *Harry and Walter go to New York*. Must modern audiences really put up with inane or violent rubbish and appear to enjoy it simply because they are supposed not to know any better? We may not be able to get the golden age back, but we can cry for it. If 'they' fail to respond we can at least appreciate the best of it, and learn from that best. This book, I hope, may help a few people to do that.

Postscript

The preceding essay was written seven years ago, but it seems to have dated in very few respects save that the prophesied decline has been a longer and more complex business than any of us imagined, the advent of such new outlets as cable and video having put back the evil day. Certainly the old pleasures of a family visit to the cinema are experienced now by almost nobody, partly because admission prices continue to skyrocket and partly because the films themselves are totally unsuitable. Thirty years ago, more than half the films on release had 'U' certificates, with a mere handful of titles labelled 'Adults Only'. Now the boot is on the other foot: the vast majority of movies are for people aged fifteen and over, and when very occasionally a 'U' film happens along, it does no business because the potential audience thinks it must be bland beyond belief.

During the same period the number of British cinemas has dwindled to a twentieth of what it was, and few indeed of those remaining make a healthy profit. This decline is more marked in Britain than anywhere else in the world, but it is scarcely surprising in a period when the cost of a reasonable seat has risen from 10 or 15p to a suburban average of £2.70 and a West End top of £4.70; this to sit in boxlike tripled or quadrupled cinemas which are uncomfortable and badly run, often with poor sound and picture quality, while the audience endures tedious advertisements and extended intervals in place of the brisk supporting programmes which some of us still remember. In some other parts of the world, probably those with more isolated communities and a less varied and attractive television service, it appears that there is still a sufficiently considerable cinema audience, though it stays more or less within the age range of 16 to 24, which producers interpret as meaning that films have to be filled with sex, violence and gutter language. This is by no means to libel all persons between 16 and 24 years old, but it does seem that those who would prefer something less excessive are prepared to patronize the cinema only in its less commercially viable art forms.

Producers with little sense of history have proved more than willing to go on spending other people's money in increasingly large amounts, and it has become clear that the best this process is likely to throw up is a couple of prestige pictures a year plus half a dozen blockbuster adventures at the level of the old newspaper comic strips. This is perhaps the most astonishing development of all. Adults thirty years ago might possibly have enjoyed *E.T.*, as they enjoyed *The Wizard of Oz*, but can you imagine them willingly sitting through *Star Wars*, *Ghostbusters* or *Gremlins*? I am not denying that when one is in the mood for something very easy these films can provide a modicum of simple enjoyment, but by and large they are hokum entertainments by and for the untrained mind, and I think one should feel just a little ashamed of submitting to them at a time when a once-great art is providing nothing more stimulating.

One way or another, the end of the cinema has been staved off for another indefinite while. British Film Year is unlikely to have much influence one way or the other. Critics and audience will continue to grit their teeth through expensive flops like *Heaven's Gate*, *Give My Regards to Broad Street* and *Dune* for the sake of the occasional product of a superior mind: *Gandhi* or *Chariots of Fire* or *A Passage to India*. How long a glamour industry can go on surviving by the skin of its teeth is obviously unsafe to predict, but in the end it is the exhibitors who will call the tune. Now beset by a greater-than-ever emphasis on home entertainment, with even the newest attractions almost simultaneously available on video, they must surely continue to close their empty halls at an even greater rate than has been recently evident; and without cinemas in which films can be seen there will eventually be no way in which producers can get their money back on big-budget enterprises. That may not be entirely a bad thing, for perhaps before too long we may see a return to wit, charm and expertise in place of the mounting excesses of the last quarter-century.

L.H.
January 1985

PPS: Two years later it seems unnecessary to update the above beyond noting an increasing break-even rate for independent films low of budget and high of brow, made specifically for a quick cinema release followed by 'minority' TV exposure. One might wish only that a greater proportion of these hybrids showed some optimism for our ailing society instead of wallowing in its lunatic shallows. Commercially, as a mass-entertainment, the cinema still needs a saviour.

L.H.
January 1987

Illustration Credits

Illustrations on the following pages appear by courtesy of the British Film Institute: 5, 17, 27, 59, 70, 79, 136, 144, 154, 173, 205, 222, 230, 243, 270, 327, 336, 342, 352, 365, 398, 432, 465, 483, 501, 518, 552, 561, 572, 581, 590, 625, 632, 650, 653, 665, 701, 712, 722, 730, 741, 770, 787, 798, 849, 910, 918, 926, 937, 943, 991, 1019, 1062, 1067, 1079, 1117